THE COLUMBIA
GRANGER'S®
INDEX TO POETRY

THE COLUMBIA GRANGER'S® INDEX TO POETRY

NINTH EDITION, COMPLETELY REVISED

INDEXING ANTHOLOGIES

PUBLISHED THROUGH JUNE 30, 1989

EDITED BY

EDITH P. HAZEN

DEBORAH J. FRYER

COLUMBIA UNIVERSITY PRESS
NEW YORK

THE COLUMBIA GRANGER'S® INDEX TO POETRY

COPYRIGHT 1904, 1918, 1929, 1940, 1945, 1953, © 1957, 1962,
1973, 1978, 1982, 1986, 1990
BY COLUMBIA UNIVERSITY PRESS

NINTH EDITION, COMPLETELY REVISED

LIBRARY OF CONGRESS CATALOGING-IN-PUBLICATION DATA

Hazen, Edith P.
  The Columbia Granger's index to poetry.

  1. Poetry—Indexes.   2. English poetry—Indexes.
I. Fryer, Deborah J.   II. Granger, Edith.   Index to
poetry.   III. Title.
PN1022.H39   1990   016.80881   90-1334
ISBN 0-231-07104-3

PRINTED IN THE UNITED STATES OF AMERICA

c 10 9 8 7 6 5 4 3 2 1

A KEY TO THE WORLD OF POETRY

THE COLUMBIA GRANGER'S® INDEX TO POETRY long ago earned its place in the hearts of everyone who regularly asked, or was asked, a number of very basic questions about poetry. Where can I find a poem whose title is the only thing about it I remember? What is the title of a poem whose first line I know? Where can I find some good poems on a subject I have to talk or write about next week? Nowhere else can such questions be so quickly, so easily, and so authoritatively answered. In this, the ninth edition of THE COLUMBIA GRANGER'S®, we are providing devoted users of the work with quick access to an even larger world of poetry than its predecessors.

In this ninth edition we have indexed over 100,000 poems. These are the poems most likely to be asked about. They appear in one or many of the almost four hundred anthologies in our list of anthologies on page xi. But searchers arrive at that list after they have asked one of several questions, and the easiest way to explain how THE COLUMBIA GRANGER'S® works is to show in detail how it answers some of these typical questions.

Where can I find a poem called "A Considered Reply to a Child"? If you go to the Title and First Line Index, which forms the great bulk of THE COLUMBIA GRANGER'S®, you'll find it listed there, with the name of its author, Jonathan Price, and with the letters BoLoP after it. This is the symbol for the anthology in which "A Considered Reply to a Child" can be found. You then look up the symbol in the List of Anthologies, where the symbols rather than the anthologies themselves are arranged alphabetically. There you will learn that you can read "A Considered Reply to a Child" in *A Book of Love Poetry*, edited by Jon Stallworthy, published by Oxford University Press in New York in 1974 and by Penguin in England under the title *The Penguin Book of Love Poetry*.

What is the title of the poem that begins "I struck the board, and cried: No More"? That question is also answered in the Title and First Line Index of THE COLUMBIA GRANGER'S®: the poem's title is "The Collar." This index also tells you that it was written by George Herbert and can be found in 30 anthologies.

Who wrote that poem that begins "You do not do, you do not do"? The Title and First Line Index tells you that Sylvia Plath wrote it. It also tells you that its title is "Daddy," and it can be found in 23 anthologies.

What poems can I find by Louise Bogan? Consult the Author Index of THE COLUMBIA GRANGER'S® and see that there are almost 50 poems by Bogan to be found in the anthologies we have indexed. Then go to the Title and First Line Index, which gives you the symbols of the anthologies, then to the List of Anthologies.

What was that poem Wordsworth wrote about a linnet? You don't know the title of the poem or the first line, but the Author Index will tell you that among the great many anthologized poems by Wordsworth there is "The Green Linnet." Again, go to the Title and First Line Index, and you'll see that it appears in four anthologies.

Where can I find some poems about the New Year? The Subject Index in THE COLUMBIA GRANGER'S® is an especially valuable tool for poetry searchers, and we have increased its value considerably in this ninth edition. In it you will find nearly a hundred poems on the New Year, including "Auld Lang Syne," by Robert Burns, and poems by Robert Lowell, John Berryman, Howard Nemerov, Edgar Guest, Robert Frost, and

Richard Wilbur. Similarly you can find poems on New York City, on old age, on illness, on brothers, on the moon (a very large number), on God, on despair, on fish, dogs, pigs, Halloween. When you have found the titles in the Subject Index, look them up in the Title and First Line Index to find their anthology symbols, then look up the symbols in the List of Anthologies.

Among more than 150 new anthologies we have indexed in the ninth edition of THE COLUMBIA GRANGER'S®, over 50 are collections of poetry translated from other languages. These additions increase the usefulness of the Subject Index enormously, unlocking a whole treasury of world poetry previously closed to poetry searchers. In this edition we have indexed poems in anthologies of poetry from Africa, Austria, Brazil, China, Finland, France, Germany, Greece, Hungary, India, Israel, Italy, Japan, Korea, Latin America, Mexico, the Netherlands, Peru, Poland, Puerto Rico, Russia, Spain; poetry in Gaelic, Hebrew, Urdu, Welsh, Yiddish; Afro-American poetry, Asian American poetry, American Indian poetry, Arab poetry, Chicano poetry, Maori poetry, Troubadour poetry.

You may find just as interesting a poem on death, or even on New York City, written by a poet from another part of the world as by an American, Canadian, or British poet.

Each collection of poetry from another country or language appears in the Subject Index under its appropriate country or language. And in the List of Anthologies we have marked these translated collections with a dagger.

Among four hundred anthologies, which should I buy first? In the List of Anthologies we have starred 40 anthologies: one star to 30 anthologies we consider excellent, two stars to those we consider the very best.

We are grateful for the expert assistance of Lillian Morrison, former Coordinator of Young Adult Services for the New York Public Library, herself a poet and anthologist; William Katz, of the School of Information and Library Services at the State University of New York at Albany, author of many reference books for libraries; and William Jay Smith, poet, translator, critic, and anthologist. They have been most generous with their time and their knowledge.

We are much indebted to Paul Lagassé and Deborah J. Fryer, who developed the format for this edition of THE COLUMBIA GRANGER'S® INDEX TO POETRY, and to Ray Fitzgerald, who patiently sorted out the complications and problems arising from merging two different computer systems. Deborah Auslaender, Melissa Solomon, Eleanor DeVane, and Virginia B. Wright brought special insights and energy to the creation of this edition from its earliest stages. William F. Bernhardt, Editor of the Fifth, Seventh, and Eighth editions of Granger's counselled willingly and wisely.

CONTENTS

A KEY TO THE WORLD OF POETRY   V

LIST OF ANTHOLOGIES   XI

ABBREVIATIONS   XXIX

TITLE AND FIRST LINE INDEX   1

AUTHOR INDEX   1503

SUBJECT INDEX   1865

LIST OF ANTHOLOGIES

Anthologies starred with two asterisks (**) are recommended for priority acquisition by small libraries, one asterisk (*) for further acquisition. Anthologies marked by a dagger (†) have been translated into English. See Preface for fuller explanation.

AA   American Anthology, An, 1787-1900. *Edmund Clarence Stedman, ed.* (1900) Houghton Mifflin Company

AAA   †Age Ago, An; a Selection of Nineteenth-Century Russian Poetry. *Alan Myers, comp. and tr.* (1988) Farrar, Straus and Giroux

AAS   Anchor Anthology of Sixteenth-Century Verse, The. *Richard S. Sylvester, ed.* (1974) Doubleday Anchor Books

ACKP   †Anthology of Contemporary Korean Poetry. *Koh Chang-soo, comp.* (1987) Seoul International Publishing House

ACP   Anthology of Catholic Poets, An. *Shane Leslie, ed.* (Rev. ed., 1952) The Macmillan Company (Later published by The Newman Press)

AH   *American Hymns Old and New, Vols. I-II. Vol. I, with music; Vol. II, notes on the hymns and biographies of the authors and composers. *Albert Christ-Janer, Charles W. Hughes, and Carleton Sprague Smith, eds.* (1980) Columbia University Press

AiP   America in Poetry. *Charles Sullivan, ed.* (1988) Harry N. Abrams

AIW   †Ain't I a Woman! a Book of Women's Poetry from around the World. *Illona Linthwaite, ed.* (1988) Peter Bedrick Books

AmFN   America Forever New; a Book of Poems. *Sara Brewton and John E. Brewton, comps.* (1968) Thomas Y. Crowell Company

AmFP   *American Folk Poetry; an Anthology. *Duncan Emrich, ed.* (1974) Little, Brown & Company

AmMo   Amazing Monsters; Verses to Thrill and Chill. *Robert Fisher, ed.* (1982) Faber and Faber

AmNP   American Negro Poetry. *Arna Bontemps, ed.* (Rev. ed., 1974) Hill and Wang

AmPA   American Poetry Anthology, The. *Daniel Halpern, ed.* (1975) Avon Books

AmPP   American Poetry and Prose. *Norman Foerster, Norman S. Grabo, Russel B. Nye, E. Fred Carlisle, and Robert Falk, eds.* (5th ed., 1970) Houghton Mifflin Company

AnAmPo   Anthology of American Poetry. *George Gesner, ed.* (1983) Avenel Books

AnAn   Antaeus Anthology, The. *Daniel Halpern, ed.* (1986) Bantam Books

AnIL   Anthology of Irish Literature, An. *David H. Greene, ed.* (1954) The Modern Library

AnOE   Anthology of Old English Poetry, An. *Charles W. Kennedy, tr.* (1960) Oxford University Press

APAS   Anthology of Poems on Affairs of State; Augustan Satirical Verse, 1600-1714. *George deF. Lord, ed.* (1975) Yale University Press

AS   American Songbag, The. *Carl Sandburg, comp.* (1927) Harcourt, Brace and Company

ASP   American Sports Poems. *R. R. Knudson and May Swenson, comps.* (1988) Orchard Books

ATCBP   †Anthology of Twentieth-Century Brazilian Poetry, An. *Elizabeth Bishop and Emanuel Brasil, eds.* (1972) Wesleyan University Press

ATF   †Among the Flowers; the Hua-chien Chi. *Lois Fusek, tr.* (1982) Columbia University Press

ATNZ   Anthology of Twentieth Century New Zealand Poetry, An. *Vincent O'Sullivan, comp.* (3d ed., 1987) Oxford University Press

AWP   **Anthology of World Poetry, An. *Mark Van Doren, ed.* (Rev. and enl. ed., 1936) Reynal & Hitchcock

AYP   †American Yiddish Poetry. *Benjamin Harshaw and Barbara Harshaw, eds.* (1986) University of California Press

BANP   Book of American Negro Poetry, The. *James Weldon Johnson, ed.* (Rev. ed., 1931) Harcourt Brace Jovanovich

BAP   Best American Poetry--1988, The. *John Ashbery, ed.* (1988) Collier Books/Macmillan Publishing Company

BeLS   Best Loved Story Poems. *Walter E. Thwing, ed.* (1941) Garden City Publishing Company

BIrV   *Book of Irish Verse, The; an Anthology of Irish Poetry from the Sixth Century to the Present. *John Montague, ed.* (1974) Macmillan Publishing Company (Also published as The Faber Book of Irish Verse)

BLA   Bread Loaf Anthology of Contemporary American Poetry, The. *Robert Pack, Sydney Lea, and Jay Parini, eds.* (1985) University Press of New England

BLPA   **Best Loved Poems of the American People, The. *Hazel Felleman, ed.* (1936) Doubleday & Company

BLPL   *Best-Loved Poems in Large Print. *Virginia S. Reiser, ed.* (1983) G. K. Hall & Company

BLRP   Best Loved Religious Poems, The. *James Gilchrist Lawson, comp.* (1933) Fleming H. Revell Company

BlSi   *Black Sister; Poetry by Black American Women, 1746-1980. *Erlene Stetson, ed.* (1981) Indiana University Press

BoLoP   *Book of Love Poetry, A. *Jon Stallworthy, ed.* (1974) Oxford University Press (Published in England under the title The Penguin Book of Love Poetry)

BoNaP   Book of Nature Poems, A. *William Cole, comp.* (1969) The Viking Press

BoS   †Book of Songs, The; the Ancient Chinese Classic of Poetry. *Arthur Waley, tr.* (1960) Grove Press

BoTP   Book of a Thousand Poems, The; a Family Treasury. *J. Murray Macbain, ed.* (1983) Peter Bedrick Books

BoWoP	Book of Women Poets from Antiquity to Now, A. *Aliki Barnstone and Willis Barnstone, eds.* (1980) Schocken Books
BPo	Black Poets, The. *Dudley Randall, ed.* (1971) Bantam Books
BrPo	British Poetry 1880-1920; Edwardian Voices. *Paul L. Wiley and Harold Orel, eds.* (1969) Appleton-Century-Crofts
BrRo	Bread and Roses; an Anthology of Nineteenth-and Twentieth-Century Poetry by Women Writers. *Diana Scott, comp.* (1982) Virago Press
BrSi	*Breaking Silence; an Anthology of Contemporary Asian American Poets.*Joseph Bruchac, ed.* (1983) The Greenfield Review Press
BwV	Burning with a Vision; Poetry of Science and the Fantastic.*Robert Frazier, ed.* (1984) Owlswick Press
BXAP	Brand-X Anthology of Poetry, The: Burnt Norton Edition. *William Zaranka, ed.* (1981) Apple-Wood Books
CaP	Canadian Poetry in English (Canadian Literature Series). *Bliss Carman, Lorne Pierce, and V. B. Rhodenizer, eds.* (Rev. and enl. ed., 1954) The Ryerson Press
CaPo	Cavalier Poets; Selected Poems. *Thomas Clayton, ed.* (1978) Oxford University Press
CAPP	Contemporary American Poetry. *A. Poulin, Jr., ed.* (4th ed., 1985) Houghton Mifflin Company
CBAP	Collins Book of Australian Poetry, The. *Rodney Hall, comp.* (1981, 1984) Fontana/Collins
CBWP 1-4	Collected Black Women's Poetry, Vols. I-IV. *Joan R. Sherman, ed.* (1988) Oxford University Press
CCP	*Contemporary Chicana Poetry; a Critical Approach to an Emerging Literature. *Marta Ester Snchez, ed.* (1985) University of California Press
CDC	Caroling Dusk; an Anthology of Verse by Negro Poets. *Countee Cullen, ed.* (1927) Harper & Brothers
CDW	Carriers of the Dream Wheel; Contemporary Native American Poetry. *Duane Niatum, ed.* (1975) Harper & Row
CenHV	Century of Humorous Verse, A, 1850-1950 (Everyman's Library). *Roger Lancelyn Green, ed.* (1959) E. P. Dutton & Company
CH	Come Hither. *Walter de la Mare, comp.* (3d ed., 1957) Alfred A. Knopf
ChER	Choice of English Romantic Poetry, A. *Stephen Spender, ed.* (1947) The Dial Press
ChTr	*Cherry-Tree, The. *Geoffrey Grigson, comp.* (1959) Phoenix House
CIP	Contemporary Irish Poetry; an Anthology. *Anthony Bradley, ed.* (New and rev. ed., 1980) University of California Press
CMoP	Chief Modern Poets of Britain and America. *Gerald DeWitt Sanders, John Herbert Nelson, and M. L. Rosenthal, eds.* (5th ed., 1970) Macmillan Publishing Company
CN	Chaos of the Night; Women's Poetry and Verse of the Second World War. *Catherine W. Reilly, ed.* (1984) Virago Press

CNA   Celebrations; a New Anthology of Black American Poetry. *Arnold Adoff, ed.* (1977) Follett Publishing Company

CoAP   Contemporary American Poets, The; American Poetry since 1940. *Mark Strand, ed.* (1969) World Publishing Company

CoAuP   †Contemporary Austrian Poetry; an Anthology. *Beth Bjorklund, ed. and tr.* (1986) Fairleigh Dickinson University Press

CoBCP   *†Columbia Book of Chinese Poetry, The, from Early Times to the Thirteenth Century. *Burton Watson, ed. and tr.* (1984) Columbia University Press

CoBLCP   †Columbia Book of Later Chinese Poetry, The. *Jonathan Chaves, ed. and tr.* (1986) Columbia University Press

CoMu   Common Muse, The; an Anthology of Popular British Ballad Poetry, XVth-XXth Century. *Vivian de Sola Pinto and Allan Edwin Rodway, eds.* (1957) Philosophical Library

CowP   Cowboy Poetry; a Gathering. *Hal Cannon, ed.* (1985) Gibbs M. Smith

CRH   Cat Will Rhyme with Hat; a Book of Poems. *Jean Chapman, ed.* (1986) Charles Scribner's Sons

CRP   Contemporary Religious Poetry. *Paul Ramsey, ed.* (1987) Paulist Press

CT   †Collected Translations. *William Jay Smith, comp.* (1985) New Rivers Press

CTC   Confucius to Cummings; an Anthology of Poetry. *Ezra Pound and Marcella Spann, eds.* (1964) New Directions

DiL   Divided Light: Father and Son Poems; a Twentieth-Century American Anthology. *Jason Shinder, ed. (1983)* The Sheep Meadow Press

DiPo   Direction of Poetry, The; an Anthology of Rhymed and Metered Verse Written in the English Language since 1975. *Robert Richman, ed.* (1988) Houghton Mifflin Company

DL   Death in Literature. *Robert F. Weir, ed.* (1980) Columbia University Press

DMF   †Defiant Muse, The; French Feminist Poems from the Middle Ages to the Present. *Domna C. Stanton, ed.* (1986) The Feminist Press

DMG   †Defiant Muse, The; German Feminist Poems from the Middle Ages to the Present. *Susan L. Cocalis, ed.* (1986) The Feminist Press

DMH   †Defiant Muse, The; Hispanic Feminist Poems from the Middle Ages to the Present. *Angel Flores and Kate Flores, eds.* (1986) The Feminist Press

DMI   †Defiant Muse, The; Italian Feminist Poems from the Middle Ages to the Present. *Beverly Allen, Muriel Kittel, and Keala Jane Jewell, eds.* (1986) The Feminist Press

DT   Dancing the Tightrope; New Love Poems by Women. *Barbara Burford, Lindsay MacRae, and Sylvia Paskin, eds.* (1988) Peter Bedrick Books

DuIn   †Dutch Interior; Postwar Poetry of the Netherlands and Flanders. *James S. Holmes and William Jay Smith, eds.* (1984) Columbia University Press

EaLo   Earth Is the Lord's, The; Poems of the Spirit. *Helen Plotz, comp.* (1965) Thomas Y. Crowell Company

EAS   English and American Surrealist Poetry. *Edward B. Germain, ed.* (1978) Penguin Books

EBEV   Everyman's Book of English Verse. *John Wain, ed.* (1981) J. M. Dent & Sons Ltd.

EBVV   Everyman's Book of Victorian Verse. *J. R. Watson, ed.* (1982) J. M. Dent & Sons Ltd.

ElL   Elizabethan Lyrics. *Norman Ault, ed.* (3d ed., 1949) William Sloane Associates (Paperback edition of 1960 published by G. P. Putnam's Sons)

ELP   English Lyric Poems, 1500-1900. *C. Day Lewis, ed.* (1961) Appleton-Century-Crofts

EnLoPo   English Love Poems. *John Betjeman and Geoffrey Taylor, comps.* (1957; paperback 1964) Faber and Faber

EnRP   English Romantic Poetry and Prose. *Russell Noyes, ed.* (1956) Oxford University Press

EnSB   English and Scottish Ballads (The Poetry Bookshelf). *Robert Graves, ed.* (1957) William Heinemann Ltd.

EOEF   *Ecstatic Occasions, Expedient Forms; 65 Leading Contemporary Poets Select and Comment on Their Poems. *David Lehman, ed.* (1987) Collier Books/Macmillan Publishing Company

ER   Early Ripening; American Women's Poetry Now. *Marge Piercy, ed.* (1987) Pandora Press

ErPo   Erotic Poetry; the Lyrics, Ballads, Idyls, and Epics of Love--Classical to Contemporary. *William Cole, ed.* (1963) Random House

ESPB   English and Scottish Popular Ballads. *Helen Child Sargent and George Lyman Kittredge, eds., from the collection of Francis James Child.* (1904, 1932, reissue, 1947) Houghton Mifflin Company

EyDe   Eye's Delight; Poems of Art and Architecture. *Helen Plotz, comp.* (1983) Greenwillow Books

FaBCIP   Faber Book of Contemporary Irish Poetry, The. *Paul Muldoon, ed.* (1986) Faber and Faber

FaBoBa   *Faber Book of Ballads, The. *Matthew Hodgart, ed.* (1965; paperback 1971) Faber and Faber

FaBoBe   Family Book of Best Loved Poems, The. *David L. George, ed.* (1952) Doubleday & Company

FaBoCh   Faber Book of Children's Verse, The. *Janet Adam Smith, comp.* (1953; paperback 1963) Faber and Faber

FaBoCo   Faber Book of Comic Verse, The. *Michael Roberts and Janet Adam Smith, eds.* (Rev. ed., 1974; paperback 1978) Faber and Faber

FaBoEE   Faber Book of Epigrams and Epitaphs, The. *Geoffrey Grigson, ed.* (1977) Faber and Faber

            Faber Book of Irish Verse, The. (1974) Faber and Faber (This book is the same as The Book of Irish Verse [BIrV]; see above)

Faber Book of Love Poems, The. (1975) Faber and Faber (This book is the same as The Gambit Book of Love Poems [GBL]; see below)

FaBoMo Faber Book of Modern Verse, The. *Michael Roberts, ed.* (4th ed., revised by Peter Porter, 1982) Faber and Faber

FaBoNo Faber Book of Nonsense Verse, The. *Geoffrey Grigson, ed.* (1979) Faber and Faber

Faber Book of Popular Verse, The. (1971) Faber and Faber (This book is the same as The Gambit Book of Popular Verse [GBP]; see below)

FaBoPa Faber Book of Parodies, The. *Simon Brett, ed.* (1984) Faber and Faber

FaBoPP Faber Book of Poems and Places, The. *Geoffrey Grigson, ed.* (1980) Faber and Faber

FaBoPV Faber Book of Political Verse, The. *Tom Paulin, ed.* (1986) Faber and Faber

FaBoRV Faber Book of Reflective Verse, The. *Geoffrey Grigson, ed.* (1984) Faber and Faber

FaBoTw Faber Book of Twentieth-Century Verse, The. *John Heath-Stubbs and David Wright, eds.* (3d ed., 1975) Faber and Faber

FaBoUs Faber Book of Useful Verse, The. *Simon Brett, ed.* (1981) Faber and Faber

FaBoWP *Faber Book of 20th Century Women's Poetry, The. *Fleur Adcock, ed.* (1987) Faber and Faber

FaBV Family Book of Verse, The. *Lewis Gannett, ed.* (1961) Harper & Row

FaFP Family Album of Favorite Poems, The. *P. Edward Ernest, ed.* (1959) Grosset & Dunlap

FaPON Favorite Poems Old and New. *Helen Ferris, ed.* (1957) Doubleday & Company

FaPoR Faber Popular Reciter, The. *Kinglsey Amis, ed.* (1978) Faber and Faber

FB Forerunners, The; Black Poets in America. *Woodie King, Jr., ed.* (1975) Howard University Press

FCEI *†From the Country of Eight Islands; an Anthology of Japanese Poetry. *Hiroaki Sato and Burton Watson, eds. and trs.* (1981) Columbia University Press

FF Fine Frenzy; Enduring Themes in Poetry. *Robert Baylor and Brenda Stokes, eds.* (2d ed., 1978) McGraw-Hill Book Company

FIA †Fiesta in Aztlan; Anthology of Chicano Poetry. *Toni Empringham, ed.* (1981) Capra Press

FiBHP Fireside Book of Humorous Poetry, The. *William Cole, ed.* (1959) Simon and Schuster

FiP Fifteen Poets; Chaucer to Arnold. (1941) Oxford University Press

FL First Lines; Poems written in youth, from Herbert to Heaney. *Jon Stallworthy, ed.* (1987) Carcanet

FM Fellow Mortals; an Anthology of Animal Verse. *Roy Fuller, comp.* (1981) Macdonald and Evans Ltd.

FOC †Face of Creation, The; Contemporary Hungarian Poetry. *Jascha Kessler, tr.* (1988) Coffee House Press

FPL Favorite Poems in Large Print. *Virginia S. Reiser, ed.* (1981) G. K. Hall & Company

FYAP Fifty Years of American Poetry; Anniversary Volume for the Academy of American Poets. Introduction by Robert Penn Warren. (1984) Harry N. Abrams

GBL Gambit Book of Love Poems, The. *Geoffrey Grigson, ed.* (1975) Gambit (Originally published in Great Britain by Faber and Faber as The Faber Book of Love Poems)

GBP Gambit Book of Popular Verse, The. *Geoffrey Grigson, ed.* (1971) Gambit (Also published in Great Britain as The Faber Book of Popular Verse)

GeTw Generation of 2000, The; Contemporary American Poets. *William Heyen, ed.* (1984) Ontario Review Press

GLP Gay & Lesbian Poetry in Our Time; an Anthology. *Carl Morse and Joan Larkin, eds.* (1988) St. Martin's Press

GN Golden Numbers. *Kate Douglas Wiggin and Nora Archibald Smith, eds.* (1902) Doubleday, Doran & Company

GOA Gift Outright, The; America to Her Poets. *Helen Plotz, ed.* (1977) Greenwillow Books

GoJo Golden Journey, The; Poems for Young People. *Louise Bogan and William Jay Smith, comps.* (1965) Reilly & Lee Company

GOS Gathering of Spirit, A; Writing and Art by North American Indian Women. *Beth Brant, ed.* (1984) Sinister Wisdom Books

GoT †Golden Tradition, The; an Anthology of Urdu Poetry. *Ahmed Ali, ed. and tr.* (1973) Columbia University Press

GoTS Golden Treasury of Scottish Poetry, The. *Hugh MacDiarmid, ed.* (1941) The Macmillan Company

GoYe Golden Year, The; the Poetry Society of America Anthology, 1910-1960. *Melville Cane, John Farrar, and Louise Townsend Nicholl, eds.* (1960) The Fine Editions Press

GOYP Going Over to Your Place; Poems for Each Other. *Paul B. Janeczko, comp.* (1987) Bradbury Press

GrPl Green Place, A; Modern Poems. *William Jay Smith, comp.* (1982) Delacorte Press/Seymour Lawrence

GTBS Golden Treasury of the Best Songs and Lyrical Poems in the English Language. *Francis Palgrave, comp.* (1929) Oxford University Press

GTBS-P *Golden Treasury of the Best Songs & Lyrical Poems in the English Language. *Francis Turner Palgrave, comp. With a fifth book selected by John Press.* (5th ed., 1964) Oxford University Press

HAP Harper Anthology of Poetry, The. *John Frederick Nims, ed.* (1981) Harper & Row

HATNAP *Harper's Anthology of 20th Century Native American Poetry. *Duane Niatum, ed.* (1988) Harper & Row

HCAP **Harvard Book of Contemporary American Poetry, The. *Helen Vendler, ed.* (1985) The Belknap Press of Harvard University Press

HeIP Heath Introduction to Poetry, The. *Joseph de Roche, ed.* (3d ed., 1988) D. C. Heath and Company

HoPM How Does a Poem Mean? *John Ciardi and Miller Williams, eds.* (2d ed., 1975) Houghton Mifflin Company

IAT In the American Tree. *Ron Silliman, ed.* (1986) The National Poetry Foundation

IDB I Am the Darker Brother; an Anthology of Modern Poems by Negro Americans. *Arnold Adoff, ed.* (1968) The Macmillan Company

IFON †Isle Full of Noises, The; Modern Chinese Poetry from Taiwan. *Dominic Cheung, ed. and tr.* (1987) Columbia University Press

IHMS I Hear My Sisters Saying; Poems by Twentieth-Century Women. *Carol Konek and Dorothy Walters, eds.* (1976) Thomas Y. Crowell Company

ILY I Like You, If You Like Me; Poems of Friendship (Margaret K. McElderry Books). *Myra Cohn Livingston, ed.* (1987) Macmillan Publishing Company

ImOP Imagination's Other Place; Poems of Science and Mathematics. *Helen Plotz, comp.* (1955) Thomas Y. Crowell Company

InPK **Introduction to Poetry, An. *X. J. Kennedy, ed.* (6th ed., 1986) Little, Brown & Company

InPS Introduction to Poetry, An. *Louis Simpson, ed.* (3d ed., 1986) St. Martin's Press

InvP Invitation to Poetry; a Round of Poems from John Skelton to Dylan Thomas. *Lloyd Frankenberg, ed.* (1956) Doubleday & Company

InW Inventing a Word; an Anthology of Twentieth-Century Puerto Rican Poetry. *Julio Marzán, ed.* (1980) Columbia University Press (in association with The Center for Inter-American Relations).

IP †Israeli Poetry; a Contemporary Anthology. *Warren Bargad and Stanley F. Chyet, comps. and trs.* (1986) Indiana University Press

IPY Irish Poetry after Yeats; Seven Poets. *Maurice Harmon, ed.* (1979) Little, Brown & Company

JB Jump Bad; a New Chicago Anthology. *Gwendolyn Brooks, ed.* (1971) Broadside Press

JCP Jacobean and Caroline Poetry; an Anthology. *T. G. S. Cain, ed.* (1981) Methuen

JLIC 1-2 †Japanese Literature in Chinese, Vols. I-II. Vol. I: Poetry and Prose in Chinese by Japanese Writers of the Early Period; Vol. II: Poetry and Prose in Chinese by Japanese Writers of the Later Period. *Burton Watson, tr.* (1975, 1976) Columbia University Press

KS Keener Sounds; Selected Poems from the Georgia Review. *Stanley W. Lindberg and Stephen Corey, eds.* (1987) The University of Georgia Press

LaA Late Augustans, The; Longer Poems of the Later Eighteenth Century (The Poetry Bookshelf). *Donald Davie, ed.* (1958) The Macmillan Company

LCAP *Longman Anthology of Contemporary American Poetry, The, 1950-1980. *Stuart Friebert and David Young, eds.* (1983) Longman

LiTA Little Treasury of American Poetry, A. *Oscar Williams, ed.* (1948) Charles Scribner's Sons

LiTB Little Treasury of British Poetry, A. *Oscar Williams, ed.* (1951) Charles Scribner's Sons

LiTM Little Treasury of Modern Poetry, A, English and American. *Oscar Williams, ed.* (3d ed., 1970) Charles Scribner's Sons

LLLT Love Is like the Lion's Tooth; an Anthology of Love Poems. *Frances McCullough, ed.* (1984) Harper & Row

LP "Language" Poetries; an Anthology. *Douglas Messerli, ed.* (1987) New Directions Publishing Corporation

LPSS †Love Poems from Spain & Spanish America. *Perry Higman, ed. and tr.* (1986) City Lights Bookstore

Ma †Manyoshu, The. Foreword by Donald Keene. (1965) Columbia University Press

MAP †Modern Arabic Poetry; an Anthology. *Salma Khadra Jayyusi, ed.* (1987) Columbia University Press

MAT Messages; a Thematic Anthology of Poetry. *X. J. Kennedy, ed.* (1973) Little, Brown & Company

MAYP *Morrow Anthology of Younger American Poets, The. *Dave Smith and David Bottoms, eds.* (1985) Quill (A Division of William Morrow & Company)

MeEL Medieval English Lyrics; a Critical Anthology. *R. T. Davies, ed.* (1964) Northwestern University Press

MeLP Metaphysical Lyrics & Poems of the Seventeenth Century; Donne to Butler. *Herbert J. C. Grierson, ed.* (1921) Oxford University Press

MePo Metaphysical Poets, The. *Helen Gardner, ed.* (1957) Penguin Books

Mes Messages; a Book of Poems. *Naomi Lewis, comp.* (1985) Faber and Faber

MexPo †Mexican Poetry; an Anthology. *Octavio Paz, comp.; Samuel Beckett, tr.* (1985) Grove Press

MHeP †Modern Hebrew Poetry. *Bernhard Frank, ed. and tr.* (1980) University of Iowa Press

MHuP †Modern Hungarian Poetry. *Mikls Vajda, ed.* (1977) Columbia University Press

MMA Men Who March Away; Poems of the First World War. *I. M. Parsons, ed.* (1965) The Viking Press

MoAB Modern American & British Poetry. *Louis Untermeyer, ed., in consultation with Karl Shapiro and Richard Wilbur.* (Rev., shorter ed., 1955) Harcourt, Brace and Company

MoAmPo Modern American Poetry. *Louis Untermeyer, ed.* (8th rev. ed., 1962) Harcourt, Brace and Company

MoBrPo Modern British Poetry. *Louis Untermeyer, ed.* (7th rev. ed., 1962) Harcourt, Brace and Company

MoBS   Modern Ballads and Story Poems. *Charles Causley, ed.* (1965) Franklin Watts (English edition, published in 1964 by Brockhampton Press Ltd., had title Rising Early)

MoCV   Modern Canadian Verse. *A. J. M. Smith, ed.* (1967) Oxford University Press

MoP   Modern Poems; an Introduction to Poetry. *Richard Ellmann and Robert O'Clair, eds.* (1976) W. W. Norton & Company

MOS   Moods of the Sea; Masterworks of Sea Poetry. *George C. Solley and Eric Steinbaugh, comps.* (1981) Naval Institute Press

MoShBr   Moon Is Shining Bright as Day, The; an Anthology of Good-humored Verse. *Ogden Nash, ed.* (1953) J. B. Lippincott Company

MOWH   Music of What Happens, The; Poems That Tell Stories. *Paul B. Janeczko, comp.* (1988) Orchard Books

MPAW   †Modern Poetry of the Arab World. *Abdullah al-Udhari, ed. and tr.* (1986) Penguin Books

MT   Made Thing, The; an Anthology of Contemporary Southern Poetry. *Leon Stokesbury, ed.* (1987) The University of Arkansas Press

NA   Nonsense Anthology, A. *Carolyn Wells, comp.* (1930) Charles Scribner's Sons (Paperback edition of 1958 published by Dover Publications)

NAAL 1-2   Norton Anthology of American Literature, The, Vols. I-II. *Nina Baym and others, eds.* (2d ed., 1985) W. W. Norton & Company

NAEL 1-2   Norton Anthology of English Literature, The, Vols. I-II. *M. H. Abrams, general ed.* (5th ed., 1986) W. W. Norton & Company

NAmP   New American Poets of the 80's. *Jack Myers and Roger Weingarten, eds.* (1984) Wampeter Press

NaP   Naked Poetry; Recent American Poetry in Open Forms. *Stephen Berg and Robert Mezey, eds.* (1969) The Bobbs-Merrill Company

NAs   Naked Astronaut, The; Poems on Birth and Birthdays. *René Graziani, ed.* (1983) Faber and Faber

NAWM 1-2   Norton Anthology of World Masterpieces, The, Vols. I-II. *Maynard Mack, general ed.* (5th ed., 1985) W. W. Norton & Company

NBLV   *Norton Book of Light Verse, The. *Russell Baker, ed.* (1986) W. W. Norton & Company

NBP   New Black Poetry, The. *Clarence Major, ed.* (1969) International Publishers Company

NeAC   New American and Canadian Poetry. *John Gill, ed.* (1971) Beacon Press

NeAP   New American Poetry, The, 1945-1960. *Donald M. Allen, ed.* (1960) Grove Press

NeIP   New Irish Poets. *Devin A. Garrity, ed.* (1948) The Devin-Adair Company

NePoEA   New Poets of England and America. *Donald Hall, Robert Pack, and Louis Simpson, eds.* (1957) Meridian Books

NePoEA-2   New Poets of England and America; Second Selection. *Donald Hall and Robert Pack, eds.* (1962) Meridian Books

NIP   *Norton Introduction to Poetry, The. *J. Paul Hunter, ed.* (3d ed., 1986) W. W. Norton & Company

NItP   †New Italian Poetry, The, 1945 to the Present; a Bilingual Anthology. *Lawrence R. Smith, ed. and tr.* (1981) University of California Press

NMM   No More Masks! an Anthology of Poems by Women. *Florence Howe and Ellen Bass, eds.* (1973) Doubleday Anchor Books

NNaP   New Naked Poetry, The; Recent American Poetry in Open Forms. *Stephen Berg and Robert Mezey, eds.* (1976) The Bobbs-Merrill Company

NoAM   *Norton Anthology of Modern Poetry, The. *Richard Ellmann and Robert O'Clair, eds.* (2d ed., 1988) W. W. Norton & Company

NOBA   *New Oxford Book of American Verse, The. *Richard Ellmann, ed.* (1976) Oxford University Press

NOBC   New Oxford Book of Canadian Verse in English, The. *Margaret Atwood, comp.* (1982) Oxford University Press

NOBE   **New Oxford Book of English Verse, The, 1250-1950. *Helen Gardner, ed.* (1972) Oxford University Press

NOBL   New Oxford Book of English Light Verse, The. *Kingsley Amis, ed.* (1978) Oxford University Press

NOBVV   New Oxford Book of Victorian Verse, The. *Christopher Ricks, ed.* (1987) Oxford University Press

NOCV   New Oxford Book of Christian Verse, The. *Donald Davie, ed.* (1981) Oxford University Press

NOEC   New Oxford Book of Eighteenth Century Verse, The. *Roger Lonsdale, ed.* (1984) Oxford University Press

NOIV   New Oxford Book of Irish Verse, The. *Thomas Kinsella, ed. and tr.* (1986) Oxford University Press

NoP   **Norton Anthology of Poetry, The. *Alexander W. Allison and others, eds.* (3d ed., 1983) W. W. Norton & Company

NOVW   New and Old Voices of Wah'kon-tah; Contemporary Native American Poetry. *Robert K. Dodge and Joseph B. McCullough, eds.* (1985) International Publishers Company

NPGG   19 New American Poets of the Golden Gate. *Philip Dow, ed.* (1984) Harcourt Brace Jovanovich

NPo   P.E.N. New Poetry I. *Robert Nye, ed.* (1986) Quartet Books

NTCP   New Treasury of Children's Poetry, A; Old Favorites and New Discoveries. *Joanna Cole, comp.* (1984) Doubleday & Company

NU   News of the Universe; Poems of Twofold Consciousness. *Robert Bly, comp.* (1980) Sierra Club Books

NYBP   New Yorker Book of Poems, The. (1969) The Viking Press. (Paperback edition of 1974 published by William Morrow & Company)

OAEL 1-2   Oxford Anthology of English Literature, The, Vols. I-II. *Frank Kermode and John Hollander, general eds.* (1973) Oxford University Press (Also published as six paperback vols.: Medieval English Literature, *J. B. Trapp, ed.;* The Literature of Renaissance England, *John Hollander*

and *Frank Kermode, eds.;* The Restoration and the Eighteenth Century, *Martin Price, ed.;* Romantic Poetry and Prose, *Harold Bloom and Lionel Trilling, eds.;* Victorian Prose and Poetry, *Lionel Trilling and Harold Bloom, eds.;* Modern British Literature, *Frank Kermode and John Hollander, eds.*)

OBAL   *Oxford Book of American Light Verse, The. *William Harmon, ed.* (1979) Oxford University Press

OBCA   *Oxford Book of Children's Verse in America, The. *Donald Hall, ed.* (1985) Oxford University Press

OBCP   Oxford Book of Christmas Poems, The. *Michael Harrison and Christopher Stuart-Clark, eds.* (1983) Oxford University Press

OBCV   Oxford Book of Canadian Verse in English and French, The. *A. J. M. Smith, ed.* (1960) Oxford University Press

OBD   Oxford Book of Death, The. *D. J. Enright, ed.* (1987) Oxford University Press

OBET   Oxford Book of English Traditional Verse, The. *Frederick Woods, ed.* (1983) Oxford University Press

OBEV   Oxford Book of English Verse, The, 1250-1918. *Sir Arthur Quiller-Couch, ed.* (New ed., rev. and enl., 1939) Oxford University Press

OBMV   Oxford Book of Modern Verse, The, 1892-1935. *William Butler Yeats, ed.* (1936) Oxford University Press

OBNC   Oxford Book of Nineteenth-Century English Verse, The. *John Hayward, ed.* (1964; reprinted, with corrections, 1965) Oxford University Press

OBNV   Oxford Book of Narrative Verse, The. *Iona Opie and Peter Opie, eds.* (1983) Oxford University Press

OBS   Oxford Book of Seventeenth Century Verse, The. *H. J. C. Grierson and G. Bullough, eds.* (1934) Oxford University Press

OBSC   Oxford Book of Sixteenth Century Verse, The. *E. K. Chambers, comp.* (1932) Oxford University Press

OBSV   Oxford Book of Satirical Verse, The. *Geoffrey Grigson, comp.* (1980) Oxford University Press

OBTV   Oxford Book of Travel Verse, The. *Kevin Crossley-Holland, ed.* (1986) Oxford University Press

OBVE   †Oxford Book of Verse in English Translation, The. *Charles Tomlinson, ed.* (1980) Oxford Univeristy Press

OBWP   *Oxford Book of War Poetry, The. *Jon Stallworthy, ed.* (1984) Oxford University Press

OBWVE   †Oxford Book of Welsh Verse in English, The. *Gwyn Jones, comp.* (1977) Oxford University Press

OFD   O Frabjous Day! Poetry for Holidays and Special Occasions. *Myra Cohn Livingston, ed.* (1977) Atheneum

OHFP   One Hundred and One Famous Poems. *Roy J. Cook, comp.* (Rev. ed., 1958) Reilly & Lee Company; reprinted 1981 by Contemporary Books

OHIP   Our Holidays in Poetry. *Mildred P. Harrington and Josephine H. Thomas, comps*. (1929) The H. W. Wilson Company

OnMSP   100 More Story Poems. *Elinor Parker, comp*. (1960) Thomas Y. Crowell Company

OnUR   Once upon a Rhyme; 101 Poems for Young Children. *Sara Corrin and Stephen Corrin, eds*. (1982) Faber and Faber

OPOP   100 Poems by 100 Poets; an Anthology. *Harold Pinter, Geoffrey Godbert, and Anthony Astbury, comps*. (1986) Grove Press

OPP   101 Patriotic Poems. (1986) Contemporary Books

OV   †Other Voice, The; Twentieth-Century Women's Poetry in Translation. *Joanna Bankier and others, eds*. (1976) W. W. Norton & Company

OxBA   Oxford Book of American Verse, The. *F. O. Matthiessen, ed*. (1950) Oxford University Press

OxBB   Oxford Book of Ballads, The. *James Kinsley, ed*. (1969) Oxford University Press

OxBC   Oxford Book of Contemporary Verse, The, 1945-1980. *D. J. Enright, comp*. (1980) Oxford University Press

OxBChV Oxford Book of Children's Verse, The. *Iona Opie and Peter Opie, eds*. (1973) Oxford University Press

OxBLMV Oxford Book of Late Medieval Verse and Prose, The. *Douglas Gray, ed*. (1985) Clarendon Press

OxBoLi Oxford Book of Light Verse, The. *W. H. Auden, ed*. (1938) Oxford University Press

OxBS   Oxford Book of Scottish Verse, The. *John MacQueen and Tom Scott, comps*. (1966) Oxford University Press

OxBSP   Oxford Book of Short Poems, The. *P. J. Kavanagh and James Michie, eds*. (1985) Oxford University Press

OxBSS   Oxford Book of Sea Songs, The. *Roy Palmer, ed*. (1986) Oxford University Press

OxBTC   *Oxford Book of Twentieth-Century English Verse, The. *Philip Larkin, ed*. (1973) Oxford University Press

OxNR   *Oxford Nursery Rhyme Book, The. *Iona Opie and Peter Opie, comps*. (1955) Oxford University Press

PAH   Poems of American History. *Burton Egbert Stevenson, ed*. (Rev. ed., 1922) Houghton Mifflin Company

Par   Parodies; an Anthology from Chaucer to Beerbohm--and After. *Dwight Macdonald, ed*. (1960) The Modern Library

PBA   †Poems from Black Africa. *Langston Hughes, ed*. (1963) Indiana University Press

PBBP   Penguin Book of Bird Poetry, The. *Peggy Munsterberg, ed*. First published by Allen Lane 1980; published in Penguin Books 1984

PBCV   †Penguin Book of Caribbean Verse in English, The. *Paula Burnett, ed*. (1986) Penguin Books

PBMUP   †Penguin Book of Modern Urdu Poetry, The. *Mahmood Jamal, ed. and tr*. (1986) Penguin Books

PBWP   **Penguin Book of Women Poets, The. *Carol Cosman, Joan Keefe, and Kathleen Weaver, eds.* (1978) Penguin Books

PChr   Poems of Christmas. *Myra Cohn Livingston, ed.* (1980) Atheneum

PCP   Postcard Poems; a Collection of Poetry for Sharing. *Paul B. Janeczko, ed.* (1979) Bradbury Press

PDV   Piping down the Valleys Wild; Poetry for the Young of All Ages. *Nancy Larrick, ed.* (1968) Delacorte Press

PeBJV   †Penguin Book of Japanese Verse, The. *Geoffrey Bownes and Anthony Thwaite, trs.* Introduction by Geoffrey Bownes. (1964) Penguin Books

PeBMYV   †Penguin Book of Modern Yiddish Verse, The. *Irving Howe, Ruth R. Wisse, and Khone Shmeruk, eds.* (1987) Viking Penguin

PeHV   Penguin Book of Homosexual Verse, The. *Stephen Coote, ed.* (1983) Penguin Books

PeNZ   Penguin Book of New Zealand Verse, The. *Ian Wedde and Harvey McQueen, eds.* (1985) Penguin Books

Per   †Peru; the New Poetry. *David Tipton, ed.* (1977) Red Dust

PeSA   †Penguin Book of South African Verse, The. *Jack Cope and Uys Krige, eds.* (1968) Penguin Books

PF   Poorhouse Fugitives, The; Self-taught Poets and Poetry in Victorian Britain. *Brian Maidment, ed.* (1987) Carcanet

PFI   †Poems from Italy. *William Jay Smith and Dana Gioia, eds.* (1985) New Rivers Press

PLW   †Poems of Love and War from the Eight Anthologies and the Ten Long Poems of Classical Tamil. *A. K. Ramanujan, comp. and tr.* (1985) Columbia University Press

PoA   Poetry Anthology, The, 1912-1977. *Daryl Hine and Joseph Parisi, eds.* (1978) Houghton Mifflin Company

PoAu 1-2   Poetry in Australia, Vols. I-II. Vol. I: From the Ballads to Brennan, *T. Inglis Moore, comp.*; Vol. II: Modern Australian Verse, *Douglas Stewart, comp.* (1965) University of California Press

PoBA   **Poetry of Black America, The; Anthology of the 20th Century. *Arnold Adoff, ed.* (1973) Harper & Row

PoE   Poetry in English; an Anthology. *M. L. Rosenthal, general ed.* (1987) Oxford University Press

PoEl 1-5   Poets of the English Language, Vols. I-V. *W. H. Auden and Norman Holmes Pearson, eds.* (1950) The Viking Press. Vol. I: Langland to Spenser; Vol. II: Marlowe to Marvell; Vol. III: Milton to Goldsmith; Vol. IV: Blake to Poe; Vol. V: Tennyson to Yeats

PoLF   Poems That Live Forever. *Hazel Felleman, ed.* (1965) Doubleday & Company

PoM   Postmoderns, The; the New American Poetry Revised. *Donald Allen and George F. Butterick, eds.* (1982) Grove Press

PoNe   Poetry of the Negro, The, 1746-1970. *Langston Hughes and Arna Bontemps, eds.* (Rev. ed., 1970) Doubleday & Company

PoPo   Portraits of Poets. *Sebastian Barker, ed.* (1986) Carcanet

PoRA	Poems to Read Aloud. *Edward Hodnett, ed.* (Rev. ed., 1967) W. W. Norton & Company
POS	Poetry of Surrealism, The; an Anthology. *Michael Benedikt, ed. and tr.* (1974) Little, Brown and Company
PoSH	Poems of the Scottish Hills; an Anthology. *Hamish Brown, comp.* (1982) Aberdeen University Press
PPP	Poetry: Past and Present. *Frank Brady and Martin Price, eds.* (1974) Harcourt Brace Jovanovich
PPR	Ploughshares Poetry Reader, The. *Joyce Peseroff, ed.* (1987) Ploughshares Books
Prf	Preferences; 51 American Poets Choose Poems from Their Own Work and from the Past. *Richard Howard, ed.* (1974) The Viking Press
PrIm	Practical Imagination, The; an Introduction to Poetry. *Northrop Frye, Sheridan Baker, and George Perkins.* (1983) Harper & Row
Pro	†Proensa; an Anthology of Troubadour Poetry. *Paul Blackburn, comp. and tr.; George Economou, ed.* (1986) Paragon House Publishers
Psk	Poetspeak; in Their Work, about Their Work. *Paul B. Janeczko, comp.* (1983) Bradbury Press
PwPP	†Postwar Polish Poetry; an Anthology. *Czeslaw Milosz, ed.* (3d ed., enl., 1983) University of California Press
PWR	Poetry Worth Remembering; an Anthology of Poetry. *Roy W. Watson, comp.* (1986) Brunswick Publishing Company
PYC	Poems for Young Children. *Caroline Royds, comp.* (1986) Doubleday & Company
QFR	Quest for Reality; an Anthology of Short Poems in English. *Yvor Winters and Kenneth Fields, eds.* (1969) The Swallow Press
RAR	Read-Aloud Rhymes for the Very Young. *Jack Prelutsky, comp.* (1986) Alfred A. Knopf
RB	Rattle Bag, The; an Anthology of Poetry. *Seamus Heaney and Ted Hughes, comps.* (1982) Faber and Faber
RFM	Room for Me and a Mountain Lion; Poetry of Open Space. *Nancy Larrick, comp.* (1974) M. Evans and Company
RHPC	**Random House Book of Poetry for Children, The. *Jack Prelutsky, ed.* (1983) Random House
RHTwFP	†Random House Book of Twentieth-Century French Poetry, The. *Paul Auster, ed.* (1982) Random House
RR	Rhythm Road; Poems to Move To. *Lillian Morrison, comp.* (1988) Lothrop, Lee & Shepard Books
SaC	Saturday's Children; Poems of Work. *Helen Plotz, comp.* (1982) Greenwillow Books
SCAP	Seventenenth-Century American Poetry. *Harrison T. Meserole, ed.* (1968) Doubleday Anchor Books
SCV	Six Centuries of Verse. *Anthony Thwaite, ed.* (1984) Thames Methuen
SD	Sprints and Distances; Sports in Poetry and the Poetry in Sport. *Lillian Morrison, comp.* (1965) Thomas Y. Crowell Company

SeCePo Seven Centuries of Poetry; Chaucer to Dylan Thomas. *A. N. Jeffares, ed.* (1955) Longmans, Green & Company

SeCP Seventeenth Century Poetry; the Schools of Donne and Jonson. *Hugh Kenner, ed.* (1964) Holt, Rinehart and Winston

SeCV 1-2 Seventeenth-Century Verse and Prose, Vols. I-II. Vol. I: 1600-1660; Vol. II: 1660-1700. *Helen C. White, Ruth C. Wallerstein, and Ricardo Quintana, eds.* (1951, 1952) The Macmillan Company

SiPS Silver Poets of the Sixteenth Century (Everyman's Library). *Gerald Bullett, ed.* (1947) J. M. Dent & Sons Ltd.

SM *Strong Measures; Contemporary American Poetry in Traditional Forms. *Philip Dacey and David Jauss, eds.* (1986) Harper & Row

SO Straight On Till Morning; Poems of the Imaginary World. *Helen Hill, Agnes Perkins, and Alethea Helbig, comps.* (1977) Thomas Y. Crowell Company

Son Sonnet, The; an Anthology. *Robert M. Bender and Charles L. Squier, eds.* (1987) Washington Square Press/Pocket Books

SOP †Salt of Pleasure: Twentieth-Century Finnish Poetry. *Aili Jarvenpa, tr.* (1983) New Rivers Press

SoSe Sound and Sense; an Introduction to Poetry. *Laurence Perrine, ed., with the assistance of Thomas R. Arp.* (6th ed., 1982) Harcourt Brace Jovanovich

SoTCo Sometime the Cow Kick Your Head; Light Year '88/9. *Robert Wallace, ed.* (1988) Bits Press

SOTW *Sleeping on the Wing; an Anthology of Modern Poetry with Essays on Reading and Writing. *Kenneth Koch and Kate Farrell.* (1981) Random House

SSI †Songs of the Saints of India. *John Stratton Hawley, ed.* (1988) Oxford University Press

STE Songs from This Earth on Turtle's Back; Contemporary American Indian Poetry. *Joseph Bruchac, ed.* (1983) The Greenfield Review Press

STP Shaking the Pumpkin; Traditional Poetry of the Indian North Americans. *Jerome Rothenberg, ed.* (Rev. ed., 1986) Alfred van der Marck Editions

StPo Story Poems, New and Old. *William Cole, ed.* (1957) The World Publishing Company

SV Singular Voices; American Poetry Today. *Stephen Berg, ed.* (1985) Avon Books

TAP *Treasury of American Poetry, The. *Nancy Sullivan, ed.* (1978) Doubleday & Company

TDD This Delicious Day. *Paul B. Janeczko, comp.* (1987) Orchard Books

TEP *Treasury of English Poetry, The. *Mark Caldwell and Walter Kendrick, eds.* (1984) Doubleday & Company

TIRV Treasury of Irish Religious Verse. *Patrick Murray, ed.* (1986) The Crossroad Publishing Company

TOF Tongues of Fire; an Anthology of Religious and Poetic Experience. *Karen Armstrong, ed.* (1987) Penguin Books

TrCP   Treasury of Christian Poetry, The. *Lorraine Eitel, comp., with Jeannine Bohlmeyer, Lynn M. Fauth, Gerald W. Healy, Daniel Taylor, and Christian Weintz.* (1982) Fleming H. Revell Company

TrGrPo   Treasury of Great Poems, English and American, A. *Louis Untermeyer, ed.* (Rev. and enl. ed., 1955) Simon and Schuster

TrJP   †Treasury of Jewish Poetry, A. *Nathan Ausubel and Marynn Ausubel, eds.* (1957) Crown Publishers

TrPWD   Treasury of Poems for Worship and Devotion, A. *Charles L. Wallis, ed.* (1959) Harper & Brothers

TSL   This Sporting Life. *Emilie Buchwald and Ruth Roston, eds.* (1987) Milkweed Editions

TSM   Toward Solomon's Mountain; the Experience of Disability in Poetry. *Joseph L. Baird and Deborah S. Workman, eds.* (1986) Temple University Press

TSS   These Small Stones. *Norma Farber and Myra Cohn Livingston, comps.* (1987) Harper & Row

TTTS   **Talking to the Sun; an Illustrated Anthology of Poems for Young People. *Kenneth Koch and Kate Farrell, eds.* (1985) The Metropolitan Museum of Art/Henry Holt and Company

TTY   3000 Years of Black Poetry. *Alan Lomax and Raoul Abdul, eds.* (1970) Dodd, Mead & Company

TV   Tangled Vines; a Collection of Mother and Daughter Poems. *Lyn Lifshin, ed.* (1978) Beacon Press

TW   Tygers of Wrath; Poems of Hate, Anger, and Invective. *X. J. Kennedy, ed.* (1981) The University of Georgia Press

TwCP   Twentieth Century Poetry; American and British (1900-1970). *John Malcolm Brinnin and Bill Read, eds.* (1963, rev. ed., 1970). McGraw-Hill Book Company (Text edition entitled The Modern Poets)

UAS   Under Another Sky; an Anthology of Commonwealth Poetry Prize Winners. *Alastair Niven, ed.* (1987) Carcanet

UL   American Poetry since 1970: Up Late. *Andrei Codrescu, ed.* (1987) Four Walls Eight Windows

UnAS   Under All Silences; Shades of Love. *Ruth Gordon, comp.* (1987) Harper & Row

UnPo   Understanding Poetry. *Cleanth Brooks and Robert Penn Warren, eds.* (4th ed., 1976) Holt, Rinehart and Winston

UnS   Untune the Sky; Poems of Music and the Dance. *Helen Plotz, comp.* (1957) Thomas Y. Crowell Company

VGW   Voice That Is Great within Us, The; American Poetry of the Twentieth Century. *Hayden Carruth, ed.* (1970) Bantam Books

VMG   †Voices of Modern Greece. *Edmund Keeley and Philip Sherrard, trs. and eds.* (1981) Princeton University Press

Vol   †Volcán; Poems from Central America. *Alejandro Murgua and Barbara Paschke, eds.* (1983) City Lights Books

VoR   Voices of the Rainbow; Contemporary Poetry by American Indians. *Kenneth Rosen, ed.* (1975) The Viking Press

VVA   Vampire in Verse, The; an Anthology. *Steven Moore, ed.* (1985) Dracula Press

VWA   †Voices within the Ark; the Modern Jewish Poets. *Howard Schwartz and Anthony Rudolf, eds.* (1980) Avon Books

WaaP   War and the Poet; an Anthology of Poetry Expressing Man's Attitudes to War from Ancient Times to the Present. *Richard Eberhart and Selden Rodman, eds.* (1945) The Devin-Adair Company

WaP   War Poets, The; an Anthology of the War Poetry of the 20th Century. *Oscar Williams, ed.* (1945) The John Day Company

WBLP   World's Best Loved Poems, The. *James Gilchrist Lawson, comp.* (1927) Harper & Row

WCI   World Comes to Iowa, The; Iowa International Anthology. *Paul Engle, Rowena Torrevillas, and Hualing Nieh Engle, eds.* (1987) Iowa State University Press

WeW   Western Wind; an Introduction to Poetry. *John Frederick Nims, ed.* (2d ed., 1983) Random House

WFTU   †Waiting for the Unicorn; Poems and Lyrics of China's Last Dynasty, 1644-1911. *Irving Yucheng Lo and William Schultz, eds.* (1986) Indiana University Press

WFTW   †Waiting for the Wind; Thirty-six Poets of Japan's Late Medieval Age. *Steven D. Carter, tr. and ed.* (1989) Columbia University Press

WGRP   World's Great Religious Poetry, The. *Caroline Miles Hill, ed.* (1954) The Macmillan Company

WiR   Wind and the Rain, The; an Anthology of Poems for Young People. *John Hollander and Harold Bloom, eds.* (1961) Doubleday & Company

WMBCH   †When My Brothers Come Home; Poems from Central and Southern Africa. *Frank Mkalawile Chipasula, ed.* (1985) Wesleyan University Press

WPE   Women Poets in English, The; an Anthology. *Ann Stanford, ed.* (1972) McGraw-Hill Book Company

WPOW   Women Poets of the World. *Joanna Bankier and Deirdre Lashgari, eds.* (1983) Macmillan Publishing Company

WS   Watchers and Seekers; Creative Writing by Black Women. *Rhonda Cobham and Merle Collins, eds.* (1988) Peter Bedrick Books

WSC   Why Am I Grown So Cold? Poems of the Unknowable. *Myra Cohn Livingston, ed.* (1982) Atheneum

WT   †Women Troubadours, The. *Meg Bogin, ed.* (1980) W. W. Norton & Company

WTO   †World Treasury of Oral Poetry, A. *Ruth Finnegan, ed.* (1978) Indiana University Press

ZPCJ   †Zen Poems of China & Japan; the Crane's Bill. *Lucien Stryk, Takashi Ikemoto, and Taigan Takayama, trs.* (1973) Grove Press

ABBREVIATIONS

abr.	abridged	*N.T.*	New Testament
ad.	adapted	*O.T.*	Old Testament
add.	additional	*orig.*	original
arr.	arranged	*par.*	paraphrase *or* paraphrased
at.	attributed	*pr.*	prose
Bk.	book	*Pt.*	part
br.	brief	*rev.*	revised
ch.	chapter	sc.	scene
comp.	compiled *or* compiler	*Sec.*	section
comps.	compilers	*sel.*	selection
cond.	condensed	*sels.*	selections
diff.	different	*sl.*	slightly
fr.	from	*st.*	stanza
frag.	fragment	*sts.*	stanzas
incl.	included *or* including	*tr.*	translator, translation, *or* translated
introd.	introduction *or* introductory		
ll.	lines	*trs.*	translators *or* translations
med.	medieval	*var.*	various
misc.	miscellaneous	*vers.*	version *or* versions
mod.	modernized *or* modern	*wr.*	wrong *or* wrongly

TITLE AND FIRST LINE INDEX

Titles and first lines are arranged in one alphabetical listing in the Title and First Line Index. Titles are distinguished by initial capital letters on the important words. All first line entries are followed by the title of the poem, if there is a title. When the title and first line of a poem are identical, or nearly so, only the title is listed, although occasionally, for purposes of clarity, the first line has been added in quotation marks and in parentheses to the title entry.

Symbols are listed after both titles and first lines. However, more complete information as to translators, acts and scenes, abridgements, and variant titles is given in the first line entry.

Indented listings below an entry have the following significance; a single indentation indicates a selection from the above work; double indentation, within parentheses, signifies a variant title or first line as used in the anthologies that follow.

Mother Goose rhymes are listed by first line only, rather than by the numerous arbitrary titles assigned to them by anthologists.

Generic title entries, such as Ode, Song, Sonnet, are followed by the first line in quotation marks for easy identification. Such entries, of course, may also be located by first line listing.

Titles and first lines beginning with "O" and "Oh" are filed separately, with cross-references where necessary. Names beginning "Mac," "Mc," and "M'" are filed as if all were spelled "Mac."

"A" (1–12), *sels.* Louis Zukofsky. VGW
  "A 11" ("River that must turn full after I stop dying."). *Fr.* 11.
  "A 4" ("Giant sparkler,/ Lights of the river."). *.r.* 4.
A, a, a, Domine Deus. David Jones. FaBoTw; NOCV
A, a noble failure, turns his critical wits on B. Names. D. J. Enright. FaBoCo
A and B. Charles Hubert Sisson. OxBC
ABC, An. *Unknown. See* New England Primer, The: In Adam's fall/ We sinned all.
A B C D. *Unknown.* OxNR
A, B, C, D, E, F, G. Alphabet. *Unknown.* FaBoUs
A, B, C, D, E, F, G, Little Robin Redbreast. *Unknown.* OxNR
A B C D Goldfish. *Unknown.* NTCP
A.B.C. of Devotion, An. *Unknown.* MeEL
A B C's in Green. Leonora Speyer. OHIP
A Cappella. Michael Pettit. GrPl
A celuy que plus eyme en mounde. *Unknown. Fr.* Lines from Love Letters, I. OBEV
  (To the One I Love Most.) MeEL
A' day aboot the hoose I work. Nocht o' Mortal Sicht. Bessie J. B. Macarthur. OxBS
A dis [h], a dis [h], a green grass. Green Grass. *Unknown.* BoTP; CH; GBP; OxBoLi; OxNR
A. E. F. Carl Sandburg. CMoP; MoAB; MoAmPo; WaaP
A. E. Housman and a Few Friends. Humbert Wolfe. BXAP; FiBHP; Par
A E I O U. Swift. BoTP
"A 11" ("River that must turn full after I stop dying."). Louis Zukofsky. *Fr.* "A" (1–12), 11. VGW
"A 4" ("Giant sparkler,/ Lights of the river."). Louis Zukofsky. *Fr.* "A" (1–12), 4. VGW
A! [*or* Ah!] fredome [*or* freedom] is a noble thing! Freedom [*or* Fredome]. John Barbour. *Fr.* The Bruce. FaBoCh; GoTS; OBEV; OxBS; TrGrPo
A ha ha ha! this world doth passe. Idle Fyno. *Unknown.* ChTr; PoEL-2

A ho! A ho!/ Love's horn doth blow. Thomas Lovell Beddoes. *Fr.* The Bride's Tragedy. ChER
A-Hunting. Jennie Dunbar. BoTP
A. "I was a Have." B. "I was a 'Have–not.' " Equality of Sacrifice. Kipling. *Fr.* Epitaphs of the War, 1914–1918. FaBoTw
A is for Alex. Line-up for Yesterday. Ogden Nash. SD
A is for axes, you very well know. The Lumberman's Alphabet. *Unknown.* AmFP
A is for the anchor we carry on the bow. The Bargeman's ABC. *Unknown.* OxBSS
A is the aftermost part of the ship. The Sailors' Alphabet. *Unknown.* AmFP
A la Bourbon. Richard Lovelace. CaPo
A la Promenade. Paul Verlaine, *tr.* by Arthur Symons. AWP; OBVE
À l'Ange Avantgardien. Francis Reginald. MoCV
"A l'usage de M. et Mme. van Gramberen." Eilean Ni Chuilleanain. *Fr.* The Rose-Geranium, IV. CIP
"À Madame, Madame B, Beauté Sexagenaire." Charles Sackville. APAS
"A, my dere, a, my dere Son." Mary Weeps for Her Child. *Unknown.* OxBSS
A peels an apple, while B kneels to God. A Primer of the Daily Round. Howard Nemerov. NYBP; SM; WeW
A Perigord pres del muralh. Bertrans de Born, *tr. fr. Provençal* by Ezra Pound. CTC
A Propos of the Wet Snow, *sel.* Nikolai Alekseyevich Nekrasov, *tr. fr. Russian* by Juliet Soskice.
  "When from dark error's subjugation." NAWM-2
À Quoi Bon Dire. Charlotte Mew. OxBTC
A. R. U. *Unknown.* AS
A soun tres chere et special. *Unknown. Fr.* Lines from Love Letters, II. OBEV
A. Stands for Absolutely Anything. Noel Coward. *Fr.* The Little Ones' A. B. C. NBLV
A stands for Archibald who told no lies. Hilaire Belloc. *Fr.* A Moral Alphabet. NoAM

A' things created have their uses. Strictures on the Economy of Nature. George Outram. FaBoCo

A to Amerous, to Adventurous, ne Angre the not to moche. The Alphabet of Aristotle. Mayster Benet. FaBoUs

A tumbled down, and hurt his Arm, against a bit of wood. Alphabet. Edward Lear. FaBoNo

A. U. C. 334: about this date. Advice to Young Ladies. A. D. Hope. NiP; NoAM; NoP

A, U, Hinny Burd. *Unknown.* GBP

A was an apple pie, B bit it, C cut it. Mother Goose. FaBoUs; OxNR

A was an archer, who shot at a frog. *Unknown.* FaBoUs; OxBChV; OxNR

A was an Army, to settle disputes. A Single-Rhyme Alphabet. *Unknown.* FaBoUs

A was once an apple-pie. An Alphabet. Edward Lear. OxBChV

A ye wha are sae guid yoursel. *See* O ye wha are sae guid yoursel.

Aa the skippers of bonny Lothen. Young Allan. *Unknown.* ESPB

Aa went te Blaydon Races, 'twas on the ninth o' June. Blaydon Races. *Unknown.* ELP

Aardvark. Julia Fields. CNA; OFD

Aardvark, The. Christopher Logue. NPo

Aaron. George Herbert. MeLP; MePo; OAEL-1; OBS

Aaron Burr's Wooing. Edmund Clarence Stedman. PAH

Aaron Hatfield. Edgar Lee Masters. *Fr.* Spoon River Anthology. LiTA

Aaron is a man of mystery. Man of Mystery. Dahlia Ravikovich, *tr. by* Warren Bargad *and* Stanley F. Chyet. IP

Aaron Nicholas, Almost Ten. Janet Campbell Hale. VoR

Aaron Stark. E. A. Robinson. MoAB; MoAmPo; Son

Abalone. *Unknown.* AS

Abalone, like inkfish. The Relaxed Abalone. Rosemarie Waldrop. InPK

Abandonado, El. *Unknown, tr. fr. Spanish by* Frank J. Dobie. AS

Abandoned, The. Mririda n'Ait Attik, *tr. fr. Berber into French by* René Euloge, *English vers. by* Daniel Halpern *and* Paula Paley. OV

Abandoned boat, An. Boncho, *tr. fr. Japanese by* Hiroaki Sato. *Fr.* Twenty-one Hokku. FCEI

Abandoned child, The. National Library. Oswald de Andrade, *tr. by* Jean R. Longland. ATCBP

Abandoned earthworks nobody tends. Su Tung-p'o, *tr. fr. Chinese by* Burton Watson. *Fr.* Eastern Slope. CoBCP

Abandoned Garden. Kikuchi Gozan, *tr. fr. Chinese by* Burton Watson. JLIC-2

Abandoned House, The. Patricia Hubbell. WSC

Abandoned House in Late Light. Chase Twichell. MAYP

Abandoned mandolin, An. Appetite of Quiet Enchantment. Martin Seymour-Smith. NPo

Abandoned, Overgrown Cemetery in the Pasture near Our House, An. Gregory Orr. MAYP

Abandoning Your Car in a Snowstorm: Rosslyn, Virginia. Michael C. Blumenthal. NoAM

Abandonment of Autos. Bruce Dawe. CBAP

Abasis. Christopher Middleton. *Fr.* Herman Moon's Hourbook. NePoEA-2

Abate, fair fugitive, abate thy speed. Daphne and Apollo. Ovid, *tr. fr. Latin by* Matthew Prior. *Fr.* Metamorphoses, I. NOEC

Abbé Liszt, The. Liszt. E. C. Bentley. *Fr.* Clerihews. UnS

Abbey Church at Bath, The. Henry Harington. FaBoEE

Abbot is painting me so true. On His Portrait. William Cowper. EyDe

Abbot of Inisfalen, The. William Allingham. GN; OnMSP; TIRV

Abbreviated Interviews with a Few Disgruntled Literary Celebrities. Reed Whittemore. FiBHP

Abdelazer, *sels.* Aphra Behn.
    "Love in fantastic [*or* fantastique] triumph sate [*or* satt]." NOBE; WPE
    (Song: "Love in fantastic triumph sate.") OBEV; TrGrPo

Abdelfatteh. E. A. Lacey. PeHV

Abdication of Fergus Mac Roy, The. Sir Samuel Ferguson. AnIL

Abdication of Noman, The. Richard Henry Stoddard. AnAmPo

Abduction, The. Stanley Kunitz. BLA; CAPP; SV

Abdul, the Bulbul Ameer. *Unknown.* AS, *with music*
    (Abdullah Bulbul Amir; or, Ivan Petrofsky Skovar.) FPL

Abdullah Bulbul Amir; or, Ivan Petrofsky Skovar. *Unknown. See* Abdul, the Bulbul Ameer.

A-Begging Buttermilk I Will Go. *Unknown.* OBET

Abel. Demetrios Capetanakis. GTBS-P; WaaP

Abel. Else Lasker-Schüler, *tr. fr. German by* Joachim Neugroschel. VWA

Abel was fair and woolly. Dan Pagis, *tr. by* Shirley Kaufman. VWA (Brothers.) *Tr. by* Bernhard Frank. MHeP

Abelard was: God is. Sic et Non. Sir Herbert Read. FaBoTw

Abel's Blood. Henry Vaughan. OBWVE

Abel's Bride. Denise Levertov. FaBoWP; VGW

Abenamar, Abenamar. *Unknown, tr. fr. Spanish by* Robert Southey. AWP

Aberdarcy: The Chaucer Road. Kingsley Amis. *Fr.* The Evans Country. NOBL

Aberdarcy: The Main Square. Kingsley Amis. *Fr.* The Evans Country. NoAM; NOBL; OxBTC

Aberdare, Llanwynno through. Glyn Cynon Wood. *Unknown, tr. by* Gwyn Williams. OBWVE

Aberdeen University 1945-49: I. Iain Crichton Smith. *Fr.* A Life. UAS

Abhorrent to all natural joys. Epigram: To Philaenis. Martial. PeHV

Abide in Me, O Lord, and I in Thee. Harriet Beecher Stowe. AH

Abide Not in the Realm of Dreams. William Henry Burleigh. AH

Abide with Me. Henry Francis Lyte. BLRP; EBVV; FaBoBe; FaFP; FaPoR; NOCV; PWR; TIRV; WBLP; WGRP

Abiding Love, The. John White Chadwick. BLPA; FaBoBe

Abiding snake. Prologue: Moments in a Glade. Alan Stephens. QFR

Abigail's Lamentation for the Loss of Mr. Harley. William Walsh. APAS

Abiku. Wole Soyinka. PBA

Abishag. Jacob Fichman, *tr. fr. Hebrew.* TrJP, *trs. by* Robert Friend, *and by* Sholom J. Kahn; VWA, *tr. by* Sholom J. Kahn

Abishag. Jacob Glatstein, *tr. fr. Yiddish by* Benjamin *and* Barbara Harshav *and* Kathryn Hellerstein. AYP

Abishag. Rainer Maria Rilke, *tr. fr. German by* Jethro Bithell. AWP

Abishag. André Spire, *tr. fr. French by* Emanuel Eisenberg. TrJP

Abishag sits in her room and writes a letter home. Abishag Writes a Letter Home. Itzig Manger, *tr. by* Ruth Whitman. VWA

Abla. Antar. *Fr.* The Mu'allaqat. AWP

Able at last to stop. Old People on the Nursing Home Porch. Mark Strand. CAPP

Abnegation. Adrienne Rich. WPE

Abner Silver's "Pu-leeze! Mr. Hemingway!" Ring Lardner. OBAL

Abnormal Is Not Courage, The. Jack Gilbert. CoAP; NPGG

Aboard a Boat at Night, Drinking with My Wife. Mei Yao-ch'en, *tr. fr. Chinese by* Burton Watson. CoBCP

Aboard a Boat, Reading Yüan Chen's Poems. Po Chü-i, *tr. fr. Chinese by* Burton Watson. CoBCP

Aboard a Ship Leaving Yokohama. Narushima Ryuhoku, *tr. fr. Chinese by* Burton Watson. JLIC-2

Aboard at a Ship's Helm. Walt Whitman. NOBA; OxBA

Aboard the Santa Maria. Gyula Illyés, *tr. fr. Hungarian by* William Jay Smith. MHuP

Abode of the nightingale is bare, The. Alone. Walter de la Mare. ChTr; EnLoPo

Abode of the Roaming Immortals. Cheng Ch'ou-yu, *tr. fr. Chinese by* Dominic Cheung. IFON

Abominable Baseball Bat, The. X. J. Kennedy. WSC

Aborigine. Hugo Williams. OBTV

Abortion. Ai. BoWoP

Abortion, An. Frank O'Hara. TAP

Abortion, The. Anne Sexton. CAPP; IHMS; MAT; NMM; SM; VGW

Abortions will not let you forget. The Mother. Gwendolyn Brooks. A Street in Bronzeville. BlSi; BPo; CAPP; FaBoWP; NMM

Abou Ben Adhem. Leigh Hunt. BeLS; BLPA; EnRP; FaBoBe; FaBV; FaFP; FaPoR; FPL; NOBE; OBEV; OHFP; PWR; WBLP; WGRP (Abou Ben Adhem and the Angel.) FaBoRV; FaPON; GN

Abou Ben Adhem's name led all the rest. Holy Order. John Basil Boothroyd. FiBHP

About. James Sherry. LP

About a fly. The Story. Charles Simic. NNaP

About a quarter to ten the door softly opened. Listening to Beethoven on the Oregon Coast. Henry Carlile. Psk

About a Year After He Got Married He Would Sit Alone in an Abandoned Shack in a Cotton Field Enjoying Himself. James Whitehead. MT

About an Excavation. Charles Reznikoff. NTCP; PCP; PrIm; VGW

About ane bank, where birdis on bewis. *At. to* Alexander Montgomerie. GoTS

About beef, for instance? Christmas. Leigh Hunt. OBCP

About Children. Phyllis McGinley. OBAL

About Feet. Margaret Hillert. RHPC

About four, a few flakes. Six Winter Privacy Poems. Robert Bly. LCAP

About her head or floating feet. My Father's Child. "Stuart Sterne." AA

About his brow the laurel and the bay. A Man! Clinton Scollard. OHIP

About in London. John Gay. *Fr.* Trivia; or, The Art of Walking the Streets of London. FaBoPP

About Marriage. Denise Levertov. NMM

About me the night, moonless, wimples the mountains. Vancouver Lights. Earle Birney. CaP

About Motion Pictures. Ann Darr. GrPl

About mountains it is useless to argue. Alpine. R. S. Thomas. BoNaP; RFM

About My Poems. Donald Justice. PoA

About one month before my thirty-third. Thinking of You. Dick Lourie. NeAC

About people, no, I don't know how they feel. Teika, *tr. fr. Japanese by* Hiroaki Sato. *Fr.* A Compendium of Good Tanka. FCEI

About Savannah. *Unknown.* PAH

About suffering they were never wrong. Musée des Beaux Arts. W. H. Auden. CMoP; FaFP; FF; GTBS-P; HAP; HeIP; InPK; InPS; LiTB; LiTM; MoAB; MoP; NAEL-2; NIP; NoAM; NOBE; NoP; PoE; PoRA; PPP; PrIm; PrIM; SCV; SeCePo; SoSe; TEP; TrCP; TrGrPo; TwCP; WeW

About the august and ancient Square. Oxford Nights. Lionel Johnson. BrPo

About the cool water. Sappho, *tr. fr. Greek by* Kenneth Rexroth. ErPo; OBVE

"About the dead, no murmur of dispraise." Elegy for a Bad Poet, Taken from Us Not Long Since. John Frederick Nims. TW

About the Fairies. Jean Ingelow. BoTP

About the Hero. Mihály Ladányi, *tr. fr. Hungarian by* Edwin Morgan. MHuP

About the hilltop how the clouds are cool. Summer Days. Roy Daniells. CaP

About the little chambers of my heart. Gone. Mary Elizabeth Coleridge. OBEV; OBNC

About the night on which a man said he would spend a 100 dollars. Epilogue: Anemone. Leslie Scalapino. *Fr.* Hmmmm. NPGG

About the Phoenix. James Merrill. NoAM

About the shark, phlegmatical one. The Maldive Shark. Herman Melville. AmPP; AnAmPo; MOS; NAAL-1; NOBA; NoP; OxBA; PoE; PoEL-5; RB; TAP; TW

About the size of an old-style dollar bill. Elizabeth Bishop. FYAP; HCAP; NoAM

About the skull of the beloved, filled. Presentation Piece. Marilyn Hacker. AmPA

About the Teeth of Sharks. John Ciardi. OBCA

About the time I miss someone. Kaya Shirao, *tr. fr. Japanese by* Hiroaki Sato. *Fr.* Twenty-one Hokku. FCEI

About the year of one B.C. Jonah and the Whale. *Unknown.* BLPA

About their prince each took his wonted seat. Pluto's Council. Tasso, *tr. fr. Italian by* Edward Fairfax. *Fr.* Godfrey of Bulloigne; or, The Recoverie of Jerusalem. OBSC

About This Book. Mechthild of Magdeburg, *tr. fr. German by* Susan L. Cocalis. DMG

About This Course. David Shapiro. PoA

About this lady many fruitful trees. The Lady with the Unicorn. Vernon Watkins. LiTB; TwCP

About those who have recognized the range of choice. It Is Difficult Now to Speak of Poetry. George Oppen. *Fr.* Of Being Numerous. NNaP

About to Die. *Gond Oral Tradition, tr. by* V. Elwin *and* S. Hivale. WTO

About twenty years ago. Wild Oats. Philip Larkin. InPS

About twilight we came to the whitewashed pub. East Coast Journey. James Keir Baxter. NoP; PeNZ

About two miles east of here. The King Cobra as Political Assassin. Ray A. Young Bear. HATNAP

About two thousand miles. Coming Home. John Stone. NIP

About us in white mist, ptarmigan. February Thaw. G. J. F. Dutton. PoSH

About women no one can know. There are some. Mary Magdalene. Saunders Lewis, *tr. by* Gwyn Morgan. OBWVE

About Women's Liberation. María Saucedo, *tr. fr. Spanish by* Toni Empringham. FIA

About Yule, when [*or* quhen] the wind blew cule. Young Waters. *Unknown.* ESPB; OxBB, *with music*

Above a clear, penetrating wind. Teika, *tr. fr. Japanese by* Hiroaki Sato. *Fr.* Eighty-four Tanka. FCEI

Above a rock. Guita Bruner. Pablo Guevara, *tr. by* Maureen Ahern *and* David Tipton. Per

Above a stretch of still unravaged weald. The Garden Party. Donald Davie. NePoEA

Above, above. Behold. *Unknown, tr. by* M. K. Pukui. WTO

Above all gifts we most should prize. Walter Savage Landor. FaBoEE

Above all, to my love I'll be attentive. Sonnet on Fidelity. Vinícius de Moraes, *tr. by* Ashley Brown. ATCBP

Above and below the ship, this blue. Becalmed. John Blight. PoAu-2

Above, below, in sky and sod. The Over-Heart. Whittier. NOCV; WGRP

Above Ben Loyal. Arthur Ball. PoSH

Above crimson leaves. Teika, *tr. by* Steven D. Carter. WFTW

Above dried-up/ river beds. Salt Gardens. Christine Busta, *tr. by* Beth Bjorklund. CoAuP

Above every seaward-facing window. The Hotel Brown Poems. John Ash. NPo

Above finespun, unruffled sheets. Lovebirds. William Jay Smith. ErPo

Above her sash. Iida Dakotsu, *tr. by* Geoffrey Bownas *and* Anthony Thwaite. PeBJV

Above in the clear. Tamenori, *tr. by* Steven D. Carter. WFTW

Above Inverkirkaig. Norman MacCraig. PoSH

Above It All. Philip Levine. NOBA

Above Lancaut, in a sequestered dell. Tintern Abbey. Edward Davies. *Fr.* Chepstow: A Poem. OBWVE

Above Machu Picchu, 129 Baker Street, San Francisco. Joseph Stroud. NPGG

Above me the abbey, grey arches on the cliff. Caedmon. Norman Nicholson. FaBoTw

Above my desk/ the Rabbi of Auschwitz. On a Drawing by Flavio. Philip Levine. VWA

Above my desk, whirring and self-important. Angel. James Merrill. CAPP; PoA

Above my face is a map. The Cloud-Mobile. May Swenson. SO

Above my half of the world. To My Unknown Friend. Irina Ratushinskaya, *tr. by* David McDuff. AIW

Above my head the apples on my grandparents' tree. Skins. Elizabeth Spires. MAYP

Above my uncle's grocery store. Door Number Four. Charlotte Pomerantz. ILY

Above Ohara/ the fallen snow has piled up. Prince Munenaga, *tr. by* Steven D. Carter. WFTW

Above, on the wall, sexy frescoes are her intentions. Pure Notations. Steve Levine. UL

Above Pate Valley. Gary Snyder. CoAP; LCAP; NaP; NoP

Above Stromness, the Hills of Hoy rise proud. Lion Gate. Vera Rich. PoSH

Above the Arno. May Swenson. NYBP

Above the branches, the frosty air pure. Humming My Verse, in My Leisure, beneath Blossoming Cassia Trees. Yün Shou-p'ing, *tr. by* Irving Lo. WFTU

Above the Bright Blue Sky, *sel.* Albert Midlane. "There's a Friend for little children." OxBChV

Above the cascade running [*or* tumbling] down the rocks. Prince Shiki, *tr. fr. Japanese.* *Fr.* Manyo Shu. FCEI, *tr. by* Hiroaki Sato; Ma

Above the Crags that fade and gloom. From a Window in Princes Street. W. E. Henley. EBVV

Above the Dock. T. E. Hulme. FaBoMo; GTBS-P

Above the Falls at Waimea. Don Johnson. MAYP

Above the fence-flowers, like a bloody thumb. Variations on Southern Themes. Donald Justice. BLA; MT; SV

Above the freeway, over the music. Jazz Station. Michael S. S. Harper. NoAM

Above the fresh ruffles of the surf. Hart Crane. *Fr.* Voyages (I–VI), I. AmPP; MoP; MOS; NAAL-2; OxBA; PoE; VGW

Above the height of Mikasa in Kasuga. *Unknown, tr. fr. Japanese.* *Fr.* Manyo Shu. Ma

Above the High. Geoffrey Grigson. EnLoPo

Above the Medway. A. J. Munby. *Fr.* The Vales of the Medway. FaBoPP

Above the north mountain-range. Empress Jito, *tr. fr. Japanese.* *Fr.* Manyo Shu. Ma

Above the pines the moon was slowly drifting. Dickens in Camp. Bret Harte. AnAmPo

Above the place where children play. A Sussex Legend. Charles Dalmon. BoTP

Above the plains. Of Only a Single Poem. G. J. F. Dutton. PoSH

Above the Pool. John Montague. NOIV

Above the pools, above the valley of fears. Élévation. Baudelaire, *tr. by* Arthur Symons. AWP

Above the quiet dock in midnight. Above the Dock. T. E. Hulme. FaBoMo; GTBS-P

Above the quiet valley and unrippled lake. Spring Oak. Galway Kinnell. BoNaP

Above the river, heavy on the heart, thousandfold hills. Written on a Painting Entitled "Misty Yangtze and Folded Hills." Su Tung-p'o, *tr. by* Burton Watson. CoBCP

Above the rocking heads of the mothers. Nelly Sachs, *tr.* by Ruth *and* Matthew Mead. PBWP

Above the roof. Landscape. Lucio Piccolo, *tr. fr. Italian by* Charles Tomlinson. *Fr.* Anna Perenna. PFI

Above the snuffle and scurry. Sometimes Music Rises. Wayne Dodd. KS

Above the sounds that echo eerily. The Unreturning Native. Basil Dowling. ATNZ

Above the stream, grunting Staoineag stands. Staoineag. Leen Volwerk. PoSH

Above the tracks. Exile. Ray di Palma. IAT

Above the treetops. Masaoka Shiki, *tr. fr. Japanese by* Burton Watson. *Fr.* Thirty-nine Haiku. FCEI

Above the turf. Golfer. Gloria A. Maxson. *Fr.* Epitaphs. SoTCo

Above the twelve mountains autumn grasses fade. Bamboo Branch Song. Ho Ching-ming, *tr.* by Jonathan Chaves. CoBLCP

Above the violent park. A Star. George MacBeth. NYBP

Above the voiceful windings of a river. At the Grave of Henry Vaughan. Siegfried Sassoon. CMoP; EaLo; GTBS-P

Above the wind the starlight is clear. Teika, *tr. fr. Japanese by* Hiroaki Sato. *Fr.* Eighty-four Tanka. FCEI

Above them spread a stranger sky. The Indian's Welcome to the Pilgrim Fathers. Lydia Huntley Sigourney. AA

Above these bleak Wyoming plains. Winter Juniper. Joseph Langland. NePoEA

Above These Cares. Edna St. Vincent Millay. NoP

Above this bramble-overarched long lane. The Clearing. Robert Graves. NYBP

Above this limitless morass. Ravel's Bolero. Gerrit Achterberg, *tr.* by James Brockway. DuIn

Above, through lunar woods a goddess flees. The Lovers. William Jay Smith. MoAmPo

Above us, stars. Beneath us, constellations. Flying at Night. Ted Kooser. InPK

Above yon sombre swell of land. The Plough. Richard Henry Horne. OBEV

Above, you paint the sky. How to Paint a Perfect Christmas. Miroslav Holub, *tr.* by George Theiner *and* Ian Milner. OBCP

Abraham. George Bogin. GOYP

Abraham. Stephen Mitchell. VWA

Abraham. Delmore Schwartz. VWA

Abraham. Eisig Silberschlag. VWA

Abraham and Hagar/ a marriage torn asunder. The Story of Abraham and Hagar. Edna Aphek, *tr.* by Yishai Tobin. VWA

Abraham and Isaac. Else Lasker-Schüler, *tr. fr. German.* BoWoP, *tr. by* Rosemarie Waldrop; VWA, *tr.* by Joachim Neugroschel.

Abraham and Sarah. Itzig Manger, *tr. fr. Yiddish by* Stephen Garrin. VWA

Abraham built a town of sod. Abraham and Isaac. Else Lasker-Schüler, *tr.* by Rosemarie Waldrop. BoWoP

Abraham Davenport. Whittier. AmPP; NoP

Abraham in Egypt. Howard Schwartz. VWA

Abraham in the land of Eden. Abraham and Isaac. Else Lasker-Schüler, *tr.* by Joachim Neugroschel. VWA

Abraham Lincoln. A. S. Ames. OHIP

Abraham Lincoln. Henry Howard Brownell. GN

Abraham Lincoln. Bryant. *See* Death of Lincoln, The.

Abraham Lincoln. Samuel Valentine Cole. OHIP

Abraham Lincoln. Edmund Clarence Stedman. PAH

Abraham Lincoln. Richard Henry Stoddard. AA; AnAmPo; FaBoBe; GN; OHIP; PAH

Abraham Lincoln. Tom Taylor. PAH

Abraham Lincoln, the Dear President. The Dear President. John James Piatt. PAH

Abraham Lincoln, the Master. Thomas Curtis Clark. OHIP

Abraham Lincoln Walks at Midnight. Vachel Lindsay. AmFN; AmPP; CMoP; FaBV; FaFP; FaPON; GOA; LiTA; MoAmPo; NOBA; OFD; OHFP; OHIP; OxBA; PAH; TAP; VGW

Abraham Sutskever. Seymour Mayne. VWA

Abraham was the name. Abraham. George Bogin. GOYP

Abraham's children played with shells. Hagar and Ishmael. Else Lasker-Schüler, *tr.* by Rosemarie Waldrop. BoWoP

Abraham's little sons played with seashells. Hagar and Ishmael. Else Lasker-Schüler, *tr.* by Joachim Neugroschel. VWA

Abram Bailey he'd three sons. Sir Lionel. *Unknown.* AmFP

Abram Brown. *Unknown.* OxNR

Abroad. Ilse Aichinger, *tr. fr. German by* Beth Bjorklund. CoAuP

Abroad as I Was Walking ("Abroad as I was walking/ Down by some green woodside"). *Unknown.* OBET

Abroad as I was walking/ All on a summer's day. Young Barnswell. *Unknown.* OBET

Abroad in the meadows to see the young lambs. Innocent Play. Isaac Watts. NOEC

Abroad on a winter's night there ran. A Christmas Legend. Frank Sidgwick. OHIP

Abroad Thoughts. Edward Blishen. NOBL

Abroad Thoughts from Home. Donald Hall. NePoEA

Abruptly All the Palm Trees. William Jay Smith. PoA

Absalom. Zerubavel Gilead, *tr. fr. Hebrew by* Dorothea Krook. VWA

Absalom. Yona Wallach, *tr. fr. Hebrew by* Warren Bargad *and* Stanley F. Chyet. IP

Absalom and Achitophel, Pt. I. Dryden. NoP; OAEL-1; SeCV-2 *Sels.*

  Achitophel: The Earl of Shaftsbury. NOBE

  "In pious times ere [*or* e'r] priestcraft did begin." FaBoPV; HAP; NoP; OAEL-1; PoE; SeCV-2

  "In the first rank of these did Zimri stand." HAP

    (Zimri ("In the first rank of These did Zimri stand.").) SeCePo

  Malcontents, The. OBS

  "Of these the false Achitophel was first." HAP; InPS; PoEL-3

    (Achitophel.) AWP, *br. sel.*; SeCePo

    (False Achitophel, The.) FiP

    (Shaftsbury.) OBS

  Popish Plot, The. ACP

  "Some by their friends, more by themselves thought wise." OBSV

  "Some of their chiefs were princes of the land." EBEV; SCV

    (Zimri ("Some of their chiefs were princes of the land").) AWP

  "With all these loads of injuries opprest." EBEV

  Zimri: The Duke of Buckingham. NOBE; OBSV

    (Zimri ("Numerous host of dreaming saints succeed.").) AWP; SeCePo

Absalom and Achitophel, Pt. II, *sels.* Dryden *and* Nahum Tate.

  "Doeg, though without knowing how or why." PoEL-3

  "Next These, a troop of busy [*or* buisy] spirits press." PPP; SeCV-2

  Og [and Doeg]. AWP; FiP; TW

  Thomas Shadwell the Poet. ChTr

  "To make quick way I'll leap o'er heavy blocks." OBSV

Absence. John Hoskyns, *sometimes at.* to John Donne. MeLP; OPOP

Absence. Richard Jago. OBEV

Absence. Ruth Kim Chun-soo, *tr. fr. Korean by* Koh Chang-soo. ACKP

Absence. Elizabeth Knies. GOYP

Absence. Walter Savage Landor. *See* Ianthe: Ianthe! you resolve [*or* are called] to cross the sea!

Absence, The. Denise Levertov. NaP

Absence. Claude McKay. CDC

Absence. Charlotte Mew. MoAB; MoBrPo

Absence. Shakespeare. *See* Being your slave, what should I do but tend.

Absence. Sir Philip Sidney. SiPS

Absence. *Unknown. See* Western Wind.

Absence, The. Sylvia Townsend Warner. MoBrPo

Absence absenting causeth me to complain. Sir Thomas Wyatt. SiPS

Absence and Presence. Fulke Greville. *See* Caelica: Absence, the noble truce.

Absence, hear thou my [*or* heare my] protestation. Absence. John Hoskyns, *sometimes at.* to John Donne. MeLP; OPOP

  (Ode: "Absence, hear thou my protestation.") EIl

  (Present in Absence.) GTBS; GTBS-P

Absence, the noble truce. Fulke Greville. *Fr.* Caelica, XLV [XLIV]. PoEL-1

  (Absence and Presence.) OBSC

Absent, The. Edwin Muir. NoAM

Absent Daughter. Barend Toerien, *tr. fr. Afrikaans by the author.* PeSA

Absent Friends. Anne Bloch. *Fr.* Separation. Mes

Absent from thee, I languish still. Earl of Rochester. BoLoP; ELP; EnLoPo; GBL; MePo; OBS; SeCePo; SeCV-2

  (Return.) NOBE; OBEV

Absent Lover. *Unknown, tr. fr. Xhosa by* A. C. Jordan. PBA

Absent, this morning. Aube Provençale. Marilyn Hacker. AmPA

Absentee, The. Denise Levertov. ER

Absinthe-Drinker, The. Arthur Symons. BrPo; FaBoTw; NOBVV

Absolute, An/ patience. The Breathing. Denise Levertov. NaP; RFM

Absolute and Abitofhell. Ronald Arbuthnott Knox. CenHV; FaBoCo

Absolute Faith. Kim Hyun-sung, *tr. fr. Korean by* Koh Chang-soo. ACKP

Absolute, pity the visionless. Address to an Absolute. Roy McFadden. NeIP

Absolute Solitude. Kim Hyun-sung, *tr. fr. Korean by* Koh Chang-soo. ACKP

Absolute zero: the locust sings. Summer. Conrad Aiken. NoAM
Absolutely abstemious ass
Absolutely abstemious ass, The. Animal Alphabet, A. Edward Lear. RB
Absolutely Ordinary Rainbow, An. Les A. Murray. CBAP
Absolution. Siegfried Sassoon. MMA
Absolution. Edward Willard Watson. AA
Absolvers, The. Robert Southey. Fr. A Vision of Judgement. EnRP
Abstemia. Gelett Burgess. NA
Abstinence. Kenneth Rosen. AmPA
Abstinence Sows Sand All Over. Blake. Fr. Gnomic Verses. EBEV;
FaBoEE; FF; GBL; TrGrPo
Abstracted, sour, as he reaches across a dish. Scylla and Charybdis.
Thomas Kinsella. OxBTC
Abstrosophy. Gelett Burgess. CenHV; NA
Absurd!/ at my age. Unknown, tr. fr. Japanese by Burton Watson. Fr.
Manyo Shu. FCEI
Abt Vogler. Robert Browning. GoTL; NAEL-2; OAEL-2; TOF; WGRP
Abu. Dudley Randall. BPo
Abu Nowas for the Barmacides. Unknown, tr. fr. Arabic by E. Powys
Mathers. Fr. The Thousand and One Nights. AWP
Abukbo. Jim Barnes. Fr. Four Things Choctaw. HATNAP
Abundant is the year, with much millet, much rice. Unknown, tr. by
Arthur Waley. BoS
Abusing Scripture, cursing Zen. Giun, tr. by Lucien Stryk and Takashi
Ikemoto. ZPCJ
Aby Kirly, the War Hero. Moyshe-Leyb Halpern, tr. fr. Yiddish by
Benjamin and Barbara Harshav. AYP
Abysmal corners will dis (be) located. Vitality. Maria Amalia Fonte
Boa, tr. by Willis Barnstone and Nelson Cerqueira. BoWoP
Abyss. X. J. Kennedy. BLA
Abyss of Death, The. Ma ruf al-Rasafi, tr. fr. Arabic by Issa Boullata and
Christopher Middleton. MAP
Acacia is drooping, The. Girl from Rafah. Samih al-Qasim, tr. by Sharif
Elmusa and Charles Doria. MAP
Acacia Tree, The. "Zelda," tr. fr. Hebrew by Bernhard Frank. MHeP
Acacias' gold and red are falling. One-sided Love. Kitahara Hakushu,
tr. by Hiroaki Sato. FCEI
Academic. Theodore Roethke. FaBoEE; OBAL
Academic Curse; an Epitaph. Wesli Court. TW
Academics? Politics? I've nothing to do with them! Liu E, tr. fr. Chinese
by Jonathan Chaves. Fr. On the Twenty-fourth: Improvisations.
CoBLCP
Acadia, sel. Joseph Howe.
"In ev'ry thought, in ev'ry wish I own." CaP
Acadian Lane. David St. John. SM
Acceleration near the Point of Impact. Joyce Carol Oates. GeTw
Accent back home, The. Unknown, tr. by Geoffrey Bownas and Anthony
Thwaite. PeBJV
Accent Schmaccent. J. F. O'Connor. SoTCo
Accept each gift, though it be small. Lines for a Wedding Gift. W.
Wesley Trimpi. NePoEA
Accept, my God, the praises which I bring. The Offering: Part One.
Mary Lee, Lady Chudleigh. WPE
Accept, my love, as true a heart. Les Estreines. Matthew Prior.
OxBSP
Accept, thou shrine of my dead saint. The Exequy. Henry King. GBL;
HAP; InPS; InvP; JCP; MeLP; NAEL-1; NoP; OBS; PoEL-2; PrIm;
QFR; SeCeP; SeCP; TEP
(Exequy on [or upon] His Wife.) BoLoP; NOBE; OBEV
(Exequy, The: To His Matchlesse Never to Be Forgotten Friend.)
MePo
Acceptance. Robert Frost. CMoP; OxBA
Acceptance Speech. Marvin Bell. AmPA
Acceptance Speech. Jayne Cortez. ER
Acceptation. Margaret Junkin Preston. PAH
Access, The. Henry Kanabus. UL
Accident, The. Len Gasparini. NeAC
Accident, The. Wu Sheng, tr. fr. Chinese by Dominic Cheung. IFON
Accident/ that took my leg, The. Mirage. A. C. Sumrall. TSM
Accident Has Occurred, The. Margaret Atwood. NMM
Accident or the gods. Subplot. Jack Butler. MT
Accidentally. Maxine W. Kumin. RHPC
Accidents. Alfred Dorn. SoTCo
Accidents of Birth. William Meredith. NoP
Accidents will happen—still, in time. A Bedtime Story. Robert Mezey.
NePoEA
(If I Should Die before I Wake.) NYBP
Acclaim the dawn of Mother's Day! Mother's Day. E. Becker. PWR
Accommodating Lion, An. Tudor Jenks. OBCA
Accompanist, The. William Matthews. BLA

Accompanying a Gift ("From thy patient, who while here"). Lizelia
Augusta Jenkins Moorer. CBWP-3
Accompanying a Gift ("One whose love will never end"). Lizelia Augusta
Jenkins Moorer. CBWP-3
Accomplices, The. Conrad Aiken. NOBA
Accordance. Henry Kanabus. UL
According to Brueghel. Landscape with the Fall of Icarus. William
Carlos Williams. Fr. Pictures from Brueghel, II. LCAP; NAAL-2;
NOAM; PPP
According to Einstein's theory of relativity. Spinning Yarns, Relatively
Speaking. Peter Payack. BWV
According to metaphysical creed. Her Education. Thomas Hood. Fr.
Miss Kilmansegg and Her Precious Leg. EBVV
According to some learn'd opinions. Irish Antiquities. Thomas Moore.
FaBoEE
"According to the Mighty Working." Thomas Hardy. CMoP
According to the silence, winter has arrived. Shepherd. William
Stafford. PoA
According to the word of the Eternal Being. L'Imprévisibilité. Zinaida
Hippius, tr. by Temira Pachmuss. PBWP
Account of the Cruelty of the Papists, An. Benjamin Harris. SCAP
Accountability. Gerrit Achterberg, tr. fr. Dutch by Adrienne Rich.
DuIn
Accountability. Paul Laurence Dunbar. PoLF
Accountability. William Stafford. LCAP; NoP
Accountant in His Bath, The ("The accountant dried his imperfect back").
Adrian Mitchell. NYBP
Accountants hover over the earth like helicopters. A Dream of
Suffocation. Robert Bly. NaP
Accountings, The. Albert Goldbarth. GeTw
Accumulation of reefs, The. The Distances. Jim Carroll. PoA
Accursed power which stands on Privilege, The. On a General Election.
Hilaire Belloc. FaBoCo; FaBoEE; NOBE; NOBL; OBSV; OxBTC
(On a Great Election.) OxBoLi
Accursed [or Accurst] the man, whom fate ordains, in spite. The Pains of
Education. Charles Churchill. Fr. The Author. FaBoCo
(Against Education.) TW
Accusation. Utahania, tr. fr. Eskimo. WTO
Accusation of the Inward Man, The. Edward Taylor. LiTA
Accused though I be without desert. Sir Thomas Wyatt. SiPS
Achaians Have Got Troy, upon This Very Day, The. Aeschylus, tr. fr.
Greek by Richmond Lattimore. Fr. Agamemnon. WaaP
Ache of Marriage, The. Denise Levertov. FF; InPK; NoAM; NOBA;
PoM; TAP
Ache of wide millions, The. Return of a Reaper. Alan Creighton.
CaP
Achieving perfection beyond the thirteen notes. On Seeing Lute Priest
Off. Enkei, tr. by Lucien Stryk and Takashi Ikemoto. ZPCJ
Achieving Perspective. Pattiann Rogers. MAYP; MT
Achilles, sel. John Gay.
"Think of dress in every light." InvP
(Song: "Think of dress in every light.") OxBSP
Achilles Deatheridge. Edgar Lee Masters. AmFN
Achilles' Heel. Herbert Scott. NAmP
Achilles in Scyros, sel. Philip Bainbrigge.
Chorus of Scyrian Maidens. PeHV
Achilles Shows Himself in the Battle by the Ships. Homer, tr. fr. Greek
by George Chapman. Fr. The Iliad, XVIII. OBS
Achilles to Lycaon. Homer, tr. fr. Greek by Richmond Lattimore. Fr.
The Iliad, XXI. WaaP
Achilles with wild fury in his heart. Homer, tr. fr. Greek by Robert
Fitzgerald. Fr. The Iliad, XXIII. OBWP
Aching. Alfonsina Storni, tr. fr. Spanish by Kate Flores. DMH
Achitophel. Dryden. See Absalom and Achitophel, Pt. I
Achitophel: The Earl of Shaftsbury. Dryden. Fr. Absalom and
Achitophel, Pt. I. NOBE
Achtung. Sappho, tr. fr. Greek by Thomas Hardy. CTC; OBVE
Achtung! Achtung! Mary Hacker. CN
A'Chuilionn. A. G. Hutchison. PoSH
Achziv, sels. Yehuda Amichai, tr. fr. Hebrew by Warren Bargad and
Stanley F. Chyet. IP
"And this is how it begins now, my late." Fr. 5.
"Clouds have come up from the south, the Nile's." Fr. 1.
"Time after time you're placed at the imagined." Fr. 4.
Acis and Galatea, sels. John Gay.
"I rage, I melt, I burn." NAEL-1
Love in Her Eyes. ELP
"O ruddier than the cherry!" ELP; NAEL-1; NOEC
(Song: "O ruddier than the cherry.") NOBE
Acknowledgement. Roberta Hill Whiteman. ER

Acme and Septimius. Catullus, *tr. by* Abraham Cowley. AWP
Acne blossoms scarlet on their cheeks. Porirua Friday Night. Sam Hunt.
   PeNZ
Acoma. William Oandasan. HATNAP
Acon. Hilda Doolittle ("H. D."). VGW
Aconite, The. A. M. Graham. BoTP
Acorn, The. *Unknown*. BoTP
Acorn. Valerie Worth. TSS
Acoustics. Susan Griffin. *Fr*. Woman and Nature. NPGG
Acquainted with the Night. Robert Frost. ChTr; CMoP; FPL; HAP;
   LiTM; MoAmPo; MoP; NoAM; NOBA; PDV; PoE; PoLF; PPP; Son;
   SoSe; TAP; TwCP; VGW; WeW
Acre of Grass, An. W. B. Yeats. CMoP; NoAM
Acrobat from Xanadu disdained all nets, The. Dan Georgakas. FF
Acrobat on the border of the sea, An. The Woman That Had More Babies
   than That. Wallace Stevens. LiTA
Acrobatics. Dan Pagis, *tr. fr. Hebrew by* Warren Bargad *and* Stanley F.
   Chyet. IP
Across a city from you, I'm with you. Adrienne Rich. *Fr*. Twenty-one
   Love Poems, XVI. GLP; PeHV
Across a pasture of yellow lillies. Blue Horses; West Winds. Anita
   Endrezze-Danielson. STE
Across a sage-grown upland. The Path of the Padres. Edith D. Osborne.
   AmFN
Across from me in the subway sat the madonna. The Madonna in the
   Subway. A. Leyeles, *tr. by* Benjamin *and* Barbara Harshav.
   AYP
Across Kansas. William Stafford. CAPP
Across North Wales. Dafydd ap Gwilym Resents the Winter. Rolfe
   Humphries. NYBP
Across one of the hills. Illuminations. Leah Goldberg, *tr. by* Robert
   Alter. OV
Across Roblin Lake, two shores away. Wilderness Gothic. Alfred W.
   Purdy. HeIP; MoCV; NOBC; NoP
Across sands as endless as the day. Globetrotter. Washington Delgado,
   tr. by David Tipton. Per
Across Space and Time. Charles Olson. PoM
Across the ages they come thundering. Say This of Horses. Minnie Hite
   Moody. PoLF
Across the barrage, the cities of Europe remember. Homage of War.
   Bruce Williamson. NeIP
Across the Bay. Donald Davie. NoAM
Across the bristled and sallow fields. The Hawk. Raymond Knister.
   OBCV
Across the brook of Time man leaping goes. Laus Mariae. Sidney
   Lanier. Son
Across the correct perspective to the painted sky. Landscape. David
   Gascoyne. FaBoMo
Across the Delaware. Will M. Carleton. PAH
Across the desk. Crocodiles. Mira Teru Kurka. UL
Across the dewy lawn she treads. Paean. Jonathan Henderson Brooks.
   CDC
Across the Eastern sky has glowed. The Crowing of the Red Cock.
   Emma Lazarus. AA
Across the face of the field. Saigyo, *tr. fr. Japanese by* Burton Watson.
   Fr. Sixty-four Tanka. FCEI
Across the field the traveling clowns. Saltimbanques. Guillaume
   Apollinaire, *tr. by* Michael Benedikt. POS
Across the flesh and feeling of soledad. Orisha. Jayne Cortez.
   BlSi
Across the floor flits the mechanical toy. Cirque d'Hiver. Elizabeth
   Bishop. InPS; LiTA
Across the frozen Bering Sea is the invisible border. Nine Below. Joy
   Harjo. ER
Across the greening lawn. A Northern Spring. Gene Baro.
   NePoEA-2
Across the hill stands erect a white man's house. Contrast. Mvula Ya
   Nangolo. WMBCH
Across the millstream below the bridge. The Blue Swallows. Howard
   Nemerov. NoP
Across the moorlands of the Not. Moorlands of the Not. *Unknown*.
   NA
Across the mud the line drags on and on. Ration Party. John Manifold.
   WaP
Across the narrow beach we flit. The Sandpiper. Celia Thaxter. AA;
   FaBoBe; FaPON; GN; OBCA; OxBChV; PWR; WBLP
Across the night. From Creature to Ghost. Pauline Hanson.
   TAP
Across the open countryside. The Unsettled Motorcyclist's Vision of His
   Death. Thom Gunn. NePoEA-2; PoA
Across the Oregon plateau. Men against the Sky. John Haines.
   LCAP

Across the page of history. Lincoln Leads. Minna Irving. OHIP
Across the plain the troop of clowns. Saltimbanques. Guillaume
   Apollinaire, *tr. by* Roger Shattuck. POS
Across the river of Asuka where the birds fly. Hitomaro, *tr. fr. Japanese
   by* Hiroaki Sato. *Fr*. Manyo Shu. FCEI
Across the river of the bird-flying Asuka. Hitomaro, *tr. fr. Japanese.
   Fr*. Manyo Shu. Ma
Across the road. Flock. Lance Henson. VoR
Across the round field, under the dark male tower. The Lovers. Alex
   Comfort. PoA
Across the sand I saw a black man stride. Jamaican Fisherman. Philip
   Sherlock. PVCV
Across the sands of Syria. The Legend of the First Cam-u-el. Arthur
   Guiterman. CenHV
Across the sea will come Adze-head. Adze-Head. *Unknown, tr. by*
   James Carney. BIrV
Across the seas of Wonderland to Mogadore we plodded. Forty Singing
   Seamen. Alfred Noyes. OnMSP
Across the sky run streaks of white light, aching. Before Olympus. John
   Gould Fletcher. MoAmPo
Across the sky the daylight crept. Coventry Patmore. *Fr*. The Angel in
   the House, II, x. GBL
Across the snow the silver bells. Silver Bells. Hamish Hendry.
   BoTP
Across the snowy pastures of the estate. The Fox Who Watched for the
   Midnight Sun. Norman Dubie. LCAP; MAYP
Across the sombre prairie sea. Prairie. Herbert Bates. AA
Across the Stony Mountains, o'er the desert's drouth and sand. The
   Crisis. Whittier. PAH
Across the stony ridges. Ballad of the Drover. Henry Lawson.
   PoAu-1
Across the Straits. Rosemary Dobson. PoAu-2
Across the street, my aunt has lost. Emergency at 8. Geof Hewitt.
   NeAC
Across the street—the freeway. Beneath the Shadow of the Freeway.
   Lorna Dee Cervantes. CCP; ER; FIA
Across the swamps and marshlands of the hours. A Sea-Change: For
   Harold. Joseph Langland. LiTM
Across the swiffling waves they went. The Cruise of the *P. C.
   Unknown*. NA
Across the tracks in Cheyenne, behind the biggest billboard. A Long Way
   outside Yellowstone. Thomas McGrath. VGW
Across the Western Ocean *or* Leave Her, Bullies, Leave Her. *Unknown*.
   AS, *with music*; OxBSS, *with music*
   (Leave Her, Johnny, Leave Her.) OxBSS
Across the winding pond, rising winds ripple the waters. The Deva-like
   Barbarian. Li Hsün, *tr. by* Lois Fusek. ATF
Across the wrack besprinkled bay. The Glaucous-Gull's Death. Daniel
   James O'Sullivan. NeIP
Across this dream of seas blue mountains fall. Between Seasons. Anne
   Welsh. PeSA
Across to the Peloponnese. James Welch. CDW
Across upon this undulated board of verdure chequered bright. David
   Jones. *Fr*. In Parenthesis: The Five Unmistakable Marks.
   NoAm
Acrostic on Wharton, An. *Unknown*. OBSV
Acrostick on Mrs. Elizabeth Hull, An. John Saffin. SCAP
Acrostick on Mrs. Winifret Griffin, An. John Saffin. SCAP
Act. Roque Dalton, *tr. fr. Spanish by* Jack Hirschman. Vol
Act, An. Kenneth Rosen. AmPA
Act, The. William Carlos Williams. SOTW; VGW
Act like a wizard. Ishikawa Takuboku, *tr. fr. Japanese by* Hiroaki Sato.
   Fr. Forty-seven Tanka in Three Lines. FCEI
Act of Faith. Arturo Trías, *tr. fr. Spanish*. InW, *tr. by* Julio Marzán
Act of Love. Robert Creeley. HAP
Act of Love. Vernon Scannell. ErPo
Act I/ Orlando hails. The Five-Minute Orlando Macbeth. George
   MacBeth. NOBL
Act Respecting Indians, An. Lenore Keeshig-Tobias. GOS
Act Six. Peter Goldsworthy. UAS
Actaeon. Rayner Heppenstall. FaBoTw
Acteon. Ovid, *tr. fr. Latin by* Arthur Golding. *Fr*. Metamorphoses, III.
   CTC
Actaeon. *Unknown. See* I Would I Were Actaeon.
Action. James Oppenheim. TrJP
Action of Electricity, The. Erasmus Darwin. *Fr*. The Economy of
   Vegetation. FaBoUs
Action of Invisible Ink, The. Erasmus Darwin. *Fr*. The Economy of
   Vegetation. FaBoUs
Action Rhyme. E. H. Adams. BoTP
Action runs left to right, The. Movies, Left to Right. Robert Sward.
   NYBP

Action shackled. Crossed Wires. Sándor Weöres, tr. by Jascha Kessler. FOC
Action Would Kill It/A Gamble. Robert Adamson. CBAP
Actions. Marcel Schwob, tr. fr. French by William Brown Meloney. TrJP
Acton Beauchamp, Herefordshire. Unknown. FaBoPP; GBP
Actor, The. Thomas Snapp. NYBP
Actors, The, sels. Nizar Qabbani, tr. fr. Arabic by Diana Der Hovanessian and Lena Jayyusi. MAP
  "June war is over, The." Fr. IX.
  "Stage is burned, The." Fr. X.
  "When a helmet becomes God in heaven." Fr. IV.
  "When ideas, when thought itself." Fr. I.
Actor's dead, and memory alone, The. J. B. Henry Cuyler Bunner. AA
Acts of Grace. Steve Orlen. NAmP
Acts passed beyond the boundary of mere wishing. Stephen Spender. OxBTC
Acts without Consequence. Steve Orlen. NAmP
Actual Vision of Morning's Extrusion. Alan Dugan. PPP
Ad Amicam. Francis Thompson. Son
Ad Coelum. William Pattison. OxBSP
Ad Coelum. Harry Romaine. BLPA; FaBoBe
Ad Finem. Heine, tr. fr. German by Elizabeth Barrett Browning. AWP
Ad Finem. Ella Wheeler Wilcox. BLPA; FPL
Ad Henricum Wottonem. Thomas Bastard. FaBoEE; FaBoPP
Ad Johannuelem Leporem, Lepidissimum, Carmen Heroicum. Unknown. FaBoNo
Ad Librum. Samuel Danforth, Jr.. SCAP
Ad Limina. Joseph Campbell. BIrV
Ad Patriam, sel. William Dudley Foulke.
  "Land of my heart,/ What future is before thee?." PGD
Ad Patriam. Clinton Scollard. PAH
Ad Tusserum. Unknown. FaBoUs
Adage, An: "Gardener's rule applies to youth and age, The." H. J. Byron. FaBoUs; NBLV
Adage Concerning a Man and an Old Book, An. Yisroel Shtern, tr. fr. Yiddish by Robert Friend. PeBMYV
Adam. Celia Dropkin, tr. fr. Yiddish by Grace Schulman. PeBMYV
Adam. Anthony Hecht. DiL
Adam. Unknown. See Adam Lay Ibounden.
Adam/ Had 'em. On the Antiquity of Microbes. Strickland W. Gillilan. NBLV
Adam, a brown old vulture in the rain. Ancient History. Siegfried Sassoon. Mes
Adam and Eve. Itzig Manger, tr. fr. Yiddish by Jacob Sonntag. TrJP
Adam and Eve. Milton. See Paradise Lost: So passed they naked on, nor shunned the sight.
Adam and Eve, sels. Karl Shapiro.
  Exile. CRP
  Recognition of Eve, The. MoAB
  Sickness of Adam, The. CRP; MoAB
Adam and Eve. C. H. Sisson. FaBoTw
Adam and Eve at the Garden Gate. Marsha Pomerantz. VWA
Adam and Eve, like us. A Circle. Theodore Spencer. NYBP
Adam and Eve, without serpent. Kendrick Smithyman. ATNZ
Adam and God. Anne Wilkinson. MoCV
Adam Bell, Clim of the Clough, and William of Cloudesly. Unknown. ESPB
  (Adam Bel, Clym of the Cloughe, and Wyllyam of Cloudesle.) OxBB
Adam Birkett took his gun. Birkett's Eagle. Dorothy S. Howard. Mes; MoBS
Adam, David, Samson, Solomon. Christine de Pisan, tr. fr. French by Sarah Spence. Fr. The Epistle to the God of Love. DMF
Adam Fallen. Milton. See Paradise Lost: Descended, Adam to the bower where Eve.
Adam Fallen. Milton. See Paradise Lost: He ended, and they both descend the hill.
Adam in Love. Stephen Mitchell. VWA
Adam, indignant, would not eat with Eve. Paradise Saved. Alec Derwent Hope. OxBC
Adam is a pupil of mine. Athlete. Don Maynard. PoAu-2
Adam is clay, the dumb. Paradise. Chana Bloch. VWA
Adam Lay Ibounden [or Ibowndyn or Ybounden]. Unknown. ChTr; CTC; HAP; InPS; NOBE; NOCV; NoP; OAEL-1; OxBLMV; OxBoLi; PoE; PoEL-1; TOF; WeW
  (Adam.) CH
  (Adam Lay Bound.) NAEL-1
  (Adam Lay in Bondage.) MeEL
  ("O Felix Culpa!") ACP
"Adam, my child, my son." Adam. Anthony Hecht. DiL

Adam on His Way Home. Robert Pack. ErPo
Adam scrivein [or scrivain], if ever it thee bifalle. To Adam, His Scribe. Chaucer. OAEL-1
  (To His Scribe Adam.) NAEL-1
  (Unto Adam, His Own Scriveyn.) OxBSP
Adam Sign, The. Muhammad Abd al-Hayy, tr. fr. Arabic by Matthew Sorenson and Alistair Elliot. Fr. Ode of Signs, I. MAP
Adam Smith. E. C. Bentley. Fr. Clerihews. FaBoCo
Adam Speaks. Milton. See Paradise Lost: Oh, why did God,/ Creator wise.
Adam, the first man, my father said, perfect. Bedtime Story. Dannie Abse. KS
Adam the goodliest man of men since born. Milton. Fr. Paradise Lost, bk. IV, ll. 323–355 abr..
  (Scene in Paradise, A.) GN
Adam to Lilith. Christopher John Brennan. Fr. Lilith. PoAu-1
Adam Unfallen. Milton. See Paradise Lost: O favorable spirit, propitious guest.
Adam was de first man and Eve was de udder. Unknown. Fr. A Metrical Version of the Bible, Said to Have Been Composed by a Negro Christian in the State of Massachusetts, and Published in Louisville, Kentucky, in 1858. FaBoUs
Adam was my grandfather. For All Blasphemers. Stephen Vincent Benét. OxBA
Adam was no fool. He knew that at his age. A Family Matter. Allen Curnow. Fr. Trees, Effigies, Moving Objects, VII. PeNZ
Adams and Liberty. Robert Treat Paine. PAH
Adam's Complaint. Denise Levertov. BoWoP; NNaP
Adam's Curse. W. B. Yeats. BIrV; CMoP; NAEL-2; NoAM; NoP; OAEL-2; SOTW; TEP
Adam's Death. Gabriel Levin. VWA
Adam's Dream. Howard Schwartz. VWA
Adam's Dying. Ridgely Torrence. FYAP
Adam's Ex. Hannah Fox. SoTCo
Adam's Footprint. Vassar Miller. MT; NePoEA
Adam's Hymn in Paradise. Joost van den Vondel, tr. fr. Dutch by Sir John Bowring. WGRP
Adam's Morning Hymn. Milton. See Paradise Lost: These are thy glorious works, Parent of good.
Adam's Song of the Visible World. Ridgely Torrence. TrPWD
Adam's Song to Heaven. Edgar Bowers. QFR
Adam's Task. John Hollander. NIP; NoP; PPP
Adapt Thyself. Shem-Tob ben Joseph Palquera, tr. fr. Hebrew by J. Chotzner. TrJP
Adaption—Year 2000. Edward Wellen. BWV
Adder's Epigrams. Colin Ellis. FaBoEE
Addict, The. Larry Rubin. GoYe
Addiction to the exceptional event. Barbarossa. Hubert Witheford. ATNZ; PeNZ
Addio a la Mamma. Noe Jitrik, tr. fr. Spanish by Yishai Tobin. VWA
Addition to Kipling's "The Dead King (Edward VII), 1910." Max Beerbohm. FaBoEE
Additional Poem, An. John Ashbery. FaBoMo
Additional Verses to Hail Columbia. Oliver Wendell Holmes. PAH
Address. Bruce Smith. Fr. In My Father's House. Son
Address. William Carlos Williams. DiL
Address to a Child during a Boisterous Winter Evening. Dorothy Wordsworth. OxBChV
  (Wind, The.) BoTP
Address to an Absolute. Roy McFadden. NeIP
Address to Children. Theodore Hook. See My little dears who learn to read.
Address to Ethiopia. Priscilla Jane Thompson. CBWP-2
Address to Lady———, Who Asked What the Passion of Love Was? Charles Morris. NOEC
Address to Miss Phillis Wheatley, An, sel. Jupiter Hammon.
  "O come you pious youth! adore." AmPP
Address to Mr. Cross, of Exeter 'Change, on the Death of the Elephant. Thomas Hood. FM
Address to My Infant Daughter, sel. Wordsworth.
  "Hast thou then survived." Par
Address to My Malay Krees. John Leyden. OBTV
Address to My Soul. Elinor Wylie. AWP; LiTM; OxBA
Address to the Dalai Lama. Antonin Artaud, tr. fr. French by Michael Benedikt. POS
Address to the Deil. Burns. EnRP; GoTS; NOEC; OAEL-1; OxBS; PoEL-4
Address to the Plebeians, An, sel. John Learmont.
  "Poor crawlin' bodies, sair neglectit." NOEC
Address to the Refugees. John Malcolm Brinnin. GOA

Address to the Scholars of New England. John Crowe Ransom. GOA; LiTM

Address to the Soul Occasioned by a Rain, An. Edward Taylor. NAAL-1; NOBA; OxBA; PoEL-3

Address to the Unco Guid, or the Rigidly Righteous. Burns. EnRP; NOBE; NOCV; NoP; OxBS; TrGrPo

Address to the Vacationers at Cape Lookout, An. William Stafford. NYBP

Address to Venus. Lucretius, tr. fr. Latin by Spenser. Fr. De Rerum Natura (On the Nature of Things), The Faerie Queene, IV, 10. AWP (Prayer to Venus.) EIL, tr. by Spenser.

Address to Venus. Spenser, fr. the Latin of Lucretius. Fr. The Faerie Queene, De Rerum Natura. AWP (Prayer to Venus.) EIL

Addressed to a Young Lady. William Cowper. See Sweet stream that winds through yonder glade.

Addressed to Haydon. Keats. See Great Spirits Now on Earth.

Ad-dressing of Cats, The. T. S. Eliot. FM

Adela Cathcart, sel. George Macdonald. Sir Lark and King Sun; a Parable. Fr. ch. 16. GN

Adelaide Neilson. William Winter. AA

Adelina Patti. Adah Isaacs Menken. CBWP-1

Adelita ("Adelita's the name of the lady"). Unknown, tr. fr. Spanish by F. S. Curtis, Jr. AS

Adepts, The. Lawrence Durrell. Fr. Eight Aspects of Melissa. ErPo

Adeste Fideles. Unknown. See O Come, All Ye Faithful.

Adew, my King, court, cuntrey, and my kin. To Henry Constable and Henry Keir. Alexander Montgomerie. OxBS

Adhesive Autopsy of Walt Whitman, The. Jonathan Williams. PoM

Adieu. Mary E. Tucker. CBWP-1

Adieu, Adieu, Forever. Priscilla Jane Thompson. CBWP-2

Adieu, adieu! my native shore. Childe Harold's Farewell to England. Byron. Fr. Childe Harold's Pilgrimage. OHFP

Adieu, dear life! here am I left alone. On My Late Dear Wife. Jonathan Richardson. NOEC

Adieu, dear object of my love's excess. Orinda to Lucasia Parting, October, 1661, at London. Katherine Philips. OBS

Adieu, fair isle! I love thy bowers. Farewell to Cuba. Maria Gowen Brooks. AA

Adieu, Farewell, Earth's Bliss[e]. Thomas Nashe. Fr. Summer's Last Will and Testament. CH; EBEV; EIL; ELP; HAP; HeIP; InvP; QFR; TEP; WeW
(Dust Hath Closed Helen's Eye.) SeCePo
(In a Time of Pestilence.) HoPM; OBEV; TrGrPo
(In Plague Time.) FaBoCh; FaPoR; OBSC
(In Time of Pestilence.) NOBE
(Litany in Time of Plague, A.) DL; NAEL-1; NoP; OAEL-1; PoRA; PPP; PrIm
(Lord, Have Mercy on Us.) ChTr
(Song: "Adieu, farewell earth's blisse.") PoEL-2
(Song in Time of Plague.) SCV

Adieu, kind Life, though thou hast often been. Departure. May Riley Smith. AA

Adieu Love, Untrue Love. Unknown. See Unfaithful Shepherdess, The.

Adieu My Lovely Nancy. Unknown. OBET

Adieu, sweet Angus, Maeve and Fand. The Passing of the Shee. John Millington Synge. BIrV; FaBoEE

Adieu the woods and waters' side. Lines on Leaving a Scene in Bavaria. Thomas Campbell. OBNC

Adieu to My Landlady, An. George Farewell. NOEC

Adieu to the alehouse, where pounds I have spent. The Bard's Reformation. Samuel Bamford. PF

Adieu to the pleasure of murder and whoring. Sir Thomas Armstrong's Last Farewell to the World. Unknown. APAS

Adieu, ye joys of La Valette! Farewell to Malta. Byron. OBTV

Adieu, you haughty maiden! Adieu, Adieu, Forever. Priscilla Jane Thompson. CBWP-2

"Adiew, madam my mother dear." Lord Maxwell's Last Goodnight. Unknown. ESPB

Adina. Harold Milton Telemaque. TTY

Adjectives. Moishe Nadir, tr. fr. Yiddish by Joseph Leftwich. TrJP

Adjuration. Charles Enoch Wheeler. AmNP; PoNe

Adjustment. Whittier. WGRP

Adjustments. H. N. Beckerman. TSM

Adlatis parke is wyde and broad. Will Stewart and John. Unknown. ESPB

Adler./ Stekel./ Freud. Three. Judah Leib Teller, tr. fr. Yiddish by Benjamin and Barbara Harshav. Fr. Psychoanalysis. AYP

Adlestrop. Edward Thomas. BrPo; CH; FaBoPP; GoJo; HAP; LiTB; NAEL-2; NOBE; OBEV; OxBTC

Adman into Toad. Frank Polite. UL

Administrator, An. Geoffrey Grigson. FaBoEE

Admiral. John Alexander Allen. NYBP

Admiral, admiral, sailing home. The Homing. John Jerome Rooney. AA

Admiral Benbow. Unknown. See Come all ye seamen bold.

Admiral Byng. Unknown. OxBSS

Admiral Hosier's Ghost. Richard Glover. NOEC

Admiral, the prisoner of your giant's. Admiral. John Alexander Allen. NYBP

Admirals All. Sir Henry Newbolt. FaPoR; MOS

Admiral's Caravan, The, sel. Charles Edward Carryl. Plaint of the Camel, The. FaPON (Camel's Complaint, The.) OBCA; OxBChV; RHPC

Admiration. Josephine D. Henderson Heard. CBWP-4

Admire Cranmer! Stevie Smith. NoAM

Admire the face of plastered stone. Quebec Farmhouse. John Glassco. NOBC

Admire the old man, admire him, admire him. Admire Cranmer! Stevie Smith. NoAM

Admire thy wreath? And wherefore should I not. To a Plagiarist. Moses ibn Ezroa, tr. by Solomon Solis-Cohen. TrJP

Admire, when you come here, the glimmering hair. Vuillard: "The Mother and Sister of the Artist." W. D. Snodgrass. CoAP

Admonition. Philip Stack. BLPA

Admonition for Spring. Louis Alexander MacKay. CaP; OBCV

Admonition to a Traveller. Wordsworth. GTBS; GTBS-P

Admonition to Montgomerie. James I, King of England. GTBS; GTBS-P; OxBS

An Admonition to Myself. Chao Meng-fu, tr. fr. Chinese by Jonathan Chaves. CoBLCP

Admonition to the Muse. Geoffrey Taylor. FaBoEE

Admonitions. Lucille Clifton. BPo; CAPP; NMM

Adolescence. W. H. Auden. See By landscape reminded once of his mother's figure.

Adolescence. Larry Levis. NAmP

Adolescence. Gregory Orr. Psk

Adolescence. Patricia K. Page. CaP; OBCV

Adolescence—I. Rita Dove. NoAM

Adolescence—II. Rita Dove. AmPA; HCAP; NoAM

Adolescence—III. Rita Dove. NoAM

Adolescence of Day. Odysseus Elytis, tr. fr. Greek by Edmund Keeley and Philip Sherrard. VMG

Adolescent Christ closes with his fingers, The. Quentin Matsys. Jaroslaw Iwaszkiewicz, tr. by Czeslaw Milosz. PwPP

Adolescent night, breath of the town, The. Midsummer. Robert Fitzgerald. PoA

Adolescents/ begin with poems. For Example. Mihály Ladányi, tr. by Jascha Kessler. FOC

Adolicus; that's a creeper rug, its small. Robin Hyde. Fr. The Houses, III. ATNZ; PeNZ

Adon 'Olam. Unknown, tr. fr. Hebrew by F. De Sola Mendes. EaLo

Adonais. William Wallace Harney. AA

Adonais; an Elegy on the Death of John Keats. Shelley. ChER; EBEV; EnRP; FiP, much abr.; HoPM; NoP; OAEL-2; PoEL-4; TrGrPo
Sels.
Go Thou to Rome. ChTr
(Grave of Keats, The.) FaBoPP
"He is made one with Nature." WGRP
"One remains, the many change and pass, The." SCV
"Peace, peace! he is not dead, he doth not sleep." OBD
(Elegy on the Death of John Keats, An.) OBNC
(Mourn Not for Adonais.) NoBE

Adonis. Hilda Doolittle ("H. D."). AWP; LiTA

Adonis, Dying. Praxilla, tr. fr. Greek by Richard Lattimore. PBWP; WPOW

Adoramus Te, Christe. David O'Bruadair, tr. fr. Irish by Thomas Kinsella. NOIV

Adoration. Mme Guyon. WGRP

Adoration of the Disk by King Akhnaten and Princess Nefer Neferiu Aten. Unknown, tr. fr. Egyptian by Robert Hillyer. Fr. Book of the Dead. AWP

"Cattle roam again across the field, The." FaPON

Adoration of the Magi, The. Christopher Pilling. OBCP

Adore we the Lord. Unknown. NOIV

Adored, invalid autumn, you will. Automne Malade. Guillaume Apollinaire, tr. by Paul Blackburn. RHTwFP

Adown the Heights of Ages. Priscilla Jane Thompson. CBWP-2

Adrian Block's Song. Edward Everett Hale. PAH

Adriani Morientis ad Animam Suam. Emperor Hadrian, tr. by Matthew Prior. OBVE; OxBSP

Adrift. Elizabeth Dickinson Dowden. WGRP

Adrift in these frictionless oceans. Flash Sleep. Robert Frazier. BWV

Adrift on an oil-drum raft. Michael Anania. *Fr.* The Riversongs of Arion, I. NoAM

Adsum. Richard Henry Stoddard. AA

Adulescentia, *sel.* Robert Fitzgerald.
"Miraculously, through prayer to Saint Anthony." SD

Adult Lullaby, An. *Unknown.* MeEL

Adulterers and customers of whores. Womanisers. John Press. BoLoP; ErPo

Adulteries, murthers, robberies, thefts. Roger Williams. SCAP

Adultery. James Dickey. CAPP; MT; TAP

Adultery at a Las Vegas Bookstore. Stephen Shu Ning Liu. BrSi

Adulthood. Nikki Giovanni. NMM

Adults Only. William Stafford. FF

Advance Guard, The. John Hay. AnAmPo

Advance of Education, The. Josephine D. Henderson Heard. CBWP-4

Advanced out toward the external from. Celestial Evening, October 1967. Charles Olson. *Fr.* The Maximus Poems. PoM

Advantages of Learning, The. Martial, *tr. fr. Latin by* Kenneth Rexroth. ErPo

Advantages of living with two cultures, The. Bonne Entente. Francis Reginald Scott. FiBHP; OBCV

Advantages of Washing, The. John Armstrong. *Fr.* The Art of Preserving Health. FaBoUs

Advent, *sel.* Brian Coffey.
"Awakening like return to Earth from Moon." CIP

Advent. William Everson. NeAP; TrCP

Advent. Anne Hartigan. CIP

Advent. Patrick Kavanagh. FaBCIP; TIRV

Advent. Christina Rossetti. TrCP

Advent; a Carol. Patric Dickinson. OBCP

Advent Lyrics. *Unknown, tr. fr. Anglo-Saxon. Fr.* Christ 1. AnOE, *tr. by* Charles W. Kennedy
"Bless earth with Thine Advent, O Saviour Christ!" *Fr.* VIII.
"Hail, O most worthy in all the world!" *Fr.* IX.
"O holy Jerusalem, Vision of peace." *Fr.* III.
". . . to the King./ Thou art the wall-stone rejected." *Fr.* I.

Advent marriage doth thee deny. Close Season for Marriage. *Unknown.* FaBoUs

Advent 1955. Sir John Betjeman. OBCP

Advent 1966. Denise Levertov. NNaP; Prf

Advent wind begins to stir, The. Advent 1955. Sir John Betjeman. OBCP

Adventure. Guy Mason. CaP

Adventurers, The. John Thompson. PoAu-2

Adventures in Bronze. Leon Stokesbury. MT

Adventures of Huckleberry Finn, The, *sel.* "Mark Twain."
Emmeline Grangerford's "Ode to Stephen Dowling Bots, Dec'd." NBLV; OBAL
(Ode to Stephen Dowling Bots, Dec'd.) FiBHP

Adventures of Isabel. Ogden Nash. CenHV; MoAmPo; MoShBr; OBAL; OBCA; OnMSP; RHPC

Adventures of Master F. I., The, *sel.* George Gascoigne.
"And if I did, what then?." EBEV; EIL; GBL; HAP; NoP; PoEL-1
(Farewell, A.) NOBE; OBSC

Adventures of Simon Swaugum, a Village Merchant, The. Philip Freneau. PoEL-4

Adventurous Muse, The. Isaac Watts. NOEC

Adversary, The. Phyllis McGinley. FaBoEE; OBCA; OxBSP

Advertisement. Oswald de Andrade, *tr. fr. Portuguese by* Jean R. Longland. ATCBP

Advertisement. *Unknown.* FaBoUs

Advertisement of a Lost Day. Lydia Huntley Sigourney. WBLP

Advertising Agency Song, The. *Unknown.* FaBoUs; NBLV

Advertising Epitaph: From Upton-on-Severn, Gloustershire. *Unknown.*
See Beneath this stone, in hope of Zion.

Advertising Epitaph: On a Quack. *Unknown.* FaBoUs

Advertising Epitaph: On One Lockyer, Inventor of a Patent Medicine. *Unknown.* FaBoUs

Advice. Yehuda Amichai, *tr. fr. Hebrew by* Ruth Nevo. VWA

Advice. Gwendolyn B. Bennett. BlSi; CDC

Advice. Langston Hughes. NBLV

Advice. Czeslaw Milosz, *tr. fr. Polish by the author.* PwPP

Advice, The. Sir Walter Ralegh. AAS; SiPS

Advice, The. Charles Sackville. FaBoUs

Advice. Ruth Stone. NMM

Advice, The. *Unknown.* APAS

Advice for good love: Don't love. Advice. Yehuda Amichai, *tr. by* Ruth Nevo. VWA

Advice from a Nightwatchman. Ian Healy. *Fr.* Poems from the Coalfields, II. PoAu-2

Advice from Euterpe. Carter Revard. VoR

Advice from Poor Robin's Almanack. *Unknown.* OBCP

Advice of an Efficiency Expert, The. Augustus Young. CIP

Advice to a Discarded Lover. Fleur Adcock. PeNZ

Advice to a Forest. Maxwell Bodenheim. TrJP

Advice to a Lady in Autumn. Earl of Chesterfield. FaBoUs

Advice to a Neighbour Girl. Yü Hsüan-chi, *tr. fr. Chinese.* PBWP, *tr. by* Kenneth Rexroth *and* Ling Chung
(For a Neighbor Girl.) BoWoP, *tr. by* Geoffrey Waters

Advice to a Painter. *Unknown.* APAS

Advice to a Prophet. Richard Wilbur. AmPP; CAPP; FYAP; MAT; MoAmPo; NYBP; OBWP; OxBC; PoE; PPP; TwCP

Advice to a Raven in Russia [December, 1812]. Joel Barlow. AmPP; NAAL-1; NOBA; OBWP; OxBA

Advice to a Young Lady. Earl of Chesterfield. *See* Advice to a Lady in Autumn.

Advice to Bores. Abraham Ibn Chasdai, *tr. fr. Hebrew by* J. Chotzner. TrJP

Advice to Colonel Valentine. Robert Graves. NYBP

Advice to Hotheads. Samuel ben Elhanan Isaac, Archevolti of Padua, *tr. fr. Hebrew by* A. B. Rhine. TrJP

Advice to Lovers. John Armstrong. *Fr.* The Oeconomy of Love; a Poetical Essay. NOEC

Advice to My Best Brother, Colonel Francis Lovelace. Richard Lovelace. CaPo

Advice to My Son. Peter Meinke. Psk

Advice to Small Children. Edward Anthony. RHPC

Advice to the Ladies. William Somervile. FaBoUs

Advice to the Ladies of London in the Choice of Their Husbands. *Unknown.* CoMu

Advice to the Old Beaux. Sir Charles Sedley. FaBoUs; SeCV-2

Advice to the Orchestra. David Wagoner. NoAM

Advice to the Painter. Matthew Prior. APAS

Advice to the Same. Sir Philip Sidney. *Fr.* Arcadia. SiPS

Advice to the Young. Miriam Waddington. NOBC

Advice to Travelers. Walker Gibson. NBLV

Advice to Young Ladies. A. D. Hope. NIP; NoAM; NoP

Adze-Head. *Unknown, tr. fr. Irish by* James Carney. BIrV

Ae Fond Kiss. Burns. ELP; EnRP; NAEL-2; OAEL-1; OBEV; PoEL-4; PPP
(Farewell to Nancy.) FaFP
(Song: "Ae fond kiss, and then we sever.") BoLoP; NOEC

Ae weet forenicht i' the yow-trummle. The Watergaw. "Hugh MacDiarmid." GoTS; NAEL-2; NoP

Aecclesiae et Reipub. William Strachey. OBTV

Aedh Tells of the Rose in His Heart. W. B. Yeats. *See* All things uncomely and broken.

Aedh Thinks of Those Who Have Spoken Evil of His Beloved. W. B. Yeats. NoAM

Aedh Wishes for the Cloths of Heaven. W. B. Yeats. MoBrPo; NoAM; OBEV

Aegean. Louis Simpson. GrPl; NYBP

Aegean Melancholy. Odysseus Elytis, *tr. fr. Greek by* Edmund Keeley *and* Philip Sherrard. VMG

Aeglamour's Lament. Ben Jonson. *See* Sad Shepherd, The; Here She Was Wont to Go.

Aelf-Scin, The. Michael McClure. PoM

Aeliana's Ditty. Henry Chettle. *Fr.* Piers Plainness' Seven Years' Prenticeship. OBSC
(Of Cupid.) EIL

Aella; a Tragycal Enterlude. Thomas Chatterton.
Sels.
Autumn. Mes
"Budding floweret blushes at the light [*or* Boddynge flourettes bloshes atte the lyghte], The."
(Mynstrelles Songe ("Boddynge flourettes bloshes atte the lyghte.").) EnRP
(Song of the Three Minstrels.) TrGrPo
Mynstrelles Songe: "Angelles bee wrogte to bee of neidher kynde." EnLoPo
"Oh! sing unto my roundelay [*or* O! Synge untoe mie roundelaie]."
CH; LiTB; Mes; NOBE
(Minstrel's Song.) HAP; TrGrPo, *sl. abr.*.
(My Love Is Dead.) WiR
(Mynstrelle's Songe ("O! synge untoe mie roundelaie").) EnLoPo; EnRP; NOEC
(Song: "O sing into my roundelay.") OBEV

Aeneas at Washington. Allen Tate. FYAP; LiTA; NoAM; NOBA; OxBA

Aeneas built, in days of yore. Edward B. Goodwin. *Fr.* Roman History in Rhyme. FaBoUs

Aeneid [*or* Eneados], The, *abr.*   Virgil, *tr. fr. Latin* by Robert Fitzgerald. NAWM-1

Sels.

Aeneas Sees Italy.   *Fr.* III, *tr. into Middle English* by Gavin Douglas. OxBLMV

"Affrayit, I glistnyt of sleip, and stert on feit."   *Fr.* II, *tr. into Middle English* by Gavin Douglas.   OBVE

"Amyd the wod his modir met thame tway."   *Fr.* I, *tr. into Middle English* by Gavin Douglas.   OBVE

"And now Aeneas charges straight at Turnus."   *Fr.* XII, *tr.* by Allen Mandelbaum.   OBWP

"And oft the owle with rufull song complain."   *Fr.* IV, *tr.* by the Earl of Surrey.   OBVE

"And Turnus than, quhar he at erth dyd ly."   *Fr.* XII, *tr. into Middle English* by Gavin Douglas.   OBVE

"Arms, and the man I sing, who forc'd by fate."   *Fr.* I, *tr.* by Dryden. OBVE

"As, sum tyme, dois the curser stert and ryn."   *Fr.* XI, *tr. into Middle English* by Gavin Douglas.   OBVE

"As this convine and ordinance was mayd."   *Fr.* VIII, *tr. into Middle English* by Gavin Douglas.   OBVE

"As when a fragment, from a mountain torn."   *Fr.* XII, *tr.* by Dryden. OBVE

"Attentively he heard us, while we spoke."   *Fr.* XI, *tr.* by Dryden. OBVE

"Batellis [*or* Batalis] and the man I will descrive."   *Fr.* I, *tr. into Middle English* by Gavin Douglas.   OBVE

   (Batalis and the Man, The.)   CTC

Battle of Actium.   *Fr.* VIII, *tr.* by Dryden.   OBS

Boat Race, The.   *Fr.* V, *tr.* by Rolfe Humphries.   SD

"Bot now the haisty, egir, and wild Dido."   *Fr.* IV, *tr. into Middle English* by Gavin Douglas.   OBVE

Boxing Match, The.   *Fr.* V, *tr.* by Rolfe Humphries.   SD

"Dear Sister, my resentment had not been."   *Fr.* IV, *tr.* by Sir John Denham.   OBVE

Destruction of Troy, The.   *Fr.* II, *tr.* by Sir John Denham.   SeCV-1

Dido among the Shades.   *Fr.* VI, *tr.* by Dryden.   OBS

Dido's Hunting.   *Fr.* IV, *tr.* by the Earl of Surrey.   OBSC

"Eneas wonderit the greitnes of Cartaige."   *Fr.* I, *tr. into Middle English* by Gavin Douglas.   OBVE

Entrance to Hell, The.   *Fr.* VI, *tr. into Middle English* by Gavin Douglas.   GoTS

"Exulting in his strength, he seems to dare."   *Fr.* XI, *tr.* by Dryden. OBVE

"Greeks' chieftains, all irked with the war, The."   *Fr.* II, *tr.* by the Earl of Surrey.   OAEL-1

"Heaven, the earth, and all the liquid mayne, The."   *Fr.* VI, *tr.* by Sir Walter Ralegh.   OBVE

"It was the time when, granted from the gods."   *Fr.* II, *tr.* by the Earl of Surrey.   NAEL-1

"It was then night: the sound[e] and quiet sleep [*or* slepe]."   *Fr.* IV, *tr.* by the Earl of Surrey.   OAEL-1; PoEL-1

"Loe! formest of a rout that follwd him."   *Fr.* II, *tr.* by the Earl of Surrey.   OBVE

"Loud report through Lybian cities goes, The."   *Fr.* IV, *tr.* by Dryden. OBVE

Marcellus.   *Fr.* VI, *tr.* by Dryden.   OBS

"Now manhood and garbroyls I chaunt."   *Fr.* I, *tr.* by Richard Stanyhurst.   BIrV; OBVE

"Onto the hallowit steid bryng in, thai cry."   *Fr.* II, *tr. into Middle English* by Gavin Douglas.   OBVE

"Prince, with wonder, sees the stately tow'rs, The."   *Fr.* I, *tr.* by Dryden.   OBVE

Prologue to Book VII, The.   *Fr.* VII, *tr. into Middle English* by Gavin Douglas.   OxBLMV; OxBS

Queen Dido Rides Out Hunting.   *Fr.* IV, *tr. into Middle English* by Gavin Douglas.   OxBLMV

"Quhen thou art careit to that cuntree."   *Fr.* III, *tr. into Middle English* by Gavin Douglas.   OBVE

"Rang'd on the line oppos'd, Antonius brings."   *Fr.* VIII, *tr.* by Dryden.   WaaP

Sixth Book of the Aeneis, The.   *Tr.* by Dryden.   SeCV-2

"There Charon stands, who rules the dreary coast."   *Fr.* VI, *tr.* by Dryden.   OBVE

"They wished [*or* whisted] all, with fixèd face attent."   *Fr.* II, *tr.* by the Earl of Surrey.   LiTB; SiPS

"Thir riveris and thir watteris kepit war."   *Fr.* VI, *tr. into Middle English* by Gavin Douglas.   OBVE

"Thus fell the King, who yet surviv'd the state."   *Fr.* II, *tr.* by Sir John Denham.   OBVE

"To my prowd foe thus, sister, humblie saye."   *Fr.* II, *tr.* by the Earl of Surrey.   OBVE

"Wee leave Creete Country; and our sayls unwrapped uphoysing."   *Fr.* III, *tr.* by Richard Stanyhurst.   OBVE

Welcome to the Sun.   *Fr.* XII, *tr. into Middle English* by Gavin Douglas.   ACP

"Whom when I saw assembled in such wise."   *Fr.* II, *tr.* by the Earl of Surrey.   PoE

Aenigma on the Six Cases.   *Unknown.*   FaBoUs

Aeolian Harp, The.   Herman Melville.   AmPP

Aeons of history float.   Prisoner. Marguerite George.   GoYe

Aerial View of Louisiana.   Cleopatra Mathis.   MAYP

Aerophorion, *sel.*   Henry James Pye.

Air Balloon, The.   NOEC

Aeroplane, The.   Jeannie Kirby.   BoTP

Aesop at Play.   Phaedrus, *tr. fr. Latin* by Christopher Smart.   AWP

Aesop, mine author, makis mention.   The Tale of the Upland Mouse and the Burgess Mouse. Robert Henryson.   OBNV

Aesop's Fable of the Frogs.   La Fontaine, *tr. fr. French* by John Hookham Frere.   OBVE

Aesthete, The.   W. S. Gilbert.   *See* Patience: Bunthorne's Song

Aesthete to the Rose, The.   *Unknown.*   BXAP

Aesthete Weasel, The.   Christian Morgenstern, *tr. fr. German* by Geoffrey Grigson.   FaBoNo

Aesthetic.   Norman Rosten.   PoA

Aesthetic Point of View, The.   W. H. Auden.   NBLV; OBAL

Aestivation [an Unpublished Poem, by My Late Latin Tutor].   Oliver Wendell Holmes.   *Fr.* The Autocrat of the Breakfast Table, *ch.* 11. NA; NOBL; OBAL

   (Intramural Aestivation, or Summer in Town, by a Teacher of Latin.) ChTr; FaBoNo

Aeterna Poetae Memoria.   Archibald MacLeish.   Son

Æthelstan King,/ Lord amongEarls.   The Battle of Brunanburh. *Unknown, tr.* by Tennyson.   OBVE; OBWP; TrGrPo; Waap.   *See also* Athelstan.

Æthelstan King, lord of eorls.   The Battle of Brunanburh.   *Unknown, tr.* by Charles W. Kennedy.   AnOE

Affable irregular, An.   The Road at My Door. W. B. Yeats.   *Fr.* Meditations in Time of Civil War, V.   BIrV; LiTB; NOBE; PoE

Affair of Honour.   George Whalley.   MoCV

Affection and Desire.   Sir Walter Ralegh.   *See* Conceit Begotten by the Eyes.

Affectionate Shepherd, The, *sels.*   Richard Barnfield.

   "As it fell upon a day."   GBL; PBBP

     (Nightingale, The.)   AWP; GTBS; GTBS-P

     (Ode, An: "As it fell upon a day.")   EiL; OBSC

     (Philomel.)   CH; NOBE; OBEV

   Daphnis to Ganymede.   EiL

   "If thou wilt love me, thou shalt be my boy."   PBBP

Affection's charm no longer gilds.   The Personified Sentimental.   Francis Bret Harte.   NA

Affirmation.   Helen Armstead Johnson.   AmNP

Afflicted by order, the minimalist disease.   To the Islands.   Howard Moss.   SM

Affliction.   Bible, *O.T.*   *Fr.* Lamentations, III: 1–15.   TrJP

Affliction.   Sir John Davies.   *Fr.* Nosce Teipsum.   NOBE; OBSC

Affliction ("Broken in pieces all asunder").   George Herbert.   JCP

Affliction ("Kill me not every day").   George Herbert.   TEP

Affliction ("When first thou didst entice to thee my heart").   George Herbert.   JCP; LiTB; MeLP; MePo; NAEL-1; NOBE; NoP; OBS; SeCP

Affliction of Margaret, The.   Wordsworth.   EnRP; GTBS; GTBS-P; PoEL-4

Affliction of Richard, The.   Robert Bridges.   QFR

Affluence—define it as.   Hezutsu Tosaku, *tr.* by Burton Watson.   FCEI

Afforestation.   E. A. Wodehouse.   FiBHP; SD

Affrayit, I glistnyt of sleip, and stert on feit.   Virgil, *tr. into Middle English* by Gavin Douglas.   *Fr.* The Aeneid [*or* Eneados], II. OBVE

Afoot.   Sir Charles G. D. Roberts.   CaP

Afoot and light-hearted I take to the open road.   Walt Whitman.   *Fr.* Song of the Open Road.   FaFP; NOBA; RFM

Afore ye tak in hand this beuk.   Lines Written in the Front of a Well-read Copy of Burns's *Songs:* To the Reader.   *Unknown.*   FaBoUs

Afraid.   Walter de la Mare.   WeW

Afraid and trackless between storm and storm.   The Hare in the Snow. Gloria Rawlinson.   ATNZ

Afraid of Life?   N. M. Rashed, *tr. fr. Urdu* by Mahmood Jamal. PBMUP

Afraid of the sun [*or* sunlight].   Advice to a Neighbour Girl. Yü Hsüan-chi.   PBWP, *tr.* by Kenneth Rexroth *and* Ling Chung

   (For a Neighbor Girl.)   BoWoP, *tr.* by Geoffrey Waters

Afraid! Of whom am I afraid?   Emily Dickinson.   OHIP; PoE

Afreet ("*Afreet* I am afraid of"). David McCord. WSC
Afresh'd with paint the shop had glare. New Storefront. Russell Atkins.
  FB
Africa. Lewis Alexander. CDC
Africa. Maya Angelou. NIP
Africa. Lucille Clifton. CNA
Africa. David Diop, *tr. fr. French by* Ulli Beier. PBA; TTY
Africa. James Russell Grant. OBTV
Africa. Claude McKay. Son
Africa. Lizelia Augusta Jenkins Moorer. CBWP-3
Africa. Adèle Naudé. PeSA
Africa/ Don't let them. Change Is Not Always Progress. Don L. Lee.
  TAP
Africa./ How many faces did i see in the mirror of your dawn?
  Corruption. Patu Simoko. WMBCH
Africa and the Caribbean. Jennifer Brown, *tr. fr. Rumanian by* Laura
  Schiff. AIW
Africa Is Made of Clay. Patu Simoko. WMBCH
Africa, my Africa. Africa. David Diop, *tr. by* Ulli Beier. PBA; TTY
Africa, you were once just a name to me. The Meaning of Africa.
  Abioseh Nicol. PBA
African. Peter Tosh. PBCV
African Affair, The. Bruce McM. Wright. AmNP; PoBA; PoNe
African Beauty. Taiwo Olaleye-Oruene. AIW
African Chief, The. Bryant. BLPA
African China. Melvin B. Tolson. PoBA
African Christmas. John Press. OBCP
African Dance. Langston Hughes. FaPON
African Dancer. Luis Palés Matos, *tr. fr. Spanish by* Perry Higman.
  LPSS
African Day. Gloria de Sant'Ana, *tr. fr. Portuguese by* Allan Francovich
  and Kathleen Weaver. PBWP
African Dirge. M. J. Chapman. PVCV
African Dream. Bob Kaufman. AmNP; PoBA
African Easter. Abioseh Nicol. PBA
African Elegy, An. Robert Duncan. NoAM
African Images. Alice Walker. InPS
African in Louisiana. Kojo Gyinaye Kyei. PBA
African Poems, *sel.* Don L. Lee.
  "We're an Africanpeople." CNA
African Sunday. Maureen Owen. UL
African Things. Victor Hernandez Cruz. InW
African Trader's Complaint, The. Dennis C. Osadebay. PBA
African Tramp, The. Geoffrey Haresnape. PeSA
Africa's Plea. Roland Tombekai Dempster. TTY
Africland. Oliver La Grone. FB
Aft on the poop deck and walking about. Strike the Bell. *Unknown.*
  OxBSS
"Aften hae I playd at the cards and the dice." The Rantin Laddie.
  Unknown. ESPB
After. Robert Browning. TrGrPo
After. Caroline Grayson. BLRP
After. William Ernest Henley. *Fr.* In Hospital, VI. BrPo
After. Ralph Hodgson. MoBrPo
After. Philip Levine. VWA
After. Philip Bourke Marston. NOBVV
After. Michael Ryan. MAYP
After. Kendrick Smithyman. ATNZ
After a bitter cold night. Winter's Tale. Norma Farber. TSS
After a black day, I play Haydn. Allegro. Tomas Transtromer, *tr. by*
  Robert Bly. EAS
After a bourbon. My Cheap Lifestyle. Eileen Myles. UL
After a damp, breathless day. It Will Pour. A. Leyeles, *tr. fr.* Benjamin
  and Barbara Harshav. AYP
After a Death. Gregory Orr. AnAn; GeTw
After a dream in which your love's fullness. The Sapphire. W. S.
  Merwin. PoA
After A. E. Housman. Peter Titheradge. *Fr.* Teatime Variations. FaBoPa
After a fearful maze where doubt. Chimera. Barbara Howes. TwCP
After a Fruitless Argument. Ishikawa Takuboku, *tr. fr. Japanese by*
  Geoffrey Bownas *and* Anthony Thwaite. PeBJV
After a Game of Squash. Samuel L. Albert. GoYe; TSL
After a heart disease, Aunt Li died. A Pair of Fireflies. Stephen Shu
  Ning Liu. BrSi
After a hundred years. Emily Dickinson. AWP; OxBA
After a Journey. Thomas Hardy. CMoP; EBEV; ELP; EnLoPo; FaBoPP;
  GBL; GTBS-P; OBNC; OxBTC; PoE; PoEL-5
After a Lecture on Keats. Oliver Wendell Holmes. AA
After a little I could not have told. The Song of the Tortured Girl. John
  Berryman. CAPP; CoAP
After a long summer of silence comes this windblown morning: Now I'll.
  Words. Dan Pagis, *tr. by* Warren Bargad *and* Stanley F. Chyet. IP

After a Long Time in the Provinces, I Returned to My Old School in My
  Late Years. Umberto Saba, *tr. fr. Chinese by* Burton Watson.
  JLIC-1
After a long winter, giving/ each other nothing. Chiyo, *tr. by* David Ray.
  BoWoP
After a month and a half without rain. August Rain. Robert Bly.
  LCAP; SV
After a Parting. Alice Meynell. NOBVV
After a Passage in Baudelaire. Robert Duncan. CMoP; PoA; PoE
After a Photo. Judith Herzberg, *tr. fr. Dutch by the author.* DuIn
After a Rain. Cha Shen-hsing, *tr. fr. Chinese by* William Schultz.
  WFTU
After a soiree, with his dark head bent. Hazlitt Sups. Katharine Day
  Little. GoYe
After a Sultry Morning. Rodney Hall. *Fr.* The Owner of My Face.
  CBAP
After a supper of mountain rice. Hometown. Luis Cabalquinto. BrSi
After a Thirties Poet. Peter Titheradge. *Fr.* Teatime Variations.
  FaBoPa
After a thousand mazes overgone. A Sleeping Youth. Keats. *Fr.*
  Endymion [a Poetic Romance]. SeCePo
After a Thousand Years. Amir Gilboa, *tr. fr. Hebrew by* Bernhard Frank.
  MHeP
After a throbbing night, the house still dark, pull. Those of Pure Origin.
  Roy Fuller. FaBoMo
After a Time. Catherine Davis. NePoEA
After a War. Chinua Achebe. UAS
After a week of physical anguish. An Evening Lull. Walt Whitman.
  NAAL-1
After a while. The Widow Perez. Gary Soto. MAYP
After a while he got used to it. Boy Hiding in a Closet. Steve Orlen.
  NAmP
After a while it dawns on us. Historical Museum, Manitoulin Island.
  Lisel Mueller. PoA
After a wind a firefly. Shiba Sonome, *tr. fr. Japanese by* Hiroaki Sato.
  Fr. Fifteen Hokku. FCEI
After a winter of seclusion. Spring Was Begging to Be Born. James
  Tate. NAmP
After Alamein. Prudence Macdonald. CN
After Algernon Charles Swinburne. Peter Titheradge. *Fr.* Teatime
  Variations. FaBoPa
After All. Donald Jeffrey Hayes. CDC
After all,/ One country, brethren! One Country. Frank Lebby Stanton.
  AA; OPP
After all and after all. After All. Donald Jeffrey Hayes. CDC
After all, Charlie, we shall see them go. Longshore Intellectual. Sean
  Lucy. CIP
After all these years. Picture from the Blitz. Lois Clark. CN
After an age when thunderbolts and hail. Louise Labé, *tr. by* Willis
  Barnstone. BoWoP
After an Eclipse of the Sun. Eugene Heimler, *tr. fr. Hungarian by* Peter
  Sherwood *and* Keith Bosley. VWA
After an hundred and thirty years' nap. On the Erection of Shakespeare's
  Statue in Westminster Abbey. Pope. FaBoEE
After an Interval. Walt Whitman. AA
After Anacreon. Lew Welch. *Fr.* Taxi Suite. NeAP; PoM
After Annunciation. Anna Wickham. MoBrPo
After Apple-picking. Robert Frost. AmPP; AnAmPo; CMoP; FPL; InPS;
  LiTA; MoAB; MoAmPo; MoP; NAAL-2; NoAM; NOBA; NU; OxBA;
  PoE; PPP; PrIM; TAP; UnPo
After Arguing against the Contention That Art Must Come from
  Discontent. William Stafford. NoAM
After Aughrim. Emily Lawless. OBEV
After Being in Love, the Next Responsibility. Jalal ed-Din Rumi, *tr. fr.*
  Persian by John Moyne *and* Coleman Barks. VWA
After Blenheim. Robert Southey. *See* Battle of Blenheim, The.
After Bombardment. John Pudney. WaP
After breakfast and they'd left for school. Divorce. Bink Noll. MAT
After Brecht. Dennis Joseph Enright. AnAn
After centuries of dissecting. Lesbian Poem. Robin Morgan. IHMS
After Christmas. Michael Richards. OBCP
After Christmas. W. H. Auden. *See* For the Time Being; a Christmas
  Oratorio: Well, So That Is That
After-Comers, The. Robert Traill Spence Lowell. AA
After dark/ Near the South Dakota border. Having Lost My Sons, I
  Confront the Wreckage of the Moon: Christmas, 1960. James
  Wright. CoAP; HCAP; NAAL-2
After Dark. Adrienne Rich. LCAP; LiTM; VGW
After Dark Vapours. Keats. EnRP; FaBoRV; TEP
  (Sonnet: "After dark vapours have oppress'd our plains.")
After Dawn. Lo Fu, *tr. fr. Chinese by* Dominic Cheung. IFON

After days of putting down my poem. January. Ellen Bryant Voigt. NoP

After Death. Charles Francis Richardson. AA

After Death. Christina Rossetti. GBL; NAEL–2; TEP

After Death. Swinburne. NOBVV

After Death in Arabia. Sir Edwin Arnold. WGRP

After death nothing is, and nothing, death. Seneca, *tr. fr. Latin by* the Earl of Rochester. *Fr.* Troades, II. EBEV; OBD; OBVE

After Dilettante Concetti. Henry Duff Traill. BXAP; CenHV; FaBoCo; Par

After dinner Erasmus. E. C. Bentley. *Fr.* Clerihews. CenHV

After dinner sit awhile. *Unknown.* FaBoUs

After dreaming some hours of the land of Cockaigne. Thomas Moore. *Fr.* The Fudge Family in Paris. BIrV

After Drinking All Night with a Friend, We Go Out in a Boat at Dawn to See Who Can Write the Best Poem. Robert Bly. NaP

After each quake. Crack in the Wall Holds Flowers. Adam David Miller. PoBA

After Eating. Po Chü-i, *tr. fr. Chinese by* Burton Watson. CoBCP

After Elegies. Jean Valentine. LCAP

After 11 years. The Most Beautiful Woman at My Highschool Reunion. Ellen Marie Bissert. GLP; PeHV

After Eli Whitney's gin. Southeast Arkanasia. Maya Angelou. SaC

After Emerson. *Unknown. See* Lives of Great Men.

After Entering Religious Life. Saigyo, *tr. fr. Japanese by* Burton Watson. *Fr.* Sixty-four Tanka. FCEI

After Ever Happily. Ian Serraillier. SO

After everyone leaves. Surely You Remember. Dahlia Ravikovich, *tr. by* Bernhard Frank. MHeP

After Experience Taught Me. W. D. Snodgrass. CAPP; CoAP; OBWP; PPP; TAP

After fifteen months you fly in. Visitation Rights. Heather Wishik. GLP

After five years. The Ownership of the Night. Larry Levis. LCAP

After Five Years. Augustus Young. BIrV

After five years passed in the country. Okura, *tr. fr. Japanese. Fr.* Manyo Shu. Ma

After Floods on the Wharfe. Andrew Marvell. *Fr.* Upon Appleton House, to My Lord Fairfax. FaBoPP

After 4 years of having known you. Lynx. Mirko Lauer, *tr. by* David Tipton. Per

After Frost. Brian Patten. EBEV

After Galen. Oliver St. John Gogarty. FaBoEE; OBMV; PoRA

After Getting Drunk, I Scribble Songs and Poems. Lu Yu, *tr. fr. Chinese by* Burton Watson. CoBCP

After-Glow, The. Mathilde Blind. OBNC

After-Glow of Pain, The. Clara Ann Thompson. CBWP-2

After Going Astray in the Underbrush. Ernst David, *tr. fr. German by* Beth Bjorklund. CoAuP

After Golgotha. Jabra Ibrahim Jabra, *tr. fr. Arabic by* Abdullah al-Udhari. MPAW

After Goliath. Kingsley Amis. NePoEA-2; NOBL; OxBTC

After Grave Deliberation. Elizabeth Flynn. NBLV

After great pain, a formal feeling comes. Emily Dickinson. AmPP; BoWoP; HAP; InPS; LiTA; MoAB; MoAmPo; NAAL-1; NAWM-2; NoAM; NOBA; NoP; PoE; PrIm; TAP; UnPo

After great storms the calm returns. Sir Thomas Wyatt. SiPS

After Greece. James Merrill. CAPP; NOBA; NYBP

After Grey Vigils. George Santayana. *Fr.* Sonnets, XLIX. AnAmPo

After Grief. Stanley Plumly. AmPA; DiL; LCAP

After half a minute of conversation. Yüan Mei, *tr. fr. Chinese by* Jonathan Chaves. *Fr.* Miscellaneous Poems on Growing Old. CoBLCP

After having slain very many beasts. Louise Labé, *tr. by* Willis Barnstone. BoWoP

After he blacked out. Scraps. Rodger Kamenetz. UL

After He Had Gone. Sylvia Townsend Warner. MoBrPo

After he had several adventures, the potato boy took the. Potchikoo Marries. Louise Erdrich. *Fr.* Old Man Potchikoo. HATNAP

After he returned home, they said. Wine Vessels: Two Labels. Yang Mu, *tr. by* Dominic Cheung. IFON

After he stripped off my clothes. Villana, *tr. by* Willis Barnstone. AIW; BoWoP

After hearing one story, he kills a wife. One Thousand and One Arabian Nights. Fei Ma, *tr. by* Dominic Cheung. IFON

After her pills the girl slept and counted. Tally. Josephine Miles. NoAM

After he's scolded. *Unknown, tr. by* Geoffrey Bownas *and* Anthony Thwaite. PeBJV

After Hilary, Age 5. Faye Kicknosway. UL

After his talking destroyed her. Antarctica. R. A. Simpson. CBAP

After his tryst. Teika, *tr. by* Steven D. Carter. WFTW

After his weary travels. "Tsuki," *tr. fr. Japanese. Fr.* Manyo Shu. Ma

After Horace. Alfred Denis Godley. NOBL

After hot loveless nights, when cold winds stream. The Sisters. Roy Campbell. BoLoP; ErPo; FaBoTw; OBMV

After Hours. Robert Mezey. NaP

After hurriedly burying all those who died. Which Chapter. Wang Jun-hua, *tr. by* Dominic Cheung. IFON

After I am dead/ Say this at my funeral. After My Death. Hayyim Nahman Bialik, *tr. by* A. C. Jacobs. VWA

After I came down from the mountain, my Lord. Moses' Account. Milan Fuest, *tr. by* André Ungar. VWA

After I died I could not close my eyes. Departure. Van K. Brock. MT

After I got religion and steadied down. "Butch" Weldy. Edgar Lee Masters. *Fr.* Spoon River Anthology. SaC

After I had cut off my hands. Intrusion. Denise Levertov. CAPP

After I Had Worked All Day. Charles Reznikoff. *Fr.* Five Groups of Verse. PrIm; VGW

After I Have Voted. Laura Jensen. AmPA

After I left the building. Meeting with Giorgio de Chirico. Wieland Schmied, *tr. by* Beth Bjorklund. CoAuP

After I read you, I thought of every mortal. Poem to the Memory of H. L. Mencken. Baron Wormser. MAYP

After it all the hunchbacked village remained. Needless Return. Dan Pagis, *tr. by* Warren Bargad *and* Stanley F. Chyet. IP

After Jena. Thomas Hardy. *Fr.* The Dynasts, *pt.* II, Act I, sc. vii. WaaP

After Jericho. R. S. Thomas. OxBC

After John Keats. Peter Titheradge. *Fr.* Teatime Variations. FaBoPa

After Johnny wear mi clothes. Johnny Tek Away Mi Wife. Slim Beckford *and* Sam Blackwood. PBCV

After Johnson's Dance. Charles Henry Souter. PoAu-1

After kicking on the swing. Li Ch'ing-chao, *tr. by* Kenneth Rexroth *and* Ling Chung. BoWoP

(Tune: Crimson Lips Adorned.) *Tr. by* C. H. Kwôck *and* Vincent McHugh. PBWP

After Labor Day. Sydney Lea. BLA; NAmP

After late evenings. After Touch. Jan Clausen. GLP

After Laughter. Grace Buchanan Sherwood. GoYe

After Li Ch'ing-chao. Anne Waldman. UL

After Long Busyness. Robert Bly. CAPP; PoA

After long journey in sun. Ear Is Not Deaf. Irene Dayton. GoYe

After Long Silence. W. B. Yeats. BoLoP; CMoP; EnLoPo; HeIP; HoPM; LiTM; NAEL-2; OAEL-2; OBMV; PPP; PrIm; UnPo

After Lorca. Robert Creeley. InPS; LCAP; NaP

After Lorca. Ted Hughes. PoA

After Love. Maxine W. Kumin. NMM; TAP

After Love. John Stone. MT

After Making Love We Hear Footsteps. Galway Kinnell. DiL; InPS; NIP; NoAM

After many scornes like these. What Hee Suffered. Ben Jonson. *Fr.* A Celebration of Charis in Ten Lyrick Peeces. SeCP

After many strange thoughts. After Working. Robert Bly. NaP

After Margrave died, nothing. History of a Literary Movement. Howard Nemerov. NePoEA; PoE

After Mass. "Michael Field." WPE

After mass father rinsed the chalice with wine. 1955. Bruce Weigl. MAYP; NAmP

After melon. *Unknown.* FaBoUs

After Midnight. Louis Simpson. CAPP; NoAM

After Midnight. Charles Vildrac, *tr. fr. French by* Jethro Bithell. AWP

After midnight I heard a scream. By Night. Robert Francis. VGW

After Midsummer. E. J. Scovell. OxBTC

After much driving. 1974—The Sounds. Christina Beer. PeNZ

After My Death. Hayyim Nahman Bialik, *tr. fr. Hebrew by* A. C. Jacobs. VWA

After My Fiftieth Birthday. Yu Kuang-chung, *tr. fr. Chinese by* Dominic Cheung. IFON

After My Grandmother's Death. Michele Roberts. AIW

After my illness, so hard to be a traveler. Yang Chi, *tr. fr. Chinese by* Jonathan Chaves. *Fr.* From Sand River to Ts'ai Rock. CoBLCP

After Night Flight. Robert Penn Warren. *See* Mortmain: In Time's concatenation and/ Carnal conventicle.

After night, the waking knowledge. Awaking. Stephen Spender. NYBP

After night there comes the day. Still He Sings. Allan Taylor. OBET

After Nightfall. William Renton. NOBVV

After night's thunder far away had rolled. Haymaking. Edward Thomas. BrPo; MoAB; MoBrPo; SeCePo

After noon, in the plaza, cries, shrill yells, running and breaking. Memorial Day. Josephine Miles. NoP

After our damp skins slid apart. Definition. Lauren Shakely. FYAP
After our Epilogue this crowd dismisses. Congreve. *Fr.* The Way of the World. NAEL-1
After our fierce loving. The Profile on the Pillow. Dudley Randall. BPo; PoBA; TAP
After Picking Rosehips. Harley Elliott. NeAC
After Plotinus. William Stafford. PoA
After Publication of Under the Volcano. Malcolm Lowry. FaBoTw
After Rabbi Akiba, Buxtorf, Herder. Commentaries on the Song of Songs. Judith Herzberg, *tr. by* Shirley Kaufman. VWA
After Rain. Hsüeh Shao-hui, *tr. fr. Chinese by* Irving Lo. WFTU
After rain. Mountain Study. Peter Van Toorn. NOBC
After rain. Patricia K. Page. NOBC; PoE
After rain, the fitful cries of wild geese fill the hall in autumn. Wu Family Thatched Hall. Cheng Hsiao-hsü, *tr. by* Irving Lo. WFTU
After rain, through afterglow, the unfolding fan. Train Ride. John Wheelwright. VGW
After Rain, Visiting the Temple of Heavenly Peace. Wang Shih-chen, *tr. fr. Chinese by* Jonathan Chaves. CoBLCP
After Reading a Child's Guide to Modern Physics. W. H. Auden. NYBP
After Reading Certain Books. Mary Elizabeth Coleridge. EaLo
After Reading *Mickey in the Night Kitchen* for the Third Time before Bed. Rita Dove. ER
After Reading Nelly Sachs. Linda Pastan. VWA
After Reading St. John the Divine. Gene Derwood. LiTM; WPE
After Reading Sylvia Plath. Alta. IHMS
After Reading *The Great American Marble Book* and Reflecting on Life's Lessons Learned at An Early. Michael Cleary. TSL
After Reading the Life of Mrs. Catherine Stubbs in Isaac Ambrose's "War with the Devils." Isaac Hann. NOCV
After Reading the Poems of Master Han Shan, *sels.* Wang Chiu-ssu, *tr. fr. Chinese by* Jonathan Chaves. CoBLCP
   "Floating, floating, the river waters."
   "This crazy man has escaped the world."
After Reading the Poetry of Yannis Ritsos. Friederike Mayröcker, *tr. fr. German by* Beth Bjorklund. CoAuP
After Rilke. Stanley Plumly. NAmP
After Robert Herrick. Peter Titheradge. *Fr.* Teatime Variations. FaBoPa
After St. Augustine. Mary Elizabeth Coleridge. TrPWD
After scanning its face again and again. John Muir on Mt. Ritter. Gary Snyder. *Fr.* Myths and Texts: Burning, VIII. NOBA
After scolding my wife. Ozaki Hosai, *tr. fr. Japanese by* Hiroaki Sato. *Fr.* One Hundred Haiku in Free Form. FCEI
After Seeing Paintings in a Small Book by T. C. Cannon (1946-1978). Alice Sadongei. HATNAP
After seven months in space, the astronauts. Down, Down, and Down. Heather McHugh. NAmP
After Shakespeare. Alex Comfort. ErPo
After sharp words from the fine mind. The Flowering Bars. Charles Donnelly. CIP
After she/ had complained about. The Proposition. Paul Blackburn. ErPo
After Sin, Penitence. F. Richard Thomas. SoTCo
After Six Thousand Years. Victor Hugo, *tr. fr. French by* Selden Rodman. WaaP
After Snow-Impromptu. Yü Chi, *tr. fr. Chinese by* Jonathan Chaves. CoBLCP
After so many deaths to breathe again. Variations on a Theme by George Herbert. Marya Zaturenska. TrPWD
After so many decades of. . . of what? To Whom It May Concern. J. V. Cunningham. FYAP
After Socrates drank hemlock. Scoop. Ernest Slyman. SoTCo
After Some Day of Decision. Reed Whittemore. NePoEA
After some years Bohemian came to this. J. V. Cunningham. VGW
After-Song. Richard Watson Gilder. AA; TrPWD
After Speaking of One Dead a Long Time. Padraic Colum. GoYe
After strenuous cultivation. To the Hosts: A Reply. Chang Ts'o, *tr. by* Dominic Cheung. IFON
After such years of dissension and strife. Dust to Dust. Thomas Hood. NBLV
   (Natural Tears.) FiBHP
After Sunset. Arthur Symons. *Fr.* At Dieppe. BrPo
After surmounting three-score and ten. My 71st Year. Walt Whitman. NAs
After Tempest. Percy MacKaye. FYAP
After ten days I come here again. On the Sixteenth Day I Visit the Temple Again. Pien Kung, *tr. by* Jonathan Chaves. CoBLCP
After Tennyson. Edward Lear. FaBoNo

After that war, when death had gone away. Joan Miró. Ruthven Todd. EAS
After the agony in the guest/ bedroom. Margaret Atwood. NeAC
After the Anonymous Swedish. Jim Harrison. VGW
After the Apocalypse, *sel.* Samih al-Qasim, *tr. fr. Arabic by* Sharif Elmusa *and* Naomi Shihab Nye. MAP
   "I feel my limbs." MAP
After the Ball. Imamu Amiri Baraka. NAAL-2
After the battle. Three Testimonies of Ayacucho. Antonio Cisneros, *tr. by* Maureen Ahern *and* David Tipton. Per
After the Battle. George Sylvester Viereck. GoYe
After the blast of lightning from the East. The End. Wilfred Owen. CH; FaBoRV; MMA
After the blaze out of the darkness. The Ferryman. László Nagy, *tr. by* George MacBeth. MHuP
After the Blitz, 1941. J. R. Ackerley. PeHV
After the brief bivouac of Sunday. The Stenographers. Patricia K. Page. CaP; HeIP; LiTM; NoAM; NoP; OBCV
After the Broken Arm. Ron Padgett. EAS
After the bronzed, heroic traveller. The Mapmaker on His Art. Howard Nemerov. NYBP
After the Burial. James Russell Lowell. AA; UnPo
After the burial-parties leave. The Hyaenas [*or* Hyenas]. Kipling. NAEL-2; OBSV
After the Centennial. Christopher Pearse Cranch. PAH
After the cloud embankments. Reconnaissance. Arna Bontemps. AmNP; BPo
After the Comanches. *Unknown.* PAH
After the Convention. Robert Lowell. NoAM
After the darkness and storm. After. Caroline Grayson. BLRP
After the Death of an Elder Klallam. Duane Niatum. CDW
After the Death of Her Daughter in Child-birth. Izumi Shikibu, *tr. fr. Japanese by* Edwin A. Cranston. PBWP
After the Deluge. House of the Living. Claude Vigée, *tr. by* Henry Braun. VWA
After the doctor checked to see. First Practice. Gary Gildner. AmPA; Psk; TSL; TW
After the door shuts and the footsteps die. A Hunt in the Black Forest. Randall Jarrell. CoAP; LCAP
After the dreadful Flood was past. The Tower of Babel. Nathaniel Crouch. OxBChV
After the earthquake, returning to the capital. Returning Home. Rai San'yo, *tr. by* Burton Watson. JLIC-2
After the end of the world. In the Middle of Life. Tadeusz Rozewicz, *tr. by* Czeslaw Milosz. PwPP
After the event the rockslide. Clarity. A. R. Ammons. HCAP; TAP
After the explosion or cataclysm, that big. The Eternal City. Archie Randolph Ammons. CAPP; EyDe; HCAP
After the eyes that looked, the lips that spake. Lincoln at Gettysburg. Bayard Taylor. *Fr.* The Gettysburg Ode. OHIP; PAH
After the Fair. Thomas Hardy. *Fr.* At Casterbridge Fair, VII. CMoP; HAP
After the Fall. Gloria Escoffery. PVCV
After the fall drive, the last. Montana Eclogue. William Stafford. NYBP
After the fall of the tree. After. Philip Levine. VWA
After the feast, my Shapcott, see. Oberon's Palace. Robert Herrick. CaPo
After the fiercest pangs of hot desire. Richard Duke. BoLoP
After the Fifth of June. Yusuf al-Khal, *tr. fr. Arabic by* May Jayyusi *and* Naomi Shihab Nye. MAP
After the Fire. Oliver Wendell Holmes. PAH
After the First Communion. Sunday Afternoon. Denise Levertov. IHMS
After the First Frost. Lew Blockcolski. VoR
After the first powerful plain manifesto. The Express. Stephen Spender. CMoP; GoJo; HeIP; LiTM; MoAB; MoBrPo; MoP; NoAM; TwCP
After the first shallows have dropped away. Daily the Ocean between Us. Patricia Goedicke. TAP
After the first sudden rain. Rains on the Island. Gabriel Preil, *tr. by* Robert Friend. VWA
After the Flight of the Earls. Fearflatha O'Gnive. NOIV
After the Flood. Pierre Jean Jouve, *tr. fr. French by* John Montague. RHTwFP
After the Flood. Sir David Lindsay. *Fr.* The Monarche. OxBS
After the Flood. Rimbaud, *tr. fr. French by* Enid Rhodes Peschal. *Fr.* Illuminations. SOTW
After the floor was grooved and tongued. Completion. Stephen Dunn. BLA
After the Funeral. Dylan Thomas. CMoP; FaBoMo; NAEL-2; NoP; OAEL-2; OBWVE

After the Gentle Poet Kobayashi Issa. Robert Hass. GeTw

After the Golden Wedding. James Kenneth Stephen. NOBVV

"She's not a faultless woman; no!" sel. EBVV

After the goldfinch. Goldfinch. John Engels. BLA

After the Guests Departed. Tsfrirah Gar, tr. fr. Hebrew by Bernhard Frank. MHeP

After the heaped piles and the cornsheaves waiting. Harvest and Consecration. Elizabeth Jennings. NePoEA-2

After the honey drops of pearly showers. The Rose. William Hammond. OBS

After the horrors of Heathrow. 747 (London-Chicago). Robert Conquest. OxBC

After the Hunt. Detlev, Freiherr von Liliencron, tr. fr. German by Ludwig Lewisohn. AWP

After the Hurricane. Samuel Hazo. GrPl

After the Industrial Revolution, All Things Happen at Once. Robert Bly. CoAP

After the Killing. Dudley Randall. CNA; SoSe

After the Kiss. Miki Rofu, tr. fr. Japanese by Geoffrey Bownas and Anthony Thwaite. PeBJV

After the Last Bulletins. Richard Wilbur. CoAP; MoAB; MoAmPo; NYBP; TrGrPo

After the Last Dynasty. Stanley Kunitz. TAP

After the Laws of Good-Bye & Autumn, sel. Eddy van Vliet, tr. fr. Dutch by James S. Holmes.

"Every soldier in the streetcar was a relation." DuIn

After the Leaves Fall. Ruth Kim Chun-soo, tr. fr. Korean by Koh Chang-soo. ACKP

After the leaves have fallen, we return. The Plain Sense of Things. Wallace Stevens. HCAP; NoAM

After the leaves have quivered and fallen. Singde, tr. fr. Chinese by William Schultz. Fr. Impressions of a Night's Stay at Shuang-lin Temple, III. WFTU

After the leg is lost, the pain remains as an emblem. Phantom Pain. Maxine Chernoff. EOEF

After the legshows and the brandies. Night Club. Louis MacNeice. OxBSP

After the light has set. The Return. George MacBeth. NYBP

After the men hunt. Dressing Game. Dennis Schmitz. NPGG

After the midnight unfolding of the White Rose. The Feast of Stephen. Kevin Nichols. OBCP

After the murder. The Last Quatrain of the Ballad of Emmett Till. Gwendolyn Brooks. CNA; PoBA; WPE

After the Night Hunt. James Dickey. PoA

After the noon hour the sky is silent on the asphalt. Brooding Afternoon in July. Andreas Okopenko, tr. fr. German by Beth Bjorklund. Fr. Summer Fragments, III. CoAuP

After the noose, and the black diary deeds. Casement's Funeral. Richard Murphy. Fr. The Battle of Aughrim. NOIV

After the palaces. May Sarton. Fr. A Nobleman's House. EyDe

After the Pangs of a Desperate Lover. Dryden. Fr. An Evening's Love, II, i. ELP

(Love's Fancy.) ErPo

After the Party. William Wise. FaPON

After the Persian. Louise Bogan. NePoAm; NYBP; PoA

After the planes unloaded, we fell down. The Dead in Europe. Robert Lowell. LiTM; NePoEA; OxBA; OxBC

After the Pleasure Party. Herman Melville. NAAL-1; PoEL-5

After the poetry of outwaiting the line-up. Mexico City, 150 Pesos to the Dollar. Jim Mitsui. BrSi

After the Pow-Wow, sel. Harold Littlebird.

"I tell him how it used to be in Paguate." STE

After the Quarrel. Paul Laurence Dunbar. AnAmPo; CDC

After the Quarrel. Barbara Gibson. FF

After the Quarrel. Priscilla Jane Thompson. CBWP-2

After the Rain. Edward A. Collier. BLRP

After the Rain. Stanley Crouch. CNA

After the Rain. Paul B. Janeczko. PCP

After the Rain. Liang Ch'i-ch'ao, tr. fr. Chinese by Cecile Chu-chin Sun. WFTU

After the rain of stars. At the Gate of the Valley. Zbigniew Herbert, tr. by Czeslaw Milosz. PwPP

After the rain the bright wide air. House on the River. Ad Zuiderent, tr. by James S. Holmes. DuIn

After the rain, the vegetables from your garden. Yang Shih-ch'i, tr. fr. Chinese by Jonathan Chaves. Fr. Libationer Hu Became Ill from Eating Sunflowers. CoBLCP

After the rapture comes, and everyone goes away. March Journal. Charles Wright. BLA

After the rare arch-poet Jonson died. Upon Mr. Ben Jonson: Epigram. Robert Herrick. CaPo

After the Rebuilding. Philip Booth. BLA

After the red leaf and the gold have gone. A Spell before Winter. Howard Nemerov. LiTM

After the Revolution. Marilyn Hacker. AmPA

After the Revolution for Jesus the Associate Professor [or a Secular Man] Prepares His Final Remarks. Miller Williams. BLA; MT

After the rooster falls from the hen. Final Soliloquy on a Randy Rooster (in a Key of Yellow). Robert Peters. BXAP

After the satyr's twilight in the park. Homecoming—Massachusetts. John Ciardi. NYBP

After the Sea-Ship. Walt Whitman. MOS

After the sea, the harbor. Sequence. Edgar Daniel Kramer. BLRP

After the Second Operation. Patricia Goedicke. TAP

After the Seizer there were ten chiefs, and there was much warfare south and east. Unknown, tr. fr. Delaware (Lenape) Indian by Daniel G. Brinton. Fr. Walam [or Wallum] Olum; or, Red Score. OBVE

After the shot the driven feathers rock. Rainbow. Robert Huff. NePoEA-2

After the Show. Sam Harrison. NeIP

After the Shower. Archibald Lampman. CaP

After the squealing brass. Saint's Parade. Robert Layzer. NePoEA

After the stars have disappeared. The Fifteenth Evening of the First Lunar Month. Li Nan, tr. by Dominic Cheung. IFON

After the stars were all hung separately. The Book of How. Merrill Moore. MoAmPo

After the Storm. Elizabeth Bartlett. GoYe

After the Storm. Henrietta Cordelia Ray. CBWP-3

After the storm, after the rain stopped pounding. Song of Napalm. Bruce Weigl. MAYP

After the sun had sunk. The Test. Michael Guttenbrunner, tr. by Beth Bjorklund. CoAuP

After the sun's eclipse. Teresa. Richard Wilbur. NoAM

After the Supper and Talk. Walt Whitman. MoAmPo; NAAL-1

After the Surprising Conversions. Robert Lowell. AmPP; HAP; NAAL-2; NePoEA; NoAM; NoP; PPP

After the sweat of swathes and the sinking madder sun. A Drink of Spring. John Ennis. CIP

After the teacher asked if anyone had a sacred place. The Sacred. Stephen Dunn. MOWH

After the test they sent an expert. School Days. William Stafford. LCAP

After the thorns I came to the first page. The Sleeping Beauty; Variation of the Prince. Randall Jarrell. PoA

After the thunder. Thunder Moth. Miyoshi Tatsuji, tr. by Geoffrey Bownas and Anthony Thwaite. PeBJV

After the tiff there was stiff silence, till. The Lovers. William Robert Rodgers. BIrV; OxBSP

After the tumult and the blood. At Vshchizh. Fyodor Ivanovich Tyutchev, tr. by Charles Tomlinson. OBWP

After the Visit. Thomas Hardy. NOBE; OBNC

After the War. Douglas Dunn. OxBC

After the War. Gleb Garbovsky, tr. fr. Russian by Joseph Langland, Tamas Aczel and Laszlo Tikos. BWV

After the War. Richard Le Gallienne. PAH

After the War. Hayim Naggid, tr. fr. Hebrew by Shlomo Vinner and Howard Schwartz. VWA

After the war—I hear men ask—what then? After the War. Richard Le Gallienne. PAH

After the whey-faced anonymity. South Country. Kenneth Slessor. CBAP

After the Winter. Claude McKay. BANP; IDB; PoBA; PoNe

After the winter thawed away, I rose. The Assignation. James Wright. NePoEA

After the words of the magnificence and doom. Country Burial. Janet Lewis. CRP

After their bells stopped. Yugo, tr. by Hiroaki Sato. FCEI

After these words the Weather-Geat prince. Beowulf's Fight with Grendel's Mother. Unknown, tr. fr. Anglo-Saxon by Michael Alexander. Fr. Beowulf. WTO

After these years of lectures heard. To a Friend, on Her Examination for the Doctorate in English. J. V. Cunningham. VGW

After they all leave. Surely You Remember. Dahlia Ravikovich, tr. by Chana Bloch. VWA

After They Have Tired of the Brilliance of Cities. Stephen Spender. FaBoMo; LiTM

After they passed I climbed. A Story. William Stafford. NNaP; RFM

After They Put Down Their Overalls. Lenrie Peters. TTY

After they've gone. Surely You Remember. Dahlia Ravikovich, tr. by Warren Bargad and Stanley F. Chyet. IP

After thirty years. Romance. Gerald Stern. CAPP

After this conversation have another. Gas. Jean Day. IAT

After this much time, it's still impossible. Spit. Charles Kenneth Williams. CAPP; NAmP; VWA

After this oracle there will be no more oracles. Last Statement for a Last Oracle. Alan Dugan. CAPP; NoAM

After those first days. Death of a Bird. Jon Silkin. NePoEA

After those reverend papers, whose soule is. To Sir H. W. at His Going Ambassador to Venice. John Donne. MeLP

(Letter to Sir H. Wotton at His Going Ambassador to Venice.) OBS

After-Thought, The. Stevie Smith. OxBC

After-Thought. Wordsworth. *See* River Duddon, The: I thought of Thee, my partner and my guide.

After throwing a parasol to the grass. Yosano Akiko, *tr. fr. Japanese by* Hiroaki Sato. *Fr.* Thirty-nine Tanka. FCEI

After thy labour, take thine ease. The Mount of the Muses. Robert Herrick. CaPo

After Tonight. Gary Soto. NoAM

After Touch. Jan Clausen. GLP

After travelling from the Imperial City. *Unknown, tr. fr. Japanese. Fr.* Manyo Shu. Ma

After trimming the split trunk of our tallest maple. The Storm. Ellen Bryant Voigt. BLA

After Trinity. John Meade Falkner. OxBTC

After Tsang Chih. Alice Notley. UL

After twenty-five years they drag you away. Mimosa. Cleopatra Mathis. MAYP

After twenty some years, one meeting with you. I Dreamt of Saichi and Woke with a Feeling of Uneasiness. Ryokan, *tr. by* Burton Watson. JLIC-2

After Twenty Years. Fadwa Tuquan, *tr. fr. Arabic.* PBWP

After twenty years I want to call it that, but was it? Rape. Joan Larkin. GLP

After twenty years of nods. The Katskills Kiss Romance Goodbye. Ishmael Reed. UL

After two sittings, now our Lady State. Andrew Marvell. *Fr.* The Last Instructions to a Painter. APAS; OBSV

After Two Years. Richard Aldington. MoBrPo

After Us. István Kormos, *tr. fr. Hungarian by* Edwin Morgan. MHuP

After W. B. Yeats. Gilbert Keith Chesterton. NOBL

After W. B. Yeats. Peter Titheradge. *Fr.* Teatime Variations. FaBoPa

After Walter de la Mare. Peter Titheradge. *Fr.* Teatime Variations. FaBoPa

After War. Ivor Gurney. OxBSP

After we, dear friends, have drunk together. Lady Otomo no Sakanoe, *tr. fr. Japanese. Fr.* Manyo Shu. Ma

After we had burned on the water a while. Voice from Danang. Thomas Dillon Redshaw. MAT

After we knew that we were dead we sat down and cried a little. The Dead. Louis Dudek. NOBC

After weeks of watching the roof leak. Gary Snyder. *Fr.* Hitch Haiku. InPK

After what felt like a lifetime of rent. Writing. Andrew Motion. DiPo

After what had/ to be said. Drunk. Carroll Arnett. VoR

After Whistler. Stanley Plumly. AnAn; NAmP

After Wings. Sarah Morgan Bryan Piatt. AA

After Winter. Sterling A. Brown. PoBA; PoNe

After winter comes. A Winter Poem. Tameie, *tr. by* Steven D. Carter. WFTW

After Work. Gary Snyder. HoPM; NNaP

After Working. Robert Bly. NaP

After years by the ocean. Sailing. Al Zolynas. TSL

After years of relative clumsiness. Arachne. Judith Kazantzis. BrRo

After years of stock-car racing, running. Miami. Daniel Mark Epstein. MAYP

After you finish your work. Ballad of Orange and Grape. Muriel Rukeyser. NoAM

After you have enriched your soul. Jonathan Swift Somers. Edgar Lee Masters. *Fr.* Spoon River Anthology. OBAL

"After you have lost me once." Rosane. Ida Hahn-Hahn, *tr. by* Susan L. Cocalis. DMG

After you left me forever. Semele Recycled. Carolyn Kizer. CAPP; InPS

After You, Madam. Alex Comfort. ErPo

After you, the killed of the Ukraine. Perets Markish, *tr. fr. Yiddish by* Leonard Wolf. *Fr.* The Mound. PeBMYV

After your death. William Knott. EAS

After you've been to bed together for the first time. Life Story. Tennessee Williams. GLP; PeHV

Aftereffects of a mother's neglects, The. Mother, Mother, Are You All There? Felicia Lamport. NBLV

Afterglow. Jorge Luis Borges, *tr. fr. Spanish by* Norman Thomas di Giovanni. NYBP

Afterglow. Jack Butler. MT

Afterglow, The. Henrietta Cordelia Ray. CBWP-3

Afterglow goldens the. The Mountain Afterglow. James Laughlin. VGW

Afterlives. Derek Mahon. CIP

Aftermath, The. Euripides, *tr. fr. Greek by* Richmond Lattimore. *Fr.* Iphigenia [*or* Iphigeneia] in Aulis. WaaP

Aftermath. Longfellow. NAAL-1; NOBA; TAP

Aftermath. Siegfried Sassoon. BrPo; MoBrPo; TrJP; WaP

Afternoon. Gerhard Fritsch, *tr. fr. German by* Beth Bjorklund. CoAuP

Afternoon. Wendell Phillips Garrison. *Fr.* Post-Meridian. AA

Afternoon. Louisa S. Guggenberger. NOBVV

Afternoon, An. Gerrit Komrij, *tr. fr. Dutch by* Jacob Lowland. DuIn

Afternoon./ Teacher and nun, bleak refugee, a stone. Street Scene. Robert Mezey. LiTM

Afternoon almost gone, The. The tide. Where Tide. Philip Booth. BLA

Afternoon: Amagansett Beach. John Hall Wheelock. BoNaP; PoRA

Afternoon arrives suddenly, The. Premonition. Tamura Ryuichi, *tr. by* Hiroaki Sato. FCEI

Afternoon at the Beach, An. Edgar Bowers. MT

Afternoon cooking in the fall sun. Robert Hass. AmPA

Afternoon dark increases with the clock, The. Late Tutorial. Vincent Buckley. PoAu-2

Afternoon Gossip, An. Priscilla Jane Thompson. CBWP-2

Afternoon in Anglo-Ireland. Bruce Williamson. NeIP

Afternoon in sultry summer, An. Amores (after Ovid). Jay Parini. MAYP

Afternoon is invading my eyes. Drunken Poem. David Helwig. NOBC

Afternoon is the snack's own seasoning. Little Pudding. Mary M. Roberts. BXAP

Afternoon late summer, in a room, An. At My Grandmother's. David Malouf. PoAu-2

Afternoon light. Who Art Thou, O Great Mountain. Dahlia Ravikovich, *tr. by* Warren Bargad *and* Stanley F. Chyet. IP

Afternoon of Grand Old Men. Sandor Csoori, *tr. fr. Hungarian by* Jascha Kessler. FOC

Afternoon on a Hill. Edna St. Vincent Millay. AnAmPo; BoTP; FaPON; GrPl; NTCP; OBCA; OxBA; PDV; TTTS

Afternoon Sleep. Robert Bly. NaP

Afternoon Sun, The. Constantine P. Cavafy, *tr. fr. Greek by* Edmund Keeley *and* Philip Sherrard. VMG

Afternoon sun on her back. Robert Pinsky. BLA

Afternoon Sunlight Plays. Kathleen Jessie Raine. PoPo

Afternoon 3. Saburoh Kuroda. EAS

Afternoon turned dark early, The. During December's Death. Delmore Schwartz. NYBP

Afternoon wears on, The. David Wright. NYBP

Afternoon with Grandmother. Barbara A. Huff. FaPON

Afternoon with the heavy hours, The. The Traveller. Allen Tate. LiTM

Afternoons/ Brought coconut smell of gorse. Sir John Betjeman. *Fr.* Summoned by Bells. FaBoPP

Afternoon's Angel. Seymour Mayne. VWA

Afternoons with Baedeker, *sels.* Osbert Lancaster.

Eireann. NOBL

English. FaBoCo; NOBL

French. FaBoCo; NOBL

Italian. FaBoCo

Manhattan. NOBL

Afterthought. Elizabeth Jennings. OBCP

Afterthoughts. Tachihara Michizo, *tr. fr. Japanese by* Geoffrey Bownas *and* Anthony Thwaite. PeBJV

Afterwake, The. Adrienne Rich. NOBA; Prf

Afterward. Gyula Illyés, *tr. fr. Hungarian by* Jascha Kessler. FOC

Afterward. Lyn Lifshin. ER

Afterward. Mary Matheson. CaP

Afterward he may take thought. The Airman. William Robert Rodgers. WaP

Afterwards. Fleur Adcock. ATNZ

Afterwards. Thomas Hardy. BoNaP; CH; ChTr; CMoP; EBEV; FaBoRV; GTBS-P; InPS; LiTB; LiTM; MoAB; MoBrPo; NOBE; NoP; OAEL-2; OBNC; PoEL-5; QFR; TOF; TrGrPo

Afterwards. Frances Ridley Havergal. BLRP

Afterwards, afterwards the wind between two mountains. David Rosenmann-Taub, *tr. by* Charles Guenther. VWA

Afterwards, the compromise. After Love. Maxine W. Kumin. NMM; TAP

Afterwards there are dogends in. Maureen Duffy. PeHV

Afterwards, They Shall Dance. Bob Kaufman. PoNe; TwCP; VGW

Afterword. Nishiwaki Junzaburo, *tr. fr. Japanese by* Hiroaki Sato. FCEI

Afterword: For Gwen Brooks, An. Don L. Lee. JB

Aftir that hervest inned had hise sheves. Hoccleve Remembers His Madness. Thomas Hoccleve. *Fr.* The Complaint. OxBLMV

Afton Water. Burns. *See* Flow Gently, Sweet Afton.

Aga Khan, The. Steve Orlen. Psk

A.G.A. to A.E. Emily Brontë. FL

Again. František Halas, *tr. fr. Czech by* Karl W. Deutsch. WaaP
Again. Glyn Jones. OBWVE
Again. Charlotte Mew. MoAB; MoBrPo
Again. Jon Stallworthy. OxBC
Again a dream-rider day. Privilegium Minus. Reinhard Priessnitz, *tr. by* Beth Bjorklund. CoAuP
Again a Neighbor Died. H. Leivick, *tr. fr. Yiddish by* Benjamin *and* Barbara Harshav. *Fr.* Clouds behind the Forest. AYP
Again and again. Masaoka Shiki, *tr. by* Geoffrey Bownas *and* Anthony Thwaite. PeBJV
Again and again I go away from you. J. Michael Yates. *Fr.* The Great Bear Lake Meditations. HoPM
Again and again I kiss thy gates at departing. Roma. Rutilius, *tr. by* Ezra Pound. CTC
Again and again I make the intolerable journey. The Repeated Journey. Thomas McGrath. NePoEA
Again and then again. the year is born. New Year's Day. Robert Lowell. AmPP; LiTM; NePoEA
Again as Evening's Shadow Falls. Samuel Longfellow. AH
Again at Christmas did we weave. Tennyson. *Fr.* In Memoriam A. H. H., LXXVIII. PChr
Again before me: A ragged sage. Homecoming. Hayyim Nahman Bialik, *tr. by* Bernhard Frank. MHeP
Again Columbia's stripes, unfurl'd. *Enterprise* and *Boxer. Unknown.* PAH
Again, day and night sit balanced. Autumn Equinox. Peter Blue Cloud. *Fr.* Within the Seasons. HATNAP
Again Everything Has Gone Quite Well. Gabriele Wohmann, *tr. fr. German by* Margaret Woodruff. DMG
Again for Hephaistos, the Last Time. Richard Howard. GLP
Again, his friend's death made the man sit still. John Berryman. NOBA
Again I hear that creaking step! My Familiar. John Godfrey Saxe. AnAmPo
Again I hold these holy letters. Finding a Yiddish Paper on the Riverside Line. Barry Spacks. SM
Again I remember. Asadullah Khan Ghalib, *tr. by* Ahmed Ali. GoT
Again I reply to the triple winds. January. William Carlos Williams. MoAB; MoAmPo
Again I see my bliss at hand. Meeting. Matthew Arnold. *Fr.* Switzerland, I. ELP
Again I see you, ah my queen. Juana. Alfred de Musset, *tr. by* Andrew Lang. AWP
Again last night I dreamed the dream called laundry. The Mad Scene. James Merrill. CoAP; NOBA; PoA; PoE; TAP
Again let me do a lot of extraordinary talking. The Song of the Militant Romance. Wyndham Lewis. FaBoTw; OxBTC
Again? New tumults in my breast? Horace. *See* Odes: IV, 1. To Venus ("Intermissa, Venus").
Again observing how my hands. Étude for Voice and Hand. Gabriel Levin. VWA
Again, oh Lord! we humbly pray. The People's Sabbath Prayer. Ebenezer Elliott. PF
Again on the morrow morning doth Sigurd the Volsung ride. Sigurd Rideth to the Glittering Heath. William Morris. *Fr.* The Story of Sigurd the Volsung, II. PoEL-5
Again one/ Again one of the seismographs. On the Death of Paul Celan (A Vindication). Doris Mühringer, *tr. by* Beth Bjorklund. CoAuP
Again rejoicing Nature sees. Burns. BoNaP
Again she learns to move. The Roan Hunter. Jana Harris. TSL
Again the ancient, meaningless. Gary Snyder. *Fr.* Myths and Texts: Logging, V. NaP
Again the call of the winter birds. Poem for Carroll, Descendant of Chiefs. Lance Henson. VoR
Again the day. If the Stars Should Fall. Samuel Allen. IDB; PoBA
Again the greyish khaki light descends. Meir Wieseltier, *tr. fr. Hebrew by* Warren Bargad *and* Stanley F. Chyet. *Fr.* Elegies by the Senses, 1. IP
Again the last ebb. Dieppe. Samuel Beckett. NOIV
Again the light of. Epitaph: Snake River. Lance Henson. VoR
Again, the morning for a male is best. How to Conceive Boys. Claude Quillet, *tr. fr. Latin by* George Sewell. *Fr.* Callipaedia; or, The Art of Getting Beautiful Children. FaBoUs
Again the native hour lets down the locks. More Sonnets at Christmas, I. Allen Tate. LiTA; LiTM; WaP
Again the summer-fevered skies. Garfield's Ride at Chickamauga. Hezekiah Butterworth. PAH
Again the time and blood consuming sun crosses its corner. A Dawn Horse. William Harmon. FYAP
Again the wood, and long with-drawing vale. To Spring. Charlotte Smith. WPE
Again the world goes open like a girl's room. February Sun. Paul Rodenko, *tr. by* James S. Holmes. DuIn

Again this morning trembles on the swift stream the image of the sun. Images. Kathleen Raine. NYBP
Again this procession of the speechless. Daybreak. W. S. Merwin. NAAL-2
Again we smelled for days on end. Again. František Halas, *tr. by* Karl W. Deutsch. WaaP
Again: who really knows. Lenny Bruce Fixes. Jotie T'Hooft, *tr. by* Scott Rollins. DuIn
Again with the boys I fought a hundred grasses. Grass Fight. Ryokan, *tr. by* Burton Watson. JLIC-2
Again your hair waves when I cry. The Years from You to Me. Paul Celan, *tr. by* Beth Bjorklund. CoAuP
Againe. Robert Herrick. SeCP
Against a Sickness: To the Female Double Principle God. Alan Dugan. NoAM
Against a somber background, blue as midnight. The Offering of the Heart Tapestry from Arras, XV Century. Rolfe Humphries. FYAP
Against Absence. Sir John Suckling. CaPo
Against an elm a sheep was tied [*or* ty'd]. The Wild Boar and the Ram. John Gay. *Fr.* Fables. FM; NOEC
Against an Old Lecher. Sir John Harington. FaBoEE
Against Blame of Woman. Gerald Fitzgerald, 4th Earl of Desmond, *tr. by* the Earl of Longford. AnIL; BIrV
Against Botticelli. Robert Hass. AmPA; NPGG
Against Broccoli. Roy Blount, Jr.. NBLV; OBAL
Against Constancy. Earl of Rochester. GBL
Against Coupling. Fleur Adcock. ATNZ
Against Dark's Harm. Anne Halley. NMM
Against deep seas blue-black like mussel-shells. Escape. Charles Spear. ATNZ
Against Education. Charles Churchill. *See* Author, The: Pains of Education, The.
Against Fruition. Sir John Suckling. CaPo; ErPo
Against Fulfillment of Desire. *Unknown.* TrGrPo
Against Gaudy-Bragging-Undoughty Daccus. John Davies of Hereford. FaBoEE
Against Homosexuality. Thomas Gilbert. *Fr.* View of the Town, A. In an Epistle to a Friend. NOEC
Against Hope. Abraham Cowley. *Fr.* The Mistress. LiTB; MeLP; OBS; SeCV-1
(On Hope.) MePo; NOBE
Against Indifference. Charles Webbe. OBEV
Against Love. Katherine Philips. BoWoP; WPE
Against Marriage to His Mistress. William Walsh. FaBoUs
Against Meaning. Andrei Codrescu. UL
Against Minoan sunlight. Wishes for Her. Denis Devlin. CIP; NOIV
Against Modesty in Love. Matthew Prior. ErPo
"Against my Love shall be, as I am now." Shakespeare. *Fr.* Sonnets, LXIII. OBSC
Against Negritude. Emanuel Corgo, *tr. fr. Portuguese by* Michael Wolfers. WMBCH
Against night's high flakes, snow. A Lullaby, a Farewell. Sonya Dorman. BWV
Against Parting. Natan Zach, *tr. fr. Hebrew by* Jon Silkin. VWA
Against Platonick Love. *Unknown.* OBS
Against Portraits. Charles Tomlinson. PoPo
Against Proud Poor Phryna. John Davies of Hereford. FaBoEE
Against Romanticism. Kingsley Amis. NePoEA; NoAM
Against Sadness. Natan Zach, *tr. fr. Hebrew by* Warren Bargad *and* Stanley F. Chyet. IP
Against Seasons. Robert Mezey. NYBP
Against Slavery. William Cowper. *See* Task, The: Time-Piece, The.
Against Starlings. Stanley Plumly. BLA
Against Still Life. Margaret Atwood. MoCV; NMM
Against Surrealism. James Wright. LCAP
Against Te Rauparaha. Alistair Campbell. *Fr.* Sanctuary of Spirits, IX. PeNZ
Against the Age. Louis Simpson. NePoEA-2
Against the Baron's Enemies. *Unknown. See* Sitteth alle stille and herkneth to me!
Against the broad sky. Takahama Kyoshi, *tr. by* Geoffrey Bownas *and* Anthony Thwaite. PeBJV
Against the burly air I strode. Genesis. Geoffrey Hill. HAP; NePoEA; OAEL-2; OxBC; TOF
Against the cherries on the hazy hilltop. Teika, *tr. fr. Japanese by* Hiroaki Sato. *Fr.* Eighty-four Tanka. FCEI
Against the clear intensity of dawn. Budding Spring. Jack Lindsay. PoAu-1
Against the day of sorrow. Trifle. Georgia Douglas Johnson. AmNP
Against the Evidence. David Ignatow. CAPP; NNaP
Against the False Magicians. Thomas McGrath. NePoEA

Against the Fear of Death. Lucretius, *tr. fr. Latin by* Rolfe Humphries. *Fr.* De Rerum Natura (On the Nature of Things), III. DL, *abr.*. ("Ah Wretch! thou cry'st, ah! miserable me.") AWP, *tr. by* Dryden; FaBoRV, *tr. by* Dryden; OAEL-1, *tr. by* Dryden; OBVE, *tr. by* Dryden.

Against the flare and descant of the gas. Warning to a Guest. John Holloway. NePoEA

Against the gentleman. The Vampire. David Galler. VVA

Against the guide of Truth. *Unknown, tr. fr. Hebrew. Fr.* Duel with Verses over a Great Man. TrJP

Against the Magpie. *Unknown.* GBP; PBBP

Against the morning glories. Kikaku, *tr. fr. Japanese by* Hiroaki Sato. *Fr.* Thirty-three Hokku. FCEI

Against the pure, reflective tiles. My Six Toothbrushes. Phyllis McGinley. GoYe

Against the rubber tongues of cows and the hoeing hands of men. Thistles. Ted Hughes. NoAM; OxBSP; OxBTC

Against the Silences to Come. Ron Loewinsohn. PoM

Against the sunset, two snipes go to the west. *Unknown, tr. by* Hiroaki Sato. FCEI

Against the white beach. Abutsu, *tr. by* Steven D. Carter. WFTW

Against the Wind. Amir Gilboa, *tr. fr. Hebrew by* Bernhard Frank. MHeP

Against the window pane. Summer Rain. Sir Herbert Read. LiTM

Against Them Who Lay Unchastity to the Sex of Women. William Habington. *Fr.* Castara, II. JCP; MePo; OBS; SeCP

Against these turbid turquoise skies. Les Ballons. Oscar Wilde. NOBVV

Against what light. Black Dada Nihilismus. Imamu Amiri Baraka. PoM

Against Whatever It Is That's Encroaching. Charles Simic. BLA

Against Winter. Elaine Feinstein. VWA

Against winter which advances. Marcabrun, *tr. by* Paul Blackburn. Pro

Against Witches. *Unknown.* GBP

Against Women. *Unknown.* MeEL

Against Women, *sel. Unknown, tr. fr. Welsh by* Gwyn Williams. "Woman is by aptitude." OBWVE

Against Women's Fashions. John Lydgate. ACP

Agamemnon ("Dear gods, set me free from all the pain.") Aeschylus, *tr. fr. Greek by* Robert Fagles. NAWM-1

Sels.

Achaians Have Got Troy, upon This Very Day, The. *Tr. by* Richmond Lattimore. WaaP

"Great Fortune is an hungry thing." *Tr. by* Gilbert Murray. AWP

God of War, Money Changer of Dead Bodies, The. *Tr. by* Richmond Lattimore. WaaP

Hymn to Zeus. *Tr. by* Gilbert Murray. WGRP

If I Were to Tell of Our Labours, Our Hard Lodging. *Tr. by* Louis MacNeice. WaaP

Signal Fire, The. *Tr. by* Dallam Simpson. CTC

Agamemnon before Troy. John Frederick Nims. Son

Agamemnon's Tomb ("Tomb/ A hollow hateful world."), *sel.* Sacheverell Sitwell. LiTB; OBMV

"One by one, as harvesters, all heavy laden." MoBrPo

Aganis the Thievis of Liddisdale. Sir Richard Maitland. GoTS

Agape the sooty collier stands. *Fr.* A Descriptive Poem, Addressed to Two Ladies at Their Return from Viewing the Mines, near Whitehaven. NOEC

Agatha Christie and Beatrix Potter. John Updike. AnAmPo

Agatha Christie to. Said. George Starbuck. OBAL

Agathon, *sel.* George Edward Woodberry.

Song of Eros. AA

Agbor Dancer. John Pepper Clark. PBA

Age. Abraham Cowley. AWP

Age. Robert Creeley. PPR

Age, An. Laura Jensen. LCAP

Age. Rae Desmond Jones. CBAP

Age. Walter Savage Landor. FaBoEE; NOBVV; PoEL-4

Age. Philip Larkin. CMoP

Age, The. Osip Mandelstam, *tr. fr. Russian by* Peter Russell. AnAn

Age. Tomioka Taeko, *tr. fr. Japanese by* Hiroaki Sato. FCEI

Age, The/ requires this task. A Different Image. Dudley Randall. BPo; CNA; FF; TAP

Age after age our bird through incense flies. Bird, Bird. Gene Derwood. LiTA

Age, and the deaths, and the ghosts. He Resigns. John Berryman. OxBSP; SM; WeW

Age and Youth. Shakespeare. *See* Passionate Pilgrim, The: Crabbed Age and Youth.

Age being mathematical, these flowers, An. Tulips. Padraic Colum. ImOP

Age cannot reach me where the veils of God. Immortality. Susan Langstaff Mitchell. TIRV

Age cannot wither her whom not gray hairs. Evening. Wendell Phillips Garrison. *Fr.* Post-Meridian. AA

Age demanded an image, The. Ezra Pound. *Fr.* Hugh Selwyn Mauberley. (Life and Contacts), II. HAP; MoAmPo; VGW

Age grips the body but the heart stays young. Love Is Bitter. *Unknown.* PeSA

Age has passed away since love, An. Asadullah Khan Ghalib, *tr. by* Ahmed Ali. GoT

Age in her embraces passed [*or* pass'd, *or* past], An. The Mistress; a Song. Earl of Rochester. EBEV; MePo; NOBE; OBS

Age in Prospect. Robinson Jeffers. MoAB; MoAmPo

Age is a quality of mind. How Old Are You? H. S. Fritsch. PoLF

Age is dull and mean, The. Men creep. For Righteousness' Sake. Whittier. PoEL-4

Age Is Ended, An. Haim Guri, *tr. fr. Hebrew by* Warren Bargad *and* Stanley F. Chyet. IP

Age Is Great and Strong, The. Victor Hugo, *tr. fr. French by* W. J. Robertson. WGRP

Age is when to a man. Samuel Beckett. *Fr.* Words and Music. BIrV; NoAM

Age Not to Be Rejected. Robert Herrick. *See* Am I despised because you say.

Age of a Dream, The. Lionel Johnson. OBMV

Age of Animals, The. *Unknown.* FaBoUs

Age of Blue Memory, The. Odysseus Elytis, *tr. fr. Greek by* Edmund Keeley *and* Philip Sherrard. VMG

Age of Bronze, The, *sel.* Byron.

"Alas, the country! how shall tongue or pen." OBSV

Age of Bronze awoke now in brutality, The. John Heath-Stubbs. *Fr.* Artorius. EBEV

Age of earth and us all chattering. Susan Howe. LP

Age of Gold. Pietro Metastasio, *tr. fr. Italian by* Ezra Pound. CTC

Age of Innocence. Graham Hough. PoRA

Age of Reason, The. Jorie Graham. NPGG

Age of Reason, The. William Langland. *Fr.* The Vision of Piers Plowman. NOCV

Age of seventy is gone, The. I Know Inside. Yüan Mei, *tr. by* Jonathan Chaves. CoBLCP

Age of Sheen, The. Dorothy Hughes. NYBP

Age of Snow, The. Márton Kalász, *tr. fr. Hungarian by* Jascha Kessler. FOC

Age of the Rubber Seals. Buland al-Haidari, *tr. fr. Arabic by* Patricia Alanah Byrne *and* Salma Khadra Jayyusi. MAP

Age of the Street, The. Anthony Howell. NPo

Aged, Aged Man, The. "Lewis Carroll." *See* Through the Looking-Glass: I'll tell thee everything I can.

Aged, bittersweet, in salt crusted, the pink meat. Smithfield Ham. Dave Smith. HCAP

Aged catch their breath, The. Wystan Hugh Auden. *Fr.* The Sea and the Mirror. LiTA

Aged Fisherman. Witter Bynner. GoYe

Aged Lover Discourses in the Flat Style, The. James Vincent Cunningham. SM

Aged Lover Renounceth Love, The. Lord Thomas Vaux. EIL; OAEL-1; PoEL-1

Aged man, that mowes [*or* mows] these fields. A Dialogue betwixt Time and a Pilgrime [*or* Pilgrim]. Aurelian Townshend. MePo; NOBE; OAEL-1; OBS; SeCP

Aged Pilot Man, The. "Mark Twain." OBAL

Aged Stranger, The. Bret Harte. AA; AmFN; AnAmPo

Aged twenty-six. Birthdays. C. J. Driver. PeSA

Aged Wino's Counsel to a Young Man on the Brink of Marriage, The. X. J. Kennedy. FF

Aged Writer, An. Roy McFadden. NeIP

Ageing Athlete, The. Neil Weiss. SD

Ageing Hunter, The. Avane, *tr. fr. Eskimo.* WTO

Ageless. Paul Eluard, *tr. fr. French by* Michael Benedikt. POS

Agency. Andrew Joron. BWV

Agent of Love. A. K. Redwing. VoR

Agents, The. Robert Conquest. EAS

Ages of Man, The. *at. to.* Abraham Ibn Ezra, *tr. fr. Hebrew by* Nina Davis Salaman. TrJP

Aghadoe. John Todhunter. AnIL

Agile voice, quick smile, and leaping eyes, An. Enid Field: In Memoriam. Gloria A. Maxson. TSM

Agincourt. Michael Drayton. BeLS; EIL; FaBoBe; FaBoCh; OBEV

Agincourt Carol, The. *Unknown.* EBEV; OAEL-1; OBET

Aging. Randall Jarrell. PoA

Aging Actress Sees Herself a Starlet on the Late Show, The. Miller Williams. MT
Aging of Clones, The. Andrew Joron *and* Robert Frazier. BWV
Aging old queers are no treat. *Unknown.* PeHV
Aging Poet, The. Hans Warren, *tr. fr. Dutch by* James S. Holmes. DuIn
Aging Poet, on a Reading Trip to Dayton, Visits the Air Force Museum and Discovers There a Plane He Once Flew, The. Richard Snyder. Psk
Agitation of the air, An. End of Summer. Stanley Kunitz. CAPP; MoAmPo; Psk; VGW
Agitato ma Non Troppo. John Crowe Ransom. OxBA
Aglaia. Nicholas Breton. *Fr.* The Passionate Shepherd. OBSC
Aglaura, *sels.* Sir John Suckling.
  "No, no, fair heretic[k], it needs must be." *Fr.* IV, i. CaPo; OBS; PrIm
  Why So Pale and Wan, Fond Lover?. *Fr.* IV, ii. AWP; ELP; FaBV; FPL; HAP; HeIP; HoPM; NOBE; OBEV; OBS; PoE; PoRA; SeCePo; TEP; TrGrPo; UnPo
    (Encouragements to a Lover.) FaFP; GTBS; GTBS-P
    (Song: "Why so pale and wan, fond lover?.") BoLoP; CaPo; EnLoPo; HeIP; InPS; JCP; MePo; PoEL-3; PrIm; SeCP; SeCV-1
Agnes. Koh Chang-soo, *tr. fr. Korean by the author.* ACKP
Agnes. Mah-do-ge Tohee. STE
Agnes Snaggletooth. X. J. Kennedy. ILY
Agnodicia, or Ignorance Banished from the Presence of Women. Catherine Des Roches, *tr. fr. French by* Dorothy Backer. DMF
Agnosco Veteris Vestigia Flammae. J. V. Cunningham. QFR; VGW
Agnosto Theo (To an Unknown God). Thomas Hardy. WGRP
Ago. Elizabeth Jennings. GOYP
Agog, in rain house-deep. Apologia. Jean Garrigue. LiTA
Agonies confirm His hour. Bahá'u'lláh in the Garden of Ridwan. Robert Hayden. PoBA
Agonies of change. Death Takes Only a Minute. Agnes Pratt. NOVW
Agonizing Memory, The. Pierre Louÿs, *tr. fr. French.* *Fr.* Chansons de Bilitis. PeHV
Agony. Giuseppe Ungaretti, *tr. fr. Italian by* Patrick Creagh. PFI
Agony, An. As Now. Imamu Amiri Baraka. AmPP; BPo; LiTM; NAAL-2; PoE; PPP
Agony in the Garden, The. Felicia Dorothea Hemans. TrCP
Agraphon. Angelos Sikelianos, *tr. fr. Greek by* Edmund Keeley *and* Philip Sherrard. VMG
Agreeable Monsters. Amy Clampitt. AnAn
Agreed that all these birds. All These Birds. Richard Wilbur. NOBA; Prf
Agreement. Kishwar Naheed, *tr. fr. Urdu by* Mahmood Jamal. PBMUP
Agreement swerves. Lyn Hejinian. UL
Agricultural Show, Flemington, Victoria, The. "Furnley Maurice." CBAP
Agriculture, *sel.* Robert Dodsley.
  Method of Preserving Hay from Being Mow-Burnt, or Taking Fire, A. FaBoUs
Agrigentum Road, The. Salvatore Quasimodo, *tr. fr. Italian by* Richard Wilbur. PFI
Ague. Sandor Csoori, *tr. fr. Hungarian by* Edwin Morgan. MHuP
Aguinaldo. Bertrand Shadwell. PAH
Ah/ Autumn wind. Song of the Pike. Sato Haruo, *tr. by* Geoffrey Bownas *and* Anthony Thwaite. PeBJV
Ah/ from the south, and from the southwest. The Breeze Comes Filling the Valley. Miyazawa Kenji, *tr. by* Hiroaki Sato. FCEI
Ah, all the sands of the earth lead unto heaven. Persian Miniature. William Jay Smith. CoAP
Ah, Are You Digging on My Grave? Thomas Hardy. BrPo; DL; MoAB; MoBrPo; NAEL-2; OBD; TEP
Ah, Be Not False. Richard Watson Gilder. AA
"Ah bed! the field where joy's peace some do see." Sir Philip Sidney. *Fr.* Astrophel and Stella, XCVIII. EnLoPo
Ah, Ben!/ Say how, or when. An Ode for Ben Jonson. Robert Herrick. AWP; InvP; SeCP; TrGrPo
  (Ode for Him, An.) CaPo; NoP; OBS; SeCV-1
Ah blackbird, giving thanks. *Unknown.* NOIV
Ah, blackbird, thou art satisfied. Blackbird, The. *Unknown, tr. by* Kuno Meyer. AnIL
Ah blessed plant! ah lucky creeper! Entwined. *Malay Oral Tradition, tr. by* R. J. Wilkinson *and* R. O. Winstedt. WTO
Ah, blessedness of work! the aimless mind. Work. Louis James Block. AA
Ah blow! thou art the last, the last! Broken Heart. Henrietta Cordelia Ray. CBWP-3
Ah Bounce! ah gentle Beast! why wouldst thou dye. Lines on Bounce. Pope. FM
Ah, broken is the golden bowl! the spirit flown forever! Lenore. Poe. AA; AmPP; AnAmPo; LiTA

Ah! changed and cold, how changed and very cold! Dead before Death. Christina Rossetti. NAEL-2
Ah child, no Persian—perfect art. Simplicity. Horace. *See* Odes: I, 38.
Ah, Chloris! Could I now but sit. Sir Charles Sedley. *See* Mulberry Garden, The: Child and Maiden.
Ah, Christ. Allen Tate. *Fr.* Sonnets at Christmas, II. HAP; LiTA; LiTM; PoNe; Son; VGW
Ah, Clemence! when I saw thee last. La Grisette. Oliver Wendell Holmes. AA
Ah Cloris! That I Now Could Sit. Sir Charles Sedley. *See* Mulberry Garden, The: Child and Maiden.
Ah, comic officer and gentleman. Elegy: E. W. L. E. Sissman. NYBP
Ah! County Guy, the hour is nigh. Serenade. Sir Walter Scott. *Fr.* Quentin Durward. GTBS; GTBS-P
  (Song: "Ah! County Guy, the hour is nigh.") CH
Ah, cruel maid, because I see. The Cruel Maid. Robert Herrick. CaPo
Ah Dalmatia, if only I could send word of your dear sons. Ante Kosovic, *tr. by* Amelia Batistich *and* Ian Wedde. PeNZ
Ah dearest Love, for how long. Mechthild von Magdeburg, *tr. fr. German.* *Fr.* The Flowering Light of the Godhead. ILwL
Ah! dearest love, sweet home of all my fears. Keats. *Fr.* Ode to Fanny. ChER
Ah, deem not when thy minstrel tunes. The Minstrel. Joseph Skipsey. PF
Ah dextrous Chirurgeons, mitigate your plan. On Having Piles. Sir Walter Scott. FaBoEE
Ah, did he climb, that man, nigher to heaven than I. Dark Rapture. "Æ." SeCePo
Ah, did you once see Shelley plain. Memorabilia. Robert Browning. FiP; NAEL-2; NOBVV; NoP; OAEL-2; OBNC; PoE; RB; SeCePo
Ah, dog. Here is my boot. Does it stink good? Timon Speaks to a Dog. Philip Hobsbaum. TW
Ah, Douglass, we have fall'n on evil days. Douglass. Paul Laurence Dunbar. Son
Ah, dry those tears; they flow too fast. To Miss———on the Death of Her Goldfish. Mr. Meredyth. FM
Ah, Fading Joy. Dryden. *Fr.* The Indian Emperor, IV, iii. ChTr; FiP
  (Song: "Ah fading joy, how quickly art thou past!") NoP
Ah! fair and lovely bloom the flowers of youth. Youth and Age. Mimnermus, *tr. by* John Addington Symonds. AWP
Ah! fair face gone from sight. Lionel Johnson. *Fr.* In Memory. OBNC; PoEL-5
Ah, fair Zenocrate, divine Zenocrate. Christopher Marlowe. *Fr.* Tamburlaine the Great, *Pt.* I, Act V, sc. ii. EBEV; PoEL-2
  (Fair Is Too Foul an Epithet.) LiTB
Ah false Amyntas, can that hour. Aphra Behn. *Fr.* The Dutch Lover. WPE
Ah, Fate! cannot a man. Fame. Emerson. AnAmPo
Ah, Faustus,/ Now hast thou but one bare hour [*or* hower] to live. Christopher Marlowe. *Fr.* Doctor Faustus, V, ii. ChTr; HeIP
  (End of Doctor Faustus, The.) PoEL-2
  (End of Faustus, The.) TrGrPo
Ah, Flood of Life on which I am a wave. Watson Kirkconnell. *Fr.* The Tide of Life. CaP
Ah, flow on, flow on. Sail Peacefully Home. Simeon Grigoryevich Frug. TrJP
Ah for the throes of a heart sorely wounded! The Damsel. Omar b. Abi Rabi'a, *tr. by* W. G. Palgrave. AWP
Ah! freedom is a noble thing! *See* A! fredome is a noble thing!
Ah, friend! 'tis true—this truth you lovers know. To Mr. Gay, Who Wrote Him a Congratulatory Letter on the Finishing His House. Pope. NOEC
Ah-fu-jung, ah-fu-jung! Wei Yüan, *tr. fr. Chinese by* Irving Lo. *Fr.* Song of Chiang-nan, VIII. WFTU
Ah! gentle, fleeting, wav'ring sprite. Emperor Hadrian, *tr. fr. Latin by* Byron. *Fr.* Hadrian's Address to His Soul When Dying. OBD; OBVE
Ah gentle shepherd, thine the lot to tend. John Dyer. *Fr.* The Fleece, I. PoEL-3
Ah! Grandmother weaves! Grandmother Sleeps. Liz Sohappy Bahe. CDW
Ah, Guillaume, my friend, and greatest of predecessors, if. To Guillaume Apollinaire. Jim Brodey, VIII. UL
Ah, happy blindness! Enion sees not the terrors of the uncertain. It Is Not So with Me. Blake. *Fr.* Vala; or The Four Zoas. SeCePo
Ah, happy who have seen Him, whom the world. Francis William Bourdillon. *Fr.* A Lost God. WGRP
Ah, happy youths, ah, happy maid. On a Picture by Poussin Representing Shepherds in Arcadia. John Addington Symonds. FaBoBe
Ah hate to see de ev'nin' sun go down. St. Louis Blues. William Christopher Handy. FF
Ah, he stood up, stood up by himself this year! Teitoku, *tr. by* Hiroaki Sato. FCEI

Ah, Heavens, intercede for me! On the Slaughter. Hayyim Nahman Bialik, *tr.* by Bernhard Frank. MHeP

Ah, how poets sing and die! Dunbar. Anne Spencer. BANP; CDC

Ah, How Sweet It Is to Love! Dryden. *Fr.* Tyrannic Love, IV, i. HoPM

Ah! Hoyland, empress of my heart. Ode to Miss Hoyland. Thomas Chatterton. BXAP

Ah! I could curse them in my woe. Revenge. Mary E. Tucker. CBWP-1

Ah, I know what happiness is! Blanche Taylor Dickinson. CDC

Ah! I remember well (and how can I). Early Love. Samuel Daniel. *Fr.* Hymen's Triumph. ErPo

Ah, if I could, I'd dwell with you tonight. A Message. George Ives. PeHV

Ah in the thunder air. Trees in the Garden. D. H. Lawrence. CMoP; MoAB; MoBrPo; NoP

Ah, is there no, no place on earth. Weariness. Mary E. Tucker. CBWP-1

Ah—it's the skeleton of a lady's sunshade. The Sunshade. Thomas Hardy. OxBTC

Ah, Jack it was, and with him little Jill. Jack and Jill. Harriet S. Morgridge. *Fr.* Mother Goose Sonnets. AA

Ah, Jesu Kri. María Sabina, *tr. fr. Mazatec Indian by* Henry Munn. *Fr.* The Chants. STP

Ah, June is here, but where is May. Unfulfillment. Frances Louisa Bushnell. AA

Ah [*or* A] kond of Swat, The. Edward Lear. CenHV; FaBoCh; FaBoCo; FaBoNo; FiBHP; NA

Ah! leave my harp and me alone. *Unknown.* SaC

Ah, Lenin, you were richt. But I'm a poet. Second Hymn to Lenin. "Hugh MacDiarmid." OAEL-2

Ah! liberal-handed lady, though. The Good Tradition. *Unknown, tr. by* Robin Flower. AnIL

Ah! light lovely lady with delicate lips aglow. At Mass. *Unknown, tr. by* Robin Flower. BIrV

Ah! little flower, upspringing, azure-eyed. Fruitionless. Ina Coolbrith. AA

Ah! little fly, alighting fitfully. Calvus to a Fly. Charles Tennyson Turner. FM; NOBVV

Ah, little road, all whirry in the breeze. The Road. Helene Johnson. AmNP; BANP; BlSi; CDC; PoNe

Ah, London! London! our delight. A Ballad of London. Richard Le Gallienne. FaBoPP

Ah, look,/ How sucking their last sweetness from the air. The Divers. Peter Quennell. MoBrPo

Ah, look at all the lonely people! Eleanor Rigby. John Lennon *and* Paul McCartney. PrIm; WTO

Ah! Love, my Master, hear me swear. Of His Death. Meleager, *tr. by* Andrew Lang. AWP

Ah! Lovely Appearance of Death! Charles Wesley. AH

Ah, Lucasta, why so bright. To Lucasta. Richard Lovelace. CaPo

Ah! lunch and. The Marunouchi Building. Nakahara Chuya, *tr. by* Geoffrey Bownas *and* Anthony Thwaite. PeBJV

Ah Ma Ma, Poppa, Leslie. Eat, Eat! Nellie Wong. ER

Ah! Matt.: old age has brought to me. Senex to Matt. Prior. James Kenneth Stephen. *Fr.* Two Epigrams. CenHV; FiBHP

Ah me,/ Was there a time. For Lucas Cranach's Eve. Adelaide Crapsey. QFR

Ah me! Am I the Swaine. George Wither. OBS

Ah me! full sorely is my heart forlorn. The School-Mistress. William Shenstone. GoTL; LaA

Ah me! How differently th'untutor'd slave. John Singleton. *Fr.* A General Description of the West Indian Islands, *Bk.* III. PBCV

Ah me! I cannot sleep at night. Foiled Sleep. "Marie Madelaine," *tr. by* Ferdinand E. Kappey. PeHV

Ah, me! I know how like a golden flower. The Grand Ronde Valley. Ella Higginson. AA

Ah me, if I grew sweet to man. The Tragic Mary Queen of Scots. "Michael Field." EnLoPo; OBMV

Ah me, my friend! it will not, will not last! William Shenstone. NOEC

Ah me, the aspidistra grows dusty behind the window pane. In North Great George's Street. "Seumas O'Sullivan." BIrV

Ah me the hand upon the body. Legerdemain. Kenneth Mackenzie. PoAu-2

Ah Me! the Mighty Love. George Frederick Cameron. CaP

Ah me! those old familiar bounds! Ode on a Distant Prospect of Clapham Academy. Thomas Hood. BXAP

Ah! might I in some humble Kentish dale. Lines Written at Cambridge, to W. R., Esquire. Phineas Fletcher. *Fr.* To My Ever-honoured Cousin W. R. Esquire. ElL

Ah, Miss Barton. Bonnie Jacobson. *Fr.* Introductions, or, What's in a Name. SoTCo

Ah, moment not to be purchased. Bayard Taylor. *Fr.* The Sunshine of the Gods. AA

Ah, more than any priest, O soul, we too believe in God. Walt Whitman. *Fr.* Passage to India. WGRP

Ah, must I leave you dear. Hasetsukabe Tori, *tr. fr. Japanese.* *Fr.* Manyo Shu. Ma

Ah my Anthea! must my heart still break? To Anthea. Robert Herrick. CaPo

Ah my city, my lady. Twentieth Telegram ("Ah my city, my lady"). Abd al-Aziz al-Maqalih, *tr. fr. Arabic by* Lena Jayyusi *and* Christopher Middleton. *Fr.* Telegrams of Tenderness for Sanaa. MAP

Ah my daughter, my grandchild! All You Others, Eat. Djurberaui, *tr. by* C. H. Berndt. WTO

Ah my dear angry [*or* deare angrie] Lord. Bitter-sweet. George Herbert. NOBE; NoP; OxBSP; TrPWD

Ah, my grandpa in Kubelnik is a simple sort of fellow. Grandpa and the Uncles. Moishe Kulbak, *tr. fr. Yiddish by* Leonard Wolf. *Fr.* Byelorussia. PeBMYV

Ah! my heart, ah! what aileth thee. To His Heart. Sir Thomas Wyatt. OBSC; SiPS

Ah my Jill loves her nakedness. Marvelous. Allan Kaplan

Ah—my *koji!* When News of Saichi's Death Arrived. Ryokan, *tr. by* Burton Watson. JLIC-2

Ah my Perilla! do'st thou grieve to see. To Perilla. Robert Herrick. CaPo; OBS; SeCP; SeCV-1

Ah, necromancy sweet! Emily Dickinson. NOBA

Ah Night! blind germ of days to be. A Ballad of High Endeavor. *Unknown.* NA

Ah! no!/ You are not a soldierly upright row! Upon a Row of Old Books and Shoes in a Pawnbroker's Window. "Furnley Maurice." CBAP

Ah no; nor I myselfe: though my pure love. Richard Barnfield. *Fr.* Sonnets, XIX. PeHV

Ah, nobody knows. Frost. Stella Benson. OxBTC

Ah Norman, my boy, my precious, my joy. Norman; or, The Fungus among Us. Bruce Bennett. SoTCo

Ah not as plains that spread into us slowly. Booty. Eileen Duggan. ATNZ

Ah, not this marble, dead and cold. Washington's Monument, February 1885. Walt Whitman. OFD

Ah nuts! It's boring reading French newspapers. Les Luths. Frank O'Hara. NoAM; NOBA

Ah! On Udo beach. Suruga Dance. *Unknown, tr. by* Geoffrey Bownas *and* Anthony Thwaite. PeBJV

Ah, our kiss—may the sea remain as it is. Wakayama Bokusui, *tr. fr. Japanese by* Hiroaki Sato. *Fr.* Forty-four Tanka. FCEI

Ah, pity love where'er it grows! The Old Man's Complaint. *Unknown.* OxBSP

Ah! poor intoxicated little knave. To a Fly, Taken out of a Bowl of Punch. "Peter Pindar." NOEC

Ah Posthumus! our years [*or* yeares] hence fly [*or* flye]. His Age, Dedicated to His Peculiar Friend, Master John Wickes, under the Name of Posthumus. Robert Herrick. CaPo; SeCP

Ah Poverties, Wincings, and Sulky Retreats. Walt Whitman. OxBSP

Ah, ra, chickera. *Unknown.* OxNR

Ah, Raleigh, when thy breath thou didst resign. Britannia and Raleigh. John Ayloffe. APAS

Ah, Robin,/ Jolly Robin. Sir Thomas Wyatt. SiPS

Ah! sad wer we as we did peace. The Turnstile. William Barnes. CH; NOBVV

Ah, see the fair chivalry come, the companions of Christ! Te Martyrum Candidatus. Lionel Johnson. ACP; OBMV; TIRV

Ah, Spain, already your tragic landscapes. The Spanish War. "Hugh MacDiarmid." CMoP; NOBC

Ah, spring comes from afar, smoky. Sunny Spring. Hagiwara Sakutaro, *tr. by* Hiroaki Sato. FCEI

Ah, spring, spring! Basho, *tr. fr. Japanese by* Burton Watson. *Fr.* Seventy-six Hokku. FCEI

Ah, stay thy treacherous hand, forbear to trace. Verses on Sir Joshua Reynolds's Painted Window at New College, Oxford. Thomas Warton the Younger. NOEC; PoEL-3

Ah! Sun-Flower ("Ah! Sun-flower, weary of time"). Blake. *Fr.* Songs of Experience. AWP; EBEV; ELP; EnRP; FaBoRV; HAP; NAEL-2; NIP; NOEC; NoP; OAEL-2; OBNC; PoE; PoEL-4; PPP; PrIm; RB; TEP; TOF; UnPo; WeW

Ah, sweet Content! where is thy mylde abode? Barnabe Barnes. *Fr.* Parthenophil and Parthenophe, LXVI. AAS
(Content.) OBSC
(Sonnet: "Ah, sweet Content! where is thy mild abode.") EIL

Ah, take these lips away; no more. Deadly Kisses. Pierre de Ronsard, *tr. by* Andrew Lang. AWP

Ah, Tam! gie me a Border burn. A Border Burn. J. B. Selkirk. *Fr.* Epistle to Tammus. PoSH

Ah, Teneriffe! Emily Dickinson. InPS

Ah, That I Were Far Away. Arthur Hugh Clough. *Fr.* Amours de Voyage, Canto III, *introd.* OBNC
(Upon Apennine Slope.) FaBoPP

Ah, that rascal love. Prince Hozumi, *tr. fr. Japanese. Fr.* Manyo Shu. Ma

Ah, that was but the wind. The Dead Bird. Andrew Young. FM

Ah, the blowfly is whining there, its maggots are eating the flesh. The Blowflies Buzz. *Unknown, tr. by* Catherine Berndt. WTO
(Djalbarmiwi's Song.) CBAP

Ah, the glorious ancestors. *Unknown, tr. by* Arthur Waley. BoS

Ah, the lovely full moon. Complaint of the Moon in the Provinces. Jules Laforgue, *tr. by* William Jay Smith. CT

Ah! the morning is grey. Chimney-Tops. *Unknown.* BoTP

Ah! the roofs. *Ambo Oral Tradition. Fr.* Five Ghost Songs. TTTS

Ah, the Sea of Grebes!/. Ietaka, *tr. by* Steven D. Carter. WFTW

Ah! the year is slowly dying. Passing of the Old Year. Mary Weston Fordham. CBWP-2

Ah! then the grassy-meäded Maÿ. Zummer Stream. William Barnes. BoNaP

Ah! there's a house that I do know. Slow to Come, Quick a-Gone. William Barnes. NOBVV

Ah, through the open door. Spring Morning. D. H. Lawrence. BrPo; CMoP; MoAB; MoBrPo

Ah! To be alone in a little cell. The Desire for Hermitage. *Unknown, tr. by* Sean O'Faolain. AnIL

Ah to be alone and uninhibited! American against Solitude. Alan Dugan

Ah, 'twas a glorious autumn night. The Two Meetings. Eugene Field. PWR

Ah, vale of woe, of gloom and darkness moulded. Rachel Morpurgo, *tr. by* Nina Davis Salaman. TrJP

Ah Were She Pitiful. Robert Greene. *Fr.* Pandosto. TrGrPo, *abr.*
(Fawnia.) OBEV; OBSC
(In Praise of His Loving and Best-beloved Fawnia.) PoEL-2

Ah what a town! Mud spurts up bursting with dirt. Budapest Elegy. István Vas, *tr. by* Edwin Morgan. MHuP

Ah! what a weary race my feet have run. Sonnet: To the River Lodon. Thomas Warton, the Younger. NOEC

Ah, what avails the sceptred race! Rose Aylmer. Walter Savage Landor. AWP; BoLoP; CH; ELP; EnLoPo; EnRP; FaFP; GBL; HAP; HeIP; HoPM; LiTB; NAEL-2; NOBE; NoP; OAEL-2; OBEV; OBNC; PoEL-4; TEP; TrGrPo; UnPo; WeW

Ah what can ail thee, knight-at-arms. *See* O what can ail thee, knight-at-arms.

Ah, what can be more stately. Walt Whitman. *Fr.* Crossing Brooklyn Ferry. AA

Ah! what is love? It is a pretty thing. The Shepherd's Wife's Song. Robert Greene. *Fr.* Greene's Mourning Garment. ElL; HAP; OBSC

Ah! what pleasant visions haunt me. The Galley of Count Arnaldos. Longfellow. OBEV

Ah, what shall I be at fifty. Tennyson. *Fr.* Maud, *Pt.* I, i. NAEL-2

Ah! what time wilt thou come? when shall that cry. The Dawning. Henry Vaughan. MePo; NOCV; TrPWD

Ah, when our last years come in sight. Last Love. Fyodor Tyutchev. AAA, *tr. by* Alan Myers

Ah, When Will Dawn Begin to Break? Shmuel Halkin, *tr. fr. Yiddish by* Hillel Halkin. PeBMYV

Ah! where the hedge athirt the hill. When We That Now Ha' Childern Wer Childern. William Barnes. NOBVV

"Ah wherefore with infection should he live." Shakespeare. *Fr.* Sonnets, LXVII. PeHV

Ah! Why, because the Dazzling Sun. Emily Brontë. BrRo
(Stars.) NAEL-2

Ah! why will my dear little girl be so cross. Washing and Dressing. Ann Taylor. FaBoUs

Ah, with the grape my fading life provide. Omar Khayyám, *tr. fr. Persian by* Edward Fitzgerald. *Fr.* The Rubáiyát of Omar Khayyám of Naishápúr. EBEV; GTBS-P

Ah! with what freedome could I once have pray'd. The Sigh. Nathaniel Wanley. OBS

Ah Woe Is Me. Sextus Propertius, *tr. fr. Latin by* F. A. Wright. *Fr.* Elegies, I, 1. AWP

Ah! would there were many in the world like you. To the Most Excellent Lady Veronica Gambara. Laura Terracina, *tr. fr. Italian by* Muriel Kittel. *Fr.* The Discourse on the Principle in All the Cantos. DMI

Ah Wretch! thou cry'st, ah! miserable me. Lucretius. *See* De Rerum Natura (On the Nature of Things): Against the Fear of Death.

Ah Wretched Me, Who Loved a Sparrow Hawk. *Unknown, tr. fr. Italian by* Muriel Kittel. DMI

Ah yah, tair um bam, boo wah. Jungle Mammy Song. *Unknown.* AS

Ah yes, I had a bear. Bear in Bed. Judith Herzberg, *tr. by* Shirley Kaufman. DuIn

Ah, Yes, I Wrote the "Purple Cow." Gelett Burgess. FiBHP
(Cinq Ans Après.) OBAL
(Confession.) FaBoNo; NBLV
(Nonsense Quatrains.) CenHV
(Sequel to the "Purple Cow.") FaBoCo

Ah yes, when love allows. Hadewijch, *tr. by* Frans van Rosevelt. PBWP

Ah! yesterday, d'ye know, I voun.' Polly Be-en Upzides wi' Tom. William Barnes. NOBVV

Ah, you are cruel. Neighbors. Anne Spencer. CDC

Ah, you beast of love. Hayden Carruth. VGW

Ah, you have much to learn, we can't know all things at twenty. Arthur Hugh Clough. *Fr.* The Bothie of Tober-na-Vuolich, *Bk.* II. FaBoPV

Ah, you mistake me, comrades, to think that my heart is steel. Arnold at Stillwater. Thomas Dunn English. PAH

Ah (you say), this is Holy Wisdom. Hilda Doolittle ("H. D."). *Fr.* Tribute to the Angels. NoAM

Ahab Mohammed. James Matthew Legaré. AA

Ahab's gaily clad fisherfriends. Evil Is No Black Thing. Sarah Webster Fabio. PoBA

Ahasuerus. Joseph Roth, *tr. fr. German by* Erna Baber Rosenfeld. VWA

Ahead I bear; the Eagle of Gál. The Lament for Urien. *Unknown, tr. fr. Middle Welsh by* Ernest Rhys. *Fr.* The Red Book of Hergest. OBMV

Ahead, the sun's face in a flaring hood. First Walk on the Moon. May Swenson. AnAn

Ahkoond of Swat, The. George Thomas Lanigan. *See* Threnody, A: "What, what, what/ What's the news from Swat?"

Ah'm goin' whah nobody knows mah name, Lawd, Lawd! Levee Moan. *Unknown.* AS

Ah'm gonna build mahself a raft. De Blues Ain' Nothin.' *Unknown.* AS

Ah'm sick, doctor-man, Ah'm sick! Calling the Doctor. John Wesley Holloway. BANP

Ahmed. James Berry Bensel. AA

Ahoy and ahoy, birds! Wings and Wheels. Nancy Byrd Turner

Ai, ai, my small red man. Song of Welcome. Hermia Harris Fraser. CaP

Aid me Bellona, while the dreadful fight. Edmund Waller. *Fr.* The Battel of the Summer-Islands. SeCV-1

Aid me, kind Muse, so whimsical a theme. The Midshipman. William Falconer. MOS

Aideen's Grave. Samuel Ferguson. NOIV

Aidenn. Katrina Trask. AA

Aids for Latin. Gordon Perry. FaBoUs

Aijö's Song. Eino Leino, *tr. fr. Finnish by* Aili Jarvenpa. SOP

Aiken Drum. *Unknown.* FaBoCh; FaBoNo; OxNR

Ailing Eagle, The. Annette von Droste-Hülshoff, *tr. fr. German by* Susan L. Cocalis *and* Gerlinde Geiger. DMG

Ailing fish moves in tired circles, An. Repose. Alfred Lichtenstein, *tr. by* Mary Zilzer. VWA

Ailing Japanese Monk, The. Hsiang Ssu, *tr. fr. Chinese by* Burton Watson. CoBCP

Ailing on my travels. Basho, *tr. by* Geoffrey Bownas *and* Anthony Thwaite. PeBJV

Aim get your sights & its sound. First Thesis. Tom Weatherly. *Fr.* Cantos, 7. PoBA

Aim straight at my heart. Krinio. Rita Boumi-Pappas, *tr. by* Eleni Fourtouni. AIW

Aim Was Song, The. Robert Frost. NoP; SoSe

Aimless. Louis Palagyi, *tr. fr. Hungarian by* Watson Kirkconnell. TrJP

Ain' Go'n' to Study War No Mo.' *Unknown.* AS

Ain't been on Market Street for nothing. Ballad of the Hoppy-Toad. Margaret Abigail Walker. BlSi; FB; HoPM

Ain't Gonna Rain, *with music. Unknown.* AS

Ain't I a Woman? Sojourner Truth. AIW; BlSi

Ain't It [*or* It's] Fine Today. Douglas Malloch. BLPA; WBLP

Ain't Nature Commonplace! Arthur Guiterman. FiBHP

Ain't No Grave Can Hold My Body Down. *Unknown.* AmFP

Air: "Arise, arise, arise!" Henry Brooke. *Fr.* Jack the Giant Queller; an Antique History. NOEC

Air: "Cat bird singing." Robert Creeley. Prf

Air: "Element that utters doves, angels and cleft flames." Kathleen Raine. MoAB; MoBrPo

Air: "Flaxen-headed cow-boy, as simple as may be, A." John O'Keefe. NOEC

Air: "For often my mammy has told." Henry Brooke. *Fr.* Jack the Giant Queller; an Antique History. NOEC

Air: "Fox may steal your hens, sir, A." John Gay. *Fr.* The Beggar's Opera, I, i. NOEC
(Soldier and a Sailor, A.) TEP
Air: "I am lost in hot fits." Amiri Baraka. SOTW
Air: "I ne'er could any lustre see." Sheridan. *Fr.* The Duenna, I, ii. NOEC
Air: "Inventory of the geodesic domes." Philip Dow. BXAP
Air: "Love of a woman, The." Robert Creeley. VGW
Air: "Naturally it is night." W. S. Merwin. CAPP; NaP
Air: "O ruddier than the cherry!" John Gay. *Fr.* Acis and Galatea. ELP; NAEL-1; NOEC
(Song: "O ruddier than the cherry.") NOBE
Air: Sentir avec Ardeur. Marie-Françoise-Catherine de Beauveau, Marquise de Boufflers, *tr. fr. French by* Ezra Pound. CTC; WPOW
Air: "Since laws were made for ev'ry degree." John Gay. *Fr.* The Beggar's Opera, III, xiii. NOEC
Air: "So full of courtly reverence." Dudley North. OxBSP
Air: "What a charming thing's a battle!" Isaac Bickerstaffe. *Fr.* The Recruiting Serjeant. NOEC
Air: "Your body is a pipeline." Tomaz Salamun, *tr. fr. Slovene by* Aleksandar Nejgebauer. VWA
Air a-gittin' cool an' coolah. Signs of the Times. Paul Laurence Dunbar. AnAmPo
Air arcs overhead. Archangel. Kit Robinson. UL
Air as the fuel of owls. Snow. Iowa. Michael Dennis Browne. NYBP
Air at night an unbroken whistling wail, The. An Autumn Night. Yu T'ung, *tr. by* Paul W. Kroll. WFTU
Air Balloon, The. Henry James Pye. *Fr.* Aerophorion. NOEC
Air by Sammartini, An. Louis Dudek. OBCV
Air, canals, plane trees, The. February. Pier Paolo Pasolini, *tr. by* Lawrence R. Smith. NItP
Air Circus. Carl Sandburg. AnAmPo
Air Drips from Rock. Yehudah Offen, *tr. fr. Hebrew by* Bernhard Frank. MHeP
Air, earth and water meet at the sea's edge. A Naked Girl Swimming. Arthur Rex Dugard Fairburn. PeNZ
Air Field. Robert Siegel. GeTw
Air fresh, as it has been for days, The. The Color of Many Deer Running. Linda Gregg. NPGG
Air gemlike, the sun so clear, The. November. Giovanni Pascoli, *tr. by* William Jay Smith. CT; PFI
Air in Newfound-land [*or* Aire in Newfoundland-land] is wholesome, good, The. The Pleasant Life in Newfoundland. Robert Hayman. NOBC
(Four Elements in Newfound-land, The.) OBTV
Air Is. John Michael Brennan. MAT
Air is, The/ Sucked clear of dross. January. H. R. Hays. EAS
Air is a mill of hooks, The. Mystic. Sylvia Plath. NYBP
Air is a smoke-tree, the wind, The. Reviewing Past Lives while Leaf-Burning. Anita Endrezze-Danielson. HATNAP
Air is clear. The furniture still, The. To a Christian Woman. Judah Leib Teller, *tr. by* Benjamin *and* Barbara Harshav. AYP
Air is cold, The. On the Way to Dakar. Blaise Cendrars, *tr. by* John Dos Passos. RHTwFP
Air is full of diamond dust tonight, The. Frozen Fire. Floris Clark McLaren. CaP
Air is high and blue yet, as we drive, The. Coming Home from Abroad. David Holbrook. OBTV
Air is like a butterfly, The. Easter. Joyce Kilmer. PDV; RHPC
Air is sweetest that a thistle guards, The. Variations: The Air Is Sweetest That a Thistle Guards. James Merrill. NePoEA
Air is thick with nerves and smoke, The. University Examinations in Egypt. D. J. Enright. OxBTC; TwCP
Air is wet, soaks, The. Monsoon History. Shirley Lim. UAS
Air New Zealand. Christian Karlson Stead. *Fr.* Clodian Songbook. PeNZ
Air of June Sings, The. Edward Dorn. NeAP; PoM
Air of the museum, The. The Frozen Hero. Thomas H. Vance. NYBP
Air Plant, The. Hart Crane. MoAB; MoAmPo; NoP
Air Raid. Peter Wild. Psk
Air-Raid Causalties: Ashridge Hospital. Patricia Ledward. CN
Air Sentry, The. Patrick Barrington. CenHV
Air Shaft. Ian Healy. *Fr.* Poems from the Coalfields, I. PoAu-2
Air stiffens to a crust, The. The Wound. Louise Glück. NoAM
Air, the dream-inspiring air, The. An Idyl of Spring. Henrietta Cordelia Ray. CBWP-3
Air Travel in Arabia. Sir Charles Johnston. OBTV
Air Traveler. Lillian Morrison. RHPC
Air Vision, The. Jakov van Hoddis, *tr. fr. German by* Charles Guenther. VWA
Air was always damp and cool, The. Home from Praying. Joseph Rolnik, *tr. by* Irving Feldman. PeBMYV

Air was soft, the ground still cold, The. April 5, 1974. Richard Wilbur. HCAP
(4/5/74.) PPR
Air was vibrant around the hills, The. Leac A'Chlarsair. Lucy Taylor. PoSH
Air, which is not anything. Elements. Carolyn Wilson Link. GoYe
Airborne dragonfly, An. Hunter's Moon. Stephen Sandy. NYBP
Aircraft are weaving the telegraph wires, The. Sunday. Philippe Soupault, *tr. by* Michael Benedikt. POS
Aircrews have had it and the war goes on. "For Whom the Bell Tolls." Gavin Ewart. WaP
Air[e] and Angels. John Donne. JCP; MeLP; MePo; NAEL-1; OAEL-1; OBS; Prf; SeCP; SeCV-1
Aire in Newfoundland. *See* Air in Newfoundland.
Aired in the sun. *Unknown, tr. by* Burton Watson. FCEI
Airedale, erect beside the chauffeur of a Rolls-Royce, An. Fashions in Dogs. E. B. White. FiBHP
Airing Books. Kametani Seiken, *tr. fr. Chinese by* Burton Watson. JLIC-2
Airing books. Masaoka Shiki, *tr. fr. Japanese by* Burton Watson. *Fr.* Thirty-nine Haiku. FCEI
Airing clothes and belongings in the courtyard. Sentimental Poem. Po Chü-i, *tr. by* Burton Watson. CoBCP
Airing Painful Memories. Yüan Chen, *tr. fr. Chinese by* Burton Watson. CoBCP
Airline Breakfast, An. William Matthews. AnAn; MAYP
Airliner. Francis Webb. CBAP
Airly Beacon. Charles Kingsley. EBVV; OBEV
Airmail Letter. Axel Schulze, *tr. fr. German by* Margitt Lehbert. WCI
Airman, The. William Robert Rodgers. WaP
Airman's Breastplate, The. Oliver St. John Gogarty. TIRV
Airplane, The ("An airplane has gigantic wings"). Rowena Bastin Bennett. FaPON
Airport. Martin Johnston. CBAP
Airport coffee tastes less of America, The. The Gulf. Derek Walcott. NoP
Airport in the Grass. X. J. Kennedy. RR
Air's advice is all, The. Prelude to Commencement. Marie De L. Welch. NYBP
Air's enveloping capacious sleeves, The. Between. Agnes Nemes Nagy, *tr. by* Alan Dixon. MHuP
Airs from the sea blown back. Ovid on the Dacian Coast. Dunstan Thompson. NYBP
Airs of Pei, *sel.* Confucius, *tr. fr. Chinese by* Ezra Pound. Efficient Wife's Complaint, The. CTC
Airs! that wander and murmur round. The Siesta. *Unknown, tr. by* Bryant. AWP
Airstrip in Essex, 1960, An. Donald Hall. LCAP; LiTM
Airy Christ, The. Stevie Smith. NOCV
Aishah Schechinah. Robert Stephen Hawker. OBNC
Aitana, my child, springtime bows. For Aitana. Rafael Alberti, *tr. by* Perry Higman. LPSS
Aix-La-Chappelle, 1945. Edgar Bowers. NePoEA
Ajanta. Muriel Rukeyser. LiTA; LiTM; MoAB; MoAmPo; NNaP
Ajax, *sel.* Sophocles, *tr. fr. Greek by* Winthrop Mackworth Praed. "Fair Salamis, the billow's roar." AWP
Ajax and Ulysses. James Shirley. *See* Contention of Ajax and Ulysses, The.
Ajax Samples, The. Laura Jensen. LCAP
Ajax the swift swerv'd never from the side. Homer, *tr. fr. Greek by* William Cowper. *Fr.* The Iliad, XIII. OBVE
Akaotu. Alistair Campbell. ATNZ
Akawense. Phyllis Wolf. STE
Akedah, The. Matti Megged, *tr. fr. Hebrew by* Howard Schwartz. VWA
Akedah, The. Aliza Shenhar, *tr. fr. Hebrew by* Linda Zisquit. VWA
Akiba. Muriel Rukeyser. VWA
Al Aaraaff, *sels.* Poe.
Song from "Al Aaraaf." AmPP; OxBA
Sonnet to Science: Prologue. AmPP; NoP; OxBA; TAP; TW
Al Capone in Alaska. Ishmael Reed. TW
Al Fitnah Muhajir. Nazzam Al Sudan. NBP
Ala. Grace Nichols. AIW
Ala, mala, mink, monk. *Unknown.* OxNR
Alabama, The. Maurice Bell. PAH
Alabama. Julia Fields. PoBA; PoNe
Alabama. Judy Dothard Simmons. CNA
Alabama Bus. Will Hairston. FaBoPV
Alabama Centennial. Naomi Long Madgett. BPo
Alabama Earth. Langston Hughes. AmFN
Alabaster legs of the lonely woman, The. The Merry Window. Francis Scarfe. EAS

Alack! 'tis melancholy theme to think. The Irish Schoolmaster. Thomas Hood. BXAP

Alajire, we ask you to be patient. *Yoruba Oral Tradition, tr. by* Ulli Beier. WTO

Alamance. Seymour W. Whiting. PAH

Alarm, The. Hildebrand Jacob. NOEC

Alarm and time clock still intrude too early. And on This Shore. M. Carl Holman. AmNP; PoBA; PoNe

Alarm sounds, The. The starting gates are empty. In the Silks. Diane Ackerman. MAYP

Alarmed Skipper, The. James Thomas Fields. AnAmPo; NBLV

Alarming New Development, An. Ron Schreiber. GLP

Alarm's Callous Racket, The. Hanny Michaelis, *tr. fr. Dutch by* André Lefevere. DuIn

Alarum. Urszula Koziol, *tr. fr. Polish by* Czeslaw Milosz. PwPP; WPOW

Alarum, The. Sylvia Townsend Warner. MoBrPo

Alas! Sadi, *tr. fr. Persian by* L. Cranmer-Byng. *Fr.* The Gulistan. AWP

Alas, Alack! Walter de la Mare. FaPON; OxBChV

Alas! alas! the while. A Night with a Holy-Water Clerk. *Unknown.* MeEL

Alas! alas! thou turn'st in vain. Claim to Love. Giovanni Battista Guarini, *tr. by* Thomas Stanley. AWP

Alas, alas, well evil I sped! Undo! *Unknown.* NOCV

Alas All for a Sparrowhawk I Sigh. *Unknown, tr. fr. Italian by* Marion Shore. PFI

Alas! and am I born for this. On Liberty and Slavery. George Moses Horton. PoNe

Alas! Carolina! J. Gordon Coogler. OBAL

Alas, dear Clio, every day. To Clio, from Rome. John Dyer. NOEC

Alas, dear heart! what hope had I. Love Me Again. *Unknown.* EIL

Alas, Death. Charles d'Orléans. OxBLMV

Alas! deceite that in truste is nowe. Trust Only Yourself. *Unknown.* MeEL

Alas, eheu, one question that sorely vexes. Ezra Pound. *Fr.* L'Homme Moyen Sensuel. OBSV

Alas! England now mourns for her poet that's gone. William McGonagall. *Fr.* Death and Burial of Lord Tennyson. OBD

Alas! for all the pretty women who marry dull men. Meditation at Kew. Anna Wickham. FaBoTw; MoBrPo

Alas for me, who loved a falcon well! A Lady Laments for Her Lost Lover, by Similitude of a Falcon. *Unknown, tr. by* Dante Gabriel Rossetti. AWP

Alas, for Peter not a helping hand. Peter Grimes at Aldeburgh. George Crabbe. *Fr.* The Borough: Peter Grimes. FaBoPP

Alas! for the South. J. Gordon Coogler. OBAL

Alas for the voyage, O High King of Heaven. Farewell to Ireland. *at. to* Saint Columcille, *tr. by* Douglas Hyde. AWP

Alas! for them, their day is o'er. Indians. Charles Sprague. GN

Alas for this unhappy night! A Song of Instruction. Te Kooti Rikirangi, *tr. by* Margaret Orbell. PeNZ

Alas for Youth. Firdausi, *tr. fr. Persian by* R. A. Nicholson. AWP

Alas, good friend, what profit can you see. Lines to a Reviewer. Shelley. OxBSP

"Alas, have I not pain enough, my friend." Sir Philip Sidney. *Fr.* Astrophel and Stella, XIV. NoP; OAEL-1

Alas, how easily things go wrong! Sweet Peril. George Macdonald. BLPA; FaBoBe

Alas! how full of fear. The Fate of the Prophets. Longfellow. *Fr.* Christus; a Mystery. WGRP

Alas How Long ("Alas how long shall I and my maidenhead lie"). *Unknown.* ErPo

Alas! How should I sing? *Unknown.* NOIV

Alas, how soon the hours are over. Plays. Walter Savage Landor. EnRP; NBLV; NoP; OxBoLi; OxBSP

Alas! I am seized by the shark, great shark! Love Is a Shark. *Unknown, tr. by* N. B. Emerson. WTO

Alas, I am so faint I may not stand. The Desertion of Beauty and Strength. *Unknown. Fr.* Everyman. ACP

Alas, I draw breath heavily. An Old Woman's Song. Akjartoq, *tr. by* Knud Rasmussen; *English vers. by* Tom Lowenstein. WPOW

Alas! if I think of her, my throat becomes. Love. Pierre Louÿs, *tr. fr. French.* Fr. Chansons de Bilitis. PeHV

Alas! Madam, for Stealing of a Kiss. Sir Thomas Wyatt. BoLoP

Alas! Mowler, the children's pride. Death of the Cat. Ian Serraillier. SO

Alas, my brothers. Hilda Doolittle ("H. D."). *Fr.* Helen in Egypt. NOBA

Alas! my child, where is the pen. The Hen. Oliver Herford. NA

Alas, my God, that we should be. Thomas Shepherd. *Fr.* For Communion with God. TrPWD

Alas, my hart will brek in three. Fearful Death. *Unknown.* MeEL

Alas, my heart is black. The New Heart. *Unknown.* WGRP

Alas, my heart! mine eye hath wronged thee. Corydon to His Phyllis. Sir Edward Dyer. EIl

Alas, my love, ye do me wrong. Lady Greensleeves. *Unknown.* GBL; PoEL-2

Alas poor Death, where does thy great strength lye? Meditations for July 25, 1666. Philip Pain. SCAP

Alas! poor Fanny! wretched girl, alas! Fanny's Removal in 1714. John Winstanley. NOEC

Alas, poor heart, I pity thee. Medieval Norman Song ("Alas, poor heart, I pity thee"). *Unknown, tr. by* John Addington Symonds. AWP

Alas, poor man, what hap have I. Sir Thomas Wyatt. SiPS

Alas, so all things now do hold [*or* thinges nowe doe holde] their peace. A Complaint by Night of the Lover Not Beloved. Earl of Surrey, *after* Petrarch. AAS; AWP; EBEV; EIL; NAEL-1; NoP; OAEL-1; OBVE; SiPS; Son; TEP   *Fr.* Sonnets to Laura: To Laura in Life, CIX *tr. by* Sir Thomas Wyatt. NAEL-1; OAEL-1; OBVE; NoP (Lover for Shamefastnesse Hideth His Desire within His Faithfull Hart, The.) AAS, 2 *versions, tr. by* Earl of Surrey. (Night.) OBSC

Alas, that ever that speche was spoken. *Unknown.* EnLoPo

Alas, that I should be. To My Infant Daughter. Yvor Winters. VGW

Alas, that I should die. Song of a Woman Abandoned by the Tribe. *Unknown, tr. by* Mary Austin. AIW; WPE

Alas! that men must see. Love and Death. Margaret Deland. AA

Alas! that such a soul should taste of death. In Memory of Arthur Clement Williams. Eloise Bibb. CBWP-4

Alas, the country! how shall tongue or pen. Byron. *Fr.* The Age of Bronze. OBSV

Alas, the days of youth fly past. Insha Allah Khan Insha, *tr. by* Ahmed Ali. GoT

Alas, the Garden Palace of my prince. *Unknown, tr. fr. Japanese. Fr.* Manyo Shu. Ma

Alas the grief, and deadly woful smart! Sir Thomas Wyatt. SiPS

Alas, the moon should ever beam. The Water Lady. Thomas Hood. CH

Alas! the time has come, old dress. Lines to an Old Dress. Mary E. Tucker. CBWP-1

Alas! they had been friends in youth. The Scars Remaining. Samuel Taylor Coleridge. *Fr.* Christabel, *pt.* II. OBNC

"Alas, 'tis true I have gone here and there." Shakespeare. *Fr.* Sonnets, CX. EBEV; OBSC; PeHV

Alas! 'Tis Very Sad to Hear. Walter Savage Landor. GTBS-P; TW; WeW

Alas, unhappy land; ill-fated spot. Dirge of the Moolla of Kotal. George Thomas Lanigan. NA

Alas! what boots it that my noble steed. On a Distant Prospect of an Absconding Bookmaker. George Rostrevor Hamilton. FaBoCo

Alas! What crime have our people committed. Song of the Exile. Huang Tsun-hsien, *tr. by* J. D. Schmidt. WFTU

Alas, what is the world? a sea of glass. Meditation 10. Philip Pain. NOBA

Alas! what shul we freres do. A Friar Complains. *Unknown.* MeEL

Alas, with what tormenting fire. Of Death. Countess of Pembroke. *Fr.* Antonius. EIl

Alas! you son of her who is short-eared. Lion. *Unknown.* PeSA

Alaska. Mary Weston Fordham. CBWP-2

Alaska. Joaquin Miller. PAH

Alaskan Drinking Song. Dave Morice. EOEF

Alaskan Fragments June 1981—Summer Solstice. Wendy Rose. HATNAP

Alaskan Mountain Poem #1. Leslie Marmon Silko. VoR

Alastor; or, The Spirit of Solitude, *sels.* Shelley. EnRP; OAEL-2
 "As an eagle grasped." ChER
 "Earth, ocean, air, belovèd brotherhood!" FiP
 "There was a poet whose untimely tomb." TOF
 "Wildly he wandered on." TOF

Alba. Samuel Beckett. BIrV

Alba. Confucius, *tr. fr. Chinese by* Ezra Pound. *Fr.* Songs of T'ang. CTC

Alba ("As cool as the pale, wet leaves"). Ezra Pound. GBL; HAP; SOTW; WeW

Alba ("When the nightingale to his mate"). Ezra Pound, *after the Provençal of* Arnaut Daniel. *Fr.* Langue d'Oc. OBVE; VGW; WeW

Alba, *sel.* Robert Tofte.
 Love's Labour Lost. EIL

Alba. Derek Walcott. GoJo; PCP

Alba after Six Years. Christopher Middleton. NePoEA-2

Alba Innominata. *Unknown, tr. fr. French by* Ezra Pound. AWP

Albatross. Lele-io-Hoku, *tr. fr. Hawaiian by* S. H. Elbert *and* N. Mahoe. WTO

Albatross. Charles Warren Stoddard. AA

Albeit the Venice girls get praise. Ballad of the Women of Paris. Villon.
AWP, *tr. by* Swinburne

"Albemarle" Cushing. James Jeffrey Roche. PAH

Albert Ayler: Eulogy for a Decomposed Saxophone Player. Stanley
Crouch. PoBA

Albert is haranguing his mother about his name. In the Heat of the
Morning. Anne Szumigalski. FaBoWP

Albert Sidney Johnston. Kate Brownlee Sherwood. PAH

Albert Sidney Johnston. Francis Orrery Ticknor. PAH

Albert Speer. W. D. Snodgrass. NoAM

Alberta. Priscilla Jane Thompson. CBWP-2

Albion Battleship Calamity, The. William McGonagall. BXAP

Albion's England, *sel.* William Warner.
Fate of Narcissus, The. OBSC

Albion's most lovely daughter sat on the banks of the. Mrs. Albion
You've Got a Lovely Daughter. Adrian Henri. OxBTC

Albuera. Thomas Hardy. *Fr.* The Dynasts, *pt.* II, Act VI, sc. iv.
WaaP

Album. Lucille Clifton. ER

Album, The. C. Day Lewis. EnLoPo; OxBTC

Album. Haim Gouri, *tr. fr. Hebrew by* Warren Bargad *and* Stanley F.
Chyet. IP

Album. Josephine Miles. FaBoWP

Album—A Runthru. Clark Coolidge. LP

Album-Leaf. Kingsley Amis. PoPo

Album Leaf. Stéphane Mallarmé, *tr. fr. French by* Keith Bosley.
OBVE

Album Leaves, *sels.* Arthur Rex Dugard Fairburn.
Back Street. ATNZ; PeNZ
Conversation in the Bush. ATNZ; PeNZ
Imperial. ATNZ
Possessor, The. PeNZ

Albumen. Tadeusz Rozewicz, *tr. fr. Polish by* Czeslaw Milosz.
PwPP

Alcaics; to H. F. B. Robert Louis Stevenson. OBEV

Alceste in the Wilderness. Anthony Hecht. PoA

Alcestis, *sel.* Euripides, *tr. fr. Greek by* A. E. Housman.
Strength of Fate, The. AWP

Alcestis. Isabel Williams Verry. GoYe

Alcestis on the Poetry Circuit. Erica Jong. AmPA

Alchemical Cupboard, The. Asa Benveniste. VWA

Alchemist, The. Louise Bogan. AWP; LLLT; MoAmPo

Alchemist, The. Richard Church. OxBTC

Alchemist, The, *sels.* Ben Jonson.
"Come on, sir. Now, you set your foot on shore." *Fr.* II, i *and* ii.
PoEL-2
"I will have all my beds blown up, not stuft." *Fr.* II, i. EBEV

Alchemist, The. Ezra Pound. CMoP; LiTA; WSC

Alchemist in the City, The. Gerard Manley Hopkins. NoP

Alchemy. Saqi Farooqi, *tr. fr. Urdu by* Mahmood Jamal.
PBMUP

Alchemy of Day, The. Anne Hébert, *tr. fr. French by* A. Poulin,
Jr. BoWoP

Alcilia, *sel.* "J. C."
Frailty of Beauty, The. ElL

Alciphron and Leucippe. Walter Savage Landor. OBEV

Alcohol. Louis MacNeice. LiTM

Alcohol Counselor/ Indian Woman. Canyon Day Woman Blues.
Geraldine Keams. GOS

Alcoholic. John Berryman. NOCV

Alcoholic. F. D. Reeve. NYBP

Alcyna met them at the outer gate. Ariosto, *tr. fr. Italian by* Sir John
Harington. *Fr.* Orlando Furioso, VII. OBVE

Alcyone. Frances Laughton Mace. AA

Aldport (Mystery Tour). Kingsley Amis. *Fr.* The Evans Country.
NOBL
(Terrible Beauty.) ErPo; NePoEA-2

Alec Yeaton's Son. Thomas Bailey Aldrich. MOS

Aleksandra Kollontay. Anja Vammelvuo, *tr. fr. Finnish by* Aili Jarvenpa.
SOP

Aleph. Stuart Z. Perkoff. VWA

Aleph Bet, The. Fay Lipshitz. VWA

Aleph the cow with wide horns. The Letters of the Book. Rose
Drachler. VWA

Alex, perhaps a colour of which neither of us had dreamt. Letter to Alex
Comfort. Dannie Abse. FaBoTw; TwCP

Alexander and Campaspe, *sels.* John Lyly.
"Cupid and my Campaspe played." *Fr.* III, v. GBL
(Apelles' Song.) TrGrPo
(Cards and Kisses.) HoPM; NOBE; OBEV
(Cupid and Campaspe.) EiL; GTBS; GTBS-P
(Cupid and My Campaspe.) HeIP; NoP; PoRA

(Song of Apelles.) OBSC
"O! [*or* Oh] for a bowl of fat canary." *Fr.* I, iii *Also in* A Mad World,
My Masters (*by* Thomas Middleton).
(Oh, for a Bowl of Fat Canary.) NoP
(Serving Men's Song, A.) NOBE; OBSC
Trico's Song. *Fr.* V, i. EiL; OBSC; PBBP; TrGrPo
(Song: "What bird so sings.") PBBP
(Spring, The.) CH
(Spring's Welcome.) OBEV
(Welcome to Spring.) NOBE

Alexander Jannai. Constantine P. Cavafy, *tr. fr. Greek by* Simon Chasen.
TrJP

Alexander Selkirk. William Cowper. *See* Verses Supposed to Be Written
by Alexander Selkirk during His Solitary Abode on the Island of Juan
Fernandez.

Alexander the Great. Iliad. Michael Casey. SoTCo

Alexander the Great. *Unknown.* CH

Alexander's Feast; or, The Power of Music [*or* Musique]. Dryden. ACP;
FaPoR; FiP; GN; GTBS; GTBS-P; LiTB; NAEL-1; NOBE; OAEL-1;
OBS; SeCV-2; TrGrPo; WiR

Alexandrian Kings, The. ("The Alexandrians turned out in force").
Constantine P. Cavafy, *tr. fr. Greek by* Edmund Keeley *and* Philip
Sherrard. VMG

Alexis, here she stayed; among these pines. William, of Hawthornden
Drummond. EiL; OBS
(Spring Bereaved.) OBEV

Alfa is nice. Her Roman eye. Safety at Forty; or, An Abecedarian Takes
a Walk. Louis Edward Sissman. Prf

Alfonso was his name; his sad cantina. Skin Diving in the Virgins. John
Malcolm Brinnin. NYBP; TAP

Alfred, A Masque, *sel.* James Thomson *and* David Mallet.
Rule, Britannia! *Fr.* II, v. FaPoR; GTBS; GTBS-P; NOEC; OBWP;
WBLP

Alfred Corning Clark. Robert Lowell. RB

Alfred Jewel, The. Robert Wells. NPo

Alfred the Harper. John Sterling. BeLS

Alfrid's Itinerary through Ireland. *Unknown, tr. fr. Irish by* James
Clarence Mangan. OBTV; TIRV

Algernon Sidney's Farewell. *Unknown.* APAS

Algonkian Burial. Alfred Goldsworthy Bailey. OBCV

Algy Met a Bear. *Unknown.* FaPON; MoShBr; RHPC

Ali. Lloyd M. Corbin, Jr. CNA; PoBA

Ali Ben Shufti. Anthony Thwaite. OxBTC

Alibazan. Laura E. Richards. OBCA

Alibi. Arthur Guiterman. BXAP

Alicante. Jacques Prévert, *tr. fr. French by* Lawrence Ferlinghetti.
BoLoP

Alice. Charles Cotton. *Fr.* Resolution in Four Sonnets, of a Poetical
Question Put to Me by a Friend, Concerning Four Rural Sisters: Alice
Is Tall and Upright as a Pine. TrGrPo

Alice B. *Unknown.* AS

Alice Brand. Sir Walter Scott. *Fr.* The Lady of the Lake, IV.
BeLS; OnMSP

Alice Corbin Is Gone. Carl Sandburg. PoA

"Alice, dear, what ails you." A Frosty Night. Robert Graves. CH;
MoAB; MoBrPo; MoBS; OxBTC

Alice Fell; or, Poverty. Wordsworth. BeLS; OBNV

Alice grown lazy, mammoth but not fat. Last Days of Alice. Allen Tate.
NAAL-2; NOBA; OxBA; UnPo

Alice Is Tall and Upright as a Pine. Charles Cotton. *Fr.* Resolution in
Four Sonnets, of a Poetical Question Put to Me by a Friend,
Concerning Four Rural Sisters, I. PoEL-3; Prf; Son
(Alice.) TrGrPo
(Two Rural Sisters.) BoLoP; EnLoPo

Alice on the croquet lawn. Matinal. Cilla McQueen. ATNZ

Alice on the croun o Bidean. On the Croun o Bidean. J. K. Annand.
PoSH

Alice Ray. Sarah Josepha Hale. AA

Alice's Adventures in Wonderland. "Lewis Carroll."
Sels.
Alice's Recitation. *Fr. ch.* 10. FaBoCo; FaBoNo; NOBL; Par
(Lobster, The, *sl. diff.*) OxBChV
"Beautiful Soup, so rich and green." *Fr. ch.* 10.
(Turtle Soup.) FaBoNo; RHPC
Evidence Read at the Trial of the Knave of Hearts. *Fr. ch.* 12.
FaBoNo; FaFP; GTBS-P; NoBVV; OxBoLi
(Silence in Court.) FaBoCo
Father William. *Fr. ch.* 5. BXAP; FaBoCo; FaBoNo; FaBoPa;
FaPON; FiBHP; FPL; GoJo; HoPM; LiTB; NOBL; NOBVV;
OxBChV; Par; PDV; PoLF; PoRA; RHPC; TrGrPo; UnPo
Fury Said to a Mouse. *Fr. ch.* 3. NoAM; NoP
(Mouse's Tale, The.) FaBoNo

"How doth the little crocodile." *Fr. ch.* 2. FaBoCh; FaBoCo;
FaBoEE; FaBoNo; FaFP; FaPON; MoShBr; NBLV; NOBL; NOBVV;
Par; RB; TTTS
(Crocodile, The.) HoPM; RHPC; TrGrPo

Mad Hatter's Song, The. *Fr. ch.* 7. FaBoNo; NOBL; Par

"Speak roughly to your little boy." *Fr. ch.* 6. FaBoCh; FaBoCo;
NBLV; Par
(Duchess's Lullaby, The.) FaBoNo
(Lullaby, A.) RHPC

"Will you walk a little faster?" said a [*or* the] whiting to a [*or* the]
snail." *Fr. ch.* 10. NoAM
(Lobster Quadrille, The.) BoTP; FaPON; MoShBr; OxBChV; Par;
RR
(Mock Turtle's Song, The.) ChTr; FaBoNo

Alice's Recitation. "Lewis Carroll." *Fr.* Alice's Adventures in
Wonderland, *ch.* 10. FaBoCo; FaBoNo; NOBL; Par
(Lobster, The, *sl. diff.*) OxBChV

Alicia's Bonnet. Elisabeth Cavazza Pullen. AA

Alien. Donald Jeffrey Hayes. AmNP

Alien, The. Gabriela Mistral, *tr. fr. Spanish by* Kate Flores. DMH

Alien. William Price Turner. OxBS

Alienation & Alliteration. Sybren Polet, *tr. fr. Dutch by* Peter Nijmeijer.
DuIn

Alison. ("Bytuene March and Averil"). *Unknown.* MeEL; NAEL-1;
NoP; OAEL-1; OBEV

Alison. ("In March and April, thereabout"). *Unknown.* HAP

Alison and Willie. *Unknown.* ESPB

Alison [*or* Allison] Gross. *Unknown.* CH; ESPB; FaBoCh; OxBB; WSC

Alisoun. *Unknown. See* Betwene March and Averil.

Aliter. Confucius, *tr. fr. Chinese by* Ezra Pound. *Fr.* Songs of Ch'en.
CTC

Alive or Not. Alfred W. Purdy. NOBC

Alive, sea cucumbers frozen in one lump. Basho, *tr. fr. Japanese by*
Burton Watson. *Fr.* Seventy-six Hokku. FCEI

Alive, this man was Manes, a common slave. Anyte, *tr. by* Willis
Barnstone. BoWoP

Alive Together. Lisel Mueller. IHMS

Alive-under my narrow. At Saya-between-the-Hills. Basho, *tr. fr.
Japanese by* Burton Watson. *Fr.* Seventy-six Hokku. FCEI

Alkali Pete Hits Town. T. J. McCoy. CowP

Alkinoos, king and admiration of men. New Coasts and Poseidon's Son.
Homer, *tr. fr. Greek by* Robert Fitzgerald. *Fr.* Odyssey, IX. WTO

All. Antoni Slonimski, *tr. fr. Polish by* Wanda Dynowska. TrJP

All The. Yona Wallach, *tr. fr. Hebrew by* Warren Bargad *and* Stanley F.
Chyet. IP

All/wrong. Charles Olson. *See* Maximus Poems, The: Songs of
Maximus.

All a green willow, willow, willow. John Heywood. EIL

All a-tremble she awoke. The Annunciation. Amrita Pritam, *tr. by*
Khushwant Singh *and* Krishna Gorowara. WPOW

All after pleasures is I rid one day. Christmas. George Herbert.
SeCV-1; TOF; TrCP

All, All a-Lonely. *Unknown.* ChTr; OxBoLi

All, All of a Piece Throughout. Dryden. *Fr.* The Secular Masque.
ChTr; ELP; HAP; InPS
(Chorus to the Gods.) OxBSP
(Song: "All, all of a piece throughout.") WeW

All Alone. Mary E. Tucker. CBWP-1

All alone from his dark sanctum the lingam fronts, affronts the sea.
Mahabalipuram. Louis MacNeice. OBTV

All alone in my little cell. *Unknown.* NOIV

All alone on the hillside. The "Grey Horse Troop." Robert William
Chambers. PAH

All along the backwater. Ducks' Ditty. Kenneth Grahame. *Fr.* The
Wind in the Willows. BoTP; FaPON; GoJo; MoShBr; NTCP;
OxBChV; PDV; RHPC

All along the rail. In Texas Grass. Quincy Troupe. PoBA

All along the valley, stream that flashest white. In the Valley of
Cauteretz. Tennyson. BoLoP; NAEL-2; NOBE

All ambitions of youth yield place to calamities. Chatting about the Past
with Huang the Elder. Hung Liang-Chi, *tr. by* Irving Lo. WFTU

All Americans are ambiguous. Shorter American Memory of the
American Character According to Santayana. Rosemarie Waldrop.
EOEF

All are architects of fate. The Builders. Longfellow. AnAmPo; FaFP;
OHFP; PWR

All are but parts of one stupendous whole. Pope. *Fr.* An Essay on Man,
Epistle I. WGRP

All are not born to soar—and ah! how few. On Imitation. Samuel
Taylor Coleridge. OxBSP

All around I heard the whispering larches. Forest Song. Sir Shane
Leslie. TIRV

All around me, the city was falling asleep. The Quick and the Dead.
Ilarie Voronca, *tr. by* Edouard Roditi. VWA

All around my house at midnight: rain. Dawn: Clear Skies. Yang Shih-
ch'i, *tr. by* Jonathan Chaves. CoBLCP

All around old Chattanooga. Freedom at McNealy's. Priscilla Jane
Thompson. CBWP-2

All around, shards of a lost tradition. A Lost Tradition. John Montague.
CIP

All around the Town, *sels.* Phyllis McGinley.
"B's the Bus." FaPON
"F is the fighting Firetruck." FaPON
"J's the jumping Jay-walker." FaPON; RHPC

All at once I see a coiled dragon forming the base of an ancient bronze
plate. Song on a Pine on Yellow Mountain. Shen Te-ch'ien, *tr. by*
Irving Lo. WFTU

All at once nature's sundry sounding pipes are stiled. Snow. Ch'ü Ta-
chün, *tr. by* Paul W. Kroll. WFTU

All at once we remember the village nights. Electricity. Sa'di Yusuf, *tr.
by* Abdullah al-Udhari. MPAW

All August we thrilled to rumors. Summer Killer. T. Alan Broughton.
MOWH

All autumn long. In a Remote Korean Village. Koh Chang-soo, *tr. by
the author.* ACKP

All beaded with dew. Gary Snyder. *Fr.* Myths and Texts: Hunting, VII.
NaP

All beauty, resonance, integrity. Le Livre Est sur la Table. John
Ashbery. EAS

All because I think of you. Silhouette. Marc Cohen. EOEF

All beginnings start right here. The Move Continuing. Al Young.
PoBA

All Being Well. W. W. Gibson. OxBTC

All beneath the white-rose tree. The Three Captains. *Unknown, tr. by*
Andrew Lang. AWP

All Bibles or sacred codes. The Voice of the Devil. Blake. *Fr.* The
Marriage of Heaven and Hell. NU

All bones but yours will rattle when I say. The Sea-Serpent. James
Robinson Planché. NA

All buildings are but monuments of death. Epigram: Fatum Supremum.
Unknown. OBS

All busy punching tickets. Crickets. David McCord. NTCP; PDV; TSS

All but Blind. Walter de la Mare. FaPON; MoAB; MoBrPo; PDV;
WeW

All Christian men in my behalf. On Sir John Calf. *Unknown.* FaBoEE

All Christians and Lay-Elders too. The Four-legg'd Elder; or, A Horrible
Relation of a Dog and an Elder's Maid. Sir John Birkenhead.
CoMu

All Christmas night upon the shelf. The Mouse. Hugh McCrae.
PoAu-1

All Clear. Cecily Pile. CN

"All clear, all clear, all clear!" after the storm in the morning. October
Morning. Mary Ursula Bethell. ATNZ

All Clowns Are Masked. Delmore Schwartz. *Fr.* The Repetitive Heart.
LiTA; OxBA

All connections. A Petite Histoire of Red Fascism. Andrei Codrescu.
UL

All craftsmen share a knowledge. They have held. Craftsmen.
V. Sackville-West. OxBTC

All creatures that live. Tabito, *tr. fr. Japanese by* Geoffrey Bownas *and*
Anthony Thwaite. *Fr.* Manyo Shu. PeBJV

All day. At Loxahatchie. Mary Oliver. KS

All day, a small mild Negro man with a broom. The Sweeper of Ways.
Howard Nemerov. HCAP

All day a strong wind blew. A Strong Wind. Austin Clarke. BoNaP;
RB

All day and all day, as I sit at my measureless turning. The Mother's
Song. Virginia Woodward Cloud. AA

All Day and All October. Laurence Lerner. PeSA

All day and every day the sea shone, steeped in its blueness. When I Was
Young. Alun Llywelyn-Williams, *tr. by* Gwyn Williams. OBWVE

All day and many days I rode. A Wish. Hamlin Garland. AA

All day and night, save winter, every weather. Aspens. Edward
Thomas. InPS

All day at the window seat. Charles Wright. *Fr.* Four Poems for the
New Year. AnAn

All day beneath the hurtling shells. The Dancers. W. W. Gibson.
MMA

All day beside the shattered tank he'd lain. Reconciliation. C. Day
Lewis. TwCP

All-day Bird, the artist, The. Claritas. Denise Levertov. VGW

All day, day after day, they're bringing them home. Homecoming.
Bruce Dawe. CBAP

All day he slept, his mouth on pennyroyal. The Soldier in the Park.
Elizabeth Riddell. CBAP

All day he stood at Weeping Cross. Karl ("All day he stood at Weeping Cross"). Charles Spear. ATNZ

All day I did the little things. The Blue Bowl. Blanche Bane Kuder. BLPA; FaBoBe

All day I follow. The Plowman. Raymond Knister. OBCV

All day I fret over wind and sand. Wu Wen, *tr. fr. Chinese by* Irving Lo. *Fr.* Starting Out on a Journey in a Windstorm, I. WFTU

All day I have been completely alone, and now the night. Separation. Derek S. Savage.

All day I have been dreaming of a dazzling stew. Ode to Food. Darrell Gray. UL

All day I have lain, foot propped. A Jogging Injury. Fleda Brown Jackson. TSL

All day I heard a humming in my ears. The Awaking of the Poetic Faculty. George Henry Boker. Son

All day I loved you in a fever, holding on to the tail of the horse. At Mid-Ocean. Robert Bly. CAPP; LLLT

All day I swing my level scythe. Scything. Basil Dowling. ATNZ

All day I tried to distinguish. Elms. Louise Glück. NoAM

All day I try out simple sums. Simultaneous Equations. Anne French. ATNZ

All day it had been raining; now, the leaves. Hunt. Melvin Walker La Follette. NePoEA

All Day It Has Rained. Alun Lewis. GTBS-P; NAEL-2; NOBE; OBWP; OBWVE; OxBTC

All day, knowing you dead. The Hours. John Peale Bishop. OxBA

All day long/ The sun shines bright. The Night Sky. *Unknown.* BoTP

All day long, I ache for spring, for spring's already gone. Seeing Spring Off. K'ang Yu-wei, *tr. by* Eugene E. Eoyang. WFTU

All day long I have been working. Madonna of the Evening Flowers. Amy Lowell. PeHV; UnAS

All day long, prismatic dazzle. Midnight. Mary Ursula Bethell. ATNZ; PeNZ

All day long roved Hiawatha. The Death of Minnehaha. Longfellow. *Fr.* The Song of Hiawatha, XX. AA

All day long the clouds formed in the peaks. First Winter Storm. William Everson. NU

All day long the guns at the forts. The Surrender of New Orleans. Marion Manville. PAH

All day long the rain would not desist. Fishermen. Gabriel Preil, *tr. by* Bernhard Frank. MHeP

All day long they have sat here. Composition in Black and White. Katha Pollitt. GrPl

All Day Long We Walked in the Fields. Odysseus Elytis, *tr. fr. Greek by* Edmund Keeley *and* Philip Sherrard. VMG

All day my father complained. Rare Rhythms. Sara London. MOWH

All day my sheep have mingled with yours. Shepherdess. Norman Cameron. *Fr.* Three Love Poems, III. GBL; OxBS

All day o'er the prairie alone I ride. The Cowboy's Soliloquy. Allen McCanless. CowP

All day pinecones drop like shot birds. Late November. Sherod Santos. Son

All day pounding nails. The Horn Blow. Jeff Tagami. BrSi

All day rain fell. Ode on Contemplating Clapham Junction. Christopher Middleton. *Fr.* Herman Moon's Hourbook. NePoEA-2

All day she hurried to get through. Mis' Smith. Albert Bigelow Paine. PoLF

All day subdued, polite. Negro Servant. Langston Hughes. VGW

All day swaying in the tower. Out from Lobster Cove. J. D. Reed. NeAC

All day the bird-song here has seemed. Random Reflections on a Summer Evening. John Hall Wheelock. NYBP

All day the black rain has fallen. Spring. Louis Johnson. *Fr.* Four Poems from the Strontium Age, III. ATNZ

All day the coast of Africa was seen. To Naples. Herbert B. Mallalieu. WaP

All day the driftwood. Driftwood Dybbuk. Barbara F. Lefcowitz. VWA

All day the geese fly south. Starting Over. Shirley Kaufman. VWA

All day the great guns barked and roared. Molly Pitcher. Laura E. Richards. PAH

All day the great planes gingerly descend. Air Field. Robert Siegel. GeTw

All day the irises have draped blue velvet. Elsdon. Freda Downie. FaBoPP

All day the light wind blew on the house. Day on Kind Continent. Robert David Cohen. NYBP

All day the mirrors kindle their brilliance. The Mirrors. Sophia de Mello Breyner Andresen, *tr. by* Allan Francovich. PBWP

All day the Nina sewed in this room. The Firstborn. Gary Soto. NPGG

All day the opposite house. The Opposite House. Robert Lowell. CMoP

All day the red spit of the chain-shot tore. Evil. Arthur Rimbaud, *tr. fr. French by* Robert Lowell. *Fr.* Eighteen-Seventy. OBWP ("Whilst the red spittle of the grape-shot sings.") WaaP, *tr. by* Norman Cameron.

All day the sun builds its temple. Dragon. Joseph Stroud. NPGG

All day the unnatural barking of dogs. The Dog. Valentin Iremonger. BIrV; NeIP

All day the waves assailed the rock. Nahant. Emerson. AA (Waves.) AmPP

All day the wind has made love. On Lake Pend Oreille. Richard Shelton. NYBP

All day they loitered by the resting ships. The *Wanderer*. John Masefield. BrPo

All day to the loose tile behind the parapet. The Wasps' Nest. George MacBeth. OxBTC

All day today the sea gulls cried. Out in the Cold. George Starbuck. NYBP

All day under acrobat. Ruins under the Stars. Galway Kinnell. LCAP; NaP

All day we hid in the woods by the river. With the Guerillas. Cecily Pile. CN

All day we travel from bed to bed, our children. Visiting the Graves. Ellen Bryant Voigt. PPR

All day we walked the streets. The Fifties. Ira Sadoff. AmPA

All Day We've Longed for Night. Sarah Webster Fabio. BlSi

All day where megaphone. Merry-go-round. Gloria Rawlinson. ATNZ

All day you didn't cry or cry out and you felt like sleeping. Tall Windows. Robert Hass. NPGG

All do not seek the exalted fire. Earth and Fire. Vernon Watkins. NYBP

All dripping in tangles green. The Tuft of Kelp. Herman Melville. ChTr; FaBoEE; FaBoRV; MOS

All else for use, One only for desire. Deo Optimo Maximo. Louise Imogen Guiney. TrPWD

All-embracing, The. Frederick William Faber. BLRP (There's a Wideness.) WBLP

All endeavor to be beautiful. Primer of Plato. Jean Garrigue. NOBA

All evening, while the summer trees were crying. Evening in Summer. Valentin Iremonger. NeIP

All eyes were on Enceladus's face. Hyperion and Saturn. Keats. *Fr.* Hyperion; a Fragment, II. SeCePo

All fathers in Western civilization must have. The Father of My Country. Diane Wakoski. NoAM; TAP

All Fellows, *sel.* Laurence Housman. "Dear love, when with a two-fold mind." WGRP

All five of them. Brahms. Michael Davidson. IAT

All fixed: early arrival at the flat. Nothing to Fear. Kingsley Amis. ErPo; OxBC

All Flesh. Francis Thompson. BrPo

All Flesh Is Grass, *sel.* Brenda G. Macrow. When I Die. PoSH

All Flesh Is Grass. Bible, *O.T. Fr.* Isaiah, XL: 6–8. TrJP

All flesh is grass, and so are feathers too. Epitaphs on Two Piping-Bullfinches of Lady Ossory's. Horace Walpole. FaBoEE; NOEC (Epitaph on Lady Ossory's Bullfinch.) ChTr

All flesh waxeth old as a garment. , Bible, Apocrypha. *Fr.* Ecclesiasticus, XIV: 17–18. OBVE

All folks, who pretend to religion and grace. The Place of the Damn'd. Swift. FaBoEE; OBSV

All for Love. Byron. *See* Oh, talk not to me of a name great in story.

All for Love, *sel.* Dryden. Cleopatra and Antony. FiP

All for Nothing. Lörinc Szabó, *tr. fr. Hungarian by* Edwin Morgan. MHuP

All gates were closed to him. What Bothered Him. David Avidan, *tr. fr. Hebrew by* Warren Bargad *and* Stanley F. Chyet. *Fr.* Samson, Our Hero, 2. IP

All gentlemen and yeomen good. Robin Hood and the Shepherd. *Unknown.* ESPB

All glory cannot vanish from the hills. The Passing of the Forest. William Pember Reeves. PeNZ

All gods and goddesses, all looked up to. Meditation on the Nativity. Elizabeth Jennings. NAs

All God's spades wear dark shades. Its Curtains. Ted Joans. PoBA

All good things. The Inner Source. Andrei Codrescu. UL

All grave old men, and souldiers they had bene, but for age. Homer, *tr. fr. Greek by* George Chapman. *Fr.* The Iliad, III. OBVE

All Greece hates. Helen. Hilda Doolittle ("H. D."). AnAmPo; BoWoP; FaBoWP; LiTM; MoAmPo; NAAL-2; NoAM; NOBA; NoP; TAP; TW

"All Green Things on the earth, bless ye the Lord!" Benedicite. Anna Callender Brackett. AA

All hail! Holy Mary, our hope and our joy! Irish Reaper's Harvest Hymn. John Keegan. TIRV

All hail, once pleasing, once inspiring shade. Lines Written in Windsor Forest. Pope. EBEV
(Hymn Written in Windsor Forest, A.) NOEC; OxBSP

All Hail the Power of Jesus' Name. Edward Perronet. NOCV
(Coronation.) WGRP

All hail! thou gorgeous sunset. Sunset. Mary Weston Fordham. CBWP-2

All Hail, Thou Noble Guest. Martin Luther, *tr. fr. German by* Arthur Tozer Russell *and* Catherine Winkworth. TrPWD

All hail! thou noble land. America to Great Britain. Washington Allston. AA

All hail! Unfurl the Stripes and Stars! God Save Our President. Francis DeHaes Janvier. PAH

All hallelujahs, Oh ye heav'nly quires. A Poem upon the Triumphant Translation of. Mrs. Anne Eliot. John Danforth. SCAP

All Hallows. Louise Glück. AmPA; HCAP; NU

All Hallows Eve. Kathryn Stripling Byer. KS

All happiness to our lord! *Unknown, tr. by* Arthur Waley. BoS

All has stilled, Magician Sleep having cast his spell. Those Last, Late Hours of Christmas Eve. Lou Ann Welte. PChr

All he owns is. Squirrel near Library. Genevieve Taggard. WPE

All heavy minds. Sir Thomas Wyatt. SiPS

All her Kamikaze friends admired my aunt. A Family Turn. William Stafford. CAPP

All hills resound with the tones of autumn. A Temple in the Hills. Yao Nai, *tr. by* Daniel Bryant. WFTU

All his beauty, wit and grace. To Joshua. Alice Thomas Ellis. OBD

All his hopes were hands, his ventures hands. The Hands. Tony Harrison. FaBoTw

All his life/ He loved to read. Flame Point. Jules Supervielle, *tr. by* Allen Mandelbaum. RHTwFP

All his life he sought one tiny bird. One Tiny Bird. Yekhi'el Mar, *tr. by* Bernhard Frank. MHeP

All holy influences dwell within. The Children Band. Sir Aubrey De Vere. OBEV

All honor to that day which long ago. Washington's Birthday. Arthur J. Burdick. OHIP

All houses wherein men have lived and died. Haunted Houses. Longfellow. PWR

All how silent and how still. Noon. John Clare. SeCePo

All human race would fain be wits. Swift. *Fr.* On Poetry; a Rhapsody. HAP; OBSV; PoEL-3

All Human Things. Peter Schroeder. BXAP

All human[e] things are subject to decay. Dryden. *Fr.* MacFlecknoe; or, A Satire [*or* Satyr] upon the True-Blue [*or-Blew*] Protestant Poet T. S. HAP; NAEL-1; NoP; OAEL-1; OBSV; OxBoLi; PoE; PPP; QFR; SCV; SeCV-2; TEP; TrGrPo
(Crown Prince of Dullness, The.) NOBE
(Poet Shadwell, The.) FiP
(Primacy of Dullness, The.) OBS

All Hungers Pass Away. Arthur Nortje. WMBCH

All Hushed and Still within the House. Emily Brontë. FaBoCh; Mes; NOBVV

All I can dream tonight is an autumn sunset. Boyhood in Tobacco Country. Robert Penn Warren. AnAn

All I can give you is broken-face gargoyles. Broken-Face Gargoyles. Carl Sandburg. AmPP; MoAmPo; OxBA

All I can offer now is a cracked china jug. Winter Offering. D. S. Savage. AmPP

All I can put my hands on, even. St. Lucy's Day. Donald Revell. BAP

All I can see, at the far side of the sky. One More Explanation for the Mystery. Pierre Reverdy, *tr. by* Michael Benedikt. POS

All I could see from where I stood. Edna St. Vincent Millay. *Fr.* Renascence. FaFP; MoAB; MoAmPo; OHFP; OHP

All I know about this man. The Man Who Made Me Love Him. Bruce Weigl. NAmP

All I know is a door into the dark. The Forge. Seamus Heaney. FaBCIP; NAEL-2

All I said was—Alexis is gorgeous. Plato, *tr. by* Peter Jay. PeHV

All I want in this creation's. Black-eyed Susie. *Unknown.* AmFP

All I wanted/ was your/ love. To Mother and Steve. Mari E. Evans. BPo; PoBA

All I wanted was to brew him rhubarb wine. My First Forty Years. Kevin Ireland. PeNZ

All I would say. On a Sea-Grape Leaf. Katherine Garrison Chapin. GrPl

All I'd wanted was to get on a train. Ishikawa Takuboku, *tr. fr. Japanese by* Hiroaki Sato. *Fr.* Forty-seven Tanka in Three Lines. FCEI

All Ignorance Toboggans into Know. E. E. Cummings. NAAL-2; NOBA; OxBA; WaP

All in a Garden Green. W. E. Henley. OBMV

All in a literary parleur. Bootie Black and the Seven Giants. Mike Cook. JB

All in All. Tennyson. *See* Idylls of the King: Merlin and Vivien.

All in Due Time. J. V. Cunningham. NIP

All in Green Went My Love Riding. E. E. Cummings. CMoP; FaBV; GoJo; HeIP; LiTA; LiTM; MoP; NoAM; NoP; OxBA; PoRA; SD

All in June. W. H. Davies. OxBSP

All in Red. Eileen Mathias. BoTP

All in the April evening [morning]. Sheep and Lambs. Katharine Tynan. BoTP; OBEV; TIRV

All in the Downs. Tom Hood. CenHV

All in the Downs the fleet was moored [*or* moor'd]. Sweet William's Farewell to Black-eyed Susan. John Gay. AmFP, *folk version*; BeLS; BoLoP; NOEC
(Black-eyed Susan.) GTBS; GTBS-P; MOS

All in the leafy darkness, when sleep had passed me by. Care. Virginia Woodward Cloud. AA

All in the merry month of May. Barbara Allen's Cruelty ("All in the merry month of May"). *Unknown.* FaBoBe
(Barbry Ellen.) PrIm

All in this pleasant evening, together come are we. Old May Song. *Unknown.* BoTP; CH

All-intellectual eye; our solar sound. James Thomson. *Fr.* To The Memory of Sir Isaac Newton. ImOP; NOEC

All Intents. Larry Eigner. VGW

All Ireland's now one vessel's company. Fearghal Og MacWard, *tr. fr. Irish. Fr.* Flight of the Earls, The, 1607. BIrV

All Is Best. Milton. *Fr.* Samson Agonistes. NOBE; OBEV; OBS; SeCePo

All is dying; hearts are breaking. Unchanging Jesus. Karl Johann Philipp Spitta, *tr. by* R. Massie. BLRP

All Is God's. Jakov de Haan, *tr. fr. Dutch by* David Soetendorp. VWA

All is passed—all that loomed ahead as evil. Reaching Forty. Abd al-Razzaq Abd al-Wahid, *tr. by* Diana Der Hovanessian *and* Lena Jayyusi. MAP

All is phantom that we mid fare. Phantasy. *Unknown.* ACP

All is quiet and the desert moon. Guard. Michael C. Martin. WaP

All is still/ Under the Pines. Under the Pines. Arthur Stanley Bourinot. OBCV

All is the same still. Earth and heaven locked in. Emily Brontë. C. Day Lewis. GTBS-P

All Is Vanity, Saith the Preacher. Byron. TrCP

All it takes is girls. To Bring Spring. George Keithley. NPGG

All its advertisements. *Unknown, tr. by* Geoffrey Bownas *and* Anthony Thwaite. PeBJV

All Jolly Fellows That Follow the Plough. *Unknown.* OBET

All joy to mortals, joy and mirth. Aphra Behn. *Fr.* Emperor of the Moon. WPE

All kings, and all their favourites [*or* favorites]. The Anniversary [*or* The Anniversarie]. John Donne. BoLoP; HAP; HoPM; JCP; LiTB; MeLP; MePo; NOBE; NoP; OAEL-1; OBS; SeCP; SeCV-1; WeW

All kings are hollow. The Cool, Cool, Country. John Shaw Neilson. PoAu-1

All-knowing God, 'Tis Thine to Know. *Unknown.* AH

All Last Night. Lascelles Abercrombie. FaBoTw

All last night I kept speaking in this. Mysteries. Terence Winch. UL

All last winter, starved cattle. An Abandoned, Overgrown Cemetery in the Pasture near Our House. Gregory Orr. MAYP

All Legendary Obstacles. John Montague. BIrV; CIP; FaBCIP; IPY; NOIV

All look and likeness caught from earth. Phantom. Samuel Taylor Coleridge. NAEL-2; OAEL-2; OxBSP; PoEL-4

All looks be pale, hearts cold as stone. A Lamentation. Thomas Campion. CH; OHIP

All love that has not friendship for its base. Upon the Sand. Ella Wheeler Wilcox. AnAmPo

All Lovely Things. Conrad Aiken. AnAmPo; PoRA

All manifestations of life are simply pain. In Lieu of a Preface to *The Great Commonwealth Book*. K'ang Yu-wei, *tr. by* Irving Lo. WFTU

All matronly in her stoop, her wings canted. The Black Angel. Henri Coulette. NYBP

All meet here with us, finally. Ostriches and Grandmothers! Amiri Baraka. NeAP

All men are brothers and each people is my own. My Song to the Jewish People. Leib Olitski, *tr. by* Jacob Sonntag. TrJP

All men are locked in their cells. Fall Down. Calvin C. Hernton. CNA; PoBA

All men are wormes: but this no man. In silke. On Court-Worme. Ben Jonson. SeCP

All men from all lands. Inscription for a Wayside Spring. Frances Cornford. BrRo

All men wait for battle and when it comes. An Apple Tree and a Pig. Emyr Humphreys. OBWVE

All middle age invisible to us, all age. The Key to the City. Anne Winters. PPR

All month a smell of burning, of dry peat. July 1914. "Anna Akhmatova," tr. by Stanley Kunitz. WPOW

All Morning. Theodore Roethke. NaP

All Morning. Terry Stokes. AmPA

All morning he lay in the tight, dark room. Signature II. Joseph Stroud. NPGG

All morning long from inside the lobby. The Enormous Aquarium. Sherod Santos. MAYP; NamP

All morning long I correct my books. Li K'ai-hsien, tr. fr. Chinese by Jonathan Chaves. Fr. Impromptu Poems. CoBLCP

All morning long we looked around the citadel. The King of Asini. George Seferis, tr. by Edmund Keeley and Philip Sherrard. VMG

All morning the beast labors up from the valley. Sibyl. Joseph Stroud. NPGG

All morning, the man roofs the house. The Hammer Falls, Is Falling. Marianne Boruch. PPR

All morning you squat in the weeds. Rescue. Ellen Bryant Voigt. NoP

All mothers' lips are stones. Prophecy of the Winds. Ahmad Faraz, tr. by Mahmood Jamal. PBMUP

All moves within the visual frame. A Monument. Charles Madge. FaBoMo

All music, sauces, feasts, delights and pleasures. Thomas Traherne. Fr. Christian Ethics. OxBSP; UnS

All must be used. Barracks Apt. 14. Theodore Weiss. CoAP; TAP

All my dark thoughts. Euclid Avenue. Charles Simic. LCAP

All my dead people. Over the Edge. Fleur Adcock. PeNZ

All my favourite characters have been. Mythology. Lawrence Durrell. OxBTC

All my friends can write them. Li K'ai-hsien, tr. fr. Chinese by Jonathan Chaves. Fr. When I Recovered from an Illness, II. CoBLCP

All my friends will come shouldering salvation. Morning-Selah. Amir Gilboa, tr. by Warren Bargad and Stanley F. Chyet. IP

All my future plans, dear. The Blue Room. Lorenz Hart. OBAL

All my life/ they have told me. To You. Frank Horne. Fr. Letters [or Notes] Found near a Suicide. BPo

"All my life I've wanted to be." Miss Crustacean. Robert Phillips. GeTw

All my life so far. Discoveries in Arizona. James Wright. NoP

All my life too lazy to try to get ahead. Ryokan, tr. by Burton Watson. JLIC-2

All My Luve, Leave Me Not. Unknown. GoTS

All my neckties. Sooner or Later. John Digby. EAS

All my past life is mine no more. Love and Life. Earl of Rochester. BoLoP; ELP; EnLoPo; FF; GBL; HAP; MePo; NOBE; OBEV; OBS; PoEL-3; SeCV-2; TrGrPo

All my plans for suicide are ridiculous. The Heart's Location. Peter Meinke. GOYP

All my pleasure is in catching of birds. The English Schoolboy. John Heywood. Fr. The Play of the Weather. ACP

All My Pretty Ones. Anne Sexton. NAAL-2; NoAM; OPOP

All my pwoblems. Maybe Dats Your Pwoblem Too. Jim Hall. MT

All my research has shown. Wyvern. Charles Connell. AmMo

All my senses, like beacon's flame. Fulke Greville. Fr. Caelica, LVI. InvP; PoEL-1; QFR

All my sex life, I had been drifting. Royston Ellis. Fr. The Cherry Boy, 1. PeHV

All my sheep/ Gather in a heap. Last Words before Winter. Louis Untermeyer. MoAmPo

All my shortcomings, in this year of grace. Dear Uncle Stranger. Conrad Aiken. NoAM; NOBA

All my stars forsake me. Song of the Night at Daybreak. Alice Meynell. CH

All my thoughts always speak to me of Love. Dante, tr. fr. Italian by Dante Gabriel Rossetti. Fr. La Vita Nuova, VI. AWP

All Nature Has a Voice to Tell. James Gilchrist Lawson. BLRP

All Nature is a temple where the alive. Correspondences. Baudelaire, tr. by Allen Tate. AWP

All nature seems at work. Slugs leave their lair. Work without Hope. Samuel Taylor Coleridge. BoNaP; EnRP; FiP; NAEL-2; NOBE; NoP; OBEV; SaC; Son; TEP
(In Springtime.) BoTP, 4 ll.

All Nearness Pauses, While a Star Can Grow. E. E. Cummings. NoAM

All Needs Met. J. H. Sammis. BLRP

All night/ you banged. To Poem. Lyn Lifshin. NeAC

All night a noise of leaping fish. The Fisher. Roderic Quinn. CBAP; PoAu-1

All night and all day the wind roared in the streets. Mid-Country Blow. Theodore Roethke. BoNaP

All Night by the Rose. Unknown. GBL; HeIP
(Rose's Scent, The.) WiR

All night fell hammers, shock on shock. A London Fete. Coventry Patmore. EBVV; HAP

All night from the roof of the chieftain. Or Ever God Created Adam. Malay Oral Tradition, tr. by R. J. Wilkinson. WTO

All night had shout of men and cry. Easter Night. Alice Meynell. BrRo; OHIP

All night I am the doe, breathing. The Strange People. Louise Erdrich. NOVW; TSL

All night I clatter upon my creed. The Wife Who Would a Wanton Be. Unknown. FaBoCo

All night I could not sleep. Unknown, tr. fr. Chinese. Fr. Tzu Yeh Songs. BoWoP, tr. by Arthur Waley.
("Nights are long and I cannot sleep.") CoBCP, tr. by Burton Watson.

All night I hear the hammers. The Students of Justice. W. S. Merwin. NaP

All Night I Heard. Gertrude MacGregor Moffatt. CaP

All night I lay awake beside you. Marthe Away (She Is Away). Kenneth Rexroth. UnAS

All night I raced the moon. Laurence Dakin. Fr. Tancred, II, i. CaP

All night I walked among your spirits, Richard. A Mourning Letter from Paris. Conrad Kent Rivers. BPo

All night I wearied utterly of the pillow of darkness. In a Wood Clearing. Wilson Pugsley MacDonald. CaP

All night I wore the phone, a dead scarf. Hello, Hello. William Matthews. PCP

All night in the flue like a trapped thing. January 25th. Maxine W. Kumin. SM

All night in winter the dogs howled. August, Ohakune. Lauris Edmond. ATNZ

All Night It Bullied You. C. K. Stead. Fr. A Small Registry of Births and Deaths. NAs

All night it humps the air. Cannery Town in August. Lorna Dee Cervantes. NoAM

All night like a star a single bulb. Late, Passing Prairie Farm. William Stafford. GOYP

All Night Long. Nina Cassian, tr. fr. Rumanian by Herbert Kuhner. VWA

All Night Long. Unknown. AS

All night long and every night. Young Night Thought. Robert Louis Stevenson. PWR

All Night Long Burned the Bridges. Yekhi'el Khazak, tr. fr. Hebrew by Bernhard Frank. MHeP

All Night Long Fooling Me. Unknown. AmFP

All night long, I couldn't fall asleep. Listening to the Rain. K'ang Hai, tr. by Jonathan Chaves. CoBLCP

All night long into my sleeping bag's head pad the blood. The Far Side of Introspection. Al Lee. CoAP

All night long the hockey pictures. To a Sad Daughter. Michael Ondaatje. GOYP; NoAM

All night long, through the starlit air and the stillness. The Cattle of His Hand. Wilbur Underwood. WGRP

All night the birds have travelled from the coast—the spring. In 62 the Starving Seabirds Reached the Center of Lima. Antonio Cisneros, tr. by Ena Hollis and David Tipton. Per

All night the blind entrance of the children. Barren Poem. Michael Ryan. AmPA

All night the bombers roared about the sky. In War. Gladys M. Haines. CN

All night, the camel-back saddle-cloth was invisible. The Next Day the Fog Was Even Worse. Yüan Mei, tr. by Jonathan Chaves. CoBLCP

All night the douanier in his sentry box. Grandchild. Maxine W. Kumin. BLA; ER

All night the long rain encloses the house. Catechism Elegy. Margaret Gibson. MAYP

All night the pimp's cars slide past the burning mill. Homage to Elvis, Homage to the Fathers. Bruce Weigl. MAYP

All night the searchlights build their towers. The Searchlights. Sylvia Lynd. CN

All night the Shabbos candles. Labor. Lucille Day. VWA

All night the sound had. The Rain. Robert Creeley. CAPP; CoAP; PoE; VGW

All night the tall young man. Merlin and the Snake's Egg. Leslie Norris. WSC

All night, the west wind blows over the capital. Snowstorm: At a Gathering at Chang Chu-fu's House. Tsung Ch'en, *tr. by* Jonathan Chaves. CoBLCP

All night the wind swept over the house. Winter Morning. William Jay Smith. BoNaP

All night they marched, the infantrymen under pack. 1935. Stephen Vincent Benét. MoAmPo

All night they whine upon their ropes and boom. Nocturne of the Wharves. Arna Bontemps. BANP; BPo; PoNe

All night, this headland. Sleepless at Crown Point. Richard Wilbur. InPK; WeW

All night upon the guarded hill. The Defence of Lawrence. Richard Realf. PAH

All night waiting, in an empty house. The Streets of Air. Malcolm Cowley. *Fr.* Blue Juniata. PoA

All-Night Waitress, The. Maura Stanton. AmPA

All-Nite Donuts. Albert Goldbarth. GeTw; MAYP

All of a Piece. Mairin Martin. SoTCo

All of a row. *Unknown.* PBBP

All of a Sudden. Teresa de Jesús, *tr. fr. Spanish by* Maria A. Proser, Arlene Scully *and* James Scully. WPOW

All of a sudden the big nasturtiums. The Big Nasturtiums. Robert Beverly Hale. BoNaP; NYBP

All of our machines need repair. Slightly Old. Bob Rosenthal. UL

All of spring's colors are found inside a brushwood gate. Strolling in Simplicity Garden for the First Time. Chin Ho, *tr.* by J. D Schmidt. WFTU

All of the Easiness Gone. Ursula Krechel, *tr. fr. German by* Susan L. Cocalis. DMG

All of Them. Qasim Haddad, *tr. fr. Arabic by* Sharif Elmusa *and* Charles Doria. MAP

All of them asleep, the suspiring everywhere is audible weight. In the House of the Judge. Dave Smith. MAYP

All of them the wind took, all of them the light lured. Alone. Hayyim Nahman Bialik, *tr. by* Jessie Sampter. TrJP

All of These. Denis Glover. PeNZ

All of us always turning away for solace. Delmore Schwartz. OxBA

All old women sometimes come to this. Old Women of Toronto. Miriam Waddington. NIP; NOBC

All on a Christmas Morning. Elizabeth Jane Coatsworth. ILY

All on one summer's evening when the fever were a-dawning. The Grey Cock. *Unknown.* FaBoBa

All on the road to Alibazan. Alibazan. Laura E. Richards. OBCA

All One in Christ. John Oxenham. BLRP

All One People. Carl Sandburg. AmFN

All one summer I thought about God. Acts without Consequence. Steve Orlen. NAmP

All or Nothing. Bayard Taylor. BXAP

All others talked as if. Caedmon. Denise Levertov. NoAM

All Our Joy Is Enough. Geoffrey Scott. OBMV

All our roads go nowhere. On Inhabiting an Orange. Josephine Miles. NoAM; PoA

All our stones like as much sun as possible. Forecast. Josephine Miles. NoAM

All out for Illinois Central. Calling Trains. *Unknown.* AmFP

All out of doors looked darkly in at him. An Old Man's Winter Night. Robert Frost. AWP; HAP; MoAB; MoAmPo; NAAL-2; NoAM; OxBA; VGW

All over America railroads ride through roses. Landscape as Metal and Flowers. Winfield Townley Scott. AmFN; GoJo

All over America women are burning dinners. What's That Smell in the Kitchen? Marge Piercy. NBLV; NIP

All over the meadow. Princess Takata, *tr. fr. Japanese. Fr.* Manyo Shu. Ma

All over the mountain. Mountain Barrier. Su Shao-lien, *tr. by* Dominic Cheung. IFON

All over the plain of the world lovers are being hurt. Christian Karlson Stead. *Fr.* Quesada, I. ATNZ; PeNZ

All over the world, I wonder, in lands that I never have trod. Meditations of a Hindu Prince. Sir Alfred Comyn Lyall. WGRP

All passes. Art alone. Austin Dobson, *after the French of* Théophile Gautier. *Fr.* Ars Victrix. CTC

All Paths Lead to You. Blanche Shoemaker Wagstaff. BLPA; FaBoBe

All patriarchs are above our understanding. Beirei, *tr. by* Lucien Stryk *and* Takashi Ikemoto. ZPCJ

All peacefully gliding. The Rapid. Charles Sangster. CaP

All people that on earth do dwell. Old Hundredth. William Kethe. FaPoR

   (Psalm C.) NOCV

   (Scotch Te Deum.) WGRP

All perished—brides and infants. Song of a Jewish Boy. "M. J.," *tr. by* A. Leyeles. TrJP

All Possession Is Theft. Lauris Edmond. PeNZ

All Praise to Thee. F. Bland Tucker. AH

All praise to Thee, my God, this night. An Evening Hymn. Thomas Ken. OBS; OxBChV

All praise your face, your verses none abuse. Horace Walpole. FaBoEE

All profits disappear: the gain. The Reckoning. Theodore Roethke. PoA

All Quiet along the Potomac. Ethel Lynn Beers, *, sometimes at. to* Lamar Fontaine. AA; AnAmPo; BeLS; FaBoBe; FaFP (Picket-Guard, The.) PAH

All right, gentlemen who cry blue murder as always. Draft of a Reparations Agreement. Dan Pagis, *tr. by* Stephen Mitchell. VWA

All right, I may have lied to you, and about you. Love, 20 Cents the First Quarter Mile. Kenneth Fearing. HAP; WeW

All right, I'll die, my spirit is strong. Fear. Vittoria Aganoor Pompili. PBWP, *tr. by* Brenda Webster

All right now, listen to me right good. Unloading Rails. *Unknown.* AmFP

All right. Try this. Northern Pike. James Wright. NAAL-2

All romance is a parody of this. The Consort. Ruthann Robson. ER

All round about the door of your house. Regret and Refusal. *Unknown, tr. by* H. J. Spinden. WTO

All round the Browns stretched forty acres of potatoes. The Brown Family. Colleen Thibaudeau. NOBC

All round the horizon black clouds appear. On a Sea-Storm nigh the Coast. Richard Steere. SCAP

All round the room I waltzed with Ellen Taylor. Ellen Taylor. *Unknown.* OBET

All Ruin Is the Same. Emanuel Litvinoff. WaP

All Saints' Day, *sel.* Margherita Guidacci, *tr. fr. Italian by* Ruth Feldman *and* Brian Swann. MAP

   "All Saints' Day; November sky." PBWP

All saints revile her, and all sober men. The White Goddess. Robert Graves. MoBrPo; NAEL-2; OAEL-2; OPOP

All Seasons in One. *Unknown.* GBL; HeIP; OBSC; TrGrPo

All seasons shall be sweet to thee. The Silent Icicles. Samuel Taylor Coleridge. *Fr.* Frost at Midnight. BoTP; FaBoRV

All-seeing Intellect, The. Phineas Fletcher. *Fr.* The Purple Island, VI. JCP

All service ranks the same with God. Service. Robert Browning. *Fr.* Pippa Passes, Introduction. TrGrPo

All Shams. *Unknown.* APAS

All silence says music will follow. Onion Bucket. Lorenzo Thomas. PoBA

All Souls. D. H. Lawrence. FaBoRV

All Souls Day. Francisco Carrillo, *tr. fr. Spanish by* Maureen Ahern *and* David Tipton. Per

All Soul's Day. Paul Celan, *tr. fr. German by* Beth Bjorklund. CoAuP

All Souls' Day. D. H. Lawrence. OBD

All Souls' Night. Frances Cornford. EnLoPo; OBD; OxBSP; OxBTC

All souls that struggle and aspire. Whittier. *Fr.* The Shadow and the Light. TrPWD

All Splendor on Earth. Karin Kiwus, *tr. fr. German by* Almut McAuley. BoWoP

All Still. William Barnes. NOBVV

All subatomic particles. Who Ordered That? W. Gregory Stewart. SoTCo

All such proclivities are tabulated. The Quiet Glades of Eden. Robert Graves. BoLoP; ErPo

All suddenly a stormy whirlwind blew. The Mask of Cupid. Spenser. *Fr.* The Faerie Queene, III, 12. OBSC (Masque of Cupid, The.)

   "Noble Mayde, still standing, all this vewd, The." PoEL-1

   "First was Fancy, like a lovely boy, The." NOBE

All-sufficient Christ, The. Bernice W. Lubke. BLRP

All-sufficing person. Poem for Potential. Fanny Howe. PPR

All summer/ they grew unseen. Shelling Jacobs Cattle Beans. Maxine W. Kumin. BLA

All summer I heard them. The Snakes of September. Stanley Kunitz. AnAn; BLA

All summer long the people knelt. At the President's Grave. Richard Watson Gilder. PAH

All that blazing day, swift-breasted swallows. Thunderstorm in South Dakota. Kay Boyle. WPE

All that blesses the step of the antelope. "Else a Great Prince in Prison Lies." Denise Levertov. NaP; PPP; VGW

All that doth flow we cannot liquid name. What Is Liquid. Margaret Cavendish, Duchess of Newcastle. FaBoUs

All That Glisters Is Not Gold. Shakespeare. *Fr.* The Merchant of Venice, II, vii. CTC

All that have two or but one ear. The Four-legg'd Quaker. *Unknown.* CoMu

All That I Am. Verna Arvey. AH

All that I am to Earth Belongs. William Baylebridge. *Fr.* Life's Testament, XI. PoAu-1

All that I do is clumsy and ill timed. The Doppelganger. Daryl Hine. OBCV

(Double-Goer, The.) MoCV

All that I had I brought. Exchanges. Ernest Dowson. OBMV

All that I had in the world. Asadullah Khan Ghalib, *tr. by* Ahmed Ali. GoT

All that I know/ Of a certain star. My Star. Robert Browning. FaPON; SoSe; TrGrPo

All that I may swynk or swet. Care Away. *Unknown.* OxBoLi

All that I ran from. The Mood. Quandra Prettyman. PoBA

All that I try to save him from. Sleep-Learning. Ruth Fainlight. NMM

All That Is Left. Basho, *tr. fr. Japanese by* Curtis Hidden Page. AWP; WaaP

("Old battle field, fresh with Spring flowers again.") AWP

All That Is Left. Michael Hartnett. NOIV

All that is left/ of the magic of the fair. The Little Trumpet. Corrado Govoni, *tr. by* Carlo L. Golino. PFI

All that is lost is the body. Counting the Losses. Barry Spacks. PPR

All That Is Lovely in Men. Robert Creeley. NaP

All that is moulded of iron. Woodworker's Ballad. Herbert Edward Palmer. OBEV

All That Is Needed. János Pilinszky, *tr. fr. Hungarian by* William Jay Smith. MHuP

All That Matters. Walter Sorell. GoYe

All that matters is to be at one with the living God. Pax. D. H. Lawrence. TrCP

All that night I walked alone and wept. Gethsemane. Arna Bontemps. CDC

All that passes descends. The Gift of Gravity. Wendell Berry. GeTw

All that running water outside. The Marshes. Jane Mayhall. TAP

All That Time. May Swenson. FF

All That We Try to Do. Steve Orlen. PPR

All That You Have Given Me, Africa. Anoma Kanié, *tr. fr. French by* Kathleen Weaver. AIW; PBWP

All That's Past. Walter de la Mare. GoJo; MoAB; NOBE; OAEL-2; OBMV; OxBTC; TrGrPo

All the afternoon there has been a chirping of birds. Free Fantasia on Japanese Themes. Amy Lowell. MoAmPo

All the awnings at home had to be pulled down. Cleaning Day. José Kozer, *tr. by* David Unger. VWA

All the bells of heaven may ring. A Child's Laughter. Swinburne. BLPL; PoLF

All the birds have come again. Spring's Arrival. *Unknown.* FaPON

All the bones of the horses rise in moonlight. Song of Returnings. William Pitt Root. GeTw

All the boys always wanted her, so. Leda's Sister and the Geese. Katharyn Machan Aal. SoTCo

All the boys of merry Lincoln. Hugh of Lincoln. *Unknown.* ACP

All the breath and the bloom of the year in the bag of one bee. Summum Bonum. Robert Browning. OHFP

All the cages are empty. The Two Selves. Margaret Avison. MoP

All the cattle are resting in the fields. Poem to the Sun ("All the Cattle are resting in the fields"). *Ancient Egyptian Oral Tradition, tr. by* Christopher Wertz. TTTS

All the cautionary tales of strange girls. Mythics. Helen Chasin. IHMS

All the Caverns of Light. Ya'akov Beser, *tr. fr. Hebrew by* Bernhard Frank. MHeP

All the crystal studded night. Mid-Winter. Sue Roe. NPo

All the day I worked and played. A Labourer's Wife. John Davidson. *Fr.* To the Street Piano. EBVV

All the days of my life. Lifelong. Rachel Boimwall, *tr. by* Gabriel Preil *and* Howard Schwartz

All the Dead Dears. Sylvia Plath. IHMS

All the dead poets know that. What the Dead Poets Know. Elizabeth Smither. ATNZ

All the Death-Room Needs. Michael Hartnett. CIP

All the different kinds of light. The Gods Must Not Know Us. Linda Gregg. NPGG

All the fields of the world. The Noonday Sun and the Shade. Muhammad al-Maghut. MPAW, *tr. by* Abdullah al-Udhari (Shade and Noon Sun.) MAP, *tr. by* May Jayyusi *and* John Heath-Stubbs

All the fishermen here remember the one. Fish Story. Henry Carlile. ASP

All the flat sea lies grey before me. Seashell. Israel Efrat, *tr. by* Bernhard Frank. MHeP

All the flies are reading microscopic books. Serious Readers. Peter Redgrove. OxBC

All the Flowers of the Spring. John Webster. *Fr.* The Devil's Law Case. EIL; ELP; LiTB; OBS; PoEL-2; PoRA (Burial, The.) CH (Nets to Catch the Wind.) TrGrPo (Vanitas Vanitatum.) NOBE; OBEV

All the forms are fugitive. Emerson. *Fr.* Woodnotes II ("As sunbeams stream through liberal space"). WGRP

All the fruit is ripe, plunged in fire, cooked. Friedrich Hölderlin, *tr. by* Robert Bly. NU

All the full-moon night in the coomb. In the Night of the Full Moon. Carl Busse, *tr. by* Jethro Bithell. AWP

All the glorious Spring makes me color blind. Sorrow. Marie Tello Phillips. GoYe

All the heaven and earth. João Cabral de Melo Neto, *tr. fr. Portuguese by* Elizabeth Bishop. *Fr.* The Death and Life of a Severino, XIV. ATCBP

All the here and all the there. Our Two Worthies. John Crowe Ransom. OBAL

All the Hills and Vales Along. Charles Hamilton Sorley. EBEV; FaBoCh; MMA; MoBrPo; OBWP

All the Hosts of Heaven. Simeon ben Isaac ben Abun of Mainz, *tr. fr. Hebrew by* Nina Davis Salaman. TrJP

All the lizards are asleep. Nature Study. Craig Raine. NoAM

All the long August afternoon. In August. William Dean Howells. GN

All the long forenoon, the loitering of insects. The Forenoon. Christopher Middleton. *Fr.* Herman Moon's Hourbook. NePoEA-2

All the materials of a poem. Lumber of Spring. Anne Ridler. NYBP

All the mill-horses of Europe. The Discovery of America. James Logie Robertson. NOBVV

All the mirrors in the world. Frank O'Hara. CAPP

All the months go past. December. Rose Fyleman. RAR

All the names I know from nurse. The Flowers. Robert Louis Stevenson. FaPON

All the new thinking is about loss. Meditation at Lagunitas. Robert Hass. AnAn; MAYP; NoP; NPGG

All the night/ And all day long. Blacksmith. B. K. Pyke. BoTP

All the night sleep came not upon my eyelids. Sapphics. Swinburne. PoEL-5

All the old familiar happiness! Song of the Water Clock at Night. Ku Hsiung, *tr. by* Lois Fusek. ATF

All the Past We Leave Behind, *with music.* Walt Whitman. AH

All the perversions of the soul. A Small Farm. Michael Hartnett. CIP

All the plenitude of a sudden so changed! Like quick cartoons of a thought. Issues of the Fall. Sydney Lea. SM

All the Pretty Little Horses. *Unknown.* AmFP; OxBoLi; TTTS

All the promises of the world are lies. The Promises of the World. Moses Ibn Ezra, *tr. fr. Hebrew by* Solomon Solis-Cohen. *Fr.* The World's Illusion. TrJP

All the Roary Night. Kenneth Patchen. LiTM

All the Same. Iftiqar Arif, *tr. fr. Urdu by* Mahmood Jamal. PBMUP

All the Same, It Would Make You Laugh. Michael Hartnett, *tr. fr. Irish by* the author. IP

All the Scenes of Nature Quicken. Christopher Smart. ELP

All the sexually active people in Westport. The Chaste Stranger. James Tate. NoAM

All the silly threatening things. The All. Yona Wallach, *tr. by* Warren Bargad *and* Stanley F. Chyet. IP

All the Sioux were defeated. Report to Crazy Horse. William Stafford. AnAn; NoAM

All the sisters of mercy. Canto Llano. Anita Endrezze-Danielson. CDW

All the skippers o Scarsburgh. Young Allan. *Unknown.* ESPB

All the Slaves. Thomas Lux. SM

All the Smoke. Eli Siegel. FiBHP

All the Spirit Powers Went to Their Dancing Place. Gary Snyder. UnPo

All the streets are named after Shakespeare. Visiting Juliet Street. Elizabeth Smither. ATNZ

All the sun's peacocks are dreaming. Song for Susannah: A Lullaby. Doris Hardie. TDD

All the things I speak of lie in the city. Things of the Earth. Ferreira Gullar, *tr. by* William Jay Smith. CT

All the things. The objects. Cold Term. Amiri Baraka. BPo; CNA; SOTW

All the time they were praying. The Death Bed. Waring Cuney. CDC

All the tough dudes. Star Boys. Richard Katrovas. NAmP

All the trees all their boughs all their leaves. Out of Sight in the Direction of My Body. Paul Éluard, *tr. by* Samuel Beckett. RHTwFP

All the trees they are so high. The Trees So High. *Unknown.* OxBoLi

All the voices of the wood called "Muriel!" Then I Saw What the Calling Was. Muriel Rukeyser. FaBoWP

All the way/ on the road to Gary. The Helmet. Philip Levine. LCAP

All the way around, outside its gates. The Other Side. Nelo Risi, *tr. by* Lawrence R. Smith. NItP

All the Way Back. Laura Riding. *Fr.* Forgotten Girlhood. RB

All the way back from the air field. Toast. Olivia FitzRoy. CN

All the Way from There to Here. Jack Gilbert. NPGG

All the way to the hospital. The Almond Tree. Jon Stallworthy. NoAM; NoP

All the way to Tir na n'Og are many roads that run. The King of Ireland's Son. Nora Hopper. AnIL

All the while, believe me, I prayed. Sappho, *tr. by* Willis Barnstone. BoWoP

All the while they were talking the new morality. The Encounter. Ezra Pound. AnAmPo

All the while we give our body and our soul. Injustice. Lucie Delarue-Mardrus, *tr. by* Barbara Johnson. DMF

All the whole world is living without war. Canzone: He Speaks of His Condition through Love. Folcachiero de' Folcachieri, *tr. by* Dante Gabriel Rossetti. AWP

All the Words. Gillian Hanscombe *and* Suniti Namjoshi. DT

All the words that I utter. Where My Books Go. W. B. Yeats. OBEV

All the World. *Unknown, tr. fr. Hebrew by* Israel Zangwill. TrJP

All the World Moved. June Jordan. NBP; PoBA

All the world shall come to serve Thee. All the World. *Unknown, tr. by* Israel Zangwill. TrJP

All the world's a school. Schoolmaster. George Rostrevor Hamilton. FaBoEE

All the World's a Stage. Sir Walter Ralegh. *See* What Is Our Life? A Play of Passion.

All the World's a Stage. Shakespeare. *Fr.* As You Like It, II, vii. FaPoR, *fr.* II, vii; FF, *fr.* II, vii; FiP, *fr.* II, vii; LiTB, *fr.* II, vii; PoLF, *fr.* II, vii; RB; TrGrPo, *fr.* II, vii.
(Seven Ages of Man, The.) FaFP

All the years waiting, the whole, barren, young. Sex. Jean Valentine. FaBoWP

All their lives in a box! What generations. The Silkworms. Douglas Stewart. CBAP; PoAu-2

All There Is to Know about Adolph Eichmann. Leonard Cohen. InPK

All These. Peter Ackroyd. NPo

All these are your essence, you are their flesh and their force. Dick Diespecker. *Fr.* Between Two Furious Oceans. CaP

All These Birds. Richard Wilbur. NOBA; Prf

All These Examples. Tom Mandel. IAT

All these [*or* those] heads these ears these eyes. Song of the Old Woman. *Unknown.* AIW, *tr. by* Paul-Emile Victor; *English vers. by* Armand Schwerner; BoWoP, *tr. by* Paul-Emile Victor; *English vers. by* Armand Schwerner; OV, *tr. by* Paul-Emile Victor; *English vers. by* Armand Schwerner

All these illegitimate babies. Valuable. Stevie Smith. OxBTC

All these maneuverings to avoid. Love's Stratagems. Donald Justice. NYBP

All these nights, all these traffic lights. Crossing with the Light. Dwight Okita. BrSi

All these on whom the sacred seal was set. An Unbeliever. Anna Hempstead Branch. WGRP

All these particles of knowledge. All These. Peter Ackroyd. NPo

All these stones, all this sadness, all. Yehuda Amichai, *tr. fr. Hebrew by* Warren Bargod *and* Stanley F. Chyet. *Fr.* Songs of the Land of Zion Jerusalem, 37. IP

All these things are in my mind also, lady; but I fear still. Hektor to Andromache. Homer, *tr. fr. Greek by* Richmond Lattimore. *Fr.* The Iliad, VI. WaaP

All things are doubly fair. Art. Théophile Gautier, *tr. by* George Santayana. AWP

All things are hushed, as Nature's self lay dead. Midnight. Dryden. ACP

All Things Be Dear but Poor Mens Labour; or, The Sad Complaint of Poor People. *Unknown.* CoMu

"All things become thee, being thine," I think sometimes. Woman. Randall Jarrell. NOBA

All things born of causes end when causes run out. To Inscribe on a Picture of a Skull I Painted. Ryokan, *tr. by* Burton Watson. FCEI; JLIC-2

All Things Bright and Beautiful. Cecil Frances Alexander. FaPoR; OHIP; OxBChV; RHPC; TIRV
(Creation, The.) FaPON

All things burn with the fire of God. Revelation. Verne Bright. BLRP; WBLP

All Things Can Tempt Me. W. B. Yeats. CMoP; OxBSP

All things come to pass. My Name Is Afrika. Keorapetse Kgositsile. PoBA

All Things Confine. Hadewijch, *tr. fr. Dutch by* Frans van Rosevelt. PBWP

All things considered we needn't dispair—I love you. When All's Said and Done. Mihály Ladányi, *tr. by* Kenneth McRobbie. MHuP

All things created, Moses writes. Josiah Chorley. *Fr.* A Metrical Index to the Bible. FaBoUs

All Things Decay and Die. Robert Herrick. CaPo

All Things Drink. Thomas Stanley, *after the Greek of* Anacreon. AWP

All things have an end. Ietaka, *tr. by* Steven D. Carter. WFTW

All Things Have Savour. *Unknown.* FaBoCo

All things have their own pace and mode of motion. E. A. Baratynsky, *tr. by* Alan Myers. AAA

All things that are on earth shall wholly pass away. The Love of God. Bernard Rascas, *tr. by* Bryant. WGRP

All things that go deep enough. The Ice Skin. James Dickey. NYBP

All things that pass. Passing and Glassing. Christina Rossetti. OBNC

All things uncomely and broken, all things worn out and old. The Lover Tells of the Rose in His Heart. W. B. Yeats. CMoP
(Aedh Tells of the Rose in His Heart.) BrPo; MoBrPo

All Things Wait upon Thee. Christina Rossetti. GN

All things within this fading world hath end. Before the Birth of One of Her Children. Anne Bradstreet. BoWoP; MAT; NAAL-1; NAs; NOBA; WPE; WPOW

All this—and the housekeeper. Hart Crane. AnAn

All this indigo, nonviolent light will triumph. Sunday Evenings. John Hollander. NYBP

All This Is My Time. Ory Bernstein, *tr. fr. Hebrew by* Warren Bargad *and* Stanley F. Chyet. IP

All this is one. My Faith. Ananda Acharya. WGRP

All this (said she) we know. Achilles Shows Himself in the Battle by the Ships. Homer, *tr. fr. Greek by* George Chapman. *Fr.* The Iliad, XVIII. OBS

All this was, was. Verses on Accepting the World. Joseph Brodsky, *tr. by* Dimitry Pospielovsky *and* Keith Bosley

All those buffalos have green horns. A Song of the Red & Green Buffalo. *Unknown, tr. by* William Whitman. STP

All those family histories. Descendancy. Tom Paulin. FaBCIP

All those heads those ears those eyes. *See* All these heads these ears these eyes.

All those seen from behind who were moving away singing. Endless Journeys. Pierre Reverdy, *tr. by* John Ashbery. POS; RHTwFP

All those summers, waiting. Waiting for You to Come By. Simon J. Ortiz. CDW

All those treasures that lie in the little bolted box. Slow Movement. William Carlos Williams. PoA

All those who are of inmost self aware. Mukhammas. Khwaja Mir Dard, *tr. by* Ahmed Ali. GoT

All those years. Good Old Body. Christine Donald. AIW

All those years. A Kinsman. Jim Wayne Miller. MOWH

All those years that you ate and changed. Peasant. W. S. Merwin. NYBP

All thoughts, all passions, all delights. Love. Samuel Taylor Coleridge. BeLS; ChER; EnRP; GTBS; GTBS-P; OBEV

All thro' the breathing night there seemed to flow. A Venetian Night. Hugo von Hofmannsthal, *tr. by* Ludwig Lewisohn. AWP

All thro' the Year. *Unknown.* BLRP

All through lunch Peter pinched at his crotch. Mission Tire Factory, 1969. Gary Soto. NPGG

All through that summer at ease we lay. The Castle. Edwin Muir. LiTB

All through that Sunday afternoon. A Kite for Michael and Christopher. Seamus Heaney. PPR

All through the fifties and sixties the land tilted. Whether It Exists. John Ashbery. KS

All through the garden I went and went. The Butterbean Tent. Elizabeth Madox Roberts. GoJo

All through the march, besides bag and blanket. Crazed Man in Concentration Camp. Agnes Gergely, *tr. by* Edwin Morgan. BoWoP; MHuP

All through the Night. *Unknown.* FaPON

All through the night. Ryokan, *tr. by* Burton Watson. FCEI

All through the night my eyes have streamed with rain. Strato, *tr. by* Sydney Oswald. PeHV

All through the Stranger's Wood. Isaac Leibush Peretz, *tr. fr. Yiddish by* Joseph Leftwich. TrJP

All through the valley, the people are whispering. Return of the Wolves. Anita Endrezze-Danielson. HATNAP

All through the windless night the clipper rolled. John Masefield. *Fr.* Dauber, VI. CMoP

All to Myself. Wilbur Dick Nesbit. BLPA

All today I lie in the bottom of the wardrobe. Yoko. Thom Gunn. NoAM

All tongues speak of him, and the bleared sights. Shakespeare. *Fr.* Coriolanus, II, i. FaBoPV

All Too Late. *Unknown.* EBEV; OAEL-1

All too late. *Unknown. See* When mine eynen misteth.
All travail of high thought. The Beginnings of Faith. Sir Lewis Morris. WGRP
All travelers [*or* travellers] at first incline. Stella's Birthday, 1721 ("All travelers at first incline"). Swift. NAEL-1; PoEL-3
All trembling in my arms Aminta lay. The Dream. Aphra Behn. *Fr.* A Voyage to the Isle of Love. PBWP
All Tropic Places Smell of Mold. Karl Shapiro. VGW
All Turns into Yesterday. *Unknown.* MeEL
All unaware, it may be. Hitomaro, *tr. fr. Japanese. Fr.* Manyo Shu. Ma
All under the leaves, the leaves of life. The Seven Virgins. *Unknown.* CH; ChTr; GBP; OBET; OBEV
All unwritten poems. I Dedicate to You. Jutta Schutting, *tr. by* Beth Bjorklund. CoAuP
All up and down in shadow-town. The Shadows. Frank Dempster Sherman. AA
All upstarts, insolent in place. The Butterfly and the Snail. John Gay. *Fr.* Fables. FM
All Virgil's idylls end in sunsets; pale. The Voice. Edmund Wilson. NYBP
All visible, visibly. Runner. W. H. Auden. SD
All walking leans to the left. Pencilled by the Rain. Peter Hooper. PeNZ
All was as it is, before the beginning began, before. Jacob. Delmore Schwartz. VWA
All was as it was when I went in. Apopemptic Hymn. Dorothy Auchterlonie. PoAu-2
All was for you: and you are dead. Beyond. Lionel Johnson. BrPo
All was in flight. The Wind Was There. Bravig Imbs. EAS
All Watched Over by Machines of Loving Grace. Richard Brautigan. MAT
All We Ask Is Justice. Mrs. Henry Linden. CBWP-4
All we do—how old are we? I must be twelve, she a little older. Still Life. C. K. Williams. NAmP
All we make is enough. All Our Joy Is Enough. Geoffrey Scott. OBMV
All we were going strong last night this time. John Berryman. FaBoMo
All week, the maid tells me, bowing. A Walk in Kyoto. Earle Birney. GoYe
All Were Too Little. George Gascoigne. *Fr.* Gascoigne's Memories. AAS; Son
All wheels; a man breathed fire. The Celebration. James Dickey. VGW
All Which Isn't Singing Is Mere Talking. E. E. Cummings. VGW
All who are sick at heart and cry in bitterness. The Garden of Song. Moses ibn Ezra, *tr. by* David Goldstein. TOF
All who have and have all can cry: "Peace!" Editorial Poem on an Incident of Effects Far-reaching. Russell Atkins. NBP
All who have loved, be sure of this from me. Richard Watson Dixon. *Fr.* Love's Consolation. OBNC
All winter long you listened for the boom. The Stoic; for Laura von Courten. Edgar Bowers. CoAP; MT; NePoEA; QFR
All winter through I bow my head. The Scarecrow. Walter de␣la␣Mare. MoBrPo; OxBTC
All winter your brute shoulders strained against collars, padding. Names of Horses. Donald Hall. CAPP; HAP; InPK; LCAP; LLLT
All wisdom and renown are worth. Summer Interlude. Lionel Stevenson. CaP
All women are beautiful as they rise. Poem for Easter. Robert Kelly. VGW
All women born are so perverse. Robert Bridges. SeCePo; TW
All women loved dance in a dying light. They Sing. Theodore Roethke. NYBP
All work and no play makes Jack a dull boy. *Unknown.* OxNR
All worldly shapes shall melt in gloom. The Last Man. Thomas Campbell. EnRP
All ye nations, pause a moment! listen to the Negro's voice. The Voice of the Negro. Lizelia Augusta Jenkins Moorer. CBWP-3
All ye poets of the age. Namby-Pamby. Henry Carey. FaBoNo; FaBoPa; NOEC; OBSV; Par
All Ye That Go Astray. Moses Ibn Ezra, *tr. fr. Hebrew by* Solomon Solis-Cohen. *Fr.* The World's Illusion. TrJP
All ye that handle harp and viol. Moses Hayyim Luzzatto, *tr. fr. Hebrew by* Nina Davis Salaman. *Fr.* Unto the Upright Praise. TrJP
All ye that lovely lovers be. Harvester's Song. George Peele. *Fr.* The Old Wives' [*or* Wife's] Tale. TrGrPo
"Lo! here we come a-reaping, a-reaping." OBSC, 4 *ll.*
All ye that pass along Love's trodden way. Dante, *tr. fr. Italian by* Dante Gabriel Rossetti. *Fr.* La Vita Nuova, II. AWP
All ye that passe by this holy place. A Second Epitaph. *Unknown.* MeEL

All ye who, far from town, in rural hall. On a Wet Summer. John Codrington Bampfylde. NOEC
All ye who love the springtime. The Dawning o' the Year. Mary Elizabeth McGrath Blake. AA
All ye woods, and trees, and bowers. The God of Sheep. John Fletcher. *Fr.* The Faithful Shepherdess, V, v. EIL; FaBoCh (To Pan.) TrGrPo
All ye young men, I pray draw near. The Gardener. *Unknown.* GBP
All year/ They have kept a careful record. The New Year for Trees. Howard Schwartz. VWA
All year long, he never visits his home town. The Merchant's Joy. Chang Yü, *tr. by* Jonathan Chaves. CoBLCP
All year, Mozart went under. To a Daughter at Fourteen Forsaking the Violin. Carole Oles. BLA
All year the flax-dam festered in the heart. Death of a Naturalist. Seamus Heaney. HAP; NoAM; OxBC; WeW
All you are doing and saying is to America dangled mirages. To a President. Walt Whitman. NAAL-1
All you can about animals as persons. What You Should Know to Be a Poet. Gary Snyder. NNaP; PoM
All you lords of Scottland ffaire. Tom Potts. *Unknown.* ESPB
All you on emigration bent. The Settler's Lament. *Unknown.* PoAu-1
All You Others, Eat. Djurberaui, *tr. fr. Aborigine by* C. H. Berndt. WTO
All you that are low-spirited, I think it won't be wrong. A New Hunting Song. *Unknown.* OBET
All you that are single and wild in your ways. Old Maids. *Unknown.* AmFP
All you that are to mirth inclin'd, come tarry here a little while. The Country Girl's Policy; or, The Cockney Outwitted. *Unknown.* CoMu
All you that delight in a frolicsome song. A New Song, Called the Frolicsome Sea Captain; or, Tit for Tat. *Unknown.* OxBSS
All you that delight to spend some time. Little John a Begging. *Unknown.* ESPB
All you that desire to here a jest. The Unfortunate Miller; or, The Country Lasses Witty Invention. *Unknown.* CoMu; OxBB
All you that in His house be here. Old Christmas. *Unknown.* OHIP
All you that to feasting and mirth are inclined. Old Christmas Returned. *Unknown.* GN; OHIP
All you violated ones with gentle hearts. For Malcolm X. Margaret Abigail Walker. BPo; CNA; PoBA; Son
All you young men an' maidens come an' listen to my song. A New Song on the Taxes. *Unknown.* WTO
All young men dream. The Bind. Wayne Brown. PBCV
All Your Fortunes We Can Tell Ye. Ben Jonson. *Fr.* The Gypsies Metamorphosed. ChTr
All yow that crye O hone! O hone! A Lementable New Ballad upon the Earle of Essex Death. *Unknown.* CoMu
Allace depairting, grund of wo. Fairweill. *Unknown.* OxBS
Allace! So Sobir Is the Micht. Mersar. OxBS
Allah ("Allah gives light in darkness"). Siegfried August Mahlmann, *tr. fr. German by* Longfellow. AWP
Allansford Pursuit, The. Robert Graves. RB
Allas, deth! Who made thee so hardy. Alas, Death. Charles d'Orléans. OxBLMV
Allas! my worthi maister honorable. Lament for Chaucer. Thomas Hoccleve. OBEV
"Allas," sche seide, "how that this manis mynde." Hue quam precipiti. Boethius, *tr. fr. Latin by* John Walton. *Fr.* The Consolation of Philosophy, I, 2. OBLMV
Allatoona. *Unknown.* PAH
Alle that beth of herte trewe. The Death of King Edward I. *Unknown.* MeEL
Allegiance is assigned. Choice. J. V. Cunningham. VGW
Allegory, An. Barcroft Henry Boake. CBAP
Allegory, An. David Ignatow. VGW
Allegory in Black. Carl Clark. JB
Allegory of Death and Night. Frank Stanford. MT
Allegory of the Adolescent and the Adult. George Barker. LiTB
Allegory of the Wolf Boy, The. Thom Gunn. OxBC
Allegro. Tomas Tranströmer, *tr. fr. Swedish by* Robert Bly. EAS
Alleluia! Christ Is Risen Today. John Henry Hopkins, Jr.. AH
Alleluya. Rubén Darío, *tr. fr. Spanish by* Lysander Kemp. TTY
Allen-a-Dale. Sir Walter Scott. *Fr.* Rokeby, III. EnRP
Allenby. Meir Wieseltier, *tr. fr. Hebrew by* Warren Bargad *and* Stanley F. Chyet. IP
Alley; an Imitation of Spenser, The. Pope. NOEC
Alley Cat School. Frank Asch. RHPC
Alley of granite arkite pillars, The. Stones: Avesbury. Daisy Aldan. PoA
Alleys. Sandra McPherson. MAYP
Allie ("Allie, call the birds in"). Robert Graves. FaPON; GoJo

Alligator, The. Mary Macdonald. RHPC

Alligator, The. Beatrice Ravenel. WPE

Alligator Bride, The. Donald Hall. EAS

Alligator chased his tail, The. The Alligator. Mary Macdonald. RHPC

Alligator on the Escalator. Eve Merriam. SO

Alligator Pie. Dennis Lee. RHPC; TDD

Alligator's Struggles with the 400 sons. *Unknown, tr. fr. Mayan by* Munro Edmonson. *Fr.* The Popol Vuh. STP

Alliteration, or the Siege of Belgrade. Alaric Alexander Watts. *See* Austrian Army, An.

"Allô!"/ said de Falla to Lalo. Intermission Greetings at the Paris Opera— 1898. David R. Slavitt. SoTCo

Allow me just one short remark. The Boa. J. J. Bell. RHPC

Alloy. Muriel Rukeyser. NoAM

All's been said. Ancient Song. Avner Trainin, *tr. by* Bernhard Frank. MHeP

All's harmony, yet everything is separate. Chokei, *tr. by* Lucien Stryk *and* Takashi Ikemoto. ZPCJ

All's ill and will be so. The Wind Is Ill. John Malcolm Brinnin. LiTA

All's Not That Simple. Shin Shalom, *tr. fr. Hebrew by* Bernhard Frank. MHeP

All's over, then: does truth sound bitter. The Lost Mistress. Robert Browning. BoLoP; FiP; NOBE; OBEV; OBNC

All's Right with the World. Gerald Massey. EBVV

All's Vast. Francis Thompson. *See* Heart, The: O nothing in this corporal earth of man.

All's Well. Harriet McEwen Kimball. AA

All's Well. Whittier. OxBSP

All's Well That Ends Well. *Unknown.* FaFP

Allthegirlsarebunched. Crystal Rowe. Mel Glenn. RR

Alluding to the One-armed Bandit. David Chapman Berry. BXAP

Allured outside by someone's plum branches in bloom. Princess Shikishi, *tr. fr. Japanese by* Hiroaki Sato. *Fr.* Seventy-eight Tanka. FCEI

Allusion to Horace; the Tenth Satire of the First Book, An. Earl of Rochester. APAS; OBS

Alluvium. Michel Deguy, *tr. fr. French by* Clayton Eshleman. RHTwFP

Alma. Tom Lehrer. NBLV

Alma Mater, Forget Me. William Cole. FiBHP

Alma Mater's Roll. Edward Everett Hale. AA

Alma; or, The Progress of the Mind, sel. Matthew Prior.
   "In Britain's isles, as Heylyn notes." NOEC

Alma Perdida. Valery Larbaud, *tr. fr. French.* CT, *tr. by* William Jay Smith; RHTwFP, *tr. by* Ron Padgett *and* Bill Zavatsky.

Alma to Her Sister. Linda Gregg. NPGG

Alma Venus, sel. Bernard O'Dowd.
   "Door of existence, beacon of our haze." PoAu-1

Almada Hill: An Epistle from Lisbon, sel. William Mickle.
   "While you, my friend, from louring wintry plains." OBTV

Almanac. May Swenson. NYBP

Almanac Verse. Samuel Danforth. SCAP

Almanac Verse. *Unknown.* SCAP

Almanack for the Year of Our Lord, 1657, An. Samuel Bradstreet. SCAP

Almería. Pablo Neruda, *tr. fr. Spanish by* Angel Flores. WaaP

Almightie Judge, how shall poore wretches brook. Judgement. George Herbert. SeCP

Almighty and everlasting God, we thank Thee. Prayer for Every Day. *Unknown, tr. by* Kweku Martin. PBA

Almighty creator and ruler as well. Hymn to the Creator. John Clare. NOBVV

Almighty crowd, thou shorten'st all dispute. Dryden. *Fr.* The Medal [*or* Medall]: Vox Populi. OBS

Almighty father! of high Heaven posses'd! The Lord's Prayer in Verse. Aaron Hill. FaBoUs

Almighty God, Fader of Hevene. A Prayer to the Trinity. *Unknown.* MeEL

Almighty God in Being Was. Silas Ballou. AH

Almighty God, Thy Constant Care. Henry Stevenson Washburn. AH

Almighty God, who fillest the recesses of the heavens. Bishop Patrick. NOIV

Almighty God, Whose Justice Like a Sun. Hilaire Belloc. TrPWD

Almighty has dealt bitterly with me, The. The Great Sad One. Uri Zvi Greenberg, *tr. by* Robert Mezey *and* Ben Zion Gold. VWA

Almighty Lord, with One Accord. Melancthon Woolsey Stryker. AH

Almighty Maker God! Isaac Watts. *Fr.* Sincere Praise. TrPWD

Almighty Sovereign of the Skies! Nathan Strong. AH

Almighty! Spake, and Gabriel Sped, Th'. George Richards. AH

Almighty! What Is Man? Solomon ibn Gabirol, *tr. fr. Hebrew by* Emma Lazarus. TrJP

Almond Blossom. Sir Edwin Arnold. GN

Almond Blossom. D. H. Lawrence. FaBoPP

Almond Blossoms. Eli Netser, *tr. fr. Hebrew by* Bernhard Frank. MHeP

Almond Tree, The. Jon Stallworthy. NoAM; NoP

Almost afraid they led her in. Transfigured. Sarah Morgan Bryan Piatt. AA

Almost always ahead of us. Frog Hunting. Peter Cooley. MAYP

Almost as much as my sins. Zimmer to His Students. Paul Zimmer. KS

Almost as though the eggs run and leap back into their shells. Remembering Fire. Rodney Jones. MAYP

Almost Aubade. Marilyn Hacker. NoAM

Almost before the princess had grown cold. The True Story of Snow White. Bruce Bennett. SM

Almost blind he takes the soft dying. The Copperhead. Linda Gregg. NAmP

Almost Dancing. Jim Simmerman. MOWH

Almost four years, and, though I merely guess. An Elegy: December, 1970. Edgar Bowers. MT

Almost Grown. Ai. MAYP

Almost happy now, he looked at his estate. Voltaire at Ferney. W. H. Auden. LiTA; LiTM

Almost Human. C. Day Lewis. NoAM

Almost I, yes, I hear. William Sydney Graham. *Fr.* The Dark Dialogues, II. OxBS

Almost Love. Magaly Sánchez, *tr. fr. Spanish by* Margaret Randall. AIW

Almost midnight. The Baal Shem sits. Saint Besht. Itzig Manger, *tr. by* Leonard Wolf. PeBMYV

Almost Ninety. Ruth Whitman. PCP

Almost Persuaded. Philip Paul Bliss. AH

Almost reluctant, we approach the block. Thumbprint. Celeste Turner Wright. Psk

Almost sheer fatigue. Early Pregnancy. Penelope Shuttle. BrRo

Almost singing, she stares past the crowd and flies. Old Woman Awaiting the Greyhound Bus. Duane Niatum. CDW

Almost-tropic night crept through my door, The. Vampire. Walter H. Kerr. VVA

Almost twenty years. Drinking Cold Water. Peter Everwine. NNaP

Almost two years now I've been sleeping. After Elegies. Jean Valentine. LCAP

Almswomen. Edmund Blunden. OBMV; OxBTC

Alnwick Castle. Fitz-Greene Halleck. AA; AnAmPo

Aloe Plant, The. Henry Harbaugh. BLPA

Aloft he guards the starry folds. The Eagle of the Blue. Herman Melville. AA

Aloft in Heavenly Mansions, Doubleyou One. The Playboy of the Demi-World: 1938. William Plomer. OxBTC; PeHV; TW

Aloft upon an old basaltic crag. Kane. Fitz-James O'Brien. PAH

Alone. "Anna Akhmatova," *tr. fr. Russian by* Stephen Berg. BoWoP

Alone. Hayyim Nahman Bialik, *tr. fr. Hebrew by* Jessie Sampter. TrJP

Alone. Chu Shu-chen, *tr. by* Kenneth Rexroth. BoWoP

Alone. Walter de la Mare. ChTr; EnLoPo

Alone. Robert Finch. CaP

Alone. Jonathan Holden. Psk

Alone. James Joyce. InvP

Alone. Elsie Laurence. CaP

Alone. Itzig Manger, *tr. fr. Yiddish by* Ruth Whitman. VWA

Alone. Poe. *See* From Childhood's Hour.

Alone. Sappho, *tr. fr. Greek by* William Ellery Leonard. AWP

Alone. Edith Jay Scovell. GBL

Alone. Richard Shelton. NYBP

Alone ("Alone! Alone!/ I sit in the solitudes of the moonshades"). *Unknown.* NA

Alone. Zoltán Zelk, *tr. fr. Hungarian by* Daniel Hoffman. MHuP

Alone, alone/ you are the eyes of midnight. The Mute City. Lazer Eichenrand, *tr. by* Gabriel Preil *and* Howard Schwartz. VWA

Alone am I, and alone I wish to be. Christine de Pisan, *tr. by* Julie Allen. BoWoP

Alone and Godless, stopped by the sudden edge. Patrick MacDonogh. *Fr.* Escape to Love. BIrV

Alone at home, naked on my bed. The Use of a Wall Mirror. Adriaan Morriën, *tr. by* James S. Holmes. DuIn

Alone, at night, with all the world. Evil Nigger Waits for Lightnin.' Amiri Baraka. NOBA

Alone at the earth's core stands each man. And Then Suddenly It's Dark. Salvatore Quasimodo, *tr. by* William Jay Smith. CT; PFI

Alone at the end of green *allées*, alone. The Statues in the Public Gardens. Howard Nemerov. EyDe

Alone by the Road's Edge. Diana O Hehir. NPGG

Alone for the evening. Bringing Flowers. Roberta Spear. AmPA

Alone, he came to his decision. Felo de Se. Vernon Scannell. OBD

Alone hunting. Deserted Farms Poem. Bruce Severy. NOVW

Alone I inhabit this white. Postponement. André du Bouchet, *tr. by* Paul Auster. RHTwFP

Alone I sit in dark bamboo. Bamboo Mile Lodge. Wang Wei, *tr. fr. Chinese* by Burton Watson. *Fr.* Twenty Views of Wang-ch'uan, 17. CoBCP

Alone I Stand. Ho Ching-ming, *tr. fr. Chinese by* Jonathan Chaves. CoBLCP

Alone I tiptoe through the stars. Star Journey. Naomi Long Madgett. BPo

Alone I walked the ocean strand. A Name in the Sand. Hannah Flagg Gould. AA

Alone in a cold autumn I stood. Midstream. Mao Tse-tung, *tr. by* Earle Birney. MoCV

Alone in an Inn at Southampton, April the 25th, 1737. Aaron Hill. NOEC

Alone in greenwood must I roam. Hollin, Green Hollin. *Unknown.* GBP

Alone in mountain fastness. Bankei, *tr. by* Lucien Stryk *and* Takashi Ikemoto. ZPCJ

Alone in my sorrow, where do my thoughts go? Thinking of My Wife. P'an Yüeh, *tr. by* Burton Watson. CoBCP

Alone in the atoning belfry how I grieve. Giotto's Campanile. Guy Butler. PeSA

Alone in the night. Stars. Sara Teasdale. FaPON

Alone in this desert under the cold moon. If I Forget Thee. Emanuel Litvinoff. TrJP; VWA

Alone is delicious. Alone. Jonathan Holden. Psk

Alone Is the Hunter. Harold Littlebird. VoR

Alone no loneliness in the dream in the quiet. Alma to Her Sister. Linda Gregg. NPGG

Alone of gods death has no love for gifts. Aeschylus, *tr. fr. Greek by* C. M. Bowra. *Fr.* Niobe. OBD

Alone on Lykaion since man hath been. Mount Lykaion. Trumbull Stickney. *Fr.* Sonnets from Greece. OxBA; Son; TrGrPo

Alone on the hill of storms. Battle of the Stars. Adah Isaacs Menken. CBWP-1

Alone on the jagged rock. November Day at McClure's. Robert Bly. NU

Alone on the lawn. The Dancing Cabman. John Bingham Morton. MoShBr; NOBL

Alone on the shore in the pause of the nighttime. The Full Heart. Robert Nichols. BoNaP

Alone on the tower. Diver. Ronald Albert Simpson. CBAP

Alone one noon on a sheet of igneous rock. Myths. Guy Butler. PeSA

Alone she climbs the small tower as spring comes to an end. The Magnolia Flower. Wei Chuang, *tr. by* Lois Fusek. ATF

Alone she feeds the white swans. The Swans of Vadstena. Ralph Gustafson. MoCV

Alone the pallid cuckoo now. Pallid Cuckoo. David Campbell. CBAP; PoAu-2

Alone the sea. Dog and Sea. Alfonsina Storni, *tr. by* Mark I. Smith. OV

Alone up here on the mountain. *Unknown.* NOIV

Alone up north, soaking this nutty bulgur for supper. Wheat. Gary Gildner. KS

Alone, upon the broad low bench, he sits. To Borglum's Seated Statue of Abraham Lincoln. Charlotte Brewster Jordan. OHIP

Alone walking/ And oft musing. The Bailey Beareth the Bell Away. *Unknown.* SeCePo

Alone walking,/ In thought pleining. Wishing My Death. *Unknown.* MeEL

Alone we are born. High Country Weather. James Keir Baxter. ATNZ

Alone with God for one sweet, solemn hour. The Quiet Hour. Louise Hollingsworth Bowman. BLRP

Along a country road he travels. Drifter's Song. Eino Leino, *tr. by* Aili Jarvenpa. SOP

Along a path in the woods. White Public Benches. Hagiwara Sakutaro, *tr. by* Hiroaki Sato. FCEI

Along a river-side, I know not where. The Washers of the Shroud. James Russell Lowell. PAH

Along a road. Rain Clouds. Elizabeth-Ellen Long. RHPC

Along a street swept clean of people. It Smashes Barricades. Anna Swirszczynska, *tr. by* Magnus Jan Krynski *and* Robert A. Maguire. PwPP

Along Ancona's hills the shimmering heat. Poppies in the Wheat. Helen Hunt Jackson. AA

Along come that F.F.V., the swiftest on the line. George Allen. *Unknown.* AmFP

Along East River and the Bronx. Ode to Walt Whitman. Federico García Lorca. PeHV

Along Highway 40, blare. The Shape of Autumn. Virginia Russ. GoYe

Along History. Muriel Rukeyser. NNaP

Along how many Main Streets have I walked. The Eternal Return. Robert Hillyer. AiP; NYBP

Along that tract of the Rio Grande. Boquillas. Greg Pape. NAmP

Along the avenue of cypresses. Giorno dei Morti. D. H. Lawrence. BrPo; FaBoRV; NOBE; SeCePo

Along the Banks. Joel Barlow. AH

Along the banks of the river. Serenade. Federico García Lorca, *tr. by* Perry Higman. LPSS

Along the blushing borders bright with dew. Spring Flowers. James Thomson. *Fr.* The Seasons: Spring. NOBE

Along the caravan routes go the camels tall. Camels in Persia. Dorothy Wellesley. OBTV

Along the cement walkway I pick up. Markings. Frank Steele. Psk

Along the coast of Tsunu. Hitomaro, *tr. fr. Japanese.* *Fr.* Manyo Shu. Ma

Along the country roadside, stone on stone. Stone Walls. Julie Mathilde Lippmann. AA

Along the dark, and silent night. The Bell-Man. Robert Herrick. OBS

Along the dark bank of the river. After the Night Hunt. James Dickey. PoA

Along the fence. Sunflowers in October. Gerhard Fritsch, *tr. by* Beth Bjorklund. CoAuP

Along the Field as We Came By. A. E. Housman. *Fr.* A Shropshire Lad, XXVI. HAP; MoAB; MoBrPo; WeW

Along the garden terrace, under which. George Meredith. *Fr.* Modern Love, XXXVII. NOBVV

Along the lake the bugle rings. Echo Reverie. Henrietta Cordelia Ray. CBWP-3

Along the line of smoky hills. Indian Summer. Wilfred Campbell. CaP; NOBC; OBCV

Along the pastoral ways I go. A Holiday. Lizette Woodworth Reese. AA

Along the path of Iware. Prince Yamakuma, *tr. fr. Japanese.* *Fr.* Manyo Shu. Ma

Along the path that skirts the wood. The Three Musicians. Aubrey Beardsley. NOBVV; OBTV

Along the path where your light feet passed. Anath. Haim Guri, *tr. by* Naomi Nir *and* Howard Schwartz. VWA

Along the river most homes here. Quatrain at Chen-chou. Wang Shih-chen, *tr. by* Jonathan Chaves. CoBLCP

Along the River, Seeing the Home of Absconded Farmers. Kao Ch'i, *tr. fr. Chinese by* Jonathan Chaves. CoBLCP

Along the river where daphnes bloom. Cup's Primitivism. Nishiwaki Junzaburo, *tr. by* Hiroaki Sato. FCEI

Along the Road. Robert Browning Hamilton. BLPA; BLPL

Along the road all shapes must travel by. Prolonged Sonnet: In the Last Days of the Emperor Henry VII. Simone dall' Antella, *tr. by* Dante Gabriel Rossetti. AWP

Along the roadside, like the flowers of gold. Whittier. *Fr.* Among the Hills. NAAL-1; OxBA; PoEL-4

Along the sea-edge, like a gnome. The Sandpiper. Witter Bynner. RHPC

Along the serried coast the Southerly raves. Sea-Grief. Dowell O'Reilly. PoAu-1

Along the shore the slimy brine-pits yawn. The Witch's Whelp. Richard Henry Stoddard. AH

Along the sprawled body of the derailed. Outside Fargo, North Dakota. James Wright. LCAP; NNaP

Along the Strand. Alfred Mombert, *tr. fr. German by* Jethro Bithell. TrJP

Along the tangled path and in the red. Manuel José Othón, *tr. by* Samuel Beckett. MexPo

Along the thousand roads of France. The Good Joan. Lizette Woodworth Reese. FaPON; MoShBr

Along the turner turnpike at a rest stop between. Poem near Midway Truck Stop. Lance Henson. STE

Along the walks the sweet queens walk their dogs. Central Park West. Jack Spicer. PeHV

Along the water the small invisible owls. Dawn near an Old Battlefield, in a Time of Peace. James Wright. AnAn

Along the Yodo. Tsurayuki, *tr. fr. Japanese by* Burton Watson. *Fr.* Kokin Shu. FCEI

Alons au bois le may cueillir. Charles d'Orléans, *tr. fr. French by* W. E. Henley. AWP

Aloof. Christina Rossetti. *See* Thread of Life, The: Irresponsive silence of the land, The.

Aloof, as if a thing of mood and whim. The Schreckhorn. Thomas Hardy. OAEL-2

Aloofe, aloofe, and come no neare. Sea Marke. John Smith. SCAP

Aloud, I said, with a slight stir of heart. Far West Once. Robert Penn Warren. BLA

Alow and aloof. The Windy Night. Thomas Buchanan Read. GN

Alpaca pictures of the previous past. Confounded Nonsense. Tom Hood. FaBoNo

Alpha November Golf Sierra Tango. Tom Clark. UL

Alphabet. Edward Lear. FaBoNo
Alphabet, An. Edward Lear. OxBChV
Alphabet, The. Karl Shapiro. NoAM; PoA; VWA
Alphabet. ("A, B, C, D, E, F, G"). *Unknown*. FaBoUs
Alphabet. ("Great A Was Alarmed at B's Bad Behavior"). *Unknown*. FaBoUs; OxNR
Alphabet Calendar of Amergin, The. *Unknown, tr. fr. Irish by* Robert Graves. BIrV
Alphabet Came to Me, The. Jerome Rothenberg. VWA
Alphabet for Auden. Carol Ann Duffy. NPo
Alphabet of, The/ the trees. The Botticellian Trees. William Carlos Williams. AmPP; LiTA
Alphabet of Aristotle, The. Mayster Benet. FaBoUs
Alphabet rejoiced to hear, The. A Literary Squabble. James Robinson Planché. CenHV
Alphabet Stew. Jack Prelutsky. RHPC
Alphabets. Seamus Heaney. NoAM
Alphonse arrives as a fifth season. A Visit from Alphonse. Paul Zimmer. GOYP
Alphonso of Castile. Emerson. NOBA
Alpine. R. S. Thomas. BoNaP; RFM
Alpine Spirit's Song. Thomas Lovell Beddoes. OBNC; OBTV
Alps. Rosanna Warren. MAYP
Alps on Alps. Pope. *See* Essay on Criticism: Little learning is a dangerous thing, A.
Already. Philippe Denis, *tr. fr. French by* Paul Auster. RHTwFP
Already autumn begins here in the mossy rocks. Thinking of "The Autumn Fields." Robert Bly. NNaP
Already batter'd, by his lee they lay. The Sea Battle. Dryden. *Fr.* Annus Mirabilis. FiP
Already blushes on thy cheek. Nemesis. Emerson. NOBA
Already dawn, before the Buddha's altar. Ozaki Hosai, *tr. fr. Japanese by* Hiroaki Sato. *Fr.* One Hundred Haiku in Free Form. FCEI
Already fallen plum-bloom stars the green. The Poor Man's Pig. Edmund Blunden. MoBrPo
Already 5 drownings 32. Riemke Ensing. *Fr.* Topographies. ATNZ
Already heavy with grief is late autumn. Random Thoughts on Autumn. Liang Ch'i-ch'ao, *tr. by* Cecile Chu-chin Sun. WFTU
Already I am no longer looked at with lechery or love. A Sunset of the City. Gwendolyn Brooks. FaBoWP; PBWP
Already it's late summer. Sunbathers go. The Divine Insect. John Hall Wheelock. GoYe; NYBP
Already, no more dreams of going to the capital. Living in Retirement at Te-ch'ing. Chao Meng-fu, *tr. by* Jonathan Chaves. CoBLCP
Already old age is wrinkling my. Sappho, *tr. by* Josephine Balmer. AIW
Already one day has detached itself from all the rest up ahead. Reunion. Charles Wright. CAPP
"Already," Said My Host. Michael Roberts. OBD
Already she seems bone thin. A Poem about Breasts. James Wright. TAP
Already the past's/ a touched-up picture. End of Term. Prunella Power. Mes
Already, the world is far behind. Already. Philippe Denis, *tr. by* Paul Auster. RHTwFP
Already this life is no fun. Drunk with Pavese. Michael Waters. NAmP
Already, through the splendour ere the morn. Virgil's Farewell to Dante. Dante, *tr. fr. Italian by* Laurence Binyon. *Fr.* Divina Commedia: Purgatorio, XXVII. FaBoTw
Already we are both fans of the green and golden dragon. A Natural History of Unicorns and Dragons My Daughter and I Have Known. William Pitt Root. SM
Already winter. Nakamura Kusadao, *tr. by* Geoffrey Bownas *and* Anthony Thwaite. PeBJV
Als I me rode this endre day. The Singing Maid. *Unknown*. MeEL
Alsace-Lorraine. Fanny Howe. IAT
Also raised/ from the noises. Paul Celan, *tr. by* Beth Bjorklund. CoAuP
Also Ulysses once—that other war. Kilroy. Peter Viereck. FF; MoAmPo
(Kilroy Was Here.) PoRA
Altar, The. George Herbert. HoPM; InPS; JCP; NAEL-1; OAEL-1; SeCP; SeCV-1; TrCP; TrGrPo
Altar Prayers. *Unknown, tr. fr. Hawaiian by* N. B. Emerson. WTO
Altars and Sacrifice. Jay Wright. FB
Altars in the Street, The. Denise Levertov. CAPP
Altarwise by Owl-Light, *sels*. Dylan Thomas. LiTM
  "Altarwise by owl-light in the half-way house." *Fr.* I. CMoP; FaBoMo; MoAB; Son
  "Death is all metaphors, shape in one history." *Fr.* II. CMoP; MoAB; Son
  "First there was the lamb on knocking knees." *Fr.* III. CMoP

"From the oracular archives and the parchment." *Fr.* IX. CMoP
"Let the tale's sailor from a Christian voyage." *Fr.* X. CMoP; FaBoMo; OAEL-2
"Now stamp the Lord's Prayer on a grain of rice." *Fr.* VII. FaBoMo
"This was the crucifixion on the mountain." *Fr.* VIII. CMoP
"What is the metre of the dictionary?." *Fr.* IV. CMoP; FaBoMo
Altarwise by owl-light in the half-way house. Dylan Thomas. *Fr.* Altarwise by Owl-Light, I. CMoP; FaBoMo; MoAB; Son
Alter! When the hills do. Emily Dickinson. AA; AmPP; FaBoBe
Altered look about the hills, An. Emily Dickinson. OxBA; PPP
Alternating Nocturne. José Juan Tablada, *tr. fr. Spanish by* Samuel Beckett. MexPo
Alternative Endings to an Unwritten Ballad. Paul Dehn. FiBHP
Alternatives. Kingsley Amis. OxBC
Alternatives. Peter Cooley. AmPA
Althea nodding all day, it has darkened. Ozaki Hosai, *tr. fr. Japanese by* Hiroaki Sato. *Fr.* One Hundred Haiku in Free Form. FCEI
Altho' a slave me is born and bred. J. B. Moreton. PVCV
Although accustomed to picking them, it always. The Woman and the Aloe. Perseus Adams. PeSA
Although across the plains of the sea I came. *Unknown, tr. fr. Japanese*. *Fr.* Manyo Shu. Ma
Although art is autonomous. On This Day I Complete My Fortieth Year. Peter Porter. NAs
Although crowds gathered once if she but showed her face. Fallen Majesty. W. B. Yeats. PoA
Although great in passing, although suddenly enlarged. Death. Sherod Santos. NAmP
Although he has no form. Mukta Bai, *tr. by* Willis Barnstone. BoWoP
Although he said it. When I Think of Him. *Unknown, tr. by* Frances Densmore. OV
Although I am on a journey. Mibu Utamaro, *tr. fr. Japanese*. *Fr.* Manyo Shu. Ma
Although I Am Taking Courses in the Language. Phyllis Janowitz. PPR
Although [*or* Altho'] I be the basest of mankind. St. Simeon Stylites. Tennyson. NOBVV; OAEL-2
Although I can see him still. The Fisherman. W. B. Yeats. CMoP; HAP; NoAM; SD
Although I Conquer All the Earth. *Unknown*. TTTS
Although I cry and though my eyes still shed. Louise Labé. BoWoP, *tr. by* Willis Barnstone
Although I do not hope to turn again. T. S. Eliot. *Fr.* Ash Wednesday. NoAM; NOBA
Although I do not know. Saigyo, *tr. by* Arthur Waley. AWP
Although I had a check. Earl of Surrey. SiPS
Although I leave Braglu, I am close to it. I Djanggawul, am paddling. Djanggawul Song-Cycle. *Aborigine Oral Tradition, tr. by* R. M. Berndt. WTO
Although I mean it, and project the meaning. The Ice-Cream Wars. John Ashbery. CAPP; PoA
Although I put away my life. Emily Dickinson. MoAmPo
Although I Remember the Sound. Robert Huff. SM
Although I shelter from the rain. The Lamentation of the Old Pensioner. W. B. Yeats. NAmP
Although I was her pupil,/ even I reproach Myrtis. Korinna, *tr. by* Willis Barnstone. BoWoP
Although I'm asleep I can't. Daughter. Kimiko Hahn. BrSi
Although it is a cold evening. At the Fishhouses. Elizabeth Bishop. CoAP; FaBoWP; HAP; HCAP; LCAP; LiTM; NAAL-2; NoP; NYBP; PoRA
Although it is night, I sit in the bathroom, waiting. Adolescence—II. Rita Dove. AmPA; HCAP; NoAM
Although it is not plainly visible to the eye. Fujiwara no Toshiyuki, *tr. fr. Japanese by* Arthur Waley. *Fr.* Kokin Shu. AWP
Although it may appear archaic. Eppur Si Muove? Robert Hillyer. GoYe
Although it's cold no clothes I wear. *Unknown*. GBP
Although it's true. An Expanded Want Ad. Brad Leithauser. MAYP
Although lamps burn along the silent streets. James Thomson ("B. V."). *Fr.* The City of Dreadful Night, III. EBVV
Although Michaelmas Daisies bloom for a very long time. Gather Ye Rosebuds. Laurence Fowler. BXAP
Although my claws weaken. Sweetness. *Unknown, tr. by* John Montague. BIrV
Although mythological or personified description. The Prefectural Engineer's Statement Regarding Clouds. Miyazawa Kenji, *tr. by* Hiroaki Sato. FCEI
Although only a fool would mock. Queen Mother to New Queen. Robert Graves. OBSV
Although she feeds me bread of bitterness. America. Claude McKay. CDC; MoP; NIP; NoAM; OPP; PoBA; PoNe; TAP; TTY
Although some are afraid that to speak of a spade as a spade is a social mistake. Rigoletto. Newman Levy. OBAL

Although the aepyornis. He "Digesteth Harde Yron." Marianne Moore. CMoP; NoAM

Although the bed, by hollow shadowing. A Simpler Thing, a Chair. Robert Mezey. NePoEA

Although the field lay cut in swaths. Timothy. Timothy Steele. InPK

Although the lattice had dropped loose. The Bride's Prelude. Dante Gabriel Rossetti. SeCePo

Although the ship's bell marks the time, it is. Concert at Sea. Hubert Creekmore. WaP

Although the sign says. The Wild Horses of Assateague Island. John Bensko. MT

Although the snow still lingers. Last Snow. Andrew Young. OxBTC

Although, those years, we squandered. A Plaint of Flowers. Ernest Sandeen. CRP

Although thy blood be frozen, and thy scalp. To a Covetous Churl. Edward May. FaBoEE

Although thy hand and faith, and good works too. Change. John Donne. Fr. Elegies, III. EBEV

Although Tormented. Kalonymos ben Judah, tr. fr. Hebrew. TrJP

Although We Do Not All the Good We Love. John Davies of Hereford. Fr. The Holy Rood. Son

Although what glitters. Two Paintings by Gustav Klimt. Jorie Graham. SV

Although you died in a distant land. Vigil. Marjorie Freeman Campbell. CaP

Although you mention Venice. For the Stranger. Carolyn Forché. MAYP

Although you move among them as a friend. The Coolin Ridge. William Bell. PoSH

Altitudes. Richard Wilbur. CMoP

Alton Locke, sel. Charles Kingsley.
Sands of Dee, The. Fr. ch. 26. BeLS; CH; EBVV; FaBoPP; FaPON; FaPoR; GN; WBLP

Alumnus Football. Grantland Rice. FPL; PoLF

Always. Guillaume Apollinaire, tr. fr. French by Roger Shattuck. POS; RHTwFP

Always. Mark Strand. BLA; CAPP

Always/ Always. Poem to My Father. Joseph Stroud. NPGG

Always/ with magpies' flights. Memorial for a Fisherman. Johannes Bobrowski, tr. by Don Bogen. AnAn

Always a new wrinkle. The Story of Your Life. Bruce Bennett. RR

Always a third one's there. The Uninvited. Dorothy Livesay. NOBC

Always at dusk, the same tearless experience. The Eyes of My Regret. Angelina Weld Grimké. CDC

Always Battling. Thomas O'Brien. NeIP

Always before, we sped in the same direction. The Queen. Kenneth Pitchford. NYBP

Always before Your Voice My Soul. E. E. Cummings. LiTA; MoAmPo

Always Begin Where You Are. Thomas Hornsby Ferril. PrIm; VGW

Always driven, always in the bite of the blast. And Yet We Are Here! Karl Wolfskehl, tr. by Carol North Valhope and Ernst Morwitz. TrJP

Always expecting the winter. In Dream: The Privacy of Sequence. Ray A. Young Bear. CDW

Always Finish. Unknown. BLPA; FaBoBe; WBLP

Always for the First Time. André Breton, tr. fr. French by Michael Benedikt. POS

Always for thirty years now. Fish Peddler and Cobbler. Kenneth Rexroth. NNaP

Always, from My First Boyhood. John Peale Bishop. VGW

Always have these clear sounds been in your ear. Poem for You. Robert Pack. NePoEA

Always he sits in his accustomed place. Habitué. Helen Frith Stickney. GoYe

Always I lay upon the brink of love. Judas. Vassar Miller. MoAmPo

Always I recall the river arbor at twilight. Tune: As in a Dream ("Always I recall the river arbor at twilight"). Li Ch'ing-chao, tr. by Burton Watson. CoBCP

Always—I tell you this they learned. House Fear. Robert Frost. Fr. The Hill Wife. VGW; WSC

Always in the Parting Year. Else Lasker-Schüler, tr. fr. German by Ralph Manheim. TrJP

Always in the past. Tameie, tr. by Steven D. Carter. WFTW

Always, in these islands, meeting and parting. Charles Brasch. Fr. The Islands, II. ATNZ

Always it was a summer afternoon. The House of Broughton Street. Mary Ann Larkin. AiP

Always it was going on. Today Is Friday. Ramon Guthrie. PoE

Always on Monday, God's name is in the morning papers. The Day after Sunday. Phyllis McGinley. MoAmPo; OBSV; UnPo

Always on the point of falling asleep. The Middle Ages. John Haines. LCAP

Always searching. Wishes, for Alix. James A. Emanuel. NIP

Always she goes like a captured wild bird. Sappho. Jack Cope. PeSA

Always she loved the sound of bells. Joan of Arc. Hugh McCrae. PoAu-1

Always She Moves from Me. Shirley Kaufman. WPE

Always so late in the day. Always. Mark Strand. BLA; CAPP

Always someone resting there. Masaoka Shiki, tr. fr. Japanese by Burton Watson. Fr. Thirty-nine Haiku. FCEI

Always the arriving winds of words. Words. W. R. Rodgers. OxBSP

Always the Following Wind. W. H. Auden. MoBrPo

Always the Melting Moon Comes. Margot Osborn. CaP

Always the same: watching. Watching War Movies. Lucien Stryk. CAPP

Always the same, when on a fated night. The Onset. Robert Frost. CMoP; MoAB; MoAmPo; OxBA; PPP

Always the setting forth was the same. Odysseus. W. S. Merwin. NOBA; NoP

Always there's some boy. Coda. Fred Johnson. CNA

Always these gallows. Mirrors. Fu'ad Rifqa, tr. by Sargon Boulus and Samuel Hazo. MAP

Always to want to. The Tortoise. Cid Corman. InPK; SM; VGW

Always too eager for the future, we. Next, Please. Philip Larkin. MoBrPo; NePoEA

Always True to You in My Fashion, sel. Cole Porter.
"If a custom-tailored vet." NBLV

Always we are going farther without ever advancing. Always. Guillaume Apollinaire, tr. by Roger Shattuck. POS; RHTwFP

Always we have believed. Disguises. Elizabeth Jennings. NePoEA-2

Always when I write I wear a mask. The Mask. Valery Larbaud, tr. by William Jay Smith. CT

Always you are there—standing. The Anima Has a Predilection. Michael Harlow. Fr. Poem Then, for Love, I. PeNZ

Always your body like a foreign country. Location. Knute Skinner. MAT

Alysoun. Unknown. See Bytuene Mersh and Averil.

Am I a king, that I should call my own. From My Arm-Chair. Longfellow. BLPA

Am I a man of the days gone by. Furuhito, tr. fr. Japanese. Fr. Manyo Shu. Ma

Am I a stone and not a sheep. Good Friday. Christina Rossetti. OFD; PoEL-5; PoEL-5

Am I alone,/ And unobserved? I am! If You're Anxious for to Shine in the High Aesthetic Line. W. S. Gilbert. Fr. Patience. NAEL-2
"If you're anxious for to shine in the high esthetic line as a man of culture." NBLV

Am I alone—or is it you, my friend? Toussaint L'Ouverture. E. A. Robinson. PoNe

Am I despised because you say. To a Gentlewoman Objecting to Him His Grey Hairs. Robert Herrick. CaPo; JCP
(Age Not to Be Rejected.) OBS

Am I failing? For no longer can I cast. George Meredith. Fr. Modern Love, XXIX. GBL

Am I mad, O noble Festus. The Distracted Puritan. Richard Corbet. OxBoLi

Am I Not the Lacemaker of Shadow. Charlotte Calmis, tr. fr. French by Mary Ann Caws. DMF

Am I really a sports fan, I ask myself. The Boxing Match. David Ignatow. ASP

Am I the slave they say. Soggarth Aroon. John Banim. TIRV

Am I the son my father and mother cherish. Yakamochi, tr. fr. Japanese. Fr. Manyo Shu. Ma

Am I thus conquered? have I lost the powers. Mary Sidney Wroth, Countess of Montgomery. Fr. Urania: Pamphilia to Amphilanthus. NAEL-1

Am I thy gold? Or purse, Lord, for thy wealth. Edward Taylor. Fr. Preparatory Meditations before My Approach to the Lord's Supper, VI. LiTA; OxBA; TAP

Am I to become profligate as if I were a blonde? Meditations in an Emergency. Frank O'Hara. CAPP; TAP

"Am I to Lose You?" Louisa S. Guggenberger. NOBVV

Am I too dangerous, that no man can let. D. B. Wyndham Lewis. Fr. If So the Man You Are. OBSV

Am I your only love—in the whole world—now? Tell Me Again. Nigâr Hanim, tr. by Tâlat S. Halman. PBWP

Am not I in blessed case. My Dear Lady. Unknown. EIL

Ama Credo. Margaret Reckord. AIW

Amagansett Beach Revisited. John Hall Wheelock. NYBP

Amagoduka at Glencoe Station. Mbuyiseni Oswald Mtshali. WMBCH

Amalek. Friedrich Torberg, tr. fr. German by Erna Baber Rosenfeld. VWA

Amanda Barker. Edgar Lee Masters. Fr. Spoon River Anthology. NoAM

Amantium Irae Amoris Redintegratio. Richard Edwards. EIL; OBEV; OBSC

Amarantha sweet and fair. To Amarantha, That She Would Dishevel Her Hair. Richard Lovelace. HoPM; MePo; NIP; NoP; OBEV; SeCP; SeCV-1; TrGrPo
   (Song: To Amarantha, that She Would Dishevel Her Hair.) CaPo; PoE
Amarillo. Alan Bernheimer. IAT
Amassing Knowledge. Mark Rich. SoTCo
Amateur and muddled, as their sex goes. The Professionals. Geoffrey Grigson. PoA
Amateur Flute, The. *Unknown.* BXAP; Par
Amateur play fell through, The. *Unknown, tr. by* Burton Watson. FCEI
Amateur Thinks, An. Stefan Themerson. NPo
Amateurs, we gathered mushrooms. Fall. Robert Hass. AmPA
A-Maying, a-Playing. Thomas Nashe. *Fr.* Summer's Last Will and Testament. EiL
Amaze. Adelaide Crapsey. QFR
Amazement fills my heart to-night. Thanksgiving. Robert Nichols. MMA
Amazing Grace. Anselm Hollo. PoM
Amazing Gracious Living on I-93. George Starbuck. PPR
Amazing monster! that, for aught I know. A Fish Answers. Leigh Hunt. *Fr.* The Fish, the Man, and the Spirit. FiBHP; NBLV
   (Fish to Man.) MoShBr
Amazing Sight! The Saviour Stands. Henry Alline. *Fr.* Christ Inviting Sinners to His Grace. AH, *with music;* CaP
Amazing thing happened to me, An. Daniil Kharms, *tr. by* George Gibian. FaBoNo
Amazons, The, *sel.* Marie-Anne Du Boccage, *tr. fr. French by* Dorothy Backer.
   "Will you never view us without distrust." DMF
Ambarvalia, *sel.* Arthur Hugh Clough.
   Pont-y-Wern. FaBoPP
Ambassador, The. Stevie Smith. Mes
Ambassador Puser the ambassador. Memorial Rain. Archibald MacLeish. AmPP; CMoP; LiTA; MoAB; MoAmPo; OBWP
Amber Bead, The. Robert Herrick. CaPo; ChTr
Amber Beads. Audrey Alexandra Brown. CaP
Amber the sky. Rokwaho. STE
Amber the wine. At the Party. Freda Laughton. NeIP
Ambergris and musk rise from the burner by the curtain. Song of Kan-chou. Ku Hsiung, *tr. by* Lois Fusek. ATF
Ambition. Morris Bishop. AmFN
Ambition. W. H. Davies. MoBrPo; TrGrPo
Ambition. Robert Herrick. CaPo
Ambition. Maggie Pogue Johnson. CBWP-4
Ambition. X. J. Kennedy. BLA
Ambition. Henrietta Cordelia Ray. CBWP-3
Ambition. Joachim Ringelnatz, *tr. fr. German by* C. Middleton. OBD
Ambition. Shakespeare *and probably* John Fletcher. *Fr.* King Henry VIII, III, ii. TrGrPo
Ambition. Nathaniel Parker Willis. OBCA
Ambition is busy with many and many. Asadullah Khan Ghalib, *tr. by* Ahmed Ali. GoT
Ambition of Ghosts, The. Rosemarie Waldrop. UL
Ambitious. Jim Gustafson. UL
Ambitious Ant, The. Amos Russel Wells. OBCA
Amboyna; or, The Cruelties of the Dutch to the English Merchants, *sel.* Dryden.
   "As needy gallants in the scriv'ners' hands." OBSV
Ambrosia of Dionysus and Semele, The. Robert Graves. NYBP
Ambulance men touched her cold, The. The Death of Marilyn Monroe. Sharon Olds. MAYP
Ambulances. Philip Larkin. FaBoTw; NAEL-2; OxBC
Ambulando. Charles Brasch. ATNZ; PeNZ
Ambuscade. Hugh McCrae. PoAu-1
Ambush. Hugo Claus, *tr. fr. Dutch by* Theo Hermans. DuIn
Ambushed by Angels. Gustav Davidson. GoYe
Ambushed myself discovered. Humility. Marie Luise Kaschnitz, *tr. by* Michael Hamburger. WPOW
Amelia Mixed the Mustard. A. E. Housman. FaBoNo; RHPC
Amen. Frederick G. Browning. BLRP
Amen. Richard W. Thomas. PoBA
Amendis to the Telyouris and Sowtaris for the Turnament Maid on Thame, The. William Dunbar. OBSV
Amendment. Thomas Traherne. SeCV-2
Amends for Ladies, *sel.* Nathaniel Field.
   Rise, Lady Mistress, Rise! EiL
   (Song: "Rise Lady Mistresse, rise.") OBS
Amergin's Songs, *sels.* Amergin. NOIV
   "Fish-teeming sea." *Fr.* III.
   "I am wind on sea." *Fr.* II.
   "I call the land of Ireland." *Fr.* I.
America. Arlo Bates. *Fr.* The Torch-Bearers. AA

America. Bryant. *See* Oh Mother of a Mighty Race.
America. Arthur Cleveland Coxe. PAH
America. Robert Creeley. MAT
America. Henry Dumas. PoBA
America. Allen Ginsberg. CAPP; CoAP; HCAP; InPS; NaP; NoAM; PoE; PoM; PPP
America. Claude McKay. CDC; MoP; NIP; NoAM; OPP; PoBA; PoNe; TAP; TTY
America. John Newlove. NOBC
America. Wendy Rose. CDW
America. Samuel Francis Smith. AA; AiP; AnAmPo; FaBoBe; FaFP; FaPON; OPP; PoLF; WBLP
America. Bayard Taylor. *Fr.* The National Ode, July 4, 1876. AA
America. Walt Whitman. GOA
America/ I/ carry/ you. The Pinta, the Nina and the Santa Maria. John Tagliabue. AmFN
America a Prophecy. Blake. OAEL-2
America; a Prophecy ("Shadowy daughter of Urthona stood before red Orc."), *sel. Blake.* OAEL-2
   Empire Is No More. EnRP
America America. Owed to America. Lawrence Durrell. OBTV
America Befriend. Henry van Dyke. *See* O Lord Our God, Thy Mighty Hand.
America Bleeds. Angelo Lewis. PoBA
America costs me. Balance Sheet with Incident. Nicholas Born, *tr. by* Margitt Lehbert. WCI
America! dear brother land! Greeting from England. *Unknown.* PAH
America for Me. Henry van Dyke. BLPA; BLPL; FaFP; OHFP; OPP; SoSe; WBLP
America Greets an Alien. John Montgomery. OPP
"America, I Love You." Bert Kalmar *and* Harry Ruby. FiBHP
America, if you were a basketball court. Stephen Vincent. ASP
America Is Hard to See. Robert Frost. AiP
America is West and the wind blowing. Archibald MacLeish. *Fr.* American Letter. AmFN
America, it is to thee. From America. James M. Whitfield. BPo
America I've given you all and now I'm nothing. America. Allen Ginsberg. CAPP; CoAP; HCAP; InPS; NaP; NoAM; PoE; PoM; PPP
America, my own! National Song. William Henry Venable. PAH
America, O Power benign, great hearts revere your name. Land of the Free. Arthur Nicholas Hosking. BLPA; OPP
America the Beautiful. Katharine Lee Bates. BLPA; EaLo; FaBoBe; FaBV; FaFP; FaPON; GOA; OPP; TAP; WBLP; WGRP
America the Beautiful. Stan Rice. NPGG
America! thou fractious nation. A Proclamation. *Unknown.* PAH
America to England. George Edward Woodberry. AA
America to Great Britain. Washington Allston. AA
America was always promises. Archibald MacLeish. *Fr.* America Was Promises. AmFN
America Was Promises, *sel.* Archibald MacLeish.
   "America was always promises." AmFN
America, watch out! Flesh Coupon. Jeff Wright. UL
America will never forgive you. H. Rap Brown. Henry Blakely. CNA
America, you are luckier. The United States. Goethe, *tr. by* Robert Bly. AiP
aMERICA, you caTNip bIN. Hymn to These Newly Abbreviated States. John Updike. SoTCo
America, you ode for reality! America. Robert Creeley. MAT
American against Solitude. Alan Dugan. SM
American Ash. Stanley Plumly. GeTw
American Bandstand. Michael Waters. MAYP
American blacks are known. Anti Apart Hate Art. Michelle T. Clinton. AIW
American Boyhood, An. Jonathan Holden. Psk
American Change. Allen Ginsberg. HCAP
American Child. Paul Engle. AmFN
American Commencement. Aram Boyajian. NeAC
American Dream, The, *sel.* Johnie Scott.
   "Speech, or dark cities screaming." NBP
American Dreams. Louis Simpson. CAPP
American Eagle, The. D. H. Lawrence. OAEL-2
American eagle is not aware he is, The. Eagle Plain. Robert Francis. AmFN
American Falls. Greg Keeler. SM
American Farm, 1934. Genevieve Taggard. VGW
American Flag, The. Joseph Rodman Drake. AA; AnAmPo; FaBoBe; FaFP; GN; OPP; PAH; WBLP
American friend using a thick British accent, An. Mecox Road. Marc Cohen. BAP
American frigate, a frigate of fame, An. Paul Jones's Victory. *Unknown.* AmFP
American frigate from Baltimore came, An. Paul Jones. *Unknown.* PAH

American Girl, An. Brander Matthews. AA
American Gothic. Samuel Allen. *See* Sometimes I feel like I will never stop.
American Heartbreak. Langston Hughes. AmPP; BPo; LiTM
American Heritage. Robert Sward. OBAL
American hero must triumph over, The. Eisenhower's Visit to Franco, 1959. James Wright. NaP
American History. Michael S. S. Harper. BPo; HCAP; NoAM
American History. W. R. Moses. LiTA
American Independence. Francis Hopkinson. PAH
American Indian, The. *Unknown.* FaBoCo; FiBHP; NBLV
American jump, American jump. *Unknown.* OxNR
American Landscape with Clouds & a Zoo. Jon Anderson. AnAn; MAYP
American Letter. Archibald MacLeish. AmPP; OxBA
American Letter, *sel.* Archibald MacLeish. AmPP; OxBA
 "America is West and the wind blowing." AmFN
American Lights, Seen from Off Abroad. John Berryman. LCAP; OBAL
American muse, whose strong and diverse heart. Stephen Vincent Benét. *Fr.* John Brown's Body. AmFN; OPP
American Names. Stephen Vincent Benét. AmFN; GOA; OBAL; OPP; OxBA
American Patriot's Prayer, The. *Unknown.* PAH
 (American Patriot's Prayer 1776, The.) OPP
American Plan. John Malcolm Brinnin. GOA
American Poet—"But Since It Came to Good. . .," The. William Hathaway. UL
American Poetry. Louis Simpson. CAPP; MoP; NoAM; NOBA; TAP
American Portrait: Old Style. Robert Penn Warren. FYAP
American Primitive. William Jay Smith. DiL; FF; InPK; MoAmPo; NePoEA; OxBSP; TwCP
American Rhapsody. Kenneth Fearing. MoAmPo
American Scenes (1904). Donald Justice. MT
American Soldier, The. Philip Freneau. TAP
American Soldier's Hymn, The. *Unknown.* PAH
American Traveller, The. "Orpheus C. Kerr." FaBoCo; OBAL
American Twilights, 1957. James Wright. CoAP
Americana Vineyard. Mildred Cousens. GoYe
Americana IX. Carl Rakosi. InPS
Americanized. Bruce Dawe. CBAP
American's a hustler, for he says so, The. A Ballad of Abbreviations. G. K. Chesterton. NOBL
Americans Are Afraid of Lizards. Karl Shapiro. AmFN
Americans are always moving on. Stephen Vincent Benét. *Fr.* Western Star. AmFN
Americans in an Orange Grove. Arthur Vogelsang. MAYP
Americans make many spectacular movies, The. The Cinema. Bill Manhire. ATNZ
Americans Playing Slow-Pitch Softball at an Airbase near Kunsan, South Korea. Halvard Johnson. TSL
Americans, rejoice. Old Song Written during Washington's Life. *Unknown.* OHIP
America's Answer. R. W. Lilliard. BLPA; OPP
America's Welcome Home. Henry van Dyke. AiP
America's Wounded Knee. Phillip William George. VoR
Americus, as he did wend. The Noble Tuck-Man. Jean Ingelow. NA
Ametas and Thestylis Making Hay-Ropes. Andrew Marvell. InvP; SeCP
Amid a vastness of autumn colors I climb the slopes. Visiting Ichijo-ji. Ito Jinsai, *tr.* by Burton Watson. JLIC-2
Amid curled leaves and green. Peach Tree with Fruit. Padraic Colum. BoNaP
Amid insect chirpings I wake. Ill in Bed. Joso, *tr. fr. Japanese by* Hiroaki Sato. *Fr.* Fifteen Hokku. FCEI
Amid my bale I bathe in bliss. A Straunge Passion of a Lover. George Gascoigne. AAS
Amid rows of tvs, screens blank as postcards from cemeteries. Utopia TV Store. Maxine Chernoff. UL
Amid the chapel's chequered gloom. Heliotrope. Harry Thurston Peck. AA
Amid the dawn's scaffolding, lines of ink and lead. Plans. Dan Pagis, *tr.* by Warren Bargad *and* Stanley F. Chyet. IP
Amid the noncommitted compounds of the mind. Metagnomy. N. H. Pritchard II. NBP
Amid the stony slapping of the waves. Barnacle Geese. Charles Higham. PoAu-2
Amid this hot green glowing gloom. Interlude. Edith Sitwell. MoAB; MoBrPo
Amid Tibetan snows the ancient lama. What Hath Man Wrought Exclamation Point. Morris Bishop. NYBP
Amidst bamboo, gate pulled shut. Nodding Off. Kao Ch'i, *tr. by* Jonathan Chaves. CoBLCP

Amidst chiseled jasper and drifting cinnabar, all in a haze. Crossing the River in Heavy Wind. Wang Shih-chen, *tr.* by Irving Lo. WFTU
Amidst fruitless activity and fat idleness. Haifa. Dovid Knut, *tr.* by Daniel Weissbort. VWA
Amidst the fairest mountain tops. Cynthia. Sir Edward Dyer. OBSC
Amien's Song. Shakespeare. *Fr.* As You Like It, IV, ii.
 (Song: "What shall he have that kill'd the dear?".") CTC
Amiens's Song. Shakespeare. *See* As You Like It: Blow, Blow, Thou Winter Wind.
Amiens's Song. Shakespeare. *See* As You Like It: Under the Greenwood Tree.
Amin, you came to Iraq, wanting to see. Poem to al-Raihani. Maruf al-Rasafi, *tr.* by Issa Boullata *and* Christopher Middleton. MAP
Aminta, *sel.* Tasso, *tr. fr. Italian.*
 "O lovely age of gold!" OBVE, *tr.* by Leigh Hunt.
 (Golden Age, The.) AWP, *tr.* by Leigh Hunt; PFI, *tr.* by Leigh Hunt.
 (Pastoral[l], A: "Oh [*or* O] happy golden age.") OAEL-1, *tr.* by Samuel Daniel; OBSC, *tr.* by Samuel Daniel; PoEL-2, *tr.* by Samuel Daniel.
Amintas and Claudia; or, The Merry Shepherdess. *Unknown.* CoMu
Amish, The. John Updike. OBAL
Amish Rug, An. Michael Longley. CIP
Ammonite, The. Jacques Hamelink, *tr. fr. Dutch by* Paul Vincent. DuIn
Amnesia. David Lehman. EOEF
Amnesiac. Mark Osaki. BrSi
Amnesiac. Sylvia Plath. NYBP
Amo, Amas. John O'Keefe. ChTr; GBL
Amoebaean Eclogues, *sel.* John Scott.
 How to Fertilize Soil. *Fr.* II. FaBoUs
Among/ of/ green. The Locust Tree in Flower. William Carlos Williams. SOTW; TTTS
Among all lovely things my love had been. Wordsworth. GBL
Among bailiffs and creditors. Wolf Bezberider. Aba Shtoltsenberg, *tr.* by Dennis Silk. PeBMYV
Among Blackberries. Michael Waters. GeTw
Among branches. Gray Glove. Roo Borson. NOBC
Among crab apple and pear, birds summon the wind. Fen-chou. T'an Ssu-t'ung, *tr.* by Timothy C. Wong. WFTU
Among Dark Trees. Mirkka Rekola, *tr. fr. Finnish by* Aili Jarvenpa. SOP
Among floating weeds, frogs. Kashiku, *tr.* by Hiroaki Sato. FCEI
Among green shades and flowering ghosts, the remembrances of love. The Two Fires. Judith Wright. MoBrPo
Among Hawks. Lance Henson. VoR
Among High Hills. William Soutar. PoSH
Among His Books. Edith Nesbit. NOBVV
Among Iron Fragments. Tuvia Ruebner, *tr. fr. Hebrew by* Robert Friend. UnAS; VWA
Among left trucks, mailbags, churns. Homing Pigeons. Ted Walker. NYBP
Among men of plain clothes. Ma Chih-yüan, *tr. fr. Chinese by* Jonathan Chaves. *Fr.* Two Poems to the Tune "Po pu tuan." CoBLCP
Among Old Houses. Ruth Dallas. ATNZ
Among our flocks of hard days. My Mother. Hayim Naggid. VWA, *tr.* by Rose Drachler.
Among our young lassies there's Muirland Meg. Muirland Meg. Burns. ErPo
Among pebbles, at the pond's edge. Grass Snake and Fish. Gyula Illyés, *tr.* by Charles Tomlinson. MHuP
Among Pelagian travellers. On the Circuit. W. H. Auden. NOBL; OxBTC
Among Philistines. R. S. Gwynn. MT; SoTCo
Among poppies in a field of maize. Death in the Corn. Detlev von Liliencron, *tr.* by C. F. MacIntyre. WaaP
Among red leaves and green mountains, white clouds fly. T'ang Yin, *tr. fr. Chinese by* Jonathan Chaves. *Fr.* Poems Inscribed on Paintings. CoBLCP
Among School Children. W. B. Yeats. AnIL; BLPL; CMoP; GTBS-P; HAP; InPS; LiTB; LiTM; MoAB; MoBrPo; MoP; NAEL-2; NAWM-2; NIP; NoAM; NOBE; NoP; OAEL-2; OAEL-2; OxBTC; PoE; PPP; PrIm; TrGrPo; WeW
Among Sharks. Al Lee. AmPA
Among snake-patterned swords Weland tasted sorrow. Deor. *Unknown, tr.* by John Wain. EBEV
Among Strangers. William Stafford. NNaP
Among the Anthropophagi. Ogden Nash. CenHV
 (Funebrial Reflections.) ImOP
Among the band of Officers was one. Wordsworth. *Fr.* The Prelude [or, Growth of a Poet's Mind]: Residence in France. ChER
Among the Beautiful Pictures. Alice Cary. BLPA
Among the Berkshire Hills. Henrietta Cordelia Ray. CBWP-3

Among the birds and moons that haunt. Deep Sea. Jules Supervielle, *tr.* by Denise Levertov. RHTwFP

Among the birds in the sky above. Nature in Couplets. Charlton Ogburn. GrPl

Among the coffee cups and soup toureens walked Beauty. Jack Spicer. PeHV

Among the Ferns. Edward Carpenter. WGRP

Among the Finger Lakes. Robert Wallace. GrPl

Among the Firs. Eugene Lee-Hamilton. NOBVV

Among the first to go are always a few. Only the Beards Are Different. Bruce Dawe. PoAu-2

Among the fleeing silverfish. Issa, *tr. fr. Japanese* by Hiroaki Sato. *Fr.* Forty-four Hokku. FCEI

Among the Flowers. Rutger Kopland, *tr. fr. Dutch* by James S. Holmes. DuIn

Among the gilded debris of the gasworks. A Thousand Times. Benjamin Péret, *tr.* by Michael Benedikt. POS

Among the greatest plagues, one is the third day ague. Of Scolding Wives and the Third Day Ague. Henricus Selyns. AiP; SCAP

Among the Grieving One Should Speak Softly. Helena Anhava, *tr. fr. Finnish* by Aili Jarvenpa. SOP

Among the guests who often stayed. Shelley. *Fr.* Peter Bell the Third. ChER

Among the high-branching, leafless boughs. The View from an Attic Window. Howard Nemerov. CoAP

Among the hillocks grows the hemp. *Unknown, tr.* by Arthur Waley. BoS

Among the Hills, *sel.* Whittier.
"Along the roadside, like the flowers of gold." NAAL-1; OxBA; PoEL-4

Among the iodoform, in twilight-sleep. The Leg. Karl Shapiro. HAP; MoAB; MoAmPo; TrGrPo; UnPo; WeW

Among the leaves the small birds sing. Lauds. W. H. Auden. *Fr.* Horae Canonicae. TrCP

Among the Millet. Archibald Lampman. CaP

Among the Myriad Voices of the Spring. George Santayana. *Fr.* Sonnets. AnAmPo

Among the Narcissi. Sylvia Plath. FaBoMo; RB; SCV

Among the Nuts. *Unknown.* BoTP

Among the offwhite walls where flowers. 2 November 1982. Alan Bold. NPo

Among the orchard weeds, from every search. Hen's Nest. John Clare. PBBP; Son

Among the oxen (like an ox I'm slow). The Nativity. C. S. Lewis. TrCP

Among the Pine Trees. Moshe Dor, *tr. fr. Hebrew* by Elaine Feinstein. VWA

Among the pines—White Stone Slope. White Stone Slope. Yang Shih-ch'i, *tr. fr. Chinese* by Jonathan Chaves. *Fr.* The Intendant Yao Shan Has Requested Six Poems on Living in the Mountains. CoBLCP

Among the plovers and the stonechats. Of Difference Does It Make. Tom Paulin. FaBCIP

Among the priceless gems and treasures rare. Pastel. Francis Saltus Saltus. AA

Among the provisions they carried. Michael Anania. *Fr.* The Riversongs of Arion, VII. NoAM

Among the rain. The Great Figure. William Carlos Williams. AiP; InPK; MoP; NoAM; QFR; TTTS

Among the Rocks. Robert Browning. *Fr.* James Lee's Wife. OxBSP

Among the Roman love-poets, possession. Note on Propertius I.5. Fleur Adcock. ATNZ; BoLoP; PeNZ

Among the rushes lived a mouse. The Needless Alarm. John Ruskin. FM

"Among the Savages. . . ." Ralph Salisbury. STE

Among the signs of autumn I perceive. Tall Ambrosia. Henry David Thoreau. PoEL-4

Among the smoke and fog of a December afternoon. Portrait of a Lady. T. S. Eliot. TwCP

Among the springs which flow from Ida's head. *Unknown, formerly at. to* Homer, *tr. fr. Greek* by Congreve. *Fr.* The Hymn to Venus. OBVE

Among the taller wood with ivy hung. The Vixen. John Clare. RB

Among the things. Antique Shop in New York. Karl Wawra, *tr.* by Beth Bjorklund. CoAuP

Among the thousand, thousand spheres that roll. Alcyone. Frances Laughton Mace. AA

Among the Worst of Men That Ever Lived. Henry David Thoreau. PoEL-4

Among them marble where the man may lie. A Thurn. John Berryman. NOBA

Among these mountains, do you know. For Allan, Who Wanted to See How I Wrote a Poem. Robert Frost. PChr

Among these tempests great and manifold. His Hope or Sheet-Anchor. Robert Herrick. CaPo

Among These Troopes of Christs Souldiers, Came. Mr. Roger Harlackenden. Edward Johnson. SCAP

Among These Turf-Stacks. Louis MacNeice. LiTB; SeCePo; WaP (Turf-Stacks.) LiTM; OBMV

Among those joys, 'tis one at eve to sail. Sailing upon the River. George Crabbe. *Fr.* The Borough, Letter IX. OBNC

Among Those Killed in the Dawn Raid Was a Man Aged a Hundred. Dylan Thomas. Son

Among trees/ my father was a spruce. Family Photograph. Gerald Vizenor. VoR

Among twenty snowy mountains. Thirteen Ways of Looking at a Blackbird. Wallace Stevens. BLPL; CMoP; HCAP; HeIP; InPK; InPS; LiTM; MoP; NAAL-2; NoAM; NOBA; NoP; PoE; RB; SOTW; TAP

Amongst the princely paragons. A Princely Ditty in Praise of the English Rose. Thomas Deloney. BoTP

Amongst the pure ones all. The Quaker's Song. *Unknown.* CoMu

Amor Loci. W. H. Auden. NOCV

Amor Mundi. Christina Rossetti. NoP; PoEL-5

Amor Mysticus. Sister Marcela de Carpio de San Felix, *tr. fr. Spanish* by John Hay. AWP

Amor Triumphans, *sel.* Arthur Symons.
Return, The. BrPo

Amor Vacui. John Fowles. AnAn

Amores, *sels.* Ovid, *tr. fr. Latin.*
Complaisant Swain, The. *Fr.* III, 14, *tr.* by F. A. Wright. AWP
Corinna, Having Tried, with Her Own Hand. *Fr.* II, 13, *tr.* by Rolfe Humphries. NAs
Corinnae Concubitus, I, 5. *Tr.* by Christopher Marlowe. EBEV; GBL; OBVE
(Elegy: "In summer's heat and mid-time of the day.") BoLoP
"Cypassis, that a thousand ways trimm'st hair." *Fr.* II, 8, *tr.* by Christopher Marlowe. EBEV
"Either she was foule, or her attire was bad." *Fr.* III, 6, *tr.* by Christopher Marlowe. OBVE
(Shameful Impotence.) ErPo
"Graecinus (well I wot) thou told'st me once." *Fr.* II, 10, *tr.* by Christopher Marlowe. EBEV
"I ask but right: let her that caught me late." *Fr.* I, 3, *tr.* by Christopher Marlowe. EBEV
"I Ovid poet of my wantonnesse." *Fr.* II, 1, *tr.* by Christopher Marlowe. OBVE
"Now ore the sea from her old love comes she." *Fr.* I, 13, *tr.* by Christopher Marlowe. OBVE
"Seeing thou art faire, I barre not thy false playing." *Fr.* III, 13, *tr.* by Christopher Marlowe. OBVE
To His Mistress. *Fr.* I, 4, *tr.* by Dryden. BoLoP; ErPo

Amores (after Ovid). Jay Parini. MAYP

Amoret. Mark Akenside. OBEV

Amoretti. Spenser. AAS
Sels.
I. "Happy ye leaves whenas those lily [*or* lilly] hands." EBEV; III. "Soverayne beauty which I doo admire, The." PoEL-1 NAEL-1; OAEL-1; PoE; Son
V. "Rudely thou wrongst my dear heart's desire." EIL
VIII. "More than most fair [*or* fayre], full of the living fire [*or* fyre]." NoP; PoE; Son; TEP; TrGrPo
X. "Unrighteous Lord of love, what law is this." NoP
XIII. "In That proud port, which her so goodly graceth." Son
XV. "Ye tradeful merchants that, with weary toil." HeIP; LiTB; NiP; OAEL-1; Son; TrGrPo
XVI. "One day as I unwarily did gaze." OAEL-1
XIX. "Merry cuckoo, messenger of spring, The." OBSC
XXII. "This holy season, fit to fast and pray." PoE
XXV. "How long shall this like dying life endure."
XXVI. "Sweet is the rose, but grows upon a brere." EIL
XXVII. "Fair proud, now tell me, why should fair be proud." Son
XXX. "My Love is like to ice, and I to fire." ErPo; FF; FPL; LiTB; TrGrPo
XXXIV. "Like as a ship, that through the ocean wide." NAEL-1; OBSC; PoE
XXXVII. "What guile [*or* guyle] is this, that those her golden tresses." NAEL-1; NoP; OBSC; Son; TrGrPo
XL. "Mark when she smiles with amiable cheer." OBSC
XLIV. "When those renowned noble peers of Greece." PoE
XLVII. "Trust not the treason of those smiling looks." TrGrPo
LIV. "Of this world's theatre in which we stay." NAEL-1; NoP; OAEL-1
LV. "So oft as I her beauty do behold." Son; TrGrPo
LVI. "Fair ye be sure, but cruel and unkind." Son
LXI. "Glorious image of the Maker's beauty, The." Son

LXII. "Weary year his race now having run, The." OBSC
LXIII. "After long storms and tempests sad assay." OAEL-1; OBSC
LXIV. "Coming [or Comming] to kiss [or kisse] her lips [or lyps], (such grace I found)." EBEV; NAEL-1; OAEL-1; Son
LXV. "Doubt which ye misdeeme, fayre love, is vaine, The." NAEL-1
LXVII. "Like [or Lyke] a huntsman after weary chase [or chace]." GBL; HeIP; NAEL-1; NoP; PoE; PoEL-1; SeCePo; Son; TrGrPo
LXVIII. "Most glorious Lord of Life [or Lyfe]! that on this day." EiL; HAP; InPS; LiTB; NAEL-1; NOCV; NoP; PoE; Son; TrPWD
  (Easter.) NoBE; OBEV
  (Easter Morning.) OHIP
LXX. "Fresh Spring, the herald of love's mighty king." AWP; ChTr; EiL; FF; HAP; InPS; NoP; OBSC; PoE; Son
  (Fresh Spring, the Herald.) LiTB
LXXI. "I joy to see how, in your drawen work." PoE
LXXII. "Oft when my spirit doth spread her bolder wings." OBSC; Son
LXXIV. "Most happy letters framed by skilfull trade." NAEL-1
LXXV. "One day I wrote her name upon the strand." AWP; BLPL; BoLoP; EBEV; EiL; FiP; GBL; HAP; HeIP; InPS; LiTB; NAEL-1; NoP; OAEL-1; PoE; SeCePo; Son; WeW
LXXVI. "Fair bosom! fraught with virtue's richest treasure." NIP
LXXVII. "Was it a dream, or did I see it plain?." NIP
LXXVIII. "Lacking my Love, I go from place to place." EiL
LXXIX. "Men call you fair [or fayre], and you do[e] credit it." AWP; FaBoBe; NAEL-1; NoP; Son
  (Sonnet: "Men call you fair, and you do credit it.") BLPL
LXXXI. "Fair [or Fayre] is my love, when her fair [or fayre] golden heares." EiL; NoP; Son
LXXXII. "Joy of my life, full oft for loving you." HeIP
LXXXIII. "Let not one sparke of filthy lustfull fyre." TEP.
LXXXIX. "Like as the culver on the bared bough." FF; GBL; PBBP; PoE
Amorgos. Nikos Gatsos, tr. fr. Greek by Edmund Keeley and Philip Sherrard. VMG
Amorix Exsul, sel. Arthur Symons.
  In the Bay. Fr. III. OBNC; PBBP
Amorous Anticipation. Jorge Luis Borges, tr. fr. Spanish by Perry Higman. LPSS
Amorous Dialogue between John and His Mistress, An. Unknown. CoMu
Amorous Leander, beautiful and young. Christopher Marlowe. Fr. Hero and Leander, First Sestiad. PeHV
Amorous Neptune. Christopher Marlowe. Fr. Hero and Leander, Second Sestiad. NOBE
Amorous of Laura's Loveliness. Sister Juana Inés de la Cruz, tr. fr. Spanish by Samuel Beckett. MexPo
Amorous shepherd lov'd a charming boy, An. Theocritus, tr. fr. Greek by Thomas Creech. Fr. Idylls, XXIII. PeHV
Amorous Temper, An. John Trumbull. Fr. The Progress of Dulness. AmPP
Amortization. Nancy G. Westerfield. SoTCo
Amos, sels. Bible O.T.
  O Ye That Would Swallow the Needy. Fr. VIII: 4–10. TrJP
Amours de Voyage. Arthur Hugh Clough. NOBVV
  Sels.
  Ah, That I Were Far Away. Fr. Canto III, introd. OBNC
    (Upon Apennine Slope.) FaBoPP
  "Dear Eustatio, I write that you may write me an answer." Fr. Canto I, i. EBVV; OBTV
  "Dulce it is, and decorum, no doubt, for the country to fall." Fr. Canto II, ii. EBVV; FaBoPV
  "Farewell, politics, utterly! What can I do? I can not." Fr. Canto III, iii. FaBoPV
  "Is it illusion? or does there a spirit from perfecter ages." Fr. Canto II, introd. -iv. EBEV
    (Spirit from Perfecter Ages.) OBNC
  Juxtaposition. Fr. Canto III, vi. OBNC
  "Only think, dearest Louisa, what fearful scenes we have witnessed!" Fr. Canto II, viii. EBVV
  "Rome disappoints me still; but I shrink and adapt myself to it." Fr. Canto I, ii. EBVV; OBTV
    (Rome.) FaBoPP
  Rome ("Rome disappoints me much"). Fr. Canto I, i. FaBoPP
  "So, I have seen a man killed!" Fr. Canto II, vii. EBVV
  "There are two different kinds, I believe, of human attraction." Fr. Canto II, xi. GTBS-P
  "Tibur is beautiful, too, and the orchard slopes, and the Anio." Fr. Canto III, xi. GTBS-P
    (So Not Seeing I Sung.) OBNC
    (Valley and Villa of Horace, The.) FaBoPP
  "Victory, Victory! Yes, ah, yes, thou republican Zion." Fr. Canto II, vi. EBVV

"What do the people say, and what does the government do?." Fr. Canto II, i. EBVV, i-iv only.; FaBoPV, i-iv only.; OBSV, i-iv only.
"When God makes a great Man he intends all others to crush him." Fr. Canto II, early variant. OBSV
"Will they fight? They say so. And will the French ?." Fr. Canto II, iii. FaBoPV
Ye Ancient Divine Ones. Fr. Canto I, x. OBNC
"Yes, we are fighting at last, it appears." Fr. Canto II, v. EBVV
Amphibians, The. Mirko Lauer, tr. fr. Spanish by David Tipton. Per
Amphibious Crocodile. John Crowe Ransom. OBAL
Amphitryon, sel. Dryden.
  "Fair Iris I love, and hourly I die." AWP
    (Mercury's Song [to Phaedra].) OxBSP; PoEL-3; SeCV-2
Amphora, The. Fyodor Sologub, tr. fr. Russian by Babette Deutsch and Avrahm Yarmolinsky. AWP
Ample heaven of fabrik sure, The. A Summer's Day. Alexander Hume. CH
Ample make this bed. Emily Dickinson. MoAB; MoAmPo; NAAL-1; OxBA; PoEL-5
Ample the air above the western peaks. After Nightfall. William Renton. NOBVV
Amputee Soldier, The. Philip Dacey. GOYP
Amsterdam. Jean Garrigue. TAP
Amsterdam. Francis Jammes, tr. fr. French by Jethro Bithell. AWP; FaPON, ll. 1–20
Amsterdam Letter. Jean Garrigue. NYBP
Amurrika! Philip Appleman. BXAP
Amused at My Own Figure while Traveling. Kikaku, tr. fr. Japanese by Hiroaki Sato. Fr. Thirty-three Hokku. FCEI
Amused contempt, is it, that scintillates. Juan de Pareja: Painted by Velazquez. Richard A. Long. AmNP
Amusing myself with rocks, I sit peering into the valley. The Temple of Bequeathed Love. Po Chü-i, tr. by Burton Watson. CoBCP
Amusing Our Daughters. Carolyn Kizer. VGW
Amy. James Matthew Legaré. AA
Amy, dieu vous sauve. Pour demander le chemin. Unknown. Fr. A Lytell Treatyse for to Lerne Englysshe and Frens. OxBLMV
Amy Elizabeth Ermyntrude Annie. Queenie Scott-Hopper. BoTP
Amy Wentworth. Whittier. AnAmPo; BeLS
Amyd the wod his modir met thame tway. Virgil, into Middle English by. Fr. The Aeneid [or Eneados], I. OBVE
Amyntas Led Me to a Grove. Aphra Behn. Fr. The Dutch Lover. ErPo
An a so de rain a-fall. A Song for England. Andrew Salkey. PBCV
An' Charlie he's my darling. Charlie He's My Darling. Burns. CH
An de beat well read. Reflection in Red. Oku Onuora. PBCV
An die Musik. David Malouf. CBAP
An' so ole Tho'nton bounced you. The Turncoat. Priscilla Jane Thompson. CBWP-2
Anabasis. "St.-John Perse," tr. fr. French by T. S. Eliot. RHTwFP
Anabasis, sel. "St.-John Perse," tr. fr. French by T. S. Eliot.
  "Such is the way of the world." Fr. IV. OBVE
Anachronism. Oliver St. John Gogarty. FYAP
Anacreon's Dove. Samuel Johnson. AWP
Anacreontic. Austin Clarke. NOIV
Anacreontic. Robert Herrick. CaPo; OxBoLi
Anacreontic. István Vas, tr. fr. Hungarian by Jascha Kessler. FOC
Anacreontic on Drinking. Abraham Cowley. See Thirsty earth soaks up the rain, The.
Anacreontic, on Parting with a Little Child. Samuel Wesley. NOEC
Anacreontic to Flip. Royall Tyler. OBAL
Anacreontics: Drinking. Abraham Cowley. See Thirsty earth soaks up the rain, The.
Anacreontics: The Epicure. Abraham Cowley. See Underneath this myrtle shade.
Anacreontics: The Swallows. Abraham Cowley. See Foolish prater, what dost thou.
Anadarko John. Carroll Arnett. VoR
Anaesthesia. Jean Valentine. TAP
Anal erotic named Herman, an. Unknown. PeHV
Analogy. Brian Higgins. FaBoTw
Analysands. Dudley Randall. BPo
Analysis of Baseball. May Swenson. ASP
Analyst. David Fisher. NPGG
Ana(Mary-Army)gram. George Herbert. OAEL-1
Anarchy and grow your own. Durham. Tony Harrison. NoAM
Anastasia McLaughlin. Tom Paulin. FaBCIP
Anastasis. Albert E. S. Smythe. CaP
Anath. Haim Guri, tr. fr. Hebrew by Naomi Nir and Howard Schwartz. VWA
Anathemata, The, sels. David Jones.
  Angle-Land. Fr. III. NoAM

"Did he meet Lud at the Fleet Gate? did count the top." EBEV

"Ship's master:/ before him, in the waist and before it." FaBoTw

Anatolia. Christine Busta, *tr. fr. German by* Beth Bjorklund. CoAuP

Anatomie of the World, An. John Donne. *See* Anatomy of the World, An.

Anatomy of a Supper. Gábor Görgey, *tr. fr. Hungarian by* Jascha Kessler. FOC

Anatomy of Baseness, The, *sel.* John Andrews.
 To the Detracted. EIL

Anatomy of Happiness, The. Ogden Nash. LiTA; TAP

Anatomy of Humor, The. Morris Bishop. NBLV

Anatomy of Melancholy, The, *sel.* Robert Burton.
 Authors Abstract of Melancholy, The. OBS

Anatomy of the World, A, *sel.* John Donne.
 First Anniversary, The. NAEL-1

Anatomy [*or* Anatomie] of the World, An: The First Anniversary, *sels.* John Donne.
 Doth Not a Tenarif, or Higher Hill. ChTr
 "She, she is dead; she's dead: when thou knowest this." JCP
 Verse and Fame. FaBoRV
 "When that rich Soule which to her heaven is gone." SeCV-1

Anatomy of the World; the First Anniversary, An. John Donne. SeCV-1

Ancestor. Thomas Kinsella. BIrV; FaBCIP; NOIV; PoE

Ancestor, The. Dave Smith. SM

Ancestor of the Hunting Heart. John Haines. BLA

Ancestors, The. Anita Barrows. VWA

Ancestors, The. John Peale Bishop. PoA

Ancestors. Rowley Habib. PeNZ

Ancestors. Dudley Randall. BPo; CNA

Ancestors. Harold Schimmel. VWA

Ancestors' Graves in Kurakawa. Joy Kogawa. BrSi

Ancestral and still fraternal. Women of All the Ages. Andrée Chédid, *tr. by* Mary Ann Caws. DMF

Ancestral Faces. Kwesi Brew. PBA

Ancestral Houses. W. B. Yeats. *Fr.* Meditations in Time of Civil War, I. LiTB; OAEL-2

Ancestral Poem. Olive Senior. PBCV

Ancestral Weight. Alfonsina Storni, *tr. fr. Spanish.* DMH, *tr. by* Kate Flores; WPOW, *tr. by* Marti Moody.

Ancestry. Stephen Crane. *Fr.* The Black Riders, XXII. AA

Anchises, Paris, and Adonis too. Spoken by Venus on Seeing Her Statue Done by Praxiteles. *Unknown.* EyDe; FaBoEE

Anchor. Maruyama Kaoru, *tr. fr. Japanese by* Hiroaki Sato. FCEI

Anchor: "Oft I must strive with wind and wave." *Unknown, formerly at. to* Cynewulf, *tr. fr. Anglo-Saxon by* Charles W. Kennedy. *Fr.* Riddles (Exeter Book). AnOE

Anchorage. Joy Harjo. HATNAP; STE

Anchorage, The. Pat Wilson. ATNZ

Anchoring, I watched him climb. Lines. Barbara Smith. TSL

Anchors Weighed. Peter McMillan. SoTCo

Anchorsmiths, The. Charles Dibdin. NOEC

Ancient. "Æ." SeCePo

Ancient and Modern Rome, *sel.* George Keate.
 "What, though oblivion in her sable shroud." OBTV

Ancient Autumn. Charles Simic. BLA

Ancient Ballad of Chevy-Chase, The. *Unknown. See* Percy out of Northumberland, The.

Ancient Barbarossa, the Kaiser Frederick old, The. Barbarossa. Friedrich Rückert, *tr. by* Elizabeth Craigmyle. AWP

Ancient bridge, and a more ancient tower, An. My House. W. B. Yeats. *Fr.* Meditations in Time of Civil War, II. LiTB

Ancient Castle, The. William Morris. *See* Golden Wings: Midways of a walled garden.

Ancient chestnut's blossoms threw, An. Alciphron and Leucippe. Walter Savage Landor. OBEV

Ancient Christmas Carol, A. *Unknown.* OHIP; PChr

Ancient Couple on Lu Mountain, The. Mark Van Doren. VGW

Ancient Custom, An. Anatoly Steiger, *tr. fr. Russian by* John Glad. VWA

Ancient Evenings. Michael Hofmann. NPo

Ancient Feeling. Wu Wei-yeh, *tr. fr. Chinese by* Jonathan Chaves. CoBLCP

Ancient Historian. Chris Wallace-Crabbe. PoAu-2

Ancient History. Arthur Guiterman. OBCA

Ancient History. Siegfried Sassoon. Mes

Ancient Law, The. André Spire, *tr. fr. French by* Stanley Burnshaw. VWA

Ancient Lights. Austin Clarke. BIrV; CMoP; IPY

Ancient Mansion, The, *sel.* George Crabbe.
 Spring to Winter. ChTr
 (In Suffolk.) FaBoPP

Ancient Mariner: The Wedding Guest's Version of the Affair from His Point of View, The. *Unknown.* FaBoPa

Ancient Monuments. John Ormond. OBWVE

Ancient Murderess Night. Anna Margolin, *tr. fr. Yiddish by* Ruth Whitman. VWA

Ancient Music. Ezra Pound. BXAP; FaBoCo; FaBoPa; FF; HeIP; LiTM; NBLV; OBAL; OxBA; Par; TW

Ancient nomadic snowman has rolled around. The Snowman. Patricia K. Page. NOBC

Ancient of Days. William Croswell Doane. AA; AH, *with music*

Ancient of Days. Anthony Rudolf. VWA

Ancient of Days, old friend, no one believes you'll come back. Stone Canyon Nocturne. Charles Wright. HCAP; LCAP

Ancient pages of the Talmud. The Talmud. Simeon Grigoryevich Frug, *tr. by* Alice Stone Blackwell. TrJP

Ancient pavilion is in ruins, The. Thoughts of the Yüeh Beauty. Sun Kuang-hsien, *tr. by* Lois Fusek. ATF

Ancient Person, for whom I. A Song of a Young Lady to Her Ancient Lover. Earl of Rochester. BoLoP; EBEV; ErPo; GBL; MePo; OPOP

Ancient Peru. Antonio Cisneros, *tr. fr. Spanish by* Maureen Ahern *and* David Tipton. Per

Ancient Pistol, peacock Payne. Tennyson. FaBoEE

Ancient Plum Tree at the K'ai-hsien Buddhist Monastery, An. Ch'ü Ta-chün, *tr. fr. Chinese by* Paul W. Kroll. WFTU

Ancient Prayer, An. Thomas H. B. Webb, *after* A Prayer Found in Chester Cathedral. BLPA; FaBoBe

Ancient Prophecy, An. Philip Freneau. PAH

Ancient readers of heaven's book, Th.' Of Cynthia. *Unknown.* OBSC

Ancient saga tells us how, An. Dead Cow Farm. Robert Graves. BrPo

Ancient Sage, The. Tennyson. WGRP

Ancient Sentiments. Hsüeh Shao-hui, *tr. fr. Chinese by* Irving Lo. WFTU

Ancient Sentiments. Wu Wei-yeh, *tr. fr. Chinese by* Irving Lo. WFTU

Ancient Song. Amir Gilboa, *tr. fr. Hebrew by* Warren Bargad *and* Stanley F. Chyet. IP

Ancient Song. Avner Trainin, *tr. fr. Hebrew by* Bernhard Frank. MHeP

Ancient Song of a Woman of Fez, An. *Unknown, tr. fr. Arabic by* Willis Barnstone. AIW; BoWoP

Ancient sowed an acorn from His mind, The. Oak. Philip Child. CaP

Ancient Speech, The. Kathleen Raine. *Fr.* Eileann Chanaidh. PoSH

Ancient story I'll tell you anon, An. King John and the Abbot of Canterbury. *Unknown.* BoTP; EnSB; GN; TrGrPo

Ancient Tear, The. Luis G. Urbina, *tr. fr. Spanish by* Samuel Beckett. MexPo

Ancient temples with their thousand pines, taken over for army camps. Improvised while Living in the Outskirts of the Capital. Taikyoku Zosu, *tr. by* Burton Watson. FCEI

Ancient Thought, The. Watson Kerr. WGRP

Ancient to Ancients, An. Thomas Hardy. CMoP; GTBS-P; LiTM; OxBTC

Ancient Virgin, An. George Crabbe. *Fr.* The Parish Register: Burials. OBNC

Ancient Wisdom, Rather Cosmic. Ezra Pound. NOBA

Ancientest of cats, truest. Hoppy. Reginald Gibbons. DiPo

Ancientness surrounds me. Death. Patty L. Harjo. VoR

Ancients of the World, The. R. S. Thomas. RB

And. Robert Creeley. LCAP

And. Ricardo Gonsalves. FIA

And a clam caught my little finger. The Little Girl That Lost a Finger. Gabriela Mistral, *tr. by* Muna Lee. FaPON

And after a Long While. Ory Bernstein, *tr. fr. Hebrew by* Warren Bargad *and* Stanley F. Chyet. IP

And after a while he'd say his head was a rose. Blossom. Stanley Plumly. GeTw; KS

And after all a slave sits out the centuries. Ghosts II. Lauris Edmond. PeNZ

And, after all, it is to them we return. Quaint Mazes. Geoffrey Hill. *Fr.* An Apology for the Revival of Christian Architecture in England, 1. NoAM

And after this quick bash in the dark. Portrait of a Young Girl Raped at a Suburban Party. Brian Patten. OxBTC

And after you have gone. The Two Nights. Nicki Jackowska. DT

And afterwards. Odeon. Aharon Amir, *tr. by* Bernhard Frank. MHeP

And afterwards, after the shedding of mucus. A Talk with My Cousin Alone. Hone Tuwhare. PeNZ

And Again. Humphrey Evans. BXAP

And again I see the long pouring headland. The Return. Alistair Campbell. ATNZ; PeNZ

And again I was like one of those little girls. Time Caught in a Net. Dahlia Ravikovich, *tr. by* Warren Bargad *and* Stanley F. Chyet. IP

And again the screech of the scaffold. Window Washer. Charles Simic. BLA

"And all her silken flanks with garlands drest." Vlamertinghe; Passing the Château, July 1917. Edmund Blunden. MMA; OBWP

And all the sails hang limp. Comes Fog and Mist. William Hart-Smith. *Fr.* Christopher Columbus. PoAu-2

And all the wickedness in this world that man might work or think. God's Mercy. William Langland. *Fr.* The Vision of Piers Plowman. NOCV

And all those horses. What She Said ("And all those horses"). Kapilar, *tr.* by A. K. Ramanujan. PLW

And already morning. The sun kisses the sown field. Star-Sown. Eli Netser, *tr.* by Bernhard Frank. MHeP

And an evening will come when I will leave. Plain Song. Benjamin Fondane. VWA, *tr.* by Matei Calinescu *and* Willis Barnstone

And And. Zoltán Zelk, *tr. fr.* Hungarian by Daniel Hoffman. MHuP

And Angling, Too. Byron. *Fr.* Don Juan. SD

And answer made King Arthur, breathing hard. Tennyson, *incorporated in* Idylls of the King *with changes, as* The Passing of Arthur. *Fr.* Morte d'Arthur. EBEV

And answer made King Arthur, breathing hard. Tennyson. *Fr.* Idylls of the King: The Passing of Arthur. EBEV

And are ye sure the news is true? The Sailor's Wife. William Julius Mickle, *also at.* to Jean Adam. BeLS; GN; GTBS; GTBS-P (There's Nae Luck about the House.) NOEC

And art thou come to this at last. Alexander McLachlan. *Fr.* To an Indian Skull. CaP

And art thou he, now "fallen on evil days." In Age. William Lisle Bowles. *Fr.* Milton: On the Busts of Milton, in Youth and Age. Son

And as for me, though that I konne [*or* can] but [*or* my wit be] lyte. Chaucer. *Fr.* Legend of Good Women, The: Prologue. CH; HeIP; ViBoPo

And as I rise slapping my feet. I Wake Thinking of Myself as a Man. Susan Griffin. GLP

And as I stood and cast aside mine eye. Lady of the Arbour. *See* Flower and the Leaf, The: And at the last I cast my mine eye aside.

And as in winter time when Jove his cold-sharpe javelins throwes. Homer, *tr. fr.* Greek by George Chapman. *Fr.* The Iliad, XII. OBVE

And as our God the beasts had given in charge. Michael Drayton. *Fr.* Noah's Flood. PBBP

And as soon as it was morning the chief priests. Bible, *N.T. Fr.* St. Mark, XV: 1-39. DL

And as we came down the staircase. Valse Oubliée. John Heath-Stubbs. OxBTC

And as we spoke the Nicene Creed we were called out. Barnfire during Church. Robert Bly. NePoEA

And as when with the West-wind's flawes the sea thrusts up her waves. Homer, *tr. fr.* Greek by George Chapman. *Fr.* The Iliad, IV. OBVE

And @ $1.13 + tx. And. Ricardo Gonsalves. FIA

And at Lake Geneva, which is in Wisconsin. At Lake Geneva. Richard Eberhart. LiTA

And at the last I cast my mine eye aside. Lady of the Arbour. *Fr.* The Flower and the Leaf. WPE ("And as I stood and cast aside mine eye.") PBBP

And Back. Rodney Bennett. BoTP

And believing she was a maid. The Faithless Wife. Federico García Lorca, *tr.* by A. L. Lloyd. BoLoP

And Bidpai said:/ the thieves have stormed. The Story. Muhammad al-Faituri, *tr.* by Sargon Boulus *and* Peter Porter. MAP

And Bidpai said:/ while the clowns laugh. Incident. Muhammad al-Faituri, *tr.* by Sargon Boulus *and* Peter Porter. MAP

And birds came crying. James Cunningham. *Fr.* The Narrator's Trance. JB

And blessed be the women who get you through. Robin Morgan. *Fr.* The Hallowing of Hell. GLP

"And Brief, Good Mother? For I am in Haste? Whither?" Dezsö Tandori, *tr. fr.* Hungarian by Daniel Hoffman. MHuP

And can I ever bid these joys farewell? Keats. *Fr.* Sleep and Poetry. TOF

And can it be, that I should gain. Free Grace. Charles Wesley. NOCV

And can the muse reflect her tear-stain'd eye. *Unknown. Fr.* Jamaica, a Poem in Three Parts, Written in That Island in the Year 1776. PBCV

And Can the Physician. *Unknown. Fr.* Robin Goodfellow, *Pt.* II. ELP (Song: "And can the physician make sick men well?.") EIL

And Canaan? How d'you get there? Dream Canaan. Aba Shtoltsenberg, *tr.* by Dennis Silk. PeBMYV

And Canst Thou, Sinner, Slight. Abby Bradley Hyde. AH

And change with hurried head has swept these scenes. Frederick Goddard Tuckerman. *Fr.* Sonnets, II, xviii. HAP; NOBA; QFR; TAP

And clearly I recall the second day's end. The Perfect Disc of the Moon. Richard Kenney. Son

And closeness, and the line between. Three inches. Distances. Albert Goldbarth. GeTw

And Death Shall Have No Dominion. Dylan Thomas. CMoP; EaLo; LiTM; MoAB; MoBrPo; NoAM; RB; SeCePo

And deep-eyed children cannot long be children. Ballad of the Outer Life. Hugo von Hofmannsthal, *tr.* by Jethro Bithell. AWP; TrJP

And did ever a man go black with sun in a Belgian swamp. Nigger. Karl Shapiro. OxBA

And Did the Animals? Mark Van Doren. VGW

And Did Those Feet in Ancient Time. Blake. *Fr.* Milton, Preface. AWP; EnRP; FaBoCh; FaBoPV; FaBV; HAP; HeIP; InPS; MAT; NAEL-2; NAWM-2; NoP; OAEL-2; PoE; PoEL-4; PoRA; PrIm; WGRP
(Jerusalem.) BoTP; EaLo; FaPoR; NOBE; NOCV; OBEV; RB; WaaP
(New Jerusalem, A.) LiTB; TrGrPo
(Prelude: "And did those feet in ancient time.") OBNC

And did we come into our own. Letter to Derek Mahon. Michael Longley. CIP; FaBCIP

And did you know. Snowflakes. Clive Sansom. OBCP

And did you not hear of a jolly young waterman. The Jolly Young Waterman. Charles Dibdin. NOEC

And did you not hear of a mirth that befell. Away to Twiver, Away, Away! *Unknown.* EIl

And did young Stephen sicken. Emmeline Grangerford's "Ode to Stephen Dowling Bots, Dec'd." "Mark Twain." *Fr.* The Adventures of Huckleberry Finn. NBLV; OBAL
(Ode to Stephen Dowling Bots, Dec'd.) FiBHP

And do our loves all perish with our frames. Immortality. Richard Henry Dana. AA; WGRP

And do they so? have they a Sense. Rom. Cap. 8 Ver. 19. Henry Vaughan. MeLP; OBS

And Don't Be Deaf to the Singing Beyond. Carter Revard. HATNAP

And don't bother telling me anything. César Vallejo, *tr.* by Robert Bly. AnAn; EAS

And dost thou faithlessly abandon me? The Unrealities. Schiller, *tr.* by James Clarence Mangan. AWP

And doun on knes anoon-ryght I me sette. This Fresshe Flour. Chaucer. *Fr.* Legend of Good Women, The: Prologue. SeCePo

And down came years one after another. Certain Years. Otto Orban, *tr.* by Jascha Kessler. FOC

And Dreams Paled. Eeva Kilpi, *tr. fr. Finnish* by Aili Jarvenpa. SOP

And Even, Even If They Take Away the Stove. Miron Bialoszewski, *tr. fr. Polish* by Czeslaw Milosz. PwPP

And Even if They Live. Meir Wieseltier, *tr. fr. Hebrew* by Bernhard Frank. MHeP

And every bird shew'd in his proper kind. Michael Drayton. *Fr.* The Owle. FM

And every prodigal greatness. The Flowering Urn. Laura Riding. LiTA

And Every Year a World. George Gascoigne. *Fr.* Gascoigne's Memories. Son

And every yeare a worlde my will did deeme. George Gascoigne. AAS

And everywhere great crowds. The Swallowing of the Earth. Gust Gils, *tr.* by James S. Holmes. DuIn

And faces, forms and phantoms, numbered not. Frederick Goddard Tuckerman. *Fr.* Sonnets, II, xix. QFR

And first Morency, far famed water, you. Standish O'Grady. *Fr.* The Emigrant. CaP

And first, the lamp-posts whose burning match-heads. Jewish Main Street. Irving Layton. CaP; VWA

And for what, except for you, do I feel love? Wallace Stevens. *Fr.* Notes toward a Supreme Fiction. NOBA

And Forgetful of Europe. Geoffrey Grigson. OBTV

And Forgive Us Our Trespasses. Aphra Behn. EBEV

And forth they yede togider, twain and twain. A Courtly Scene and a Sudden Storm. Chaucer. *Fr.* The Floure and the Leafe. OxBLMV

And from the Citie Tegea there came the Paragone. Ovid, *tr. fr. Latin* by Arthur Golding. *Fr.* Metamorphoses, X. OBVE

And God created the great whales, and each. Milton. *Fr.* Paradise Lost, *Bk.* VII, *ll.* 391–416. MOS

And God looked down at God that day. My God, My God, Look upon Me. Chad Walsh. *Fr.* The Psalm of Christ. TrCP

And God said, let the waters generate. Milton. *Fr.* Paradise Lost, *Bk.* VII, *ll.* 387–505. (Creation of the Animals.) FM

And God saw that the wickedness of man was great. Bible, *O.T. Fr.* Genesis, VI: 5-22. NAWM-1

And God stepped out on space. The Creation. James Weldon Johnson. BANP; CDC; FaBV; MoAmPo; PoBA; PoRA; TrCP

And Grow. John Hay. WaP

And Hannah prayed, and said. Hannah's Thanksgiving. Bible, *O.T. Fr.* First Samuel, II: 1–10. BoWoP

And haply, bason'd in some unsunn'd cleft. Samuel Taylor Coleridge. *Fr.* To a Young Friend. ChER

And Happy Am I. Syd Scroggie. PoSH

And hast thou left old Jemmy in the lurch? A Satire upon the French King. Thomas Brown. APAS

And hath he finish'd life's brief sum. My Uncle Tum. Elijah Ridings. PF

And Have the Bright Immensities. Howard Chandler Robbins. AH

And have we done with war at last? Two Fusiliers. Robert Graves. MMA

And have we lost another friend? John Close. Fr. In Respectful Memory of Mr. Yarker. FaBoCo

And He Answered Them Nothing. Richard Crashaw. MePo

And he is risen? Well, be it so. A Drizzling Easter Morning. Thomas Hardy. CMoP

And he said, So is the kingdome of God. Bible, N.T. Fr. St. Mark, IV: 26-32. OBVE

And he said, So soule doth magnifie the Lord. Bible, N.T. Fr. St. Mark, IV: 26-32. OBVE

And he showed me a pure river of water of life. There Shall Be No Night. Bible, N.T. Fr. Revelation, XXII: 1-5. TrGrPo

And he went unto Ramah. There he met. The Dance of Saul with the Prophets. Saul Tchernichowsky, tr. by I. M. Lask. TrJP

And heed not them that warn or chide thee. Hark! The Rosy Days Are Numbered. Moses Ibn Ezra, tr. fr. Hebrew by Solomon Solis-Cohen. Fr. Wine-Songs. TrJP

And here am I alone, still listening. In the Evening. Countess Lara, tr. by Muriel Kittel. DMI

And here face down beneath the sun. You, Andrew Marvell. Archibald MacLeish. AWP; CMoP; FaBV; FYAP; HAP; HeIP; HoPM; LiTA; LiTM; MoAB; MoAmPo; MoP; NAAL-2; NoAM; NOBA; NoP; OxBA; PoRA; PPP; PrIm; SoSe; TrGrPo; TwCP; WeW

And here fair freedom shall forever reign. Leander. Hugh Henry Brackenridge and Philip Freneau. Fr. The Rising Glory of America. AiP

And here I wish my soul died with my breath. Ovid, tr. fr. Latin by Henry Vaughan. Fr. Tristium, III, 3a. OBVE

And here is dear old Boston. The New Order. Phyllis McGinley. AmFN

And here the cross on the window means myself. The Once-in-Passing. Louis MacNeice. Fr. A Hand of Snapshots. FaBCIP

And here the precious dust is laid [or layd]. Maria Wentworth. Thomas Carew. CaPo; JCP; MeLP; MePo; OBD; OBS; SeCV-1 (Inscription on the Tombe of the Lady Mary Wentworth, The.) OBS

And here's the child's Dad. Unknown. OxNR

And here's the happy, bounding flea. The Flea. Roland Young. RHPC

And, Hinges. Ted Greenwald. LP

And Hiram of Tyre sent his servants unto Solomon. Bible, O.T. Fr. First Kings, V: 1-5, 11-14. EyDe

And his son Judas, who was called Maccabeus. Judas Maccabeus. Bible, Apocrypha. Fr. First Maccabees, III: 1-9. TrJP

And how are the rats doing in the maze? Progress Report. Charles Simic. GeTw

And how beguile you? Death has no repose. James Elroy Flecker. Fr. The Golden Journey to Samarkand, II. OxBTC

And how to distinguish the alien. Gran Mal. Kathryn Rantala. BWV

And how will I forget. Eyes. Clarisse Nicoïdski, tr. by Stephen Levy. VWA

And I a beginner. Answer to Yo/ Question. Sonia Sanchez. BPo

And I Am Old to Know. Pauline Hanson. TAP

And I awoke. A lidded coffin—fingers. Never. Afanasi Afanasievich Fet, tr. by Alan Myers. AAA

And I bowed my body and beheld all about. William Langland. Fr. The Vision of Piers Plowman. CTC (Vision of Nature, A.) PoEL-1

And I bowed [or is bowede] my body and beheld all about [or bihelde al aboute]. A Vision of Nature. William Langland. Fr. The Vision of Piers Plowman. CTC; PoEL-1

And I call Him. Sweet Father. Malka Heifetz-Tussman, tr. by Kathryn Hellerstein. AYP

"And I fare you well, Lady Ouncebell." Lord Lovel. Unknown. ESPB

And I fell in love with a woman so tall that. From the Travels of Gulliver. Suniti Namjoshi. GLP

And I have come upon this place. L'An Trentiesme de Mon Eage. Archibald MacLeish. LiTM; MoP; NOBA (In My Thirtieth Year.) MoAmPo

And I have learned how diving's done. Fantasia. Dorothy Livesay. MoCV; OBCV

And I have never been mild. I Am Not a Honey-Hearted Child. Leyzer Volf, tr. by Robert Friend. PeBMYV

And I hear the pad of feet to the union hall. Thomas McGrath. Fr. Letter to an Imaginary Friend, Part One, II, 2. NNaP

And I hear the pad of feet to the union hall. Thomas McGrath. Fr. Letter to an Imaginary Friend, Part Two, II, 2. NNaP

And I, I was a good child on the whole. Elizabeth Barrett Browning. Fr. Aurora Leigh. BrRo

And I made myself a surrogate wedding-day. The Sisters. Nicki Jackowska. BrRo

And I ran away. Faker. Malka Heifetz-Tussman, tr. by Kathryn Hellerstein. AYP

And I remember Spain. Louis MacNeice. Fr. Autumn Journal. OBWP

And I rode the Greyhound down to Brooklyn. Wild Strawberry. Maurice Kenny. HATNAP; NOVW; STE

And I saw a new heaven and a new earth. The New Jerusalem. Bible, N.T. Fr. Revelation, XXI: 1-6, 10-12, 21, 23-25. TrGrPo

And I say nothing—no, not a word. My Sister Jane. Ted Hughes. OnUR; SO

And I should go and I should do and. Risen Matters. Clark Coolidge. UL

And I standing in the shade. Petition. R. S. Thomas. FaBoMo

And I thought of how impossibly alone we were. After a Game of Squash. Samuel L. Albert. GoYe; TSL

And I took her down by the river. The Faithless Wife. Federico García Lorca. ErPo, tr. by Robert O'Brien

And I took myself for a walk in the woods that day. Family Outing—a Celebration. Nicki Jackowska. BrRo

And I was born with you, wasn't I, Blues? The Blues Don't Change. Al Young. NPGG

And I with only a reed in my hands. Memory I. George Seferis, tr. by Edmund Keeley and Philip Sherrard. VMG

And I, woman, cloaked in blues. I, Woman. Irma McClaurin. BlSi

And ich bowede my body and bihelde al aboute. See And I bowed my body and beheld all about.

And if an eye may save or slay. Sir Thomas Wyatt. SiPS

And if any man should ask me. Deliverance. Frances Ellen Watkins Harper. WPOW

And if death were only the eyelid. The Never Again. Charles Dobzynski, tr. by Anita Barrows. VWA

And if he ever should come back. The Last Words. Maurice Maeterlinck, tr. by Frederick York Powell. AWP

And if he should come again. Ylen's Song. Richard Hovey. Fr. The Birth of Galahad. AA

And if I did, what then? George Gascoigne. Fr. The Adventures of Master F. I.. EBEV; EIL; GBL; HAP; NoP; PoEL-1 (Farewell, A.) NOBE; OBSC

And if I lived in those olden times. Anonymous. Victor Hernandez Cruz. UL

And if I loved you Wednesday. Thursday. Edna St. Vincent Millay. PoA

And if I talk nicely to my son—what good does it do? My Only Son. Moyshe-Leyb Halpern, tr. by Benjamin and Barbara Harshav and Kathryn Helle. AYP

And if, in the rush of your days. Arteriosclerosis. Jacob Glatstein, tr. by Benjamin and Barbara Harshav. AYP

And if Moyshe-Leyb, the poet, tells [or Should tell or recounted how]. Memento Mori. Moyshe-Leyb Halpern, tr. by Benjamin and Barbara Harshav and Kathryn Helle. AYP

And if our lives spill. Philip Dow. NPGG

And if the dead, and the dead. The Conspirators. Frederic Prokosch. LiTM; PrIm; WaP

And if the soul. George Seferis, tr. fr. Greek by Edmund Keeley and Philip Sherrard. Fr. Mythistorima, IV. VMG

And if tonight my soul may find her peace. Shadows. D. H. Lawrence. OxBTC

And if ye stand in doubt. John Skelton. Fr. Colin Clout. NAEL-1; OAEL-1

And, if you asked of him to say. Charles Stuart Calverley. Fr. Gemini and Virgo. FiBHP

And if you would ask me "Where do you find your songs." Hanukah. Jakov de Haan, tr. by David Soetendorp. VWA

And I'm thinking how to get out. History. Myra Cohn Livingston. RHPC

And in conclusion I'll say. Goodbye. Bella Akhmadulina, tr. by Barbara Einzig. BoWoP

And in September, O what keen delight. September. Folgore Da San Gimignano, tr. fr. Italian by Dante Gabriel Rossetti. Fr. Sonnets of the Months. AWP

And in September, O what keen delight! Sonnets of the Months: September. Folgore da San Geminiano, tr. by Dante Gabriel Rossetti. AWP; SD

And in spite of it all I must. Yehuda Amichai, tr. fr. Hebrew by Warren Bargod and Stanley F. Chyet. Fr. Songs of the Land of Zion Jerusalem, 38. IP

And in That Drowning Instant. A. M. Klein. VWA

And in that land dwells a king. Sir Cawline. Unknown. ESPB

And in the 51st Year of That Century, While My Brother Cried in the Trench, While My Enemy Glared from the Cave. Hyam Plutzik. RB

And in the frosty season, when the sun. On the Frozen Lake. Wordsworth. *Fr.* The Prelude [or, Growth of a Poet's Mind]: Childhood and School-Time. FaBoCh; GN

And in the Hanging Gardens. Conrad Aiken. MoAB; MoAmPo

And in the Human Heart, *sels.* Conrad Aiken. Son Bend as the Bow Bends. *Fr.* I. Green, Green, and Green Again. *Fr.* XXVIII.

And in the midst of all, a fountaine stood. Spenser. *Fr.* The Faerie Queene: The Bower of Bliss.

And in the morning the king loved you most. Arcanum One. Gwendolyn MacEwen. MoCV

And in their holiness made power. Winkte. Maurice Kenny. GLP

And in this swyving there nas noon hir pere. The Continuation of *The Cook's Tale.* William Zaranka. BXAP

And is he gone, whom these arms held but now. Quaerit Jesum Suum Maria. Richard Crashaw. ACP

And Is It Night? Are they thine eyes that shine? *Unknown.* EIL; GBL

And is our life, a life wherein we borrow. Matthew X. 28. Roger Wolcott. SCAP

And is the great cause lost beyond recall? Faith. Ada Cambridge. PoAu-1

And is the water come? Sure't cannot be. Upon Sir John Lawrence's Bringing Water over the Hills. Sir John Suckling. CaPo

And is there care in heaven? and is there love. Spenser. *Fr.* The Faerie Queene, II, 8. NOCV; OAEL-1 (Guardian Angels.) OBSC

And is there then no earthly place. Thomas Moore. *Fr.* Rhymes on the Road. OBSV; OBTV

And is this—Yarrow?—This the stream. Yarrow Visited. Wordsworth. EnRP; GTBS; GTBS-P

And Ishmael crouch'd beside a crackling briar. Ishmael. Herbert Edward Palmer. OBEV

And it all died down. From My Lai the Thunder Went West. Richard Ryan. CIP

And It Came to Pass at Midnight. Yannai, *tr. fr. Hebrew.* TrJP

And it came to pass in those days, that there went out a decree from Caesar Augustus. Bible, *N.T. Fr.* St. Luke, II. NAWM-1

And it is hard to tell one. To a Friend Who Wouldn't Bother to Strain His Noodleboard because Even So It Is Hard to Go Hunting When Your Rifle Is Blunt and Love Is Soft as an Old blanket. Jacob Glatstein, *tr. by* Benjamin *and* Barbara Harshav. AYP

And it seemed, while we waited, he began to walk. Geoffrey Hill. *Fr.* Mercian Hymns, XXX. NoAM; NoP

And it shall come to pass in the end of days. In the End of Days. Bible, *O.T. Fr.* Isaiah, II: 2–4. TrJP

And it shall come to pass when the days shall grow long. When the Days Shall Grow Long. Hayyim Nahman Bialik, *tr. by* A. M. Klein. TrJP

And it was ancient, quiet, lean and brass. I Drove Through This Old World This Afternoon. Clark Coolidge. LP

And it was on the third day in the morning. H. Leivick, *tr. fr. Yiddish by* Benjamin *and* Barbara Harshav. *Fr.* The Wolf. AYP

And it's forty miles to Nicut Hill. Prince Robert. *Unknown.* AmFP

And it's hard to see the mountains. Can I Say. Dolly Bird. WPOW

And it's three score and ten boys and men were lost from Grimsby town. Three Score and Ten. *Unknown.* OxBSS

And Jesus Don't Have Much Use for His Old Suitcase Anymore. Tom Kryss. NeAC

And Joseph was brought down to Egypt. Bible, *O.T. Fr.* Genesis, XXXIX-XLVI: 6. NAWM-1

And Joshua looks down on my face. Joshua's Face. Amir Gilboa. VWA, *tr. by* Shirley Kaufman.

And June. ? György Somlyó, *tr. fr. Hungarian by* Jascha Kessler. FOC

And just by crossing the short sea. Channel Crossing. George Barker. GTBS-P

And last night a man came in. Spring Street Bar. Mei-Mei Berssenbrugge. WPOW

And Later by Myself. Ory Bernstein, *tr. fr. Hebrew by* Warren Bargad *and* Stanley F. Chyet. IP

And learn O voyager to walk. Seafarer. Archibald MacLeish. NoP

And Lightly, like the Flowers. Pierre de Ronsard, *tr. fr. French by* W. E. Henley. AWP

And, like a bird at rest. National Anthem. Egbert Martin. PVCV

And, like a dying lady, lean and pale. The Waning Moon. Shelley. CH; ChER; OxBSP; TrGrPo (Moon, The.) FaBoCh; OBEV

And like thy father sing in tunefulness. A Barren Soul. Joseph Ezobi, *tr. fr. Spanish by* D. I. Friedmann. *Fr.* The Silver Bowl. TrJP

And lo! a monstrous herd of swine appears. Morgante and the Boars. Luigi Pulci, *tr. by* Byron. PFI

And, lo! leading a blessed host comes one. Lincoln. Harriet Monroe. *Fr.* Commemoration Ode. AA

And Los and Enitharmon builded Jerusalem weeping. Vala, Night the Ninth Being the Last Judgment. Blake. *Fr.* Vala; or The Four Zoas. OAEL-2

And Los beheld the mild Emanation, Jerusalem, eastward bending. In Deadly Fear. Blake. *Fr.* Jerusalem. SeCePo

And Love Hung Still. Louis MacNeice. *Fr.* Trilogy for X, II. CIP; GBL; MoBrPo

And maddening—it's all by someone else! Mirabell's Books of Number. James Merrill. *Fr.* The Changing Light at Sandover. NAAL-2

"And Man is left alone with Man." 'Tis well! At the Worst. Israel Zangwill. WGRP

And many voices marshalled in one hymn. Thomas Lovell Beddoes. NOBVV

And Marie said, My soule doth magnifie the Lord. Bible, *N.T. See* St. Luke: Magnificat, The.

And mathematics, fresh as May. Edmund Blunden. *Fr.* Reliques. ImOP

And me happiest when I compose poems. The Birth of Tragedy. Irving Layton. MoCV; NoAM; NoP; OBCV

And me my winter's task is drawing over. Frederick Goddard Tuckerman. *Fr.* Sonnets, V, xiv. QFR

And mightier grew the joy to meet full-faced. Swimming. Swinburne. *Fr.* Tristram of Lyonesse. GN

And Mr. Ferritt. Judith Wright. MoBrPo

And Monelle said: I will speak to you of actions. Actions. Marcel Schwob, *tr. by* William Brown Meloney. TrJP

And Monelle said: I will speak to you of moments. Moments. Marcel Schwob, *tr. by* William Brown Meloney. TrJP

And Monelle said: I will speak to you of things dead. Things Dead. Marcel Schwob, *tr. by* William Brown Meloney. TrJP

And much fruit, the swan. See in the Midst of Fair Leaves. Marianne Moore. MoAB

And my bat and my ball. B Is for Baseball. Scott Bates. SoTCo

And my love has come to me. Wendell Berry. *Fr.* 9 Verses of the Same Song. LLLT

And My Mama Used to Tell Me. *Unknown, tr. fr. Italian by* Muriel Kittel. DMI

And my poor fool is hang'd! No, no, no life! Death of Lear. Shakespeare. *Fr.* King Lear, V, iii. FiP

And my young sweetheart sat at board with me. Alfred Mombert, *tr. by* Ludwig Lewisohn. AWP

And Naomi said/ Unto her two daughters-in-law. Naomi and Ruth. Bible, *O.T. Fr.* Ruth, I: 8-17. TrJP

And night and distant travel; for the train. Last Evening. Rainer Maria Rilke, *tr. by* J. B. Leishman. OBWP

And no one knows what became of him, Crazi Levi. Crazi Levi. Rokhl Korn, *tr. by* Seymour Levitan. PeBMYV

And Noah was six hundred years old when the flood of waters. Bible, *O.T. Fr.* Genesis, VII: 6-IX: 17. NAWM-1

"And Now." John Basil Boothroyd. FiBHP

And now a fig for the lower house. Patrick Carey. JCP

And now Aeneas charges straight at Turnus. Virgil, *tr. fr. Latin, tr. by* Allen Mandelbaum. *Fr.* The Aeneid [or Eneados], XII. OBWP

And now all Nature seem'd in Love. On a Bank [or Banck] as I Sate [or Sat] a-Fishing; a Description of the Spring. Sir Henry Wotton. OBS; SeCP (May Day, A.) CH

And now. An attempt. Behold the Lilies of the Field. Anthony Hecht. NePoEA-2

And now as the iron rinds over. Skunk Cabbage. Mary Oliver. KS

And now at last. Robert E. Lee. Stephen Vincent Benét. *Fr.* John Brown's Body. AmFN

And now at length the joyful time drew on. Endymion's Convoy. Michael Drayton. *Fr.* Endimion and Phoebe. OBSC

And now, behold! as at the approach of the morning. The Celestial Pilot. Dante, *tr. fr. Italian by* Longfellow. *Fr.* Divina Commedia: Purgatorio, II. WGRP

And now both bands in close embraces met. Heaps on Heaps. Matthew Concanen. *Fr.* A Match at Football. SD

And now Eurynome had bath'd the king. Homer, *tr. fr. Greek by* George Chapman. *Fr.* Odyssey, XXIII. OBVE

"And Now Farley Is Going to Sing *While I Drink a Glass of Water!*" Albert Goldbarth. GeTw

And now four days the sun had seen our woes. The Great Fire. Dryden. *Fr.* Annus Mirabilis. FiP

And, now gives Time, her states description. George Chapman. *Fr.* Euthymiae Raptus; or, The Teares of Peace. PoEL-2

And now he roams the boundaries of my orchard. Patios of Ithaca. Mirko Lauer, *tr. by* David Tipton. Per

And now his well-known row the master bore. Homer, *tr. fr. Greek by* Pope. *Fr.* Odyssey, XXI. OBVE

And now I, Meleager, am among them. Meleager, *tr. by* Peter Whigham. PeHV

And now, kind friends, what I have wrote. Julia A. Moore. FaBoCo; FiBHP

And now love sang: but his was such a song. Willowwood ("And now love sang: but his was such a song"). Dante Gabriel Rossetti. *Fr.* The House of Life, L. NAEL-2; OAEL-2

And now man-slaughtering Pallas took in hand. Homer, *tr. fr. Greek by* George Chapman. *Fr.* Odyssey, XXII. OBVE (End of the Suitors, The.) OBS

And now my pampered beast. Epitaph for My Cat. Jean Garrigue. TAP

And now one prayer. *Unknown, tr. fr. Old Norse by* William Morris *and* Eirikur Magnusson. *Fr.* The Elder Edda: The Lay [*or* Short Lay] of Sigurd. OBVE

"And now," said the Governor, gazing abroad on the piled-up store. First Thanksgiving Day. Margaret Junkin Preston. PAH

And now she cleans her teeth into the lake. Camping Out. William Empson. CMoP; FaBoMo; OxBTC

And now take thought, my sonnet, who is he. Sonnets of the Months: Conclusion. Folgore da San Geminiano, *tr. by* Dante Gabriel Rossetti. AWP

And now th'art set wide ope, the spear's sad art. I Am the Door. Richard Crashaw. NAEL-1

And, now that every thing may in the proper place. Michael Drayton. *Fr.* Polyolbion, Fourteenth Song. FM

And now the book is closed. Anne Waldman *and* Ted Berrigan. *Fr.* Memorial Day; a Collaboration. EAS

And now the dark comes on, all full of chitter noise. The Sound of Night. Maxine W. Kumin. BoNaP; WPE

And now the green household is dark. In the Tree House at Night. James Dickey. NoP

And now the heart/ overflows its beats. Beginning. Marcos Rodríguez Frese, *tr. by* Julio Marzán. InW

And now the Queene of women had intent. Homer, *tr. fr. Greek by* George Chapman. *Fr.* Odyssey, XXI. OBVE

And now the riverbank. For the last time. Marina Tsvetayeva, *tr. fr. Russian by* Paul Schmidt. *Fr.* The Daughter of Jairus, II. BoWoP

And now the riverbank. I cling. Marina Tsvetayeva, *tr. fr. Russian by* Paul Schmidt. *Fr.* The Daughter of Jairus, III. BoWoP

And now the sea-scoured temptress, having failed. The Re-Birth of Venus. Geoffrey Hill. NePoEA

And now the sun that through the horizon peeps. Christopher Marlowe. *Fr.* Hero and Leander, Second Sestiad. OAEL-1

And now the trembling light. Shoreham: Twilight Time. Samuel Palmer. OAEL-2 (Twilight Time.) FaBoPP

And now the words. Mourning Song. Robert Pearl, *tr. by* Armand Schwerner. STP

And now there is nothing left to celebrate. George Barker. *Fr.* Pacific Sonnets, XII. LiTM

And now there is the lively sound. Baby's Awake Now. Bill Berkson. UL

And now they nigh approachèd to the stead. The Mermaids. Spenser. *Fr.* The Faerie Queene, II, 12. ChTr

And now 'tis time; for their officious haste. Heroique Stanzas, Consecrated to the Glorious Memory of His Most Serene and Renowned Highnesse, Oliver, Late Lord Protector of This Common-Wealth. Dryden. SeCV-2

"And now to God the Father," he ends. In Church. Thomas Hardy. *Fr.* Satires of Circumstance, II. BrPo; InPK; MoAB; MoBrPo; SCV

And now to overcome what? Acceptance Speech. Jayne Cortez. ER

And now to the abyss I pass. Andrew Marvell. *Fr.* Upon Appleton House, to My Lord Fairfax. OAEL-1

And now, unveiled, the toilet stands displayed. The Toilet. Pope. *Fr.* The Rape of the Lock, I. OBVE

And now was Paris come/ From his high towres. Homer, *tr. fr. Greek by* George Chapman. *Fr.* The Iliad, VI. OBVE

And now we walked along the solid mire. Dante, *tr. fr. Italian by* Robert Lowell. *Fr.* Divina Commedia: Inferno, XV. OBVE

And now where're he strayes. Richard Crashaw. *Fr.* Saint[e] Mary Magdalene; or, The Weeper. FaBoCo; Par

And now you tell me (it's your voice). Equality. Armanda Guiducci, *tr. by* Muriel Kittel. DMI

And Now You're Ready Who While She Was Here. J. V. Cunningham, *after the Greek of* Skythinos. *Fr.* Five Epigrams. OBVE; TW (Epigram: "And now you're ready who while she was here.") ErPo

And O and O. Song of Spring. Keats. BoTP

And of all that was theirs only the letters were left. Haim Guri, *tr. by* Warren Bargad *and* Stanley F. Chyet. IP

And of Columbus. Horace Gregory. GOA; OFD

And of the Azazmeh too, it would seem. Of the Azazmeh Too. Haim Guri, *tr. by* Warren Bargad *and* Stanley F. Chyet. IP

And of trees and the river. Muscle and Bone of Song. Hone Tuwhare. ATNZ

And oft the owle with rufull song complaind. Virgil, *tr. fr. Latin by* the Earl of Surrey. *Fr.* The Aeneid [*or* Eneados], IV. OBVE

And oh! the jay our nest did yield. Day's Work a-Done. William Barnes. SaC

And oh, to think the sun can shine. Adelaide Neilson. William Winter. AA

And on My Eyes Dark Sleep by Night. "Michael Field." OBMV

And on My Return. Haim Guri, *tr. fr. Hebrew by* Mark Elliott Shapiro. VWA

And on that day, upon the heavenly scarp. Upon the Heavenly Scarp. A. M. Klein. *Fr.* The Psalter of Avram Haktani. PoA

And on the porch, across the upturned chair. Sonnet: The Poet at Seven. Donald Justice. MT

And on the Very First Day. Benjamin Péret, *tr. fr. French by* Michael Benedikt. POS

And on the wall was limned a mouldering corse. On the Wall. Immanuel di Roma, *tr. by* Solomon Solis-Cohen. TrJP

And on this day, which poets unto thee. Ovid, *tr. fr. Latin by* Henry Vaughan. *Fr.* Tristium, V, 3. OBVE

And on This Shore. M. Carl Holman. AmNP; PoBA; PoNe

And once again I was within that house. The Dream. John Peale Bishop. LiTA; LiTM

And one morning while in the woods I stumbled suddenly upon the thing. Between the World and Me. Richard Wright. AmNP; IDB; LiTM; MoP; PoBA

And One Shall Live in Two. Jonathan Henderson Brooks. PoNe

"And other wond'rous works were done." Ascension of Our Lord Jesus Christ. Christopher Smart. *Fr.* Hymns and Spiritual Songs, XIV. NOCV

And Paradise does come. Joy. Gavin Bantock. OxBTC

And Paris be it or Helen dying. A Fragment on Death. Villon, *tr. by* Swinburne. CTC (Fragment of Death.) AWP

And Pergamos,/ City of the Phrygians. Euripides, *tr. fr. Greek by* Hilda Doolittle ("H. D."). *Fr.* Iphigenia [*or* Iphigeneia] in Aulis. AWP; OBVE;

And Perhaps. Roger Giroux, *tr. fr. French by* Paul Auster. RHTwFP

And power and pain. Paul Celan, *tr. by* Beth Bjorklund. CoAuP

"And pray, who are you?" The Tax-Gatherer. John Banister Tabb. GN

And Ride in Triumph through Persepolis. Christopher Marlowe. *Fr.* Tamburlaine the Great, pt. I, Act II, sc. v. TrGrPo

And Ronda with the old windows of the posadas. Yes. James Joyce. *Fr.* Ulysses. FF

And Ruth said, Intreat me not to leave. Bible, O.T. *Fr.* Ruth, I: 16-17. FF (Ruth to Naomi.) TrGrPo

And Samson grew old in days. Samson. Amir Gilboa, *tr. by* Stephen Mitchell. VWA

And "Science" said. The Dunce. Walter de la Mare. ImOP

And see th' expected hour is on the wing. Propsect of the Future Glory of America. John Trumbull. AmPP

And seeing the multitudes, he went up. Bible, N.T. *Fr.* St. Matthew, V-VII. NAWM-1

And several strengths from drowsiness campaigned. The Sermon on the Warpland. Gwendolyn Brooks. BPo; LiTM; NOBA; PoBA

And shall we ever seek in vain. All Alone. Mary E. Tucker. CBWP-1

And she/ pouring red wine into my glass. Don't Think. Ahmad Faraz, *tr. by* Mahmood Jamal. PBMUP

And she aloof to laughter—till I don't know. Big, Fat Summer—and the Lean and Hard. Frederick Bock. NYBP

And she, being old, fed from a mashed plate. Old Woman. Iain Crichton Smith. FaBoTw; OxBTC

And she is beautiful, our daughter. To Our Daughter. Jennifer Armitage. BrRo

And She Was Bad. Marvin Wyche, Jr. AmNP

And She Washed His Feet with Her Tear[e]s, and Wiped Them with the Hairs of Her Head. Sir Edward Sherburne, *after the Italian of* Giambattista Marina. ChTr; MeLP; OBS (Magdalen, The.) ACP (Proud Egyptian Queen, The.) OxBSP

And shores and strands and naked piers. Henry James at Newport. Weldon Kees. PoA

And should I thank you, my dear skin. Gratitude. Annette Lynch. FF

And silence/ which proves. Monument to Pushkin. Joseph Brodsky. VWA, *tr. by* Dimitry Pospielovsky *and* Keith Bosley

And silence/ which proves. The End of Man Is His Beauty. Amiri Baraka. AmNP

And since I was silent and lived in chaste timidity. Confession. Louise Otto-Peters, *tr. by* Susan L. Cocalis *and* Gerlinde Geiger. DMG

And so a sword was driven. The Ravine. Yves Bonnefoy, *tr. by* Anthony Rudolf. RHTwFP

And so an easier life our Cyclops drew. Theocritus, *tr. fr. Greek. Fr.* Idylls, XI. OBVE, *tr. by* Elizabeth Barrett Browning. (Cyclops, The.) AWP

And so depart into dark. Homage to Ezra Pound. Gilbert Highet. Par (Homage.) BXAP

And so for nights. The Night-blooming Cereus. Robert Hayden. CAPP; FB; NoP; NU

And so I cross into another world. New Heaven and Earth. D. H. Lawrence. CMoP

And so I somehow-nohow played. Robert Browning. *Fr.* Fifine at the Fair. Par

And so I speak/ in place of that primordial cry. Monique Laederach, *tr. fr. French by* Charles Guenther. *Fr.* Penelope. BoWoP

And so must I lose her whose mind. Prothalamium. Donagh MacDonagh. BIrV; NeIP

And so, one day when the tide was away out. Pat Wilson. ATNZ

And so, the closer he looks at things, the farther away they seem. The New Physics. Al Zolynas. BWV

And so the day beginning. A. J. Seymour. *Fr.* For Christopher Columbus, V. PBCV

And So the Oracles. Eeva-Liisa Manner, *tr. fr. Finnish by* Jaakko A. Ahokas. *Fr.* Cambrian, VII. OV

And so the things the country wants to see. Local Politics. Robert Pinsky. MAYP

And so they buried Lincoln? Strange and vain. Cenotaph of Lincoln. James Thompson McKay. OHIP

And so they found that the gold of the olive-root had dripped. The Autopsy. Odysseus Elytis, *tr. by* Edmund Keeley *and* Philip Sherrard. VMG

And So They Withered. Manfred Winkler, *tr. fr. Hebrew by* Bernhard Frank. MHeP

And so to a chambre full solacious. Dame Music. Stephen Hawes. *Fr.* The Pastime of Pleasure. PoEL-1

And so we two [*or* too] came where the rest have come. The Question. F. T. Prince. BoLoP; GTBS-P; PeSA

And so we went. Night Walk. Eli Netser, *tr. by* Bernhard Frank. MHeP

And so, wine and meat markets are proscribed. Shu Wei, *tr. fr. Chinese by* Irving Lo. *Fr.* The Price of Rice, IV. WFTU

And so you found that poor room dull. Appearances. Robert Browning. OxBSP

And so you marry, offering your youth. To a Bride-to-Be. Natalie Clifford Barney, *tr. by* Barbara Johnson. DMF

And so your landscape became old, even. Landscape Left Behind. Gerrit Kouwenaar, *tr. by* Adrian Henri. DuIn

And some chose trade they fared the better. The Entertainment Industry. William Langland. *Fr.* The Vision of Piers Plowman. NOCV

"And something that. . . . that is theirs—no longer ours." The Dispossessed. John Berryman. VGW

And sometimes I am sorry when the grass. Peace. Patrick Kavanagh. FaBCIP

And sometimes in the cool night I see you are an animal. Ode for Soft Voice. Michael McClure. NeAP

And sometimes the speech. Invisible Trumpets Blowing. E. J. Pratt. *Fr.* Brébeuf and His Brethren. CaP

And spoke: coopers, craftsmen, shepherds. Great God Paused among Men. Daniel Berrigan. MAT

And, star and system rolling past. Tennyson. *Fr.* In Memoriam A. H. H., Epilogue. ImOP

And still, at sea all night, we had a sense. Samos. James Merrill. *Fr.* Scripts for the Pageant. HCAP

And still I lie here. Song of the Invisible Corpse in the Field. Gregory Orr. AnAn

"And still," I say, and wait. Princess Shikishi, *tr. fr. Japanese by* Hiroaki Sato. *Fr.* Seventy-eight Tanka. FCEI

And still they come and go: and this is all I know. Picture-Show. Siegfried Sassoon. CMoP

And still we stood and stared far down. Therefore Is the Name of It Called Babel. Sir Osbert Sitwell. MMA

And still you lie. We Can Try Again Another Day. Judith Kazantzis. DT

And still you paint, and still I stand. The Painter's Mistress. James Elroy Flecker. BrPo

And such exactly she would be: whatever is superfluous. Nike. Ernest Bryll, *tr. by* Czeslaw Milosz. PwPP

And Summer mornings the mute child, rebellious. Eleven. Archibald MacLeish. HAP; WeW

And summer turns her head with its dark tangle. Ralegh's Prizes. Robert Pinsky. DiPo; MAYP

And sun on the roof, and the memory of Fiesole. Open Window in Florence. Leah Goldberg, *tr. by* Bernhard Frank. MHeP

And that question which I have not asked. The Last. Ezra Zussman, *tr. by* D. Shnayorson. VWA

And the Age Ended. W. H. Auden. *Fr.* In Time of War, XII. Son

And the Age of Snow came. The ravaging migration came. The Age of Snow. Márton Kalász, *tr. by* Jascha Kessler. FOC

And the Americans put Pound in a cage. The Cage. John Berryman. PoA

And the angel, taking some pains, told. Joseph's Suspicion. Rainer Maria Rilke, *tr. by* J. B. Leishman. TrCP

And the bitter storm augments; the wild winds wage. John Josselyn. SCAP

And the child, mine. Expectation. Aliza Shenhar, *tr. by* Linda Zisquit. VWA

And the Children. Peter Ackroyd. NPo

And the Cock Begins to Crow. Richard K. Avery. AH

And the Communists have nothing to offer but fat cheeks and eyeglasses and lying policemen. Kral Majales. Allen Ginsberg. PoM

And the cunning of the poem, that it consumes the world. Max Hölzer, *tr. by* Beth Bjorklund. CoAuP

And the curtains, the lamp. True to a Dream. Donald Petersen. NePoEA-2

And the days/ of Sarah were. The Days of Sarah. Benyamin Galai, *tr. by* Bernhard Frank. MHeP

And the days are not full enough. Ezra Pound. PCP; RB

And the Dervish spat. The Dervish. Muhammad al-Faituri, *tr. by* Sargon Boulus *and* Peter Porter. MAP

And the Earth Rebelled. Yuri Suhl, *tr. fr. Yiddish by* Max Rosenfeld. TrJP

And "the earth under our feet." At Kenneth Burke's Place. William Carlos Williams. NOBA

And the emphasis. Anne-Marie Albiach, *tr. fr. French by* Keith Waldrop. *Fr.* Enigma, IX. RHTwFP

And the euphorbia. December 1974: a Lament. Abdur-Rahman Slade Hopkinson. PBCV

And the Fete Continues. Jacques Prévert, *tr. fr. French by* Lawrence Ferlinghetti. RHTwFP

And the first among them. Stony Brook Tavern. Ken Belford. NeAC

And the first grey of morning fill'd the east. Sohrab and Rustum. Matthew Arnold. OBNV

And the ground spoke when she was born. For Alva Benson, and for Those Who Have Learned to Speak. Joy Harjo. HATNAP

And the ladies dress in silk. On the High Cost of Dairy Products. James McIntyre. FiBHP

And the lemon is tall. The sun is tall, and descends. Lemon. Mario Satz, *tr. by* Willis Barnstone. VWA

And the light, a wakened heyday of air. November Sunday Morning. Alvin Feinman. CoAP

And the Lord God planted a garden eastward in Eden. Bible, *O.T. Fr.* Genesis, II: 8–22. OAEL-1

And the Lord Was Not in the Whirlwind. Louis MacNeice. *Fr.* Visitations: VII. EaLo

And the Love of Laughter. Bruce Andrews. LP

And the mist: and the rain in the west: and the wind steady. The Omelet of A MacLeish. Edmund Wilson. NYBP; Par

And the mother, closing the exercise book. Poets Seven Years Old. Rimbaud, *tr. by* Kenneth Koch *and* Georges Guy. SOTW

And the next I remembered I'm on a table. The Loser. Charles Bukowski. ASP

And the Old Folks Said. Diane Mei Lin Mark. BrSi

And the Old Women Gathered. Mari E. Evans. BlSi; PoBA

And the place of their waiting a long burrow. David Jones. *Fr.* In Parenthesis. FaBoMo

And the rain came. And the water came. Chamutal Reich. *Fr.* Three Poems in Black and White, 3. WCI

And the Same Words. David Ignatow. NNaP

And the Seventh Dream Is the Dream of Isis. David Gascoyne. EAS

And the Silver Turns into Night. Nathan Yonathan, *tr. fr. Hebrew by* Richard Flantz. VWA

And the snake was/ talking to Eve. An Old Story. Rena Lee. VWA

And the stones in the Prague cemetery were so bored. The Drunken Stones of Prague. David Scheinert, *tr. by* Edouard Roditi. VWA

And the stranger at last stood before the monument of lava and anger. The Stone and the Blade of Grass in the Warsaw Ghetto. David Scheinert, *tr. by* Edouard Roditi. VWA

And the streams here, ledge to ledge. Lights among Redwood. Thom Gunn. OBTV

And the sun wields mercy. The Sun Wields Mercy. Charles Bukowski. MAT

And the traveller hopes: let me be far from any. Journey to Iceland. W. H. Auden. PoA

And the trunk: "So sweet those words to me that I." Pier delle Vigne. Dante, tr. fr. Italian by John Ciardi. Fr. Divina Commedia: Inferno, XII. HoPM

And the two reservist guys went. Look, don't shoot. The Poem on Our Mother, Our Mother Rachel. Avot Yeshurun, tr. by Harold Schimmel. VWA

And the voice said: Walk. Little Falls. Robert Hogg. MoCV

And the way goes on in the worn earth. Archibald MacLeish. Fr. Conquistador. NoAM

And the whole earth was of one language, and of one speech. Bible, O.T. Fr. Genesis, XI: 1-9. EyDe; NAWM-1

And the wingspan? Wingspan. Bartolo Cattafi, tr. by Lawrence R. Smith. NItP

And the woman sat on. About Women's Liberation. María Saucedo, tr. by Toni Empringham. FIA

And the World's Face. Julian Symons. WaP

And then? Colors and names of colors. No Way of Knowing. John Ashbery. AnAn

And then he would lift this finest. Out-of-the-Body Travel. Stanley Plumly. AmPA; DiL; GeTw; LCAP

And then I pressed the shell. The Shell. James Stephens. BoNaP; BoTP; CH; CMoP; MoAB; MoBrPo; MOS; MoShBr

And then I sat me down, and gave the rein. Gustav Rosenhane, tr. by Sir Edmund Gosse. AWP

And then in mid-May the first morning of steady heat. Late Spring. Robert Hass. GeTw; MAYP

And Then It Rained. Mark Van Doren. BoNaP

And Then No More. Friedrich Rückert, tr. fr. German by James Clarence Mangan. BIrV; BLPA

And then one day Hershey played by the door. You Are a Jew! Delmore Schwartz. Fr. Genesis. TrJP

And Then Suddenly It's Dark. Salvatore Quasimodo, tr. fr. Italian by William Jay Smith. CT; PFI

And then the knife. Song of the Hanged. Eléni Vakaló, tr. by James Damaskos. PBWP

And then the old inhabitants, so kind. Fishing Village. Louis Dudek. Fr. Provincetown. MoCV

And then went down to the ship. Ezra Pound. Fr. Cantos, I. AmPP; CMoP; LiTA; MoAB; MoAmPo; MoP; NoAM; NoP; OBVE; PoE; TrGrPo; VGW

And then, without his knowing, sweet sleep descended down. The Marriage in Eden. William Williams, tr. fr. Welsh by Lewis Saunders and Gwyn Jones. Fr. A View of Christ's Kingdom. OBWVE

And there are times truly. An Underdeveloped Country. D. J. Enright. NOBL

And there came two angels to Sodom at even. Bible, O.T. Fr. Genesis, XIX: 1-38. HoPM

"And there goes the bell for the third month." The Fight of the Year. Robert McGough. OBCP

And there I found a gray and ancient ass. Pegasus Lost. Elinor Wylie. MoAmPo

And there I was. Not a dictionary. Northwest Airlines. Fred Chappell. HoPM

And there is nothing at all—neither fear. Natalya Gorbanevskaya, tr. by Daniel Weissbort. BoWoP; OV

And there shall come forth a rod out of the stem of Jesse. The Rod of Jesse. Bible, O.T. Fr. Isaiah, XI: 1-11. AWP; OBVE; TrJP

And there she's leand her back to a thorn. The Cruel Mother. Unknown. ESPB

And there they were: with fire everywhere. A New Dance. S. E. Anderson. NBP

"And There Was a Great Calm." Thomas Hardy. ChTr; CMoP; FaBoRV; LiTM; OAEL-2

And there was great mourning in Israel in every place. Great Mourning. Bible, Apocrypha. Fr. First Maccabees, I: 25-28. TrJP

And there were in the same country shepherds abiding in the field. Bible, N.T. Fr. St. Luke, II: 8-14. PChr

And there were spring-faced cherubs that did sleep. The Sea of Death. Unknown. CH

And these mountains which my eyes have seen. Seven Metal Mountains. Bible, Pseudepigrapha. Fr. Enoch, LII: 6-9. TrJP

And these too I want to remember. I Shall Remember. Jacob Glatstein, tr. by Benjamin and Barbara Harshav. AYP

And they both lived happily ever after. After Ever Happily. Ian Serraillier. SO

And they have drown'd thee then at last! poor Phillis! On the Death of a Favourite Old Spaniel. Robert Southey. FM

And they have thrust our shattered dead away in foreign graves. The Martyrs of the Maine. Rupert Hughes. PAH

And they have to get it right. We just need. John Ashbery. HCAP

And they stopped before that bad sculpture of a fisherman. Maximus, to Gloucester, Sunday, July 19. Charles Olson. Fr. The Maximus Poems. NAAL-2

And they were there in the City of Fire, enflamed. JuJu. Askia Muhammad Touré. PoBA

And this/ is all there is. Yakamochi, tr. fr. Japanese by Burton Watson. Fr. Manyo Shu. FCEI

And This Happened ("And this happened in Prague many years ago. Through the wall"). Haim Guri, tr. fr. Hebrew by Warren Bargad and Stanley F. Chyet. IP

And this happened in Prague many years ago, on a cold grey day. At the Train Station. Haim Guri, tr. by Warren Bargad and Stanley F. Chyet. IP

And this is England! June's undarkened green. This Is England. Laurence Binyon. BoTP

"And this is freedom!" cried the serf. Bondage. "Owen Innsley." AA

And this is good old Boston. A Boston Toast. At. to John Collins Bossidy. BLPA; CenHV. See also I come from the city of Boston. (Boston.) AmFN

And this is how it begins now, my late. Yehuda Amichai, tr. fr. Hebrew by Warren Bargad and Stanley F. Chyet. Fr. Achziv, 5. IP

And this is how you live: a woman, children. A Primary Ground. Adrienne Rich. NNaP

And This Is Love. Paula Reingold. IHMS

And this is the organ which was made last. Skinning-the-Cat. Dennis Schmitz. NPGG

And this is the song that the white woman sings. Goosey Goosey Gander—by Various Authors (Kipling's Version). William Percy French. CenHV

And this is the way the baby woke. The Way the Baby Woke. James Whitcomb Riley. AA

And this is the way they ring. Ringing the Bells. Anne Sexton. FF; HCAP; PoE; TAP; VGW

And this is where. Ian Wedde. Fr. Angel. PeNZ

And this, ladies and gentlemen, whom I am not in fact. The Suicide. Louis MacNeice. FaBCIP

And this reft house is that the which he built. On a Ruined House in a Romantic Country. Samuel Taylor Coleridge. Fr. Sonnets Attempted in the Manner of Contemporary Writers. FaBoPa; Par; Son

And this, then, is the place where Romans trod. Manchester. John Bolton Rogerson. PF

And those black rocks which overhung the stream. Black Rocks. C. H. Sisson. DiPo

And Thou Art Dead. Byron. PoEL-4

(Elegy on Thyrza.) GTBS; GTBS-P

And thou art gone, most loved, most honored friend. On the Late S. T. Coleridge. Washington Allston. AA

And thou art now no longer near! To the Parted One. Goethe, tr. by Christopher Pearse Cranch. AWP

And thou, Dalhousie, the Great God of War. Unknown. FaBoCo

And Thou, Expectant. Amado Nervo, tr. fr. Spanish by Samuel Beckett. MexPo

And Thou, O Lord! by whom are seen. Whittier. Fr. The Eternal Goodness. TrPWD

And thou wert sad—yet I was not with thee. Lines on Hearing That Lady Byron Was Ill. Byron. EBEV

And Thou! whom earth still holds, and will not yield. Wordsworth. William Wilberforce Lord. Fr. Ode to England. AA

And thou! whose sense, whose humour, and whose rage. Inscriptio. Pope. OxBSP

And through the Caribbean Sea. Margaret Danner. BPo

And thus as we were talking to and fro. Complaint of the Common Weill of Scotland. Sir David Lindsay. Fr. The Dreme. GoTS

(Compleynt of the Comoun Weill of Scotland, The.) OxBS

And thus continuing, she said. Wordsworth. Fr. The Sailor's Mother. Par

And thus declared that Arab lady. Solomon and the Witch. W. B. Yeats. NoAM

And Thus in Nineveh. Ezra Pound. VGW

And thus the people every year. Attack of the Squash People. Marge Piercy. NBLV

And thus went out this lamp of light. An Account of the Cruelty of the Papists. Benjamin Harris. SCAP

And to begin again, the night was dark and dreary, and. Sister Water. Robert Penn Warren. MT

And to Her-Without-Bounds I send. Tribal Memories. Robert Duncan. Fr. Passages. NOBA

And to Private Ball it came. David Jones. Fr. In Parenthesis. OBWVE

And to render harmless a bomb or the like. Holding the Thought of Love. Bernadette Mayer. BAP

And to the Young Men. Merrill Moore. MoAmPo

And Tomorrow Wend Our Ways. *Malay Oral Tradition, tr. by* R. J. Wilkinson *and* R. O. Winstedt. WTO

And Truly It Is a Most Glorious Thing. William Bradford. AH

And Turnus than, quhar he at erth dyd ly. Virgil, *tr. into Middle English by* Gavin Douglas. *Fr.* The Aeneid [*or* Eneados], XII. OBVE

And two birdchildren. Poem for Thel—the Very Tops of Trees. Joseph Major. NBP

And upon returning to his home town, he found a sea. Odysseus. Haim Guri, *tr. by* Bernhard Frank. MHeP

And "Ut Pictura Poesis" Is Her Name. John Ashbery. InPS

And Was Not Improved. Lerone Bennett, Jr. CNA; PoBA

And wasna he a roguey. The Piper o' Dundee. *Unknown.* OxBS

And We Conquered. Rob Penny. PoBA

And we love Art for Art's sake. Art for Art's Sake. Marc Blitzstein. *Fr.* The Cradle Will Rock. TrJP

And we were speaking easily and all the light stayed low. In Judgment of the Leaf. Kenneth Patchen. UnAS; VGW

And we will lace the. God Send Easter. Lucille Clifton. CNA

And welcom now (Great Monarch) to your own. Dryden. *Fr.* Astraea Redux. OBS

And were it for thy profit, to obtain. On Change of Weathers. Francis Quarles. OxBSP

And what a charm is in the rich hot scent. Among the Firs. Eugene Lee-Hamilton. NOBVV

And What About the Children. Audre Lorde. PoBA

And what are we to do with the horses. Answer. Leah Goldberg, *tr. by* Robert Friend. VWA

And what are you that, wanting you. The Philosopher. Edna St. Vincent Millay. CMoP

And what if all Nature ratify this merciless outrage? *Unknown.* FM

And what if now I told you this, let's say. At a Reading. J. D. McClatchy. DiPo

And what if someone comes and says: Here's the harp. Play for me on this harp. I've Come to the Simplest Words. Amir Gilboa, *tr. by* Warren Bargad *and* Stanley F. Chyet. IP

And what is left for the others. What Is Left? István Vas, *tr. by* Emery George. VWA

And what is life? A Primer for Schoolchildren. Richard Weber. CIP

And what is love? It is a doll dress'd up. Modern Love. Keats. OBNC

And what is love? Misunderstanding, pain. J. V. Cunningham. CRP; HAP; HoPM; PoA

And what is so rare as a day in June? James Russell Lowell. *See* What is so rare as a day in June?

And what now, wood thrush. Ietaka, *tr. by* Steven D. Carter. WFTW

And What of Me? Liz Sohappy Bahe. CDW

And what of the journey where the head of Wu meets the tail of Ch'u? Wang Shih-chen, *tr. fr. Chinese by* Daniel Bryant. *Fr.* On the River. WFTU

And what of you? You also shall not say. Insights. Catherine Davis. NePoEA; QFR

And what shall I be today, what. Faye Kicknosway. ER

And what shall I bring back from such a voyage. Voyage. Stanislaw Wygodski, *tr. by* Isaac Komem. VWA

And What Shall You Say? Joseph Seamon Cotter, Jr.. BANP; CDC; PoBA; PoNe

And What though Winter Will Pinch Severe. Sir Walter Scott. *Fr.* Old Mortality, *ch.* 19. EnRP

And what was the big room he walked in? Before a Fall. Geoffrey Grigson. EAS

And what will they remember when. "A Midsummer Night's Dream" in Regent's Park. Derwent May. Mes

And What with the Blunders. Kenneth Patchen. NaP

And when/ the cold white ness. Query. Ebon Dooley. PoBA

And When I go up as a pilgrim in winter, to recover. 1980. Abraham Sutskever, *tr. fr. Yiddish by* Cynthia Ozick. *Fr.* Poems from a Diary. PeBMYV

And When I Lamented. Heine, *tr. fr. German by* Emma Lazarus. *Fr.* Homeward Bound. TrJP

And when I lie between the standing walls. What She Didn't Say. Ory Bernstein, *tr. by* Warren Bargad *and* Stanley F. Chyet. IP

And when I pay death's duty. Robin Blaser. NeAP

And when it comis to the ficht. Bruce Addresses His Army. John Barbour. *Fr.* The Bruce. GoTS

And when suddenly it hit me. Just Looking, Thank You. Leonard Nathan. BLA

And when that ballad lady went. A Road in Kentucky. Robert Hayden. LCAP

And when the light is exact. Feeling of Time. Giuseppe Ungaretti, *tr. by* Isabella Gardner. PFI

And when the rain had gone away. The Bug. Marjorie Barrows. RHPC

And when the sun puts out his lamp. To the Mountains. Henry David Thoreau. PoEL-4

And when they asked her what she wanted to be. Vocation. Judith Herzberg, *tr. by* Manfred Wolf. DuIn; WPOW

And when they came together in one place. Homer, *tr. fr. Greek by* Tennyson. *Fr.* The Iliad, IV. OBVE

And when thou hast on foot the purblind hare. Poor Wat. Shakespeare. *Fr.* Venus and Adonis. OBSC

And when we die at last. Heaven and Hell. Nalungiaq, *tr. by* Edward Field. DL; STP

And when you have forgotten the bright bedclothes. When You Have Forgotten Sunday: The Love Story. Gwendolyn Brooks. BPo; FF; WPOW

And when you try to sleep. For Bill. Geof Hewitt. NeAC

And Where Do You Stand on the National Question. Tom Paulin. CIP; FaBCIP

"And where have you been, my Mary?" The Fairies of the Caldon-Low. Mary Howitt. BeLS

And where the plankton is falling. Retrieval System. Peter Porter. AnAn

And while his gray voice drones on from the front desk. Scrut Gets Marty Crowe for Social Studies. George Roberts. TSL

And While We Are Waiting. Carolyn M. Rodgers. JB

And whilst the outer lake beneath the lash. Shelley. *Fr.* The Witch of Atlas. PBBP

And Who Has Seen a Fair Alluring Face. George Peele. ErPo

And who has seen the moon, who has not seen. Moonrise. D. H. Lawrence. LiTM; PoA

And who shall separate the dust. Common Dust. Georgia Douglas Johnson. AmNP; PoBA; TTY

And why does Gratt teach English? Why, because. Professor Gratt. Donald Hall. OBAL

And why not I, as hee. To Himselfe and the Harpe. Michael Drayton. OBS

And why not the hedge of geysers the obelisk of hours the smooth scream. Sentence. Aimé Césaire, *tr. by* Clayton Eshleman *and* Annette Smith. RHTwFP

And why so coffined in this vile disguise. John Cleveland. *Fr.* The King's Disguise. JCP

And why to me this, thou lame Lord of fire. An Execration upon Vulcan. Ben Jonson. SeCP

And Will He Not Come Again. Shakespeare. *Fr.* Hamlet, IV, v. PoEL-2
(Ophelia's Songs, 2 ("And will he not come again").) TrGrPo

And will she never hold her tongue. The Power of Silence. W. H. Davies. BrPo

And will they always be so tender, her. Swift Love, Sweet Motor. Hildegarde Flanner. WPE

And will they cast the altars down. In Portugal, 1912. Alice Meynell. NOCV

"And will you cut a stone for him." The Stone. W. W. Gibson. MoBrPo

And wilt thou have me fashion into speech. Elizabeth Barrett Browning. *Fr.* Sonnets from the Portuguese, XIII. BrRo

And Wilt Thou Leave Me Thus? Sir Thomas Wyatt. ElL; EnLoPo; NAEL-1; SiPS
("And wylt thou leve me thus?") AAS
(Lover's Appeal, The.) GTBS; GTBS-P

And with March a Decade in Bolinas. Joanne Kyger. UL

And with what body do they come? Emily Dickinson. OBD

And without her having stooped to seduce her jailers. The Thunder's Son. Aimé Césaire, *tr. by* Michael Benedikt. POS

And worth the blossoms that acacias. Poplar Tree. Padraic Colum. NePoAm

And would you gather turds. A History of Love. William Carlos Williams. VGW

And Would You See My Mistress' Face? *At. to* Thomas Campion. OBSC

"And would you sign my copy sir?" "A Scotch?" The Poet at Fifty. Laurence Lerner. PeSA

And would'st thou reach, rash scholar mine. Zeal and Love. John Henry, Cardinal Newman. TW

And wylt thou leve me thus? Sir Thomas Wyatt. *See* And Wilt Thou Leave Me Thus?

And, yeah, brothers. I Sing of Shine. Etheridge Knight. BPo

And Yet. Kadya Molodovsky, *tr. fr. Yiddish by* Seymour Levitan. VWA

And Yet. Arthur B. Rhinow. BLRP

And Yet. Errol B. Sloan. BLRP

And yet a kiss (like blubber)'d blur and slip. Love and Death. John Frederick Nims. HoPM; SM; WeW (Finisterre.) KS

And yet but lately have I seen, e'en here. A Winter-Piece. Ambrose Philips. SeCePo

And yet hath prayer, the heav'n-breathing foliage of faith. Ethick. Robert Bridges. *Fr.* The Testament of Beauty, IV. OxBTC

And yet I cannot reprehend the flight. Samuel Daniel. *Fr.* To Delia. OBEV

And yet not long ago. *Unknown. Fr.* Vox Populi, Vox Dei. FaBoPV

And yet one arrives somehow. Arrival. William Carlos Williams. AnAmPo

And yet the driving mirror shows me plain. To His Coy Mistress. W. J. Webster. BXAP

And yet the southern whale does some time come. The Whales. Marguerite Young. WPE

And yet the woman, who all things remembers. Metamorphoses of the Vampire. Baudelaire, *tr. by* Arthur Symons. VWA

And yet this great wink of eternity. Hart Crane. *Fr.* Voyages (I–VI), II. AmPP; HAP; LiTM; MoAB; MoAmPo; MOS; OxBA; PoE; PPP; UnPo; VGW

And Yet We Are Here! Karl Wolfskehl. *tr. fr. German by* Carol North Valhope *and* Ernst Morwitz. TrJP

And yet we should consider how we go forward. An Old Man on the River Bank. George Seferis, *tr. by* Edmund Keeley *and* Philip Sherrard. VMG

And yet, where would we be without the American culture. Goodbye Nkrumah. Diane DiPrima. PoM

And yet whiteness. A Sketch for a Modern Love Poem. Tadeusz Rozewicz, *tr. by* Czeslaw Milosz. PwPP

And yet you experienced the flames of Hell. Proof. Czeslaw Milosz, *tr. by the author.* TOF

And you are dead. The earth has not yet covered you. Isaac Leybush Peretz. Moyshe-Leyb Halpern, *tr. by* Kathryn Hellerstein. VWA

And you, big rocket. November the Fifth. Leonard Clark. OnUR

And you came back. Samar Attar. *Fr.* The Return of the Dead. PBWP

And You, Helen. Edward Thomas. BoLoP; OBWVE

And you, Italy, one day I knelt. Valery Larbaud, *tr. fr. French by* William Joy Smith. *Fr.* Europe, X. CT

And you my daughter. Daughter. Mary Dorcey. AIW

And you never liked parties. The Table. Carlos Drummond de Andrade, *tr. by* Elizabeth Bishop. ATCBP

"And you, Sir Poet, shall you make, I pray." The Poet and the Child. Winifred Howells. AA

And you, whate'er your Fav'rite does, approve. Albius Tibullus, *tr. fr. Latin by* John Dart. *Fr.* Odes, I, 4. PeHV

And You Woods. Shin Dong-jip, *tr. fr. Korean by* Koh Chang-soo. ACKP

And you'll say a nation totters. G. D. H. Cole. *Fr.* Civil Riot. OxBTC

And you're dead. And you've not been covered by the ground. Yitskhok Leybush Perets. Moyshe-Leyb Halpern, *tr. by* John Hollander. PeBMYV

An Andalusian Exile. Ahmad Shauqi, *tr. fr. Arabic by* M. Mustafa Badawi *and* John Heath-Stubbs. MAP

Andalusian merchant, that returns, The. *Unknown. Fr.* Wonders. FaBoCh

Andalusian Sereno, The. Francis Saltus Saltus. AA

Andante, ma Non Assai. Rufinus Domesticus, *tr. fr. Greek by* Dudley Fitts. ErPo

Andonis, My Daughter. Thomas Peacock. VoR

Andraitx—Pomegranate Flowers. D. H. Lawrence. NoP

André Chénier. Marina Tsvetayeva, *tr. fr. Russian by* Tom Paulin. FaBoPV

Andrea del Sarto. Robert Browning. CTC; NAEL-2; NOBVV; NoP; OAEL-2; PoE; PoEL-5

Andreas, *sel. Unknown, tr. fr. Anglo-Saxon by* Charles W. Kennedy. St. Andrew's Voyage to Mermedonia. AnOE

Andrée Rexroth. Kenneth Rexroth. PrIm; VGW

André's Request to Washington. *Unknown.* PAH

Andrew. Thomas William Parsons. AA

Andrew and Maudlin, Rebecca and Will. A Ballad of Andrew and Maudlin. *Unknown.* CoMu

Andrew Gear of Sunderland. *Unknown.* FaBoCo

Andrew Jackson. Martha Keller. AmFN

Andrew Lammie. *Unknown. See* At Fyvie's yetts there grows a flower.

Andrew M'Crie. Robert Fuller Murray. CenHV; FaBoCo

Andrew Rose. *Unknown.* OxBSS

Andrew Rykman's Prayer, *sels.* Whittier. TrPWD

"Make my mortal dreams come true."

"Pardon, Lord, the lips that dare."

Androgynous child whose hair curls into flowers. The Total Influence or Outcome of the Matter: The Sun. Marge Piercy. WPOW

Andromache, *sel.* Euripides, *tr. fr. Greek by* George Allen. Chorus: The Kings of Troy. WaaP

Andromache's Lamentation. Homer, *tr. fr. Greek by* Congreve. *Fr.* The Iliad, XXIV. OBVE

Andromache's Wedding. Sappho, *tr. fr. Greek by* Willis Barnstone. BoWoP

Andromeda/ forgot. Sappho, *tr. by* Willis Barnstone. BoWoP

Andromeda. Thomas Bailey Aldrich. AA

Andromeda. Gerard Manley Hopkins. EBEV; FaBoMo; LiTB

Andromeda. James Jeffrey Roche. AA

Andromeda, by Perseus saved and wed. Aspecta Medusa. Dante Gabriel Rossetti. OxBSP

Andujar in the Pique of His Career. Bob McKenty. SoTCo

Andy-Diana DNA Letter. Andrew Weiman. HAP

Andy's Gone with Cattle. Henry Lawson. PoAu-1

Ane Ballat of Our Lady. William Dunbar. *See* Ballad of Our Lady.

Ane doolie sessoun to ane cairfull dyte. The Testament of Cresseid. Robert Henryson. GoTS; OxBLMV; OxBS

Ane Sang of the Birth of Christ, with the Tune of Baw Lula Low. Martin Luther, *tr. fr. German by* John Wedderburn. ChTr

Ane Satire [*or* Satyre] of the Three [*or* Thrie] Estaitis, *sels. Sir David Lindsay.*
"Have I nocht made ane honest shift." GoTS
"My patent pardouns ye may see." OBSV

Ane Supplication in Contemptioun of Syde Taillis. Sir David Lyndsay. GoTS

Ane to Anither. Duncan Glen. PoSH

Anear the centre of that northern crest. James Thomson ("B. V."). *Fr.* The City of Dreadful Night, XXI. GTBS-P (City's Queen, The.) NOBE

Anecdote for Fathers. Wordsworth. EnRP

Anecdote from William IV Street. D. J. Enright. OxBC

An Anecdote of Love. John Clare. NOBVV

Anecdote of the Jar. Wallace Stevens. AmPP; CMoP; HCAP; HeIP; HoPM; InPK; LiTA; MoAB; MoAmPo; MoP; NAAL-2; NAWM-2; NIP; NoAM; NOBA; NoP; OxBA; OxBSP; PoA; PPP; PrIm; SOTW; TAP; UnPo

Anecdote of the Prince of Peacocks. Wallace Stevens. SOTW

Anecdote That Went with It, The. Ray DiPalma. LP

Anemic pictures! Legend. Jules Laforgue, *tr. by* Louis Simpson. Prf

Anesthetist is singing, The. In the Operating Room. Alden Nowlan. NOBC

Angel, The. Blake. *Fr.* Songs of Experience. CH; EnRP; LiTB

Angel, The. Alfred Hayes. TrJP

Angel, The. Galway Kinnell. NoAM

Angel. Brad Leithauser. DiPo; FYAP; MAYP

Angel. James Merrill. CAPP; PoA

Angel, The. Pinhas Sadeh, *tr. fr. Hebrew by* Bernhard Frank. MHeP

Angel/ three years we waited intently for him, The. George Seferis, *tr. fr. Greek by* Edmund Keeley *and* Philip Sherrard. *Fr.* Mythistorima, I. VMG

Angel, *sel.* Ian Wedde.
"And this is where." PeNZ

Angel and Stone. Howard Nemerov. NYBP

Angel and the girl are met, The. The Annunciation. Edwin Muir. CMoP; CRP; NOCV

Angel came by night, The. Adsum. Richard Henry Stoddard. AA

Angel came to me, An. O Simplicitas. Madeleine L'Engle. *Fr.* Three Songs of Mary. OBCP; PChr

Angel came to me and said, An. Memorable Fancy, A ("Angel came to me and said"). Blake. *Fr.* The Marriage of Heaven and Hell. NU

Angel came to me and stood by my bedside, An. Nightmare, with Angels. Stephen Vincent Benét. MAT

Angel Describes Truth, An. Ben Jonson. *Fr.* Hymenaei. OBS

Angel Eye of Memory. John Malcolm Brinnin. PoA

Angel in the House, The. Coventry Patmore.
Sels.
"Across the sky the daylight crept." *Fr.* II, x. GBL
Attainment, The. *Fr.* I, iii. FaBoEE
Cathedral Close, The. *Fr.* I, i. EBVV
(Salisbury; the Cathedral Close.) EBVV; FaBoPP
County Ball, The. *Fr.* II, iii. EBVV
"I vow'd unvarying faith; and she." *Fr.* II, xi. NoBVV
(Constancy Rewarded.) OxBSP
In Love, at Stonehenge. FaBoPP
Kiss, The. BoLoP; EnLoPo; FiBHP; NOBVV, II, viii.

Love at Large. EBVV, I, ii; NOBVV, I, ii.
Love Serviceable. *Fr.* I, vi. EnLoPo
Married Lover, The. *Fr.* II, xii. OBEV; TrGrPo
Perspective. *Fr.* II, i. FaBoEE; GBL
Rainbow, The. *Fr.* II, iii. GTBS-P
Revelation, The. *Fr.* I, viii. OxBSP
   ("Idle poet, here and there, An.") EnLoPo; GBL; GTBS-P; HAP;
   OBNC
Sahara. EBVV
Spirit's Epochs, The. *Fr.* I, viii. EBEV; GBL; OxBSP
Tribute, The. *Fr.* I, iv. EBEV; OBNC
"'Twas when the spousal time of May." *Fr.* II, vii. GBL
"Whir'd off at last, for speech I sought." *Fr.* II, xi. GBL
Angel, king of streaming morn. Sun. Henry Rowe. OBEV
Angel Michael, The. Anath Bental, *tr. fr. Hebrew by* Howard Schwartz.
   VWA
Angel of Death, The. *Unknown.* AmFP
Angel of Death Is Always with Me, The. Morton Marcus. NAmP
Angel of Patience, The. Whittier. WGRP
Angel of Peace, Thou Hast Wandered Too Long. Oliver Wendell Holmes.
   AH
Angel of poets,/ Tell us how. Prayer for All Poets at This Time. Irwin
   Edman. TrPWD
Angel [*or* Angell] saith to Joseph mild, The. For Innocents' Day. Luke
   Wadding. NOIV; TIRV
Angel, robed in spotless white, An. Dawn. Paul Laurence Dunbar.
   AmNP; AnAmPo; PoLF; PoNe
Angel said to me, the: "Why are you laughing?" Sarah. Delmore
   Schwartz. VWA
Angel slide your hand. A Poem in Yellow after Tristan Tzara. Jerome
   Rothenberg. PoM; RHTwFP
Angel Spirits of Sleep. Robert Bridges. CH
   (Spirits.) OBEV
Angel Surrounded by Paysans. Wallace Stevens. HCAP; LCAP; PPP
Angel That Presided o'er My Birth, The. Blake. *Fr.* Gnomic Verses.
   InPK; NAs; OxBSP; RB; TrGrPo
Angel-Thief, The. Oliver Wendell Holmes. AnAmPo
Angel told Mary, An. Harry Behn. PChr
Angel Unawares, An. *Unknown.* BLRP
Angel with a voice like summer show'rs, An. Repose. Henrietta
   Cordelia Ray. CBWP-3
Angel with Horn. Margit Szécsi, *tr. fr. Hungarian by* Jascha Kessler.
   FOC
Angel with the Sun Dial (Cathedral at Chartres), The. Christine Busta, *tr.*
   fr. German by Beth Bjorklund. CoAuP
Angela Davis. Alice S. Cobb. BlSi
Angela Davis, the Virgin Mary, and I. To Mainz! Ursula Krechel, *tr. by*
   Susan L. Cocalis. DMG
Angela Honey (she wrote) I would it were not so. From Lois in London.
   Angela McCabe. AmPA
Angelica and the Ork. Ariosto, *tr. fr. Italian by* Sir John Harington. *Fr.*
   Orlando Furioso, X. OBSC
Angelica has gain'd the dell. Robert Dunbar. *Fr.* The Caraguin.
   PBCV
Angelica the Doorkeeper. *Unknown, tr. fr. Serbian by* Anne Pennington.
   RB
Angelical whites of your eyes, The. Susan. Robin Magowan. EAS
Angell saith to Joseph mild, The. *See* Angel saith to Joseph mild, The.
Angelles bee wrogte to bee of neidher kynde. Mynstrelles Songe.
   "Angelles bee wrogte to bee of neidher kynde." Thomas Chatterton.
   Fr. Aella; a Tragycal Enterlude. EnLoPo
Angelo Orders His Dinner. Bayard Taylor. AnAmPo; BXAP; Par
Angels. Dannie Abse. PoA
Angels. Richard Burns. VWA
Angels, The. William Drummond of Hawthornden. *Fr.* Flowers of Sion.
   GN
   (Nativitie, The.) OBS
Angels, The. Richard Eberhart. BLA
Angels. Gertrude Hall. AA
Angels, The. Mirko Lauer, *tr. fr. Spanish by* David Tipton. Per
Angels, The. Paul Ramsey. CRP
Angels. Anne Szumigalski. Mes; NOBC
Angels, The. Marguerite Young. WPE
Angels/ might fall that way. Snowfall: Four Variations. George
   Amabile. NYBP
Angels and ministers of grace defend us! Shakespeare. *Fr.* Hamlet, I,
   iv. EBEV
Angels are bending, The. W. B. Yeats. NOBVV
Angels, as well as birds, on silent wing. On Angels. W. W. Eustace
   Ross. MoCV

Angels Came a-Mustering, The. *Unknown, tr. fr. Hebrew by* Israel
   Zangwill. EaLo; TrJP
Angels' eyes, whom veils cannot deceive, The. Of the Blessed Sacrament
   of the Altar. Robert Southwell. OBEV
Angels, from the realms of glory. Nativity. James Montgomery.
   NOCV
Angels have no memory. God's Language. Ruth Fainlight. VWA
Angels in Heav'n, as we may say. A Poem upon the Caelestial Embassy.
   Richard Steere. SCAP
Angels in the House. Jerred Metz. VWA
Angels in Winter. Nancy Willard. LCAP
"Angels, it seems, don't always know." Lyn Hejinian. UL
Angel's Message, The. Clara Ann Thompson. CBWP-2
Angels of Buena Vista, The. Whittier. BeLS; PAH
Angels, pulled into light—provoking the air, fall here. What Memory
   Reveals. Susan Wheeler. BAP
Angel's Song. Charles Causley. OBCP
Angels' Song, The. Edmund Hamilton Sears. *See* It Came upon the
   Midnight Clear.
Angels Sung a Carol, The. Edward Taylor. AH
Angels take approaches, The. Some enter by root. The Angels. Paul
   Ramsey. CRP
Angel's Visit, The. Eugene Field. PWR
Angels walking under the palm trees. A Little Carol of the Virgin. Lope
   de Vega. PChr
Angelus inquit pastoribus. Now the Most High Is Born. James Ryman.
   MeEL
Angelus-Time near Dublin. William Bedell Stanford. NeIP
Anger. Charles *and* Mary Lamb. FaBoBe
Anger. Robert Creeley. NaP
Anger does this. Changing the Children. Maxine W. Kumin. ER
Anger in its time and place. Anger. Charles *and* Mary Lamb. FaBoBe
Anger Lay by Me All Night Long. Elizabeth Daryush. RB
Anger rises with metal filings, The. A Man All Grown Up Is Supposed
   To. Terry Stokes. AmPA
Anger so hot, so thick and clotted. Sarcophagus. Paul Mariani. BLA
Anger that breaks a man down into boys, The. César Vallejo, *tr. by*
   Robert Bly. EAS
Angered, may I be near a glass of water. Sapphics against Anger.
   Timothy Steele. SM
Anger's Freeing Power. Stevie Smith. OxBC
Anges Sont Blancs, Les. George Seferis, *tr. fr. Greek by* Edmund Keeley
   and Philip Sherrard. VMG
Anghiari is medieval, a sleeve sloping down. The Journey. James
   Wright. CAPP; NoAM; PoE
Angina Pectoris. W. R. Moses. LiTA
Angle-Land. David Jones. *Fr.* The Anathemata, III. NoAM
Angle of Geese. N. Scott Momaday. CDW; HATNAP; NOVW; QFR
Angle of Vision. Robert Rendall. OxBTC
Angler, The. Thomas Buchanan Read. AnAmPo
Anglers, The. Yekhi'el Mar, *tr. fr. Hebrew by* Bernhard Frank. MHeP
Angler's Invitation, The. Thomas Tod Stoddart. GN
Angler's Reveille, The. Henry Van Dyke. *Fr.* The Toiling of Felix.
   GN
Anglers Song, The, (*in* Izaak Walton's The Compleat Angler), *sel.*
   William Basse. OBS
   "As inward love breeds outward talk." SD
Angler's Song, The. John Dennys. *Fr.* The Secrets of Angling. ElL
Anglers Song (*in* Izaak Walton's The Compleat Angler), The. William
   Basse. OBS
Angler's Wish, An. Henry van Dyke. AA
Angles. Dixie Partridge. TSM
Anglican curate in want, An. Ronald Arbuthnott Knox. FaBoNo
Anglican firelight. The Other Voice. Tom Paulin. FaBCIP
Anglicized Utopia. W. S. Gilbert. OBSV
Angling. David Gullette. PPR
Anglo-American Chainpoem. *Unknown.* EAS
Anglo-Eire Vignette. Patric Stevenson. NeIP
Anglo-Irishman's Complaint, An. *Unknown.* AnIL
Anglo Saxon Street. Earle Birney. HeIP; NOBC
Anglo-Swiss, or a Day among the Alps, *sel.* William Plomer.
   "Away she flies and he follows." RR
Angola Question Mark. Langston Hughes. BPo; TTY
Angrier than my now occasional. A Preface to the Memoirs. James
   Merrill. NOBA
Angry Children. Carole Stewart. WS
Angry, is he, a wasp drinking water. Taigi, *tr. fr. Japanese by* Hiroaki
   Sato. *Fr.* Twenty-nine Hokku. FCEI
Angry Poet, The. Frank O'Connor, *tr. fr. Irish.* CIP
Angry young husband called Bicket, An. John Galsworthy. CenHV

Angst-ridden amorist, Fred, An. The Love Song of J. Alfred Prufrock. J. Walker. BXAP
Anguilla, Adina. A Sea-Chantey. Derek Walcott. RB
Anguish. Stéphane Mallarmé, tr. fr. French by Arthur Symons. AWP
Anguish of a naked body is more terrible, The. A Prayer to the Lord Ramakrishna. James Wright. NNaP
Anguish of the earth absolves our eyes, The. Absolution. Siegfried Sassoon. MMA
Anguish'd Doubt Broods over Eden, The. Christopher John Brennan. Fr. Lilith. PoAu-1
Anguished I remain. The Final Dance. Bernice Zamora. CCP
Anima. Diana O Hehir. NPGG
Anima Has a Predilection, The. Michael Harlow. Fr. Poem Then, for Love, I. PeNZ
Anima quodammodo omnia. Translation. Howard Nemerov. CRP
Animae Supersiti. Charles Spear. ATNZ
Animal. Max Eastman. FYAP
Animal Acts. Charles Simic. LCAP
Animal Alphabet, A. Edward Lear. RB
Animal bones and some mossy tent rings. Lament for the Dorsets. Alfred W. Purdy. NoAM; NoP
Animal Crackers. Christopher Morley. FaPON
Animal Fair. Unknown. AS, with music; AS; BLPA; BLPA; FaBoBe; FPL; MoShBr; NTCP; RHPC
Animal House, The. Sandy Brechin. Mes
Animal Howl, The. "M. J.", tr. fr. Polish by A. Leyeles. TrJP
Animal I wanted, the. Kenneth Patchen. VGW
Animal Kingdom. Sydney Clouts. PeSA
Animal Magnetism; the Pseudo-Philosopher Baffled. Laurence Hynes Halloran. NOEC
Animal Mood. Judah Leib Teller, tr. fr. Yiddish by Benjamin and Barbara Harshav. AYP
Animal Pictures. Lawrence Locke. GrPl
Animal runs, it passes, it dies, The. And it is the great cold. Death Rites II. Unknown, tr. by C. M. Bowra. TTY
Animal Song. Alfredo Giuliani, tr. fr. Italian by Lawrence R. Smith. NItP
Animal Song. Heather McHugh. AnAn; MAYP
Animal Store, The. Rachel Lyman Field. PDV
Animal That Drank Up Sound, The. William Stafford. VGW
Animal, Vegetable and Mineral. Louise Bogan. FM
Animal willows of November. The Willows of Massachusetts. Denise Levertov. NAAL-2
Animals, The. Stephen Berg. NaP
Animals, The. Josephine Jacobsen. GoYe
Animals. Robinson Jeffers. NU
Animals, The. Edwin Muir. CMoP; CRP; EBEV; HeIP; MoBrPo; NoP
Animals, The. Linda Pastan. ER
Animals, The. Charles Simic. GeTw
Animals. Walt Whitman. See Song of Myself: I think I could turn and live with animals.
Animals are coming, The. Songs to Welcome the Society of the Mystic Animals. Unknown, tr. by Jerome Rothenberg and Richard Johnny John. STP
Animals Are Passing from Our Lives. Philip Levine. CAPP; CoAP; NOBA; SM; TAP; TW
Animals are silent in the hold, The. Noah's Song. Evan Jones. PoAu-2
Animals' Arrival, The. Elizabeth Jennings. PBWP
Animals' Carol, The. Charles Causley. NAs
Animal's Crusade, The. H. H. ter Balkt, tr. fr. Dutch by Scott Rollins. DuIn
Animals do not sleep. At night. The Face of the Horse. Nikolai Alekseevich Zabolotsky, tr. by Daniel Weissbort. RB
Animals have no names. A Walk. Nikolai Alekseevich Zabolotsky, tr. by Daniel Weissbort. RB
Animals in That Country, The. Margaret Atwood. NoAM; NoP
Animals in the Ark, The. Unknown. Fr. The Deluge. ChTr; GBP
Animals live in darkness, The. World of Darkness. Robert Chatain. PoA
Animals own a fur world. Adults Only. William Stafford. FF
Animals Sick of the Plague, The. Marianne Moore, ad. fr. La Fontaine. InPS
Animals, that day, behaved with odd foreboding, The. The Tremors at Balvano. Norman Williams. KS
Animals that look at us like children, The. The Dying Animals. Gavin Ewart. OBD
Animals That Stand in Dreams, sel. Harley Elliott. Panda, The. NeAC
Animals we have seen, all marvelous creatures, The. The Park in Milan. William Jay Smith. CoAP

Animals will never know, The. If They Spoke. Mark Van Doren. ImOP
Animas, Las. Mario Luzi, tr. fr. Italian by I. L. Salomon. PFI
Animated glass that drawest nigh. Grievous Peril of a Gallant in Moth Metaphor. Luis de Sandoval y Zapata, tr. by Samuel Beckett. MexPo
Animula. T. S. Eliot. CRP; LiTB; NAs
Animula. W. S. Merwin. CAPP
Animula vagula blandula. Conrad Aiken. FaBoNo; OBAL
Animula Vagula, Blandula. Emperor Hadrian, tr. fr. Latin by Henry Vaughan. FaBoRV
Anishinabe children sing songs of sleep. For the Children. Thomas Peacock. VoR
Anishinabe Grandmothers. Gerald Vizenor. VoR
Anita and Giovanni. Henrietta Cordelia Ray. CBWP-3
Ank'hor Vat. Denis Devlin. BIrV; CIP; IPY; NOIV
Anklet Song. Unknown, tr. fr. Hawaiian by N. B. Emerson. WTO
Ankotarinya. Unknown, tr. fr. Aranda by T. G. H. Strehlow. CBAP
Ann and the Fairy Song. Walter de la Mare. Fr. A Child's Day. FaBV
Ann, Ann!/ Come! quick as you can! Alas, Alack! Walter de la Mare. FaPON; OxBChV
Ann Eleanor, a child of ten. A Small Elegy. Richard Snyder. PCP
Ann stood and watched the combers race to shore. Andrew Merkel. Fr. Tallahassee. CaP
Anna. Burns. TrGrPo
Anna. Joe Johnson. CNA
Anna Elise. Unknown. OxNR
Anna Livia Plurabelle. William Rossa Cole. Fr. A Mini-Samizdat of New River Rhymes. SoTCo
Anna Perenna, sel. Lucio Piccolo, tr. fr. Italian by Charles Tomlinson. Landscape. PFI
Anna Playing in a Graveyard. Caroline Gilman. OBCA
Annabel Lee. Poe. AA; AiP; AmPP; AnAmPo; AWP; BeLS; BLPA; CH; DL; FaFP; FaPON; FPL; HeIP; LiTA; NAAL-1; NOBA; NoP; OBCA; OnMSP; OPOP; OxBA; PrIm; TAP; TrGrPo; WBLP
Annales, sel. Quintus Ennius, tr. fr. Latin by John Wight. Like a Shower of Rain. WaaP
Annan Water ("Annan's Water's waiding deep"). Unknown. CH
Anne. Lizette Woodworth Reese. AA
Anne and the Peacock. Noel Welch. FF
Anne Boleyn. Eloise Bibb. CBWP-4
Anne Hutchinson's Exile. Edward Everett Hale. PAH
Anne Rutledge. Edgar Lee Masters. Fr. Spoon River Anthology. AmFN; CMoP; FaFP; HAP; LiTA; LiTM; MoAmPo; MoP; NoAM; NOBA; NoBA; OFD; OHFP; OxBA; TrGrPo
Anne says she dreams sometimes—and so do I. Silent Hill. Zilpha Keatley Snyder. WSC
Annemarie Fischer: Portrait of Robbert. Jan Kuijper, tr. fr. Dutch by Jacob Lowland. DuIn
Annette came through the meadows. Henrietta Cordelia Ray. CBWP-3
Annette Myers; or, A Murder in St. James's Park. Unknown. OxBoLi
Annex no next time or anxiety or brood or bid. Recommend. Jackson MacLow. LP
Anniad, The. Gwendolyn Brooks. BlSi
Annie. Guillaume Apollinaire, tr. fr. French by William Meredith. RHTwFP
Annie and Rhoda, sisters twain. The Sisters. Whittier. AWP
Annie and Willie's Prayer. Sophia P. Snow. BeLS; BLPA
Annie Bolanny. Unknown. ChTr
Annie Died the Other Day. E. E. Cummings. ErPo
Annie Laurie. William Douglas, revised by Lady Jane Scott. FaBoBe; FaBV; FaFP; GN; WBLP
Annie, my first-born, gentle child. To Annie. Mary E. Tucker. CBWP-1
Annihilation. Conrad Aiken. GBL; MoAB; MoAmPo
Annihilation of Nothing, The. Thom Gunn. NePoEA-2
Anniversary, The. William Dickey. GOYP
Anniversary [or The Anniversarie], The. John Donne. BoLoP; HAP; HoPM; JCP; LiTB; MeLP; MePo; NOBE; NoP; OAEL-1; OBS; SeCP; SeCV-1; WeW
Anniversary. Odysseus Elytis, tr. fr. Greek by Edmund Keeley and Philip Sherrard. VMG
Anniversary, An. Thomas Hardy. OxBTC
Anniversary. Heine, tr. fr. German by Alistair Elliot. OBD
Anniversary. Ted Kooser. SM
Anniversary. Richmond Lattimore. NYBP
Anniversary. Giancarlo Majorino, tr. fr. Italian by Lawrence R. Smith. NItP
Anniversary, The. Roberta Spear. MAYP
Anniversary. John Wain. NePoEA-2; TwCP

Anniversary. Daniel Weissbort. VWA
Anniversary Approaches, An; of the Birth of God. David Wright. *Fr.* On the Margin. NAs
Anniversary of Death, An. John Wieners. PoM
Anniversary of the Air. Michael Waters. NAmP
Anniversary on the Hymeneals of My Noble Kinsman, Thomas Stanley, Esquire, An. Richard Lovelace. CaPo
Anniversary Poem for the Cheyennes Who Fell at Sand Creek. Lance Henson. VoR
Anniverse; an Elegy, The. Henry King. JCP
Anno Aetatis XXXV. Emmanuel Hocquard, *tr. fr. French by* Michael Palmer. RHTwFP
Anno Domini, *sel.* Craig Raine.
    Birth. NAs
Anno 1829. Heine, *tr. fr. German by* Charles Stuart Calverley. AWP; OBVE
Annot Lyle's Song. Sir Walter Scott. *Fr.* The Legend of Montrose, *ch.* 6. EnRP
Annotations of Auschwitz, *sel.* Peter Porter.
    "London is full of chickens, on electric spits." OxBTC
Announced by all the trumpets of the sky. The Snow-Storm. Emerson. AA; AmPP; AnAmPo; BLPL; BoNaP; FaBoBe; GN; LiTA; NAAL-1; NOBA; NoP; OHFP; OxBA; PoE; PoEL-4; PoLF; Prf; TAP; TrGrPo; UnPo; WiR
Announcer, The. Austin Straus. TSL
Annual Gaiety. Wallace Stevens. MoAB; MoAmPo
Annual Legend. Winfield Townley Scott. CoAP; LiTA; LiTM; WaP
Annul Wars. Rabbi Nahman of Bratzlav, *tr. fr. Hebrew by* Jacob Sloan. TrJP
Annunciation. John Donne. *Fr.* La Corona. TrCP
Annunciation, The. Edwin Muir. CMoP; CRP; NOCV
Annunciation, The. Amrita Pritam, *tr. fr. Punjabi by* Khushwant Singh *and* Krishna Gorowara. WPOW
Annunciation. Rainer Maria Rilke, *tr. fr. German by* James Blair Leishman. OBVE
Annunciation. Kay Smith. NIP
Annunciation, The. *Unknown.* MeEL
Annunciation over the Shepherds, *sel.* Rainer Maria Rilke, *tr. fr. German by* M. D. Herter Norton.
    "Look up, you men. Men there at the fire." PChr
Annunciations. Geoffrey Hill. NePoEA-2
Annus Mirabilis, *sels.* Dryden.
    "By viewing Nature, Natures hand-maid, Art." MOS
    Fire of London, The. ChTr
    Fourth Day's Battle, The. OBS
    Great Fire, The. FiP
    New London, The. FaBoCh; OBS
    (London.) SeCePo
    (London after the Great Fire, 1666.) NOBE
    "Now van to van the foremost squadrons meet." OBWP
    Sea Battle, The. FiP
    "Swell'd with our late successes on the foe." EBEV
    "Yet London, empress of the northern clime." NAEL-1
Annus Mirabilis. Philip Larkin. NBLV; NIP; NOBL; OBAL
Anonymous. Victor Hernandez Cruz. UL
Anonymous. John Banister Tabb. AA
Anonymous as cherubs. Richard Wilbur. *Fr.* Two Voices in a Meadow. NBLV; UnPo
    (Milkweed.) CRP
Anonymous days transact to know. The Word I Like White Paint Considered. James Sherry. LP
Anonymous Drawing. Donald Justice. CoAP; EyDe; HeIP; NePoEA-2
Anonymous—nor needs a name. Anonymous. John Banister Tabb. AA
Anonymous water can slide under the ground. Explanations. Lucille Clifton. GeTw
Another. Thomas Lovell Beddoes. Son
Another. Ellen Marie Bissert. PeHV
Another ("As loving hind. . ."). Anne Bradstreet. *See* Letter to Her Husband, Absent upon Public Employment, A ("as loving hind. ").
Another. Abraham Cowley, *after the Greek of* Anacreon. *See* Epicure ("Underneath this myrtle shade, The").
Another ("As I beheld a winters evening air"). Richard Lovelace. SeCP
Another ("The centaur, siren I forgo"). Richard Lovelace. CaPo; PoEL-3
Another. Matthew Prior. *See* Epigram: "Yes, every poet is a fool."
Another and another and. Theodore Weiss. DiPo
Another and another and another. James Henry. NOBVV
Another and the Same. Samuel Rogers. *Fr.* Human Life. OBNC

Another armored animal—scale. The Pangolin. Marianne Moore. HAP; NoAM; NOBA; PBWP
Another Birthday. Ben Jonson. *See* Ode to Sir William Sydney, on His Birth-Day.
Another Breed. Delmira Agustini, *tr. fr. Spanish by* Kate Flores. DMH
Another Canto. John Bingham Morton. FaBoPa
Another Catalogue Item. David Avidan, *tr. fr. Hebrew by* Warren Bargad *and* Stanley F. Chyet. *Fr.* Traveling in the City, 12. IP
Another Coast. David Wojahn. MAYP
Another Complaint of Lord Pierrot. Jules Laforgue, *tr. fr. French by* William Jay Smith. CT
Another conference year has passed. To the Conference. Mrs. Henry Linden. CBWP-4
Another cove of shale. On the Marginal Way. Richard Wilbur. CoAP; NOBA
Another dawn, leaden. Words. Philip Levine. VWA
Another Day. Isabella Maria Brown. PoNe
Another day drags its obscenities. My Friends, This Storm. Kizito Z. Muchemwa. WMBCH
Another day let slip! Its hours have run. The Wasted Day. Robert Fuller Murray. EBVV
Another day of standstill heat. Sheridan. Robert Lowell. DiL
Another Death. D. E. Borrell. FF
Another dreadful tale of woe as I will here unfold. Annette Myers; or, A Murder in St. James's Park. *Unknown.* OxBoLi
Another Easter. John Ridland. SM
Another Epitaph on an Army of Mercenaries. "Hugh MacDiarmid." InPK; MoP; NAEL-2; NIP; NoAM; OBWP; RB
Another [Epitaph on the Lady Mary Villiers]. Thomas Carew. CaPo; SeCV-1
Another evening we sprawled about discussing. Charles on Fire. James Merrill. CAPP
Another Face. Ray A. Young Bear. CDW
Another for the Briar Rose. William Morris. NOBVV
Another four I've left yet to bring on. The Four Seasons of the Year. Anne Bradstreet. SCAP
Another Full Moon. Ruth Fainlight. BrRo
Another Grace for a Child. Robert Herrick. *See* Grace for a Child.
Another guest that winter night. Prophetess. Whittier. *Fr.* Snow-bound; a Winter Idyl. AA
Another high jumper. A Kind of Thanks. Joseph C. Fischer. *Fr.* From the XXIII Summer Olympics, the Poet as Report, XVI. TSL
Another hill town. Hotel Paradiso e Commerciale. John Malcolm Brinnin. NYBP; TwCP
Another. In Defence of Their Inconstancie. Ben Jonson. *See* In the Person of Womankind (In Defense of Their Inconstancy).
Another Kind of Burning. Ruth Fox. NYBP
Another knight smote Saint Thomas in that self wound. Becket's Diadem. *Unknown.* ACP
Another Ladyes Exception Present at the Hearing. Ben Jonson. *Fr.* A Celebration of Charis in Ten Lyrick Peeces. SeCP
Another land, another age, another self. Covered Bridge. Robert Penn Warren. AiP
Another Letter to Lord Byron. David R. Slavitt. SM
Another Life. Frank Bidart. HCAP
Another Life. Derek Walcott. PBCV
Another Lineage. Delmira Agustini, *tr. fr. Spanish by* Perry Higman. LPSS
Another look like his mixed me up again. Yosano Akiko, *tr. fr. Japanese by* Hiroaki Sato. *Fr.* Thirty-nine Tanka. FCEI
Another Night in the Ruins. Galway Kinnell. CoAP
Another Night on the Porch Swing. Cathleen Quirk. NMM
Another November. Stanley Plumly. AnAn; LCAP
Another Ode to the North-East Wind. *Unknown.* Par
Another of Seafarers, Describing Evil Fortune. *Unknown.* OxBSS
Another of the placid beauties! Natalya Nikolayevna Goncharov. Don Coles. NOBC
Another of the Same. Sir Walter Ralegh. SiPS
Another Old Song. Barney Bush. STE
Another Poem about the Madness of Women. Tom Wayman. NOBC
Another Poem for Me. Etheridge Knight. NNaP
Another Poem on Absalom. Nathan Yonathan, *tr. fr. Hebrew by* Fichard Flantz. VWA
Another Prince Is Born. Adrian Mitchell. NAs
Another Reading. Nicki Jackowska. DT
Another Reply to "In Flanders Fields." J. A Armstrong. BLPA
Another road. It seems sometimes. The Idiot. Keith Wilson. Psk
Another round of farting. Issa, *tr. fr. Japanese by* Hiroaki Sato. *Fr.* Forty-four Hokku. FCEI
Another Sarah. Anne Porter. TTTS

Another sate near him, whose harp of gold. Fenton Johnson. *Fr.* The Vision of Lazarus. BANP

Another season centers on this place. The Gourd Dancer. N. Scott Momaday. CDW; STE

Another September. Thomas Kinsella. BIrV; CIP; FaBCIP

Another shall hang from the gallows' height. *Unknown, tr. fr. Anglo-Saxon. Fr.* The Fortunes of Men. PBBP

Another shout from the wharves. Hilda Doolittle ("H. D."). *Fr.* Helen in Egypt. NOBA

Another side, umbrageous grots and caves. Milton. *Fr.* Paradise Lost, *Bk.* IV, *ll.* 257–294. (Paradise.) OBS

Another Small Town in Georgia. Bin Ramke. NAmP

Another Song. Beaumont *and* Fletcher. *See* Knight of the Burning Pestle. The: Jillian of Berry.

Another Song. Donald Justice. NePoEA-2; VGW

Another Song. William Ross. GoTS

Another Song about That Same Dead Person or Mole—Whichever it Was. *Unknown, tr. fr. Seneca Indian by* Jerome Rothenberg *and* Richard Johnny John. STP

Another Song of the Same Woman, to Some Partridges, Sent to Her Alive. Florencia del Pinar, *tr. fr. Spanish by* Julie Allen. BoWoP

Another Spirit Advances. Jules Romains, *tr. fr. French by* Joseph T. Shipley. AWP

Another Spring, Another Year. Anja Vammelvuo, *tr. fr. Finnish by* Aili Jarvenpa. SOP

Another Sunday Morning. Derek Mahon. CIP

Another Sunday Morning. Carter Revard. VoR

Another Sunday morning comes. Wendell Berry. *Fr.* Sabbaths, I. BLA

Another Testimony. Dan Pagis, *tr. fr. Hebrew by* Warren Bargad *and* Stanley F. Chyet. IP

Another Time. W. H. Auden. OxBA

Another Time. Ory Bernstein, *tr. fr. Hebrew by* Bernhard Frank. MHeP

Another to the Maids. Robert Herrick. OHIP

Another to the Same. Horace. *See* Odes: I, 5. "What slender youth bedewed with liquid odours" ("Quis multa gracilis").

Another to Urania. Benjamin Colman. SCAP

Another transparent skin has grown. Felix Pollak. *Fr.* Tunnel Visions, IV. TSM

Another Tribute to Wyatt. Earl of Surrey. *See* In the rude age when seyence was not so rife.

Another True Maid. Matthew Prior. FaBoEE

Another turn around the sun. Pheasant. Nishiwaki Junzaburo, *tr. by* Hiroaki Sato. FCEI

Another uncle/ was a pathological liar. Family 8. Lyn Lifshin. NeAC

Another Voice. Paolo Volponi, *tr. fr. Italian by* Lawrence R. Smith. NItP

Another Way. Ambrose Bierce. AA

Another While. Morris Jacob Rosenfeld, *tr. fr. Yiddish.* TrJP

Another Woman. Rosemary Norman. DT

Another Year. Frances Ridley Havergal. *See* Another Year Is Dawning.

Another year! another deadly blow! November, 1806. Wordsworth. OBWP

Another year, another return. New Year. Alfred Corn. BAP

Another Year Come. W. S. Merwin. NYBP; OFD; PCP

Another year I enter. A New Year's Promise. *Unknown.* BLRP

Another Year Is Dawning. Frances Ridley Havergal. WBLP (Another Year.) BLRP

Another year it may betide. *Unknown.* HAP

Another year like a frail flower is bound. Written in Autumn. Thomas Cole. AiP

Another youthful advocate of truth and right has gone. To the Memory of J. Horace Kimball. "Ada." BlSi

Anseo. Paul Muldoon. CIP; FaBoPV

An Answer. Ahmad al-Mushari al-Udwani, *tr. fr. Arabic by* Hilary Kilpatrick *and* Charles Doria. MAP

Answer. Leah Goldberg, *tr. fr. Hebrew by* Robert Friend. VWA

Answer, The. George Herbert. FaBoRV; TEP

Answer, The. Robinson Jeffers. CMoP; GoYe

Answer, The. John Montague. CIP; TIRV

Answer, The. Sara Teasdale. PoA

Answer, The. Chuck Wachtel. UL

Answer for Hope. Richard Crashaw. *See* Dear hope! earth's dowry, & heav'ns debt!.

Answer in Verse for Someone Studying in Ingolst, An, *sels.* Argula von Grumbach, *tr. fr. German by* Susan L. Cocalis. DMG
Argula's Answer.
Verses against Argula.

Answer Is, The. Hugues C. Pernath, *tr. fr. Dutch by* James S. Holmes. DuIn

Answer Me. Adah Isaacs Menken. CBWP-1

Answer of Mr. Waller's Painter to His Many New Advisers, The. *Unknown.* APAS

Answer that ye made to me, my dear, The. Sir Thomas Wyatt. SiPS

Answer to a Child's Question. Samuel Taylor Coleridge. EnRP; FaBoBe; OxBChV

Answer to a Lady Advising Me to Retirement, An. Lady Mary Wortley Montagu. TEP

Answer to a Man's Question, An, "What Can I Do about Women's Liberation?" Susan Griffin. GLP

Answer to All Problems, The. Marge Piercy. SoTCo

Answer to Another Persuading a Lady to Marriage, An. Katherine Philips. HAP; WeW
(To One Persuading a Lady to Marriage.) OBEV

Answer to Cloe [*or* Chloe] Jealous. Matthew Prior. NOBE; SeCePo
(Better Answer to Cloe [*or* Chloe] Jealous, A.) AWP; ELP; NAEL-1; NOEC; PoEL-3

Answer to Marlowe. Sir Walter Ralegh. *See* If all the world and love were young.

Answer to – – –'s Professions of Affection. Byron. OxBSP

Answer to the Parson, An. Blake. FaBoEE; NBLV; OxBoLi

Answer to Thomas Barry, An. Pierce Fitzgerald, *tr. fr. Irish by* Joan Keefe. TIRV

Answer to Voznesensky and Evtushenko. Frank O'Hara. NNaP; PoM

Answer to Yo/ Question. Sonia Sanchez. BPo

Answer was, The. On the Way to Language. Michael Palmer. LP; NPGG

Answered Prayers. Ella Wheeler Wilcox. PWR

Answerers. William Stafford. CAPP

Answering Dance. William Pitt Root. MAYP

Answering Li Ying Who Showed Me His Poems about Summer Fishing. Yü Hsüan-chi, *tr. fr. Chinese.* BoWoP, *tr. by* Geoffrey Waters

Answers. Elizabeth Jennings. NePoEA; OxBSP; OxBTC

Answers flag like wilted lettuce. Questions & Answers. A. L. Lazarus. SoTCo

Ant, The. Richard Lovelace. CaPo

Ant, The. ("Ant has made himself illustrious, The"). Ogden Nash. FaBV; OBAL

Ant-Heap, The. A. C. Benson. EBVV

Ant-Hills. "Marian Douglas." OBCA

Ant on the tablecloth, An. Departmental. Robert Frost. GoYe; HeIP; HoPM; MoAB; MoAmPo; NAAL-2; NOBA; NOBL; OBAL; SoSe

Ant-seething city, city full of dreams. The Seven Old Men. Baudelaire, *tr. by* Roy Campbell. OBVE

Ant Sun, The. Christopher Middleton. *Fr.* Herman Moon's Hourbook. NePoEA-2

Ant Trap, The. Joe Rosenblatt. NOBC

Ant Village, The. Marion Edward *and* Dorothy Grider. FaPON

Antaeus; a Fragment. Wilfred Owen. PeHV

Antaeus (The Prodigious Builders). Roger Dutcher. BWV

Antarctic Muse, The. Thomas Perry. OBTV

Antarctica. Ronald Albert Simpson. CBAP

Ante-bellum Negro prayed, The. Must Be Freed. Lizelia Augusta Jenkins Moorer. CBWP-3

Ante-Bellum Sermon, An. Paul Laurence Dunbar. BPo

Ante Mortem. Robinson Jeffers. MoAmPo

Ante Mortem. Syd Scroggie. PoSH

Ante-natal Dream. Patrick Kavanagh. NAs

Antenora. "Hugh MacDiarmid." SeCePo

Anteroom: Geneva. Denis Devlin. CIP

Anteroom was just a modern lobby, The. In Hell. Mark Jarman. BLA

Anterotics. William Ernest Henley. *Fr.* In Hospital, XXVI. BrPo

Anthea bade me tie her shoe. The Shoe-tying. Robert Herrick. CaPo

Anthem: "America, if you were a basketball court." Stephen Vincent. ASP

Anthem: "Let us praise our Maker, with true passion extol Him." W. H. Auden. NOCV

Anthem: "Our bones will all be built into the runway." Gavin Ewart. NPo

Anthem for Doomed Youth. Wilfred Owen. BrPo; ChTr; CMoP; CMOP; EBEV; FaBoMo; FaBoRV; FaFP; GTBS-P; HAP; HeIP; HoPM; InPK; InPS; LiTM; MoAB; MoBrPo; MoP; NAEL-2; NoAM; NOBE; NoP; OAEL-2; OBEV; OBWP; OxBTC; PoE; PPP; SCV; SeCePo; Son; SoSe; TrGrPo; WaP; WeW

Anthologistics. Arthur Guiterman. NBLV

Anthology. Manuel Bandeira, *tr. fr. Portuguese by* Jean R. Longland. ATCBP

Anthology of Nouns. Parker Tyler. PoA

Anthology Poem. Petra von Morstein, *tr. by* Rosemarie Waldrop. BoWoP

Anthracite. Bartolo Cattafi, *tr. fr. Italian by* Lawrence R. Smith. NItP
Anthropology. Anselm Hollo. UL
Anthropology: Cricket at Kano. Stewart Brown. OBTV
Anthropophagites See a Sign on NC Highway 177 That Looks like Heaven, The. Jonathan Williams. OBAL
Anthropos apteros for days. The Labyrinth. W. H. Auden. LiTA
Anti-aircraft seen from a certain distance. Dam Neck, Virginia. Richard Eberhart. LiTA; MoAB; WaP
Anti Apart Hate Art. Michelle T. Clinton. AIW
Anti-Cupid. Catharina Regina von Greiffenberg, *tr. fr. German by* Susan L. Cocalis *and* Gerlinde Geiger. DMG
Anti-Love Poems. Elizabeth Brewster. NOBC
Anti-Memoirs. Simon Schuchat. UL
Anti-Nostalgia. Henryk Grynberg, *tr. fr. Polish by* Isaac Komem. VWA
Anti-Racist Person. Marsha Prescod. AIW
Anti-Semanticist, The. Everett Hoagland. BPo
Anti-Short Story. Rae Armantrout. IAT
Antichrist. Edwin Muir. EaLo
Antichrist, or the Reunion of Christendom; an Ode. G. K. Chesterton. FaBoCo; NOBE; NOBL; OBSV; SeCePo
Antichrist, playing his lissome flute and merry. Armageddon. John Crowe Ransom. LiTA
Anticipation. Emily Brontë. OBNC
Anticipation. Lord De Tabley. ELP
Anticipation. Joseph Tusiani. GoYe
Anticipation of Sharks. Diane Wakoski. MAT
Antigone. Sophocles, *tr. fr. Greek by* Robert Fagles. NAWM-1
Antigone ("My own flesh and blood—"). Sophocles, *tr. fr. Greek.* NAWM-1, *tr. by* Robert Fagles.
  Thebes of the Seven Gates, *sel. Tr. by* Dudley Fitts *and* Robert Fitzgerald. WaaP
Antigone and Oedipus. Henrietta Cordelia Ray. BlSi; CBWP-3
Antigone I. Herbert Martin. PoBA
Antigone VI. Herbert Martin. PoBA
Antigonish. Hughes Mearns. *See* Little Man Who Wasn't There, The.
Antipastoral Memory of One Summer, An. Dave Smith. MAYP; MT
Antipathy. Rowland Watkyns, *after the Latin of* Martial. FaBoEE
Antiphonal Hymn in Praise of Inanna. Enheduanna, *tr. fr. Sumerian.* BoWoP, *ad. by* Aliki *and* Willis Barnstone.
Antiplatonick, The. John Cleveland. MePo; SeCP
Antiquary, The. Joseph Campbell. OxBTC
Antiquary. John Donne. EBEV; FF
Antiquary, The, *sels.* Sir Walter Scott.
  "Herring loves the merry moonlight, The." *Fr.* 40. FaBoCh, 1 *st..*
    Red Harlaw. *Fr. ch.* 40. OxBB
  Why Sit'st Thou by That Ruin'd Hall. *Fr. ch.* 10. EnRP
Antique Harvesters. John Crowe Ransom. MoAB; MoAmPo; NoP; OxBA
Antique Indian should be Henry James, The. American Plan. John Malcolm Brinnin. GOA
Antique Shop. Carl Carmer. FaPON
Antique Shop in New York. Karl Wawra, *tr. fr. German by* Beth Bjorklund. CoAuP
Antiques. Walter de la Mare. PoA
Antiques fill their house. Wormrunner's Curse. Sonya Dorman. BWV
Antiquity of Freedom, The. Bryant. AA
Antiseptic Baby and the Prophylactic Pup, The. Strictly Germ-proof. Arthur Guiterman. BLPA; TrJP
Antithin. Sándor Weöres, *tr. fr. Hungarian by* Richard Lourie. MHuP
Antlered forests, the. The. Ank'hor Vat. Denis Devlin. BIrV; CIP; IPY; NOIV
Antonina. Felix Mnthali. WMBCH
Antonio. Laura Elizabeth Richards. MoShBr; OBCA; PDV; RHPC
Antonius, *sel.* Countess of Pembroke.
  Of Death. EIL
Antonville. Peter Seaton. LP
Antony and Cleopatra. Henri Coulette. NePoEA
Antony and Cleopatra. William Haines Lytle. *See* I am dying, Egypt, dying.
Antony and Cleopatra. Shakespeare.
  Sels.
  "Barge she sat in, like a burnish'd throne, The." *Fr.* II, ii. SCV
    (Cleopatra.) LiTB
    (Cleopatra's Barge.) TrGrPo
  Cleopatra's Lament. *Fr.* V, ii. UnPo
  Death of Antony. *Fr.* IV, xv. FiP
  Death of Cleopatra. *Fr.* V, ii. FiP
    (Cleopatra's Death.) TrGrPo
    (Immortal Longings.) FaBoRV
  Drinking Song, A. *Fr.* II, vii. OBSC

"Eros, thou yet behold'st me?." *Fr.* IV, xiv. EBEV
"Miserable change now at my end, The." *Fr.* IV, xiii. EBEV
"My desolation does begin to make." *Fr.* V, ii. OBD
Antony to Cleopatra. William Haines Lytle. AA; BeLS
Antony's Oration [over Caesar's Body]. Shakespeare. *Fr.* Julius Caesar, III, iii. LiTB; TrGrPo
    (Mark Antony Addresses the Mob.) FaPoR
Antrim. Robinson Jeffers. BIrV; NOBA; VGW
Ants. Mary Ann Hoberman. RAR
Ants. Ramón López Velarde, *tr. fr. Spanish by* Samuel Beckett. MexPo
Ants. Yusuf al-Sa'igh, *tr. fr. Arabic by* Diana Der Hovanessian *with* Salma Khadra Jayyusi. MAP
Ants, Although Admirable Are Awfully Aggravating. Walter Rollin Brooks. RHPC
Ants and Others. Adrien Stoutenburg. FYAP; NYBP
Ants and the Sun. Khalil Khouri, *tr. fr. Arabic by* Sharif Elmusa *and* Christopher Middleton. MAP
Ants are walking under the ground, The. The People. Elizabeth Madox Roberts. GoJo; RHPC
Ants at the Olympics, The. Richard Digance. RHPC
Ants gnaw his flesh. The Arab Refugee. Abdul Wahab al-Bayati, *tr. by* Abdullah al-Udhari. MPAW
Ants Live Here. Lilian Moore. RAR
Ants look up as I trot by. Dog's Song. Robert Wallace. TDD
Ants stopped coming. Ozaki Hosai, *tr. fr. Japanese by* Hiroaki Sato. *Fr.* One Hundred Haiku in Free Form. FCEI
Antwerp and Bruges. Dante Gabriel Rossetti. OBTV
Antwerp: Musée Des Beaux-Arts. Alan Ross. NYBP
Antwerp to Ghent. Dante Gabriel Rossetti. *Fr.* A Trip to Paris and Belgium. OBTV
Anvil—God's Word, The. John Clifford. BLPA
Anxious bird in the lush, The. The Age of Reason. Jorie Graham. NPGG
Anxious Dead, The. John McCrae. OHIP
Anxious Farmer, The. Burges Johnson. BoNaP
Anxiously chirps the cicada. *Unknown, tr. by* Arthur Waley. BoS
Any clear thing that blinds us with surprise. Fishnet. Robert Lowell. HCAP
Any Complaints? Vernon Scannell. OxBTC
Any country is only a way of failing. Considerations. David Helwig. NOBC
Any fool knows a Br'er in a rocker. Br'er Sterling and the Rocker. Michael S. S. Harper. LCAP
Any man makin' a living by punchin' cows. The Dying Times. Ross Knox. CowP
Any Man to His Secretary. Hilary Corke. ErPo
Any Man's Advice to His Son. Kenneth Fearing. CMoP
Any moment now I'll knock my master down. Keisen, *tr. by* Lucien Stryk *and* Takashi Ikemoto. ZPCJ
Any niche is my college. A Hedge Schoolmaster. Padraic Fallon. CIP
Any of the several names. Eulogy for Populations. Ron Welburn. PoBA
Any Part of Piggy. Noel Coward. NBLV
Any point in that wood. The Plantation. Seamus Heaney. FaBCIP
Any Saint. Francis Thompson. MoBrPo
Any Soul to Any Body. Cosmo Monkhouse. NOBVV
Any Time. William Stafford. LCAP
Any Time, What May Hit You. T. R. Hummer. MAYP
Any Wife or Husband. Carol Haynes. BLPA
Any Wife to Any Husband. Robert Browning. OBNC
Anyone could hunt the old dog. The One to Grieve. Rudy Thomas. GOYP
Anyone Lived in a Pretty How Town. E. E. Cummings. CMoP; FPL; HAP; InPK; LiTA; LiTM; MoAB; MoAmPo; NAAL-2; NIP; NiP; NOBA; NoP; PoA; PrIm; RB; TAP; TwCP; VGW; WeW
Anyone who has ever lived. Why I Can't Write My Autobiography. Rodger Kamenetz. VWA
Anyone who swallows foolishly. Pons de Capdueill, *tr. by* Paul Blackburn. Pro
Anyone with quiet pace who. Walking West. William Stafford. RB
Anything Goes. Cole Porter. OBAL
Anything that promises good. First Hymn. John Gill. NeAC
Anzac Ceremony. Kendrick Smithyman. ATNZ
Anzac Cove. Leon Gellert. PoAu-1
Aodh Ruadh O'Domhnaill. Thomas MacGreevy. CIP; OBMV
Aoibhinn, A Leabhráin, Do Thriall. *Unknown, tr. fr. Irish by* Flann O'Brien. BIrV
Apart/ meant —licking stick good golly. If. Bruce Andrews. *Fr.* I Guess Work the Time Up. IAT
Apart from my sisters, estranged. Cinderella. Olga Broumas. InPK

Apart from Oneself. Alejandra Pizarnik, *tr. fr. Spanish by* Yishai Tobin. VWA

Apart, thank Heaven, from all to do. The Owl. Walter de la Mare. OxBSP

Apartment Cats. Thom Gunn. GrPl

Apartment House. Gerald Raftery. AmFN

Apathy. Eeva-Liisa Manner, *tr. fr. Finnish by* Jaakko A. Ahokas. *Fr.* Cambrian, VI. OV

Ape, Lion, Fox and Ass, An. *Unknown.* OBET

Apelles' Song. John Lyly. *See* Alexander and Campaspe: Cupid and my Campaspe played.

Apeneck Sweeney spread his knees. Sweeney among the Nightingales. T. S. Eliot. AmPP; AnAmPo; CMoP; FaBoMo; HAP; HeIP; InvP; LiTA; LiTM; MoP; NAAL-2; NAEL-2; NoAM; NOBA; NOBE; NoP; OBMV; OxBA; PPP; WeW

Apes yawn and adore their fleas in the sun, The. The Jaguar. Ted Hughes. LiTM

Apex. Nate Salsbury. NBLV

Aphorism. "Novalis," *tr. fr. German by* Charles E. Passage. NU

Aphrodisiac, The. Medbh McGuckian. FaBCIP

Aphrodite!/ Aphrodite of the blue sleep. Blue Sleep. Winifred Bryher. PoA

Aphrodite,/ my Cape Town lady. To Like, to Love. Anne Sexton. AnAn

Apis! the men you boxed with, grateful that you. The World's Worst Boxer. Lucilius, *tr. by* Humbert Wolfe. SD

Apocalypse. D. J. Enright. OBSV

Apocalypse. Jean Lipkin. VWA

Apocalypse. Francis Ernest Kobina Parkes. PBA

Apocalypse and Resurrection. John Clifford Bayliss. EAS

Apocrypha. Stanley Moss. VWA

Apocrypha. János Pilinszky, *tr. fr. Hungarian.* FOC, *tr. by* Jascha Kessler; MHuP, *tr. by* Ted Hughes.

Apocrypha. Charles Simic. AnAn

Apollinaire thought/ he had. Opinions about the Painter de Chirico. Wieland Schmied, *tr. by* Beth Bjorklund. CoAuP

Apollo. James Wright. LCAP

Apollo 8. John Berryman. AnAn

Apollo and Daphne. William Robert Rodgers. ErPo; LiTB

Apollo and Daphne, *sel.* Paul Whitehead.
  Hunting Song. OxBoLi

Apollo and Daphne. Yvor Winters. Son

Apollo and Marsyas. Zbigniew Herbert, *tr. fr. Polish by* Czeslaw Milosz. PwPP

Apollo kept my father's sheep. A Daughter of Admetus. T. Sturge Moore. FaBoTw

Apollo now, Sol's carman, drives his stud. Evening; an Elegy. Horace Smith. BXAP

Apollo sings, his harpe resounds; give roome. Upon Master Fletcher's Incomparable Playes. Robert Herrick. OBS

Apollo spacecraft one hundred miles high. Heartland. Paul Engle. WCI

Apollo walks the deep roads back in the hills. Translation into the Original. Jack Gilbert. NPGG

Apollyonists, The, *sel.* Phineas Fletcher.
  Cambridge and the Cam. FaBoPP

Apologia. Jean Garrigue. LiTA

Apologia Addressed to Ireland in the Coming Days. W. B. Yeats. *See* Know that I would accounted be.

Apologia pro Poemate Meo. Wilfred Owen. FaBoRV; LiTM; MoAB; MoBrPo; NAEL-2

Apologia Pro Vita. June Siegel. SoTCo

Apologia Pro Vita Sua. A. R. Ammons. CAPP; HCAP; NOBA

Apologia Pro Vita Sua. Samuel Taylor Coleridge. EnRP; OxBSP

Apologia pro, Vita Sua. Pope. *Fr.* Epistle to Dr. Arbuthnot. NOBE

Apologia pro Vita Sua. Sedulius Scottus, *tr. fr. Latin by* Helen Waddell. BIrV

Apologie for Having Loved Before, An. Edmund Waller. MePo

Apologist's Evening Prayer, The. C. S. Lewis. TrCP

Apologizing for going to. The No More Apologizing the No More Little Laughing Blues. Lyn Lifshin. ER

Apologue. Tony Connor. BoLoP

Apology. Anthony Cronin. CIP

Apology, The. Emerson. AmPP; AnAmPo

Apology. Amiq Hanafi, *tr. fr. Urdu by* Mahmood Jamal. PBMUP

Apology. Vassar Miller. NePoEA

Apology, An. William Morris. *Fr.* The Earthly Paradise. AWP; EBVV; LiTB; NAEL-2; NoP; OAEL-2; OBNC

Apology. Duane Niatum. HATNAP

Apology, An. Diane Wakoski. TAP

Apology. Richard Wilbur. Psk

Apology for a Short Speech, An. Abdul Wahab al-Bayati, *tr. fr. Arabic by* Abdullah al-Udhari. MPAW

Apology for Actors, An, *sel.* Thomas Heywood.
  Author to His Booke, The. OBS

Apology for Apostasy? Etheridge Knight. NeAC

Apology for Bad Dreams. Robinson Jeffers. AmPP; LiTA; MoAB; MoAmPo; NOBA; OxBA

Apology for the Foregoing Hymn, An. Richard Crashaw. JCP

Apology for the Revival of Christian Architecture in England, An, *sels.* Geoffrey Hill.
  Idylls of the King. *Fr.* 11. FaBoRV; NoAM; PoE
  Laurel Axe, The. *Fr.* 9. NAEL-2; NoAM; NoP; PoE
  Quaint Mazes. *Fr.* 1. NoAM

Apology for Understatement. John Wain. NePoEA-2; OxBTC

Apology of Genius. Mina Loy. QFR

Apology of the Young Scientists. Celia Dimmette. GoYe

Apology: Why Do I Write Today? William Carlos Williams. OxBA

Apon the midsummer evin, mirriest of nichtis. The Tretis of the Tua Mariit Wemen and the Wedo. William Dunbar. GoTS; OxBS

Apopemptic Hymn. Dorothy Auchterlonie. PoAu-2

Apostasy. Aus of Kuraiza, *tr. fr. Arabic by* Hartwig Hirschfeld. TrJP

Apostasy of One and But One Lady, The. Richard Lovelace. CaPo

Apostate, The. A. E. Coppard. OBMV

Apostles of the hidden sun. The Last Supper. Oscar Williams. FaFP; LiTA; LiTM

Apostrophe to a Dead Friend. Maxine W. Kumin. CAPP

Apostrophe to the Island of Cuba. James Gates Percival. PAH

Apostrophe to the Ocean. Byron. *See* Childe Harold's Pilgrimage: Ocean, The.

Apostrophe to the Parret. E. H. Burrington. FaBoPP

Apothegms and Counsels. Colette Inez. EOEF

Apotheosis. Jules Laforgue, *tr. fr. French by* William Jay Smith. CT

Appalachian Convalescence. Robert Conquest. OxBC

Appalachian Front. Robert Lewis Weeks. AmFN; NYBP

Apparel of green woods and meadows gay. On Revisiting Cintra after the Death of Catarina. Luis de Camões, *tr. by* Richard Garnett. AWP

Apparelled as a Paynim in pilgrim's wise. The Palmer. William Langland. *Fr.* The Vision of Piers Plowman. ACP

Apparent Failure. Robert Browning. NAEL-2; NOBE

Apparently/ You hate most of the people. Longterm Hatred. David Avidan, *tr. by* Warren Bargad *and* Stanley F. Chyet. IP

Apparently insignificant, An. The Quarry. László Kálnoky, *tr. by* Jascha Kessler. FOC

Apparently with no surprise. Emily Dickinson. AmPP; NAAL-1; NoP; PPP; SoSe; TrGrPo

Apparition, The. John Donne. EnLoPo; GBL; HeIP; MePo; NAEL-1; NAWM-1; NOBE; NOBL; OAEL-1; OBD; OBEV; OBS; PoE; SCV; SeCP; SeCV-1

Apparition. W. E. Henley. *Fr.* In Hospital, XXV. BrPo; TrGrPo

Apparition, The. Herman Melville. NoP

Apparition, The. Otto Orban, *tr. fr. Hungarian by* Edwin Morgan. MHuP

Apparition, The. Stephen Phillips. OBEV

Apparition of His Mistress[e] Calling Him to Elizium [*or* Elysium], The. Robert Herrick. CaPo; SeCP; SeCV-1

Apparition of these faces in the crowd, The. In a Station of the Metro. Ezra Pound. AmPP; HAP; HeIP; InPK; MoAB; MoAmPo; MoP; NAAL-2; NIP; NoAM; NOBA; NoP; OxBA; PoE; TAP; UnPo; VGW; WeW

Apparitions. Thomas Bailey Aldrich. AnAmPo

Apparitions, The. W. B. Yeats. CMoP; LiTM

Appeal, The. Kipling. OBD

Appeal. Noémia da Sousa, *tr. fr. Portuguese.* TTY, *tr. by* Dorothy Guedes *and* Phillippa Rumsey; WPOW, *tr. by* Alan Ryder

Appeal by Unemployed Ex-Service Men, An. *Unknown.* OBET

Appeal to Cats in the Business of Love, An. Thomas Flatman. EnLoPo; GBL; HAP

Appeal to Harold, The. H. C. Bunner. AA

Appeal to My Countrywomen, An. Frances E. W. Harper. BlSi

Appeal to the Moongod Nanna-Suen to Throw Out Lugalanne. Enheduanna, *tr. fr. Sumerian by* Aliki *and* Willis Barnstone. BoWoP

Appealing to the Imagination. Ad Zuiderent, *tr. fr. Dutch by* Scott Rollins. DuIn

Appear, O Mother, was the perpetual cry. Wilfred Watson. MoCV

Appear out of nowhere. Small Towns. Alejandro Murguía. FIA

Appearance. Norman H. Russell. STE

Appearance and Reality. John Hollander. OBAL

Appearances. Robert Browning. OxBSP

Appearances. Ben King. AnAmPo

Appendix to the Anniad. Gwendolyn Brooks. BlSi

Appetite, The. Yom Kippur: Fasting. Ruth Whitman. OFD

Appetite of Quiet Enchantment. Martin Seymour-Smith. NPo

Applauding youths laughed with young prostitutes. The Harlem Dancer. Claude McKay. BANP; BPo; FF; NoAM; Son; TAP

Applause and cheers for the opening. Salon Chronicle. Rigoberto Paredes, *tr. by* Walter Martínez. Vol

Applause flutters onto the open air. A Snapshot for Miss Bricka Who Lost in the Semi-final Round of the Pennsylvania Lawn Tennis Tournament. Robert Wallace. SD

Apple, The. Judah Halevi, *tr. fr. Hebrew by* Robert Mezey. UnAS

Apple, The. *at. to* Plato, *tr. fr. Greek.* WeW

Apple, The. Tadeusz Rozewicz, *tr. fr. Polish by* Czeslaw Milosz. PwPP

Apple, The. Ray Smith. TrCP

Apple a day, An. Health Food. *Unknown.* FaBoUs

Apple-Barrel of Johnny Appleseed, The. Vachel Lindsay. AmFN; OxBA

Apple Blight. Paul Zimmer. VGW

Apple Blossom. Louis MacNeice. RB

Apple-blossom, a great spread of it. And Where Do You Stand on the National Question. Tom Paulin. CIP; FaBCIP

Apple Blossoms. Henry Adams Parker. BoTP

Apple blossoms look like snow. A Comparison. John Farrar. FaPON

Apple Dumplings. Mary E. Tucker. CBWP-1

Apple Dumplings and a King, The. "Peter Pindar." OBSV

Apple Fell in the Night and a Wagon Stopped, An. James McMichael. PPR

Apple for the sea, marble narcissus flower, An. Mahmoud Darwish, *tr. fr. Arabic by* Lena Jayyusi *and* Christopher Middleton. *Fr.* Beirut. MAP

Apple Gathering, An. Christina Rossetti. NAEL-2; OBNC

Apple Harvest. Helen Leuty. BoTP

Apple Hell. Mark Van Doren. PoA

Apple Orchard in the Spring, An. William Martin. GN; PWR

Apple Peeler. Robert Francis. LCAP

Apple-pie, apple-pie. *Unknown.* OxNR

Apple Poem. Vernon Scannell. NPo

Apple Rhyme, The. Madeleine Nightingale. BoTP

Apple-Seed John. Lydia Maria Child. OHIP

Apple Song. Frances Frost. FaPON

Apple Tree, The. James Keir Baxter. OxBC

Apple-Tree, The. Brian Vrepont. PoAu-2

An Apple Tree and a Pig. Emyr Humphreys. OBWVE

Apple Trees, The. Louise Glück. HCAP

Apple Trees Apple Trees Apple Trees. Nelo Risi, *tr. fr. Italian by* Lawrence R. Smith. NItP

Apple Trees at Olema, The. Robert Hass. NAmP; NPGG

Apple Wassail. *Unknown.* OBET

Apples. Donald Hall. LCAP

Apples. Shirley Kaufman. NMM

Apples. Swift. *Fr.* Verses for Fruitwomen. AnYI

Apples. Michael Waters. GeTw

Apples. Itamar Ya'oz-kest, *tr. fr. Hebrew by* Bernhard Frank. MHeP

Apples are seasoned, The. Apple Song. Frances Frost. FaPON

Apples Be Ripe. *Unknown.* GBP

Apples, bright on the leafless bough. Apple Hell. Mark Van Doren. PoA

Apples in New Hampshire. Marie Emilie Gilchrist. BoNaP

Apples of gold, in silver pictures shrined. Edward Taylor. *Fr.* Preparatory Meditations before My Approach to the Lord's Supper, XLII. NAAL-1

Applicant, The. Sylvia Plath. MAT; NAAL-2; NaP; NMM; NOBA; TwCP

Application for a Grant. Anthony Hecht. SaC

Apply for the position (I've forgotten now for what) I had. In Order To. Kenneth Patchen. NaP

Appoggiatura. Donald Jeffrey Hayes. AmNP; PoBA; PoNe

Appointed in the newe Moon. Jason and Medea. John Gower. *Fr.* Confessio Amantis, V. ACP

Appointment, The. Maxine W. Kumin. NMM

Appointment, The. Leonard Alfred George Strong. OxBTC

Appraisal. Sara Teasdale. MoAmPo

Appreciation. Thomas Bailey Aldrich. AA

Apprehension this spring. the leaves, the leaves. Homage and Lament for Ezra Pound in Captivity. Robert Duncan. NOBA

Apprentice at the Feast, The. Peter Redgrove. NPo

Apprentice in the shop across from me, The. A Short Winter Tale. Natan Zach, *tr. by* Peter Everwine *and* Shula Starkman. VWA

Apprentice Painter, The. Jack Myers. AmPA

Apprentices. Robin Munro. PoSH

Approach, The, *sel.* Thomas Traherne.
"O Lord, I wonder at thy lov." TrPWD

Approach. Tristan Tzara, *tr. fr. French.* POS, *tr. by* Michael Benedikt; RHTWFP, *tr. by* Lee Harwood.

Approach of Pharaoh, The. Caedmon, *tr. fr. Anglo-Saxon by* C. W. Kennedy. *Fr.* Genesis. ACP; WaaP

Approach of the Storm, The. *Unknown, tr. fr. Chippewa Indian by* Frances Densmore. OBVE; TTTS

Approach to a City. William Carlos Williams. PoRA

Approach to the bar, The. Pole Vaulter. David Allan Evans. ASP; TSL

Approach to Thebes, The. Stanley Kunitz. PoA

Approaches, The. W. S. Merwin. NOBA; Prf

Approaching. Lan Ling, *tr. fr. Chinese by* Dominic Cheung. IFON

Approaching by the gate (Class of '79). Views of the Favorite Colleges. John Malcolm Brinnin. LiTA; MoAB

Approaching Death. Prince Otsu, *tr. fr. Chinese by* Burton Watson. JLIC-1

Approaching death. William Carlos Williams. *Fr.* Asphodel, That Greeny Flower. FaBoMo

Approaching Silence, The. Gyula Illyés, *tr. fr. Hungarian by* William Jay Smith. MHuP

Approaching South Lake, I already begin to dread the journey. Passing through South Lake Again. Li E, *tr. by* Shirleen S. Wong. WFTU

Approximate Man, *sel.* Tristan Tzara, *tr. fr. French by* Paul Auster. RHTwFP

"Sunday solid lid above the boilings of bubbling blood." *Fr.* I, *tr. by* Michael Benedikt. POS

Approximately. Diane Ward. LP

Après le Bain. William Carlos Williams. OBAL

Après-midi d'un Faune, L', *sel.* Stéphane Mallarmé, *tr. fr. French by* Aldous Huxley. AWP

"Proud of my music, let me often make." ErPo

Après un Rêve. Martin Seymour-Smith. NPo

Apricot about to fade, raindrops quiet now. Things Seen. Yüan Mei, *tr. by* Jonathan Chaves. CoBLCP

Apricot Garden in Blossom. Yin O, *tr. fr. Chinese by* Lois Fusek. ATF

Apricot Tree. Magda Isanos, *tr. fr. Rumanian by* Willis Barnstone *and* Matei Calinescu. BoWoP

Apricot trees form a grove. Pien Kung, *tr. fr. Chinese by* Jonathan Chaves. *Fr.* Mooring at K'ou-ch'üeh, I. CoBLCP

April. Obadiah Cyrus Auringer. AA

April. Remy Belleau, *tr. fr. French by* Andrew Lang. AWP

April. Vidame de Chartres, *tr. fr. French by* Swinburne. AWP

April. Lucille Clifton. RAR

April. Linda Pastan. Psk

April. Ezra Pound. CMoP

April. Henrietta Cordelia Ray. CBWP-3

April. Folgore Da San Gimignano, *tr. fr. Italian by* Dante Gabriel Rossetti. *Fr.* Sonnets of the Months. PFI

April. Sara Teasdale. FaPON; PDV

April. Samuel Thompson. BIrV

April. Jean Valentine. TAP

April. Sir William Watson. *See* Song: "April, April,/ Laugh thy girlish laughter."

April. Nathaniel Parker Willis. AnAmPo

April. Yvor Winters. RFM

April. Charles Wright. CAPP; MT

April again, and it is a year again. Sidney Keyes. FL; WaP

April again, and its message unvaried, the same old impromptu. The Burden of Junk. John Glassco. OBCV

April, and a fool's good day. April Notebook. Christian Karlson Stead. PeNZ

April and Dying. Anne Reeve Aldrich. AA

April and May. Emerson. *Fr.* May-Day. GN; OHIP

April, and no one able to calculate. Patrick Kavanagh. *Fr.* The Great Hunger. IPY

April, April,/ Laugh thy girlish laughter. Sir William Watson. OBEV; TrGrPo

(April.) BoTP; FaBV

(Song to April.) GN

April cold with dropping rain. April and May. Emerson. *Fr.* May-Day. GN; OHIP

April Day, An. Joseph Seamon Cotter, Jr.. CDC

April, 1885. Robert Bridges. OxBSP; OxBTC

April Fantasie. Ellen Mackay Hutchinson Cortissoz. AA

April 5, 1974. Richard Wilbur. HCAP

4/5/74. Richard Wilbur. *See* Air was soft, the ground still cold, The.

April Fool, The. Eugene Field. PWR

April Fool. Joan Drew Ritchings. SoTCo
April Fools' Day. Yusef Komunyakaa. MAYP
April Fool's Day, or St. Mary Egypt. John Berryman. *Fr.* Dream Songs. NaP
April Fourth. Robert Mezey. NaP
April, Glengarry. Philip Coxon. PoSH
April Hill, The. Janet Lewis. CRP
April in England. Robert Browning. *See* Oh! to be in England.
April Interval I. Marilyn Hacker. BLA
April Inventory. W. D. Snodgrass. CAPP; CoAP; HAP; LiTM; NePoEA; NoAM; NoP; TAP; TwCP
April is a very unkind month, I am telling you. The Wasted Land. Edward Pygge. FaBoPa
April is in my mistress' face. All Seasons in One. *Unknown*. GBL; HeIP; OBSC; TrGrPo
April is no month for burials. Rite of Spring. Leo Kennedy. CaP
April is the cruellest month, breeding. The Waste Land. T. S. Eliot. AmPP; CMoP; FaBoMo; HAP; LiTA; LiTM; MoAB; MoAmPo; MoP; NAAL-2; NAEL-2; NAWM-2; NoAM; NOBA; NOBE; NoP; OAEL-2; OxBA; OxBTC; PoE; TAP; UnPo
April May July. And June. ? György Somlyó, *tr. by* Jascha Kessler. FOC
April Mortality. Léonie Adams. MoAB; MoAmPo
April Mortality, *sel.* Léonie Adams. MoAB; MoAmPo
"With all the drifting race of men." TrGrPo
April 1940. Patrick Maybin. NeIP
April, 1942. Mark Van Doren. WaP
April 1962. Paul Goodman. VGW
April Notebook. Christian Karlson Stead. PeNZ
April One. Alicia Ostriker. ER
April, pride of woodland ways. April. Remy Belleau, *tr. by* Andrew Lang. AWP
April Rain. Robert Loveman. BoTP; TrJP
April Rain Song. Langston Hughes. FaPON; NTCP; OBCA; PDV; RHPC
April 68. Sam Cornish. CNA
4/13/79. Lewis Warsh. UL
April this year, not otherwise. Song of a Second April. Edna St. Vincent Millay. CMoP; OxBA
April Woman. Salma Khadra Jayyusi, *tr. fr. Arabic by the author and* Charles Doria. MAP
April. You hearken, my fellow. Earth's Lyric. Bliss Carman. AnAmPo
Aprill. Spenser. *Fr.* The Shepheardes [*or* Shepeards *or* Shepherd's] Calender. NAEL-1; PoEL-1
  ("Tell me, good Hobbinoll, what garres thee greete?.") OBEV; OBSC; PoEL-1
  Elisa ("Ye dainty nymphs, that in this blessed brook"). OBSC
  (Lay to Eliza, The.) NOBE
  Ditty, A: In Praise of Eliza, Queen of the Shepherds. OBEV
  (Ditty, A: "See where she sits upon the grassy green.") FaBoCh
Aprille is of al the months moste dyr. Burialle of the Dede. Martin Fagg. BXAP
Aprilly. Bert Leston Taylor. OBAL
Apron of Flowers, The. Robert Herrick. CaPo; SeCV-1
Apron Strings. Marge Piercy. TAP
Aprons of Silence. Carl Sandburg. NOBA
Aquarium. George T. Wright. NYBP
Aquellos Vatos. Tino Villanueva. FIA
Arab and His Donkey, An. *Unknown.* NBLV
Arab came to the river side, An. An Arab and His Donkey. *Unknown.* NBLV
Arab Love-Song, An. Francis Thompson. AWP; MoAB; MoBrPo
Arab Refugee, The. Abdul Wahab al-Bayati, *tr. fr. Arabic by* Abdullah al-Udhari. MPAW
Arab Song. Richard Henry Stoddard. AA
Arab to His Favorite Steed, The. Caroline Elizabeth Norton. BeLS
Arab Traveler in a Space Ship, An. Muhammad al-Maghut, *tr. fr. Arabic.* MAP, *tr. by* Jayyusi *and* John Heath-Stubbs; MPAW, *tr. by* Abdullah al-Udhari
Arabesque. Fred Johnson. PoBA
Arabesque: Five Poems for Women without Children, *sels.* Mary Mackey. ER
 First Position.
 Grande Jetée.
 Second Position.
Arabia. John Meade Falkner. OxBTC
Arabic Script. Anthony Thwaite. OBTV
Arabs complain—or so I have been told. For the Rain It Raineth Every Day. Robert Graves. NYBP

Arab's Farewell to His Horse, The. Caroline Elizabeth Norton. *See* My beautiful! My beautiful! that standest meekly by.
Arachne. Rose Terry Cooke. AA
Arachne. William Empson. InvP; OBMV
Arachne. Judith Kazantzis. BrRo
Arac's Song. W. S. Gilbert. *Fr.* Princess Ida. FiBHP
Aran Islands. Irving Layton. NeAC
Aranda Song. *Unknown, tr. fr. Aranda by* T. G. H. Strehlow. CBAP
Ararat. Peter Cooley. KS
Ararat. Dan Pagis, *tr. fr. Hebrew by* Warren Bargad *and* Stanley F. Chyet. IP
Arawak Prologue. Basil McFarlane. PBCV
Arawata Bill, *sels.* Denis Glover.
 Camp Site. ATNZ; PeNZ
 River Crossing, The. ATNZ; PeNZ
 Scene, The. ATNZ
 Search, The. ATNZ
 Soliloquies. ATNZ
 To the Coast. ATNZ
 "With his weapon a shovel." PeNZ
Arbasto, *sels.* Robert Greene.
 Doralicia's Song. OBSC
 Whereat Erewhile I Wept, I Laugh. ElL
Arbeit Macht Frei. Dennis Schmitz. AnAn; NPGG
Arbitrary Destiny. Robert Desnos, *tr. fr. French by* Michael Benedikt. POS
Arbor Amoris. Villon, *tr. fr. French by* Andrew Lang. AWP
Arbor Day Tree, An. *Unknown.* OHIP
Arbor Vitae. Coventry Patmore. *Fr.* The Unknown Eros, II, iii. OBNC; SeCePo
Arbour, The. Anne Brontë. EBVV
Arbuckle Jones. Peter Wesley-Smith. TDD
Arc. Tom Clark. UL
Arc Inside and Out, The. A. R. Ammons. NoP
Arcades, *sels.* Milton.
 Nymphs and Shepherds. ELP
  (Song: "Nymphs and shepherds dance no more.") FiP
 "O'er [*or* O're] the smooth enameled green." OBEV; TrGrPo
  (Song: "O'er the smooth enamelled green.") OxBSP
Arcades Ambo. Charles Stuart Calverley. BXAP
Arcadia. Sir Philip Sidney.
 Sels.
 Advice to the Same. SiPS
 Complaint of Love. PoEL-1; SiPS
 Country Song, A. OBSC; SiPS
 Cupid. SiPS
 Echo. SiPS
 Geron and Histor. SiPS
 Get Hence Foule Griefe. PoEL-1
  (Contentment.) SiPS
 Graven Thoughts. SiPS
 In Vain, Mine Eyes. SiPS
 Love and Jealousy. SiPS
 Love and Reason. SiPS
 My Sheep Are Thoughts. SiPS
 My True Love Hath My Heart [and I Have His]. BoLoP; CH; FaBoBe; GBL; PoE; PoEL-1; TrGrPo
  (Arcadian Duologue.) SiPS
  (Bargain, The.) NOBE; OBEV
  (Ditty, A: "My true love hath my heart, and I have his.") AWP; GTBS; GTBS-P
  (Heart Exchange.) LiTB
  (Sonnet: "My true love hath my heart.") ElL
  (True Love.) ChTr; OBSC
 Night. SiPS
 Old Age. SiPS
 Rural Poesy. ElL
 Sapphics. SiPS
 Shepherd Song. SiPS
 Shepherd's Tale, A. SiPS
 Since So Mine Eyes. SiPS
 Sleep. OBSC; SiPS
  (Sonnet: "Lock up, fair lids, the treasure of my heart.") ElL
 Solitariness. OBSC; SiPS
 Sweeter Saint I Serve, A. SiPS
 Tale for Husbands, A. SiPS
 What Tongue Can Her Perfections Tell?. SiPS
 When Two Suns Do Appear. SiPS
 Why Fear to Die?. SiPS
 Wronged Lover, The. SiPS

Ye Goat-herd Gods. HAP; NAEL-1; NOBE; NoP; OAEL-1
   (Double Sestine.) LiTB; PoEL-1
Arcadia was of old (said he) a State. Rhotus on Arcadia. John Chalkhill.
   Fr. Thealma and Clearchus. OBS
Arcadian Duologue. Sir Philip Sidney. See Arcadia: My True Love Hath
   My Heart [and I Have His].
Arcana Sylvarum. Charles De Kay. AA
Arcanum One. Gwendolyn MacEwen. MoCV
Archaeological Picnic, The. Sir John Betjeman. EnLoPo
Archaeology. Katha Pollitt. MAYP
Archaeology of Love, The. Richard Murphy. EnLoPo
Archaic Song of Dr. Tom the Shaman. Unknown, tr. fr. Nootka Indian by
   Jerome Rothenberg. STP
Archaic Torso of Apollo. Rainer Maria Rilke, tr. fr. German.
   NAWM-2, tr. by Stephen Mitchell; NU, tr. by Robert Bly
Archangel. Kit Robinson. UL
Archangel's silver panties glint as he flies, The. Michael. Sandra
   McPherson. LCAP
Archbishop Tait. Unknown. ChTr; FaBoNo
Archer, The. Clinton Scollard. FaPON
Archer, The. A. J. M. Smith. OBCV
Archer (acquainted with brilliance), The. The Access. Henry Kanabus.
   UL
Archer is wake, The! Peace on Earth. William Carlos Williams.
   LiTA
Archery. Walter de la Mare. FaBoNo
Archery Instructor. Richard Aldridge. TSL
Archibald MacLeish Suspends the Five Little Pigs. Louis Untermeyer.
   Fr. Mother Goose Up-to-Date. MoAmPo
Ar(chibald')s Poetica. Alan Ribback. BXAP
Archie o [or of] Cawfield. Unknown. AmFP; ESPB; OxBS
Archie o Cawfield. Unknown. ESPB
Archin' here and arrachin' there. Water Music. "Hugh MacDiarmid."
   GoTS
Arching perfectly-plucked eyebrows. Kirsten. Hugo Williams. Fr.
   Calling Your Name in the Zoo. NPo
Architect. Louise Townsend Nicholl. EyDe
Architectural Masks. Thomas Hardy. EyDe
Archy and Mehitabel, sels. Don Marquis.
   Archy at the Zoo. NBLV; OBAL
   Archy Confesses. FiBHP
   Cheerio My Deario. FaBoCo
   Hen and the Oriole, The. FiBHP
   Old Trouper, The. FaBoCo
   Song of Mehitabel, The. FiBHP
   Wail of Archy, The. FiBHP
   Warty Bliggens, the Toad. FiBHP
Archy, the Cockroach, Speaks. Don Marquis. Fr. Certain Maxims of
   Archy. FaPON
Archys Life of Mehitabel, sel. Don Marquis.
   Ballade of the Under Side. InvP
Arctic Convoy. James King Annand. OxBS
Arctic honey blabbed over the report causing darkness, The. Leaving the
   Atocha Station. John Ashbery. CAPP
Arctic moon hangs overhead, The. The Wolf Cry. Lew Sarett. FaPON;
   RHPC
Arctic Ox, The. Marianne Moore. NYBP
Arctic Tern in a Museum. Effie Lee Newsome. PoNe
Arctic Vision, An. Bret Harte. PAH
Arcturus is his other name. Emily Dickinson. FaBV; NOBA
Arcturus, the bear driver. Night Sky. Louise Erdrich. HATNAP
Arcuconspicilla oves looks for perditas. She Lost Her Sheep. J. Moyr
   Smith. FaBoNo
Ardan Mór. Francis Ledwidge. See As I was climbing Ardan Mor.
Arden is not Eden, but Eden's rhyme. In Arden. Charles Tomlinson.
   OxBC
Ardent in love and cold in charity. A Man's Sliding Mood. Mary
   Elizabeth Fullerton. CBAP
Ardently down the backs of cousins. Hair. Maxine Silverman. VWA
Ardour and Memory. Dante Gabriel Rossetti. Fr. The House of Life,
   LXIV. OAEL-2
Are all such off'rings, as are crusht, and bruis'd. Francis Quarles.
   FaBoEE
Are all these stones. Close-up. A. R. Ammons. PoA
Are needed to put a frame around the landscape. Windows. William
   Dickey. KS
". . . Are not molesters of women" the book says. Pocket Guide for
   Service Men. Hubert Creekmore. WaP
Are sorrows hard to bear,—the ruin. Burdens. Edward Dowden.
   NOBVV

Are the desolate, dark weeks. These. William Carlos Williams.
   MoAB; MoAmPo; MoP; NOBA; NoP; OxBA
". . . Are the horns of the hall on fire?" The Battle of Finnsburg.
   Unknown, tr. by Charles W. Kennedy. AnOE
Are there birds twittering under the earth. Under the Earth. Abraham
   Sutskever, tr. by Ruth Whitman. VWA
Are there favoring ladies above thee? Valse Jeune. Louise Imogen
   Guiney. AA
Are there no gods of heaven and earth? Unknown, tr. fr. Japanese. Fr.
   Manyo Shu. Ma
Are there not twelve whole hours in every day. The Day of Denial.
   Jones Very. NOBA
Are there others too. What She Said. Venkorran, tr. by A. K.
   Ramanujan. PLW
Are these ashes in my hand. Hilda Doolittle ("H. D."). Fr. Sigil, XII.
   AnAn
Are these mellifluous sheep. Strictly Bucolic. Charles Simic. PPR
Are These Moods of Mine Memory. Yona Wallach, tr. fr. Hebrew by
   Warren Bargad and Stanley F. Chyet. IP
Are these the honors they reserve for me. Columbus in Chains. Philip
   Freneau. PAH
Are these the pope's grand tools? On the Murder of Sir Edmund Berry
   Godfrey. Unknown. APAS
Are these the unheard voices. The Voice of Blooming. Yip Wai-lim, tr.
   by Dominic Cheung. IFON
Are these truly the fisher-maids. Tanabe Akiniwa, tr. fr. Japanese. Fr.
   Manyo Shu. Ma
Are they clinging to their crosses. Antichrist, or the Reunion of
   Christendom; an Ode. G. K. Chesterton. FaBoCo; NOBE; NOBL;
   OBSV; SeCePo
Are They Dancing. Edward Dorn. NeAP; PoM
Are they exiles here from the rest of the world? What Do the Birds
   Think? Alfred W. Purdy. MoCV
Are They Shadows [That We See]? Samuel Daniel. Fr. Tethy's Festival.
   CH; EIL; InvP; NoP
   (Shadows.) NOBE; OBSC
   (Song: "Are they shadowes that we see?.") PoEL-2
Are Those Two Stars. Giles Fletcher the Elder. Fr. Licia, XLIII.
   Son
Are We Not the People, sel. Al-Samau'al Ibn Adiya, tr. fr. Arabic by
   Hartwig Hirschfeld.
   "Now listen to boasting which leaves the heart dazed." TrJP
Are we quite cut off from Thee? The Trial. Gershom Scholem tr. by
   Jonathan Griffin, VWA
Are we unfathomable night. Hilda Doolittle ("H. D."). Fr. Sigil, XVIII.
   AnAn
"Are Ye Right There, Michael?" (A Lay of the Wild West Clare.).
   William Percy French. WTO
Are you a glass of milk, rich and cold? Song for the Moon. Nazik al-
   Mala'ika, tr. by Matthew Sorenson and Christopher Middleton.
   MAP
Are you a trailor, or are you a trolley? Are You You? Edmund Vance
   Cook. PWR
Are you alive? The Pool. Hilda Doolittle ("H. D."). CMoP
Are you almost disgusted with life, little man? How to Be Happy.
   Unknown. BLPA
Are you asking where I'm going with these sad faces. Poem with the
   Final Tune. Julia de Burgos, tr. by Julio Marzán. InW
"Are you asleep?" After the Kiss. Miki Rofu, tr. by Geoffrey Bownas
   and Anthony Thwaite. PeBJV
"Are you awake, Gemelli." Star-Talk. Robert Graves. BoNaP; GoJo;
   MoBrPo; OxBTC
Are You Glad? Mongol Oral Tradition, tr. by C. R. Bawden.
   WTO
Are you going to Whittingham Fair? Whittingham Fair. Unknown.
   GBP
Are you he who would assume a place to teach or be a poet here in the
   States? Walt Whitman. Fr. By Blue Ontario's Shore, Sec. XII.
   FaBoPV
Are you hot there too? Black Muslim Boy in a Hospital. James A.
   Emanuel. PoNe
Are You looking for us? We are here. The 151st Psalm. Karl Shapiro.
   EaLo; VWA
Are you out, woman of the lean pelt. Ire. R. S. Thomas. OxBSP
"Are you ready, O Virginia." The Call to the Colors. Arthur Guiterman.
   PAH
Are you ready? soul said again. Two Trinities. Kenneth Mackenzie.
   CBAP
Are you so weary? Come to the window. Wind in the Grass. Mark Van
   Doren. FaBV

Are you standing at "Wit's End Corner." Wit's End Corner. Antoinette Wilson. BLRP

"Are You Still There." Joy Harjo. NOVW

Are You the New Person Drawn toward Me? Walt Whitman. OxBSP; PPP

Are you the woman. Secret Woman. Meiling Jin. WS

Are you what your faire lookes expresse? Thomas Campion. AAS

Are you worsted in a fight? Laugh It Off. Henry Rutherford Elliot. WBLP

Are You You? Edmund Vance Cook. PWR

Are you You or Me or It? Hello Up There. Marge Piercy. NBLV

Are your sorrows hard to bear? The Length of Life. Amos Russel Wells. PWR

Areas. Leslie Scalapino. NPGG

Arena, The. Hubert Witheford. ATNZ

Arena dust rusted by four bulls' blood to a dull redness. The Goring. Sylvia Plath. OBTV

Ares. Albert Ehrenstein, *tr. fr. German by* Babette Deutsch *and* Avram Yarmolinsky. TrJP

Ares at last has quit the field. Under Which Lyre, a Reactionary Tract for the Times. W. H. Auden. MoAB; MoBrPo; NOBL

Arethusa, The. Prince Hoare. FaPoR

Arethusa. Shelley. EnRP; GN; WiR

Argalus and Parthenia, *sels.* Francis Quarles.
    Authour's Dreame, The. OBS
    Hos Ego Versiculos. OBS, *See also* Man's Mortality *sl. diff. vers. at.* to Simon Wastell, *fr.* Microbiblion.

Argent Solipsism. Howard Blake. PoA

Argenteuil County. Peter Dale Scott. MoCV

Argentine gaucho named Bruno, An. *Unknown.* NOBL

Argoed. T. Gwynn Jones, *tr. fr. Welsh by* Anthony Conran. OBWVE

Argonauts, The. D. H. Lawrence. NoAM

Arguing That There Are Inconsistencies between Men's Tastes and Their Censure When They Accuse Women. Sister Juana Inés de la Cruz, *tr. fr. Spanish by* Muriel Kittel. DMH

Argula's Answer. Argula von Grumbach, *tr. fr. German by* Susan L. Cocalis. *Fr.* An Answer in Verse for Someone Studying in Ingolst. DMG

Argument, The. Samuel Butler. *Fr.* Hudibras, I, 1. EBEV; NAEL-1; OAEL-1; SeCV-2

Argument, An. Thomas Moore. BoLoP; EnLoPo; OxBSP

Argument against Metaphor. Gad Hollander. VWA

Argument of Democritus Platonissans, or the Infinitie of Worlds, The. Henry More. SeCV-2

Argument of His Book, The. Robert Herrick. AWP; CaPo; EBEV; HAP; HeIP; InVP; JCP; NAEL-1; NoP; OAEL-1; OBS; PoE; PoEL-3; PoRA; SeCePo; SeCP; SeCV-1; TEP; TrGrPo; TTTS

Argument One: The Lady Shews How She Is Foresaken for a Piece of Wood. Judith Emlyn Johnson. TSL

Arguments against restraint, The. To His Dear Friend, Bones. Jay Parini. MAYP

Aria. Rolfe Humphries. NYBP

Aria. Delmore Schwartz. ErPo

Aria for Flute and Oboe. Joseph Langland. NePoEA

Aria Senza da Capo. Robert Finch. MoCV

Ariake, Japanese friend, I regard. To Ariake Kambara. Norman Rosten. NYBP

Ariana. Franklin Benjamin Sanborn. AA

Arid Husband, The. E. L. T. Mesens. EAS

Arid that country and high, anger of sun on the mountains, but. Rattlesnake Country. Robert Penn Warren. NAAL-2

Aridity. "Michael Field." OBMV

Ariel. David Campbell. CBAP; PoAu-2

Ariel. Sylvia Plath. CMoP; HCAP; HeIP; LCAP; MoP; NAAL-2; NoAM; NOBA; NoP; PBWP; PoE

Ariel in the Cloven Pine. Bayard Taylor. AA

Ariel, one true. Thoughts about My Daughter before Sleep. Sandra Hochman. TV

Ariel to Miranda:—Take. With a Guitar, to Jane. Shelley. EnRP; OAEL-2
    (To a Lady, with a Guitar.) GTBS; GTBS-P

Ariel was glad he had written his poems. The Planet on the Table. Wallace Stevens. HAP; HCAP

Ariel's Dirge. Shakespeare. *See* Tempest, The: Full fathom [*or* fadom] five thy father lies.

Ariel's Song: "Come unto these yellow sands." Shakespeare. *See* Tempest, The: Come unto these yellow sands.

Ariel's Song: "Full fathom five thy father lies." Shakespeare. *See* Tempest, The: Full fathom [*or* fadom] five thy father lies.

Ariel's Song: "Where the bee sucks, there suck I." Shakespeare. *See* Tempest, The: Where the bee sucks, there suck I.

Arion. Pushkin, *tr. fr. Russian by* Alan Myers. AAA

Ariosto. Osip Mandelstam, *tr. fr. Russian by* W. S. Merwin *and* Clarence Brown. OBVE

Arise and go now to the city of slaughter. The City of Slaughter. Hayyim Nahman Bialik, *tr. by* A. M. Klein. TrJP

Arise and Pick a Posy. *Unknown.* OBET

Arise and See the Glorious Sun. Francis Hopkinson. AH

Arise, Arise. *Unknown.* OBET

Arise, arise, arise! Henry Brooke. *Fr.* Jack the Giant Queller; an Antique History. NOEC

Arise faint Muse bring one heart-melting verse. An Elegie on the Deploreable Departure of the Honered and Truely Religious Chieftain John Hull. John Saffin. SCAP

Arise from your rope-strung bed, Clabe Mott. Clabe Mott. James Still. GrPl

Arise, my soul, on wings enraptured, rise. Thoughts on the Works of Providence. Phillis Wheatley. NAAL-1

Arise, My Soul! With Rapture Rise! Samuel J. Smith. AH

Arise, O Glorious Zion. William G. Mills. AH

Arise, O soul, and gird thee up anew. A Challenge. James Benjamin Kenyon. AA

Arise up on thy feet, O Quiet Heart! He Biddeth Osiris to Arise from the Dead. *Unknown, tr. fr. Egyptian by* Robert Hillyer. *Fr.* Book of the Dead. AWP

Arise ye daughters of a land. The Women's Marseillaise. F. E. M. Macaulay. BrRo

Arise, Ye Saints of Latter Days. *Unknown.* AH

Arisen from what childhood. The Phoenix of Mozart. Claude Vigée, *tr. by* Anthony Rudolf. VWA

Aristeides. Antipater of Sidon, *tr. fr. Greek by* Charles Whibley. AWP

Aristocrats. Keith Douglas. FaBoMo; NAEL-2; NePoEA; NoAM; OBWP

Aristomenis, son of Menelaos. A Prince from Western Libya. C. P. Cavafy, *tr. by* Edmund Keeley *and* Philip Sherrard. VMG

Aristophanes' Symposium. Rita Mae Brown. IHMS

Aristotle was a little man with/ eyes like a lizard. Humanities Lecture. William Stafford. NNaP; NoAM

Arithmetic. Aleksander Wat, *tr. fr. Polish by* Czeslaw Milosz. PwPP

Arithmetic ("Arithmetic is where numbers fly like pigeons in and out of your head"). Carl Sandburg. FaPON; ImOP; RHPC

Arithmetic on the Frontier. Kipling. OBWP

Arizona. Sharlot M. Hall. PAH

Arizona. *Unknown.* AmFP

Arizona Highways. James Welch. CDW; NoAM

Arizona Nature Myth. James Michie. NOBL

Arizona Village. Robert Stiles Davieau. AmFN

Arizona wind dries out my nostrils, The. The Hitchhiker. Ai. GeTw

Arjuna said:/ How shall I in battle against Bhisma. *Unknown, tr. fr. Sanskrit by* Franklin Edgerton. *Fr.* The Bhagavad-Gita. DL

Ark, The, *sels.* Jay Macpherson.
    Ark Anatomical. NOBC
    Ark Apprehensive. NOBC
    Ark Artefact. NOBC
    Ark Articulate. NOBC
    Ark Astonished. NOBC
    Ark Overwhelmed. NOBC
    Ark Parting. NOBC
    Ark to Noah. NOBC; PoA

Ark Anatomical. Jay Macpherson. *Fr.* The Ark. NOBC

Ark Apprehensive. Jay Macpherson. *Fr.* The Ark. NOBC

Ark Artefact. Jay Macpherson. *Fr.* The Ark. NOBC

Ark Articulate. Jay Macpherson. *Fr.* The Ark. NOBC

Ark Astonished. Jay Macpherson. *Fr.* The Ark. NOBC

Ark noisy with children, The. Noah. Chana Bloch. VWA

Ark of the Covenant. Louise Townsend Nicholl. ImOP

Ark Overwhelmed. Jay Macpherson. *Fr.* The Ark. NOBC

Ark Parting. Jay Macpherson. *Fr.* The Ark. NOBC

Ark to Noah. Jay Macpherson. *Fr.* The Ark. NOBC; PoA

Arkansas Traveller. Charles Wright. MT

Arlington Cemetery Looking toward the Capitol. Winthrop Palmer. GoYe

Arlo Will. Edgar Lee Masters. *Fr.* Spoon River Anthology. LiTA

Arm, Arm, Arm, Arm! John Fletcher. *Fr.* The Mad Lover, V, iv. ElL

Arm for a pillow, fragrance of hair. Wakayama Bokusui, *tr. fr. Japanese by* Hiroaki Sato. *Fr.* Forty-four Tanka. FCEI

Arm for my pillow. Cold in the Grass. Kenko, *tr. by* Steven D. Carter. WFTW

Arm in Arm. Louis Simpson. PBCV

Arm Wrestling with My Father. Jack Driscoll. GOYP
Armada, The. Macaulay. BeLS; FaBoCh; FaPoR; GN; WBLP
Armada, 1588, The. John Wilson. OxBChV
Armada, The [a Fragment] ("Attend, all ye who list to hear our noble
  England's praise."), *sel.* Macaulay. BeLS; FaBoCh; FaPoR; GN;
  WBLP
  "Night sank upon the dusky beach, and on the purple sea." OBNC
Armadillo[—Brazil], The. Elizabeth Bishop. CAPP; HCAP; MoP;
  NAAL-2; NoAM; NOBA; NoP; NYBP; SM; TAP; VGW
Armageddon. John Crowe Ransom. LiTA
Armchairs. Dan Pagis, *tr. fr. Hebrew.* IP, *tr. by* Warren Bargad *and*
  Stanley F. Chyet; MHeP, *tr. by* Bernhard Frank
Arme, Arme, Arme, Arme, great Neptune rowze, awake. John Smith of
  His Friend Master John Taylor. John Smith. SCAP
Armed Vision. N. P. van Wyck Louw, *tr. fr. Afrikaans by* Jack Cope *and*
  Uys Krige. PeSA
Armed we go. . . we are the dancers. A Tryptych for Jan Bockelson.
  John Oliver Simon. NeAC
Armful, The. Robert Frost. CMoP; OxBSP
Armies Enter Cuailnge, The. *Unknown, tr. fr. Irish by* Thomas Kinsella.
  Fr. The Táin. NOIV
Armies in the Fire. Robert Louis Stevenson. *Fr.* A Child's Garden of
  Verses. EBVV
Arming of Pigwiggen, The. Michael Drayton. *See* Nymphidia:
  Pigwiggin Arms Himself.
Armistice. Paul Dehn. OxBTC
Armistice. Sophie Jewett. AA
Armistice. Thomas Lodge. *See* For Pity, Pretty Eyes, Surcease.
Armistice Day. Charles Causley. NAEL-2; OBWP
Armistice Day. John Freeman. MMA; OPP
Armor. James Dickey. CoAP
Armor. Sharon Olds. InPS
Armorer's Daughter, The. Debora Greger. MAYP
Armorer's Song, The. Harry Bache Smith. AA; OHIP
Armorial. Ralph Gustafson. MoCV
Armoury, An. Alcaeus, *tr. fr. Greek by* Gilbert Highet. WaaP
Arms/ spiral/ in clinical. The Dance. Maud Sulter. DT
Arms and the Boy. Wilfred Owen. BrPo; CMoP; FaFP; HAP; LiTB;
  LiTM; MoAB; MoBrPo; OAEL-1; OAEL-2; OxBSP; PoE; WaP;
  WeW
Arms, and the man I sing, who forc'd by fate. Virgil, *tr. fr. Latin, tr. by*
  Dryden. *Fr.* The Aeneid [*or* Eneados], I. OBVE
Arms at my side like some inadequate sign. Mountain Town—Mexico.
  Eldon Grier. NOBC
Arms finned-out across the water. The Drowned. David Bottoms.
  MT
Arms reversed and banners craped. A Dirge for McPherson. Herman
  Melville. PAH; PoEL-5
Arms seem clumsy at first, The. The Fever Toy. Charles Wright.
  AmPA
Arms spread, a frog floats. Chiri, *tr. by* Hiroaki Sato. FCEI
Arms stretching from the precipice, finally. Koseisoku, *tr. by* Lucien
  Stryk *and* Takashi Ikemoto. ZPCJ
The *Armstrong* at Fayal. Wallace Rice. PAH
Army, The. Hagiwara Sakutaro, *tr. fr. Japanese by* Hiroaki Sato.
  FCEI
Army Corps on the March, An. Walt Whitman. AiP; InPS; PoLF
Army Correspondent's Last Ride. George Alfred Townsend. AA
Army marched by for days and was admired by all, The. The Decimation
  before Phraata. Alan Dugan. AnAn
Army, Navy. *Unknown.* OxNR
Army of the Lord. I'm a Soldier in the Army of the Lord. *Unknown.*
  AmFP
Army returned home wet with sunlight, The. One Night Away from Day.
  John Digby. EAS
Army was ours that spring, The. Landing in England. North Pickenham.
  Coman Leavenworth. *Fr.* Norfolk Memorials, I. LiTA
Arnold at Stillwater. Thomas Dunn English. PAH
Arnold, I must tell you. A Confidence. Juan Gonzalo Rose, *tr. by* Ena
  Hollis. Per
Arnold, the Vile Traitor ("Arnold the name, as heretofore"). *Unknown.*
  PAH
Around, above my bed, the pitch-dark fly. Truth. Howard Nemerov.
  HoPM; LiTM
Around, around the sun we go. Mother Goose's Garland. Archibald
  MacLeish. AnAmPo; OBAL
Around her shrine no earthly blossoms blow. La Madonna dell' Acqua.
  John Ruskin. NOBVV
Around islands of jade and malachite. The Wave Symphony. Arthur
  Davison Ficke. *Fr.* Four Japanese Paintings. PoA

Around it the furze-clad hills arise. The Mountain Altar. Brian
  O'Higgins. TIRV
Around me roar and crash the pagan isms. The Pagan Isms. Claude
  McKay. BPo
Around me the images of thirty years. The Municipal Gallery Revisited.
  W. B. Yeats. GTBS-P; LiTB; OxBTC
Around my garden the little wall is low. Losing a Slave-Girl. Po Chü-i,
  tr. by Arthur Waley. AWP
Around Thanksgiving. Rolfe Humphries. OFD
Around the battlements go by. War on the Periphery. George Johnston.
  NOBC
Around the Campfire. Andrew Hudgins. MOWH; MT
Around the Corner. Laura Riding. *Fr.* Forgotten Girlhood. RB
Around the Corner ("Around the corner I have a friend"). Charles Hanson
  Towne. PoLF
Around the fire one wintry night. The Beggar Man. Lucy Aikin.
  OxBChV
Around the fireplace, pointing at the fire. On Falling Asleep by Firelight.
  William Meredith. NoAM; NYBP
Around the gleaming map of Europe. Autobahnmotorwayautoroute.
  Adrian Mitchell. RB
Around the headland, at the end. The Lives of Gulls and Children.
  Howard Nemerov. NePoEA
Around the house stood an. Grandmothers Land. William Oandasan.
  HATNAP
Around the house the flakes fly faster. Birds at Winter Nightfall.
  Thomas Hardy. MoBrPo
Around the inlet. Cold Reeds around the Inlet. Joben, *tr. by* Steven D.
  Carter. WFTW
Around the little park. Back to Life. Thom Gunn. NoP
Around the quays, kicked off in twos. Fishing Boats in Martigues. Roy
  Campbell. FaBoEE; FaBoPP; OxBSP
Around the rick, around the rick. *Unknown.* OxNR
Around the Rough and Rugged Rocks the Ragged Rascal Rudely Ran.
  John Ashbery. InPS
Around the World. Gary Lenhart. UL
Around this lovely valley rise. Midsummer. John Townsend
  Trowbridge. AA
Around us speeches of birds. I tremble. Lines to a Tree. Judah Leib
  Teller, *tr. by* Gabriel Preil *and* Howard Schwartz. VWA
Around us summer wrote its last farewell. September Afternoon.
  Margaret Haley Carpenter. GoYe
Around were all the roses red. Spleen. Paul Verlaine, *tr. by* Ernest
  Dowson. AWP
Arouse, arouse, ye friends of right. The World Hymn. James Gilchrist
  Lawson. WBLP
Arraigned before his worldly gods. The Execution of Cornelius Vane.
  Sir Herbert Read. BrPo
Arraignment. Helen Gray Cone. AA
Arraignment of a Lover, The. George Gascoigne. AAS
Arraignment of Paris, The, *sels.* George Peele.
  "Welladay, welladay, poor Colin, thou art going to the ground." EiL
  (Shepherd's Dirge, The.) OBSC
  Fair and Fair. EiL; OBEV
  (Oenone and Paris.) NOBE
  (Song of Oenone and Paris.) OBSC
  O Gentle Love. EiL
  (Colin's Passion of Love.) OBSC
  Oenone's Complaint. EiL; OBSC
Arran. *Unknown, tr. fr. Old Irish.* ChTr, *tr. by* Kenneth Jackson,
  FaBoCh, *tr. by* Kuno Meyer; FaBoPP, *tr. by* Kenneth Jackson
Arrange the scene with only a shade of difference. An Incident. Douglas
  Le Pan. MoCV
Arranged by two's as peaches are. Nine Nectarines and Other Porcelain.
  Marianne Moore. OxBA
Arranged on the opposite porch is a male. Hilaire Kirkland. *Fr.*
  Observations, I. PeNZ
Arrangements with Earth for Three Dead Friends. James Wright. NIP
Arras. P. K. Page. MoCV; OBCV
Arrayed at night, like fingers stretched through bars. The Lead Plates at
  the Rom Press. Abraham Sutskever, *tr. by* Neal Kozodoy.
  PeBMYV
Arrest of Oscar Wilde at the Cadogan Hotel, The. Sir John Betjeman.
  CMoP; EBEV; InvP; MoBrPo; MoP; NoAM; NoP; OxBTC
Arria to Poetus. Mary E. Tucker. CBWP-1
Arrival/ departure: what difference? Sanso, *tr. by* Lucien Stryk *and*
  Takashi Ikemoto. ZPCJ
Arrival, The. Alexander McLachlan. *Fr.* The Emigrant. NOBC
Arrival. John Wain. EBEV
Arrival. William Carlos Williams. AnAmPo

Arrival and Departure. Charles Eglington. PeSA
Arrival at Santos. Elizabeth Bishop. FaBoWP; OxBC
Arrival at the Waldorf. Wallace Stevens. HCAP
Arrival in Hell. Ricarda Huch, tr. fr. German by Susan C. Strong. PBWP
Arrival, New York Harbor. Robert Peters. GOA
Arrival of the Bee Box, The. Sylvia Plath. FaBoMo; FaBoWP; HCAP; NaP
Arrivals at a Watering-Place. Winthrop Mackworth Praed. NOBL
Arrivals, Departures. Philip Larkin. MoBrPo
Arrive. The Ladies from the Ladies' Betterment League. The Lovers of the Poor. Gwendolyn Brooks. CAPP; MoP; NAAL-2; NoAM; NOBA
Arrived from scattered cities, several lands. Shipment to Maidanek. Ephim G. Fogel. OBWP; TrJP
Arrived upon the downs of asphodel. Classic Encounter. "Christopher Caudwell." OxBTC
Arrives like a jinn, instantly. Resuscitation Team. U. A. Fanthorpe. FaBoWP
Arriving. Daniel Halpern. HoPM
Arriving. Gabriel Preil, tr. fr. Hebrew by Robert Friend. VWA
Arriving at Hangchou. Yüan Mei, tr. fr. Chinese by Jonathan Chaves. CoBLCP
Arriving in Lo-yang Again. Shao Yung, tr. fr. Chinese by Burton Watson. CoBCP
Arriving was their passion. The Tourists. C. Day Lewis. OBTV
Arrogance. Walter de la Mare. OxBSP
Arrogance Repressed. Sir John Betjeman. FiBHP
Arrow and the Song, The. Longfellow. AA; AnAmPo; FaFP; PWR
Arrow of Desire, The. Gond Oral Tradition, tr. by V. Elwin and S. Hivale. WTO
Arrow rides upon the sky, An. Samuel Allen
Arrowhead Christian Center and No-Smoking Luncheonette. Janet Sylvester. MAYP
Arrows. William Heyen. SM
Arrows of the narrow moon flock down direct, The. Communion of Saints: The Poor Bastard under the Bridge. Marie Ponsot. VGW
Arrowy Dreams. Witter Bynner. GOA
Arroyo. Tom Weatherly. PoBA
Ars. Marina Tsvetayeva, tr. fr. Russian by Willis Barnstone and Edward Brown. BoWoP
Ars Amoris. James Vincent Cunningham. QFR
Ars Longa. Which is crueller. The Peacock Room. Robert Hayden. FB
Ars Poetica. Cees Buddingh', tr. fr. Dutch by James Brockway. DuIn
Ars Poetica. X. J. Kennedy. ErPo
Ars Poetica. Archibald MacLeish. AmPP; AWP; CMoP; FPL; HAP; HeIP; HoPM; InPK; InPK; LiTA; LiTM; MoAB; MoAmPo; NAAL-2; NIP; NOBA; NoP; OxBA; PoA; PoRA; SoSe; TAP; WeW
Ars Poetica? Czeslaw Milosz, tr. fr. Polish by Lillian Vallee. AnAn
Ars Poetica. József Tornai, tr. fr. Hungarian by Jascha Kessler. FOC
Ars Poetica. Arturo Trías, tr. fr. Spanish by Julio Marzán. InW
Ars Poetica. Victor van Vriesland, tr. fr. Dutch by Adriaan J. Barnouw. TrJP
Ars Poetica. Adam Wazyk, tr. fr. Polish by Isaac Komem. VWA
Ars Poetica. Charles Wright. AnAn
Ars Poetica about Ultimates. Tram Combs. TwCP
Ars Poetica: 4. Herman de Coninck, tr. fr. Dutch by James S. Holmes. DuIn
Ars Victrix, sel. Austin Dobson, after the French of Théophile Gautier. "All passes. Art alone." CTC
Arsenal at Springfield, The, sel. Longfellow. AmPP; WaaP
Message of Peace, A. WBLP
Arsenic. Howard Moss. CoAP; NYBP
Arson. Peter Goldsworthy. UAS
Arson and Cold Lace. Worth Long. NBP
Art. Hjalmar Flax, tr. fr. Spanish by Julio Marzán. InW
Art. Théophile Gautier, tr. fr. French by George Santayana. AWP
Art. Herman Melville. AmPP; NAAL-1; NOBA
Art. Lilla Cabot Perry. AA
Art, sel. James Thomson.
   "Singing is sweet; but be sure of this." NOBVV
Art. Unknown. BLPA; NBLV
Art, I. Alfred Noyes. OBEV
Art and Heart. Ella Wheeler Wilcox. AnAmPo
Art as meagre as a quilt, An. The Spare Quilt. John Peale Bishop. GOA
Art for Art's Sake. Marc Blitzstein. Fr. The Cradle Will Rock. TrJP

Art has nothing to do with perfect circles. Christian Karlson Stead. Fr. Walking Westward. ATNZ
Art, II. Alfred Noyes. OBEV
Art. It cures affliction. As lights go down and. Farewell Performance. James Merrill. BAP
Art McCooey. Patrick Kavanagh. CIP; FaBCIP
Art Market: Leopoldville. Michael Jackson. ATNZ
Art Master, An. John Boyle O'Reilly. AA
Art of Angling, The, sels. Thomas Barker. FaBoUs
   Baits for Various Fish.
   How to Catch Trout.
   Methods of Cooking Trout.
Art of Being Second, The. J. Bernlef, tr. fr. Dutch by Peter Nijmeijer. DuIn
Art of Biography, The. E. C. Bentley. Fr. Clerihews. CenHV; FiBHP; NOBL
Art of Clay, The. Duane Niatum. HATNAP
Art of Cookery, The, sel. William King.
   "Far from the parlour have your kitchen plac'd." FaBoUs
Art of Dancing, The, sels. Soame Jenyns. FaBoUs
   "Dare I in such momentous points advise."
   "Now haste, my Muse, pursue thy destin'd way."
Art of days art of nights. No Grounds for Prosecution. André Breton, tr. by Paul Auster. RHTwFP
Art of Holding On, The. Dwight Okita. BrSi
Art of losing isn't hard to master, The. One Art. Elizabeth Bishop. CAPP; DiPo; HAP; NAAL-2; NoAM; PoE; SM; SoSe
Art of Love, The, sel. Kenneth Koch.
   "To win the love of women one should first discover." NNaP
Art of Love, The, sels. Ovid, tr. fr. Latin.
   "Attend, ye nymphs, by wedlock unconfin'd." Tr. by Congreve. FaBoUs
   "Kiss, if you can: Resistance if she make." Tr. by Dryden. ErPo
   "You, who in Cupid's rolls inscribe your name." Tr. by Dryden. FaBoUs
Art of Making Puddings, The, sel. William King.
   "Sometimes the frugal matron seems in haste." FaBoUs
Art of Picasso, The. Salvador Dali, tr. fr. Spanish by David Gascoyne. EAS
Art of Poetry, The, sels. Horace, tr. fr. Latin.
   "As woods whose change appeares." Tr. by Ben Jonson. OBVE
   "Should some ill painter, in a wild design." Tr. by John Oldham. OBVE
Art of Poetry, An. James McAuley. NOCV
Art of Politics, The, sel. James Bramston.
   Time's Changes. NOEC
Art of Preserving Health, The, sels. John Armstrong.
   Advantages of Washing, The. FaBoUs
   Dangers of Sexual Excess, The. FaBoUs
   Madness. NOEC
   Transience. NOEC
   Urban Pollution. NOEC
Art of Surrender, The. David Wagoner. KS
Art of the Sonnet, sels. Gil Orlovitz.
   "If I could rise and see my father young." DiL
   "Night comes. Day runs for its life into my eyes." PoA
Art of War, The, sel. Joseph Fawcett.
   Feast of Blood, The. NOEC
Art of Wenching, The, sel. Unknown.
   "Be punctual then to know." NOEC
Art photographer alone, The. Quantum. Martin Johnston. CBAP
Art Poétique. Paul Verlaine, tr. fr. French by Arthur Symons. AWP
Art thou a Statist in the van. A Poet's Epitaph. Wordsworth. EnRP
Art thou afraid the adorer's prayer. Walter Savage Landor. GBL
Art Thou Gone in Haste? Unknown, at. to John Webster and William Rowley. Fr. The Thracian Wonder, I, i. EiL; ELP; OxBoLi
   (Chase, The.) CH
   (Love Pursued.) GBL
   (Pursuit of Love.) ChTr
Art thou gone so far. Ode: The Spirit Wooed. Richard Watson Dixon. OBNC
Art thou not hungry for thy children, Zion. To Zion. Judah Halevi, tr. by Maurice Samuel. AWP
Art thou pale for weariness. To the Moon. Shelley. BoNaP; ChER; GTBS; GTBS-P; PPP; TrGrPo; TTTS
   (Fragment: To the Moon.)
Art thou poor, yet hast thou golden slumbers? Thomas Dekker and others. Fr. The Pleasant Comedy of Patient Grissell [or Grissel or Grissill]. HAP; InPS; UnPo
   (Basket-Maker's Song, The.) OBSC; TrGrPo

(Happy Heart, The.) GTBS; GTBS-P; RB

(Sweet Content.) CH; EiL; OBEV

Art thou some wingëd Sprite, that, fluttering round. To a Maple Seed. Lloyd Mifflin. AA

Art Thou That She. *Unknown.* OxBSP

Art thou the grave of Charidas? If for Arimmas' son. Callimachus, *tr. fr. Greek by* A. M. Young. *Fr.* Epigrams, XV. OBD

Art Thou the Same. Frances Dorr Tatnall. AA

Artegall and Radigund. Spenser. *Fr.* The Faerie Queene, V, 5. OBSC

Artemidora! Gods invisible. The Death of Artemidora. Walter Savage Landor. *Fr.* Pericles and Aspasia, LXXXV. EnRP; OBNC

Artemis. Rita Boumi-Pappas, *tr. fr. Greek by* Eleni Fourtouni. AIW

Artemis. Peter Davison. ErPo

Artemis. Dulcie Deamer. PoAu-1

Artemisia Tiger, The. Chang Yü, *tr. fr. Chinese by* Jonathan Chaves. *Fr.* Four Poems On the Ch'ung-wu Festival. CoBLCP

Arteries Juicy with Blood. Osip Mandelstam, *tr. fr. Russian by* James Greene. *Fr.* Lines Concerning the Unknown Soldier. NAs

Arteriosclerosis. Jacob Glatstein, *tr. fr. Yiddish by* Benjamin *and* Barbara Harshav. AYP

Arthritic farmer and a calf watch Dr. Graves, The. These Obituaries of Rattlesnakes Being Eaten by the Hogs. Roger Weingarten. AmPA

Arthritis. Jan Glading. TSM

Arthur. Ogden Nash. FiBHP; NoP

Arthur. Tom Paulin. FaBCIP

Arthur. William Winter. AA

Arthur Hugh Clough. Richard O'Connell. *Fr.* Lives of the Poets. SoTCo

Arthur Mitchell. Marianne Moore. PoNe; RR

Arthur O'Bower has broken his bands [*or* band]. The Wind. *Unknown.* FaBoCh; GBP; OxNR

(High Wind, The.) ChTr

Arthur Ridgewood, M.D. Frank Marshall Davis. BPo

Arthur wes forwunded, wunder ane swithe. The Passing of Arthur. Layamon. *Fr.* The Brut. PoE

Arthur's Seat, *sel.* Thomas Mercer. "Where is the gallant race that rose." OxBS

Artichoke. Henry Taylor. MAYP; MT

Artichoke for Montesquieu, An. Jorie Graham. NPGG

Articles of War. Dunstan Thompson. WaP

Artifact. Edith Purevich. GOS

Artifice Afire. René Daumal, *tr. fr. French by* Michael Benedikt. POS

Artificer. X. J. Kennedy. TwCP

Artificial Beauty. Lucianus, *tr. fr. Greek by* William Cowper. AWP

Artificial Teeth. Solyman Brown. *Fr.* Dentologia; a Poem on the Diseases of the Teeth and Their Proper Remedies. FaBoUs

Artillerie [*or* Artillery]. George Herbert. InPS; NoP; PoEL-2; SeCV-1

Artillery Shoot. James Forsyth. WaP

Artisan, The. Alice Brown. TrPWD

Artist, An. Robinson Jeffers. VGW

Artist, The. Stanley Kunitz. CAPP

Artist, The. *Unknown, tr. fr. Aztec Indian by* Denise Levertov. STP

Artist, The. William Carlos Williams. InPS; LCAP; NYBP; RB

Artist and Ape. Gordden Link. GoYe

Artist is the creator of beautiful things, The. Oscar Wilde. *Fr.* The Picture of Dorian Gray. NAEL-2

Artist must leave these woods now, The. The Departure. Reed Whittemore. TAP

Artist on Penmaenmawr, The. Charles Tennyson Turner. FaBoPP; OBNC

Artist, that underneath my table. The Spider. Edward Littleton. NOEC

Artist, The: disciple, abundant, multiple, restless. The Artist. *Unknown, tr. by* Denise Levertov. STP

Artists East and West. Diana Chang. BrSi

Artless Talk. Takamura Kotaro, *tr. fr. Japanese by* Geoffrey Bownas *and* Anthony Thwaite. PeBJV

Artorius, *sels.* John Heath-Stubbs. EBEV

"Age of Bronze awoke now in brutality, The."

"It was the virgin Zennora, who dwelt."

Art's Variety. David McFadden. NeAC

Arundel Tomb, An. Philip Larkin. NePoEA-2; PPP

As a bathtub lined with white porcelain. The Bathtub [*or* Bath Tub]. Ezra Pound. NIP; WeW

As a Beauty I Am Not a Star. Anthony Euwer. *Fr.* The Limeratomy. InvP

(Face, The.) OBAL

(My Face.) FaFP; PoLF

As a Bell in a Chime. Robert Underwood Johnson. AA

As a Black child I was a dreamer. Conrad Kent Rivers. *See* As a child I bought a red scarf.

As a boy/ I sometimes lifted. Peter Turrini, *tr. by* Beth Bjorklund. CoAuP

As a boy I left my father, ran off to other lands. Ryokan, *tr. by* Burton Watson. JLIC-2

As a boy I studied literature. Ryokan, *tr. by* Burton Watson. JLIC-2

As a boy with a richness of needs I wandered. Clifford Dyment. OxBTC

As a Buddhist tried for months. Genitori. David Ray. TW

As a child/ I bought a red scarf. Four Sheets to the Wind and a One-Way Ticket to France. Conrad Kent Rivers. BPo; IDB; PoBA; PoNe ("As a Black child I was a dreamer.") AmNP

As a child. I Knocked My Head against the Wall. Anna Swirszczynska, *tr. by* Czeslaw Milosz. PwPP

As a child holds a pet. Port Bou. Stephen Spender. OBTV; TwCP

As a child I was. Woman. Elouise Loftin. PoBA

As a child, Mary Callahan admired. From Our Mary to Me. Alice Fulton. PPR

As a child of cedar, hemlock, and the sea. No One Remembers Abandoning the Village of White Fir. Duane Niatum. CDW

As a child running loose. Learning to Speak. Peter Everwine. NNaP

As a Child Seeing a Cardinal. John Gill. NeAC

As a child, they could not keep me from wells. Personal Helicon. Seamus Heaney. FaBCIP; IPY

As a critic the poet Buchanan. On Robert Buchanan, Who Attacked Him under the Pseudonym of "Thomas Maitland." Dante Gabriel Rossetti. FaBoEE

As a dare-gale skylark scanted in a dull cage. The Caged Skylark. Gerard Manley Hopkins. CMoP; FM; LiTM; MoAB; MoBrPo; OBMV; PBBP; Son; SoSe

As a fond mother, when the day is o'er. Nature. Longfellow. AA; BoNaP; FaBoBe; FPL; PoLF; TAP; TrGrPo

As a friend to the children commend me the yak. The Yak. Hilaire Belloc. FaBV; FaPON; MoBrPo; NA; NBLV; NoAM; NOBL; OxBChV

As a gray hawk's eyes. Hawk's Eyes. Yvor Winters. PoA

As a hungry fledgling, who sees and hears. Vittoria da Colonna, *tr. by* Brenda Webster. WPOW

As a lamp of fine crystal, wonderfully wrought. Radclyffe Hall. *Fr.* Forgotten Island. PeHV

As a little fat man of Bombay. *Unknown.* OxBChV

As a little white snake. What He Said. Catti Natanar, *tr. by* A. K. Ramanujan. PLW

As a Man Walks. Louis Simpson. CAPP

As a man who soon must be without. Hunger. Gaspara Stampa, *tr. by* Brenda Webster. WPOW

As a member of the force, you must consider what force. A Police Manual. David Wagoner. AnAn

As a mirror on which has set. Mohammad Taqi Mir, *tr. by* Ahmed Ali. GoT

As a mote in at a minster door, so mighty were its jaws. Jonah. *Unknown. Fr.* Patience. ACP

As a naked man I go. In Waste Places. James Stephens. MoAB; MoBrPo

As a Plane Tree by the Water. Robert Lowell. CMoP; CoAP; LiTM; MoAB; MoAmPo; NePoEA; NOBA; OxBA; TrGrPo

As a Possible Lover. Imamu Amiri Baraka. AmNP

As a queen sits down, knowing that a chair will be there. Walking to Sleep. Richard Wilbur. LCAP; NYBP

As a rule, man is a fool. Man Is a Fool. *Unknown.* FaFP

As a rule, the patients I know do not pace. Their Patients. Robert Pinsky. *Fr.* Essay on Psychiatrists, XVII. NoAM

As a Seal upon Thy Heart. Bible, *O.T. Fr.* The Song of Solomon, VIII: 6-7. TrJP

("Set me as a seal on your heart.") BoWoP, *ad. by* Willis Barnstone.

As a signet of carbuncle in a setting of gold. Music. Bible, Apocrypha. *Fr.* Ecclesiasticus, XXXII: 5-6. TrJP

As a sloop with a sweep of immaculate wing on her delicate spine. Buick. Karl Shapiro. CMoP; HoPM; MoAB; RR; TrGrPo

As a teenager I would drive Father's. Running on Empty. Robert Phillips. InPK

As a torn paper might seal up its side. The Pruned Tree. Howard Moss. NYBP

As a twig trembles, which a bird. She Came and Went. James Russell Lowell. AA; AnAmPo

As a warbler flits from one plum twig to another. Teika, *tr. fr. Japanese by* Hiroaki Sato. *Fr.* A Compendium of Good Tanka. FCEI

As a white candle. The Old Woman. Joseph Campbell. AWP; MoBrPo; OxBTC

As a white stone draws down the fish. Behaviour of Fish in an Egyptian Tea Garden. Keith Douglas. FaBoMo; OBTV; RB

As a young man, Potchikoo sometimes embarrassed his. How Potchikoo Got Old. Louise Erdrich. *Fr.* Old Man Potchikoo. HATNAP

As Adam Early in the Morning. Walt Whitman. OxBA

As Aesop was with boys at play. Aesop at Play. Phaedrus, *tr. by* Christopher Smart. AWP

As Ah walked oot, yah Sunday morn. Bleeberrying. Jonathan Denwood. MoBS

As an American traveler I have. Internal Migration: On Being on Tour. Alan Dugan. NoAM

As an eagle grasped. Shelley. *Fr.* Alastor; or, The Spirit of Solitude. ChER

As an egg, when broken, never. Thomas Holley Chivers. *Fr.* To Allegra Florence in Heaven. BXAP

As an imperial officer, I collect the taxes. A Ballad of Hu-hsi. Shih Jun-chang, *tr. by* William Shultz. WFTU

As an individual penance when my nothing speaks. "Space Is Not Merely a Background for Events, But Possesses an Autonomous Structure." A. Einstein. Alan Dugan. CAPP

As an intruder I trudged with careful innocence. Old Mansion. John Crowe Ransom. HeIP; NOBA; OxBA

As an old man. John Oliver Simon. BWV

As an old traveller, I am indebted to paper-bound thrillers. Calling Spring VII-MMMC. Ogden Nash. FaBoCo

"As an unperfect actor on the stage." Shakespeare. *Fr.* Sonnets, XXIII. InvP; Son

As Ann came in one summer's day. The Sleeper. Walter de la Mare. MoAB; MoBrPo

As, at a railway junction, men. Sic Itur. Arthur Hugh Clough. EBVV

As at noone Dulcina rested. On Dulcina. *At. to* Sir Walter Ralegh. CoMu

As at return of tide the total weight of ocean. Arthur Hugh Clough. *Fr.* The Bothie of Tober-na-Vuolich, *Bk.* IX. FaBoPV

As at the railing of a bridge. Moment. Zoltán Zelk, *tr. by* Daniel Hoffman. MHuP

As autumn mists. Tsurayuki, *tr. fr. Japanese by* Burton Watson. *Fr.* Kokin Shu. FCEI

As autumn wears on. Tamenori, *tr. by* Steven D. Carter. WFTW

As aw was gannin to Durham. Durham Old Women. *Unknown.* GBP

As aw wur hurryin' on i' th' dark. Ten Heawrs a Day. Joseph Burgess. PF

As bad as a dyer's. *Unknown*, *tr. by* Geoffrey Bownas *and* Anthony Thwaite. PeBJV

As Bad as a Mile. Philip Larkin. InPK; OxBC; OxBSP

As banked clouds. Saigyo, *tr. fr. Japanese by* Burton Watson. *Fr.* Sixty-four Tanka. FCEI

As billows upon billows roll. The Surrender at Appomattox. Herman Melville. PAH

As Birds Are Fitted to the Boughs. Louis Simpson. BoLoP; NePoEA

As black as ink and isn't ink. *Unknown.* OxNR

As boring as the fact of a marvelous friend. The Rainy Season. William Meredith. NePoEA

As bryght Phebus, scheyn soverane hevynnys[e]. The Prologue to Book VII. Virgil, *tr. into Middle English by* Gavin Douglas. *Fr.* The Aeneid [*or* Eneados], VII. OxBLMV; OxBS

As bubbles are baked. Spending the Night. Maxine W. Kumin. CAPP

As by Fire. Ella Wheeler Wilcox. AnAmPo

As by the instrument she took her place. Virtuosa. Mary Ashley Townsend. AA

As cages, think of department stores and certain zoos. Cages. Marvin Solomon. NYBP

As Camels Who Have Become Thirsty. Ilmi Bowndheri, *tr. fr. Somali by* M. F. Abdillahi *and* B. W. Andrzejewski. WTO

As careful mothers do to sleeping lay. On the Deputy of Ireland's Child. Sir John Davies. FaBoEE

As casual as cow-dung. A Stone. Richard Wilbur. *Fr.* Two Voices in a Meadow. CRP

As Catholics make of the Redeemer. Brand Speaks. Ibsen, *tr. fr. Norwegian by* C. H. Herford. *Fr.* Brand. WGRP

As Children Together. Carolyn Forché. NAmP; NoAM

As Chloris [*or* Cloris] full of harmless thoughts. Earl of Rochester. ErPo; TEP

As clever Tom Clinch, while the rabble was bawling. Clever Tom Clinch Going to Be Hanged. Swift. CoMu; FaBoBa; NOIV

As Cloe came into the room t'other day. A Lover's Anger. Matthew Prior. ErPo

As commanded, I looked for my origin. The Search. Michael Hamburger. VWA

As Concerning Man. Alexander Radcliffe. OBSV

As convicts go, when it is time, to cells. The Convict. Anthony Frisch. CaP

As cool as the pale wet leaves. Alba. Ezra Pound. GBL; HAP; SOTW; WeW

As cruel as a Turk: Whence came. On Mammon. Herman Melville. *Fr.* Clarel. OxBA

As custome was, the pepill far and neir. The Assembly of the Gods. Robert Henryson. *Fr.* The Testament of Cresseid. PoEL-1

A dainty a sight as ever I did see! Ballade of Boys Bathing. Frederick William Rolfe. PeHV

As darkness/ is my shelter. The Voice of the Power of This World. Gregory Hall. NU

As Day Begins to Wane. Helena Coleman. CaP

As day did darken on the dewless grass. The Wind at the Door. William Barnes. ELP; GBL; GTBS-P; PoEL-4

As day fades away. Emperor Hanazono, *tr. by* Steven D. Carter. WFTW

As day nears its end. Ietaka, *tr. by* Steven D. Carter. WFTW

As Dick and I. Lines Left at Mr. Theodore Hook's House in June, 1834. "Thomas Ingoldsby." FaBoUs

As Difference Blends into Identity. Josephine Miles. NoAM

As doctors give physic by way of prevention. For My Own Monument. Matthew Prior. OBEV

(For His Own Epitaph.) FaBoEE

As doth his heart who travels far from home. To a Young Child. Eliza Scudder. AA

As Down a Lone Valley. Timothy Dwight. AH

As down the rapid Po I chanced to glide. On Descending the River Po. William Parsons. OBTV

As down the torrent of an angry flood. The Story of the Pot and the Kettle. Charles Montagu. APAS

As down through Cupid's garden for pleasure I did walk. The 'Prentice Boy. *Unknown.* AmFP

As down through Moore's field one evening I went. The Silk Weaver's Daughter. *Unknown.* AmFP

As down thru Sally's garden one evening as I chanced to stray. Sally's Garden. *Unknown.* AmFP

As due by many titles I resign[e]. John Donne. *Fr.* Holy Sonnets, II. JCP; MePo; OBS

As dyed in blood the streaming vines appear. Woodbines in October. Charlotte Fiske Bates. AA

As even little children know. Euro-Squawk. Joan Van Poznak. SoTCo

As, even today, the airman, feeling the plane sweat. Icarus. Valentin Iremonger. BIrV; CIP; NeIP

As evening comes. Sanetomo, *tr. fr. Japanese by* Burton Watson. *Fr.* Twenty-four Tanka. FCEI

As evening comes. Shunzei, *tr. fr. Japanese by* Burton Watson. *Fr.* Thirty Tanka. FCEI

As evening falls the autumn wind is cold. *Unknown, tr. fr. Japanese.* *Fr.* Manyo Shu. Ma

As Expected. Thom Gunn. GLP

As fair as morn, as fresh as May. *Unknown.* GBL

As far as one can see. Teika, *tr. by* Steven D. Carter. WFTW

As far as sleeping goes. *Unknown, tr. fr. Japanese by* Burton Watson. *Fr.* Manyo Shu. FCEI

As far as statues go, so far there's not. From Trollope's Journal. Elizabeth Bishop. FaBoPV; GOA

As far as the eye can see. Teika, *tr. by* Geoffrey Bownas *and* Anthony Thwaite. PeBJV

As far away as distant China. Teika, *tr. fr. Japanese by* Hiroaki Sato. *Fr.* A Compendium of Good Tanka. FCEI

As fine a piece of furniture. Central. Ted Kooser. Psk

As fire, unfound ere pole approaches pole. William Baylebridge. *Fr.* Love Redeemed, LXXXVIII. PoAu-1

As flame streams upward, so my longing thought. He Made Us Free. Maurice Francis Egan. AA

As Flows the Rapid River. Samuel Francis Smith. AH

As for me/ I have seen Llywelyn. A Day Which Endures Not. A. G. Prys-Jones, *tr. by* Anthony Conran. OBWVE

As for me. Requiem for My Mother. Keorapetse Kgositsile. WMBCH

"As for me I am a child of the god of the mountains." This Poem Is for Bear. Gary Snyder. *Fr.* Myths and Texts: Hunting, VI. NoBA; NU

("Bear down under the cliff, A.") HCAP; NaP

As for me, I can take. Tamatsukuribe Hirome, *tr. fr. Japanese.* *Fr.* Manyo Shu. Ma

As for Me, I Delight in the Everyday Way. Joseph Stroud. NPGG

As for me, my Nanna ignores me. Condemning the Moongod Nanna. Enheduanna. BoWoP, *ad. by* Aliki *and* Willis Barnstone

As for my life, I've led it. A Placid Man's Epitaph. Thomas Hardy. MoBrPo
As for people—well. Tsurayuki, *tr. fr. Japanese by* Burton Watson. *Fr.* Kokin Shu. FCEI
As for Poets. Gary Snyder. CAPP
A's for the anchor that swings at our bow. The Sailors' Alphabet. *Unknown.* AmFP; OxBSS, *with music*
As for the birds and the beasts, the men in bygone times. William Langland. *Fr.* The Vision of Piers Plowman, Passus XII. PBBP
As for the Quince. Nuala Ni Dhomhnaill, *tr. fr. Irish by* Paul Muldoon. CIP
As Fowlers Lie in Wait. , Bible, *O.T.. Fr.* Jeremiah, V: 26-31. TrJP
As Freedom Is a Breakfastfood. E. E. Cummings. CMoP; LiTA; LiTM; MAT; NOBA; OxBA; TAP; VGW
As from an [*or* their] ancestral oak. Similes for Two Political Characters of 1819. Shelley. FaBoPV; RB; TW
(To Sidmouth and Castlereagh.) NAEL-2
As from the Dorset shore I travell'd home. The White Horse of Westbury. Charles Tennyson Turner. EBEV
As gay for you to take your father's ax. To a Young Wretch. Robert Frost. OFD
As Gentle Dews Distill. George Rogers. AH
As grit swirls in the wind the word spreads. The Center of Attention. Daniel Hoffman. FYAP; UnPo
As hang two mighty thunderclouds. The Guns in the Grass. Thomas Frost. PAH
As hath been, lo, these many generations. First Travels of Max. John Crowe Ransom. MoAmPo
As He Came near Death. Roy Fisher. FaBoMo; OBD
As he climbs down our hill, my kestrel rises. Esyllt. Glyn Jones. OBWVE
As he enters the house. *Unknown, tr. by* Geoffrey Bownas *and* Anthony Thwaite. PeBJV
As he left the ship he saw this, only this. The Descent of the Vulture. Marya Zaturenska. WPE
As he listened. Waka on Kyosei's Raindrop Sound. Dogen, *tr. by* Lucien Stryk *and* Takashi Ikemoto. ZPCJ
As he moves the mine-detector. Hunting Civil War Relics at Nimblewill Creek. James Dickey. GOA
As he said vanity, so vain say I. The Vanity of All Worldly Things. Anne Bradstreet. NoP; SCAP
As he that loves oft looks on the dear form. On the "Vita Nuova" of Dante. Dante Gabriel Rossetti
As he trudged along to school. The Story of Johnny Head-in-Air. Heinrich Hoffmann. OxBChV
As Hermes once took to his feathers light. On a Dream. Keats. EnRP
As Holy Kirke makes mind. The Nativity. *Unknown.* MeEL
As honest Jacob on a night. The Patriarch. Burns. CoMu
As honey in wine/ wine, honey. Meleager, *tr. by* Peter Whigham. PeHV
As I am,/ I should be able. Missing Beat. Carolyn M. Rodgers. JB
As I am a Rhymer. On My Joyful Departure from the City of Cologne. Samuel Taylor Coleridge. FaBoCo; InvP; OBTV; TW
(On My Joyful Departure from the Same City.) NBLV
As I Am My Father's. Rose Drachler. VWA
As I am not. Posterity. Cyril Dabydeen. BrSi
As I am unhappy. Yosano Akiko, *tr. by* Glenn Hughes *and* Yozan T. Iwasaki. WPOW
As I beheld a winters evening air. Another ("As I beheld a winters evening air"). Richard Lovelace. SeCP
As I behold you motionless. Death and the Knight (1513). Nikos Gatsos, *tr. by* Edmund Keeley *and* Philip Sherrard. VMG
"As I cam in by boney Glasgow town." Glasgow Peggie. *Unknown.* ESPB
As I cam in by Dunidier. The Battle of Harlaw. *Unknown.* ESPB
As I cam thro the Garrioch land. The Battle of Harlaw. *Unknown.* ESPB
As I Came Down from Lebanon. Clinton Scollard. AA
As I Came Down Mount Tamalpais. Clarence Thomas Urmy. AA
As I came down Talbingo Hill. Bullocky Bill. *Unknown.* PoAu-1
As I came down the Cano'gate. Merry May the Keel Row. *Unknown.* GBP
As I came home through Drury's woods. Cold Fear. Elizabeth Madox Roberts. WPE
As I Came in by Fiddich-Side. *Unknown.* RB
(Willie Macintosh.) ESPB
As I Came O'er Cairney Mount. Burns. CoMu
As I came o'er the Devil's Stair. Southward Bound. J. F. A. Burt. PoSH
As I came out of the New York Public Library. Nuns in the Wind. Muriel Rukeyser. NNaP

As I came over London Bridge. Geordie. *Unknown.* OBET
As I Came Over the Grey, Grey Hills. Joseph Campbell. AnIL
As I came over Windy Gap. Running to Paradise. W. B. Yeats. OxBoLi
As I came round the harbor buoy. The Long White Seam. Jean Ingelow. GN; NOBVV
As I came through the desert thus it was. James Thomson ("B. V."). *Fr.* The City of Dreadful Night, IV. LiTB
As I came through the Valley of Despair. Through the Valley. Ella Wheeler Wilcox. AnAmPo
As I came to the edge of the woods. Come In. Robert Frost. AmPP; BoNaP; FaBV; LiTA; LiTM; MoAB; MoAmPo; NOBA; NoP; TrGrPo
As I came to the sea wall that August day. On the Sea Wall. C. Day Lewis. SeCePo
As I come hulking. Crumbs. Donald Finkel. BLA
As I did the washing one day. The Shirt of a Lad. *Unknown, tr. by* Anthony Conran. OBWVE
As I did walk abroad one time. The Mourning Conquest; or, The Woman's Sad Complaint, and Doleful Cry to See Her Love in Fainting Fits to Lye. *Unknown.* CoMu
As I did walke my selfe alone. King James and Brown. *Unknown.* ESPB
As I do zew, wi' nimble hand. Lwonesomeness. William Barnes. NOBVV
As I drive my parents home through the snow. Driving My Parents Home at Christmas. Robert Bly. CAPP
As I drive through farm country. Driving through Farm Country at Sunset. Diane Ackerman. NIP
As I drive to the junction of lane and highway. At Castle Boterel. Thomas Hardy. EBEV; GTBS-P; NOBE; OBNC; PoE; SCV
As I Ebb'd with the Ocean of Life. Walt Whitman. AmPP; NAAL-1; NOBA; PrIm; TAP
As I enter the backlane with a fruit vendor. By the River. Koh Chang-soo, *tr. by the author.* ACKP
As I gaed down to Collistown. The Cunning Clerk. *Unknown.* OxBB
As I gaed in by the Duke o' Athole's gates. The Duke o' Athole's Nurse. *Unknown.* OxBB
As I gaze afar. Blossoms at Their Height. Kaneyoshi, *tr. by* Steven D. Carter. WFTW
As I gaze, the moon dims. Princess Shikishi, *tr. fr. Japanese by* Hiroaki Sato. *Fr.* Seventy-eight Tanka. FCEI
As I get older, I like quiet sitting. Quiet Sitting. Wang Chiu-ssu, *tr. by* Jonathan Chaves. CoBLCP
As I Gird on for Fighting. A. E. Housman. CMoP
As I go to bed, I think. Tomorrow I Will Heat the Sauna. Eeva Kilpi, *tr. by* Aili Jarvenpa. SOP
As I Grew Older. Langston Hughes. AmPP; BANP
As I grow old, and weaker grow my eyes. Yüan Mei, *tr. fr. Chinese by* Jonathan Chaves. *Fr.* Moments of Fullfillment—Writing Down Miscellaneous. CoBLCP
As I grow older. White Dwarf. A. R. Ammons. CAPP
As I grow used to the mattress of moss. Princess Shikishi, *tr. fr. Japanese by* Hiroaki Sato. *Fr.* Seventy-eight Tanka. FCEI
As I hear it, now when there is company. Grandmother and Grandson. W. S. Merwin. NePoEA-2
As I in hoary [*or* hoarie] winter's night stood shivering in the snow. The Burning Babe. Robert Southwell. ACP; CH; ElL; FaBoCh; HAP; HeIP; InPS; LiTB; MePo; NAEL-1; NAs; NOBE; NOCV; NoP; OAEL-1; OBCP; OBEV; OBSC; PoEL-2; Prf; RB; SeCePo; TOF; TrCP; TrGrPo
As I lay asleep in Italy. Shelley. *Fr.* The Mask of Anarchy. EnRP; Mes; OBSV; RB; SCV
As I lay awake. Teika, *tr. by* Steven D. Carter. WFTW
As I lay, fullness of praise. The Rattle Bag. Dafydd ap Gwilym, *tr. by* Joseph Clancy. NBLV; RB
As I lay musing all alone/ upon my resting bed. The Poore [*or* Poor] Man Payes [*or* Pays] for All. *Unknown.* CoMu; OBET
As I Lay Musing ("As I lay musing all alone"). *Unknown.* CoMu (Friar in the Well, The.) ESPB
As I lay musing in my bed. The Praise of Sailors. *Unknown.* OxBSS
As I Lay Quiet. Margaret Widdemer. GoYe
As I Lay Sleeping. *Unknown.* TrGrPo
As I Lay with My Head in Your Lap Camerado. Walt Whitman. AnAmPo; NAAL-1; OxBA
As I leaned at my window. The Song of Samuel Sweet. Charles Causley. OBNV
As I leaned to retrieve. The Savage Beast. William Carlos Williams. TW
As I lie in bed. Joseph Seamon Cotter, Jr.. BANP

As I listened from a beach-chair in the shade. Their Lonely Betters. W. H. Auden. GoJo; NAEL-2; NoAM

As I look around, I see a weir of waves. Teika, *tr. fr. Japanese by Hiroaki Sato*. *Fr. A Compendium of Good Tanka*. FCEI

As I look at the moon. Saigyo, *tr. fr. Japanese by Burton Watson*. *Fr. Sixty-four Tanka*. FCEI

As I look from the isle, o'er its billows of green. Sun and Shadow. Oliver Wendell Holmes. AnAmPo

As I look out from the desk window. Laura St. Martin. FF

As I look out, there are neither blossoms nor crimson leaves. Teika, *tr. fr. Japanese by Hiroaki Sato*. *Fr. Eighty-four Tanka*. FCEI

As I look, the moon has moved West. Teika, *tr. fr. Japanese by Hiroaki Sato*. *Fr. Eighty-four Tanka*. FCEI

As I look, there's no place for my thoughts to go. Princess Shikishi, *tr. fr. Japanese by Hiroaki Sato*. *Fr. Seventy-eight Tanka*. FCEI

As I Looked at a Lake, My Thoughts Turned to a Certain Friend. Chu Yün-ming, *tr. fr. Chinese by Jonathan Chaves*. CoBLCP

As I looked, the poplar rose in the shining air. The Deceptive Present, the Phoenix Year. Delmore Schwartz. BoNaP

As I looked, winter came. Princess Shikishi, *tr. fr. Japanese by Hiroaki Sato*. *Fr. Seventy-eight Tanka*. FCEI

As I my little flock on Ister Bank. Shepherd Song. Sir Philip Sidney. *Fr. Arcadia*. SiPS

As I one evening [*or* ev'ning] sat before my cell. Artillerie [*or* Artillery]. George Herbert. InPS; NoP; PoEL-2; SeCV-1

As I one morning shaving sat. The Cat and the Boot; or, An Improvement upon Mirrors. *Unknown*. FaBoUs

As I pass over Mount Shiotsu. Kanamura, *tr. fr. Japanese*. *Fr. Manyo Shu*. Ma

As I pass through my incarnations in every age and race. The Gods of the Copybook Headings. Kipling. FaPoR; NoAM; OBSV; OHFP; OPOP; OxBTC; TW

As I pass'd [*or* passed] by a river side [*or* riverside]. The Carnal and the Crane. *Unknown*. ESPB; OBET

As I passed by a willow tree. The Willow Tree. *Unknown*. OBET

As I pick young herbs for you. Teika, *tr. fr. Japanese by Hiroaki Sato*. *Fr. A Compendium of Good Tanka*. FCEI

As I picked it up. Taigi, *tr. by Peter Beilenson*. TSS

As I reach to close each book. Against the Evidence. David Ignatow. CAPP; NNaP

As I retire, each day, with myself. First Telegram ("As I retire, each day, with myself"). Abd al-Aziz al-Maqalih, *tr. fr. Arabic by Lena Jayyusi and Christopher Middleton*. *Fr. Telegrams of Tenderness for Sanaa*. MAP

As I rode out by Tom Sherman's bar-room. The Dying Cowboy. *Unknown*. FaBoBa

As I roll back from you. Blank Verse for a Fat Demanding Wife. Jim Lindsey. TW

As I roved by the dockside one evening so rare. Fiddler's Green. John Conolly. OxBSS

As I roved out impatiently. In the Ringwood. Thomas Kinsella. CMoP; FaBCIP

As I roved out on a May morning. Johnny's the Lad I Love. *Unknown*. OxBoLi

As I roved out on a summer's morning. Castle Hyde. *Unknown*. FaBoPP

As I roved out one summer's morning, speculating most curiously. Colleen Rue. *Unknown*. BIrV

As I rowed out to the light-house. The Light-House Keeper's White-Mouse. John Ciardi. PDV

As I rummaged thro' the attic. My Trundle Bed. J. G. Baker. BLPA; FaBoBe

As I Sat at My Spinning-Wheel. *Unknown*. CoMu

As I Sat at the Café. Arthur Hugh Clough. *Fr. Spectator ab Extra (also in Dipsychus)*. ELP; FaBoCo; FiBHP; GTBS-P, 3 *sts.*; NBLV; OxBoLi
(How Pleasant It Is to Have Money.) NOBE; OAEL-2
(So Pleasant It Is to Have Money.) SeCePo

As I sat by my window last evening. Miss Foggerty's Cake. *Unknown*. BLPA; NBLV

As I sat down one evening. The Frozen Logger. *Unknown*. OBAL

As I sat down to breakfast in state. The Country Clergyman's Trip to Cambridge. Macaulay. OBSV; OxBoLi

As I sat in a lonesome grove. The Little Dove. *Unknown*. AmFP

As I sat in the gloaming. The Voice. Walter de la Mare. WSC

As I Sat on a Sunny Bank. *Unknown*. ChTr; OxBoLi, *abr;* OxNR, *abr*
(Sunny Bank.) GBP

As I Sat under a Sycamore Tree. *Unknown*. LiTB
(I Saw Three Ships.) ACP

As I sd to my/ friend. I Know a Man. Robert Creeley. CAPP; InPS; MAT; NOBA; OxBSP; PoM; PPP

As I searched for cherry blossoms. Teika, *tr. fr. Japanese by Hiroaki Sato*. *Fr. A Compendium of Good Tanka*. FCEI

As I see it, T'ao Yüan-ming. The Supervisor, Han Chün-mei, Has Shown Me Five Poems He Has Written. Tai Piao-yüan, *tr. by Jonathan Chaves*. CoBLCP

As I sent over the water. *Unknown*. PBBP

As I sit by the ruddy oak fire. Nestle-down Cottage. Mary Weston Fordham. CBWP-2

As I sit looking out of a window of the building. The Instruction Manual. John Ashbery. HAP; InPS; MoP; NeAP; NoAM; NOBA; PoM; SOTW; WeW

As I sit on a log here in the woods among the clean-faced beeches. Choir Practice. Ernest Crosby. AA

As I sit worn and weary. *Unknown*, *tr. fr. Japanese*. *Fr. Manyo Shu*. Ma

As I Sit Writing Here. Walt Whitman. NAAL-1

As I sleep somewhere near a mountain away from home. Princess Shikishi, *tr. fr. Japanese by Hiroaki Sato*. *Fr. Seventy-eight Tanka*. FCEI

As I stand by the winter sea. By the Sea on a Winter Day. Koh Chang-soo, *tr. by the author*. ACKP

As I Step over a Puddle at the End of Winter, I Think of an Ancient Chinese Governor. James Wright. CAPP; NaP

As I stood/ Ling'ring upon the threshold, half-concealed. Xantippe. Amy Levy. BrRo

As I stood at the door. The College of Surgeons. James Stephens. AnIL

As I strayed in the shade of the Buachaille. The Last of the Grand Old Masters. Tom Patey. PoSH

As I strole the city, oft I. Swift. *Fr. The Legion Club*. BIrV

As I strolled out one evening just as the sun went down. The Farmer and the Shanty Boy. *Unknown*. AmFP

As I strolled out one evening upon a dark career. The Fire Ship. *Unknown*. OxBSS

As I talk with learned people. A Spade Is Just a Spade. Walter Everette Hawkins. PoBA

As I travel, there are no flowers. No Flowers. Ch'ien Ch'ien-i, *tr. by Jonathan Chaves*. CoBLCP

As I traveled from the city. Salah Fa'iq, *tr. by Patricia Alanah Byrne and Salma Khadra Jayyusi*. MAP

As I wait for him to come. *Unknown*, *tr. by Geoffrey Bownas and Anthony Thwaite*. PeBJV

As I wait for you in the grass with lilies. Yosano Akiko, *tr. fr. Japanese by Hiroaki Sato*. *Fr. Thirty-nine Tanka*. FCEI

As I walk out of the *La Belle*. Simply. Laura Chester. NPGG

As I walk through the streets. F. S. Flint. TrPWD

As I walk'd thinking through a little grove. Catch: On a Wet Day. Franco Sacchetti, *tr. by Dante Gabriel Rossetti*. AWP
(On a Wet Day.) BoNaP

As I walked between Bolton and Bury. The New Bury Loom. *Unknown*. OBET

As I Walked [*or* Walk'd] by Myself. *Unknown*. ChTr; FaBoEE; OxBSP; OxNR
(Song on King William III, A.) NA

As I walked down by the river. A Ballad for Katharine of Aragon. Charles Causley. FaBoTw; NePoEA

As I walked down yon meadow, I carelessly did stray. A British Man-of-War. *Unknown*. OBET

As I walked fforth one morninge. Christopher White. *Unknown*. ESPB

As I walked forth one morning fair. The Wanton Seed. *Unknown*. OBET

As I walked forth one summer's morn, all in the month of June. Brave Collier Lads. *Unknown*. OBET

As I walked one May morning. Down by the Riverside. *Unknown*. OBET

As I Walked Out in the Streets of Laredo. *Unknown*. AS, *with music*
(Cowboy's Lament, The.) ChTr; FaFP; GBP
(Streets of Laredo, The.) AmFP; RB

As I Walked Out One Evening. W. H. Auden. FF; HeIP; InPK; LiTM; NoAM; NOBE; NoP; PrIm; RB; TwCP; UnPo
(Song: "As I walked out one evening.") MoAB; MoBrPo; OAEL-2

As I walked out one evening, all in the month of May. The Banks of Claudy. *Unknown*. AmFP

As I walked out one evening down by the Strawberry Lane. Captain Wedderburn's Courtship. *Unknown*. AmFP

As I walked out one May morning,/ One May morning betimes. Searching for Lambs. *Unknown*. OBET

As I walked out one May morning,/ One May morning early. Seventeen
  Come Sunday. *Unknown.* OBET
As I walked out one May morning,/ When May was all in bloom. The
  Royal Fisherman. *Unknown.* GBP
As I walked out one May morning/ When May was white in bloom.
  Cupid the Ploughboy. *Unknown.* OBET
As I walked out one May morning,/ When the small birds sang so sweet.
  The Lover Proved False. *Unknown.* AmFP
As I walked out one midsummer's morning. The Banks of Sweet
  Primroses. *Unknown.* ELP
As I Walked Out One Morning. *Unknown.* AmFP
As I walked out one morning/ All in the month of May. The Banks of
  Claudy. *Unknown.* OBET
As I walked out one morning for pleasure. Git Along Little Dogies.
  Unknown. MoShBr
As I walked out one morning in May. Archie o Cawfield. *Unknown.*
  AmFP
As I walked out one morning, just as day was dawning. As I Walked Out
  One Morning. *Unknown.* AmFP
As I walked out one morning on the fourteenth of July. The Mower.
  Unknown. CoMu; OBET
As I Walked Out One Night. *Unknown.* Mes
  (Sailor's Return, The.) OxBoLi
As I walked out that sultry night. Full Moon. Robert Graves. NOBE
As I walked over the western plain. Legend. Charles Causley. TOF
As I walked the heights of Meelin on a tranquil autumn day. The Fairy
  Harpers. James B. Dollard. CaP
As I Walked through the Meadows. *Unknown.* OBET
As I walked with my friend. Columbus. Louis Simpson. Mes
As I wandered in the forest. Wild Flower's Song. Blake. BoTP
As I wandered on the beach. The Great Blue Heron. Carolyn Kizer.
  CoAP; NePoEA-2; WPE
As I wandered round the homestead. My Mother's Prayer. T. C.
  O'Kane. BLPA; FaBoBe
As I Was. János Pilinszky, *tr. fr. Hungarian by* Ted Hughes. MHuP
As I was a-going to Strawberry Fair. Strawberry Fair. *Unknown.*
  OBET
As I was a-gwine down the road. Turkey in the Straw. *Unknown.* AS,
  with music; FaFP; GBP
As I was a-hoeing, a-hoeing my lands. The Six Badgers. Robert Graves.
  GoJo; GrPl; WSC
As I was a-roaming for pleasure one day. The Little Mohea. *Unknown.*
  AmFP
As I was a-roving one morning in spring. The Mantle So Green.
  Unknown. AmFP
As I was a-walkin' down Paradise Street. Blow the Man Down.
  Unknown. AS
As I was a-walking/ One morning in spring. The Pretty Ploughboy.
  Unknown. GBP
  (Lark in the Morning, The.) ChTr
As I was a-walking down Wapping. Ratcliffe Highway. *Unknown.*
  OxBSS
As I was a walking, I cannot tell where. Narcissus, Come Kiss Us!
  Unknown. ErPo
As I was a-walking on Westminster Bridge. *Unknown.* OxNR
As I was a-walking on yon far distant shore. The Indian Lass.
  Unknown. OBET
As I was a-walking one midsummer's morning. The Plains of Waterloo.
  Unknown. OBET
As I was a-walking [or walked out] one morning for pleasure. Whoopee-
  Ti-Yi-Yo. *Unknown.* AS, *with music;* FaPON
  (Git Along, Little Dogies.) MoShBr
As I was a-walking one morning in the spring. The Sign of the Bonny
  Blue Bell. *Unknown.* OBET
As I was a-walking the other day. The Shoemaker. *Unknown.* FaPON
As I was a-walking to Nottingham Fair. Nottingham Fair. *Unknown.*
  AmFP
As I was cast in my ffirst sleepe. Young [or Younge] Andrew.
  Unknown. ESPB; OxBB
As I was climbing Ardán Mór. The Herons. Francis Ledwidge. ACP
  (Ardan Mór.) AWP
As I was coming down the stair. *Unknown.* CenHV
As I was driving my waggon one day. Gee Ho, Dobin. *Unknown.*
  CoMu
As I was fishing off Pondy Point. Jim Desterland. Hyam Plutzik. RB;
  VGW
As I was going along, long, long. Mother Goose. OxNR
As I was going by Charing Cross. *Unknown.* CH; FaBoCh; OxNR
  (King Charles the First.) GBP

As I was going down the lane. Ballad of No Proper Man. Daniel
  Hoffman. MAT
As I was going o'er London Bridge. Mother Goose. OxNR
As I was going o'er Tipple Tine. *Unknown.* OxNR
As I was going out one day down by the Clarence Dock. Heave Away,
  My Johnny. *Unknown.* OxBSS
As I was going over Mulberry Mountain. Mulberry Mountain.
  Unknown. AmFP
As I was going to Banbury. *Unknown.* OxNR
As I was going to Bethlehem town. Bethlehem Town. Eugene Field.
  WBLP
As I was going to Derby. The Derby Ram. *Unknown.* FaBoNo; GBP;
  OxNR
  (Wonderful Derby Ram, The.) BoTP
As I was going to St. Ives. Mother Goose. NTCP; OxNR
As I Was Going to Saint Ives. Daniel Hoffman. NYBP
As I was going to sell my eggs. Mother Goose. OxNR
As I was going to town. Me Alone. Lula Lowe Weeden. CDC
As I was going up Pippen Hill. Mother Goose. OxNR
As I was going up the hill. *Unknown.* OxNR
  (Jack the Piper.) ChTr; GBP
As I was going up the stair. The Little Man Who Wasn't There. Hughes
  Mearns. FaFP; FaPON
  (Antigonish.) BLPL; NBLV; PoLF
  (Case, A.) OnUR
  (I Met a Man.) OnUR
  (Little Man, The.) RHPC
  (Man Who Wasn't There, The.) PYC
As I was hiking past the woods, the cool and sleepy summer woods. Out
  There Somewhere. Henry Herbert Knibbs. BLPA
As I Was Laying on the Green. *Unknown.* FiBHP
As I was leaving Albion's shore, mist-covered. Konstantin Nikolayevich
  Batyushkov, *tr. by* Alan Myers. AAA
As I was letting down my hair. The Lady with Technique. Hughes
  Mearns. *Fr.* Later Antigonishes. FiBHP
As I was musing by myself alone. Mirth and Melancholy. Margaret
  Cavendish, Duchess of Newcastle. WPE
As I was sitting in my chair. The Perfect Reactionary. Hughes Mearns.
  NTCP
As I was spittin' into the Ditch aboard o' the *Crocodile.* "Soldier an'
  Sailor Too." Kipling. MOS
As I Was Standing in the Street. *Unknown.* NTCP
As I was strolling lonely in the Backs. In the Backs. James Kenneth
  Stephen. NOBVV
As I was travelling toward the city of satisfactions. The City of
  Satisfactions. Daniel Hoffman. Prf
As I was waiting for the bus. Sight Unseen. Kingsley Amis. ErPo;
  NePoEA-2; NoAM
As I was walkin' an' a-ramblin' one day. The Wild Rippling Water.
  Unknown. FaBoBa
As I Was Walkin' down Wexford Street. *Unknown.* AS
As I was walkin' the jungle round, a-killin' of tigers an' time. Guy
  Wetmore Carryl. BXAP; NBLV; Par
As I was walking. Memorable Fancy, A ("As I was walking among the
  fires of hell."). Blake. *Fr.* The Marriage of Heaven and Hell.
  NU
As I was walking. Kore. Robert Creeley. InPS; PoE
As I was walking all alane [or alone]. The Twa Corbies. *Unknown.*
  AWP; CH; ELP; EnSB; ESPB; FaBoBa; FaBoCh; GoTS; GTBS;
  GTBS-P; HAP; InPK; NoP; OBEV; OxBS; PBBP; PPP; RB; SeCePo;
  UnPo
As I was walking [or wa'king] all alone [or alane]. The Wee Wee Man.
  Unknown. CH; EBEV; ELP; ESPB; FaBoCh; GBP; OAEL-1, *with
  music;* OxBB, *with music*
As I was walking along-long-long. Singing in the Spring. Ivy O.
  Eastwick. RAR
As I was walking down by the seashore. The Lover's Lament for Her
  Sailor. *Unknown.* AmFP
As I was walking down Covent Garden. The Buck's Elegy. *Unknown.*
  OBET
As I was walking I met a woman. An Old Air. F. R. Higgins. AnIL
As I was walking in a field of wheat. *Unknown.* OxNR
As I was walking in the fields last Tuesday of all days. The Slender Lad.
  Unknown, tr. by Kenneth Hurlstone Jackson. OBWVE
As I was walking in the park. The Neutral. Wrenne Jarman. CN
As I was walking mine alane. Archie o [or of] Cawfield. *Unknown.*
  ESPB; OxBS
As I was walking one midsummer morning. O Dear O. *Unknown.*
  ErPo

As I was walking one morn at my ease. What's the Life of a Man? *Unknown.* OBET

As I was walking one morning in spring. I Shall Be Married on Monday Morning. *Unknown.* ErPo

As I was walking out one morning, I met a buxom lass. Buxom Lass. *Unknown.* ErPo

As I was walking up the street. O Mally's Meek, Mally's Sweet. Burns. GN

As I went a-walking one fine summer's morning. The Shoofly. Felix O'Hare. AmFP

As I went by a dyer's door. The Dyer. *Unknown.* ChTr; OxNR

As I went by St. James's, I heard a bird sing. An Excellent New Ballad Called the Prince of Darkness. *Unknown.* APAS

As I went down the hill along the wall. Meeting and Passing. Robert Frost. OxBA

As I went down the hill I heard. The Voice. Norman Gale. OHIP

As I went down the village green. Ducks. Norman Ault. BoTP

As I Went Down to David's Town. George Craig Stewart. AH

As I went down to Dymchurch Wall. In Romney Marsh. John Davidson. EBVV; FaBoPP; GoTS; OxBTC

As I went down to the huckleberry picnic. The Kicking Mule. *Unknown.* AmFP

As I went down to the mowin' field. Fod. *Unknown.* AmFP

As I went on Yol Day. Jankin, the Clerical Seducer. *Unknown.* MeEL
(Jolly Jankin.) OxBLMV

As I went out a crow. The Last Word of a Bluebird. Robert Frost. FaPON; GoJo; GrPl; SO

As I went out a-walking to breathe the pleasant air. Rolly Trudum. *Unknown.* AmFP

As I went out one May morning. Bird in a Cage. *Unknown.* AS, *with music;* GBP

As I went out, so I came in. *Unknown.* GBP

As I went out walking for pleasure one day. The Little Mohea. *Unknown.* AmFP

As I went over London Bridge. *Unknown.* ChTr

As I went over the water. *Unknown.* OxNR

As I went over Tipple Tyne. *Unknown.* ChTr

As I went owre the Hill o' Hoos. *Unknown.* GBP

As I went through the marshes. A Doe at Evening. David Herbert Lawrence. BrPo

As I Went to Bonner. *Unknown.* OxBoLi; OxNR

As I went to Totnam. The Maid of Tottenham. *Unknown.* CoMu

As I went up by Ovillers. Ballad of the Three Spectres. Ivor Gurney. OBWP

As I went up the Brandy hill. *Unknown.* OxNR

As I went up the garden. *Unknown.* BoTP

As I went up the humber jumber. *Unknown.* FaBoNo

As I went up to Craigbilly Fair. Craigbilly Fair. *Unknown.* ChTr; GBP

As I went walking one fine Sunday. Coati-Mundi. William Jay Smith. ILY

As I wer readen ov a stwone. Readen ov a Head-Stwone. William Barnes. CH

As I work at the pump, the wind heavy. Mother. Seamus Heaney. NAs

As if a cloud were sailing. Lady Otomo no Sakanoe, *tr. fr. Japanese. Fr.* Manyo Shu. Ma

As if a one-room schoolhouse were all we knew. An Amish Rug. Michael Longley. CIP

As If a Phantom Caress'd Me. Walt Whitman. GBL

As if fixed by a long habit of thought. The Garrotted Man. Barry Goldensohn. NAmP

As if going into battle, the knapsack. Bushfire. Philip Salom. UAS

As if her face were made of glass! She. The Standing Woman. Peter Rosei. CoAuP

As if his eye had no boundaries, at night. Inside God's Eye. Pattiann Rogers. NAmP

As if hit on a thousand times. Asteroid Lil. Steve Sneyd. BWV

As if I carried a charm. Her Going. Shirley Kaufman. PCP

As if I didn't have enough. Small Aircraft. Bella Akhmadulina, *tr. by* Daniel Halpern. BoWoP

As if in a presence of an intelligence. The Cold. Charles Simic. HCAP

As if in that far Pentecostal day. The Living. Gloria A. Maxson. *Fr.* Two Guitars. TSM

As if it were/ forever that they move, that we. Merritt Parkway. Denise Levertov. AmPP; NeAP; PoM

As if it were a relic. Tsurayuki, *tr. by* Geoffrey Bownas *and* Anthony Thwaite. PeBJV

As if it were a scene made-up by the mind. Often I Am Permitted to Return to a Meadow. Robert Duncan. CAPP; CMoP; HeIP; NOBA; NU

As if it's been waiting until he can't have it. Eating. Reginald Gibbons. MAYP

As if my thoughts were secretly listened to. Ishikawa Takuboku, *tr. fr. Japanese by* Hiroaki Sato. *Fr.* Forty-seven Tanka in Three Lines. FCEI

As if of wax. The Pear. Vinícius de Moraes, *tr. by* Ashley Brown. ATCBP

As if some irremediable poison. London. J. R. Rowland. CBAP

As if somebody ordered it. Tashkent Breaks into Bloom. "Anna Akhmatova," *tr. by* Richard McKane. BoWoP

As if the first time. Ernst David, *tr. by* Beth Bjorklund. CoAuP

As if the mind could choose. Perennials. Judith Kitchen. KS

As if the sky could no longer hold its color. The Evening Light along the Sound. Sherod Santos. NAmP

As if the sun were winding round a spool, this. Thin Places. Clark Coolidge. LP

As if the trees were not indifferent. Gathered at the River. Denise Levertov. PPR; SV

As if to foreshadow. *Unknown, tr. fr. Japanese. Fr.* Manyo Shu. Ma

As if to say that I may die. Hitomaro, *tr. fr. Japanese. Fr.* Manyo Shu. Ma

As if to say the land will prosper. *Unknown, tr. fr. Japanese. Fr.* Manyo Shu. Ma

As if touching a boil a willow bends. Basho, *tr. fr. Japanese by* Burton Watson. *Fr.* Seventy-six Hokku. FCEI

As if we swam in air. Word of Snow. Tony Beyer. *Fr.* Surviving the Journey. ATNZ

As if with wardens posted. *Unknown, tr. fr. Japanese. Fr.* Manyo Shu. Ma

As If You Had Never Been. Richard Eberhart. EyDe

As imperceptibly as grief. Emily Dickinson. CMoP; LiTA; NAAL-1; NOBA; NoP; PBWP; PoE; PoEL-5; QFR

As in a dream of flood from which we rose intact but alone. The Break. Elizabeth Nancy Sargent. NYBP

As in a duskie and tempestuous night. William Drummond of Hawthornden. OBS

As in a pot the milk turns sour. The Shattering of Love. *Gond Oral Tradition, tr. by* V. Elwin *and* S. Hivale. WTO

As in a Rose-Jar. Thomas S. Jones, Jr. PoLF

As in a thunderstorm at night. Waiting. Robert Pack. GOYP

As in a Watteau fete of rose and silver blue. The Tempest. Marya Zaturenska. MoAmPo

As in the age of shepherd king and queen. Dans l'Allée. Paul Verlaine, *tr. by* Arthur Symons. AWP

As in the autumn paddies rice stalks lean only one way. Princess Tajima, *tr. fr. Japanese by* Hiroaki Sato. *Fr.* Manyo Shu. FCEI

As in the cool-air'd road I come by. My Love's Guardian Angel. William Barnes. GBL; PoEL-4

As in the depths of an ancient cavern. The Ancient Tear. Luis G. Urbina, *tr. by* Samuel Beckett. MexPo

As in the gardens, all through May, the rose. His Lady's Tomb. Pierre de Ronsard, *tr. by* Andrew Lang. AWP

As in the house I sate [*or* sat]. Poverty. Thomas Traherne. Prf; TEP; TrCP

As in the lonely night. The Setting of the Moon. Giacomo Leopardi, *tr. by* John Heath-Stubbs. PFI

As in the Midst of Battle There Is Room. George Santayana. *Fr.* Sonnets. AnAmPo; AWP

As in your innocent eyes last night. Birthday Poem, November 4th. John Thompson, Jr. WaP

As ink is spilt on paper. Asadullah Khan Ghalib, *tr. by* Ahmed Ali. GoT

As into the Garden Elizabeth Ran. A. E. Housman. NBLV

As inward love breeds outward talk. The Anglers Song (*in* Izaak Walton's The Compleat Angler,). William Basse. OBS; SD

As Is the Sea Marvelous. E. E. Cummings. MOS

As it[t] befel[l] in midsum[m]ertime [*or* midsumer-time]. Sir Andrew Bart[t]on. *Unknown.* AmFP, 2 *vers.;* EnSB; ESPB; OxBB

As it befell on a bright holiday. The Bitter Withy. *Unknown.* ChTr; FaBoBa; GBP; NOCV; NoP; OBET

As it befell upon one time. Hughie Grame. *Unknown.* ESPB (Hughie Graham.) OxBB, *with music*

As it begins to dawn, I almost take for daybreak. Teika, *tr. fr. Japanese by* Hiroaki Sato. *Fr.* A Compendium of Good Tanka. FCEI

As it fell on a holy day. John Dory. *Unknown.* ESPB; OxBSS, *with music*

As it fell one holy-day [*or* on a light holyday *or* high holyday]. Little Musgrave and Lady Barnard. *Unknown.* ErPo; ESPB; FaBoBa; InvP; OBET; OxBB

As it fell out in a long summer's day. Fair Margaret and Sweet William ("As it fell out in a long summer's day"). *Unknown.* ESPB, A *and* B *vers.*; OxBB, *with music*

As it fell out on a holiday. Holy Well, The ("As it fell out on a holiday"). *Unknown.* OBET

As it fell out on a holy day [*or* upon a bright holiday *or* upon one day]. The Bitter Withy. *Unknown.* FaBoBa; NOCV; NoP ("As it fell out upon one day.") OBET

As it fell out one May morning. Holy Well, The ("As it fell out one May morning"). *Unknown.* FaBoCh; GBP; NOCV

As it fell out upon a day [*or* one day]. Dives and Lazarus ("As it fell out upon a day"). *Unknown.* ELP; ESPB; FaBoBa; OBET; OxBB

As it fell out upon one day. *Unknown. See* As it fell out on a holy day.

As it fell upon a day. A Vision of Truth. J. C. Squire. NOBL

As it fell upon a day. Richard Barnefield. *Fr.* The Passionate Pilgrim. GBL; PBBP

(Nightingale, The.) AWP; GTBS; GTBS-P

(Ode, An.) EiL; OBSC

(Philomel.) CH; NOBE; OBEV

As it is true that I, like all, must die. Scene-Shifter Death. Mary Devenport O'Neill. NeIP

As It Looked Then. E. A. Robinson. CMoP

As it wanders. The Little Brown Celery. George MacBeth. TSS

As It Was. John Mander. Mes

As It Was. Lilla Cabot Perry. *Fr.* Meeting after Long Absence, II. AA

As it's such a sweat. *Unknown, tr. by* Geoffrey Bownas *and* Anthony Thwaite. PeBJV

As itt beffell in midsumer-time. Sir Andrew Barton. *Unknown.* ESPB; OxBB

As Jack, the jolly plowboy, was plowing of his land. The Jolly Plowboy. *Unknown.* AmFP

As Jack walked out of London city. Jack the Jolly Tar. *Unknown.* AmFP

As Jock the Leg and the merry merchant. Jock the Leg and the Merry Merchant. *Unknown.* ESPB

As Joe Gould says in. E. E. Cummings. FiBHP

As Joseph Was a-Walking [*or* a-Waukin']. *Unknown.* BoTP; OHIP

(Cherry Tree Carol, The.) PChr

(Christmas Carol.) GN

As Julia once a-slumbering lay. The Captived Bee; or, The Little Filcher. Robert Herrick. CaPo

As Kingfishers Catch Fire [Dragonflies Draw Flame]. Gerard Manley Hopkins. CMoP; EaLo; EBEV; EBVV; FaBoMo; LiTM; NAEL-2; NOBVV; NOCV; NoP; PoE; PrIm; RB

As Lambs into the Pen. Dorothy Wellesley. FaBoTw

As lamps burn silent, with unconscious light. Modesty. Aaron Hill. OxBSP

As landscapes richen after rain, the eye. Foliage of Vision. James Merrill. VGW

As lark ascending. Praying. P. J. Kavanagh. OxBSP

As late I journey'd o'er the extensive plain. Life. Samuel Taylor Coleridge. EnRP

As late I lay within an arbour sweet. A Poem of a Maid Forsaken. *Unknown.* PBBP

As lately I travelled towards Gravesend. The Seaman's Compass. Laurence Price. OxBSS

As laurel leaves that cease not to be green. The Promise of a Constant Lover. *Unknown.* EiL

As life improved, their poems. Postscript. R. S. Thomas. FaBoMo; OxBC

As life runs on, the road grows strange. Sixty-eighth Birthday. James Russell Lowell. OxBSP; PCP; PoEL-5

As Life What Is So Sweet? *Unknown.* OxBSP

As little Jenny Wren/ Was sitting by the shed. Mother Goose. OxNR

As long as Don Oldani. Incompatibility. Luciano Erba, *tr. by* Lawrence R. Smith. NItP

As long as I continue weeping. Louise Labé, *tr. by* Joan Keefe *and* Richard Terdiman. PBWP

As long as I go forth on ships that sail. A Seaman's Confession of Faith. Harry Hibbard Kemp. TrPWD

As long as I live. Lady Kasa, *tr. fr. Japanese by* Burton Watson. *Fr.* Manyo Shu. FCEI

As long as I live. Me. Walter de la Mare. FaPON; RHPC

As long as I remained asleep. Bahadur Shah Zafar, *tr. by* Ahmed Ali. GoT

As long as the word kept its distance and metaphor could double for the sensible. Anno Aetatis XXXV. Emmanuel Hocquard, *tr. by* Michael Palmer. RHTwFP

As long as we look forward, all seems free. The Western Approaches. Howard Nemerov. HCAP; TAP

As Long as You're Happy. Jack Myers. NAmP

As long as you've got inherited provisions stored in your cellar. Comic Verse. Takamura Kotaro, *tr. by* Hiroaki Sato. FCEI

As love and I, late harbour'd in one inn. Michael Drayton. GBL

As love is cause of joy. Love. Anthony Munday. *Fr.* Zelanto, the Fountain of Fame. OBSC

As loving hind that (hartless) wants her deer. Letter to Her Husband, Absent upon Public Employment, A. Anne Bradstreet. OxBA; WPE

(Another ("As loving hind. . .").) SCAP

As mad sexton's bell, tolling. Song on the Water. Thomas Lovell Beddoes. *Fr.* Death's Jest Book. FaBoCh

As many, Mother, are your moods and forms. Bernard O'Dowd. *Fr.* The Bush. PoAu-1

As Mars and Minerva were viewing of some implements. Under the Rose. *Unknown.* OBET

As May came to the Kuroshio off Mount Kinka. Spouting Whale. Takamura Kotaro, *tr. by* Hiroaki Sato. FCEI

As May was opening the rosebuds. Birth of the Foal. Ferenc Juhász, *tr. by* David Wevill. RB

As me and me marrer was gannin' te work. The Collier's Rant. *Unknown.* OBET

"As men from men." Despondency Corrected. Wordsworth. *Fr.* The Excursion, IV. EnRP

As men who fought for home and child and wife. The Battle of Oriskany. Charles D. Helmer. PAH

As men who see a city fitly planned. Proofs of Buddha's Existence. *Unknown.* WGRP

As much as I've made vers and canso. Aimeric de Peguilhan, *tr. by* Paul Blackburn. Pro

As much as someone could plow in one day. Breeze Nomadly Coupling Summer Sounds (Precision Insects Chomping). Bill Knott. PPR

As Much as You Can. Constantine P. Cavafy, *tr. fr. Greek by* Edmund Keeley *and* Philip Sherrard. RB; VMG

As much for the seatide ages of my sons. The Alchemical Cupboard. Asa Benveniste. VWA

As my daughter approaches graduation. The Month of June: 13½. Sharon Olds. BLA

As my eyes search the prairie. Spring Song. *Unknown, tr. by* Frances Densmore. OBVE

As my mind in fancy wanders. The Negro Has a Chance. Maggie Pogue Johnson. CBWP-4

As my new life begins, I start smiling at the people around me. Farewell to Kurdistan. Rosemary Tonks. OxBTC

As My Way Passed through T'ung-ch'uan. Tai Piao-yüan, *tr. fr. Chinese by* Jonathan Chaves. CoBLCP

As "Name of individual, partnership, or corporation to whom paid." Royalties. D. J. Enright. NOBL

As Nature H——'s clay was blending. On a Certain Effeminate Peer. John Winstanley. FaBoEE

As near beauteous Boston lying. A New Song. *Unknown.* PAH

As near Portobello lying. Admiral Hosier's Ghost. Richard Glover. NOEC

As needy gallants in the scriv'ners' hands. Dryden. *Fr.* Amboyna; or, The Cruelties of the Dutch to the English Merchants. OBSV

As New and as Old. Martin Carter. PBCV

As Night Comes On. Cecil Cobb Wesley. GoYe

As night drew on, and, from the crest. Winter Night. Whittier. *Fr.* Snow-bound; a Winter Idyl. TrGrPo

As oceans are to porpoises. The Snowfish. Edward Field. GrPl

As Ocean's Stream. Fyodor Ivanovich Tyutchev, *tr. fr. Russian by* Babette Deutsch *and* Avrahm Yarmolinsky. AWP

As o'er my latest book I pored. Printer's Error. P. G. Wodehouse. FiBHP

As o'er the hill we roam'd at will. Wanderers. Charles Stuart Calverley. CenHV

As o'er thy loved one now in grief ye bendeth. Solace. Josephine D. Henderson Heard. CBWP-4

As oft as I behold and see. Earl of Surrey. SiPS

As often as some where before my feet. Francis Daniel Pastorius. SCAP

As old age approaches. Yün Shou-p'ing, *tr. fr. Chinese by* Jonathan Chaves. *Fr.* A Lament for Myself. CoBLCP

As on a Darkling Plain. Henry Taylor. MT

As on a window late I cast mine eye. Love-Joy. George Herbert. OAEL-1

As on Euphrates shady banks we lay. George Sandys. *Fr.* Paraphrase on the Psalms of David: Psalme CXXXVI. OBS

As on the bank the poor fish lies. The Restless Heart. *Unknown.* WGRP

As on the Cross, the Saviour hung. Deep Spring. *Unknown.* AmFP

As on the gauzy wings of fancy flying. Oliver Wendell Holmes. *Fr.* The Iron Gate. AA

As on the Heather. Reinmar von Hagenau, *tr. fr. German by* Jethro Bithell. AWP

As on the highway's quiet edge. Coast, The: Norfolk. Frances Cornford. OxBTC

As once, if not with light regard. Ode on the Poetical Character. William Collins. EnRP; NAEL-1; NOEC; OAEL-1; PoE; PoEL-3; TEP

As once in black[e] I disrespected walked. On a Maid [*or* Maide] of Honour Seen by a Scholar in Somerset Garden. Thomas Randolph. JCP; MePo

As once in heaven Dante looked back down. The Backward Look. Howard Nemerov. OxBC

As one abandoned on a barren shore. To Rotenham. August, Graf von Platen, *tr. by* Reginald Bancroft Cooke. PeHV

As one advances up the slow ascent. Solitude. Philip Henry Savage. AA

As one, at midnight, wakened by the call. W. W. Gibson. MoBrPo

As one but hears the rumbling thunder. Kuramochi Chitose, *tr. fr. Japanese. Fr.* Manyo Shu. Ma

As one by one the singers of our land. The Succession. Frances Laughton Mace. AA

As One Non-Combatant to Another. George Orwell. OxBTC

As One Put Drunk into the Packet-Boat. John Ashbery. HAP; HCAP

As one that for a weary space has lain. The Odyssey. Andrew Lang. OBEV; OBNC; PoLF; PoRA

As One Who Bears beneath His Neighbor's Roof. Robert Hillyer. MoAmPo

As one who came with ointments sweet. Spikenard. Laurence Housman. TrPWD

As one who cleaves the circumambient air. Timon of Archimedes. Charles Battell Loomis. NA

As one who dreams, in a light sleep, may hear. La Belle Morte. Conrad Aiken. VVA

As one who follows a departing friend. Last Days. Elizabeth Stoddard. AA

As one who hangs down-bending from the side. A Dedicated Spirit. Wordsworth. *Fr.* The Prelude [*or,* Growth of a Poet's Mind]: Summer Vacation. SeCePo

As one who has sailed across an unknown sea. The Solitary. Rainer Maria Rilke, *tr. by* C. F. MacIntyre. TrJP

As one who held herself a part. Sister. Whittier. *Fr.* Snow-bound; a Winter Idyl. AA

As one who, long by wasting sickness worn. Hope. William Lisle Bowles. EnRP

As One Who Wanders into Old Workings. C. Day Lewis. FaBoMo; LiTM

As other men, so I myself do muse. Michael Drayton. *Fr.* Idea, IX. JCP; Son

As our king lay musing on his bed. King Henry Fifth's Conquest of France. *Unknown.* ESPB

(Henry V's Conquest of France.) OBET

As over muddy shores a dragon flock. The Fear. Lascelles Abercrombie. OBMV

As Oyster Nan Stood by Her Tub. *Unknown.* CoMu

As Pants the Hart. Nahum Tate. TIRV

As Parmigianino did it, the right hand. Self-Portrait in a Convex Mirror. John Ashbery. HCAP; NAAL-2

As patience paints the flower red, so grass. And Grow. John Hay. WaP

As people have told from mouth to mouth. *Unknown, tr. fr. Japanese. Fr.* Manyo Shu. Ma

As pilot well expert in perilous wave. Spenser. *Fr.* The Faerie Queene, II, 7. OAEL-1

(Cave of Mammon, The.) PoEL-1

"At length they came into a larger space," *fr. sts.* 21-32. FiP

As pools beneath stone arches take. John Drinkwater. PoA

As power and wit will me assist. Sir Thomas Wyatt. SiPS

As praiseworthy/ the power of breathing. Lorine Niedecker. VGW

As proper mode of quenching legal lust. Gerald Massey. NOBVV

As Ralph and Nick i'th'field were plowing. The Plowman. *Unknown.* APAS

As red as a starling's his peepers. Opium-Den. *Malay Oral Tradition, tr. by* R. J. Wilkinson *and* R. O. Winstedt. WTO

As Regis asserts they resemble one another. The Murderers of Kings. Zbigniew Herbert, *tr. by* John Carpenter *and* Bogdana Carpenter. AnAn

As Rimbaud said, I thought today sitting in the library. Leslie Scalapino. *Fr.* Hmmmm. NPGG

As riper years approach us. Glimpses of Infancy. Priscilla Jane Thompson. CBWP-2

As rising from the vegetable World. James Thomson. *Fr.* The Seasons: Spring. PoEL-3

As Rochefoucauld his maxims drew. Verses on the Death of Dr. Swift, D.S.P.D., Occasioned by Reading a Maxim in Rochefoucauld. Swift. NOEC; PoEL-3; TEP

As round as an apple, as deep as a cup. Mother Goose. OxNR

As round as an apple, as deep as a pail. *Unknown.* OxNR

As round the rose's heart the golden threads. Soul Incense. Henrietta Cordelia Ray. CBWP-3

As round their dying father's bed. The Father and His Children. *Unknown.* OxBChV

As round this earthly globe the oceans pour. Fyodor Ivanovich Tyutchev, *tr. by* Alan Myers. AAA

As Sand. Natan Zach, *tr. fr. Hebrew by* Jon Silkin. VWA

As sea-foam blown of the winds, as blossom of brine that is drifted. "Home, Sweet Home," with Variations ("As sea-foam blown of the winds, as blossom of brine that is drifted"). H. C. Bunner. *Fr.* Home. CenHV; OBAL

As seventh sign, the antique heavens show. Feast of the Ram's Horn. Harvey Shapiro. VGW

As Severn lately in her ebbs that sank. The Severn. Michael Drayton. *Fr.* The Baron's War, Canto I. ChTr

As Shadows Cast by Cloud and Sun. Bryant. AH

As Shakespeare couldn't write his plays. By Deputy. Arthur St. John Adcock. CenHV

As She Feared It Would Be. Lilla Cabot Perry. *Fr.* Meeting after Long Absence, I. AA

As she shook her little fist. The Death of the Novel. David Young. AmPA

As shines the sunbeam through dark clouds. Hope. Mary E. Tucker. CBWP-1

As ships, becalmed at eve, that lay. Qua Cursum Ventus. Arthur Hugh Clough. MOS; OBEV

As shows the air when with a rainbow graced. Upon Julia's Ribband. Robert Herrick. CaPo

As silent as a mirror is believed. Legend. Hart Crane. InPS; OxBA

As simple an act. Way Out West. Imamu Amiri Baraka. NeAP; PoBA

As sinewy as biltong, as narrow. My Grandmother. Perseus Adams. PeSA

As Sir Launfal made morn through the darksome gate. Sir Launfal and the Leper. James Russell Lowell. *Fr.* The Vision of Sir Launfal, *Pt.* I. GN

As Sisyphus against the infernal steep. Byron. *Fr.* English Bards and Scotch Reviewers. OBSV

As slow I climb the cliff's ascending side. At Tynemouth Priory, after a Tempestuous Voyage. William Lisle Bowles. Son

As slow our ship her foamy track. The Journey Onwards. Thomas Moore. GTBS; GTBS-P; SeCePo

As slowly and sadly I strayed by the river. Lost Jimmie Whalen. *Unknown.* AmFP

As soft as silk, as white as milk. Mother Goose. GBP; OxNR

As some brave admiral, in former war. The Disabled Debauchee. Earl of Rochester. BoLoP; HAP; NAEL-1; NOBL; OBSV; PPP; WeW

(Maim'd Debauchee, The.) PoEL-3

As some day it may happen that a victim must be found. Ko-Ko's Song ("As some day it may happen that a victim must be found"). W. S. Gilbert. *Fr.* The Mikado. LiTB

As some fond virgin, whom her mother's care. Epistle to Miss [*or* Miss Teresa] Blount, on Her Leaving the Town after the Coronation. Pope. BoLoP; EBEV; NAEL-1; NOBE; NOEC; NoP; OPOP; PoEL-3; PPP

As some heroes bold, I will unfold, together were conversing. Grand Conversation on Brave Nelson. *Unknown.* OBET

As Some Mysterious Wanderer of the Skies. Henry Jerome Stockard. AA

As sometimes in a dead man's face. Tennyson. *Fr.* In Memoriam A. H. H., LXXII. LiTB

As soon as April pierces to the root. Chaucer. *See* Canterbury Tales, The: Prologue.

As soon as he came home, straightway Pygmalion did repair. Pygmalion's Statue Comes to Life. Ovid, *tr. fr. Latin by* Arthur Golding. *Fr.* Metamorphoses, X. OAEL-1

As soon as I could I have called you together. The Queen's Speech. Arthur Mainwaring. APAS

As soon as I lie down in my soft bed. Louise Labé, *tr. by* Willis Barnstone. BoWoP

As soon as I saw I was naked. Will the Real Me Please Stand Up? A. L. Hendricks. PVCV

As soon as I'm in bed at night. Mrs. Brown. Rose Fyleman. BoTP; OxBChV

As soon as it blows, autumn grass and trees wither. Teika, *tr. fr. Japanese* by Hiroaki Sato. *Fr.* A Compendium of Good Tanka. FCEI

As soon as the day is shoved. Change of Scene. Ellen Warmond, *tr. by* Manfred Wolf. OV

As soon as the idea of the Flood had subsided. After the Flood. Rimbaud, *tr. fr. French* by Enid Rhodes Peschal. *Fr.* Illuminations. SOTW

As soone as wee to bee begvnne. *Unknown.* OBD

As spring has come when the mist trails. Kamo Taruhito, *tr. fr. Japanese. Fr.* Manyo Shu. Ma

As Spring the Winter Doth Succeed. Anne Bradstreet. AH

As sultry as the cruising hum. Muted Music. Robert Penn Warren. KS

As, sum tyme, dois the curser stert and ryn. Virgil, *tr. into Middle English* by Gavin Douglas. *Fr.* The Aeneid [*or* Eneados], XI. OBVE

As summer ends and leaves fall like dust. A Cantor's Dream before the High Holy Days. Martin Robbins. VWA

As supple as a tiger's skin. The Prayer Rug. Sara Beaumont Kennedy

As sure as shooting. From the Brothers Grimm to Sister Sexton to Mother Goose; One Transmogrification. David Cummings. BXAP

"As surely as I hold your hand in mine." Brown Boy to Brown Girl. Countee Cullen. PoBA

As swift as the moon. Tonna, *tr. by* Steven D. Carter. WFTW

As swift greyhound pups run wildly away. A Valediction: Forbidding Whining. David Shevin. SoTCo

As that Arabian bird (whom all admire). William Browne. *Fr.* Britannia's Pastorals, I, Song 4. OAEL-1

As the Allied tanks trod Germany to shard. May, 1945. Peter Porter. OxBC

As the bat flies. Masaoka Shiki, *tr. by* Geoffrey Bownas *and* Anthony Thwaite. PeBJV

As the beaver/ loves the willow. Beaver Love. Geoffrey Ursell. UAS

As the birds come in Spring. The Poet and His Songs. Longfellow. AnAmPo

As the black storm upon the mountain-top. Residence in London. Wordsworth. *Fr.* The Prelude [*or,* Growth of a Poet's Mind], VII. HAP, *short sel.;* PoEL-4

"From these sights/ Take one,—that ancient festival, the Fair." HAP

"Genius of Burke! forgive the pen seduced." FaBoPV

"Rise up, thou monstrous ant-hill on the plain." HAP

Fair below Helvellyn, The. FaBoPP

Young Wordsworth's London, The. FaBoPP

As the body denies the means to look. Pernette Du Guillet, *tr. by* Joan Keefe *and* Richard Terdiman. PBWP

As the Botanist. Mariella Bettarini, *tr. fr. Italian* by Muriel Kittel. DMI

As the brown mowers strode across the field. The Swathe Uncut. John Hewitt. NeIP

As the cassias blossom. What Her Girl Friend Said ("As the cassias blossom"). Peyanar, *tr. fr. Tamil* by A. K. Ramanujan. *Fr.* Nine on Happy Reunion, 6. PLW

As the cat. William Carlos Williams. FaPON; InPS; InvP; NoP; PDV; RR; TTTS

As the chameleon, who is known. The Chameleon. Matthew Prior. OBSV

As the clouds that are so light. The Clouds That Are So Light. Edward Thomas. FaBoTw

As the coin of her ear-ring. June Song of a Man Who Looks Two Ways. Leslie Daiken. NeIP

As the companion is dead. Vigil. Cecília Meireles, *tr. by* James Merrill. ATCBP

As the crest of some slow-arching wave. Lincolnshire Shores. Tennyson. *Fr.* Idylls of the King: The Last Tournament. FaBoPP

As the Crow Flies, Let Him Fly, *sel.* Samuel Hoffenstein.

"Early bird may catch the worm, The." NBLV

As the Day Breaks. Ernest McGaffey. AA

As the day stands when the Sun begins to glow. Dante, *tr. fr. Italian. Fr.* Divina Commedia: Purgatorio, XXVII. NAWM-1, *tr. by* John Ciardi.

As the days go by. Taking the Cool in the Shade of the Trees. Tamemasa, *tr. by* Steven D. Carter. WFTW

As the Dead Prey upon Us. Charles Olson. NeAP

As the deep blue of heaven brightens into stars. God's Promises. *Unknown.* BLRP

As the deer begin to hide. What He Said ("As the deer begin to hide"). Peyanar, *tr. fr. Tamil* by A. K. Ramanujan. *Fr.* Nine on Happy Reunion, 5. PLW

As the dust from the wet dream of a nation. Written in Unbridled Repugnance near Sioux Falls, Alabama—April 30, 1974. A. K. Redwing. VoR

As the evening shower clears. Miura Chora, *tr. fr. Japanese* by Hiroaki Sato. *Fr.* Sixteen Hokku. FCEI

As the fat sheriff who's taken. Sneaking in the State Fair. Kevin Fitzpatrick. RR

As the first congress. First and Last. Bruce Severy. NOVW

As the flute and strings cease playing, there's only laughter and clamor. Poem in Response. Liu Shih, *tr. by* Irving Lo. WFTU

As the fog lifts over. Snacks. Ronald P. Tanaka. BrSi

As the forest absorbs. Snow Fall. Koh Chang-soo, *tr. by* the author. ACKP

As the gods began one world, and man another. Snakecharmer. Sylvia Plath. NePoEA-2

As the golden grass burns out. September Evening, 1938. William Plomer. SeCePo

As the gook woman howls. In the Mourning Time. Robert Hayden. BPo

As the guests arrive at my son's party. Rite of Passage. Sharon Olds. MAYP

As the hand moves over the harp, and the strings speak. Inspiration. *Unknown, tr. fr. Greek* by J. Rendel Harris. *Fr.* Solomon, VI. WGRP

As the hart panteth after the water brooks. Psalm XLII ("As the hart panteth after the water brooks"). Bible *O.T. Fr.* Psalms. AWP; TrJP

(My Soul Thirsteth for God.) TrGrPo

(Search, The, XLII *and* XLIII *Moulton, Modern Reader's Bible*) WGRP

As the holy grouth grene. Green Groweth the Holly. *Unknown.* OxBLMV

As the image of the sun. Estuary. Ted Walker. NYBP

As the insect from the rock. The Making of Man. John White Chadwick. AA

As the lovely new flowers. What She Said ("As the lovely new flowers"). Allur Nanmullai, *tr. by* A. K. Ramanujan. PLW

As the mist clears away. Tamehide, *tr. by* Steven D. Carter. WFTW

As the Mist Leaves No Scar. Leonard Cohen. NoP

As the moon sinks on the mountain-edge. *Unknown, tr. fr. Japanese. Fr.* Manyo Shu. Ma

As the morning glory. Moritake, *tr. by* Geoffrey Bownas *and* Anthony Thwaite. PeBJV

As the mountain torrents roar and roar again. Hitomaro, *tr. fr. Japanese. Fr.* Manyo Shu. Ma

As the mute nightingale in closest groves. To the Blessed Virgin Mary. Gerald Griffin. TIRV

As the night deepens. Yoshimoto, *tr. by* Steven D. Carter. WFTW

As the night grows late. Emperor Kogon, *tr. by* Steven D. Carter. WFTW

As the night wears on. Tamekane, *tr. by* Steven D. Carter. WFTW

As the old year ends. Yoshimoto, *tr. by* Steven D. Carter. WFTW

As the poets have mournfully sung. The Aesthetic Point of View. W. H. Auden. NBLV; OBAL

As the poor end of each dead day drew near. He Liked the Dead. Malcolm Lowry. OxBTC

As the proud horse with costly trappings gay. Shortening Sail. William Falconer. *Fr.* The Shipwreck, II. MOS

As the Queen and Prince Albert, so buxom and all pert. Old England Forever and Do It No More. *Unknown.* GBP

As the rains of spring. Lady Izumi, *tr. by* Edwin A. Cranston. PBWP

As the seasons change. Yakamochi, *tr. fr. Japanese. Fr.* Manyo Shu. Ma

As the seed waits eagerly watching for its flower and fruit. Night VIII (The Eternal Man). Blake. *Fr.* Vala; or The Four Zoas. PoE

As the sin that was sweet in the sinning. Barry Pain. *Fr.* The Poets at Tea, III. Par

As the single pang of the blow, when the metal is mingled well. Tropic Rain. Robert Louis Stevenson. OBTV

As the slanting sun drowsed lazily. Cape Coloured Batman. Guy Butler. PeSA

As the stars hide in the light before daybreak. Avoiding News by the River. W. S. Merwin. NaP

As the stores close, a winter light. February Evening in New York. Denise Levertov. NoAM

As the story goes,/ the Jews bought for themselves. The Jews in Hell. Isaac Goldemberg, *tr. by* David Unger. VWA

As the sun came up, a ball of red. *Unknown, tr. by* Robert Wyndham. ILY

As the sun declined the snow at our feet. Prose Poem. Humphrey Jennings. EAS

As the sun, its globe compressed in. Rannoch Moor. Malcolm MacGregor. PoSH

As the sun that lights creation. Africa. Lizelia Augusta Jenkins Moorer. CBWP-3

As the sunbeams stream through liberal space. Emerson. *Fr.* Woodnotes II ("As sunbeams stream through liberal space"). OHIP

As the sunlight in the sky. For the Cultural Campaign. Chimedin Jigmed, *tr. by* C. R. Bawden. WTO

As the swamp cooler breathes. A Sale of Smoke. Roberta Spear. AmPA

As the sweet sweat of roses in a still. The Comparison. John Donne. ErPo; TEP

As the Team's Head-Brass. Edward Thomas. GTBS-P; MMA; NAEL-2; OBWP; OxBTC; PoE; RB

As the tenth month comes to a river district. P'eng Sun-yü, *tr. fr. Chinese by* Daniel Bryant. *Fr.* Mooring in the Evening at Plum Village, II. WFTU

As the tides flow, in the rain. Buson, *tr. fr. Japanese by* Hiroaki Sato. *Fr.* Eighty-seven Hokku. FCEI

As the Transatlantic tourists. The Doves of Venice. Laurence Hutton. AA

As the tree does not end. Appearance. Norman H. Russell. STE

"As the twig is bent, the tree's inclined." Her Precious Leg. Thomas Hood. *Fr.* Miss Kilmansegg and Her Precious Leg. NOBVV

As the used anger drips from his hands like blood. The Murderer. Paul Petrie. NYBP

As the war-trumpet drowns the rustic flute. Pindar. Antipater of Sidon, *tr. by* John Addington Symonds. AWP

As the warrior reaches up. Sanetomo, *tr. fr. Japanese by* Burton Watson. *Fr.* Twenty-four Tanka. FCEI

As the wind at play with a spark. Louisa May Alcott. Louise Chandler Moulton. AA

As the Window Darkens. Laura Jensen. LCAP

As the Word came to prophets of old. Prophets for a New Day. Margaret Abigail Walker. BPo

As the World Turns. Larry Mollin. NeAC

As the *yu*-cloth is dyed fast and deep. Hitomaro, *tr. fr. Japanese*. *Fr.* Manyo Shu. Ma

As there, along the elmy hedge, I go. Troubles of the Day. William Barnes. GTBS-P

As there are taped sororal presents and psychological reversals. It Was Miss Scarlet with the Candlestick in the Billiard Room. Bernadette Mayer. UL

As they came from the East. Kings and Stars. John Erskine. TrCP

As they came in by the Eden side. The Slaughter of the Laird of Mellerstain. *Unknown*. ESPB

As they carry the white paddy of their land. What Her Girl Friend Said to Him, Trying to Dissuade Him from His Long Journey. *Unknown*, *tr. by* A. K. Ramanujan. PLW

As they sat and talked beneath the boundary trees. Married Love. Sherod Santos. Son

As they surround the house, there is no mistaking. Concert. Otto Orban, *tr. by* William Jay Smith. MHuP

As they were. Confirmation Day. Juliane Windhager, *tr. by* Beth Bjorklund. CoAuP

As things be/come. Word Poem (Perhaps Worth Considering). Nikki Giovanni. PoBA

As this convine and ordinance was mayd. Virgil, *tr.into Middle English by* Gavin Douglas. *Fr.* The Aeneid [*or* Eneados], VIII. OBVE

As Thomas was cudgell'd [*or* cudgel'd] one day by his wife. Swift. FaBoEE
(Cudgeled Husband, The.) NBLV

As those of old drank mummia. Mummia. Rupert Brooke. BrPo

As those we love decay, we die in part. On the Death of a Particular Friend. James Thomson. *Fr.* On the Death of Mr. William Aikman the Painter. OBEV

As those who are not athletic at breakfast day by day. Nature Morte. Louis MacNeice. NoAM

As though an aged person were to wear. Elegy for the Monastery Barn. Thomas Merton. VGW

As Though It Had Never Been. Sándor Weöres, *tr. fr. Hungarian by* Jascha Kessler. FOC

As though my own mother had died. Aleksandra Kollontay. Anja Vammelvuo, *tr. by* Aili Jarvenpa. SOP

As though our hides were the paper. Marginalia. György Somlyó, *tr. by* Jascha Kessler. FOC

As though you never lived. Sa'di Yusuf, *tr. fr. Arabic by* Sargon Boulus *and* Naomi Shihab Nye. *Fr.* Three Dispositions Regarding One Woman, III. MAP

As thro' the Land at Eve. Tennyson. *Fr.* The Princess, *Pt.* I. LiTB

As through earth's garden once I strayed. The Crushed Flower. Mary E. Tucker. CBWP-1

As through the Void we went I heard his plumes. The Doors. Lloyd Mifflin. AA

As thus the snows arise, and foul and fierce. Winter ("As thus the snows arise, and foul and fierce"). James Thomson. *Fr.* The Seasons: Winter. SeCePo

As Thy Days. Grant Colfax Tullar. BLRP

As Thy Days So Shall Thy Strength Be. "George Klingle." BLRP

As Time One Day by Me Did Pass. Henry Vaughan. MeLP; SeCV-1

As to a bird's song she were listening. Deaf. H. C. Bunner. AA

As to a sacrament/ Quiet I go. Love's Language. Donagh MacDonagh. NeIP

As to Being Alone. James Oppenheim. TrJP

As to His Choice of Her. Wilfrid Scawen Blunt. *Fr.* The Love Sonnets of Proteus, VIII. Son

As to kidnap the Congress has long been my aim. General Howe's Letter. *Unknown*. PAH

As to my own concerns, it seems odd, given. Peroration, Concerning Genius. Robert Pinsky. *Fr.* Essay on Psychiatrists, XX. NoAM

As to the blooming prime. To Favonius. Edmund Bolton. OBSC

As Toilsome I Wander'd Virginia's Woods. Walt Whitman. NAAL-1

As Tom the porter went up Ludgate Hill. Tom the Porter. John Byrom. NOEC

As Tommy Snooks and Bessy Brooks. Mother Goose. OxNR

As tongueless Echo in the pastoral vale. To the Greek Anthologists. George Rostrevor Hamilton, *after the Greek of* Satyros. FaBoEE

As t'other night in bed I thinking lay. The Dream of the Cabal; a Prophetical Satire. *Unknown*. APAS

As Tranquil Streams. Marion Franklin Ham. AH

As true as I was born into. Halfway. Maxine W. Kumin. GoYe

As two men were a-walking, down by the sea-side. The Duke of Grafton. *Unknown*. ChTr; GBP

As unto the bow the cord is. Hiawatha's Wooing. Longfellow. *Fr.* The Song of Hiawatha, X. NeLS

As virtuous men pass mildly away. A Valediction: Forbidding Mourning. John Donne. BLPL; FF; HAP; HeIP; HoPM; InPS; JCP; LiTB; MeLP; MePo; NAEL-1; NIP; NOBE; NoP; OAEL-1; OBS; PoE; PoEL-2; PPP; PrIm; SeCP; SeCV-1; SoSe; TEP; UnPo; WeW

As vonce I valked by a dismal swamp. The Old Cove. Henry Howard Brownell. PAH

As wave after wave of the turbulent sea. A. K. Tolstoy, *tr. by* Alan Myers. AAA

As We Are So Wonderfully Done with Each Other. Kenneth Patchen. ErPo; UnAS

As we came through the gate to look at the few new lambs. Ravens. Ted Hughes. InPS; NAs

As We Dance Round. *Unknown*. CH

As we eat crushed strawberry ice. Seamstress at St. Léon. Gillian Clarke. *Fr.* A Journal from France. OBTV

As we get older we do not get any younger. Chard Whitlow. Henry Reed. BXAP; FaBoCo; FaBoNo; FaBoPa; FiBHP; LiTM; MoBrPo; NBLV; NOBL; NoP; OxBTC; Par; UnPo

As we go about the toils of life. As We Sow We Shall Reap. Maggie Pogue Johnson. CBWP-4

As we go fast, rowing the huge ship. Hanishi Mitoshi, *tr. fr. Japanese*. *Fr.* Manyo Shu. Ma

As we lay musing in our beds. The Seamen's Distress. *Unknown*. OxBSS
(Mermaid, The.) ESPB

As we live, we are transmitters of life. We Are Transmitters. D. H. Lawrence. OxBTC

As we loll on white sand in Barbados. The Calvinist's Caribbean. Donald Hall. SoTCo

As we paced along/ Upon the giddy footing of the hatches. Shakespeare. *Fr.* King Richard III, I, iv. MOS

As we row round the jutting beaches. Kurohito, *tr. fr. Japanese*. *Fr.* Manyo Shu. Ma

As we rowed from our ships and set foot on the shore. The Savages. Josephine Miles. LiTM

As we rush, as we rush in the train. In the Train. James Thomson ("B. V."). *Fr.* Sunday at Hampstead. BoTP; OBEV

As we sailed on the water blue. Whisky Johnny. *Unknown*. AS

As we say farewell to autumn. Yün Shou-p'ing, *tr. fr. Chinese by* Jonathan Chaves. *Fr.* Chrysanthemums. CoBLCP

As We Sow We Shall Reap. Maggie Pogue Johnson. CBWP-4

As we speed out of youth's sunny station. Life's Journey. Ella Wheeler Wilcox. PWR

As we stood at the cliff's edge. Against the Wind. Amir Gilboa, *tr. by* Bernhard Frank. MHeP

As we stood on the crushed stone. A Conversation. Barbara Howes. IHMS

As we was sailing on the main. The *Caesar's* Victory. *Unknown.* OxBSS

As we wax older on this earth. The Things That Are More Excellent. Sir William Watson. OHFP

As we went/ I felt a scruple, which I durst not vent. The Poet Questions Peace. George Chapman. *Fr.* Euthymiae Raptus; or, The Teares of Peace. JCP

As we were marching to Quebec. Marching to Quebec. *Unknown.* AmFP

As we withered ferns. Ballade of Dead Friends. E. A. Robinson. AA

As wearied pilgrims, once possessed. His Own Epitaph. Robert Herrick. CaPo

As Weary Pilgrim, Now at Rest. Anne Bradstreet. NAAL-1; PoEL-3; SCAP

(Longing for Heaven.) AnAmPo; LiTA

As Well as They Can ("As well as it can, the hooked fish while it dies"). A. D. Hope. GrPl

As, when a beauteous nymph decays. Stella's Birthday, 1725. Swift. NOEC

As When a Child. Charles Lamb. Son

As when a fragment, from a mountain torn. Virgil, *tr. fr. Latin, tr. by* Dryden. *Fr.* The Aeneid [*or* Eneados], XII. OBVE

As When a Man. Tennyson. *Fr.* A Dream of Fair Women. ChER

As when a Scout/ through dark and desart wayes with peril gone. Milton. *Fr.* Paradise Lost, *Bk.* III, *ll.* 543–571.

(New Worlds.) OBS

As, when a tree's cut down, the secret root. Prologue to "The Tempest." Dryden. NoP

As when an architect some palace wall. Homer, *tr. fr. Greek by* William Cowper. *Fr.* The Iliad, XVI. OBVE

As when desire, long darkling, dawns, and first. Bridal Birth. Dante Gabriel Rossetti. *Fr.* The House of Life, II. OBVE

As when devouring flames some forest seize. Homer, *tr. fr. Greek by* William Cowper. *Fr.* The Iliad, II. OBVE

"As When Emotion Too Far Exceeds Its Cause." Gloria C. Oden. AmNP

As when far off the warbled strains are heard. LaFayette. Samuel Taylor Coleridge. EnRP

As when into the garden paths by night. Old Age. Frederick Tennyson. NOBVV

As when it happ'neth that some lovely town. Sonnet: Content and Resolute. William Drummond of Hawthornden. JCP

As when of frequent bees. Homer, *tr. fr. Greek by* George Chapman. *Fr.* The Iliad, II. OBVE

As when rooting in a bin. Dick, a Maggot. Swift. NBLV; TW

As when some dire usurper Heav'n provides. The Fire of London. Dryden. *Fr.* Annus Mirabilis. ChTr

As When Some Hungry Fledgling Hears and Sees. Vittoria da Colonna, *tr. fr. Italian.* BoWoP, *tr. by* Barbara Howes; PBWP, *tr. by* Lynne Lawner; PFI, *tr. by* Barbara Howes

As when some wayfaring man passing a wood. A Devonshire Walk. William Browne. *Fr.* Britannia's Pastorals, I, Song 5. FaBoPP

As When the Blowfish Perishing. Linda Gregg. NPGG

As when the bright cerulean firmament. Sir John Davies. *Fr.* The Gulling Sonnets. Son

As, when the squire and tinker, Wood. Prometheus. Egan Swift. FaBoPV

As when the winds, ascending by degrees. Homer, *tr. fr. Greek by* Pope. *Fr.* The Iliad, IV. OBVE

As when, to one who long hath watched, the morn. John Codrington Bampfylde. NOEC

As when two men have loved a woman well. Lost on Both Sides. Dante Gabriel Rossetti. *Fr.* The House of Life, XCI. NoP; SeCePo

As when two monarchs of the brindled breed. Paul Whitehead. *Fr.* Gymnasiad, The, or Boxing Match. NOEC

As wild oxen bellowed. What He Said ("As wild oxen bellowed"). Peyanar, *tr. fr. Tamil by* A. K. Ramanujan. *Fr.* Nine on Happy Reunion, 3. PLW

As William and Mary stood by the seaside. William and Mary. *Unknown.* AmFP

As winds blow over white dewdrops. Teika, *tr. fr. Japanese by* Hiroaki Sato. *Fr.* A Compendium of Good Tanka. FCEI

As winter comes, the sound from the valley stream stops. Princess Shikishi, *tr. fr. Japanese by* Hiroaki Sato. *Fr.* Seventy-eight Tanka. FCEI

As Winter, fleeing. The Fearless. Mortimer J. Adler. PoA

As wishing all about us sweet. On St. Winefred. Gerard Manley Hopkins. SaC

As with Gladness Men of Old. William Chatterton Dix. FaPoR

As with heaped bees at hiving time. Robert Louis Stevenson. NOBVV

As with the dapper terns, or that sole cloud. Trolling for Blues. Richard Wilbur. BAP

As with varnished red and glistening. Casualty. W. E. Henley. *Fr.* In Hospital, XIII. BrPo

As withereth the primrose by the river. A Palinode. Edmund Bolton. EIL; InvP; OBSC; PoEL-2; PrIm

As Women of Our Race. Mrs. Henry Linden. CBWP-4

As woods whose change appeares. Horace, *tr. fr. Latin by* Ben Jonson. *Fr.* The Art of Poetry. OBVE

As Wulfstan said on another occasion. Speech for the Repeal of the McCarran Act. Richard Wilbur. CMoP; GOA

As ye go through these palm-trees. A Song of the Virgin Mother. Lope de Vega, *tr. by* Ezra Pound. AWP

As ye see, a mountaine lion fare. Sarpedon's Speech. Homer, *tr. fr. Greek by* George Chapman. *Fr.* The Iliad, II. OBS

As years do grow, so cares increase. To Mistress Anne Cecil, upon Making Her a New Year's Gift, January 1, 1567-8. William Cecil, Lord Burghley. EIL; OBSC

As Yet. Vicente Rodríguez Nietzche, *tr. fr. Spanish by* Julio Marzán. InW

As yonder lamp in my vacated room. The Lamp. Charles Whitehead. OBEV

As you advance in years you long. Of Change of Opinions. Victor Plarr. NOBVV

As you all know, tonight is the night of the full moon. 12 o'Clock News. Elizabeth Bishop. OxBC

As You Came from the Holy Land. John Ashbery. CAPP

As You Came from the Holy Land, *sel.* Sir Walter Ralegh.

"But true love is a durable fire." OBD

As You [*or* Ye] Came from the Holy Land of Walsingham. *Unknown, sometimes at. to* Sir Walter Ralegh. AAS; ChTr; EIL; EnLoPo; GBL; HAP; InPS; NoP; OBEV; PoEL-2; PrIm; RB; TrGrPo

(Holy Land of Walsingham, The.) EnSB

(Walsingham[e].) BoLoP; FaBoCh; LiTB; NOBE; OBSC; PPP

As you came with me in silence. Changes. Seamus Heaney. FaBCIP

As You Come In. Anne Marriott. NOBC

As you drank deep as Thor, did you think of milk or wine? Fish Food. John Wheelwright. LiTA; MOS

As you grow older, it gets colder. View to the North. May Swenson. ER

As you haven't asked me for advice. Plug. Edmund Vance Cooke. PWR

As you, honoured Lord, travelled all the way. Mushimaro, *tr. fr. Japanese.* *Fr.* Manyo Shu. Ma

As You Leave Me. Etheridge Knight. FF; MT; NNaP

As You Like It, *sels.* Shakespeare.

All the World's a Stage. *Fr.* II, vii. FaPoR, II, vii; FF, II, vii; FiP, II, vii; LiTB, II, vii; PoLF, II, vii; RB; TrGrPo, II, vii.

(Seven Ages of Man, The.) FaFP

Amien's Song. *Fr.* IV, ii.

(Song: "What shall he have that kill'd the dear?") CTC

Blow, Blow, Thou Winter Wind. *Fr.* II, vii. AWP; CH; ChTr; EIL; ELP; GBL; GTBS; GTBS-P; HeIP; InPS; LiTB; NAEL-1; NOBE; NoP; OAEL-1; OBEV; PrIm; TrGrPo; WiR

(Amiens's Song.) OBSC

(Blow, Thou Winter Wind.) FaFP

(Song: "Blow, blow, thou winter wind.") CTC; FiP; PoEL-2

(Songs of the Greenwood: "Blow, blow, thou winter wind.") TrGrPo

It Was a Lover and His Lass. *Fr.* V, iii. AWP; CH; EIL; ELP; GBL; GTBS; GTBS-P; HeIP; InPS; LiTB; NAEL-1, V, iii; NAEL-1; NOBE; NoP; OBEV; RB; TTTS

(Country Song.) TrGrPo

(Pages' Song, The.) OBSC; SeCePo

(Song: "It was a lover and his lass.") CTC; FiP

Motley's the Only Wear. *Fr.* II, vii. TrGrPo

Orlando's Rhymes. *Fr.* III, ii. CTC; OBSC

Under the Greenwood Tree. *Fr.* II, v. AWP; BoNaP; BoTP; CH; EIL; ELP; FaBoBe; FaFP; FaPON; GN; GTBS; GTBS-P; HeIP; HoPM; InPS; LiTB; NAEL-1; NoP; OAEL-1; OBEV; OHIP; TTTS; UnPo; WiR

(Amiens's Song.) OBSC

(Song: "Under the greenwood tree.") CTC; FiP
(Songs of the Greenwood.) TrGrPo
Uses of Adversity, The. *Fr.* II, i. LiTB; TrGrPo
As You Like It. Theodore Weiss. TAP
As You Pass High Upon. Sandro Penna, *tr. fr. Italian by* Henry Taylor. PFI
As you plaited the harvest bow. The Harvest Bow. Seamus Heaney. FaBCIP; NoAM
As you read, a white bear leisurely. To the Reader. Denise Levertov. AmPP; PoM; VGW
As you see, sister, I am weary. The Closing Door. Antonia Pozzi, *tr. by* Muriel Kittel. DMI
As you set out for Ithaka. Ithaka. Constantine P. Cavafy, *tr. by* Edmund Keeley *and* Philip Sherrard. VMG
As you went away. Abutsu, *tr. by* Steven D. Carter. WFTW
As you will know. What It Means to Be Naked. Bill Manhire. ATNZ
As yung Awrora with cristall haile. The Fenyeit Freir of Tungland. William Dunbar. OxBLMV
Asante Sana, Te Te. Thadious M. Davis. BlSi
Asbestos-suited Man in Hell, The. Gordon Challis. ATNZ
Ascend my shoulders, firmly keep thy seat. Formerly *at.* to Homer, *tr. fr. Greek by* Thomas Parnell. *Fr.* The Battle of the Frogs and Mice. OBVE
Ascendancy. Herbert A. Simmons. NBP
Ascending Red Cedar Moon. Duane Niatum. CDW
Ascending the mountain, I let my eyes roam. Climbing to the Peak of Yang-t'ai Mountain to View the Ming Tombs. Wang P'eng-yün, *tr. by* Kang-i Sun Chang. WFTU
Ascension. Denis Devlin. BIrV
Ascension [*or* Ascention]. John Donne. *Fr.* La Corona. OBS; Son
Ascension. Kaneko Mitsuharu, *tr. fr. Japanese by* Geoffrey Bownas *and* Anthony Thwaite. PeBJV
Ascension Hymn, *sel.* Henry Vaughan.
"Dear, beauteous death! the jewel of the just." OBD
"Dust and clay." SeCV-1; TrCP
Ascension: 1925, The. John Malcolm Brinnin. InPK
Ascension of Our Lord Jesus Christ. Christopher Smart. *Fr.* Hymns and Spiritual Songs, XIV. NOCV
Ascension Thursday. Saunders Lewis, *tr. fr. Welsh by* Gwyn Morgan. OBWVE
Ascent. Donald G. Saunders. PoSH
Ascent to the Sierras. Robinson Jeffers. OxBA
Ascention. John Donne. OBS
Ascetic, The. Victor James Daley. PoAu-1
Ascot Waistcoat. David McCord. FiBHP; NBLV
(Sportif.) NYBP
Ase I me rod this ender day. The Five Joys of Mary. *Unknown.* MeEL
Ash. Kim Hyun-sung, *tr. fr. Korean by* Koh Chang-soo. ACKP
Ash falls on the roof. Mother. Erica Jong. TV
Ash-Glory. Paul Celan, *tr. fr. German by* Joachim Neugroschel. VWA
Ash on an old man's sleeve. T. S. Eliot. *Fr.* Four Quartets: Little Gidding, II. FaBoTw
Ash pail has stopped dripping, The. Boncho, *tr. fr. Japanese by* Hiroaki Sato. *Fr.* Twenty-one Hokku. FCEI
Ash Wednesday. T. S. Eliot. LiTA; MoAB; MoAmPo; OxBA; VGW *Sels.*
"Although I do not hope to turn again." NoAM; NOBA
"At the first turning of the second stair." NOBA
Ash Wednesday. Christina Rossetti. TrCP
Ashby. John Reuben Thompson. AA
Ashcake. Thomas Nelson Page. AA
Ashen feelers of the frigid morrow, The. The Specter. Ernst Hardt, *tr. by* Jethro Bithell. AWP
Ashen man on ashen cliff above the salt halloo. Statue against a Clear Sky. Wallace Stevens. *Fr.* New England Verses. EyDe
Ashes. Vasco Popa, *tr. fr. Serbo-Croatian by* Anne Pennington. *Fr.* Games. RB
Ashes. Brian Turner. ATNZ
Ashes of Life. Edna St. Vincent Millay. BLPL; FaBoBe
Ashes of Roses. Elaine Goodale Eastman. AA
Ashes of roses, forsythia bones. Changes of Life. Constance Urdang. VWA
Ashes to NASA, dust to space. Heaven Can't Wait. Robert N. Feinstein. SoTCo
Ashkelon. Anthony Rudolf. VWA
Ashkelon is not cut off with the remnant of a val ley. Judith. Adah Isaacs Menken. CBWP-1

Ashland Tragedy, The. Elijah Adams. AmFP
Ashokan. Dachine Rainer. NePoAm
Ashtabula Disaster, The. Julia A. Moore. OBAL
Asian Desert. Dorothy Wellesley. OBMV
Asian Peace Offers Rejected without Publication. Robert Bly. NaP
Asians Dying, The. W. S. Merwin. CoAP; HCAP; NaP; NOBA; NYBP
Aside. Alan Dugan. PoA
Aside. R. S. Thomas. OxBC
Asides. Paul Valéry, *tr. fr. French by* William Jay Smith. CT
Asides on the Oboe. Wallace Stevens. FaBoMo; MoAB; MoAmPo
A-Sitting on a Gate. "Lewis Carroll." *See* Through the Looking-Glass: I'll tell Thee everything I can see.
Ask, and Ye Shall Receive. Mrs. Havens. BLRP
Ask Buddha—he doesn't know. Unzan, *tr. by* Lucien Stryk *and* Takashi Ikemoto. ZPCJ
Ask even at the world's end. On Frost. Wang Fu-chih, *tr. by* Irving Lo. WFTU
Ask in one life no more. Word by Night. Charles Brasch. ATNZ; PeNZ
Ask, is it well, O thou consumed of fire. The Burning of the Law. Meïr of Rothenburg, *tr. by* Nina Davis Salaman. TrJP
Ask no more, my truth to prove. Winter Song. Elizabeth Tollet. NOEC
Ask Me No More [the Moon May Draw the Sea]. Tennyson. *Fr.* The Princess, *Pt.* VI. GBL; LiTB; NAEL-2; OBNC; PoEL-5; TrGrPo
Ask Me No More Where Jove Bestows. Thomas Carew. AWP; ELP; HAP; NAEL-1; PoE; PoRA; SeCePo; TEP
(Song: "Ask [*or* Aske] me no more where Jove bestows.") CaPo; CH; EnLoPo; FaFP; GBL; HeIP; HoPM; InPS; LiTB; MeLP; MePo; NOBE; NoP; OBEV; OBS; PoEL-3; PPP; SeCP; SeCV-1; TrGrPo
Ask me no more, why there appears. Pyms Anarchy. *At.* to Thomas Jordan. OBS
Ask me not for the semblance of my loue. She Dwelt among the Untrodden Ways. J. C. Squire. BXAP
Ask me not of the heart's. Mohammad Taqi Mir, *tr. by* Ahmed Ali. GoT
Ask me why I send you here. The Primrose. *At.* to Robert Herrick. FaBoUs; OBEV
Ask night how it feels to be dark. To Be Black, to Be Lost. Hannah Kahn. GoYe
Ask no return for love that's given. Horace Gregory. *Fr.* Chorus for Survival, XIV. VGW
(Ask No Return.) MoAmPo
Ask not overmuch for fair. He That Loves a Rosy Cheek. Heinrich von Rugge, *tr. by* Jethro Bithell. AWP
Ask not the cause why sullen Spring. Song to a Fair Young Lady, Going Out of the Town in the Spring. Dryden. OBEV; OBS
Ask not why hearts turn magazines of passions. A Funeral Elogy, upon Mrs. Anne Bradstreet. John Norton. SCAP
Ask the Empresse of the night. The Magnet. Thomas Stanley. MePo; NOBE
Ask the Mountains. Phil George. NOVW
Ask the west wind why it keeps up its lament. Withered Willows. Wang Fu-chih, *tr. by* Irving Lo. WFTU
Ask you what provocation I have had? Pope. *Fr.* Epilogue to the Satires [*or* 1738], Dialogue II. OBSV
(Defence of Satire.) NOEC
(Power of Ridicule, The.) NOBE
Asked "Did you hear it?" *Unknown, tr. by* Geoffrey Bownas *and* Anthony Thwaite. PeBJV
Asked, "How old?" a child shows its palm. Issa, *tr. by* Hiroaki Sato. FCEI
Askest, "How long thou shalt stay?" The Visit. Emerson. AnAmPo; NOBA
Askest thou of these graves? They'll tell thee. Gheluvelt. Robert Bridges. BrPo
Asking for Ruthie. Judy Grahn. ER; NMM
Asking what, asking what?—all a boy's afternoon. Debate: Question, Quarry, Dream. Robert Penn Warren. VGW
Asleep. Wilfred Owen. MMA
Asleep. William Winter. AA
Asleep at the Switch. George Hoey. BeLS
Asleep he wheezes at his ease. Roger the Dog. Ted Hughes. RHPC
Asleep in the Arms of Mother Night. Andrew Joron. BWV
Asleep, My Love? Shakespeare. *Fr.* A Midsummer Night's Dream, V, i. CTC
Asleep while the children howl and the house burns. Goddess. Judith Johnson Sherwin. BoWoP
Asleep, you turn. Hot Bath in an Old Hotel. Paula Rankin. MT

A-sleepin' at length on the sand. The Sea Serpent. Wallace Irwin. FiBHP
Asmodai. Geoffrey Hill. NePoEA
Asolando, sels. Robert Browning.
　"At the midnight in the silence of the sleep-time." FaBV; FiP; NOBE; OBNC; OHFP; TEP; TrGrPo
　(Epilogue: "At the midnight in the silence of the sleep-time.") NAEL-1
　"Poet's age is sad, The: for why?" OAEL-2
Aspatia's Song. Beaumont and Fletcher. See Maid's Tragedy, The.
Aspect of Love, Alive in the Ice and Fire, An. Gwendolyn Brooks. BPo; CAPP; TAP
Aspecta Medusa. Dante Gabriel Rossetti. OxBSP
Aspects. Norman MacCaig. OxBS
Aspects of Eve. Linda Pastan. CRP
Aspects of Now, sel. Gwyn Williams.
　"Today has it all, sunshine." OBWVE
Aspects of Robinson. Weldon Kees. CoAP; NaP; NYBP
Aspects of Spring in Greater Boston. George Starbuck. Fr. Poems from a First Year in Boston, II. NYBP
Aspects of the Pines. Paul Hamilton Hayne. AA
Aspects of the World like Coral Reefs. William Bronk. VGW
Aspen and the Stream, The. Richard Wilbur. NYBP
Aspens. Edward Thomas. InPS
Aspens yesterday, The. Did You Not See. Alex Kuo. BrSi
Asphalt morning found him, The; he was dead. Raccoon on the Road. Joseph Payne Brennan. GoYe
Asphodel. David Malouf. CBAP
Asphodel, That Greeny Flower, sels. William Carlos Williams.
　"Approaching death." FaBoMo
　"Of asphodel, that greeny flower." CMoP
Aspiration. Mário de Andrade, tr. fr. Portuguese by John Nist. TTY
Aspiration. Adah Isaacs Menken. CBWP-1
Aspiration. Henrietta Cordelia Ray. CBWP-3
Aspiring Man, by learned pens. Brief Essay on Man. Arthur Guiterman. OBAL
Aspiring Poet. Koh Chang-soo, tr. fr. Korean by the author. ACKP
Ass, The. Moses Mendes. Fr. The Chaplet. TrJP
Ass-Face. Dame Edith Sitwell. OBMV
Ass in the Lion's Skin, The ("An ass put on a lion's skin and went"). Aesop, tr. fr. Greek by William Ellery Leonard. AWP
Ass will with his long ears fray, An. Samuel Butler. FaBoEE
Assailant. John Raven. BPo
Assassination, The. Robert Hillyer. MoAmPo; OFD
Assassination, The. Donald Justice. CAPP
Assassination. Don L. Lee. AmNP; FF; NeAC; OFD; PoBA
Assassination Poems. John Ridland. MAT; OFD
Assassin's Fatal Error, The. Lawrence Raab. AmPA
Assault on the Fortress, The. Timothy Dwight. PAH
Assemble, all ye maidens, at the door. Elegy on a Lady, Whom Grief for the Death of Her Betrothed Killed. Robert Bridges. OBEV
Assemble the stone fragments from the shattering of forward. Clubs Are Trump. Benjamin Péret, tr. by Michael Benedikt. POS
Assembled Whole, The. René Char, tr. fr. French by William Jay Smith. CT
Assembling of the Fays, The. Joseph Rodman Drake. Fr. The Culprit Fay. GN
Assembling the Model. Peter Payack. BWV
Assembly: Harlem School. Eugene T. Maleska. GoYe
Assembly of Ladies, The, sel. Lady of the Assembly.
　Palace of Pleasant Regard, The. WPE
Assembly of the Gods, The. Robert Henryson. Fr. The Testament of Cresseid. PoEL-1
Asses' milk, half a pint, take at seven, or before. Advice to a Lady in Autumn. Earl of Chesterfield. FaBoUs
　(Advice to a Young Lady.) NOEC
"Asshole" and "shit" were always on her lips. A Lady. W. D. Snodgrass. TW
Assignation, The. Juana de Ibarbourou, tr. fr. Spanish by Brian Swann. PBWP
Assignation, The, sel. Poe.
　To One in Paradise. AA; AmPP; BLPL; BoLoP; LiTA; OBEV; OxBA; PoLF; TAP; TrGrPo
Assignation, The. James Wright. NePoEA
Assignation with a Somnambulist. John Manifold. CBAP
Assimilation. Eeva-Liisa Manner, tr. fr. Finnish by Aili Jarvenpa. SOP
Assistance, The. Paul Blackburn. NeAP; PoM
Assistant editor of Crewel World, The. The New York Woman. L. E. Sissman. MAT

Associated Press called it, The. A Sirventes against the Management of the Mammoth Supermarket in Toulouse. Chuck Wachtel. UL
Ass's hoof alone can hold, An. On Burning a Dull Poem. Swift. TW
Assume/ that being human. On the Speed of Sight. Raymond DiZazzo. BWV
Assuming that 98% of it's invisible. Cosmology and Us. Thomas M. Disch. BWV
Assumption, The. Sir John Beaumont. ACP
Assumption. Padraic Fallon. BIrV; NOIV
Assumption about the Harlem Brown Baby. Salih Michael Fisher. GLP
Assunpink and Princeton. Thomas Dunn English. PAH
Assurance. Josephine D. Henderson Heard. CBWP-4
Assurance. William Stafford. CAPP
Assurbanipal loved me. The Birth of Aisha and Her Death. Abd al-Bayyati, tr. by Sargon Boulus and Christopher Middleton. MAP
Assynt. Alan Gilchrist. PoSH
Assyrian came down like the wolf on the fold, The. The Destruction of Sennacherib. Byron. BeLS; BLPA; BLPL; EnRP; FaBoBe; FaBoCh; FaFP; FaPON; FaPoR; FF; GN; HAP; HeIP; InPS; NoP; OBWP; OnMSP; PoLF; RB; TrCP; WBLP; WeW; WGRP
Assyrian King in peace, with foul desire, The. The Portrait of Henry VIII. Earl of Surrey. ACP
　(Sardanapalus.) SiPS
　("Thassyryans king, in peas with fowle desyre.") AAS
Aster. Plato, tr. fr. Greek by Peter Jay. PeHV
Asteroid Lil. Steve Sneyd. BWV
Astolfo Visits the Moon. Ariosto, tr. fr. Italian by Sir John Harington. Fr. Orlando Furioso, XXXIV. PFI
Astonished poplars hide. Paysage Moralisé. John Hollander. ErPo; NePoEA
Astræa. Whittier. AA
Astraea at the Capitol. Whittier. PAH
Astraea Redux, sels. Dryden. OBS
　"And welcom now (Great Monarch) to your own."
　"Now with a general peace the world was blest."
Astride on steel. Motorcycle. Benjamin Sturgis Pray. GoYe
Astrologer's Song, An. Kipling. MoBrPo
Astronaut's Widow. Steve Sneyd. BWV
Astronomer's Journal, An. Jane Shore. PoA
Astronomers of Mont Blanc, The. Edgar Bowers. PoA; QFR
Astronomy. A. E. Housman. OBWP
Astrophel, sel. Spenser.
　"Such skill, matcht with such courage as he had." OBWP
Astrophel and Stella, sels. Sir Philip Sidney. AAS; SiPS (Sonnets, I–CVIII and 9 Songs)
Sonnets.
I. "Loving in truth, and fain in verse my love to show." AWP; BLPL; EBEV; GBL; HAP; InPS; LiTB; NAEL-1; NoP; OAEL-1; OBSC; PoE; SeCePo; Son; TEP; TrGrPo
II. "Not at the first sight, nor with a dribbed shot." NAEL-1; OAEL-1
III. "Let dainty wits cry on the Sisters nine." OAEL-1; OBSC; SiPS; Son
V. "It is most true that eyes are formed to serve." NAEL-1; OAEL-1; OBSC; Son
VI. "Some lovers speak, when they their muses entertain." NAEL-1; Son
VII. "When Nature made her chief work, Stella's eyes." NAEL-1; NIP; Son
IX. "Queen Virtue's court, which some call Stella's face." NAEL-1
X. "Reason, in faith thou art well served, that still." NAEL-1
XI. "In truth, O Love, with what a boyish kind." ElL; InvP; PoE
XIV. "Alas, have I not pain enough, my friend." NoP; OAEL-1
XV. "You that do search for every purling spring." NAEL-1; OAEL-1; OBSC; Son
XVI. "In nature apt to like when I did see." NAEL-1
XVIII. "With what sharp checks I in myself am shent." NAEL-1
XX. "Fly, fly, my friends, I have my death wound; fly." OAEL-1; TEP
XXI. "Your words, my friend, right helpful caustics, blame." NAEL-1; PoE; TEP
XXII. "In highest way of heaven the Sun did ride." OBSC; Son
XXV. "Wisest scholar of the wight most wise, The." NoP; OAEL-1
XXVI. "Though dusty wits dare scorn astrology." OAEL-1; Son
XXVIII. "You that with allegory's curious frame." OAEL-1
XXX. "Whether the Turkish new-moon minded be." PoE
XXXI. "With how sad steps, O [or Oh] Moon, thou climb'st the skies!" AWP; BoLoP; CH; ChTr; ElL; EnLoPo; GBL; HAP; HeIP; InPS; InvP; MAT; NAEL-1; NoP; OBSC; PoE; PoEL-1; PoRA; PPP; Son; TEP; TrGrPo; WeW

(His Lady's Cruelty.) OBEV
(Languishing Moon, The.) BoNaP
(To the Sad Moon.) NOBE
XXXIII. "I might—unhappy word—oh me, I might." OAEL-1; OBSC
XXXVII. "My mouth doth water, and my breast doth swell." NAEL-1; Son
XXXIX. "Come sleep! O sleep, the certain knot of peace." EiL; NAEL-1; NIP; NoP; OBSC; PoE; PoRA; PPP; SCV; Son; TEP; TrGrPo
(Sleep.) OBEV
(To Sleep.) NOBE
XLI. "Having this day my horse, my hand, my lance." HAP; NAEL-1; OBSC; PoE; Son
XLV. "Stella oft sees the very face of woe." InPS; NAEL-1; PoE
XLVII. "What, have I thus betrayed my liberty?." GBL; NAEL-1; NoP; PoEL-1
(Yoke of Tyranny, The.) TrGrPo
XLVIII. "Soul's joy, bend not those morning stars from me." NoP
XLIX. "I on my horse, and Love on me, doth try." NAEL-1; NoP; OAEL-1; PoE
LII. "Strife is grown between Virtue and Love, A." NAEL-1; NoP
LIII. "In martial sports I had my cunning tried." NAEL-1
LIV. "Because I breathe not love to every one." InPS; OBSC; TrGrPo
LVI. "Fie, school of patience, fie, your lesson is." NAEL-1
LIX. "Dear, why make you more of a dog than me?." GBL; PrIm
LXI. "Oft with true sighs, oft with uncallèd tears." NAEL-1
LXIII. "O grammar-rules, O now your virtues show."
(Grammar-Rules.) FaBoUs
LXIV. "No more, my dear, no more these counsels try." OBSC
LXV. "Love, by sure proof I may call thee unkind." Son
LXVIII. "Stella, the only planet of my light." OBSC
LXIX. "O joy too high for my low style to show!" NAEL-1; TrGrPo
LXXI. "Who will in fairest book of Nature know." InPS; NAEL-1; NoP; OAEL-1; PoE
LXXII. "Desire, though thou my old companion art." NAEL-1
LXXIII. "Love still a boy and oft a wanton is." Son
LXXIV. "I never drank of Aganippe well." HeIP; NAEL-1; OBSC; Son
LXXXI. "O kiss, which dost those ruddy gems impart." NAEL-1; Son
LXXXII. "Nymph of the garden where all beauties be." InvP; PoE
LXXXIII. "Good brother Philip, I have borne you long." PBBP
LXXXIV. "Highway, since you my chief Parnassus be." EiL; OBSC
(Highway, The.) LiTB; OBEV
LXXXVII. "When I was forced from Stella ever dear." NAEL-1
LXXXIX. "Now that of absence the most irksome night." NAEL-1
XC. "Stella, think not that I by verse seek fame." OBSC
XCI. "Stella, while now by honor's [or honor's] cruel might." NAEL-1; PoE
XCVIII. "Ah bed! the field where joy's peace some do see." EnLoPo
XCIX. "When far-spent night persuades each mortal eye." OBSC; PoE; Son
C. "O tears, no tears, but rain from beauty's skies." Son
CIV. "Envious wits, what hath been mine offense." PoE; Son
CVII. "Stella! since thou so right a princess art." NoP
CVIII. "When sorrow (using mine own fire's might)."
CIX. "Thou blind man's mark, thou fool's self-chosen snare." Sometimes considered part of Astrophel and Stella ErPo; HeIP; PPP
(Desire.) LiTB; NOBE
CX. "Leave me, O Love, which reachest but to dust.", Sometimes considered part of Astrophel and Stella FaBoRV; GBL; HeIP; LiTB; NIP; PPP; SeCePo; Son
(Splendidis Longum Valedico Nugis.) NOBE
Songs.
First Song: "Doubt you to whom my Muse these notes intendeth." OBSC
(To Stella.) EiL
Third Song: "If Orpheus voyce had force to breathe such musickes love." PoEL-1
Fourth Song: "Only joy, now here you are." EiL; GBL; HAP; InvP; NAEL-1; NoP; OBSC
Sixth Song: "O you that hear this voice." OBSC
Eighth Song: "In a grove most rich of shade." OBSC; SiPS
Eleventh Song: "Who is it that this dark night." EiL; NAEL-1; OBSC; PoE; PoEL-1; TEP
(Underneath My Window.) SeCePo
(Voices at the Window.) NOBE; OBEV
Asunder shall the clouds be rolled. The Day of Judgment. Dugald Buchanan. GoTS
Aswelay. Norman Henry Pritchard II. PoBA
A-swell within her billowed skirts. The Mad Woman of Punnet's Town. L. A. G. Strong. MoBrPo

Asylum, The, sel. Hayden Carruth.
"Winds; words of the wind; rumor of great walls pierced." Fr. II. SM
Asylum. John Freeman. OBMV
Asylum under my tread all this day. Samuel Beckett. Fr. Echo's Bones. NOAM
At a Bach Concert. Adrienne Rich. NePoEA; NIP; SM
At a Child's Baptism. Vassar Miller. GoJo
At a Chinaman's Grave. Wing Tek Lum. BrSi
At a Concert of Music. Conrad Aiken. MoAB; MoAmPo; UnS
At a Country Fair. John Holmes. MoShBr
At a Country Hotel. Howard Nemerov. PoRA
At a Danse Macabre. Charles Spear. ATNZ; PeNZ
At a Farewell Party for Fujiwara no Yoshino. Emperor Junna, tr. fr. Chinese by Burton Watson. JLIC-1
At a Fishing Settlement. Alistair Campbell. ATNZ
At a Fragrance of Plums. Basho and Shita Yaba, tr. fr. Japanese by Burton Watson. FCEI
At a Friends' Meeting. Mary Elizabeth Coleridge. WPE
At a grass hut I eat smartweed. Kikaku, tr. fr. Japanese by Hiroaki Sato. Fr. Thirty-three Hokku. FCEI
At a high place. Landscape: 7. Ono Tozaburo, tr. by Hiroaki Sato. FCEI
At a Loss. Moshe Dor, tr. fr. Hebrew by Bernhard Frank. MHeP
At a Loss. James L. Weil. GoYe
At a Low Mass for Two Hot-Rodders. X. J. Kennedy. Psk
At a March against the Vietnam War. Robert Bly. EAS
At a Parade. F. T. Prince. WaP
At a party of university people. Double Exposure. Ian Young. NeAC; PeHV
At a party they cry, "Oh, here comes Carol!" Dirty Work on the Appellation Trail. William Rossa Cole. SoTCo
At a Pause in a Country Dance. Thomas Hardy. Mes
At a pleasant evening party I had taken down to supper. Ferdinando and Elvira. W. S. Gilbert. FaBoCo; FaBoNo; FiBHP
At a Potato Digging. Seamus Heaney. CIP; IPY
At a Private Showing in 1982. Maxine W. Kumin. SV
At a Reading. Thomas Bailey Aldrich. AnAmPo; OBAL
At a Reading. J. D. McClatchy. DiPo
At a Ruined Croft. John Manson. PoSH
At a Solemn Music[k]. Milton, sel. GTBS; GTBS-P; HeIP; NOBE; OBEV; OBS; PoEL-3
"Blest pair of Sirens, pledges of Heaven's joy." UnS
At a springe wel under a thorn. The Spring under a Thorn. Unknown. MeEL
At a Summer Hotel. Isabella Gardner. GrPl
At a Time. Ray Mathew. PoAu-2
At a Vacation Exercise [in the College], sel. Milton.
"Hail native language, that by sinews weak." JCP; OBS
At a Watering-Place. Thomas Hardy. Fr. Satires of Circumstance, V. BrPo; CMoP
At a Welsh Waterfall. Gerard Manley Hopkins. See It was a hard thing to undo this knot.
At a Window. Carl Sandburg. FaBoBe; TrPWD
At Aberdeen. George Macdonald. See Here lie I, Martin Elginbrodde.
At Akitio. James Keir Baxter. ATNZ
At alarming bell daybreak, before. Eiléan Ní Chuilleanáin. Fr. Site of Ambush. CIP
At all the corners. Unknown, tr. by Geoffrey Bownas and Anthony Thwaite. PeBJV
At an eagle's nest on dead camphor. Boncho, tr. fr. Japanese by Hiroaki Sato. Fr. Twenty-one Hokku. FCEI
At an Exhibition of Historical Paintings, Hobart. Vivian Smith. CBAP
At an Inn. Thomas Hardy. NOBVV
At anchor in Hampton Roads we lay. The Cumberland. Longfellow. AA; PAH
At Annika's Place. Siv Widerberg, tr. fr. Swedish by Verne Moberg. NTCP
At another year. Birthday on the Beach. Ogden Nash. ASP
At April. Angelina Weld Grimké. BlSi
At Arley. Andrew Young. FaBoPP
At Arrow Rapids, the water spashes foam. Wang T'ing-hsiang, tr. fr. Chinese by Jonathan Chaves. Fr. Traveling by Boat. CoBLCP
At Autumn Cove, so many white monkeys. Autumn Cove. Li Po, tr. by Burton Watson. CoBCP; TTTS
At Baia. Hilda Doolittle ("H. D."). LiTA; NAAL-2; NOBA
At Ballyshannon, Co. Donegal. William Allingham. FaBoPP; NoBVV
At Barstow. Charles Tomlinson. MoP; NoAM; TwCP
At Beautyes barre as I dyd stande. The Arraignment of a Lover. George Gascoigne. AAS

At Beltane, when ilk body bownis. Peblis to the Play. *Unknown.*
GoTS
At bend of bay. Old Sailor Looking at a Container Ship. Robert Carson.
AiP
At Bessemer. Philip Levine. BLA
At Best. John Boyle O'Reilly. AA
At Bethlehem. John Banister Tabb. *Fr.* The Child. AA
At Bickford's. Gerald Stern. CAPP
At Birth. Anthony Thwaite. NePoEA-2
At *Bon* we dance. *Unknown, tr. by* Geoffrey Bownas *and* Anthony
Thwaite. PeBJV
At break of day we leave the western gate. After Rain, Visiting the
Temple of Heavenly Peace. Wang Shih-chen, *tr. by* Jonathan
Chaves. CoBLCP
At Breakfast. Ida M. Mills. BoTP
At breakfast. On Certain Mornings Everything Is Sensual. David Jauss.
GOYP
At Brill on the hill. *Unknown.* GBP; OxNR
At Bungendore. James McAuley. PoAu-2
At Candlemas. Charles Causley. OBCP
At Carbis Bay. Arthur Symons. FaBoPP
At Carmel. Mary Austin. AmFN
At Carmel Highlands. Janet Lewis. PoA
At Casterbridge Fair, *sels.* Thomas Hardy.
After the Fair. *Fr.* VII. CMoP; HAP
Ballad-Singer, The. *Fr.* I. BoLoP
Former Beauties. *Fr.* II. NoAM; OBMV; OBNC
At Castle Boterel. Thomas Hardy. EBEV; GTBS-P; NOBE; OBNC;
PoE; SCV
At Castor Bay. Sam Hunt. PeNZ
At Chadwicks Bar and Grill. Lance Henson. HATNAP; STE
At Ch'ang-ku, Reading: To Show to My Man Pa. Li Ho, *tr. fr. Chinese
by* Burton Watson. CoBCP
At Chappaqua. Joel Benton. AA
At Christmas-Tide. Henrietta Cordelia Ray. CBWP-3
At Christmas time so long ago. The Little Fir Tree. Margaret Rose.
BoTP
At Christmas, when old friends are meeting. Good Will to Men—
Christmas Greetings in Six Languages. Dorothy Brown Thompson.
OBCP
At Church Next Sunday. *Unknown.* BLRP
At Cockcrow. Lizette Woodworth Reese. TrPWD
At Common Dawn. Vivian Locke Ellis. CH
At Communion. Madeleine L'Engle. TrCP
At Cooloolah. Judith Wright. MoBrPo
At counters where I eat my lunch. Marble-Top. E. B. White. FiBHP;
OBAL
At court I met it, in clothes brave enough. On Something, That Walks [*or*
Walkes] Somewhere. Ben Jonson. NAEL-1; OxBSP; PoE; SeCP;
SeCV-1
At court I'm asked so much I'm sick. Aimeric de Peguilhan, *tr. by* Paul
Blackburn. CoBCP
At Cove on the Crooked River ("At cove at our camp in the open
canyon"). William Stafford. LiTM; NaP
At Creçy by Somme in Ponthieu. Creçy. Francis Turner Palgrave.
BeLS
At Dante's Grave. Ezra Zussman, *tr. fr. Hebrew by* D. Shnayorson.
VWA
At Darien Bridge. James Dickey. NoP
At Dawn. Arthur Symons. OBNC
At dawn a knot of sea-lions lies off shore. Animals. Robinson Jeffers.
NU
At Dawn, Climbing the Heavenly Pillar Peak of Myst, *sel.* Hsü Chung-
hsing, *tr. fr. Chinese by* Jonathan Chaves.
"I shake my robe—and mists disperse, leaving clear autumn sky."
CoBLCP
At dawn crowed the cock. Cock. Aharon Amir, *tr. by* Bernhard Frank.
MHeP
"At dawn," he said, "I bid them all farewell." The Volunteer. Elbridge
Jefferson Cutler. AA
At dawn I climb a river tower to its very highest storey. Wang Shih-chen,
tr. fr. Chinese by Daniel Bryant. *Fr.* Chen-chou Quatrains, III.
WFTU
At dawn I gathered up the bones in the fields. Written after the Revolt.
Ogasawara Gokyo, *tr. by* Burton Watson. JLIC-2
At dawn I squat on the garage. Sound. Jim Harrison. VGW
At dawn of day I saw a man stand by a grog saloon. The Drunkard's
Doom. *Unknown.* AS
At dawn of the day the Creator. Gaspara Stampa, *tr. by* J. Vitiello.
BoWoP

At dawn setting out from a cassia and orchid shore. Picking Rushes.
Unknown, tr. by Burton Watson. CoBCP
At dawn she lay with her profile at that angle. Daybreak. Stephen
Spender. BoLoP
At dawn the cornering taxis cast. New York. William Logan. EOEF
At Dawn the Light Will Come. N. P. Van Wyk Louw, *tr. fr. Afrikaans
by* Uys Krige *and* Jack Cope. PeSA
At dawn the ridge emerges massed and dun. Attack. Siegfried Sassoon.
MoBrPo; NOBE; OxBTC
At dawn the sea monster slept. Explorations/ Bronchitis: The Rosario
Beach House. Aleida Rodríguez, *tr. by* Toni Empringham. FIA
At Dawn the Virgin Is Born. Lope de Vega, *tr. fr. Spanish by* W. S.
Merwin. PChr
At dawn three shearsmen. Bernie's Quick-Shave (1968). Sydney Lea.
MAYP
At Daybreak. Siegfried Sassoon. PeHV
At daybreak/ a white sail goes by. In the Hospital at the Suma Seashore.
Masaoka Shiki, *tr. fr. Japanese by* Burton Watson. *Fr.* Thirty-nine
Haiku. FCEI
At daybreak frogs begin. Sensetsu, *tr. by* Hiroaki Sato. FCEI
At daybreak when plovers call. Taigi, *tr. fr. Japanese by* Hiroaki Sato.
Fr. Twenty-nine Hokku. FCEI
At daybreak, when the falcon claps his wings. Ballad Written for a
Bridegroom. Villon, *tr. by* Swinburne. AWP
At day's light. In Autumn. Jon Anderson. AmPA
At dead of night, after an evening ball. The Duchess of York's Ghost.
Unknown. APAS
At dead of night, the sailors sprawled on deck. Nearing La Guaira.
Derek Walcott. TTY
At Delft. Charles Tomlinson. NYBP
At Delphos shrine one did a doubt propound. Upon Master Edmund
Spenser. Francis Beaumont. FaBoEE
At Devlin's Siding. Barcroft Henry Boake. CBAP
At Dieppe, *sels.* Arthur Symons.
After Sunset. BrPo
Grey and Green. FaBoPP; NOBVV
Rain on the Down. BrPo; OBNC
At dinner, in that careful rouge of light. Anniversary. Ted Kooser. SM
At Dinner, She Is Hostess. George Meredith. *Fr.* Modern Love, XVII.
HeIP; NOBVV; NoP; PoE; Son
At Dirty Dick's and Sloppy Joe's. Song of the Master and Boatswain.
W. H. Auden. *Fr.* The Sea and the Mirror. BoLoP; MOS
(Master and Boatswain.) FaBoTw
At discos where I eavesdrop. Vampirella. Elaine Equi. UL
At Dover Cliffs. William Lisle Bowles. EnRP
At Drugger's Head, without a puff. From a Tobacco Wrapper.
Unknown. FaBoUs
At Dunbar, Castle or Arcade. Double Feature. Robert Hayden. NoAM
At Dunwich. Anthony Thwaite. MoBS
At dusk/ from the island in the river. If the Owl Calls Again. John
Haines. BoNaP; CoAP; HeIP; LCAP; NU
At dusk heavy clouds grieve the long day. Poem to the Tune of "Tsui hua
yin." Li Ch'ing-chao, *tr. by* Marsha Wagner. WPOW
At dusk the first stars appear. Stars. Gary Soto. TDD
At dusk they'd ask. Site. Meir Wieseltier, *tr. by* Warren Bargad *and*
Stanley F. Chyet. IP
At each level. Lamb and Bear; Jet Landing. Laurence Lieberman. DiL
At each step lies a coffin. Progress. "Miraji", *tr. by* Mahmood Jamal.
PBMUP
At Eagle Farm I stand at the passenger gate. Flights. Roger McDonald.
CBAP
At Early Morn. Binga Dismond, *fr. the French of* Catulle Mendes.
PoNe
At early morning, clear and cold. The Troopship. Lionel Johnson.
EBVV
At Ease. Walter de la Mare. GTBS-P
At Easter Time. Laura Elizabeth Richards. OHIP
At eight I was brilliant with my body. Black Hair. Gary Soto. NPGG
At 8:00 he rises, bathes, and dresses. Mr. Eliot's Day. Robert Francis.
NYBP
At eight stealing a mirror glance. Li Shang-yin, *tr. by* Burton Watson.
CoBCP
At Eighteen Cataracts, the rocks are jagged teeth. A Ballad of One
Hundred Fathoms. Shih Jun-chang, *tr. by* William Shultz. WFTU
At eighteen, the U.S. Navy eye chart. The Pornography Box. Dave
Smith. DiL
At eighteen when I worked in oology. Oxford Street Museum. Margo
Lockwood. PPR
At eighty-six she takes to pressing flowers. Foxfire. Nancy Willard.
IHMS

At Elsdon. George Chatt. FaBoPP
At End. Louise Chandler Moulton. PWR
At Epidaurus. Lawrence Durrell. LiTB; OBTV
At Euston. A. M. Harbord. PoSH
At Eutaw springs the valiant died. To the Memory of the Brave
    Americans. Philip Freneau. AiP; AmPP; PoLF
    (Eutaw Springs.) AA; AnAmPo; BeLS; PAH
At Evans Street. Janet Frame. ATNZ
At even, when the hour drew nigh at which we say farewell. Strato, tr.
    by Sydney Oswald. PeHV
At evening, sitting on this terrace. Bat. D. H. Lawrence. BrPo;
    GTBS-P; HAP; OAEL-1; OAEL-2; OBTV
At evening the horse comes down unled. The Shadow of Himself.
    William Renton. NOBVV
At Evening Time, sel. Hayyim Nahman Bialik, tr. fr. Hebrew by
    Bernhard Frank.
    "Between clouds of fire and clouds of blood." MHeP
At evening when the lamp is lit. The Land of Story-Books. Robert
    Louis Stevenson. FaBoBe; FaPON; PWR
At every hour I wake. Night. Aldo Camerino, tr. by Anita Barrows.
    VWA
At every step there was. Mohammad Taqi Mir, tr. by Ahmed Ali. GoT
At every stroke his brazen fins do take. The Whale. John Donne. Fr.
    The Progress[e] of the Soul[e]. ChTr
At every trotting sound of a horse's hoofs. Unknown, tr. fr. Japanese.
    Fr. Manyo Shu. Ma
At Farringford. Tennyson. Fr. To the Rev. F. D. Maurice. FaBoPP
At Fifteen I Went Off to the Army. Unknown, tr. fr. Chinese by Burton
    Watson. CoBCP
At fifteen Jean Calvin made a list. Preposterous. Jim Hall. MT
At fifty, I approach myself. In a Dream. David Ignatow. PoA
At First. C. H. Sisson. OxBC
At first blush, discomfiting. Diehard. Judith Moffett. PoA
At first I prayed for Light. The Larger Prayer. Edna D. Cheney.
    BLRP; WGRP
At first I thought a pest. Armour's Undermining Modesty. Marianne
    Moore
At first I thought I would feel. Nothing Could Take Away the Bear-
    King's Image. Ray A. Young Bear. HATNAP
At first I was given centuries. Margaret Atwood. HAP; NMM; WPOW
At first I was worried about you. When I Held You to My Chest, You
    Fit. Jack Myers. AmPA
At first I went apart. And now I see. Tammuz. Rayner Heppenstall.
    WaP
At first it is a constellation. Interior. H. C. Artmann, tr. by Beth
    Bjorklund. CoAuP
At first it was as though you had passed. Many Wagons Ago. John
    Ashbery. HCAP
At first light. Bird Theater. Robert Wallace. TDD
At first my mother would be shy. In the Ocean. Patricia Goedicke.
    TSL; TV
At first my territory was a wood. The Wall. David Gascoyne. PoPo
At first nothing is. Nothing Is. Sun-Ra. PoBA
At First Sight. Robert Graves. FaBoEE; OxBSP
At first the river's very small. The Growing River. Rodney Bennett.
    BoTP
At first there all sea-water on the topland. On the Creation and Ontogony.
    Unknown, tr. fr. Delaware (Lenape) Indian by C. S. Rafinesque. Fr.
    Walam [or Wallum] Olum; or, Red Score. LiTA
"At first there were men, all sorts of men, and not one at a time." Her
    Words from the Corner. Ory Bernstein, tr. by Warren Bargad and
    Stanley F. Chyet. IP
At first we heard the jingling of her ornaments. Egyptian Dancer at
    Shubra. Bernard Spencer. NoAM
At first we sat imprisoned in this place. Conversation in Black and White.
    May Sarton. GoYe
At first we see the tiny leaves. The Strawberry. Maggie Pogue Johnson.
    CBWP-4
At first, what flew hard from my grandfather's mouth. The Wind of Late
    Summer. Pamela Stewart. NAmP
At first when I heard the old song. I Heard the Old Song. B. W.
    Vilakazi. PeSA
At first when we saw a girl. Sunday Afternoon. Philip Levine. NaP
At five in the afternoon. Lament for Ignacio Sánchez Mejías. Federico
    García Lorca. NAWM-2, tr. by Stephen Spender and J. L. Gili;
    OBVE, tr. by A. L. Lloyd
At five in the morning, as jolly as any. The Miner's Doom. Unknown.
    AmFP
At five this morn, when Phoebus raised his head. Tunbridge Wells. Earl
    of Rochester. FaBoPP; OBSV

At Flores in the Azores, Sir Richard Grenville lay. Tennyson. Fr. The
    Revenge. BeLS; EBVV; FaBoCh; FaPoR; OBWP; OnMSP; PoaRA
At focus in the national. The Monument and the Shrine. John Logan.
    LCAP
At Fotheringay. Robert Southwell. PoEL-2
At 4:00 a.m., I drove to American Falls. American Falls. Greg Keeler.
    SM
At four in the morning the smoke of the forded river. While We Slept.
    David Wolff. TrJP
At four it would still be dark. Spring. Robert Grenier. Fr. A
    Sequence/ 28 Separate Poems. IAT
At four o'clock. Roosters. Elizabeth Bishop. LiTM
At four o'clock it's dark. In Winter. Michael Ryan. MAYP
At 4:30 AM/ she rose. Ntozake Shange. Fr. For Colored Girls Who
    Have Considered Suicide When the Rainbow Is Enuf. BoWoP
At 14th Street and First Avenue. Strawberries in Mexico. Ron Padgett.
    EAS
At fourth watch a single star peers over a cloud. The Dying Lamp. Li
    Chien, tr. by Hsin-sheng C. Kao. WFTU
At Francis Allen's on the Christmas eve. The Epic. Tennyson.
    NAEL-2
At Fredericksburg. John Boyle O'Reilly. PAH
At Frost's Grave. Dave Smith. BLA
At Fyvie's yetts there grows a flower. The Trumpeter of Fyvie.
    Unknown. OxBB
    (Andrew Lammie.) ESPB
At Galway Races. W. B. Yeats. SD
At Gesthemane. Ruth Kim Chun-soo, tr. fr. Korean by Koh Chang-soo.
    ACKP
At Gettysburg full anonymity. Yugoslav Cemetery. Celeste Turner
    Wright. WPE
At Gibraltar. George Edward Woodberry. AA; GN
At Glastonbury. Henry Kingsley. PoRA
At Glendalough lived a young saint. St. Kevin. At. to Samuel Lover.
    WTO
At God's Command. Joseph Rolnik, tr. fr. Yiddish by Keith Bosley.
    VWA
At Golgotha I stood alone. Edwin John Ellis. Fr. Himself. OBMV
At Grandfather's. Clara Doty Bates. OBCA
At Grass. Philip Larkin. HAP; NePoEA; OxBTC; RB; SD; WeW
At Great Torrington, Devon. Unknown. FaBoCo; FaBoEE
At Guaracara Park. Eric Roach. PBCV
At Gull Lake; August, 1810. Duncan Campbell Scott. NOBC; OBCV
At Hadleigh, Suffolk. Unknown. FaBoCo
At half-past five—the earth cooling. Bachelor Farmer. Roger McDonald.
    CBAP
At half past three, a single bird. Emily Dickinson. MoAmPo; NAWM-2;
    OxBA
At Half Past Three in the Afternoon. Jon Stallworthy. EOEF
At Hallowmas, whan nights grow lang. Hallow-Fair. Robert Fergusson.
    OxBS
At Henry's bier let some thing fall out well. John Berryman. Fr. Dream
    Songs. NoP
At her departure his disdain return'd. Homer, tr. fr. Greek by Dryden.
    Fr. The Iliad, I. OBVE
At her doorway Mrs. Mayle. The Lavender Bush. Elizabeth Fleming.
    BoTP
At Her Fair Hands. Walter Davison. EIL
    (Ode: "At her fair hands how have I grace entreated.") BoLoP;
    OBSC
At her step the water-hen. Dante Gabriel Rossetti. FM
At his estate/ in St. Alban near Basel. Mark Tobey's Legacy. Wieland
    Schmied, tr. by Beth Bjorklund. CoAuP
At His Father's Grave. John Ormond. FaBoTw; OBD; OBWVE
At his incipient sun. First Love. Stanley Kunitz. GOYP
At home alone, O Nomades. Home, Sweet Home, with Variations, III.
    H. C. Bunner. CenHV; OBAL
At home, as in no other city, here. Oxford. Keith Douglas. NePoEA
At home at Annika's place. At Annika's Place. Siv Widerberg, tr. by
    Verne Moberg. NTCP
At Home in Dakar. Margaret Danner. BlSi; FB
At home, in my flannel gown, like a bear to its floe. 90 North. Randall
    Jarrell. CAPP; CoAP; FYAP; MoAB; MT; NAAL-2; NoAM; NOBA;
    TAP
At Home the Green Remains. John Figueroa. PBCV
At home the hagi flowers of autumn. Lady Otomo no Tamura, tr. fr.
    Japanese. Fr. Manyo Shu. Ma
At human footfalls a frog. Ko'oku, tr. by Hiroaki Sato. FCEI
At Hung-tung Mountain, the war-drums sounded. To the Filial Son,
    Ts'ui. Hsü Pen, tr. by Jonathan Chaves. CoBLCP

At insular café tables under awnings. Green Coconuts: Rio. Lawrence Durrell. OBTV
At It. R. S. Thomas. OxBC
At Ithaca. Hilda Doolittle. VGW
At its margin. Ode to Arnold Schoenberg. Charles Tomlinson. NePoEA-2
At Iwashiro I bind. Prince Arima, tr. fr. Japanese. Fr. Manyo Shu. Ma
   ("At Iwashiro I tie together branches of a beach pine"), tr. by Hiroaki Sato. FCEI
At Jacob's well a stranger sought. Jacob's Well. Unknown. OBET
At Kaya in Tamba. Buson, tr. fr. Japanese by Hiroaki Sato. Fr. Eighty-seven Hokku. FCEI
At Kenneth Burke's Place. William Carlos Williams. NOBA
At Kfar Kana. Charles Causley. TOF
At Kino Viejo, Mexico. Alberto Ríos. NoAM
At Kirk Yetholm. Dave Calder. PoSH
At Kisheneff two wicked men. Russia's Resentment. Lizelia Augusta Jenkins Moorer. CBWP-3
At Knaresborough. Donald Davie. NePoEA
At Kresge's Diner in Stonefalls, Arkansas. Edward Hirsch. SM
At Lai Family Village, the spring is beautiful. Walking Outside the City Walls. Pien Kung, tr. by Jonathan Chaves. CoBLCP
At Lake Geneva. Richard Eberhart. LiTA
At Lake Lietzen; or, The Search for Identity. Gerald Bisinger, tr. fr. German by Beth Bjorklund. CoAuP
At Large in the Eighties. Louis Johnson. ATNZ
At Lascaux they've shut the caves. Nancy Sullivan. Fr. Two Orgasms, II. NIP
At Last. Syd Scroggie. PoSH
At Last. Katrina Trask. AA
At Last. Whittier. TrPWD; WGRP
At last a juggler is led out under the stars. The Initiate. W. S. Merwin. NNaP
At last I can figure out the nature of that whisking sound. Fate in Incognito. Michael Benedikt. OBAL
At last I found the monastery. A young. Abstinence. Kenneth Rosen. AmPA
At last I have the right to say hello to all these beings I do not know. The Musician of Saint-Merry. Guillaume Apollinaire, tr. by Michael Benedikt. POS
At last I put off love. He Abjures Love. Thomas Hardy. OBNC
At last I touch the distant edge of eternity. Absolute Solitude. Kim Hyun-sung, tr. by Koh Chang-soo. ACKP
At last it has leaked out—thin men are the cause of everything. Antithin. Sándor Weöres, tr. by Richard Lourie. MHuP
At last love has come. I would be more ashamed. Sulpicia, tr. by Aliki and Willis Barnstone. BoWoP
At last, my old, inveterate foe. To Melancholy. Countess of Winchilsea. WPE
At last, O thou serene retreat. To Retirement. Luis de León, tr. by Thomas Walsh. TrJP
At last she calls to mind where hangs a piece. Troy Depicted. Shakespeare. Fr. The Rape of Lucrece. OBSC
At last the beef appears in sight. Edward Chicken. Fr. The Collier's Wedding. NOEC
At last the cure, I bid farewell to pain. Oblivion. Ibrahim Naji, tr. by Issa Boullata and John Heath-Stubbs. MAP
At Last the Secret Is Out. W. H. Auden. InPS; SeCePo
At last, the train will lurch in. Return. Mary Dorcey. AIW
At last to be identified! Resurgam. Emily Dickinson. WGRP
At last Wayman gets the girl into bed. Wayman in Love. Tom Wayman. NIP; NOBC
At Last We Killed the Roaches. Lucille Clifton. CAPP; NIP
At last withdraw your cruelty. Sir Thomas Wyatt. SiPS
At last year's Jungle Olympics. The Ants at the Olympics. Richard Digance. RHPC
At last you yielded up the album, which. Lines on a Young Lady's Photograph Album. Philip Larkin. EnLoPo; HAP; OAEL-2; WeW
At Least. Don Mattera. WMBCH
At least 100 seabirds attended my grandmother's funeral. My Grandmother's Funeral. Thomas Lux. WeW
At least a hundred times. For Edward Hicks. David Helwig. NOBC
"At least, at least in his dreams"—so thinking. Yosano Akiko, tr. fr. Japanese by Hiroaki Sato. Fr. Thirty-nine Tanka. FCEI
"At least let it burn just as it burns!"—that way I feel. Yosano Akiko, tr. fr. Japanese by Hiroaki Sato. Fr. Thirty-nine Tanka. FCEI
"At least we can meet at the Indian Market." Promise! Mafika Pascal Gwala. WMBCH
At Leeds. Unknown. FaBoCo

At leisure, idling patiently, lost. Idling. István Vas, tr. by Jascha Kessler. FOC
At length, by so much importunity pressed. The Lover; a Ballad. Lady Mary Wortley Montagu. NAEL-1; NoP
At length, my Lord, I have the bliss. Thomas Moore. Fr. The Fudge Family in Paris. OBSV
At length nigh to the sea they drew. Spenser. Fr. The Faerie Queene, V, 2. NoP
At Length the Busy Day Is Done. Francis Hopkinson. AH
At length the long-expected morning came. The Voyage. Denis Florence MacCarthy. Fr. The Voyage of St. Brendan. TIRV
At length the soft nocturnal minutes fly. The Bricklayer's Labours. Robert Tatersal. NOEC
At length the term's ending. A Letter. Sir Arthur Quiller-Couch. CenHV
At length their long kiss severed, with sweet smart. Nuptial Sleep. Dante Gabriel Rossetti. Fr. The House of Life, VI. EBVV; NAEL-2; NOBVV
At Length There Dawns the Glorious Day, with music. Ozora Stearns Davis. AH
At length they came into a larger space. Spenser. Fr. The Faerie Queene: As pilot well expert in perilous wave. FiP
At length 'tis done, the glorious conflict's done. On the Late Successful Expedition against Louisbourg. Francis Hopkinson. PAH
At length we have settled a pastor. Wanted, a Minister's Wife. Unknown. BLPA
At length with jostling, elbowing, and the aid. Byron. Fr. The Vision of Judgment. OBSV
At liberty I sit and see. The Lover in Liberty Smileth at Them in Thraldom, That Sometime Scorned His Bondage. Unknown. ElL
At life's most testing moment, when. Mikhail Yurevich Lermontov, tr. by Alan Myers. AAA
At Lincoln. Oscar Fay Adams. AA
At Lindos. May Sarton. WPE
At Long Last. Lindsay Patterson. CNA
At Lord's. Francis Thompson. EBVV; OxBSP
At Loschwitz above the city. The Birch-Tree at Loschwitz. Amy Levy. TrJP
At low tide like this how sheer the water is. The Bight. Elizabeth Bishop. FaBoWP; HCAP; NAAL-2; NYBP; RB
At Loxahatchie. Mary Oliver. KS
At Luca Signorelli's Resurrection of the Body. Jorie Graham. HCAP
At Magnolia Cemetery. Henry Timrod. See Ode: "Sleep sweetly in your humble graves."
At Majority. Adrienne Rich. NePoEA-2
At Marshfield. William Cleaver Wilkinson. Fr. Webster; an Ode. AA
At Mass. Vachel Lindsay. VGW
At Mass. Unknown, tr. fr. Irish by Robin Flower. BIrV
At Matyne houre in midis of the nicht. Honour with Age. Walter Kennedy. OxBS
At Melville's Tomb. Hart Crane. HAP; MoAmPo; MoP; MOS; NAAL-2; NoAM; NoP; PoA; TAP; UnPo; VGW
At Mexican Springs. Laura Tohe. STE
At Mid-Ocean. Robert Bly. CAPP; LLLT
At midday the birds doze. The Hermit Picks Berries. Maxine W. Kumin. RFM
At midday they looked up and saw their death. George Barker. Fr. Pacific Sonnets, VII [or IX]. LiTM; WaP
At midday when the sea's visible. Wakayama Bokusui, tr. fr. Japanese by Hiroaki Sato. Fr. Forty-four Tanka. FCEI
At Midnight. Ted Kooser. GOYP
At Midnight. Frank Dempster Sherman. AA
At midnight by the stream I roved. Lewti. Samuel Taylor Coleridge. EnRP
At midnight Death dismissed the chancellor. Lines on the Death of Bismarck. John Jay Chapman. PoEL-5
At midnight down by the rivulets of asphalt. North Wind. Benjamin Péret, tr. by Michael Benedikt. POS
At midnight, flaking down like chromium. Closing Time. David Wagoner. NYBP
At midnight I woke up [or awoke]. Clams. Ishigaki Rin, tr. by Hiroaki Sato. FCEI; PBWP
At midnight, in his guarded tent. Fitz-Greene Halleck. Fr. Marco Bozzaris. AA; AnAmPo; BeLS; GN; HoPM; WBLP
At midnight in the alley. The Tom-Cat. Don Marquis. PoRA
At midnight, in the month of June. The Sleeper. Poe. AA; AmPP; AnAmPo; LiTA; NAAL-1; NOBA; OxBA; PoEL-4; TAP; TrGrPo
At Midnight's Hour I Raised My Head. Henry David Thoreau. PoEL-4
At midnight's scrawl, the fog has. The Harbor of Illusion. Charles Bernstein. UL

At Midsummer. Norman Dubie. MAYP; NoAM
At minus tide the music. Poke-Pole Fishing. Dennis Schmitz. AmPA
At Misaka, the Pass of the Gods. Kamutobe Kooshio, *tr. fr. Japanese. Fr.* Manyo Shu. Ma
At Monday dawn, I climbed into my skin. Diary. David Wagoner. CoAP
At morning light the ark lay grounded fast. A Problem in History. Robert Wallace. CRP
At morning we all look out. Hedge Life. James Dickey. LCAP
At most [*or* moost] mischief. My Lute and I. Sir Thomas Wyatt. MeEL; SiPS
At Mount Rushmore I looked up into one. X. J. Kennedy. *Fr.* Edgar's Story. OFD
At Mrs. Alefounder's. Barbara Howes. AnAn
At My Country Home in Chung-nan. Wang Wei, *tr. fr. Chinese* by Burton Watson. CoBCP
At My Father's Grave. John Ciardi. SM
At My Father's Grave. "Hugh MacDiarmid." GTBS-P
At my father's wake. Desmet, Idaho, March 1969. Janet Campbell Hale. STE; VoR
At My Grandmother's. David Malouf. PoAu-2
At my home. Lady Kasa, *tr. fr. Japanese* by Burton Watson. *Fr.* Manyo Shu. FCEI
At my house small mosquitoes. Basho, *tr. fr. Japanese* by Burton Watson. *Fr.* Seventy-six Hokku. FCEI
At My Mother's Bedside. Marcia Lee Masters. WPE
At my mountain home. Tonna, *tr.* by Steven D. Carter. WFTW
At My Nativity. Shakespeare. *Fr.* King Henry IV, Pt. I, III, i. NAs
At my side. Wakayama Bokusui, *tr.* by Geoffrey Bownas *and* Anthony Thwaite. PeBJV
At My Wedding. Yankev-Yitskhok Segal, *tr. fr. Yiddish* by Grace Schulman. PeBMYV
At my window, I pull the curtains wide. A Visitation. W. D. Snodgrass. SM
At my windowpane a bird. That Is All I Heard. "Yehoash," *tr.* by Isidore Goldstick. TrJP
At Naniwa Bay/ frost freezes on the shore reeds. Cold Reeds around an Inlet. Tameshige, *tr.* by Steven D. Carter. WFTW
At Nature's Shrine. Henrietta Cordelia Ray. CBWP-3
At new age fifty. A Phoenix at Fifty. Lawrence Ferlinghetti. NAs
At Night. Bella Akhmadulina, *tr. fr. Russian* by Daniel Halpern *and* Albert Todd. BoWoP
At Night. Rachel Boimwall, *tr.* by Gabriel Preil *and* Howard Schwartz. VWA
At Night. Frances Cornford. MoBrPo
At Night. Aileen Fisher. RAR
At Night. Margherita Guidacci, *tr. fr. Italian* by Marina La Palma. WPOW
At Night. Alice Meynell. CH
At Night. George Edgar Montgomery. AA
At Night. Georg Trakl, *tr. fr. German* by Joachim Neugroschel. AnAn
At night/ he'd lie in bed. Louis B. Russell. Bruce Guernsey. InPK
At night/ yes night. Loneliness. Amjad Nasir, *tr.* by May Jayyusi *and* Charles Doria. MAP
At night, alone, the animals came and shone. The Animals. Josephine Jacobsen. GoYe
At night and in the wind and the rain. Refugees. Chaim Grade, *tr.* by Marc Kaminski. VWA
At night, as drough the mead I took my way. To Me. William Barnes. PoEL-4
At night Babylon is remembered. Apocalypse. Jean Lipkin. VWA
At night, by the fire. Domination of Black. Wallace Stevens. AmPP; MoAB; MoAmPo; OxBA
At night Chinamen jump. Frank O'Hara. NoAM; NOBA; SM
At night, distracted, over the town. Fir Tree. Wayne Brown. UAS
At Night, Hearing Someone Singing in the House Next Door. Mei Yao-ch'en, *tr. fr. Chinese* by Burton Watson. CoBCP
At night I always think of Mickey. Dear Mickey. Dahlia Ravikovich, *tr.* by Warren Bargad *and* Stanley F. Chyet. IP
At night, I do not know who I am. Mysteries. Dannie Abse. PoPo
At night I follow bell and chant. Staying Overnight at Spirit-Source Temple. Wen Cheng-ming, *tr.* by Jonathan Chaves. CoBLCP
At night I have wings. Night Flight. Franz Richter, *tr.* by Beth Bjorklund. CoAuP
At night I sit, uneasy and unhappy. To Yung-erh. Li Tung-yang, *tr.* by Jonathan Chaves. CoBLCP
At night in each other's arms. Love's Vision. Edward Carpenter. WGRP
At night, in the fish-light of the moon, the dead wear our white shirts. Homage to Paul Cézanne. Charles Wright. NAAL-2

At night, in the Museum Art School. Life Drawing. Steve Orlen. BLA
At Night in the Wood. Nancy M. Hayes. BoTP
At night, in west wind. Ma Chih-yüan, *tr. fr. Chinese* by Jonathan Chaves. *Fr.* Two Poems to the Tune "Chin-tzu ching." CoBLCP
At night my shoes look at me. My Mother's Shoes. Rayzel Zychlinska, *tr.* by Marc Kaminsky. VWA
At night secretly a worm. Basho, *tr. fr. Japanese* by Burton Watson. *Fr.* Seventy-six Hokku. FCEI
At night, sometimes, when I cannot sleep. 11 rue Daguerre. John Montague. FaBCIP
(Chosen Light, A.) IPY
At night the cat goes out to cry out. Paw. Paul Eluard, *tr.* by Michael Benedikt. POS
At night, the coffeepot stands upended in the rack. Parachute. Dwight Okita. BrSi
At night the day is constantly woken up. Work. Andrei Codrescu. EAS
At night the gold and black slashed bees come. Gold and Black. Michael Ondaatje. NoP
At night the most private of a dog's long body groan. Birth of Sound. Michael Ondaatje. HeIP
At night the sand wears a corsage of flesh. Casino Beach. Thomas Rabbitt. MAYP
At night, the skies clear of mist and rain. Mountain Hawthorns. Wei Ch'eng-pan, *tr.* by Lois Fusek. ATF
At night the wallpaper shakes. At Night. Margherita Guidacci, *tr.* by Marina La Palma. WPOW
At night they pound the vermilion newt. Painting Her Nails. Yang Wei-chen, *tr.* by Jonathan Chaves. CoBLCP
At night, Uncle Avram looked after the horses. Uncle Avram Pastures the Horses. Moishe Kulbak, *tr. fr. Yiddish* by Leonard Wolf. *Fr.* Byelorussia. PeBMYV
At night what things will stalk abroad. Lux in Tenebris. Katharine Tynan. TrPWD
At night when ale is in. Of Drunkenness. George Turberville. NBLV; NoP
At night when dying proceeds to sever all seams. Landscape of Screams. Nelly Sachs, *tr.* by Michael Roloff. NYBP
At night, when the black water-hen. The Heron. John Lyle Donaghy. NeIP
At night while. Black Warrior. Norman Jordan. PoBA
At Nightfall. Charles Hanson Towne. BLPA; FaBoBe
At nine from behind the door. Serenade for Strings. Dorothy Livesay. NAs
At nine in the morning there passed a church. Faintheart in a Railway Train. Thomas Hardy. CTC; EnLoPo
At ninety-nine, snowy side-locks. Gen of Kohoin, *tr.* by Lucien Stryk *and* Takashi Ikemoto. ZPCJ
At noon I watch the sun shine. Carlo Betocchi, *tr. fr. Italian* by I. L. Salomon. *Fr.* Little Diary on Growing Old. PFI
At noon, in the dead centre of a faith. Desertmartin. Tom Paulin. CIP; FaBCIP
At noon in the desert a panting lizard. At the Bomb Testing Site. William Stafford. CAPP; CoAP; LiTM; NoAM; NoP; OBWP; RB
At noon of night, and at the night's pale end. Apparitions. Thomas Bailey Aldrich. AnAmPo
At noon she waited for her shadow. The Blind Woman. Lucha Corpi. CCP
At noon the sun puffed up, outsize. Francis Webb. PoAu-2
At noon they talk of evening and at evening. Cypresses. Robert Francis. LCAP
At noon, Tithonus, withered by his singing. The Wedding. Conrad Aiken. CMoP; TAP
At noon today, I woke from a nightmare. Mexico, 1940. Ai. NoAM
At North Farm. John Ashbery. HCAP; PoE
At Nuclear Medicine. Dixie Partridge. TSM
At number one, i' Bowton's Yard, mi gronny keeps a skoo. Bowton's Yard. Samuel Laycock. PF
At once whatever happened starts receding. Whatever Happened? Philip Larkin. Son
At once with him they rose. Hell ("At once with him they rose"). Milton. *Fr.* Paradise Lost, *Bk.* II, *ll.* 475–628. OBS
At once with resolution held. John Trumbull. *Fr.* M'Fingal. AmPP
At one glance/ I loved you. Mihri Hatun, *tr.* by Tâlat S. Halman. PBWP
At 100 Mile House the cowboys ride in rolling. The Cariboo Horses. Alfred W. Purdy. HeIP; NOBC
At one the wind rose. Night-Music. Philip Larkin. InPS
At one time. A Sometimes Love Poem. George Leong. BrSi
At Only That Moment. Alan Ross. ErPo

At our awful Sovereign's word. *Unknown, tr. fr. Japanese. Fr.* Manyo Shu. Ma
At our dread Sovereign's word. Yuki Yakamaro, *tr. fr. Japanese. Fr.* Manyo Shu. Ma
At our ease. Pagan Fires. Tawfiq Zayyad, *tr. by* Sharif Elmusa *and* Charles Doria. MAP
At Pakiri Beach. David Mitchell. PeNZ
At Paris it was, at the Opera there. Aux Italiens. "Owen Meredith." BeLS; BLPA; BLPL; FaBoBe
At Parting. Ho Sun, *tr. fr. Chinese by* Burton Watson. CoBCP
At Parting. Anne Ridler. CN
At Pavia, a visitation of some sorrow. Boethius' dungeon. Geoffrey Hill. *Fr.* Mercian Hymns, XVIII. FaBoMo
At Peach Blossom Bank is Peach Blossom Retreat. Song of Peach Blossom Retreat. T'ang Yin, *tr. by* Jonathan Chaves. CoBLCP
At Penshurst [Another]. Edmund Waller. OAEL-1; SeCV-1
At Perigord near to the wall. A Perigord pres del muralh. Bertrans de Born, *tr. by* Ezra Pound. CTC
At Piccadilly Circus. Vivian de Sola Pinto. OBMV
At Polwart on the Green. Polwart on the Green. Allan Ramsay. NOEC
At Pompeii. Shelley. *Fr.* Ode to Naples. FaBoPP
At Port Royal, *sel.* Whittier. PAH
Song of the Negro Boatman. GN
At Potterne, Wiltshire. *Unknown.* FaBoCo
At present I still have. Exit Lines. George Jonas. NeAC
At Prime Jesus was y-led. William of Shoreham. *Fr.* Hours of the Passion. ACP
At Quebec. Jean Blewett. CaP
At Quincey's moat the squandering village ends. Almswomen. Edmund Blunden. OBMV; OxBTC
At Rest in the Blast. Marianne Moore. MoAB; MoAmPo
At Richmond the people walked along by the river. Mr. Symons at Richmond, Mr. Pope at Twickenham. Julian Symons. WaP
At Robert Fergusson's Grave, October 1962. Robert Garioch. OxBS
At Rochdale. Ian Young. NeAC
At Rochecoart/ Where the hills part. Provincia Deserta. Ezra Pound. OxBA
At Saint Patrick's Purgatory. Donnchadh Mor O'Dala, *tr. fr. Irish by* Sean O'Faolain. AnIL; TIRV
At Sainte-Marguerite. Trumbull Stickney. LiTA; OxBA
At Sasanami/ the pines are just as they were. Tameuji, *tr. by* Steven D. Carter. WFTW
At Saya-between-the-Hills. Basho, *tr. fr. Japanese by* Burton Watson. *Fr.* Seventy-six Hokku. FCEI
At school, during class. Graffiti in a University Restroom: "Killing People Is Easier than Writing Poetry." Jim Mitsui. BrSi
At school I scribbled in the margin of my atlas. The Study of Geography, or History. Lauris Edmond. UAS
At Sea. James Whitcomb Riley. MOS
At Sea. Yona Wallach, *tr. fr. Hebrew by* Warren Bargad *and* Stanley F. Chyet. IP
At sea in the dome of St. Paul's. Homage to Wren. Louis MacNeice. EyDe
At Set of Sun. Mary Ashley Townsend. AA
At seven, on the dock next door. In the Shadows of Early Sunlight. Robert Wallace. TDD
At seven, when I go to bed. A Child's Thought. Robert Louis Stevenson. BoTP
At seventeen your. Maryuma. Frank Lamont Phillips. AmNP
At several times the speed of light. Gemini Jones. Willard R. Espy. FaBoUs
At Shakespeare's Grave. Irving Browne. AA
At Shelley's birth. To Shelley. John Banister Tabb. AA
At Shoanji, an old temple of the Jodo sect. Shoan Temple. Takamura Kotaro, *tr. by* Hiroaki Sato. FCEI
At Shoraku-ji in Omi, First Poem of the Year. Kishun Ryuki, *tr. fr. Japanese by* Burton Watson. FCEI
At six I lived for spells. What For. Garrett Kaoru Hongo. MAYP
At six o'clock. The Sound of Morning in New Mexico. Reeve Spencer Kelley. AmFN
At six o'clock we were waiting for coffee. A Miracle for Breakfast. Elizabeth Bishop. LiTA
At six, when April chills our hands and feet. Elektra on Third Avenue. Marilyn Hacker. MAYP
At six years old I had before mine eyes. Old Man. James Henry. NOBVV
At sixteen I came West, riding. A Living Pearl. Kenneth Rexroth. LiTM
At sixteen I joined the army. Homecoming. Michael Sheridan. NAmP

At Sixty. Sándor Weöres, *tr. fr. Hungarian by* Jascha Kessler. FOC
At sixty, it might be well to start. The Collector. Desirée Flynn. BrRo
At some point in the pageant there is a moment. Endless Variation. John Ashbery. BLA
At stated .ic times. Composed in the Composing Room. Franklin Pierce Adams. NIP; OBAL
At Staufen. Michael Hamburger. VWA
At Su K'wa K'e there used to bloom a flower. Lost Love. *Unknown, tr. by* H. J. Spinden. WTO
At Su Terrace Viewing the Past. Li Po, *tr. fr. Chinese by* Burton Watson. CoBCP
At summer eve, when Heaven's ethereal bow. Thomas Campbell. *Fr.* The Pleasures of Hope. EnRP
At sundown I got in. Métro Balard-Charenton. Peter Handke, *tr. by* Beth Bjorklund. CoAuP
At sundown the little birds. *Unknown, tr. by* Geoffrey Bownas *and* Anthony Thwaite. PeBJV
At Sunset. Ivy O. Eastwick. BoTP
At Sunset. Henrietta Cordelia Ray. CBWP-3
At Sunset. Margaret Elizabeth Munson Sangster. PWR
At sunset. The Other Side. Linda Hogan. ER
At sunset I have a vision of 10,000 carabaos. The New Manong. Luis Syquia. BrSi
At sunset my foot outreached the mounting Pacific's. Swimming in the Pacific. Robert Penn Warren. ASP
At sunset, when the night-dews fall. The Snail. James Reeves. TSS
At Swindon. Reginald Brett. PeHV
At table yonder sits the man we seek. At the Mermaid Inn. Charles Lotin Hildreth. AA
At Taieri Mouth. James Keir Baxter. ATNZ
At Takadachi in Oshu. Basho, *tr. fr. Japanese by* Burton Watson. *Fr.* Seventy-six Hokku. FCEI
At Takase Mountain. Tamekane, *tr. fr. Japanese by* Steven D. Carter. WFTW
At Tara today, in this awful hour. St. Patrick's Hymn before Tara. James Clarence Mangan. EnRP
At Tauba's death I swore. Lamenting Tauba. Laila Akhyaliyya, *tr. by* Willis Barnstone. BoWoP
At Tea. Thomas Hardy. *Fr.* Satires of Circumstance, I. BrPo
At tea in cocktail weather. Publisher's Party. Phyllis McGinley. OBAL
At ten a clock, when I the fire rake. Francis Daniel Pastorius. SCAP
At ten A.M. the young housewife. The Young Housewife. William Carlos Williams. HeIP; NAAL-2; NoP; TAP
At ten I wanted fame. I had a comb. Behind Grandma's House. Gary Soto. NAmP
At ten I was wheeled in a chair. The Summer Anniversaries. Donald Justice. AnAn
At Thames faire port. Praise of Poets. William Browne. *Fr.* Britannia's Pastorals, II, Songs 1 *and* 2. OBS
At That Moment. Raymond R. Patterson. PoBA
At that moment you were leaning. Commerce in the Caucasus. Ishihara Yoshiro, *tr. by* Hiroaki Sato. FCEI
At that soft pale hour. Encounter in Jerusalem. Fay Lipshitz. VWA
At That Time. Alfred Gong, *tr. fr. German by* Beth Bjorklund. CoAuP
At The Abbey Theatre (Imitated from Ronsard). William Butler Yeats. Son
At the Airport. John Malcolm Brinnin. MoAB
At the airport, ready to leave on my little trip. The Fear of Flying. Mona Van Duyn. NMM
At the alder-darkened brink. Hamlen Brook. Richard Wilbur. BLA; CAPP
At the Algonquin. Howard Moss. Psk
At the Altar. Robert Lowell. *Fr.* Between the Porch and the Altar, IV. InPK
At the Altar-Rail. Thomas Hardy. *Fr.* Satires of Circumstance, IX. BrPo; MoAB; MoBrPo
At the Aquarium. Max Eastman. FaPON; WGRP
At the Art Exhibit. Manfred Winkler, *tr. fr. Hebrew by* Bernhard Frank. MHeP
At the Art Gallery. Koh Chang-soo, *tr. fr. Korean by the author.* ACKP
At the back of the houses there is the wood. The House in the Wood. Randall Jarrell. LCAP
At the Back of the North Wind, *sel.* George Macdonald. Baby, The. *Fr.* 23. FaPON
   (Where Did You Come From.) BLPA; FaFP; OxBChV
At the bad time, nothing betrays outwardly the harsh findings. December Blues. Robert Pinsky. MAYP
At the Badr Trench. Safiya bint Musafir, *tr. fr. Arabic by* Bridget Connelly *and* Deirdre Lashgari. WPOW
At the Ball! Charles Henry Webb. OBAL

At the Ball Game. William Carlos Williams. CMoP; MoP; NoAM; NOBA; OxBA; PoE
At the Band Concert. John Malcolm Brinnin. PoA
At the barren heart of midnight. Nocturn: "At the barren heart of midnight." William Ernest Henley. *Fr.* In Hospital, XXVII. BrPo
At the base of the earth, a face. Sick Face at the Base of the Earth. Hagiwara Sakutaro, *tr. by* Geoffrey Bownas *and* Anthony Thwaite. PeBJV
At the Battery Sea-Wall. Clifford James Laube. GoYe
At the beginning I noticed. A Stone Diary. Pat Lowther. NOBC
At the beginning of heaven and earth. Hitomaro, *tr. fr. Japanese. Fr.* Manyo Shu. Ma
At the beginning of winter a cold spirit comes. *Unknown, tr. by* Arthur Waley. BoWoP
At the bidding of my great Sovereign. Yakamochi, *tr. fr. Japanese. Fr.* Manyo Shu. Ma
At the big trumpet, we must all put on. Rise and Shine. Richmond Lattimore. NYBP
At the blackboard I had missed. Zimmer's Head Thudding against the Blackboard. Paul Zimmer. PCP
At the Body Club. X. J. Kennedy. SoTCo
At the bolted doors of the crumbs of property. Property. Jacob Glatstein, *tr. by* Benjamin *and* Barbara Harshav. AYP
At the Bomb Testing Site. William Stafford. CAPP; CoAP; LiTM; NoAM; NoP; OBWP; RB
At the bottom of the ground a face emerging. Sickly Face at the Bottom of the Ground. Hagiwara Sakutaro, *tr. by* Hiroaki Sato. FCEI
At the Bottom of the Well. Louis Untermeyer. GoJo
At the British Museum. Richard Aldington. MoBrPo
At the British War Cemetery, Bayeux. Charles Causley. NAEL-2; OBWP; OxBC
At the Bus Stop: Eurydice. David Ferry. PPR
At the Cannon's Mouth. Herman Melville. PAH
At the Cantina. Gary Soto. MAYP
At the Carnival. Anne Spencer. BANP; BlSi; CDC; PoNe
At the Cascade. Henrietta Cordelia Ray. CBWP-3
At the Cavour. Arthur Symons. NOBVV; OxBSP
At the Cedars. Duncan Campbell Scott. CaP; NOBC
At the center of that parade. Saltimbanques. Pierre Reverdy, *tr. by* Michael Benedikt. POS
At the center of the earth. *Unknown, tr. by* Jerome Rothenberg. STP
At the ceremonies. Civil Marriage. Cecilia Bustamante, *tr. by* David Tipton. Per
At the ceremony of *Emobo.* Ceremony. Kattie M. Cumbo. BlSi
At the Ch'ang Family Well. Wu Chia-chi, *tr. fr. Chinese by* John E. Wills, Jr.. *Fr.* Ten Miscellaneous Poems on Tung-t'ao, VIII. WFTU
At the city gates in the New Year season, a hundred skills are displayed. A Caged Tiger: A Ballad. Huang Ching-jen, *tr. by* Daniel Bryant. WFTU
At the close of a winter day. The Rhyme of the Three Captains. Kipling. BeLS
At the Closed Gate of Justice. James David Corrothers. BANP
At the Cochise Tourist Pavilion. Maura Stanton. NAmP
At the coming of the New Year. Prince Funado, *tr. fr. Japanese. Fr.* Manyo Shu. Ma
"At the Corner of Muck and Myer." Paul Violi. UL
At the corner of the reed fence. *Unknown, tr. fr. Japanese by* Hiroaki Sato. *Fr.* Manyo Shu. FCEI
At the corner of Wood Street, when daylight appears. The Reverie of Poor Susan. Wordsworth. CH; EnRP; GTBS; GTBS-P; OxBoLi; WiR
At the country inn, thousands of peach trees. Inscribed on a Painting ("At the country inn, thousands of peach trees"). T'ang Yin, *tr. by* Jonathan Chaves. CoBLCP
At the court of the miracle-working Rabbi of Sadagora. Father. Rose Ausländer, *tr. by* Ewald Osers. VWA
At the cross her station keeping. Stabat Mater. *At. to* Jacopone da Todi. WGRP
At the cross-roads I came upon the delinquent moon. Templeogue. Blanaid Salkeld. NeIP
At the Crossroads. Thomas Kinsella. NoAM
At the crossroads/ of my gaping dreams. Trembling. Aliza Shenhar, *tr. by* Linda Zisquit. VWA
At the crossroads. Jealousy. Valerie Sinason. DT
At the cry of the first bird. The Crucifixion. *Unknown, tr. by* Kuno Meyer. TIRV
At the Dark Hour. Paul Dehn. BoLoP; WaP
At the dark street corner. Guilt, Desire and Love. James Baldwin. GLP

At the dawn I seek Thee. Morning Song. Solomon ibn Gabirol, *tr. by* Nina Davis Salaman. TrJP
At the dawn of your life, you ate gruel. Cheng Hsieh, *tr. fr. Chinese by* Jonathan Chaves. *Fr.* Mourning for My Son Jun-erh. CoBLCP
At the dead end of a road twisting snakelike. Party at Bannon Brook. Alden Nowlan. NeAC
At the Discharge of Cannon Rise the Drowned. Hubert Witheford. ATNZ; PeNZ
At the Dog Show. Christopher Morley. MoShBr
At the door of his hut sat Massasoit. The Peace Message. Burton Egbert Stevenson. PAH
At the door of Mercy Sighing. Thomas Mackellar. AH
At the Door of the Native Studies Director. Robert H. Davis. HATNAP
At the door on summer evenings. Longfellow. *See* Song of Hiawatha, The: Hiawatha's Childhood.
At the Doors. Der Nistor, *tr. fr. Yiddish by* Joseph Leftwich. TrJP
At the Draper's. Thomas Hardy. *Fr.* Satires of Circumstance, XII. BrPo; MoAB; MoBrPo; OBD
At the earliest ending of winter. Not Ideas about the Thing but the Thing Itself. Wallace Stevens. HAP; HCAP; LCAP; TAP
At the Edge. Denise Levertov. NAAL-2
At the edge of all the ages. The Song of Finis. Walter de la Mare. MoBrPo
At the edge of the forest. On the Meatwheel. Dick Gallup. UL
At the Edge of the Jungle. Patrick Lane. NOBC
At the edge of the page the pen. Houses. Dan Pagis, *tr. by* Warren Bargad *and* Stanley F. Chyet. IP
At the edge of the Sea of Serenity. Instamatic The Moon February 1973. Edwin Morgan. BWV
At the edge of the window that limits space. Javier Sologuren, *tr. by* Maureen Ahern *and* David Tipton. Per
At the edge of the woods where people. At Woods' Edge. Ory Bernstein, *tr. by* Warren Bargad *and* Stanley F. Chyet. IP
At the edge of tide. The Sandpiper. Frances Mary Frost. RHPC
At the Edge of Town. William Stafford. NNaP
At the end a/ "The Prisoner of Zenda." The Prisoner of Zenda. Richard Wilbur. NBLV
"At the end, he listened only to." Late Stravinsky Listening to Late Beethoven. Stephen Spender. AnAn
At the end of a little sloping street, I recognize. Valery Larbaud, *tr. fr. French by* William Joy Smith. *Fr.* Europe, XI. CT
At the end of a long-walled garden. The Cottage Hospital. Sir John Betjeman. GTBS-P; MoBrPo; NoAM; NOBE; OBD; UnPo
At the end of a melancholy world. The End of the World. João Cabral de Melo Neto, *tr. by* James Wright. ATCBP
At the end of autumn. Mototoshi, *tr. by* Geoffrey Bownas *and* Anthony Thwaite. PeBJV
At the end of Avenue B. The Flower Farm. Greg Pape. NAmP
At the end of life paralysis or those creeping teeth. Bog and Candle. Robert David Fitzgerald. CBAP
At the end of my yard there is a vat. *Unknown.* ChTr
At the end of October. The Snake. Wendell Berry. GeTw
At the end of Spring. Yü Hsüan-chi, *tr. fr. Chinese by* Geoffery Waters. BoWoP
At the end of Tarriers' Lane, which was the street. Wm. Brazier. Robert Graves. NOBL
At the End of the Affair. Maxine W. Kumin. TAP
At the end of the battle. Masses. César Vallejo, *tr. by* Lynn C. Jacox *and* Perry Higman. LPSS
At the end of the bough! Sweet Apple. James Stephens. CMoP
At the end of the day. Nothing Strange. Tom Kryss. NeAC
At the end of the garden. Pumpkins. John Cotton. BoNaP
At the end of the garden walk. The Cold Green Element. Irving Layton. NOBC; NoP; OBCV
At the end of the journey we built. Journeys. Meg Campbell. PeNZ
At the end of the path a schoolhouse. My Tea. Kenneth Rosen. NAmP
At the end of the road. The Story of the Unknown Man. Samih al-Qasim, *tr. by* Abdullah al-Udhari. MPAW
At the end of the road, in a drab chapel. Mother Tongue. Jon Stallworthy. NoAM
At the end of the row. The Objection to Being Stepped On. Robert Frost. NBLV
At the end of the Second World War. A Broken Bowl. Chan Ch'e, *tr. by* Dominic Cheung. IFON
At the End of the Street of Stars. Pierre Reverdy, *tr. fr. French by* Michael Benedikt. POS
At the end of the third act, poetry gutters down. After Shakespeare. Alex Comfort. ErPo
At the end of the war I arose. The Driver. James Dickey. VGW
At the End of Things. Arthur Edward Waite. WGRP
At the Entrance. Douglas Stewart. CBAP

At the equinox when the earth was veiled in a late rain. Continent's End. Robinson Jeffers. AWP; FaBV; ImOP

At the Executed Murderer's Grave. James Wright. HCAP

At the far end of a trip north. Nooksack Valley. Gary Snyder. NaP

At the feast of Belshazzar and a thousand of his lords. The Handwriting on the Wall. Knowles Shaw. BLPA

At the Ferry. U. A. Fanthorpe. FaBoWP

At the Ferry in Kuwana. Chiyojo, tr. fr. Japanese by Hiroaki Sato. Fr. Seventeen Hokku. FCEI

At the Ferry on the Miya River. Shiba Sonome, tr. fr. Japanese by Hiroaki Sato. Fr. Fifteen Hokku. FCEI

At the field's edge. The White Hare. Lilian Bowes-Lyon. OxBTC

At the Fillmore. Philip Levine. NNaP

At the first hour from dawn. Journey through the Night. John Holloway. NePoEA

At the first strokes of the fiddle bow. The Wheel. Wendell Berry. GeTw

At the first turning of the second stair. T. S. Eliot. Fr. Ash Wednesday. NOBA

At the Fishhouses. Elizabeth Bishop. CoAP; FaBoWP; HAP; HCAP; LCAP; LiTM; NAAL-2; NoP; NYBP; PoRA

At the Five Corners. Blaise Cendrars, tr. fr. French by Anselm Hollo. RHTwFP

At the Flying School. Leonard Trawick. SoTCo

At the foot of Meetinghouse Hill. Bricking the Church. Robert Morgan. MAYP

At the foot of the bank, many fragrant grasses. The Cowherd. Yabu Kozan, tr. by Burton Watson. JLIC-2

At the foot of the Cathedral of Burgos. Autobiography. Gloria Fuertes, tr. by Philip Levine. AnAn; PBWP

At the foot of yonder mountain where the fountains do flow. The Green Briar Shore. Unknown. AmFP

At the ford, while grass-green frogs. Charming the Moon. James DenBoer. MAT

At the Fountain. Marcabrun, tr. fr. French by Harriet Waters Preston. AWP

At the Fox Glacier Hotel. James Keir Baxter. ATNZ

At the frontier the long train slows to a stop. The Frontier. John Hewitt. BIrV

At the Garden Gate. David McCord. FaPON; ILY

At the Gate. Chaucer. Fr. Troilus and Criseyde [or Criseide]. SeCePo

At the Gate in the Middle of My Life. Linda Gregg. NAmP

At the gate of old Granada, when all its bolts are heard. The Lamentation for Celin. Unknown, tr. by John Gibson Lockhart. AWP

At the Gate of the Valley. Zbigniew Herbert, tr. fr. Polish by Czeslaw Milosz. PwPP

At the gathered ends of rooty paths. The Island in the Evening. Fairfield Porter. PoA

At the Golden Ball and Lillie's Head. To Saffold's Customers. At. to John Case. FaBoUs

At the Grave of Burns. Wordsworth. EnRP

At the Grave of Henry James. W. H. Auden. LiTA; NoP

At the Grave of Henry Vaughan. Siegfried Sassoon. CMoP; EaLo; GTBS-P

At the Grave of Walker. Joaquin Miller. AA; AnAmPo

At the great sky. Mitsune, tr. by Geoffrey Bownas and Anthony Thwaite. PeBJV

At the Great Wall of China. Edmund Blunden. GTBS-P

At the Grey Round of the Hill. W. B. Yeats. RB

At the Hacienda. Bret Harte. AA

At the head of Wear Water about twelve at noon. The North Country Collier. Unknown. OxBSS

At the headland of Kashima. Mushimaro, tr. fr. Japanese. Fr. Manyo Shu. Ma

At the Heich Kirk-Yaird, sel. Alastair MacKie. Passin Ben Dorain. PoSH

At the Holi festival of color. Mirabai, tr. by Willis Barnstone and Usha Nilsson. BoWoP

At the hour shaped for him Scyld departed. Unknown, tr. fr. Anglo-Saxon by Michael Alexander. Fr. Beowulf. OBD

At the hour when the heat of the day is overcome. Dante, tr. fr. Italian by John Ciardi. Fr. Divina Commedia: Purgatorio NAWM-1

At the house where the Saburu girl. Yakamochi, tr. fr. Japanese. Fr. Manyo Shu. Ma

At the Indian Killer's Grave. Robert Lowell. NOBA; VGW

At the instant of drowning he invoked the three sisters. The Three Fates. Rosemary Dobson. BoWoP

At the Jaffé Memorial Fountain, Botanic Gardens. Frank Ormsby. CIP

At the Jewish Cemetery in Prague. Oscar Levertin, tr. fr. Swedish by Richard Burns and Göran Printz-Pahlson. VWA

At the Jewish Museum. Linda Pastan. VWA

At the jungle's edge, torn open. Lan Nguyen; the Uniform of Death, 1971. David Mura. BrSi

At the Keyhole. Walter de la Mare. MoAB; MoBrPo

At the king's gate the subtle noon. Coronation. Helen Hunt Jackson. AA; BeLS; GN

At the Klamath Berry Festival. William Stafford. InPK

At the lads who where lightfoot. Observation by a Formerly Rose-Lipt Maiden. Joyce LaMers. SoTCo

At the Lake—Remembering My Dead Son, Yü. Pien Kung, tr. fr. Chinese by Jonathan Chaves. CoBLCP

At the Landing. Maura Stanton. NAmP

At the large foot of a fair hollow tree. The Country-Mouse. Abraham Cowley, after the Latin of Horace. OBVE; SeCP

At the last moment I. Elegy for an Android. D. M. Thomas. BWV

At the last, tenderly. The Last Invocation. Walt Whitman. MoAmPo; OBD; OxBA; OxBSP; PoEL-5; TrGrPo; TrPWD (Imprisoned Soul, The.) OBEV; WGRP

At the Long Island Jewish Geriatric Home. Jorie Graham. NPGG

At the long tables of time. The Jugs. Paul Celan, tr. by Christopher Middleton. OBVE

At the Loom. Robert Duncan. Fr. Passages. VGW

At the meeting of the icy silences. Waterfall. Pierre Reverdy, tr. by Mark Rudman. RHTwFP

At the Mermaid Inn. Charles Lotin Hildreth. AA

At the Mid Hour of Night. Thomas Moore. GTBS; GTBS-P; NOBE; OBEV; OBNC; PoEL-4

At the midnight in the silence of the sleep-time. Robert Browning. Fr. Asolando. FaBV; FiP; NOBE; OBNC; OHFP; TEP; TrGrPo (Epilogue: "At the midnight in the silence of the sleep-time.") NAEL-1

At the Millinery Shop. Daniel Mark Epstein. MAYP

At the Moated Grange. Shakespeare. See Measure for Measure: Take, O Take Those Lips Away.

At the Monument to Pierre Louÿs. Richard Howard. EOEF

At the Mountain of the Mysterious Tomb. Wu Wei-yeh, tr. fr. Chinese by Jonathan Chaves. CoBLCP

At the mouth of Wu-ling Stream. Riding a Boat on Wu-ling Stream. Tao-chi, tr. by Jonathan Chaves. CoBLCP

At the Movie: Virginia, 1956. Ellen Bryant Voigt. NoAM

At the muezzin's call for prayer. Ad Coelum. Harry Romaine. BLPA; FaBoBe

At the Museum. John Malcolm Brinnin. EyDe

At the National Air and Space Museum. Janice Townley Moore. TSM

At the National Gallery. Judith Kazantzis. AIW

At the Nature-Strip. Judith Rodriguez. CBAP

At the New Year. Kenneth Patchen. LiTM

At the news from Fal's high plain I cannot sleep. Geoffrey Keating, tr. by Thomas Kinsella. NOIV

At the next table, two carry on. Carrying On. Leonard Nathan. BLA

At the Ninth Hour. John Lancaster Spalding. Fr. God and the Soul. AA

At the Ocean's Verge. Ralph Gustafson. OBCV

At the officers' table, for half an hour afterwards, port. Class Incident from Graves. Alan Brownjohn. OxBTC

At the old concert hall on the Bowery. She Is More to Be Pitied than Censured. William B. Gray. BeLS; BLPA

At the Opening of Chikubu's Collection of Haikai. Onitsura, tr. fr. Japanese by Hiroaki Sato. Fr. Twenty-three Hokku. FCEI

At the palace of Kukuri. Unknown, tr. fr. Japanese. Fr. Manyo Shu. Ma

At the park. Returned from California. Simon J. Ortiz. HATNAP

At the Party. W. H. Auden. OxBSP

At the Party. Freda Laughton. NeIP

At the Pauwels. Diane Glancy. CRP

At the Piano. Andrew Hudgins. MOWH

At the Piano. Swinburne. See Heptalogia, The: John Jones.

At the Place of the Roman Baths. "Richard Scrace." CaP

At the Place of the Sea. Annie Johnson Flint. BLPA

At the Playground. William Stafford. LCAP

At the Poem Society a black-haired man stands up to say. Fresh Air. Kenneth Koch. NeAP; NNaP

At the point of separating out. Marcabrun, tr. by Paul Blackburn. Pro

At the point of shining feathers. The Night a Sailor Came to Me in a Dream. Diane Wakoski. TAP; VGW

At the Polo-Ground. Samuel Ferguson. NOIV

At the Portal. Frances Ridley Havergal. BLRP

At the post house lodge, plum flowers scattering. Tune: Treading on Grass. Ou-yang Hsiu, *tr.* by Burton Watson. CoBCP

At the post office he sees Joe McInnes. Quiet Desperation. Louis Simpson. SV

At the post station. *Unknown, tr. fr. Japanese by* Hiroaki Sato. *Fr.* Manyo Shu. FCEI

At the President's Grave. Richard Watson Gilder. PAH

At the prison's gate. Oil Painting. Walter Martínez, *tr. by the author.* Vol

At the Protestant Museum. Hugh Maxton. CIP

At the rising, climbing, southern limit there are clouds. Teika, *tr. fr. Japanese by* Hiroaki Sato. FCEI

At the River Tower Parting from My Younger Brother, Fu-ling. Wu Wei-yeh, *tr. fr. Chinese by* Jonathan Chaves. CoBLCP

At the road's end glimmer the station lights. Fetching the Wounded. Laurence Binyon. MMA

At the roadside. Saigyo, *tr. by* Geoffrey Bownas *and* Anthony Thwaite. PeBJV

At the Roman Baths, Bath. Edward Lucie-Smith. NePoEA-2

At the round earths imagined corners, blow. John Donne. *Fr.* Holy Sonnets, VII. BLPL; EaLo; EBEV; FaBoRV; HAP; HeIP; InPS; JCP; LiTB; MeLP; MePo; NAEL-1; NAWM-1; NOBE; NoP; OAEL-1; OBD; OBS; PoE; PoEL-2; PPP; QFR; SeCP; SeCV-1; Son; TEP; TOF

(Blow Your Trumpets.) ChTr

At the round earth's imagined corners let. The Last Judgment. Giuseppe Gioacchino Belli, *tr. by* Anthony Burgess. OBD; PFI

At the St. Louis Institute of Music. Ronald Wallace. GOYP

At the Salvation Army. Simon J. Ortiz. *Fr.* From Sand Creek. STE

At the San Francisco Airport. Yvor Winters. AiP; HeIP; InPK; NIP; NOBA; QFR

At the Sea's Edge. Gwen Harwood. CBAP

At the Seaside. Robert Louis Stevenson. NTCP; OxBChV

At the Shelter-Stone. Brenda G. Macrow. PoSH

At the Ship. Richard Percival Lister. FiBHP

At the shouts and cheers. *Unknown, tr. by* Geoffrey Bownas *and* Anthony Thwaite. PeBJV

At the Shrine. Richard Kendall Munkittrick. AA

At the siege of Belle Isle. Mother Goose. OxNR

At the Sign-Painter's. Jared Carter. FYAP

At the Slackening of the Tide. James Wright. MOS; UnPo; VGW

At the Smithville Methodist Church. Stephen Dunn. BLA

At the song's beginning. Violet. John Hollander. FYAP

At the sound of my voice. My One Voice. Bob Perelman. IAT

At the spring. To Light. Linda Hogan. ER; HATNAP

At the stand where we ate fish. Peter Rosei, *tr. by* Beth Bjorklund. CoAuP

At the summit of perception. Prince Henry the Navigator. Sydney Clouts. PeSA

At the Swings. Henry Taylor. MT

At the Table Island. *Unknown, tr. fr. Japanese. Fr.* Manyo Shu. Ma

At the table she used to sew at. Sorting It Out. Philip Booth. PPR

At the Telephone Club. Henri Coulette. CoAP

At the Tennis Club. I. L. Martin. SD

At the Theater. Rachel Lyman Field. FaPON

At the Theater. A. P. Herbert. FiBHP

At the third hour always. Rain. Paul Murray. BIrV

At the time it seemed unimportant: he was lying. The Day. Roy Fuller. OxBTC

At the time of Matines, Lord, thu were itake. The Hours of the Passion. *Unknown.* MeEL

At the time of puberty I had obsessions. Ralph Chubb. *Fr.* The Sun Spirit. PeHV

At the time of the white dawn. Song of the Fallen Deer. *Unknown, tr. by* Frank Russell. OBVE

At the time when blossoms. *Unknown, tr. fr. Chinese by* Arthur Waley. *Fr.* Tzu Yeh Songs. BoWoP

At the time when the earth became hot. Birth of Sea and Land Life. Keaulumoku, *tr. fr. Hawaiian by* M. W. Beckwith. *Fr.* Kumulipo, The; a Creation Chant. WTO

At the tip of the old pier a boat trembled. Observation on a Small Harbor outside the Military Zone. Abba Kovner, *tr. by* Bernhard Frank. MHeP

At the Tomb of Rachel. "Yehoash," *tr. fr. Yiddish by* Isidore Goldstick. TrJP

At the Tomb of Washington. Clinton Scollard. OHIP

At the top of a low hill. Hampstead; the Horse Chestnut Trees. Thom Gunn. NoP

At the top of my street the attorneys abound. Conversation in Craven Street, Strand. James Smith *and* Sir George Rose. FaBoCo

At the top of the house the apples are laid in rows. Moonlit Apples. John Drinkwater. BoNaP; BoTP; OBMV; OxBTC; PoRA

At the top of the stairs. Beatrix Is Three. Adrian Mitchell. NAs

At the top of the years I stand. Muttering. Sándor Weöres, *tr. by* Jascha Kessler. FOC

At the top of this ridge I could whistle happily. Descending the Ridge of Flying Clouds. T'ang Hsien-Tsu, *tr. by* Jonathan Chaves. CoBLCP

At the topmost peak, one thatch hut. Visiting a Recluse on West Mountain and Not Finding Him In. Ch'iu Wei, *tr. by* Burton Watson. CoBCP

At the Tourist Center in Boston. Margaret Atwood. NoP

At the track the horses run. The Track. Nicholas Christopher. MAYP

At the Train Station. Haim Guri, *tr. fr. Hebrew by* Warren Bargad *and* Stanley F. Chyet. IP

At the Treatment Center. Jerome Sala. UL

At the Turning Point of Life. Gyula Illyés, *tr. fr. Hungarian by* William Jay Smith. MHuP

At the Un-National Monument along the Canadian Border. William Stafford. HAP; HeIP

At the upper course of the river. *Unknown, tr. fr. Japanese. Fr.* Manyo Shu. Ma

At the Vent Haven Museum in Fort Mitchell. "And Now Farley Is Going to Sing *While I Drink a Glass of Water!*" Albert Goldbarth. GeTw

At the very beginning of creation. I Was That Woman. Debjani Chatterjee. WS

At the Wailing Wall. Aidan Carl Mathews. CIP

At the Waldron Court Apartments. Adventures in Bronze. Leon Stokesbury. MT

At the Washing of My Son. David Ray. DiL

At the Well. Malka Heifetz-Tussman, *tr. fr. Yiddish by* Marcia Falk. VWA

At the Western Shore. Sarah Youngblood. IHMS

At the Western Wall. Barbara F. Lefcowitz. VWA

At the windows, you look out. Synthesizing Several Abstruse Concepts with an Experience. Carol Poster. BXAP

At the Woodpile. Raymond Henri. SaC

At the wood's mouth. The Gibber. Theodore Roethke. *Fr.* The Lost Son. NAAL-2

At the World's Last Outpost. Robert Desnos, *tr. fr. French by* Michael Benedikt. POS

At the Worst. Israel Zangwill. WGRP

At the Worst ("And Man is left alone with Man." 'Tis well. . ."), *sel.* Israel Zangwill. WGRP

At the worst place in the hills above the city. The Birthday Dream. James Dickey. NAs

At the "Ye That Do Truly." Charles Williams. NOCV

At the Zoo. Alan Alexander Milne. FaPON

At the Zoo. Thackeray. NTCP; OxBChV

At the Zoo. Israel Zangwill. TrJP

At thee the Mocker sneers in cold derision. The Maid of Orleans. Schiller, *tr. by* James Clarence Mangan. AWP

At Thermopylae. Simonides. WaaP

At these high words great heaven began to shake. A Prayer Brings Rain. Tasso, *tr. fr. Italian by* Edward Fairfax. *Fr.* Godfrey of Bulloigne; or, The Recoverie of Jerusalem. OBSC

At thieves I bark; at lovers wag my tail. *Unknown, after the Latin of* Joachim du Bellay. FaBoEE

At Thirty Years. Byron. *Fr.* Don Juan, I. FiP

At this Adonis smiles as in disdain. Shakespeare. *Fr.* Venus and Adonis. EBEV

At this dilapidated hut. Boncho, *tr. fr. Japanese by* Hiroaki Sato. *Fr.* Twenty-one Hokku. FCEI

At this hour of nightfall. Havdala. Amir Gilboa, *tr. by* Warren Bargad *and* Stanley F. Chyet. IP

At this hour the soul floats weightlessly. Poor Angels. Edward Hirsch. MAYP

At this late date. Keiun, *tr. by* Steven D. Carter. WFTW

At this moment hundreds of women. The Watch. Marge Piercy. GeTw

At this moment in time. They Flee from Me That Sometime Did Me Seek. Gavin Ewart. OxBC

At this old monastery, long corridors are lost in the shade. The Jasper Cloud Monastery. Wu Wen, *tr. by* Chang Yin-nan. WFTU

At this range, it's really monumental. Grass. Alfred Corn. MAYP

At this remote village, I have no neighbors. Chang Yü, *tr. by* Jonathan Chaves. CoBLCP

At this th' impatient hero sowrly smil'd. Homer, *tr. fr. Greek by* Dryden. *Fr.* The Iliad, I. OBVE

At this time I find the bed very arid. The Reason for Poetry. Nancy Morejón, *tr. by* Anita Whitney. WPOW

At this time of the year when the white-clouded Tatsuta Hill. Mushimaro, *tr. fr. Japanese.* Fr. Manyo Shu. Ma

At this year's end too. Prince Munenaga, *tr. by* Steven D. Carter. WFTW

At those who come to my grave with flowers, I can but laugh. One of the Dead Speaks. Cahit Sitki Taranci, *tr. by* Nermin Menemencioglu. OBD

At 3 a.m. I run my tongue. Death's Head. Phyllis Gotlieb. NOBC

At three in the morning. Pointed Boots. Christopher Middleton. *Fr.* Herman Moon's Hourbook. NePoEA-2

At Thurgarton Church, *sel.* George Barker.
"I enter and find I stand." PoPo

At thy nativity a glorious quire. Milton. *Fr.* Paradise Regained, *Bk.* I, *ll.* 242-254. PChr

At Times. Cheryl Moskowitz. DT

At times each poet imagines himself. Poetry's Buried. Meir Wieseltier, *tr. by* Warren Bargad *and* Stanley F. Chyet. IP

At times I almost believed it: madness. Emily Dickinson's Sestina for Molly Bloom. Barbara F. Lefcowitz. SM

At times I resort, beyond man's discerning. Wind: "At times I resort, beyond man's discerning." *Unknown, formerly at. to* Cynewulf, *tr. fr. Anglo-Saxon. Fr.* Riddles (Exeter Book). AnOE

At times I see it, present. A Bright Day. John Montague. CIP; FaBCIP

At times in the course of history. Lesson on the Facts of Life. Karin Kiwus, *tr. by* Susan L. Cocalis. DMG

At times it is like watching a face you have just met. The Way It Sometimes Is. Henry Taylor. MT

At times it seemed the country itself was a cloud. England. Mary Jo Salter. DiPo

At times the heart looks toward open fields. Near Twelve Mile Point. Lance Henson. HATNAP

At times the rose, at times the hue. Mohammad Taqi Mir, *tr. by* Ahmed Ali. GoT

At times you fall silent. Wakayama Bokusui, *tr. fr. Japanese by* Hiroaki Sato. *Fr.* Forty-four Tanka. FCEI

At Timon's villa let us pass a day. Pope. *Fr.* Moral Essays: To Richard Boyle, Earl of Burlington: Of the Uses of Riches. NOEC; OAEL-1; OBSV; PoEl-3; PPP
(Timon's Villa) PoE

At Toledo. Arthur Symons. BrPo

At tourist shrines where history is tracked. Near Myth. Marian Gleason. SoTCo

At Tripod Lake on that day His Majesty quit this world. Ballad of Yüan-yüan. Wu Wei-yeh, *tr. by* Jonathan Chaves. CoBLCP

At Tripolis. Constance Carrier. WPE

At Twelfth Night twilight now. Twelfth Night. Philip Booth. NePoEA

At twelve bell answers bell. Angelus-Time near Dublin. William Bedell Stanford. NeIP

At 12 o'clock in the afternoon. Meleager, *tr. by* Sydney Oswald. PeHV

At twenty-one Jupe ran away. Slave Story. Hodding Carter. PoNe

At twenty she was brilliant and adored. Pathedy of Manners. Ellen Kay. SoSe

At Twilight. Peyton Van Rensselaer. AA

At twilight. The Servant of Others. Kathleen Spivack. ER

At twilight amidst the currents of water. Chamutal Reich. *Fr.* Three Poems in Black and White, 2. WCI

At twilight I went into the street. Descending Figure. Louise Glück. AnAn; FaBoWP; GeTw

At two a.m. a thing, jumping out of a manhole. News Report. David Ignatow. ErPo; TwCP

At Tynemouth Priory, after a Tempestuous Voyage. William Lisle Bowles. Son

At Upton-on-Severn. *Unknown.* FaBoCo; FaBoEE

At Veronica's. Robert Peterson. NeAC

At Viscount Nelson's lavish funeral. 1805. Robert Graves. FaBoCh; OBSV

At Vshchizh. Fyodor Ivanovich Tyutchev, *tr. fr. Russian by* Charles Tomlinson. OBWP

At War. Russell Atkins. AmNP

At War. Charles Madge. FaBoMo

At water's edge, clouds float up. Night of the Fourteenth. Ho Ching-ming, *tr. by* Jonathan Chaves. CoBLCP

At wave-bright Naniwa. Lady Otomo no Sakanoe, *tr. fr. Japanese. Fr.* Manyo Shu. Ma

At Wednesbury there was a cocking. The Wednesbury Cocking. *Unknown.* EnSB; FaBoBa

At which time I close my Roger Fry, successfully. A Window Seat. Albert Goldbarth. NAmP

At whiles (yea oftentimes) I muse over. Dante, *tr. fr. Italian by* Dante Gabriel Rossetti. *Fr.* Vita Nuova, La, IX. AWP

At Wonder Donut. Laureen Mar. BrSi

At Woodlawn I heard the dead cry. Theodore Roethke. *Fr.* The Lost Son. DiL; HAP; HCAP; LiTM; VGW
(Flight, The.) NAAL-2; RB; TrGrPo

At Woods' Edge. Ory Bernstein, *tr. fr. Hebrew by* Warren Bargad *and* Stanley F. Chyet. IP

At Woodward's Gardens. Robert Frost. ImOP; PoA

At words poetic, I'm so pathetic. You're the Top. Cole Porter. OBAL; UnPo

At work his arms wave like a windmill. The Secretary. Peter Redgrove. OxBTC

At Year's End. Richard Wilbur. *See* Now winter down's the dying of the year.

At Yellow Crane Tower Taking Leave of Meng Hao-jan. Li Po, *tr. fr. Chinese by* Burton Watson. CoBCP

At your door. Weariness in the Evening of January Thirty-Second. Isam Mahfouz, *tr. by* Sargon Boulus *and* Samuel Hazo. MAP

At your entreaty, I at last have writ. Maidenhead. "Ephelia." WPE

At your house, at the end of your roof. House. Saibara, *tr. by* Hiroaki Sato. FCEI

At your light side trees shy. William Knott. EAS

At Your Naked Back. Anadad Eldan, *tr. fr. Hebrew by* Bernhard Frank. MHeP

At your silver wedding in '64 we gave. Psycho. Peter Olds. PeNZ

Atalanta. Jan Kemp. ATNZ

Atalanta in Calydon, *sels.* Swinburne.
Before the Beginning of Years. FaFP; HeIP; LiTB; NAEL-2; NoP
(Chorus: "Before the beginning of years.") EBVV; OBEV
(Man.) TrGrPo
"Who hath given man speech? or what hath set therein." OAEL-2
"Maiden, and mistress of the months and stars." PoEL-5
When the Hounds of Spring [Are on Winter's Traces]. FaBoBe; HeIP; LiTB; NAEL-2; NoP; PoE; PrIm; TEP; TrGrPo
(Chorus: "When the hounds of spring are on winter's traces.") AWP; CTC; EBVV; FaBoBe; GTBS-P; GTBS-P; HAP; HeIP; LiTB; NOBE; NoP; OAEL-2; OBEV; PrIm; TEP; TrGrPo; WeW
(Hounds of Spring, The.) FaBV

Atalanta in Camden-Town. "Lewis Carroll." CenHV

Atameros. John Beevers. EAS

Atami. Chugan Engetsu, *tr. fr. Chinese by* Burton Watson. FCEI; JLIC-2

Atavism. Elinor Wylie. PoA

Até. Claude Royet-Journoud, *tr. fr. French by* Keith Waldrop. RHTwFP

Athalie, *sel.* Jean Racine, *tr. fr. French by* Charles Randolph.
"God whose goodness filleth every clime, The." WGRP

Athanasia. Oscar Wilde. BrPo

Atheist's Tragedy, The, *sels.* Cyril Tourneur.
Epitaph on a Soldier. EiL
Soldier's Death, A. SeCePo
"Walking next day upon the fatal shore." WaaP
Soldier's Death, A. SeCePo

Atheling Grange; or, The Apotheosis of Lotte Nussbaum. William Plomer. OBNV

Athelstan the king, captain of earls. Brunanburg. *Unknown, tr. by* Kemp Malone. PoE. *See also* Aethelstan.

Athelstane. Priscilla Jane Thompson. CBWP-2

Athens. Milton. *See* Paradise Regained: Look once more ere we leave this specular Mount.

Athirst for spiritual good. The Prophet. Pushkin. AAA, *tr. by* Alan Myers

Athirst in spirit, through the gloom. The Prophet. Pushkin, *tr. by* Babette Deutsch *and* Avrahm Yarmolinsky. AWP; EaLo

Athlete. Don Maynard. PoAu-2

Athlete, one vacation, An. An Accommodating Lion. Tudor Jenks. OBCA

Athletes. Walker Gibson. SD

Athletic Employment. *Unknown.* SD

Athol Brose. Thomas Hood. FaBoCo

Athwart the sky a lowly sigh. London. John Davidson. NOBE; OBNC

Atlanta Exposition Ode. Mary Weston Fordham. CBWP-2

Atlantic Charter, A.D. 1620-1942. Francis Brett Young. AmFN

Atlantic Charter: 1942. Francis Brett Young. OPP

Atlantic is a sea of bones. Lucille Clifton. ER

Atlantic is a stormy moat, and the Mediterranean, The. The Eye. Robinson Jeffers. LiTA; LiTM; NoAM; NOBA; OxBA; WaP

Atlantis. Hart Crane. *Fr.* The Bridge, VIII. LiTM

Atlantis, *sel.* Louis Dudek.
Marine Aquarium, The. MoCV

Atlantis. Maura Stanton. NAmP
Atlas, The, *sels.* Kenneth Slessor. PoAu-2
  Dutch Seacoast.
  King of Cuckooz, The.
  Mermaids.
  Post-Roads.
AtLeastItIsnta. S. L. A. B. S. for George Herbert. George Starbuck.
  SoTCo
Atoll in the Mind, The. Alex Comfort. LiTB; LiTM; SeCePo
Atom from Atom. Emerson. *Fr.* Fragments on Nature and Life.
  ImOP
Atomic Bomb. Tsuchiya Kyutai, *tr. fr. Chinese by* Burton Watson.
  JLIC-2
Atomic Courtesy. Ethel Jacobson. FaFP
Atomic Pantoum. Peter Meinke. SM
Atonement, The. Milton. *See* Paradise Lost: Father, Thy word is past,
  man shall find grace.
Atop a tower I pitched a silken thing. Parachuting Thoor Ballylee.
  William Zaranka. BXAP
Atop its mound frosted white. "Among the Savages. ." Ralph
  Salisbury. STE
A-traipsin' from a shindig, I unsaddles. Agamemnon before Troy. John
  Frederick Nims. Son
Atrocious Pun, An. *Unknown.* RHPC
Atropos. Hilaire Kirkland. *Fr.* Clotho, Lachesis, Atropos, III. PeNZ
Attaché Case, The. George Bogin. PPR
Attack, The. Thomas Buchanan Read. PAH
Attack. Siegfried Sassoon. MoBrPo; NOBE; OxBTC
Attack me, Father, now. Prayer for Peace. Johnstone G. Patrick.
  TrPWD
Attack of the Crab Monsters. Lawrence Raab. AmPA; NoP
Attack of the Squash People. Marge Piercy. NBLV
Attainment. Madison Cawein. WGRP
Attainment, The. Coventry Patmore. *Fr.* The Angel in the House, I, iii.
  FaBoEE
Attainment. Ella Wheeler Wilcox. WGRP
Attempt. Ilse Aichinger, *tr. fr. German by* Beth Bjorklund. CoAuP
Attempt, An. Adam Wazyk, *tr. fr. Polish by* Czeslaw Milosz. PwPP
Attempt at a Description of a Supper of Various Heads in Paris, France.
  Jacques Prévert, *tr. fr. French by* Michael Benedikt. POS
Attempt at Jealousy, An. Craig Raine. NoAM
Attempt at Jealousy, An. Marina Tsvetayeva, *tr. fr. Russian by* Robert
  Perelman *and* Aleksandar Petrov. WPOW
Attend, all ye who list to hear our noble England's praise. The Armada.
  Macaulay. BeLS; FaBoCh; FaPoR; GN; WBLP
Attend my fable if your ears be clean. Roy Campbell. *Fr.* The
  Wayzgoose. OBSV
Attend my lays, ye ever honour'd nine. An Hymn to the Morning.
  Phillis Wheatley. TAP
Attend, ye mournful Parents, while. Another to Urania. Benjamin
  Colman. SCAP
Attend, ye nymphs, by wedlock unconfin'd. Ovid, *tr. fr. Latin by*
  Congreve. *Fr.* The Art of Love. FaBoUs
Attend you and give ear a while, and you shall understand. The Honour
  of Bristol. *At. to* Laurence Price. OxBSS
Attend, Young Friends, While I Relate. *Unknown.* AmFP
Attention. Adrienne Rich. TAP
Attention, architect! Message from a Mouse, Ascending in a Rocket.
  Patricia Hubbell. RHPC
Attention, there he goes now with his pen. Icily. René Daumal, *tr. by*
  Michael Benedikt. POS
Attentive eyes, fantastic heed. A Poet. Thomas Hardy. NoAM
Attentively he heard us, while we spoke. Virgil, *tr. fr. Latin by* Dryden.
  Fr. The Aeneid [*or* Eneados], XI. OBVE
Attic, The. Charles Bruce. *Fr.* The Flowing Summer. CaP
Attic, The. Henri Coulette. NePoEA-2; PoRA
Attic Dance. Joan Drew Ritchings. RR
Attic Landscape, The. Herman Melville. AnAmPo; NOBA; OBAL
Attic maid! with honey fed. To the Swallow. William Cowper, *after the
  Greek of* Euenus. OBVE
Attic, The ("The attic and the cedar closet—nostalgia!"). Richard
  Eberhart. *Fr.* Burr Oaks. MoAB
Atticus ("How did they fume, and stamp, and roar, and chafe"). Pope.
  Fr. Epistle to Dr. Arbuthnot. TW
Atticus ("Peace to all such! but were there one whose fires"). Pope. *Fr.*
  Epistle to Dr. Arbuthnot. AWP; InPK; NoBE; SeCePo
Attired in black, spangled with flames of fire. The Spirit of Night.
  Thomas Rogers. EiL
Attis. Catullus, *tr. fr. Latin by* Peter Whigham. OBVE
Attitudes and Beliefs. Anne Stevenson. ER

Attractions of a Fashionable Irish Watering-Place, The. Francis Sylvester
  Mahony. FaBoPP
Atween the world o' licht. Scotland. William Soutar. OxBS
Au Bout du Temps. Andrei Codrescu. UL
Au Jardin des Plantes. John Wain. NePoEA-2; OxBTC
Au Tombeau de Mon Père. Ronald McCuaig. PoAu-2
Aubade: Desert, The. Frederick Bock. PoA
Aubade: Donna Anna to Juan, Still Asleep. Richard Howard. PoA
Aubade: "Hark! hark! the lark at heaven's gate sings." Shakespeare. *See*
  Cymbeline: Hark! Hark! the Lark.
Aubade: "Hours before dawn we were woken by the quake." William
  Empson. FaBoMo; FaBoTw; LiTB; OxBTC
Aubade: "I work all day, and get half drunk at night." Philip Larkin.
  OPOP; SoSe
Aubade: "In the early morning." Linda Pastan. TV
Aubade: "Jane, Jane,/ Tall as a crane." Dame Edith Sitwell. CMoP;
  MoAB; MoBrPo; MoP; NoAM; PoRA
Aubade: Lake Erie. Thomas Merton. NYBP
Aubade: "Lark now leaves his watery [*or* wat'ry] nest, The." Sir William
  Davenant. *See* Lark Now Leaves His Water [*or* Wat'ry] Nest.
Aubade: "Leave me, dawn! I'm in wretched fettle." Richard Moore.
  SoTCo
Aubade: "Million stars are dreaming out, A." Frank O'Hara. SM
Aubade: "Night's ride's over." Anselm Hollo. UL
Aubade: N.Y.C. Robert Wallace. HoPM
Aubade: "She wakes long before he does. A fierce shock." Mekeel
  McBride. MAYP
Aubade: "Stay, O sweet, and do not rise." See Stay, O sweet . . . .
Aubade: "Today above the gull's call." Louise Glück. AnAn
Aubade: "What dawn is it?" Karl Shapiro. VGW
Aubade for Hope. Robert Penn Warren. MoAmPo
Aubade Triste. Agnes Mary Frances Robinson. NOBVV
Aube Provençale. Marilyn Hacker. AmPA
Aubrey Bodine's crosswater shot of Menchville. The Perspective and
  Limits of Snapshots. Dave Smith. MAYP
Auburn. Goldsmith. *Fr.* The Deserted Village. SeCePo
  (Sweet Auburn.) LiTB; NOBE
  (Village, The.) TrGrPo
Auburn. Paul Verlaine, *tr. fr. French by* Lawrence M. Bensky.
  ErPo
Aucassin and Nicolette, *sel. Unknown, tr. fr. French by* Andrew Lang.
  Who Would List. CTC
"Auchanachie Gordon is bonny and braw." Lord Saltoun and
  Auchanachie. *Unknown.* ESPB
Auction. William Heyen. MAYP
Auction Sale, The. Henry Reed. MoBrPo
Auctioneer. Carl Sandburg. PDV
Auctioneer of parting, The. Emily Dickinson. PoEL-5
Auctioneer's Handbill, An. William Hall. FaBoUs
Auden at Milwaukee. Stephen Spender. AiP
Auden, MacNeice, Day Lewis, I have read them all. British Leftish
  Poetry, 1930-40. "Hugh MacDiarmid." CMoP; FaBoTw; NoAM
Auden's Funeral. Stephen Spender. AnAn
Audience with the emperor, Hall of Inherited Brilliance. Presented to
  Piao, the Prince of Pai-ma. Ts'ao Chih, *tr. by* Burton Watson.
  CoBCP
Audley Court. Tennyson. NOBVV
Audubon, *sels.* Robert Penn Warren.
  Love and Knowledge. *Fr.* VI.
  Tell Me a Story. *Fr.* VII.
  Was Not the Lost Dauphin. *Fr.* I.
Audubon, Drafted. Amiri Baraka. PPP; TTY
Auf dem Wasser zu Singen. Stephen Spender. EnLoPo
Auf meiner Herzliebsten Äugelein. Heine, *tr. fr. German by* Richard
  Garnett. AWP
Auf Wiedersehen. Donald Jeffrey Hayes. CDC
Augmentation of the Unknown. Yannis Ritsos, *tr. fr. Greek by* Kimon
  Friar *and* Kostas Myrsiades. AnAn
Augsburg Adoration, The. Randall Jarrell. NYBP
Auguries of Innocence, *sels.* Blake. BLPL; EBEV; EnRP; FaBoCh;
  FaBV; FaFP; FaPoR; FM; LiTB; OAEL-1; OBNC; OxBoLi; PoEL-4;
  RHPC; TrGrPo
  "Robin Redbreast in a cage, A." OxBoLi, *sl. abr.*
  (Three Things to Remember.) FaPON; MoShBr
  To See a World in a Grain of Sand. ImPK; InPK; OAEL-2; RB;
  WGRP
Augury. W. H. Oliver. PeNZ
August. Eunice Fallon. BoTP
August. Robert Frost. BXAP
August. Izi Kharik, *tr. fr. Yiddish by* Leonard Wolf. PeBMYV

August. Louis MacNeice. LiTM
August. Katharine Pyle. OBCA
August. Henrietta Cordelia Ray. CBWP-3
August. Adrienne Rich. CAPP; NNaP; PBWP
August. Folgore Da San Gimignano, *tr. fr. Italian by* Dante Gabriel
    Rossetti. *Fr.* Sonnets of the Months. CTC
August ("Sixth was August, The."). Spenser. *Fr.* The Faerie Queene,
    VII, 7. GN
August ("Tell me, Perigot"). Spenser. *Fr.* The Shepheardes [*or*
    Shepeards *or* Shepherd's*]* Calender.
   It Fell upon a Holy Eve. InvP
    (Roundelay, A: "It fell upon a holy eve.") ElL
August. Swinburne. WiR
August. Celia Thaxter. FaPON
August. John Updike. *Fr.* A Child's Calendar. OBCA; RHPC
August. Elinor Wylie. MoAB; MoAmPo
August/Fresno 1973. Roberta Spear. AmPA
August at the Lake. David Young. AmPA
August 18. Joanne Kyger. PoM
August for the People. W. H. Auden. WaP
    (Birthday Poem.) NAs
August from My Desk. Roland Flint. AmFN
August, goldenrod blowing. We walk. Maple Syrup. Donald Hall.
    CAPP
August heat. Gerald Vizenor. VoR
August Heat. *Unknown.* RAR
August heat swaddles the cemetery. Voices. Celia Gilbert. ER
August is nearly over, the people. Louis MacNeice. *Fr.* Autumn
    Journal. CMoP
August Midnight, An. Thomas Hardy. BrPo; NOBVV
August Night. Gerhard Fritsch, *tr. fr. German by* Beth Bjorklund.
    CoAuP
August Night. Sara Teasdale. MoAmPo
August Night, 1953. Elizabeth B. Harrod. NePoEA
August 1914. Isaac Rosenberg. EBEV; NOBE; OBWP; OPOP;
    OxBTC
August 1968. Wystan Hugh Auden. OxBSP
August 1964. Ferreira Gullar, *tr. fr. Portuguese by* William Jay Smith.
    CT
August, Ohakune. Lauris Edmond. ATNZ
August on Sourdough, a Visit from Dick Brewer. Gary Snyder.
    SOTW
August Rain. Robert Bly. LCAP; SV
August 6, 1945. City of Hiroshima. The Day after Trinity. Richard
    Oyama. BrSi
August sun hangs low above the city. Return. Mark Vinz. GOYP
August 'twas, the twenty-fifth. Bar's Fight, August 28, 1746. Lucy
    Terry. BlSi; BPo; PoNe
August 24, 1963—1:00 A.M.—Omaha. Donna Whitewing. NOVW
August 2. Norman Jordan. PoBA
August Was Foggy. Gary Snyder. NNaP
August wind rides Spain tonight in a fierce saddle, The. Casa de Pollos.
    Kathleen Fraser. AmPA
Augusto Ngangula. Costa Andrade, *tr. fr. Portuguese by* Michael
    Wolfers. WMBCH
August's dense astronomy fits itself, all stars. Patricia Hampl. *Fr.*
    Resort, VII. NAmP
Augustus was a chubby lad. The Story of Augustus, Who Would Not
    Have Any Soup. Heinrich Hoffmann. FaBoUs; GoJo; MoShBr;
    NBLV; OxBChV; RHPC
Auld Daddy Darkness. James Ferguson. OxBChV
Auld Deil cam to the man at the pleugh, The. The Farmer's Curst Wife.
    Unknown. ESPB, B *vers.*
Auld Hammus knapped his whunstane chips. A Border Forecast.
    William Landles. PoSH
Auld House, The. William Soutar. OxBS
Auld Lang Syne. Burns. AWP; BLPL; EnRP; FaFP; GoTS; LiTB;
    NAEL-2; NOBE; OBEV; OxBS; PoLF; TEP
Auld Lang Syne. John White Chadwick. *See* It singeth low in every
    heart.
Auld Man's Mear's Dead, The. Patrick Birnie. GoTS
Auld Matrons. *Unknown.* ESPB
Auld mune on her back, The. Leander Stormbound. Sydney Goodsir
    Smith. OxBS
Auld Noah was at hame wi' them a.' Parley of Beasts. "Hugh
    MacDiarmid." MoBrPo; MoP; NoAM; NoP; OBMV
Auld Robin Gray. Lady Anne Lindsay. AIW; BeLS; CH; GoTS; GTBS;
    GTBS-P; NOEC; OBEV; WPE
Auld Sang. William Soutar. OxBS
Auld Seceder Cat, The. *Unknown. See* There was a Presbyterian cat.

Auld wife sat at her ivied door, The. Charles Stuart Calverley. BXAP;
    CenHV; FaBoCo; FiBHP; NA; NBLV; Par; WiR
Auld wumman cam' in, a mere rickle o' banes, An. Old Wife in High
    Spirits. "Hugh MacDiarmid." CMoP; OxBTC; PoE
Auncient Acquaintance, Madam, The. John Skelton. AAS; PoEL-1
Aunt Eliza. Harry Graham. ChTr; FaFP; NA
Aunt Helen. T. S. Eliot. AnAmPo; OBAL; PoA
Aunt Jane. Alden Nowlan. SoSe
Aunt Jane Allen. Fenton Johnson. IDB; PoBA; PoNe
Aunt Jane, of whom I dreamed the nights it thundered. Aunt Jane.
    Alden Nowlan. SoSe
Aunt Jemima of the Ocean Waves. Robert Hayden. LCAP; PoBA
Aunt Jennifer's Tigers. Adrienne Rich. CAPP; FaBoWP; HeIP; InPK;
    NIP; NoAM; NoP; SM
Aunt Julia. Norman MacCaig. RB
Aunt Laura Moves toward the Open Grave of Her Father. Joseph De
    Roche. HeIP
Aunt Leaf. Mary Oliver. TDD
Aunt Liza/ Yes? Me, Colored. Peter Abrahams. *Fr.* Tell Freedom.
    PBA
Aunt Lucrezia. Alistair Campbell. ATNZ
Aunt Mary. Robert Stephen Hawker. OHIP
Aunt Maud. Harry Graham. *See* I had written to Aunt Maud.
Aunt Nerissa's Muffin. Wallace Irwin. FiBHP
Aunt Rose—now—might I see you. To Aunt Rose. Allen Ginsberg.
    LiTM; NAAL-2; NoP; PoE; VGW
Aunt Sponge and Aunt Spiker. Roald Dahl. RHPC
Aunt Tabitha. Oliver Wendell Holmes. CenHV
Aunt Zillah Speaks. Herbert Edward Palmer. FaBoTw
Auntie Bridge and Uncle Pat. Geoffrey Lehmann. *Fr.* Ross's Poems.
    CBAP
Auntie, did you feel no pain. Harry Graham. *Fr.* Some Ruthless
    Rhymes, III. CenHV
Aura Amara, L.' Arnaut Daniel, *tr. fr. Provençal by* Ezra Pound. CTC
Auras of Delight. Coventry Patmore. *Fr.* The Unknown Eros. ACP
Auras on the Interstates. Gerald Vizenor. STE
Aurelia. Robert Nichols. OBMV
Aureng-Zebe, *sels.* Dryden.
    "Our author by experience finds it true." FiP; OBS; OxBoLi; SeCV-2
    When I Consider Life. *Fr.* IV, i. FiP
Aurora. Timothy Steele. DiPo
Aurora, *sels.* William Alexander, Earl of Stirling.
    "Cleare moving cristall, pure as the Sunne beames." *Fr.* XXV.
    OxBS
    I Envy Not Endymion. *Fr.* XXIX. Son
     (Sonnet: "I envy not Endymion now no more.") ElL
    I Hope, I Fear. *Fr.* LXVIII. Son
    "Ile give thee leave my love, in beauties field." *Fr.* XXVI. OxBS
    "Let others of the world's decaying tell." ElL
    "O happy Tithon! if thou know'st thy harp." OBEV
    Oh, If Thou Knew'st How Thou Thyself Dost Harm. *Fr.* XXXIII.
     Son
     (Sonnet: "Oh, if thou knew'st how thou thyself dost harm.") ElL
     (To Aurora.) FaFP; GTBS; GTBS-P
    "When in her face mine eyes I fix." ElL
Aurora Borealis. Edouard Roditi. EAS
Aurora gazed from out her shell-pink bower. Sunrise Thought. Henrietta
    Cordelia Ray. *Fr.* A Group of Musings. CBWP-3
Aurora, lady grey. A Simple Pastoral. George Alexander Stevens.
    NOEC
Aurora Leigh, *sels.* Elizabeth Barrett Browning.
    "And I, I was a good child on the whole." BrRo
    "Books, books, books!" WPOW
    "Critics say that epics have died out, The." PBWP
    Florence. FaBoPP
    "I felt the wind soft from the land of souls." OBTV
    "I had a little chamber in the house." FaBoPP
    "I learnt the collects and the catechism." TEP
    "I mused/ Up and down, up and down, the terraced streets." OBTV
    "Of writing many books there is no end;." NOBVV
    Olives and Mountains. *Fr.* VII. FaBoPP
    Reading. GN
    "Then, land!—then, England! oh, the frosty cliffs." FaBoPP;
     NAEL-2
    "There is it!/ You play beside a death-bed like a child.'" BrRo
    "Truth, so far, in my book; the truth which draws." WGRP
    Tuscan Life. *Fr.* VII. FaBoPP
Auroras of Autumn, The, *sels.* Wallace Stevens.
    "Farewell to an idea. A cabin stands." *Fr.* II. CMoP; HCAP
    "Farewell to an idea. The mother's face." *Fr.* III. CMoP; HCAP

"Is there an imagination that sits enthroned." *Fr.* VII. CMoP; HCAP
"It is a theatre floating through the clouds." *Fr.* VI. CMoP; HCAP
"This is where the serpent lives, the bodiless." *Fr.* I. CMoP; PoE
"Unhappy people in a happy world, An." *Fr.* X. CMoP
Auschwitz, *sel.* Elizabeth Wyse.
   "What big heavy doors!" CN
Auschwitz from Colombo. Anne Ranasinghe. VWA
Auspex. James Russell Lowell. PoEL-5; TAP
Auspice of Jewels. Laura Riding. LiTA
Auspicious night. Courtesan with Fan. Elizabeth Spires. MAYP
Austere the Music of My Songs. Fyodor Sologub, *tr. fr. Russian by*
   Babette Deutsch and Avrahm Yarmolinsky. AWP
Australasia, *sel.* William Charles Wentworth.
   "Land of my birth! though now, alas! no more." PoAu-1
Australia. Alec Derwent Hope. NoAM; NoP
Australia. Bernard O'Dowd. PoAu-1
Australia 1970. Judith Wright. CBAP; NoAM
Australian, The. Arthur H. Adams. PoAu-1
Australian Dream, The. David Campbell. CBAP
Australian Transcripts, *sels.* "Fiona Macleod." FM
   Bell-Bird, The.
   Mid-Noon in January.
   Wood-Swallows, The.
Australia's best-kept dead-end road. Women on the Road to Pine Gap.
   Wendy Poussard. AIW
Australia's on the Wallaby. *Unknown.* PoAu-1
Austrian Army, An. *At. to* Alaric Alexander Watts. FaBoCo; FiBHP;
   NOBL
   (Alliteration, or the Siege of Belgrade.) ChTr
   (Siege of Belgrade, The.) BLPA
Austrian Poem 1979/80. Peter Handke, *tr. fr. German by* Beth Bjorklund.
   CoAuP
Autant En Emporte le Vent. Marguerite de Navarre, *tr. fr. French by*
   Aline Allard. PBWP
Autet e bas. Arnaut Daniel, *tr. fr. Provençal by* Ezra Pound. CTC
Authentic, The! Shadows of it. Matins. Denise Levertov. AmPP;
   FaBoWP; IHMS; MoP; NoAM; NOBA
Author, The, *sels.* Charles Churchill.
   "Gods! with what pride I see the titled slave." OBSV
   Pains of Education, The. FaBoCo
   (Against Education.) TW
   "When with much pains this boasted learning's got." OBSV
Author Apologizes to a Lady for His Being a Little Man, The.
   Christopher Smart. BoLoP
Author Consults a Critic and Sells His Manuscript, The. Francis Hawling.
   Fr. The Signal; or, A Satire against Modesty. NOEC
Author Loving These Homely Meats, The. John Davies of Hereford. *Fr.*
   The Scourge of Folly. EIL; FaBoNo; Son
   (Buttered Pippin-Pies.) ChTr
   (Homely Meats.) FaBoCh
Author of *Christine,* The. Richard Howard. CoAP
Author, of His Own Fortune, The. Sir John Harington. FaBoEE
Author of light, revive my dying spright. Thomas Campion. AAS
Author to Her Book, The. Anne Bradstreet. AmPP; AnAmPo; InPK;
   NAAL-1; NOBA; NoP; OxBA; PoE; SCAP; TAP
Author to His Body on Their Fifteenth Birthday, 29.ii.80, The. Howard
   Nemerov. NAs; NoAM
Author to His Book, The. George Alsop. SCAP
Author to His Booke, The. Thomas Heywood. *Fr.* An Apology for
   Actors. OBS
Author to His Wife, of a Woman's Eloquence, The. Sir John Harington.
   BoLoP; ErPo
Author to the Reader, The. Randall Jarrell. OxBC
Author Unknown. William Montgomerie. OxBS
Authority. William Reed Huntington. AA
Authority is a disease, and cure. Samuel Butler. FaBoEE
Authors Abstract of Melancholy, The. Robert Burton. *Fr.* The Anatomy
   of Melancholy. OBS
Authors and actors and artists and such. Bohemia. Dorothy Parker.
   AnAmPo; NBLV
Author's Apology, The. T. Carmi, *tr. fr. Hebrew by* Marcia Falk. VWA
Author's Epitaph, The. *Unknown.* FiBHP
Author's Epitaph, Made By Himself, The. Sir Walter Ralegh. *See* Even
   Such Is Time.
Author's Epitaph, Written by Himself, An. Abel Evans. FaBoEE
Authors of the Town, The, *sel.* Richard Savage. TAP
   "First, let me view what noxious nonsense reigns." OBSV
Author's Reply, The. Sir Carr Scroope. APAS
Author's Resolution, The. George Wither. *See* Shall I, wasting in
   despair.

Authorship. James Ball Naylor. *See* King David and King Solomon.
Authour's Dreame, The. Francis Quarles. *Fr.* Argalus and Parthenia.
   OBS
Auto-da-Fe. Kevin Ireland. ATNZ
Auto Mobile. A. R. Ammons. FF; OBAL
Auto Wreck. Karl Shapiro. CMoP; FF; LiTM; NIP; RB; VGW
Autobahnmotorwayautoroute. Adrian Mitchell. RB
Autobiographia Literaria. Frank O'Hara. CAPP; NNaP; NOBA; TTTS
Autobiographical. Abraham Moses Klein. MoCV; NoAM
Autobiographical Flashback: Puma and Pokeweed. Jim Barnes. NOVW
Autobiographical Fragment. Kingsley Amis. NePoEA-2
Autobiographies. Derek Mahon. FaBCIP
Autobiography. Sonja Akesson, *tr. fr. Swedish by* Ingrid Claréus.
   BoWoP
Autobiography. Patricia Beer. PoPo
Autobiography. Charles Causley. LiTM; Son
Autobiography. Mbella Sonne Dipoko. TTY
Autobiography. Janet Dubé. BrRo
Autobiography. Gloria Fuertes, *tr. fr. Spanish by* Philip Levine. AnAn;
   PBWP
Autobiography. Jacob Glatstein, *tr. fr. Yiddish by* Benjamin and Barbara
   Harshav. AYP
Autobiography. Thom Gunn. NoAM
Autobiography. Louis MacNeice. FaBCIP; NOIV; RB
Autobiography. Dan Pagis, *tr. fr. Hebrew.* IP, *tr. by* Warren Bargad
   and Stanley F. Chyet; MHeP, *tr. by* Bernhard Frank; VWA, *tr. by*
   Robert Friend
Autobiography, An. Ernest Rhys. OBEV; OBWVE
Autobiography, Chapter XVII: Floating the Big Piney. Jim Barnes.
   HATNAP
Autobiography, Chapter XLII: Three Days in Louisville. Jim Barnes.
   HATNAP
Autobiography: Hollywood. Charles Reznikoff. *Fr.* Going To and Fro
   and Walking Up and Down. VWA
Autobiography: Last Chapter. Jim Barnes. CDW
Autobiography of a Lungworm. Roy Fuller. MoP; NoAM; NoP; OxBC
Autobiography of a Sloppy Sluggard. Kuan Kuan, *tr. fr. Chinese by*
   Dominic Cheung. IFON
Autochthon. Sir Charles G. D. Roberts. CaP
Autocrat of the Breakfast Table, The, *sels.* Oliver Wendell Holmes.
   Aestivation [an Unpublished Poem, by My Late Latin Tutor]. *Fr. ch.*
     11. NA; NOBL; OBAL
   (Intramural Aestivation, or Summer in Town, by a Teacher of Latin.)
     ChTr; FaBoNo
   Chambered Nautilus, The. *Fr. Ch.* 4. AA; AmPP; FaBoBe; FaFP;
     FPL; GN; HoPM; LiTA; MOS; NOBA; NoP; OHFP; PoEL-5; PoLF;
     PrIm; WGRP
   Contentment. *Fr.* 11. AmPP; OxBA
   Deacon's Masterpiece, The; or, The Wonderful "One-Hoss Shay." *Fr.*
     ch. 11. AmPP; BeLS; FaBoBe; FaFP; FPL; LiTA; MoShBr; NOBA;
     OBAL; OBCA; OHFP; OxBA; PoLF; PoRA; TAP; WBLP
   (Wonderful "One-Hoss Shay," The.) BeLS; FaBoBe
   Living Temple, The. AA, 7.
   Voiceless, The. AA, 12.
Autograph, An. James Russell Lowell. AA
Autograph, An. Whittier. AA
Autograph Book/ Prophecy. Anne Halley. NMM
Autograph on the Soul, The. Adah Isaacs Menken. CBWP-1
Autolycus as Peddler. Shakespeare. *Fr.* The Winter's Tale, IV, iii.
   OAEL-1
   (Autolycus's Song ("Lawn as white as driven snow").) OBSC
   (Come Buy! Come Buy!) EIL
   (Pedlar, The.) WiR
   (Pedlar's Song, The.) CH
Autolycus Sings. Shakespeare. *See* Winter's Tale, The: When daffodils
   begin to peer.
Autolycus's Song ("Jog on, jog on, the footpath way"). Shakespeare.
   See Winter's Tale, The: Jog On, jog on, the footpath way.
Autolycus's Song ("Lawn as white as driven snow"). Shakespeare. *See*
   Winter's Tale, The: Autolycus as Peddler.
Autolycus's Song ("When daffodils begin to peer"). Shakespeare. *See*
   Winter's Tale, The: When daffodils begin to peer.
Autolycus's Song ("Will you buy any tape"). Shakespeare. *See* Winter's
   Tale, The: Will you buy any tape.
Automatic fingers write, The. Séance. Francis King. PoA
Automne Malade. Guillaume Apollinaire, *tr. fr. French by* Paul
   Blackburn. RHTwFP
Automobile, The. Russell Edson. LCAP
Automobile Mechanics. Dorothy Walter Baruch. FaPON
Automobiles/ In/ a/ row. Stop-Go. Dorothy Walter Baruch. FaPON

Autonomous. Mark Van Doren. LiTA
Autonomy. Wislawa Szymborska, tr. fr. Polish by Czeslaw Milosz. PwPP
Autopsy, The. Odysseus Elytis, tr. fr. Greek by Edmund Keeley and Philip Sherrard. VMG
Autosonic Door. Dorothy Brown Thompson. GoYe
Autumn. Bella Akhmadulina, tr. fr. Russian by Barbara Einzig. BoWoP; OV
Autumn. Guillaume Apollinaire, tr. fr. French by W. S. Merwin. POS; RHTwFP
Autumn. E. A. Baratynsky, tr. fr. Russian by Alan Myers. AAA
Autumn. D. R. Beeton. PeSA
Autumn. Roy Campbell. GTBS-P; MoBrPo; OBMV; OxBTC
Autumn. William Carpenter. Psk
Autumn. Chang Yü, tr. fr. Chinese by Jonathan Chaves. Fr. The Four Seasons in the Mountains. CoBLCP
Autumn. Thomas Chatterton. Fr. Aella; a Tragycal Enterlude. Mes
Autumn ("I love the fitful gust"). John Clare. BoTP
Autumn ("Summer is gone and all the merry noise"). John Clare. SaC
Autumn ("Thistledown's flying, The"). John Clare. BoNaP; HAP; NU; PoEL-4; WeW
Autumn. Walter de la Mare. OxBTC
Autumn. Jacob Glatstein, tr. fr. Yiddish by Benjamin and Barbara Harshav. AYP
Autumn. Florence Hoatson. BoTP
Autumn. Thomas Hood. BLPL; LiTB; OBEV
    (Ode: Autumn.) OAEL-2; OBNC; PoEL-4; UnPo
Autumn. Patricia Hubbell. PDV
Autumn. T. E. Hulme. FaBoMo; SeCePo
Autumn. Ietaka, tr. fr. Japanese by Steven D. Carter. WFTW
Autumn. Walter Savage Landor. See Ianthe: Mild is the parting year, and sweet.
Autumn. Philip Levine. NNaP
Autumn. A. Leyeles, tr. fr. Yiddish by Benjamin and Barbara Harshav. AYP
Autumn. Detlev von Liliencron, tr. fr. German by Ludwig Lewisohn. AWP
Autumn. Itzig Manger, tr. fr. Yiddish. TrJP, trs. by Ruth Whitman and by Joseph Leftwich; VWA, tr. by Ruth Whitman.
Autumn. Thomas Nashe. Fr. Summer's Last Will and Testament. EIL; OAEL-1; OBSC; QFR; TrGrPo
Autumn. Nishiwaki Junzaburo, tr. fr. Japanese by Hiroaki Sato. FCEI
Autumn. Pushkin, tr. fr. Russian by Max Eastman. AWP
Autumn. Rainer Maria Rilke, tr. fr. German by C. F. MacIntyre. TrJP
Autumn. Christina Rossetti. BrRo
Autumn. Vernon Scannell. OxBTC
Autumn. Thomas William Shapcott. CBAP
Autumn. Princess Shikishi, tr. fr. Japanese by Hiroaki Sato. PBWP
Autumn. Stevie Smith. See He Told His Life Story to Mrs Courtly.
Autumn. William Jay Smith. NePoAM
Autumn. Spenser. Fr. The Faerie Queene, VII, 7. GN
Autumn. Wallace Stevens. FL
Autumn ("List to the sad wind, drearily moaning"). Priscilla Jane Thompson. CBWP-2
Autumn ("Sun shines bright, but sadly, The"). Priscilla Jane Thompson. CBWP-2
Autumn. Rabindranath Tagore. WGRP
Autumn. Tamura Ryuichi, tr. fr. Japanese by Hiroaki Sato. FCEI
Autumn. James Thomson. Fr. The Seasons.
    Autumnal Moon, The. NOBE
    (Autumn ("Western sun withdraws the shorten'd day, The").) NOBE
Autumn ("But see the fading many-colour'd woods"). EnRP
    "Fled is the blasted verdure of the fields."
    "Here the rude clamour of the sportsman's joy." PBBP
    "Poor is the triumph o'er the timid hare." EnRP; FM; PBBP
Autumn ("I at my window sit, and see"). Unknown. NOEC
Autumn ("Woman full of wile"). Unknown.
Autumn. Jean Starr Untermeyer. MoAmPo
Autumn. Frances Winwar. GoYe
Autumn. Humbert Wolfe. ILY, st. 1; PoLF
Autumn; a Dirge. Shelley. CH
Autumn, a Visit to the Byodo-in Temple. Gensei, tr. fr. Chinese by Burton Watson. JLIC-2
Autumn, Again Grass. José Hidalgo, tr. fr. Spanish by Brady Earnhart. WCI
Autumn air banishes lingering rains, The. A Mid-Autumn Night. Chao Chih-hsin, tr. by Michael S. Duke. WFTU
Autumn air snatches me out of a solitary man's dream. On the Twenty-Second Night of the Seventh Month, Facing the Moon at Listening-to-the-Water Studio. Ch'en Pao-shen, tr. by Irving Lo. WFTU

Autumn; an Ode. Charles Gullans. NePoEA
Autumn Begins in Martins Ferry, Ohio. James Wright. CAPP; HCAP; InPK; InPS; NaP; NoAM; TSL
Autumn Birds. John Clare. PBBP
Autumn Blitz. Frances Cornford. CN
Autumn Breeze, An. William Hamilton Hayne. AA
Autumn burgeons, sounds rise everywhere. Autumn Night—Sleepless. Wu Wei-yeh, tr. by Jonathan Chaves. CoBLCP
Autumn Burial; a Meditation. Charles Gullans. QFR
Autumn Chapter in a Novel. Thom Gunn. FaBoMo; OxBTC
Autumn chrysanthemums. Tsurayuki, tr. fr. Japanese by Burton Watson. Fr. Kokin Shu. FCEI
Autumn colors/ on the leaves. Autumn Plants, Flowers, Bamboo, Rocks. Yün Shou-p'ing, tr. by Jonathan Chaves. CoBLCP
Autumn colors trickle through the gauze curtains. A Woman's Room in Autumn. Yüan Hung-tao, tr. by Jonathan Chaves. CoBLCP
Autumn constellations, The. Moon Festival. Tu Fu, tr. by Kenneth Rexroth. NaP
Autumn Cove. Li Po, tr. fr. Chinese by Burton Watson. CoBCP; TTTS
Autumn, Crystal Eye. Margot Ruddock. OBMV
Autumn, Dark Wanderer. Elizabeth Daryush. QFR
Autumn Day. Rainer Maria Rilke, tr. fr. German by C. F. MacIntyre. TrJP
Autumn Day, An. Clara Ann Thompson. CBWP-2
Autumn Day at the Home of Prince Nagaya. Hironiwa, tr. fr. Chinese by Burton Watson. JLIC-1
Autumn day its course has run—the Autumn evening falls, The. Charlotte Brontë. NOBVV
Autumn Day Stroll in the Country. Kokan Shiren, tr. fr. Chinese by Burton Watson. JLIC-2
Autumn Dusk. Empress Eifuku, tr. fr. Japanese by Steven D. Carter. WFTW
Autumn Equinox. Peter Blue Cloud. Fr. Within the Seasons. HATNAP
Autumn Evening. George Anthony. EAS
Autumn Evening. Shotetsu, tr. fr. Japanese by Steven D. Carter. WFTW
Autumn Evening. Tameshige, tr. fr. Japanese by Steven D. Carter. WFTW
Autumn evening is for whisperers, The. Three Poets at Yuyama. Unknown, tr. by Hiroaki Sato. FCEI
Autumn Fancies. Unknown. FaPON
Autumn feels slowed down, The. Paula Becker to Clara Westhoff. Adrienne Rich. NAAL-2
Autumn gone, the past distant in the great sky. Teika, tr. fr. Japanese by Hiroaki Sato. Fr. Eighty-four Tanka. FCEI
"Autumn has come."/ —so the wind proclaims. Teika, tr. by Steven D. Carter. WFTW
Autumn has come; crimson leaves have fallen. Teika, tr. fr. Japanese by Hiroaki Sato. Fr. A Compendium of Good Tanka. FCEI
Autumn has turned the dark trees toward the hill. Quail in Autumn. William Jay Smith. Psk
Autumn hath all the summer's fruitful treasure. Autumn. Thomas Nashe. Fr. Summer's Last Will and Testament. EIL; OAEL-1; OBSC; QFR; TrGrPo
Autumn hills. Gyodai, tr. by Geoffrey Bownas and Anthony Thwaite. PeBJV
Autumn, I think, now. Fall. Mary Ursula Bethell. ATNZ
Autumn Idleness. Dante Gabriel Rossetti. Fr. The House of Life, LXIX. GBL; OAEL-2
Autumn Imagined. Donald Davie. PoA
Autumn Impressions, sels. Cha Shen-hsing, tr. fr. Chinese by William Schultz. WFTU
    "Chrysanthemum pistils daily yellow." Fr. III.
    "Cricket chirrups near my bed, A." Fr. I.
Autumn in California. Charles West. SoTCo
Autumn in Gaol. Tsuboi Shigeji, tr. fr. Japanese by Geoffrey Bownas and Anthony Thwaite. PeBJV
Autumn in the West. William Davis Gallagher. AA
Autumn, Iowa City. Edwin Thumboo. WCI
Autumn is about to leave. In an Abandoned Garden. Nishiwaki Junzaburo, tr. by Hiroaki Sato. FCEI
Autumn is always a time. What Is There for Us. Arto Melleri, tr. by Aili Jarvenpa. SOP
Autumn is in the air. London Interior. Harold Monro. BrPo
Autumn is the blue of the wall: being sheltered by little deaths. Apart from Oneself. Alejandra Pizarnik, tr. by Yishai Tobin. VWA
Autumn is weary, halt, and old. The October Redbreast. Alice Meynell. MoBrPo
Autumn Journal, sels. Louis MacNeice.

"And I remember Spain." OBWP

"August is nearly over, the people." CMoP

"Conferences, adjournments, ultimatums." FaBoPV; OxBTC; WaP

"Nightmare leaves fatigue." AnIL; BIrV; CIP; FaBCIP

"Shelley and jazz and lieder and love and hymn-tunes." NOBL

Week to Christmas, A. TIRV

Autumn Leaves. Clara Ann Thompson. CBWP-2

Autumn Leaves, The. *Unknown.* NA

Autumn Leaves. Charles H. Webb. OBAL

Autumn leaves are falling, The. The Autumn Leaves. *Unknown.* NA

Autumn Leaves Are Virgin Mary. Unsi al-Haj, *tr. fr. Arabic by* Patricia Alanah Bryne and Salma Khadra Jayyusi. MAP

Autumn made colors burn, The. Venus Khoury-Gata, *tr. by* Willis Barnstone. BoWoP

Autumn met me today as I walked over Castle Hill. The Stand-to. Cecil Day Lewis. OBWP

Autumn mists/ don't rise up this morning! *Unknown, tr. fr. Japanese by* Burton Watson. *Fr.* Kokin Shu. FCEI

Autumn Morning, An. *Unknown.* BoTP

Autumn Morning. Adeline White. BoTP

Autumn Morning at Cambridge. Frances Cornford. PoRA

Autumn Morning in Shokoku-ji, An. Gary Snyder. *Fr.* Four Poems for Robin. HAP; NNaP; NoAM; NOBA; NoP; SOTW; VGW

Autumn Mushrooms. Kenneth Mackenzie. CBAP

Autumn Music. Gabriel Preil, *tr. fr. Hebrew by* Howard Schwartz. VWA

Autumn Night. Michizane, *tr. fr. Chinese by* Burton Watson. JLIC-1

Autumn Night. Tanaka Fuyuji, *tr. fr. Japanese by* Geoffrey Bownas and Anthony Thwaite. PeBJV

Autumn Night, An. Yu T'ung, *tr. fr. Chinese by* Paul W. Kroll. WFTU

Autumn night grows late, The. Princess Shikishi, *tr. fr. Japanese by* Hiroaki Sato. *Fr.* Seventy-eight Tanka. FCEI

Autumn night: I question. Taigi, *tr. fr. Japanese by* Hiroaki Sato. *Fr.* Twenty-nine Hokku. FCEI

Autumn Night—Sleepless. Wu Wei-yeh, *tr. fr. Chinese by* Jonathan Chaves. CoBLCP

Autumn 1940. W. H. Auden. LiTA

Autumn on Nan-Yueh, *sel.* William Empson.

"I said I wouldn't fly again." PoPo

Autumn on the Upper Thames. William Morris. *See* Fair Is the World.

Autumn-pallid sun looks down, The. The End Is Now. "Marie Madelaine", *tr. by* Ferdinand E. Kappey. PeHV

Autumn Plants, Flowers, Bamboo, Rocks. Yün Shou-p'ing, *tr. fr. Chinese by* Jonathan Chaves. CoBLCP

Autumn Poem, An. Emperor Kogon, *tr. fr. Japanese by* Steven D. Carter. WFTW

Autumn Rain. D. H. Lawrence. BrPo

Autumn Rain. Kenneth Rexroth. NU

Autumn rain! The. River Messages. Yen Hsüan, *tr. by* Lois Fusek. ATF

Autumn rains,/ Autumn rains. Tune: A Song to Induce Laughter. Wu Hsi-ch'i, *tr. by* Frederick P. Brandauer. WFTU

Autumn Refrain. Wallace Stevens. LiTA

Autumn resumes the land, ruffles the woods. The Laurel Axe. Geoffrey Hill. *Fr.* An Apology for the Revival of Christian Architecture in England, 9. NAEL-2; NoAM; NoP; PoE

Autumn River. T'ang Hsien-Tsu, *tr. fr. Chinese by* Jonathan Chaves. CoBLCP

Autumn Rivulets, *sel.* Walt Whitman.

There Was a Child Went Forth. NAAL-1

Autumn Robin, The. John Clare. BoTP

Autumn Scene. Basil Dowling. BoNaP

Autumn season comes to the country, The. Yang Chi, *tr. fr. Chinese by* Jonathan Chaves. *Fr.* Living in Master Fang's Garden. CoBLCP

Autumn seems to cry for thee, The. Helen. "Susan Coolidge." AA

Autumn Sequel, *sel.* Louis MacNeice.

"To work. To my own office, my own job." *Fr.* IV. FaBCIP

Autumn Sequence. Adrienne Rich. VGW

Autumn Shade. Edgar Bowers. MT

Autumn sky between the leaf and bough. Man Falling. Zoltán Zelk, *tr. by* Daniel Hoffman. MHuP

Autumn sky has detached itself, The. Kikaku, *tr. fr. Japanese by* Hiroaki Sato. *Fr.* Thirty-three Hokku. FCEI

Autumn so soon. Kyoroku, *tr. by* Geoffrey Bownas and Anthony Thwaite. PeBJV

Autumn Song. Margaret Rose. BoTP

Autumn Song. Johann Ludwig Tieck, *tr. fr. German by* James Clarence Mangan. AWP

Autumn Song, An. Wang Fu-chih, *tr. fr. Chinese by* Irving Lo. WFTU

Autumn Song on Perry Street. Lloyd Frankenberg. GrPl

Autumn Squall—Lake Erie. Lola Ingres Russo. AmFN

Autumn storm dying, The. Hara Sekitei, *tr. by* Geoffrey Bownas and Anthony Thwaite. PeBJV

Autumn sunlight, The. Shotetsu, *tr. by* Steven D. Carter. WFTW

Autumn Testament, *sels.* James Keir Baxter.

"Father Lenin, you understood the moment." *Fr.* 18. ATNZ

"Rata blooms explode, the bow-legged tomcat, The." *Fr.* 42. ATNZ; PeNZ

"Spider crouching on the ledge above the sink, The." *Fr.* 48. ATNZ; PeNZ

"To pray for an easy heart is no prayer at all." *Fr.* 22. ATNZ

"To wake up with a back sore from the hard mattress." *Fr.* 7. ATNZ

"To wish to climb a ladder to the loft." *Fr.* 12. PeNZ

Autumn: the ninth year of Yüan Ho. The Temple. Po Chü-i, *tr. by* Arthur Waley. OBMV

Autumn Thoughts, *sels.* Han Yü, *tr. fr. Chinese by* Burton Watson. CoBCP

"Leaves fall turning turning to the ground." *Fr.* 8.

"This morning I can't seem to get out of bed." *Fr.* 6.

"When white dew descends on the hundred grasses." *Fr.* 2.

Autumn Thoughts. Lu Yu, *tr. fr. Chinese by* Burton Watson. CoBCP

Autumn Thoughts. Ma Chih-yüan, *tr. fr. Chinese by* Jonathan Chaves. *Fr.* To the Tune "T'ien ching sha." CoBLCP

Autumn Thoughts. Mary E. Tucker. CBWP-1

Autumn, Thurlby Domain. Charles Brasch. ATNZ

Autumn-time has come, The. My Triumph. Whittier. NOBA

Autumn time is with us, The. Autumn in the West. William Davis Gallagher. AA

Autumn upon us was rushing, The. Ravings. Tom Hood. BXAP; Par

Autumn Vista. Li Meng-yang, *tr. fr. Chinese by* Jonathan Chaves. CoBLCP

Autumn Walk, An. Witter Bynner. GoYe

Autumn Warrior. Barney Bush. HATNAP

Autumn was cold in Plymouth town. Her Picture. Ellen Mackay Hutchinson Cortissoz. AA

Autumn Wind. Akera Kanko, *tr. fr. Japanese by* Burton Watson. FCEI

Autumn Wind, The. John Clare. BoNaP

Autumn Wind. Ruth Dallas. *Fr.* Letter to a Chinese Poet, VIII. PeNZ

Autumn Wind, The ("Autumn wind rises; white clouds fly"). Emperor Wu Ti, *tr. fr. Chinese by* Arthur Waley. FaBoCh

Autumn wind:/ Everything I see. Takahama Kyoshi, *tr. by* Geoffrey Bownas and Anthony Thwaite. PeBJV

Autumn wind:/ Eyes distended. Watanabe Suiha, *tr. by* Geoffrey Bownas and Anthony Thwaite. PeBJV

Autumn wind, The/ flutters the long sleeves. A Travel Poem. Teika, *tr. by* Steven D. Carter. WFTW

Autumn wind—/ I open out. Kato Shuson, *tr. by* Geoffrey Bownas and Anthony Thwaite. PeBJV

Autumn wind came stealing. The Thief. Irene F. Pawsey. BoTP

Autumn wind is and is not as of old, The. Teika, *tr. fr. Japanese by* Hiroaki Sato. *Fr.* A Compendium of Good Tanka. FCEI

Autumn wind rises. Song of the Autumn Wind. Liu Ch'e, *tr. by* Burton Watson. CoBCP

Autumn wind rises; white clouds fly. Autumn wind. Emperor Wu-Ti, *tr. by* Arthur Waley. FaBoCh

Autumn wind: ten thousand trees wither. The Stone on the Hilltop. Lu Yu, *tr. by* Burton Watson. CoBCP

Autumn winds blow along the river. The Grain-Barge Wife. Wu Chia-chi, *tr. by* Jonathan Chaves. CoBLCP

Autumn winds blow in from Chieh-shih Mountain. Sadness in the Autumn Chambers. Yün Shou-p'ing, *tr. by* Jonathan Chaves. CoBLCP

Autumnal. Ernest Dowson. EBVV; OBNC

Autumnal Consummation. Patric Stevenson. NeIP

Autumnal Equinox. Edward E. Wilson. MOWH

Autumnal Moon, The. James Thomson. *Fr.* The Seasons: Autumn. NOBE

(Autumn ("Western sun withdraws the shorten'd day, The").) NOBE

Autumnal Ode. Aubrey Thomas De Vere. OBNC

Autumnal Song. Walter Savage Landor. *See* Very True, the Linnets Sing.

Autumnal Spring Song. Vassar Miller. NePoEA

Autumnal[l], The. John Donne. *Fr.* Elegies, IX. InPS; JCP; PoEL-2; SeCV-1; TEP

Autumn's bright moon. Kaga no Chiyo, *tr. by* R. H. Blyth. PBWP

"Autumn's come"—"The year's half gone." Teika, *tr. fr. Japanese by* Hiroaki Sato. *Fr.* A Compendium of Good Tanka. FCEI

Autumn's deep, The—my neighbor. Basho, *tr. fr. Japanese by* Burton Watson. *Fr.* Seventy-six Hokku. FCEI

Autumn's Fragrance. Kim Hyun-sung, *tr. fr. Korean by* Koh Chang-soo. ACKP

Autumn's Mirth. Samuel Minturn Peck. GN
Autumn's Poem. Kim Hyun-sung, tr. fr. Korean by Koh Chang-soo. ACKP
Autumn's Processional. Dinah Maria Mulock Craik. GN
Autumn's wind on suthering wings, The. The Autumn Wind. John Clare. BoNaP
Autumnus. Joshua Sylvester. EiL; OBS; SoSe
Aux Italiens. "Owen Meredith." BeLS; BLPA; BLPL; FaBoBe
Availability/ doesn't mean. Anne-Marie Albiach, tr. fr. French by Keith Waldrop. Fr. Enigma, I. RHTwFP
Avalanche. Adrien Stoutenburg. NYBP
Avalon. Audrey McGaffin. NePoAm
Avant Garde. Louis Dudek. Fr. Provincetown. MoCV
Avarice. George. FaBoRV; LiTB
Avarice. Anthony Hecht. OxBSP
Avast, honest Jack! now, before you get mellow. The Battle of Erie. Unknown. PAH
Ave atque Vale. Dryden. Fr. Sigismonda and Guiscardo. OBS
Ave atque Vale. Swinburne. NAEL-2; NOBE; OAEL-2; OBEV; OBNC
Ave atque Vale. Unknown. Malay Oral Tradition, tr. by R. J. Wilkinson and R. O. Winstedt. WTO
Ave atque Vale. Rosamund Marriott Watson. NOBE; OAEL-2; OBEV; OBNC
Ave, Caesar. W. E. Henley. Fr. In Hospital, XIV. BrPo
Ave Caesar. Robinson Jeffers. FaBoPV; MoP; NoAM; NOBA; OxBA; OxBSP
Ave Maria. Hart Crane. Fr. The Bridge, I. NoAM; NOBA
Ave Maria. Barbara Ferland. PBCV
Ave Maria. Frank O'Hara. HCAP; NAAL-2; NNaP; NoP; PoM
Ave Maria! Maiden mild! Hymn to the Virgin. Sir Walter Scott. Fr. The Lady of the Lake, III. EnRP
Ave Maris Stella ("Ave maris stella, the star of the sea"). Unknown. CTC
Ave! Nero Imperator. Duffield Osborne. AA
'Ave you 'eard o' the Widow at Windsor. The Widow at Windsor. Kipling. BrPo; NAEL-2; NoAM; NoP
Avenge, O Lord, thy slaughtered [or slaughter'd] saints, whose bones. On the Late Massacre or Massacher in Piedmont or Piemont. Milton. AWP; GTBS; GTBS-P; HAP; HeIP; LiTB; NAEL-1; NOBE; NoP; OBWP; SOW; OAEL-2; PPP; Son; UnPo; WaaP; WeW
   (Sonnet: "Avenge, O Lord, thy slaughtered saints, whose bones.") OAEL-1; TW
   (Sonnet: On the Late Massacre in Piedmont.) JCP; NOCV; OBS
Avenge, O Lord, thy slaughtered Saint Bernards. On the Late Mass of Curs in Piedmont. David Shevin. SoTCo
Avengers, The. Edwin Markham. MoAmPo
Avenida Abancay. Julio Ortega, tr. fr. Spanish by David Tipton. Per
Avenue Bearing the Initial of Christ into the New World, The, sels. Galway Kinnell.
   "Behind the Power Station on 14th, the held breath." Fr. 14. NaP
   "Children set fires in ashbarrels." NaP, 9.
   "First Sun Day of the year. Tonight." NaP, 4.
   "Fishmarket closed, the fishes gone into flesh, The." NaP, 11.
   "In sunlight on the Avenue." LiTM, 2.
   "In the pushcart market, on Sunday." NaP, 6.
   "Pcheek pcheek pcheek pcheek pcheek." Fr. 1. LiTM; NePoEA-2
   "Promise was broken too freely, The." NaP, 8.
Avenue Y. Anita Barrows. VWA
Avenues, The. David St. John. MAYP
Average Man, The. Margaret E. M. Sangster. WBLP
Aviary. Medbh McGuckian. FaBCIP
Aviemore. Janet Waller. PoSH
Avocado. John Logan. CAPP
Avoid and pass us by, O curse. An Imprecation against Foes and Sorcerers. Unknown, tr. by A. A. MacDonnell. WSC
Avoid the reeking herd. The Eagle and the Mole. Elinor Wylie. AWP; BoWoP; LiTA; LiTM; MoAB; MoAmPo; UnPo
Avoidances. Ron Welburn. PoBA
Avoiding News by the River. W. S. Merwin. NaP
Avondale Mine Disaster, The. Unknown. AmFP
Avremele, when will we have our own child? Abraham and Sarah. Itzig Manger, tr. by Stephen Garrin. VWA
Aw/ You so ugly. Ugly Chile. Clarence Williams. TW
Aw was young and lusty. Sair Fyel'd, Hinny. Unknown. GBP
Awa te the hulls, awa. Feels. J. C. Milne. PoSH
Awaits no solar quadriga. The Welcome. Freda Laughton. NeIP
Awake./ Your youth is passing like smoke. A Lamentation. Carl Rakosi. VWA
Awake! Jack Black. BXAP
Awake. Mary Elizabeth Coleridge. OBNC
Awake! Bible, O.T. Fr. The Song of Solomon, IV: 16. FaPON

Awake! W. R. Rodgers. LiTM; WaP
Awake! Walther von der Vogelweide, tr. fr. German by Jethro Bithell. AWP
Awake, Aeolian lyre, awake. The Progress of Poesy. Thomas Gray. AWP; EnRP; GTBS; GTBS-P; NOEC; OBEV
Awake, alone, aware. Insomniac Poem. Ron Loewinsohn. NeAP
Awake, arise,/ Pull out your eyes. Mother Goose. OxNR
Awake! arise! shake off thy dreams! To My Native Land. James Clarence Mangan. AnIL
Awake, arise, the hour is come. A Radical War Song. Macaulay. OBSV
Awake! arise, ye men of might! To Arms. Park Benjamin. PAH
Awake, Arise, You Drowsy Sleeper. Unknown. AmFP
Awake, Awake! Thomas Campion. ELP
Awake! Awake! The Bells. William Young. Fr. Wishmakers' Town. AA
Awake, awake, good people all. May Carol. Unknown. OBET
Awake! awake! my gallant friends. The Battle of Tippecanoe. Unknown. PAH
Awake, awake, my little boy! The Land of Dreams. Blake. BeLS; CH
Awake, awake, my Lyre! A Supplication. Abraham Cowley. Fr. Davideis. GTBS, fr. III; GTBS-P, fr. III.
Awake, awake, O Church of God! The Clarion-Call. Unknown. BLRP
Awake, awake! thou heavy sprite. Awake, Awake! Thomas Campion. ELP
Awake, awake, ye drowsy souls. New Year's Carol. Unknown. OBET
Awake but not yet up, too early morning. Out of Sleep. Allen Curnow. ATNZ
Awake, faire Muse; for I intend. William Browne. OBS
Awake! flower of the forest, sky-treading bird of the prairie. Calling One's Own. Unknown, tr. by Charles Fenno Hoffman. AnAmPo
Awake! for morning in the bowl of night. Omar Khayyám, tr. fr. Persian by Edward Fitzgerald. Fr. The Rubáiyát of Omar Khayyám of Naishápúr. Mes; NOBVV
Awake! For Sweeney in pyjamas bright. Awake! Jack Black. BXAP
Awake (great Sir) the Sun shines heer. On New-Year's Day 1640, to the King. Sir John Suckling. SeCV-1
Awake, like a hippopotamus with eyes bulged. Monday. William Stafford. NYBP
Awake, mine eyes, see Phoebus bright arising. Unknown. EiL; PBBP
Awake, My Fair. Judah Halevi, tr. fr. Hebrew by Alice Lucas. TrJP
Awake, My Heart, to Be Loved. Robert Bridges. GTBS-P; MoAB; MoBrPo; NOBE; OBEV
Awake, My Lute! C. S. Lewis. CenHV; FaBoNo
Awake, my St. John! leave all meaner things. Pope. Fr. An Essay on Man, Epistle I. NAEL-1; NoP; PoEL-3
   (Wild Garden, The.) PrIm, fr. ll. 1–16.
Awake, My Soul! Philip Doddridge. WGRP
Awake, My Soul. Moses Ibn Ezra, tr. fr. Hebrew by Solomon Solis-Cohen. Fr. Wine-Songs. TrJP
Awake, my soul, and with the sun. Morning Hymn. Thomas Ken. FaFP; OBS
Awake My Soul, Betimes Awake. Isaac Chanler. AH
Awake, My Soul! In Grateful Songs. Andrew Fowler. AH
Awake, my soul; stretch every nerve. Awake, My Soul! Philip Doddridge. WGRP
Awake, O rain, O sun, O night. Ending. Unknown, tr. by K. Luomala. WTO
Awake! Oh, north wind. Awake! Bible, O.T. Fr. The Song of Solomon, IV: 16. FaPON
Awake sound sleeper! hark, what dismal knells. Upon the Death of His Much Esteemed Friend Mr. Jno Saffin Junr. Grindall Rawson. SCAP
Awake! The day is coming now. Awake! Walther von der Vogelweide, tr. by Jethro Bithell. AWP
Awake to the cold light. March. Hart Crane. BoNaP
Awake, ye forms of verse divine! The National Paintings. Fitz-Greene Halleck and Joseph Rodman Drake. Fr. The Croaker Papers. AA
Awake! ye joyful strains, awake! Ode to David's Harp. Isaac Rosenberg. FL
Awake ye muses nine, sing me a strain divine. A Valentine. Emily Dickinson. FL
Awake, ye nations, slumbering supine. Sonnets Written in the Fall of 1914. George Edward Woodberry. PAH
Awake yee westerne nymphs, arise and sing. Samuel Danforth. SCAP
Awakened by a horse's fart, I see a firefly in the air. Issa, tr. fr. Japanese by Hiroaki Sato. Fr. Forty-four Hokku. FCEI
Awakened by someone gnashing his teeth. Issa, tr. fr. Japanese by Hiroaki Sato. Fr. Forty-four Hokku. FCEI
Awakened under stick and kwatz. Hakutei, tr. by Lucien Stryk and Takashi Ikemoto. ZPCJ

Awakened War God, The. Margaret Widdemer. WGRP
Awakening. Robert Bly. NaP
Awakening, The. Robert Creeley. NeAP
Awakening. John Haines. EAS
Awakening, The. Angela Morgan. OHIP
Awakening. Antonia Pozzi, tr. fr. Italian by Brenda Webster. OV
Awakening. Lil Milagro Ramírez, tr. fr. Spanish by Barbara Paschke. VoI
Awakening. Henrietta Cordelia Ray. CBWP-3
Awakening. Margaret E. Sangster. AA
Awakening. Lucien Stryk. CAPP; SV
Awakening—/ Voices of birds. Nelly Sachs, tr. by Ruth and Matthew Mead. PBWP
Awakening like return to Earth from Moon. Brian Coffey. Fr. Advent. CIP
Awakening of Man, The. Robert Browning. Fr. Paracelsus, V. WGRP
Awakening of the People, The. Gerald Massey. PF
Awaking. Stephen Spender. NYBP
Awaking muscle of a race asleep. Maceo. Luis Lloréns Torres. InW, tr. by Julio Marzán
Awaking of the Poetic Faculty, The. George Henry Boker. Son
A-walking and a-talking. The Cuckoo. Unknown. OBET, B vers
Award. Ray Durem. BPo; IDB; PoBA; SoSe; TTY
Aware. D. H. Lawrence. BoNaP; MoBrPo; NoAM
Aware Aware. Tram Combs. TwCP
Aware that summer baked the water clear. Skykomish River Running. Richard Hugo. PoA
Aware that your body cannot follow. Lady Izumi, tr. fr. Japanese by Hiroaki Sato. Fr. Fifty-one Tanka. FCEI
Aware to the dry throat of the wide hell in the world. King David Dances. John Berryman. OxBC; OxBSP
Awareness. Don L. Lee. PoBA
Away. Walter de la Mare. NoP
Away! Robert Frost. NOBA
Away. James Whitcomb Riley. BLRP; WGRP
Away,/ out/ beyond. Into the Wind. Barbara J. Petoskey. TSL
Away above a Harborful. Lawrence Ferlinghetti. Fr. A Coney Island of the Mind. BoLoP; ErPo; PoM
Away! away!/ Tempt me no more, insidious Love. The Complaint. Mark Akenside. OBEV
Away, away in the Northland. A Legend of the Northland. Phoebe Cary. OBCA; OnMSP
Away, away, O breeze of the spring. Insha Allah Khan Insha, tr. by Ahmed Ali. GoT
Away beyond the Jarboe house. Strange Tree. Elizabeth Madox Roberts. BoNaP; FaPON; GrPl; WSC
Away by the haunts of the Yang-tse-boo. The Rhyme of the Kipperling. Sir Owen Seaman. CenHV
Away, Delights. Beaumont and Fletcher. Fr. The Captain, III, iv. EiL; NOBE; OBEV
    (Sad Song, The.) GBL
Away despair; my gracious Lord doth heare. The Bag. George Herbert. SeCP
Away down deep and away up high. At the Playground. William Stafford. LCAP
Away down into the shadowy depths of the Real I once lived. Myself. Adah Isaacs Menken. CBWP-1
Away, for we are ready to a man! James Elroy Flecker. Fr. The Golden Journey to Samarkand. NOBE
Away from earth and its cares set free. Eternity. Josephine D. Henderson Heard. CBWP-4
Away from Home. Unknown. PWR
Away from home, in Fushimi village. Princess Shikishi, tr. fr. Japanese by Hiroaki Sato. Fr. Seventy-eight Tanka. FCEI
Away from home: over the dewdrops fragile on my pillow. Princess Shikishi, tr. fr. Japanese by Hiroaki Sato. Fr. Seventy-eight Tanka. FCEI
Away from the direction of falling blossoms. Teika, tr. fr. Japanese by Hiroaki Sato. Fr. Eighty-four Tanka. FCEI
Away from the sight of my dear wife. Akahito, tr. fr. Japanese. Fr. Manyo Shu. Ma
Away from you three or four years. Back from Green Dragon. Mei Yao-ch'en, tr. by Burton Watson. CoBCP
Away! Go back to where you spent the night! Surdas, tr. by John Stratton Hawley and Mark Juergensmeyer. SSI
Away in a Manger. At. to Martin Luther. AH, with music
    (Cradle Hymn.) BoTP; FaPON; OHIP
Away; let nought to Love displeasing. Winifreda. Unknown. OBEV
Away loose-reined careers of poetry! Urian Oakes. Fr. An Elegie upon the Death of the Reverend Mr. Thomas Shepard. NOCV
Away, Melancholy. Stevie Smith. OxBTC; PBWP

Away she flies and he follows. William Plomer. Fr. Anglo-Swiss, or a Day among the Alps. RR
Away! the moor is dark beneath the moon. Stanzas—April, 1814. Shelley. ChER; EnRP; FiP; OBNC
    (Remorse.) OBEV
Away to Twiver, Away, Away! Unknown. EiL
Away up high in the Sierry Petes. The Sierry Petes. Gail Gardner. CowP
Away, useless trifles! Of the Sad Lot of the Humanists in Paris. George Buchanan. GoTS
Away Vane World. Alexander Montgomerie. NOCV
Away with all whimsical bubbles of air. Botany Bay. John Freeth. NOEC
Away with silks, away with lawn. Clothes Do but Cheat and Cozen Us. Robert Herrick. CaPo; ErPo
Away with these self-loving lads. Fulke Greville. Fr. Caelica, LII. (Cynthia.) OBSC
    (Of His Cynthia.) EiL; ELP; NoP
"Away with you, away with you, James de Grant!" James Grant. Unknown. ESPB
Away, ye gay landscapes, ye gardens of roses! Lachin y Gair. Byron. OxBS
Away yee barb'rous woods; how ever yee be plac't. Michael Drayton. Fr. Polyolbion, Third Song. OBS
Away, you who rattle at my door. Unknown, tr. fr. Japanese. Fr. Manyo Shu. Ma
Aweary Am I. Abu-l-Ala al-Maarri, tr. fr. Arabic by R. A. Nicholson. AWP
Awéé. Nia Francisco. STE
Awesome are the works of God. The Works of God. Moses ibn Ezra, tr. by Solomon Solis-Cohen. TrJP
Awesome beyond speech. Hitomaro, tr. fr. Japanese. Fr. Manyo Shu. Ma
Awful Mother, The. Susan Griffin. NPGG
Awful shadow of some unseen power, The. Hymn to Intellectual Beauty. Shelley. BLPL; EnRP; HAP; HeIP; NAEL-2; NoP; OAEL-2; OBNC; PoE; TOF
Awhile in the dead of the winter. Seasons and Times. William Barnes. NOBVV
Awkward was she yesterday. The Maiden. Peter Hille, tr. by Jethro Bithell. AWP
Ax was sharpe, the stokke was harde, The. Epigram on the Year 1390-1. Unknown. NIP
Axe angles, An/ From my neighbor's ashcan. Junk. Richard Wilbur. HAP; NoP; SaC; SM; WeW
Axe Handles. Gary Snyder. CAPP; NoAM
Axe has cut the forest down, The. Conquest. Elizabeth J. Coatsworth. AmFN
    (Wilderness Is Tamed, The.) FaPON
Axe-Helve, The. Robert Frost. OxBA
Axe of the Pioneer, The. Isabella Valancy Crawford. CaP
Axe rings in the wood, The. Remembered Morning. Janet Lewis. WPE
Axeltree, The. Gene Van Troyer. BWV
Axes/ After whose stroke the wood rings. Words. Sylvia Plath. HCAP; LCAP; NAAL-2; PoE
Axes Rust, The. Jan G. Elburg, tr. fr. Dutch by Koos Schuur. DuIn
Axioms. Gad Hollander. VWA
Axolotl, The. David McCord. FiBHP; OBAL
Ay. Tennyson. Fr. Window, The; or, The Song of the Wrens. PBBP
Ay: A Gift of Elephants. Mutamociyar, tr. fr. Tamil by A. K. Ramanujan. PLW
Ay, ay, Oay—the winds that bend the brier! Tristram's Song. Tennyson. Fr. Idylls of the King: The Last Tournament. FaBoRV
Ay [or Aye], besherewe yow [or beshrew you!] be [or by] my fay. Mannerly Margery Mylk and Ale. John Skelton. AAS; FaBoNo; NAEL-1; NoP
Any [or Aye], but to die, and go we know not where. Shakespeare. Fr. Measure for Measure, III, i. OBD; RB
Ay, buzz and buzz away. Dost thou suppose. Luther to a Bluebottle Fly. Eugene Lee-Hamilton. Fr. Imaginary Sonnets. Son
Ay chinga! God. Bob Perelman. IAT
Ay! drop the treacherous mask! throw by. Butler's Proclamation. Paul Hamilton Hayne. PAH
Ay, Dwainie!—My Dwainie! Dwainie. James Whitcomb Riley. Fr. The Flying Islands of the Night. AA
Ay: His Hill. Mutamociyar, tr. fr. Tamil by A. K. Ramanujan. PLW
Ay, his mother was a mad one. The Sad Boy. Laura Riding. RB
Ay, it is fitting on this holiday. Ode in Memory of the American Volunteers Fallen for France. Alan Seeger. PAH

Ay, let it rest! And give us peace. The Gospel of Peace. James Jeffrey Roche. PAH

Ay me, alas, heigh ho, heigh ho! Thomas Weelkes. FaBoCh; OxBoLi

Ay me, alas! the beautiful bright hair. Canzone: His Lament for Selvaggia. Cino da Pistoia, tr. by Dante Gabriel Rossetti. AWP

Ay me, me, I sigh to see the scythe afield. A Proper Sonnet, How Time Consumeth All Earthly Things. At. to Thomas Proctor. FaBoRV; OBSC
(How Time Consumeth All Earthly Things.) ChTr; ElL
(Sic Transit.) TrGrPo

Ay me, how many perils doe unfold. Spenser. Fr. The Faerie Queene, I, 8. OAEL-1

Ay me! whilst thee the shores and sounding seas. Milton. Fr. Lycidas. Prf

"Ay, not at home, then, didst thou say?" A Call on Sir Walter Raleigh. Sarah Morgan Bryan Piatt. AA

Ay, Oliver! I was but seven, and he was eleven. Echo and the Ferry. Jean Ingelow. EBVV

Ay or Nay? Ralph Schomberg. Fr. The Judgment of Paris. TrJP

Ay, shout and rave, thou cruel sea. Herndon. Silas Weir Mitchell. PAH

Ay, tear her tattered ensign down! Old Ironsides. Oliver Wendell Holmes. AA; AiP; AnAmPo; BLPA; FaBoBe; FaFP; FaPON; FPL; GN; GOA; MOS; NAAL-1; OPP; PAH; PWR; TAP

Ay—There It Is! Emily Brontë. ChER

Ay, this is freedom!—these pure skies. The Hunter of the Prairies. Bryant. AA

Ay, 'Tis Thus. Unknown, tr. fr. Hebrew by Israel Zangwill. TrJP

Ay, 'twas here, on this spot. Atalanta in Camden-Town. "Lewis Carroll." CenHV

Ay! Unto thee belong. Theocritus. Annie Fields. AA

Ay Waukin O. Burns. See Simmer's a Pleasant Time.

Ayaiyaja/ This why, I wonder. It Is Hard to Catch Trout. Piuvkaq. WTO

Aye, at that time our days wer but vew. Childhood. William Barnes. NOBVV

Aye, aye, lads, we fought 'em. "Off Manilly." Edmund Vance Cooke. PAH

Aye, but to die. . . See Any, but to die. . . .

"Aye! I am a poet and upon my tomb." And Thus in Nineveh. Ezra Pound. VGW

"Aye, squire," said Stevens, "they back him at evens." How We Beat the Favourite. Adam Lindsay Gordon. CBAP

Aye, the good man, kind father, best of friends. "Bona de Mortuis." Thomas Lovell Beddoes. TW

Aye, There's Hills. Hamish Brown. PoSH

Aye up at the feast, by Melhill's brow. Melhill Feast. William Barnes. OBNC

Aye Waukin' O! Unknown. GoTS

Aye! What a thing is the passing of Cronos, the angular-minded. John Cowper Powys. Fr. The Ridge. OBWVE

Ayee! Ai! This is heavy earth on our shoulders. Burying Ground by the Ties. Archibald MacLeish. Fr. Frescoes for Mr. Rockefeller's City, III. GOA; MoAmPo

Ayii, Ayii,/ I walked on the ice of the sea. Unknown. RFM

Ayii, Ayii/ The great sea has set me in motion. Unknown. RFM

Aylmer's Field, sel. Tennyson.

Leolin and Edith. GN

Ayohu Kanogisdi. Carroll Arnett. STE

Azalea, The. Coventry Patmore. Fr. The Unknown Eros. ELP; GBL

Azaleas arranged, and by them. Basho, tr. fr. Japanese by Burton Watson. Fr. Seventy-six Hokku. FCEI

Azaleas—whitest of white! White Azaleas. Harriet McEwen Kimball. AA

A-zellen meat-weare I shall get noo meat. Shop o' Meat-Weare. William Barnes. NOBVV

Aziola, The. Shelley. EBEV; PBBP

Azouou. Mririda n'Ait Attik, tr. fr. Berber into French. WPOW

Azra, The. Heine, tr. fr. German by John Hay. AWP

Aztec City, The. Eugene Fitch Ware. AA

Aztec sacrifice, An. Le Musée Imaginaire. Charles Tomlinson. NePoEA-2

Azure. Louis Zukofsky. IAT

Azure, I come! from the caves of death withdrawn. Helen, the Sad Queen. Paul Valéry, tr. by Joseph T. Shipley. AWP

Azure screen is pulled aside, An. Thoughts of the Yüeh Beauty. Lu Ch'ien-i, tr. by Lois Fusek. ATF

Azure sky, An. Christmas. "Mary I." BoTP

Azure Striation Swirls beyond the Stones. Marilyn Hacker. Fr. La Fontaine de Vaucluse, I. Son

Azure striation swirls beyond the stones. La Fontaine de Vaucluse. Marilyn Hacker. FYAP

Azured [or Azur'd] vault, the crystal circles bright, The. James I, King of England. ElL; SeCePo
(Heaven and Earth.) ChTr

Azzoomm, azzoomm loud and strong. Riding in an Airplane. Dorothy W. Baruch. FaPON

B

B. Larry Eigner. NeAP

B Is for Baseball. Scott Bates. SoTCo

B Negative. X. J. Kennedy. NePoEA-2

B stands for Bear. When bears are seen. Hilaire Belloc. Fr. A Moral Alphabet. NoAM

B, taught by Pope to do his good by stealth. A Misconception. James Russell Lowell. OBAL

Ba Cottage. Andrew Young. OxBSP

Baa, baa, black sheep, have you any wool? Mother Goose. FaBoBe; FaFP; OxNR

Baa, baa, black sheep, where'd you leave your lamb? Unknown. AmFM

Baal Shem Tov. A. M. Klein. CaP; TrJP

Bab-Lock-Hythe. Laurence Binyon. SD

Babe. Maud Sulter. WS

Babe & Lou. Franz Douskey. ASP

Babe Didrikson. Grantland Rice. ASP

Babe is born all of a May, A. Unknown. Fr. Three Christmas Carols, I. ACP

Babe Ruth. Damon Runyon. ASP

Babe was laid in the Manger, The. A Nativity. Kipling. NAs

Babe, with a cry brief and dismal, The. Edward Gorey. OBAL

Babes in the Wood, The ("My dear, do you know"). Unknown. OxBChV; PBBP

Babes in the Wood, The ("Now ponder well your parents dear"). Unknown. OBNV
(Children in the Wood, The.) EnSB

Babi Yar. Lev Ozerov, tr. fr. Russian by Daniel Weissbort. VWA

Babiaantje, The. F. T. Prince. MoBrPo

Babies, The. Mark Strand. GeTw; NYBP

Babies Haven't Any Hair. Samuel Hoffenstein. NBLV

Babies of Yesterday. The Raging Generation. Mbuyiseni Oswald Mtshali. WMBCH

Baboon. Unknown, tr. fr. Hottentot. PeSA

Baboon. Unknown, tr. fr. Yoruba by Ulli Beier. Fr. Hunter Poems of the Yoruba. RB

Baboon. Zulu Oral Tradition, tr. by C. and W. Leslav. WTO

Baboon, The. Rhydwen Williams, tr. fr. Welsh by R. Gerallt Jones. OBWVE

Baboon 2. Unknown, tr. fr. Hottentot. PeSA

Babushka. Edith M. Thomas. OnMSP

Baby. Elaine Goodale Eastman. AA

Baby. Jung Han-mo, tr. fr. Korean by Koh Chang-soo. ACKP

Baby,/ You shall be free. Kadia the Young Mother Speaks. Jessie E. Sampter. TrJP

Baby, The. George Macdonald. Fr. At the Back of the North Wind, 23. FaPON
(Where Did You Come From.) BLPA; FaFP; OxBChV

Baby. Joyce Carol Oates. GeTw

Baby, The. James Reaney. Fr. A Sequence in Four Keys. NAs

Baby. John Shea. SoTCo

Baby, The. Ann Taylor. OHIP

Baby, The/ was made in a cell. The Nursery. Fanny Howe. UL

Baby and I. Unknown. OxNR

Baby and Mary. Unknown. NA

Baby at my breast, The. Against Dark's Harm. Anne Halley. NMM

Baby, baby, naughty baby. Mother Goose. NOBL; OxNR

Baby Beds. Unknown. BoTP

Baby brought us luck, The. Lucky. Cathy Song. BrSi

Baby Cobina. Gladys May Casely Hayford. CDC

Baby, depend upon it. Shade. Charles Lynch. CNA

Baby got here once who before, A. The Rampage. C. K. Williams. GeTw

Baby Hilary, Sir Edmund, The. Kathleen Leland Baker. NBLV
Baby I am, A. Awéé.' Nia Francisco. STE
Baby, if you love me. Down and Out. Langston Hughes. PoE
Baby I'm sick. I need. Night Thoughts: Baby & Demon. Gwen Harwood. CBAP
Baby is born [or borne], us bliss [or blis] to bring, A. Dear Son, Leave Thy Weeping. Unknown. CTC
(Jesus Comforts His Mother.) MeEL
Baby-Land. George Cooper. BoTP
Baby Lon; or, The Bonnie Banks o' Fordie. Unknown. See There were three ladies lived in a bower.
Baby loves to play with me. Hide and Seek. Phyllis Drayson. BoTP
Baby lying on his mother's breast, A. Man's Pillow. Irving Browne. AA
Baby picked from an ash barrel by the night police, The. Chicago Boy Baby. Carl Sandburg. NAs
Baby Pictures of Famous Dictators. Charles Simic. GeTw; WeW
Baby Running Barefoot. D. H. Lawrence. NoP
Baby Sardine, A. Spike Milligan. OnUR
Baby sat on the window-seat. Baby and Mary. Unknown. NA
Baby Seed Song. Edith Nesbit. FaPON
Baby-Sermon, A. George Macdonald. OxBChV
Baby-Sitting. Gillian Clarke. FaBoWP
Baby Song. Thom Gunn. Fr. Three Songs. AnAn; NAS; RB
Baby sparrows. Kikaku, tr. by Geoffrey Bownas and Anthony Thwaite. PeBJV
Baby Talk. Anna Bird Stewart. RHPC
Baby Ten Months Old Looks at the Public Domain, A. William Stafford. NYBP
Baby Toes. Carl Sandburg. FaPON
Baby Tortoise. D. H. Lawrence. CMoP
Baby Verse, A. Unknown. See Tit, tat, toe.
Baby Villon. Philip Levine. CoAP; NaP
Baby wades alone across the lawn, The. Errantry. Robert Fitzgerald. NYBP
Baby you know I get high. Not Quite Spring. Lyn Lifshin. NeAC
Babyhood. Josiah Gilbert Holland. Fr. Bitter-sweet. AA
Babylon. Ralph Hodgson. BrPo
Babylon ("King and Queen of Contelón"). Unknown. ChTr
Babylon. Unknown. See There were three ladies lived in a bower.
Babylon and Sion (Goa and Lisbon). Luis de Camões, tr. fr. Portuguese by Richard Garnett. AWP
Babylon, O Babylon. Pablo Guevara, tr. fr. Spanish by David Tipton. Per
Babylon; or, The Bonnie Banks o' Fordie. Unknown. AmFP; ESPB; OxBB, with music.
Babylon Revisited. Imamu Amiri Baraka. BPo; MoP; NoAM; TW
Baby's Awake Now. Bill Berkson. UL
Baby's Baking. Evaleen Stein. RAR
Baby's Dance, The. At. to Ann Taylor and to Mother Goose. OxBChV; OxNR
Baby's Debut, The. Horace Smith and James Smith. Par
Baby's Drinking Song. James Kirkup. NTCP
Baby's feet, like sea-shells pink, A. Swinburne. Fr. Étude Réaliste, I. FaPON; WeW
Baby's Room. Jung Han-mo, tr. fr. Korean by Koh Chang-soo. ACKP
Babysitters, The. Sylvia Plath. NoP
Baccalaureate. David McCord. BXAP; NBLV; OBAL
Bacchae, sel. Euripides, tr. fr. Greek by Gilbert Murray.
Home of Aphrodite, The. AWP
Bacchanal. Peter De Vries. BXAP; NBLV; NIP; NOBL; OBAL
Bacchanal. Irving Layton. OBCV
Bacchanalia; or, The New Age, sels. Matthew Arnold.
"Epoch ends, the world is still, The." Fr. II. OAEL-2
First-born Star, The. FaBoRV
Bacchus. Emerson. AmPP; AWP; LiTA; NOBA; OBEV; OxBA; PoEL-4
Bacchus, sels. William Empson. NoAM; PoCH
"God who fled down with a standard yard, The." PoA
"Herm whose length measured degrees of heat, The." PoA
Bacchus in Tuscany, sels. Francesco Redi, tr. fr. Italian by Leigh Hunt.
Bacchus on Beverages. PFI
Bacchus's Opinion of Wine, and Other Beverages. AWP; OBVE
Bacchus, let me drink no more. A Hymn to Bacchus. Robert Herrick. JCP
Bacchus must now his power resign. A Drinking-Song. Henry Carey. OBEV
Bacchus on Beverages. Francesco Redi, tr. fr. Italian by Leigh Hunt.
Fr. Bacchus in Tuscany. PFI

Bacchus, the father of drunken Nowls. The Man in the Moon Drinks Clarret. Unknown. CoMu
Bacchus's Opinion of Wine, and Other Beverages. Francesco Redi, tr. fr. Italian by Leigh Hunt. Fr. Bacchus in Tuscany. AWP; OBVE
Bacchylides. George Meason Whicher. AA
Bach. Eeva-Liisa Manner, tr. fr. Finnish by Aili Jarvenpa. SOP
Bachelor, The/ Gives humblest thanks. Unknown, tr. by Geoffrey Bownas and Anthony Thwaite. PeBJV
Bachelor. William Meredith. NoAM
Bachelor Bold and Young. Unknown. AmFP
Bachelor Farmer. Roger McDonald. CBAP
Bachelor Hall. Eugene Field. BLPA; FPL
Bachelors and Language, sel. Andreas Okopenko, tr. fr. German by Beth Bjorklund.
"Hannelore will thus be my wife." CoAuP
Bachelors' Buttons. Maud Morin. BoTP
Bachelor's-Buttons. William Jay Smith. DiPo
Bachelor's Complaint, The. Unknown. AmFP
Bachelor's Hand, The. Russell Edson. AnAn
Bachelor's Song, The. Thomas Flatman. See How happy a thing were a wedding.
Back. Weldon Kees. NaP; PrIm
Back. Angela McCabe. AmPA
Back. Robert Mezey. AmPA
Back/ and forth/ on the swing. Tautology. Nelo Risi, tr. by Lawrence R. Smith. NItP
Back Again for the Holidays. Sir John Betjeman. Fr. Summoned by Bells. FaBoPP
Back Again from Yucca Flats. Reeve Spencer Kelley. AmFN
Back Again, Home. Don L. Lee. BPo
Back Always. Clark Coolidge. UL
Back and Forth. Lucy Sprague Mitchell. FaPON
Back and forth. As in a swing. When there's. Amir Gilboa, tr. by Warren Bargad and Stanley F. Chyet. IP
Back and forth, back and forth. Fall 1961. Robert Lowell. OBWP; VGW
Back and Side Go Bare, Go Bare. at. to William Stevenson and also to John Still. Fr. Gammer Gurton's Needle. HeIP; InvP; LiTB; NAEL-1
(Drinking Song.) WiR, at. to John Still.
(In Praise of Ale.) TrGrPo, at. to John Still.
(Of Jolly Good Ale and Old.) EiL
(Song of Ale, A.) OBSC
Jolly Good Ale and Old. NoP; OBEV; TrGrPo
Back at my home. Home. Miki Rofu, tr. by Geoffrey Bownas and Anthony Thwaite. PeBJV
Back Country. Joyce Carol Oates. Psk
Back from camp that morning. What Saundra Said about Being Short. Jim Hall. MOWH
Back from Green Dragon. Mei Yao-ch'en, tr. fr. Chinese by Burton Watson. CoBCP
Back from the festival. Unknown, tr. by Geoffrey Bownas and Anthony Thwaite. PeBJV
Back from the fields. Unknown, tr. by Burton Watson. FCEI
Back from the kill. Contest. Florence Victor. SD
Back from the line one night in June. Corporal Stare. Robert Graves. BrPo
Back from the palace of a famous king. The Larkin Automatic Car Wash. Gavin Ewart. NoAM
Back from the Paved Way. Robert David Fitzgerald. PoAu-2
Back from the trebly crimsoned field. Wanted—A Man. Edmund Clarence Stedman. AnAmPo; PAH
Back from the Word-Processing Course, I Say to My Old Typewriter. Michael C. Blumenthal. GOYP; NoAM
Back here the fall, spreading down the hills. Ember Week, Reseda. Stephen Yenser. EOEF
Back home. Manong Federico Delos Reyes and His Golden Banjo. Al Robles. BrSi
Back home the black women are all beautiful. W. W. Imamu Amiri Baraka. HeIP; NBP; NOBA; PoBA
Back in back of the back country. Alabama. Judy Dothard Simmons. CNA
Back in my country after fifteen years of exile. A New House. Bertolt Brecht, tr. by Michael Hamburger. AnAn
Back in tachanka days, when Red and Green. Makhno's Philosophers. John Manifold. CBAP
Back in the dear old thirties' days. The Poet of Bray. John Heath-Stubbs. NOBL
Back in the Return, sel. Huw Menai.
"Where shall the eyes a darkness find." OBWVE
Back in the States. Louis Stimson. PBCV

Back in the Twenties, Filippo Marinetti, Italian Futurist. The Glass Hat. László Kálnoky, *tr.* by Jascha Kessler. FOC

Back in the years when Phlagstaff, the Dane, was monarch. The Rejected "National Hymns." "Orpheus C. Kerr." OBAL

Back into the Garden. Sarah Webster Fabio. BlSi

Back Lane. R. D. Murphy. PoAu-2

Back of the beating hammer. The Thinker. Berton Braley. BLPA; WBLP

Back of the dam, under. The Town of Hill. Donald Hall. CAPP; TAP

Back of the door the child is playing that. Resolution. W. S. Merwin. NYBP

Back of the head resting on the pillow was not wasted, The. For She. Carla Harryman. LP

Back on Times Square, Dreaming of Times Square. Allen Ginsberg. PoE

Back out of all this now too much for us. Directive. Robert Frost. AmPP; BLPL; CMoP; HAP; InPS; LiTA; LiTM; MAT; MoAB; MoAmPo; NAAL-2; NoAM; NOBA; NoP; PoE; PPP; PrIm

Back Road Farm. Charles Bruce. CaP

Back Room Joys. Justin Richardson. FiBHP

Back Seat Dodge '38, The. Patrick Conrad, *tr. fr. Dutch by* Peter Nijmeijer. DuIn

Back Street. Arthur Rex Dugard Fairburn. *Fr.* Album Leaves. ATNZ; PeNZ

Back then, my father still big. Johnson Brothers Ltd. Rutger Kopland, *tr.* by Ria Leigh-Loohuizen. DuIn

Back there: the library, walled. The Burning of Paper instead of Children. Adrienne Rich. NAAL-2

Back through clouds. Train Tune. Louise Bogan. RR

Back through East Flatbush, a raw grave. Burial in Cypress Hills. Amy Clampitt. AnAn

Back through the Looking Glass to This Side. John Ciardi. NBLV

Back to Africa. Louise Bennett. PBCV

Back to back, stud poker & an open/ pot. Twin Aces. Keith Wilson. Psk

Back to Base. Jenny Joseph. BrRo

Back to Dublin. R. A. D. Ford. CaP; MoCV

Back to each other, graves do not boast. Graves as Exercises. Elizabeth Smither. ATNZ

Back to Griggsby's Station. James Whitcomb Riley. BLPA; BLPL

Back to Hometown Kingston. James Berry. PBCV

Back to Life. Thom Gunn. NoP

Back to silent big soap flakes. Don't Hope to Gain by What Has Preceded. Joanne Kyger. PoM

Back to the bewildering vision. Kinship. Sir Charles G. D. Roberts. CaP

Back to the flower-town, side by side. In Memory of Walter Savage Landor. Swinburne. PoEL-5

Back to the Ghetto. Jacob Glatstein, *tr. fr. Yiddish by* Joseph Leftwich. TrJP

Back to the green deeps of the outer bay. The Herring Weir. Sir Charles G. D. Roberts. *Fr.* Songs of the Common Day. NOBC

Back to Town. John Hollander. NoAM

Back when it took all day to come up. Hearing. W. S. Merwin. NoAM

Back will go the head with the dark curls. Castanets. Bernard Spencer. WeW

Back wings, The/ of the. Between Walls. William Carlos Williams. HoPM; SOTW; TAP; VGW

Back Yard, July Night. William Cole. BoNaP

Backdrop: The dining room at Stonington. James Merrill. *Fr.* The Book of Ephraim. NoAM

Backed correctly into a corner. A Cappella. Michael Pettit. GrPl

Backed up against time. Venus Khoury-Gata, *tr.* by Carol Cosman. OV

Backgrounds to Italian Paintings: Fifteenth Century. Anne Ridler. WPE

Backing into the Fan Mail (Unreceived). Dick Gallup. UL

Backlash Blues, The. Langston Hughes. BPo

Backra one fo go a hebben? Query. Michael McTurk. PBCV

Backroad leafmold stonewall chipmunk. Silent Poem. Robert Francis. CRP; LCAP

Backtracking/ Fifty miles past Bakersfield. Visiting Father. Genny Lim. BrSi

Backward among the dusky years. Compassion. Thomas Hardy. FM

Backward & down into inbetween as Vicki says. Mean Drunk Poem. Sharon Thesen. NOBC

Backward—Forward. *Unknown.* BLRP

Backward Look, The. Howard Nemerov. OxBC

Backward Spring, A. Thomas Hardy. PPP

Backward, turn backward, O time, in your flight. Rock Me to Sleep, [Mother]. Elizabeth Akers Allen. AA; AnAmPo; BLPA; BLPL; FaBoBe; FaFP; OBCA; WBLP

Backward we look regretful, forward we glance with dread. Resurgam. W. Nelson Bitton. BLRP

Backwards and upside down in the twilight, that. I Cannot Forget the Woman in the Mirror. Sharon Olds. ER

Backwoods Hero, A, *sel.* Alexander McLachlan. "Where yonder ancient willow weeps." CaP

Backyard. Alice Notley. UL

Backyard Swing. Janet Campbell Hale. STE

Bacon was carved thin, The. Landscape of Domestic Life. David Graham. KS

Bacon's Epitaph, Made by His Man. *At.* to John Cotton. PAH; SCAP

Bad and Good. Alexander Resnikoff. NTCP

Bad at the bourse. Galician Winter. Aba Shtoltsenberg, *tr.* by Dennis Silk. PeBMYV

Bad Bishop Jegon. *Unknown.* GBP

Bad breed of the natives with their hates, The. D. C. Karl Shapiro. NYBP

Bad company is a disease. Rowland Watkyns. FaBoEE

Bad Craftsmen. Victor Segalen, *tr. fr. French by* Nathaniel Tarn. RHTwFP

Bad deal you made, Almagro, A. Question of Time. Antonio Cisneros, *tr.* by David Tipton. Per

Bad Dream. Louis MacNeice. FaBCIP; NoAM

Bad Dreamer, The. Antonin Artaud, *tr. fr. French by* Michael Benedikt. POS

Bad Dreams, *sel.* Robert Browning. OxBSP "This was my dream! I saw a forest." *Fr.* III. OAEL-2

Bad Habit, The. Charles Henri Ford. EAS

Bad hands tear me from Mama. Earthquake. Malka Heifetz-Tussman, *tr.* by Kathryn Hellerstein. AYP

Bad Kittens, The. Elizabeth J. Coatsworth. FaPON; OBCA

Bad Man Ballad. *Unknown.* AmFP

Bad Mirror. Hermann Jandl, *tr. fr. German by* Beth Bjorklund. CoAuP

Bad Morning. Langston Hughes. OBAL

Bad Mother, The. Susan Griffin. NPGG

Bad news has come to town, bad news is carried. Montcalm and Wolfe. *Unknown.* AmFP

Bad Old Days, The. Kenneth Rexroth. NNaP; NoAM

Bad quartos were my first love. Bibliographer. Josephine Miles. FaBoWP

Bad Season Makes the Poet Sad, The. Robert Herrick. CaPo; LiTB; NAEL-1; PrIm

Bad Sleeper, A. Paul Verlaine, *tr. fr. French by* François Pirou. PeHV

Bad Sport. Beth Kalikoff. TSL

Bad-tempered, I got back. Ryota, *tr.* by Geoffrey Bownas *and* Anthony Thwaite. PeBJV

Badger ("When midnight comes a host of dogs and men"), *sel.* John Clare. EnRP; HAP; LiTB; NoP; NU; OAEL-2; PoEL-4; PoE; PrIM; WeW; WiR

Badger ("Badger grunting on his woodland track, The"), *longer version* FM; InPS

Badgers, The. Eden Phillpotts. BoTP

Badgers are boring, the trees are so trivial, The. Country Matters. Gavin Ewart. SoTCo

Badman of the Guest Professor. Ishmael Reed. BPo

Baedeker for Metaphysicians. Brian Higgins. FaBoTw

Baffled Knight, The. *Unknown. See* There was a knight and he was young.

Baffling Picture. Lajos Kassák, *tr. fr. Hungarian by* Edwin Morgan. MHuP

Bag, The. George Herbert. SeCP

Bag of Tools, A. R. L. Sharpe. BLPA

Bag Woman. Dudley Randall. NoAM

Bagatelles. Steve Orlen. NAmP

Bagel, The. David Ignatow. CAPP; FF; TwCP

Baggot Street Deserta. Thomas Kinsella. CIP; CMoP; FaBCIP; IPY; NoAM

Bagman O'Reilly's Curse. Les A. Murray. TW

Bagpipe Music. "Hugh MacDiarmid." OAEL-2

Bagpipe Music. Louis MacNeice. CMoP; GTBS-P; LiTB; LiTM; MoP; NAEL-2; NBLV; NoAM; NOBE; NOBL; NoP; OAEL-2; OBSV; OxBTC; RB; SeCePo

Bags of Meat. Thomas Hardy. FM; RB

Bags Packed and We Expected This. Ramona Wilson. VoR

Bah! I have sung women in three cities. Cino. Ezra Pound. VGW

Bahamas. George Oppen. NYBP

Bahá'u'lláh in the Garden of Ridwan. Robert Hayden. PoBA
Baii. Jim Barnes. *Fr.* Four Things Choctaw. HATNAP
Bailey Beareth the Bell Away, The. *Unknown.* SeCePo
Bailiff's Daughter of Islington, The. *Unknown.* AmFP; ESPB; FaBoBa;
     GN; OBET; OxBB, *with music;* OxBoLi
Bairnies cuddle doon at nicht, The. Cuddle Doon. Alexander Anderson.
     GN; OHFP
Bait [e], The. John Donne. ErPo; HoPM; InPK; InPS; NAEL-1; NIP;
     OAEL-1; PoRA; RB; SD; TEP
Bait-Gathering. Angus Martin. NPo
Baith Gud [e] and Fair and Womanlie [*or*] Womanly. *Unknown.* GoTS;
     OxBS
Baits for Various Fish. Thomas Barker. *Fr.* The Art of Angling.
     FaBoUs
Baja. Gerald Stern. SV
Bajan Litany. Bruce St. John. PBCV
Baked the day she suddenly dropped dead. Book Ends. Tony Harrison.
     Fr. The School of Eloquence, I. DiPo; NAEL-2; NoAM
Baker. Gloria A. Maxson. *Fr.* Epitaphs. SoTCo
Baker's Boy, The. Mary Effie Lee Newsome. CDC
Baker's Dozen of Wild Beasts, A, *sels.* Carolyn Wells. OBCA
     Bath-Bunny, The.
     Corn-Pone-y, The.
     Cream-Puffin, The.
     Mince-Python, The.
Baker's Duzzen uv Wize Sawz, A. Edward Rowland Sill. FaBoBe;
     FaFP
Baker's Tale, The. "Lewis Carroll." *Fr.* The Hunting of the Snark.
     EBEV; NAEL-2
Balaam. John Keble. OBNC
Balaam's Blessing. Bible, O.T. *Fr.* Numbers, XXIV: 5–9. TrGrPo
Balaclava. *Unknown.* OBET
Balade and Roundel to Master Somer. Thomas Hoccleve. OxBLMV
Balade de Bon Conseill. Chaucer. TrGrPo
Balade: "Hide [*or* Hyd], Absalon, thy gilte tresses clere." Chaucer. *See*
     Legend of Good Women, The: Prologue: Hyd, Absalon, thy gilte
     tresses clear.
Balade Simple. John Lydgate. GBL
Balalaika. Norman Dubie. AmPA
Balance. Philip Schultz. MAYP
Balance Sheet with Incident. Nicholas Born, *tr. fr. German by* Margitt
     Lehbert. WCI
Balanced a row of peas on it. My Grandaddy Mostly with His Knife.
     David Huddle. GrPl
Balanced Bait in Handy Pellet Form, A. Allen Curnow. ATNZ
Balancing spaces are not disturbed, The. The Known Soldier. Kenneth
     Patchen. WaaP
Balankin was as gude a mason. Lamkin. *Unknown.* ESPB
Balboa. Nora Perry. PAH
Balboa, the Entertainer. Imamu Amiri Baraka. NoAM
Balcony with Birds, A. Howard Moss. NePoEA
Bald. Bill Zavatsky. UL
Bald-bare, bone-bare, and ivory yellow: skull. The U. S. Sailor with the
     Japanese Skull. Winfield Townley Scott. LiTM; WaP
Bald Cavalier, The. *Unknown.* OxBChV
Bald heads forgetful of their sins. The Scholars. W. B. Yeats. CMoP;
     NoP; OAEL-2; PoA
Bald trees neatly stand row upon row. Strolling in the Moonlight. Ch'en
     San-li, *tr. by* Irving Lo. WFTU
Balder, *sel.* Sydney Thompson Dobell.
     Chanted Calendar, A. BoTP; OBEV
     (Procession of the Flowers, The.) GN
Balder Dead, *sel.* Matthew Arnold.
     Second Asgard, The. FiP
Balder's Wife. Alice Cary. AA
Baldpate Pond. E. F. Weisslitz. NYBP
Baldy Bane. William Sydney Graham. NePoEA
Bale-fire kindled in the night, A. Carlyle and Emerson. Montgomery
     Schuyler. AA
Balearic Idyll. Frederick Packard. FiBHP
Balena, The. *Unknown.* OxBSS
Balgu Song. *Unknown, tr. fr. Balgu by* Clancy McKenna. CBAP
Balin and Balan. Tennyson. *Fr.* Idylls of the King.
     Vivien's Song ("But now the wholesome music of the wood").
     OAEL-2
Balkis was in her marble town. Song. Lascelles Abercrombie. *Fr.*
     Judith. MoBrPo
Ball, A. Moishe Kulbak, *tr. fr. Yiddish by* Leonard Wolf.
     PeBMYV
Ball and the Club, The. Forbes Lindsay. SD

Ball dances in, The. For Hoyt Wilhelm. Joel Oppenheimer. ASP
Ball of fire shoots through the tamarack, A. The Scarlet Tanager. Joel
     Benton. AA
Ball Poem, The. John Berryman. ASP; CoAP; FF; MoAmPo; NoAM;
     NOBA; NoP
Ball will bounce, but less and less, A. Juggler. Richard Wilbur.
     CMoP; LiTM; MoAB; NePoEA; NYBP; TAP
Ball would lift, The. When I Got It Right. Carl Lindner. TSL
Ballad, A: "All the World's a Stage." Victor Gray. NBLV
Ballad: "Altho' a slave me is born and bred." J. B. Moreton. PVCV
Ballad, A: "As I was walkin' the jungle round, a-killin' of tigers an' time."
     Guy Wetmore Carryl. BXAP; NBLV; Par
Ballad: "Auld wife sat at her ivied door, The." Charles Stuart Calverley.
     BXAP; CenHV; FaBoCo; FiBHP; NA; NBLV; Par; WiR
Ballad: Between the Boxcars, *sel.* Robert Penn Warren.
     I Can't Even Remember the Name. CRP
Ballad: "He went with another." Gabriela Mistral, *tr. by* Muriel Kittel.
     AIW
Ballad: "Hundred ballads I have written, A." Christine de Pisan, *tr. by*
     Joan M. Ferrante. DMF
Ballad: "I put my hat upon my head." Samuel Johnson. NOBL
Ballad: "It was Earl Haldan's daughter." Charles Kingsley. GN
Ballad: "My lady was found mutilated." Leonard Cohen. OBCV
Ballad: "O what is that sound. . ." W. H. Auden. *See* O What Is That
     Sound [Which So Thrills the Ear].
Ballad: "Of all the girls that e'er were seen." John Gay. CoMu; ErPo
Ballad: "Oh, come my joy, my soldier boy." Henry Treece. WaP
Ballad: "Shoot, comrades." Jacob Glatstein, *tr. by* Benjamin *and* Barbara
     Harshav. AYP
Ballad: "They were a man's words, a ballad of an old time." James Still.
     MT
Ballad: "What's that approaching like dust like poverty." Charles Simic.
     LCAP
Ballad against the Enemies of France. Villon, *tr. fr. French by*
     Swinburne. AWP
Ballad by Hans Breitmann. Charles Godfrey Leland. BXAP; CenHV;
     NOBL
Ballad Called Perkins's Figary, A. *Unknown.* APAS
Ballad Called the Haymarket Hectors, A. *Unknown.* APAS
Ballad for a Boy, A. William Johnson Cory. FaPoR; OxBChV
Ballad for Gloom. Ezra Pound. LiTM; MoAmPo
Ballad for Katharine of Aragon, A. Charles Causley. FaBoTw; NePoEA
Ballad for the Unknown Soldier. Allan Taylor. OBET
Ballad from the Seven Dials Press, A. *Unknown.* CoMu
Ballad in "G," A. Eugene Fitch Ware. PoLF
Ballad, November 1680, Made upon Casting the Bill against the Duke of
     York, A. *Unknown.* APAS
Ballad of a Barber, The. Aubrey Beardsley. NOBVV
Ballad of a Bun, A. Sir Owen Seaman. CenHV
Ballad of a General. Paul Snoek, *tr. fr. Dutch by* John Stevens Wade.
     DuIn
Ballad of a Mine, A. Robin Skelton. MoBS
Ballad of a Nun, A. John Davidson. BeLS; MoBrPo; OnMSP
Ballad of a Perennially Misunderstood Man. Gust Gils, *tr. fr. Dutch by*
     Manfred Wolf. DuIn
Ballad of a Springtime River: Presented to Wang the Elder, A. Hung
     Liang-chi, *tr. fr. Chinese by* William Schultz. WFTU
Ballad of a Strange Thing. Howard Phelps Putnam. OxBA
Ballad of Abbreviations, A. Gilbert Keith Chesterton. NOBL
Ballad of Agincourt, The. Michael Drayton. *See* Agincourt.
Ballad of All the Trades, A. *Unknown.* CoMu; ErPo
Ballad of an Empty Table. Tom Kryss. NeAC
Ballad of an Old Woman. Frank A. Collymore. PVCV
Ballad of Andrew and Maudlin, A. *Unknown.* CoMu
Ballad of Another Ophelia. David Herbert Lawrence. ChTr
Ballad of Baby Bell, The. Thomas Bailey Aldrich. AnAmPo
Ballad of Badmen. Owen Dodson. FB
Ballad of Banners (1944), The. John Lehmann. MoBS
Ballad of Barnaby, The. W. H. Auden. OBNV
Ballad of Bedlam. *Unknown.* NA
Ballad of Billie Potts, The. Robert Penn Warren. NOBA; OxBA
Ballad of Billy Rose, The. Leslie Norris. MoBS
Ballad of Birmingham. Dudley Randall. BPo; HeIP; InPK; MoP; NIP;
     NoAM
Ballad of Blossom, The. Mona Van Duyn. EOEF; SM
Ballad of Bouillabaisse, The, *sel.* Thackeray. OBEV; OBTV
     "This Bouillabaisse a noble dish is." FaBoUs
Ballad of Bunker Hill, The. Edward Everett Hale. PAH
Ballad of Calvary Street. James Keir Baxter. ATNZ

Ballad of Ch'ao-chou, The. Huang Tsun-hsien, *tr. fr. Chinese by* J. D. Schmidt. WFTU
Ballad of Chickamauga, The. Maurice Thompson. PAH
Ballad of Christmas, A. Walter de la Mare. OBCP
Ballad of Constancy. *Unknown, tr. fr. Spanish by* Perry Higman. LPSS
Ballad of Culinary Frustration. Phyllis McGinley. FiBHP
Ballad[e] of Dead Ladies. Villon, *tr. fr. French by* Dante Gabriel Rossetti. AWP; CTC; FaFP; OBVE; PoRA; PrIm
Ballad of Dead Men's Bay, The. Swinburne. MOS
Ballad of Dead Yankees, The. Donald Petersen. HeIP
Ballad of Don Juan Tenorio and the Statue of the Comendador. Roy Campbell. PeSA
Ballad of East and West, The. Kipling. BeLS; BLPL; BrPo; FaBoBe; FaBV; FaPoR; OBNV
Ballad of Faith. William Carlos Williams. OBAL
Ballad of Fat Margot. Augustus Young. CIP
Ballad of Father Gilligan, The. William Butler Yeats. EaLo; EBVV; MoBrPo; OnYI; PoRA
Ballad of Fisher's Boardinghouse, The. Kipling. PoRA
Ballad of François Villon, A. Swinburne. PoEL-5; PoRA
Ballad of Going Down to the Store, A. Miron Bialoszewski, *tr. fr. Polish by* Czeslaw Milosz. PwPP
Ballad of Good Counsel. Chaucer. *See* Flee fro the press and dwelle with sooth fastnesse.
Ballad of Hampstead Heath, The. James Elroy Flecker. MoBrPo
Ballad of Heaven, A. John Davidson. BeLS
Ballad of Hector in Hades. Edwin Muir. MoP; NoAM; NOBE
Ballad of Hell, A. John Davidson. HoPM; MoBrPo
(Christmas Eve.) EBVV; OHIP
"Ballad of Helmut Franze, The." Jerome Sala. UL
Ballad of Herman's Rose, *sels.* Arvo Turtiainen, *tr. fr. Finnish by* Aili Jarvenpa. SOP
"Finally I understood Rose's death." *Fr. V.* Helsinki.
"There where the Kulo Saari bridge." *Fr. I.*
"Where could I find the words." *Fr. III.*
Ballad of Heroes, A. Austin Dobson. OHIP
Ballad of High Endeavor, A. *Unknown.* NA
Ballad of Hiram Hover, The. Bayard Taylor. AnAmPo; BXAP; FaBoCo; OBAL
Ballad of Hu-hsi, A. Shih Jun-chang, *tr. fr. Chinese by* William Shultz. WFTU
Ballad of Human Life. Thomas Lovell Beddoes. BeLS
Ballad of Ira Hayes. Peter La Farge. MAT
Ballad of Ishmael Day, The. *Unknown.* PAH
Ballad of John Cable and Three Gentlemen. W. S. Merwin. CoAP; NePoEA; NOBA
Ballad of Keith of Ravelston, The. Sydney Thompson Dobell. *Fr.* A Nuptial Eve. CH; OBEV
Ballad of Kynd Kittok, The. William Dunbar. GoTS; OxBoLi
Ballad[e] of Ladies' Love, Number Two. Villon, *tr. by* John Payne. ErPo
Ballad of Lager Bier, The. Edmund Clarence Stedman. OBAL
Ballad of London, A. Richard Le Gallienne. FaBoPP
Ballad of Longwood Glen, The. Vladimir Nabokov. NYBP
Ballad of Luna, Luna. Federico García Lorca, *tr. fr. Spanish by* William B. Logan. SOTW
Ballad of Manila Bay, A. Sir Charles G. D. Roberts. PAH
Ballad of Mary Baldwin, The. Stephen Sandy. MAT
Ballad of Master McGrath, A. *Unknown.* FaBoBa
Ballad of Mr. Cooke, The. Bret Harte. AnAmPo
Ballad of Mrs. Noah, The. Robert Duncan. MoP; NoAM; NOBA
Ballad of My Beautiful Lady. *Unknown, tr. fr. Spanish by* Perry Higman. LPSS
Ballad of Nat Turner, The. Robert Hayden. BPo; SM; VGW
Ballad of New Orleans, The. George Henry Boker. PAH
Ballad of No Proper Man. Daniel Hoffman. MAT
Ballad of O'Bruadir, The. Frederick Robert Higgins. OBMV
Ballad of One Hundred Fathoms, A. Shih Jun-chang, *tr. fr. Chinese by* William Shultz. WFTU
Ballad of Orange and Grape. Muriel Rukeyser. NoAM
Ballad of Oriskany, The. Obadiah Cyrus Auringer. AA
Ballad of Our Lady ("Hail sterne superne! Hail in eterne"), *sel.* William Dunbar. ACP
(Ane Ballat of Our Lady.) OxBS
(Hymn to Mary, A.) MeEL
"Empryce of prys, imperatrice." EBEV
Ballad of Paco Town, The. Clinton Scollard. PAH
Ballad of Past Meridian, A. George Meredith. OAEL-2

Ballad of Peach Blossom Spring. Yüan Mei, *tr. fr. Chinese by* Jonathan Chaves. CoBLCP
Ballad of Persse O'Reilly, The. James Joyce. *Fr.* Finnegans Wake. FaBoBa; LiTB
Ballad of Private Chadd, The. A. A. Milne. CenHV
Ballad of Queensland (Sam Holt), A. G. H. Gibson. PoAu-1
Ballad of Reading Gaol, The, *sels.* Oscar Wilde. BeLS; MoBrPo; NOBE; OAEL-2; OBMV; OBNC; OBNV
Sels.
"For oak and elm have pleasant leaves." NoAM
"He did not wear his scarlet coat." MoBrPo; NoAM; NOBE; NOBVV; OBMV; OBNC
"In Debtor's Yard the stones are hard." NOBVV
In Reading Gaol by Reading Town. FaFP; LiTB
"There is no chapel on the day." EBVV; NoAM; TIRV
Yet Each Man Kills the Thing He Loves. TEP; TrGrPo
Ballad of Red Fox, The. Melvin Walker La Follette. NePoEA
Ballad of Redhead's Day, A. Richard Butler Glaenzer. PAH
Ballad of Remembrance, A. Robert Hayden. AmNP; BPo; IDB; PoBA; PoNe
Ballad of Rodborough Common, The. Jenny Joseph. NPo
Ballad of Rudolph Reed, The. Gwendolyn Brooks. RB
Ballad of Sally in Our Alley, The. Henry Carey. *See* Of all the girls that are so smart.
Ballad of Selling a Child. Wang Chiu-ssu, *tr. fr. Chinese by* Jonathan Chaves. CoBLCP
Ballad of Sir Brian and the Three Wishes, The. Newman Levy. FiBHP
Ballad of Sir John Franklin, A. George Henry Boker. AA; AnAmPo; OnMSP
Ballad of Sue Ellen Westerfield, The. Robert Hayden. AmPP; NoAM
Ballad of Sweet P, The. Virginia Woodward Cloud. PAH
Ballad of the Bayonet, A. Ernest Bryll, *tr. fr. Polish by* Czeslaw Milosz. PwPP
Ballad of the Boston Tea-Party, A. Oliver Wendell Holmes. PAH
Ballad of the Bread Man. Charles Causley. RB
Ballad of the Bushman. Ellen Duggan. PeNZ
Ballad of the Canal. Phoebe Cary. AnAmPo
Ballad of the Conemaugh Flood, A. Hardwick Drummond Rawnsley. PAH
Ballad of the Cool Fountain. *Unknown, tr. fr. Spanish by* Edwin Honig. BoWoP
Ballad of the Courtier and the Country Clown, A. *Unknown.* CoMu
Ballad of the D-Day Dodgers. *Unknown.* WTO
Ballad of the Dark Ladie, The. Samuel Taylor Coleridge. EnRP
Ballad of the Days of the Messiah. A. M. Klein. TrJP
Ballad of the Deserted Mansion. Kao Ch'i, *tr. fr. Chinese by* Jonathan Chaves. CoBLCP
Ballad of the Despairing Husband. Robert Creeley. NeAP; NoP; OBAL; SM
Ballad of the Dreamy Girl. Edith Roseveare, *tr. fr. Chinese.* Mes
Ballad of the Drinker in His Pub. N. P. van Wyck Louw, *tr. fr. Afrikaans by* Uys Krige, Jack Cope *and* Ruth Miller. PeSA
Ballad of the Drover. Henry Lawson. PoAu-1
Ballad of the Electric Eel. Wayne Brown. PBCV
Ballad of the Emeu, The. Bret Harte. NBLV
Ballad of the Epiphany. Charles Dalmon. OnMSP
Ballad of the Faded Field. Robert Burns Wilson. AA
Ballad of the Fatherless Boy. Wang Chiu-ssu, *tr. fr. Chinese by* Jonathan Chaves. CoBLCP
Ballad of the Ferocious Tiger. Hsü Pen, *tr. fr. Chinese by* Jonathan Chaves. CoBLCP
Ballad of the Flood. Edwin Muir. MoBS
Ballad of the French Fleet, A. Longfellow. AA; PAH
Ballad of the Frozen Field, The. Dabney Stuart. MT
Ballad of the Gibbet. Villon, *tr. fr. French by* Andrew Lang. AWP
Ballad of the Girl from Lan-ling. Chin Ho, *tr. fr. Chinese by* J. D. Schmidt. WFTU
Ballad of the Golden Bowl. Sara Henderson Hay. OnMSP
Ballad of the Good Lord Nelson, A. Lawrence Durrell. ErPo; LiTM
Ballad of the Goodly Fere. Ezra Pound. CMoP; LiTA; LiTM; MoAB; MoAmPo; MoBS; OFD; PoRA; TrCP; TrGrPo
Ballad of the Government Granary Clerk. Ho Ching-ming, *tr. fr. Chinese by* Jonathan Chaves. CoBLCP
Ballad of the Great London Fog. Huang Tsun-hsien, *tr. fr. Chinese by* J. D. Schmidt. WFTU
Ballad of the Harp-Weaver, The. Edna St. Vincent Millay. WSC
Ballad of the Hidden Dragon. *Unknown, tr. fr. Chinese.* WTO
Ballad of the Hoppy-Toad. Margaret Abigail Walker. BlSi; FB; HoPM
Ballad of the Icondic. John Ciardi. OBAL

Ballad of the Landlord. Langston Hughes. HCAP; NOBA
Ballad of the Londoner. James Elroy Flecker. EnLoPo
Ballad of the Lords of Old Time. Villon, *tr. fr. French by* Swinburne. AWP
Ballad of the Merchant. Hsü Pen, *tr. fr. Chinese by* Jonathan Chaves. CoBLCP
Ballad of the Mermaid. Charles Godfrey Leland. *See* Noble Ritter Hugo, Der.
Ballad of the Morning Streets. Imamu Amiri Baraka. CNA; SOTW; TTTS
Ballad of the Mouse. Robert Wallace. NYBP
Ballad of the Neighborhood Shaman. Kao Ch'i, *tr. fr. Chinese by* Jonathan Chaves. CoBLCP
Ballad of the Oedipus Complex. Lawrence Durrell. FaBoCo
Ballad of the Outer Life. Hugo von Hofmannsthal, *tr. fr. German by* Jethro Bithell. AWP; TrJP
Ballad of the Oysterman, The. Oliver Wendell Holmes. AnAmPo; FaFP; MOS; MoShBr
Ballad of the Righteous Tiger, A. Sung Wan, *tr. fr. Chinese by* William Schultz. WFTU
Ballad of the Rising in the North, A. *Unknown.* ACP
Ballad of the Stonegut Sugar Works. James Keir Baxter. PeNZ
Ballad of the Store Clerk. Gerrit Achterberg, *tr. fr. Dutch by* James S. Holmes. DuIn
Ballad of the Strange and Wonderful Storm of Hail, A. *Unknown.* CoMu
Ballad of the Tempest. James Thomas Fields. AnAmPo; BeLS; BLPL; FaBoBe; PoLF
Ballad of the Ten Casino Dancers. Cecília Meireles, *tr. fr. Portuguese by* James Merrill. ATCBP; BoWoP; OV
Ballad of the Three Spectres. Ivor Gurney. OBWP
Ballad of the Two Tapsters. Vernon Watkins. MoBS
Ballad of the White Glow, The. Itzig Manger, *tr. fr. Yiddish by* Leonard Wolf. PeBMYV
Ballad of the White Horse, The, *sel.* Gilbert Keith Chesterton. "Before the gods that made the gods." ACP
Ballad of the Women of Paris. Villon, *tr. fr. French by* Swinburne. AWP
Ballad of Trees and the Master, A. Sidney Lanier. AA; AnAmPo; FPL; LiTA; NOBA; OxBA; PoEL-5; PoLF; WGRP
Ballad of Villon and Fat Madge, The. Villon, *tr. fr. French by* Swinburne. OBVE
Ballad of William Bloat, The. *Unknown.* NOBL
Ballad of William Sycamore, The. Stephen Vincent Benét. MoAmPo; PoRA
Ballad of Yi River. Ho Ching-ming, *tr. fr. Chinese by* Jonathan Chaves. CoBLCP
Ballad of Yüan-yüan. Wu Wei-yeh, *tr. fr. Chinese by* Jonathan Chaves. CoBLCP
Ballad of Yukon Jake, The. Edward E. Paramore, Jr.. BeLS; BLPA
Ballad on the Taxes, A. Edward Ward. OxBoLi
Ballad on the Times, A. Henry Hall. APAS
Ballad-Singer, The. Thomas Hardy. *Fr.* At Casterbridge Fair, I. BoLoP
Ballad to a Traditional Refrain. Maurice James Craig. BIrV; SeCePo; TIRV
Ballad to the Tune of Bateman, A. Sir Charles Sedley. CoMu
Ballad [*or* Ballade] upon a Wedding, A ("I tell thee, Dick, where I have been"), *sel. Sir John* Suckling. CaPo; CoMu; EBEV; FaBoBa; InvP; JCP; NoP; OBS; Par; SeCP; SeCV-1
Bride, The. TrGrPo
Ballad upon the Popish Plot, A. John Gadbury. CoMu
Ballad Which Anne Askew Made and Sang When She Was in Newgate, The. Anne Askew. WPE
Ballad with an Ancient Refrain. *Unknown.* NA
Ballad Written for a Bridegroom. Villon, *tr. fr. French by* Swinburne. AWP
Ballade: "Lone am I, and would be." Christine de Pisan, *tr. by* Tom Vaughan. AIW
Ballade: "Pretty maid she died, she died, in love-bed as she lay, The." Paul Fort, *tr. by* Frederick York Powell. AWP
Ballade by the Fire. E. A. Robinson. AnAmPo
Ballade de Marguerite. *Unknown, tr. fr. French by* Oscar Wilde. AWP
Ballade des Belles Milatraisses. Rosalie Jonas. BlSi
Ballade d'une Grande Dame. G. K. Chesterton. OxBoLi
Ballade Made in the Hot Weather. W. E. Henley. MoBrPo
Ballade of Andrew Lang. Dugald Sutherland MacColl. CenHV
Ballade of Bones. Alfred Dorn. SoTCo
Ballade of Boys Bathing. Frederick William Rolfe. PeHV
Ballade of Dead Actors. W. E. Henley. EBVV; OBMV

Ballade of Dead Friends. E. A. Robinson. AA
Ballade of England. Louis MacNeice. NYBP
Ballade of Evolution, A. Grant Allen. EBVV
Ballade of Expansion. Hilda Johnson. PAH
Ballade of Faith. Tom MacInnes. CaP
Ballade of Good Counsel. Chaucer. *See* Flee fro the press and dwelle with sooth fastnesse.
Ballade of Illegal Ornaments. Hilaire Belloc. ACP
Ballade of Islands, A. Lucy Catlin Robinson. AA
Ballade of Lawn Tennis, A. Franklin Pierce Adams. SD
Ballade of Liquid Refreshment. E. C. Bentley. FaBoCo
Ballade of Lost Objects. Phyllis McGinley. CRP; NBLV; PoRA
Ballade of Sayings. W. S. Merwin. NNaP
Ballade of Suicide, A. G. K. Chesterton. FiBHP; NBLV
Ballade of the Armada, A. Austin Dobson. FaPoR
Ballade of the Back Road. Ron Block. SM
Ballade of the Grindstones. Judith Johnson Sherwin. SM
Ballade of the Nurserie, A. John Twig. NA
Ballade of the Poetic Life. J. C. Squire. OBMV
Ballade of the Scottyshe Kynge, A. John Skelton. CoMu; FaBoBa
Ballade of the Under Side. Don Marquis. *Fr.* Archys Life of Mehitabel. InvP
Ballade on Eschatology. Sister Mary Madeleva. GoYe
Ballade to His Mistress. Villon, *tr. fr. French by* Norman Cameron. WeW
Ballade to My Psychoanalyst. Kenneth Lillington. FiBHP
Ballade to Our Lady of Czestochowa. Hilaire Belloc. ACP
Ballade to Rosamund. Chaucer. *See* Madame, ye been of alle beautee shrine.
Ballade Tragique à Double Refrain. Max Beerbohm. OBSV
Ballade un Peu Banale. A. J. M. Smith. MoCV
Ballade which Villon Made. Donagh MacDonagh. TIRV
Ballat o the Hingit. Villon, *tr. fr. French by* Tom Scott. OBVE
Ballat o the Leddies o Langsyne. Villon, *tr. fr. French by* Tom Scott. OBVE
Ballata: Concerning a Shepherd-Maid. Guido Cavalcanti, *tr. fr. Italian by* Dante Gabriel Rossetti. AWP
Ballata II: "Fair women I saw passing where she passed." Guido Cavalcanti, *tr. by* Ezra Pound. PFI
Ballata: He Reveals, in a Dialogue, His Increasing Love for Mandetta. Guido Cavalcanti, *tr. fr. Italian by* Dante Gabriel Rossetti. AWP
Ballata: He Will Gaze upon Beatrice. Dante, *tr. fr. Italian by* Dante Gabriel Rossetti. AWP
Ballata: His Talk with Certain Peasant Girls. Franco Sacchetti, *tr. fr. Italian by* Dante Gabriel Rossetti. AWP
Ballata: In Exile at Sarzana. Guido Cavalcanti, *tr. fr. Italian by* Dante Gabriel Rossetti. AWP
Ballata II: Last Song: from Exile. Guido Cavalcanti, *tr. fr. Italian by* G. S. Fraser. PFI
Ballata V: "Light do I see within my Lady's eyes." Guido Cavalcanti, *tr. by* Ezra Pound. CTC; PFI
Ballata: Of a Continual Death in Love. Guido Cavalcanti, *tr. fr. Italian by* Dante Gabriel Rossetti. AWP
Ballata: Of His Lady among Other Ladies. Guido Cavalcanti, *tr. fr. Italian by* Dante Gabriel Rossetti. AWP
Ballata: Of True and False Singing. *Unknown, tr. fr. Italian by* Dante Gabriel Rossetti. AWP
Ballata: One Speaks of the Beginning of His Love. *Unknown, tr. fr. Italian by* Dante Gabriel Rossetti. AWP
Ballatetta. Ezra Pound. NIP; VGW
Ballet Blanc. Katha Pollitt. SM
Ballet [*or* Ballit] of de Boll Weevil, De. *Unknown.* AS; NOBA
Ballet of the Fifth Year, The. Delmore Schwartz. MoAB; OxBA; TwCP
Ballgame, The. Imamu Amiri Baraka. DiL
Ballinderry. *Unknown.* WTO
Balliol Rhymes, *sels. Var. authors.*
"First come I. My name is Jowett." Henry Charles Beeching. CenHV; FaBoCo; FaBoEE; NOBL
"I am a most superior person." Henry Charles Beeching. CenHV
"I am Andrew Cecil Bradley." Cecil Arthur Spring-Rice. CenHV
"I am Branson; Nature's laws." Henry Charles Beeching *and* John Bowyer Nichols. FaBoEE
"I am featly-tripping Lee." Henry Charles Beeching. CenHV; FaBoEE
"I am Huxley, blond and merry." John Bowyer Buchanan Nichols. CenHV
"I am rather tall and stately." *Unknown.* FaBoEE; NOBL
"I am the Dean, and this is Mrs. Liddell." *Unknown.* FaBoEE
"I am the Dean of Christ Church, Sir." Cecil Arthur Spring-Rice. CenHV; FaBoCo; FaBoEE; NOBL
"I'm the great Sir William Anson." *Unknown.* FaBoEE

"My name is George Nathaniel Curzon." John William Mackail *and* Cecil Arthur Spring-Rice. FaBoCo; FaBoEE; NOBL

"Old tips come out as good as new." John William Mackail. CenHV

"Positivists ever talk in s-/Uch an epic style as Dawkins." John William Mackail. FaBoEE

"Roughly, so to say, you know." John William Mackail. CenHV

"Upright and shrewd, more woo'd of fame." Henry Charles Beeching. CenHV

Ballit of de Boll Weevil, De. *Unknown. See* Ballet of de Boll Weevil, De.

Balloon, The. Karla Kuskin. PDV

Balloon ascends on that path it finds in the air, A. Coming to Know. William Stafford. BLA

Balloon Faces. Carl Sandburg. CMoP; PoE

Balloon Man, The. Rose Fyleman. BoTP

Balloon Man, The. E. Herbert. BoTP

Balloon Seller, The. Elizabeth Fleming. BoTP

Balloons. Dan Pagis, *tr. fr. Hebrew by* Bernhard Frank. MHeP

Balloons. Sylvia Plath. FaBoWP; PoE

Balloons hang on wires in the Marigold Gardens, The. Balloon Faces. Carl Sandburg. CMoP; PoE

Ballot, The. John Pierpont. AA

Ballroom Dancing Class. Phyllis McGinley. MoShBr

Ball's Bluff. Herman Melville. OBWP

Balls in an over, six you know. Aids for Latin. Gordon Perry. FaBoUs

Ballydavid Pier. Thomas Kinsella. BIrV; FaBCIP

Ballykinlar: May 1940. Patrick Maybin. NeIP

Ballynahinch. George Canning. FaBoCo

Ballyshannon foundered off the coast of Cariboo, The. Etiquette. William Schwenck Gilbert. CenHV; FaBoCh; FaBoCo; FiBHP

Ballywaire. Tom Paulin. FaBCIP

Balme. Spenser. *Fr.* The Faerie Queene, I, 11. CH

Balmoral balconies are tossed in gloom. Death of a Comic Opera Composer. Peter Porter. *Fr.* Baroque Quatrains. AnAn

Balow, my Babe, weep not for me. The New Balow. *Unknown.* CoMu

Balsham Bells. Kenrick Prescot. NOEC

Balthasar. Charles Spear. ATNZ

Balthasar's Song. Shakespeare. *See* Much Ado about Nothing

Balulalow. John James *and* Robert Wedderburn. EaLo; OBEV

Bam, Bam, Bam. Eve Merriam. PDV

Bambini picking daisies in the new spring grass. Daisies of Florence. Kathleen Jessie Raine. NYBP

Bamboo. Hagiwara Sakutaro, *tr. fr. Japanese by* Hiroaki Sato. FCEI

Bamboo. William Plomer. PeSA

Bamboo and Oak. Miyazawa Kenji, *tr. fr. Japanese by* Sato. FCEI

Bamboo bed, rattan pillow, A. Chu Yün-ming, *tr. fr. Chinese by* Jonathan Chaves. *Fr.* Miscellaneous Poems Written in My Studio on an Autumn Day. CoBLCP

Bamboo Branch Song. Ho Ching-ming, *tr. fr. Chinese by* Jonathan Chaves. CoBLCP

Bamboo Branch Song. Liu Yü-hsi, *tr. fr. Chinese by* Burton Watson. CoBCP

Bamboo Branch Song. Wang Fu-chih, *tr. fr. Chinese by* Irving Lo. WFTU

Bamboo Branch Song of Han-chia. Wang Shih-chen, *tr. fr. Chinese by* Jonathan Chaves. CoBLCP

Bamboo Branch Song of the Seacoast. Yang Wei-chen, *tr. fr. Chinese by* Jonathan Chaves. CoBLCP

Bamboo Branch Song of West Lake. Yang Wei-chen, *tr. fr. Chinese by* Jonathan Chaves. CoBLCP

Bamboo fishing coat, purple official gown. Feelings in Nature ("Bamboo fishing coat, purple official gown"). Ma Chih-yüan, *tr. fr. Chinese by* Jonathan Chaves. *Fr.* Four Poems to the Tune "Ch'ing-chiang yin," IV. CoBLCP

Bamboo frond, The. Sanetomo, *tr. fr. Japanese by* Burton Watson. *Fr.* Twenty-four Tanka. FCEI

Bamboo Grass. *Unknown, tr. fr. Japanese by* Hiroaki Sato. FCEI

Bamboo grass in front of the Oji Shrine, The. Emperor Go-Shirakawa, *tr. fr. Japanese by* Hiroaki Sato. *Fr.* Ryojin Hisho. FCEI

Bamboo Mile Lodge. Wang Wei, *tr. fr. Chinese by* Burton Watson. *Fr.* Twenty Views of Wang-ch'uan, 17. CoBCP

Bamboo Villa, The. Shen Chou, *tr. fr. Chinese by* Jonathan Chaves. CoBLCP

Bamboos cast blurred shadows, the shadows of trees lengthen. Sitting Up at Night. Ku T'ai-ch'ing, *tr. by* Pao Chia-lin. WFTU

Banana. Charles G. Bell. ErPo

Banana leaves are burning. "Containing Communism." Charlie Cobb. PoBA

Bananananananananana. William Cole. RHPC

Bananas. Yu T'ung, *tr. fr. Chinese by* Paul W. Kroll. WFTU

Bananas ripe and green, and ginger-root. The Tropics in New York. Claude McKay. AmNP; NoAM; PoBA; PoNe; TTY

Banbury Fair. Edith G. Millard. BoTP

Band in the Pines, The. John Esten Cooke. AA

Band Music. John Fuller. NePoEA-2

Band of carousers sits crammed in a tavern, A. In the Tavern. Moishe Kulbak, *tr. by* Leonard Wolf. PeBMYV

Band of Gideon, The. Joseph Seamon Cotter, Jr.. BANP; CDC

Band of the bold were gathered together, The. The Parting of the Red Sea. *Unknown, tr. fr. Anglo-Saxon by* Charles W. Kennedy. *Fr.* Exodus. AnOE

Band Played On, The. John F. Palmer. OBAL

Band Played Waltzing Matilda, The. Eric Bogle. OBET

Bandaged rain turned and left, The. Autumn. Tamura Ryuichi, *tr. by* Hiroaki Sato. FCEI

Banded Cobra, The. C. Louis Leipoldt, *tr. fr. Afrikaans by* Uys Krige, Jack Cope *and* Ruth Miller. PeSA

Bandit chief composes a tanka, The. Buson, *tr. fr. Japanese by* Hiroaki Sato. *Fr.* Eighty-seven Hokku. FCEI

Bando warriors are skilled with their bows. *Unknown, tr. by* Hiroaki Sato. FCEI

Bandog, The. Walter de la Mare. BrPo

Bang, bang, bang. The History of the Flood. John Heath-Stubbs. MoBS; OxBTC

Bangkok. F. R. Scott. MoCV; OBCV

Bangladesh. Kaifi A'Zmi, *tr. fr. Urdu by* Mahmood Jamal. PBMUP

Banished, dispossessed dead, The. Litany of the Rooms of the Dead. Franz Werfel, *tr. by* Edith Abercrombie Snow. TrJP

Banished Duke of Grantham, The. *Unknown.* EnSB

Banished from the Palace. Prince Nakao, *tr. fr. Chinese by* Burton Watson. JLIC-1

Banished Gods, The. Derek Mahon. OxBC

Banishment, The. Milton. *See* Paradise Lost: So spake our Mother Eve, and Adam heard.

Banishment from Ur. Enheduanna, *tr. fr. Sumerian by* W. W. Hallo *and* J. J. A. van Dijk. BoWoP

Banjo, The. Robert Winner. FF

Banjo Player, The. Fenton Johnson. BANP; PoNe

Banjo Song, A. Paul Laurence Dunbar. AnAmPo

Bank foyer is plush, The. People pass. Incident. Felix Pollak. TSM

Bank of spring clouds, rain swelling the stream, A. Going Out to the Country on a Boat Trip. Kao Ch'i, *tr. by* Jonathan Chaves. CoBLCP

Bank Thief, The. J. R. Farrell. BeLS; BLPA

Bankers Are Just like Anybody Else, except Richer. Ogden Nash. LiTA

Banking Coal. Jean Toomer. PoNe

Bankis of Helicon, The, *sel. Unknown.*
"Declair, ye bankis of Helicon." OxBS

Bankrupt. Cortlandt W. Sayres. PoLF

Banks fou, braes fou. *Unknown.* GBP

Banks o'Doon, The. Burns. BoLoP; OBEV; PrIM; TrGrPo

Banks of a River, The. Abraham Sutskever, *tr. fr. Yiddish by* Ruth Whitman. VWA

Banks of Champlain, The. *Unknown.* AmFP

Banks of Claudy, The. *Unknown.* AmFP; OBET

Banks of Dee, The. *Unknown.* AmFP

Banks of Newfoundland ("My bully boys of Liverpool"), The. *Unknown.* GBP

Banks of Newfoundland ("Oh may you bless your happy lot that lies secure on shore"), The. *Unknown.* OxBSS

Banks of Newfoundland ("You rambling boys of Liverpool I'll have you to beware"), The. *Unknown.* OxBSS

Banks of Sacramento, The. *Unknown.* AS

Banks of Sweet Dundee, The. *Unknown.* AmFP

Banks of Sweet Primroses, The. *Unknown.* ELP

Banks of the Condamine, The. *Unknown.* FaBoBa; GBP; PoAu-1

Banks of the Gaspereaux, The. *Unknown.* AmFP

Banks of the Nile, The. *Unknown.* OBET

Banks of Wye, The, *sels.* Robert Bloomfield. OBNC
Coracle Fishers, The.
Meandering Wye.

Banneker. Rita Dove. NoAM

Banner of England, not for a season, O banner of Britain, hast thou. The Defence of Lucknow. Tennyson. BeLS

Banner of Freedom high floated unfurled, The. The *United States* and *Macedonian. Unknown.* PAH

Banner of the Jew, The. Emma Lazarus. AA; TrJP

Banquet. Gloria Evans Davies. NPo

Banquet, The. Keats. *Fr.* Lamia. SeCePo

Banquet, A. Sotades, *tr. fr. Greek by* Charles Duke Yonge. FaBoUs

Banquet-cups, of many a hue and shape, The. The Respite. Maria Gowen Brooks. *Fr. Zophiël.* AA

Bansha Peeler wint won night, A. The Peeler and the Goat. *Unknown.* AnIL

Bantams in Pine-Woods. Wallace Stevens. CMoP; InPS; NoAM; NOBA; OxBA; UnPo

Baptism. Charles G. Bell. AmFN

Baptism. Claude McKay. PBCV; PoNe

Baptism. Dale Zieroth. NOBC

Baptist, The. William Drummond of Hawthornden. *See* Last and greatest herald of Heaven's King, The.

Baptize me again. Only the Eyes. Marie Luise Kaschnitz, *tr. by* Susan L. Cocalis. DMG

Bar close as you can, and bolt fast too your door. No Lock against Lechery. Robert Herrick. CaPo

Bar Giamaica, 1959-60. Charles Wright. EOEF

Bar is closed and I come, The. Night on Clinton. Robert Mezey. AmPA; NaP

Bar is crossed, The; but Death—the pilot—stands. Becalmed. John Banister Tabb. AA

Bar Kochba. Emma Lazarus. TrJP

Bar Mitzvah. Isaac Goldemberg, *tr. fr. Spanish by* David Unger. VWA

Bar of steel—it is only, A. Carl Sandburg. *Fr.* Smoke and Steel. AiP

Bar on the Piccola Marina, A. Noel Coward. NBLV

Bar-Room Matins. Louis MacNeice. EaLo; NYBP

Barabbas, Judas Iscariot. The Morning After. Dorothy Wellesley. OBMV

Barbadoes, *sels.* M. J. Chapman. PBCV
   "Still sparkles here the glory of the west."
   "While the noon-lustre o'er the land is spread."

Barbados, *sels.* Nathaniel Weekes. PBCV
   "Virtues of the cane must now be sung, The."
   "When frequent rains, and gentle show'rs descend."

Barbara. Mary Moran. GOS

Barbara. Jacques Prévert, *tr. fr. French by* Lawrence Ferlinghetti. RHTwFP

Barbara. Alexander Smith. GoTS

Barbara Allan ("It was about the Martinmas time"). *Unknown.* EnSB

Barbara Allen ("Down in London where I was raised"). *Unknown.* FaBoBa

Barbara Allen ("In London City where once I did dwell"). *Unknown.* BeLS

Barbara Allen ("In Scarlet Town where I was born"). *Unknown.* FaFP

Barbara Allen ("Twas early in the month of May"). *Unknown.* OBET

Barbara Allen's Cruelty ("All in the merry month of May"). *Unknown.* FaBoBe

Barbara Allen's Cruelty ("In Scarlet Town where I was born"). *Unknown.* OBEV

Barbara Frietchie. Whittier. AiP; AnAmPo; BeLS; BoTP; CTC; FaBoBe; FaBV; FaFP; FaPON; FaPoR; FPL; GN; NOBA; OBAL; OBCA; PAH; PoLF; TrGrPo; WBLP

Barbara shed her clothes and stuffed them. Barbara. Mary Moran. GOS

Barbara's Land Revisited—August 1978. Geary Hobson. STE

Barbarian Chieftain, The. Mao Wen-hsi, *tr. fr. Chinese by* Lois Fusek. ATF

Barbarian Prayer. Sandor Csoori, *tr. fr. Hungarian by* Edwin Morgan. MHuP

Barbarians. John Fowles. AnAn

Barbarians must we always be? Observing a Vulgar Name on the Plinth of an Ancient Statue. Walter Savage Landor. EyDe

Barbarossa. Friedrich Rückert, *tr. fr. German.* AWP, *tr. by* Elizabeth Craigmyle; WSC, *tr. by* John W. Thomas.

Barbarossa. Hubert Witheford. ATNZ; PeNZ

Barb'd blossoms of the guarded gorse. A Song of Winter. Emily Jane Pfeiffer. OBWVE

Barbecue Service. James Applewhite. MT

Barbed wire awaits you, the wasp, the viper, the bright, The. Edoardo Sanguineti, *tr. fr. Italian by* Lawrence R. Smith. *Fr.* Purgatory of Hell. NItP

Barbed Wire Fence Meditates upon the Goldfinch, A. Don McKay. NOBC

Barber, The. John Gray. NOBVV

Barber, barber, shave a pig. Mother Goose. OxNR

Barber shaved the mason, The. *Unknown.* OxNR

Barber shop is blank, The. Through the Barber Shop Window. Violet Anderson. CaP

Barber's, The. Walter de la Mare. GoJo

Barbershop. Martin Gardner. RHPC

Barbie Doll. Marge Piercy. CAPP; NIP

Barbra Allen ("In London City where I once did dwell"). *Unknown.* AS, *with music.*

Barbry Ellen. *Unknown.* ("All in the merry month of May"). PrIm

Barbury Camp. Charles Hamilton Sorley. FL

Bard. Gavin Bantock. FaBoTw

Bard, The. Blake. *See* Songs of Experience: Hear the Voice of the Bard!

Bard, The, *sel.* Thomas Gray. EnRP; GTBS; GTBS-P; NOBE; NOEC; OAEL-1
   Pindaric Ode, A. SeCePo

Bard, The. James Shirley. ErPo

Bard a Pindaric Ode, The. Thomas Gray. EnRP; GTBS; GTBS-P; NOBE; NOEC; OAEL-1

Bard is buried here, not strong, but sweet, A. The Epitaph of Eusthenes. Edward Cracroft Lefroy, *after the Greek of* Theocritus. *Fr.* Echoes from Theocritus, XXVIII. AWP, *abr.*

Bard is nature's favourite, The. She has made. Genius. James Waddington. PF

Bard who is singing of Wollombi Jim, The. Jim the Splitter. Henry Clarence Kendall. PoAu-1

Bard whom pilf'red pastorals reknown, The. Pope. *Fr.* Epistle to Dr. Arbuthnot. OBSV

Bards, The. Walter de la Mare. FaBoNo; NOBL

Bard's Chant. James Shirley. *Fr.* Saint Patrick for Ireland. ACP

Bard's Family, A. Peruncittiranar, *tr. fr. Tamil by* A. K. Ramanujan. PLW

Bards of passion and of mirth. Keats. ChER; EnRP; OBEV (Ode on the Poets.) GTBS; GTBS-P

Bard's Reformation, The. Samuel Bamford. PF

Bard's Song, The. Sir Robert Stapylton. SeCePo

Bare Almond-Trees. D. H. Lawrence. FaBoPP; OBTV

Bare Arms of Trees, The. John Tagliabue. Psk

Bare branches tremble, The. Tzu Yeh, *tr. by* Kenneth Rexroth *and* Ling Chung. WPOW

Bare bulb, a scatter of nails, The. An Ulster Twilight. Seamus Heaney. CIP

Bare earth it is, the way to my love. The Hour's Late. Abba Kovner, *tr. by* Warren Bargad *and* Stanley F. Chyet. IP

Bare-handed, I hand the combs. Stings. Sylvia Plath. NaP

Bare room, The. Lost. David Fisher. NPGG

Bare root of the bean is pink, The. What She Said. Allur Nanmullai, *tr. by* A. K. Ramanujan. PLW

Bare skin is my wrinkled sack. The Shrouded Stranger. Allen Ginsberg. NeAP

Bare soul will tramp, The. Footprints. Hamish Brown. PoSH

Bare Tree and Poetry. Ruth Kim Chun-soo, *tr. fr. Korean by* Koh Chang-soo. ACKP

Bare trees, The/ alternate. Larry Eigner. PoM

Barefoot and ragged, with neglected hair. On a Fair Beggar. Philip Ayres. EnLoPo; OBS

Barefoot Boy, A. James Whitcomb Riley. FaFP

Barefoot Boy, The, *sels.* Whittier. AA; FaBoBe; FaFP; FPL; GN; LiTA; OBAL; OBCA; OHFP; PoLF; WBLP, *abr.*
   "Blessings on thee, little man." AnAmPo; FaPON
   "Oh for boyhood's painless play." AiP

Barefoot boy, A! I mark him at his play. A Barefoot Boy. James Whitcomb Riley. FaFP

Barefoot Days. Rachel Field. FaPON

Barefoot I went and made no sound. The Viper. Ruth Pitter. FaBoTw

Barefoot, in unaccustomed clouts or skirts of raw muslin. The New Saddhus. Robert Pinsky. MAYP

Barefoot on the shore. On the Shore. Aila Meriluoto, *tr. by* Aili Jarvenpa. SOP

Barefoot through the bazaar. Sindhi Woman. Jon Stallworthy. OxBC

Barefoot tramp on a stone, A. On My Wandering Flute. Abraham Sutskever, *tr. by* Ruth Whitman. VWA

Barefoot vagabond on a stone, A. In the Sack of the Wind. Abraham Sutskever, *tr. by* Chana Bloch. PeBMYV

Barefoot without a stitch she walks. Dance with Banderillas. Richard Duerden. NeAP

Barely a twelvemonth after. Horses, The ("Barely a twelvemonth after"). Edwin Muir. HAP; HeIP; MoBrPo; MoP; NoAM; NOBE; NoP; OAEL-2; OxBTC; PoE; RB; TEP; WeW

Barely acceptable in grammar. Man and Wife Is One Flesh. Ann Deagon

Barely anything to say, everything said. But you break. Michael Palmer. UL

Barely did the dust settle. Taking Off. Ron Rogers. NOVW
Barely, rarely, comest thou. Shelley. *See* Rarely, Rarely, Comest Thou.
Barely tolerated, living on the margin. Soonest Mended. John Ashbery. HCAP; NAAL-2; Prf
Barely twelve years old. In Memory of My Arab Grandmother. Evelyn Arcad Zerbe. WPOW
Bargain, The. Sir Philip Sidney. *See* Arcadia: My True Love Hath My Heart [and I Have His].
Barge glided, The. Vision. Israel Zangwill. TrJP
Barge she sat in, like a burnish'd throne, The. Shakespeare. *Fr.* Antony and Cleopatra, II, ii. SCV
   (Cleopatra.) LiTB
   (Cleopatra's Barge.) TrGrPo
Bargeman's ABC, The. *Unknown.* OxBSS
Barges on the Hudson. Babette Deutsch. WPE
Barges, Rivers. Hans Tentije, *tr. fr. Dutch by* Scott Rollins. DuIn
Bark leaps love-fraught from the land, The. The Thousand Islands. Charles Sangster. *Fr.* St. Lawrence and the Saguenay. NOBC; OBCV
Bark smells like pineapple. Foxtail Pine. Gary Snyder. NaP; NU
Barking sound the shepherd hears, A. Fidelity. Wordsworth. FM
Barks the melancholy dog. Wakeful in the Township. Elizabeth Riddell. PoAu-2
Barley-Break, A. Sir John Suckling. CaPo; SeCV-1
Barley-Break; or, Last in Hell. Robert Herrick. CaPo
Barley straw's good fodder. *Unknown.* FaBoUs
Barmenissa's Song. Robert Greene. FaBoRV
Barn, The. Wendell Berry. EyDe
Barn, The. Edmund Blunden. MoBrPo; SeCePo
Barn, The. Elizabeth J. Coatsworth. OBCP
Barn, The. Seamus Heaney. HAP
Barn, The. Stephen Spender. CMoP
Barn, The. Edward Thomas. EyDe
Barn Fire. Thomas Lux. LCAP; NAmP
Barn in Winter, The. Claire Harris MacIntosh. CaP
Barn is full of mice, The. Peter Rosei, *tr. by* Beth Bjorklund. CoAuP
Barnacle Geese. Charles Higham. OBAL
Barney Bodkin broke his nose. *Unknown.* OxNR
Barney Google. Billy Rose. OBAL
Barney McGee. Richard Hovey. AnAmPo; OBAL
Barney's Invitation. Philip Freneau. PAH
Barnfire during Church. Robert Bly. NePoEA
Barnfloor and Winepress. Gerard Manley Hopkins. ACP
Barns grow slowly out of the dark. Lenox Christmas Eve 68. Sam Cornish. CNA
Barns huddle over the horns. November Harvest. Anita Endrezze-Danielson. HATNAP
Barnsley and District. Donald Davie. NoAM; OxBC
Barnyard, The. *Unknown.* AmFP
Barnyard Melodies. Fred Emerson Brooks. OBAL
Baron has decided to mate the monster, The. The Bride of Frankenstein. Edward Field. CoAP; HeIP
Baron o [*or of*] Leys, The. *Unknown.* ESPB; OxBB
Baron of Brackley, The. *Unknown.* ESPB; ESPB, A *and* B *vers.*
   (Baron of Braikley, The.) OxBB
Baron of Braikley, The. *Unknown.* *See* Doon Deeside cam Inverey.
Baron of Buchlyvie. Buchlyvie. *Unknown.* GBP; TW
Baron of Smaylho'me rose with day, The. The Eve of Saint John. Sir Walter Scott. EnRP; PoEL-4
Baron of the sea, the great tropic, A. The Marvel. Keith Douglas. RB
Baron Renfrew's Ball. Charles Graham Halpine. PAH
Baron Tells of His Last Experience, The. Jacob Glatstein, *tr. fr. Yiddish by* Benjamin *and* Barbara Harshav. AYP
Baroness Mu Impeded in Her Wish to Help Famine Victims in Wei. Confucius, *tr. fr. Chinese by* Ezra Pound. *Fr.* Yung Wind. CTC
Baron's Last Banquet, The. Albert Gorton Greene, *tr. by* Alice Fletcher. AA; AnAmPo; BeLS
Baron's War, The, *sel.* Michael Drayton.
   Severn, The. *Fr.* Canto I. ChTr
Baroque-handled and sharp. The Compasses. George MacBeth. NePoEA-2
Baroque Quatrains, *sels.* Peter Porter. AnAn
   Death of a Comic Opera Composer.
   Queer Assayers of the Frontier, The.
Baroque Wall-Fountain in the Villa Sciarra, A. Richard Wilbur. AmPP; CAPP; NAAL-2; NePoEA; NoP; NYBP; TwCP
Barques we ride on over the sea. The Trees. Bill Manhire. PeNZ
Barquisimeto, Venezuela, October 27, 1561. Ai. *Fr.* The Gilded Man, II. AnAn

Barracks Apt. 14. Theodore Weiss. CoAP; TAP
Barracks-square, washed clean with rain, The. In Barracks. Siegfried Sassoon. FaBoTw
Barracuda. Joseph MacInnis. RR
Barrage. Richard Aldington. BrPo
Barred Islands. Philip Booth. NePoEA
Barrel Organ, The. Daniel Mark Epstein. *Fr.* Homage to Mallarmé. DiPo
Barrel-Organ, The. Alfred Noyes. BLPL; BoTP; FaBV; MoBrPo; PoRA
Barrel-Organ, The. Arthur Symons. NOBVV
Barrels of blue potato-spray, The. Spraying the Potatoes. Patrick Kavanagh. BIrV; FaBCIP; IPY; NoP
Barren. Rachel, *tr. fr. Hebrew by* L. V. Snowman. TrJP
Barren Area, A. Hagiwara Sakutaro, *tr. fr. Japanese by* Hiroaki Sato. FCEI
Barren cross-ties of penny-whistle twigs. Affirmation. Helen Armstead Johnson. AmNP
Barren Moors, The. William Ellery Channing. AA
Barren Poem. Michael Ryan. AmPA
Barren Shore, The. Coventry Patmore. GBL
Barren Soul, A. Joseph Ezobi, *tr. fr. Spanish by* D. I. Friedmann. *Fr.* The Silver Bowl. TrJP
Barren Spring. Dante Gabriel Rossetti. *Fr.* The House of Life, LXXXIII. EBVV; NoP; OAEL-2; OBNC; PoEL-5
Barren Tree, The, *sel.* Llewelyn Wyn Griffith.
   "From his own solitude to the world unheeding." OBWVE
Barren Woman. Sylvia Plath. OxBSP
Barricade—a wall—a stronghold, A. The Breech. Michael McClure. NeAP
Barricades. Michael S. S. Harper. PoBA
Barrier, The. Claude McKay. BANP
Barrier guard's brazier, The. Buson, *tr. fr. Japanese by* Hiroaki Sato. *Fr.* Eighty-seven Hokku. FCEI
Barrier stone has rolled away, The. Easter. Edwin L. Sabin. OHIP
Bars. Nicolás Guillén, *tr. fr. Spanish by* Perry Higman. LPSS
Bar's Fight, August 28, 1746. Lucy Terry. BlSi; BPo; PoNe
Bars on Eighth Avenue in Harlem, The. Harlem Gallery: From the Inside. Larry Neal. BPo
Barter. Sara Teasdale. FaBV; FaPON; SoSe
Barter. Margaret Widdemer. WGRP
Bartholdi Statue, The. Whittier. PAH
Bartholomew Benjamin Bunting. The Singular Sangfroid of Baby Bunting. Guy Wetmore Carryl. NA
Barthram's Dirge. *Unknown.* FaBoRV
Bartleme Fair. George Alexander Stevens. ELP; NOEC
Bartley Costello, eighty years old. Gaeltacht. Pearse Hutchinson. BIrV
Bartol. Amos Bronson Alcott. AA
Baruch, *sel.* Bible, Apocrypha.
   Path of Wisdom, The. *Fr.* III: 9–IV: 4. TrJP
Baryshnikov leaps higher than your heart. Ballet Blanc. Katha Pollitt. SM
Base Details. Siegfried Sassoon. FF; HeIP; MMA; MoBrPo; OxBSP; SoSe
Base metal hanger by your master's thigh! One Writing against His Prick. *Unknown.* TW
Base Stealer, The. Robert Francis. GoJo; NTCP; RHPC; SD; TSL
Base Words Are Uttered. W. H. Auden. OxBSP
Baseball. Gail Mazur. PPR
Baseball. Frank Dempster Sherman. OBCA
Baseball and Writing. Marianne Moore. BoWoP
Baseball Canto. Lawrence Ferlinghetti. ASP
Baseball Note. Franklin P. Adams. SD
Baseball's Sad Lexicon. Franklin P. Adams. FaFP; SD
Based on its rock of right your empire lies. Joel Barlow. *Fr.* The Columbiad. OPP
Bases. Rae Armantrout. BAP
Bashert, *sel.* Irena Klepfisz.
   "These words are dedicated to those who died." ER
Bashful Earthquake, The, *sel.* Oliver Herford.
   "If this little world to-nigh." AA
Basho, coming. The Snow Party. Derek Mahon. CIP; FaBCIP; FaBoPV; OxBC
Basia, *sel.* Johannes Secundus, *tr. fr. Latin by* Thomas Stanley.
   "Not always give a melting kiss." *Fr.* VIII. OBVE
Basic. Ray Durem. PoNe
Basil. Gibbons Ruark. MT
Basilisk, The. Philip Child. CaP

Baskerville, Perpetua, Garamond. The Printer. Linda Pastan. KS
Basket Catch. Bart Schneider. TSL
Basket-Maker's Song, The. Thomas Dekker *and others.* See Pleasant
    Comedy of Patient Grissell [*or* Grissel *or* Grissill], The: Art thou
    poor, yet hast thou golden slumbers?
Basket of dirty clothes, A. Repetition of Words and Weather. Ruth
    Stone. BoWoP
Basket of Walnuts, A. George MacBeth. NPo
Basketball. Nikki Giovanni. RHPC
Basketball. Stephen Vincent. NeAC
Basketball: A Retrospective. Stephen Dunn. ASP
Basketball Season Begins. Norbert Krapf. TSL
Basketball Star. Karama Fufuka. RHPC
Baskets of ripe fruit in air. Gardener Janus Catches a Naiad. Dame
    Edith Sitwell. MoAB; MoBrPo
Bass Culture. Linton Kwesi Johnson. PBCV
Bastard, The, *sel.* Richard Savage.
    "In gayer hours, when high my fancy ran." NOEC; OBSV
Bat, The. Frank Jacobs. RHPC
Bat. D. H. Lawrence. BrPo; GTBS-P; HAP; OAEL-1; OAEL-2; OBTV
Bat, The. Ruth Pitter. FM
Bat, The. Theodore Roethke. GoJo; OBCA; PDV; PYC; RHPC; WSC
Bat, The. Edith Sitwell. FaBoMo
Bat, The. Roberta Spear. AmPA; MAYP
Bat, The. Ellen Bryant Voigt. MAYP
Bat Angels. Larry Levis. AmPA
Bat, bat, come under my hat. Mother Goose. OxNR
Bat in the Bedroom, The. Robert Crum. MOWH
Bat is born, A. Bats. Randall Jarrell. GrPl; NTCP; NU; OBCA; RFM
Bat is dun, with wrinkled wings, The. Emily Dickinson. FM; NAAL-1
Bat on the Road, A. Seamus Heaney. PoE
Batalis and the Man, The. Virgil. *See* Batellis. . .
Batata and rice. Tiempo Muerto. Ricardo Alonso. SaC
Batchelor leads an easy life, A. Good and Bad Wives. *Unknown.*
    CoMu
Batellis [*or* Batalis] and the man I will descrive. Virgil, *tr. into Middle*
    English by Gavin Douglas. *Fr.* The Aeneid [*or* Eneados], I.
    OBVE
    (Batalis and the Man, The.) CTC
Bath, The. Harry Graham. CenHV
Bath, The. Joel Oppenheimer. NeAP
Bath, The. Gary Snyder. CAPP; DiL; NNaP; TAP
Bath-Bunny, The. Carolyn Wells. *Fr.* A Baker's Dozen of Wild Beasts.
    OBCA
Bath in Pylos, The. Gábor Devecseri, *tr. fr. Hungarian by* Robert
    Graves. MHuP
Bath; or, The Western Lass, The, *sel.* Thomas D'Urfey.
    Dialogue, between Crab and Gillian. NOEC
Bath over, on a chair. Early Autumn Evening. Rokunyo, *tr. by* Burton
    Watson. JLIC-2
Bathe me O God in thee, mounting to thee. Walt Whitman. *Fr.* Passage
    to India. TrPWD
Bathed and fresh, the innkeeper's son. The Net. Joseph Rolnik, *tr. by*
    Irving Feldman. PeBMYV
Bathers, The. W. S. Merwin. PoE
Bathers, The. Karl Shapiro. ASP
Bathing. Sara Boyes. DT
Bathing in the roaring white waterfall. A Hunter Once, Now an Ascetic.
    Marippittiyar, *tr. by* A. K. Ramanujan. PLW
Bathing of Oisin's Head, The. *Unknown, tr. fr. Early Modern Irish by*
    Eoin MacNeill. AnIL
Bathing Song. Anne Ridler. NYBP
Bathing the Aged. Paul Monette. AmPA
Bathing with Father. Doug Fetherling. NeAC
Bathos, The. Richard Porson. FaBoEE
Bathroom Walls. Maura Stanton. PPR
Baths of Rome and Babylon. A City Song. John Hanlon Mitchell. CaP
Bathsheba came out to the sun. Telling the Bees. Lizette Woodworth
    Reese. AA
Bathtub [*or* Bath Tub], The. Ezra Pound. NIP; WeW
Bathtub is white and full of strips, The. The Stones of Time. Kenneth
    Koch. *Fr.* Days and Nights, II. NoAM
Bathtubs. Richmond Lattimore. NYBP
Batle of Otterbourne, The. *Unknown. See* Battle of Otterburn, The.
Batlonim. Yankev Fridman, *tr. fr. Yiddish by* Ruth Whitman.
    PeBMYV
Bats, The. Robert Hillyer. GoYe
Bats. Randall Jarrell. GrPl; NTCP; NU; OBCA; RFM
Bats. Dave Smith. NoAM
Bats are creepy; bats are scary. The Bat. Frank Jacobs. RHPC
Bats in a birdless country. Birdless Country. Shimazaki Toson, *tr. by*
    Burton Watson. FCEI

Batt he gets children, not for love to reare 'em. Upon Batt. Robert
    Herrick. FaBoEE
Battel of the Summer-Islands, The, *sel.* Edmund Waller.
    "Aid me Bellona, while the dreadful fight." SeCV-1
Batter my heart, three person'd God; for you. John Donne. *Fr.*
    Holy Sonnets, XIV. BLPL; EaLo; EBEV; FaFP; FF; HAP;
    HeIP; HoPM; InPK; InPS; JCP; LiTB; MeLP; MePo; NAEL-1;
    NIP; NOBE; NoP; OAEL-1; OBS; PoE; PoEL-2; PPP; PrIm;
    SeCePo; SeCP; SeCV-1; Son; SoSe; TEP; TOF; TrCP; TrGrPo;
    TrPWD
Batter'd, wreck'd old man, A. Prayer of Columbus. Walt Whitman.
    AmPP; WGRP
Battered roof where stars went tripping, A. The Sleepers. Frederick
    William Harvey. MMA
Batteries Out of Ammunition. Kipling. *Fr.* Epitaphs of the War, 1914–
    1918. MMA
Battery grides and jingles, The. The Day's March. Robert Nichols.
    MMA
Battery Moving Up to a New Position from Rest Camp: Dawn. Robert
    Nichols. MMA
Battle, The. Chu Yuan, *tr. fr. Chinese by* Arthur Waley. WaaP
Battle, A. Isabella Valancy Crawford. NOBC
Battle, The. W. H. Davies. BrPo
Battle. Robinson Jeffers. *See* Forseen for so many years.
Battle, The. Louis Simpson. InPS; OBWP; PVCV
Battle Autumn of 1862, The. Whittier. PAH
Battle Ballad, A. Francis Orrery Ticknor. PAH
Battle Cry. William Henry Venable. PAH
Battle Cry [*or* Battle-Cry] of Freedom, The. George Frederick Root.
    AnAmP; FaBoBe; PAH
Battle-Field, The. Bryant. AA; AnAmPo; FPL; PoLF
Battle-Field, The. PAH
Battle Hymn. Michael Altenburg, *tr. fr. German by* Catherine
    Winkworth. WGRP
Battle Hymn of the [American] Republic, The. Julia Ward Howe.
    AA; AH, *with music;* AnAmPo; BLPA; CH; EaLo; FaBoBe; FaFP;
    FaPON; FaPoR; GN; NOBA; NOCV; OBWP; OHIP; OPP; PAH;
    PWR; SCV; TAP; WBLP; WGRP; WPE
Battle Hymn of the Spanish Rebellion. L. A. MacKay. OBCV
Battle in the Clouds, The. William Dean Howells. PAH
Battle of Actium. Virgil, *tr. fr. Latin, tr. by* Dryden. *Fr.* The Aeneid
    [*or* Eneados], VIII. OBS
Battle of Agincourt, The. Michael Drayton. *See* Fair stood the wind for
    France.
Battle of Antietam Creek, The. *Unknown.* AmFP
Battle of Argoed Llwyfain, The. Taliesin, *tr. fr. Welsh by* Anthony
    Conran. OBWVE
Battle of Aughrim, The, *sels.* Richard Murphy.
    Casement's Funeral. NOIV
    "Deep red bogs divided." CIP
    Green Martyrs. NOIV
    Orange March. NOIV
    Planter. BIrV
    Rapparees. BIrV; NOIV
    "Who owns the land where musket-balls are buried." IPY
    Wolfhound. NOIV
Battle of Baltimore, The. *Unknown.* PAH
Battle of Bennington, The. Thomas P. Rodman. PAH
Battle of Blenheim, The. Robert Southey. BeLS; EnRP; FaBoPV;
    FaBV; FaPoR; FPL; GN; OBNC; OBWP; PoLF; TrGrPo; WBLP
Battle of Bothwell Bridge, The. *Unknown.* OxBB, *with music*
Battle of Bridgewater, The. *Unknown.* PAH
Battle of Brunanburh, *sels. Unknown, tr. fr. Anglo-Saxon by* Tennyson.
    OBVE; OBWP; TrGrPo; WaaP
    "Æthelstan King, lord of eorls." *Tr. by* Charles W. Kennedy.
    AnOE
    "Then the Northmen fled in their nailed ships." PBBP
Battle of Bull Run, The. *Unknown.* AmFP
Battle of Bunker Hill, The. *Unknown.* PAH
Battle of Charleston Harbor, The. Paul Hamilton Hayne. PAH
Battle of Charlestown, The. Henry Howard Brownell. PAH
Battle of Erie, The. *Unknown.* PAH
Battle of Eutaw, The. William Gilmore Simms. PAH
Battle of Finnsburg, The. *Unknown, tr. fr. Anglo-Saxon by* Charles W.
    Kennedy. AnOE
Battle of Flodden, The. *Unknown. Fr.* Scotish Feilde.
    OxBLMV
Battle of Gettysburg, The. Stephen Vincent Benét. *Fr.* John
    Brown's Body. BeLS
Battle of Glentilt (1847), The. Sir Douglas Maclagan. PoSH
Battle of Harlaw, The. *Unknown.* ESPB
Battle of Ivry, The. Macaulay. *See* Now glory to the Lord of Hosts.

Battle of King's Mountain, The. *Unknown.* PAH

Battle of La Prairie, The. William Douw Schuyler-Lighthall. PAH

Battle of Lake Champlain, The. Philip Freneau. PAH

Battle of Lookout Mountain, The. George Henry Boker. PAH

Battle of Lovell's Pond, The. Longfellow. PAH

Battle of Maldon, The. *Unknown, tr. fr. Anglo-Saxon by* Charles W. Kennedy. AnOE; OAEL-1; OBWP, *tr. by* Kevin Crossley-Holland.

Battle of Manila, The. Richard Hovey. PAH

Battle of Monmouth, The. Thomas Dunn English. PAH

Battle of Monmouth, The. "R. H." PAH

Battle of Morris' Island, The. *Unknown.* PAH

Battle of Murfreesboro, The. Kinahan Cornwallis. PAH

Battle of Muskingum; or, The Defeat of the Burrites, The. William Harrison Safford. PAH

Battle of Navarino, The. *Unknown.* CoMu

Battle of New Orleans, The. Thomas Dunn English. PAH

Battle of New Orleans, The. *Unknown.* AmFP

Battle of Oriskany, The. Charles D. Helmer. PAH

Battle of Otterburn [*or* Otterbourne *or* Oterborne], The, *sel. Unknown.* ESPB, (A, B *and* C *vers.*); OnMSP

(Battle of Otterbourne, The.) FaBoCh; GoTS; OxBB, *with music*

"It fell abowght the Lamasse tyde." OxBS

Battle of Philiphaugh, The. *Unknown.* ESPB

Battle of Plattsburg, The. *Unknown.* PAH

Battle of Plattsburg Bay, The. Clinton Scollard. PAH

Battle of Queenstown, The. William Banker, Jr.. PAH

Battle of Shiloh, The. *Unknown.* AmFP

Battle of Similes. *Malay Oral Tradition, tr. by* R. J. Wilkinson *and* R. O. Winstedt. WTO

Battle of Sole Bay, The. *Unknown.* GBP

(Song on the Duke's Late Glorious Success over the Dutch, A.) OxBSS

Battle of Somerset. Cornelius C. Cullen. PAH

Battle of Stonington on the Seaboard of Connecticut, The. Philip Freneau. PAH

Battle of the Baltic. Thomas Campbell. EnRP; FaPoR; GN; GTBS; GTBS-P; OBEV

Battle of the *Bonhomme Richard* and the *Serapis*. Walt Whitman. *Fr.* Song of Myself, XXXV-XXXVI. MOS; RB; UnPo

Battle of the Cowpens, The. Thomas Dunn English. PAH

Battle of the Frogs and Mice, The, *sel. Formerly at. to* Homer, *tr. fr. Greek by* Thomas Parnell.

"Ascend my shoulders, firmly keep thy seat." OBVE

Battle of the Jarama, The. Pablo Neruda, *tr. fr. Spanish by* Angel Flores. WaaP

Battle of the Kegs, The. Francis Hopkinson. AnAmPo; OBAL

(British Valor Displayed.) PAH

Battle of the King's Mill. Thomas Dunn English. PAH

Battle of the Stars. Adah Isaacs Menken. CBWP-1

Battle of Tippecanoe, The. *Unknown.* PAH

Battle of Trenton, The. *Unknown.* PAH

Battle of Valparaiso, The. *Unknown.* PAH

Battle of Waterloo, The. Byron. *See* Childe Harold's Pilgrimage: There was a sound of revelry by night.

Battle of Waun Gaseg, The. Llywelyn ab y Moel, *tr. fr. Welsh by* H. Idris Bell. OBWVE

Battle Pledge. *Somali Oral Tradition, tr. by* M. Laurence. WTO

Battle Problem. William Meredith. NYBP

Battle rent a cobweb diamond-strung, The. Range-finding. Robert Frost. MoP; NIP; NoAM; NoP; OBWP; RB

Battle Report. Bob Kaufman. AmNP; TTY

Battle Royal between Dr. Sherlock, Dr. South, and Dr. Burnet, The. William Pittis. APAS

Battle Scene. Aricil Kilar, *tr. fr. Tamil by* A. K. Ramanujan. PLW

Battle ships arrayed by the estuary. The Song of the Boat Trackers. Ch'en Wei-sung, *tr. by* Madeline Chu. WFTU

Battle Song. Macuilxochitl, *tr. fr. Nahuatl Indian by* Catherine Rodriquez-Nieto. WPOW

Battle Song. Robert Burns Wilson. PAH

Battle-Song of the *Oregon*. Wallace Rice. PAH

Battle Songs of the King Tshaka. *Unknown, tr. fr. Zulu.* PeSA

Battle, The ("But as they left the dark'ning heath"). Sir Walter Scott. *Fr.* Marmion, VI. ELP

Battle, The ("By this, though deep the evening fell"). Sir Walter Scott. *Fr.* Marmion, VI. PoEL-4

Battle, The ("Not far advanc'd was morning day"). Sir Walter Scott. *Fr.* Marmion, VI. EnRP

Battle waged strong, The. The Release. Adah Isaacs Menken. CBWP-1

Battle Won Is Lost. Phil George. GrPl; NOVW

Battledore. John Gray. NOBVV

Battlefield. Richard Aldington. MMA; OBWP

Battlefield of Dreams. Okamoto Jun, *tr. fr. Japanese by* Geoffrey Bownas *and* Anthony Thwaite. PeBJV

Battles nor songs can from oblivion save. Immortality. Lizette Woodworth Reese. AA

Batuschka. Thomas Bailey Aldrich. AnAmPo

Batyushkov. Osip Mandelstam, *tr. fr. Russian by* W. S. Merwin *and* Clarence Brown. OBVE

Baucis. Erinna, *tr. fr. Greek by* Richard Garnett. AWP

Baucis and Philemon. Katherine Hoskins. PoA

Baucis and Philemon. Ovid. *See* Metamorphoses: Philemon and Baucis.

Baucis and Philemon; Imitated from the Eighth Book of Ovid. Swift. GN; NOEC; OAEL-1

Baudelaire. Delmore Schwartz. TwCP; VGW

Baudelaire in Brussels. Anthony Cronin. BIrV

Bavarian Gentians. D. H. Lawrence. CMoP; CMoP; FaBoCh; FaBoMo; GoJo; GTBS-P; GTBS-P; HAP; InPK; InPK; InPS; LiTB; MoP; NAEL-2; NoAM; NOBE; NoP; OAEL-2, 2 *versions;* PoE; SOTW; TTTS

Bawl of a steer, The. The Cowboy's Life. *At. to* James Barton Adams. AmFN

Baxter Bickerbone of Burlington. On Learning to Adjust to Things. John Ciardi. OBCA

Bay, The. James Keir Baxter. ATNZ; PeNZ

Bay at Shiga, The. Ietaka, *tr. fr. Japanese by* Steven D. Carter. WFTW

Bay Fight, The. Henry Howard Brownell. PAH

Bay is not blue but somber yellow, The. Self-Criticism in February. Robinson Jeffers. AmPP

Bay of Biscay, The. *Unknown.* AmFP

Bay of Tsunu, The. Hitomaro, *tr. fr. Japanese by* Kenneth Rexroth. UnAS

Bay Poem. Lance Henson. VoR

Bay Psalm Book, The, *sels.*

"O Blessed man, that in th'advice." SCAP

"O Thou my soule, Jehovah blesse." SCAP

"O Give yee thanks unto the Lord." SCAP

"I to the hills lift up mine eyes." OBCA

"Heavens doe declare/ The majesty of God, The." SCAP

"Lord to me a shepherd is, The." OBCA

Bay was anchor, sky, The. Offshore. Philip Booth. SD

Bayadere, The. Francis Saltus Saltus. AA

Baying Hounds, The. Mary Gilmore. PoAu-1

Bayonet and the Needle, The. Eliezer Steinbarg, *tr. fr. Yiddish by* Curt Leviant. VWA

Bayonets. Jacob Glatstein, *tr. fr. Yiddish by* Benjamin *and* Barbara Harshav. AYP

Bayonne Turnpike to Tuscarora. Allen Ginsberg. NNaP

BC:AD. U. A. Fanthorpe. OBCP

Be a guide—this is a boat rowing in the traceless waves. Princess Shikishi, *tr. fr. Japanese by* Hiroaki Sato. *Fr.* Seventy-eight Tanka. FCEI

Be a Monster. Roy Fuller. AmMo

Be Absolute for Death. Shakespeare. *Fr.* Measure for Measure, III, i. FaBoRV

Be always in time. *Unknown.* OxNR

Be assured, the Dragon is not dead. Vanity. Robert Graves. GTBS-P

Be-Bop Boys. Langston Hughes. OBAL

Be Careful. *Unknown.* NBLV

Be careful, then, and be gentle about death. All Souls' Day. D. H. Lawrence. OBD

Be careful what/ You say or do. Zoo Manners. Eileen Mathias. BoTP

Be composed—be at ease with me—I am Walt Whitman. To a Common Prostitute. Walt Whitman. MoAmPo

Be Cool, Baby. Rob Penny. PoBA

Be Daedalus. Nanina Alba. PoBA; PoNe

Be dark, be deep, wait there for me between. The Upper Lake. Francis Stuart. NeIP

Be Different to Trees. Mary Carolyn Davies. FaPON; OHIP

Be dumb ye infant chimes, thump not the metal. Great Tom. Richard Corbet. OxBoLi

Be ever meek and humble, nor essay. The Meek and the Proud. Abraham ibn Chasdai, *tr. by* J. Chotzner. TrJP

Be extra careful by this door. The Whisperer. Mark Van Doren. MoAmPo

Be Fair. Eugène Guillevic, *tr. fr. French by* John Montague. RHTwFP

Be Frugal. Richard Church. OxBSP; OxBTC

Be glaid, al ye that luvaris bene. Four May Poems: "Be glaid, al ye that luvaris bene." *Unknown.* OxBS

Be Glorified Eternally. Balthasar Hoffman, *tr. fr. German by* Sheema Z. Buehne. AH

Be good. For Starters. Victoria McCabe. CRP

Be governour baith guid and gratious. To the Queen. Lord Darnley. OxBS

Be happy, be happy again. Song of Delight. Shao Yung, *tr. by* Burton Watson. CoBCP

Be happy for me, girls,/ my mother-in-law is dead! *Unknown, tr. by* Willis Barnstone. BoWoP

Be his memory forever green and rich. Baal Shem Tov. Abraham Moses Klein. CaP; TrJP

Be in me as the eternal moods. Doria. Ezra Pound. MoAB; MoAmPo

Be it right or wrong, these men among. The Nut-brown Maid. *Unknown.* OBEV; OBSC

Be it so, for I submit; his doom is fair. Milton. *Fr.* Paradise Lost, *Bk.* X, *ll.* 770-1114. NAWM-1

Be just (domestick monarchs) unto them. George Alsop. SCAP

Be kind and tender to the Frog. The Frog. Hilaire Belloc. FaBoBe; FaBV; FaPON; FiBHP; GoJo; MoShBr; NA; NTCP; OxBChV; RHPC

Be kind, good sir, and I'll lift my sark. Confucius, *tr. fr. Chinese by* Ezra Pound. *Fr.* Songs of Cheng. CTC

Be kind to her. To End Her Fear. John Freeman. OBMV

Be kind to me. Sappho, *tr. by* Mary Barnard. PeHV

Be kind to the panther! for when thou wert young. The Panther. *Unknown.* NA

Be kind to yourself, it is only one. Who Be Kind To. Allen Ginsberg. NNaP

Be life what it has been, and let us hold. To His Wife. Ausonius, *tr. by* Terrot Reaveley Glover. AWP

Be like the Bird. Victor Hugo, *tr. fr. French.* FaPON

Be like the water. The Poet's Counsel. Philippe Soupault, *tr. by* Michael Benedikt. POS

Be Merry. *Unknown.* RB

Be merry, all birds, today. Ay. Tennyson. *Fr.* Window, The; or, The Song of the Wrens. PBBP

"Be mine," I begged on bended knee. Did She Say "Hmp—mp" instead of "Mp—hmp"? Willard R. Espy. SoTCo

Be mute, this autumn; gather in the world. In March. Philip Martin. PoAu-2

Be Near Me. Tennyson. *Fr.* In Memoriam A. H. H., L. ELP; HAP; HeIP; LiTB; NOCV; NoP; PoEL-5; SCV

Be near to me, O white shadowless Light of my soul's swift venture. Psalm to the Holy Spirit. A. M. Sullivan. TrPWD

Be Never Discouraged. Daniel C. Colesworthy. PWR

Be Not Afeard: The Isle is Full of Noises. Shakespeare. *Fr.* The Tempest, III, ii. RB
(Caliban.) FiP
(To Dream Again.) TrGrPo

Be not afraid of every stranger. A Spell. George Peele. *Fr.* The Old Wives' [*or* Wife's] Tale. ChTr

Be not concerned, O my Sovereign. Princess Minabe, *tr. fr. Japanese. Fr.* Manyo Shu. Ma

Be not deceived by life, O Asad. Asadullah Khan Ghalib, *tr. by* Ahmed Ali. GoT

Be not deceived by the surge. Mohammad Taqi Mir, *tr. by* Ahmed Ali. GoT

Be not dismayed, whate'er betide. God's Goodness. C. D. Martin. WBLP

Be not frighted with our fashion. All Your Fortunes We Can Tell Ye. Ben Jonson. *Fr.* The Gypsies Metamorphosed. ChTr

Be not hasty. Kojima, *tr. fr. Japanese. Fr.* Manyo Shu. Ma

Be not proud, but now incline. The Changes to Corinna. Robert Herrick. JCP

Be not proud of your sweet body. *Gond Oral Tradition, tr. by* V. Elwin *and* S. Hivale. WTO

Be Not Silent. David ben Meshullam, *tr. fr. Hebrew.* TrJP

Be not sparing. Herrings. Swift. *Fr.* Verses for Fruitwomen.

Be not thou so foolish nice. Invitation to Dalliance. *Unknown.* FaBoEE

Be not too certain, life! The Hill. Horace Holley. WGRP

Be not too proud, imperious dame. The Defiance. Thomas Flatman. OBS

Be of good cheer, spirit of Myrrha! To a Courtesan a Thousand Years Dead. Paul Eldridge. PoA

Be Off! Stevie Smith. OxBC

Be pitiful, my God! Mea Culpa. "Ethna Carbery." TrPWD

Be plain in dress and sober in your diet. Lady Mary Wortley Montagu. FaBoEE

Be Present at Our Table, Lord. *at. to* John Cennick. BLRP

Be proud as Spaniards! Leap for pride ye fleas! On Donne's Poem "To a Flea." Samuel Taylor Coleridge. FM

Be punctual then to know. *Unknown. Fr.* The Art of Wenching. NOEC

Be Quiet, Sir! *Unknown.* ErPo

Be, rather than be called, a child of God. On an Infant Which Died before Baptism. Samuel Taylor Coleridge. OBD

Be reasonable, my pain, and think with more detachment. Inward Conversation. Baudelaire, *tr. by* Robert Bly. InPK

Be Sad, My Heart. Francis Quarles. NIP

Be silent with me, as all bells are silent! Ingeborg Bachmann, *tr. by* Beth Bjorklund. CoAuP

Be staid; be careful; and be not too free. Week-end. Harold Monro. SeCePo

Be Still. William Ward Ayer. BLRP

Be Still as You Are Beautiful. Patrick MacDonogh. NeIP

Be still: be still: nor dare. A Holy Hill. "Æ." AWP

Be Still Heart. Nilene O. A. Foxworth. AIW

Be still, my soul, be still; the arms you bear are brittle. A. E. Housman. *Fr.* A Shropshire Lad, XLVIII. MoAB; MoBrPo; NOBVV; OAEL-2; OBNC; TrGrPo

Be Still. The Hanging Gardens Were a Dream. Trumbull Stickney. LiTA

Be still, while the music rises about us: the deep enchantment. At a Concert of Music. Conrad Aiken. MoAB; MoAmPo; UnS

Be Strong. Maltbie Davenport Babcock. AH, *with music;* BLPA; FaBoBe; FaFP; OHFP; PWR; WBLP

Be strong like a mansion built. Sakatabe Obitomaro, *tr. fr. Japanese. Fr.* Manyo Shu. Ma

Be strong this way. Hercules Musarum. Robert Kelly. BAP

Be sure you paint. Alluding to the One-armed Bandit. D. C. Berry. BXAP

Be Swift O Sun. R. A. K. Mason. PeNZ

Be Thankful unto Him. Bible, *O.T. See* Psalms: Psalm C ("Make a joyful noise. . .").

Be the Best of Whatever You Are. Douglas Malloch. BLPA

Be the mistress of my choice. What Kind of Mistress He Would Have. Robert Herrick. CaPo; TrGrPo

Be then your counsels, as your subject, great. To the Federal Convention. Timothy Dwight. PAH

Be thou at peace this night. Edward Davison. CH

Be Thou My Guide. Florence Earle Coates. TrPWD

Be thou my vision, O Lord of my heart. *Unknown, tr. by* Eleanor Hull. TIRV

Be thou our country's Chief. A National Hymn. John William De Forest. *Fr.* Miss Ravenel's Conversion. OPP

Be thou praised, my Lord, with all Thy creatures. Praise of Created Things. Saint Francis of Assisi. FaPON

Be thou then my beauty named. Thomas Campion. AAS

Be True [*or* Be True Thyself]. Horatius Bonar. FaBoBe; GN; PWR

Be True to Your Condition in Life. John Audelay. MeEL

Be Useful. George Herbert. GN

Be vengeance wholly left to powers divine. Conversion. Dryden. *Fr.* The Hind and the Panther, III. ACP
(Worldly Vanity.) FiP

Be wary, lad; the road up which you go. To a Negro Boy Graduating. Eugene T. Maleska. PoNe

Be wary of the loathsome troll. The Troll. Jack Prelutsky. RHPC

Be White Man's slave. The Marital Problem. Sonja Åkesson, *tr. by* Joanna Bankier. OV

Be who you are and will be. For Each of You. Audre Lorde. CNA

Be with me, Beauty, for the fire is dying. On Growing Old. John Masefield. CMoP; FaFP; FPL; LiTB; LiTM; MoAB; MoBrPo; PoLF; PoRA

Be With Me, Lord. George Macdonald. *Fr.* Diary of an Old Soul. TrCP

Be with me, Luis de San Angel, now. Ave Maria. Hart Crane. *Fr.* The Bridge, I. NoAM; NOBA

Be with us, Lord, at eventide. Grace at Evening. Edwin McNeill Poteat. TrPWD

Be Ye in Love with April-Tide. Clinton Scollard. AA

Be you to others kind and true. Our Saviour's Golden Rule. Isaac Watts. OxBChV

Beach, The. Robert Graves. OxBSP

Beach at Evening, The. David Ferry. TDD

Beach at this evening full, The. The Beach at Evening. David Ferry. TDD

Beach at Veracruz, The. George Bowering. NeAC

Beach Burial. Kenneth Slessor. CBAP; PoAu-2

Beach Glass. Amy Clampitt. FaBoWP; NoAM

Beach Homos, The. Forrest Anderson. PeHV

Beach House, The. James Keir Baxter. ATNZ

Beach in August, The. Weldon Kees. VGW

Beach is beautiful; and there grow, The. Kuramochi Chitose, *tr. fr. Japanese. Fr.* Manyo Shu. Ma

Beach on Aegina is a bit tawdry, although, The. Happening on Aegina. John Logan. CAPP

Beach Rainbow. Takahashi Shinkichi, *tr. fr. Japanese by* Geoffrey Bownas *and* Anthony Thwaite. PeBJV

Beach Stones. Lilian Moore. TSS

Beach Talk. Norman MacCaig. PoA

Beach Women, The. Robert Pinsky. PPR

Beachcomber. George Mackay Brown. OxBC

Beached on the meadow, close by the sea's/ Accustomed lap. The Old Boat. Lenore Pratt. CaP

Beaches, The, *sels.* Robin Hyde.
    "Close under here, I watched two lovers once." *Fr.* VI. ATNZ; FaBoWP; PeNZ
    "Cool and certain, their oars will be lifted in dusk." *Fr.* VII. PeNZ

Beaches are full of dirty nails after rain. Coming Back. "Shake" Keane. PBCV

Beachy Head, *sel.* Charlotte Smith.
    "I once was happy, when, while yet a child." WPE

Beacons of the fishing-boats, The. *Unknown, tr. fr. Japanese by* Geoffrey Bownas *and* Anthony Thwaite. *Fr.* Manyo Shu. PeBJV

Beadle's Testimony, The. Jerome Rothenberg. NNaP

Beads, The. Jaime Jacinto. BrSi

Beads around/ my neck. African Images. Alice Walker. InPS

Beads of death. The Image. Tamura Ryuichi, *tr. by* Hiroaki Sato. FCEI

Beagles. W. R. Rodgers. FaBoTw; SD

Beak, The. Elizabeth Smither. ATNZ

Beak of the Dove, The. Juan Gonzalo Rose, *tr. fr. Spanish by* David Tipton. Per

Beaks of Eagles, The. Robinson Jeffers. NOBA

Beale Street. Langston Hughes. PPP

Beam of Light, A. John Jerome Rooney. AA

Beams. Audre Lorde. NoAM

Bean Eaters, The. Gwendolyn Brooks. AIW; BlSi; GrPl; HAP; HeIP; MAT; NoP; PoBA; PoE; PrIm; TAP; TTY; WeW

Bean Spasms. Ted Berrigan. EAS

Bean-Stalk, The. Edna St. Vincent Millay. WSC

Beanfield, The. John Clare. BoTP

Beans in blossom with their spots of jet, The. Field Path. John Clare. OxBSP

Beanstalk, Meditated Later, The. Judith Wright. NoAM

Bear, The. Robert Frost. MoAB; MoAmPo; NoAM

Bear, The. Ted Hughes. FaBoMo

Bear, The. Galway Kinnell. CAPP; CoAP; InPS; NNaP; RFM; TAP; VGW

Bear, The. N. Scott Momaday. CDW; HATNAP; NOVW

Bear, The. Ann Stanford. WSC

Bear: A Totem Dance As Seen by Raven. Peter Blue Cloud. HATNAP

Bear and the Squirrels, The. Christopher Pearse Cranch. OBCA

Bear at the door, begging, The. Snow White and Rose Red. Debora Greger. BAP

Bear cub, chained and tethered to a stake, A. Squaring the Circle. Louis O. Coxe. NYBP

Bear Dance. Ron Rogers. STE

Bear down lightly. To Destiny. *Unknown, tr. by* Frances Herskovits. EaLo

Bear down under the cliff, A. Gary Snyder. *Fr.* Myths and Texts: Hunting. HCAP; NaP

Bear him, comrades, to his grave. Burial of Barber. Whittier. PAH

Bear, however hard he tries, A. Teddy Bear. A. A. Milne. OnUR

Bear Hunt, The. Margaret Widdemer. FaPON

Bear Hunting. Aua, *tr. fr. Eskimo.* WTO

Bear in Bed. Judith Herzberg, *tr. fr. Dutch by* Shirley Kaufman. DuIn

Bear in mind. Drum. Langston Hughes. MoAmPo

Bear in mind. Catmint. Eric Clough Taylor. CRH

Bear me to Dictaeus. Acon. Hilda Doolittle ("H. D."). VGW

Bear on the Delhi Road, The. Earle Birney. HeIP; MoCV; NoAM; NOBC; NoP; NYBP; PrIm

Bear part with me most straight and pleasant tree. Morea's Sonnet. Mary Sidney Wroth, Countess of Montgomery. *Fr.* Urania. WPE

Bear puts both arms around the tree above her, The. The Bear. Robert Frost. MoAB; MoAmPo; NoAM

Bear Ropin' Buckaroo. S. Omar Barker. CowP

Bear sleeps in a cellar hole, A. New Hampshire. Donald Hall. LCAP; NePoEA-2

Bear Song, *sels.* Sándor Rákos, *tr. fr. Hungarian by* Jascha Kessler. FOC
    To the Animal Lover.
    To the Bear.
    To the Hunter.

Bear [*or* Bare] that breathes [*or* breaks] the northern blast, The. Upon a Wasp Chilled [*or* Child] with Cold. Edward Taylor. NAAL-1; NOBA; NOCV; PoEL-3

Bear Who Came to Dinner, The. Adrien Stoutenburg. SO

Bear who eats with a silver spoon, A. Animal Acts. Charles Simic. LCAP

Bear with me, Master, when I turn from Thee. Edith Lovejoy Pierce. TrPWD

Bearded grass waves in the summer breeze, The. Death and Night. James Benjamin Kenyon. AA

Bearded Lady. Bernice Zamora. CCP

Bearded man seated on a camp-stool, A. The Photographer. Louis Simpson. LCAP

Bearded Oaks. Robert Penn Warren. LiTM; MoAmPo; MoP; NAAL-2; NoAM; NOBA; PoA; PoE; TAP; TwCP

Bearer of Evil Tidings, The. Robert Frost. MoP; NoAM

Bearer of finches and clouds, pale atmosphere. Oxygen. Joan Swift. NYBP

Bearing their birds and gardens on their hats. L'Après Midi d'une Fille aux Cheveux de Lin. Ronald McCuaig. PoAu-2

Bearing white myrrh and incense, autumn melts. From a Book of Hours. Charles Spear. ATNZ

Bears. Arthur Guiterman. PoRA

Bears. Adrienne Rich. NePoEA; NYBP

Bears are kept by hundreds within fences, are fed cracked, The. Elizabeth's War with the Christmas Bear. Norman Dubie. LCAP; MAYP; NoAM

Bear's Blood. Ileana Malancioiu, *tr. fr. Rumanian by* Stavros Deligiorgis. BoWoP

Bear's Song, The. *Unknown, tr. fr. Haida Indian by* Constance Lindsay Skinner. *Fr.* Three Songs from the Haida. AWP

Beast, The. Brian Patten. AmMo

Beast, The. Theodore Roethke. SO

Beast and bird must bow aside. Epilogue for a Masque of Purcell. Adrienne Rich. NePoEA; NYBP

Beast in Man, The. George Clutesi. HATNAP

Beast in the Space, The. William Sydney Graham. FaBoTw; PoA

Beast, I've known you. Ode to an Alien. Diane Ackerman. BWV

Beast Section, The. Welton Smith. PoBA

Beast stands at my eye, A. The Naked Land. Kenneth Patchen. EAS

Beast That Rode the Unicorn, The. Conny Hannes Meyer, *tr. fr. German by* Herbert Kuhner. VWA

Beasts. Richard Wilbur. AmPP; LCAP; NU; PPP; TwCP

Beasts and Birds. Adelaide O'Keeffe. OxBChV

Beasts in their major freedom. Beasts. Richard Wilbur. AmPP; LCAP; NU; PPP; TwCP

Beasts onely capable of sense, enjoy. John Ford. *Fr.* The Broken Heart, IV, ii. PoEL-2

Beat! Beat! Drums! Walt Whitman. AnAmPo; FaBV; FPL; InPK; InPS; NAAL-1; NoP; OBWP; PoLF

Beat hell out of it. Episode 17. Wiiliam Carlos Williams. *Fr.* Paterson. OxBA

Beat on proud billowes, Boreas blow. Loyalty Confin'd. Sir Roger L'Estrange. OBS

Beat Poem by an Academic Poet. Vassar Miller. WPE

Beat the drums of skins. War Comes. Zalman Schneour, *tr. by* Joseph Leftwich. TrJP

Beat the drums of tragedy for me. Fantasy in Purple. Langston Hughes. BANP; CDC

Beat the knife on the plate and the fork on the can. Going In to Dinner. Edward Shanks. OBMV; OxBTC

Beata l'Alma. Sir Herbert Read. FaBoMo

Beaten/ to the privy. *Unknown, tr. by* Burton Watson. FCEI

Beaten, beaten, beaten, beaten. The Copper Song. H. H. Fraser. CaP

Beaten like an old hound. Mad Day in March. Philip Levine. NYBP

Beating, The. T. R. Hummer. MAYP; MT

Beating, The. Ann Stanford. WPE

Beating the Drum. Ruth Dallas. *Fr.* Letter to a Chinese Poet. ATNZ

Beating their wings. *Unknown, tr. fr. Japanese by* Geoffrey Bownas *and* Anthony Thwaite. *Fr.* Kokin Shu. PeBJV

Beatitudes, The. Bible, *N.T. See* St. Matthew: Blessed are the poor[e] in spirit for theirs is the kingdom[e] of heaven.

Beatrice, *sel.* Joseph Sheridan Le Fanu.
    "Hush! oh ye billows." TIRV

Beatrice's Last Words. Shelley. *Fr.* The Cenci. FiP

Beatrix Is Three. Adrian Mitchell. NAs

Beatus Vir. Richard Le Gallienne. OHIP

Beaucourt Revisited. A. P. Herbert. MMA

Beaufort, fair Beaufort, thou art a favored spot. General Robert Smalls. Josephine D. Henderson Heard. CBWP-4

Beauregard. Catherine Anne Warfield. PAH

Beau's Receipt for a Lady's Dress, The. *Unknown.* CoMu

Beau's Reply. William Cowper. FaBoCh

Beauté, La. Baudelaire, *tr. fr. French by* Lord Alfred Douglas. AWP

Beauteous Ethel's father has a, The. A Piazza Tragedy. Eugene Field. FiBHP; NBLV

Beauteous, Yea Beauteous More than These. Christopher Smart. *Fr.* A Song to David. EaLo

Beautie and the life, The. *See* Beauty and the life, The.

Beauties of Santa Cruz, The, *sel.* Philip Freneau.
  "Sick of thy northern glooms, come, shepherd, seek." AmPP
Beautiful. William Allen Bixler. WBLP
Beautiful, The. John Aylmer Dorgan. AA
Beautiful, The. Mary E. Tucker. CBWP-1
Beautiful, The. F. S. Woodley. PeHV
Beautiful always the littoral line. The Innocent. Gene Derwood. WaP
Beautiful American Word, Sure, The. Delmore Schwartz. LiTA; VGW
Beautiful and blond they come, the Californians. The Californians.
  Theodore Spencer. NYBP; TW
Beautiful are the fingers of the loved one. When She Plays upon the Harp
  or Lute. Moses ibn Ezra, *tr. by* Solomon Solis-Cohen. TrJP
Beautiful as the flying legend of some leopard. Judith of Bethulia. John
  Crowe Ransom. FaBoMo; FYAP; LiTA; LiTM; NoAM; NOBA
Beautiful as the pomegranate is the white face of Ophrah. The Hot Flame
  of My Grief. Moses ibn Ezra, *tr. by* Solomon Solis-Cohen. TrJP
Beautiful Black Men. Nikki Giovanni. BPo; NMM
Beautiful Black Women. Imamu Amiri Baraka. BPo; PoM
Beautiful boys curve and writhe, The. Young Wrestlers. Grace Butcher.
  ASP
Beautiful cashier's white face has risen once more, The. Before the [*or* a]
  Cashier's Window in a Department Store. James Wright. CoAP;
  MAT; NYBP
Beautiful Changes, The. Richard Wilbur. CMoP; CoAP; HCAP; InPS;
  PoE
Beautiful city, infected, like a sore, A. Nameless. Natan Zach, *tr. by*
  Warren Bargad *and* Stanley F. Chyet. IP
Beautiful Creatures Brief as These. Douglas G. Jones. MoCV
Beautiful Dead Leaf. Takamura Kotaro, *tr. fr. Japanese by* Hiroaki Sato.
  FCEI
Beautiful, delicate bright gazelle, The. Walter James Turner. OBMV
Beautiful Evelyn Hope is dead! Evelyn Hope. Robert Browning.
  TrGrPo
Beautiful evening, early summer, A. It's Time. Ian Wedde. *Fr.*
  Earthly: Sonnets for Carlos, 2. ATNZ
Beautiful excess of Jesus on the waters, The. To Swim, to Believe.
  Maxine W. Kumin. TSL
Beautiful eyes of the dead, The. Carried Away. Anne Elder. CBAP
Beautiful faces are those that wear. Beautiful Things. Ellen Palmer
  Allerton. BLPA; PWR; WBLP
Beautiful girl said something in your praise, A. To a Friend on His
  Marriage. F. T. Prince. LiTM
Beautiful habitations, auras of delight! Auras of Delight. Coventry
  Patmore. *Fr.* The Unknown Eros. ACP
Beautiful heights, joy of the world, city of a great king. Jerusalem.
  Judah Halevi, *tr. by* David Goldstein. TOF
Beautiful is fair, the just is fair, The. Fair and Unfair. Robert Francis.
  VGW
Beautiful is she, this woman. Love Song. *Unknown, tr. by* Constance
  Lindsay Skinner. *Fr.* Three Songs from the Haida. AWP
Beautiful Is the Loved One. Moses ibn Ezra, *tr. fr. Hebrew by* Solomon
  Solis-Cohen. TrJP
Beautiful is the moon-lit night. Yotsuna, *tr. fr. Japanese. Fr.* Manyo
  Shu. Ma
Beautiful is the South. Tune: Remembering the South. Singde, *tr. by*
  William Schultz. WFTU
Beautiful ladies through the orchard pass. Les Demoiselles de Sauve.
  John Gray. NOBVV
Beautiful Lady Yü, The. Ku Hsiung, *tr. fr. Chinese by* Lois Fusek.
  ATF
Beautiful Lady Yü, The. Li Hsün, *tr. fr. Chinese by* Lois Fusek.
  ATF
Beautiful Lady Yü, The. Lu Ch'ien-i, *tr. fr. Chinese by* Lois Fusek.
  ATF
Beautiful Lady Yü, The. Mao Wen-hsi, *tr. fr. Chinese by* Lois Fusek.
  ATF
Beautiful Lady Yü, The. Sun Kuang-hsien, *tr. fr. Chinese by* Lois Fusek.
  ATF
Beautiful Lady Yü, The. Yen Hsüan, *tr. fr. Chinese by* Lois Fusek.
  ATF
Beautiful Land of Nod, The. Ella Wheeler Wilcox. PWR
Beautiful Lawn Sprinkler, The. Howard Nemerov. PCP
Beautiful, lo, the summer clouds. Song of the Blue-Corn Dance.
  Unknown, tr. by Natalie Curtis. WTO
Beautiful Meals. T. Sturge Moore. BoTP
Beautiful mother is bending, The. Nativity Song. Jacopone da Todi.
  OHIP
Beautiful must be the mountains whence ye come. Nightingales. Robert
  Bridges. BrPo; CMoP; LiTB; LiTM; MoAB; MoBrPo; NOBE;
  OAEL-1; OBEV; OBMV; OBNC; PBBP; TrGrPo; UnPo
Beautiful, my delight. To Be Sung on the Water. Louise Bogan. PrIm;
  VGW

Beautiful natural blossoms. To a Beautiful Pear Tree. James Wright.
  HAP
Beautiful Necessity, The, *sel.* Claude Bragdon.
  Point, the Line, the Surface and Sphere, The, , 2 *ll.* ImOP
Beautiful Night, A. Thomas Lovell Beddoes. *Fr.* Fragments Intended
  for the Dramas. ChER
Beautiful Ohio. James Wright. CAPP
Beautiful place is the town of Lo-yang, A. Lo-yang. Emperor Ch'ien
  Wen-ti, *tr. by* Arthur Waley. AWP
Beautiful Poultry. Ian Wedde. ATNZ
Beautiful rain falls, the unheeded angel, The. In Time. Kathleen Jessie
  Raine. WPE
Beautiful Ruined Orchard, The. Daniel Berrigan. FYAP
Beautiful Sea, The. Mary E. Tucker. CBWP-1
Beautiful, seen through holes. Issa, *tr. by* Geoffrey Bownas *and* Anthony
  Thwaite. PeBJV
Beautiful! Sir, you may say so. Thar is n't her match in the country.
  Chiquita. Bret Harte. AA; AnAmPo
Beautiful Slave, The. Giovanni Battista Marino, *tr. fr. Italian by* Dana
  Gioia. PFI
Beautiful Snow, The. John Whittaker Watson. BLPA; WBLP
Beautiful snow falls on a bed, A. Philip Dacey. SM
Beautiful Soup, so rich and green. "Lewis Carroll." *Fr.* Alice's
  Adventures in Wonderland, *ch.* 10.
  (Turtle Soup.) FaBoNo; RHPC
Beautiful Spring Scene, The. Ho Ning, *tr. fr. Chinese by* Lois Fusek.
  ATF
Beautiful star in heav'n so bright. Star of the Evening. James M.
  Sayles. Par
Beautiful sun that giveth us light. Beautiful. William Allen Bixler.
  WBLP
Beautiful Sunday. "Jake Falstaff." BoNaP
Beautiful sunlight has come. Taigi, *tr. fr. Japanese by* Hiroaki Sato.
  Fr. Twenty-nine Hokku. FCEI
Beautiful Swimmer, The. Walt Whitman. PeHV
Beautiful, tender, wasting away for sorrow. Luscious and Sorrowful.
  Christina Rossetti. PoEL-5; SeCePo
Beautiful—the sky. Issa, *tr. fr. Japanese by* Hiroaki Sato. *Fr.* Forty-
  four Hokku. FCEI
Beautiful the strong man in his strength. Tempora Mutantur. Charles
  Brasch. *Fr.* Night Cries, Wakari Hospital. ATNZ
Beautiful thing/ I saw you. William Carlos Williams. *Fr.* Paterson.
  CMoP
Beautiful Things. Ellen Palmer Allerton. BLPA; PWR; WBLP
Beautiful, through clear skies newly blue. Spring Landscape. Melvin
  Walker La Follette. NePoEA-2
Beautiful Toilet, The. Ezra Pound, *after the Chinese.* OBVE
Beautiful, tragical faces. Piccadilly. Ezra Pound. AnAmPo
Beautiful trees make paths beneath themselves. Juan Chi, *tr. fr. Chinese*
  by Burton Watson. *Fr.* Singing of Thoughts. CoBCP
Beautiful Urinals of Paris, The. C. D. Wright. MT
Beautiful was the appearance of Cormac in that assembly. Cormac Mac
  Airt Presiding at Tara. *Unknown, tr. by* Douglas Hyde
Beautiful, The! what is not perfect here below. The Beautiful. Mary E.
  Tucker. CBWP-1
Beautiful, which mocked his fond pursuing, The. The Beautiful. John
  Aylmer Dorgan. AA
Beautiful Woman. Dale Zieroth. NOBC
Beautiful woman, a cup of wine, and a garden, A. Joy of Life. Moses
  ibn Ezra, *tr. fr. Hebrew by* Solomon Solis-Cohen. *Fr.* The Book of
  Tarshish. TrJP
Beautiful woman, you crown the hours. Beautiful Woman. Dale Zieroth.
  NOBC
Beautiful women—we've vowed to be lovers! Liu E, *tr. fr. Chinese by*
  Jonathan Chaves. *Fr.* On the Twenty-fourth: Improvisations.
  CoBLCP
Beautiful World, The. W. Lomax Childress. OHIP
Beautiful you rise upon the horizon of heaven. The Hymn to the Sun.
  Akhenaton, *tr. by* J. E. Manchip White. TTY
Beautifull Young Nymph Going to Bed, A. Swift. NIP; NOEC; OPOP
Beautifull Mistress, A. Thomas Carew. OBS
Beautifully Janet slept. Janet Waking. John Crowe Ransom. CMoP;
  InPK; MoAB; MoAmPo; MoP; NAAL-2; NoAM; NoP; OBD; PoE;
  RB; TAP
Beauty. "Badawi al-Jabal," *tr. fr. Arabic by* Matthew Sorenson *and* John
  Heath-Stubbs. MAP
Beauty. Laurence Binyon. MoBrPo
Beauty. Abraham Cowley. LiTB; PoEL-2; TrGrPo
Beauty. "E-Yeh-Shure." FaPON
Beauty. Sir Richard Fanshawe, *after the Italian of* Giovanni Battista
  Guarini. *See* Il Pastor Fido: Of Beauty.
Beauty. Peter Hille, *tr. fr. German by* Jethro Bithell. AWP

Beauty. Christopher Marlowe. *Fr.* Tamburlaine the Great, *pt.* I, Act V. TrGrPo

Beauty. Isaac Rosenberg. TrJP

Beauty. Spenser. *Fr.* An Hymne in Honour of Beautie. OBSC

Beauty. Thomas Stanley, *after the Greek of* Anacreon. AWP; OBVE

Beauty. *Unknown. Fr.* The Passionate Pilgrim, XIII. OBSC

Beauty. Walt Whitman. WeW

Beauty. Elinor Wylie. NAAL-2; OxBA

Beauty—a beam, nay, flame. Fading Beauty. Giovanni Battista Marino, *tr. by* Samuel Daniel. AWP

Beauty, a silver dew that falls in May. *Unknown.* OBSC

Beauty, Alas, Where Wast Thou Born. *At.* to Thomas Lodge *and to* Robert Greene. EIL

Beauty all stainless, a pearl of a maiden, A. The Geraldine's Daughter. Egan O'Rahilly, *tr. by* James Clarence Mangan. AnIL

Beauty and Love. Andrew Young. GBL

Beauty and Sadness. Cathy Song. MAYP; NoAM

Beauty and Terror. Lesbia Harford. CBAP; PoAu-1

Beauty and the Beast. Rita Dove. NoAM

Beauty and the Bird. Dante Gabriel Rossetti. FM

Beauty and the Illiterate. Odysseus Elytis, *tr. fr. Greek by* Edmund Keeley *and* Philip Sherrard. VMG

Beauty [*or* Beautie], and the life, The. William Drummond of Hawthornden. EIL; PoEL-2
(Her Passing.) OBEV

Beauty, Arise! Thomas Dekker *and others. Fr.* The Pleasant Comedy of Patient Grissell [*or* Grissel *or* Grissill]. EIL
(Bridal Song, A ("Beauty arise, show forth thy glorious shining!").) OBSC; TrGrPo

Beauty as a Shield. Elsie Robinson. BLPA

Beauty Bathing. Anthony Munday. *See* Primaleon of Greece: Beauty Sat Bathing by a Spring.

Beauty—be not caused—it is. Emily Dickinson. TAP

Beauty clear and fair. John Fletcher. *Fr.* The Elder Brother, III, v. OBEV; OBS

Beauty does not walk through lovely days. Beauty and Terror. Lesbia Harford. CBAP; PoAu-1

Beauty Extoll'd. *At.* to Henry Noel *and to* William Strode. ChTr; ELP; OBS

Beauty goes into the butcher's shop. A Woman Shopping. Denis Glover. ATNZ

Beauty Imposes. John Shaw Neilson. PoAu-1

Beauty in flesh is a mirage, a bubble. Ballade of Bones. Alfred Dorn. SoTCo

Beauty in the old way of life. New Way, Old Way. David W. Martinez. NOVW

Beauty in Trouble. Robert Graves. NYBP

Beauty in woman; the high will's decree. Sonnet: He Compares All Things with His Lady, and Finds Them Wanting. Guido Cavalcanti, *tr. by* Dante Gabriel Rossetti. AWP

Beauty in Worship. *Unknown. Fr.* A Poem in Defence of the Decent Ornaments of Christ-Church, Oxon, Occasioned by a Banbury Brother, Who Called Them Idolatries. OBS

Beauty Is a Witch. Shakespeare. *Fr.* Much Ado about Nothing, II, i. TrGrPo

Beauty is but a vain and doubtful good. Beauty. *Unknown. Fr.* The Passionate Pilgrim, XIII. OBSC

Beauty is never satisfied. Mythmaking. Kathleen Spivack. NMM

Beauty Is Not Bound. Thomas Campion. *See* Give beauty all her right.

Beauty is not caused—it is. Emily Dickinson. LiTA

Beauty is seen. Beauty. "E-Yeh-Shure." FaPON

Beauty is still immortal in our eyes. The Immortal. Marjorie Pickthall. CaP

Beauty, it would be a great wrong. On a Lady Named Beloved. Anne de Rohan, *tr. by* Dorothy Backer. DMF

Beauty no other thing is than a beam. The Definition of Beauty. Robert Herrick. CaPo

Beauty of, The/ the terrible faces. Apology: Why Do I Write Today? William Carlos Williams. OxBA

Beauty of Dawn, The. Felix Mnthali. WMBCH

Beauty of Israel is slain [*or* slaine] upon thy high places, The. Bible, *O.T. Fr.* Second Samuel. OBVE; OBWP
(David's Lament.) ChTr, I: 19-27; FF, I: 19-27; TrGrPo, I: 19-27; TrJP, I: 19-27.
(David's Lament for Saul and Jonathan.) AWP
(How Are the Mighty Fallen.) WaaP

Beauty of Job's Daughters, The. Jay Macpherson. MoCV; NOBC

Beauty of manhole covers, The—what of that? Manhole Covers. Karl Shapiro. AmFN; GoJo; NoAM

Beauty of My Land Peers Warily, The. Dennis Brutus. WMBCH

Beauty of the flowers faded, The. Komachi, *tr. fr. Japanese by* Burton Watson. *Fr.* Kokin Shu. FCEI

Beauty of the Friend it was that taught me, The. Makhfi, *tr. by* Paul Whalley. WPOW

Beauty of the northern dawns, The. Christine. John Milton Hay. AA

Beauty of the Ship, The. Walt Whitman. MOS

Beauty of the Stars, The. Moses Ibn Ezra, *tr. fr. Hebrew by* Solomon Solis-Cohen. TrJP

Beauty of the unused, The. Unspeakable. Margaret Avison. NOBC

Beauty of Things, The. Robinson Jeffers. PoA

Beauty Rohtraut. Eduard Friedrich Mörike, *tr. fr. German by* George Meredith. AWP; OBVE

Beauty Sat Bathing by a Spring. Anthony Munday. *Fr.* Primaleon of Greece. EIL
(Beauty Bathing.) NOBE; OBEV
(Colin.) GTBS; GTBS-P
(To Colin Clout.) OBSC

Beauty screws her new. Rewrite. E. A. Markham. PBCV

Beauty shall be freed. Asadullah Khan Ghalib, *tr. by* Ahmed Ali. GoT

Beauty, Since You So Much Desire. Thomas Campion. ErPo; OAEL-1

Beauty, sweet Love, is like the morning dew. Samuel Daniel. *Fr.* To Delia. NOBE; OBEV; OBSC
(Sonnet: "Beauty, sweet love, is like the morning dew.") EIL

Beauty That All Night Long, A. Jalal ed-Din Rumi, *tr. fr. Persian by* Edward Fitzgerald. AWP

Beauty! thou art a wanderer on the earth. Behold, O Aspasia! I Send You Verses. Walter Savage Landor. *Fr.* Pericles and Aspasia, CXC. OBNC

Beauty, thou wild fantastic ape. Beauty. Abraham Cowley. LiTB; PoEL-2; TrGrPo

Beauty, Time and Love. Samuel Daniel. *See* To Delia: Fair is my love, and cruel as she's fair.

Beauty Too of Twisted Trees, A. Philip Sherlock. PBCV

Beauty was hers that glowed like autumn mountains. Hitomaro, *tr. fr. Japanese. Fr.* Manyo Shu. Ma

Beauty's Hands Are Cool. Karle Wilson Baker. GoYe

Beaver Love. Geoffrey Ursell. UAS

Beaver Moon—The Suicide of a Friend. Mary Oliver. GOYP

Beaver Pond. Anne Marriott. NOBC

Beaver roars hoarse with meltin' snows. James Russell Lowell. *Fr.* The Biglow Papers: 2d Series, No. X. PoEL-5

Beaver Skin. Antonio Porta, *tr. fr. Italian by* Lawrence R. Smith. NItP

Beaver's Story, The. Vernon Watkins. NYBP

Becalmed. John Blight. PoAu-2

Becalmed. John Banister Tabb. AA

Because. James McAuley. CBAP

Because. B. W. Vilakazi, *tr. fr. Zulu.* PeSA

Because a destiny most. Here Are Told the Misfortunes of Women. Christine de Pisan, *tr. fr. French by* Sarah Spence. *Fr.* The Book of Fortune's Changes. DMF

Because a lady asks me, I would tell. A Lady Asks Me. Guido Cavalcanti, *tr. by* Ezra Pound. PFI

Because all this food is grown in the store. Picketing Supermarkets. Tom Wayman. NIP

Because as they cut it was that special green, they decided. Two Brothers in a Field of Absence. Cynthia MacDonald. NIP

Because beer tingles. Beer Drops. Melba Joyce Boyd. BlSi

Because both Dad and Mom. Let Me Tell You about Myself. Tomioka Taeko, *tr. by* Hiroaki Sato. FCEI

Because everything I build is built on the miracle. The Miracle. Chaim Grade, *tr. by* Ruth Whitman. VWA

Because everything will be deserted then. Apocrypha. János Pilinszky, *tr. by* Jascha Kessler. FOC

Because fog engulfs. Myoe, *tr. fr. Japanese by* Burton Watson. *Fr.* Ten Tanka. FCEI

Because for one night you don't come. *Unknown, tr. fr. Japanese by* Burton Watson. *Fr.* Kangin Shu. FCEI

Because Going Nowhere Takes a Long Time. Kenneth Patchen. NaP

Because he had spoken harshly to his mother. Revelation. Robert Penn Warren. LiTA; NoAM

Because he is young. Okura, *tr. fr. Japanese by* Arthur Waley. *Fr.* Manyo Shu. AWP

Because He Liked to Be at Home. Kenneth Patchen. NaP

Because He Lives. Adele Lathrop. BLRP

Because he puts the compromising chart. Zola. E. A. Robinson. OxBA

Because he sent a head of cattle on. The Island and the Cattle. Nicholas Moore. EAS

Because he sometimes bored himself with thought. Hank. Stephen Tapscott. PPR

Because he studied texts. The Poor Shammes of Berditchev. Rochelle Ratner. VWA

Because he was a butcher and thereby. Reuben Bright. Edwin Arlington Robinson. AnAmPo; MoAB; MoAmPo; NOBA; NoP; Son; TAP; TrGrPo

Because he's one-eyed. The Greeks Are Blinding Polyphemus. Gyorgy Raba, *tr. by* Jascha Kessler. FOC

Because his madness had outgrown the world. The Kabbalist. Deborah Eibel. VWA

Because his nose and face were one festering sore. Orf. Ted Hughes. NoAM

Because his soup was cold, he needs must sulk. House-Mates. Leon Gellert. CBAP

Because I am a woman. Muse Poem. Kathryn Van Spanckeren. FF

Because I am broke again. Luck's Shining Child. George Garrett. MT

Because I am human and unable to be near a god. *Unknown, tr. fr. Japanese by* Hiroaki Sato. *Fr.* Manyo Shu. FCEI

Because I am idolatrous and have besought. Ernest Dowson. ACP; OxBSP

"Because I am mad about women." The Wild Old Wicked Man. W. B. Yeats. AnIL; CMoP

Because I believe in the community of little children. The Massacre of the Innocents. William Jay Smith. EaLo

"Because I breathe not love to every one." Sir Philip Sidney. *Fr.* Astrophel and Stella, LIV. InPS; OBSC; TrGrPo

Because I Could Not Dump. Andrea Paterson. BXAP

Because I could not stop for death. Emily Dickinson. AmPP; AWP; BoWoP; CMoP; DL; FF; FPL; HAP; HeIP; InPK; LiTA; LiTM; Mes; MoAB; MoAmPo; MoP; NAAL-1; NAWM-2; NIP; NoAM; NoP; OBD; OxBA; PBWP; PoE; PoEL-5; SCV; SoSe; SOTW; TAP; UnPo; WeW; WGRP; WPE (Chariot, The.) AnAmPo

Because I Deeply Praised. Angelos Sikelianos, *tr. fr. Greek by* Edmund Keeley *and* Philip Sherrard. VMG

Because I Did Not Want to Ask. Jolanda Insana, *tr. fr. Italian by* Keala Jane Jewell. DMI

Because I do not always know. A Prayer for Charity. Edwin O. Kennedy. TrPWD

Because I do not hope to turn again. Ash-Wednesday. T. S. Eliot. LiTA; MoAB; MoAmPo; OxBA; VGW

Because I do not know where you are. Elegies for Prince Atsumichi ("Because I do not know where you are"). Lady Izumi, *tr. fr. Japanese by* Hiroaki Sato. *Fr.* Fifty-one Tanka. FCEI

Because I feel that, in the Heavens above. To My Mother. Poe. OxBA

Because I fell asleep. Komachi, *tr. fr. Japanese by* Burton Watson. *Fr.* Kokin Shu. FCEI

Because I had loved so deeply. Compensation. Paul Laurence Dunbar. AmNP; BPo; PoNe

Because I had reproached him where he failed. Jausbert de Puycibot, *tr. by* Paul Blackburn. Pro

Because I have been given much. Because of Thy Great Bounty. Grace Noll Crowell. TrPWD

Because I know deep in my own heart. Pauli Murray. BlSi

Because I Liked You Better. A. E. Housman. GBL; NOBVV; OxBTC; PeHV

Because I Live. Evelyn Ames. GoYe

Because I loved someone. *Unknown, tr. fr. Japanese by* Burton Watson. *Fr.* Kokin Shu. FCEI

Because I once beat you up. For a Far-out Friend. Gary Snyder. NeAP; PoM

Because I Paced My Thought. John Hewitt. CIP

Because I set no snare. Michael's Song. W. W. Gibson. BoTP

Because I sit eating cherries. Cherries. Lucien Stryk. CAPP

Because I think not ever to return. Ballata: In Exile at Sarzana. Guido Cavalcanti, *tr. by* Dante Gabriel Rossetti. AWP

Because I used to shun. The Spark. Joseph Mary Plunkett. AWP

Because in Destroying He Creates. Alain Delahaye, *tr. fr. French by* Paul Auster. RHTwFP

Because in This Sorrowing Statue of Flesh. Kenneth Patchen. NaP

Because in Vietnam the vision of a Burning Babe. Advent 1966. Denise Levertov. NNaP; Prf

Because insect blood flows and seeps in. An Impression of Early Summer. Hagiwara Sakutaro, *tr. by* Hiroaki Sato. FCEI

Because it is an imperative voiced. Duelling Platitudes. Tom Disch. SoTCo

Because it is lunchtime. Planting Trout in the Chicago River. Dennis Schmitz. AnAn; NPGG

Because it is the day of Palms. Palm Sunday: Naples. Arthur Symons. BrPo

Because it is windy, a woman. Blackbirds. Susan Mitchell. NAmP

Because language dreams in metaphors. Charming. William Matthews. MAYP

Because limits are set. Teika, *tr. fr. Japanese by* Hiroaki Sato. *Fr.* A Compendium of Good Tanka. FCEI

Because mine eyes are fashioned so. Vagabonds. "Marie Madelaine," *tr. by* Ferdinand E. Kappey. PeHV

Because mine eyes can never have their fill. Ballata: He Will Gaze upon Beatrice. Dante, *tr. by* Dante Gabriel Rossetti. AWP

Because my country is beautiful. A Guerrilla's Word. Javier Heraud, *tr. by* Maureen Ahern. Per

Because my grief seems quiet and apart. Robert Nathan. TrJP

Because my home village is close to Mount Yoshino. Teika, *tr. fr. Japanese by* Hiroaki Sato. *Fr.* A Compendium of Good Tanka. FCEI

Because my shelter must not be known. Cricket. No Ch'ŏn-myŭng, *tr. by* Ko Won. PBWP

Because no one has ever asked. Mythology. Michael Waters. MAYP

Because of body's hunger are we born. Sehnsucht. Anna Wickham. MoBrPo

Because of Clothes. Laura Riding. LiTA

Because of long depression and a sudden urge. Midnight and Ten Minutes. Shlomo Vinner, *tr. by* Laya Firestone *and* Howard Schwartz. VWA

Because of the change of key midway in "Come Back to Sorrento." Song of Reasons. Robert Pinsky. AnAn; HCAP

Because of the fragrance. Sakaki, or a Sacred Tree. Kagura, *tr. by* Hiroaki Sato. FCEI

Because of the slanderous tongues. Princess Tajima, *tr. fr. Japanese. Fr.* Manyo Shu. Ma

Because of the steepness. Mountain Brook. Elizabeth J. Coatsworth. RHPC

Because of Thy Great Bounty. Grace Noll Crowell. TrPWD

Because of you, I'm an heiress. A Daughter's House. Norma Hope Richman. GOYP

Because of your errant love for a maid. *The wife of* Isonokami Otomaro, *tr. fr. Japanese. Fr.* Manyo Shu. Ma

Because of your long neck. Deer. No Ch'ŏn-myŭng, *tr. by* Ko Won. PBWP

Because on the branch that is tapping my pane. In the Hospital. Arthur Guiterman. WGRP

Because one dead man does not make a summer. Brief Thunder at Sharpeville. Arthur Nortje. WMBCH

Because One Is Always Forgotten. Carolyn Forché. ER; MAYP

Because one's husband is different from one's self. Causes. Mona Van Duyn. SM

Because our being grows in mind. For the Opening of the William Dinsmore Briggs Room. Yvor Winters. CRP

Because peacocks moved like you. What He Said ("Because peacocks moved like you"). Peyanar, *tr. fr. Tamil by* A. K. Ramanujan. *Fr.* Nine on Happy Reunion, 2. PLW

Because Pearl's 95. Sitting Around Waiting for Your Cat to Die. Bonnie Jacobson. SoTCo

Because people's words are rampant and the rumor pains me. Princess Tajima, *tr. fr. Japanese by* Hiroaki Sato. *Fr.* Manyo Shu. FCEI

Because river-fog. Kiyowara Fukuyabu, *tr. fr. Japanese by* Arthur Waley. *Fr.* Shui Shu. AWP

Because river-fog. River-Fog. Kiyowara Fukuyabu, *tr. by* Arthur Waley. AWP; FaPON

Because she breathed too wildly in the sun. The Sixth Hell. Jerome Rothenberg. *Fr.* The Seven Hells of Jigoku Zoshi. NNaP

Because She Would Ask Me Why I Loved Her. Christopher John Brennan. CBAP

Because Sometimes You Can't Always Be So. Kenneth Patchen. NaP

Because spring's here. Yakamochi, *tr. fr. Japanese by* Burton Watson. *Fr.* Manyo Shu. FCEI

Because talk in the town. Why Rosalie Did It. Jim Wayne Miller. MOWH

Because the cithole hath a thousand tones. Soul-Severance. St. John Emile Clavering Hankin. FaBoPa

Because the light this morning is recondite. Cold Glow: Icehouses. David Wojahn. MAYP

Because the moon became my mother. Joseph Stroud. NPGG

Because the paint is not the shadow of branches. Camouflage. John Manifold. WaP

Because the papers meanly ignore me. Zishe Landau, *tr. by* Irving Feldman. PeBMYV

Because the pleasure-bird whistles after the hot wires. January 1939. Dylan Thomas. EAS

Because the sadness of the mode rests. For Dulcimer and Doubled Voice. Jordan Smith. KS

Because the shadows are sepia. 1930. Kathleen Fraser. NPGG

Because the warden is a cousin, my. Deer Hunt. Judson Jerome. RFM

Because the warm honey. Sanctuary. Bruce Boyd. NeAP

Because their fathers had been drilled. The Last Republicans. Austin Clarke. CIP

Because there are avenues. After Tonight. Gary Soto. NoAM

Because there is safety in derision. The Apparitions. W. B. Yeats. CMoP; LiTM

Because there was a man somewhere in a candystripe silk shirt. Homage to the Empress of the Blues. Robert Hayden. CNA; HCAP; LCAP; PoBA; PoNe

Because there was disquiet in the wind. This Poor Man. W. J. Gruffydd, *tr. by* Gwyn Jones. OBWVE
Because there was no other place. Flee on Your Donkey. Anne Sexton. NYBP
Because there's a Monarch butterfly/ on my foot. By Return Mail. Vivienne Joseph. ATNZ
Because they are not. The Deceptrices. William Carlos Williams. NYBP
Because they bloom, because I look at them. At the Opening of Chikubu's Collection of Haikai. Onitsura, *tr. fr. Japanese by* Hiroaki Sato. *Fr.* Twenty-three Hokku. FCEI
Because they were prisoners. The Pilots. Denise Levertov. InPS
Because They Were Very Poor That Winter. Kenneth Patchen. NaP
Because, this month, when napkins, pretty spoons. Roman Presents. Martial, *tr. by* James Michie. OBCP
Because this village. Tameyo, *tr. by* Steven D. Carter. WFTW
Because thou canst not see. The Philosopher to His Mistress. Robert Bridges. LiTM; PoEL-5
Because Thou Did'st Give. Harry Morris. CRP
Because time is a fiction in the mind. Miklos Radnoti. Willis Barnstone. VWA
Because time kept. Pre Domina. Jean Lipkin. PeSA
Because time subdues sharp angles and closes wounds. Burial. Paulin Joachim, *tr. by* Oliver Bernard. TTY
Because We Are Not Taken Seriously. Stephen Dunn. KS
Because we breathe the same birds of sand. Brotherhood. José Luis Vega, *tr. by* Julio Marzán. InW
Because we do. Together. Paul Engle. RHPC
Because We Do Not See. *Unknown.* BLRP
Because we live in the browning season. Kopis'taya. Paula Gunn Allen. HATNAP; STE
Because we suspected/ the pillow would say "I know." Lady Ise, *tr. by* Etsuko Terasaki *and* Irma Brandeis. AIW; BoWoP
Because we were baffled. The White Bird. Wilfred Watson. MoCV
Because you are going. Emily Dickinson. MoAmPo
Because you are simple people, kindly and romantic. Fourth Act. Robinson Jeffers. LiTA; WaP
Because You Asked about the Line between Prose and Poetry. Howard Nemerov. WeW
Because you died in autumn. Notes for an Elegy: for John Gardner. Linda Pastan. AnAn
Because you have increased my hurt. The Storm. Robert David Cohen. NYBP
Because you have shared the white bread. Your Body's Bread. Andras Fodor, *tr. by* Jascha Kessler. FOC
Because you have thrown off your prelate lord. On the New Forcers of Conscience Under the Long Parliament. Milton. FaBoPV; NAEL-1; Son
Because you once beat me up. Melon-Slaughterer; or, A Sick Man's Praise for a Well Woman. Robert Peters. BXAP
Because you passed, and now are not. A Ballad of Heroes. Austin Dobson. OHIP
Becket, *sels.* Tennyson.
  Duet. GBL
  "Over! the sweet summer closes." GBL
Becket's Diadem. *Unknown.* ACP
Beckett Kit, The. Linda Gregg. AmPA
Beckie, my luve!—What is't, ye twa-faced tod? George Campbell Hay. OxBS
Beckon Me, Ye Cuillins. K. G. P. Hendrie. PoSH
Becoming a Dad. Edgar A. Guest. BLPL; PoLF
Becoming a Nun. Erica Jong. MAYP
Becoming an Eskimo isn't hard once you must. Bum's Rush. Michael Dransfield. CBAP
Bed, The. Ray DiPalma. LP
Bed, The. A. D. Hope. NoAM; OxBC; OxBSP
Bed, The. James Merrill. NePoEA
Bed, The. Dennis Saleh. NeAC
Bed, The. Karl Shapiro. NYBP
Bed Book, The, *sels.* Sylvia Plath.
  "Most beds are beds." PYC
  "These are the beds." RHPC
Bed creaks, The. Senryu. Pat Nolan. UL
Bed in Summer. Robert Louis Stevenson. GoJo; NBLV; OxBChV
Bed of Campanula, A. "John Crichton." CaP
Bed Time. Peter Davison. UnPo
Bed-time. Thomas Hood. BoTP
Bed-Time. L. Alma Tadema. BoTP
Bed without a Woman, A. Raymond Souster. ErPo
Bedford Level. John Dyer. *Fr.* The Fleece, II. FaBoPP
Bedlam; a Poem on His Majesty's Happy Escape from His German Dominions, *sel. Unknown.*
  "What mean these loud aerial cracks I hear?" NQEC

Bedlam Hills. Vivian Smith. PoAu-2
Bedlamite, The. Thomas Mozeen. NOEC
Bedouin Song. Bayard Taylor. AA; AnAmPo; FaBoBe
Bedouin springs from his horse, A. Into the Book. Martin Grossman. VWA
Bedouins of the Skies, The. James Benjamin Kenyon. AA
Bedpost, The. Robert Graves. SO
Bedraggled Ostrich. Takamura Kotaro, *tr. fr. Japanese by* Geoffrey Bownas *and* Anthony Thwaite. PeBJV
Bedrock. Gary Snyder. PoE
Bedroom Window, The. Fleur Adcock. ATNZ
Beds are made close to a wall flat. Saturday Morning. Richard Howard. ErPo
Beds of Fleur-de-Lys, The. Charlotte Perkins Gilman. AA
Bedtime. Eleanor Farjeon. RAR
Bedtime. Denise Levertov. IHMS; NaP; SM; TwCP
Bedtime Story. Dannie Abse. KS
Bedtime Story. Lou Lipsitz. VGW
Bedtime Story. George MacBeth. MoP; NePoEA-2; SoSe
Bedtime Story, A. Robert Mezey. NePoEA
Bedtime Story. Lilian Moore. NTCP; RAR
Bedtime Story. Charles Simic. AnAn
Bedtime Story for My Son. Peter Redgrove. NePoEA-2
Bee, The. James Dickey. SoSe
Bee, The. Emily Dickinson. GN; MoAB; MoAmPo
Bee, The. John Fandel. GoYe
Bee, The. Charles Fitz-Geffry. *Fr.* Sir Francis Drake. EIL
Bee, The. Henry Hawkins. ACP
Bee. X. J. Kennedy. OBCA
Bee and the Petunia, The. Katherine Hoskins. ErPo
Bee his burnished carriage, a. Emily Dickinson. NOBA
Bee! I'm expecting you! Emily Dickinson. SO; SOTW; TTTS
Bee in a bloom on the long hand of a floral, A. Keep in a Cool Place. Allen Curnow. ATNZ
Bee-keeper kissed me, The. *Unknown, tr. by* W. S. Merwin. BoWoP
Bee-logic: each small life. Kindergarten. Dennis Schmitz. NPGG
Bee Meeting, The. Sylvia Plath. HCAP; InPS; PPP; WPE
Bee-Orchis, The. Andrew Young. ChTr
Bee Song. Carl Sandburg. PDV
Bee, the Ant, and the Sparrow, The. Nathaniel Cotton. OxBChV
Bee upon a briar-rose hung, A. The Flesh-Fly and the Bee. Coventry Patmore. FaBoEE
Bee Wassail. *Unknown.* OBET
Bee-Wisp, The. Charles Tennyson Turner. FM
Beech, The. Andrew Young. BoNaP
Beech Leaves. James Reeves. OnUR
Beech leaves caught in a moment gust, The. Departure. Edmund Blunden. OxBSP
Beehive. Jean Toomer. IDB; PoBA; TTY
Beehive Cell. Richard Murphy. CIP
Beekeeper's Daughter, The. Sylvia Plath. IHMS
Beela by the Sea. Leroy F. Jackson. RHPC
Been in the Pen So Long. *Unknown.* AS
Been on the hummer since ninety-four. A. R. U. *Unknown.* AS
Beeny Cliff. Thomas Hardy. OBNC; RB
Beer. George Arnold. AA; OBAL
Beer, *sel.* Charles Stuart Calverley. BXAP; CenHV; FaBoCo
  "But hark! a sound is stealing on my ear." FiBHP
Beer Bottle. Ted Kooser. SM
Beer Drops. Melba Joyce Boyd. BlSi
Bees, The. Lola Ridge. FaPON
Bees and a honeycomb in the dried head of a horse. In Tall Grass. Carl Sandburg. PoA
Bees and lilies there were. Bring the Day! Theodore Roethke. CRP
Bees are black, with gilt surcingles. Emily Dickinson. NAAL-1
Bees Awater. Robert Morgan. WeW
Bees, bees of paradise. Bee Wassail. *Unknown.* OBET
Bees build around red liver. A Poor Christian Looks at the Ghetto. Czeslaw Milosz, *tr. by the author.* NIP; PwPP
Bees build in the crevices, The. The Stare's Nest by My Window. W. B. Yeats. *Fr.* Meditations in Time of Civil War, VI. BIrV; GTBS-P; InPS; LiTB; NOBE
  ("Bees in the crevices, The.") FaBoPV
Bees have four wings. Wings. Aileen Fisher. RAR
Bees in the clover are making honey, and I am making my hay, The. The Mower in Ohio. John James Piatt. AA
Bees in the crevices, The. William Butler Yeats. *See* Meditations in Time of Civil War: Stare's Nest by My Window, The.
Bees in the late summer sun. Bee Song. Carl Sandburg. PDV
Bees inside Me. Laura Chester. NPGG
Bees over the gooseberry bushes. The Bees. Lola Ridge. FaPON

Bees, six tiny legs and wings all lovely. What She Said ("Bees, six tiny legs and wings all lovely"). Orampokiyar, *tr. fr. Tamil by* A. K. Ramanujan. *Fr.* Five on the Riverside Cane, 1. PLW

Bees that have been hiving above the church pond, The. James Keir Baxter. *Fr.* Jerusalem Sonnets, II. ATNZ; PeNZ

Beethoven. Zbigniew Herbert, *tr. fr. Polish by* John Carpenter *and* Bogdana Carpenter. AnAn

Beethoven. Henrietta Cordelia Ray. CBWP-3

Beethoven. John Hall Wheelock. PoA

Beethoven's Death Mask. Stephen Spender. OxBTC

Beetle, The, *sel.* James Whitcomb Riley.
"Shrilling locust slowly sheathes, The." FaPON

Beetle loves his unpretending track, The. Wordsworth. *Fr.* Liberty. FaBoCo; FiBHP; Par

Beetle on the Shasta Daylight. Shirley Kaufman. NYBP; WPE

Beetlebombs make jelly jam. Makers. Nancy Dingman Watson. RAR

Beets Poem, The ("Beets: now there's a subject"). Katharyn Machan Aal. ER

Before. Albert Goldbarth. MAYP

Before. William Ernest Henley. *Fr.* In Hospital, IV. BrPo; MoBrPo

Before/ and After. Jewel C. Latimore. JB

Before/ I opened my mouth. On Reading Poems to a Senior Class at South High. David Chapman Berry. SoSe

Before a bomb buried. Salman. Tawfiq Zayyad, *tr. by* Sharif Elmusa *and* Charles Doria. MAP

Before a Cashier's Window in a Department Store. James Wright. *See* Beautiful cashier's white face has risen once more, The.

Before a Corpse. Manuel Acuña, *tr. fr. Spanish by* Samuel Beckett. MexPo

Before a Fall. Geoffrey Grigson. EAS

Before a Funeral. Lauris Edmond. ATNZ

Before a Journey. Robert Wells. NPo

Before a Saint's Picture. Walter Savage Landor. OxBChV

Before Action. Leon Gellert. CBAP

Before Action. William Noel Hodgson. WGRP

Before Agincourt. Shakespeare. *See* King Henry V: Now Entertain Conjecture of a Time.

Before an audible sound, an almost recognizable. Prelude to Memorial Song: 100 Years Later. Phillip William George. VoR

Before an Old Painting of the Crucifixion. N. Scott Momaday. QFR

Before autumn's swift clouds the moon bounds to and fro. Early Darkness. Gyula Illyés, *tr. by* William Jay Smith. MHuP

Before balance, before counting, before. Man Dancing with a Baby. Susan Stewart. NAmP

Before Bannockburn. John Barbour. *Fr.* The Bruce. OxBS

Before Bannockburn. Burns. *See* Scots Wha Hae [wi' Wallace Bled].

Before Breakup on the Chena outside Fairbanks. David McElroy. Psk

Before Breughel the Elder. Aleksander Wat, *tr. fr. Polish by* Czeslaw Milosz. PwPP

Before Chia-yu Pass gathers the evening fog. Upon Arriving at Ili, Recalling What I Saw on the Road. Hung Liang-chi, *tr. by* Irving Lo. WFTU

Before Chilembwe Tree. Jack A. Mapanje. WMBCH

Before Dawn. Horace Hamilton. NYBP

Before dawn i rose thirsty. Other. Lance Henson. VoR

Before dawn passing Chiang-k'ou town. Fan Tseng-hsiang, *tr. fr. Chinese by* J. P. Seaton. *Fr.* Random Verses from a Boat, IV. WFTU

Before Day. Siegfried Sassoon. WGRP

Before daybreak, before dew breaks. Youth. Barend Toerien, *tr. by the author.* PeSA

Before Death. Alfonso Quijada Urías, *tr. fr. Spanish by* Barbara Paschke. Vol

Before Disaster. Yvor Winters. HoPM; QFR

Before entering I drink a glass. Visit to the Juvenile Penitentiary. Hermann Gail, *tr. by* Beth Bjorklund. CoAuP

Before Gereint, foe's affliction. Gereint ab Erbin. *Unknown, tr. by* Joseph P. Clancy. OBWVE

Before Gion Shrine, determined to drive away poverty. Nakajima Soin, *tr. fr. Chinese by* Burton Watson. *Fr.* Miscellaneous Songs of the Four Seasons East of the Kamo. JLIC-2

Before God's footstool to confess. Thy Best. Henry Cole. PWR

Before he died. Equena, *tr. by* James Koller. STP

Before he turned to stone. Coma. Christopher Logue. NPo

Before Him weltered like a shoreless sea. Judgment Day. William Dean Howells. AA

Before history. Brightness. Heather McHugh. GeTw

Before I am completely shriven. Single Vision. Stanley Kunitz. CAPP

Before I began life this time. Last Poem. Ted Berrigan. UL

Before I began to burn. Interval with Fire. Dorothy Livesay. CaP

Before I called him by name. Flower. Ruth Kim Chun-soo, *tr. by* Koh Chang-soo. ACKP

Before I could tell time, I'd sit and wait. The Cuckoo Clock. Maura Stanton. PPR

Before I crossed the sound. The Paps of Jura. Andrew Young. PoSH

Before I Die. Mihály Váci, *tr. fr. Hungarian by* Alan Dixon. MHuP

Before I drove Davy to nursery school. To the Woodville Depot. D. C. Berry. MT

Before I got my eye put out. Emily Dickinson. LiTA; LiTM; PoE

Before I had a face. The Man Who Buys Hides. Dennis Schmitz. LCAP

Before I Knocked and Flesh Let Enter. Dylan Thomas. FaBoTw; RB

Before I know it, winter and spring depart. Lamenting the Dead. P'an Yüeh, *tr. by* Burton Watson. CoBCP

Before I laughed with him. What She Said. Maturai Eruttalan Centamputan, *tr. by* A. K. Ramanujan. BoLoP

Before I melt. The Snowflake. Walter de la Mare. RHPC; TSS

Before I set sail, I will not fail. Skin the Goat's Curse on Carey. *Unknown.* FTBV; TW

Before I sigh my last gasp, let me breathe. The Will. John Donne. EBEV; LiTB; MePo

Before I Was Born. Solomon ibn Gabriol, *tr. fr. Hebrew by* David Goldstein. TOF

Before I woke I knew her gone. Robert Nichols. *Fr.* The Flower of Flame. OBMV

Before I woke, the customed thews. Male Torso. Christopher Middleton. NePoEA-2

Before I'm awake, the dreamlike. If the Cardinals Were like Us. Sandra McPherson. AnAn

Before Life and After. Thomas Hardy. FaBoRV

Before lying in the churchyard you poise on outstretched wings. De Cultu Virginis. Nanni Balestrini, *tr. by* Lawrence R. Smith. NItP

Before man came to blow it right. The Aim Was Song. Robert Frost. NoP; SoSe

Before me on my track. Kisakibe Isoshima, *tr. fr. Japanese.* *Fr.* Manyo Shu. Ma

Before meat/ O Thou, who kindly doth provide. A Poet's Grace. Burns. TrPWD

Before Mine Eye. George Gascoigne. *Fr.* Gascoigne's Memories. Son

Before mine eye to feele my greedy will. George Gascoigne. AAS

Before morning you shall be here. Alba. Samuel Beckett. BIrV

Before my back was bent I was eloquent. *Unknown, tr. fr. Welsh by* Gwyn Jones. *Fr.* Hateful Old Age. OBWVE

Before my bright window. Winter. Mani Leib, *tr. by* Keith Bosley. VWA

Before my drift-wood fire I sit. Burning Drift-Wood. Whittier. MOS

Before my face the picture hangs. Upon the Image of Death. Robert Southwell. CH; EIL; NOBE; OBD, *sh. vers.*; OBSC

Before my feet the ploughshare rolls the earth. Winter Ploughing. William Everson. NU

Before my goblet of wine, I watch half the sun go down. Climbing Ch'ing-shuo Tower at Yün-chung. Chu Yi-tsun, *tr. by* Irving Lo. WFTU

Before my lady's window gay. Medieval Norman Song ("Before my lady's window gay"). *Unknown, tr. by* John Addington Symonds. AWP

Before my light goes out for ever if God should give me a choice of graces. Impenitentia Ultima. Ernest Dowson. BrPo

Before Olympus. John Gould Fletcher. MoAmPo

Before our eyes a pageant rolled. After the Centennial. Christopher Pearse Cranch. PAH

Before our skates had touched the pond that day. On Cedar Lake, 1957. Ruth F. Brin. TSL

Before Parting. Swinburne. NOBVV

Before Passover. Seymour Mayne. NOBC

Before Play. Vasco Popa, *tr. fr. Serbo-Croatian by* Anne Pennington. *Fr.* Games. RB

Before priests transubstantiate. At the Body Club. X. J. Kennedy. SoTCo

Before Rereading Shakespeare's Sonnets. T. Sturge Moore. BrPo

Before St. Anno. A Good Bishop. *Unknown, tr. by* William Taylor. WGRP

Before Salamis. William Bedell Stanford. NeIP

Before Sentence Is Passed. R. P. Blackmur. LiTA

Before she has her floor swept. Portrait by a Neighbor. Edna St. Vincent Millay. FaPON; MoShBr; OBCA; PDV

Before she saw him in the wood. The Quickening. Stella Weston Tuttle. GoYe

Before sixteen. First Love. Carl Lindner. TSL

Before Sleep. Fleur Adcock. *Fr.* Night-Piece, II. PeNZ

Before Sleep. Anne Ridler. CN

Before Sleeping. *Unknown.* *See* Matthew, Mark, Luke, and John/ Bless the bed that I lie on.

Before Spring. P. A. Ropes. BoTP

Before Suicide. "Sahir Ludhianvi," *tr. fr. Urdu by* Mahmood Jamal. PBMUP

Before sunrise. Song for My Name. Linda Hogan. STE

Before Sunrise in Winter. Edward Rowland Sill. AA
Before the/ red blossoms. Masaoka Shiki, *tr. fr. Japanese by* Burton Watson. *Fr.* Fifteen Haiku. FCEI
Before the Actual Cold. Ray A. Young Bear. VoR
Before the Anæsthetic; or, A Real Fright. Sir John Betjeman. SeCePo
Before the barn-door crowing. John Gay. *Fr.* The Beggar's Opera, II, i. ErPo; OxBSP; PBBP; PoEL-3
Before the Bath. Corinna Marsh. RAR
Before the Beginning of Years. Swinburne. *Fr.* Atalanta in Calydon. FaFP; HeIP; LiTB; NAEL-2; NoP
(Chorus: "Before the beginning of years.") EBVV; OBEV
(Man.) TrGrPo
Before the Big Storm. William Stafford. NaP
Before the Birth of One of Her Children. Anne Bradstreet. BoWoP; MAT; NAAL-1; NAs; NOBA; WPE; WPOW
Before the blond horsemen rode into our village. An Event. Edward Field. CoAP
Before the bright sun rises over the hill. The Gleaner. Jane Taylor. OxBChV
Before the Carnival. Thom Gunn. NePoEA
Before the [*or* a] Cashier's Window in a Department Store. James Wright. MAT; NYBP
Before the cathedral in grandeur rose. How the Great Guest Came. Edwin Markham. BeLS; BLPA; BLPL
Before the day ends. The Last Farewell. Miyazawa Kenji, *tr. by* Hiroaki Sato. FCEI
Before the day is everywhere. Martha Blake. Austin Clarke. TIRV
Before the Day of Wrath. Louis Johnson. *Fr.* Four Poems from the Strontium Age, I. ATNZ
Before the Fall. Milton. *See* Paradise Lost: She, as a veil down to the slender waist.
Before the falling summer sun. Musings. William Barnes. HAP; NOBE; OBNC
Before the Feast of Shushan. Anne Spencer. BANP; BlSi
Before the Flowers of Friendship Faded Faded, *sel.* Gertrude Stein. "I love my love with a v." PeHV
Before the gate of Little Su. Bamboo Branch Song of West Lake. Yang Wei-chen, *tr. by* Jonathan Chaves. CoBLCP
Before the gate, served up on a platter. The Yomyo Stupa. Zotan, *tr. by* Lucien Stryk *and* Takashi Ikemoto. ZPCJ
Before the glare o' dawn I rise. The Shearer's Wife. Louis Esson. PoAu-1
Before the gods that made the gods. G. K. Chesterton. *Fr.* The Ballad of the White Horse. ACP
Before the Great Void, we burn the fragrant incense. To Purity and Truth. *Unknown, tr. by* William C. White. TrJP
Before the Last Battle. *Unknown, tr. fr. Irish by* Thomas Kinsella. *Fr.* The Táin. NOIV
Before the light of evening can go out. Charles Brasch. *Fr.* Home Ground, XIII. PeNZ
Before the Mirror, *sel.* Swinburne. "Glad, but not flush'd with gladness." OBEV
Before the Monkey's Cage. Edna Becker. RAR
Before the Mountain. Elizabeth Libbey. AmPA
Before the Mountains Were Brought Forth. Christina Rossetti. *Fr.* Later Life, I. Son
Before the Pacific. Blanca Varela, *tr. fr. Spanish by* Willis Barnstone. BoWoP
Before the Paling of the Stars. Christina Rossetti. TrCP
Before the Poetry Reading. Louis Simpson. OxBC
Before the press scarce one could see. To His Book. Robert Herrick. OxBSP
Before the Rain. Thomas Bailey Aldrich. GN
Before the Rain. Amélie Rives. AA
Before the Roman came to Rye or out to Severn strode. The Rolling English Road. G. K. Chesterton. FaBoCh; NOBE; NOBL; OBEV; OBMV; OxBTC
Before the seas again divide. Walter Adolphe Roberts. PVCV
Before the Shrine of the Filial Marquis. Inscribed on a Painting. Ni Tsan, *tr. by* Jonathan Chaves. CoBLCP
Before the sixth day of the next new year. On the Cards and Dice. Sir Walter Ralegh. RB
(Prognostication upon Cards and Dice, A.) SiPS
Before the solemn bronze Saint Gaudens made. An Ode in Time of Hesitation. William Vaughn Moody. AnAmPo; OxBA; PAH
Before the starry threshold of Jove's court. Comus. Milton. OAEL-1
Before the Statue of Apollo. Saul Tchernichowsky, *tr. fr. Hebrew by* L. V. Snowman. TrJP
Before the Storm. Richard Dehmel, *tr. fr. German by* Ludwig Lewisohn. AWP
Before the Storm. Kenneth O. Hanson. CoAP
Before the Stuff Comes Down. Gary Snyder. HeIP

Before the sun goes down. Astrid Hjertenaes Andersen, *tr. by* Nadia Christensen. BoWoP
Before the Sun Rises. Sarah Kirsch, *tr. by German by* Gordon Brotherston *and* Gisela Brotherston. OV
Before the sun rose at yester-dawn. Kitty Bhan. Edward Walsh. ACP
Before the Thaw. John Gill. NeAC
Before the thing begins we have. Poetry Reading. Vernon Scannell. NOBL
Before the tigerish soldiers leave, tigerish bailiffs arrive. A Lament for Those Who Hanged Themselves. Cheng Chen, *tr. by* William Schultz. WFTU
Before the War. Marilyn Hacker. AmPA
Before the war. From Our Album. Lawson Fusao Inada. AmPA
Before the war all that was different. Magic. Judith Herzberg, *tr. by the author.* DuIn
Before the World Was Made. W. B. Yeats. GTBS-P
Before Their Tanks. Tawfiq Zayyad, *tr. fr. Arabic by* Sharif Elmusa *and* Charles Doria. MAP
Before, there is water. Water. Edmond Jabès, *tr. by* Anthony Rudolf. VWA
Before, there was one. Birth. Constance Urdang. VWA
Before They Made Things Be Alive They Spoke. Lucario Cuevish, *tr. fr. Luiseño Indian by* Jerome Rothenberg. STP
Before they ripen into diffused spirits. Katerina Anghelaki-Rooke, *tr. by* Kimon Friar. NU
Before this feminine landscape I feel. Ecstasy. Paul Eluard, *tr. by* Michael Benedikt. POS
Before this fever of the almost cold. Mirror. Peter De Vries. PoA
Before this longing. Her Longing. Theodore Roethke. NAAL-2; NU
Before this tyme in Kentschire it befell. The Unicornis Tale. *Unknown. Fr.* The Talis of the Fyve Bestis. OxBLMV
Before thy door too long of late. III, 10. Extremum Tanain. Horace, *tr. fr. Latin by* Austin Dobson. *Fr.* Odes. AWP
Before Vespasian's regal throne. Death of Gaudentis. "Harriet Annie." WBLP
Before Vicksburg. George Henry Boker. PAH
Before Waterloo. Thomas Hardy. *See* Dynasts, The: Eve of Waterloo, The.
Before we know, the year passes, so many stumbles! Sitting in a Circle, Speaking Our Thoughts. Michizane, *tr. by* Burton Watson. JLIC-1
Before we shall again behold. Endimion Porter and Olivia. Sir William Davenant. MeLP; MePo; NOBE
(Song: "Before we shall again behold.") MeLP
(Song: Endimion Porter and Olivia.) OBS
Before we've had our fill. Narihira, *tr. fr. Japanese by* Burton Watson. *Fr.* Kokin Shu. FCEI
Before you I have cried in vain. To a Man of the World. Betty Paoli, *tr. by* Susan L. Cocalis *and* Gerlinde Geiger. DMG
Before you know what years are made of they are lost. Little Girl Blue. "Yvonne." TSL
Before you step out. I Hope I Don't Have You Next Semester, But. Edwin S. Godsey. HoPM
Before you were conceived. The Miracle. Maureen Hawkins. AIW; WS
Before your mouth was fringed with hair. Epigram: On a Slanderer. Martial. PeHV
Before Your Waking. Anna Gréki, *tr. fr. French by* Anita Barrows. WPOW
Beg a ten cent mista. Version. Dennis Scott. PBCV
Beg-Innish. J. M. Synge. MoBrPo
Beg Parding. *Unknown.* ChTr
Bega. Marjorie Pickthall. CaP
Began drinking sake at fifteen. Kikaku, *tr. fr. Japanese by* Hiroaki Sato. *Fr.* Thirty-three Hokku. FCEI
Begetting. Dorothea Spears. PeSA
Begetting of Cain, The. Hyam Plutzik. VWA
Beggar, The. Muhammad al-Ghuzzi, *tr. fr. Arabic by* May Jayyusi *and* John Heath-Stubbs. MAP
Beggar, The. Adrian Mitchell. FaBoTw
Beggar, The. Thomas Moss. NOEC
Beggar. Murano Shiro, *tr. fr. Japanese by* Geoffrey Bownas *and* Anthony Thwaite. PeBJV
Beggar, The. *Unknown.* OBET
Beggar at the Gate, The. Ian Wedde. PeNZ
Beggar Boy, The. Cecil Frances Alexander. OxBChV
"Beggar," he sayes. Little John a Begging. *Unknown.* ESPB
Beggar I came and cried my say, A. Mohammad Taqi Mir, *tr. by* Ahmed Ali. GoT
Beggar in patched robe stands in my doorway, A. Liu-K'o-chuang, *tr. fr. Chinese by* Burton Watson. *Fr.* Ten Poems Recording Things that Happened at the Ye. CoBCP
Beggar-Laddie, The. *Unknown.* ESPB
Beggar Maid, The. Tennyson. BeLS; BoTP; OnMSP

Beggar Man, The. Lucy Aikin. OxBChV
Beggar shouts his martial wares, The. The Beggar. Adrian Mitchell. FaBoTw
Beggar to Beggar Cried. W. B. Yeats. CMoP; NoAM
Beggar to Burgher. Arthur Rex Dugard Fairburn. PeNZ
Beggar to Mab, the Fairy [or Fairie] Queen, The. Robert Herrick. CaPo; WSC
Beggar to the graveyard hied, A. Poverty. *Unknown, tr. fr. Sanskrit by* Arthur Ryder. *Fr.* The Panchatantra. AWP
Beggar Wind, The. Mary Austin. BoNaP
Beggar Woman, The. William King. NOEC
Beggar Woman of Naples, The. Max Jacob, *tr. fr. French by* John Ashbery. RHTwFP
Beggarman's Song, A, *sel. Unknown, tr. fr. Gaelic by* Frank O'Connor. "Would God that I and my darling." WTO
Beggars. Francis Davidson. CH
Beggars. Ella Higginson. AA
Beggars and Kings. W. S. Merwin. AnAn
Beggars Are Coming to Town, The. Mother Goose. *See* Hark, hark, the dogs do bark.
Beggars have no one, The. Mirza Mohammad Rafi Sauda, *tr. by* Ahmed Ali. GoT
Beggars in the stories of old. Fairy Tales. Itzig Manger, *tr. by* Miriam Waddington. VWA
Beggar's Opera, The ("If poverty be a title to poetry, I am sure nobody can dispute mine."), *sels.* John Gay. OAEL-1
  "Fox may steal your hens, sir, A." *Fr.* I, i. NOEC
    (Soldier and a Sailor, A.) TEP
  "Since laws were made for ev'ry degree." *Fr.* III, xiii. NOEC
  Highwaymen, The. *Fr.* II, i. WiR
  "If the heart of a man is deprest [or depressed] with cares." *Fr.* II, ii. ELP; EnLoPo; HeIP; NAEL-1
    (Would You Have a Young Virgin?.) TEP
  Modes of the Court, The. *Fr.* III, iv. HeIP
  "O Polly, you might have toy'd and kist." *Fr.* I, i. EnLoPo
  "Before the barn-door crowing." *Fr.* II, i. ErPo; OxBSP; PBBP; PoEL-3
  "Can love be controlled by advice?." *Fr.* I, viii. OxBSP
  "If any wench Venus's girdle wear." *Fr.* I, i. PoEL-3
  "Thus when the swallow, seeking prey." *Fr.* II, ii. PoEL-3
  "Were I laid on Greenland's coast." *Fr.* I, i. EnLoPo; NAEL-1; OxBoLi; PoEL-3
    (Macheath and Polly.) NOEC
    (Over the Hills and Far Away.) NOBE; PrIm
  What Shall I Do to Show How Much I Love Her?. *Fr.* I, vii. TEP
  Youth's the Season. *Fr.* II, i. WiR
    (Youth and Love.) NOBE
Beggar's Serenade. John Heath-Stubbs. BoLoP; ErPo
Begging A.I.D. David Rubadiri. WMBCH
Begging Another, on Colour of Mending the Former. Ben Jonson. *Fr.* A Celebration of Charis in Ten Lyrick Peeces. PoEL-2; SeCP
Begging food, I went to the city. Dialogue in a Dream. Ryokan, *tr. by* Burton Watson. FCEI; JLIC-2
Begin and end in inhaling exhaling. Too Short. Meir Wieseltier, *tr. by* Warren Bargad *and* Stanley F. Chyet. IP
Begin before birth with swept-back fins. The Matin Pandemoniums. Richard Eberhart. NYBP
Begin by parting your hair. Parting; a Game. Lynn Sukenick. NMM
Begin, ephebe, by perceiving the idea. Wallace Stevens. *Fr.* Notes toward a Supreme Fiction. NOBA
Begin Summer. Ingrid Jonker, *tr. fr. Afrikaans by* Jack Cope *and* Uys Krige. PeSA
Begin to charm, and as thou strok'st mine ears. To Music. Robert Herrick. CaPo
Begin unto my God with timbrels. With Timbrels. Bible, Apocrypha. *Fr.* Judith. TrJP
Beginner, The. Kipling. *Fr.* Epitaphs of the War, 1914–1918. FaBoTw
Beginner/ Perpetual beginner. What Can I Tell My Bones? Theodore Roethke. AmPP; NOBA
Beginners. Walt Whitman. AA
Beginning. Jacob Glatstein, *tr. fr. Yiddish by* Benjamin *and* Barbara Harshav. AYP
Beginning. Kurt Klinger, *tr. fr. German by* Beth Bjorklund. CoAuP
Beginning. Alden Nowlan. NeAC; NIP; NOBC
Beginning. Marcos Rodríguez Frese, *tr. fr. Spanish by* Julio Marzán. InW
Beginning. David Rokeah, *tr. by* Robert Mezey. VWA
Beginning, The. Wallace Stevens. VGW
Beginning/ each day. Peter Zumpf, *tr. by* Beth Bjorklund. CoAuP
Beginning and an End, A. Edouard Roditi. VWA
Beginning by Example, *sel.* Christopher Gilbert.
  Blue. FYAP

Beginning explains since dew the day, The. Since Dew the Day. Hugues C. Pernath, *tr. by* James S. Holmes. DuIn
Beginning I will praise a fine beginning. The Goods She Can Carry: Canticle of Her Basket Made of Reeds. Gibbons Ruark. MAYP
Beginning in half darkness. The Morning Track. Edward Parone. NYBP
Beginning my fortieth year. Beyond the Presidency. Morgan Gibson. FF
Beginning My Studies. Walt Whitman. NAAL-1; OxBA
Beginning of a Long Poem on Why I Burned the City, The. Lawrence Benford. NBP; TTY
Beginning of an Undergraduate Poem. *Unknown.* FaBoCo
Beginning of art, The. Basho, *tr. by* Geoffrey Bownas *and* Anthony Thwaite. PeBJV
Beginning of autumn, The. Basho, *tr. by* Geoffrey Bownas *and* Anthony Thwaite. PeBJV
Beginning of Love. Tanikawa Shuntaro, *tr. fr. Japanese by* Hiroaki Sato. FCEI
Beginning of Spring—A Stroll with My Wife. Hsü Chün-ch'ien, *tr. fr. Chinese by* Burton Watson. CoBCP
Beginning of the Day, The. Lin Huan-ch'ang, *tr. fr. Chinese by* Dominic Cheung. IFON
Beginning of the End, The. Jon Stallworthy. OxBC
Beginning, The: Some landscape & words about nature. Kirk Lonegren's Home Movie Taking Place Just North of Prince George, with Sound. Sharon Thesen. NOBC
Beginning Speech. "Adunis," *tr. fr. Arabic by* Lena Jayyusi *and* John Heath-Stubbs. MAP
Beginning storm sets my blood racing. Lives. Cyril Dabydeen. BrSi
Beginning the Year at Rosebud, S.D. Roberta Hill. CDW
Beginning to Autumn: A Poem to Send to Tzu-yu. Su Tung-p'o, *tr. fr. Chinese by* Burton Watson. CoBCP
Beginning to dangle beneath. In the Marble Quarry. James Dickey. AmFN; NoP
Beginning to End. Carla Harryman. LP
Beginning to Squall. May Swenson. RFM
Beginning with C in the dank school basement. Mr. Brunt. Robert Siegel. GeTw
Beginnings. Erez Biton, *tr. fr. Hebrew by* Judith Katz. VWA
Beginnings, *sel.* Robert Hayden.
  "Plowdens, Finns." CNA
Beginnings. *Unknown, tr. fr. Mayan by* Munro Edmonson. *Fr.* The Popol Vuh. STP
Beginnings of Faith, The. Sir Lewis Morris. WGRP
Beginnings of the Fugitive, The. Louis Aragon, *tr. fr. French by* Joachim Neugroschel. POS
Begins the crying. Guitar. Federico García Lorca, *tr. by* Keith Waldrop. InPK
Begins with the *ooo ooo* of a mourning dove. Holy Thursday. Charles Wright. AnAn; GeTw
Begot by butchers, but by bishops bred. On Cardinal Wolsey. *Unknown.* FaBoCo
Begotten by the meeting of rock with rock. Sea Holly. Conrad Aiken. LiTM
Begotten of the Spleen. Charles Simic. LCAP
Begun before Easter. . ./ Sign of the Fish. Thomas McGrath. *Fr.* Letter to an Imaginary Friend, Part Two, VI, 4. NNaP
Behave, my sorrow! let's have no more scenes. Meditation. Baudelaire, *tr. by* Richard Howard
Behaviorally. Anselm Hollo. UL
Behaviour of Fish in an Egyptian Tea Garden. Keith Douglas. FaBoMo; OBTV; RB
Behaviour of Money. Bernard Spencer. LiTB
Behind a cloud of green gauze is her jadelike face. Willow Branches. Chang Pi, *tr. by* Lois Fusek. ATF
Behind a web of bottles, bales. The Gombeen. Joseph Campbell. BIrV
Behind an unfrequented glade. Matthew Prior. *Fr.* The Turtle and the Sparrow. PBBP
Behind Bars. Hugo Claus, *tr. fr. Dutch by* Theo Hermans. DuIn
Behind Bars, *sel.* Fadwa Tuqan, *tr. fr. Arabic by* Hatem Hussaini. "My mother's phantom hovers here." *Fr.* I. OV
Behind glass, my room is neat. Out of Chaos Out of Order Out. Michele Roberts. BrRo
Behind Grandma's House. Gary Soto. NAmP
Behind her not the quivering of a leaf. Circe. A. D. Hope. PPP
Behind him lay the gray Azores. Columbus. Joaquin Miller. AA; AnAmPo; BeLS; FaBoBe; FaFP; FaPON; GN; MOS; OHFP; OPP; PAH; PPP
Behind him spreads the horizoned shore. On a Landscape of Sestos. Carlos Baker. *Fr.* A Visit to the Art Gallery. EyDe
Behind him the hotdogs split and drizzled. Suicide off Egg Rock. Sylvia Plath. PPP
Behind his dinner jacket. He's Doing Natural Life. Conyus. PoBA

Behind its snout like a huge button. Photo of the Author with a Favorite Pig. William Matthews. BLA

Behind King's Chapel what the earth has kept. At the Indian Killer's Grave. Robert Lowell. NOBA; VGW

Behind me—dips eternity. Emily Dickinson. PBWP

Behind me I do not see the ancient men. Song on Climbing Yu-chou Gate Tower. Ch'en Tzu-ang, *tr. by* Burton Watson. CoBCP

Behind my parents' house. Ikutamabe Tarukuni, *tr. fr. Japanese by* Geoffrey Bownas *and* Anthony Thwaite. *Fr.* Manyo Shu. PeBJV

Behind shut doors, in shadowy quarantine. The First Time. Karl Shapiro. ErPo; SM; VGW

Behind, sun, before, shadow! Silhouette. Annette M'Baye, *tr. by* Kathleen Weaver. PBWP

Behind That Wall My Roommate Fucks His Girl. Geof Hewitt. NeAC

Behind that white brow. To a Dead Journalist. William Carlos Williams. QFR

Behind the calm famous faces knowledge of what crimes? Collapsible. Tom Raworth. EAS

Behind the door. Interrogation. Sándor Rákos, *tr. by* Daniel Hoffman. MHuP

Behind the door, nothing, behind the curtain. To Open. Antonio Porta, *tr. by* Lawrence R. Smith. NItP

Behind the fair familiar face. Seasoning. Paul Humphrey. SoTCo

Behind the Falls. William Stafford. RFM

Behind the gate of light. Season of Beginning and End. Zuhur Dixon, *tr. by* Patricia Alanah Byrne *and* Salma Khadra Jayyusi. MAP

Behind the Glass Wall. Harold Norse. PeHV

Behind the granite church. Fugue. Constance Carrier. GoYe

Behind the house the upland falls. After the Pleasure Party. Herman Melville. NAAL-1

Behind the Kokusai Theatre in Nihonmachi. Dreams in Progress. Richard Oyama. BrSi

Behind the Log, *sel.* E. J. Pratt.
  "There is a language in a naval log." MoCV

Behind the mountain ledge. *Unknown, tr. fr. Japanese by* Geoffrey Bownas *and* Anthony Thwaite. *Fr.* Manyo Shu. PeBJV

Behind the New Jersey shore. Obon by the Hudson. Richard Oyama. BrSi

Behind the Power Station on 14th, the held breath. Galway Kinnell. *Fr.* The Avenue Bearing the Initial of Christ into the New World, 14. NaP

Behind the wall of St. John's in the city. The Garden at St. John's. May Swenson. NePoEA

Behind you/ a riot of pallid orphans. Small Country. Claribel Alegría, *tr. by* Aliki *and* Willis Barnstone. BoWoP

Behind your fan. *Unknown, tr. fr. Japanese by* Burton Watson. *Fr.* Kangin Shu. FCEI

Behold. *Unknown, tr. fr. Hawaiian by* M. K. Pukui. WTO

Behold! a giant am I! The Windmill. Longfellow. MoShBr

Behold a hag whom Life denies a kiss. Opportunity. Madison Cawein. AA

Behold, a silly [*or* little] tender babe. New Prince, New Pomp. Robert Southwell. ELP; GN; NOBE; NOCV; OBSC; OHIP; TrCP

Behold, a virgin shall conceive. The Messiah. Bible, *O.T. Fr.* Isaiah, VII: 14–25. AWP

Behold a woman! The Justified Mother of Men. Walt Whitman. OHIP

Behold a Wonder Here! *Unknown.* OBSC; TrGrPo

"Behold another singer!" Criton said. "Song to the Gods, Is Sweetest Sacrifice." Annie Fields. AA

Behold, four Kings in majesty rever'd. The Playing Cards. Pope. *Fr.* The Rape of the Lock, III. ChTr

Behold from sluggish winter's arm. Primo Vere. Giosuè Carducci, *tr. by* John Bailey. AWP

Behold, from the land of the farther suns. Stephen Crane. *Fr.* The Black Riders, XXIX.

Behold, God is great, and we know him not. Bible, *O.T. Fr.* Job, XXXVI: 26–30, 32. ImOP

Behold he comes to make thy people groan. Pasquin to the Queen's Statue at St. Paul's. William Shippen. APAS

Behold her seven hills loom white. Resurge San Francisco. Joaquin Miller. PAH

Behold her, single in the field. The Solitary Reaper. Wordsworth. AWP; BLPL; CH; ChER; EnRP; FaBoCh; FaPoR; FiP; GN; HAP; HeIP; InPS; LiTB; NAEL-2; NOBE; NoP; OAEL-2; OBEV; OBNC; PoEL-4; PoRA; PPP; SCV; SoSe; TEP; TrGrPo; UnPo; WeW (Reaper, The.) GTBS; GTBS-P

Behold him now his genuine colours wear. Sonnet: To the Departing Spirit of an Alienated Friend. Anna Seward. PeHV

Behold, how eager this our little boy. Of the Boy and Butterfly. Bunyan. OxBChV

Behold, how good and how pleasant it is. Psalm CXXXIII ("Behold, how good and how pleasant. . ."). Bible, *O.T. Fr.* Psalms. AWP

(Psalm CXXXIII: "Beholde, how good and joyfull a thinge it is.") OBVE, *tr. by* Miles Coverdale.
(To Dwell Together in Unity.) TrJP

Behold! in various throngs the scribbling crew. Byron. *Fr.* English Bards and Scotch Reviewers. EnRP; OAEL-2

Behold, love, thy power how she despiseth! Sir Thomas Wyatt. GBL

Behold me before all a man of good sense. The Pretty Red-Head. Guillaume Apollinaire, *tr. by* Roger Shattuck. POS

Behold me waiting—waiting for the knife. Before. William Ernest Henley. *Fr.* In Hospital, IV. BrPo; MoBrPo

Behold, my dearest, how the fragrant rose. To Her Love. Edward May. FaBoEE

Behold, my Samsons are returning, and the gates of Gaza are on their shoulders. My Samsons. Haim Guri, *tr. by* Mark Elliott Shapiro. VWA

Behold, my servant shall deal prudently. The Song of The Suffering Servant. Bible, *O.T. Fr.* Isaiah, LII: 13-LIII: 12. NAWM-1

Behold, O Aspasia! I Send You Verses. Walter Savage Landor. *Fr.* Pericles and Aspasia, CXC. OBNC

Behold, O Man. Spenser. *Fr.* The Faerie Queene, II, 6. ElL

Behold once more with serious labor here. To the Reader. Samuel Daniel. OBSC
(To His Reader.) OBSC

Behold, One of Several Little Christs. Kenneth Patchen. NaP

Behold the birds of heaven. God Provides. , Bible, *N.T.. Fr.* St. Matthew, VI: 26-34. BLRP

Behold the brand of beauty tossed! The Dancer. Edmund Waller. TrGrPo

Behold the child, by Nature's kindly law. Pope. *Fr.* An Essay on Man, Epistle II. FaBoRV

Behold the critic, pitched like the *castrati*. Pipling. Theodore Roethke. *Fr.* Three Epigrams, 1. NBLV; TW

Behold the Deeds! H. C. Bunner. NBLV

Behold the dental artist's bright array. Artificial Teeth. Solyman Brown. *Fr.* Dentologia; a Poem on the Diseases of the Teeth and Their Proper Remedies. FaBoUS

Behold the duck. The Duck. Ogden Nash. MoShBr; RB

Behold the ever-tim'rous hare. April. Samuel Thompson. BIrV

Behold the fatal day arrive! Swift. *Fr.* Verses on the Death of Doctor Swift [D.S.P.D., Occasioned by Reading a Maxim in Rochefoucauld]. SCV

Behold the flag! Is it not a flag? The Rejected "National Hymns." "Orpheus C. Kerr." OBAL

Behold, the grave of a wicked man. Why? Stephen Crane. *Fr.* The Black Riders, XXV. AA

Behold, the Grave of a Wicked Man. Stephen Crane. *Fr.* The Black Riders, XXV. TAP

Behold the hippopotamus! The Hippopotamus. Ogden Nash. FaBV; OnUR

Behold the house of Sir William Forbes. The Pentland Hills. *Unknown.* GBP

Behold the Lilies of the Field. Anthony Hecht. NePoEA-2

Behold the man alive in me. Ecce Homo. Witter Bynner. WGRP

Behold the Manly Mesomorph. W. H. Auden. OxBSP

Behold, the Meads. Guillaume de Poitiers, *tr. fr. French by* Harriet Waters Preston. AWP

Behold the mighty dinosaur. The Dinosaur. Bert Leston Taylor. ImOP

Behold the Mount of Olives and the Greek cloister. Jerusalem. Antoni Slonimski, *tr. by* Isaac Komen. VWA

Behold the portal: open wide it stands. The Garden Where There Is No Winter. Louis James Block. AA

Behold the ravens on the trees. Contentment. Benjamin Schlipf. BLRP

Behold, the Shade of Night Is Now Receding. Saint Gregory the Great, *tr. fr. Latin by* Ray Palmer. AH

Behold the tormented and the fallen angel. Beethoven. John Hall Wheelock. PoA

Behold the wonders of the mighty deep. The Sea. *Unknown.* NA; RHPC

Behold the works of William Morris. *Unknown.* BXAP; Par

Behold this brief hexagonal. Text. Audrey Wurdemann. FYAP

Behold this needle when the arctic stone. On the Needle of a Sundial. Francis Quarles. OBS; TrGrPo

Behold this ruin! 'Twas a skull. To a Skeleton. Anna Jane Vardhill. BLPA

Behold those wingèd images. A Legend of the Hive. Robert Stephen Hawker. EBVV

Behold, thou art fair. Bible, *O.T. Fr.* The Song of Solomon, IV: 1-7. TrJP

Behold three Kings come from the East. For Twelfth Day. Luke Wadding. TIRV

Behold through the veil of distance a pleasing image. Jonathan. Rachel, *tr. by* L. V. Snowman. TrJP

Behold, we have gathered together our battleships, near and afar. "Mene, Mene, Tekel, Upharsin." Madison Cawein. PAH

Behold with Joy. Elhanan Winchester. AH

Behold within our Hayden Planetarium. Ode to the Hayden Planetarium. Arthur Guiterman. ImOP

Behold, within the leafy shade. The Sparrow's Nest. Wordsworth. EnRP

Behold yon breathing prospect bids the muse. Spring ("Behold yon breathing prospect bids the muse"). James Thomson. *Fr.* The Seasons: Spring. PoE

Behold yon hill, how it is swell'd with pride. Describes the Place Where Cynthia Is Sporting Herself. Philip Ayres. EnLoPo

Behold young Raphael coming back. Raphael. Priscilla Jane Thompson. CBWP-2

Beholde me, I pray thee, with all thine whole reson. Wofully Araide. *Unknown.* MeEL

Beholding element, in whose pure eye. The Aspen and the Stream. Richard Wilbur. NYBP

Bei Hennef. David Herbert Lawrence. BrPo

Beim Schlafengehen. K. O. Arvidson. *Fr.* The Four Last Songs of Richard Strauss at Takahe Creek above the Kaipara. ATNZ

Being a boy from the hills, brought up. The Welshman in Exile Speaks. T. H. Jones. OBWVE

Being a Giant. Robert Mezey. GrPl

Being a Jew means running forever to God. To Be a Jew. Aaron Zeitlin, *tr. by* Robert Friend. PeBMYV

Being a modest man, you wanted. For My Father. Philip Whalen. DiL

Being a woman, I am. The Wife Speaks. Mary Stanley. PeNZ

Being asked by an intimate party. His Answer to "Her Letter." Bret Harte. AnAmPo

Being at last on our way. Departure. William Hart-Smith. *Fr.* Christopher Columbus. PoAu-2

Being awake still and not unhappy. Selichos. Francis Landy. VWA

Being Aware. Dennis Cooper. GLP; UL

Being black's all the same. Black Is Black. David Macfield, *tr. by* Jack Hirschman. Vol

Being Born Is Important. Carl Sandburg. NAs

Being Called For. Rosemary Dobson. CBAP; Mes

Being drunk upstairs and listening. Green Revolutions. Barbara Guest. FaBoWP

Being Forsaken of His Friend He Complaineth. "E. S." EIL

Being Herded Past the Prison's Honor Farm. David Wagoner. SoSe

Being his resting place. A Dog Sleeping on My Feet. James Dickey. NAAL-2

Being in thought of love, I chanced to see. Ballata: He Reveals, in a Dialogue, His Increasing Love for Mandetta. Guido Cavalcanti, *tr. by* Dante Gabriel Rossetti. AWP

Being one day at my window all alone. The Visions. Petrarch, *tr. fr. Italian by* Edmund Spenser. *Fr.* Sonnets to Laura: Songs. AWP; PFI

Being Refused Local Credit. Paula Rankin. MAYP

Being Sad. Orban Veli Kanik, *tr. fr. Turkish by* Talat Sait Halman. LLLT

Being Somebody. Edwin Honig. TAP

Being to Timelessness as It's to Time. E. E. Cummings. HAP; UnAS

Being with Men. Linda Gregg. NPGG

Being with you. Margaret Atwood. *Fr.* The Circle Game. MoCV

Being without quality. Vox Humana. Thom Gunn. NePoEA-2

Being witless it said no prayer. The Death of an Angel. Russell Edson. LCAP

Being you, you cut your poetry from wood. The Egg Boiler. Gwendolyn Brooks. PoBA

"Being your slave, what should I do[e] but tend." Shakespeare. *Fr.* Sonnets, LVII. HAP; OBEV; PeHV; PoEL-2 (Absence.) GTBS; GTBS-P

Beinn A' Ghlo. Bill Tulloch. PoSH

Beinn Naomh, *sel.* Kathleen Jessie Raine. Summit, The. *Fr.* IV. OxBS

Beirut, *sel.* Mahmood Darwish, *tr. fr. Arabic by* Lena Jayyusi *and* Christopher Middleton. "Apple for the sea, marble narcissus flower, An." MAP

Beirut. Ahmad Faraz, *tr. fr. Urdu by* Mahmood Jamal. PBMUP

Beirut. Sami Mahdi, *tr. fr. Arabic by* Abdullah al-Udhari. MPAW

Beirut-Hell Express, The, *sel.* Etel Adnan. "Human race is going to the cemetery, The." WPOW

Bel m'es quan lo vens m'alena. Arnaut Daniel, *tr. fr. French by* Harriet Waters Preston. AWP

Belated Violet, A. Oliver Herford. AA

Belden Hollow. Leslie Nelson Jennings. GoYe

Beleaguered City, The. Longfellow. AnAmPo

Belfast. Donald Revell. SM

Belfast Confetti. Ciaran Carson. CIP

Belfast Linen. *Unknown. See* In a mean abode in Shankill Road.

Belfast Lough. *Unknown, tr. fr. Irish by* John Montague. BIrV

Belfry, The. Laurence Binyon. CH

Belief. Archie Randolph Ammons. GOA

Belief/ As unbelief before, Shakes us by fits. Belief and Unbelief. Robert Browning. *Fr.* Bishop Blougram's Apology. FaBV

Belief. Josephine Miles. FaBoWP; MoP; NoAM; TAP

Belief. Ella Wheeler Wilcox. PWR

Belief and Unbelief. Robert Browning. *Fr.* Bishop Blougram's Apology. FaBV

Believe and Take Heart. John Lancaster Spalding. AA

Believe in me, for I believe in you. Unchastity. Hugues C. Pernath, *tr. by* James S. Holmes. DuIn

"Believe in me," the Prophet cried. Infallibility. Thomas Stephens Collier. AA

Believe It. John Logan. AnAn; CAPP; LCAP

Believe me, every hour e'en yet I dream. To Schmidlein. August, Graf von Platen, *tr. by* Reginald Bancroft Cooke. PeHV

Believe me, I say to the gentleman with the pince-nez. In the Library. Elizabeth Brewster. OBCV

Believe Me, If All Those Endearing Young Charms. Thomas Moore. BLPA; ELP; EnRP; FaBoBe; FaBV; FaFP; FPL; LiTB; NAEL-2; OBNC; PoEL-4; TEP; WBLP

Believe me, knot of gristle, I bleed like a tree. Give Way, Ye Gates. Theodore Roethke. CMoP

Believe me, Love, this vagrant life. To Cordelia. Joseph Stansbury. CaP; NOBC

Believe me, sir, I'd like to spend whole days. Martial, *tr. by* J. V. Cunningham. OBVE

Believe Not. Isaac Leibush Peretz, *tr. fr. Yiddish by* Solomon Liptzin. TrJP

Believe not that the world is for naught, made. Believe Not. Isaac Leibush Peretz, *tr. by* Solomon Liptzin. TrJP

Believing in Those Inexorable Laws. Muriel Rukeyser. Son

Belinda lived in a little white house. The Tale of Custard the Dragon. Ogden Nash. FaPON; OBCA; PoRA; PYC (Custard the Dragon.) OnUR

Belisarius. Longfellow. PoEL-5; WiR

Bell, A. Clinton Scollard. AA

Bell and drum on the south river bank. Following the Rhymes of Chiang Hui-shu. Su Tung-p'o, *tr. by* Burton Watson. CoBCP

Bell-Bird, The. "Fiona Macleod." *Fr.* Australian Transcripts. FM

Bell-Birds. Henry Clarence Kendall. PoAu-1

Bell has rung, the sign, The. Lady Kasa, *tr. fr. Japanese by* Geoffrey Bownas *and* Anthony Thwaite. *Fr.* Manyo Shu. PeBJV

Bell has rung twelve times, A. Savannah, Sleepless. Richard Tillinghast. BLA

Bell horses, bell horses, what time of day? Mother Goose. BoTP; OxNR

Bell lily blooming under a shrub in the summer field, A. Lady Otomo no Sakanoe, *tr. fr. Japanese by* Hiroaki Sato. *Fr.* Manyo Shu. FCEI

Bell-Man, The. Robert Herrick. OBS

Bell-man of night, if I about shall go. Cock-Crow. Robert Herrick. PBBP

Bell of Ste. Anne Des Monts, The. Leo Cox. CaP

Bell-rope that gathers God at dawn, The. The Broken Tower. Hart Crane. AmPP; CMoP; LiTM; MoAB; MoAmPo; NoAM; NOBA; NoP; OxBA; TrGrPo

Bell sounds are buried. Song of Sungbuk. Jung Han-mo, *tr. by* Koh Chang-soo. ACKP

Bell sounds penetrate the mountain mist. Rising Early with My Son Chih to Leave Tung-ming Ch'an Monastery. Huang Tsung-hsi, *tr. by* Lynn Struve. WFTU

Bell Speech. Richard Wilbur. MoAB; MoAmPo

Bell-Toll. Pierre Reverdy, *tr. fr. French by* Michael Benedikt. POS

Bell Too Heavy to Ring. Tom Kryss. NeAC

Bell Tower. Léonie Adams. MoAB; MoAmPo

Bell wakes me at 6 in the pale spring dawn, The. Letter from Pretoria Central Prison. Arthur Nortje. WMBCH

Bella and the Golem. Rossana Ombres, *tr. fr. Italian by* Edgar Pauk. VWA

Bella was young and Bella was fair. Unhappy Bella. *Unknown.* ErPo

Bella Dame sans Mercy, La, *sel. At. to* Alain Chatier, *French tr. at. to* Richard Ros. Lady Resists the Lover's Pleas, The. OxBLMV

Belle de Jour. George Melly. FaBoPa

Belle of the Balkans, The. Newman Levy. FiBHP

Belle of the Ball-Room, The. Winthrop Mackworth Praed. *Fr.* Every-Day Characters. EnRP; FaBoCo

Bellerin' and Bawlin.' Linda Ash. CowP

Bellerophon, *sel.* Euripides, *tr. fr. Greek by* John Addington Symonds. There Are No Gods. EaLo

Belles of the eighties were soft, The. Reflections Outside of a Gymnasium. Phyllis McGinley. SD

Bellflower spilling a candlesnuffer's dark hints. Of. Debora Greger. EOEF

Bellies bitter with drinking the/ Weak tears. Final Chorus. Archibald MacLeish. *Fr.* Panic. MoAmPo

Bellman, The. Robert Herrick. CaPo; CH; OBS

Bellman's Song, The. *Unknown.* EBEV; ElL; SeCePo

Bellow of good Master Bull, The. Ballade un Peu Banale. A. J. M. Smith. MoCV

Bellower with the antlers. Suibne Geilt. NOIV

Bellows Maker of Oxford, The. John Hoskyns. FaBoEE

Bells, The. Poe. AA; AnAmPo; FaFP; FaPON; FPL; GN; LiTA; OBAL; OBCA; OHFP; PoLF; RR; TAP; WBLP

"Hear the sledges with the bells," *st.* 1. FaPON

Bells. Duncan Campbell Scott. CaP

Bells, The. *Unknown.* FiBHP

Bells, The. William Young. *Fr.* Wishmakers' Town. AA

Bells and drums lie cold, The. Song of the Water Clock at Night. Wei Chuang, *tr.* by Lois Fusek. ATF

Bells are booming down the bohreens. Ireland with Emily. Sir John Betjeman. GTBS-P; OxBTC

Bells Are Calling for Me, The. László Nagy, *tr. fr. Hungarian by* Jascha Kessler. FOC

Bells Are Ringing for Me and Chagall, The. Terence Winch. UL

Bells are tolling, The. Lady Kasa, *tr. fr. Japanese.* *Fr.* Manyo Shu. Ma

Bells assault the maiden air, The. Ou Phrontis. Charles Causley. NePoEA

Bells at Midnight, The. Thomas Bailey Aldrich. PAH

Bells, bells—worms cannot touch their lips. The Bells Are Calling for Me. László Nagy, *tr.* by Jascha Kessler. FOC

Bells for John Whiteside's Daughter. John Crowe Ransom. CMoP; FF; HAP; HeIP; HoPM; InPK; InPS; LiTA; LiTM; MoAB; MoAmPo; MoP; NAAL-2; NIP; NoAM; NOBA; NoP; OxBA; PoE; PPP; PrIm; RB; SoSe; TAP; UnPo; VGW; WeW

Bells have wide mouths and tongues, but are too weak. Upon a Ring of Bells. Bunyan. CH

Bells of Grey Crystal. Dame Edith Sitwell. OxBSP

Bells of Heaven, The. Ralph Hodgson. BoTP; BrPo; EaLo; GoJo; LiTM; MoAB; MoBrPo; NOBE; OBEV; OxBSP

Bells of London, The. *Unknown.* BoTP; OxNR; PoRA

Bells of Lynn, The. Longfellow. AA

Bells of Ostend, The. William Lisle Bowles. *See* Sonnet: "How sweet the tuneful bells' responsive peal!"

Bells of St. Michael. Mary Weston Fordham. CBWP-2

Bells of San Blas, The. Longfellow. OxBA

Bells of Shandon, The. Francis Sylvester Mahony. ACP; CH; ChTr; OBEV

Bells of Sunday rang us down, The. John Ciardi. WaP

Bells of waiting Advent ring, The. Christmas. Sir John Betjeman. OBCP; OxBTC

Bells of Youth, The. "Fiona Macleod." BoTP

Bells ov Alderburnham, The. William Barnes. EBVV

Belly and Tubs Went Out in a Boat. Clyde Watson. RAR

Belly Dancer. Diane Wakoski. NIP; NoAM

Belly Dancer in the Nursing Home, The. Ronald Wallace. GOYP

Belly of the Land, The. Luci Tapahonso. STE

Belly Woman's Lament. Lillian Allen. PBCV

Belmore. Anthony Howell. NPo

Belonging to a New Family. Mohammad Bennis, *tr. fr. Arabic by* Sharif Elmusa *and* Charles Doria. MAP

Beloved, The. Paul Eluard. *See* She is standing on my lids.

Beloved. Iyamide Hazeley. WS

Beloved, The. David Roberts, *tr. fr. Welsh by* H. Idris Bell. OBWVE

Beloved,/ my parents mock me. Freely, from a Song Sung by Jewish Women of Yemen. Stephen Levy. VWA

Beloved,/ What does it take to put a house in order? Don Mager. *Fr.* Letters from a Married Man. GLP

Beloved, and he sweetly thus goes on. A Pulpit to Be Let. *Unknown.* APAS

Beloved dog, in from the wet. Birthday. James Merrill. NAs

Beloved friends! More glorious times than ours. To My Friends. Schiller, *tr.* by James Clarence Mangan. AWP

Beloved, gaze in thine own heart. The Two Trees. W. B. Yeats. BrPo; OAEL-2

Beloved, it is good. Dream Song. *Unknown, tr.* by Francis Densmore. OBVE

Beloved, let us once more praise the rain. Conrad Aiken. *Fr.* Preludes for Memnon; or, Preludes to Attitude. LiTA; UnPo

Beloved, may your sleep be sound. W. B. Yeats. BoLoP; FaBoTw; OBMV

Belovéd, my Belovéd, when I think. Elizabeth Barrett Browning. *Fr.* Sonnets from the Portuguese, XX. Son; WPE

Beloved one, my lord. *Unknown, tr. fr. Japanese by* Burton Watson. *Fr.* Manyo Shu. FCEI

Beloved person must I think, The. Ki no Akimine, *tr. fr. Japanese by* Arthur Waley. *Fr.* Kokin Shu. AWP

Belovéd, thou hast brought me many flowers. Elizabeth Barrett Browning. *Fr.* Sonnets from the Portuguese, XLIV. EBVV; OBNC; WPE

Beloved, you are like thread in the loom. Ancient Feeling. Wu Wei-yeh, *tr.* by Jonathan Chaves. CoBLCP

Beloved, you are sleeping still. Watching You Sleep under Monet's Water Lilies. Gibbons Ruark. SM

Beloved's Image, The. *Unknown, tr. fr. Hawaiian by* M. W. Beckwith. WTO

Below fair Peebles, on the river's side. Alexander Pennecuik. *Fr.* A Marriage betwixt Scrape, Monarch of the Maunders, and Blobberlips, Queen of the Gypsies. NOEC

Below Hekla. Selima Hill. FaBoWP

Below Incense Burner Peak I built a new mountain dwelling. A New Thatched Hall. Po Chü-i, *tr.* by Burton Watson. CoBCP

Below lies one whose name was traced in sand. My Epitaph. David Gray. EBVV

Below Loughrigg. Fleur Adcock. PeNZ

Below me on the road, the blackbirds. Blackbird Sestina. Candice Warne. SM

Below me the city was in flames. The Improved Binoculars. Irving Layton. NOBC

Below Mount T'ui K'oy, Home of the Gods, Todos Santos Cuchumatán, Guatemalan Highlands. Joseph Stroud. NPGG

Below the boulder where I sit. Joso, *tr. fr. Japanese by* Hiroaki Sato. *Fr.* Fifteen Hokku. FCEI

Below the dancing larches freckled. Joseph Gordon MacLead. *Fr.* Men of the Rocks. OxBS

Below the down the stranded town. A Cinque Port. John Davidson. BrPo

Below the gardens and the darkening pines. At Carmel Highlands. Janet Lewis. PoA

Below the Great Wall-the watering hole. The Horse-Watering Hole. Yang Wei-chen, *tr.* by Jonathan Chaves. CoBLCP

Below, the river scrambled like a goat. God's Little Mountain. Geoffrey Hill. NePoEA

Below the Surface-Stream. Matthew Arnold. NOBVV; OxBSP

Below the thunders of the upper deep. The Kraken. Tennyson. AmMo; NAEL-2; NoP; OAEL-2; OBNC; PoEL-5; TOF; WiR; WSC

Below thir stanes lie Jamie's banes. On a Noisy Polemic. Burns. FaBoEE

Belshazzer's Feast. Eloise Bibb. CBWP-4

Be'mi'ster. William Barnes. EBVV

Ben Alder 1963-1977. Des Hannigan. PoSH

Ben Battle was a soldier bold. Faithless Nelly Gray. Thomas Hood. BXAP; EnRP; FaBoCo; NA; NOBL

Ben Bolt. Thomas Dunn English. AA; AnAmPo; FaBoBe; FaFP

Ben Franklin munched a loaf of bread while walking down the street. Benjamin Franklin 1706-1790. Rosemary *and* Stephen Vincent Benét. FaPON

Ben Hall was out on the Lachlan side. The Death of Ben Hall. Will H. Ogilvie. PoAu-1

Ben Hur, *sel.* Lew Wallace.
"Wake not, but hear me, love!" AA

Ben. Johnsons Sociable Rules for the Apollo. Ben Jonson, *tr. fr. Latin by* Alexander Brome. SeCV-1

Ben Jonson. Swinburne. *Fr.* Sonnets of English Dramatic Poets. Son

Ben Jonson Entertains a Man from Stratford. Edwin Arlington Robinson. AmPP; MoAB; MoAmPo

Ben Milam. William H. Wharton. PAH

Ben Nevis is a mountain. The Harlot. Hamish Brown. PoSH

Bench of Boors, The. Herman Melville. AnAmPo; NAAL-1; OBAL

Benches are broken, the grassplots brown and bare, The. South End. Conrad Aiken. CMoP; HoPM; OxBA

Bend after bend, the long embankment. Tao-chi, *tr.* by Jonathan Chaves. CoBLCP

Bend as the Bow Bends. Conrad Aiken. *Fr.* And in the Human Heart, I. CMoP; Son

Bend back thy bow, O Archer, till the string. The Archer. A. J. M. Smith. OBCV

Bend in the River. Simon J. Ortiz. HATNAP

Bend low again, night of summer stars. Summer Stars. Carl Sandburg. RFM

Bend low, O dusky night. To-Night. Louise Chandler Moulton. AA

Bend willow, willow bend down deep. Willow Bend and Weep. Herbert Clark Johnson. PoNe

Bending, I bow my head. Combing. Gladys Cardiff. CDW; STE

Bending neither to the rain. November Third. Miyazawa Kenji, *tr.* by Geoffrey Bownas *and* Anthony Thwaite. PeBJV

Bending the Bow. Robert Duncan. CAPP

Bendix. John Updike. AnAmPo; NYBP

Beneath a churchyard yew. O Sweet Anne Page. William Shenstone. SeCePo

Beneath a clear sky. Emperor Hanazono, *tr.* by Steven D. Carter. WFTW

Beneath a holm repaired two jolly swains. Corydon and Thyrsis. Virgil, *tr. fr. Latin by* Dryden. *Fr.* Eclogues, VII. AWP

Beneath a myrtle shade. Song of the Zambra Dance. Dryden. *Fr.* The Conquest of Granada, *Pt.* I, Act III, sc. i. ErPo; PoEL-3 (Zambra Dance, The.) SeCV-2

Beneath a striped umbrella. Song of the Darkness. John Bricuth. SM

Beneath a thundery glaze. W. J. Turner. *Fr.* The Seven Days of the Sun. OBMV

Beneath all the statistics. New York. Federico García Lorca, *tr. by* Robert Bly. NU

Beneath him with new wonder now he views. Milton. *Fr.* Paradise Lost, *bk.* IV, *ll.* 205–268. PPP

Beneath its morning caul, this ravaged land. Dakota Badlands. Elizabeth Landeweer. AmFN

Beneath my palm-trees, by the riverside. Song of the Indian Maid, The. Keats. *Fr.* Endymion.
    O sorrow/ why dost borrow. NOBE

Beneath our consecrated elm. The New-come Chief. James Russell Lowell. *Fr.* Under the Old Elm, III. PAH

Beneath our eaves the moonbeams play. Moon and Candle-light. William Renton. NOBVV

Beneath our feet, the shuddering bogs. On Yes Tor. Sir Edmund William Gosse. CH

Beneath the Apple of Paradise in Iowa. Joanna Salamon, *tr. fr. Polish by* Christopher Wertz. WCI

Beneath the blistering tropical sun. Wheeler's Brigade at Santiago. Wallace Rice. PAH

Beneath the branch of the green may. Medieval Norman Song ("Beneath the branch of the green may"). *Unknown, tr. by* John Addington Symonds. AWP

Beneath the burning brazen sky. The Ute Lover. Hamlin Garland. AA

Beneath the Cypress Shade. Thomas Love Peacock. *See* Grave of Love, The.

Beneath the deep my broken timbers lie. The Spirit of the *Bluenose*. Claire Harris MacIntosh. CaP

Beneath the evening gold. Golden. Francisco A. de Icaza, *tr. by* Samuel Beckett. MexPo

Beneath the fabric of leaves. The Spring. Ellen Bryant Voigt. MAYP

Beneath the leaf a green insect, and frost upon the leaf. The Tiniest of Lives. Chin Jen-Jui, *tr.* by Irving Lo. WFTU

Beneath the Malebolge lies Hastings Street. Christ Walks in This Infernal District Too. Malcolm Lowry. MoCV; NOBC

Beneath the marmalade, muffins, and tea. Sunday Review Section. Baron Wormser. MAYP

Beneath the Memnonian shadows of Memphis, it rose from the slime. The Reed. Henry Bernard Carpenter. AA

Beneath the midnight moon of May. The Night Watch. William Winter. AA

Beneath the Mound. R. T. Smith. STE

Beneath the new green. Nagachika, *tr. by* Steven D. Carter. WFTW

Beneath the sagging roof. Ezra Pound. *Fr.* Hugh Selwyn Mauberley (Life and Contacts), X. MoAmPo

Beneath the same bush rests his brother. Epitaphs on Two Piping-Bullfinches of Lady Ossory's. Horace Walpole. FaBoEE

Beneath the shadow of dawn's aerial cope. Hope and Fear. Swinburne. FaBoBe

Beneath the Shadow of the Freeway. Lorna Dee Cervantes. CCP; ER; FIA

Beneath the shadow of Tongariro mountain. A Song of Yearning. Kohine Whakarua Ponika, *tr. by the author*. PeNZ

Beneath the Shrine of the Three Loyal Ones. Wen Cheng-ming, *tr. fr. Chinese by* Jonathan Chaves. *Fr.* Improvised on Horseback to Say Good-bye to Those Who Are Seeing Me Off. CoBLCP

Beneath the silent eaves, a tinkling as of jade. The Studio for Listening to the Snow. Yang Chi, *tr. by* Jonathan Chaves. CoBLCP

Beneath the snow the broad sad wastelands. Winter Day. Susannah Fried, *tr. by* Anthony Rudolf. VWA

Beneath the umbrageous shadow of a shade. A Pastoral; in the Modern Style. "Worcester." NOEC

Beneath the willow wound round with ivy. Hops. Boris Pasternak, *tr. by* Jon Stallworthy *and* Peter France. BoLoP; TTTS

Beneath their flames, cities of candelabra. The Chestnut Avenue at Alton House. Charles Tomlinson. FaBoTw

Beneath these alien stars. Pioneer Woman. Vesta Pierce Crawford. AiP

Beneath these fruit-tree boughs that shed. The Green Linnet. Wordsworth. EnRP; GTBS; GTBS-P; PBBP

Beneath these plains. West of Chicago. John Dimoff. RFM

Beneath these poppies buried deep. Epitaph on Robert Southey. Thomas Moore. FaBoCo; FaBoEE

Beneath these shades, beside yon winding steam. On Visiting the Graves of Hawthorne and Thoreau. Jones Very. TAP

Beneath this smooth stone by the bone of his bone. *Unknown*. FaBoEE

Beneath this sod lie the remains. Epitaph on a Young Poet Who Died before Having Achieved Success. Amy Lowell. OBAL

Beneath this stone a Poet Laureate lies. Epitaph on William Whitehead. *Unknown*. FaBoEE

Beneath this stone does William Hazlitt lie. W. H. *Eheu!* Samuel Taylor Coleridge. FaBoEE

Beneath this stone in hopes of Zion. At Upton-on-Severn. *Unknown*. FaBoCo; FaBoEE
    (Advertising Epitaph: From Upton-on-Severn, Gloustershire.) FaBoUs

Beneath this stone lies the body of Hengist. Hengest Cyning. Jorge Luis Borges, *tr. by* Norman Thomas di Giovanni. NYBP

Beneath this tent, clutching this glass of beer. Blues for an Old Blue. Walker Gibson. NYBP

Beneath those parts, where stretching to its bound. The Process of Conception. Claude Quillet, *tr. fr. Latin by* George Sewell. *Fr.* Callipaedia; or, The Art of Getting Beautiful Children. FaBoUs

Beneath thy spell, O radiant summer sea. The Sea's Spell. Susan Marr Spalding. AA

Beneath Thy Wing. Hayyim Nahman Bialik, *tr. fr. Hebrew by* Helena Frank. TrJP

Beneath Time's roaring cannon. When the Mississippi Flowed in Indiana. Vachel Lindsay. CMoP

Beneath yon birch with silver bark. The Ballad of the Dark Ladie. Samuel Taylor Coleridge. EnRP

Beneath yon larkspur's azure bells. The Blue-Bird. Herman Melville. BLPL; NOBA

Beneath yon ruin'd abbey's moss-grown piles. Thomas Warton, the Younger. *Fr.* The Pleasures of Melancholy. NOEC

Benedicite. Anna Callender Brackett. AA

Benedicite, What Dreamed I This Night? *Unknown*. HAP; PoEL-1 (Dream, A.) OBSC

Benediction. Bible, *O.T. Fr.* Numbers, VI: 24–26. TrGrPo (Blessing of the Priests.) TrJP
    ("Lorde blesse the and kepe the, The,," *tr. by* William Tyndale) OBVE, VI: 24–27.

Benediction. William Freedman. VWA

Benediction. Donald Jeffrey Hayes. AmNP; PoNe

Benediction. Bob Kaufman. PoNe

Benediction. Stanley Kunitz. VGW

Benediction. Myra Sklarew. VWA

Benediction. Mark Turbyfill. PoA

Benediction for the Felt. *Mongol Oral Tradition, tr. by* C. R. Bawden. WTO

Benediction for the Tent. *Mongol Oral Tradition, tr. by* C. R. Bawden. WTO

Beneficent but blind, my blood. The Prayer of the Arab Physician. Monk Gibbon. TIRV

Benefits and Abuse of Alcohol, The. Eubulus, *tr. fr. Greek by* Richard Cumberland. FaBoUs; NBLV

Benefits of Sorrow. Lizelia Augusta Jenkins Moorer. CBWP-3

Bengal. "Sahir Ludhianvi," *tr. fr. Urdu by* Mahmood Jamal. PBMUP

Bengal. *Unknown. See* Limerick: "There once was a man of Bengal."

Bengal Tiger, The. Michael Spence. SoTCo

Benicasim. Sylvia Townsend Warner. OBWP

Benighted to the Foothills of the Cairngorms. Olive Fraser. PoSH

Benign Neglect/ Mississippi, 1970. Primus St. John. PoBA

Benjamin Franklin 1706-1790. Rosemary *and* Stephen Vincent Benét. FaPON

Benjamin Franklin Hazard. Edgar Lee Masters. *Fr.* The New Spoon River. GOA

Benjamins' Lamentation for Their Sad Loss at Sea, by Storms and Tempests, The. *Unknown*. OxBSS

Bennachie. Charles Murray. PoSH

Bennington. William Henry Babcock. PAH

Bens camp by the road-side, The. Passin Ben Dorain. Alastair MacKie. *Fr.* At the Heich Kirk-Yaird. PoSH

Bent. Martin Carter. PBCV

Bent Branches. Amjad Nasir, *tr. fr. Arabic by* May Jayyusi *and* Charles Doria. MAP

Bent double, like old beggars under sacks. Dulce et Decorum Est. Wilfred Owen. CMoP; DL; FaBoPV; FaBoTw; FaBV; FF; HeIP; HoPM; InPK; InvP; LiTB; LiTM; MMA; MoAB; MoBrPo; NAEL-2; NIP; NoAM; NoP; OAEL-2; OBWP; PoE; PPP; PrIm; TW; UnPo; WaP

Bent old men and women and dirty children scavenging. Environment. Lionel Kearns. NOBC

Bent over, staggering in panic or despair. Tableau. Judith Wright. CBAP

Bent Sae Brown, The. *Unknown.* ESPB

Bent Willows. Li Chien, *tr. fr. Chinese by* Hsin-sheng C. Kao. WFTU

Bents and Broom, The. *Unknown.* OxBB

Beowulf. Kingsley Amis. FaBoCo; OxBC

Beowulf ("Lo! we have listened to many a lay."), *sels. Unknown, tr. fr. Anglo-Saxon.* OAEL-1, *tr. by* Charles W. Kennedy

  "At the hour shaped for him Scyld departed." *Tr. by* Michael Alexander. OBD

Beowulf and Wiglaf Slay the Dragon. *Tr. by* Charles W. Kennedy. AnOE

Beowulf's Death. *Tr. by* Charles W. Kennedy. AnOE

Beowulf's Fight with Grendel's Mother. *Tr. by* Michael Alexander. WTO

Fire-Dragon and the Treasure, The. *Tr. by* Charles W. Kennedy. AnOE

Funeral Pyre, The. *Tr. by* Charles W. Kennedy. AnOE

Grendel. *Tr. by* Burton Raffel. NU

Last Survivor's Speech, The. *Tr. by* Alfred David. NAEL-1

Lay of Finn, The. *Tr. by* Charles W. Kennedy. AnOE

  "Oft in the hall I have heard my people." *Tr. by* Charles W. Kennedy. HeIP

  "So Hrothgar's men lived happy in his hall." *Tr. by* Burton Raffel. PoE

Tale of Sigemund, The. *Tr. by* Charles W. Kennedy. AnOE

Beowulf and Wiglaf Slay the Dragon. *Unknown, tr. fr. Anglo-Saxon by* Charles W. Kennedy. *Fr.* Beowulf. AnOE

Beowulf's Death. *Unknown, tr. fr. Anglo-Saxon by* Charles W. Kennedy. *Fr.* Beowulf. AnOE

Beowulf's Fight with Grendel's Mother. *Unknown, tr. fr. Anglo-Saxon by* Michael Alexander. *Fr.* Beowulf. WTO

Beppo; a Venetian Story ("'Tis known, at least it should be, that throughout."), *sels.* Byron. NOBL, *abr.;* OBNV, *abr.;* OBSV

  "England! with all thy faults I love thee still." UnPo

  Italy. SeCePo

  (Italy versus England.) NOBE

Bequest of His Heart, A. Alexander Scott. OBEV

Berck-Plage, *sel.* Sylvia Plath.

  "Wedding-cake face in a paper frill, A." OBD

Bereaved. James Whitcomb Riley. AA

Bereaved Child's First Night. Frances Bellerby. FaBoWP

Bereaved Maid, The. *Unknown. See* Lully, lullay [*or* lulley], lully, lullay [*or* lully].

Bereaved of mind by a weird truck. The Department. Allen Grossman. PPR

Bereaved Swan, The. Stevie Smith. FaBoNo; FaBoTw

Bereavement. Elizabeth Barrett Browning. WPE

Bereavement of the Fields. Wilfred Campbell. CaP

Bereft. Robert Frost. LiTM; MoAB; MoAmPo; OxBA; SoSe

Bereft. Thomas Hardy. BoLoP; NoAM

Bereft. Josephine D. Henderson Heard. CBWP-4

Berg, The. Herman Melville. AmPP; LiTA; NOBA; NoP; PoEL-5; TAP

Berlin Interior with Jews, 1939. Lynn Emanuel. MAYP

Bermudas. Andrew Marvell. AWP; CH; ChTr; FaBoCh; GN; JCP; MePo; MOS; NAEL-1; NOBE; NOCV; NoP; OBEV; OBS; OBTV; PAH; PoE; RB; SeCP; SeCV-1

Bernie's Quick-Shave (1968). Sydney Lea. MAYP

Berries. Walter de la Mare. MoBrPo

Berries, The. William Heyen. GeTw; MAYP

Berry Picking. Irving Layton. HeIP; MoCV; NoP

Berstein disc jockey. Ten O'Clock News. Simon J. Ortiz. NOVW

Bert Schultz. Colin Thiele. PoAu-2

Berthe Morisot. Anne Waldman. UL

Beryl. Lyn Lifshin. NeAC

"Beshrew that heart that makes my heart to groan." Shakespeare. *Fr.* Sonnets, CXXXIII. InvP

Beside a chapel I'd a room looked down. Dread. J. M. Synge. BoLoP; MoBrPo; OxBSP

Beside a Deathbed. Vassar Miller. MT

Beside a dewless, noonday mugwort. Santen, *tr. by* Hiroaki Sato. FCEI

Beside a green meadow a stream used to flow. The Cow and the Ass. Ann Taylor *and* Jane Taylor. BoTP

Beside a narrow trail in the blue. Dream of the Lynx. John Haines. NU

Beside green water. Enjoying Retirement ("Beside green water"). Ma Chih-yüan, *tr. fr. Chinese by* Jonathan Chaves. *Fr.* Three Poems to the Tune "Ssu-k'uai yü," 2. CoBLCP

Beside her ashen hearth she sate her down. The Fortunate One. Harriet Monroe. AA

Beside him in the old Ford pickup. Driving Lesson. Michael Pettit. MOWH

Beside his heavy-shouldered team. Bullocky. Judith Wright. CBAP; PoAu-2; SeCePo

Beside his wife at Passover in spring. Passover Eve. Fania Kruger. GoYe

Beside me,—in the car,—she sat. Natura Naturans. Arthur Hugh Clough. HAP; NOBVV

Beside me she sat, hand hooked and hovering. An Egyptian Passage. Theodore Weiss. TAP

Beside My Grandmother. Al Lee. SM

Beside that tent and under guard. Geronimo. Ernest McGaffey. AA; PAH

Beside the Bed. P. J. Kavanagh. NPo

Beside the Bed. Charlotte Mew. MoAB; MoBrPo; OxBSP; TrGrPo; WPE

Beside the bed where parting life was laid. The Village Preacher. Goldsmith. *Fr.* The Deserted Village. TrGrPo

Beside the broad, gray Thames one lies. Laleham: Matthew Arnold's Grave. Lionel Johnson. FaBoPP

Beside the Brokenstraw or Licking Creek. John Chapman. Richard Wilbur. OxBC

Beside the idle summer sea. William Ernest Henley. OBNC

Beside the landsman knelt a dame. The Manor Lord. George Houghton. AA

Beside the Line of Elephants. Edna Becker. RHPC

Beside the lone river. Little Big Horn. Ernest McGaffey. PAH

Beside the pounding cataracts. The City of the End of Things. Archibald Lampman. NOBC; OBCV

Beside the rail, despite the gale. The Missing Link. Oliver Herford. CenHV

Beside the river—waterbirds, in the river—fish. Li K'ai-hsien, *tr. fr. Chinese by* Jonathan Chaves. *Fr.* Impromptu Poems. CoBLCP

Beside the road. Basho, *tr. by* Kenneth Koch *and* Harold Henderson. TTTS

Beside the Road. Ken Belford. NeAC

Beside the road the *wu t'ung* tree. Wu Chia-chi, *tr. fr. Chinese by* John E. Willis, Jr. *Fr.* Miscellaneous Poems, I. WFTU

Beside the Seaside, *sel.* Sir John Betjeman.

  "Green shutters, shut your shutters! Windyridge." OxBTC

Beside the slew the poplars play. A Prairie Water Colour. Duncan Campbell Scott. OBCV

Beside the sycamore, in hesitating. Within an Emerald. Salvador Díaz Mirón, *tr. by* Samuel Beckett. MexPo

Beside the ungathered rice he lay. The Slave's Dream. Longfellow. FaPoR; NAAL-1; PoNe

Beside the wine. Claustrophobia. Sean O Riordain, *tr. by* Thomas Kinsella. NOIV

Beside yon straggling fence that skirts the way. The Village Schoolmaster. Goldsmith. *Fr.* The Deserted Village. BeLS; EnRP; FaFP; GoTL; LaA; NOEC; NoP; OAEL-1; PoEL-3; TEP

Besides he was a shrewd Philosopher. Hudibras the Sectarian ("Besides he was a shrewd Philosopher"). Samuel Butler. *Fr.* Hudibras, I, 1. SeCePo

Besides the autumn poets sing. Emily Dickinson. OxBA

Besieged. Zalman Schneour, *tr. fr. Yiddish by* Joseph Leftwich. TrJP

Bespoke for weeks, he turned up some morning. Thatcher. Seamus Heaney. FaBCIP; IPY

Bess. William Stafford. NNaP; NoP

Bess My Badger. Ted Hughes. Mes

Besse Bunting. *Unknown.* MeEL

Bessie Carmichael School health day fair. Pan-Asian Holiday Tour. Luis Syquia. BrSi

Bessy Bell and Mary Gray. Mother Goose. OxNR

Bessy [*or* Bessie] Bell and Mary Gray. Mother Goose. ESPB; OxBB; OxNR

Best, The. Elizabeth Barrett Browning. OxBSP

Best? Siv Widerberg, *tr. fr. Swedish by* Verne Moberg. NTCP

Best and brightest, come away. The Invitation. Shelley. GTBS; GTBS-P; OBEV

  (Invitation, to Jane, The.) CH

  (To Jane: The Invitation.) NAEL-2

Best Cowboy Movie, The. Elizabeth Smither. PeNZ

Best dance is the dance of the eastern clans, The. *Somali Oral Tradition, tr. by* B. W. Andrzejewski *and* I. M. Lewis. WTO

Best Friend, The. W. H. Davies. OBMV

Best Loved of Africa. Margaret Danner. PoBA; PoNe

Best of All, The. Fanny Crosby. BLRP

Best of All, The. Margaret G. Rhodes. BoTP

Best of All. *Unknown.* WBLP

Best of All. J. M. Westrup. BoTP

Best of all is to be idle. Against Whatever It Is That's Encroaching. Charles Simic. BLA

Best of both worlds being got, The. Poets' Corner. Robert Graves. FaBoEE

Best of poetry comes from the destitute, but my pocket is not yet empty, The. Chao Yi, *tr. fr. Chinese* by Irving Lo. *Fr.* On Poetry, V. WFTU

Best of thy sex! if sacred friendship can. To Phylocles, Inviting Him to Friendship. "Ephelia." WPE

Best Old Fellow in the World, The. *Unknown.* AmFP

Best Religion, The. Heine, *tr. fr. German* by Emma Lazarus. *Fr.* Tannhäuser. TrJP

"Best scene/ in the whole play!" *Unknown, tr.* by Burton Watson. FCEI

Best slave, The. Alcestis on the Poetry Circuit. Erica Jong. AmPA

Best Slow Dancer, The. David Wagoner. NoAM

Best solace of my lonely hours! To Poesy. John Critchley Prince. PF

Best Thing, The. Jacques Roubaud, *tr. fr. French* by Neil Baldwin. RHTwFP

Best Thing in the World, The. Elizabeth Barrett Browning. EBVV; NOBVV

Best Time for Conception, The. Claude Quillet, *tr. fr. Latin* by George Sewell. *Fr.* Callipaedia; or, The Art of Getting Beautiful Children. FaBoUs

"Best way to go, The," said my muffled-up friend. March Hares. Walter de la Mare. FaBoNo

Bestiary. A. M. Klein. OBCV

Bestiary, A. Kenneth Rexroth. OBAL

Bestiary, A ("Man who found the aardvark, The."), *sels. Kenneth* Rexroth. OBAL
   Deer. HoPM; PBBP
   Fox. NNaP
   Herring. HoPM
   Horse. NNaP
   Lion. HoPM
   Raccoon. NNaP
   (Racoon.) FiBHP
   Vulture. NNaP
   Wolf. NNaP
   You. HoPM

Bestiary, The, *sels. Unknown, tr. fr. Middle English.*
   Nature of the Eagle, The. PBBP
   Nature of the Turtle Dove, The. PBBP
   Whale, The. *Tr.* by Richard Wilbur. CRP

Bestiary for the Fingers of My Right Hand. Charles Simic. AmPA; LCAP

Bestow, O Lord, thy gracious pardon. Fyodor Tyutchev, *tr.* by Alan Myers. AAA

Bestow this day on us the grace. The Festival of the Nativity. Richard De Ledrede, *tr.* by Robert Wyse Jackson. TIRV

Bête Humaine. Francis Brett Young. CH

Beth Gêlert. William Robert Spencer. BeLS
   (Beth Gêlert; or, The Grave of the Greyhound.) BLPA; OBNV

Bethel. A. J. H. Duganne. PAH

Bethlehem. William Canton. *See* Carol: "When the herd[s] were watching."

Bethlehem Town. Eugene Field. WBLP

Bethou me, said sparrow, to the crackled blade. Wallace Stevens. *Fr.* Notes toward a Supreme Fiction. LiTM

Bethsabe Bathing. George Peele. *See* David and Bethsabe: Bethsabe's Song.

Bethsabe's Song. George Peele. *Fr.* David and Bethsabe, sc. i. GBL; NOBE; NoP; OBSC; OxBoLi; OxBSP; PoEL-2; RB; TEP

Betjeman at the Post Office. Stanley J. Sharpless. FaBoPa

Betjeman, 1984. Charles Causley. FaBoCo; NOBL; OxBTC

Betray no surprise. Whisper in Agony. Jules Supervielle, *tr.* by D. J. Enright. OBD

Betrayal. Sidney Lanier. *Fr.* The Jaquerie. AA

Betrayal. Sherod Santos. NAmP

Betrayal. John Banister Tabb. ACP

Betrayal. Sir Thomas Wyatt. *See* How Should I Be So Pleasant.

Betrayal of Christ in Tucson and Brussels, The. David Wojahn. NAmP

Betrayal of the Rose, The. Edith Matilda Thomas. AA

Betrayed by friend dragged from the garden hailed. Ecce Homunculus. R. A. K. Mason. ATNZ; PeNZ

Betrayed Maiden, The. *Unknown.* OBET

Betrothal, A. Edith Jay Scovell. GBL

Betrothed. Louise Bogan. LLLT

Betsy Baker. *Unknown.* OxNR

Betsy, if pencil erasers could sing. 110 Year Old House. Ed Ochester. Psk

Betsy Jane's Sixth Birthday. Alfred Noyes. ILY

Betsy says a friend of hers. The Bookkeepers Talk Baseball. Jim Daniels. SoTCo

Betsy's Battle Flag. Minna Irving. OPP; PAH

Better a day in Oxbridge. Stanley J. Sharpless. BXAP

Better Answer to Cloe [*or* Chloe] Jealous, A. Matthew Prior. *See* Dear Cloe how blubbered is that pretty face!

Better born than married, misled. The Grandmother. Wendell Berry. MT; SaC

Better Come Drink Wine with Me, *sels.* Po Chü-i, *tr. fr. Chinese* by Burton Watson. CoBCP
   "Don't go climbing up to the blue clouds."
   "Don't go hide in the deep mountains."
   "Don't go into the realm of red dust."
   "Don't go off and be a farmer."

Better disguised than the leaf-insect. The Lake. Ted Hughes. FaBoTw; NYBP

Better it were had you borne black earth, o mother, rather than me. Mother of Man. Vesna Parun, *tr.* by Mary Coote. PBWP

Better never trouble Trouble. Trouble. David Keppel. FaFP; FPL; PoLF; WBLP

Better not go to these deep woods. The Great Fountains. Anne Hébert, *tr.* by Willis Barnstone. BoWoP

Better not to go back to the village. The Malefic Return. Ramón López Velarde, *tr.* by Samuel Beckett. MexPo; OBVE

Better one bird in hand than ten in the wood. Of Birds and Birders. John Heywood. PBBP

Better one thin frail line of friendship in a letter. The Letter. John Blight. CBAP

Better Resurrection, A. Christina Rossetti. NOBVV; TrPWD

Better than a closet martinet. What Happened? John Wieners. PoM

Better than Gold ("Better than grandeur, better than gold"). Abram Joseph Ryan. FaFP

Better than granite, Spoon River. Aaron Hatfield. Edgar Lee Masters. *Fr.* Spoon River Anthology. LiTA

Better than to say things like a wise fellow. Tabito, *tr. fr. Japanese* by Hiroaki Sato. *Fr.* Manyo Shu. FCEI

Better the book against the rock. Three Poems about Children. Austin Clarke. CIP

Better they never learned to read! The Misogynist. Jean Morgan. FF

Better Things. George Macdonald. PWR

Better to be the rock above the river. La Crosse at Ninety Miles an Hour. Richard Eberhart. AmFN

Better to close the book and say good-night. The Double Autumn. James Reeves. OxBSP

Better to live as a rogue and a bum. Mahsati, *tr.* by Deirdre Lashgari. AIW; WPOW

Better to see your cheek grown hollow. Madman's Song. Elinor Wylie. MoAB; MoAmPo; PoRA

Better to smell the violet cool than sip. Better Things. George Macdonald. PWR

Better to Spit on the Whip than Stutter Your Love like a Worm. Colette Inez. TW

Better trust all and be deceived. Faith. Frances Anne Kemble. FaBoBe

Better Way, The. "Susan Coolidge." OPP

Better Way, The. Walter Leaf. FaBoCo

Better, Wiser and Happier. Ella Wheeler Wilcox. WBLP

Betty at the Party. *Unknown.* BOTP; OnUR

Betty Blue. Mother Goose. OxNR

Betty Botter bought some butter. *Unknown.* OxNR

Betty Fuller cried and said, Hit me. A Local Man Remembers Betty Fuller. James Whitehead. MT

Betty Pringle's Pig. Mother Goose. OxNR

Betty Zane. Thomas Dunn English. PAH

Betuix twell houris and ellevin. The Amendis to the Telyouris and Sowtaris for the Turnament Maid on Thame. William Dunbar. OBSV

Between. Agnes Nemes Nagy, *tr. fr. Hungarian* by Alan Dixon. MHuP

Between. Tomioka Taeko, *tr. fr. Japanese* by Sato. FCEI

Between a Contractor and His Wife. *Unknown.* NOEC

Between a sunny bank and the sun. Two Houses. Edward Thomas. FaBoCh

Between a wicked rhinoceros trail. Minor Mythology. David Avidan, *tr.* by Warren Bargad *and* Stanley F. Chyet. IP

Between an Unemployed Artist and His Wife. *Unknown.* NOEC

Between August and November. Koh Chang-soo, *tr. fr. Korean by the author.* ACKP

Between Birthdays. Ogden Nash. OnUR

Between Botallack and the light. A Ballad of a Mine. Robin Skelton. MoBS

Between Cellini's Perseus and the Sabine Rape. More Nudes for Florence. Harold Witt. ErPo

Between clouds of fire and clouds of blood. Hayyim Nahman Bialik, *tr. fr. Hebrew* by Bernhard Frank. *Fr.* At Evening Time. MHeP

Between dawn and the Opera. Clandestine Work. Iwan Goll, *tr. by* Anthony Rudolf. VWA

Between decision and ensuing act. Birdwatcher. Henry Treece. WaP

Between each layer of tattered, broken flesh. Burial Detail. Andrew Hudgins. MT

Between Evening and Night. Gerhard Fritsch, *tr. fr. German by* Beth Bjorklund. CoAuP

Between extremities. Vacillation. W. B. Yeats. NoAM

Between fields of popcorn. "America, I Love You." Bert Kalmar *and* Harry Ruby. FiBHP

Between five and fifty. Praise. Jane Cooper. TAP

Between great coloured vanes the butterflies. Wings. Judith Wright. CBAP

Between grief on my knees and death on my feet. Choice. Abd al-Aziz al-Maqalih, *tr. by* Lena Jayyusi *and* Christopher Middleton. MAP

Between Hard Rocks and Savage Winds I Try. Vittoria da Colonna, *tr. fr. Italian by* Muriel Kittel. DMI

Between her and me there was a table. Czeslaw Milosz, *tr. fr. Polish by the author*. *Fr.* Bobo's Metamorphosis, VIII. PwPP

Between Here and Illinois. Ralph Pomeroy. Psk

Between him and me, I feel. Bi-Lingual. Sylvia Paskin. DT

Between Jejuri and the Railway Station. Arun Kolatkar. UAS

Between ladder and north wall. Attempt. Ilse Aichinger, *tr. by* Beth Bjorklund. CoAuP

Between Leaps. Brad Leithauser. MAYP

Between Life and Death. Frantisek Gottlieb, *tr. fr. Czech by* Ewald Osers. VWA

Between Love and Death. Frank Stanford. MT

Between Me and Anyone Who Can Understand. Sharon Scott. JB

Between me and the rising sun. Cobwebs. E. L. M. King. BoTP

Between me and the sunset, like a dome. The Man against the Sky. E. A. Robinson. AmPP; CMoP; LiTA; OxBA

Between me and the wood. Ark Artefact. Jay Macpherson. *Fr.* The Ark. NOBC

Between Mobile and Galveston. Annie. Guillaume Apollinaire, *tr. by* William Meredith. RHTwFP

Between mountains coils a city. Wind. Abba Kovner, *tr. by* Warren Bargad *and* Stanley F. Chyet. IP

Between my finger and my thumb. Digging. Seamus Heaney. BIrV; CIP; InPS; IPY; NAEL-2; TwCP

Between myself and the apple tree. Complaint on Solipsism. Gyula Illyés, *tr. by* William Jay Smith. MHuP

Between Ourselves. Audre Lorde. WPOW

Between painting a roof yesterday and the hay. Independence Day. Wendell Berry. OFD

Between pond and sheepbarn, by maples and watery birches. A Sister on the Tracks. Donald Hall. BLA

Between rebellion as a private study and the public. Last Poem. Charles Donnelly. BIrV

(Poem: "Between rebellion as a private study and the public.") CIP

Between Rivers and Seas. Lance Henson. VoR

Between sea-foam and the tide. To a Boy. Nancy Morejón, *tr. by* Kathleen Weaver. AIW

Between Seasons. Anne Welsh. PeSA

Between Talcy and Mer. Carole Oles. BLA

Between the cloud and the ground. Clouds and Clay. Valerie Gillies. PoSH

Between the dark and the daylight. If. Franklin P. Adams. OBAL

Between the dark and the daylight. The Children's Hour. Longfellow. AA; AnAmPo; FaBoBe; FaBV; FaFP; FaPON; FPL; OBAL; OBCA; OHFP; PoEL-5; PoLF; WBLP

Between the dark silent trees. Dionysius. Sophia de Mello Breyner Andresen, *tr. by* Allan Francovich. PBWP

Between the earth and the drowned platinum. The Battle of the Jarama. Pablo Neruda, *tr. by* Angel Flores. WaaP

Between the earth and the sky. The Inheritance. Sami Mahdi, *tr. by* May Jayyusi. MAP

Between the falling leaf and rose-bud's breath. The Term of Death. Sarah Morgan Bryan Piatt. AA

Between the fosse and inner wall. The Defender. Arthur M. Sampley. GoYe

Between the freeway/ and the gray conning towers. A Walk with Tom Jefferson. Philip Levine. BAP

Between the gardening and the cookery. A Bookshop Idyll. Kingsley Amis. NePoEA; OxBTC

Between the ghetto's slumber. The Casbah. Mamdouh Udwan, *tr. by* May Jayyusi *and* Naomi Shihab Nye. MAP

Between the midnight and the morn. The Secret Muse. Roy Campbell. PeSA

Between the mountains and the sea. Santa Barbara. Francis Fisher Browne. AA

Between the perfect. Somewhere the Equation Breaks Down. Daniel Berrigan. NYBP

Between the Porch and the Altar ("Meeting his mother makes him lose ten years."), *sel.* Robert Lowell. NePoEA

At the Altar. *Fr.* IV. InPK

Between the Quay of San Nicolas and the Sea. Antonio Cisneros, *tr. fr. Spanish by* David Tipton. Per

Between the railway and the mine. The Blackberry. Norman Nicholson. MoBrPo

Between the rough hills of gabbro and the cold sea. In Our Time. Michael Roberts. WaP

Between the rusted railways. One Plant for Man-made Oil. Ono Tozaburo, *tr. by* Hiroaki Sato. FCEI

Between the shrubs in the farmyard struts. A Turkey. Hugo Claus, *tr. by* Theo Hermans. DuIn

Between the Sunken Sun and the New Moon. Paul Hamilton Hayne. AA

Between the tides. The Bourgeois Are Beasts. Pablo Guevara, *tr. by* Ena Hollis *and* David Tipton. Per

Between the Traveller and the Setting Sun. Henry David Thoreau. PoEL-4

Between the two main destinations. Mohammad Taqi Mir, *tr. by* Ahmed Ali. GoT

Between the under and the upper blue. Seagulls. Robert Francis. RFM

Between the Walls of the Valley. Elisabeth Peck. AmFN

Between the walls, the brim. Terce. James McMichael. PoA

Between the White Stone Canyons. Anadad Eldan, *tr. fr. Hebrew by* Bernhard Frank. MHeP

Between the World and Me. Richard Wright. AmNP; IDB; LiTM; MoP; PoBA

Between their sandspit ends. Barred Islands. Philip Booth. NePoEA

Between them is the land of broken colors. The Black Horse Rider. Pierre Loving. EAS

Between thirty and forty, one is distracted by the five lusts. On Being Sixty. Po Chü-i, *tr. by* Arthur Waley. AWP

Between this wall and that I place. Ah, When Will Dawn Begin to Break? Shmuel Halkin, *tr. by* Hillel Halkin. PeBMYV

Between town and the. The Quarry Pool. Denise Levertov. VGW

Between trains, on this day of snow. At the Roman Baths, Bath. Edward Lucie-Smith. NePoEA-2

Between Two Furious Oceans, *sel.* Dick Diespecker.

"All these are your essence, you are their flesh and their force." CaP

Between two golden tufts of summer grass. Lying in the Grass. Sir Edmund William Gosse. EBVV

Between two mighty hills a sheer. The Eagle. "Fiona Macleod." *Fr.* Transcripts from Nature. FM

Between two rivers. Island. Langston Hughes. HCAP

Between Two Worlds. Rosemary Thomas. NYBP

Between Us. Stephen Berg. NaP

Between Us. James Merrill. PoE

Between us. Nizar Qabbani, *tr. by* Lena Jayyusi *and* W. S. Merwin. MAP

Between Vicksburg and Rolling Fork. Road. D. C. Berry. MT

Between Walls. William Carlos Williams. HoPM; SOTW; TAP; VGW

Between Words. Gary Soto. NAmP

Between You and Me. Samuel Hazo. GOYP

Between You and Me. Fahmida Riaz, *tr. fr. Urdu by* Mahmood Jamal. PBMUP

Between You and Me. Shmu'el Shatal, *tr. fr. Hebrew by* Bernhard Frank. MHeP

Between you and me on the overlook. Two in Twilight. Eugenio Montale, *tr. by* William Arrowsmith. AnAn

Betweens. Norman MacCaig. EAS

Betwene Merch and Averil. *See* Bytuene Mersh and Averil.

"Betwixt mine eye and heart a league is took." Shakespeare. *Fr.* Sonnets, XLVII. EyDe

Betwixt the quarters, flows a golden sea. Battle of Actium. Virgil, *tr. fr. Latin, tr. by* Dryden. *Fr.* The Aeneid [*or* Eneados], VIII. OBS

Betwixt two ridges of plowed-land sat Wat. The Hunting of the Hare. Margaret Lucas, Duchess of Newcastle. FM

Beverley Maid and the Tinker, The. *Unknown.* CoMu

Beverly Hills, Chicago. Gwendolyn Brooks. VGW

Bewail not much, my parents! me, the prey. Lucian, *tr. by* William Cowper. OBD

Bewail with me, all ye that have professed. On the Death of Phillips. *Unknown.* OBSC

Bewailing in my chamber thus allone. He Sees His Beloved. James I, King of Scotland. *Fr.* The Kingis Quair. GoTS; PoEL-1

Bewar, squier, yeman, and page. A Warning to Those Who Serve Lords. *Unknown.* MeEL

Beware: Do Not Read This Poem. Ishmael Reed. BPo; CNA; NIP; NoP; PoBA; WSC

Beware Fair Maide. *At. to* Joshua Sylvester. OBS

Beware, My Child. Shel Silverstein. PDV

Beware, My Successor. Loren C. Eiseley. BWV
Beware of age. Charles Hubert Sisson. *Fr.* The Regrets. PoPo
Beware of Dogmas. Ebenezer Elliott. FaBoEE
Beware of Figs. Nicophon, *tr. fr. Greek by* Charles Duke Yonge. FaBoUs
Beware of my heart: it is. Shamsuddin Mohammad Vali, *tr. by* Ahmed Ali. GoT
Beware of Ruins. Alec Derwent Hope. NoAM
Beware of the man who denounces ambition. Seventeen Warnings in Search of a Feminist Poem. Erica Jong. AmPA
Beware of the Poison. Hazel Williams. WS
Beware of thinking nothing's there. Virtual Particles. Frank Wilczek. NBLV
Beware, Soul Brother. Chinua Achebe. UAS
Beware the Months of Fire. Patrick Lane. NeAC
Bewick and Graham. *Unknown.* ESPB
Bewick and the Graeme, The. *Unknown. See* Gude Lord Graeme is to Carlisle gone.
Bewick Finzer. E. A. Robinson. CMoP; MoAB; MoAmPo; NAAL-2; PPP
Bewildered in our buying throng. Patrum Propositum. Robert Fitzgerald. GOA
Bewildered with the broken tongue. Words in Time. Archibald MacLeish. PoRA
Bewilderingly, from wildly shaken cloud. Internal Firesides. Mathilde Blind. FM
Bewilderment at the Entrance of the Fat Boy into Eden, A. Daryl Hine. NOBC; OBCV
Bewley's Oriental Café, Westmoreland Street. Paul Durcan. CIP
Bewteis of the Fute-Ball, The. *Unknown.* FaBoCo; GoTS; OxBS
Bewty of hir amorus ene, The. Off Womanheid Ane Flour Delice. *Unknown.* OxBS
Beyond. Vicente Aleixandre, *tr. fr. Spanish by* Perry Higman. LPSS
Beyond. Aimé Césaire, *tr. fr. French by* Clayton Eshleman *and* Annette Smith. RHTwFP
Beyond. Lionel Johnson. BrPo
Beyond. Hannah Parker Kimball. AA
Beyond. *Unknown.* PWR
Beyond/ restless children littering popcorn. Cowboy-Boot Sale. Norma Thomas Colvin. TSM
Beyond all this, the wish to be alone. Wants. Philip Larkin. GTBS-P; NoP
Beyond, beneath, within, wherever blood. A Quintina of Crosses. Chad Walsh. TrCP
Beyond Feith Buidhe. Hamish Brown. PoSH
Beyond Kerguelen. Henry Clarence Kendall. PoAu-1
Beyond Logic. Lo Fu, *tr. fr. Chinese by* Dominic Cheung. IFON
Beyond Love. Octavio Paz, *tr. fr. Spanish by* Perry Higman. LPSS
Beyond Magdalen and by the Bridge, on a place called there the Plain. By Magdalen Bridge, Oxford. Gerard Manley Hopkins. FaBoPP
Beyond Memory. Monny De Boully, *tr. fr. Serbo-Croatian by* Aleksander Nejgebauer. VWA
Beyond my sight, deep into the darkness. Song of the Lamp. Maruyama Kaoru, *tr. by* Hiroaki Sato. FCEI
Beyond my window in the night. A Town Window. John Drinkwater. BoTP
Beyond Nagel's Funeral Parlor. "The Elizabethans Called It Dying." James Schuyler. NeAP; PoM
Beyond New York the sun rolls down. The Yellow-White Glow. H. Leivick, *tr. by* Benjamin *and* Barbara Harshav. AYP
Beyond number/ are the fools, who simply cannot see. Nanak, *tr. by* John Stratton Hawley *and* Mark Juergensmeyer. SSI
Beyond Possession. Elizabeth Jennings. NePoEA
Beyond Recall. Mary Emily Bradley. AA
Beyond Religion. Lucretius, *tr. fr. Latin by* William Ellery Leonard. AWP
Beyond the Alps. Robert Lowell. NOBA
Beyond the Atlas roams a glutton. The Glutton. Robert Graves. CMoP; TW
Beyond the back door. Ito Sachio, *tr. by* Geoffrey Bownas *and* Anthony Thwaite. PeBJV
Beyond the Beaten Way. George Sands Johnson. PWR
Beyond the blind, the rain rattles down. Tune: Ripples Sifting Sand. Li Yü, *tr. by* Burton Watson. CoBCP
Beyond the bourn of mortal death and birth. At Last. Katrina Trask. AA
Beyond the Chagres. James Stanley Gilbert. PoLF
Beyond the choric gestures of the olive. Greece. Derek Walcott. AnAn
Beyond the doorway of the tiny room. Blue Homespun. Frank Oliver Call. CaP
Beyond the edge of the sepia. Lament for a Cricket Eleven. Kenneth Allott. OxBTC
Beyond the End. Denise Levertov. NeAP; VGW

Beyond the fence she hesitates. Midwife Cat. Mark Van Doren. CRH
Beyond the fences. Hawking. Shotetsu, *tr. by* Steven D. Carter. WFTW
Beyond the foot of the bed: a seascape whose ocean. On Motel Walls. David Wagoner. BLA; DiPo
Beyond the great valley an odd instinctive rising. Ascent to the Sierras. Robinson Jeffers. OxBA
Beyond the green railings there is a small garden. Song of the River City. Chang Pi, *tr. by* Lois Fusek. ATF
Beyond the hour we counted rain that fell. Old Countryside. Louise Bogan. HAP; LiTA; WPE
Beyond the Hunting Woods. Donald Justice. NePoEA; NYBP
Beyond the Imaginary Garden. Gabriel Preil, *tr. fr. Hebrew by* Bernhard Frank. MHeP
Beyond the inmost barriers of the brain. The Owl. Edward Davison. PoA
Beyond the last gate, where I made my first halt. On Scafell Pike. Ted Walker. NYBP
Beyond the last horizon's rim. The Hills of Rest. A. B. Paine. WGRP
Beyond the last house, where home was. American Portrait: Old Style. Robert Penn Warren. FYAP
Beyond the Last Lamp Near Tooting Common. Thomas Hardy. NOBE; OBNC
Beyond the low marsh-meadows and the beach. The Pines and the Sea. Christopher Pearse Cranch. AA
Beyond the murk that swallows me. Irene Rutherford McLeod. *Fr.* Rebel. WGRP
Beyond the Nigger ("Beyond the outstretched hands"). Sterling Plumpp. PoBA
Beyond the Potomac. Paul Hamilton Hayne. PAH
Beyond the Presidency. Morgan Gibson. FF
Beyond the scrub pine ridges, beyond Pisgah. Forever Mountain. Fred Chappell. BLA
Beyond the sea, I know not where. Vivérols. David Starr Jordan. AA
Beyond the soft violet fog. Bird. Jung Han-mo, *tr. by* Koh Chang-soo. ACKP
Beyond the sphere which spreads to widest space. Dante, *tr. fr. Italian by* Dante Gabriel Rossetti. *Fr.* La Vita Nuova, XXIX. AWP; CTC
Beyond the stone wall. Jug Brook. Ellen Bryant Voigt. MAYP; MT
Beyond the system's fall. The FTL Addict Fixes. Bruce Boston. BWV
Beyond the Tapestries. Norma Farber. GoYe
Beyond the temple, a hidden cliff. Yang Shih-ch'i, *tr. fr. Chinese by* Jonathan Chaves. *Fr.* A Group of Officials. CoBLCP
Beyond the turning sea's far foam. At War. Russell Atkins. AmNP
Beyond the vague Atlantic deep. Our Mother Tongue. Richard Monckton Milnes. GN
Beyond the waves rearing a thousandfold. Hitomaro, *tr. fr. Japanese. Fr.* Manyo Shu. Ma
Beyond the white dust flushed by the carriers. Patrol; Buonamary. Bernard Gutteridge. WaP
Beyond these cypresses. MS. Found in a Bottle. Yang Mu, *tr. by* Dominic Cheung. IFON
Beyond Time. Mieczyslaw Jastrun. PwPP
Beyond us, the Garden of Gethsemane. The Betrayal of Christ in Tucson and Brussels. David Wojahn. NAmP
Beyond Wars. David Morton. PAH
Beyond Winter. Emerson. RHPC
Beyond Words. Robert Frost. TW; WeW
Bhagavad-Gita, The, *sels. Unknown, tr. fr. Sanskrit.*
  "Arjuna said:/ How shall I in battle against Bhisma." *Tr. by* Franklin Edgerton. DL
  "Learn from me, Son of Kunti! also this." *Tr. by* Sir Edwin Arnold. TOF
  "Nay, but of such an one." *Tr. by* Sir Edwin Arnold. TOF
  "Sovereign soul, The/ Of him who lives self-governed and at peace." *Tr. by* Sir Edwin Arnold. TOF
  "Steadfast a lamp burns sheltered from the wind." *Tr. by* Sir Edwin Arnold. TOF
  "Yet hard/ the travail is for such as bend their minds." *Tr. by* Sir Edwin Arnold. TOF
Bhil woman tasted them, plum after plum, The. Mirabai, *tr. by* John Stratton Hawley *and* Mark Juergensmeyer. SSI
Bi-Lingual. Sylvia Paskin. DT
Biafra. L. V. Mack. PoBA
Bianca among the Nightingales. Elizabeth Barrett Browning. BrRo; GTBS-P
Bianca's First Steps in the Arts. K. Schippers, *tr. fr. Dutch by* Peter Nijmeijer. DuIn
Bible, The, *sel.* David Levi, *tr. fr. Italian by* Mary A. Craig. "Thou, Zion, old and suffering." TrJP
Bible, The. Lizelia Augusta Jenkins Moorer. CBWP-3
Bible, The. Sir Walter Scott. *See* Monastery, The: Sir Walter Scott's Tribute.

Bible is an antique volume, The. Emily Dickinson. NAAL-1; NoP

Bible opens then closes real hard, A. Empty Streams of Autumn. Ray A. Young Bear. NOVW

Bible says Sennacherib's campaign was spoiled, The. C. S. Lewis. TrCP

Bible soothes the harried soul, The. Travelling Companions. Richard Armour. GrPl

Bible Story. Charles Causley. TOF

Bibliographer. Josephine Miles. FaBoWP

Bibliolaters, *sel.* James Russell Lowell.
   God Is Not Dumb. WGRP

Bibliomaniac's Prayer, The. Eugene Field. AA

Bibliophile, The. Max Jacob, *tr. fr. French by* Ron Padgett. RHTwFP

Bibliotheca Bodleiana. Geoffrey Grigson. GBL

Bibulous eagle behind me at the ball game, The. One to Nothing. Carolyn Kizer. OBAL

"Biby's" Epitaph. *Unknown. See* Muvver was barfin' 'er biby one night.

Bicause I have the still kept fro lyes and blame. Petrarch, *tr. by* Sir Thomas Wyatt. OBVE

Bickering of vowels on the buses, The. An Irish Childhood in England: 1951. Eavan Boland. CIP

Bicylcalamity. Edmund W. Peters. SD

Bicycle, The. Stan Rice. NPGG

Bicycle, The. David Wojahn. NAmP

Bicycle Rider, The. Thomas William Shapcott. CBAP

Bicycles go by in twos and threes, The. Inniskeen Road: July Evening. Patrick Kavanagh. CIP; FaBCIP; IPY; MoP; NoAM; NoP

Bicycles! Tricycles! John Banister Tabb. OBAL

Bicycling Song. Henry Charles Beeching. *See* With lifted feet, hands still.

Bid a strong ghost stand at the head. A Prayer for My Son. W. B. Yeats. EBEV; NAs; TIRV

Bid me not go where neither suns nor show'rs. William Cartwright. OBS

Bid me remember, O my gracious Lord. Mary Elizabeth Coleridge. *Fr.* Death. TrPWD

Bid me to live, and I will live. To Anthea, Who May Command Him Anything. Robert Herrick. CaPo; GTBS; GTBS-P; JCP; NOBE; OAEL-1; OBEV; OBS; SeCP; SeCV-1; TrGrPo

Bid your Papa Goodnight. Sweet exhibition! Mrs. Hopley, on Seeing Her Children Say Goodnight to Their Father. Gerard Manley Hopkins. FaBoEE

Bidean Nam Bian. A. M. Dobson. PoSH

Bifocal. William Stafford. RB

Biftek aux Champignons. Henry Augustin Beers. AA

Big. Dorothy Aldis. RAR

Big Baboon, The. Hilaire Belloc. MoBrPo; MoShBr

Big Bell in Zion, The. Theodore Henry Shackleford. BANP

Big Ben is cracked, we needs must own. To Disraeli. Shirley Brooks. NOBL

Big Bessie Throws Her Son into the Street. Gwendolyn Brooks. VGW

Big Billie Potts was big and stout. The Ballad of Billie Potts. Robert Penn Warren. NOBA; OxBA

Big blue-jean, the summer-bored boy next door, The. Carry Me Back. John Holmes. AmFN

Big box,/ Little box. *Unknown.* OxNR

Big Boy came. Catch. Langston Hughes. NoAM

Big breakers roll over the sea. Breakers over the Sea. *Malay Oral Tradition, tr. by* R. O. Winstedt. WTO

Big Brother. Elizabeth Madox Roberts. FaPON

Big brown hen and Mrs. Duck, The. A Little Talk. *Unknown.* RAR

Big bull-dyke, surly and sallow, A. *Unknown.* PeHV

Big cat teases a butterfly, A. Issa, *tr. fr. Japanese by* Hiroaki Sato. *Fr.* Forty-four Hokku. FCEI

Big-city streets. New York in a Jewish Mood. Judah Leib Teller, *tr. by* Benjamin *and* Barbara Harshav. AYP

Big Daddy Lipscomb, who used to help them up. Say Goodbye to Big Daddy. Randall Jarrell. ASP; PoNe

Big Dam. William Robert Moses. AmFN

Big Dog. Anselm Hollo. UL

Big Engines, The. Jack Kerouac. *Fr.* Mexico City Blues, 146. NeAP

Big farm girl with the dumb prophetic body, The. Bitter Harvest. Alistair Campbell. ATNZ; PeNZ

Big, Fat Summer—and the Lean and Hard. Frederick Bock. NYBP

Big feet,/ Black feet. Feet. Irene Thompson. BoTP

Big field brings a heavy crop, The. *Unknown, tr. by* Arthur Waley. BoS

Big Fine Woman from Ruleville. Jayne Cortez. ER

Big Friend of the Stones. Steve Orlen. Psk

Big Fun. Diane Burns. STE

Big grey elephant, A. Just Jumbo. Eileen Mathias. BoTP

Big guns again. Imperator Victus. Hart Crane. OxBA

Big High and Lonesome, The. Baxter Black. CowP

Big House, The. Paul Muldoon. NoAM

Big house,/ Little house. *Unknown.* OxNR

Big impression left on me, The. My Answer. Ralph Adamo. MT

Big Man. Mason Jordan Mason. PoNe

Big Momma. Don L. Lee. BPo; CNA

Big Nasturtiums, The. Robert Beverly Hale. BoNaP; NYBP

Big-nose looks best in mountain-coarse clothes. My Man Pa Replies. Li Ho, *tr. by* Burton Watson. CoBCP

Big old houses have passed away. Sometimes I Think of Maryland. Jodi Braxton. CNA

Big One, The. Luis Cabalquinto. BrSi

Big pine's darkening, The. Ozaki Hosai, *tr. fr. Japanese by* Hiroaki Sato. *Fr.* One Hundred Haiku in Free Form. FCEI

Big Rabbit goes to see his baby. *Unknown, tr. by* Jerome Rothenberg. STP

Big Ralph from Rolfe had a black Corvette. The True Ballad of the Great Race to Gilmore City. Phil Hey. Psk

Big rat, big rat, Do not gobble our [*or* don't eat my] millet! *Unknown.* BoS, *tr. by* Arthur Waley; CoBCP, *tr. by* Burton Watson.

Big Rock Candy Mountains, The ("On a summer day in the month of May"). *Unknown.* NOBA

Big Rock Candy Mountains, The ("One evening as the sun went down [*or* when the sun was low]"). *Unknown.* AmFP; ChTr; GBP; OBAL; TTTS, *shorter vers.*

Big rocks into pebbles. Rocks. Florence Parry Heide. NTCP

Big Sheep Knocks You About. Sharon Bryan. MAYP; PPR

Big Steamers. Kipling. Par

Big steel tourist shield says maybe, The. On a Field Trip at Fredericksburg. Dave Smith. GeTw; HCAP

Big stones of the cistern behind the barn, The. Twilights. James Wright. LCAP; NaP

Big Trimmer, The. Ronald P. Tanaka. BrSi

Big trucks for steel beams. Trucks. James Sterling Tippett. FaPON

Big trucks with apples. Country Trucks. Monica Shannon. FaPON

Big Turtle, A. *Unknown.* RAR

Big water main, The. In War. Mason Jordan Mason. PoNe

Big Willie's back from the war. Right Where He Left Off. Craig Weeden. ASP

Big Wind. Theodore Roethke. AmPP; CMoP; GoJo; InvP; NoP; VGW

Big with great purposes and proud, they sat. Homer, *tr. fr. Greek by* William Cowper. *Fr.* The Iliad, VIII. OBVE

Big yellow trolley limbers along. There Are So Many Ways of Going Places. Leslie Thompson. FaPON

Big young bareheaded woman, A. Proletarian Portrait. William Carlos Williams. AnAmPo; OBAL; TAP

Bigerlow. *Unknown.* AS

Bigger Day, The. G. E. Bishop. WBLP

Bigger than earth, certainly. What She Said ("Bigger than earth, certainly"). Tevakulattar, *tr. by* A. K. Ramanujan. PLW

Biggest Killing, The. Edward Dorn. VGW

Bight, The. Elizabeth Bishop. FaBoWP; HCAP; NAAL-2; NYBP; RB

Biglow Papers, The, *sels.* James Russell Lowell.
  1st Series, No. I.
    Letter, A ("Thrash away, you'll hev to rattle"). AmPP; OxBA (Mr. Hosea Biglow Speaks.) PAH
  1st Series, No. II.
    Letter, A ("This kind o' sogerin' ain't a mite like our October trainin' "). OxBA
  1st Series, No. III.
    What Mr. Robinson Thinks. AA; AmPP; PAH
  1st Series, No. V.
    Debate in the Sennit, The. PAH
  1st Series, No. VII.
    Candidate's Letter, The. AA
  2d Series, Introduction.
    Courtin', The. AA; AmPP; BeLS; NOBA; OBAL
  2d Series, No. II.
    Jonathan to John. PAH
  2d Series, No. IV.
    Rev. Homer Wilbur's "Festina Lente." OBAL
  2d Series, No. VI.
    Sunthin' in the Pastoral Line.
    (Spring.)
  2d Series, No. X.
    Mr. Hosea Biglow to the Editor of the Atlantic Monthly. AA, *abr.* ("Beaver roars hoarse with meltin' snows.") PoEL-5

Bigness of cannon, The. La Guerre. E. E. Cummings. MoAB; MoAmPo

Bignonia blossoms on both shores, a streamful of water. In a Boat on the Cha River. Chang Yü, *tr. by* Jonathan Chaves. CoBLCP

Bigots at home, and infidels abroad. Epigram on the Play-House at Amsterdam. William Parsons. OBTV

Bile Them Cabbage Down. *Unknown.* AmFP

Bill. Peter Kocan. CBAP

Bill/ exists. A Personality Sketch: Bill. Ronda Davis. JB
Bill/ Was ill. Careless Talk. Mark Hollis. FiBHP; NBLV
Bill and Joe. Oliver Wendell Holmes. AA
Bill Bailey, Won't You Please Come Home. Hughie Cannon. OBAL
Bill Bubble in a bowler hat. All the Way Back. Laura Riding. *Fr.*
 Forgotten Girlhood. RB
Bill Jones had been the shining star upon his college team. Alumnus
 Football. Grantland Rice. FPL; PoLF
Bill the Bachelor lived by himself. Bachelors' Buttons. Maud Morin.
 BoTP
Bill the Whaler. Will Lawson. PoAu-1
Billie Holiday's burned voice. Canary. Rita Dove. ER
Billows in love's stormy sea, The. Insha Allah Khan Insha, *tr. by* Ahmed
 Ali. GoT
Billowy headlands swiftly fly, The. Battle-Song of the *Oregon.* Wallace
 Rice. PAH
Billy. Harry Graham. *See* Some Ruthless Rhymes: Tender-heartedness.
Billy Boy. Dorothy King. BoTP
Billy Boy. *Unknown.* AmFP; BLPA; HoPM; OBET
Billy Budd, Foretopman, *sel.* Herman Melville.
 Billy in the Darbies. HAP; NAAL-1; NAWM-2; NOBA; OxBoLi;
 PoEL-5
Billy Could Ride. James Whitcomb Riley. ASP
Billy Grimes. *Unknown.* AmFP
Billy in one of his nice new sashes. Tender-heartedness. Harry Graham.
 Fr. Some Ruthless Rhymes, II. FaFP; NA; NBLV; RHPC
 (Billy.) FaBoCo
Billy in the Darbies. Herman Melville. *Fr.* Billy Budd, Foretopman.
 HAP; NAAL-1; NAWM-2; NOBA; OxBoLi; PoEL-5
Billy Ray Smith. Ogden Nash. ASP
Billy the Kid. *Unknown.* FaBoBe
Billy was born for a horse's back! Billy Could Ride. James Whitcomb
 Riley. ASP
Biltong. James Twala. WMBCH
Bim Bam. Dorothy Rosenberg. PoNe
Binary. Bob Perelman. LP
Bind, The. Wayne Brown. PBCV
Bind us the Morning, mother of the stars. Thefts of the Morning. Edith
 Matilda Thomas. AA
Bind-Weed. "Susan Coolidge." GN
Bind your straight hair. Thessalian. Winifred Bryher. PoA
Binding has some golden grillwork which imprisons cockatoos, The. The
 Bibliophile. Max Jacob, *tr. by* Ron Padgett. RHTwFP
Bindweed, The. Walter de la Mare. BrPo
Bingen on the Rhine. Caroline Elizabeth Norton. BeLS; BLPA;
 WBLP
Bingo. *Unknown.* CH; TTTS
Binni the Meshuggener. Danny Siegel. VWA
Binnorie; or, The Two Sisters. *Unknown.* OBEV; PoE; TrGrPo
Binoculars I'd meant for birds. Between Leaps. Brad Leithauser.
 MAYP
Binsey Poplars (Felled 1879). Gerard Manley Hopkins. BoNaP; BrPo;
 EBVV; ELP; FaBoPP; InPS; Mes; NAEL-2; NoAM; NoP; RB
Biographical Note. Gabriel Preil, *tr. fr. Hebrew by* Howard Schwartz.
 VWA
Biography. Amiri Baraka. TAP
Biography. Charles Bruce. CaP
Biography, *sels.* Ernst Jandl. CoAuP
 "Death/ Coming."
 "Lifeboat/ drown."
 "Weather or not/ born."
Biography. Abraham Moses Klein. TrJP
Biography, *sel.* John Masefield.
 "Other bright days of action have seemed great." OxBTC
Biography. Michael Ondaatje. NoAM
Biography. Maura Stanton. MAYP
Biography for Traman, *sel.* Winfield Townley Scott.
 "Let us record/ The evenings when we were innocents of twenty."
 ErPo
Biography of a Still LIfe. Charles Edward Eaton. KS
Biography of an Agnostic. Louis Ginsberg. TrJP
Biography of Southern Rain. Kenneth Patchen. VGW
Biological, The/ and dynastic phenomenon. The Art of Picasso.
 Salvador Dali, *tr. by* David Gascoyne. EAS
Bio-poetic Statement. Carroll Arnett. STE
Biothanatos. Joseph Beaumont. OBS
Biped. Dan Pagis, *tr. fr. Hebrew by* Warren Bargad *and* Stanley F.
 Chyet. IP
Biplane, The. Steve Orlen. GOYP
Birch begins to crack its outer sheath, The. A Young Birch. Robert
 Frost. BoNaP; LiTA

Birch, hazel, oak, beech, holly. Ramble. Anthony Howell. NPo
Birch-Tree at Loschwitz, The. Amy Levy. TrJP
Birch Trees. John Richard Moreland. OHIP; RHPC
Birches. Robert Frost. AmPP; CMoP; FaBV; FPL; HeIP; LiTA; LiTM;
 MoAB; MoAmPo; MoP; NAAL-2; NIP; NoAM; NoP; OxBA; PoLF;
 PoRA; RB; TAP; TrGrPo
Birches stand in their beggar's row, The. February; the Boy Breughel.
 Norman Dubie. LCAP
Birches that dance on the top of the hill, The. Parenthood. John
 Chipman Farrar. OHIP
Bird, The. "Adunis," *tr. fr. Arabic by* Abdullah al-Udhari. MPAW
Bird, The. Robert Greacen. NeIP
Bird, The. Moyshe-Leyb Halpern, *tr. fr. Yiddish.* AYP, *tr. by* Benjamin
 and Barbara Harshav; PeBMYV; *tr. by* John Hollander; PPP, *tr. by*
 John Hollander.
Bird, The. Samuel Hoffenstein. FiBHP
Bird. Jung Han-mo, *tr. fr. Korean by* Koh Chang-soo. ACKP
Bird, The. Max Michelson. TrJP
Bird. Agnes Nemes Nagy, *tr. fr. Hungarian by* Bruce Berlind. BoWoP
Bird. Shotetsu, *tr. fr. Japanese by* Steven D. Carter. WFTW
Bird, The. Charles Simic. AmPA
Bird, The. Louis Simpson. NePoEA-2
Bird, The. Henry Vaughan. FM; OBEV; PoE; PoEL-2; SeCV-1
Bird and beast. What She Said ("Bird and Beast"). Nannakaiyar, *tr. by*
 A. K. Ramanujan. PLW
Bird and the Muse. Marya Zaturenska. PoA
Bird and the Tree, The. Ridgely Torrence. PoNe
Bird at Dawn, The. Harold Monro. BoTP; MoBrPo
Bird at Night. Marion Ethel Hamilton. GoYe
Bird Bath, The. Florence Hoatson. BoTP
Bird, Bird. Gene Derwood. LiTA
Bird, bird don't edge me in. The Reply. Theodore Roethke. NoP;
 NYBP
Bird bobs/ Branch creaks. Minimal. Roland Jooris, *tr. by* Peter
 Nijmeijer. DuIn
Bird calls me, A. The Bird. Charles Simic. AmPA
Bird came down the walk, A. Emily Dickinson. AmPP; BLPL; CMoP;
 FaPON; FF; FM; GoJo; InvP; LiTA; LiTM; Mes; MoAmPo; NAAL-1;
 NoAM; NOBA; NoP; NTCP; OBAL; OBCA; OxBA; PDV; PoLF;
 PoRA
Bird came with a crutch under his wing, A. The Bird. Moyshe-Leyb
 Halpern, *tr. by* Benjamin *and* Barbara Harshav. AYP
Bird Catcher, The. *Unknown, tr. fr. Egyptian by* Ulli Beier. TTY
Bird-Catcher's Song. Jacques Prévert, *tr. fr. French by* Mark Strand *and*
 Jean Ballard. POS
Bird comes, A/ delicately as a little girl. Yosano Akiko, *tr. fr. Japanese
 by* Kenneth Rexroth *and* Ikuko Atsumi. WPOW
Bird flew tangent-wise to the open window, A. The Bird. Robert
 Greacen. NeIP
Bird flies and I gum it to a concept, A. Letter to Anne Ridler. George
 Sutherland Fraser. OxBS
Bird flies away quietly, A. Wakayama Bokusui, *tr. fr. Japanese by*
 Hiroaki Sato. *Fr.* Forty-four Tanka. FCEI
Bird flying past my head said previous previous, The. Conrad Aiken.
 Fr. Time in the Rock [or, Preludes to Definition], LXII. VGW
Bird in a Cage. *Unknown.* AS, *with music;* GBP
Bird in flight parts from the old wood, The. Yüan Mei, *tr. fr. Chinese by*
 Jonathan Chaves. *Fr.* Five Poems on Returning to Hangchou.
 CoBLCP
Bird in my bower, A. Francis Howard Williams. AA
Bird in my heart is calling through a far-fled, tear-grey sea, The. Blanid's
 Song. Gordon Bottomley. *Fr.* The Crier by Night. BrPo
Bird in Search of a Cage, A. Robert Pack. NePoEA
Bird in the Hand, A. Vassar Miller. CRP
Bird is calling from the willow, A. *Unknown.* *Fr.* Four Glosses.
 NOIV
Bird is lost, The. Yardbird's Skull. Owen Dodson. AmNP; CNA; IDB;
 PoBA; VGW
Bird is my neighbor, a whimsical fellow and dim, The. The Crane Is My
 Neighbor. John Shaw Neilson. CBAP; PoAu-1
Bird is tangled in a tree, A. Wilhelm Busch. OBD
Bird kept saying that birds had once been men, The. On an Old Horn.
 Wallace Stevens. LiTA
"Bird Lives": Charles Parker in St. Louis. Michael S. S. Harper.
 AmPA
Bird Mertsyfint, The. Moyshe-Leyb Halpern, *tr. fr. Yiddish by* Benjamin
 and Barbara Harshav. AYP
Bird of Dawning, The. Shakespeare. *See* Hamlet:
 Some say that ever 'gainst that season comes.
Bird of Juno glories in his plumes, The. Verses under a Peacock
 Portrayed in Her Left Hand. Robert Greene. PBBP

Bird of My Being, The. Israel Efrat, *tr. fr. Hebrew by* Bernhard Frank. MHeP

Bird of Night, The. Randall Jarrell. RFM

Bird of omen, A. Shot. Itamar Ya'oz-kest, *tr. fr. Hebrew by* Bernhard Frank. *Fr.* Ordeal by Fire. MHeP

Bird of Paradise, The. W. H. Davies. BrPo

Bird of Passage. Ida Hahn-Hahn, *tr. fr. German by* Susan L. Cocalis. DMG

Bird of Power. Jim Tollerud. VoR

Bird of the bitter bright grey golden morn. A Ballad of François Villon. Swinburne. PoEL-5; PoRA

Bird of the moths! that radiant wing. The Butterfly. Robert Stephen Hawker. EBVV

Bird of the wilderness. The Skylark. James Hogg. GN; PBBP

Bird of the woodland, sing me a song. To the Mock-Bird. Mary Weston Fordham. CBWP-2

Bird on the wire was an accident, The. Falling in Love. Jon Anderson. MAYP

Bird-Scene at a Rural Dwelling, A. Thomas Hardy. FM

Bird-shaped island, with secretive bird-voices. New Guinea. James McAuley. NOCV; PoAu-2

Bird sings free and clear, alone, The. The Street Drummer. Moyshe-Leyb Halpern, *tr. by* John Hollander. PeBMYV

Bird sings the selfsame song, A. The Selfsame Song. Thomas Hardy. CMoP; PBBP

Bird Sings to Establish Frontiers, A. Jack Gilbert. NPGG

Bird Song, The. Mrs. Henry Linden. CBWP-4

Bird Song. Betsy Rosenberg. VWA

Bird swerved dapple-white in the blue sky, The. Winged in Gold. Euros Bowen, *tr. by the author.* OBWVE

Bird that fell out of the nest, A. Ernst Schönwiese, *tr. by* Beth Bjorklund. CoAuP

Bird that flies so sweetly, The. Bird-Catcher's Song. Jacques Prévert, *tr. by* Mark Strand *and* Jean Ballard. POS

Bird that flies to climates crisper, The. Spring. Oscar Williams. LiTA

Bird that I don't know, A. A Country Life. Randall Jarrell. MoAmPo

Bird Theater. Robert Wallace. TDD

Bird tills the soil, The. Lightning Victory. René Char, *tr. by* W. S. Merwin. RHTwFP

Bird voices gently calling. Kyogoku Tamekane, *tr. fr. Japanese by* Burton Watson. *Fr.* Twenty-three Tanka. FCEI

Bird Was Singing, A. Dietmar von Aist, *tr. fr. German by* Jethro Bithell. AWP

Bird watchers top my honors list. Up from the Egg; the Confessions of a Nuthatch Avoider. Ogden Nash. FiBHP; PoRA

Bird-Window-Flying. Tess Gallagher. NAmP

Bird with a Broken Wing, The. Hezekiah Butterworth. WBLP

Bird with bone on the outside, The. The Eggs. Peter Redgrove. NAs

Bird-witted. Marianne Moore. CMoP; FM; NAAL-2

Bird-Woman. Rachel McAlpine. PeNZ

Bird-Woman of the ultra-world. Lilith. Iwan Goll. VWA

Bird Woman they call me. The One Who Skins Cats. Paula Gunn Allen. GOS

Birdcatcher, The. Ralph Hodgson. MoBrPo

Birdie McReynolds. Samuel Hoffenstein. BXAP; NBLV

Birdie with a yellow bill, A. Time to Rise. Robert Louis Stevenson. OxBChV

Birdies' Breakfast, The. *Unknown.* BoTP

Birdies, can there be any doubt. November. James Reaney. *Fr.* A Suit of Nettles. OBCV

Birdless Country. Shimazaki Toson, *tr. fr. Japanese by* Burton Watson. FCEI

Birdless heaven, seadusk, one lone star, A. Tutto è Sciolto. James Joyce. OBMV

Birds, The, *sel.* Aristophanes, *tr. fr. Greek by* Swinburne.
   Chorus of Birds. AWP
   (Grand Chorus of Birds.) PoEL-5

Birds, The. Blake. CH

Birds, The. Samuel Taylor Coleridge. *See* Do you ask what the birds say?

Birds. Robinson Jeffers. InPS; VGW

Birds. "Llywelyn." PoAu-2

Birds. Ruth Miller. PeSA

Birds, *sel.* "St.-John Perse," *tr. fr. French by* Robert Fitzgerald.
   "Birds, birds held by long affinity close to man's frontiers." *Fr.* VIII. RHTwFP

Birds, The. David Posner. NYBP

Birds, The, *sel.* Sir John Collings Squire.
   "O let your strong imagination turn." PBBP

Birds. Richard Henry Stoddard. AA; AnAmPo

Birds, The. *Unknown.* PChr

Birds, The. *Unknown, Aborigine Oral Tradition. Fr.* Moon-Bone Song [*or* Cycle]. WTO

Birds. *Unknown, tr. fr. Arabic by* E. Powys Mathers. *Fr.* The Thousand and One Nights. AWP

Birds, The/ confused by the angle. December Eclipse. Margo Lockwood. Psk

Birds/ cruel neverending chirping. Subnarcosis. Andrea Zanzotto, *tr. by* Lawrence R. Smith. NItP

Birds against the April wind, The. What the Birds Said. Whittier. NOBA

Birds all the sunny day. Nest Eggs. Robert Louis Stevenson. FM

Birds and bees and butterflies. Out of Doors. E. North. BoTP

Birds and Fishes. Robinson Jeffers. NAAL-2; NoP

Birds and periodic blood. 5:30 A.M. Adrienne Rich. NMM; NOBA

Birds and Roses Are Birds and Roses. William Heyen. GeTw

Birds and sunlight. Yellow. De Leon Harrison. PoBA

Birds are burning, The. Invasion. "Adunis," *tr. by* Abdullah al-Udhari. MPAW

Birds Are Drowsing on the Branches. Leah Rudnitsky, *tr. fr. Yiddish by* David G. Roskies. VWA

Birds are flowers flying. Mirrorment. Archie Randolph Ammons. PCP

Birds are gone to bed the cows are still, The. Hares at Play. John Clare. RB

Birds are our angels—out of heaven. Birds. Llywelyn." PoAu-2

Birds, The—are they worth remembering? Wingtip. Carl Sandburg. PCP

Birds are singing round my window. Birds. Richard Henry Stoddard. AA; AnAmPo

Birds aroused. Landscape. Judah Leib Teller, *tr. by* Benjamin *and* Barbara Harshav. AYP

Birds at a Mountain Home. Emperor Fushimi, *tr. fr. Japanese by* Steven D. Carter. WFTW

Birds at dawn fly around in confusion now you are gone, The. Lament for Te Heuheu Herea. Te Heuheu Tukino, *tr. by* Margaret Orbell. PeNZ

Birds at Winter Nightfall. Thomas Hardy. MoBrPo

Birds' Ball, The. Charles William Bardeen. BLPA

Birds, birds, birds. Beat Poem by an Academic Poet. Vassar Miller. WPE

Birds, birds held by long affinity close to man's frontiers. "St.-John Perse," *tr. fr. French by* Robert Fitzgerald. *Fr.* Birds, VIII. RHTwFP

Bird's call this morning was a fine bird call, The. *Unknown, tr. by* Hiroaki Sato. FCEI

Birds called warblers are fancy mountain birds, The. *Unknown, tr. by* Hiroaki Sato. FCEI

Birds come like fishes out of the air, The. Prey to Prey. David Rowbotham. CBAP

Birds drip from the trees. Daybreak. Bert Meyers. EAS

Bird's-Eye View of the Tool and Die Co. John Ashbery. AnAn

Birds feed on birds, beasts on each other prey. Wretched Man. 2nd Earl of Rochester. *Fr.* A Satire against [Reason and] Mankind. SeCePo

Birds Flying. Alistair Paterson. ATNZ

Birds gathered for the great black migration. Icarian Is the Sea. Hans Tentije, *tr. by* Scott Rollins. DuIn

Birds go fluttering in the air, The. The Silent Snake. *Unknown.* BoTP; FaPON

Birds have stripped, The. The Burial. Glover Davis. SM

Birds I beheld building nests in the bushes. William Langland. *Fr.* The Vision of Piers Plowman, Passus XI. PBBP

Birds in a whirl, drift to the rooftops. Gary Snyder. *Fr.* Myths and Texts: Hunting, III. NaP

Birds in flight switch places above and below a hypothetical bar. Bases. Rae Armantrout. BAP

Birds in Snow. Hilda Doolittle. PoA

Birds in the Fens. Michael Drayton. *See* Polyolbion: Duck, and Mallard first, the falconers onely sport, The.

Birds in the first light twitter and whistle, The. A Little Morning Music. Delmore Schwartz. BoNaP; NYBP

Birds in the high Hall-garden. Tennyson. *Fr.* Maud, *pt.* I. NAEL-2

Birds in the Night. Luis Cernuda, *tr. fr. Spanish by* Erskine Lane. PeHV

Birds' Lament. John Clare. PoEL-4

Bird's Nest, A. Erez Biton, *tr. fr. Hebrew by* Judith Katz. VWA

Bird's Nest, The. John Drinkwater. PDV

Bird's Nest, The. Elizabeth Turner. OHIP

Birds Nest in My Arms, The. Gloria Fuertes, *tr. fr. Spanish by* Kate Flores. DMH

Birds' Nests. John Clare. OAEL-2; OxBSP

Birds' Nests. Millicent Seager. BoTP

Birds' Nests. Edward Thomas. HeIP

Birds' Nests. *Unknown.* BoTP
Birds of America, The. James Richard Broughton. AmFN
Birds of Arles, The. David Fisher. NPGG
Birds of Bethlehem, The. Richard Watson Gilder. AA
Birds of Killingworth, The (The Poet's Tale). Longfellow. *Fr.* Tales of a Wayside Inn, *pt.* I. OnMSP; OxBA
"Do you ne'er think what wondrous beings these?." *Fr.* 2 *sts.*.WBLP
Birds of 9th Ave, The. Alma Denny. SoTCo
Birds of omen dark and foul. Annot Lyle's Song. Sir Walter Scott. *Fr.* The Legend of Montrose, *ch.* 6. EnRP
Birds of Paradise, The. John Peale Bishop. GoJo
Birds of Passage. Longfellow. AnAmPo
Birds of Scotland, The, *sel.* James Grahame.
"With earliest spring, while yet in mountain cleughs." PBBP
Birds of the Island Palace, The. Hitomaro, *tr. fr. Japanese. Fr.* Manyo Shu. Ma
Birds of Tin, The. Charles Madge. EAS
Birds on a Blighted Tree. Grace Schulman. AnAn
Birds on the School Windowsill, The. Evelyn Dainty. BoTP
Birds' Rondel, The. Chaucer. *See* Parlement of Foules, The: Now Welcom[e], Somer [*or* Summer].
Birds sang in the wet trees, The. Wet Evening in April. Patrick Kavanagh. PoPo
Birds sang sweet as ony bell, The. Sir Aldingar. *Unknown.* ESPB
Birds saw the people walking along, The. The Birds. *Aborigine Oral Tradition. Fr.* Moon-Bone Song [*or* Cycle]. WTO
Birds scream with mama's voice. Sigmund Freud at the Age of Eighty-Two. Judah Leib Teller, *tr. fr. Yiddish by* Benjamin *and* Barbara Harshav. *Fr.* Psychoanalysis. AYP
Birds sing the song of sadjoy. Autumn. Jacob Glatstein, *tr. by* Benjamin *and* Barbara Harshav. AYP
Birds stayed not their singing. Armistice Day. John Freeman. MMA; OPP
Birds that migrated, The. The Fifteenth Telegram ("Birds that migrated"). Abd al-Aziz al-Maqalih, *tr. fr. Arabic by* Lena Jayyusi *and* Christopher Middleton. *Fr.* Telegrams of Tenderness for Sanaa. MAP
Birds their love-notes warble, The. Alice Ray. Sarah Josepha Hale. AA
Birds their quire apply; airs, vernal airs, The. Milton. *Fr.* Paradise Lost, *Bk.* IV, *ll.* 264–268.
(Eternal Spring, The.) GN
Birds, trees and flow'rs they bring to me. J. C. Squire. *Fr.* The Swallow. BXAP
Birds turned, The. Wrapped Hair Bundles. Tauhindauli. STE
Birds Waking. W. S. Merwin. NOBA
Birdsong. Burns Singer. FaBoTw
Birdsville Track, The, *sel.* Douglas Stewart.
"Oh the corrugated-iron town." CBAP
Birdwatcher. Henry Treece. WaP
Birdwatchers of America. Anthony Hecht. HoPM; NoAM; NOBA; PPP
Birdwatching at Fan Lake. Anita Endrezze-Danielson. HATNAP
Birkett's Eagle. Dorothy S. Howard. Mes; MoBS
Birks of Aberfeldy, The. Burns. CTC
Birlinn Chlann-Raghnaill. Alexander MacDonald, *tr. fr. Gaelic by* "Hugh MacDiarmid." GoTS
Birmingham. Julia Fields. *Fr.* Poems: Birmingham 1962–1964. PoBA; PoNe
Birmingham. Louis MacNeice. CMoP; MoAB; MoBrPo
Birmingham. Margaret Abigail Walker. PoBA
Birmingham and Wolverhampton. James Woodhouse. *Fr.* The Life and Lucubrations of Crispinus Scriblerus. NOEC
Birmingham Jail. *Unknown. See* Down in the Valley.
Birmingham 1963. Raymond R. Patterson. CNA; PoBA
Birmingham Sunday. Langston Hughes. PoNe
Birth. Edith Bruck, *tr. fr. Italian by* Ruth Feldman *and* Brian Swann. BoWoP
Birth. Cecilia Bustamante, *tr. fr. Spanish by* David Tipton. Per
Birth, A. James Dickey. NOBA
Birth, The. Rosemary Dobson. PoAu-2
Birth. Amir Gilboa, *tr. fr. Hebrew.* OFD, *tr. by* Robert Mezey *and* Shula Starkman; VWA, *tr. by* Stephen Mitchell.
Birth. Langston Hughes. NAs
Birth. Gabriela Melinescu, *tr. fr. Rumanian by* Willis Barnstone *and* Matei Calinescu. BoWoP
Birth. Harold Monro. *Fr.* Strange Meetings. PoA
Birth. Craig Raine. *Fr.* Anno Domini. NAs
Birth. Grace Raymond. AA
Birth. Takahashi Shinkichi, *tr. fr. Japanese by* Geoffrey Bownas *and* Anthony Thwaite. PeBJV
Birth. Constance Urdang. VWA
Birth. Eddy van Vliet, *tr. fr. Dutch by* Peter Nijmeijer. DuIn

Birth (al-Maulid). Muhammad al-Mahdi al-Majdhoub, *tr. fr. Arabic by* Salma Khadra Jayyusi *and* Charles Doria. MAP
Birth-Bond, The. Dante Gabriel Rossetti. *Fr.* The House of Life, XV. Son
Birth by Anesthesia. George Scarbrough. GoYe
Birth-Dues. Robinson Jeffers. MoAB; MoAmPo
Birth in a Narrow Room, The. Gwendolyn Brooks. BlSi; NAs; PoNe
Birth Is. John Figueroa. PBCV
Birth of a Country. Agnes Gergely, *tr. fr. Hungarian by* Emery George. VWA
Birth of a Great Man. Robert Graves. NYBP
Birth of a Shark, The. David Wevill. TwCP
Birth of a Son. Sam Hunt. PeNZ
Birth of Aisha and Her Death, The. Abd al-Bayyati, *tr. fr. Arabic by* Sargon Boulus *and* Christopher Middleton. MAP
Birth of Galahad, The, *sel.* Richard Hovey.
Ylen's Song. AA
Birth of Jesus, The. Josephine D. Henderson Heard. CBWP-4
Birth of John Henry, The. Melvin Beaunearus Tolson. *Fr.* Harlem Gallery. BPo; TTY
Birth of Love. Robert Penn Warren. UnPo
Birth of Moshesh, The. David Granmer T. Bereng, *tr. fr. Sotho by* Dan Kunene *and* Jack Cope. PeSA; TTY
Birth of Potchikoo, The. Louise Erdrich. *Fr.* Old Man Potchikoo. HATNAP
Birth of Rainbow. Ted Hughes. AnAn; NAs
Birth of Robin Hood, The. *Unknown.* OAEL-1; OxBB
Birth of Sea and Land Life. Keaulumoku, *tr. fr. Hawaiian by* M. W. Beckwith. *Fr.* Kumulipo, The; a Creation Chant. WTO
Birth of Shaka, The. Mbuyiseni Oswald Mtshali. WMBCH
Birth of Sound. Michael Ondaatje. HeIP
Birth of the Cool. C. D. Wright. MT
Birth of the Foal. Ferenc Juhász, *tr. fr. Hungarian by* David Wevill. RB
Birth of the Squire; an Eclogue, The. John Gay. NAEL-1; NOEC; PoEL-3
Birth of Time, The. Josephine D. Henderson Heard. CBWP-4
Birth of Tragedy, The. Irving Layton. MoCV; NoAM; NoP; OBCV
Birth of Venus. Constance Urdang. NAs
Birth Report. X. J. Kennedy. *Fr.* Snapshots. NAs
Birthday. Earle Birney. NAs
Birthday. John Ciardi. NAs
Birthday, The. Philip Dacey. AmPA
Birthday, The. Louis Johnson. ATNZ
Birthday. P. J. Kavanagh. NAs
Birthday. D. H. Lawrence. NAs
Birthday. James Merrill. NAs
Birthday, A. Edwin Muir. NAs
Birthday, A. Christina Rossetti. AWP; BLPL; CH; FaFP; InvP; LiTB; NA; NAEL-2; NOBE; NOBVV; OAEL-2; OBEV; PoE; TrGrPo; TTTS; WiR; WPE
Birthday. William Stafford. NAs
Birthday. Manfred Winkler, *tr. fr. Hebrew by* Bernhard Frank. MHeP
Birthday. Yevgeny Yevtushenko, *tr. fr. Russian by* Peter Levi *and* Robin Milner-Gulland. NAs
Birthday Cake. Aileen Fisher. PDV
Birthday Candle, A. Donald Justice. NYBP
Birthday Card for a Psychiatrist. Mona Van Duyn. IHMS
Birthday Child, The. Rose Fyleman. FaPON
Birthday Dream, The. James Dickey. NAs
Birthday Gift, A. Stephen Dunn. BLA
Birthday Gifts. Herbert Asquith. OFD
Birthday greetings/ From a friend. Birthday Wishes to a Physician. Lizelia Augusta Jenkins Moorer. CBWP-3
Birthday in Hospital, A. Elizabeth Jennings. NAs
Birthday Memorial to Seventh Street, A. Audre Lorde. CNA
Birthday Ode to Mr. Alfred Austin, A. Sir Owen Seaman. NOBL
Birthday of but a single pang. Emily Dickinson. NAs; OFD
Birthday on the Beach. Ogden Nash. ASP
Birthday Poem. W. H. Auden. *See* August for the People.
Birthday Poem, A. James Simmons. OxBSP
Birthday Poem. Al Young. NPGG
Birthday Poem from Venice. Patricia Beer. OxBC
Birthday Poem, November 4th. John Thompson, Jr. WaP
Birthday Prayer, A. John Finley. TrPWD
Birthday Sonnet. Elinor Wylie. MoAB; MoAmPo
Birthday Verses Written in a Child's Album. James Russell Lowell. OxBChV
Birthday Visit. P. J. Kavanagh. NPo
Birthday Wishes to a Husband. Lizelia Augusta Jenkins Moorer. CBWP-3
Birthday Wishes to a Minister of the Gospel. Lizelia Augusta Jenkins Moorer. CBWP-3

Birthday Wishes to a Physician. Lizelia Augusta Jenkins Moorer. CBWP-3
Birthdays. Hilde Domin, *tr. fr. German by* Tudor Morris. BoWoP
Birthdays. C. J. Driver. PeSA
Birthdays. Mary Ann Hoberman. RAR
Birthdays from the ocean one desert april noon. That "Craning of the Neck." Isabella Gardner. WPE
Birthdays? yes, in a general way. Sincere Flattery of R. B. James Kenneth Stephen. FaBoPa; NOBL; Par
Birthnight; to F, The. Walter de la Mare. NAs
Birthplace. Duane Big Eagle. STE
Birthplace, The. Robert Frost. EyDe; OFD
Birthplace, The. Seamus Heaney. FaBCIP
Birthplace. Tahereh Saffarzadeh, *tr. fr. Farsi by* Deirdre Lashgari. AIW; WPOW
Birthplace; New Rochelle. George Oppen. DiL
Birthplace Revisited. Gregory Corso. NeAP; PoM; VGW
Birthright. John Drinkwater. CH; OxBTC
Birthright. Geraldine Kudaka. BrSi
Bishop/ High priest of Grenada. Lament for Maurice Bishop. Howard Fergus. PBCV
Bishop Blomfield's First Charge to His Clergy. *At. to* Sydney Goodsir Smith. FaBoEE
Bishop Blougram's Apology, *sel.* Robert Browning. OBNC; PoEL-5 Belief and Unbelief. FaBV
Bishop Doane on His Dog. George Washington Doane. BLPA; FaBoBe
Bishop Hatto. Robert Southey. *See* Summer and autumn had been so wet, The.
Bishop James A. Shorter. Josephine D. Henderson Heard. CBWP-4
Bishop of Atlanta: Ray Charles, The. Julian Bond. AmNP; CNA
Bishop of Canterbury, The. *Unknown.* AmFP
Bishop of Chester, The. On Dr. Keene, Bishop of Chester. Thomas Gray. FaBoEE
Bishop of El Salvador is dead, murdered by no one knows who, The. Rusia en 1931. Robert Hass. AnAn; MAYP
Bishop of Rum-ti-Foo, The. W. S. Gilbert. CenHV
Bishop Orders His Tomb at Saint Praxed's Church, The. Robert Browning. AWP; EBVV; FiP; HAP; HeIP; NAEL-2; NAWM-2; NOBVV; NoP; OAEL-2; OBAL; PoE; PPP; PrIm; TEP
Bishop Orders His Tomb in St. Praxed's. Morris Bishop. OBAL
Bishop sat in lordly state and purple cap sublime, The. Tangmalangaloo. P. J. Hartigan. PoAu-1
Bishop seduces the world with his voice, The. The Bishop of Atlanta: Ray Charles. Julian Bond. AmNP; CNA
Bishop tells us, The: "When the boys come back." "They." Siegfried Sassoon. CMoP; NAEL-2; OBSV; OBWP
Bishop Winterbourne. Walter de la Mare. FaBoNo
Bishop's hand on a widow's breast, A. Russell Lucas. BXAP
Bishop's Harp, The. Robert Mannyng. ACP
Bishop's See, The. *Unknown.* CoMu
Bison, The. Hilaire Belloc. FaBoNo; NA; NoAM
Bit an apple on its red. Green Red Brown and White. May Swenson. VGW
Bit of color against the blue, A. A Song for Our Flag. Margaret E. M. Sangster. FaFP
Bit of Colour, A. Horace Smith. BoTP
Bit of talcum, A. Reflection on Babies. Ogden Nash. FaBoUs; NBLV
Bit of yarrow and then of rue, A. Bouquet in Dog Time. Hayden Carruth. GrPl
Bitch-Kitty, The. Jonathan Williams. PoM
Bite, and the taste of tongues. The Empty Pain-Killer Bottles. Tom Raworth. EAS
Bite deep and wide, O Axe, the tree. Isabella Valancy Crawford. *Fr.* Malcolm's Katie. OBCV
Biting air. Winter Days. Gareth Owen. OBCP
Biting hard pears, arguing. Ozaki Hosai, *tr. fr. Japanese by* Hiroaki Sato. *Fr.* One Hundred Haiku in Free Form. FCEI
Biting Through. Traise Yamamoto. BrSi
Bits of shrapnel trying to huddle together. Gun Emplacement. Maruyama Kaoru, *tr. by* Geoffrey Bownas *and* Anthony Thwaite. PeBJV
Bits of Straw. John Clare. *See* Song: "I peeled bits of straw and I got switches too."
Bitten to dust are the savage feathers of fire. To a Seaman Dead on Land. Kay Boyle. PoA
Bitter air, The. Aura Amara, L'. Arnaut Daniel, *tr. by* Ezra Pound. CTC
Bitter batter boop! The Last Cry of the Damp Fly. Dennis Lee. NTCP
Bitter bitter. A Judezmo Writer in Turkey Angry. Stephen Levy. VWA
Bitter Bread. Osip Mandelstam, *tr. fr. Russian by* James Greene. VWA
Bitter for Sweet. Christina Rossetti. GBL
Bitter Harvest. Alistair Campbell. ATNZ; PeNZ

Bitter Herbs. Alta. NMM
Bitter Herbs. Sharon A. Stern. TSM
Bitter king in anger to be gone, A. Like an Old Proud King in a Parable. Arthur James Marshall Smith. OBCV
Bitter rain in my courtyard. Wu Tsao, *tr. by* Kenneth Rexroth *and* Ling Chung. BoWoP
Bitter Sanctuary. Harold Monro. FaBoMo; LiTB; OBMV
Bitter sight—/ I watch and my tears. Sanetomo, *tr. fr. Japanese by* Burton Watson. *Fr.* Twenty-four Tanka. FCEI
Bitter Sonnet to a Cup of Coffee. Ricardo Castorrivas, *tr. fr. Spanish by* Cecilia Guidos. Vol
Bitter-sweet. George Herbert. NOBE; NoP; OxBSP; TrPWD
Bitter-sweet, *sels.* Josiah Gilbert Holland.
    Babyhood.
    Babyhood. AA
    "For Summer's bloom and Autumn's blight." TrPWD
Bitter—that I should not have decayed. Teika, *tr. fr. Japanese by* Hiroaki Sato. *Fr.* A Compendium of Good Tanka. FCEI
Bitter the sea's taste, bitter when. Statues. Agnes Nemes Nagy, *tr. by* Daniel Hoffman. MHuP
Bitter the storm to-night. Vikings, The ("Bitter the storm to-night"). *Unknown.* ChTr
Bitter the wind tonight. Vikings, The ("Bitter the wind tonight"). *Unknown, tr. by* John Montague. BIrV
Bitter was it, Oh to view. *Unknown. Fr.* A Lament for the Priory of Walsingham. ChTr
Bitter wind taxes the will, A. In the American Tree. Kit Robinson. IAT
Bitter Winter. Franco Fortini, *tr. fr. Italian by* Lawrence R. Smith. NItP
Bitter Withy, The. *Unknown.* ChTr; FaBoBa; GBP; NOCV; NoP ("As it fell out upon one day.") OBET
Bitter year it was, A. What woman ever. The Wreath. Robert Graves. BoLoP
Bittern, I'm sorry to see you stretched. The Yellow Bittern. Cathal Buidhe Mac Giolla Ghunna. NOIV, *tr. by* Thomas Kinsella
Bitterness of days like these we know, The. Salutamus. Sterling Allen Brown. CDC
Bitweene Merch and Averil. *See* Betwene March and Averil.
Bivouac of the Dead, The. Theodore O'Hara. AA; AnAmPo; BLPA; PAH
Bivouac on a Mountain Side. Walt Whitman. AA; AiP; ChTr; OxBA; PoLF
Bix to Buxtehude to Boulez. The Victor Dog. James Merrill. NoAM; NoP
Bix's sound. For Leon Bismarck Beiderbecke (1903-1931). Michael Horovitz. NPo
Bizarre Apollo, half what Henry dreamed. Apollo 8. John Berryman. AnAn
Black. Marcelin Pleynet, *tr. fr. French by* John Ashbery. RHTwFP
Black/ wings sun glanced. Leaving Smoke's. Gordon Henry. STE
Black A, white E, red I, green U, blue O—vowels. Vowels. Rimbaud, *tr. by* Kenneth Koch. SOTW; TTTS
Black absence hides upon the past. John Clare. EnLoPo; NOBVV
Black Aggie. Norman Andrew Kirk. TSM
Black All Day. Raymond R. Patterson. PoBA
Black and glossy as a bee and curled was my hair. Ambapali, *tr. by* A. L. Basham. WPOW
Black and tan—yeah, black and tan. Dancing Gal. Frank Marshall Davis. FB
Black and White. Leonard Adame. SoSe
Black and White. Tom Schmidt. NeAC
Black and yellow. Bumble Bee. Margaret Wise Brown. PDV
Black Angel, The. Katerina Anghelaki-Rooke, *tr. fr. Greek by* Gail Holst-Weirhaft. WCI
Black Angel, The. Henri Coulette. CoAP; NYBP
Black Army, The. S. E. K. Mqhayi, *tr. fr. Xhosa by* C. M. Mcanyangwa *and* Jack Cope. PeSA
Black Art. Imamu Amiri Baraka. BPo
Black Art, The. Anne Sexton. PoA
Black as a battering-ram the massive head. Buffalo. Roy Daniells. CaP
Black as a chimney is his face. "Sooeep!" Walter de la Mare. BoTP
Black as the centre of an eye, the centre, a blackness. Marina Tsvetayeva, *tr. fr. Russian by* Elaine Feinstein *and* Angela Livingston. *Fr.* Insomnia. PBWP
Black ash. Pine Point, You Are. Gordon Henry. STE
Black Bagatelles, *sels.* Rodney Hall. CBAP
    My Coffin Is a Deckchair.
    October.
    They're Dying Just the Same in Station Homesteads.
    World Is a Musician's Cliff House, The.
Black Banderillas. Robert Marteau, *tr. fr. French by* Anne Winters. RHTwFP

Black bear does a strange and shuffling dance, The. Bear: A Totem Dance As Seen by Raven. Peter Blue Cloud. HATNAP

Black Bear sang, drumming on a log. Moon of Huckleberries. Phillip William George. VoR

Black bear sits alone, A. Galway Kinnell. *Fr.* Lastness. DiL

Black beauty, which above that common light. Sonnet of Black Beauty. Herbert of Cherbury. MePo

Black biplane crashes into [*or* through] the window, The. Gregory Orr. GeTw; MAT

Black, black, black is the color of my true love's hair. Black Is the Color. *Unknown.* FF

Black, black cloud, A. William Carlos Williams. FL

Black Blues. Bloke Modisane. PBA

Black Book, The, *sel.* John Berryman.

"Grandfather, sleepless in a room upstairs." VGW

Black Book of Carmarthen, The, *sel. Unknown, tr. fr. Welsh by* Ernest Rhys.

Song of the Graves, The. OBMV

Black Bourgeoisie. Amiri Baraka. BPo

Black Boy. Norman Rosten. TrJP

Black boy/ let me get up from the white man's table of fifty sounds. Melvin B. Tolson. PoBA; PSI

Black boy, the night hides you. Black Boy. Norman Rosten. TrJP

Black Bread. Tom Paulin. CIP

Black brother, think you life so sweet. Time to Die. Ray Garfield Dandridge. BANP; PoBA

Black Bud. Michael Smith. PBCV

Black Bull of Aldgate. Tennyson. TW

Black Buoy. Robert H. Davis. HATNAP

Black Cascade. Philippe Jaccottet, *tr. fr. French by* Michael Hamburger. RHTwFP

Black cat, sweet brother. For James Baldwin. Kay Boyle. NMM

Black cat yawns, The. Cat. Mary Britton Miller. CRH; RHPC

Black centipedal bugs. Letter with a Black Border. Sandra McPherson. GeTw

Black Church on Sunday. Joseph M. Mosley, Jr. NBP

Black Cloud, The. W. H. Davies. RB

Black cock crowed, The. Two o'Clock. Katharine Pyle. *Fr.* The Wonder Clock. OBCA

Black copper sun paled the hunter's cheeks, The. Winter Conversation. Nishiwaki Junzaburo, *tr. by* Hiroaki Sato. FCEI

Black Cottage, The. Robert Frost. VGW

Black Crispus Attucks taught. Dark Symphony. Melvin B. Tolson. AmNP; PoNe

Black crosses on the skyline, like a squad heedless of levies. Erris Coast, 1943. Hugh Connell. NeIP

Black, crumbling rock. Dead scree. The dolorous wind. Climb in Torridon. Brenda G. Macrow. PoSH

Black Cry. José Craveirinha, *tr. fr. Portuguese by* Eduardo Mondlane. WMBCH

Black Dada Nihilismus. Imamu Amiri Baraka. PoM

Black Dog. Ray A. Young Bear. CDW

Black Dog, Red Dog. Stephen Dobyns. NAmP

Black Draftee from Dixie, The. Carrie Williams Clifford. BlSi

Black Earth. Marianne Moore. FaBoMo

Black-eyed Susan. John Gay. *See* All in the Downs the fleet was moor'd.

Black-eyed Susie. *Unknown.* AmFP

Black eyes if you seem dark. To Her Eyes. Herbert of Cherbury. JCP; OBS

Black Faced Sheep, The. Donald Hall. LCAP; SV

Black Fear. Elizabeth Woody. STE

Black Finger, The. Angelina Weld Grimké. AmNP; PoBA

Black Flags Are Fluttering. David Vogel, *tr. fr. Hebrew by* A. C. Jacobs. VWA

Black flies kept nagging in the heat, The. Tao and Unfitness at Inistiogue on the River Nore. Thomas Kinsella. FaBCIP

"Black folks have got to be superhuman." A Poem about Beauty, Blackness, Poetry. Linda Brown Bragg. CNA

Black fool, why winter here? These frozen skies. Advice to a Raven in Russia [December, 1812]. Joel Barlow. AmPP; NAAL-1; NOBA; OBWP; OxBA

Black, frost-cold distance, sparsely honey-combed. Space. Edward Rowland Sill. AnAmPo

Black Girl. Paul-Jean Toulet, *tr. fr. French by* William Jay Smith. CT

Black girl black girl. Blackberry Sweet. Dudley Randall. HAP; InPS; NBP; WeW

(Black Magic.) CNA; PoBA

Black Girl Goes By, A. Emile Roumer, *tr. fr. French by* Edna Worthley Underwood. TTY

Black greyed into white a nightmare of bicycling. That Which We Call a Rose. Michael Dransfield. CBAP

Black Hair. Gary Soto. NPGG

Black hair. Yosano Akiko, *tr. fr. Japanese. Fr.* Thirty-nine Tanka. FCEI, *tr. by* Hiroaki Sato; UnAS, *tr. by* Kenneth Rexroth.

Black Hat, The. Clayton Eshleman. VGW

Black Hawk in Hiding. George Keithley. NPGG

Black Hills Survival Gathering, 1980. Linda Hogan. STE

Black history. The Living Truth. Sterling Plumpp. PoBA

Black Hole of Calcutta, The. Ebenezer Elliott. PF

Black Horse Rider, The. Pierre Loving. EAS

Black I am and much admired. Mother Goose. OxNR

Black in blazonry means. The Buffalo. Marianne Moore. PoA

Black iron fence closes the graves in, A. Visiting Emily Dickinson's Grave with Robert Francis. Robert Bly. LCAP

Black is a political word. The Word. Fyna Dowe. WS

Black Is a Soul. Joseph Blanco White. IDB; PoBA

Black Is Best. Larry Thompson. PoBA

Black Is Black. David Macfield, *tr. fr. Spanish by* Jack Hirschman. Vol

Black is; slavery was; I am. This Child Is the Mother. Gloria C. Oden. BlSi

Black is the beauty of the brightest day. To Entertain Divine Zenocrate. Christopher Marlowe. *Fr.* Tamburlaine the Great, *Pt.* II, Act II, sc. iii. ChTr

Black Is the Color. *Unknown.* FF

Black Is the Colour. *Unknown.* GBP

Black is the first nail I ever stepped on. Negritude. James A. Emanuel. BPo; CNA

Black is the night. What Is Black? Mary O'Neill. NTCP

Black is what the prisons are. The African Affair. Bruce McM. Wright. AmNP; PoBA; PoNe

Black Jack Davey. *Unknown. See* There were three gipsies a-come to my door.

Black Jackets. Thom Gunn. HeIP; NAEL-2; TwCP

Black Jam for Dr. Negro. Mari E. Evans. BPo; PoBA

Black Jess. Peter Kane Dufault. NYBP

Black Jewel, The. W. S. Merwin. CAPP

Black Joy. Hans Arp, *tr. fr. French by* Michael Benedikt. POS

Black key. White key. Unrelenting Flood. William Matthews. GeTw

Black Lady in an Afro Hairdo Cheers for Cassius. R. Ernest Holmes. ASP

Black lake, black boat, two black, cut-paper people. Crossing the Water. Sylvia Plath. CAPP; HCAP; RB

Black Lightning. Arthur Sze. BrSi

Black, long-tailed, The. The Yellow Season. William Carlos Williams. MoAB; MoAmPo

Black Lotus. Alicia Loy Johnson. NBP

Black luggie, lammer bead. Against Witches. *Unknown.* GBP

Black Madonna, The. Albert Rice. CDC

Black Magdalens. Countee Cullen. BANP

Black Magic. Dudley Randall. *See* Black girl, black girl.

Black Magic. Sonia Sanchez. BPo

Black Mail. Alice Walker. AmPA

Black Majesty. Countee Cullen. PoBA; VGW

Black Mammies. John Wesley Holloway. BANP

Black Man, A. Sam Cornish. CNA; PoBA

Black man is hugging me around the throat from behind, A. Father and Son. David Ignatow. DiL

Black Man Talks of Reaping, A. Arna Bontemps. AmNP; BANP; BPo; CDC; FB; IDB; PoBA; PoNe

Black Man's Feast. Sarah Webster Fabio. PoBA; PoNe

Black Man's Son, The. Oswald Durand, *tr. fr. French by* Edna Worthley Underwood. TTY

Black Maps. Mark Strand. PoA

Black Marigolds. Bilhana, *formerly at. to* Chauras, *tr. fr. Sanskrit by* E. Powys Mathers. AWP; ErPo, *abr.*

Black men bleeding to death inside themselves. Eulogy for Alvin Frost. Audre Lorde. CNA

Black Mesa, The. James Merrill. PoA

Black Mesa. Ron Rogers. STE

Black milk of dawn [*or* daybreak] we drink it at dusk [*or* nightfall]. Death Fugue. Paul Celan. TrJP, *tr. by* Clement Greenberg; VWA, *tr. by* Joachim Neugroschel

(Fugue of Death.) OBVE, *tr. by* Christopher Middleton

Black Money. Tess Gallagher. GeTw

Black Mother. Viriato da Cruz, *tr. fr. Portuguese by* Margaret Dickinson. WMBCH

Black mother. Dream of the Black Mother. Marcelino dos Santos, *tr. by* Philippa Rumsey. WMBCH

Black Muslim Boy in a Hospital. James A. Emanuel. PoNe

Black Muzzle. Su Tung-p'o, *tr. fr. Chinese by* Burton Watson. CoBCP

Black Narcissus. Gerald William Barrax. PoBA

Black Night./ White snow. Alexander Blok, *tr. fr. Russian by* Babette Deutsch *and* Avrahm Yarmolinsky. *Fr.* The Twelve. AWP

Black November Turkey, A. Richard Wilbur. LCAP; MoAB; NAAL-2

Black of brow, with cheeks aglow. A Glance. *Unknown*, *tr. by* Thomas Kinsella. NOIV
Black of my hair, The. Teika, *tr. by* Steven D. Carter. WFTW
Black one, last as usual, swings her head, The. Fetching Cows. Norman MacCaig. OxBC
Black-Out. Valentine Ackland. CN
Black-out, The. Mary Désirée Anderson. CN
Black-out. Robinson Jeffers. LiTA; LiTM; WaP
Black Panther, The. John Hall Wheelock. FF; LiTM
Black Patch on Lucasta's Face, A. Richard Lovelace. CaPo; SeCP
Black Pebble, The. James Reeves. PDV
Black People! Imamu Amiri Baraka. BPo
Black people think. Awareness. Don L. Lee. PoBA
Black People: This Is Our Destiny. Imamu Amiri Baraka. CNA
Black people, we rainclouds. We Rainclouds. Marvin Wyche, Jr. AmNP
Black pitchy night, companion of my woe. Michael Drayton. *Fr.* Idea's Mirrour, XLV. OBSC
Black Plateau, The. W. S. Merwin. NNaP
Black Poet, White Critic. Dudley Randall. BPo
Black poets should live—not leap. For Black Poets Who Think of Suicide. Etheridge Knight. CNA; HeIP; InPK; PoBA
Black Power. Alvin Saxon. PoBA
Black Power Poem. Ishmael Reed. BPo
Black Pride. Margaret Goss Burroughs. BlSi
Black Queen on the red King. Solitaire. John Updike. SoTCo
Black reapers with the sound of steel on stones. Reapers. Jean Toomer. BPo; CDC; HAP; MoP; NoAM; PoBA; PPP; WeW
Black Regiment, The. George Henry Boker. AnAmPo; GN; PAH
Black Riders, The, *sels.* Stephen Crane.
　Ancestry. *Fr.* XXII. AA
　"Behold, from the land of the farther suns." *Fr.* XXIX. AA
　Behold, the Grave of a Wicked Man. *Fr.* XXV. TAP
　"Black riders came from the sea." *Fr.* I. NAAL-2; TAP
　　(Black Riders, The.) AA
　Blades of Grass, The. *Fr.* XVIII. MoAmPo
　Book of Wisdom, The. *Fr.* XXXVI. HoPM; MoAmPo
　"God fashioned the ship of the world carefully." *Fr.* VI. MOS
　God in Wrath, A. *Fr.* XIX. OxBSP; TAP
　"God lay dead in heaven." *Fr.* LXVII. AmPP
　"I saw a man pursuing the horizon." *Fr.* XXIV. AmPP; FF; HoPM; LiTA; LiTM; MAT; MoAmPo; NOBA
　I Stood upon a High Place. *Fr.* IX. LiTA
　"I walked in a desert." *Fr.* XLII. NAAL-2
　In the Desert. *Fr.* III. FaBoEE; LiTM; NOBA; OxBSP; TAP
　　(Heart, The.) HoPM; MoAmPo; TAP
　"It Was Wrong to Do This" Said the Angel. *Fr.* LIV. LiTA
　Learned Man, A. *Fr.* XX. LiTA; MoAmPo
　"Man feared that he might find an assassin, A." *Fr.* LVI. NAAL-2
　Man Saw a Ball of Gold in the Sky, A. *Fr.* XXXV. LiTA
　"Many red devils ran from my heart." *Fr.* XLVI. TAP
　Many Workmen. *Fr.* XXXI. LiTA; TAP
　"Ocean said to me once, The." *Fr.* XXXVIII. MOS
　Scaped. *Fr.* LXV. AA
　"Should the wide world roll away." *Fr.* X. AmPP
　Think as I Think. *Fr.* XLVII. WeW
　Why? *Fr.* XXV. AA
　Youth in Apparel That Glittered, A. *Fr.* XXVII. LiTA; NAAL-2
　　(Content.) AA
　　(Youth, A.) MoAmPo
Black Rock of Kiltearn. Andrew Young. FaBoTw; RB
Black Rocks. Laureen Mar. BrSi
Black Rocks. Charles Hubert Sisson. DiPo
Black Rook in Rainy Weather. Sylvia Plath. LiTM; NAAL-2; NePoEA-2; NIP; SM
Black Rose. "Zelda," *tr. fr. Hebrew by* Bernhard Frank. MHeP
Black Sampson, The. Josephine D. Henderson Heard. CBWP-4
Black Sea really was extremely black, The. When the Sovereign Asks. Sirkka Turkka, *tr. by* Aili Jarvenpa. SOP
Black shadows fall. Birds of Passage. Longfellow. AnAmPo
Black Sheep. Richard Burton. AA
Black Silk. Tess Gallagher. FaBoWP; MAYP; NAmP
Black Sister. Kattie M. Cumbo. BlSi
Black Sketches. Don L. Lee. NeAC
Black skin against bright green. Black Sister. Kattie M. Cumbo. BlSi
Black skull-caps. Dying under a Fall of Stars. Mark Elliott Shapiro. VWA
Black-smocked smiths, smattered with smoke. Blacksmiths. *Unknown.* RR; WiR
Black Snake, The. Patricia Hubbell. PDV
Black Soldier's Civil War Chant. *Unknown. See* Ole Abe (God bless his ole soul!).

Black Song. Murano Shiro, *tr. fr. Japanese by* Geoffrey Bownas *and* Anthony Thwaite. PeBJV
Black Song. Amin Nakhla, *tr. fr. Arabic by* Matthew S. Sorenson. MAP
Black Soul of the Land. Lance Jeffers. FB
Black spirits and white, red spirits and gray. Thomas Middleton. *Fr.* The Witch, V, i. WSC
Black Spring. Robert Lowell, *ad. fr. Russian of* Innokenti Annensky. NaP
Black spruce and Norway pine. Pare Lorentz. *Fr.* The River. AmFN
Black Star Line. Henry Dumas. CNA; PoBA
Black steel carcass in a field of sheep, A. Scrap Iron. Raymond Durgnat. PCP
Black storm clouds have risen in the sky. Surdas, *tr. by* John Stratton Hawley *and* Mark Juergensmeyer. SSI
Black Students. Julia Fields. NBP
Black Study. Michael S. Harper. CAPP
Black Sun, The. Nikos Gatsos, *tr. fr. Greek by* Edmund Keeley *and* Philip Sherrard. *Fr.* Four Songs. VMG
Black swallows swooping or gliding. The Skaters. John Gould Fletcher. ASP; MoAmPo; SD
Black Swan, The. Randall Jarrell. CAPP; CMoP; PoE
Black Taffy. Peggy Susberry Kenner. JB
Black Tambourine. Hart Crane. InPK; InPS; NoAM; OxBA; OxBSP; PPP; TAP
Black Thing. *Unknown.* CoMu
Black Thread. Bartolo Cattafi, *tr. fr. Italian by* Lawrence R. Smith. NItP
Black Tower, The. W. B. Yeats. CMoP
Black Tragedy lets slip her grim disguise. Masks. Thomas Bailey Aldrich. AA
Black trees. The banks fill with shadow. For My Father. Stephen Berg. DiL
Black Trumpeter. Henry Dumas. PoBA
Black Truth. Brenda Agard. WS
Black Veins. Hans Arp, *tr. fr. French by* Michael Benedikt. POS
Black Venus of the Dead, what Sun of Night. Elegy for Dylan Thomas. Dame Edith Sitwell. PoA
Black Walnut Tree, The. Mary Oliver. CAPP
Black Warrior. Norman Jordan. PoBA
Black was the color of the peddler's wagon. Needles and Pins. Mark Van Doren. SO
Black was the without eye. Two Legends. Ted Hughes. *Fr.* Crow. PoE
Black Water and Bright Air. Constance Carrier. SD
Black water. White waves. Furrows snowcapped. Seamus Heaney. *Fr.* Station Island, VII. NoAM
Black Wedding Song, A. Gwendolyn Brooks. CNA
Black within, and red without. Mother Goose. GBP; OxNR
Black Woman. Naomi Long Madgett. BlSi; FB; PoBA
Black Woman. Nancy Morejón, *tr. fr. Spanish by* Lisa E. Davis. DMH
Black Woman. Léopold Sédar Senghor, *tr. fr. French by* Anne Atik. TTY
Black Woman Out Dere. Nefertiti Gayle. WS
Black, yes, but beautiful. Sweet paradox. The Beautiful Slave. Giovanni Battista Marino, *tr. by* Dana Gioia. PFI
Blackberries sweet and dusty. Someplace Else. Marge Piercy. NeAC
Blackberry, The. Norman Nicholson. MoBrPo
Blackberry Eating. Galway Kinnell. InPK
Blackberry Fold. *Unknown. See* It's of a rich squire in Bristol doth dwell.
Blackberry-picking. Seamus Heaney. BoNaP
Blackberry Sweet. Dudley Randall. HAP; InPS; NBP; WeW
Blackberry Winter. John Crowe Ransom. AnAmPo; OxBA; PoRA
Blackberrying. Sylvia Plath. HAP; HCAP; NAAL-2; NoAM; NOBA; NYBP
Blackbird, The. Phyllis Drayson. BoTP
Blackbird, The. W. E. Henley. *Fr.* Echoes. MoBrPo; TrGrPo
Blackbird. Rutger Kopland, *tr. fr. Dutch by* Ria Leigh-Loohuizen. DuIn
Blackbird, The. D. M. Mulock. BoTP
Blackbird, The. Su Shao-lien, *tr. fr. Chinese by* Dominic Cheung. IFON
Blackbird, The. Tennyson. FM; PBBP
Blackbird, The ("Ah, blackbird, thou art satisfied"). *Unknown, tr. fr. Middle Irish by* Kuno Meyer. AnIL
Blackbird, The ("In midst of woods or pleasant grove"). *Unknown.* EIL
Blackbird, The. *Unknown.* NOIV
Blackbird, The. Humbert Wolfe. BoTP; FaPON; GoJo; GrPl; RHPC
Blackbird, blackbird in the cage. The Bird and the Tree. Ridgely Torrence. PoNe
Blackbird calls in grief, The. *Unknown.* NOIV
Blackbird of Derrycairn, The. *Unknown, tr. fr. Irish by* Austin Clarke. BIrV; NeIP

Blackbird Sestina. Candice Warne. SM
Blackbird Singing, A. R. S. Thomas. OBWVE
Blackbirds. Susan Mitchell. NAmP
Blackbirds and Thrushes. *Unknown.* GBP
Blackbird's Song. *Unknown.* GBP
Blackcaps pipe among the reeds, The. Before the Rain. Amélie Rives.
AA
Blackcock, The. Joanna Baillie. PBBP
Blacken thy heavens, Jove. Prometheus. Goethe, *tr. by* John S. Dwight.
AWP
Blackened and bleeding, helpless, panting, prone. Chicago. Bret Harte.
AiP; PAH
Blackening the offing. Joso, *tr. fr. Japanese by* Hiroaki Sato. *Fr.*
Fifteen Hokku. FCEI
Blackfish Poem. Milton Acorn. NeAC
Blackfriars. Eleanor Farjeon. OxBChV
Blackie Thinks of His Brothers. Stanley Crouch. PoBA
Blackleg. Kendrick Smithyman. ATNZ
Blackleg Miners, The. *Unknown.* GBP; OBET
Blacklisted. Carl Sandburg. SaC
Blackmen: Who Make Morning. Angela Jackson. CNA
Blackness of one quarter lights up the mauve of three, The. The
Northland in Cold. Li Ho, *tr. by* Burton Watson. CoBCP
Blackpool Breezes. *Unknown.* CoMu
Blacks in frame houses. Song: I Want a Witness. Michael S. S. Harper.
CAPP
Blackshawled women of New Mexico, The. Old Women beside a
Church. Keith Wilson. Psk
Blacksmith. B. K. Pyke. BoTP
Blacksmith, The ("A blacksmith, courted me, nine months and better").
Unknown. OBET
Blacksmith Pain. Otto Julius Bierbaum, *tr. fr. German by* Jethro Bithell.
AWP
Blacksmiths, The. *Unknown.* RB; RR; TW, *mod. vers. by* Wesli Court;
WiR
(Swarte-smeked Smithes.) HAP
Blacksmith's boy went out with a rifle, The. Legend. Judith Wright.
RB; SO
Blacksmith's Song, The. *Unknown.* GBP
Blackstone Rangers, The. Gwendolyn Brooks. NoAM; PoBA
Blackthorn. Euros Bowen, *tr. fr. Welsh by the author.* OBWVE
Blackwater Mountain. Charles Wright. CAPP; GeTw
Blade of a knife, The. Richard Murphy. IPY
Blade of Grass Sings to the River, The. Leah Goldberg, *tr. fr. Hebrew by*
Robert Friend. TrJP
Blades. Charles Kenneth Williams. GeTw
Blades of Grass, The. Stephen Crane. *Fr.* The Black Riders, XVIII.
MoAmPo
Blades of Harden, The. Will H. Ogilvie. *Fr.* Whaup o' the Reed.
GoTS
Bladyn's Song of Cloten. C. M. Doughty. *Fr.* The Dawn in Britain.
PoEL-5
Blah, Blah, Blah. Ira Gershwin. OBAL
Blair, to make his mother screech. Fresh Brats. X. J. Kennedy. SoTCo
Blake Leads a Walk on the Milky Way. Nancy Willard. OBCA
Blake Mistake, The. Sandie Castle. UL
Blake shuts his eyes. Life Mask. Charles Brasch. PeNZ
Blakeney people, The. The People of Blakeney. *Unknown.* GBP
Blakewater hath a broad bridge stretched across. Salford Bridge —That
Popular Resort of the Great Unwashed. William Billington. PF
Blame me not, Sweet, if here and there. Alibi. Arthur Guiterman.
BXAP
Blame not my cheeks, though pale with love they be. Thomas Campion.
AAS; UnPo
Blame Not My Lute for He Must Sound [*or* Sownde]. Sir Thomas Wyatt.
AAS; EBEV; EiL; NAEL-1; OAEL-1; PoE; SiPS
(Lute Obeys, The.) OBSC; QFR
"Blame not thyself too much," I said, "nor blame." Tennyson. *Fr.* The
Princess, *Pt.* VII. NAEL-2
Blame was all. Khwaja Mir Dard, *tr. by* Ahmed Ali. GoT
Blaming Sons. T'ao Ch'ien, *tr. fr. Chinese by* Burton Watson. CoBCP
Blancheflour and Jellyflorice. *Unknown.* ESPB
Blanid's Song. Gordon Bottomley. *Fr.* The Crier by Night. BrPo
Blank Book Letter, The. Samuel Greenberg. LiTA
Blank faces smile and nod. Waiting for the Rain. Felix Mnthali.
WMBCH
Blank the screens. Partial View of a Supernova. Terry A. Garey.
BWV
Blank Verse for a Fat Demanding Wife. Jim Lindsey. TW
Blantyre Explosion, The. *Unknown.* OBET
Blasphemies, The. Louis MacNeice. FaBCIP
Blast of War, The. Shakespeare. *See* King Henry V:
Once more unto the breach, dear friends, once more.

Blast of wind, a momentary breath, A. Barnabe Barnes. *Fr.* A Divine
Century of Spiritual Sonnets. EBEV
(Life of Man, The.) OBSC
Blast ripped off the railroad man's, The. Field Hospital, 1945. Andras
Fodor, *tr. by* Jascha Kessler. FOC
Blasted Herb, The. Meshech Weare. PAH
Blasted with sighs, and surrounded with tears. Twicknam [*or*
Twickenham] Garden. John Donne. EBEV; EnLoPo; FaBoPP;
MeLP; MePo; OBS; OPOP; PoE; PoEL-2; SeCP; TEP
Blasting from Heaven. Philip Levine. CoAP
Blasts rip newspaper grey Mannahatta's mid day air spires. Friday the
Thirteenth. Allen Ginsberg. NNaP
Blatant as factory buildings. Marina Tsvetayeva, *tr. fr. Russian by*
Elaine Feinstein *and* Angela Livingstone. *Fr.* Poem of the End.
PBWP
Blauen Veilchen der Aügelein, Die. Heine, *tr. fr. German by* James
Thomson. AWP
Blaydon Races. *Unknown.* ELP
Blazing Heart, The. Alice Williams Brotherton. AA
Blazing noon, fierce, unrelenting noon!, The. William Hosack. *Fr.* The
Isle of Streams; or, the Jamaica Hermit. PBCV
Blazing white shirts of the white men, The. Race Riot, Tulsa, 1921.
Sharon Olds. MAYP
Blazon Columbia's emblem. Columbia's Emblem. Edna Dean Proctor.
GN
Bleached wood massed in bone piles. Kalaloch. Carolyn Forché.
AmPA; AnAn; NOAM
Bleak. Sándor Weöres, *tr. fr. Hungarian by* Jascha Kessler. FOC
Bleak season was it, turbulent and bleak. The Sunbeam Said, Be Happy.
Wordsworth. *Fr.* The Recluse, I. FaBoRV
Bleak the February light. Kingdom of Heaven. Léonie Adams. MoAB;
MoAmPo
Bleat of Protest. Mildred Weston. FiBHP
Bled/ holding on/ to details. Monogram 23. Martina Werner, *tr. by*
Rosemarie Waldrop. BoWoP
Bleeberrying. Jonathan Denwood. MoBS
Bleecker Street. Jean Garrigue. TAP
Bleed Through. Joy Harjo. ER
Bleeder. Stephen Dobyns. NAmP
Blenheim, *sel.* John Philips.
War Poetry. NOEC
Blennerhassett's Island. Thomas Buchanan Read. *Fr.* The New Pastoral.
PAH
Bless earth with Thine Advent, O Saviour Christ! *Unknown, tr. fr. Anglo-
Saxon.* *Fr.* Christ 1: Advent Lyrics, VIII. AnOE, *tr. by* Charles W.
Kennedy
Bless Him ("Bless Him, O constant companions"). *Unknown, tr. fr.
Hebrew by* Israel Abrahams. TrJP
Bless the four corners of this house. House Blessing. Arthur Guiterman.
TrPWD
Bless the Lord, O my soul/ O Lord my God. Bible, *O.T.* Psalm CIV.
NAWM-1; OHIP, *abr.;* TrJP
(Hymn of the World Without, *Moulton Modern Reader's Bible*)
WGRP
"So is this great and wide sea." *Fr.* 25-28. MOS
Bless the Lord, O my soul: and all that is within me. Bible, *O.T.* Psalm
CIII. AWP
("O Thou my soule, Jehovah blesse," *Bay Psalm Book.*) SCAP
("Praise, my soul, the King of heaven.")
(Psalm CIII: "Praise the Lord, O my soul," *paraphrased by* Henry
Francis Lyte.)
Bless Thou this year, O Lord! A Prayer for a Happy New Year. Andrew
Stuart Currie Clarke. BLRP
Bless you, bless you. The Price of Giving Too Much. Vanparanar, *tr.
by* A. K. Ramanujan. PLW
Bless you, bless you, burnie-bee [*or* bonnie-bee]. Mother Goose. BoTP;
OxNR
Bless you, earth. Earth's Bounty. Auvaiyar, *tr. by* A. K. Ramanujan.
PLW
Bless you, friend. Listen. What She Said to Her Girl Friend When She
Returned from the Hills. Kapilar, *tr. by* A. K. Ramanujan. PLW
Bless you God our God. The Fringes. Harris Lenowitz. VWA
Bless you. Listen to me. What She Said to Her Girl Friend, Her Foster-
Mother within Earshot. Kapilar, *tr. by* A. K. Ramanujan. PLW
Bless you, Mother. On the Appeal from the Race of Sheba: II. Léopold
Sédar Senghor, *tr. by* John Reed *and* Clive Wake. TTY
Bless you, Mother, listen. What Her Friend Said to the Foster-Mother
(Who Is Guarding Her Carefully). Kapilar, *tr. by* A. K. Ramanujan.
PLW
Bless'd art Thou, O Lord of all. Prayer before Sleep. Alice Lucas.
TrJP
Blessed. Soné, *tr. fr. Hebrew by* David Kuselewitz. TrJP

Blessed/ are the injured animals. Blessing. Linda Hogan. STE
Blessed above women/ shall Jael the wife of Heber the Kenite be. Bible, *O.T. Fr.* Judges: The Song of Deborah, V:24-31. WPOW
Blessed and Resting Uncle. Harley Elliott. NeAC
Blessed angell not a word replies, The. Ariosto, *tr. fr. Italian by* Sir John Harington. *Fr.* Orlando Furioso, XIV. OBVE
Blessed are the poor[e] in spirit for theirs is the kingdom[e] of heaven. Bible, *N.T. Fr.* St. Matthew, V: 3-10. OBVE (Beatitudes, The.)
Blessed are they of the Easter faith. Easter Beatitudes. Clarence M. Burkholder. BLRP
Blessed are they that have eyes to see. Some Blesseds. John Oxenham. WGRP
Blessed are they who sow but do not reap. Blessed. Soné, *tr. by* David Kuselewitz. TrJP
Blessed Are Those Who Sow and Do Not Reap. Avraham Ben-Yitzhak, *tr. fr. Hebrew by* A. C. Jacobs. VWA
Blessed Art Thou, O Lord. *Unknown, tr. fr. Hebrew by* Theodor H. Gaster. *Fr.* The Dead Sea Scrolls. TrJP
Blessed Assurance. Fanny Crosby. AH
Blessed be that lady bright. A Cause for Wonder. *Unknown.* MeEL
Blessed be the English and all their ways and works. Jobson's Amen. Kipling. OBTV
Blessed Be the Holy Will of God. *Unknown, tr. fr. Irish by* Douglas Hyde. TIRV
Blessed Bible, sacred treasure. The Best of All. Fanny Crosby. BLRP
Blessed by the day which bids my grief subside. To Mr. William Long, On His Recovery from a Dangerous Illness, 1785. William Hayley. Son
Blessed Comforter Divine. Lydia Huntley Sigourney. AH
Blessed Damozel, The. Dante Gabriel Rossetti. AWP; BLPL; EBVV; LiTB; NAEL-2; NOBE; NOBVV; NoP; OAEL-2; OBEV; OBNC; OHFP; PoE; PoEL-5; TEP; TrGrPo
Blessed Event. Ada Jackson. CN
Blessed Is Everyone. *Unknown.* AH
Blessed Is God. Bible, Apocrypha, *tr. fr. Greek by* D. C. Simpson. *Fr.* Tobit, XIII. TrJP
Blessed is he who has found the break-weed. Handful of Ashes. Ilya Rubin, *tr. by* Linda Zisquit. VWA
Blessed is the man that walketh not in the counsel of the ungodly [or wicked]. Bible, *O.T.* Psalm I. AWP
(Happy Is the Man.) TrJP
("O blessed man, that in th' advice," *Bay Psalm Book)* SCAP
(Tree and the Chaff, The.) WGRP
Blessed land of Judea! thrice hallowed of song. Palestine. Whittier. WBLP
Blessed Lord, What It Is to Be Young. David McCord. NTCP
Blessed Mary. *Unknown.* OxBSP
Blessed Mary, moder virginal. A Short Prayer to Mary. *Unknown.* MeEL
Blessed Match, The. Hannah Senesh, *tr. fr. Yiddish.* TrJP
Blessed Name, The. George W. Bethune. *See* There Is No Name So Sweet on Earth.
Blessed Offendour: who thyself haist try'd. To Saint Mary Magdalen ("Blessed Offendour: who thyself haist try'd"). Henry Constable. PoEL-2
Blessed poster girl leaned out, The. The Poster Girl. Carolyn Wells. BXAP
Blessed the match that was burned. The Blessed Match. Hannah Senesh. TrJP
Blessed Trinity have pity! Childless. Giolla Brighde MacNamee. BIrV, *tr. by* Frank O'Connor
Blessed Virgin Compared to the Air We Breathe, The. Gerard Manley Hopkins. BrPo; NOBVV
Blessed with a joy that only she. The Gift of God. E. A. Robinson. MoAB; MoAmPo; OxBA
Blessing. Linda Hogan. STE
Blessing, The. Carolyn Kizer. CAPP
Blessing, A. Mekeel McBride. MAYP; SM
Blessing. Melvin Wilk. VWA
Blessing, A. James Wright. CAPP; GrPl; InPK; InPS; LLLT; NAAL-2; NaP; NoAM; NOBA; NoP; PoE; PPP; TwCP
Blessing a Bride and Groom; a Wedding Night Poem. Robert Peters. BXAP
Blessing for the Blessed, A, *sel.* L. Alma Tadema. "When the sun has left the hill-top." BoTP
Blessing his handiwork, his drawbridge closed. Artificer. X. J. Kennedy. TwCP
Blessing in Disguise, A. John Ashbery. PoM
Blessing Mrs. Larkin. Margery Swett Mansfield. GoYe
Blessing of St. Francis, The. Sister Maura. CaP
Blessing of the Firstborn. Howard Schwartz. VWA

Blessing of the Priests. Bible, *O.T. See* Numbers: Benediction.
Blessing on Little Boys. Arthur Guiterman. TrPWD
Blessing on you, Mrs. Larkin, for planting my trees! A. Blessing Mrs. Larkin. Margery Swett Mansfield. GoYe
Blessing the Hounds. Mary Winter. GoYe
Blessing without Company. *Unknown.* BPo
Blessings in abundance come. The Good-Night, or Blessing. Robert Herrick. CaPo
Blessings [*or* Blessing] on the hand of women! The Hand That Rocks the Cradle Is the Hand That Rules the World. William Ross Wallace. BLPL; FaFP; PoLF; WBLP
Blessings on thee, little man. Whittier. *Fr.* The Barefoot Boy. AA; AnAmPo; FaBoBe; FaPON; FPL; GN; LiTA; OBAL; OBCA; OHFP; PoLF; WBLP
Blessings That Remain, The. Annie Johnson Flint. BLRP
Blest are the pure in heart. Purity of Heart. John Keble. BLRP
Blest are your North parts, for all this long time. To Mr. I. L. John Donne. SeCP
Blest as th' immortal gods is he. Fragment of Sappho. *Unknown, tr. by* Ambrose Philips
Blest be Mother bind your hand on my head on the eve. The Poem on the Guilt. Avot Yeshurun, *tr. by* Harold Schimmel. VWA
Blest be the day, and blest the month and year. Petrarch, *tr. fr. Italian. Fr.* Sonnets to Laura: To Laura in Life, XLVII, *tr. by* Joseph Auslander. NAWM-1
("Father in heaven, after each lost day," *tr. by* Bernard Bergonzi) NAWM-1
Blest Be the Wondrous Grace. George Barrell Cheever. AH
Blest, Blest and Happy He. *Unknown.* GBL; GoTS
Blest hour of peace, of poetry, and love! John Critchley Prince. *Fr.* The Poet's Sabbath. PF
Blest is t' bride at t' sun shines on. Wedding and Funeral. *Unknown.* GBP
Blest is the man who loves and after early play. Boys and Sport. Solon, *tr. by* John Addington Symonds. PeHV
Blest Is the Man Whose Tender Breast. Abijah Davis. AH
Blest leaf! whose aromatic gales dispense. Isaac Hawkins Browne. *Fr.* A Pipe of Tobacco. BXAP; Par
Blest pair of Sirens, pledges of heaven's joy. Milton. *Fr.* At a Solemn Music[k]. GTBS; GTBS-P; HeIP; NOBE; OBEV; OBS; PoEL-3; UnS
Blest the infant Babe. Wordsworth. *Fr.* The Prelude [or, Growth of a Poet's Mind]: School-Time. TOF
Bleue Maison. Edmund Blunden. BrPo
Blight. Arna Bontemps. BANP; CDC
Blight. Emerson. NOBA; NoP
Blight of Love, The. Mary E. Tucker. CBWP-1
Blight rests in your face, The. To a Publisher. Cut-out. Imamu Amiri Baraka. NeAP
Blighted apples will not shine. Apple Blight. Paul Zimmer. VGW
"Blighters." Siegfried Sassoon. CMoP; FaBoTw; MMA; MoP; NoAM; OxBSP
Blimps and Nightingales. Richard Moore. SoTCo
Blind Adolphus. Angela McCabe. AmPA
Blind as the song of birds. Lines to a Blind Girl. Thomas Buchanan Read. AA
Blind Bartimaeus at the gates. Jericho's Blind Beggar. Longfellow. WBLP
Blind Beggar, The. *Unknown.* AmFP
Blind Boy, The. Colley Cibber. GTBS; GTBS-P; NOEC; OxBChV
Blind Boy's Pranks, The. William Thom. OBEV
Blind Date. Conrad Aiken. DL
Blind-drunk/ New Year caller, A. Yomono Akara, *tr. by* Geoffrey Bownas *and* Anthony Thwaite. PeBJV
Blind girl, A. Black Lightning. Arthur Sze. BrSi
Blind Girl. W. S. Merwin. NePoEA-2
Blind girl singing on the radio, A. Singing in the Dark. Irma Wassall. PoNe
Blind, I Speak to the Cigarette. Joanne de Longchamps. GoYe
Blind Leading the Blind, The. Lisel Mueller. IHMS
Blind Linnet, The. Robert Williams Buchanan. FM
Blind Louise. George Washington Dewey. AA
Blind Love. Shakespeare. *See* O me! what eyes hath love put in my head.
Blind Man. Michael Hamburger. NePoEA-2
Blind Man, The, *sel.* Judith Wright.
Country Dance. CBAP
Blind man, A. I can stare at him. A Solitude. Denise Levertov. NePoEA-2
Blind man asked me, A. Huda Na mani, *tr. fr. Arabic by* Lena Jayyusi. *Fr.* To You, III. MAP
Blind Man at the Fair, The. Joseph Campbell. AWP

Blind man, blind man. Mother Goose. OxNR
Blind Man Lay beside the Way. *Unknown.* AS
Blind-Man's Buff. Blake. WiR
Blind, mean-minded, A. Tulsidas, *tr. by* John Stratton Hawley *and* Mark
  Juergensmeyer. SSI
Blind Men and the Elephant, The. John Godfrey Saxe. BLPA; BoTP;
  FaBoBe; FPL; OBCA; OnMSP; OnUR; WBLP
Blind men, blind men. *Unknown, tr. by* Arthur Waley. BoS
Blind Mr. Klugel loves the baritone of Mr. Cantini. The Follies. Daniel
  Mark Epstein. MAYP
Blind Musician, The. Ali Mahmud Taha, *tr. fr. Arabic by* Issa Boullata
  and Thomas G. Ezzy. MAP
Blind Old Woman. Clarence Major. PoBA
Blind Psalmist, The. Elizabeth Clementine Kinney. AA
Blind Samson. William Plomer. PeSA
Blind Sheep, The. Randall Jarrell. NYBP; OBAL
Blind Steersmen. Francis Ernest Kobina Parkes. PBA
Blind Thamyris, and blind Maeonides. Ode to the Human Heart. Laman
  Blanchard. NA; NOBL
Blind Upholsterer, The. Stanley Cook. NPo
Blind with love, my daughter. Pain for a Daughter. Anne Sexton.
  SoSe; TV; WeW
Blind Woman, The. Lucha Corpi. CCP
Blinded Bird, The. Thomas Hardy. CMoP; EaLo; LiTM
Blinded parson gingering down the neo-Gothic steps, A. The Four.
  Geoffrey Grigson. WaP
Blindest and most frantic prayer. The Deserter. Edward Rowland Sill.
  AnAmPo
Blindest buzzard that I know, The. A Sketch. Christina Rossetti.
  GTBS-P
Blinding spot burned on the snow, A. Mistress of the Matchless Mine.
  Clyde Robertson
Blinding sun at ten o'clock, The. The Church. Edwin Ford Piper.
  WGRP
Blindman's Buff. Peter Viereck. LiTM; MoAmPo
Blindness. Delmira Agustini, *tr. fr. Spanish by* D. M. Pettinella.
  PBWP
Blindness of Samson, The. Milton. *Fr.* Samson Agonistes. LiTB
  "I, dark in light, exposed," 5 *ll.* TrGrPo
Blinking eyes of the grazing ox, The. Peasant and Ox. Shin Dong-jip,
  tr. by Koh Chang-soo. ACKP
Bliss. Eleanor Farjeon. RHPC
Bliss. George Johnston. NOBC
Bliss for which our spirits pine, The. The True Heaven. Paul Hamilton
  Hayne. WGRP
Bliss of man, The (could pride that blessing find). Pope. *Fr.* An Essay
  on Man, Epistle I. NOEC; NU
Bliss of Sunday, The. László Nagy, *tr. fr. Hungarian by* Edwin Morgan.
  MHuP
"Blissful" quoth I, "may this be true?" The Queen of Courtesy.
  Unknown. Fr. Pearl. ACP
Blistered and dry was the desert I trod. The Palm. Roy Campbell.
  MoBrPo
Blizzard, The. Eugene Ware. CowP
Bloated/ on rotten eggs. The Skunk. Philip Dow. BXAP
Bloated Biggaboon, The. Henry Cholmondeley-Pennell. NA
Block City. Robert Louis Stevenson. EyDe; FaPON; NTCP
Block the cannon; let no trumpets sound! Sunset Horn. Myron
  O'Higgins. AmNP; PoNe
Blocked by Snow. Wu Wei-yeh, *tr. fr. Chinese by* Marie Chan. WFTU
Blocked by thick branches. Tamekane, *tr. by* Steven D. Carter. WFTW
Blockhouse. Olga Kirsch, *tr. fr. Afrikaans by* Jack Cope. PeSA
Blocking the Pass. Charles Madge. FaBoMo
Blocks, The. Clark Coolidge. IAT
Blocks, The/ which are the buildings and walls. Comforted by Limestone.
  Edward Dorn. *Fr.* Oxford. NOBA
Blocks. Frank O'Hara. EAS; HCAP
Blocks of dawn crumble, The. White Blocks. Hans Arp, *tr. by* Michael
  Benedikt. POS
Blodwen,/ Her name like the hours. Her Name like the Hours. Gloria
  Evans Davies. OBWVE
Blok: Let Me Learn the Poem. Aram Boyajian. NeAC
Blond. Joseph de Roche. HeIP
Blond in gray and black and silver. Stay Beautiful. Jeff Wright.
  UL
Blond stones all round-sided. Morning at Point Dume. May Swenson.
  DiPo
Blonde hair at the edge of the pavement. Mitching. Michael Smith.
  CIP
Blondel. Clarence Urmy. AA
Blood. Ray Bremser. NeAP
Blood. Barney Bush. STE

Blood, The. Nina Cassian, *tr. fr. Rumanian.* VWA, *tr. by* Herbert
  Kuhner; WPOW, *tr. by* Laura Schiff
Blood Countess, The, *sel.* Robert Peters.
  "Blood stains the feather." VVA
Blood falling in drops to the earth. Where Are the Men Seized in This
  Wind of Madness? Alda do Espírito Santo, *tr. by* Alan Ryder.
  TTY; WPOW
Blood flows from my brow, The. Meir Wieseltier, *tr. fr. Hebrew by*
  Warren Bargad *and* Stanley F. Chyet. *Fr.* Wintry Dawn, 12. IP
Blood flows in me, but what does it have to do. Living by the Red River.
  James Wright. NNaP
Blood has soaked the bone which hides the stone, The. Clive James. *Fr.*
  Peregrine Prykke's Pilgrimage. FaBoPa
"Blood Horse, The." "Barry Cornwall." GN
Blood Is Thicker than Water. Wallace Rice. PAH
Blood Marksman and Kureldei the Marksman. *Tatar (Turkic) Oral
  Tradition, tr. fr. German and Russian versions by* Norman Cohn.
  WTO
Blood on the Sails. Phil *and* June Colclough. OBET
Blood-red the aloes flank. Farm Gate. Uys Krige, *tr. by* Uys Krige *and*
  Jack Cope. PeSA
Blood River Day. Dennis Brutus. WMBCH
Blood-Sister. Adrienne Rich. NAAL-2; NoP
Blood stains the feather. Robert Peters. *Fr.* The Blood Countess. VVA
Blood-strained Banders, The. *Unknown.* AmFP
Blood, the Note "B." Yves Bonnefoy, *tr. fr. French by* Anthony Rudolf.
  RHTwFP
Blood thudded in my ears. I scuffed. First Confession. X. J. Kennedy.
  NePoEA-2; PPP
Blood will not serve. A Poem for Heroes. Julia Fields. CNA
Blood, wine, and glee. The Dance of the Sword. *Unknown, tr. by* Tom
  Taylor. WaaP
Bloodhounds look like sad old judges, The. Nice Day for a Lynching.
  Kenneth Patchen. PoNe
Bloods and bucks of this lewd town, The. Horace. *See* Odes: I, 25.
  Ribald Romeos Less and Less Berattle ("Parcius iunctas quatiunt
  fenestras").
Bloody, A/ egg yolk. A burnt hole. Out of the Sea, Early. May
  Swenson. RFM
Bloody and a sudden end, A. John Kinsella's Lament for Mrs. Mary
  Moore. W. B. Yeats. CMoP; LiTM; MoAB; NoP; OAEL-2; RB
Bloody, and stained, and with mothers' cries. The Innocents. Jay
  Macpherson. OBCV
Bloody Brother, The, *sels.* Robert H. Fletcher *and others.*
  Drinking Song. *Fr.* II, ii. ElL
  Take, Oh, Take Those Lips Away. *Fr.* V, ii, *st.* 1 *also in*
  Shakespeare's Measure for Measure. NoP
  (Song: "Take, oh take those Lips away.") PoEL-2
Bloody Conquests of Mighty Tamburlaine, The. Christopher Marlowe.
  Fr. Tamburlaine the Great, *pt.* II, Act IV, sc. iii. ChTr
  (Emperor of the Threefold World.) TrGrPo
Bloody Pause. Astra. BrRo
Bloody Sire, The. Robinson Jeffers. CMoP; LiTM; PoA
Bloody trunk [*or* Bloudy trunck] of him who did possess[e], The. The
  Fall. Sir Richard Fanshawe, *after the Italian of* Giovanni Battista
  Guarini. *Fr.* Il Pastor Fido. MePo; OBS
  (Great Favorit Beheaded, A.) OBVE
Bloom is result. To Meet a flower. Emily Dickinson. PoEL-5
Bloom Street. Angela McCabe. AmPA
Bloomfield, Inc. Richard Katrovas. NAmP
Blooming everywhere. Tamehide, *tr. by* Steven D. Carter. WFTW
Blooming Sally. *Unknown.* OBET
Blooms such as wither at finger-touch. Brian Coffey. *Fr.* Muse, June,
  Related. BIrV
Blossom, The. Blake. *Fr.* Songs of Innocence. GoJo; PBBP
Blossom [*or* Blossome], The. John Donne. AWP; LiTB; MeLP;
  NAEL-1; OBS; SeCP; UnPo
Blossom. Stanley Plumly. GeTw; KS
Blossom, The. Shakespeare. *See* Love's Labour's Lost: On a Day—
  Alack the Day.
Blossom, butterfly, a girl's cheeks. Just a Little Wind. Ruth Kim Chun-
  soo, *tr. by* Koh Chang-soo. ACKP
Blossom drops, and that, A. Issa, *tr. fr. Japanese by* Hiroaki Sato. *Fr.*
  Forty-four Hokku. FCEI
Blossom is in her hair. Flowers. *Gond Oral Tradition, tr. by* V. Elwin
  and S. Hivale. WTO
Blossom of the almond trees. Almond Blossom. Sir Edwin Arnold.
  GN
Blossom of the Soul, The. Robert Underwood Johnson. AA
Blossom Time. Wilbur Larremore. AA
Blossom to the roots, The. Emperor Sutoku, *tr. by* Geoffrey Bownas *and*
  Anthony Thwaite. PeBJV

Blossoming peach trees among the bamboos: patches of moistened red. South Lake in the Rain. Li E, *tr. by* Shirleen S. Wong. WFTU
Blossoming plum. Teika, *tr. by* Steven D. Carter. WFTW
Blossoms. Frank Dempster Sherman. OBCA
Blossoms at Evening. Empress Eifuku, *tr. fr. Japanese by* Steven D. Carter. WFTW
Blossoms, at least wait. Tsurayuki, *tr. fr. Japanese by* Burton Watson. *Fr.* Kokin Shu. FCEI
Blossoms at Their Height. Kaneyoshi, *tr. fr. Japanese by* Steven D. Carter. WFTW
Blossoms bloom, I don't wanna die, but this illness. Raizan, *tr. fr. Japanese by* Hiroaki Sato. *Fr.* Thirteen Hokku. FCEI
Blossoms bright, the moon dark, shadowed in thin mist. Tune: Deva-like Barbarian ("Blossoms bright, the moon dark, shadowed in thin mist"). Li Yü, *tr. by* Burton Watson. CoBCP
Blossoms closed into buds, The. Adam's Dream. Howard Schwartz. VWA
Blossoms crowd the branches: too beautiful to endure. Spring-gazing Song. Hsüeh T'ao, *tr. by* Carolyn Kizer. BoWoP
Blossoms have fallen, The. Princess Shikishi, *tr. by* Donald Keene. BoWoP
Blossoms of plum. Teika, *tr. by* Steven D. Carter. WFTW
Blossoms of the wood have scattered their spring crimson. Tune: Crows Crying at Night. Li Yü, *tr. by* Burton Watson. CoBCP
Blossoms of water reeds take wing like willow floss, The. On Hearing a Cricket in the Boat. Sung Wan, *tr. by* William Schultz. WFTU
Blot in the 'Scutcheon, A, *sel.* Robert Browning. Earl Mertoun's Song. OBEV
Blow Away the Morning Dew. *Unknown.* OBET
Blow, blow over me, sweet-scented breath. Wind of the Prairie. Grace Clementine Howes. GoYe
Blow, Blow, Thou Winter Wind. Shakespeare. *Fr.* As You Like It, II, vii. AWP; CH; ChTr; EIL; ELP; GBL; GTBS; GTBS-P; HeIP; InPS; LiTB; NAEL-1; NOBE; NoP; OAEL-1; OBEV; PrIm; TrGrPo; WiR (Amiens's Song.) OBSC
(Blow, Thou Winter Wind.) FaFP
(Song: "Blow, blow, thou winter wind.") CTC; FiP; PoEL-2
(Songs of the Greenwood: "Blow, blow, thou winter wind.") TrGrPo
Blow, blow, ye spicy breezes. Ambrose Bierce. *Fr.* The Devil's Dictionary. OBAL
Blow, bugle, blow! Bugle Song of Peace. Thomas Curtis Clark. WBLP; WGRP
Blow, Bugle, Blow. Tennyson. *See* Princess, The: Splendor Falls [on Castle Walls], The.
Blow muffled through years of, The. Marina Tsvetayeva, *tr. fr. Russian by* Elaine Feinstein. *Fr.* Epitaph, IV. OV
Blow, Northern Wind. *Unknown.* GBL; OBEV
Blow one bred blow two, my friends. Rekayi Tangwena. Mudereri Kadhani. WMBCH
Blow out the candles of your cake. For K. R. on Her Sixtieth Birthday. Richard Wilbur. NoP
"Blow out the light," they said, they said. Temper. Rose Fyleman. OxBChV
Blow out, you bugles, over the rich dead. Dead, The ("Blow out, you bugles, over the rich dead!"). Rupert Brooke. *Fr.* 1914, III. WGRP
Blow softly down the valley. The King of Ireland's Cairn. "Ethna Carbery." WPE
Blow softly, through, upon the hush. The Veery-Thrush. Joseph Russell Taylor. AA
Blow the Candle Out ("Come all ye jolly boatswain boys"). *Unknown.* AmFP
Blow the Candle Out ("It was late one Saturday evening"). *Unknown.* FaBoBa
Blow the fire, blacksmith. Mother Goose. OxNR
Blow the Man Down ("As I was a-walkin' down Paradise Street"). *Unknown.* AS
Blow the Man Down ("Come all you young fellows who follow the sea"). *Unknown.* OxBSS, *vers.* I, *with music.*
Blow the Man Down ("I'll put on my boots and I'll blow the man down"). *Unknown.* AmFP; OxBSS, *vers.* 2.
Blow the Stars Home. Eleanor Farjeon. PDV
Blow, Thou Winter Wind. Shakespeare. *See* As You Like It: Blow, Blow, Thou Winter Wind.
Blow Thy Horn, Hunter. *Unknown.* OxBLMV
Blow, wind, blow! and go, mill, go! Mother Goose. OxNR
Blow wind of heaven. Henjo, *tr. by* Geoffrey Bownas *and* Anthony Thwaite. PeBJV
Blow, Winds. Shakespeare. *Fr.* King Lear, III, ii. TrGrPo (Lear's Speech to the Storm.) TW
Blow Ye Winds. *Unknown.* OxBSS
Blow Ye Winds in the Morning. *Unknown.* AmFP

Blow Your Trumpets. John Donne. *See* Holy Sonnets: At the round earths imagined corners, blow.
Blowflies Buzz, The. *Unknown, tr. fr. Djambarbingu dialect by* Catherine Berndt. WTO
Blowing Bubbles. William Allingham. GN
Blowing Bubbles. Margaret Hillert. RAR
Blowing hard at the bus stop. Transit. Margaret Avison. FaBoWP
Blowing the evening sun. Ozaki Hosai, *tr. fr. Japanese by* Hiroaki Sato. *Fr.* One Hundred Haiku in Free Form. FCEI
Blowing wind, The. Mitsune, *tr. by* Geoffrey Bownas *and* Anthony Thwaite. PeBJV
Blowing wind's companion, A. Boncho, *tr. fr. Japanese by* Hiroaki Sato. *Fr.* Twenty-one Hokku. FCEI
Blown[e] in the morning, thou shalt fade ere noon. A Rose. Sir Richard Fanshawe, *after the Italian of* Giovanni Battista Guarini. *Fr.* Il Pastor Fido. OBEV; OBS; PoEL-2; SeCePo (Rose of Life, The.) AWP
Blown in the wind the silver river. Inscribed on a Snowscape. Yün Shou-p'ing, *tr. by* Jonathan Chaves. CoBLCP
Blown out of the prairie in twilight and dew. Coyote. Bret Harte. AnAmPo
Blows the Wind Today. Robert Louis Stevenson. *Fr.* Songs of Travel. CH; PoSH
(To S. R. Crockett.) EBVV; FaBoPP; NOBE; OBNC
Blubber Lips. Jim Daniels. TDD
Blue. Christopher Gilbert. *Fr.* Beginning by Example. FYAP
Blue/ on/ blue. Pinay. Virginia Cerenio. BrSi
Blue Alert. Eve Merriam. PCP
Blue and gold morning of paper propaganda, The. Magaiça. Noémia da Sousa, *tr. by* Margaret Dickinson. WMBCH
Blue and the Gray, The. Francis Miles Finch. AA; AnAmPo; BLPA; BLPL; FaBoBe; OPP; PAH; WBLP
Blue and White. Mary Elizabeth Coleridge. OBEV
Blue Animals, The. Jon Anderson. AmPA; SM
Blue are the beautiful skies! Sweeping the Skies. Elizabeth Anna Hart. CenHV
Blue Arm. Bernard Spencer. NoAM
Blue as the blowpipe's petal of flame. Blue Flag. Dorothy Donnelly. NYBP
Blue-Bird, The. Herman Melville. BLPL; NOBA
Blue-Bird, The. Alexander Wilson. AA
Blue Black. Bloke Modisane. PBA
Blue-black flare at the bottom, The. Blue Bottle. Patricia Hampl. NAmP
Blue-black mountains are etched, The. The Chance. Arthur Sze. BrSi
Blue Blood. James Stephens, *after the Irish of* David O'Bruaidar. MoAB; MoBrPo; OBMV
Blue, blue is the grass about the river. The Beautiful Toilet. Ezra Pound, *after the Chinese.* OBVE
Blue Blue Your Collar. *Unknown, tr. fr. Chinese by* Burton Watson. CoBCP
Blue Bog Children. Roger Weingarten. AmPA
Blue Bonnets over the Border. Sir Walter Scott. *See* Monastery, The: Border Ballad.
Blue Booby, The. James Tate. AmPA; EAS; NoAM; NoP
Blue Book 42. Steve Benson. IAT
Blue Bottle. Patricia Hampl. NAmP
Blue boughs, green fruit. The Furnished Room. James Merrill. NOBA
Blue Bowl, The. Blanche Bane Kuder. BLPA; FaBoBe
Blue-Butterfly Day. Robert Frost. RFM
Blue calf tethered. *Gond Oral Tradition, tr. by* V. Elwin *and* W. Hivale. WTO
Blue Chinese carpet, The. Leading to your Hands. Patricia Hampl. NAmP
Blue Coat, A. Gertrude Stein. *Fr.* Tender Buttons. PBWP
Blue crane fishing in Cooloolah's twilight, The. At Cooloolah. Judith Wright. MoBrPo
Blue Crest of Fondness. Unsi al-Haj, *tr. fr. Arabic by* Sargon Boulus *and* Alistair Elliot. MAP
Blue Cuckoo. *Unknown, tr. fr. Yoruba by* Ulli Beier. *Fr.* Hunter Poems of the Yoruba. RB
Blue day, A/ a blue jay. March. Elizabeth J. Coatsworth. PDV; RHPC
Blue Day Journey, The. Gwyn Jones. OBWVE
Blue, dew-drenched. Gardens for the Fire and the Rain. Muhammad al-Asad, *tr. by* Lena Jayyusi *and* Charles Doria. MAP
Blue eagle and the demon of the steppes, The. The Staircase with a Hundred Steps. Benjamin Péret, *tr. by* David Gascoyne. EAS
Blue expanse of hyacinthine bloom, The. Memories of a Dorset Childhood in the 1730's. Thomas Cole. *Fr.* The Life of Hubert. NOEC
Blue Ey'd Mary. *Unknown.* CoMu

Blue-eyed and bright of face but waning fast. Staff-Nurse: New Style.
  W. E. Henley. *Fr.* In Hospital, X. BrPo
Blue-eyed Girl. *Unknown.* AmFP
Blue-eyed Mary. Mary E. Wilkins Freeman. OBCA
Blue-eyed Precinct Worker, The. Henri Coulette. MAT
Blue Flag. Dorothy Donnelly. NYBP
Blue Flag, The. Chris Miller. FaBoPa
Blue Flame, The. Amryl Johnson. WS
Blue-Fly, The. Robert Graves. CMoP; NAEL-2; NoAM; NYBP
Blue Fly. Joaquim Maria Machado de Assis, *tr. fr. Portuguese by* Frances
  Ellen Bruckland. TTY
Blue Funk. Joel Oppenheimer. NeAP
Blue-geese, white-geese, you may say. Hilda Doolittle ("H. D."). *Fr.*
  The Flowering of the Rod. NOBA
Blue Girls. John Crowe Ransom. ChTr; CMoP; GBL; LiTA; MoAB;
  MoAmPo; NoAM; PrIm; RB; TAP; VGW; WeW
Blue Glass. Fleur Adcock. FaBoWP
Blue go up and blue go down. American Lights, Seen from Off Abroad.
  John Berryman. LCAP; OBAL
Blue-green bamboo, white sand, village on the river. A Trip to the
  Village of the River of White Sand. Tao-chi, *tr. by* Jonathan Chaves.
  CoBLCP
Blue gulf all around us. The Burial of the Dane. Henry Howard
  Brownell. AA
Blue Heron, The. Theodore Goodridge Roberts. CaP; NOBC; OBCV
Blue hill is my desire, The. Hwang Chin-i, *tr. by* Ko Won. PBWP
Blue Hills beneath the Haze. Charles Goodrich Whiting. AA
Blue-Hole, The. Charles G. Bell. GrPl
Blue Homespun. Frank Oliver Call. CaP
Blue Horse, The. Melvin Walker La Follette. NePoEA
Blue Horses. Ed Roberson. PoBA
Blue Horses; West Winds. Anita Endrezze-Danielson. STE
Blue in the west the mountain stands. Vickery's Mountain. E. A.
  Robinson. MoAmPo
Blue is Our Lady's colour. Blue and White. Mary Elizabeth Coleridge.
  OBEV
Blue is this night of stars. Inquietude. Pauli Murray. BlSi
Blue Island Intersection. Carl Sandburg. MoAmPo
Blue Jay, The. D. H. Lawrence. FM
Blue Jay [*or* Bluejay]. Robert Francis. LCAP; PCP
Blue jay, fly to my windowsill! Invitation. Harry Behn. FaPON
Blue jay scuffling in the bushes follows, The. On the Move. Thom
  Gunn. CMoP; HAP; LiTM; NePoEA-2; NoP; OAEL-2; OxBTC;
  PoE; PPP; TwCP
Blue jay with a crest on his head, The. The Blue Jay. D. H. Lawrence.
  FM
Blue Jeaned Rock Queen in Search of Happiness on a Blind Thursday at
  1/3 Speed and Crying, A. A. K. Redwing. VoR
Blue Juniata, *sel.* Malcolm Cowley.
  Streets of Air, The. PoA
Blue laguna rocks and quivers, The. Port of Holy Peter. John Masefield.
  OBMV
Blue landing lights make. Our Ground Time Here Will Be Brief.
  Maxine W. Kumin. ER
Blue Lantern. Cathy Song. MAYP
Blue Light, The. Tom Dent. UL
Blue light is the night harbor-slip. Louis Zukofsky. *Fr.* 29 Poems, 27.
  PoE
Blue light, morning. This Decoration. Hayden Carruth. NNaP
Blue like Death. James Welch. CDW
Blue Mason Jars. Keith Abbott. UL
Blue Meridian, The, *sel.* Jean Toomer. PoNe
  Brown River, Smile. AmNP; PoBA
Blue mists surround the mountains now. Lines Written on a Farewell
  View of the Franconia Mountains at Twilight. Henrietta Cordelia
  Ray. CBWP-3
Blue Moles. Sylvia Plath. NePoEA-2
Blue Monday. *Unknown.* AmFP
Blue Moonshine. Francis G. Stokes. NA
Blue Mountain. Roberta Hill. VoR
Blue mountains to the north of the walls. Taking Leave of a Friend. Li
  Po, *tr. by* Ezra Pound. RB; SOTW
Blue Mud Shoal. Yang Shih-ch'i, *tr. fr. Chinese by* Jonathan Chaves.
  Fr. Ten Scenes at the Hsiao Family Stone Pulp. CoBLCP
Blue Night Road. Tanaka Fuyuji, *tr. fr. Japanese by* Geoffrey Bownas
  and Anthony Thwaite. PeBJV
Blue of my eyes faded tonight, The. At Night. Georg Trakl, *tr. by*
  Joachim Neugroschel. AnAn
Blue Owl Song. Alfred Kittner, *tr. fr. German by* Herbert Kuhner.
  VWA
Blue Rain. Alistair Campbell. ATNZ
Blue Rapids. Lu Yu, *tr. fr. Chinese by* Burton Watson. CoBCP
Blue Ridge. Ellen Bryant Voigt. AnAn; MAYP; NoAM

Blue robe on their shoulder [s], A. The Seven Fiddlers. Sebastian
  Evans. EBVV; OnMSP
Blue Room, The. Lorenz Hart. OBAL
Blue roses ring the fire brigade. Higher Love. Jeff Wright. UL
Blue Ruth: America. Michael S. S. Harper. PoBA
Blue shadow of dawn settles, The. A Blessing. Mekeel McBride.
  MAYP
Blue sky, blue noon, and the secret line if flung. The Sounding. Conrad
  Aiken. AnAmPo
Blue sky, cold wild-geese crying. Empty Begging Bowl. Ryokan, *tr. by*
  Burton Watson. JLIC-2
Blue sky has died, the yellow sky rises, The. Ballad of the Great London
  Fog. Huang Tsun-hsien, *tr. by* J. D. Schmidt. WFTU
Blue Sleep. Winifred Bryher. PoA
Blue smoke eclipsed, the. Eclipse. Amir Rashidd. NBP
Blue Sparks in Dark Closets. Richard Snyder. Psk
Blue Specks. Nurunnessa Choudhury, *tr. fr. Bengali by the author and*
  Paul Joseph Thompson. AIW
Blue Springs, Georgia. Ree Young. GOYP
Blue Spruce. Mark Halliday. PPR
Blue Stones. Larry Levis. DiL
Blue Swallows, The. Howard Nemerov. NoP
Blue-Tail Fly, The. *Unknown.* FaFP; GBP
Blue Tanganyika. Lebert Bethune. PoBA
Blue toads are dying all over Minnesota. Walking through a Cornfield in
  the Middle of Winter I Stumble over a Cow Pie and Think of the
  Sixties Press. Barbara Hart. BXAP
Blue Train for the South—but the Green Train for us, The. The Green
  Train. E. V. Rieu. SO
Blue Tropic. Luis Cabalquinto. BrSi
Blue unsolid tongue, if you could talk. The Overturned Lake. Charles
  Henri Ford. EAS
Blue water; upon it two possible movements. The Landfall. James
  Dickey. PoA
Blue Waves. David St. John. MAYP
Blue West, The. Dahlia Ravikovich, *tr. fr. Hebrew by* Chana Bloch.
  PBWP
Blue Whale, The. Robert Watson. MAT
Blue Winter. Robert Francis. LCAP
Bluebeard's Closet. Rose Terry Cooke. AA
Bluebell. Geoffrey Taylor. NeIP
Bluebells. Olive Enoch. BoTP
Bluebells. Juliana Horatia Ewing. BoTP
Bluebells. P. A. Ropes. BoTP
Bluebells for Love. Patrick Kavanagh. FaBCIP; IPY
Blueberry Man. David Bergman. GLP
Bluebird &/ honeymoon over. Spring. Reed Bye. TTTS
Bluebird lives in yonder tree, A. To Miguel de Cervantes Saavadra.
  Richard Kendall Munkittrick. AA
Bluejay. Robert Francis. *See* Blue Jay.
Blueline. Ken Belford. NeAC
Bluely, bluely, styles from stone chimneys crippling smoke. In Memory
  of My Father. James Agee. DiL
Blueness of night, The. The Listening Rock. Ray A. Young Bear.
  NOVW
Blueprint. D. B. Steinman. GoYe
Blues. John Fuller. NOBL
Blues/ Never climb a hill. Get Up, Blues. James A. Emanuel. AmNP;
  PoBA
Blues and Bitterness. Lerone Bennett, Jr. FF; PoBA
Blues' Body. Richard Katrovas. NAmP
Blues Don't Change, The. Al Young. NPGG
Blues for an Old Blue. Walker Gibson. NYBP
Blues for Benny Kid Paret. Dave Smith. ASP
Blues for Bessie. Myron O'Higgins. PoNe
Blues for Old Dogs. Paul Zimmer. BLA
Blues for Sister Sally. Lenore Kandel. NMM
Blues is the black o' the face, The. Black Blues. Bloke Modisane.
  PBA
Blues lady/ with the beaded face. Grinding Vibrato. Jayne Cortez. BlSi
Blues meant Swiss-Up, The. Riding across John Lee's Finger. Stanley
  Crouch. PoBA
Blues Note. Bob Kaufman. CNA; PoBA
Blues Today, The. Mae Jackson. PoBA
Bluff Henry the Eighth to six spouses was wedded. Henry VIII.
  Unknown. FaBoUs
Bluffalo, The. Jane Yolen. RHPC
Bluish, pale, The. Moontan. Mark Strand. NYBP
Blum. Dorothy Aldis. MoShBr
Blundering. Jutta Schutting, *tr. fr. German by* Beth Bjorklund. CoAuP
Blunt, flat faces. Ruins. Judah Leib Teller, *tr. by* Benjamin *and* Barbara
  Harshav. AYP
Blunt good looks cut out day. Passing Strange. Alan Bernheimer. UL

Blurry Cow. Chase Twichell. MAYP

Blurt, Master Constable, *sels.* Thomas Middleton.
  Midnight. EIL; SeCePo
  True Love Ditty, A. EIL

Blush as of roses, A. Le Marais du Cygne. Whittier. PAH

Blush is on the flower, and the bloom is on the tree, The. My Own Cáilin Donn. George Sigerson. FaBoBe

Blustered by icy winds the boulders grown pointed. Staying at Horai Temple. Basho, *tr. fr. Japanese by* Burton Watson. *Fr.* Seventy-six Hokku. FCEI

Blyth Aberdeane, throw beriall of all tounis. To Aberdein. William Dunbar. FaBoPP

Blythsome Bridal, The. *At. to* Frances Sempill. GBP

"Bo" is a sound bordering on "bourgeois." "Bounded" to "Bower" for "E." Tina Darragh. LP

Bo-peep/ Little Bo-peep. *Unknown.* OxNR

Bo peeper. *Unknown.* OxNR

Bo-talee rode easily among his enemies. The Fear of Bo-talee. N. Scott Momaday. STE

Boa, The. J. J. Bell. RHPC

Boadicea; an Ode. William Cowper. BeLS; FaPoR

Boar of Badenoch and the Sow of Atholl, The. Naomi Mitchison. PoSH

Board Meets, The. John Gloag. FiBHP

Board of War has quelled the mutiny, The. To the Minister Liu. Yu Hsüan-chi, *tr. by* Geoffrey Waters. BoWoP

Boarder, The. Louis Simpson. InPK; SM

Boarding, The. Denis Johnson. MAYP

Boarding nettings are triced for fight, The. Jack Creamer. James Jeffrey Roche. PAH

Boar's Head Carol, The. *Unknown.* MeEL

Boast not proud English, of thy birth and blood. Roger Williams. GOA; SCAP

Boast of heraldry, the pomp of pow'r, The. Thomas Gray. *Fr.* Elegy Written in a Country Churchyard. OBD

Boast of Masopha. Z. D. Mangoaela, *tr. fr. Sotho.* PeSA

Boasting of Sir Peter Parker, The. Clinton Scollard. PAH

Boat, The. Caroline Gilman. OBCA

Boat, The. Robert Pack. CoAP; DiL; NePoEA-2; SM

Boat-Haven, Co. Mayo. Geoffrey Taylor. NeIP

Boat is chafing at our long delay, The. John Davidson. OBEV

Boat-load of emigrant Huns, A. Wreck of the Deutschland, The, *parody.* David Annett. BXAP

Boat moored, lunch in a lonely village, The. The Dappled Horse. Mei Yao-ch'en, *tr. by* Burton Watson. CoBCP

Boat on the Serchio, The, *sel.* Shelley.
  "Our boat is asleep on Serchio's stream." Mes

Boat Poem. Bernard Spencer. FaBoTw; OxBTC

Boat Race, The. Virgil, *tr. fr. Latin by* Rolfe Humphries. *Fr.* The Aeneid [*or* Eneados], V. SD

Boat Sails Away, The. Kate Greenaway. MoShBr

Boat Song, A. Saint Columbanus, *tr. fr. Latin.* NOIV

Boat Song. Henrietta Cordelia Ray. CBWP-3

Boatie Rows, The. *Unknown.* OxBSS, *ad. by* John Ewen

Boating on Feng Stream on the Double Fifth. Chang Hui-yen, *tr. fr. Chinese by* Michael Duke. WFTU

Boatman, The. Jay Macpherson. MoCV; OBCV

Boatman, have they crossed? "Not all." Doom Ferry. Sir Arthur Quiller-Couch. EBVV

Boatman he can dance and sing, The. Dance the Boatman. *Unknown.* AiP

Boatman's Song, The. Thomas Hardy. *Fr.* The Dynasts, *pt.* I, Act V, sc. vii. WaaP

Boatmen/ how late you've come! Song of the Transport Workers. Pien Kung, *tr. by* Jonathan Chaves. CoBLCP

Boats Are Afloat, The. Chu Hsi, *tr. fr. Chinese by* Kenneth Rexroth. NaP

Boats at Night. Edward Shanks. CH

Boats in a Fog. Robinson Jeffers. MOS; NAAL-2; NoP; OxBA

Boats like huge bright birds, The. Camp Evergreen. Jane Kenyon. PPR

Boats of orchid-wood float on the river. Gathering Lotus with Singing Girls. Mo Shih-lung, *tr. by* Jonathan Chaves. CoBLCP

Boats sail on the rivers. The Rainbow. Christina Rossetti. *Fr.* Sing-Song. OxBChV

Boats sail upstream and downstream alike, The. Poem to the Sun ("The boats sail upstream and downstream alike"). *Ancient Egyptian Oral Tradition, tr. by* Christopher Wertz. TTTS

Boats that carry sugar. Freight Boats. James S. Tippett. FaPON

Boatswain's Call, The. *Unknown.* OxBSS

Bob Anderson, My Beau. *Unknown.* PAH

Bob-ing split-able heads. Solitary Visions of a Kaufmanoid. James Cunningham. JB

Bob Robin. Mother Goose. OxNR

Bob Southey! You're a poet—poet-laureate. Byron. *Fr.* Don Juan. CTC; EnRP; OAEL-2; OBSV
  (Dedication to the Poet Laureate.) FiP
  (Southey and Wordsworth.) TrGrPo

Bob Thin; or, the Poorhouse Fugitive, *sel.* William James Linton. Life and Adventure of Bob Thin, The. PF

Bob was bathing in the Bay. Harry Graham. *Fr.* Some Ruthless Rhymes, V. CenHV

Bobber. Raymond Carver. GeTw

Bobbing in the waters of the womb. The Buddha in the Womb. Erica Jong. MAYP

Bobbing with the crowds. The Urban Experience: Part One. Lew Blockcolski. VoR

Bobby Blue. John Drinkwater. FaPON

Bobby Orr's marble. High Stick. Billy Collins. ASP

Bobby Shaftoe's gone to sea. Mother Goose. GBP; OxNR

Bobby's First Poem. Norman Gale. FiBHP; MoShBr

Bobo, a nasty boy, was changed into a fly. Czeslaw Milosz, *tr. fr. Polish by the author. Fr.* Bobo's Metamorphosis, VII. PwPP

Bobolinks, The. Christopher Pearse Cranch. AA; GN

Bobo's Metamorphosis, *sels.* Czeslaw Milosz, *tr. fr. Polish by the author.* PwPP
  "Between her and me there was a table." *Fr.* VIII.
  "Bobo, a nasty boy, was changed into a fly." *Fr.* VII.
  "I liked him as he did not look for an ideal object." *Fr.* V.

Bob's Lane. Edward Thomas. PoE

Boccherini's Tomb. István Vas, *tr. fr. Hungarian by* William Jay Smith. MHuP

Boddynge flourette bloshes. Thomas Chatterton. *Fr.* Aella.
  (Mynstrelle's Song: "Boddynge flourettes bloshes atte the lyghte, The.") EnRP
  (Song of the Three Minstrels.) TrGrPo

Bodega, Goodbye. Edwin Honig. NoAM

Bodies on fire. Black Hills Survival Gathering, 1980. Linda Hogan. STE

Bodiless, nameless God. Prayer of the Young Stoic. Stephen P. Dunn. TrPWD

Body, The. William Bronk. VGW

Body, The. Robert Herrick. CaPo

Body, The. Hanny Michaelis, *tr. fr. Dutch by* Manfred Wolf. DuIn

Body, The. Yona Wallach, *tr. fr. Hebrew by* Warren Bargad *and* Stanley F. Chyet. IP

Body, a resonant bowl, The. A Fugue. Ellen Bryant Voigt. KS

Body black in the rock spine of Quinag. Marry the Lass? Andrew Greig. PoSH

Body, blind with sleep, A. Statue. Gerrit Achterberg, *tr. by* Adrienne Rich. DuIn

Body Fished from the Seine. Gregory Corso. SM

Body full of bees. "I Don't Hear Any Melody Breathing I Hear." John Gill. NeAC

Body is like a November birch facing the full moon, The. Solitude Late at Night in the Woods. Robert Bly. VGW

Body Is like Roots Stretching, The. Charles Reznikoff. VWA

Body is the soul's poor house, or home, The. The Body. Robert Herrick. CaPo

Body Is the Victory and the Defeat of Dreams, The. Katerina Anghelaki-Rooke, *tr. fr. Greek by* Philip Ram. WPOW

Body leaning slightly back, the arms held firm and straight, The. Sonata. John Fuller. DiPo

Body lies under the ground. Gavin Bantock. OxBTC

Body, long oppressed, The. This Corruptible. Elinor Wylie. MoAB; MoAmPo

Body my house. Question. May Swenson. HeIP; LiTM; NePoEA; PrIm; SM; VGW

Body of a fourteen year old caught playing politics, The. No Man's Land. Gloria Escoffery. PVCV

Body of a Rook. David Wevill. MoCV

Body of John. R. A. K. Mason. ATZN; PeNZ

Body of my love is a familiar country, The. Mary Stanley. PeNZ

Body of Summer. Odysseus Elytis, *tr. fr. Greek by* Edmund Keeley *and* Philip Sherrard. VMG

Body perishes, the heart stays young, The. Old Age. *Zulu Oral Tradition, tr. by* H. Tracey. WTO

Body Politic, The. Donald Hall. NePoEA

Body, Remember. C. P. Cavafy, *tr. fr. Greek by* Edmund Keeley *and* Philip Sherrard. VMG

Body Work. Melinda Goodman. ER

Body's Beauty. Dante Gabriel Rossetti. *Fr.* The House of Life, LXXVIII. OAEL-2; Son; TrGrPo
  (Lilith.) PoEL-5

Body's desire that knows no end. In Adoration of Love. Takamura Kotaro, *tr. by* Hiroaki Sato. FCEI

Body's products become, The. Dido. John Ashbery. *Fr.* Two Sonnets. VGW

Boedromion. Alfred Gong, *tr. fr. German by* Beth Bjorklund. CoAuP

Boethius at Cavalzero. John Macoubrie. CRP

Bofors A. A. Gun, The. Gavin Ewart. WaP

Bog. Leen Volwerk. PoSH

Bog and Candle. Robert David Fitzgerald. CBAP

Bog-Face. Stevie Smith. RB

Bog Queen. Seamus Heaney. AnAn; NoAM

Bogeyman, The. Jack Prelutsky. RHPC

Boggy wood as full of springs as trees, A. The Idea of Entropy at Maenporth Beach. Peter Redgrove. FaBoMo

Bogland. Seamus Heaney. FaBCIP; HeIP; IPY; NoAM; NOIV; NoP

Bogs, purgatory, wolves and ease, by fame. Barten Holyday. FaBoEE

Bogus-Boo, The. James Reeves. AmMo; RHPC

Bohemia. Dorothy Parker. AnAmPo; NBLV

Bohemian Hymn, The. Emerson. WGRP

Bohemians, The. Ivor Gurney. MMA

Boil water, my lads. Naga Okimaro, *tr. fr. Japanese. Fr.* Manyo Shu. Ma

Boiling Falls. Liu E, *tr. fr. Chinese by* Jonathan Chaves. CoBLCP

Bois de Boulogne. Ahmad Shauqi, *tr. fr. Arabic by* M. Mustafa Badawi *and* John Heath-Stubbs. MAP

Bolakins was a very fine mason. Lamkin. *Unknown.* AmFP

Bold Adventures of Captain Ross. *Unknown.* OxBSS

Bold, amiable, ebon outlaw, grave and wise. To a Crow. Robert Burns Wilson. AA

Bold Captain of the Body-Guard. Zagonyi. George Henry Boker. PAH

Bold Dragoon, A. ("In the dragon's ride from out of the north"). *Unknown.* OBET

Bold Dragoon, The ("My father is a knight and a man of high renown"). *Unknown.* OBET

Bold General Wolfe. *Unknown.* OBET

Bold Jack Donahue. *Unknown.* AmFP

Bold Lanty was in love, you see, with lively Rosie Carey. Lanty Leary. *Unknown.* ChTr

Bold outlines are drawn to encompass. Charcoal. Wilson Harris. PVCV

Bold Pedlar and Robin Hood, The. *Unknown.* AmFP; ESPB

Bold *Princess Royal. Unknown.* OxBSS

Bold Reynard the Fox. *Unknown.* OBET

Bold Troubleshooters. Peter Veale. NOBL

Bolding Vedas! Shanks New Nisa! Place-Names of China. Alan Bennett. FaBoPa; NOBL

Boldness[e] in Love. Thomas Carew. CaPo; ErPo; MePo; SeCV-1

Boll Weevil Song. *Unknown.* AS

Boll-weevil's coming, and the winter's cold. November Cotton Flower. Jean Toomer. CDC; MoP; NoAM; UnPo

Bolsheviks. Aba Shtoltsenberg, *tr. fr. Yiddish by* Stanley Kunitz. PeBMYV

Bolsum Brown. *Unknown.* AS

Bolt and bar the shutter. Mad as the Mist and Snow. W. B. Yeats. ChTr

Bolted Room. A. Leyeles, *tr. fr. Yiddish.* AYP, *tr. by* Benjamin *and* Barbara Harshav; PeBMYV, *tr. by* Leonard Wolf.

Bomb Disposal, The. Ciaran Carson. CIP

Bomb-disposal/ combed the area. Peace-Time. Mervyn Morris. PVCV

Bomb Incident. Barbara Catherine Edwards. CN

Bomb Is Made, The. Keith Sinclair. PeNZ

Bomb Story (Manchester, 1942). Margery Lea. CN

Bombardment. Richard Aldington. MMA

Bombardment. D. H. Lawrence. MMA

Bombardment of Bristol, The. *Unknown.* PAH

Bombed Church. Elizabeth Berridge. CN

Bomber, The. Beatrice R. Gibbs. CN

Bomber, The ("Bomber climb out on the roof"). Robert Lowell. WaaP

Bombers, The. Sarah Churchill. CN

Bombers. C. Day Lewis. CMoP; MoAB

Bon Mot, A. *Unknown.* ErPo

"Bon soir, ma chérie." Comrades in Arms: Conversation Piece. *Unknown.* ErPo

Bon, the sixteenth night. Lyrics of the Bon Dance. *Unknown, tr. by* Geoffrey Bownas *and* Anthony Thwaite. PeBJV

"Bona de Mortuis." Thomas Lovell Beddoes. TW

Bondage. "Owen Innsley." AA

Bondage. Hubert Witheford. ATNZ

Bondmen of Mizraim/ Were our fathers. Flowering Without End. Stefan Zweig, *tr. fr. German by* Eden *and* Cedar Paul. *Fr.* Jeremiah. TrJP

Bone-aged is my white horse. Brenda Chamberlain. NeIP (Talysarn.) OBWVE

Bone and Skin, two millers thin. On Two Monopolists. John Byrom. FaBoCo; FaBoEE

Bone China. R. P. Lister. NYBP

Bone-Flower Elegy. Robert Hayden. NoAM

Bone Step-Women, The. Brenda Marie Osbey. ER

Bone that has no marrow, The. Emily Dickinson. TAP

Bone Thoughts on a Dry Day: Chicago. George Starbuck. GoYe; NYBP; TwCP

Bone Yard. Jim Barnes. CDW

"Boneless tongue, so small and weak, The." The Tongue. Phillips Burrows Strong. WBLP

Bones. Walter de la Mare. FiBHP

Bones, The. W. S. Merwin. LiTM; NePoEA-2

Bones. Carl Sandburg. MOS

Bones in the child. Warm. Robert Grenier. IAT

Bones in the grass beneath the dream body. Dried Bones under the Pine. Etsudo, *tr. by* Lucien Stryk *and* Takashi Ikemoto. ZPCJ

Bones of Chuang Tzu, The. Chang Heng, *tr. fr. Chinese by* Arthur Waley. AWP

"Dead man answered me, The," *sel.* OBD

Bones of Incontention, The. Robert David Cohen. NYBP

Bones of My Father, The. Etheridge Knight. DiL

Bones of our fathers, The. Talking to the Townsfolk in Ideal, Georgia. Isaac J. Black. CNA

Bones tuned, the body sings. He Hola. Keri Hulme. PeNZ

Boneset, why are you blooming. Sanetomo, *tr. fr. Japanese by* Burton Watson. *Fr.* Twenty-four Tanka. FCEI

Bonfire, The. Robert Frost. InvP

Bonfire of my Indian summer burns, The. Indian Summer. Mani Leib, *tr. by* John Hollander. PeBMYV

Bongaloo, The. Spike Milligan. AmMo

Bonhoeffer in his skylit cell. Christmas Trees. Geoffrey Hill. NOCV

The *Bonhomme Richard* and *Serapis.* Philip Freneau. PAH

Bonie Doon. Burns. *See* Ye banks and braes o' Bonnie Doon.

Bonita. Tristan Tzara, *tr. fr. French by* Michael Benedikt. POS

Bonnard; a Novel. Richard Howard. CoAP; NYBP

Bonne Entente. F. R. Scott. FiBHP; OBCV

Bonnets So Blue. *Unknown.* OBET

Bonnie Annie (A *and* B *vers.*). *Unknown.* ESPB

Bonnie Annie Livieston. *Unknown.* OxBB

Bonnie Blue Flag, The. Annie Chambers Ketchum. PAH

Bonnie Blue Flag. Harry McCarthy. AnAmPo

Bonnie Bower, The. *Unknown. See* My love he built me a bonnie bower.

Bonnie Broukit Bairn, The. "Hugh MacDiarmid." FaBoCh; HAP; InPS

Bonnie Earl of Moray [*or* Murray], The. *Unknown. See* Ye Highland and ye lawlands.

Bonnie [*or* Bonny] George [*or* James] Campbell. *Unknown.* AmFP; CH; ELP; EnRP; ESPB; FaBoBa; GBP; GoTS; NoP; OxBB, *with music;* OxBoli

("O it's up in the Highlands.") ESPB

Bonnie House o' Airlie, The. *Unknown.* ESPB; OBEV; OxBB, *with music;* OxBS

Bonnie James Campbell. *Unknown.* ESPB

Bonnie Kilmeny. James Hogg. *Fr.* The Queen's Wake. OBEV

(Bonny Kilmeny Gaed Up the Glen.) GoTS

Bonnie Laddie's Lang a-Grouwin', The. *Unknown.* OxBS

Bonnie lassie, will ye go. The Birks of Aberfeldy. Burns. CTC

Bonnie Lesley. Burns. CTC; GTBS; GTBS-P; NOBE; OBEV

Bonniest Bairn in a' the Warl', The. Robert Ford. GN

Bonniest lass that ye meet neist, The. For A' That an' A' That. *At. to* Burns. CoMu

Bonny at Morn. *Unknown.* GBP

Bonny Baby Livingston. *Unknown.* ESPB

Bonny Barbara Allan ("In Scarlet Town where I was born"). *Unknown.* TrGrPo

Bonny Barbara Allan ("It was [in and] about the merry month of May"). *Unknown.* AWP; BoLoP; CH; ESPB, A *and* B *vers.*; HeIP; LiTB; NoP; OxBB, *with music.*

Bonny Barbara Allan ("Oh, in the merry month of May"). *Unknown.* AmFP

Bonny Bee Hom. *Unknown.* ESPB

Bonny Birdy, The. *Unknown.* ESPB

Bonny Brown Girl, The. *Unknown. See* I am as brown as brown can be.

Bonny Bunch of Roses O, The. *Unknown.* FaBoBa; OxBoLi

Bonny Cravet, The. Mother Goose. OxNR

Bonny [*or* Bonnie] Dundee. Sir Walter Scott. *Fr.* The Doom of Devorgoil, II, ii. EnRP; FaBoCh; OxBoLi; OxBS; Par

Bonny Earl o' Moray, The. *Unknown. See* Ye Highlands and ye Lawlands.

Bonny Earl of Livingston, The. *Unknown. See* Oh we were sisters seven, Maisry.

Bonny Earl of Murray, The. *Unknown.* ESPB, A *vers.*; FaBoBa; OBEV; OxBB, *with music;* OxBB; PrIM
Bonny fine maid of a noble degree, A. Robin Hood and Maid Marian. *Unknown.* ESPB
Bonny Grey, The. *Unknown.* GBP
"Bonny heir, and the well-faird heir, The." The Heir of Linne. *Unknown.* ESPB, B *vers.*
Bonny Heyn, The. *Unknown. See* Bonny Hind, The.
Bonny Hind, The. *Unknown.* ESPB
  (Bonny Heyn, The.) OxBB
Bonny John Seton. *Unknown.* ESPB
Bonny Keel Laddie, The. *Unknown.* GBP
Bonny Kilmeny Gaed Up the Glen. James Hogg. *See* Bonnie. . .
Bonny Lass of Anglesey, The. *Unknown.* ESPB, A *and* B *vers.*
Bonny Lassie O! John Clare. CH
Bonny Lizie Baillie. *Unknown.* ESPB
Bonny Moorhen, The. *Unknown.* GBP
Bonsai [*or* Bonzai] tree, The. A Work of Artifice. Marge Piercy. IHMS; Psk
Bonum Est Mihi Quod Humiliasti Me. Earl of Surrey. SiPS
Bonus. A. R. Ammons. HCAP
Bony. Simon J. Ortiz. CDW
Bood is beabig brighdly, love, The. To Bary Jade. Charles Follen Adams. OBAL
Boogie Chant and Dance. *Unknown, tr. by* Ewald Osers. RR
"Boogie with O. O. Gabugah." Al Young. NPGG
Boogie-woogie Ballads. St. Clair McKelway. PoNe
Book, A ("There is no frigate like a book"). Emily Dickinson. *See* There is no frigate like a book.
Book, The. William Drummond of Hawthornden. CH
Book, The. Waddie Mitchell. CowP
Book, The. Henry Vaughan. JCP; SeCV-1
Book Ends. Tony Harrison. *Fr.* The School of Eloquence, I. DiP; NAEL-2; NoAM
Book I Held Grew Cold, The. Ernst Toller, *tr. fr. German by* Ashley Dukes. TrJP
Book lay unread in my lap, The. Going Home. Maurice Kenny. STE
Book-Lender's Lament. *Unknown.* FaBoUs
Book Moth: "A moth ate a word. To me it seemed." *Unknown, formerly at. to* Cynewulf, *tr. fr. Anglo-Saxon by* Charles W. Kennedy. *Fr.* Riddles (Exeter Book). AnOE
Book of Ephraim, The, *sels.* James Merrill. NAAL-2
  "Backdrop: The dining room at Stonington." NoAM
  "Life like the periodical not yet." HCAP
  Lost in Translation. HCAP
  "Zero hour. Waiting yet again." HCAP
Book of Fortune's Changes, The, *sel.* Christine de Pisan, *tr. fr. French by* Sarah Spence.
  Here Are Told the Misfortunes of Women. DMF
Book of Gawain, The. Jack Spicer. *Fr.* The Holy Grail. PoM
Book of God's Madness, The, *sel.* Ralph Chubb.
  "Liveliest effigy of the human race." PeHV
Book of Hours, The, *sel.* Rainer Maria Rilke, *tr. fr. German.*
  "O Lord, grant each his own, his own death indeed." *Tr. by* J. B. Leishman. OBD
Book of hours, The. The Hours. Paul Ramsey. CRP
Book of How, The. Merrill Moore. MoAmPo
Book of Hunting, *sels.* Julians Barnes. WPE
  "Time of grease beginneth at Midsummer day."
  "When ye hunt at the roe, then shall ye see there."
  "Wheresoever ye fare by frith or by fell."
Book of Job and a Draft of a Poem to Praise the Paths of the Living, The. George Oppen. NNaP
Book of Juniper, The. Tom Paulin. FaBCIP
Book of Kells, The. Padraic Colum. BIrV
Book of Kells, The. Howard Nemerov. EaLo
Book of Lies, The. James Tate. SM
Book of Los, The, *sel.* Blake.
  Immortal, The. *Fr. ch.* 2. LiTB
Book of Music, A. Jack Spicer. PoM
Book of Mysteries, The. Anthony Barnett. VWA
Book of Persephone, The. Robert Kelly. PoM
  Sels.
  Dance, The. *Fr.* 17.
  "Earth is a woman who imagines us. She sings." *Fr.* 10.
  Fourth Ode to Persephone. *Fr.* 16.
  Glade, The. *Fr.* 18.
  "Persephone is the woman buried." *Fr.* 11.
  Second Ode to Persephone. *Fr.* 9.
  Third Ode to Persephone. *Fr.* 14.
  Versions. *Fr.* 12.

Book of Roses, The, *sel.* Said Aql, *tr. fr. Arabic.*
  "My ecstasy is that I have met you." *Tr. by* Matthew Sorenson *and* Naomi Shihab Nye. MAP
Book of Tarshish, The, *sel.* Moses ibn Ezra, *tr. fr. Hebrew by* Solomon Solis-Cohen.
  Joy of Life. TrJP
Book of the Dead. *Unknown, tr. fr. Egyptian by* Robert Hillyer.
  Sels.
  Adoration of the Disk by King Akhnaten and Princess Nefer Neferiu Aten. AWP
    "Cattle roam again across the field, The." FaPON
  Dead Man Ariseth and Singeth a Hymn to the Sun, The. AWP
  He Approacheth the Hall of Judgment. AWP
  He Asketh Absolution of God. AWP
  He Biddeth Osiris to Arise from the Dead. AWP
  He Cometh Forth into the Day. AWP
  He Commandeth a Fair Wind. AWP
  He Defendeth His Heart against the Destroyer. AWP
  He Embarketh in the Boat of Ra. AWP
  He Entereth the House of the Goddess Hathor. AWP
  He Establisheth His Triumph. AWP
  He Holdeth Fast to the Memory of His Identity. AWP
  He Is Declared True of Word. AWP
  He Is like the Lotus. AWP; EaLo
    (Death as a Lotus Flower.) TTY, *tr. by* Ulli Beier.
  He Is like the Serpent Saka. AWP
  He Kindleth a Fire. AWP
  He Knoweth the Souls of the East. AWP
  He Knoweth the Souls of the West. AWP
  He Maketh Himself One with Osiris. AWP
  He Maketh Himself One with the God Ra. *Tr. by* Robert Hillyer.
  He Maketh Himself One with the Only God, Whose Limbs Are the Many Gods. AWP
  He Overcometh the Serpent of Evil in the Name of Ra. AWP
  He Prayeth for Ink and Palette That He May Write. AWP
  He Singeth a Hymn to Osiris, the Lord of Eternity. AWP
  He Singeth in the Underworld. AWP
  He Walketh by Day. AWP
  Other World, The. AWP; OBD
Book of the defeated man. Qasim Haddad, *tr. fr. Arabic by* Sharif Elmusa *and* Charles Doria. *Fr.* Standing While We Die. MAP
Book of the Duchesse, The, *sel.* Chaucer.
  Dream, The. FiP; PBBP
Book of the Two Married Women and the Widow, The, *sel.* William Dunbar.
  Widow Speaks, The. PoEL-1
Book of the Yellow Castle. Michael Palmer. LP
Book of Thel, The. Blake. ChER; EnRP; NAEL-2; NoP; OAEL-2; OBNC; PoE; PoEL-4; TEP
  Sels.
  "O little cloud," the virgin said, "I charge thee tell to me."" OBD
  Secrets of the Earth, The. NOBE
  Thel's Motto, 4 *ll.* ChTr
Book of True Love, The, *sel.* Juan Ruiz, Archpriest of Hita, *tr. fr. Spanish by* Hubert Creekmore.
  "When you're together with her, and you have a good excuse." ErPo
Book of verses underneath the bough, A. Omar Khayyám, *tr. fr. Persian by* Edward Fitzgerald. *Fr.* The Rubáiyát of Omar Khayyám of Naishápúr. HoPM; NOBE; OBEV
  (Quatrains.) SeCePo
Book of Wisdom, The. Stephen Crane. *Fr.* The Black Riders, XXXVI. HoPM; MoAmPo
Book of Yolek, The. Anthony Hecht. BLA
Book Our Mothers Read, The. Whittier. *Fr.* Miriam. BLRP
Book Review. Russell Davies. FaBoEE
Book Rises Out of the Fire, The. Edmond Jabès, *tr. fr. French by* Rosemarie Waldrop. VWA
Book was writ of late called *Tetrachordon,* A. On the Detraction Which Followed upon My Writing Certain Treatises. Milton. PoE; Son
Book-Worms, The. Burns. ChTr; FaBoEE; FiBHP
Book Years. Bob Perelman. LP
Book you made, The. Love. Patrick Lane. NeAC
Booker T. and W. E. B. Dudley Randall. MoP; NoAM
Booker Washington Trilogy, The, *sels.* Vachel Lindsay.
  John Brown. *Fr.* II. MoAmPo
  Simon Legree—a Negro Sermon. *Fr.* I. LiTA; TAP
    (Negro Sermon, A—Simon Legree.) MoAmPo
Booking clerk believes in the doctrine, The. The Station Master. Arun Kolatkar. UAS
Bookkeepers Talk Baseball, The. Jim Daniels. SoTCo
Bookmark. St. Theresa of Avila. *See* Lines Written in Her Breviary.
Bookra. Charles Dudley Warner. AA

Books. Wordsworth. *Fr.* The Prelude [or, Growth of a Poet's Mind], V. EnRP; OAEL-2

"He who in his youth." TOF

There Was a Boy ("There was a boy, ye knew him well"). ChER; FaBoCh; FaBoRV; FiP; OBNC; PoE; PoEL-4
(Winander Lake.) FiP

Books, books, books! Elizabeth Barrett Browning. *Fr.* Aurora Leigh. WPOW

Books Fall Open. David McCord. OBCA

Books from strange libraries. Abroad. Ilse Aichinger, *tr. by* Beth Bjorklund. CoAuP

Books on the printed wall. Night before a Journey. Charles Causley. PoPo

Bookshop Idyll, A. Kingsley Amis. NePoEA; OxBTC

Bookworm, The. Sacha Rabinovitch. NPo

Boom! Howard Nemerov. LiTM; NBLV; NIP

Boom/ The shrill whistle of the wolf. Bird of Power. Jim Tollerud. VoR

Boom above my knees lifts, and the boat, The. Sailing to an Island. Richard Murphy. IPY

Boomer Johnson. Henry Herbert Knibbs. CowP

Boomerang. David Cram. SoTCo

Boomerang. John Perreault. EAS

Boomerang, The. Adriano Spatola, *tr. fr. Italian by* Lawrence R. Smith. NItP

Boon, A. William Meredith. NePoEA

Boon Nature to the woman bows. The Tribute. Coventry Patmore. *Fr.* The Angel in the House, I, iv. EBEV; OBNC

Boone. Susan Mitchell. NAmP

Boosting the Booster ("Boost your city, boost your friend"). *Unknown.* WBLP

Boot and Saddle("Boot, saddle, to horse, and away!"). Robert Browning. *Fr.* Cavalier Tunes, III. SoSe

Booth Killed Lincoln. *Unknown.* AmFP; OFD; OPP

Booth led boldly with his big bass drum. General William Booth Enters into Heaven. Vachel Lindsay. AmPP; CMoP; LiTA; LiTM; MoAB; MoAmPo; NOBA; OxBA; PoA; PoE; TAP; TrGrPo; WGRP

Booths knew nothing either. They built themselves in. The Old Sipsey Valley Road. Thomas Rabbitt. MT

Bootie Black and the Seven Giants. Mike Cook. JB

Boots. Kipling. BLPA; FaPoR; FPL; MoBrPo

Boots,/ Shoes. *Unknown.* OxNR

Boots and Saddles. Nicolas Saboly, *tr. fr. Provençal.* OHIP

Boots and Shoes. Lilian McCrea. BoTP

Boots are being polished. Where Will You Be? Patricia Parker. GLP

Booty. Eileen Duggan. ATNZ

Booze Turns Men into Women. Bernadette Mayer. UL

Bop Lyrics. Allen Ginsberg. OBAL

Boquillas. Greg Pape. NAmP

Bora Ring. Judith Wright. NoAM

Borborygms! Borborygms! Valery Larbaud, *tr. by* William Jay Smith. CT

Bordello, *sels.* Lewis Turco.
Rick De Travaille. SM
Simon Judson. SM

Border, The. Edwin Muir. Mes

Border Ballad, A. Thomas Love Peacock. BXAP

Border Ballad. Sir Walter Scott. *Fr.* The Monastery, *ch.* 25. GN

Border Burn, A. J. B. Selkirk. *Fr.* Epistle to Tammus. PoSH

Border Forecast, A. William Landles. PoSH

Border March. Sir Walter Scott. *See* March, march, Ettrick and Teviotdale.

Border Mountain Moon. Lu Yu, *tr. fr. Chinese by* Burton Watson. CoBCP

Border River. Alfred Goldsworthy Bailey. CaP

Bordering Manuscript. James Applewhite. PoA

Bored. Horatio Brown. PeHV

Bored by Ascham and Zeno. The Glad Eye. Paul Muldoon. NoAM

Bored with his wife that fatal day. The Brockton Murder; a Page out of William James. Knute Skinner. TW

Boredom of seething crudities rises rancorously to your chest, The. Tonic. Tristan Tzara, *tr. by* Michael Benedikt. POS

Boredom, the sadness, and no one to take by the hand, The. Mikhail Yurevich Lermontov, *tr. by* Alan Myers. AAA

Bores hed in hondes I bring, The. The Boar's Head Carol. *Unknown.* MeEL

Borgia, thou once wert [*or* were] almost too august. On Seeing a Hair of Lucretia Borgia. Walter Savage Landor. HAP; WeW
(On Lucretia Borgia's Hair.) EnRP

Boring Days. Aba Shtoltsenberg, *tr. fr. Yiddish by* Dennis Silk. PeBMYV

Boring executors approach their locks, The. Poem against Catholics. James Fenton *and* John Fuller. OBSV

Boring Orbit, The. Samih al-Qasim, *tr. fr. Arabic by* Abdullah al-Udhari. MPAW

Born/ given a name. Vita with Postcript. Ilse Tielsch, *tr. by* Beth Bjorklund. CoAuP

Born a girl child. She. Sista Roots. WS

Born Again. Forugh Farrokhzad, *tr. fr. Persian by* Jascha Kessler *and* Amin Banani. PBWP

Born by a whim. Signature. Dorothy Livesay. OBCV

Born here, you never lived. Tsurayuki, *tr. fr. Japanese by* Burton Watson. *Fr.* Kokin Shu. FCEI

Born I was to be old. Anacreontic. Robert Herrick. CaPo; OxBoLi

Born[e] I was to meet with age. On Himself [e]. Robert Herrick. ChTr; FaBoEE; SeCV-1

Born in a fence-corner. Tumbling Mustard. Malcolm Cowley. AmFN

Born in a hovel, trained in hardship's school. Abraham Lincoln. A. S. Ames. OHIP

Born in a notch of the high mountains where. Chant Royal. Robert Morgan. SM

Born in a trance, we wake, observe, inquire. Another and the Same. Samuel Rogers. *Fr.* Human Life. OBNC

Born in my mouth, the naked beast leaned out. A Warning to My Love. David Wagoner. NePoEA-2

Born in the garret, in the kitchen bred. A Sketch from Private Life. Byron. OBNC

Born in the purple the red grouse cry. The Kingship of the Hills. Will H. Ogilvie. PoSH

Born in the quarter-night, brash. Delta Traveller. Charles Wright. AmPA; LCAP

Born in wealth and wealthily nursed. Thomas Hood. *Fr.* Miss Kilmansegg and Her Precious Leg. EBVV

Born into the world. Tamesuke, *tr. by* Steven D. Carter. WFTW

Born, nurtured, wedded, prized, within the pale. La Fayette. Dolly Madison. AiP; PAH

Born of the sorrowful of heart. For Paul Laurence Dunbar. Countee Cullen. *Fr.* Four Epitaphs. CDC

Born over there, in mist, not even God. Grandfather. Willis Barnstone. VWA

Born to cling to this human road. Cheng Chen, *tr. fr. Chinese by* Irving Lo. *Fr.* Responding to Yüan-ming's "Drinking Wine" Poems, XI. WFTU

Born to these gentle stones and grass. Urn Burial. Ted Hughes. EBEV

Born Tying Knots. Samuel Makidemewabe, *tr. fr. Cree Indian by* Howard Norman. STP

Born under the sign of Cancer. Under the Sign of Cancer. Carolyne Wright. NAmP

Born was the island. *Unknown.* WTO

Born with all arms, he sought a separate peace. The Deserter. John Manifold. CBAP; WaP

Born with the Vices. Thomas D'Urfey. OBS

Born without a Chance. Edmund Vance Cooke. BLPA

Born Yesterday. Philip Larkin. NAs

Borne on a whispered sigh. Fallen Leaves. Kathryn Munro Tupper. CaP

Borning Room, The. Michael S. S. Harper. CAPP

Borough, The, *sels.* George Crabbe.
Caroline, The. *Fr.* Letter XI. SeCePo
"Now is it pleasant in the summer-eve." *Fr.* Letter IX. FM
Peter Grimes. *Fr.* Letter XXII. EnRP; OBNV; PoEL-4; TEP
(Poor of the Borough, The; Peter Grimes.) NoP
"He built a mud-wall'd hovel, where he kept." SaC
Peter Grimes at Aldeburgh. FaBoPP
"Priest attending, found he spoke at times, The." PoE
"Thus by himself compelled to live each day." NOBE; OBNC; SeCePo
Sailing upon the River. *Fr.* Letter IX. OBNC
Schools. *Fr.* Letter XXIV. CTC
Slum Dwelling, A. *Fr.* Letter XVIII. OBNC
Suffolk Shore, The. *Fr.* Letter XXIII. FaBoPP
Vicar, The. *Fr.* Letter III. OBSV
"But let applause be dealt in all we may." OBNC
Winter Views Serene. *Fr.* Letter IX. OBNC

Borrow 50 from George. How to Get to Canada. Ted Berrigan. UL

"Borrowed." *Unknown. See* They borrowed a bed to lay his head.

Borrowed is all glory. Mohammad Taqi Mir, *tr. by* Ahmed Ali. GoT

Borrowed light went through the dark, The. Jack Rabbit. Adrien Stoutenburg.

Borrowed wings on his ankles. Perseus. Louis MacNeice. LiTM

Borrower of Salt, The.   Oscar Williams.   *Fr.* Variations on a Theme, III. LiTA

Borrowing Days, The.   *Unknown.*   GBP

Bosho's Old Hut.   Kikaku, *tr. fr. Japanese by* Hiroaki Sato.   *Fr.* Thirty-three Hokku.   FCEI

Bos'n Hill.   John Albee.   AA

Bosnia. November. And the mountain roads.   Sarajevo.   Lawrence Durrell.   GTBS-P; OBTV

Bosom/ that was meant to bloom, A.   I'll Tell You What a Flapper Is. Anne Hobson Freeman.   GrPl

Bosom of, A/ green buds.   Mare Nostrum.   Joel Oppenheimer. NeAP

Boss, The.   James Russell Lowell.   OBAL; SaC

Boss he had a yaller gal.   Git Along Down to Town.   *Unknown.* AmFP

Boss knows what shape I'm in, The. He tells me.   Drunk Last Night with Friends, I Go to Work Anyway.   Philip Dow.   InPK; NPGG

Boss's Wife, The.   *Unknown.*   CBAP

Boston.   John Collins Bossidy.   FaBoCo; FaBoEE; NBLV, *at. to* Samuel C. Bushnell; OBAL, *at. to* Samuel C. Bushnell; OxBoLi, *at. to* Samuel C. Bushnell.   *See also* I come from the city of Boston.

Boston.   John Collins Bossidy.   *See* And this is good old Boston.

Boston.   John Boyle O'Reilly.   PAH

Boston.   E. A. Robinson.   AnAmPo

Boston Ballad, A.   Walt Whitman.   OBAL

Boston Burglar, The.   *Unknown.*   AmFP

Boston Charlie.   Walt Kelly.   FiBHP; GoJo

Boston College team has gold helmets, under which the, The.   The Hockey Poem.   Robert Bly.   TSL

Boston Evening Transcript, The.   T. S. Eliot.   InPK

Boston has a festival.   In the Public Garden.   Marianne Moore. NOBA

Boston Hymn.   Emerson.   OPP; PAH; WGRP

Boston in Distress.   *Unknown.*   NOEC

Boston, Lincolnshire.   *Unknown.*   FaBoPP; GBP

Boston. Lord God, the ocean never to windward.   Aspects of Spring in Greater Boston.   George Starbuck.   *Fr.* Poems from a First Year in Boston, II.   NePoEA-2; NYBP

Boston Toast, A.   *At. to* John Collins Bossidy.   BLPA; CenHV

Boswell by my bed.   Reading in War Time.   Edwin Muir.   WaP

Bosworth Field, *sel.*   Sir John Beaumont.
   Richard III's Speech.   JCP

Bot now the haisty, egir, and wild Dido.   Virgil, *tr. into Middle English by* Gavin Douglas.   *Fr.* The Aeneid [*or* Eneados], IV.   OBVE

Bot of ane bowrd in to bed I sall yow breif yit.   William Dunbar.   *Fr.* The Tretis of the Tua Mariit Wemen and the Wedo.   EBEV

Botanic Garden, The, *sels.*   Erasmus Darwin.
   Economy of Vegetation, The.   *Fr. pt.* I.
      Steam Power.   NOEC
   Loves of the Plants, The.   *Fr. pt.* II.
      Vegetable Loves.   SeCePo
      Nightmare.   NOEC

Botany Bay.   John Freeth.   NOEC

Botany Bay.   *Unknown.*   PoAu-1

Both blossoms and trees.   Moon on a Spring Dawn.   Sanetaka, *tr. by* Steven D. Carter.   WFTW

Both Cherokee and Samek saw you, and tell.   Bear Dance.   Ron Rogers. STE

Both Earth and Heaven.   Huda Namani, *tr. fr. Arabic by* Lena Jayyusi *and* John Heath-Stubbs.   MAP

Both Erato the Muse or Lyric Poetry and Mime.   Mock Translation from the Greek.   Alan Dugan.   PPR

Both fields and mountains.   Joso, *tr. fr. Japanese by* Hiroaki Sato.   *Fr.* Fifteen Hokku.   FCEI

Both gentlemen, or yoemen bould.   A True Tale of Robin Hood. *Unknown.*   ESPB

Both have whiskers—I mean, the cat's wife, too.   Raizan, *tr. fr. Japanese by* Hiroaki Sato.   *Fr.* Thirteen Hokku.   FCEI

Both my child.   Teitoku, *tr. by* Nobuyuki Yuasa.   OFD

Both of Us Together and Each Apart.   Yehuda Amichai, *tr. fr. Hebrew by* Bernhard Frank.   MHeP

Both Plutarch and Pausanius tell a story.   Kleomedes.   David Wright. MoP

Both skyed.   Japanese Print.   Austin Clarke.   IPY; NOIV

Both Strangers.   Jamil Sidqi al-Zahawi, *tr. fr. Arabic by* Issa Boullata *and* Christopher Middleton.   MAP

Both were so shy.   Robert Canzoneri.   HoPM

Both you two have.   To the Yew and Cypress to Grace His Funeral. Robert Herrick.   QFR

Bothered by Something.   Ryokan, *tr. fr. Chinese by* Burton Watson. JLIC-2

Bothie of Tober-na-Vuolich, The, *sels.*   Arthur Hugh Clough.
   "Ah, you have much to learn, we can't know all things at twenty."   *Fr. Bk.* II.   FaBoPV
   "As at return of tide the total weight of ocean."   *Fr. Bk.* IX.   FaBoPV
   "Nodding and beckoning across, observed of Attaché and Guardsman."   *Fr. Bk.* I.   FaBoPV
   "There is a stream, I name not its name."   *Fr. Bk.* III.   BoNaP (Highland Glen near Loch Ericht, A.)   FaBoPP
   "This is the letter of Hobbes the kilted and corpulent hero."   *Fr. Bk.* IX. FaBoPV

Bothwell Bridge.   *Unknown.*   *See* O Billie, billie, bonny billie.

Botticellian Trees, The.   William Carlos Williams.   AmPP; LiTA

Bottle, The.   Al Levine.   GrPl

Bottle, coarse tumbler, loaf of bread.   Still Life.   Walter de la Mare. EyDe

Bottle Creek Blues.   Sam Hunt.   PeNZ

Bottle-neck/ oh I'd.   Tribute to Nervous.   Kit Robinson.   IAT

"Bottle Should Be Plainly Labeled 'Poison.' "   Sara Henderson Hay. GoYe

Bottled message is twisted in the bottle, The.   The Guard, 8.   Lyn Hejinian.   LP

Bottled [New York].   Helene Johnson.   BlSi; CDC; PoBA

Bottles are empty, the breakfast was good, The.   The Morning After. Heine, *tr. by* Louis Untermeyer.   ErPo

Bottom clawed out of a canvas boat, The.   Two Sons Drowning.   Roger Weingarten.   NAmP

Bottom of a green arras extends a vocabulary, The.   Various Meanings. Jackson MacLow.   LP

Bottom of loneliness, The.   Joso, *tr. fr. Japanese by* Hiroaki Sato.   *Fr.* Fifteen Hokku.   FCEI

Bottomless pits. There's one in Castleton.   National Trust.   Tony Harrison.   NAEL-2

Bottom's Dream.   Philip Dow.   NPGG

Bottom's Song.   Shakespeare.   *Fr.* A Midsummer Night's Dream, III, i. CTC; PBBP

Boudoir Feeling.   Hsü Ts'an, *tr. fr. Chinese by* Irving Lo.   WFTU

Boudoir Lament.   Yü Hsüan-chi, *tr. by* Geoffrey Waters.   BoWoP

Bough bent, The.   Quarry.   Itamar Ya'oz-kest, *tr. by* Bernhard Frank. MHeP

Boughs do shake and the bells do ring, The.   Harvest Song.   *Unknown.* BoTP; OxNR

Boughs, the boughs are bare enough, The.   Winter with the Gulf Stream. Gerard Manley Hopkins.   CMoP; NoAM

Bought/ from the flower-peddler's tray.   Tune: Magnolia Blossom.   Li Ch'ing-chao, *tr. by* C. H. Kwôck *and* Vincent McHugh.   PBWP

Bought at the drug store, very cheap; and later pawned.   Green Light. Kenneth Fearing.   PoE; VGW

Bought Embrace, A.   G. S. Fraser.   WaP

Bought Locks.   Martial, *tr. fr. Latin by* Sir John Harington.   AWP

Boulder Dam.   May Sarton.   SaC

Boulevard, The.   Léon-Paul Fargue, *tr. fr. French by* Lydia Davis. RHTwFP

Bounce ball! Bounce ball!   Song for a Ball-Game.   Wilfrid Thorley. BoTP

Bounce, buckram, velvet's dear.   *Unknown.*   OxNR

Bounce to Fop; an Heroick Epistle from a Dog at Twickenham to a Dog at Court.   Pope.   FM

Bounced from class to class, I hug the walls.   As the Botanist.   Mariella Bettarini, *tr. by* Muriel Kittel.   DMI

Bouncing! bouncing! on the beds.   In the Motel.   X. J. Kennedy.   RHPC

Bound.   Theodore Roethke.   PoA

Bound and free.   Eudaimon.   Kathleen Jessie Raine.   PBWP

Bound hand and foot he lies.   Sacrifice.   H. Leivick, *tr. by* Robert Friend.   PeBMYV

Bound in a moonlight circle.   The 49 Stomp.   Lew Blockcolski.   VoR

Bound No'th Blues.   Langston Hughes.   AmNP

Bound to a boy's swift feet, hard blades of steel.   River Skater.   Winifred Welles.   SD

Bound to my heart as Ixion to the wheel.   Dirge for the New Sunrise. Dame Edith Sitwell.   *Fr.* Three Poems of the Atomic Bomb.   CMoP; EaLo; MoAB; MoBrPo; SeCePo

Boundaries.   Roberta Spear.   MAYP

Boundaries of the plastic arts, The.   Bianca's First Steps in the Arts.   K. Schippers, *tr. by* Peter Nijmeijer.   DuIn

Boundaries too small. No space in which to step.   In a Small Country. Uuno Kailas, *tr. by* Aili Jarvenpa.   SOP

Boundary.   A. L. Hendricks.   PBCV

"Bounded" to "Bower" for "E."   Tina Darragh.   LP

Boundless Moment, A.   Robert Frost.   NAAL-2

Bounty.   Josephine Miles.   NoAM

Bounty of Jehovah Praise, The.   George Sandys.   AH

Bounty of Our Age, The. Henry Farley. FaBoCh; FaBoEE; SeCePo
Bouquet in Dog Time. Hayden Carruth. GrPl
Bouquet of Belle Scavoir. Wallace Stevens. MoAB; MoAmPo
Bourbons. Walter Savage Landor. OBSV
Bourgeois Are Beasts, The. Pablo Guevara, tr. fr. Spanish by Ena Hollis and David Tipton. Per
Bourne, The. Christina Rossetti. ELP; OBNC
Bourtree, bourtree, crookit rung. The Elder, or Bourtree. Unknown. GBP
   (Elder Tree, The.) ChTr
Bout with Burning. Vassar Miller. LiTM; MoAmPo; MT; NePoEA
Bow Down, Mountain. Norma Farber. AH
Bow down my soul in worship very low. St. Isaac's Church, Petrograd. Claude McKay. AmNP; PoBA
   (Russian Cathedral.) CDC
Bow down. (Prostrates himself.). János Pilinszky, tr. fr. Hungarian by Jascha Kessler. Fr. Three Poems. FOC
Bow Down Your Head and Cry. Unknown. WTO
Bow to me, bow to me. Fever. Robert Browning. Fr. The Dance of Death. FL
Bow-wow, says the dog. Mother Goose. OxNR
Bow, wow, wow,/ Whose dog art thou? Mother Goose. OxNR
Bowed by the weight of centuries he leans. The Man with the Hoe. Edwin Markham. AA; AnAmPo; BLPA; BLPL; EaLo; FaFP; LiTA; MoAmPo; OHFP; PrIm; SaC; TrGrPo; WBLP; WGRP
Bower of Bliss, The. Spenser. Fr. The Faerie Queene, II, 12. PoEL-1
   "And in the midst of all, a fountaine stood."
   "Eftsoones they heard a most melodious sound." NOBE; OBSC; SCV
   "Thence passing forth, they shortly do arruve." FiP
Bower of Peace, The. Robert Southey. Fr. Ode Written during the War with America, 1814, PAH.
Bowge of Courte, The. John Skelton. AAS
Bowge of Courte, The ("In Autumpne, whan the sonne in Vyrgyne."), sel. John Skelton. AAS
Dreamer Meets Riot, The. OxBLMV
Bowl of gruel and greens, beard wet from steam and snivel, A. Mocking Myself. Chao Yi, tr. by Shirleen S. Wong. WFTU
Bowl of Roses, A. W. E. Henley. MoBrPo
Bowlegged peasant and his ox receding, A. Autumn. Guillaume Apollinaire, tr. by W. S. Merwin. POS; RHTwFP
Bowling-Green, The, sel. William Somervile.
   "Where fair Sabrina's wand'ring currents flow." NOEC
Bowman listens to a cuckoo, A. Kaya Shirao, tr. fr. Japanese by Hiroaki Sato. Fr. Twenty-one Hokku. FCEI
Bowton's Yard. Samuel Laycock. PF
Box cars run by a mile long. Work Gangs. Carl Sandburg. SaC
Box Step. Bruce Bennett. SoTCo
Boxcar Poem, The ("The boxcars drift by"). David Young. AmPA
Boxer. Joseph P. Clancy. SD
Boxers. Armando, tr. fr. Dutch by James S. Holmes. DuIn
Boxer's Face, The. Lucilius, tr. fr. Greek by Humbert Wolfe. SD
Boxes break, The/ At the corners. Christmas Ornaments. Valerie Worth. PChr
Boxing Match, The. David Ignatow. ASP
Boxing Match, The. Virgil, tr. fr. Latin, tr. by Rolfe Humphries. Fr. The Aeneid [or Eneados], V. SD
Boxing the Fox. Pearse Hutchinson. CIP
Boxing towards My Birth. Jack Driscoll. TSL
Boy, A. John Ashbery. DiL; NeAP
Boy, The. Ruth Dallas. ATNZ
Boy, The. Eugene Field. NA
Boy Actor, The. Noel Coward. OxBTC
Boy and a Roll, A. Jacob Glatstein, tr. fr. Yiddish by Benjamin and Barbara Harshav. Fr. From the Nursery. AYP
Boy and the Deer, The. Andrew Peynetsa, Zuni Oral Tradition, tr. by Dennis Tedlock. STP
Boy and the Dream, The. Anna Wickham. AIW
Boy and the Flute, The. Björnstjerne Björnson, tr. fr. Norwegian by Sir Edmund Gosse. AWP
Boy and the Geese, The. Padraic Fiacc. NeIP
Boy and the Lantern, The. Evaristo Ribera Chevremont, tr. fr. Spanish by Julio Marzán. InW
Boy and the Mantle, The. Unknown. ESPB; OxBB
Boy and the Parrot, The. John Hookham Frere. OxBChV
Boy and the Shrike, The. Umberto Saba, tr. fr. Italian by Felix Stefanile. PFI
Boy and the Snake, The. Charles and Mary Lamb. OxBChV
Boy at Target Practice; a Contemplation. W. R. Moses. NYBP
Boy at the Window. Richard Wilbur. Mes; NoP
Boy became enamoured of a shrike, A. The Boy and the Shrike. Umberto Saba, tr. by Felix Stefanile. PFI
Boy Breaking Glass. Gwendolyn Brooks. AiP; MoP; NAAL-2; NoAM; NoP

Boy! bring an ounce of Freeman's best. Isaac Hawkins Browne. Fr. A Pipe of Tobacco. Par
   (Boy! Bring an Ounce.) BXAP
Boy, bring me candles on a silver salver. Candles. Hélène Swarth, tr. by Jonathan Crewe. WPOW
Boy Brittan. Forceythe Willson. PAH
Boy brought in the logs to start the fire, The. Mesón Brujo. E. A. Lacey. PeHV
Boy Changed into a Stag Cries Out at the Gate of Secrets, The. Ferenc Juhász, tr. fr. Hungarian by Kenneth McRobbie. MHuP
Boy claims he saw you on a bicycle last week, A. The Use of Fiction. Naomi Shihab Nye. MAYP
Boy Died in My Alley, The. Gwendolyn Brooks. NoAM
Boy drove into the city, his wagon loaded down, A. The Little Black-eyed Rebel. Will M. Carleton. FaPON; PAH
Boy eats a roll with butter, A. A Boy and a Roll. Jacob Glatstein, tr. fr. Yiddish by Benjamin and Barbara Harshav. Fr. From the Nursery. AYP
Boy Fishing, The. Edith Jay Scovell. FaBoWP
Boy from his bedroom-window, The. At Ballyshannon, Co. Donegal. William Allingham. FaBoPP; NoBVV
Boy from Rome, Da. T. A. Daly. FaPON
Boy had been alone for fifteen days, The. Keeping the Horses. Roy Scheele. MOWH
Boy had run all the way home, The. Mending Crab Pots. Dave Smith. GeTw; MT
Boy He Had an Auger, A. Unknown. AS
Boy Hiding in a Closet. Steve Orlen. NAmP
Boy, I detest the Persian pomp. Horace. See Odes: I, 38. Simplicity.
Boy, I hate their empty shouts. I, 38. Simplicity. Horace, tr. fr. Latin. Fr. Odes. InPK; NBLV
   ("Ah child, no Persian—perfect art.") OBVE, tr. by Gerard Manley Hopkins.
   (Chicago Analogue.) NBLV, tr. by Keith Preston.
   ("Dear Lucy, you know what my wish is.")
     (Victorian Paraphrase, A.) NBLV, tr. by Thackeray.
   (Fie on Eastern Luxury.) InPK, tr. by Hartley Coleridge.
   (Myrtle for Two.) NBLV, tr. by George F. Whicher.
   (Persian Fopperies.) AWP, tr. by William Cowper.
   (Persicos Odi: Pocket Version.) NBLV
   (Preference Declared, The, tr. by Eugene Field) InPK; NBLV
   (Simplicity.) OBVE, tr. by William Cowper.
   (To his Servant.) NBLV, tr. by Christopher Smart.
   (Victorian Paraphrase, A.) NBLV, tr. by Thackeray.
Boy in Ice. Laurie Lee. NYBP
Boy is as old as the stars, A. To My God in His Sickness. Philip Levine. NNaP
Boy looked out of eyes like Euclid's eyes, The. Form Was the World. Maurice English. NYBP
Boy-mad no longer. Rufinus Domesticus, tr. by Alan Marshfield. PeHV
Boy-Man. Karl Shapiro. NYBP; SoSe
Boy Mozart could compose, The. Prolific. William Matthews. BLA
Boy named Simon sojourned in a dale, A. Simple Simon. Harriet S. Morgridge. AA
Boy of fifteen, A. Honi Soit Qui Mal Y Pense. Ian Young. PeHV
Boy of Quebec, The. Kipling. See There was a young boy [or man] of Quebec.
Boy; or, Son of Rip-off, The. Malcolm Glass. BXAP
Boy, presuming on his intellect, A. At Woodward's Gardens. Robert Frost. ImOP; PoA
Boy Reciter, The. David Everett. See Tall Oaks from Little Acorns Grow.
Boy rehearsing the Continental Stroll, The. American Bandstand. Michael Waters. MAYP
Boy Remembers in the Field. Raymond Knister. CaP; NOBC
Boy Riding Forward Backward. Robert Francis. LCAP
Boy Serving at Table, The. John Lydgate. OxBChV
Boy Shepherds' Simile, The. David Bottoms. MT
Boy should have an open fireplace, A. A Boy's Need. Herbert Clark Johnson. PoNe
Boy sits in the classroom, The. Learning Experience. Marge Piercy. FF; NoAM
Boy stood in the supper-room, The. Unknown. CenHV
Boy stood on the burning deck, The. Casabianca. Felicia Dorothea Hemans. BeLS; BLPA; FaBoBe; FaBoPa; FaFP; FaPON; FPL; WBLP
Boy stood on the burning deck, The/ Eating peanuts by the peck. Peanuts. Unknown. FaFP
Boy stood on the burning deck, The/ His feet were covered with blisters. Unknown. FaBoPa
Boy stood on the burning deck, The/ His fleece was white as snow. Familiar Lines. Unknown. FiBHP

Boy stoops, picking greens with his mother, A. Greens. David Ray. SM; VGW

Boy that is good, The [or A]. The Description of a Good Boy. Henry Dixon. OxBChV; OxNR, st. 1

Boy that is truthful and honest, A. The Boy We Want. Unknown. WBLP

Boy, the giant beauty. Instruction in the Art. Philip Booth. SD

Boy Thirteen, A. Jeff Irish. DL

Boy waits on the top step, his hand on the door, The. Black Dog, Red Dog. Stephen Dobyns. NAmP

Boy Wandering in Simms' Valley. Robert Penn Warren. SoSe

Boy was lying upside-down from me, The. Too Dark. Mark McCloskey. PoA

Boy watched the sun, The. Driving Home after a Funeral. Gregory Orr. GeTw

Boy We Want, The. Unknown. WBLP

Boy Who Became Sky, The. David Wagoner. AnAn

Boy who fell into the Morning Glory Pool, The. Morning Glory Pool. Sandra McPherson. LCAP

Boy Who Laughed at Santa Claus, The. Ogden Nash. CenHV

Boy Who Smells like Cocoa, A. Robert Hershon. NeAC

Boy who throws the ball, The. The Beadle's Testimony. Jerome Rothenberg. NNaP

Boy with a Cart, The, sel. Christopher Fry. "In our fields, fallow and burdened, in grass and furrow." LiTB

Boy with a Hammer. Russell Hoban. PCP

Boy with His Hair Cut Short. Muriel Rukeyser. LiTM; MoAB; NoAM; TwCP; VGW; WPE

Boy with yellow hair, his clothes in place, A. War Memento (Somewhere in France 1915). Roger Hecht. CRP

Boyang the Wandering Recluse. Al Robles. BrSi

Boycott. Khalil Mutran, tr. fr. Arabic by Issa Boullata and Thomas G. Ezzy. MAP

Boyhood in Tobacco Country. Robert Penn Warren. AnAn

Boyhood of Christ, The. Saint Columbanus. NOIV

Boyne Water, The. Unknown. FaPoR; NOIV

Boys, The. Oliver Wendell Holmes. WBLP

Boys. Winifred M. Letts. TIRV

Boys/ I don't promise you nothing. Admonitions. Lucille Clifton. BPo; CAPP; NMM

Boys and girls come out to play. Mother Goose. OxNR

Boys and girls crying with hunger, all over the village. A Painting of Peach Blossom Spring. Shen Chou, tr. by Jonathan Chaves. CoBLCP

Boys and Sport. Solon, tr. fr. Greek by John Addington Symonds. PeHV

Boys. Black. Gwendolyn Brooks. CNA

Boys, by Girls Held in Their Thighs. John Peale Bishop. ErPo

Boys' cocks, Diodore. Strato, tr. by Thomas Meyer. PeHV

Boys flying kites haul in their white-winged birds. Words. Unknown. PoLF

Boys in October. Irving Layton. OBCV

Boys in sporadic but tenacious droves. The Horse Chestnut Tree. Richard Eberhart. CMoP; LiTM; MoAB; MoAmPo; NePoAm

Boys like puppets dangling. Spring Is a Looping-free Time. Martin Robbins. SD

Boys Make Men. Unknown. PWR

Boy's Mother, A. James Whitcomb Riley. OHIP

Boy's Need, A. Herbert Clark Johnson. PoNe

Boys of Ch'ien-t'ang practice riding the bore, The. Song of Surfing on the Bore. Cheng Hsieh, tr. by Jonathan Chaves. CoBLCP

Boys of Mullabaun [or Mullaghbawn], The. Unknown. BIrV; GBP

Boys of Sanpete County, The. Unknown. AmFP

Boys of These Men Full Speed. Muriel Rukeyser. NNaP

Boys of Tyre are beautiful, The. Meleager, tr. by Peter Whigham. PeHV

Boys of Wexford, The. Unknown. ELP

Boy's Place, A. Rose Burgunder. PDV

Boy's Prayer, A. Henry Charles Beeching. See Prayers.

Boy's Song, A. James Hogg. BoTP; CH; FaPON; FaPoR; ILY; MoShBr; OBEV; OnUR; OxBChV; WiR

Boy's Will, Joyful Labor without Pay, and Harvest Home, sel. Robert Penn Warren. Work. SaC

Boysick (by gadzooks thunderstruck), The. The Honey Lamb. Jonathan Williams. PoM

Bozzy and Piozzi, sel. "Peter Pindar." Introduction and Anecdotes. PoEL-3

Braced against the rise and fall of ocean. Korea Bound, 1952. William Childress. AmFN

Braced in the sinewy vigour of thy breed. The Horse and His Rider. Joanna Baillie. NOEC

Bracelet, The. John Peck. AnAn

Bracelet: To Julia, The. Robert Herrick. OBEV; TrGrPo

Bracken fern. Unknown, tr. by Geoffrey Bownas and Anthony Thwaite. PeBJV

Bracken Hills in Autumn. "Hugh MacDiarmid." NoP

Brackish reach of shoal off Madaket, A. The Quaker Graveyard in Nantucket. Robert Lowell. CMoP; HAP; LiTM; MoAB; MoP; MOS; NAAL-2; NoAM; NOBA; NoP; OxBA; TAP; UnPo

Braddan Vicarage. Thomas Edward Brown. FaBoPP

Braddock's Fate, with an Incitement to Revenge. Stephen Tilden. PAH

Brady. Unknown. AS

Braemar. Galway Kinnell. PoA

Braes o' Yarrow, The. Unknown. See Late at e'en, drinkin' the wine.

Braes of Yarrow, The. John Logan. GTBS; GTBS-P

Braes of Yarrow, The. Unknown. ESPB; OxBB

Brag, sweet tenor bull. Basil Bunting. Fr. Briggflatts [An Autobiography], I. NoAM; PoE

Bragatelle. K. F. Lazarus. SoTCo

Brahma. Emerson. AA; AmPP; AWP; EaLo; HAP; LiTA; NOBA; NoP; OBEV; OxBA; PoE; PoRA; TAP; TrGrPo; UnPo; WGRP

Brahma. Andrew Lang. BXAP; CenHV; FaBoCo; NOBL

Brahma, the World Idea. Unknown. tr. fr. Sanskrit by Romesh Dutt. Fr. Vedic Hymns. WGRP

Brahms. Michael Davidson. IAT

Brahms/ stabbed me in the ear. St. Julien's Eve. James Cunningham. JB

Braid Claith. Robert Fergusson. GoTS; NOEC; OxBS

Brain Cells, The. Donald Hall. TAP

Brain-Cry. Jean Daive, tr. fr. French by Paul Auster. RHTwFP

Brain—cut off, The. Flood. Judah Leib Teller, tr. fr. Yiddish by Benjamin and Barbara Harshav. Fr. Three Poems of Nightmare. AYP

Brain Drain. "The Mighty Chalkdust." PBCV

Brain forgets, but the blood will remember, The. The Dark Chamber. Louis Untermeyer. MoAmPo

Brain is wider than the sky, The. Emily Dickinson. MoAB; MoAmPo; MoP; NAAL-1; NAWM-2; OxBA

Brain itself in its skull, The. Harsh Climate. Charles Simic. LCAP

Brain, the blood, the busy thews, The. William Baylebridge. Fr. Life's Testament, II. PoAu-1

Brain, within its groove, The. Emily Dickinson. NoAM; NOBA

Brains inflate collapse. Saltimbanques. Tristan Tzara, tr. by Michael Benedikt. POS

Brainstorm. Howard Nemerov. HAP; SM

Brainwashing Dramatized. Don Johnson. PoNe

Brakes, like young stag's horns, come up in Spring, The. London versus Epping Forest. John Clare. Fr. Child Harold. FaBoPP

Bramble Jam. Irene F. Pawsey. BoTP

Branch, The. Stanley Moss. DiL

Branch of may, it does look gay, A. May Song. Unknown. OBET

Branch of Nettle Enters through the Window, A. André Breton, tr. fr. French by David Antin. POS; RHTwFP

Branch of the apple-tree from Emain, A. Unknown, tr. fr. Old Irish by Kuno Meyer. Fr. The Voyage of Bran. AnIL

Branches Back Into. Ken Belford. NeAC

Branches of the locusts shade the chattering orioles, The. Echoing Heaven's Everlastingness. Wei Chuang, tr. by Lois Fusek. ATF

Branches of the vine-bean, The. Unknown, tr. by Arthur Waley. BoS

Branches ripped by a storm tide. Walking the Beach. Sarah Youngblood. IHMS

Branchy leafy oak-tree, The. Sweeney Praises the Trees. Unknown, tr. by Seamus Heaney. RB

Brand. Paul Celan, tr. fr. German by Beth Bjorklund. CoAuP

Brand, sel. Ibsen, tr. fr. Norwegian by C. H. Herford. Brand Speaks. WGRP

Brandish't sword of God before them blaz'd, The. Milton. Fr. Paradise Lost, Bk. XII, ll. 633–649. (Expulsion from Paradise.) ChTr

Brandy Glass, The. Louis MacNeice. FaBCIP

Branwell's Sestina. James Reaney. Fr. A Suit of Nettles. MoCV

Branwen's Starling. R. Williams Parry, tr. fr. Welsh by Gwyn Jones. OBWVE

Brasília. Sylvia Plath. CAPP

Brass and parrot feathers. Oshun, the River Goddess. Yoruba Oral Tradition, tr. by Ulli Beier. WTO

Brass Horse, The. Drummond Allison. FaBoTw

Brass Spittoons. Langston Hughes. AmNP; BANP; MoAmPo; NoAM

Brass Tacks. Denise Levertov. InPS

Brassica (oleracea) is a cabbage. Cabbage. Rosemary Norman. BrRo

Brat, tied up, The. Issa, tr. by Hiroaki Sato. FCEI

Brats. X. J. Kennedy. NBLV

Bratslaver to His Scribe, The. Jacob Glatstein, *tr. fr. Yiddish by* Leonard Wolf. PeBMYV

Bratslav Rabbi to His Scribe, The. Jacob Glatstein, *tr. fr. Yiddish by* Jacob Sloan. TrJP

Brave and high-souled Pilgrims, you who knew no fears. Thanksgiving Day. Annette Wynne. OHIP

Brave as a falcon and as merciless. The Falcon. Wilfrid Scawen Blunt. *Fr.* The Love Sonnets of Proteus, II. ACP

Brave as a postage stamp. Sporting Goods. Philippe Soupault, *tr. by* Rosemarie Waldrop. RHTwFP; TTTS

Brave at Home, The. Thomas Buchanan Read. AnAmPo

Brave Collier Lads. *Unknown.* OBET

Brave Donahue. *At. to.* Jack Donahue. PoAu-1

Brave flowers, that I could gallant it like you. A Contemplation upon Flowers. Henry King. BoNaP; ELP; MeLP; MePo; NoP; OBEV; OBS; SeCP; TrGrPo

Brave hero prizes his sword, the beauty her mirror, The. Airing Books. Kametani Seiken, *tr. by* Burton Watson. JLIC-2

Brave infant of Saguntum, clear[e]. To the Immortal Memory and Friendship of That Noble Pair, Sir Lucius Cary and Sir Henry Morison. Ben Jonson. NAEL-1; NOBE; NoP; OAEL-1; OBS; PoEL-2; SeCP; SeCV-1

Brave lads in olden musical centuries. Alcaics; to H. F. B. Robert Louis Stevenson. OBEV

Brave liegeman like you, A. Kanamura, *tr. fr. Japanese. Fr.* Manyo Shu. Ma

Brave little bird that fears not God, A. The Meadow Lark. Hamlin Garland. AA

Brave Man, The. Wallace Stevens. SOTW

Brave Man and Brave Woman. Mrs. Henry Linden. CBWP-4

Brave man has ambitions wide as the four seas, The. Poem without a Category ("The brave man has ambitions wide as the four seas"). T'ao Ch'ien, *tr. by* Burton Watson. CoBCP

Brave New World. Archibald MacLeish. NOBA; OFD; OxBA

Brave New World. Shakespeare. *Fr.* The Tempest, V, i. TrGrPo

Brave news is come to town. *Unknown.* OxNR

Brave Old Duke of York, The. *Unknown. See* O the grand old Duke of York.

Brave Old Oak, The. Henry Fothergill Chorley. FaBoBe

Brave Old Ship, the *Orient*, The. Robert Traill Spence Lowell. AA; FaBoBe

Brave Old World. Elisabeth Lambert. FaFP

Brave Paulding and the Spy. *Unknown*

Brave Rover. Max Beerbohm. NBLV

Brave Teuton, though thy awful name. Schemmelfennig. Bret Harte. OBAL

Brave weathercock, I see thou'lt set thy nose. Upon the Weathercock. Bunyan. OxBChV

Brave Wolfe. *Unknown.* PAH

Brave young city by the Balboa seas, The. Twilight at the Heights. Joaquin Miller. AA

Brave youth, to whom Fate in one hour. For a Picture Where a Queen Laments over the Tomb of a Slain Knight. Thomas Carew. CaPo

Bravely from Fairyland he rode, on furlough. The Broken Girth. Robert Graves. BIrV

Bravery runs in my family. Coward. A. R. Ammons. OBAL

Bravest Battle, The. Joaquin Miller. WBLP

Bravest names for fire and flames, The. General John. W. S. Gilbert. NA

Braving the Wilds All Unexplored, *with music.* Robert Freeman. AH

Brawling of a sparrow in the eaves, The. The Sorrow of Love. W. B. Yeats. NAEL-2; OAEL-2; TEP

Brazen Image. Anne Hartigan. CIP

Brazen Tongue. William Rose Benét. MoAmPo

Brazil. Tony Harrison. *Fr.* Sentences. OBTV

Brazil, January 1, 1502. Elizabeth Bishop. FaBoWP; NoAM

Brazilian Fazenda. Patricia K. Page. FaBoWP

Brazilian Rain Forest. Gyula Illyés, *tr. fr. Hungarian by* William Jay Smith. MHuP

Brazilian Tragedy. Manuel Bandeira, *tr. fr. Portuguese by* Elizabeth Bishop. ATCBP

Brazos River, The. *Unknown.* PrIm

Bread. Stanley Burnshaw. TrJP

Bread. Stephen Corey. KS

Bread. Mahmoud Darwish, *tr. fr. Arabic by* Lena Jayyusi *and* Christopher Middleton. MAP

Bread. James Dickey. LCAP

Bread. Nancy Keesing. PoAu-2

Bread. W. S. Merwin. EAS

Bread. Gabriela Mistral, *tr. fr. Spanish by* Allan Francovich *and* Kathleen Weaver. WPOW

Bread. Susan Mitchell. NAmP

Bread. H. E. Wilkinson. BoTP

Bread and a Pension. Louis Johnson. ATNZ; PeNZ

Bread and Music. Conrad Aiken. *See* Discordants: Music I heard with you was more than music.

Bread and Wine, *sel.* Friedrich Hölderlin, *tr. fr. German by* Robert Bly. "Oh friend, we arrived too late." NU

Bread Hot from the Oven, The. John Thompson. NOBC

Bread is a lovely thing to eat. Lovely Things. H. M. Sarson. BoTP

Bread Is Born. Anne Hébert, *tr. fr. French by* Maxine W. Kumin. BoWoP

Bread of Heaven, on Thee We Feed. Josiah Conder. TrCP

Bread of Our Affliction, The. Martin Grossman. VWA

Bread rises, The. Homage to Guillaume Apollinaire. Blaise Cendrars, *tr. by* Anselm Hollo. RHTwFP

Bread that bringeth strength I want to give, The. I Shall Not Pass Again This Way. *Unknown.* BLRP; WBLP

Breadth. Circle. Desert. Monarch. Month. Wisdom. John Hollander. PoA

Breadwinner, The. Amrita Pritam, *tr. fr. Punjabi by* Charles Brasch *and* Amrita Pritam. OV

Break, The. Elizabeth Nancy Sargent. NYBP

Break and trail home. The Girl I Left behind Me. *Unknown.* AmFP

"Break, Break, Break." J. C. Squire. *See* Fly, Muse, thy wanted themes, no longer seek.

Break, Break, Break. Tennyson. AWP; BLPL; CH; DL; FaBoBe; FaBV; FaPoR; FF; FiP; GoJo; GTBS-P; HAP; HeIP; LiTB; MOS; NAEL-2; NIP; NOBE; NOBVV; NoP; OBNC; PoEL-5; PoRA; PrIm; PWR; RB; TEP; TrGrPo; WBLP; WeW

Break—break it open; let the knocker rust. Dedication to the Generation Knocking at the Door. John Davidson. BrPo

Break forth, break forth, O Sudbury town. Lydia. Lizette Woodworth Reese. AA

Break, kid. You get one chance. Clean. Lance Newman. ASP

Break not his sweet repose. A Soldier's Grave. John Albee. AA

Break not my loneliness, O Wanderer! The Dove's Loneliness. George Darley. OBNC

Break not the slumbers of the bride. An Hymeneal Song on the Nuptials of the Lady Anne Wentworth and the Lord Lovelace. Thomas Carew. CaPo

Break of Day. John Shaw Neilson. PoAu-1

Break of Day. *Unknown. At. to* John Donne. ElL; TrGrPo

Break of Day in the Trenches. Isaac Rosenberg. BrPo; FaBoMo; GTBS-P; MMA; MoBrPo; NAEL-2; NIP; NoAM; NOBE; NoP; OAEL-2; OBWP; PoA; SeCePo; VWA; WaaP; WaP

Break thou my heart, ah, break it. Arab Song. Richard Henry Stoddard. AA

Break Thou the Bread of Life. Mary Artemisia Lathbury. AH

Break-up, The. Abraham Moses Klein. NOBC

Break-up, The. László Nagy, *tr. fr. Hungarian by* George MacBeth. MHuP

Breakdown, The. Sherod Santos. MAYP; SM

Breake now my heart and dye! Oh no, she may relent. Thomas Campion. AAS

Break[e] of Day. John Donne. ErPo; LiTB; NAEL-1

Breakers of the Ise Sea, The. Lady Kasa, *tr. fr. Japanese by* Geoffrey Bownas *and* Anthony Thwaite. *Fr.* Manyo Shu. PeBJV

Breakers of the ocean, The. Sanetomo, *tr. by* Geoffrey Bownas *and* Anthony Thwaite. PeBJV

Breakers over the Sea. *Malay Oral Tradition, tr. by* R. O. Winstedt. WTO

Breakfast. W. W. Gibson. OBMV; OxBTC

Breakfast. Thom Gunn. OxBC

Breakfast. Everette Maddox. MT

Breakfast for Barbarians, A. Gwendolyn MacEwen. NOBC

Breakfast in Bed (Influenza in War-time). Donald McDonald. PBCV

Breakfast more than he could want. A World War II Premium from Battle Creek. John Caddy. TSL

Breakfast Song in Time of Diet. Stoddard King. OBAL

Breakfast with Gerard Manley Hopkins. Anthony Brode. BXAP; FaBoPa; FiBHP; NOBL; Par

Breakfasting alone in Karachi, Delhi, Calcutta. Solitary Travel. Louis MacNeice. OBTV

Breaking. Alexander Allan. PoAu-2

Breaking, The. Zsuzsa Beney, *tr. fr. Hungarian by* Jascha Kessler. *Fr.* A Broken Glass. FOC

Breaking a branch off my cherry tree. Kikaku, *tr. by* Hiroaki Sato. FCEI

Breaking and spreading for a bed. *the wife of* Go Dan-ochi, *tr. fr. Japanese. Fr.* Manyo Shu. Ma

Breaking Days. Sara Boyes. DT

Breaking Green. Michael Ondaatje. NOBC

Breaking Ground in Me. Tom Kryss. NeAC

Breaking of the Glass, The. Abdallah al-Tayyib, tr. fr. Arabic by Salma Khadra Jayyusi and Christopher Middleton. MAP

Breaking Off from Waiting. Clarisse Nicoïdski, tr. fr. Judezmo by Stephen Levy. VWA

Breaking off rock azaleas. Lady Izumi, tr. fr. Japanese by Hiroaki Sato. Fr. Fifty-one Tanka. FCEI

Breaking Out. A. R. Ammons. CAPP

Breaking Point. Sylvia Auxier. GoYe

Breaking Silence. Janice Mirikitani. BrSi

Breaking the morning ice on the well's bucket was no great hardship. On the Pilgrim's Way in Kent, as It Leads to the Coldrum Stones. Asphodel. BrRo

Breaking the Precepts. Yasin Taha Hafiz, tr. fr. Arabic by Sharif Elmusa and Christopher Middleton. MAP

Breaking through the first door, he found. Seven Dreams. John Clifford Bayliss. EAS

Breaking Tradition. Janice Mirikitani. BrSi

Breaking waves dashed high, The. The Landing of the Pilgrim Fathers [in New England]. Felicia Dorothea Hemans. BeLS; BLPA; FaBoBe; FaBV; FaFP; FaPON; GN; OHIP; OPP; PAH; WBLP; WPE (Pilgrim Fathers, The.) BoTP

Breakings. Henry Taylor. GrPl

Breaklight. Lucille Clifton. CAPP

Breaks up in obelisks on the river. Ice. Ai. FYAP

Breakthrough. Carolyn M. Rodgers. BPo

Breakthrough. John Sinclair. NBP

Breakwaters. Ted Walker. NYBP

Breast/ below ground. The Dance. Robert Kelly. Fr. The Book of Persephone, 17. PoM

Breast/ Is best. Note on Feeding. Unknown. FaBoUs

Breastdown fluttering in the breeze. Sparrow in Winter. Takahashi Shinkichi, tr. by Lucien Stryk and Takashi Ikemoto. NU

Breasts. Maxine Chernoff. UL

Breasts. Tess Gallagher. AmPA

Breasts. Donald Hall. OBAL

Breasts. Charles Simic. NNaP

Breasts of a barmaid of Crale, The. Unknown. NOBL

Breasts of Mnasidice, The. Pierre Louÿs, tr. fr. French. Fr. Chansons de Bilitis. PeHV

Breasts of the Queen Are Turned out of Wood, The. Stanislaw Grochowiak, tr. fr. Polish by Czeslaw Milosz. PwPP

Breath, A. "Madeline Bridges." AA

Breath. James Dickey. SM

Breath. Reginald Gibbons. MAYP

Breath. Heather McHugh. GeTw

Breath. Mark Strand. HCAP

Breath can fan love's flame to burning. A Breath. "Madeline Bridges." AA

Breath in My Nostrils. Lance Jeffers. CNA

Breath is on my face when the cloudy sun. Breath. James Dickey. SM

Breath of Air, A. James Wright. NOBA

Breath of Hampstead Heath. Edith M. Thomas. AA

Breath of life imbued those few dim days, The. Jessie Redmond Fauset. CDC

Breath of my life, The—no less. Meleager, tr. by Peter Whigham. PeHV

Breath of Spring. Ryokan, tr. fr. Japanese by Burton Watson. FCEI; JLIC-2

Breath on the Oat. Joseph Russell Taylor. PAH

Breathe and blow. Dragon Smoke. Lilian Moore. RAR

Breathe Dust. Fred Wah. NOBC

Breathe in experience, breathe out poetry. Poem Out of Childhood. Muriel Rukeyser. NMM

Breathe not, hid Heart: cease silently. To an Unborn Pauper Child. Thomas Hardy. FaBoRV; GTBS-P; LiTB; NAs

Breathe, trumpets, breathe. George Lunt. AA

Breathers, The. James Reiss. AmPA

Breathes there a man with hide so tough. Samuel Hoffenstein. FiBHP

Breathes There the [or a] Man [with Soul So Dead]. Sir Walter Scott. Fr. The Lay of the Last Minstrel, VI. BLPA; EnRP; FaFP; FPL; OPP; OxBS

Breathing, The. Denise Levertov. NaP; RFM

Breathing do I draw that air to me. Song of Breath. Peire Vidal, tr. by Ezra Pound. AWP

Breathing his last music, Mozart is supposed. Lost Letter to James Wright, with Thanks for a Map of Fano. Gibbons Ruark. MAYP; MT

Breathing seems much easier at nighttime. A. A. Fet, tr. by Alan Myers. AAA

Breathing something German at the end. The Gift to Be Simple. Howard Moss. ImOP; Psk; TwCP

Breathing Space July. Tomas Tranströmer, tr. fr. Swedish by Robert Bly. RB

Breathing the Strong Smell. Harold Norse. PeHV

Breathless. Wilfred Noyce. OBTV

Breathless she stood, her graceful head bent low. Listening Nydia. Henrietta Cordelia Ray. CBWP-3

Breathless, we flung us on the windy hill. The Hill. Rupert Brooke. MoBrPo; OxBTC; Son

Breaths. Birago Diop, tr. fr. French by Anne Atik. TTY

Brébeuf and His Brethren, sels. E. J. Pratt. Invisible Trumpets Blowing. CaP Martyrdom of Brébeuf and Lalemant, 16 March 1649, The. NOBC; OBCV ("Less than two hours it took the Iroquois.") OBCV

Brébeuf and His Brethren. F. R. Scott. NOBC

Brecon Beacons and the Black Mountains, The. Henry Vaughan. FaBoPP

Bred up at home, full early I begun. Pope. Fr. The Second Epistle of the Second Book of Horace Imitated. TOF

Bredon Hill. A. E. Housman. Fr. A Shropshire Lad, XXI. BrPo; EBVV; FaBoPP; MoAB; MoBrPo; NAEL-2; SoSe

Breech, The. Michael McClure. NeAP

Breed of Athletes, The. Euripides, tr. fr. Greek by Moses Hadas. SD

Breed's described, The: Now, Satire, if you can. Daniel Defoe. Fr. The True-born Englishman, II. OBSV

Breeze, The. Li Nan, tr. fr. Chinese by Dominic Cheung. IFON

Breeze and Billow. Albert Durrant Watson. CaP

Breeze Comes Filling the Valley, The. Miyazawa Kenji, tr. fr. Japanese by Hiroaki Sato. FCEI

Breeze has swelled the whitening sail, The. Song of the Pilgrims. Thomas Cogswell Upham. PAH

Breeze is blowing, The. Unknown, tr. by A. Armstrong and R. Nagata. WTO

Breeze is on the bluebells, The. Bluebells. Juliana Horatia Ewing. BoTP

Breeze Nomadly Coupling Summer Sounds (Precision Insects Chomping). Bill Knott. PPR

Breeze Swept Through, A. Luci Tapahonso. GOS

Breeze was crisp and the sea lay blue, The. The Pirates' Fight. Joseph Schull. Fr. The Legend of Ghost Lagoon. CaP

Breezes blowing/ through the little clumps. Yakamochi, tr. fr. Japanese by Burton Watson. Fr. Manyo Shu. FCEI

Breezes went steadily thro' the tall pines, The. Nathan Hale. Unknown. PAH

Breezeways in the tropics winnow the air. A Letter from the Caribbean. Barbara Howes. CoAP; UnPo

Breitmann in Politics, sel. Charles Godfrey Leland. "Dere's a liddle fact in hishdory vitch few hafe onnershtand." OBAL

Brennan on the Moor. Unknown. AmFP; FaBoBa; GBP

Brennhaum. Ezra Pound. Fr. Hugh Selwyn Mauberley. (Life and Contacts). MoAmPo

Brent; a Poem to Thomas Palmer Esq, sels. William Diaper. FaBoPP "Had mournful Ovid been to Brent condemned." OBSV "Happy are you, whom Quantock overlooks." NOEC; OBSV

Br'er Sterling and the Rocker. Michael S. S. Harper. LCAP

Brereton Omen, The, sel. Felicia Dorothea Hemans. "Yes! I have seen the ancient oak." CTC

Brest Left Behind. John Chipman Farrar. PAH

Bretagne had not her peer. In the province far or near. Lady of Castlenoire. Thomas Bailey Aldrich. BeLS

Breton Afternoon. Ernest Dowson. OBNC

Breughel's Winter. Walter De la Mare. SeCePo

Brevities. Siegfried Sassoon. PoLF

Brew your potion, mix your spell. Comrade in Arms. Tom Inglis Moore. PoAu-2

Brewer, A. Unknown. FaBoCo

Brewer's Man, The. L. A. G. Strong. FaBoCo; FiBHP

Brewing of Soma, The ("Fagots blazed, the caldron's smoke, The."), sel. Whittier. PoEL-4 "Dear Lord and Father of Mankind." AH, with music; NOCV; TrPWD

Brewing Stone, The. Lo Fu, tr. fr. Chinese by Dominic Cheung. IFON

Brewing Tea at Moon Pond. Chang Yü, tr. fr. Chinese by Jonathan Chaves. Fr. Seven Poems on Living in the Mountains: Seeing Off. CoBLCP

Breyten Breytenbach May Look at the Moon. "Lucebert," tr. fr. Dutch by Larry Ten Harmsel. DuIn

Brian O'Linn. Unknown. FaBoBa; FaBoNo; NBLV; RB (Bryan O'Lynn.) GBP

Brick, The. Paul Roche. NYBP
Brick distinguishes this country. Amsterdam Letter. Jean Garrigue. NYBP
Brick plant like a school. The winter set, The. L. E. Sissman. *Fr.* Parents in Winter. DiL
Brickbat for Krazy Kat, A. K. Schippers, *tr. fr. Dutch by* Peter Nijmeijer. DuIn
Bricking the Church. Robert Morgan. MAYP
Bricklayer tells the busdriver, The. The Continuity. Paul Blackburn. NeAP
Bricklay'r throws his trowel by, The. Religion and the Lower Classes. Evan Lloyd. *Fr.* The Methodist. NOEC
Bricklayer's Labours, The. Robert Tatersal. NOEC
Bricks. Wang Jun-hua, *tr. fr. Chinese by* Dominic Cheung. IFON
Brickster, The. *Unknown.* OBET
Bridal bed, The. Above it. Jenny Mastoraki, *tr. by* Nick Germanacos. PBWP
Bridal Birth. Dante Gabriel Rossetti. *Fr.* The House of Life, II. Son
Bridal Couch. Donald J. Lloyd. NIP
Bridal Pair, The. William Young. *Fr.* Wishmakers' Town. AA
Bridal Piece. Louise Glück. SM
Bridal Song, A ("Beauty arise, show forth thy glorious shining!"). Thomas Dekker *and others.* See Beauty arise, show forth thy glorious shining.
Bridal Song ("Cynthia, to thy power"). Beaumont *and* Fletcher. *Fr.* The Maid's Tragedy, I, ii. OBEV
Bridal Song ("Hold back thy hours"). Beaumont *and* Fletcher. *Fr.* The Maid's Tragedy, I, ii. ElL; ErPo; TrGrPo
Bridal Song ("Now, sleep! bird fast"). George Chapman. *Fr.* The Masque of the Middle Temple and Lincoln's Inn. ElL; OxBSP
Bridal Song ("O come! soft rest of cares"). Chapman. *Fr.* Hero and Leander, Fifth Sestiad. NOBE; OBEV
Bridal Song, A ("Roses, their sharp spines being gone"). John Fletcher *and* Shakespeare. *Fr.* The Two Noble Kinsmen, I, i. ElL; NOBE; OBSC
Bridal Song to Amala. Thomas Lovell Beddoes. *Fr.* Death's Jest Book. ChER, *fr.* IV, iii; GBL, *fr.* IV, iii; OBNC, *fr.* IV, iii.
(Epithalamia.) PoEL-4
(Song: "We have bathed, where none have seen us.") ChER; NOBVV; OBNC
Bride, The. Bella Akhmadulina, *tr. fr. Russian.* AIW; BoWoP, *tr. by* Stephan Stepanchev
Bride, The. Ambrose Bierce. AA
Bride, A. Harry Fainlight. BoLoP
Bride, The. D. H. Lawrence. NoAM; OxBTC
Bride, The. Sir John Suckling. *Fr.* A Ballad [*or* Ballade] upon a Wedding. TrGrPo
Bride cam' out o' the byre, The. A Wooed and Married and. Alexander Ross. OxBS
Bride loved old words, and found her pleasure marred. J. V. Cunningham. *Fr.* Five Epigrams. OBAL
Bride of Corinth, The. Goethe, *tr. fr. German by* Christopher Middleton, W. E. Aytoun *and* Theodore Martin. VVA
Bride of Frankenstein, The. Edward Field. CoAP; HeIP
Bride of Lammermoor, The, *sel.* Sir Walter Scott.
Lucy Ashton's Song. *Fr. ch.* 3. EnRP; GoTS; NOBE; OBEV; OxBS
(Look Not Thou.) OxBSP
Bride of the Disappearing Man, *sels.* Gregory O'Brien. ATNZ
Fable, The.
Light, The.
Bride Song. Christina Rossetti. *Fr.* The Prince's Progress. OBEV; WPE
Bridegroom. Gerrit Achterberg, *tr. fr. Dutch by* James S. Holmes. DuIn
Bridegroom, The. Kipling. *Fr.* Epitaphs of the War, 1914–1918. FaBoEE
Bridegroom Dick, *sel.* Herman Melville.
"Where's Commander All-a-Tanto?" PoEL-5
Bridegroom of Cana, The. Marjorie Pickthall. CaP; TrCP
Brides, The. A. D. Hope. HAP
Bride's Farewell: Two Songs. *Gond Oral Tradition, tr. by* V. Elwin *and* S. Hivale. WTO
Bride's Hours, A. Jean Valentine. FaBoWP
Bride's Prelude, The. Dante Gabriel Rossetti. SeCePo
Bride's Song, The. William Cory. OBTV
Bride's Toilette, The. Ellen Mackay Hutchinson Cortissoz. AA
Bride's Tragedy, The, *sels.* Thomas Lovell Beddoes.
"A ho! A ho!/ Love's horn doth blow." ChER
Poor Old Pilgrim Misery. EnRP
Bridestones. Ted Hughes. AnAn
Bridge. A. R. Ammons. CoAP; NAAL-2

Bridge, The, *sels.* Hart Crane. LiTA; NAAL-2
Atlantis. *Fr.* VIII. LiTM
Ave Maria. *Fr.* I. NoAM; NOBA
Cape Hatteras. *Fr.* IV. InPS; MoAB; MoAmPo
"Nasal whine of power whips a new universe." MoAB
(Power.) MoAmPo
Cutty Sark. *Fr.* III. FaBoMo
Powhatan's Daughter. *Fr.* II.
Dance, The. LiTM; MoAB; MoAmPo; OxBA
Harbor Dawn, The. AmPP; CMoP; FaBV; GOA; LiTM; MoAB; MoAmPo; NoAM; NOBA; OxBA; PrIm; TrGrPo
River, The. AmPP; CMoP; GOA; MoAB; MoAmPo; NOBA; OxBA; PrIm
("Down, down—born pioneers in time's despite.") TrGrPo
Van Winkle. AmPP; FaBV; MoAB; MoAmPo
Quaker Hill. *Fr.* VI. LiTM; NAAL-2
Southern Cross. NAAL-2
Three Songs. *Fr.* V.
National Winter Garden. ErPo; InPS; LiTM; NAAL-2; OxBA
To Brooklyn Bridge. AiP; AmPP; BLPL; CMoP; EyDe; HAP; HeIP; InPS; LiTA; LiTM; MoAB; MoAmPo; NoAM; NOBA; NoP; OxBA; PoE; PrIm; TAP; WeW
(Proem: To Brooklyn Bridge.) AmFP; AmPP; CMoP; HAP; HeIP; NoAM; NoP; TAP; WeW
Tunnel, The. *Fr.* VII. CMoP; MAT; MoAB; MoAmPo; OxBA
Virginia. NAAL-2
Bridge, The. Khalil Hawi, *tr. fr. Arabic by* Diana Der Hovanessian *and* Lena Jayyusi. MAP
Bridge, The. Leopold Staff, *tr. fr. Polish by* Czeslaw Milosz. PwPP
Bridge, The. Katri Vala, *tr. fr. Finnish by* Aili Jarvenpa. SOP
Bridge all-at-once-/ without-future, A. A Built Bridge, Footnotes. Carolyn Stoloff. SoTCo
Bridge, and a hot concrete road, A. The Desert of Love. János Pilinszky, *tr. by* Ted Hughes *and* János Csokits. MHuP; OBVE
Bridge broken, The. Taigi, *tr. by* Geoffrey Bownas *and* Anthony Thwaite. PeBJV
Bridge from Brooklyn, The, *sel.* Raymond Henri.
"Roebling, his life and mind reprieved enough." EyDe
Bridge-Guard in the Karroo. Kipling. OBWP
Bridge of Death, The. *Unknown, tr. fr. French by* Andrew Lang. AWP
Bridge of Drifted Fragrance, The. Wu Wen, *tr. fr. Chinese by* Chang Yin-nan. *Fr.* Poems on Yi Garden: Written for Mr. Juan-t'ing, III. WFTU
Bridge of Heraclitus, The. George Reavey. BIrV
Bridge of Sighs, The. Thomas Hood. BeLS; EBEV; EnRP; FaPoR; FPL; GTBS; GTBS-P; OBEV; WBLP
Bridge Poem, The. Kate Rushin. GLP
Bridge was frozen, The. Winter Landscape with a Girl in Brown Shoes. Sherod Santos. AnAn
Bridges and Tunnels. Beth Bentley. EyDe
Bridges are essential in a place. Covered Bridge. Robert Peter Tristram Coffin. AmFN
Bridges hang stretched with cool fear on steel ropes. New York Everywhere. Berysh Vaynshteyn, *tr. fr. Yiddish by* Benjamin *and* Barbara Harshav. *Fr.* New York Everywhere. AYP
Bridgework. Annette Lynch. FF
Bridging Hour in Wesciv. Brian W. Aldiss. BWV
Brief Autumnal. *Unknown, tr. fr. Greek by* Dudley Fitts. WeW
Brief Discourse: That Woman's Excellence Surpasses Man's. Marie de Romieu, *tr. fr. French by* Dorothy Backer. DMF
Brief Elegie on My Dear Son John, A. John Saffin. SCAP
Brief Encounter. Winfield Townley Scott. GOYP
Brief Essay on Man. Arthur Guiterman. OBAL
Brief Farewell. Anthony Delius. PeSA
Brief harp of the larches. To Friend-Tree of Counted Days. René Char, *tr. by* William Carlos Williams. RHTwFP
Brief History. Olga Hampel Briggs. GoYe
Brief History of Imbecility, A, *sels.* Takamura Kotaro, *tr. fr. Japanese by* Hiroaki Sato. FCEI
Cooperative Council.
Day of Pearl Harbor, The.
Sculpting in the Imperial Presence.
Brief is this mortal life. Yakamochi, *tr. fr. Japanese.* *Fr.* Manyo Shu. Ma
Brief Journey West, The. Howard Nemerov. NoAM
Brief Landing. Sarah Kirsch, *tr. fr. German by* Gerda Mayer. OV
Brief meeting, the east wind has no will of its own, A. On a Rainy Evening: Written in Playful Imitation of Yi-shan's "Untitled Poems." Li Tz'u-ming, *tr. by* Daniel Bryant. WFTU
Brief, on a flying night. Chimes. Alice Meynell. BoTP; CH; MoBrPo; WPE

Brief Reflections on an Ancient and Beautiful City on the Coast of the Mediterranean Sea. Mahmoud Darwish, *tr. fr. Arabic by* Abdullah al-Udhari. MPAW

Brief Thunder at Sharpeville. Arthur Nortje. WMBCH

"The Brigade Must Not Know, Sir!" *Unknown.* PAH

Brigadier. Arthur James Marshall Smith. MoCV

Briggflatts [An Autobiography], *sels.* Basil Bunting.
"Brag, sweet tenor bull." *Fr.* I. NoAM; PoE
Coda. OAEL-2
"Grass caught in willow tells the flood's height." *Fr.* IV. FaBoMo
"Light lifts from the water." *Fr.* V. OAEL-2; PoPo

Bright Abandon. Tessa Sweazy Webb. GoYe

Bright and beautiful art thou. October. Mary Weston Fordham. CBWP-2

Bright are the days which the Fates hold in store for us. To William (Whom We Have Missed). P. G. Wodehouse. NOBL

Bright are the flowers. *Unknown, tr. by* Arthur Waley. BoS

Bright are the heavens, the narrow bay serene. The Indian's Grave. George J. Mountain. CaP

Bright as the day, and like the morning fair. Cloe. George Granville. FaBoCo; FaBoEE; NIP

Bright as the light that burns at night. Venetia. Adah Isaacs Menken. CBWP-1

Bright Babe! whose awfull beautyes make. In the Glorious Epiphanie of Our Lord God. Richard Crashaw. PoEL-2

Bright Be the Place of Thy Soul! Byron. HoPM

Bright berries on the roadside. On the March. Richard Aldington. BrPo

Bright-bodied hounds run silent, The. Death of a Unicorn. Jane Yolen. BWV

Bright books! the perspectives to our weak sights. To His Books. Henry Vaughan. QFR

Bright breaks the warrior o'er the ocean wave. The Ocean Wanderer. *Unknown.* NA

Bright bright!/ bright bright bright! Myoe, *tr. fr. Japanese by* Burton Watson. *Fr.* Ten Tanka. FCEI

Bright Clouds. Edward Thomas. BrPo

Bright-coloured, mirror-plated, strung with lights. Merry-go-round. James McAuley. CBAP

Bright Day, A. William Henry Davies. OBWVE

Bright Day, A. John Montague. CIP; FaBCIP

Bright drips the morning from its trophied nets. Sonnet of Fishes. George Barker. FaBoMo; Son

Bright Flower! whose home is everywhere. To the Daisy. Wordsworth. EnRP

Bright-green acacia tree, decked with the fragrance, The. The Acacia Tree. "Zelda," *tr. by* Bernhard Frank. MHeP

Bright-haired Spirit! Golden Brow! Onward to Far Ida. George Darley. *Fr.* Nepenthe. OBNC

Bright Hillside, The. Rhoda Coghill. NeIP

Bright, hot day, A. Late June. The bus from Rome. La Banditaccia, 1979. Rika Lesser. MAYP

Bright House. Fukao Sumako, *tr. fr. Japanese by* Kenneth Rexroth *and* Ikuko Atsumi. UnAS

Bright is the ring of words. Robert Louis Stevenson. *Fr.* Songs of Travel. BrPo; OBNC; TrGrPo

Bright mirror I braved, The: the devil in it. Cleopatra to the Asp. Ted Hughes. EBEV

Bright moon: a crab, The. Kito, *tr. fr. Japanese by* Hiroaki Sato. *Fr.* Twenty-four Hokku. FCEI

Bright Moon: after an Illness. Onitsura, *tr. fr. Japanese by* Hiroaki Sato. *Fr.* Twenty-three Hokku. FCEI

Bright moon born of the sea. Watching the Moon with Thoughts of Far Away. Chang Chiu-ling, *tr. by* Burton Watson. CoBCP

Bright moon illumines the night-prospect, A. *Unknown, tr. by* Arthur Waley. BoWoP

Bright moon lifts from the Mountain of Heaven, The. The Moon at the Fortified Pass. Li Po, *tr. by* Witter Bynner *and* Kiang Kang-hu. WaaP

Bright moon: on the straw mat. Kikaku, *tr. fr. Japanese by* Hiroaki Sato. *Fr.* Thirty-three Hokku. FCEI

Bright moon slowly, slowly rises, The. The "Slowly, Slowly" Poem. Yüan Hung-tao, *tr. by* Jonathan Chaves. CoBLCP

Bright moon: strolling around the pond all night long. Basho, *tr. fr. Japanese by* Burton Watson. *Fr.* Seventy-six Hokku. FCEI

Bright moon, when did you appear? Tune: Prelude to Water Music. Su Tung-p'o, *tr. by* Burton Watson. CoBCP

Bright moonlight. Kawabata Bosha, *tr. by* Geoffrey Bownas *and* Anthony Thwaite. PeBJV

Bright moonlight floods the steps like a cascade of water. Deva-like Barbarian. Sun Kuang-hsien, *tr. by* Lois Fusek. ATF

Bright New Missouri. Steve Sneyd. BWV

Bright on the banners of lily and rose. Welcome to the Nations. Oliver Wendell Holmes. PAH

Bright portalles of the skie. An Hymne of the Ascension. William Drummond of Hawthornden. OBS

Bright ran thy line, O Galloway. Lord Galloway. Burns. OxBoLi

Bright rays of lofty Phaeton shine, The. Immortal Springtime and Its Tokens. Bernardo de Balbuena, *tr. fr. Spanish by* Samuel Beckett. *Fr.* Grandeza Mexicana. MexPo

Bright red blossoms burst from the ripened lotus pods. The Beautiful Lady Yü. Yen Hsüan, *tr. by* Lois Fusek. ATF

Bright sea washed beneath her feet, The. The Return. Annie Fields. AA

Bright shadows of true Rest! some shoots of blisse. Son-Dayes. Henry Vaughan. SeCP

Bright shines the new terrace. *Unknown, tr. by* Arthur Waley. BoS

Bright shines the sun; play, beggars, play! In Praise of a Beggar's Life. "A. W." ElL; TrGrPo
(Song in Praise of a Beggar's Life, A.) OBSC

Bright Sparkles in de Churchyard. *Unknown.* AA

Bright Star, Would I Were Steadfast as Thou Art! Keats. BLPL; EnLoPo; GBL; GTBS; GTBS-P; HAP; InPK; InPS; LiTB; NAEL-2; NAWM-2; NIP; OAEL-2; PoE; PPP; PrIm; SCV; Son; TrGrPo

Bright they shone on earth below. *Unknown, tr. by* Arthur Waley. BoS

Bright town, tossed by waves of time to a hill. Ode to Swansea. Vernon Watkins. OBWVE

Bright tulips, we do know. To a Bed of Tulips. Robert Herrick. CaPo

Bright vocabularies are transient as rainbows. Precious Moments. Carl Sandburg. MoAmPo

Bright wanderer, fair coquette of heaven. Lines Written in the Bay of Lerici. Shelley. NAEL-2; OAEL-2

Bright Was the Morning. Thomas D'Urfey. OBS

Bright waves scour the wound of Carthage, The. Rome Remember. Sidney Keyes. MoAB

Bright white street lights, The. Allegory in Black. Carl Clark. JB

Bright—Young-Autumn's delicate gold cupolas ignite. Young-Autumn. A. Leyeles, *tr. by* Benjamin *and* Barbara Harshav. AYP

Brightest and Best of the Sons of the Morning. Reginald Heber. GN; WGRP

Brightest of the Bright, The. Egan O'Rahilly, *tr. fr. Irish by* James Clarence Mangan. BIrV

Brightest threads on life's pathway, The. Home and Mother. Hettye Rayburn Ramsey. PWR

Brightly colored for a new season. Merry-go-round. Oliver Jenkins. GoYe

Brightly shone the sun in my hut. Those Who Lost Everything. David Diop, *tr. by* Langston Hughes. PBA

Brightly the sun of summer shone. Memory. Anne Brontë. EBVV

Brightness. Denis Glover. PeNZ

Brightness. Heather McHugh. GeTw

Brightness as a Poignant Light. David Ignatow. DiL

Brightness most bright I beheld on the way, forlorn. Egan O'Rahilly, *tr. by* Thomas Kinsella. NOIV

Brightness: not even a wind blowing. Miura Chora, *tr. fr. Japanese by* Hiroaki Sato. *Fr.* Sixteen Hokku. FCEI

"Brigid is a caution, sure!"—What's that ye say? Her Sister. Moira O'Neill. AIW; OxBTC

Brignall Banks. Sir Walter Scott. *Fr.* Rokeby, III. EnRP; OBEV
(Edmund's Song.) PoRA
(Outlaw, The.) GTBS; GTBS-P

Brilliant beard of ice, A. Icicles. Robert Pinsky. BLA; SM

Brilliant-bellied newt flashes, The. Summer Matures. Helene Johnson. BlSi; CDC; PoNe

Brilliant, bright—the flowers of the cold season! The Pavilion for Listening to Fragrance. Chang Yü, *tr. by* Jonathan Chaves. CoBLCP

Brilliant Day, A. Charles Tennyson Turner. NOBVV

Brilliant fierce eagles. The Lancet. Denis Devlin. NOIV

Brilliant kernel of the night, The. Robert Louis Stevenson. *Fr.* The Light-Keeper. EBVV

Brilliant minds were legion by the gate of the ancestral kingdom. Wang P'eng-yün, *tr. fr. Chinese by* Kang-i Sun Chang. *Fr.* Random Thoughts upon Reading History, Hastily Composed. WFTU

Brilliant seaside glitters its farewell, The. A Summer Gone. Howard Moss. NePoEA

Brilliant stills of food, the cozy, The. Sonnet: The Ladies' Home Journal. Sandra M. Gilbert. NIP

Brilliantly lighted halls resound. A Ball. Moishe Kulbak, *tr. by* Leonard Wolf. PeBMYV

Brilliantly Speculating. Hanny Michaelis, *tr. fr. Dutch by* James S. Holmes. DuIn

Brindabella. Douglas Stewart. PoAu-2

Bring a leaf to me. Invitation Standing. Paul Blackburn. VGW

Bring a Torch, Jeanette, Isabella.   Nicolas Saboly, *tr. fr. Provençal.*
    OHIP
"Bring an old towel," said Pa.   Buying a Puppy.   Leslie Norris.   ILY
Bring cypress, rosemary and rue.   Grover Cleveland.   Joel Benton.   PAH
Bring Daddy home.   *Unknown.*   OxNR
Bring down the moon for genteel Janet.   Goodbye Now, or, Pardon My
    Gauntlet.   Ogden Nash.   FiBHP
Bring flowers, to strew again.   Ode for Decoration Day.   Henry Peterson.
    OHIP
Bring Good Ale.   *Unknown.   See* Bring Us In Good Ale.
Bring Kateen-beug and Maurya Jude.   Beg-Innish.   J. M. Synge.
    MoBrPo
Bring me a cup of good red wine.   Rinaldo.   Henry Peterson.   AA
Bring me a letter, postman!   The Postman.   Alice Todd.   BoTP
Bring me men to match my mountains.   Sam Walter Foss.   *Fr.* The
    Coming American.   AmFN; BLPA; FaBoBe
Bring me my rose-buds, drawer, come.   A Frolic.   Robert Herrick.
    FaBoEE
Bring Me the Cup.   Moses Ibn Ezra, *tr. fr. Hebrew by* Solomon Solis-
    Cohen.   *Fr.* Wine-Songs.   TrJP
Bring me the sunflower to plant in my garden here.   The Sunflower.
    Eugenio Montale, *tr. by* Maurice English.   PFI
Bring me the sunset in a cup.   Emily Dickinson.   MoAmPo; NOCV
Bring me to the blasted oak.   Crazy Jane and the Bishop.   W. B. Yeats.
    CMoP; LiTM
Bring me wine, but wine which never grew.   Bacchus.   Emerson.
    AmPP; AWP; LiTA; NOBA; OBEV; OxBA; PoEL-4
Bring now the last flower in to warm this room.   At My Mother's
    Bedside.   Marcia Lee Masters.   WPE
Bring, O Morn, thy music! Bring, O night, thy hushes! "Who Wert and
    Art and Evermore Shalt Be."   William Channing Gannett.   TrPWD
Bring out the tall tales now that we told.   Ghost Story.   Dylan Thomas.
    OBCP
Bring that red mouth of yours.   Madrigal de Verano.   Federico García
    Lorca, *tr. by* Paul Blackburn.   ErPo
Bring the biggest bath you've seen.   The Song of the Bath.   Margaret
    Gibbs.   BoTP
Bring the camera closer in.   Focus.   Documentary.   Joseph Stroud.
    NPGG
Bring the comb and play upon it!   Marching Song.   Robert Louis
    Stevenson.   BoTP; FaPON
Bring the Day!   Theodore Roethke.   CRP
Bring the good old bugle, boys, we'll sing another song.   Marching
    through Georgia.   Henry Clay Work.   FaPoR; PAH
Bring the holy crust of bread.   Charmes.   Robert Herrick.   WSC
Bring the North.   William Stafford.   LCAP
Bring the War Home.   William Matthews.   GeTw
Bring the Wine!   Li Po, *tr. fr. Chinese by* Burton Watson.   CoBCP
Bring Them Not Back.   James Benjamin Kenyon.   AA
Bring to me then all passionate, crimson flowers.   She Plans Her Funeral.
    Louise Morey Bowman.   CaP
Bring Torches.   Alexander Maitland Stephen.   CaP
Bring Us In Good Ale.   *Unknown.*   CH; EBEV; FaBoCo; MeEL;
    OAEL-1
    (Bring Good Ale.)   SeCePo
Bring your first song.   Ietaka, *tr. by* Steven D. Carter.   WFTW
Bringer of sun, arrower of evening, star-begetter and moon-riser.   Hymnal.
    Harold Vinal.   TrPWD
Bringing Flowers.   Roberta Spear.   AmPA
Bringing flowers with it.   Kunaikyo, *tr. by* Geoffrey Bownas *and* Anthony
    Thwaite.   PeBJV
Bringing Up Babies.   Roy Fuller.   RHPC
Brisk Chaunticleer his matins had begun.   A Morning-Piece; or, An Hymn
    for the Hay-Makers.   Christopher Smart.   NOEC
Brisk Young Widow, A.   *Unknown.*   OBET
Brissit brawnis and broken banis.   The Bewteis of the Fute-Ball.
    Unknown.   FaBoCo; GoTS; OxBS
Bristol.   Richard Savage.   FaBoPP
Bristol and Clifton.   Sir John Betjeman.   CMoP
Bristol Channel, The.   T. E. Brown.   NOBVV
Bristowe Tragedie: or, The Dethe of Syr Charles Bawdin.   Thomas
    Chatterton.   EnRP; OxBB
Britain.   Goldsmith.   *Fr.* The Travel[l]er; or, A Prospect of Society.
    NOEC
Britannia.   James Thomson.   *See* Seasons, The: Summer.
Britannia and Raleigh.   John Ayloffe.   APAS
Britannia now lament for our hero that is dead.   Lamentation on the Death
    of the Duke of Wellington.   *Unknown.*   OBET
Britannia rules the waves.   On a Parisian Boulevard.   James Kenneth
    Stephen.   *Fr.* England and America.   NOBL
Britannia to Columbia.   Alfred Austin.   *See* What is the voice I hear.
Britannia's Baby.   D. H. Lawrence.   NAs

Britannia's daughters, much more fair than nice.   Edward Young.   *Fr.*
    Love of Fame, the Universal Passion, Satire V.   OBSV
Britannia's gallant streamers.   Yankee Thunders.   *Unknown.*   PAH
Britannia's isles proclaim.   To the First of August.   Ann Plato.   BlSi
Britannia's Pastorals, *sels.*   William Browne.
    "As that Arabian bird (whom all admire)."   *Fr.* I, Song 4.   OAEL-1
    Celadyne's Song.   *Fr.* III, Song 1.   OBS
    Course of the Tavy, The.   *Fr.* I, Song 2.   FaBoPP
    Devonshire Walk, A.   *Fr.* I, Song 5.   FaBoPP
    Frolic Mariners of Devon, The.   *Fr.* II, Song 3.   ChTr
    Gentle Nymphs, Be Not Refusing.   *Fr.* I, Song 3.   EIL
    Glide Soft, Ye Silver Floods.   EIL, II, Song 1.
    "Mounting lark, day's herald, got on wing, The."   *Fr.* I, Song 3.
        PBBP
    "Muses' friend, The (grey-eyed Aurora), yet."   *Fr.* II, Song 2.   JCP
    Praise of Poets.   *Fr.* II, Songs 1 *and* 2.   OBS
    Shall I Tell You Whom I Love?.   *Fr.* II, Song 2.   EIL
    "So shuts the marigold her leaves."   *Fr.* III, Song 1.   ChTr, *short sel..*
        (Memory.)   OBEV
Brither-men wha eftir us live on.   Ballat o the Hingit.   Villon, *tr. by* Tom
    Scott.   OBVE
British Army now carries two rifles, The.   Identification in Belfast (I.R.A.
    Bombing).   Robert Lowell.   OxBC
British Grenadier, The.   *Unknown.*   PAH
British Grenadiers, The.   *Unknown.*   OxBoLi
British Journalist, The.   Humbert Wolfe.   FaBoEE; FiBHP; OxBTC
British Leftish Poetry, 1930-40.   "Hugh MacDiarmid."   CMoP; FaBoTw;
    NoAM
British Lyon Roused, The.   Stephen Tilden.   PAH
British Man-of-War, A.   *Unknown.*   OBET
British Museum Reading Room, The.   Louis MacNeice.   LiTM; MoAB;
    MoBrPo; NOBE; SeCePo; WaP
British Prison Ship, The, *sel.*   Philip Freneau.
    Hospital Prison Ship, The.   *Fr.* III.   AmPP
British, the Ethiopians, and the Italians are squabbling, The.   Our Country
    Is Divided.   Faarah Nuur, *tr. by* B. W. Andrzejewski *and* I. M.
    Lewis.   WTO
British Valor Displayed.   Francis Hopkinson.   *See* Battle of the Kegs,
    The.
Britomart at Isis' Church.   Spenser.   *Fr.* The Faerie Queene, V, 7.   PoE
Britomart in the House of Busirane.   Spenser.   *Fr.* The Faerie Queene:
    The Legend of Britomartis, or of Chastitie, III, 11–12.   FiP
Briton, A.   Herman de Coninck, *tr. fr. Dutch by* Theo Hermans.   DuIn
Britons grown big with pride.   A Poem Containing Some Remarks on the
    Present War.   *Unknown.*   PAH
Brittain's Ida, *sel.*   Phineas Fletcher.
    "Fond men! whose wretched care the life soon ending."   EIL
Brittan's Remembrancer, *sel.*   George Wither.
    "I know that if thou please thou canst provide."   SeCV-1
Brittle beauty [*or* beautie], that nature made so frail[e].   Earl of Surrey.
    AAS; EnLoPo; SiPS; TrGrPo
    (Frailty and Hurtfulness of Beauty, The.)   HoPM
Brittle hollow stalks of sunflower, The.   Nature Green Shit.   Gary
    Snyder.   LCAP
Brittle streets, with midnight walking flung, The.   Sonnet on a Still Night.
    J. V. Cunningham.   PoA
"Broad acres, sir."   You hear them in my talk.   At Knaresborough.
    Donald Davie.   NePoEA
Broad and ample he warms himself.   *Unknown, tr. by* Thomas Kinsella.
    NOIV
Broad and far-reaching, the level plain.   Rhyme-Prose on the Desolate
    City.   Pao Chao, *tr. by* Burton Watson.   CoBCP
Broad August burns in milky skies.   Day-Dreams.   William Canton.
    NOBVV
Broad-Ax, The.   Walt Whitman.   *Fr.* Song of the Broad-Ax.   MoAmPo
Broad-backed hippopotamus, The.   The Hippopotamus.   T. S. Eliot.
    AWP; HoPM; LiTB; NAEL-2; OBMV; VGW
Broad bars of sunset-slanted gold.   Ballad of the Faded Field.   Robert
    Burns Wilson.   AA
Broad-based, broad-fronted, bounteous, multiform.   Ben Jonson.
    Swinburne.   *Fr.* Sonnets of English Dramatic Poets.   Son
Broad beach, The/ Sea wind and the sea's irregular rhythm.   Afternoon:
    Amagansett Beach.   John Hall Wheelock.   BoNaP; PoRA
Broad Gulf-Stream, great stretch of time.   Separate Time.   Anna Hajnal,
    tr. by Edwin Morgan.   MHuP
Broad is the gate and wide the path.   The Bath.   Harry Graham.   CenHV
Broad Is the Road.   Isaac Watts.   AH, *with music;* AmFP
Broad leaves turn themselves on the trees.   Mother Dies.   Saito Mokichi,
    tr. by Hiroaki Sato.   FCEI
Broad Meadow.   Alain Delahaye, *tr. fr. French by* Paul Auster.
    RHTwFP
Broad shadows fall. On all the mountain side.   A Sunset at Les
    Éboulements.   Archibald Lampman.   OBCV

Broad sun, The. The Far-Farers. Robert Louis Stevenson. BoTP
Broadax. Nishiwaki Junzaburo, *tr. fr. Japanese by* Hiroaki Sato. FCEI
Broads. David R. Slavitt. BXAP
Broadway. Carl Sandburg. AiP
Broadway. Walt Whitman. NAAL-1
Brobdingnag. Adrien Stoutenburg. NYBP
Brocade and rush hat [*or* sedge-hat that] you loved, The. Emperor
    Go-Shirakawa, *tr. fr. Japanese. Fr.* Ryojin Hisho. FCEI, *tr. by*
    Hiroaki Sato; PeBJV, *tr. by* Geoffrey Bownas *and* Anthony Thwaite.
Brocade sedge-hat you loved, The. Emperor Go-Shirakawa. *See* Ryojin
    Hisho: Brocade and rush hat you loved, The.
Brocaded Sash. *Unknown, tr. fr. Japanese by* Hiroaki Sato. FCEI
Brocades left at the treetops ceased to be, The. Princess Shikishi, *tr. fr.*
    Japanese by Hiroaki Sato. *Fr.* Seventy-eight Tanka. FCEI
Brocadós and Damasks, and Tabbies, and Gawzes. An Excellent New
    Song on a Seditious Pamphlet. Swift. CoMu
Brock. Paul Muldoon. NoAM
Brocks snuffle from their holt within. The Badgers. Eden Phillpotts.
    BoTP
Brockton Murder; a Page out of William James, The. Knute Skinner.
    TW
Broken, The. W. S. Merwin. LCAP
Broken. Zana. TSM
Broken altar, Lord, thy servant rears, A. The Altar. George Herbert.
    HoPM; InPS; JCP; NAEL-1; OAEL-1; SeCP; SeCV-1; TrCP; TrGrPo
Broken Appointment, A. Thomas Hardy. GBL; NAEL-2; NoAM;
    NOBVV; NoP
Broken Bowl, A. Chan Ch'e, *tr. fr. Chinese by* Dominic Cheung. IFON
Broken Bowl, The. James Merrill. PoA
Broken-down Digger, The. *Unknown.* PoAu-1
Broken-down Squatter, The. *Unknown.* PoAu-1
Broken-down taboos, The. Paul Celan, *tr. by* Beth Bjorklund. CoAuP
Broken-Face Gargoyles. Carl Sandburg. AmPP; MoAmPo; OxBA
Broken faces. Vestige. Jung Han-mo, *tr. by* Koh Chang-soo. ACKP
Broken from the bursting bough. The Apple. Ray Smith. TrCP
Broken Girth, The. Robert Graves. BIrV
Broken Glass, A, *sels.* Zsuzsa Beney, *tr. fr. Hungarian by* Jascha
    Kessler. FOC
Breaking, The.
Color, The.
Reflections.
Broken Heart, The. Thomas Beedome. OBS
Broken Heart, The. John Donne. EBEV
Broken Heart, The, *sels.* John Ford.
    "Beasts onely capable of sense, enjoy." *Fr.* IV, ii. PoEL-2
    Can You Paint a Thought?. *Fr.* III, ii. InvP; PoEL-2
    "Oh [*or* O], no more, no more, too late." *Fr.* IV, iii. GBL; PoEL-2
        (Love's Martyrs.) NOBE
        (Oh No More, No More.) ELP
        (Song: "Oh no more, no more, too late.") OBS; OxBSP; SeCePo
    "Glories, pleasures, pomps, delights, and ease." *Fr.* V, iii. OBS
Broken Heart. Henrietta Cordelia Ray. CBWP-3
Broken Heart, Broken Machine. Richard E. Grant. PoBA
Broken-hearted Gardener, The. *Unknown.* ChTr; GBP
Broken Home, The. James Merrill. HAP; HCAP; MoP; NAAL-2;
    NoAM; NOBA; NYBP; PPP; WeW
Broken Home. William Stafford. NNaP
Broken in pieces all asunder. Affliction ("Broken in pieces all asunder").
    George Herbert. JCP
Broken Lampstand, The. Wu Wei-yeh, *tr. fr. Chinese by* Jonathan
    Chaves. CoBLCP
Broken Mirror, The. Jacques Prévert, *tr. fr. French by* Michael Benedikt.
    POS
Broken mirror, The. X, Oh X. Mark Simpson. GOYP
Broken Off by the Music. John Yau. EOEF
Broken pillar of the wing jags from the clotted shoulder, The. Hurt
    Hawks. Robinson Jeffers. AmPP; CMoP; FYAP; FYAP; LiTA;
    LiTM; MoAB; MoAmPo; MoP; NAAL-2; NoAM; NOBA; NoP;
    OxBA; PrIm; RB; TAP; UnPo
Broken plaster wings. Caged Wings: First Impressions from the Boat
    Alcatraz Island/ Indian Land, 1970. Wendy Rose. NOVW
Broken Sky. Carl Sandburg. PCP
Broken sods, a whipped flag, The. A Burial. Seamus Deane. CIP
Broken String, The. *Unknown, tr. fr. Bushman by* W. H. I. Bleek.
    PeSA
Broken the pot, there's still the jar. Loves of the Birds. *Malay Oral*
    Tradition, tr. by R. J. Wilkinson *and* R. O. Winstedt. WTO
Broken Token, The. *Unknown. See* Pretty Fair Maid, A.
Broken Tower, The. Hart Crane. AmPP; CMoP; LiTM; MoAB;
    MoAmPo; NoAM; NOBA; NoP; OxBA; TrGrPo
Broken Treaties, FBI, What civil rights?! Keep a Dime. Debra Swallow.
    GOS

Broken wagon wheel that rots away beside the river, A. Pioneers.
    Charles Badger, Jr. Clark. FaBoBe
Broken were our axes. *Unknown, tr. by* Arthur Waley. BoS
Brome, brome on hill. The Broomfield Hill. *Unknown.* CH
Broncho Dan halts midway of the stream. A Health at the Ford. Robert
    Cameron Rogers. AA; FaBoBe
Bronco Busting, Event #1. May Swenson. ASP; RR
Brontosaurus. Gail Kredenser. RHPC
Bronx. Joseph Rodman Drake. AnAmPo
Bronze god running, The. At Guaracara Park. Eric Roach. PBCV
Bronze Head, A. W. B. Yeats. LiTB
Bronze of bells aroused by the night sky, The. Christmas. Mani Leib,
    tr. by John Hollander. PeBMYV
Bronze Rider, Wellington, The. Robin Hyde. ATNZ
Bronze soldier hitches a bronze cape, The. In Memoriam Francis
    Ledwidge. Seamus Heaney. CIP; FaBCIP; NoAM
Bronze Statuette of Kwan-yin, A. Charles Wharton Stork. GoYe
Bronzer than leaf green, see, the abrupt plover. 1943. Naomi Mitchison.
    CN
Bronzes. Carl Sandburg. EyDe
Bronzeville Man with a Belt in the Back. Gwendolyn Brooks. IDB;
    PoBA
Brooch, The. Chang Hsian-hua, *tr. fr. Chinese by* Valeria Doran. WCI
Brooding Afternoon in July. Andreas Okopenko, *tr. fr. German by* Beth
    Bjorklund. *Fr.* Summer Fragments, III. CoAuP
Brooding Grief. D. H. Lawrence. CMoP; PoE
Brooding Likeness. Louise Glück. MAYP
Brooding of Sigurd, The. William Morris. *Fr.* The Story of Sigurd the
    Volsung. SeCePo
Brooding on the eightieth letter of *Fors Clavigera*. Geoffrey Hill. *Fr.*
    Mercian Hymns, XXV. HAP; PoE
Brooding upon its unexerted power. Gas and Hot Air. Morris Bishop.
    OBAL
Brook, The. William Wilberforce Lord. AA
Brook, The. Tennyson. *Fr.* The Brook; an Idyl. BoNaP; BoTP; FaBV;
    FaPON; GN; GoJo; PWR
    (Brook's Song, The.) FaBoBe; FaFP
Brook, The. Edward Thomas. OAEL-2
Brook, The, *sel.* William Bull Wright.
    "Through his million veins are poured." AA
Brook glides on to the river, The. Reverie. Henrietta Cordelia Ray.
    CBWP-3
Brook in February, The. Sir Charles G. D. Roberts. BoNaP; OBCV
Brook in the City, A. Robert Frost. OxBA
Brook in Winter, The. James Russell Lowell. *Fr.* The Vision of Sir
    Launfal, Prelude to Pt. II. GN
Brook Song. James Herbert Morse. AA
Brook, The; an Idyl, *sel.* Tennyson.
    Brook, The. BoNaP; FaBV; FaPON; GN; GoJo
    (Brook's Song, The.) FaBoBe; FaFP
Brook, would thou couldst flow. Brook Song. James Herbert Morse.
    AA
Brookfield, *sel.* William E. Marshall.
    "But see this happy village festival." CaP
Brooklet, The. Joseph Skipsey. PF
Brooklyn at Santiago, The. Wallace Rice. PAH
Brooklyn Bridge, The. Edna Dean Proctor. PAH
Brooklyn Bridge. Sir Charles G. D. Roberts. PAH
Brooklyn Heights. John Wain. LiTM; OBTV; OxBTC
Brooklyn Theater Fire, The. *Unknown.* AmFP
Brook's Song, The. Tennyson. *See* I come from haunts of coot and
    hern.
Broom Balancing. Kathleen Fraser. RHPC
Broom, Green Broom. *Unknown.* LiTB; OxBoLi; PoRA
Broom of Cowdenknows, The, A *and* B *vers. Unknown.* ESPB
Broom out the floor now, lay the fender by. June. Francis Ledwidge.
    BIrV; NOIV
Broom pods crackling in the heat. A Picture. D. C. Cuthbertson.
    PoSH
Broom Squire's Song, The. *Unknown.* OxNR
Broomfield Hill, The. *Unknown.* AmFP; CH; ESPB, A *and* B *vers.*;
    OxBB, *with music.*
Broomfield Wager, The. *Unknown.* OBET
Brooms. Charles Simic. AmPA; LCAP; NNaP; NNaP, *early version*
Broomstick bat, The. Stickball. Virginia Schonborg. RHPC
Broomstick Train, The, *sel.* Oliver Wendell Holmes.
    "Look out! Look out, boys! Clear the track!" FaPON
Brother, The. Peter Everwine. FYAP; NNaP
Brother. Jewel C. Latimore. JB
Brother, The. Semion Yakovlevich Nadson, *tr. fr. Russian by* H.
    Badanes. TrJP
Brother Alberto, one hot summer day. Pietro Aretino. PeHV

Brother and Sister. "Lewis Carroll." ChTr; FaBoNo
Brother and Sister. "George Eliot."
  Sels.
  "But sudden came the barge's pitch-black prow." NOBVV
  I Cannot Choose but Think upon the Time. *Fr.* I. GN; Son
  "Long hears have left their writing on my brow." *Fr.* II. GN
  "Our brown canal was endless to my thought." NOBVV
  "Our mother bade us keep the trodden ways." *Fr.* III. GN
  School Parted Us. *Fr.* XI. Son
  "Those long days measured by my little feet." NOBVV
  "We had the selfsame world enlarged for each." *Fr.* IX. GN
Brother and Sisters. Judith Wright. FaBoWP
Brother Astolfo sated appetite. Pietro Aretino. PeHV
Brother Baptis' on Woman Suffrage. Rosalie Jonas. BlSi
Brother, Can You Spare a Dime? E. Y. Harburg. SaC
Brother, come! And What Shall You Say? Joseph Seamon Cotter, Jr..
  BANP; CDC; PoBA; PoNe
Brother Fire. Louis MacNeice. MoAB; MoP; NoAM; NOBE; WaaP
Brother Green. *Unknown.* AmFP
Brother, Hast Thou Wandered Far. James Freeman Clarke. AH
Brother-in-Law, The. Larry Rubin. MT; TW
Brother Jonathan, Brother Kafka. Vincent O'Sullivan.
  Sels.
  "Figure who stands on the beach, A." *Fr.* 27. PeNZ
  "Last things/ the turning leaves slip in the wind." *Fr.* 40. PeNZ
  "Magpie vicious or mute on his frozen tree, The." *Fr.* 42. ATNZ
  "On the day my father died a flame-tree." *Fr.* 8. ATNZ
  "There is a day when elaborate weathers ease down." *Fr.* 43. ATNZ
  "To be in a place for spring and not have lived its winter." *Fr.* 13.
    ATNZ; PeNZ
  "Young bee falls between my window, A." *Fr.* 32. ATNZ
Brother Jonathan's Lament for Sister Caroline. Oliver Wendell Holmes.
  PAH
Brother of mine, good monk with cowled head. Thomas à Kempis.
  Lizette Woodworth Reese. AA
Brother Symmes conversed with her on the ship. Anne Stanford. *Fr.*
  The Covenant of Grace. CRP
Brother, Though from Yonder Sky. James Henry Bancroft. AH
Brother to the firefly. Morning Light. Mary Effie Lee Newsome.
  AmNP; CDC; PoBA; PoNe
Brotherhood. José Luis Vega, *tr. fr. Spanish by* Julio Marzán. InW
Brotherhood. "J. J. W." PeHV
Brotherhood is not by the blood certainly, The. Speech to Those Who Say
  Comrade. Archibald MacLeish. OxBA
Brothers. Robert Currie. Psk
Brothers. James Weldon Johnson. BANP
Brothers, The. Edwin Muir. GTBS-P; HeIP; Mes; NoP; PrIm
Brothers. Dan Pagis. *See* Abel was pure and woolly.
Brothers, The. Charles Sprague. AA
Brothers/ brothers/ everywhere. Utopia. Jewel C. Latimore. BPo
Brothers and men that shall after us be. Ballad of the Gibbet. Villon, *tr.*
  by Andrew Lang. AWP
Brothers, blessed in number. Montefiore in Vilna. Leyzer Volf, *tr. by*
  Robert Friend. PeBMYV
Brothers in blood! They who this wrong began. To the United States of
  America. Robert Bridges. PAH
Brothers Lacôte, The. Louis Aragon, *tr. fr. French by* Michael Benedikt.
  POS
Brothers, my teeth hurt. Strictly for Posterity. Charles Simic. NNaP
Brothers Together in Winter. Harley Elliott. NeAC
Brothers, we glory in this blinding hour. Three Poems for Kaddish.
  Robert Lowell. PPR
Brought back from the tedium of dying. Return of a Popular Statesman.
  Vincent Buckley. CBAP
Brought here in slave ships and pitched overboard. Love Your Enemy.
  Yusef Iman. BPo; TTY
Brought low in Kyoto. How to Survive Nuclear War. Maxine W.
  Kumin. PPR
Brought to bed by sickness, cut off from men. Replying to a Poem from
  My Cousin Hui-lien. Hsieh Ling-yün, *tr. by* Burton Watson.
  CoBCP
Brought up as I was to ask of the weather. Point Grey. Daryl Hine.
  NOBC
Broughty Wa's. *Unknown.* ESPB
Brow, brow, brenty. *Unknown.* OxNR
Brow of Nephin, The. *Unknown, tr. fr. Modern Irish by* Douglas Hyde.
  AnIL
Brow of night is stricken and turns frosty, The. Pheasant. Sándor Rákos,
  tr. by Alan Dixon. MHuP
Brown Adam. *Unknown.* ESPB; OxBB
Brown and furry. The Caterpillar. Christina Rossetti. *Fr.* Sing-Song.
  BoTP; FaPON; GoJo; OxBChV; RHPC

Brown arms of the mothering plateau, The. The Lowveld. Charles
  Eglington. PeSA
Brown Baby Blues. Una Marson. PBCV
Brown Baby Cobina, with his large black velvet eyes. Baby Cobina.
  Gladys May Casely Hayford. CDC
Brown Bear, The. Mary Austin. FaPON
Brown Boy to Brown Girl. Countee Cullen. PoBA
Brown, brittle, wait-a-bit weeds. The Indian Cave Jerry Ramsey Found.
  William Stafford. NoAM
Brown bunny sits inside his burrow. The Rabbit. Edith King. BoTP
Brown-dappled fawn, The. The Fawn in the Snow. William Rose Benét.
  MoAmPo
Brown earth-line meets gray heaven. In November. Anne Reeve
  Aldrich. AA
Brown enormous odor he lived by, The. The Prodigal. Elizabeth
  Bishop. CoAP; InvP; LCAP; LiTM; MoAB; NYBP; PPP; TwCP
Brown-faced nurse has murmured something unintelligible, The.
  Microcosmos. Susan Miles. OxBTC
Brown Family, The. Colleen Thibaudeau. NOBC
Brown field jabbed a finger into the grove of cottonwoods, A. Firefly.
  George Uba. BrSi
Brown Frog, The. Mary K. Robinson. BoTP
Brown Girl, The. *Unknown.* ELP; ESPB, (A *and* B *vers.*); OBET
Brown girl chanting Te Deums on Sunday. Ruth. Pauli Murray. NMM
Brown Girl Dead, A. Countee Cullen. TAP
Brown in the snow, a car with a heater. Strangers. William Stafford.
  NNaP
Brown Is My Love. *Unknown.* EIL; GBL; OBSC
Brown like Us. Gary Soto. NPGG
Brown lived at such a lofty farm. Brown's Descent; or, The Willy-Nilly
  Slide. Robert Frost. MoAmPo; PoRA
Brown o' San Juan. "Home, Sweet Home," with Variations ("Brown o'
  San Juan"). H. C. Bunner. *Fr.* Home. OBAL
Brown of Ossawatomie. Whittier. PAH
Brown old man with a green thumb, A. He Was. Richard Wilbur.
  SaC
Brown owl sits in the ivy bush, The. The Great Brown Owl. Jane
  Euphemia Browne. OxBChV
Brown Oxen Knoll. Chu Yi-tsun, *tr. fr. Chinese by* Irving Lo. *Fr.*
  Quatrains on Peking's Western Suburb, VI. WFTU
Brown paper worn next to the skin. B. L. Howarth. BXAP
Brown Penny. W. B. Yeats. BoLoP; CMoP; ELP; FaBoCh; LLLT
Brown River, Smile. Jean Toomer. *Fr.* The Blue Meridian. AmNP;
  PoBA
Brown Robin. *Unknown.* ESPB; OxBB
Brown Robyn's [*or* Robin's] Confession. *Unknown.* ACP; CH; ESPB;
  GBP
Brown, sad-coloured hillside, where the soil, A. The Sower. Sir Charles
  G. D. Roberts. CaP; OBCV
Brown seas, black seas, seas of marvel. The Seyes. Raymond Queneau,
  tr. by Teo Savory. RHTwFP
Brown semicolons move doggedly. The Ant Trap. Joe Rosenblatt.
  NOBC
Brown Thrush, The. Lucy Larcom. BoTP; FaPON; OBCA
Brownies' Celebration, The. Palmer Cox. OBCA
Browning. Robert Louis Stevenson. NOBVV
Browning at Asolo. Robert Underwood Johnson. AA
Browning makes the verses. Browning. Robert Louis Stevenson.
  NOBVV
Browning, old fellow. In a Copy of Browning. Bliss Carman.
  AnAmPo
Brownish green moss has grown into the side of gray blue rock. This
  Rocky Land. Väinö Kirstinä, *tr. by* Aili Jarvenpa. SOP
Brown's Descent; or, The Willy-Nilly Slide. Robert Frost. MoAmPo;
  PoRA
Brown's wife, herself a normal type. Family Life. Allan M. Laing.
  FiBHP
Browny Bee. Irene F. Pawsey. BoTP
Browny Hen, The. Irene F. Pawsey. BoTP
Browsing in *Roget's Thesaurus.* R. P. Dickey. SoTCo
Br-r-r-am-m-m, rackety-am-m, om, am. What the Motorcycle Said.
  Mona Van Duyn. NIP
Bruadar and Smith and Glinn. A Curse. *Unknown, tr. by* Douglas Hyde.
  BIrV
Bruce, The, *sels.* John Barbour.
  Before Bannockburn. OxBS
  Bruce Addresses His Army. GoTS
  Bruce Consults His Men. GoTS
  Freedom [*or* Fredome]. FaBoCh; GoTS; OBEV; OxBS; TrGrPo
  "Storys to rede ar delitabill." OxBS
Bruce and the Spider. Bernard Barton. BeLS
Bruce Consults His Men. John Barbour. *Fr.* The Bruce. GoTS
Bruckner. James Camp. MAT

Bruised by the masseur's final whack. Health and Fitness. J. B. Morton. FaBoCo

Bruised Titans, The. Keats. *Fr.* Hyperion; a Fragment. OBNC

Bruisers of England, the men of tremendous renown, The. The Fancy. William Rose Benét. SD

Brumana. James Elroy Flecker. BrPo

Brummell at Calais. John Glassco. MoCV

Brunanburg. *Unknown, tr. fr. Anglo-Saxon by* Kemp Malone. PoE

Brush in rocks, draw a stream. Yün Shou-p'ing, *tr. fr. Chinese by* Jonathan Chaves. Landscape. CoBLCP

Brush Up Your Shakespeare. Cole Porter. OBAL

Brushed by the shadows of the dead. Dusk. Guillaume Apollinaire, *tr. by* Dudley Fitts. RHTwFP

Brushes and paints are all I have. Quatrains. Gwendolyn B. Bennett. CDC

Brushing aside the clouds. Miura Chora, *tr. fr. Japanese by* Hiroaki Sato. *Fr.* Sixteen Hokku. FCEI

Brushing away the dust, I opened the broken box. In a Book-Box I Found the Lost Manuscript of a Poem. Chang Yü, *tr. by* Jonathan Chaves. CoBLCP

Brushing back the curls from your famous brow. The Copulating Gods. Carolyn Kizer. CAPP; Prf

Brushwood bones. Boncho, *tr. by* Geoffrey Bownas *and* Anthony Thwaite. PeBJV

Brusque shoulders and bluff beard. Tudor Portrait. Richmond Lattimore. EyDe

Brussels and Oxford. William Hurrell Mallock. EBVV

Brussels in Winter. W. H. Auden. OBTV; OxBTC

Brut, The, *sel.* Layamon.
　Passing of Arthur, The. PoE

Bruton Town. *Unknown.* EnSB

Bryan, Bryan, Bryan, Bryan. Vachel Lindsay. CMoP; LiTA; OxBA; OxBoLi

Bryan O'Lynn. *Unknown. See* Brian O'Linn.

Bryan's Last Battle. *Unknown.* AmFP

Bryant. James Russell Lowell. *Fr.* A Fable for Critics. NOBA; TAP

Brynbwrla. Kingsley Amis. *Fr.* The Evans Country. NOBL

B's the Bus. Phyllis McGinley. *Fr.* All around the Town. FaPON

Buachaille Etive Mor and Buachaille Etive Beag. Naomi Mitchison. PoSH

Bubble, The. John Banister Tabb. AA

Bubble; a Song, The. Robert Herrick. CaPo

Bubble Burs, De. Fyna Dowe. WS

Bubble Gum. Nina Payne. RHPC

Bubble still a bubble now de bubble burs, De. Bubble Burs, De. Fyna Dowe. WS

Bubbles. Bill Berkson. UL

Bubbles. George Garrett. MT

Bubbles. L. Nicholson. BoTP

Bubbles. Carl Sandburg. TDD

Bubbles soar and die in the sterile bottle, The. Notes for the Chart in 306. Ogden Nash. NYBP

Bubbling Wine. Abu Zakariya, *tr. fr. Arabic by* A. J. Arberry. TTY

Bucharest. Veijo Meri, *tr. fr. Finnish by* Aili Jarvenpa. SOP

Buchenwald, 1945. Ai. *Fr.* He Kept On Burning, II. AnAn

Buchlyvie. *Unknown.* GBP; TW

Buck. Michael S. S. Harper. CAPP

Buck has a headache. Tony ate. The Garden of Earthly Delights. Charles Simic. NoP

Buck Up. Felicia Lamport. SoTCo

Buckdancer's Choice. James Dickey. HeIP; NoAM; NOBA; NoP; NYBP; PoNe

Buckee Bene. *Unknown.* CH

Bucket, The. Samuel Woodworth. *See* How dear to my heart. . . .

Bucket of Sea-Serpents. Howard Ant. GoYe

Buckin' Horse Ballet. Lucky Whipple. CowP

Bucking Bronco. *Unknown.* AmFP

Buckingham Palace. A. A. Milne. OxBChV; PDV

Buckinghamshire. *Unknown.* GBP

Buckle the spur and belt again. Lofty Lane. Edwin Gerard. PoAu-1

Bucko-Mate. Samuel Schierloh. GoYe

Buck's Elegy, The. *Unknown.* OBET

Buckskin Flats. Gordon Eastman. CowP

Bucolic. Simon Rae. NPo

Bucolic Eclogues, *sel.* Ethel Anderson.
　Waking, Child, While You Slept. PoAu-2; WPE

Bucolic Funeral. Justo Sierra, *tr. fr. Spanish by* Samuel Beckett. MexPo

Bud, The/ stands for all things. Saint Francis and the Sow. Galway Kinnell. CAPP; FYAP; InPK; NIP; RB

Bud fantasies, dreams of an ear of corn. Paean to Eve's Apple. James Liddy. CIP

Budapest. Judd Teller, *tr. fr. Yiddish by* Grace Schulman. PeBMYV

Budapest Elegy. István Vas, *tr. fr. Hungarian by* Edwin Morgan. MHuP

Buddha. Arno Holz, *tr. fr. German by* William Ellery Leonard. AWP

Buddha. Herman Melville. HeIP

Buddha at Kamakura. Francis Hastings Kipling. OBTV

Buddha himself, The. *Unknown, tr. by* Geoffrey Bownas *and* Anthony Thwaite. PeBJV

Buddha in the Womb, The. Erica Jong. MAYP

Buddha is not more strange. In a Warm Bath. Carl Rakosi. TAP

Buddha preached the twelve divisions. Ryokan, *tr. by* Burton Watson. JLIC-2

Buddha's Birthday: April 8, 1819. Issa, *tr. fr. Japanese by* Nobuyuki Yuasa. *Fr.* Oraga Haru. OFD

Buddha's Death Day: February 15, 1815. Issa, *tr. fr. Japanese by* Nobuyuki Yuasa. *Fr.* Oraga Haru. OFD

Buddhist monastery across a stone bridge, A. I Went to Gold Mountain to Visit a Ch'an Master. Mo Shih-lung, *tr. by* Jonathan Chaves. CoBLCP

Buddhist Monk Cut and Burned His Own Flesh to Make the Rains Stop, A. Hsü Wei, *tr. fr. Chinese by* Jonathan Chaves. CoBLCP

Buddhist Priest, A. Ho Xuan Huong, *tr. fr. Vietnamese by* Nguyen Ngoc Bich *and* Burton Raffel. PBWP

Budding floweret blushes at the light, The. Thomas Chatterton. *Fr.* Aella; a Tragycal Enterlude.
　(Mynstrelles Songe ("Boddynge flourettes bloshes atte the lyghte.").) EnRP
　(Song of the Three Minstrels.) TrGrPo

Budding grass is like a soft mist, The. Song of the Southern Country. Ou-yang Chiung, *tr. by* Lois Fusek. ATF

Budding plums of Yüeh are bursting open in the chill, The. Deva-like Barbarian. Ho Ning, *tr. by* Lois Fusek. ATF

Budding Spring. Jack Lindsay. PoAu-1

Budding-Time Too Brief. Evaleen Stein. AA

Budding wild plum has yet to burst, The. In Praise of Merit. Mao Wen-hsi, *tr. by* Lois Fusek. ATF

Buddy and I left home, A. Young Fellers. R. O. Munn. CowP

Budgie Finds His Voice. Wendy Cope. FaBoPa

Budging the sluggard ripples of the Somme. Hospital Barge at Cérisy. Wilfred Owen. OBTV; RB

Budmouth Dears. Thomas Hardy. *Fr.* The Dynasts, *pt.* III, Act II, sc. i. CH

Buds. Elizabeth Jane Coatsworth. TSS

Buds from winter's frost-work lift, The. The Coming of Spring. Henrietta Cordelia Ray. CBWP-3

Buen Matina. Sir John Salusbury. ElL

Buena Vista. Albert Pike. PAH

"Bueno," Which in Spanish Means Good. Nyle A. Henderson. CowP

Buffalo. Florence Earle Coates. PAH

Buffalo. Roy Daniells. CaP

Buffalo. Henry Dumas. PoBA

Buffalo. Charles Eglington. PeSA

Buffalo, The. Marianne Moore. PoA

Buffalo. *Unknown, tr. fr. Yoruba by* Ulli Beier. *Fr.* Hunter Poems of the Yoruba. RB

Buffalo Bill's [Defunct]. E. E. Cummings. AmPP; CMoP; HeIP; InPK; LiTA; NAAL-2; NOBA; OBD; OxBSP; PoE; RB; TAP; VGW

Buffalo Boy. Lance Henson. STP

Buffalo Boy. *Unknown.* AmFP

Buffalo breathed quietly inside, The. The Crow-Children Walk My Circles in the Snow. Ray A. Young Bear. CDW

Buffalo, buffalo, buffalo, buffalo. Death Chant. Peter Bluecloud. VoR

Buffalo Creek. John Le Gay Brereton. PoAu-1

Buffalo Dusk. Carl Sandburg. GOA; OBCA; PDV; RFM; RHPC

Buffalo—Isle of Wight Power Cable. Anselm Hollo. PoM

Buffalo Marrow on Black. Lance Henson. STE

Buffalo Skinners, The. *Unknown.* AmFP; AS, *with music;* GBP; RB

Buffalo Trace. Robert Morgan. GeTw

Buffaloes are gone, The. Buffalo Dusk. Carl Sandburg. GOA; OBCA; PDV; RFM; RHPC

Buffel's Kop. Roy Campbell. PeSA

Buffeted and blown. Emperor Fushimi, *tr. by* Steven D. Carter. WFTW

Bufo. Pope. *Fr.* Epistle to Dr. Arbuthnot. OBSV

Bug, The. Marjorie Barrows. RHPC

Bug, flower, bird on slipware fired and fluted. Syrinx. James Merrill. HCAP

Bug in a Jug. *Unknown.* RHPC

Bug Sat in a Silver Flower, A. Karla Kuskin. RHPC

Bugle calls coiling through the rocky valley. A Northern Legion. Sir Herbert Read. SeCePo

Bugle Song. Tennyson. *See* Princess, The: Splendor Falls [on Castle Walls], The.

Bugle Song of Peace. Thomas Curtis Clark. WBLP; WGRP

Bugle sounds the measured call to prayers, The. Sunday: New Guinea. Karl Shapiro. AmFN

Bugler boy from barrack (it is over the hill), A. The Bugler's First Communion. Gerard Manley Hopkins. NoAM; PeHV

Bugler sent a call of high romance, The. The Last Post. Robert Graves. MMA

Bugler's First Communion, The. Gerard Manley Hopkins. NoAM; PeHV

Bugles!/ And the great nation thrills and leaps to arms! The Call of the Bugles. Richard Hovey. AA; AnAmPo

Bugs, sels. Mary Ann Hoberman. OBCA
    Cockroach.
    Combinations.

Bugs. Will Stokes. MoShBr

Bugville team was surely up against a rocky game, The. Casey—Twenty Years Later. S. P. McDonald. BLPA

Buick. Karl Shapiro. CMoP; HoPM; MoAB; RR; TrGrPo

Buik of Alexander, The, sel. John Barbour.
    Prologue to the Avowis of Alexander. OxBS

"Build at Kallundborg by the sea." Kallundborg Church. Whittier. BeLS

Build for yourself a strong-box. Then Laugh. Bertha Adams Backus. BLPA; PWR; WBLP

"Build me a nation," said the Lord. Then and Now. Frances Ellen Watkins Harper. PWR

Builder, The. Francis Sherman. CaP

Builder builded a temple, A. Two Temples. Hattie Vose Hall. BLPA

Builder, in building the little house. The Kitchen Chimney. Robert Frost. EyDe

Builder of Continents, The. "Ping Hsin," tr. fr. Chinese by Kai-yu Hsu. Fr. The Stars. WPOW

Builders, The, sel. Henry van Dyke.
    "Grant us the knowledge that we need." TrPWD

Builders, The. Longfellow. AnAmPo; FaFP; OHFP; PWR

Builders, The. Judith Wright. SeCePo

Builder's Lesson, A. John Boyle O'Reilly. PoLF; PWR

Building, The. As You Come In. Anne Marriott. NOBC

Building. I. E. Dickenga. PWR

Building a poem is like building a house. To Build a Poem. Christine E. Hemp. GOYP

Building a Sano boat-bridge. Teika, tr. fr. Japanese by Hiroaki Sato. Fr. A Compendium of Good Tanka. FCEI

Building a Skyscraper. James S. Tippett. OnUR

Building Bridges. Solomon Mahaka. WMBCH

Building for Eternity. N. B. Sargent. BLPA

Building in Stone. Sylvia Townsend Warner. MoBrPo

Building of a New Church, The. Unknown. EyDe

Building of the Ship, The, sels. Longfellow.
    "Then the Master." NAAL-1; OHFP
    "Thou, too, sail on, O Ship of State!" MOS
    (O Ship of State.) FaFP
    (Republic, The.) AA; OPP; PAH; WGRP
    (Sail On, O Ship of State.) FaPON
    (Ship of State, The.) FaBoBe; OHIP

Building of the Skyscraper, The. George Oppen. GOA

Building Programme. Kendrick Smithyman. ATNZ

Building Society Blues. Roger Roughton. EAS

Building the Barricade. Anna Swirszczynska, tr. fr. Polish by Magnus Jan Krynski and Robert A. Maguire. PwPP

Building the Bridge. Will Allen Dromgoole. WeW

Buildings, The. Wendell Berry. EyDe

Buildings are all womanly, The. Their roofs. The Buildings. Wendell Berry. EyDe

Built Bridge, Footnotes, A. Carolyn Stoloff. SoTCo

Buke of the Howlat, The, sel. Sir Richard Holland.
    "Roye Robert the Bruss the rayke he avowit, The." OxBS
    (Douglas and the Bruce's Heart.) OxBLMV

Bulb, A. Richard Kendall Munkittrick. AA

Bulbs strung along. Christmas Lights. Valerie Worth. PChr

Bulbul, The ("The bulbul hummeth like a book"). Sir Owen Seaman. NA

Bulbul in the garden, The. Khwaja Haider Ali Atish, tr. by Ahmed Ali. GoT

Bulge, The. George Johnston. MoCV

Bulge of light sits on that shelf, A. A Truth in Two Halves. Norman MacCaig. PoPo

Bulging rampart streaked with pink and jade, The. The Watchers. Charles Spear. PeNZ

Bulkeley, Hunt, Willard, Hosmer, Meriam, Flint. Hamatreya. Emerson. AmPP; HeIP; MAT; NOBA; NoP; OxBA; PoEL-4; Prlm; TAP

Bull, The. Ralph Hodgson. BrPo; LiTM; MoAB; MoBrPo; OBMV; OxBTC

Bull, The. Freda Laughton. NeIP

Bull, A. Ahmad Nadeem Qasmi, tr. fr. Urdu by Mahmood Jamal. PBMUP

Bull, The. Victoria Mary Sackville-West. WPE

Bull, The. William Carlos Williams. LiTM; NoP; TwCP

Bull, The. Judith Wright. GrPl; PoAu-2

Bull be took bad, Th', says old Sam—wunnot fancy 'is fodder. From My Rural Pen. T. S. Watt. FiBHP

Bull Calf, The. Irving Layton. InPK; OBCV

Bull-Dog! Cole Porter. ASP

Bull-Fights. H. Leivick, tr. fr. Yiddish by Benjamin and Barbara Harshav. AYP

Bull Moses, The. Ted Hughes. NoP

Bull Rider's Advice, The. David Allan Evans. TSL

Bull, the fleece are cranm'd, and not a room, The. Audley Court. Tennyson. NoBVV

Bull-voiced young fellow of Pawling, A. Hog-calling Competition. Morris Bishop. RHPC

Bullard's Song, The. Unknown. OBET

Bulldozer, The. Donald A. Stauffer. WaP

Bulldozers. Frederick Dec. PCP

Bulldozers come, they rip, The. The Development. Marge Piercy. NBLV

Bullfight. Miroslav Holub, tr. fr. Czech by Ian and Jarmila Milner. RB

Bullfrog. Ted Hughes. NYBP; RFM

Bullfrogs. David Allan Evans. Psk

Bullocky. Judith Wright. CBAP; PoAu-2; SeCePo

Bullocky Bill. Unknown. PoAu-1

Bullrush Basket. Jan Kuijper, tr. fr. Dutch by Jacob Lowland. DuIn

Bull's eyes and targets. Unknown. OxNR

Bully, The. At. to Earl of Rochester and to Thomas D'Urfey. InvP

Bully, A. Malay Oral Tradition, tr. by R. J. Wilkinson. WTO

Bum. W. Dayton Wedgefarth. BLPA

Bumble Bee. Margaret Wise Brown. PDV

Bumble bees! Don't worry about the bumble bees. Raw Honey. Lewis MacAdams. UL

Bumi. Imamu Amiri Baraka. PoBA

Bump on his forehead?, The. Make for Him a Revolution, If You Can! Moyshe-Leyb Halpern, tr. fr. by Benjamin and Barbara Harshav. AYP

Bumpety, bumpety, bump. Fan, the Filly. Wilfrid Thorley. BoTP

Bumpity doun in the corrie gaed whuddran the pitiless whun stane. Sisyphus. Robert Garioch. PoSH

Bums, on Waking. James Dickey. NYBP

Bum's Rush. Michael Dransfield. CBAP

Bunch Grass #37. Robert Sund. NU

Bunch of Grapes, The. George Herbert. NAEL-1; TOF

Bunch of keys the keys to such beautifully old-fashioned fantastic creatures, A. Tercets. Louis Aragon, tr. by Michael Benedikt. POS

Bunch of Larks, The. Robert Leighton. EBVV

Bunch of the boys were whooping it up in the Malamute saloon, A. The Shooting of Dan McGrew. Robert W. Service. BeLS; FaBoBe; FaFP; FPL; PoLF; PoRA; RB

Bunches of Grapes. Walter de la Mare. GoJo; GrPl; MoShBr; OxBChV

Bundle of orange flames, A. Old Miniatures. Leo Vroman. VWA

Bundle of Truths—A Parody, A. Alexander Rodger. PF

Bundles. Carl Sandburg. MoAmPo

Bungaloid Growth. Colin Ellis. FaBoEE

Bungalows, The. John Ashbery. CoAP

Bunker Hill. George Henry Calvert. BeLS; FaBoBe; PAH

Bunker's Hill, or the Soldier's Lamentation. John Freeth. NOEC

Bunky Boy Bunky Boy Who's My Little Bunky Boy. Larry Mollin. NeAC

Bunnies are a feeble folk, The. A Bunny Romance. Oliver Herford. OBCA

Bunny creeps out and caresses his nose. Bunny Rabbit. Unknown. BoTP

Bunny Rabbit. Unknown. BoTP

Bunny Romance, A. Oliver Herford. OBCA

Bunthorne's Song [The Aesthete]. W. S. Gilbert. Fr. Patience. EBVV; FiBHP; LiTB; OAEL-2

Bunyip, The. Douglas Stewart. AmMo

Bunyip and the Whistling Kettle, The. John Manifold. LiTB; PoAu-2; WaP

Buonaparte. Tennyson. Son

Buoy-Bell, The. Charles Tennyson Turner. Son

Buoy like a man in a red sou'wester, A. Beginning to Squall. May Swenson. RFM

Burd Ellen and Young Tamlane. Unknown. ESPB

Burd Helen was her mother's dear. Broughty Wa's. Unknown. ESPB

Burd Isabel and Earl Patrick. Unknown. ESPB

Burden, The. Francesca Yetunde Pereira. PBA

Burden of Decision, The. Peter Everwine. NNaP

Burden of Egypt, The, *sel.* Richard Monckton Milnes.
"Tranquil above the rapids, rocks, and shoals." OBTV
Burden of Junk, The. John Glassco. OBCV
Burden of Love, The. "Owen Innsley." AA
Burdened with family feelings, I went. Burnt. Boris Slutsky, *tr. by* Daniel Weissbort. VWA
Burdened with raindrops. An Autumn Poem. Emperor Kogon, *tr. by* Steven D. Carter. WFTW
Burdens. Edward Dowden. NOBVV
Burdens of All, The. Frances Ellen Watkins Harper. PWR
Bureaucratic Limerick ("The Bureau of Labor Statistics"). William Harmon. OBAL
Burgeis, thou haste so blowen atte the cole. Too Much Sex. *Unknown.* MeEL
Burgeoning anew in spring. *Unknown, tr. fr. Japanese.* Fr. Manyo Shu. Ma
Burgess was drunk when he was admitted. The Hospital—Retrospections. Kenneth Mackenzie. CBAP
Burgesses of Calais, The. Laurence Minot. ACP
Burglar Bill. "F. Anstey." CenHV; FiBHP
Burglar of Babylon, The. Elizabeth Bishop. InPS; NYBP; RB
Burial, The. Glover Davis. SM
Burial, A. Seamus Deane. CIP
Burial. Paulin Joachim, *tr. fr. French by* Oliver Bernard. TTY
Burial. Hone Tuwhare. ATNZ
Burial. Mark Van Doren. MoBS
Burial. Alice Walker. AmPA; PrIm
Burial, The. John Webster. *See* Devil's Law Case, The: All the Flowers of the Spring.
Burial at Sea. Edwin John Pratt. *Fr.* The *Roosevelt and the* Antinoe. CaP
Burial Detail. Andrew Hudgins. MT
Burial, Green, A. Marcia Southwick. MAYP
Burial in Cypress Hills. Amy Clampitt. AnAn
Burial in Flanders, The. Robert Nichols. PeHV
Burial of a Fairy Queen. Mary E. Tucker. CBWP-1
Burial of a Fisherman in Hydra. Grace Schulman. BoWoP
Burial of an Irish President. Austin Clarke. BIrV; IPY
Burial of Barber. Whittier. PAH
Burial of King Cormac, The. Sir Samuel Ferguson. AnIL; NOIV; TIRV
Burial of Latané, The. John Reuben Thompson. PAH
Burial of Moses, The. Cecil Frances Alexander. BeLS; BLPA; BLRP; GN; WBLP
Burial of Sir John Moore after [*or* at] Corunna, The. Charles Wolfe. ChTr; EnRP; FaBoPa; FaBoRV; FaFP; FaPoR; GN; GTBS; GTBS-P; NOBE; OBEV; OBWP; OnYI; PoRA; PWR; WaaP; WBLP
Burial of the Bachelor, The. *Unknown.* FaBoPa
Burial of the Dane, The. Henry Howard Brownell. AA
Burial of the Dog. Susan Musgrave. NoAM
Burial of the Linnet, The. Juliana Horatia Ewing. OxBChV
Burial of the Spirit of a Young Poet. Richard Hughes. MoBrPo
Burial of the Young Love. Waring Cuney. BANP
Buriall. Henry Vaughan. SeCV-1
Burialle of the Dede. Martin Fagg. BXAP
Burials. George Crabbe. *Fr.* The Parish Register, *pt.* III. OAEL-1, *abr.*
Lady of the Manor, The. NOBE; OBNC
Ancient Virgin, An. OBNC
Burials. Geoffrey Grigson. PoA
Buried at Springs. James Schuyler. CoAP; PoM
Buried beneath his poems, here lies. The Wandering Jew. Benjamin Fondane, *tr. by* Edouard Roditi. VWA
Buried in noontime traffic. The Glade. Robert Kelly. *Fr.* The Book of Persephone, 18. PoM
Buried in the shades of horrid night. On His Late Espoused Saint. Sir Kenelm Digby. ACP
Buried Life, The. Matthew Arnold. NAEL-2; OAEL-2
Buried Stream, The. James Keir Baxter. OxBC
Buried under a flat stone, but beside. Patty, 1949–1961. Sharon Mayer Libera. IHMS
Burke and Wills. Ken Barratt. PoAu-2
Burlesque. John Skoyles. NAmP
Burlesque Ode, on the Author's Clearing a New House of Some Workmen, A, *sel.* George Keate.
"Midst the fair range of buildings which, new-reared." NOEC
Burlington will now no more, The. The California Zephyr. Ernest Kroll. RR
Burly, dozing humble-bee. The Humble-Bee. Emerson. AA; AnAmPo; FaPON; FM; GN; NOBA; OxBA
Burma Hills. Bernard Gutteridge. WaP
Burn drowns steadily in its own downpour, The. Waterfall. Seamus Heaney. HeIP

Burn Out Burn Quick. Abraham Reisen, *tr. fr. Yiddish by* Joseph Leftwich. TrJP
Burn Ovid with the rest. Lovers will find. Penal Law. Austin Clarke. BoLoP; GTBS-P; IPY; NOIV
Burn stilly, thou; and come with me. To a Candle. Walter de la Mare. ELP
Burncombe Hollow. William Barnes. OBNC
Burned Bridge, The. Ruth Stone. WPE
Burned in this element. Letter II. William Sydney Graham. NePoEA
Burnet's Character. *Unknown.* APAS
Burning. Galway Kinnell. CoAP
Burning, The. N. Scott Momaday. HATNAP
Burning. Gary Snyder. *Fr.* Myths and Texts. NeAP; *Sels.* PoM
"After scanning its face again and again. John Muir on Mt. Ritter." *Fr.* VIII. NOBA
"He's out stuck in a bird's craw." *Fr.* IV. NaP
"If, after attaining Buddhahood, anyone in my land."" *Fr.* X. NaP
"Night here, a covert." *Fr.* IX. NaP
Second Shaman Song. *Fr.* I. NeAP; NOBA; PoM
"Sourdough mountain called a fire in." *Fr.* XVII. NAAL-2; NaP; NoP
"Spikes of new smell driven up nostrils." *Fr.* XIII. NaP
"Stone-flake and salmon." *Fr.* XV. NaP
Burning a Book. William Stafford. BLA
Burning against the Wind. Judith Minty. GeTw
Burning and Fathering; Accounts of My Country. Jack Gilbert. NPGG
Burning Babe, The. Robert Southwell. ACP; CH; EiL; FaBoCh; HAP; HeIP; InPS; LiTB; MePo; NAEL-1; NAs; NOBE; NOCV; NoP; OAEL-1; OBCP; OBEV; OBSC; PoEL-2; Prf; RB; SeCePo; TOF; TrCP; TrGrPo
Burning Bright. Lillian Morrison. TSS
Burning Bush. Martin Feinstein. TrJP
Burning Bush, The. Norman Nicholson. EaLo; SeCePo
Burning Drift-Wood. Whittier. MOS
Burning Hills. Michael Ondaatje. NoAM; NOBC; NoP
Burning in the Night. Thomas Clayton Wolfe, *arr. in verse by* John S. Barnes. AmFN
Burning Incense. Yu T'ung, *tr. fr. Chinese by* Paul W. Kroll. WFTU
Burning Love Letters. Howard Moss. HoPM
Burning Mountain. W. S. Merwin. NYBP
Burning of Auchindown. *Unknown. See* Willie Macintosh.
Burning of Jamestown, The. Thomas Dunn English. PAH
Burning of Paper instead of Children, The. Adrienne Rich. LCAP; NAAL-2
Burning of the Barns of Ayr, The. Henry the Minstrel. *Fr.* The Wallace. OxBLMV
Burning of the Law, The. Meïr of Rothenburg, *tr. fr. Hebrew by* Nina Davis Salaman. TrJP
Burning of the Leaves, The. Laurence Binyon. GTBS-P; NOBE; OxBTC
Burning of the Temple, The. Isaac Rosenberg. FaBoMo; TrJP
Burning Out. Robert Long. NAmP
Burning Sand of Sinai. Nelly Sachs, *tr. fr. German by* Keith Bosley. VWA
Burning Ship. Jaroslav Seifert, *tr. fr. Czech by* Jeffrey Fiskin *and* Erik Vestville. AnAn
Burning Ship, The. Margit Szécsi, *tr. fr. Hungarian by* Laura Schiff. MHuP
Burning Shit at An Khe. Bruce Weigl. MAYP
Burning sun and clouds. Emperor Kogon, *tr. by* Steven D. Carter. WFTW
Burning, The—at first—would be probably worst. Heaven and Hell. James Kenneth Stephen. CenHV
Burning the Cat. W. S. Merwin. NIP
Burning the Christmas Greens. William Carlos Williams. LiTM; MoP; NAAL-2; NoAM; NOBA
Burning the Letters. Gwendolyn Grew. HoPM
Burning the Letters. Randall Jarrell. MoAB; MoAmPo
Burning the Root. Margaret Gibson. MAYP
Burning the Small Dead. Gary Snyder. NNaP
Burning the Tomato Worms. Carolyn Forché. AmPA
Burning upon some hidden shore. The Lighthouse. Marjorie Wilson. BoTP
Burnished, burned-out, still burning as the year. The Public Garden. Robert Lowell. NoP; PoRA; TAP
Burnished Day, Conch of the Voice. Odysseus Elytis, *tr. fr. Greek by* Edmund Keeley *and* Philip Sherrard. VMG
Burnished silver mask hangs in white air, The. On a Celtic Mask by Henry Moore. Horace Gregory. PoA
Burnout in the Overshoot. A. R. Ammons. BLA
Burns. Fitz-Greene Halleck. AA; AnAmPo
Burns. Sandra Hoben. TV
Burnt. Boris Slutsky, *tr. fr. Russian by* Daniel Weissbort. VWA
Burnt Bush, The. Jack R. Clemo. FaBoTw

Burnt Child, The. W. S. Merwin. NoAM

Burnt Debris. Thomas Sessler, *tr. fr. German* by Herbert Kuhner. VWA

Burnt eyes burned, The. For a Lost Night. Tachihara Michizo, *tr. by* Hiroaki Sato. FCEI

Burnt has been the heart. Asadullah Khan Ghalib, *tr. by* Ahmed Ali. GoT

Burnt in the fireplace. Buson, *tr. fr. Japanese* by Hiroaki Sato. *Fr.* Eighty-seven Hokku. FCEI

Burnt Norton. T. S. Eliot. *Fr.* Four Quartets. CMoP; LiTM; MoAB; MoAmPo; NAAL-2; PoE

  "Words move, music moves." *Fr.* V.UnS

Burnt Ship, A. John Donne. EBEV; InPK; OBWP; WaaP

Burr Oaks, *sel.* Richard Eberhart.

  Attic, The ("The attic and the cedar closet—nostalgia!"). MoAB

Burro once, sent by express, A. Advice to Travelers. Walker Gibson. NBLV

Burro with the Long Ears. *Unknown, tr. fr. Navajo Indian* by Hilda Faunce Wetherill. FaPON

Burrowing deep into earth until the grave is complete. Wolf. Peter Blue Cloud. HATNAP; VoR

Burrowing into my dreams. Morning Sounds. Saqi Farooqi, *tr. by* Mahmood Jamal. PBMUP

Burst of iris so that, A. Iris. William Carlos Williams. InPS; LCAP; WeW

Burst of steam from the pipes in the morning startles me, A. The Two of Cups. Emmett Jarrett. NeAC

Bury Her at Even. "Michael Field." OBMV

Bury Him Deep. Thomas Lovell Beddoes. TW

Bury it, and sift. Lost Love. Edward Rowland Sill. AnAmPo

Bury Me in a Free Land. Frances Ellen Watkins Harper. BPo

Bury me in the overcoat if I die. E. K.'s Will. Sandor Csoori, *tr. by* Jascha Kessler. FOC

Bury Me Not on the Lone Prairie. *Unknown.* AS; FaBV; FaFP (Dying Cowboy, The.) FaBoBe

Bury the dragon's teeth! Bury Them. Henry Howard Brownell. PAH

Bury Them. Henry Howard Brownell. PAH

Bury your heart in some deep green hollow. Saturday Market. Charlotte Mew. WPE

Burying. Judith Herzberg, *tr. fr. Dutch by the author.* DuIn

Burying Blues for Janis. Marge Piercy. GeTw; NeAC

Burying Ground by the Ties. Archibald MacLeish. *Fr.* Frescoes for Mr. Rockefeller's City, III. GOA; MoAmPo

Burying Uncle Salomon. David Avidan, *tr. fr. Hebrew* by Warren Bargad *and* Stanley F. Chyet. IP

Bus, The. Leonard Cohen. HeIP

Bus, The. "Peter." BoTP

Bus Depot Reunion. David Allan Evans. TSL

Bus driver. We Thank You! L. E. Cox. BoTP

Bus halts its long brawl, The. At Kfar Kana. Charles Causley. TOF

Bus Ride. Lenore Kandel. NMM

Bus Ride. Selma Robinson. *Fr.* Ferry Ride. FaPON

Bus Stop. Donald Justice. CAPP; FYAP; LCAP

Bus Trip, The. Joel Oppenheimer. NeAP

Busby, Whose Verse No Piercing Beams, No Rays. Richard Moore. TW

Bush, The, *sels.* Bernard O'Dowd.

  "As many, Mother, are your moods and forms." PoAu-1

  "To other eyes and ears you are a great." CBAP

Bush, a gathering smoke, The. Blackthorn. Euros Bowen, *tr. by the author.* OBWVE

Bush Christening, A. A. B. Paterson. PoAu-1

Bush Clover. Shin Dong-jip, *tr. fr. Korean* by Koh Chang-soo. ACKP

Bush clovers must have shed their flowers. Teika, *tr. fr. Japanese by* Hiroaki Sato. *Fr.* A Compendium of Good Tanka. FCEI

Bush-Fiddle, The. Judith Green. PoAu-2

Bush Justice. Charles Harpur. CBAP

Bush land scrub land. The Country North of Belleville. Alfred W. Purdy. NOBC

Bush Section, A, *sel.* B. E. Baughan.

  "Logs, at the door, by the fence; broadcast over the paddock." ATNZ; PeNZ

Bush, The. Yes. It burned like they say it did. Deuteronomy. Robert Bringhurst. NOBC

Bush was on that dump, A. The Burnt Bush. Jack R. Clemo. FaBoTw

Bushed. Earle Birney. MoCV; NoAM; NOBC; NoP; OBCV

Bushed. Charles Lillard. NOBC

Bushed. Barry McKinnon. NOBC

Bushes and Briars. *Unknown.* OBET

Bushes lean in the wind, The. Need of an Angel. Raymond Souster. CaP

Bushfeller, The. Eileen Duggan. ATNZ

Bushfire. Philip Salom. UAS

Bushman's Song, A. Andrew Barton Paterson. PoAu-1

Bushranger, A. Kenneth Slessor. CBAP

Bushrangers, The. Edward Harrington. PoAu-1

Business, The. Robert Creeley. CAPP

Business. Mihály Ladányi, *tr. fr. Hungarian* by Jascha Kessler. *Fr.* Sketchbook. FOC

Business Is Business. Berton Braley. WBLP

Business Life, The. David Ignatow. NNaP; TW

Business Man's Prayer, A. William Ludlum. BLRP

Business men with awkward hips. The City. Sir John Betjeman. TEP

Business of the lambing ewes would make me, The. Eagles over the Lambing Paddock. Ernest G. Moll. PoAu-2

Business Partners. Brenda Agard. WS

Businessman of Alicante, The. Philip Levine. NaP

Buson, Goshun, Kinkoku. Artists East and West. Diana Chang. BrSi

Busses are bright yellow and have brought, The. The Dream about Junior High School in America. Dick Lourie. NeAC

Bussy d'Ambois, *sels.* George Chapman.

  "Ile sooth his plots: and strow my hate with smiles." *Fr.* IV, ii. PoEL-2

  "Now all the peacefull regents of the night." *Fr.* II, ii. PoEL-2

  "Now shall we see, that nature hath no end." *Fr.* V, ii. PoEL-2

Bustan, The. Sadi, *tr. fr. Persian* by Sir Edwin Arnold. AWP Dancer, The.

  Great Physician, The.

Buster Keaton & the Cops. George Keithley. NPGG

Bustle in a house, The. Emily Dickinson. FaBV; FPL; HAP; HeIP; NAAL-1; NoP; OBD; OxBA; PoEL-5; PoLF; WGRP

Busts and Bosoms Have I Known. *Unknown.* ErPo

Busy. Yüan Mei, *tr. fr. Chinese* by Jonathan Chaves. CoBLCP

Busy ant works hard all day, The. Ants, Although Admirable Are Awfully Aggravating. Walter Rollin Brooks. RHPC

Busy, curious, thirsty fly! On a Fly Drinking out of [*or* from] His Cup. William Oldys. FaFP; OBEV; TrGrPo

Busy Heart, The. Rupert Brooke. MoBrPo

Busy in study be thou, child. Demeanour. *Unknown.* OxBChV

Busy is the life of the weaving woman! Song of the Weaving Woman. Yüan Chen, *tr. by* Wu-chi Liu. SaC

Busy Old Fool. Ian Kelso. BXAP

Busy [*or* Busie] old fool, unruly sun. The Sun [*or* Sunne] Rising. John Donne. BoLoP; FF; GBL; HAP; HeIP; InPS; InvP; JCP; LiTB; MeLP; MePo; NAEL-1; NIP; NOBE; NoP; OAEL-1; PoE; PoEL-2; PPP; SCV; SeCePo; SeCP; SeCV-1; SoSe; TEP; TrGrPo; WeW

Busy, the winter clouds. Shiba Sonome, *tr. fr. Japanese* by Hiroaki Sato. *Fr.* Fifteen Hokku. FCEI

Busy with love, the bumble bee. Meleager, *tr. by* Peter Whigham. BoLoP

Busy yellow bee, after his mighty quest, A. *Unknown.* NOIV

But/ there was/ in that murky dim pond. Sher Imdad Ali's Tadpole. Saqi Farooqi, *tr. by* Mahmood Jamal. PBMUP

But a fisherman's daughters. Tabito, *tr. fr. Japanese.* *Fr.* Manyo Shu. Ma

But a large quantity of brandy. A Small Faculty Stag for the Visiting Poet. Earle Birney. OxBC

But a little while ago. Winter and Spring. *Unknown.* BoTP

But ae braithless note. Sydney Goodsir Smith, *after the French of* Tristan Corbiére. *Fr.* The Gangrel Rymour and the Pairdon of Sanct Anne. OBVE

But another day I touch your hand. Warm hand. Your Hand in Mine. Vicente Aleixandre, *tr. by* Perry Higman. LPSS

But are these landscapes to be imagined. Ronald Johnson. *Fr.* Letters to Walt Whitman, IX. VGW

But as I lay this other night waking. Sir Thomas Clanvowe. *Fr.* The Cuckoo and the Nightingale. PBBP

But as they left the dark'ning heath. Battle, The ("But as they left the dark'ning heath"). Sir Walter Scott. *Fr.* Marmion, VI. ELP

But Bacchus was not so content: he quyght forsooke their land. King Midas. Ovid. *Fr. Latin* by Arthur Golding. *Fr.* Metamorphoses, XI. CTC

"But be contented: when that fell arrest." Shakespeare. *Fr.* Sonnets, LXXIV. NAEL-1; OBSC; Son

But black is the colour of my true love's hair. Black Is the Colour. *Unknown.* GBP

But can see better there, and laughing there. "Pygmies Are Pygmies Still, Though Percht on Alps." Gwendolyn Brooks. PoNe

But could it come up into a limestone so correct, teeth. Manlius to Coeymans. Clark Coolidge. LP

But did not paradise itself contain. Age of Innocence. Graham Hough. PoRA

But do not let us quarrel any more. Andrea del Sarto. Robert Browning. CTC; NAEL-2; NOBVV; NoP; OAEL-2; PoE; PoEL-5

But do the threat'ning clouds precipitate. A Method of Preserving Hay from Being Mow-Burnt, or Taking Fire. Robert Dodsley. *Fr.* Agriculture. FaBoUs

But does every man feel like this at forty. The Second Life. Edwin Morgan. OxBS

But doesn't heaven. England, Autumn. Wayne Brown. PBCV

But don't call Mother Damnable names. Around the Corner. Laura Riding. *Fr.* Forgotten Girlhood. RB

But don't you know it, my dear. Looking at a Picture on an Anniversary. Thomas Hardy. EyDe

But Dwell in Darkness. George Chapman. *Fr.* A Coronet for His Mistress Philosophy, II. Son

But ere sterne conflict mixt both strengths, faire Paris stept before. Homer, *tr. fr. Greek by* George Chapman. *Fr.* The Iliad, III. OBVE

But Fear Thou Not, O Jacob. , Bible, *O.T..* *Fr.* Jeremiah, XLVI: 27-28. TrJP

But for a breathing-space the witch. The Witch. W. W. Gibson. *Fr.* Skye. PoSH

But for a brief/ Moment, a poised minute. A Grasshopper. Richard Wilbur. HAP; HoPM; WeW

But for a hair's breadth. Happiness. Hermann Jandl, *tr. by* Beth Bjorklund. CoAuP

But for a jackdaw's shadow. First Light. P. J. Kavanagh. NPo

But for an hour's sleep in a filthy bed. Recall. Reed Whittemore. NYBP

But for Lust. Ruth Pitter. FaBoTw; OxBTC

But for the broken firing pin. Spider Reeves. Henry Carlile. Psk

But for the steady wash of rain. No Country You Remember. Robert Mezey. FF

But for your terror. To Death. Oliver St. John Gogarty. FaBoEE; OBD; OBMV

But give me for my soul, those beauteous maids. Those Beauteous Maids. Moses ibn Ezra, *tr. by* Solomon Solis-Cohen. TrJP

But give them me, the mouth, the eyes, the brow! Orpheus and Eurydice. Robert Browning. CTC

But God has no machine. Eclogue: Queen Elizabeth's Day. John Davidson. BrPo

But God's Own Descent. Robert Frost. *Fr.* Kitty Hawk. EaLo

But grant I may relapse, for want of grace. Pope. *Fr.* The Second Epistle of the Second Book of Horace Imitated. TOF

But grant, the virtues of a temp'rate prime. Life's Last Scene. Samuel Johnson. *Fr.* Vanity of Human Wishes, The: The Tenth Satire of Juvenal Imitated. SeCePo

But gratious [*or* gracious] God, how well dost thou provide. Dryden. *Fr.* The Hind and the Panther, I. TrPWD
(Church's Testimony, The.) ACP

But half of me is woman grown. To a Vagabond. Constance Davies Woodrow. CaP

But hark! a sound is stealing on my ear. Charles Stuart Calverley. *Fr.* Beer. FiBHP

But hark! the cry is Astur. Horatius. Macaulay. *Fr.* Lays of Ancient Rome. OBWP

But hark! The sharp beat of the Afric drum. William Hosack. *Fr.* The Isle of Streams; or, the Jamaica Hermit. PBCV

But hark! What hubbub now is this that comes. Charles Harpur. *Fr.* The Temple of Infamy. PoAu-1

But he his wonted pride. Milton. *Fr.* Paradise Lost, *Bk.* I, *ll.* 527–699.
(Satan and His Host.) OBS

But He Was Cool; or, He Even Stopped for Green Lights. Don L. Lee. AmNP; BPo; MoP; PoBA

But hear. If you stay, and the child be born. In the Restaurant. Thomas Hardy. *Fr.* Satires of Circumstance, XI. BrPo; MoAB; MoBrPo

"But hold y. hold y. " says Robin. The Jolly Pinder of Wakefield. *Unknown.* ESPB, (B *vers.*)

But How It Came from Earth. Conrad Aiken. MoAB; MoAmPo

But how many merry monthes be in the yeere? Robin Hood and the Curtal Friar. *Unknown.* ESPB

But how shall we this union well expresse? In What Manner the Soule Is United to the Body. Sir John Davies. *Fr.* Nosce Teipsum. LiTB; PoEL-2
(Soul and the Body, The.) CTC; NOBE; OBSC

But I Am Growing Old and Indolent. Robinson Jeffers. NOBA; TAP

But I Do Not Need Kindness. Gregory Corso. NeAP

But I knew it: a verse is a magic helmet. The Seven-League Boots. Ilarie Voronca, *tr. by* Willis Barnstone *and* Matei Calinescu. VWA

But I Shall Weep. Beatrice Redpath. CaP

But I think the king of that country comes out from his tireless host. The Gospel of Labor. Henry van Dyke. WGRP

But I was dead, an hour or more. Escape. Robert Graves. BrPo; MoBrPo

But I Wonder. Aileen Fisher. RAR

But I'd go today. Ultimatum. Philip Larkin. *Fr.* Poetry of Departures. FL

But if a man should eat green figs at noon. Beware of Figs. Nicophon, *tr. by* Charles Duke Yonge. FaBoUs

But if I look the ice is gone from the lake. Spring of the Thief. John Logan. CAPP; NNaP

But if I tell you how my heart swings wide. Sunflower Sonnet Number One. June Jordan. SM; Son

But if I were to have a lover, it would be someone. The Faithful Wife. Barbara L. Greenberg. SM

But if there be a power too just and strong. Dryden. *Fr.* Religio Laici. NOCV

But in the crowding darkness not a word did they say. The Old-Marrieds. Gwendolyn Brooks. AmNP; PoBA

But in the dome of mighty Mars the red. Chaucer. *Fr.* The Canterbury Tales: The Knight's Tale, *mod. version by* Dryden. OBWP

But in the end one tires of the high-flown. About the Phoenix. James Merrill. NoAM

But it was right that she. His Wife. Shirley Kaufman. LCAP

But it won't be that way. Hilda Doolittle ("H. D."). *Fr.* Sigil, XVI. AnAn

But, John, have you seen the world, said he. Angle of Vision. Robert Rendall. OxBTC

But, knowing now that they would have her speak. The Defense of Guenevere. William Morris. NAEL-2; TEP

But let applause be dealt in all we may. George Crabbe. *Fr.* The Borough: The Vicar. OBNC

But lo! at length the day is lingered out. Francis Thompson. *Fr.* Sister Songs. OBMV

But, lo! from forth a copse that neighbours by. Shakespeare. *Fr.* Venus and Adonis. FM
(Courser, The.) OBSC
(Courser and the Jennet, The.) NOBE

But lo! The reaking surface of the vale. John Singleton. *Fr.* A General Description of the West Indian Islands, *Bk.* II. PBCV

But to we see, we touch, sayeth John. Of the Holy Eucharist. *Unknown.* ACP

But Look. Nelly Sachs, *tr. fr. German by* Ruth Mead *and* Matthew Mead. OV

But look/ look at him out there. What Her Friend Said. Kapilar, *tr. by* A. K. Ramanujan. PLW

But look a trial down from some far height. Full Vision. Henrietta Cordelia Ray. CBWP-3

But look! o'er the fall see the angler stand. The Angler. Thomas Buchanan Read. AnAmPo

But love curdles to milk in this climate. Harbour. Edward Kamau Brathwaite. PBCV

But love whilst that thou mayst be loved again. Samuel Daniel. *Fr.* To Delia. ElL; NoP; OBSC

But mark you well the words I say. Horatio Nelson Huggins. *Fr.* Hiroona. PBCV

But mind, but thought/ If these have been the master part of us. Life and Thought. Matthew Arnold. *Fr.* Empedocles on Etna, II. FiP

But most beautiful of all is the Un-found Island. The Most Beautiful. Guido Gozzano, *tr. by* Victoria Pesce. TTTS

But most by numbers judge a poet's song. Pope. *Fr.* Essay on Criticism, *pt.* II. FaBoUs; HAP; NIP
(Poetical Numbers.) SeCePo

But most of all subdued, or fearful least. James Hurdis. *Fr.* The Favourite Village. OBNC

But my good little man, you have made a mistake. To a Boy-Poet of the Decadence. Sir Owen Seaman. CenHV; FiBHP

But nearer night than you, my younger. Solomon and Morolph, Their Last Encounter. Oscar Levertin, *tr. by* Richard Burns *and* Göran Printz-Pahlson. VWA

But no, the familiar symbol, as that the. Conrad Aiken. *Fr.* Time in the Rock [*or,* Preludes to Definition], XCII. VGW

But not on a shell, she starts. The Paltry Nude Starts on a Spring Voyage. Wallace Stevens. HCAP

But now at thirty years my hair is grey. Growing old. Byron. *Fr.* Don Juan, I. NOBE; SCV

But now Athenian mountains they descry. William Falconer. *Fr.* The Shipwreck, III. GoTL

"But now farewell. I am going a long way." Tennyson, *Incorporated in* Idylls of the King *with changes, as* The Passing of Arthur. *Fr.* Morte d'Arthur. FaBoRV

But now more serious let me grow. Matthew Green. *Fr.* The Spleen. PoEL-3

But now Mr. Ferritt. And Mr. Ferritt. Judith Wright. MoBrPo

But now my Muse toyled with continuall care. Richard Barnfield. *Fr.* Sonnets, XX. PeHV

But now, no longer deaf to honour's call. Homer, *tr. fr. Greek by* Pope. *Fr.* The Iliad, VI. OBVE

But now the dentist cannot die. Andrew Lang. CenHV

But now the gentle dew-fall sends abroad. Looking Down on Nether Stowey. Samuel Taylor Coleridge. *Fr*. Fears in Solitude. FaBoPP
But now the salmon-fishers moist. Carrying Their Coracles. Andrew Marvell. *Fr*. Upon Appleton House, to My Lord Fairfax. ChTr
But now the wholesome music of the wood. Vivien's Song ("But now the wholesome music of the wood"). Tennyson. *Fr*. Idylls of the King: Balin and Balan. OAEL-2
But, O immortals! What had I to plead. Christopher Smart. *Fr*. Hymn to the Supreme Being on Recovery from a Dangerous Fit of Illness. NOEC
But O, my Muse, what numbers wilt thou find. A Poem to His Grace the Duke of Marlborough. Joseph Addison. *Fr*. The Campaign. OBWP
But O! the freedom, pleasure and the ease. On Giving Up Smoking. Lawrence Spooner. *Fr*. A Looking-Glass for Smokers. NOEC
But of all the plagues, the greatest is untold. Juvenal, *tr. fr. Latin by* Dryden. *Fr*. Satires, VI. OBSV
But oh! how different is each sight and sound. Forest Thoughts. Sir Roger Casement. TIRV
But Once. Theodore Winthrop. AA
But once upon a time. Cranach. Sir Herbert Read. BrPo; FaBoMo
But one apocalyptic lion's whelp (in flesh). There Is No Opera like "Lohengrin." John Wheelwright. NYBP
But only to be memories of spiritual gate. Immortality. Samuel Greenberg. LiTA
But peaceful was the night. Milton. *Fr*. On the Morning of Christ's Nativity. FaBoCh
But Perhaps. Nelly Sachs, *tr. fr. German by* Ruth *and* Matthew Mead. BoWoP
But piteous things we are—when I am gone. Robert Nichols. *Fr*. Sonnets to Aurelia. OBMV
"But plett a wand o bonnie birk." Sweet William's Ghost. *Unknown*. ESPB
But pretty though as/ roses is. Three Sayings from Highlands, North Carolina. Jonathan Williams. OBAL
But Robin he walkes in the greene fforest. Robin Hood and the Butcher. *Unknown*. ESPB
But see here comes thy reverend Sire. Milton. *Fr*. Samson Agonistes. EBEV
But see the fading many-colour'd woods. Autumn ("But see the fading many-colour'd woods"). James Thomson. *Fr*. The Seasons: Autumn. EnRP
But see this happy village festival. William E. Marshall. *Fr*. Brookfield. CaP
But Sgurr nan Gillean the best Sgurr of them. Sgurr Nan Gillean. Sorley MacLean. *Fr*. The Cuillin. PoSH
But, sires o word forgat I in my tale. Chaucer. *Fr*. The Canterbury Tales: The Pardoner's Tale. EBEV
But some one will ask, "How are the dead raised?" Bible, *N.T*. *Fr*. First Corinthians, XV: 35-57. DL
"But Still in Israel's Paths They Shine." Carter Revard. VoR
But still the thunder of Los peals loud and thus the thunder's cry. Blake. *Fr*. Jerusalem. OAEL-2
But sudden came the barge's pitch-black prow. "George Eliot." *Fr*. Brother and Sister. NOBVV
But sweet sister death has gone debauched today and stalks. David Jones. *Fr*. In Parenthesis. OBWP
But teeming women, when desire grows strong. Cravings during Pregnancy. M. Saint-Marthe, *tr. fr. French*. *Fr*. Paedotrophiae; or, The Art of Bringing Up Children. FaBoUs
But that from slow dissolving pomps of dawn. Darkness. Arthur Hugh Clough. OxBSP
But That Is Another Story. Donald Justice. CoAP; NePoEA-2
But that Thou art my wisdom, Lord. Submission. George Herbert. JCP
"But that was nothing to what things came out." Welsh Incident. Robert Graves. CMoP; NOBE; OxBTC; WSC
But the Copperbelt night is a snake. The Leader. Dorothy Livesay. MoCV
But the last black horse of all. The Last Ones. Robin Hyde. ATNZ; PeNZ
But the men who are now dying. Breakthrough. John Sinclair. NBP
But the morn to the noon hath fallen, and the afternoon to the eve. The Brooding of Sigurd. William Morris. *Fr*. The Story of Sigurd the Volsung. SeCePo
But the vast pile th' amazed vulgar views. The Destruction of Troy. Virgil, *tr. fr. Latin by* Sir John Denham. *Fr*. The Aeneid [*or* Eneados], II. SeCV-1
But Thee, but Thee, O sovereign Seer of time. Sidney Lanier. *Fr*. The Crystal. TrPWD
But Then and There the Sun Bore Down. N. Scott Momaday. CDW
But then came the angels. Les Enfants du Paradis. Doris Mühringer, *tr. by* Beth Bjorklund. CoAuP

But then what do you know about the rights of suffocated genitals. Mariella Bettarini, *tr. fr. Italian by* Muriel Kittel. *Fr*. Paternal. DMI
But there is no black jaw which cannot be broken by our word. Kenneth Patchen. *Fr*. The Journal of Albion Moonlight. NaP
But there was/ once/ a time. Eléni Vakaló, *tr. by* John Stathatos. WPOW
But they know that my country. They Know. Tawfiq Zayyad, *tr. by* Sharif Elmusa *and* Charles Doria. MAP
But they're crazy, I'm telling you. Those Zionists. Crescenzo Del Monte, *tr. by* Barbara Garvin. VWA
But this by sure experiment we know. Ovid, *tr. fr. Latin by* Dryden. *Fr*. Metamorphoses: Of the Pythagorean Philosophy. FM
But this fruit-dish (I suppose it is for fruit). A Good Thing. Ray Mathew. CBAP
But, this I found. Robert Norwood. *Fr*. The Man of Kerioth, V. CaP
But this is learning; to have skill to throw. Learning. George Chapman. *Fr*. Euthymiae Raptus; or, The Teares of Peace. SeCePo
But this, so feminine? Donald Davie. *Fr*. The Forests of Lithuania. OxBTC
But thou, false infidel! shall writhe. Byron. *Fr*. The Giaour. VVA
But thou, Israel, My servant. Israel, My Servant. , Bible, *O.T*.. *Fr*. Isaiah, XLI: 8-16. TrJP
But thou my deere sweet-sounding lute be still. Richard Lynche. *Fr*. Diella, XVI. AAS
But Troy, alas, me thought above them all. Troy. Thomas Sackville. *Fr*. Induction to "A Mirror for Magistrates." SeCePo
But true love is a durable fire. Sir Walter Ralegh. *Fr*. As You Came from the Holy Land. OBD
But 'twas a time when Europe was rejoiced. Wordsworth. *Fr*. The Prelude [or, Growth of a Poet's Mind]: Cambridge and the Alps. FaBoPV
But twelve short years you lived, my son. His Son. Callimachus, *tr. by* G. B. Grundy. AWP
But Venus first. Sister Juana Inés de la Cruz, *tr. fr. Spanish by* Samuel Beckett. *Fr*. First Dream. BoWoP; MexPO
But was there time? No. The Ikons of the Dead. George Barker. NPo
But we are set to strive to make our mark. Frederick Goddard Tuckerman. *Fr*. Sonnets, III, xv. TrCP
But we must build our walls, for what we are. Ultimatum. Philip Larkin. FL
But We Shall Bloom. Haim Guri, *tr. fr. Hebrew by* David Kuselewitz. TrJP
But well away, so is mine heart woe. To Chaucer. Thomas Hoccleve. *Fr*. De Regimine Principum. ACP
But We'll Make Another One. Nanni Balestrini, *tr. fr. Italian by* Lawrence R. Smith. NItP
But what is happening I see. The Birds of Arles. David Fisher. NPGG
But What Is the Reader to Make of This? John Ashbery. InPS
But when I looked further. Maps to Nowhere. David Rosenberg. VWA
But when I waked, I saw that I saw not. A Storm at Sea. John Donne. *Fr*. The Storm. NOBE
But when it was my turn to wrestle with the angel. Under the Ladder to Heaven. Elizabeth Fenton. NMM
But when that comely he covered his wits. The Temptation of Sir Gawain. *Unknown, tr. fr. Middle English by* Brian Stone. *Fr*. Sir Gawain and the Green Knight. ACP
But when the golden-thron'd Aurora made. *Unknown, formerly at. to* Homer, *tr. fr. Greek by* Congreve. *Fr*. The Hymn to Venus. OBVE
But when the next day brake from underground. Percivale's Quest. Tennyson. *Fr*. Idylls of the King: The Holy Grail. OAEL-2
But when the water roars around us. The Ocean. Louis Dudek. *Fr*. Provincetown. MoCV
But when with her white horses day shone fair. Salamis. Aeschylus, *tr. fr. Greek by* G. M. Cookson. *Fr*. The Persians. WaaP
But where began the change; and what's my crime? George Meredith. *Fr*. Modern Love, X. PoEL-5
But where to find the happiest spot below. The First, Best Country. Goldsmith. *Fr*. The Travel[l]er; or, A Prospect of Society. GN
"But who are [*or* art] thou, with curious beauty graced." Opportunity. Machiavelli, *tr. by* James Elroy Flecker. AWP; PFI
But who is this, what thing of sea or land? Delilah. Milton. *Fr*. Samson Agonistes. SeCePo
But who shall parcel out. Wordsworth. *Fr*. The Prelude [or, Growth of a Poet's Mind]: School-Time. TOF
But who the melodies of morn can tell? Nature and the Poets. James Beattie. *Fr*. The Minstrel. SeCePo
But who tipped the sand out of your shoes. Burning Sand of Sinai. Nelly Sachs, *tr. by* Keith Bosley. VWA
But whoso may, thrice happy man him hold. Spenser. *Fr*. An Hymn of Heavenly Beauty. WGRP
But why are you sleeping, your wispy black hair. Anima. Diana O Hehir. NPGG

"But why do you go?" said the lady, while both sate under the yew. Lord Walter's Wife. Elizabeth Barrett Browning. BeLS; HAP

But why is Father Larkin talking to the dead? David Jones. *Fr.* In Parenthesis. PoE

But word is come to Warrington. Sir John Butler. *Unknown.* ESPB

But yesterday and he was one of us. To the New Ordained. John D. Sheridan. TIRV

But yesterday the earth drank like a child. A Letter to His Friend Isaac. Judah Halevi, *tr. by* Emma Lazarus. TrJP

But yesterday, when from the bath he stept. Strato, *tr. by* Sydney Oswald. PeHV

But you can Life upon the Poor bestow. To a Good Physician. William Wycherley. ACP

But You, My Darling, Should Have Married the Prince. Kathleen Spivack. AmPA; NMM

But you, Thomas Jefferson. Brave New World. Archibald MacLeish. NOBA; OFD; OxBA

"But, you're so/ different," they said of. The Photograph the Cat Licks. Beatrice Walter. NMM

Butch once remarked to me how sinister it was. That Pull from the Left. Louise Erdrich. NoAM

"Butch" Weldy. Edgar Lee Masters. *Fr.* Spoon River Anthology. SaC

Butcher, The. Hugo Williams. OxBTC

Butcher, a bald guy, The. Kicking from Centre Field. David McFadden. NeAC

Butcher and Co., *sel.* Vincent O'Sullivan. ATNZ.

"Butcher in sunlight picking at teeth with a combend."

Butcher Boy, The. *Unknown.* AmFP

Butcher carves veal for two, The. The Butcher. Hugo Williams. OxBTC

Butcher Shop. Charles Simic. AmPA; InPK; LCAP; NNaP

Butcherboy. Tom Schmidt. NeAC

Butcher's Wife, The. Louise Erdrich. HATNAP

Butchery. Sandra McPherson. LCAP

Buteo Regalis. N. Scott Momaday. NOVW

Butler's Proclamation. Paul Hamilton Hayne. PAH

Butter. Tom Schmidt. NeAC

Butterbean Tent, The. Elizabeth Madox Roberts. GoJo

Buttercup, A. *Unknown.* BoTP

Buttercup nodded and said good-by. August. Celia Thaxter. FaPON

Buttercups. Wilfrid Thorley. FaPON

Buttercups. *Unknown.* BoTP

Buttercups about the rocks and the sky. The Pass. John Logan. LCAP

Buttercups and Daisies. Mary Howitt. BoTP; OHIP; OxBChV

Buttercups golden and gay. Buttercups. *Unknown.* BoTP

Buttered Pippin-Pies. John Davies of Hereford. *See* Scourge of Folly, The: Author Loving These Homely Meats, The.

Butterflies. Chang Yü, *tr. fr. Chinese by* Jonathan Chaves. *Fr.* Twelve Miscellaneous Poems on the Fang Garden. CoBLCP

Butterflies and dragonflies come in succession. Cheng Chen, *tr. fr. Chinese by* Irving Lo. *Fr.* Miscellaneous Poems Composed While Drinking Wine, X. WFTU

Butterflies, butterflies. Corn-grinding Song. *Unknown*, *tr. by* Natalie Curtis. AWP

Butterflies darting. Saigyo, *tr. fr. Japanese by* Burton Watson. *Fr.* Sixty-four Tanka. FCEI

Butterflies don't sit. Bush Clover. Shin Dong-jip, *tr. by* Koh Chang-soo. ACKP

Butterflies flutter and flit o'er the bay. Unique among Girls. Malay Oral Tradition, *tr. by* R. J. Wilkinson *and* R. O. Winstedt. WTO

Butterfly. Peter Armstrong. PCP

Butterfly, The. Margaret Avison. OBCV

Butterfly. Afanasi Afanasievich Fet, *tr. fr. Russian by* Alan Myers. AAA

Butterfly, The. Pavel Friedmann, *tr. fr. Czech by* Dennis Silk. VWA

Butterfly, The. Robert Stephen Hawker. EBVV

Butterfly, The. Alice Archer James. AA

Butterfly. D. H. Lawrence. NoAM; SOTW; TTTS

Butterfly, The. Ron Padgett. *Fr.* Three Animals. TTTS

Butterfly, The. Margaret Rose. BoTP

Butterfly, The. Clinton Scollard. RAR

Butterfly. William Jay Smith. GoJo

Butterfly. Tsuboi Shigeji, *tr. fr. Japanese by* Geoffrey Bownas *and* Anthony Thwaite. PeBJV

Butterfly, a [*or* the] cabbage-white, The. Flying Crooked. Robert Graves. FaBoMo; LiTM; OxBSP; PCP; RB; TwCP

Butterfly and the Caterpillar, The. Joseph Lauren. OnMSP

Butterfly and the Snail, The. John Gay. *Fr.* Fables. FM

Butterfly Bones; or, Sonnet against Sonnets. Margaret Avison. LiTM

Butterfly, butterfly, butterfly, butterfly. Butterfly Song. *Unknown*, *tr. by* Frances Densmore. OBVE

Butterfly comes and takes a butterfly, A. Issa, *tr. fr. Japanese by* Hiroaki Sato. *Fr.* Forty-four Hokku. FCEI

Butterfly dying right in front, A. Natsume Seibi, *tr. fr. Japanese by* Hiroaki Sato. *Fr.* Twenty-seven Hokku. FCEI

Butterfly in Church, A. George Marion McClellan. BANP

Butterfly it's, The/ a crazy toy. Butterfly. Peter Armstrong. PCP

Butterfly Maidens. Lahpu, *tr. fr. Hopi Indian by* Natalie Curtis. WTO

Butterfly: now in front. Chiyojo, *tr. fr. Japanese by* Hiroaki Sato. *Fr.* Seventeen Hokku. FCEI

Butterfly on Rock. Irving Layton. NoAM; NOBC

Butterfly, one summer morn, A. The Butterfly and the Caterpillar. Joseph Lauren. OnMSP

Butterfly settles on the neckplate, A. Buson, *tr. fr. Japanese by* Hiroaki Sato. *Fr.* Eighty-seven Hokku. FCEI

Butterfly Song. *Unknown*, *tr. fr. Acoman Indian by* Frances Densmore. OBVE

Butterfly, the wind blows sea-ward, strong beyond the garden wall! Butterfly. D. H. Lawrence. NoAM; SOTW; TTTS

Butterfly: what's it dreaming of. Chiyojo, *tr. fr. Japanese by* Hiroaki Sato. *Fr.* Seventeen Hokku. FCEI

Butterfly's Ball, The. William Roscoe. OnUR; OxBChV; RHPC

Butterfly's Ball and the Grasshopper's Feasts, The. The Peacock "At Home." Catherine Ann Dorset. OxBChV

Butternut and walnut. Hillside Pause. Catharine Morris Wright. GoYe

Buttock against buttock. Dogs. Tu Kuo-ch'ing, *tr. by* Dominic Cheung. IFON

Button to chin. *Unknown.* FaBoUs; OxNR

Buttons. Walter de la Mare. FaBoNo

Buttons, a farthing a pair. Mother Goose. OxNR

Buwaib/ Buwaib. The River and Death. Badr Shakir al-Sayyah, *tr. by* Abdullah al-Udhari. MPAW

Buwayb/ Buwayb. Death and the River. Badr Shakir al-Sayyah, *tr. by* Lena Jayyusi *and* Christopher Middleton. MAP

Buxom is the peach-tree. *Unknown*, *tr. by* Arthur Waley. BoS

Buxom Lass. *Unknown.* ErPo

Buxom Young Dairy Maid, The. *Unknown.* OBET

Buxom young fellow from London came down, A. Nine Times a Night. *Unknown.* OBET

Buxton, Fyrish, Cove-an-John, Bush Lot, Mahaica. Guyana not Ghana. Marc Matthews. PBCV

Buy a fresh chicken. Sweet 'n Sour. Genny Lim. BrSi

Buy me a Kyoto comb, yes, a Kyoto comb! *Unknown*, *tr. by* Hiroaki Sato. FCEI

Buy Me an Ounce and I'll Sell You a Pound. E. E. Cummings. OxBA

Buy One Now. Dennis Joseph Enright. NOBL

Buy the paper, take it home. Coming and Going. Mitchell Goodman. VGW

Buy tobacco, buy tobacco. *Unknown.* PBBP

Buy Us a Little Grain. Christine Lavant, *tr. fr. German by* Michael Hamburger. WPOW

Buying a Puppy. Leslie Norris. ILY

Buying a Record. Robert Peters. BXAP

Buying a Shop on Dizengoff. Erez Biton, *tr. fr. Hebrew by* Judith Katz. VWA

Buz, Quoth the Blue Fly. Ben Jonson. *Fr.* Oberon, the Fairy Prince. NA; TEP

("Buzz, quoth the blue fly," *sl. diff.*) OxNR

(Catch, A.) EIL

(Satyrs' Catch, The.) FaBoNo; FM

Buzz. Jim Tollerud. VoR

Buzz Buzz, the Blue Flies. *Unknown*, *tr. fr. Chinese by* Burton Watson. CoBCP

Buzz, buzz the bluebottles. *Unknown*, *tr. by* Arthur Waley. BoS

Buzz in the Window ("Buzz frantic"). Ted Hughes. *Fr.* Orts. NoAM

Buzz Plane, The. Robert Francis. TW

Buzz, quoth the blue fly. Ben Jonson. *See* Oberon, the Fairy Prince: Buz, Quoth the Blue Fly.

Buzz saw snarled and rattled in the yard, The. "Out, Out." Robert Frost. DL; FF; HAP; HeIP; NAAL-2; OxBA; RB; SoSe; UnPo; VGW; WeW

Buzzard. Michael Daugherty. PoSH

Buzzard. George Garrett. MT

Buzzards over Pondy Woods, The. Pondy Woods. Robert Penn Warren. MoAmPo

Bwagamoyo. Lebert Bethune. PoBA

By/ birds/ bird flocks. Divination. Jerred Metz. VWA

By a bank as I lay. Dawn. *Unknown.* OBSC; PBBP

By a Bank of Pinks and Lilies. *Unknown.* ErPo

By a Chapel as I Came. *Unknown.* ChTr; GBP

By a clear well, within a little field. Of Three Girls and of Their Talk. Boccaccio, *tr. fr. Italian by* Dante Gabriel Rossetti. *Fr.* Sonnets. AWP; PFI

By a clump of grass. Issa, *tr. fr. Japanese by* Hiroaki Sato. *Fr.* Forty-four Hokku. FCEI

By a dismal cypress lying. A Song from the Italian. Dryden. *Fr.* The Kind Keeper. SeCV-2

By a flat rock on the shore of the sea. The Rock. *Unknown, tr. by* Geoffrey Grigson. ChTr; GBL

By a great, swift water. Aleksander Wat, *tr. fr. Polish by* Czeslaw Milosz. *Fr.* Persian Parables. PwPP

By a Lake in Minnesota. James Wright. AmFN

By a loading bay that smells of millet. Whitman at a Grain Depot. James Reiss. AnAn

By a peninsula the painter sat. Conduct. Samuel Greenberg. LiTA

By a peninsula the wanderer sat and sketched. Emblems of Conduct. Hart Crane. LiTA; LiTM

By a poorer probability. White Noise. Andrew Joron. BWV

By a quiet little stream on an old mossy log. The Frog and the Bird. Vera Hessey. BoTP

By a route obscure and lonely. Dream-Land. Poe. AmPP; AnAmPo; LiTA; NAAL-1; NOBA; OxBA (Dreamland.) TAP

By a Waterfall. David Wagoner. BLA

By a window overlooking tv antennas and bakery. Reflections on the Death of a Parrot. Jaime Jacinto. BrSi

By a window where evening silence falls. Wakayama Bokusui, *tr. fr. Japanese by* Hiroaki Sato. *Fr.* Forty-four Tanka. FCEI

By a winter river a crow's pecking. Water Lowers and Stones Show. Kito, *tr. fr. Japanese by* Hiroaki Sato. *Fr.* Twenty-four Hokku. FCEI

By accident I broke a rice bowl. Ishikawa Takuboku, *tr. fr. Japanese by* Hiroaki Sato. *Fr.* Forty-seven Tanka in Three Lines. FCEI

By Achmelvich Bridge. Norman MacCaig. OxBS

By airplane you can't leave right away. Thank You, America. Joanna Salamon, *tr. by* Christopher Wertz. WCI

By all means sing of love, but if you do. The Truest Poetry Is the Most Feigning; or, Ars Poetica for Hard Times. W. H. Auden. NYBP

By all-star orchestra, they dine in space. Space Shuttle. Diane Ackerman. MAYP

By all the glories of the day. Before Action. William Noel Hodgson. WGRP

By all the published facts in the case. About Children. Phyllis McGinley. OBAL

By all the routes under heaven. Yakamochi, *tr. fr. Japanese. Fr.* Manyo Shu. Ma

By Aloeswood Pavilion, you once walked in your stocking feet. Responding to a Poem on T'ai-po Pavilion at Colored Stone. Chao Yi, *tr. by* Irving Lo. WFTU

By an unfortunate error a number of lines. Errata Slip. Jared Carter. SoTCo

By and by. Epitaph on a Waiter. David McCord. NBLV; NIP; OBAL

By April mist. Spring Song. Katharine O'Brien. GoYe

By archy/ the roach that scurries. Ballade of the Under Side. Don Marquis. *Fr.* Archys Life of Mehitabel. InvP

By Arthur's Dale as late I went. Bonny Bee Hom. *Unknown.* ESPB

By Babel's Streams *with music.* Philip Freneau. AH

By-Blows. Mark Jarman. NAmP

By Blue Ontario's Shore, *sels.* Walt Whitman.
"Are you he who would assume a place to teach or be a poet here in the States?." *Fr. sec.* XII. FaBoPV
Poet, The. *Fr. sec.* IX–XVII. MoAmPo

By bluster, graft, and doing people down. A Tribute to the Founder. Kingsley Amis. NePoEA-2

By Canoe through the Fir Forest. James Dickey. NYBP

By Cavité on the bay. The Battle of Manila. Richard Hovey. PAH

By chance I composed "Ascending the Clouds," by chance I grew tired of flying. Kung Tzu-chen, *tr. fr. Chinese by* Shirleen S. Wong. *Fr.* Miscellaneous Poems of the Year *Chi-hai*, CXXXV. WFTU

By chance I find a strand of your hair. Wakayama Bokusui, *tr. fr. Japanese by* Hiroaki Sato. *Fr.* Forty-four Tanka. FCEI

By channels of coolness the echoes are calling. Bell-Birds. Henry Clarence Kendall. PoAu-1

By Chickamauga's crooked stream the martial trumpets blew. The Ballad of Chickamauga. Maurice Thompson. PAH

By Clyde's bonny banks where I sadly did wander. The Blantyre Explosion. *Unknown.* OBET

By Cobequid Bay. Alexander Louis Fraser. CaP

By Cool Siloam's Shady Rill. Reginald Heber. ELP; NOCV

By dark severance the apparition head. Painted Head. John Crowe Ransom. LiTA; LiTM; NoAM; OxBA (Painting: A Head.) MoAB; MoAmPo

By Day. Paul Celan, *tr. fr. German by* Joachim Neugroschel. AnAn

By day and also by night and you are. Ian Wedde. *Fr.* Earthly: Sonnets for Carlos, 10. ATNZ; PeNZ

By day Golgotha sleeps, but when night comes. Night at Gettysburg. Don C. Seitz. OHIP

By day she woos me, soft, exceeding fair. The World. Christina Rossetti. BoWoP

By day the bat is cousin to the mouse. The Bat. Theodore Roethke. GoJo; OBCA; PDV; PYC; RHPC; WSC

By day the fields and meadows cry. The Poet's Call. Thomas Curtis Clark. WGRP

By day your high gates are closed. Seal of Fire. Mordecai Temkin, *tr. by* Jeremy Garber. VWA

By death's favor. Epitaph on an Engraver. Henry David Thoreau. EyDe

By Deputy. Arthur St. John Adcock. CenHV

By dint of color. A Dab of Color. Theodore Weiss. VGW

By divination came the Dorians. In Arcadia. Lawrence Durrell. MoBrPo

By duty bound and not by custom led. To the Memory of My Dear and Ever Honored Father Thomas Dudley Esq. Anne Bradstreet. NAAL-1

By ear, she sd. I, Maximus of Gloucester, to You ("By ear, she sd"). Charles Olson. *Fr.* The Maximus Poems, NeAP.

By-Election Idyll. Peter Dickinson. FiBHP

By every ebb of the river-side. Pisgah. Willard Austin Wattles. WGRP

By fall the vines have crawled out. Pumpkin. Robert Morgan. GeTw

By fate, not option, frugal Nature gave. Xenophanes. Emerson. NOBA

By favorable breezes fanned. Cythère. Paul Verlaine, *tr. by* Arthur Symons. AWP

By feathers green, across Casbeen. The Phoenix. A. C. Benson. OBEV

By Fiat of Adoration. Oscar Williams. LiTM

By flash in sunshine "to reduce contrast." Snapshot of Adam. James Merrill. EOEF

By Frazier Creek Falls. Gary Snyder. GOA; InPS

By Godde and Seynt Johne I sweare ye. The Eternale Footeman's Tale. George Moor. BXAP

By good luck a few days back. the Monk of Montaudon, *tr. by* Paul Blackburn. Pro

By Goose Lake Mountain, rice and miller grown fat. Shrine Festival. Wang Chia, *tr. by* Burton Watson. CoBCP

By granting charters of peace. An Anglo-Irishman's Complaint. *Unknown.* AnIL

By Hakone Road/ I cross over. Sanetomo, *tr. fr. Japanese by* Burton Watson. *Fr.* Twenty-four Tanka. FCEI

By Hallucination Visited. Robert Horan. EAS

By hand-drawn cart, an excursion at evening. Lotus Lake. Ts'ao P'i, *tr. by* Burton Watson. CoBCP

By hard journeys in a dead land. Omphalos: The Well. Sean Jennett. NeIP

By Heaven! *Unknown, tr. fr. Chinese by* Burton Watson. CoBCP

By Heaven 'tis false, I am not vain. The Defiance. Aphra Behn. EnLoPo

By Heaven's! 'twas bravely done! Spoken Extempore. Earl of Rochester. SeCePo

By Her Aunt's Grave. Thomas Hardy. *Fr.* Satires of Circumstance, III. BrPo; MoAB; MoBrPo

By her the heaven is in his course contained. Scudamor in the Temple of Venus. Spenser. *Fr.* The Faerie Queene, IV, 10. PoE

By Heraclides. *Unknown, tr. fr. Greek by* William Cowper. OBVE

By his commandment hee maketh the snow to fall apace. Bible, Apocrypha. *Fr.* Ecclesiasticus, XLIII: 13–26. OBVE

By illness pent in lime-tree bower. Lines Written near Linton, on Exmoor. Daniel Hoffman. BXAP

By its own wind, a small butterfly. Chiyojo, *tr. fr. Japanese by* Hiroaki Sato. *Fr.* Seventeen Hokku. FCEI

By itself and from a distance. The Brick. Paul Roche. NYBP

By June our brook's run out of song and speed. Hyla Brook. Robert Frost. BoNaP

By landscape reminded once of his mother's figure. Wystan Hugh Auden. MoP (Adolescence.) NoAM

By late afternoon the light. Orchard. John Engels. BLA

By late evening she was cleaning the sink. Variegation. Janet Sutherland. DT

By late in spring the cottonmouths and rattlers. Coon Hunt, Sixth Month (1955). Sydney Lea. MAYP

By leave of my eyes that watched the bereaving. Pledge. Avraham Shlonsky, *tr. by* Francis Landy. VWA

By Logan's streams that rin sae deep. Logan Braes. John Mayne. OxBS

By love was my eye opened. How Beautiful You Are: 3. Elaine Edelman. IHMS

By Magdalen Bridge, Oxford. Gerard Manley Hopkins. FaBoPP

By miracles exceeding power of man. Crucifying. John Donne. *Fr.* La Corona. OBS; Son

By moonlight. Conversation Piece. Robert Graves. GrPl

By morning star and quarter moon. The Last Buckaroo. Dick Gibford. CowP

By myself I walk today. Tiny Catullus. Steve Levine. UL

By myself walking. Hypochondriacus. Charles Lamb. BXAP

By nature I love to dress my hair. Hsü Pen, tr. fr. Chinese by Jonathan Chaves. Fr. Five Things Sought For——In the Manner of Han Wo. CoBLCP

By Nebo's lonely mountain. The Burial of Moses. Cecil Frances Alexander. BeLS; BLPA; BLRP; GN; WBLP

By Night. Robert Francis. VGW

By night around my temple grove. Buddha. Arno Holz, tr. by William Ellery Leonard. AWP

By night on my bed I sought him whom my soul loveth. On My Bed I Sought Him. , Bible, O.T.. Fr. The Song of Solomon, III: 1-5. TrJP

("In my bed at night.") BoWoP, ad. by Willis Barnstone.

By night they haunted a thicket of April mist. Spectral Lovers. John Crowe Ransom. GBL; HeIP

By night we linger'd [or lingered] on the lawn. Tennyson. Fr. In Memoriam A. H. H., XCV. HAP; NoP; OBNC; PoEL-5; TOF

By none but me can the tale be told. The White Ship. Dante Gabriel Rossetti. OBNV

By noon, as I recall, the sky was clear. Rural Colloquy with a Painter. Timothy Steele. CRP

By Now. Ralph Salisbury. STE

By Now I Am So Tired of Waiting. Gaspara Stampa, tr. fr. Italian by Muriel Kittel. DMI

By now I bet he's dead which suits me fine. Bleeder. Stephen Dobyns. NAmP

By now I should be entering on the supreme stage. Pilgrim's Problem. Clive Staples Lewis. TrCP

By now you will have met. Voice. W. S. Merwin. NNaP

By numbers here from shame or censure free. Samuel Johnson. Fr. London: A Poem in Imitation of the Third Satire of Juvenal. NOEC; OBSV

(Poverty in London.) ChTr

By order/ shapes take shape. Nanak, tr. by John Stratton Hawley and Mark Juergensmeyer. SSI

By our first strange and fatal interview. On His Mistress [or Mistris]. John Donne. Fr. Elegies, XVI. BoLoP; EBEV; LiTB; NAEL-1; PoEL-2

(Elegie XVI: On His Mistress.) SeCP

(Elegy on His Mistress.) GBL; MeLP; MePo; SeCV-1

(To His Mistress Desiring to Travel with Him as His Page.) NOBE

By pain of stone and wearing down of bronze. Upon This Rock. Ruthven Todd. PoA

By post, news from the capital. Hearing of the Earthquake in Kyoto. Rai San'yo, tr. by Burton Watson. JLIC-2

By-Products. Baron Wormser. MAYP

By Rail through the Earthly Paradise, Perhaps Bedfordshire. Denise Levertov. NNaP

By reason of despair we set forth behind you. The Murder of Moses. Karl Shapiro. EaLo

By Return Mail. Vivienne Joseph. ATNZ

By runnels and sea-dipped clover, easing. Green Island. William Logan. MAYP

By Saint [or Saynt] Mary, my lady. To Mistress [or Maystres] Isabell Pennell. John Skelton. Fr. The Garlande [or Garlands] of Laurell. AAS; InPS; NAs; NOBE; OBEV; OBSC; OxBoLi; PoEL-1; TrGrPo; TTTS

(In Praise of Isabel Pennell.) CH

By St. Thomas Water. Charles Causley. Mes

By Sandy Waters. Jesse Stuart. AmFN

By Saturday I said you would be better on Sunday. The Operation. Robert Creeley. NaP

By sea, by land, harass us. Boycott. Khalil Mutran, tr. by Issa Boullata and Thomas G. Ezzy. MAP

By Sea to Santiago. Unknown. See Men may leue alle gamys.

By sloth on sorrow fathered. Lollocks. Robert Graves. ChTr; RB

By some derision of wild circumstance. Reunion. E. A. Robinson. NOBA

By some peculiar force centrifugal. To a Book. Elinor Wylie. LiTA

By some sad means, when reason holds no sway. Philip Freneau. Fr. The House of Night. PoEL-4

By special lens, photo-electric cells. A Different Speech. Louise Townsend Nicholl. ImOP

By spring banks waterplants are green. The Painting "Solitary Fisherman by a Spring River. . . ." Ni Tsan, tr. by Jonathan Chaves. CoBLCP

By Stubborn Stars, sel. Kenneth Leslie.

"Silver herring throbbed thick in my seine, The." ErPo; OBCV

(Sonnet: "Silver herring throbbed thick in my seine, The.") NOBC

By such an all-embalming summer day. Near Helikon. Trumbull Stickney. LiTA

By sundown we came to a hidden village. Conquerors. Henry Treece. GOYP; OBWVE

By Talland Church as I did go. The Planted Heel. Sir Arthur Quiller-Couch. EBVV

By That Long Scan of Waves. Walt Whitman. NAAL-1

By that swamp's shore. Unknown, tr. by Arthur Waley. BoS

By that the Manciple hadde his tale al ended. The Parson's Prologue. Chaucer. Fr. The Canterbury Tales. NAEL-1

By that withering oak. Daybreak. Frank Lamont Phillips. CNA

By the Arno. Oscar Wilde. EBVV

By the Babe Unborn. G. K. Chesterton. NAs

By the Babylonish waters. By the Waters of Babylon. Heine, tr. fr. German by Charles Godfrey Leland. Fr. Hebrew Melodies. TrJP

By the beard of the Prophet the Bashaw swore. How We Burned the Philadelphia. Barrett Eastman. PAH

By the Beautiful Ohio. Joan LaBombard. SM

By the Bivouac's Fitful Flame. Walt Whitman. NoAM; NoP; OxBA; PoE

By the blue taper's trembling light. A Night-Piece on Death. Thomas Parnell. NOEC

By the blue wooden sea. Switchback. Dame Edith Sitwell. PBWP

By the Boat House, Oxford. Anne Stevenson. FaBoWP

By the Bridge. Ted Walker. NYBP

By the brilliant ramp. 3 A.M. John Updike. AnAmPo

By the brink of the river I'd often walk. The Midnight Court. Brian Merriman, tr. by Thomas Kinsella. NOIV

By the clearing at the Eastern Gate. Unknown, tr. by Arthur Waley. BoS

By the Conemaugh. Florence Earle Coates. PAH

By the crumbling fire we talked. Witness. John Montague. CIP

By the day I perish in the barrel. Diogenes. Katerina Anghelaki-Rooke, tr. by Peter Dreyer. OV

By the Deep Nine. Unknown. ChTr

By the Deep Sea. Byron. See Childe Harold's Pilgrimage: Ocean, The.

By the dry road the fathers cough and spit. The Brief Journey West. Howard Nemerov. NoAM

By the eastern sea. Ishikawa Takuboku, tr. fr. Japanese by Hiroaki Sato. Fr. Forty-seven Tanka in Three Lines. FCEI

By the Exeter River. Donald Hall. MoBS

By the fierce flames of love I'm in a sad taking. Royall Tyler. TAP

By the Fire. Mother Goose. OxNR

By the Fire-Side. Robert Browning. EBVV; OAEL-2

By the Fireside. Afanasi Afanasievich Fet, tr. fr. Russian by Alan Myers. AAA

By the first hour we knew the day's luck. Rituals along the Arkansas. William Mills. MT

By the Flat Cup. Horace, tr. fr. Latin. Fr. Odes (I,31). CTC

By the Flooded Canal. John Ashbery. BLA; NPo

By the flow of the inland river. The Blue and the Gray. Francis Miles Finch. AA; AnAmPo; BLPA; BLPL; FaBoBe; OPP; PAH; WBLP

By the Ford. Edward Thomas. OxBSP

By the four-storied tower of a middle school. Forenoons. Ernst Jandl, tr. by Beth Bjorklund. CoAuP

By the gas-fire, kneeling. Olga Poems. Denise Levertov. LCAP; NNaP

By the gate with star and moon. Medallion. Sylvia Plath. HeIP; NoP; SM

By the glim of a midwinterish early morning. Son and Father. C. Day Lewis. EaLo

By the Graveyard, Luskentyre. Norman MacCaig. NPo

By the great stones we chose our ground. In Love, at Stonehenge. Coventry Patmore. Fr. The Angel in the House. FaBoPP

By the highway the stream downslope. Runoff. Archie Randolph Ammons. PPP

By the Hoof of the Wild Goat. Kipling. Fr. Plain Tales from the Hills. OBNC

By the Iowa River. Satoru Sato, tr. fr. Japanese by the author. WCI

By the Isar, in the twilight. River Roses. David Herbert Lawrence. BrPo; CMoP; GBL; OAEL-2; ViBoPo

By the Klondike River. Alan Coren. OnUR

By the lamplit stall I loitered, feasting my eyes. Sight. W. W. Gibson. MoBrPo

By the light of the flares. Unknown, tr. fr. Japanese by Burton Watson. Fr. Manyo Shu. FCEI

By the light of the Moon God. Prince Yuhara, tr. fr. Japanese. Fr. Manyo Shu. Ma

By the light or dark. Kunaikyo, tr. by Geoffrey Bownas and Anthony Thwaite. PeBJV

By the little river. The Willows. Walter Prichard Eaton. FaPON; OHIP

By the Margin of the Great Deep. "Æ." OBEV

By the margin of the ocean, one morning [or one pleasant evening] in the month of June. The Bonny Bunch of Roses O. Unknown. FaBoBa; OxBoLi

By the merest chance, in the twilight gloom. What My Lover Said. Homer Greene. AA

By the Moon ("By the moon we sport and play"). *At.* to John Lyly *and to* Thomas Ravenscroft. *Fr.* The Mayde's Metamorphosis. CH
(Fairy Dances.) EiL
(Urchin's Dance, The.) BoTP

By the new Boot's, a tool-chest with flagpoles. Aberdarcy: The Main Square. Kingsley Amis. *Fr.* The Evans Country. NoAM; NOBL; OxBTC

By the newly bulldozed logging road, for a hundred yards. Working against Time. David Wagoner. MAT

By the North Gate, the wind blows full of sand. Lament of the Frontier Guard. Li Po, *tr.* by Ezra Pound. OBVE; OBWP; VGW; WaaP

By the North Sea, *sels.* Swinburne.
"Land that is lonelier than ruin, A." *Fr.* I. PoEL-5
Suffolk. *Fr.* III. FaBoPP
Where Dunwich Used to Be. *Fr.* VI. FaBoPP

By the Old Castle at Komoro. Shimazaki Toson, *tr. fr. Japanese by* Geoffrey Bownas *and* Anthony Thwaite. PeBJV

By the old Moulmein Pagoda, lookin' eastward to [*or* lazy at] the sea. Mandalay. Kipling. BrPo; FaBV; FPL; LiTB; MoBrPo; NOBE; OBTV; TrGrPo

By the Pacific Ocean. Joaquin Miller. AA

By the Pasture Bars. George Sands Johnson. PWR

By the Pool at the Third Rosses. Arthur Symons. *Fr.* In Ireland, II. FaBoPP; OBNC

By the Potomac. Thomas Bailey Aldrich. PAH; Son

By the public hook for the private eye. River Song. Weldon Kees. PPP

By the purple haze that lies. Indian Summer. Susanna-Strickland Moodie. CaP

By the Rio Grande. The Rio Grande. Sacheverell Sitwell. SeCePo

By the River. Koh Chang-soo, *tr. fr. Korean by the author.* ACKP

By the River. Wang An-shih, *tr. fr. Chinese by* Burton Watson. CoBCP

By the River Ashley, *sels.* Mary Ursula Bethell.
"Hour is dark. The river comes to its end, The." *Fr.* VI. ATNZ; PeNZ
"Sauntering home from church we lingered." *Fr.* IV. PeNZ
"That bridge from the city, that was Waimakariri." *Fr.* V. PeNZ

By the River Eden. Kathleen Jessie Raine. NYBP

By the riverbank idly I pick white-budded reeds. Thoughts South of the Yangtze. Yü Hu, *tr.* by Burton Watson. CoBCP

"By the Rivers of Babylon." Mary Weston Fordham. CBWP-2

By the rivers [*or* waters] of Babylon [*or* Babel], there we sat down. Bible, *O.T.* Psalms CXXXVII. AWP; NAWM-1; OAEL-1; TrJP
("As by the streams of Babylon," *paraphrased by* Thomas Campion.) OAEL-1
("As on Euphrates shady banks we lay," *paraphrased by* George Sandys.) OBS
("By the rivers of Babel we sate," *The Geneva Bible.*) OAEL-1
("By the waters of Babylon we sat down [*or* downe] and wept [*or* weapte].") AWP; OBVE, *tr.* by Miles Coverdale.
("Nigh seated where the river flows," *paraphrased by* the Countess of Pembroke.) OAEL-1
("On the floodis of Babiloyne there we saten," *Second Wycliffite Version.*) OAEL-1
("On the proud banks of great Euphrates' flood," *paraphrased by* Richard Crashaw.) OAEL-1
("Sitting by the streams that glide," *paraphrased by* Thomas Carew.) OAEL-1
("Upon the rivers of Babylon, there we sat and wept," *The Douay-Rheims Version.*) OAEL-1
("When as we sat all sad and desolate," *paraphrased by* Francis Bacon.) OAEL-1
("When on Euphrates' banks we sate," *paraphrased by* Sir John Denham.) OAEL-1
("When we, our weary limbs to rest," *paraphrased by* Nahum Tate *and* Nicholas Brady.) OAEL-1
("Whenas we sat in Babylon," *paraphrased by* Thomas Sternhold *and* John Hopkins.) OAEL-1
Song of Exile, A, *sel. Fr.* 1-6. TrGrPo

By the Road. Geoffrey Grigson. OxBTC

By the road to the contagious hospital. Spring and All. William Carlos Williams. CMoP; HAP; InPK; InPS; LiTM; MoP; NAAL-2; NoAM; NOBA; OxBA; PoE; QFR; TAP
(Poem: "By the road to the contagious hospital.") MoAB; MoAmPo; UnPo

By the Roadside in My Birthplace. Basho, *tr. fr. Japanese by* Burton Watson. *Fr.* Seventy-six Hokku. FCEI

By the roots of my hair some god got hold of me. The Hanging Man. Sylvia Plath. HCAP

By the rude bridge that arched the flood. Concord Hymn. Emerson. AA; AiP; AmFN; AmPP; AWP; BLPA; BLPL; FaBoBe; FaFP; FaPON; FaPoR; GN; GOA; HAP; HeIP; LiTA; NOBA; NoP; OBWP; OHFP; OPP; OxBA; PAH; TAP; TrGrPo; WaaP

(Hymn: "By the rude bridge that arched the flood.") AnAmPo
(Hymn Sung at the Completion of the Concord Monument.) NAAL-1
By the rude bridge that arched the flood. Concord Hymn. Emerson. AA; AmFN; AmPP; AWP; BLPA; BLPL; FaBoBe; FaFP; FaPON; FaPoR; GN; GOA; HAP; HeIP; LiTA; NOBA; NoP; OBWP; OHFP; OxBA; PAH; TAP; TrGrPo; WaaP

By the sad waters of separation. Exile. Ernest Dowson. BoLoP; BrPo

By the Saltings. Ted Walker. NYBP

By the Sea. Emily Dickinson. *See* I started early, took my dog.

By the Sea. Richard Watson Dixon. OBNC

By the Sea. Cynthia Macdonald. ER

By the Sea. Christina Rossetti. BoNaP; MOS; NOBVV

By the Sea on a Winter Day. Koh Chang-soo, *tr. fr. Korean by the author.* ACKP

By the sea-shore of Mitsu, that reminds one. Tajihi Kasamaro, *tr. fr. Japanese. Fr.* Manyo Shu. Ma

By the shores of Gitche [*or* Gitchee] Gumee. Hiawatha's Childhood. Longfellow. *Fr.* The Song of Hiawatha. FaPON; OHFP; WBLP
("At the door on summer evenings.") BoTP
("Downward through the evening twilight.") FaBV

By the side of a green stagnate pool. George Alexander Stevens. CoMu; ErPo

By the side of a murmuring stream an elderly gentleman sat. The Elderly Gentleman. George Canning. NA

By the Sluice. Anthony Thwaite. PoPo

By the southern woods I have built my hut. Watching Fish in the Water. Suemochi, *tr.* by Burton Watson. JLIC-1

By the spring pond, deep and wide. Duckweed Pond. Wang Wei, *tr.* by Burton Watson. CoBCP

By the Statue of King Charles at Charing Cross. Lionel Johnson. BrPo; FaBoRV; MoBrPo; NOBE; OBEV; OBMV; OBNC; PoEL-5

By the time it comes to me. The Sparrows. Peter Cooley. NAmP

By the time you read this. Letter. W. S. Merwin. HAP

By the time you swear you're his. Unfortunate Coincidence. Dorothy Parker. BXAP; FaBoUs; NoP

By the Tomb Gate are thorn-trees. Unknown, *tr.* by Arthur Waley. BoS

By the Waterfall. Friedrich Adler, *tr. fr. German by* Jethro Bithell. TrJP

By the Waters of Babylon. Benjamin Fondane, *tr. fr. French by* Edouard Roditi. VWA

By the Waters of Babylon. Heine, *tr. fr. German by* Charles Godfrey Leland. *Fr.* Hebrew Melodies. TrJP

By the Waters of Babylon, *sels.* Emma Lazarus. WPE
Currents.
Exodus (August 3, 1492), The.

By the waters of Babylon we sat down and wept. Super Flumina Babylonis. Swinburne. PoEL-5

By the waters of Life we sat together. An Old Man's Idyl. Richard Realf. AA

By the wayside. Edmond Jabès, *tr. fr. French by* Rosemarie Waldrop. *Fr.* Fall and Exile, IV. RHTwFP

By the wayside, on a mossy stone. Old. Ralph Hoyt. AA

By the wayside, three crows sat on a cross. Adam on His Way Home. Robert Pack. ErPo

By the well side. Morning-Glories. Rokunyo, *tr.* by Burton Watson. JLIC-2

By the wells. Zippora Returns to Moses at Rephidim. Rose Drachler. VWA

By the willows of the Eastern Gate. Unknown, *tr.* by Arthur Waley. BoS

By the wireless I can hear. Wireless. Rodney Bennett. BoTP

By the Wood. Robert Nichols. MMA

By Then You'd Dressed. Imre Oravecz, *tr. fr. Hungarian by* Jascha Kessler. FOC

By these slow shadows and the frosted air. Calvinist Autumnal. Elizabeth B. Harrod. NePoEA

By this cold shuddering fit of fear. The Glen of Silence. "Hugh MacDiarmid." CMoP

By this he knew she wept with waking eyes. George Meredith. *Fr.* Modern Love, I. EnLoP; HeIP; NAEL-2; NOBVV; NoP; OAEL-2; PoE; PoEL-5; Son
(End of Love, The.) HoPM

By this, Leander, being near the land. Christopher Marlowe. *Fr.* Hero and Leander, Second Sestiad. EBEV; ErPo

By this, though deep the evening fell. Battle, The ("By this, though deep the evening fell"). Sir Walter Scott. *Fr.* Marmion, VI. PoEL-4

By this time long-gowned Lumen walked abroad. William Rankins. *Fr.* Satyrus Peregrinans. OBSV

By those soft tods of wool [I]. A Conjuration, to Electra. Robert Herrick. GBL; PoEL-3

By thys fyre I warme my handys. The Months. Unknown. ChTr

By Tre, Pol and Pen. Cornishmen. Unknown. FaBoUs

By two black eyes my heart was won. Unknown. FaBoCo

By viewing Nature, Natures hand-maid, Art. Dryden. *Fr.* Annus Mirabilis. MOS
By Vows of Love Together Bound, *with music.* Eleazar Thompson Fitch. AH
By Wauchopeside. "Hugh MacDiarmid." EBEV
By Way of Preface. Edward Lear. *See* How Pleasant to Know Mr. Lear.
By way of pretext. Yakamochi, *tr. fr. Japanese by* Arthur Waley. *Fr.* Manyo Shu. AWP
By ways remote and distant waters sped. On the Burial of His Brother. Catullus, *tr. by* Aubrey Beardsley. AWP
By what appalling dim upheaval. Simon Gerty. Elinor Wylie. OBAL
By what bold passion am I rudely led. Sir William Davenant. *Fr.* Gondibert, I, 3. OBS
By what name will they call. The Diaspora. Jack Myers. NAmP
By what sends. Children's Rhymes. Langston Hughes. BPo
By World Laid Low. *Unknown, tr. fr. Irish.* ChTr
By yellow Chame, where all the Muses reign. Cambridge and the Cam. Phineas Fletcher. *Fr.* The Apollyonists. FaBoPP
By Yon Bonny Banks or Thereabout. Vonna Adrian. SoTCo
By younde the Brugge on thi right hand. The Way to Jerusalem. *Unknown.* OBTV
By your breasts. Conversation between the Chevalier de Chamilly and Mariana Alcoforado in the Manner of a Song of Regret. The Three Marias, *tr. by* Helen R. Lane. BoWoP
By your leave. Deathbed Verse. Jippensha Ikku, *tr. by* Hiroaki Sato. FCEI
By your unnumbered charities. Hospital for Defectives. Thomas Blackburn. GTBS-P; OxBTC
Bye Baby Bother. Stevie Smith. TW
Bye, baby bunting. Mother Goose. OxNR
Bye Baby Walnut. Norma Farber. TSS
Bye, bye, baby bunting/ Your daddy's gone a-hunting. *Unknown.* OxNR
Byelorussia, *sels.* Moishe Kulbak, *tr. fr. Yiddish by* Leonard Wolf. PeBMYV
    Grandfather Dying.
    Grandpa and the Uncles.
    Nastasya.
    Uncle Avram Pastures the Horses.
    Winter at Night in the Old Hut.
Byfield Rabbit, The. Katherine Hoskins. SaC
By'm By. *Unknown.* AS
B'york! but it's lovely under the leaf. Spring Song. Donald Finkel. NYBP
Byrnies, The. Thom Gunn. MoP; NePoEA-2; NoAM; OxBTC
Byron. J. Gordon Coogler. OBAL
Byron, *sel.* Joaquin Miller.
    In Men Whom Men Condemn as Ill. PoLF
Byron Recollected at Bologna. Samuel Rogers. *Fr.* Italy. OBNC
By's beard the Goat, by his bush-tail the Fox. Of Kate's Baldness. John Davies of Hereford. FaBoEE
Bystander, The. Rosemary Dobson. CBAP; Mes
Bystanders. William Matthews. TW
Bytuene [*or* Bytwene *or* Betwene *or* Bitwene *or* Bitweene] Mersh [*or* March *or* Mershe] and [*or* ant] Averil. Alison. *Unknown.* MeEL; NAEL-1; NoP; OAEL-1; OBEV
    (Alisoun.) CTC
    (Alysoun.) HAP; HeIP
Byzantium. W. B. Yeats. CMoP; EBEV; FaBoMo; HAP; InPS; LiTM; MoAB; MoBrPo; MoP; NAEL-2; NAWM-2; NIP; NoAM; NOBE; NoP; OAEL-2; OxBTC; PoE; PPP; SeCePo; TEP
Byzantium Burning. Jack Gilbert. NPGG

C

C. Louis Aragon, *tr. fr. French by* William Jay Smith. CT
C. C. Rider. *Unknown.* AS
C. G. Jung's "First Years." Thomas Kinsella. IPY
C Is for Charms. Eleanor Farjeon. WSC
C. L. M. John Masefield. LiTM; MoBrPo; OxBTC
C Stands for Civilization. Kenneth Fearing. TrJP
Ca' the Yowes. Burns. EnRP
    (Hark! the Mavis.) OBEV
Ca' the Yowes to the Knowes. Isobel Pagan. OBEV
Ca' the Yowes to the Knowes. *Unknown.* OxBS
Cabbage. Rosemary Norman. BrRo
Cabeza, if anyone knew all about civilization, it was you. Czeslaw Milosz, *tr. fr. Polish by the author and* Peter Dale Scott. *Fr.* Throughout Our Lands, XIV. PwPP
Cabin Creek Flood, The. *Unknown.* AmFP
Cabin in Minnesota, A. Marvin Bell. HoPM

Cabin North of It All, The. James McMichael. AmPA
Cabinet, A. Eugène Guillevic, *tr. fr. French by* Teo Savory. RHTwFP
Cabinet of Seeds Displayed, A. Howard Nemerov. CRP; KS
Cable Hymn, The. Whittier. PAH
Cable Ship, The. Harry Edmund Martinson, *tr. fr. Swedish by* Robert Bly. RB
Cables entangling her. She Is Far from the Land. Thomas Hood. FaBoNo; WiR
Caboose Thoughts. Carl Sandburg. CMoP
Cachalot, The, *sels.* Edwin John Pratt.
    "Thousand years now had his breed, A." MoCV; OBCV
    "Where Cape Delgado strikes the sea." CaP; MoCV
Cache la Poudre. James Galvin. AnAn
Cachikel Woman. Vidaluz Meneses, *tr. fr. Spanish by* David Volpendesta. Vol
Cackle, cackle, Mother Goose. *Unknown.* OxNR; PBBP
Cackling, smelling of camphor, crumbs of pink icing. Muse. David Wagoner. PoA
Cacoëthes Scribendi. Oliver Wendell Holmes. AA; NBLV
Cactus towers, straight and tall, The. In Mexico. Evaleen Stein. AA
Cactuses, The. Hubert Witheford. ATNZ
Cadaver Politic. Tom Paulin. FaBCIP
Cadenza. Ted Hughes. CMoP; NYBP
Cadenza. Miriam Waddington. CaP
Cader Idris at Sunset. Charles Tennyson Turner. FaBoPP
Caedmon. Denise Levertov. NoAM
Caedmon. Norman Nicholson. FaBoTw
Caedmon's Hymn. Caedmon. OAEL-1
Caedmon's Hymn. *tr. fr. Anglo-Saxon.* EBEV, *tr. by* Sally Purcell; OAEL-1; TEP, *tr. by* Walter Kendrick.
Caelia, *sels.* William Browne. Son
    Lo, I the Man. *Fr.* I.
    So Sat the Muses. *Fr.* IV.
Caelia, *sel.* Sir David Murray.
    "Ponder thy cares, and sum them all in one." EIL
Caelica, *sels.* Fulke Greville.
    "Absence, the noble truce." *Fr.* XLV [XLIV]. PoEL-1
        (Absence and Presence.) OBSC
    "All my senses, like beacon's flame." *Fr.* LVI. InvP; PoEL-1; QFR
    "Away with these self-loving lads." *Fr.* LII.
        (Cynthia.) OBSC
        (Of His Cynthia.) EIL; ELP; NoP
    "Caelica, I overnight was finely used." *Fr.* XXXVIII. AAS; Son
        (Sonnet: "Caelica, I overnight was finely used.") JCP
    "Caelica, when I did see you every day." *Fr.* LXIII. AAS
    "Cupid, thou naughty boy, when thou wert loathed." *Fr.* XII. Son
    "Down in the depth of mine iniquity." *Fr.* XCIX [C]. QFR
        (Sonnet: "Downe in the depth of mine iniquity.") OBS
    "Earth with thunder torn[e], with fire blasted, The." *Fr.* LXXXVI [LXXXVII]. AAS; QFR
        (Sonnet: "Earth with thunder torn, with fire blasted, The.") JCP
    "Eternall Truth, almighty, infinite." *Fr.* XCVII [XCVIII].
        (Sonnet: "Eternall Truth, almighty, infinite.") OBS
    "Faction, that ever dwells." *Fr.* XXIX.
        (Love and Fortune.) OBSC
    "Farewell, sweet boy; complain not of my truth." *Fr.* LXXXIV [LXXXV]. FaBoRV; GBL; QFR; Son
        (Farewell to Cupid.) OBSC
    "Fie [*or* Fye], foolish Earth, think[e] you the heaven wants glory." *Fr.* XVI. PoEL-1; Son
        (Love's Glory.) OBSC
    "Golden age was when the world was young, The." *Fr.* XLIV. OAEL-1
    "I, with whose colors [*or* colours] Myra dressed [*or* dress'd] her head." *Fr.* XXII. GBL; HAP; InvP; QFR
        (Myra.) EIL; NOBE; OBEV; OBSC
        (To Myra.) LiTB
    "In night, when colors [*or* colours] all to black[e] are cast." *Fr.* C. AAS; OAEL-1; QFR; Son
    "In the time when herbs and flowers." *Fr.* LXXVI.
        (Caelica and Philocell.) OBSC
    "In the window of a grange." *Fr.* LXXIV.
        (Love and Honour.) OBSC
    "In those years when our sense, desire and wit." *Fr.* XCVI. NOCV
    "Love is the peace, whereto all thoughts do[e] strive." *Fr.* LXXXV. AAS
        (Sonnet: "Love is the peace, whereto all thoughts do strive.") JCP
    "Love, the delight of all well-thinking minds." *Fr.* I. GBL; OBSC
    "Man, dream[e] no more of curious mysteries." *Fr.* LXXXVIII [LXXXIX]. MePo; QFR
        (Sonnet: "Man, dream[e] no more of curious mysteries.") JCP; OBS
    "Manicheans did no idols make, The." *Fr.* LXXXIX. NOCV

"Men, that delight to multiply desire." *Fr.* XCIV.
  (Sonnet: "Men, that delight to multiply desire.") OBS
"More than most fair, full of that heavenly fire." *Fr.* III. EIL
  (To His Lady.) OBSC
"Nurse-life wheat, within his greene huske growing, The." *Fr.* XL. AAS
  (Sonnet: "Nurse-life wheat within his green husk growing, The.")
  JCP
  (Youth and Maturity.) OBSC
"O false and treacherous Probability." *Fr.* CIII [CIV]. AAS
  (Sonnet: "O false and treacherous Probability.") OBS
"Sion lies [*or* Syon lyes] waste, and thy Jerusalem." *Fr.* CIX [CX].
  NoP; PoEL-1
"Three things there be in man's opinion dear[e]." *Fr.* CV [CVI].
  LiTB; NOCV; PoEL-1
  (Sonnet: "Three things there be in mans opinion deare.") OBS
"When all this All doth pass from age to age." *Fr.* LXIX. EBEV
"Whenas [*or* When as] man's life, the light of human[e] lust." *Fr.*
  LXXXVII [LXXXVIII]. LiTB; MePo; PoEL-1
  (Sonnet: "When as man's life, the light of human lust.") OBS
"Who grace, for zenith had, from which no shadowes grow." *Fr.*
  LXXXIII. PoEL-1
  (Despair.) OBSC
"World, that all contains, is ever moving, The." *Fr.* VII.
  (Change.) OBSC
"Wrapped up, O Lord, in man's degeneration." *Fr.* XCVIII [XCIX].
  QFR
"You little stars that live in skies." *Fr.* IV. EIL; NoP
  (His Lady's Eyes.) OBSC
"You that seek what life is in death." *Fr.* LXXXII [LXXXIII].
  (Time and Eternity.) OBSC
Caelica and Philocell. Fulke Greville. *See* Caelica: In the time when
  herbs and flowers.
Caelica, I overnight was finely used. Fulke Greville. *Fr.* Caelica,
  XXXVIII. AAS; Son
  (Sonnet: "Caelica, I overnight was finely used.") JCP
Caelica, when I did see you every day. Fulke Greville. *Fr.* Caelica,
  LXIII. AAS
Caenlochan. Helen B. Cruickshank. PoSH
Caernarfon, 2 July 1969. T. Glynne Davies, *tr. fr. Welsh by* Joseph P.
  Clancy. OBWVE
Caesar. W. S. Merwin. LCAP; NaP
Caesar. Paul Valéry, *tr. fr. French by* C. F. MacIntyre. WaaP
Caesar, afloat with his fortunes! The Turtle. *Unknown.* PAH
Caesar, serene Caesar, your foot on all. Caesar. Paul Valéry, *tr. by* C.
  F. MacIntyre. WaaP
Caesar's Victory, The. *Unknown.* OxBSS
Caesura. Kenneth Mackenzie. CBAP
Café. Hala Baykov. Mes
Cafe in Warsaw. Allen Ginsberg. HAP
Café Tableau. May Swenson. ErPo
Cafe: 3 A.M. Langston Hughes. GLP; HCAP
Cage, The. John Berryman. PoA
Cage, The. David Gascoyne. EAS
Cage, The. John Montague. CIP; FaBCIP
Cage, The. James Stephens. OxBTC
Cage, The. Avner Treinin, *tr. fr. Hebrew by* A. C. Jacobs. VWA
Caged Bird, The. Arthur Symons. BrPo
Caged in old woods, whose reverend echoes wake. Captivity. Samuel
  Rogers. OBNC
Caged Rats. Ebenezer Elliott. EBEV
Caged Skylark, The. Gerard Manley Hopkins. CMoP; FM; LiTM;
  MoAB; MoBrPo; OBMV; PBBP; Son; SoSe
Caged Tiger: A Ballad, A. Huang Ching-jen, *tr. fr. Chinese by* Daniel
  Bryant. WFTU
Caged Wings: First Impressions from the Boat Alcatraz Island/ Indian
  Land, 1970. Wendy Rose. NOVW
Cages. Marvin Solomon. NYBP
Cain. Irving Layton. MoCV
Cain Shall Not Slay Abel Today on Our Good Ground. Malcolm Lowry.
  OBCV
Cain the Immortal. Yusuf al-Khal, *tr. fr. Arabic by* Sargon Boulus *and*
  Samuel Hazo. MAP
Cain's eyes are not gracious to God. Abel. Else Lasker-Schüler, *tr. by*
  Joachim Neugroschel. VWA
Cain's Song. Donald Finkel. VWA
Caint call your name. The Hermit Cackleberry Brown, on Human Vanity.
  Jonathan Williams. OBAL; PoM
Caique. Angelos Sikelianos, *tr. fr. Greek by* Edmund Keeley *and* Philip
  Sherrard. VMG
Cairngorm, November 1971. Martyn Berry. PoSH
Cairo Jag. Keith Douglas. NePoEA
Cakes and Ale. *Unknown.* FaFP
Cakewalkman. Sam Abrams. UL

Cala-Achí! Ha! Aha! Yeha! Ahau! Wow! Achí! *Unknown, tr. fr. Mayan*
  by Nathaniel Tarn. *Fr.* Rabinal-Achí, IV. STP
Calabash wherein she served my food, The. The Serving Girl. Gladys
  May Casely Hayford. CDC
Calais, August 15, 1802. Wordsworth. NAs
Calamiterror, *sel.* George Barker.
  "Meandering abroad in the Lincolnshire meadows day." *Fr.* VI. EAS
Calamity, my great laborer. Repose in Calamity. Henri Michaux, *tr. by*
  W. S. Merwin. RHTwFP
Calamity of seals begins with jaws, The. Seals at High Island. Richard
  Murphy. CIP; IPY
Calculation, The. David Wagoner. NYBP
Calcutta. Gábor Garai, *tr. fr. Hungarian by* Daniel Hoffman. MHuP
Calder, A. Karl Shapiro. EyDe
Calder Valley: At the Top of the Ainleys. Stanley Cook. NPo
Caldwell of Springfield. Bret Harte. PAH
Caledonia. Colleen J. McElroy. BlSi
Caledonia. Anthony Powell. NOBL
Calendar. Cecil Bødker, *tr. fr. Danish by* Nadia Christensen *and*
  Alexander Taylor. BoWoP
Calendar is ironic, The. The stripper dances. The Dancing Sunshine
  Lounge. Thomas Rabbitt. MAYP
Calendar of Oengus, The, *sel. Unknown.*
  "This sad world we inhabit." NOIV
Calendar Rhyme. Flora Willis Watson. BoTP
Calenture. Alastair Reid. NYBP; PrIm
Calf-deep in spruce dust. Dulcimer Maker. Carolyn Forché. SaC
Calf-Path, The. Sam Walter Foss. PoLF
Caliban. Shakespeare. *See* Tempest, The: Be Not Afeard: The Isle is
  Full of Noises.
Caliban in the Coal Mines. Louis Untermeyer. MoAmPo; PDV; TrJP
Caliban upon Setebos; or, Natural Theology in the Island. Robert
  Browning. AWP; EBEV; NAEL-2; NOBVV; NoP; OAEL-2; WGRP
Caliban's Song. Jane Yolen. BWV
Calico-pale paddocks through the window, The. Song for Past Midnight.
  Geoffrey Lehmann. CBAP
Calico Pie. Edward Lear. FaBoCh; FaPON; PYC; TrGrPo
Califas/ baby blue skies. Heading for Eugene. Lorenza Schmidt. FIA
California. Thomas Lake Morris. AA
California. Lydia Huntley Sigourney. PAH
California. *Unknown.* AS
California. Bernice Zamora. CCP
California Dead. G. E. Murray. MAYP
California Dreaming. Charles Wright. CAPP
California Hills in August. Dana Gioia. DiPo; InPK
California Oaks, The. Yvor Winters. GOA
California Phrasebook, The. Dennis Schmitz. AmPA; NPGG
California Quail in January. Will C. Jumper. GrPl
California song, A. Song of the Redwood-Tree. Walt Whitman. AmPP
California Winter. Karl Shapiro. AiP
California Winter, *sel.* Karl Shapiro.
  "This land grows the oldest living things." AmFN
California Zephyr, The. Ernest Kroll. RR
Californian, The. *Unknown.* AmFP
Californians, The. Theodore Spencer. NYBP; TW
Caliph shot a gazelle, The. Humorous Verse. Abu Dolama, *tr. by* Raoul
  Abdul. TTY
Calisto, *sel.* John Crowne.
  "Kind lovers, love on." OxBSP
Call, The. James Dickey. NePoEA-2
Call, The. John Hall. MeLP; MePo; OBS
Call, The. Thomas O. Mordaunt, *formerly at. to* Scott. *See* Sound,
  Sound the Clarion.
Call, The. Jules Supervielle, *tr. fr. French.* NU, *tr. by* Geoffrey
  Gardner
Call, The. *Unknown.* OBEV
"Call All." *Unknown.* PAH
Call all hands to man the capstan, see the cable is all clear. Rolling
  Home. *Unknown.* OxBSS
Call and assemble together Aotearoa. Call Together. Kohine Whakarua
  Ponika, *tr. by* Sam Karetu. PeNZ
Call—call—and bruise the air. Expression. Isaac Rosenberg. MoBrPo
Call down the hawk from the air. The Hawk. William Butler Yeats.
  PoA
Call for the Robin Redbreast and the Wren. John Webster. *Fr.* The
  White Devil, V, iv. ChTr; EBEV; FaBoCh; HAP; HeIP; NoP;
  PoEL-2; PoRA; PrIm; RB; SeCePo
  (Cornelia's Song.) OBS; TrGrPo
  (Dirge, A: "Call for the robin-redbreast and the wren.") EIL; LiTB;
  NOBE; OBEV
  (Land Dirge, A.) CH; GTBS; GTBS-P
Call from the Afterworld. Jozef Habib Gerez, *tr. fr. Turkish by* Musa
  Moris Farhi *and* Anthony Rudolf. VWA

Call him drunken Ira Hayes, he won't answer any more.   Ballad of Ira Hayes.   Peter La Farge.   MAT

Call Him the Lover and call me the Bride.   The Song the Body Dreamed in the Spirit's Mad Behest.   William Everson.   ErPo

Call in the Midst of the Crowd, A, *sel.*   Alfred Corn.
   Fire: The People.   NAAL-2

Call is for belief, The.   The Fundament Is Shifted.   Abbie Huston Evans.   NYBP

Call It a Good Marriage.   Robert Graves.   BoLoP

Call it a louse—I'm.   Cid Corman.   VGW

Call it neither love nor spring madness.   Without Name.   Pauli Murray.   AmNP; PoBA; PoNe

Call it not vain; they do not err.   The Minstrel Responds to Flattery.   Sir Walter Scott.   *Fr.* The Lay of the Last Minstrel, V.   OBNC

Call it our craziness even.   Roots.   Lucille Clifton.   CAPP

Call Martha Corey.   The Trial.   Longfellow.   *Fr.* Giles Corey of the Salem Farms.   PAH

Call me bad when me start walk de streets.   Eighties, De.   Frederick Williams.   PBCV

Call me Ishmael and listen.   Ishmael.   Gabriel Levin.   VWA

Call me no more.   His Lachrimae or Mirth, Turn'd to Mourning.   Robert Herrick.   SeCV-1

Call me no more, O gentle stream.   To a River in the South.   Sir Henry Newbolt.   CH

Call Me Not Back from the Echoless Shore.   *Unknown.*   BLPA

Call Me Not Dead.   Richard Watson Gilder.   WGRP

Call me not false, beloved.   The Bridegroom.   Kipling.   *Fr.* Epitaphs of the War, 1914–1918.   FaBoEE

Call me Zamboni. Nights my job is hockey.   Rink Keeper's Sestina.   George Draper.   PrIm

Call not thy wanderer home as yet.   Germinal.   "Æ."   BIrV; MoBrPo; OBEV; OBMV

Call of Nature, The.   Tony Harrison.   NoAM

Call of the Bugles, The.   Richard Hovey.   AA; AnAmPo

Call of the Christian, The.   Whittier.   NOCV

Call of the River Nun, The.   Gabriel Okara.   PBA

Call of the Wild, The.   Robert W. Service.   CaP

Call on Sir Walter Raleigh, A.   Sarah Morgan Bryan Piatt.   AA

Call Out My Number.   Julia de Burgos, *tr. fr. Spanish by* Julio Marzán.   InW

Call the cows home!   Thunder.   Walter de la Mare.   BoNaP

Call the Horse, Marrow.   *Unknown.*   OBET

Call the roller of big cigars.   The Emperor of Ice-Cream.   Wallace Stevens.   AmPP; AnAmPo; CMoP; FaBoMo; FF; HAP; HCAP; HeIP; InPK; LiTA; MoP; NAAL-2; NAWM-2; NIP; NoAM; NOBA; NoP; OPOP; OxBA; PoE; TAP; WeW

Call the seller of used cars.   Sunday Service.   Michael Heffernan.   BXAP

Call Them Back.   Chris Petrakos.   GOYP

Call to Action, A.   Callinus, *tr. fr. Greek by* T. F. Higham.   WaaP

Call to Action, A.   Ch'iu Chin, *tr. fr. Chinese by* Kenneth Rexroth *and* Ling Chung.   PBWP

Call to Arms, A.   Mary Raymond Shipman Andrews.   PAH

Call to Arms.   Tso Yen-nien, *tr. fr. Chinese by* Burton Watson.   CoBCP

Call to Pentecost, A.   Inez M. Tyler.   BLRP

Call to the Colors, The.   Arthur Guiterman.   PAH

Call to the Strong, The.   William Pierson Merrill.   BLRP

Call Together.   Kohine Whakarua Ponika, *tr. fr. Maori by* Sam Karetu.   PeNZ

Called Back.   Emily Dickinson.   *See* Just lost, when I was saved!

Called out on Christmas Eve for a working-party.   Devil on Ice.   Donald Davie.   NoAM

Called Proud.   Walter Savage Landor.   GBL

Caller Herrin'.   Lady Nairne.   OxBS

Caller rain rase abune.   Douglas Young.   OBVE

Callicles' Song.   Matthew Arnold.   *See* Through the black, rushing smoke-burst.

Calligram, 15 May 1915.   Guillaume Apollinaire, *tr. fr. French by* O. Bernard.   OBWP

Calligraphy Practice.   Ou-yang Hsiu, *tr. fr. Chinese by* Burton Watson.   CoBCP

Calling.   H. Edgar Hix.   SoTCo

Calling all butterflies of every race.   From a Milkweed Pod.   Robert Frost.   KS
   (Pod of the Milkweed.)   LiTM

Calling black people.   SOS.   Imamu Amiri Baraka.   BPo; CNA; PoBA

Calling Lucasta from Her Retirement.   Richard Lovelace.   CaPo

Calling on Peadar O'Donnell at Dungloe.   John Hewitt.   CIP

Calling One's Own.   *Unknown, tr. fr. Ojibwa Indian by* Charles Fenno Hoffman.   AnAmPo

Calling out the station name as if singing.   Ishikawa Takuboku, *tr. fr. Japanese by* Hiroaki Sato.   *Fr.* Forty-seven Tanka in Three Lines.   FCEI

Calling Spring VII-MMMC.   Ogden Nash.   FaBoCo

Calling the Doctor.   John Wesley Holloway.   BANP

Calling, the heron flies athwart the blue.   The Creek-Road.   Madison Cawein.   AA

Calling the Roll.   Nathaniel Graham Shepherd.   *See* "Corporal Green!" the orderly cried.

Calling the Scientists Home.   Wendy Rose.   BWV

Calling to mind[e], mine eie long went about [*or* my eyes went long about].   The Excuse.   Sir Walter Ralegh.   AAS; SiPS

Calling to my mind [*or* minde] since first my love begun.   Michael Drayton.   *Fr.* Idea, LI.   NOBE; OBSC; PoEL-2

Calling Trains.   *Unknown.*   AmFP

Calling Your Name in the Zoo, *sels.*   Hugo Williams.   NPo
   Elaine.
   Gladys.
   Kirsten.
   Noelle.
   Them.
   Tracy & Co.

Calliope.   *Unknown.*   AS

Calliope in the Labour Ward.   Elaine Feinstein.   BrRo

Calliope's Nymph Brings the Poet to the Palace to Honour.   Gawin Douglas.   *Fr.* The Palace [*or* Palice] of Honor [*or* Honour].   OxBLMV

Callipaedia; or, The Art of Getting Beautiful Children, *sels.*   Claude Quillet, *tr. fr. Latin by* George Sewell.   FaBoUs
   Best Time for Conception, The.
   How to Conceive Boys.
   Process of Conception, The.

Calls of a clapper rail far into the night.   Princess Shikishi, *tr. fr. Japanese by* Hiroaki Sato.   *Fr.* Seventy-eight Tanka.   FCEI

Calm.   Aldo Camerino, *tr. fr. Italian by* Anita Barrows.   VWA

Calm.   Robert Hass.   NAmP

Calm after Storm.   Frank Yerby.   AmNP

Calm and Full the Ocean.   Robinson Jeffers.   WaP

Calm and knowing ways.   Tabito, *tr. fr. Japanese by* Geoffrey Bownas *and* Anthony Thwaite.   *Fr.* Manyo Shu.   PeBJV

Calm and solemn is the midnight!   Labour.   "Marie".   PF

Calm as that second summer which precedes.   Charleston.   Henry Timrod.   AA; AmPP; AnAmPo; NOBA; OxBA; PAH; TAP

Calm, The/ Cool face.   Suicide's Note.   Langston Hughes.   CDC

Calm Death, God of crossed hands and passionless eyes.   Death.   George Pellew.   AA

Calm down, my sorrow, we must move with care.   Meditation.   Baudelaire, *tr. by* Robert Lowell.   InPK; NAWM-2

Calm is all nature as a resting wheel.   Written in Very Early Youth.   Wordsworth.   EnRP

Calm is the landscape when the storm has passed.   Peace in the Welsh Hills.   Vernon Watkins.   GTBS-P; OxBTC

Calm Is the Morn.   Tennyson.   *Fr.* In Memoriam A. H. H., XI.   ChTr; EBEV; ELP; FaBoRV; FiP; HeIP; LiTB; NOBE; NoP; OBNC; PoEL-5; TrGrPo
   (Lincolnshire Wolds and Lincolnshire Sea.)   FaBoPP

Calm martyr of a noble cause.   Jefferson Davis.   Walker Meriwether Bell.   PAH

Calm Morning at Sea.   Sara Teasdale.   MOS

Calm on the bosom of thy God.   Felicia Dorothea Hemans.   *Fr.* The Siege of Valencia.   OBEV

Calm, on the Listening Ear of Night.   Edmund Hamilton Sears.   AH

Calm Soul of All Things! [Make It Mine].   Matthew Arnold.   *Fr.* Lines Written in Kensington Gardens.   TrPWD; WGRP

Calm [*or* Calme] was the day, and through the trembling air [*or* ayre].   Prothalamion.   Spenser.   *Fr.* AAS; AWP; ChTr; EBEV; EIL; FaBoPP; GTBS; GTBS-P; HAP; LiTB; Mes; NIP; OBSC; PPP; SeCePo

Calm was the even, and clear [*or* cleer] was the sky.   Dryden.   *Fr.* An Evening's Love, IV, i.   FF; SeCV-2

Calm was the evening and clear was the sky.   Amintas and Claudia; or, The Merry Shepherdess.   *Unknown.*   CoMu

Calm Winter Sleep.   Hilary Corke.   NYBP

Calme, The.   John Donne.   MePo; MOS

Calme was the day.   *See* Calm was the day.

Calmly beside her tropic strand.   Charleston.   Paul Hamilton Hayne.   PAH

Calmly in the twilight made.   Muted.   Paul Verlaine, *tr. by* C. F. MacIntyre.   UnAS

Calmly We Walk through This April's Day.   Delmore Schwartz.   *Fr.* The Repetitive Heart.   LiTM; PrIm; OPOP
   (For Rhoda.)   MoAB; MoAmPo; OxBA
   (Time Is the Fire.)   LiTA

Calumny.   Frances Sargent Osgood.   AA

Calvary.   Padraig De Brun, *tr. fr. Irish by* Máire Mhac an tSaoi.   TIRV

Calvary.   E. A. Robinson.   MoAmPo; OFD; Son; WGRP

Calvary. Libby Stopple. GoYe
Calvary. *Unknown.* AH
Calvary and Easter. Susan Coolidge. WBLP
   (Easter Song, An.) BLRP
Calverly's. E. A. Robinson. NoAM
Calvin in the Casino. Turner Cassity. NIP
Calvinist Autumnal. Elizabeth B. Harrod. NePoEA
Calvinist Sang. Alexander Scott. OxBS
Calvinist's Caribbean, The. Donald Hall. SoTCo
Calv'ry's tragedy is ended. The Empty Tomb. Clara Ann Thompson.
   CBWP-2
Calvus to a Fly. Charles Tennyson Turner. FM; NOBVV
Calypso/ Is a bit of a dipso. Forever Ambrosia. Christopher Morley.
   OBAL
Calypsomania. Anthony Brode. FiBHP
Calypso's Island. Archibald MacLeish. MoAB; NoP
Calypso's Song to Ulyssess. Adrian Mitchell. GBL
Calyx of the Oboe Breaks, The. Conrad Aiken. NYBP
   (Music.) AnAmPo
Cam' Ye By [the Salmon Fishers]. *Unknown.* CH; GBP
Cambodia Witness. Lisa Vice. ER
Cambrian, *sels.* Eeva-Liisa Manner, *tr. fr. Finnish by* Jaakko A. Ahokas.
   And So the Oracles. *Fr.* VII. OV
   Apathy. *Fr.* VI. OV
   "If they wanted freedom." *Fr.* V. PBWP
   "To move over shifting borders." *Fr.* I. PBWP
   "Turn the page of stone and there." *Fr.* III. PBWP
Cambrian Swain, The. Edward Davies. *Fr.* Chepstow: A Poem.
   OBWVE
Cambridge and the Alps. Wordsworth. *Fr.* The Prelude [or, Growth of a
   Poet's Mind], VI. FiP; ImOP; PoEL-4
   "But 'twas a time when Europe was rejoiced." FaBoPV
   Crossing the Alps. OBTV; RB
   Imagination ("Imagination—here the power so called"). FiP
   "'Tis told by one whom stormy waters threw." ImOP
   "When from the Vallais we had turned." TOF
Cambridge and the Cam. Phineas Fletcher. *Fr.* The Apollyonists.
   FaBoPP
Cambridge Elegy. Sharon Olds. BLA
Cambridge Ladies Who Live in Furnished Souls, The. E. E. Cummings.
   Fr. Sonnets—Realities. AmPP; HeIP; MoP; NAAL-2; NoAM;
   NoAM; NOBA; NoP; OBAL; OxBA; Son; TAP
Cambridge Songs, *sel. Unknown, tr. fr. Latin by* Willis Barnstone.
   "Wind is this." BoWoP
Camden Magpie. Hugh McCrae. PoAu-1
Camden, most reverend head, to whom I owe. To William Camden.
   Ben Jonson. AWP; JCP; NAEL-1; OBS; SeCV-1
Came a stranger late among us. In Memory of James M. Rathel.
   Josephine D. Henderson Heard. CBWP-4
Came in my full youth to the midnight cave. Ajanta. Muriel Rukeyser.
   LiTA; LiTM; MoAB; MoAmPo; NNaP
Came the morning of that day. Sumter. Edmund Clarence Stedman.
   PAH
Came to lakes; came to dead water. A Field of Light. Theodore
   Roethke. LiTM; TwCP
Came to me. Rudaki, *tr. by* Basil Bunting. BoLoP; OBVE
Came You Not from Newcastle. *Unknown.* GBP
Camel. Laila Akhyaliyya, *tr. fr. Arabic by* Willis Barnstone. BoWoP
Camel, The. Al-Munsif al-Wahaybi, *tr. fr. Arabic by* Salma Khadra
   Jayyusi *and* Naomi Shihab Nye. MAP
Camel. Alan Brownjohn. RHPC
Camel, The. Ogden Nash. CenHV
Camel at the close of day, The. The Kneeling Camel. Anna Temple
   Whitney. BLPA
   (Submission and Rest.) BLRP
Camel has a single hump, The. The Camel. Ogden Nash. CenHV
Camel-Rider, The. *Unknown, tr. fr. Arabic by* Wilfrid Scawen Blunt.
   AWP
Camellia drops and spills, A. Buson, *tr. fr. Japanese by* Hiroaki Sato.
   Fr. Eighty-seven Hokku. FCEI
Camellia, yes, and plum, yes. Yosano Akiko, *tr. fr. Japanese by* Hiroaki
   Sato. *Fr.* Thirty-nine Tanka. FCEI
Camelopard, The. Hilaire Belloc. FaBoNo
Camel's Complaint, The. Charles Edward Carryl. *See* Canary-birds feed
   on sugar and seed.
Camel's hump is an ugly lump, The. The Hump. Kipling. *Fr.* Just-So
   Stories. OxBChV
Camels in Persia. Dorothy Wellesley. OBTV
Camels, the Kings' Camel, The. Leslie Norris. PChr
   (Camels of the Kings.) OBCP
Cameo, The. Edna St. Vincent Millay. FYAP; LiTA; MoAmPo; UnPo;
   WPE
Cameo No. II. June Jordan. BPo

Camera. Ted Kooser. Psk
Camera at the crossing sees the city. Gauley Bridge. Muriel Rukeyser.
   NNaP
Camera Obscura, The. John Addington Symonds. NOBVV
Camerados. Bayard Taylor. AnAmPo; Par; UnPo
Camões, alone, of all the lyric race. Luis de Camões. Roy Campbell.
   FaBoTw; PeSA
Camoes and the Debt. Sophia de Mello Breyner Andresen, *tr. fr.*
   Portuguese by Willis Barnstone *and* Nelson Cerqueira. BoWoP
Camouflage. John Manifold. WaP
Camouflaged Troop-Ship. Amy Lowell. AiP
Camp. Patrick Anderson. OBCV
Camp Evergreen. Jane Kenyon. PPR
Camp in the Prussian Forest, A. Randall Jarrell. CMoP; MoAmPo;
   OBWP; OxBC
Camp Notes, *sels.* Mitsuye Yamada. WPOW
   In the Outhouse.
   On the Bus.
Camp of Souls, The. Isabella Valancy Crawford. NOBC
Camp Site. Denis Glover. *Fr.* Arawata Bill. ATNZ; PeNZ
Camp within the West, The. Roderic Quinn. PoAu-1
Campaign, The, *sel.* Joseph Addison.
   Poem to His Grace the Duke of Marlborough, A. OBWP
Campaign. Ciaran Carson. CIP
Campaign, The. Josephine Miles. WPE
Campaign Promise. Henry Taylor. TW
Campfire Extinguished. Raymond Roseliep. InPK; SM
Campi Flegrei. Barend Toerien, *tr. fr. Afrikaans by the author.* PeSA
Campidoglio. Robert Garioch, *after* Guiseppe Belli. OBVE
Camping Out. William Empson. CMoP; FaBoMo; OxBTC
Camping Out on Rainy Mountain. Jim Barnes. CDW
Campion white, The. The Lamp Flower. Margaret Cecilia Furse.
   BoTP
Camptown. John Ciardi. WaP
Camptown Races, The. Stephen Collins Foster. AnAmPo
   (Gwine to Run All Night; or, De Camptown Races.) OBAL
Campus, The. David Posner. NYBP
Campus on the Hill, The. W. D. Snodgrass. AiP; LiTM; NIP; NoAM;
   TAP; TwCP
Can a sad song take the place of crying? Sad Song. *Unknown, tr. by*
   Burton Watson. CoBCP
Can America be reckoned as the country of the free? The Negro Ballot.
   Lizelia Augusta Jenkins Moorer. CBWP-3
Can freckled August, drowsing warm and blonde. The Rain-Crow.
   Madison Cawein. AA
Can. Hist. Earle Birney. OxBC
Can I easily say. Sisters. Adrienne Rich. IHMS
Can I explain this to you? Your eyes. The Knife. Keith Douglas.
   NoAM
Can I Forget? ("Can I forget the sickle mune."). Sydney Goodsir Smith.
   SeCePo
Can I forget the sweet days that have been. Days That Have Been. W.
   H. Davies. FaBoPP
Can I forget thee? No, while mem'ry lasts. On Parting with a Friend.
   Mary Weston Fordham. CBWP-2
Can I not come to Thee, my God, for these. To His Ever-loving God.
   Robert Herrick. TrPWD
Can I not sin, but thou wilt be. To His Conscience. Robert Herrick.
   NAEL-1; NoP; PoEL-3
Can I not sing but "hoy." The Jolly Shepherd. *Unknown.* NOBE
Can—I—poet. For Some Poets. Mae Jackson. PoBA
Can I Say. Dolly Bird. WPOW
Can I see another's woe. On Another's Sorrow. Blake. *Fr.* Songs of
   Innocence. AWP; EnRP; FaBV; PoEL-4
"Can I Tempt You to a Pond Walk?" James Schuyler. PoA
Can I, who have for others oft compiled. Of My Dear Son [*or* Deare
   Sonne], Gervase Beaumont. Sir John Beaumont. JCP; NOBE; OBS
Can it be growing colder when I begin. Adrienne Rich. *Fr.* Twenty-one
   Love Poems, XIX. GLP; NAAL-2
Can it be right to give what I can give? Elizabeth Barrett Browning. *Fr.*
   Sonnets from the Portuguese, IX. CTC; Son
Can it be that the moon has changed? Narihira, *tr. by* Geoffrey Bownas
   and Anthony Thwaite. PeBJV
Can it be true, that we can meet. Slumbering Passion. Josephine D.
   Henderson Heard. CBWP-4
Can Life Be a Blessing. Dryden. *Fr.* Troilus and Cressida. SeCePo
   (Song: "Can life be a blessing.") NoP; SeCV-2
Can life's best consciousness of joy. Questioning. Henrietta Cordelia
   Ray. CBWP-3
Can. Lit. Earle Birney. NOBC
Can love be controlled by advice? John Gay. *Fr.* The Beggar's Opera,
   I, viii. OxBSP
Can one love a boulder. Highland Loves. Rennie McOwan. PoSH

Can only a spring rain so drench. *Unknown, tr. fr. Japanese. Fr.* Manyo Shu. Ma

Can the lover share his soul. W. J. Turner. OBMV

Can the Mole Take. Cecil Day Lewis. OBMV

Can the prime of youth come back to me? Tabito, *tr. fr. Japanese. Fr.* Manyo Shu. Ma

Can there be a moon in heaven to-night. Isabelle. James Hogg. BXAP; Par

Can these movements which move themselves. Belly Dancer. Diane Wakoski. NIP; NoAM

Can this night be tonight? Samantabhadra Facing Westward. Ho Shao-chi, *tr. by* Irving Lo. WFTU

Can u walk away from ugly. Positives for Sterling Plumpp. Don L. Lee. JB; PoBA

Can we fail to be touched by the thought. Sanctuary. John Basil Boothroyd. FiBHP

Can We Make It Next Weekend Instead? Willard R. Espy. SoTCo

Can we not force from widowed [*or* widdowed] poetry. An Elegy upon the Death of the Dean of St. Paul's, Doctor John Donne. Thomas Carew. CaPo

(Elegie upon the Death of the Deane of Paul's, Dr. John Donne, An.) MeLP; MePo; OBS; SeCP; SeCV-1

(Elegy upon the Death of Doctor Donne, Dean of Paul's, An.) PoE

(Elegy upon the Death of the Dean of Paul's, Dr. John Donne, An.) JCP; NAEL-1; NoP

Can ye play me Duncan Gray. Duncan Gray. Burns. CoMu; ErPo

Can Ye Sew Cushions? *Unknown.* FaBoCh

Can You Change a Shilling? Toni Del Renzio. EAS

Can You Hear Me, Thinktank Two? Thomas M. Disch. BWV

Can you hear the music of the letters of the alphabet? Life of the Letters. Emily Borenstein. VWA

Can you imagine. Ms World. Caeia March. DT

Can you imagine this poet. Delete? Yes/No? Edmund Pennant. SoTCo

Can you make me a cambric shirt. *Unknown.* OxNR

Can You Paint a Thought? John Ford. *Fr.* The Broken Heart, III, ii. InvP; PoEL-2

Can you recall an ode to June. A Drawing-Room Ballad. Henry Duff Traill. CenHV

Can your foreigner's nose smell mullets. Who Among You Knows the Essence of Garlic? Garrett Kaoru Hongo. InPS

Can Zone; or, The Good Food Guide. Rika Lesser. MAYP

Cana. Thomas Merton. TrCP

Cana Revisited. Seamus Heaney. FaBoMo

Canaan. Muriel Spark. NYBP

Canada-I-O ("There was a gallant lady all in her tender youth"). *Unknown.* AmFP

Canada-I-O ("Come all ye jolly lumbermen and listen to my song"). *At. to* Ephraim Braley. AmFP

Canada's Natural Resource. Midnight Sun. GOS

Canadian Authors Meet, The. F. R. Scott. NOBC; OBCV

Canadian Boat Song. *At. to* John Galt *and also to* "Christopher North." BLPA; CaP; FaBoCh; FaPoR; GoTS; OBEV; OBNC; OxBS

Canadian Exile, The. Antoine Gerin-Lajoie, *tr. fr. French-Canadian by* John Boyd. CaP

Canadian Farmer. Genevieve Bartole. CaP

Canadian Herd-Boy, The. Susanna-Strickland Moodie. OBCV

Canadian Prairies View of Literature, The. David Donnell. NOBC

Canadian Rossignol, The. Edward William Thomson. CaP

Canadians. Ivor Gurney. FaBoTw

Canal Bank, The. James Stephens. GrPl

Canal Bank Walk. Patrick Kavanagh. CIP; CMoP; FaBoTw; IPY; MoBrPo; NoAM

Canal Street. John Wheelwright. PoA

Canaries were his hobby. The Glass Blower. James Scully. NYBP; TwCP

Canary. Rita Dove. ER

Canary, The. Ogden Nash. FiBHP; RHPC

Canary, The. Elizabeth Turner. OxBChV

Canary-birds feed on sugar and seed. The Plaint of the Camel. Charles Edward Carryl. *Fr.* The Admiral's Caravan. BoTP; FaPON

(Camel's Complaint, The.) OBCA; OxBChV; RHPC

Canary yellow, The. Playing Horses. Tadeusz Rozewicz, *tr. by* Czeslaw Milosz. PwPP

Canberra in April. J. R. Rowland. PoAu-2

Cancer. Hans Verhagen, *tr. fr. Dutch by* Peter Nijmeijer. DuIn

Cancer Cells, The. Richard Eberhart. HAP; LiTM

Cancer's a Funny Thing. John Burdon Sanderson Haldane. OxBTC

Cancion: "O love, I never, never thought." Juan II of Castile, *tr. by* George Ticknor. AWP

Cancion: "When I am the sky." Denise Levertov. PoM

Candaules, King of Lydia. The Queen of Lydia. C. H. Sisson. OxBC

Candelaria and the Sea Turtle. Gladys Cardiff. HATNAP

Candid Man, The. Stephen Crane. *Fr.* War Is Kind, IX. MoAmPo

Candid morn already lifts on high, The. Morning. José Manuel Martínez de Navarrete, *tr. by* Samuel Beckett. MexPo

Candida ("Candida is one today"). Patrick Kavanagh. NAs

Candidate, The. Thomas Gray. PPP

Candidate: Now, Mr. Echo, will you vote for me? By-Election Idyll. Peter Dickinson. FiBHP

Candidate's Letter, The. James Russell Lowell. *Fr.* The Biglow Papers: 1st Series, No. VII. AA

Candle. Jacob Isaac Segal, *tr. fr. Yiddish by* Seymour Mayne. VWA

Candle, A. Sir John Suckling. ErPo

Candle, a Saint, The. Wallace Stevens. PoRA

Candle dies, and incense fades by the closed curtains, A. Speaking of Love. Wei Chuang, *tr. by* Lois Fusek. ATF

Candle Has Slept in Its Own Flame, A. Lo Chih-ch'eng, *tr. fr. Chinese by* Dominic Cheung. IFON

Candle in a long street, A. Hamra Night. Sa'di Yusuf, *tr. by* Abdullah al-Udhari. MPAW

Candle Indoors, The. Gerard Manley Hopkins. LiTB; LiTM; PoEL-5

Candle, Lamp & Firefly. Tess Gallagher. NAmP

Candle lit in darkness of black waters, A. On the Lake. Victoria Mary Sackville-West. OBMV

Candle of Brief Times, The. Anadad Eldan, *tr. fr. Hebrew by* Bernhard Frank. MHeP

Candle Song. Anna Elizabeth Bennett. GoYe

Candle takes the first desperate, The. Homage to Chagall. Duane Niatum. CDW

Candlelight Fisherman, The. *Unknown.* OxBSS

Candlemas. Alice Brown. AA

Candlemas Day. Sister Mary Madeleva. CRP

Candles. Sylvia Plath. NMM

Candles. Hélène Swarth, *tr. fr. Dutch by* Jonathan Crewe. WPOW

Candles Draw Well after All, The. Laura Jensen. LCAP

Candles gutter and burn out, The. Winter Night. Arthur Rex Dugard Fairburn. ATNZ

Candles inhale their own flame, The. Despair. László Kálnoky, *tr. by* Edwin Morgan. MHuP

Candles. Red tulips, ninety cents the bunch. Evening Musicale. Phyllis McGinley. OBAL; Son

Candles splutter, The; and the kettle hums. The Still Small Voice. A. M. Klein. OBCV

Candy/ Is dandy. Reflections on Ice-breaking. Ogden Nash. AiP; BLPL; FaBoCo; FaFP; LiTM; NBLV; NoP; OBAL

Candystore in Washington Heights, A. James Reiss. AnAn

Cane Fields, The. Rita Dove. *Fr.* Parsley, I. NoAM

Cane of Ch'iung Bamboo, The. Hsü Chung-hsing, *tr. fr. Chinese by* Jonathan Chaves. CoBLCP

Canedolia. Edwin Morgan. FaBoCo; PoSH

Canefield and the Sea, The. João Cabral de Melo Neto, *tr. fr. Portuguese by* Louis Simpson. ATCBP

Canine Mother ("Canine fingers, mother, wife, ox"). Dacia Maraini, *tr. fr. Italian by* Muriel Kittel. DMI

Canis Major. Robert Frost. *Fr.* A Sky Pair. MoAB; MoAmPo

Canner, Exceedingly Canny, A. Carolyn Wells. FaPON

Cannery, The. Lucien Stryk. CAPP

Cannery Town in August. Lorna Dee Cervantes. NoAM

Cannibal Future. Gyula Illyés, *tr. fr. Hungarian by* Jascha Kessler. FOC

Cannibal Hymn, The. *Unknown, tr. fr. Egyptian by* Samuel A. B. Mercer. TTY

Cannibalism. Diana Chang. WPOW

Cannibals' Grace before Meat, The. Charles Dickens. FaBoNo

Cannily/ the mists smoor. Kythans. Stewart McGavin. PoSH

Cannon Arrested. Michael S. Harper. CNA

Cannon Park. Mark St. Germain. PCP

Cannon's brazen lips are cold, The. To Pius IX. Whittier. TW

Canny bord ower there. Rape. Tom Pickard. FaBoTw

Canny moment, lucky fit. The Nativity Chant. Sir Walter Scott. *Fr.* Guy Mannering. ChTr; FaBoCh; NAs

Canoe. Patrick Anderson. SD

Canoe, The. Isabella Valancy Crawford. *See* Said the Canoe.

Canoe-hauling Chant. *Unknown, tr. by* Apirana Ngata. WTO

Canoe Song at Twilight. Laura E. McCully. CaP

Canoe Speaks, The, *sel.* Robert Louis Stevenson. "On the great streams the ships may go." SD

Canoe-Trip. Douglas Le Pan. CaP; OBCV

Canogait kirkyaird in the failing year. At Robert Fergusson's Grave, October 1962. Robert Garioch. OxBS

Canonical black-coats, like birds of a feather. Vox Clero. *Unknown.* APAS

Canonical Hours. William Dickey. CoAP

Canonicus and Roger Williams. *Unknown.* PAH

Canonization, The. John Donne. BLPL; ElL; EnLoPo; HAP; JCP; LiTB; MePo; NAEL-1; NAWM-1; NIP; NOBE; NoP; OAEL-1; OBS; PoE; PoEL-2; PPP; SeCePo; SeCP; SeCV-1; TrGrPo; UnPo
(Canonisation, The.) SeCePo; TEP
Canopic Jar. Rika Lesser. MAYP
Canopus. Bert Leston Taylor. FiBHP; NOBL
Canopy of nerve ends. Epiderm. Michael Dransfield. CBAP
Canst thinke the cargoe wherewith ship is fraught. Upon the Decease of Mrs. Anne Griffin. John Fiske. SCAP
Canst thou by searching find out God? Job's Comforters. Bible, *O.T.* Fr. Job, XI: 7–8 *Moulton, Modern Reader's Bible.* WGRP
Canst Thou Draw Out Leviathan with an Hook. Allen Curnow. ATNZ; PeNZ
Canst thou draw out Leviathan with an hook[e]? Bible, *O.T. Fr.* Job. MOS (XLI: 1–10); OBVE (XLI).
(Leviathan, XLI: 1–21) TrGrPo
Canst thou imagine where those spirits live. Shelley. *Fr.* Prometheus Unbound, II, ii. WSC
Canst thou indeed be he that still would sing. Dante, *tr. fr. Italian by* Dante Gabriel Rossetti. *Fr.* La Vita Nuova, XIII. AWP
Canst thou love and lie alone? The Courtier's Good-Morrow to His Mistress. *Unknown.* EIL
Canst thou love me, lady? Love. Charles Stuart Calverley. FiBHP
Cant. Imamu Amiri Baraka. NAAL-2
Can't. Harriet Prescott Spofford. PAH
Can't believe it. April One. Alicia Ostriker. ER
Can't make excuses for you, Cinque. Cinque. Janet Campbell Hale. VoR
"Can't say that now, you have little spring." Yosano Akiko, *tr. fr. Japanese by* Hiroaki Sato. *Fr.* Thirty-nine Tanka. FCEI
"Can't see out of my left eye." Spinning. Alfred W. Purdy. NoAM; NoBC
Can't we find some way/ to meet again. To Ibn Zaidun. Wallada, *tr. by* James Monroe *and* Deirdre Lashgari. WPOW
Can't you see it there. Sogi, *tr. by* Steven D. Carter. WFTW
Cante Hondo. Ellen de Young Kay. NePoEA
Cantelope, The. Bayard Taylor. AnAmPo
Canter has two stride patterns, one on the right lead and one on the left, The. The Flying Change. Henry Taylor. MAYP
Canterbury Tales, The, *sels.* Chaucer.
  Clerk's Tale, The.
    Patient Griselda, *mod. by* Edward Hodnett. PoRA
  Cook's Tale, The. BXAP
  Epilogue of the Man of Law's Tale, The.
    Shipman, The. ACP
  "Fair was this yonge wyf, and therwithal." EBEV
  Franklin's Prologue, The. NAEL-1; OAEL-1
  Franklin's Tale, The. NAEL-1; OAEL-1
  Friar's Prologue, The. PoE
  Friar's Tale, The. PoE
  Introduction to the Franklin's Prologue, The. NAEL-1
  Introduction to the Man of Law's Prologue. FiP
  Introduction to the Pardoner's Prologue, The. NAEL-1; NoP
  Knight's Tale, The.
    "But in the dome of mighty Mars the red," *mod. version by* Dryden. BWP
  Manciple's Tale, The.
    Lat Take a Cat. ChTr
    Controlling the Tongue. OxBChV
  Miller's Prologue, The.
    ("Whan that the knight had [*or* hadde] thus his tale ytold.") NAEL-1; OAEL-1
  Miller's [*or* Milleres] Tale, The. NAEL-1; OAEL-1; OxBoLi
    ("Sometime ago there was a rich old codger," *mod. vers. by* Nevill Coghill.) TEP
    ("There used to be a rich old oaf who made," *mod. vers. by* Theodore Morrison.) NAWM-1
    "Fair was this yonge wyf, and therwithal," *sel.* EBEV
  Nun's Priest's Prologue, The. OAEL-1
    (" 'Stop!' cried the kinght. 'No more of this good sir!' ") NAWM-1
  Nun's Priest's Tale, The. FiP; NAEL-1; NoP; PoEL-1; TrGrPo, *orig. and mod. vers. by* Frank Ernest Hill.
    (Cock and the Hen, The.) OBNV
    ("Once a poor widow, aging year by year," *mod. version by* Theodore Morrison.) NAWM-1
    ("Once, long ago, set close beside a wood.") TrGrPo
    ("There liv'd, as authors tell, in days of yore.") OBVE
      Chauntecleer. FiP
      "His comb was redder than the fine coral." PBBP
    "There liv'd, as authors tell, in days of yore," *mod. version by* Dryden. OBVE

Pardoner's Prologue, The. NAEL-1; NoP; OAEL-1; PoE
  ("In churches," said the Pardoner, "when I preach," *mod. vers. by* Theodore Morrison.) NAWM-1
Pardoner's Tale, The. FiP; HAP; NAEL-1; NoP; OAEL-1; PoE; PoEL-1
  ("It's of three rioters I have to tell," *mod. vers. by* Nevill Coghill) SCV
  ("There was a company of young folk living," *mod. vers. by* Theodore Morrison) NAWM-1
  Death and the Three Revellers. OBNV
  "But, sires o word forgat I in my tale." EBEV
  "This olde man gan looke in his visage." OBD
Parson's Prologue, The. NAEL-1
Prioress's Tale, The. ACP
Prologue. NoP; OAEL-1; PPP, *abr.*
  Clerk of Oxford, The. InPS; TrGrPo
    ("Student came from Oxford town also, A," *mod. vers. by* Louis Untermeyer.) TrGrPo
  "Knyght ther[e] was, and that a worthy man, A." InPS; TrGrPo, *orig. and mod. version by* Louis Untermeyer.
  "Miller was a stout carl, for the nones, The." TrGrPo
    ("Miller, stout and sturdy as the stones, The," *mod. vers. by* Louis Untermeyer.) TrGrPo
  "Monk ther was, a fair for the maistrye [*or* maistrie], A." CTC, *abr. ;* TrGrPo
    ("Monk there was, a monk of mastery, A," *mod. vers. by* Louis Untermeyer.) TrGrPo
  Poor Parson, The. ACP; NOCV; WGRP
    (Good Parson, The, *mod. by* H.C. Leonard) WGRP
  Prioress, The. CTC, *abr.*
    (Madam Eglantine.) NOBE
    ("There also was a nun, a Prioress," *mod. vers. by* Louis Untermeyer.) TrGrPo
  "Sergeant of the Lawe, war and wys, A." CTC, *abr.*
  Shipman, The. MOS
  "This Pardoner had hair as yellow as wax," *mod. vers. by* Nevill Coghill SCV
  "Whan that Aprill[e] with his shoures [*or* shower] soote," *br. sels.* ChTr; CTC, *abr.;* FiP; InPS; NAEL-1; NIP; NoP; OAEL-1; PoE; SCV; TrGrPo
    (As soon as April pierces to the root, *mod. vers. by* Theodore Robinson) NAWM-1
    (When April with Its Sweet Showers.) PrIm
    (When in April the Sweet Showers Fall, *mod. vers. by* Nevill Coghill) TEP
    (When the Sweet Showers of April Follow March, *mod. vers. by* Louis Untermeyer) TrGrPo
  "Good Wif [*or* Wyf] was ther of biside [*or* bisyde] Bathe, A." EBEV; InPS
    (Good Wyf was Ther of Bisyde Bathe, A.) TrGrPo
    ("There was a Wife from Bath, a well-appearing," *mod. vers. by* Louis Untermeyer.) TrGrPo
  "With him ther was his sone, a young Squyer." TrGrPo
    ("With him there was his son, a youthful Squire," *mod. vers. by* Louis Untermeyer) TrGrPo
  "Marchant was ther with a forked berd, A." CTC, *abr.*
Prologue of the Prioress's Tale, The.
  Two Invocations of the Virgin, II. ACP
Prologue to Sir Thopas. Par
  ("Whan said was al this miracle, every man.") NAEL-1
Prologue to the Man of Law's Tale. FiP
Prologue to the Miller's Tale. NAWM-1
Prologue to the Second Nun's Tale, The.
  Two Invocations of the Virgin, I. ACP
Sir Thopas. Par
  (Sir Thopas's Tale.) NAEL-1
  (Tale of Sir Thopas.) BXAP
Wife of Bath's Prologue, The. NAEL-1; OAEL-1; OxBoLi, *abr.*
  (Prologue to the Wife of Bath's Tale, The.) PoEL-1
  "If poor (you say) she drains her husband's purse," *mod. version by* Pope. OBSV
  "My fifthe housbonde, god his soule blesse!" FiP
Wife of Bath's Tale, The. NAEL-1; OAEL-1
Cantica: Our Lord Christ: Of Order. St. Francis of Assisi, *also at. to* Jacopone da Todi, *tr. fr. Italian by* Dante Gabriel Rossetti. AWP; OBVE; PFI
Canticle. Joseph Bruchac. NOVW
Canticle. James McAuley. PoAu-2
Canticle. Michael McClure. NeAP; PoM
Canticle. David Shapiro. TTTS
Canticle for Xmas Eve. David Wagoner. SM

Canticle of Created Things. Saint Francis of Assisi, *tr. fr. Italian by* Henry Taylor. PFI

Canticle of Darkness. Wilfred Watson. MoCV

Canticle of the Sun. Saint Francis of Assisi, *tr. fr. Italian by* Maurice Francis Egan. WGRP

Canticle to Apollo, A. Robert Herrick. CaPo

Canticle to the Waterbirds, A. William Everson. NeAP; PoM

Cantico del Sole. Saint Francis of Assisi, *tr. fr. Italian by* Ezra Pound. CTC

Cantico del Sole. Ezra Pound. OBAL

Canto Amor. John Berryman. CoAP; MoAmPo; VGW

Canto Cantare Cantavi Cantatum. Rita Mae Brown. PeHV

Canto 5: Coon Fire. Tom Weatherly. PoBA

Canto Llano. Anita Endrezze-Danielson. CDW

Canto 7: First Thesis. Tom Weatherly. PoBA

Cantor sings, The. Yom Kippur. Lucille Day. VWA

Cantor was reading [*or* would chant] Psalms, The. Requiem after Seventeen Years. Dahlia Ravikovich. IP, *tr. by* Warren Bargad *and* Stanley F. Chyet; VWA, *tr. by* Chana Bloch

Cantor's Dream before the High Holy Days, A. Martin Robbins. VWA

Cantos, *sels.* Ezra Pound.
  "And then went down to the ship." *Fr.* I. AmPP; CMoP; LiTA; MoAB; MoAmPo; MoP; NoAM; NoP; OBVE; PoE; TrGrPo; VGW
  "Ed ascoltando al leggier mormorio." *Fr.* LXXXI. PoE
  "Eleanor (she spoiled in a British climate)." *Fr.* VII. NoAM; NOBA
  "From the colour the nature,'." *Fr.* XC. VGW
  "Hang it all, Robert Browning." *Fr.* II. AmPP; HAP; MoAB; MoAmPo; NoAM; NOBA; OxBA; PoA
  "Has he tempered the viol's wood." *Fr.* LXXXII. HAP
  "I sat on the Dogana's steps." *Fr.* III. TAP
  "Kung walked/ by the dynastic temple." *Fr.* XIII. CMoP; FaBoMo; PoE
  "Oh to be in England now that Winston's out." *Fr.* LXXX. PoA
  Said Jim X. . . *Fr.* XII. NAs
  "Scientists are in terror, The." *Fr.* CXV. FaBoMo
  "Serenely in the crystal jet." *Fr.* LXXIV. PoE
  "So that the vines burst from my fingers." *Fr.* XVII. InPS; NAAL-2; OBMV
  "Then a partridge-shaped cloud over dust storm." *Fr.* CXIII. NYBP
  "Tudor indeed is gone and every rose." *Fr.* LXXX. FaBoTw
  "What thou lovest well remains." *Fr.* LXXXI. CMoP; FaBoTw; MoAB; NOBE; OxBA; ViBoPo
  "Who even dead, yet hath his mind entire!" *Fr.* XLVII. CMoP; PoE; VGW
  With Usura. *Fr.* XLV. CMoP; LiTM; NAAL-2; NOBA; PoE; TW
  "Zeus lies in Ceres' bosom." *Fr.* LXXXI. FaBoMo; MoP; NAAL-2; NoAM; NOBA; VGW

Cantos, *sels.* Tom Weatherly. PoBA
  Coon Fire. *Fr.* 5.
  First Thesis. *Fr.* 7.
  Gullfish. *Fr.* 4.

Canute at Ely, *sel. Unknown.*

Cnut's Song. PoE

Canyon Day Woman Blues. Geraldine Keams. GOS

Canzone: "Consider the three functions of the tongue." Marilyn Hacker. NoAM, *abr.*

Canzone: Donna Mi Priegha. Guido Cavalcanti, *tr. fr. Italian by* Ezra Pound. CTC

Canzone: He Beseeches Death for the Life of Beatrice. Dante, *tr. fr. Italian by* Dante Gabriel Rossetti. AWP

Canzone: He Speaks of His Condition through Love. Folcachiero de' Folcachieri, *tr. fr. Italian by* Dante Gabriel Rossetti. AWP

Canzone: His Lament for Selvaggia. Cino da Pistoia, *tr. fr. Italian by* Dante Gabriel Rossetti. AWP

Canzone: His Portrait of His Lady, Angiola of Verona. Fazio degli Uberti, *tr. fr. Italian by* Dante Gabriel Rossetti. AWP

Canzone: "I crisscross my feelings with a view." Anne Waldman. UL

Canzone: Lady Asks Me, A. Guido Cavalcanti, *tr. fr. Italian by* Ezra Pound. PFI

Canzone: "Love, which is least sure and most dared, the pure, keen." Peyton Houston. *Fr.* Sonnet Variations, CVI, ii. Son

Canzone: "No better lost than any other woman." Marilyn Hacker. NoAM

Canzone: Of His Dead Lady. Giacomino Pugliesi, *tr. fr. Italian by* Dante Gabriel Rossetti. AWP

Canzone: Of His Love, with the Figure of a Sudden Storm. Prinzivalle Doria, *tr. fr. Italian by* Dante Gabriel Rossetti. AWP

Canzone: Of the Gentle Heart. Guido Guinicelli, *tr. fr. Italian by* Dante Gabriel Rossetti. AWP; CTC; OBVE; PFI

Canzone: "Strained daybreak breaks in past the blinds." Lorenzo Thomas. UL

Canzone: To Love and to His Lady. Guido delle Colonne, *tr. fr. Italian by* Dante Gabriel Rossetti. AWP

Canzone: "When shall we learn, what should be clear as day." W. H. Auden. LiTA

Canzonet. *Unknown.* EIl

Canzonetta. Antonia Pozzi, *tr. fr. Italian by* Brenda Webster. OV

Canzonetta: A Bitter Song to His Lady. Pier Moronelli da Fiorenza, *tr. fr. Italian.* AWP, *tr. by* Dante Gabriel Rossetti; OBVE, *tr. by* Dante Gabriel Rossetti

Canzonetta: He Will Neither Boast nor Lament to His Lady. Jacopo da Lentino, *tr. fr. Italian by* Dante Gabriel Rossetti. AWP

Canzonetta: Of His Lady, and of His Making Her Likeness. Jacopo da Lentino, *tr. fr. Italian by* Dante Gabriel Rossetti. AWP

Canzonetta: Of His Lady in Absence. Giacomino Pugliesi, *tr. fr. Italian by* Dante Gabriel Rossetti. AWP

Cap and Bells, The. W. B. Yeats. BrPo; ChTr; MoAB; MoBrPo; NoAM; NoP; OnMSP; RB; WSC

Cap so tall, A. *Unknown, tr. by* Arthur Waley. BoS

Cap tipped back, propped by a window, still can't settle down. Sitting Outdoors. Lu Yu, *tr. by* Burton Watson. CoBCP

Capability Brown. William Cowper. SaC

Cape Ann. T. S. Eliot. *Fr.* Landscapes, V. GoJo; NAEL-2; NoAM; RB

Cape Ann; a View. John Malcolm Brinnin. NYBP

Cape Breton. Elizabeth Bishop. InPS

Cape Canaveral. Outer Space Haiku. Thomas M. Disch. BWV

Cape Coast Castle Revisted. Jo Ann Hall-Evans. BlSi

Cape Cod. George Santayana. AnAmPo

Cape Cod girls they've got no combs. The Codfish Shanty. *Unknown.* GBP

Cape Coloured Batman. Guy Butler. PeSA

Cape Hatteras. Hart Crane. *Fr.* The Bridge, IV. InPS; MoAB; MoAmPo
  "Nasal whine of power whips a new universe." MoAB
  (Power.) MoAmPo

Capes. Frederica Goldsmith. TSM

Capilano ("Capilano, in the canyon"). A. M. Maitland. CaP

Capital. Heather McHugh. MAYP

Capital at Shiga, The. Tadanori, *tr. by* Geoffrey Bownas *and* Anthony Thwaite. PeBJV

Capital ship for an ocean trip, A. The *Walloping Window-Blind,* . Charles Edward Carryl. *Fr.* Davy and the Goblin, *ch.* 8. NA; NBLV; OBCA
  (Nautical Ballad, A.) FaPON; OBAL
  ("Oh, a capital ship for an ocean trip.") MoShBr

Capital Square. Patrick Anderson. OBCV

Capitals Are Rocked, The. Nikolai Alekseyevich Nekrasov, *tr. fr. Russian by* Babette Deutsch *and* Avrahm Yarmolinsky. AWP

Cap'n, I Believe *with music. Unknown.* AS

Capped arbiter of beauty in this street. Hart Crane. *Fr.* For the Marriage of Faustus and Helen, III. FaBoMo; LiTM

Capri as Cloud. Karl Wawra, *tr. fr. German by* Beth Bjorklund. CoAuP

Capriccio Dramatico, Il, *sel. Lorenzo da Ponte, tr. fr. Italian by* John Mazzinghi.
  To an Artful Theatre Manager. TrJP

Capriciousness ("Capricious was the guest of another day"). Chin Jen-Jui, *tr. fr. Chinese by* Irving Lo. WFTU

Capsized on the bed. Trying On for Size. Mary Dorcey. AIW

Captain, The, *sels.* Beaumont *and* Fletcher.
  Away, Delights. *Fr.* III, iv. EIl; NOBE; OBEV
  (Sad Song, The.) GBL
  Tell Me Dearest, What is Love?. EIl

Captain, The. Tennyson. MOS

Captain, The. Blanca Varela, *tr. fr. Spanish by* Lynne Alvarez. WPOW

Captain, The. Jon Manchip White. NePoEA

Captain,/ what are you doing. George Simic. Charles Simic. DiL

Captain/ the rockets, the open forces of the waterfall threaten us. Monsieur AA, Antiphilosopher. Tristan Tzara, *tr. by* Richard Howard. RHTwFP

Captain Arthur Phillip and the Birds. Lex Banning. PoAu-2

Captain Barton's Distress on Board the *Lichfield. Unknown.* OxBSS

Captain bold in [*or* from] Halifax, that [*or* who] dwelt in country quarters, A. Unfortunate Miss Bailey. George Colman, the Younger. FiBHP; GBP
  (Miss Bailey's Ghost.) FaBoBa; OxBoLi

Captain Bover. *Unknown.* GBP

Captain Bunker. *Unknown.* AmFP

Captain Car. *Unknown. See* Edom o' Gordon.

Captain Car; *or,* Edom o Gordon. *Unknown.* ESPB

Captain Carpenter. John Crowe Ransom. FaBoMo; HoPM; LiTA; LiTM; MoAB; MoAmPo; MoP; NoAM; NOBA; OxBA; TwCP

Captain Chilver's gone to sea. The Benjamins' Lamentation for Their Sad Loss at Sea, by Storms and Tempests. *Unknown.* OxBSS

Captain Craig, *sel.* Edwin Arlington Robinson.
"I doubt if ten men in all Tilbury Town." PoEL-5

Captain Death. *Unknown.* CoMu

Captain Glen's Unhappy Voyage to New Barbary. *Unknown.* OxBSS

Captain Hall. *Unknown.* GBP

Captain Hawk scourged clean the seas. The Hemp. Stephen Vincent Benét. FL

Captain is drinking rum, The. Anchor. Maruyama Kaoru, *tr. by* Hiroaki Sato. FCEI

Captain James. *Unknown.* OxBSS

Captain Jinks. *Unknown.* BLPA; FaFP

Captain Jones' Invitation. Philip Freneau. MOS

Captain Kidd ("Oh, my name was Robert Kidd, as I sailed, as I sailed"). *Unknown.* MoShBr

Captain Kidd ("You captains brave and bold, hear our cry, hear our cry"). *Unknown.* AmFP

Captain Kid's Farewell to the Seas; or, The Famous Pirate's Lament. *Unknown.* OxBSS

Captain Mansfield's Fight with the Turks at Sea. *Unknown.* OxBSS

Captain Michael. Park Je-chun. WCI

Captain of the *Shannon* came sailing up the bay, The. The *Shannon* and the *Chesapeake.* Thomas Tracy Bouvé. PAH

Captain of the Western wood. Madroño. Bret Harte. AA

Captain or colonel, or knight in arms. When the Assault Was Intended to the City. Milton. GTBS; GTBS-P; NoP; Son
(Sonnet: "Captain or colonel or knight in arms.") OAEL-1

Captain Reece. William Schwenck Gilbert. CenHV; FiBHP; GN

Capt. Smith and Pocahontas. Eloise Bibb. CBWP-4

Captain Spud and His First Mate, Spade. John Ciardi. OBCA

Captain Stood on the Carronade, The. Frederick Marryat. *Fr.* Snarleyyow; or, The Dog Fiend. MOS

Captain Stratton's Fancy. John Masefield. MoBrPo; OBEV

Captain Sword. Leigh Hunt. GN

Captain: the weathervane's rusted. Widow's Walk. Elizabeth Spires. MAYP

Captain Ward and the *Rainbow. Unknown.* ESPB; OBET; OxBSS

Captain Wattle and Miss Roe. Charles Dibdin. OxBoLi

Captain! we often heretofore. To Our House-Dog Captain. Walter Savage Landor. PoEL-4

Captain Wedderburn's Courtship ("As I walked out one evening down by the Strawberry Lane"). *Unknown.* AmFP; ESPB, A *and* B. *vers.*

Captain's Daughter, The. James Thomas Fields. *See* We were crowded in the cabin.

Captain's Feather, The. Samuel Minturn Peck. AA

Captive. Peretz Hirshbein, *tr. fr. Yiddish by* Joseph Leftwich. TrJP

Captive. Marion Strobel. ErPo

Captive Dove, The. Anne Brontë. EBVV

Captive Escaped in the Wilds of America Addressed to the Honorable Mrs. O'Neill, The. Charlotte Smith. Son

Captive of Love. Ovid, *tr. fr. Latin by* Christopher Marlowe. *Fr.* Elegies, I, 2. AWP

Captive Ships at Manila, The. Dorothy Paul. PAH

Captive Stone, The. Jim Barnes. CDW

Captived Bee; or, The Little Filcher, The. Robert Herrick. CaPo

Captive's Hymn, The. Edna Dean Proctor. PAH

Captivity. Louise Erdrich. HATNAP; NoAM

Captivity, The, *sel.* Goldsmith.
O Memory, Thou Fond Deceiver. *Fr.* I. OxBSP
(Memory.) OBEV

Captivity. Samuel Rogers. OBNC

Captivity Narrative, September 1981. Adrian C. Louis. STE

Capture of Edwin Alonzo Boyd, The. Peter Miller. MoCV

Capture of Little York. *Unknown.* PAH

Caput apri refero. The Boar's Head Carol. *Unknown.* MeEL

Capystranus. *Unknown.* OxBLMV

Car, The. Robert Creeley. RR

Car, A. Lan Ling, *tr. fr. Chinese by* Dominic Cheung. IFON

Car Cemetery, The. Ciaran Carson. CIP

Car/ I give you over to. Car Wash. Myra Cohn Livingston. NTCP

Car conveys us where we've been, The. Moving between Beloit and Monroe. Bink Noll. GrPl

Car coughing moves with. The Car. Robert Creeley. RR

Car goes slowly around the curve, now, The. Peter Rosei, *tr. by* Beth Bjorklund. CoAuP

Car is also, A/ a high-speed hermitage. Portrait of the Autist as a New World Driver. Les A. Murray. CBAP

Car is heavy with children, The. The Road Back. Anne Sexton. NYBP

Car Wash. Myra Cohn Livingston. NTCP

Caraguin, The, *sel.* Robert Dunbar.
"Angelica has gain'd the dell." PBCV

Carat of the first radiance. Lightning Bug. Robert Morgan. GeTw

Caravaggio Dying, Porto Ercole, July 1610, Aged 36, *sel.* Edward Lucie-Smith.
"My own head. Seen in mirrors. Cleanly axed." *Fr.* II. PeHV

Caravan. Michael Longley. CIP; FaBCIP

Caravan, The. Gwendolyn MacEwen. MoCV

Caravan, The. Madeleine Nightingale. BoTP

Caravans. Irene Thompson. BoTP

Caravati's Junkyard. Elizabeth Morgan. GrPl

Caravati's Salvage: Richmond, Virginia. Dave Smith. KS

Carbon or/ silicon. Syrup. Steve Rasnic Tem. BWV

Carcassonne. Gustave Nadaud, *tr. fr. French by* John R. Thompson. BLPA; FaBoBe

Card comes to tell you, A. Non Piangere, Liù. Peter Porter. OxBC

Card Game; Kinjiro Sawada, A. Patricia Y. Ikeda. BrSi

Card of licence A B C the viceroy of India was a queen in the majority of cases. The New Republic. Marcelin Pleynet, *tr. by* John Ashbery. RHTwFP

Card-Players, The. Philip Larkin. OxBC

Card-Players, The. David Ray. VGW

Card table in the library stands ready, A. Lost in Translation. James Merrill. *Fr.* The Book of Ephraim. FYAP; HCAP; NAAL-2; NoAM

Cardinal Bembo's Epitaph on Raphael. Thomas Hardy, *after* Pietro Bembo. EyDe; FaBoEE

Cardinal Bird, The. William Davis Gallagher. AA

Cardinal Fisher. John Heywood. ACP

Cardinal Ideograms. May Swenson. OBCA

Cardinal is perched upon a bat, A. World Champions. William Jay Smith. ASP

Cardinal Newman. Christina Rossetti. NAEL-2

Cardinal Wolsey's Farewell. Shakespeare *and probably* John Fletcher. *See* King Henry VIII: Wolsey's Farewell to His Greatness.

Cardinal's Dog, The. John Glassco. MoCV

Cardinals in the Ice Age. John Engels. BLA

Cards and Kisses. John Lyly. *See* Alexander and Campaspe: Cupid and my Campaspe played.

Care. Virginia Woodward Cloud. AA

Care. Josephine Miles. NYBP

Care. Richard Murphy. IPY

Care and heavy thought weigh me down. Estat ai en greu cossirier. Beatriz de Dia, *tr. by* Paul Blackburn. ErPo

Care Away ("Care away, away, away,/ Care away for evermore!"). *Unknown.* OxBoLi

Care-Charmer Sleep. Bartholomew Griffin. *Fr.* Fidessa, More Chaste than Kind, XV. AAS; NIP
(Sleep.) OBSC

Care-charmer sleep[e], son[ne] of the sable night. Samuel Daniel. *Fr.* To Delia. AAS; GTBS; GTBS-P; InPS; NAEL-1; NOBE; NoP; OBSC; TrGrPo
(Care-charmer Sleep.) LiTB; NiP; OAEL-1; Son
(Sonnet: "Care-charmer sleep[e], son[ne] of the sable night.") EiL; PoEL-2

Care-charming Sleep [Thou Easer of All Woes]. John Fletcher. *Fr.* The Tragedy of Valentinian, V, ii. ELP; FaBoRV; OxBSP; TrGrPo
(Into Slumbers.) SeCePo
(Song: "Care-charming sleep, thou easer of all woes.") OBS; PoEL-2
(Song to Sleep.) OxBoLi
(To Sleep.) PoRA

Care of Bees, The. Virgil, *tr. fr. Latin by* Dryden. *Fr.* Georgics, IV. FaBoUs

Care thy father once bestowed on me, The. To My Nephew, J. B. Clement Barksdale. OxBSP

Careening/ I'm roaming. Creaming. Elizabeth McKim. ER

Career Women Who Marry Today. Ned Pastor. SoTCo

Careering on a downslope from the bail. Blackleg. Kendrick Smithyman. ATNZ

Careers. Marjorie Welish. UL

Careful Angler, The. Robert Louis Stevenson. SD; SoSe

Careful! Even moonlit dewdrops. Waka. Sogyo, *tr. by* Lucien Stryk *and* Takashi Ikemoto. ZPCJ

Careful: my knife drills your soul. The Killer. A'yunini, *tr. by* Jerome Rothenberg. STP

Careful [l] observers may foretell the hour. A Description of a City Shower. Swift. HeIP; MAT; NAEL-1; NOEC; NoP; OAEL-1; OBSV; PoE; PPP; SeCePo; TEP; UnPo

Carefully she opened her tunic. The Breasts of Mnasidice. Pierre Louÿs, *tr. fr. French.* *Fr.* Chansons de Bilitis. PeHV

Careless/ but not fearless. Walter Lew. *Fr.* Urn I: Silent for Twenty-five Years, the Father of My Mother Advises Me. BrSi

Careless and still. The Rabbit Hunter. Robert Frost. ASP

Careless Content. John Byrom. NOEC

Careless for an instant I closed my child's fingers in the jamb. Fingers in the Door. David Holbrook. NePoEA-2

Careless Gallant, The. Thomas Jordan. CoMu; HAP; OxBoLi
   (Coronemus Nos Rosis Antequam Marcescant.) OBEV
   (Epicure, The, Sung by One in the Habit of a Town Gallant.) NOBE
Careless Good Fellow, The. John Oldham. APAS; SeCV-2
Careless Love. Stanley Kunitz. WaP
Careless Love. *Unknown. AS, with music; UnPo
Careless Talk. Mark Hollis. FiBHP; NBLV
Careless Willie. *Unknown.* FaPON
Carelesse Nurse Mayd, The. Thomas Hood. FaBoNo
Carentan O Carentan. Louis Simpson. CoAP; MoBS; NOBA; OBWP;
   PoE; PrIm; RB
Cares of Majesty, The. Shakespeare. *Fr.* King Henry IV, Pt. II, III, i.
   LiTB
   (O Gentle Sleep.) FaBoRV
   (Soliloquy on Sleep.) FiP
Caress, The. Juana de Ibarbourou, *tr. fr. Spanish by* Perry Higman.
   LPSS
Caressing one another noise. Mohammad Taqi Mir, *tr. by* Ahmed Ali.
   GoT
Cargoes. John Masefield. BLPL; CMoP; FaBV; FaPON; FaPoR; InPK;
   LiTM; MoAB; MoBrPo; MOS; NOBE; OBEV; OBMV; PoRA; TEP
Cargoes of the Radanites. Harry Alan Potamkin. TrJP
Carhop floated up, The. Chicken. Dave Etter. MAT
Caria and Philistia considered. Cry Faugh! Robert Graves. MoBrPo
Cariboo Horses, The. Alfred W. Purdy. HeIP; NOBC
Caries. Solyman Brown. *Fr.* Dentologia; a Poem on the Diseases of the
   Teeth and Their Proper Remedies. FaBoUs
Carious Exposure. Gladys Cardiff. CDW
Carissima Joannissima, ave. Letter from the Alpes-Maritimes. Marilyn
   Hacker. EOEF
Carl Hamblin. Edgar Lee Masters. *Fr.* Spoon River Anthology.
   CMoP; LiTA; LiTM; OBSV
Carle He Came o'er the Croft, The. Allan Ramsay. OxBS
Carlino! what art thou about, my boy? To My Child Carlino. Walter
   Savage Landor. NoP
Carlos, keep calm, love. Don't Kill Yourself. Carlos Drummond de
   Andrade, *tr. by* Elizabeth Bishop. ATCBP
Carlyle and Emerson. Montgomery Schuyler. AA
Carlyle combined the lit'ry life. Thomas Carlyle. *Unknown.* FiBHP
Carlyle on Burns. William Jeffrey. *Fr.* On Glaister's Hill. OxBS
Carmel Point. Robinson Jeffers. NAAL-2; NoAM; NoP
Carmelite. Raymond Murray, *tr. fr. Irish by the author.* TIRV
Carmen. Victor Hernandez Cruz. PoBA
Carmen. Newman Levy. FiBHP
Carmen Bellicosum. Guy Humphreys McMaster. AA; GN; PAH
Carmen Elegiacum. Thomas Morton. SCAP
Carmen Possum. *Unknown.* BLPA; NBLV
Carmen Saeculare. Charles Hubert Sisson, *after the Latin of* Horace.
   OBVE
Carmina Amico, *sels.* Edward James. PeHV
   "He had a many-coloured glance like flowers."
   "You have returned. You have returned, my joy."
Carmina Burana, *sel. Unknown, tr. fr. Latin by* Willis Barnstone.
   "I loved/ secretly." BoWoP
Carmina XXII. Catullus. *See* Suffenus, whom so well you know.
Carnal and the Crane, The. *Unknown.* ESPB; OBET
Carnal Knowledge. Thom Gunn. BoLoP
Carnal Knowledge. Gwen Harwood. CBAP
Carnation Milk ("Carnation milk is the best in the land"). *Unknown.*
   InPK
   (Virtues of Carnation Milk, The.) OBAL
Carnation, The ("May this carnation announce to [*or* tell] you").
   Guillaume Apollinaire, *tr. fr. French.* POS, *trs. by* Michael Benedikt
   and Roger Shattuck.
Carnations and Butterflies. Pope. *Fr.* The Dunciad. NOEC
Carnival is over, The. The high tents. Sunday Night in Santa Rosa.
   Dana Gioia. GrPl
Carnival Songs, *sel.* Lorenzo de' Medici, *tr. fr. Italian by* Richard
   Aldington.
   Triumph of Bacchus and Ariadne. CTC
Carol: "Deep in the fading leaves of night." William Robert Rodgers.
   OBCP
Carol: Five Joys of the Virgin, The. *Unknown.* ACP
Carol: "Garden and gardener He made." Thomas Kinsella. TIRV
Carol: "I was a lover of turkey and holly." Anne Wilkinson. OBCV
Carol: "Mary laid her Child among." Norman Nicholson. OBCP
Carol: "Mary, the mother, sits on the hill." Langdon E. Mitchell. OHIP
Carol: "My heart of gold as true as steel." *Unknown. See* My heart of
   gold.
Carol: "My lady went to Canterbury [*or* Caunterbury]." *Unknown.*
   FaBoCo; FaBoNo
   (Nonsense Song, A.) OxBLMV
Carol: "Now is the world withdrawn all." Howard Nemerov. TrCP

Carol: "There was a boy bedded in bracken." John Short. FaBoCh;
   FaBoTw
Carol: "Villagers all, this frosty tide." Kenneth Grahame. *See* Wind in
   the Willows, The: Villagers all, this frosty tide.
Carol: "When the herd[s] were watching." William Canton. OHIP
Carol, every violet has. Alfred Noyes. *Fr.* The Flower of Old Japan.
   MoBrPo
Carol for Advent. John Heath-Stubbs. OxBC
Carol for Children, A. Ogden Nash. EaLo
Carol for St. Stephen's Day, A. *Unknown. See* Seynt Stevene was a clerk
Carol for the Last Christmas Eve. Norman Nicholson. OBCP
Carol for Twelfth Day, A. *Unknown.* OHIP
Carol in Praise of the Holly and Ivy. *Unknown.* OHIP
Carol, in the Park, Chewing on Straws. Judy Grahn. *Fr.* The Common
   Woman, IV. PeHV; WPOW
Carol of Agincourt, A. *Unknown. See* Our king went forth to
   Normandy.
Carol of Death, The. Walt Whitman. *See* Memories of President
   Lincoln: When Lilacs Last in the Dooryard Bloom'd.
Carol of Death, The. Walt Whitman. *Fr.* When Lilacs Last in the
   Dooryard Bloom'd. DL; SCV
Carol of Patience. Robert Graves. OBCP
Carol of St. George, A. *Unknown.* MeEL
Carol of the Birds. *Unknown, tr. fr. French.* OHIP
Carol of the Brown King. Langston Hughes. PChr
Carol of the Numbers. *Unknown.* AmFP
Carol of the Poor Children, The. Richard Middleton. OBCP
Carol of the Russian Children. *Unknown, tr. fr. Russian.* OHIP
Carol of the Three Kings. William Stanley Merwin. PChr
Carol Singers, The. Margaret G. Rhodes. BoTP
Carol to Catherine. Sister Juana Inés de la Cruz, *tr. fr. Spanish by* Kate
   Flores. DMH
Carolina. Henry Timrod. PAH
Carolina mourns to-day. For he, the gifted. Tribute to Capt. F. W.
   Dawson. Mary Weston Fordham. CBWP-2
Caroline, The. George Crabbe. *Fr.* The Borough, Letter XI. SeCePo
Caroline and Her Young Sailor Bold. *Unknown.* AmFP
Caroline beside the Sundial. Kevin Ireland. ATNZ
Caroline of Edinboro' Town. *Unknown.* AmFP
Carousel, The. Gloria C. Oden. AmNP; PoBA
Carp and trout, roach and grayling. Crusade in Europe. Carla Lanyon
   Lanyon. CN
Carp are secrets, The. Lifting Illegal Nets by Flashlight. William
   Stafford. NNaP
Carp pennant, The. *Unknown, tr. by* Geoffrey Bownas *and* Anthony
   Thwaite. PeBJV
Carpe Diem. Thomas Lodge. *See* Robert, Second Duke of Normandy:
   Pluck the Fruit and Taste the Pleasure.
Carpe Diem. Shakespeare. *See* Twelfth Night: O [*or* Oh] Mistress Mine
   [Where Are You Roaming?].
Carpe Diem. C. K. Stead. ATNZ
Carpenter. George Mackay Brown. OxBC
Carpenter, The. George Macdonald. TrPWD
Carpenter, The. Mary Brent Whiteside. TrCP
Carpenter is intent on the pressure of his hand, The. El Greco: Espolio.
   Earle Birney. MoCV
Carpenter, mechanic, and I. Fall. Sydney Lea. BLA
Carpenter's Complaint, The. Edward Baugh. PVCV
Carpenter's made a hole, The. A Hole in the Floor. Richard Wilbur.
   NOBA; SoSe
Carpenter's Son, The. A. E. Housman. *Fr.* A Shropshire Lad, XLVII.
   MoAB; MoBrPo
Carpenter's son, carpenter's son. Craftsman. Luci Shaw. TrCP
Carpenter's Wife, The ("O whare hae ye been, my dearest dear").
   Unknown. OAEL-1; OxBB
Carpenter's Wife, The ("Well met, well met, my own true love").
   Unknown. OBET
Carpet-Weavers' Lament, The. *Unknown.* OBET
Carpets cover many floors where I come from. To Vietnam. Charlie
   Cobb. PoBA
Carravagio. Janet Hamill. UL
Carrefour. Amy Lowell. BoWoP
Carriage brushes through the bright, The. Solo for Ear-Trumpet. Dame
   Edith Sitwell. MoAB; MoBrPo
Carriage from Sweden, A. Marianne Moore. HAP; LiTA; LiTM;
   MoAB; TwCP; WeW
Carrickfergus. Louis MacNeice. AnIL; FaBCIP; FaBoPP; NAEL-2;
   NoAM; NOIV
Carried Away. Anne Elder. CBAP
Carried her unprotesting out the door. The Rites for Cousin Vit.
   Gwendolyn Brooks. *Fr.* The Womanhood, VI. BPo; HAP; WeW;
   WPE

Carried overhead and wished upon. Teika, *tr. fr. Japanese* by Hiroaki Sato. *Fr.* Eighty-four Tanka. FCEI
Carrier Indians. Ken Belford. NOBC
Carrier Letter. Hart Crane. BoLoP
Carriers of the Dream Wheel. N. Scott Momaday. CDW
Carrion, A. Baudelaire, *tr. fr. French* by Allen Tate. AWP
Carrion. Harold Monro. *Fr.* Youth in Arms, IV. MMA
Carrion Comfort. Gerard Manley Hopkins. CMoP; HeIP; LiTB; NAEL-2; NoAM; NoP; OAEL-2; PoE; PoEL-5; PPP; Son; TEP; TOF
Carrion Crow, The. Thomas Lovell Beddoes. *See* Death's Jest Book: Old Adam, the Carrion Crow.
Carrion crow flew over Bayswater, A. A Crow in Bayswater. John Heath-Stubbs. PoPo
Carrion crow sat upon an oak, The. Mother Goose. OxNR; PBBP, *sl. diff. version, with 2 add. sts*
Carrion-eater's nobility calls back from God, The. A Dreamed Realization. Gregory Corso. NeAP; PoM; VGW
Carrot Crazy. Edward Watkins. SoTCo
Carrots tried to be mushrooms, The. Their songs cried to the sonnet. Echo. Steve Benson. IAT
Carrouse to the Emperor, the Royal Pole, and the Much-wronged Duke of Lorrain, A. *Unknown.* CoMu
Carrousel Tune. Tennessee Williams. NBLV; OBAL
Carry Her over the Water. W. H. Auden. FaBoTw; RB
Carry me ackee go a Linstead market. Linstead Market. *Unknown.* PBCV
Carry Me Back. John Holmes. AmFN
Carry Me Back to Old Virginny. James A. Bland. FaBoBe; FaFP (Old Virginny.) FaBV
Carry me back to old Virginny. Notes for a Southern Road Map. Phyllis McGinley. NBLV
Carry me back to Ole Virginny. First Families Move Over! Ogden Nash. FaBoCo
Carry me out. Discharged. W. E. Henley. *Fr.* In Hospital, XXVIII.
Carry your garden. The Serpent Muses. Peggy Henderson. NMM
Carry your grief alone. Alone. Robert Finch. CaP
Carrying a hammer on a quiet street. The Planting. Harley Elliott. NeAC
Carrying a parasol and singing. Having Followed the Sound of Rain into the Mountain but Found No Rain. Lo Fu, *tr.* by Dominic Cheung. IFON
Carrying fresh water with both hands. Ozaki Hosai, *tr. fr. Japanese* by Hiroaki Sato. *Fr.* One Hundred Haiku in Free Form. FCEI
Carrying from the courtyard. Song of the Cricket. Lo Fu, *tr.* by Dominic Cheung. IFON
Carrying generations of lust on his tiny feet. Agent of Love. A. K. Redwing. VoR
Carrying his wife on his back a frog. Jokushi, *tr.* by Hiroaki Sato. FCEI
Carrying mother on my back. Ishikawa Takuboku, *tr.* by Geoffrey Bownas *and* Anthony Thwaite. PeBJV
Carrying my world. Father. Myra Cohn Livingston. NTCP
Carrying On. Leonard Nathan. BLA
Carrying Their Coracles. Andrew Marvell. *Fr.* Upon Appleton House, to My Lord Fairfax. ChTr
Carrying their packages of groceries in particular. Old Men and Old Women Going Home on the Street Car. Merrill Moore. MoAmPo
Cars/ In the Park. Central Park Tourney. Mildred Weston. AmFN
Cars are wicked, poets think. Man on Wheels. Karl Shapiro. PCP
Cars in Caracas, The. John Updike. RR
Cars in the mirror come swiftly forward, The. Rear Vision. William Jay Smith. NYBP
Cars Once Steel and Green, Now Old. Louis Zukofsky. VGW
Cartagena de Indias. Earle Birney. MoCV
Carter, The. *Unknown.* OBET
Carthon; a Poem. James Macpherson. EnRP
Carthusians. Ernest Dowson. NAEL-2
Cartload of Shoes, A. Abraham Sutskever, *tr. fr. Yiddish* by David G. Roskies. VWA
Cartographers, The. Heather Allen. KS
Cartwheels. Mary Lonnberg Smith. AIW
Caruso: a voice. Sleeping with Women. Kenneth Koch. PoM
Carved by a mighty race whose vanished hands. The Sphinx Speaks. Francis Saltus Saltus. AA
Carved in cheap marble, milky & veined. The Lamb. Keith Wilson. Psk
Carved into Buddha's form. Ozaki Hosai, *tr. fr. Japanese* by Hiroaki Sato. *Fr.* One Hundred Haiku in Free Form. FCEI
Carved on an Areca Nut. Ho Xuan Huong, *tr. fr. Vietnamese* by Nguyen Ngoc Bich *and* Burton Raffel. PBWP
Carved out of granite. One Rose of Stone. Keith Wilson. GOYP
Carver, The. Lucille Clifton. CAPP

Carving on the jamb of an embrasure, A. The Priory of St. Saviour, Glendalough. Donald Davie. OxBC
Caryatid. Léonie Adams. LiTM
Caryophyllaceae, The/ like a scroungy. Spring Coming. A. R. Ammons. HeIP; InPK
Casa d'Amunt. Alastair Reid. NePoEA
Casa de Pollos. Kathleen Fraser. AmPA
Casa Nuestra, *sel.* Marco Martos, *tr. fr. Spanish* by David Tipton. "Sometimes I visit the city." Per
Casabianca. Elizabeth Bishop. FaBoWP; OxBSP
Casabianca. Felicia Dorothea Hemans. BeLS; BLPA; FaBoBe; FaBoPa; FaFP; FaPON; FPL; WBLP
Casablanca Time Again. Joy Howard. DT
Casanova's Ankle ("Casanova was turned by an ankle"). Elizabeth Smither. ATNZ; PeNZ
Casbah, The. Mamdouh Udwan, *tr. fr. Arabic* by May Jayyusi *and* Naomi Shihab Nye. MAP
Cascade, The. Edgell Rickword. FaBoTw
Cascadilla Falls. A. R. Ammons. NIP; NOBA
Cascando. Samuel Beckett. NOIV
Case, The. Hoffman Reynolds Hays. EAS
Case, A. Hughes Mearns. *See* As I was going up the stair.
Case at Sessions, A. Walter Savage Landor. OBSV
Case for the Miners, The. Siegfried Sassoon. SaC
Case of Ample Ora: Sweetness and Light, The. Pamela White Hadas. BLA
"Case of Assault, A." Lydia Stephanou, *tr. fr. Modern Greek* by Kimon Friar. BoWoP
Case to the Civilians, A. *Unknown.* FaBoEE
Cased in your bone and plaster. The Succubus. Harriet Rose. BrRo
Casement's Funeral. Richard Murphy. *Fr.* The Battle of Aughrim. NOIV
Casey at the Bat. Ernest Lawrence Thayer. AiP; AnAmPo; BeLS; BLPA; FaBoBe; FaFP; FaPON; FPL; OBAL; OBCA; PoRA; SD
Casey Jones. Edward Vincent Swart. PeSA
Casey Jones. *Unknown.* AS, *with music;* BeLS; FaBV; OxBoLi; RR; TrGrPo
Casey Jones has left today. Casey Jones. Edward Vincent Swart. PeSA
Casey—Twenty Years Later. S. P. McDonald. BLPA
Casey's Daughter at the Bat. Al Graham. ASP
Casey's Revenge. James Wilson. BLPA; OnMSP
Cash Only, No Refund, No Return. Daniel Mark Epstein. MAYP
Cashel of Munster. *At. to* William English, *tr. fr. Irish* by Sir Samuel Ferguson. BIrV; GBL; OBEV
Casida of the Rose. Federico García Lorca, *tr.* by Robert Bly. NU
Casino Beach. Thomas Rabbitt. MAYP
Casket Song, A. Shakespeare. *See* Merchant of Venice, The: Tell Me Where Is Fancy [*or* Fancie] Bred.
Cassamen and Dowsabell. Michael Drayton. *Fr.* The Shepherd's Garland, Eclogue VIII (1593 ed.). OBSC
Cassandra. Louise Bogan. HAP; MoAmPo; PBWP; VGW
Cassandra. Robinson Jeffers. HeIP; LiTA; LiTM; WaP
Cassandra. E. A. Robinson. CMoP; LiTA; LiTM; NoAM; OxBA
Cassandra Southwick. Whittier. AnAmPo; PAH
Cassia hall has collapsed, The. The Deserted Estate at South Garden. Hsü Pen, *tr.* by Jonathan Chaves. CoBLCP
Cassinus and Peter. Swift. OAEL-1; PPP
Cassius Hueffer. Edgar Lee Masters. *Fr.* Spoon River Anthology. OxBA
Cast a cold eye. W. B. Yeats. *Fr.* Under Ben Bulben. FaBoEE
Cast Down, but Not Destroyed. *Unknown.* PAH
"Cast down your bucket where you are." Atlanta Exposition Ode. Mary Weston Fordham. CBWP-2
Cast Off, The. Marge Piercy. NoAM
Cast on 120 stitches,/ Rep. to the end of the row. On a Grey-haired Old Lady Knitting at an Orchestral Concert. "Furnley Maurice." CBAP
Cast on the field from their full height. Second Shadow. Theodore Roethke. PoA
Cast on the water by a careless hand. The Cocoa-Tree. Charles Warren Stoddard. AA
Cast out, amid so many companions. The Comet. Emil Makai, *tr.* by André Ungar. VWA
Cast Rose. Anna Hajnal, *tr. fr. Hungarian* by Jascha Kessler. *Fr.* Images. FOC
Cast Thy Bread upon the Waters. Phoebe A. Hanaford. AH
Cast thy bread upon the waters. Bible, *O.T. Fr.* Ecclesiastes, XI. AWP, 1-6; OBVE, 1-8.
Castanets. Bernard Spencer. WeW
Castara, *sels.* William Habington.
    Against Them Who Lay Unchastity to the Sex of Women. *Fr.* II. JCP; MePo; OBS; SeCP

"Nox Nocti Indicat Scientiam." *Fr.* III. ACP; JCP; MeLP; MePo; NOBE; OBEV; OBS
Reward of Innocent Love, The. *Fr.* II. ACP
To Castara, upon Beautie. *Fr.* II. SeCP
To Roses in the Bosom[e] of Castara. *Fr.* I. EnLoPo; MeLP; OBEV; SeCP
Upon Thought Castara May Die. *Fr.* I. ACP
Castara, see that dust, the sportive wind. To Castara, upon Beautie. William Habington. *Fr.* Castara, II. SeCP
Castaway, The. William Cowper. ELP; EnRP; FiP; HeIP; MOS; NAEL-1; NOBE; NOEC; NoP; OAEL-1; PoE; PoEL-3; PPP
Castaway. John Nerber. PoA
Castaway, A, *sel.* Augusta Davies Webster.
"Well, well, I know the wise ones talk and talk." BrRo
Castellated, tall. The Bat. Edith Sitwell. FaBoMo
Castiglione has many a frontier. The Road to Bologna. Roy Macnab. PeSA
Castilian Mother Speaks, The. Baldomero Fernández Moreno, *tr. fr. Spanish by* Perry Higman. LPSS
Casting. Howard Nemerov. OxBSP
Casting, up a salt creek in the sea-rank air. San Pedro Road. Robert Hass. GeTw
Castle, The. Sidney Alexander. PoNe
Castle, The. Edwin Muir. LiTB
Castle by the Sea, The. Ludwig Uhland, *tr. fr. German by* Longfellow. AWP
Castle Hyde. *Unknown.* FaBoPP
Castle of Indolence, The, *sels.* James Thomson.
"In lowly dale, fast by a river's side." *Fr.* I. EnRP; NOEC
(Land of Indolence, The.) SeCePo
"Sometimes the pencil, in cool airy halls." PoEL-3, I.
Castle to castle. Caernarfon, 2 July 1969. T. Glynne Davies, *tr. by* Joseph P. Clancy. OBWVE
Castles. A. Leyeles, *tr. fr. Yiddish.* AYP, *tr. by* Benjamin *and* Barbara Harshav; TrJP, *tr. by* Joseph Leftwich; VWA, *tr. by* Keith Bosley
Castles in the Sand. Dorothy Baker. BoTP
Castles with lofty. Soldier's Song. Goethe, *tr. fr. German by* Bayard Taylor. *Fr.* Faust. AWP
Castleside Song. Wang Ch'ang-ling, *tr. fr. Chinese by* Burton Watson. CoBCP
Castoff Skin. Ruth Whitman. InPK
Casts across otherwise unavailable fields. Sentences My Father Used. Charles Bernstein. LP
Casual glance on me, The. Old Essex Door. Agnes MacCarthy Hickey. GoYe
Casual Man, The. Denis Glover. *Fr.* Sings Harry. ATNZ
Casual Wear. James Merrill. NIP
Casualties. Frances Cornford. CN
Casualty. Seamus Heaney. FaBoPV; IPY; NAEL-2; PoE
Casualty. William Ernest Henley. *Fr.* In Hospital, XIII. BrPo
Casualty. Robert Nichols. MMA
Casualty. Diana Witherby. CN
Cat. Dorothy Walter Baruch. CRH
Cat. Alan Brownjohn. CRH
Cat, The. Charles Stuart Calverley. *Fr.* Sad Memories. ChTr
Cat, The. W. H. Davies. CRH; NOBE
Cat. Eleanor Farjeon. OnUR
Cat. Michael Hamburger. PoPo
Cat, The. Oliver Herford. FaBV
Cat, The. Marie Luise Kaschnitz, *tr. fr. German by* Susan L. Cocalis. DMG
Cat. Kitahara Hakushu, *tr. fr. Japanese by* Hiroaki Sato. FCEI
Cat, The. William Matthews. AmPA
Cat. Mary Britton Miller. CRH; RHPC
Cat, The. Ogden Nash. CRH
Cat. Joe Rosenblatt. NOBC
Cat. Vernon Scannell. CRH
Cat, A. Edward Thomas. BrPo
(She Had a Name.) OxBSP
Cat. J. R. R. Tolkien. CRH
Cat!/ Scat! Cat. Eleanor Farjeon. OnUR
Cat and Mouse. Ted Hughes. EaLo; OxBSP
Cat and the Bird, The. George Canning. ChTr
Cat and the Boot; or, An Improvement upon Mirrors, The. *Unknown.* FaBoUs
Cat and the Fish, The. Thomas Gray. *See* 'Twas on a lofty vase's side.
Cat and the Moon, The. W. B. Yeats. CMoP; CRH; FaBoCh; GoJo; TTTS
Cat and the Weather. May Swenson. HAP; WeW
Cat as Cat, The. Denise Levertov. NOBA
Cat at the Cream. *Unknown.* GBP

Cat at the end of the world, The. A Vision. Sándor Weöres, *tr. by* Jascha Kessler. FOC
Cat Ballerina Assoluta. Emilie Glen. GoYe
Cat bird singing. Robert Creeley. Prf
Cat brushes past, The. Burns. Sandra Hoben. TV
Cat by the fireside, purring, A. Herbs in the Attic. Marilyn Nelson Waniek. MAYP
Cat Came Back, The. *Unknown.* CRH
Cat came fiddling out of a barn, A. *Unknown.* BoTP
Cat curls in a whorl, The. Circle Sleeper. Jean H. Marvin. CRH
Cat Goddesses. Robert Graves. NYBP; OxBSP
Cat Got Your Tongue? Janet Sutherland. DT
Cat Heard the Cat-Bird, The. John Ciardi. SO
Cat, if you go outdoors you must walk in the snow. On a Night of Snow. Elizabeth J. Coatsworth. CRH; MoAmPo; MoShBr; OBCA
Cat in Cold Weather, The. Rai San'yo, *tr. fr. Japanese by* Burton Watson. FCEI; JLIC-2
Cat in Despondency, A. *Unknown.* RHPC
Cat in distress, A. Verses on a Cat. Shelley. FL
Cat in the Dovecot. Avner Trainin, *tr. fr. Hebrew by* Bernhard Frank. MHeP
Cat in the Snow. Aileen Fisher. NTCP
Cat Kisses. Bobbi Katz. RAR
Cat May Look at a King, A. *Unknown.* OxBoLi
Cat Merchant, The. Yisroel Rabon, *tr. fr. Yiddish by* Robert Friend. PeBMYV
Cat Morgan Introduces Himself. T. S. Eliot. NOBL
Cat of Cats, The. William Brighty Rands. OxBChV; RHPC
Cat on my bosom, The. The Cat as Cat. Denise Levertov. NOBA
Cat on the Porch at Dusk. Dorothy Harriman. GoYe
Cat or Stomp. Laura Tohe. STE
Cat Poem. Bernice Zamora. CCP
Cat runs races with her tail, The. John Clare. *Fr.* Signs of Winter. OAEL-2
(Signs of Winter.) BoNaP; WiR
Cat said, A/ on the corner. Vietnam #4. Clarence Major. FF; PoBA
Cat sat asleep by the side of the fire, The. *Unknown.* OxNR
Cat sat quaintly by the fire, A. Hearth. Peggy Bacon. FaPON
Cat sits on the pavement by the house, A. The Lonely Man. Randall Jarrell. OxBC
Cat so close, The. The Ambition of Ghosts. Rosemarie Waldrop. UL
"Cat spreads herself, The." Six Haiku for Graham V. Phillips Who First Said the First One. Robert Phillips. GrPl
Cat takes a look at the weather. Cat and the Weather. May Swenson. HAP; WeW
Cat that comes to my window sill, The. That Cat. Ben King. AnAmPo; CRH; FiBHP
Cat That Followed His Nose, The. John Kaye Kendall. CenHV
Cat that someone found sat in a construction scene and screamed, The. The Cat. Marie Luise Kaschnitz, *tr. by* Susan L. Cocalis. DMG
Cat was once a weaver, The. What the Gray Cat Sings. Arthur Guiterman. MoShBr
Cat went here and there, The. The Cat and the Moon. W. B. Yeats. CMoP; CRH; FaBoCh; GoJo; TTTS
Cat Who Aspired to Higher Things, The. X. J. Kennedy. TDD
Cat! who hast pass'd thy grand climacteric. To a Cat. Keats. FaBoCh
(On Mrs. Reynolds's Cat.) FM
Cat, who sleeps upon the mat, The. The Stray. Barbara Euphan Todd. CRH
Cat Will Rhyme with Hat. Spike Milligan. CRH
Cat with yellow eyes doesn't yet realize, The. Getting Up. Stephen Dobyns. MAYP
Cataclysmic if it were so. "What You See Is Me." Barbara Gibbs. NYBP
Catacombs. István Vas, *tr. fr. Hungarian by* Jascha Kessler. VWA
Catalogue. Hilde Domin, *tr. fr. German by* Tudor Morris. VWA
Catalogue. Rosalie Moore. CRH
Catalogue, *sel.* Rosalie Moore.
"Cats sleep fat and walk thin." NTCP
Catalogue Army. Naomi Shihab Nye. MAYP
Cataloguing, The. Simon Rae. NPo
Catalpa Tree. Miriam Waddington. MoCV; OBCV
"Catamount Tavern" is lively to-night, The. Parson Allen's Ride. Wallace Bruce. PAH
Cataract. Margoret Smith. NYBP
Cataract of Lodore, The. Robert Southey. GN; OxBChV; TEP; WBLP
Cataract of Lodore, The, *sel.* Robert Southey.
"From its sources which well." RR
Cataract, whirling to the precipice, The. John Clare. BoNaP
Catastrophe (Chimbote), The. Julio Ortega, *tr. fr. Spanish by* David Tipton. Per
Catch, A. Henry Aldrich. *See* If all be true that I do think.
Catch, The. Raymond Carver. ASP

Catch. Robert Francis. ASP; HeIP; InPK
Catch, The. Brewster Ghiselin. HAP
Catch. Langston Hughes. NoAM
Catch, A. Ben Jonson. *See* Oberon, the Fairy Prince: Buz, Quoth the Blue Fly.
Catch. Ethna McKiernan. TSL
Catch. Mother Goose. OxNR
Catch, A. Richard Henry Stoddard. AA
Catch, A. Tom Hood. CenHV
Catch, The. Richard Wilbur. BLA; DiPo
Catch a floater, catch an eel. Beela by the Sea. Leroy F. Jackson. RHPC
Catch a Little Rhyme. Eve Merriam. OBCA; PDV
Catch by the Hearth, A. *Unknown.* OHIP
Catch him coming off the thing after a state of the union. Strategies. Welton Smith. NBP; PoBA
Catch him, crow! Carry him, kite! *Unknown.* OxNR
Catch, my Uncle Jack said. Elizabeth. Michael Ondaatje. NoAM
Catch not my breath, O clamorous heart. Tennyson. *Fr.* Maud, *Pt.* I, xvi. NAEL-2
Catch: On a Wet Day. Franco Sacchetti, *tr. fr. Italian by* Dante Gabriel Rossetti. AWP
Catch the blues song. Transformation. Quincy Troupe. CNA
Catch What You Can. Jean Garrigue. VGW
Catching One Clear Thought Alive. Paula Gunn Allen. WPOW
Catching the water that drips. Sparrow Bathing. Ono Tozaburo, *tr. by* Hiroaki Sato. FCEI
Catechism Elegy. Margaret Gibson. MAYP
Catechism, 1958. W. M. Ransom. CDW
Caterpillar. Kitahara Hakushu, *tr. fr. Japanese by* Hiroaki Sato. FCEI
Caterpillar. R. E. Rashley. CaP
Caterpillar, The. Christina Rossetti. *Fr.* Sing-Song. BoTP; FaPON; GoJo; OxBChV; RHPC
Caterpillar, The. Miller Williams. MT
Caterpillar and the Ant, The. Allan Ramsay. SeCePo
Catfish, Mudcat, Ducky, Coot. The Song of Snohomish. William S. Wallace. ASP
Catharine of Arragon. Eloise Bibb. CBWP-4
Cathay. Paul-Jean Toulet, *tr. fr. French by* William Jay Smith. CT
Cathedral, A. Stanislav Vinaver, *tr. fr. Serbo-Croatian by* Vasa D. Mihailovich. VWA
Cathedral Close, The. Coventry Patmore. *Fr.* The Angel in the House, I, i. EBVV
(Salisbury; the Cathedral Close.) EBVV; FaBoPP
Cathedral in the Thrashing Rain. Takamura Kotaro, *tr. fr. Japanese by* Hiroaki Sato. FCEI
Cathedral Is, The. John Ashbery. InPK
Catherine. Karla Kuskin. NTCP; PDV
Catherine, describing a perfect circle. Virgin Martyrs. John Heath-Stubbs. OxBC
Catherine said "I think I'll bake." Catherine. Karla Kuskin. NTCP; PDV
Cathexis. F. J. Bryant, Jr. PoBA
Cathleen. *Unknown, tr. fr. Irish by* Thomas MacIntyre. BIrV
Cathleen Sweeping. George Johnston. NOBC
Catholic Bells, The. William Carlos Williams. CMoP; NOBA; OxBA
Catholic Church, The. Dryden. *Fr.* The Hind and the Panther, II. OBS
Catkins fall and the orioles' cries fade at sundown, The. Sand of Silk-Washing Stream. Ou-yang Chiung, *tr. by* Lois Fusek. ATF
Catkins flying: floating white snow. Ma Chih-yüan, *tr. fr. Chinese by* Jonathan Chaves. *Fr.* Two Poems to the Tune "Chin-tzu ching." CoBLCP
Catkins, like caterpillars slung arow. Lost Lane. Dorothy Wellesley. WPE
Catmint. Eric Clough Taylor. CRH
Cato, sel. Joseph Addison.
Cato's Soliloquy. *Fr.* V, i. WBLP
Cato. C. H. Sisson. NOCV
Cato's Soliloquy. Joseph Addison. *Fr.* Cato, V, i. WBLP
Cats, The. Samuel Exler. GOYP
Cats. Eleanor Farjeon. PDV; RHPC
Cats. Robert Francis. RR
Cats, The. Weldon Kees. NaP
Cats, The. Kurt Klinger, *tr. fr. German by* Beth Bjorklund. CoAuP
Cats. Louis MacNeice. *Fr.* Nature Notes. FaBCIP
Cats and Dogs. N. M. Bodecker. RAR
Cats and Dogs. Howard Moss. OBAL
Cats and kittens, kittens and cats. Country Barnyard. Elizabeth J. Coatsworth. CRH; RHPC
Cat's Conscience, A. *Unknown.* PoLF
Cats Crept Up on Me Slowly. Ursula Laird. Mes
Cat's eye marble is green, The. Backyard. Alice Notley. UL

Cats have gone off to hunt, The. Last winter. The Cats. Samuel Exler. GOYP
Cats like Angels. Marge Piercy. CAPP
Cat's Meat. Harold Monro. OBMV
Cat's Menu. Richard Shaw. CRH; RHPC
Cats of Campagnatico, The. Peter Porter. OBTV
Cats of Kilkenny, The. *Unknown.* RHPC
Cats of Santa Anna, The. Tasso, *tr. fr. Italian by* Barbara Howes. PFI
Cat's purr, A. At the Loom. Robert Duncan. *Fr.* Passages. VGW
Cats purr. I Speak, I Say, I Talk. Arnold L. Shapiro. GrPl
Cat's sitting at the window darkness, The. Today. György Somlyó, *tr. by* Jascha Kessler. FOC
Cats sleep/ Anywhere. Cats. Eleanor Farjeon. PDV; RHPC
Cats sleep fat and walk thin. Rosalie Moore. *Fr.* Catalogue. CRH; NTCP
Cat's Song, The. *Unknown.* GBP
Cats walk neatly. Cats. Robert Francis. RR
Cattail fluff. Porous. William Carlos Williams. NYBP
Cattle. Peter Skrzynecki. CBAP
Cattle Brand. János Pilinszky, *tr. fr. Hungarian by* William Jay Smith. MHuP
Cattle carry on their horns. Perets Markish, *tr. by* Leonard Wolf. PeBMYV
Cattle in the common field, The. On the Heights. Walter Savage Landor. FaBoEE
Cattle is selected, The. Mamparra M'gaiza. José Craveirinha, *tr. by* Margaret Dickinson. WMBCH
Cattle of His Hand, The. Wilbur Underwood. WGRP
Cattle roam again across the field, The. *Unknown, tr. fr. Egyptian by* Robert Hillyer. *Fr.* Book of the Dead: Adoration of the Disk by King Akhnaten and Princess Nefer Neferiu Aten. FaPON
Cattle Sale. Philip Salom. UAS
Cattle Show. "Hugh MacDiarmid." FaBoMo; GoTS; HAP; MoBrPo; OBMV; OxBTC
Cattle Thief, The. Emily Pauline Johnson. WPOW
Cattle-trains edge along the river, bringing morning on a white vibration. Ceiling Unlimited. Muriel Rukeyser. MoAmPo
Catullus to Lesbia. James Reeves. ErPo
Caughnawaga Beadwork Seller, The. William Douw Lighthall. CaP
Caught. Gaston Dubois. ASP
Caught and composed, motionless blue, behind. The Desire of Water. Mark Jarman. PoA
Caught at hanger's ends the limp. Goodwill, Inc. Dennis Schmitz. AmPA
Caught behind Words. Robin Gathany Shea. TSM
Caught between two streams of traffic, in the gloom. T. S. Eliot. Robert Lowell. NoAM; NOBA
Caught in a net, a desperate, thrashing lion. The Lion and the Mouse. Eliezer Shteynbarg, *tr. by* Leonard Wolf. PeBMYV
Caught in the centre of a soundless field. Myxomatosis. Philip Larkin. CMoP; MoP; NoAM; NoP
Caught in the glib catcher's net. Sockeye Salmon. Ronald Hambleton. CaP; OBCV
Caught on the shoulders of Bunn Mhor on a slope. Soaring. Cal Clother. PoSH
Caught still as Absalom. Chagrin. Isaac Rosenberg. MoBrPo; VWA
Caught without wife and mother, child. Getting Drunk with Daughter. Robert Huff. NePoEA-2
Cauld blows the wind frae north to south. Cold Blows the Wind. John Hamilton. CH
Cauld, cauld is Alnack. Benighted to the Foothills of the Cairngorms. Olive Fraser. PoSH
Cauld Cornwood. *Unknown.* GBP
Cauld Lad of Hilton, The *or* The Wandering Spectre. *Unknown.* OxBoLi
Cauld Lad's Song, The. *Unknown. See* Wae's me, wae's me.
Cause and Effect. Matthew Prior. *See* On his deathbed poor Lubin lies.
cause: "Brain is wider than the sky, The." Emily Dickinson. MoAB; MoAmPo; MoP; NAAL-1; NAWM-2; OxBA
Cause for Wonder, A. *Unknown.* MeEL
Cause nobody deals with Aretha—a mother with four children. Poem for Aretha. Nikki Giovanni. BPo; PoBA
Cause of this stab in my side. The Tryst. *Unknown, tr. by* Joseph P. Clancy. OBWVE
Causes. Mona Van Duyn. SM
Causes are in Time, The; only their issue. The Allegory of the Wolf Boy. Thom Gunn. OxBC
Caution Prevents Accidents. Meir Wieseltier, *tr. fr. Hebrew.* IP, *tr. by* Warren Bargad *and* Stanley F. Chyet; MHeP, *tr. by* Bernhard Frank NePoEA-2
Caution to Poets, A. Matthew Arnold. FaBoUs
Cautionary Limerick. *Unknown.* FaBoUs; NBLV
Cautionary Tale, A. Anne Wilkinson. OBCV

Cautionary Verses to Youth of Both Sexes. Theodore Hook. OxBChV
Cautious Gunslinger, The. An Idle Visitation. Edward Dorn. *Fr.*
　　Gunslinger. NOBA
Cautiously the sun rose over the wet sand [*or* shone on the damp sand].
　　Caution Prevents Accidents. Meir Wieseltier. IP, *tr. by* Warren
　　Bargad *and* Stanley F. Chyet; MHeP, *tr. by* Bernhard Frank
Cavafy in Redondo. Mark Jarman. NAmP
Cavalier. Richard Bruce. CDC
Cavalier Tunes, *sel.* Robert Browning.
　　Boot and Saddle("Boot, saddle, to horse, and away!"). *Fr.* III. SoSe
"Cavaliere d'Occidente" wavers, The. Voyage. Cesare Vivaldi, *tr. by*
　　Lawrence R. Smith. NItP
Cavalier's Escape, The. George Walter Thornbury. FaBoBe; GN
Cavalier's Song, The. William Motherwell. GN
Cavalry Crossing a Ford. Walt Whitman. AA; AiP; AmPP; ChTr; HeIP;
　　InPK; InPS; MoP; NAAL-1; NoAM; NoP; OxBA; PPP; TAP; UnPo
Cave, The. Glenn Ward Dresbach. RFM
Cave, The. Arthur Rex Dugard Fairburn. ATNZ; PeNZ
Cave-Boy, The. Laura Elizabeth Richards. FaPON
Cave-Drawing, The. Vernon Watkins. LiTB
Cave Drawings. László Benjámin, *tr. fr. Hungarian by* Edwin Morgan.
　　MHuP
Cave of Despair, The. Spenser. *Fr.* The Faerie Queene, I, 9. OBNV
"Ere long they come, where that same wicked wight." NOBE; OAEL-1
Cave of Gold Essence in Ning-tu, The. T'ang Hsien-Tsu, *tr. fr. Chinese
　　by* Jonathan Chaves. CoBLCP
Cave of Mammon, The. Spenser. *See* Faerie Queene, The:
　　As pilot well expert in perilous wave.
Cave of Night, The, *sel.* John Montague.
　　"Rifled honeycomb, the." CIP
Cave we found, but vacant all within, The. Homer, *tr. fr. Greek by* Pope.
　　Fr. Odyssey, IX. OBVE
Caved-in cardboard box, The. Words, like Spiders. P. Wolny. PCP
Cavern, The. Charles Tomlinson. CMoP
Caverns there were within my mind, which sun. Wordsworth. *Fr.* The
　　Prelude [*or,* Growth of a Poet's Mind]: Residence at Cambridge.
　　FaBoPP
Caves. David Baker. MAYP
Caves, The. Janice Gould. GOS
Caw, caw, caw. Poem/Ditty-Bop. Carolyn M. Rodgers. JB
Caw Caw Caw. The Sea and Ourselves at Cape Ann. Lawrence
　　Ferlinghetti. PoM
Caw Caw the Crows Caw Caw. *Unknown, tr. fr. Seneca Indian by*
　　Jerome Rothenberg *and* Richard Johnny John. STP
"Caw," said the rook. Birds' Nests. Millicent Seager. BoTP
Caxtons are mechanical birds with many wings. A Martian Sends a
　　Postcard Home. Craig Raine. NAEL-2; NoAM; NoP
CCC, The ("CCC campers near West Cummington"). Thomas Whitbread.
　　NYBP
Cease rude Boreas blust'ring railers. The Tempest. *Unknown.* AmFP
Cease your labors, lovers of boys. *Unknown.* PeHV
Ceaseless flows that beck. *Unknown, tr. by* Arthur Waley. BoS
Ceaseless wanderers from of old, the puppeteers. The Puppeteers.
　　Tadamichi, *tr. by* Burton Watson. JLIC-1
Ceaselessly the weaver, Time. The Weaver. William H. Burleigh.
　　BLPA
Cecil Beaton,/ Though not schooled at Eton. Margaret Blaker. SoTCo
Cecil County. Ron Welburn. PoBA
Cecilia. Julio Ortega, *tr. fr. Spanish by* David Tipton. Per
Cedar. Robert Morgan. GeTw
Cedar and jagged fir. The Lonely Land. A. J. M. Smith. CaP; NOBC
Cedar at first, then a splay of staghorn put to the torch. Burning the Root.
　　Margaret Gibson. MAYP
Cedar Mountain. Annie Fields. PAH
Cedar Needles. Chase Twichell. MAYP
Cedar River, The. Reginald Gibbons. MAYP
Cedars of Lebanon, The. Alphonse Marie Louis de Lamartine, *tr. fr.
　　French by* Toru Dutt. AWP
Ceiling, The. Theodore Roethke. EyDe
Ceiling of hell was fastened with thick gold nails, The. The Wallpaper of
　　Mr. R. K. Max Jacob, *tr. by* Andrei Codrescu. RHTwFP
Ceiling Unlimited. Muriel Rukeyser. MoAmPo
Celadyne's Song. William Browne. *Fr.* Britannia's Pastorals, III, Song
　　1. OBS
Celan. Asya, *tr. fr. Yiddish by* Gabriel Preil *and* Howard Schwartz.
　　VWA
Celan. Anthony Barnett. VWA
Celandine. Edward Thomas. OxBTC
Celebrants chanted, The. Four Ways of Dying. Steve Chimombo.
　　WMBCH
Celebrants, The, came chanting, "God is dead!" The Death of God.
　　Howard Nemerov. OxBC; OxBSP

Celebrated Return. Clarence Major. AmNP
Celebrating the Freak. Cynthia MacDonald. Psk
Celebration. Leonard Cohen. ErPo
Celebration, The. James Dickey. VGW
Celebration. Alonzo Lopez. ILY
Celebration. Sybren Polet, *tr. fr. Dutch by* James S. Holmes. DuIn
Celebration. Ray A. Young Bear. CDW
Celebration: Birth of a Colt. Linda Hogan. HATNAP; NOVW
Celebration for My Mother. Wendy Rose. CDW
Celebration for the Cold Snap. Carolyne Wright. NAmP
Celebration in the Plaza, The. Adrienne Rich. NePoEA
Celebration 1982. Terri Meyette. GOS
Celebration of Charis in Ten Lyrick Peeces, A ("Let it not your wonder
　　move."), *sels.* Ben Jonson. SeCP
　　Another Ladyes Exception Present at the Hearing. SeCP
　　Begging Another, on Colour of Mending the Former. PoEL-2; SeCP
　　Clayming a Second Kisse by Desert. SeCP
　　Her Man Described by Her Owne Dictamen. SeCP
　　His Discourse with Cupid. SeCP
　　His Excuse for Loving. JCP; PoEL-2; QFR; SeCP; SeCV-1
　　How He Saw Her. QFR; SeCP; SeCV-1
　　Triumph of Charis, The. CTC; EBEV; EIL; ELP; InvP; JCP; LiTB;
　　　NOBE; NoP; OBEV; OPOP; PoEL-2; PrIm; SeCP; SeCV-1
　　(Her Triumph.) CTC; EBEV; EIL; JCP; PoEL-2; PrIm; SeCP;
　　　SeCV-1
　　Urging Her of a Promise. SeCP
　　What Hee Suffered. SeCP
Celebration of the Nadir. János Pilinszky, *tr. fr. Hungarian by* William
　　Jay Smith. MHuP
Celebrations. Austin Clarke. IPY
Celery. Ogden Nash. FaBoUs; FaPON; RHPC; TDD
Celeste Dancing. Frances Sargent Osgood. AnAmPo
Celestial. Michael Pettit. MOWH
Celestial choir, enthron'd in realms of light. To His Excellency, General
　　Washington. Phillis Wheatley. NAAL-1; OFD; WPE
　　(His Exceilency General Washington.) PoNe
Celestial City, The. Giles Fletcher the Younger. *Fr.* Christ's Victory
　　and Triumph: Christ's Triumph after Death, IV. NOBE; OBD; OBS
Celestial Evening, October 1967. Charles Olson. *Fr.* The Maximus
　　Poems. PoM
Celestial Love. Buonarroti Michelangelo, *tr. fr. Italian by* John
　　Addington Symonds. AWP
Celestial Passion, The. Richard Watson Gilder. AA
Celestial Pilot, The. Dante, *tr. fr. Italian by* Longfellow. *Fr.* Divina
　　Commedia: Purgatorio, II. WGRP
Celestial Surgeon, The. Robert Louis Stevenson. BrPo; EBVV;
　　MoBrPo; TrGrPo; TrPWD; WGRP
Celestial Wisdom. Juvenal, *tr. fr. Latin by* Samuel Johnson. *Fr.* Satires,
　　X. AWP
Celia. Ellen Bass. NMM
Celia Bleeding, to the Surgeon. Thomas Carew. SeCP
Celia Celia. Adrian Mitchell. FaBoEE
Celia, Celia, your name is like cilia. Celia. Ellen Bass. NMM
Celia's Home-coming. Agnes Mary Frances Robinson. OBEV
Celimena, of my heart. Damon and Celimena. Dryden. *Fr.* An
　　Evening's Love, V, i. InvP
Cell, The. George Rostrevor Hamilton. TrPWD
Cell, brick, cement, bars, walls, hard. Cells. Mary Bennett. GOS
Cell by cell the baby made herself, the cells. Sara in Her Father's Arms.
　　George Oppen. NNaP
Cell Lay Inside Her Body, The. Murray Edmond. *Fr.* A Patching
　　Together, 3. NAs
Cell of Himself, The. Arthur Freeman. TwCP
Cell Song. Etheridge Knight. NNaP; PoBA
Cellars and Attics. Malka Heifetz Tussman, *tr. fr. Yiddish by* Kathryn
　　Hellerstein. AYP
Cellars with collected sorted jackets gloom in tallow candles. Division
　　Street. Berysh Vaynshteyn, *tr. fr. Yiddish by* Benjamin *and* Barbara
　　Harshav. *Fr.* New York Everywhere. AYP
Cello, The. Richard Watson Gilder. AA
Cello Entry. Paul Celan, *tr. fr. German by* Joachim Neugroschel. VWA
Cello sobs, the symphony begins, The. The Festival. Frederic Prokosch.
　　LiTA; WaP
Cells. Mary Bennett. GOS
Cells Breathe in the Emptiness. Galway Kinnell. NaP; VGW
Cells hold mock convention in the brain, The. Lobotomy. Kenneth
　　Pitchford. PoA
Celluloid of a photograph holds them well, The. Six Young Men. Ted
　　Hughes. OBWP
Celtic Albatross, The. Alan Bold. NPo
Celtic Cross. Norman MacCaig. OxBS
Celtic Cross, The. Thomas D'Arcy Magee. TIRV
Celtic Fringe, The. Stevie Smith. FaBoNo

Celtic Lyric, The. J. C. Squire. BXAP

Celts, The. Thomas D'Arcy Magee. TIRV

Celts, The. Stevie Smith. NoP

Cement-grey floors and walls. On the Island. Dennis Brutus. WMBCH

Cemeteries are places for departed souls. Lines Written at the Grave of Alexander [or Alexandre] Dumas. Gwendolyn B. Bennett. CDC; PoNe

Cemetery, A. Emily Dickinson. *See* This quiet dust was gentlemen and ladies.

Cemetery at Academy, California, The. Philip Levine. NaP; NYBP

Cemetery in New Mexico, A. Alfred Alvarez. VWA

Cemetery in Pernambuco ("Nobody lies in this earth"). João Cabral de Melo Neto, *tr. fr. Portuguese by* Jane Cooper. ATCBP

Cemetery in Pernambuco ("This is a marine cemetery"). João Cabral de Melo Neto, *tr. fr. Portuguese by* Jane Cooper. ATCBP

Cemetery Nights. Stephen Dobyns. NAmP; SV

Cemetery of Childhood. Joaquim Cardozo, *tr. fr. Portuguese by* Elizabeth Bishop. ATCBP

Cemetery of Orange Trees in Crete, The. Gerald Stern. CAPP

"Cemetery stone New England autumn, The." Voices of Heroes. Horace Gregory. OFD

Cenci, The, *sels.* Shelley. EnRP
  Beatrice's Last Words. FiP
  Cenci's Curse upon His Daughter, The. TW

Cenci's Curse upon His Daughter, The. Shelley. *Fr.* The Cenci. TW

Cenotaph, The. Charlotte Mew. MMA; WPE

Cenotaph of Lincoln. James Thompson McKay. OHIP

Censorship. John Ciardi. NBLV; TW

Censorship. Arthur Waley. OxBTC; WaP

Centaur. Max Jacob, *tr. fr. French by* Armand Schwerner. RHTwFP

Centaur, The. May Swenson. FaBoWP; GrPl; NMM; SO; TwCP

Centaur, siren [or syren], I forgo [or foregoe], The. Another ("The centaur, siren I forgo"). Richard Lovelace. CaPo; PoEL-3

Centaur Song. Hilda Doolittle ("H. D."). VGW

Centaur Song. Stanley Moss. DiL

Centaurs, The. James Stephens. AmMo

Centaur's Bath, The. Luis G. Urbina, *tr. fr. Spanish by* Samuel Beckett. MexPo

Centenarian's Story, The. Walt Whitman. CTC

Centenary's Day. Marcus Garvey. PBCV

Centennial Hymn. Bryant. PAH

Centennial Hymn. Whittier. AA; OPP; PAH

Centennial Meditation of Columbia, The, *sel.* Sidney Lanier. PAH
  Dear Land of All My Love. GN

Center, The. Roger Giroux, *tr. fr. French by* Paul Auster. RHTwFP

Center of Attention, The. Daniel Hoffman. FYAP; UnPo

Centerfold Reflected in a Jet Window. Sandra McPherson. GeTw; MAYP

Centipede, The. A. P. Herbert. CenHV

Centipede, The. Ogden Nash. FaPON

Centipede, A. *Unknown.* OnUR

Centipede adown the street, The. Archy at the Zoo. Don Marquis. *Fr.* Archy and Mehitabel. NBLV; OBAL

Centipede along the threshold crept, The. Thomas Hood. *Fr.* The Haunted House. EBEV; SeCePo; WiR

Centipede is not complete, The. About Feet. Margaret Hillert. RHPC

Centipede is not quite nice, The. The Centipede. A. P. Herbert. CenHV

Centipede was happy quite, A. A Centipede. *Unknown.* OnUR
  (Puzzled Centipede, The.) FaPON

Central. Ted Kooser. Psk

Central Heating. Pierre Reverdy, *tr. fr. French by* Michael Benedikt. POS

Central Heating System. Stephen Spender. GrPl

Central Park. Robert Lowell. LiTM

Central Park *Some People (3 P.M.).* Nancy Morejón, *tr. fr. Spanish by* Sylvia Carranza. PBWP

Central Park Tourney. Mildred Weston. AmFN

Central Park West. Stanley Moss. PCP

Central Park West. Jack Spicer. PeHV

Centre in a kingdom is absurd, A. God Bless Karl Marx. C. H. Sisson. NPo

"Centre of Earth!" a Chinaman he said. The Chinaman. Christina Rossetti. FL

Centre of equal daughters, equal sons. America. Walt Whitman. GOA

Century and eight more years, A. The Four Directions. Emerson Blackhorse Mitchell. NOVW

Century has gone by, A. Secret. Raquel Jodorowsky, *tr. by* Kate Flores. DMH

Century Piece for Poor Heine, A. John Logan. NNaP

Century since, out in the West, A. Betty Zane. Thomas Dunn English. PAH

Ceremonial Band, The. James Reeves. OnUR

Ceremonies for Candlemas[se] Eve. Robert Herrick. CaPo; JCP; OBS

Ceremonies for Christmas[se] ("Come, bring with a noise."), *sel.* Robert Herrick. GN; OHIP; TEP
  "Wassail the trees, that they may bear." PChr

Ceremony. Al-Munsif al-Wahaybi, *tr. fr. Arabic by* Salma Khadra Jayyusi *and* Naomi Shihab Nye. MAP

Ceremony. Kattie M. Cumbo. BlSi

Ceremony. Jack Dann. BWV

Ceremony/ the triumph. Ray DiPalma. *Fr.* Planh, VI. IAT

Ceremony. Jewel L. Latimore. BlSi

Ceremony. Vassar Miller. NePoEA

Ceremony. William Stafford. LCAP

Ceremony. Richard Wilbur. CoAP; MoP; NAAL-2; NoAM

Ceremony after a Fire Raid. Dylan Thomas. CMoP; WaP

Ceremony must be found, The. Speaking of Poetry. John Peale Bishop. LiTA; OxBA

Ceremony of Sending, *sel. Unknown, tr. fr. Osage Indian by* Barbara Tedlock.
  Hidden People and the Star People, The. STP

Ceremony upon Candlemas Eve. Robert Herrick. OBCP

Cernunnos. Hugh Maxton. CIP

Certain acts survive. I recall. A Victory. R. T. Smith. MOWH

Certain Americans refuse to return. Change. Phyllis Janowitz. EOEF

Certain Bend, A. William Stafford. CAPP

Certain bones are from other bones distinguished. Discoveries of Bones and Stones. Geoffrey Grigson. OBTV

Certain Choices. Richard Shelton. Psk

Certain dark underground eyes. Picture of Loot. Alan Sillitoe. OxBTC

Certain Days. Israel Efrat, *tr. fr. Hebrew by* Bernhard Frank. MHeP

Certain days wash ashore from the sea. Good Memory. Sotero Rivera-Avilés, *tr. by* Julio Marzán. InW

Certain Dead. John Haines. LCAP

Certain great statesman, whom all of us know, A. Ballynahinch. George Canning. FaBoCo

Certain Lady, A. Dorothy Parker. NIP

Certain Man, A. Abraham Chalfi, *tr. fr. Hebrew by* Bernhard Frank. MHeP

Certain Maxims of Archy, *sels.* Don Marquis. OBAL
  Archy, the Cockroach, Speaks. FaPON
  "I once heard the survivors." NBLV

Certain Mercies. Robert Graves. GTBS-P

Certain moments will never change, nor stop being. Thinking about the Past. Donald Justice. MT

Certain painter, leaving in the morning, A. The Saddled Ass. La Fontaine, *tr. by* Deems Taylor. NBLV

Certain parting does not wait its hour. Penelope. Ursula Vaughn Williams. CN

Certain pasha, dead five thousand years, A. A Turkish Legend. Thomas Bailey Aldrich. GN

Certain Peace, A. Nikki Giovanni. CNA

Certain people would not clean their buttons. The Bohemians. Ivor Gurney. MMA

Certain poets/ have written good poems. On the Poet's Leer. David Ray. NePoEA-2

Certain Presbyterian Pair, A. The Presbyterian Wedding. *Unknown.* CoMu; ErPo

Certain presuppositions are altered. Upland. A. R. Ammons. NOBA

Certain Sandpiper, A. X. J. Kennedy. TDD

Certain Slant of Light, A. Emily Dickinson. *See* There's a certain slant of light.

Certain Sonnets, *sel.* Sir Philip Sidney.
  "Oft have I mused, but now at length I find." EIL; GBL; NOBE; OBSC; SiPS

Certain things here are quietly American. Midsummer. Derek Walcott. NAEL-2

Certain True Woords Spoken Concerning One Benet Corbett after Her Death. Richard Corbett. SeCP

Certain words disappear from a language. Louisiana Perch. Ron Padgett. UL

Certain Years. Otto Orban, *tr. fr. Hungarian by* Jascha Kessler. FOC

Certain young gourmet of Crediton, A. Charles Cuthbert Inge. CenHV

Certain Young Lady, A. Washington Irving. FaBoBe

Certain youthful lady in Thoulouse, A. Sonnet: Of the Eyes of a Certain Mandetta. Guido Cavalcanti, *tr. by* Dante Gabriel Rossetti. AWP

Certainly there was something to their stories. Childe Roland, etc. Elder Olson. OBAL

"Certainties are arrived at only on foot." Accordance. Henry Kanabus. UL

Certainty before Lunch. John Berryman. LCAP; OxBC

Certified Copy. Ann Deagon. NIP

Cerulean and jet, the Tuareg. Anthropology: Cricket at Kano. Stewart Brown. OBTV

Cervantes, Dostoievsky, Poe. A Poem Intended to Incite the Utmost Depression. Samuel Hoffenstein. FaBoCo

Cervera. Bertrand Shadwell. PAH

Cerveteri road. Elena Clementelli, *tr. fr. Italian by* Ruth Feldman *and* Brian Swann. *Fr. Etruscan Notebook.* PBWP

Cessation of War. Ellodë Collins. CN

'Cession's stahted on de gospel way, De. A Spiritual. Paul Laurence Dunbar. BPo

Cetewayo, chief of the Zulus. Footnote. Anthony Delius. PeSA

Ceylon. Nishiwaki Junzaburo, *tr. fr. Japanese by* Sato. FCEI

Cézanne. Rose Ausländer, *tr. fr. German by* Beth Bjorklund. CoAuP

Cézanne. Gertrude Stein. TAP

Cha, me tired of men whistling at me. Girl Talk. Monique Griffiths. WS

Chacago. Amy Lowell. FL

Chaeronean Plutarch, to thy deathless praise. Plutarch. Agathias, *tr. by* Dryden. AWP

Chaff, The. W. S. Merwin. PPP

Chaffinch flies fast, The. Cherry Tree. Ivy O. Eastwick. BoTP

Chagrin. Isaac Rosenberg. MoBrPo; VWA

Chahcoal Man. *Unknown.* AS

Chain, The. Christine Craig. AIW

Chain. Audre Lorde. BlSi; ER

Chain Gang Blues. *Unknown.* WTO

Chain of Pearl, A, *sel.* Lady Diana Primrose. Fourth Pearl: Temperance, The. WPE

Chained by stern duty to the rock of state. Lincoln. S. Weir Mitchell. PAH

Chained in the market-place he stood. The African Chief. Bryant. BLPA

Chains, my good lord: in your raised brows I read. Tennyson. *Fr.* Columbus. OFD

Chains that bind my thinking, The. The Searching. Alice S. Cobb. BlSi

Chair, The. Theodore Roethke. TDD

Chair, Dog, and Clock. Hilary Corke. NYBP

Chair she sat in, like a burnished throne, The. A Game of Chess. T. S. Eliot. *Fr. The Waste Land, II.* SCV

Chair squeaks in a high wind, The. Nostalgias. Derek Mahon. FaBCIP

Chair That Is Filled, The. Carrie Biggs. PWR

Chairman of many committees. Clubwoman. Mary Carter Smith. PoNe

Chairs. Valerie Worth. NTCP

Chairs above the Danube. Szabolcs Várady, *tr. fr. Hungarian by* William Jay Smith. MHuP

Chairs, tables, lamps, chandeliers. The Final Night. Ali Sardar J'afri, *tr. by* Mahmood Jamal. PBMUP

Chalk Angel, The. Dennis Schmitz. NPGG

Chalk-Pit, The. Edward Thomas. BrPo

Challenge. Sterling A. Brown. CDC

Challenge. Samuel Hazo. SD

Challenge, A. James Benjamin Kenyon. AA

Challenge, The. Grenville Kleiser. BLRP

Challenge. Ada Negri, *tr. fr. Italian by* Muriel Kittel. DMI

Challenge, The. Pope. PoEL-3

Challenge comes, The. The Challenge. Grenville Kleiser. BLRP

Challengers. Alfred Dorn. GoYe

Chamber Music. James Joyce. *Poems indexed separately by titles and first lines.*

Chamber-Pot Rhyme. *Unknown.* GBP

Chambered Nautilus, The. Oliver Wendell Holmes. *Fr. The Autocrat of the Breakfast Table, Ch. 4.* AA; AmPP; FaBoBe; FaFP; FPL; GN; HoPM; LiTA; MOS; NOBA; NoP; OHFP; PoEL-5; PoLF; PrIm; WGRP

Chambermaid's Second Song, The. W. B. Yeats. ErPo

Chambers of Jerusalem. Yehuda Karni, *tr. by* Jeremy Garber. VWA

Chameleon, The. A. P. Herbert. FaPON

Chameleon, The. Matthew Prior. OBSV

Chameleon changes his color, The. The Chameleon. Sir Alan Patrick Herbert. FaPON

Chameleons saw an arc of color, The. The Lord's Chameleons. Peter Klappert. AmPA

Chamois, The. Hilaire Belloc. FaBoNo

Champ de Manœuvres. Sir Herbert Read. BrPo

Champagne. Rita Dove. MAYP

Champagne. Medbh McGuckian. FaBCIP

Champagne Rosée. John Kenyon. OBEV

Champion of those who groan beneath. To William Lloyd Garrison. Whittier. PAH

Champs d'Honneur. Ernest Hemingway. AiP; PoA

Chance, The. Arthur Sze. BrSi

Chance adjustment of my car mirror, A. In a Mirror. Marcia Stubbs. MAT

Chance Meeting. Susan Griffin. NPGG

Chancellor's Nightmare, The. W. S. Gilbert. *See* Iolanthe: Nightmare.

Chancery Suit, A. Sir George Rose. *See* Mr. Leach made a speech.

Chances, The, *sel.* John Fletcher.
  "Merciless love, whom nature hath denied." *Fr.* III, ii. GBL

Chances, The. Wilfred Owen. MMA; OxBTC

Chances of Rhyme, The. Charles Tomlinson. FaBoMo; PoA

Chances "R." Allen Ginsberg. HCAP

Chandeliers hemorrhage, Tritons, The. Figures in a Ruined Ballroom. George Hitchcock. VGW

Ch'ang-an. Ho Ching-ming, *tr. by* Jonathan Chaves. CoBLCP

Ch'ang-an—one slip of moon. Tzu-yeh Song. Li Po, *tr. by* Burton Watson. CoBCP

Chang Liang's face was like an old woman's. Impromptu. Wu Wei-yeh, *tr. by* Jonathan Chaves. CoBLCP

Change./ like if u were a match I wd light u. A Poem to Complement Other Poems. Don L. Lee. BPo

Change. Ellen Bass. ER

Change, The. Samuel Chimsoro. WMBCH

Change, The. Abraham Cowley. *Fr.* The Mistress. MeLP; MePo; OBS; SeCP; SeCV-1

Change. John Donne. *Fr.* Elegies, III. EBEV

Change. Earl of Essex. *See* Change Thy Mind since She Doth Change.

Change. Robert Graves. OxBTC

Change. Fulke Greville. *See* Caelica: World, that all contains, is ever moving, The.

Change. William Dean Howells. AA

Change. Phyllis Janowitz. EOEF

Change. Raymond Knister. CaP; OBCV

Change, The. Matabaruka. PVCV

Change, The. David O'Bruadair, *tr. fr. Irish by* Austin Clarke. BIrV

Change and Immutability. Syd Scroggie. PoSH

Change in Style, A. Eochadh O'Hussey. NOIV

Change in the Year, A. Wordsworth. *See* It is the first mild day of March.

Change Is Not Always Progress. Don L. Lee. TAP

Change Me, Some God, into that Breathing Rose. Wordsworth. Son

Change, move, dead clock, that this fresh day. Small Prayer. Weldon Kees. PoA; VGW

Change of Address. Kathleen Fraser. NYBP

Change of Color. Kathinka Zitz-Halein, *tr. fr. German by* Susan L. Cocalis *and* Gerlinde Geiger. DMG

Change of Scene. Ellen Warmond, *tr. fr. Dutch by* Manfred Wolf. OV

Change Should Breed Change. William Drummond of Hawthornden. OBEV

Change [Thy Mind since She Doth Change]. Earl of Essex. EIL; OBSC

Change-up. Don L. Lee. CNA; PoBA

Changed. Charles Stuart Calverley. FiBHP; NoBVV

Changed and not changed. Three million years. Fossil, 1975. Janet Lewis. CRP

Changed is the scene: the peace. La Noche Triste. Robert Frost. FL

Changeful Beauty. *Unknown, tr. fr. Greek by* Andrew Lang. EnLoPo

Changeless Shore. Sarah Leeds Ash. GoYe

Changeling, The. Marilyn Davis. TSM

Changeling, The. Charlotte Mew. CH

Changeling, The, *sels.* Thomas Middleton. PoEL-2
  "Here we are, if you have any more." *Fr.* V, iii.
  "What makes your lip so strange?." *Fr.* III, iv.

Changeling VIII. Kristjana Gunnars. NOBC

Changelings. Mary Potter Thacher Higginson. AA

Changes. Robert Bulwer-Lytton. PoLF

Changes. Seamus Heaney. FaBCIP

Changes, The. Robert Pinsky. NPGG

Changes around the Bay. Michael Palmer. NPGG

Changes of Life. Constance Urdang. VWA

Changes to Corinna, The. Robert Herrick. JCP

Changing. Mary Ann Hoberman. RHPC

Changing, *sel.* Liv Ullmann.
  "I was born in a small hospital in Tokyo. Mama says." TV

Changing at York. Tony Harrison. NPo

Changing foot prints. Witchcraft. Nora Naranjo-Morse. GOS

Changing guests, each in a different mood, The. Inclusiveness. Dante Gabriel Rossetti. *Fr.* The House of Life, LXIII. NAEL-2

Changing Light at Sandover, The, *sels.* James Merrill. NAAL-2
  Book of Ephraim, The.
  Mirabell's Books of Number.

Changing of the Guard. Charles G. Ballard. NOVW
Changing the Children. Maxine W. Kumin. ER
Changing the Tire. Lorrie Goldensohn. NAmP
Changing water. Adding aspirin. Nitrogen, potash or. Flowers. Kathleen Fraser. TV
Changsha Shoe Factory. Willis Barnstone. SaC
Channel Crossing. George Barker. GTBS-P
Channel Firing. Thomas Hardy. BrPo; CMoP; EBEV; HAP; HeIP; LiTB; MoP; NAEL-2; NIP; NoAM; NoP; OAEL-2; OxBTC; PoE; PoEL-5; PoRA; PrIm; RB; SoSe; UnPo; WaaP
Channel moon went down, as ignorance, The. The Outlanders. Andrew Glaze. NYBP
Channel Passage, A. Rupert Brooke. MOS
Channel U.S.A.—Live. Adrien Stoutenburg. AmFN
Channing. Amos Bronson Alcott. AA
Chanson. Pernette du Guillet, tr. fr. French by Joan Keefe and Richard Terdiman. PBWP
Chansons d'Automne. Paul Verlaine, tr. fr. French by Arthur Symons. AWP
Chansons de Bilitis, sels. Pierre Louÿs, tr. fr. French. PeHV
   Agonizing Memory, The.
   Breasts of Mnasidice, The.
   Complaisant Friend, The.
   Love.
   Meeting, The.
   Penumbra.
Chansons Innocentes, sels. E. E. Cummings.
   "In just-/ spring when the world is mud." Fr. I. AmPP; FaBV; FaPON; HeIP; MoAB; MoAmPo; MoShBr; NIP; NoP; PrIm; SoSe; WeW
   (In Just-.) InPK
   "Little tree." Fr. II. NTCP; OBCP; PChr; PDV
Chant for Reapers. Wilfrid Thorley. OBEV
Chant for Young/Brothas and Sistuhs, A. Sonia Sanchez. BPo
Chant Out of Doors, A. Marguerite Wilkinson. TrPWD
Chant-Pagan. Kipling. FaBoPV
Chant Royal. Robert Morgan. SM
Chant to Io. Tiwai Paraone, tr. fr. Maori by A. Alpers. WTO
Chanted Calendar, A. Sydney Thompson Dobell. Fr. Balder. BoTP; OBEV
   (Procession of the Flowers, The.) GN
Chanticleer. Margaret Irvin. PoAu-2
Chanting Cherubs—A Group by Greenough, The. Richard Henry Dana. AA
Chanting in Tibet has not ceased, The. Moiré. Michael McClure. EAS
Chanting Poems. Wang Chiu-ssu, tr. fr. Chinese by Jonathan Chaves. CoBLCP
Chanting sun, as ever, rivals, The. Goethe, tr. fr. German by Louis MacNeice. Fr. Faust, Pt. I. NAWM-2
Chanting the Square Deific. Walt Whitman. NAAL-1
Chants, The, sel. María Sabina, tr. fr. Mazatec Indian by Henry Munn.
   "Ah, Jesu Kri." STP
Chants Communal, sel. Horace Logo Traubel.
   What Can I Do?. TrJP
"Chaos is purple," you said. Purple Chaos. Alistair Campbell. ATNZ
Chapel, as the pivot of this valley, The. For the Altarpiece of the Roseau Valley Church, Saint Lucia. Derek Walcott. NoP
Chaperon, The. H. C. Bunner. AA; AnAmPo
Chaplet, The, sels. Moses Mendes. TrJP
   Ass, The.
   Philanderer, The.
Chaplet of Southernwood, A, sel. John Gambril Nicholson.
   "I love him wisely if I love him well." PeHV
Chaplinesque. Hart Crane. CMoP; LiTM; MoP; NAAL-2; NoAM; NOBA; OxBA; VGW
Chapter Heading. Ernest Hemingway. PoA
Chapter of Kings, The. John Collins. FaBoUs
Character, A. Charlotte Fiske Bates. AA
Character. Emerson. AA; LiTA; OxBSP
Character, A, sel. Tennyson.
   "With a half-glance upon the sky." Mes
Character, indistinct, entered, A. Thomas Kinsella. Fr. Songs of the Psyche, I. NoAM
Character of a Certain Whig, The. William Shippen. APAS
Character of a Critic. Charles Churchill. Fr. The Rosciad. NOEC
Character of a Good Parson, The. Dryden. NOCV
Character of a Happy Life, The. Sir Henry Wotton. ElL; GTBS; GTBS-P; LiTB; NOBE; OBEV; OBS; TrGrPo
Character of a landscape stands always in a mysterious relation, The. Charles Madge. EAS
Character of a Roundhead, The. Unknown. FaBoPV
Character of a Trimmer, The. Unknown. APAS

Character of Holland, The. Andrew Marvell. ChTr; NOBL; OBSV; OBTV
Character of Holland, The, abr. sel. Andrew Marvell. NOBL
   "Holland, that scarce deserves the name of land." ChTr; OBSV
Character of Love Seen as a Search for the Lost, The. Kenneth Patchen. NaP; VGW
Character of Sir Robert Walpole, The. Swift. FaBoEE; PoE
Character of the Happy Warrior. Wordsworth. EnRP; FaBoBe; FaFP; LiTB
   (The Happy Warrior.) OHFP
Charade. Winthrop Mackworth Praed. GN
Charade. Unknown. OxNR
Charcoal. Wilson Harris. PBCV
Charcoalman, The. John Townsend Trowbridge. AnAmPo
Chard Whitlow. Henry Reed. BXAP; FaBoCo; FaBoNo; FaBoPa; FiBHP; LiTM; MoBrPo; NBLV; NOBL; NoP; OxBTC; Par; UnPo
Charge. Christopher Gilbert. MAYP
Charge, The. Denise Levertov. NePoEA-2
Charge, A. Herbert Trench. OBEV
Charge, The. Jay Wright. DiL; FB
Charge at Santiago, The. William Hamilton Hayne. PAH
Charge by the Ford, The. Thomas Dunn English. PAH
Charge of the Light Brigade, The. Tennyson. BeLS; BLPA; FaBoBe; FaBV; FaFP; FaPON; FaPoR; FPL; GN; HoPM; NAEL-2; NIP; NOBVV; OBWP; OHFP; PrIm; TEP; WBLP
Charge that Heaven gave, The. Unknown, tr. by Arthur Waley. BoS
Charge to the Poets, A, sel. William Whitehead.
   "If nature prompts you, or if friends persuade." OBSV
Charged with liquid effervescence. The Wineglass. E. A. Baratynsky, tr. by Alan Myers. AAA
Chariot, The. Emily Dickinson. See Because I could not stop for death.
Chariot Wheel, A. Auvaiyar, tr. fr. Tamil by A. K. Ramanujan. PLW
Charis guesse, and doe not misse. Clayming a Second Kisse by Desert. Ben Jonson. Fr. A Celebration of Charis in Ten Lyrick Peeces. SeCP
Charis one day in discourse. Urging Her of a Promise. Ben Jonson. Fr. A Celebration of Charis in Ten Lyrick Peeces. SeCP
Charitable Stranger, The. Tom Riley. SoTCo
Charitas Nimia; or, The Dear[e] Bargain. Richard Crashaw. JCP; MePo; NOCV
Charité Espérance et Foi. Earle Birney. OxBC
Charity. Connie Bensley. FaBoWP
Charity. Henrietta Cordelia Ray. CBWP-3
Charity. Unknown. BLPA
Charity lotteries for dream houses, The. Judith Wright. Fr. Habitat, VI. CBAP
Charity Overcoming Envy. Marianne Moore. NYBP
Charlemagne. Longfellow. FaFP
Charles Augustus Fortescue. Hilaire Belloc. NoAM
Charles Carville's Eyes. E. A. Robinson. AnAmPo; CMoP; OxBA; TAP
Charles Darwin Pays a Visit, December 1971. Michael Ondaatje. HeIP
Charles Donnelly, sel. Donagh MacDonagh.
   "Of what a quality is courage made." CIP
Charles Guiteau, 2 vers. Unknown. AmFP
Charles Harpur in his journals long ago. Extinct Birds. Judith Wright. PBWP
Charles J. Correll/ Sang in no chorale. Louis Phillips. SoTCo
Charles! my slow heart was only sad, when first. Sonnet to a Friend Who Asked, How I Felt When the Nurse First Presented My Infant to Me. Samuel Taylor Coleridge. EnRP
Charles on Fire. James Merrill. CAPP
Charles river reaps here like a sickle, The. Professor Kelleher and the Charles River. Desmond O'Grady. CIP
Charles Sumner. Henrietta Cordelia Ray. CBWP-3
Charles the First, sels. Shelley.
   "Heigho! the lark and the owl!" Fr. sc. v. PBBP
   "Widow bird sate mourning for her love, A." ELP; GTBS; GTBS-P
   (Song, A: "Widow bird sate mourning for her love, A.") NOBE; OBNC; OxBSP; PoEL-4
   (Widow Bird, A.) BoTP; CH; FaPON
Charles the King, our Emperor, the Great. The Song of Roland. Unknown, tr. by Frederick Goldin. NAWM-1, abr.
Charles II. Andrew Marvell. See Last Instructions to a Painter, The: Paint last the King, and a dead shade of night.
Charles II. Unknown. FaBoEE
Charles XII of Sweden. Samuel Johnson. See Vanity of Human Wishes, The: The Tenth Satire of Juvenal Imitated: On what foundation stands the warrior's pride.
Charles used to watch Naomi, taking heart. Laboratory Poem. James Merrill. CAPP; InPK; MAT; NePoEA-2; TwCP
Charleston. Richard Watson Gilder. PAH
Charleston. Paul Hamilton Hayne. PAH

Charleston. Henry Timrod. AA; AmPP; AnAmPo; NOBA; OxBA; PAH; TAP

Charleston Garden, A. Henry Bellamann. PoLF

Charleston in the 1860s. Adrienne Rich. CoAP; NAAL-2

Charley Barley, butter and eggs. *Unknown.* OxNR

Charley, Charley. *Unknown.* OxNR

Charley Coleman told me this. Incident. Karl Kopp. GOYP

Charley du Bignon. Mary E. Tucker. CBWP-1

Charley Warlie had a cow. *Unknown.* OxNR

Charley's Green Guide. Michael Holstein. SoTCo

Charlie Chaplin went to France. *at. to* Carl Withers. FaFP; MoShBr

Charlie didn't want to be pushed down. Dummy, 51, to Go to Museum. Ventriloquist Dead at 75. May Swenson. BAP

Charlie, He's My Darling. Burns. CH; FaBoPV

Charlie MacPherson. *Unknown.* ESPB

Charlie Piecan. L. Murray *and* F. Leigh. OxBoLi

Charlie Wolf used to whittle skinning knives. Halcyon Days. Jim Barnes. CDW

Charlie's Sad Date. Rafael Alberti, *tr. fr. Spanish by* Mark Strand. AnAn

Charlotte Brontë. "Susan Coolidge." OBCA

Charlotte Brontë said, "Wow, sister! *What* a man! Victor Gray. NOBL

Charlotte Corday. Charles Tomlinson. OxBC

Charlotte, Her Book. Elizabeth Bartlett. FaBoWP

Charlotte Nicholls. Jack R. Clemo. NAs

Charlottie liv'd on a mountain top in a bleak and lonely spot. The Frozen Girl. *Unknown.* AS

Charm, A. Dryden. ChTr

Charm, A. Robert Herrick. ChTr

Charm. Miklós Radnóti, *tr. fr. Hungarian by* Steven Polgar, Stephen Berg *and* S. J. Marks. LLLT

Charm, The. Shakespeare. *See* Macbeth: Thrice the Brinded Cat Hath Mewed.

Charm, A. *Unknown, tr. fr. Anglo-Saxon by* Richard Hammer. RB

Charm a single charm is doubtful, A. Nothing Elegant. Gertrude Stein. *Fr.* Tender Buttons. PBWP

Charm against a Magpie, A. *Unknown.* ChTr

Charm against the Toothache, A. John Heath-Stubbs. NePoEA; TwCP

Charm: Bleeding. *Unknown.* FaBoUs

Charm: Burns. *Unknown.* FaBoUs

Charm: Corns. *Unknown.* FaBoUs

Charm for Lighting the Fire, A. *Unknown, tr. fr. Irish by* Thomas Kinsella. NOIV

Charm for Love and Lasting Affection, A. *Unknown, tr. fr. Irish by* Thomas Kinsella. NOIV

Charm: Hiccups. *Unknown.* FaBoUs

Charm is the measure of attraction's power. What Is Charm? Louisa Carroll Thomas. BLPA

Charm Mary put on the butter, The. A Charm for Love and Lasting Affection. *Unknown, tr. by* Thomas Kinsella. NOIV

Charm me asleep, and melt me so. Robert Herrick. *Fr.* To Music [*or* Musique], to Becalm [e] His Fever. CaPo; GoJo; OBEV; OBS; QFR; SeCV-1; UnS

Charm of my life, my dearest care. Martial, *tr. by* Brian Hill. PeHV

Charm of rouge on fragile cheeks, The. Maquillage. Arthur Symons. OxBSP

Charm'd with a drink which Highlanders compose. Athol Brose. Thomas Hood. FaBoCo

Charme. Ben Jonson. *See* Masque of Queens, The: Witches' Charms, The.

Charme, or an Allay for Love, A. Robert Herrick. FaBoCh; FaBoUs

Charmed as a brown wicker nest. Reflections on a Womb Which Is Called "Vacant." Jeanine Hathaway. IHMS

Charmer Turned Ascetic, A. Marippittiyar, *tr. fr. Tamil by* A. K. Ramanujan. PLW

Charmes. Robert Herrick. WSC

Charmides, *sel.* Edmund St. Gascoigne Mackie. "Up leaps the lark. Delightful Spring once more." PeHV

Charming. William Matthews. MAYP

Charming Beauty Bright. *Unknown.* AmFP

Charming oysters I cry. Oysters. Swift. ErPo

Charming the Moon. James DenBoer. MAT

Charming, the movement of girls about a May-pole in May. Men Working. Edna St. Vincent Millay. SaC

Charming Woman, The. Helen Selina Sheridan. WPE

Charmion's Lament. Eloise Bibb. CBWP-4

Charms for a Sudden Stitch. *Unknown, tr. fr. Anglo-Saxon by* Charles W. Kennedy. AnOE

Charms for Unfruitful Land. *Unknown, tr. fr. Anglo-Saxon by* Charles W. Kennedy. AnOE

Charms of Nature, The. Joseph Warton. *Fr.* Enthusiast, The; or, The Lover of Nature. SeCePo

Charms, that call down the moon from out her sphere. To Music, to Becalm a Sweet-sick Youth. Robert Herrick. CaPo

Charnwood Forest. Michael Drayton. *Fr.* Polyolbion, Sixth and Twentieth Song. FaBoPP

Charon. Louis MacNeice. FaBCIP; FaBoTw

Charon: I shall be a scandal on your ferry. Rebel. Juana de Ibarbourou, *tr. by* Kate Flores. DMH

Charon! Thou slave! Thou fool! Thou Cavalier! A Mock Charon. Richard Lovelace. CaPo

Charon's Cosmology. Charles Simic. GeTw; HCAP; NoP

Chartist Chorus, A. Ernest Charles Jones. PF

Chartivel, *sel.* Marie de France, *tr. fr. French by* Arthur O'Shaughnessy. "Hath any loved you well, down there." EnLoPo; WPOW

(Song from "Chartivel.") AWP

Chartres. Raymond Henri. *Fr.* View of the Cathedral. EyDe

Charwoman. Ben Belitt. SaC

Chase, The. W. H. Davies. BrPo

Chase, The. Sir Walter Scott. *Fr.* The Lady of the Lake, I. EnRP

Chase, The, *sel.* William Somervile. Hare-hunting. NOEC

Chase, The. *Unknown, at. to* John Webster *and* William Rowley. *See* Thracian Wonder, The: Art Thou Gone in Haste?

Chase Henry. Edgar Lee Masters. OBD

Chased from my calling to this hackneyed trade. James Kennedy. *Fr.* The Exile's Reveries. NOEC

Chasing joy. Mathematician. Bruce Boston. BWV

Chasm. A. R. Ammons. OBAL

Chaste Arabian Bird, The. John Wilmot, 2nd Earl of Rochester. ErPo

Chaste Florimel. Matthew Prior. BoLoP; ErPo

Chaste Maid in Cheapside, A, *sel.* Thomas Middleton. Parting. ElL

Chaste, pious, prudent Charles the Second. The History of Insipids. John Freke. APAS

Chaste Stranger, The. James Tate. NoAM

Chaste trees, dark-clustered, The. A Leaf in Love and War. Veripatiya Kamakkanniyar, *tr. by* A. K. Ramanujan. PLW

Chastity. Milton. *Fr.* Comus; a Masque Presented at Ludlow Castle. OBS

Chateau Papineau. Susan Frances Harrison. CaP

Chateaux en Espagne. Henrietta Cordelia Ray. CBWP-3

Chatter of birds two by two. Prairie Waters by Night. Carl Sandburg. NAAL-2

Chatter of the dawn orioles breaks her dream of love, The. The Beautiful Lady Yü. Ku Hsiung, *tr. by* Lois Fusek. ATF

Chattering finch and water-fly. The Skeleton. G. K. Chesterton. FaBoTw

Chattering swallow! what shall we. The Swallow. Thomas Stanley. AWP

Chatterton. Rina Hands. Mes

Chatting about the Past with Huang the Elder. Hung Liang-Chi, *tr. fr. Chinese by* Irving Lo. WFTU

Chaucer. Benjamin Brawley. BANP

Chaucer. Longfellow. AA; AWP; HeIP; InvP; NOBA; NoP; OBEV; OxBA; PoE; PoRA; PrIm; Son; TAP; TrGrPo

Chaucer, Langland, Douglas, Dunbar with all your. Ode to the Medieval Poets. W. H. Auden. PoA

Chaunt of the Brazen Head, The, *sel.* Winthrop Mackworth Praed. "I think the thing you call Renown." OBSV

Chauntecleer. Chaucer. *Fr.* The Canterbury Tales: The Nun's Priest's Tale. FiP

Chayem-Shmyl, a steak-knife in his hand. In a "Speakeasy"—the Flower Girl. Moyshe-Leyb Halpern, *tr. by* Benjamin *and* Barbara Harshav. AYP

Che Fece. Il Gran Rifiuto. Constantine P. Cavafy, *tr. fr. Greek by* Edmund Keeley *and* Philip Sherrard. VMG

Cheat of Cupid; or, The Ungentle Guest, The. Robert Herrick, *after* Anacreon. AWP; OBVE

Chebutykin. Dick Davis. NPo

Check. James Stephens. AnIL; OnUR; RHPC

Check to Song. "Owen Meredith." *See* I dream'd that I walked in Italy.

Cheddar Pinks. Robert Bridges. SeCePo

Cheer and salute for the Admiral, and here's to the Captain bold, A. The Men behind the Guns. John Jerome Rooney. AA; BLPA; FaBoBe; PAH

Cheer, cheer for old Notre Dame. The Notre Dame Victory March. John Shea. ASP

Cheer for the Consumer. Nixon Waterman. OBAL

Cheer up, cheer up! my own Jeannette, tho' far away I go. Jeannot's Answer. Charles Jefferys. BLPA

Cheer up, cheer up, you sons of toil, and listen to my song. Striking Times. *Unknown.* OBET

Cheer up, my young men all; let nothing fright you. Brave Wolfe. *Unknown.* PAH

Cheered with this hope, to Paris I returned. Wordsworth. *Fr.* The Prelude [or, Growth of a Poet's Mind]: Residence in France. PoEL-4

Cheerfu' supper done, wi' serious face, The. The Cotter's Saturday Night. Burns. BeLS; EnRP; FaBoBe; PoLF; WGRP

Cheerful arn he blaws in the marn, The. The Cheerful Horn. *Unknown.* CH

Cheerful Chilterns, The. Frank Sidgwick. BXAP

Cheerful Horn, The. *Unknown.* CH

Cheerful Welcome, A. *Unknown.* MeEL

Cheerily Man. *Unknown.* RR

Cheerio My Deario. *Fr.* Archy and Mehitabel. FaBoCo

Cheers, Cheers for Old Cha Cha Ass ("Cheers, cheers for old Patchogue High"). Walta Borawski. GLP

Cheese. Mark Irwin. SoTCo

Cheese it is a peevish elf. *Unknown.* FaBoUs

Cheetie-Poussie-Cattie, O. *Unknown. See* There Was a Wee Bit Mousikie.

Chelmsfords Fate. Benjamin Tompson. SCAP

Chelsea. Robert Long. NAmP

Chemicals ripen the citrus. In California. Donald Davie. NoAM

Chemistry of Character, The. Elizabeth Dorney. BLPA

Chen-chou Quatrains, *sels.* Wang Shih-chen, *tr. fr. Chinese by* Daniel Bryant. WFTU

"At dawn I climb a river tower to its very highest storey." *Fr.* III.

"Most of the houses along the river are those of fisherfolk." *Fr.* IV.

Ch'en-hsi County. Ho Ching-ming, *tr. fr. Chinese by* Jonathan Chaves. CoBLCP

Cheng-tao Temple. Tai Piao-yüan, *tr. fr. Chinese by* Jonathan Chaves. CoBLCP

Chepstow: A Poem, *sels.* Edward Davies. OBWVE

Cambrian Swain, The.

Tintern Abbey.

Chercheuses de Poux, Les. Rimbaud, *tr. fr. French by* T. Sturge Moore. *Fr.* Illuminations. AWP

Cherokee, The. Mary Weston Fordham. CBWP-2

Cherokee Dean, The. Norman H. Russell. STE

Cherrie-ripe. Robert Herrick. *See* Cherry-ripe.

Cherries, *sel.* Edward Brathwaite.

So When the Hammers of the Witnesses of Heaven Are Raised All Together. NAs

Cherries. Zalman Schneour, *tr. fr. Yiddish by* Joseph Leftwich. TrJP

Cherries. Lucien Stryk. CAPP

Cherries; a Parable, The. Thomas Moore. OBSV

Cherries are blooming. Joben, *tr. by* Steven D. Carter. WFTW

Cherries bloom on distant hills. Teika, *tr. fr. Japanese by* Hiroaki Sato. *Fr.* A Compendium of Good Tanka. FCEI

Cherries, cuckoo. Sampu, *tr. by* Geoffrey Bownas *and* Anthony Thwaite. PeBJV

Cherry. Gene Baro. ErPo

Cherry. Hagiwara Sakutaro, *tr. fr. Japanese by* Hiroaki Sato. FCEI

Cherry and pear are white. The Crowns. John Freeman. CH

Cherry and the Slae, The, *sel. at. to* Alexander Montgomerie.

"About ane bank, where birdis on bewis." GoTS

Cherry blossom spring festival. Sushi-Okashi and Green Tea with Mitsu Yashima. Al Robles. BrSi

Cherry-Blossom Wand, The. Anna Wickham. MoBrPo

Cherry blossoms. Narihira, *tr. fr. Japanese by* Burton Watson. *Fr.* Kokin Shu. FCEI

Cherry blossoms, The. Spring. Princess Shikishi, *tr. by* Hiroaki Sato. PBWP

Cherry Blossoms at Shiga, The. Kaneyoshi, *tr. fr. Japanese by* Steven D. Carter. WFTW

Cherry blossoms must have opened. Teika, *tr. fr. Japanese by* Hiroaki Sato. *Fr.* A Compendium of Good Tanka. FCEI

Cherry Boy, The, *sels.* Royston Ellis. PeHV

"All my sex life, I had been drifting." *Fr.* 1.

"It was an international rage." *Fr.* 6.

Cherry Fair, The. *Unknown. See* Farewell, This World.

Cherry flowers. *Unknown, tr. fr. Japanese by* Burton Watson. *Fr.* Kokin Shu. FCEI

Cherry Ice. Donna Masini. ER

Cherry-lipped Adonis. Richard Barnfield. *Fr.* Cynthia, XVII. Son

Cherry-lipt Adonis in his snowie shape. Richard Barnfield. *Fr.* Sonnets, XVII. PeHV

Cherry petals/ like the tears. Saigyo, *tr. fr. Japanese by* Burton Watson. *Fr.* Sixty-four Tanka. FCEI

Cherry red kind of washed-out. Bruce Andrews. *Fr.* Confidence Trick. IAT

Cherry-ripe. Robert Herrick. CaPo; CH; ELP; OBEV; TEP (Cherrie-ripe.) SeCV-1

Cherry Robbers. D. H. Lawrence. MoAB; MoBrPo

Cherry Tree. Ivy O. Eastwick. BoTP

Cherry Tree, The. Thom Gunn. GLP; Psk

Cherry-Tree Carol, The. *Unknown.* AmFP, 4 *vers.*; ChTr; EBEV, A *and* B *vers.*; ELP; EnSB; ESPB; FaBoBa; GBP; HeIP; OAEL-1, *with music*; OBCP; OBET; OFD; OnMSP; OxBB, *with music*; OxBoLi; TrGrPo

(Joseph Was an Old Man.) OBCP

See also As Joseph Was a-Walking [*or* a-Waukin'].

Cherry Trees, The. Edward Thomas. NAEL-2; OBWP

Cherry year, A. *Unknown.* OxNR

Cherrylog Road. James Dickey. CoAP; HAP; HCAP; InPS; MT; NAAL-2; NIP; NYBP; PrIm; TwCP; WeW

Cherubic Pilgrim, The. "Angelus Silesius", *tr. fr. German.* WGRP

Chesapeake. Gerta Kennedy. NYBP

Chesapeake and *Shannon* ("The *Chesapeake* so bold"). *Unknown.* PAH

(*Shannon* and *Chesapeake*.) OxBSS

"Chessie," the Chesapeake and Ohio's. Our Flag Was Still There. Richard Tillinghast. MAYP

Chest of Perote, The. Joaquín Arcadio Pagaza, *tr. fr. Spanish by* Samuel Beckett. MexPo

Chestnut Avenue at Alton House, The. Charles Tomlinson. FaBoTw

Chestnut Buds. Evelyn M. Williams. BoTP

Chestnut tree stands in the line of sight, A. St. Asaph's. Kingsley Amis. OxBTC

Chestnut vendor, The. Karl Szelki. PCP

Chestnut's a fine tree, The. A Christmas-Tree Song. Rodney Bennett. BoTP

Chestnuts Are Falling, The. Lilian Moore. RR

Chevy Chase. *Unknown.* FaBoBa; GN; OBET

Chevy Chase. *Unknown.* EnSB; OxBB, *sl. diff. vers.*

Chewing Chawing Gum. *Unknown.* AmFP

Chez Brébant. Francis Alexander Durivage. AA

Chez Jane. Frank O'Hara. CoAP; NeAP; NoAM; NOBA; PoA; PoE

Chez Madame. Sam Harrison. NeIP

Chez-Nous. Albert Gordon Austin. PoAu-2

Chi Tzu of Yen Ling Hangs Up His Sword. Yang Mu, *tr. fr. Chinese by* Dominic Cheung. IFON

Ch'i-yü-ko. *Unknown, tr. fr. Chinese by* Burton Watson. CoBCP

Chia Mountain Monastery. Chu Yi-tsun, *tr. fr. Chinese by* Irving Lo. *Fr.* Quatrains on Peking's Western Suburb, VIII. WFTU

Chiapas. Gary Soto. NoAM

Chiaroscuro. Carole Bergé. ErPo

Chic desolation of the/ factory. The Emergency Room. David Fisher. NPGG

Chic Freedom's Reflection. Alice Walker. InPS; NMM

Chicago. Bret Harte. AiP; PAH

Chicago. John Boyle O'Reilly. PAH

Chicago. Lola Ridge. PoA

Chicago. Carl Sandburg. AiP; AmPP; AnAmPo; BLPL; CMoP; FaBV; LiTM; MoAB; MoAmPo; MoP; NoAM; NOBA; NoP; OxBA; PoA; TAP; UnPo; VGW; ViBoPo

Chicago. Whittier. PAH

Chicago Analogue. Horace. *See* Odes: I, 38. Simplicity.

Chicago Boy Baby. Carl Sandburg. NAs

Chicago "Defender" Sends a Man to Little Rock, The. Gwendolyn Brooks. AmNP; PoBA

Chicago Exposition Ode. Mary Weston Fordham. CBWP-2

Chicago "Manuel of Style" is really neat, The. John Tranter. *Fr.* Crying in Early Infancy, LXXI. NoAM

Chicago: Near West-Side Renewal. Dennis Schmitz. AmPA

Chicago Odyssey, The. Jim Barnes. NOVW

Chicago Picasso, The. Gwendolyn Brooks. *Fr.* Two Dedications. BPo; EyDe; LiTM

Chicago Poem. Lew Welch. NeAP; PoM

Chicago ran a fever of a hundred and one that groggy Sunday. The Shooting of John Dillinger outside the Biograph Theater July 22, 1934. David Wagoner. CoAP; FYAP; RB; SM

Chicago, Summer Past. Richard Snyder. Psk

Chick! my naggie. *Unknown.* OxNR

Chickadee, The. Emerson. FaPON

Chicken. Dave Etter. MAT

Chicken. Dennis Kelly. PeHV

Chicken. *Unknown, tr. fr. Yoruba by* Ulli Beier. *Fr.* Hunter Poems of the Yoruba. RB

Chicken blessed and caressed. *Unknown. Fr.* A Collection of Hymns. . .of the Moravian Brethren. NOEC

Chicken. How shall I tell you what it is. A Presentation of Two Birds to My Son. James Wright. DiL; PPP

Chicken-Licken. Maya Angelou. FF

Chicken Poem, The. Don Welch. MOWH
Chicken wants, The. *Unknown, tr. by* Geoffrey Bownas *and* Anthony Thwaite. PeBJV
Chickens, The. *Unknown. See* Said the first little chicken.
Chickens a-crowin' on Sourwood Mountain. Sourwood Mountain. *Unknown.* AS, *with music;* GBP
Chickens the Weasel Killed. William Stafford. NaP
Chickory. Zerubavel Gal'ed, *tr. fr. Hebrew.* TrJP
Chide, chide no more away. Expectation. Thomas Stanley. OBS
Chief. Michael S. Harper. PPR
"Chief, The." W. E. Henley. *Fr.* In Hospital, XV. BrPo
Chief defect of Henry King, The. Henry King, Who Chewed Bits of String, and Was Early Cut Off in Dreadful Agonies. Hilaire Belloc. CenHV; FaBoNo; FaBoUs; NBLV
Chief Leschi of the Nisqually. Duane Niatum. CDW; STE
Chief of the West, Darkling, The. David Knight. MoCV
Chief Petty Officer. Charles Causley. OxBTC
Chiefe use then in man of that he knowes, The. Fulke Greville. *Fr.* Of Human Learning. OBS
Chiefly, it is blue. People use. A Vacation on Earth. Thomas M. Disch. BWV
Chiefly to Mind Appears. C. Day Lewis. MoAB; MoBrPo
Chieftain Iffucan of Azcan in caftan. Bantams in Pine-Woods. Wallace Stevens. CMoP; InPS; NoAM; NOBA; OxBA; UnPo
Chieftain to the Highlands bound, A. Lord Ullin's Daughter. Thomas Campbell. BeLS; BoTP; EnRP; FaPON; FaPoR; GN; GTBS; GTBS-P; WBLP
Chieko Mounting on the Wind. Takamura Kotaro, *tr. fr. Japanese by* Geoffrey Bownas *and* Anthony Thwaite. PeBJV
Child, A. Charles *and* Mary Lamb. *See* Child's plaything for an hour, A.
Child. E. N. Sargent. NYBP
Child, A. Richard Watson Gilder. AA
Child, The. Donald Hall. NePoEA-2
Child, The. George Keithley. NPGG
Child. Sylvia Plath. HCAP; PBWP
Child, The. Ivor Popham. EaLo
Child, The, *sels.* John Banister Tabb. AA
  At Bethlehem.
  To his Mother.
  "Where were ye, Birds, that bless His name."
Child,/ You are my brother. The Mists Are Rising Now. Hasye Cooperman. GoYe
Child, A/ Curious and innocent. To Robert Louis Stevenson. W. E. Henley. MoBrPo
Child, The. George Edward Woodberry. *Fr.* Wild Eden, XXX. AA
Child (a boy) bouncing, A. To. William Carlos Williams. OBAL
Child, and all children. To a Christmas Two-Year-Old. Luci Shaw. TrCP
Child and Boatman. Jean Ingelow. *Fr.* Songs on the Voices of Birds. FM
Child and Maiden. Sir Charles Sedley. *Fr.* The Mulberry Garden. GTBS; GTBS-P
  ("Ah, Cloris! Could I now but sit.") OBS
  (Song: "Ah Cloris! That I could now sit.") SeCV-2
  (To Chloris.) OBEV
Child and the Mariner, The. W. H. Davies. CH
Child and the Shadow, The. Elizabeth Jennings. NePoEA-2
Child awaits the angel, The. The Angel. Alfred Hayes. TrJP
Child Bearers, The. Anne Sexton. BoWoP
Child Beater. Ai. BoWoP
Child begins to walk, The. Poem for the Sandman. James Tate. NAmP
Child-Bride, The. Joyce Carol Oates. GeTw
Child Built a Castle, A. Ya'akov Beser, *tr. fr. Hebrew by* Bernhard Frank. MHeP
Child chases a butterfly, A. Lilac Blossoms. Ruth Kim Chun-soo, *tr. by* Koh Chang-soo. ACKP
Child Compassion, The. Margot Ruddock. OBMV
Child Crying. Anthony Thwaite. NePoEA-2
Child crying in the night, A. Unintelligible Terms. Charles Simic. NoP
Child, Do Not Throw This Book About. Hilaire Belloc. NoAM
  (Dedication on the Gift of a Book to a Child.) EBEV
Child Dying, The. Edwin Muir. FaBoTw; GTBS-P; RB
Child Explains Dying, A. Robert Crum. PPR
Child Harold, *sels.* John Clare.
  London versus Epping Forest. FaBoPP
  Northamptonshire Fens. FaBoPP
  Stanzas from "Child Harold." OBNC
  (In Epping Forest.) FaBoPP
Child has a vision of the happy army, The. The Happy Army. Peter Bland. ATNZ
Child has never been older, The. Late Winter Snow. Brian Turner. ATNZ

Child I carry on my back, The. Shiba Sonome, *tr. fr. Japanese by* Hiroaki Sato. *Fr.* Fifteen Hokku. FCEI
Child I do not have, The. The Second Heart. Ellen Wittlinger. TV
Child I left your class to have, The. For Elizabeth Bishop. Sandra McPherson. GeTw; MAYP
Child, I warn thee in all wise. Symon's Lesson of Wisdom for All Manner of Children. *Unknown.* OxBChV
Child, I will give you rings to wear. Declaration. Arthur Symons. *Fr.* Violet. BrPo
Child in a Blue Linen Dress. Helen Sorrells. MOWH
Child in Prison, A. Gofraidh Fionn O'Dalaigh. NOIV
Child in the 80's, A. Derwent May. OBD
Child in the Street, The. John James Piatt. AA
Child is born, A. Life. Jean Follain, *tr. by* Keith Waldrop. RHTwFP
Child is father of the man, The. Ode: Intimations of Immortality from Recollections of Early Childhood. Wordsworth. AWP; BLPL; ChER; EnRP; FaBoRV; FiP; HAP; HeIP; InvP; LiTB; NAs; NoBE; NoP; OAEL-2; OBEV; OBNC; PoE; PoEL-4; PPP; PrIm; TEP; TrGrPo
  (Ode on Intimations of [*or* on] immortality.) FaFP; GTBS; GTBS-P; OHFP
"Child Is Father to the Man, The." Gerard Manley Hopkins. FaBoCo; NOBVV
  (Triolet.) NOBL
Child is holy and most wise, The. The Child. Ivor Popham. EaLo
Child Is Introduced to the Cosmos at Birth, The. *Unknown, tr. fr. Omaha Indian by* Alice Fletcher. AnAmPo
  (Ho! Ye Sun, Moon, Stars.) PrIM
Child is like a rare bird, A. Praise of a Child. *Yoruba Oral Tradition, tr. by* Ulli Beier *and* B. Gbadamosi. WTO
Child is like a sailor cast up by the sea, The. Lucretius, *tr. fr. Latin by* C. H. Sisson. *Fr.* De Rerum Natura (On the Nature of Things). NAs
Child is not dead, The. The Child Who Was Shot Dead by Soldiers at Nyanga. Ingrid Jonker, *tr. by* Jack Cope *and* Uys Krige. PeSA
Child is on my shoulders, The. Laughing Child. Carl Sandburg. PCP
Child, is thy father dead? Ebenezer Elliott. PF; SaC
Child jumps out of a willow, A. Issa, *tr. by* Hiroaki Sato. FCEI
Child-King, The. Morris Wintchevsky, *tr. fr. Yiddish by* Alter Brody. TrJP
Child Labor. Charlotte Perkins Gilman. AnAmPo
Child Life. Mary E. Tucker. CBWP-1
Child like mustard seed, The. War-Baby. D. H. Lawrence. NAs
Child listen/ I am singing. White-arm, *tr. by* W. S. Merwin *after* Robert Lowie. STP
Child Maurice. *Unknown.* ESPB, A, B *and* D *vers.*
  (Childe Maurice.) TrGrPo
Child might be hiding in the ship, The. Hide and Seek. Penelope Shuttle. NPo
Child most infantine, A. A Child of Twelve. Shelley. *Fr.* The Revolt of Islam, II. GN
Child-Musician, The. Austin Dobson. GN
Child Naming Flowers. Robert Hass. MAYP; NPGG
Child Next Door, The ("The child next door has a wreath on her hat"). Rose Fyleman. FaPON
Child Noryce is a clever young man. Child Maurice. *Unknown.* ESPB, B *vers.*
Child not yet is lulled to rest, The. Cradle-Song at Twilight. Alice Meynell. NOBVV
Child of death. Praises of the King of Oyo. *Yoruba Oral Tradition, tr. by* Ulli Beier. WTO
Child of Loneliness. Norman Gale. WGRP
Child of maize! Red Monkey. *Unknown, tr. fr. Yoruba by* Ulli Beier. *Fr.* Hunter Poems of the Yoruba. RB
Child of My Winter Born. William DeWitt Snodgrass. *Fr.* Heart's Needle, I. MoAmPo
Child of Our Time. Eavan Boland. CIP
Child of patient industry. Invitation to the Bee. Charlotte Smith. OxBChV
Child of silence and shadow. Yvonne Caroutch, *tr. by* David Cloutier. BoWoP
Child of sin and sorrow. Exhortation. Thomas Hastings. AA
Child of the Romans. Carl Sandburg. NAAL-2
Child of the season of adventure, child of the heart. Child. E. N. Sargent. NYBP
Child of the World. Edna L. S. Barker. GoYe
Child of To-Day, A. James Buckham. AA
Child of Twelve, A. Shelley. *Fr.* The Revolt of Islam, II. GN
Child on the Judgment Seat, The. Elizabeth Rundle Charles. BLPA
Child on Top of a Greenhouse. Theodore Roethke. LCAP; VGW
Child Owlet. *Unknown.* ESPB

Child Plays, The. Katri Vala, *tr. fr. Finnish by* Aili Jarvenpa. SOP

Child Reads an Almanac, The ("The child reads on; her basket of eggs stands by"). Francis Jammes, *tr. fr. French by* Ludwig Lewisohn. AWP; FaPON

Child returns to teach you nothing, The. Broad Meadow. Alain Delahaye, *tr. by* Paul Auster. RHTwFP

Child said, A *What is the grass?.* Walt Whitman. *Fr.* Song of Myself, VI. NoP

  (Grass.) BLPL

  (Leaves of Grass, VI *and* XX) AA

Child saw the bombers skate, The. Come to the Stone. Randall Jarrell. VGW

Child says, "Nammu, Nammu", A. Issa, *tr. by* Hiroaki Sato. FCEI

Child Scribbles, The. Nizar Qabbani, *tr. fr. Arabic by* Diana Der Hovanessian *and* Lena Jayyusi. MAP

Child should always say what's true, A. Whole Duty of Children. Robert Louis Stevenson. FaBoUs; NBLV; OxBChV

Child skipping jump on the quay at the mill, A. Poor Old Horse. David Holbrook. NePoEA-2

Child Taken from the Mother, The. Minnie Bruce Pratt. GLP

Child That Has a Cold, A. Thomas Dibdin. ChTr; FaBoNo

Child, the current of your breath is six days long. Unknown Girl in the Maternity Ward. Anne Sexton. MoP; NAs; NoAM

Child to His Sick Grandfather, A. Joanna Baillie. NOEC

Child was taught, A. On Pretext. Charles Simic. PPR

Child Waters. *Unknown.* ESPB, A *and* B *vers.;* FaBoBa; OBET; OxBB

Child, weary of thy baubles of to-day. The Human Plan. Charles Henry Crandall. AA

Child Who Was Shot Dead by Soldiers at Nyanga, The. Ingrid Jonker, *tr. fr. Afrikaans by* Jack Cope *and* Uys Krige. PeSA

Child, who went gathering the flowers of death. Haroun Al-Rachid for Heart's-Life. *Unknown, tr. fr. Arabic by* E. Powys Mathers. *Fr.* The Thousand and One Nights. AWP

Child with a Cockatoo. Rosemary Dobson. CBAP

Child with a stupid expression watches a crack in a window, A. Sorcery. René Daumal, *tr. by* Michael Benedikt. POS

Child with a wrench is, A/ moving. A Junkie with a Flute in the Rain. David Fisher. NPGG

Child with Six Fingers. Carol Muske. AmPA

Child with the hungry eyes. Beggars. Ella Higginson. AA

Child, you were conceived in my upstairs room. To a Child Born in Time of Small War. Helen Sorrells. WPE

Childbirth. Ted Hughes. NAs

Childcity, Aprilcity. Paris. Gregory Corso. VGW

Childe Harold's Farewell to England. Byron. *Fr.* Childe Harold's Pilgrimage. OHFP

Childe Harold's Pilgrimage, *sels.* Byron.

  Childe Harold's Farewell to England. OHFP

  Dedication: To Ianthe. OBNC

  Dying Gladiator, The. *Fr.* IV. NOBE

  Fame. *Fr.* IV. FiP

  "He that has sail'd upon the dark blue sea." *Fr.* II. MOS

  "I stood in Venice on the Bridge of Sighs." *Fr.* IV. EnRP, *abr.;* OBTV, *abr.*.

  (On the Bridge of Sighs.) FaBoPP, 4 *sts.*

  "Is thy face like thy mother's, my fair child!" *Fr.* III. ChER, 15 *sts.;* EnRP; OAEL-2, *abr.*.

  It Is the Hush of Night. *Fr.* III. LiTB

    Lake Leman ("Clear, placid Leman! thy contrasted lake"). OBNC, *sl. diff. sel.*

  "Lake Leman woos me with its crystal face." *Fr.* III. InPS

  (Lake Leman.) PoEL-4

  Ocean, The. *Fr.* IV. PoEL-4

  (Apostrophe to the Ocean.) OHFP; WBLP

  (By the Deep Sea.) OBNC, *shorter sel.*

  (Deep and Dark Blue Ocean.) ChTr

  (Ocean, The.) FaBV; TrGrPo

  (Roll On, Thou Deep and Dark Blue Ocean.) FaPON; FiP

  (Sea, The.) BLPL; FaBoBe; LiTB

  ("There is a pleasure in the pathless woods.") MOS

  (To the Ocean.) GN; WGRP

  "Oh love! no habitant of earth thou art." *Fr.* IV. OAEL-2

  (Fatal Spell, The.) OBNC

  "Oh, thou! in Hellas deemed of heavenly birth." *Fr.* I. NAEL-2, *much abr.*

  "On, on the vessel flies, the land is gone." *Fr.* XIV–XIX. OBTV

  Poet and the World, The. *Fr.* III. SeCePo

  Rome by Metella's Tomb. *Fr.* IV. FaBoPP

  "Stop! for thy tread is on an empire's dust!" *Fr.* III. InPS

  "There was a sound of revelry by night." *Fr.* III. EBEV; OBWP

  (Battle of Waterloo, The.) FaFP

  (Eve of Waterloo, The.) BeLS; FaBoBe; FaBoCh; FaBV; NOBE; OBNC

  (Night before the Battle of Waterloo, The.) WBLP

  (Night before Waterloo, The.) GN

  (Waterloo.) FiP; TrGrPo; WaaP

  To Eddleston. *Fr.* II. PeHV

  Wandering Outlaw, The. *Fr.* III. FiP

Childe Maurice. *Unknown.* See Child Maurice.

Childe Roland, etc. Elder Olson. OBAL

"Childe Roland to the Dark Tower Came." Robert Browning. NAEL-2; NOBVV; NoP; OAEL-2; OBNV; PoE; PPP

Childe Rolandine. Stevie Smith. BrRo

Childe Watters in his stable stoode. Child Waters. *Unknown.* ESPB; FaBoBa; OxBB

Childheart, time alone is not enough. A Late Spring. James Scully. NYBP

Childhood. Jens Baggesen, *tr. fr. Danish by* Longfellow. AWP

Childhood. William Barnes. NOBVV

Childhood. Edith Bruck, *tr. fr. Italian by* Anita Barrows. VWA

Childhood. Frances Cornford. FaBoWP; OxBSP; OxBTC

Childhood. Donald Justice. AnAn; LCAP

Childhood. Jewel C. Latimore. JB

Childhood. Donagh MacDonagh. NeIP

Childhood. Edwin Muir. CMoP; HeIP; NoP; SeCePo

Childhood. Sir Herbert Read. BrPo

Childhood. Rainer Maria Rilke, *tr. fr. German by* M. D. Herter Norton. SOTW

Childhood. David Rokeah, *tr. fr. Hebrew by* Bernhard Frank. MHeP

Childhood. Maura Stanton. MAYP; SM

Childhood. Thomas Traherne. TrGrPo

Childhood. Margaret Abigail Walker. IHMS; PBWP; PoBA; Son; WPOW

Childhood and School-Time. Wordsworth. *Fr.* The Prelude [or, Growth of a Poet's Mind], I. CH; GN; HAP; NOBE; NOBE; NoP; NoP; NU; OBNC; PoE; SCV

  (Introduction—Childhood and School-Time.) PoEL-4

  (On the Solitary Fells around Hawkshead.) FaBoPP

  "Dust as we are, the immortal spirit grows." SCV

  In Patterdale. FaBoRV

  Influence of Natural Objects. AWP

  "Oh [*or* O] there is a blessing in this gentle breeze." EnRP; OAEL-2

  On the Frozen Lake. FaBoCh; GN

  On Ullswater. FaBoPP; RB

  On Windermere; Bowness Bay and Belle Isle. FaBoPP

  One Summer Evening ("One summer evening (led by her) I found"). FiP; NU

  Skating. TOF

  "So through the darkness and the cold we flew." CH; SD

  Was It for This. RB

  "Wisdom and spirit of the universe!" NOBE

  Wordsworth Skates on Esthwaite Water. FaBoPP

Childhood Fled. Charles Lamb. EnRP

Childhood in Jacksonville, Florida. Jane Cooper. TAP

Childhood is not from birth to a certain age and at a certain age. Childhood Is the Kingdom Where Nobody Dies. Edna St. Vincent Millay. FaBoWP

Childhood of a Spy. Dick Davis. DiPo

Childhood of an Equestrian, The. Russell Edson. AmPA

Childhood remembrances [*or* memories] are always a drag. Nikki-Rosa. Nikki Giovanni. AIW; AmNP; BlSi; HeIP; IHMS; MoP; PoBA; TAP

Childhood Summers. Helena Anhava, *tr. fr. Finnish by* Aili Jarvenpa. SOP

Childhood's Retreat. Robert Duncan. NoAM

Childish Game, A. Reinmar von Hagenau, *tr. fr. German by* Jethro Bithell. AWP

Childish Prank, A. Ted Hughes. OAEL-2; OxBC

Childish Things. William Stafford. BLA

Childless. Giolla Brighde MacNamee, *tr. fr Irish by* Frank O'Connor. BIrV

Childless Father, The. Wordsworth. CH

Childless Witch, A. Raquel Chalfi, *tr. fr. Hebrew by* Alexandra Meiri *and* Myra Glazer Schotz. VWA

Children, The/ who cried. *Unknown, tr. fr. Japanese by* Hiroaki Sato. *Fr.* Manyo Shu. FCEI

Children, The. Charles Monroe Dickinson. AA

Children. Russell Edson. AmPA

Children, The. Qasim Haddad, *tr. fr. Arabic by* Sharif Elmusa *and* Charles Doria. MAP

Children, The. William Heyen. GeTw

Children, The. Susan MacDonald. IHMS

Children. Sandra McPherson. AnAn; FaBoWP

Children. Bill Manhire. ATNZ; PeNZ

Children, The. Vincent O'Sullivan. ATNZ
Children. Pantiyan Arivutai Nampi, *tr. fr. Tamil by* A. K. Ramanujan. PLW
Children. Laura Riding. *Fr.* Forgotten Girlhood. RB
Children. Su Tung-p'o, *tr. fr. Chinese by* Burton Watson. CoBCP
Children. Teaching the Children. Myra Sklarew. CRP
Children/ They teach to walk. Training on the Shore. Shlomo Vinner, *tr. by* Laya Firestone *and* Howard Schwartz. VWA
Children, The. Constance Urdang. CoAP; IHMS
Children among the Hills. Linda Gregg. NPGG
Children among the Tombstones. John Russell Hervey. ATNZ
Children and Sir Nameless, The. Thomas Hardy. NoP
Children are dumb to say how hot the day is. The Cool Web. Robert Graves. AWP; GTBS-P; MoP; NAEL-2; NIP; NoAM; NoP; OxBTC; PoA; PrIm; SCV
Children are shouting. Ozaki Hosai, *tr. fr. Japanese by* Hiroaki Sato. *Fr.* One Hundred Haiku in Free Form. FCEI
Children Band, The. Sir Aubrey De Vere. OBEV
Children begin at green dawn nimbly to build. The Altars in the Street. Denise Levertov. CAPP
Children, behold the chimpanzee. The Chimpanzee. Oliver Herford. CenHV; FaBV; FiBHP; NA
Children believe in clover, magic numbers. The Sacred Children. H. R. Hays. EAS
Children born of fairy stock. I'd Love to Be a Fairy's Child. Robert Graves. BoTP; FaPON; PDV
Children called, The. Itamar Ya'oz-kest, *tr. fr. Hebrew by* Bernhard Frank. *Fr.* Ordeal by Fire. MHeP
Children, children, come and look. Jack-in-the-Boat. Allen Curnow. ATNZ
Children, Children Everywhere. Jack Prelutsky. RHPC
Children conceived when two nightgowns. The Submarine Bed. John Peale Bishop. LiTA
Children cried: "Mummy!", The. Massacre of the Innocents. Tadeusz Rózewicz, *tr. by* Jan Darowski. OBD
Children dear, was it yesterday. Matthew Arnold. *Fr.* The Forsaken Merman. BoTP
Children do not ask the proper questions. Leaping into the Gulf. Patricia Beer. OxBC
Children, do you ever. My Other Me. Grace Denio Litchfield. AA
Children don't know what worry means! Children. Su Tung-p'o, *tr. by* Burton Watson. CoBCP
Children enter, The. Sundown at Darlington 1878. Lance Henson. VoR
Children go forward with their little satchels, The. The School Children. Louise Glück. AmPA; HCAP; WeW
Children I told you I tell you our sun was a hail of gold! Summers Ago. Isabella Gardner. CAPP
Children, if you dare to think. Warning to Children. Robert Graves. FaBoCh; FaFP; NoP; OAEL-2; SO
Children in the Wood, The. *Unknown. See* Now ponder well, you parents dear.
Children know how to do it, The. Feeding the Fire. Donald Finkel. VWA
Children March, The. Elizabeth Riddell. CBAP
Children of a Grieved Mother. Shauqi Abi Shaqra, *tr. fr. Arabic by* Abdullah al-Udhari. MPAW
Children of Auschwitz. Naum Korzhavin, *tr. fr. Russian by* Daniel Weissbort. VWA
Children of dreams are in terror, The. A Text for These Distracted Times. Rodney Hall. CBAP
Children of Greenock, The. William Sydney Graham. FaBoTw
Children of Israel prayed for bread, The. Old Sam's Wife. *Unknown.* ChTr
Children of Light. Robert Lowell. CMoP; MoAB; NAAL-2; OxBA
Children of Lir. Susan Howe. *Fr.* White Foolscap/Book of Cordelia. LP
Children of Love. Harold Monro. MoBrPo
Children of Stare, The, *sel.* Walter de la Mare. BrPo
"Winter is fallen early." Mes
Children of the cold sun and the broken horizon. The City. Ben Maddow. WaP
Children of the Heavenly King. John Cennick. WGRP
Children of the Night, The. E. A. Robinson. OxBA
Children of the Owl and the Pussy-Cat, The. Edward Lear. FaBoNo
Children of the Poor, The. Gwendolyn Brooks. *Fr.* The Womanhood, I. PoA, *complete;* WPE, 1 *and* 2.
What Shall I Give. BPo, 2 *only.*
Children of the Sun. Fenton Johnson. BANP
Children of the world are on the march, The. The Children March. Elizabeth Riddell. CBAP

Children of yesterday. Song of Hope. Mary Artemisia Lathbury. BLPA
Children picking up our bones. A Postcard from the Volcano. Wallace Stevens. HAP; HCAP; LiTA; NoAM; WeW
Children: Private Ward. William Ernest Henley. *Fr.* In Hospital, XVIII. BrPo
Children set fires in ashbarrels. Galway Kinnell. *Fr.* The Avenue Bearing the Initial of Christ into the New World, 9. NaP
Children sleep at night. Children. Laura Riding. *Fr.* Forgotten Girlhood. RB
Children, the Sandbar, That Summer. Muriel Rukeyser. LCAP
Children They, The. Angelika Mechtel, *tr. fr. German by* Susan L. Cocalis. DMG
Children they move stand, The. Clear. Angelo Lewis. PoBA
Children Waking: Indian Hill Station. Ralph Nixon Currey. PeSA
Children walk. City. Jane Stembridge. NMM
Children Walking Home from School through Good Neighborhood. Donald Justice. DiPo
Children wandered up and down, The. The Cruise of the *Mystery*. Celia Thaxter. OBCA
Children we have not borne. To My Daughter the Junkie on a Train. Audre Lorde. CNA
Children were frightened by crescendoes, The. A Fete. Larry Eigner. NeAP
Children were shouting together, The. Frolic. "Æ." BoTP; FaPON; MoBrPo
Children who love more than they hate. Families. Thomas Blackburn. OxBSP
Children, why do you fear, why turn away? For Miriam. Marjorie Oludhe Macgoye. WPOW
Children, you are very little. Good and Bad Children. Robert Louis Stevenson. *Fr.* A Child's Garden of Verses. EBVV; FaBoCh; FaFP; NBLV; OxBChV; PWR
Children's Bells, The. Eleanor Farjeon. BoTP; CH
Children's Carnival. Juliane Windhager, *tr. fr. German by* Beth Bjorklund. CoAuP
Children's Carol, The. Eleanor Farjeon. PChr; RHPC
Children's Crusade, The. Philip Levine. NaP
Children's Crusade 1939. Bertolt Brecht, *tr. fr. German by* Michael Hamburger. MoBS
Children's Elegy. Muriel Rukeyser. *Fr.* Eighth Elegy. LCAP
Children's Games. Abraham Reisen, *tr. fr. Yiddish by* Leonard Wolf. PeBMYV
Children's Hour, The. Longfellow. AA; AnAmPo; FaBoBe; FaBV; FaFP; FaPON; FPL; OBAL; OHFP; PoEL-5; PoLF; WBLP
Children's Letters, The. Dorothy Livesay. NOBC
Children's Party, The. Eiluned Lewis. CN
Children's Rhymes. Langston Hughes. BPo
Children's Song. Arye Sivan, *tr. fr. Hebrew by* David Shevin. VWA
Children's Song, The. *Unknown.* FaPON
Children's voices in the orchard. New Hampshire. T. S. Eliot. *Fr.* Landscapes, I. FaBoCh; GTBS-P; NoAM; RB; WeW
Child's a plaything for an hour, A. Parental Recollections. Charles *and* Mary Lamb. OxBSP
(Child, A.) OBEV
Child's Blackness. Jean Follain, *tr. fr. French by* Keith Waldrop. RHTwFP
Child's Calendar, A, *sels.* John Updike.
August. OBCA; RHPC
May. OBCA
Child's castle crumbles; hot air shimmers, The. Mercury Bay Eclogue. M. K. Joseph. ATNZ; PeNZ
Child's Christmas Carol, A. Christine Chaundler. BoTP
Child's Christmas Day, A. *Unknown.* OBCP
Child's Christmas without Jean Cocteau, A. David Fisher. NPGG
Child's cough scratches at my heart, The—my head. New York— December, 1931. Babette Deutsch. ImOP
Child's Day, A, *sel. Walter de la Mare.*
Ann and the Fairy Song. FaBV
Child's Dream, The. Susan Ludvigson. MAYP
Child's Evening Prayer, A. Samuel Taylor Coleridge. *See* Ere on my bed my limbs I lay.
Child's eyes to see. The Vision Clear. J. M. Westrup. BoTP
Child's First Grief, The. Felicia Dorothea Hemans. BLPA
Child's foot is not yet aware it's a foot, The. To the Foot from Its Child. Pablo Neruda, *tr. by* Alistair Reid. RB
Child's Game. Judson Jerome. DuDa
Child's Garden of Verses, A, *sels.* Robert Louis Stevenson.
Armies in the Fire. EBVV
Good and Bad Children. EBVV; FaBoCh; FaFP; OxBChV
Lamplighter, The. EBVV; OxBChV; SaC
Winter Time. EBVV; MoBrPo; OxBChV
Child's Grace, A. Burns. FaBoCh; FaPON; MoShBr

Child's Grace Robert Herrick. *See* Here a little child I stand.
Child's Grave, Hale County, Alabama. Jim Simmerman. BLA
Child's Grave Marker, A. Ted Kooser. GOYP
Child's Laughter, A. Swinburne. BLPL; PoLF
Child's Mirror, A. Judith Herzberg, *tr. fr. Dutch by the author.* DuIn
Child's Morning Prayer, A. J. Kirby. BoTP
Child's Natural History, *sels.* Oliver Herford.
  Mon-Goos, The. AA
  Some Geese. FiBHP; NA
Child's Pet, A. William Henry Davies. CH; RB
Child's Prayer, A. William Canton. BoTP
Child's Prayer, A. Siegfried Sassoon. BoTP
Child's Prayer, A. John Banister Tabb. FaPON
Child's Prayer, A. Francis Thompson. *See* Little Jesus, wast Thou
  shy.
Child's Prayer, A. *Unknown.* BLRP; BoTP
Child's Present, A. Robert Herrick. *See* Go pretty child, and bear
  this flower.
Child's Question, A. Emma Huntington Nason. AA
Child's Return, The. Phyllis Allfrey. PBCV
Child's Sight, The. Hy Sobiloff. VGW
Child's Song. Gerald Gould. BoTP
Child's Song. Robert Lowell. RB
Child's Song in Spring. Edith Nesbit. BOTP; OHIP; OxBChV
Child's Song of Christmas, A. Marjorie Lowry Christie Pickthall.
  BoTP
Child's Talk in April. Christina Rossetti. GN
Child's Thought, A. Robert Louis Stevenson. BoTP
Child's Thought of God, A. Elizabeth Barrett Browning. FaPON
Child's Thought of Harvest, A." "Susan Coolidge." OHIP
Child's Visit to the Biology Lab, A. Kathleen Spivack. AmPA
Child's Winter Evening, A. Gwen John. CH
Child's wisdom is in saying, The. The Child's Sight. Hy Sobiloff.
  VGW
Child's Wish, A. Abram Joseph Ryan. AA
Child's Wish Granted, The. George Parsons Lathrop. AA
Child's World, The. William Brighty Rands. *See* Great, wide, beautiful,
  wonderful world.
Chile. Susan Griffin. NPGG
Chile. Roberto Vargas, *tr. fr. Spanish by* Alejandro Murguía. Vol
Chilean Elegies: 5, The. The Interior. Tom Wayman. NOBC
Chiliasm. Richard Eberhart. EaLo
Chill, A. Christina Rossetti. BoTP
Chill dewdrops are like frozen pearls, The. Lotus Leaf Cup. Wen T'ing-
  yün, *tr. by* Lois Fusek. ATF
Chill New England sunshine, The. The Death of Goody Nurse. Rose
  Terry Cooke. PAH
Chill on the grain, we can't put up our padded quilts. Visiting My Father.
  Rai San'yo, *tr. by* Burton Watson. JLIC-2
Chilled by the Blasts of Adverse Fate. Jacob Duché. AH
Chilled by the present, its gloom and its noise. W. H. Auden. *Fr.*
  Sonnets from China, XVIII. PPP
Chilled in this Irish pub I wish my loves. John Berryman. *Fr.* Dream
  Songs. FaBoMo; LCAP
Chilled into a serenity. To an Icicle. Blanche Taylor Dickinson. CDC
Chilled with salt dew, tossed on dark waters deep. A Mermaiden.
  Thomas Hennell. FaBoTw
Chilling moon, A. Taigi, *tr. by* Geoffrey Bownas *and* Anthony Thwaite.
  PeBJV
Chillingham. Mary Elizabeth Coleridge. BoTP
Chilly and thirsty. Peeling Pears at Midnight. Lo Fu, *tr. by* Dominic
  Cheung. IFON
Chilly now: insects pestering round the lights. Autumn Night. Tanaka
  Fuyuji, *tr. by* Geoffrey Bownas *and* Anthony Thwaite. PeBJV
Chilly walls with sharp steel hooks. Berysh Vaynshteyn, *tr. fr. Yiddish by*
  Benjamin *and* Barbara Harshav. *Fr.* Guys of the Volye. AYP
Chilterns, The. Rupert Brooke. MoBrPo
Chimera, The. Dino Campana, *tr. fr. Italian by* William Weaver. PFI
Chimera, The. Théophile Gautier, *tr. fr. French by* William Jay Smith.
  CT
Chimera. Mary Ann Henn. SoTCo
Chimera. Barbara Howes. TwCP
Chimera, The. Alfred Mombert, *tr. fr. German by* Erna Baber Rosenfeld.
  VWA
Chimes. Alice Meynell. BoTP; CH; MoBrPo; WPE
Chimes. Dante Gabriel Rossetti. OBNC
Chimes for Yahya. James Merrill. AnAn
Chimney, breathing a little smoke, A. February. James Schuyler.
  NeAP
Chimney of my neighbour's house. Soliloquy to Absent Friends.
  Douglas G. Jones. MoCV
Chimney Sweeper, The. *Unknown.* AmFP

Chimney Sweeper ("A little black thing among the snow"), The. Blake.
  Fr. Songs of Experience. NAEL-2; NAWM-2; NOEC; OAEL-2;
  PPP; RB; SaC; TEP
Chimney Sweeper, The ("When my mother died I was very young").
  Blake. *Fr.* Songs of Innocence. CH; EnRP; FaBoPV; FF; HeIP;
  InPK; NAEL-2; NAWM-2; NOEC; OAEL-2; OxBChV; PoE; PPP;
  SaC; SoSe; TEP
Chimney-Sweeper's Complaint, The ("A chimney-sweepers' boy am I").
  Mary Alcock. NOEC
Chimney-Tops. *Unknown.* BoTP
Chimneys: colder. Reindeer Report. U. A. Fanthorpe. OBCP
Chimneys, rank on rank, The. Evening. Richard Aldington. MoBrPo;
  SeCePo
Chimpanzee, The/ Is a most embarrassing animal to see. Muriel Sly.
  FiBHP
Chimpanzee, The. Oliver Herford. CenHV; FaBV; FiBHP; NA
Chin buried in the collar of my overcoat. Ishikawa Takuboku, *tr. fr.*
  Japanese by Hiroaki Sato. *Fr.* Forty-seven Tanka in Three Lines.
  FCEI
Ch'in Chia's Wife's Reply. *Unknown, tr. fr. Chinese by* Arthur Waley.
  BoWoP
China. William Empson. OBTV
Chinaman, The. Christina Rossetti. FL
Chinaman's Chance, A. Marilyn Chin. BrSi
Chinaman's Chance, A. Alex Kuo. UL
China's got a machine. The Latest in Guillotines. Giuseppe Giusti, *tr.*
  by Nigel Dennis. PFI
Chinashop at seaborde. Civility a Bogey. Margaret Avison. NOBC
Chinatown. Chiang Hsun, *tr. fr. Chinese by* Dominic Cheung. IFON
Chinatown Chant. Tom MacInnes. CaP
Chinatown Games. Wing Tek Lum. BrSi
Chinatown Talking Story. Kitty Tsui. BrSi; ER
Chinese Ballad. Mao Tse-tung, *tr. fr. Chinese by* William Empson.
  Mes
Chinese Banquet, A. Kitty Tsui. GLP
Chinese Banyan, The. William Meredith. NePoEA
Chinese Camp, Kamloops (circa 1883). Andrew Suknaski. NOBC
Chinese Checkers. Arleen Cohen. TSL
Chinese know the space inside us, The. The Intimate Earth. Pamela
  Kircher. KS
Chinese Mural, A. Carlos Baker. *Fr.* A Visit to the Art Gallery.
  EyDe
Chinese Nightingale, The. Vachel Lindsay. MoAmPo
Chinese Poems: Arthur Waley. "C. A. Fair." PeSA
Chinese Restaurant. Ernest Slyman. SoTCo
Chinese sleeps under his running horse, The. Coolie. Yoshioka Minoru,
  tr. by Hiroaki Sato. FCEI
Chinese Song. Federico García Lorca, *tr. fr. Spanish by* William Jay
  Smith. *Fr.* Songs of Childhood. CT
Chinese Space. Mei-Mei Berssenbrugge. BAP
Chinese, to whom the eighteenth-century English, The. The Fashionable
  Heart. Jack Gilbert. NPGG
Chinese Winter. F. R. Higgins. BIrV
Ching a Ring. James Robinson Planché. NOBL
Ch'ing-ming Nostalgia. Yung Tzu, *tr. fr. Chinese by* Dominic Cheung.
  IFON
Ching-wei. Ku Yen-wu, *tr. fr. Chinese by* J. P. Seaton. WFTU
Ch'ing-yang Ford. *Unknown, tr. fr. Chinese by* Burton Watson. CoBCP
Chinless and slouched, gray-faced, and slack of jaw. For an Early
  Retirement. Donald Hall. TW
Chinoiserie. Charles Wright. AmPA
Chinoiseries. Amy Lowell. PoRA
Chip. George Starbuck. OBAL
Chip on His Shoulder, A. *Unknown.* BLPA; WBLP
Chipmunk, The. Randall Jarrell. *See* In and out the bushes, up the ivy.
Chipmunk, The. Ogden Nash. NIP
Chipmunk can't drag it along. Alonzo Gonzales, *tr. by* Jerome
  Rothenberg. STP
Chipmunk chewing the Chippendale. Exit, Pursued by a Bear. Ogden
  Nash. NYBP
Chipmunk was standing. Alonzo Gonzales, *tr. by* Jerome Rothenberg.
  STP
Chipmunk's Day, The. Randall Jarrell. OBCA; RHPC
Chipmunks jump, and/ Greensnakes slither. Valentine. Donald Hall.
  GrPl; LLLT; NTCP; PCP
Chipmunk's Song, The. Randall Jarrell. *See* In and out the bushes, up
  the ivy.
Chipped away, the moon disappears. Buson, *tr. fr. Japanese by* Hiroaki
  Sato. *Fr.* Eighty-seven Hokku. FCEI
Chippewa Love Song. *Unknown, tr. fr. Chippewa Indian by* Frances
  Densmore. BoWoP, *ad. by* Willis Barnstone
Chips fly off around them. Only Statues Don't Shy Away. Tsfrirah Gar,
  tr. by Bernhard Frank. MHeP

Chiqui and Terra Nova. Jessica Hagedorn. UL
Chiquita. Bret Harte. AA; AnAmPo
Chirp Chirp the Katydids. *Unknown, tr. fr. Chinese by* Burton Watson. CoBCP
Chisel Grows Heavy, The. Jon Silkin. PoPo
Chisel in hand stood a sculptor boy. Life Sculpture. George Washington Doane. BLPA; OHFP; WBLP
Chisizas I, The. Guy C. Z. Mhone. WMBCH
"Chkk! chkk!" hopper-grass. Confucius, *tr. fr. Chinese by* Ezra Pound. *Fr.* Shao and the South. CTC
Chloe,/ In verse by your command I write. A Letter from Artemisia in the Town to Chloe in the Country. Earl of Rochester. PoE
Chloe. Burns. GN
Chloe. Pope. *See* Moral Essays: Epistle to a Lady: Of the Characters of Women.
Chloe Divine. Thomas D'Urfey. OBEV
Chloe, why wish you that your years. To Chloe, Who Wished Herself Young Enough for Me. William Cartwright. JCP; MePo; OBS
(To Chloe.) LiTB, *4 sts.*
(To Chloe, who for His Sake Wished Herself Younger.) OBEV, *2 sts.*
Chloe's a nymph in flowery groves. Chloe Divine. Thomas D'Urfey. OBEV
Chloris, *sels.* William Smith.
Feed, silly sheep. *Fr.* III. Son
"Some in their harts their mistris colours bears." *Fr.* XXIX. AAS
To the Most Excellent and Learned Shepherd, Colin Clout, *dedication* AAS; Son
Chloris and Hilas. Made to a Saraban. Edmund Waller. SeCV-1
Chloris Farewell. Edmund Waller. OBS
Chloris, forbear a while. Henry Bold. GBL
Chloris in the Snow. William Strode. *See* I saw fair Chloris walk alone.
Chloris, since first our calm of peace. To Chloris, upon a Favour Received. Edmund Waller. OxBSP
Chloris, 'Tis Not in Your Power. Sir George Etherege. OBS
Chloris, when I to thee present. *Unknown.* OBS
Chocolate Cake. Nina Payne. RHPC
Chocolate Chocolate. Arnold Adoff. RHPC
Chocolate Easter bunny. Patience. Bobbi Katz. RHPC
Chocolate Milk. Ron Padgett. TTTS
Chocolate Soldiers, The. Calvin Forbes. MAT; MAYP
Chocolates. Louis Simpson. InPS; LCAP; Mes; OxBC
Cheeses me boue er plach yoang. Foreign Literature. Thackeray. FaBoNo
Choice. Abd al-Aziz al-Maqalih, *tr. fr. Arabic by* Lena Jayyusi *and* Christopher Middleton. MAP
Choice, The. Hilary Corke. NYBP
Choice. Emily Dickinson. *See* Of all the souls that stand create.
Choice, A. Edward de Vere, 17th Earl of Oxford. OBSC
Choice. J. V. Cunningham. VGW
Choice, The. John Masefield. *Fr.* Lollingdon Downs, VIII. MoAB; MoBrPo
Choice. Angela Morgan. PoLF
Choice, The. John Pomfret. NOEC
Choice, The. Dante Gabriel Rossetti. *Fr.* The House of Life, LXXIII. GTBS-P; OBEV
Choice, The. Nahum Tate. OxBSP
Choice, The. *Unknown, tr. fr. Ten'a Indian by* John W. Chapman. OV
Choice, The. George Wither. OBEV
Choice, The. W. B. Yeats. CMoP; NoAM; OxBSP; OxBTC
Choice of the Cross, The. Dorothy L. Sayers. *Fr.* The Devil to Pay. TrCP
Choice of Weapons, A. Stanley Kunitz. LiTM; VGW
Choice soul, in whom, as in a glass, we see. The Doom of Beauty. Michelangelo, *tr. by* John Addington Symonds. AWP
Choir Invisible, The. "George Eliot." EBVV; OBNC; OHFP; WBLP; WGRP
Choir of Day, The. Blake. *See* Milton: Thou hearest the nightingale begin the song of spring.
Choir of spirits on a cloud, A. William Baylebridge. *Fr.* Life's Testament, XVII. PoAu-1
Choir Practice. Ernest Crosby. AA
Chomei at Toyama. Basil Bunting. OxBTC
Choo a choo a choo tooth. The Cannibals' Grace before Meat. Charles Dickens. FaBoNo
Chook, chook, chook, chook, chook. *Unknown.* OxNR; RAR
Chookaloski Mare. Lucky Whipple. CowP
Choose me your valentine. To His Mistress. Robert Herrick. OFD
Choose now among this fairest number. William Browne. GBL
Choose Something like a Star. Robert Frost. MoAB; MoAmPo
Choose the darkest part o' the grove. Incantation to Oedipus. Dryden. *Fr.* Oedipus, III, i. OFD; WSC
(Spell, A.) WiR

Choosing a Death. Alberta Turner. LCAP
Choosing a Mast. Roy Campbell. FaBoTw; PeSA
Choosing a Name. Charles *and* Mary Lamb. OxBChV
Choosing a Name. Anne Ridler. NOBE
Choosing a Wet-Nurse. M. Saint-Marthe, *tr. fr. French. Fr.* Paedotrophiae; or, The Art of Bringing Up Children. FaBoUs
Choosing Coffins. Raymond Souster. MoCV
Choosing Craft. May Swenson. ASP
Choosing "sage" as a name for sake. Tabito, *tr. fr. Japanese by* Hiroaki Sato. *Fr. Manyo Shu.* FCEI
Choosing Shoes. ffrida Wolfe. PYC
Choosing the Devil. Linda Gregg. NPGG
Choosing to Think of It. Stephen Dunn. AnAn
Chop-Cherry. Robert Herrick. EnLoPo
Chop, chop they cut the hardwood. *Unknown, tr. by* Arthur Waley. BoS
Chopin Nocturne. Jacob Glatstein, *tr. fr. Yiddish by* Benjamin *and* Barbara Harshav *and* Kathryn Helle. AYP
Chopin's Minute Waltz. Gerda Mayer. DT
Chopping Fire-Wood. Robert Pack. NePoEA-2
Chopping with an ax. Buson, *tr. fr. Japanese by* Hiroaki Sato. *Fr.* Eighty-seven Hokku. FCEI
Chopping Wood. Dave Smith. SM
Chops Are Flyin. Stanley Crouch. NBP
Choral Symphony Conductor. Carol Coates. CaP
Chorale: "Often had I found her fair." A. D. Hope. ErPo
Chords, *sels.* Eugenio Montale, *tr. fr. Italian by* Jonathan Galassi. PFI
Oboe. *Fr.* V.
Violins. *Fr.* I.
Chords knotted together like insane nouns. Tom Clark. *Fr.* You, IV. EAS
Choric Song of the Lotus-Eaters. Tennyson. *See* Lotos-Eaters, The: There Is Sweet Music Here.
Chorus: "All ye that handle harp and viol." Moses Hayyim Luzzatto, *tr. fr. Hebrew by* Nina Davis Salaman. *Fr.* Unto the Upright Praise. TrJP
Chorus: "And Pergamos,/ City of the Phrygians." Euripides, *tr. fr. Greek by* Hilda Doolittle ("H.D."). *Fr.* Iphigenia [*or* Iphigeneia] in Aulis. AWP; OBVE
Chorus: "Before the beginning of years." Swinburne. *See* Atalanta in Calydon: Before the Beginning of Years.
Chorus: "Big Engines, The." Jack Kerouac. *Fr.* Mexico City Blues, 146. NeAP
Chorus: "Essence of Existence, The." Jack Kerouac. *Fr.* Mexico City Blues, 182. NeAP
Chorus: "Fair Salamis, the billow's roar." Sophocles, *tr. fr. Greek by* Winthrop Mackworth Praed. *Fr.* Ajax. AWP
Chorus: "Glenn Miller and I were heroes." Jack Kerouac. *Fr.* Mexico City Blues, 179. NeAP
Chorus: "Got up and dressed up." Jack Kerouac. *Fr.* Mexico City Blues, 113. NeAP
Chorus: "Great Fortune is an hungry thing." Aeschylus, *tr. fr. Greek by* Gilbert Murray. *Fr.* Agamemnon. AWP
Chorus: "How dost thou wear and weary out thy days." Samuel Daniel. *Fr.* The Tragedie of Philotas. OBSC
Chorus: "If I drink water while this doth last." Thomas Love Peacock. *Fr.* Crotchet Castle. NBLV
Chorus: "In the ocean there's a very sad turtle." Jack Kerouac. *Fr.* Mexico City Blues, 229. PoM
Chorus: "Kings of Troy, The. Euripides, *tr. fr. Greek by* George Allen. *Fr.* Andromache. WaaP
Chorus: "Love's multitudinous boneyard." Jack Kerouac. *Fr.* Mexico City Blues, 230. NeAP
Chorus: "Nobody knows the other side." Jack Kerouac. *Fr.* Mexico City Blues, 127. NeAP
Chorus: "Oh, may my constant feet not fail." Sophocles, *tr. fr. Greek by* Robert Whitelaw. *Fr.* Oedipus the King [*or* Oedipus Rex]. WGRP
Chorus: "Old Man Mose." Jack Kerouac. *Fr.* Mexico City Blues, 221. NeAP
Chorus: "Only awake to Universal Mind." Jack Kerouac. *Fr.* Mexico City Blues, 183. NeAP
Chorus: "Praised be man, he is existing in milk." Jack Kerouac. *Fr.* Mexico City Blues, 228. NeAP
Chorus: "Saints, I give myself up to thee." Jack Kerouac. *Fr.* Mexico City Blues, 219. NeAP
Chorus: "Spring all the Graces of the age." Ben Jonson. *Fr.* Neptune's Triumph. OBS
Chorus: "Summer holds, The: upon its glittering lake." W. H. Auden. *Fr.* The Dog beneath the Skin. OxBTC
Chorus: "Sweet are the ways of death to weary feet." Lord De Tabley. *Fr.* Medea. OBEV
Chorus: "Then thus we have beheld." Samuel Daniel. *Fr.* Cleopatra. OBSC

Chorus: "To throw away the key and walk away." W. H. Auden. *See* Paid on Both Sides: Walking Tour, The.

Chorus: "Void that's highly embraceable, The." Jack Kerouac. *Fr.* Mexico City Blues, 225. NeAP

Chorus: "We do not wish anything to happen." T. S. Eliot. *Fr.* Murder in the Cathedral. OxBTC

Chorus: "We have not been happy, my Lord, we have not been too happy." T. S. Eliot. *Fr.* Murder in the Cathedral. OxBTC

Chorus: "What man is he that yearneth." Sophocles, *tr. fr. Greek by* A. E. Housman. *Fr.* Oedipus at Colonus. AWP

Chorus: "Wheel of the quivering Meat, The." Jack Kerouac. *Fr.* Mexico City Blues, 211. NeAP; PoM

Chorus: "When the hounds of spring are on winter's traces." Swinburne. *See* Atalanta in Calydon: When the Hounds of Spring [Are on Winter's Traces].

Chorus: "Who hath given man speech? or what hath set therein." Swinburne. *Fr.* Atalanta in Calydon. OAEL-2

Chorus: "World's great age begins anew, The." Shelley. *See* Hellas: Choruses from "Hellas."

Chorus: "Worlds on worlds are rolling ever." Shelley. *See* Hellas: Choruses from "Hellas."

Chorus: "You are the town and we are the clock." W. H. Auden. *Fr.* The Dog beneath the Skin. OxBTC

Chorus for Survival, *sel.* Horace Gregory.
  "Ask no return for love that's given." *Fr.* XIV. VGW
  (Ask No Return.) MoAmPo

Chorus from "Hellas." Shelley. *See* Hellas: Choruses from "Hellas."

Chorus from "The Rock." T. S. Eliot. *Fr.* The Rock, III. LiTB

Chorus of Angels. Cardinal Newman. *Fr.* The Dream of Gerontius. NOCV; PoEL-5

Chorus of Birds. Aristophanes, *tr. fr. Greek by* Swinburne. *Fr.* The Birds. AWP

Chorus of Satyrs, Driving Their Goats. Euripides, *tr. fr. Greek by* Shelley. *Fr.* Cyclops. AWP

Chorus of Scyrian Maidens. Philip Bainbrigge. *Fr.* Achilles in Scyros. PeHV

Chorus of the Rescued. Nelly Sachs, *tr. fr. German.* VWA, *tr. by* Harry Zohn; WPOW, *tr. by* Ruth Mead *and* Matthew Mead

Chorus of the Unborn. Nelly Sachs, *tr. fr. German by* Ruth Mead *and* Matthew Mead. NYBP

Chorus of the Years. Thomas Hardy. *See* Dynasts, The: Field of Waterloo, The.

Chorus Primus: Wise Counsellors. Fulke Greville. *Fr.* Mustapha. OBS

Chorus Quintus: Tartarorum. Fulke Greville. *Fr.* Mustapha. OBS

Chorus Sacerdotum. Fulke Greville. *Fr.* Mustapha. HAP; InvP; JCP; LiTB; MePo; NAEL-1; NOBE; OAEL-1; OBS; PoEL-1; PPP; SeCePo

Chorus Speaks Her Words as She Dances, The. Linda Gregg. AnAn; NPGG

Chorus Tertius: Of Time; Eternitie. Fulke Greville. *Fr.* Mustapha. OBS

Eternity's Speech against Time. JCP

Chorus to the Gods. Dryden. *See* Secular Masque, The: All, All of a Piece Throughout.

Choruses from "Hellas." Shelley. *Fr.* Hellas.
  "Darkness has dawned in the east." *Fr.* 3.EnRP
  "Life may change, but it may fly not." *Fr.* 1.EnRP
  "World's great age begins anew, The." *Fr.* 4.EnRP; FiP; HeIP; NAEL-2; PoE; TEP
  (Chorus: "World's great age begins anew, The.") EBEV; HAP; NOBE; NoP; OAEL-2; PoEL-4
  (Chorus from "Hellas.") AWP
  (Final Chorus, The.) SeCePo
  (Hellas.) ChTr; OBEV
  (New World, A.) TrGrPo
  "Worlds on worlds are rolling ever." EnRP; NoP; TEP
  (Chorus: "Worlds on worlds are rolling ever.") NAEL-2
  (Worlds on Worlds.) HeIP

Chosen. W. B. Yeats. BoLoP; CMoP

Chosen—Kalgoorlie, 1894, The. Fay Zwicky. VWA

Chosen Light, A. John Montague. *See* At night, sometimes when I cannot sleep.

Chosen of God. Stefan Zweig, *tr. fr. German by* Eden *and* Cedar Paul. *Fr.* Jeremiah. TrJP

Chosen People, The. W. N. Ewer. FaBoEE

Chosen Three, on Mountain Height, The. David H. Ela. AH

Chou and the South, *sel.* Confucius, *tr. fr. Chinese by* Ezra Pound.
  "In the South be drooping trees." CTC

Chou and the South. *Unknown, tr. fr. Chinese by* Ezra Pound. *Fr.* Shi King. CTC

Chou it is that continues the footsteps here below. *Unknown, tr. by* Arthur Waley. BoS

Chough, The. James Reaney. OBCV

Chough. Rex Warner. PoRA

Chough and crow to roost are gone, The. The Outlaw's Song. Joanna Baillie. OBEV

Chough, said a dictionary, The. The Chough. James Reaney. OBCV

Christ./ May I die at night. Robert Lowell. OBD

Christ and Satan, *sel. Unknown, tr. fr. Anglo-Saxon by* Charles W. Kennedy.
  Lamentations of the Fallen Angels. AnOE

Christ and the Little Ones. Julia Gill. BLPA

Christ and the Pagan. John Banister Tabb. TrCP

Christ, by dark clouds of worldliness concealed. Prayer before Meat. Una W. Harsen. TrPWD

Christ Calls Man Home. *Unknown.* MeEL

Christ Child, The. Mary Weston Fordham. CBWP-2

Christ child lay on Mary's lap, The. G. K. Chesterton. BoTP; FaFP; OBCP; OHIP

Christ Church Meadows, Oxford. Donald Hall. NYBP

Christ Climbed Down. Lawrence Ferlinghetti. VGW

Christ comes to mind and comes across the mind. Burns Singer. *Fr.* Sonnets for a Dying Man, XXXIX. NePoEA-2

Christ Complains to Sinners. *Unknown.* MeEL

Christ Crucified. Richard Crashaw. OBEV

Christ for the World! We Sing. Samuel Wolcott. AH

Christ hath a garden walled around. Isaac Watts. FaBoCh

Christ How My Circumspect Heart. Gillian Hanscombe *and* Suniti Namjoshi. DT

Christ I Wudint Know Normal if I Saw It When. Bill Bissett. NOBC

Christ in Alabama. Langston Hughes. PoBA

Christ in the Clay-Pit. Jack R. Clemo. GTBS-P

Christ in the Universe. Alice Meynell. ACP; MoBrPo; NOBE

Christ Inviting Sinners to His Grace, *sel.* Henry Alline.
  Amazing Sight! The Saviour Stands. AH, *with music;* CaP

Christ is a nigger. Christ in Alabama. Langston Hughes. PoBA

Christ Is Arisen. Goethe, *tr. fr. German. Fr.* Faust. TrCP
  (Easter Chorus.) WGRP, *tr. by* Bayard Taylor.

Christ Is Risen! Mrs. D. H. Dugan. BLRP

Christ is the Fact of facts, the Bible's Theme. The Greatest Person in the Universe. Daniel L. Marsh. BLRP

Christ keep the Hollow Land. William Morris. *Fr.* The Hollow Land. ChTr
  (Song: "Christ keep the Hollow Land.") PoEL-5

Christ made a trance on Friday view. Good Friday. *Unknown.* ChTr

Christ made [*or* maketh] to man a fair present. Divine Love. *Unknown.* OAEL-1
  (Christ's Gift to Man.) ACP
  (Love Unlike Love.) MeEL

Christ, My Beloved. William Baldwin. EiL; ELP; NOCV
  (Spouse to the Beloved, The.) OBSC
  (Spouse to the Younglings, The.) OxBSP

Christ, my Life, my Only Treasure. During His Courtship. Charles Wesley. NOCV

Christ of His gentleness. In the Wilderness. Robert Graves. CH; MoAB; MoBrPo; SeCePo

Christ of Judea, look thou in my heart! Richard Watson Gilder. *Fr.* Credo. TrPWD

Christ of the Andes, The, *sel.* Edwin Markham.
  "O Christ of Olivet, you hushed the wars." TrPWD

Christ 1, *sel. Unknown, tr. Anglo-Saxon.* AnOE, *tr. by* Charles W. Kennedy
  Advent Lyrics.
    "Hail, O most worthy in all the world!" *Fr.* IX.
    "O holy Jerusalem, Vision of peace." *Fr.* III.
    "Bless earth with Thine Advent, O Saviour Christ!" *Fr.* VIII.
    ". to the King./ Thou art the wall-stone rejected." *Fr.* I.

Christ risen was rarely recognized by sight. For They Shall See God. Luci Shaw. TrCP

Christ the Lord is risen to-day. Easter Hymn. Charles Wesley. OHIP

Christ, the Man. W. H. Davies. WGRP

Christ! These are her angels! The Unicorn and the Lady. Jean Garrigue. NYBP

Christ 3, *sel. Unknown, tr. fr. Anglo-Saxon by* Charles W. Kennedy.
  Last Judgment, The. AnOE

Christ to His Spouse *or* The Beloved to the Spouse. William Baldwin. EiL; NOCV; OBSC

Christ to seek the lost was sent. Sympathy. Lizelia Augusta Jenkins Moorer. CBWP-3

Christ 2, *sel.* Cynewulf, *tr. fr. Anglo-Saxon by* Charles W. Kennedy. Voyage of Life, The. AnOE; MOS

Christ Walking on the Water. W. R. Rodgers. AnIL; MoAB

Christ Walks in This Infernal District Too. Malcolm Lowry. MoCV; NOBC

Christ was born on Christmas day. Thomas Helmore. OHIP

Christ was your lord and captain all your life. To His Father. Robinson Jeffers. DiL

Christ washed the feet of Judas! The Feet of Judas. George Marion McClellan. BANP; PoNe
Christ, wha'd ha'e been Chief Rabbi gin he lik't. Up to Date. "Hugh MacDiarmid." FaBoCo
Christ, when a child, a garden made. A Legend. At. to Peter Ilich Tchaikovsky, tr. by Nathan Haskell Dole. OHIP
Christ, whose glory fills the skies. Morning Hymn. Charles Wesley. TOF
Christabel ("'Tis the middle of night by the castle clock."), sels. Samuel Taylor Coleridge. CH, ll. 1-65; EnRP; FiP, (I); GoTL; NAEL-2; OAEL-2; SeCePo, ll. 1-70; VVA, (I)
  Christabel and Geraldine. Fr. pt. I. PeHV
  In the Touch of This Bosom There Worketh a Spell. Fr. pt. I. RB
  Scars Remaining, The. Fr. pt. II. OBNC
Christabel and Geraldine. Samuel Taylor Coleridge. Fr. Christabel, pt. I. PeHV
Christchurch Bells. Unknown. OBET
Christchurch, N. Z. Earle Birney. OxBC
Christendom. Thomas Traherne. PoEL-2
Christening, A. Donald Davie. OxBC
Christening-Day Wishes for My God-Child. Robert P. Tristram Coffin. OFD
Christenings. Peter Porter. NAs
Christian, Be Up. Robert Nathan. AH
Christian constellations run, The. The Circle. Lizelia Augusta Jenkins Moorer. CBWP-3
Christian Ethics. Thomas Traherne. OxBSP
  Sels.
  "All music, sauces, feasts, delights and pleasures." UnS
  Contentment. NOCV
  ("For man to act as if his soul did see.") NOCV
Christian Freedom. George Matheson. TrPWD
Christian Life, The. Samuel Longfellow. WGRP
Christian Pilgrim's Hymn, The. William Williams. See Guide Me, O Thou Great Jehovah.
Christiana. Peter Redgrove. OxBC
Christianite. William Stafford. NoAM
Christians at War. John F. Kendrick. TW
Christians awake, salute the happy morn. A Hymn for Christmas Day. John Byrom. NOCV; PoEL-3
Christian's "Good-Night", The. Sarah Doudney. BLPA
Christians have always been pilgriming. "Faith and Practice." John Balaban. GOA
Christian's New-Year Prayer, The, sel. Ella Wheeler Wilcox.
  "If my vain soul needs blows and bitter losses." TrPWD
Christian's Reply to the Philosopher, The ("Good in graves as heavenly seed are sown, The."), sel. Sir William Davenant. MeLP
  Life and Death. OBS
Christina. Louis MacNeice. BoLoP
Christina. Yona Wallach, tr. fr. Hebrew by Warren Bargad and Stanley F. Chyet. IP
Christine. John Milton Hay. AA
Christine to Her Son. Christine de Pisan, tr. fr. French by Barbara Howes. BoWoP
Christmas. Sir John Betjeman. OBCP; OxBTC
Christmas. George Herbert. SeCV-1; TOF; TrCP
Christmas. Leigh Hunt. OBCP
Christmas. Koh Chang-soo, tr. fr. Korean by the author. ACKP
Christmas. Mani Leib, tr. fr. Yiddish by John Hollander. PeBMYV
Christmas. "Mary I." BoTP
Christmas. Shakespeare. See Hamlet: Some say that ever 'gainst that season comes.
Christmas. Nahum Tate. See While Shepherds Watched [Their Flocks by Night].
Christmas and Common Birth. Anne Ridler. FaBoTw
Christmas and Death. Janet Frame. PeNZ
Christmas Antiphones, sel. Swinburne.
  "Thou whose birth on earth." TrPWD
Christmas at Freelands. James Stephens. TIRV; TrCP
Christmas at Melrose. Leslie Pinckney Hill. BANP
Christmas at Sea. Robert Louis Stevenson. BLPL; BrPo; CH; EBVV; FaBoBe; FaBV; Mes; MOS; OBTV
Christmas Bells. Longfellow. AH, with music; AnAmPo; BLRP; FaFP; FaPON; OBCP; PChr, st. 1; WBLP
Christmas bells, awake and ring. Christmas Morning. Harry Behn. PChr
Christmas Bills. Joseph Hatton. OBCP
Christmas Card. Ted Hughes. OBCP
Christmas Carol, A: "Angel told Mary, An." Harry Behn. PChr
Christmas Carol: As Joseph Was a Walking. Unknown. See As Joseph Was a-Walking [or a-Waukin'].
Christmas Carol: "Babe is born all of a May, A." Unknown. ACP

Christmas Carol, A: "Christ child lay on Mary's lap, The." G. K. Chesterton. BoTP; FaFP; OBCP; OHIP
Christmas Carol: "Christ was born on Christmas day." Thomas Helmore. OHIP
Christmas Carol, A: "Close to a quarter of a century since then." T. H. Parry-Williams, tr. fr. Welsh by Joseph P. Clancy. OBWVE
Christmas Carol, A: "Everywhere, everywhere, Christmas tonight!" Phillips Brooks. See Everywhere, everywhere, Christmas tonight.
Christmas Carol: "From the starry heav'ns descending." J. R. Newell. BLRP
Christmas Carol: "God bless the master of this house." Unknown. BoTP; OHIP
Christmas Carol: "I walk today, the pain of childbirth in each step." Rosario Murillo, tr. fr. Spanish by Barbara Paschke. Vol
Christmas Carol, A ("In the bleak mid-winter."), sel. Christina Rossetti. ChTr; InPS; NOBVV; OHIP
  My Gift. Fr. st. 5. FaPON; PChr
Christmas Carol: "Lacking samite and sable." May Probyn. ACP
Christmas Carol: "Man, be merry, I thee rede." Unknown. ACP
Christmas Carol: Moonless Darkness Stands Between. Gerard Manley Hopkins. OBCP
Christmas Carol, A: "So now is come our joyful'st feast." George Wither. OBS
Christmas Carol: "Thank God, thank God, we do believe." Christina Rossetti. PChr
Christmas Carol, A: "There's a song in the air!" Josiah Gilbert Holland. AA; GN; OHIP
Christmas Carol: "This night there is a child born." Unknown. ACP
Christmas Carol: "Three outas from the bleak Karoo." D. J. Opperman, tr. fr. Afrikaans by Anthony Delius. PeSA
Christmas Carol, A: "Thys ender nyght." Unknown. TrGrPo, abr.
Christmas Carol, A: "Villagers all, this frosty tide." Kenneth Grahame. See Wind in the Willows, The: Villagers all, this frosty tide.
Christmas Carol, A: "When Christ was born in Bethlehem." Unknown, tr. by Longfellow. OHIP
Christmas Caroll Sung to the King in the Presence at White-Hall, A ("What sweeter music [or musick] can we bring."), sel. Robert Herrick. GoJo; PChr, st. 1
Christmas Carols. Patricia Beer. OxBC
Christmas Carols. Longfellow. BoTP
Christmas Childhood, A, sel. Patrick Kavanagh. AnIL; FaBCIP; IPY
  "My father played the melodion." PChr; RB
Christmas come tomorrow. Christmas with the Holy Family. Susan Cavin. GLP
Christmas comes but once a year. Mother Goose. OxNR
Christmas Comes to Moccasin Flat. James Welch. CDW; MAT; NoAM
  ("Christmas comes like this: wise men.")
Christmas Creek. Henry Clarence Kendall. CBAP
Christmas Day. Roy Fuller. OBCP
Christmas Day. Christopher Smart. See Hymns and Spiritual Songs: Nativity of Our Lord and Saviour Jesus Christ, The.
Christmas Day. Andrew Young. OBCP
Christmas Day in the Workhouse. George R. Sims. BeLS; BLPA
Christmas Day Is Come. Luke Wadding. TIRV
Christmas Day; the Family Sitting. John Meade Falkner. NOCV; OxBTC
Christmas declares the glory of the flesh. Christmas and Common Birth. Anne Ridler. FaBoTw
Christmas Dinner. Michael Rosen. OBCP
Christmas dinner was at two, The. A Summer Christmas in Australia. Douglas Sladen. OBCP
Christmas 1898, sel. Sir Lewis Morris.
  "'Tis nigh two thousand years." TrPWD
Christmas Eve. A. R. Ammons. NAs
Christmas Eve. Patricia Beer. OBCP
Christmas Eve. Charlotte Druitt Cole. BoTP
Christmas Eve. John Davidson. See Letter from my love today! A.
Christmas Eve. Cecil Day Lewis. EaLo
Christmas Eve. Eugene Field. OHIP
Christmas Eve. Lizelia Augusta Jenkins Moorer. CBWP-3
Christmas Eve. Karl Shapiro. NYBP
Christmas Eve. Robert Siegel. GeTw
Christmas Eve. Edna Kingsley Walla. BoTP
Christmas-Eve and Easter-Day, sel. Robert Browning.
  Earth Breaks Up. TrCP
Christmas Eve, and twelve of the clock. The Oxen. Thomas Hardy. BoTP; CMoP; EBEV; HAP; InPK; InPK; LiTM; MoAB; MoBrPo; MoP; NoAM; NoAM; NOBE; OAEL-2; OBCP; OxBTC; PChr; PPP; RB; SoSe; TOF; WeW
Christmas Eve—Another Ceremony. Robert Herrick. OHIP

Christmas Eve in France. Jessie Redmond Fauset. BANP
Christmas Eve in Nineteen-fourteen. Christmas 1914. Mike Harding. OBET
Christmas Eve in Whitneyville, 1955. Donald Hall. DiL; UnPo
Christmas Eve Service at Midnight at St. Michael's. Robert Bly. NNaP
Christmas Eve, South, 1865. Mary E. Tucker. CBWP-1
Christmas Eve under Hooker's Statue. Robert Lowell. CAPP; FF; OxBA
Christmas Everywhere. Phillips Brooks. BLRP; FaFP; OHFP; PWR; WBLP
  (Christmas Carol, A: "Everywhere, everywhere, Christmas tonight!") OHIP
Christmas Family Reunion. Peter De Vries. NBLV; NOBL
Christmas Folk-Song, A. Lizette Woodworth Reese. FaPON; OBCA; OHIP; OnMSP; TrCP
Christmas Ghost, A. Priscilla Jane Thompson. CBWP-2
Christmas Ghost-Story, A. Thomas Hardy. OBWP
Christmas Hymn, A. Cecil Frances Alexander. *See* Once in Royal David's City.
Christmas Hymn, A. Alfred Domett. GN; WGRP
Christmas Hymn. Sister Juana Inés de la Cruz, *tr. fr. Spanish by* Samuel Beckett. MexPo
Christmas Hymn. *Unknown, tr. fr. Irish by* Douglas Hyde. TIRV
Christmas Hymn, A. Richard Wilbur. OBCP; OFD; PChr; TrCP
Christmas in Biafra (1969). Chinua Achebe. UAS
Christmas in England ("Heap on more wood!—the wind is chill") Time. Sir Walter Scott. *Fr.* Marmion, *introd. to* VI. OBCP
Christmas in Penang. John Leyden. OBTV
Christmas in the Heart. *Unknown.* OHIP
Christmas in the Wood. Frances Mary Frost. TrCP
Christmas is coming [*or* a-coming],/ The geese are getting fat. *Unknown.* NTCP; OxNR; PChr
Christmas is in the air. Five Days Old. Francis Webb. PoAu-2
Christmas Is Really for the Children. Steve Turner. OBCP
Christmas Landscape. Laurie Lee. OBCP
Christmas Legend, A. Frank Sidgwick. OHIP
Christmas Letter Home. George Sutherland Fraser. OxBTC
Christmas Lights. Valerie Worth. PChr
Christmas Lullaby for a New-born Child. Yvonne Gregory. AmNP
Christmas Mass for a Little Atheist Jesus. Claude Maillard, *tr. fr. French by* Maxine *and* Judith Kumin. BoWoP
Christmas Message, A. Gavin Ewart. FaBoMo
Christmas Morn. *Unknown. See* Shall I tell you who [*or* what] will come.
Christmas Morning. Harry Behn. PChr
Christmas Morning. Elizabeth Madox Roberts. MoAmPo; PChr
Christmas Morning I. Carol Freeman. PChr; PoBA; TTY
  (Gift.) PoNe
Christmas Mourning. Vassar Miller. MoAmPo
Christmas Night. B. E. Milner. BoTP
Christmas Night. Lawrence Sail. OBCP
Christmas Night in the Quarters, *sel.* Irwin Russell.
  Fust Banjo, De. AA; BLPA
Christmas Night of '62. William Gordon McCabe. AA
Christmas night: the solstice storm. The Narrows of Birth. William Everson. PoM
Christmas 1959 et Cetera. Gerald William Barrax. OFD; PChr
Christmas 1942. Eric Irvin. PoAu-2
Christmas 1914. Mike Harding. OBET
Christmas 1970. Spike Milligan. OBCP
Christmas 1962. Paul Mariah. GLP
Christmas: 1924. Thomas Hardy. FaBoEE; OBCP
Christmas Now Is Drawing Near. *Unknown.* OBET
Christmas Ornaments. Valerie Worth. PChr
Christmas Package, A, *sels.* David McCord.
  "My stocking's where." PChr; RHPC
  "That broken star." PChr
Christmas Party, The. Adeline White. BoTP
Christmas Poem. Vinícius de Moraes, *tr. fr. Portuguese by* Ashley Brown. ATCBP
Christmas Prayer, A. George Macdonald. PChr
Christmas Prayer, A. Robert Louis Stevenson. TrCP
Christmas Present, The. Patricia Hubbell. PDV
Christmas Reply to the Phylosopher, The. Sir William Davenant. MeLP
Christmas Revel, A. Dafydd Bach ap Madog Wladaidd, *tr. fr. Welsh.* OBWVE
Christmas Rhyme, A. George Sands Johnson. PWR
Christmas Rose, The. C. Day Lewis. TIRV

Christmas Rush, The. Clara Ann Thompson. CBWP-2
Christmas, season of streamers, coloured lights. Christmas Story (1980). Pat Arrowsmith. BrRo
Christmas Sermon, A, *sel.* Robert Louis Stevenson.
  To Be Honest, to Be Kind. PoLF
Christmas Shopping. Louis MacNeice. OBCP
Christmas Silence, The. Margaret Deland. OHIP
Christmas Song. *At. to* Eugene Field. BoTP; OHIP
Christmas Song, A. *Unknown.* BoTP
Christmas Sonnet, A. E. A. Robinson. EaLo
Christmas, South, 1866. Mary E. Tucker. CBWP-1
Christmas Story (1980). Pat Arrowsmith. BrRo
Christmas Thank You's. Mick Gowar. OBCP
Christmas, the Year One, A.D. Sara Henderson Hay. PoRA
Christmas Thoughts, by a Modern Thinker. William Hurrell Mallock. NOBVV
Christmas Times. Maggie Pogue Johnson. CBWP-4
Christmas Tree, The. Patricia Beer. OBCP
Christmas Tree, A. William Burford. SoSe
Christmas Tree. Stanley Cook. OBCP
Christmas Tree, The. Peter Cornelius. PChr
Christmas Tree. Aileen Fisher. PDV
Christmas Tree, The. Lizelia Augusta Jenkins Moorer. CBWP-3
Christmas Tree, The. Frederick Morgan. BLA
Christmas Tree, The. Isabel de Savitzsky. BoTP
Christmas Tree. Laurence Smith. OBCP
Christmas Tree in the Nursery, The. Richard Watson Gilder. OHIP
Christmas-Tree Song, A. Rodney Bennett. BoTP
Christmas Trees, The. Mary Frances Butts. OHIP
Christmas Trees. Geoffrey Hill. NOCV
Christmas twigs crispen and needles rattle, The. New Year's Poem. Margaret Avison. LiTM; NOBC; OBCV
Christmas Verse, A. "Kay." BoTP
Christmas was in the air and all was well. Karma. E. A. Robinson. AmPP; CMoP; HeIP; MoAB; MoAmPo; OFD; TrCP
Christmas Wish, A. Rose Fyleman. BoTP
Christmas with the Holy Family. Susan Cavin. GLP
Christofo Colombo was a hungry man. Mysterious Biography. Carl Sandburg. OFD
Christoph. Charles Spear. ATNZ
Christophe. Russell Atkins. PoNe
Christopher Columbus, *sels.* William Hart-Smith. PoAu-2
  Cipangu.
  Comes Fog and Mist.
  Departure.
  Space.
  Waterspout, The.
Christopher Marlowe. Michael Drayton. *Fr.* To Henry Reynolds, of Poets and Poesy. ChTr
Christopher Marlowe. Swinburne. *Fr.* Sonnets of English Dramatic Poets. Son; TrGrPo
Christopher of the Shenandoah, A. Edith Matilda Thomas. PAH
Christopher Robin goes/ Hoppity, hoppity. Hoppity. A. A. Milne. FaBV; NTCP
Christopher Street Liberation Day, June 28, 1970. Fran Winant. PeHV
Christopher White. *Unknown.* ESPB
Christo's. Paul Muldoon. CIP
Christ's Bounty. *Unknown, tr. fr. Irish by* Brendan Kennelly. TIRV
Christ's Descent into Hell. Rainer Maria Rilke, *tr. fr. German by* James Wright *and* Sarah Youngblood. Prf
Christ's Gift to Man. *Unknown. See* Christ made [*or* maketh] to man a fair present.
Christ's Kirk on the Green. *At. to* James V, King of Scotland. OxBS
Christ's Life Our Code. Benjamin Copeland. AH
Christ's Prayer in Gethsemane. *Unknown.* SeCePo
Christ's Reply. Edward Taylor. *See* God's Determinations: Peace, peace, my hony [*or* honey], do not cry.
Christ's Resurrection and Ascension. Philip Doddridge. NOCV
Christ's Tear Breaks My Heart. *Unknown.* MeEL
Christ's teeth ascended with him into heaven. The Linen Workers. Michael Longley. CIP; FaBCIP
Christ's Victory and Triumph, *sels.* Giles Fletcher the Younger.
  Christ's Triumph after Death, IV.
    Celestial City, The. NOBE; OBD; OBS
    Easter Morn. EiL; NOCV
    Halcyon's Nest, The. FaBoPP
  Christ's Victory in Heaven, I.
    Excellency of Christ. WGRP
    Mercy Pleads for Mankind. JCP

Christ's Victory on Earth, II.
"His haire was blacke and in small curls did twine." SeCV-1
Wooing Song. EIL; OBEV
Christus; a Mystery, sel. Longfellow.
Fate of the Prophets, The. *Fr.* I, Introitus. WGRP
Christus Mattaeum et Discipulos Alloquitur. Sir Edward Sherburne.
ACP
Christus natus est! the cock. The Animals' Carol. Charles Causley.
NAs
Chrome Babies Eating Chocolate Snowmen in the Moonlight. A. K.
Redwing. VoR
Chromo. Sarah Webster Fabio. CNA
Chronicle. A. Q. Urías, *tr. fr. Spanish by* Barbara Paschke. Vol
Chronicle, A. *Unknown.* BLPL; NA
Chronicle; a Ballad, The. Abraham Cowley. SeCV-1
Chronicle "Green Sheet" dries out, The. News. Dennis Schmitz.
NPGG
Chronicle of Lima. Antonio Cisneros, *tr. fr. Spanish by* Maureen Ahern
and David Tipton. Per
Chronicler, The. Alexander Bergman. TrJP
Chronique Scandaleuse. Richard Augustine Chima. WMBCH
Chronology. Turner Cassity. PoA
Chronos, Chronos, mend thy pace. The Secular Masque. Dryden.
NAEL-1; PoE; PoEL-3; PrIm; SeCV-2
Chrysalides. Thomas Kinsella. BIrV
Chrysalis, A. Mary Emily Bradley. AA
Chrysanthemum and the Sword, The. Tu Yeh, *tr. fr. Chinese by* Dominic
Cheung. IFON
Chrysanthemum didn't spill a dewdrop, The. Basho, *tr. fr. Japanese by*
Burton Watson. *Fr.* Seventy-six Hokku. FCEI
Chrysanthemum pistils daily yellow. Cha Shen-hsing, *tr. fr. Chinese by*
William Schultz. *Fr.* Autumn Impressions, III. WFTU
Chrysanthemums. Martin Seymour-Smith. NPo
Chrysanthemums/ in the coffin-vase. Still Life. Rose Ausländer, *tr. by*
Beth Bjorklund. CoAuP
Chrysanthemums bloom among masons' stones. In Hatchobori. Basho,
tr. fr. Japanese by Burton Watson. *Fr.* Seventy-six Hokku.
FCEI
Chrysanthemums have all withered. Ozaki Hosai, *tr. fr. Japanese by*
Hiroaki Sato. *Fr.* One Hundred Haiku in Free Form. FCEI
Chrysanthemums, Rowers ("The chrysanthemums/ that stand in the vase on
the table"). Hans Faverey, *tr. fr. Dutch by* J. M. Coetzee. DuIn
Chuang Tzu and Hui Tzu. The Joy of Fishes. Chuang Tzu, *tr. by*
Thomas Merton. Mes
Chuangtzu Poem No. 6. Park Je-chun, *tr. fr. Korean by* Koh Chang-soo.
ACKP
Chuck Will's Widow Song. *Unknown.* BPo
Chüeh-chü. Tu Fu, *tr. fr. Chinese by* Burton Watson. CoBCP
"Chuff! chuff! chuff!" An' a mountain-bluff. A Song of Panama. Damon
Runyon. PAH
Chug! Puff! Chug! Tugs. James S. Tippett. FaPON
Chums. Arthur Guiterman. RAR
Chung-i Temple, The, *sel.* Wen Cheng-ming, *tr. fr. Chinese by* Jonathan
Chaves.
"This little courtyard—the wind is pure." CoBLCP
Chunks of night. Shadows. Patricia Hubbell. TDD
Church,/ Chapel. *Unknown.* OxNR
Church, The. Edwin Ford Piper. WGRP
Church, The. Jules Romains, *tr. fr. French by* Jethro Bithell.
WGRP
Church and State. W. B. Yeats. CMoP
Church and the World marched far apart, The. The Church Walking with
the World. Matilda Caroline Edwards. BLPA
Church at little Winwick, The. Winwick, Lancashire. *Unknown.*
GBP
Church Bell in the Night, The. *Unknown. See* Sweet little bell.
Church Bells, The. Mrs. Henry Linden. CBWP-4
Church Bells. Clara Ann Thompson. CBWP-2
Church bells ring—it is the Sabbath day, The. The Lifting of the Cloud.
Thomas McDonagh. TIRV
Church Burning: Mississippi. James A. Emanuel. PoBA; PoNe
Church-Floor [*or* Floore], The. George Herbert. EBEV; MeLP;
OAEL-1; OBS; SeCePo
Church Going. Philip Larkin. CMoP; GTBS-P; HeIP; LiTM; MoBrPo;
MoP; NAEL-2; NePoEA; NIP; NoAM; NoP; OAEL-2; PPP; PrIm;
SCV; TwCP; UnPo
Church is a business, and the rich, The. After Lorca. Robert Creeley.
InPS; LCAP; NaP
Church is an iceberg, The. Winter Night. Charles Simic. HCAP
Church is blossoming in green, The. Meditation at Stuyvesant Church.
Judah Leib Teller, *tr. by* Benjamin *and* Barbara Harshav. AYP
Church Lock and Key. George Herbert. OxBSP

Church Monuments. George Herbert. HAP; JCP; NAEL-1; NOCV;
NoP; OAEL-1; PoE; QFR
Church Mouse commends: tapeworms and slugs grow wings. Critics and
Poets. Geoffrey Grigson. FaBoEE
Church-Music[k]. George Herbert. OxBSP; SeCV-1; UnS
Church of a Dream, The. Lionel Johnson. OAEL-2; OBMV
Church of England, The. Dryden. *Fr.* The Hind and the Panther.
OBS
Church of England's Glory, The. *Unknown.* APAS
Church of San Antonio de la Florida, The. Paul Petrie. NYBP
Church of the Revolution, The. Hezekiah Butterworth. PAH
Church of Vice-Morcate, The. View by Color Photography on a
Commercial Calendar. William Carlos Williams. LCAP
Church on Comiaken Hill, The. Richard Hugo. LCAP; Prf; SM
Church Poem. Joyce Carol Thomas. CNA
Church Romance, A. Thomas Hardy. FaBoTw; NOBE; OxBTC
Church the Garden of Christ, The. Isaac Watts. NOCV
Church Today, The. Sir William Watson. WGRP
Church tower crowned the town, A. The Glass Town. Alastair Reid.
NYBP
Church Universal, The. Samuel Longfellow. WGRP
Church Walking with the World, The. Matilda Caroline Edwards.
BLPA
Church Windows, The. George Herbert. *See* Lord, how can man preach
thy eternal word.
Church-Windows, The. *Unknown. Fr.* A Poem in Defence of the Decent
Ornaments of Christ-Church, Oxon, Occasioned by a Banbury
Brother, Who Called Them Idolatries. OBS
Churches are best for prayer, that have least light. Dark Churches. John
Donne. *Fr.* A Hymn [*or* Hymne] to Christ, at the Author's Last
Going into Germany. FaBoRV
Churches, lord, all the dark churches, The. Crag Jack's Apostasy. Ted
Hughes. EaLo
Churches of Rome and of England, The. Dryden. *See* Hind and the
Panther, The: Milk white Hind, immortal and unchang'd, A.
Church's one foundation, The. Battle Hymn of the Spanish Rebellion.
Louis Alexander MacKay. OBCV
Church's One Foundation, The. Samuel John Stone. WGRP
Church's Restoration, The. Sir John Betjeman. FaBoPa
Church's Testimony, The. Dryden. *See* Hind and the Panther, The:
But gratious [*or* gracious] God, how well dost thou provide.
Churchyard. Robert Hass. NAmP; NPGG
Churchyard leans to the sea with its dead, The. The Old Churchyard of
Bonchurch. Philip Bourke Marston. EBVV; OBNC
Churchyard of St. Mary Magdalene, Old Milton. John Heath-Stubbs.
NePoEA
Churchyard on the Sands, The. Lord De Tabley. CH, *abr.;* FaBoPP;
GBL; OBNC
Churl that wants another's fare, The. The Dog in the River. Phaedrus,
tr. by Christopher Smart. AWP
Churning the compost, dazed. To Earth. James Applewhite.
PoA
Chyrsanthemums, *sel.* Yün Shou-p'ing, *tr. fr. Chinese by* Jonathan
Chaves.
"As we say farewell to autumn." CoBLCP
Cibber! write all thy verses upon glasses. Pope. FaBoEE
Cicada, The. H. M. Green. PoAu-1
Cicada, The. Ou-yang Hsiu, *tr. fr. Chinese by* Arthur Waley.
AWP
Cicada. Adrien Stoutenburg. NYBP; RFM
Cicada shrieks, The. Yoshitsune, *tr. by* Geoffrey Bownas *and* Anthony
Thwaite. PeBJV
Cicada voices rising continually, far away. Teika, *tr. fr. Japanese by*
Hiroaki Sato. *Fr.* Eighty-four Tanka. FCEI
Cicadas in brambled foliage, The. The House-Builders. Kamala Das.
PBWP
Cicadas shrieking. Matsumoto Takashi, *tr. by* Geoffrey Bownas *and*
Anthony Thwaite. PeBJV
Cider and Vesalius. John Peck. AmPA
Cider Song. Mildred Weston. BoNaP
Cigales. Richard Wilbur. NePoEA; NOBA
Cigar Smoke, Sunday, after Dinner. Louise Townsend Nicholl. FYAP
Cigarette, The. Jules Laforgue, *tr. fr. French by* William Jay Smith.
CT
Cigarette, A. *Mongol Oral Tradition, tr. by* C. R. Bawden. WTO
Cigarette for the Bambino. Gavin Ewart. WaP
Cigarette is dead, The. Ozaki Hosai, *tr. fr. Japanese by* Hiroaki Sato.
Fr. One Hundred Haiku in Free Form. FCEI
Cigarette my girl is smoking, A. Jealousy. *Malay Oral Tradition, tr. by*
R. J. Wilkinson *and* R. O. Winstedt. WTO
Cigarette Poem, The. Faye Kicknosway. IHMS
Cigarette smoke floated. Milne's Bar. Norman MacCaig. FaBoTw
Cigarettes Will Spoil Yer Life. *Unknown.* AS

Cigars droop in sickly fingers. Thanksgiving, Growing Older. William Doreski. KS

Cill Chais. *Unknown, tr. fr. Irish by* Thomas Kinsella. NOIV

Cimabuella. Bayard Taylor. BXAP

Cincirinella Had a Mule. *Unknown, tr. by* Maria Cimino. FaPON

Cincophrenicpoet. Bob Kaufman. PoNe

Cinderella. Olga Broumas. InPK

Cinderella. Randall Jarrell. LCAP; NAAL-2

Cinderella. Jan Kemp. ATNZ

Cinderella. Ruby C. Saunders. BlSi

Cinderella. Anne Sexton. HeIP; InPS; NAAL-2

Cinema. Kurt Klinger, *tr. fr. German by* Beth Bjorklund. CoAuP

Cinema, The. Bill Manhire. ATNZ

Cinema at the Lighthouse. Henri Coulette. *Fr.* The War of the Secret Agents, VI. NePoEA-2

Cinema is cruel, The. An Image of Leda. Frank O'Hara. HCAP

Cinéma Vérité. Dorothy Walters. IHMS

Cinnabar Well—I don't know where it is. Searching for Herb Brazier and Cinnabar Well. Tao-chi, *tr. by* Jonathan Chaves. CoBLCP

Cinnamon Peeler, The. Michael Ondaatje. NOBC

Cino. Ezra Pound. VGW

Cinq Ans Après. Gelett Burgess. *See* Ah, Yes, I Wrote the "Purple Cow."

Cinquain: A Warning. Adelaide Crapsey. *See* Just now/ Out of the strange.

Cinque. Janet Campbell Hale. VoR

Cinque Port, A. John Davidson. BrPo

Cinque Ports, The. *Unknown.* FaBoUs

Cipangu. William Hart-Smith. *Fr.* Christopher Columbus. PoAu-2

Circe. Lord De Tabley. NOBVV

Circe. Hilda Doolittle ("H. D."). PoRA

Circe. William Gibson. PoA

Circe. A. D. Hope. PPP

Circe. Louis MacNeice. OBMV

Circe/ Mud Poems, *sel.* Margaret Atwood.
   "Men with the heads of eagles." NoAM

Circle, And, and in this circle, another. A Circular Cry. Edmond Jabès, *tr. by* Anthony Rudolf. VWA

Circle, The. Carol Coates. CaP

Circle, The. Jean Garrigue. LiTA

Circle, The. Lizelia Augusta Jenkins Moorer. CBWP-3

Circle, A. Theodore Spencer. NYBP

Circle, a Square, a Triangle and a Ripple of Water. Jane Cooper. TAP

Circle Begins, A. Harold Littlebird. STE

Circle Game, The, *sels.* Margaret Atwood. MoCV
   "Being with you."
   "Returning to the room."
   "Summer again."

Circle of Struggle. William Pitt Root. NYBP

Circle of Thorns. Amryl Johnson. WS

Circle Sleeper. Jean H. Marvin. CRH

Circle to the left, Old Brass Wagon. Old Brass Wagon. *Unknown.* AS

Circled by trees, ringed with the faded folding chairs. The Tennis. E. B. White. ASP

Circles. Carl Sandburg. AmFN

Circles never fully round, but change, The. Perspective of Co-ordination. Arthur Davison Ficke. PoA

Circling, around a thousand sails and water. Approaching. Lan Ling, *tr. by* Dominic Cheung. IFON

Circling on high, in the cloudless sky. On the Plains. Frances Brooks. *Fr.* Intaglios. AA

Circling shadow on the measured dial, The. Chronology. Turner Cassity. PoA

Circling upon his star. The Sleepwalker. Nelly Sachs, *tr. by* Michael Hamburger. BoWoP; NYPE

Circuit closes, The. House and heart. Winter Night. Louis O. Coxe. NYBP

Circuit Judge, The. Edgar Lee Masters. *Fr.* Spoon River Anthology. FaBoEE

Circular Cry, A. Edmond Jabès, *tr. fr. French by* Anthony Rudolf. VWA

Circular Roads. Kizito Z. Muchemwa. WMBCH

Circulation, The. Thomas Washbourne. NOCV

Circulation of the Blood, The. Sir Richard Blackmore. *Fr.* Creation. FaBoUs

Circumambulation of Mt. Tamalpais. Andrew Hoyem. PoA

Circumcision, The. Linda Zisquit. VWA

Circumstance. Thomas Bailey Aldrich. AA

Circumstance. Alice Bowen. GOS

Circus, The. Milton Kaplan. GoYe

Circus, The. Elizabeth Madox Roberts. FaPON

Circus Animals' Desertion, The. W. B. Yeats. CMoP; FaBoMo; FaBoTw; LiTB; MAT; MoP; NAEL-2; NAWM-2; NIP; NoAM; NOBE; NOIV; NoP; OAEL-2; OxBTC; PrIm; TEP

Circus at the Barber's Shop. Kendrick Smithyman. PeNZ

Circus Dancer, The. Celia Dropkin, *tr. fr. Yiddish by* Grace Schulman. PeBMYV; VWA, *tr. by* Howard Schwartz

Circus Garland, A, *sels.* Rachel Lyman Field.
   Equestrienne. OBCA
   Gunga. OBCA
   Parade. OBCA
   Performing Seal, The. OBCA; RHPC

Circus of battleships carrying heavy laughter, A. Celebrated Return. Clarence Major. AmNP

Circus; or One View of It, The. Theodore Spencer. RR

Circus Parade, The. Katharine Pyle. OBCA

Circus-Postered Barn, The. Elizabeth J. Coatsworth. MoAmPo

Circus Ringmaster's Apology to God, The. Norman Dubie. MAYP

Circus runaway, tattooed from head to toe in yellow. Finding the Tattooed Lady in the Garden. Pattiann Rogers. MT

Circus Song. Patricia Goedicke. TV

Circus was never meant for children, The. Circus. Milton Kaplan. GoYe

Cirque d'Hiver. Elizabeth Bishop. InPS; LiTA

Cirrus bow of surf is blown, The. A Fantasy of Little Waters. James Scully. NYBP

Cissie. Lotte Kramer. CN

Cit, a Common-Council-Man by place, The. What Is't to Us? Charles Churchill. *Fr.* Night; an Epistle to Robert Lloyd. SeCePo

Citation and Examination of William Shakespeare, The, *sel.* Walter Savage Landor.
   Maid's Lament, The. OBEV; OBNC

Cities, The. "Æ." OBMV

Cities and Science. David McCord. AmFN

Cities and Seas. Norman Jordan. PoNe

Cities and Thrones and Powers. Kipling. *Fr.* Puck of Pook's Hill. GoJo; NOBE; OBNC; OxBTC; PoEL-5

Cities and towns, ye haunts of wretchedness! Industrial Evils. Joseph Cottle. *Fr.* Malvern Hills. NOEC

Cities are walled. It is a cruel land. Memory. Babette Deutsch. PoA

Cities are washed into time, The. John Oliver Simon. NeAC

Cities behind Glass. Linda Hogan. STE

Cities break up, The. The Desert. "Adunis", *tr. by* Abdullah al-Udhari. MPAW

Cities burn behind us; the lake glitters. Nostalgia of the Lakefronts. Donald Justice. BAP

Cities Drowned. Sir Henry Newbolt. CH

Cities Have Fallen, The. Fragano Ledgister. PBCV

Cities of dream wander under the bark of a December forest, The. A December Forest. Vesna Krmpotic, *tr. by* Vasa D. Mihailovich. WPOW

Citizen. Chris Wallace-Crabbe. CBAP

Citizen myself, or personal friend. Allen Tate. *Fr.* More Sonnets at Christmas. WaP

Citizen of—the World, A. Donald McDonald. PBCV

Citizen's Dissertation on His Neighborhood, A. Avraham Shlonsky, *tr. fr. Hebrew by* Bernhard Frank. MHeP

Citizenship; Form 8889512, Sub-Section Q. G. K. Chesterton. OxBoLi

Cit's Country Box, The. Robert Lloyd. NOEC

City, The. "Æ." WGRP

City, The. W. H. Auden. *Fr.* The Quest. Son

City, The. Sir John Betjeman. TEP

City, The. Charles Brasch. *Fr.* Nineteen Thirty-Nine. ATNZ

City. Joseph Bruchac. CDW

City, The. C. P. Cavafy, *tr. fr. Greek by* Edmund Keeley and Philip Sherrard. VMG

City, The. Robert Creeley. LCAP

City. Dovid Hofshteyn, *tr. fr. Yiddish by* Leonard Wolf. PeBMYV

City, The. David Ignatow. PCP

City, The. James Thomson ("B. V."). *See* City of Dreadful Night, The: Lo, thus, as prostrate, "In the dust I write."

City, The. Ben Maddow. WaP

City, The. Frank Mason North. *See* Where Cross the Crowded Ways of Life.

City. Jane Stembridge. NMM

City. Joseph Stroud. NPGG

City a Wrecked Ship, The. Amal Dunqul, *tr. fr. Arabic by* Sharif Elmusa *and* Thomas G. Ezzy. MAP

City Afternoon. John Ashbery. HeIP; InPK

City Afternoon. Barbara Howes. AmFN

City!/ You called me from afar. City. Dovid Hofshteyn, *tr. by* Leonard Wolf. PeBMYV

City asleep. The City Dump. Felice Holman. RHPC

City bred. Moon. Frances Horovitz. BrRo

City built in darkness and cold air, A. Peter Levi. *Fr.* Pancakes for the Queen of Babylon. CRP

City by the Sea, The. Josephine D. Henderson Heard. CBWP-4

City Child, The. Tennyson. BoTP; OxBChV

City, City. Marci Ridlon. RHPC

City Clerk, The. Thomas Ashe. EBVV

City clocks point out the hours, The. Belfast: High Street. Padraic Colum. NePoAm

City defenseless by day one sees desolation, A. Amir Gilboa, *tr. by* Warren Bargad *and* Stanley F. Chyet. IP

City Dump, The. Felice Holman. RHPC

City Eclogue, A. "W. J." NOEC

City Flower, A. Austin Dobson. TEP

City folks sit back in their reclining chairs. Easy Chairs and Saddle Sores. Ross Knox. CowP

City Gent. Craig Raine. NoAM

City Girl in the Country. Elizabeth Smither. PeNZ

City Hall. Belle Randall. CRP

City Highway. Judah Leib Teller, *tr. fr. Yiddish by* Benjamin *and* Barbara Harshav. AYP

City in the Sea *or* The Doomed City, The. Poe. AA; AmPP; AnAmPo; LiTA; MAT; MOS; NAAL-1; NOBA; NoP; OxBA; PoE; PoEL-4; SCV; TAP; TrGrPo

City is of Night, The; perchance of Death. James Thomson ("B. V."). *Fr.* The City of Dreadful Night, I. EBVV; LiTB; PoEL-5; ViBoPo

City Johannesburg. Mongane Wally Serote. WMBCH

City Lights. Rachel Lyman Field. FaPON; PDV; RHPC

City Lights: I Took That Picture. Steve Albert. PPR

City Limits, The. A. R. Ammons. CAPP; HCAP; MoP; NAAL-2; NoAM; NOBA; NoP

City, Lord, Where Thy Dear Life, The. William E. Dudley. AH

City: Midnight, The. Bruce Dawe. PoAu-2

City Mouse and the Garden Mouse, The. Christina Rossetti. *Fr.* Sing-Song. BoTP; FaBoBe; FaPON; NTCP

City of Baltimore, The. Unknown. OxBSS

City of Beggars, The. Alfred Hayes. WaP

City of Dreadful Night, The, *abr., sels.* James Thomson ("B. V."). OBNC

"Although lamps burn along the silent streets." *Fr.* III. EBVV

"Anear the centre of that northern crest." *Fr.* XXI. GTBS-P (City's Queen, The.) NOBE

"As I came through the desert thus it was." *Fr.* IV. LiTB

"City is of Night, The; perchance of Death." *Fr.* I. EBVV; LiTB; PoEL-5; ViBoPo

"He stood alone within the spacious square." *Fr.* IV. NOBVV; WiR

"I wandered in a suburb of the north." *Fr.* XVIII. NOBVV

"Large glooms were gathered in the mighty fane." *Fr.* XIV. EBEV; OAEL-2

"Mighty river flowing dark and deep, The." *Fr.* XIX. EBVV

"Lo, thus, as prostrate, "In the dust I write."" GoTS; OxBS; ViBoPo (City, The.) NOBE

"What men are they who haunt these fatal glooms." *Fr.* XI. EBVV

City of Dreadful Night, The. James Thomson. GoTS; NOBE; OBNC; OxBS

City of Esteli, The. June 10. Magdalena de Rodriguez, *tr. by* Nina Serrano. WPOW

City of God. Samuel Johnson. AA; WGRP

City of God, The. Francis Turner Palgrave. WGRP

City of Golf, The. Robert Fuller Murray. SD

City of Light. Nahum Bomze, *tr. fr. Yiddish by* Gabriel Preil *and* Howard Schwartz. VWA

City of Nara of good blue clay, The. Ono no Oyu, *tr. fr. Japanese by* Hiroaki Sato. *Fr.* Manyo Shu. FCEI

City of Prague, The. William Jeffery Prowse. CenHV

City of San Salvador. Tirso Canales, *tr. fr. Spanish by* Juan Felipe Herrera. Vol

City of Satisfactions, The. Daniel Hoffman. Prf

City of Slaughter, The. Hayyim Nahman Bialik, *tr. fr. Hebrew by* A. M. Klein. TrJP

City of tense and stricken faces. Jackson, Mississippi. Margaret Walker. FB

City of the End of Things, The. Archibald Lampman. NOBC; OBCV

City, Oh, City! Jack Prelutsky. RHPC

City Park. Remco Campert, *tr. fr. Dutch by* John Scott *and* Graham Martin. DuIn

City Pigeons. Helen Chasin. WeW

City planners. To the New Annex to the Detroit County Jail. Richard W. Thomas. PoBA

City Rises, The. James Cunningham. JB

City Roofs. Charles Hanson Towne. BLPA

City [San Francisco]. Langston Hughes. AmFN; PDV; RHPC

City shuffles through the snow, the whirling snow, and I, indifferent, The. Dead of Winter. Anthony Towne. NYBP

City Singers, The. John L. Owen. PF

City Song, A. John Hanlon Mitchell. CaP

City Songs. Mark Van Doren. NYBP

City Sparrow. Jane Mayhall. TAP

City-Storm. Harold Monro. MoBrPo

City streets and pavements receive me. In the Aging City. Fadwa Tuqan, *tr. by* Patricia Alanah Byrne, Salma Khadra Jayyusi, *and* Naomi Shihab Nye. MAP

City streets coil around me, The. Jaikur and the City. Badr Shakir al-Sayyah, *tr. by* Lena Jayyusi *and* Christopher Middleton. MAP

City Traffic. Eve Merriam. PDV

City Tree, The. Isabella Valancy Crawford. CaP

City Trees. Edna St. Vincent Millay. FaPON

City Walk-up, Winter 1969. Carolyn Forché. MAYP

City was flooded with light, The. The Continental College of Beauty. Mark Strand. BLA

City where I was born, Radautz in Bukovina, cast me out when I was/ ten, The. The Souvenir. Dan Pagis, *tr. by* Warren Bargad *and* Stanley F. Chyet. IP

City which thou seest no other deem, The. Rome ("The City which thou seest no other deem"). Milton. *Fr.* Paradise Regained, *Bk.* IV, *ll.* 44–108. OBS

City, whose streets are wavering reflections. Canal Street. John Wheelwright. PoA

City without Walls. W. H. Auden. NYBP

City yawns, The. Sunrise. Frank Asch. RHPC

City's Crown, The. William Dudley Foulke. WGRP

City's Queen, The. James Thomson ("B. V."). *See* City of Dreadful Night, The: Anear the centre of that northern crest.

Civil Defense. Kenneth Burke. OBAL

Civil Elegies, *sel.* Dennis Lee.

"Often I sit in the sun and brooding over the city, always." NOBC

Civil Irish and Wild Irish. Laoiseach Mac an Bhaird, *tr. fr. Late Middle Irish by* Kenneth Jackson. AnIL

Civil Marriage. Cecilia Bustamante, *tr. fr. Spanish by* David Tipton. Per

Civil Marriage, *sel.* Pablo Guevara, *tr. fr. Spanish by* Maureen Ahern *and* David Tipton.

"I remember." Per

Civil Riot, *sel.* G. D. H. Cole.

"And you'll say a nation totters." OxBTC

Civil Service, The. William Langland. *Fr.* The Vision of Piers Plowman. NOCV

Civil War, *sel.* Austin Clarke.

"They are the spit of virtue now." NOIV

Civil War. Charles Dawson Shanly. PAH

Civil Wars, The, *sel.* Samuel Daniel.

"It was upon the twilight of that day." *Fr.* VIII. OBWP

Civile, res ago. See, Will, 'Ere's a Go. *Unknown.* ChTr; FaBoNo

Civilian. Josephine Miles. WPE

Civilian for a pause of hours. Goodmorning with Light. John Ciardi. WaP

Civilisation is hooped together, brought. Meru. W. B. Yeats. NoAM; OAEL-2; PoA

Civilities. Thomas Whitbread. SD

Civilities of Lamplight. Charles Tomlinson. OxBC

Civility a Bogey. Margaret Avison. NOBC

Civilization. Tom Schmidt. NeAC

Civilization and Its Discontents. John Ashbery. LCAP; TwCP

Civilized. Ahmad Nadeem Qasmi, *tr. fr. Urdu by* Mahmood Jamal. PBMUP

Civilized, crying how to be human again: this will tell you how. Signpost. Robinson Jeffers. GoYe

Clabe Mott. James Still. GrPl

Clack your beaks you cormorants and kittiwakes. A Canticle to the Waterbirds. William Everson. NeAP; PoM

Clacking and gouging when huddled. Snapshot of a Crab-Picker among Barrels Spilling Over, Apparently at the End of Her Shift. Dave Smith. NoAM

Clad All in White. Abraham Cowley. *Fr.* The Mistress. SeCV-1

Clad in the wealthy robes his genius wrought. On Shakespeare and Voltaire. Thomas Holcroft. NOEC

Claflin's Alumni. Lizelia Augusta Jenkins Moorer. CBWP-3

Claim, The. Edith Nesbit. NOBVV

Claim to Love. Giovanni Battista Guarini, *tr. fr. Italian by* Thomas Stanley. AWP

Clair de Lune. Anthony Hecht. NYBP

Clair de Lune. Jules Laforgue, *tr. fr. French by* William Jay Smith. CT

Clair de Lune. Paul Verlaine, *tr. fr. French by* Arthur Symons. AWP

Clamb ape mountain backwards. To Be Quicker. Don L. Lee. JB

Clamming. Reed Whittemore. NYBP; TAP

Clamour of the wind making music. Saint Columcille, *tr. by* John Montague. BIrV

Clams. Ishigaki Rin, *tr. fr. Japanese by* Hiroaki Sato. FCEI; PBWP

Clan Meeting: Births and Nations: A Blood Song. Michael S. Harper. NoAM

Clancy of the Overflow. Andrew Barton Paterson. PoAu-1

Clandestine Work. Iwan Goll, *tr. fr. French by* Anthony Rudolf. VWA

Clanking of the chain is now, The. Mohammad Taqi Mir, *tr. by* Ahmed Ali. GoT

Clap, clap the double nightcap on! William Gifford. Walter Savage Landor. FaBoEE; GTBS-P

Clap hands, clap hands/ Hie, Tommy Randy. *Unknown.* OxNR

Clap hands, clap hands/ Till father comes home. *Unknown.* OxNR

Clap hands, Daddy comes/ With his pocket full of plums. *Unknown.* OxNR

Clap hands, Daddy's coming/ Up the waggon way. *Unknown.* OxNR

Clap Your Hands for Herod. Josef Hanzlik, *tr. fr. Czech by* Ian Milner. OBCP

Clapping the door to, in the little light. Charwoman. Ben Belitt. SaC

Clare de Kitchen. *Unknown.* BLPA

Clarel, *sels.* Herman Melville.
  Of Rome. OxBA
  On Mammon. OxBA
  Prelusive. AmPP
  Sodom. AmPP
  Ungar and Rolfe. OxBA

Clarence ("Clarence Lee from Tennessee"). Shel Silverstein. OBCA

Clarence Mangan. Thomas Kinsella. CIP

Clarence Short Bull died. Sitting Bull's Will versus the Sioux Treaty of 1868 and Monty Hall. A. K. Redwing. VoR

Clarendon had law and sense. On the Young Statesmen. Charles Sackville. APAS

Clari, the Maid of Milan, *sel.* John Howard Payne.
  Home, Sweet Home. AA; BLPA; FaBoBe; FaFP; WBLP

Clarimonde. Théophile Gautier, *tr. fr. French by* Lafcadio Hearn. *Fr.* Taches Jaunes, Les. AWP; VVA

Clarion-Call, The. *Unknown.* BLRP

Claritas. James Camp. SoTCo

Claritas. Denise Levertov. VGW

Clarity. A. R. Ammons. HCAP; TAP

Clark Colven and his gay ladie. Clerk Colvill. *Unknown.* EnSB; ESPB; FaBoBa; GBP; OxBB

Clark Sanders. *Unknown. See* Clerk Saunders.

Clarrie Smythe let's call him there was one of him. Them. Vincent O'Sullivan. ATNZ

Clash of salutation. As keels thrust into shingle. Geoffrey Hill. *Fr.* Mercian Hymns, XVI. NoAM; NoP

Clasp you the God within yourself. The Last Round. Anna Wickham. MoBrPo

Clasped Hands. Philippe Soupault, *tr. fr. French by* Michael Benedikt. POS

Clasping of Hands. George Herbert. PoEL-2

Class Incident from Graves. Alan Brownjohn. OxBTC

Class of 19—— Frederick Dec. PCP

Class Song of '91. Eloise Bibb. CBWP-4

Class was history, that's, The. Before. Albert Goldbarth. MAYP

Classic. A. R. Ammons. NOBA

Classic Ballroom Dances. Charles Simic. GeTw; LCAP

Classic Case, A. Gilbert Sorrentino. NeAP

Classic Encounter. "Christopher Caudwell." OxBTC

Classic landscapes of dreams are not, The. The Snowfall. Donald Justice. CRP; NePoEA-2; VGW

Classic Ode, A. Charles Battell Loomis. NA

Classic Scene. William Carlos Williams. NAAL-2; OxBA

Classic Waits for Me, A. E. B. White. BXAP; NYBP; Par

Classical engine of death moves my day, The. Hurrying me. Burning and Fathering; Accounts of My Country. Jack Gilbert. NPGG

Classical Idyll, A. Avraham Huss, *tr. by* Mark Elliott Shapiro. VWA

Classical Quatrain, A. Paul Goodman. VGW

Classical Style, The. Michael Palmer. NPGG

Classical warfare. Ian Hamilton Finlay. *Fr.* Monostichs de la Guerre de Petite-Sparte. PoPo

Classics Revisited, The. Mirko Lauer, *tr. fr. Spanish by* David Tipton. Per

Classroom in October. Elias Lieberman. GoYe

Claude Allen. *Unknown.* AmFP

Claudio's Lament: "Pardon, goddess of the night." Shakespeare. *Fr.* Much Ado about Nothing. OBSC
  (Song: "Pardon, goddess of the night.") CTC

Claudius Gilbert. John Wilson. SCAP

Claudy. James Simmons. CIP

Claus von Stauffenberg. Thom Gunn. OBWP

Claustrophobia. Sean O Riordain, *tr. fr. Irish by* Thomas Kinsella. NOIV

Clavering. E. A. Robinson. OxBA

Clay is the word and clay is the flesh. Patrick Kavanagh. *Fr.* The Great Hunger, I. FaBCIP; IPY; NoAM; OxBTC

Clay Jug, The. Kabir, *ad. fr.* Hindi by Robert Bly. NU

Clay, sand, and rock, seem of a diff'rent birth. Barten Holyday. FaBoEE

Clayfeld believed indulging in one's whims. Clayfeld's Glove. Robert Pack. BLA

Clayfeld's Anniversary Song. Robert Pack. BLA

Clayfeld's Daughter Reveals Her Plans. Robert Pack. BLA

Clayfeld's Glove. Robert Pack. BLA

Clayfeld's Twin. Robert Pack. BLA

Clayming a Second Kisse by Desert. Ben Jonson. *Fr.* A Celebration of Charis in Ten Lyrick Peeces. SeCP

Clean. Lance Newman. ASP

Clean as a lady. Tulip. Humbert Wolfe. MoBrPo

Clean birds by sevens. A Charm against a Magpie. *Unknown.* ChTr
  (Dove, The.) GBP

Clean de ba'n an' sweep de flo.' Uncle Eph's Banjo Song. James Edwin Campbell. BANP

Clean Hands. Austin Dobson. TrPWD

Clean in the light, with nothing to remember. Aspects. Norman MacCaig. OxBS

Clean Men. Stanislaw Grochowiak, *tr. fr. Polish by* Czeslaw Milosz. PwPP

Clean sky, empty of bird wings. Snow in Iowa City. Jayanta Mahapatra. WCI

Clean the spittoons, boy. Brass Spittoons. Langston Hughes. AmNP; BANP; MoAmPo; NoAM

Clean thin hollow of breast. Reflections. Anita Barrows. NMM

Cleaning a Fish. Dave Smith. NoAM

Cleaning Day. José Kozer, *tr. fr. Spanish by* David Unger. VWA

Cleaning the Fish. Robert Pack. SM

Cleaning the Well. Fred Chappell. MT

Cleaning Up. Edward Dyson. PoAu-1

Cleaning woman opened the rusty door, A. The Church of San Antonio de la Florida. Paul Petrie. NYBP

Cleanliness. Charles *and* Mary Lamb. OxBChV

Cleanly rush of the mountain air, The. The Dead Knight. John Masefield. CH; GTBS-P

Cleanly, sir, you went to the core of the matter. A Correct Compassion. James Kirkup. FaBoTw; ImOP; OxBTC; SeCePo

Cleanness, *sel. Unknown, tr. fr. Middle English by* Brian Stone.
  "He who would acclaim Cleanness in becoming style." NOCV

Cleansing Fires. Adelaide Anne Procter. WGRP

Cleanthes of Andros, The. To a Greek Ship in the Port of Dublin. William Bedell Stanford. NeIP

Clear. Angelo Lewis. PoBA

Clear Air of October, The. Robert Bly. NaP

Clear and Cool. Charles Kingsley. *Fr.* The Water Babies. BoNaP; GN; OxBChV

Clear and gentle stream! Robert Bridges. BrPo

Clear and glittering bright. *Unknown, tr. by* Arthur Waley. BoS

Clear and high, a mountain. The Hike. Neil Weiss. SD

Clear and loud. Hitomaro, *tr. fr. Japanese by* Geoffrey Bownas *and* Anthony Thwaite. *Fr.* Manyo Shu. PeBJV

Clear are the Huai currents, I see the river's depth. Mooring My Boat at Pan-ch'a. Shen Te-ch'ien, *tr. by* Marie Chan. WFTU

Clear as air, the western waters. The Grave of Rury. Thomas Rolleston. AnIL

Clear autumn scene is fresh, The. Song of the Water Clock at Night. Mao Hsi-chen, *tr. by* Lois Fusek. ATF

Clear Bright. Li Ch'ing-chao, *tr. fr. Chinese by* Kenneth Rexroth. BoWoP

Clear bright morning, with its scented air, The. The Fair Morning. Jones Very. NOBA

Clear brown eyes, kindly and alert, with 12-20 vision, The. Portrait. Kenneth Fearing. MoAmPo

Clear cool note of the cuckoo which has ousted the legitimate nest-holder, The. Sincere Flattery of W. W. (Americanus). James Kenneth Stephen. FiBHP; NOBL; Par
(Imitation of Walt Whitman.) FaBoPa
Clear current, craggy boulders. Written on the Oi River. Rokunyo, tr. by Burton Watson. JLIC-2
Clear dawn graces the morning of the Cold Food Festival, A. Sand of Silk-Washing Stream. Wei Chuang, tr. by Lois Fusek. ATF
Clear disk of the sun, The. Revisit. John Engels. BLA
Clear [or Cleere] had the day been [or bin] from the dawn [or dawne]. Michael Drayton. Fr. Muses' Elysium [or Elizium]. BoTP
(Fine Day, A.) GN
(Sixt Nimphall, The.) OBS
Clear is the bottom of the lake. Yakamochi, tr. fr. Japanese. Fr. Manyo Shu. Ma
Clear laughter of African children. Thoughts after Work. David Rubadiri. WMBCH
Clear Midnight, A. Walt Whitman. HAP; OxBSP
Clear moon arcs, The. Red Rock Ceremonies. Anita Endrezze-Danielson. VoR
Clear moon brightly shining in the night. Unknown, tr. fr. Chinese by Burton Watson. Fr. Nineteen Old Poems of the Han, VII. CoBCP
Clear Night. Charles Wright. GeTw; MT
Clear nights, the massive. War Bride. Douglas Worth. FF
Clear, noon sky at midsummer is God's eye, A. Cosmic Eye. A. K. Redwing. VoR
Clear ocean seems, The. The Double Vision of Manannan. Unknown, tr. by John Montague. BIrV
Clear or Cloudy, Sweet as April Showering. Unknown. ElL; OBSC
Clear, placid Leman! thy contrasted lake. Lake Leman ("Clear, placid Leman! thy contrasted lake"). Byron. Fr. Childe Harold's Pilgrimage: It Is the Hush of Night. OBNC, sl. diff. sel.
Clear pond, The. Then and Now. Kapilar, tr. by A. K. Ramanujan. PLW
Clear Shell, A. Frances Bellerby. FaBoWP
Clear—the senses bright—sitting in the black chair—Rocker. Michael McClure. Fr. Peyote Poem. NeAP
Clear the trail, you short-horn pilgrims, hunt your hole or climb a tree. Alkali Pete Hits Town. T. J. McCoy. CowP
Clear the Way. John Montague. FaBCIP
Clear the way and build the road! The Road. Zalman Schneour, tr. by Joseph Leftwich. TrJP
Clear-toned cicadas have exhausted their voices, The. Princess Shikishi, tr. fr. Japanese by Hiroaki Sato. Fr. Seventy-eight Tanka. FCEI
Clear transparent sea with light, The. Horatio Nelson Huggins. Fr. Hiroona. PBCV
Clear water has no front or back. Chiyojo, tr. fr. Japanese by Hiroaki Sato. Fr. Seventeen Hokku. FCEI
Clear water in a brilliant bowl. The Poems of Our Climate. Wallace Stevens. NoP; OxBA; TrGrPo; TwCP
Clear water of the imperial pond, The. Ise Tayu, tr. by Kenneth Rexroth and Ikuko Atsumi. BoWoP
Clear waters unchanged. Saigyo, tr. fr. Japanese by Burton Watson. Fr. Sixty-four Tanka. FCEI
Clear weather of juniper, The. Sloe Gin. Seamus Heaney. FaBCIP
Clear wind—what is it? The. Lotus Viewing. Su Tung-p'o, tr. by Burton Watson. CoBCP
Clear Winter. Pierre Reverdy, tr. fr. French by John Ashbery. POS; RHTwFP
Clearances, sels. Seamus Heaney. CIP
"Cool that came off sheets just off the line, The." Fr. V.
"In the last minutes he said more to her." Fr. VII.
"When all the others were away at Mass." Fr. /III.
Cleare moving cristall, pure as the Sunne beames. William Alexander, Earl of Stirling. Fr. Aurora, XXV. OxBS
Cleared Land, A, sel. Robin Fulton.
More than People. PoSH
Clearing, The. Peter Everwine, after the Nahuatl Indian. NNaP
Clearing, The. Robert Graves. NYBP
Clearing at Dawn. Li Po, tr. fr. Chinese by Arthur Waley. AWP
Clearing brush away. Taking to the Woods. Henry Taylor. MAYP; MT
Clearings. Blaise Cendrars, tr. fr. French by John Dos Passos. RHTwFP
Clearly he would notice: in my eyes. Elegies for Prince Atsumichi ("Clearly he would notice: in my eyes"). Lady Izumi, tr. fr. Japanese by Hiroaki Sato. Fr. Fifty-one Tanka. FCEI
Clearly I see the pebbles in the water. Unknown, tr. fr. Japanese. Fr. Manyo Shu. Ma
Clearsightedness. Andrew Salkey. PBCV
Clearwater Beach, Florida. William Matthews. BLA
Cleat curved you curved the spider, The. Lapstrake. Ted Greenwald. LP
Cleator Moor. Norman Nicholson. FaBoTw

Cleavage. A. R. Ammons. OBAL
Cleere had the day bin from the dawne. See Clear had the day been from the dawn.
Cleitagoras. Leonidas of Tarentum, tr. fr. Greek by William M. Hardinge. AWP
Clementine. Percy Montross. See In a cavern [or cabin], in a canyon.
Cleomenes, sel. Dryden.
No, No, Poor Suffering Heart. Fr. II, ii. LiTB; QFR; ViBoPo
(One Happy Moment.) OBEV
(Song: "No, no, poor suff'ring Heart no Change endeavour.") SeCV-2
Cleon ("Cleon the poet from the sprinkled isles"). Robert Browning. OAEL-2
Cleonicos. Edward Cracroft Lefroy, after the Greek of Theocritus. Fr. Echoes from Theocritus, XXVII. AWP
Cleopatra. "Anna Akhmatova," tr. fr. Russian by D. M. Thomas. AIW
Cleopatra, sels. Samuel Daniel.
"Then thus we have beheld." OBSC
"O fearfull, frowning nemesis." PoEL-2
Cleopatra. Mary Mackey. AIW
Cleopatra. Shakespeare. See Antony and Cleopatra: Barge she sat in, like a burnish'd throne, The.
Cleopatra. William Wetmore Story. AA
Cleopatra. Swinburne. BeLS
Cleopatra and Antony. Dryden. Fr. All for Love. FiP
Cleopatra Dying. Thomas Stephens Collier. BLPA; BLPL; FaBoBe
Cleopatra to the Asp. Ted Hughes. EBEV
Cleopatra, washed up nude, sprawled. Remu. Wayne Brown. UAS
Cleopatra, who thought they maligned her. Newton Mackintosh. NA
Cleopatra's Barge. Shakespeare. See Antony and Cleopatra: Barge she sat in, like a burnish'd throne, The.
Cleopatra's Death. Shakespeare. See Antony and Cleopatra: Death of Cleopatra.
Cleopatra's Lament. Shakespeare. Fr. Antony and Cleopatra, V, ii. UnPo
Cleric black and layman white are plainly far apart. In Early Spring, While at the Temple at Bamboo Ravine Mountain. Doji, tr. by Burton Watson. JLIC-1
Cleric Courts His Lady, A. Unknown. MeEL
Clerical Cabal, The. Unknown. APAS
Clerical Oppressors. Whittier. PAH
Clerihew: "Cecil Beaton,/ Though not schooled at Eton." Margaret Blaker. SoTCo
Clerihew: "Charles J. Correll/ Sang in no chorale." Louis Phillips. SoTCo
Clerihew: "Dorothy Parker/ Knew the darker." Martha H. Freedman. SoTCo
Clerihew: "Frederick the Great/ Accepted quite late." H. F. Cascorbi. SoTCo
Clerihew: "Guillaume Apollinaire/ Didn't care." Margaret Blaker. SoTCo
Clerihew: "Henry David Thoreau/ Rhymed his name with Burrow." Peg Russell. SoTCo
Clerihew: "Henry James/ Only liked dames." Martha H. Freedman. SoTCo
Clerihew: "Jan Vermeer/ liked to paint a tankard of beer." Vonna Adrian. SoTCo
Clerihew: "John Henry, Cardinal Newman." Maurice Sagoff. SoTCo
Clerihew: "Joseph Mallord Turner/ no slow learner." Vonna Adrian. SoTCo
Clerihew: "Mata Hari/ Was later sorry." Paul Curry Steele. SoTCo
Clerihew: Nicolsons, The. Roberta Simone. SoTCo
Clerihew: "Orson Welles/ Suffered from eating spells." Edmund Conti. SoTCo
Clerihew: "Oscar Wilde/ Married and fathered a child." Maurice Sagoff. SoTCo
Clerihew: "Said Henry VIII/ Accepting his fate." Edmund Conti. SoTCo
Clerihew: "Said Jean Arp's wife to Mary Martin." Lila Zeiger. SoTCo
Clerihew: "Scarlett O'Hara/ in time came to care a." Patricia Bunge. SoTCo
Clerihew: "Spinoza/ Collected curiosa." Unknown. NOBL
Clerihew: "Wandering Ulysses/ While returning to his Mrs." Roberta Simone. SoTCo
Clerihew: "When Georges Seurat." Lila Zeiger. SoTCo
Clerihew: "William F. Buckley/ Writes pluckley." Edmund Conti. SoTCo
Clerihews, sels. E. C. Bentley.
"Adam Smith." FaBoCo
"After dinner Erasmus." CenHV
"Art of Biography, The." CenHV; FiBHP; NOBL
"Dear me!" exclaimed Homer. FiBHP
"Dr. Clifford." CenHV
"George the Third." FaBoCo; FiBHP; NOBL; OxBoLi

"Great Duke of Wellington, The." CenHV

"I am not Mahomet." NOBL

"I quite realized," said Columbus." FiBHP

"If only Mr. Roosevelt." CenHV

"Intrepid Ricardo, The." CenHV

"John Stuart Mill." FaBoCo; FiBHP
   (J. S. Mill.) OxBoLi

Liszt. UnS

"Mr. Bernard Shaw." CenHV

"Mr. Hilaire Belloc." CenHV

"No," said Charles Peace." NOBL

"No, sir," said General Sherman." NOBL

"People of Spain think Cervantes, The." CenHV; FiBHP

"Sir Christopher Wren." CenHV; FaBoCo; FiBHP; MoShBr; NBLV

"Sir Humphry Davy." CenHV; FaBoCo; ImOP

"Sir Walter Raleigh." CenHV

"There exists no proof as." NOBL

"What I like about Clive." CenHV; NOBL
   (Lord Clive.) MoShBr

"When Alexander Pope." FiBHP

Clerimont's Song. Ben Jonson. *See* Epicoene; or, The Silent Woman: Still to Be Neat [Still to Be Drest (*or* Dressed)].

Clerk Colvill. *Unknown.* EnSB; ESPB; FaBoBa; GBP; OxBB

Clerk of Oxford, The. Chaucer. *Fr.* The Canterbury Tales: Prologue. InPS; TrGrPo
   ("Student came from Oxford town also, A," *mod. vers.* by Louis Untermeyer) TrGrPo

Clerk Saunders. *Unknown.* ESPB, A, B *and* F *vers.*; FaBoBa; OBEV; OxBS
   (Clark Sanders.) OxBB

"Is there ony room at your head, Saunders?" *sel.* OBD

Clerk Ther Was of Cauntebrigge Also, A. Walter William Skeat. BXAP; Par

Clerk ther was of Oxenford also, A. The Clerk of Oxford. Chaucer. *Fr.* The Canterbury Tales: Prologue. InPS; TrGrPo
   ("Student came from Oxford town also, A," *mod. vers.* by Louis Untermeyer.) TrGrPo

Clerke ther was, a puissant wight was hee, A. Ye Clerke of Ye Wethere. *Unknown.* BXAP

Clerks, The. E. A. Robinson. AA; AnAmPo; MoAB; MoAmPo; NAAL-2; PoEL-5

Clerks pretend to be shepherds, and under, The. Peire Cardenal, *tr. by* Paul Blackburn. Pro

Clerk's Song II. Norman H. Russell. NOVW

Clerk's Tale, The. Chaucer. *Fr.* The Canterbury Tales. Patient Griselda, *mod.* by Edward Hodnett PoRA

Clerk's Twa Sons o Owsenford, The. *Unknown.* ESPB

Clevedon Church. Andrew Lang. GoTS, *abr.*

Cleveland Lyke Wake Dirge, The. *Unknown. See* This ae nighte [*or* ean night], This ae nighte.

Clever man builds a city, A. Woman. *Unknown, tr. fr. Chinese* by H. A. Giles. *Fr.* Shi King. AWP

Clever Peter and the Ogress. Katharine Pyle. OBCA

Clever River, The. Eliezer Shteynbarg, *tr. fr. Yiddish* by Leonard Wolf. PeBMYV

Clever Skipper, The. *Unknown.* AmFP

Clever Tom Clinch Going to Be Hanged. Swift. CoMu; FaBoBa; NOIV

Clever Woman, A. Mary Elizabeth Coleridge. BrRo

Cliches with worn welt combined. On a Lover of Books. Geoffrey Grigson. FaBoEE

Click Go the Shears, Boys. *Unknown.* PoAu-1

Click ticks and she a, A. Clock and Mommie. Jacob Glatstein, *tr. fr. Yiddish* by Benjamin *and* Barbara Harshav. *Fr.* From the Nursery. AYP

Clickbeetle. Mary Ann Hoberman. RHPC

Clickety-clack. Song of the Train. David McCord. FaPON; NTCP

Clickstone. Rokwaho. STE

Cliff gave way and the slope shifted ground, The. The Trees in the Road. James Still. GrPl

Cliff Klingenhagen. E. A. Robinson. AmPP; AnAmPo; MoAB; MoAmPo; Son

Cliff-locked port and a bluff sea wall, A. Reid at Fayal. John Williamson Palmer. PAH

Cliff of the Ancient Tomb, The. Chang Yü, *tr. fr. Chinese* by Jonathan Chaves. *Fr.* Seven Poems on Living in the Mountains: Seeing Off. CoBLCP

Cliff Rose, The. Ernest Fewster. CaP

Cliff-Top, The. Robert Bridges. BoNaP; BoTP

Clifford, we've grown too far apart. Postcards of the Hanging: 1869. Andrew Hudgins. MOWH

Cliffs/ Cliffs. Thorn Piece. Amy Lowell. PeHV

Cliffs at Manzanilla, The. Jan Carew. PBCV

Cliffs that rise a thousand feet. Sailing Homeward. Chan Fang-sheng, *tr. by* Arthur Waley. AWP; FaBoCh

Cliffside pavilion juts out from the treetops, A. Spending the Night at Monk Ch'ao Yün's Retreat on Mount Lung-men. Li E, *tr. by* Shirleen S. Wong. WFTU

Clifton. Joan Larkin. GLP

Clifton Chapel. Sir Henry Newbolt. OBEV

Clifton Grove, *sel.* Henry Kirke White.
   "Lo! in the West, fast fades the ling'ring light." OBNC

Climate of Paradise, The. Louis Simpson. NOBA

Climate of Thought, The. Robert Graves. MoAB

Climax of passion, the dancers are trembling, The. Rumba. José Zacarías Tallet, *tr. by* Sangodare Akanji. TTY

Climb at court for me that will. Seneca. *See* Thyestes: Stond [*or* Stand] who so list upon the slipper toppe.

Climb in Torridon. Brenda G. Macrow. PoSH

Climb to Snowdon, The. Wordsworth. *Fr.* The Prelude [*or*, Growth of a Poet's Mind]: Conclusion ("It was a close, warm, breezeless summer night"). FaBoRV

Climb Up, The. Yisroel-Yankev Schwartz, *tr. fr. Yiddish* by Seymour Levitan. *Fr.* Kentucky. PeBMYV

Climbed up, devoured. In her beak. Cat in the Dovecot. Avner Trainin, *tr. by* Bernhard Frank. MHeP

Climber Surveys His Mountain, The. Hugh Ouston. PoSH

Climbers, The. Elizabeth Jennings. NePoEA

Climbers. Musaemura Bonus Zimunya. WMBCH

Climbers are fools, forget. Magma. G. J. F. Dutton. PoSH

Climbin up de mountain. Trouble Oh. *Unknown.* PBCV

Climbing. Tom Clark. UL

Climbing. Gloria Fuertes, *tr. fr. Spanish* by Philip Levine. PBWP

Climbing. Jennifer Maiden. CBAP

Climbing Ch'ing-shuo Tower at Yün-chung. Chu Yi-tsun, *tr. fr. Chinese* by Irving Lo. WFTU

Climbing, climbing, the path of stones. Temple of the Ocean of Awakening. Shen Chou, *tr. by* Jonathan Chaves. CoBLCP

Climbing from the Lethal dead. Orpheus. Yvor Winters. NOBA; VGW

Climbing Gannett. Roberta Hill Whiteman. HATNAP

Climbing high, sadly I gaze at the Mountain of Eight Immortals. Passing by Huai-yin I Have Feelings. Wu Wei-yeh, *tr. by* Jonathan Chaves. CoBLCP

Climbing in Glencoe. Andrew Young. SD

Climbing Mount Yang. Yüan Hung-tao, *tr. fr. Chinese* by Jonathan Chaves. CoBLCP

Climbing northward. The Herds. W. S. Merwin. NaP; NYBP

Climbing P'iao-miao Peak. Wu Wei-yeh, *tr. fr. Chinese* by Jonathan Chaves. CoBLCP

Climbing Rope, The. Alice V. Stuart. PoSH

Climbing T'ai Mountain. Yüan Mei, *tr. fr. Chinese* by Anthony C. Yu. WFTU

Climbing the Mountain. Chiang Hsun, *tr. fr. Chinese* by Dominic Cheung. IFON

Climbing the peaks of Tsukuba. Mushimaro, *tr. fr. Japanese*. *Fr.* Manyo Shu. Ma

Climbing the rutted path, the lights of the town. The Phases of Darkness. Paul Petrie. TAP

Climbing the staircase. Simplicity. Louis Simpson. Prf

Climbing the stairway gray with urban midnight. Effort at Speech. William Meredith. Prf; SM; WeW

Climbing through the January snow, into the Lobo canyon. Mountain Lion. D. H. Lawrence. Mes; OBTV; OxBTC; RB; RFM

Climbing to the Peak of Yang-t'ai Mountain to View the Ming Tombs. Wang P'eng-yün, *tr. fr. Chinese* by Kang-i Sun Chang. WFTU

Climbing to the Top of the City Walls at Kan-yü. Wang T'ing-hsiang, *tr. fr. Chinese* by Jonathan Chaves. CoBLCP

Climbing to the Very Top of Swallow Rock Once Again, in an Early Morning Rain. Wang Shih-chen, *tr. fr. Chinese* by Daniel Bryant. WFTU

Climbing up the hillside beneath the summer stars. Man in Nature. William Roscoe Thayer. AA

Climbing You. Erica Jong. PoA

Climbing Zero Gully. David J. Morley. PoSH

Climbs hobbling. A Very Old Woman. Clayton Eshleman. MAT

Clime of the brave! the high heart's home. New England. George Denison Prentice. AA

Cling to Me. John Le Gay Brereton. PeHV

Clinging to my breast, no stronger. Spinster's Lullaby. Vassar Miller. BoWoP; NMM

Clinging to this transient life. Prince Omi, *tr. fr. Japanese*. *Fr.* Manyo Shu. Ma

Clinic Day. Jo Barnes. BrRo

Clinical. William Ernest Henley. *Fr.* In Hospital, XI. BrPo

Clinics. Michael Bachstein. TSM

Clink, clink, clinkety-clink. The Milkman. Clive Sansom. BoTP

Clink of the Ice, The. Eugene Field. AnAmPo
Clinton South of Polk. Carl Sandburg. AmFN
Clio's Protest. Sheridan. FaBoEE
Clip-clop go water-drops and bridles ring. Nude in a Fountain. Norman MacCaig. OxBS
Clipped the nails, the fingers. Ozaki Hosai, tr. fr. Japanese by Hiroaki Sato. Fr. One Hundred Haiku in Free Form. FCEI
Clippety cloppety,/ Cesare Borgia. Chip. George Starbuck. OBAL
Clitoris is a kind of brain, A. Alice Notley. UL
Cloak, The. Violet Anderson. CaP
Clobber the Lobber. Felicia Lamport. RR
Clock, The. Felice Holman. GrPl
Clock. Harold Monro. BrPo
Clock, The. Mauro Moto, tr. fr. Portuguese by Mark Strand. ATCBP
Clock-a-Clay. John Clare. EBEV; EBVV; FaPON; LiTB; NAEL-2; OAEL-2; OBNC; PoEL-4
　(Clock-o'-Clay.) TrGrPo
Clock and Mommie. Jacob Glatstein, tr. fr. Yiddish by Benjamin and Barbara Harshav. Fr. From the Nursery. AYP
Clock gleams, The. 1941. Everette Maddox. MT
Clock in the Square, A. Adrienne Rich. HeIP
Clock is striking autumn at the apple vendor's fair, The. Autumn. Patricia Hubbell. PDV
Clock-o'-Clay. John Clare. See Clock-a-Clay.
Clock of my days winds down, The. The Alligator Bride. Donald Hall. EAS
Clock on Hancock Street. June Jordan. FaBoWP
Clock on the War, The. Samih al-Qasim, tr. fr. Arabic by Abdullah al-Udhari. MPAW
Clock says, The, "When will it be morning?" After Lorca. Ted Hughes. PoA
Clock shows nearly five, The. To a Salesgirl, Weary of Artificial Holiday Trees. James Wright. NYBP
Clock stopped, A. Emily Dickinson. AmPP; NAAL-1; NoP; PoEL-5
Clock stops ticking, The. Stroke. Mike Lowery. Psk
Clock strikes in the cold, A. Song of the Water Clock at Night. Sun Kuang-hsien, tr. by Lois Fusek. ATF
Clock without Hands. John Frederick Nims. PoA
Clocked with the sun and by his journey paced. Homestead—Winter Morning. Mary Ballard Duryee. GoYe
Clocks. Louis Ginsberg. TrJP
Clocks. Malka Locker, tr. fr. Yiddish by Jeremy Garber. VWA
Clocks are sorry, the clocks are very sad, The. Psalm and Lament. Donald Justice. DiPo
Clocks begin, civicly simultaneous, The. At Delft. Charles Tomlinson. NYBP
Clock's Song, The. Rose Hawthorne Lathrop. AA
Clock's untiring fingers wind the wool of darkness, The. Louis MacNeice. MoAB; MoBrPo
　(Cradle Song for Miriam.) NAs
Clocks were running as usual so they waited only. The Fathers of a Star. Zbigniew Herbert, tr. by Czeslaw Milosz. PwPP
Clockwork beings, winding out their lives. Insects. Isidor Schneider. TrJP
Clockwork Doll. Dahlia Ravikovich, tr. fr. Hebrew by Chana Bloch. OV
Clockwork skating Wordsworth on the ice, A. Xmas for the Boys. Gavin Ewart. OBSV
Clod and the Pebble, The. Blake. Fr. Songs of Experience. EnLoPo; EnRP; FaBV; InPS; NAEL-2; NOBE; NoP; OBNC; OxBSP; PoE; PrIm; RB; SCV; TEP; TrGrPo
Clod of earth in his shovel, The. Tending the Garden. Eric Pankey. MOWH
Clodian Songbook, sels. Christian Karlson Stead.
　"Air New Zealand." PeNZ
　"End of scene Catullus." ATNZ
　"Fucking, I feel at one with the world." PeNZ
Clods of earth. Naito Meisetsu, tr. by Geoffrey Bownas and Anthony Thwaite. PeBJV
Cloe ("Bright as the day, and like the morning fair."). George Granville. FaBoCo; FaBoEE; NIP
Cloe. George Granville. See Cloe's the wonder of her sex.
Cloe, blooming sweet as May. To Cloe. Hildebrand Jacob. NOEC
Cloe, by your command, in verse I write. A Letter from Artemisa in the Town, to Cloe, in the Country. Earl of Rochester. SeCV-2
Cloe's the wonder of her sex. To Cloe. George Granville. FaBoEE (at. to Charles Sackville); NBLV
　(Cloe.) OxBSP
Clog with a broken thong. Masaoka Shiki, tr. fr. Japanese by Burton Watson. Fr. Thirty-nine Haiku. FCEI
Clogged ashtray a dead lung, A. Grass, Grass. George Bowering. NeAC

Cloister. Conrad Aiken. See Preludes for Memnon; or, Preludes to Attitude: So, in the evening, to the simple cloister.
Cloistered. Alice Brown. AA
Cloisters. Anthony Barnett. VWA
Clonakilty. Unknown. FaBoEE
Clonfeacle. Paul Muldoon. CIP
Clonmel Jail. Unknown, tr. fr. Irish by Valentin Iremonger. BIrV
Cloudburst an' soarin' mune. Cloudburst and Soaring Moon. "Hugh MacDiarmid." NoAM
Cloosmit the herring, hosts in the night. Ko-Ishin-Mit Goes Fishing. George Clutesi. HATNAP
Clora, come view my soul and tell. The Gallery. Andrew Marvell. MeLP; NoP; OBS; PoE
Clorinda and Damon. Andrew Marvell. SeCP
Cloris, I cannot say your eyes. To Cloris. Sir Charles Sedley. BoLoP
Cloris, it is not thy disdaine. To the Tune of, In Fayth I Cannot Keepe My Father's Sheepe. Sidney Godolphin. OBS
　(Song: "Chloris, it is not thy disdaine.") MeLP
Close by the basement door-step. A Toad. Elizabeth Akers Allen. OBCA
Close by those meads, for ever crowned with flow'rs. Pope. Fr. The Rape of the Lock, III. FiP; OxBoLi, sl. abr.
　(Hampton Court.) FaBoPP, shorter sel.; OBSV, shorter sel.
Close Clan, The. Mark Van Doren. GoYe
Close his eyes; his work is done! Dirge for a Soldier. George Henry Boker. AA; AnAmPo; PAH; WaaP
Close in the hollow bank she lies. The Stockdove. Ruth Pitter. SeCePo
Close keep your lips, if that you meane. To Women, to Hide Their Teeth, if They Be Rotten or Rusty. Robert Herrick. FaBoUs
Close now the door; shut down the light. The Supremer Sacrifice. "Furnley Maurice." CBAP
Close now thine eyes, and rest secure. A Good-Night. Francis Quarles. OBS; TrGrPo
Close of Day, The. Wesley Curtright. CDC
Close of day. Kyorai, tr. fr. Japanese by Burton Watson. Fr. Twenty Hokku. FCEI
Close on the edge of a midsummer dawn. A Shadow of the Night. Thomas Bailey Aldrich. AA
Close Quarters. John Banister Tabb. OBAL
Close Season for Marriage. Unknown. FaBoUs
Close the cloth-plant spreads its fibres. Unknown, tr. by Arthur Waley. BoS
Close the dim eyes, for expression hath left them. Lines on a Dead Girl. Priscilla Jane Thompson. CBWP-2
Close thine eyes, and sleep secure. On a Quiet Conscience. Charles I, King of England. CH
Close to a quarter of a century since then. T. H. Parry-Williams, tr. by Joseph P. Clancy. OBWVE
Close to a tape shop. Sentiment. Sa'di Yusuf, tr. by Lena Jayyusi and Naomi Shihab Nye. MAP
Close to death. Saito Mokichi, tr. by Geoffrey Bownas and Anthony Thwaite. PeBJV
Close to Home. Frank Steele. MOWH
Close to nature my brother, your thoughts ring softly. To an Indian Poet. Patty L. Harjo. VoR
Close to the gates a spacious garden lies. Homer, fr. fr. Greek by Pope. Fr. Odyssey, VII. OBVE
　(Gardens of Alcinous, The.) OAEL-1.
Close to the sod. Snowdrop. Anna Bunston de Bary. BoTP
Close under here, I watched two lovers once. Robin Hyde. Fr. The Beaches, VI. ATNZ; FaBoWP; PeNZ
Close-up. A. R. Ammons. PoA
Close-up. Heather McPherson. PeNZ
Close up the casement, draw the blind. Shut Out That Moon. Thomas Hardy. BrPo; CMoP; NoAM; NOBE
Close up they're seen in fine detail. A Painting of One Hundred Wild Geese. Tai Piao-yüan, tr. by Jonathan Chaves. CoBLCP
Close-ups of Summer. Norman MacCaig. OxBC
Close Your Eyes! Arna Bontemps. AmNP; CDC; FB; PoBA; PoNe
Close your eyes. Pussy Willows. Aileen Fisher. RAR
Closed Door, The. Theodosia Pickering Garrison. BLPA
Closed Door, The. Muhammad al-Faituri, tr. fr. Arabic by Sargon Boulus and Peter Porter. MAP
Closed Doors. Marie Thorson. PWR
Closed eyes can't see the white roses. Give Them the Flowers Now. Unknown. WBLP
Closed is that curious ear by Death's cold hand. Thomas Gray's View of Nature. William Mason. Fr. The English Garden, III. NOEC
Closed, it sleeps. Safety Pin. Valerie Worth. TSS
Closed like confessionals, they thread. Ambulances. Philip Larkin. FaBoTw; NAEL-2; OxBC
Closed System, The. Larry Eigner. VWA

Closed window looks down, A. Ka 'Ba. Amiri Baraka. BPo; CNA; TAP

Closed World, The. Denise Levertov. NoP

Closedown. Kendrick Smithyman. ATNZ

Closer First to Earth. Anne Hazlewood-Brady. IHMS

Closer I come to their huge black-and-white sides, the, less, The. Being Herded Past the Prison's Honor Farm. David Wagoner. SoSe

Closes and courts and lanes. John Davidson. BrPo

Closest to men, thou pitying Son of Man. To Jesus of Nazareth. Frederic Lawrence Knowles. TrPWD

Closing Album, The, *sels.* Louis MacNeice.
    Cushendun. FaBCIP
    Dublin. OBTV

Closing Door, The. Antonia Pozzi, *tr. fr. Italian by* Muriel Kittel. DMI

Closing of the Rodeo, The. William Jay Smith. AiP; ASP; GOA; NePoEA; SaC; SD; TwCP

Closing Piece. Rainer Maria Rilke, *tr. fr. German by* M. D. Herter Norton. PCP

Closing Prayer. Johnstone G. Patrick. TrPWD

Closing Scene, The. Thomas Buchanan Read. AA; AnAmPo

Closing the House. Jim Wayne Miller. MT

Closing Time. James Michie. NePoEA-2

Closing Time. David Wagoner. NYBP

Clote (Water-Lily, The). William Barnes. ELP; PoEL-4

Cloth of Gold. Francis Reginald. MoCV

Cloth-plant grew till it covered the thorn bush, The. *Unknown, tr. by* Arthur Waley. *Fr.* Shih Ching. BoS
    (Widow's Lament.) BoWoP

Cloth-plant on that high mound, The. *Unknown, tr. by* Arthur Waley. BoS

Cloth socks, straw sandals, robe of coarse cloth. Walking to the Temple of Precious Light. Wen Cheng-ming, *tr. by* Jonathan Chaves. CoBLCP

Cloth was laid in the Vorkhouse hall, The. The Workhouse Boy. *Unknown.* GBP

Clothed in yellow, red and green. *Unknown.* OxNR

Clother of the lily, feeder of the sparrow. They Toil Not neither Do They Spin. Christina Rossetti. TrPWD
    (Prayer: "Clother of the lily, feeder of the sparrow.") OBD

Clothes, The. Rayzel Zychlinska, *tr. fr. Yiddish by* Marc Kaminsky. VWA

Clothes Do but Cheat and Cozen Us. Robert Herrick. CaPo; ErPo

Clothes in which you saw me, The. The Clothes. Rayzel Zychlinska, *tr. by* Marc Kaminsky. VWA

Clothes-Line, The. Charlotte Druitt Cole. BoTP

Clothes make no sound when I tread ground. The Swan: "Clothes make no sound when I tread ground." *Unknown, formerly at. to Cynewulf, tr. fr. Anglo-Saxon by* Geoffrey Grigson. *Fr.* Riddles (Exeter Book). ChTr; RB

Clothes Make the Man. Jack Conway. NBLV

Clothes Maketh the Man. Theodore Weiss. NoAM

Clothes Pit, The. Douglas Dunn. OxBTC

Clothespins. Stuart Dybek. ASP

Clothing's New Emperor, The. Donald Finkel. NePoEA

Clotho. Hilaire Kirkland. *Fr.* Clotho, Lachesis, Atropos, I. PeNZ

Clotho, Lachesis, Atropos, *sels.* Hilaire Kirkland. PeNZ
    Atropos. *Fr.* III.
    Clotho. *Fr.* I.
    Lachesis. *Fr.* II.

Cloud, The. Edwin Muir. OBTV

Cloud, The. Shelley. BLPL; ChER; EnRP; FaPON; GN; ImOP; LiTB; NAEL-2; NoP; OHFP; PoEL-4; PWR; TrGrPo

Cloud/ A white horse stands up. Pop Tune. Louis Aragon, *tr. by* Michael Benedikt. POS

Cloud, a reminder of my lover, The. Teika, *tr. fr. Japanese by* Hiroaki Sato. *Fr.* A Compendium of Good Tanka. FCEI

Cloud and water, lonely, desolate. Mooring at Night at the River Mouth, I Heard a Flute. Wang Shih-chen, *tr. by* Jonathan Chaves. CoBLCP

Cloud-backed heron will not move, The. The Heron. Vernon Watkins. GTBS-P; TwCP; UnPo

Cloud Burst. Hubert Witheford. ATNZ

Cloud capped peaks fill the eyes. On a Visit to Ch'ung Chen Taoist Temple. Yu Hsüan-chi, *tr. by* Kenneth Rexroth *and* Ling Chung. PBWP

Cloud Chamber, The. Arthur Sze. BrSi

Cloud clings, The. *Unknown, tr. fr. Japanese. Fr.* Manyo Shu. Ma

Cloud—cloud—cloud—hurls. It. Gary Snyder. LCAP

Cloud Country. James Merrill. NePoEA

Cloud doth gather, the green wood roar, The. Thekla's Song. Schiller, *tr. fr. German by* Samuel Taylor Coleridge. *Fr.* The Piccolomini. AWP

Cloud drifting over the brows, The. Hitomaro, *tr. fr. Japanese. Fr.* Manyo Shu. Ma

Cloud Factory, The. John Haines. EAS

Cloud Fantasy. Henrietta Cordelia Ray. CBWP-3

Cloud fell at noon, A. Flying. Sa'di Yusuf, *tr. by* Abdullah al-Udhari. MPAW

Cloud-Fish, The. Rudolf Bayer, *tr. fr. German by* Beth Bjorklund. CoAuP

Cloud-Flower Lullaby, The. *Unknown, tr. fr. Tewa Indian by* H. J. Spinden. WTO

Cloud in the morning. Fate. W. S. Merwin. KS

Cloud in Trousers, A. Vladimir Mayakovsky, *tr. fr. Russian by* Peter Bogdanoff. SOTW

Cloud is the post office between continents, The. To Modigliani to Prove to Him That I Am a Poet. Max Jacob, *tr. by* Wallace Fowlie. TrJP

Cloud-maidens that float on forever. Song of the Clouds. Aristophanes, *tr. fr. Greek by* Oscar Wilde. *Fr.* The Clouds. AWP

Cloud-Mobile, The. May Swenson. SO

Cloud moved close, A. The bulk of the wind shifted. The Visitant. Theodore Roethke. CMoP; PoE; RB; UnPo

Cloud no bigger than a button, A. Old Champagne Glass. Eddy van Vliet, *tr. by* Theo Hermans. DuIn

Cloud of dust on the long white road, A. The Teams. Henry Lawson. CBAP; PoAu-1

Cloud of esters escapes as Elena splits an orange, A. The Romance of Citrus. Christy Sheffield Sanford. UL

Cloud of witnesses, A. To whom? To what? A Fanfare for the Makers. Louis MacNeice. NOBE

Cloud Parade, The. Laura Jensen. LCAP

Cloud-piles o'er Kona's sea whet my joy, The. Fathomless Is My Love. Kalola, *tr. by* N. B. Emerson. WTO

Cloud possessed the hollow field, A. The High Tide at Gettysburg. Will Henry Thompson. AA; AnAmPo; BeLS; BLPA; FaBoBe; PAH

Cloud-puffball, torn tufts, tossed pillows. That Nature Is a Heraclitean Fire and of the Comfort of the Resurrection. Gerard Manley Hopkins. BrPo; FaBoMo; GTBS-P; LiTB; MoAB; NoP; OAEL-2; PoE; PoEL-5; TEP

Cloud River. Charles Wright. GeTw; MT

Cloud Shadow. Lilian Moore. TDD

Cloud Song. Henrietta Cordelia Ray. CBWP-3

Cloud Spots. Steven Lavoie. UL

Cloud was hidden by the sun as she steeped tea, A. Floating. Michael Brownstein. UL

Cloudburst and Soaring Moon. "Hugh MacDiarmid." NoAM

Cloudburst and steady downpour now. Gifts of Rain. Seamus Heaney. IPY

Clouded Morning, The. Jones Very. NOBA

Clouded with snow. Winter. Walter de la Mare. OAEL-2; OBMV

Cloudless Morning, A. Dov Khomsky, *tr. fr. Hebrew by* Bernhard Frank. MHeP

Clouds, The, *sel.* Aristophanes, *tr. fr. Greek by* Oscar Wilde.
    Song of the Clouds. AWP

Clouds. Rupert Brooke. BrPo; OBEV; OBMV; OxBTC

Clouds, The. William Croswell. AA

Clouds. Philip Levine. LCAP

Clouds, The. João Cabral de Melo Neto, *tr. fr. Portuguese by* Ashley Brown. ATCBP

Clouds, The. Mirabai, *tr. fr. Medieval Hindi, English version by* Robert Bly. NU

Clouds. Jutta Schutting, *tr. fr. German by* Beth Bjorklund. CoAuP

Clouds, The. Arthur Vogelsang. MAYP

Clouds, The. William Carlos Williams. VGW

Clouds/ of the summer, The. Striped Canvas. Robert Grenier. IAT

Clouds and Clay. Valerie Gillies. PoSH

Clouds and the stars didn't wage this war, The. For the Record. Adrienne Rich. CAPP; NIP

"Clouds and water block the way home." The Ailing Japanese Monk. Hsiang Ssu, *tr. by* Burton Watson. CoBCP

Clouds are hair, The. The Clouds. João Cabral de Melo Neto, *tr. by* Ashley Brown. ATCBP

Clouds are swept into the sunset—a sky beyond the sky. Chu Yün-ming, *tr. fr. Chinese by* Jonathan Chaves. *Fr.* Poem Inscribed on a Landscape Painting. CoBLCP

Clouds are swirling, clouds are straying. Phantoms of the Steppe. Pushkin, *tr. by* Edna Worthley Underwood. WSC

Clouds Are the First Fatalities, The. Yehuda Amichai, *tr. fr. Hebrew by* Bernhard Frank. MHeP

Clouds at the border are white in a pale autumn sky, The. Deva-like Barbarian. Yin O, *tr. by* Lois Fusek. ATF

Clouds behind the Forest, *sels.* H. Leivick, *tr. fr. Yiddish by* Benjamin *and* Barbara Harshav. AYP
    Again a Neighbor Died.

"Clouds behind the forest come close to the tops of the trees."
  Open up, Gate.
Clouds behind the forest come close to the tops of the trees. H. Leivick,
  tr. fr. Yiddish by Benjamin and Barbara Harshav. Fr. Clouds behind
  the Forest. AYP
Clouds burn, the sun sets, The. Wakayama Bokusui, tr. fr. Japanese by
  Hiroaki Sato. Fr. Forty-four Tanka. FCEI
Clouds darken the plain. Hand. Edouard Roditi. EAS
Clouds darken, then disperse. Boating on Feng Stream on the Double
  Fifth. Chang Hui-yen, tr. by Michael Duke. WFTU
Clouds dissolve into blueness. Hearing of the End of the War. Richard
  Tillinghast. MAYP
Clouds fill the sky. The Morning after. . .Love. Kattie M. Cumbo.
  BlSi
Clouds from Matiatia Bay. The Uses of Clouds. Gregory O'Brien.
  ATNZ
Clouds from the peak. Tameko, tr. by Steven D. Carter. WFTW
Clouds have come up from the south, the Nile's. Yehuda Amichai, tr. fr.
  Hebrew by Warren Bargad and Stanley F. Chyet. Fr. Achziv, 1. IP
Clouds Have Left the Sky, The. Robert Bridges. CH
Clouds in the sky at twilight. The Violin Calls. Florence Randal
  Livesay. CaP
Clouds lift off Flagstaff, The. Listening to the Mountain. Brian Turner.
  ATNZ
Clouds like wolves above the roasted mountains. The Indigo Eater.
  "Lucebert," tr. by Scott Rollins. DuIn
Clouds, lingering yet, extend in solid bars. Composed by the Side of
  Grasmere Lake. Wordsworth. ChER
Clouds now and then. Basho, tr. by Geoffrey Bownas and Anthony
  Thwaite. PeBJV
Clouds of Evening. Robinson Jeffers. MoAmPo
Clouds of May rain have closed into one, The. Princess Shikishi, tr. fr.
  Japanese by Hiroaki Sato. Fr. Seventy-eight Tanka. FCEI
Clouds on the Sea. Ruth Dallas. Fr. Letter to a Chinese Poet, IV.
  PeNZ
Clouds over Islands. James Seay. MT
Clouds scattered across the sky all so far away. The Words. Lee
  Harwood. EAS
Clouds shouldered a path up the mountains, The. The Drought. Gary
  Soto. NoAM
Clouds that are barely still clouds. Clouds. Jutta Schutting, tr. by Beth
  Bjorklund. CoAuP
Clouds That Are So Light, The. Edward Thomas. FaBoTw
Clouds that drift so far and free. The Wife's Thoughts. Hsü Kan, tr. by
  Burton Watson. CoBCP
Clouds, the source of rain, one stormy night, The. Lost in Heaven.
  Robert Frost. MoAmPo
Clouds were fishbone, The. Walden in July. Donald Junkins. NYBP
Clouds, which rise with thunder, slake, The. All's Well. Whittier.
  OxBSP
Clouds' Work. Ferreira Gullar, tr. fr. Portuguese by Paul Blackburn.
  ATCBP
Cloudy Bay. Ellen Duggan. PeNZ
Cloudy Day. Jimmy Santiago Baca. InPS
Clove, salmon knocking. For Lerida. David St. John. AmPA; AnAn
Clover, The. Margaret Deland. AA
Clover, The. James Whitcomb Riley. AnAmPo
Clover. John Banister Tabb. AA
Clover-burr was two feet high, and the billabongs were full, The. Irish
  Lords. Charles H. Souter. PoAu-1
Clover Flower, The. Ali Abdallah Khalifa, tr. fr. Arabic by Lena Jayyusi
  and Alistair Elliot. MAP
Clown, The. Dorothy Aldis. PDV
Clown, The. Janet Frame. ATNZ; PeNZ
Clown, The. Donald Hall. NYBP
Clown, and All the Sea behind Him. Vincent O'Sullivan. ATNZ
Clown of Karahamba used to crumble, The. Kol-Nidre. Moyshe-Leyb
  Halpern, tr. by Benjamin and Barbara Harshav and Kathryn Helle.
  AYP
Clownlike, happiest on your hands. You're. Sylvia Plath. FaBoTw;
  FaBoWP; NAs; RB
Clowns, The. Jules Laforgue, tr. fr. French by William Jay Smith. CT
Clown's Song, The. Shakespeare. See Twelfth Night: Come Away,
  Come Away, Death.
Cloying sea envelopes man at birth, A. Adventure. Guy Mason. CaP
Clubs Are Trump. Benjamin Péret, tr. fr. French by Michael Benedikt.
  POS
Clubwoman. Mary Carter Smith. PoNe
Clucking Hen, The. Unknown. BoTP
Clue, The. Charlotte Fiske Bates. AA
Clues to Displaced Persons. Mark Jarman. BLA
Clumped murmuring above a sump of loam. The Woodlot. Amy
  Clampitt. HCAP

Clumsy clot of shadow in the fold, A. A Moth. Henry Bellyse Baildon.
  NOBVV
Clumsy in his drunken joints. Animal Pictures. Lawrence Locke. GrPl
Clusters in Thy vineyard turn to gold, O God, The. Grape-gathering.
  Avraham Shlonsky, tr. by I. M. Lask. TrJP
Clusters of cold-weather blossoms. Ch'ien Ch'ien-i, tr. fr. Chinese by
  Jonathan Chaves. Fr. In Lamplight, Watching My Wife Preparing a
  Flower. CoBLCP
Clusters of ruins on vine-shoots of steel. Grave at Cassino. Noah Stern,
  tr. by Harold Schimmel. VWA
Clusters of water chestnuts are blooming on the pond. Immortal at the
  River. Yin O, tr. by Lois Fusek. ATF
Clyde's Water[s], diff. versions. Unknown. ESPB, A and B vers.;
  OxBB, with music.
Cnut's Song. Unknown. Fr. Canute at Ely. PoE
Co-operation. J. Mason Knox. BLPA
Co ye to? Tanks. Mirko Lauer, tr. by David Tipton. Per
Coach,/ Carriage. Unknown. OxNR
Coach has taught her how to swing, The. Instruction. Conrad Hilberry.
  ASP
Coach is at the door at last, The. Farewell to the Farm. Robert Louis
  Stevenson. BoTP; FaPON
Coach-wheels crunch, The. Unknown, tr. by Arthur Waley. BoS
Coachman's Yarn, The. Edwin James Brady. PoAu-1
Coal. Audre Lorde. BlSi; CNA; NoAM; NoP; PoBA
Coal Diggin' Blues. Unknown. AmFP
Coal Fire in Winter, A. Thomas McGrath. NU
Coal Loadin' Blues. Unknown. AmFP
Coal Miner's Goodbye, A. Unknown. AmFP
Coal-Owner and the Pitman's Wife, The. Unknown. CoMu
Coal-white bird appeares this spring, A. Almanac Verse. Samuel
  Danforth. SCAP
Coalmen, The. László Nagy, tr. fr. Hungarian by Tony Connor. MHuP
Coals raked out on hearthstones writhe like men. Where We Are.
  Judson Mitcham. KS
Coarse/ jocosity/ catches the crowd. Archy Confesses. Don Marquis.
  Fr. Archy and Mehitabel. FiBHP
Coarse Old Maid, The. Leyzer Volf, tr. fr. Yiddish by Robert Friend.
  PeBMYV
Coast hills at Sovranes Creek, The. The Place for No Story. Robinson
  Jeffers. AiP
Coast, The: Norfolk. Frances Cornford. OxBTC
Coast to Coast. Adrienne Rich. NIP
Coast View, A, sel. Charles Harpur.
  "Dead city walls may pen us in, but still." CBAP
Coastguard House, The. Robert Lowell; fr. ad. the Italian of Eugenio
  Montale. NAP
Coastline. Elaine Feinstein. BrRo
Coat, A. W. B. Yeats. CMoP; LiTM; NAEL-2; NoAM; OxBSP;
  PoEL-5
Coat of Arms. Alan Dugan. DiL
Coati-Mundi. William Jay Smith. ILY
Coaxin.' Joseph Ramsbottom. PF
Cob, thou nor soldier, thief, nor fencer art. To Pertinax Cob. Ben
  Jonson. JCP
"Cobalt and umber and ultramarine." The Paint Box. Emile Victor Rieu.
  RHPC; SO
Cobalt water. Winter Time. Robert Louis Stevenson. ER
Cobb Would Have Caught It. Robert Fitzgerald. GrPl; HAP; InvP; SD;
  TwCP; WeW
Cobbe's Prophecies. Unknown. NA
Cobbler, The. Unknown. BoTP
Cobbler, cobbler, mend my shoe. Mother Goose. OxNR
Cobbler's Song, The. at. to Charles Tilney. Fr. Locrine. OBSC
Cobbles live in the house next door, The. Neighbors. Mary Ann
  Hoberman. ILY
Coble o Cargill, The. Unknown. ESPB
Coblerone I'm told, A. Mutton and Leather. Unknown. CoMu
Cobra is the night image of a chinese water-print. North Express. Joyce
  Mansour, tr. by the author. WPOW
Cobwebs. E. L. M. King. BoTP
Cobwebs. Christina Rossetti. NAEL-2
Cobwebs and dust have long. Hut near Desolated Pines. Alistair
  Campbell. ATNZ
Cocaine Lil [and Morphine Sue]. Unknown. AS; GBP; MAT; OxBoLi;
  RB
Cock. Aharon Amir, tr. fr. Hebrew. MHeP, tr. by Bernhard Frank
Cock, The. Ewa Lipska, tr. fr. Polish by Peter Jay and Geri Lipschultz.
  VWA
Cock-a-doodle-do! 'tis the bravest game. Cock-throwing. Martin
  Lluellyn. PBBP
Cock a doodle doo!/ My dame has lost her shoe. Mother Goose. BoTP;
  OxNR

Cock-a-doodle-doo the brass-lined rooster goes [*or* says].   Dog.   John
  Crowe Ransom.   InPS; LiTA; OBAL
Cock-a-Hoop.   Isabella Gardner.   WPE
Cock and his hen perching in the night, A.   The Cock and the Hen.   John
  Heywood.   PBBP
Cock and the Bull, The.   Charles Stuart Calverley.   BXAP; FaBoCo;
  FaBoNo; FaBoPa; NA; Par
Cock and the Fox, The.   La Fontaine, *tr. fr. French by* Elizur Wright.
  AWP
Cock and the Hen, The.   Chaucer.   *See* Canterbury Tales, The: Nun's
  Priest's Tale, The.
Cock and the Hen, The.   John Heywood.   PBBP
Cock before Dawn.   Norman MacCaig.   OxBC
Cock, cock, cock, cock.   *Unknown.*   OxNR
Cock-Crow.   Ralph Nixon Currey.   PeSA
Cock-Crow.   Robert Herrick.   PBBP
Cock-Crow.   Edward Thomas.   GTBS-P; MoAB; MoBrPo; OxBSP; RB
Cock-crowing.   Henry Vaughan.   MePo; OAEL-1; PBBP; SeCV-1
Cock Crows, The.   Saibara, *tr. fr. Japanese by* Hiroaki Sato.   FCEI
Cock crows, The.   Depression before Spring.   Wallace Stevens.   OBAL;
  SOTW
Cock crows in the morn, The.   Mother Goose.   PBBP
Cock doth crow, The/ To let you know.   Mother Goose.   OxNR
Cock doth crow, the wind doth blow, The.   Mother Goose.   GBP
Cock gaed to Rome, seeking shoon, seeking shoon, The.   *Unknown.*
  PBBP
Cock has crowed, The.   *Unknown, tr. by* Arthur Waley.   BoS
Cock is crowing, The.   Written in March.   Wordsworth.   BoNaP; BoTP;
  EnRP; FaPON; GoJo; NAEL-2; NTCP; PYC; UnPo
  (Merry Month of March, The.)   MoShBr
Cock of Glory is the *coq français*, The.   The French, 1870-1871.
  Unknown.   FaBoEE
Cock of the Game, The.   *Unknown.*   OBET
Cock Robin got up early.   *Unknown.*   BoTP; OxNR; PBBP
Cock shall crow, The.   Robert Louis Stevenson.   TrGrPo
Cock-throwing.   Martin Lluellyn.   PBBP
Cockaigne: A Dream.   L. E. Sissman.   DiPo
Cockcrow.   Ted Hughes.   AnAn
Cocker of Snooks, A.   Phyllis Gotlieb.   NOBC
Cockies of Bungaree.   *Unknown.*   PoAu-1
Cockle-Shell and Sandal-Shoon.   Herbert T. J. Coleman.   CaP
Cockles and Mussels.   *Unknown.*   ELP
Cockney of the North, The.   Harry Graham.   CenHV
Cockpit in the Clouds.   Dick Dorrance.   FaPON; RHPC
Cockroach.   Mary Ann Hoberman.   *Fr.* Bugs.   OBCA
Cockroaches.   Kaye Starbird.   RHPC
Cocks in the north at dawn.   Dawn in the Cockloft.   José Juan Tablada,
  tr. by Samuel Beckett.   MexPo
Cock's on the wood pile, The.   *Unknown.*   OxNR
Cocktail is a pleasant drink, The.   R-E-M-O-R-S-E.   George Ade.
  FiBHP; NBLV; OBAL
Cocoa Morning.   Bob Kaufman.   AmNP
Cocoa-Tree, The.   Charles Warren Stoddard.   AA
Coconut, The.   "Ande."   FiBHP
Coconut.   Mario Satz, *tr. fr. Spanish. by* Willis Barnstone.   VWA
Coconut.   Shimazaki Toson, *tr. fr. Japanese by* Geoffrey Bownas *and*
  Anthony Thwaite.   PeBJV
Coconut, The.   Shimazaki Toson, *tr. fr. Japanese by* Burton Watson.
  FCEI
Coconut for Katerina, A.   Sandra McPherson.   LCAP
Cocoon.   Ishigaki Rin, *tr. fr. Japanese by* Ayusawa Takako.   WPOW
Cocoon.   David McCord.   OBCA
Cocooning, The.   Frédéric Mistral, *tr. fr. Provençal by* Harriet Waters
  Preston.   *Fr.* Mirèio.   AWP
Coda.   Basil Bunting.   *Fr.* Briggflatts [An Autobiography].   OAEL-2
Coda, *sel.*   Marilyn Hacker.
  "Did you love well what very soon you left?."   NoAM
Coda.   Fred Johnson.   CNA
Coda.   Louis MacNeice.   FaBCIP
Coda.   Ezra Pound.   NOBA
Coda.   Shafiq al-Kamali, *tr. fr. Arabic by* Sargon Boulus *and* Christopher
  Middleton.   MAP
Coda.   James Tate.   AmPA; NYBP
Coda.   William Carlos Williams.   NOBA
Coda: Greed Part 12—Looking for Beethoven in Las Vegas.   Diane
  Wakoski.   ER
Coda: Revising History.   Paul Mariani.   MAYP
Coda: The Higher Keys, *sel.*   James Merrill.
  "Empty perfection, as I take you in."   NoAM
Code, The.   Robert Frost.   OBNV; PoA; UnPo
Code of Morals, A.   Kipling.   FaBoCo
Codes.   Diana Chang.   BrSi
Codex.   Clark Coolidge.   IAT

Codex.   Stephen Rodefer.   IAT; UL
Codex Minor.   Rachel Hadas.   EOEF
Codfish lays ten thousand eggs, The.   Advertisement.   *Unknown.*
  FaBoUs
  (Codfish, The.)   RHPC
Codfish Shanty, The.   *Unknown.*   GBP
Codicil.   Mabel MacDonald Carver.   GoYe
Codicil.   Ruth Stone.   BoWoP
Codicil.   Derek Walcott.   MoP; NoAM
Coelia, *sels.*   William Percy.
  "Judged by my goddess' doom to endless pain."   *Fr.* I.   Son
  "Relent, my dear yet unkind Coelia."   *Fr.* XVII.   AAS; Son
  "It shall be said [*or* sayd] I died [*or* dy'de] for Coelia."   *Fr.* XIX.   EiL
Coesper erat: tunc lubriciles ultravia circum.   Mors Iabrochii.   *Unknown.*
  NA
Coeur de Lion to Berengaria.   Theodore Tilton.   AA
Coffee.   J. V. Cunningham.   MoAmPo; PrIm; VGW
Coffee, The/ the cigarettes.   Canyon Day Woman Blues.   Geraldine
  Keams.   GOS
Coffee and jasmine on a tray.   Convalescence.   James McAuley.   CBAP
Coffee cups cool on the Vicar's harmonium.   A Game of Consequences.
  Paul Dehn.   ErPo; FiBHP; NOBL
Coffee-House Philosopher, The.   Giuseppe Gioacchino Belli, *tr. fr. Italian
  by* Harold Norse.   PFI
Coffee-stained, knife-cut tablecloth.   Amy Károlyi, *tr. fr. Hungarian by*
  Laura Schiff.   *Fr.* The Third House, V.   OV
Coffin, The.   Heine, *tr. fr. German by* Louis Untermeyer.   AWP
Coffin bearing the face of a boy, A.   A Mirror for the Twentieth Century.
  "Adunis", *tr. by* Abdullah al-Udhari.   MPAW
Coffin-Worm, The.   Ruth Pitter.   MoBrPo
Cognition, Language, Poetry.   László Nagy, *tr. fr. Hungarian by* Jascha
  Kessler.   FOC
Coiffed in a crown of thorns.   Glory.   Jacques Prévert, *tr. by* Michael
  Benedikt.   POS
Coiled like a lyncher's rope.   Portrait in Georgia.   Jean Toomer.
  NAAL-2
Coilyear, gudlie in feir, tuke him be the hand, The.   *Unknown.*   *Fr.* Rauf
  Coilyear.   OxBS
Coin in the Fist.   Florence Kerr Brownell.   GoYe
Coins handsome as Nero's; of good substance and weight.   Geoffrey Hill.
  Fr. Mercian Hymns, XI.   FaBoMo; HAP; NoAM
Cokkils.   Sydney Goodsir Smith.   OxBS; PoA
Col. Bascombe had in his garden a boiler.   Englishry.   W. G. Shepherd.
  NPo
Cold.   Brian Coffey.   CIP
Cold.   Robert Francis.   LCAP; PoA
Cold, The.   Lance Henson.   CDW
Cold.   Dorothy Roberts.   NOBC
Cold, The.   Charles Simic.   HCAP
Cold and brilliant streams the sunlight on the wintry banks of Seine.
  Funeral of Napoleon I.   Sir John H. Hagarty.   CaP
Cold and Heat.   *Unknown, tr. fr. Hawaiian by* M. W. Beckwith.   WTO
Cold and silent, the dew deep in the night.   Tune: Cuckoo Sky.   Singde,
  tr. by Julie Landau.   WFTU
Cold and starry darkness moans, A.   Ghosts.   Harry Behn.   RHPC
Cold and the colors of cold: mineral, shell.   Cold.   Robert Francis.
  LCAP; PoA
Cold April, A.   *Unknown.*   FaBoUs
Cold Are the Crabs.   Edward Lear.   FaBoNo; GoJo; NAEL-2
  (Sonnet, A: "Cold are the crabs that crawl on yonder hills.")   CenHV
Cold as no love, and wild with all negation.   Stevie Smith.   FaBoEE
Cold as no plea.   The Death Sentence.   Stevie Smith.   NoP
Cold as the breath of winds that blow.   Lucasta's World.   Richard
  Lovelace.   CaPo; SeCP
Cold as the thin Marquis who bit when kissing.   The Lucifer.   Guy
  Glover.   CaP
Cold autumn winds cut sharply at her grief, The.   Jade Butterflies.   Wen
  T'ing-yün, *tr. by* Lois Fusek.   ATF
Cold beams chinking.   Equinoctial.   István Vas, *tr. by* Jascha Kessler.
  FOC
Cold black soup.   Swan Song.   Morton Marcus.   NAmP
Cold blast at the casement beats, The.   The Heart's Summer.   Epes
  Sargent.   AA
Cold-blooded Creatures.   Elinor Wylie.   ImOP; OxBSP
Cold-blooded in warm waters, my Nurse.   Among Sharks.   Al Lee.
  AmPA
Cold blows the blast—the night's obscure.   George Colman the Younger.
  Fr. Maid of the Moor, The; or, The Water-Fiends.   NOEC
Cold blows the northern wind.   *Unknown, tr. by* Arthur Waley.   BoS
Cold Blows the Wind.   John Hamilton.   CH
Cold blows the wind to my true-love [*or* tonight, sweetheart].   The
  Unquiet Grave.   *Unknown.*   FaBoBa; OBET

Cold blows the winter wind: 'tis Love. Love at the Door. Meleager, *tr.*
   by John Addington Symonds. AWP
Cold chain of life presseth heavily on me tonight, The. Adah Isaacs
   Menken. CBWP-1
Cold, clear, and blue, the morning heaven. The Morning Star. Emily
   Brontë. ChTr
Cold, coiled line of mottled lead, A. Massasauga. Hamlin Garland.
   AA
Cold! Cold!/ Wide Lurg Plain is cold tonight. *Unknown.* NOIV
Cold, cold!/ Cold tonight is broad Moylurg. A Song of Winter.
   Unknown, tr. by Kuno Meyer. AnIL; CH
Cold, cold is the north wind and rude is the blast. The Battle of Lovell's
   Pond. Longfellow. PAH
Cold, cold the year draws to its end. Old Poem. *Unknown, tr. by* Arthur
   Waley. AWP; BoWoP
Cold Colloquy. Patrick Anderson. *Fr.* Poem on Canada, V. CaP;
   NOBC
Cold comes about, The. North Dakota, North Light. N. Scott Momaday.
   HATNAP
"Cold coming we had of it, A." Journey of the Magi. T. S. Eliot.
   EaLo; FaBoCh; FaBoMo; FaFP; HAP; HeIP; InPK; LiTA; LiTM;
   MoAB; MoAmPo; NAEL-2; NIP; NOCV; NoP; OBCP; OBMV;
   OxBTC; PChr; PoE; SoSe; TAP; TrGrPo; TwCP
Cold days sit where it's warm. Written on the Wall of Pan-shan Temple.
   Wang An-shih, *tr. by* Burton Watson. CoBCP
Cold, deserted and silent. *Unknown.* *Fr.* Winter on Black Mingo.
   FiBHP
Cold dew of heaven has fallen, The. Lady Otomo no Sakanoe, *tr. fr.*
   Japanese. *Fr.* Manyo Shu. Ma
Cold drool on his chin, warm drool in his lap, a sigh. A Dimpled Cloud.
   Frederick Seidel. FYAP
Cold earth slept below, The. Shelley. ChER; EnRP
Cold Fear. Elizabeth Madox Roberts. WPE
Cold Fire. George Starbuck. NYBP
Cold Fly. Yang Wan-li, *tr. fr. Chinese by* Burton Watson. CoBCP
Cold Front, A. William Carlos Williams. NAs
Cold Glow: Icehouses. David Wojahn. MAYP
Cold Green Element, The. Irving Layton. NOBC; NoP; OBCV
Cold grey walls. San Francisco County Jail Cell B-6. Conyus. PoBA
Cold has put blue horses where lambs were, The. Blue Horses. Ed
   Roberson. PoBA
Cold Heaven, The. W. B. Yeats. AWP; CTC; GTBS-P; HAP; NoAM;
   OAEL-2; OxBSP; RB; TEP; WeW
Cold holds its own, inside and out. Si Monumentum Requiris. Daryl
   Hine. EOEF
Cold in the earth   and the deep snow piled above thee. Remembrance.
   Emily Brontë. BLPL; BoLoP; BoWoP; CH; EBEV; EnLoPo; FaFP;
   HAP; LiTB; NAEL-2; NOBE; NoBVV; NoP; OBNC; PBWP; PoE;
   PoEL-5; TEP; TrGrPo; WeW; WPE
   (R. Alcona to J. Brenzaida.) BrRo; EBVV; OPOP
Cold in the Grass. Kenko, *tr. fr. Japanese by* Steven D. Carter. WFTW
Cold Irish Earth, The. Knute Skinner. InPK
Cold Iron. Kipling. OnMSP
Cold Is the North Wind. *Unknown, tr. fr. Chinese by* Burton Watson.
   CoBCP
Cold is the winter. The wind is risen. *Unknown.* NOIV
Cold limbs of the air, The. A Mountain Wind. "Æ." AWP
Cold Logic. Barney Hutchinson. SD
Cold Miao, the Savage Miao, rose up in revolt, The. On Hearing That on
   the Sixteenth Day of the Tenth Month the Magistrate of Li-po, Chiang
   Hsiao-yün, *tzu* Chia-ku, of Shao-hsing/ Attacked the Rebels. Cheng
   Chen, *tr. by* William Schultz. WFTU
Cold mist, sparse. Evening Bell from Misty Temple. Ma Chih-yüan, *tr.*
   fr. Chinese by Jonathan Chaves. *Fr.* Three Poems to the tune "Lo-
   mei Feng," 2. CoBLCP
Cold moon: a white sheet. Kaya Shirao, *tr. fr. Japanese by* Hiroaki Sato.
   Fr. Twenty-one Hokku. FCEI
Cold moon: amidst dead trees. Suburb ("Cold moon: amidst dead trees").
   Buson, *tr. fr. Japanese by* Hiroaki Sato. *Fr.* Eighty-seven Hokku.
   FCEI
Cold moon hangs to the sky by its horn, The. The Night of the Dance.
   Thomas Hardy. BrPo
Cold moon led us coldly, The. Shooting Ducks in South Louisiana.
   Richard Tillinghast. MAYP
Cold moon—the sound of the bridge. Taigi, *tr. fr. Japanese by* Hiroaki
   Sato. *Fr.* Twenty-nine Hokku. FCEI
Cold morning early. Two Mornings. Lawrence McGaugh. PoBA
Cold morning, in a public men's room. Winter: 1955. Takahashi
   Mutsuo, *tr. by* Hiroaki Sato. FCEI
Cold Night. Ch'en Shih-tao, *tr. fr. Chinese by* Burton Watson. CoBCP
Cold night/ pasania nuts rolling down. Kyotai, *tr. fr. Japanese by* Burton
   Watson. *Fr.* Sixteen Hokku. FCEI

Cold Night. A. Leyeles, *tr. fr. Yiddish by* Benjamin *and* Barbara
   Harshav. AYP
Cold Night. Nakahara Chuya, *tr. fr. Japanese by* Geoffrey Bownas *and*
   Anthony Thwaite. PeBJV
Cold Night, A. Bernard Spencer. WaP
Cold night: I keep a vigil. Issa, *tr. fr. Japanese by* Hiroaki Sato. *Fr.*
   Forty-four Hokku. FCEI
Cold-night Moon—In the Manner of Meng Tung-yeh. Huang Tsung-hsi,
   tr. fr. Chinese by Lynn Struve. WFTU
Cold night, the sidewalk we walk on icy, A. Christmas Eve Service at
   Midnight at St. Michael's. Robert Bly. NNaP
Cold Nights. Basho, *tr. fr. Japanese by* Burton Watson. *Fr.* Seventy-six
   Hokku. FCEI
Cold nights outside the taverns in Wyoming. Accountability. William
   Stafford. LCAP; NoP
Cold Oxford unfamiliar now, around. Above the High. Geoffrey
   Grigson. EnLoPo
Cold penetrates to the river's shore. To the Tune "Flowers in the Rain."
   Yang Shen, *tr. by* Jonathan Chaves. CoBLCP
Cold rain beats the river, the wind's contrary, too, A. A Contrary Wind.
   Ho Shao-chi, *tr. by* J. D. Schmidt. WFTU
Cold rain swirls savagely. Night Song of a Traveller. Tachihara
   Michizo, *tr. by* Geoffrey Bownas *and* Anthony Thwaite. PeBJV
Cold Reeds around an Inlet. Tameshige, *tr. fr. Japanese by* Steven D.
   Carter. WFTW
Cold Reeds around the Inlet. Joben, *tr. fr. Japanese by* Steven D. Carter.
   WFTW
Cold remote islands, The. Night. Louise Bogan. UnPo
Cold Rendering, A. *Unknown.* BXAP
Cold, Sharp Lamentation. Douglas Hyde, *tr. fr. Irish by* Lady Gregory.
   OBMV
Cold shuttered loveless star, skulker in clouds. News of the World I
   ("Cold shuttered loveless star, skulker in clouds"). George Barker.
   LiTB
Cold slope is standing in darkness, The. December Night. W. S.
   Merwin. CAPP
Cold, smoldering, The. A Love Dirge to the Whitehouse. Bob Fletcher.
   NBP
Cold soft drinks. Sho Nuff. Nilene O. A. Foxworth. AIW
Cold Spring, A. Elizabeth Bishop. TwCP
Cold spring day. Kawahigashi Hekigoto, *tr. by* Geoffrey Bownas *and*
   Anthony Thwaite. PeBJV
Cold stings your bare cheeks and arms, The. To a Cactus Seller. Anwar
   Shaul, *tr. by* Yoffee Berkovitz. VWA
Cold Term. Amiri Baraka. BPo; CNA; SOTW
Cold transparent male is on my fork, The. Sonnet to Vauxhall. Thomas
   Hood. PoEL-4
Cold was the night wind, drifting fast the snows fell. The Widow.
   Robert Southey. NOEC
Cold-Weather Love. Ronald G. Everson. MoCV
Cold wind at evening, A. Ballad of Yi River. Ho Ching-ming, *tr. by*
   Jonathan Chaves. CoBLCP
Cold wind, my wife is dead, what really matters though. boy, it's cold.
   Anniversary. Giancarlo Majorino, *tr. by* Lawrence R. Smith. NItP
Cold wind stirs the blackthorn, A. Endure Hardness. Christina Rossetti.
   NOBVV
Cold winds swept the mountain's height, The. The Mother in the Snow-
   Storm. Sebald Smithon. MoCV
Cold winter's in the wood. In the Wood. Eileen Mathias. BoTP
Colder Fire. Robert Penn Warren. *Fr.* To a Little Girl, One Year Old,
   in a Ruined Fortress. LiTM
Colder than the snow. Joso, *tr. fr. Japanese by* Hiroaki Sato. *Fr.*
   Fifteen Hokku. FCEI
Coldly, sadly descends. Rugby Chapel. Matthew Arnold. PoEL-5;
   WGRP
Coldness, The. Jon Silkin. VWA
Cold's the wind, and wet's the rain. Drinking Song. Thomas Dekker.
   Fr. The Shoemaker's Holiday. TrGrPo
   (Hey Derry Derry.) SeCePo
   (Saint Hugh.) OBSC
   (Troll the Bowl!) EIl
Cole Porter's Son. Gerrit Henry. EOEF
Cole, that unwearied prince of Colchester. Variations of [*or* on] an Air:
   After Alfred Lord Tennyson. G. K. Chesterton. FaBoPa; NOBL;
   Par
Cole Younger. *Unknown.* AmFP; BeLS
Colebrook Dale, *sel.* Anna Seward.
   "While neighbouring cities waste the fleeting hours." NOEC
Colenso Rhymes for Orthodox Children. Bret Harte. OBAL
Coleridge. Medbh McGuckian. CIP
Coleridge. R. S. Thomas. TOF
Coleridge. Theodore Watts-Dunton. Son

Coleridge caused his wife unrest. Theme and Variation. Peter De Vries. NYBP

Coleridge Crossing the Plain of Jars; 1833. Norman Dubie. LCAP

Coleridge received the Person from Porlock. Thoughts about the Person from Porlock. Stevie Smith. FaBoCo; NAEL-2; NoAM; NoP

Cole's Island. Charles Olson. *Fr.* The Maximus Poems. PoM

Colin. Anthony Munday. *See* Primaleon of Greece: Beauty Sat Bathing by a Spring.

Colin Clout, *sels.* John Skelton.
　"And if ye stand in doubt." NAEL-1; OAEL-1
　"Doctors that learned be." OBSV
　Prelates, The. TrGrPo

Colin Clout's Come Home Again, *sels.* Spenser.
　Colin Clout at Court. OBSC
　Her Heards Be Thousand Fishes. ChTr
　"Of loves perfection perfectly to speake." OAEL-1

Colin, my dear and most entire beloved. To the Most Excellent and Learned Shepherd, Colin Clout. William Smith. *Fr.* Chloris. AAS; Son

Colin, my deare, when shall it please thee sing. November. Spenser. *Fr.* The Shepheardes [*or* Shepeards *or* Shepherd's] Calender. PoEL-1

Dido My Dear, Alas, Is Dead. ChTr

Colin, you can tell my words are crippled now. James Keir Baxter. *Fr.* Jerusalem Sonnets, XXXVII. PeNZ

Colin's Passion of Love. George Peele. *See* Arraignment of Paris, The: O Gentle Love.

Coliseum, The. Poe. AmPP; NOBA

Colkelbie Sow, *sel. Unknown.*
　"Penny lost in the lak, The." OxBS

Collage for Richard Davis—Two Short Forms, A. De Leon Harrison. PoBA

Collapsars. Sandra McPherson. LCAP

Collapsible. Tom Raworth. EAS

Collapsible lover, the spider in iniquitousness, The. Anthology of Nouns. Parker Tyler. PoA

Collar, The. George Herbert. AWP; BLPL; EaLo; EBEV; HAP; HeIP; InPS; JCP; LiTB; MeLP; MePo; NAEL-2; NOBE; NOCV; NoP; OAEL-1; OBS; OBWVE; PoE; PoEL-2; PoRA; PPP; SCV; SeCePo; SeCP; SeCV-1; TEP; TOF; TrGrPo; WeW

Collarbone of a Hare, The. W. B. Yeats. OxBTC; RB

Collect the silver on a Sunday. The Lucky Coin. Austin Clarke. NeIP

Collected Time. Otto Laaber, *tr. fr. German by* Beth Bjorklund. CoAuP

Collecting Antiques. Cheng Hsieh, *tr. fr. Chinese by* Jonathan Chaves. CoBLCP

Collection of Emblemes, Ancient and Moderne, A, *sel.* George Wither.
　"Why, silly Man! so much admirest thou." SeCV-1

Collection of Hymns. of the Moravian Brethren, A, *sels. Unknown.*
　"Chicken blessed and caressed." NOEC
　"What does a bird in Cross's air." NOEC

Collection of umbrellas, A. Grains of Sand on a Radio. K. Schippers, *tr. by* Peter Nijmeijer. DuIn

Collective Portrait, The. Robert Finch. MoCV

Collective Shot, A. Jaime Suárez Quemain, *tr. fr. Spanish by* Wilfredo Castaño. Vol

Collector, The. Desirée Flynn. BrRo

Collector, The. Raymond Souster. ErPo; OBCV

Collector of lost beads, buttons, bird bones. The Pack Rat. Robert Pack. PPP

Collector of the Sun, The. Dave Smith. SM

Collectors are abroad, the nets are spread. At the Museum. John Malcolm Brinnin. EyDe

Colleen Rue. *Unknown.* BIrV

College Cat, The. Alfred Denis Godley. CenHV

College Colonel, The. Herman Melville. AA; OBWP

College of Surgeons, The. James Stephens. AnIL

Colley's Run-I-O. *Unknown.* AmFP

Collier, The. Vernon Watkins. FaBoTw; OBWVE

Collier Lad's Lament, The. *Unknown.* OBET

Collier Lass, The. Frankie Armstrong. BrRo

Colliers' March, The. John Freeth. OBET

Collier's Rant, The. *Unknown.* OBET

Collier's Wedding, The, *sel.* Edward Chicken.
　"At last the beef appears in sight." NOEC

Collier's Wife, The. D. H. Lawrence. OxBTC

Collision: two seconds before, I saw the dark. Night Mare. Anita Endrezze-Danielson. STE

Colloam. P. Inman. LP

Colloque Sentimental. Paul Verlaine, *tr. fr. French by* Ernest Dowson. BrPo
　(Sentimental Conversation.) WSC, *tr. by* Lloyd Alexander

Colloquial. Rupert Brooke. BrPo

Colloquy. Weldon Kees. NaP; NYBP

Colloquy at Peniel. W. S. Merwin. NePoEA

Colloquy in Black Rock. Robert Lowell. CAPP; MoAB; MoAmPo; NAAL-2

Colloquy of Silences, A. Michael Heffernan. SM

Colloquy with a King-Crab. John Peale Bishop. LiTA

Colloquy with God, A. Sir Thomas Browne. *Fr.* Religio Medici. OBS

Collusion between a Alegaiter and a Water-Snaik. J. W. Morris. NA

Colobus Monkey. *Unknown, tr. fr. Yoruba by* Ulli Beier. *Fr.* Hunter Poems of the Yoruba. RB

Cologne. Samuel Taylor Coleridge. FaBoEE; NBLV; OBTV; TW

Cologne. Hilde Domin, *tr. fr. German by* Tudor Morris. VWA

Colombine. Hugh McCrae. PoAu-1

Colombo. March. The city white fire. Auschwitz from Colombo. Anne Ranasinghe. VWA

Colonel, The. Carolyn Forché. InPS; OBWP

Colonel B. Afforestation. E. A. Wodehouse. FiBHP; SD

Colonel Chartres. John Arbuthnot. *See* Her continueth to rot.

Colonel Cold strode up the line. Winter Warfare. Edgell Rickword. OBWP; OxBTC

Colonel Ellsworth. Richard Henry Stoddard. PAH

Colonel Fantock. Dame Edith Sitwell. MoAB; MoBrPo; OBMV

Colonel Fazackerley. Charles Causley. OnUR; RHPC

Colonel from Cheltenham stopped everyone, A. W. H. Auden. *Fr.* A Happy New Year. OBSV

Colonel in a casual voice, The. Gallantry. Keith Douglas. NAEL-2; NoAM; OBWP

Colonel rode by his picket-line, The. The Two Wives. William Dean Howells. AA

Colonels here in solemn manner meet, The. Thomas Brown. FaBoEE

Colonel's Soliloquy, The. Thomas Hardy. OBWP

Colonial cemetery wears, The. All Souls Day. Francisco Carrillo, *tr. by* Maureen Ahern *and* David Tipton. Per

Colonial Set. Alfred Goldsworthy Bailey. OBCV

Colonialism ("The colonialist governments"). Cabdullaahi Qarshe, *tr. fr. Somali by* J. W. Johnson. WTO

Colonists/ unearth their wealth. Shaman Breaks. Gerald Vizenor. HATNAP

Colonization in Reverse. Louise Bennett. PBCV

Colonus' Praise. Sophocles, *tr. fr. Greek by* W. B. Yeats. *Fr.* Oedipus at Colonus. OBVE

Colophon. Oliver St. John Gogarty. OBMV

Colophon for Lan-t'ing Hsiu-hsi. John Peck. AmPA

Colophon Written on the Flyleaf of a Book Sent to My Several Friends at Hsi-ling. Wu Hsi-ch'i, *tr. fr. Chinese by* Frederick P. Brandauer. WFTU

Color, The. Zsuzsa Beney, *tr. fr. Hungarian by* Jascha Kessler. *Fr.* A Broken Glass. FOC

Color—caste—denomination. Emily Dickinson. EaLo; TAP

Color it/ blue funk. Chromo. Sarah Webster Fabio. CNA

Color of Honey. Anne Waldman. TV

Color of Many Deer Running, The. Linda Gregg. NPGG

Color of silence is the oyster's color, The. Earliness at the Cape. Babette Deutsch. FYAP; NYBP

Color of stone when leaves are yellow, The. Autumn. William Jay Smith. NePoAm

Color of the flowers, The/ has faded. Komachi, *tr. by* Kenneth Rexroth. BoWoP

Color of the grave is green, The. Emily Dickinson. PoE

Color "yellow" comes from "light bay", The. "Yea" to "Yill" for "W." Tina Darragh. LP

Colorado Sand Storm, A. Eugene Fieldson, Jr.. LiTA; WaP

Colorado Trail, The. *Unknown.* AS

Colored Hats. Gertrude Stein. *Fr.* Tender Buttons. TTTS

Colored pictures. Charles Olson. *Fr.* The Maximus Poems, I. NoAM

Colored pictures/ of all things to eat: dirty. Charles Olson. *Fr.* The Maximus Poems: Songs of Maximus, I. NeAP; NoAM

Colorful frames are erected beside the Yellow River, The. Li K'ai-hsien, *tr. fr. Chinese by* Jonathan Chaves. *Fr.* Watching the Swinging. CoBLCP

Coloring high means that the strange reason is in front. An Umbrella. Gertrude Stein. *Fr.* Tender Buttons. TTTS

Colorless./ No sound, no hue passed by. Immobile. A. Leyeles, *tr. by* Benjamin *and* Barbara Harshav. AYP

Colors. Yevgeny Yevtushenko, *tr. fr. Russian by* Robin Milner-Gulland *and* Peter Levi. LLLT

Colors fade, The. Upon Listening to the Third Brandenburg Concerto. Gerhard Fritsch, *tr. by* Beth Bjorklund. CoAuP

Colors for Mama. Barbara Mahone. CNA; PoBA

Colors in the sun, colors at night, the Army, Navy and Marines. The Lagoon. Ashton Greene. NePoAm

Colors of childhood. Description of a Landscape. Erich Fried, *tr. by* Beth Bjorklund. CoAuP

Colors of Night, The. N. Scott Momaday. STE

Colors of the country, powerful river.   At the River Tower Parting from My Younger Brother, Fu-ling.   Wu Wei-yeh, *tr.* by Jonathan Chaves.   CoBLCP

Colors of the Dark One have penetrated Mira's body, The.   Why Mira Can't Go Back to Her Old House.   Mirabai, *tr.* by Robert Bly.   NU

Colors of the Windows, The.   Pierre Reverdy, *tr. fr. French by* Michael Benedikt.   POS

Colors on the elephant's body, The.   What She Said to Her Friend ("The colors on the elephant's body").   Kapilar, *tr.* by A. K. Ramanujan.   PLW

"Colors," she said, "are never so fine."   The Green and the Black.   Anthony Bailey.   NYBP

Colors shifting.   Time of Fish Dying.   Gabriela Melinescu, *tr.* by Stavros Deligiorgis.   BoWoP

Colors—the time will come.   Without Colors.   Gerrit Kouwenaar, *tr.* by Koos Schuur.   DuIn

Colors we depend on are, The.   The Love Bit.   Joel Oppenheimer.   PoM

Colosseum.   Harold Norse.   TrJP

Colossus, The.   Sylvia Plath.   CAPP; FaBoWP; HCAP; LiTM; NePoEA-2; NoAM; NOBA; NoP; TAP

Colour.   Adeline White.   BoTP

Colour it cherry-red and call it Death-Wish Valley—that's the message.   Loveliest of Counties, Shropshire Now.   Ian Sainsbury.   BXAP

Colour meant nothing.   Anyone.   To an Expatriate Friend.   Mervyn Morris.   PBCV

Colour-Scheme.   Edward Baugh.   PBCV

Colour Symphony.   Catherine Brewster Toosey.   CN

Coloured lanterns lit the trees, the grass, The.   Episode of a Night of May.   Arthur Symons.   *Fr.* Scènes de la Vie de Bohème.   BrPo; OBTV

Coloured long-shore fishermen unfurl, The.   The Gamblers.   Anthony Delius.   PeSA

Coloured nights, The.   Colour Symphony.   Catherine Brewster Toosey.   CN

Colours of Love, The.   Denis Devlin.   IPY

Colours of the setting sun, The.   The Sliprails and the Spur.   Henry Lawson.   PoAu-1

Coltish horseplay of the locker room, The.   The Feast of Stephen.   Anthony Hecht.   HAP; KS; NoAM; NoP

Coltrane must understand how.   Soul.   D. L. Graham.   PoBA

Columbia.   Timothy Dwight.   OPP; PAH

Columbia.   *Unknown.*   AmFP

Columbia, all hail!   Chicago Exposition Ode.   Mary Weston Fordham.   CBWP-2

Columbia, appear! To thy mountains ascend.   Perry's Victory—A Song.   *Unknown.*   PAH

Columbia, Columbia, to glory arise.   Columbia.   Timothy Dwight.   OPP; PAH

Columbia, the Gem of the Ocean.   David T. Shaw.   FaBoBe

Columbia, Trust the Lord.   *Unknown.*   AH

Columbiad, The, *sels.*   Joel Barlow.
    "Based on its rock of right your empire lies."   OPP
    "Eager he look'd. Another train of years."   *Fr.* X.   AmPP

Columbian poet, whom we've all respected.   Letter to an American Visitor.   Alex Comfort.   OxBTC

Columbia's Agony.   "Orpheus C. Kerr."   OBAL

Columbia's Emblem.   Edna Dean Proctor.   GN

Columbine, The.   Jones Very.   NOBA

Columbus.   Arthur Hugh Clough.   AmFN

Columbus.   Edward Everett Hale.   PAH

Columbus.   Joaquin Miller.   AA; AnAmPo; BeLS; FaBoBe; FaFP; FaPON; GN; MOS; OHFP; OPP; PAH; PPP

Columbus.   Ogden Nash.   NoP; OFD

Columbus.   Muriel Rukeyser.   GOA

Columbus.   Schiller, *tr. fr. German by* Erika Gathmann Koessler.   OFD

Columbus.   Lydia Huntley Sigourney.   AA; PAH

Columbus.   Louis Simpson.   Mes

Columbus, *sel.*   Tennyson.
    "Chains, my good lord: in your raised brows I read."   OFD

Columbus and the Mayflower.   Richard Monckton Milnes.   PAH

Columbus and the Mermaids.   Elizabeth Jane Coatsworth.   GOA

Columbus at the Convent.   John Townsend Trowbridge.   PAH

Columbus Circle at dusk—mixture of flesh and stone.   January 30.   A. Leyeles, *tr. fr. Yiddish by* Benjamin *and* Barbara Harshav.   *Fr.* Fabius Lind's Diary.   AYP

Columbus Day.   Jimmie Durham.   HATNAP

Columbus discovered America.   A Concise History of the World.   Ira Sadoff.   AmPA

Columbus Dying.   Edna Dean Proctor.   PAH

Columbus in Chains.   Philip Freneau.   PAH

Columbus is remembered by young men.   And of Columbus.   Horace Gregory.   GOA; OFD

Columbus looked; and still around them spread.   The First American Congress.   Joel Barlow.   PAH

Columbus looks towards the New World.   Space.   William Hart-Smith.   *Fr.* Christopher Columbus.   PoAu-2

Columbus may have worked the wind.   America Is Hard to See.   Robert Frost.   AiP

Columbus Reaches Juana, 1492.   Ralph Gustafson.   NOBC

Columbus sailed the ocean blue.   *Unknown.*   FaBoUs

Columbus to Ferdinand.   Philip Freneau.   OBCA; PAH

Column of mosquitoes, A.   Kyotai, *tr. fr. Japanese by* Burton Watson.   *Fr.* Sixteen Hokku.   FCEI

Columns.   Meir Wieseltier, *tr. fr. Hebrew by* Warren Bargad *and* Stanley F. Chyet.   IP

Columns and Caryatids.   Carolyn Kizer.   WPE

Colville 1964.   Kendrick Smithyman.   PeNZ
    (Colville.)   ATNZ

Com home againe!   Christ Calls Man Home.   *Unknown.*   MeEL

Coma.   Christopher Logue.   NPo

Coma.   Dennis Schmitz.   NPGG

Comanche Ghost Dance: An Impression.   Lance Henson.   VoR

Comarnad it is a very bonny place.   Richie Story.   *Unknown.*   ESPB

Comb, The.   Walter de la Mare.   FaBoRV

Combat, The.   Edwin Muir.   CMoP; LiTB; Mes; MoBrPo; NOBE

Combat, The.   Thomas Stanley.   AWP

Combat.   Clementina Suárez, *tr. fr. Spanish by* Magaly Fernández.   VoI

Combat.   C. K. Williams.   AnAn

Combat raged not long, but ours the day, The.   The Burial of Latané.   John Reuben Thompson.   PAH

Combe, The.   Edward Thomas.   FM; GTBS-P; RB

Combe Florey.   Paul Durcan.   FaBCIP

Combed by the cold seas, Bering and Pacific.   Love Letter from an Impossible Land.   William Meredith.   WaP

Combinations.   Mary Ann Hoberman.   *Fr.* Bugs.   OBCA

Combines crossed the wheat field, The.   Wheat.   Diane Glancy.   CRP

Combing.   Gladys Cardiff.   CDW; STE

Combing My Hair in the Hall.   Alberto Rios.   NAmP

Comcomly's Skull.   Jim Barnes.   STE

Come!   William Barnes.   CH

Come/ Home.   The Shortest and Sweetest of Songs.   George Macdonald.   NOBVV

"Come a little nearer, Doctor, thank you, let me take the cup."   The Old Sergeant.   Forceythe Willson.   AA; BeLS

Come again to the place.   After the Visit.   Thomas Hardy.   NOBE; OBNC

Come all fair maids both far and near and listen unto me.   Tragic Verses.   *Unknown.*   CoMu

Come all gallant [*or* you gallant] seamen that unite a meeting.   The Death of Nelson.   *Unknown.*   OxBoLi
    (New Song Composed on the Death of Lord Nelson, A.)   CoMu

Come, all my good people, and listen to my song.   Tittery-Irie-Aye.   *Unknown.*   AmFP

Come all my jolly seamen, likewise the landsmen, too.   The *Cumberland* and the *Merrimac*. . . .   *Unknown.*   AmFP

Come all of you blooming country lads and listen unto me.   Country Hirings.   *Unknown.*   OBET

Come all old maids that are squeamish.   Eurynome.   Jay Macpherson.   OBCV

Come all that loves good company.   The Merry Hoastess.   *Unknown.*   CoMu

Come all ye bold Americans, to you the truth I tell.   The Surrender of Cornwallis.   *Unknown.*   PAH

Come all ye bold undaunted ones who brave the winter's frost.   Fifteen Ships on Georges Banks.   *Unknown.*   AmFP

Come all ye British tars, lend an ear, lend an ear.   Admiral Byng.   *Unknown.*   OxBSS

Come All Ye Fair and Tender Ladies.   *Unknown.*   AmFP

Come all ye foreign strolling gentry.   Four Epigrams on the Naturalization Bill.   John Byrom.   NOBL

Come all ye gentle Christians [*or* Christian people], wherever you may be.   Charles Guiteau.   *Unknown.*   AmFP, *2 versions.*

Come, all ye good people, my story to hear.   Poor Ellen Smith.   *Unknown.*   AmFP

Come all ye jolly boatsman boys.   Blow the Candle Out.   *Unknown.*   AmFP

"Come all ye jolly fellows, who delight in a gun."   Polly Vaughn.   *Unknown.*   AmFP

Come all ye jolly lumbermen and listen to my song.   Canada-I-O ("Come all ye jolly lumbermen and listen to my song").   *at. to* Ephraim Braley.   AmFP

Come, all ye jolly sailors bold.   The *Arethusa*.   Prince Hoare.   FaPoR

Come all ye jolly shepherds.   When the Kye Comes Hame.   James Hogg.   OxBS

Come all ye knights, ye knights of Molites.   The Sons of Levi.   *Unknown.*   AmFP

Come all ye lads who know no fear. Barney's Invitation. Philip Freneau. PAH

Come all ye Lewiston fac'try girls. The Factory Girl's Come-All-Ye. *Unknown.* AmFP; OBAL

Come All Ye Mourning Pilgrims. John A. Granade. AH

Come, All Ye People. George R. Seltzer. AH

Come all ye railroad section men. Jerry, Go an' Ile That Car. *Unknown.* AS

Come, all ye seamen [*or* you sailors] bold. The Death of Admiral Benbow. *Unknown.* CoMu; GBP

(Admiral Benbow.) EnSB

Come all ye sons of Brittany. Braddock's Fate, with an Incitement to Revenge. Stephen Tilden. PAH

Come all ye true-born Irishmen, a story I will tell. The *City of Baltimore.* *Unknown.* OxBSS

Come all ye [*or* you] true born shanty-boys, wherever you may be [*or* whoever that ye be]. The Jam on Gerry's Rock. *Unknown.* AmFP; AS, *with music;* FaBoBa

Come all ye valiant seamen. The Man-of-War's Garland. *Unknown.* OxBSS

Come all ye wits, that with immortal rhymes. Invites Poets and Historians to Write in Cynthia's Praise. Philip Ayres. Son

Come all ye Yankee sailors, with swords and pikes advance. The *Constellation* and the *Insurgente.* *Unknown.* PAH

Come all ye young people and all my relations. Mr. Davis's Experience. *Unknown.* AmFP

Come all you blessed Christians dear. A Ballad from the Seven Dials Press. *Unknown.* CoMu

Come all you bold sailors that follow the lakes. Red Iron Ore. *Unknown.* AS

Come all you bonny boys. The Bullard's Song. *Unknown.* OBET

Come all you brave Americans. Brave Paulding and the Spy. *Unknown*

Come all you brave boys whose courage is bold. A Copy of Verses Composed by Captain Henry Every. *Unknown.* OxBSS

Come, all you brave gallants, and listen a while. Robin Hood and the Butcher. *Unknown.* ESPB

Come all you brave sailors, that sails on the Main. The Famous Fight at Malago; or, The Englishmen's Victory over the Spaniards. *Unknown.* CoMu; OxBSS

Come all you brave seamen that ploughs on the main. Captain Barton's Distress on Board the *Lichfield.* *Unknown.* OxBSS

Come all you brave soldiers, both valiant and free. On Independence. Jonathan Mitchell Sewall. PAH

Come all you brave young shanty-boys. James Whaland. *Unknown.* AS

Come all you British hearts of oak, and listen unto me. The Glorious Victory of Navarino! *Unknown.* CoMu

Come all you cockers, far and near. The Bonny Grey. *Unknown.* GBP

Come all you fair gallants, fair gallants attend. Pretty Polly of Topsham. *Unknown.* AmFP

Come all you fine young fellows with hearts so warm and true. Flat River Girl. *Unknown.* AS

Come all you focsle lawyers that always take deli ght. The Merchant Shipping Act. *Unknown.* CoMu

Come all you gallant heroes, I'd have you lend an ear. Major André. *Unknown.* AmFP

Come all you gallant poachers, that ramble free from [*or* void of] care. Van Dieman's Land. *Unknown.* CoMu; FaBoBa; OBET; OBTV

Come all you girls and all you boys. Kitty Morey. *Unknown.* AmFP

Come all you good people/ From all over the World. Lula Vires. *Unknown.* AmFP

Come all you hearty roving blades, and listen to my song. The Frolicsome Parson Outwitted. *Unknown.* CoMu

Come all you heroes, where'er you be. The Dying Sergeant. *Unknown.* AmFP

Come all you jolly cowboys and listen to my song. The Buffalo Skinners. *Unknown.* GBP; RB

Come all you jolly fellows, come listen to my song. The Shanty Boys and the Pine. *Unknown.* AmFP

Come all you jolly freighters that ever hit the road. Freighting from Wilcox to Globe. *Unknown.* AmFP

Come all you jolly-hearted sailors. False Nancy. *Unknown.* AmFP

Come all you jolly highwaymen and outlaws of the land. Bold Jack Donahue. *Unknown.* AmFP

Come all you jolly lumbermen, and listen to my song. Colley's Run-I-O. *Unknown.* AmFP

Come all you jolly lumbermen, I'd have you for to know. The Banks of the Gaspereaux. *Unknown.* AmFP

Come all you jolly ploughmen. The Painful Plough. *Unknown.* OBET

Come all you jolly railroad men, and I'll sing you if I can. Way Out in Idaho. *Unknown.* AmFP

Come all you jolly seamen who plough that restless deep. Jimmy Judge. *Unknown.* AmFP

Come all you jolly shanty boys that work the shanty and go. Turner's Camp on the Chippewa. *Unknown.* AmFP

Come all you jolly travellers that's out of work, just mind. Cockies of Bungaree. *Unknown.* PoAu-1

Come all you Lachlan men, and a sorrowful tale I'll tell. The Streets of Forbes. *Unknown.* CBAP

Come all you lads of high renown and listen to my story. Country Statutes. *Unknown.* OBET

Come all you loyal Unionists, wherever you may be. Virginia's Bloody Soil. *Unknown.* AmFP

Come all you maids that live at a distance. I Live Not Where I Love. *Unknown.* OBET

Come all you married couples gay. The Dunmow Flitch of Bacon. *Unknown.* OBET

Come all you married seamen bold, a few lines to you I'll write. The Dockyard Gate. *Unknown.* OxBSS

Come all you men and maidens. Rufus Mitchell's Confession. *Unknown.* AmFP

Come all you muckers and gather here. Casey Jones. *Unknown.* See Come all you rounders. . . .

Come all you noble, bold commanders. Captain James. *Unknown.* OxBSS

Come all you people from every land. Ellen Flannery. *Unknown.* AmFP

Come all you pretty fair maids. Green Willow, Green Willow. *Unknown.* AmFP

Come all you pretty fair maids, I pray you attend. My New Garden Field. *Unknown.* AmFP

Come all you rounders [*or* muckers] if you want [*or* for I want you] to hear. Casey Jones. *Unknown.* AmFP; AS, *with music;* BeLS; FaBV; OxBoLi; RR; TrGrPo

Come all you sailors bold. The Death of Admiral Benbow. *Unknown.* CoMu; GBP

Come, all you sailors of the southern waters. Phantoms All. Harriet Prescott Spofford. AA

Come all you saucy landladies, what makes you look so gay? The Royal Light Dragoon. *Unknown.* OBET

Come all you sons of Erin, attention now I crave. Morrissey and the Russian Sailor. *Unknown.* AS

Come all you sons of freedom and listen to my theme. Once More a-Lumbering Go. *Unknown.* AmFP

Come, all you sons of Liberty, that to the seas belong. The *General Armstrong.* *Unknown.* PAH

Come all you Sussex heroes with courage stout and bold. The Smuggler's Victory. *Unknown.* OxBSS

Come all you swaggering farmers, whoever you may be. The Times Have Altered. *Unknown.* CoMu

Come all you thoughtless young men, a warning take by me. The Murder of Maria Marten. W. Corder. CoMu; OBET

Come All You Tonguers. *Unknown.* PeNZ

Come all you valiant heroes and listen unto me. A New Song on the Total Defeat of the French Fleet. *Unknown.* OxBSS

Come all you valiant sailors of courage stout and bold. The Sailor's Lamentation. *Unknown.* OxBSS

Come all you wild and wicked youths. Van Dieman's Land. *Unknown.* OBET

Come all you wild young men. The Valiant Sailor. *Unknown.* OxBSS

Come all you wild young people and listen to my song. Young Edwin in the Lowlands Low. *Unknown.* OBET

Come all you young and handsome ladies. Little Sparrow. *Unknown.* AmFP

Come all you young fellows that follow the gun. Young Molly Ban. *Unknown.* FaBoBa

Come all you young fellows who follow the sea. Blow the Man Down. *Unknown.* OxBSS, *with music.*

Come All You Young Ladies and Gentlemen. *Unknown.* OBET

Come all you young ladies and make no delay. *Unknown.* OxNR

Come all you young maidens I pray you attend. Sally Munro. *Unknown.* OxBSS

Come all you young people/ That live far and near. The Murder of Goins. *Unknown.* AmFP

Come all you young people, a story I will tell. Naomi (Omie) Wise. *Unknown.* AmFP

Come all you young people who handle the gun. Shooting of His Dear. *Unknown.* OxBoLi

Come, all young girls, pay attention to my noise. Kansas Boys. *Unknown.* AS

Come all young men and ladies, come fathers and mothers, too. The Rowan County Crew. At. to James William Day. AmFP

Come all young men and maidens, come listen to my rhyme. Caroline of Edinboro' Town. *Unknown.* AmFP

Come, all young men, taking warning by me. Married and Single Life. *Unknown.* AmFP

Come along, boys, and listen to my tale. The Old Chisholm Trail. *Unknown.* BeLS; FaBoBe

Come along in then, little girl! From a Very Little Sphinx. Edna St. Vincent Millay. OBAL

Come along, 'tis the time, ten or more minutes past. Arthur Hugh Clough. *Fr.* Spectator ab Extra. OBSV

Come and let me make thee glad. The Builder. Francis Sherman. CaP

Come and let us live my deare. Catullus, *tr. by* Richard Crashaw. OBVE

Come and listen to the chiming. Bells of St. Michael. Mary Weston Fordham. CBWP-2

"Come and see! Come and see!" What the Thrush Says. Queenie Scott-Hopper. BoTP

"Come and you shall see." Shadow. Ann Mars. GoYe

Come, arm ye! Come, arm ye! The Garibaldi Hymn. Luigi Mercantini. WBLP

Come at dawn, good friend. *Unknown, tr. by* Willis Barnstone. BoWoP

Come away,/ Make no delay. Dooms-Day. George Herbert. JCP; OBD; SeCP; SeCV-1

Come Away, Come Away, Death. Shakespeare. *Fr.* Twelfth Night, II, iv. EIL; ELP; GBL; NOBE; NoP
(Clown's Song, The.) CTC
(Come Away, Death.) PoRA
(Dirge: "Come away, come away, death.") OBEV
(Dirge of Love.) GTBS; GTBS-P
(Feste's Song ("Come away, come away, death").) OBSC
(Love's Despair.) TrGrPo
(Song: "Come away, come away, death.") FiP; PoEL-2

Come Away, Come, Sweet Love. At. to John Dowland. NAEL-1; OBSC; PoEL-2
(To His Love.) EIL; ELP; GBL

Come away, Death. Shakespeare. *See* Twelfth Night: Come Away, Come Away, Death.

Come away to the skies. For His Wife, on Her Birthday. Charles Wesley. NOCV

Come away with me, Tom. The Invitation. Charles Kingsley. NOBVV

Come Back. Henry William Herbert. AA

Come Back. W. S. Merwin. NaP

Come back and bring my life again. Come Back. Henry William Herbert. AA

Come Back Blues. Michael S. S. Harper. PoBA

Come back to me! my life is young. Karazah to Karl. Adah Isaacs Menken. CBWP-1

Come back me, O ye, my children. Mother's Recall. Mary Weston Fordham. CBWP-2

Come back, ye wandering Muses, come back home. On the Hellenics. Walter Savage Landor. *Fr.* The Hellenics. EnRP

Come balmy sleep! tired Nature's soft resort! To Sleep. Charlotte Smith. Son; WPE

Come boyes, fill us a bumper, we'l make the Nation roare. The Courtier's Health; or, Merry Boys of the Times. *Unknown.* CoMu

"Come brave honest Jack Tar, once more will you venture?" Jack Tar. *Unknown.* OxBSS

Come, Break with Time. Louise Bogan. MoAmPo

Come, break your heart, then, with the world's beauty. Sic Transit Gloria Mundi. James Wreford Watson. CaP

Come, brethren of the water. The Powte's Complaint. *Unknown.* GBP

Come, bring the children. Let them. Summer Solstice. Peter Blue Cloud. *Fr.* Within the Seasons. HATNAP

Come, bring with a noise. Ceremonies for Christmas. Robert Herrick. GN; OBCP; OHIP
(Yule Log.) TEP

Come, brother, and tell me your life. Jorge Rebelo, *tr. by* Margaret Dickinson. WMBCH

Come, brother, come. Let's lift it. Cotton Song. Jean Toomer. BPo; CDC

Come, Brother, turn with me from pining thought. The Soul. Richard Henry Dana. AnAmPo

Come, brothers! rally for the right! The Bonnie Blue Flag. Annie Chambers Ketchum. PAH

Come, butter, come. Mother Goose. OxNR

Come Buy! Come Buy! Shakespeare. *See* Winter's Tale, The: Autolycus as Peddler.

Come buy my fine wares. Apples. Swift. *Fr.* Verses for Fruitwomen. AnYI

Come, cheer up, my lads, like a true British band. *Unknown.* PAH

Come, cheer up, my lads! 'tis to glory we steer. Heart of Oak. David Garrick. NOEC; OxBoLi

Come, Cheerful Day! Thomas Campion. AAS; EIL

Come child, and with your sunbeam gaze assign. The Green Eye. James Merrill. PoA

Come, children, hear the joyful sound. The Big Bell in Zion. Theodore Henry Shackleford. BANP

Come, children, listen to me now. The Cow. *Unknown.* FaBoUs

Come Christmas. David McCord. PChr

Come, come away, to the Tavern I say. *Unknown.* OBS

Come, come dear Night! Love's mart of kisses. Epithalamion Teratos. Chapman. *Fr.* Hero and Leander, Fifth Sestiad. EIL

Come, come fill up your glasses. The British Grenadier. *Unknown.* PAH

Come, come, Flipote; it's time I left this place. Tartuffe. Molière, *tr. by* Richard Wilbur. NAWM-2

Come, come, I say. Onitsura, *tr. by* Geoffrey Bownas *and* Anthony Thwaite. PeBJV

Come, come, let's go home, look at today's sun. *Unknown, tr. by* Hiroaki Sato. FCEI

Come, come, my love, the bush is growing. With Garments Flowing. John Clare. GBL

Come, come, no time for lamentation now. Milton. *Fr.* Samson Agonistes. FiP
(Death of Samson.) ChTr
(No Time for Lamentation Now.) FaBoRV

"Come, come," said Tom's father, "at your time of life." A Joke Versified. Thomas Moore. FaBoCo

Come, come, what doe I here? Henry Vaughan. MePo; SeCV-1

Come, cousin Cuba, me yerry some news. Quaco Sam. *Unknown.* PBCV

"Come!" cried Helen, eager Helen. Sisters. Eleanor Farjeon. FaPON

"Come," cried the Voice, "it is already Spring." Mary, Mary. Anthony C. Deane. FaBoPa

Come, cropper lads of great renown. The Cropper Lads. *Unknown.* OBET

Come, cuddle your head on my shoulder, dear. The Beautiful Land of Nod. Ella Wheeler Wilcox. PWR

Come, cut thy throte, and have thy throte-ball out! Lovers' Debouchment. William Zaranka. BXAP

Come dally me, darling, dally me with kisses. Psyche to Cupid: Her Ditty. James Richard Broughton. ErPo

Come dance a jig. Mother Goose. OxNR

Come Dance with Kitty Stobling. Patrick Kavanagh. FaBCIP; MoP; NoAM

Come, dark-eyed Sleep, thou child of Night. And on My Eyes Dark Sleep by Night. "Michael Field." OBMV

Come, day, glad day, day running out of the night. Glad Day. Louis Untermeyer. TrJP

Come, dear children, let us away. The Forsaken Merman. Matthew Arnold. BeLS; EBEV; FaBoCh; FaPoR; FiP; GN; MOS; NAEL-2; OBNV

Come, dear old comrade, you and I. Bill and Joe. Oliver Wendell Holmes. AA

Come, Death, I'd have a word with thee. Motley. Walter de la Mare. HoPM; MMA

Come, Death—My Lady Is Dead. At. to Charles, Duc d' Orléans. MeEL

Come, doleful owl, the messenger of woe. *Unknown.* PBBP

Come Down. George Macdonald. TrPWD

Come down at dawn from windless hills. Sunrise on Rydal Water. John Drinkwater. LiTM

Come down, come down to the Square. The Cat That Followed His Nose. John Kaye Kendall. CenHV

Come Down, Darkness. Muhammad Mahdi al-Jawahiri, *tr. fr. Arabic by* Christopher Tingley *and* Christopher Middleton. MAP

Come down from heaven to meet me when my breath. Siegfried Sassoon. MoBrPo

Come down from the Cross, my soul, and save thyself. Descent from the Cross. "Michael Field." WPE

Come down from your heights. Warning. Ursula Krechel, *tr. by* Susan L. Cocalis. DMG

Come down, O Christ, and help me! reach thy hand. E Tenebris. Oscar Wilde. BrPo; MoBrPo; NAEL-2; Son; TIRV; TrPWD

Come Down, O Maid, [from Yonder Mountain Height]. Tennyson. *Fr.* The Princess, *Pt.* VII. EBVV; FF; GTBS-P; NAEL-2; NOBVV; OAEL-2; OBEV; OBNC
(Idyl, An.) TrGrPo
(Song: "Come down, O maid, from yonder mountain height.")

Come down, ye graybeard mariners. A Cry from the Shore. Ellen Mackay Hutchinson Cortissoz. AA

Come, each death-doing dog who dares venture his neck. Hot Stuff. Edward Botwood. PAH

Come evening once again, season of peace. William Cowper. *Fr.* The Task, IV. NAEL-1

Come, Every Soul. John H. Stockton. AH

Come! fill a fresh bumper, for why should we go. Ode for a Social Meeting. Oliver Wendell Holmes. OBAL

Come, fill the beaker, while we chaunt a pean of old days. Fort Duquesne. Florus B. Plimpton. PAH

Come, fill the cup, and in the fire of spring. Omar Khayyám, *tr. fr. Persian by* Edward Fitzgerald. *Fr.* The Rubáiyát of Omar Khayyám of Naishápúr. FaBoRV; FaBV; TEP; WGRP

Come fleetly, come fleetly, my hookabadar. Cossimbazar. Henry Sambrooke Leigh. NA

Come, follow, follow me. The Fairies. *Unknown.* BoTP

Come, follow me by the smell. Onyons. Swift. *Fr.* Verses for Fruitwomen. BIrV; FaBoUs

Come forth from thy oozy couch. Imitation of Julia A. Moore. "Mark Twain." OBAL

Come forth, old lion, from thy den. On Himself. Walter Savage Landor. FaBoEE

Come forth, you workers! Réveille. Lola Ridge. WPE

Come forthe, sire sergeaunt, with your stately mace. The Dance. *Unknown, tr. fr. French by* John Lydgate. *Fr.* The Dance of Death. PoEL-1

Come, freemen of the land. Put It Through. Edward Everett Hale. PAH

Come, freighted heart, within this port. Lovemusic. Carolyn Kizer. ErPo

Come, friendly bombs, and fall on Slough. Slough. Sir John Betjeman. MoBrPo; NoAM

Come friends and listen to my song. The Three Tall Men. *Unknown.* OBET

Come, Friends and Neighbors, Come. Lewis Hartsough. AH

Come, friends, if you will listen, a story I will tell. The Sherman Cyclone. *Unknown.* AmFP

Come from a distant country. At Birth. Anthony Thwaite. NePoEA-2

Come from my first, ay, come! Charade. Winthrop Mackworth Praed. GN

Come from Thy Palace. Thomas Randolph. *Fr.* The Conceited Pedlar. OxBSP

Come gather 'round me, cowboys. The Flyin' Outlaw. Curley W. Fletcher. CowP

Come, Gaze with Me upon This Dome. E. E.. NoAM; OxBA

Come, Gentle Death! Thomas Watson. *Fr.* Hecatompathia; or, Passionate Century of Love. EIL

Come, gentle sleep, death's image though thou art. Thomas Warton the Younger, *tr. by* Wordsworth. OBVE

Come, gentlemen all, and listen a while. Robin Hood and the Bishop. *Unknown.* ESPB

Come, gentlemen Tories, firm, loyal, and true. Sir Henry Clinton's Invitation to the Refugees. Philip Freneau. PAH

Come gie's a sang, Montgomery cry'd. Tullochgorum. John Skinner. GoTS; OxBS

Come, Gorgo, put the rug in place. "Michael Field." *Fr.* Variations on Sappho. PeHV

Come, guard this night the Christmas-pie. Christmas Eve — Another Ceremony. Robert Herrick. OHIP

Come, Happy Children,. *Unknown.* AH

Come Harken unto Me. *Unknown.* AH

Come, hear the tale of love's romance. Mir Sirajuddin Siraj, *tr. by* Ahmed Ali. GoT

"Come here, come here, you freely feed." Kemp Owyne. *Unknown.* ESPB

(Kempion.) OxBB, *with music*

Come here, Denise. Denise. Robert Beverly Hale. GrPl

Come here, little girl, come here. David Avidan, *tr. by* Bernhard Frank. MHeP

Come Here, Little Robin. *Unknown.* BoTP

"Come here, my boy; hould up your head." The Irish Schoolmaster. James A. Sidney. FiBHP

Come here, said my hostess, her face making room. A Literary Dinner. Vladimir Nabokov. FiBHP; OBAL

Come here, thou proud pretender unto arts. There's Life in a Mussel; a Meditation. George Farewell. NOEC

Come here, you niguramus. Dolly's Lesson. *Unknown.* FaBoUs

Come Hither. John Clare. NoP

Come hither all sweet maidens soberly. Sonnet: On a Picture of Leander. Keats. EnRP

Come hither and behold this lady's face. Laura Sleeping. Louise Chandler Moulton. AA

Come hither, Child! and rest. Villanelle of Sunset. Ernest Dowson. BrPo

Come hither, Evan Cameron! The Execution of Montrose. William Edmonstoune Aytoun. OnMSP

Come hither lads, and hearken, for a tale there is to tell. The Day Is Coming, *parody.* Sir Walter Besant. CenHV

Come hither lads, and hearken, for a tale there is to tell. The Day Is Coming. William Morris. WGRP

Come Hither, My Dear One. John Clare. ELP

Come hither, Sir John, my picture is here. On a Lady Who Beat Her Husband. *Unknown.* FiBHP

Come hither, Topham, come, with a hey, with a hey. A Raree Show. Stephen College. APAS

Come hither, womankind and all their worth. Kissing. Herbert of Cherbury. EnLoPo; ViBoPo

Come hither ye dreamers of dreams. The Vision. Daniel Defoe. APAS

Come hither, ye who thirst. Come Hither. John Clare. NoP

Come Hither, You That Love. John Fletcher. ELP

Come, hoist the sail, the fast let go! The Pleasure-Boat. Richard Henry Dana. AnAmPo

Come Holy Spirit, Dove Divine. Adoniram Judson. AH

Come, holy tortoise shell. Sappho, *tr. by* Willis Barnstone. BoWoP

Come Home. *Unknown, tr. fr. Zulu by* Jack Cope. PeSA

Come Home, Come Home! Arthur Hugh Clough. HAP

Come Home from the Movies. Lucille Clifton. CAPP

Come home with me a little space. Christmas at Melrose. Leslie Pinckney Hill. BANP

Come home with white gulls waving across gray. Winter Landscape. Stephen Spender. MoAB; MoBrPo

Come, Hooker, come forth of thy native soile. Yee Shall Not Misse of a Few Lines in Remembrance of Thomas Hooker. Edward Johnson. SCAP

Come, human dogs, interfertilitate. The Eugenist. Robert Graves. FaBoEE

Come, I will make the continent indissoluble. For You, O Democracy. Walt Whitman. OPP; TrGrPo

Come In. Robert Frost. AmPP; BoNaP; FaBV; LiTA; LiTM; MoAB; MoAmPo; NOBA; NoP; TrGrPo

Come In. Isaiah Shembe, *tr. fr. Zulu by* H. Tracey. WTO

Come in at the low-silled window. Being Called For. Rosemary Dobson. CBAP; Mes

Come in, Aunt Jemima. De Wintah Styles. Maggie Pogue Johnson. CBWP-4

Come in light variable and with calm. Susan Howe. PPR

Come in sweet grief. Tricked Again. Ridhiana. NBP

Come in, the ford is roaring on the plain. Enid's Song. Tennyson. *Fr.* Idylls of the King: Geraint and Enid. FaBoRV

Come in the garden. The Snowman. E. M. Adams. BoTP

Come in this hour to set my spirit free. Before Day. Siegfried Sassoon. WGRP

Come in, Tom longtail, come short hose and round. *Unknown.* EBEV

Come inside the weather. By Hallucination Visited. Robert Horan. EAS

Come into Animal Presence. Denise Levertov. HeIP; NaP; NU

Come into dinner squalls the dame. Snaps for Dinner, Snaps for Breakfast, and Snaps for Supper. George Moses Horton. OBAL

Come into the garden. Mohammad Taqi Mir, *tr. by* Ahmed Ali. GoT

Come into the garden, Kate. The Tryst. E. V. Knox. CenHV

Come into the garden, Maud. Tennyson. *Fr.* Maud, I, xxii. EBVV; FaBV; FiP; NOBE; NOBVV; OAEL-2; PoE (Maud.) OBEV

(Song: "Come into the garden, Maud.") AWP

"Come into the hall with me, George." The Kiss. George Bogin. MOWH

Come into the orchard, Anne. Swinburne. FaBoNo

Come, John, sit thee down I have somewhat to say. An Amorous Dialogue between John and His Mistress. *Unknown.* CoMu

Come jolly sailors join with me. The Lucky Sailor; or, The Sailor's Invitation to Go with Admiral Anson. *Unknown.* OxBSS

Come keen iambicks with your badger's feet. John Cleveland. *Fr.* The Rebel [*or* Rebell] Scot. OBS

Come knock your heads against this stone. Blake. TEP

Come lads and listen to my song, a song of honest toil. The English Labourer. *Unknown.* OBET

Come, Landlord, Fill the Flowing Bowl. *Unknown.* OxBoLi

Come lasses and lads, take leave of your dads. The Rural Dance about the Maypole. *Unknown.* GBP; OxBoLi; RR

Come Laugh with Me. *Gond Oral Tradition, tr. by* V. Elwin *and* S. Hivale. WTO

Come learn with me the fatal song. The Mighty Heart. Emerson. *Fr.* Woodnotes II ("As sunbeams stream through liberal space"). AA

Come leave the loathed stage. Ode to Himsel[f]e. Ben Jonson. NAEL-1; OAEL-1; OBS; SeCP

Come let us also raise our hands to pray. Faiz Ahmad Faiz, *tr. by* Mahmood Jamal. PBMUP

Come let us be going my brothers. Come Home. *Unknown, tr. by* Jack Cope. PeSA

Come! let us draw the curtains. Humbert Wolfe. *Fr.* Autumn. ILY; PoLF

Come, let us drink away the time. A Song of Sack. *at. to* Charles Cotton. OBS

Come, let us go a-roaming! Travellers. Arthur St. John Adcock. BoTP

Come, let us hide ourselves in caves. A Stubborn Back — And Nothing More. H. Leivick, *tr. by* Robert Friend. PeBMYV

Come, let us join this festal lay. Rally Song. Mary Weston Fordham. CBWP-2

Come, let us mourn. Crucifixion of the Word. Ahmad Faraz, tr. by Mahmood Jamal. PBMUP

Come, let us now resolve at last. The Reconcilement. John Sheffield. OBEV

Come, let us pity those who are better off than we are. The Garret. Ezra Pound. AnAmPo; SOTW

Come let us plant the apple tree. The Planting of the Apple-Tree. Bryant. AA; GN; OHIP

Come let us rejoice. About Savannah. Unknown. PAH

Come, let us sigh a requiem over love. Robert Nichols. Fr. Sonnets to Aurelia. OBMV

Come, let us sing! it is time for summer. For an Eskimo. Annie Charlotte Dalton. CaP

Come, let us tell the weeds in ditches. Last Hill in a Vista. Louise Bogan. FaBoWP

Come, Let Us Tune Our Loftiest Song. Robert A. West. AH

Come, let us walk. Spring in Virginia. Ramona Wilson. VoR

Come let's begin to revel't out. Unknown. BoTP

Come, let's go climb on that jasmine-mantled rock. What Her Girlfriends Said to Her. Okkur Macatti, tr. by A. K. Ramanujan. BoWoP

Come, let's to bed. Mother Goose. GBP; OxBoLi; OxNR

Come lie down next to me and rest. And Later by Myself. Ory Bernstein, tr. by Warren Bargad and Stanley F. Chyet. IP

Come light and listen, you gentlemen all. Robin Hood and the Beggar, I. Unknown. ESPB

Come, list and hark, the bell doth toll. The Passing Bell. Thomas Heywood. Fr. The Rape of Lucrece. FaBoRV

Come list you gallant Englishmen who ramble at your ease. Loss of the Amphitrite. Unknown. OxBSS

Come listen a while and give ear to my song. Hard Times. Unknown. AmFP

Come listen a while, you gentlemen all. Robin Hood Newly Revived. Unknown. ESPB

Come, listen all unto my song. How Cyrus Laid the Cable. John Godfrey Saxe. AnAmPo; PAH

Come listen all ye feeling people while this sad story I relate. The Wreck of the Northfleet. Unknown. OxBSS

Come listen, and hear me tell/ the end of a tale so true. The Lass of Lynn's New Joy, for Finding a Father for Her Child. Unknown. CoMu

Come listen and I'll tell you. The Yankee Privateer. Arthur Hale. PAH

Come listen awhile, and I'll sing you a song. The Silly Old Man. Unknown. CoMu; TW

Come listen awhile with attention. Bold Adventures of Captain Ross. Unknown. OxBSS

Come listen, good neighbors of every degree. The Liberty Pole. Unknown. PAH

Come listen, good people, to what I shall say. A Ballad Called Perkins's Figary. Unknown. APAS

Come listen, O Love, to the voice of the dove. The Voice of the Dove. Joaquin Miller. AA

Come listen to another song. The Old Scottish Cavalier. William Edmonstoune Aytoun. GN

Come listen to me, you gallants so free. Robin Hood and Allen [or Allin] -a-Dale. Unknown. ESPB; FaBoBe; GBP; MoShBr

Come, listen to my story, ye landsmen, one and all. Raging Canawl. Unknown. AS

Come, listen to my tragedy, good people, young and old. Mary Wyatt and Henry Green. Unknown. AmFP

Come listen to the story of brave Lathrop and his men. The Lamentable Ballad of the Bloody Brook. Edward Everett Hale. PAH

Come listen, ye Whigs, to my pitiful moan. The Salamanca Doctor's Farewell. Unknown. APAS

Come, little babe, come, silly soul. Nicholas Breton. NOBE; OBEV
(Sweet Lullaby, A.) EiL; OBSC

Come, little cottage girl, you seem. Barry Pain. Fr. The Poets at Tea, VI. Par

Come, little Drummer Boy, lay down your knapsack here. The Soldiers' Friend. George Canning and John Hookham Frere. Par

Come, little John, tell me the lovely tale. Whom Jesus Loved. John Barford. PeHV

Come, Little Leaves. George Cooper. FaPON
(Wind and the Leaves, The.) BoTP

Come Live with Me. Naomi Marks. BXAP

Come, live with me and be my love. C. Day Lewis. Fr. Two Songs BoLoP; NBLV; NoAM; OBMV
(Song: "Come, live with me and be my love.") NIP; NoP

"Come live with me and be my love." Bacchanal. Peter De Vries. BXAP; NBLV; NIP; NOBL; OBAL

Come live with me [e] and be [e] my love. The Bait [e]. John Donne. ErPo; HoPM; InPK; InPS; NAEL-1; NIP; OAEL-1; PoRA; RB; SD; TEP

Come live with me and be my love. That Strain Again. Ronald Hambleton. CaP

Come, live with me and be my love. Samuel Hoffenstein. Fr. Invocation. NBLV

Come live with me[e] and be my Love. The Passionate Shepherd to His Love. Christopher Marlowe. AAS; AWP; BoLoP; CTC; EiL; ELP; FaBoBe; FaFP; FF; FPL; GTBS; GTBS-P; HAP; HeIP; HoPM; InPK; InPS; LiTB; NAEL-1; NBLV; NIP; NOBE; NoP; OAEL-1; OBEV; OBSC; PoE; PoLF; PoRA; PPP; RB; SCV; SeCePo; TrGrPo; TTTS; WeW
(Shepherd to His Love, The.) GN
(Shepherd's Plea, The.) SiPS

Come live with me and be my whore. The Wooing Rogue. Unknown. CoMu

Come live with me and be my wife. The Passionate Shepherd to His Love. Delmore Schwartz. NIP

Come, love, for now the night and day. Song for Autumn. Andrew Young. GBL

Come, Love, Let's Walk. Unknown. EiL

Come lovely and soothing death. Walt Whitman. Fr. Memories of President Lincoln: When Lilacs Last in the Dooryard Bloom'd. SCV
(Carol of Death, The.) DL

Come, lovely Muse, desert for me. Samuel Hoffenstein. BXAP

Come loyal Britons all rejoice with joyful acclamations. English Courage Displayed; or, Brave News from Admiral Vernon. Unknown. OxBSS

Come, Madam, come, all rest my powers defy. Going to Bed. John Donne. Fr. Elegies, XIX. EBEV; LiTB; NAEL-1; PPP

Come! Marget, come!—the team is at the gate! The Country Lovers; or, Isaac and Marget Going to Town, on a Summer's Morning. George Smith. NOEC

Come marvel at my ox. Song of Praise for an Ox. Abraham Sutskever, tr. by Ruth Whitman. VWA

Come, me canny Tynesiders, an' lissen. The Strike. Unknown. OBET

Come, mint me up the golden gorse. The Casual Man. Denis Glover. Fr. Sings Harry. ATNZ

Come, Muse, migrate from Greece and Ionia. The Muse in the New World. Walt Whitman. Fr. Song of the Exposition. MoAmPo

Come muster, my lads, your mechanical tools. The New Roof. Francis Hopkinson. PAH

Come, my brothers. The Only Tourist in Havana Turns His Thoughts Homeward. Leonard Cohen. MoCV; MoP

Come, my Celia, let us prove. Ben Jonson. Fr. Volpone, III, vii. EiL; OBVE; TEP
(Come, My Celia.) FaBV; FF; HeIP; NoP; TrGrPo
(Song to Celia.) ErPo; JCP; OAEL-1, with music; OBS; SeCP; SeCV-1

Come (my dear) whilst youth conspires. Time Recover'd. Thomas Stanley, after the Italian of Girolamo Casone. OBVE

Come my friends and listen unto me. The Parson Grocer. Unknown. CoMu

Come my friends come. Call from the Afterworld. Jozef Habib Gerez, tr. by Musa Moris Farhi and Anthony Rudolf. VWA

Come, my little Robert, near. Cleanliness. Charles and Mary Lamb. OxBChV

Come, my Lucasia, since we see. Friendship's Mystery; to My Dearest Lucasia. Katherine Philips. PeHV

Come, my men, let us hasten to Yamato! Okura, tr. fr. Japanese. Fr. Manyo Shu. Ma

"Come my own one, come my fond one." The Saucy Sailor. Unknown. OBET

Come, my pretty little Muse. On My Pretty Marten. Charles Cotton. FM

Come, my songs, let me express our baser passions. Ezra Pound. Fr. Lustra. PoA
(Further Instructions.) TwCP

Come, my tan-faced children. Pioneers! O Pioneers! Walt Whitman. FaBoBe; OPP

Come, mysterious night. A Hymn to Night. Max Michelson. TrJP

Come Nataki dance with me. Dance Poem. Nikki Giovanni. RR

Come near come nearer. Out of the Depths I Cry unto You, O Death! Tawfiq Sayigh, tr. by Anne Royal and Samuel Hazo. MAP

"Come, neighbours, no longer be patient and quiet." The Riot; or, Half a Loaf Is Better than No Bread. Hannah More. NOEC

Come night. News from Mount Amiata. Robert Lowell. NaP

Come not again! I dwell with you. The Flown Soul. George Parsons Lathrop. AA

Come Not Near My Songs. Unknown, tr. fr. Shoshone Indian by Mary Austin. AWP; WPE

Come not the earliest petal here, but only. Quiet. Marjorie Pickthall.
  NOBC; OBCV
Come Not the Seasons Here. Edwin John Pratt. NoP
Come Not When I Am Dead. Tennyson. FaBoRV; GBL
  (Go By.) OBNC
Come now, and let us wake them: time. *Unknown, tr.* by Jethro Bithell.
  AWP
Come now behold. The Glory of and Grace in the Church Set Out.
  Edward Taylor. *Fr.* God's Determinations. AmPP
Come now each gen'rous feeling heart. The Framework-knitters
  Lamentation. *Unknown.* CoMu
Come now! the victorious kings. *Unknown, tr.* by Arthur Waley. BoS
Come now! You supercilious detractors of America. Meredith Phyfe.
  Edgar Lee Masters. *Fr.* The New Spoon River. GOA
Come, O come, my life's delight. My Life's Delight. Thomas Campion.
  EIL; InvP; OBSC; TrGrPo
Come, O Friend, to Greet the Bride. Solomon Halevi Alkabez, *tr. fr.*
  Hebrew into German by Heine; *English vers. by* Louis Untermeyer.
  TrJP
Come, O Lord, Like Morning Sunlight. Milton S. Littlefield. TrPWD
Come, O Sabbath Day. Gustav Gottheil. AH
Come, O thou traveller unknown. Wrestling Jacob. Charles Wesley.
  NOBE; NOCV; NOEC; OBEV; PoEL-3; SeCePo; TOF
Come o'er the hills, and pass unto the wold. A Winter Hymn—to the
  Snow. Ebenezer Jones. OBNC
Come o'er the stream, Charlie. McLean's Welcome. James Hogg.
  OxBS
Come, oh come in pious Laies. A Hymne I: Generall Invitation to Praise
  God. George Wither. *Fr.* Hallelujah; or, Britain's Second
  Remembrancer. SeCV-1
Come on, come on! and where you go. Ben Jonson. *Fr.* Pleasure
  Reconciled to Virtue. NAEL-1
Come on! Come on! This hillock hides the spire. Sunday Afternoon
  Service in St. Enodoc Church, Cornwall. Sir John Betjeman.
  NOCV
Come On Home. Sharon Scott. JB
Come On In. *Unknown.* SD
Come On in, the Senility Is Fine. Ogden Nash. AiP
Come on, my fellow pilgrims, come. *At. to.* Sarah Lancaster. AmFP
Come on, Nathan, let's not think today. Nakhman of Bratslav to His
  Scribe. Jacob Glatstein, *tr.* by Benjamin *and* Barbara Harshav.
  AYP
Come on out of there with your hands up, Charlie. Patriotic Ode on the
  Fourteenth Anniversary of the Persecution of Charlie Chaplin. Bob
  Kaufman. PoBA
"Come on" sayd sche, "this ordenance to vysyte." Calliope's Nymph
  Brings the Poet to the Palace to Honour. Gawin Douglas. *Fr.* The
  Palace [*or* Palice] of Honor [*or* Honour]. OxBLMV
Come on, sir; here's the place. Stand still. How fearful. Dover, the
  Samphire Cliff. Shakespeare. *Fr.* King Lear, IV, vi. FaBoPP
Come on, sir. Now, you set your foot on shore. Ben Jonson. *Fr.* The
  Alchemist, II, i *and* ii. PoEL-2
Come on then, ye dwellers by nature in darkness. Chorus of Birds.
  Aristophanes, *tr. fr.* Greek by Swinburne. *Fr.* The Birds. AWP
  (Grand Chorus of Birds.) PoEL-5
Come, on thy swaying feet. The Spirit of the Fall. Danske Bedinger
  Dandridge. AA
Come on, ye critics! Find one fault who dare. On Mr. Edward Howard,
  upon His British Princes. Charles Sackville. OBSV
Come, Ophrah, fill my cup—but not with wine. The Splendor of Thine
  Eyes. Moses ibn Ezra, *tr.* by Solomon Solis-Cohen. TrJP
Come out and climb the garden path. Luriana, Lurilee. Charles Elton.
  Mes
Come out come out come out. Moon Eclipse Exorcism. *Unknown, tr.* by
  Armand Schwerner. STP
Come out, come out, this sunny day. Hay-Time. C. M. Lowe. BoTP
Come Out, Come Out, Ye Souls That Serve. Christopher John Brennan.
  Fr. The Wanderer. PoAu-1
Come out for a while and look from the outside in. Christmas Eve. C.
  Day Lewis. EaLo
Come Out into the Sun. Robert Francis. NYBP
Come out of Crete/ and find me here. Sappho, *tr.* by Guy Davenport.
  OBVE
Come out of the Golden Gate. Old Counsel. Herman Melville.
  FaBoRV
Come out of the shrubs now. Hagar to Ishmael. Deborah Eibel. VWA
Come out of your body among us & we're all one. How to Get Grizzly
  Spirit. *Unknown, tr.* by James Koller. STP
Come out, 'tis now September. The Ripe and Bearded Barley.
  Unknown. BoNaP; ChTr; GBP
Come over the born bessy. A Songe betwene the Quenes Majestie and
  Englande. William Birche. CoMu

Come Painter, you and I, you know, dare do. Old England. Nahum
  Tate. APAS
Come Peace, on snowy pinions. Ode to Peace. Mary Weston Fordham.
  CBWP-2
Come, Philomele, that sing'st of ravishment. Shakespeare. *Fr.* The Rape
  of Lucrece. PBBP
Come pity me, young maidens all. Disconsolate Judy's Lamentation.
  Unknown. OxBSS
Come play with me. To a Squirrel at Kyle-na-no. W. B. Yeats.
  FaPON; FM; PDV; RHPC
Come play with me said the sun. Play. Frank Asch. NTCP
Come praise Colonus' horses, and come praise. Colonus' Praise.
  Sophocles, *tr. fr.* Greek by W. B. Yeats. *Fr.* Oedipus at Colonus.
  OBVE
Come, Precious Soul. *Unknown.* AH
Come rede me, dame, come tell me, dame. Nine Inch Will Please a
  Lady. Burns. ErPo
Come, rejoice, 'tis Easter Day! Christ Is Risen! Mrs. D. H. Dugan.
  BLRP
Come right in this house, Will Johnson! Mrs. Johnson Objects. Clara
  Ann Thompson. AIW; BlSi; CBWP-2
Come, rouse up, ye bold-hearted Whigs of Kentucky. Old Tippecanoe.
  Unknown. PAH
Come rouse ye, my lads, though no land we are near. The Sailor's
  Christmas Day. *Unknown.* OxBSS
Come rude Boreas, blustering railer, list ye landsmen all to me. Rude
  Boreas. *Unknown.* OBET
"Come saddle me my fastest steed." Geordie. *Unknown.* AmFP
Come, Said My Soul. Walt Whitman. NOBA
"Come!" said Old Shellover. Old Shellover. Walter de la Mare. BoTP;
  OxBChV
Come, saints and sinners, hear me tell. A Parody. Frederick Douglass.
  Fr. Narrative of the Life of an American Slave. NAAL-1; NAWM-2
Come sheathe your swords! my gallant boys. Sergeant Champe.
  Unknown. PAH
Come, Shepherds, Come! John Fletcher. *Fr.* The Faithful Shepherdess,
  I, iii. EIL; ErPo
Come, Silence, thou sweet reasoner. Silence. James Herbert Morse.
  AA
Come, sit thee down by these cool streams. Then Lose in Time Thy
  Maidenhead. *Unknown.* ErPo
Come, sleep. Francis Beaumont *and* Fletcher. *Fr.* The Woman-Hater.
  EIL; ELP
Come sleep, and with the sweet deceiving. Come, sleep. Francis
  Beaumont *and* Fletcher. *Fr.* The Woman-Hater. EIL; ELP
"Come sleep! O sleep, the certain knot of peace." Sir Philip Sidney. *Fr.*
  Astrophel and Stella, XXXIX. EIL; NAEL-1; NIP; NoP; OBSC;
  PoE; PoRA; PPP; SCV; Son; TEP; TrGrPo
  (Sleep.) OBEV
  (To Sleep.) NOBE
Come slowly, Eden. Emily Dickinson. CMoP
Come Slowly, Paradise. James Benjamin Kenyon. AA
Come, sons of Mars, who thirst for blood. A Drinking-Song, against All
  Sorts of Disputes in Drinking. William Wycherley. SeCV-2
Come, sons of summer, by whose toil [e]. The Hock-Cart, or Harvest
  Home. Robert Herrick. CaPo; EBEV; FaBoPV; JCP; NAEL-1;
  OBS; SeCP; SeCV-1
Come soon. Letter to a Friend. Lilian Moore. ILY
Come, sound up your trumpets and beat up your drums. The Young Earl
  of Essex's Victory over the Emperor of Germany. *Unknown.*
  ESPB; OBET
Come, spread foam rubber on the floor. I Can't Have a Martini, Dear, but
  You Take One. Ogden Nash. PoRA
Come spur [*or* spurre] away. An Ode to Mr. [*or* Master] Anthony
  Stafford to Hasten Him into the Country. Thomas Randolph.
  NOBE; OBEV; OBS
Come, stack arms, men! Pile on the rails. Stonewall Jackson's Way.
  John Williamson Palmer. AA; PAH
Come, stir the fire. Safe. James Walker. OBCP
Come, Stumpy, old man, we must shift while we can. The Broken-down
  Squatter. *Unknown.* PoAu-1
Come! supper is ready. The Good Moolly Cow. Eliza Lee Follen.
  OBCA
Come swallow your bumpers, ye Tories, and roar. Massachusetts Song of
  Liberty. *At. to* Mrs. Mercy Warren. PAH
Come take up your hats, and away let us haste. The Butterfly's Ball.
  William Roscoe. OnUR; OxBChV; RHPC
Come, the wind may never again. A D.G.C. to J. Emily Brontë.
  BrRo, 1st; EnLoPo, 1st.
Come then, and like two doves with silv'rie [*or* silvery] wings. The
  Apparition of His Mistress [e] Calling Him to Elizium [*or* Elysium].
  Robert Herrick. CaPo; SeCP; SeCV-1

Come then! and while the slow icicle hangs. Henry Vaughan. *Fr.* To His Retired Friend, an Invitation to Brecknock.

Come then, as ever, like the wind at morning! Invocation to Youth. Laurence Binyon. OBEV

Come, then, cuckoo. *Unknown, tr. by* Geoffrey Bownas *and* Anthony Thwaite. PeBJV

Come, then, my men. Emperor Ojin, *tr. fr. Japanese by* Geoffrey Bownas *and* Anthony Thwaite. *Fr.* Manyo Shu. PeBJV

Come think with me: the Paris sky, the giant meadow-saffron. Memory of France. Paul Celan, *tr. by* Joachim Neugroschel. AnAn

Come, Thou Almighty King. Charles Wesley. WGRP

Come, thou monarch of the vine. A Drinking Song. Shakespeare. *Fr.* Antony and Cleopatra, II, vii. OBSC

Come thou, who art the wine and wit. His Winding-Sheet. Robert Herrick. CaPo; OBEV

Come through the quiet fields; April again. April 1940. Patrick Maybin. NeIP

Come to guard us, come to bless us. The Triple Benison. Henrietta Cordelia Ray. CBWP-3

Come to Me. *Gond Oral Tradition, tr. by* V. Elwin *and* S. Hivale. WTO

Come to me, angel of the weary hearted! To Sleep. Frances Sargent Osgood. AA

Come to me, Beloved. Homo Factus Est. Digby Mackworth Dolben. TrPWD

Come to me broken dreams and all. The Still Voice of Harlem. Conrad Kent Rivers. CNA; IDB; PoBA

Come to me, Eros, if you needs must come. To the God of Love. E. V. Knox. NOBL

Come to me from Crete to this holy temple. Sappho, *tr. by* Richmond Lattimore. WPOW

Come to me, grief, for ever. A Funerall Song. *Unknown.* CH

Come to me in my dreams, and then. Longing. Matthew Arnold. FPL; PoLF

Come to me in the night—we shall sleep closely together [*or* Let us sleep entwined]. Else Lasker-Schüler. BoWoP, *tr. by* Michael Gillespie; OV, *tr. by* Robert Alter; TrJP, *tr. by* Michael Gillespie

Come to me in the silence of the night. Echo. Christina Rossetti. BoLoP; CH; EBVV; ELP; GBL; NOBE; NoP; OAEL-2; OBNC; PoE; PoEL-5

Come to me, my dearest. *Unknown, tr. fr. Japanese. Fr.* Manyo Shu. Ma

Come to me tonight. Emperor Fushimi, *tr. by* Steven D. Carter. WFTW

Come to me when the swelling wind assails the wood with a sealike roar. Late Light. Edmund Blunden. EnLoPo

Come to my window in the evening twilight. Sunset. Hayyim Nahman Bialik, *tr. by* Helena Frank. TrJP

Come to see me through the spaces. *Unknown, tr. fr. Japanese by* Hiroaki Sato. *Fr.* Manyo Shu. FCEI

Come to Sunny Prestatyn. Sunny Prestatyn. Philip Larkin. NoAM

Come to term the started child shocks. Mustipara: Gravida 5. Marie Ponsot. VGW

Come to the festal board tonight. The Festal Board. *Unknown.* BLPA

Come to the judgment, golden threads. The Judgment of the May. Richard Watson Dixon. OBNC

Come to the Stone. Randall Jarrell. VGW

Come to the window & see sweet dawn shine on this wonder; a man. Bottom's Dream. Philip Dow. NPGG

Come to think of it. Ishikawa Takuboku, *tr. fr. Japanese by* Hiroaki Sato. *Fr.* Forty-seven Tanka in Three Lines. FCEI

Come to your heaven, you heavenly choirs [*or* quires]. New Heaven, New War[re]. Robert Southwell. MePo; NOBE; NoP; OBSC

Come townsmen all and women too. Funny Rigs of Good and Tender-hearted Masters. *Unknown.* OBET

Come trotting up. Foal. Mary Britton Miller. PDV

"Come, try your skill, kind gentlemen." The Gipsy Girl. Ralph Hodgson. MoBrPo

Come Turn to Mee, Thou Pretty Little One. *Unknown.* CoMu

Come unto Me, When Shadows Darkly Gather. Catharine H. Watterman. AH

Come unto me, ye heroes. Saratoga Song. *Unknown.* PAH

Come unto these yellow sands. Shakespeare. *Fr.* The Tempest, I, ii. BoTP; CH; EiL; HeIP; OBEV; OBSC; TTTS

(Ariel's Song: "Come unto these yellow sands.") CTC; FaBoCh; GN; GoJo; NOBE; TEP

(Song: "Come unto these yellow sands.") PoEL-2

Come up England by a different line. I Remember, I Remember. Philip Larkin. FaBoPP; NOBL

Come Up from the Fields, Father. Walt Whitman. AnAmPo; MoAmPo; OBWP; OxBA; PPP; UnPo

Come Up, Methuselah. C. Day Lewis. OBMV

Come up, my horse, to Budleigh Fair. *Unknown.* OxNR

Come up to me at early dawn. Invitation. Solomon ibn Gabirol, *tr. by* Israel Zangwill. TrJP

Come, virgin tapers of pure wax. Richard Crashaw. NOCV

Come visit my pancake collection. The Pancake Collector. Jack Prelutsky. OBCA

Come, walk with me. Emily Brontë. NOBVV

Come, Walter Savage Landor, come this way. Landor. John Albee. AA

Come, warm your hands. Driftwood. Witter Bynner. FYAP

Come Wary One. Ruth Manning-Sanders. CH

Come, we shepherds [*or* shepheards], whose blest sight. In the Holy Nativity of Our Lord God. Richard Crashaw. NAEL-1; PoEL-2; SeCV-1

(Holy Nativity of Our Lord God, The.) WGRP

(Hymn[e] of the Nativity.) HAP; MeLP; MePo; OBS

Come, wed me, Lady Singleton. Lady "Rogue" Singleton. Stevie Smith. FaBoWP; OxBSP

Come wench, are we almost at the well. Fair Maiden. George Peele. *Fr.* The Old Wives' [*or* Wife's] Tale. PoEL-2

Come, when no graver cares employ. To the Rev. F. D. Maurice. Tennyson. GTBS-P; NOBVV

Come when the leaf comes, angle with me. The Angler's Invitation. Thomas Tod Stoddart. GN

Come when you're called. Mother Goose. OxNR

"Come, wife," said good old Farmer Gray. The Little Dog under the Wagon. *Unknown.* PoLF

Come, "Will," let's be good friends again. Sunshine after Cloud. Josephine D. Henderson Heard. CBWP-4

Come with Me. Robert Bly. NoAM; NOBA

Come with me and you may see. A Christmas Rhyme. George Sands Johnson. PWR

Come with me at dawn. Dawncall. Niyi Osundare. UAS

Come with me into those things that have felt this despair for so long. Come with Me. Robert Bly. NoAM; NOBA

Come with Me into Winter's Disheveled Grass. Karen Swenson. GrPl

Come with me to the City of Slaughter, come, enter its courtyards. Hayyim Nahman Bialik, *tr. fr. Hebrew by* Bernhard Frank. *Fr.* In the City of Slaughter. MHeP

Come with rain, O loud Southwester! To the Thawing Wind. Robert Frost. OxBA

Come with the Spring-time, forth fair maid, and be. The Meddow Verse; or, Aniversary to Mistris Bridget Lowman. Robert Herrick. SeCV-1

Come, worthy Greek, Ulysses, come. Ulysses and the Siren. Samuel Daniel. EiL; HAP; NAEL-1; NOBE; NoP; OBEV; OBSC; PoE; PoEL-2; TEP

Come, Ye Disconsolate. Thomas Moore. WGRP

Come, ye heavy states of night. *Unknown.* OBSC

Come, Ye Lads, Who Wish to Shine. *Unknown.* PAH

Come ye old English huntsmen that love noble sport. The Old Pack. *Unknown.* APAS

Come, ye thankful people, come. Harvest Home. Henry Alford. WGRP

Come you, cartoonists. Halsted Street Car. Carl Sandburg. NAAL-2

Come you fatall sisters three. Whipping Cheare. *Unknown.* FaBoBa

Come you gallants all, to you I do call. Robin Hood's Chase. *Unknown.* ESPB

Come, You Pretty False-eyed Wanton. Thomas Campion. ELP; OBSC

Come, You Whose Loves Are Dead. Francis Beaumont *and* Fletcher. *Fr.* The Knight of the Burning Pestle, IV, iv. EiL

Comedian as the Letter C, The. Wallace Stevens. OxBA

Comedian, holding a chunk of flaming shale, The. Why That's Bob Hope. William Hathaway. NAmP; SM

Comedy of Art: Henri de Toulouse Lautrec, The. Richard Howard. AnAn

Comely and capable one of our race. On the Portrait of a Woman about to Be Hanged. Thomas Hardy. CMoP

Comes a brown. Corkby, Part Two. Jerome Rothenberg. NNaP

Comes a cry from Cuban water. Cuba Libre. Joaquin Miller. PAH

Comes a time. The Poet in Old Age Fishing at Evening. Desmond O'Grady. CIP

Comes Fog and Mist. William Hart-Smith. *Fr.* Christopher Columbus. PoAu-2

Comes home dull with coal-dust deliberately. Her Husband. Ted Hughes. OxBC

Comes not the springtime here. Come Not the Seasons Here. Edwin John Pratt. NoP

Comes often to my memory. Sonnet: Comes Often to My Memory. Dante, *tr. by* Frederick Morgan. PFI

Comes the deer to my singing. Hunting-Song. *Unknown, tr. by* Natalie Curtis. AWP

Comes the lure of green things growing. Afoot. Sir Charles G. D. Roberts. CaP

Comes the time. Algonkian Burial. Alfred Goldsworthy Bailey. OBCV

Comes the time when it's later. A Wicker Basket. Robert Creeley. CAPP; HAP; MoP; NoAM; NoP; SM
Comes walking barefoot. Sojourner Truth. Robert Hayden. *Fr.* Stars. CNA
Comes Winter, the Sea Hunting. Norman Dubie. MAYP
Comet, The. Thomas Lovell Beddoes. FL
Comet, The. Emil Makai, *tr. fr. Hungarian by* André Ungar. VWA
Comet, The. Michael Palmer. NPGG
Comet, The. Paolo Volponi, *tr. fr. Italian by* Lawrence R. Smith. NItP
Comet at Yell'ham, The. Thomas Hardy. CMoP; GBL
Comets and Princes. Samuel Johnson. FaBoEE
Comfort. Margaret Widdemer. GoYe
Comfort for the Sick Child. Gregory O'Brien. ATNZ
Comfort in Puirtith. Helen B. Cruickshank. OxBS
Comfort is nothing, you say. Moving Out. Robley Wilson, Jr.. KS
Comfort me with stars, not apples. Star Drill. Tom Inglis Moore. PoAu-2
Comfort of the Fields. Archibald Lampman. CaP
Comfort of the Trees, The. Richard Watson Gilder. PAH
Comfort thyself, my woful heart. Sir Thomas Wyatt. SiPS
Comfort to a Youth That Had Lost His Love. Robert Herrick. NOBE; OBEV
Comfort ye, comfort ye my people. Bible, *O.T. Fr.* Isaiah, XL: 1–11. EaLo; OBVE, (1-8); TrJP, (1-5).
Comfortable Strangers. Terence Winch. UL
Comfortably fixed for clothing and food, children married off. Half in the Family, Half Out. Po Chü-i, *tr. by* Burton Watson. CoBCP
Comforted by Limestone. Edward Dorn. *Fr.* Oxford. NOBA
Comforters, The. Dora Sigerson Shorter. CH
Comic Adventures of Old Mother Hubbard and Her Dog, The. Sarah Catherine Martin. *See* Old Mother Hubbard.
Comic Miseries. John Godfrey Saxe. AnAmPo
Comic Verse. Takamura Kotaro, *tr. fr. Japanese by* Hiroaki Sato. FCEI
Comical Revenge, The, *sel.* Sir George Etherege.
"Ladies, though to your conquering eyes." *Fr.* V, iii. OBS; OxBSP
Comin' thro' the Rye ("Comin' thro' the rye, poor body"). Burns. OxBS
Comin' thro' the Rye ("Gin a body meet a body"). Burns. FaFP; LiTB; WBLP
Coming. Philip Larkin. MoBrPo; OxBTC
Coming Across. Mehri, *tr. fr. Farsi by* Deirdre Lashgari. WPOW
Coming American, The, *sel.* Sam Walter Foss.
"Bring me men to match my mountains." AmFN; BLPA; FaBoBe
Coming and Going. Mitchell Goodman. VGW
Coming and Going. Louis Johnson. ATNZ
Coming and going, life and death. Gizan, *tr. by* Lucien Stryk *and* Takashi Ikemoto. ZPCJ
Coming and going, no fixed lodging. Impromptu Poem in Yün-chien. Zekkai Chushin, *tr. by* Burton Watson. FCEI
Coming around the corner of a dark trail. what was wrong with the valley? The Inquisitors. Robinson Jeffers. MoAmPo
Coming around the corner of a dream. Cockaigne: A Dream. Louis Edward Sissman. DiPo
Coming around the Horn. John A. Stone. AmFP
Coming at an end, the lovers. A Book of Music. Jack Spicer. PoM
Coming Awake. D. H. Lawrence. BrPo
Coming Back. Joseph Bruchac. CDW
Coming Back. Linda Gregg. NPGG
Coming Back. "Shake" Keane. PVCV
Coming Back Home. Ray A. Young Bear. CDW
Coming back one evening through deserted fields. Through All Your Abstract Reasoning. Brian Patten. FaBoTw
Coming back over the col between. Strength through Joy. Kenneth Rexroth. FYAP; VGW
Coming Back to America. James Dickey. NYBP
Coming back to this generous island. Returning to Store Bay. Barbara Howes. Psk
Coming by a mountain path. Basho, *tr. fr. Japanese by* Burton Watson. *Fr.* Seventy-six Hokku. FCEI
Coming by evening through the wintry city. At a Bach Concert. Adrienne Rich. NePoEA; NIP; SM
"Coming, coming!" Kyorai, *tr. fr. Japanese by* Burton Watson. *Fr.* Twenty Hokku. FCEI
Coming down into an air brown as whiskey, the plane. Autobiography, Chapter XLII: Three Days in Louisville. Jim Barnes. HATNAP
Coming Down to It. Malcolm Glass. BXAP
Coming Events. John Montague, *tr. fr. Chinese.* FaBCIP
Coming from the south. Six Ten Sixty-nine. Conyus. PoBA
Coming Home. Philip Levine. CAPP
Coming Home. Rai San'yo, *tr. fr. Japanese by* Burton Watson. FCEI; JLIC-2

Coming Home. John Stone. NIP
Coming Home. Brian Turner. PeNZ
Coming Home at Night in the Snow. Yanagawa Koran, *tr. fr. Chinese by* Burton Watson. JLIC-2
Coming Home from Abroad. David Holbrook. OBTV
Coming Home from Camp. Lonny Kaneko. BrSi
Coming home, I find you still in bed. Abortion. Ai. BoWoP
Coming Home in March. Harold Littlebird. STE; VoR
Coming home late through the smoky. Coming Home. Brian Turner. PeNZ
Coming home on a summer night. Small Moon. Howard Nemerov. PCP
Coming home with the last load I ride standing. Emergency Haying. Hayden Carruth. NNaP
Coming Homeward out of Spain. Barnabe Googe. EIL
Coming, I don't enter at the gate. Gyoko, *tr. by* Lucien Stryk *and* Takashi Ikemoto. ZPCJ
Coming in again, you know the town by boards it makes eyes touch. Autobiography: Last Chapter. Jim Barnes. CDW
Coming in front of a mirror store. Ishikawa Takuboku, *tr. fr. Japanese by* Hiroaki Sato. *Fr.* Forty-seven Tanka in Three Lines. FCEI
Coming into the high room again after years. Late Spring. W. S. Merwin. AnAn
Coming into the store at first angry. The Man Who Finds That His Son Has Become a Thief. Raymond Souster. NOBC; OBCV
Coming into Your Room. John Lehmann. PoPo
Coming of Age. John Logan. DiL
Coming of Age in the County Jail. Carter Revard. VoR
Coming of Age in "The Movement." Wendy Rose. ER
Coming of Arthur, The. Tennyson. *Fr.* Idylls of the King. Merlin's Riddling. FaBoRV
Coming of Christ, The. *Unknown.* ACP
Coming of Dusk upon a Village in Haiti, The. Henry Rago. HoPM
Coming of Good Luck, The. Robert Herrick. FaBoEE; JCP; OxBSP
Coming of His Feet, The. Lyman W. Allen. BLPA
Coming of Light, The. Mark Strand. HCAP
Coming of Spring, The. Nora Perry. PWR
Coming of Spring, The. Henrietta Cordelia Ray. CBWP-3
Coming of that limpid star is twice, The. Louise Labé, *tr. by* Willis Barnstone. BoWoP
Coming of the Cold, The. Theodore Roethke. OBCP
Coming of the King, The. *Unknown. See* Yet if his majesty, our sovereign [*or* soveraign] Lord.
Coming of the Plague, The. Weldon Kees. NaP; VGW
Coming of the White Man, The. Patrick Anderson. *Fr.* Poem on Canada. MoCV
"Wide was the land." CaP
Coming of War; Actaeon, The. Ezra Pound. CMoP; PoA; PoE
Coming of Winter, The. Jules Laforgue, *tr. fr. French by* William Jay Smith. CT
Coming of Wisdom with Time, The. W. B. Yeats. FaBoEE; SoSe
Coming Out. Jacqueline Lapidus. IHMS
Coming out of the dark of the short night. Buson, *tr. fr. Japanese by* Hiroaki Sato. *Fr.* Eighty-seven Hokku. FCEI
Coming out of the house on a fresh March morning. March 1st. Kathleen Spivack. NYBP
Coming out of the mountains of a summer evening. St. Gervais. Michael Roberts. FaBoCh
Coming out of the privy. Buson, *tr. fr. Japanese by* Hiroaki Sato. *Fr.* Eighty-seven Hokku. FCEI
Coming out with your clutch of postcards. Leaving the Tate. Fleur Adcock. ATNZ
Coming Suddenly to the Sea. Louis Dudek. NOBC
Coming to an end and leaving the moon as a keepsake. Teika, *tr. fr. Japanese by* Hiroaki Sato. *Fr.* Eighty-four Tanka. FCEI
Coming [*or* Comming] to kiss [*or* kisse] her lips [*or* lyps], (such grace I found.) Amoretti, LXIV. Spenser. EBEV; NAEL-1; OAEL-1; Son
Coming to Know. William Stafford. BLA
Coming to the Surface. Jack Myers. NAmP
Coming to This. Mark Strand. HCAP
Coming together. Recreation. Audre Lorde. NIP; NoP
Coming toward me. A Man Walking through the Snow. Shotetsu, *tr. by* Steven D. Carter. WFTW
Coming Up and Falling Down. Stephen Vincent. NeAC
Coming up England by a different line. I Remember, I Remember. Philip Larkin. NOBL
Coming upon it unawares. Pittsburgh. Witter Bynner. AmFN
Coming Woman, The. Mary Weston Fordham. CBWP-2
Comings, goings, hard to settle down. Seeing Off Wang Yüan-chao— Reprise. Wu Wei-yeh, *tr. by* Jonathan Chaves. CoBLCP

Commander Lowell. Robert Lowell. DiL; VGW
Commanding Elephants. Philip Levine. NaP
Commemoration. Claude McKay. BANP
Commemoration. Sir Henry Newbolt. FaBoTw
Commemoration Ode, *sels.* Harriet Monroe.
    Democracy. AA
    Lincoln. AA
    Washington. AA; FaBoBe
    (Two Heroes.) OHIP
Commemorative of a Naval Victory. Herman Melville. AiP; HAP;
    MOS; UnPo
Commencement. Constance Carrier. WPE
Commendations of Mistress Jane Scrope, The. John Skelton. *Fr.*
    Phyllyp Sparowe [*or* Philip Sparrow]. OBSC
Commendatory Verses to Edmund Spenser's Fairy Queen, *sel.* Sir Walter
    Ralegh.
    Vision upon This Conceit of the Fairy Queen, A. Son
Comment. Dorothy Parker. *Fr.* Some Beautiful Letters. AnAmPo;
    NBLV; NIP; OBAL
Comment on Ethnopoetics and Literacy. Wendy Rose. ER
Commentaries on the Song of Songs. Judith Herzberg, *tr. fr. Dutch by*
    Shirley Kaufman. VWA
Commentary Applied to Spiritual Things. Saint John of the Cross, *tr. fr.*
    Spanish by K. Kavanaugh *and* O. Rodrigues. TOF
Comments. Peggy Susberry Kenner. JB
Commerce in the Caucasus. Ishihara Yoshiro, *tr. fr. Japanese by* Hiroaki
    Sato. FCEI
Coming to kisse her lyps. *See* Coming to kiss her lips.
Commingling sky, A. Freely Espousing. James Schuyler. NeAP; NoP
Commiserating with the Poor. Li K'ai-hsien, *tr. fr. Chinese by* Jonathan
    Chaves. CoBLCP
Commission. Ezra Pound. BoLoP; NIP; OPOP; TwCP
Commissioner bet me a pony, The—I won. Songs of the Squatters.
    Robert Lowe. PoAu-1
Committee, The. C. Day Lewis. CMoP
Committee, The—now a permanent body. Dream. Marianne Moore.
    NYBP
Committee's fat, The. Un-American Investigators. Langston Hughes.
    BPo
Commodity of the heart, The. Mohammad Taqi Mir, *tr. by* Ahmed Ali.
    GoT
Common Bill. *Unknown.* AmFP; AS, *with music*
Common Blessings. Thomas Curtis Clark. TrPWD
Common Conditions, *sel. Unknown.*
    Lustily, Lustily. OxBSS
Common Cormorant [*or* Shag], The. Christopher Isherwood. ChTr;
    FaBoCh; FaBoCo; FaBoNo; FiBHP; NBLV; PYC; RHPC
Common Dawn. Guy Butler. PeSA
Common Dust. Georgia Douglas Johnson. AmNP; PoBA; TTY
Common Form. Kipling. *Fr.* Epitaphs of the War, 1914–1918.
    FaBoEE; FaBoTw
Common Grave, The. James Dickey. CoAP
Common Ground, A. Denise Levertov. PoM
Common Inference, A. Charlotte Perkins Gilman. AA; WGRP
Common Living Dirt, The. Marge Piercy. GeTw
Common Lot, The. Adelbert Sumpter Coats. TrPWD
Common Man, The. Arthur James Marshall Smith. NOBC
Common Occurrence, A. Priscilla Jane Thompson. CBWP-2
Common Poem, A. Carolyn M. Rodgers. CNA
Common Road, The. Silas H. Perkins. BLPA; FaBoBe
Common Sailor, The. *Unknown.* OxBSS
Common Sense. Thomas Field. AA
Common Sense. Harry Graham. *See* "There's been an accident," they
    said.
Common Song, A. Ya Hsien, *tr. fr. Chinese by* Dominic Cheung. IFON
Common Woman, The, *sels.* Judy Grahn.
    Carol, in the Park, Chewing on Straws. *Fr.* IV. PeHV; WPOW
    Ella, in a Square Apron, along Highway 80. *Fr.* II. NMM
Commonplace. James Joyce. FL
Commonplace, The. Walt Whitman. MoAmPo; TrGrPo
Commonplace Day, A. Thomas Hardy. NOBVV
Commons' Petition to Charles II, The. Earl of Rochester. FaBoCo
Commonwealth of the Bees, The. Shakespeare. *Fr.* King Henry V.
    GN
Commotion of these waves, however strong, cannot disturb, The. Louis
    Dudek. *Fr.* Europe. OBCV
Communal. Mary Elizabeth Fullerton. PoAu-1
Communication. Elizabeth Jennings. NePoEA
Communication in Whi-te. Don L. Lee. BPo
Communication of His Thirtieth Birthday. Marvin Bell. CoAP
Communication to Nancy Cunard, A. Kay Boyle. PoNe

Communication to the City Fathers of Boston. George Starbuck. NYBP
Communion. Edward Dowden. TrPWD
Communion. David Ignatow. CAPP
Communion. J. L. Spicer. BLRP
Communion. John Banister Tabb. WGRP
Communion Hymn, A. Alice Freeman Palmer. TrPWD
Communion Hymn. George Seaver. TIRV
Communion of Saints: The Poor Bastard under the Bridge. Marie Ponsot.
    VGW
Communism. Franco Fortini, *tr. fr. Italian by* Lawrence R. Smith. NItP
Communism. Ella Wheeler Wilcox. AnAmPo
Commuter ("Commuter—one who spends his life"). E. B. White.
    NBLV
    (Commuters.) FaBoCo
Commuters. Edward Hirsch. NAmP
Commuters. E. B. White. *See* Commuter.
Como lo Siento. Lorna Dee Cervantes. NoAM
Companion, The. E. A. Robinson. NoAM
Companion of her lord till death. *Unknown, tr. by* Arthur Waley. BoS
Companions. Charles Stuart Calverley. FaBoCo; NA; NOBL
Companions, The. Howard Nemerov. NYBP
Company in Loneliness. *Unknown.* NOIV
Company of mountains, an upthrust of mountains, A. Kinloch Ainort.
    Sorley MacLean. PoSH
Company of vessels on the sea, A. Battle Problem. William Meredith.
    NYBP
Comparatives. N. Scott Momaday. SM
Compared to a tree, compared to a dead man. Myopia. Giancarlo
    Majorino, *tr. by* Lawrence R. Smith. NItP
Compared to the transcendental realm, the world under the roofed-in-cave
    is somber. Unachieved. Philip Lamantia. BAP
Comparison, A. William Cowper. OxBSP
Comparison, The. John Donne. ErPo; TEP
Comparison, A. John Farrar. FaPON
Comparison, A. Agnes Nemes Nagy, *tr. fr. Hungarian by* Alan Dixon.
    MHuP
Comparison, The, *sel. Unknown.*
    "Let dirty streets be paved with flow'ry green." NOEC
Comparison and Complaint, The. Isaac Watts. TrPWD
Comparison of Hands One Day Late Summer El Sobrante. Wendy Rose.
    HATNAP
Comparison of the Life of Man, A. Richard Barnfield. OBSC; OxBSP
Comparisons. Christina Rossetti. OxBChV
Compasses, The. George MacBeth. NePoEA-2
Compassion. Thomas Hardy. FM
Compassion for the Farmers. Li K'ai-hsien, *tr. fr. Chinese by* Jonathan
    Chaves. CoBLCP
Compassion is pungent. Flowers of the Foothills and Mountain Valleys.
    Alice Notley. UL
Compassionate eyes had our brave John Brown. John Brown; a Paradox.
    Louise Imogen Guiney. PAH
Compassionate Fool, The. Norman Cameron. GTBS-P; OxBSP;
    OxBTC; RB
Compatience perses, reuth and marcy stoundes. The Passion of Jesus.
    Unknown. MeEL
Compel Them to Come In. Leonard Dodd. BLRP
Compelled to Love. Walter Stone. ErPo
Compendium of Good Tanka, A, *sels.* Teika, *tr. fr. Japanese by* Hiroaki
    Sato. FCEI
    "About people, no, I don't know how they feel."
    "As a warbler flits from one plum twig to another."
    "As far away as distant China."
    "As I look around, I see a weir of waves."
    "As I pick young herbs for you."
    "As I searched for cherry blossoms."
    "As it begins to dawn, I almost take for daybreak."
    "As soon as it blows, autumn grass and trees wither."
    "As winds blow over white dewdrops."
    "Autumn has come; crimson leaves have fallen."
    "Autumn wind is and is not as of old, The."
    "Autumn's come"—"The year's half gone.""
    "Because limits are set."
    "Because my home village is close to Mount Yoshino."
    "Bitter—that I should not have decayed."
    "Building a Sano boat-bridge."
    "Bush clovers must have shed their flowers."
    "Cherries bloom on distant hills."
    "Cherry blossoms must have opened."
    "Cloud, a reminder of my lover, The."
    "Crimson leaves flow in Tatsuta River."
    "Dew at the tip of a leaf."

"Dew on my sleeves, The."
"Didn't we make a vow."
"Do not let it be known."
"Dream broken by the sound of a mallet."
"Even in a remote place eightfold heaps."
"Everyone else has changed to a flowery robe."
"Faintly, in the dawn moonlight."
"Flower's color has passed, The."
"From now on may it go on falling."
"From tomorrow, who will visit."
"Frost has touched the bamboo grass."
"Had I expected this?."
"I remember, I burn brushwood."
"I suffer enough, now it would all be the same."
"I will return and look on Matsushima once again."
"Ice on my laid-out sleeve still frozen, The."
"If by chance someone asks."
"If I can't twist my thread with yours."
"If I must, I'll have to pick them haphazardly."
"If you do not come, must I sleep alone."
"In a winter-seared forest."
"In Akishino is it raining on the villages."
"In May rain, the smoke from the seaweed."
"In the autumn paddies, the roof mats for the makeshift."
"In the evening my thoughts go toward the end of the clouds."
"In Yatano Field the reeds have turned color."
"Is it because autumn dew has collected."
"Its dark green—what if it should be unable to resist."
"It's the start of spring, they say."
"Just because you said, "I'll come right away.""
"Like a mountain stream whose rapids are blocked."
"Like the foam on the ever-flowing Thinking River."
"Like the white dewdrop that forms at the leaf-tip."
"Like trees buried in the shallows of Natori River."
"Lodging in a hut where the Naniwa men burn reeds."
"Loneliness has no special color."
"Long as the foot-wearying mountain."
"Looking at it, just thinking about it."
"Looking at the moon, I feel sad."
"Lovely rock buried under the seaweed, A."
"My love affair is like the clumps of bush clover."
"My thought grows like rock azaleas."
"Not many days have passed."
"Now, today, I'll lose myself."
"On a spring day when boundless light."
"On Mount Moru where both white dew."
"On this trip I couldn't even come with offerings."
"One who's unkind is like you, The."
"Parting from you, I go to Inaba."
"People of the hundred-acre palace, The."
"Pity, how the dew must spill from grass leaves."
"Plum blossoms are hard to make out."
"Princess Tatsuta's headband loosened."
"Rampant rank reed, to repress it I try."
"Since our parting when the moon at dawn looked unfriendly."
"Since the mountain cherries began to bloom."
"Since the sparse bush clover began to flower."
"So far apart our meetings."
"Spring passed, and summer it seems has come."
"Tears of wild geese crying, The."
"Those early-rice paddies by the hill."
"Though false rumors pop up as at a fair."
"Though the space may be short."
"Throughout the land, blossoms are in their prime."
"To my hut overgrown with burdocks."
"Tomorrow I'll come again to this wild path."
"Under a willow by the road."
"Unexpectedly cool, in summer clothes."
"Unheard of even in the age of mighty gods."
"Weir that winds have made in a mountain stream, The."
"What should I do? If only I had a hut."
"When day breaks, must I go over the mountain ridge again."
"When evening falls, the autumn wind rustles."
"When I hear deep in the mountains."
"White chrysanthemums they've set up at Fukiage."
"Wild geese departing, their wings in white clouds, The."
"Wild geese lured by the autumn wind."
"Will I see it again."
"Would the moon ever tell us to grieve."
"Years and months, The."
"Your Majesty's reign will never end."
Compensation. James Edwin Campbell. BANP
Compensation. Thomas Stephens Collier. AA

Compensation. Paul Laurence Dunbar. AmNP; BPo; PoNe
Compensation. Emerson. AmPP; FPL; LiTA; NOBA; TAP
Compensation. Robinson Jeffers. MoAB; MoAmPo
Compensation. Henrietta Cordelia Ray. CBWP-3
Competing not so much with one another. Watching Gymnasts. Robert Francis. RR
Competitors, The. Gerald William Barrax. KS
Complacencies of the peignoir, and late. Sunday Morning. Wallace Stevens. AmPP; AmPP; BLPL; CMoP; HAP; HCAP; HeIP; InPS; LiTA; LiTM; MoAB; MoAmPc; MoP; NAAL-2; NAWM-2; NIP; NoAM; NOBA; NoP; OxBA; PoA, *early version*; PoA; PoE; QFR; TAP; WeW
Complacent Cliff-Dweller, The. Margaret Fishback. PoLF
"Complaine my lute, complaine on him." A Pleasant New Ballad of Two Lovers. *Unknown.* CoMu
Complaint, The. Mark Akenside. OBEV
Complaint. Joseph Deericks Bennett. LiTA
Complaint, The, *sel.* Thomas Hoccleve.
  Hoccleve Remembers His Madness. OxBLMV
Complaint. Alistair Paterson. *Fr.* Incantations for Warriors, XXII. PeNZ
Complaint. William Carlos Williams. QFR
Complaint, A. Wordsworth. NOBE; PoEL-4
Complaint. James Wright. NOBA; TAP; VGW
Complaint about Exile, A. Mairi MacLeod, *tr. fr. Gaelic by* Joan Keefe. PBWP
Complaint after Psycho-Analysis. Edgell Rickword. PoPo
Complaint by Night of the Lover Not Beloved, A. Earl of Surrey, , *after* Petrarch. AAS; AWP; EBEV; EIL; NAEL-1; OAEL-1; OBVE; SiPS; Son; TEP
Complaint of a Lover Forsaken of His Love, The. *Unknown. See* Poor soul sat sighing beside a sycamore tree, The.
Complaint of a Lover Rebuked. Petrarch. *See* Sonnets to Laura: To Laura in Life.
Complaint of a Young Girl. Wang Chung-ju, *tr. fr. Chinese by* Kenneth Rexroth. PCP
Complaint of Chaucer to His Empty Purse, The. Chaucer. NAEL-1
  (Complaint of Chaucer to His Purse, The.) OAEL-1
  (Complaint to His Purse, The.) NoP
  (Compleinte of Chauser to His Empty Purs, The Chaucer's Complaint to His Empty Purse.) TrGrPo, 2 *vers.*
  (Song to His Purse for the King, A.) MeEL
Complaint of Henry Duke of Buckingham, The. Thomas Sackville. *See* Induction to "A Mirror for Magistrates."
Complaint of Love. Sir Philip Sidney. *Fr.* Arcadia. PoEL-1; SiPS
Complaint of New Amsterdam, The. Jacob Steendam. PAH
Complaint of Rosamond, The, *sels.* Samuel Daniel.
  Henry's Lament. OBSC
  Lonely Beauty. CTC; OBSC
  Rosamond's Appeal. OBSC
Complaint of the Absence of Her Lover Being upon the Sea. Henry Howard, Earl of Surrey. AAS; EIL; ELP; GBL; OBEV
Complaint of the Common Weill of Scotland. Sir David Lindsay. *Fr.* The Dreme. GoTS
  (Compleynt of the Comoun Weill of Scotland, The.) OxBS
Complaint of the Fair Armoress [*or* Armouress], The. Villon, *tr. fr. French by* Swinburne. AWP; CTC; OBVE
Complaint of the Grandparents. Donald Justice. BLA; CAPP
Complaint of the King of Thule. Jules Laforgue, *tr. fr. French by* William Jay Smith. CT
Complaint of the Moon in the Provinces. Jules Laforgue, *tr. fr. French by* William Jay Smith. CT
Complaint of the Morpethshire Farmer, The. Basil Bunting. CTC
Complaint of the Oblivion of the Dead. Jules Laforgue, *tr. fr. French by* William Jay Smith. CT
Complaint of Troilus, The. Chaucer. *Fr.* Troilus and Criseyde [*or* Criseide], V. NOBE; OBEV
Complaint on Solipsism. Gyula Illyés, *tr. fr. Hungarian by* William Jay Smith. MHuP
Complaint that His Ladie after She Knew of His Love Kept Her Face Alway Hidden from Him,. Earl of Surrey. *See* I never saw you madam, lay [*or* sawe my Ladye] laye apart.
Complaint to His Purse. Chaucer. *See* To you, my purs, and to noon other wight.
Complaints of Poverty, The, *sel.* Nicholas James.
  "May poverty, without offence, approach." NOEC
Complaisant Friend, The. Pierre Louÿs, *tr. fr. French. Fr.* Chansons de Bilitis. PeHV
Complaisant Swain, The. Ovid, *tr. fr. Latin by* F. A. Wright. *Fr.* Amores, III, 14. AWP
Complaynt. Anne Waldman. UL
Compleat Anglers, The. Dennis Scott. UAS

Compleinte of Chauser to His Empty Purs, The. Chauser's Complaint to His Empty Purse. Chaucer. *See* To you, my purs, and to noon other wight.
Complete Balancing Weather Meets. Ted Greenwald. LP
Complete Cynic, The. Keith Preston. NBLV
Complete in Thee, No Work of Mine. Aaron R. Wolfe. AH
Complete Introductory Lectures on Poetry, The. Bernadette Mayer. UL
Complete Misanthropist, The. Morris Bishop. FiBHP; FPL; TW
Complete Thought. Barrett Watten. IAT
Completion. Stephen Dunn. BLA
Complexity was never your strong suit. The Response of Telemachus. Sanford Pinsker. SoTCo
Compleynt of the Comoun Weill of Scotland, The. Sir David Lindsay. *See* Dreme, The: Complaint of the Common Weill of Scotland.
Complicity. Tess Gallagher. GeTw
Complicity killed you. I know. I know. Closer First to Earth. Anne Hazlewood-Brady. IHMS
Compliment, The. William Habington. ACP
Compliment to the Ladies, A. Blake. BXAP
Compliment upon a crutch, A. To a Lady, with a Present of a Walking-Stick. John Hookham Frere. FaBoUs
Compline. Donald Davie. *Fr.* Horae Canonicae. CRP
Components. Roger McDonald. CBAP
Compose compose beds. Sacred. Gertrude Stein. OBAL
Composed at Neidpath Castle, the Property of Lord Queensberry, 1803. Wordsworth. GTBS; GTBS-P
Composed by the Seaside, near Calais, August, 1802. Wordsworth. EnRP; Son
Composed by the Side of Grasmere Lake. Wordsworth. ChER
Composed, generally defined. The Map. Mark Strand. NYBP
Composed in the Composing Room. Franklin Pierce Adams. NIP; OBAL
Composed in the Tower before his execution. "More Light! More Light!" Anthony Hecht. CoAP; HAP; NePoEA-2; NoAM; NOBA; NoP; OBWP; RB; SM; SoSe; TwCP; UnPo; VGW; VWA
Composed near Calais, on the Road Leading to Ardres, August 7, 1802. Wordsworth. FaBoPV
Composed on a Journey Homeward; the Author Having Received Intelligence of the Birth of a Son. Samuel Taylor Coleridge. Son
Composed on a Moonlit Night Outing on Ancient West, *sels.* Shu Wei, *tr. fr. Chinese by* Barry L. Gartell. WFTU
"I neither trim the sail nor tend the mast." *Fr.* II.
"Wind comes up, clouds depart, the moon just overhead, The." *Fr.* I.
Composed on a Spring Day and Shown to Yang Tzu-sha, *sel.* Chang Hui-yen, *tr. fr. Chinese by* An-yan Tang.
"Spring breeze is a loafer, The." WFTU
Composed on the Theme "Willows by the Riverside." Yü Hsüan-chi, *tr. fr. Chinese.* WPOW, *tr. by* Jan W. Walls
Composed upon an Evening of Extraordinary Splendour and Beauty. Wordsworth. EnRP; OAEL-2
Composed upon Westminster Bridge, September 3, 1802. Wordsworth. AWP; BLPL; ChTr; EnRP; EyDe; FaBoCh; FaBoPP; FaBoRV; FaBV; FaFP; FF; HAP; HeIP; InPK; InPS; InvP; NAEL-2; NAWM-2; NoP; OAEL-2; OBNC; PoE; PoEL-4; PoLF; PrIm; Son; TEP; TrGrPo; UnPo; WeW
Composed While Ill. Basho, *tr. fr. Japanese by* Burton Watson. *Fr.* Seventy-six Hokku. FCEI
Composed While under Arrest. Mikhail Yurevich Lermontov, *tr. fr. Russian by* Max Eastman. AWP
Composer's Winter Dream, The. Norman Dubie. LCAP
Composition. Peter Blue Cloud. VoR
Composition for Words and Paint. Fleur Adcock. ATNZ
Composition in Black and White. Katha Pollitt. GrPl
Composition in Glass, for. Michael Harlow. ATNZ
Composition of Pat Young, The. Pat Young. Kenneth Mackenzie. PoAu-2
Composition 1. Francisco Carrillo, *tr. fr. Spanish by* Maureen Ahern *and* David Tipton. Per
Compost. James Grainger. *Fr.* The Sugar Cane. NOEC
(How to Fertilize Soil.) FaBoUs
Compost Heap, The. Vernon Watkins. NYBP
Compound earths in structural compositions are Palus Putredinis. Edoardo Sanguineti, *tr. fr. Italian by* Lawrence R. Smith. *Fr.* Laborintus. NItP
Compound Eye, The. Peter Davison. SM
Compound Eye, The. Sandra McPherson. AnAn
Compounded in confusion. The New Litany. Rita Mae Brown. PeHV
Comprehensive. Carol Ann Duffy. NPo
Compromised by sorrow. Elegy for Chief Sealth. Duane Niatum. CDW
Compulsive Qualifications, *sels.* Richard Howard. PoA
"Richard, may I ask a question? What is an episteme?."
"Richard, what will it be like when you ask the questions?."
Computation, The. John Donne. OxBSP

Computative Oak. Ruth Berman. BWV
Computer. Otto Orban, *tr. fr. Hungarian by* Emery George. VWA
Computer Iterates the Greater Trumps, The. Gene Wolfe. BWV
Computer was supposed to be a carpenter Tuesday, The. Computative Oak. Ruth Berman. BWV
Computer's First Christmas Card, The. Edwin Morgan. FaBoCo; NIP; PChr
Comrade. Philippe Soupault, *tr. fr. French by* Pat Nolan. RHTwFP
Comrade in Arms. Tom Inglis Moore. PoAu-2
Comrade Jesus. Sarah Norcliffe Cleghorn. WGRP
Comradery. Madison Cawein. AA
Comrades. Henry Ames Blood. AA
Comrades. Henry R. Dorr. PAH
Comrades as We Rest Within. Ronald Hambleton. CaP
Comrades in Arms: Conversation Piece. *Unknown.* ErPo
Comrades, leave me here a little, while as yet 'tis early morn. Locksley Hall. Tennyson. BLPL; EBEV; FaBoBe; FaFP; NAEL-2; OAEL-2
Comrades of risk and rigour long ago. Prisoners. Frederick William Harvey. MMA
Comrades, the morning breaks, the sun is up. Hafiz, *tr. fr. Persian by* Richard Le Gallienne. *Fr.* Odes, II. AWP
Comrades, you may pass the rosy. The Lay of the Lovelorn. William Edmonstoune Aytoun *and* Sir Theodore Martin. FaBoCo
(Cry of the Lovelorn, The.) CenHV
Comrades, you may pass the rosy. The Lay of the Lovelorn. William Edmonstoune Aytoun *and* Sir Theodore Martin. CenHV; FaBoCo
Comreigh Critter, The. Gerrit Komrij, *tr. fr. Dutch by* Jacob Lowland. DuIn
Comus; a Masque Presented at Ludlow Castle ("Before the starry threshold of Jove's court"). Milton. OAEL-1, *with music.*
Sels.
Chastity. OBS
Comus's Praise of Nature. PoEL-3
Echo. ELP; OBEV; OBS
(Lady Sings, The.) NOBE
(Lady's Song.) TrGrPo
Sabrina. OBS
Sabrina Fair. EBEV; ELP; FaBoCh, *much abr.;* GN; PoEL-3
(Sabrina.) CH, *abr.;* NOBE; OBEV
"Star that bids the shepherd fold, The." FaBoCh; OBEV
(Comus' Invocation to His Readers.) TrGrPo
(Comus Speaks.) NOBE
(Invocation of Comus, The.) OBS, *longer sel..*
(Mask, A.) FiP
Temperance and Virginity. OBS
"To the ocean now I fly." OBEV; OBS
(Farewell of the Attendant Spirit.) TrGrPo
(Spirit Epiloguizes, The.) NOBE
Concealment: Ishi, the Last Wild Indian, The. William Stafford. NaP
Conceit Begotten by the Eyes. Sir Walter Ralegh. SiPS
(Affection and Desire.) OBSC
Conceit upon the Feet. William Zaranka. BXAP
Conceited Man. *Gond Oral Tradition, tr. by* V. Elwin *and* S. Hivale. WTO
Conceited Pedlar, The, *sel.* Thomas Randolph.
Come from Thy Palace. OxBSP
Conceits, *sels.* Arlo Bates. AA
Kitty's Laugh.
Kitty's "No."
Conceiving of the universe as a big cookie. The Rooster. Li Nan, *tr. by* Dominic Cheung. IFON
Concentred here th' united wisdom shines. The Federal Convention. *Unknown.* PAH
Concentric. Richard Kostelanetz. TAP
Conception. Waring Cuney. BANP
Conception. Sandra McPherson. NAmP
Conception. Josephine Miles. FaBoWP
Conception is interesting, The: to see, as though reflected. Wet Casements. John Ashbery. NAAL-2; PoM
Concepts and Their Bodies (The Boy in the Field Alone). Pattiann Rogers. MAYP; MT
Concerning Cork. Alan Bold. NPo
Concerning Death, *sel.* Sister Mary Madeleva.
I Ask My Teachers. CRP
Concerning Kavin. Bliss Carman. AnAmPo
Concerning One Responsible Negro with Too Much Power. Nikki Giovanni. BPo
Concerning the Awakening of My Soul. Henriëtte Roland-Holst, *tr. fr. Dutch by* Jonathan Crewe. WPOW
Concerning the Dead Women: The Munitions Plant Explosion: June, 1918. Elizabeth Libbey. AmPA
Concerning the Nature of Love. Lucretius, *tr. fr. Latin by* Dryden. *Fr.* De Rerum Natura (On the Nature of Things), IV. ErPo

Concerning the Stone. Gregory Orr. AnAn
Concerning Unnatural Nature: An Inverted Form. Hollis Spurgeon Summers. ErPo
Concerning your letter in which you ask. With Mercy for the Greedy. Anne Sexton. CAPP; HCAP; TOF
Concert. Robert Morgan. TDD
Concert. Otto Orban, *tr. fr. Hungarian by* William Jay Smith. MHuP
Concert. Helen G. Quigless. NBP
Concert. Robert Sward. VGW
Concert at Sea. Hubert Creekmore. WaP
Concert at the Station. Osip Mandelstam, *tr. fr. Russian by* Andrew Glaze. VWA
Concert-hall creaked like a full-dress shirt, The. Unfamiliar Quartet. Stephen Vincent Benét. AnAmPo
Concert-hall was crowded the night of the Crash, The. Paper Anniversary. Muriel Rukeyser. NoAM
Concert Party. Siegfried Sassoon. MMA
Concert Scene. John Logan. NePoEA-2
Conch. Raymond Queneau. OBD
Conchobor, what are you thinking, you. *Unknown, tr. fr. Irish by* Thomas Kinsella. *Fr.* Exile of the Sons of Uisliu. NOIV
Concierge at the front gate where relatives, The. Aeterna Poetae Memoria. Archibald MacLeish. Son
Concierge's old lady and the concierge will be looking the other way, The. Monday Christine Street. Guillaume Apollinaire, *tr. by* Michael Benedikt. POS
Concise History of the World, A. Ira Sadoff. AmPA
Conclusion: "Did you love well what very soon you left?" Marilyn Hacker. *Fr.* Coda. NoAM
Conclusion, The: "Even such is time." Sir Walter Ralegh. *See* Even Such Is Time.
Conclusion: "I came to pay you a visit, but you were sad and I empty-handed." Manfred Winkler, *tr. by* Bernhard Frank. MHeP
Conclusion: "If what began (look far and wide) will end." John Frederick Nims. PoA
Conclusion: "Image dance of change, An." Siegfried Sassoon. MoBrPo
Conclusion: "It was a close, warm, breezeless summer night." Wordsworth. *Fr.* The Prelude [or, Growth of a Poet's Mind], XIV [XIII]. PoEL-4
"Oh! yet a few short years of useful life." EBEV; OBNC; PoEL-4
Climb to Snowdon, The. FaBoRV
(Snowdon Sunrise, The.) FaBoPP
"It was a summer's night, a close warm night." PoEL-4
Conclusion: "Now have I brought a woork to end." Ovid. *See* Metamorphoses: Now have I brought a woork to end which neither Joves fierce [or feerce] wrath.
Concord Hymn. Emerson. AA; AiP; AmFN; AmPP; AWP; BLPA; BLPL; FaBoBe; FaPP; FaPON; FaPoR; GN; GOA; HAP; HeIP; LiTA; NOBA; NoP; OBWP; OHFP; OPP; OxBA; PAH; TAP; TrGrPo; WaaP
Concrete Cat. Dorthi Charles. InPK
Concrete Mixers. Patricia Hubbell. PDV; RHPC
Concrete somersaults cleanly in a bridge. Calder Valley: At the Top of the Ainleys. Stanley Cook. NPo
Condemn'd to hope's delusive mine. On the Death of Mr. [or Dr.] Robert Levet, a Practiser in Physic. Samuel Johnson. EBEV; HeIP; InPS; NOBE; NOEC; NoP; OAEL-1; OBEV; PoEL-3; PPP; SCV; TEP
Condemned, The. Enrique Gonzáles Martínez, *tr. fr. Spanish by* Samuel Beckett. MexPo
Condemned, The. Edward Howland. AA
Condemned, The. Edmond Jabès, *tr. fr. French by* Jack Hirschman. VWA
Condemned [or Condemn'd] to hope's delusive mine. On the Death of Mr. [or Dr.] Robert Levet, a Practiser in Physic. Samuel Johnson. EBEV; HeIP; InPS; NAEL-1; NOBE; NOEC; NoP; OAEL-1; OBEV; PoE; PoEL-3; PPP; SCV; TEP
Condemning the Moongod Nanna. Enheduanna, *tr. fr. Sumerian, ad. by* Aliki *and* Willis Barnstone. BoWoP
Condition, The. T. Carmi, *tr. fr. Hebrew by* Peter Everwine *and* Shula Starkman. VWA
Condition of Desire. Harry Mathews. EOEF
Conditions. José Luis Vega, *tr. fr. Spanish by* Julio Marzán. InW
Condo Girl. Elaine Equi. UL
Condom salesman tries them on like shoes, The. The No. Philip Dacey. NAmP
Condoms keep catching at the river's skirt. In Mysterious Ways. Faye Kicknosway. GeTw
Condors. Padraic Colum. GoJo
Conduct. Samuel Greenberg. LiTA
Conductor when he receives a fare, The. The Passenjare. Isaac H. Bromley. FiBHP
Conductor's cocked twig turns out, The. Orchestra. Reg Saner. KS

Conductor's hands were black with money, The. Charon. Louis MacNeice. FaBCIP; FaBoTw
Conemaugh. Elizabeth Stuart Phelps Ward. PAH
Coney Island Life, A. James L. Weil. AmFN
Coney Island of the Mind, A, *sels.* Lawrence Ferlinghetti.
Away above a Harborful. ErPo
"Constantly risking absurdity." CAPP; LiTM; NeAP; PoM; TAP
"Frightened/ by the sound of my own voice." TAP
Funny Fantasies Are Never So Real as Oldstyle. ErPo
In Golden Gate Park That Day. RB
In Goya's Greatest Scenes. FF; HeIP; LiTM; NeAP; NoAM; PoM; TAP
"Pennycandystore beyond the El, The." CAPP; HeIP; PoM; TAP
"Poet's yes obscenely seeing, The." LiTM
"Sometime during eternity." CAPP; NoAM
"This life is not a circus where." PPP
"Wounded wilderness of Morris Graves, The." NeAP
Confab. Kenneth Rosen. AmPA
Confections. Paul Éluard, *tr. fr. French by* Samuel Beckett. RHTwFP
Conference among ourselves we called, A. George Gascoigne. *Fr.* The Fruits of War. OBWP
Conference of the Birds, The, *sels.* Faridu'ddin Attar, *tr. fr. Persian by* Afkham Darbandi *and* Dick Davis. TOF
"Dervish wept to feel the violence of, A."
"Hallaj's corpse was burnt and when the flame."
"In India lives a bird that is unique."
Conferences, adjournments, ultimatums. Louis MacNeice. *Fr.* Autumn Journal. FaBoPV; OxBTC; WaP
Confess, Marpessa. Robert Graves. TEP
"Confess, my daughter." "I'm ashamed to start." The Good Spiritual Father. Giuseppe Gioacchino Belli, *tr. by* Miller Williams. PFI
Confess We All, before the Lord. John Wilson. AH
Confessio Amantis, *sels.* John Gower.
Jason and Medea. *Fr.* V. ACP
Parting of Venus and Old Age, The. *Fr.* VIII. PoEL-1
Confessio Fidei. Dryden. *See* Hind and the Panther, The: Private Judgement Condemned.
Confession. Gelett Burgess. *See* Ah, Yes, I Wrote the "Purple Cow."
Confession. Lucille Clifton. GeTw
Confession, The. Peter Cooley. AmPA
Confession. Donald Jeffrey Hayes. CDC
Confession. George Herbert. JCP
Confession, A. Robert Mezey. AmPA; NaP
Confession. Charles, Duc d' Orléans. *See* My Ghostly Father, I me confess.
Confession. Louise Otto-Peters, *tr. fr. German by* Susan L. Cocalis *and* Gerlinde Geiger. DMG
Confession, The. "Thomas Ingoldsby." FiBHP
Confession, A. Paul Verlaine, *tr. fr. French by* Arthur Symons. WGRP
Confession, The. Wen Yi-tuo, *tr. fr. Chinese.* ChTr
Confession of a Stolen Kiss. Charles, Duc d' Orléans. *See* My Ghostly Father, I me confess.
Confession of Faith. Imre Csanádi, *tr. fr. Hungarian by* Edwin Morgan. MHuP
Confession of Faith. Elinor Wylie. MoAmPo
Confession Overheard in a Subway. Kenneth Fearing. LiTA; LiTM; WaP
Confession Stone, The. Owen Dodson. TTY
Confession to Settle a Curse. Rosemarie Waldrop. TW
Confessional. Frank Bidart. GLP
Confessional Poetry. Tony Harrison. DiPo
Confessions. Robert Browning. ELP; GTBS-P; NOBE; NOBVV
Confessions of Gerrit. Gerrit Henry. BAP
Confessions of the Life Artist. Thom Gunn. CMoP
Confessor, The. Giuseppe Gioacchino Belli, *tr. fr. Italian by* Harold Norse. ErPo
Confidence, A. Juan Gonzalo Rose, *tr. fr. Spanish by* Ena Hollis. Per
Confidence. *Unknown.* BLRP
Confidence Trick, *sels.* Bruce Andrews.
"Cherry red kind of washed-out." IAT
"Equality demands no less; history begins with old man crying." LP
Confines of a city block, The. Construction. Karl Shapiro. PCP
Confirmation. Art Lange. UL
Confirmation, The. Edwin Muir. OxBS
Confirmation, The. Karl Shapiro. ErPo
Confirmation Day. Juliane Windhager, *tr. fr. German by* Beth Bjorklund. CoAuP
Confirmers, The. A. R. Ammons. TAP
Confiscating Salt. Wang An-shih, *tr. fr. Chinese by* Burton Watson. CoBCP
Conflict, The. Cecil Day Lewis. LiTB; LiTM; MoAB; MoBrPo; NoP
Conflict. Francis Reginald Scott. CaP
Conflict of Convictions, The. Herman Melville. NOBA

Conformers, The. Thomas Hardy. Mes
Confound it! aw ne'er wur so woven afore. The Shurat Weaver's Song. Samuel Laycock. PF
Confounded Nonsense. Tom Hood. FaBoNo
Confrontations with the Devil in the Form of Love, *sel.* Judy Grahn. "My name is Judith meaning." ER
Confronting a longing. Poem to My Death. Julia de Burgos, *tr. by* Grace Schulman. BoWoP
Confronting the wind, late autumn trees. Drunk, Facing Crimson Leaves. Po Chü-i, *tr. by* Burton Watson. CoBCP
Confused. Chang Ts'o, *tr. fr. Chinese by* Dominic Cheung. IFON
Confusion. Victor Hernandez Cruz. UL
Confusion. Christopher Hervey. BXAP; Par
Congealed vapors surge in vast space. Seeing off Editor Wang Chou-tz'u and Secretary Lin Shih-lai. Wang Shih-chen, *tr. by* Jonathan Chaves. CoBLCP
Congo, The. Vachel Lindsay. CMoP; FaFP; LiTA; MoAB; MoAmPo; NOBA; OxBA; PoNe; PoRA; TAP
Congratulations. Shunzei, *tr. fr. Japanese by* Burton Watson. *Fr.* Thirty Tanka. FCEI
Congratulations on a New House. Basho, *tr. fr. Japanese by* Burton Watson. *Fr.* Seventy-six Hokku. FCEI
Coniagui Women. Audre Lorde. NAAL-2
Conies had their hiding-place, The. He "Had Not Where to Lay His Head." Frances Ellen Watkins Harper. PWR
Conjecture, A. Charles Francis Richardson. AA
Conjugation. Patricia Hubbell. ILY
Conjuration. Agnes Gergely, *tr. fr. Hungarian by* Emery George. VWA
Conjuration, to Electra, A. Robert Herrick. GBL; PoEL-3
Conjuring Roethke. James Tate. OBAL
Connais-Tu le Pays? Richard Shelton. NYBP
Connection. Caroline Halliday. DT
Connection, The. Daniil Kharms, *tr. fr. Russian by* George Gibian. FaBoNo
Connoisseur of Chaos. Wallace Stevens. LiTM
Connoisseur of pearl, A. African China. Melvin B. Tolson. PoBA
"Conquer the gloomy night of thy sorrow." Defiance. Solomon ibn Gabirol, *tr. by* Emma Lazarus. TrJP
Conquered Banner, The. Abram Joseph Ryan. AA; AnAmPo; PAH
Conqueror Worm, The. Poe. *Fr.* Ligeia *prose tale.* AA; AnAmPo; AWP; BLPL; LiTA; NOBA; OBD
Conquerors. Henry Treece. GOYP; OBWVE
Conqueror's Grave, The. Bryant. AA
Conquest. Elizabeth Jane Coatsworth. AmFN
Conquest *or* His Lady's Might. Philippe Desportes. AWP
Conquest, The. Oliver St. John Gogarty. OBMV
Conquest. Georgia Douglas Johnson. AmNP
Conquest of Granada, The, *sels.* Dryden.
    "They who have best succeeded on the stage." *Fr. pt.* II. FiP; SeCV-2
    Love. *Fr. pt.* II, Act III, sc. iii. FiP
    Song of the Zambra Dance. *Fr. pt.* I, Act III, sc. i. ErPo; PoEL-3 (Zambra Dance, The.) SeCV-2
Conquistador, *sel.* Archibald MacLeish.
    "And the way goes on in the worn earth." NoAM
Conrad. Antoni Slonimski, *tr. fr. Polish by* Isaac Komem. VWA
Conrad in Twilight ("Conrad, Conrad, aren't you old"). John Crowe Ransom. OxBA
Conscience. Melech Ravitch, *tr. fr. Yiddish by* Keith Bosley. VWA
Conscience. Sir Edward Sherburne. ACP
Conscience. Charles William Stubbs. BLPA
Conscience and Remorse. Paul Laurence Dunbar. AnAmPo
Conscience-Curst! The. "F. Anstey." CenHV
Conscience-Keeper, The. William Young. *Fr.* Wishmakers' Town. AA
Conscience's Song. Robert Wilson. *See* Three Ladies of London, The: New Brooms.
Conscientious Objector. Edna St. Vincent Millay. WPOW
Conscientious Objector, The. Karl Shapiro. OxBA
Conscious. Wilfred Owen. MMA
Consciousness. Agnes Nemes Nagy, *tr. fr. Hungarian by* Jascha Kessler. FOC
Consciousness ("Consciousness enclosed in itself every separate birch"). Czeslaw Milosz, *tr. fr. Polish by* Robert Hass. AnAn
Consecration, A. John Masefield. MoAB; MoBrPo
Consecration. Benjamin Schmolck. BLRP
Consecration. Susan Stewart. NAmP
Consecration of the Corn Tortilla. Ricardo Castorrivas, *tr. fr. Spanish by* David Volpendesta. Vol
Consecration of the House. Wolfe Seymour Fairbridge. PoAu-2
Consejos y Documentos al Rey Dom Pedro, *sel.* Santob de Carrion, *tr. fr. Spanish.*
    Jewish Poet Counsels a King, A. TrJP

Conservative, A. Charlotte Perkins Gilman. AA
Conserves. David Mus. *Fr.* The Joy of Cooking. PoA
Conserving the Magnitude of Uselessness. A. R. Ammons. NoAM
Consider. Christina Rossetti. GN
Consider a coral or guano atoll. Manichean Geography I. Tom Paulin. FaBCIP
Consider a Move. Michael Ryan. MAYP; SM
Consider a new habit—classical. Arras. P. K. Page. MoCV; OBCV
Consider Famous Men, Dai Bach. Idris Davies. OBWVE
Consider for a moment how the body of a dancer. Female Dancer. James Camp. Son
Consider Icarus, pasting those sticky wings on. To a Friend Whose Work Has Come to Triumph. Anne Sexton. InPK
Consider me a memory, a dream that passed away. Recessional. Georgia Douglas Johnson. CDC; PoNe
Consider, O my soul, what morn is this! A Meditation for Christmas. Selwyn Image. OBEV
Consider, praise, remember all of these. All of These. Denis Glover. PeNZ
Consider the case of the many-minded men. Friday Evening. Sean Lucy. CIP
Consider the egg. It's a miracle. Eggomania. Felicia Lamport. NBLV
Consider the Lilies. William Channing Gannett. *See* He Hides within the Lily.
Consider the lowering Lynx. Langford Reed. CenHV
Consider the mysterious salt. In Time like Air. May Sarton. NYBP
Consider the sages who pulverize boulders. P Is for Paleontology. Milton Bracker. FiBHP
Consider the sea's listless chime. The Sea-Limits. Dante Gabriel Rossetti. MOS; NAEL-2; OAEL-2
Consider the three functions of the tongue. Marilyn Hacker. NoAM, *abr.*
Consider the will to love. Training for the Apocalypse. Gloria Frym. UL
Consider them both in paradise. W. H. Auden & Mantan Moreland. Al Young. NPGG
Consider These, for We Have Condemned Them. C. D. Lewis. LiTB; LiTM; SeCePo
Consider this:/ A man who feels for the people. Liberal. Vincent O'Sullivan. *Fr.* The Pilate Tapes. ATNZ
Consider This and in Our Time. W. H. Auden. FaBoMo; LiTB
Consider this barbarian coast. At Akitio. James Keir Baxter. ATNZ
Consider this small dust, here in the glass. Hour Glass, The ("Consider this small dust, here in the glass"). Ben Jonson. BLPL; LiTB
Consider Well. Sir Thomas More. ACP
Considerable Speck, A. Robert Frost. MoAB; MoAmPo; OBAL; PPP
Considerate Crocodile, The. Amos R. Wells. OBCA
Consideration for Others. Christopher Smart. *See* Hymns for the Amusement of Children: Mutual Subjugation.
Considerations. David Helwig. NOBC
Considerations, *sel.* Kendrick Smithyman.
    "High in the afternoon the dove." ATNZ
Consideratus Considerandus. John Saffin. SCAP
Considered Reply to a Child, A. Jonathan Price. BoLoP
Considering Coldly, Impartially. César Vallejo, *tr. fr. Spanish by* Perry Higman. LPSS
Considering the Bleakness. Moyshe-Leyb Halpern, *tr. fr. Yiddish by* Richard J. Fein. VWA
Considering the Snail. Thom Gunn. GrPl; LiTM; NAEL-2; NePoEA-2; TwCP
Consignee of silent storms and unseen lightning. Lynx. R. A. D. Ford. CaP
Consolation. Arthur Guiterman. BXAP
Consolation. Gyula Illyés, *tr. fr. Hungarian by* Charles Tomlinson. MHuP
Consolation, A. Shakespeare. *See* Sonnets: XXIX. "When, in disgrace with fortune and men's eyes."
Consolation. Earl of Surrey. AAS; EBEV; EnLoPo; NOBE; OBSC; SiPS; TEP
Consolation. W. B. Yeats. OxBSP
Consolation, The. Edward Young. *Fr.* Night Thoughts, Night IX. NOEC
Consolation in War. Lewis Mumford. NYBP
Consolation of Philosophy, The, *sels.* Boethius, *tr. fr. Latin.*
    "Happy he whose eyes have view'd." *Fr.* III, 12, *tr. by* Samuel Johnson. OBVE
    "Happy that first white age! when wee." *Fr.* II, 5, *tr. by* Henry Vaughan. OBVE
    Happy Too Much. *Fr.* II, *tr. by* Elizabeth I, Queen of England. CTC
    Huc omnes pariter. *Fr.* III, 2, *tr. by* John Walton. OBLMV
    Hue quam precipiti. *Fr.* I, 2, *tr. by* John Walton. OBLMV

"O thou whose pow'r o'er moving worlds presides." *Fr.* III, 9, *tr. by* Samuel Johnson. OBVE; TrPWD

"Though countless as the grains of sand." *Fr.* II, 2, *tr. by* Samuel Johnson. OBVE

Consolations. Paul Ramsey. *Fr.* Three Epigrams. CRP

Consolations of Art. Roy Fuller. OxBC

Consolations of Philosophy. Derek Mahon. BIrV; CIP

Consolatory! St. John Emile Clavering Hankin. CenHV

Consolatory Poem Dedicated unto Mr. Cotton Mather, A. Nicholas Noyes. SCAP

Consolatrice. René Daumal, *tr. fr. French by* Michael Benedikt. POS

Consoling Wu Te-cheng on the Death of His Son. Shen Chou, *tr. fr. Chinese by* Jonathan Chaves. CoBLCP

Consort, The. Ruthann Robson. ER

Consorting with Angels. Anne Sexton. NMM

Conspirators, The. Frederic Prokosch. LiTM; PrIm; WaP

Constable Calls, A. Seamus Heaney. *Fr.* Singing School. FaBoPV; IPY; NOIV

Constance Kent. *Unknown.* OBET

Constancy. Samuel Daniel. *Fr.* Hymen's Triumph. OBSC

Constancy. Earl of Rochester. OBEV; OBS

Constancy. Sir Thomas Wyatt. OBSC; SiPS
(Perdye I Saide Yt Not.) PoEL-1

Constancy of a Lover, The. George Gascoigne. QFR

Constancy Rewarded. Coventry Patmore. *See* Angel in the House, The: I vow'd unvarying faith; and she.

Constancy to an Ideal Object. Samuel Taylor Coleridge. NAEL-2

Constancye. Sidney Godolphin. MePo

Constant, The. A. R. Ammons. HAP; WeW

Constant Bridegrooms, The. Kenneth Patchen. LiTM; NaP

Constant Cannibal Maiden, The. Wallace Irwin. AnAmPo; OBAL

Constant cry against an old order, The. Polo Ponies Practicing. Wallace Stevens. ASP

Constant Defender. James Tate. MAYP

Constant Farmer's Son, The. *Unknown.* OBET

Constant Labor, A. James W. Thompson. BPo

Constant Love Even beyond Death. Francisco de Quevedo, *tr. fr. Spanish by* Perry Higman. LPSS

Constant Lover, The. Louis Simpson. NYBP

Constant North, The. J. F. Hendry. OxBS

Constant Penelope sends to thee, careless Ulysses. Ovid. EnLoPo; GBL; NAEL-1; OAEL-1

Constant to none, but ever false to me. Thomas Campion. AAS

Constant X, The. Onlie X. Fanny Howe. PPR

Constantine's Vision of the Cross. Cynewulf, *tr. fr. Anglo-Saxon by* Charles W. Kennedy. *Fr.* Elene. AnOE

Constantly I hear the mountain's deep grievances. Chi Tzu of Yen Ling Hangs Up His Sword. Yang Mu, *tr. by* Dominic Cheung. IFON

Constantly near you, I never in my entire. The Horse Show. William Carlos Williams. CMoP; NOBA; TAP; VGW

Constantly risking absurdity. Lawrence Ferlinghetti. *Fr.* A Coney Island of the Mind. CAPP; LiTM; NeAP; PoM; TAP

Constellation, The. Henry Vaughan. SeCV-2

Constellation and the *Insurgente,* The. *Unknown.* PAH

Constipation. Ronald Wallace. MOWH

Constitution and the *Guerrière,* The. *Unknown.* AmFP; PAH

Constitution's Last Fight, The. James Jeffrey Roche. PAH

Constricted by my tortured thought. Prayer before Study. Theodore Roethke. TrPWD

Constructed Space, The. W. S. Graham. PoA

Construction. Karl Shapiro. PCP

Constructive Criticism. May Richstone. SoTCo

Consumed. James Tate. MAT

Consumer's Report, A. Peter Porter. FaBoCo; NOBL

Consummate Happiness. Wordsworth. *Fr.* The Prelude [or, Growth of a Poet's Mind]: Summer Vacation. OBNC

Consummation. Thomas Traherne. SeCV-2

Consummation of their lawless pleasure, The. Their Beginning. Constantine P. Cavafy, *tr. by* John Mavrogordato. PeHV

Consumptive, The. Priscilla Jane Thompson. CBWP-2

Contact. John F. Deane. TIRV

Contact. Dorothy Livesay. CaP

Container, The. Cid Corman. VGW

"Containing Communism." Charlie Cobb. PoBA

Contemplate all this work of Time. Tennyson. *Fr.* In Memoriam A. H. H., CXVIII. FF

Contemplation. John Frederick Nims. InPK

Contemplation. Francis Thompson. BrPo

Contemplation ("This morning saw I, fled the shower."), *sel.* Francis Thompson. BrPo
"Nature one hour appears a thing unsexed." OBNC

Contemplation of Our State in Our Deathbed. John Donne. *Fr.* Of the Progresse of the Soule; the Second Anniversarie. OBS

Contemplation of the Heavens. Bill Manhire. PeNZ

Contemplation upon Flowers, A. Henry King. BoNaP; ELP; MeLP; MePo; NoP; OBEV; OBS; SeCP; TrGrPo

Contemplations ("Some time now past in the autumnal tide.") Anne Bradstreet. AmPP; PoEL-3, *abr.;* SCAP; WPE, *abr.*
Sels.
"I wist not what to wish, yet sure thought I." PBWP
"Mariner that on smooth waves doth glide, The." WPOW
"O Time the fatal wrack of mortal things." PBWP; WPOW
"Shall I then praise the heavens, the trees, the earth." PBWP
"Silent alone, where none or saw, or heard." PBWP
"So he that saileth in this world of pleasure." WPOW
"When I behold the heavens as in prime." PBWP

Contemplative Sentry, The. W. S. Gilbert. *Fr.* Iolanthe. FiBHP

Contemporania, *sel.* Ezra Pound.
Tenzone. PoA

Contemporary. Hortense Flexner. PoA

Contemporary Muse, The. Edgell Rickword. OBSV

Contemporary Native American Poetry. Jim Barnes. NOVW

Contemporary Song. Theodore Spencer. LiTA

Contempt for the World, *sel. Bernard of Morlas.*
"Scarcely believe things shameful to utter which yet I shall speak of." *Fr. bk.* III. PeHV

Contempt for the World. Bernard of Cluny. *See* Scarcely believe things shameful to utter.

Contempt of Poetry, The. Spenser. *See* Shepheardes [*or* Shepeards *or* Shepherd's] Calender, The: October.

Contempt of the World. *Unknown. See* Where are those that were before us.

Contemptuous of his home beyond. A Frog's Fate. Christina Rossetti. NOBVV

Contend in a sea which the land partly encloses. The Yachts. William Carlos Williams. AmPP; CMoP; HeIP; LiTA; LiTM; MoAB; MoAMPo; MoP; MOS; NoAM; NOBA; NoP; OxBA; PoE; PPP

Contending with her streams, renascent stars. Aria for Flute and Oboe. Joseph Langland. NePoEA

Content. Barnabe Barnes. *See* Parthenophil and Parthenophe: Ah, sweet Content! where is thy mylde abode?

Content. Thomas Campion. OBSC

Content. Stephen Crane. *See* Black Riders, The: Youth in Apparel That Glittered, A.

Content. Earl of Essex. *See* Happy Were He.

Content. Lord Thomas Vaux. *See* When all is done and said, in the end this you shall find.

Content. Geffrey Whitney. EIL
(Song: "In crystal towers and turrets richly set.") ACP

Content and Rich. Robert Southwell. OBSC

Content Thyself with Thy Estate. *Unknown.* EIL

Content within his wigwam warm. Canonicus and Roger Williams. *Unknown.* PAH

Contention between Four Maids Concerning That Which Addeth Most Perfection to That Sex. Sir John Davies. SiPS

Contention betwixt a Wife, a Widow, and a Maid, A. Sir John Davies. OBSC; SiPS

Contention of Ajax and Ulysses, The, *sel.* James Shirley.
Glories of Our Blood and State, The. *Fr. sc.* iii. ChTr; FaBoRV; HAP; InvP; JCP; NoP; OBD, OBS; PoRA; PPP; TrGrPo; WaaP
(Death the Leveller.) BLPL; FaPoR; FF; GTBS; GTBS-P; LiTB; NOBE; OBEV; UnPo
(Dirge: "Glories of our blood and state, The.") ACP; AWP; OAEL-1; PoEL-2

Contentment. Charles Stuart Calverley. NOBVV

Contentment. Nathaniel Cotton. OxBChV

Contentment. Oliver Wendell Holmes. AnAmPo; PWR

Contentment. Oliver Wendell Holmes. *Fr.* The Autocrat of the Breakfast Table, 11. AmPP; OxBA

Contentment. Mark Osaki. BrSi

Contentment. Benjamin Schlipf. BLRP

Contentment. Sir Philip Sidney. *See* Arcadia: Get Hence Foule Griefe.

Contentment. Thomas Traherne. *Fr.* Christian Ethics. NOCV
("For man to act as if his soul did see.") NOCV

Contentment is a sleepy thing. Contentment. Thomas Traherne. *Fr.* Christian Ethics. NOCV
("For man to act as if his soul did see.") NOCV

Contentment of Willoughby, The. Frances Alexander. GoYe

Contest. Susan Bright. TSL

Contest. Florence Victor. SD

Contest of Nerves, The. Patricia Traxler. TV

Contest Snake, The. Cheng Hsieh, *tr. fr. Chinese by* Jonathan Chaves. CoBLCP

Continental College of Beauty, The. Mark Strand. BLA

Continental Crossing. Dorothy Brown Thompson. AmFN
Continent's End. Robinson Jeffers. AWP; FaBV; ImOP
Continual Conversation with a Silent Man. Wallace Stevens. LiTM; NoP
Continually. Herbert Zand, tr. fr. German by Beth Bjorklund. CoAuP
Continuation of a Long Poem of These States, sel. Allen Ginsberg.
    S.F. Southward. NAAL-2
Continuation of The Cook's Tale, The. William Zaranka. BXAP
Continuaunce/ of remembraunce. A Lover Left Alone. Unknown.
    MeEL
Continued. Matthew Arnold. Son
Continuing City, The. Laurence Housman. WGRP
Continuity. "Æ." MoBrPo
Continuity, The. Paul Blackburn. NeAP
Continuous, a medley of old pop numbers. The Songs. Martin Bell. FF
Continuously, as their name tells. Akahito, tr. fr. Japanese. Fr. Manyo
    Shu. Ma
Continuum. Denise Levertov. LCAP
Contours of Fixation, The. Weldon Kees. NaP
Contra Mortem. Hayden Carruth. PoA
Contra Mortem, sel. Hayden Carruth.
    "Wherever shadow falls wherever the drowning." PoA
Contradictions: Tracking Poems, sels. Adrienne Rich. ER
    "Heart of cold. Bones of cold. Scalp of cold." Fr. 2.
    "I came out of the hospital like a woman." Fr. 11.
    "In a bald skull sits our friend in a helmet." Fr. 22.
    "Tobacco fields lie fallow the migrant pickers, The." Fr. 20.
Contraries. Sándor Weöres, tr. fr. Hungarian by Jascha Kessler. FOC
Contrary Theses (I). Wallace Stevens. OxBA
Contrary to popular belief, the lowest circle of hell is not. Pan Cogito's
    Thoughts on Hell. Zbigniew Herbert, tr. by Adam Czerniawski.
    FaBoPV
Contrary Waiter, The. Edgar Parker. RHPC
Contrary Wind, A. Ho Shao-chi, tr. fr. Chinese by J. D. Schmidt.
    WFTU
Contrast, The. Helen Gray Cone. AA
Contrast. Mvula Ya Nangolo. WMBCH
Contrast; the Parrot and the Wren, The. Wordsworth. FM
Contre Jour. Elizabeth Bartlett. FaBoWP
Contretemps, The. Thomas Hardy. CMoP; LiTM
Controlling the Tongue. Chaucer. Fr. The Canterbury Tales: The
    Manciple's Tale. OxBChV
Controls, The. Harrison Fisher. UL
Conundrum. Carl Clark. JB
Conundrum of the Workshops, The. Kipling. MoBrPo
Convalescence. Noël Coward. TTTS
Convalescence. James McAuley. CBAP
Convent of Pleasure, The, sel. Margaret Cavendish, Duchess of
    Newcastle.
    My Cabinets Are Oyster-Shells. ELP
    (Song: "My cabinets are oyster-shells.") WPE
Convent Threshold, The. Christina Rossetti. NoP
Convention Song. Unknown. PAH
Convergence of the Many. René Char, tr. fr. French by Thomas Merton.
    RHTwFP
Convergence of the Twain (Lines on the Loss of the Titanic, The).
    Thomas Hardy. BrPo; FaBoTw; HeIP; InPK; InPS; LiTB; LiTM;
    MoAB; MoBrPo; MoP; MOS; NAEL-2; NIP; NoAm; NoP; OAEL-2;
    OxBTC; PrIm; TEP
Conversation. John Berryman. LiTA; LiTM; WaP
Conversation. Buson, tr. fr. Japanese. NTCP
Conversation. Rose Fyleman. BoTP
Conversation, A. Barbara Howes. IHMS
Conversation. Rutger Kopland, tr. fr. Dutch by Ria Leigh-Loohuizen.
    DuIn
Conversation. David McCord. GrPl; SO
Conversation. Louis MacNeice. TEP
Conversation. Gyorgy Raba, tr. fr. Hungarian by Jascha Kessler. VWA
Conversation, A. Dylan Thomas. RFM
Conversation at the Bend in the Road. Buland al-Haidari, tr. fr. Arabic by
    Abdullah al-Udhari. MPAW
Conversation between the Chevalier de Chamilly and Mariana Alcoforado
    in the Manner of a Song of Regret. The Three Marias, tr. fr.
    Portuguese by Helen R. Lane. BoWoP
Conversation brings us so close! Opening. Looking into a Face. Robert
    Bly. CAPP; NOBA
Conversation by the Body's Light. Jane Cooper. ER
Conversation in Avila. Phyllis McGinley. EaLo
Conversation in Black and White. May Sarton. GoYe
Conversation in Craven Street, Strand. James Smith and Sir George Rose.
    FaBoCo
Conversation in the Bush. Arthur Rex Dugard Fairburn. Fr. Album
    Leaves. ATNZ; PeNZ
Conversation in the Drawing Room, The. Weldon Kees. EAS

Conversation of Prayer, The. Dylan Thomas. EBEV; GTBS-P; NoP
Conversation Piece. Arthur Freeman. ErPo
Conversation Piece. Robert Graves. GrPl
Conversation with a Countryman. Antoni Slonimski, tr. fr. Polish by
    Isaac Komen. VWA
Conversation with an Angel. Wanda Barford. Mes
Conversation with Mr. Yao, A. Sung Chang-kyung. WCI
Conversation with Rain. Louise D. Gunn. GoYe
Conversation with Washington. Myra Cohn Livingston. OFD
Conversational. Unknown. FiBHP
Conversations. Ory Bernstein, tr. fr. Hebrew by Bernhard Frank. MHeP
Conversations are simple, The: about food. Under the Window: Ouro
    Preto. Elizabeth Bishop. NYBP
Conversations from Childhood: the Victrola. Joseph Langland. SM
Conversations in Courtship, sel. Unknown, tr. fr. Egyptian into Italian by
    Boris de Rachewiltz; tr. into English by Ezra Pound.
    "Darling, you only, there is no duplicate." CTC
Conversations in Mayan. Alonzo Gonzales Mó, tr. fr. Mayan by Allan F.
    Burns. STP
Conversing. Lan Ling, tr. fr. Chinese by Dominic Cheung. IFON
Conversion. Frances Angermayer. PoLF
Conversion. Dryden. Fr. The Hind and the Panther, III. ACP
    (Worldly Vanity.) FiP
Conversion. Geof Hewitt. NeAC
Conversion. T. E. Hulme. FaBoMo; OxBSP
Convert, The. Margaret Danner. BPo
Convert's but a fly, that turns about, A. Samuel Butler. FaBoEE
Convex face of the black countries, The. The First Psalm. Bertolt
    Brecht, tr. by Robert Bly. NU
Convict, The. Anthony Frisch. CaP
Convict of Clonmel, The. Unknown, tr. fr. Irish by Jeremiah Joseph
    Callanan. AnIL; SD
Convict Song, The. Alfred Cruickshank. PBCV
Convict's Lament on the Death of Captain Logan, A. Unknown. PoAu-1
Convinced by Sorrow. Elizabeth Barrett Browning. Fr. The Cry of the
    Human. BLRP; WBLP
Convoy, The. Juan Antonio Corretjer, tr. fr. Spanish by Julio Marzán.
    InW
Convoy. William Jay Smith. WaP
Convulsions came; and, where the field. The Apparition. Herman
    Melville. NoP
Coo-Coo. Unknown. AS
Coo-pe-coo. Unknown. PBBP
Coogan's Wood. Francis Stuart. NeIP
Cook, The. Ray A. Young Bear. CDW
Cook crows—cock-a-doodle-doo!—the east grows bright, The. On the
    Hall of Precious Virtue. Yang Shih-ch'i, tr. by Jonathan Chaves.
    CoBLCP
Cook sleeps, A. On her lap a bowl of thickened material. The
    Thickening. Russell Edson. NAmP
Cooking Eggs. Dave Smith. AnAn; BLA
Cooking the Rice. Angelika Mechtel, tr. fr. German by Susan L. Cocalis.
    DMG
Cook's Tale, The. Chaucer. Fr. The Canterbury Tales. BXAP
Cooks who'd roast a sucking-pig. Roasted Sucking Pig. Unknown.
    BXAP
Cooky-Nut Trees, The. Albert Bigelow Paine. OBCA
Cool and certain, their oars will be lifted in dusk. Robin Hyde. Fr. The
    Beaches, VII. PeNZ
Cool and fresh. Boncho, tr. by Geoffrey Bownas and Anthony Thwaite.
    PeBJV
Cool beneath the Summer Moon. Shotetsu, tr. fr. Japanese by Steven D.
    Carter. WFTW
Cool breezes—I sleep by the open window. Unknown, tr. fr. Chinese by
    Burton Watson. Fr. Tzu Yeh Songs. CoBCP
Cool, Cool, Country, The. John Shaw Neilson. PoAu-1
Cool, cool, the moon too is white. The Night Grew Late in Kuzuha
    Village in Hirakata. Onitsura, tr. fr. Japanese by Hiroaki Sato. Fr.
    Twenty-three Hokku. FCEI
Cool Day in July. Alice Mattison. PPR
Cool Gold Wines of Paradise, The. Robert Farren. SeCePo
Cool in summer's heat. The Well: Two Songs. Gond Oral Tradition, tr.
    by V. Elwin and S. Hivale. WTO
Cool it Mag. Margaret Are You Drug. George Starbuck. InPK; MAT
Cool Mule. Dale A. Schreiber. SoTCo
Cool Nights of October. David Wojahn. NAmP
Cool of bamboo invades my room, The. Restless Night. Tu Fu, tr. by
    Burton Watson. CoBCP
Cool red rose and a pink cut pink, A. Red Roses. Gertrude Stein. Fr.
    Tender Buttons. TTTS
Cool shades and dews are round my way. A Scene on the Banks of the
    Hudson. Bryant. AnAmPo
Cool shadows blanked dead cities, falling. Falling. Bob Kaufman. PoBA

Cool sky opens like a hand, The. William Blake Sees God. Roy McFadden. NeIP

Cool small evening shrunk to a dog bark and the clank of a bucket, A. Full Moon and Little Frieda. Ted Hughes. OxBC; OxBSP

Cool summer: mountains took on steeper slopes. Destruction of the Fifth Planet. Brian W. Aldiss. BWV

Cool that came off sheets just off the line, The. Seamus Heaney. *Fr.* Clearances, V. CIP

Cool to our bodies, the fresh linen pleats. Newness. Tom Paulin. FaBCIP

Cool Tombs. Carl Sandburg. AmPP; BLPL; CMoP; HAP; HeIP; MoAB; MoAmPo; MoP; NAAL-2; NoAM; NOBA; OPP; OxBSP; PoLF; TAP; TrGrPo

Cool Web, The. Robert Graves. AWP; GTBS-P; MoP; NAEL-2; NIP; NoAM; NoP; OxBTC; PoA; PrIm; SCV

Coole Park and Ballylee, 1931. W. B. Yeats. CMoP; GTBS-P; NoAM; NOIV; OBMV; PPP

Coole Park, 1929. W. B. Yeats. OAEL-2; OBMV

Cooled down at last. Emperor Fushimi, *tr. by* Steven D. Carter. WFTW

Cooler than the wind. Tameyo, *tr. by* Steven D. Carter. WFTW

Coolie. Yoshioka Minoru, *tr. fr. Japanese by* Hiroaki Sato. FCEI

Coolie Chinee, The. Septimus Winner. OBAL

Coolin Ridge, The. William Bell. PoSH

Cooling Off in the Evening. Onitsura, *tr. fr. Japanese by* Hiroaki Sato. *Fr.* Twenty-three Hokku. FCEI

Coolness creeping through the willows, rain upon the flowers. K'uang Chou-yi, *tr. by* Irving Lo. WFTU

Coolness: separating from a bell. Buson, *tr. fr. Japanese by* Hiroaki Sato. *Fr.* Eighty-seven Hokku. FCEI

Coon Can (Poor Boy). *Unknown.* AS

Coon Fire. Tom Weatherly. *Fr.* Cantos, 5. PoBA

Coon Hunt. Thomas Rabbitt. MT

Coon Hunt, Sixth Month (1955). Sydney Lea. MAYP

Coon Song. A. R. Ammons. MoP; NOBA

Cooney Potter. Edgar Lee Masters. *Fr.* Spoon River Anthology. SaC

Cooper. James Russell Lowell. *Fr.* A Fable for Critics. NOBA; OxBA; TAP

Cooper & Bailey Great London Circus, The. Robert Hershon. MAT

Cooper o' Dundee, The. *Unknown.* CoMu

Cooper, whose name is with his country's woven. Red Jacket. Fitz-Greene Halleck. AA; AnAmPo

Cooperative Council. Takamura Kotaro, *tr. fr. Japanese by* Hiroaki Sato. *Fr.* A Brief History of Imbecility. FCEI

Cooper's Hill. Sir John Denham. SeCP; SeCV-1

Cooper's Hill ("Sure there are poets which did never dream."), *sels. Sir John* Denham. SeCP; SeCV-1

  "Here have I seen the king, when great affairs." PoE

  "Here should my wonder dwell, and here my praise." NAEL-1

  "My eye descending from the Hill, surveys." OAEL-1

  (Thames from Cooper's Hill, The.) OBS; SeCePo

  "There Faunus and Sylvanus keep their courts." JCP

Cootchie. Elizabeth Bishop. FaBoWP; NIP

Cop, The/ with a cold. High-cool//2. James Cunningham. JB

Cop holds me up like a fish, The. Fish. Larry Levis. AmPA

Copacetic Mingus. Yusef Komunyakaa. MAYP

Copernican System, The. Thomas Cunningham. FaBoUs

Cophetua. "Hugh MacDiarmid." OxBS

Coplas about the Soul Which Suffers with Impatience to See God, *sel.* Saint John of the Cross, *tr. fr. Spanish by* Roy Campbell.

  "I live without inhabiting/ Myself." OBVE

Copper cobra comes out of his slit, The. The Banded Cobra. C. Louis Leipoldt, *tr. by* Uys Krige, Jack Cope *and* Ruth Miller. PeSA

Copper-green Phillip. Captain Arthur Phillip and the Birds. Lex Banning. PoAu-2

Copper Song, The. Hermia Harris Fraser. CaP

Copperhead, The. David Bottoms. MAYP

Copperhead, The. Linda Gregg. NAmP

Coppersmith. Richard Murphy. IPY

Coptic Poem ("A Coptic deputation, going to Ethiopia"). Lawrence Durrell. FaBoCo

Copulating Gods, The. Carolyn Kizer. CAPP; Prf

Copy. Ben-Zion Tomer, *tr. fr. Hebrew by* Bernhard Frank. *Fr.* Song Sequence. MHeP

Copy of an Intercepted Despatch from His Excellency Don Strepitoso Diabolo. Thomas Moore. OBSV

Copy of Non Sequitors, A. *Unknown.* FaBoNo

Copy of Verses, A. John Wilson. SCAP

Copy of Verses Composed by Captain Henry Every, A. *Unknown.* OxBSS

Copy of Versus on Jefferys the Seaman, A. *Unknown.* OxBSS

Coquette, The. Aphra Behn. TrGrPo

Coquettes with doctors; hoards her breath. The Old Beauty. Phyllis McGinley. FaBoEE

Coracle, The. Lucan, *tr. fr. Latin by* Sir Walter Ralegh. ChTr

Coracle Fishers, The. Robert Bloomfield. *Fr.* The Banks of Wye. OBNC

Coral Grove, The. James Gates Percival. AA; GN

Coral Reef, The. Laurence Lieberman. CoAP

Corda Concordia, *sel.* Edmund Clarence Stedman.

  Quest. AA

Cordate head meanders through himself, The. Pit Viper. N. Scott Momaday. CDW; HATNAP; NOVW

Cordial Advice. *Unknown.* OxBSS

'Cordin to de present perdicament. Subtlety. Bruce St. John. PBCV

Cordoba. Asher Mendelsohn. VWA

Cordon Negro. Essex Hemphill. GLP

Cordova. Ibn Zaydun, *tr. fr. Arabic by* H. A. R. Gibb. AWP

Cords made out of calls. Links. Guillaume Apollinaire, *tr. by* Michael Benedikt. POS

Corduroy road, unfit for biking. Course of Life. Franz Richter, *tr. by* Beth Bjorklund. CoAuP

Corfou. Richard Monckton Milnes. *Fr.* The Ionian Islands. OBTV

Coridon and Phillis. Robert Greene. *Fr.* Perimedes [*or* Perimedes, the Blacksmith]. OBSC

Coridon's Song. John Chalkhill

Corinna Bathes. George Chapman. *Fr.* Ovid's Banquet of Sense. OBSC

Corinna, from Athens, to Tanagra. Walter Savage Landor. *Fr.* Pericles and Aspasia, XLIV. OBEV

  (Corinna to Tanagra.) OBNC

  (Corinna, to Tanagra, from Athens.) NOBE

Corinna, Having Tried, with Her Own Hand. Ovid, *tr. fr. Latin by* Rolfe Humphries. *Fr.* Amores, II, 13. NAs

Corinna in Vendome. Pierre de Ronsard, *tr. fr. French by* Robert Mezey. BoLoP; ErPo

Corinna, pride of Drury-Lane. A Beautiful Young Nymph Going to Bed. Swift. NIP; NOEC; OPOP

Corinna to Tanagra. Walter Savage Landor. *See* Pericles and Aspasia: Corinna, from Athens, to Tanagra.

Corinna, to Tanagra, from Athens. Walter Savage Landor. *See* Pericles and Aspasia: Corinna, from Athens, to Tanagra.

Corinnae Concubitus, I, 5. Ovid, *tr. fr. Latin by* Christopher Marlowe. *Fr.* Amores. EBEV; GBL; OBVE

  (Elegy: "In summer's heat and mid-time of the day.") BoLoP

Corinna's Going a-Maying. Robert Herrick. BoNaP; CaPo; GN; HAP; InPS; JCP; NAEL-1; NiP; NOBE; NoP; OAEL-1; OBEV; OBS; PoE; PoEL-3; PPP; PrIm; SeCP; SeCV-1; TEP; TrGrPo

Corinne at the Capitol. Felicia Dorothea Hemans. BrRo

Coriolan, *sel.* T. S. Eliot.

  Triumphal March. OBWP; WaaP

Coriolanus, *sels.* Shakespeare.

  "All tongues speak of him, and the bleared sights." *Fr.* II, i. FaBoPV

  "He that will give good words to thee, will flatter." *Fr.* I, i. FaBoPV

Corkby, Part Two. Jerome Rothenberg. NNaP

Cormac Mac Airt Presiding at Tara. *Unknown, tr. fr. Irish by* Douglas Hyde. BIrV

Cormorant boats, The. Tameyo, *tr. by* Steven D. Carter. WFTW

Cormorant has, The. Tails and Heads. Suzanne Knowles. RB

Cormorant in His Element, The. Amy Clampitt. InPK

Cormorant still screams, The. Late. Louise Bogan. PBWP; VGW

Cormorants. John Blight. CBAP

Corn, The. Daniel David Moses. HATNAP

Corn-blossom maidens. Masahongva, *tr. by* Natalie Curtis. WTO

Corn Cañon. Patric Stevenson. NeIP

Corn does not hurry, and the black grape swells. Second Wisdom. Henry Morton Robinson. GoYe

Corn-grinding Song. *Unknown, tr. fr. Laguna Indian by* Natalie Curtis. AWP

Corn-grinding Song. *Unknown, tr. fr. Tewa Indian by* N. Barnes. WTO

Corn Harvest, The. William Carlos Williams. *Fr.* Pictures from Brueghel, VII. PPP

Corn has stood ripe on the stalks for months, The. The Frost in the Corn. Robert McAlmon. AiP

Corn Husker, The. Pauline Johnson. CaP

Corn-Planter. Maurice Kenny. NOVW; STE

Corn-Pone-y, The. Carolyn Wells. *Fr.* A Baker's Dozen of Wild Beasts. OBCA

Corn Rigs Are Bonnie. Burns. *See* It was upon a Lammas night.

Corn Song, The. John Wesley Holloway. BANP

Corn-Song, The. Whittier. GN; OHIP

Corn swaying in the rhythm of the wind. Death in the Woods. Harold Littlebird. NOVW

Cornbush, the name Cornbush. Elfriede Gerstl, tr. by Beth Bjorklund.
  CoAuP
Corncrakes. Louis MacNeice. Fr. Nature Notes. FaBCIP
Cornelia, sel. Thomas Kyd.
  Of Fortune, abr. EIL
Cornelian, The. Byron. PeHV
Cornelia's Song. John Webster. See White Devil, The: Call for the
  Robin Redbreast and the Wren.
Corner. Amal Dunqul, tr. fr. Arabic by Sharif Elmusa and Thomas G.
  Ezzy. MAP
Corner bank has lost a great window, The. High Wind at the Battery.
  Ralph Pomeroy. NYBP
Corner Knot, The. Robert Graves. NYBP
Corner Lot. Sharon Bryan. MAYP
Corner of Pain and Anguish, there's a worn old house. The Sweatshop.
  Morris Jacob Rosenfeld, tr. by Aaron Kramer. PeBMYV
Corner Stone, The. Walter de la Mare. BrPo
Cornered and trapped, The. For Mack C. Parker. Pauli Murray. PoBA
Cornet, The. Earl of Surrey. See I never saw you madam, lay [or sawe
  my Ladye] laye apart.
Cornfield. Leo Cox. CaP
Cornfield, The. Elizabeth Madox Roberts. GoJo
Cornfield Myth. Mary Goose. STE
Cornfields in Accra. Ama Ata Aidoo. WPOW
Cornhusk bag. Talking Designs. Liz Sohappy Bahe. CDW
Cornish Emigrant's Song, The. Robert Stephen Hawker. EBVV
Cornish Magic. Ann Durell. FaPON
Cornishmen. Unknown. FaBoUs
Cornwallis led a country dance. The Dance. Unknown. PAH
Cornwallis's Surrender. Unknown. PAH
Corona. Paul Celan, tr. fr. German by Joachim Neugroschel. VWA
Corona. Marilyn Hacker. BLA
Coronach. Alexander Scott. OxBS
Coronach. Sir Walter Scott. Fr. The Lady of the Lake, III. CH; EnRP;
  GTBS; GTBS-P; OHIP; TrGrPo; WiR
Coronary Thrombosis. William Price Turner. OxBS
Coronation. Helen Hunt Jackson. AA; BeLS; GN
Coronation. Edward Perronet. See All Hail the Power of Jesus' Name.
Coronation Day at Melrose. Peter Bladen. PoAu-2
Coronemus Nos Rosis Antequam Marcescant. Thomas Jordan. See Let
  us drink and be merry.
Coroner's Jury. L. A. G. Strong. OxBTC
Coronet, The. Andrew Marvell. MeLP; MePo; NAEL-1; NOCV; NoP;
  OBS; PoE; SeCV-1; TOF
Coronet for His Mistress Philosophy, A, sels. George Chapman.
  But Dwell in Darkness. Fr. II. Son
  Love Flows Not from My Liver. Fr. III. Son
  Muses That Sing Love's Sensual Empery. Fr. I. EIL; Son
  (Love and Philosophy.) OBSC; SeCePo
"Corporal Green!" the orderly cried. Roll-Call. Nathaniel Graham
  Shepherd. AA; OHIP
  (Calling the Roll.) OBCA
Corporal Pym. Walter de la Mare. FaBoEE
Corporal Stare. Robert Graves. BrPo
Corporate Entity. Archibald MacLeish. OBAL
Corposant. Peter Redgrove. NePoEA-2; OxBTC
Corps d'Esprit. Heather McHugh. AmPA
Corpse, The. Salvador Díaz Mirón, tr. fr. Spanish by Samuel Beckett.
  MexPo
Corpse, The. María Isabel de los Ángeles Ruano, tr. fr. Spanish by
  Barbara Paschke. Vol
Corpse-bearing. Thomas Ashe. EBVV; NOBVV
Corpse, clad with carefulness. Of Misery. Thomas Howell. EIL; FF
Corpse has walked across my shadow, A. Into the Known. Tess
  Gallagher. AnAn
Corpse-Keeper, The. Unknown, tr. fr. Catalan by W. S. Merwin.
  BoWoP
Corpse of a Cat, The. Hagiwara Sakutaro, tr. fr. Japanese by Hiroaki
  Sato. FCEI
Corpse rotted from its exhibiting noose, The. The Example. Salvador
  Díaz Mirón, tr. by Samuel Beckett. MexPo
Corpse was there, brothers and sisters, The. The Corpse. María Isabel
  de los Ángeles Ruano, tr. by Barbara Paschke. Vol
Corpses in the Wood. Ernst Toller, tr. fr. German by E. Ellis Roberts.
  TrJP
Corpus Christi Carol, The ("Heron flew east, the heron flew west, The").
  Unknown. GBP
Corpus Christi Carol ("Lully, lullay [or lulley], lully, lullay [or lully]."
  Unknown. ChTr; GBP; MeEL; NAEL-1; NOBE; NoP; OAEL-1;
  OBD; SCV
Corpus Christi Carol ("Over yonder's a park"). Unknown. GBP
Corral, The. Earle Thompson. STE
Correct Compassion, A. James Kirkup. FaBoTw; ImOP; OxBTC; SeCePo

Correggio's Cupolas at Parma. Aubrey Thomas De Vere. Son
Correlated Greatness. Francis Thompson. See Heart, The: O nothing in
  this corporal earth of man.
Correspondence:/ when I have sad thoughts. Lady Ise, tr. by Etsuko
  Terasaki and Irma Brandeis. BoWoP
Correspondence. Henri Coulette. DiPo
Correspondence between Mr. Harrison in Newcastle and Mr. Sholto Peach
  Harrison in Hull. Stevie Smith. FaBoNo; NBLV; OxBC
Correspondence School Instructor Says Goodbye to His Poetry Students,
  The. Galway Kinnell. NoAM; NOBA; NoP; TAP
Correspondences. Baudelaire, tr. fr. French by Allen Tate. AWP
Correspondences. Robert Duncan. PoM
Corridor, The. Thom Gunn. NePoEA
Corridor, The. E. A. Robinson. AnAmPo
Corridors of the soul! Rebirth. Antonio Machado, tr. by Robert Bly.
  NU
Corries. Janet M. Smith. PoSH
Corroded flat as hills allow. Bedlam Hills. Vivian Smith. PoAu-2
Corrupt Man in the French Pub, The. Brian Higgins. OxBTC
Corruption. Patu Simoko. WMBCH
Corruption. Henry Vaughan. JCP; NAEL-1; NOCV; OAEL-1; OBS; Prf;
  SeCP; SeCV-1
Corruption of Metals. Sonya Dorman. BWV
Corrymeela. "Moira O'Neill." AWP
Corsair, The, sel. Byron.
  Sunset over the Aegean. Fr. III. OBNC
Corsons Inlet. A. R. Ammons. CoAP; MoP; NAAL-2; NoAM; NOBA;
  NoP; PoE; PPP
Cortège. Paul Verlaine, tr. fr. French by Arthur Symons. AWP; OBVE
Cortege for Colette. Jean Garrigue. NYBP
Coruisk. Walter Chalmers Smith. PoSH
Corydon and Thyrsis. Virgil, tr. fr. Latin by Dryden. Fr. Eclogues, VII.
  AWP
Corydon to His Phyllis. Sir Edward Dyer. EIL
Corydon's Farewell, on Sailing in the Late Expedition Fleet. Unknown.
  NOEC
Cosmic Eye. A. K. Redwing. VoR
Cosmic Fabric, The. Yakov Petrovich Polonsky, tr. fr. Russian by
  Avrahm Yarmolinsky and Cecil Cowdery. EaLo
Cosmic Leviathan, that monstrous fish. Cosmogony. Edgell Rickword.
  FaBoTw
Cosmic Tapestry. Anna Kiss, tr. fr. Hungarian by Jascha Kessler. FOC
Cosmogony. David Chapman Berry. BXAP
Cosmogony. Edgell Rickword. FaBoTw
Cosmology. Phyllis Gotlieb. BWV
Cosmology and Us. Thomas M. Disch. BWV
Cossimbazar. Henry Sambrooke Leigh. NA
Cost, The. Anthony Hecht. OxBC
Cost of Pretending, The. Peter Davison. TW
Cost of Seriousness, The. Peter Porter. NoAM
Cosy fire is bright and gay, The. Barry Pain. Fr. The Poets at Tea, IV.
  Par
Cot, The. Grover Amen. NYBP
Côte d'Azur. Katherine Hoskins. NYBP
Cotignac Again ("Cotignac is full of spies"). Charles Hubert Sisson.
  NPo
Cottage, The. Jones Very. OxBA
Cottage at Chigasaki, The. Edmund Blunden. OBTV
Cottage Hospital, The. Sir John Betjeman. GTBS-P; MoBrPo; NoAM;
  NOBE; OBD; UnPo
Cottage in the Wood, A. Russell Edson. LCAP
Cottage party is long past, The. Thirteen Years. Ilse Aichinger, tr. by
  Beth Bjorklund. CoAuP
Cottage Street, 1953. Richard Wilbur. CAPP; FaBoMo; HCAP
Cottager to Her Infant, The. Dorothy Wordsworth. CH; OxBChV; TTTS
Cottager's Complaint, on the Intended Bill for Enclosing Sutton-Coldfield,
  The. John Freeth. NOEC; OBET
Cotter's Saturday Night, The. Burns. BeLS; EnRP; FaBoBe; PoLF;
  WGRP
Cotton. Harry Edmund Martinson, tr. fr. Swedish by Robert Bly. RB
Cotton blankets left in the cold. Liu E, tr. fr. Chinese by Jonathan
  Chaves. Fr. On the Fifteenth Day of the Eighth Month. CoBLCP
Cotton blouse your mother said, the. McDonogh Day in New
  Orleans. Marcus B. Christian. AmNP; PoNe
Cotton Boll, The. Henry Timrod. AA; AmPP
Cotton Song. Jean Toomer. BPo; CDC
Cottonmouth Country. Louise Glück. CoAP; GeTw
Cottonmouth white faces survey the marshes. Okeechobee. John Allison.
  GrPl
Cottontail. George Bogin. MOWH
Cottonwood, willow, and briar. Leaves like Fish. Gladys Cardiff.
  CDW

Coughing in a shady grove. Ipecacuanha. George Canning. ChTr; FaBoNo

Coughing up blood. Differences. Ray A. Young Bear. NU

Could a little spring rain. *Unknown, tr. fr. Japanese by* Burton Watson. *Fr.* Manyo Shu. FCEI

Could all this be forgotten? Yes, a schism. Keats. *Fr.* Sleep and Poetry. ChER

Could but this be brought into your ken. Technique. Langdon Elwyn Mitchell. *Fr.* To a Writer of the Day. AA

Could every time-worn heart but see Thee once again. To the Child Jesus. Henry van Dyke. TrPWD

Could he have made Priscilla share. Llewellyn and the Tree. Edwin Arlington Robinson. BeLS

Could Homer come himself, distressed and poor. Epigram on the Refusal of the University of Oxford to Subscribe to His Translation of Homer. William Cowper. TW

Could I but retrace. Tanka (I–VIII). Lewis Alexander. CDC

Could I remove the stones from the river? Song of Longing. *Gond Oral Tradition, tr. by* V. Elwin *and* S. Hivale. WTO

Could I Say I Touched You. Harold Littlebird. VoR

Could I take me to some cavern for mine hiding. O for the Wings of a Dove. Euripides, *tr. fr. Greek by* Gilbert Murray. *Fr.* Hippolytus. AWP

Could I tell you how it is. Evelyn Searching. Denise Panek. GOS

Could it be, Bud. For Bud. Michael S. Harper. PoE

Could it be I wait. Teika, *tr. by* Steven D. Carter. WFTW

Could It Have Been a Shadow? Monica Shannon. FaPON; RHPC

Could Man Be Drunk for Ever. A. E. Housman. *Fr.* A Shropshire Lad. LiTM; NAEL-2; OBMV; PPP

Could mortal lip divine. Emily Dickinson. RB

Could my quiet ship take you in. *Unknown, tr. fr. Japanese. Fr.* Manyo Shu. Ma

Could my longings have. Black Rose. "Zelda," *tr. by* Bernhard Frank. MHeP

Could not once blinding me, cruel, suffice? Samson to His Delilah. Richard Crashaw. TrGrPo

Could she come back who has been dead so long. Separation. Alice Learned Bunner. *Fr.* Vingtaine, I. AA

Could we have those trees cleared out of the way? Mode Z. Barrett Watten. LP

Could ye come back to me, Douglas, Douglas. Douglas, Douglas, Tender and True. Dinah Maria Mulock Craik. BLPA

Could you bid an acorn. Lover's Reply to Good Advice. Richard Hughes. MoBrPo

Could you catch a little fish, son. Father and Son. Richard Eberhart. DiL

Could you hush the drums a bit. In the Middle of the Road. Jacob Glatstein, *tr. by* Benjamin *and* Barbara Harshav. AYP

Could you indeed come lightly. Song for a Departure. Elizabeth Jennings. GOYP

Could you register birds. Holocaust. Myra Sklarew. CRP

Could you, so arrantly of earth, so cool. Animal. Max Eastman. FYAP

Could you tell me the way to Somewhere. Somewhere. Walter de la Mare. FaPON

Couldn't you have died. Squared by Walls. László Nagy, *tr. by* Tony Connor. MHuP

Couldst thou, Great Fairy, give to me. The Pines. Harriet Prescott Spofford. AA

Could'st thou (O Earth) live thus obscure, and now. George Alsop. SCAP

Councell Given to Master Bartholmew Withipoll. George Gascoigne. AAS

Council of Horses, The. John Gay. GN

Council of Satan, The. Milton. *See* Paradise Lost: So Satan spake, and him Beëlzebub.

Councils. Marge Piercy. NeAC

Counsel. Naomi Lewis. Mes

Counsel of Moderation, A. Francis Thompson. MoBrPo

Counsel to Girls. Robert Herrick. *See* Gather ye rosebuds while ye may.

Counsel to Girls. Archibald Stodart-Walker. *Fr.* The Moxford Book of English Verse. CenHV

Counsel to Unreason. Léonie Adams. PoA

Counsels of Sigrdrifa. *Unknown, tr. fr. Old Norse by* William Morris *and* Eirikr Magnusson. *Fr.* The Elder Edda. AWP (Part of the Lay of Sigrdrifa.) OBVE

Count each affliction, whether light or grave. Sorrow. Aubrey Thomas De Vere. BLPA; WGRP

Count has moved me by Sir Arramon Luc d'Esparro, The. Bertrans de Born, *tr. by* Paul Blackburn. Pro

Count me o'er earth's chosen heroes—they were souls that stood alone. James Russell Lowell. *Fr.* The Present Crisis. WGRP

Count not his broken pledges as a crime. Lloyd George. *Unknown.* FaBoCo

Count on dead fingers of time the years that pass. Poem for Garcia Lorca. George Woodcock. NOBC

Count Orlo in England. Jon Manchip White. NePoEA

Count the sighs, and count the teares. The Broken Heart. Thomas Beedome. OBS

Count the white horses you meet on the way. White Horses. Eleanor Farjeon. PDV

Count them. The Onus of Mercy. Yehuda Amichai, *tr. by* Warren Bargad *and* Stanley F. Chyet. IP

Count up those books whose pages you have read. Indolence. Vernon Watkins. FaBoTw

Count William's Escapade. Guillaume de Poitiers, *tr. fr. Provençal by* Hubert Creekmore. ErPo

Count Your Blessings. Mrs. Henry Linden. CBWP-4

Counted Out. Ilse Aichinger, *tr. fr. German by* Beth Bjorklund. CoAuP

Countee Cullen. Eugene T. Maleska. PoNe

Countenance like lightning, why do you stand. Colloquy at Peniel. W. S. Merwin. NePoEA

Counter-Attack. Siegfried Sassoon. BrPo; MoBrPo; WaP

Counter-Revolution. W. H. Oliver. ATNZ; PeNZ

Counterblast against Garlic, A. Horace, *tr. fr. Latin by* Roswell Martin Field. *Fr.* Epodes, III. NBLV

Counterpart, The. Elizabeth Jennings. LiTM; TOF

Counterparts. Stephen Dobyns. PoA

Counterpoint, A. Robert Creeley. NeAP

Counterpoint. Owen Dodson. PoNe

Countershadow, The. Philip Booth. NYBP

Countess Laura. George Henry Boker. BeLS

Countesse of Douglas out of her boure she came, The. The Knight of Liddesdale. *Unknown.* ESPB

Counting. Fenton Johnson. AmNP

Counting-out Rhyme. Edna St. Vincent Millay. GoJo; InPK; MoShBr; TTTS

Counting-out Rhyme. *Unknown.* ChTr; GBP

Counting-out Rhymes. *Unknown.* FaPON

Counting Sheep. Russell Edson. LCAP

Counting Small-boned Bodies. Robert Bly. CAPP; EAS; NaP

Counting-Song. *Unknown, tr. fr. Japanese by* Geoffrey Bownas *and* Anthony Thwaite. PeBJV

Counting the Beats. Robert Graves. ELP; GBL; GTBS-P; HAP; OxBTC; WeW

Counting the dewdrops that vie in falling off. Princess Shikishi, *tr. fr. Japanese by* Hiroaki Sato. *Fr.* Seventy-eight Tanka. FCEI

Counting the fleabites while suckling her baby. Issa, *tr. by* Hiroaki Sato. FCEI

Counting the Losses. Barry Spacks. PPR

Counting the Mad. Donald Justice. CAPP; FF; NePoEA; NIP; UnPo

Countless are the mountains in Yamato. Emperor Jomei, *tr. fr. Japanese. Fr.* Manyo Shu. Ma

Countless gold of a merry heart, The. Riches. Blake. TrGrPo

Countless great lords and statesmen of past regimes, The. Thoughts on T'ien-chin Bridge. Shao Yung, *tr. by* Burton Watson. CoBCP

Countless stars, which to our human eye, The. The Starry Host. John Lancaster Spalding. *Fr.* God and the Soul. AA

Countless tears I've shed, yet. Tears. Prince P. A. Vyazemsky, *tr. by* Alan Myers. AAA

Countless things escape easily out of me. Afternoon 3. Saburoh Kuroda. EAS

Countrie men of England, who live at home with ease. Saylors for My Money. Martin Parker. CoMu

Countries grow old and fall apart. Psalms. Yankev-Yitskhok Segal, *tr. by* Grace Schulman. PeBMYV

Countries tears, be ye my spring, The; my hill. To the Memory of the Learned and Reverend, Mr. Jonathan Mitchell. Francis Drake. SCAP

Country, The/ was back in the hands of the patriots. Fred Levinson. AmPA

Country and Town. Charles Morris. NOEC

Country Barnyard. Elizabeth J. Coatsworth. CRH; RHPC

Country Bedroom, The. Frances Cornford. MoBrPo

Country Boy in Winter, A. Sarah Orne Jewett. OBCA

Country Burial. Janet Lewis. CRP

Country Burying (1919). Robert Penn Warren. LiTM

Country Child, The. Irene Thompson. BoTP

Country Clergy, The. Ronald Stuart Thomas. GTBS-P; OxBTC

Country Clergyman's Trip to Cambridge, The. Macaulay. OBSV; OxBoLi

Country clouds scatter four ways. Written on a Summer Night. Kan Sazan, *tr. by* Burton Watson. JLIC-2

Country Club Romance, A. Derek Walcott. OxBC

Country Curate, The. Henry Taylor. NOEC

Country Dance. Edward Baugh. PBCV
Country Dance. Dame Edith Sitwell. MoP; NoAM
Country Dance, A. Charles Tennyson Turner. NOBVV
Country Dance. Judith Wright. *Fr.* The Blind Man. CBAP
Country Doctor, The. Will M. Carleton. BLPA
Country Faith, The. Norman Gale. BoTP; OBEV; WGRP
Country Fiddler, The. John Montague. FaBCIP
Country folk who pass have said to me, The. The Grave. John Lyle Donaghy. NeIP
Country Girl's Policy; or, The Cockney Outwitted, The. *Unknown.* CoMu
Country Glee. Thomas Dekker. *See* Sun's Darling, The: Haymakers, Rakers.
Country God, A. Edmund Blunden. MoBrPo
Country Gods. Cometas, *tr. fr. Greek by* T. F. Higham. FaBoCh
Country Greeting. Frank Steele. Psk
Country Gulliver, A. The Reports Come In. J. D. Reed. NYBP
Country Hirings. *Unknown.* OBET
Country Hotel. Brian Turner. ATNZ
Country House, The. Louis Simpson. NOBA
Country Justice, The, *sels.* John Langhorne. LaA
  Gypsies. NOEC
  Poor, The. NOEC
Country lad and bonny lass, A. Have-at a Venture. *Unknown.* CoMu; ErPo
Country Life. Horace, *tr. fr. Latin by* Dryden. *Fr.* Epodes, II. AWP
Country Life, A. Randall Jarrell. MoAmPo
Country Life: To His Brother, Master Thomas Herrick, A. Robert Herrick. CaPo; SeCP; SeCV-1
Country Lovers; or, Isaac and Marget Going to Town, on a Summer's Morning, The. George Smith. NOEC
Country Man, The, *sel.* George Farewell.
  "Crunking crane heard high amongst the clouds, The." NOEC
Country Matters. Gavin Ewart. SoTCo
Country-Mouse, The. Abraham Cowley, *after the Latin of* Horace. OBVE; SeCP
Country Mouse and the City Mouse, The. Richard Scrafton Sharpe. OxBChV
Country Night. Rocco Scotellaro, *tr. fr. Italian by* Lawrence R. Smith. NItP
Country North of Belleville, The. Alfred W. Purdy. NOBC
Country Nun. Geoff Page. CBAP
Country of hunchbacks!—where the strong, straight spine. Sonnet to Gath. Edna St. Vincent Millay. BoWoP; CMoP; MoAB; MoAmPo
Country of No Lack. Jean Starr Untermeyer. MoAmPo
Country of rubble, country of brush—rocks. Face. Eugène Guillevic, *tr. by* Teo Savory. RHTwFP
Country of Water. Bernice Ames. WPE
Country Pleasures. Martial, *tr. fr. Latin by* F. A. Wright. AWP
Country Press. Rosemary Dobson. FaBoWP
Country Reverie. Carol Coates. CaP
Country rings around with loud alarms, The. The Militia. Dryden. *Fr.* Cymon and Iphigenia. OBSV
Country road—/ boys whacking at a snake. Masaoka Shiki, *tr. fr. Japanese by* Burton Watson. *Fr.* Thirty-nine Haiku. FCEI
Country Roads. Rolf Jacobsen, *tr. by* Robert Bly. NU
Country roads are yellow and brown. Street Lanterns. Mary Elizabeth Coleridge. BoTP; PoRA
Country Scene, *sels.* Wu Wei-yeh, *tr. fr. Chinese by* Jonathan Chaves. CoBLCP
  "Fading, sick, again I hear of war."
  "River Ching flows rapidly, The."
Country Song. Nicholas Breton. *See* Shall we go dance the hay? The hay?
Country Song. Shakespeare. *See* As You Like It: It Was a Lover and His Lass.
Country Song, A. Sir Philip Sidney. *Fr.* Arcadia. OBSC; SiPS
Country Stars. William Meredith. GrPl
Country Statutes. *Unknown.* OBET
Country Store, The. *Unknown.* BLPA
Country Summer. Léonie Adams. GoJo; LiTM; MoAB; MoAmPo; TrGrPo
Country that draws fifty foot of water, A. Description of Holland. Samuel Butler. OBTV
Country Thought. Sylvia Townsend Warner. MoBrPo
Country Towns. Kenneth Slessor. CBAP; PoAu-2
Country Trucks. Monica Shannon. FaPON
Country vegetables scorn, The. Vegetables. Eleanor Farjeon. FaPON
Country Villa. Jean Garrigue. TAP
Country Walk, A. Thomas Kinsella. CIP; CMoP
Country Ways. Marcia Lee Masters. *Fr.* Impressions of My Father, I. GoYe
Country Wedding (A Fiddler's Story), The. Thomas Hardy. UnPo
Country without a Mythology, A. Douglas Le Pan. MoCV; NOBC
Country Woman Elegy. Margaret Gibson. MT
Country Wooing, *sel.* J. C. Squire.
  "So lay the youth with Mary in his arms." BXAP
Countryman's Return, The. Dylan Thomas. OxBTC
Countryman's Wooing, A. Theocritus, *tr. fr. Latin by* Charles Stuart Calverley. ErPo
Countrymen of England who live at home at ease. Sailors for My Money. Martin Parker. OxBSS
Country's Crisis, The. Brian Merriman, *tr. fr. Modern Irish by* David Marcus. *Fr.* The Midnight Court. BIrV
Country's depressed, I'm depressed, The. Sexy Food Stamps. Jeffrey Miller. UL
Countryside in France. Hans Andreus. DuIn
Countrywoman of Mine, A. Elaine Goodale Eastman. AA
County Ball, The. Coventry Patmore. *Fr.* The Angel in the House, II, iii. EBVV
County Ball, The, *sel.* Winthrop Mackworth Praed.
  County Member, The. OBNC
County Mayo, The. Anthony Raftery, *tr. fr. Irish by* James Stephens. AnIL
County Member, The. Winthrop Mackworth Praed. *Fr.* The County Ball. OBNC
County of Mayo, The. *At. to* Thomas Flavell, *tr. fr. Irish by* George Fox. BIrV; OBEV
County Roads. Thomas Rabbitt. MAYP
Coup-clock Clicks, The. Brian Meeks. PBCV
Coup de Grace, The. Edward Rowland Sill. AA; PPP
Coup d'Etat. Ruth Herschberger. LiTA
Couple, The. Ana Blandiana, *tr. fr. Rumanian by* author and William M. Murray. WPOW
Couple, The. Sandra Hochman. NYBP
Couple. Walter Stone. NYBP
Couple of kids, A. Cottontail. George Bogin. MOWH
Couple Overheard, The. William Meredith. HoPM; TW
Couplet. Donald Hall. ASP; TSL
Couplets. Natalie Clifford Barney, *tr. fr. French by* Barbara Johnson. DMF
Couplets, XX. Robert Mezey. FYAP; NU
Courage. Matthew Arnold. OAEL-2
Courage. Stopford Brooke. WGRP
Courage. Paul Gerhardt, *tr. fr. German by* John Wesley. WGRP
Courage. Sadi, *tr. fr. Persian by* Sir Edwin Arnold. *Fr.* The Gulistan. AWP
Courage, a Tale. Thom Gunn. GLP
Courage brother! do not stumble. Trust in God. Norman Macleod. *Fr.* Trust in God and Do the Right. BLRP
Courage, brother! do not stumble. Trust in God and Do the Right. Norman Macleod. BLRP
Courage, dear Moll! and drive away despair. À Madame, Madame B, Beauté Sexagenaire. Charles Sackville. APAS
Courage for the Pusillanimous. Paul Roche. GoYe
"Courage!" he said, and pointed toward the land. The Lotos-Eaters. Tennyson. ChTr; FiP; LiTB; NAEL-2; NoP; OAEL-2; OnMSP; PoEL-5; TEP
Courage, I told myself, gather courage. Song of the Hammer. Armanda Guiducci, *tr. by* Muriel Kittel. DMI
Courage Means Running. William Empson. LiTB
Courage, my soul, now learn to wield. A Dialogue between the Resolved Soul and Created Pleasure. Andrew Marvell. MeLP; MePo; OAEL-1; OBS; SeCP; SeCV-1
Courage, my Soul! now to the silent wood. Peace. Bhartrihari, *tr. by* Paul Elmer More. AWP
Courage: your tongue has left. Stutterer. Alan Dugan. NYBP
Coureurs de Bois. Douglas Le Pan. CaP; MoCV; NOBC
Couriers, The. Sylvia Plath. LCAP
Course, The. Robert Huff. CoAP
Course bread and water's most their fare. Roger Williams. SCAP
Course of a Day in a Summer Garden, The. Peter Handke, *tr. fr. German by* Beth Bjorklund. CoAuP
Course of a Particular, The. Wallace Stevens. HCAP; QFR
Course of a Year, The. George Sands Johnson. PWR
Course of Life. Franz Richter, *tr. fr. German by* Beth Bjorklund. CoAuP
Course of the Tavy, The. William Browne. *Fr.* Britannia's Pastorals, I, Song 2. FaBoPP
Courser, The. Shakespeare. *See* Venus and Adonis: But, lo! from forth a copse that neighbours by.
Courser and the Jennet, The. Shakespeare. *See* Venus and Adonis: But, lo! from forth a copse that neighbours by.
Court, The. *Unknown.* APAS

Court considered the country's crisis, The. The Country's Crisis. Brian Merriman, *tr. fr. Modern Irish by* David Marcus. *Fr.* The Midnight Court. BIrV

Court is kept att leeue London, The. Hugh Spencer's Feats in France. *Unknown.* ESPB

Court ladies may board a boat, The. Hitomaro, *tr. fr. Japanese. Fr.* Manyo Shu. Ma

Court Lady, A. Elizabeth Barrett Browning. BeLS

Court of Sapience, *sel.* John Lydgate.
  "Farewell Mercy, farewell thy piteous grace." PoEL-1

Courteous kind gallants all. Sir Walter Rauleigh His Lamentation. *Unknown.* CoMu

Courteous Knight, The. *Unknown. See* There was a knight and he was young.

Courteous pagan shall condemne, The. Roger Williams. SCAP

Courteously self-assured, although alone. Charlotte Corday. Charles Tomlinson. OxBC

Courtesan with Fan. Elizabeth Spires. MAYP

Courtesies of good-morning and good-evening. On Dwelling. Robert Graves. CMoP; FaBoMo; OxBSP

Courtesy. Hilaire Belloc. ACP

Courthouse Square. Herbert Merrill. AmFN

Courtier's a Riddle, A. Ralph Schomberg. *Fr.* The Judgment of Paris. TrJP

Courtier's Good-Morrow to His Mistress, The. *Unknown.* EIL

Courtier's Health; or, Merry Boys of the Times, The. *Unknown.* CoMu

Courtier's Life, The. Sir Thomas Wyatt. FaBoEE

Courtin', The. James Russell Lowell. *Fr.* The Biglow Papers: 2d Series, Introduction. AA; AmPP; AnAmPo; BeLS; NOBA; OBAL

Courtly Scene and a Sudden Storm, A. Chaucer. *Fr.* The Floure and the Leafe. OxBLMV

Courtship, The. George Ella Lyon. MOWH

Courtship. Diana O Hehir. NPGG

Courtship. Mark Strand. HCAP

Courtship of Miles Standish, The ("In the old colony days, in Plymouth the land of the Pilgrims."), *sels. Longfellow.* AiP, *st.* 1; BeLS
  Expedition to Wessagusset, The. *Fr.* PAH.
  War-Token, The. PAH

Courtship of the Yonghy-Bonghy-Bo, The. Edward Lear. EnLoPo; FaBoNo; NA; OAEL-2; OnMSP; WiR

Courtyard in Winter. John Montague. IPY

Courtyard, quiet, The. Rainy Night. Ho Ching-ming, *tr. by* Jonathan Chaves. CoBLCP

Courtyards in Delft. Derek Mahon. CIP; FaBCIP

Cousin, it's of you I always dream. El Sueño de la Razón. Jane Cooper. FaBoWP

Cousin Jack Song. *at. to* Charley Tregonning. AmFP

Cousin Nancy. T. S. Eliot. AnAmPo; OBAL; OxBSP

Covenant. Paul Auster. VWA

Covenant, The. James Cunningham. JB

Covenant of Grace, The, *sel.* Anne Stanford.
  "Brother Symmes conversed with her on the ship." CRP

Coventry Carol. *Unknown.* ELP; MeEL; OFD; PChr
  (Lully, Lulla.) TTTS

Coventry Carol, The. *Unknown.* MeEL

Cover Her Face. Thomas Kinsella. CIP; IPY

Cover my eyes with your palm. Ruth Miller. *Fr.* Cycle. PeSA

Cover myself with the quilt. Ishikawa Takuboku, *tr. fr. Japanese by* Hiroaki Sato. *Fr.* Forty-seven Tanka in Three Lines. FCEI

Covered boat, A. *Unknown, tr. by* Burton Watson. FCEI

Covered Bridge. Robert Peter Tristram Coffin. AmFN

Covered Bridge. Robert Penn Warren. AiP

Covered with snow, the herd, with none to guide. Without the Herdsman. Diotimus, *tr. by* John William Burgon. AWP

Covered with yellow leaves. Memory Gardens. Allen Ginsberg. NNaP

Covering All Bases. Evelyn Thomas. TSM

Covers. Nikki Giovanni. RAR

Covetousness. Peter Idley. OxBChV

Covey of cotton-dressed, apple-breasted girls, A. Wax. Winfield Townley Scott. ErPo

Covey struts across the chrome-green roof, The. California Quail in January. Will C. Jumper. GrPl

Cow, The. Oliver Herford. *Fr.* More Animals. NA

Cow, The. Janet Reed McFatter. GrPl

Cow, The. Ogden Nash. CenHV; NBLV; NoP; RB; RHPC

Cow, The. Bernard O'Dowd. PoAu-1

Cow, The. Jack Prelutsky. RHPC

Cow, The. Theodore Roethke. FiBHP; OBAL; OBCA

Cow, The. Robert Louis Stevenson. BrPo; FaPON; FM; NTCP; OxBChV; PWR

Cow, The. Ann Taylor. OxBChV

Cow, The. *Unknown.* FaBoUs

Cow and a calf, A. *Unknown.* OxNR

Cow and the Ass, The. Ann Taylor *and* Jane Taylor. BoTP

Cow Ate the Piper, The. *Unknown.* GBP

Cow-Boy's Song, The. Anna Maria Wells. OBCA

Cow-Chace, The. John André. PAH

Cow Dance. Bruce Beaver. PoAu-2

Cow eats green grass, The. Response to Rimbaud's Later Manner. T. Sturge Moore. OBMV

Cow in Apple Time, The. Robert Frost. MoAB; MoAmPo; OxBSP; PoLF

Cow is of the bovine ilk, The. The Cow. Ogden Nash. CenHV; NBLV; NoP; RB; RHPC

Cow is too well known, I fear, The. The Cow. Oliver Herford. *Fr.* More Animals. NA

Cow-lady, or sweet lady-bird. Lines to a Lady-Bird. Lord De Tabley. FM

Cow low'd sadly o'er the distant gate, The. Rose and Cushie. Charles Tennyson Turner. Mes

Cow mainly moos as she chooses to moo, The. The Cow. Jack Prelutsky. RHPC

Cow of Our Time, A. Tom Disch. EOEF

Cow Pissing. Robert Morgan. GeTw

Cow Slips Away, The. Ben King. AnAmPo

Cow walks away from him, The. Thomas in the Fields. Lois Moyles. NYBP

Coward. A. R. Ammons. OBAL

Coward, The. Kipling. *Fr.* Epitaphs of the War, 1914–1918. FaBoEE; FaBoTw

Coward, The. Eve Merriam. TrJP

Coward,—of heroic size. Grizzly. Bret Harte. AA; AnAmPo

Cowards die many times before their deaths. Shakespeare. *Fr.* Julius Caesar, II, ii. FF
  (That Men Should Fear.) TrGrPo

Cowards fear to die, but courage stout. On the Snuff of a Candle. Sir Walter Ralegh. FaBoEE; OBD; SiPS

Cowboy, The. John Antrobus. AA; FaBoBe; FaPON

Cowboy. *Unknown.* ChTr

Cowboy and his trusty pal, A. The Cowboy's Dream. Bruce Kiskaddon. CowP

Cowboy-Boot Sale. Norma Thomas Colvin. TSM

Cowboy Song. Charles Causley. NePoEA; PoRA

Cowboy stands beneath, The. Vaquero. Edward Dorn. NeAP; PoM

Cowboy's Christmas Ball, The. Larry Chittendon. CowP

Cowboys, come and hear a story of Roy Bean in all his glory. Roy Bean. *Unknown.* AnAmPo; BeLS; OBAL

Cowboy's Dance Song, The. James Barton Adams. CowP

Cowboy's Dream, The. Bruce Kiskaddon. CowP

Cowboy's Favorite. Barney Nelson. CowP

Cowboy's Lament, The. *Unknown. See* As I Walked Out in the Streets of Laredo.

Cowboy's Lament, The Smoky Mountains. *Unknown.* AmFP

Cowboy's Life, The. *At. to* James Barton Adams. AmFN

Cowboy's Life Is a Very Dreary Life, The. *Unknown.* AmFP

Cowboy's Prayer, A. Badger Clark. CowP

Cowboy's Prayer, The. Curley W. Fletcher. CowP

Cowboy's Soliloquy, The. Allen McCanless. CowP

Cowboy's Toast. Dick Gibford. CowP

Cowherd, The. Yabu Kozan, *tr. fr. Chinese by* Burton Watson. JLIC-2

Cowherd, since parting with the Princess Weaver, The. Okura, *tr. fr. Japanese by* Hiroaki Sato. *Fr.* Manyo Shu. FCEI

Cowherd's Song: In Imitation of Chang Chi, A. Li E, *tr. fr. Chinese by* Irving Lo. WFTU

Cowhorn-crowned, shockheaded, cornshuck-bearded. The Knight, Death, and the Devil. Randall Jarrell. WeW

Cowper's Tame Hare. Norman Nicholson. RB

Cowper's Three Hares. Charles Tennyson Turner. FM

Cows. Stanley Plumly. AnAn

Cows. James Reeves. NTCP

Cows and Logs. Harold Otto. CowP

Cows at Night, The. Hayden Carruth. SV

Cows bring in the last light, The. The Black Plateau. W. S. Merwin. NNaP

Cows! Cows! With ears like mouths of telephones! Band Music. John Fuller. NePoEA-2

Cows graze. Horses Graze. Gwendolyn Brooks. CNA

Cows in Vatra Dornii lumber on the grass-wet, The. Hertza. Benjamin Fondane, *tr. by* Matei Calinescu *and* Willis Barnstone. VWA

Cows near the Graveyard, The. Howard Nelson. NU

Cows of Heaven, The. Saleem Barakat, *tr. fr. Arabic by* Lena Jayyusi *and* Naomi Shihab Nye. MAP

Cows once believed that if you stand in a pond, The. The Silver Coin. Trish Reeves. PPR

Cows they had, many, like heavy clouds drifting in the meadow. The Wheelbarrow. Russell Edson. LCAP

Coy Lass Dress'd Up in Her Best, The. *Unknown*. ErPo

Coy Nature (which remain'd, though [*or* tho] aged grown). Abraham Cowley. *Fr.* Ode upon Doctor Harvey. Par; PoEL-2

Coy Shepherdess; or, Phillis and Amintas, The. *Unknown*. CoMu

Coyote. Bret Harte. AnAmPo

Coyote, The. Carter Revard. NOVW; VoR

Coyote/ running. Sweat Song. Peter Blue Cloud. STE; VoR

Coyote and the Locust, The. *Unknown*. *See* Locust, locust, playing a flute.

Coyote, Coyote, Please Tell Me. Peter Blue Cloud. STE

Coyote Fragments. Lance Henson. HATNAP

Coyote kicks back. Agnes. Mah-do-ge Tohee. STE

Cozzo Grillo. Herbert B. Mallalieu. WaP

Crab. Fleur Adcock. ATNZ

Crab. François Dodat, *tr. fr. French by* Bert *and* Odette Meyers. TSS

Crab-Legged Flower, The. Lo Fu, *tr. fr. Chinese by* Dominic Cheung. IFON

Crab Orchard Sanctuary, Late October. Thomas Kinsella. IPY

Crab shops and fishing village—in an out of the way place. Inscribed on a Painting. Ts'ao Chen-chi, *tr. by* William H. Nienhauser, Jr.. WFTU

Crab Tree, The. Oliver St. John Gogarty. AnIL

Crabbed Age and Youth. Shakespeare. *Fr.* The Passionate Pilgrim, XII. GBL; InPS; LiTB; OBEV

    (Age and Youth.) EiL

    (Madrigal, A: "Crabbed age and youth.") GTBS; GTBS-P

    (Youth and Age.) OBSC

Crabbing. Norman Levine. CaP; OBCV

Crabs. Marge Piercy. NBLV

Crack, The. Michael Goldman. NYBP

Crack in the Wall Holds Flowers. Adam David Miller. PoBA

Crack is moving down the wall, The. Weldon Kees. *Fr.* Five Villanelles, I. SM

Crack ran through our hearthstone long ago, A. The Refugees. Edwin Muir. NoAM

Crack—recall it vividly as first fabric. Light. Richard Kenney. Son

Crack soldiers get no sleep, The. Li K'ai-hsien, *tr. fr. Chinese by* Jonathan Chaves. *Fr.* Songs of the Frontier. CoBLCP

Cracked cedar, The. Elephants. Patrick Lane. NeAC

Cracked is the very foundation. Epigram: To Charinus, a Catamite. Martial. PeHV

Cracking whips, off to the wine shop. The Streets of Ch'ang-an. Ch'u Kuang-hsi, *tr. by* Burton Watson. CoBCP

Cracks in eight log buildings, counting sheds. Montana Ranch Abandoned. Richard Hugo. CAPP

Cracks on the walls, The. Star Blanket. Ray A. Young Bear. CDW

Cradle Hymn. Martin Luther. *See* Away in a Manger.

Cradle Hymn, A. Isaac Watts. OBEV; OxBChV; PoEL-3

Cradle Song, A: "Angels are bending, The." W. B. Yeats. NOBVV

Cradle Song: "Clock's untiring fingers wind the wool of darkness, The." Louis MacNeice. MoAB; MoBrPo

    (Cradle Song for Miriam.) NAs

Cradle Song: "Come here, little girl, come here." David Avidan, *tr. by* Bernhard Frank. MHeP

Cradle Song, A: "Come, little babe, come, silly soul." Nicholas Breton. NOBE; OBEV

    (Sweet Lullaby, A.) EiL; OBSC

Cradle Song, A: "O men from the fields." Padraic Colum. TIRV

    (Lullaby.) WTO

Cradle Song: "Curled like a hoop in sleep." Lawrence Durrell. NAs

Cradle Song: "From groves of spice." Sarojini Naidu. FaPON

    (Hindu Cradle Song.) BoTP

Cradle Song, A: "Golden slumbers kiss your eyes." Thomas Dekker *and others*. *See* Pleasant Comedy of Patient Grissell [*or* Grissel *or* Grissill], The: Golden Slumbers.

Cradle Song: "Imagine lamenting our longing, no." Yona Wallach, *tr. by* Leonore Gordon. VWA

Cradle Song: "Lullaby, my little one." Carl Michael Bellman. FaPON

Cradle Song, A: "Sleep baby sleep!/ Thy father watches the sheep." *Unknown*. *See* Sleep, Baby, Sleep ("Sleep baby sleep!/ Thy father watches the sheep").

Cradle Song: "Sleep, my child, my little daughter." *Unknown, tr. by* Joseph Leftwich. TrJP

Cradle Song: "Sleep, sleep, beauty bright." Blake. EnRP; FPL; OBEV; PoLF

Cradle Song, A: "Sweet dreams, form a shade." Blake. *Fr.* Songs of Innocence. EnRP; OBCP

Cradle Song: "What does little birdie say?" Tennyson. *Fr.* Sea Dreams. BOTP; OxBChV

Cradle Song at Bethlehem. E. J. Falconer. BoTP

Cradle-Song at Twilight. Alice Meynell. NOBVV

Cradle Song for Miriam. Louis MacNeice. *See* Cradle Song: "Clock's untiring fingers wind the wool of darkness, The."

Cradle Song of the Elephants. Adriano Del Valle, *tr. fr. Spanish by* Alida Malkus. FaPON

Cradle Will Rock, The, *sel.* Marc Blitzstein.

    Art for Art's Sake. TrJP

Cradled and warm, fur-warm, in the she-wolf's lair. Wolf-Boy. David Malouf. CBAP

Craftsman, The. Marcus B. Christian. PoNe

Craftsman. Luci Shaw. TrCP

Craftsman. Lajos Kassák, *tr. fr. Hungarian by* Edwin Morgan. MHuP

Craftsmen. V. Sackville-West. OxBTC

Crafty Farmer, The. *Unknown*. AmFP; ESPB

Crafty Miss of London; or, The Fryar Well Fitted, The. *Unknown*. CoMu; OxBB

Crafty rats, tricking me forever, gnawing holes in the wall. Night Thoughts. Ozaki Bunki, *tr. by* Burton Watson. JLIC-2

Crag, The. Joaquín Arcadio Pagaza, *tr. fr. Spanish by* Samuel Beckett. MexPo

Crag Jack's Apostasy. Ted Hughes. EaLo

Craggy rocks, crouching like elephants. Climbing Mount Yang. Yüan Hung-tao, *tr. by* Jonathan Chaves. CoBLCP

Craigbilly Fair. *Unknown*. ChTr; GBP

Cramped like sardines on the Queens, and sedated. Tourists. Howard Moss. FiBHP; NYBP

Cranach. Sir Herbert Read. BrPo; FaBoMo

Cranberry Song, The. Barney Reynolds. AmFP

Crane, The, *sel.* Saleem Barakat, *tr. fr. Arabic by* Lena Jayyusi *and* Naomi Shihab Nye.

    Dilana and Diram. MAP

Crane. Maruyama Kaoru, *tr. fr. Japanese by* Hiroaki Sato. FCEI

Crane. Joseph Langland. NYBP

Crane, The. Charles Tomlinson. MoBrPo

Crane from the shore standing at the top of the steps, The. Going Alone to Spend a Night at the Hsien-Yu Temple. Po Chü-i, *tr. by* Arthur Waley. Mes

Crane Is My Neighbor, The. John Shaw Neilson. CBAP; PoAu-1

Crane Lodge. Wu Wen, *tr. fr. Chinese by* Chang Yin-nan. *Fr.* Poems on Yi Garden: Written for Mr. Juan-t'ing, II. WFTU

Cranes, The. Po Chü-i, *tr. fr. Chinese by* Arthur Waley. OBVE

Cranes fly calling towards Sakurada Fields. Kurohito, *tr. fr. Japanese. Fr.* Manyo Shu. Ma

Cranes of Ibycus, The. Emma Lazarus. AA

Cranial Nerves, The. *Unknown*. FaBoUs

Crankadox leaned o'er the edge of the moon, The. Craqueodoom. James Whitcomb Riley. OBAL

    (Spirk Troll-Derisive.) NA

Cranmer. Charles Hubert Sisson. FaBoTw

Cranmer's Prophecy of Queen Elizabeth. Shakespeare *and probably* John Fletcher. *Fr.* King Henry VIII, V, v. WGRP

Cranston Near the City Line. Ted Berrigan. UL

Crapshooters. Carl Sandburg. VGW

Craqueodoom. James Whitcomb Riley. OBAL

    (Spirk Troll-Derisive.) NA

Cras amet qui nunquam amavit, quiquam amavit cras Moriatur. Refrains. John Hollander. AnAn

Crash. Things to Do in Providence. Ted Berrigan. UL

Crashed through the woods that lumbering Coach. The dust. The Last Coachload. Walter de la Mare. SeCePo

Crass Times Redeemed by Dignity of Souls, *sel.* Peter Viereck.

    "Tenderness of dignity of souls, The." HoPM

Craswall. Roland Mathias. OBWVE

Craven. Sir Henry Newbolt. PAH

Craving of Samuel Rouse for clearance to create, The. The Slave and the Iron Lace. Margaret Danner. AmNP; BPo

Cravings during Pregnancy. M. Saint-Marthe, *tr. fr. French. Fr.* Paedotrophiae; or, The Art of Bringing Up Children. FaBoUs

Crawl Blues. Vincent McHugh. ErPo

Crawl, laugh. Issa, *tr. by* Nobuyuki Yuasa. OFD

Crawlers, The. Keaulumoku, *tr. fr. Hawaiian by* M. W. Beckwith. *Fr.* Kumulipo, The; a Creation Chant. WTO

Crawlin' aboot like a snail in the mud. The Image o' God. Joe Corrie. OxBS

Crayon House. Muriel Rukeyser. EyDe

Crayons. Marchette Chute. RAR

Crazed. Walter de la Mare. OxBSP

Crazed. Mary E. Tucker. CBWP-1

Crazed Chieko no longer utters words. Chieko Mounting on the Wind. Takamura Kotaro, *tr. by* Geoffrey Bownas *and* Anthony Thwaite. PeBJV

Crazed Girl, The. W. B. Yeats. InPS; Son

Crazed Man in Concentration Camp. Agnes Gergely, *tr. fr. Hungarian by* Edwin Morgan. BoWoP; MHuP

Crazi Levi. Rokhl Korn, *tr. fr. Yiddish by* Seymour Levitan. PeBMYV

Crazy/ to be alive in such a strange. Lawrence Ferlinghetti. FF

Crazy Arithmetic. D'Arcy Wentworth Thompson. FaBoCo

Crazy as hell and typical of us. Making Contact. John Manifold. CBAP

Crazy Bill to the Bishop. Robert Peters. BXAP

Crazy bookcase, placed before, A. Epilogue to the Breakfast-Table Series. Oliver Wendell Holmes. *Fr.* The Poet at the Breakfast Table. AA

Crazy Horse Monument. Peter Blue Cloud. HATNAP

Crazy Horse Returns to South Dakota. Harley Elliott. NeAC

Crazy Horse: The Last Morning. Lance Henson. VoR

Crazy Jane and Jack the Journeyman. W. B. Yeats. CMoP

Crazy Jane and the Bishop. W. B. Yeats. CMoP; LiTM

Crazy Jane Grown Old Looks at the Dancers. W. B. Yeats. CMoP; EBEV

Crazy Jane on God. W. B. Yeats. CMoP; EBEV; MoAB; OxBTC

Crazy Jane on the Day of Judgment. W. B. Yeats. CMoP; SOTW

Crazy Jane on the Mountain. W. B. Yeats. CMoP

Crazy Jane Reproved. W. B. Yeats. CMoP

Crazy Jane Talks with the Bishop. W. B. Yeats. BoLoP; CMoP; EBEV; ErPo; InPK; MoP; NAEL-2; NoAM; NoP; OAEL-2; PoE; PPP; TOF

Crazy ladies are singing again, The. The Belly Dancer in the Nursing Home. Ronald Wallace. GOYP

Crazy Lady, The. Kurt Klinger, *tr. fr. German by* Beth Bjorklund. CoAuP

Crazy Movie. Gregorio Barrios, *tr. fr. Spanish by* Toni Empringham. FIA

Crazy Song to the Air of "Dixie." "Andy Lee." AS

Crazy tugs, The. East River. Rosemary Thomas. AmFN

Crazy Weather. John Ashbery. AnAn; PoE

Crazy World, The. William Gay. PoAu-1

Creak, creak, loom and shuttle, hidden beyond the trees. Hearing Loom and Shuttle. Yü Chi, *tr. by* Jonathan Chaves. CoBLCP

Cream of phosphorescent light, A. Jonah. Aldous Huxley. ChTr

Cream-Puffin, The. Carolyn Wells. *Fr.* A Baker's Dozen of Wild Beasts. OBCA

Cream Song, The. Apirana Ngata, *tr. fr. Maori by* Margaret Orbell. PeNZ

Creamcheese babies square and downy as bolsters. The Peaceable Kingdom. Marge Piercy. TwCP

Creaming. Elizabeth McKim. ER

Created, The. Jones Very. NOCV; QFR

Created Clay. Maimee Lee Brown. PWR

Created for whose sake? The praying. Don't Sit under the Apple Tree with Anyone Else but Me. Robert Pack. FF

Created purely from glass the saint stands. In Piam Memoriam. Geoffrey Hill. NePoEA-2; OxBC

Creation, The. Cecil Frances Alexander. *See* All Things Bright and Beautiful.

Creation. Ambrose Bierce. AA

Creation, *sel.* Sir Richard Blackmore. Circulation of the Blood, The. FaBoUs

Creation, The. Abraham Cowley. *Fr.* Davideis, I. OBS

Creation. Mary Weston Fordham. CBWP-2

Creation, The. James Weldon Johnson. BANP; CDC; FaBV; MoAmPo; PoBA; PoRA; TrCP

Creation, The ("And God stepped out on space."), *sel. James Weldon Johnson.* BANP; CDC; FaBV; MoAmPo; PoBA; PoRA; TrCP
Up from the Bed of the River. EaLo

Creation. Louise Townsend Nicholl. GoYe

Creation. *Maori Oral Tradition, tr. by* Richard Taylor. WTO

Creation, According to Coyote, The. Simon J. Ortiz. CDW; HATNAP

Creation of Light, The. Sister Maura. CRP

Creation of Man. *Maori Oral Tradition, tr. by* John White. WTO

Creation of My Lady, The. Francesco Redi, *tr. fr. Italian by* Sir Edmund Gosse. AWP

Creation of the Animals. Milton. *See* Paradise Lost: And God said, let the waters generate.

Creation of the Child. Susan Litwack. VWA

Creation of the Inaudible, The. Pattiann Rogers. KS

Creation of the World, The. Éva Tóth, *tr. fr. Hungarian by* Laura Schiff. AIW

Creation's and Creator's crowning good. To the Body. Coventry Patmore. *Fr.* The Unknown Eros, XL. OAEL-2; PoEL-5

Creation's Lord, We Give Thee Thanks. William deWitt Hyde. AH

Creations mildest charms are there combined. Britain. Goldsmith. *Fr.* The Travel[l]er; or, A Prospect of Society. NOEC

Creative Force. Maude Miner Hadden. GoYe

Creative Process, The. Mark Akenside. *Fr.* The Pleasures of Imagination, II. NOEC

Creator of Infinities. Chadwick Hansen. AH

Creator Spirit, by whose aid. Veni Creator Spiritus. *At. to* Charlemagne *and to* Hrabanus Maurus, *paraphrased by* Dryden. AWP; FaPoR; SeCV-2; WGRP

Creator Spirit come. Pagan Rites. Paul Goodman. *Fr.* North Percy. DiL

Creatrix. Anna Wickham. MoBrPo

Creature. Sándor Rákos, *tr. fr. Hungarian by* Daniel Hoffman. MHuP

Creature half horse, half human, A. Centaur Song. Stanley Moss. DiL

Creature in the Classroom, The. Jack Prelutsky. RHPC

Creature of flame, out of. Prayer to the White Lady. László Nagy, *tr. by* George MacBeth. MHuP

Creature to pet and spoil, A. Kob Antelope. *Unknown, tr. fr. Yoruba by* Ulli Beier. *Fr.* Hunter Poems of the Yoruba. RB; WTO

Creatures all eyes and brows, and tresses streaming. Correggio's Cupolas at Parma. Aubrey Thomas De Vere. Son

Creatures of Early Morning. Naomi Lewis. Mes

Creatures speak in sounds. Simone Weil, *tr. fr. French by* Carol Cosman. *Fr.* Random Thoughts on the Love of God. OV

Creatures that we met this morning, The. Discovery of the New World. Carter Revard. VoR

Creçy. Francis Turner Palgrave. BeLS

Credential, A. Philip Hobsbaum. NPo

Creditor, The. Louis MacNeice. EaLo

Credo. Zona Gale. TrPWD

Credo. Brewster Ghiselin. PoA

Credo, *sel.* Richard Watson Gilder.
"Christ of Judea, look thou in my heart!" TrPWD

Credo. Robinson Jeffers. MoAB; MoAmPo

Credo. Georgia Douglas Johnson. PoBA

Credo. Denise Levertov. *Fr.* Mass for the Day of St. Thomas Didymus. AIW

Credo. Jean Lipkin. AIW

Credo. John Oxenham. BLRP

Credo. E. A. Robinson. AmPP; CMoP; LiTM; MoAmPo; NAAL-2; OxBA; TAP; TrCP; WGRP

Creed. Walter Lowenfels. PoNe

Creed, A. Norman Macleod. WGRP

Creed, A. Edwin Markham. BLPA; BLPL; FaBoBe; FaFP

Creed, A. John Masefield. WGRP

Creed. Anne Spencer. CDC

Creed. Mary Ashley Townsend. BLPA; FaBoBe

Creed of Mr. Nicholas Culpeper. Patricia Beer. OxBC

Creeds. Karle Wilson Baker. WGRP

Creeds of the Bells. George W. Bungay. PWR

"Cree. ee. ee. ee. eak." Winter Piece. Guido Gozzano, *tr. by* Charles Tomlinson. PFI

Creek, The. W. W. Eustace Ross. MoCV; OBCV

Creek of the Four Graves, The, *sels.* Charles Harpur.
"I verse a settler's tale of olden times." CBAP
"Settler in the olden times went forth, A." PoAu-1

Creek-Road, The. Madison Cawein. AA

Creek, shining, The. The Creek. W. W. Eustace Ross. MoCV; OBCV

Creep into thy narrow bed. The Last Word. Matthew Arnold. FiP; NOBE; OAEL-2; OBNC; PoEL-5; TrGrPo

Creeper, The. Tom Schmidt. NeAC

Creeper grows over thorn. Alba. Confucius, *tr. fr. Chinese by* Ezra Pound. *Fr.* Songs of T'ang. CTC

Creeps in half wanton, half asleep. Wagner. Rupert Brooke. FaBoTw; NOBL

Creide's Lament for Cael. *Unknown.* NOIV

Créide's Lament for Dínertech. *Unknown.* NOIV

Cremation of Sam McGee, The. Robert W. Service. BLPL; FaFP; NOBC; OBNV; PoLF

Crematorium. Sir John Betjeman. PoA

Crematorium, The. Geoffrey Grigson. NPo

Creole Girl. Leslie Morgan Collins. PoNe

Creole Slave-Song, A. Maurice Thompson. AA

Crepe de Chine. Tennessee Williams. NYBP

Crêpes Flambeau. Tess Gallagher. MAYP

Crept side by side beyond the thresh. Vassar Miller. NePoEA

Crepuscular. Richard Howard. TwCP

Crescent Moon. Gabriele D'Annunzio, *tr. fr. Italian by* George Campster. PFI

Crescent Moon. William Renton. NOBVV

Crescent moon with silver sheen aglow, The. Sunset Thought. Henrietta Cordelia Ray. *Fr.* A Group of Musings. CBWP-3

Cresseid's Complaint against Fortune. Robert Henryson. *Fr.* The Testament of Cresseid. MeEL

Cressid. Nora Perry. AA
Cressida's Leprosy. Robert Henryson. *Fr.* The Testament of Cresseid. SeCePo
Crest Jewel, The. James Stephens. AnIL; MoAB; MoBrPo
Crested and ruffed and stiff with whistling frills. Ganymede. William Plomer. PeHV
Crests/ beyond the cry. Brain-Cry. Jean Daive, *tr. by* Paul Auster. RHTwFP
Crete. Greek Archipelagoes. Patrick Leigh-Fermor. OBTV
Crethis. Callimachus, *tr. fr. Greek by* Richard Garnett. AWP
Crevice! shouts the emperor in his sleep, A. The Emperor's Dream. Zbigniew Herbert, *tr. by* Czeslaw Milosz. PwPP
Crew Cut. David McCord. SD
Crew-cuts. Donald Hall. MAT
Crew Practice on Lake Bled, in Jugoslavia. James Scully. NYBP
Crib, The. Robert Finch. OBCP
Cricket, The. Vincent Bourne, *tr. fr. Latin by* William Cowper. PoLF
Cricket. *Unknown, tr. fr. Japanese by* Hiroaki Sato. FCEI
Cricket. No Ch'ŏn-myŭng, *tr. fr. Korean by* Ko Won. PBWP
Cricket, The. Frederick Goddard Tuckerman. FM; NOBA; QFR
Cricket; an Heroic Poem, *sel.* James Dance.
  "When the returning sun begins to smile." NOEC
Cricket and the greshope wenten hem to fight, The. Nonsense. *Unknown.* EBEV
Cricket and the Machine Gun, The. Yu Kuang-chung, *tr. fr. Chinese by* Dominic Cheung. IFON
Cricket chirps in a scarecrow's sleeve, A. Kaai Chigetsu, *tr. fr. Japanese by* Hiroaki Sato. *Fr.* Thirteen Hokku. FCEI
Cricket chirrups near my bed, A. Cha Shen-hsing, *tr. fr. Chinese by* William Schultz. *Fr.* Autumn Impressions, I. WFTU
Cricket is in the hall, The. *Unknown, tr. by* Arthur Waley. BoS
Cricket Kept the House, The. Edith M. Thomas. OBCA
Cricket Match. David Cram. SoTCo
Cricket Music, *sel.* Lörinc Szabó, *tr. fr. Hungarian by* Edwin Morgan.
  "What happened? My dear, don't cry. The thing." MHuP
Cricket on a rubbish-tip, A. Winter Cricket. John Heath-Stubbs. OBCP
Cricket singing, A. Masaoka Shiki, *tr. fr. Japanese by* Burton Watson. *Fr.* Thirty-nine Haiku. FCEI
Cricket sings on Twelfth-night, The. Natalya Gorbanevskaya, *tr. by* Daniel Weissbort. OV
Crickets. David McCord. NTCP; PDV; TSS
Crickets. David Rigsbee. KS
Crickets. Aram Saroyan. MAT
Crickets. Valerie Worth. RHPC
Crickets—/ as the cold of the night. Saigyo, *tr. fr. Japanese by* Burton Watson. *Fr.* Sixty-four Tanka. FCEI
Crickets/ Crickets/ Crickets. Crickets. Aram Saroyan. MAT
Crickets/ in the corner of the garden. Masaoka Shiki, *tr. fr. Japanese by* Burton Watson. *Fr.* Thirty-nine Haiku. FCEI
Crickets/ Talk/ In the tall/ Grass. Crickets. Valerie Worth. RHPC
Crickets and locusts, cicadas. Rosalía de Castro, *tr. by* Benjamin M. Woodbridge, Jr.. PBWP
Cricket's angry, furious!, The. Cricket. Kagura, *tr. by* Hiroaki Sato. FCEI
Crickets chirp at my bedside, The. *Unknown, tr. fr. Japanese. Fr.* Manyo Shu. Ma
Crickets in the Fields, The. Edward Rowland Sill. AnAmPo
Crickets in the thickets, The. But I Wonder. Aileen Fisher. RAR
Crickets sang, The. Emily Dickinson. SOTW
Crier, The. Michael Drayton. ElL; InvP
  (Cryer, The.) PoEL-2
Crier, The. Philip Kahclamet, *tr. fr. Wishram Chinook Indian by* Dell Hymes. STP
Crier by Night, The, *sel.* Gordon Bottomley.
  Blanid's Song. BrPo
Crier-to-Heaven. Yanagawa Seigan, *tr. fr. Chinese by* Burton Watson. JLIC-2
Cries of crickets, The. Ietaka, *tr. by* Steven D. Carter. WFTW
Cries still linger on the battlefield. Kingdom of Silence. Amir Gilboa, *tr. by* Warren Bargad *and* Stanley F. Chyet. IP
Crime. Philip Dacey. NAmP
Crime at Its Best. Stoddard King. NBLV
Crime Club. Weldon Kees. NaP
Crimes of Lizzie Borden, The. *Unknown. See* Lizzie Borden took an axe.
Crimes of Lugalanne. Enheduanna, *tr. fr. Sumerian by* BoWoP, *ad. by* Aliki *and* Willis Barnstone
Crimes of Passion: The Phone Caller. Terry Stokes. AmPA
Crimes of Passion: The Slasher. Terry Stokes. AmPA
Crimp and whorl of conch, The. A Mantelpiece of Shells. Ruthven Todd. NYBP

Crimson berry, A. Masaoka Shiki, *tr. by* Geoffrey Bownas *and* Anthony Thwaite. PeBJV
Crimson Cherry Tree, The. Henry Treece. WaP
Crimson Leaves. Joben, *tr. fr. Japanese by* Steven D. Carter. WFTW
Crimson leaves flow in Tatsuta River. Teika, *tr. fr. Japanese by* Hiroaki Sato. *Fr.* A Compendium of Good Tanka. FCEI
Crimson Lute That Comest in the Dawn. Sister Juana Inés de la Cruz, *tr. fr. Spanish by* Samuel Beckett. MexPo
Crimson nor yellow roses, nor. Eros D'Aute. Theodore Wratislaw. GBL
Crimson roses burn and glow, The. Vigil. Richard Dehmel, *tr. by* Ludwig Lewisohn. AWP
Crimson Tent. John Dos Passos. PoA
Crimson tomato. Saito Mokichi, *tr. by* Geoffrey Bownas *and* Anthony Thwaite. PeBJV
Crinog, melodious is your song. To Crinog. *Unknown, tr. by* Kuno Meyer. AnIL
Crip. Norman Andrew Kirk. TSM
Cripple, The. Khalil Khouri, *tr. fr. Arabic by* Sharif Elmusa *and* Christopher Middleton. MAP
Cripple Creek. *Unknown.* AmFP
Cripple Dick upon a stick. *Unknown.* OxNR
Cripple for Life; or, The Poor Volunteer, The. *Unknown.* AmFP
Cripple in Sight. John Crosson. TSM
Crippler, The. Danny Siegel. VWA
Cripples. Nina Cassian, *tr. fr. Rumanian by* Herbert Kuhner. VWA
Cripples. J. D. Reed. NeAC
Crisis, The. Robert Creeley. FF; PPP
Crisis, The. Whittier. PAH
Crisis is part of me. October Poem. Tamura Ryuichi, *tr. by* Geoffrey Bownas *and* Anthony Thwaite. PeBJV
Crisp, The/ pale green. Salad La Raza. Janet Campbell Hale. VoR
Crispus Attucks. Robert Hayden. CNA
Crispus Attucks. John Boyle O'Reilly. PAH
Crispus Attucks McCoy. Sterling Allen Brown. BPo
Critic, A. Walter Savage Landor. ChTr; FaBoEE
Critic. Elwyn Brooks White. *Fr.* Definitions. NBLV
Critic advises, A. Black Poet, White Critic. Dudley Randall. BPo
Critic leaves at curtain fall, The. Critic. E. B. White. *Fr.* Definitions. NBLV
Critic of the days of yore, The. Narcissus and Some Tadpoles. Victor James Daley. PoAu-1
Critic on the Hearth, The. L. E. Sissman. TW
Critical Observations. Archibald MacLeish. OBAL
Critics. Martial, *tr. fr. Latin by* Sir John Harington. AWP
Critics, The. Theodore Spencer. NYBP
Critics. Swift. *See* On Poetry; a Rhapsody: Hobbes clearly proves that every creature.
Critics and Connoisseurs. Marianne Moore. AmPP; CMoP; FaBoWP; NoAM; NOBA; OxBA
Critics and Poets. Geoffrey Grigson. FaBoEE
Critics cry unfair, The. In Defense of Black Poets. Conrad Kent Rivers. BPo
Critics: in your sight. Sister Juana Inés de la Cruz, *tr. fr. Spanish by* Judith Thurman. *Fr.* A Satirical Romance. PBWP
Critics say that epics have died out, The. Elizabeth Barrett Browning. *Fr.* Aurora Leigh. PBWP
Critics sipping cups of tea. Obituary. Anthony Brode. FiBHP
Critter. W. M. Ransom. CDW
Croak of a raven hoar, The! Mammon Marriage. George Macdonald. BoLoP; EBVV
Croaker Papers, The, *sels.* Fitz-Greene Halleck *and* Joseph Rodman Drake.
  Man Who Frets at Worldly Strife, The. AA
  National Paintings, The. AA
  Ode to Fortune. AA
Croaking, crying, the frogs form a kingdom. A Night at My Lodge. Ch'en San-li, *tr. by* Irving Lo. WFTU
Crocodile, A. Thomas Lovell Beddoes. *Fr.* The Last Man. FM; NOBVV; OBTV; RB
Crocodile, The. "Lewis Carroll." *See* Alice's Adventures in Wonderland: How doth the little crocodile.
Crocodile, The. Oliver Herford. OBCA
Crocodile. William Jay Smith. OBCA
Crocodile once dropped a line, A. The Crocodile. Oliver Herford. OBCA
Crocodile wept bitter tears, The. Crocodile. William Jay Smith. OBCA
Crocodiles. Mira Teru Kurka. UL
Crocus, The. Walter Crane. RHPC
Crocus armies from the dead, The. Veni Coronaberis. Geoffrey Hill. DiPo; NoP

Crocus Night. James Schuyler. PoM
Crocus, while the days are dark, The. Round the Year. Coventry Patmore. BoTP
    (Year, The.) EBVV
Crocuses, The. Frances E. W. Harper. BlSi
Crocuses. Anna M. Platt. BoTP
Crocuses in the Square. Extras. Richard Burton. AA
Crofters few but crafty. Shore Tullye. Robert Rendall. OxBS
"Crom Cruach and his sub-gods twelve." The Burial of King Cormac. Sir Samuel Ferguson. AnIL; NOIV; TIRV
Cromek [or On Cromek]. Blake. FaBoCo; FiBHP
Cromwell Dead. Andrew Marvell. See Poem upon the Death of Oliver Cromwell, A: I saw him dead, a leaden slumber lyes [or lies].
Cromwell, I charge thee, fling away ambition. Ambition. Shakespeare and probably John Fletcher. Fr. King Henry VIII, III, ii. TrGrPo
Cromwell, I did not think to shed a tear. Wolsey. Shakespeare and probably John Fletcher. Fr. King Henry VIII. FaBoRV
Cromwell, our chief of men, who through a cloud. To the Lord General Cromwell. Milton. FaBoPV; NAEL-1; NoP; OBS; Son; TrGrPo
Crooked/ beneath a denim. Dreams. Charles Cooper. PoBA
Crooked bank still winds to something new, The. Sneyd Davies. Fr. A Voyage to Tintern Abbey. NOEC
Crooked gables. In Chagall's Village. Rose Ausländer, tr. by Ewald Osers. VWA
Crooked paths go every way, The. The Goat Paths. James Stephens. AWP; CH; GoJo; LiTB; UnPo
Croon on Hennacliff, A. Robert Stephen Hawker. NOBVV
Crop plane stalls its engines, The. The Hours. Susan Tichy. MAYP
Cropdusting, The. William Zaranka. BXAP
Cropper Lads, The. Unknown. OBET
Croppy Boy, The. William B. McBurney. TIRV
Croppy Boy, The. Unknown. AmFP; AnIL; FaBoBa; NOIV; OxBoLi
Crops are all in and the peaches are rotting, The. Plane Wreck at Los Gatos (Deportee). Woody Guthrie. PrIm; WTO
Cross. Langston Hughes. AmNP; BANP; IDB; LiTM; PoBA; PoLF; SoSe; TAP
Cross, The. Charles Nelson Pace. BLRP
Cross, The. Allen Tate. AWP; MoAmPo; OxBA
Cross at the morning. Once and Upon. Madeline Gleason. NeAP
Cross-eyed Lover, The. Donald Finkel. Prf
Cross-fade of grief to nothingness. The Unoccupied Zone. Louis Aragon, tr. by Louis MacNeice. RHTwFP
Cross is such a simple thing, The. The Cross. Charles Nelson Pace. BLRP
Cross leaves marks the tree we fancy, A. An Owl Is an Only Bird of Poetry. Robert Duncan. NeAP; PoM
Cross-legged in my pinafore. That Mulberry Wine. Janet Sylvester. MAYP
Cross-legged on his bed. Son. James A. Emanuel. PoNe
Cross of Gold, The. David Gray. AA
Cross of Snow, The. Longfellow. HeIP; NOBA; OxBA; TAP
Cross Patch/ Draw the latch. Mother Goose. ChTr; GBP; OxNR
Cross Talk. Cyril Cusack. TIRV
Cross, the Cross, The. Tortoise-Shell. D. H. Lawrence. CMoP; FM; NAEL-2; OAEL-2
Cross, the Cross is tainted, the! O most Just. The Temptation of Saint Anthony. Arthur Symons. BrPo
Cross, the icon, The. The Paradox. Francesca Yetunde Pereira. PBA
Cross Ties. X. J. Kennedy. HoPM
Cross Was His Own, The. Unknown. BLPA
Crossbow wanted a child. The Children's Crusade. Philip Levine. NaP
Crosscauseway, Bristo Street, and Potterrow. Green Breeks. Douglas Dunn. FaBoPV
Crosse of Jesu Christ be ever oure spede. An A.B.C. of Devotion. Unknown. MeEL
Crossed Apple, The. Louise Bogan. HeIP
Crossed Swords, The. Nathaniel Langdon Frothingham. AA
Crossed Wires. Sándor Weöres, tr. fr. Hungarian by Jascha Kessler. FOC
Crossroads. Martin Staples Shockley. FF
Crosses. Faiz Ahmad Faiz, tr. fr. Urdu by Mahmood Jamal. PBMUP
Crosses. Robert Herrick. CaPo
Crossing. Anthony Barnett. VWA
Crossing, The. Paul Blackburn. NYBP
Crossing. Philip Booth. AmFN; GOA
Crossing a Creek. Herbert Clark Johnson. PoNe
Crossing Alone the Nighted Ferry. A. E. Housman. FaBoRV; GTBS-P; NOBE; NoP; OxBSP
Crossing at Fredericksburg, The. George Henry Boker. PAH
Crossing Brooklyn Ferry. Walt Whitman. AmPP; InPS; LiTA; MoP; NAAL-1; NoAM; NOBA; NoP; TAP

Crossing Brooklyn Ferry ("Flood-tide below me! I see you face to face!"), sel. Walt Whitman. AmPP; LiTA; NoAM; NOBA; NoP; TAP
    "Ah, what can be more stately." AA
Crossing Cook Straight. James Keir Baxter. ATNZ
Crossing Hakone Pass. Rai Mikisaburo, tr. fr. Chinese by Burton Watson. JLIC-2
Crossing Kansas by Train. Donald Justice. AiP; NYBP
Crossing Lake Biwa. Geppa, tr. fr. Japanese by Lucien Stryk and Takashi Ikemoto. ZPCJ
Crossing Nation. Allen Ginsberg. AiP
Crossing Ontario. Robert Grenier. IAT
Crossing Over. William Meredith. NoAM
Crossing Portsmouth Bridge. Alan Chong Lau. BrSi
Crossing Several Mountain Ridges on My Way to P'u-ch'eng from Chiang-shan after a Snowfall. Chiang Shih, tr. fr. Chinese by Irving Lo. WFTU
Crossing Ta-yü Mountain Ridge. Chu Yi-tsun, tr. fr. Chinese by Irving Lo. WFTU
Crossing the Alps. Wordsworth. Fr. The Prelude [or, Growth of a Poet's Mind]: Cambridge and the Alps. OBTV; RB
Crossing the Atlantic. Anne Sexton. MOS; NoAM
Crossing the Bar. Tennyson. BLRP; DL; EBVV; FaBoRV; FaBV; FaFP; FaPoR; FF; FiP; FPL; HeIP; LiTB; MOS; NAEL-2; NOBE; NOBVV; NoP; OAEL-2; OBEV; OBNC; OHFP; PoLF; PoRA; PWR; SoSe; TEP; TrCP; TrGrPo; WBLP; WGRP
Crossing the Border into Canada. Joy Harjo. STE
Crossing the bridge I met my ghost. That Night. Oliver Bernard. PoPo
Crossing the County Line. Elizabeth Randall-Mills. GoYe
Crossing the Frontier. Li Meng-yang, tr. fr. Chinese by Jonathan Chaves. CoBLCP
Crossing the Park. Howard Moss. NYBP
Crossing the plain, black with the ashes. Ambush. Hugo Claus, tr. by Theo Hermans. DuIn
Crossing the Plains. Joaquin Miller. AA; AnAmPo; GN
Crossing the ridge, the woodcutter loses his way. Li K'ai-hsien, tr. fr. Chinese by Jonathan Chaves. Fr. Describing My Feelings upon Encountering Snow. CoBLCP
Crossing the River. Yang Shih-ch'i, tr. fr. Chinese by Jonathan Chaves. CoBLCP
Crossing the River at Kuan-yin Gate after Rain. Wang Shih-chen, tr. fr. Chinese by Daniel Bryant. WFTU
Crossing the River in Heavy Wind. Wang Shih-chen, tr. fr. Chinese by Irving Lo. WFTU
Crossing the Sento River. Masso, tr. fr. Chinese by Lucien Stryk and Takashi Ikemoto. ZPCJ
Crossing the shallow holdings high above sea. The Hungry Grass. Donagh MacDonagh. BIrV; NeIP
Crossing the street. The Broken Home. James Merrill. HAP; HCAP; MoP; NAAL-2; NoAM; NOBA; NYBP; PPP; WeW
Crossing the Tropics. Herman Melville. AA
Crossing the Water. Sylvia Plath. CAPP; HCAP; RB
Crossing the Yangtze in a Strong Wind. Wang Shih-chen, tr. fr. Chinese by Jonathan Chaves. CoBLCP
Crossing there under the trees with leaden pace. False Enchantment. Jean Starr Untermeyer. MoAmPo
Crossing this lake at night in a shell canoe. Maine Lake at Night. Harry Morris. CRP
Crossing with the Light. Dwight Okita. BrSi
Crotalus. (Francis Bret Harte). AA
Crotchet Castle, sels. Thomas Love Peacock.
    Priest and the Mulberry-Tree, The. BoTP; GN; OnMSP
Crouched beneath a snowbound sky. The Grey Ones. Louis MacNeice. CMoP
Crouched in its giant green the Indian hid. Vacant Lot. Dudley Randall. NoAM
Crouched in the chirping. Friederike Mayröcker, tr. by Beth Bjorklund. CoAuP
Crouched in the yard. Ellen Bryant Voigt. MAYP
Crouched on one knee one. Autumn Warrior. Barney Bush. HATNAP
Crouched on the pavement close by Belgrave Square. West London. Matthew Arnold. FF; Son
Crouched up beneath a crowd of Grampian hills. Highland Shooting Lodge. Maurice Lindsay. PoSH
Crouching—the cold under the medicine kettle. Waiting on Basho as He Lay Ill. Joso, tr. fr. Japanese by Hiroaki Sato. Fr. Fifteen Hokku. FCEI
Crow, The. Mrs. Alexander. BoTP
Crow, The. Rita Boumi-Pappas, tr. fr. Modern Greek by Kimon Friar. PBWP
Crow, The. Robert Creeley. TW
Crow, The. Russell Hoban. TDD

Crow, *sels.* Ted Hughes. PoE
  Dawn's Rose.
  Littleblood.
  That Moment.
  Two Legends.
Crow. Kenneth Rosen. NAmP
Crow and Pie. *Unknown.* ESPB
Crow and the Fox, The. La Fontaine, *tr. fr. French by* Edward Marsh. AWP
Crow and the Nighthawk, The. Watson Kirkconnell. CaP
Crow Blacker than Ever. Ted Hughes. TEP
Crow-Children Walk My Circles in the Snow, The. Ray A. Young Bear. CDW
Crow, crow, get out of my sight. *Unknown.* PBBP
Crow cry of eyes that fists in mourning grind into. The Eyes. Michel Deguy, *tr. by* Clayton Eshleman. RHTwFP
Crow in Bayswater, A. John Heath-Stubbs. PoPo
Crow, in pulpit lone and tall. In the Pauper's Turnip-Field. Herman Melville. OxBSP; PoEL-5
Crow in the cage in the dining-room, The. The Crow. Robert Creeley. TW
Crow in the night, A. Emperor Kogon, *tr. by* Steven D. Carter. WFTW
Crow Jane. Imamu Amiri Baraka. PoM
Crow on the fence. *Unknown.* PBBP
Crow Resting. Edward Pygge. BXAP; FaBoPa
Crow sat perched upon an oak, A. The Crow and the Fox. La Fontaine, *tr. by* Edward Marsh. AWP
Crow, Straight Flier, but Dark. Laya Firestone. VWA
Crow that feeds on the rice, A. Prince Takamiya, *tr. fr. Japanese. Fr.* Manyo Shu. Ma
Crow will tumble up and down, The. Crows in Spring. John Clare. EnRP
Crow wipes its beak on young grass, A. Boncho, *tr. fr. Japanese by* Hiroaki Sato. *Fr.* Twenty-one Hokku. FCEI
Crow wordlessly flew away, A. Ozaki Hosai, *tr. fr. Japanese by* Hiroaki Sato. *Fr.* One Hundred Haiku in Free Form. FCEI
Crowd, The. John Masefield. OxBTC
Crowd at the ball game, The. At the Ball Game. William Carlos Williams. CMoP; MoP; NoAM; NOBA; OxBA; PoE
Crowd back the hills and give me room. Soul Lifted. Albert Durrant Watson. CaP
Crowd eager for faith, A. Avenida Abancay. Julio Ortega, *tr. by* David Tipton. Per
Crowd fear: blown paper and uprooted ferns. The Spring Festival on the River. John Peck. AmPA
Crowd of love's torments, A. Mohammad Taqi Mir, *tr. by* Ahmed Ali. GoT
Crowded Circle, The. Claude Royet-Journoud, *tr. fr. French by* Keith Waldrop. RHTwFP
Crowded steps, a sea of white faces. Sacrifice. Thomas Kinsella. IPY
Crowded Ways of Life. Walter S. Gresham. BLPA
Crowdieknowe. "Hugh MacDiarmid." InPS; NoP; OxBS
Crowds. Virginia Schonborg. RHPC
Crowds of shuffling feet pass over the bridge. The Goddess Chiao. *Unknown, tr. by* Burton Watson. CoBCP
Crowds pushing. Crowds. Virginia Schonborg. RHPC
Crowing of the Red Cock, The. Emma Lazarus. AA
Crown me with roses whilest I live. Abraham Cowley, *after the Greek of* Anacreon. *Fr.* The Epicure ("Underneath this myrtle shade"). OBVE
Crown of Days. *Unknown, tr. fr. Hebrew by* Herbert Loewe. TrJP
Crown of Happiness. Anne Hébert, *tr. fr. French by* Willis Barnstone. BoWoP
Crown of Hatred and Love. Ferenc Juhász, *tr. fr. Hungarian by* Kenneth McRobbie. MHuP
Crown of ivy! I submit my head, A. On Receiving a Crown of Ivy from the Same. Leigh Hunt. Son
Crown of Sonnets Dedicated to Love, A, *sel. Mary Sidney Wroth, Countess of Montgomery.*
  In This Strange Labyrinth How Shall I Turn?. NAEL-1
Crown of Windflowers, A. Christina Rossetti. OxBChV
Crown Prince of Dullness, The. Dryden. *See* MacFlecknoe; or, A Satire [*or* Satyr] upon the True-Blue [*or*-Blew] Protestant Poet T. S: All human[e] things are subject to decay.
Crowned, girdled, garbed and shod with light and fire. Christopher Marlowe. Swinburne. *Fr.* Sonnets of English Dramatic Poets. Son; TrGrPo
Crowned Poet, A. Anne Reeve Aldrich. AA
Crowned with flowers, I saw fair Amarillis. *Unknown.* EnLoPo
Crowning a bluff where gleams the lake below. Pontoosuce. Herman Melville. NOBA

Crowns, The. John Freeman. CH
Crows, The. Louise Bogan. FaBoWP
Crows, The. David McCord. MoAmPo
Crows. Marge Piercy. CAPP
Crows. Charles Simic. GeTw
Crows, The. Maria Valli. CBAP
Crows. William Witherup. PCP
Crows are cawing from the ancient trees. Spirit of the Yellow River. Chang Pi, *tr. by* Lois Fusek. ATF
Crows are come again to pick my eyes, The. Soliloquy on Death. F. K. Fiawoo. PBA
Crows came in, The. Caw Caw the Crows Caw Caw. *Unknown, tr. by* Jerome Rothenberg *and* Richard Johnny John. STP
Crows crowd croaking overhead. Summer Evening. John Clare. BoTP
Crow's Ditty. *Unknown.* GBP
Crow's First Lesson. Ted Hughes. MoP; NoAM
Crows in Spring. John Clare. EnRP
Crow's Letter, The. Saijo Yaso, *tr. fr. Japanese by* Geoffrey Bownas *and* Anthony Thwaite. PeBJV
Crows mark, The. African Day. Gloria de Sant'Ana, *tr. by* Allan Francovich *and* Kathleen Weaver. PBWP
Crow's Nest. Richard F. Armknecht. GoYe
Crows nesting in abandoned tents. On 19 December 1853, the Rebels Are Approaching the Capital. Chiang Ch'un-lin, *tr. by* Irving Lo. WFTU
Crow's Way. Duane Niatum. CDW
Crucified and the Verminous Man, The. Itzig Manger, *tr. fr. Yiddish by* Leonard Wolf. PeBMYV
Crucified Lord, you swim upon your cross. Lachrimae Verae. Geoffrey Hill. *Fr.* Lachrimae, I. NAEL-2; NoAM; NoP
Crucified to the World. *Unknown.* MeEL
Crucifix, The. Daniel Berrigan. CRP
Crucifix, The. Sir Herbert Read. BrPo
Crucifixion. Eva Gore Booth. WGRP
Crucifixion. Waring Cuney. BANP
Crucifixion, The. Mary Weston Fordham. CBWP-2
Crucifixion. "Marie Madelaine," *tr. fr. German by* Ferdinand E. Kappey. PeHV
Crucifixion, The. ("At the cry of the first birds"). *Unknown, tr. fr. Irish by* Kuno Meyer. TIRV
Crucifixion, The. ("I syke when I singe"). *Unknown.* MeEL
Crucifixion ("They crucified my Lord"). *Unknown.* BPo; TAP; TrGrPo
Crucifixion of the Word. Ahmad Faraz, *tr. fr. Urdu by* Mahmood Jamal. PBMUP
Crucifixion to the World by the Cross of Christ. Isaac Watts. *See* When I Survey the Wondrous Cross.
Cruciform. Winifred Welles. NYBP
Crucifying. John Donne. *Fr.* La Corona. OBS; Son
Crude Foyer. Wallace Stevens. LiTM
Cruel arrows gone, The. Fleche. Larry Eigner. VGW
Cruel Boys. Gary Soto. MOWH; NPGG
Cruel Brother, The. *Unknown.* AmFP; ESPB; OxBB
Cruel, Clever Cat. Geoffrey Taylor. ChTr; FaBoEE
Cruel Maid, The. Robert Herrick. CaPo
Cruel Mother, The. *Unknown.* AmFP; ESPB, (A, B, C *and* P *vers.*); FaBoBa; InPK; OBET; OxBB, *with music*
Cruel night stands in the stable door, The. Young Johnstone. *Unknown.* ESPB, A *vers.*
Cruel Photograph without Light at Daybreak. Mirko Lauer, *tr. fr. Spanish by* David Tipton. Per
Cruel Sister, The. ("There were two sisters sat in a bour"). *Unknown.* OxBB, *with music.*
Cruel Sister, The. *Unknown. See* There was an old woman lived on the seashore.
Cruel: under a helmet, a cricket. Basho, *tr. fr. Japanese by* Burton Watson. *Fr.* Seventy-six Hokku. FCEI
Cruel You Be. George Puttenham. EiL
Cruelty. T. R. Hummer. MAYP
Cruelty and rain could be expected. The House on 15th S.W. Richard Hugo. CAPP
Cruelty has a human heart. Divine Image, A ("Cruelty has a human heart"). Blake. *Fr.* Songs of Experience. ChTr; NAEL-2; NoP; OBNC; RB; TEP
Cruelty of ages past affects us now, The. MMDCCXIII½. Lorenzo Thomas. UL
Cruise, The, *sel.* Robert Dunbar.
  "Summit gain'd how glorious the reward, The." PBCV
Cruise of the Fair American, The. *Unknown.* PAH
Cruise of the *Monitor*, The. George Henry Boker. PAH

Cruise of the *Mystery*, The. Celia Thaxter. OBCA
Cruise of the *P. C.*, The. *Unknown.* NA
Crum Appointment, The. Lizelia Augusta Jenkins Moorer. CBWP-3
Crumbled rock of London is dripping under, The. Roy Fuller. PoA
Crumbling a dark leaf between darker fingers. Midewiwan. Phyllis Wolf. STE
Crumbling and weathered, their features half-erased. Small Park in East Germany: 1969. Gerda Mayer. OBTV
Crumbling centuries are thrust, The. Jewels. Austin Clarke. MoAB
Crumbling is not an instant's act. Emily Dickinson. AmPP; NOBA; PPP
Crumbs. Donald Finkel. BLA
Crumbs for the robin; well he knew. The Robin. William Bell Scott. FM
Crumbs or the Loaf. Robinson Jeffers. CMoP
Crunch and Lick. Dorothy Aldis. RAR
Crunking crane heard high amongst the clouds, The. George Farewell. *Fr.* The Country Man. NOEC
Crusade in Europe. Carla Lanyon Lanyon. CN
Crusaders knew the Holy Places, The. Jenny Mastoraki, *tr. by* Nikes Germanakos. BoWoP; PBWP
Cruse, The. Louise Townsend Nicholl. NYBP
Crush the manroot, swallow what you desire. Learning the Spells; a Diptych. Anita Endrezze-Danielson. CDW
Crushed by that just contempt his follies bring. On Poet Ninny. John Wilmot, 2nd Earl of Rochester. APAS
Crushed by the waves upon the crag was I. Sea Dirge. Archias of Byzantium, *tr. by* Andrew Lang. AWP
Crushed Flower, The. Mary E. Tucker. CBWP-1
Crushing of a thousand petals, Lord, The. The Poet Prays. Grace Noll Crowell. TrPWD
Crusoe in England. Elizabeth Bishop. HCAP
Crust of bread and a corner to sleep in, A. Life. Paul Laurence Dunbar. AmNP; AnAmPo; CDC
Crustaceans. Roy Fuller. NoAM
Crutches. Robert Herrick. CaPo
Cry. Zoltán Zelk, *tr. fr. Hungarian by* Daniel Hoffman. MHuP
Cry-Bird Journey, The. Stan Rice. NPGG
Cry, crow. Hayden Carruth. NNaP; Son
Cry Faugh! Robert Graves. MoBrPo
Cry for a Disused Synagogue in Booysens. Mannie Hirsch. VWA
Cry for Light, A. *Unknown.* BLRP
Cry from the Canadian Hills, A. Lilian Leveridge. BLPA
Cry from the Ghetto, A. Morris Jacob Rosenfeld, *tr. fr. Yiddish by* Charles Weber Linn. TrJP
Cry from the Shore, A. Ellen Mackay Hutchinson Cortissoz. AA
Cry in Distress, A. Bible, *O.T. See* Psalms: Psalm XXII ("My God, my God.").
Cry in my mouth wakes me, The (thirty years later). It Comes during Sleep. Philip Dow. NPGG
Cry left your mouth, A. Mouth. Clarisse Nicoïdski, *tr. by* Stephen Levy. VWA
Cry, little one. Maria Enchained. Juana Castro, *tr. by* Kate Flores. DMH
Cry Mercy. Charles Brasch. ATNZ
Cry of an Aged One, The. Ray Fraser. NeAC
Cry of Generations, The. Mordechai Husid, *tr. fr. Yiddish by* Seymour Mayne *and* Rivka Augenfeld. VWA
Cry of the Age, The. Hamlin Garland. WGRP
Cry of the Child, The. William Zaranka. BXAP
Cry of the Children, The ("Do ye hear the children weeping, O my brothers."), *sel. Elizabeth Barrett* Browning. EBVV
  "They look up with their pale and sunken faces." OBD
Cry of the cicada dies away with the setting sun, The. Immortal at the River. Mao Wen-hsi, *tr. by* Lois Fusek. ATF
Cry of the crickets, The. Saigyo, *tr. by* Geoffrey Bownas *and* Anthony Thwaite. PeBJV
Cry of the Daughter of My People, The. Bible, *O.T. Fr.* Jeremiah, VIII: 18-23. TrJP
Cry of the Dreamer, The. John Boyle O'Reilly. BLPA
Cry of the Gravediggers, The. Jacob Glatstein, *tr. fr. Yiddish by* Benjamin *and* Barbara Harshav. AYP
Cry of the Human, The, *sel. Elizabeth Barrett* Browning. Convinced by Sorrow. BLRP; WBLP
Cry of the Lovelorn, The. William Edmonstoune Aytoun *and* Sir Theodore Martin. *See* Comrads, you may pass the rosy.
Cry of the Peoples, The. Alter Brody. TrJP
Cry of those being eaten by America, The. Those Being Eaten by America. Robert Bly. CoAP; NaP
Cry out for Sakhr when a dove with necklaces. Elegy for Her Brother Sakhr. Al-Khansa, *tr. by* Willis Barnstone. BoWoP

Cry reverberates across the water, The. Cry. Zoltán Zelk, *tr. by* Daniel Hoffman. MHuP
Cry That Kills the Senses: Meditation after a Nightmare, The. Susan Tichy. ER
Cry, The, is: "Back to God!" Without respite. The Homeward Journey. Leonard Aaronson. TrJP
Cry to Arms, A. Henry Timrod. PAH
Cry to Mary, A. Saint Godric. MeEL
Cry went through me like a stab of a knife, A. W. H. Auden. *Fr.* A Happy New Year. OBSV
Cryer, The. Michael Drayton. *See* Crier, The.
Crying. Galway Kinnell. NTCP
Crying Asia! that famous place. The Marriage of Hector and Andromache. Sappho, *tr. by* Guy Davenport. OBVE
Crying in Early Infancy, *sels.* John Tranter.
  "Chicago 'Manuel of Style' is really neat, The." *Fr.* LXXI. NoAM
  "Giving up women is worse than animal laxatives." *Fr.* XVIII. NoAM
  "It's bad luck with a coughing baby." CBAP
  "Spy bears his bald intent like a maniac, The." CBAP
  "Sweat is a style of the body." *Fr.* XCIII. NoAM
  "They burn the radio and listen to the blues." *Fr.* V. NoAM
Crying only a little bit. Crying. Galway Kinnell. NTCP
Crying Uncle. Tom Hansen. TSL
Cryogenetic wings. Bridging Hour in Wesciv. Brian W. Aldiss. BWV
Crystal, The. George Barker. LiTM; OBMV
Crystal, The. Titus Munson Coan. AA
Crystal. Faye Kicknosway. IHMS
Crystal, The, *sel.* Sidney Lanier.
  "But Thee, but Thee, O sovereign Seer of time." TrPWD
Crystal Bridge, The. Lucha Corpi. CCP
Crystal Cabinet, The. Blake. CH; FaBoCh; OAEL-2; OBNC; PoEL-4
Crystal curtains rolled-up have cleared the dense mist. Chiang Ch'un-lin, *tr. by* Irving Lo. WFTU
Crystal Gazer, The. Sara Teasdale. MoAmPo
Crystal Lithium, The. James Schuyler. PoM
Crystal parting the meads. The River in the Meadows. Léonie Adams. MoAB; MoAmPo
Crystal Rowe. Mel Glenn. RR
Crystallization of color spreads, A. Aurora Borealis. Edouard Roditi. EAS
Crystals like Blood. "Hugh MacDiarmid." HAP; NoP; RB
C.S.A. Commissioners, The. *Unknown.* PAH
Cú Chuimne in his youth. Epitaph for Cú Chuimne. *Unknown, tr. by* Thomas Kinsella. NOIV
Cu Chuimne in youth. *Unknown, tr. by* John V. Kelleher. BIrV
Cuba. Thomas MacDermot. PBCV
Cuba. Paul Muldoon. CIP; PPR
Cuba. Harvey Rice. PAH
Cuba. Edmund Clarence Stedman. PAH
Cuba, disheveled, naked to the waist. On a Monument to Martí. Walter Adolphe Roberts. PBCV; TTY
Cuba Libre. Joaquin Miller. PAH
Cuba, 1962. Ai. AmPA
Cuba to Columbia. Will M. Carleton. PAH
Cubana bird touched down, The. Waiting for Fidel. John Agard. PBCV
Cube, A/ i.e. a box. Somewhat Minimal. Roland Jooris, *tr. by* James S. Holmes. DuIn
Cubes. Mary Elizabeth Fullerton. PoAu-1
Cubical Domes, The. David Gascoyne. EAS
Cubist Portrait. Marjorie Allen Seiffert. PoA
Cubs of bears a living lump appear, The. The Phoenix Self-born. Ovid, *tr. fr. Latin by* Dryden. *Fr.* Metamorphoses, XV. ChTr
Cuchulain Comforted. W. B. Yeats. CMoP; LiTM; OAEL-2; TOF
Cuchulain's Fight with the Sea. W. B. Yeats. *See* Death of Cuchulain, The.
Cuchulain's Lament over Fardiad. *Unknown, tr. by* George Sigerson. AnIL
Cuckoo, The. Patrick Reginald Chalmers. CenHV
Cuckoo. Robert Desnos, *tr. fr. French by* Armand Schwerner. RHTwFP
Cuckoo, The. Gerard Manley Hopkins. MoAB; MoBrPo; OxBSP; PBBP; RB; TTTS
  (Fragment, The ("Repeat that, repeat").) FM
Cuckoo. Roland Jooris, *tr. fr. Dutch by* Theo Hermans. DuIn
Cuckoo, The. Edward Thomas, *tr. fr. Spanish.* BrPo; OBD
Cuckoo, The ("A-walking and a-talking"). *Unknown.* OBET, B *vers.*
Cuckoo, The ("Cuckoo is a bonny [*or* fine *or* funny *or* merry *or* pretty] bird, The"). *Unknown.* AmFP; ChTr; FSW; GBP; OBET, 2 *vers.*; OxNR; PBBP.
  See also O the cuckoo she's a pretty bird.

Cuckoo, The ("In April/ Come he will"). *Unknown.* BoTP

Cuckoo ("In former days my father and mother"). *Unknown, formerly at. to Cynewulf, tr. fr. Anglo-Saxon by* Charles W. Kennedy. *Fr.* Riddles (Exeter Book). AnOE

Cuckoo. *Unknown. See* Summer [*or* Summer] is icumen [*or* y-comen] in.

Cuckoo. Andrew Young. ChTr

Cuckoo—, The/ Its call stretching. Basho, *tr. by* Geoffrey Bownas *and* Anthony Thwaite. PeBJV

Cuckoo—/ I've yet to hear him. Saigyo, *tr. fr. Japanese by* Burton Watson. *Fr.* Sixty-four Tanka. FCEI

Cuckoo,/ repeating his cry, The. Kyogoku Tamekane, *tr. fr. Japanese by* Burton Watson. *Fr.* Twenty-three Tanka. FCEI

Cuckoo and the Nightingale, The, *sel.* Sir Thomas Clanvowe. "But as I lay this other night waking." PBBP

Cuckoo called, The. Sanesada, *tr. by* Geoffrey Bownas *and* Anthony Thwaite. PeBJV

Cuckoo calls out, A. Tameie, *tr. by* Steven D. Carter. WFTW

Cuckoo, cherry tree. *Unknown.* PBBP

Cuckoo-Clock. Robert Desnos, *tr. fr. French by* Michael Benedikt. POS

Cuckoo Clock, The. Maura Stanton. PPR

Cuckoo comes in April, The. *Unknown.* OxNR

Cuckoo, cuckoo/ What do you do? *Unknown.* OxNR; PBBP

Cuckoo, cuckoo!/ Is it thy double note I hear. Cuckoo. Andrew Young. ChTr

Cuckoo, cuckoo, cherry tree. *Unknown.* OxNR

Cuckoo fades away, A. Basho, *tr. fr. Japanese by* Burton Watson. *Fr.* Seventy-six Hokku. FCEI

Cuckoo, glad cuckoo, Oh! where wilt thou rest to-night? Cuckoo Song. Henrietta Cordelia Ray. CBWP-3

Cuckoo is a bonny [*or* fine *or* merry] bird, The. The Cuckoo. *Unknown.* AmFP; ChTr; OBET, (2 *vers.*); OxNR; PBBP *See also* O the cuckoo she's a pretty bird.

Cuckoo is on the mulberry-tree, The. *Unknown, tr. by* Arthur Waley. BoS

Cuckoo, noisy among the Shenbaka flowers. Andal, *tr. by* Willis Barnstone. BoWoP

Cuckoo, scabbëd gowk. *Unknown.* PBBP

Cuckoo sings/ at right angles, The. Kyorai, *tr. fr. Japanese by* Burton Watson. *Fr.* Twenty Hokku. FCEI

Cuckoo Song. Henrietta Cordelia Ray. CBWP-3

"Cuckoo! The," cried my child, the while I slept. The Oocuck. Justin Richardson. FiBHP

Cuckoo-throb, the heartbeat of the Spring, The. Ardour and Memory. Dante Gabriel Rossetti. *Fr.* The House of Life, LXIV. OAEL-2

Cuckoo Waltz. *Unknown.* AS

Cuckoo, what are you. Shunzei, *tr. fr. Japanese by* Burton Watson. *Fr.* Thirty Tanka. FCEI

Cuckoo, when the lambkins bleat, The. The Cuckoo. Patrick Reginald Chalmers. CenHV

Cuckoos. Andrew Young. ChTr

Cuckoo's double note, The. Wiltshire Downs. Andrew Young. GTBS-P; OxBTC

Cuckoo's voice lays itself over the water, A. Basho, *tr. fr. Japanese by* Burton Watson. *Fr.* Seventy-six Hokku. FCEI

Cuddie [*or* Cuddy], for shame hold up thy heavy[e] head. October. Spenser. *Fr.* The Shepheardes [*or* Shepeards *or* Shepherd's] Calender. NAEL-1; OAEL-1 (Contempt of Poetry, The.) OBSC

Cuddle Doon. Alexander Anderson. GN; OHFP

Cudgeled Husband, The. Swift. *See* Epigram: "As Thomas was cudgell'd [*or* cudgel'd] one day by his wife."

Cuento. Carlos Cumpian. FIA

Cuernavaca. Ory Bernstein, *tr. fr. Hebrew by* Warren Bargad *and* Stanley F. Chyet. *Fr.* Poems from Mexico. IP

Cui Bono? Thomas Carlyle. WGRP

Cuillin, The, *sel.* Sorley MacLean. Sgurr Nan Gillean. PoSH

Cuisine Bourgeoise. Wallace Stevens. LiTA

Culbin Sands. Andrew Young. GTBS-P; OxBS; OxBTC

Cullen ("Cullen renounced his cradle at fifteen"). Patricia K. Page. CaP

Culloden and After. Iain Crichton Smith. OxBS

Culprit Fay, The. Joseph Rodman Drake. AnAmPo

Culprit Fay, The, *sels.* Joseph Rodman Drake. Assembling of the Fays, The. GN Elfin Song. AA Fairy Dawn. GN Fairy in Armor, A. FaPON

Fay's Crime, The. GN

Fay's Departure, The. GN (First Quest, The.) AA

Fay's Sentence, The. AA

Fay's Sentence, The. GN "If the spray-bead gem be won." GN

Second Quest, The. AA

Throne of the Lily-King, The. GN

Cult of the Celtic, The. Anthony C. Deane. BXAP; NOBL

Cultivate Your Men. Edwin Waugh. PF

Cultivated Signals types. Footnote to Enright's "Apocalypse." Martin Bell. FaBoMo

Cultivation. Mrs. Henry Linden. CBWP-4

Cultivation of Christmas Trees, The. T. S. Eliot. OFD

Cultural Exchange. Langston Hughes. BPo; PoBA; PoNe

Cultural Notes. Kenneth Fearing. CMoP; PoE

Culture/ What does a fool do with culture? With a Fool. Malka Heifetz-Tussman, *tr. by* Marcia Falk. PeBMYV

Culture in the Slums. W. E. Henley. CenHV

"Culture of a people, The." Anthropology. Anselm Hollo. UL

Cultured gentleman, mature, congenial, refined. Personal. Samuel Yellen. NYBP

Cultured Girl Again, The. Ben King. FiBHP; OBAL

Cum here, Mandy, what's you chewin.' When Daddy Cums from Wuk. Maggie Pogue Johnson. CBWP-4

Cum, listen w'ile yore Unkel sings. 'Ittle Touzle Head. Ray Garfield Dandridge. BANP

Cumberbunce, The. Paul West. NA

Cumberland, The. Longfellow. AA; PAH

Cumberland and the *Merrimac,* The. *Unknown.* AmFP

Cumberland Gap. *Unknown.* AmFN

Cumberland Station. Dave Smith. HCAP; MAYP

The *Cumberland*'s Crew. *Unknown.* AmFP

Cummerbund, The. Edward Lear. CenHV; OBTV

Cumnor Hall. William Julius Mickle. BeLS; OxBB

Cumulus Clouds. Sheryl L. Nelms. TDD

Cun-ne-wa-bum—"one who looks on stars." Portrait of a Cree. "Katherine Hale." CaP

Cunard Liner 1940. Phyllis Shand Allfrey. CN

Cunning and art he did not lack. The Allansford Pursuit. Robert Graves. RB

Cunning as a woman beautiful as a snake shy as an idol. Another Poem on Absalom. Nathan Yonathan, *tr. by* Fichard Flantz. VWA

Cunning Clerk, The. *Unknown.* OxBB

Cunning Cobbler Done Over, The. *Unknown.* CoMu

Cunning, wise, cautious, folly is, by which. Upon the Most Useful Knowledge, Craft or Cunning, Which Is More Wisdom, as 'Tis Less Wit. William Wycherley. SeCV-2

Cup, The. John Oldham. AWP

Cup, The. Judith Wright. FaBoWP

Cup and Rose. Nizar Qabbani, *tr. fr. Arabic by* Diana Der Hovanessian *and* Lena Jayyusi. MAP

Cup capsizes along the formica, A. In the Snack-Bar. Edwin Morgan. FF

Cup in hand the bashful beauty. Shamsuddin Mohammad Vali, *tr. by* Ahmed Ali. GoT

Cup of Happiness, The. Gilbert Thomas. TrPWD

Cup of wine as clear as water, A. New Year's Eve in the Year *Keng-tzu.* Chu Hsiao-tsang, *tr. by* Li Chi *and* Michael Patrick O'Connor. WFTU

Cupbearer, O victorious Falcon, come! Qorratu'l-Ayn, *tr. fr. Farsi by* Deirdre Lashgari. *Fr.* He the Beloved. WPOW

Cupbearer Speaks, The. Goethe, *tr. fr. German by* John Weiss. *Fr.* West-Easterly Divan, *Bk.* 9. PeHV

Cupbearer, take your wine away. Abu al-Qasim al-Shabbi, *tr. fr. Arabic by* Sargon Boulus *and* Christopher Middleton. *Fr.* Song of Ecstasy. MAP

Cupboard, The. Walter de la Mare. FaPON; NTCP

Cupid. Sir Philip Sidney. *Fr.* Arcadia. SiPS

Cupid. *Unknown.* EiL

Cupid a Plowman. Moschus. *See* His lamp his bow and quiver laid aside.

Cupid and Campaspe. John Lyly. *See* Alexander and Campaspe: Cupid and my Campaspe played.

Cupid and Death, *sel.* James Shirley. Victorious Men of Earth. OBS; TrGrPo (Last Conqueror, The.) GTBS; GTBS-P

Cupid and my Campaspe played. John Lyly. *Fr.* Alexander and Campaspe, III, v. GBL (Apelles' Song.) TrGrPo (Cards and Kisses.) HoPM; NOBE; OBEV (Cupid and Campaspe.) EiL; GTBS; GTBS-P

(Cupid and My Campaspe.) HeIP; NoP; PoRA
(Song of Apelles.) OBSC
Cupid and Venus. Mark Alexander Boyd. *See* Fra Bank to Bank, Fra Wood to Wood I Rin.
Cupid as he lay among. The Wounded Cupid. Robert Herrick. AWP; OBVE; OFD
Cupid Defends Women. Thomas Hoccleve. *Fr.* The Letter of Cupid. OxBLMV
Cupid did cry, his mother chid him so. The Compliment. William Habington. ACP
Cupid Far Gone. Richard Lovelace. CaPo; OPOP
Cupid in a Bed of Roses. *Unknown.* ElL
Cupid the Ploughboy. *Unknown.* OBET
Cupid, thou naughty boy, when thou wert loathed. Fulke Greville. *Fr.* Caelica, XII. Son
Cupid Turned Plowman. Moschus, *tr. fr. Greek by* Matthew Prior. AWP
Cupidon. William Jay Smith. NePoEA
Cupids Call. James Shirley. ErPo
Cupid's Darts. Sir Alan Patrick Herbert. CenHV
Cupid's Indictment. John Lyly. *Fr.* Galathea. ElL
(Song of Diana's Nymphs, A.) OBSC
Cupid's Revenge, *sel.* Francis Beaumont *and* Fletcher.
Lovers Rejoice! ElL
Cupping her chin and lying there, the Bren. Defensive Position. John Manifold. MoBrPo
Cup's Primitivism. Nishiwaki Junzaburo, *tr. fr. Japanese by* Hiroaki Sato. FCEI
Cup's rotation has, The. Mohammad Taqi Mir, *tr. by* Ahmed Ali. GoT
Cur foretells the knell of parting day, The. Ambrose Bierce. *Fr.* The Devil's Dictionary. OBAL
Curate Thinks You Have No Soul, The. St. John Lucas. BLPA
Curb for stubborn steed. Earliest Christian Hymn. Clement of Alexandria, *tr. by* Edward H. Plumptre. WGRP
Cure. Alan Brownjohn. PoPo
Cure, The. Medbh McGuckian. FaBCIP
Cure at Porlock, A. Amy Clampitt. NoAM
Cure for Fault Finding, A, *sel.* Strickland W. Gillilan.
"Just stand aside, and watch yourself go by." PWR
Cure for Poetry, A. *Unknown, after the Latin of* George Buchanan.
Curé in his windy gown, The. Saint Francis. John Peale Bishop. EaLo
Cure me with quietness. For Sleep, or Death. Ruth Pitter. TrPWD
Curfew. Paul Eluard, *tr. fr. French by* Quentin Stevenson. BoLoP
Curfew. Longfellow. AA; AnAmPo; OxBA
Curfew. Bee Bee Tan. ER
Curfew Breakers, The. Samuel Chimsoro. WMBCH
Curfew Must Not Ring Tonight. Rose Hartwick Thorpe. BeLS; BLPA; BLPL; FaBoBe; FaPON; WBLP
Curfew tolls the knell of parting day, The. Diversions of the Re-Echo Club. Carolyn Wells. OBAL
Curfew tolls the knell of parting day, The. Elegy Written in a Country Churchyard. Thomas Gray. AWP; DL; EBEV; EnRP; FaBoBe; FaBoPP; FaBoPV; FaBoRV; FaFP; FaPoR; FPL; GN; GTBS; GTBS-P; HAP; HeIP; InPK; InPK; InPS; LaA; LiTB; NAEL-1; NOBE; NOEC; NoP; OAEL-1; OBEV; OHFP; PoE; PoEL-3; PoLF; PPP; PrIm; SCV; TEP; TrGrPo; UnPo
Curfew tolls the knell of parting day, The. If Gray Had Had to Write His Elegy in the Cemetery of Spoon River Instead of in That of Stoke Poges. J. C. Squire. BXAP; FaBoPa
Curing Homosexuality. Jim Everhard. GLP
Curio's rich sideboard seldom sees the light. On a Stingy Beau. John Winstanley. FaBoEE
Curiosity. Alastair Reid. SoSe
Curiosity, *sels.* Charles Sprague.
Fiction. AA
News, The. AA
Curiosity-Shop, The. Peter Redgrove. OxBC
Curious child, who dwelt upon a tract, A. Wordsworth. *Fr.* The Excursion, IV. WGRP
Curious, compelling way in which the light, The. Winter Light. Jon Anderson. AnAn
Curious, curious Tiggady Rue. Tiggady Rue. David McCord. WSC
Curious Discourse That Passed between the Twenty-five Letters at Dinner-Time, A. *Unknown.* FaBoUs
Curious fly. Bug in a Jug. *Unknown.* RHPC
Curious is this stonework! The Fates destroyed it. The Ruin. *Unknown, tr. by* Gavin Bone. EBEV
Curious knot God made in paradise, A. Upon Wedlock and Death of Children. Edward Taylor. AmPP; NAAL-1; NoP

Curious twists, The. Energy for a New Thang. Ernie Mkalimoto. NBP
Curled like a hoop in sleep. Lawrence Durrell. NAs
Curliest Thing, The. *Unknown.* BoTP
Curling them around. Cutting Greens. Lucille Clifton. CAPP
Curly Locks! Curly Locks! wilt thou be mine? Mother Goose. OxNR
Curr dhoo, curr dhoo. Mother Goose. OxNR
Current, The. James Merrill. NYBP
Current freed for a while. Listening to Confucius. Henryk Grynberg, *tr. by* Issac Komem. VWA
Currents. Emma Lazarus. *Fr.* By the Waters of Babylon. WPE
Curricle and hansom, The. The Great Garret, or 100 Wheels. James McMichael. AmPA
Curriculum Vitae. Ingeborg Bachmann, *tr. fr. German by* Jerome Rothenberg. BoWoP
Curse, The. John Donne. TW
Curse, A. Irving Feldman. TW
Curse, The. Robert Francis. TW
Curse. Robert Greacen. TW
Curse, The. John Hollander. UnPo
Curse, The. John Millington Synge. ChTr; FaBoCo; FaBoEE; NOIV; TW
Curse, A. *Unknown, tr. fr. Irish by* Douglas Hyde. BIrV
Curse against the Owner, A. Barton Sutter. TW
Curse for a Nation, A. Elizabeth Barrett Browning. WPE; WPOW
Curse God and Die, You Said to Me. Archibald MacLeish. *Fr.* J. B.. EaLo
Curse him who digs in yellow leaves. Academic Curse; an Epitaph. Wesli Court. TW
Curse of Cromwell, The. W. B. Yeats. BIrV; SeCePo
Curse of Kehama, The, *sels.* Robert Southey.
Kehama's Curse. OBNC
Love Indestructible. OBNC
Curse of the Cat Woman. Edward Field. WeW
Curse on Mine-Owners, A. *Unknown.* TW
Curse on the star, dear Harry, that betrayed. An Epistle from a Half-Pay Officer in the Country to His Friend in London. Richardson Pack. NOEC
Curse on Uruk, A. Enheduanna, *tr. fr. Sumerian by* Aliki *and* Willis Barnstone. BoWoP
Curse, The; a Song. Robert Herrick. CaPo
Curse upon Edward, The. Thomas Gray. OBEV
Curse upon that faithless maid, A. Aphra Behn. *Fr.* Emperor of the Moon. WPE
Cursed Be the Day. , Bible, *O.T.* *Fr.* Jeremiah, XX: 14-18. TrJP
Cursing the First Book. John Woods. SoTCo
Cursive crawl, the squared-off characters, The. Writing. Howard Nemerov. NYBP
Curtain! Paul Laurence Dunbar. CenHV
Curtain. Lance Henson. VoR
Curtain Curtain. André Breton, *tr. fr. French by* Michael Benedikt. POS
Curtain falls; the play is done, The. It's Going Out. Heine, *tr. by* Alistair Elliot. OBD
Curtain hooks sway gently in the spring breeze. Wu Hsi-ch'i, *tr. by* Frederick P. Brandauer. WFTU
Curtains drawn back, the door ajar. Robinson at Home. Weldon Kees. CoAP; NYBP
Curtains in the House of the Metaphysician, The. Wallace Stevens. PoA
Curtains in the solemn room, The. Solitude. Arthur Rex Dugard Fairburn. ATNZ
Curtains Now Are Drawn, The. Thomas Hardy. CMoP
Curtains of rock. Orpheus in the Underworld. David Gascoyne. FaBoTw
Curtains were half drawn, the floor was swept, The. After Death. Christina Rossetti. GBL; NAEL-2; TEP
Curvd lines toe-drawn, round cornerd squares, The. Hop, Skip, and Jump. Gary Snyder. LCAP
Curves of a woman's body. Landscape. Horiguchi Daigaku, *tr. by* Geoffrey Bownas *and* Anthony Thwaite. PeBJV
Curving, leaping line of light, A. Prairie Fires. Hamlin Garland. OBCA
Cushendall. *Unknown.* WTO
Cushendun. Louis MacNeice. *Fr.* The Closing Album. FaBCIP
Cushy cow, bonny, let down thy milk. Mother Goose. GBP; OxNR
Custard the Dragon. Ogden Nash. *See* Belinda lived in a little white house.
Custer. Edmund Clarence Stedman. PAH
Custer Lives in Humbolt County. Janet Campbell Hale. STE; VoR
Custer Must Have Learned to Dance. Elizabeth Woody. STE
Custer's Last Charge. Frederick Whittaker. OnMSP; PAH; PoLF
Custody of the Eyes, The. Carolyne Wright. NAmP

Custom of the World, The. Louis Simpson. BoLoP
Customer's blowing, A. All-Nite Donuts. Albert Goldbarth. GeTw; MAYP
Customs. Juan Gelman, *tr. fr. Spanish by* Yishai Tobin. VWA
Customs Change. *Unknown.* OxBChV
Customs Station at Weed Lake, The. Cha Shen-hsing, *tr. fr. Chinese by* William Schultz. WFTU
Cut. Sylvia Plath. CAPP; TAP
Cut branches back for a day. Trail Crew Camp at Bear Valley. 9000 Feet. Gary Snyder. HCAP
Cut Flower, A. Karl Shapiro. BoNaP; HAP; WeW
Cut flowers riding the skin of this river, The. Self Portrait as Both Parties. Jorie Graham. BLA
Cut from the green hedge a forked hazel stick. The Diviner. Seamus Heaney. FaBCIP
Cut Grass. Philip Larkin. NoAM; OxBC; PrIm; RB
Cut Lilac. Tony Beyer. ATNZ
Cut the Grass. A. R. Ammons. CAPP; HAP; PPP; TAP; WeW
Cut them on Monday, you cut them for health. *Unknown.* OxNR
Cut thistles in May. *Unknown.* FaBoUs; OxNR
Cutstone Pond. Chao Meng-fu, *tr. fr. Chinese by* Jonathan Chaves. *Fr.* Twenty-Eight Poems Inscribed on T'ien-kuan Mountai. CoBLCP
Cutter risen from the mollusks, it is a god, A. The Memoirs. Carl Rakosi. PoA
Cutting Beetle-Blighted Ponderosa Pine. Jonathan Holden. KS
Cutting Edge, The. Philip Levine. NYBP
Cutting Greens. Lucille Clifton. CAPP
Cutting Off, The. Uri Zvi Greenberg, *tr. fr. Hebrew by* Bernhard Frank. MHeP
Cutting past the front. Emperor Hanazono, *tr. by* Steven D. Carter. WFTW
Cutting that jungle road from Lugardville. Surveyor. Guy Butler. PeSA
Cutting Wood on Shell Creek. Gretel Ehrlich. MAYP
Cuttings ("Sticks-in-a-drowse droop over sugary loam"). Theodore Roethke. HCAP; LCAP; MoP; NAAL-2; NoAM; NOBA; TAP; UnPo
Cuttings ("This urge, wrestle, resurrection of dry sticks"). Theodore Roethke. CAPP; HCAP; LCAP; MoP; NAAL-2; NoAM; NOBA; TAP; UnPo
Cutty Sark. Hart Crane. *Fr.* The Bridge, III. FaBoMo
Cutty Wren, The. *Unknown.* GBP; OxBoLi; WiR
Cuvier Light. Pat Wilson. ATNZ
Cwmrhydyceirw Elegiacs. Vernon Watkins. PoA
Cyanide jar seals life, as someone move, The. Butterfly Bones; or, Sonnet against Sonnets. Margaret Avison. LiTM
Cyclamen, The. Arlo Bates. AA
Cyclamens. "Michael Field." NOBVV
Cycle. Langston Hughes. FaPON
Cycle. Sean Jennett. WaP
Cycle, *sels.* Ruth Miller. PeSA
"Cover my eyes with your palm."
"Dropped leaf, The."
"To eat pain like bread is a condition."
Cycle for Mother Cabrini, A, *sel.* John Logan.
"Saint, who overlaps." CRP
Cycle sings, A. Nature. Walter Stone. NYBP
Cycle was closed and rounded, A. Bennington. William Henry Babcock. PAH
Cycle's complete, The. Exit from the Garden of Delights. Aharon Amir, *tr. by* Bernhard Frank. MHeP
Cycles, Cycles. Suzanne Berger Rioff. NMM
Cyclist, The. Marge Piercy. NoAM
Cyclists, The. Amy Lowell. WPE
Cyclone at Sea, A. William Hamilton Hayne. AA
Cyclops, *sels.* Euripides, *tr. fr. Greek by* Shelley. AWP
Chorus of Satyrs, Driving Their Goats.
"One with eyes the fairest."
Cyclops. Ovid. *See* Metamorphoses: More whyght thou art than primrose leaf my Lady Galatee.
Cyclops, The. Theocritus. *See* Idylls: And so an easier life our Cyclops drew.
Cyder, *sels.* John Philips.
How to Catch Wasps. FaBoUs
Pruning. FaBoUs
Cymbals clash. Harlem Sounds: Hallelujah Corner. William Browne. AmNP
Cymbals crash, The. A Victory Dance. Alfred Noyes. PoLF
Cymbeline, *sels.* Shakespeare.
Fear No More the Heat o' the Sun. *Fr.* IV, ii. AWP; CH; ChTr; EBEV; EIL; ELP; FaFP; FF; GBL; HAP; HeIP; InPS; LiTB; Mes; NAEL-1; NoP; OBD; PoRA; PrIm; QFR; RB; SCV; SoSe; TrGrPo

(Dirge: "Fear no more the heat o' the sun.") OAEL-1
(Dirge for Fidele.) NOBE
(Fidele.) GTBS; GTBS-P; OBEV
(Fidele's Dirge.) FaBoCh; OBSC
(Song: "Fear[e] no more the heat[e] o' the sun.") CTC; FiP; PoE; PoEL-2
Hark! Hark! the Lark. *Fr.* II, iii. AWP; BoTP; CH; ChTr; FaBoCh; FaBV; FaFP; FaPON; HeIP; LiTB; NIP; NoP; PrIm; TrGrPo
(Aubade: "Hark! hark! the lark at heaven's gate sings.") OBEV
(Morning Song, A.) GN
(Song: "Hark! hark! the lark at heaven's gate sings.") EIL; FiP
(Song to Imogen.) GN
"With fairest flowers,/ Whilst summer lasts." *Fr.* IV, ii. EBEV; RB
Cymbeline, Tempest, Much Ado, Verona. Memoria Technica for the Plays of Shakespeare. *Unknown.* FaBoUs
Cymochles and Phaedria. Spenser. *Fr.* The Faerie Queene, II, 6. OBSC
Cymon and Iphigenia ("Old as I am, for ladies' love unfit."), *sels.* Dryden. OBNV
Militia, The. OBSV
Power of Love, The. OBS
Cymru. David Gwenallt Jones, *tr. fr. Welsh by* Gwyn Jones. OBWVE
Cynara. Ernest Dowson. *See* Non Sum Qualis Eram Bonae sub Regno Cynarae [*or* Cynara].
Cynderaxa kind and good. Trim's Song: The Fair Kitchen-Maid. Sir Richard Steele. *Fr.* The Funeral. OBSC
Cynic, The ("Whoever to finding fault inclines."), *sel.* St. George Tucker. OBAL
"Once at a merry wedding feast." NBLV
Cynical Portraits. Louis Paul. NBLV
Cynicus to W. Shakspere. James Kenneth Stephen. *Fr.* Two Epigrams. CenHV
Cynotaph, The. "Thomas Ingoldsby." *Fr.* The Ingoldsby Legends. FM
Not a Sous Had He Got. FaBoCo
Cynthia, *sels.* Richard Barnfield.
Cherry-lipped Adonis. *Fr.* XVII. Son
Sighing, and Sadly Sitting by My Love. *Fr.* XI. Son
Cynthia. Sir Edward Dyer. OBSC
Cynthia. Fulke Greville. *See* Caelica: Away with these self-loving lads.
Cynthia Lodgepole's Bum Rap ("Cynthia Lodgepole// looked over her shoulder"). Bruce Berlind. SoTCo
Cynthia Matz, with my finger in your cunt. Each Day. David Ignatow. NNaP
Cynthia on Horseback. Philip Ayres. EnLoPo
Cynthia, Queen of seas and lands. The Mariner's Song. Sir John Davies. OBSC
Cynthia, to thy power. Bridal Song ("Cynthia, to thy power"). Francis Beaumont *and* Fletcher. *Fr.* The Maid's Tragedy, I, ii. OBEV
Cynthia's Revels, *sels.* Ben Jonson.
Glove, The. *Fr.* IV. EIL; GBL
Hymn to Diana. *Fr.* V, vi. AWP; CH; ChTr; EIL; GTBS; GTBS-P; HAP; HeIP; NOBE; NoP; OAEL-1; OBEV; OBS; PoRA; QFR; SeCP; TrGrPo; WiR
(Hesperus' Hymn[e] to Cynthia.) JCP; SeCV-1
(Hesperus' Song.) GN
(Hymn: "Queen and huntress, chaste, and fair.") InPS
(Hymn to Cynthia.) PoE; PrIm; SeCePo
(Hymne, The: "Queene and huntress, chaste, and faire.") PoEL-2
Slow, Slow, Fresh Fount. *Fr.* I, ii. ChTr; EIL; ELP; InPS; NoP; OAEL-1; OBS; PrIm
(Echo's Lament for Narcissus.) CH
(Echo's [*or* Eccho's] Song.) JCP; SeCV-1; TrGrPo
(Song: "Slow, slow fresh fount, keep time with my salt tears.") OxBSP; PoEL-2; SeCP
Cypassis, that a thousand ways trimm'st hair. Ovid. *tr. fr. Latin by* Christopher Marlowe. *Fr.* Amores, II, 8. EBEV
Cypress. Friederike Mayröcker, *tr. fr. German by* Beth Bjorklund. CoAuP
Cypress Grove. Austin Clarke. IPY
Cypress stood up like a church, The. Bianca among the Nightingales. Elizabeth Barrett Browning. BrRo; GTBS-P
Cypress swamp around me wraps its spell, The. Down the Bayou. Mary Ashley Townsend. AA
Cypresses, The. Jon Anderson. NAmP
Cypresses. Robert Francis. LCAP
Cypresses. D. H. Lawrence. FaBoPP; NAEL-2
Cyriack, this three years' day these eyes, though clear. To Mr. Cyriack Skinner upon His Blindness. Milton. OBS; Son
(To Cyriack Skinner ("Cyriack, this three years' day").) TrGrPo

Cyriack, whose grandsire, on the royal bench. To Cyriack Skinner.
  ("Cyriack, whose grandsire") Milton. GTBS; GTBS-P; NoP; OBEV;
  Son
  (Sonnet: "Cyriack, whose grandsire, on the royal bench.") OBS
Cythera. David Ferry. DiPo
Cythera. Suniti Namjoshi. AIW
Cythère. Paul Verlaine, tr. fr. French by Arthur Symons. AWP
Cytogenetics Lab. Lucille Day. BWV
Cywdd to Morvydd, The. Daffyd ap Gwilym, tr. fr. Welsh. NOEC
Czar's Last Christmas Letter: A Barn in the Urals, The. Norman Dubie.
  NoAM
Czestochowa, Jasna Gora, Auschwitz, Nova Huta. Lolek. John Jordan.
  TIRV

D

D Blues. Calvin C. Hernton. PoBA
D. C. Karl Shapiro. NYBP
D-Dawn. Margaret McGarvey. GoYe
D. G. C. to J. A. Emily Brontë. BrRO, 1 st.; EnLoPo, 1 st.
D. H. Lawrence and James Joyce. Humbert Wolfe. FaBoEE
D is for Dog. W. H. Davies. OxBSP
D-2 Horse Wrangler. D. J. O'Malley. See One day I thought I'd have
  some fun.
D-Y Bar. James Welch. CDW; STE
Da Silva Gives the Cue. Walter Hart Blumenthal. TrJP
Dab of Color, A. Theodore Weiss. VGW
Dabbling in the Dew. Unknown. CH
Daccus is all bedaub'd with golden lace. Against Gaudy-Bragging-
  Undoughty Daccus. John Davies of Hereford. FaBoEE
Dachshunds ("The dachshund leads a quiet life"). William Jay Smith.
  OBAL
Dactylic Heart That in Me Is a Rebel, The. Amelia Rosselli, tr. fr. Italian
  by Muriel Kittel. DMI
Dad. Elaine Feinstein. AIW; VWA
Dad and the Cat and the Tree. Kit Wright. OnUR
Dad had some talent. Real Talent. Sheryl L. Nelms. TDD
Dada would have liked a day like this. Lawrence Ferlinghetti. Fr.
  Pictures of a Gone World, sec. 23. NeAP
Daddy. Lucille Clifton. NIP
Daddy. Sylvia Plath. BoWoP; CAPP; CMoP; CoAP; HCAP; HeIP;
  InPK; InPS; LiTM; MoP; NAAL-2; NaP; NIP; NMM; NoAM; NOBA;
  NoP; OPOP; PoE; PrIm; TW; TwCP; UnPo
Daddy and Mummy. Life Story. Tomioka Taeko, tr. fr. Harry and Lynn
  Guest and Kajima Shozo. WPOW
Daddy eat dog shark, malingay. Dog Shark. Unknown. PBCV
Daddy Fell into the Pond. Alfred Noyes. FaPON; PDV; RHPC
Daddy fixed breakfast [or the breakfast]. Mummy Slept Late and Daddy
  Fixed Breakfast. John Ciardi. PDV; RHPC
"Daddy, how old is Groucho Marx?" A Child in the 80's. Derwent
  May. OBD
Daddy made Evangeline and me. Elevation. Robert Morgan. MOWH
Daddy sits/ in his brown. Sunflowers and Saturdays. Melba Joyce Boyd.
  BlSi
Daddyboy/ trickster hero. Daring. Carol Konek. IHMS
Dae what ye wull ye canna parry. "Hugh MacDiarmid." Fr. A Drunk
  Man Looks at the Thistle. EBEV
Daedalus. Ovid, tr. fr. Latin by Arthur Golding. Fr. Metamorphoses,
  VIII. CTC
  ("Now in this while gan Daedalus a weariness to take.") OBVE
Daedalus. Alastair Reid. NYBP
Daedalus. Angelos Sikelianos, tr. fr. Greek by Edmund Keeley and Philip
  Sherrard. VMG
Daemon, The. Louise Bogan. NYBP
Daemon, The, sel. Mikhail Yurevich Lermontov, tr. fr. Russian by
  Babette Deutsch and Avrahm Yarmolinsky.
  "On the sightless seas of ether." AWP
Daemon Lover, The. Unknown. See Demon Lover, The.
Daffodil. Waldo Williams, tr. fr. Welsh by Gwyn Jones. OBWVE
Daffodils. Michael Heffernan. SM
Daffodils. Lizette Woodworth Reese. AA
Daffodils. P. A. Ropes. BoTP
Daffodils, The. Wordsworth. See I Wandered Lonely as a Cloud.
Daffodil's Return. Bliss Carman. CaP
Daffy-down-dilly is new come to town [or Daffadowndilly has come up to
  town]. Mother Goose. NTCP; OxNR
Daft Days, The. Robert Fergusson. NOEC
Dafydd ap Gwilym Resents the Winter. Rolfe Humphries. NYBP
Dagger. Mikhail Yurevich Lermontov, tr. fr. Russian by Max Eastman.
  AWP

Dagger, The ("A dagger rests in a drawer"). Jorge Luis Borges, tr. fr.
  Spanish by Norman Thomas di Giovanni. NYBP
Dago shovelman sits by the railroad track, The. Child of the Romans.
  Carl Sandburg. NAAL-2
Daguerreotype Taken in Old Age. Margaret Atwood. BoWoP; NoAM
Dahlias. Padraic Colum. GoJo
Dahn the Plug'ole. Unknown, tr. by Robert Bly. RB
  ("Biby's" Epitaph.) FiBHP
Dahomey. Audre Lorde. NAAL-2
Dai horse neighs against the bleak wind of Etsu, The. South-Folk in Cold
  Country. Ezra Pound, after the Chinese. OBVE
Daikon Song. Rai Kyohei, tr. fr. Chinese by Burton Watson. JLIC-2
Daily Delights. Hameed Said, tr. fr. Arabic by Lena Jayyusi and Naomi
  Shihab Nye. MAP
Daily going out, The. Waterpot. Grace Nichols. PBCV
Daily Grind, The. Fenton Johnson. AmNP
Daily Manna, The. Sara Henderson Hay. GoYe
Daily News. Tom Clark. EAS
Daily Preparations. Leo Vroman. DuIn
Daily Round of the Spinster. Rosario Castellanos, tr. fr. Spanish by Kate
  Flores. DMH
Daily routine. Masaoka Shiki, tr. fr. Japanese by Burton Watson. Fr.
  Thirty-nine Haiku. FCEI
Daily Space. João Cabral de Melo Neto, tr. fr. Portuguese by W. S.
  Merwin. ATCBP
Daily the Drum. Anne Wilkinson. NOBC
Daily the neighbour's dog is withdrawn to the park. Hilaire Kirkland.
  Fr. Observations, II. PeNZ
Daily the Ocean between Us. Patricia Goedicke. TAP
Daily the wind-flowers age, and so do I. Weaving Love-Knots. Hsüeh
  T'ao, tr. by Carolyn Kizer. BoWoP
Daily Trials. Oliver Wendell Holmes. PoEL-5
Daily Wages. Amrita Pritam, tr. fr. Punjabi by the author and Charles
  Brasch. PBWP
Daily walked the fair and lovely. The Azra. Heine, tr. by John Hay.
  AWP
"Daily with You." Annie Johnson Flint. BLRP
Daintiness of her attire is especially nice in summer, The. Sand of Silk-
  Washing Stream. Li Hsün, tr. by Lois Fusek. ATF
Dainty fine bird, that art encaged there. Prisoners. Unknown. EIL
Dainty little maiden, whither would you wander? The City Child.
  Tennyson. BoTP; OxBChV
Dainty Miss Apathy. Pooh! Walter de la Mare. HAP
Dainty water-weeds, growing up-stream. Hitomaro, tr. fr. Japanese. Fr.
  Manyo Shu. Ma
Daisies, The. Bliss Carman. AnAmPo; BoNaP
Daisies. Alden Nowlan. NeAC
Daisies, The. James Stephens. AWP
Daisies. Valerie Worth. PCP
Daisies. Andrew Young. GoJo
Daisies and Grasses. Unknown. BoTP
Daisies of Florence. Kathleen Jessie Raine. NYBP
Daisies so bright. Daisies and Grasses. Unknown. BoTP
Daisy, The. Burns. See To a Mountain Daisy.
Daisy, The, sel. James Montgomery.
  "There is a flower, a little flower." BoTP
Daisy, The. Tennyson. EnLoPo; NOBVV; OBNC; PoEL-5
Daisy. Francis Thompson. AWP; BeLS; BrPo; FaBV; MoAB; MoBrPo;
  OBEV; OBNC
Daisy. William Carlos Williams. MoAB; MoAmPo
Daisy, The. Marya Zaturenska. GrPl; MoAmPo
Daisy and Lily. Waltz. Edith Sitwell. Fr. Façade. RR
Daisy Fraser. Edgar Lee Masters. Fr. Spoon River Anthology. CMoP;
  HAP; PoE
Daisy Pinks. Alistair Campbell. ATNZ
Daisy's Song. Keats. BoNaP
Dakota Badlands. Elizabeth Landeweer. AmFN
Dakota: Five Times Six. Joseph Hansen. NYBP
Dakota Land. Unknown. AS
Dakota: October, 1822, Hunkpapa Warrior. Rod Taylor. WeW
Dakota Wheat-Field, A. Hamlin Garland. OBCA
Dalesman's Litany, The. Unknown. OBET
Daley's Dorg Wattle. W. T. Goodge. PoAu-1
Dalliance of the Eagles, The. Walt Whitman. AA; AmPP; FM; HAP;
  HeIP; NAAL-1; NoP; PPP; PrIm; TAP
Dalmatian Ballad. Doris Mühringer, tr. fr. German by Beth Bjorklund.
  CoAuP
Dalyaunce. Unknown. CH
Dam Bellona, The. Der Blinde Junge. Mina Loy. QFR
Dam, Glen Garry, The. Robert Symmens. PoSH
Dam Neck, Virginia. Richard Eberhart. LiTA; MoAB; WaP

Damaged Aria, The. Pamela Stewart. NAmP
Damages, Two Hundred Pounds. Thackeray. OBSV
Dame, dame! the watch is set. The Witches' Charms. Ben Jonson. *Fr.*
  The Masque of Queens. EiL
  (Witches' Sabbath, The.) WSC
  Witches' Charm, The. FaBoCh
  (Charme.) FM
Dame, get up and bake your pies. *Unknown.* BoTP; OxNR
Dame Guillelma, several knights travelling by dark. Guillelma de Rosers,
  tr. by Meg Bogin. WT
"Dame, how the moments go." The Bride's Toilette. Ellen Mackay
  Hutchinson Cortissoz. AA
Dame Jane a sprightly nun and gay. The Penitent Nun. John Lockman.
  ErPo
Dame Liberty Reports from Travel. Dorothy Cowles Pinkney. GoYe
Dame Music. Stephen Hawes. *Fr.* The Pastime of Pleasure. PoEL-1
Dame Nature. Spenser. *Fr.* The Faerie Queene, VII, 7. PoEL-1
Dame, said the Panther, times are mended well. Dryden. *Fr.* The Hind
  and the Panther, II. PoEL-3
Dame Trot and her cat. Mother Goose. BoTP; OxNR
Dame Wiggins of Lee and Her Seven Wonderful Cats. *At. to* Richard
  Scrafton Sharpe, *and to* Mrs. Pearson. FaBoBe; FaBoNo; OxBChV
Damelus' [*or* Damelias'] Song to His Diaphenia. *At. to* Henry Constable
  and also to Henry Chettle. *See* Diaphenia.
Dames of France are fond and free, The. The Girl I Left behind Me.
  Thomas Osborne Davis. FaBoBe; FaFP
Damit blackman. Domestics. Kattie M. Cumbo. BlSi
Dammit it's almost fall again. An Empty Mailman Drowns in the Country
  Road. Hans Lodeizen, *tr. by* James S. Holmes. DuIn
Dammit, they get pulled up all the time. *Unknown, tr. fr. Japanese by*
  Hiroaki Sato. *Fr.* Inutsukuba Shu. FCEI
Dammitty-hammitty. All of a Piece. Mairin Martin. SoTCo
Damn/ ache/ again. Arthritis. Jan Glading. TSM
Damn it all! all this our South stinks peace. Sestina: Altaforte. Ezra
  Pound. CMoP; FaBoTw; LiTA; MoAB; MoAmPo; NOBA; SoSe;
  SOTW
Damn that celibate farm, that cracker-box house. Censorship. John
  Ciardi. NBLV; TW
Damn Yankees, *sel.* Richard Adler *and* Jerry Ross.
  Heart. ASP
Damn you, you dark poisons. Sleep. Georg Trakl, *tr. by* Joachim
  Neugroschel. AnAn
Damnation follows death in other men. On Poets. Pope. FaBoEE
Damnation of Vancouver, *sel.* Earle Birney.
  Speech of the Salish Chief. OBCV
Damned Minoan crevices, that I clog them up! Paranoia in Crete.
  Gregory Corso. NeAP
Damned ship lurched and slithered, The. Quiet and quick. A Channel
  Passage. Rupert Brooke. MOS
Damned Women. Baudelaire, *tr. fr. French by* Roy Campbell. BoLoP
Damocles. Robert Graves. NYBP
Damon and Celimena. Dryden. *Fr.* An Evening's Love, V, i. InvP
Damon and Cupid. John Gay. EnLoPo
Damon and Pythias. Robert Creeley. LCAP
Damon come drive thy flocks this way. Clorinda and Damon. Andrew
  Marvell. SeCP
Damon forbear, and don't disturb your Muse. The Court. *Unknown.*
  APAS
Damon the Mower. Andrew Marvell. JCP; NAEL-1; OAEL-1
Damp clouds press on the window, the lamp about to die. Martyred
  Widow Liu of Hai-ling: A Ballad. Cheng Hsieh, *tr. by* Jan *and*
  Yvonne Walls. WFTU
Damp fallen leaves smell of ripe bananas, The. Walking Home at Night.
  Daniel Weissbort. VWA
Damp sky is eating your hair, The. The Kiss. Bill Manhire. ATNZ
Damp swell of dunes that turn into flour, The. A New Genesis.
  Avraham Shlonsky, *tr. by* Francis Landy. VWA
Dampe, The. John Donne. SeCP
Damsel, The. Omar b. Abi Rabi'a, *tr. fr. Arabic by* W. G. Palgrave.
  AWP
Dan Ellis's Boys. *Unknown.* AmFP
Dan, the Dust of Masada Is Still in My Nostrils. Ruth Whitman. VWA
Danaë. Barbara Howes. WPE
Dance, The. *At. to* Thomas Campion. EiL; FaBoCh
Dance, The. Hart Crane. *Fr.* The Bridge: Powhatan's Daughter.
  LiTM; MoAB; MoAmPo; OxBA
Dance, The. Gareth Alban Davies, *tr. fr. Welsh by* Gwyn Jones.
  OBWVE
Dance, The. Robert Duncan. NeAP
Dance. Haim Guri, *tr. fr. Hebrew by* Warren Bargad *and* Stanley F.
  Chyet. IP

Dance, The. Jim Gustafson. UL
Dance, The. Daniel Halpern. MAYP
Dance, The. Robert Kelly. *Fr.* The Book of Persephone, 17. PoM
Dance, The. Morton Marcus. NAmP
Dance. N. M. Rashed, *tr. fr. Urdu by* Mahmood Jamal. PBMUP
Dance, The. Spenser. *See* Faerie Queene, The: Dance of the Graces,
  The.
Dance, The. Mark Strand. GeTw
Dance, The. Maud Sulter. DT
Dance, The. *Unknown.* PAH
Dance, The. *Unknown, tr. fr. French by* John Lydgate. *Fr.* The Dance
  of Death. PoEL-1
Dance. Lula Lowe Weeden. CDC
Dance, The. William Carlos Williams. AmPP; CMoP; GoJo; GrPl;
  HAP; HeIP; InPK; LiTM; MoP; NAAL-2; NIP; NoAM; NoAm;
  NOBA; NoP; OxBA; PoE; PrIm; SoSe; TAP; WeW
Dance a baby diddy. Mother Goose. OxNR
Dance a Ghost. "Chrystos." GOS
Dance and Eye Me (Wicked)ly My Breath a Fixed Sphere. Rochelle
  Owens. NMM
Dance begins with the sun descending, The. Marrakech. Richard
  Eberhart. LiTM
Dance Calls. *Unknown.* RR
Dance Chant, A. *Unknown, tr. fr. Iroquois Indian by* E. S. Parker.
  WGRP
Dance Chant, A. *Unknown, tr. by* D. G. Brinton. WGRP
Dance, dance in this museum case. Love Song to Eohippus. Peter
  Viereck. MoAmPo
Dance, dance, snail! Emperor Go-Shirakawa, *tr. fr. Japanese by* Hiroaki
  Sato. *Fr.* Ryojin Hisho. FCEI
  ("Dance, dance, little snail!") PeBJV, *tr. by* Geoffrey Bownas *and*
  Anthony Thwaite.
Dance Figure. Ezra Pound. HeIP; MoAB; MoAmPo
Dance for Ma Rainey, A. Al Young. NBP
Dance for Militant Dilettantes, A. Al Young. PoBA
Dance grows, The. The Dead. Jay Wright. FB
Dance Hymn. Isaiah Shembe, *tr. fr. Zulu by* B. G. M. Sundkler. WTO
Dance in the township hall is nearly over, The. Country Dance. Judith
  Wright. *Fr.* The Blind Man. CBAP
Dance Instructions for a Young Girl. Kimiko Hahn. BrSi
Dance is on the Bridge of Death, The. The Bridge of Death. *Unknown,*
  tr. by Andrew Lang. AWP
Dance, little baby, dance up high. The Baby's Dance. *At. to* Ann
  Taylor, *and to* Mother goose. OxBChV; OxNR
Dance of blue-bells in the shady places, A. Sweet Surprises. Sarah
  Doudney. BoTP
Dance of Death, The, *sels.* Robert Browning.
  Fever. FL
  Madness. FL
Dance of Death, The, *sels. Unknown, tr. fr. French by* John Lydgate.
  Dance, The. PoEL-1
  "Sir Emperour, lorde of al the ground." OxBLMV
Dance of Despair, The. Hayyim Nahman Bialik, *tr. fr. Hebrew by* A. M.
  Klein. TrJP
Dance of Dust, The. Louis Untermeyer. BXAP
Dance of Love, The. Sir John Davies. *Fr.* Orchestra; or, A Poem[e] of
  Da[u]ncing. EiL; SeCePo
Dance of Saul with the Prophets, The. Saul Tchernichowsky, *tr. fr.*
  Hebrew by I. M. Lask. TrJP
Dance of the Abakweta. Margaret Danner. PoNe
Dance of the Daughters of Herodias, The. Arthur Symons. BrPo
Dance of the Elephants, The. Michael S. Harper. LCAP
Dance of the Graces, The. Spenser. *Fr.* The Faerie Queene, VI, 10.
  OBSC
  (Dance, The.) TrGrPo
Dance of the Infidels. Al Young. PoBA
Dance of the Macabre Mice. Wallace Stevens. CMoP; NOBA; OxBA
Dance of the Rain, The. Eugène Marais, *tr. fr. Afrikaans by* Jack Cope
  and Uys Krige. PeSA
Dance of the Rain Gods. *Unknown, tr. fr. Cora Indian by* Anselm Hollo.
  STP
Dance of the Sevin Deidly Synnis, The. William Dunbar. GoTS; OxBS;
  PoE
Dance of the Sword, The. *Unknown, tr. fr. Breton by* Tom Taylor.
  WaaP
Dance on Pushback. James Still. GrPl
Dance Poem. Nikki Giovanni. RR
Dance Script with Electric Ballerina. Alice Fulton. KS
Dance Song. Angelo Poliziano, *tr. fr. Italian by* John Heath-Stubbs. PFI
Dance Song. *Unknown, tr. fr. Chinese by* Arthur Waley. FaBoCh
Dance-Song of the Lightning. *Unknown, tr. fr. Hottentot.* PeSA

Dance the Boatman. *Unknown.* AiP
Dance, Thumbkin, dance. Mother Goose. OxNR
Dance to your [or thee] daddy. Mother Goose. OBET; OxNR (2 *vers.*)
Dance with Banderillas. Richard Duerden. NeAP
Dancer!/ A one-headed drum. A Poet to a Dancer. Auvaiyar, *tr. by* A. K. Ramanujan. PLW
Dancer, The. Joseph Campbell. OBMV
Dancer, The. Sadi, *tr. fr. Persian by* Sir Edwin Arnold. *Fr.* The Bustan. AWP
Dancer. Roy Scheele. GOYP
Dancer, The. W. J. Turner. OBMV
Dancer, The. Edmund Waller. TrGrPo
Dancer, The. Al Young. PoBA
Dancer from the Dance, The. Suzanne Juhasz. IHMS
Dancers, The. W. W. Gibson. MMA
Dancers at the Moy. Paul Muldoon. BIrV
Dancers Exercising. Amy Clampitt. NoAM
Dancers Inherit the Party, The. Ian Hamilton Finlay. FF
Dancer's Life, A. Donald Justice. LCAP
Dancers of Colbek, The. Robert Mannyng. *Fr.* Handling Sin. PoE
Dancers with cane whistles. Memory. Elizabeth Cook-Lynn. *Fr.* Journey, II. HATNAP
Dances of Death, *sel.* Aleksandr Aleksandrovich Blok, *tr. fr. Russian by* Jon Stallworthy *and* Peter France.
   "Night, street, a lamp, a chemist's window." OBVE
Dancing, The. Gerald Stern. DiL
Dancing. Yang Kuei-fei, *tr. fr. Chinese by* Florence Ayscough *and* Amy Lowell. FaPON
Dancing at Whitsun. Austin John Marshall. OBET
Dancing Bear, The. Rachel Lyman Field. NTCP
Dancing Bear, The. Albert Bigelow Paine. OBCA
Dancing Bear, The. Robert Southey. FM
Dancing Cabman, The. J. B. Morton. MoShBr; NOBL
Dancing Faun, The. Robert Cameron Rogers. AA
Dancing Gal. Frank Marshall Davis. FB
Dancing Girl, A. Frances Sargent Osgood. *See* Celeste Dancing.
Dancing-Girl's Song. Kshetrayya, *tr. fr. Telugu by* Tambimuttu *and* R. Appalaswamy. BoWoP
Dancing on the edge of a razor blade. Ming the Merciless. Jessica Hagedorn. BrSi
Dancing on the Shore. M. M. Hutchinson. BoTP
Dancing on Water. Harold Bond. TSM
Dancing Partners. Philip Child. CaP
Dancing School. Jonathan Holden. Psk
Dancing Sea, The. Sir John Davies. *Fr.* Orchestra; or, A Poem[e] of Da[u]ncing. ChTr
Dancing Seal, The. W. W. Gibson. OnMSP
Dancing Songs, *sels. Unknown.* PBCV
   "Hipsaw! my dea! you no do like a-me!" *Fr.* I.
   "Tajo, tajo, tajo! tajo, my mackey massa!" *Fr.* II.
Dancing Sunshine Lounge, The. Thomas Rabbitt. MAYP
Dancing Teepees. Calvin O'John. NOVW
Dancing the Shout to the True Gospel; or, The Song Movement Sisters Don't Want Me to Sing. Rita Mae Brown. NMM; PeHV
Dandelion. Hilda Conkling. FaPON; PDV; RHPC
Dandelion: from time to time. Chiyojo, *tr. fr. Japanese by* Hiroaki Sato. *Fr.* Seventeen Hokku. FCEI
Dandelion Puff, The. Mary K. Robinson. BoTP
Dandelion stares, The. The Little Dandelion. Lula Lowe Weeden. CDC
Dandelions. John Albee. AA
Dandelions. Louis MacNeice. *Fr.* Nature Notes. FaBCIP
Dandelions. Craig Raine. NoAM
Dandelions, The. *Unknown.* BoTP
Dandelions for Chains ("Dandelions meet me wherever I am"). Sarah Kirsch, *tr. fr. German by* Michael Hamburger. WPOW
Dandelions purr in their sleep. Of Dandelions & Tourists. Joe Rosenblatt. NOBC
Dandelions, wrecked on their stems, The. Late Dandelions. Ben Belitt. NYBP
Dandy Horse, The. *Unknown.* OBET
Dandy O, The. *Unknown.* CoMu
Dane-Geld. Kipling. OxBTC
Danebury. *Unknown.* PeHV
Danger is silent in the bloodless square. Capital Square. Patrick Anderson. OBCV
Dangerous. Dorothy Aldis. RAR
"Dangerous Condition": Sign on Inner-City House. Russell Atkins. CNA
Dangerous, yet felicitous. *Unknown, tr. by* Hiroaki Sato. FCEI
Dangers of drifting while driving in a daze, The. In a Motion. Laura Chester. NPGG
Dangers of Foot-ball, The. John Gay. *Fr.* Trivia; or, The Art of Walking the Streets of London. SD

Dangers of Sexual Excess, The. John Armstrong. *Fr.* The Art of Preserving Health. FaBoUs
Dangling sacred cords. Tameie, *tr. by* Steven D. Carter. WFTW
Daniel. Vachel Lindsay. ChTr
Daniel and Abigail. Miguel de Barrios. TrJP
Daniel at Breakfast. Phyllis McGinley. OBSV
Daniel Boone. Stephen Vincent Benét. AmFN; GOA
Daniel Boone. Arthur Guiterman. FaPON; MoShBr
Daniel Gray. Josiah Gilbert Holland. AA
Daniel Jazz, The. Vachel Lindsay. *See* Darius the Mede was a king and a wonder.
Daniel Webster. Oliver Wendell Holmes. PAH
Daniel Webster's Horses. Elizabeth J. Coatsworth. AmFN; MoAmPo; OBCA
Danish Cradle Song, A. *Unknown.* BoTP
Danish Wit. John Hollander. NBLV
Dank, limber verses, stuft with lakeside sedges. Some of Wordsworth. Walter Savage Landor. ChTr
Dankwerts, scholarship boy from the slums. Living? Our Supervisors Will Do That for Us! David Holbrook. NePoEA-2
Danny. Malcolm Cowley. PoM
Danny Deever. Kipling. BrPo; EBVV; FaBoBa; FaPoR; FPL; GTBS-P; InPS; LiTB; MoBrPo; NAEL-2; NoAM; NOBE; NOBVV; OxBoLi; OxBTC; PoLF; SCV; SeCePo; TEP; TrGrPo; UnPo; WaaP
Danny Murphy. James Stephens. BoTP; OnUR
Danny's Wooing. David McKee Wright. PoAu-1
Dans l'Allée. Paul Verlaine, *tr. fr. French by* Arthur Symons. AWP
Danse Russe. William Carlos Williams. CMoP; InPS; NOBA; NoP; PoE; PPP; TAP
Dante, *sel.* Robert Duncan.
   "I know a little language of my cat, tho Dante says." PoM
Dante. Longfellow. AA
Dante. Michelangelo Buonarroti, *tr. fr. Italian by* Longfellow. AWP; PFI
Dante. Henrietta Cordelia Ray. CBWP-3
Dante, a sigh that rose from the heart's core. To Dante Alighieri: He Reports, in a Feigned Vision, the Successful Issue of Lapo Gianni's Love. Guido Cavalcanti, *tr. by* Dante Gabriel Rossetti. AWP
Dante Alighieri, a dark oracle. Inscription for a Portrait of Dante. Boccaccio, *tr. fr. Italian by* Dante Gabriel Rossetti. *Fr.* Sonnets. AWP
Dante Alighieri, Cecco, your good friend. Sonnet: To Dante Alighieri on the Last Sonnet of the Vita Nuova. Cecco Angiolieri da Siena, *tr. by* Dante Gabriel Rossetti. AWP
Dante Alighieri, if I jest and lie. Sonnet: To Dante Alighieri (He Writes to Dante, Then in Exile at Verona, Defying Him as No Better Than Himself). Cecco Angiolieri da Siena, *tr. by* Dante Gabriel Rossetti. AWP
Dante Alighieri in Becchina's praise. Sonnet: He Rails against Dante, Who Had Censured His Homage to Becchina. Cecco Angiolieri da Siena, *tr. by* Dante Gabriel Rossetti. AWP
Dante Études, *sel.* Robert Duncan.
   Work, The. CAPP
Dante had the right idea. If Justice Moved. Bettie M. Sellers. KS; TW
Dante, if thou within the sphere of Love. To Dante in Paradise, after Fiammetta's Death. Boccaccio, *tr. fr. Italian by* Dante Gabriel Rossetti. *Fr.* Sonnets. AWP
Dante, whenever this thing happeneth. To Dante Alighieri: He Conceives of Some Compensation in Death. Cino da Pistoia, *tr. by* Dante Gabriel Rossetti. AWP
Danube to the Severn gave, The. Tennyson. *Fr.* In Memoriam A. H. H., XIX. FF; GTBS-P; NoP
   (Hushing of the Wye, The.) FaBoPP
Daphnaïda, *sel.* Spenser.
   "She fell away in her first ages spring." OBEV
Daphne. Bliss Carman. OBCV
Daphne. Thomas Samuel Jones, Jr. OHIP
Daphne. John Lyly. *Fr.* Midas. EiL
   (Song of Daphne to the Lute, A.) OBSC
Daphne. Selden Rodman. PoNe
Daphne. Swift. NOBL
Daphne and Apollo. Ovid, *tr. fr. Latin by* Matthew Prior. *Fr.* Metamorphoses, I. NOEC
Daphne knows, with equal ease. Daphne. Swift. NOBL
Daphne Stillorgan. Denis Devlin. CIP
Daphnis to Ganymede. Richard Barnfield. *Fr.* The Affectionate Shepherd. EiL
Dappled Horse, The. Mei Yao-ch'en, *tr. fr. Chinese by* Burton Watson. CoBCP
Dappled sky, a world of meadows, A. Jean Ingelow. *Fr.* Divided. OBNC
Darby and Joan. St. John Honeywood. AA
Darby and Joan were dressed in black. *Unknown.* OxNR

Dardanelles 1916. Padraic Fallon. CIP
Dare I dislike the green pond for the reflection of my unkempt hair?
    Ch'en Pao-shen, *tr.* by Irving Lo. WFTU
Dare I in such momentous points advise. Soame Jenyns. *Fr.* The Art of
    Dancing. FaBoUs
Dare to Do Right. George Lansing Taylor. PWR
Dare we despair? Through all the nights and days. He Leads Us Still.
    Arthur Guiterman. OHIP
Daredevil. Kirby Congdon. PeHV
Dareios. C. P. Cavafy, *tr. fr. Greek by* Edmund Keeley *and* Philip
    Sherrard. AnAn; VMG
Darest Thou Now O Soul. Walt Whitman. AA; TrGrPo; WGRP
Darien. Sir Edwin Arnold. PAH
Daring. Carol Konek. IHMS
Darius Green and His Flying-Machine. John Townsend Trowbridge.
    AnAmPo; BeLS; BLPL; FaBoBe; MoShBr; OBAL; OBCA; OxBChV;
    PoLF
Darius the Mede was a king and a wonder. Daniel. Vachel Lindsay.
    ChTr
    (Daniel Jazz, The.) TrGrPo
Dark, The. William Heyen. EyDe
Dark abdomen upraised. Answering Dance. William Pitt Root. MAYP
Dark accurate plunger down the successive knell. The Subway. Allen
    Tate. NOBA
Dark an' stormy may come de wedder. Slave Marriage Ceremony
    Supplement. *Unknown.* BPo; TAP
Dark and bolted room. Bolted Room. A. Leyeles, *tr.* by Leonard Wolf.
    PeBMYV
Dark and Falling Summer, The. Delmore Schwartz. NYBP
Dark and more dark the shades of evening fell. Sonnet: Composed after a
    Journey across the Hamilton Hills, Yorkshire. Wordsworth. ChER
Dark Angel, The. Lionel Johnson. ACP; GTBS-P; LiTB; MoBrPo;
    NOBE; NOBVV; OAEL-2; OBMV
Dark Area. Russell Atkins. FB
Dark as the clouds of even. The Black Regiment. George Henry Boker.
    AnAmPo; GN; PAH
Dark as the spring river, the earth. Farm Wife. Ellen Bryant Voigt.
    MT
Dark as wells, his eyes. Long Person. Gladys Cardiff. CDW; STE
Dark Beauty. Said Aql, *tr. fr. Arabic by* Matthew Sorenson *and* Naomi
    Shihab Nye. MAP
Dark Birds, The. Bert Meyers. VWA
Dark, black robe. Invitation (To the Night and All Other Things Dark).
    Ronda Davis. JB
Dark, bolted room. Bolted Room. A. Leyeles, *tr.* by Benjamin *and*
    Barbara Harshav. AYP
Dark branches. Alaskan Mountain Poem #1. Leslie Marmon Silko.
    VoR
Dark Brother, The. Lewis Alexander. CDC
Dark brother touches me, The. Will Inman. *Fr.* 108 Tales of a Po
    'Buckra. GLP
Dark brown is the river. Where Go the Boats? Robert Louis Stevenson.
    FaBoBe; FaBoCh; GoJo; Mes; NTCP; OxBChV; PYC
Dark Centre. Norman MacCaig. NPo
Dark Chamber, The. Louis Untermeyer. MoAmPo
Dark Château, The. Walter de la Mare. BrPo
Dark Churches. John Donne. *Fr.* A Hymn [*or* Hymne] to Christ, at the
    Author's Last Going into Germany. FaBoRV
Dark Conclusions. Ruth Stone. BoWoP
Dark Country, A. Derek Mahon. BIrV
Dark curtain of rain sweeps slowly over the sunlit mountain, A. Summer
    Rain in Mountains. Robert Penn Warren. AnAn
Dark Danny. Ivy O. Eastwick. FaPON
Dark, dark, far mists rise. Things Seen. Wang Shih-chen, *tr.* by
    Jonathan Chaves. CoBLCP
Dark, dark is the night, now it wholly. The War of 1793. Diodata
    Saluzzo, *tr.* by Muriel Kittel. DMI
Dark, deep, and cold the current flows. Plaint. Ebenezer Elliott. OBD;
    OBEV
Dark, deeply. A red. Inside the River. James Dickey. PoA
Dark Dialogues, The, *sels.* William Sydney Graham. OxBS
    "Almost I, yes, I hear." *Fr.* II.
    "Now in the third voice." *Fr.* III.
Dark Earth and Summer. Edgar Bowers. QFR
Dark Eleanor and Henry sat at meat. The Rose of the World. John
    Masefield. PoRA
Dark eleventh hour, The. Ulster. Kipling. FaBoPV
Dark eyed/ O woman of my dreams. Dance Figure. Ezra Pound. HeIP;
    MoAB; MoAmPo
Dark-eyed Gentleman, The. Thomas Hardy. MoAB; MoBrPo; NBLV;
    UnPo
Dark Eyes at Forest Hills. I. L. Martin. SD

Dark fell the night, the watch was set. Alfred the Harper. John Sterling.
    BeLS
Dark figures, lunged ahead, The. The Moral. Theodore Weiss. Prf
Dark Flows the River. Arthur Stanley Bourinot. CaP
Dark foreboding haunts me lest I die, A. Thomas MacDermot. *Fr.* San
    Gloria. PBCV
Dark Forest, The. Edward Thomas. NoP
"Dark fragrance, sparse shadows." Night of the Fifteenth, Second Month.
    Yüan Mei, *tr.* by Jonathan Chaves. CoBLCP
Dark Girl Dressed in Blue, The. *Unknown.* BeLS
Dark gray clouds, The. Natalia M. Belting. PDV
Dark green truck on the cement platform, The. Train Window. Robert
    Finch. OBCV
Dark grey. This Urn Contains Earth from German Concentration Camps.
    Audre Lorde. ER
Dark-haired girl, who holds my thoughts entirely, The. Peggy Browne.
    Turlough Carolan, *tr.* by Austin Clarke. BIrV
Dark Hand, A. Itzig Manger, *tr. fr. Yiddish by* David G. Roskies *and*
    Hillel Schwartz. VWA
Dark Hills, The. E. A. Robinson. AiP; FaFP; GoJo; HAP; LiTA; LiTM;
    MoAB; MoAmPo; NoAM; WeW
Dark House. Tennyson. *See* In Memoriam A. H. H.: Dark house, by
    which once more I stand.
Dark House, The. *Unknown.* NTCP
Dark house, by which once more I stand. Tennyson. *Fr.* In Memoriam
    A. H. H., VII. EBEV; GTBS-P; HAP; HeIP; NOBE; NoP; OBD;
    OBNC; PeHV; PoEL-5; SCV; UnPo
    (Dark House.) LiTB
Dark in the cubicle boxed from snow-darkness of night. History during
    Nocturnal Snowfall. Robert Penn Warren. DiPo
Dark in the Reich of the Blond. William Heyen. MAYP
Dark is dreaming, The. Good Night, Good Night. Dennis Lee. RAR
Dark is kind and cozy, The. God's Dark. John Martin. PoLF
Dark is no more than a blanket, The. Wind. Hamish Brown. PoSH
Dark is the face of Harriet. Harriet Tubman. Margaret Abigail Walker.
    PoNe
Dark is the forest and deep, and overhead. The Dark Forest. Edward
    Thomas. NoP
Dark is the sapphire night. Half-Light. Jean Percival Waddell. CaP
Dark is the stair, and humid the old walls. The Belfry. Laurence
    Binyon. CH
Dark jade clouds over cliffs and canyons coil in distant shapes. The
    Government Pond. Yao Nai, *tr.* by Daniel Bryant. WFTU
Dark lintels, the blue and foreign stones, The. Adrienne Rich. *Fr.*
    Twenty-one Love Poems, XXI. GLP; NoAM
Dark Lord of Savaiki, The. Alistair Campbell. ATNZ; PeNZ
Dark Mirage. "Badawi al-Jabal," *tr. fr. Arabic by* Christopher Tingley
    and Richard Wilbur. MAP
Dark Morning, The. Thomas Merton. PoA
Dark Mountains. Milton Lockyer, *tr. fr. Yindjibarndi by* Frank Wordick.
    CBAP
Dark Night, The. Saint John of the Cross, *tr. fr. Spanish.* WeW, *tr.* by
    John Frederick Nims
    (Obscure Night of the Soul, The.) AWP, *tr.* by Arthur Symons;
    OBMV, *tr.* by Arthur Symons
Dark night: a child begins weeping. Boncho, *tr. fr. Japanese by* Hiroaki
    Sato. *Fr.* Twenty-one Hokku. FCEI
Dark November night, A. Late. The back door wide. Pets. Ted Hughes.
    CRH
Dark o'clock. The Bed. Ray DiPalma. LP
Dark of winter, eleventh month. Ryokan, *tr.* by Burton Watson. JLIC-2
Dark one are you restless. The Armies Enter Cuailnge. *Unknown, tr. fr.
    Irish by* Thomas Kinsella. *Fr.* The Táin. NOIV
Dark Phrases. Ntozake Shange. *Fr.* For Colored Girls Who Have
    Considered Suicide When the Rainbow Is Enuf. BISi
Dark Pines under Water. Gwendolyn MacEwen. NOBC
Dark Planet, The. John Heath-Stubbs. OAEL-2
Dark plume fetch me from yon blasted yew, A. Return. Wordsworth.
    Fr. The River Duddon. HAP
Dark, puckered hole: a purple carnation. Sonnet: To the Asshole.
    Rimbaud *and* Paul Verlaine, *tr.* by J. Murat *and* W. Gunn. PeHV
Dark Rapture. "Æ." SeCePo
Dark Romance. Lucha Corpi, *tr. fr. Spanish by* Catherine Rodriguez-
    Nieto. CCP; WPOW
Dark Rosaleen. *at. to* Owen Roe MacWard *and to* Hugh O'Donnell, *tr.
    fr. Irish by* James Clarence Mangan. ACP; AnIL; AWP; BIrV; CH;
    EnRP; NOIV; OBEV
Dark Rosaleen, *sels.* David McKee Wright. PoAu-1
    "My Love is the voice of a song." *Fr.* IX.
    "On a shining silver morning long ago." *Fr.* I.
Dark Scent of Prayer, The. Rose Drachler. VWA
Dark Sea. Maruyama Kaoru*tr. fr. Japanese by* Hiroaki Sato. FCEI

Dark sea-shelter. Far from the Beach. Alda do Espírito Santo, *tr. by* Kathleen Weaver. OV

Dark Shadows. John Hall. NBP

Dark sky blowing over, A. The Elm's Home. William Heyen. MAYP

Dark socket of the year, The. My Mother's Body. Marge Piercy. ER

Dark Song. A. R. Ammons. MAT

Dark Song. Dame Edith Sitwell. CMoP; FaBoTw; PBWP

Dark Stag, The. Isabella Valancy Crawford. NOBC

Dark Stream. Ingrid Jonker, *tr. fr. Afrikaans by* Jake Cope *and* William Plomer. OV

Dark streets are deserted, The. After Midnight. Louis Simpson. CAPP; NoAM

Dark swimmers, The. Larry Eigner. PoM

Dark Symphony. Melvin B. Tolson. AmNP; PoNe

Dark Testament. Pauli Murray. AmNP; BlSi

Dark theme keeps me here, A. In Evening Air. Theodore Roethke. CAPP; NYBP; TAP

Dark, thinned, beside the wall of stone. In Time of Grief. Lizette Woodworth Reese. AA

Dark thoughts are my companions. I have wined. J. V. Cunningham. QFR; TW; VGW

Dark-time. The little ones like bees. Little Lullaby. Irving Feldman. NYBP

Dark to me is the earth. Dark to me are the heavens. The Desolate City. *Unknown, tr. by* Wilfrid Scawen Blunt. AWP; OBEV

Dark violet plum, A. Poetry. Abraham Sutskever, *tr. by* Chana Bloch. PeBMYV

Dark was the day for Childe Rolandine the artist. Childe Rolandine. Stevie Smith. BrRo

Dark Was the Night. *Unknown.* AmFP

Dark waters churn amongst us. C. G. Jung's "First Years." Thomas Kinsella. IPY

Dark Way Home: Survivors, The. Michael S. Harper. CNA

Dark Welcome, The. James Keir Baxter. *Fr.* Five Sestinas, III. ATNZ; PeNZ

Dark whispers. Night Gives Old Woman the Word. Gail Tremblay. HATNAP

Dark wind is blowing, A. Winnie Song. Lucille Clifton. ER

Dark-Winged Swallows Will Return, The. Gustavo Adolfo Bécquer, *tr. fr. Spanish by* Perry Higman. LPSS

Dark Wings. James Stephens. PoA

Dark Wood. Ian Wedde. ATNZ

Darkened bedroom, the double bed, The. Driving Wheel. Sherley Anne Williams. BlSi

Darkened farmhouse is asleep, The. Saving the Harvest. Geoffrey Lehmann. CBAP

Darkened hut outlined againt the sky, A. The Sunrise of the Poor. Robert Burns Wilson. AA

Darkened in the Soul. Napa, *tr. fr. Eskimo.* WTO

Darkened Windows. Ronald Bottrall. PoA

Darkening Garden, The. *Unknown.* BoTP

Darkening Hotel Room. Alfred Corn. MAYP

Darkening mountains are distant. Kikaku, *tr. fr. Japanese by* Hiroaki Sato. *Fr.* Thirty-three Hokku. FCEI

Darkening the azure roof of Nero's world. Domine Quo Vadis? Sir William Watson. WGRP

Darkening was like riches in the room, The. From a Childhood. Rainer Maria Rilke. TTTS, *tr. by* M. D. Herter Norton

Darkling Chicken, The. Robert Peters. BXAP

Darkling Elves, The. Jack Prelutsky. RHPC

Darkling I listen; and for many a time. Keats. *Fr.* Ode to a Nightingale. OBD

Darkling Thrush, The. Thomas Hardy. BrPo; CMoP; EBVV; FaFP; FPL; HAP; InPS; LiTB; LiTM; MoAB; MoBrPo; MoP; NAEL-2; NIP; NoAM; NOBE; NOBVV; NoP; OAEL-2; OBEV; OBNC; PBBP; PoE; PPP; RB; SoSe; TEP; TOF; TrGrPo; UnPo; WaP

Darkly in vesper stillness. An Earthquake Somewhere Else. Vivienne Finch. TSM

Darkmotherscream. Andrei Voznesensky, *tr. fr. Russian by* Robert Bly *and* Vera Dunham. NU

Darkness. Byron. EnRP; LiTB; NAEL-2; OAEL-2; OPOP; PoE; PoEL-4; TEP

Darkness. Joseph Campbell. BIrV

Darkness. Bartolo Cattafi, *tr. fr. Italian by* Lawrence R. Smith. NItP

Darkness. Arthur Hugh Clough. OxBSP

Darkness, The. Lionel Johnson. BrPo

Darkness./ Thick, lumpy. January 28. A. Leyeles, *tr. fr. Yiddish by* Benjamin *and* Barbara Harshav. *Fr.* Fabius Lind's Diary. AYP

Darkness and death? Nay, Pioneer, for thee. Walt Whitman. Francis Howard Williams. AA

Darkness and stars i' the mid-day! they invite. A Rhapsody. Henry Vaughan. NAEL-1

Darkness begins a/ retreat. After Christmas. Michael Richards. OBCP

Darkness comes out of the earth. Twilight. D. H. Lawrence. OBMV

Darkness crumbles away, The. Break of Day in the Trenches. Isaac Rosenberg. BrPo; FaBoMo; GTBS-P; MMA; MoBrPo; NAEL-2; NIP; NoAM; NOBE; NoP; OAEL-2; OBWP; PoA; SeCePo; VWA; WaaP; WaP

Darkness encloses the concert hall. Choral Symphony Conductor. Carol Coates. CaP

Darkness falls like a wet sponge. The Picture of Little J.A. in a Prospect of Flowers. John Ashbery. CAPP; PPP

Darkness falls short by an hour. Felicia's Café. Medbh McGuckian. FaBCIP

Darkness has called to darkness, and disgrace. As a Plane Tree by the Water. Robert Lowell. CMoP; CoAP; LiTM; MoAB; MoAmPo; NePoEA; NOBA; OxBA; TrGrPo

Darkness has dawned in the east. Shelley. *Fr.* Hellas: Choruses from "Hellas", 3. EnRP

Darkness invades the shallows of the street. Evening Tide. X. J. Kennedy. TDD

Darkness is closing around us, The. In Orbit. Henry Taylor. BXAP

Darkness is falling through darkness. The Hermit. Robert Bly. CAPP

Darkness is not dark, nor sunlight the light of the sun. Foal. Vernon Watkins. OxBTC

Darkness lifts, imagine, in your lifetime, The. The Undertaking. Louise Glück. FaBoWP

Darkness like a guillotine, The. Nightfall on Sedgemoor. Andrew Young. FaBoPP

Darkness marks the distance where river meets ocean. Autumn River. T'ang Hsien-Tsu, *tr. by* Jonathan Chaves. CoBLCP

Darkness Music. Muriel Rukeyser. BoWoP

Darkness presses all around, The. Government! Tuta Nihoniho, *tr. by* A. Armstrong. WTO

Darkness refuses the amnesia. Night Crackles. Elizabeth Woody. STE

Darkness reigned. Sacrifice. Nana Issaia, *tr. by* Helle Tzalopoulou Barnstone. BoWoP

Darkness slowly lifts. Morning. Sami Mahdi, *tr. by* May Jayyusi. MAP

Darkness: the rain sluiced down; the mire was deep. The Redeemer. Siegfried Sassoon. MMA; WGRP

Darkness was a richness in the room, The. From a Childhood. Rainer Maria Rilke, *tr. by* C. F. MacIntyre. TrJP

Darkness wears off, and, dawning into light. The Figures on the Frieze. Alastair Reid. ErPo; NYBP

Darky Sunday School. *Unknown.* OxBoLi

Darling, at the beautician's you buy. A Valentine for a Lady. Lucilius, *tr. by* Dudley Fitts. OFD

Darling! Because My Blood Can Sing. E. E. Cummings. InvP; OxBA

Darling Cory. *Unknown.* AmFP

Darling, each morning a blooded rose. Corinna in Vendome. Pierre de Ronsard, *tr. by* Robert Mezey. BoLoP; ErPo

"Darling," he said, "I never meant." Forgetfulness! Josephine D. Henderson Heard. CBWP-4

Darling, how long before this breath will cease? Evanishings. Mary E. Tucker. CBWP-1

Darling, I am growing old. Silver Threads among the Gold. Eben Eugene Rexford. FaFP

Darling I steal, and with hushed footsteps slow. Midnight at Baiae; a Dream Fragment of Imperial Rome. John Addington Symonds. PeHV

Darling, I won't be your hot love. Sulpicia, *tr. by* Aliki *and* Willis Barnstone. BoWoP

Darling, If You Only Knew. Edward Newman Horn. ErPo

Darling of the world is come, The. Robert Herrick. *Fr.* A Christmas Caroll Sung to the King in the Presence at White-Hall. PChr

Darling, the plates have been cleared away. Beauty and the Beast. Rita Dove. NoAM

Darling, you only, there is no duplicate. *Unknown, tr. fr. Egyptian into Italian by* Boris de Rachewiltz; *tr. into English by* Ezra Pound. *Fr.* Conversations in Courtship. CTC

Darned Mounseer, The. W. S. Gilbert. *Fr.* Ruddigore. NOBL

Dar's a lazy, sorta hazy. Sprin' Fevah. Ray Garfield Dandridge. BANP

Dar's a skool in West Virginny. To Professor Byrd Prillerman. Maggie Pogue Johnson. CBWP-4

Dar's plenty t'ings to write erbout. Dat Mule ob Brudder Wright's. Maggie Pogue Johnson. CBWP-4

Dart, The. *Unknown.* GBP

Dart, here's a man. The River Dart. *Unknown.* GBP

Dart of Izdabel prevails, The! 'twas dipped. The Dying Indian. Joseph Warton. NOEC

Darting over the cedar brakes. Yakamochi, *tr. fr. Japanese by* Burton Watson. *Fr.* Manyo Shu. FCEI

Dartmoor: Sunset at Chagford. T. E. Brown. NOBVV

Dartmouth Winter-Song. Richard Hovey. AA

Darwin and Mendel laid on man the chains. Progress. David McCord. ImOP
Darwin in 1881. Gjertrud Schnackenberg. NoAM; SM
Darwin on Species. *Unknown.* FaBoUs
Darwinism in the Kitchen. *Unknown.* FiBHP; NBLV
Darwinity. Herman Charles Merivale. NA
Das Kapital. Imamu Amiri Baraka. PoM
Das Liebesleben. Thom Gunn. ErPo
Dash back that ocean with a pier. Tennyson. *Fr.* Mechanophilus. FaBoCo
Dash for the Colors, The. Frederick G. Webb. BeLS
Dashing thro' the snow in a one-horse open sleigh. Jingle Bells. James S. Pierpont. FaFP
Dasius, chucker-out/ at the Turkish Baths. Martial, *tr.* by Peter Porter. OBVE
Dat Mule ob Brudder Wright's. Maggie Pogue Johnson. CBWP-4
Dat Sunshine Special comin' around de bend. C. C. Rider. *Unknown.* AS
Data, data, data. Transfigured Night. Ralph Gustafson. MoCV
Dates. *Unknown, tr. fr. Arabic by* E. Powys Mathers. *Fr.* The Thousand and One Nights. AWP; FaPON
Dates on bridges, The. History and Abstraction. Thomas Lux. AmPA
Datur Hora Quieti. Sir Walter Scott. GTBS; GTBS-P
Dauber, *sels.* John Masefield.
  "All through the windless night the clipper rolled." *Fr.* VI. CMoP
  Rounding the Horn. *Fr.* VI. MoAB; MoBrPo
Daufuskie. Mari E. Evans. BlSi
Daughter. Mary Dorcey. AIW
Daughter. Kimiko Hahn. BrSi
Daughter. Ellen Bryant Voigt. MT
"Daughter, how the door is creaking." Evening Prayer. Arthur Fitger, *tr.* by Jethro Bithell. AWP
Daughter-my-mother. The Blessing. Carolyn Kizer. CAPP
Daughter of Admetus, A. T. Sturge Moore. FaBoTw
Daughter of Debate, The. Elizabeth I, Queen of England. *See* Doubt of Future Foes, The.
Daughter of earth and child of the wave be appeased. William Everson. *Fr.* Tendril in the Mesh, IV. NoAM
Daughter of Egypt, veil thine eyes! Bayard Taylor. AA
Daughter of Jairus, The, *sels.* Marina Tsvetayeva, *tr. fr. Russian by* Paul Schmidt. BoWoP
  "And now the riverbank. For the last time." *Fr.* VII.
  "And now the riverbank. I cling." *Fr.* III.
  "I catch the movement of his lips." *Fr.* V.
  "Our last bridge." *Fr.* VIII.
  "Past factory workshops, empty." *Fr.* IX.
  "Rain. A heavy mane." *Fr.* XII.
  "To lose it all at once." *Fr.* XI.
Daughter of Jove, relentless power. Hymn to Adversity. Thomas Gray. EnRP; GTBS; GTBS-P
Daughter of Mendoza, The. Mirabeau Buonaparte Lamar. AA
Daughter of Night, chaotic Queen! Ode to the German Drama. *Unknown.* NOEC
Daughter of the Regiment, The. Clinton Scollard. PAH
Daughter of th'Italian heaven! Corinne at the Capitol. Felicia Dorothea Hemans. BrRo
Daughter, take this amulet. Mwana Kupona Msham, *tr. fr. Swahili by* J. W. T. Allen. *Fr.* Poem to Her Daughter. AIW, *ad. by* Deirdre Lashgari; WPOW, *ad. by* Deirdre Lashgari.
Daughter to that good Earl, once President. To the Lady Margaret Ley. Milton. GTBS; GTBS-P; OBEV
  (Sonnet: "Daughter to that good Earl, once president.") OBS
Daughter who has never been here, The. Empty Backstreet in a Small Southern Town. T. R. Hummer. NAmP
Daughterly. Kathleen Spivack. TV
Daughters. Astra. BrRo
Daughter's House, A. Norma Hope Richman. GOYP
Daughters, in the wind's boisterous roughing. Vernal Equinox. Ruth Stone. MoAmPo
Daughters of Blum, The. Charles Wright. CoAP; SM
Daughters of Jove, whose voice is melody. Hymn to Selene. *Unknown, tr. fr. Greek by* Shelley. *Fr.* Homeric Hymns. AWP
Daughters of the Horseleech, The. Stanley Kunitz. TW
Daughters of the Seraphim led round their sunny flocks, The. The Book of Thel. Blake. EnRP; NoP; OAEL-2; OBNC; PoEL-4; TEP
Daughters of Time, the hypocritic Days. Days. Emerson. AA; AmPP; AnAmPo; HAP; HeIP; LiTA; NAAL-1; NOBA; NoP; OxBA; OxBSP; PoE; PoEL-4; TAP; TrGrPo
Daughters of War. Isaac Rosenberg. BrPo
Daughter's Rebellion, The. Francis Hopkinson. PAH
Dauncing (bright Lady) then began to bee. Sir John Davies. *Fr.* Orchestra; or, A Poem[e] of Da[u]ncing. PoEL-2
D'Avalos' Prayer. John Masefield. MOS; TrPWD

Davening. Rochelle Ratner. VWA
Daventry Wonder, The. "Agricola." NOEC
David. Earle Birney. CaP; NOBC
David. Linda Pastan. CRP
David and Bethsabe, *sel.* George Peele.
  Bethsabe's Song. *Fr.* sc. i. GBL; NOBE; NoP; OBSC; OxBoLi; OxBSP; PoEL-2; RB; TEP
  (Bethsabe Bathing.) EiL; TrGrPo
David and Delilah. Clark Stillman. SoTCo
David and Goliath. Nathaniel Crouch. OxBChV
David and Goliath. Priscilla Jane Thompson. CBWP-2
David and I that summer cut trails on the Survey. David. Earle Birney. CaP; NOBC
David and Jonathan. Abraham Cowley. *Fr.* Davideis, II. PeHV
David Drummond's destinie. The Coble o Cargill. *Unknown.* ESPB
David Garrick. Goldsmith. *Fr.* Retaliation. NOEC
David Hume ate a swinging great dinner. On the Author of the *Treatise of Human Nature.* James Hay Beattie. FaBoCo
David Hume, Dying, Talks to Boswell. Alan Bold. NPo
David Lowston. *Unknown.* PeNZ
David the king was grieved and moved. David's Lamentation. William Billings. AmFP
Davideis, *sels.* Abraham Cowley.
  Creation, The. *Fr.* I. OBS
  David and Jonathan. *Fr.* II. PeHV
  Power of Numbers, The. *Fr.* I. OBS
  Supplication, A. GTBS, III; GTBS-P, III.
  "With sober pace an heav'nly Maid walks in." *Fr.* III. SeCV-1
David's Lament. Bible, *O.T. See* Second Samuel: Beauty of Israel is slain [*or* slaine] upon thy high places, The.
David's Lament for Jonathan. Peter Abelard, *tr. fr. Latin by* Helen Waddell. PeHV
David's Lament for Saul and Jonathan. Bible, *O.T. See* Second Samuel: Beauty of Israel is slain [*or* slaine] upon thy high places, The.
David's Lamentation. William Billings. AmFP
Davis Matlock. Edgar Lee Masters. *Fr.* Spoon River Anthology. LiTA; LiTM
Davus, I detest. Horace. *See* Odes: I, 38. Simplicity.
Davy and the Goblin, *sels.* Charles Edward Carryl.
  My Recollectest Thoughts. *Fr. ch.* 7. NA
  Robinson Crusoe. *Fr. ch.* 11. AA
  (Robinson Crusoe's Story.) BeLS; FiBHP; PoRA
  Walloping Window-Blind, The. NA, *ch.* 8; NBLV, *ch.* 8; OBCA, *ch.* 8.
  (Nautical Ballad, A.) FaPON; OBAL
  ("Oh, a capital ship for an ocean trip.") MoShBr
Davy Crockett in his woodman dress. Lament for the Alamo. Arthur Guiterman. AmFN
Davy Davy Dumpling. *Unknown.* OxNR; RAR
Dawn. Louis Aragon, *tr. fr. French by* Lou Lipsitz *and* Jean Gillou. POS
Dawn. Sir John Betjeman. FL
Dawn. Gordon Bottomley. BoTP; MoBrPo
Dawn/ rose like a hand at the edge of dark. Crazy Horse: The Last Morning. Lance Henson. VoR
Dawn. Paul Laurence Dunbar. AmNP; AnAmPo; PoLF; PoNe
Dawn. John Ford. *Fr.* The Lover's Melancholy. OBEV, *fr.* V, i.
Dawn. Federico García Lorca, *tr. fr. Spanish by* William B. Logan. SOTW
Dawn. Juana de Ibarbourou, *tr. fr. Spanish by* Perry Higman. LPSS
Dawn. Philippe Jaccottet, *tr. fr. French by* W. S. Merwin. RHTwFP
Dawn. John Masefield. BrPo
Dawn, *sel.* Harold Monro.
  God. WGRP
Dawn. Eileen Myles. UL
Dawn. Constance Ortmayer. SaC
Dawn. Alejandra Pizarnik, *tr. fr. Spanish by* Alina Rivero. VWA
Dawn. Rachel, *tr. fr. Hebrew by* A. M. Klein. TrJP
Dawn. Rimbaud, *tr. fr. French by* Enid Rhodes Peschel. *Fr.* A Season in Hell. TTTS
Dawn. Rimbaud, *tr. fr. French by* Enid Rhodes Peschal. *Fr.* Illuminations. SOTW
Dawn. Frederick George Scott. CaP
Dawn. David Shevin. VWA
Dawn. Shunzei, *tr. fr. Japanese by* Burton Watson. *Fr.* Thirty Tanka. FCEI
Dawn. Lucien Stryk. CAPP
Dawn, The. Tennyson. NAEL-2
Dawn. *Unknown.* OBSC; PBBP
Dawn. *Malay Oral Tradition, tr. by* R. J. Wilkinson. WTO
Dawn. Ella Wheeler Wilcox. PWR
Dawn. William Carlos Williams. MoAB; MoAmPo

Dawn: a good wind blows from the sea. Semantic. Robert Conquest. TEP

Dawn: and foot on the cold stair treading. Aubade for Hope. Robert Penn Warren. MoAmPo

Dawn and night of fighting, lovers like actual wars. Sonnet: Kamikaze. Bernadette Mayer. UL

Dawn; and the jew's-harp's sawing seesaw song. Pilots, Man Your Planes. Randall Jarrell. MoAB; MoAmPo

Dawn Blossoms. Empress Eifuku, tr. fr. Japanese by Steven D. Carter. WFTW

Dawn. Blueness comes down. A Stool at the Head of My Bed. Kadya Molodovsky, tr. by Irving Feldman. PeBMYV

Dawn Boy's Song. Unknown, tr. fr. Navajo Indian by Washington Matthews. FaBV

Dawn breaking as I woke. Alba. Derek Walcott. GoJo; PCP

Dawn breaks, snow patches lie on the slopes. After Snow-Impromptu. Yü Chi, tr. by Jonathan Chaves. CoBLCP

Dawn breezes are clear, The. Song of the Fisherman. Ku Hsiung, tr. by Lois Fusek. ATF

Dawn came wild with rain, and all day long, The. Moonlight on Lake Sydenham. Wilson Pugsley MacDonald. CaP

Dawn Cherries. Hezutsu Tosaku, tr. fr. Japanese by Burton Watson. FCEI

Dawn: Clear Skies. Yang Shih-ch'i, tr. fr. Chinese by Jonathan Chaves. CoBLCP

Dawn comes cold, The: the haystack smokes. Dawn. John Masefield. BrPo

Dawn cried out: the brutal voice of a bird. In All These Acts. William Everson. NoP

Dawn drizzle [or Dawndrizzle] ended dampness steams from. Anglo Saxon Street. Earle Birney. HeIP; NOBC

Dawn. First light tearing. Clouds. Philip Levine. LCAP

Dawn from the foretop! Dawn from the barrel! The Ice-Floes. Edwin John Pratt. CaP

Dawn Has Yet to Ripple In. Melville Cane. MoAmPo

Dawn Hippo. Sydney Clouts. PeSA

Dawn Horse, A. William Harmon. FYAP

Dawn: I half-open the gate. Spring. Chang Yü, tr. fr. Chinese by Jonathan Chaves. Fr. The Four Seasons in the Mountains. CoBLCP

Dawn in a tree of birds, A. Kenneth Rexroth. InPK

Dawn in Britain, The, sels. C. M. Doughty.
   Bladyn's Song of Cloten. PoEL-5
   Gauls Sacrifice, The. FaBoTw
   Hymn to the Sun. FaBoTw
   Roman Officer Writes, A. FaBoTw

Dawn in January. Lance Henson. CDW

Dawn in New York comes. Dawn. Federico García Lorca, tr. by William B. Logan. SOTW

Dawn in the Cockloft. José Juan Tablada, tr. fr. Spanish by Samuel Beckett. MexPo

Dawn in the Heart of Africa. Patrice Emery Lumumba. PBA; TTY

Dawn is blue at the window, The. Hagar Leaves Abraham's House. Itzig Manger, tr. by Leonard Wolf. PeBMYV

Dawn is grey here, she went on to tell him, The. It was not always like this. Henri Michaux, tr. fr. French by Richard Ellmann. Fr. I Am Writing to You from a Far-Off Country, III. RHTwFP

Dawn is, in essence, sinister as fire. Dew. Jennifer Maiden. CBAP

Dawn is smiling on the dew that covers, The. The Genesis of Butterflies. Victor Hugo, tr. by Andrew Lang. AWP

Dawn Journey. Yi Shun-ting, tr. fr. Chinese by Timothy C. Wong. WFTU

Dawn moon struggles to shine its light, The. On Failing the Examination. Meng Chiao, tr. by Burton Watson. CoBCP

Dawn near an Old Battlefield, in a Time of Peace. James Wright. AnAn

Dawn of a pleasant morning in May. Lee to the Rear. John Randolph Thompson. PAH

Dawn of Day. William Browne. Fr. The Shepherd's Pipe. EIL

Dawn of Day, The. Keaulumoku, tr. fr. Hawaiian by M. W. Beckwith. Fr. The Kumulipo; a Creation Chant. WTO

Dawn of Jaffa Pigeons, A. Eli Bachar, tr. fr. Hebrew by Jeremy Garber. VWA

Dawn of Love, The. Henrietta Cordelia Ray. BlSi; CBWP-3

Dawn of the Space Age. John Ciardi. OBAL

Dawn on the East Coast. Alun Lewis. OBWP

Dawn on the Lievre, The. Archibald Lampman. CaP

Dawn peeled mists. The Rose. Mary R. Gaumond. TSM

Dawn peered through the pines as we dashed at the ford. Riding with Kilpatrick. Clinton Scollard. PAH

Dawn shakes the candle, shoots a flame. May It Be. Boris Pasternak, tr. by C. M. Bowra. TrJP

Dawn Snow. Huang Ching-jen, tr. fr. Chinese by Daniel Bryant. WFTU

Dawn spreads out its colors before my boat has barely left the shore. Leaving Southern Screen Hill at Dawn and Crossing the Lake. Li E, tr. by Irving Lo. WFTU

Dawn that cares for nobody. February. W. S. Merwin. NNaP

Dawn the sun steadily rose. The One Who Is Within. Nia Francisco. STE

Dawn Wail for the Dead. Kath Walker. CBAP

Dawn Walk. Edward Hirsch. MAYP; NAmP

Dawn was apple-green, The. Green. D. H. Lawrence. GBL; MoBrPo; PoA

Dawn was breaking. Little Song of Seville. Federico García Lorca, tr. fr. Spanish by William Jay Smith. Fr. Songs of Childhood. CT

Dawn, with its scant. Jack Yazzie's Girl. Pamela Stewart. NAmP

Dawncall. Niyi Osundare. UAS

Dawndrizzle ended dampness steams from. See Dawn drizzle ended dampness steams from.

Dawning. Richard Watson Dixon. NOBVV

Dawning, The. Henry Vaughan. MePo; NOCV; TrPWD

Dawning Fair, Morning Wonderful. Unknown. AH

Dawning o' the Year, The. Mary Elizabeth McGrath Blake. AA

Dawning of morn, the daylight's sinking, The. Thee, Thee, Only Thee. Thomas Moore. GBL; OBNC

Dawning sun; The/ Shines down on the dunes. Siilenboor. Mongol Oral Tradition, tr. by C. R. Bawden. WTO

Dawn's Awake, The! Otto Leland Bohanan. BANP

Dawn's Carol. Henrietta Cordelia Ray. CBWP-3

Dawns I Have Seen. Ivor Gurney. FaBoPP

Dawn's precise pronouncement waits, The. The Edge of Day. Laurie Lee. NYBP

Dawn's Rose. Ted Hughes. Fr. Crow. PoE

Day, The. Peter Ackroyd. NPo

Day, The. George M. Brady. NeIP

Day, The. Roy Fuller. OxBTC

Day, The. John Glassco. MoCV

Day. Khairi Mansour, tr. fr. Arabic by Lena Jayyusi and Charles Doria. MAP

Day. Cecil Arthur Spring-Rice. BoTP

Day, The/ is ready to close. Saturday Night in the Village. Giacomo Leopardi, tr. by Robert Lowell. OBVE

Day, a night, an hour of sweet content, A. Content. Thomas Campion. OBSC

Day after Chasing Porcupines. James Welch. NoAM

Day after Conference, The. Josephine D. Henderson Heard. CBWP-4

Day after Day. Rabindranath Tagore. Fr. Gitanjali, LXXVI. OBMV

Day after day it goes on. How Much Longer? Robert Mezey. OBWP

Day after day, O lord of my life, shall I stand before thee face to face? Day after Day. Rabindranath Tagore. Fr. Gitanjali, LXXVI. OBMV

Day after day the sticky mixture stayed. Remembering Mincemeat. George MacBeth. NPo

Day after day they caught rain in the smoke-hole. Two Animals, One Flood. Diane Glancy. STE

Day after decapitation, The. The Head. Padraic Fallon. CIP

Day after Saying Goodby to Mototada, The. Rai San'yo, tr. fr. Chinese by Burton Watson. JLIC-2

Day after Sunday, The. Phyllis McGinley. MoAmPo; OBSV; UnPo

Day after Trinity, The. Richard Oyama. BrSi

Day agone, as I rode sullenly, A. Dante, tr. fr. Italian by Dante Gabriel Rossetti. Fr. La Vita Nuova, IV. AWP

Day and Night. Lewis Alexander. CDC

Day and Night. Leyb Kvitko, tr. fr. Yiddish by Allen Mandelbaum and Harold Rabinowitz. PeBMYV

Day and Night. James Stephens. BoTP

Day and Night. Fyodor Ivanovich Tyutchev, tr. fr. Russian by Alan Myers. AAA

Day and night are never weary. Greek Epigram. Ezra Pound. MoAB; MoAmPo

Day and Night Handball. Stephen Dunn. AmPA

Day and night I wander widely through the wilderness of thought. God. Gamaliel Bradford. WGRP

Day and night my thoughts incline. The Jar. Richard Henry Stoddard. AA

Day and night, rain, the wind razes. That Sleepless Flame. Roberto Obregón, tr. by Tina Alvarez Robles. Vol

Day and night she dances. Shulamit in Her Dreams. Marcia Falk. VWA

Day and then a week passed by, A. The Cardinal Bird. William Davis Gallagher. AA

Day arrives of the autumn fair, The. A Sheep Fair. Thomas Hardy. Prf

Day at the beach. Littoral. Hjalmar Flax, tr. by Julio Marzán. InW

Day at the Farm, A. "L. J." BoTP

Day Aviva Came to Paris, The. Irving Layton. MoCV

Day before April, The. Mary Carolyn Davies. BoTP; FaPON

Day before Christmas. Marchette Chute. NTCP

Day before the holidays began, The. One Christmas-Time. Wordsworth. Fr. The Prelude [or, Growth of a Poet's Mind]: France. RB

Day before the houses sank beneath the waves, The. The Day the Houses Sank. Constance Urdang. MAT

Day before yesterday the street was a street. That Street of Mine. Yekhi'el Mar, tr. by Bernhard Frank. MHeP

Day Begins, A. Denise Levertov. NaP

Day Begins at Governor's Square Mall. Leon Stokesbury. MAYP; MT

Day begins to droop, The. Winter Nightfall. Robert Bridges. MoAB; MoBrPo; OBEV

Day-Breakers [or Daybreakers], The. Arna Bontemps. AmNP; CDC; IDB; PoBA; PoNe

Day breaks, your mind aches, The. For No One. John Lennon and Paul McCartney. WTO

Day by Day. Julia Harris May. BLRP

Day by day I float my paper boats/ one by one down the running stream. Paper Boats. Rabindranath Tagore. FaPON

Day by Day the Manna Fell. Josiah Conder. TrCP

Day by day the Organ-Builder in his lonely chamber wrought. The Legend of the Organ-Builder. Julia Caroline Ripley Dorr. BeLS; BLPA; FaBoBe

Day concludes burning, The. Desmond O'Grady. Fr. The Dying Gaul. CIP

Day creeps down. The moon is creeping up. The Man on the Dump. Wallace Stevens. HAP; NAWM-2; NoAM

Day dawns with scent of must and rain, The. Mirror in February. Thomas Kinsella. CIP; FaBCIP; GTBS-P; NoAM

Day does not come with violence. Deer in Aspens. Kay DeBard Hall. GoYe

Day drags by with textbooks, The. The Schoolbus Comes before the Sun. Robert Currie. TDD

Day draws to an end, The. The Author's Apology. T. Carmi, tr. by Marcia Falk. VWA

Day-Dreams. William Canton. NOBVV

Day Dreams, or Ten Years Old. Margaret Johnson. BLPA

Day ending/ and again it starts. Kyotai, tr. fr. Japanese by Burton Watson. Fr. Sixteen Hokku. FCEI

Day Flight. Jack Davis. CBAP

Day for Anne Frank, A. C. K. Williams. GeTw

Day Glo Question of Identity, The. Jeffrey Miller. UL

Day goes down red darkling, The. Desolate. Gerald Massey. EBVV

Day had awakened all things that be. Daybreak. Shelley. GN

Day had fled, the moon arose, The. George Gordon McCrae. Fr. Mamba the Bright-eyed. PoAu-1

Day had lapsed to twilight, The. Teatime Variations: After A. E. Housman. Peter Titheradge. FaBoPa

Day has her star, as well as Night. The Two Stars. W. H. Davies. MoBrPo

Day has pleasures of its own, The. I Love the Night. Matilda Caroline Edwards. PWR

Day he first spoke to me of love, The. When He Spoke to Me of Love. M. A. Mokhomo, tr. by Dan Kunene and Jack Cope. PeSA

Day I go, The/ to pick arrowhead. Unknown, tr. fr. Japanese by Burton Watson. Fr. Manyo Shu. FCEI

Day I met you I tore up, The. Nizar Qabbani, tr. by Lena Jayyusi and W. S. Merwin. MAP

Day I Once Dreamed, The. Pat Arrowsmith. AIW

Day I put him off the sun outside, The. Long Tour: The Country Music Star Explains Why He Put off the Bus and Fired a Good Lead Guitar in West Texas. James Whitehead. MT

Day in a Long Hot Summer, A. Yuri Kageyama. BrSi

Day in Autumn, A. R. S. Thomas. BoNaP

Day in, day out. Yosami, tr. fr. Japanese. Fr. Manyo Shu. Ma

Day in France, A. David Holbrook. OBTV

Day in June, A ("And what is so rare as a day in June?"). James Russell Lowell. Fr. The Vision of Sir Launfal, Prelude to Pt. I. FaPON

Day in melting purple dying. Song of Egla. Maria Gowen Brooks. AA

Day in My Union Suit, A. Michael Pettit. MAYP

Day in the City, A. L. E. Sissman. NYBP

Day in the Life, A. Stef Pixner. BrRo

Day is a Negro, The. Day and Night. Lewis Alexander. CDC

Day is again begun. Unrest. Richard Watson Dixon. OBNC

Day is broke, The! Melpomene, begone. Iter Boreale. Robert Wild. APAS

Day is cold, and dark, and dreary, The. The Rainy Day. Longfellow. AWP; FPL; PoLF

Day is colorless like Swiss characters in a novel, The. For Guillaume Apollinaire. William Meredith. CoAP

Day Is Coming, The, parody. Sir Walter Besant. CenHV

Day Is Coming, The. William Morris. WGRP

Day is curled about again, The. An Anniversary on the Hymeneals of My Noble Kinsman, Thomas Stanley, Esquire. Richard Lovelace. CaPo

Day is dark, The. Sehnsucht; or, What You Will. "Corinna." FiBHP

Day is dark and dreary, The. If. Franklin P. Adams. OBAL

Day Is Done, The. Phoebe Cary. AnAmPo; BXAP; OBAL

Day Is Done, The. Longfellow. AnAmPo; BLPA; FaBoBe; FaFP; FPL; NOBA; OHFP; OxBA; PoRA; PWR; TrGrPo

Day is drawing to its fall, A. First Sight of Her and After. Thomas Hardy. PoEL-5

Day Is Dying in the West. At. to Mary Artemisia Lathbury. AH, with music; WGRP

Day is ended, The. Ere I sink to sleep. All's Well. Harriet McEwen Kimball. AA

Day Is Gone, The. Keats. EnRP

Day is great and strong, The. World without Peculiarity. Wallace Stevens. HCAP

Day is late enough you could stand, The. American Ash. Stanley Plumly. GeTw

Day is long; the worn noon dreams, The. Noon's Dream-Song. Eugene Lee-Hamilton. NOBVV

Day is o'er and twilight's shade, The. Gerarda. Eloise Bibb. CBWP-4

Day is o'er! yet pleasure, commerce, gain, The. Thomas Cleaver. Fr. Night. PF

Day Is Past and Gone, The, with music. John Leland. AH (Evening Shade.) AmFP

Day is past, the sun is set, The. Evening. Thomas Miller. OxBChV

Day is quenched, and the sun is fled, The. A Song of Doubt. Josiah Gilbert Holland. WGRP

Day is so pretty, The. Duet. Ruth Krauss. RR

Day is the children's friend. The Prejudice against the Past. Wallace Stevens. LiTM

Day is turning ghost, The. A Commonplace Day. Thomas Hardy. NOBVV

Day is warm, The. June. Aileen Fisher. PDV

Day it comes, it goes, The. Ravidas, tr. by John Stratton Hawley and Mark Juergensmeyer. SSI

Day Lady Died, The. Frank O'Hara. CAPP; HCAP; MoP; NAAL-2; NeAP; NoAM; NOBA; NoP; PoE; PoM; SOTW

Day later than he said in the letter, A. The Light Passages. Debora Greger. MAYP

Day lay like a pearl on her lap, The. Diane di Prima. Fr. Loba. ER

Day like blank paper, The. The Six Hundred Thousand Letters. Harvey Shapiro. VWA

Day-long cold hard rain drove, The. Surviving. James Welch. CDW; HATNAP; STE

Day my father and Jack Grimes, The. Dreamers and Flyers. Joan LaBombard. MOWH

Day my poems, The. Mahmoud Darwish, tr. by Abdullah al-Udhari. MPAW

Day of anger after the holy night, The. News from a Pacified Area. James Keir Baxter. OxBC

Day of Atonement. Jack Myers. VWA

Day of Battle, The. A. E. Housman. Fr. A Shropshire Lad, LVI. OHIP; WaaP

Day of Denial, The. Jones Very. NOBA

Day of Doom, The. Michael Wigglesworth. NAAL-1, abr.; SCAP "Then to the bar, all they drew near," sel. OBCA

Day of glory! Welcome day! The Fourth of July. John Pierpont. OPP; PAH

Day of God! Thou Blessed Day. Hannah Flagg Gould. AH

Day of hunting done. Twilight in California. Philip Dow. AmPA

Day of Inverlochy, The. Iain Lom, tr. fr. Gaelic. GoTS

Day of Judgement, The. Swift. BIrV; FaBoRV; NOBE; NOEC; OAEL-1; OBSV; PPP; TW

Day of Judgement [or Judgment]; an Ode, The. Isaac Watts. HAP; NOBE; NOEC; NoP; OBEV; SeCePo

Day of Judgment, The. Dugald Buchanan, tr. fr. Gaelic. GoTS

Day of Judgment, The. Thomas of Celano. See Hears't thou, my soul, what serious things.

Day of My Death, The. Pier Paolo Pasolini, tr. fr. Italian by Lawrence R. Smith. NItP

Day of my double birth, if such the year. John Thelwall. Fr. Lines Written at Bridgewater, 27 July 1797. NOEC

Day of Pearl Harbor, The. Takamura Kotaro, tr. fr. Japanese by Hiroaki Sato. Fr. A Brief History of Imbecility. FCEI

Day of Renewal. Louis MacNeice. NAs

Day of Resurrection, The. Saint John of Damascus, tr. fr. Greek by John Mason Neale. TrCP

Day of sunny face and temper, A. Big Bessie Throws Her Son into the Street. Gwendolyn Brooks. VGW

Day of tender memory, A. Memorial Day. Emma A. Lent. WBLP

Day of the fête, The—and what a day for it. School Cadets. Anne Elder. CBAP

Day of the Pancreas, The. David McFadden. NeAC

Day of the Parade. Alan Chong Lau. BrSi

Day of the Sentry, The. David St. John. AnAn

Day of These Days. Laurie Lee. BoNaP

Day of wrath, that day of burning. Dies Irae. Thomas of Celano, tr. by Abraham Coles. AA

Day of Wrath, that dreadful day, The. The Day of Judgment. Thomas of Celano, tr. by Wentworth Dillon. TIRV

Day on Kind Continent. Robert David Cohen. NYBP

The day recedes. Seventh Telegram ("The day recedes"). Abd al-Aziz al-Maqalih, tr. fr. Arabic by Lena Jayyusi and Christopher Middleton. Fr. Telegrams of Tenderness for Sanaa. MAP

Day she visited the dissecting room, The. Two Views of a Cadaver Room. Sylvia Plath. CMoP; GoYe

Day Song. Lance Henson. HATNAP

Day that ends the world will be the one, The. Like a Whisper. Ethan Ayer. GoYe

Day That I Have Loved. Rupert Brooke. FPL; PoLF

Day that I was christened, The. Godmother. Dorothy Parker. PoRA

Day that my dear came to us, The. Early Mornings. Unknown, tr. by Louis Untermeyer. AS

Day the big tree went, The. The Tree. Pat Wilson. ATNZ

Day the birds were lifted from my shoulders, The. The Nest. Marvin Bell. CAPP

Day the buds opened, I returned, The. Sparrow. Shin Dong-jip, tr. by Koh Chang-soo. ACKP

Day the dancer in the loud red dress, The. Burlesque. John Skoyles. NAmP

Day the Emperor treated me, The. Etsuzan, tr. fr. Chinese by Lucien Stryk and Takashi Ikemoto. ZPCJ

Day the fat woman, The. The Beach in August. Weldon Kees. VGW

Day the Houses Sank, The. Constance Urdang. MAT

Day, The? Memorial. Grape Sherbet. Rita Dove. MOWH

Day the rose petals scattered, The. Memory of a Rose. Koh Chang-soo, tr. by the author. ACKP

Day the Tide, The. Philip Booth. CoAP

Day the two old women were dissecting two birds, The. Richard Brought His Flute. Nancy Morejón, tr. by Kathleen Weaver. AIW

Day the wind was hardly, A. Letter VI. William Sydney Graham. FaBoMo

Day the Winds, The. Josephine Miles. FaBoWP

Day the world was O.K, The. O.K. Ann Ziety. DT

Day They Busted the Grateful Dead, The. Richard Brautigan. MAT

Day They Cleaned Up the Border El Salvador, February, 1981, The. Wendy Rose. HATNAP

Day they laid your grandfather away, The. Second Wind. Fred Chappell. MT

Day they strung the cable from America to Europe, The. Cotton. Harry Edmund Martinson, tr. by Robert Bly. RB

Day Thou Gavest, Lord, Is Ended, The. John Ellerton. EBVV; FaPoR

Day time failed began as usual, The. Burial of a Fisherman in Hydra. Grace Schulman. BoWoP

Day transports fallen snows, muddied, mildewed, ruined, The. Spring over the City. Anne Hébert, tr. by Kathleen Weaver. PBWP

Day Twenty-three. Victor Coleman. NOBC

Day was cloudy. No one could come to a decision, The. The Last Day. George Seferis, tr. by Edmund Keeley and Philip Sherrard. VMG

Day was here when it was his to know, The. The New Tenants. E. A. Robinson. NoAM

Day when Charmus ran with five, The. A Mighty Runner. E. A. Robinson. OBAL; SD

Day when I yearn for home, A. Ishikawa Takuboku, tr. by Geoffrey Bownas and Anthony Thwaite. PeBJV

Day when it will not matter, The. The Day. John Glassco. MoCV

Day Which Endures Not, A. A. G. Prys-Jones, tr. fr. Welsh by Anthony Conran. OBWVE

Day will come when I will, The. A Farewell to a Southern Melody. Huang O, tr. by Kenneth Rexroth and Ling Chung. BoWoP

Day will come when you will cease to know, The. Warning. Robert Frost. AnAmPo

Day will come, when't shall be said, The. Swift. Fr. The Life and Character of Dean Swift. NOIV

Day will return with a fresher boon, A. A Song of Faith. Josiah Gilbert Holland. WGRP

Day will rise and the sun from eastward. George Campbell Hay. OxBS

Day will soon be gone, The. Fujiwara no Michinobu, tr. fr. Japanese by Curtis Hidden Page. Fr. Hyaku-Nin-Isshu. AWP

Day with sky so wide, A. The Motion of the Earth. Norman Nicholson. ImOP

Day with the Foreign Legion, A. Reed Whittemore. CoAP; LiTM; NePoEA

Day you, The/ came into the ice without shoes. Counted Out. Ilse Aichinger, tr. by Beth Bjorklund. CoAuP

Day you appeared I began to speak, The. To Your Question. Duane Niatum. CDW

Day You Are Born, The. Cathy Song. BrSi

Day You Are Reading This, The. William Stafford. PoA

Day you came, The. Breasts. Tess Gallagher. AmPA

Day you came naked to Paris, The. The Day Aviva Came to Paris. Irving Layton. MoCV

Day Zimmer Lost Religion, The. Paul Zimmer. InPK

Daybreak. Frances Cornford. FM

Daybreak. Galway Kinnell. LCAP

Daybreak. Longfellow. BOTP; FPL; PoLF; PWR

Daybreak. W. S. Merwin. NAAL-2

Daybreak. Bert Meyers. EAS

Daybreak. Phillip Yellowhawk Minthorn. STE

Daybreak. Frank Lamont Phillips. CNA

Daybreak. Carl Sandburg. PDV

Daybreak. Shelley. GN

Daybreak. Samuel Francis Smith. See Morning Light Is Breaking, The.

Daybreak. Stephen Spender. BoLoP

Daybreak. See Break of Day.

Daybreak/ On the corn shoots. Onitsura, tr. by Geoffrey Bownas and Anthony Thwaite. PeBJV

Daybreak/ whales trumpet. Kyotai, tr. fr. Japanese by Burton Watson. Fr. Sixteen Hokku. FCEI

Daybreak: a white fish. Basho, tr. fr. Japanese by Burton Watson. Fr. Seventy-six Hokku. FCEI

Daybreak: at the tips of wheat blades, spring frost. Leaving Itami in Early February. Onitsura, tr. fr. Japanese by Hiroaki Sato. Fr. Twenty-three Hokku. FCEI

Daybreak, big waves, the clear sky. Ozaki Hosai, tr. fr. Japanese by Hiroaki Sato. Fr. One Hundred Haiku in Free Form. FCEI

Daybreak comes first. Daybreak. Carl Sandburg. PDV

Daybreak in a Garden. Siegfried Sassoon. BoTP

Daybreak in Alabama. Langston Hughes. AmFN; CNA

Daybreak: in its madder-red. Kito, tr. fr. Japanese by Hiroaki Sato. Fr. Twenty-four Hokku. FCEI

Daybreak: the household slept. Father and Child. Gwen Harwood. CBAP; WPE

Daybreak upon the hills! Peace. Adeline D. T. Whitney. PAH

Daydream. A. S. J. Tessimond. SeCePo

Daydreamers. Norma L. Davis. PoAu-2

Daylight Saving Time. Phyllis McGinley. RHPC

Daylights. Rosanna Warren. MAYP; NoAM

Daylong this tomcat lies stretched flat. Esther's Tomcat. Ted Hughes. OxBC

Days. Emerson. AA; AmPP; AnAmPo; HAP; HeIP; LiTA; NAAL-1; NOBA; NoP; OxBA; OxBSP; PoE; PoEL-4; TAP; TrGrPo

Days. Philip Larkin. EBEV; FaBoMo; Mes; OxBC; OxBSP; RB; TOF

Days accumulate; the more snow falls. Princess Shikishi, tr. fr. Japanese by Hiroaki Sato. Fr. Seventy-eight Tanka. FCEI

Days Ago. Dianne Hai-Jew. BrSi

Days and Nights, sels. Kenneth Koch. NoAM

"I certainly have lost something." Fr. V.
Stones of Time, The. Fr. II.

Days and the Giants, The. Unsi al-Haj, tr. fr. Arabic by Abdullah al-Udhari. MPAW

Days are cold, the nights are long, The. The Cottager to Her Infant. Dorothy Wordsworth. CH; OxBChV; TTTS

Days are sad, it is the holy tide, The. The Holy Tide. Frederick Tennyson. OBEV

Days are short, The. January. John Updike. PDV; RHPC

Days Clinging to the City, The. Alfredo Giuliani, tr. fr. Italian by Lawrence R. Smith. NItP

Days Count Again, The. Alfred Gesswein, tr. fr. German by Beth Bjorklund. CoAuP

Days dawn on us that make amends for many. The Interpreters. Swinburne. PoEL-5

Days Drawing In. Edith Jay Scovell. CN

Day's End. Lesbia Harford. PoAu-1

Days fail: night broods over afternoon, The. Edith Jay Scovell. Fr. The First Year. FaBoWP
(Days Drawing In.) CN

Days Gone By, The. James Whitcomb Riley. OBCA

Days grow and the stars cross over, The. Darkness Music. Muriel Rukeyser. BoWoP

Days grow shorter, the nights grow longer, The. Ella Wheeler Wilcox. BLPA; FPL

Day's grown old, the fainting sun, The. Evening. Charles Cotton. PoEL-3; WiR
(Evening Quatrains.) ChTr
(Summer Evening.) TrGrPo

Days have kept on coming, The. Daddy. Lucille Clifton. NIP

Days in White. Ingeborg Bachmann, tr. fr. German. BoWoP, tr. by Daniel Huws; CoAuP, tr. by Beth Bjorklund

Days I've got. Unknown, tr. by Burton Watson. FCEI

Days like this, off Jake's, the August fog. Jake's Wharf. Philip Booth. NYBP

Day's March, The. Robert Nichols. MMA

Day's not enough for my idle meandering, The. Perets Markish, tr. by Leonard Wolf. PeBMYV

Days of 1896. Constantine P. Cavafy, tr. fr. Greek by Edmund Keeley and Philip Sherrard. PeHV

Days of 'Forty-nine, The. Unknown. PAH

Days of misfortune pass and are gone. Unknown, tr. by Geoffrey Dunlop. OBD

Days of My Youth. St. George Tucker. AA

Days of 1956. Robin Magowan. EAS

Days of 1941 and '44. James Merrill. GLP

Days of 1978. Gerald Stern. CAPP

Days of 1964. James Merrill. CoAP; HCAP; NAAL-2; PoE

Days of Our Youth, The. Unknown, tr. fr. Arabic by Wilfrid Scawen Blunt. AWP

Days of Rain; the Rivers Have Overflowed. Su Tung-p'o, tr. fr. Chinese by Burton Watson. CoBCP

Days of Sarah, The. Benyamin Galai, tr. fr. Hebrew by Bernhard Frank. MHeP

Days of spring are here, The! the eglantine. Hafiz, tr. fr. Persian by Gertrude Lowthian Bell. Fr. Odes, X. AWP

Days of the Unicorns, The. Phyllis Webb. NOBC

Days pass easy over these ancient hills. We Are a People. Lance Henson. VoR

Days Pass: Men Pass. Stephen Vincent Benét. AnAmPo

Days shorten, the south blows wide for showers now, The. Salmon-fishing. Robinson Jeffers. ASP; SD

Day's sweetest moments are at dawn. Dawn. Ella Wheeler Wilcox. PWR

Days That Have Been. W. H. Davies. FaBoPP

Days, the Months, the Years, The. Diego Valeri, tr. fr. Italian by Michael Palma. PFI

Days through Starch and Bluing. Alice Fulton. GOYP

Day's too beautiful, The. First Love. Robert Polito. PPR

Days Too Short. W. H. Davies. MoBrPo

Days went by, The. I took up the old days. Tuscan Life. Elizabeth Barrett Browning. Fr. Aurora Leigh, VII. FaBoPP

Days Were Great as Lakes. David Vogel, tr. fr. Hebrew by A. C. Jacobs. VWA

Days when fir trees reared and shook. Kate and I. Susan Navarre Tarrant. TDD

Day's Work a-Done. William Barnes. SaC

Dayseye hugging the earth, The. Daisy. William Carlos Williams. MoAB; MoAmPo

Dayspring. Luis G. Urbina, tr. fr. Spanish by Samuel Beckett. MexPo

Daytime. Outside. Closeup. Not Allowed to Make a Movie in This Country. David Avidan, tr. fr. Hebrew by Warren Bargad and Stanley F. Chyet. Fr. Traveling in the City, 18. IP

Dazzle. Dorothy Roberts. NOBC

Dazzle on the sea, my darling, The. Leaving Barra. Louis MacNeice. EBEV

Dazzled. Arthur Sze. BrSi

Dazzled blood, The. Faustus Triumphant. Thom Gunn. FaBoMo

Dazzled [or Dazel'd] thus with height of place. Upon the Sudden Restraint of the Earl[e] of Somerset, Then Falling from Favor [or Favour]. Sir Henry Wotton. ELP; JCP; MePo; NOBE; NoP; OBS; SeCP

De Aegypto. Ezra Pound. VGW

De Ambiente. Tatiana de la Tierra. GLP

De Amore. Ernest Dowson. OBNC
"Lord over life and all the ways of breath," sel. TrPWD

De Black Girl. Unknown. GBP

De Blues Ain' Nothin'. Unknown. AS

De Civitate Hominum. Thomas MacGreevy. CIP

De Coenatione Micae. Martial, tr. fr. Latin by Robert Louis Stevenson. FaBoCh

De Consolatione Philosophiae. Boethius. See Consolation of Philosophy, The.

De Consulatu Stilichonis, sel. Claudian, tr. fr. Latin by Osbern Bokenham.
Rome Araieth Stilico in Vesture of the Consul. OxBLMV

De Contemptu Mundi, sels. Bernard of Cluny, tr. fr. Latin by John Mason Neale.
Jerusalem the Golden. WGRP, shorter sel..
"Scarcely believe things shameful to utter which yet I shall speak of." PeHV

De Cultu Virginis. Nanni Balestrini, tr. fr. Italian by Lawrence R. Smith. NItP

De Cunjah Man. James Edwin Campbell. BANP

De Day befo' Thanksgibin.' Maggie Pogue Johnson. CBWP-4

De Dheepfol.' Sarah Pratt McLean Greene. AA

De Guiana, Carmen Epicum. George Chapman. OBSC

De Gustibus, sel. Robert Browning. InPS
"What I love best in all the world." OBTV
(Italy of the South.) FaBoPP

De Gustibus. St. John Emile Clavering Hankin. CenHV

De Imagine Mundi. John Ashbery. FaBoMo

De massa ob de sheepfol.' Sheepfol', De. Sarah Pratt McLean Greene. AA

De Morte. Sir Henry Wotton. OBS; OxBSP

De Naevo in Facie Faustinae. Thomas Bastard. FaBoEE

De Ole Sheep Dey Know de Road. Unknown. BPo

De Ponto, sels. Ovid, tr. fr. Latin by Henry Vaughan. OBVE
"Shall I complain or not? Or shall I mask." Fr. Elegy IV, 3a.
"You have consum'd my language, and my pen." Fr. Elegy III, 7.

De Profundis, sel. Elizabeth Barrett Browning.
"Whatever's lost, it first was won." TrPWD

De Profundis. László Kálnoky, tr. fr. Hungarian by Edwin Morgan. MHuP

De Profundis. "Hugh MacDiarmid." SeCePo

De Profundis. Dorothy Parker. ErPo; NAAL-2

De Profundis. Bible, O.T. See Psalms: Psalm CXXX ("Out of the depths. . .").

De Profundis. Walter de la Mare. OBD

De Profundis. Amos Niven Wilder. TrPWD

De Puero Balbutiente. Thomas Bastard. See Methinks 'Tis Pretty Sport [to Hear a Child].

De Regimine Principum, sels. Thomas Hoccleve.
Hoccleve Meets an Old Beggar. OxBLMV
Lament for Chaucer. OxBLMV
"O maister deere and fader reverent!" EBEV
To Chaucer. ACP

De Rerum Natura. Andrei Codrescu. UL

De Rerum Natura (On the Nature of Things), sels. Lucretius, tr. fr. Latin.
Address to Venus. Fr. The Faerie Queene, IV, 10, tr. by Spenser. AWP
(Prayer to Venus.) ElL, tr. by Spenser.
Against the Fear of Death. Fr. III, tr. by Rolfe Humphries. DL, abr..
("Ah Wretch! thou cry'st, ah! miserable me.") AWP, tr. by Dryden; FaBoRV, tr. by Dryden; OAEL-1, tr. by Dryden; OBVE, tr. by Dryden.
"Child is like a sailor cast up by the sea, The." Tr. by C. H. Sisson. NAs
Concerning the Nature of Love. Fr. IV, tr. by Dryden. ErPo
"Delight of humane kind, and gods above." Fr. I, tr. by Dryden. OBVE
No Single Thing Abides. Tr. by W. H. Mallock. AWP; ImOP, abr.
"Now since the members of the world we view." Fr. I, tr. by Thomas Creech. OBVE
Suave Mari Magno. Fr. II, tr. by W. H. Mallock. AWP
What Has This Bugbear Death. Fr. III, tr. by Dryden. CTC; OBD

De Roberval, sels. John Hunter-Duvar.
"Here, then, we stand, on the Canadian shore." CaP
La Belle Sauvage. OBCV

De Sade. John Fuller. NBLV

De Se. John Weever. FaBoEE

De Tea Fabula. Sir Arthur Quiller-Couch. CenHV

De Titanic. Unknown. AS

Deacon Brown's Conclusion. George Sands Johnson. PWR

Deacon Morgan. Naomi Long Madgett. BlSi

Deacon's Masterpiece, The; or, The Wonderful "One-Hoss Shay." Oliver Wendell Holmes. Fr. The Autocrat of the Breakfast Table, ch. 11. AmPP; BeLS; FaBoBe; FaFP; FPL; LiTA; MoShBr; NOBA; OBAL; OBCA; OHFP; OxBA; PoLF; PoRA; TAP; WBLP
(Wonderful "One-Hoss Shay," The.) BeLS; FaBoBe

Deacon's wife was a bit desirish, The. Pride of Ancestry. Robert Frost. OBAL

Dead, The. Mathilde Blind. WGRP

Dead, The ("Blow out, you bugles, over the rich dead!"). Rupert Brooke. Fr. 1914, III. WGRP

Dead, The ("These hearts were woven"). Rupert Brooke. *Fr.* 1914, IV. BrPo; CH; LiTB; MMA; PoA

Dead, The. C. Day Lewis. TwCP

Dead, The. Louis Dudek. NOBC

Dead, The. Charles Heavysege. *See* How Great unto the Living Seem the Dead!

Dead. Lionel Johnson. BrPo; OBNC; PoEL-5

Dead, The. Gloria A. Maxson. *Fr.* Two Guitars. TSM

Dead, The. David Morton. PAH

Dead, The. Salvatore Quasimodo, *tr. fr. Italian by* Jack Bevan. PFI

Dead, The. A. J. M. Smith. NOBC

Dead, The. Mark Strand. HeIP

Dead, The. Jones Very. AA; AnAmPo; HAP; NOBA; OxBA; TAP

Dead, The. Jay Wright. FB

Dead abide with us, The! Though stark and cold. The Dead. Mathilde Blind. WGRP

Dead and the Living One, The. Thomas Hardy. MMA

Dead are a cadmium blue, The. Charles Wright. *Fr.* Homage to Paul Cézanne. HCAP

Dead at Clonmacnois [*or* Clonmacnoise], The. Angus O'Gillan, *tr. fr. Irish by* Thomas William Rolleston. AnIL; FaBoPP; OBEV; OBMV

Dead Baby, The. William Carlos Williams. NAAL-2

Dead beast, turned up, The. The Well-travelled Roadway. John Newlove. NeAC

Dead before Death. Christina Rossetti. NAEL-2

Dead Bird. David R. Slavitt. BXAP

Dead Bird, The. Andrew Young. FM

Dead Birds. Rutger Kopland, *tr. fr. Dutch by* Ria Leigh-Loohuizen. DuIn

Dead birds fell, but no one had seen them fly, The. Some Dreams They Forgot. Elizabeth Bishop. NoAM

Dead Boy. John Crowe Ransom. CMoP; FaBoMo; LiTA; Mes; NoAM; NoP; OBD; OxBA; PoE; TwCP

Dead boy living among men as a man, A. A Head. James Schuyler. PoM

Dead Bride, The. Geoffrey Hill. TW

Dead Brother, The. *Unknown.* EnSB

Dead Butterfly, The. Denise Levertov. NoP

Dead by the Side of the Road, The. Gary Snyder. HAP; InPS

Dead Center. Chester Kallman. PoA

Dead Center. Ruth Whitman. NYBP

Dead Child, The. Ernest Dowson. BrPo

Dead Cities Speak to the Living Cities, The. Edmond Fleg, *tr. fr. French by* Anthony Rudolf. VWA

Dead city walls may pen us in, but still. Charles Harpur. *Fr.* A Coast View. CBAP

Dead Cleopatra lies in a crystal casket. Conrad Aiken. *Fr.* Discordants, IV. PoA

Dead Color. Charles Wright. HCAP; LCAP

Dead Conquerors, The. Antonio Cisneros, *tr. fr. Spanish by* David Tipton. Per

Dead Cow Farm. Robert Graves. BrPo

Dead Crab, The. Andrew Young. FaBoTw; FM; OBD; RB

Dead dandelions, bald as drumsticks. Dandelions. Craig Raine. NoAM

Dead! dead! the Child I lov'd so well! On the Death of His Son. Charles Wesley. NOCV

Dead Dog. Vernon Scannell. OxBC

Dead Eagle, The. Thomas Campbell. EnRP; OBTV

Dead Embryos. Judit Tóth, *tr. fr. Hungarian by* Laura Schiff. MHuP; WPOW

Dead Faith, The. Fanny Heaslip Lea. WGRP

Dead Feast of the Kol-Folk, The. Whittier. PoEL-4

Dead Fiddle, The. Humbert Wolfe. TrJP

Dead Fires. Jessie Redmond Fauset. BANP; PoNe

Dead Fly. Eiléan Ní Chuilleanáin. CIP

Dead fly husk. Ishida Hakyo, *tr. by* Geoffrey Bownas *and* Anthony Thwaite. PeBJV

Dead Gentile women in greatcoats. Itsik Fefer, *tr. by* Leonard Wolf. PeBMYV

Dead, gently he lies on the flowers of the coffin. Improvisation of the Dead Boy. Mário de Andrade, *tr. by* Richard Eberhart. ATCBP

Dead Girl. Anna Hajnal, *tr. fr. Hungarian by* Jascha Kessler. *Fr.* Images. FOC; VWA

Dead Hand. W. S. Merwin. CAPP; InPK

Dead hangs the fruit on that tall tree. Burial of the Spirit of a Young Poet. Richard Hughes. MoBrPo

Dead have remembered, the. Posthumous Rehabilitation. Tadeusz Rozewicz, *tr. by* Adam Czerniawski. FaBoPV

Dead heat rises for weeks, The. In the Middle of August. Edward Hirsch. MAYP

Dead here look upon the light from caves, The. Girod Street Cemetery: New Orleans. Harry Morris. GoYe

Dead Heroes. Karoniaktatie. STE

Dead Heroes, The. Isaac Rosenberg. MoBrPo

Dead Horse, The. Cecília Meireles, *tr. fr. Portuguese by* James Merrill. ATCBP; PBWP

Dead Horse, The. *Unknown.* AS

Dead Host's Welcome, The. John Fletcher. *Fr.* The Lover's Progress, III, i. TrGrPo

Dead in Europe, The. Robert Lowell. LiTM; NePoEA; OxBA; OxBC

Dead in Queens lean westward from their stones, The. A Day in the City. L. E. Sissman. NYBP

Dead in the cold, a song-singing thrush. Last Rites. Christina Rossetti. OxBChV; RHPC

Dead in the Sierras. Joaquin Miller. AA

Dead in via, The. La Préface. Charles Olson. PoM

Dead in Wars and in Revolutions. Mary Devenport O'Neill. NeIP

Dead is Columba: the world's arch. Saint Columba. Lionel Johnson. TIRV

Dead! Is it possible? He, the bold rider. Custer's Last Charge. Frederick Whittaker. OnMSP; PAH; PoLF

Dead is the roll of the drums. Abraham Lincoln. Henry Howard Brownell. GN

Dead Jews, dead Jews, just points now an underground. Dime Call. Albert Goldbarth. VWA

Dead Knight, The. John Masefield. CH; GTBS-P

Dead Lamb, A. Allen Curnow. ATNZ

Dead Leaf, A. Howard Moss. NYBP

Dead leaves, one-time fair, The. A Word to the West End. Thomas Ashe. EBVV

Dead lemon like a cowled old woman crouching in the cold, A. For *Under the Volcano.* Malcolm Lowry. NOBC

Dead Liebknecht, The. "Hugh MacDiarmid," *after the German of* Rudolf Leonhard. FaBoPV; OBVE

Dead, long dead. Tennyson. *Fr.* Maud, *pt.* II, v. OAEL-2

Dead Love. Mary Mathews Adams. AA

Dead Love. Elizabeth Siddal. NOBVV

Dead man, A/ who never caused others to die. W. H. Auden. *Fr.* Marginalia. OAEL-2

Dead man answered me, The. Chang Heng, *tr. fr. Chinese by* Arthur Waley. *Fr.* The Bones of Chuang Tzu. OBD

Dead Man Ariseth and Singeth a Hymn to the Sun, The. *Unknown, tr. fr. Egyptian by* Robert Hillyer. *Fr.* Book of the Dead. AWP

Dead Man Dragged from the Sea, The. Carl Gardner. PoBA

Dead Man's Dump ("Plunging limbers over the shattered track, The."), *sel.* Isaac Rosenberg. BrPo; FaBoMo; GTBS-P; LiTM; MMA; NAEL-2; NoAM; NoP; OBWP; TrJP; VWA; WaP

"None saw their spirits' shadow shake the grass." OBD

Dead man's mother is buying flowers, The. Chronicle. Alfonso Quijada Urías, *tr. by* Barbara Paschke. VoI

Dead Man's Song, Dreamed by One Who Is Alive. Paulinaoq, *tr. fr. Eskimo.* WTO

Dead Marine. Louis O. Coxe. WaP

Dead Marten, The. Walter Savage Landor. FM

Dead Men, The. Sophia de Mello Breyner Andresen, *tr. fr. Portuguese by* Allan Francovich. PBWP

Dead men are wisest, for they know. The Wise. Countee Cullen. PoNe

Dead men of 'ninety-two, also of 'ninety-three. Rimbaud, *tr. by* Norman Cameron. WaaP

Dead Mole, A. Andrew Young. FM; GTBS-P; OxBSP

Dead Moon, The. Danske Bedinger Dandridge. AA

Dead Musicians. Siegfried Sassoon. BrPo

Dead of My Songs, The. István Agh, *tr. fr. Hungarian by* Alan Dixon. MHuP

Dead of the Wilderness, The. Hayyim Nahman Bialik, *tr. fr. Hebrew by* Maurice Samuel. AWP

Dead of Winter. Anthony Towne. NYBP

Dead of winter: crows are black. Buson, *tr. fr. Japanese by* Hiroaki Sato. *Fr.* Eighty-seven Hokku. FCEI

Dead on the War Path. *Unknown, tr. fr. Tewa Indian by* H. J. Spinden. OBD; WTO

Dead! One of them shot by the sea in the east. Mother and Poet. Elizabeth Barrett Browning. NAEL-2

Dead Past, A. *at. to.* C. C. Munson. BLRP; WBLP

Dead people come to visit tonight. Elegies for Prince Atsumichi ("Dead people come to visit tonight"). Lady Izumi, *tr. fr. Japanese by* Hiroaki Sato. *Fr.* Fifty-one Tanka. FCEI

Dead Pig, The. *Unknown.* FaBoNo

Dead Player, The. Burns. AA

Dead Poet, The. Lord Alfred Bruce Douglas. PeHV

Dead Poet, The. Alfred W. Purdy. NOBC

Dead Poet in the Mountains. Michael Guttenbrunner, *tr. fr. German by* Beth Bjorklund. CoAuP

Dead poets stalk the air. Rainy Night at the Writers' Colony. Josephine Jacobsen. TAP

Dead Ponies. Brenda Chamberlain. OBWVE; WPE

Dead President, The. Edward Rowland Sill. PAH

Dead scents I couldn't bear bore. Year of the Bird. Brian Swann. AmPA

Dead Sea, The. Henryk Grynberg, *tr. fr. Polish* by Isaac Komem. VWA

Dead Sea Scrolls, The, *sels. Unknown, tr.fr. Hebrew.* TrJP
Blessed Art Thou, O Lord. *Tr.* by Theodor H. Gaster.
Lo, I Am Stricken Dumb. *Tr.* by Theodor H. Gaster.
My Soul in the Bundle of Life. *Tr.* by E. Margaret Rowley, *fr. the French vers..*
Though Mine Eye Sleep Not. *Tr.* by Theodor H. Gaster.

Dead Seal. Alfred W. Purdy. MoCV; MoP

Dead Seal near McClure's Beach, The. Robert Bly. NNaP; NU

Dead Shall Be Raised Incorruptible, The. Galway Kinnell. NOBA; PoE
In the Twentieth Century of My Trespass on Earth, *sel.* TW

Dead shall rise again, The. The Raising of Lazarus. Lucille Clifton. CNA

Dead shalt thou lie; and nought. Achtung. Sappho, *tr.* by Thomas Hardy. CTC; OBVE

Dead sheep/ beside the highway. Preparations. Leslie Marmon Silko. VoR

Dead Sheep, The. Andrew Young. FM

Dead Singer, The. Mary Ashley Townsend. AA

Dead Sister, The. Caroline Gilman. OBCA

Dead Skunk. Richard Eberhart. BLA

Dead smell the rain gives, The. Cut Lilac. Tony Beyer. ATNZ

Dead Soldier. Nicolás Guillén, *tr. fr. Spanish* by Langston Hughes. TTY

Dead Soldier, A. George Edgar Montgomery. AA

Dead Soldiers. James Fenton. NoAM; OBTV; OBWP

Dead Solomon, The. John Aylmer Dorgan. AA

Dead Sparrow, The. William Cartwright. CH

Dead squid, A. Masaoka Shiki, *tr. fr. Japanese* by Burton Watson. *Fr.* Thirty-nine Haiku. FCEI

Dead stare out of empty sockets, The. The Dead. A. J. M. Smith. NOBC

Dead Statesman, A. Kipling. *Fr.* Epitaphs of the War, 1914–1918. FaBoEE; NBLV

Dead Still. Andrei Voznesensky, *tr. fr. Russian* by Richard Wilbur. BoLoP

Dead Tribune, The. Denis Florence MacCarthy. ACP

Dead Waters. Manuel Gutiérrez Nájera, *tr. fr. Spanish* by Samuel Beckett. MexPo

Dead Weasel, A. David Helwig. NOBC

Dead "Wessex" the Dog to the Household. Thomas Hardy. FM

Dead Witness, The. Buland al-Haidari, *tr. fr. Arabic.* MAP, *tr. by* Patricia Alanah Byrne *and* Salma Khadra Jayyusi; MPAW, *tr. by* Abdullah al-Udhari

Dead woman lay in her first night's grave, The. The Dead and the Living One. Thomas Hardy. MMA

Dead Words, The. Vernon Watkins. LiTM

Dead young man stood up in his grave, The. Articles of War. Dunstan Thompson. WaP

Deader they die here, or at least. Fall Comes in Back-Country Vermont. Robert Penn Warren. NYBP; VGW

Deadfall. Martha Keller. GoYe

Deadly Dance, The. *Unknown, tr. fr. Aztec Indian* by Edward Kissam. STP

Deadly Kisses. Pierre de Ronsard, *tr. fr. French* by Andrew Lang. AWP

Deadly Weapon. Beatrix Gates. GLP

Deadman's Dirge. George Darley. *See* Syren Songs: Sea-Ritual, The.

Dead's right grain, The. The Future and the Ancestor. Andrée Chedid, *tr. by* Samuel Hazo *and* Mirène Ghossein. WPOW

Deadsong. Don Domanski. NOBC

Deaf. H. C. Bunner. AA

Deaf. Barry O. Higgs. PeSA

Deaf and Blind, The. Paul Éluard, *tr. fr. French* by Paul Auster. RHTwFP

Deaf-and-Dumb School. Anthony Delius. PeSA

Deaf children were monkey-nimble, fish-tremulous and sudden, The. Deaf School. Ted Hughes. NoP

Deaf, giddy, helpless, left alone. On His Own Deafness. Swift. BIrV; FaBoEE

Deaf is like. Deaf. Barry O. Higgs. PeSA

Deaf-Mute in the Pear Tree. P. K. Page. NoAM; PoE

Deaf School. Ted Hughes. NoP

Deaf to God, who calls and walks. Doomsday Morning. Genevieve Taggard. MoAmPo

Deaf to the bustle of the street, soporifically. The Jewish Cemetery. César Tiempo, *tr.* by Angela McEvan-Alvarado. VWA

Deafening noise! Tachibana Akemi, *tr. fr. Japanese* by Burton Watson. *Fr.* Thirty Tanka. FCEI

Deafening tic-tic-tic of the clock, The. Loneliness. Loyal Shegonee. NOVW

Deafness. Richard Ryan. BIrV

Deal table where he wrote, so small and plain, The. The Birthplace. Seamus Heaney. FaBCIP

Dealer, bewitched by gain-promising dreams, A. Bush Justice. Charles Harpur. CBAP

Dean and prebendary, A. The Battle Royal between Dr. Sherlock, Dr. South, and Dr. Burnet. William Pittis. APAS

Dean-bourn, a Rude River in Devon, by Which Sometimes He Lived ("Dean-bourn, farewell; I never look to see"). Robert Herrick. SeCV-1

(To Dean-bourn, a Rude River in Devon, by which Sometimes He Lived.) CaPo; FaBoPP

Dean Inge. Humbert Wolfe. FaBoEE

(On Dean Inge.) ChTr

Dean of Paul's did search for his wife, The. Fragment of a Song on the Beautiful Wife of Dr. John Overall. *Unknown.* BoLoP

Dear/ Diana. Andy-Diana DNA Letter. Andrew Weiman. HAP

Dear——/ Hi, you can be in my new poem, if you're a Yankees fan. The History of the Human Body// Winfield's Infield Hit// The Lassitude of the Infinite. Elinor Nauen. UL

Dear Alice! you'll laugh when you know it. The Talented Man. Winthrop Mackworth Praed. EnRP; FiBHP; NOBL

Dear Ann, wherever you are. For Ann Scott-Moncrieff. Edwin Muir. GTBS-P

Dear architect of fine *Chateaux en l'air.* To William Hayley, Esq.: In Reply to His Solicitation to Write with Him in a Literary Work. William Cowper. Son

Dear as the Moon. *Gond Oral Tradition, tr.* by V. Elwin *and* S. Hivale. WTO

Dear Auntie/ Oh, what a nice jumper. Christmas Thank You's. Mick Gowar. OBCP

Dear, back my wounded heart restore. The Divorce. Thomas Stanley. MeLP

Dear, beauteous death! the jewel of the just. Henry Vaughan. *Fr.* Ascension Hymn. OBD

Dear Bill,/ When I search the past for you. A Letter to William Carlos Williams. Kenneth Rexroth. NNaP

Dear Black Head. *Unknown, tr.* by Sir Samuel Ferguson. BIrV
(Cean Dubh Deelish.) GBL; SeCePo

Dear Bob. Spring Training. Robert Polito. PPR

Dear Body. Janine Canan. UL

Dear Boy, What a superlative day for a funeral. Micheál Mac Liammóir. Paul Durcan. FaBCIP

Dear boy, you will not hear me speak. Pangloss's Song [A Comic-Opera Lyric]. Richard Wilbur. MoP; NBLV; NoAM

Dear Brethren, Are Your Harps in Tune? Eunice Smith. AH

Dear Brook, farewell! To-morrow's noon again. Wordsworth. *Fr.* An Evening Walk. EnRP

Dear brother, would you know the line. A Letter. Emerson. OxBA

Dear cell, the Martian winter ends. Love Letter from Mars. John Ciardi. BWV

Dear child, first-born, what I could give outright. Hand-Shadows. Jarold Ramsey. NIP

Dear child, my daughter, who stood. Lady Otomo no Sakanoe, *tr. fr. Japanese. Fr.* Manyo Shu. Ma

Dear child of nature, let them rail! To a Young Lady. Wordsworth. EnRP

Dear child, these words which briefly I declare. The Maiden's Best Adorning. *Unknown.* OxBChV

Dear Child Whom I Begot. J. V. Cunningham. NAs

"Dear children," they asked in every town. The Wise Men Ask the Children the Way. Heine, *tr.* by Geoffrey Grigson. OBCP
(Kings from the East, The.) ChTr

Dear Cleo, I can't complain about your absence. To the Muse. Philip Whalen. PoM

Dear Clive, I've meant to scribble you a letter. Letter to Myself. Christopher Reid. FaBoPa

Dear Cloe [*or* Chloe], how blubbered is that pretty face! Answer to Cloe [*or* Chloe] Jealous. Matthew Prior. NOBE; SeCePo
(Better Answer to Cloe [*or* Chloe] Jealous, A.) AWP; ELP; NAEL-1; NOEC; PoEL-3

Dear Comfort, when you come today. Through the Eye of the Needle. Mani Leib, *tr.* by John Hollander. PeBMYV

Dear common flower, that grow'st beside the way. James Russell Lowell. *Fr.* To the Dandelion. AnAmPo; FaPON, 2 *sts.*; GN; NAAL-1

Dear Craoibhin Aoibhin, look into our case.   At The Abbey Theatre (Imitated from Ronsard).   W. B. Yeats.   Son

Dear critic, who my lightness so deplores.   To a Captious Critic.   Paul Laurence Dunbar.   BPo

Dear Cynthia, though thou bear'st the name.   To Cynthia. On Her Changing.   Sir Francis Kynaston.   MePo

Dear Dave: Rain five days and I love it.   Letter to Wagoner from Port Townsend.   Richard Hugo.   NNaP

Dear, dear, dear.   The Thrush's Song.   Unknown, tr. by William MacGillivray.   CH

Dear Denise: Long way from, long time since Boulder.   Letter to Levertov from Butte.   Richard Hugo.   NNaP

Dear Dennice: I'm this close but the pass is tough this year.   Letter to Scanlon from Whitehall.   Richard Hugo.   NNaP

Dear doll.   The Doll.   Margarete Beutler, tr. by Susan L. Cocalis and Gerlinde Geiger.   DMG

Dear Dolly, stay thy scampering joints one minute.   Ode to a Country Hoyden.   "Peter Pindar."   NOEC

Dear Dove, that bear'st to my sole-laboring ark.   Ad Amicam.   Francis Thompson.   Son

Dear Emily, my tears would burn your page.   To Emily Dickinson.   Yvor Winters.   Son

Dear Eustatio, I write that you may write me an answer.   Arthur Hugh Clough.   Fr. Amours de Voyage, Canto I, i.   EBVV; OBTV

Dear, farewell, a little while.   Anacreontic, on Parting with a Little Child.   Samuel Wesley.   NOEC

Dear Father/ hear and bless.   Margaret Wise Brown.   PDV

Dear father and dear mother: Let me crave.   Erotion.   Martial, tr. by Kirby Flower Smith.   AWP

Dear Father Christmas.   Russell Davies.   FaBoPa

Dear Father (heavenly).   I Look at Your Land.   Aila Meriluoto, tr. by Aili Jarvenpa.   SOP

Dear father I slept like a lion and then when the innocent sun had searched me.   Letter from the Mountain Sanitarium.   Alfredo Giuliani, tr. by Lawrence R. Smith.   NItP

Dear Father, Look Up.   "Orpheus C. Kerr."   OBAL

Dear father, mother, sister, come listen while I tell.   The Ashland Tragedy.   Elijah Adams.   AmFP

"Dear Father, tell me, Why are worms?"   Why?   Walter de la Mare.   FiBHP

Dear fellow-artist, why so free.   To a Young Beauty.   W. B. Yeats.   CMoP

Dear fellow castaway, the cruise ships.   Weathering the Depths.   Al Lee.   AmPA

Dear Female Heart.   Stevie Smith.   FaBoEE

Dear Fergusson—They've Ramsay's statue clean.   Letter to Robert Fergusson.   Alexander Scott.   OxBS

Dear Folks.   Patrick Kavanagh.   FaBoTw

Dear Frank, with fancy, fire and style.   Upon an Ingenious Friend, Over-Vain.   Thomas Fitzgerald.   OxBSP

Dear Friend,/ I hear this town does so abound.   An Epistolary Essay from M. G. to O. B. upon Their Mutual Poems.   John Wilmot, 2nd Earl of Rochester.   APAS

Dear friend! Believe me, Love's not always blind.   Love Has Eyes.   William Forster.   CBAP

Dear friend, I fear my heart will break.   Out of French.   Sir Charles Sedley.   FaBoEE

Dear Friend, since you have chosen to associate.   Tennyson's Poems.   Josephine D. Henderson Heard.   CBWP-4

Dear [or Deare] friend, sit down: the tale is long and sad.   Love Unknown.   George Herbert.   JCP; Prf

Dear friend, the here-there emphasis is made.   Letter.   Janet Frame.   PeNZ

Dear Friend, Whose Presence in the House.   James Freeman Clarke.   AH

Dear Friends/ Winter has come here.   A Letter.   Jenny Joseph.   NPo

Dear friends, let your disease be what God will.   Saffold's Cures.   At. to Thomas Saffold.   FaBoUs

Dear friends, we are gathered together.   A Tribute to the Bride and Groom.   Priscilla Jane Thompson.   CBWP-2

Dear Fronto, famed alike in peace and war.   Country Pleasures.   Martial, tr. by F. A. Wright.   AWP

Dear galway/ it is flooding here, in missouri.   A Poem to Galway Kinnell.   Etheridge Knight.   NNaP

Dear gentle soul, who went so soon away.   Luis de Camões, tr. by Roy Campbell.   BoLoP

Dear George,/ At last the blowfly's buzz retreats.   Letter to a Friend.   John Thompson.   PoAu-2

Dear Gill I ne'er thought till last night.   The New Married Couple; or, A Friendly Debate between the Country Farmer and His Buxome Wife.   Unknown.   CoMu

Dear God,/ give us a flood of water.   The Prayer of the Little Ducks.   Carmen Bernos de Gasztold.   PDV

Dear God, I humbly pray.   Prayer of a Beginning Teacher.   Ouida Smith Dunnam.   TrPWD

Dear God our Father, at Thy knee confessing.   For Deeper Life.   Katharine Lee Bates.   TrPWD

Dear Godmother, —Another year, time for the rendezvous.   Queen Charming.   Pamela White Hadas.   BLA

Dear gods, set me free from all the pain.   Agamemnon.   Aeschylus, tr. by Robert Fagles.   NAWM-1, complete

Dear Grandmamma, with what we give.   Grandmamma's Birthday.   Hilaire Belloc.   FiBHP

Dear, had the world in its caprice.   Respectability.   Robert Browning.   EnLoPo

Dear Happy Souls.   Eunice Smith.   AH

Dear Harp of My Country.   Thomas Moore.   AnIL; EnRP; NOIV

Dear Harriet.   Naked Poetry.   Peter Cooley.   SM

Dear heart, I shall not altogether die.   Non Omnis Moriar.   Manuel Gutiérrez Nájera, tr. by Samuel Beckett.   MexPo

Dear, heavn-designing soul!   To a Young Gentle-Woman, Councel Concerning Her Choice.   Richard Crashaw.   OBS

Dear hope! Earth's dowry and heaven's debt!   For Hope.   Richard Crashaw.   LiTB
(Answer for Hope.)   MeLP
(M. Crashaw's Answer for Hope.)   OBS; SeCV-1
(On Hope.)   MePo; NOBE

Dear Horace! be melted to tears.   Epistle, from Algiers, to Horace Smith.   Thomas Campbell.   OBTV

Dear, I must be gone.   Parting.   W. B. Yeats.   FaBoTw

Dear, if unsocial privacies obsess me.   J. V. Cunningham.   VGW

Dear, If You Change.   Unknown.   ElL; EnLoPo; InvP; OBSC
(Deare, If You Change.)   PoEL-2

Dear, if you love me, hold me most your friend.   Alice Duer Miller.   AA

Dear———, I'll gie ye some advice.   To an Artist.   Burns.   EyDe

Dear J. D.: One should think of Chief Joseph here.   Letter to Reed from Lolo.   Richard Hugo.   NNaP

Dear Jim: This is as far as I ever chased a girl.   Letter to Welch from Browning.   Richard Hugo.   NNaP

Dear John.   Lindsay MacRae.   DT

Dear John, Dear Coltrane.   Michael S. S. Harper.   AmPA; GeTw; NIP

Dear John: This is a Dear John letter from booze.   Letter to Logan from Milltown.   Richard Hugo.   NNaP

Dear John, whoever now takes pen to write.   James McAuley.   Fr. A Letter to John Dryden.   CBAP

Dear Jonno.   A Trip on the Staten Island Ferry.   Audre Lorde.   CNA

Dear kindly Sergeant Krupke.   Gee, Officer Krupke.   Stephen Sondheim.   OBAL

Dear Knight, how great a drudge is he.   Hudibras and Milton Reconciled.   William Somervile.   NOEC

Dear Kong.   Fay Wray to the King.   Judith Rechter.   NMM

Dear Land of All My Love.   Sidney Lanier.   Fr. The Centennial Meditation of Columbia.   GN

Dear Land of Hope, thy hope is crowned.   Land of Hope and Glory.   Arthur Christopher Benson.   FaPoR

Dear Lela is my joy and crown.   Lela's Charms.   L. A. J. Moorer.   CBWP-3

Dear letters, fond letters.   Love Letters.   Josephine D. Henderson Heard.   CBWP-4

Dear little bog-face.   Bog-Face.   Stevie Smith.   RB

Dear little Dorothy, she is no more.   Dorothy.   Rose Hawthorne Lathrop.   AA

Dear little Mosca.   Xenia.   Eugenio Montale, tr. by G. Singh.   OBD

Dear little tree that we plant to-day.   An Arbor Day Tree.   Unknown.   OHIP

Dear Lizbie Browne.   To Lizbie Browne.   Thomas Hardy.   ELP; NOBVV

Dear Lord! accept a sinful heart.   Self-Acquaintance.   William Cowper.   NOCV

Dear Lord and Father of Mankind.   Whittier.   Fr. The Brewing of Soma.   AH, with music; NOCV; TrPWD

Dear Lord, Behold Thy Servants.   Hosea Ballou I.   AH

Dear Lord, I do not hesitate.   A Business Man's Prayer.   William Ludlum.   BLRP

Dear Lord! Kind Lord!   Love's Prayer.   James Whitcomb Riley.   AA

Dear Lord, receive my son, whose winning love.   Of His Dear Son, Gervase.   Sir John Beaumont.   Fr. Of My Dear Son, Gervase Beaumont.   OBEV

Dear Lord, thy table is outspread.   The Master's Invitation.   Anson Davies Fitz Randolph.   AA

Dear Lord, Whose serving-maiden.   Josephine Preston Peabody.   TrPWD

Dear Lord's best interpreters, The.   In Earthen Vessels.   Whittier.   BLRP

Dear lords of life, stump-toothed, with ragged breath.   Geoffrey Hill.   Fr. The Mystery of the Charity of Charles Péguy.   DiPo

"Dear love, dost thou sleep fairly?"   Parting at Morning.   Dietmar von Aist, tr. by Frank C. Nicholson.   AWP

Dear [or Deare] love, for nothing less[e] than thee. The Dream[e]. John Donne. EIL; InvP; LiTB; MeLP; MePo; OAEL-1; OBEV; OBS; SeCP; TOF

Dear love, when with a two-fold mind. Laurence Housman. *Fr.* All Fellows. WGRP

"Dear love, why should you weep." A Lost World. Robert Graves. NYBP

Dear Lucy, you know what my wish is. Horace. *See* Odes: I, 38. Simplicity.

Dear Madam, did you never gaze. On Mites; to a Lady. Stephen Duck. FM

Dear Madam, you have seen this play. At the Theater. A. P. Herbert. FiBHP

Dear Maiden. Heine, *tr. fr. German by* John Todhunter. AWP

Dear Mama. Letter. Langston Hughes. PoE

Dear Mamma, if you just could be. A Lesson for Mamma. Sydney Dayre. OBCA; OxBChV

Dear man from the city. What Her Girl Friend Said when He Sent a Flattering Minstrel on His Behalf. Orampokiyar, *tr. by* A. K. Ramanujan. PLW

Dear marshes, by no hand of man/ Laboriously sown. Flood-Time on the Marshes. Evaleen Stein. AA

Dear Martin Folkes, dear scholar, brother, friend. John Byrom. *Fr.* A Full and True Account of a Horrid and Barbarous Robbery. NOBL

Dear Marvin: Months since I left broke down and sobbing. Letter to Bell from Missoula. Richard Hugo. NNaP

Dear Mary, thou didst see thy first-born Son. Prayer to Mother Mary. Padriac Pearse. TIRV

"Dear me!" exclaimed Homer. E. C. Bentley. *Fr.* Clerihews. FiBHP

Dear me! what signifies a pin. The Pin. Ann Taylor. OxBChV

Dear Men and Women. John Hall Wheelock. NYBP; Prf

Dear Messrs. Tippins, what is feared by you. Reply to a Creditor. George Harding. FaBoUs

Dear Mickey. Dahlia Ravikovich, *tr. fr. Hebrew by* Warren Bargad *and* Stanley F. Chyet. IP

Dear Mike: We didn't have a chance. Our starter had no change. Letter to Mantsch from Havre. Richard Hugo. TSL

Dear Miss. Herman Gladwin. PeNZ

Dear Miss Dix, I am a young man of half-past thirty-seven. Two and One Are a Problem. Ogden Nash. FiBHP

Dear Miss Miller. Letter to a Substitute Teacher. Gary Gildner. Psk

Dear Mister Congressman. Bob Dylan. MAT

Dear Mistress, do not grieve for me. Leo to His Mistress. Henry Dwight Sedgwick. BLPA

"Dear Molly, why so oft in tears?" ("Quid sles, asterie"). Horace, *tr. fr. Latin. Fr.* Odes, III, 7. OBVE, *tr. by* George Stepney.

Dear Mom. Paul Zarzyski. TSL

Dear Monsters. Anna Margolin, *tr. fr. Yiddish by* Marcia Falk. PeBMYV

Dear Mother. Emmett Jarrett. NeAC

Dear Mother. Ebba M. Leaf. PWR

Dear Mother dear. Mother-land'scape (Letters). William Harmon. PPR

Dear Mother, dear Mother, the Church is cold. The Little Vagabond. Blake. *Fr.* Songs of Experience. NBLV; OBSV

Dear Mother, I attempt to write you a letter. A Letter from School. Thomas Love Peacock. FaBoUs

"Dear Mother," said a little fish. The Little Fish That Would Not Do as I Was Bid. Ann Taylor *and* Jane Taylor. OHIP

Dear mothers. That There Should Be Laughter. Innocent Banda. WMBCH

Dear Mr. Editor: I wish to say. A Grievance. James Kenneth Stephen. BXAP; FaBoPa; Par

Dear Mr. Noman, does it ever strike you. On Noman, a Guest. Hilaire Belloc. FaBoEE

Dear murdered comrades, not in vain. Tulips from Their Blood. Edwin Brooks. NBP

Dear native brook! wild streamlet of the west! Sonnet: To the River Otter. Samuel Taylor Coleridge. ChER; OAEL-2
(To the River Otter.) Son

Dear native regions, I foretell. Wordsworth. FL

Dear, near and true—no truer Time himself. Tennyson. OxBSP

Dear Night! this world's defeat. Henry Vaughan. *Fr.* The Night. TrGrPo

Dear Nona, Christmas comes from far. Christmas in Penang. John Leyden. OBTV

Dear Norman. Carol Ann Duffy. NPo

Dear object of defeated care! Lines Written beneath a Picture. Byron. OxBSP

Dear object of my love, whose manly charms. Pretty Maids Beware!!! *Unknown.* CoMu

Dear object of my love, whose pow'rful charms. Sarah Hazard's Love Letter. John Ellis. NOEC

Dear Obour/ Our crossing was without. A Letter from Phillis Wheatley. Robert Hayden. NoAM

Dear! of all happy in the hour, most blest. Safety. Rupert Brooke. *Fr.* 1914, II. BrPo; EnLoPo

Dear old equivocal and closest friend. The Author to His Body on Their Fifteenth Birthday, 29.ii.80. Howard Nemerov. NAs; NoAM

Dear old man's verse, The. *Unknown, tr. fr. Japanese. Fr.* Manyo Shu. Ma

Dear Old Stockholm. Al Young. NPGG

Dear, on a day of dumb rain. Rain. Howard Moss. ErPo

Dear one, forgive my appearing before you like this. A Victorian Hangman Tells His Love. Bruce Dawe. NoAM

Dear Paulus it's a busy trade of late. Lines Descriptive of Thomson's Island. Benjamin Lynde. SCAP

Dear Phoebus, hear my only vow. The Poetess's Bouts-Rimés. *Unknown.* NOEC

Dear Possible. Laura Riding. LiTA

Dear President, The. John James Piatt. PAH

Dear Queenie, though it breaks my heart. The Handmaid of Religion. Edgell Rickword. OBSV

Dear Reader. Peter Meinke. Psk

Dear Reader. James Tate. EAS

Dear reliques of a dislodg'd soul, whose lack. Death's Lecture at the Funeral of a Young Gentleman. Richard Crashaw. SeCP

Dear Reynolds! as last night I lay in bed. Epistle to John Hamilton Reynolds. Keats. OBNC

Dear Saint Brigid of The Kine. Invocation to Saint Bride. John Irvine. TIRV

Dear Samson,/ I put your hair. Love Letter. Carole C. Gregory. AIW; BlSi

Dear San: Everybody doesn't write poetry. Feeling and Form. Marilyn Hacker. NoAM

Dear Saviour, If These Lambs Should Stray. Abby Bradley Hyde. AH

Dear school of my childhood. Lines to an Old School-House. Priscilla Jane Thompson. CBWP-2

Dear singer. A Guide to Patrons. Alattur Killar, *tr. by* A. K. Ramanujan. PLW

Dear singer of our fathers' day. To John Greenleaf Whittier. William Hayes Ward. AA

Dear Sir—You wish to know my notions. The Candidate's Letter. James Russell Lowell. *Fr.* The Biglow Papers: 1st Series, No. VII. AA

Dear Sir, your astonishment's odd. A Reply. *Unknown.* FaBoCo; NBLV; NOBL

Dear Sirs:/ Of course I'll come. I've packed my galoshes. In Response to Executive Order 9066: All Americans of Japanese Descent Must Report to Relocation Centers. Dwight Okita. BrSi

Dear Sirs: Is it not time we formed a Boston. Communication to the City Fathers of Boston. George Starbuck. NYBP

Dear sister! Dear Ismene! How many evils. Antigone. Sophocles, *tr. by* T. H. Banks. NAWM-1, *complete*

Dear Sister, my resentment had not been. Virgil, *tr. fr. Latin by* Sir John Denham. *Fr.* The Aeneid [*or* Eneados], IV. OBVE

Dear Smith, the sleest, paukie thief. To James Smith. Burns. HoPM

Dear Son, Leave Thy Weeping. *Unknown.* CTC

Dear soul be strong! Richard Crashaw. *Fr.* On a Prayer Book Sent to Mrs. M.R. ErPo

Dear steps may die away. Room. Robert Finch. MoCV

Dear stranger, reading this small, true book. Strength to War. Stephen Stepanchev. WaP

Dear sugar, dear tea, and dear corn. The Four Dears. Ebenezer Elliott. SaC

Dear these three who have come to see me. In Praise of Three Young Men. Lochlann Og O Dalaigh. NOIV

Dear things! we would not have you learn too much. Womankind. Gerald Massey. NOBVV

Dear Thomas, didst thou never pop. A Simile. Matthew Prior. NOEC

Dear, Though the Night Is Gone. W. H. Auden. BoLoP; InvP

Dear, though to part it be a hell. To Dianeme ("Dear, though to part it be a hell"). Robert Herrick. CaPo

Dear, though your mind stand so averse. Hear Me Yet. *Unknown.* EIL

Dear to me were the three sides. The Wife of Aed mac Ainmirech, King of Ireland, Laments Her Husband. *Unknown, tr. by* Myles Dillon. AnIL

Dear to my soul! then leave me not forsaken! Henry Constable. *Fr.* Diana. AAS; OBSC
(Sonnet: "Dear to my soul! then leave me not forsaken!") EIl

Dear Uncle Stranger. Conrad Aiken. NoAM; NOBA

Dear urge no more that killing cause. To One That Pleaded Her Own Want of Merit. Thomas Stanley. OBS
(To Celia Pleading Want of Merit.) MeLP

Dear, when I did from you remove. Lord Herbert of Cherbury. EIl

Dear, when the sun is set. Give Me Not Tears: Joy. Rose Hawthorne Lathrop. AA

Dear, when we sit in that high, placid room. Touché. Jessie Redmond Fauset. BlSi; CDC

Dear, when you see my grave. Give Me Not Tears: Despair. Rose Hawthorne Lathrop. AA

Dear Whizz, I remember you at St. Mark's in '39. To Auden on His Fiftieth. Richard Eberhart. NAs

Dear Whoever-You-Are-That-You-Are. A Letter from the Pygmies. Theodore Weiss. VGW

"Dear, why make you more of a dog than me?" Sir Philip Sidney. *Fr.* Astrophel and Stella, LIX. GBL; PrIm

Dear, why should you command me to my rest. *See* Deare, Why should you command me to my rest.

Dear wife and bosom friend I hat seen hart. Gary Gildner. *Fr.* Letters from Vicksburg, XII. SM

Dear wife, last midnight, whilst I read. Dibdin's Ghost. Eugene Field. AA

Dear wife, let me have a fire made. Sir T. J.'s Speech to His Wife and Children. *Unknown.* CoMu

Dear Wordsworth. William Hathaway. UL

Dear World. Paula Gunn Allen. HATNAP

Dear, you are in my hands like dough. Twisting. Circus Song. Patricia Goedicke. TV

Dear youth, too early lost, who now art laid. On the Death of a Young and Favorite Slave. Martial, *tr. by* Goldwin Smith. AWP

Deare, If You Change. *Unknown. See* Dear, If You Change.

Deare love for nothing lesse than thee. *See* Dear love for nothing less than thee.

Deare [*or* Dear], why should you command [*or* commaund] me to my rest. Michael Drayton. *Fr.* Idea, XXXVII. AAS; NOBE; OBSC; PoEL-2; Son

(Night and Day.) LiTB

(Sonnet: "Dear, why should you command me to my rest.") ElL

Dearest Barry. An Answer to Thomas Barry. Pierce Fitzgerald, *tr. by* Joan Keefe. TIRV

Dearest Evelyn, I often think of you. The Jungle Husband. Stevie Smith. FaBoWP; NBLV; RB

Dearest Friend, Thou Art in Love. Heine, *tr. fr. German by* Emma Lazarus. *Fr.* Homeward Bound. TrJP

Dearest, I did not think four years ago. To Helen. Winthrop Mackworth Praed. NOBVV

Dearest, if I almost cease to weep for you. Love's Guerdons. Edith Nesbit. NOBVV

Dearest, it was a night. The Birthnight; to F. Walter de la Mare. NAs

Dearest love, do you remember. When This Cruel War Is Over. Charles C. Sawyer. AmFP

Dearest of thousands, now the time drawes neere. His Charge to Julia at His Death. Robert Herrick. SeCV-1

"Dearest Papa," says my boy to me. The Legend of the Easter Eggs. Fitz-James O'Brien. BeLS

Dearest Reader. Michael Palmer. NPGG

Dearest Spot on Earth, The. W. T. Wrighton. FaBoBe

Dearest, when your lovely head. But I Shall Weep. Beatrice Redpath. CaP

Death./ The death of a million. Ron Loewinsohn. NeAP

Death. Maltbie Davenport Babcock. *See* Why be afraid of death, as though your life were breath?

Death. E. A. Baratynsky, *tr. fr. Russian by* Alan Myers. AAA

Death. Maxwell Bodenheim. TrJP

Death. George Boleyn, *also at. to* Anne Boleyn. *See* O Death, Rock Me Asleep.

Death. Emily Brontë. EBVV; OBNC

Death. Howard Byatt. FF

Death. Madison Cawein. AA

Death. John Clare. GTBS-P

Death, *sel.* Mary Elizabeth Coleridge.

"Bid me remember, O my gracious Lord." TrPWD

Death. John Donne. *See* Holy Sonnets: Death be not proud, though some have called thee.

Death. Thomas Flatman. OBD

Death. Roy Fuller. NoAM

Death. Patty L. Harjo. VoR

Death. George Herbert. JCP; MePo; NAEL-1; NoP; OBS; SeCP; SeCV-1

Death/ Coming. Ernst Jandl. *Fr.* Biography. CoAuP

Death. Ruth Kim Chun-soo, *tr. fr. Korean by* Koh Chang-soo. ACKP

Death. William Knott. EAS

Death. Jeffrey Miller. UL

Death. Sean O Riordain, *tr. fr. Irish by* Thomas Kinsella. NOIV

Death. James Oppenheim. WGRP

Death. George Pellew. AA

Death. Sherod Santos. NAmP

Death. William Bell Scott. NOBVV

Death. John Stone. MT

Death. *Gond Oral Tradition, tr. by* V. Elwin *and* S. Hivale. WTO

Death. *Unknown.* BLPA; FPL

Death. *Unknown, tr. fr. Welsh by* Aneirin Talfan Davies. OBWVE; RB

Death. William Carlos Williams. NAAL-2; OxBA; VGW

Death. W. B. Yeats. OxBSP

Death/ Is nothing to us, has no relevance. Against the Fear of Death. Lucretius, *tr. fr. Latin by* Rolfe Humphries. *Fr.* De Rerum Natura (On the Nature of Things), III. DL, *abr.*

("Ah Wretch! thou cry'st, ah! miserable me.") AWP, *tr. by* Dryden; FaBoRV, *tr. by* Dryden; OAEL-1, *tr. by* Dryden; OBVE, *tr. by* Dryden.

Death Again. T. Hope. BXAP

Death, always cruel, Pity's foe in chief. Dante, *tr. fr. Italian by* Dante Gabriel Rossetti. *Fr.* La Vita Nuova, III, b. AWP

Death and Burial of Lord Tennyson, *sel.* William McGonagall.

"Alas! England now mourns for her poet that's gone." OBD

Death, and change, and darkness everlasting. Where Dunwich Used to Be. Swinburne. *Fr.* By the North Sea, VI. FaBoPP

Death and Co. Sylvia Plath. CMoP; FF; LCAP; PrIm

Death and Doctor Hornbook. Burns. OxBS

Death and Empedocles 444 B.C. Horace Gregory. PoA

Death, and it is broken. The Instrument. Kathleen Jessie Raine. PoA

Death and Life of a Severino, The, *sels.* João Cabral de Melo Neto, *tr. fr. Portuguese by* Elizabeth Bishop. ATCBP

"All the heaven and earth." *Fr.* XIV.

"My name is Severino." *Fr.* I.

"Whom are you carrying." *Fr.* II.

Death and Love. Ben Jonson. *See* Sad Shepherd, The: Though I Am Young and Cannot Tell.

Death and Night. James Benjamin Kenyon. AA

Death and Resurrection. George Croly. WGRP

Death and Resurrection. Priscilla Jane Thompson. CBWP-2

Death and the Bridge. Robert Lowell. HCAP

Death and the Cobbler. *Unknown.* APAS

Death and the Fool, *sel.* Hugo von Hofmannsthal, *tr. fr. German by* Michael Hamburger.

"When a man sleeps, often his dream will break." OBD

Death and the Knight (1513). Nikos Gatsos, *tr. fr. Greek by* Edmund Keeley *and* Philip Sherrard. VMG

Death and the Lady. Léonie Ada:ns. MoAB; MoAmPo

Death and the Plowman. Sidney Keyes. OxBTC

Death and the River. Badr Shakir al-Sayyah, *tr. fr. Arabic by* Lena Jayyusi *and* Christopher Middleton. MAP

Death and the Three Revellers. Chaucer. *Fr.* The Canterbury Tales: The Pardoner's Tale. OBNV

Death and the Woodman. La Fontaine, *tr. fr. French by* Edward Marsh. OBD

Death-angel smote Alexander McGlue, The. Mr. Slimmer's Funeral Verses for the *Morning Argus.* "Max Adeler." CenHV

(Out of the Hurly-Burly.) OBAL

Death as a Lotus Flower. *Unknown. See* Book of the Dead: He Is like the Lotus.

Death as History. Jay Wright. PoBA

Death at Daybreak. Anne Reeve Aldrich. AA

Death at the headlands, Hesiod, long ago. Hesiod, 1908. Alexander Mair. GoTS

Death be not proud, though some have called thee. John Donne. *Fr.* Holy Sonnets, X. ChTr; DL; ElL; FaBoRV; FaBV; FaFP; FF; FPL; HAP; HeIP; InPK; InPS; InvP; JCP; LiTB; MeLP; MePo; NAEL-1; NAWM-1; NIP; NOBE; NoP; OAEL-1; OBD; OBS; PoE; PoEL-2; PoRA; PPP; PrIm; SCV; SeCP; SeCV-1; TEP; TrGrPo; WeW (Death.) OBEV

Death be not proud, thy hand gave not this blow. Lucy Harington, Countess of Bedford. WPE

Death, become a shewolf. Crown of Happiness. Anne Hébert, *tr. by* Willis Barnstone. BoWoP

Death-Bed, A. James Aldrich. AA

Death Bed, The. Waring Cuney. CDC

Death-Bed, The. Thomas Hood. EnRP; GTBS; GTBS-P; NOBE; OBD; OBEV; OBNC

Death Bed. Thomas Kinsella. CIP

Death-Bed, The. Siegfried Sassoon. LiTM; MMA

Death-Bed Poem. Jakusho, *tr. fr. Chinese by* Burton Watson. JLIC-1

Death-Bed Reflections of Michel-Angelo. Hartley Coleridge. EyDe

Death-Bed Song. *Unknown.* AmFP

Death before forty's no bar. Lo! Obit on Parnassus. F. Scott Fitzgerald. NBLV; NYBP; PrIm

Death by Drowning. Elizabeth Brewster. NOBC

Death by Rarity. Marguerite Young. LiTA

Death by Water. T. S. Eliot. *Fr.* The Waste Land, IV. OBVE

Death Came for Michael Rockinghorse. Natan Zach, *tr. fr. Hebrew by* Warren Bargad *and* Stanley F. Chyet. IP

Death Camp. Irena Klepfisz. GLP

Death-cell, A? The shack of the coastguards. The Coastguard House. Robert Lowell. NaP

Death Chant. Peter Blue Cloud. VoR

Death-Charade. Jacob Glatstein, *tr. fr. Yiddish by* Benjamin *and* Barbara Harshav. AYP

Death Circus, The. John Tranter. CBAP

Death comes in quantity from solved. The Tolerance of Crows. Charles Donnelly. CIP

Death Crown. Robert Morgan. MT

Death designs swirl high above faces that are of disbelief. War Walking Near. Ray A. Young Bear. CDW

Death devours all lovely things. Passer Mortuus Est. Edna St. Vincent Millay. CMoP; FaBoWP; MoAmPo; OBD; OxBA

Death did not come black and cringing. Icarus. Jane Yolen. BWV

Death did not come to my mother. Conception. Josephine Miles. FaBoWP

Death does away with sickness; Hell cures chance. Consolations. Paul Ramsey. *Fr.* Three Epigrams. CRP

Death, Don't Be Boring. Roy Kelly. BXAP

Death for the Dark Stranger. Thomas McGrath. VGW

Death from Cancer. Robert Lowell. *Fr.* In Memory of Arthur Winslow. TwCP

Death Fugue. Paul Celan, *tr. fr. German.* TrJP, *tr. by* Clement Greenberg; VWA, *tr. by* Joachim Neugroschel (Fugue of Death.) OBVE, *tr. by* Christopher Middleton

Death gallops up the bridge of red railtie girders. Death and the Bridge. Robert Lowell. HCAP

Death has got something to be said for it. Delivery Guaranteed. Kingsley Amis. OBD

Death hath deprived me of my dearest friend. A Remembrance of My Friend Mr. Thomas Morley. John Davies of Hereford. OxBSP

Death himself. LMFBR. Gary Snyder. PoM

Death I recant, and say, unsaid by me. Elegy on Mistress Boulstred. John Donne. JCP

Death, I repent. Kathleen Jessie Raine. *Fr.* Two Invocations of Death, I. OxBTC (Invocation of Death.) MoAB

Death, if thou wilt, fain would I plead with thee. A Dialogue. Swinburne. PoEL-5

Death in Leamington. Sir John Betjeman. NoP; RB

Death in Life. Lord Thomas Vaux. *See* How can the tree but waste and wither away.

Death in Madrid. To Ernest Hemingway. Abdul Wahab al-Bayati, *tr. by* Abdullah al-Udhari. MPAW

Death in Spring, A. Amir Gilboa, *tr. fr. Hebrew by* Warren Bargad *and* Stanley F. Chyet. IP

Death in the Aquarium. Richard Hugo. AnAn

Death in the Corn. Detlev von Liliencron, *tr. fr. German by* C. F. MacIntyre. WaaP

Death in the Desert, A. Charles Tomlinson. FF

Death in the Family, A. Bill Manhire. ATNZ

Death in the Home. T. Sturge Moore. BrPo

Death in the Woods. Harold Littlebird. NOVW

Death in this tomb his weary bones hath laid. Death's Epitaph. Philip Freneau. *Fr.* The House of Night. AA, *br. sel.*

Death in Yorkville. Langston Hughes. PoBA

Death Invited. May Swenson. WPE

Death Invoked. Philip Massinger. *Fr.* The Emperor of the East. ACP (Sad Song, A.) OBS

Death is a dialogue between. Emily Dickinson. WGRP

Death Is a Door. Nancy Byrd Turner. BLPA

Death is a five o'clock door forever changing time. Kwa Mama Zetu Waliotuzaa. Sonia Sanchez. ER

Death Is a Second Cousin Dining with Us Tonight. Geraldine Kudaka. BrSi

Death is all metaphors, shape in one history. Dylan Thomas. *Fr.* Altarwise by Owl-Light, II. CMoP; MoAB; Son

Death is another milestone on their way. The Funeral. Stephen Spender. CMoP; MoAB; MoBrPo; NoAM

Death is before me today. Dying. A. Alvarez. VWA

Death is great. Closing Piece. Rainer Maria Rilke, *tr. by* M. D. Herter Norton. PCP

Death is more than. One X. E. E. Cummings. FaBoMo

Death is only an old door. Death Is a Door. Nancy Byrd Turner. BLPA

Death is stronger than all the governments Death Snips Proud Men. Carl Sandburg. CMoP

Death is the cook of nature, and we find. Margaret Cavendish, Duchess of Newcastle. *Fr.* Nature's Cook. PBWP

Death is the strongest of all living things. Warning to One. Merrill Moore. MoAmPo; TrGrPo

Death killed the rich. *Yoruba Oral Tradition, tr. by* W. Abimbola. WTO

Death King, The. Anne Sexton, *tr. fr. Czech by* Jeffrey Fiskin *and* Erik Vestville. AnAn

Death-Lace. David Ray. MAT

Death lay in ambush. Christopher Okigbo. *Fr.* Distances. TTY

Death lies on her like an untimely frost. Frost on the Flower. Shakespeare. *Fr.* Romeo and Juliet, IV, v. FaBoRV

Death Looks Down. Linda Gregg. NPGG

Death May Be Very Gentle. Oliver St. John Gogarty. PoRA

Death, my lifes Mistress, and the soveraign Queen. To His Mistress for Her True Picture. Lord Herbert of Cherbury. SeCP

Death never troubled Damocles. Damocles. Robert Graves. NYBP

Death News. Allen Ginsberg. MoP

Death of a Bird. Jon Silkin. NePoEA

Death of a Ceiling. Medbh McGuckian. DT

Death of a Comic Opera Composer. Peter Porter. *Fr.* Baroque Quatrains. AnAn

Death of a Dog. Peter Bland. ATNZ

Death of a Dove. Nurunnessa Choudhury, *tr. fr. Bengali by the author and* Paul Joseph Thompson. AIW

Death of a Friend. Pauli Murray. PoBA

Death of a Grandparent. Mrs. Jennette Bonneau. Mary Weston Fordham. CBWP-2

Death of a Hind. Alasdair Maclean. PoSH

Death of a man is like the fall of a mighty nation, The. The Fall. Czeslaw Milosz, *tr. by* Czeslaw Milosz *and* Lillian Vallee. OBD

Death of a Naturalist. Seamus Heaney. HAP; NoAM; OxBC; WeW

Death of a Negro Poet, The. Conrad Kent Rivers. BPo

Death of a Parent, The. Linda Pastan. BLA

Death of a Poet. Charles Causley. OxBTC

Death of a Prominent Business Man. Louis MacNeice. FL

Death of a Ram. Sedulius Scottus, *tr. fr. Latin.* NOIV

Death of a Soldier, The. Wallace Stevens. OBWP; OFD; OxBSP; QFR

Death of a Son. Jon Silkin. FF; GTBS-P; MoP; NePoEA; OxBTC; VWA

Death of a Toad, The. Richard Wilbur. CMoP; LiTM; MoP; NAAL-2; NoAM; NoP; PoA

Death of a Unicorn. Jane Yolen. BWV

Death of a Vermont Farm Woman. Barbara Howes. MoAmPo; SM

Death of a Warrior, The. Jenny Mastoraki, *tr. fr. Modern Greek by* Kimon Friar. BoWoP

Death of a Whale. John Blight. CBAP; OBD; PoAu-2

Death of a Young Son by Drowning. Margaret Atwood. BoWoP; NIP; NOBC

Death of Admiral Benbow, The ("Come all you sailors bold"). *Unknown.* CoMu; GBP

Death of Admiral Benbow, The ("O we sailed to Virginia and thence to New York"). *Unknown.* OxBSS

Death of Adonis, The. Philip Ayres, *after the Greek of* Theocritus. OBVE

Death of Alexander, The. *Unknown.* GoTS; OxBS

Death of an Aircraft. Charles Causley. MoBS

Death of an Angel, The. Russell Edson. LCAP

Death of an Elephant, The. Gianfranco Pagnucci. NU

Death of an Irishwoman. Michael Hartnett. CIP

Death of an Old Man, The. Michael Hamburger. NePoEA

Death of an Ox. Abraham Sutskever, *tr. fr. Yiddish by* Ruth Wisse. PeBMYV

Death of Antony. Shakespeare. *Fr.* Antony and Cleopatra, IV, xv. FiP

Death of Artemidora, The. Walter Savage Landor. *Fr.* Pericles and Aspasia, LXXXV. EnRP; OBNC

Death of Atahuallpa, The. Valery Larbaud, *tr. fr. French by* William Jay Smith. CT

Death of Azron, The. Alice Wellington Rollins. AA

Death of Ben Hall, The. Will H. Ogilvie. PoAu-1

Death of Buckingham, The. Pope. *See* Moral Essays: Duke of Buckingham, The.

Death of Cleopatra. Shakespeare. *Fr.* Antony and Cleopatra, V, ii. FiP (Cleopatra's Death.) TrGrPo (Immortal Longings.) FaBoRV

Death of Colman, The. Thomas Frost. PAH

Death of Cuchulain, The. W. B. Yeats. ChTr (Cuchulain's Fight with the Sea.) AnIL

Death of Daphnis, The. Theocritus, *tr. fr. Greek by* Charles Stuart Calverley. *Fr.* Idylls, I. AWP

Death of David, The. Hayyim Nahman Bialik, *tr. fr. Hebrew by* Herbert Danby. TrJP, *ad. by* Sholom J. Kahn

Death of Digenes Akritas, The. John Heath-Stubbs. NePoEA

Death of Don Pedro, The. *Unknown, tr. fr. Spanish by* John Gibson Lockhart. AWP

Death of Dr. King. Sam Cornish. CNA; OFD; PoBA

Death of Europe, The. Charles Olson. NeAP

Death of Eurydice and Orpheus' Journey to Hell, The. Ovid, *tr. fr. Latin by* George Sandys. *Fr.* Metamorphoses. JCP

Death of faithful Dobbin I deplore, The. An Elegy on the Death of Dobbin, the Butterwoman's Horse. Francis Fawkes. NOEC

Death of Fathers, The. Theodore Weiss. DiL; SV

Death of Floyd Collins, The. Clark Coolidge. LP

Death of Friends, The. Adele Levi. GoYe

Death of Gaudentis. "Harriet Annie." WBLP

Death of General Pike, The. Laughton Osborn. PAH

Death of General Uncebunke, The; a Biography in Little, sel. Lawrence Durrell.
    "My uncle sleeps in the image of death." FaBoMo

Death of God, The. Howard Nemerov. OxBC; OxBSP

Death of Goody Nurse, The. Rose Terry Cooke. PAH

Death of Grant, The. Ambrose Bierce. AA

Death of Guillaume Apollinaire, The. Tristan Tzara, tr. fr. French. POS, tr. by Michael Benedikt; RHTwFP, tr. by Lee Harwood.

Death of Haidée, The. Byron. Fr. Don Juan, IV. FiP

Death of Hamlet. Shakespeare. See Hamlet: I am dead, Horatio. Wretched queen, adieu!

Death of Harrison, The. Nathaniel Parker Willis. PAH

Death of Hector, The. Homer, tr. fr. Greek by George Chapman. Fr. The Iliad, XXII. OBS

Death of Hoel, The. Thomas Gray. NOEC

Death of Jefferson, The. Hezekiah Butterworth. PAH

Death of Justice, The. Walter Everette Hawkins. PoBA

Death of King Edward I, The. Unknown. MeEL

Death of King Edward VII, The. Unknown. OxBoLi

Death of King George V. Sir John Betjeman. See "New King Arrives in His Capital by Air."—Daily Newspaper.

Death of Kings, The. Shakespeare. Fr. King Richard II: Let's Talk of Graves. TrGrPo

Death of Leander, The. Thomas Hood. Fr. Hero and Leander. EnRP

Death of Lear. Shakespeare. Fr. King Lear, V, iii. FiP

Death of Leonidas, The. George Croly. BeLS

Death of Lesbia's Bird, The. Catullus, tr. fr. Latin by Samuel Taylor Coleridge. AWP
    (Death of the Starling, The.) PBBP

Death of Lincoln, The. Bryant. NAAL-1; TAP
    (Abraham Lincoln.) PAH
    (To the Memory of Abraham Lincoln.) OHIP

Death of Little Boys. Allen Tate. LiTA; MoAB

Death of Lord Warriston, The. Unknown. OxBB

Death of Lovers, The. Baudelaire, tr. fr. French by Roy Campbell. OBD

Death of Lyon, The. Henry Peterson. PAH

Death of Marilyn Monroe, The. Sharon Olds. MAYP

Death of Minnehaha, The. Longfellow. Fr. The Song of Hiawatha, XX. AA

Death of Morgan, The. Unknown. FaBoBa

Death of Moses, The. Margit Szécsi, tr. fr. Hungarian by Laura Schiff. OV

Death of Moses, The. Unknown, tr. fr. Hebrew by Alice Lucas. TrJP

Death of My Aunt. Unknown. OxBoLi

Death of Myth-making, The. Sylvia Plath. PoA

Death of Nelson, The. Unknown. OxBoLi
    (New Song Composed on the Death of Lord Nelson, A.) CoMu

Death of Old Joe Yazzie, The. Ron Rogers. STE

Death of Othello. Shakespeare. Fr. Othello, V, ii. FiP

Death of Parcy Reed, The. Unknown. ESPB

Death of Peter Esson, The. George Mackay Brown. NePoEA-2

Death of Poetry, The. Livia Candiani, tr. fr. Italian by Muriel Kittel. DMI

Death of Potchikoo, The. Louise Erdrich. Fr. Old Man Potchikoo. HATNAP

Death of Queen Jane, The. Unknown. AmFP, 2 vers.; ESPB (A vers.); OBET
    ("Queen Jeanie, Queen Jeanie, travel'd six weeks and more.") ESPB, B vers.

Death of Rimbaud. David Fisher. NPGG

Death of Robert, Earl of Huntingdon, sel. Anthony Munday.
    "Weep, weep, ye woodmen! wail." CH
    (Dirge: "Weep, weep, ye woodmen, wail.") CTC; OBSC
    (Robin Hood's Funeral.) WiR
    (Song: "Weep, weep, ye woodmen, wail.") EiL

Death of Robin Hood, The. Unknown. EnSB

Death of Saint Guthlac. Cynewulf, tr. fr. Anglo-Saxon. Fr. Guthlac. ACP

Death of Samson. Milton. See Samson Agonistes: Come, come, no time for lamentation now.

Death of Samuel Adams, The. Unknown. AmFP

Death of Sir Nihil, book the nth. Tywater. Richard Wilbur. CMoP; LiTA; LiTM; MoAB

Death of Slavery, The. Bryant. AA

Death of Sohrab, The ("He spoke; and Sohrab smiled on him, and took"). Matthew Arnold. Fr. Sohrab and Rustum. FiP

Death of Somoza, The. Ernesto Mejía Sánchez, tr. fr. Spanish by Alejandro Murguía. Vol

Death of Southwell, The, sel. John Logan.
    "Topcliffe's horses shake." CRP

Death of Tammuz, The. Saul Tchernichowsky, tr. fr. Hebrew by L. V. Snowman. TrJP

Death of Tammuz, The. Saul Tchernichowsky, tr. fr. Hebrew by Mark Elliot Shapiro. VWA

Death of the Ball Turret Gunner, The. Randall Jarrell. CAPP; CMoP; FF; HAP; HeIP; HoPM; InPK; LCAP; LiTM; MoAmPo; MT; NAAL-2; NAs; NIP; NoAM; NOBA; NoP; OBD; OBWP; OxBA; PoE; PPP; PrIm; RB; SoSe; TAP; UnPo; VGW; WaaP; WaP

Death of the Beloved, The. Rainer Maria Rilke, tr. fr. German by J. B. Leishman. OBD

Death of the Bird, The. A. D. Hope. PoAu-2

Death of the Bosun's Mate. Louis Johnson. PeNZ

Death of the Bronx, The. Chana Bloch. MAYP

Death of the Cat. Ian Serraillier. SO

Death of the Craneman, The. Alfred Hayes. LiTA; WaP

Death of the Day. Walter Savage Landor. NoP

Death of the Epileptic Poet Yesenin, The. Aram Boyajian. NeAC

Death of the Factory Child, The. John Critchley Prince. PF

Death of the First Man, The. Nancy Sullivan. NIP

Death of the Flowers, The. Bryant. AA; AnAmPo; BLPL; BoNaP; GN; OBCA; PoLF; WBLP

Death of the Gods; an Ode Written in Imitation of Pindar, The. L. Ker. NOEC

Death of the Hired Man, The. Robert Frost. AmPP; CMoP; HeIP; HoPM; MoAB; MoAmPo; NAAL-2; NoP; OxBA; SoSe; TrGrPo

Death of the Horses by Fire. Tess Gallagher. NAmP

Death of the Kapowsin Tavern. Richard Hugo. CAPP; NAAL-2

Death of the Lincoln Despotism. Unknown. PAH

Death of the Lord of the Flies. Lucebert, tr. fr. Dutch by Larry Ten Harmsel. DuIn

Death of the Moon, The. David Wagoner. PoA

Death of the Novel, The. David Young. AmPA

Death of the Sheriff, The. Robert Lowell. MoAB; MoAmPo
    (Noli Me Tangere, The.) LCAP

Death of the Shoemaker, The. Ahmad Dahbur, tr. fr. Arabic by Lena Jayyusi and Charles Doria. MAP

Death of the Starling, The. Catullus. See Pity! mourn in plaintive tone.

Death of the Trackstar. William Meissner. TSL

Death of the Vaudevillian, The. Mark Sanders. SoTCo

Death, of thee do I make my moan. To Death, of His Lady. Villon, tr. by Dante Gabriel Rossetti. AWP

Death of Venus, The. Robert Creeley. NOBA

Death of Vitellozzo Vitelli, The. Irving Feldman. TwCP

Death of Warren, The. Epes Sargent. PAH

Death of Will, The. Charles Tomlinson. OxBC

Death of Wolfe, The. Unknown. PAH

Death of Wyatt, The. Earl of Surrey. SiPS
    ("Dyvers thy death doo dyverslye bemone.") AAS

Death of Yeats, The. George Barker. LiTB

Death on a Live Wire. Michael Baldwin. MoBS

Death ("Once he will miss, twice he will miss"). Unknown, tr. fr. Arabic by E. Powys Mathers. Fr. The Thousand and One Nights. AWP

Death rides a horse in the sky. The Angel. Pinhas Sadeh, tr. by Bernhard Frank. MHeP

Death Rites II. Unknown, tr. by C. M. Bowra. TTY

Death Room, The. Robert Graves. NYBP

Death, Said Remco. Bert Schierbeek, tr. fr. Dutch by Charles McGeehan. DuIn

Death Seed. Ricarda Huch, tr. fr. German by Susan C. Strong. PBWP

Death Sentence, The. Stevie Smith. NoP

Death shall be death forever unto thee. Forever Dead. Sappho, tr. by William Ellery Leonard. AWP

Death; She Was Always Here. Yona Wallach, tr. fr. Hebrew by Leonore Gordon. VWA

Death, since I find not one with whom to grieve. Canzone: He Beseeches Death for the Life of Beatrice. Dante, tr. by Dante Gabriel Rossetti. AWP

Death sitting, death standing. Koho, tr. by Lucien Stryk and Takashi Ikemoto. ZPCJ

Death Snips Proud Men. Carl Sandburg. CMoP

Death Song, A. Paul Laurence Dunbar. BANP; CDC; PoLF; PoNe

Death Song. Robert Stephen Hawker. OBNC

Death Song. Alonzo Lewis. PAH

Death Song, A. William Morris. NAEL-2

Death Song for Owain ab Urien. Taliesin, tr. fr. Welsh by Anthony Conran. OBWVE

Death Songs. L. V. Mack. PoBA

Death Songs ("I'll keep your shirt white"). *Unknown, tr. fr. Turkish by* Reza Baraheni *and* Zahra-Soltan Shokoohtaezeh. BoWoP

Death Songs ("I'm the snow on mountains"). *Unknown, tr. fr. Turkish by* Reza Baraheni *and* Zahra-Soltan Shokoohtaezeh. BoWoP

Death Sonnet I. Gabriela Mistral, *tr. fr. Spanish by* David Garrison. BoWoP

Death Stairs/Life House. Jack Hand. TSM

Death Stands above Me. Walter Savage Landor. EnRP; LiTB; NOBE; NoP; OBNC; OxBSP; PoEL-4; SoSe

  (On Death.) OAEL-2; TrGrPo

Death stretched down two hands. Casualty. Diana Witherby. CN

Death Sweet. Thomas Lovell Beddoes. NOBVV

Death Takes Only a Minute. Agnes Pratt. NOVW

Death, that struck when I was most confiding. Death. Emily Brontë. EBVV; OBNC

Death the Consequence of the Fall. Dryden. *Fr.* The State of Innocence. NOCV

Death, the friend behind phenomenon. A Game of Chance. Howard Moss. PoA

Death the Leveller. James Shirley. *See* Contention of Ajax and Ulysses, The: Glories of Our Blood and State, The.

Death, Thou Hast Seized Me. Isaac Luzzatto, *tr. fr. Hebrew by* Nina Davis Salaman. TrJP

Death, that was once an uncouth, hideous thing. Death. George Herbert. JCP; MePo; NAEL-1; NoP; OBS; SeCP; SeCV-1

Death, though [*or* tho] I see him not, is near. Age. Walter Savage Landor. FaBoEE; NOBVV; PoEL-4

Death, thou'rt a cordial old and rare. The Stirrup-Cup. Sidney Lanier. AA; AmPP; AnAmPo

Death to the Lady said. Death and the Lady. Léonie Adams. MoAB; MoAmPo

Death to Us, A. Jon Silkin. NePoEA

Death to Van Gogh's Ear! Allen Ginsberg. NaP; VGW

Death took my father. Manos Karastefanís. James Merrill. TAP

Death-Wake or Lunacy, The, *sel.* Thomas Tod Stoddart.

  Mirthful Lunacy. *Fr.* Lunacy. OBNC

Death Was a Woman. Sydney King Russell. GoYe

Death was at hand. Death. Sean O Riordain, *tr. by* Thomas Kinsella. NOIV

Death was there, sitting by the roadside. Climbing. Gloria Fuertes, *tr. by* Philip Levine. PBWP

Death, when you come to me, tread with a footstep. So Might It Be. John Galsworthy. BLPL; PoLF

Death, who one day taketh all. Epitaph for a Persian Kitten. Miriam Vedder. CRH

Death, why hast thou made life so hard to bear. Canzone: Of His Dead Lady. Giacomino Pugliesi, *tr. by* Dante Gabriel Rossetti. AWP

Death, why so cruel [*or* soe crewill]? What! no other way. Bacon's Epitaph, Made by His Man. *at. to* John Cotton. PAH; SCAP

Death Will Come and Will Have Your Eyes. Cesare Pavese, *tr. fr. Italian by* Norman Thomas Di Giovanni. AWP

Death will go there. Death. Ruth Kim Chun-soo, *tr. by* Koh Chang-soo. ACKP

Death will make his entry into your body which is so beautiful. Death. *Gond Oral Tradition, tr. by* V. Elwin*and* S. Hivale. WTO

Death with his sad hands. Death of Rimbaud. David Fisher. NPGG

Death you are a dreadful fellow. Death, Don't Be Boring. Roy Kelly. BXAP

Deathbed, A. John Hawthorn. *Fr.* The Journey and Observations of a Countryman. NOEC

Deathbed Verse. Jippensha Ikku, *tr. fr. Japanese by* Hiroaki Sato. FCEI

Deathless Aphrodite, throned in flowers. Ode to Aphrodite. Sappho, *tr. by* William Ellery Leonard. AWP

Death's but one more to-morrow. Thou art gray. Of One Who Seemed to Have Failed. S. Weir Mitchell. AA

Death's Epitaph. Philip Freneau. *Fr.* The House of Night. AA, *br. sel.*

Death's Head. Phyllis Gotlieb. NOBC

Death's head on your hand you neede not weare, A. Thomas Dudley, Ah! Old Must Dye. *Unknown.* SCAP

Death's Jest Book, *sels.* Thomas Lovell Beddoes.

  Bridal Song to Amala. ChER, IV, iii; GBL, IV, iii; OBNC, IV, iii. (Epithalamia.) PoEL-4

    (Song: "We have bathed, where none have seen us.") ChER; NOBVV; OBNC

  Dirge: "Swallow leaves her nest, The." *Fr.* I. PoEL-4

    (Song from the Waters.) NOBE

    (Voice from the Waters, A.) OBNC

    ("We do lie beneath the grass.") ELP; NOBE; OBNC; WiR

  "Who findeth comfort in the stars and flowers." OBNC

  "Fair and bright assembly, A: never strode." *Fr.* II, iii. CTC

  "If thou wilt ease thine heart." *Fr.* II. EnRP

  (Dirge: "If Thou wilt ease Thine heart.") LiTB; OBNC; PoEL-4

  (Wolfram's Dirge.) NOBE; OBEV

  Old Adam, the Carrion Crow. *Fr.* V, iv. ChER; EBEV; EnRP; LiTB; OAEL-2; PBBP; PoEL-4

    (Carrion Crow, The.) TrGrPo; WiR

    (Old Adam.) ELP

    (Song: "Old Adam, The carrion crow.") ChER; EBEV; LiTB; OAEL-2; PBBP; PoEL-4

  Song on the Water. FaBoCh

  "Squats on a toad-stool under a tree." *Fr.* III, ii. InVP; OBD

    (Song by Isbrand.) InVP; NOBVV; OBNC; PrIM

  To Sea. *Fr.* I, i. CH

  We Do Lie beneath the Grass. *Fr.* V, iv. ELP

    (Dirge: "We do lie beneath the grass.") NOBVV; OBNC; WiR

    (Sibilla's Dirge.) NOBE

Death's Lecture at the Funeral of a Young Gentleman. Richard Crashaw. SeCP

Death's the Classic Look. John Ciardi. PoA

Death's Transfiguration. Israel Zangwill. TrJP

Death's Vision, *sel.* John Reynolds.

  Mysteries Revealed after Death. NOEC

Death's Warning to Beauty. *Unknown, tr. fr. Early Modern Irish by* Robin Flower. AnIL

Deathward. John Lyle Donaghy. BIrV

Deathwatch. Michael S. S. Harper. AmPA; PoBA

Debate between Arjuna and Sri Krishna. *Unknown, tr. by* Swami Prabhavananda *and* Christopher Isherwood. WaaP

Debate in the Sennit, The. James Russell Lowell. *Fr.* The Biglow Papers: 1st Series, No. V. PAH

Debate not who I am. Hitomaro, *tr. fr. Japanese. Fr.* Manyo Shu. Ma

Debate: Question, Quarry, Dream. Robert Penn Warren. VGW

Debits and Credits, *sel.* Kipling.

  We and They. NoAM

Debora Sleeping. William Logan. MAYP

Deborah as Scion. James Dickey. SV

Deborah Lee. Yvonne. CNA

Debout, *sel.* Tchicaya U Tam'si, *tr. fr. French by* E. S. Yntema.

  "Here is the stream again under the rainbow." PBA

Debridement. Michael S. Harper. NoAM

Debridement: Operation Harvest Moon: *On Repose.* Michael S. Harper. GeTw

Debris clud. P. Inman. IAT

Debt, The. Paul Laurence Dunbar. AmNP; BANP; CDC; SoSe

Debt. *Gond Oral Tradition, tr. by* V. Elwin *and* S. Hivale. WTO

Debt is paid, The. The Past. Emerson. FaBoCh; FPL; LiTA; PoEL-4; TAP

Debts. Robert Long. NAmP

Debutante was sitting in the parlor of her flat, A. Song: "Don't Tell Me What You Dreamt Last Night." Franklin Pierce Adams. FiBHP

Decade, A. Amy Lowell. MoAmPo

Decanter of Madeira, Aged 86, to George Bancroft, Aged 86, A. Silas Weir Mitchell. AA

Decay. George Herbert. SeCP; SeCV-1

Decay of a People, The. William Gilmore Simms. AA

Decay of Piety. Wordsworth. TrCP

Decayed Time. Jean Wahl, *tr. fr. French by* Charles Guenther. VWA

Deceased. Cid Corman. PCP; VGW

Deceased, The. Keith Douglas. FaBoTw

Deceav'd and undeceav'd to be. The Self-Deceaver. Thomas Stanley. OBVE

Deceiving world, that with alluring toys. A Palinode. Robert Greene. *Fr.* Greene's Groatsworth of Wit. OBSC

December. John Clare. OBCP

December. Robert Francis. LCAP

December. Rose Fyleman. RAR

December. Josephine D. Henderson Heard. CBWP-4

December. Maurice Kenny. HATNAP; STE

December. Ron Padgett. EAS

December. Henrietta Cordelia Ray. CBWP-3

December. Folgore da San Gimignano, *tr. fr. Italian by* Dante Gabriel Rossetti. *Fr.* Sonnets of the Months. PFI

December. Gary Snyder. InPS

December among the Vanished. W. S. Merwin. NaP

December, and the closing of the year. Christmas Eve in Whitneyville, 1955. Donald Hall. DiL; UnPo

December at Yase. Gary Snyder. *Fr.* Four Poems for Robin. NoAM

December Blues. Robert Pinsky. MAYP

December Day, Hoy Sound. George Mackay Brown. OxBS

December Day in Honolulu. Galway Kinnell. AnAn

December Eclipse. Margo Lockwood. Psk

December 15, 1811. Poem for My Family: Hazel Griffin and Victor Hernandez Cruz. June Jordan. BPo

December Forest, A. Vesna Krmpotic, *tr. fr. Croatian by* Vasa D. Mihailovich. WPOW
December Fragments. Richmond Lattimore. PChr
December Morning. Fleur Adcock. ATNZ
December, my dear, on the road to Nijmegen. The Road to Nijmegen. Earle Birney. OBCV
December narrows our day to a thread of light. Song in the Cold Season. Samuel French Morse. PoA
December Night. W. S. Merwin. CAPP
December, nightfall at three-thirty. Swan. Donald Hall. LCAP
December 1974: a Lament. Abdur-Rahman Slade Hopkinson. PBCV
December: Of Aphrodite. W. S. Merwin. NePoEA
December pools, latent, crosshatched. Instructions for Fishing the Eel. Dennis Schmitz. AnAn
December: Prayer to St. Nicholas. John Heath-Stubbs. OBCP
December Stillness. Siegfried Sassoon. CMoP
December sun sits low over hedgegrows, glitter. What Shines in Winter Burns. T. R. Hummer. MAYP; MT
December: the trees chafing. Mile Hill. Dennis Schmitz. LCAP
December 30th. Ivor Gurney. NAEL-2
December 20th 1965, the sun. Frédérique, or How I Became a Historian. Herman de Coninck, *tr. by* James S. Holmes. DuIn
December 21st. Jean Valentine. LCAP
December 24 and George McBride Is Dead. Richard Hugo. HoPM
December 27, 1966. L. E. Sissman. DiPo; SM
Decent docent doesn't doze, The. History of Education. David McCord. OBAL
Deception. Alfred Corn. PoA
Deception. Josephine D. Henderson Heard. CBWP-4
Deceptions. René Daumal, *tr. fr. French by* Michael Benedikt. POS
Deceptions. Philip Larkin. CMoP; ErPo; GTBS-P; NePoEA
Deceptive Grin of the Gravel Porters, The. Gavin Ewart. FaBoMo
Deceptive Present, the Phoenix Year, The. Delmore Schwartz. BoNaP
Deceptrices, The. William Carlos Williams. NYBP
Decimation before Phraata, The. Alan Dugan. AnAn
Decision, The. Camille Bélot, *tr. fr. French by* Beth Archer. *Fr.* The Unwed Mother. DMF
Decision, The. Owen Dodson. PoNe
Decision, The. Theodore Roethke. CRP; VGW
Decision, A. Edith Södergran, *tr. fr. Swedish by* Jaakko O. Ahokas. PBWP
Deck of Cards, A. Gail Mazur. PPR
Deck thyself, maiden. Esthonian Bridal Song. Johann Gottfried von Herder, *tr. by* W. Taylor. AWP
Deck us all with Boston Charlie. Boston Charlie. Walt Kelly. FiBHP; GoJo
Decks. Robert Phillips. GeTw
Decks awash,/ Mast-top dipping. Archilochus, *tr. by* Guy Davenport. OBVE
Declaimer, The. Henry Baker. NOEC
Declair, ye bankis of Helicon. *Unknown. Fr.* The Bankis of Helicon. OxBS
Declamatory Poem. Max Jacob, *tr. fr. French by* Michael Brownstein. RHTwFP
Declaration. Arthur Symons. *Fr.* Violet. BrPo
Declaration, The. Nathaniel Parker Willis. AnAmPo; OBAL
Declaration of Independence. Michael Brownstein. UL
Declare, my pretty maid. The Philanderer. Moses Mendes. *Fr.* The Chaplet. TrJP
Declension. Stephen Sandy. PoA
Decline and Fall of a Roman Umpire. Ogden Nash. SD
Decline of an Empire. Dan Pagis, *tr. fr. Hebrew by* Warren Bargad *and* Stanley F. Chyet. IP
Declining of a Gallant, The. *Unknown.* FaBoUs
Decorating the Soldiers' Graves. Minot Judson Savage. OHIP
Decoration. Mary Ursula Bethell. ATNZ; PeNZ
Decoration. Louise Bogan. MoAB; MoAmPo
Decoration. Thomas Wentworth Higginson. AA; OHIP
Decoration Day. George Hurlbut Barbour. OHIP
Decoration Day. Josephine D. Henderson Heard. CBWP-4
Decoration Day. Julia Ward Howe. OHIP
Decoration Day. Longfellow. OHIP
Decorations. Nishiwaki Junzaburo, *tr. fr. Japanese by* Hiroaki Sato. FCEI
Decorations climbing up the loft on a wobbly ladder. My Christmas; Mum's Christmas. Sarah Forsyth. OBCP
Decoy. John Ashbery. PoM
Decoys, The. W. H. Auden. CMoP; PoE
Decrees of God, The. Chao Ying-tou, *tr. fr. Chinese by* William C. White. TrJP
Decrepit Old Gasman, A. *Unknown.* FaFP
(Limerick: "Decrepit old gas man named Peter, A.") SoSe
Dedicated, The. Philip Larkin. OxBC

Dedicated Dancing Bull and the Water Maid, The, *sel.* Stevie Smith. "Hop hop, thump thump." WPE
Dedicated Spirit, A. Wordsworth. *Fr.* The Prelude [or, Growth of a Poet's Mind]: Summer Vacation. SeCePo
Dedicated to Dr. W. H. Sheppard. Maggie Pogue Johnson. CBWP-4
Dedicated to F. W. Ernest Hemingway. ASP
Dedicated to the Right Rev'd D. A. Payne. Mary Weston Fordham. CBWP-2
Dedication, A, *sel.* Karin Boye, *tr. fr. Swedish by* Nadia Christensen. "I feel your steps in the hall." PBWP
Dedication: "Bob Southey! You're a poet—poet-laureate." Byron. *Fr.* Don Juan. CTC; EnRP; OAEL-2; OBSV
(Dedication to the Poet Laureate.) FiP
(Southey and Wordsworth.) TrGrPo
Dedication, A: "Dear, near and true—no truer Time himself." Tennyson. OxBSP
Dedication: "Had there been peace there never had been riven." Drummond Allison. FaBoTw
Dedication, A: "Hans, there are moments when the whole mind." James Merrill. CAPP
Dedication, A: "He was, through boyhood's storm and shower." G. K. Chesterton. FiBHP
Dedication, The: "Health to great Gloucester—from a man unknown." Charles Churchill. OBSV
(Dedication to the Sermons, The.) QFR
Dedication: "Holy Jesus, Thou art born." Victoria Saffelle Johnson. TrPWD
Dedication: "I would the gift I offer here." Whittier. *Fr.* Songs of Labor. OxBA
Dedication, A: "Life of my learning, fire of all my Art." Mary Elizabeth Coleridge. TrPWD
Dedication, A: "My new-cut ashlar takes the light." Kipling. PoEL-5
Dedication II: "Strongest and the noblest argument, The." Sir John Davies. *Fr.* Nosce Teipsum. SiPS
Dedication: "Tall unpopular men." Oliver St. John Gogarty. OBMV
Dedication: "These words are dedicated to those who died." Irena Klepfisz. *Fr.* Bashert. ER
Dedication, A: "They are rhymes rudely strung with intent less." Adam Lindsay Gordon. CBAP; PoAu-1
Dedication: "They shall not die in vain," we said." Ralph Gustafson. CaP
Dedication: "Thou, whose unmeasured temple stands." Bryant. BLRP
(How Amiable Are Thy Tabernacles!) TrPWD
Dedication to Ianthe. Byron. *Fr.* Childe Harold's Pilgrimage. OBNC
Dedication: To Leigh Hunt, Esq. Keats. *See* To Leigh Hunt, Esq.
Dedication I: "To that clear majesty which in the north." Sir John Davies. *See* Nosce Teipsum: To Queen Elizabeth.
Dedication: "Unto the blithe and lordly fellowship." Folgore Da San Gimignano, *tr. fr. Italian by* Dante Gabriel Rossetti. *Fr.* Sonnets of the Months. AWP
Dedication: "When I have ended, then I see." Laurence Housman. TrPWD
Dedication: "You whom I could not save." Czeslaw Milosz, *tr. by the author.* PwPP
Dedication Day. Maggie Pogue Johnson. CBWP-4
Dedication Day Poem. Lizelia Augusta Jenkins Moorer. CBWP-3
Dedication of the Cook. Anna Wickham. MoBrPo
Dedication of the Illustrations to Blair's "Grave," *sel.* Blake.
Door of Death, The. ChTr
(To the Queen.) EnRP
Dedication on the Gift of a Book to a Child. Hilaire Belloc. *See* Child, Do Not Throw This Book About.
Dedication to G**** H******* Esq., A, *sel.* Burns. "Morality, thou deadly bane." OBSV
Dedication to Hunger, *sels.* Louise Glück. AnAn; FaBoWP; GeTw
Deviation, The. *Fr.* IV.
Eros. *Fr.* III.
From the Suburbs. *Fr.* I.
Grandmother. *Fr.* II.
Sacred Objects. *Fr.* V.
Dedication to My Wife, A. T. S. Eliot. BoLoP; FF
Dedication to the Final Confrontation. Lloyd M. Corbin, Jr.. PoBA
Dedication to the Generation Knocking at the Door. John Davidson. BrPo
Dedication to the Poet Laureate. Byron. *See* Don Juan: Bob Southey! You're a poet—poet-laureate.
Dedication to the Sermons, The. Charles Churchill. *See* Dedication, The: "Health to great Gloucester—from a man unknown."
Dedications, I: To His Very Friend, Master Richard Martin. Sir John Davies. *Fr.* Orchestra; or, A Poem[e] of Da[u]ncing. SiPS
Dedications, II: To the Prince. Sir John Davies. *Fr.* Orchestra; or, A Poem[e] of Da[u]ncing. SiPS

Dedications [*of Orchestra*], *sels.* Sir John Davies. SiPS
  To His Very Friend, Master Richard Martin. *Fr.* I.
  To the Prince. *Fr.* II.
Dedications [of Orchestra], I: To His Very Friend, Master Richard Martin. Sir John Davies. SiPS
Dedications [of Orchestra], II: To the Prince. Sir John Davies. SiPS
Dedicatory Ode, *sel.* Hilaire Belloc.
  They Say That in the Unchanging Place. PoLF
Dedicatory: "Somewhere, sometime, in an April twilight." Willa Cather. WPE
Dedicatory Sonnet to S. T. Colerige. Hartley Coleridge. OAEL-2; Son
Dee dee dee dee dee wee weee eeeeee wee we. Communication in White. Don L. Lee. BPo
Deean Tractorman, Clear, The. Edith Anne Robertson. OxBS
Deean Tractorman, Deleerit, The. Edith Anne Robertson. OxBS
Deed of Lieutenant Miles, The. Clinton Scollard. PAH
Deed that takes place in winter, The. Famine Winter. Hans Vlek, *tr. by* James S. Holmes. DuIn
Deeds of Valor at Santiago. Clinton Scollard. PAH
Deeds That Might Have Been, The. Wilfrid Scawen Blunt. *Fr.* In Vinculis. TrGrPo
Deem as ye list, upon good cause. Sir Thomas Wyatt. SiPS
Deem not, because you see me in the press. George Santayana. *Fr.* Sonnets, XI. TrGrPo
Deem not, devoid of elegance, the sage. Sonnet: Written in a Blank Leaf of Dugdale's "Monasticon." Thomas Warton the Younger. SeCePo (Written in a Blank Leaf of Dugdale's "Monasticon.") Son
Deep, The. John Gardiner Calkins Brainard. AA
Deep affections of the breast, The. The Parrot. Thomas Campbell. FM
Deep and Dark Blue Ocean. Byron. *See* Childe Harold's Pilgrimage: Ocean, The.
Deep and wise was Shang. *Unknown, tr. by* Arthur Waley. BoS
Deep asleep, perfect immobility, no apparent evidence of consciousness or of dream. Waking Jed. C. K. Williams. DiL
Deep blue of the earth, The. In the Arab House. Al-Munsif al-Wahaybi, *tr. by* Salma Khadra Jayyusi *and* Naomi Shihab Nye. MAP
Deep calleth unto deep. Dial Call. Christopher Morley. NBLV
Deep cradled in the fringed mow to lie. Theophany. Evelyn Underhill. WGRP
Deep Dark Night, The. Tennyson. *Fr.* The Devil and the Lady. SeCePo
Deep Dark River. Lloyd Roberts. CaP
Deep Gratitude. Niu Chiao, *tr. fr. Chinese by* Lois Fusek. ATF
Deep in a distant bay, and deeply hidden. The Lonely Isle. Claudian, *tr. by* Howard Mumford Jones. AWP
Deep in a Rose's glowing heart. Sent with a Rose to a Young Lady. Margaret Deland. AA
Deep in a vale, a stranger now to arms. The American Soldier. Philip Freneau. TAP
Deep in a vale where rocks on every side. Gustav Rosenhane, *tr. by* Sir Edmund Gosse. AWP
Deep in a windless/ wood. Buson, *tr. by* Harry Behn. WSC
Deep in Alabama earth. Alabama Earth. Langston Hughes. AmFN
Deep in clouds, the winds' home. Up and Down. Sándor Weöres, *tr. by* Jascha Kessler. FOC
Deep in love. Bhavabhuti, *tr. by* W. S. Merwin *and* J. Moussaieff Masson. LLLT
Deep in mountain caves. Scenes in a Silver Mine. Tachibana Akemi, *tr. fr. Japanese by* Burton Watson. *Fr.* Thirty Tanka. FCEI
Deep in my heart I hear them, the gaunt hounds pacing. The Hounds of the Soul. Louis Ginsberg. TrJP
Deep in my soul there roared the crashing thunder. Calm after Storm. Frank Yerby. AmNP
Deep in the air the past appears. The Greeks. Tom Clark. PoA
Deep in the back ways of my mind I see them. My Great-Grandfather's Slaves. Wendell Berry. GeTw
Deep in the bamboo grove. Haritsu, *tr. by* Hiroaki Sato. FCEI
Deep in the brown bosom. Bangkok. F. R. Scott. MoCV; OBCV
Deep in the fading leaves of night. W. R. Rodgers. OBCP
Deep in the family shrine. Kyorai, *tr. fr. Japanese by* Burton Watson. *Fr.* Twenty Hokku. FCEI
Deep in the forest there is a pond. After the Anonymous Swedish. Jim Harrison. VGW
Deep in the Georgia night when all. Georgia Towns. Daniel Whitehead Hicky. AmFN
Deep in the grass there lies a dead gazelle. Maytime. *Unknown, tr. fr. Chinese by* L. Cranmer-Byng. *Fr.* Shi King. AWP
Deep in the heart of the forest the lily of Yorrow is growing. The Lily of Yorrow. Henry van Dyke. AA
Deep in the leafy fierceness of the wood. Apollo and Daphne. Yvor Winters. Son
Deep in the Mountain. Saibara, *tr. fr. Japanese by* Hiroaki Sato. FCEI

Deep in the mountains, the pine door isn't aware of spring. Princess Shikishi, *tr. fr. Japanese by* Hiroaki Sato. *Fr.* Seventy-eight Tanka. FCEI
Deep in the mountains, through the pine door closed. Princess Shikishi, *tr. fr. Japanese by* Hiroaki Sato. *Fr.* Seventy-eight Tanka. FCEI
Deep in the shady sadness of a vale. Keats. *Fr.* Hyperion; a Fragment, I. ChER; FiP; PoEL-4
  (Saturn.) OBNC; TrGrPo
Deep in the Siberian mine. Message to Siberia. Pushkin, *tr. by* Max Eastman. AWP; TTY
Deep in the study. The Phoenix. Ogden Nash. CenHV
Deep in the temple. Shoha, *tr. by* Geoffrey Bownas *and* Anthony Thwaite. PeBJV
Deep in the wave is a coral grove. The Coral Grove. James Gates Percival. AA; GN
Deep in the winter plain, two armies. Two Armies. Stephen Spender. OBWP; OxBTC; WaP
Deep in the wood I made a house. August. Katharine Pyle. OBCA
Deep in the woods we'll go. Heart of the Woods. Wesley Curtright. PoNe
Deep in these Ozark hills, dark-limbed. Caves. David Baker. MAYP
Deep in this grave her bones remain. Reflections, Written on Visiting the Grave of a Venerated Friend. Ann Plato. BlSi
Deep in your cheeks. Origins. Keorapetse Kgositsile. PoBA
Deep into autumn. Red Leaves. Tameshige, *tr. by* Steven D. Carter. WFTW
Deep into the midst of a great, dark, wood. The Snail's Lesson. Priscilla Jane Thompson. CBWP-2
Deep into the night. Empress Eifuku, *tr. by* Steven D. Carter. WFTW
Deep lane, poor families; I have few friends. At the End of Spring. Yü Hsüan-chi, *tr. by* Geoffrey Waters. BoWoP
Deep loneliness/ was something I was used to. Tamemasa, *tr. by* Steven D. Carter. WFTW
Deep Love, A. Mao Wen-hsi, *tr. fr. Chinese by* Lois Fusek. ATF
Deep music of the ancient forest! Sancta Silvarum. Lionel Johnson. BrPo
Deep on the convent-roof the snows. St. Agnes' Eve. Tennyson. LiTB; OBEV
Deep peace, pure white of the moon to you. "Fiona Macleod." *Fr.* Invocation of Peace. BoTP
Deep prolonged entry with the strong pink cock. She Loves. Olga Broumas. GLP
Deep red bogs divided. Richard Murphy. *Fr.* The Battle of Aughrim. CIP
Deep River ("Deep river, my home is over Jordan"). *Unknown.* BPo; TAP
Deep rolls the thunder. *Unknown, tr. by* Arthur Waley. BoS
Deep scarred. Not by Wind Ravaged. Hone Tuwhare. ATNZ
Deep Sea. István Kormos, *tr. fr. Hungarian by* Edwin Morgan. MHuP
Deep Sea. Jules Supervielle, *tr. fr. French by* Denise Levertov. RHTwFP
Deep-Sea Fishing. "Hugh MacDiarmid." SeCePo
Deep Sea Soundings. Sarah Williams. WGRP
Deep Sea Tug. Harry Robertson. OxBSS
Deep snow that, The. Saigyo, *tr. fr. Japanese by* Burton Watson. *Fr.* Sixty-four Tanka. FCEI
Deep Spring. *Unknown.* AmFP
Deep-sworn Vow, A. W. B. Yeats. CMoP; OAEL-2; PCP; PoE; UnPo
Deep Well, *sel.* Roland Robinson.
  "I am at Deep Well where the spirit-trees." CBAP
Deep well knows it certainly, The. World-Secret. Hugo von Hofmannsthal, *tr. by* Charles Wharton Stork. TrJP
Deep within the backlands I walked along the road. The Song of the Wild Dove. Cassiano Ricardo, *tr. by* Jean R. Longland. ATCBP
Deep wooden note, A. Overheard. Denise Levertov. PoM
Deeper, running. Mackerel. Wayne Brown. UAS
Deeper than sleep but not so deep as death. Night Feeding. Muriel Rukeyser. NMM; WPE
Deeply repentant of my sinful ways. Gaspara Stampa, *tr. by* Lorna de'Lucchi. WPOW
Deer, The. Asya, *tr. fr. Yiddish by* Gabriel Preil *and* Howard Schwartz. VWA
Deer, The. Mary Austin. FaPON
Deer. John Drinkwater. CH
Deer. No Ch'ön-myüng, *tr. fr. Korean by* Ko Won. PBWP
Deer. Kenneth Rexroth. *Fr.* A Bestiary. HoPM; PBBP
Deer among Cattle. James Dickey. CAPP
Deer and the Snake, The. Kenneth Patchen. MoAmPo
Deer are gentle and graceful. Deer. Kenneth Rexroth. *Fr.* A Bestiary. HoPM; PBBP
Deer at the Red Sea. Abraham Sutskever, *tr. fr. Yiddish by* Chana Bloch. PeBMYV

Deer at the Roadside. Iain Crichton Smith. *Fr.* Deer on the High Hills—a Meditation. PoSH

Deer carcass hangs from a rafter, The. Gathering the Bones Together. Gregory Orr. AmPA; GeTw; Psk

Deer feed on. Upon Leaving the Parole Board Hearing. Conyus. PoBA

Deer Fence. Wang Wei, *tr. fr. Chinese* by Burton Watson. *Fr.* Twenty Views of Wang-ch'uan, 5. CoBCP

Deer Hunt. Judson Jerome. RFM

Deer Hunt, Salt Lake Valley. Helen Handley. GrPl

Deer in Aspens. Kay DeBard Hall. GoYe

Deer in the Bush. Chana Bloch. MAYP

Deer in the morning look edgy and lost. Natsume Seibi, *tr. fr. Japanese* by Hiroaki Sato. *Fr.* Twenty-seven Hokku. FCEI

Deer is humble, lovely as God made her, The. The Deer and the Snake. Kenneth Patchen. MoAmPo

Deer Isle. Philip Booth. VGW

Deer Lay Down Their Bones, The. Robinson Jeffers. NoAM

Deer, lightning, bluebird, toad. Beneath the Mound. R. T. Smith. STE

Deer-of-the-Waters: he laboured hard on his grammar. Red Indian Corpse. Peter Redgrove. OxBC

Deer on the High Hills—a Meditation, *sel.* Iain Crichton Smith. Deer at the Roadside. PoSH

Deer Sing, *sel.* Confucius, *tr. fr. Chinese* by Ezra Pound. Fraternitas. CTC; OBVE

Deer Song. Leslie Silko. VoR

Deer that seeks the *hagi* flowers for mate, A. *Unknown, tr. fr. Japanese.* *Fr.* Manyo Shu. Ma

Deer that weds, The. *Unknown, tr. fr. Japanese* by Burton Watson. *Fr.* Manyo Shu. FCEI

Deer were bounding like blown leaves, The. Fire on the Hills. Robinson Jeffers. CMoP

Deer which lives, The. Onakatomi Yoshinobu, *tr. fr. Japanese* by Arthur Waley. *Fr.* Shui Shu. AWP

Deer whose legs you try to hit, The. Fairy Tale. Gust Gils, *tr.* by Koos Schuur. DuIn

Deer's Cry, The. Saint Patrick. *See* I arise today.

Deevil's Waltz, The. Sydney Goodsir Smith. FaBoTw

Defeat. Witter Bynner. PoNe

Defeat, A. Denise Levertov. PBWP

Defeat and Victory. Wallace Rice. PAH

Defeat at the Hands of Alien Scholars. Bruce Boston. BWV

Defeat may serve as well as victory. Victory in Defeat. Edwin Markham. BLPL; PoLF

Defeat of the Norsemen, The, *sel.* Sedulius Scottus, *tr. fr. Latin.* "Heavens, ocean, and all earth, rejoice!" NOIV

Defeat of the Rebels. Robert Graves. WaP

Defence of Lawrence, The. Richard Realf. PAH

Defence of Lucknow, The. Tennyson. BeLS

Defence of Poetry, A. Giolla Brighde Mac Con Midhe. NOIV

Defence of Satire. Pope. *See* Epilogue to the Satires [*or* 1738]: Ask you what provocation I have had?

Defence of the Alamo. Joaquin Miller. *See* Defense of the Alamo, The.

Defence of the Moon. Antoni Slonimski, *tr. fr. Polish* by Czeslaw Milosz. PwPP

Defend It. Agnes Nemes Nagy, *tr. fr. Hungarian* by Alan Dixon. MHuP

Defend Us, Lord, from Every Ill. John Hay. AH

Defender, The. Arthur M. Sampley. GoYe

Defender of his country, The—the founder of liberty. Epitaph on Washington. *Unknown.* OHIP

Defense of Guenevere, The. William Morris. NAEL-2; TEP

Defense of the Alamo, The. Joaquin Miller. BeLS; FaBoBe; PAH (Defence of the Alamo.) OnMSP; PAH

Defense Rests. Vassar Miller. MoAmPo

Defensive Position. John Manifold. MoBrPo

Defiance, The. Aphra Behn. EnLoPo

Defiance, The. Thomas Flatman. OBS

Defiance. Solomon ibn Gabirol, *tr. fr. Hebrew* by Emma Lazarus. TrJP

Deficiency, A. Ute Erb, *tr. fr. German* by Susan L. Cocalis. DMG

Defiled Is My Name Full Sore. *At. to* Anne Boleyn. WPE

Defining It for Vanessa. Colleen J. McElroy. ER

Defining Love. Francisco de Quevedo, *tr. fr. Spanish* by Perry Higman. LPSS

Definition. Lauren Shakely. FYAP

Definition for Blk/Children. Sonia Sanchez. PoBA

Definition of Beauty, The. Robert Herrick. CaPo

Definition of Blue. John Ashbery. CAPP; NAAL-2

Definition of Love, The. Andrew Marvell. BLPL; BoLoP; EBEV; GBL; HoPM; InPS; JCP; LiTB; MeLP; MePo; NAEL-1; NOBE; NoP; OAEL-1; OBEV; OBS; PoEL-2; SeCePo; SeCP; SeCV-1; TEP; TrGrPo; UnPo

Definition of Nature. Eugene B. Redmond. PoBA

Definition of the Soul. Boris Pasternak, *tr. fr. Russian* by Babette Deutsch. TrJP

Definitions, *sel.* E. B. White. Critic. NBLV

Definitions of the Word *Gout.* Tina Koyama. BrSi

Definitive Declaration. Louis Aragon, *tr. fr. French* by Michael Benedikt. POS

Defoliated Leaves. Yehuda Amichai, *tr. fr. Hebrew* by Bernhard Frank. MHeP

Deformed Mistress, The. Sir John Suckling. BXAP; ErPo

Deftly, admiral, cast your fly. W. H. Auden. GTBS-P

Degas. Paul Monette. AmPA

Degenerate Age, A. Solomon Ibn Gabirol, *tr. fr. Hebrew* by Emma Lazarus. TrJP

Degenerate Douglas! O the unworthy lord! Composed at Neidpath Castle, the Property of Lord Queensberry, 1803. Wordsworth. GTBS; GTBS-P

Degli Sposi. Rika Lesser. FYAP; UnAS

Degree Four. Nathaniel Mackey. BAP

Degrees of Gray in Philipsburg. Richard Hugo. CAPP; CoAP; NAAL-2; NoAM; NoP

Deh 'Pon Um Again. Michael McTurk. PBCV

Deid is now that divour (*or* dyvour) and dollin in erd. The Widow Speaks. William Dunbar. *Fr.* The Book of the Two Married Women and the Widow [*or* The Tua Mariit Wemen and the Wedo]. PoEL-1

(Widow Has Buried Her Second Husband.) OxBLMV

Deid sall ye ligg, and ne'er a memorie. Douglas Young, *after the Greek of* Sappho. OBVE

Deidre's Lament for the Sons of Usnach. *Unknown. See* Deirdre's Lament for the Sons of Usnach.

Deigne at my hands this crown of prayer and praise. La Corona. John Donne. OBS

De'il cam fiddling through the town, The. The Exciseman. Burns. GoTS

Deir El Bahari: Temple of Hatshepsut. D. J. Enright. OBTV

Deirdre. James Stephens. AWP; CMoP; OBMV; PoRA

Deirdre and the Poets. Ewart Milne. NeIP

Deirdre's [*or* Deidre's] Lament for the Sons of Usnach. *Unknown, tr. fr. Irish* by Sir Samuel Ferguson. NOIV; SeCePo

Deirdre's Song at Sunrise. Sister Maura. CaP

Deity of Love Incorporate, A. Edward Taylor. *Fr.* Preparatory Meditations before My Approach to the Lord's Supper, XI. TAP

Déjà, Indeed. John Updike. SoTCo

Déjà Vu. Shirley Kaufman. LCAP

Dejection. Robert Bridges. QFR

Dejection; an Ode. Samuel Taylor Coleridge. EnRP; FiP; HeIP; LiTB; NAEL-2; NAWM-2; NOBE; NoP; OAEL-2; OBNC; PoE; PoEL-4; PPP; SeCePo, *st.* 1; TOF

Dekunle, handsome man, hail! Omobayode Arowa, *tr. fr. Yoruba.* *Fr.* Dirge for Fajuyi. WTO

Del Cascar. William Stanley Braithwaite. BANP; CDC

Delacroix pentit Chopin's heid. Ye Mongers Aye Need Masks for Cheatrie. Sydney Goodsir Smith. OxBS

Delay. Charlotte Fiske Bates. AA

Delay. Elizabeth Jennings. NePoEA; OxBTC

Delayed Action. Christian Morgenstern, *tr. fr. German* by W. D. Snodgrass *and* Lore Segal. RB

Delayed till she had ceased to know. Emily Dickinson. AA

Delerium: Jesting at Illness. Yüan Mei, *tr. fr. Chinese* by J. P. Seaton. WFTU

Delete? Yes/No? Edmund Pennant. SoTCo

Delfica. Gérard de Nerval, *tr. fr. French* by Andrew Hoyem. NU

Delgadina. *Unknown, tr. fr. Spanish* by Lysander Kemp. DMH

Delia. Samuel Daniel. *See* To Delia.

Delia Holmes ("Delia, Delia, why didn't you run?"). *At. to* "Whistling Bill" Ruff. AmFP

Delia Very Angry. *Unknown.* NOEC

Deliberately, long ago/ the carcasses. From an Old House in America. Adrienne Rich. NNaP

Delicate breast. Flower-Market Quay. Pierre Reverdy, *tr.* by Michael Benedikt. POS

Delicate corner shot, The. Civilities. Thomas Whitbread. SD

Delicate eyes that blinked blue Rockies all ash. On Neal's Ashes. Allen Ginsberg. CAPP; PoM

Delicate fabric of bird song, A. May Day. Sara Teasdale. BoNaP

Delicate girl was eager to air, The. Princess Elizabeth of Bohemia, as Perdita. Frank O'Hara. PoA

Delicate grasses, faint wind on the bank. A Traveler at Night Writes His Thoughts. Tu Fu, *tr.* by Burton Watson. CoBCP

Delicate Mother Kangaroo. D. H. Lawrence. GrPl

Delicate, Plummeting Bodies, The. Stephen Dobyns. FYAP

Delicate river grasses spread into the tangled undergrowth. Ripples Sifting Sand. Huang-fu Sung, *tr.* by Lois Fusek. ATF

Delicate sound of a moth; a page turning. The Moths. Sean O Riordain, *tr. by* Thomas Kinsella. NOIV

Delicate weave of clever talk, The. Entr'acte. Anna Margolin, *tr. by* Marcia Falk. PeBMYV

Delicate yellow willows are enfolded in cloudy mist, The. Eight-beat Barbarian Tune. Yen Hsüan, *tr. by* Lois Fusek. ATF

Delicate young Negro stands, A. Anonymous Drawing. Donald Justice. CoAP; EyDe; HeIP; NePoEA-2

Delicious beauty that doth lie. John Marston. EIL

Delight. J. Bernlef, *tr. fr. Dutch by* James S. Holmes. DuIn

Delight in books from evening. Francis Daniel Pastorius. SCAP

Delight in Disorder. Robert Herrick. CaPo; EBEV; EnLoPo; ErPo; FaBV; FF; GTBS; GTBS-P; HAP; HeIP; InPK; InPS; JCP; LiTB; NAEL-1; NIP; NOBE; NoP; OAEL-1; OBEV; OBS; PoE; PoRA; PPP; PrIm; SeCePo; SeCP; SeCV-1; TEP; TrGrPo; WeW

Delight in the High-Flying Orioles. Hsüeh Chao-yün, *tr. fr. Chinese by* Lois Fusek. ATF

Delight in the High-Flying Orioles. Mao Wen-hsi, *tr. fr. Chinese by* Lois Fusek. ATF

Delight in the High-Flying Orioles. Wei Chuang, *tr. fr. Chinese by* Lois Fusek. ATF

Delight of crossing a summer river. At Kaya in Tamba. Buson, *tr. fr. Japanese by* Hiroaki Sato. *Fr.* Eighty-seven Hokku. FCEI

Delight of humane kind, and gods above. Lucretius, *tr. fr. Latin by* Dryden. *Fr.* De Rerum Natura (On the Nature of Things), I. OBVE

Delight of Solitariness, The. Sir Philip Sidney. *See* Arcadia: Solitariness.

Delight Song of Tsoai-Talee, The. N. Scott Momaday. CDW; GrPl; InPK; STE

Delighted that Jippo Has Come to See Me in My Illness. Rai San'yo, *tr. fr. Chinese by* Burton Watson. FCEI; JLIC-2

Delightful at night, quiet during the day. Miura Chora, *tr. fr. Japanese by* Hiroaki Sato. *Fr.* Sixteen Hokku. FCEI

Delightful, book, your trip. Aoibhinn, A Leabhráin, Do Thriall. *Unknown, tr. by* Flann O'Brien. BIrV

Delightful change from the town's abode. Barnyard Melodies. Fred Emerson Brooks. OBAL

Delightful I think it to be in the bosom of an isle. St. Columcille's Island Hermitage. *Unknown, tr. by* Kenneth Jackson. AnIL

Delights of the Door, The. Francis Ponge, *tr. fr. French by* Robert Bly. NU

Delilah. Kipling. BrPo

Delilah. Milton. *Fr.* Samson Agonistes. SeCePo

Delilah Aberyswith was a lady—not too young. Delilah. Kipling. BrPo

Delineaments of the Giants, The. William Carlos Williams. *See* Paterson: Paterson lies in the valley under the Passaic Falls.

Delinquent Travellers, The. Samuel Taylor Coleridge. OBTV

Delirium in Vera Cruz. Malcolm Lowry. FaBoTw; OxBTC

Deliverance. Barbara Crooker. TSL

Deliverance. Frances Ellen Watkins Harper. WPOW

Deliverance from a Fit of Fainting. Anne Bradstreet. TAP

Deliverance is not for me in renunciation. Rabindranath Tagore. *Fr.* Gitanjali, LXXIII. WGRP

Deliverance of Argos, The. Adelaïde-Gillette Dufresnoy, *tr. fr. French by* Dorothy Backer. DMF

Deliverance of Jehovah, The. Bible, *O.T. See* Psalms: Psalm XXVII ("The Lord is my light. ").

Deliverer, The. Milton. *See* Samson Agonistes: Oh [*or* O], how comely it is, and how reviving.

Delivering Children. David Holbrook. NePoEA-2

Delivery Guaranteed. Kingsley Amis. OBD

DeLiza Spend the Day in the City ("DeLiza drive the car to fetch, Alexis"). June Jordan. NoAM

Dell, The. Gavin Ewart. OxBC

Dell's hounds leap like the damned around the trunk. Coon Hunt. Thomas Rabbitt. MT

Delos. Bernard Spencer. NoAM

Delta, The. Michael Dennis Browne. NYBP

Delta lies unchanged, flat, The. Aerial View of Louisiana. Cleopatra Mathis. MAYP

Delta Traveller. Charles Wright. AmPA; LCAP

Delug'd with tears, by what you heard before. To My Honoured Patron Humphery Davie. Benjamin Tompson. SCAP

Deluge. John Clare. BoNaP

Deluge, The, *sel. Unknown.*
Animals in the Ark, The. ChTr; GBP

Deluge, The. *Unknown, tr. fr. Delaware (Lenape) Indian by* C. S. Rafinesque. *Fr.* Walam [*or* Wallum] Olum; or, Red Score. LiTA

Deluge 1939, The. Saunders Lewis, *tr. fr. Welsh by* Gwyn Morgan. OBWVE

Delusions of the days that once have been. Longfellow. *Fr.* Giles Corey of the Salem Farms. PAH

Delve deep amongst the musty muniments. Nicolas Gatineau. Arthur Stanley Bourinot. CaP

Dem Belly Full. Legon Cogil *and* Carlton Barrett. PBCV

Dem say/ who say? Black Bud. Michael Smith. PBCV

Dem say him born. For Don Drummond. Lorna Goodison. PBCV

Dem youths now a days. De Youths. Nefertiti Gayle. WS

Demagogue, The. Phyllis McGinley. FaBoEE

Demands nothing threatens nothing. Study: A Hand. Gyorgy Raba, *tr. by* Jascha Kessler. FOC

Demands of the Muse. Vernon Watkins. PoA

Deme as Ye List Uppon Goode Cause. Sir Thomas Wyatt. PoEL-1

Demeanour. *Unknown.* OxBChV

Demension Trumps (21). The Computer Iterates the Greater Trumps. Gene Wolfe. BWV

Dementia Praecox. Morris Bishop. PoA

Demiurge's Laugh, The. Robert Frost. OxBA

Democracy. Harriet Monroe. *Fr.* Commemoration Ode. AA

Democratic Barber; or, Country Gentleman's Surprise, The. John Parrish. NOEC

Democritus and Heraclitus ("Democritus, dear droll, revisit Earth"). Matthew Prior. OxBSP

Demolition, The. Anne Stevenson. OxBSP

Demon. Ahmad Faraz, *tr. fr. Urdu by* Mahmood Jamal. PBMUP

Demon-Lover, The. James Abraham Hillhouse. *Fr.* Hadad. AA

Demon-Lover. Sylvia Paskin. DT

Demon Lover, The. Adrienne Rich. IHMS

Demon Lover, The. *Unknown.* EnSB; HAP; LiTB; MAT; UnPo; WeW

Demon of the Mirror, The. Bayard Taylor. BeLS

Demons. Aimé Césaire, *tr. fr. French by* Michael Benedikt. POS

Denial, A. Elizabeth Barrett Browning. GBL; OBNC

Denial. George Herbert. JCP; NAEL-1; NOBE; NoP; OAEL-1 (Deniall.) MePo; PoEL-2; TOF

Denied: the secret notebook of roots. Lessons. Mekeel McBride. NAmP

Denise. Robert Beverly Hale. GrPl

Denise: A Letter Never Sent. Henri Coulette. *Fr.* The War of the Secret Agents, VIII. NePoEA-2

Denmark. Humbert Wolfe. OBTV

Denouement. Ruth Stone. BoWoP

Dense on the stream the vapours lay. The Mowers: An Anticipation of the Cholera, 1848. Charles MacKay. EBVV

Dense ravine, no inch, A. Portola Valley. Amy Clampitt. EOEF

Dense, the white cloud of moths whirling. Hitler Spring. Eugenio Montale, *tr. by* William Arrowsmith. AnAn

Density. Roland Jooris, *tr. fr. Dutch by* Peter Nijmeijer. DuIn

Dentist, A. *Unknown.* FaBoCo; FaBoEE (Epitaph on a Dentist.) OxBoLi

Dentists continue to water their lawns even in the rain. The Great Society. Robert Bly. NoAM

Dentist's Window, A. James Keir Baxter. OxBC

Dentologia; a Poem on the Diseases of the Teeth and Their Proper Remedies, *sels.* Solyman Brown. FaBoUs
Artificial Teeth.
Caries.
Tartar.
Value of Dentistry, The.

Denunciation, A. Mahammed Abdille Hassan, *tr. fr. Somali by* B. W. Andrzejewski. WTO

Denunciation; or, Unfrock'd Again. Philip Whalen. NeAP

Denzel Brush zipped up his periscope and treed the bartender. Errant. John Godfrey. UL

Deo gracias [*or* gracias], Anglia. The Agincourt Carol. *Unknown.* EBEV; OAEL-1; OBET (Carol of Agincourt, A.) MeEL

Deo Optimo Maximo. Louise Imogen Guiney. TrPWD

Deodand, The. Anthony Hecht. DiPo; NoAM

Deor. *Unknown, tr. fr. Anglo-Saxon.* EBEV, *tr. by* John Wain; TEP, *tr. by* Walter Kendrick

Deor's Lament. *Unknown, tr. fr. Anglo-Saxon by* Charles W. Kennedy. AnOE; OAEL-1

Depairt, depairt, depairt [*or* Departe, departe, departe]. Lament of the Master of Erskine. Alexander Scott. GBL (Lament, 1547, A.) CH

Depart from Me. Mary Elizabeth Coleridge. TrPWD

Departe, departe, departe. *See* Depairte, depairte, depairte.

Departed, The. John Banister Tabb. AA

"Departed Friend, A." Julia A. Moore. FiBHP

Departed friend, I do not come. Exequy: To Peter Allt. Kildare Dobbs. OBCV

Departing Geese. Yoshida no Kenko, *tr. fr. Japanese by* Steven D. Carter. WFTW

Departing leaves. Falling Leaves. Ch'iao Lin, *tr. by* Dominic Cheung. IFON

Departing spring: a boat with brushwood. Buson, *tr. fr. Japanese by* Hiroaki Sato. *Fr.* Eighty-seven Hokku. FCEI

Departing spring: birds cry. Basho, *tr. fr. Japanese by* Burton Watson. *Fr.* Seventy-six Hokku. FCEI

Departing spring: I've lost the eyeglasses. Buson, *tr. fr. Japanese by* Hiroaki Sato. *Fr.* Eighty-seven Hokku. FCEI

Departing spring: on the carriage. Buson, *tr. fr. Japanese by* Hiroaki Sato. *Fr.* Eighty-seven Hokku. FCEI

Departing wild geese. Issa, *tr. fr. Japanese by* Hiroaki Sato. *Fr.* Forty-four Hokku. FCEI

Departing Words to a Son. Robert Pack. GOYP

Department, The. Allen Grossman. PPR

Departmental. Robert Frost. GoYe; HeIP; HoPM; MoAB; MoAmPo; NAAL-2; NOBA; NOBL; OBAL; SoSe

Departure. Kingsley Amis. NePoEA

Departure. Ory Bernstein, *tr. fr. Hebrew by* Bernhard Frank. MHeP

Departure. Edmund Blunden. OxBSP

Departure. Van K. Brock. MT

Departure. Carolyn Forché. AnAn

Departure, The. Kevin Hart. UAS

Departure. William Hart-Smith. *Fr.* Christopher Columbus. PoAu-2

Departure. Genny Lim. BrSi

Departure. Edna St. Vincent Millay. MoAmPo

Departure. Erika Mitterer, *tr. fr. German by* Beth Bjorklund. CoAuP

Departure, The. William Vaughn Moody. AnAmPo

Departure, The. Robert Pack. NePoEA

Departure. Coventry Patmore. *Fr.* The Unknown Eros, I, viii. ACP; NOBE; OBEV; OBNC; SeCePo

Departure. Pierre Reverdy, *tr. fr. French by* Michael Benedikt. POS

Departure, The. Jeremy Robson. VWA

Departure. May Riley Smith. AA

Departure, The. Frank Steele. GOYP

Departure, The. Reed Whittemore. TAP

Departure; an Elegy, The. Henry King. SeCP

Departure in Middle Age. Roland Mathias. CRP; OBWVE

Departure in the Dark. C. Day Lewis. TwCP

Departure of '82. Sa'di Yusuf, *tr. fr. Arabic by* Lena Jayyusi *and* Naomi Shihab Nye. MAP

Departure of the Good Daemon, The. Robert Herrick. FaBoRV

Departure (Southampton Docks: October 1899). Thomas Hardy. Son

Departure's Girl-Friend. W. S. Merwin. LCAP

Deportation. "M. B." *tr. fr. Polish by* A. Leyeles. TrJP

Deportation. Judah Leib Teller, *tr. fr. Yiddish by* Benjamin *and* Barbara Harshav. AYP

Deportation Order. Franco Fortini, *tr. fr. Italian by* Lawrence R. Smith. NItP

Deposition. Kevin Ireland. ATNZ

Deposition by John Wilmot, A. Vincent McHugh. ErPo

Deposition from Love, A. Thomas Carew. CaPo; MeLP; OBS

Deposition of the Burden, The. Tadeusz Rozewicz, *tr. fr. Polish by* Czeslaw Milosz. PwPP

Depot, The. Lewis Turco. GrPl

Depot Blues. *Unknown.* AmFP

Depot in Rapid City. Roberta Hill. BoWoP

Depreciating Her Beauty. Wilfrid Scawen Blunt. *Fr.* The Love Sonnets of Proteus, VI. OBMV

Depressed by the Death of the Horse That He Bought from Robert Bly. Henry Taylor. BXAP

Depressing to dismount the siege-machines. Bertrans de Born, *tr. by* Paul Blackburn. Pro

Depression. Robert Bly. NaP

Depression. Wendy Cope. FaBoWP

Depression before Spring. Wallace Stevens. OBAL; SOTW

Deprived of his enemy, shrugged to a standstill. John Berryman. *Fr.* Dream Songs. CAPP; LCAP

Deprived of the green of that exclusive golf course, the scotch. Epistle to the Gentiles. Alfred Hayes. TrJP

Depths, The. Denise Levertov. NaP; NU

Depths of Sorrow, The. *Gond Oral Tradition, tr. by* V. Elwin *and* S. Hivale. WTO

Der Abschied. May Sarton. ER

Der Blinde Junge. Mina Loy. QFR

Der lived a king inta da aste. King Orfeo. *Unknown.* ESPB; OxBB, *with music;* OxBoLi

Der Mond ist aufgegangen. Heine, *tr. fr. German by* James Thomson. AWP

Deranged. Padraic Fiacc. NeIP

Derby Ram, The ("As I was going to Derby"). *Unknown.* FaBoNo; GBP; OxNR

Derby Ram, The ("Oh, as I went down to Derby Town"). *Unknown.* AmFP

Derelict. Young E. Allison. BLPA; FaBoBe; FaFP; OnMSP

Derelict, The. Lucius Harwood Foote. AA

Derelict. Kipling. BrPo; NoAM

Derelict. Elisabeth Cavazza Pullen. AA

Dere's a beeg jam up de reever, w'ere rapide is runnin' fas.' The Log Jam. William Henry Drummond. NOBC

Dere's a liddle fact in hishdory vitch few hafe onnershtand. Charles Godfrey Leland. *Fr.* Breitmann in Politics. OBAL

Dere's No Hidin' Place Down Dere. *Unknown.* BPo

Derivations, *sel.* Jenny Joseph.
  Watching a Child Watching a Witch. AIW

Dermis. Anthony McNeill. PBCV

Derry. Seamus Deane. CIP

Derry Morning. Derek Mahon. NOIV

Dervish, The. Muhammad al-Faituri, *tr. fr. Arabic by* Sargon Boulus *and* Peter Porter. MAP

Dervish wept to feel the violence of, A. Faridu'ddin Attar, *tr. fr. Persian by* Afkham Darbandi *and* Dick Davis. *Fr.* The Conference of the Birds. TOF

Dervorgilla's supremely lovely daughter. Portrait with Background. Oliver St. John Gogarty. OBMV

Derwent; an Ode, *sel.* John Carr.
  Memories of Childhood. NOEC

Des a little cabin. A Little Cabin. Charles Bertram Johnson. BANP

Descartes. Mark Insingel. DuIn

Descartes and the Stove. Charles Tomlinson. FaBoMo

Descartes at Daybreak. Aidan Carl Mathews. CIP

Descend, embrace this daughter. Dialogue with the Dead. Amelia Rosselli, *tr. by* Lawrence R. Smith. NItP

Descend, Fair Sun! George Chapman. *Fr.* The Masque of the Middle Temple and Lincoln's Inn. EIL

Descend from Heav'n Urania, by that name. Milton. *Fr.* Paradise Lost, *bk.* VII, *ll.* 1-39. EBEV; NAEL-1; OAEL-1; TOF
  (Invocation to Urania.) FiP; OBS

Descend from that pneumatic pedestal. To a Loudmouth Pontificator. Ray Mizer. TW

Descend, Ye Nine. Pope. *Fr.* Ode on St. Cecilia's Day. GN

Descendancy. Tom Paulin. FaBCIP

Descendant of the ancestor Kao-yang. Encountering Sorrow. *Unknown, tr. by* Burton Watson. CoBCP

Descended, Adam to the bower where Eve. Milton. *Fr.* Paradise Lost, *bk.* XII, *ll.* 607-649.
  (Adam Fallen.) NOCV

Descended of an ancient line ("Tyrrhena regum progenies"). Horace, *tr. fr. Latin. Fr.* Odes, III, 29. NOCV
  (Happy the Man, *st.* 8 *only.*) FaPoR
  (Horat. Ode 29. Book 3.) SeCV-2
  ("In time to come, if such a crime should be.")
  (To Maecenas.) AWP, *tr. by* Dryden; OBVE, *tr. by* Dryden; SeCV-1, *tr. by* Dryden.

Descending. Valentin Iremonger. *See* Going Down the Mountain.

Descending. Robert Pack. NePoEA-2

Descending Figure. Louise Glück. AnAn; FaBoWP; GeTw

Descending the Ridge of Flying Clouds. T'ang Hsien-Tsu, *tr. fr. Chinese by* Jonathan Chaves. CoBLCP

Descent, The. William Carlos Williams. HAP; MoAB; WeW

Descent for the Lost. Philip Child. CaP

Descent from the Cross. "Michael Field." WPE

Descent into Hell, The. William Langland. *Fr.* The Vision of Piers Plowman. PoEL-1

Descent of Abu Nuwas. Hasab al-Shaikh Jafar, *tr. fr. Arabic by* Diana Der Hovanessian *and* Salma Khadra Jayyusi. MAP

Descent of the Child, The. Susan Langstaff Mitchell. TIRV

Descent of the Vulture, The. Marya Zaturenska. WPE

Descent of Winter (Section 10/30), The. William Carlos Williams. InPK

Descent on Middlesex, The. Peter St. John. PAH

Describe porcelain and I was touching the cool gleam of white sink. Tender Arc. Diane Ward. LP

Describes Rationally the Irrational Effects of Love. Sister Juana Inés de la Cruz, *tr. fr. Spanish by* Samuel Beckett. MexPo

Describes the Place Where Cynthia Is Sporting Herself. Philip Ayres. EnLoPo

Describing a Suit. Hafiz Ibrahim, *tr. fr. Arabic by* Christopher Tingley *and* Christopher Middleton. MAP

Describing My Feelings upon Encountering Snow, *sel.* Li K'ai-hsien, *tr. fr. Chinese by* Jonathan Chaves.
  "Crossing the ridge, the woodcutter loses his way." CoBLCP

Describing My Feelings While Living in Retirement by the Riverside: Seven Poems to the Tune "Ch'ing-p'ing-yüeh." Yang Chi, *tr. fr. Chinese by* Jonathan Chaves. CoBLCP

Describing My Feelings While Living in the Spring Quarters at Chiang-ning: Four Poems to the Tune "Ching-p'ing-yëh", *sel.* Yang Chi, *tr. fr. Chinese by* Jonathan Chaves. CoBLCP
   "Wild singing and drunken dancing."

Description, A. Lord Herbert of Cherbury. OPOP; SeCP

Description of a City Shower, A. Swift. HeIP; MAT; NAEL-1; NOEC; NoP; OAEL-1; OBSV; PoE; PPP; SeCePo; TEP; UnPo

Description of a Good Boy, The. Henry Dixon. OxBChV; OxNR, *st.* 1

Description of a Landscape. Erich Fried, *tr. fr. German by* Beth Bjorklund. CoAuP

Description of a New England Spring. John Josselyn. SCAP

Description of a Plaza, a Monument and Allegories in Bronze. Antonio Cisneros, *tr. fr. Spanish by* David Tipton. Per

Description of a Strange (and Miraculous) Fish, A. Martin Parker. CoMu

Description of an American Billionaire. Hermann Gail, *tr. fr. German by* Beth Bjorklund. CoAuP

Description of an Author's Bedchamber, A. Goldsmith. BIrV

Description of an Irish Feast, The. Hugh MacGowran. *See* O'Rourke's noble fare [*or* O'Rourke's revel rout].

Description of Beauty, A ("O beauty (beams, nay, flame)."), *sel.* Samuel Daniel, *after the Italian of* Giambattista Marini. OBSC
   Enjoy Thy April Now. ElL; ELP

Description of Elizium, The. Michael Drayton. *Fr.* Muses' Elysium [*or* Elizium]. OAEL-1
   (Poet's Paradise, The.) WiR, *much abr.*

Description of His Ugly Lady, A. Thomas Hoccleve. MeEL

Description of Holland. Samuel Butler. OBTV

Description of London, A. John Bancks. NOEC

Description of Maidenhead, A. Earl of Rochester. NOBL

Description of Sir Geoffrey Chaucer, The. Robert Greene. *Fr.* Greene's Vision. CTC; OBSC
   (Sir Geoffrey Chaucer.) FaBoCh

Description of Spring in London, A. *Unknown.* NOEC

Description of Spring, Wherein Each Thing Renews Save Only the Lover. Earl of Surrey. *See* Soote Season, The.

Description of the Contrarious Passions in a Lover. Petrarch. *See* Sonnets to Laura: To Laura in Life.

Description of the Morning, A. Swift. EBEV; FF; HAP; HeIP; InPS; NOBE; NOEC; NoP; OAEL-1; PPP; Prf; SoSe; TEP; WeW

Description of Tyme, A. Alexander Montgomerie. OxBS

Description of Wallace, A. Henry the Minstrel. *Fr.* The Wallace, IX. GoTS
   (Schir William Wallace.) OxBS

Descriptive Piece for April, 1853, A. Chiang Ch'un-lin, *tr. fr. Chinese by* Irving Lo. WFTU

Descriptive Poem, Addressed to Two Ladies at Their Return from Viewing the Mines, near Whitehaven, A, *sel.* John Dalton.
   Agape the sooty collier stands. NOEC

Dese Bones Gwine to Rise Again. *Unknown.* AS, *with music;* OxBoLi

Desert, The. "Adunis", *tr. fr. Arabic by* Abdullah al-Udhari. MPAW

Desert, The. Al-Munsif al-Wahaybi, *tr. fr. Arabic by* Salma Khadra Jayyusi *and* Naomi Shihab Nye. MAP

Desert. Agnes Gergely, *tr. fr. Hungarian by* Emery George. VWA

Desert afternoon. Alone. Zoltán Zelk, *tr. by* Daniel Hoffman. MHuP

Desert around. Desert. Treason of Sand. Hemda Roth, *tr. by* Mariana Potasman. VWA

Desert Claypan. Frederick Macartney. PoAu-1

Desert Flowers. Keith Douglas. FaBoTw

Desert in the Sea. Brian Swann. AmPA

Desert is full of powerful winds, The. Parting Chant. T'an Ssu-t'ung, *tr. by* Timothy C. Wong. WFTU

Desert Lark, The. Eugène Marias, *tr. fr. Afrikaans by* Uys Krige *and* Jack Cope. PeSA

Desert Madness. A. Leyeles, *tr. fr. Yiddish by* Benjamin *and* Barbara Harshav. AYP

Desert March. Gerda Norvig. VWA

Desert moves out on half the horizon, The. The Supper after the Last. Galway Kinnell. NOBA

Desert of Love, The. János Pilinszky, *tr. fr. Hungarian by* Ted Hughes *and* János Csokits. MHuP; OBVE

Desert Places. Robert Frost. AmPP; CMoP; InPK; MoAB; MoAmPo; MoP; NAAL-2; NoAM; NOBA; OxBA; PoE; PPP; RB; TAP; UnPo

Desert River. Patricia Benton. GoYe

Desert Shipwreck. Barbara Leslie Jordan. GoYe

Desert Stone. Miriam Waddington. VWA

Desert Tortoise. Byrd Baylor. RHPC

Desert Warfare. Michael Longley. CIP

Desert Wind. Malka Heifetz-Tussman, *tr. fr. Yiddish by* Kathryn Hellerstein. AYP

Deserted and scorned, the proud Marlborough sate. The False Favorite's Downfall. *Unknown.* APAS

Deserted Beach. Ruth Dallas. ATNZ

Deserted Buildings under Shefford Mountain. John Glassco. OBCV

Deserted city, residence of Ch'en emperors. The Residence of the Emperors of Ch'en. Yang Wei-chen, *tr. by* Jonathan Chaves. CoBLCP

Deserted Estate at South Garden, The. Hsü Pen, *tr. fr. Chinese by* Jonathan Chaves. CoBLCP

Deserted Farms Poem. Bruce Severy. NOVW

Deserted Home, A. Sidney Royse Lysaght. CH

Deserted Homestead, The. Loren C. Eiseley. PoA

Deserted House, The. Mary Elizabeth Coleridge. BoTP; CH

Deserted House, *sel.* Dorothy Wellesley.
   "He is not dead nor liveth." OBMV

Deserted Mountain, The. *Unknown, tr. fr. Irish by* John Montague. BIrV

Deserted mountain, streams and stones, A. Searching for the Ruins of the Pavilion of the Drunken Old Man. Yang Shih-ch'i, *tr.* Jonathan Chaves. CoBLCP

Deserted Plantation, The. Paul Laurence Dunbar. AnAmPo

Deserted Room. Erich Fried, *tr. fr. German by* Beth Bjorklund. CoAuP

Deserted Shrine. Avner Treinin, *tr. fr. Hebrew by* E. A. Levenston. VWA

Deserted Village, The, *sels.* Goldsmith. BeLS; EnRP; FaFP; GoTL; LaA; NOEC; NoP; OAEL-1; PoEL-3; TEP
   Auburn. SeCePo
   (Sweet Auburn.) LiTB; NOBE
   (Village, The.) TrGrPo
   "Even now the devastation is begun." EBEV
   "Ill fares the land, to hastening ills a prey." OBSV
   "O luxury! Thou curst by Heaven's decree." BIrV
   "Sweet Auburn! parent of the blissful hour." EBEV
   "Sweet smiling village, loveliest of the lawn." NOIV
   Village Parson, The. WGRP
   (Village Preacher, The.) TIRV
   Village Preacher, The. TrGrPo
   Village Schoolmaster, The. TrGrPo
   "Yes! let the rich deride, the proud disdain." OBSV

Deserted Village, The. "Robin Hyde." ATNZ; PeNZ; WPE

Deserted Well, The. Yusuf al-Khal, *tr. fr. Arabic by* Sargon Boulus *and* Naomi Shihab Nye. MAP

Deserter, The. Joseph Seamon Cotter, Jr. CDC

Deserter, The. A. E. Housman. OBMV

Deserter, The. John Manifold. CBAP; WaP

Deserter, The. Edward Rowland Sill. AnAmPo

Deserter, The. Stevie Smith. FaBoWP

Deserter's Lamentation, The. John Philpot Curran. FaBoRV; SeCePo

Desertion of Beauty and Strength, The. *Unknown. Fr.* Everyman. ACP

Desertion of the Women and Seals, The. George Mackay Brown. OxBC

Desertmartin. Tom Paulin. CIP; FaBCIP

Desideria. Wordsworth. *See* Surprised by Joy [Impatient as the Wind].

Desiderium. Phineas Fletcher. *Fr.* The Purple Island, I. OBS

Design. Robert Frost. BLPL; CMoP; HeIP; InPK; InPS; MoP; NAAL-2; NIP; NoAM; NOBA; NoP; PPP; PrIm; Son; SoSe; TAP

Design, The. Clarence Major. PoBA

Design. Peter Redgrove. OxBC

Design for Mediæval Tapestry. Abraham Moses Klein. CaP

Designer sits, head in hand, The. Design. Peter Redgrove. OxBC

Desirable Property, A. Vivienne Joseph. ATNZ

Desire. "Æ." OBMV; TIRV; TrPWD

Desire. Matthew Arnold. WGRP

Desire. Isaac de Botton, *tr. fr. Judezmo by* Stephen Levy. VWA

Desire ("The knight knocked at the castle gate"). William Cornish. Mes; OBSC
   (Knight and the Lady, The.) NOBE

Desire ("You and I and Amyas"). William Cornish. OBSC
   (Latet Languis.) OBEV

Desire. Gary Eddy. KS

Desire. Dinah Livingstone. AIW

Desire. Mary Mackey. ER

Desire. Sir Philip Sidney. *See* Astrophel and Stella: CIX. "Thou blind man's mark, thou fool's self-chosen snare."

Desire. Judah Leib Teller, *tr. fr. Yiddish by* Benjamin *and* Barbara Harshav. AYP

Desire and Revenge. Lawrence Raab. BLA

Desire for a woman took hold of me in the night. *Unknown.* LLLT

Desire for Hermitage, The. *Unknown, tr. fr. Old Irish by* Sean O'Faolain. AnIL

Desire is a witch. C. Day Lewis. CMoP

Desire Is Dead. D. H. Lawrence. FaBoEE

Desire makes you. Ann Smith, *tr. by* Joanna Bankier. OV

Desire may be dead. Desire Is Dead. D. H. Lawrence. FaBoEE

Desire of Water, The. Mark Jarman. PoA
Desire that all men have is all my love. Love and Marriage. Ray
   Mathew. PoAu-2
"Desire, though thou my old companion art." Sir Philip Sidney. *Fr.*
   Astrophel and Stella, LXXII. NAEL-1
Desire was a quotation from someone. Michael Palmer. UL
Desiree,/ I find it most bitter that you. Denise: A Letter Never Sent.
   Henri Coulette. *Fr.* The War of the Secret Agents, VIII. NePoEA-2
Desires. Connie Bensley. FaBoWP
Desire's Government. "A. W." EiL
Desires of Men and Women. John Berryman. LiTM
Desirous, in the lighted sound of his dreams. Fear Makes the Spectator.
   Cees Nooteboom, *tr.* by Peter Nijmeijer. DuIn
Desk, The. David Bottoms. BLA; MAYP; MT
Desk, The. Cid Corman. VGW
Desks. Dave Smith. HCAP
Desmet, Idaho, March 1969. Janet Campbell Hale. STE; VoR
Desnos Reading the Palms of Men on Their Way to the Gas Chambers.
   Stephen Berg. VWA
Desolate. Sydney Thompson Dobell. OBNC
Desolate. Claude McKay. CDC
Desolate. Gerald Massey. EBVV
Desolate and lone. Lost. Carl Sandburg. AmPP; CMoP; PDV
Desolate City, The. *Unknown, tr. fr. Arabic by* Wilfrid Scawen Blunt.
   AWP; OBEV
Desolate Lover, The. Eileen Shanahan. NeIP
Desolate poems of chaotic times—could I bear. Ch'ien Ch'ien-i, *tr. fr.*
   Chinese by Jonathan Chaves. *Fr.* Miscellaneous Feelings at West
   Lake. CoBLCP
Desolate rhythm of dying recurs, The. Fall. Michael Smith. CIP
Desolate that cry as though world were unworthy. Chough. Rex Warner.
   PoRA
Desolate Valley, The. Thomas Pringle. OBTV
Desolation. E. A. Baratynsky, *tr. fr. Russian by* Alan Myers. AAA
Desolation. Amy Lowell. PoA
Desolation. *Unknown, tr. fr. Welsh by* Aneirin Talfan Davies. OBWVE
Desolation in Zion. Bible, *O.T. Fr.* Lamentations, I: 12–17. TrJP
"Desolation Is a Delicate Thing." Elinor Wylie. MoAmPo
Despair. Fulke Greville. *See* Caelica: Who grace, for zenith had, from
   which no shadowes grow.
Despair. László Kálnoky, *tr. fr. Hungarian by* Edwin Morgan. MHuP
Despair. Denise Levertov. NNaP
Despair. Spenser. *Fr.* The Faerie Queene, I, 9. SeCePo
Despair and Hope. Israel Zangwill. TrJP
Despair inspires me, moods guide my hand. Canada's Natural Resource.
   Midnight Sun. GOS
Despair of all, and hope for none! Despair and Hope. Israel Zangwill.
   TrJP
Despair of the Sun. Robert Desnos, *tr. fr. French by* Michael Benedikt.
   POS
Despairing Lover, The. William Walsh. ELP; FaBoCh; NBLV; NOBL;
   OxBoLi
Despisals. Muriel Rukeyser, *tr. fr. Greek by* Edmund Keeley. AnAn;
   NMM; Prf
Despise the World. *Unknown.* MeEL
Despised and Rejected. Katharine Lee Bates. TrCP
Despite myself I become so childish. Kaai Chigetsu, *tr. fr. Japanese by*
   Hiroaki Sato. *Fr.* Thirteen Hokku. FCEI
Despondency Corrected. Wordsworth. *Fr.* The Excursion, IV. EnRP
Desponding Phyllis [*or* Phillis] was endu'd. Phyllis; or, The Progress of
   Love. Swift. OAEL-1; OBSV; PoE
   (Phillis; or, The Progress of Love.) PoEL-3
Desponding Soul's Wish, The. John Byrom. *See* My Spirit Longeth for
   Thee.
Despot treads thy sacred sands, The. Carolina. Henry Timrod. PAH
Despot's heel is on thy shore, The. My Maryland. James Ryder Randall.
   AA; AnAmPo; FaBoBe; FaFP; PAH
Destination or an origin?, A. Infinity Effect at the Hôtel Soubise. Alfred
   Corn. EOEF
Destinations. Josephine Jacobsen. WPE
Destined for greatness, he lies on his stomach, a pacifier. Pages of an
   Album. Dan Pagis, *tr.* by Warren Bargad *and* Stanley F. Chyet. IP
Destined to war from very infancy. Gabriello Chiabrera, *tr. by*
   Wordsworth. *Fr.* Epitaphs. AWP; PFI
Destinie. Abraham Cowley. MeLP
Destiny. Sir Edwin Arnold. PoLF
Destiny. Matthew Arnold. NOBVV; OxBSP
Destiny. Eloise Bibb. CBWP-4
Destiny. Angela Figueroa-Aymerich, *tr. fr. Spanish by* Kate Flores.
   DMH
Destiny. Amalia Guglielminetti, *tr. fr. Italian by* Muriel Kittel. DMI
Destiny. Harrison Smith Morris. AA
Destiny of Nations, The, *sels.* Samuel Taylor Coleridge.

" 'Even so' (the exulting Maiden said)." ChER
"For what is Freedom, but the unfettered use." EnRP
Destiny of the Poet. Claude Vigée, *tr. fr. French by* Anthony Rudolf.
   VWA
Destroyer of Destroyers, The. Wallace Rice. PAH
Destroying Angel. Hilary Corke. NYBP
Destruction. Joanne Kyger. UL
Destruction of Jerusalem by the Babylonian Hordes, The. Isaac
   Rosenberg. VWA
Destruction of Letters. Babette Deutsch. WPE
Destruction of Sennacherib, The. Byron. BeLS; BLPA; BLPL; EnRP;
   FaBoBe; FaBoCh; FaFP; FaPON; FaPoR; FF; GN; HAP; HeIP; InPS;
   NoP; OBWP; OnMSP; PoLF; RB; TrCP; WBLP; WeW; WGRP
Destruction of the Fifth Planet. Brian W. Aldiss. BWV
Destruction of Troy, The. Virgil, *tr. fr. Latin by* Sir John Denham. *Fr.*
   The Aeneid [*or* Eneados], II. SeCV-1
Destructive caries comes with secret stealth. Caries. Solyman Brown.
   Fr. Dentologia; a Poem on the Diseases of the Teeth and Their Proper
   Remedies. FaBoUs
Desultory Thoughts on My Old Home. Yu T'ung, *tr. fr. Chinese by* Paul
   W. Kroll. WFTU
Detachment is a virtue, teachers say. Ballade on Eschatology. Sister
   Mary Madeleva. GoYe
Detail. Mary Ursula Bethell. ATNZ; PeNZ
Detail, The. Cid Corman. PCP
Detail from an Annunciation by Crivelli. Rosemary Dobson. PoAu-2
Details. Dezsö Tandori, *tr. fr. Hungarian by* Daniel Hoffman. MHuP
Detectives from the vice squad. Cafe: 3 A.M. Langston Hughes. GLP;
   HCAP
Determination. John Henrik Clarke. CNA; PoBA
Determinism. Maurice Evan Hare. *See* There once was a man [*or* There
   was a young man] who said, "Damn!"
Determinism. Lyn Hejinian. LP
Detour. Harold Bond. TSM
Detour. Michael Longley. CIP
Detroit. Donald Hall. AmFN
Detroit City. Jill Witherspoon Boyer. CNA
Detroit Conference of Unity and Art. Nikki Giovanni. HoPM
Detroit Hymns, Christmas Eve. Jim Daniels. SoTCo
Detroit just sits there. The Idea of Detroit. Jim Gustafson. UL
Deuce, a Roast of Scraggy Quails, a Bit, The. Francesco Berni, *tr. fr.*
   Italian by Lorna de' Lucci. PFI
Deuteronomy. Robert Bringhurst. NOBC
Deuteronomy, *sels.* Bible, *O.T.*
   "For the Lordes parte is his folke." *Fr.* XXXII: 9-15, *tr.* by William
   Tyndale. OBVE
   Give Ear, Ye Heavens. *Fr.* XXXII: 1-43. TrJP
Deva-like Barbarian. Ho Ning, *tr. fr. Chinese by* Lois Fusek. ATF
Deva-like Barbarian, The. Li Hsün, *tr. fr. Chinese by* Lois Fusek. ATF
Deva-like Barbarian. Mao Hsi-chen, *tr. fr. Chinese by* Lois Fusek. ATF
Deva-like Barbarian. Niu Chiao, *tr. fr. Chinese by* Lois Fusek. ATF
Deva-like Barbarian. Sun Kuang-hsien, *tr. fr. Chinese by* Lois Fusek.
   ATF
Deva-like Barbarian. Wei Ch'eng-pan, *tr. fr. Chinese by* Lois Fusek.
   ATF
Deva-like Barbarian. Wei Chuang, *tr. fr. Chinese by* Lois Fusek. ATF
Deva-like Barbarian. Wen T'ing-yün, *tr. fr. Chinese by* Lois Fusek.
   ATF
Deva-like Barbarian. Yin O, *tr. fr. Chinese by* Lois Fusek. ATF
Devastated land, and I searched. The Catastrophe (Chimbote). Julio
   Ortega, *tr.* by David Tipton. Per
Devastation. Peter Russell. NPo
Developing a Wife. Andrew Taylor. CBAP
Development. D. J. Enright. OxBSP
Development, The. Marge Piercy. NBLV
Development of Idiocy, A. Ebenezer Jones. OBNC
Deviation, The. Louise Glück. *Fr.* Dedication to Hunger, IV. AnAn;
   GeTw
Deviator, The. Bertram J. Warr. OBCV
Devil, A. Zbigniew Herbert, *tr. fr. Polish by* Czeslaw Milosz. RB
Devil and the Angel, The, *sel.* Rosemary Dobson.
   Methuselah. PoAu-2
Devil and the Governor, The, *sel.* William Forster.
   "In New South Wales, as I plainly see." CBAP; PoAu-1
Devil and the Lady, The, *sel.* Tennyson.
   Deep Dark Night, The. SeCePo
Devil-Dancers, The. William Plomer. PeSA
Devil, having nothing else to do, The. On Lady Poltagrue, a Public Peril.
   Hilaire Belloc. FaBoCo; MoBrPo
Devil! I tell thee without nubbs or jubbs. After Reading the Life of Mrs.
   Catherine Stubbs in Isaac Ambrose's "War with the Devils." Isaac
   Hann. NOCV

Devil in Hades we're told was chained, The. Hell in Texas. *Unknown.* CowP

Devil in Texas, The. *Unknown.* NBLV; RB

Devil Is an Ass, The, *sel.* Ben Jonson.
   "Have you seen but a bright lily grow." FaBoCh
   (So Sweet Is She.) GN
   (So White, So Soft, So Sweet.) TrGrPo

Devil now knew his proper cue, The. Shelley. *Fr.* Peter Bell the Third. OBSV

Devil on Ice. Donald Davie. NoAM

Devil to Pay, The, *sel.* Dorothy L. Sayers.
   Choice of the Cross, The. TrCP

Devil was more generous than Adam, The. Samuel Butler. FaBoEE

Devil, we're told, in hell was chained, The. Hell in Texas. *Unknown.* BLPA

Devilish and the dark, the dying and diseas'd, The. "The Rounded Catalogue Divine Complete." Walt Whitman. NAAL-1

Devilish Mary. *Unknown.* AmFP

Devils. Norman Mailer. OBAL

Devil's Advice to Story-Tellers, The. Robert Graves. LiTM; MoP; NAEL-2; NoAM

Devil's Bag, The. James Stephens. WSC

Devil's Daughter, The. Lucha Corpi, *tr. fr. Spanish by the author and* Catherine Rodríguez-Nieto. *Fr.* The Marina Poems, III. CCP; OV

Devil's Dictionary, The, *sels.* Ambrose Bierce. OBAL
   "Blow, blow, ye spicy breezes."
   "Cur foretells the knell of parting day, The."
   "Fiercely the battle raged, and, sad to tell."
   "Hail, holy Lead!—of human feuds the great."
   "Megaceph, chosen to serve the State."
   "Once I seen a human ruin."
   " 'One night,' a doctor said, 'last fall.' "
   "Spelling reformer indicted, A."
   "There's a man with a nose."

Devil's Law Case, The, *sel.* John Webster.
   All the Flowers of the Spring. EiL; ELP; LiTB; OBS; PoEL-2; PoRA
   (Burial, The.) CH
   (Nets to Catch the Wind.) TrGrPo
   (Vanitas Vanitatum.) NOBE; OBEV

Devil's Nine Questions, The. *Unknown.* AmFP; WSC

Devil's Thoughts, The. Robert Southey *and* Samuel Taylor Coleridge. FaBoCo, *abr;* OBSV; OxBoLi, *abr.*

Devoide of reason, thrale to hopeles ire. Thomas Lodge. *Fr.* Phyllis, XXXI *after the French of* Pierre de Ronsard. AAS

Devonshire Scenes. Coventry Patmore. *Fr.* Tamerton Church-Tower or First Love. FaBoPP

Devonshire Song, A. *At. to* William Strode. OBS; PoEL-2, *sl. diff. vers.*

Devonshire Walk, A. William Browne. *Fr.* Britannia's Pastorals, I, Song 5. FaBoPP

Devotion. Thomas Campion. *See* Follow Thy Fair Sun [Unhappy Shadow].

Devotion. Thomas Campion. *See* Follow Your Saint [Follow with Accents Sweet].

Devotional Sonnet. Timothy Steele. CRP

Devotions of the Fowls, *sel.* John Lydgate.
   "Then I heard a voice celestial." PBBP

"Devouring Time, blunt thou the lion's paws [lyons pawes]." Shakespeare. *Fr.* Sonnets, XIX. AWP; ChTr; EBEV; MAT; NAEL-1; OAEL-1; OBSC; PoE; PoEL-2; TrGrPo

Devout Fits. John Donne. *See* Holy Sonnets: Oh, to vex me, contraries [*or* contraryes] meet in one.

Devout Lover, A. Thomas Randolph. HoPM; OBEV

Devout Man Prays to His Relations, The. William Herebert. MeEL

Devout Prayer of the Passion, A. *Unknown.* MeEL

Dew. Jennifer Maiden. CBAP

Dew. Charles Reznikoff. *See* Let other people come as streams.

Dew and the frost, the. Tameuji, *tr. fr. Japanese by* Steven D. Carter. WFTW

Dew at the tip of a leaf. Teika, *tr. fr. Japanese by* Hiroaki Sato. *Fr.* A Compendium of Good Tanka. FCEI

Dew for flowers, mist for grass! The Taoist Nun. Chang Pi, *tr. by* Lois Fusek. ATF

Dew is gleaming in the grass, The. Among the Millet. Archibald Lampman. CaP

Dew is on the grasses, dear, The. Youth. Georgia Douglas Johnson. BANP; PoNe

Dew is on the heather, The. The Captain's Feather. Samuel Minturn Peck. AA

Dew it trembles on the thorn, The. Silent Love. John Clare. EnRP

Dew of the rouge-flower, The. Kaga no Chiyo, *tr. by* R. H. Blyth. PBWP

Dew on a Dusty Heart. Jean Starr Untermeyer. MoAmPo

Dew on it. Ryokan, *tr. fr. Japanese by* Burton Watson. FCEI

Dew on my sleeves, The. Teika, *tr. fr. Japanese by* Hiroaki Sato. *Fr.* A Compendium of Good Tanka. FCEI

Dew on roses. Ma Chih-yüan, *tr. fr. Chinese by* Jonathan Chaves. *Fr.* Three Poems to the tune "Lo-mei Feng", 3. CoBLCP

Dew on the bamboos. *Unknown, tr. by* E. Powys Mathers. LLLT

Dew on the leek. *Unknown, tr. fr. Japanese by* Burton Watson. CoBCP

Dew Sat on Julia's Hair. Robert Herrick. ELP

Dew, scatter if you will. Teika, *tr. fr. Japanese by* Hiroaki Sato. *Fr.* Eighty-four Tanka. FCEI

Dew that formed remains, The. Lady Izumi, *tr. fr. Japanese by* Hiroaki Sato. *Fr.* Fifty-one Tanka. FCEI

Dew, the rain and moonlight, The. A Net to Snare the Moonlight. Vachel Lindsay. PoLF

Dew was falling fast, the stars began to blink, The. The Pet Lamb. Wordsworth. OxBChV

Dewey and His Men. Wallace Rice. PAH

Dewey at Manila. Robert Underwood Johnson. PAH

Dewey in Manila Bay. R. V. Risley. PAH

Dews drop slowly and dreams gather, The: unknown spears. The Valley of the Black Pig. W. B. Yeats. ChTr

Dews of summer night[e] did fall[e], The. Cumnor Hall. William Julius Mickle. BeLS; OxBB

Dewy vapors are like tiny insects, The. On the Night of the Fourteenth of the Eleventh Month Setting Out for Nanchang by Boat on a Moonlit Night. Ch'en San-li, *tr. by* Irving Lo. WFTU

Dey Got Each and de Udder's Man. *Unknown.* WTO

Dey had a gread big pahty down to Tom's de othah night. The Party. Paul Laurence Dunbar. AmNP

Dey is times in life when Nature. When de Co'n Pone's Hot. Paul Laurence Dunbar. AnAmPo; BANP

Dey lynched him, shore dey lynched him. Paternal. Ernest J. Wilson, Jr. PoNe

Dey tell me Joe Turner he done come. Joe Turner Blues. *Unknown.* AS

Dey was hard times jes fo' Christmas round our neighborhood one year. An Indignation Dinner. James David Corrothers. BANP; PoNe

Dey was talkin' in de cabin, dey was talkin' in de hall. When Dey 'Listed Colored Soldiers. Paul Laurence Dunbar. BPo

Dey's a so't o' threatenin' feelin' in de blowin' of de breeze. Soliloquy of a Turkey. Paul Laurence Dunbar. BPo

Deze eatin' folks may tell me ub de gloriz ub spring lam'. Hog Meat. Daniel Webster Davis. BANP

Diagnosis of our hist'ry proves, A. The Rejected "National Hymns. "Orpheus C. Kerr." OBAL

Diakka, The. Gerald Massey. NOBVV

Dial around forth enough means that there since. Clark Coolidge. *Fr.* Polaroid. IAT

Dial Call. Christopher Morley. NBLV

Dial is dark, 'tis but half-past one, The. A Rhyme of the Sun-Dial. William Bell Scott. NOBVV

Dial Tone, The. Howard Nemerov. NYBP

Dialect Quatrain. Marcus B. Christian. AmNP

Dialog. Jean Garrigue. AnAn

Dialog outside the Lakeside Grocery. Ishmael Reed. UL

Dialogue. Buland al-Haidari, *tr. fr. Arabic by* Patricia Alanah Byrne *and* Salma Khadra Jayyusi. MAP

Dialogue. Jeannie Ebner, *tr. fr. German by* Beth Bjorklund. CoAuP

Dialogue, A. George Herbert. MePo; OBEV; OBS; SeCV-1

Dialogue, A. David Ignatow. NNaP

Dialogue. Marie de Ventadour, *tr. fr. Provençal by* Joan M. Ferrante. DMF

Dialogue. Erika Mitterer, *tr. fr. German by* Beth Bjorklund. CoAuP

Dialogue, A. Lizelia Augusta Jenkins Moorer. CBWP-3

Dialogue. Howard Nemerov. NYBP

Dialogue. Adrienne Rich. TAP

Dialogue, A. Swinburne. PoEL-5

Dialogue after Enjoyment. Abraham Cowley. BoLoP

Dialogue between a Squeamish Cotting Mechanic and His Sluttish Wife, in the Kitchen. Edward Ward. *Fr.* Nuptial Dialogues. NOEC

Dialogue, between Crab and Gillian. Thomas D'Urfey. *Fr.* The Bath; or, The Western Lass. NOEC

Dialogue between King William and the Late King James on the Banks of the Boyne, A. Charles Blount. APAS

Dialogue between Strephon and Daphne, A. John Wilmot, 2d Earl of Rochester. SeCV-2

Dialogue between the Resolved Soul and Created Pleasure, A. Andrew Marvell. MeLP; MePo; OAEL-1; OBS; SeCP; SeCV-1
Dialogue between the Soul and [the] Body, A. Andrew Marvell. HAP; INPS; JCP; MeLP; MePo; NAEL-1; NoP; OAEL-1; OBS; PoEL-2; PPP; SeCP; SeCV-1; TEP; WeW
Dialogue between Thyrsis and Dorinda, A. Andrew Marvell. SeCP
Dialogue betwixt God and the Soul, A. At. to Sir Henry Wotton. MeLP; OBS
Dialogue betwixt Time and a Pilgrime [or Pilgrim], A. Aurelian Townshend. MePo; NOBE; OAEL-1; OBS; PoEL-2; SeCP
Dialogue I'll tell you as true as my life, A. The Coal-Owner and the Pitman's Wife. Unknown. CoMu
Dialogue in a Dream. Ryokan, tr. fr. Japanese by Burton Watson. FCEI; JLIC-2
Dialogue: Lover and Lady. Ciullo d'Alcamo, tr. fr. Italian by Dante Gabriel Rossetti. AWP
Dialogue of Self and Soul, A. W. B. Yeats. CMoP; FaBoMo; LiTB; LiTM; MoBrPo; NAEL-2; NoAM; PoE
Dialogue of the Night of the Roses. Zuhur Dixon, tr. fr. Arabic by Patricia Alanah Byrne and Salma Khadra Jayyusi. MAP
Dialogue of Watching, A. Kenneth Rexroth. UnAS
Dialogue—2 Dollmakers. Gregory Corso. NeAP
Dialogue with Herz. Antonio Porta, tr. fr. Italian by Lawrence R. Smith. NItP
Dialogue with the Dead. Amelia Rosselli, tr. fr. Italian by Lawrence R. Smith. NItP
Dialogues 4 1 Voice Only. Doug Fetherling. NeAC
Diameter of the Bomb Was Thirty Centimeters, The. Yehuda Amichai, tr. fr. Hebrew. MHeP, tr. by Bernhard Frank
    (Lament: "Diameter of the bomb was thirty centimeters, The.")
    VWA, tr. by Ruth Nevo
Diamond Cut Diamond. Ewart Milne. FaBoCh; NeIP
Diamond of a morning, A. Morning Song. Sara Teasdale. AnAmPo
Diamonds are forever so I gave you quartz. The Hardness Scale. Joyce Peseroff. LLLT; PPR
Dian, Isis, Artemis, whate'er thy name. W. J. Turner. Fr. The Seven Days of the Sun. OBMV
Diana, sels.
    "Dear to my soul! then leave me not forsaken!" AAS; OBSC
    ("Sonnet: "Dear to my soul! then leave me not forsaken!'") ElL
    "Fair sun, if you would have me praise your light." OBSC
    "Grace full of grace, though in these verses here." OBSC
    "Hope, like the hyaena [or hyena], coming to be old." EnLoPo; OBSC; Son
    "If ever Sorrow spoke from soul that loves." ElL
    "Miracle of the world, I never will deny." OBSC
    "My tears are true, though others be divine." OBSC
    "Needs must I leave and yet needs must I love." InvP; OBSC
    "Not that thy hand is soft, is sweet, is white." OBSC
    "Ready to seek out death in my disgrace." OBSC
    Resolved to Love. Son
    "If ever Sorrow spoke from soul that loves." ElL
    "My lady's presence makes the roses red." ElL; NIP; OBSC
    "Sun, his journey ending in the west, The." OBSC
    "To live in hell, and heaven to behold." AAS; OBSC; Son
    "Whilst Echo cries [or eccho cryes], 'What shall become of me[e]?' " AAS; OBSC
    "You secret vales, you solitary fields." OBSC
Diana, sel. Jorge de Montemayor, tr. fr. Spanish by Bartholomew Young. ElL
    "Shepherd, who can pass such wrong."
Diana. Sir Walter Ralegh. OBSC
Diana Fitzpatrick Mauleverer James. Miss James. A. A. Milne. MoShBr
Diana guardeth our estate. Hymn to Diana. Catullus, tr. by Richard Claverhouse Jebb. AWP
Diana, naked in the shadowy pool. Petrarch, tr. by Morris Bishop. PFI
Diana's Hunting-Song. Dryden. Fr. The Secular Masque. NOBE; SeCePo
Diane de Poitiers, Josephine and Pompadour. Mother Goose Rhyme. Kenneth Rexroth. ErPo
Diapered in hospital linen. The Recovery Room: Lying-in. Helen Chasin. IHMS
Diaphenia. At. to Henry Constable and also to Henry Chettle. CH; ElL; GTBS; GTBS-P; NOBE
Diary. David Wagoner. CoAP
Diary of a Church Mouse. Sir John Betjeman. OxBTC
Diary of a Palestinian Wound, sel. Mahmoud Darwish, tr. fr. Arabic by Lena Jayyusi and Christopher Middleton.
    "We do not need to be reminded." MAP

Diary of a Prisoner. Lo Ch'ing, tr. fr. Chinese by Dominic Cheung. IFON
Diary of a Raccoon. Gertrude Ryder Bennett. GoYe
Diary of an Old Soul, sels. George Macdonald. TrCP
    Be With Me, Lord.
    That Thou Art Nowhere to Be Found.
    This Day Be with Me.
Diary of Days for Adjoa. Jackie Kay. DT
Diary of the Sailors of the North, A. David Shulman, tr. fr. Hebrew by the author. VWA
Diary of the Waning Moon, The, sel. Abutsu the Nun, tr. fr. Japanese by Edwin O. Reischauer.
    "Shore wind is cold on my travel clothes, The." PBWP
Diaspora, The. W. H. Auden. See How he survived them they could never understand.
Diaspora, The. Jack Myers. NAmP
Diaspora Jews. Rachel Boimwall, tr. by Gabriel Preil and Howard Schwartz. VWA
Dibdin's Ghost. Eugene Field. AA
Dic Siôn Dayfydd. Thomas Jacob Thomas, tr. fr. Welsh by H. Idris Bell. OBWVE
Dicamus Bona Verba. Albius Tibullus, tr. fr. Latin by Constance Carrier. NAs
Dick, a Maggot. Swift. NBLV; TW
Dick and Jane. Judith Kroll. AmPA
Dick Hairbrain Learns the Social Graces. John Trumbull. Fr. The Progress of Dulness. AmPP
"Dick, I marvel much why in every plat." The "Gloria Patri." John Heywood. ACP
Dick is the one with the weenie. Dick and Jane. Judith Kroll. AmPA
Dick o' the Cow. Unknown. ESPB; OxBB
Dick Turpin and Black Bess. Unknown. AmFP
Dick Turpin's Ride ("Dick Turpin bold! Dick, hie away"). Unknown. OBET
(My Bonny Black Bess.) CoMu
Dickens in Camp. Bret Harte. AnAmPo
Dickery, dickery, dare. Mother Goose. OxNR
Dicky-Birds. Natalie Joan. BoTP
"Dictates of nature prove school-knowledge weak, The." Repentance. George Alexander Stevens. NOEC
Dictators, The. Jaime Suárez Quemain, tr. fr. Spanish by Jack Hirschman. VoI
Dictionary Black. Sista Roots. WS
Dictionary Is an Historian: A Found Political Poem, The. Judith McCombs. IHMS
Did all the lets and bars appear. The March into Virginia. Herman Melville. BLPL; HAP; LiTA; NAAL-1; NoP; PoE; TAP; TrGrPo; WaaP
Did any seer of ancient time forbode. The Steam Threshing-Machine. Charles Tennyson Turner. OBNC
Did but the law appoint us one. A Popular Functionary. Charles Dibdin. NOEC
Did Chaos form,—and water, air, and fire. Genesis. John Hall Ingham. AA
Did every one of the three hundred poets have a teacher? Sung Hsiang, tr. fr. Chinese by Irving Lo. Fr. On Poetry, I. WFTU
Did he meet Lud at the Fleet Gate? did count the top. David Jones. Fr. The Anathemata. EBEV
Did he strike soundings off Vecta Insula? Angle-Land. David Jones. Fr. The Anathemata, III. NoAM
Did I do it. Scrapping Limits. Salma Khadra Jayyusi, tr. by the author and Charles Doria. MAP
Did I evah tell you, Sonny. Uncle Jimmie's Yarn. Priscilla Jane Thompson. CBWP-2
Did I ever tell you that Mrs. McCave. Too Many Daves. "Dr. Seuss." OBCA; RHPC
Did I ever think. Ono no Takamura, tr. fr. Japanese by Arthur Waley. Fr. Kokin Shu. AWP
Did I ever think. Saigyo, tr. fr. Japanese by Burton Watson. Fr. Sixty-four Tanka. FCEI
Did I follow Truth wherever she led. Herman Altman. Edgar Lee Masters. Fr. Spoon River Anthology. OxBA
Did I hear you ask. Saigyo, tr. fr. Japanese by Burton Watson. Fr. Sixty-four Tanka. FCEI
Did I my lines intend for public[k] view. Countess of Winchilsea. NAEL-1; WPOW
Did I not tell you, avoid the path. Mohammad Taqi Mir, tr. by Ahmed Ali. GoT
Did I reach the pinnacle of success. Willis Beggs. Edgar Lee Masters. Fr. The New Spoon River. SaC
Did I stand on the bald top of Nefin. The Brow of Nephin. Unknown, tr. by Douglas Hyde. AnIL

Did I this morn devoutly pray. Self-Examination. *Unknown.* FaBoUs
Did it go wrong just about a hundred. Counter-Revolution. W. H. Oliver. ATNZ; PeNZ
Did it not signal. Tameuji, *tr. fr. Japanese by* Steven D. Carter. WFTW
Did it perhaps. Joben, *tr. fr. Japanese by* Steven D. Carter. WFTW
Did ivver ye see the like o' that? Pride. Violet Jacob. OxBS
Did men living long ago. Hitomaro, *tr. fr. Japanese. Fr.* Manyo Shu. Ma
Did my father curse his father for his lust I wonder. The Young Man Thinks of Sons. R. A. K. Mason. ATNZ; PeNZ
Did my hand ever touch your hair? Birth. Takahashi Shinkichi, *tr. by* Geoffrey Bownas *and* Anthony Thwaite. PeBJV
Did Not. Thomas Moore. BoLoP; ErPo
Did Not the Heavenly Rhetoric of Thine Eye. Shakespeare. *Fr.* Love's Labour's Lost, IV, iii. LiTB; Son
Did one look at what one saw. Hart Crane. AnAn
Did our best moment last. Emily Dickinson. NOBA
Did She Say "Hmp—mp" instead of "Mp—hmp"? Willard R. Espy. SoTCo
Did Shriner die or make it to New York? A Disappearance in West Cedar Street. L. E. Sissman. TwCP
Did somebody give you a pat on the back? Pass. Edmund Vance Cooke. PWR
Did the cuckoo pity me in the sky. Princess Shikishi, *tr. fr. Japanese by* Hiroaki Sato. *Fr.* Seventy-eight Tanka. FCEI
Did the gentle night agree with you. Good Morning? Heavenly Madam Ping. Fritzi Harmsen van Beek, *tr. by* Greta Kilburn. DuIn
Did the harebell loose her girdle. Emily Dickinson. FaBV
Did the people of Viet Nam. What Were They Like? Denise Levertov. HeIP; NIP; OBWP; VGW; WPE
Did they catch as it were in a Vision at shut of the day. Jezreel. Thomas Hardy. NoP
"Did they dare, did they dare, to slay Owen Roe O'Neil?" Lament for the Death of Eoghan Ruadh O'Neill. Thomas Osborne Davis. NOIV
Did they send me away from my cat and my wife. Gunner. Randall Jarrell. OFD
Did We Laugh or Did We Cry? Patu Simoko. WMBCH
Did ye ever hear o guid Earl o Bran. Earl Brand. *Unknown.* ESPB
Did ye ever sleep at the foot o' the bed. Sleepin' at the Foot o' the Bed. Luther Patrick. BLPA
Did You? William Cole. RHPC
"Did You Call Me, Father?" Mary E. Tucker. CBWP-1
Did you come here? *Unknown, tr. fr. Japanese by* Burton Watson. *Fr.* Kokin Shu. FCEI
Did you eever iver ever. Hand-clapping Rhyme. *Unknown.* NTCP
Did you ever. Backyard Swing. Janet Campbell Hale. STE
Did you ever come to the place. Mother's Love. Ross B. Clapp. WBLP
Did You Ever, Ever, Ever. *Unknown.* AS, *with music*; FaBoNo; GBP
Did You Ever Go Fishing? *Unknown.* RHPC
Did you ever hear about Cocaine Lil? Cocaine Lil [and Morphine Sue]. *Unknown.* AS; GBP; MAT; OxBoLi; RB
Did You Ever Hear an English Sparrow Sing? Bertha Johnston. BLPA
Did you ever hear of Captain Wattle? Captain Wattle and Miss Roe. Charles Dibdin. OxBoLi
Did you ever hear of Editor Whedon. Daisy Fraser. Edgar Lee Masters. *Fr.* Spoon River Anthology. CMoP; HAP; PoE
Did you ever hear tell of sweet Betsy from Pike. Sweet Betsy from Pike. *Unknown.* FaBoBa
Did you ever hear the story 'bout Willy the Weeper? Willy the Weeper. *Unknown.* AS
Did you ever look. Raccoons. Aileen Fisher. PDV
Did you ever make some small success. You Too. Edmund Vance Cooke. PWR
Did you ever see an alligator. Arlo Will. Edgar Lee Masters. *Fr.* Spoon River Anthology. LiTA
Did you ever sit and ponder, sit and wonder, sit and think. Life's a Funny Proposition after All. George M. Cohan. PoLF
Did you ever think as the hearse rolls by. The Hearse Song. *Unknown.* AS, B *vers.*
Did you ever think you'd like to. Honest, Wouldn't You? *Unknown.* WBLP
Did you go at all to Chicago? The Stockyard. J. C. Squire. OxBTC
Did you have relatives. Endless Nights of Rain. Greg Pape. NAmP
Did you hear of the curate who mounted his mare. The Priest and the Mulberry-Tree. Thomas Love Peacock. *Fr.* Crotchet Castle. BoTP; GN; OnMSP
Did you hear of the fight at Corinth. The Eagle of Corinth. Henry Howard Brownell. PAH
Did you love well what very soon you left? Marilyn Hacker. *Fr.* Coda. NoAM
Did You Not See. Alex Kuo. BrSi
Did you see me walking by the Buick Repairs? Frank O'Hara. TTTS

Did you see my wife, did you see, did you see. *Unknown.* OxNR
Did you tackle that trouble that came your way. How Did You Die? Edmund Vance Cooke. BLPA; OHFP; PWR
Did your mother ever wear a hat. Taint. Liz Socolow. PPR
Didactic Piece. Louise Bogan. NoAM
Didactic Sonnet. Melvin Walker La Follette. NePoEA; PoA
Diddle, diddle, dumpling, my son John. Mother Goose. BoTP; OxNR
Diddlety, diddlety, dumpty. Mother Goose. OxNR
Didn't acknowledge receipt. The Suicide. Joyce Carol Oates. Psk
Didn't My Lord Deliver Daniel? *Unknown.* AH
Didn't we make a vow. Teika, *tr. fr. Japanese by* Hiroaki Sato. *Fr.* A Compendium of Good Tanka. FCEI
Didn't you say we should trace. Before Chilembwe Tree. Jack A. Mapanje. WMBCH
Dido. John Ashbery. *Fr.* Two Sonnets. VGW
Dido among the Shades. Virgil, *tr. fr. Latin by* Dryden. *Fr.* The Aeneid [*or* Eneados], VI. OBS
Dido My Dear, Alas, Is Dead. Spenser. *Fr.* The Shepheardes [*or* Shepeards *or* Shepherd's] Calender: November. ChTr
Dido: Swarming. Kathleen Spivack. PoA
Dido's Farewell. Linda Pastan. GOYP
Dido's Hunting. Virgil, *tr. fr. Latin by* the Earl of Surrey. *Fr.* The Aeneid [*or* Eneados], IV. OBSC
Didst thou not find the place inspired. Upon My Lady Carlisle's Walking in Hampton Court Garden. Sir John Suckling. CaPo; NoP
Didymus. Louis MacNeice. EaLo
Die Bauernhochzeit. Kendrick Smithyman. ATNZ
Die blauen Veilchen der Äugelein. Heine, *tr. fr. German by* James Thomson. AWP
Die, die my shriek, you will not be heard. Die My Shriek. Aaron Kushniroff, *tr. by* Joseph Leftwich. TrJP
Die for a thing like that? Ishikawa Takuboku, *tr. fr. Japanese by* Hiroaki Sato. *Fr.* Forty-seven Tanka in Three Lines. FCEI
Die is cast, and we must part, The. The Parting. Josephine D. Henderson Heard. CBWP-4
Die is cast, come weal, come woe, The. Marriage. Mary Weston Fordham. CBWP-2
Die Lotusblume ängstigt. Heine, *tr. fr. German by* James Thomson. AWP
Die My Shriek. Aaron Kushniroff, *tr. fr. Yiddish by* Joseph Leftwich. TrJP
Die Not, Fond Man. *Unknown.* EIL
Die, pussy, die. *Unknown.* OxNR
Die Rose, die Lilie, die Taube, die Sonne. Heine, *tr. fr. German by* Richard Garnett. AWP
(Love's Resume.) TrJP, *tr. by* "J. F. C."
(Rose and the lily, the moon and the dove, The.) NAWM-2, *tr. by* P. G. L. Webb
Die Welt ist dumm, die Welt ist blind. Heine, *tr. fr. German by* James Thomson. AWP
Die, wild country, like the eaglehawk. Australia 1970. Judith Wright. CBAP; NoAM
"Died. . ." Elizabeth Barrett Browning. NOBVV
Died/ at thirty-five, not even. The Juggler. Austin Straus. TSL
Died from fatigue, three laundresses together all. *Unknown.* FaBoEE
Died of Love. *Unknown.* OBET
Died, Sir Charles Wetherell's laundress, honest Sue. *Unknown.* FaBoEE
Diehard. Judith Moffett. PoA
Diella, *sels.* Richard Lynche.
"But thou my deere sweet-sounding lute be still." *Fr.* XVI. AAS
Love's Despair. *Fr.* XIII. EIL
Soon as the Azure-colored Gates. *Fr.* II. Son
"What sugred termes, what all-perswading arte." *Fr.* IV. AAS
(What Sugared Terms.) Son
Dieppe. Samuel Beckett. NOIV
Dies Irae. Thomas of Celano, *tr. fr. Latin.* AA, *tr. by* Abraham Coles; AwP, *tr. by* Richard Crashaw.
Diesel and Shale. Cyril Tawney. OxBSS
Diesel trucks past the Scrovegni chapel. Ian Wedde. *Fr.* Earthly: Sonnets for Carlos, 31. PeNZ
Diet, The. Maureen Burge. AIW; BrRo
Diet of Poland, A Satire, The, *sel.* Daniel Defoe.
"In northern climes where furious tempests blow." OBTV
Dietary Advice. *Unknown.* FaBoUs
Dieu Qu'il la Fait. Charles, Duc d' Orléans, *tr. fr. French by* Ezra Pound. AWP
Difference, The. Guido Gozzano, *tr. fr. Italian by* Carol L. Golino. PFI
Difference. T. H. Jones. OBWVE
Difference, The. Stoddard King. OBAL
Difference, The. Tadhg Dall O'Huiginn, *tr. fr. Irish by* Robin Flower. BIrV
Difference between despair, The. Emily Dickinson. NAAL-1; NoP; QFR

Difference between poetry and rhetoric, The.   Power.   Audre Lorde.
     GLP; NoAM
Difference of Zoos, A.   Gregory Corso.   VGW
Differences.   Kath McKay.   DT
Differences.   Ray A. Young Bear.   NU
Differences between rich and poor, king and queen.   Rank.   Lincoln
     Kirstein.   OBWP
Different.   Clere Parsons.   FaBoTw
Different Bicycles.   Dorothy W. Baruch.   FaPON
Different Door, A.   X. J. Kennedy.   CRH
Different from me entirely: male, foreign.   Man.   Armanda Guiducci, tr.
     by Muriel Kittel.   DMI
Different Image, A.   Dudley Randall.   BPo; CNA; FF; TAP
Different Speech, A.   Louise Townsend Nicholl.   ImOP
Different task remains, A; the secret paths.   Poetic Genius.   Mark
     Akenside.   Fr. The Pleasures of Imagination, IV.   NOEC
Different their voices, different their eyes.   Men Who Hunger.   Yisroel
     Shtern, tr. by Robert Friend.   PeBMYV
Different wind, taller skies, A.   Footsteps of Spring.   Hayyim Nahman
     Bialik, tr. by Ruth Nevo.   VWA
Difficult Adjustment, A.   Lauris Edmond.   FaBoWP
Difficult road, The.   Kokuo, tr. fr. Japanese by Lucien Stryk and Takashi
     Ikemoto.   ZPCJ
Difficult to recall an emotion that is dead.   The Patient Is Rallying.
     Weldon Kees.   NaP
Difficulties of Translation, The.   Gawin Douglas.   Fr. Prologues to the
     Aeneid, Bk. I, Prologue.   GoTS
Difficulties, the impossibilities, The.   Robert Lowell.   Fr. Mexico, 1.
     HCAP
Difficulty of Parting, The.   Hsüeh Chao-yün, tr. fr. Chinese by Lois
     Fusek.   ATF
Difficulty to think at the end of day, The.   A Rabbit as King of the
     Ghosts.   Wallace Stevens.   NoAM; SOTW; TTTS
Difficulty was, it was, The.   In the Beginning Was a Word.   Robert
     Graves.   PoA
Difficulty with all, The.   Knight, with Umbrella.   Elder Olson.
     FiBHP
Diffugere Nives.   Horace.   See Odes: IV, 7. "The snow dissolv'd no
     more is seen" ("Diffugere nives").
Dig for Her the Narrow Bed.   Robert Wallace.   SoTCo
Dig My Grave.   Unknown.   AmFP
Digger for Gold, The.   Abraham Chalfi, tr. fr. Hebrew by Bernhard
     Frank.   MHeP
Diggers, The.   W. S. Merwin.   EAS
Digger's Song, The.   Gerrard Winstanley.   FaBoPV
Digging.   Donald Hall.   CAPP
Digging.   Seamus Heaney.   BIrV; CIP; InPS; IPY; NAEL-2; TwCP
Digging.   Edward Thomas.   BrPo; MoAB; MoBrPo; OxBTC
Digging a compost hole.   Another Easter.   John Ridland.   SM
Digging and building tire men out.   Poem of the Western Fields.   Wu
     Wei-yeh, tr. by Jonathan Chaves.   CoBLCP
Digging earth for puddles, she would wake stranded.   Steps.   Roberta
     Hill.   VoR
Digging for China.   Richard Wilbur.   GoJo; GrPl; TwCP
Digging for Indians.   Gary Gildner.   AmPA
Digging In.   Marge Piercy.   CAPP
Digging Out the Roots.   Duane Niatum.   STE
Dignified and thin.   Unitas.   Edward Gold.   ASP
Dignified things, may I your leaves implore.   To the Respective Judges.
     Unknown.   APAS
Dignity of Labor, The.   Robert Bersohn.   NBLV
Dilana and Diram.   Saleem Barakat, tr. fr. Arabic by Lena Jayyusi and
     Naomi Shihab Nye.   Fr. The Crane.   MAP
Dilection.   Ernst Jandl, tr. fr. German by Beth Bjorklund.   CoAuP
Dilemma.   Patricia Beer.   OxBC
Dilemma.   David Ignatow.   VGW
Dilemma of the Elm.   Genevieve Taggard.   MoAmPo
Dilettante, The: A Modern Type.   Paul Laurence Dunbar.   AnAmPo
Diligent in the burnt fields above the sea.   Find.   Josephine Miles.   NoP;
     WPE
Dillar, a dollar, A,/ A ten o'clock scholar.   Mother Goose.   FaBoBe;
     FaFP; OxNR
Dilly Dilly.   Unknown.   OxNR
Dilly Dilly Piccalilli.   Clyde Watson.   NTCP
Dilly Song, The.   Unknown.   See I'll sing you one-O [or twelve O].
Dim afternoon December afternoon.   December.   Robert Francis.
     LCAP
Dim, as the borrow'd beams of moon and stars.   Dryden.   Fr. Religio
     Laici.   OAEL-1; SeCV-2
     (Reason and Religion.)   FiP
     (Reason and Revelation.)   OBS

Dim boy claps because the others clap, The.   The Freaks at Spurgin Road
     Field.   Richard Hugo.   LCAP; NoAM; SM
Dim deep of a yellow evening slides, The.   Vision.   E. E. Cummings.
     FL
Dim, dim the light from the small window.   Cheng Chen, tr. fr. Chinese
     by William Schultz.   Fr. Reading beside Ox Tail River, II.   WFTU
Dim, gradual thinning of the shapeless gloom.   The Troops.   Siegfried
     Sassoon.   CMoP
Dim light of daybreak now.   Dawn Wail for the Dead.   Kath Walker.
     CBAP
Dim light to the sou'ward, The.   Sunrise.   Ben King.   AnAmPo
Dim reading in a white book.   Inwards.   Yehudah Offen, tr. by Bernhard
     Frank.   MHeP
Dim the light in your faces: be passionless in the room.   The Image.
     Richard Hughes.   OBMV
Dim vales—and shadowy floods.   Fairyland.   Poe.   NAAL-1
Dim wind pillared the hills: stiller than mist it seemed.   Sunrise Trumpets.
     Joseph Auslander.   TrJP
Dime Call.   Albert Goldbarth.   VWA
Dime store. The goldfish swam in the murky.   Kite.   Laura Jensen.
     LCAP
Dimidium Animae Meae.   Charles A. Brady.   GoYe
Dimly in the dawn mist.   Unknown, tr. fr. Japanese by Geoffrey Bownas
     and Anthony Thwaite.   Fr. Kokin Shu.   PeBJV
Dimly Outlined by a Police Artist.   Charles Simic.   PPR
Dimme eyes, deaf ears, cold stomach shew.   Verses Found in Thomas
     Dudley's Pocket after His Death.   Thomas Dudley.   SCAP
Dimmed Observation.   Abba Kovner, tr. fr. Hebrew by Warren Bargad
     and Stanley F. Chyet.   IP
Dimpled and flushed and dewy pink he lies.   Baby.   Elaine Goodale
     Eastman.   AA
Dimpled Cloud, A.   Frederick Seidel.   FYAP
Din of work is subdued, The.   W. H. Auden.   FaBoMo; GLP; NoAM
Dined with Auden. He'd been at Milwaukee.   Auden at Milwaukee.
     Stephen Spender.   AiP
Diners in the Kitchen, The.   James Whitcomb Riley.   OBAL
Ding dang, bell rang.   Unknown.   OxNR
Ding Dong.   A. C. Hilton.   BXAP; Par
Ding-Dong!   Unknown.   BoTP
Ding Dong.   Unknown.   Fr. Swetnam, the Woman-Hater.   EIL
Ding, dong, bell,/ Pussy's in the well.   Mother Goose.   OxNR
Dingle Bank.   Edward Lear.   FaBoNo
Dingle dingle doosey.   Unknown.   OxNR
Dingty diddelty.   Mother Goose.   OxNR
Dingy donkey, formal and unchanged, A.   John Hookham Frere.
     FaBoCo
Dining-Room Tea.   Rupert Brooke.   BrPo; MoBrPo
Dining with his older daughter.   Waiters.   Mary Ann Hoberman.   RHPC
Dinkey-Bird, The.   Eugene Field.   AA; AmMo; NA
Dink's Song.   Unknown.   ErPo; OxBoLi
Dinky.   Theodore Roethke.   OBAL; OBCA; RHPC; SM
Dinner at the Mongoloid's.   Larry Rubin.   MT
Dinner Guest: Me.   Langston Hughes.   BPo
Dinner Party 1940.   Philip Sherlock.   PBCV
Dino.   Michael Lassell.   Fr. Times Square Poems.   GLP
Dino Campana and the Bear.   Edward Hirsch.   MAYP
Dinogad's Petticoat ("Dinogad's speckled petticoat").   Unknown, tr. fr.
     Welsh by Gwyn Williams.   OBWVE; RB
Dinosaur, The.   Bert Leston Taylor.   ImOP
Dinosaur, an ancient beast, The.   So Big!   Max Fatchen.   AmMo
Dinosaur died, and small, The.   The Naked Ape.   John Updike.   EOEF
Dinosaur Spring.   Marilyn Nelson Waniek.   ER; MAYP
Dinosaurs.   Abba Kovner, tr. fr. Hebrew by Warren Bargad and Stanley
     F. Chyet.   IP
Dinosaurs.   Carolyn Stoloff.   NYBP
Dinosaurs.   Valerie Worth.   NTCP
Dinosaurs are not all dead, The.   Steam Shovel.   Charles Malam.
     NTCP; PYC; RHPC
Dinosaurs lived so long ago.   Unfortunately.   Bobbi Katz.   RAR
Dinosaurs wept angry tears.   Dinosaurs.   Abba Kovner, tr. by Warren
     Bargad and Stanley F. Chyet.   IP
Dinosaurus courteously, The.   Leaving the Dance.   Alexander Whitaker.
     NIP
Diodorus is nice, isn't he, Philocles?   Meleager, tr. by Peter Whigham.
     PeHV
Diodorus Siculus.   Unknown.   ErPo
Diogenes.   Katerina Anghelaki-Rooke, tr. fr. Greek by Peter Dreyer.   OV
Diogenes.   Morris Bishop.   NBLV
Diogenes.   Arthur Rex Dugard Fairburn.   PeNZ
Diogenes, that wise old bird.   The Complete Cynic.   Keith Preston.
     NBLV

Dion of Tarsus. *Unknown, tr. fr. Greek by* Alma Strettell. AWP

Dionysius. Sophia de Mello Breyner Andresen, *tr. fr. Portuguese by* Allan Francovich. PBWP

Dionysus. Irving Layton. ErPo

Dionysus as Psychiatrist. Robert Pinsky. *Fr.* Essay on Psychiatrists, X. HCAP

Dioramacist does not know, The. The Museum of the Second Creation. Sandra McPherson. LCAP

Dip, dip, allebadar. *Unknown.* GBP

Dip, dip, dip. *Unknown.* GBP

Dip your pipe and gently blow. Blowing Bubbles. Margaret Hillert. RAR

Dipper, The. Phoebe Hesketh. PoSH

Dipping our fingers in cups of cherry ice. Cherry Ice. Donna Masini. ER

Dipsychus, *sels.* Arthur Hugh Clough.
  "As I sat at the café, I said to myself." *Fr. pt.* II, sc. ii, *also in* Spectator ab Extra. ELP; FaBoCo; FaBoPV; FiBHP; GTBS, 3 *sts.*; NOBVV; OAEL-2; OxBoLi
  (How Pleasant It Is to Have Money.) NOBE
  (So Pleasant It Is To Have Money.) SeCePo
  I Dreamt a Dream. *Fr. pt.* I, sc. v. NAEL-2
  "There is no God," the wicked saith. *Fr. Pt.* I, sc. v. NAEL-2; NOBVV
  (There Is No God.) BLPL; NOBE
  "Yet I could think, indeed, the perfect call." *Fr. pt.* II, sc. v. OBNC

Diptych. Velma West Sykes. IHMS

Dirce. Walter Savage Landor. *Fr.* Pericles and Aspasia, CCXXX. AWP; CTC; EBEV; EnRP; FaBoEE; GBL; HAP; LiTB; NOBE; NoP; OAEL-2; OBEV; OBNC; OxBSP; PoEL-4; PoRA; TrGrPo; WeW

Dirdum drum. The Cat's Song. *Unknown.* GBP

Direct Address. Amy Gerstler. UL

Direction. Barbara Guest. WPE

Direction. Roberta Hill. CDW

Direction. Alonzo Lopez. NOVW

Directions. William Matthews. AmPA

Directions for Dreamfishing. Martin Johnston. CBAP

Directions for Making a Birth-Day Song, *sel.* Swift.
  To Form a Just and Finish'd Piece. NAs

Directions in Our Blood. Barney Bush. HATNAP

Directions that you took. Old Haven. Jean Garrigue. WPE

Directions to a Rebel. W. R. Rodgers. LiTM

Directions to the Nomad. James Welch. CDW

Directive. Robert Frost. AmPP; BLPL; CMoP; HAP; InPS; LiTA; LiTM; MAT; MoAB; MoAmPo; NAAL-2; NoAM; NOBA; NoP; PoE; PPP; PrIm

Directory that runs from B to V, A. Changing at York. Tony Harrison. NPo

Diretro al Sol. Charles G. Bell. NePoAm

Dirge: "Body lies under the ground." Gavin Bantock. OxBTC

Dirge, A: "Call for the robin-redbreast and the wren." John Webster.
  See White Devil, The: Call for the Robin Redbreast and the Wren.

Dirge: "Calm on the bosom of thy God." Felicia Dorothea Hemans. *Fr.* The Siege of Valencia. OBEV

Dirge: "Come away, come away, death." Shakespeare. *See* Twelfth Night: Come Away, Come Away, Death.

Dirge: "Fear no more the heat o' the sun." Shakespeare. *See* Cymbeline: Fear No More the Heat o' the Sun.

Dirge: "Glories of our blood and state, The." James Shirley. *See* Contention of Ajax and Ulysses, The: Glories of Our Blood and State, The.

Dirge: "Her house is become like a man dishonored." Bible, *Apocrypha. Fr.* First Maccabees, II: 8-14. TrJP

Dirge: "I make this dirge for you Miss Mary Binning I miss you." *Unknown, tr. by* Armand Schwerner. BoWoP

Dirge: "If Thou wilt ease Thine heart." Thomas Lovell Beddoes. *See* Death's Jest Book: If thou wilt ease thine heart.

Dirge: "It is the endless dance of the dead." Quincy Troupe. PoBA

Dirge: Metrical Feet. Samuel Taylor Coleridge. FaBoUS; NIP; OxBChV; SoSe

Dirge, A: "Naiad, hid beneath the bank." William Johnson Cory. OBNC

Dirge: "1-2-3 was the number he played but today the number came 3-2-1." Kenneth Fearing. FF; HeIP; HoPM; NIP; PoRA; RB; TrJP

Dirge, A: "Rough wind, that moanest loud." Shelley. ChTr; EnRP; NAEL-2; NOBE; PoRA; SoSe; TEP; TrGrPo; WiR

Dirge: "Softly!/ She is lying/ With her lips apart." Charles Gamage Eastman. AA

Dirge: "Swallow leaves her nest, The." Thomas Lovell Beddoes. *Fr.* Death's Jest Book, I. PoEL-4
  (Song from the Waters.) NOBE
  (Voice from the Waters, A.) OBNC
  ("We do lie beneath the grass.") ELP; NOBE; OBNC; WiR

Dirge: "We do lie beneath the grass." Thomas Lovell Beddoes. *See* Death's Jest Book: We Do Lie beneath the Grass.

Dirge: "Weep, weep, ye woodmen, wail." Anthony Munday. *See* Death of Robert, Earl of Huntingdon: Weep, weep, ye woodmen! wail.

Dirge: "Welladay, welladay, poor Colin, thou art going to the ground." George Peele. *Fr.* The Arraignment of Paris. EIL

Dirge: "What shall her silence keep?" Madison Cawein. AA

Dirge, A: "Why were you born when the snow was falling?" Christina Rossetti. ChTr; EBVV; NOBVV

Dirge for a Soldier. George Henry Boker. AA; AnAmPo; PAH; WaaP

Dirge for Ashby. Margaret Junkin Preston. PAH

Dirge for Fajuyi, *sel.* Omobayode Arowa, *tr. fr. Yoruba.*
  "Dekunle, handsome man, hail!" WTO

Dirge for Fidele. Shakespeare. *See* Cymbeline: Fear No More the Heat o' the Sun.

Dirge for McPherson, A. Herman Melville. PAH; PoEL-5

Dirge for One Who Fell in Battle [*or* Dirge]. Thomas William Parsons. AA; GN; PAH

Dirge; for the Barrel-Organ of the New Barbarism. Louis Aragon, *tr. fr. French by* Selden Rodman. WaaP

Dirge for the New Sunrise. Dame Edith Sitwell. *Fr.* Three Poems of the Atomic Bomb. CMoP; EaLo; MoAB; MoBrPo; SeCePo

Dirge for the Ninth of Ab. *Unknown, tr. fr. Hebrew by* Nina Davis Salaman. TrJP

Dirge for the Year. Shelley. GN

Dirge for Three Trumpets. *Unknown.* EAS

Dirge for Two Veterans. Walt Whitman. AnAmPo; MoAmPo; PoEL-5

Dirge in "Cymbeline." William Collins. *See* To fair Fidele's grassy tomb.

Dirge in Woods. George Meredith. FF; NAEL-2; OBEV; OBNC; OPOP; WiR

Dirge is sung, the ritual said, The. I. H. B. William Winter. AA

Dirge of Alaric the Visigoth. Edward Everett. BeLS

Dirge of Love. Shakespeare. *See* Twelfth Night: Come Away, Come Away, Death.

Dirge of the Moolla of Kotal. George Thomas Lanigan. NA

Dirge of the Three Queens. John Fletcher *and* Shakespeare. *See* Two Noble Kinsmen, The: Urns and Odours Bring Away!

Dirge Sung at Death. *Unknown, tr. fr. Maori by* John White. WTO

Dirge upon the Death of the Right Valiant Lord, Bernard Stuart, A. Robert Herrick. SeCV-1

Dirge without Music. Edna St. Vincent Millay. CMoP; DL; LiTA; TrGrPo

Dirge Written for a Drama. Thomas Lovell Beddoes. EnRP

Dirigible, The. Ralph Wilhelm Bergengren. FaPON

Dirigible, The. Chris Wallace-Crabbe. CBAP

Dirindina the discontented. The Discontented Woman. *Unknown, tr. by* Muriel Kittel. DMI

Dirt road rose abruptly through a wood, The. Snake Hill. Jay Parini. MAYP

Dirt sticks under fingernails. Pulling Weeds. Eric Chock. BrSi

Dirtiest Man in the World, The. Shel Silverstein. OBCA

Dirty-billed Freeze Footy, The. Judith Hemschemeyer. TV

Dirty Floor, The. Edward Field. *See* Floor Is Dirty, The.

Dirty fog is swirling in the wake, A. Aboard the Santa Maria. Gyula Illyés, *tr. by* William Jay Smith. MHuP

Dirty Little Accuser, The. Norman Cameron. OxBS

Dirty money and the sleazy hearts, The. The Matadors. Josephine Jacobsen. TAP

Dirty picture, a photograph, possibly a tintype, A. Floor. C. K. Williams. GeTw; NAmP

Dirty river by religious explorers, The. Mystic River. John Ciardi. NYBP

Dirty Word, The. Karl Shapiro. CoAP; InPK; PoA

Dirty Work on the Appellation Trail. William Rossa Cole. SoTCo

Dîs Aliter Visum; or, Le Byron de Nos Jours. Robert Browning. NAEL-2

Dis Long Time, Gal. *Unknown.* PBCV

Dis Mornin', Dis Evenin', So Soon. *Unknown.* AS

Dis sun are hot. This Sun Is Hot. *Unknown.* BPo

Dis Time No Stan' Like befo' Time. James Martinez. PVCV

Disabled. Wilfred Owen. BrPo; CMoP; FF; InPS; LiTM; MMA; MoP; NAEL-2; NIP; NoAM; OBWVE; OxBTC; WaP

Disabled Debauchee, The. Earl of Rochester. BoLoP; HAP; NAEL-1; NOBL; OBSV; PPP; WeW

Disagreeable Man, The. W. S. Gilbert. FiBHP

Disagreements. John Hollander. AnAn

Disappearance in West Cedar Street, A. L. E. Sissman. TwCP

Disappearing in a glimpse! Impressions at the Vulture Peak. Chou Meng-tieh, *tr. by* Dominic Cheung. IFON

Disappointed Sailor, The. *Unknown.* OxBSS

Disappointed Shrimper, The. P. A. Ropes. BoTP

Disappointment, A. Joanna Baillie. NOEC

Disappointment. Thomas Stephens Collier. AA

Disappointment. John Boyle O'Reilly. ACP

Disappointment, The. Jane Taylor. FaBoUs

Disappointment. Mary E. Tucker. CBWP-1

Disappointment—His Appointment. Edith Lillian Young. BLRP; WBLP

Disarmed. Laura Redden Searing. AA

Disarticulated/ arm torn out. Last Affair: Bessie's Blues Song. Michael S. Harper. HCAP; LCAP

Disaster, The. Bruce Bennet. RR

Disaster. Charles Stuart Calverley. CenHV; FM; NBLV

Disaster. Meiling Jin. WS

Disaster frowned. The Martyr. Ibrahim Tuqan, *tr. by* Lena Jayyusi *and* John Heath-Stubbs. MAP

Disasters numb within us, The. Life at War. Denise Levertov. NMM; VGW

Discard myself—just the thought is bitter. Elegies for Prince Atsumichi ("Discard myself—just the thought is bitter"). Lady Izumi, *tr. fr. Japanese by* Hiroaki Sato. *Fr.* Fifty-one Tanka. FCEI

Discharged. W. E. Henley. *Fr.* In Hospital, XXVIII.

Disciple, The. Oscar Wilde. OAEL-2

Disciples of light have never invented anything, The. The Great Days of the Poet. Robert Desnos, *tr. by* Michael Benedikt. POS

Discipline. George Herbert. FPL; LiTB; MeLP; MePo; NAEL-1; NOBE; NOCV; NoP; OBEV; OBS; PoLF; SeCePo; TrGrPo

Discipline is the workshop. Nanak, *tr. by* John Stratton Hawley *and* Mark Juergensmeyer. SSI

Disciplined by wind and snow. Eun, *tr. by* Lucien Stryk *and* Takashi Ikemoto. ZPCJ

Disciplined in the school of hard campaigning. Horace. *See* Odes: III, 2. "Let the youth hardened by a sharp soldier's life" ("Angustam amice").

Disco Chinatown. Yuri Kageyama. BrSi

Discomfort in High Places. Sydney Tremayne. PoSH

Disconnection, The. Rita Mae Brown. IHMS

Disconsolate and sad. Platonick Love. Lord Herbert of Cherbury. OBS

Disconsolate I/ from the thinning line. Witness to Death. Richmond Lattimore. VGW

Disconsolate Judy's Lamentation. *Unknown.* OxBSS

Discontented Student, The. St. George Tucker. OBAL

Discontented Woman, The. *Unknown, tr. fr. Italian by* Muriel Kittel. DMI

Discontents in Devon. Robert Herrick. CaPo; OxBSP; SeCV-1

Discordants, *sels.* Conrad Aiken. "Dead Cleopatra lies in a crystal casket." *Fr.* IV. PoA "Music I heard with you was more than music." *Fr.* I. AWP; BLPL; CMoP; FaFP; LiTA; LiTM; NOBA; OxBA; PoRA (Bread and Music.) MoAB; MoAmPo

Discourse of the Wanderer, and an Evening Visit to the Lake. Wordsworth. *Fr.* The Excursion, IX. EnRP

Discourse on the Principle in All the Cantos, The, *sel.* Laura Terracina, *tr. fr. Italian by* Muriel Kittel. To the Most Excellent Lady Veronica Gambara. DMI

Discovered in Mid-Ocean. Stephen Spender. *See* He will watch the hawk with an indifferent eye.

Discovered in the act. *Unknown, tr. fr. Japanese by* Geoffrey Bownas *and* Anthony Thwaite. PeBJV

Discoverer. James Michie. DiPo

Discoverer, The. Edmund Clarence Stedman. AA; AnAmPo

Discoveries. Vernon Watkins. LiTM; WaP

Discoveries in Arizona. James Wright. NoP

Discoveries of Bones and Stones. Geoffrey Grigson. OBTV

Discovering. Sharon Scott. JB

Discovering God Is Waking One Morning. John L'Heureux. BoNaP

Discovering My Daughter. Dabney Stuart. SM

Discovering Your Subject. Pattiann Rogers. MT

Discovery. Hilaire Belloc. OxBSP

Discovery, The. Gwendolyn MacEwen. NOBC

Discovery, The. J. C. Squire. *See* There was an Indian, who had known no change.

Discovery of America, The. James Logie Robertson. NOBVV

Discovery of LSD a True Story, The. Anselm Hollo. PoM

Discovery of San Francisco Bay. Richard Edward White. PAH

Discovery of the New World. Carter Revard. VoR

Discovery of the Pacific, The. Thom Gunn. HeIP

Discovery of This Time. Archibald MacLeish. LiTA; WaP

Discreet. Maria Flook. EOEF

Discreet, not cryptic. I write to you from the garden. A Message. Fleur Adcock. DiPo

Discretions of Alcibiades. Robert Pinsky. NPGG

Discriminator, The. Vernon Scannell. OxBC

Discussing Poetry with Shu-yüan. K'ang Yu-wei, *tr. fr. Chinese by* Irving Lo. WFTU

Discussion of Poetry to Demonstrate to the Students the Coming of a New Age, A. Cheng Chen, *tr. fr. Chinese by* William Schultz. WFTU

Discussion of the Vicissitudes of History under a Pine Tree, A. Katha Pollitt. MAYP

Disdain. Sir Thomas Wyatt. *See* If in the World There Be More Woe.

Disdain me not without desert. Sir Thomas Wyatt. SiPS

Disdain Me Still. William Herbert, Earl of Pembroke. EIL

Disdainful Mistress, The. *Malay Oral Tradition, tr. by* R. J. Wilkinson *and* R. O. Winstedt. WTO

Disdaining butterflies. The Woman Who Loved Worms. Colette Inez. NMM

Diseases of Bath; a Satire, The, *sel. Unknown.* "If to the Pump Room in the morn we go." NOEC

Diseases of the Moon. Doug Fetherling. NeAC

Disembarking at Quebec. Margaret Atwood. PoE

Disenchantment. Charles Leonard Moore. AA

Disfigurement. Yannis Ritsos, *tr. fr. Greek by* Edmund Keeley. AnAn

Disguise upon disguise, and then disguise. Soul unto Soul Glooms Darling. Charles Leonard Moore. AA

Disguised in my mouth as a swampland. In the Morning. Jayne Cortez. BISi

Disguises. Thomas Edward Brown. WGRP

Disguises. Elizabeth Jennings. NePoEA-2

Disgusted by everything alive I withdrew into the. Aleksander Wat, *tr. fr. Polish by* Czeslaw Milosz. *Fr.* Songs of a Wanderer, II. PwPP

Disgusted with crimes that are piffling and messy. Crime at Its Best. Stoddard King. NBLV

Dish for a Poet, A. *Unknown.* OBCP

Dish for the bishop, a crushed and bitter dish, A. Almería. Pablo Neruda, *tr. by* Angel Flores. WaaP

Dishonest Miller, The. *Unknown.* AmFP

Dishonor. Edwin Denby. ErPo

Dishonorable Seaman's Grave. Hans Lodeizen, *tr. fr. Dutch by* James S. Holmes. DuIn

Dishwasher, The. Judith Herzberg, *tr. fr. Dutch by* John Rudge. DuIn

Disillusion. E. A. Baratynsky, *tr. fr. Russian by* Alan Myers. AAA

Disillusion. Maureen Burge. AIW; BrRo

Disillusion. *Unknown, tr. fr. Tewa Indian by* H. J. Spinden. WTO

Disillusioned. "Lewis Carroll." CenHV

Disillusionment. René Daumal, *tr. fr. French by* Michael Benedikt. POS

Disillusionment. Virginia Graham. NBLV

Disillusionment of Ten o'Clock. Wallace Stevens. AnAmPo; CMoP; FF; InPS; NAAL-2; NoAM; OxBA; RB; SOTW; TTTS

Disinherited, The, *sel.* Mary Gilmore. "Sudden autumn winds, like hounds, The." PoAu-1

Disinherited, The. Charles Spear. ATNZ; PeNZ

Disintegrating at low speeds. To Live at the Speed of Biography. Yona Wallach, *tr. by* Warren Bargad *and* Stanley F. Chyet. IP

Disintegration. Richard Kostelanetz. InPK

Disinterment. James Sherry. UL

Dislike for Flowers, A. Michael Cadnum. KS

Dislike of Nature. Ono Tozaburo, *tr. fr. Japanese by* Hiroaki Sato. FCEI

Dislike of Tasks. Richmond Lattimore. SaC

Dismantled Ship, The. Walt Whitman. AmPP; MOS; NoP; OxBA

Dismiss the instruments that for your pleasure. Music in Venice. Louis Simpson. NYBP

Dismiss your apprehension, pseudo bard. At Shakespeare's Grave. Irving Browne. AA

Dismissal. Thomas Campion. *See* Mountebank's Mask, The: Hours of Sleepy Night, The.

Dismissing Progress and Its Progenitors. George Reavey. EAS

Dismissing reports and men, he put pressure on the wax. Geoffrey Hill. *Fr.* Mercian Hymns, XIV. HAP

Disobedience. A. A. Milne. NTCP

Disorder. A. Leyeles, *tr. fr. Yiddish by* Leonard Wolf. PeBMYV

Dispart the frost-white boughs, and lo! Promised Land. Charles Spear. ATNZ

Dispatch Number Nine. Doug Fetherling. NeAC

Dispatch Number Sixteen. Doug Fetherling. NeAC

Dispatch Number Sixty. Doug Fetherling. NeAC

Dispensary, The, *sels.* Sir Samuel Garth. OBSV

"How impotent a deity am I!"

"Oft has this planet rolled around the sun."

"This wight all mercenary projects tries."

Dispensing Morning Balm. Gabriel Okara. UAS

Dispersion and Convergence. Tom Clark. UL

Displacement, The. Hubert Witheford. ATNZ

Display thy breasts, my Julia: there let me. Upon Julia's Breasts. Robert Herrick. CaPo; NoP

Disposal. W. D. Snodgrass. CAPP

Disposed to wed, e'en while you hasten, stay. George Crabbe. *Fr.* The Parish Register: Marriages. FaBoUs

Disposing of a Pregnant Daughter. *Unknown. Fr.* The Fyftene Joyes of Maryage. OxBLMV

Disposition No. 1. Shafiq al-Kamali, *tr. fr. Arabic by* Sargon Boulus *and* Christopher Middleton. MAP

Dispossessed, The. John Berryman. VGW

Dispossessed. Janice Gould. GOS

Dispossessed, The. Thomas Kinsella. NOCV

Dispossessions. Jane Cooper. FaBoWP

Dispraise of Absalom, The. *Unknown, tr. fr. Irish by* Robin Flower. BIrV

Dispraise of Love, and Lovers' Follies. "A. W." EIL; OBSC; TrGrPo

Dispute between Women, A. *Unknown, tr. fr. Eskimo by* Tom Lowenstein. STP

Dispute of the Heart and Body of François Villon, The. Villon, *tr. fr. French by* Swinburne. AWP; OBVE

Dispute over Suicide, A. *Unknown, tr. fr. Egyptian by* T. Eric Peet. TTY

Disquieting Muses, The. Sylvia Plath. NMM; TV

Disregard. Ai. NoAM

Disrobe, my love. Nizar Qabbani, *tr. by* Diana Der Hovanessian *and* Lena Jayyusi. MAP

Dissatisfaction with Metaphysics. William Empson. CMoP

Dissembler. Charles Shaw. GoYe

Dissenters' Thanksgiving for the Late Declaration, The. *Unknown.* APAS

Dissolution, The. John Donne. SeCV-1

Dissolution. Jacob Glatstein, *tr. fr. Yiddish by* Benjamin *and* Barbara Harshav. AYP

Dissolving, the coals shift. Rain swaddles us. The Ruin. Charles Tomlinson. NePoEA-2

Distaff, The. Erinna, *tr. fr. Greek by* Marylin Arthur. WPOW

Distaff, my care, I promise thee and swear. To My Distaff. Catherine Des Roches, *tr. by* Dorothy Backer. DMF

Distance. Anthony Delius. PeSA

Distance. Peter Everwine. NNaP

Distance between Bodies, The. Bill Manhire. ATNZ

Distance doesn't matter, Francisco. Extracts: From the Journal of Elisa Lynch. Maura Stanton. AmPA

Distance from Me to You, The. Dov Khomsky, *tr. fr. Hebrew by* Bernhard Frank. MHeP

Distance from Satan to God, The. Apathy. Eeva-Liisa Manner, *tr. fr. Finnish by* Jaakko A. Ahokas. *Fr.* Cambrian, VI. OV

Distance is swept by the smooth. Radar. Alan Ross. FF

Distance of a City. James Berry. PBCV

Distance sheltered upon tubes of foam. The Ghost of the Cargo Boat. Pablo Neruda, *tr. by* Donald D. Walsh. WSC

Distance Spills Itself. Yocheved Bat-Miriam, *tr. fr. Hebrew by* Robert Friend. VWA

Distance that the dead have gone, The. Emily Dickinson. AnAmPo; OBD

Distances, The. Jim Carroll. PoA

Distances. Katherine Gallagher. AIW

Distances. Albert Goldbarth. GeTw

Distances. Richard Hugo. CAPP

Distances. Jeremy Kingston. NYBP

Distances, The. W. S. Merwin. NOBA

Distances, *sel.* Christopher Okigbo.
"Death lay in ambush." TTY

Distances, The. Charles Olson. NAAL-2; NeAP; NoP

Distances to the Friend, The. Jonathan Williams. NeAP

Distant and long have I waited without going. To Mackinnon of Strath. Iain Lom. GoTS

Distant as the Duchess of Savoy. *Unknown.* MeEL

Distant clouds churn the waters. River Messages. Chang Pi, *tr. by* Lois Fusek. ATF

Distant Drum, The. Calvin C. Hernton. FF; TTY

Distant from warblers all day. Buson, *tr. fr. Japanese by* Hiroaki Sato. *Fr.* Eighty-seven Hokku. FCEI

Distant Fury of Battle, The. Geoffrey Hill. NoP

Distant Love. Shotetsu, *tr. fr. Japanese by* Steven D. Carter. WFTW

Distant Mountains. Ou-yang Hsiu, *tr. fr. Chinese by* Burton Watson. CoBCP

Distant Orgasm, The. James Tate. AmPA

Distant range of the mountains, like a shark's lower jaw, The. Fire. Kondo Azuma, *tr. by* Geoffrey Bownas *and* Anthony Thwaite. PeBJV

Distant Roads. Wu Wei-yeh, *tr. fr. Chinese by* Jonathan Chaves. CoBLCP

Distant Runners, The. Mark Van Doren. GOA; LiTA; LiTM; MoAmPo

Distant sailboat never quite, A. Kyorai, *tr. fr. Japanese by* Burton Watson. *Fr.* Twenty Hokku. FCEI

Distant Seychelles are not so remote, The. Eireann. Osbert Lancaster. *Fr.* Afternoons with Baedeker. NOBL

Distant View. Uys Krige, *tr. fr. Afrikaans by* Uys Krige *and* Jack Cope. PeSA

Distant View of England from the Sea. William Lisle Bowles. EnRP

Distant View of the Sea, A. Tamekane, *tr. fr. Japanese by* Steven D. Carter. WFTW

Distant wind blows as I stand alone, A. While on an Evening Stroll Outside the Gates, I Stood Alone Looking Out on the Water. Li Tz'u-ming, *tr. by* Daniel Bryant. WFTU

Distant Winter, The. Philip Levine. VGW

Distich. Shuraikh, *tr. fr. Arabic.* TrJP

Distichs. John Hay. AnAmPo

Distil not poison in mine ears. John Hall. OxBSP

Distillation. Richard Hovey. AnAmPo

Distilled Water. M. K. Joseph. ATNZ; PeNZ

Distinction. Mark A. de Wolfe Howe. AA

Distinctions. Charles Tomlinson. CMoP

Distinguish carefully between these two. The Justice of the Peace. Hilaire Belloc. NOBVV; OBSV

Distracted. Pedro Salinas, *tr. fr. Spanish by* Perry Higman. LPSS

Distracted Puritan, The. Richard Corbet. OxBoLi

Distracted the Mother Said to Her Boy. Gregory Harrison. Mes

Distracted with care. The Despairing Lover. William Walsh. ELP; FaBoCh; NBLV; NOBL; OxBoLi

Distraction. A. R. Ammons. CAPP

Distraction. Henry Vaughan. SeCP

Distractions and the Human Crowd. Stevie Smith. OxBC

Distress. Susan Griffin. NPGG

Distressed Men of War. *Unknown.* OxBSS

Distribution of Honours for Literature. Walter Savage Landor. FaBoEE

Distrust. Robert Herrick. CaPo

Disturb me not, oh bouyant youths! *Unknown, tr. by* John White. WTO

Disturbed by consciousness. Satori. Gayl Jones. BlSi

Disturbed, the cat. *Unknown, tr. by* Geoffrey Bownas *and* Anthony Thwaite. PeBJV

Disturbing the Sallies Forth. Clark Coolidge. UL

Disturbing to have a person. Barbara Guest. FaBoWP

Disused Shed in Co. Wexford, A. Derek Mahon. AnAn; CIP; FaBCIP; FaBoPV; NOIV; OxBC

Disused Temple, The. Norman Cameron. OxBS; OxBTC

Ditchdigger's Tears, The, *sel.* Pier Paolo Pasolini, *tr. fr. Italian by* Lawrence R. Smith.
"Only loving, only knowing." NItP

Dithering towards the horizon. Horizon without Landscape. Tom Lowenstein. VWA

Dithyramb in Retrospect. Peter Hopegood. PoAu-2

Ditty, A. John Day. *Fr.* Humour Out of Breath. EIL

Ditty: Below the Frontier. Shen Te-ch'ien, *tr. fr. Chinese by* Marie Chan. WFTU

Ditty: "Cock shall crow, The." Robert Louis Stevenson. TrGrPo

Ditty, A: "I went into my garden to gather some herbs." Bertha Jacobs, *tr. by* Jonathan Crewe. WPOW

Ditty: "If this town should tumble down." Audrey Beecham. CN

Ditty, A: In Praise of Eliza, Queen of the Shepherds. Spenser. *Fr.* The Shepheardes [*or* Shepeards *or* Shepherd's] Calender: Aprill. OBEV
(Ditty, A: "See where she sits upon the grassy green.") FaBoCh

Ditty, A: "My true love hath my heart, and I have his." Sir Philip Sidney. *See* Arcadia: My True Love Hath My Heart [and I Have His].

Ditty, A: "O holy Love, religious saint!" Sir Robert Chester. *Fr.* Love's Martyr. EIL

Ditty, A: "See where she sits upon the grassy green." Spenser. *See* Shepheardes [*or* Shepeards *or* Shepherd's] Calender, The: Aprill.

Ditty in Imitation of the Spanish ["Entre Tanto Que L'Avril"], A. Lord Herbert of Cherbury. EIL; OBS

Ditty of the Six Virgins, The. Thomas Watson. *See* Honourable Entertainment Given to the Queen's Majesty in Progress at Elvetham, 1591, The: With Fragrant Flowers We Strew the Way.

Diuturnal Infirmity of Hope. Sister Juana Inés de la Cruz, *tr. fr. Spanish by* Samuel Beckett. MexPo

Divan, The. Richard Henry Stoddard. AA

Dive could come who was its fledgling first, The. Nijinsky. Parker Tyler. PoA

Diver, The. Robert Hayden. AmPP; BPo; MOS

Diver, The. John Frederic Herbin. CaP

Diver, The. Ben Howard. SM

Diver, The. Edward Leslie Mayo. CoAP

Diver, The. Leonard E. Nathan. ErPo

Diver, The. W. W. Eustace Ross. NOBC; OBCV

Diver. R. A. Simpson. CBAP

Divers. Charles Ghigna. TSL

Divers, The. Peter Quennell. MoBrPo

Divers' Death, The. Alison Brackenbury. DiPo

Divers Doth Use. Sir Thomas Wyatt. NAEL-1; SiPS; Son

("Dyvers dothe use as I have heard and kno.") AAS

Divers thy death do diversely bemoan. The Death of Wyatt. Earl of Surrey. SiPS

("Dyvers thy death doo dyverslye bemone.") AAS

Diversions of the Re-Echo Club. Carolyn Wells. OBAL

Diverting History of John Gilpin, The. William Cowper. *See* John Gilpin.

Dives and Lazarus ("As it fell out upon a day"). *Unknown.* ELP; ESPB; FaBoBa; OBET; OxBB

Dives and Lazarus ("There was a man in olden times"). *Unknown.* AmFP

Dives and Laz'us. *Unknown.* TTY

Dives, when you and I go down to Hell. To Dives. Hilaire Belloc. OBSV

Divide your bread in two. Heavenly Jerusalem, of the Earth. Leah Goldberg, *tr. by* Robert Friend. VWA

Divided. David Gray. AA

Divided, *sel.* Jean Ingelow.

"Dappled sky, a world of meadows, A." OBNC

Divided Heart, The. George Wither. *Fr.* Fair Virtue, the Mistress of Philarete. TrGrPo

Dividends. Hubert Creekmore. WaP

Divina Commedia, *sels.* Dante, *tr. fr. Italian.*

Inferno. NAWM-1, *tr. by* John Ciardi.

"And now we walked along the solid mire." *Fr.* XV. OBVE

Francesca of Rimini. *Fr.* V. PFI

Gates of Hell, The. *Fr.* III. PFI

"Like fire-flies that the peasant on the hill." *Fr.* XXVI. Prf

"Now the hard margin bears us on, while steam." PeHV

Pier delle Vigne. *Fr.* XII. HoPM

"Through men you enter the city of lament." *Fr.* III. OBD

Ugolino. *Fr.* XXXII-XXXIII. AnAn; FaBoPV; PFI, *fr.* XXXIII.

Paradiso.

"Glory of Him who moves all things rays forth, The." *Fr.* I. NAWM-1, *tr. by* John Ciardi.

"Glory of the great all-mover goes, The." *Fr.* I. OBD

"Piercing brightness of the living ray, The." *Fr.* XXXIII. TOF, *tr. by* Dorothy L. Sayers *and* Barbara Reynolds.

Saint Bernard's Hymn of Praise to the Virgin Mary. *Fr.* XXXIII. PFI

Saints in Glory, The. *Fr.* XXXI. WGRP

"That sun that breathed love's fire into my youth." *Fr.* III. NAWM-1, *tr. by* John Ciardi.

"Then, in the form of a white rose, the host." *Fr.* XXXI-XXXIII. NAWM-1, *tr. by* John Ciardi.

Purgatorio.

"As the day stands when the Sun begins to glow." *Fr.* XXVII. NAWM-1, *tr. by* John Ciardi.

"At the hour when the heat of the day is overcome." *Fr.* XIX. NAWM-1, *tr. by* John Ciardi.

Celestial Pilot, The. *Fr.* II. WGRP

"Earnest to explore within and all around." *Fr.* XXVIII. OBVE

"For better waters now the little bark." *Fr.* I-II. NAWM-1, *tr. by* John Ciardi.

Lady Clothed in Flame, The. *Fr.* III. PFI

Oderisi D'Agobbio on Pride. *Fr.* IX. PFI

Virgil's Farewell to Dante. *Fr.* XXVII. FaBoTw

"When the Septentrion of the First Heaven." *Fr.* XXX-XXXI. NAWM-1, *tr. by* John Ciardi.

Divina Commedia (*poems introductory to* Longfellow's *tr. of the* Divine Comedy, I-VI.) Longfellow. AmPP; HAP, (I); OBEV, (I); OxBA; Son, (I); TAP

Divination. Jerred Metz. VWA

Divination by a Daffadill [*or* Daffodil]. Robert Herrick. CaPo; OBS; SeCV-1

Divine Abundance. *Unknown.* BLRP

Divine Awe. George Edward Woodberry. *Fr.* Wild Eden, XVI. AA

Divine Blacksmith, The. Matthew Prior. FaBoNo

Divine Century of Spiritual Sonnets, A, *sels.* Barnabe Barnes.

"Blast of wind, a momentary breath, A." EBEV

(Life of Man, The.) OBSC

God's Virtue. NOCV; OBSC

(Sonnet: "World's bright comforter, whose beamsome light, The.") EIL

No More Lewd Lays. Son

Divine destroyer, pity me no more. A la Bourbon. Richard Lovelace. CaPo

Divine Hand, The. William Williams. *See* Guide Me, O Thou Great Jehovah.

Divine Image, A ("Cruelty has a human heart"). Blake. *Fr.* Songs of Experience. ChTr; NAEL-2; NoP; OBNC; RB; TEP

Divine Image, The ("To mercy, pity, peace, and love"). Blake. *Fr.* Songs of Innocence. BoTP; EnRP; NAEL-2; NOBE; NOEC; NoP; OAEL-2; OBNC; PoE; PoEL-4; PPP; TEP; WGRP

Divine Insect, The. John Hall Wheelock. GoYe; NYBP

Divine Love. Michael Benedikt. AmPA; CoAP

Divine Love. *Unknown.* OAEL-1

Divine Love. Charles Wesley. *See* Love Divine, All Loves Excelling.

Divine Meditations, *sels.* William Alabaster. Son

Night, the Starless Night of Passion, The. *Fr.* I.

Up to Mount Olivet. *Fr.* VI.

Divine name, brief and compendious. Song to the Most Holy Name of Jesus. Fernando de Córdova y Bocanegra, *tr. by* Samuel Beckett. MexPo

Divine Office of the Kitchen, The. Cecily Hallack. BLRP; PoLF

Divine prince, born and descended. Lady Otomo no Sakanoe, *tr. fr. Japanese by* Hiroaki Sato. *Fr.* Manyo Shu. FCEI

Divine prince of eight thousand spears, The/ great ruler of our land. Songs Exchanged between Prince Okuninushi and Princess Nunakawa ("The divine prince of eight thousand spears/ great ruler of our land"). *Unknown, tr. fr. Japanese by* Hiroaki Sato. *Fr.* The Kojiki. FCEI

Divine prince of eight thousand spears/ because I am a woman. Songs Exchanged between Prince Okuninushi and Princess Nunakawa ("Divine prince of eight thousand spears"). *Unknown, tr. fr. Japanese by* Hiroaki Sato. *Fr.* The Kojiki. FCEI

Divine Rapture. Francis Quarles. *See* Emblems: My Beloved Is Mine, and I Am His; He Feedeth among the Lillies.

Divine Rose, That in a Pleasant Garden. Sister Juana Inés de la Cruz, *tr. fr. Spanish by* Samuel Beckett. MexPo

Divine September, the moon wanes. After the Flood. Pierre Jean Jouve, *tr. by* John Montague. RHTwFP

Divine winds upon the waters, The. Hai. Stuart Z. Perkoff. VWA

Divine Wooer, The, *sel.* Phineas Fletcher.

"Me Lord? can'st Thou mispend." TrPWD

Divinely shapen cup, thy lip. On a Greek Vase. Frank Dempster Sherman. AA

Divinely Superfluous Beauty. Robinson Jeffers. HeIP; MoAmPo

Diviner, The. Seamus Heaney. FaBCIP

Diviners, The. Mary Oliver. WPE

Diving for Pearls. Traise Yamamoto. BrSi

Diving into the Wreck. Adrienne Rich. CAPP; HCAP; HeIP; InPK; InPS; MoP; MOS; NAAL-2; NIP; NoAM; NOBA; NoP

Divinities. W. S. Merwin. PoA

Division. John Ratti. NYBP

Division of Parts, The. Anne Sexton. NePoEA-2

Division Street. Berysh Vaynshteyn, *tr. fr. Yiddish by* Benjamin *and* Barbara Harshav. *Fr.* New York Everywhere. AYP

Divorce, *sels.* Tove Ditlevsen, *tr. fr. Danish by* Ann Freeman. OV

"He would/ in the case of a divorce." *Fr.* I.

"It is not easy." *Fr.* III.

Divorce. Adam Koehn. AiP

Divorce. Bink Noll. MAT

Divorce, The. Thomas Stanley. MeLP

Divorce. Anna Wickham. MoBrPo

Divorce of a Lover, The ("Divorce me nowe good death"). George Gascoigne. AAS

Divorce Song. *Unknown, tr. fr. Tsimshian Indian by* Carl Cary. STP

Divorced, but friends again at last. The Onion, Memory. Craig Raine. NAEL-2; NoAM; NoP

Dixie. Daniel Decatur Emmett. AnAmPo; FaFP; FaPON; TrGrPo

Dixie. Albert Pike. AA; PAH

Dixon, a Choctaw, twenty years of age. A Savage. John Boyle O'Reilly. AA

Dizziness. Shin Dong-jip, *tr. fr. Korean* by Koh Chang-soo. ACKP

Djalbarmiwi's Song. *Unknown. See* Ah, the blowfly is whining there, its maggots are eating the flesh.

Djanggawul Song-Cycle. *Aborigine Oral Tradition, tr.* by R. M. Berndt. WTO

Do. Melvin B. Tolson. *See* Libretto for the Republic of Liberia: On the Founding of Liberia.

Do' a-stan'in' on a jar, fiah a-shinnin' thoo. Howdy, Honey, Howdy! Paul Laurence Dunbar. PoLF

Do all the good you can. A Rule. John Wesley. FaFP

Do alley cats go. Alley Cat School. Frank Asch. RHPC

Do any thing anything you will. Pigeon. Elouise Loftin. CNA

Do as they do in the Isle of Man. The Isle of Man. *Unknown.* GBP

Do As You Would Be Done By. Matilda Caroline Edwards. PWR

Do [*or* Doe] but consider this small dust. Hourglass [*or* The Houre-Glasse], The ("Do but consider this small dust"). Ben Jonson. EnLoPo; NIP; OAEL-1; SeCP

Do diddle di do. Jim Jay. Walter de la Mare. BrPo; CenHV; SD; SO

Do gorillas have birthdays? Questions My Son Asked Me, Answers I Never Gave Him. Nancy Willard. LCAP

Do I believe in Angels? Yes. The Angel's Visit. Eugene Field. PWR

Do I give off in the wee. The Sickness of Friends. Henri Coulette. NYBP

Do I have the right to end. I Have the Right. Ana Blandiana, *tr. by* Laura Schiff. OV

Do I prefer to forget it? This middle stretch. Day of Renewal. Louis MacNeice. NAs

"Do I see a hat in the road?" I said. The Old Sussex Road. Ian Serraillier. NTCP

Do I sleep? do I dream? Further Language from Truthful James. Bret Harte. FaBoCo; NOBL
(Truthful James.) CenHV

Do I sleep? Do I dream? De Tea Fabula. Sir Arthur Quiller-Couch. CenHV

Do I venture away too far. Keith Douglas. NePoEA

Do I wake up, or lie here torpid. Consciousness. Agnes Nemes Nagy, *tr. by* Jascha Kessler. FOC

Do It Now. Berton Braley. BLPA; FaFP; WBLP

Do It Now! *Unknown.* BLPA; FaFP; WBLP

Do It Right. Samuel O. Buckner. WBLP

"Do it up!" The wife of Mikata Shami, *tr. fr. Japanese. Fr.* Manyo Shu. Ma

Do It Yrself. Larry Eigner. NeAP; PoM

Do Li A. *Unknown.* GBP

"Do look at those pigs as they lie in the straw." The Pigs. Jane Taylor. FM

Do, Lord, Remember Me. *Unknown.* AmFP

Do nettles mar the month of May. Nettles in May. Euros Bowen, *tr. by the author.* OBWVE

Do Not Accompany Me. Shimon Halkin, *tr. fr. Hebrew* by Ruth Nevo. VWA

Do not account that for thine own. Isabella Whitney. *Fr.* Sweet Nosegay, A, or Pleasant Posy. WPE

Do Not Ask. Christine Lavant, *tr. fr. German* by Michael Hamburger. WPOW

Do not ask how, before cock-crow, my sister had departed. My Sister. Muhammad al-Ghuzzi, *tr.* by May Jayyusi *and* John Heath-Stubbs. MAP

Do not ask me, charming Phillis. By a Bank of Pinks and Lilies. *Unknown.* ErPo

Do Not Ask of Me, My Love. Faiz Ahmad Faiz, *tr. fr. Urdu* by Mahmood Jamal. PBMUP

Do not ask, sir, why this weary woman. Sonnet, Freely Adapted, for J. R. S. Bernice Zamora. CCP

Do not ask: where? We Go. Karl Wolfskehl. TrJP, *tr.* by Carol North Valhope *and* Ernst Morwitz; VWA, *tr.* by Harry Zohn

Do not assume I came out on Christopher Street. Assumption about the Harlem Brown Baby. Salih Michael Fisher. GLP

Do not bathe her in blood. An Abortion. Frank O'Hara. TAP

Do not be angry if I tell you. The Sofa. Medbh McGuckian. FaBCIP

Do not be faithless to me. Shamsuddin Mohammad Vali, *tr. fr. Urdu* by Ahmed Ali. GoT

Do not be greedy, wander not from land to land. The Gipsy. Vali Mohammad Nazir, *tr.* by Ahmed Ali. GoT

Do not burn the brake. *Unknown, tr. fr. Japanese. Fr.* Manyo Shu. Ma

Do not chafe at social rules. The Lonely Cloud of Care. Coventry Patmore. *Fr.* The Victories of Love, II, vii. FaBoRV

Do not come down the ladder. Susan Howe. LP

Do not come too close, nor touch. A Shift of Emphasis. Lauris Edmond. *Fr.* Two Birth Poems, I. ATNZ

Do not come when I am dead. My Hereafter. Juanita de Long. WGRP

Do not conceal[e] thy radiant eyes. To Cynthia, on Concealment of Her Beauty. Sir Francis Kynaston. MeLP; MePo; NOBE; OBS

Do not conceive that I shall here recount. A Virgin Declares Her Beauties. Francesco da Barberini, *tr. by* Dante Gabriel Rossetti. AWP; ErPo

Do not crouch to-day and worship. The Present. Adelaide Anne Procter. WGRP

Do Not, Daughter. *Unknown, tr. fr. Spanish* by Kate Flores. DMH

Do not despair. For Johnny. John Pudney. OBWP

Do not despair, my sister, of a brother's process. Under Our Own Wings. Nellie Wong. BrSi

Do Not Die. W. S. Merwin. CAPP

Do not disdain, O straight up-raised pine. Graven Thoughts. Sir Philip Sidney. *Fr.* Arcadia. SiPS

Do not doubt my love. Pledge. N. M. Rashed, *tr. by* Mahmood Jamal. PBMUP

Do Not Embrace Your Mind's New Negro Friend. William Meredith. WaP

Do not enforce the tired wolf. Prelude to an Evening. John Crowe Ransom. EAS; MoAB; MoAmPo; OxBA

Do Not Expect Again a Phoenix Hour. C. Day Lewis. CMoP; FaBoMo; LiTB; LiTM; MoAB; MoBrPo; NoAM; OxBTC; PoRA

Do not fear to put thy feet. The River-God's Song ("Do not fear to put thy feet"). John Fletcher. *Fr.* The Faithful Shepherdess, III, i. FaPON; MoShBr
(Song: "Do not fear to put thy feet.") ElL; OBS

Do not fill postcards with memories. Face Lost in the Wilderness. Fadwa Tuqan, *tr.* by Patricia Alanah Byrne, Salma Khadra Jayyusi, *and* Naomi Shihab Nye. MAP

"Do not force me with present favor." Hsi. Lady Wang Wei, *tr.* by Burton Watson. CoBCP

Do Not Go Gentle ("Do not go gentle into Death's esteemed vale"). Tim Hopkins. BXAP

Do Not Go Gentle into That Good Night. Dylan Thomas. DL; FaFP; FF; HAP; HeIP; HoPM; InPK; InPS; LiTM; MoAB; MoBrPo; MoP; NAEL-2; NIP; NoAM; NOBE; NoP; OAEL-2; OBD; OxBTC; PoE; PrIm; RB; SCV; SoSe; TEP; TOF; TW; TwCP; UnPo; WeW

Do not hinder my path. Song of the Wind. Munir Niazi, *tr.* by Mahmood Jamal. PBMUP

Do not hold my few years. So We've Come at Last to Freud. Alice Walker. IHMS

Do not hurry; have faith. Have Faith. Edward Carpenter. WGRP

Do not imagine that the exploration. The Discovery. Gwendolyn MacEwen. NOBC

Do not jump on ancient uncles. Rules. Karla Kuskin. RHPC

Do not leave me, Lord, do not let the field lie fallow. Prayer for the Useless Days. Edith Lovejoy Pierce. TrPWD

Do not let any woman read this verse! Deirdre. James Stephens. AWP; CMoP; OBMV; PoRA

Do not let it be known. Teika, *tr. fr. Japanese* by Hiroaki Sato. *Fr.* A Compendium of Good Tanka. FCEI

Do not lie there in the darkness silent. Thunderhead. Archibald MacLeish. AnAmPo

Do Not Lock Your House. Doris Mühringer, *tr. fr. German* by Beth Bjorklund. CoAuP

Do not look for him. Leonard Cohen. HeIP

Do not lose sight. You Who Occupy Our Land. Manuela Margarido, *tr. by* Allan Francovich. WPOW

Do not love me, my friend. Flavien Ranaivo, *tr. fr. French* by Miriam Koshland. PBA

Do Not, Oh, Do Not Prize. *Unknown.* ElL; OBSC
(Pride Is the Canker.) TrGrPo

Do not pay too much attention to the stupid old body. The Stupid Old Body. Edward Carpenter. WGRP

Do not pay too much attention to the wandering lunatic mind. The Wandering Lunatic Mind. Edward Carpenter. WGRP

Do not place frill or border or bouquet. At the Jewish Cemetery in Prague. Oscar Levertin, *tr. by* Richard Burns *and* Göran Printz-Pahlson. VWA

Do not rumple my top-knot. The Coy Lass Dress'd Up in Her Best. *Unknown.* ErPo

Do not say that time once gone can never be returned! Yüan Mei, *tr. fr. Chinese* by Jonathan Chaves. *Fr.* Moments of Fullfillment—Writing Down Miscellaneous. CoBLCP

Do Not Show Your Love. Said Aql, *tr. fr. Arabic by* Matthew Sorenson *and* Naomi Shihab Nye. MAP

Do not stifle me with the strange scent. Alien. Donald Jeffrey Hayes. AmNP

Do not suddenly break the branch, or. Usk. T. S. Eliot. *Fr.* Landscapes, III. FaBoCh; NOCV; RB

Do not suppose that I do not fear death. The Fear of Death. Elizabeth Jennings. OBD

"Do not take a bath in Jordan." Scotch Rhapsody. Dame Edith Sitwell. TwCP

Do not take your piece. Bio-poetic Statement. Carroll Arnett. STE

Do not tether a horse. *Unknown, tr. fr. Japanese.* Fr. Manyo Shu. Ma

Do Not Think. Carol Freeman. CNA

Do not think I am not grateful for your small. Gratitude. Louise Glück. FaBoWP; HeIP

Do not think you are the only one in his perspective. At the Art Gallery. Koh Chang-soo, *tr. by the author.* ACKP

Do not till too big a field. *Unknown, tr. by* Arthur Waley. BoS

Do not torment me, lady. *Unknown.* NOIV

Do Not Torment Me, Woman ("Do not torment me, woman, for your honour's sake do not pursue me"). *Unknown, tr. fr. Late Middle Irish by* Kenneth Jackson. AnIL

Do not torment me, woman, let us set our minds at one. Reconciliation. *Unknown, tr. by* Kenneth Jackson. AnIL

Do not trust him gentle lady. The Gipsy's Warning. *Unknown.* BeLS

Do Not Turn Away. Kumeroa Ngoingoi Pewhairangi, *tr. fr. Maori by* Sam Karetu. PeNZ

Do not wake the sick birds. H. Leivick, *tr. fr. Yiddish by* Benjamin *and* Barbara Harshav. *Fr.* The Sick Birds. AYP

Do not waste your pity, friend. A Wasted Sympathy. Winifred Howells. AA

Do not weep maiden, for war is kind. War Is Kind, I (title poem). Stephen Crane. *Fr.* The Wayfarer. AnAmPo; AmPP; FPL; LiTA; LiTM; NAAL-2; NOBA; OBWP; PoLF; TAP; WaaP

Do not worry if I scurry from the grill-room in a hurry. Cupid's Darts. A. P. Herbert. CenHV

Do Nothing till You Hear from Me. David Henderson. CNA; PoBA

Do skyscrapers ever grow tired. Skyscrapers. Rachel Field. FaPON

Do something. Widowhood. Malka Heifetz-Tussman. AYP, *tr. by* Kathryn Hellerstein; PeBMYV, *tr. by* Marcia Falk

Do the Baby Cake-Walk. Clyde Watson. NTCP

Do the courtiers even now. Nakatomi Yakamori, *tr. fr. Japanese.* Fr. Manyo Shu. Ma

Do the Dead Know What Time It Is? Kenneth Patchen. HoPM; MoAmPo

Do the vast oceans die? *Unknown, tr. fr. Japanese.* Fr. Manyo Shu. Ma

Do the wife and baby travelling to see. The Sick Nought. Randall Jarrell. OxBA

Do these words mean what I assume they mean? Hootali Ajignat. William Dickey. BLA

Do They Whisper behind My Back? Delmore Schwartz. LiTA

Do we indeed desire the dead. Tennyson. *Fr.* In Memoriam A. H. H., LI. OBD

Do we reach the sea with clocks. The Deaf and Blind. Paul Éluard, *tr. by* Paul Auster. RHTwFP

Do ye hear the children weeping, O my brothers. The Cry of the Children. Elizabeth Barrett Browning. EBVV

Do ye indeed speak righteousness, O congregation? Psalm LVIII ("Do ye indeed speak righteousness. . ."). Bible, *O.T. Fr.* Psalms. (Psalm LVIII: "Do ye indeed speak righteousness, O congregation?" *paraphrased by* the Countess of Pembroke) NOCV (Psalm LVIII: Si Vere Utique: "And call ye this to utter what is just," *paraphrased by* the Countess of Pembroke) BoWoP; NAEL-1; WPE

Do ye ken hoo to fush for the salmon? Master and Man. Sir Henry Newbolt. OxBTC

Do you/ dig ray/ charles. Ray Charles. Sam Cornish. CNA

Do you ask me how I prove. The Heart's Proof. James Buckham. BLRP; WBLP

Do you ask me what I think of. What I Think of Hiawatha. J. W. Morris. Par

Do you ask what the birds say? The sparrow, the dove. Answer to a Child's Question. Samuel Taylor Coleridge. EnRP; FaBoBe; OxBChV (Birds, The.) BoTP

Do you blame me that I loved him? A Double Standard. Frances Ellen Watkins Harper. BlSi; PWR

Do you come to me to bend me to your will. A Woman to Her Lover. Christina Walsh. BrRo

Do you desire our love to endure? Lady Otomo no Sakanoe, *tr. fr. Japanese.* Fr. Manyo Shu. Ma

Do you ever look in the looking-glass. Robert, Who Is Often a Stranger to Himself. Gwendolyn Brooks. RAR

Do you ever think of me, Kitty Kline? Kitty Kline. *Unknown.* AmFP

Do You Fancy Me? Dinah Butler. AIW

Do You Fear the Wind? Hamlin Garland. AA

Do you feel your heart discouraged as you pass along the way? When Thou Passest through the Waters. Henry Crowell. BLRP

Do you forget the shifting hole. To a Defeated Saviour. James Wright. NePoEA

Do you have a sweet thought, Cerinthus. Sulpicia, *tr. fr. Latin by* Aliki *and* Willis Barnstone. BoWoP

Do you hear the blue owl shriek? Blue Owl Song. Alfred Kittner, *tr. by* Herbert Kuhner. VWA

Do you hear the cry as the pack goes by. Wind-Wolves. William D. Sargent. RHPC

"Do you herd sheep?" old gramma sighed. How Low Is the Lowing Herd. Walt Kelly. FiBHP

Do you know how the people of all the land. From Potomac to Merrimac. Edward Everett Hale. PAH

Do you know me now? From the Ballad of Evil. N. P. van Wyck Louw, *tr. by* Anthony Delius. PeSA

Do you know of just one habitation. Nikolai Alekseyevich Nekrasov, *tr. fr. Russian by* Alan Meyers. *Fr.* Reflections by a Main Entrance. AAA

Do you know of the dreary land. The River Fight. Henry Howard Brownell. PAH

Do you know Paul, Paul Pine (he's nine). Friend. Felice Holman. ILY

Do you know that once. Overnight Guest. Ramona Wilson. VoR

Do you know that your soul is of my soul such part. To My Son. Margaret Johnston Grafflin. SoSe (Like Mother, like Son.) BLPA

Do you know the old man who. The Wild Flower Man. Lu Yu, *tr. by* Kenneth Rexroth. NaP

Do you know there's lots of people. Get into the Boosting Business. *Unknown.* WBLP

Do you know what. Fancy. Robert Creeley. NOBA

Do You Know What I Mean? Jack Myers. NAmP

Do you know what is bad? Bad and Good. Alexander Resnikoff. NTCP

Do you know where I got my song? My Song. Hayyim Nahman Bialik, *tr. by* Ruth Nevo. VWA

Do you know why rivers grip their banks tightly? Beyond Logic. Lo Fu, *tr. by* Dominic Cheung. IFON

Do you know you have asked for the costliest thing. A Woman's Question. Lena Lathrop, *wr. at to* Elizabeth Barrett Browning. BLPA; WBLP

Do you lazily nurse your knee and muse? What Are You Doing? Edmund Vance Cooke. PWR

Do you like marigolds? Marigolds. Louise Driscoll. BoTP

Do you look for a rainbow, Love, in this wet weather. Wet Weather. Patricia Low. VGW

Do you love me. Question. *Unknown.* RHPC

"Do you mind the news while we eat?" Dinner Party 1940. Philip Sherlock. PBCV

Do you need an explanation. The Russian God. Prince P. A. Vyazemsky, *tr. by* Alan Myers. AAA

Do you ne'er think what wond'ous beings these? Longfellow. *Fr.* Tales of a Wayside Inn: Birds of Killingworth, The (The Poet's Tale), 2 *sts.* WBLP

"Do you not find something very strange about him?" The Assassination. Robert Hillyer. MoAmPo; OFD

Do you not hear her song. Daphne. Thomas Samuel Jones, Jr. OHIP

"Do you not hear the Aziola cry?" The Aziola. Shelley. EBEV; PBBP

Do you not see that we pitched our tent on the banks of night. Female. Muhammad al-Ghuzzi, *tr. by* May Jayyusi *and* John Heath-Stubbs. MAP

"Do you not wish to renounce the Devil?" Armand Lanusse, *tr. by* Langston Hughes. PoNe; TTY

Do you, now, as the news becomes known. Pay-off. Kenneth Fearing. CMoP

Do You Plan to Speak Bantu? Ogden Nash. FiBHP

Do you remember/ That afternoon. W. E. Henley. BrPo

Do you remember. Friend. Hone Tuwhare, *tr. by* Kumeroa Ngoingoi Pewhairangi. PeNZ

Do you remember/ How you won. To James. Frank Horne. *Fr.* Letters [*or* Notes] Found near a Suicide. BPo

Do you remember an inn. Tarantella. Hilaire Belloc. CH; FaBoCh; MoBrPo; MoShBr; OBMV; RB; RR

Do you remember how I beat on the door. A Door. W. S. Merwin. EAS; LCAP

Do You Remember Me? Walter Savage Landor. Fr. Ianthe. EnRP

("Do you remember me? or are you proud?.") OBNC

(Ianthe's Question.) OBEV

Do you remember Mr. Goodbeare, the carpenter. Elegy for Mr. Goodbeare. Sir Osbert Sitwell. MoBrPo

Do you remember, my sweet, absent son. The Child's Wish Granted. George Parsons Lathrop. AA

Do You Remember 1926? Idris Davies. OBWVE

Do you remember that day of the roaring storm. Mountaineering Bus. Rennie McOwan. PoSH

Do You Remember That Night? Unknown, tr. fr. Irish by Eugene O'Curry. BIrV

Do you remember the lizard? The Lizard. Rona Murray. NOBC

Do you remember the meadow-field. The Meadow-Field. Charles Sangster. Fr. Pleasant Memories. OBCV

Do you remember, when you were first a child. Message from Home. Kathleen Jessie Raine. ImOP; WPE

Do you say/ its progesterone. What Do You Say When a Man Tells You, You Have the Softest Skin. Mary Mackey. FF

Do you see this grain of sand. A Grain of Sand. Frances Ellen Watkins Harper. PWR

Do you still remember? On the faces. Postscript. János Pilinszky, tr. by Edwin Morgan. MHuP

Do You Think? Josephine D. Henderson Heard. CBWP-4

Do you think/ you must work signs. Instructions for the Messiah. Myra Sklarew. VWA

Do you think of me at all. Dead "Wessex" the Dog to the Household. Thomas Hardy. FM

Do you think we skip. The Zobo Bird. Frank A. Collymore. AmMo; GoJo

"Do you think you will hug the shore, Captain, to-day?" Hugging the Shore. Mary E. Tucker. CBWP-1

Do you want to know his name? The Porch. R. S. Thomas. NOCV

Do you wish the world were better? Better, Wiser and Happier. Ella Wheeler Wilcox. WBLP

Do Your Best. Mrs. Henry Linden. CBWP-4

DOA in Dulse. Diane Burns. STE

Doan't You Be What You Ain't. Edwin Milton Royle. BLPA

Dobbin. George Bowering. NOBC

Docker. Seamus Heaney. HeIP; MoP; NOIV; TW

Dockyard Gate, The. Unknown. OxBSS

Doctor. See also Dr.

Doctor asked him if he dreamed at night, The. The Patient. Nicholas Moore. EAS

Doctor Bill Williams. Ernest Walsh. InvP

Doctor Bottom was preparing to leave. Medical Aid. Walter Hard. BXAP

Doctor, doctor, it fits real fine. Vet's Rehabilitation. Ray Durem. PoBA

Doctor Emmanuel ("Doctor Emmanuel Harrison-Hyde"). James Reeves. RHPC

Doctor Faustus. Geoffrey Hill. NePoEA-2

Doctor Faustus ("Not marching in the fields of Trasimene."), sels. Christopher Marlowe. NAEL-1; OAEL-1

"Ah, Faustus,/ Now hast thou but one bare hour [or hower] to live." Fr. V, ii. ChTr; HeIP

(End of Doctor Faustus, The.) PoEL-2

(End of Faustus, The.) TrGrPo

"Was this the face that launched a thousand ships?" Fr. V, i. EBEV; GBL; HeIP; NIP; TrGrPo

(Face of Helen, The.) FaBV

(Helen.) BLPL; FaFP; LiTB

(Helen of Troy.) FF

"Where are you damn'd?" Fr. I, iii. OBD

Doctor Fell. Thomas Brown, after the Latin of Martial. ChTr; FaBoCo; FaBoEE; FaFP; MoShBr; NBLV; OBVE; OxNR

Doctor Foster is a good man. Unknown. OxNR

Doctor Foster went to Gloucester [or Glo'ster]. Mother Goose. OxBoLi; OxNR

Doctor Frolic. Robert Pinsky. NoAM

Doctor Johnson. Soame Jenyns. FaBoEE; OBSV

Doctor loves the patient, The. The Bed. A. D. Hope. NoAM; OxBC; OxBSP

Doctor Major. Lionel Johnson. BrPo

Doctor punched my vein, The. Scyros. Karl Shapiro. HoPM; LiTA; LiTM; WaP

Doctor said, count to ten, The. Flight. Ruth Whitman. SO

Doctor Who Sits at the Bedside of a Rat, The. Josephine Miles. VGW

Doctor, you say there are no haloes. Monet Refuses the Operation. Lisel Mueller. FYAP

Doctors attended behind each chair. W. H. Auden. Fr. A Happy New Year. OBSV

Doctors' Row. Conrad Aiken. HAP

Doctor's Story, The. Will M. Carleton. BLPA

Doctors tender of their fame, The. Swift. Fr. Verses on the Death of Doctor Swift [D.S.P.D., Occasioned by Reading a Maxim in Rochefoucauld]. NOBL

Doctors that learned be. John Skelton. Fr. Colin Clout. OBSV

Document. Tuvia Ruebner, tr. by Harold Schimmel. VWA

Documentary. Joseph Stroud. NPGG

Documentary on Airplane Glue, A. David Henderson. MAT

Documentary on Brazil, The. Alfred Corn. MAYP

Documentation. Michael Palmer. NPGG

Dodder twines around the huang-po tree, The. The Woman Née Wu. Wu Chia-chi, tr. by Jonathan Chaves. CoBLCP

Dodder vine trails with the long wind, The. Old Chüeh-chü. Unknown, tr. by Burton Watson. CoBCP

Doddledy, doodledy, doodledy, dan. Unknown. OxNR

Dodger, The. Unknown. AmFP; GBP

Dodo, The. Hilaire Belloc. ChTr

Dodo. Henry Carlile. Psk

Dodo used to walk around, The. The Dodo. Hilaire Belloc. ChTr

Dodona's Oaks Were Still. Patrick MacDonogh. NeIP

Doe. Philip Dow. NPGG

Doe at Evening, A. D. H. Lawrence. BrPo

Doe of the mountains east. Mother/ Deer/ Lady. Harold Littlebird. VoR

Doeg, though without knowing how or why. John Dryden and Nahum Tate. Fr. Absalom and Achitophel: Part II. PoEL-3

Does a tear fall from the eye. Tragedy. Howard Moss. NePoEA

Does anybody listen to advice? Senior Poet. Robert Pinsky. Fr. Three on Luck. AnAn

Does anything get more tangled and higgeldy-piggeldy than the days. A Post-Impressionist Susurration for the First of November, 1983. Hayden Carruth. BLA

Does he not know how. Princess Shikishi, tr. fr. Japanese by Hiroaki Sato. Fr. Seventy-eight Tanka. FCEI

Does he think of me in the merry throng. The Question. Josephine D. Henderson Heard. CBWP-4

Does It Matter? Siegfried Sassoon. MoBrPo; WaP

Does it wear a yarmulka. What Is a Jewish Poem? Myra Sklarew. CRP; VWA

Does its pounding pierce the sun in the sky? Wakayama Bokusui, tr. fr. Japanese by Hiroaki Sato. Fr. Forty-four Tanka. FCEI

Does man love Art? Man visits Art, but squirms. The Chicago Picasso. Gwendolyn Brooks. Fr. Two Dedications. BPo; EyDe; LiTM

Does morning always have to come? The Second Hymn to the Night. "Novalis," prose poem version, tr. fr. German by Robert Bly. Fr. Hymns to the Night. NU

Does mother get praised as often as she should. The Woman Back in the Kitchen. Nicholas Lloyd Ingraham. PWR

Does nature bear a tyrant's breast? John Langhorne. Fr. Owen of Carron. FaBoCo

Does nelis have a glass chin? Boxers. Armando, tr. by James S. Holmes. DuIn

Does one really have to fret. Shinsho, tr. by Lucien Stryk and Takashi Ikemoto. ZPCJ

Does the Eagle know what is in the pit? Thel's Motto. Blake. Fr. The Book of Thel. ChTr (4 ll.)

Does the lily flower open? Star Song of the Bushman Women. Unknown, tr. by W. H. I. Bleek. PeSA

Does the moon say "Grieve!" Saigyo, tr. fr. Japanese by Burton Watson. Fr. Sixty-four Tanka. FCEI

Does the road wind up-hill all the way? Uphill [or Up-Hill]. Christina Rossetti. BLPA; CH; EBVV; FaBoBe; FaBoRV; FPL; HAP; InPK; NAEL-2; NOBE; NoP; OAEL-2; OBD; OBEV; OBNC; PoE; PoRA; PPP; TrCP; TrGrPo; WeW; WGRP; WiR; WPE

Does the Spearmint Lose Its Flavor on the Bedpost Overnight? Billy Rose. OBAL

Does the typewriter type. Truth. Susan Fromberg Schaeffer. IHMS

Doesn't he realize/ that I am not/ like the swaying kelp. Komachi, tr. by Kenneth Rexroth and Ikuko Atsumi. BoWoP; WPOW

Dog. David Chapman Berry. BXAP

Dog, The. Frederick William Faber. FM

Dog. Lawrence Ferlinghetti. HoPM
Dog, The. Oliver Herford. FaBV
Dog, The. Valentin Iremonger. BIrV; NeIP
Dog. Ingrid Jonker, tr. fr. Afrikaans by Jack Cope and William Plomer. PBWP
Dog, The. Li Nan, tr. fr. Chinese by Dominic Cheung. IFON
Dog. Harold Monro. MoBrPo
Dog. John Crowe Ransom. InPS; LiTA; OBAL
Dog. William Jay Smith. GoJo
Dog, A. Gertrude Stein. Fr. Tender Buttons. TTTS
Dog, The. Gerald Stern. BLA
Dog, The. Unknown. WBLP
Dog, The. W. H. Davies. MoBrPo
Dog and Sea. Alfonsina Storni, tr. fr. Spanish by Mark I. Smith. OV
Dog barked; then the woman stood in the doorway, The. Roan Stallion. Robinson Jeffers. BeLS
Dog barks, A. Somewhere else, another dog barks. Two Dogs. Ruth Kim Chun-soo, tr. by Koh Chang-soo. ACKP
Dog barks from a cloud, The. Adolescence. Gregory Orr. Psk
Dog beneath the Skin, The, sels. Wystan Hugh Auden. OxBTC
"Summer holds, The: upon its glittering lake."
"You are the town and we are the clock."
Dog body and cat mind, The. Jenny Joseph. BrRo
Dog called Sesamë slewed out. Stray Dog, near Ecully. Margaret Avison. OBCV; PoA
Dog Child, The. Keaulumoku, tr. fr. Hawaiian by M. W. Beckwith. Fr. Kumulipo, The; a Creation Chant. WTO
Dog Creek Mainline ("Dog Creek: cat track and bind splay"). Charles Wright. AmPA; LCAP
Dog Day Vespers. Charles Wright. LCAP
Dog, Dog in My Manger. George Barker. LiTM
Dog emerges from the flies, A. Nino, the Wonder Dog. Roy Fuller. FF
Dog Hospital. Peter Wild. AmPA
Dog in San Francisco, A. Michael Ondaatje. GOYP
Dog in the River, The. Phaedrus, tr. fr. Latin by Christopher Smart. AWP
Dog is a faithful, intelligent friend, The. The Song Called "His Hide Is Covered with Hair." Hilaire Belloc. FaBoNo; FM
Dog is man's best friend, The. An Introduction to Dogs. Ogden Nash. MoShBr
Dog loved its churlish life, The. Lupercalia. Ted Hughes. CMoP
Dog means dog. Blum. Dorothy Aldis. MoShBr
Dog must see your corpse, The. The last thing that you feel. Dog Prospectus. Peter Redgrove. OxBC
Dog Named Ego, the Snowflakes as Kisses, A. Delmore Schwartz. LiTA; LiTM
Dog of Art, The. Denise Levertov. MoP; NoAm
Dog On the Road. Ory Bernstein, tr. fr. Hebrew by Bernhard Frank. MHeP
Dog Poem, A. Saqi Farooqi, tr. fr. Urdu by Mahmood Jamal. PBMUP
Dog Poisoner, The. Keith Wilson. MOWH
Dog Prospectus. Peter Redgrove. OxBC
Dog Sacrifice at Lake Ronkonkoma. William Heyen. AmPA
Dog scatters her body in sleep, The. Biography. Michael Ondaatje. NoAM
Dog Shark. Unknown. PBCV
Dog Sleeping on My Feet, A. James Dickey. NAAL-2
Dog Star Sale. Douglas Crase. BAP
Dog stops barking after Robinson has gone, The. Robinson. Weldon Kees. MoP; NaP; NYBP
Dog Story. James Steel Smith. SoTCo
Dog, that has ten years of breath, A. The Last Years. William Henry Davies. FM
Dog that is beat has a right to complain, The. On Sir Henry Clinton's Recall. Unknown. PAH
Dog, The. The book. The glass. Poem Following Discussion of Brain. Stan Rice. NPGG
Dog-tired, suisired, will now my body down. The Poet's Final Instructions. John Berryman. SM; Son; VGW
Dog trots freely in the street, The. Dog. Lawrence Ferlinghetti. HoPM
Dog was there, outside her door, The. The Dog. W. H. Davies. MoBrPo
Dog who knew the winter felt no spleen, The. The Watcher. Ruth Stone. NYBP
Dog will come when he is called, The. Beasts and Birds. Adelaide O'Keeffe. OxBChV
Dog will often steal a bone, A. A Cat's Conscience. Unknown. PoLF
Dog with daisies for eyes, The. The Dog of Art. Denise Levertov. NoAM

Dog with Schoolboys. Jean Follain, tr. fr. French by Keith Waldrop. RHTwFP
Dog writes on the window with his nose, The. Early Spring. Philip Whalen. TDD
Dog Yoga. Charles Wright. LCAP
Dogchain Gang, The. Stan Rice. NPGG
Doggerel by a Senior Citizen. W. H. Auden. NBLV; NOBL
Dogget Gap. Unknown. AmFP
Doggies went to the mill, The. Unknown. BoTP; OxNR
Dogknotting in Quezaltenango. Vincent O'Sullivan. PeNZ
Dogrose. Patric Stevenson. NeIP
Dog's, A/ body zipped. At the Crossroads. Thomas Kinsella. NoAM
Dogs. Susan Griffin. NPGG
Dogs. Tu Kuo-ch'ing, tr. fr. Chinese by Dominic Cheung. IFON
Dogs and Cats and Bears and Bats. Jack Prelutsky. RHPC
Dogs and Weather. Winifred Welles. FaPON
Dogs are quite a bit like people. Dog. William Jay Smith. GoJo
Dogs Are Shakespearean, Children Are Strangers. Delmore Schwartz. NoAM
Dog's Death, A. Sir John Collings Squire. FM
Dog's Death. John Updike. Psk
Dogs in the Morning Light. Bruce Dawe. NoAM
Dogs in the Storm. Michael Waters. NAmP
Dogs of Dawn. Berysh Vaynshteyn, tr. fr. Yiddish by Benjamin and Barbara Harshav. Fr. Guys of the Volye. AYP
Dog's Song. Robert Wallace. TDD
Dogwood Blossoms. Peter Blue Cloud. STE
Dogwood Blossoms. George Marion McClellan. BANP
Dogwood flakes. Variations Done for Gerald Van de Wiele. Charles Olson. NeAP; NoAM; NoP
Doing, a Filthy Pleasure Is, and Short. Petronius Arbiter, tr. fr. Latin by Ben Jonson. BoLoP; ErPo; LLLT; OBVE
(Fragment of Petronius, A.) OxBSP
Doing my wash. Wash Day. Larry Mollin. NeAC
Doing Nothing. Dennis Saleh. SoTCo
Doing the Dubhs. Unknown. PoSH
Dole of the King's Daughter, The. Unknown, tr. fr. French by Oscar Wilde. AWP
Dolgelley Hotel, The. Thomas Hughes. CenHV; FaBoCo
Doll, The. Margarete Beutler, tr. fr. German by Susan L. Cocalis and Gerlinde Geiger. DMG
Doll, The. Peyton Houston. Fr. Sonnet Variations, XVII. Son
Doll, The. Gregory Orr. AmPA
Doll. Fahmida Riaz, tr. fr. Urdu by Mahmood Jamal. PBMUP
Doll as well, A. Unknown, tr. by Geoffrey Bownas and Anthony Thwaite. PeBJV
Doll, don't be too proud of those eyes. To Vanity. Darwin T. Turner. PoNe
Doll in the doll-maker's house, A. The Dolls. W. B. Yeats. BrPo; CMoP; NoAM; PoE
Dollar-green Cadillac limousine, A. Moguls and Monks. Lewis MacAdams. UL
$. Abelardo. FIA
Dolls. David St. John. LCAP
Dolls, The. W. B. Yeats. BrPo; CMoP; NoAM; PoE
Doll's hair concealing, A. Partial Resemblance. Denise Levertov. CoAP; NaP
Dolls' Wash, The. Juliana Horatia Ewing. OxBChV
Dolly's Lesson. Unknown. FaBoUs
Dolomites. J. C. Milne. PoSH
Dolor. Josephine Miles. FaBoWP
Dolor. Theodore Roethke. AmPP; CMoP; HCAP; HeIP; HoPM; LiTM; MoP; NoAM; OxBSP; PoA
Dolphin. Robert Lowell. NoAM; NOBA
Dolphin plunge, fountain play. Louis MacNeice. SO
Dolphins, The. Carol Ann Duffy. NPo
Dolphin's Return, The. Unknown. OxBSS
Dom Pedro, The. Unknown. AmFP
"Domaine Public." Geoffrey Hill. OxBC
Dome of Sunday, The [or A]. Karl Shapiro. CMoP; CoAP; LiTM; MoAB; MoAmPo; NoAM; OxBA; WaP
Dome Poem. Dave Smith. PoA
Domed with the azure of heaven. Vapour and Blue. Wilfred Campbell. CaP
Domestic Asides; or, Truth in Parentheses. Thomas Hood. EnRP
Domestic: Climax. Merrill Moore. ErPo
Domestic Poems, sel. Thomas Hood.
Serenade, A. NBLV
Domestic Quarrel. Sally McInerney. GrPl
Domestic Scene. Michael Hartnett. BIrV

Domestic Science. *Unknown*. WBLP

Domestic Stones (fragment), The. Hans Arp, *tr. fr. French by* David Gascoyne. EAS

Domestic Storm, A. Priscilla Jane Thompson. CBWP-2

Domesticated Stones. Hans Arp, *tr. fr. French by* Michael Benedikt. POS

Domestics. Kattie M. Cumbo. BlSi

Domicilium. Thomas Hardy. FaBoPP; FL

Domination as Another Form of Weakness. David Avidan, *tr. fr. Hebrew by* Bernhard Frank. MHeP

Domination of Black. Wallace Stevens. AmPP; MoAB; MoAmPo; OxBA

Dominatrix. Clifford Young. VVA

Domine, Quo Vadis? *Unknown*. ACP

Domine Quo Vadis? Sir William Watson. WGRP

Domineering Eagle and the Inventive Bratling, The. Guy Wetmore Carryl. OBAL

Dominic Francis Xavier Brotherton-Chancery. Gavin Ewart. OxBC

Dominica Pentecostes. Aubrey Thomas De Vere. TIRV

Dominion of Australia, The. Brunton Stephens. PoAu-1

Dominus Illuminatio Mea. Richard Doddridge Blackmore. OBEV

Domus Caedet Arborem. Charlotte Mew. PBWP

Don. Anthony McNeill. PBCV

Don Baty, the Draft Register. Muriel Rukeyser. NNaP

Don Giovanni, *sel.* Lorenzo Da Ponte, *tr. fr. Italian by* Natalie MacFarren.

  "Giovinette, Che Fate All'Amore." TrJP

Don Giovanni on His Way to Hell. Jack Gilbert. NPGG

Don Giovanni on His Way to Hell II ("How could they think women a creation?"). Jack Gilbert. NPGG

Don Juan, *sels.* Byron.

  And Angling, Too. SD

  At Thirty Years. *Fr.* I. FiP

  Death of Haidée, The. *Fr.* IV. FiP

  "Bob Southey! You're a poet—poet-laureate." CTC; EnRP; OAEL-2; OBSV

  (Dedication to the Poet Laureate.) FiP

  (Southey and Wordsworth.) TrGrPo

  Donna Julia. *Fr.* I. PoEL-4

  Evening, *after* Sappho *Fr.* III. TrGrPo

  (Hesperus the Bringer.) AWP

  "Fourth day came, but not a breath of air, The." *Fr.* II. ChER

  "I would to heaven that I were so much clay." *Fr. on the back of the poet's MS of* I. CTC; FiP; NAEL-2; NOBL; NoP; OAEL-2; OxBSP; PrIm

  Growing old. *Fr.* I. NOBE; SCV

  Gulbeyaz. *Fr.* V. PoEL-4

  Haidée. *Fr.* IV. SeCePo

  Haidée and Don Juan. *Fr.* II. OBNC

  "Hail, Muse! et caetera.—We left Juan sleeping." *Fr.* III. OAEL-2

  "I know that what our neighbours call *longueurs*.." *Fr.* II. OBSV

  "I want a hero: an uncommon want." *Fr.* I. EnRP; NAEL-2, *abr.*; NoP; OAEL-2, *abr.*; PoE, *abr.*.

  "I wonder if his appetite was good?." *Fr.* V. OAEL-2

  "In her first passion woman loves her lover." *Fr.* I. ErPo

  "In the great world—which, being interpreted." *Fr.* XI. OxBoLi

  Isles of Greece, The. *Fr.* III. AWP; ChTr; FaPoR; FiP; LiTB; NOBE; OBEV; OBTV

  "Juan embark'd—the ship got under way." *Fr.* II. MOS

  Juan in England. *Fr.* XI. FiP

  "Juan knew several languages—as well." *Fr.* XI. OAEL-2

  Lady Adeline Amundeville. *Fr.* XIII. PoEL-4

  "Let there be light!" said God, and there was light!" *Fr.* VII. OBWP

  "Milton's the prince of poets—so we say." *Fr.* III. NOBL; OAEL-2

  My Days of Love Are Over. *Fr.* I. OBNC

  "O love! O glory! what are you who fly." *Fr.* VII. OAEL-2

  "Oh Wellington! (Or "Villainton," for Fame)." *Fr.* IX. OBSV; OxBoLi

  (On Wellington.) FiP

  "Oh ye! who teach the ingenuous youth of nations." *Fr.* II. EnRP

  "Old Lambro pass'd unseen a private gate." *Fr.* III. EnRP

  "Over the stones still rattling, up Pall Mall." NOBL, XI.

  Poetical Commandments. *Fr.* I. FiP; OxBoLi

  (Poet's Credo.) SeCePo

  Romantic to Burlesque. *Fr.* IV. EnRP; FiP; OAEL-2

  "Sagest of women, even of widows, she." *Fr.* I. NOBL

  "Shore looked wild, without a trace of man, The." *Fr.* II. HAP

  "They were alone once more; for them to be." *Fr.* IV. EBEV

  "Though somewhat large, exuberant, and truculent." *Fr.* IX. OAEL-2

  "'Tis thus with people in an open boat." *Fr.* II. FaBoPV

"To our theme.—The man who has stood on the Acropolis." *Fr.* XI. InPS; OBSV

"'Twas on a summer's day—the sixth of June." *Fr.* I. PPP

"Where is the world!" cries Young at eighty." *Fr.* XI. FaBoPV

"Why call the miser miserable?." *Fr.* XII. UnPo

"You know, or you don't know, that great Bacon saith." NOBL, XIV.

"Young unmarried man, with a good name, A." NOBL, XII.

Don Juan. Lucius Harwood Foote. AA

Don Juan. D. H. Lawrence. PoA

Don Juan had got out on Shooter's Hill. Juan in England. Byron. *Fr.* Don Juan, XI. FiP

Don Juan has ever the grand old air. Don Juan. Lucius Harwood Foote. AA

Don Juan in Hell. Baudelaire, *tr. fr. French by* James Elroy Flecker. AWP

Don Juan in Winter. Michael Mott. KS

Don Juan's Address to the Sunset. Robert Nichols. OBMV

Don Larsen's Perfect Game. Paul Goodman. ASP

Don Leon, *sel. Unknown*.

  "Then, say, was I or nature in the wrong." PeHV

Don' Let Yo' Watch Run Down. *Unknown*. AS

Don Quixote. Craven Langstroth Betts. AA

Don Quixote. Ben-Zion Tomer, *tr. fr. Hebrew by* Bernhard Frank. MHeP

Don Quixote in England, *sel.* Henry Fielding.

  Hunting Song. OxBoLi

Don Quixote's Credo. W. H. Auden. *Fr. Man of La Mancha.* AnAn

Don Quixote's Farewell. W. H. Auden. *Fr. Man of La Mancha.* AnAn

Don Surly, to aspire the glorious name. On Don Surly. Ben Jonson. FaBoEE; NAEL-1

Don Wellman wrote asking me if I would write. Radical Coherency. David Antin. UL

Doña Gabriela made the front. Saints, and Their Care. Alberto Rios. UL

Donahue's Sister. Thom Gunn. NoAM

Donal[l] Oge [*or* Og]: Grief of a Girl's Heart. *Unknown, tr. fr. Modern Irish by* Lady Gregory. GBL; PBWP; RB

Donald. Henry Abbey. AA

Donald, he's come to this town. Dugall Quin. *Unknown*. ESPB

Donald of the Isles. *Unknown. See* Lizie Lindsay.

Done Begging. Ryokan, *tr. fr. Japanese by* Burton Watson. FCEI

Done For. Rose Terry Cooke. AA

Done Is a Battle. William Dunbar. NoP

  (On the Resurrection of Christ.) NOCV; OxBS; PoEL-1

  (Resurrection of Chirst, The.) OxBLMV

Done playing the lute, but still full of feeling. Pien Kung, *tr. fr. Chinese by* Jonathan Chaves. *Fr. Paintings,* II. CoBLCP

Done to death by slanderous tongues. Shakespeare. *Fr. Much Ado about Nothing,* V, iii. CTC

  (Claudio's Lament: "Done to death by slanderous tongues.") OBSC

Done with a long day's begging. Ryokan, *tr. by* Burton Watson. JLIC-2

Done with myself, I asked. Coma. Dennis Schmitz. NPGG

Donegal Hush Song, A. Cathal O'Byrne. TIRV

Dong Jin. Park Je-chun, *tr. fr. Korean by* Koh Chang-soo. ACKP

Dong with a Luminous Nose, The. Edward Lear. AmMo; CenHV; ChTr; EBVV; FaBoCo; FaBoNo; FaBV; NOBVV; PoEL-5; WiR

Donibristle Moss Moran Disaster, The. *Unknown*. WTO

Donkey, The. G. K. Chesterton. ACP; FaBV; FaPoR; FPL; InPK; MoBrPo; OBEV; PoLF; RB; WGRP

Donkey, The. Rose Fyleman. BoTP

Donkey, The. Theodore Roethke. GrPl; OBCA; RAR

Donkey, The. *Unknown*. RHPC

Donkey. Mark Van Doren. EaLo

Donkey and the Lapdog, The. La Fontaine, *tr. fr. French by* Marianne Moore. OBVE

Donkey doctor came covered with rain, The. Big Friend of the Stones. Steve Orlen. Psk

Donkey, donkey, do not bray. *Unknown*. OxNR

Donkey Will Carry You, A. Jakov Steinberg, *tr. fr. Hebrew by* Mark Elliott Shapiro. VWA

Donna Anna Writes to Her Sister. Tom Disch. SoTCo

Donna Julia. Byron. *Fr.* Don Juan, I. PoEL-4

Donna Mi Priegha. Guido Cavalcanti. *See* Canzone: Donna Mi Priegha.

Donne, the delight of Phoebus, and each Muse. To John Donne. Ben Jonson. NAEL-1; OBS; SeCV-1

Donner Party, The, *sel.* George Keithley.

  "Old Graves fell asleep." NPGG

Donnybrook. James Stephens. TIRV

Donought would have everything. Ebenezer Elliott. NOBVV

Don's Holiday. George Rostrevor Hamilton. FaBoCo

Don't ape what must be born in one. The Donkey and the Lapdog. La Fontaine, *tr.* by Marianne Moore. OBVE

Don't Ask. Chin Jen-Jui, *tr. fr. Chinese* by Irving Lo. WFTU

Don't ask a geologist about rocks. No More Soft Talk. Diane Wakoski. FF; IHMS

Don't ask about the Six Dynasties of the Sui Palace. Wang T'ing-hsiang, *tr. fr. Chinese* by Jonathan Chaves. *Fr.* Song of Wu-ch'eng. CoBLCP

Don't ask any questions! Drunk among the Flowers. Mao Wen-hsi, *tr.* by Lois Fusek. ATF

Don't ask from where you came. Setting Off. Fu'ad Rifqa, *tr.* by Abdullah al-Udhari. MPAW

Don't ask me for a date. Rendezvous in the Cave. Ahmad Abd al-Muti Hijazi, *tr.* by Sargon Boulus *and* Peter Porter. MAP

Don't ask me if these knives are real. Dreaming Winter. James Welch. NOVW

Don't ask me what to wear. Sappho, *tr.* by Mary Barnard. PBWP

Don't Ask Me Who I Am. James A. Randall, Jr.. BPo

Don't be afraid of dying. The glass of water. Couplets, XX. Robert Mezey. FYAP; NU

Don't be afraid, she tells us. Dogs. Susan Griffin. NPGG

Don't be fed up by it all, please! Keep turning! May It Not Run Down. Anna Hajnal, *tr.* by Jascha Kessler. FOC

Don't Be Foolish Pray. *Unknown.* CoMu

Don't be in a hurry, Miranda. For My Daughter. Judith Kazantzis. AIW

Don't blame me, ladies, if I've loved. No sneers. Louise Labé. BoWoP, *tr.* by Willis Barnstone
  ("Don't scold me, ladies, if I have loved.") PBWP, *tr.* by Carol Cosman

Don't bother/ The fight's fixed. Wrestling with the Angel. Jacques Prévert, *tr.* by Michael Benedikt. POS

Don't bother a bit, you are only a dream you are having. A Real Question Calling for a Solution. Robert Penn Warren. PPP

Don't bother telling me about the programs. TV. John Forbes. CBAP

Don't bring the curtain down. Hamlet. Abdul Wahab al-Bayati, *tr.* by Abdullah al-Udhari. MPAW

Don't Call Me Mama. Carole Stewart. WS

Don't Call Me Pedant. Berta Freistadt. DT

Don't Call Me Sir Call Me Strong. Kitty Tsui. ER

Don't call to me father. To My Dead Father. Frank O'Hara. CAPP; DiL

"Don't Care" and "Never Mind." John Kendrick Bangs. FaFP

Don't care didn't care. *Unknown.* GBP

"Don't Care" is no friend of mine. "Don't Care" and "Never Mind." John Kendrick Bangs. FaFP

Don't care where you come from. African. Peter Tosh. PBCV

Don't come forth from our mouth. Word and Afterword. Ingeborg Bachmann, *tr.* by Beth Bjorklund. CoAuP

Don't Count. Ory Bernstein, *tr. fr. Hebrew* by Warren Bargad *and* Stanley F. Chyet. IP

Don't curse your hands. A Manifesto for the Faint-Hearted. Carole Oles. SM

Don't cut the bamboo grass under the elm. *Unknown, tr. fr. Japanese* by Hiroaki Sato. FCEI

Don't cut the shrub on Idemi Beach. *Unknown, tr. fr. Japanese* by Hiroaki Sato. *Fr.* Manyo Shu. FCEI

Don't, Don't. Huan Fu, *tr. fr. Chinese* by Dominic Cheung. IFON

Don't dress for it. Chiyo, *tr.* by David Ray. BoWoP

Don't drink the beer that's brewed in Pennsylvania. O Rolling. Three Mile Island. Maureen Owen. UL

Don't drive me out of my mind. Second Honeymoon. *Unknown, tr.* by Augustus Young. BIrV

Don't escort the big chariot. *Unknown, tr.* by Arthur Waley. BoS

Don't Ever Cross a Crocodile. Kaye Starbird. PDV

Don't Ever Seize a Weasel by the Tail. Jack Prelutsky. RHPC

Don't expect me to believe. The Ammonite. Jacques Hamelink, *tr.* by Paul Vincent. DuIn

Don't fancy for a moment. To One Who Hankers after Buddhahood. Bunan, *tr.* by Lucien Stryk *and* Takashi Ikemoto. ZPCJ

Don't Forget. Stephen Berg. PoA

Don't Forget. Alice Sadongei. HATNAP

Don't forget the crablike/ hands. The Hands. Denise Levertov. NeAP; PoM

Don't forget when the sticks are ready for picking. Don't Forget. Alice Sadongei. HATNAP

Don't get the wrong idea. Eyewitness. Rodney Hall. PoAu-2

Don't Give Up. *Unknown.* FaFP

Don't give up hoping when the ship goes down. Hang to Your Grit! Louis E. Thayer. WBLP

Don't go. Larry Eigner. PoM

Don't go!/ now with the night so far gone. *Unknown, tr. fr. Japanese* by Burton Watson. *Fr.* Manyo Shu. FCEI

Don't go anywhere without me. In the Arc of Your Mallet. Jalal ed-Din Rumi, *tr.* by John Moyne *and* Coleman Barks. UnAS

Don't go climbing up to the blue clouds. Po Chü-i, *tr. fr. Chinese* by Burton Watson. *Fr.* Better Come Drink Wine with Me. CoBCP

Don't go hide in the deep mountains. Po Chü-i, *tr. fr. Chinese* by Burton Watson. *Fr.* Better Come Drink Wine with Me. CoBCP

Don't go into the realm of red dust. Po Chü-i, *tr. fr. Chinese* by Burton Watson. *Fr.* Better Come Drink Wine with Me. CoBCP

Don't go looking for fairies. Fairies. Eleanor Farjeon. RAR

Don't go off and be a farmer. Po Chü-i, *tr. fr. Chinese* by Burton Watson. *Fr.* Better Come Drink Wine with Me. CoBCP

"Don't go so fast," I called. The Walk. Celia Gilbert. PPR

Don't Grow Old, *sel.* Allen Ginsberg. DiL
  Father Death Blues. SM

Don't hand me over with a word, Toihau. Reply to a Marriage Proposal. Irihapeti Rangi te Apakura, *tr.* by Roger Oppenheim *and* Allen Curnow. PBWP

Don't Hope to Gain by What Has Preceded. Joanne Kyger. PoM

Don't keep your heart from resenting me. In Reply ("Don't keep your heart from resenting me"). Lady Izumi, *tr. fr. Japanese* by Hiroaki Sato. *Fr.* Fifty-one Tanka. FCEI

Don't Kill Yourself. Carlos Drummond de Andrade, *tr. fr. Portuguese* by Elizabeth Bishop. ATCBP

Don't kiss me, my love. Kill Me. Anna Swirszczynska, *tr.* by Czeslaw Milosz. PwPP

Don't Knock the Rawleigh's Man. Vincent O'Sullivan. PeNZ

Don't know why I. Angola Question Mark. Langston Hughes. BPo; TTY

Don't laugh because it's muddy—year-end wine brewed in country homes. A Trip to Mountain West Village. Lu Yu, *tr.* by Burton Watson. CoBCP

"Don't lay your trip on me, ladies." No Dead Ends. Cathleen Quirk. PPR

"Don't leave me, ever!" she said. Wakayama Bokusui, *tr.* by Hiroaki Sato. FCEI

Don't let me lose you. How Tuesday Began. Kathleen Fraser. NYBP

Don't Let That Horse. Lawrence Ferlinghetti. RB

Don't let the sun go out! Sunbeams. Avner Trainin, *tr.* by Bernhard Frank. MHeP

Don't let them die out. Now Poem. For Us. Sonia Sanchez. CNA; PoBA

Don't lie down again. Lying Down. *Unknown, tr.* by Franz Boas. STP

Don't lock me in wedlock, I want. About Marriage. Denise Levertov. NMM

Don't look for bridges to people. February 15. A. Leyeles, *tr. fr. Yiddish* by Benjamin *and* Barbara Harshav. *Fr.* Fabius Lind's Diary. AYP

Don't Look Now but Mary Is Everybody. Peter Viereck. LiTA

Don't look, the woman says. Tarantula. Diana O Hehir. NPGG

Don't love me, my sweet. Song of a Common Lover. Flavien Ranaivo, *tr.* by Alan Ryder. TTY

Don't make so much. First Position. Mary Mackey. *Fr.* Arabesque: Five Poems for Women without Children. ER

Don't mention others' shortcomings. Mottoes. Basho, *tr. fr. Japanese* by Burton Watson. *Fr.* Seventy-six Hokku. FCEI

Don't mind the train or the rollin' sea. The Grey Funnel Line. Cyril Tawney. OBET

Don't need metaphors for the city. Want Ad. Bruce Boston. BWV

Don't neglect the quiet hour. Communion. J. L. Spicer. BLRP

Don't offend. Song of the Breed. Carroll Arnett. STE

Don't play too much, don't play. The Accompanist. William Matthews. BLA

Don't pull that bud, it yet may grow. To George Pulling Buds. Adelaide O'Keeffe. FaBoUs

Don't Quit. *Unknown.* BLPA; FPL

Don't Say. Moshe Yungman, *tr. fr. Yiddish* by Marcia Falk. VWA

Don't Say You Like Tchaikowsky. Paul Rosner. FiBHP

Don't scold me ladies, if I have loved. *See* Don't blame me ladies, if I have loved.

Don't seek me where the myrtles bloom! My Camping Ground. Morris Jacob Rosenfeld, *tr.* by Aaron Kramer. TrJP

Don't Show Me. Ruth Beker. VWA

Don't sing: a song. Drops of Gall. Gabriela Mistral, *tr.* by David Garrison. BoWoP

Don't sing of crimson flowers or wings of the dragonfly. Nakano Shigeharu, *tr. by* Geoffrey Bownas *and* Anthony Thwaite. PeBJV

Don't sing "The Song of Everlasting Sorrow." Ma-wei. Yüan Mei, *tr. by* Jonathan Chaves. CoBLCP

Don't Sit under the Apple Tree with Anyone Else but Me. Robert Pack. FF

Don't Sleep. Ingrid Jonker, *tr. fr. Afrikaans by* Elizabeth Jones. WPOW

Don't sleep! for your paddle fell into the water and your spear. Song of Parents Who Want to Wake Up Their Son. *Unknown.* TTTS

Don't sleep, look! Don't Sleep. Ingrid Jonker, *tr. by* Elizabeth Jones. WPOW

Don't Smile. Robin Gathany Shea. TSM

Don't steal. Thou'lt never thus compete. Ambrose Bierce. NBLV

Don't suppose that the weightless phantom. The Titans. Betti Alver, *tr. by* Willis Barnstone *and* Felix Oinas. BoWoP

Don't sweep away this green after the rain. Moss below the Stairs. Kao Ch'i, *tr. by* Jonathan Chaves. CoBLCP

Don't take the cups and dishes. Instructions for the Waitress. Yehuda Amichai, *tr. by* Warren Bargad *and* Stanley F. Chyet. IP

Don't Talk to Me about Bread. E. A. Markham. PBCV

Don't talk to me about trees having branches and roots. On Trees. Alan Dugan. NoAM

Don't talk to me no words. Relocation. Simon J. Ortiz. NOVW

Dont Tell Bad Dreams Says Tita's Mother. John Oliver Simon. NeAC

Don't tell me how difficult the Way. Hofuku Seikatsu, *tr. by* Lucien Stryk *and* Takashi Ikemoto. ZPCJ

Don't Tell Me That I Talk Too Much! Arnold Spilka. RHPC

Don't Tell Me What You Dreamt Last Night. Franklin Pierce Adams. FiBHP

Don't tell people how it was. Lady Izumi, *tr. fr. Japanese by* Hiroaki Sato. *Fr.* Fifty-one Tanka. FCEI

Don't tell them about my. Secret. Maria Teresa Horta, *tr. by* Suzette Macedo. OV

Don't tell your friends about your indigestion. Of Tact. Arthur Guiterman. MoShBr

Don't Think. Ahmad Faraz, *tr. fr. Urdu by* Mahmood Jamal. PBMUP

Don't think/ that I don't know. Sous-Entendu. Anne Stevenson. OxBSP

Don't think about useless things. *Unknown, tr. fr. Japanese. Fr.* Manyo Shu.

Don't think it won't come to you. Watching a Child Watching a Witch. Jenny Joseph. *Fr.* Derivations. AIW

Don't throw your arms around me in that way. Footnote to John II: 4. R. A. K. Mason. ATNZ; PeNZ

Don't touch me. The Hermaphrodite's Song. Lorna Mitchell. BrRo

"Don't touch me!" I scream at passers-by. Natalya Gorbanyevskaya, *tr. by* Daniel Weissbort. LLLT

Don't touch that fruit, Eve. Paradise Lost. Stanley J. Sharpless. BXAP

Don't Trouble Trouble. Mark Guy Pearse. WBLP

Don't Trust Anyone over Thirty. Wilhelm Szabo, *tr. fr. German by* Beth Bjorklund. CoAuP

Don't wait for the wind to blow you through the door. Moving In. Paul Engle. PoA

Don't walk beside the Big Carriage. *Unknown, tr. fr. Chinese by* Burton Watson. CoBCP

Don't Wanna Be. Sonia Sanchez. CNA

Don't waste your time in looking for. Long Gone. Jack Prelutsky. RHPC

"Don't wear that snake." The Rattlesnake Band. Robert J. Conley. STE

Don't wilt and brood on things. *Unknown, tr. fr. Japanese by* Hiroaki Sato. *Fr.* Manyo Shu. FCEI

Don't worry/ One night we'll find that deserted kinema. If Life's a Lousy Picture, Why Not Leave before the End. Roger McGough. OxBTC

Don't worry about growing old. Prayerwheel: 2. David Meltzer. NeAP

Don't worry baby. Broken Heart, Broken Machine. Richard E. Grant. PoBA

"Don't worry!" he says. *Unknown, tr. by* Burton Watson. FCEI

Don't Worry if Your Job Is Small. *Unknown.* RHPC

Dont Worry Yr Hair. Bill Bissett. NOBC

Don't write poems about what's happening. Looking for Poetry. Carlos Drummond de Andrade, *tr. by* Mark Strand. AnAn

Don't You Be like the Foolish Virgin. *Unknown.* AH

Don't you care for my love? she said bitterly. Intimates. D. H. Lawrence. BoLoP; NBLV; OxBSP

Don't you love my baby, mam. Infant Song. Charles Causley. NAs; OxBC

Don't you remember sweet Alice, Ben Bolt. Ben Bolt. Thomas Dunn English. AA; AnAmPo; FaBoBe; FaFP

Don't you see the ships a-coming? The Rolling Sailer. *Unknown.* OxBSS

Don't you think it's probable. Little Talk. Aileen Fisher. FaPON

Don't you trouble trouble till trouble troubles you. Don't Trouble Trouble. Mark Guy Pearse. WBLP

Don'ts. D. H. Lawrence. LiTB; LiTM; OxBoLi

Doodling on the margin. Poem for Putzi Hanfstaengel. Evangeline Paterson. CN

Dooley Is a Traitor. James Michie. NePoEA-2; OxBTC

Doom Ferry. Sir Arthur Quiller-Couch. EBVV

Doom is dark and deeper than any sea-dingle. The Wanderer. W. H. Auden. CMoP; LiTB; MoP; NoAM; RB; SOTW; WeW

Doom of Beauty, The. Michelangelo Buonarroti, *tr. fr. Italian by* John Addington Symonds. AWP

Doom of Devorgoil, The, *sel.* Sir Walter Scott.
Bonny [*or* Bonnie] Dundee. *Fr.* II, ii. EnRP; FaBoCh; OxBoLi; OxBS; Par

Doomed in the depths to dwell. Thanksgiving. David Abenatar Melo, *tr. by* Henry Hart Milman. TrJP

Doomed ship weighs anchor, out she is bound, The. The Unseaworthy Ship. J. Smith. OxBSS

Dooms-Day George Herbert. JCP; SeCP; SeCV-1
"Come away." OBD, *br. sel.*

Doomsday Morning. Genevieve Taggard. MoAmPo

Doon Deeside cam Inverey. The Baron of Braikley. *Unknown.* OxBB

Door, The. W. H. Auden. *Fr.* The Quest. Son

Door, The. Robert Creeley. NaP; NeAP; NoAM; PoM; VGW

Door, The. Robert Graves. LiTB

Door, A. W. S. Merwin. CAPP; EAS; LCAP

Door, The. Mark Strand. NoAM

Door, The. L. A. G. Strong. MoBrPo

Door, The. Charles Tomlinson. PoA

Door and Window Bolted Fast. Mani Leib, *tr. fr. Yiddish by* Joseph Leftwich. TrJP

Door behind me was you, The. Tom Clark. *Fr.* You, I. EAS

Door closed, The. The Sweat. Nila NorthSun. STE

Door closed against the splinters. Old Seawoman. Gordon LeClaire. CaP

Door half open, The. In the Winter Dark. Dan Gerber. KS

Door is before you again and the shrieking, The. The Door. Mark Strand. NoAM

"Door is shut fast, The." Who's In. Elizabeth Fleming. BoTP; RHPC

Door it opened slowly, The. Story of Isaac. Leonard Cohen. VWA

Door-latch rusted, A. Issa, *tr. fr. Japanese by* Hiroaki Sato. *Fr.* Forty-four Hokku. FCEI

Door Number Four. Charlotte Pomerantz. ILY

Door of Death, The. Blake. *Fr.* Dedication of the Illustrations to Blair's "Grave." ChTr
(To the Queen.) EnRP

Door of existence, beacon of our haze. Bernard O'Dowd. *Fr.* Alma Venus. PoAu-1

Door of Hope, The. Lizelia Augusta Jenkins Moorer. CBWP-3

Door opened and a gust of mandolins, A. Jack and the Beanstalk. Kenneth Rosen. NAmP

Door opens, The. My Guests. Faiz Ahmad Faiz, *tr. by* Mahmood Jamal. PBMUP

Door opens in the gray wall, A. Dreaming of the Castle. Endre Vészi, *tr. by* Jascha Kessler. FOC

Door slam, The. After the First Frost. Lew Blockcolski. VoR

Door still swinging to, and girls revive, The. A Dream of Fair Women. Kingsley Amis. FF; NoAM; OAEL-2

Door sunk in a hillside, with a bolt, A. The Icehouse in Summer. Howard Nemerov. MoP; NoAM

Door that someone opened wide, The. The Message. Jacques Prévert, *tr. by* John Frederick Nims. WeW

Door was bolted and the windows of my porch, The. The Milkman. Isabella Gardner. CAPP

Door was shut, as doors should be, The. Jack Frost. "Gabriel Setoun." BoTP

Doorbell buzzed, The. It was past three o'clock. The Australian Dream. David Campbell. CBAP

Doorbells. Rachel Lyman Field. FaPON

Doors, The. Lloyd Mifflin. AA

Doors. Thérèse Plantier, *tr. fr. French by* Willis Barnstone *and* Elene Kolb. BoWoP

Doors are locked, The. House. For Sale. Leonard Clark. RHPC

Doors flapped open in Ulysses' house, The. The Return ("The doors flapped open in Ulysses' house"). Edwin Muir. CMoP

Doors Have Opened, The. Tristan Tzara, *tr. fr. French by* Michael Benedikt. POS

Doors of that city are ninety feet high, The. The Retarded Children Find a World Built Just for Them. Diana O Hehir. NPGG

Doors open, The/ and the heat undoes itself. In the Beach House. Anne Sexton. PPP

Doors, where my heart was used to beat. Tennyson. *Fr.* In Memoriam A. H. H., CXIX. NoP; OBNC; PoEL-5; SCV

Doorstep, Lightning, Waif-Dreaming. James Dickey. CAPP

Doorway, The. Lin Huan-ch'ang, *tr. fr. Chinese by* Dominic Cheung. IFON

Doorway to Time in Three Voices. Luis Palés Matos, *tr. fr. Spanish by* Rachel Benson. InW

Dopefiends Trip. Hector Angulo. FIA

Doppelganger, The. Daryl Hine. OBCV
(Double-Goer, The.) MoCV

Dora Markus. Eugenio Montale, *tr. fr. Italian by* Alfred Corn. PFI

Dora versus Rose. Austin Dobson. NOBL; PDV

Dora Williams. Edgar Lee Masters. *Fr.* Spoon River Anthology. HAP

Doralicia's Song. Robert Greene. *Fr.* Arbasto. OBSC

Dorchester Giant, The. Oliver Wendell Holmes. FaPON; OnMSP

Doré knew this overhang. View from the Gorge. Ben Belitt. NYBP

Doretha wore the short blue lace last night. The Reception. June Jordan. FaBoWP; NMM

Doria. Ezra Pound. MoAB; MoAmPo

Doric. Anghelos Sikelianos, *tr. fr. Greek by* Edmund Keeley *and* Philip Sherrard. ErPo; VMG

Doricha. Poseidippus, *tr. fr. Greek by* E. A. Robinson. AWP; FaBoEE; OBVE

Dorinda's sparkling wit, and eyes. Charles Sackville. OBEV; OBS; SeCePo; SeCV-2
(On Dorinda.) OxBSP
(On the Countess of Dorchester.) APAS

Doris. Congreve. NOEC

Doris and Philemon, *sel.* J. C. Squire.
"Now the declining fulgent orb of day." BXAP

Dormouse, The. Charlotte Druitt Cole. BoTP

Doron's Description of Samela. Robert Greene. *Fr.* Menaphon. PoEL-2
(Samela.) EiL; GBL; NOBE; OBEV; OBSC

Doron's Jigge. Robert Greene. *Fr.* Menaphon. PoEL-2
(Jig, A.) EiL

Dorothy. Rose Hawthorne Lathrop. AA

Dorothy Parker/ Knew the darker. Martha H. Freedman. SoTCo

Dorothy Q. Oliver Wendell Holmes. AA; NOBA

Dorothy Wordsworth, dying, did not want to read. My Sisters, O My Sisters. May Sarton. ER

Dory Miller. Sam Cornish. CNA

Dose of a mere, The. The Discovery of LSD a True Story. Anselm Hollo. PoM

Dosn't thou 'ear my 'erse's legs, as they canters awaäy. Northern Farmer. Tennyson. NAEL-2

Dosser in Springtime, The. Douglas Stewart. ErPo

Dost deem him weak that owns his strength is tried? The Strong. John Vance Cheney. AA

Do'st see how unregarded now. Sir John Suckling. CaPo; ELP

"Dost tha hear my horse's feet, as he canters away?" Lord Tennyson and Lord Melchett. D. H. Lawrence. FaBoEE

Dost thou remember ever, for my sake. Mathilde Blind. *Fr.* Love in Exile. OBNC

Dostoevsky. Jacob Glatstein, *tr. fr. Yiddish by* Benjamin *and* Barbara Harshav. AYP

Dostoievsky's Daughters. Michael Hamburger. NAs

Doth Not a Tenarif, or Higher Hill. John Donne. *Fr.* An Anatomy [or Anatomie] of the World: The First Anniversary. ChTr

Doth some one say that there be gods above? There Are No Gods. Euripides, *tr. fr. Greek by* John Addington Symonds. *Fr.* Bellerophon. EaLo

Doth then the world go thus, doth all thus move? William Drummond of Hawthornden. GTBS; GTBS-P

D'Où Venons Nous? Que Sommes Nous? Où Allons No, *sels.* A. L. Hendricks. PBCV
"I touch jig-saw fragments."
"Looking out toward the stars."
"Woman in the garden gathers lilacs, A."

Double. Rae Armantrout. LP

Double, The. Irving Feldman. NYBP

Double Agent. Heather McHugh. AnAn

Double Autumn, The. James Reeves. OxBSP

Double Axe, The. Anne Hazlewood-Brady. IHMS

Double Ballad of Good Counsel, A. Villon, *tr. fr. French by* Swinburne. AWP

Double Ballade of Primitive Man. Andrew Lang *and* Edward Burnett Tylor. CenHV

Double-barreled Ding-Dong-Bat. Dennis Lee. RHPC

Double boiler fixed on fiery wheels, A. On Shakespeare Critics. A. D. Hope. *Fr.* Dunciad Minor, *bk.* V. OxBC

Double, double toil and trouble. Song of the Witches. Shakespeare. *Fr.* Macbeth: Thrice the Brinded Cat Hath Mewed. RHPC

Double Dutch. Walter de la Mare. CRH

Double Elegy. Michael S. Harper. NoAM

Double Exposure. Ian Young. NeAC; PeHV

Double Feature. Robert Hayden. NoAM

"Double flesh/ Double way." Freud: Dying London, He Recalls the Smoke of His Cigar Beginning to Sing. James Schevill. TAP

Double-Goer, The. Daryl Hine. *See* Doppelganger, The.

Double-headed Snake, The. John Newlove. MoCV

Double Jade Ring Grievance. Chang Ts'o, *tr. fr. Chinese by* Dominic Cheung. IFON

Double L and single T. The Spelling of Elliot. *Unknown.* FaBoUs

Double Looking Glass, The. A. D. Hope. CBAP

Double Mock Sonnet. Charles O. Hartman. SM

Double Monologue. Adrienne Rich. NePoEA-2

Double Occupancy—Sahara Style. Ned Pastor. SoTCo

Double Ode. Muriel Rukeyser, *tr. by* Edmund Keeley. AnAn; LCAP

Double Play, The. Robert Wallace. SD

Double Semi-Sestina. George Starbuck. SM

Double Sestine. Sir Philip Sidney. *See* Arcadia: Ye Goat-herd Gods.

Double Shame, The. Stephen Spender. LiTB; LiTM

Double Sonnet. Anthony Hecht. SM; Son

Double Standard, The. Franklin Pierce Adams. OBAL

Double Standard, A. Frances Ellen Watkins Harper. BlSi; PWR

Double-Take. Fleur Adcock. ATNZ

Double Take at Relais de L'Espadon. Thadious M. Davis. BlSi

Double Transformation, The. Goldsmith. OBNV

Double Vision of Manannan, The. *Unknown, tr. fr. Irish by* John Montague. BIrV

Doubly Employed. Giancarlo Majorino, *tr. fr. Italian by* Lawrence R. Smith. NItP

Doubt. Margaret Deland. TrPWD

Doubt. Fernand Gregh, *tr. fr. French by* Ludwig Lewisohn. WGRP

Doubt. Helen Hunt Jackson. WGRP

Doubt. Pat Nolan. UL

Doubt. Robert Cameron Rogers. AA

Doubt. Tennyson. *See* In Memoriam A. H. H.:
You say, but with no touch of scorn.

Doubt. Clara Ann Thompson. CBWP-2

Doubt crept into a heart one day, A. Doubt. Clara Ann Thompson. CBWP-2

Doubt no longer miracles. Miracles. Arna Bontemps. PoNe

Doubt of Future Foes, The. Elizabeth I, Queen of England. CTC; NAEL-1; PBWP; WPE
(Daughter of Debate, The.) OBSC

Doubt of Martyrdom, A. Sir John Suckling. *See* Sonnet: "Oh! [*or* O!] for some honest lover's ghost."

Doubt which ye misdeeme, fayre love, is vaine, The. Spenser. *Fr.* Amoretti, LXV. NAEL-1

Doubt you to whom my Muse these notes intendeth. Sir Philip Sidney. *Fr.* Astrophel and Stella. OBSC
(To Stella.) EiL

Doubter, The. Richard Watson Gilder. TrPWD

Doubter's Prayer, The. Anne Brontë. TrPWD; WGRP

Doubtful Choice, A. Edward de Vere, 17th Earl of Oxford. *See* Choice, A.

Doubting. Louis Simpson. NNaP

Doubtless a way there is of grasping whole. Thomas Hardy Considers the Newly-Published Special Theory of Relativity. Brian W. Aldiss. BWV

Doubts. Rupert Brooke. CH

Douglas and the Bruce's Heart. Sir Richard Holland. *See* Buke of the Howlat, The:
Roye Robert the Bruss the rayke he avowit, The.

Douglas, Douglas, Tender and True. Dinah Maria Mulock Craik. BLPA

Douglas Tragedy, The. *Unknown. See* Earl Brand (The Douglas Tragedy).

Douglass. Paul Laurence Dunbar. Son

Douglass was someone who. Frederick Douglass: 1817-1895. Langston Hughes. BPo

Doun throw the sea. Cokkils. Sydney Goodsir Smith. OxBS; PoA

Dour thing in olive trees, The. Olive Trees. Bernard Spencer. NoAM
Dousing clean a thousand old cares. A Night with a Friend. Li Po, *tr. by* Burton Watson. CoBCP
Dove. Norma Farber. PChr
Dove, The. Judah Halevi, *tr. fr. Hebrew by* Amy Levy. TrJP
Dove, A. Ted Hughes. OxBC
Dove, The. Ewan MacColl. OBET
Dove, The. *Unknown. See* Clean birds by sevens.
Dove alone expresses, The. Thomas Campion. *Fr.* What Harvest Half So Sweet Is. PBBP
Dove Apologizes to His God for Being Caught by a Cat, The. Anthony Eaton. PeSA
Dove it is a pretty bird, she sings as she flies, The. The Dove. Ewan MacColl. OBET
Dove-Late Afternoon, A. Jutta Schutting, *tr. fr. German by* Beth Bjorklund. CoAuP
"Dove-Love." Judith Wright. NoAM
Dove of Dacca, The. Kipling. GN
Dove of liberty sat on an egg, The. The American Eagle. D. H. Lawrence. OAEL-2
Dove of New Snow, The. Vachel Lindsay. MoAmPo
Dove of rarest worth, A. The Dove. Judah Halevi, *tr. by* Amy Levy. TrJP
Dove purrs—over and over the dove, The. "Dove-Love." Judith Wright. NoAM
Dove returns, The; it found no resting place. Where We Must Look for Help. Robert Bly. NePoEA
Dove says, Coo, coo, The. Mother Goose. BoTP; OxNR; PBBP
Dove stays in the garden, The. *Ambo Oral Tradition. Fr.* Five Ghost Songs. TTTS
Dove walks with sticky feet, The. Kenneth Patchen. NaP
Dover Beach. Matthew Arnold. AWP; BLPA; EaLo; EBVV; FaBoBe; FaBoPP; FaBoRV; FaBV; FaFP; FF; FiP; FPL; GTBS-P; HAP; HeIP; HoPM; InPK; InPS; InVP; InVP; LiTB; MAT; MOS; NAEL-2; NIP; NOBE; NOBVV; NoP; NU; OAEL-2; OBNC; OPOP; PoE; PoEL-5; PoRA; PPP; Prf; PrIm; SCV; SeCePo; TOF
"Dover Beach"—a Note to That Poem. Archibald MacLeish. FF
Dover Bitch, The. Anthony Hecht. BXAP; MAT; NBLV; NePoEA-2; NIP; NOBA; NOBL; OBAL; PPP; UnPo; VGW
Dover, Sandwich, and Winchelsea. The Cinque Ports. *Unknown.* FaBoUs
Dover, the Samphire Cliff. Shakespeare. *Fr.* King Lear, IV, vi. FaBoPP
Dover to Munich. Charles Stuart Calverley. NOBL, *abr.*; OBTV
Doves. E. J. Falconer. BoTP
Doves. Joachim Neugroschel. VWA
Doves. Jutta Schutting, *tr. fr. German by* Beth Bjorklund. CoAuP
Doves, The. Katharine Tynan. AWP
Doves flit by in their flocks of thousands. Sick unto Death of Love. *Malay Oral Tradition, tr. by* R. J. Wilkinson *and* R. O. Winstedt. WTO
Dove's Loneliness, The. George Darley. OBNC
Doves of Venice, The. Laurence Hutton. AA
Dove's Song in Winter. *Zulu Oral Tradition, tr. by* B. W. Vilakazi. WTO
Dowager. John Montague. AnAn; IPY
Dowager Semibreve sat by the fire, The. First Lessons in Musical Time. *Unknown.* FaBoUs
Dowie Houms o' Yarrow, The. *Unknown.* GoTS; OBEV; OBS; OxBS (Braes o' Yarrow, The.) ESPB
Down/ a/ deep/ well. The Grasshopper. David McCord. GrPl
Down/ Down into the fathomless depths. Black Is a Soul. Joseph Blanco White. IDB; PoBA
Down a blackened alley. La Llorona. Greg Pape. AmPA
Down a street in the town where I went. Shapes, Vanishings. Henry Taylor. MAYP
Down and Out. Clarence Leonard Hay. BeLS; BLPA
Down and Out. Langston Hughes. PoE
Down at the Docks. Kenneth Koch. PrIm; VGW
Down at the hall at midnight sometimes. Dance. Lula Lowe Weeden. CDC
Down Below. Joan Aiken. WSC
Down below the town-gate. *Unknown, tr. by* Arthur Waley. BoS
Down by the brook which glides through yonder vale. Robin; a Pastoral Elegy. John Dobson. NOEC
Down by the church-way walk, and where the brook. An Ancient Virgin. George Crabbe. *Fr.* The Parish Register. OBNC
Down by the gate of the orchard. Spring Whistles. Lucy Larcom. OBCA
Down by the meadows, chasing butterflies. *Unknown.* BoTP

Down by the ocean side where ships were sailing. The Nightingales of Spring. *Unknown.* AmFP
Down by the river. *Unknown.* OxNR
Down by the Riverside. *Unknown.* OBET
Down by the Salley Gardens. W. B. Yeats. CMoP; CTC; EBVV; EnLoPo; NAEL-2; NoAM; OBEV; PoEL-5; PrIm; SoSe (Old Song Resung, An.) MoAB; MoBrPo
Down by the Station, Early in the Morning. John Ashbery. HCAP
Down by the waterside stand a house and a plat. *Unknown.* GBP
Down by the weeping willow. Florella; or, The Jealous Lover. *Unknown.* AmFP
Down by the Wild Mustard River. The Wild Mustard River. *Unknown.* AmFP
Down by yon garden green. The Laird of Wariston. *Unknown.* ESPB
"Down cellar," said the cricket. The Potatoes' Dance. Vachel Lindsay. FaPON
Down! Down! Eleanor Farjeon. NTCP
Down down across the open sea to Shikoku. Ancestors' Graves in Kurakawa. Joy Kogawa. BrSi
Down, Down, and Down. Heather McHugh. NAmP
Down, down—born pioneers in time's despite. Hart Crane. *Fr.* The Bridge: Powhatan's Daughter. TrGrPo
Down, Down Derry Down. *Unknown.* AS
Down, down, in millions, blending. The Snow-Flakes. Priscilla Jane Thompson. CBWP-2
Down drop of the blackbird, The. Three Spring Notations on Bipeds. Carl Sandburg. AWP
Down East Drama. David H. Green. SoTCo
Down flew the shaft of the god. A Love Affair. Arnold Bennett. OxBTC
Down from his post in the tower. Across the Straits. Rosemary Dobson. PoAu-2
Down from the branches. Emperor Hanazono, *tr. by* Steven D. Carter. WFTW
Down from the Country. John Blight. CBAP
Down here now/ summer's burnt skeins. In Blanco County. Russell T. Fowler. NOBC
Down in a Coal Mine. J. B. Geoghegan. AmFP
Down in a deep dark ditch sat an old cow munching a beanstalk. Hexameter and Pentameter. *Unknown.* ChTr; FaBoNo
Down in a garden olden. The Rose's Cup. Frank Dempster Sherman. AA
Down in a meadow fresh and gay. Picking Lilies. *Unknown.* OBET
Down in Carlisle there lived a lady. The Lady of Carlisle. *Unknown.* AmFP
Down in Dallas. X. J. Kennedy. FF; OFD
Down in Dumbarton there wonnd a rich merchant. Bonnie Annie (B *vers.*). *Unknown.* ESPB
Down in front of Casey's old brown wooden stoop. The Sidewalks of New York. James W. Blake. BLPA; FaBoBe
Down in green valleys a town in Yorkshire. Bonnets So Blue. *Unknown.* OBET
Down in history we find it and in grandest works of art. Negro Heroines. Lizelia Augusta Jenkins Moorer. CBWP-3
Down in London where I was raised. Barbara Allen. *Unknown.* FaBoBa
Down in our cellar on a Monday and a Tuesday. Old Ellen Sullivan. Winifred Welles. FaPON
Down in St. Louis at 12th and Carr. Brady. *Unknown.* AS
Down in some lone valley, in some lonesome place. Pretty Saro. *Unknown.* AmFP
Down in some lonesome piney grove. Lonesome Dove. *Unknown.* AmFP
Down in the bleak December bay. The Mayflower. Erastus Wolcott Ellsworth. AA; FaBoBe; PAH
Down in the cabin all things were gay. Thwarted. Priscilla Jane Thompson. CBWP-2
Down in the deep, dumb worlds are waiting, silent. Letter to My Wife. Miklós Radnóti, *tr. by* Emery George. VWA
Down in the dell. Sunrise. Henrietta Cordelia Ray. *Fr.* Idyl. BlSi; CBWP-3
Down in the depth of mine iniquity. Fulke Greville. *Fr.* Caelica, XCIX [C]. QFR (Sonnet: "Downe in the depth of mine iniquity.") OBS
Down in the Forest. *Unknown.* OBET
Down in the Frantic Mountains. A Survey. William Stafford. RB
Down in the grassy hollow. Merry Little Men. Kathleen M. Chaplin. BoTP
Down in the hole we go, boys. Lament while Descending a Shaft. *Unknown.* AmFP

Down in the jungle/ Living in a tent. *Unknown.* WTO

Down in the Lonesome Garden. *Unknown.* BPo

Down in the meadow, sprent with dew. Revelation. Alice Brown. *Fr.* The Road to Castaly. WGRP

Down in the mine, in the dark, dismal drift. Only a Miner. *Unknown.* AmFP

Down in the south, by the waste without sail on it. Beyond Kerguelen. Henry Clarence Kendall. PoAu-1

Down in the valley. Red Leaves on a Buried Tree. Shotetsu, *tr. by* Steven D. Carter. WFTW

Down in the Valley. *Unknown.* AS, *with music;* FaFP; WTO (Birmingham Jail.) GBP

Down in the water meadows Riley. Riley. Charles Causley. SO

Down in the west the shadows rest. Canoe Song at Twilight. Laura E. McCully. CaP

Down in yon garden sweet and gay. Willy Drowned in Yarrow. *Unknown.* GTBS; GTBS-P

Down in Yonder Meadow. *Unknown.* CH

Down [or Downe] lay the shepherd swain. Hye Nonny Nonny Noe. *Unknown.* FaBoCo; NOBL

Down Loudon Lanes, with swinging reins. Mosby at Hamilton. Madison Cawein. PAH

Down mountain roads like scars across a fist. At Tripolis. Constance Carrier. WPE

Down near the end of a wandering lane. A Rhyme of the Dream-Maker Man. William Allen White. PoLF

Down on My Luck. Arthur Rex Dugard Fairburn. ATNZ; PeNZ

Down one of Baghdad's lanes I went. Both Strangers. Jamil Sidqi al-Zahawi, *tr. by* Issa Boullata *and* Christopher Middleton. MAP

Down streams of centuries grown old. Women of My Land. Frankie Armstrong. BrRo

Down stucco sidestreets. Dublinesque. Philip Larkin. NoAM; OxBC

Down swept the chill wind from the mountain peak. The Brook in Winter. James Russell Lowell. *Fr.* The Vision of Sir Launfal: Prelude to Pt. II. GN; OnMSP

Down the ass-tuft the dew drips, drips. *Unknown, tr. fr. Japanese by* Hiroaki Sato. *Fr.* Inutsukuba Shu. FCEI

Down the assembly line they roll and pass. The Brides. Alec Derwent Hope. HAP

Down the Bayou. Mary Ashley Townsend. AA

Down the blue night the unending columns press. Clouds. Rupert Brooke. BrPo; OBEV; OBMV; OxBTC

Down the centuries, eternal. From a Venetian Sequence. Adèle Naudé. PeSA

Down the close, darkening lanes they sang their way. The Send-off. Wilfred Owen. BrPo; LiTB; MoAB; MoBrPo; OBWP; OBWVE; OxBTC; RB

Down the coast south of here. Earth. Jim Tollerud. VoR

Down the dawn-brown. The Current. James Merrill. NYBP

Down the dead streets of sun-stoned Frederiksted. The Virgins. Derek Walcott. OxBC; SoSe

Down the deep steps of stone, through iron doors. Judgment. William Rose Benét. AnAmPo

Down the dripping pathway dancing through the rain. Rainy Song. Max Eastman. FaBoBe

Down the Glimmering Staircase. Siegfried Sassoon. *Fr.* Vigils. PoLF

Down the goldenest of streams. Mater Amabilis. Emma Lazarus. OHIP

Down the green hill-side fro' the castle window. Lady Jane. Sir Arthur Quiller-Couch. FiBHP

Down the lane by the Butts in the headlights. Delivering Children. David Holbrook. NePoEA-2

Down the Little Big Horn. Francis Brooks. PAH

Down the long hall she glistens like a star. Venus of the Louvre. Emma Lazarus. AA

Down the M4. Dannie Abse. OxBC

Down the Mississippi. John Gould Fletcher. AmFN; LiTA

Down the mountain into the path of darkness. Lady Izumi, *tr. fr. Japanese by* Hiroaki Sato. *Fr.* Fifty-one Tanka. FCEI

Down the mountain road. Sprigs of Blossoms. Tamemasa, *tr. by* Steven D. Carter. WFTW

Down the Nile. Robert Lowell. HCAP

Down the picket-guarded lane. How Are You, Sanitary? Bret Harte. AnAmPo

Down the quiet eve. Music ("Down the quiet eve"). William Ernest Henley. *Fr.* In Hospital, XXIII. BrPo

Down the road my hand walks naked on five legs. Hand Etc. Gerrit Kouwenaar, *tr. by* Peter Nijmeijer. DuIn

Down the road someone is practicing scales. Sunday Morning. Louis MacNeice. FaBCIP; FaBoMo; HeIP; LiTB; MoAB; MoBrPo; NAEL-2; NIP; Son

Down the rock chute into the tombs of the kings. This Is the Life. Louis MacNeice. NoAM

Down the white steps, into the night, she came. Victory. Lionel Johnson. NOBVV

Down the wintry mountain. Dinah Maria Mulock Craik. *Fr.* Highland Cattle. GN

Down the Wolf river. Feasts of Death, Feasts of Love. Stuart Z. Perkoff. NeAP

Down the world with Marna! The Wander-Lovers. Richard Hovey. AA

Down the Yellowstone, the Milk, the White and Cheyenne. Pare Lorentz. *Fr.* The River. AmFN

Down There. Robert Marteau, *tr. fr. French by* John Montague. RHTwFP

Down there a poor woman. The Potter. *Unknown, tr. by* Halim El-Dabh. TTY

Down there where I was. The Story of My Life. Carroll Arnett. NOVW; VoR

Down through the ancient Strand. Scherzando. William Ernest Henley. *Fr.* London Voluntaries, III. BrPo

Down through the snow-drifts in the street. The Boy. Eugene Field. NA

Down through the spheres there came the Name of One. The Path of the Stars. Thomas S. Jones, Jr. WGRP

Down through Venetian blinds the morning air. News from Paris. Charles Spear. ATNZ

Down to Sleep. Helen Hunt Jackson. GN

Down to the Puritan marrow of my bones. Elinor Wylie. *Fr.* Wild Peaches. BoWoP

(Puritan Sonnet, IV.) FPL; MoAB; MoAmPo; TrGrPo

Down to the Sacred Wave. Samuel Francis Smith. AH

Down toward the deep-blue water, marching to throb of drum. Your Lad, and My Lad. Randall Parrish. PAH

Down, up—a single dot of red. Pitch-Ball. Yang Chi, *tr. fr. Chinese by* Jonathan Chaves. *Fr.* Ten Poems on the Tuan-yang Festival. CoBLCP

Down valley a smoke haze. Mid-August at Sourdough Mountain Lookout. Gary Snyder. HAP; InPK; MAT; NaP; NoP; TAP

Down, Wanton, Down! Robert Graves. BoLoP; CMoP; ErPo; FaBoTw; HeIP; InPK; LiTM; MoP; NAEL-2; NoAM; NoP; OAEL-2; PoE; TEP

Down where New York's a-glare at night. Exiles. Patrick O'Connor. TIRV

Down Wind against the Highest Peaks. Clarence Major. NBP

Down with the lambs. *Unknown.* OxNR

Down with the rosemary and bay[e]s. Ceremonies for Candlemas[se] Eve. Robert Herrick. CaPo; JCP; OBS

Down with the rosemary, and so. Ceremony upon Candlemas Eve. Robert Herrick. OBCP

Down, you mongrel, Death! The Poet and His Book. Edna St. Vincent Millay. MoAmPo

Downe to the king's most bright-kept baths they went. Homer. *See* Odyssey

Downfall of Charing Cross, The. *Unknown.* FaBoCo

Downfall of Piracy, The. *at. to* Benjamin Franklin. PAH

Downfall of the Chancellor, The. *Unknown.* APAS

Downfall of the Gael, The. Fearflatha O'Gnive, *tr. fr. Late Middle Irish by* Sir Samuel Ferguson. AWP

Downfall of the Tyrant, The. Bible, *O.T. Fr.* Isaiah, XIV:4–19. TrGrPo

Downhill [or Down hill] I came, hungry, and yet not starved. The Owl. Edward Thomas. ChTr; EBEV; FaBoRV; FaBoTw; FF; GTBS-P; LiTB; MoP; NAEL-2; NIP; NoAM; NOBE; NoP; OAEL-2; OBWVE; PoE; RB; SoSe; UnPo

Downing his drink to toasts of cut-rate jokes. 3 for 25. William Jay Smith. WaP

Downpour fills the heavens, The. First Rain. Tsfrirah Gar, *tr. by* Bernhard Frank. MHeP

Downright Country-Man; or, The Faithful Dairy Maid, The. *Unknown.* CoMu

Downs and tender-tinted cliffs are lost, The. The Needles' Lighthouse from Keyhaven, Hampshire. Charles Tennyson Turner. FaBoPP

Downs will lose the sun, white alyssum, The. Head and Bottle. Edward Thomas. BrPo

Downstairs, a door. Summer Storm. John Montague. IPY

Downstream. Thomas Kinsella. FaBCIP

Downstream they have killed the river and built a dam. The Fish Counter at Bonneville. William Stafford. AmFN

Downtown-Boy Uptown. David Henderson. PoNe

Downward through the evening twilight. Longfellow. *See* Song of Hiawatha, The: Hiawatha's Childhood.
Downwards. Charles Kenneth Williams. GeTw
Dow's Flat. Bret Harte. AnAmPo; FaBoBe
Dowsed coals fume and hiss after your meal, The. The Book of Yolek. Anthony Hecht. BLA
Doxology. Josephine D. Henderson Heard. CBWP-4
Doxology. Bert Leston Taylor. OBAL
Doxy, oh! thy glaziers shine. The Maunder's Praise of His Strowling Mort. *Unknown.* OxBoLi
Doze, The. James Reeves. AmMo
Dozen Amish men and women on the beach, A. Looking at a Photograph on My Forty-Fourth Birthday. Carl Dennis. BLA
Dozen machines, A. A Time for Building. Myra Cohn Livingston. PDV
Dozens of wrangling sparrows have built their. Power Transformer. Ian Wedde. *Fr.* Earthly: Sonnets for Carlos, 26. ATNZ; PeNZ
Dozing, thoughts interminable in paths of dream. Teika, *tr. fr. Japanese by* Hiroaki Sato. *Fr.* Eighty-four Tanka. FCEI
Dr. *See also* Doctor.
Dr. Birch and His Young Friends, *sel.* Thackeray. End of the Play, The. FaFP; GN
Dr. Clifford. E. C. Bentley. *Fr.* Clerihews. CenHV
"Dr. Halley never eat any thing." Edmond Halley. Roy Fuller. OxBC
Dr. Joseph Goebbels. W. D. Snodgrass. *Fr.* The Führer Bunker. "Stand back, make way, you mindless scum,.." TW
"Say goodbye to the help, the ranks." CAPP
Dr. Newman with the crooked pince-nez. Robert Graves. *Fr.* Grotesques. CMoP
Dr. Potatohead Talks to Mothers. Judith Johnson Sherwin. MoP
Dr. Sigmund Freud Discovers the Sea Shell. Archibald MacLeish. SoSe
Dr. Unlikely, we love you so. Horror Movie. Howard Moss. NePoEA-2
Dr. Wild's Ghost. *Unknown.* APAS
Dracula. Steve Kowit. VVA
Draft Horse, The. Robert Frost. CMoP; HeIP; HoPM; PoE
Draft of a Reparations Agreement. Dan Pagis, *tr. fr. Hebrew.* VWA, *tr. by* Stephen Mitchell
Draft Riot, The. Charles De Kay. PAH
Drafted Vulture, The. João Cabral de Melo Neto, *tr. fr. Portuguese by* W. S. Merwin. ATCBP
Drafts for a Quatrain. Edmund Wilson. OBAL
Drag Race. Dave Smith. AnAn
Dragged along by scarlet dolphins through a sea of soot in darkness. I Am Being Dragged by Red Dolphins. István Kormos, *tr. by* Edwin Morgan. MHuP
Dragging a rake through layers of my sleep. Finding the Pistol. Gibbons Ruark. MAT
Dragging across. Iida Dakotsu, *tr. by* Geoffrey Bownas *and* Anthony Thwaite. PeBJV
Dragging his hunger through the sky. The Vulture. Samuel Beckett. *Fr.* Echo's Bones. NOAM
Dragging in Winter. David McElroy. AmPA
Dragon, The. Mary Mullineaux. BoTP
Dragon, The. Spenser. *Fr.* The Faerie Queene, I, 11. SeCePo
Dragon. Joseph Stroud. NPGG
Dragon Country: To Jacob Boehme. Robert Penn Warren. PPP
Dragon-Fly, The. Walter Savage Landor. OBEV
Dragon-fly and I together, The. Two of a Trade. Samuel Willoughby Duffield. AA
Dragon hatched a cockatrice, The. China. William Empson. OBTV
Dragon Mouth Cliff. Chao Meng-fu, *tr. fr. Chinese by* Jonathan Chaves. *Fr.* Twenty-Eight Poems Inscribed on T'ien-kuan Mountai. CoBLCP
Dragon of the Seas, The. Thomas Nelson Page. PAH
Dragon Skate. Gladys Cardiff. CDW
Dragon Smoke. Lilian Moore. RAR
Dragon Song. Park Je-chun, *tr. fr. Korean by* Koh Chang-soo. ACKP
Dragon that our seas did raise his crest, The. Of the Great and Famous. Sir Francis Drake, and of My Little-Little Selfe. Robert Hayman. CH; FaBoCh; NoP
Dragon-Tiger Terrace. Yang Shih-ch'i, *tr. fr. Chinese by* Jonathan Chaves. CoBLCP
Dragonflies' resting place. Issa, *tr. fr. Japanese by* Hiroaki Sato. *Fr.* Forty-four Hokku. FCEI
Dragonfly, The. Louise Bogan. HeIP; NIP
Dragonfly, A. Eleanor Farjeon. FaPON; OnUR; PDV; RHPC
Dragonfly. Florence Page Jaques. RAR
Dragonfly, The. Howard Nemerov. PoA
Dragonfly, The. Theodore Harding Rand. CaP
Dragonfly, A/ Is very thin. Dragonfly. Florence Page Jaques. RAR

Dragonfly catches a fly, A. Joso, *tr. fr. Japanese by* Hiroaki Sato. *Fr.* Fifteen Hokku. FCEI
Dragonfly-Mother, The. Denise Levertov. InPS
Dragonfly—unable to get hold of a grass blade. Basho, *tr. fr. Japanese by* Burton Watson. *Fr.* Seventy-six Hokku. FCEI
Dragons, The/ tell me how to move. Chinese Checkers. Arleen Cohen. TSL
Dragons, The. Gerrit Komrij, *tr. fr. Dutch by* Jacob Lowland. DuIn
Dragon's Hoard, The. J. R. R. Tolkien. AmMo
Draining the Ornamental Lake. Simon Rae. NPo
Drake he's in his hammock an' a thousand mile away. Drake's Drum. Sir Henry Newbolt. FaBoCh; FaPoR; OBMV; PoRA
Drake, who the world hast conquered like a scroll. To the Noble Sir Francis Drake. Thomas Beedome. OxBSP
Drake's Drum. Sir Henry Newbolt. FaBoCh; FaPoR; OBMV; PoRA
Drama's vitallest expression is the common day. Emily Dickinson. NOBA
Dramatic Fragment. Trumbull Stickney. OxBA
Dramatic Monologue in the Speaker's Own Voice. Vassar Miller. TSM
Drank lonesome water. Lonesome Water. Roy Helton. AmFN; MoAmPo
Drank tonight at Eastern Slope, sobered up, drank again. Tune: Immortal at the River. Su Tung-p'o, *tr. by* Burton Watson. CoBCP
Draped in khaki, Jurgis. Jurgis Petrakas, the Workers' Angel, Organizes the First Miner's Strike in Exeter, Pennsylvania. Anthony Petrosky. FYAP
Drat my hateful birthday. Sulpicia, *tr. by* John Dillon. PBWP
Draw a historical parallel. Entrance Exams. "Cuthbert Bede." FaBoNo
Draw a little closer, comrades! The Fisherman's Story. Henrietta Cordelia Ray. CBWP-3
Draw a pail of water. *Unknown.* BoTP; MoShBr; OxNR
Draw closer to me, God, than were I one. Prayer of an Unbeliever. Lizette Woodworth Reese. TrPWD
Draw me nere [or near], draw me nere [or near]. *Unknown.* EBEV (Jolly Jugger, The.) NoP
(Magician and the Baron's Daughter, The.) MeEL
Draw near [or neer]/ You lovers that complain. The Exequies. Thomas Stanley. MeLP; OBS
Draw near, young men, and learn of me. McAfee's Confession. *Unknown.* AmFP
Draw neer/ You lovers that complain. *See* Draw near/ You lovers that complain.
Drawer, The. George MacBeth. NePoEA-2
Drawing. James Sherry. LP
Drawing a Banana. Myra Schneider. CN
Drawing his/ sparrow-hunting bow. Saigyo, *tr. fr. Japanese by* Burton Watson. *Fr.* Sixty-four Tanka. FCEI
Drawing on Kreisler. James Sherry. LP
Drawing-Room Ballad, A. Henry Duff Traill. CenHV
Drawing Wildflowers. Jorie Graham. NPGG
Drawings of the Song Animals. Duane Niatum. HATNAP
Drawn blinds and flaring gas within. In Bohemia. Arthur Symons. BrPo
Drawn by old Homer's hand, the rose. Helen like the Rose. Evan Lloyd. *Fr.* The Powers of the Pen. OBWVE
Drawn by Stones, by Earth, by Things That Have Been in the Fire. Marvin Bell. CAPP
Drawn by the memory of your face I turn to look. Teika, *tr. fr. Japanese by* Hiroaki Sato. *Fr.* Eighty-four Tanka. FCEI
Drawn on by moonlight. Kyogoku Tamekane, *tr. fr. Japanese by* Burton Watson. *Fr.* Twenty-three Tanka. FCEI
Drawn out into the light. Negative. Yoshioka Minoru, *tr. by* Hiroaki Sato. FCEI
Drayman, The. Walt Whitman. *Fr.* Song of Myself, XIII. PoNe "Oxen that rattle the yoke and chain or halt in the leafy shade." FM
Dread. J. M. Synge. BoLoP; MoBrPo; OxBSP
Dread are the death-pale Kings. Still-Heart. Frank Pearce Sturm. OBMV
Dread imperial command, The. Mononobe Akimochi, *tr. fr. Japanese.* *Fr.* Manyo Shu. Ma
Dreaded Road. Abd al-Razzaq Abd al-Wahid, *tr. fr. Arabic by* Diana Der Hovanessian *and* Lena Jayyusi. MAP
Dreadful as hurricanes, athwart the main. The West Indies. James Montgomery. PBCV
Dreadful case of murder, A. Execution of Alice Holt. *Unknown.* OxBoLi
Dreadful Dinotherium he, The. Hilaire Belloc. *Fr.* A Moral Alphabet. NOBL
Dreadful Doings of Jelly Belly, The. Dennis Lee. RAR

Dreadful dullness will characterize the coming day, A. Ebony Life. Robert Desnos, *tr. by* Michael Benedikt. POS
Dreadful Fate of Naughty Nate, The. john Kendrick Bangs. OBCA
"Dreadful Has Already Happened, The." Mark Strand. HCAP; NoAM
Dreadful order, The. Mononobe Akimochi, *tr. fr. Japanese by* Geoffrey Bownas *and* Anthony Thwaite. *Fr.* Manyo Shu. PeBJV
Dreadnought, The. *Unknown.* AmFP; OxBSS
Dream, A. Bella Akhmadulina, *tr. fr. Russian by* Jean Valentine *and* Olga Carlisle. BoWoP
Dream, A [*or* The]. William Allingham. BIrV; NOBVV
Dream, A. Matthew Arnold. GBL; GTBS-P; OBTV; SeCePo
Dream, The. Aphra Behn. *Fr.* A Voyage to the Isle of Love. PBWP
Dream, The. "Brian Bendo." NOEC
Dream, The. John Peale Bishop. LiTA; LiTM
Dream, A. Blake. *Fr.* Songs of Innocence. CH; EnRP
Dream, The. Louise Bogan. InPK; LiTA; LiTM; MAT; MoAB; MoAmPo; NoAM
Dream, A, *sel.* Burns.
   Guid-Mornin to Your Majesty! NAs
Dream, The. Byron. BeLS; ChER; TEP
Dream, The. Chaucer. *Fr.* The Book of the Duchesse. FiP; PBBP
Dream, A. Hugh Connell. NeIP
Dream. Elizabeth Cook-Lynn. *Fr.* Journey, I. HATNAP
Dream, The. Robert Creeley. BAP
Dream. Richard Watson Dixon. EBEV; NOBVV
Dream. Stephen Dobyns. MAYP
Dream[e], The. John Donne. EIL; InvP; LiTB; MeLP; MePo; OAEL-1; OBEV; OBS; SeCP; TOF
Dream. Norman Dubie. NAmP
Dream. Solomon Edwards. PoNe
Dream. Joseph Eliyia, *tr. fr. Greek by* Rae Dalven. VWA
Dream, The. David Ignatow. CoAP; MAT; NNaP; VWA
Dream. Nana Issaia, *tr. fr. Modern Greek by* Helle Tzalopoulou Barnstone. BoWoP
Dream, A. Maggie Pogue Johnson. CBWP-4
Dream[e], The. Ben Jonson. NOBE
Dream, A. Keats. *Fr.* The Fall of Hyperion, I. OAEL-2; OBNC
Dream, A. Elizabeth Clementine Kinney. AA
Dream. Emperor Kogon, *tr. fr. Japanese by* Steven D. Carter. WFTW
Dream, The. Li Nan, *tr. fr. Chinese by* Dominic Cheung. IFON
Dream, The. M. Y. Lermontov, *tr. fr. Russian by* Alan Myers. AAA
Dream. Josephine Miles. PoA
Dream. Marianne Moore. NYBP
Dream, A. Muhammad al-Ghuzzi, *tr. fr. Arabic by* May Jayyusi *and* John Heath-Stubbs. MAP
Dream, The. Paul Petrie. TAP
Dream, The. Theodore Roethke. LLLT; NoP; NYBP; UnPo
Dream, The. Sir Edward Sherburne. OxBSP
Dream. Shotetsu, *tr. fr. Japanese by* Steven D. Carter. WFTW
Dream, A, *sels.* Rachel Speght. WPE
   "I sought, I found, she asked me what I would."
   "My grief, quoth I, is called Ignorance."
   "Quoth she, I wish I could prescribe your help."
   "Upon a sudden, as I gazing stood."
Dream, The. May Swenson. *Fr.* Poet to Tiger. GLP
Dream, A. Charles Tomlinson. OxBC
Dream. Malka Heifetz Tussman, *tr. fr. Yiddish by* Kathryn Hellerstein. AYP
Dream. *Unknown, tr. fr. Eskimo by* Armand Schwerner. STP
Dream, A. *Unknown. See* Benedicite, What Dreamed I This Night?
Dream, A. Sándor Weöres, *tr. fr. Hungarian by* Jascha Kessler. FOC
Dream, A. Charles Williams. OBEV
Dream. Harold Witt. SM
Dream about an Aged Humorist, A. Aaron Zeitlin, *tr. fr. Yiddish by* Ruth Whitman
Dream about Junior High School in America, The. Dick Lourie. NeAC
Dream about Our Master, William Shakespeare, The. Hyam Plutzik. Mes; RB
Dream about Sunsets. Annabelle Hébert. GrPl
Dream after dream I see the wrecks that lie. Posted. John Masefield. Son
Dream after Touring the Tokyo Tokei. Joy Kogawa. BrSi
Dream always went back to a lonely village by the mountain, The. For a Memory. Tachihara Michizo, *tr. by* Hiroaki Sato. FCEI
Dream and the Song. James David Corrothers. BANP
Dream as Calculation, The. Barry Goldensohn. NAmP
Dream as Reported, A. Virginia Earle. GoYe
Dream Barker. Jean Valentine. PrIm; VGW
Dream behind the. Here. Bob Orr. PeNZ
Dream Boogie. Langston Hughes. AmPP; HCAP; RR
Dream broken by the sound of a mallet. Princess Shikishi, *tr. fr. Japanese by* Hiroaki Sato. *Fr.* Seventy-eight Tanka. FCEI

Dream Called Life, The. Pedro Calderón de la Barca, *tr. fr. Spanish by* Edward Fitzgerald. AWP
Dream Canaan. Aba Shtoltsenberg, *tr. fr. Yiddish by* Dennis Silk. PeBMYV
Dream Data. Robert Duncan. NeAP
Dream Deferred. Langston Hughes. *See* Lenox Avenue Mural: Harlem ("What happens to a dream deferred").
Dream, Dump-Heap, and Civilization. Robert Penn Warren. NoP
Dream Fairy, The. Thomas Hood. BoTP
Dream Fantasy. "Fiona Macleod." WGRP
Dream Farmer. Jill Witherspoon Boyer. CNA
Dream Feast (Three Poems), The. Anita Endrezze-Danielson. VoR
Dream fluently, still brothers, who when young. To the Etruscan Poets. Richard Wilbur. OxBC
Dream in a dream the heavy soul somewhere. Canto Amor. John Berryman. CoAP; MoAmPo; VGW
Dream is a cocktail at Sloppy Joe's, The. Havana Dreams. Langston Hughes. PoNe
"Dream is the thought in the ghost, The." George Meredith. *Fr.* A Faith on Trial. WGRP
Dream is vague, The. Beale Street. Langston Hughes. PPP
Dream it was in which I found myself, A. The Dream Called Life. Pedro Calderón de la Barca, *tr. by* Edward Fitzgerald. AWP
Dream Kiss, The. Karoline von Günderode, *tr. fr. German by* Susan L. Cocalis. DMG
Dream-Land. Poe. AmPP; AnAmPo; LiTA; NAAL-1; NOBA; OxBA (Dreamland.) TAP
Dream Land. Christina Rossetti. BrRo
Dream-Language of Fergus, The. Medbh McGuckian. CIP
Dream-Love. Christina Rossetti. CH; HAP; PoEL-5
Dream not, o soul, that easy is the task. Help. Whittier. Son
Dream not of noble service elsewhere wrought. Life's Common Duties. Minot Judson Savage. WBLP
Dream not, poor poet, that th' ephemeral breath. Henry F. Lott. PF
Dream of a Baseball Star. Gregory Corso. SD; VGW
Dream of a Boy Who Lived at Nine Elms, The. William Brighty Rands. OxBChV
Dream of a Girl Who Lived at Sevenoaks, The. William Brighty Rands. OxBChV
Dream of Artemis, A, *sel.* Francis Ledwidge.
   "God, whose kindly hand doth sow." TrPWD
Dream of Barcelona: My Ancient World. Takahashi Mutsuo, *tr. fr. Japanese by* Hiroaki Sato. FCEI
Dream of Burial, A. James Wright. NaP
Dream of Dakiki, The. Firdausi, *tr. fr. Persian by* A. V. Williams Jackson. WGRP
Dream of Death, A. "Owen Innsley." AA
Dream of Death, A. W. B. Yeats. GBL
Dream of dolorous women stole my sleep, A. Vampire Bride. Felix Stefanile. VVA
Dream of Elfland, A. Henrietta Cordelia Ray. CBWP-3
Dream of Eugene Aram [the Murderer], The. Thomas Hood. BeLS; EnRP
Dream of Fair Women, A. Kingsley Amis. FF; NoAM; OAEL-2
Dream of Fair Women, The. Carl Dennis. BLA
Dream of Fair Women, A, *sel.* Tennyson.
   As When a Man. ChER
Dream of Flowers, A. Titus Munson Coan. AA
Dream of Gerontius, The, *sels.* Cardinal Newman.
   Chorus of Angels. NOCV; PoEL-5
   (Fifth Choir of Angelicals.) NOBVV
   "Jesu, Maria—I am near to death." ACP
Dream of Governors, A. Louis Simpson. NYBP
Dream of Horses, A. Ted Hughes. NePoEA-2
Dream of Husbands, A. Alberto Ríos. NoAM
Dream of Jealousy, A. Seamus Heaney. FaBCIP
Dream of Judgement, A. Douglas Dunn. OxBC
Dream of Rebirth. Roberta Hill Whiteman. CDW
Dream of Roaming, A. Sándor Weöres, *tr. fr. Hungarian by* Jascha Kessler. FOC
Dream of Suffocation, A. Robert Bly. NaP
Dream of the Artfairy. Carl Morse. GLP
Dream of the Artisan, The. G. R. Emerson. PF
Dream of the Black Mother. Marcelino dos Santos, *tr. fr. Portuguese by* Philippa Rumsey. WMBCH
Dream of the Cabal; a Prophetical Satire, The. *Unknown.* APAS
Dream of the Cross, The ("I would tell a marvellous vision"). *Unknown, tr. fr. Anglo-Saxon by* Sally Purcell. EBEV
Dream of the Forgotten Lover. Lucia Fox, *tr. fr. Spanish by* R. Maghan. BoWoP

Dream of the Lynx. John Haines. NU
Dream of the night, The. Narihira, *tr. by* Geoffrey Bownas *and* Anthony Thwaite. PeBJV
Dream of the Rood, A. *At.* to Cynewulf, *tr. fr. Old English by* Charles W. Kennedy. AnOE; OAEL-1
Dream of the Rood, The (*"Hwaet!* A dream came to me"). *Unknown.* NOCV, *tr. by* Michael Alexander
Dream of the Rood, The ("I am remembering in the long ago"). *Unknown, tr. fr. Anglo-Saxon.* ACP
Dream of the Unknown, The. Shelley. *See* I dreamed [*or* dream'd] that, as I wandered by the way.
Dream of the walls of a cave. The Fossil. John Lyle Donaghy. NeIP
Dream of Venus, A. Bion, *tr. fr. Greek by* Leigh Hunt. AWP
Dream of wandering in woods with. Susan Howe. LP
Dream of Winter. George Mackay Brown. FaBoTw
Dream of Women, A. Carolyn Maisel. IHMS
Dream of Wrecks, A. Shakespeare. *Fr.* King Richard III, I, iv. ChTr
Dream on stone. Afternoon's Angel. Seymour Mayne. VWA
Dream- or angel-honey. Kinsey Report. Jutta Schutting, *tr. by* Beth Bjorklund. CoAuP
Dream, or the Type of the Rising Sun, A. Jean Adams. NOEC
Dream Palace, The. Kaiseki, *tr. fr. Chinese by* Lucien Stryk *and* Takashi Ikemoto. ZPCJ
Dream-Pedlary. Thomas Lovell Beddoes. BoTP; CH; EnRP; FaBoBe; HAP; LiTB; NOBE; OBEV; OBNC; PoEL-4; TrGrPo; WiR
Dream, ploughman, of what agriculture brings. Elegy for the Lost Parish. Douglas Dunn. DiPo
Dream Record: June 8, 1955. Allen Ginsberg. NOBA
Dream Sequence, Part 9. Naomi Long Madgett. BPo
Dream-Ship, The. Eugene Field. AnAmPo
Dream Ship, The. W. K. Holmes. BoTP
Dream Song. Lewis Alexander. PoBA; PoNe
Dream Song. *Unknown, tr. fr. Pawnee Indian by* Francis Densmore. OBVE
Dream Songs, *sels.* John Berryman.
April Fool's Day, or St. Mary Egypt. NaP
"At Henry's bier let some thing fall out well." NoP
"Chilled in this Irish pub I wish my loves." FaBoMo; LCAP
"Deprived of his enemy, shrugged to a standstill." CAPP; LCAP
Elegy for W. C. W., the Lovely Man, An. NoP
"Father being the loneliest word in the one language." DiL
"Filling her compact and delicious body." BoLoP; CAPP; HAP; HCAP; NoP; OBAL; OPOP; WeW
"Full moon. Our Narragansett gales subside." CoAP
"Glories of the world struck me, made me aria, once, The." HCAP
"God bless Henry. He lived like a rat." CAPP
"He lay in the middle of the world, and twitcht." HCAP; NoP; PoE
"He stared at ruin. Ruin stared straight back." CAPP; HCAP
"He yelled at me in Greek." FYAP
Henry hates the world. What the world to Henry. NaP
"Henry sats in de bar and was odd." HCAP
Henry's Confession. LCAP; MoP; NAAL-2; NoAM; PoE; TwCP
"Henry's mind grew blacker the more he thought." FaBoMo; NOBA
"Henry's pelt was put on sundry walls." MoP; NoAM
His Helplessness. NoP
"How this woman came by the courage, how she got." TAP
"Huffy Henry hid the day." CAPP; HCAP; NoP; PoE
"I am, outside. Incredible panic rules." CAPP
"I am the little man who smokes and smokes." WeW
"I can't get him out of my mind, out of my mind." NoP
"I don't operate often. When I do." NaP
"I have moved to Dublin to have it out with you." MoP; NoAM
"Ill lay he long, upon this last return." TAP
"I'm cross with god who has wrecked this generation." FaBoMo
"Irish have the thickest ankles in the world, The." TAP
Lay of Ike, The. LCAP
"Let us suppose, valleys and such ago." NaP; PPP
"Life, friends, is boring. We must not say so." CAPP; HAP; HCAP; HeIP; LiTM; MoP; NaP; NoAM; NOBA; PrIm; TAP; TwCP
"Love her he doesn't but the thought he puts." FaBoMo
"Marker slants, flowerless, day's almost done, The." CAPP; DiL; HCAP
"Peter's not friendly. He gives me sideways looks.." CAPP
Sabbath. LCAP
"Seedy Henry rose up shy in de world." HCAP
So Long? Stevens. HAP; HCAP; NOBA
"Some good people, daring and subtle voices." HCAP
"Supreme my holdings, greater yet my need." CRP
"That dark brown rabbit, lightness in his ears." TwCP

"There are voices, voices. Light's dying. Birds have quit." CAPP
"There sat down, once, a thing on Henry's heart." CAPP; HAP; HCAP; NoP; PoE
"This world is gradually becoming a place." MoP; NoAM; NOBA
"Three 'coons come at his garbage. He be cross." LCAP
"Three limbs, three seasons smashed; well, one to go." HCAP
"Turning it over, considering, like a madman." MoP; NoAM
"Weather was fine, The. They took away his teeth." CAPP
"Welcome, grinned Henry, welcome fifty-one!" TAP
"You couldn't bear to grow old, but we grow old." TAP
"Your face broods from my table, Suicide." TAP
Dream, The ("I dreamed that buried in my fellow clay."). *Unknown.* NOEC
Dream, The ("Last night I had a dream bad 'cess to my dreaming."). *Unknown.* WTO
Dream, The ("Last night I supped on lobster; it nearly drove me mad."). *Unknown.* OxBoLi
Dream Time. Anthony Thwaite. DiPo
Dream 2: Brian the Still-Hunter. Margaret Atwood. BoWoP
Dream Variation [*or* Variations]. Langston Hughes. AmNP; CDC; HAP; IDB; NAAL-2; NOBA; PoBA; PoNe; WeW
Dream vision, Breyten, the print, A. The Hartlaub Gull. H. C. ten Berge, *tr. by* Greta Kilburn. DuIn
Dream with Fred Astaire. Bill Berkson. UL
Dream within a Dream, A. Poe. AmPP; AnAmPo; BLPL; GBL; NOBA; OxBA; TAP; TrGrPo
"I stand amid the roar," *sel.* ChTr
Dream within a Song, A. Henrietta Cordelia Ray. CBWP-3
Dream you're smiling. I Dream. Jacques Roubaud, *tr. by* Robert Kelly. RHTwFP
Dreame, The. John Donne. *See* Dream, The.
Dreamed Realization, A. Gregory Corso. NeAP; PoM; VGW
Dreamer, The. Thomas Nunan. WBLP
Dreamer Meets Riot, The. John Skelton. *Fr.* The Bowge of Courte. OxBLMV
Dreamer of Dreams. William Herbert Carruth. PoLF
Dreamers. Siegfried Sassoon. BrPo; MoBrPo; NoAM; Son
Dreamers and Flyers. Joan LaBombard. MOWH
Dreaming America. Joyce Carol Oates. GeTw
Dreaming animal cries out, The. Nearly Nameless. Márton Kalász, *tr. by* Jascha Kessler. FOC
Dreaming in the Shanghai Restaurant. D. J. Enright. OBTV
Dreaming in the Trenches. William Gordon McCabe. AA
Dreaming of Amaro. Michizane, *tr. fr. Chinese by* Burton Watson. JLIC-1
Dreaming of Li Po. Tu Fu, *tr. fr. Chinese by* Burton Watson. CoBCP
Dreaming of Master Chung-lu. K'ang Hai, *tr. fr. Chinese by* Jonathan Chaves. CoBLCP
Dreaming of the Bones, *sel.* W. B. Yeats. At the Grey Round of the Hill. RB
Dreaming of the Castle. Endre Vészi, *tr. fr. Hungarian by* Jascha Kessler. FOC
Dreaming of the South. Huang-fu Sung, *tr. fr. Chinese by* Lois Fusek. ATF
Dreaming of the South. Niu Chiao, *tr. fr. Chinese by* Lois Fusek. ATF
Dreaming of the South. Wen T'ing-yün, *tr. fr. Chinese by* Lois Fusek. ATF
Dreaming Trout, The. Charles Bruce. *Fr.* The Flowing Summer. CaP
Dreaming Winter. James Welch. NOVW
Dreaming with a Friend. Stephen Berg. NaP
Dreaming you say thank you. Voices That Have Filled My Day. Fay Chiang. BrSi
Dreamland, *sel.* Charles Mair.
"We are not wholly blest who use the earth." CaP
Dreamland. Poe. *See* Dream-Land.
Dreamlike leap, A. For the Record. Roy Blount, Jr.. OBAL
Dreams. Anne Bloch. Mes
Dreams. Charles Cooper. PoBA
Dreams. Victor James Daley. PoAu-1
Dreams, The. Eugene Field. AnAmPo
Dreams. Nikki Giovanni. CNA; PoBA
Dreams. Robert Herrick. CaPo; HAP; NAEL-1; OxBSP
Dreams. Langston Hughes. RHPC
Dreams. Poe. AmPP; OxBA; TAP
Dreams. Arthur Symons. PoA
Dreams. Israel Zangwill. TrJP
Dreams are old before you, The. It Is Finished. Barney Bush. STE
"Dreams Are the Royal Road to the Unconscious." Paul Goodman. PoA

Dreams fled away, this country bedroom, raw. Another September. Thomas Kinsella. BIrV; CIP; FaBCIP

Dreams go fast and far. To Dark Eyes Dreaming. Zilpha Keatley Snyder. RHPC

Dreams in Progress. Richard Oyama. BrSi

Dreams in War Time, *sel.* Amy Lowell. "I dug a grave under an oak-tree." BoWoP

Dreams of Auschwitz. Boris Slutsky, *tr. fr. Russian by* Daniel Weissbort. VWA

Dreams of Beauty. Adah Isaacs Menken. CBWP-1

Dreams of Snakes, Chocolate and Men. Christy Sheffield Sanford. UL

Dreams of the Dreamer, The. Georgia Douglas Johnson. CDC

Dreams of the One, The. Lörinc Szabó, *tr. fr. Hungarian by* Edwin Morgan. MHuP

Dreams of Water. Donald Justice. LCAP; NYBP

Dreams Old and Nascent. D. H. Lawrence. WGRP

Dreams, said the dog. Dialog. Jean Garrigue. AnAn

Dreams that delude with flying shade men's minds. We Are Such Stuff as Dreams. Petronius Arbiter, *tr. by* Howard Mumford Jones. AWP

Dreams, Yellow Lions. Alistair Campbell. ATNZ

Dreamscape. Roger Zelazny. BWV

Dreamscape in Kümmel. Harold Witt. NYBP

Dreamt I today the dream of yesternight. George Santayana. *Fr.* Sonnets. AnAmPo

Dreamtime I You Dog You. Thulani Davis. ER

Dreamwater. Hilde Domin, *tr. fr. German by* Tudor Morris. VWA

Dreamy crags with raucous voices croon, The. Hymn to the Sunrise. *Unknown.* NA

Dreamy in a darkling bar. Ode to a Nightingale. Roy Kelly. BXAP

Dreary and brown the night comes down. Columbus at the Convent. John Townsend Trowbridge. PAH

Dreary Black Hills, The ("Kind friends, you must pity my horrible tale"). *Unknown.* AmFP

Dreary Black Hills, The ("Roundhouse in Cheyenne is filled every night, The"). *Unknown.* AS

Dreary Change, The. Sir Walter Scott. FaBoPP; NAEL-2; OAEL-2; OBNC

Dreary lay the long road, dreary lay the town. The Toy Band. Sir Henry Newbolt. BoTP

Dred of deth, sorow of sin. In His Utter Wretchedness. John Audelay. MeEL

Dree Night, The. *Unknown.* ChTr

Dregs. Ernest Dowson. OBMV; SeCePo

Dreidel Song. Efraim Rosenzweig. RAR

Dreme, The, *sels.* Sir David Lindsay.
Complaint of the Common Weill of Scotland. GoTS
(Compleynt of the Comoun Weill of Scotland, The.) OxBS
Of the Realme of Scotland. OxBS

Drenched at times is your listening. Not for You. Ory Bernstein, *tr. by* Bernhard Frank. MHeP

Drenched earth has a warm, sweet radiance all her own, The. The Robin's Egg. Annie Charlotte Dalton. CaP

Drenching night drags on: no sleep or snore, The. Egan O'Rahilly, *tr. by* Thomas Kinsella. NOIV

Drenching rain hisses down, cooling the evening. Days of Rain; the Rivers Have Overflowed. Su Tung-p'o, *tr. by* Burton Watson. CoBCP

Dresden. Ciaran Carson. CIP

Dress, The. Dahlia Ravikovich, *tr. fr. Hebrew by* Bernhard Frank. MHeP

Dress, The. Mark Strand. GeTw

Dress Me, Dear Mother. Avraham Shlonsky, *tr. fr. Hebrew by* Robert Mezey. VWA

Dress me in green. *Unknown, tr. by* Willis Barnstone. BoWoP

Dress of Fire, A. Dahlia Ravikovich, *tr. fr. Hebrew by* Chana Bloch. VWA

Dress that my brother has put on is thin, The. Lady Otomo no Sakanoe, *tr. fr. Japanese by* Arthur Waley. *Fr.* Manyo Shu. AWP

Dresscessional, A. Carolyn Wells. WBLP

Dressed in his clumsy, stiff, aquatic clothes. The Diver. Edward Leslie Mayo. CoAP

Dressed man and a naked man, A. George Orwell. EBEV

Dressed to Kill. Clarence Major. UL

Dressed up in my melancholy. M. Carl Holman. AmNP; PoNe

Dresses. Kathleen Fraser. NMM

Dressing Game. Dennis Schmitz. NPGG

Dressing Stations, The. Norman Dubie. AmPA

Dried Apple Pies. *Unknown.* BLPA

Dried bean-cake: $1.00. Pay the Bill. Ch'iao Lin, *tr. by* Dominic Cheung. IFON

Dried Bones under the Pine. Etsudo, *tr. fr. Chinese by* Lucien Stryk *and* Takashi Ikemoto. ZPCJ

Dried Fruit. Philip Dow. BXAP

Dried sinks and hot. Caravati's Junkyard. Elizabeth Morgan. GrPl

Dried thistles hide his face. Gathering Mushrooms. Alistair Campbell. ATNZ

Dried up old cactus. June. Elaine Feinstein. BrRo

Drift descends like rattling dust, The. Avalanche. Adrien Stoutenburg. NYBP

Drift-Wood. Clara Ann Thompson. CBWP-2

Drifter off Tarentum, A. Kipling. *Fr.* Epitaphs of the War, 1914–1918. FaBoEE; MMA

Drifters. Bruce Dawe. CBAP; NoAM

Drifter's Song. Eino Leino, *tr. fr. Finnish by* Aili Jarvenpa. SOP

Drifting. Thomas Buchanan Read. AA; AnAmPo; GN

Drifting. Andrew Salkey. PPR

Drifting. Kathleen Spivack. IHMS

Drifting and innocent and like snow. Christmas Letter Home. G. S. Fraser. OxBTC

Drifting night in the Georgia pines. O Daedalus, Fly Away Home. Robert Hayden. HAP; IDB; PoBA; PoNe; WeW

Drifting off the wheel of a past. First Spring. Duane Niatum. HATNAP

Drifting on the wind, and through. A Fall of Rain at Miti-Miti. Hone Tuwhare. ATNZ

Drifting outside in a pall of smoke. Forever. Raymond Carver. GeTw

Drifting Sands and a Caravan. Yolande Langworthy. BLPA

Drifting to meet us on the darkening stage. Downstream. Thomas Kinsella. FaBCIP

Drifts That Bar My Door. Adah Isaacs Menken. CBWP-1

Driftwood. Witter Bynner. FYAP

Driftwood. Daniel Smythe. RFM

Driftwood Dybbuk. Barbara F. Lefcowitz. VWA

Driftwood from a Ship. Galway Kinnell. AnAn

Drill, The. Harry Brown. WaaP

Drill Man Blues. George Sizemore. AmFP; WTO

Drilling in Russell Square. Edward Shanks. OBMV

Drink. William Carlos Williams. OxBA

Drink and dance and laugh and lie. The Flaw in Paganism. Dorothy Parker. NBLV

Drink! drink! to whom shall we drink? The Old Man's Carousal. James Kirke Paulding. AA

Drink, Friends. Moses Ibn Ezra, *tr. fr. Hebrew by* Solomon Solis-Cohen. *Fr.* Wine-Songs. TrJP

Drink from My Empty Cup. Zindzi Mandela. WMBCH

Drink, gossips mine! we drink no wine. Medieval Norman Song ("Drink, gossips mine!"). *Unknown, tr. by* John Addington Symonds. AWP

Drink me. Thirst. Musa Moris Farhi. VWA

Drink of Milk, A. John Montague. FaBCIP

Drink of Spring, A. John Ennis. CIP

Drink of Water, A. Seamus Heaney. FaBCIP; OxBC

Drink On. Mary E. Tucker. CBWP-1

Drink to-day, and drown all sorrow. Drinking Song. John Fletcher *and others.* *Fr.* The Bloody Brother, II, ii. EIL

Drink to me only with thine eyes. To Celia ("Drink to me only with thine eyes"). Ben Jonson. BoLoP; EnLoPo; FaBoBe; FaBV; FaFP; FPL; GTBS; GTBS-P; InPK; LiTB; NOBE; OBEV; OBS; OBVE; PoLF; TEP; TrGrPo
(Song: To Celia.) AWP; EIL; ELP; GBL; HeIP; NAEL-1; NoP; OAEL-1; PoE; PoEL-2; PrIm; SeCP; SeCV-1

Drink, unhappy lover, drink. Meleager, *tr. by* Peter Whigham. PeHV

Drinke and be merry, merry, merry boyes. Thomas Morton. SCAP

Drinking. Chu Yün-ming, *tr. fr. Chinese by* Jonathan Chaves. CoBLCP

Drinking. Abraham Cowley, *after the Greek of* Anacreon. BLPL; FF; MePo; NOBE; OBEV; OBVE; SeCePo; SeCP; SeCV-1; TrGrPo
(Anacreontic on Drinking.) SeCePo
(Anacreontics: Drinking.) HeIP
(Thirsty Earth, The.) WiR

Drinking Alone in the Moonlight. Li Po, *tr. fr. Chinese by* Amy Lowell *and* Florence Ayscough. AWP

Drinking as only you know how. Poetry Reading in the Iowa City Railroad Station. Carlos Cortínez, *tr. by* Miller Williams. WCI

Drinking at Night with Yen Kung-mou. Shen Chou, *tr. fr. Chinese by* Jonathan Chaves. CoBLCP

Drinking at the Cave Mouth. Tsung Ch'en, *tr. fr. Chinese by* Jonathan Chaves. CoBLCP

Drinking Cold Water. Peter Everwine. NNaP

Drinking Fountain. Marchette Chute. RAR

Drinking is done, the lamps extinguished, The. New Year's Eve. Wen Cheng-ming, *tr. by* Jonathan Chaves. CoBLCP

Drinking, singing. The Shop. Wu Sheng, *tr. by* Dominic Cheung. IFON

Drinking Song. Louis Aragon, *tr. fr. French by* Michael Benedikt. POS

Drinking Song. Burns. *See* Jolly Beggars, The: See the smoking bowl before us.

Drinking-Song, A. Henry Carey. OBEV

Drinking Song. Thomas Dekker. *Fr.* The Shoemaker's Holiday. TrGrPo

    (Hey Derry Derry.) SeCePo

    (Saint Hugh.) OBSC

    (Troll the Bowl!) EIL

Drinking Song. John Fletcher *and others. Fr.* The Bloody Brother, II, ii. EIL

Drinking Song. Louise Geneviève de Sainctonge, *tr. fr. French by* Dorothy Backer. DMF

Drinking Song, A. Shakespeare. *Fr.* Antony and Cleopatra, II, vii. OBSC

Drinking Song. Sheridan. *Fr.* The School for Scandal. NOIV

Drinking Song. James Kenneth Stephen. NOBL

Drinking Song. *At. to* William Stevenson *and also to* John Still. *See* Gammer Gurton's Needle: Back and Side Go Bare, Go Bare.

Drinking Song, A ("If ever your spirits are damp, low"). *Unknown.* FaBoUs

Drinking Song ("She tells me with claret she cannot agree"). *Unknown.* NOBL

Drinking Song, A. W. B. Yeats. BoLoP; OAEL-2

Drinking-Song, against All Sorts of Disputes in Drinking, A. William Wycherley. SeCV-2

Drinking strong genmai tea. After Li Ch'ing-chao. Anne Waldman. UL

Drinking Tea. Chang Ts'o, *tr. fr. Chinese by* Dominic Cheung. IFON

Drinking the Sun of Corinth. Odysseus Elytis, *tr. fr. Greek by* Edmund Keeley *and* Philip Sherrard. VMG

Drinking the Wind. Tan Ying, *tr. fr. Chinese by* Kenneth Rexroth *and* Ling Chung. WPOW

Drinking Wine. Mo Shih-lung, *tr. fr. Chinese by* Jonathan Chaves. CoBLCP

Drinking Wine, *sels.* T'ao Ch'ien, *tr. fr. Chinese by* Burton Watson. CoBCP

    "Fall chrysanthemums have beautiful colors." *Fr.* VII.

    "I built my hut in a place where people live." *Fr.* V.

    "Prosperity and decline have no fixed dwelling." *Fr.* I.

    "Way's been lost for a thousand years, The." *Fr.* III.

Drinking Wine: Second Series. Ch'ien Ch'ien-yi, *tr. fr. Chinese by* Ronald Miao. WFTU

Drinking Wine with Yoshiyuki and Being Very Happy. Ryokan, *tr. fr. Japanese by* Burton Watson. FCEI; JLIC-2

Drip drip, the rain on paulownia leaves. Pouring Out My Feelings after Parting from Yüan Chen. Po Chü-i, *tr. by* Burton Watson. CoBCP

Dripping dew of the foot-wearying mountain, The. Lady Ishikawa, *tr. fr. Japanese by* Hiroaki Sato. *Fr.* Manyo Shu. FCEI

Dripping June, A. *Unknown.* FaBoUs

Drips surprise, The. They talk too. Fag-End. Philip O'Connor. EAS

Drive, The. Janet Reed McFatter. GrPl

Drive a Tractor. *Unknown.* NBLV

Drive Imagining. Arthur Vogelsang. MAYP

Drive-ins are out, to start with. Movie-Going. John Hollander. CoAP

Drive on, sharp wings, and cry above. The Redshanks. Julian Bell. OBMV

Drive on the Peninsula, A. Brian Turner. ATNZ

Driven by a myriad-mile wind, I come and go. Written on Board a Ship on the Yellow Sea, When a Japanese Friend Asked Me for a Poem. Ch'iu Chin, *tr. by* Pao Chia-lin. WFTU

Driven from the soil of France, a female came. Sonnet: September 1, 1802. Wordsworth. ChER

Driven in by autumn's sharpening air. Wordsworth. *Fr.* The Redbreast. PBBP

Driver, The. James Dickey. VGW

Driver in Italy, The. Nicholas Christopher. MAYP

Driver rubbed at his nettly chin, The. To the Four Courts, Please. James Stephens. BIrV; MoAB; MoBrPo; UnPo

Driver wasn't even aware, The. Examination of Conscience before Going to Sleep. T. Carmi, *tr. by* Stephen Mitchell. OBD

"Driver, what stream is it?" I asked, well knowing. The Lordly Hudson. Paul Goodman. CoAP; VGW

Drivers are washing the concrete mixers, The. Concrete Mixers. Patricia Hubbell. PDV; RHPC

Drivin' Steel. *Unknown.* AS

Drivin' steel, drivin' steel. Hammer Man. *Unknown.* AS

Driving. Myra Cohn Livingston. RR

Driving a prairie, we see a mill far off. Distances. Richard Hugo. CAPP

Driving at Dawn. William Heyen. SaC

Driving Cattle to Casas Buenas. Roy Campbell. PeSA

Driving Cross-Country. X. J. Kennedy. TwCP

Driving down from the turf bog in the rain. Merchandise. Sean Jennett. NeIP

Driving down the concrete artery. The White Man Pressed the Locks. James C. Kilgore. InPK

Driving, driven. The Driver in Italy. Nicholas Christopher. MAYP

Driving Home after a Funeral. Gregory Orr. GeTw

Driving Home the Cows. Kate Putnam Osgood. AA; BeLS; PAH

Driving huge bulls up the hill. Ozaki Hosai, *tr. fr. Japanese by* Hiroaki Sato. *Fr.* One Hundred Haiku in Free Form. FCEI

Driving, I come for a while. Late at Night. William Stafford. NNaP

Driving in Oklahoma. Carter Revard. HATNAP; VoR

Driving in the Park. *Unknown.* OxBoLi

Driving into Enid. Michael Van Walleghen. FYAP

Driving into the Storm: The Art of Poetry. Ian Wedde. ATNZ

Driving keel, cut from the forest—look—travels the current, The. A Boat Song. Saint Columbanus. NOIV

Driving late at night I pass. Sleep. Dana Naone. CDW

Driving Lesson. Michael Pettit. MOWH

Driving My Parents Home at Christmas. Robert Bly. CAPP

Driving Saw-Logs on the Plover. *Unknown.* AS

Driving south and travelling. Maintrunk Country Roadsong. Sam Hunt. PeNZ

Driving the new road to Buck's Lake. Coming of Age. John Logan. DiL

Driving through Coal Country in Pennsylvania. Jonathan Holden. GOYP

Driving through Farm Country at Sunset. Diane Ackerman. NIP

Driving through Minnesota during the Hanoi Bombings. Robert Bly. NoP

Driving through New England. Lucille Clifton. GOA

Driving through Tennessee. Charles Wright. CAPP

Driving to the Beach. Joanna Cole. RHPC

Driving to Town Late to Mail a Letter. Robert Bly. BoNaP; CAPP; HeIP; InPK; NaP; VGW

Driving toward the Lac Qui Parle River. Robert Bly. LCAP; NaP; NoP

Driving Wheel. Shirley Anne Williams. BlSi

Driving with my mother. For My Mother's Mother. Judith McDaniel. TV

Drizzling Easter Morning, A. Thomas Hardy. CMoP

Drone of airplane neared, and dimmed away, The. Immanent. Walter de la Mare. PoA

Drone *v.* Worker. Ebenezer Elliott. FaBoPV; OBSV

Droning a drowsy syncopated tune. The Weary Blues. Langston Hughes. FaBV; MoP; NoAM; NOBA; NoP; PoNe

Droop under doves' wings silent, breathing shapes. The Night Nurse Goes Her Round. John Gray. OBNC

Drooping, the labourer-ox. Winter ("Drooping, the labourer-ox"). James Thomson. *Fr.* The Seasons: Winter. FM

Drop a Pebble in the Water. James William Foley. BLPA

Drop a Stone. *Unknown.* PWR

Drop by drop, seventy-seven winters. Keso, *tr. by* Lucien Stryk *and* Takashi Ikemoto. ZPCJ

Drop by drop, the water clock drips sadly in the cold. A Deep Love. Mao Wen-hsi, *tr. by* Lois Fusek. ATF

Drop down, drop down, white snowflakes! Winter's Song. *Unknown.* BoTP

Drop, drop, slow tears. Phineas Fletcher. EIL; OBS; OxBSP

Drop fell on the apple tree, A. Emily Dickinson. BoNaP

Drop of Dew, A. Shmuel Halkin, *tr. fr. Yiddish by* Jacob Sonntag. TrJP

Drop of Ink, A. Joseph Ernest Whitney. AA

Drop of sepia in the fragrant vase, The. Dusk. Abraham Z. Lopez-Penha, *tr. by* Thomas Walsh. TrJP

Drop, one drop, how sweetly one fair drop, A. On Dives. Richard Crashaw. ACP

Drop the Wires. Hugh Seidman. AmPA

Droplet of Man, A. Hans Arp, *tr. fr. French by* Michael Benedikt. POS

Dropped leaf, The. Ruth Miller. *Fr.* Cycle. PeSA

Dropped petals of a broken lotus-moon. No Less than Prisoners. Frederick Thomas Bennett Macartney. CBAP

Dropped the door-bolt thong. *Unknown, tr. by* Geoffrey Bownas *and* Anthony Thwaite. PeBJV

Dropping back with the ball ripe in my palm. The Passer. George Abbe. SD

Dropping Your Aitches. Joseph Warren Beach. NYBP

Drops of dew. On the Impermanence of Life. Saigyo, *tr. fr. Japanese by* Burton Watson. *Fr.* Sixty-four Tanka. FCEI

Drops of Gall. Gabriela Mistral, *tr. fr. Spanish by* David Garrison. BoWoP

Drops of pattering rain, The. Jakuren, *tr. by* Geoffrey Bownas *and* Anthony Thwaite. PeBJV

Drosophila wing of the morning moon, The. Mushroom Hunting in Late August, Peterborough, N.H. Michael C. Blumenthal. MAYP

Drought. Oumar Ba, *tr. fr. French by* Kathleen Weaver. PBWP

Drought, The. Cheng Min, *tr. fr. Chinese by* Kai-yu Hsu. OV

Drought. David Holbrook. OxBTC

Drought. Frederick E. Laight. OBCV

Drought, The. Gary Soto. NoAM

Drought Breaks, The. Fleur Adcock. ATNZ

Drought Year. Judith Wright. NoAM

Drove-Road, The. W. W. Gibson. OxBTC

Drover, A. Padraic Colum. AnIL; AWP; MoBrPo; OBMV; RB

Droving Man. Thea Astley. PoAu-2

Drowned, The. David Bottoms. MT

Drowned, The. Norman MacCaig. OxBC

Drowned, The. Stephen Spender. MOS

Drowned at the Bottom of a Boring Dream. Joyce Mansour, *tr. fr. French by* Albert Herzing. DMF

Drowned Children, The. Louise Glück. HCAP

Drowned Lady, The. *Unknown.* ChTr

Drowned Mariner, The. Longfellow. AA

Drowned Sailor. Neufville Shaw. CaP

Drowning. Jacques Roubaud, *tr. fr. French by* Robert Kelly. RHTwFP

Drowning in Spain. Tom Schmidt. NeAC

Drowning is not so pitiful. Emily Dickinson. CMoP; OxBSP

Drowning of Conaing, The. *Unknown, tr. fr. Old Irish by* Frank O'Connor. AnIL

Drowsily come the sheep. Slumber Song. Louis V. Ledoux. FaPON

Drowsy Herodotus holds him there, The. Ancient Historian. Chris Wallace-Crabbe. PoAu-2

Drowsy sun went slowly to his rest, The. Evening. James Stephens. MoBrPo

Drug of the incomprehensible. The Bad Habit. Charles Henri Ford. EAS

Drug Store. Karl Shapiro. CMoP; OxBA; TwCP

Drugged. Walter de la Mare. BrPo

Drugs Made Pauline Vague. Stevie Smith. FaBoWP

Drugstore Conscience. Tristan Tzara, *tr. fr. French by* Michael Benedikt. POS

Druid, The. John Banister Tabb. AA

Druid Stones at Kensaleyre. Richard Hugo. AnAn

Drum. Langston Hughes. MoAmPo

Drum-footed black elephant's calf, The. What Her Friend Said Criticizing Him to Give Her Strength. Kuriyiraiyar, *tr. by* A. K. Ramanujan. PLW

Drum for Ben Boyd, A, *sel.* Francis Webb. Papuan Shepherd, A. PoAu-2

Drum Majah, De. Ray Garfield Dandridge. BANP

Drum on your drums, batter on your banjos. Jazz Fantasia. Carl Sandburg. AiP; MoAB; MoAmPo; PoNe

Drum sounds from the high city wall as the lampwick burns, The. Wang Kuo-wei, *tr. by* Ching-i Tu. WFTU

Drum that the watchman beats, The. *Unknown, tr. fr. Japanese. Fr.* Manyo Shu. Ma

Drum; the Narrative of the Demon of Tedworth, The. Dame Edith Sitwell. FaBoTw

Drum thumps, faraway, A. The House-Slave. Mervyn Morris. PBCV

Drumdelgie. *Unknown.* GBP

Drumdrumdrum, A. The Wall. Gwendolyn Brooks. *Fr.* Two Dedications. PoBA

"South of success and east of gloss and glass are." PoNe

Drumlin Prayer. Tom MacIntyre. CIP

Drumlin Woodchuck, A. Robert Frost. GoYe; NoAM; NOBA

Drummer-Boy and the Shepherdess, The ("Drummer-boy, drummer-boy, where is your drum?"). William Brighty Rands. MoShBr

Drummer Boy of Shiloh, The. *Unknown.* AmFP

Drummer Hodge. Thomas Hardy. AWP; BrPo; EBEV; GTBS-P; HAP; InPS; MoP; NAEL-2; NoAM; NOBVV; NoP; OBWP; WeW

Drumming and dancing in the gulley. *Unknown, tr. by* Arthur Waley. BoS

Drumochter. Anne B. Murray. PoSH

Drumrolled gusts of love. Summer. Javier Heraud, *tr. by* Maureen Ahern. Per

Drums. Martha Chosa. NOVW

Drums/ Then again drums. A. J. Seymour. PBCV

Drums and bells jingle. *Unknown, tr. by* Arthur Waley. BoS

Drums and horns rouse the river town. Shih Jun-chang, *tr. fr. Chinese by* William Shultz. *Fr.* Songs on Accompanying the Governor-General, I. WFTU

Drums gather and humble us beyond escape. Belief. A. R. Ammons. GOA

Drums in Scotland. Richard Hugo. LCAP

Drunk. Carroll Arnett. VoR

Drunk among the Flowers. Mao Wen-hsi, *tr. fr. Chinese by* Lois Fusek. ATF

Drunk and senseless in his place. Ramon. Bret Harte. BeLS

Drunk as drunk on turpentine. Pablo Neruda, *tr. by* Christopher Logue. BoLoP

Drunk, Climbing to the Peak of Iron Tomb on Wei Mountain. Li K'ai-hsien, *tr. fr. Chinese by* Jonathan Chaves. CoBLCP

Drunk, Facing Crimson Leaves. Po Chü-i, *tr. fr. Chinese by* Burton Watson. CoBCP

Drunk, he leans back in his boat. Wu Chen, *tr. fr. Chinese by* Jonathan Chaves. *Fr.* Paintings of Fishermen, II. CoBLCP

Drunk I have been. And drunk I was that night. To Laura Phelan: 1880-1906. Leon Stokesbury. MAYP; MT

Drunk in the Furnace, The. W. S. Merwin. CAPP; LiTM; MAT; MoP; NAAL-2; NePoEA-2; NoAM; NoP; PoE; SM; TwCP

Drunk Last Night with Friends, I Go to Work Anyway. Philip Dow. InPK; NPGG

Drunk Man Looks at the Thistle, A, *sels.* "Hugh MacDiarmid."
   "Dae what ye wull ye canna parry." EBEV
   Farewell to Dostoevski. NAEL-2
   Yet Ha'e I Silence Left. NAEL-2

Drunk with Pavese. Michael Waters. NAmP

Drunkard, A. Fei Ma, *tr. fr. Chinese by* Dominic Cheung. IFON

Drunkard, The. Philip Levine. NePoEA-2

Drunkard, The. Bible, *O.T. Fr.* Proverbs, XXIII: 29-35. TrJP

Drunkard and the Pig, The. *Unknown.* OBAL

Drunkard cannot meet a cork, A. Emily Dickinson. InPS

Drunkards, The. Malcolm Lowry. NYBP

Drunkards, The ("The drunkards are rolling in slowly"). Jalal ed-Din Rumi, *ad. fr. Persian by* Robert Bly. NU

Drunkard's Doom, The. *Unknown.* AS

Drunkard's Wife, The. Mary E. Tucker. CBWP-1

Drunken Americans. John Ashbery. HCAP

Drunken Dee, The. Syd Scroggie. PoSH

Drunken Fisherman, The. Robert Lowell. AmPP; CMoP; LiTA; LiTM; NOBA; OxBA; VGW

Drunken Gentleman, The. Hsüeh Chao-yün, *tr. fr. Chinese by* Lois Fusek. ATF

Drunken Gentleman, The. Ku Hsiung, *tr. fr. Chinese by* Lois Fusek. ATF

Drunken Gentleman, The. Yin O, *tr. fr. Chinese by* Lois Fusek. ATF

Drunken Lover. Owen Dodson. AmNP

Drunken Man, The. Steve Orlen. MAYP

Drunken night in my house with a, A. Dream Record: June 8, 1955. Allen Ginsberg. NOBA

Drunken Poem. David Helwig. NOBC

Drunken Rose, The. Amarou, *tr. fr. Sanskrit by* E. Powys Mathers. AWP

Drunken Satyr from Newton County Tells How He Met Daphne, A. Michael Burns. SoTCo

Drunken Stones of Prague, The. David Scheinert, *tr. fr. French by* Edouard Roditi. VWA

Drunken Streets. Malka Locker, *tr. fr. Yiddish by* Jeremy Garber. VWA

Drunken sun, The/ totters among the clouds. Orgy (That Is, Vegetable Market, at Sarno). Gina Labriola, *tr. by* Edgar Pauk. WPOW

Drunkenness of Pain, The. Aliza Shenhar, *tr. fr. Hebrew by* Linda Zisquit. VWA

Dry. Samuel Hoffenstein. BXAP

Dry August and warm. *Unknown.* FaBoUs

Dry brown coughing beneath their feet, The. Beverly Hills, Chicago. Gwendolyn Brooks. VGW

Dry earth near this salt sea, The. Laocoön. Wilson Harris. PBCV

Dry Gapa dingy general store. Western Town. David Wadsworth Cannon, Jr.. PoNe

Dry Leaves, Dry Leaves. *Unknown, tr. fr. Chinese by* Burton Watson. CoBCP

Dry leaves, soldier, dry leaves, dead leaves. The Wars. Conrad Aiken. *Fr.* The Soldier, I. WaaP

Dry Loaf. Wallace Stevens. NOBA; OxBA; PoRA

Dry-Point. Philip Larkin. CMoP

Dry River Bed. Andrew Salkey. PBCV

Dry Rock Number. Tina Reid. AIW

Dry Root in a Wash. Simon J. Ortiz. HATNAP

Dry Salvages, The. T. S. Eliot. *Fr.* Four Quartets. AiP; LiTB; NoP; OxBA; SeCePo

Dry vine leaves burn in an angle of the wall. The Thousand Things. Christopher Middleton. NePoEA-2

Dry Your Tears, Africa! Bernard Dadié, *tr. fr. French by* Donatus Ibe Nwoga. TTY

Dryad Song. Margaret Witter Fuller. WGRP

Dryad's home was once the tree, A. On Sivori's Violin. Frances Sargent Osgood. AA

Drynaun Dhun, The. *Unknown.* GBP

Du Bartas: His Divine Weeks and Works, *sels.* Joshua Sylvester.
   Fifth Day of the First Week, The.
      "Pretty lark, climbing the welkin clear." PBBP
   Seventh Day of the First Week, The.
      "There on his knee, behind a box tree shrinking." PBBP

Du bist wie eine Blume. Heine, *tr. fr. German.* *Fr.* Homeward Bound. AWP, *tr. by* Kate Freiligrath Kroeker.
   ("Thou Seemest Like a flower.") TrJP, *tr. by* Emma Lazarus.

Dual, The. Richard Lovelace. CaPo

Dual Site, The. Michael Hamburger. NePoEA-2; TwCP

Duality. Arthur Sherburne Hardy. AA

Duality. Katherine Thayer Hobson. GoYe

Dublin. Louis MacNeice. *Fr.* The Closing Album. CIP; FaBoPP; OBTV; OxBTC

Dublin Bay. Ewart Milne. NeIP

Dublin Made Me. Donagh MacDonagh. NeIP; OxBTC

Dublinesque. Philip Larkin. NoAM; OxBC

Dubrovnik Poem (Emilio Tolentino). Anthony Rudolf. VWA

Duc and Duchess de Guermantes loved Swann, The. Visit. Norman Dubie. *Fr.* The Duchess' Red Shoes, II. AnAn

"Ducats take, the! I'll sign the bond today." Two Argosies. Wallace Bruce. AA

Duchess after the Burial, The. Norman Dubie. *Fr.* The Duchess' Red Shoes, IV. AnAn

Duchess of Malfi, The, *sels.* John Webster. NAEL-1 *(complete)*
   Hark, Now Everything Is Still. *Fr.* IV, ii. ElL; HAP; NoP; OBD; QFR; SeCePo
      (Hark.) CH
      (Hearke, Now Every Thing Is Still.) OBS
      (Shrouding of the Duchess of Malfi, The.) NOBE; OBEV
   "I am come to make thy tomb." *Fr.* IV, ii. ChTr
   Madman's Song, The. *Fr.* IV, ii. ElL
      (Song: "O, let us howl some heavy note.") InvP
   "What death?" *Fr.* IV, ii. OBD
   "What hideous noyse was that?" *Fr.* IV, ii. PoEL-2
   "Yond's the Cardinall's window: This fortification." *Fr.* V, iii. PoEL-2

Duchess of York's Ghost, The. *Unknown.* APAS

Duchess' Red Shoes, The, *sels.* Norman Dubie. AnAn
   Duchess after the Burial, The. *Fr.* IV.
   "Swann had gone to the estate that afternoon to tell his." *Fr.* III.
   "Swann has visited the Duc and Duchess de Guermantes." *Fr.* I.
   Visit. *Fr.* II.

Duchess's Lullaby, The. "Lewis Carroll." *See* Alice's Adventures in Wonderland: Speak roughly to your little boy.

Duck, The. Richard Digance. RHPC

Duck. John Lyle Donaghy. BIrV

Duck, The. Edith King. BoTP

Duck, The. Ogden Nash. MoShBr; RB

Duck. Valerie Worth. NTCP

Duck and a drake, A. Mother Goose. OxNR

Duck, and Mallard first, the falconers onely sport, The. Michael Drayton. *Fr.* Polyolbion, Five and Twentieth Song. FM
   (Birds in the Fens.) ChTr

Duck and the Kangaroo, The. Edward Lear. ILY; OxBChV

Duck-chasing. Galway Kinnell. TwCP; VGW

Duck in Central Park. Frances Higginson Savage. GoYe

Duck Pond at Mini's Pasture, a Dozen Years Later, The. Philip Dow. AmPA; NPGG

Duck who had got such a habit of stuffing, A. The Notorious Glutton. Ann Taylor. OxBChV

Ducking: After Maupassant. Dave Smith. AnAn

Ducks. Norman Ault. BoTP

Ducks. Frederick William Harvey. OnUR
   "Yes, ducks are valiant things," *sel.* BoTP

Ducks along the reedy shore, The. Prince Shiki, *tr. fr. Japanese by* Hiroaki Sato. *Fr.* Manyo Shu. FCEI

Ducks are dabbling in the rain. Ducks in the Rain. James S. Tippett. RAR

Ducks are like our cousins, The. Rustic Landscape. Paul Snoek, *tr. by* James S. Holmes. DuIn

Ducks' Ditty. Kenneth Grahame. *Fr.* The Wind in the Willows. BoTP; FaPON; GoJo; MoShBr; NTCP; OxBChV; PDV; RHPC

Ducks in the Rain. James S. Tippett. RAR

Duckweed Pond. Wang Wei, *tr. fr. Chinese by* Burton Watson. CoBCP

Duct Tape Psalm. Greg Keeler. SoTCo

Dude Wrangler, The. Gail Gardner. CowP

Dudes. Nick Johnson. CowP

Due of the Dead, The. Thackeray. OBWP

Duel, The. Eugene Field. BeLS; CenHV; FaBoBe; FaFP; FaPON; FPL; MoShBr; OBAL; OBCA; OHFP; OnMSP; PoLF; PoRA; RHPC

Duel among the Roses. Paul Snoek. *tr. fr. Dutch by* Alasdair MacKinnon. DuIn

Duel in the Park. Lisa Grenelle. GoYe

Duel with Verses over a Great Man, *sels. Unknown, tr. fr. Hebrew.* TrJP
   "Against the guide of Truth."
   "Forgive us, son of Amram, be not wroth."
   "Here lies a man, and still no man."
   "Thou fool profane, be silent!"
   "Thou Guide to doubt, be silent evermore."
   "What thought ye to burn, when ye kindled the pyre."

Duelling Platitudes. Tom Disch. SoTCo

Duellist, The, *sel.* Charles Churchill.
   "First (entitled to the place), The." OBSV

Duenna, The, *sels.* Sheridan.
   "I ne'er could any lustre see." *Fr.* I, ii. NOEC
   "Give Isaac the nymph who no beauty can boast." NOIV

Duet. Ruth Krauss. RR

Duet, A. T. Sturge Moore. OBEV

Duet. Tennyson. *Fr.* Becket. GBL

Duet, The. Ella Wheeler Wilcox. AnAmPo

Dug-out, The. Siegfried Sassoon. CH; MoBrPo; OHIP; WaaP; WaP

Dugall Quin. *Unknown.* ESPB

Duino Elegies, *sels.* Rainer Maria Rilke, *tr. fr. German by* Stephen Mitchell.
   "Who, if I cried out, would hear me among the angels?." *Fr.* I. NAWM-2
   "Why, if this interval of being can be spent serenely." *Fr.* IX. NAWM-2

Duke Is the Lad to Frighten a Lass, The. Thomas Moore. TW

Duke o' Athole's Nurse, The ("As I gaed in by the Duke o' Athole's gates"). *Unknown.* OxBB

Duke of Athole's Nurse, The ("Where shall I gang, my ain true love?"). *Unknown.* ESPB

Duke of Athole's Nurse, The ("Ye are the Duke of Athol's nurse"). *Unknown.* ESPB

Duke of Buckingham, The. Pope. *Fr.* Moral Essays, Epistle III. NOBE
   (Death of Buckingham, The.) FiP

Duke of Gordon's Daughter, The ("The Duke of Gordon has three daughters"). *Unknown.* ESPB

Duke of Grafton, The. *Unknown.* ChTr; GBP

Duke of Marlborough, The. *Unknown.* OBET

Duke of Plaza-Toro, The. W. S. Gilbert. *Fr.* The Gondoliers. FaPON; FiBHP

Duke of York's Statue, The. Walter Savage Landor. FaBoEE

Duke William ("Duke William and a nobleman, heroes of England's nation"). *Unknown.* OxBSS

Duke William was a wench's son. Song of Duke William. Hilaire Belloc. FaBoNo

Duke's Song, The. Mary Sidney Wroth, Countess of Montgomery. *Fr.* Urania. WPE

Dulce et Decorum Est. Wilfred Owen. CMoP; DL; FaBoPV; FaBoTw; FaBV; FF; HeIP; HoPM; InPK; InvP; LiTB; LiTM; MMA; MoAB; MoBrPo; NAEL-2; NIP; NoAM; NoP; OAEL-2; OBWP; PoE; PPP; PrIm; TW; UnPo; WaP

Dulce it is, and *decorum*, no doubt, for the country to fall. Arthur Hugh Clough. *Fr.* Amours de Voyage, Canto II, ii. EBVV; FaBoPV

Dulcimer Maker. Carolyn Forché. SaC

Dulcinea walks. Christian Karlson Stead. *Fr.* Quesada, IV. ATNZ

Dull as I was, to think that a court fly. A Black Patch on Lucasta's Face. Richard Lovelace. CaPo; SeCP

"Dull day, A." Wait till Then. Mark Van Doren. SO

Dull evening in a run-down village, A. Earth Poem. Mahmoud Darwish, *tr. by* Abdullah al-Udhari. MPAW

Dull heap, that thus thy head above the rest dost rear. Stonehenge. Michael Drayton. *Fr.* Polyolbion, Third Song. FaBoPP

Dull Is My Verse. Walter Savage Landor. PoEL-4

Dull masses of dense green. Down the Mississippi. John Gould Fletcher. AmFN; LiTA

Dull people, A. From Colony to Nation. Irving Layton. NOBC

Dull soul aspire. To the Soul. John Collop. TrGrPo

Dull, Sullen Prisoners. Pope. *See* Elegy to the Memory of an Unfortunate Lady: Most souls, 'tis true, but peep out once an age.

Dull swish of runners. Landing. Antonia Pozzi, tr. by Brenda Webster. OV

Dull to myself and almost dead to these. The Bad Season Makes the Poet Sad. Robert Herrick. CaPo; LiTB; NAEL-1; PrIm

Dull unwashed windows of eyes. A Poem Some People Will Have to Understand. Imamu Amiri Baraka. BPo; NOBA

Dulled by the slow glare of the yellow bulb. A Wartime Dawn. David Gascoyne. LiTM

Dullest people I knew, The. When I Was Dying. William Hathaway. UL

Dum Vivimus Vigilamus. Charles Henry Webb. AA

Dumain's Rhymes. Shakespeare. *See* Love's Labour's Lost: On a Day— Alack the Day.

Dumb,/ Bloodied, the severed. A Grafted Tongue. John Montague. BIrV; CIP

Dumb are the trumpets, cymbals. Solomon. Heine, tr. by Emma Lazarus. TrJP

Dumb Dick. Leslie A. Fiedler. ErPo

Dumb genius blows. From Another Room. Gregory Corso. NeAP

Dumb Oxen. Sister Mary Madeleva. *Fr.* Of Mary. CRP

Dumb Soldier, The. Robert Louis Stevenson. OxBChV

Dumb World, The. W. H. Davies. OBWVE; OxBTC

Dumbfounding, The. Margaret Avison. NOBC

Dumbo rescue report: the weather was dirty. Time Zones for Forty-four. Donald A. Stauffer. WaP

Dummer the shepherd sacrific'd. Cotton Mather. SCAP

Dummy, 51, to Go to Museum. Ventriloquist Dead at 75. May Swenson. BAP

Dump, The. Greg Kuzma. PoA

Dumplings before cherries. Teitoku, tr. by Geoffrey Bownas and Anthony Thwaite. PeBJV

Dumpy and obese—a woman. Israel Efrat, tr. fr. Hebrew by Bernhard Frank. *Fr.* Written in a Public Restaurant. MHeP

Dumpy Ducky. Lucy Larcom. OBCA

Dun-Colour [or Dun-Color]. Ruth Pitter. FM; PoRA

Dunbar. Anne Spencer. BANP; CDC

Duncan and his brother was playing pool. Brady. *Unknown.* AS

Duncan Gray ("Can ye [or you] play me Duncan Gray"). Burns. CoMu; ErPo

Duncan Gray ("Duncan Gray cam here to woo"). Burns. GoTS; GTBS; GTBS-P

Dunce, The. Walter de la Mare. ImOP

Dunce, The. Jacques Prévert, tr. fr. French by Lawrence Ferlinghetti. RHTwFP

Dunce, The. *Unknown.* OxNR

Dunce Song 6. Mark Van Doren. DuDa

Dunciad, The, *sels.* Pope.
  Carnations and Butterflies. NOEC
  "Mighty mother, and her son who brings, The." *Fr.* I. OBSV; PoE
  "Next bidding all draw near on bended knees." *Fr.* IV. OBSV
  Triumph of Dullness [or Dulness], The. *Fr.* IV. EBEV; FaBoPV; FiP; NOBE; NOEC; NoP; SCV
  (Reign of Chaos, The.) FiP
  "Yet, yet a moment, one dim ray of light." *Fr.* IV. NAEL-1; OAEL-1; PoEL-3
  Young Traveller Is Presented to the Goddess Dulness, A. *Fr.* IV. NOEC

Dunciad Minor, *sels.* A. D. Hope.
  "Now Muse assist me, aptly to describe." *Fr. bk.* V. BXAP
  On Shakespeare Critics. *Fr. bk.* V. OxBC

Dundonnel Mountains. Andrew Young. PoSH

Dunes are graying that were blackest. Aubade: The Desert. Frederick Bock. PoA

Dungeon horrible, on all sides round, A. Milton. *Fr.* Paradise Lost, *Bk.* I, *ll.* 61-74. OBD

Dunlavin Green. *Unknown.* FaBoBa

Dunmow Flitch of Bacon, The. *Unknown.* OBET

Dunna thee tell me it's his'n, mother. Whether or Not. D. H. Lawrence. MoBrPo

Dunno speak, dunno laugh, Tommy, husht. Sorrowin.' Joseph Ramsbottom. PF

Duns Scotus's Oxford. Gerard Manley Hopkins. EBEV; EyDe; FaBoPP; GTBS-P; NAEL-2; NoAM; OBMV; PoEL-5

Duomo, Milan. Raymond Henri. *Fr.* View of the Cathedral. EyDe

Duplicity of Women, The. John Lydgate. MeEL

Durable Material. Hans Vlek, tr. fr. Dutch by James S. Holmes. DuIn

Duraluminum dove dives, The. Summary of the Distance between the Bomber and the Objective. Walter Benton. WaP

Durand of Blonden. Ludwig Uhland, tr. fr. German by James Clarence Mangan. AWP

Durban, Birmingham. Question and Answer. Langston Hughes. BPo

Dürer; Innsbruck, 1495. "Ern Malley." CBAP

Dürer would have seen a reason for living. The Steeple-Jack. Marianne Moore. *Fr.* Part of a Novel, Part of a Poem, Part of a Play. BoWoP; CMoP; FaBoMo; FaBoWP; HAP; InPS; NoAM; NOBA; NoP; OxBA; PBWP; WeW; WPE

Durham. Tony Harrison. NoAM

"Durham," "Devonia," "Allendale,"—their houses, those. A Summer Cloud. Waldo Williams, tr. by Joseph P. Clancy. OBWVE

Durham Field. *Unknown.* ESPB

Durham Lock-out, The. *Unknown.* CoMu

Durham Old Women. *Unknown.* GBP

Duriesdyke. Swinburne. OxBB

During a Bombardmant by V-Weapons. Roy Fuller. OxBSP

During December's Death. Delmore Schwartz. NYBP

During dinner, out on the balcony. Indian Summer. Leo Vroman, tr. by James S. Holmes. DuIn

During His Courtship. Charles Wesley. NOCV

During Music. Arthur Symons. NOBVV

During my glorious. Distraction. A. R. Ammons. CAPP

During one period I remember. Eveningsong 2. Ramona Wilson. VoR

During the Day He Held a Low-level Position. Wilhelm Szabo, tr. fr. German by Beth Bjorklund. CoAuP

During the Depression my grandmother. One Foot in the Door. Anne Elder. CBAP

During the early winter. Poem for Shane on Her Brother's Birthday. Donald T. Sanders. TTTS

During the ebb I wrote words in the sand. Fame. Kahlil Gibran, tr. by Adnan Haydar and Michael Beard. MAP

During the Great Debates, he tried a joke. Campaign Promise. Henry Taylor. TW

During the holidays. Holidays. Eva Mylonas, tr. by Kimon Friar. BoWoP

During the Pageant at Medicine Lodge. Charles G. Ballard. NOVW; VoR

During the plague I came into my own. Tarantula or the Dance of Death. Anthony Hecht. CoAP; OBD

During the season of cut organs we. Initiation. Jayne Cortez. PoBA

During the third mile. Joan Benoit. Rina Ferrarelli. ASP

During the War. Marvin Bell. CAPP

During the winter she began. Division. John Ratti. NYBP

During Wind and Rain. Thomas Hardy. CMoP; ELP; GTBS-P; HAP; Mes; NAEL-2; NIP; OAEL-2; OxBTC; PoE; PPP; QFR; TEP; TOF

Dusk. Guillaume Apollinaire, tr. fr. French by Dudley Fitts. RHTwFP

Dusk. Ken Belford. NeAC

Dusk. Angelina Weld Grimké. CDC

Dusk. James Harrison. TDD

Dusk. Maruyama Kaoru, tr. fr. Japanese by Hiroaki Sato. FCEI

Dusk. Abraham Z. Lopez-Penha, tr. fr. Spanish by Thomas Walsh. TrJP

Dusk. Gabriela Mistral, tr. fr. Spanish by David Garrison. BoWoP

Dusk. Marcia Southwick. MAYP

Dusk./ Above the/ water hang the. Swan and Shadow. John Hollander. InPK; NoP; PoA

Dusk/ no dawns, and silver linings. No Dawns. Julianne Perry. PoBA

Dusk comes on. Desert Wind. Malka Heifetz-Tussman, tr. by Kathryn Hellerstein. AYP

Dusk descends early in midday. What Is Your Life? Hannu Mäkelä, tr. by Aili Jarvenpa. SOP

Dusk falls with a chill. Winter. Masayori, tr. by Steven D. Carter. WFTW

Dusk falters over shelf and chair. God Save the Stock. Charles Spear. ATNZ

Dusk, first lights coming on. Window-Dreaming with SAS. Haim Guri, tr. by Warren Bargad and Stanley F. Chyet. IP

Dusk grew on the window. Taking the Train Home. William Matthews. GeTw

Dusk in the Country. Harry Edmund Martinson, tr. fr. Swedish by Robert Bly. RB

Dusk in the Domain. Dorothea MacKellar. PoAu-1

Dusk in the still yard, cut from the same pattern. Tune: Bitter Longing. Wu Tsao, tr. by Julie Landau. WFTU

Dusk in Winter. W. S. Merwin. NaP

Dusk: Mallards on the Charles River. Michael C. Blumenthal. BLA

Dusk of Horses, The. James Dickey. LiTM; NYBP

Dusk over the lake. Virgil Hutton. InPK

Dusk over the lake. Dusk. James Harrison. TDD

Dusk Song. William H. A. Moore. BANP

Dusk, the sea is between colors. Postcard. Pamela Stewart. NAmP

Dusk was best. Searching. Shooting. B. H. Fairchild. TDD

Dusky night rides down the sky, The. Hunting Song. Henry Fielding. *Fr.* Don Quixote in England. OxBoLi

Dust. "Æ." WGRP

Dust. Rupert Brooke. MoBrPo; OxBTC

Dust. Waring Cuney. CDC

Dust, The. Gertrude Hall. AA

Dust. P. A. Ropes. BoTP

Dust. André Spire, *tr. fr. French by* Jethro Bithell. TrJP

Dust. Kathleen Spivack. BoWoP

Dust. Randolph Hughes. CBAP; PoAu-2

Dust,/ Through which. Dust. Waring Cuney. CDC

Dust always blowing about the town. A Peck of Gold. Robert Frost. PDV; SO

Dust and clay. Ascension-Hymn ("Dust and clay"). Henry Vaughan. SeCV-1; TrCP

Dust as we are, the immortal spirit grows. Wordsworth. *Fr.* The Prelude [or, Growth of a Poet's Mind]: Childhood and School-Time. SCV

Dust Bowl. Robert A. Davis. IDB

Dust Bowl. Langston Hughes. PoA

Dust cools easily. South Texas Summer Rain. Rebecca Gonzales. AiP

Dust has settled on the walls, The. The Dust Is Upon Us. N. M. Rashed, *tr. by* Mahmood Jamal. PBMUP

Dust Hath Closed Helen's Eye. Thomas Nashe. *See* Summer's Last Will and Testament: Adieu, Farewell, Earth's Bliss[e].

Dust in the room, The. Deserted Room. Erich Fried, *tr. by* Beth Bjorklund. CoAuP

Dust Is Upon Us, The. N. M. Rashed, *tr. fr. Urdu by* Mahmood Jamal. PBMUP

Dust now is the old-fashioned house. Hart Crane. AnAn

Dust of all the saints of the ages, The. Cymru. David Gwenallt Jones, *tr. by* Gwyn Jones. OBWVE

Dust of Snow. Robert Frost. CMoP; MoShBr; OxBA; OxBSP; PDV; PrIm; RHPC; SoSe; TAP; UnPo; WeW

Dust of Timas, The. Sappho, *tr. fr. Greek by* E. A. Robinson. AWP

Dust on my hair and face. Irrigation. Susan Tichy. MAYP

Dust on Spring Street. Louis Grudin. NoP

Dust silvers and a wind from the corner, The. Dark Centre. Norman MacCaig. NPo

Dust thou art, but dust carefully. Ralph Hodgson. *Fr.* Flying Scrolls. FaBoTw

Dust to Dust. Walter de la Mare. TrPWD

Dust to Dust. Thomas Hood. NBLV

Dust Will Settle, The. Luci Tapahonso. STE

Duster, dust away, my friend. Dust. André Spire, *tr. by* Jethro Bithell. TrJP

Dusting. Rita Dove. HCAP; MAYP

Dusting of the Books, The. Dorothy Hughes. GoYe

Dusting off the board, I sit down happily to play. Wei-ch'i Chess. Li K'ai-hsien, *tr. by* Jonathan Chaves. CoBLCP

Dustman, The. Clive Sansom. BoTP

Dustman, The. *Unknown.* BoTP

Dusty Answer, A. George Meredith. *See* Modern Love: Thus piteously Love closed what he begat.

Dusty light falls through windows. Cities behind Glass. Linda Hogan. STE

Dusty road is mine to tread, A. Pedlar Jim. Florence Hoare. BoTP

Dutch, The. George Canning. *See* In matters of commerce the fault of the Dutch.

Dutch April. Daniel Halpern. GrPl

Dutch in the Medway, The. Andrew Marvell. *Fr.* The Last Instructions to a Painter. OBS

Dutch Interior. May Sarton. SM

Dutch Lover, The, *sels.* Aphra Behn.
  Amyntas Led Me to a Grove. ErPo
  "Ah false Amyntas, can that hour." WPE

Dutch Lullaby, A. Eugene Field. *See* Wynken, Blynken, and Nod.

Dutch Picture, A. Longfellow. MoShBr

Dutch Proverb, A. Matthew Prior. FaBoEE; NOEC

Dutch Seacoast. Kenneth Slessor. *Fr.* The Atlas. PoAu-2

Dutch Ship. Rai San'yo, *tr. fr. Chinese by* Burton Watson. JLIC-2

Dutchess of Monmouth's Lamentation for the Loss of Her Duke, The. *Unknown.* CoMu; FaBoBa

Dutty Tough. Louise Bennett. PVCV

Duty. Arthur Hugh Clough. EBVV

Duty. Emerson. *Fr.* Voluntaries, III. FaFP; GN

Duty. Ellen S. Hooper. BLPA

Duty, or Truth at Work. Lizelia Augusta Jenkins Moorer. CBWP-3

Duty—that's to say, complying. Duty. Arthur Hugh Clough. EBVV

Duty to Death, LD. Dick Roberts. WaP

Dvonya. Louis Simpson. NNaP; NOBA

Dwainie. James Whitcomb Riley. *Fr.* The Flying Islands of the Night. AA

Dwarf barefooted, chanting, The. The Peasants. Alun Lewis. LiTM

Dwarf of Disintegration. Oscar Williams. LiTM; PoCH

Dwarf of the Hill Caves, The. Lupenga Mphande. WMBCH

Dwarf pines; the wild plum on the wind-grassed shore. Colloquy with a King-Crab. John Peale Bishop. LiTA

Dwarfed limb, A. The Copperhead. David Bottoms. MAYP

Dwell, awful Silence, on the shady hills. Pan Piping. Plato, *tr. by* Thomas Stanley. FaBoEE

Dwelling, The. Moshe Dor, *tr. fr. Hebrew by* Dennis Johnson. VWA

Dwelling-Place, The. Henry Vaughan. MeLP; OBS; TrPWD; WGRP

Dwellings of Our Dead, The. Arthur H. Adams. ATNZ

Dwindling Forest of Arden, The. Michael Drayton. *Fr.* Polyolbion, Thirteenth Song. FaBoPP

D'ye ken John Peel with his coat so gay [*or* gray]? John Peel. John Woodcock Graves. CH; OxBoLi; SD

D'ye ken the big village of Balmaquhapple. The Village of Balmaquhapple. James Hogg. FaBoCo; FaBoPP

Dyer, The. *Unknown.* ChTr; OxNR

Dying. A. Alvarez. VWA

Dying. Adah Isaacs Menken. CBWP-1

Dying. Robert Pinsky. HCAP; MAYP

Dying. John Stigall. CRP

Dying Airman, The. *Unknown.* AS, *with music*; FaBoNo; FaFP; OxBoLi; RB

Dying: An Introduction. L. E. Sissman. NYBP

Dying Animals, The. Gavin Ewart. OBD

Dying at the Edge of Death. Hameed Said, *tr. fr. Arabic by* Diana Der Hovanessian *and* Lena Jayyusi. MAP

Dying Away. William Meredith. NoAM

Dying Californian, The. *Unknown.* AmFP

Dying Child, The. John Clare. EnRP; TrGrPo

Dying Child's Request, The. Hannah Flagg Gould. OBCA

Dying Christian to His Soul, The. Pope. *See* Vital spark of heavenly flame!

Dying Cowboy, The ("As I rode out by Tom Sherman's bar-room"). *Unknown.* FaBoBa

Dying Cowboy, The. *Unknown.* *See* "O [*or* Oh] bury me not on the lone prairie."

Dying day pinches the tot. Daily News. Tom Clark. EAS

Dying Father's Farewell, The. Berryman Hicks. *See* Time Is Swiftly Rolling On, The.

Dying firelight slides along the quirt, A. The End of the Weekend. Anthony Hecht. FaBoMo; HAP; LiTM; NePoEA-2; SM; WeW

Dying Garden, The. Howard Nemerov. Psk

Dying Gaul, The, *sel.* Desmond O'Grady. BIrV
  "Day concludes burning, The." CIP

Dying Girl, The. Mary Weston Fordham. CBWP-2

Dying Gladiator, The. Byron. *Fr.* Childe Harold's Pilgrimage, IV. NOBE

Dying Hobo, The. *Unknown.* AmFP

Dying Hogger, The. *Unknown.* AS

Dying in the Street. Amryl Johnson. WS

Dying Indian, The. Joseph Warton. NOEC

Dying Lamp, The. Li Chien, *tr. fr. Chinese by* Hsin-sheng C. Kao. WFTU

Dying Lover, The. Richard Henry Stoddard. AnAmPo

Dying Man in His Garden, The. George Sewell. GTBS; GTBS-P

Dying Mine Brakeman, The. Orville Jenks. AmFP

Dying—or so one heard. In Memoriam M. Tambimuttu. Derek Stanford. NPo

Dying Prostitute, The; an Elegy. Thomas Holcroft. NOEC

Dying Sergeant, The. *Unknown.* AmFP

Dying Speech of an Old Philosopher. Walter Savage Landor. *See* Last Fruit Off an Old Tree, The: I Strove with None.

Dying Stockman, The. *Unknown.* PoAu-1

Dying sun, shine warm a little longer! Lament for Pasiphae. Robert Graves. FaBoTw

Dying Swan, The. T. Sturge Moore. OBMV; SeCePo

Dying Swan, The. Tennyson. PBBP; WiR

Dying Swan, The. *Unknown.* ChTr

Dying Thief. Itzig Manger, *tr. fr. Yiddish by* Stephen Garrin. VWA

Dying tiger—moaned for drink, A. Emily Dickinson. InPK

Dying Times, The. Ross Knox. CowP

Dying under a Fall of Stars. Mark Elliott Shapiro. VWA

Dying Viper, A. "Michael Field." FM

Dying Wife to Her Husband, A. Moses ibn Ezra, *tr. fr. Hebrew.* TrJP

Dying Words of Stonewall Jackson, The. Sidney Lanier. PAH
Dying Year, The. Clara Ann Thompson. CBWP-2
Dyke-Builder, The. Henry Treece. LiTB; WaP
Dykes, The. Kipling. OBWP
Dykes in the Garden. Sharon Barba. PeHV
Dylan, Who Is Dead. Samuel Allen. PoBA
Dynamite Song. *Unknown.* AmFP
Dynasts, The, *sels.* Thomas Hardy.
  After Jena. *Fr. pt.* II, Act I, sc. vii. WaaP
  Albuera. *Fr. pt.* II, Act VI, sc. iv. WaaP
  Boatman's Song, The. *Fr. pt.* I, Act V, sc. vii. WaaP
  Budmouth Dears. *Fr. pt.* III, Act II, sc. i. CH
  Eve of Waterloo, The. *Fr. pt.* III, Act VI, sc. viii. OAEL-2; OBWP
    (Before Waterloo.) MoAB
  Field of Talavera, The. *Fr. pt.* II, Act IV, sc. iv. CMoP
  Field of Waterloo, The. FaBoCh
    (Chorus of the Years.) CMoP
    ("Yes, the coneys are scared by the thud of hoofs.") WaaP
  Men Who March Away. *Fr. pt.* I, Act I, sc. i. CH
  Night of Trafalgar, The. *Fr. pt.* I, Act V, sc. vii. ChTr; FaBoCh;
    MoBrPo; MOS; OBMV
    (Trafalgar.) CH
Dyvers dothe use as I have heard and kno. Sir Thomas Wyatt. *See*
  Divers Doth Use.
Dyvers thy death doo dyverslye bemone. Earl of Surrey. *See* Divers thy
  death do diversely bemoan.

E

E/ ee/ eei/ eeio. Perfection. Ernst Jandl, *tr. by* Beth Bjorklund. CoAuP
E/ it almost twelve. Sticky Fingers. Robert Grenier. IAT
E=MC^2. Morris Bishop. ImOP
E Flat. Peter Olds. ATNZ
E hó hì ura bhì. Waulking Song: Two. Minnie Bruce Pratt. GLP
E. Jarvis-Thribb (17) and Keith's Mum. On the Tercentenary of Milton's
  Death. Gavin Ewart. OxBC
E. K.'s Will. Sandor Csoori, *tr. fr. Hungarian by* Jascha Kessler.
  FOC
E ou o youyou you i e ou o, A. Bonita. Tristan Tzara, *tr. by* Michael
  Benedikt. POS
E. P. Ode Pour l'Election de Son Sepulchre. Ezra Pound. *See* Hugh
  Selwyn Mauberley. (Life and Contacts): For three years, out of key
  with his time.
E Questo il Nido in Che la Mia Fenice? A. D. Hope. OxBC
E-ri-e, The. *Unknown.* AS
E stands for egg. Hilaire Belloc. *Fr.* A Moral Alphabet. NoAM
E Tenebris. Oscar Wilde. BrPo; MoBrPo; NAEL-2; Son; TIRV; TrPWD
È, the Feasting Florentines. Daniel Hoffman. VGW
E Uni Que A The Hi A Tho, Father. Roberta Hill. VoR
'E was sittin' on a door-step. The Road to Vagabondia. Dana Burnet.
  PoLF
'E was warned agin 'er. The Sergeant's Weddin.' Kipling. OxBTC
Each a Part of All. Augustus Wright Bamberger. WBLP
Each and All. Emerson. AA; AmPP; AnAmPo; AWP; BLPL; NAAL-1;
  NOBA; OHFP; OxBA; TAP; WGRP
Each beast can choose his fere according to his mind. Of a Lady That
  Refused to Dance with Him. Earl of Surrey. SiPS
Each Bird Walking. Tess Gallagher. FaBoWP; MAYP; SV
Each birthday wish. The Wish. Ann Friday. RAR
Each body has its art, its precious prescribed. "Still Do I Keep My Look,
  My Identity. ." Gwendolyn Brooks. PoA
Each care-worn face is but a book. The Strangers. Jones Very.
  AnAmPo; OxBA
Each dawn is clear. Gary Snyder. *Fr.* Myths and Texts: Logging, VIII.
  NaP
Each Day. David Ignatow. NNaP
Each Day. Sister Maura. CRP
Each day, a certain hour. In Disguise. Joseph Rolnik, *tr. by* Keith
  Bosley. VWA
Each day brings its toad, each night its dragon. Jerome. Randall Jarrell.
  PPP
Each Day Does That. Jon Anderson. NAmP
Each day I live, each day the sea of light. Poem against the Rich.
  Robert Bly. NOBA
Each day I walk with wonder. Clinton Scollard. TrPWD
Each day into the upper air. Election Reflection. M. Keel Jones.
  NBLV
Each day is a full. After My Grandmother's Death. Michele Roberts.
  AIW
Each day is an iceberg. Nightdream. Charles Wright. CAPP; LCAP

Each day the earth turns, each day. As for Me, I Delight in the Everyday
  Way. Joseph Stroud. NPGG
Each day the tide withdraws; chills us; pastes. Wreaths. Geoffrey Hill.
  PoA
Each day was like another. Ballad of the Hidden Dragon. *Unknown.*
  WTO
Each day's morning tastes of thinking of you. Every Day that I Love
  You. Teresita Fernández, *tr. by* Margaret Randall. AIW
Each dockpost comes with a pelican. Clearwater Beach, Florida.
  William Matthews. BLA
Each evening, shortly after sunset. The Migration of Darkness. Peter
  Payack. BWV
Each face in the street is a slice of bread. Bread. W. S. Merwin. EAS
Each face its own phantom. Cartagena de Indias. Earle Birney. MoCV
Each Found Himself at the End Of. . . Ebbe Borregaard. NeAP
Each gesture. A Reason. Robert Creeley. NaP
Each golden note of music greets. Moonlight Song of the Mocking-Bird.
  William Hamilton Hayne. AA
Each grain of sand has an architecture, but. Proposition II. Keith
  Waldrop. InPK
Each hour has some glory all its own. The Hour's Glory. Henrietta
  Cordelia Ray. CBWP-3
Each house had its ghost. Sigmund Freud. Howard Nemerov. PoA
Each in His Own Tongue. William Herbert Carruth. BLPA; OHFP;
  WBLP; WGRP
Each is beautiful. Tell Our Daughters. Besmilr Brigham. IHMS
Each known mile comes late. The Train Runs Late to Harlem. Conrad
  Kent Rivers. IDB; PoBA
Each lover's longing leads him naturally. To Dante Alighieri: He
  Interprets Dante's Dream. Cino da Pistoia, *tr. by* Dante Gabriel
  Rossetti. AWP
Each man has/ his own way. The End Bit. Jim Burns. FF
Each man me telleth I change most my devise. Sir Thomas Wyatt. SiPS
Each man to his forced march; this is mine. Hitchhiker. Jack Marshall.
  NYBP
Each moment. Wind and Impulse. Duane Big Eagle. STE
Each moment of the long-liv'd day. Catullus, *tr. by* Tom Brown. OBVE
Each More Melodious Note I Hear. Henry David Thoreau. OxBSP
Each Morning. Amiri Baraka. *Fr.* Hymn for Lanie Poo. IDB; PoBA
Each morning a wren comes. Kaai Chigetsu, *tr. fr. Japanese by* Hiroaki
  Sato. *Fr.* Thirteen Hokku. FCEI
Each morning the birds awake me. Morning Vigil. Phillip William
  George. VoR
Each morning they bring me the condemned man's brekker. Analogy.
  Brian Higgins. FaBoTw
Each morning when I lit the coke furnace. The Morgue. James Keir
  Baxter. ATNZ
Each night for seven nights beyond the gulf. The Oleaster. Robert
  Graves. OBTV
Each night I send off several newly built ships. Recent Status. Park Je-
  chun, *tr. by* Koh Chang-soo. ACKP
Each night this house sinks into the shadows. Shadows. Linda Pastan.
  BLA
Each object by a few short years how changed! A Visit to the Author's
  Paternal Seat. Richard Polwhele. *Fr.* The Influence of Local
  Attachment. NOEC
Each of the dozen saints is bound. Martyrdom: A Love Poem. Bin
  Ramke. KS
Each of them must have terrified. In Memory of the Utah Stars. William
  Matthews. GeTw; MAYP; Psk
Each of us is like Balboa: once in all our lives do we. Rare Moments.
  Charles Henry Phelps. AA
Each of us like you. Adonis. Hilda Doolittle ("H. D."). AWP; LiTA
Each pale Christ stirring underground. Words for a Resurrection. Leo
  Kennedy. OBCV
Each person lies in their bed, restless. Tonight Everyone in the World Is
  Dreaming the Same Dream. Susan Litwack. VWA
Each poet with a different talent writes. Earl of Roscommon. *Fr.* An
  Essay on Translated Verse. FaBoUs
Each prisoner is so sad in the glare. The Line-up. Joan Swift. SM
Each Saturday, our father downtown to work. Arrowhead Christian Center
  and No-Smoking Luncheonette. Janet Sylvester. MAYP
Each shining light above us. The Light of Love. John Hay. AnAmPo
Each soldier as he passes looks at their breasts. Namkwin Pul. Bernard
  Gutteridge. WaP
Each storm-soaked flower has a beautiful eye. Rain. Vachel Lindsay.
  CMoP
Each subtlety hard for the pedant to solve. Coming Across. Mehri, *tr.
  by* Deirdre Lashgari. WPOW
Each time a star falls. The Famous Archer. Park Je-chun, *tr. by* Koh
  Chang-soo. ACKP
Each time a wave rolls in. Buson, *tr. fr. Japanese by* Hiroaki Sato. *Fr.*
  Eighty-seven Hokku. FCEI

Each time, greenbones, you pressed the neat trigger. Boy at Target Practice; a Contemplation. W. R. Moses. NYBP

Each time he gives a thrust, the juice squishes. *Unknown, tr. by* Hiroaki Sato. FCEI

Each time his will abdicated. Possession. Lynne Lawner. ErPo

Each time I return to this place. The Marsh. Marcia Southwick. MAYP

Each time I send you into the sky. Preparing for Weather. Carole Oles. BLA

Each time the doors to her room were opened. Combing My Hair in the Hall. Alberto Rios. NAmP

Each time they break. Kaneyoshi, *tr. by* Steven D. Carter. WFTW

Each time they meet, they make squishy noises. *Unknown, tr. by* Hiroaki Sato. FCEI

Each time they roll in. Shiba Sonome, *tr. fr. Japanese by* Hiroaki Sato. *Fr.* Fifteen Hokku. FCEI

Each time we lose grief, friend, we are free from joy & cross into eternity. Goodbye "Hello." Philip Dow. NPGG

Each to Each. Melville Cane. GoYe

Each traveller prays, "Let me be far from any." Journey to Iceland. W. H. Auden. OBTV; PoA

Each way the turn. The Turn. Robert Creeley. LCAP

Each with each has borne in patience. To Edom. Heine. TrJP

Each writes long letters. Absent Friends. Anne Bloch. *Fr.* Separation. Mes

Each year for a short season. Folk Wisdom. Thomas Kinsella. TwCP

Each year I have a birthday. A Giant's Cake. Evelina San Garde. BoTP

Each year on this day. Blood River Day. Dennis Brutus. WMBCH

Each year, the court expands. The Old Pro's Lament. Paul Petrie. TAP

Eachie, peachie, pearie, plum. *Unknown.* GBP

Eadwacer. *Unknown, tr. fr. Anglo-Saxon.* PBWP, *tr. by* Kemp Malone; WPE

(Wulf and Eadwacer.) BoWoP, *tr. by* Willis Barnstone *and* Elene Kolb; CIP, *ad. by* Richard Ryan; TrGrPo

Eager he look'd. Another train of years. Joel Barlow. *Fr.* The Columbiad, X. AmPP

Eager note on my door said "Call me," The. Frank O'Hara. CAPP; EAS; NoAM; NoBA

Eager Spring. Gordon Bottomley. MoBrPo

Eager Street. Kendra Kopelke. AiP

Eager to breathe out. Mocking Song against Qaqortingneq. Piuvkaq. WTO

Eagerly/ Like a woman hurrying to her lover. Four Glimpses of Night. Frank Marshall Davis. AmNP; NoP; PoBA; PoNe

Eagle, An. Umar Abu Risha, *tr. fr. Arabic by* Issa Boullata *and* Thomas G. Ezzy. MAP

Eagle. Tom Bowker. PoSH

Eagle, The. "Fiona Macleod." *Fr.* Transcripts from Nature. FM

Eagle. Robin Skelton. NOBC

Eagle, The. Tennyson. BoTP; CH; FaBoCh; FaPON; FF; FiP; FM; GN; GoJo; GTBS-P; HeIP; InPK; NAEL-2; NOBVV; NoP; NTCP; OAEL-2; OxBSP; PBBP; PDV; PrIm; RHPC; SeCePo; TrGrPo; UnPo; WiR

Eagle, The. Andrew Young. PoSH

Eagle above Us, The. Santiago Altamirano, *tr. fr. Cora Indian by* Anselm Hollo. STP

Eagle and the Beetle, The. La Fontaine, *tr. fr. French by* Elizur Wright. OBVE

Eagle and the Mole, The. Elinor Wylie. AWP; BoWoP; LiTA; LiTM; MoAB; MoAmPo; UnPo

Eagle and Vulture, The. Thomas Buchanan Read. PAH

Eagle, did ye see him fall, The? The Eagle's Fall. Charles Goodrich Whiting. AA

Eagle-Feather Fan, The. N. Scott Momaday. CDW; STE

Eagle for an Emperor. Falconry. Anne Wilkinson. MoCV; OBCV

Eagle has moved down to the foot of the mountain, The. An Eagle. Umar Abu Risha, *tr. by* Issa Boullata *and* Thomas G. Ezzy. MAP

Eagle in New Mexico, *sel.* David Herbert Lawrence.

"Towards the sun, towards the south-west." RB

Eagle is my power, The. The Eagle-Feather Fan. N. Scott Momaday. CDW; STE

Eagle of Corinth, The. Henry Howard Brownell. PAH

Eagle of Pengwern. *Unknown, tr. fr. Welsh by* Gwyn Williams. PBWP

Eagle of the armies of the West, The. The Flight of the War-Eagle. Obadiah Cyrus Auringer. AA

Eagle of the Blue, The. Herman Melville. AA

Eagle Plain. Robert Francis. AmFN

Eagle Poem. Joy Harjo. HATNAP

Eagle so caught in some bursting cloud, An. Shelley. *Fr.* Prometheus Unbound. PBBP

Eagle soars in the summit of heaven, The. T. S. Eliot. *Fr.* The Rock. OBMV

Eagle Song. Gordon Bottomley. *Fr.* Suilven and the Eagle. MoBrPo

Eagle, stooping from yon snow-blown peaks, The. Whittier. GOA

Eagle That Is Forgotten, The. Vachel Lindsay. AWP; CMoP; LiTA; MoAB; MoAmPo; NOBA; OxBA

Eagle Valor, Chicken Mind. Robinson Jeffers. LiTA; OxBA; OxBSP; WaP

Eagle! why soarest thou above that tomb? Spirit of Plato. *Unknown, tr. by* Shelley. AWP; OBVE

(Plato's Tomb.) FaBoCh

Eagles, The. Jones Very. TAP

Eagles. Elizabeth Woody. STE

Eagles and Isles. W. W. Gibson. PoSH

Eagle's eye is the strongest eye, The. The Great Way of the Man. Norman H. Russell. NOVW

Eagle's Fall, The. Charles Goodrich Whiting. AA

Eagles gather on the place of death, The. The Eagles. Jones Very. TAP

Eagles have practically left America, The. Inability to Depict an Eagle. Richard Eberhart. GOA

Eagle's nest on the head of an old redwood, An. The Beaks of Eagles. Robinson Jeffers. GOA

Eagles of coral. The Footsteps. C. P. Cavafy, *tr. by* Edmund Keeley *and* Philip Sherrard. VMG

Eagles over the Lambing Paddock. Ernest G. Moll. PoAu-2

Eagle's shadow runs across the plain, The. Zebra. "Isak Dinesen." GoJo; RFM

Eagle's Song, The. Mary Austin. GOA

Eagle's Song, The. Richard Mansfield. PAH

Eagles, that wheel above our crests. The Cedars of Lebanon. Alphonse Marie Louis de Lamartine, *tr. by* Toru Dutt. AWP

Eaper Weaper. *Unknown.* FaBoNo; OxBoLi

Ear, The. Louis MacNeice. OxBSP

Ear Ear. Concrete Cat. Dorthi Charles. InPK

Ear Is Not Deaf. Irene Dayton. GoYe

Ear the answer, The. The Hill of Intrusion. William Sydney Graham. NePoEA

Earl and Lady Chatham, The. Bonnie Jacobson. *Fr.* Introductions, or, What's in a Name. SoTCo

Earl Bothwell. *Unknown.* ESPB

Earl Brand. *Unknown.* ESPB, A, B, *and* F. *vers.*

Earl Brand ("O did you ever hear of the brave Earl Brand."). *Unknown.* OxBB

Earl Brand. *Unknown.* ("Sweet William rode up to the old man's gate"). AmFP

Earl Brand (The Douglas Tragedy). *Unknown.* FaBoBa

Earl Crawford. *Unknown.* ESPB

Earl March look'd on his dying child. The Maid of Neidpath. Thomas Campbell. GoTS; GTBS; GTBS-P

Earl Mar's Daughter. *Unknown.* GN

Earl Mertoun's Song. Robert Browning. *Fr.* A Blot in the 'Scutcheon. OBEV

Earl o' Quarterdeck, The. George Macdonald. BeLS

Earl of Aboyne, The. *Unknown.* ESPB

Earl of Errol, The. *Unknown.* ESPB

Earl of Mar's Daughter, The. *Unknown.* CH; ESPB

Earl of Surrey to Geraldine, The. Michael Drayton. OBSC

Earl of Westmoreland, The. *Unknown.* ESPB

Earl of Wigton had three daughters, The. Richie Story. *Unknown.* ESPB

Earl Percie of Northumberland. Chevy Chase. *Unknown.* EnSB

Earl Rothes. *Unknown.* ESPB

Earl stood on two legs when he had one to spare. Cash Only, No Refund, No Return. Daniel Mark Epstein. MAYP

Earle Douglasse for this day doth with the Percies stand, The. Michael Drayton. *Fr.* Polyolbion, Two and Twentieth Song. OBS

Earlier in the evening the moon. The Moon. Robert Creeley. VGW

Earliest before sunrise. Susan Howe. LP

Earliest Christian Hymn. Clement of Alexandria, *tr. fr. Greek by* Edward H. Plumptre. WGRP

Earliest Spring. William Dean Howells. OBEV

Earliest Spring. Denise Levertov. LCAP

Earliness at the Cape. Babette Deutsch. FYAP; NYBP

Early April on Broadway, south of Union Square. Seeing Off a Friend. Stephen Dobyns. AnAn

Early Autumn. Joben, *tr. fr. Japanese by* Steven D. Carter. WFTW

Early Autumn. Keiun, *tr. fr. Japanese by* Steven D. Carter. WFTW

Early Autumn. Onitsura, *tr. fr. Japanese by* Hiroaki Sato. *Fr.* Twenty-three Hokku. FCEI

Early Autumn. Shotetsu, *tr. fr. Japanese by* Steven D. Carter. WFTW

Early Autumn Evening. Rokunyo, *tr. fr. Chinese by* Burton Watson. JLIC-2

Early Bacon. Archibald Stodart-Walker. *Fr.* The Moxford Book of English Verse. CenHV

Early before the day doth spring. Of Astraea. Sir John Davies. *Fr.* Hymns of Astraea. TrGrPo

Early bird got up and whet his beak, The. A Birthday Ode to Mr. Alfred Austin. Sir Owen Seaman. NOBL

Early bird may catch the worm, The. Samuel Hoffenstein. *Fr.* As the Crow Flies, Let Him Fly. NBLV

Early blossoms—could a single. Permanence in Change. Goethe, *tr. by* John Frederick Nims. HoPM

Early Bluebird, An. Maurice Thompson. AA

Early Copper. Carl Sandburg. HeIP

Early Darkness. Gyula Illyés, *tr. fr. Hungarian by* William Jay Smith. MHuP

Early Death. Hartley Coleridge. OBEV

Early dew woos the half-opened flowers, An. Haroun's Favorite Song. *Unknown, tr. fr. Arabic by* E. Powys Mathers. *Fr.* The Thousand and One Nights. AWP

Early Discoveries. David Malouf. CBAP

Early Dutch. Jennie M. Palen. GoYe

Early, each morning, Martha Blake. Martha Blake at Fifty-one. Austin Clarke. CIP; IPY; NOIV

Early early early. Mississippi Mornings. Tom Dent. UL

Early, Early in the Spring. *Unknown.* OBET

Early Electric! With what radiant hope. The Metropolitan Railway. Sir John Betjeman. EBEV; OxBTC

Early Evening Quarrel. Langston Hughes. UnPo

Early have a miser's insinuating rub, The. Timers. Flora J. Arnstein. GoYe

Early I rose. *Unknown, tr. by* Mary Austin. AWP; LiTA

Early Illinois Winter, An. Alex Kuo. BrSi

Early in March we pitched our scar. Winterward. William Stafford. SM

Early in the Morning. Louis Simpson. LCAP

Early in the morning. Small Is Beautiful. Liu K'o-hsiang, *tr. by* Dominic Cheung. IFON

Early in the morning. A Watering Rhyme. P. A. Ropes. BoTP

Early in the Morning You Lean. Yehuda Amichai, *tr. fr. Hebrew by* Bernhard Frank. MHeP

Early in the spring when the snow is all gone. A Trip to the Grand Banks. Amos Hanson. AmFP

Early in the Springtime. *Unknown.* OBET

Early January. W. S. Merwin. VGW

Early Losses; a Requiem. Alice Walker. BISi

Early Love. Samuel Daniel. *Fr.* Hymen's Triumph. ErPo

Early Love. Herbert Scott. MOWH; NAmP

Early Lynching. Carl Sandburg. MoAmPo

Early Meadow-Rue. Stanley Plumly. LCAP

Early Morn. W. H. Davies. CH

Early Morning, The. Hilaire Belloc. BoNaP; BoTP; OxBSP

Early morning. Ojisan after the Stroke; Three Notes to Himself. Tina Koyama. BrSi

Early morning Meadow Song. Charles Dalmon. CH

Early morning over Rouen, hopeful. Rouen. May Wedderburn Cannan. NAEL-2; OBWP; OxBTC

Early morning road, a dog, An. Ozaki Hosai, *tr. fr. Japanese by* Hiroaki Sato. *Fr.* One Hundred Haiku in Free Form. FCEI

Early Morning Roundup. Owen Barton. CowP

Early morning smoke smoulders over a city field in a December dawn. Negro Geo'ge. Berysh Vaynshteyn, *tr. fr. Yiddish by* Benjamin *and* Barbara Harshav. *Fr.* Negroes. AYP

Early Mornings. *Unknown, tr. by* Louis Untermeyer. AS

Early, my God, without delay. Isaac Watts. AmFP

Early News. Anna Maria Pratt. AA

Early Nightingale. John Clare. PBBP

Early October, maple trees. Players. Ruth Roston. TSL

Early on a Monday morning. Kevin Barry. *Unknown.* AS

Early on the morning of Monday. Omens. *Unknown, tr. by* A. Carmichael. RB

Early One Morning. *Unknown.* ChTr

Early one morning. Voodoo on the Un-Assing of Janis Joplin. Carolyn M. Rodgers. JB

Early one morning in the spring. The Disappointed Sailor. *Unknown.* OxBSS

Early one morning, just as the sun was rising. Early One Morning. *Unknown.* ChTr

Early Ones, The. William Stafford. CAPP

Early pleasures please best, some old voice whispers. Firstness. Richard Tillinghast. BLA

Early Pregnancy. Penelope Shuttle. BrRo

Early Rebels, The. Mervyn Morris. PVCV

Early Rising. John Godfrey Saxe. AnAmPo; BLPL; PoLF

Early September. Americans Playing Slow-Pitch Softball at an Airbase near Kunsan, South Korea. Halvard Johnson. TSL

Early Snow. Lo Fu, *tr. fr. Chinese by* Dominic Cheung. IFON

Early Spring. Eloise Bibb. CBWP-4

Early Spring. Sidney Keyes. MoBrPo

Early Spring. Philip Whalen. TDD

Early spring's sweet blush, The. Early Spring. Eloise Bibb. CBWP-4

Early Summer: At the Riverside, *sel.* Li K'ai-hsien, *tr. fr. Chinese by* Jonathan Chaves.

"Not a day goes by without someone borrowing books from me." CoBLCP

Early Summer in the Year *Jen-tzu.* Yün Shou-p'ing, *tr. fr. Chinese by* Jonathan Chaves. CoBLCP

Early Summer, *Jen-tzu* Year, in Playful Imitation of Ts'ao Yün-hsi. Yün Shou-p'ing, *tr. fr. Chinese by* Irving Lo. WFTU

Early Summer, Paying a Second Visit to the Kankantei of the Kansho-in in the Toei. Rokunyo, *tr. fr. Chinese by* Burton Watson. JLIC-2

Early Summer Sea-Tryst. Frederick Macartney. CBAP

Early sun on Beaulieu water. Youth and Age on Beaulieu River, Hants. Sir John Betjeman. FaBoTw; TwCP

Early Sunday Morning. John Stone. MT

Early Supper. Barbara Howes. GoJo; GrPl; SM

Early that afternoon, as we keep. The "Portland" Going Out. W. S. Merwin. NYBP

Early thou goest forth, to put to rout. To a "Tenting" Boy. Charles Tennyson Turner. OBNC

Early Thoughts of Marriage. Nathaniel Cotton. OxBChV

Early to bed and early to rise. *Unknown.* FaBoBe; FaBoUs

Early to bed and early to rise. New Proverb. Shirley Brooks. FaBoNo

Early Unfinished Sketch. Austin Clarke. ErPo

Early, up without breakfast. Moving. Janet Reed McFatter. GrPl

Early wagons left no sign, The. The Trail into Kansas. W. S. Merwin. GOA

Early Waking. Léonie Adams. LiTM

Early we set out from Ch'en-hsi ferry. Ch'en-hsi County. Ho Ching-ming, *tr. by* Jonathan Chaves. CoBLCP

Early winter. Naito Meisetsu, *tr. by* Geoffrey Bownas *and* Anthony Thwaite. PeBJV

Early Winter. Weldon Kees. NaP

Earlye, Earlye, in the Spring. *Unknown.* AmFP

Earnest, earthless, equal, attuneable. Spelt from Sibyl's Leaves. Gerard Manley Hopkins. BrPo; CMoP; FaBoMo; LiTM; NOBVV; OAEL-2; PrIm; TOF

Earnest Liberal's Lament, The. Ernest Hemingway. OBAL; OBSV

Earnest to explore within and all around. Dante, *tr. fr. Italian by* Shelley. *Fr.* Divina Commedia: Purgatorio, XXVIII. OBVE

Earning a Dinner. Matthew Prior. NBLV

Ears. Sonja Akesson, *tr. fr. Swedish by* Joanna Bankier. WPOW

Ears, alert like dogs and like stars. Sharp Hour. Judah Leib Teller, *tr. by* Benjamin *and* Barbara Harshav. AYP

Ears deaf, eyes blind: Void's. On Wisdom. Hakuin, *tr. by* Lucien Stryk *and* Takashi Ikemoto. ZPCJ

Ears Hear. Lucia *and* James L. Hymes, Jr. RAR

Ears in the Turrets Hear. Dylan Thomas. FaBoTw

Earth. Margaret Atwood. PoE

Earth. Philippe Denis, *tr. fr. French by* Paul Auster. RHTwFP

Earth, The. Emerson. AA

Earth. Kahlil Gibran, *tr. fr. Arabic by* Adnan Haydar *and* Michael Beard. MAP

Earth, The. David Gwenallt Jones, *tr. fr. Welsh by* Dyfnallt Morgan. OBWVE

Earth. Jim Tollerud. VoR

Earth, The. Jones Very. AnAmPo; OxBA

Earth ("Grasshopper, your fairy song"). John Hall Wheelock. LiTA; MoAmPo

Earth ("Planet doesn't explode, A"). John Hall Wheelock. LiTM; OBD; SoSe

Earth, The/ is a wonderful. Poem for Friends. Quincy Troupe. PoBA

Earth a flower. For Nothing. Gary Snyder. NNaP

Earth Abideth Forever, The. Bible, *O.T. Fr.* Ecclesiastes, I: 4-7. FaPON

Earth and Fire. Wendell Berry. FF

Earth and Fire. Vernon Watkins. NYBP

Earth and I Gave You Turquoise. N. Scott Momaday. CDW; HATNAP; NOVW; UnPo

Earth and Sky. Euripides, *tr. fr. Greek by* C. M. Bowra. EaLo

Earth and sky black. Camp Site. Denis Glover. *Fr.* Arawata Bill. ATNZ; PeNZ

Earth and water air. Martha Graham. James Laughlin. RR

Earth and water, air and stars. Immortality. "Nicolai Maksimovich Minsky," *tr. by* Babette Deutsch. TrJP

Earth around him, The: he within his life. Adam in Love. Stephen Mitchell. VWA

Earth—as though I had entered. Earth. Philippe Denis, *tr. by* Paul Auster. RHTwFP

Earth Asks and Receives Rain, The. Phyllis Haring. PeSA

Earth Breaks Up. Robert Browning. *Fr.* Christmas-Eve and Easter-Day. TrCP

Earth Buried. Kenneth Mackenzie. CBAP

Earth conceived and in windows, The. On a Clear Night. Ya'ir Hurvits, *tr. by* Bernhard Frank. MHeP

Earth Cycle Dream, The. Phillip Yellowhawk Minthorn. STE

Earth darkens and is beaded. Quod Tegit Omnia. Yvor Winters. QFR

Earth does not ever grow fat, The. Ngoni Burial Song. *Unknown.* PeSA

Earth does not understand her child. The Return. Edna St. Vincent Millay. LiTA; MoAB; MoAmPo; MoP; NoAM; OxBA

Earth draws her breath so gently, heaven bends. The Marriage of Earth and Heaven. Jay Macpherson. OBCV

Earth Dweller. William Stafford. LCAP

Earth Felicities, Heavens Allowances. Richard Steere. SCAP

Earth from her winter slumber breaks. Decoration Day. Julia Ward Howe. OHIP

Earth gets its price for what Earth gives us. James Russell Lowell. *Fr.* The Vision of Sir Launfal, Prelude to *Pt.* I. OnMSP

Earth goes on the earth glittering in gold, The. Inscribed in Melrose Abbey. *Unknown.* FaBoEE; FaBoRV

Earth ("Grasshopper, your fairy song"). John Hall Wheelock. LiTA; MoAmPo

Earth grown old, yet still so green. Advent. Christina Rossetti. TrCP

Earth has borne a little son. The Aconite. A. M. Graham. BoTP

Earth has not anything to show more fair. Composed upon Westminster Bridge, September 3, 1802. Wordsworth. AWP; BLPL; ChTr; EnRP; EyDe; FaBoCh; FaBoPP; FaBoRV; FaBV; FaFP; FF; HAP; HeIP; InPK; InPS; InvP; NAEL-2; NAWM-2; NoP; OAEL-2; OBNC; PoE; PoEL-4; PoLF; PrIm; Son; TEP; TrGrPo; UnPo; WeW (Sonnet Composed upon Westminster Bridge, September 3, 1802.) FiP

Earth has not anything to show more fair. On Mrs. W—— Nicolas Bentley. FiBHP

Earth Has Shrunk in the Wash. William Empson. CMoP

Earth holds the sunlit. For Spring. Douglas G. Jones. NOBC

Earth in Spring, The. Judah Halevi, *tr. fr. Hebrew by* Edward G. King. TrJP

Earth is a beautiful place, The. The Third Sermon on the Warpland. Gwendolyn Brooks. BPo

Earth is a place on which England is found, The. Geography. G. K. Chesterton. *Fr.* Songs of Education. OBSV

Earth is a woman who imagines us. She sings. Robert Kelly. *Fr.* The Book of Persephone, 10. PoM

Earth Is as Blue as an Orange, The. Paul Eluard, *tr. fr. French by* Michael Benedikt. POS

Earth is dark where you rest. Dark Earth and Summer. Edgar Bowers. QFR

Earth is the Lord's, and the fullness thereof, The. Psalm XXIV ("The Earth is the Lord's."). Bible, *O.T. Fr.* Psalms. AWP; EaLo; FaPON (1-4); TrJP (Lift Up Your Heads.) TrGrPo

Earth issues forth from Earth forcibly. Earth. Kahlil Gibran, *tr. by* Adnan Haydar *and* Michael Beard. MAP

Earth keeps some vibration going, The. Fiddler Jones. Edgar Lee Masters. *Fr.* Spoon River Anthology CMoP; LiTA; NoAM; OxBA; TAP; TrGrPo

Earth, Late Choked with Showers, The. Thomas Lodge. *Fr.* Scilla's Metamorphosis. EiL (Melancholy.) OBSC

Earth lies here in giant folds and creases, The. High Wheat Country. Elijah L. Jacobs. AmFN

Earth, My Likeness. Walt Whitman. OxBA

Earth now is green, and heaven is blue. To the Spring. Sir John Davies. *Fr.* Hymns of Astraea. EiL

Earth-Ocean. Guillaume Apollinaire, *tr. fr. French.* POS, Michael Benedikt

Earth, ocean, air, belovèd brotherhood! Shelley. *Fr.* Alastor; or, The Spirit of Solitude. EnRP; FiP; NAEL-2; OAEL-2

Earth out of Earth. *Unknown.* MeEL

Earth, paved, freezes, The. In the "Trocadero." Max Hölzer, *tr. by* Beth Bjorklund. CoAuP

Earth Poem. Mahmoud Darwish, *tr. fr. Arabic by* Abdullah al-Udhari. MPAW

Earth Poems, *sel.* Javier Heraud, *tr. fr. Spanish by* Maureen Ahern. "I want two geraniums." Per

Earth Psalm. Denise Levertov. PPP

Earth puts her colours by. P. H. B. Lyon. BoTP

Earth rais'd up her head. Earth's Answer. Blake. *Fr.* Songs of Experience. EnRP; InPS; NAEL-2; NAWM-2; NOEC; OAEL-2; PoE

Earth rebelled, The./ The good and patient earth. And the Earth Rebelled. Yuri Suhl, *tr. by* Max Rosenfeld. TrJP

Earth, receive an honoured guest. W. H. Auden. *Fr.* In Memory of W. B. Yeats. ChTr; FaBoRV; FaBoTw (4 *sts.); Mes*

Earth rolls on through empty space, its journey's never done, The. The Ramble-eer. *Unknown.* PoAu-1

Earth runs furrows under my skin, The. New Graveyard: Jerusalem. Shirley Kaufman. VWA

Earth Scrapes Us. Mahmoud Darwish, *tr. fr. Arabic by* Lena Jayyusi *and* Christopher Middleton. *Fr.* Poems after Beirut, I. MAP

Earth seems a desolate mother, The. March. Charles Henry Webb. AA

Earth sees in thee. To Sultan Murad II. James Clarence Mangan. NOIV

Earth shows her face to the moon, The. Eclipse II. Linda Hogan. HATNAP

Earth, Sky. Sydney Clouts. PeSA

Earth Song. Thomas Peacock. VoR

Earth to earth, and dust to dust. Death and Resurrection. George Croly. WGRP

Earth Took of Earth. *Unknown.* HAP

Earth Trembles Waiting. Blanche Shoemaker Wagstaff. PoLF

Earth tremor. I felt an earth tremor. On the Wallowy. Laura Chester. NPGG

Earth Tremor in Lugano. James Kirkup. NYBP

Earth turns, The/ like a rainbow. When You Read This Poem. Pinkie Gordon Lane. BlSi

Earth Walk. William Meredith. MAT

Earth was form'd, but in the womb as yet, The. Milton. *Fr.* Paradise Lost, *Bk.* VII, *ll.* 276–309. MOS

Earth was green, the sky was blue, The. A Green Cornfield. Christina Rossetti. BoTP

Earth was young, the world was fair, The. The Saxon Legend of Language. Mary Weston Fordham. CBWP-2

Earth will be going on a long time, The. Lute Music. Kenneth Rexroth. TAP

Earth, with all its fullness, is the Lord's, The. Poor for Our Sakes. Mary Brainerd Smith. BLRP

Earth with thunder torn[e], with fire blasted, The. Fulke Greville. *Fr.* Caelica, LXXXVI [LXXXVII]. AAS; QFR (Sonnet: "Earth with thunder torn, with fire blasted, The.") JCP

Earth Worm, The. Denise Levertov. NOBA

Earthborn. Peter McArthur. CaP

Earthen *K'ang*, An. Sung Wan, *tr. fr. Chinese by* William Schultz. *Fr.* Songs Composed in Prison, II. WFTU

Earthen Stove, An. Sung Wan, *tr. fr. Chinese by* William Schultz. *Fr.* Songs Composed in Prison, VI. WFTU

Earthly Illusion. Louise Leighton. GoYe

Earthly Paradise, The, *sels.* William Morris. Apology, An. AWP; EBVV; LiTB; NAEL-2; NoP; OAEL-2; OBNC October. OBNC "Of Heaven or Hell I have no power to sing." OPOP Outlanders, The. EBVV (Minstrels and Maids.) GN Prologue: The Wanderers. EBVV Road of Life, The. OBNC "Under a bent when the night was deep." PChr

Earthly roses at God's call have made, The. On the Death of a Pious Lady. Olof Wexionius, *tr. by* Sir Edmund Gosse. AWP

Earthly: Sonnets for Carlos, *sels.* Ian Wedde. "By day and also by night and you are." *Fr.* 10. ATNZ; PeNZ "Diesel trucks past the Scrovegni chapel." *Fr.* 31. PeNZ "If thy wife is small bend down to her and.'" *Fr.* 9. ATNZ; PeNZ "In time a message back, like this, to say." *Fr.* 18. ATNZ It's Time. *Fr.* 2. ATNZ "Land-Mine Casualty Amman 1970." *Fr.* 37. ATNZ Madonna. *Fr.* 1. ATNZ Paradiso Terrestre. *Fr.* 3. ATNZ Power Transformer. *Fr.* 26. ATNZ; PeNZ "Precocious spring how beautiful you are!" *Fr.* 27. ATNZ "Right now the elm seeds whisper to the ground." *Fr.* 39. ATNZ

Earthquake. R. A. D. Ford. NOBC

Earthquake. Malka Heifetz-Tussman, *tr. fr. Yiddish by* Kathryn Hellerstein. AYP

Earthquake. Kokan Shiren, *tr. fr. Chinese by* Burton Watson. FCEI; JLIC-2

Earthquake, *sel.* Li K'ai-hsien, *tr. fr. Chinese by* Jonathan Chaves. "Earthquake covered Shansi and Shensi, The." CoBLCP

Earthquake, The. *Unknown, tr. fr. Zuni Indian by* K. Kennedy. WTO

Earthquake. Sándor Weöres, *tr. fr. Hungarian by* Jascha Kessler. FOC

Earthquake covered Shansi and Shensi, The. Li K'ai-hsien, *tr. fr. Chinese by* Jonathan Chaves. *Fr.* Earthquake. CoBLCP

Earthquake of 1886, The. Josephine D. Henderson Heard. CBWP-4

Earthquake Somewhere Else, An. Vivienne Finch. TSM

Earth's Answer. Blake. *Fr.* Songs of Experience. EnRP; InPS; NAEL-2; NAWM-2; NOEC; OAEL-2; PoE

Earth's Bondman. Betty Page Dabney. GoYe

Earth's Bounty. Auvaiyar, *tr. fr. Tamil by* A. K. Ramanujan. PLW

Earth's Children Cleave to Earth. Bryant. AnAmPo

Earth's first Adam, he lay in the grass. Adam and Eve. Itzik Manger, *tr. by* Jacob Sonntag. TrJP

Earth's Lyric. Bliss Carman. AnAmPo

Earth's shadow crosses the full-/moon. Lunar Eclipse. Diane Glancy. STE

Earthsleep. Fred Chappell. KS

Earthworm, The. Harry Edmund Martinson, *tr. fr. Swedish by* Robert Bly. RB

Earthworms. Parody. Martha Paley Francescato, *tr. by* Willis Barnstone. BoWoP

Earthy Anecdote. Wallace Stevens. CMoP; GoJo; RB; RFM

Eartly [*or* Earthly] nourris [*or* nouris *or* nourice] sits and sings, An. The Great Silkie of Sule Skerry. *Unknown.* ChTr; ESPB; FaBoBa; FaBoCh; GBP; MAT; MOS
(Grey Selchie of Sule Skerry, The.) OxBB

Ease. William Cowper. *Fr.* The Task, I. TEP

Ease is the pray'r of him who, in a whaleboat. Sapphics: At the Mohawk-Castle, Canada. Thomas Morris. NOEC

Easier to encapsulate your lives. Granddaughter. Adrienne Rich. *Fr.* Grandmothers. NAAL-2

Easily to the old. Exit. Wilson Pugsley MacDonald. CaP

Easiness of August night, The. To the Summer Sweethearts. Sydney Lea. NAmP

East Anglian Bathe. Sir John Betjeman. NoP; SD

East Anglian Fen. George Crabbe. *Fr.* Tales of the Hall. FaBoPP

East Coast—Canada. Elizabeth Brewster. CaP

East Coast Journey. James Keir Baxter. NoP; PeNZ

East Coker. T. S. Eliot. *Fr.* Four Quartets. HAP; PPP; VGW

East is a clear violet mass, The. A Street Scene. Lizette Woodworth Reese. OBCA

East London. Matthew Arnold. WGRP

East looking down from the Chieh-shih. Viewing the Ocean. Ts'ao Ts'ao, *tr. by* Burton Watson. CoBCP

East of the eastern ocean. Song of a Dream Journey over the Vast Sea. Yang Wei-chen, *tr. by* Jonathan Chaves. CoBLCP

East of the salt village, low and narrow. Wu Chia-chi, *tr. by* Jonathan Chaves. CoBLCP

East River. Rosemary Thomas. AmFN

East St. Louis Blues. *Unknown.* AmFP

East Texas. Leon Stokesbury. SM

East the ocean, west the Himalaya. A Eulogy of the Sagely Virtue of His Imperial Majesty Emperor Shih-tsu. Chao Meng-fu, *tr. by* Jonathan Chaves. CoBLCP

East Wind asperges Boston with Lynn's sulphurous brine, An. Father. John Wheelwright. DiL; UnPo

East wind churns the ground, whirling upwards elm tree pods, The. Stopping Overnight at Black Dragon River. Singde, *tr. by* William Schultz. WFTU

East wind, knowing I plan to walk through the hills, The. On the Road to Hsin-ch'eng. Su Tung-p'o, *tr. by* Burton Watson. CoBCP

East wind rises in hurried gusts, The. Sorrow on Gazing at the River. Niu Chiao, *tr. by* Lois Fusek. ATF

East wind stirs fine dust on the roads. Rhyming with Tzu-yu's "Treading the Green." Su Tung-p'o, *tr. by* Burton Watson. CoBCP

East winds to greet my mother when we came. Escorting My Mother Home. Rai San'yo, *tr. by* Burton Watson. FCEI; JLIC-2

East wind's whistlin' cauld an' shrill, The. A Schule Laddie's Lament on the Lateness of the Season. James Logie Robertson. NOBVV

Easter. Mary Carolyn Davies. OHIP

Easter ("I got me flowers to straw [*or* strew] Thy Way"). George Herbert. BoTP; CH; FaBoCh; NAEL-1; NOBE; OBEV; OBS; OHIP; TrGrPo

Easter ("Rise, heart, thy Lord is risen. Sing his praise"). George Herbert. NAEL-1; SeCV-1; TrCP

Easter. Joyce Kilmer. PDV; RHPC

Easter. Howard Nemerov. NoP

Easter. Frank O'Hara. EAS

Easter. Edwin L. Sabin. OHIP

Easter. C. H. Sisson. OxBSP

Easter. Spenser. *See* Amoretti: LXVIII. "Most glorious Lord of Life [*or* Lyfe]! that on this day."

Easter again, and a small rain falls. The Other Side of the River. Charles Wright. MT

Easter Beatitudes. Clarence M. Burkholder. BLRP

Easter Bonnet, The. Clara Ann Thompson. CBWP-2

Easter Bunny Blues or All I Want for Xmas Is the Loop, The. Ebon Dooley. PoBA

Easter Canticle, An. Charles Hanson Towne. OHIP; TrPWD

Easter Carol. George Newell Lovejoy. OHIP

Easter Carol. Henrietta Cordelia Ray. CBWP-3

Easter Carol, An. Christina Rossetti. OHIP

Easter Chick, An. Thirza Wakley. BoTP

Easter Chorus. Goethe. *See* Faust: Christ Is Arisen.

Easter Communion. Gerard Manley Hopkins. BrPo; OFD

Easter dawn! Morning, Noon, And. Hawley Truax. NYBP

Easter duck and Easter chick. Some Things That Easter Brings. Elsie Parrish. RAR

Easter Eve. Muriel Rukeyser. VGW

Easter Garland, An. Carol Rumens. FaBoWP

Easter has come around. W. D. Snodgrass. *Fr.* Heart's Needle, VI. CAPP; NePoEA

Easter Hymn. A. E. Housman. EaLo; EBEV; MoAB; OFD

Easter Hymn. An. Richard Le Gallienne. OHIP

Easter Hymn. Charles Wesley. OHIP

Easter Island. Frederick George Scott. OBCV

Easter Light, The. Clara Ann Thompson. CBWP-2

Easter lilies! Can you hear. On Easter Day. Celia Thaxter. FaPON

Easter Monday. Christina Rossetti. NOCV

Easter Morn. Giles Fletcher the Younger. *Fr.* Christ's Victory and Triumph: Christ's Triumph after Death, IV. EIL; NOCV

Easter Morn. Josephine D. Henderson Heard. CBWP-4

Easter Morning. A. R. Ammons. HCAP; NAAL-2; NoAM; NoP

Easter Morning. Spenser. *See* Amoretti: LXVIII. "Most glorious Lord of Life [*or* Lyfe]! that on this day."

Easter Night. Alice Meynell. BrRo; OHIP

Easter, 1916. W. B. Yeats. BrPo; CMoP; FaBoMo; FaBoPV; FaPoR; HAP; HeIP; InPS; LiTM; MoAB; MoP; NAEL-2; NAWM-2; NIP; NoAM; NOBE; NOIV; NoP; OAEL-2; OBWP; OxBTC; PoE; PPP

Easter, 1923. John G. Neihardt. OHIP

Easter; or, Spring-Time. Lizelia Augusta Jenkins Moorer. CBWP-3

Easter Poem. Kathleen Jessie Raine. LiTB

Easter Praise. Rodney Bennett. BoTP

Easter Song, An. Susan Coolidge. *See* Calvary and Easter.

Easter Song. Mary Artemisia Lathbury. OHIP

Easter Sunday. Sedulius Scottus, *tr. fr. Latin by* Helen Waddell. OFD

Easter Sunday, 1945. G. A. Borgese. NePoAm

Easter Thought. Leo Cox. CaP

Easter Week. Charles Kingsley. OHIP

Easter Wings. George Herbert. HAP; HeIP; InPK; InPS; LiTB; MeLP; MePo; NAEL-1; NIP; NoP; OAEL-1; OBS; PoE; PoEL-2; PPP; SeCP; TEP; TOF; TrCP; WeW

Eastern Evangelic Planet, *sel.* Carlos de Sigüenza y Góngora, *tr. fr. Spanish by* Samuel Beckett.
Invocation and Proposition. MexPo

Eastern guard tower. Etheridge Knight. BPo; MoP; NeAC; SM; TAP

Eastern hills—dense and lush. Rai San'yo, *tr. fr. Chinese by* Burton Watson. *Fr.* Reading Books, VI. FCEI; JLIC-2

Eastern mountains/ and western mountains. Yüan Hung-tao, *tr. fr. Chinese by* Jonathan Chaves. *Fr.* Passing by the Hot Springs at Hua-ch'ing Palace. CoBLCP

Eastern neighbor, western neighbor. Yang Chi, *tr. fr. Chinese by* Jonathan Chaves. *Fr.* Scenes. CoBLCP

Eastern Slope, *sels.* Su Tung-p'o, *tr. fr. Chinese by* Burton Watson. CoBCP
"Abandoned earthworks nobody tends."
"I planted rice before Spring Festival."
"Little stream used to cross my land, A."

Eastern Tempest. Edmund Blunden. MoBrPo

Eastmuir king, and Wastmuir king. Fause Foodrage. *Unknown.* ESPB

Eastward, etched in purple by a sun. Appalachian Convalescence. Robert Conquest. OxBC

Eastward I Stand, Mercies I Beg. *Unknown, tr. fr. Anglo-Saxon by* Sarah Plotz. EaLo

Easy as a Bat. *Gond Oral Tradition, tr. by* V. Elwin *and* S. Hivale. WTO

Easy as cove-water rustles its pebbles and shells. Part of a Letter. Richard Wilbur. CMoP

Easy Chairs and Saddle Sores. Ross Knox. CowP

Easy River, they call it. Tamekane, *tr. by* Steven D. Carter. WFTW

Easy thing, O Power Divine, An. The Things I Miss. Thomas Wentworth Higginson. TrPWD

Eat/ 300 feet. The Anthropophagites See a Sign on NC Highway 177 That Looks like Heaven. Jonathan Williams. OBAL

Eat and drink. Sun-Watchers. Abba Kovner, *tr. by* Warren Bargad *and* Stanley F. Chyet. IP

Eat and Walk. James Norman Hall. BLPA

Eat, Eat! Nellie Wong. ER

Eat garlic every day. The Latest Diet. Jim Young. SoTCo

Eat-It-All Elaine. Kaye Starbird. PDV; RHPC

"Eat my cake, eat," cried the young. To the Last Wedding Guest. Horace Gregory. NYBP

Eat no green apples or you'll droop. Advice to Small Children. Edward Anthony. RHPC

Eat with Care. *Unknown.* FaBoUs

Eat your banana, Annie dear. Sales Talk for Annie. Morris Bishop. NBLV

Eaten Heart, The. *Unknown, tr. fr. Middle English by* Pearl London. *Fr.* The Knight of Curtesy. TrGrPo

Eaters saddened every heart in Tenejapa, The. A Story of the Eaters. Santiago Mendes Zapata, *tr. by* W. S. Merwin. STP

'Eathen, The. Kipling. OxBTC

Eating. Reginald Gibbons. MAYP

Eating Bamboo-Shoots. Po Chü-i, *tr. fr. Chinese by* Arthur Waley. OBVE

Eating Lechon, with My Brothers and Sisters. Luis Cabalquinto. BrSi

Eating Poetry. Mark Strand. CAPP; GrPl; MAT; MoP; NoAM; PPP; TAP

Eating the living germs of grasses. Song of the Taste. Gary Snyder. CAPP; LCAP

Eau-Forte. F. S. Flint. OxBTC

Eaves. Ellis Jones, *tr. fr. Welsh by* Anthony Conran. OBWVE

Eavesdropper, The. Bliss Carman. AnAmPo

Ebb. John Lyle Donaghy. NeIP

Ebb. Edna St. Vincent Millay. AnAmPo

Ebb/ with the flow. Daufuskie. Mari E. Evans. BlSi

Ebb and Flow. George William Curtis. AA

Ebb and Flow, The. Edward Taylor. AmPP; SCAP

Ebb on, tide, moving swiftly outwards! Invalid's Song. Harata Tangikuku, *tr. by* Margaret Orbell. PeNZ

Ebb slips from the rock, the sunken, The. Night. Robinson Jeffers. AWP; LiTA; MoAmPo; NOBA; OxBA

Ebb Tide. Marjorie Pickthall. CaP

Ebb Tide, The. Robert Southey. OBNC

Ebb-tide to me as to the sea; old age brings me reproach [*or* Ebb tide has come for me:/My life drifts downward]. The Hag of Beare. *Unknown.* BIrV, *tr. by* John Montague; OBVE, *tr. by* Lady August Gregory; PBWP, *tr. by* John Montague

Ebbed and flowed the muddy Pei-ho by the gulf of Pechili. Blood Is Thicker than Water. Wallace Rice. PAH

Ebony Life. Robert Desnos, *tr. fr. French by* Michael Benedikt. POS

Ecce Homo. Witter Bynner. WGRP

Ecce Homo. David Gascoyne. *Fr.* Miserere. LiTM; OBWP

Ecce Homunculus. R. A. K. Mason. ATNZ; PeNZ

Ecce in Deserto. Henry Augustin Beers. AA

Ecce Puer. James Joyce. BIrV; EBEV; MoP; NAs; NoAM; OPOP; TrCP

Eccentric old person of Slough, An. George Robey. CenHV

Eccho, The. Richard Leigh. MePo

Ecchoing Green, The. Blake. *See* Echoing Green, The.

Ecclesiastes. G. K. Chesterton. MoBrPo; OxBSP

Ecclesiastes. Peter Goldsworthy. UAS

Ecclesiastes. Joseph Langland. NePoEA

Ecclesiastes. Derek Mahon. BIrV; CIP

Ecclesiastes, *sels. Bible, O.T.*
   "Cast thy bread upon the waters." *Fr.* XI. AWP, (1-6); OBVE, (1-8).
   Earth Abideth Forever, The. *Fr.* I: 4-7. FaPON
   "I returned, and saw under the sun." *Fr.* IX: 11-12. Prf
   "It Is Better. . ." *Fr.* VII: 1-9. TrJP
   Light Is Sweet, The. *Fr.* XI: 7. FaPON
   Remember Now Thy Creator. *Fr.* XII: 1-8. AWP; ChTr; OBVE
     (Remember Then Thy Creator.) TrJP
     (Youth and Age.) TrGrPo
   To Everything There Is a Season. *Fr.* III: 1-8. FF; OBVE
     ("For everything there is a season.") DL
     (Time for Everything, A.) TrGrPo
   "Vanity of vanities, saith the Preacher, vanity of vanities; all is vanity." *Fr.* I: 2-11. FaBoPV; TrJP, (I: 2-9).

Ecclesiastical Chronicle, An, *sel.* John Heath-Stubbs.
   "Year of Our Lord two thousand one hundred and seven, The." NOBL

Ecclesiastical Sonnets, *sels.* Wordsworth.
   Inside of King's College Chapel, Cambridge. *Fr. pt.* III, XLIII. EnRP; OBNC
   Mutability. *Fr.* III, XXXIV. EBEV; EnRP; HeIP; InPK; LiTB; NOBE; NoP; OAEL-2; OBEV; PoEL-4; Prlm
   Trepidation of the Druids. Son

Ecclesiasticus, *sels. Bible, Apocrypha.*
   "All flesh waxeth old as a garment." *Fr.* XIV: 17–18. OBVE
   "By his commandment hee maketh the snow to fall apace." *Fr.* XLIII: 13–26. OBVE
   "Let us now praise famous men." *Fr.* XLIV: 1–15. ChTr; OBVE
     (Our Fathers.) TrJP
   Music. *Fr.* XXXII: 5–6. TrJP

O Death. *Fr.* XLI: 1-4. TrJP

Test of Men, The. *Fr.* XXXVI: 5-8. TrJP

Ech, Sic a Pairish. *Unknown.* FaBoCo; FiBHP

Eche man me telleth I chaunge moost my devise. Sir Thomas Wyatt. AAS

Echo. Steve Benson. IAT

Echo. Leonard Clark. Mes

Echo. Walter de la Mare. OBMV

Echo. Alfred Gong, *tr. fr. German by* Beth Bjorklund. CoAuP

Echo. Elizabeth Stanton Hardy. GoYe

Echo. Viscountess Grey of Fallodon. CH

Echo. Milton. *Fr.* Comus; a Masque Presented at Ludlow Castle. ELP; OBEV; OBS
   (Lady Sings, The.) NOBE
   (Lady's Song.) TrGrPo

Echo. Thomas Moore. ELP

Echo. Christina Rossetti. BoLoP; CH; EBVV; ELP; GBL; NOBE; NoP; OAEL-2; OBNC; PoE; PoEL-5

Echo. John Godfrey Saxe. AnAmPo

Echo. Sir Philip Sidney. *Fr.* Arcadia. SiPS

Echo. Mildred Weston. BoNaP

Echo. Zoltán Zelk, *tr. fr. Hungarian by* Barbara Howes. MHuP

Echo always mocks the sound, The. Rabindranath Tagore. *Fr.* Epigrams. PoA

Echo and the Ferry. Jean Ingelow. EBVV

Echo Canyon. *Unknown.* AmFP

Echo, I ween, will in the wood reply. A Gentle Echo on Woman. Swift. FaBoCo; NBLV; NU

Echo of insects where the lamplight thins. At Ch'ang-ku, Reading: To Show to My Man Pa. Li Ho, *tr. by* Burton Watson. CoBCP

Echo of Mandela. Zindzi Mandela. WMBCH

Echo Poem. M. Allan. FiBHP

Echo Reverie. Henrietta Cordelia Ray. CBWP-3

Echo, the beating of the tide. Prophecy on Lethe. Stanley Kunitz. PoA

Echo to a Rock. Lord Herbert of Cherbury. PoEL-2

Echo ("Two poles. We didn't disagree."). Michael Palmer. IAT

Echo ("Which in a dry season might"). Michael Palmer. IAT

Echo ("Which resound. Re-sounds. Where first would"). Michael Palmer. IAT

Echoes. Thomas Moore. *See* How sweet the answer Echo makes.

Echoes. José Peón y Contreras, *tr. fr. Spanish by* Samuel Beckett. MexPo

Echoes. W. E. Henley.
Sels.
   Blackbird, The. *Fr.* VIII. MoBrPo; TrGrPo
     (To A. D.) HoPM
   "I am the Reaper," *Fr.* V. OBNC
   Margarita Sorori [I. M.]. *Fr.* XXXV. MoBrPo; NOBE; OBEV; OBNC; TrGrPo; WGRP
     (Late Lark, A.) PoRA
   On the Way to Kew. *Fr.* XXXVIII. MoBrPo; TrGrPo
   "Out of the night that covers me." *Fr.* IV. NOBE; OBNC
     (Invictus.) BLPA; FaBoBe; FaBV; FaFP; FaPoR; FPL; HoPM; LiTB; MoBrPo; OBEV; OBMV; OHFP; TEP; TrGrPo; MGRP
   We'll Go No More a—Roving. *Fr.* VIII. MoBrPo

Echoes are soundless. Transformations. Orkhan Muyassar, *tr. by* Lena Jayyusi *and* Samuel Hazo. MAP

Echoes from Theocritus, *sels.* Edward Cracroft Lefroy, *after the Greek of* Theocritus.
   Cleonicos. *Fr.* XXVII. AWP
   Epitaph of Eusthenes, The. *Fr.* XXVIII. AWP
   Flute of Daphnis, The. *Fr.* XXIII. AWP
   Grave of Hipponax, The. *Fr.* XXX. AWP
   Monument of Cleita, The. *Fr.* XXIX. AWP
   Sacred Grove, A. *Fr.* XXIV. AWP
   Sylvan Revel, A. *Fr.* XXV. AWP
   Thyrsis. *Fr.* XXVI. AWP

Echoes of Childhood. Alice Corbin. PoNe

Echoes of the hymns return. Grandfather's Sermon and Michael Smith. E. A. Markham. PBCV

Echoing Cliff, The. Andrew Young. PoSH

Echoing [*or* Ecchoing] Green, The. Blake. *Fr.* Songs of Innocence. BoTP; CH; NAEL–2; PoE; UnPo; WiR

Echoing Heaven's Everlastingness. Ku Hsiung, *tr. fr. Chinese by* Lois Fusek. ATF

Echoing Heaven's Everlastingness. Mao Wen-hsi, *tr. fr. Chinese by* Lois Fusek. ATF

Echoing Heaven's Everlastingness. Niu Chiao, *tr. fr. Chinese by* Lois Fusek. ATF

Echoing Heaven's Everlastingness. Wei Chuang, *tr. fr. Chinese by* Lois Fusek. ATF

Echoing high/ in the tips of the pines. Emperor Fushimi, *tr. by* Steven D. Carter. WFTW

Echoing Old Man Mu's Poem. Wang Shih-chen, *tr. fr. Chinese by* Jonathan Chaves. CoBLCP

Echoing with the cries. Yakamochi, *tr. fr. Japanese by* Burton Watson. *Fr.* Manyo Shu. FCEI

Echo's Bones. Samuel Beckett. *Fr.* Echo's Bones. NOAM
Echo's Bones.
Vulture, The.

Echo's Complaint. Henrietta Cordelia Ray. CBWP-3

Echo's Lament for Narcissus. Ben Jonson. *See* Cynthia's Revels: Slow, Slow, Fresh Fount.

Echo's [*or* Eccho's] Song. Ben Jonson. *See* Cynthia's Revels: Slow, Slow, Fresh Fount.

Eclipse, The. Jacques Prévert, *tr. fr. French by* Michael Benedikt. POS

Eclipse. Anita Endrezze-Danielson. CDW

Eclipse. Bin Ramke. NAmP

Eclipse. Amir Rashidd. NBP

Eclipse. Ed Roberson. PoNe

Eclipse. Tomaz Salamun, *tr. fr. Slovene by* Michael Scammel *and* Veno Taufer. VWA

Eclipse, The. Henry Vaughan. OxBSP

Eclipse of Faith, The. Theodore Dwight Woolsey. AA

Eclipse II. Linda Hogan. HATNAP

Eclipses. Nancy Sullivan. TAP

Eclogue IV: The Poet. Charles Jenner. AWP

Eclogue between the Motherless. Louis MacNeice. FaBCIP

Eclogue for Christmas, An. Louis MacNeice. FaBoMo; NoAM; OBMV

Eclogue: "Late 'twas in June, the fleece when fully grown." Michael Drayton. *Fr.* The Shepherd's Garland, Eclogue IX (1606 ed.). OBSC

Eclogue: "Lycon begin—begin the mournful tale." William Diaper. *Fr.* Nereides; or, Sea-Eclogues. SeCePo

Eclogue: Queen Elizabeth's Day. John Davidson. BrPo

Eclogue to Mr. Johnson, An, *sel.* Thomas Randolph.
Poetry and Philosophy. OBS

Eclogue: "What makes you look so black, so glum, so cross?" Edward Lear. FaBoNo

Eclogues, *sel.* Alexander Barclay.
Winter. *Fr.* V. OxBLMV

Eclogues. Dennis Schmitz. NPGG

Eclogues, *sels.* Virgil, *tr. fr. Latin.*
Corydon and Thyrsis. *Fr.* VII, *tr. by* Dryden. AWP
Lycidas and Moeris. *Fr.* IX, *tr. by* Dryden. AWP
Messiah, The. *Fr.* IV. AWP, *tr. by* Dryden.
Shepherd's Gratitude, The. *Fr.* I, *tr. by* Charles Stuart Calverly. AWP

Ecole St. Luc. Ray Fraser. NeAC

Ecolgue IV. Andrea Zanzotto, *tr. fr. Italian by* Lawrence R. Smith. NItP

Ecology. Ernesto Cardenal, *tr. fr. Spanish by* Alejandro Murguía. Vol

Economics. Alvin Aubert. MT

Economics. Mona Van Duyn. SM

Economics Lesson. Rocco Scotellaro, *tr. fr. Italian by* Paul Vangelisti. PFI

Economy, Convenience, Good Taste. Tom Disch. SoTCo

Economy of Vegetation, The. Erasmus Darwin. *Fr.* The Botanic Garden, *pt.* I.
Action of Electricity, The. FaBoUs
Action of Invisible Ink, The. FaBoUs
Protection of Plants, The. FaBoUs
Steam Power. NOEC

Ecstasy, The. John Donne. BoLoP; FPL; HAP; InPS; JCP; LiTB; NAEL-1; NOBE; NoP; OAEL-1; OBEV; PoE; PrIm; TEP; TOF; TrGrPo

Ecstasy. Paul Eluard, *tr. fr. French by* Michael Benedikt. POS

Ecstasy. Duncan Campbell Scott. CaP

Ecstasy. Hélène Swarth, *tr. fr. Dutch by* Jonathan Crewe. WPOW

Ecstasy. Rachel Annand Taylor. GoTS

Ecstasy. Walter James Turner. CH

Ecstasy. *Unknown. See* Oh, When Shall I See Jesus?

Ecstatic bird songs pound. Dawn. William Carlos Williams. MoAB; MoAmPo

Ectoplasm in the air! A partial eclipse. The History of the World. Roger Weingarten. NAmP

Eczema. David R. Slavitt. TW

Ed ascoltando al leggier mormorio. Ezra Pound. *Fr.* Cantos, LXXXI. PoE

Eddi, priest of St. Wilfrid. Eddi's Service. Kipling. OBCP

Eddington's universe goes phut. Richard Tolman's Universe. Leonard Bacon. ImOP

Eddi's Service. Kipling. OBCP

Eden. Lev Mak, *tr. fr. Russian by* Daniel Weissbort. VWA

Eden. Thomas Traherne. PoEL-2; SeCV-2; TrGrPo

Eden Gate. Allen Curnow. ATNZ

Eden Is a Zoo. Margaret Atwood. WPE

Edenhall. "Susan Coolidge." OBCA

Edenlike as your name. Edge. John Montague. IPY

Edgar A. Guest Considers "The Old Woman Who Lived in a Shoe" and the Good Old Verities at the Same Time. Louis Untermeyer. *See* Mother Goose Up-to-Date: Edgar A. Guest Considers "The Good Old Woman Who Lived in a Shoe" and the Good Old Truths Simultaneously.

Edgar's Story, *sel.* X. J. Kennedy.
"At Mount Rushmore I looked up into one." OFD

Edge. Robert D. Fitzgerald. CBAP

Edge. John Montague. IPY

Edge. Sylvia Plath. FaBoWP; HCAP; NAAL-2; PoE; TAP

Edge, The. Lola Ridge. OnYI

Edge-Hill; or, The Rural Prospect Delineated and Moralised, *sel.* Richard Jago.
Iron Industry in Birmingham, The. NOEC

Edge of Autumn, The. Michael Anania. NoAM

Edge of Day, The. Laurie Lee. NYBP

Edge of our bed was a wide grid, The. Sisters in Arms. Audre Lorde. ER

Edge of the cancer, The. Front Lines. Gary Snyder. PoE

Edi be thu, Hevene Quene. In Praise of Mary. *Unknown.* MeEL

Edinburgh after Flodden, *sel.* William Edmonstoune Aytoun.
"Then the Provost he uprose." OBWP

Edinburgh from the Pentland Hills. Sir Walter Scott. *Fr.* Marmion, IV. FaBoPP

Edith. William Ellery Channing. AA

Edith. Andreas Okopenko, *tr. fr. German by* Beth Bjorklund. CoAuP

Edith, the silent stars are coldly gleaming. Edith. William Ellery Channing. AA

Editor sat in his easy chair, The. The Editor's Tragedy. St. John Emile Clavering Hankin. CenHV

Editor Whedon. Edgar Lee Masters. PoE

Editor Whedon. Edgar Lee Masters. *Fr.* Spoon River Anthology. CMoP; FaBoEE; NOBA; OBSV; OxBA

Editorial Poem on an Incident of Effects Far-reaching. Russell Atkins. NBP

Editor's Tragedy, The. St. John Emile Clavering Hankin. CenHV

Editor's Wooing, The. "Orpheus C. Kerr." OBAL

Edmond Halley. Roy Fuller. OxBC

Edmonton, thy cemetery. Stevie Smith. OxBTC

Edmund Burke. Goldsmith. *See* Retaliation: Here lies our good Edmund, whose genius was such.

Edmund Davie 1682; Annagram. Benjamin Tompson. SCAP

Edmund Pollard. Edgar Lee Masters. *Fr.* Spoon River Anthology. ErPo

Edmund's Song. Sir Walter Scott. *See* Rokeby: Brignall Banks.

Edna St. Vincent Millay Exhorts Little Boy Blue. Louis Untermeyer. *Fr.* Mother Goose Up-to-Date. MoAmPo

Edom. Isaac Watts. AmFP

Edom o' Gordon. *Unknown.* OxBB

Educated Love Bird, The. Peter Newell. FiBHP

Educating the Body. Kevin Ireland. ATNZ

Education. Don L. Lee. AmNP

Education by Stone. João Cabral de Melo Neto, *tr. fr. Portuguese by* James Wright. ATCBP

Education of Nature, The. Wordsworth. *See* Lucy: Three Years She Grew in Sun and Shower.

Education regarding chills is not well handled in this country, The. Henri Michaux, *tr. fr. French by* Richard Ellmann. *Fr.* I Am Writing to You from a Far-Off Country, XII. RHTwFP

Edvard Munch. Charles Wright. HCAP

Edward [*or* Edward, Edward]. *Unknown.* AmFP; CH; EBEV; ELP; EnRP; ESPB; FaBoBa; FaPoR; GoTS; HAP; HoPM; InPK; InPS; LiTB; Mes; NAEL-1; NOBE; NoP; OBEV; OxBB; OxBS; PoEL-1; PoRA; PrIm; SoSe; TrGrPo; TW; WeW

Edward/ Paterson has grown older. William Carlos Williams. *Fr.* Paterson, *Bk.* V. NoAM

"Edward back from the Indian Sea." Neglectful Edward. Robert Graves. BrPo; MoBrPo

Edward Lear. W. H. Auden. InvP

Edward Lear in February. Christopher Middleton. TwCP

Edward the Dyke and Other Poems, *sel.* Judy Grahn.
"In the place where." PeHV

Edward the Third had seven sons. The Ballad of Banners (1944). John Lehmann. MoBS

Edwardus Comes Clarendoniae. Bibliotheca Bodleiana. Geoffrey Grigson. GBL

Edwin Dickinson's Perspective. William Corbett. PPR

Edwin in the Lowlands Low. *Unknown.* AmFP

Eek!/ Her legs are caught in something. The Orlando Commercial. George MacBeth. NOBL

Eel, The. Ogden Nash. FaBV; FaPON; NTCP

Eels and Tortoises. William Diaper, *after the Greek of* Oppian. *See* Halieutica: Strange the formation of the eely race.

Eemis-Stane, The. "Hugh MacDiarmid." NAEL-2

E'en as a lovely flower. Du bist wie eine Blume. Heine, *tr. fr. German. Fr.* Homeward Bound. AWP, *tr. by* Kate Freiligrath Kroeker. ("Thou Seemest Like a flower.") TrJP, *tr. by* Emma Lazarus.

E'en as the flowers do wither. *Unknown.* OBSC

E'en as the sculptor chisels patiently. The Tireles Sculptor. Henrietta Cordelia Ray. CBWP-3

E'en this, Lord, didst thou bless. Insomnia. John Banister Tabb. TrPWD

Eena, meena, mina, mo. *Unknown.* OxNR

Eenie, meenie, mackeracka. *Unknown.* OxNR

Eenie, meenie, minie, mo. Counting-out Rhymes. *Unknown.* FaPON

Eenity, feenity, fickety, feg. *Unknown.* OxNR

Eeny, weeny, winey, wo. *Unknown.* OxNR

E'er since the time the Judge on high. The Prophet. Mikhail Yurevich Lermontov, *tr. by* Alan Myers. AAA

Ef I had wings like Noah's dove. Dink's Song. *Unknown.* ErPo; OxBoLi

Effendi. Michael S. Harper. CNA; PoBA

Effervescence and Evanescence. Keith Preston. OBAL

Efficiency Apartment. Gerald William Barrax. PoBA

Efficient Wife's Complaint, The. Confucius, *tr. fr. Chinese by* Ezra Pound. *Fr.* Airs of Pei. CTC

Effie. Sterling A. Brown. BANP

Effingham, Grenville, Raleigh, Drake. Admirals All. Sir Henry Newbolt. FaPoR; MOS

Effort at Speech. William Meredith. Prf; SM; WeW

Effort at Speech between Two People. Muriel Rukeyser. FYAP; MoAB; MoAmPo; TrGrPo; TrJP; TwCP; WeW

Eftsoones they heard a most melodious sound. Spenser. *Fr.* The Faerie Queene: The Bower of Bliss. NOBE; OBSC; SCV

Eftsoons they saw an hideous host array'd. Sea Monsters. Spenser. *Fr.* The Faerie Queene, II, 12. ChTr

Egan O Rahilly. *Unknown, tr. fr. Irish by* James Stephens. EBEV; OBMV; SeCePo

Egg, The. George Bowering. NeAC

Egg, The. Clarence Day. NBLV

Egg, The. Jean Follain, *tr. fr. French by* W. S. Merwin. RHTwFP

Egg-and-Dart. Robert Finch. OBCV

Egg and the Machine, The. Robert Frost. MoAmPo

Egg Boiler, The. Gwendolyn Brooks. PoBA

Egg for Easter, An. Irene F. Pawsey. BoTP

Egg grew human, The. James Weigel, Jr. *Fr.* Testaments, I. TSM

Egg is a grand thing for a journey, An. How the Hen Sold Her Eggs to the Stingy Priest. Nancy Willard. LCAP

Egg sat on the workbench, The. The Egg. George Bowering. NeAC

Egg Thoughts. Russell Hoban. *See* I do not like the way you slide.

Egg won't roll well, An. An Airline Breakfast. William Matthews. AnAn; MAYP

Eggleston was a taxi-driver. Cynical Portraits. Louis Paul. NBLV

Eggomania. Felicia Lamport. NBLV

Eggplants Have Pins and Needles, The. Novella Matveyeva, *tr. fr. Russian by* Daniel Weissbort. WPOW

Eggs, The. Peter Redgrove. NAs

Eggs for Breakfast. Irene F. Pawsey. BoTP

Eggs from a chain store grocery. One No. 7. John Frederick Frank. GoYe

Egnatius has fine teeth, and those. Catullus, *tr. by* Walter Savage Landor. OBVE

Ego. Philip Booth. TwCP

Ego. Norman MacCaig. GTBS-P

Ego. Robert Siegel. GeTw; PoA

Ego. Annie Vivanti, *tr. fr. Italian by* Muriel Kittel. DMI

Ego Dominus Tuus. W. B. Yeats. CMoP

Ego Tripping. Nikki Giovanni. MoP; Psk

Egocentric. Stevie Smith. FaBoNo

Egoism. W. Craddle. FiBHP

Egoisme à Deux. Louisa S. Guggenberger. NOBVV

Egoist Dead, The. Elizabeth Brewster. CaP

Egotism. Edward Sandford Martin. AA

Egret. André Breton, *tr. fr. French by* Michael Benedikt. POS

Egrets. Judith Wright. GoJo

Egrets poise among the white iris on the cold bank. The Fisherman. Ho Ning, *tr. by* Lois Fusek. ATF

Egypt, divided by the river Nile. Milton. *Fr.* Paradise Lost, *Bk.* XII, *ll.* 157–235. FaBoPV

Egypt, Tobago. Derek Walcott. AnAn

Egyptian Dancer. Terence Tiller. OBTV

Egyptian Dancer at Shubra. Bernard Spencer. NoAM

Egyptian Lotus, The. Arthur Wentworth Hamilton Eaton. AA

Egyptian Passage, An. Theodore Weiss. TAP

Egyptian Pulled Glass Bottle in the Shape of a Fish, An. Marianne Moore. PBWP

Egyptian Serenade. Ali Mahmud Taha, *tr. fr. Arabic by* Issa Boullata *and* Thomas G. Ezzy. MAP

Egyptian Tomb, The. William Lisle Bowles. OBTV

Egyptians say, the sun has twice, The. Samuel Butler. *Fr.* Hudibras, II, 3. ImOP

Egypt's Might Is Tumbled Down. Mary Elizabeth Coleridge. CH

Eheu Fugaces. "Thomas Ingoldsby." FaBoEE; OxBoLi

Eia, with handbells, jews' harps, risible. Geoffrey Hill. *Fr.* Hymns to Our Lady of Chartres. DiPo

Eichmann. Audrey Beecham. CN

Eight Aspects of Melissa, *sels.* Lawrence Durrell.
   Adepts, The. ErPo
   Visitations. MoBrPo

8-Ball at the Twilite. David Baker. MAYP

Eight-Beat Barbarian Tune. Sun Kuang-hsien, *tr. fr. Chinese by* Lois Fusek. ATF

Eight-beat Barbarian Tune. Yen Hsüan, *tr. fr. Chinese by* Lois Fusek. ATF

Eight Days in April. Marilyn Hacker. ER

Eight Feet. Ku Yen-wu, *tr. fr. Chinese by* J. P. Seaton. WFTU

Eight hands across, form a ring. Mississippi Sawyer. *Unknown.* AmFP

Eight hundred days. Lady Kasa, *tr. fr. Japanese by* Burton Watson. *Fr.* Manyo Shu. FCEI

Eight hundred of them, and this as ordinary. An Evening in November. Anne French. ATNZ

Eight-legged aerialists, The. Spiders. Diane Ackerman. MAYP

Eight Lines for a Script Girl. George Jonas. NeAC

Eight Oars and a Coxswain ("Eight oars compel"). Arthur Guiterman. ASP; SD

Eight o'Clock. A. E. Housman. BrPo; CMoP; InPK; MoAB; MoBrPo; MoP; NoAM; NoP; OxBSP; PoE; SoSe; TrGrPo

Eight Poems for August. Lance Henson. NOVW

Eight Sandbars on the Takano River. Gary Snyder. NOBA; NoP; VGW

Eight-toes, teetering. Magpie. Peter Davison. GrPl

Eight, we stand around our mother. Her Oak. Malka Heifetz-Tussman, *tr. by* Kathryn Hellerstein. AYP

Eight Witches. B. J. Lee. RHPC

Eight years ago this May. A Spring Night in Shokoku-ji. Gary Snyder. *Fr.* Four Poems for Robin. NNaP; NoAM; NOBA; NoP; SOTW; VGW

Eight years gone & the welfare building is a parking ramp. Balance. Philip Schultz. MAYP

Eighteen. Maria Banus, *tr. fr. Rumanian by* Willis Barnstone *and* Matei Calinescu. BoWoP; VWA

1808 Wordsworth dies from fall while hiking in Scotland. Other Lives of the Romantics. Jane Flanders. SoTCo

1887. A. E. Housman. *Fr.* A Shropshire Lad, I. FaPoR; NIP; NOBVV; PrIm; UnPo

1805. Robert Graves. FaBoCh; OBSV

1805 Gratiot. Richard Hugo. PPR

Eighteen-Forty-Three. *Unknown.* FaBoCo

1894 in London. Charles Spear. ATNZ

1892-1941. Louis Zukofsky. PoA

1801. Wordsworth. Son

Eighteen-Seventy. Arthur Rimbaud, *tr. fr. French. Sels.*
   Evil. *Tr. by* Robert Lowell. OBWP
   ("Whilst the red spittle of the grape-shot sings.") WaaP, *tr. by* Norman Cameron.
   Napoleon after Sedan. *Tr. by* Robert Lowell. FaBoPV; OBWP
   Poster of Our Dazzling Victory at Saarbrucken, A. *Tr. by* Robert Lowell. FaBoPV; OBWP
   Sleeper in the Valley, The. *Tr. by* Robert Lowell. OBWP
   ("There's a green hollow where a river sings.") AWP, *tr. by* Ludwig Lewisohn.
   ("Through a green gorge the river like a fountain.") WaaP, *tr. by* Seldman Rodman.
   To the French of the Second Empire. *Tr. by* Robert Lowelrl. FaBoPV; OBWP

Eighteen sixty nine being the date of the year [*or* and the year]. A Ballad of Master McGrath. *Unknown.* FaBoBa (Master McGrath.) OBET
1863, my great grandmother. Generations. Judy Dothard Simmons. CNA
18,000 Feet. Ed Roberson. PoNe
Eighteen Verses Sung to a Tatar Reed Whistle, *sels.* Ts'ai Yen, *tr. fr. Chinese by* Kenneth Rexroth *and* Ling Chung.
  "I have no desire to live, but I am afraid of death." *Fr.* XI. WPOW
  "I never believed that in my broken life." *Fr.* XIII. BoWoP; WPOW
  "I was born in a time of peace." *Fr.* I. BoWoP; PBWP; WPOW
  "Seventeenth stanza, The. My heart aches, my tears fall." *Fr.* XVII. WPOW
  "Sun sets, The. The wind moans." *Fr.* VII. BoWoP; WPOW
  "Tatar chief forced me to become his wife, A." *Fr.* II. WPOW
Eighteen years. Horses. Melech Ravitch, *tr. by* Seymour Levitan. PeBMYV
Eighteenth of October, The. The Fire of Frendraught. *Unknown.* ESPB; OxBB
Eightfold camellia blossom that opens on my tongue full of love. Forecome and Come. Takahashi Mutsuo, *tr. fr. Japanese by* Hiroaki Sato. *Fr.* Ode in 1,000 Lines. FCEI
Eightfold fence of Izumo where clouds rise. Susano-o's Song. *Unknown, tr. fr. Japanese by* Hiroaki Sato. *Fr.* The Kojiki. FCEI
Eighth Air Force. Randall Jarrell. CAPP; FF; MoP; NoAM; NOBA; NoP; OBWP; SM
Eighth child of an eighth child, your wilful advent. Birth of a Great Man. Robert Graves. NYBP
Eighth day was the wedding, The. The First Wedding in the World. Joel Rosenberg. VWA
Eighth Elegy, *sel.* Muriel Rukeyser.
  Children's Elegy. LCAP
Eighth Song: "In a grove most rich of shade." Sir Philip Sidney. *Fr.* Astrophel and Stella. OBSC; SiPS
Eighties Becoming, The. Bob Rosenthal. UL
Eighties, De. Frederick Williams. PBCV
Eighty and nine with their captain. The Charge by the Ford. Thomas Dunn English. PAH
Eighty are the harbours. *Unknown, tr. fr. Japanese. Fr.* Manyo Shu. Ma
Eighty-eight, my head's pure white. Seiko, *tr. by* Lucien Stryk *and* Takashi Ikemoto. ZPCJ
Eighty-four Tanka. Teika, *tr. fr. Japanese by* Hiroaki Sato. FCEI *Sels.*
  "Above a clear, penetrating wind."
  "Above the wind the starlight is clear."
  "Against the cherries on the hazy hilltop."
  "As I look out, there are neither blossoms nor crimson leaves."
  "As I look, the moon has moved West."
  "At the rising, climbing, southern limit there are clouds."
  "Autumn gone, the past distant in the great sky."
  "Away from the direction of falling blossoms."
  "Carried overhead and wished upon."
  "Cicada voices rising continually, far away."
  "Coming to an end and leaving the moon as a keepsake."
  "Dew, scatter if you will."
  "Dozing, thoughts interminable in paths of dream."
  "Drawn by the memory of your face I turn to look."
  "Even her heart again a stranger's."
  "Evening voices of cicadas, The."
  "Fading, desolate: at the autumn coloring."
  "Floating bridge of dreams this spring night, The."
  "For the one I await the path must have ended."
  "Great sky hazy with scents of plum blossoms, The."
  "He does not come, but I wait."
  "Here again, another useless sign of the floating world."
  "Hint at the hilltop of the moon, A."
  "How can I forget?—spring hazes lost."
  "How many autumns have I passed."
  "I lifted her hair strand by strand."
  "If only I had my phantom to send to you."
  "In May rains the water, the waves."
  "In my birthplace, the garden and the hedges."
  "In the past too, hearts have separated from hearts."
  "Izumi River: like the bubbles on a pole."
  "Lamplight in the window at slow dawn, A."
  "Light of the moon that crosses the Plain of Heaven, The."
  "Like some ailing leaf."
  "Like tinkling gems, neither dewdrops nor tears stay."
  "Loneliness is more intense with frost than with snow."
  "Look, this must be love that fills the sky!"
  "Lush emerald the summer color becomes."
  "Missives, fleeting, my lover's only trace."
  "Mists above the crimson leaves."
  "More melancholy than the bright moon."
  "My thoughts, useless dreams in midair."
  "Neglectful, I have not died of love."
  "Negligently the day opens before I have time to sleep."
  "No shade for halting the horse to shake my sleeves."
  "Not like an ordinary cloud."
  "On his way home, he may be watching this."
  "On my way home at dusk."
  "On the sea god's plain the waves and the sky merge."
  "Only one or two nights since winter came."
  "Orange flowers scatter in a village."
  "Plain of Heaven, think of it, The."
  "Regarding my infants as friends from old days."
  "Relished as cooler than usual tonight."
  "Retaining the colors of snow and moon."
  "Rippling, a wind from the Bay of Grebes."
  "Rising sun casts the same light, The."
  "Scent of the plum blossoms, The."
  "Snow falling in quantities and the valley deep, The."
  "So light the sleeves of this cicada-wing robe."
  "Somehow my heart settles on the hill's rim."
  "Sound of pine winds and their color are one, The."
  "Stalling ox, shuffling, swirls up dust, A."
  "Straw mattress: the Bridge Princess of Uji."
  "Suddenly darkening, the sky beyond my eaves."
  "Take it as a pledge: a dewdrop on a lotus leaf."
  "They become fragrant, and the Spring ends."
  "Thinking of the past I wake."
  "Through a rift in evening rainclouds."
  "Traveler's sleeves fluttered by an autumn wind, A."
  "Troubled throughout the year."
  "Turning and turning, these summer days, to my regret."
  "Unable to settle through the long unending night."
  "Under the lamplight that grows feeble."
  "Under the lower leaves of hydrangea fireflies cluster."
  "Wakeful for last year's call that I loved."
  "Well into the distance young leaves of grass undulate."
  "When there's love as unrecognized as a lily."
  "While we bring to dawn the flower and the moon."
  "Wind passes, the mirror of blossoms clouds, A."
  "With no more fragrance, the *sakaki*, its voice."
  "Woods again holing up for winter, under snow."
  "Yearning for the moon hazy."
  "You, weary of the waves rolling into autumn."
'Eighty-nine was bad. Graves at Elkhorn. Richard Hugo. UnPo
Eighty-seven Hokku. Buson, *tr. fr. Japanese by* Hiroaki Sato. FCEI *Sels.*
  "As the tides flow, in the rain."
  At Kaya in Tamba.
  "Bandit chief composes a tanka, The."
  "Barrier guard's brazier, The."
  "Burnt in the fireplace."
  "Butterfly settles on the neckplate, A."
  "Camellia drops and spills, A."
  "Chipped away, the moon disappears."
  "Chopping with an ax."
  "Coming out of the dark of the short night."
  "Coming out of the privy."
  "Coolness: separating from a bell."
  "Dead of winter: crows are black."
  "Departing spring: a boat with brushwood."
  "Departing spring: I've lost the eyeglasses."
  "Departing spring: on the carriage."
  "Distant from warblers all day."
  "Each time a wave rolls in."
  "Even the floating weeds sink."
  "Evening downpour: clutching grass blades."
  "Evening wind: the water strikes."
  "Flowing in the spring rain."
  "Flying kite, in the spot in the sky, A."
  "Footfall of someone I wait for, The."
  "For white plum blossoms."
  "From the acorns on a round tray."
  "Gleaners walk toward where the sunlight is, The."
  "Huge gate and its heavy doors, A."
  "I buy scallions and go home through leafless trees."
  "I look around: humans like green stalks."
  "I mistook a warbler for a sparrow."
  "In a water pail, nodding at each other."
  "In an old pond a frog."
  "In an old pond a sandal lies sunken."
  "In the autumn dusk a woman."

"In the candlelight in my hand."
"In the pear orchard someone stands."
"Into the darkness of an old well."
"Leaving my gate, I too am someone."
"Lightning spills a noise."
"Lonely—still, I've forgotten."
"Looking at a passing cloud."
"Love in many forms."
"May rain: in front of a wide river."
"May rain: paddy by paddy."
"May rain: the muddy water thrusts."
"Moon about to set, The."
"Moon at heaven's center."
"Morning glories: a single flower."
"Mosquito whirs each time, A."
"Mountains are low, The."
"Mountains darkened, The."
"Mountains, darkening, have robbed."
"Not yet dark, but stars glitter."
Old Man's Thoughts, An ("Lonelier still than last year").
"Path ending, a fragrance, The."
"Peony in a wide garden."
"Rape flowers: the moon in the east."
"Roof repairman steps on dead leaves, The."
"Settled on a temple bell and asleep."
"Short night: on a hairy caterpillar."
"Shower silently wets the roots, A."
"Sitting at an edge."
"Sparks from a stonemason."
"Spring at dusk."
"Spring rain: small clams."
"Spring rain: telling stories."
"Spring sea sloshes, The."
"Spring water flows through the mountainless land."
"Spring water flows, wetting violets."
"Stonemason cools his chisels, The."
Suburb ("A woodland of silent oak trees").
Suburb ("Cold moon: amidst dead trees").
Suburb ("Heat haze: a bug I don't know").
"Summer mountains: across the span of Kyoto."
"Swimming, a frog looks as if."
"That the autumn has come."
"Though divorced, she steps."
"Waking from a nap."
"Walking a flatland and weary."
"Warrior walks, A."
"Waving flies off a sick man's shoulders."
"White dew: one drop on each prickle."
"Winter wind: blowing pebbles."
"Winter wind: pebbles in a plowed field."
"Winter wind: the voice of water."
"Young leaves have left Fuji, The."
Eighty years, a day's journey. Guan, tr. by Lucien Stryk and Takashi Ikemoto. ZPCJ
Eighty years ago a woman passed. Tomorrow Is a Birthday. Gwendolen Haste. GoYe
Eighty years, and I've added another. First Poem of the Year. Kishun Ryuki, tr. by Burton Watson. FCEI
Eileann Chanaidh, sel. Kathleen Raine.
   Ancient Speech, The. PoSH
Eileen Aroon, sel. Gerald Griffin.
   "When like the rising day." OBEV
Eileen of four. The Clock's Song. Rose Hawthorne Lathrop. AA
Ein feste Burg ist unser Gott. Martin Luther, tr. by M. Woolsey Stryker. CTC
Ein Fichtenbaum steht einsam. Heine, tr. fr. German by James Thomson. AWP
Eine Kleine Snailmusik. May Sarton. NBLV
Einem alten Architekten in Rom. Joseph Brodsky, tr. fr. Russian by George L. Kline. AnAn
Einstein, sel. Archibald MacLeish.
   "He lies upon his bed." ImOP
Einstein's Exile in an Old Dutch Winter. Norman Dubie. NAmP
Eire. David O'Bruadair, tr. fr. Irish by Austin Clarke. BIrV
Eireann. Osbert Lancaster. Fr. Afternoons with Baedeker. NOBL
Eisenhower's Visit to Franco, 1959. James Wright. NaP
Either get out of my house or conform to my tastes, woman. Martial, tr. by James Michie. FaBoEE
Either she was foule, or her attire was bad. Ovid, tr. fr. Latin by Christopher Marlowe. Fr. Amores, III, 6. OBVE
   (Shameful Impotence.) ErPo
Either to keep the thinking in. Country Ways. Marcia Lee Masters. Fr. Impressions of My Father, I. GoYe

Either you will. Prospective Immigrants Please Note. Adrienne Rich. AiP; GOA; VGW
"Ej Blot til Lyst." William Morton Payne. AA
Ejected Wife, The. Unknown, tr. fr. Chinese by Arthur Waley. OBVE
El-a-noy. Unknown. AS
El Abandonado. Unknown, tr. by Frank J. Dobie. AS
El Aghir. Norman Cameron. See Sprawled on the bags and the crates in the rear of the truck.
El Alamein. Steve Crow. HATNAP
El Alamein Revisited. Roy Macnab. PeSA
El Capitan-General. Charles Godfrey Leland. AA
El Dorado. Richard Ryan. BIrV
El Greco. Edward Leslie Mayo. HoPM
El Greco: Espolio. Earle Birney. MoCV
El-Hajj Malik El-Shabazz. Robert Hayden. CNA; PoBA
El Hombre. William Carlos Williams. CMoP; LiTA
El Ropero. Antonio di Montorio. TrJP
El Sueño de la Razón. Jane Cooper. FaBoWP
El Vaquero. Lucius Harwood Foote. AA
Elaboration, The. Bill Manhire. ATNZ
Elaine. Hugo Williams. Fr. Calling Your Name in the Zoo. NPo
Elais Cairel, I want to know. Isabella, tr. by Meg Bogin. WT
Elan. Sándor Weöres, tr. fr. Hungarian by William Jay Smith. MHuP
Elba. Gerrit Kouwenaar, tr. fr. Dutch by Peter Nijmeijer. DuIn
Elbow-queen on the windowsill, The. Woman at the Window. Ernst Jandl, tr. by Beth Bjorklund. CoAuP
Elbows in wine-slops, news of the ocean isles. Cipangu. William Hart-Smith. Fr. Christopher Columbus. PoAu-2
Elder Brother, The, sel. John Fletcher.
   "Beauty clear and fair." Fr. III, v. OBEV; OBS
Elder Edda, The, sels. Unknown, tr. fr. Old Norse by William Morris and Eirikr Magnusson.
   Counsels of Sigrdrifa. AWP
    (Part of the Lay of Sigrdrifa.) OBVE
   First Lay of Gudrun, The. Tr. by William Morris and Eirikr Magnusson. AWP
    Gudrun Laments over Sigurd. OBVE
   Lay [or Short Lay] of Sigurd, The. Tr. by William Morris and Eirikur Magnusson. AWP
    "And now one prayer." OBVE
   Voluspo. Tr. by Henry Adams Bellows. AWP
"Elder Father, though thine eyes." The Holy of Holies. Gilbert Keith Chesterton. WGRP
Elder, or Bourtree, The. Unknown. GBP
   (Elder Tree, The.) ChTr
Elder Sister, The. Sharon Olds. NIP
Elder sister,/ Who is it coming, in the loft? Family. Tanikawa Shuntaro, tr. by Geoffrey Bownas and Anthony Thwaite. PeBJV
Elder Tree, The. Unknown. See Bourtree, bourtree, crookit rung.
Elderberry Flute Song. Peter Blue Cloud. STE
Elderly Gentleman, The. George Canning. NA
"Elderly mermaid, I sneeze in your lasagne." Footnote. Christopher Logue. NPo
Elder's Reproof to his Wife, An. 'Abdillaahi Muuse, tr. fr. Somali by B. W. Andrzjewski and I. M. Lewis. TTY; WTO
Eldest is calling, The. Tip-of-the-Single-Feather. Velema, tr. by B. H. Quain. WTO
Eldest son bestrides him, The. The Undertaker's Horse. Kipling. FaBoNo; FM
Eldorado. Poe. AmPP; AnAmPo; AWP; FaBoBe; FaBoCh; FPL; NOBA; NoP; OxBA; RR; TAP; WiR
Eleanor———. Hayden Carruth. AnAn
Eleanor Rigby. John Lennon and Paul McCartney. PrIm; WTO
Eleanor (she spoiled in a British climate). Ezra Pound. Fr. Cantos, VII. NoAM; NOBA
Eleanora Duse, sel. Amy Lowell.
   Seeing You Stand Once More before My Eyes. Son
Eleazar Wheelock. Richard Hovey. OBAL
Elect. Mary Ursula Bethell. PeNZ
Elected Knight, The. Unknown, tr. fr. Danish by Longfellow. AWP
Elected Silence. Siegfried Sassoon. MoBrPo
Elected Silence, sing to me. The Habit of Perfection. Gerard Manley Hopkins. ACP; BrPo; LiTB; MoAB; MoBrPo; MoP; NoAM; NoP; OBEV; OBMV; PoRA; RB; TrGrPo; UnS, st.1.
Election 1960. James Keir Baxter. ATNZ
Election Reflection. M. Keel Jones. NBLV
Election Songs. Yoruba Oral Tradition, tr. by Ulli Beier. WTO
Election Speech for the Presidency of the United States of Chinamerica. David Avidan, tr. fr. Hebrew by Warren Bargad and Stanley F. Chyet. IP
Election Time. Unknown. FaBoPa
Electra. Francis Howard Williams. AA
Electric Cop, The. Victor Hernandez Cruz. PoBA

Electric Eel, The. Ron Padgett. *Fr.* Three Animals. TTTS
Electric Storm. Michael C. Martin. WaP
Electric Telegraph, The. Thomas Baker. *Fr.* The Steam Engine; or, The Power of the Flame. FaBoUs
Electricity. Sa'di Yusuf, *tr. fr. Arabic by* Abdullah al-Udhari. MPAW
Electricity Is Funny! John Currier. GrPl
Electrocution. Lola Ridge. WPE
Electronic baby born to be. Dream after Touring the Tokyo Tokei. Joy Kogawa. BrSi
Elegance. Christopher Smart. *Fr.* Hymns for the Amusement of Children, XIII. NOCV
Elegant use of foliage and grace, An. More. Gertrude Stein. *Fr.* Tender Buttons. PBWP
Elegiac. James Gates Percival. AA
Elegiac Stanzas. Wordsworth. NAEL-2; PoE
Elegiac Stanzas Suggested by a Picture of Peele Castle, in a Storm [Painted by Sir George Beaumont]. Wordsworth. ChER; EnRP; FaBoPP; GTBS; GTBS-P; NoP; OAEL-2; OBNC
Elegiack Verse on[,] An./Mr. Elijah Corlet. Nehemiah Walter. SCAP
Elegie: Going to Bed. John Donne. *See* Elegies
Elegie: His Parting from Her. John Donne. *See* Elegies: His Parting from Her.
Elegie V: His Picture. John Donne. *See* Elegies: His Picture.
Elegie, An: "Let me be what I am, as Virgil cold." Ben Jonson. PoEL-2; SeCP
Elegie, An: "Love, give me leave to serve thee, and be wise." Thomas Randolph. MePo
Elegie: "Nature's lay ideot, I taught thee to love." John Donne. *See* Elegies: Nature's lay idiot, I taught thee to love.
Elegie Made by Mr. Aurelian Townshend in Remembrance of the Ladie Venetia Digby, An. Aurelian Townshend. SeCP
Elegie XVI: On His Mistress. John Donne. *See* Elegies: On His Mistress [*or* Mistris].
Elegie, An: "Though beautie be the marke of praise." Ben Jonson. *See* Elegy, An: "Though beauty be the mark of praise."
Elegie XIX: To His Mistris Going to Bed. John Donne. *See* Elegies
Elegie on the Depleareable Departure of the Honered and Truely Religious Chieftain John Hull, An. John Saffin. SCAP
Elegie on the Lady Jane Pawlet, Marchion: of Winton, An. Ben Jonson. SeCP
Elegie upon That Reverend. Mr. Thomas Shepard, An ("Oh! That I were a poet now in grain!"), *sel.* Urian Oakes. SCAP
"Away loose-reined careers of poetry!" NOCV
Elegie upon the Death of the Dean [*or* Deane] of [St.] Paul's, Dr. John Donne, An. Thomas Carew. *See* Can we not force from widowed poetry.
Elegie upon the Death of the Lord Hastings, An. Sir John Denham. SeCV-1
Elegies. André Marie de Chénier, *tr. fr. French by* Arthur Symons. AWP
Sels.
"Every Man has his sorrows; yet each still." *Fr.* I.
"Well, I would have it so. I should have known." *Fr.* III.
"White nymph wandering in the woods by night, A." *Fr.* II.
Elegies. John Donne.
Sels.
Autumnal[l], The. *Fr.* IX. InPS; JCP; PoEL-2; SeCV-1; TEP
Change. *Fr.* III. EBEV
Going to Bed. *Fr.* XIX. EBEV; LiTB; NAEL-1; PPP
His Parting from Her. *Fr.* XII. EBEV
(Elegie: His Parting from Her.) OBS
His Picture. *Fr.* V. MePo
(Elegie V: His Picture.) MeLP; OBS
Jealousy. *Fr.* I. FF
Love's Progress. *Fr.* XVIII. LiTB; OAEL-1
"Nature's lay idiot, I taught thee to love." *Fr.* VII. NoP
(Elegie: "Nature's lay ideot, I taught thee to love.") SeCP
On His Mistress [*or* Mistris]. *Fr.* XVI. BoLoP; EBEV; LiTB; NAEL-1; PoEL-2
(Elegie XVI: On His Mistress.) SeCP
(Elegy on His Mistress.) GBL; MeLP; MePo; SeCV-1
(To His Mistress Desiring to Travel with Him as His Page.) NOBE
Perfume, The. *Fr.* IV. SeCP
Elegies. Ovid, *tr. fr. Latin.*
Sels.
Captive of Love. *Fr.* I, 2, *tr. by* Christopher Marlowe. AWP
Lente, Lente. *Fr.* I, 14, *tr. by* Kirby Flower Smith. AWP
To Verse Let Kings Give Place. *Fr.* XV, *tr. by* Christopher Marlowe. ChTr
Elegies. Sextus Propertius, *tr. fr. Latin.* AWP
Sels.
Ah Woe Is Me. *Fr.* I, 1, *tr. by* F. A. Wright.

Hylas. *Fr.* I, 20, *tr. by* F. A. Wright.
Revenge to Come. *Fr.* III, 25, *tr. by* Kirby Flower Smith.
Elegies by the Senses, *sel.* Meir Wieseltier, *tr. fr. Hebrew by* Warren Bargad *and* Stanley F. Chyet.
"Again the greyish khaki light descends." *Fr.* 1. IP
Elegies for Her Daughter, Ko-Shikibu ("That she may know I love her and miss her"). Lady Izumi, *tr. fr. Japanese by* Hiroaki Sato. *Fr.* Fifty-one Tanka. FCEI
Elegies for Prince Atsumichi. Lady Izumi, *tr. fr. Japanese by* Hiroaki Sato. *Fr.* Fifty-one Tanka. FCEI
Sels.
"Because I do not know where you are".
"Clearly he would notice: in my eyes".
"Dead people come to visit tonight."
"Discard myself—just the thought is bitter."
"I miss your voice as you talked to me."
"I wish I could see you like this snow."
"It would console me to see you."
"No dreams through the night."
"One body, but heart shattered into a thousand pieces."
"Though my heart isn't a summer field."
"You are gone, and I have nothing unhappy to remember."
Elegies for the Hot Season. Sandra McPherson. AmPA
Elegies, or the Stations of the Other Time. Ahmad Abd al-Muti Hijazi, *tr. fr. Arabic by* May Jayyusi *and* Naomi Shihab Nye. MAP
Elegy XI: "Ah me, my friend! it will not, will not last!" William Shenstone. NOEC
Elegy: "Along the tangled path and in the red." Manuel José Othón, *tr. by* Samuel Beckett. MexPo
Elegy: "And if our lives spill." Philip Dow. NPGG
Elegy: "April again, and it is a year again." Sidney Keyes. FL; WaP
Elegy: "Clear and gentle stream!" Robert Bridges. BrPo
Elegy [*or* Elegye]: "An Constant to none, but ever false to me." Thomas Campion.
Elegy: "Death be not proud, thy hand gave not this blow." Lucy Harington, Countess of Bedford. WPE
Elegy, An: December, 1970. Edgar Bowers. MT
Elegy: "Do not look for him." Leonard Cohen. HeIP
Elegy: E. W. Louis Edward Sissman. NYBP
Elegy: "Extinguished are my years of carefree laughter." Pushkin, *tr. by* Alan Myers. AAA
Elegy: "Fled is the swiftness of all the white-footed ones." Joseph Auslander. TrJP
Elegy: "Floods of tears well from my deepest heart, The." Immanuel di Roma, *tr. by* J. Chotzner. TrJP
Elegy: "Friend, whose unnatural early death." David Gascoyne. FaBoTw; TwCP
Elegy: "Gnu up at the zoo, The." John Hall Wheelock. NYBP
Elegy: "He has held." Perevin Muruvalar, *tr. by* A. K. Ramanujan. PLW
Elegy XXIII: "How does it help me if, with flawless art." Louise Labé, *tr. by* Raymond Oliver. WPOW
Elegy: "I die for Your holy word without regret." Antonio Enriquez Gomez. TrJP
Elegy: "I know but will not tell." Alan Dugan. CAPP; DiL
Elegy: "I must wait for a stranger to knock on my door." David Ignatow. NNaP
Elegy: "I remember the feel of a hammer." Robert Winner. DiL
Elegy: "I stood between two mirrors when you died." William Jay Smith. NePoEA
Elegy: "I visit once again." Pushkin, *tr. by* Alan Myers. AAA
Elegy: "If he found a little liquor." Auvaiyar, *tr. by* A. K. Ramanujan. PLW
Elegy: "In pain she bore the son who her embrace." Moses Ibn Ezra, *tr. by* Solomon Solis-Cohen. TrJP
Elegy: "In summer's heat and mid-time of the day." Ovid. *See* Amores: Corinnae Concubitus, I, 5.
Elegy: Ise Lamenting the Death of Empress Onshi. Lady Ise, *tr. fr. Japanese by* Etsuko Terasaki *and* Irma Brandeis. BoWoP
Elegy: "Let day, let night, come no more." Auvaiyar, *tr. by* A. K. Ramanujan. PLW
Elegy: "Let them bury your big eyes." Edna St. Vincent Millay. *Fr.* Memorial to D. C., V. CMoP; MoAB; MoAmPo; PoRA
Elegy, The: "Madam, no more! The time has come to eat." A. D. Hope. ErPo; NoP
Elegy VII: "Me happy, night, night full of brightness." Ezra Pound. *Fr.* Homage to Sextus Propertius. ErPo; InvP; VGW
Elegy: "Morning after death on the bar was calm." Paul Henderson. ATNZ
Elegy IX: "My dear, observe the rose! though she desire it." William Bell. NePoEA
Elegy: "My father was born with a spade in his hand and traded it." John Ciardi. DiL

Elegy: "My prime of youth is but a frost of cares." Chidiock Tichborne. *See* My prime of youth is but a frost of cares.

Elegy: "My thoughts impelled me to the resting-place." Moses Ibn Ezra, *tr. by* Emma Lazarus. TrJP

Elegy: "Newspaper appears in the morning, The." Khalifa al-Wugayyan, *tr. by* Lena Jayyusi *and* John Heath-Stubbs. MAP

Elegy: "No more, no more Jewish townships in Poland." Antoni Slonimski, *tr. by* Isaac Komem. VWA

Elegy, An: "Noon is beautiful, The: the perfect wheel." Yvor Winters. VGW

Elegy: "Nor Hammond's love nor Shenstone's was sincere." John Maclaurin. NOEC

Elegy X: "Now Christendom bids her cathedrals call." William Bell. NePoEA

Elegy: "O money, money, tell me why." N. M. Yazykov, *tr. by* Alan Myers. AAA

Elegy: "O [*or* Oh] snatch'd away in beauty's bloom!" Byron. EnRP; FiP; GTBS; GTBS-P

Elegy: "O spare a tear for poor Tom Hood." Martin Fagg. *See* O spare a tear for poor Tom Hood.

Elegy: "Out on the roads of sky the moon stands poised." Roy McFadden. NeIP

Elegy: "Pages of history open, The." Sandra M. Gilbert. PoA

Elegy: "People's wrath finds no expression, The." N. M. Yazykov, *tr. by* Alan Myers. AAA

Elegy: "Proud freedom's noble inspiration." N. M. Yazykov, *tr. by* Alan Myers. AAA

Elegy V: Separation of Man from God. George Barker. FaBoTw; LiTB

Elegy, An: "She fell away in her first ages spring." Spenser. *Fr.* Daphnaïda. OBEV

Elegy: "Since the beginning of heaven and earth." Yakamochi. *Fr.* Manyo Shu. Ma

Elegy: Summer-House on the Mound. Robert Bridges. GoTL

Elegy: "They are lang deid, folk that I used to ken." Robert Garioch. OxBS

Elegy: "This bright burning pyre." Auvaiyar, *tr. by* A. K. Ramanujan. PLW

Elegy: "Those reckless hosts rush to the wells." Baruch of Worms. TrJP

Elegy, An: "Though beauty be the mark of praise." Ben Jonson. NoP; OBEV; QFR

Elegy: To Spring, *sel.* Michael Bruce.
    "Farewell, ye blooming fields! ye cheerful plains!" NOEC

Elegy: "Today, because I am not dead." Vincent O'Sullivan. ATNZ

Elegy: "Tonight the moon is high, to summon all." William Bell. FaBoTw

Elegy: "Were you, as old prints have shown." John Frederick Nims. BLA

Elegy: "When in the mirror of a permanent tear." Gene Derwood. *See* When in the mirror of a permanent tear.

Elegy: "When the old ones die." Karoniaktatie. STE

Elegy: "Whenever we touched, I thought of the Lying-in Hospital." Robert Layzer. NePoEA

Elegy: "While walking at dusk in a strange city." Pinhas Sadeh, *tr. by* Gabriel Preil *and* Howard Schwartz. VWA

Elegy: "Who keeps the owl's breath? Whose eyes desire?" David St. John. LCAP

Elegy: "Who would I show it to." W. S. Merwin. HCAP

Elegy: "Whole tribe dies, A." Duane Big Eagle. STE

Elegy: "Wind won't come to draw smiles in dream sand, The." Yehuda Amichai, *tr. by* Warren Bargad *and* Stanley F.Chyet. IP

Elegy: "Wood is bare, The: a river-mist is steeping." Robert Bridges. EBVV

Elegy: Woods, The. Sa'di Yusuf, *tr. fr. Arabic by* Sargon Boulus *and* Naomi Shihab Nye. MAP

Elegy: "Yes, I experienced youth." Wu Sheng, *tr. by* Dominic Cheung. IFON

Elegy: "Young will not wear it, The." Kutavayir Kirattanar, *tr. by* A. K. Ramanujan. PLW

Elegy. Frank Bidart. HCAP
    Sels.
    Light. *Fr.* IV.
    Lineage. *Fr.* V.

Elegy. Alistair Campbell.
    Sels.
    Laid-out Body, The. *Fr.* 8. ATNZ
    Now He Is Dead. *Fr.* 2. ATNZ

Elegy and Flame. Horace Gregory. FYAP

Elegy and Kaddish. David Rosenmann-Taub, *tr. fr. Spanish by* Charles Guenther. VWA

Elegy before Death. Edna St. Vincent Millay. CMoP; LiTA; LiTM

Elegy for a Bad Poet, Taken from Us Not Long Since. John Frederick Nims. TW

Elegy for a Countryman. Padraic Fallon. NeIP

Elegy for a Dead Soldier. Karl Shapiro. HAP; LiTM; OBWP; OxBA; WaaP; WaP
    Sel.
    "Underneath this wooden cross there lies." OFD

Elegy for a Diver. Peter Meinke. Psk

Elegy for a Forest Clear-Cut by the Weyerhaeuser Company. David Wagoner. NoAM

Elegy for a Man Who Died and Died. Mamdouh Udwan, *tr. fr. Arabic by* May Jayyusi *and* Naomi Shihab Nye. MAP

Elegy for a Nature Poet. Howard Nemerov. BoNaP; HoPM

Elegy for a Puritan Conscience. Alan Dugan. CAPP; SM

Elegy for a School-Friend. Augustus Young. BlrV

Elegy for a Schoolmate. Vincent O'Sullivan. ATNZ; PeNZ

Elegy for a Woman of No Importance. Nazik al-Mala'ika, *tr. fr. Arabic by* Chris Knipp *and* Mohammad Sadiq. OV

Elegy for Aisha. Abd al-Wahhab al-Bayyati, *tr. fr. Arabic by* Sargon Boulus *and* Christopher Middleton. MAP

Elegy for Alfred Hubbard. Tony Connor. SoSe

Elegy for an Android. D. M. Thomas. BWV

Elegy for an Estrangement. John Holloway. NePoEA

Elegy for an Unknown Soldier. James K. Baxter. ATNZ

Elegy for Bella, Sarah, Rosie, and All the Others. Sonya Dorman. GOA

Elegy for Bob Marley, An. William Matthews. MAYP

Elegy for Chief Sealth. Duane Niatum. CDW

Elegy for Delina. Albert Rowe. CRH

Elegy for Dylan Thomas. Edith Sitwell. PoA

Elegy for Frank Stanford. Thomas Lux. AnAn

Elegy for Her Brother Sakhr. Al-Khansa, *tr. fr. Arabic.* BoWoP, *tr. by* Willis Barnstone; WPOW, *tr. by* Bridget Connelly

Elegy (for Himself). Moses Rimos of Majorca, *tr. fr. Hebrew by* Israel Abrahams. TrJP

Elegy for Himself. Chidiock Tichborne. *See* My prime of youth is but a frost of cares.

Elegy for His Daughter Ellen. Goronwy Owen, *tr. fr. Welsh by* George Borrow. OBWVE

Elegy for Hölderlin, An. Fu'ad Rifqa, *tr. fr. Arabic by* Abdullah al-Udhari. MPAW

Elegy for Jack Bowman. Joseph Bruchac. CDW

Elegy for Jane. Theodore Roethke. AmPP; CAPP; CoAP; FF; HAP; HCAP; InPK; InPS; LiTM; MoAB; MoAmPo; NoP; PoE; TAP; TwCP; WeW

Elegy for John Wilborg. Sylvester Pollet. SoTCo

Elegy for Lyn James. Leslie Norris. OBWVE

Elegy for Maria Alves. Joaquim Cardozo, *tr. fr. Portuguese by* Elizabeth Bishop. ATCBP

Elegy for María Belén Chacón. Emilio Ballagas, *tr. fr. Spanish by* Perry Higman. LPSS

Elegy for Minor Poets. Louis MacNeice. FaBCIP

Elegy for Mr. Goodbeare. Sir Osbert Sitwell. MoBrPo

Elegy for My Father. Howard Moss. CoAP; DiL; LiTM; NePoEA; VWA

Elegy for My Father, *sels.* Mark Strand. DiL; GeTw; LCAP
    Empty Body, The. UnPo
    New Year, The. UnPo
    Your Shadow. Prf

Elegy for My Father, *sel.* Irving Wexler.
    "When Friday nights are lucky, you." DiL

Elegy for My Mother. Richard Katrovas. SM

Elegy for Myself. Ching An, *tr. fr. Chinese by* Irving Lo. WFTU

Elegy for N. N. Czeslaw Milosz. SV

Elegy for Our Dead. Edwin Rolfe. WaP

Elegy for the Duke of Marmalade. Luis Palés Matos, *tr. by* Julio Marzán. InW

Elegy for the Forgotten Oldsmobile. Adrian C. Louis. STE

Elegy for the Giant Tortoises. Margaret Atwood. BoWoP

Elegy for the Lost Parish. Douglas Dunn. DiPo

Elegy for the Monastery Barn. Thomas Merton. VGW

Elegy for the Other. Cleopatra Mathis. MT

Elegy for the Silent Voices and the Joiners of Everything. Kenneth Patchen. NaP

Elegy for the Wife of a Friend. Yü Hsüan-chi, *tr. fr. Chinese by* Geoffrey Waters. BoWoP

Elegy for the Young Corpse. José Luis Villatoro, *tr. fr. Spanish by* Tony Ryan. Vol

Elegy for Two Banjos. Karl Shapiro. LiTA; TrJP; WaP

Elegy for W. C. W., the Lovely Man, An. John Berryman. *Fr.* Dream Songs. NoP

Elegy for William Soutar. William Montgomerie. OxBS

Elegy for Wright & Hugo. Norman Dubie. NoAM

Elegy for Yards, Pounds, and Gallons. David Wagoner. PoA

Elegy in a Country Churchyard. G. K. Chesterton. FaPoR; MMA; MoBrPo; OBWP; OxBSP; TrGrPo

Elegy in a Presbyterian Burying-Ground. Robert Noble Denison Wilson.
  BlrV
Elegy in a Theatrical Warehouse. Kenneth Fearing. NYBP
Elegy in Memory of the Worshipful Major Thomas Leonard Esq, An.
  Samuel Danforth, Jr.. SCAP
Elegy in the Orongorongo Valley. Hubert Witheford. ATNZ
Elegy Is Preparing Itself, An. Donald Justice. CRP; HoPM
Elegy Just in Case. John Ciardi. TwCP
Elegy, Montreal Morgue. Goodridge MacDonald. CaP
Elegy of a Bronze Age Man, The. Zoltán Jékely, *tr. fr. Hungarian by*
  Edwin Morgan. MHuP
Elegy of Fortinbras. Zbigniew Herbert, *tr. fr. Polish by* Czeslaw Milosz.
  FaBoPV; PwPP
Elegy of the Hogs. H. H. ter Balkt, *tr. fr. Dutch by* Scott Rollins. DuIn
Elegy on a Lady, Whom Grief for the Death of Her Betrothed Killed.
  Robert Bridges. OBEV
Elegy on a Nordic White Protestant. John Gould Fletcher. PoNe
Elegy on Albert Edward the Peacemaker. *Unknown.* CoMu
Elegy on an Australian Schoolboy, *sel.* Zora Cross.
  "O brother in the restless rest of God!" PoAu-1
Elegy on Any Lady by George Moore. Max Beerbohm. FaBoEE
Elegy on Ben Jonson, An. John Cleveland. MeLP; OBS
Elegy on Captain Matthew Henderson, *sel.* Burns.
  "Mourn, ye wee songsters o' the wood." PBBP
Elegy on Cynddylan, The, *sel. Unknown, tr. fr. Welsh by* Kenneth
  Hurlstone Jackson.
  "Stand out, maids, and look on the land of Cynddylan." OBWVE
Elegy on Gordon Barber. Gene Derwood. FaFP
  (Elegy: "When in the mirror of a permanent tear.") LiTA; LiTM
Elegy on His Mistress. John Donne. *See* By our first strange and fatal
  interview.
Elegy on Mistress Boulstred. John Donne. JCP
Elegy on My Father. Allen Curnow. ATNZ
Elegy on Shakespeare. William Basse. FaBoRV; OBS
Elegy on That [*or* the] Glory of Her Sex, Mrs. Mary Blaize, An.
  Goldsmith. FaBoNo; NA
Elegy on the Death of a Mad Dog, An. Goldsmith. *Fr.* The Vicar of
  Wakefield, *ch.* 17. BeLS; BLPA; FaBoBe; FaBoCh; FaBoCo; FaFP;
  FPL; GN; NA; NBLV; NOBE; NOEC; NOIV; OBNV; TEP
Elegy on the Death of Dobbin, the Butterwoman's Horse, An. Francis
  Fawkes. NOEC
Elegy on the Death of Furuhi, An. Okura. DL
Elegy on the Death of Her Husband. Anne Howard. WPE
Elegy on the Death of His Mistress Hoor Tal'at. Momin Khan Momin, *tr.
  fr. Urdu by* Ahmed Ali. GoT
Elegy on the Death of John Keats, An. Shelley. *See* Adonais; an Elegy
  on the Death of John Keats: Peace, peace! he is not dead, he doth not
  sleep.
Elegy on the Dust. Thom Gunn. NoAM
Elegy on the Eve. George Barker. WaaP
Elegy on the Glory of Her Sex, Mrs. Mary Blaize, The. Goldsmith.
Elegy on the Lady Jane Paulet, An, *sel.* Ben Jonson.
  "How did she leave the world? with what contempt?." OBD
Elegy on the Late King of Patagonia, An. St. John Emile Clavering
  Hankin. CenHV
Elegy on Thomas Hood. Martin Fagg. FaBoPa; NOBL
  (Elegy: "O spare a tear for poor Tom Hood.") BXAP
Elegy on Thyrza. Byron. *See* And Thou Art Dead.
Elegy, or Friend's Passion for His Astrophil [*or* Astrophel], An, *sels.*
  Matthew Royden.
On Sir Philip Sidney. EiL
  "Upon the branches of those trees." PBBP
Elegy over a Tomb. Lord Herbert of Cherbury. EiL; MeLP; MePo;
  NOBE; OBEV; OBS; OBWVE; PoEL-2; QFR
Elegy, to an Old Beauty, An. Thomas Parnell. NOEC
Elegy to Li Shuang-tse. Chiang Hsun, *tr. fr. Chinese by* Dominic
  Cheung. IFON
Elegy to the Memory of an Unfortunate Lady ("O Ever beauteous, ever
  friendly, tell"). Pope. ACP
Elegy to the Memory of an Unfortunate Lady ("What beckoning ghost,
  along the moonlight shade."), *sels.* Pope. ACP; FiP; NOBE;
  NOEC; OAEL-1; OBEV; TEP
Sels.
  "Most souls, 'tis true, but peep out once an age." CH
  (Dull, Sullen Prisoners.) FaBoRV
  "What beck'ning ghost, along the moonlight shade." OBD
Elegy to the Sioux. Norman Dubie. MAYP
Elegy upon His Tomb in Herndon-Hill Church, Erected by His Wife, Who
  Speaks, An. James Howell. OBWVE
Elegy upon the Death of Doctor Donne, Dean of Paul's, An. Thomas
  Carew. *See* Elegy upon the Death of the Dean of [St.] Paul's, Dr.
  John Donne, An.

Elegy upon the Death of That Holy Man of God Mr. John Allen, An.
  Edward Taylor. PoEL-3
Elegy upon the Death of the Dean of [St.] Paul's, Dr. John Donne, An.
  Thomas Carew. CaPo; JCP; NoP
  (Elegie upon the Death of the Deane of Pauls, Dr. John Donne, An.)
  MeLP; MePo; OBS; SeCP; SeCV-1
  (Elegy upon the Death of Doctor Donne, Dean of Paul's, An.)
  OAEL-1
On the Death of Donne, *sel.* NOBE
Elegy upon the Most Incomparable King Charles the First, An, *sel.* Henry
  King.
  "Thou from th' enthroned martyrs blood-stain'd line." OBS
Elegy Written at the Sea-Side, and Addressed to Miss Honoria Sneyd.
  Anna Seward. PeHV
Elegy Written in a Country Churchyard. Thomas Gray. AWP; DL;
  EBEV; EnRP; FaBoBe; FaBoPP; FaBoPV; FaBoRV; FaFP; FaPoR;
  FPL; GN; GTBS; GTBS-P; HAP; HeIP; InPK; InPS; LaA; LiTB;
  NOBE; NOEC; NoP; OAEL-1; OBEV; OHFP; PoEL-3; PoLF; PPP;
  PrIm; SCV; TEP; TrGrPo; UnPo; WBLP; WeW
Sels.
  "Boast of heraldry, the pomp of pow'r, The." OBD
  "Here rests his head upon the lap of earth." FaBoPV
Elegy Written in a Country Coal-Bin. Christopher Morley. OBAL
Elegy, Written with His Own Hand in the Tower before His Execution.
  Chidiock Tichborne. *See* Tichborne's Elegy.
Elegy Wrote in the Tower, 1554. John Harington. EiL
Elegye, An: "Constant to none, but ever false to me." Thomas Campion.
  AAS
Elektra on Third Avenue. Marilyn Hacker. MAYP
Element. P. K. Page. MoCV
Element that utters doves, angels and cleft flames. Air. Kathleen Jessie
  Raine. MoAB; MoBrPo
Elemental. D. H. Lawrence. NoP
Elementary. Jim Tollerud. VoR
Elementary Cosmogony. Charles Simic. NNaP
Elementary Scene, The. Randall Jarrell. CMoP; LCAP; PoE
Elementary School Classroom in a Slum, An. Stephen Spender.
  FaBoMo; FF; LiTB; MoAB; MoBrPo; NIP; TrGrPo; TwCP; UnPo
Elementary school for six years. Autobiography of a Sloppy Sluggard.
  Kuan Kuan, *tr. by* Dominic Cheung. IFON
Elementary Thoughts, *sels.* Nelo Risi, *tr. fr. Italian by* Gavin Ewart.
  PFI
  "Loud voices are needed." *Fr.* XXI.
  "To deny what we know." *Fr.* XX.
Elements, The. William Henry Davies. MoBrPo
Elements. Arthur Rex Dugard Fairburn. ATNZ
Elements, The. Tom Lehrer. FaBoUs
Elements. Carolyn Wilson Link. GoYe
Elements have merged into solicitude, The. The Racer's Widow. Louise
  Glück. AmPA; ASP; GeTw; NYBP; SM
Elements of Grammar. Calvin C. Hernton. NBP
Elements of San Joaquin, The ("Wind sprays pale dirt into my mouth,
  The."), *sels.* Gary Soto. NPGG
Rain. NoAM
Wind. NoAM
Elena's Song. Sir Henry Taylor. *Fr.* Philip van Artevelde, II. OBEV
Elene, *sels.* Cynewulf, *tr. fr. Anglo-Saxon by* Charles W. Kennedy.
  AnOE
Constantine's Vision of the Cross.
Helena Embarks for Palestine.
Elephant, The. A. E. Housman. *See* Tail behind a trunk in front, An.
Elephant, The. Herbert Asquith. BoTP
Elephant, The. Hilaire Belloc. BoTP
Elephant. Alan Brownjohn. OnUR
Elephant, The. E. J. Falconer. BoTP
Elephant. Louis Johnson. ATNZ
Elephant, *sel.* Pablo Neruda, *tr. fr. Spanish.*
  "Gross innocent." TTTS
Elephant, The. Dan Pagis, *tr. fr. Hebrew by* Bernhard Frank. MHeP
Elephant ("Elephant, a spirit in the bush"). *Unknown, tr. fr. Yoruba by*
  Ulli Beier. *Fr.* Hunter Poems of the Yoruba. RB
Elephant, The ("Elephant carries a great big trunk, The"). *Unknown.*
  OnUR; RAR
Elephant [II], The ("Elephant hunter, take your bow!"). *Unknown, tr. fr.
  Gabon Pigmy by* C. M. Bowra. TTY
Elephant [I], The ("Elephant who brings death."). *Unknown, tr. fr.
  Yoruba by* Gbadamosi *and* Ulli Beier. TTTS; TTY
Elephant ("Tall-topped acacia"). *Unknown.* PeSA
Elephant, ancient general, scarred, The. The Elephant. Dan Pagis, *tr. by*
  Bernhard Frank. MHeP
Elephant beaten with candy and little pops and chews. A Sound.
  Gertrude Stein. *Fr.* Tender Buttons. TTTS

Elephant carries a great big trunk, The. Elephant, The. *Unknown.* OnUR; RAR

Elephant is in love with the millimeter, The. What the Violins Sing in Their Baconfat Bed. Hans Arp, *tr.* by John Frederick Nims. WeW

Elephant is like a wall, The. The Elephant. E. J. Falconer. BoTP

Elephant Is Slow to Mate, The. D. H. Lawrence. LiTB; LiTM; PPP; TEP

Elephant of long service to a circus, An. The Retirement of the Elephant. Russell Edson. AmPA

Elephant of Moissel, hear my pious prayer. Léopold Sédar Senghor, *tr. fr. French by* Ellen Conroy Kennedy. *Fr.* Return of the Prodigal Son. GrPl

Elephant, or the Force of Habit, The. A. E. Housman. NOBL (Elephant, The.) FaBV

Elephant Rock. Primus St. John. PoBA

Elephant, the huge old beast, The. The Elephant Is Slow to Mate. D. H. Lawrence. LiTB; LiTM; PPP; TEP

Elephant who brings death. Elephant [I], The ("Elephant who brings death."). *Unknown, tr.* by Gbadamosi *and* Ulli Beier. TTTS; TTY

Elephants. Patrick Lane. NeAC

Elephants Are Different to Different People. Carl Sandburg. MoAmPo

Elephants Dying, The. Michael C. Blumenthal. NoAM

Elephants from the Sea. Ian Young. NeAC

"Elephants in bed," my daughter says. Vision. Louis Johnson. PeNZ

Elephant's in love with the millimeter, The. What Violins Are Singing in Their Beds of Lard. Hans Arp, *tr.* by Michael Benedikt. POS

Elephants May Parade before Your House. *Gond Oral Tradition, tr.* by V. Elwin *and* S. Hivale. WTO

Elephants walking. Holding Hands. Lenore M. Link. FaPON; MoShBr; NTCP; RAR; RHPC

Eletelephony. Laura Richards. FaPON; GoJo; MoShBr; NBLV; NTCP; OBCA; OnUR; OxBChV; PDV; PYC; RHPC

Elevated stammers and clatters, the 7:10, The. Jazz Vamp. Maurice B. Cloud. VVA

Élévation. Baudelaire, *tr. fr. French by* Arthur Symons. AWP

Elevation. Robert Morgan. MOWH

Elevator Landscapes, *sels.* Stephen Vincent. NeAC
  Floor: Five.
  Floor: O.

Elevator Man Adheres to Form, The. Margaret Danner. PoBA; PoNe

Elevator operator. Mr. 'Gator. N. M. Bodecker. NTCP; OnUR

Elevator rises, Negro men, The. Poem to Negro and Whites. Maxwell Bodenheim. PoNe

Eleven. Archibald MacLeish. HAP; WeW

Eleven Addresses to the Lord, *abr., sels.* John Berryman. OxBC
  "Master of beauty, craftsman of the snowflake." *Fr.* I. UnPo
  Prayer for the Self, A. *Fr.* VIII. PPP
  "Sole watchman of the flying stars, guard me." *Fr.* III. UnPo

"1100 Exposition." Newletter from My Mother. Michael S. Harper. PoBA

Eleven o'clock, and the curtain falls. End of the Comedy. Louis Untermeyer. PoA

11 rue Daguerre. John Montague. FaBCIP

Eleven-thirty and hot. The Cyclist. Marge Piercy. NoAM

Eleven years ago I left for good. Elegy for My Mother. Richard Katrovas. SM

Eleventh Song: "Who is it that this dark night." Sir Philip Sidney. *Fr.* Astrophel and Stella. EiL; NAEL-1; OBSC; PoE; PoEL-1; TEP
  (Underneath My Window.) SeCePo
  (Voices at the Window.) NOBE; OBEV

Elf and the Dormouse, The. Oliver Herford. AA; FaBoBe; FaPON; OnMSP; RHPC

Elf-light, owl-light. Dusk in the Domain. Dorothea MacKellar. PoAu-1

Elf Night. Ron Rogers. STE

Elfer Hill. *Unknown, tr. fr. Danish by* Robert Jamieson. AWP

Elfin Knight, An. Joseph Rodman Drake. BoTP

Elfin Knight, The ("Go tell him to clear me one acre of ground"). *Unknown.* AmFP; WSC

Elfin Knight, The ("Elphin Knight sits on yon hill, The"). *Unknown.* ESPB

Elfin Pedlar, The. George Darley. BoTP

Elfin People Fill the Tubes, The. Winifred M. Letts. BoTP

Elfin Song. Joseph Rodman Drake. *Fr.* The Culprit Fay. AA

Elfin Town. Rachel Lyman Field. WSC

Eli, Eli. Judith Wright. CBAP

Eli, Eli, lama sabacthani? At the Ninth Hour. John Lancaster Spalding. *Fr.* God and the Soul. AA

Eli the Thatcher. Max Beerbohm *and* William Rothenstein. FaBoNo

Elijah Speaking. Doug Fetherling. NOBC

Elijah's mantle fell upon. A Little Song of Work. Sarah Elizabeth Sprouse. BLRP

Elinda's [*or* Ellinda's] Glove. Richard Lovelace. CaPo; OBS

Elinor Wylie fell in love with Shelley. A Thought in Time. Robert Hillyer. NYBP

Elisa ("Ye dainty nymphs, that in this blessed brook"). Spenser. *Fr.* The Shepheardes [*or* Shepeards *or* Shepherd's] Calender: Aprill. OBSC (Lay to Eliza, The.) NOBE

Elise, I have your valentine with the red shoes, I have. A Grandfather's Last Letter. Norman Dubie. MOWH

Elixir, The. George Herbert. BoTP; FaBoCh; GN; NoP; OHIP; SeCV-1; TrGrPo; WGRP

Eliza and Anne were extremely distress'd. The Bird's Nest. Elizabeth Turner. OHIP

Eliza in Uncle Tom's Cabin. Eloise Bibb. CBWP-4

Eliza Telefair. Jocelyn Macy Sloan. GoYe

Elizabeth. Caroline Griffin. DT

Elizabeth. Valentin Iremonger. *See* Elizabeth fridgidly stretched.

Elizabeth. Michael Ondaatje. NoAM

Elizabeth. Sylvia Townsend Warner. MoAB; MoBrPo

Elizabeth Cried. Eleanor Farjeon. ILY

Elizabeth, Elspeth, Betsy, and Bess. Mother Goose. OxNR

Elizabeth, frigidly stretched. This Houre Her Vigill. Valentin Iremonger. CIP; NOIV; OxBTC
  (Elizabeth.) NeIP

Elizabeth in Italy. Richard Weber. BoLoP

Elizabeth of Bohemia. Sir Henry Wotton. *See* You meaner Beauties of the night.

"Elizabeth the Beloved." Elizabeth. Sylvia Townsend Warner. MoAB; MoBrPo

Elizabethan Tragedy; a Footnote. Howard Moss. NePoEA

"Elizabethans Called It Dying, The." James Schuyler. NeAP; PoM

Elizabeth's War with the Christmas Bear. Norman Dubie. LCAP; MAYP; NoAM

Elk at Black Fork Canyon. Tom Sleigh. PPR

Elk Camp. Raymond Carver. TSL

Elk Ghosts: A Birth Memory. Dave Smith. GeTw

Elk on Mutability, The. John Bensko. MT

Elk, The Whelk, The. Robert Williams Wood. NBLV

Elk Uncovers the Heavens, The. John Bensko. MT

Ella, fell a/ Maple tree. Picnic. Hugh Lofting. GoJo

Ella, in a Square Apron, along Highway 80. Judy Grahn. *Fr.* The Common Woman, II. NMM

Ella Mi Fu Rapita! Gavin Ewart. NoAM

Ella Speed. *Unknown.* AmFP

Ellas and the Statues. Gülten Akin, *tr. fr. Turkish by* Nermin Menemencioglu. PBWP

Ellen Flannery. *Unknown.* AmFP

Ellen Taylor. *Unknown.* OBET

Ellen West. Frank Bidart. NAAL-2; PPR

Ellery Street. David Ferry. PPR

Ellie Mae Leaves in a Hurry. Peter Klappert. SM

Ellinda's Glove. Richard Lovelace. *See* Elinda's Glove.

Elliott Hawkins. Edgar Lee Masters. *Fr.* Spoon River Anthology. OxPA

Ellsworth. *Unknown.* PAH

Elm. Sylvia Plath. NoAM; NOBA; NoP

Elm is turned to crystal, The. Weather. William Meredith. NYBP

Elm lets fall its leaves before the frost, The. The Pine. Augusta Webster. OHIP

Elm Speaks, The. Sylvia Plath. *See* I know the bottom she says.

Elms. Louise Glück. NoAM

Elms are bad, sinister trees. Breakwaters. Ted Walker. NYBP

Elms have to fight, The. Home Movies. Carter Revard. VoR

Elm's Home, The. William Heyen. MAYP

Elms of the Eastern Gate. *Unknown, tr.* by Arthur Waley. BoS

Eloisa. Pope. *Fr.* Eloisa to Abelard. SeCePo

Eloïsa to Abelard. Pope. NAEL-1; PoEL-3; TEP

Eloisa to Abelard ("In these deep solitudes and awful cells."), *sels.* Pope. PoEL-3; TEP
  Eloisa. SeCePo
  Vestal, The. ACP

Elongated line of a river, An. Boncho, *tr. fr. Japanese by* Hiroaki Sato. *Fr.* Twenty-one Hokku. FCEI

Eloquent between the formal hedges. Affair of Honour. George Whalley. MoCV

Elphin Knight, The. ("The Elphin knight sits on yon hill"). *Unknown.* ESPB

Elsa Wertman. Edgar Lee Masters. *Fr.* Spoon River Anthology. MoP; NoAM; OxBA

Elsa's Eyes. Louis Aragon, *tr. fr. French by* William Jay Smith. CT

Elsdon. Freda Downie. FaBoPP

"Else a Great Prince in Prison Lies." Denise Levertov. NaP; PPP; VGW

Elsewhere. Linda Pastan. VWA

Elsewhere. Derek Walcott. BAP

Elsewheres. Donald Justice. LCAP

Elsie Marley is grown so fine. *Unknown.* OxNR

Elul in Galilee. Leah Goldberg, *tr. fr. Hebrew* by Bernhard Frank. MHeP

Elusive Maid, The. Abraham ibn Chasdai, *tr. fr. Hebrew* by J. Chotzner. TrJP

Elustrious Dame whose vertues rare doe shine. An Acrostick on Mrs. Elizabeth Hull. John Saffin. SCAP

Elver Fishers. Ivor Gurney. FaBoPP

Elves' Dance, The. *at. to* John Lyly *and to* Thomas Ravenscroft. *Fr.* The Mayde's Metamorphosis. CH; FaPON

Elvin's Blues. Michael S. Harper. BPo

Elwha River, The. Gary Snyder. NoAM

Elysee. Larry Eigner. VGW

Elysium is as far as to. Emily Dickinson. GrPl; MoAB; MoAmPo; OxBA; WPE
(Suspense.) AWP

Emanations. Hameed Said, *tr. fr. Arabic* by Lena Jayyusi *and* Naomi Shihab Nye. MAP

Emancipation. Maltbie Davenport Babcock. BLRP; WBLP

Emancipation. Priscilla Jane Thompson. CBWP-2

Emancipation. *Unknown.* BLPA; FPL

Emancipation Day. Lizelia Augusta Jenkins Moorer. CBWP-3

Emancipation from British Dependence. Philip Freneau. PAH

Emancipation of George-Hector (a Colored Turtle), The. Mari E. Evans. AmNP

Emancipators, The. Randall Jarrell. PoA; WaP

Emaricdulfe. "E. C." ElL
Sels.
"E. C."
My Heart Is like a Ship. *Fr.* XXIX. Son
Within Her Hair. *Fr.* VI. Son

Embalm, O Muse, in an appropriate lay. The Holiday. Thomas Frank Bignold. OBTV

Embankment [*or* Fantasia of a Fallen Gentleman], The. T. E. Hulme. EBEV; FaBoMo; GTBS-P; OxBSP; OxBTC

Embarcation. Thomas Hardy. BrPo; OBWP

Embarkation, The. Longfellow. *Fr.* Evangeline, PAH. BeLS

Embarrassed, you reach God's door. Ceremony. Al-Munsif al-Wahaybi, *tr.* by Salma Khadra Jayyusi *and* Naomi Shihab Nye. MAP

Embarrassing Episode of Little Miss Muffet, The. Guy Wetmore Carryl. FaPON; OBCA; OnMSP

Embassy of doves, An. Late. Helen Salz. GoYe

Ember Week, Reseda. Stephen Yenser. EOEF

Embers of the day are red, The. Evensong. Robert Louis Stevenson. TrPWD

Emblazoned bleak in austral skies. Southern Cross. Herman Melville. LiTA

Emblem of England's ancient faith. To an Oak Tree. Sir Walter Scott. *Fr.* Waverley, 29. OBNC

Emblem of Two Foxes, An. Barry Spacks. HoPM

Emblems. Douglas Dunn. FaBoMo

Emblems, *sels.* Francis Quarles.
"My soul, thy love is dear: 'twas thought a good." *Fr.* V, 4. OAEL-1
"Great All in All, that art my rest, my home." *Fr.* IV, 3. TrPWD
Like to the Arctic Needle. *Fr.* V, 4. EBEV; NOCV; OAEL-1
(I Am My Beloved's, and His Desire Is towards Me.) OBS
My Beloved Is Mine, and I Am His; He Feedeth among the Lillies. *Fr.* V, 3. MeLP; MePo; NOBE; OBEV; OBS; TrGrPo, abr.; TrGrPo
(Divine Rapture.) OBEV
Wherefore Hidest Thou Thy Face, and Holdest Me for Thine Enemie? *Fr.* III, 7. MePo; OBS
Wilt Thou Set Thine Eyes upon That Which Is Not? *Fr.* II, 5. OBS
(False World, Thou Liest.) SeCePo

Emblems. Allen Tate. AWP; VGW

Emblems mean nothing. Like the Sea, Kisses. Vicente Aleixandre, *tr.* by Perry Higman. LPSS

Emblems of Conduct. Hart Crane. LiTA; LiTM

Emblems of Love, *sels.* Lascelles Abercrombie.
"What shall we do for Love these days?." CH; MoBrPo
Small Fountains. CH
Hymn to Love. OBEV
Song: "Balkis was in her marble town." MoBrPo
Vashti.
Woman's Beauty. MoBrPo

Embodied close, the lab'ring Grecian train. Homer, *tr. fr. Greek* by Pope. *Fr.* The Iliad, V. OBVE

Embodiment of what, The. Arthur Gregor. TAP

Embrace me,/ My sweet embraceable carrot. Carrot Crazy. Edward Watkins. SoTCo

Embrace the Blade. Joyce Mansour, *tr. fr. French* by Carol Cosman. PBWP

Embracing low-falutin. The Countryman's Return. Dylan Thomas. OxBTC

Embracing the young mother from behind. Peyanar, *tr. fr. Tamil* by A. K. Ramanujan. *Fr.* Seven Said by the Foster-Mother, 2. PLW

Embracing this woman. Peyanar, *tr. fr. Tamil* by A. K. Ramanujan. *Fr.* Seven Said by the Foster-Mother, 5. PLW

Embro to the Ploy. Robert Garioch. OxBS

Embroidery. Catherine Nomura Crystal. AiP

Embroidery, An. Denise Levertov. NMM; NU

Embryo. Mary Ashley Townsend. AA

Emer, he is your man, now. Fand Yields Cuchulain to Emer. *Unknown*, *tr.* by Sean O'Faolain. AnIL

Emerald, The. James Merrill. *Fr.* Up and Down. CAPP

Emerald cages a jungle, The. Prologue for a Bestiary. Ronald Perry. NePoEA-2

Emerald is as green as grass, An. Flint. Christina Rossetti. *Fr.* Sing-Song. OxBChV; RHPC

Emeralds are singing on the grasses, The. How Many Heavens. Dame Edith Sitwell. TrCP

Emergency at 8. Geof Hewitt. NeAC

Emergency Haying. Hayden Carruth. NNaP

Emergency Maker, The. David Wagoner. NePoEA-2

Emergency Poem 1973. Cyn Zarco. UL

Emergency Room, The. David Fisher. NPGG

Emerges daintily, the skunk. The Wood Weasel. Marianne Moore. CMoP

Emerging from the inmost hideout. Splendor. Shin Shalom, *tr.* by Abraham Birman. VWA

Emerging from the nose. Issa, *tr.* by Geoffrey Bownas *and* Anthony Thwaite. PeBJV

Emeritus, The. Leonard Nathan. MOWH

Emeritus, n. Henri Coulette. FF

Emerson. Amos Bronson Alcott. AA

Emerson. Mary Mapes Dodge. AA

Emerson. James Russell Lowell. *See* Fable for Critics, A: There comes Emerson first, whose rich words, every one.

Emerson. Henrietta Cordelia Ray. CBWP-3

Emerson thought the bride had one eye. New England, Springtime. Norman Dubie. NAmP

Emigrant, The, *sels.* Alexander McLachlan.
Arrival, The. NOBC
"Old England is eaten by Knaves." NOBC; OBCV

Emigrant, The, *sels.* Standish O'Grady.
"And first Morency, far famed water, you." CaP
Old Nick in Sorel. OBCV
Winter in Lower Canada. NOBC; OBCV

Emigrant Ship, The. Henry Dalton. PVCV

Emigrant Song. "S. Ansky," *tr. fr. Yiddish* by Joseph Leftwich. TrJP

Emigration. Anita Barrows. NMM

Emigration of the Fairies, The, *sel.* John Hunter-Duvar.
"First halt. They heard within a sugar patch." CaP

Emigravit. Helen Hunt Jackson. AA

Emigré Jewess. Gabriela Mistral, *tr. fr. Spanish* by Kate Flores. DMH

Emigrés, The. Ted Walker. OBTV

Emilia/ strung the lines of white laundry. Short Biography of a Washerwoman. Yolanda Ulloa. AIW

Emily Brontë. C. Day Lewis. GTBS-P

Emily Carr. Wilfred Watson. MoCV; NOBC; OBCV

Emily Dickinson. Michael Longley. CIP

Emily Dickinson, Bismarck and the Roadrunner's Inquiry. Ray A. Young Bear. HATNAP

Emily Dickinson Postage Stamp. Lynn Strongin. NMM

Emily Dickinson's Sestina for Molly Bloom. Barbara F. Lefcowitz. SM

Emily Geiger. *Unknown.* BLPL; PoLF

Emily Hardcastle, Spinster. John Crowe Ransom. CMoP; OxBSP

Emily wandered through town and folks said that she saw. Old Emily. Hyacinthe Hill. GoYe

Emily's Haunted Housman. David Cummings. BXAP

Eminence becomes you. Now when the rock is struck. To T. S. Eliot. Emanuel Litvinoff. VWA

Eminent Critic. John Frederick Nims. TW

Emma. Yvonne. CNA
(Premonition (in a Voice My Mother Called "Not Your Own").) TV

Emmeline Grangerford's "Ode to Stephen Dowling Bots, Dec'd." "Mark Twain." *Fr.* The Adventures of Huckleberry Finn. NBLV; OBAL

Emmett Till. James A. Emanuel. CNA; NIP; PoBA

Emmonsail's Heath in Winter. John Clare. PoEL-4

Emmonsales Heath was the last rim of the world. John Clare and the Acts of Enclosure. Neil Curry. NPo

Emmy ("Emmy's exquisite youth and her virginal air"). Arthur Symons. OBNC

Empathy. Agnes Pratt. NOVW

Empathy for David Winfield. David Shapiro. BAP

Empedocles came coughing through the smoke. To the Thoughtful Reader. William Meredith. NoAM

Empedocles on Etna, *sels.*   Matthew Arnold.
   "Far far from here."   *Fr.* I, 2.   GTBS-P
    (Song of Callicles, The ("Far, far from here").)   FiP
   "It is so small a thing."   *Fr.* I, 2.   OBEV
   Life and Thought.   FiP, II.
   Song for Apollo.
   Song of Callicles, The ("Through the black, rushing smoke-burst").   *Fr.*
    II.   NOBE; OAEL-2; OBEV
    (Callicles' Song.)   ChTr
    (Not Here, O Apollo.)   FaBoRV
    (Song for Apollo.)   FiP
    (Song of the Muses, The.)   WiR
Empedocles on Etna.   Herbert B. Mallalieu.   PoA
Emperor, The.   Tamura Ryuichi, *tr. fr. Japanese by* Hiroaki Sato.   FCEI
Emperor, The.   Tu Fu, *tr. fr. Chinese by* E. Powys Mathers.   AWP
Emperor Hadrian to His Soul, The.   Hadrian, *tr. by* Stevie Smith.   OBVE
Emperor Nap he would set off, The.   The March to Moscow.   Robert
   Southey.   FaBoCo
Emperor of Ice-Cream, The.   Wallace Stevens.   AmPP; AnAmPo; CMoP;
   FaBoMo; FF; HAP; HCAP; HeIP; InPK; LiTA; MoP; NAAL-2;
   NAWM-2; NIP; NoAM; NOBA; NOP; NoP; OPOP; OxBA; PoE;
   TAP; WeW
Emperor of the East, The, *sel.*   Philip Massinger.
   Death Invoked.   ACP
    (Sad Song, A.)   OBS
Emperor of the Moon, *sels.*   Aphra Behn.
   "All joy to mortals, joy and mirth."   WPE
   "Curse upon that faithless maid. A."   WPE
   "When maidens are young, and in their spring."   FF
Emperor of the Southern Ch'i favored one lovely lady, The.   Immortal at
   the River.   Mao Hsi-chen, *tr. by* Lois Fusek.   ATF
Emperor of the Threefold World.   Christopher Marlowe.   *See*
   Tamburlaine the Great: Bloody Conquests of Mighty Tamburlaine,
   The.
Emperor Ojin's Song.   *Unknown, tr. fr. Japanese by* Hiroaki Sato.   *Fr.*
   The Kojiki.   FCEI
Emperor Wen.   Hsüeh Shao-hui, *tr. fr. Chinese by* Irving Lo.   WFTU
Emperor Worm, The.   Poe.   *See* Lo! 'tis a gala night.
Emperor (you've heard?) went by this road, The.   King of Kings.   Hubert
   Witheford.   ATNZ
Emperor's city, a place of fame and profit, The.   A Quiet House in
   Ch'ang-lo Ward.   Po Chü-i, *tr. by* Burton Watson.   CoBCP
Emperor's Dream, The.   Zbigniew Herbert, *tr. fr. Polish by* Czeslaw
   Milosz.   PwPP
Empire Builders.   Archibald MacLeish.   OxBA
Empire Clock, The.   Bernard Spencer.   OBTV
Empire Is No More.   Blake.   *Fr.* America; a Prophecy.   EnRP
Empire of Dreams.   Charles Simic.   LCAP
"Empire be lost or won, An!"   Whitman's Ride for Oregon.   Hezekiah
   Butterworth.   PAH
Employment ("He that is weary, let him sit.").   George Herbert.   JCP;
   OBS; SeCP; TEP
Employment ("If as a flowre doth spread and die.").   George Herbert.
   SeCV-1
Emplumada.   Lorna Dee Cervantes.   NoAM
Empress Brand Trim: Ruby Reminisces, The.   Sherley Anne Williams.
   BlSi
Empryce of prys, imperatrice.   William Dunbar.   *Fr.* Ballad of Our Lady.
   EBEV
Emptied with weeping.   At the Badr Trench.   Safiya bint Musafir, *tr. by*
   Bridget Connelly *and* Deirdre Lashgari.   WPOW
Empties Coming Back.   Angelo de Ponciano.   BLPA
Emptiness of Man, The.   João Cabral de Melo Neto, *tr. fr. Portuguese by*
   Galway Kinnell.   ATCBP
Empty Apartment, The.   Aaron Zeitlin, *tr. fr. Yiddish by* Ruth Whitman.
   VWA
Empty as death and slow as pain.   The Lesser Evil.   George Orwell.
   OBTV
Empty astronauts.   Stone Stars.   Jack Dann.   BWV
Empty at the corners.   John Gibson's Bat.   Michael S. S. Harper.   AnAn
Empty at the Heart of Things.   Frank Polite.   UL
Empty Backstreet in a Small Southern Town.   T. R. Hummer.   NAmP
Empty Bed Blues.   Bessie Smith.   OBAL; UnPo
Empty Begging Bowl.   Ryokan, *tr. fr. Chinese by* Burton Watson.
   JLIC-2
Empty Body, The.   Mark Strand.   *Fr.* Elegy for My Father.   UnPo
Empty carousel in a deserted place, An.   The Carousel.   Gloria C. Oden.
   AmNP; PoBA
Empty Dwelling Places.   Kenneth Patchen.   PoA
Empty Glen, The.   R. Crombie Saunders.   OxBS
Empty hills, no one in sight.   Deer Fence.   Wang Wei, *tr. fr. Chinese by*
   Burton Watson.   *Fr.* Twenty Views of Wang-ch'uan, 5.   CoBCP
Empty Holds a Question.   Pat Folk.   GOYP

Empty House, The.   Walter de la Mare.   BrPo
Empty House, The.   Russell Hoban.   WSC
Empty House, The.   Harold Monro.   BrPo
Empty House, The.   Stephen Spender.   NYBP; PCP
Empty house, The.   Tabito, *tr. fr. Japanese by* Geoffrey Bownas *and*
   Anthony Thwaite.   *Fr.* Manyo Shu.   PeBJV
Empty House, The.   Max Williams.   CBAP
Empty, I echo to the least footfall.   Barren Woman.   Sylvia Plath.
   OxBSP
Empty, illusory life.   The Enchanted Region; or, Mistaken Pleasures.
   Walter Harte.   EBEV
Empty Kettle.   Louis Oliver.   HATNAP; STE
Empty Mailman Drowns in the Country Road, An.   Hans Lodeizen, *tr. fr.*
   Dutch by James S. Holmes.   DuIn
Empty my heart, Lord, of daily vices.   Theodore Spencer.   TrPWD
Empty Pain-Killer Bottles, The.   Tom Raworth.   EAS
Empty perfection, as I take you in.   James Merrill.   *Fr.* Coda: The Higher
   Keys.   NoAM
Empty Pitchforks.   Thomas Lux.   NAmP
Empty Promises.   Chang Ts'o, *tr. fr. Chinese by* Dominic Cheung.
   IFON
Empty Room Is Still an Empty Room, The.   Hans Andreus, *tr. fr. Dutch*
   by Johanna H. Prins.   DuIn
Empty sands spread out without limit, The.   Song of the Wine Spring.
   Sun Kuang-hsien, *tr. by* Lois Fusek.   ATF
Empty Streams of Autumn.   Ray A. Young Bear.   NOVW
Empty Threat, An.   Robert Frost.   RFM
Empty Tomb, The.   Clara Ann Thompson.   CBWP-2
Empty Valley, The.   John Russell Hervey.   ATNZ
Empty Vessel.   "Hugh MacDiarmid."   FaBoTw; NoP; OxBS
Empty Woman, The.   Gwendolyn Brooks.   IHMS
Emptying the boat, they all climbed up.   Ozaki Hosai, *tr. fr. Japanese by*
   Hiroaki Sato.   *Fr.* One Hundred Haiku in Free Form.   FCEI
Emulate Han, emulate Tu, emulate the bearded Su.   Sung Hsiang, *tr. fr.*
   Chinese by Irving Lo.   *Fr.* On Poetry, V.   WFTU
Emulation, The.   Sarah Fyge Egerton.   NOEC
Emus.   Mary Elizabeth Fullerton.   PoAu-1
En Bateau.   Paul Verlaine, *tr. fr. French by* Arthur Symons.   AWP
En Garde, Messieurs.   William Lindsey.   AA
En las Internas Entrañas.   St. Theresa of Avila, *tr. fr. Spanish by* Father
   Benedict Zimmerman.   WPOW
En Passant.   Andrei Codrescu.   UL
En Route.   Duncan Campbell Scott.   NOBC; OBCV
En Route.   Georg Trakl, *tr. fr. German by* Joachim Neugroschel.   AnAn
En route to the picnic they drive through their history.   Picnic: the
   Liberated.   M. Carl Holman.   PoBA; PoNe
Enacting someone's notion of themselves.   Aunt Jemima of the Ocean
   Waves.   Robert Hayden.   LCAP; PoBA
Enamel Girl, The.   Genevieve Taggard.   MoAmPo
Enamored so of form, of calculation.   Of the Mathematician.   Alice Clear
   Matthews.   GoYe
Enamoured Architect of Airy Rhyme.   Thomas Bailey Aldrich.   AA
Enamoured of the Miniscule.   Michael Hartnett.   BIrV
Enarmoured, here in English, we're.   The Touble With In.   Heather
   McHugh.   NAmP
Encantadas, The, *sel.*   Richard Kenney.
   "One might as well conceive this story in the cirrose."   EOEF
An Enchanted Bird.   "Zelda", *tr. fr. Hebrew by* Bernhard Frank.   MHeP
Enchanted Region; or, Mistaken Pleasures, The.   Walter Harte.   EBEV
Enchanted Shell, The.   Henrietta Cordelia Ray.   CBWP-3
Enchanted Shirt, The.   John Hay.   BLPA; GN
Enchanted Spring, The.   George Darley.   BoNaP
Enchantment.   Lewis Alexander.   PoBA
Enchantment, The.   Thomas Otway.   OBEV
Enchantment, The.   Theocritus, *tr. fr. Greek by* Thomas Creech.   *Fr.*
   Idylls, II.   CTC; OBVE
Enchantment of my past existence.   V. A. Zhukovsky, *tr. by* Alan Myers.
   AAA
Enchantress, touch no more that strain.   Music and Memory.   John Albee.
   AA
Encinctured with a twine of leaves.   The Fruit Plucker.   Samuel Taylor
   Coleridge.   CH
   (Fragment: "Encinctured with a twine of leaves.")   OBNC
   (In a Moonlight Wilderness.)   FaBoCh
Enclosed, self-possessed one spreads his wings across the lake, The.   The
   Flamingo.   Saleem Barakat, *tr. by* Lena Jayyusi *and* Naomi Shihab
   Nye.   MAP
Enclosed the lacquered, coiling snake.   The Zoo in the City.   Sara Van
   Alstyne Allen.   GoYe
Enclosed with a Letter to My Family.   Yang Shih-ch'i, *tr. fr. Chinese by*
   Jonathan Chaves.   CoBLCP
Enclosure, The.   Jules Supervielle, *tr. fr. French by* James Kirkup.
   RHTwFP

Encolpius. Thom Gunn. *Fr.* Three Songs. AnAn
Encomium upon a Parliament, An. Daniel Defoe. APAS
Encompass me, my lover. The Constant North. J. F. Hendry. OxBS
Encompassed by a thousand nameless fears. As Day Begins to Wane.
　Helena Coleman. CaP
Encounter, The. Paul Blackburn. NeAP
Encounter. Denis Devlin. BIrV
Encounter. Geraldine Hammond. IHMS
Encounter. Uys Krige, *tr. fr. Afrikaans by the author.* PeSA
Encounter, An. A. Leyeles, *tr. fr. Yiddish by* Benjamin *and* Barbara
　Harshav. AYP
Encounter, The. Ezra Pound. AnAmPo
Encounter, The. Edgell Rickword. OxBTC
Encounter in a Glass. David Wright. NPo; PoPo
Encounter in Jerusalem. Fay Lipshitz. VWA
Encounter in Safed. Moshe Yungman, *tr. fr. Yiddish by* Gabriel Preil *and*
　Howard Schwartz. VWA
Encountering Fire Again in the Fifth Month. Huang Tsung-hsi, *tr. fr.*
　Chinese by Lynn Struve. WFTU
Encountering Fire in Early Spring, 1662. Huang Tsung-hsi, *tr. fr.*
　Chinese by Lynn Struve. WFTU
Encountering Sorrow. *Unknown, tr. fr. Chinese by* Burton Watson.
　CoBCP
Encounters. Faiz Ahmad Faiz, *tr. fr. Urdu by* Mahmood Jamal. PBMUP
Encouragement. Mrs. Henry Linden. CBWP-4
Encouragement to Exile. Petronius Arbiter, *tr. fr. Latin by* Howard
　Mumford Jones. AWP
Encouragements to a Lover. Sir John Suckling. *See* Aglaura: Why So
　Pale and Wan, Fond Lover?
End, The, *sel.* Tristan Corbière, *tr. fr. French by* C. F. MacIntyre.
　"Well, all these seamen—sailors and skippers—they." OBD
End, The. Walter Savage Landor. *See* Last Fruit Off an Old Tree, The:
　I Strove with None.
End, The. Sharon Olds. NIP
End, The. Wilfred Owen. CH; FaBoRV; MMA
End, The. Wallace Rice. AA
End, An. Christina Rossetti. FaBoRV; GBL
End Bit, The. Jim Burns. FF
End came as I drove it down the road, The. Last of the Poet's Car.
　Tony Connor. OxBTC
End came easy for most of us, The. The Man from Washington. James
　Welch. CDW; HATNAP; NoAM; NOVW
End Is Near the Beginning, The. David Gascoyne. EAS
End Is Now, The. "Marie Madelaine", *tr. fr. German by* Ferdinand E.
　Kappey. PeHV
End, Middle, Beginning. Anne Sexton. PoE
End of a Century. Jean Follain, *tr. fr. French by* W. S. Merwin.
　RHTwFP
End of a Course. I. A. Richards. CRP
End of a Dynasty, The. Zbigniew Herbert, *tr. fr. Polish by* Czeslaw
　Milosz. FaBoPV; PwPP
End of a long stillness. Dawn in January. Lance Henson. CDW
End of a Summer Sunday. Andreas Okopenko, *tr. fr. German by* Beth
　Bjorklund. *Fr.* Summer Fragments, I. CoAuP
End of a War, The. Sir Herbert Read. OBMV; WaP
End of a Year. Robert Lowell. HCAP
End of Another Home Holiday. D. H. Lawrence. EBEV;
　FaBoMo
End of April, The. Robert Fuller Murray. CenHV
End of August. Gregory Orr. MAYP
End of Autumn. Julio Ortega, *tr. fr. Spanish by* Ena Hollis *and* David
　Tipton. Per
End of Being, The. Seneca, *tr. fr. Latin by* H. C. Leonard. WGRP
End of Clonmacnois, The. *Unknown, tr. fr. Irish by* Frank O'Connor.
　CIP
End of Doctor Faustus, The. Christopher Marlowe. *See* Doctor Faustus:
　Ah, Faustus,/ Now hast thou but one bare hour [*or* hower!] to live.
End of Exploring, The. David Campbell. SeCePo
End of Fall, The. Francis Ponge, *tr. fr. French by* Robert Bly. NU
End of Faustus, The. Christopher Marlowe. *See* Doctor Faustus: Ah,
　Faustus,/ Now hast thou but one bare hour [*or* hower!] to live.
End of His Work, The. Robert Herrick. CaPo
End of It, The. Francis Thompson. NOBVV; OxBSP
End of life's journey, The. Asadullah Khan Ghalib, *tr. by* Ahmed Ali.
　GoT
End of Love, The. George Meredith. *See* Modern Love: By this he
　knew she wept with waking eyes.
End of Man Is Death, The. Moses Ibn Ezra, *tr. fr. Hebrew by* Solomon
　Solis-Cohen. TrJP
End of Man Is His Beauty, The. Amiri Baraka. AmNP
End of May, The. William Morris. NOBVV
End of my journey, The. Mitsune, *tr. by* Geoffrey Bownas *and* Anthony
　Thwaite. PeBJV

End of Play. Robert Graves. EBEV
End of scene Catullus. Christian Karlson Stead. *Fr.* Clodian Songbook.
　ATNZ
End of Solitude. Kim Hyun-sung, *tr. fr. Korean by* Koh Chang-soo.
　ACKP
End of Sorrow, The. Edmond Fleg, *tr. fr. French by* Humbert Wolfe.
　Fr. The Wall of Weeping. TrJP
End of Steel. Thomas Saunders. CaP
End of Summer. Stanley Kunitz. CAPP; MoAmPo; Psk; VGW
End of Summer, The. Edna St. Vincent Millay. BoNaP
End of Summer, The. Judith Minty. GeTw
End of Summer. Berl Pomerantz, *tr. fr. Hebrew by* Harold Schimmel.
　VWA
End of Summer. Shlomoh Tan'ee, *tr. fr. Hebrew by* Bernhard Frank.
　MHeP
(End) of Summer (1966). William Knott. EAS
End-of-Summer Poem. Rowena Bastin Bennett. FaPON
End of Term. Prunella Power. Mes
End of the Affair. Geoffrey Grigson. GBL
End of the Book, The. Moyshe-Leyb Halpern, *tr. fr. Yiddish by* Benjamin
　and Barbara Harshav. AYP
End of the Comedy. Louis Untermeyer. PoA
End of the Flower World (A.D. 2300). Stanley Burnshaw. TrJP
End of the Ice Age. Paul Snoek, *tr. fr. Dutch by* Alasdair MacKinnon.
　DuIn
End of the Indian Poems, The. Stanley Plumly. GOA
End of the Parade, The. William Carlos Williams. NYBP
End of the Play, The. Thackeray. *Fr.* Dr. Birch and His Young Friends.
　FaFP; GN
End of the Season on a Stormy Day—Oban. Iain Crichton Smith.
　NePoEA-2
End of the Seers' Convention. Kenneth Fearing. LiTA
End of the Street, The. John Haines. LCAP
End of the Suitors, The. Homer. *See* Odyssey: And now man-
　slaughtering Pallas took in hand.
End of the Third Lunar Month, The. Kaneyoshi, *tr. fr. Japanese by*
　Steven D. Carter. WFTW
End of the Trip. David Avidan, *tr. fr. Hebrew by* Warren Bargad *and*
　Stanley F. Chyet. *Fr.* Traveling in the City, 19. IP
End of the Way, The. Harriet Cole. BLRP
End of the Weekend, The. Anthony Hecht. FaBoMo; HAP; LiTM;
　NePoEA-2; SM; WeW
End of the World, The. Gordon Bottomley. BrPo; CH; MoBrPo
End of the World. Else Lasker-Schüler, *tr. fr. German by* Willis
　Barnstone *and* Michael Gillespie. BoWoP
End of the World, The. Thomas McGrath. SM
End of the World, The. Archibald MacLeish. BLPL; CMoP; HoPM;
　InPK; LiTM; MAT; MoAB; MoAmPo; NoAM; NOBA; OBAL;
　OxBA; Son; TAP; TrGrPo; VGW
End of the World, The. João Cabral de Melo Neto, *tr. fr. Portuguese by*
　James Wright. ATCBP
End of the World. Jakov van Hoddis, *tr. fr. German by* Edouard Roditi.
　VWA
End of Winter in a Mountain Village. Yaguchi Kensai, *tr. fr. Chinese by*
　Burton Watson. JLIC-2
End of winter seeped up, The. Julian Barely Misses Zimmer's Brains.
　Paul Zimmer. GOYP
End Song. Ruth Krauss. LLLT
End Song. Shlomoh Tan'ee, *tr. fr. Hebrew by* Bernhard Frank. MHeP
End to Everything, The. Paul Eluard, *tr. fr. French by* Michael Benedikt.
　POS
End was more of a melting, The. The Death of Will. Charles
　Tomlinson. OxBC
End was quick and bitter, The. Quick and Bitter. Yehuda Amichai.
　BoLoP, *tr. by* Assia Gutmann; IP, *tr. by* Warren Bargad *and* Stanley
　F. Chyet
Endimion and Phoebe, *sels.* Michael Drayton. OBSC
　Endymion's Convoy.
　Phoebe on Latmus.
Endimion Porter and Olivia. Sir William Davenant. MeLP; MePo;
　NOBE
Ending, The. Paul Engle. NYBP
Ending. Gavin Ewart. NBLV; OxBSP
Ending. Norman Jordan. PoNe
Ending. *Unknown, tr. fr. Hawaiian by* K. Luomala. WTO
Endless. Muriel Rukeyser. NYBP
Endless Chain, An. Abraham Reisen, *tr. fr. Yiddish by* Keith Bosley.
　VWA
Endless Journeys. Pierre Reverdy, *tr. fr. French by* John Ashbery. POS;
　RHTwFP
Endless Nights of Rain. Greg Pape. NAmP
Endless Song, The. Ruth McEnery Stuart. OBAL
Endless Variation. John Ashbery. BLA

Endlessly over the water. The Sweetness of Nature. *Unknown*, *tr. by* Frank O'Connor. TIRV

Endlessly, time-honoured irritant. Dry-Point. Philip Larkin. CMoP

Ends of the Hibiscus burgeon, The. Song of a Sick Child. *Malay Oral Tradition*, *tr. by* R. J. Wilkinson *and* R. O. Winstedt. WTO

Ends of Things, The. Amir Gilboa, *tr. fr. Hebrew by* Warren Bargad *and* Stanley F. Chyet. IP

Endurance. Carolyn Forché. NAmP; SV

Endurance Test. Dacre Balsdon. FiBHP

Endure Hardness. Christina Rossetti. NOBVV

Endure what life God gives and ask no longer span. Sophocles, *tr. fr. Greek by* W. B. Yeats. *Fr.* Oedipus at Colonus. OBMV

Enduring is the bust of bronze. The Duke of York's Statue. Walter Savage Landor. FaBoEE

Endymion. Longfellow. AA

Endymion, *sel.* John Lyly.
Fairy Song, A. OBSC

Endymion [a Poetic Romance], *sels.* Keats.
Hymn to Pan. *Fr.* I. ChER; PoEL-4
Life Again. SeCePo
"Muse of native land! loftiest Muse!" *Fr.* IV. EnRP
"O Moon! the oldest shades 'mong oldest trees." *Fr.* III. EnRP
"O sovereign power of love! O grief! O balm!" *Fr.* II. EnRP; OBNC
Sleeping Youth, A. SeCePo
Song of the Indian Maid ("O Sorrow,/ Why dost borrow"). *Fr.* IV. NOBE; OBEV
(O Sorrow!, *abr.*) CH
Song of the Indian Maid, The ("Beneath my palm-trees, by the riverside"). NOBE
"Thing of beauty is a joy forever, A." *Fr.* I. BLPL; CTC; EnRP; FaBV; FaFP; FiP; LiTB; NIP; OBNC; PrIm

Endymion's Convoy. Michael Drayton. *Fr.* Endimion and Phoebe. OBSC

Eneados. Virgil. *See* Aeneid, The.

Eneas wonderit the greitnes of Cartaige. Virgil, *into Middle English by*. *Fr.* The Aeneid [*or* Eneados], I. OBVE

Enemies,/ take care. A Chariot Wheel. Auvaiyar, *tr. by* A. K. Ramanujan. PLW

Enemy Action. N. K. Cruikshank. CN

Enemy forces are in wild flight, The. Defeat of the Rebels. Robert Graves. WaP

Enemy of life, decayer of all kind, The. Sir Thomas Wyatt. OxBSP; SiPS

Enemy's Eyes, The. Emma Lee Warrior. HATNAP

Enemy's Portrait, The. Thomas Hardy. EyDe; TW

Enemy's Testament, The. Etel Adnan, *tr. fr. French by the author*. OV

Energetic Women. D. H. Lawrence. InPS

Energy. Victor Hernandez Cruz. PoBA

Energy for a New Thang. Ernie Mkalimoto. NBP

Enfant perdu. Heine, *tr. fr. German by* Lord Houghton. AWP

Enfeebled: I've bitten on the sand in seaweed. Basho, *tr. fr. Japanese by* Burton Watson. *Fr.* Seventy-six Hokku. FCEI

Enfors we us with all our might. A Carol of St. George. *Unknown*. MeEL

Enfranchising cable, silvered by the sea. Granite and Steel. Marianne Moore. NYBP

Engine Driver, The. "G. S. O." BoTP

Engine Driver's Story, The. William Wilkins. BeLS

Engine Failure. Timothy Corsellis. WaP

Engine screams and Murphy, inside. The. Thomas Kinsella. FaBCIP

Engineer, The. João Cabral de Melo Neto, *tr. fr. Portuguese by* William Jay Smith. CT

Engineer's Story, The. *Unknown*. BeLS

Engines grumble behind the mist. Fly Past Alderney. Lois Clark. CN

Engingines, The. Paul Goodman. RR

England. William Cowper. *Fr.* The Task, II. FiP

England. Richard Edwin Day. AA

England. George Edgar Montgomery. AA

England. Marianne Moore. FaBoWP; LiTA; MoAB; MoAmPo

England. John Henry, Cardinal Newman. ACP

England. Mary Jo Salter. DiPo

England. *Unknown*. FaBoEE; OxBSP

England and America, *sels.* James Kenneth Stephen.
On a Parisian Boulevard. NOBL
On a Rhine Steamer. NOBL; OBTV; TW

England and America, 1863. Richard Monckton Milnes. EBVV

England and America in 1782. Tennyson. PAH

England and Switzerland 1802. Wordsworth. *See* Two voices are there; one is of the sea.

England, Autumn. Wayne Brown. PBCV

England! awake! awake! awake! Blake. *Fr.* Jerusalem, IV, Prologue. EnRP; NoP
(Prelude: "England! awake! awake! awake!".) OBNC

England, 1802 ("Great men have been among us"). Wordsworth. *See* Great Men Have Been Among Us.

England, 1802 ("It is not to be thought of"). Wordsworth. *See* It Is Not to Be Thought Of [That the Flood].

England, 1802 ("Milton! Thou should'st be living at this hour"). Wordsworth. *See* Milton! thou should'st be living at this hour.

England, 1802 ("This was written immediately after my return from"). Wordsworth. *See* This was written immediately after my return from.

England, 1802 ("When I have borne in memory") Wordsworth. *See* When I Have Borne in Memory.

England Expects? Sir Owen Seaman. NOBL

England, I stand on thy imperial ground. At Gibraltar. George Edward Woodberry. AA; GN

England in 1819. Shelley. EnRP; FaBoPV; FF; MAT; NAEL-2; NAWM-2; NOBE; NoP; OAEL-2; Son; TrGrPo; TW; UnPo
(Sonnet: England in 1819.) FiP; PPP; SeCePo

England, look up! Thy soil is stained with blood. Martyrdom of Father Campion. Henry Walpole. ACP

England, My England. W. E. Henley. BLPL; MoBrPo; OBEV; PoLF

England, my England—you have been my tutrix. W. H. Auden. *Fr.* Letter to Lord Byron. OBSV

England! my persecuted isle. George Richardson. *Fr.* Patriotism. PF

England, Table, Hamlet, and I. Stefan Themerson. NPo

England! the time is come when thou shouldst wean. Wordsworth. Son

England, unlike junior nations. Remember Suez? Adrian Mitchell. OxBTC

England, we love thee better than we know. Gibralter. Richard Chenevix Trench. OBTV

England! with all thy faults I love thee still. Byron. *Fr.* Beppo; a Venetian Story. UnPo

England, with all thy faults, I love thee still. England. William Cowper. *Fr.* The Task, II. FiP

England with its baby rivers and little towns, each with its abbey or its cathedral. England. Marianne Moore. LiTA; MoAB; MoAmPo

"England, you had better go." Voices against England in the Night. Stevie Smith. CN

England's Darling; or, Great Britain's Joy and Hope on That Noble Prince James, Duke of Monmouth. *Unknown*. CoMu

England's Great Loss by a Storm of Wind. *Unknown*. OxBSS

England's Heroical Epistles, *sel.* Michael Drayton.
King Henry to Rosamond. OBSC

England's ingratitude still blots. What Jenner Said on Hearing in Elysium That Complaints Had Been Made of His Having a Statue [in Trafalgar Square]. Shirley Brooks. EyDe; FaBoEE

England's lads are miniature men. Boy-Man. Karl Shapiro. NYBP; SoSe

England's Sovereigns in Verse. *Unknown*. BLPA

England's sun was slowly setting. Curfew Must Not Ring Tonight. Rose Hartwick Thorpe. BeLS; BLPA; BLPL; FaBoBe; FaPON; WBLP

England's Triumph. *Unknown*. CoMu

English. Osbert Lancaster. *Fr.* Afternoons with Baedeker. FaBoCo; NOBL

English, The. *Unknown*. GBP

English Are Frosty, The. Alice Duer Miller. *Fr.* The White Cliffs. PoLF

English Ballad, on the Taking of Namur by the King of Great Britain, 1695, An. Matthew Prior. PoEL-3

English Bards and Scotch Reviewers, *sels.* Byron.
"As Sisyphus against the infernal steep." OBSV
"Behold! in various throngs the scribbling crew." EnRP; OAEL-2
"Illustrious Holland! hard would be his lot." OBSV
"When some brisk youth, the tenant of a stall." PF
William Lisle Bowles. OBNC

English Beach Memory: Mr. Thuddock. Sir Osbert Sitwell. NYBP

English Cemetery, The. Franco Fortini, *tr. fr. Italian by* Lawrence R. Smith. NItP

English Courage Displayed; or, Brave News from Admiral Vernon,. *Unknown*. OxBSS

English Fog, The. John Dyer. *Fr.* The Fleece. TrGrPo

English Garden, The, *sels.* William Mason.
How to Build a Ha-ha. FaBoUs
Thomas Gray's View of Nature. *Fr.* III. NOEC

English Girl. *Unknown*, *tr. fr. Chinese by* E. Powys Mathers. OBMV

English History in Rhyme, or a Rhyming Epitome of the History of England, from B.C. 55 to A.D. 1872, *sel.* Edward B. Goodwin.
"Growth of Heptarchy we trace, The." FaBoUs

English Labourer, The. *Unknown*. OBET

English lad, who, reading in a book, An. Keats. Lizette Woodworth Reese. AA

English Language, The. William Wetmore Story. GN

English Liberal. Geoffrey Taylor. FaBoEE

English man fell in love, An. On the State of Englishness (A Fairy Tale). Deborah Levy. DT

English Poetry. Samuel Daniel. *Fr.* Musophilus; or, Defence of All
　Learning. OBSC
　(Heavenly Eloquence.) NOBE
English Schoolboy, The. John Heywood. *Fr.* The Play of the Weather.
　ACP
English Succession, The. *Unknown.* OxBChV
English Thornton. Edgar Lee Masters. *Fr.* Spoon River Anthology.
　OxBA
English—ugh! Tsuboi Shigeji, *tr. fr. Japanese by* Geoffrey Bownas *and*
　Anthony Thwaite. PeBJV
English Was Only a Second Language. Walta Borawski. GLP
English Weather. Wendy Cope. SoTCo
English Wood, An. Robert Graves. BrPo
Englishman, The. W. S. Gilbert. *Fr.* H. M. S. Pinafore. NOBL
Englishman in Italy, The ("Fortù, fortù, my beloved one."), *sel.* Robert
　Browning. PoEL-5
　Piano di Sorrento. FaBoPP; SeCePo
　(Englishman in Italy, The ["Time for rain! for your long hot dry
　　autumn"].) SeCePo
Englishman in Italy, The ["Time for rain! for your long hot dry autumn"].
　Robert Browning. *See* Englishman in Italy, The: Piano di Sorrento.
Englishman in the old days, An. Carl Sandburg. *Fr.* The People, Yes,
　sec. 11. FYAP
Englishman on the French Stage, The. Sir Owen Seaman. OBTV
Englishman with an Atlas; or, America the Unpronounceable, An. Morris
　Bishop. GOA
Englishry. W. G. Shepherd. NPo
Engraved on the case. Gold Watch. Patrick Kavanagh. InPS
Engraved on the Collar of a Dog, Which I Gave to His Royal Highness.
　Pope. *See* I am His Highness' dog at Kew.
Enid Field: In Memoriam. Gloria A. Maxson. TSM
Enid's Song. Tennyson. *Fr.* Idylls of the King: Geraint and Enid.
　FaBoRV
Enigma, *sels.* Anne-Marie Albiach, *tr. fr. French by* Keith Waldrop.
　RHTwFP
　"And the emphasis." *Fr.* IX.
　"Availability/ doesn't mean." *Fr.* I.
　"For if it's a theme state it." *Fr.* II.
　"Unspecifiable/ the inexhaustible novel, The." *Fr.* IV.
Enigma. Jessie Redmond Fauset. PoNe
Enigma. Hugh McCrae. PoAu-1
Enigma, An. Poe. Son
Enigma Variations, The. Paul Petrie. NYBP
Enigma was plagued with vertigo, The. Romance. Richard Stull.
　EOEF
Enigmas. Pablo Neruda, *tr. fr. Spanish by* Robert Bly. NU
Enigmatic moon has at long last died, The. Stevedore. Leslie Morgan
　Collins. AmNP
Enigmatical, tremulous. The Barrel-Organ. Arthur Symons. NOBVV
Enion Replies from the Caverns of the Grave. Blake. *Fr.* Vala; or The
　Four Zoas, The Four Zoas. OBNC
Enitharmon Revives with Los. Blake. *Fr.* Vala; or The Four Zoas, The
　Four Zoas. OBNC
Enitharmon's Song. Blake. *See* Vala; or The Four Zoas: Enitharmon
　Revives with Los.
Enjoy Thy April Now. Samuel Daniel, *after the Italian of* Giambattista
　Marini. *Fr.* A Description of Beauty. EiL; ELP
Enjoy your time, my soul! another race. Enjoyment. Theognis, *tr. by*
　John Hookham Frere. AWP
Enjoying Retirement ("Beside green water"). Ma Chih-yüan, *tr. fr.*
　Chinese by Jonathan Chaves. *Fr.* Three Poems to the Tune "Ssu-
　k'uai yü," 2. CoBLCP
Enjoying Retirement ("The wine just purchased"). Ma Chih-yüan, *tr. fr.*
　Chinese by Jonathan Chaves. *Fr.* Three Poems to the Tune "Ssu-
　k'uai yü," 1. CoBLCP
Enjoyment. Theognis, *tr. fr. Greek by* John Hookham Frere. AWP
Enjoyment, The. *Unknown.* ErPo
Enkindled Spring, The. D. H. Lawrence. NoAM
Enmeshed in steel stands a stone. The Captive Stone. Jim Barnes.
　CDW
Ennui. Langston Hughes. OBAL; OBCA
Ennui. Peter Viereck. NYBP
Enoch, *sels.* Bible, *Pseudepigrapha.* TrJP
　Seven Metal Mountains. *Fr.* LII: 6–9. TrJP
　Wisdom's Plight. *Fr.* XLII: 1–3.
Enoch. Jones Very. HAP
Enoch Arden, *sel.* Tennyson. BeLS
　November in the Isle of Wight. FaBoPP
Enoch Arden. Tennyson. BeLS
Enormous Aquarium, The. Sherod Santos. MAYP; NAmP
Enormous cloud-mountains that form over Point Lobos and into the sunset.
　Clouds of Evening. Robinson Jeffers. MoAmPo

Enormous Hand, The. Jorge de Lima, *tr. fr. Portuguese by* June Jordan.
　ATCBP
Enormous white rose of marble towered alone, The. The Rose of Marble
　and the Rose of Iron. Robert Desnos, *tr. by* Michael Benedikt. POS
Enos Slaughter. Jim Lavella Havelin. ASP
Enough! Bunyan. *See* Pilgrim's Progress, The: He that is down needs
　fear no fall.
Enough. Digby Mackworth Dolben. EBVV
Enough. Donald Finkel. BLA
Enough. Arthur Gregor. TAP
Enough. Tom Masson. OBAL
Enough. Marianne Moore. NOBA
Enough; and leave the rest to fame. Andrew Marvell. OBEV
Enough blarney about love and death! Failure. Alfred Gong, *tr. by* Beth
　Bjorklund. CoAuP
"Enough!" I say. Lady Shii, *tr. fr. Japanese by* Burton Watson. *Fr.*
　Manyo Shu. FCEI
Enough! Let this season end. Enough. Arthur Gregor. TAP
Enough of a day has come to pass. Inner-City Lullaby. Russell Atkins.
　CNA
Enough of those who study the oblique. A Good Resolution. Roy
　Campbell. OBSV
Enough of Thought, Philosopher, *sel.* Emily Brontë.
　"O for the time when I shall sleep." OBD
Enough, She Said. Yusuf al-Khal, *tr. fr. Arabic by* Abdullah al-Udhari.
　MPAW
"Enough," she said. But the dust still rained around [*or* about] her. Dust.
　Randolph Stow. CBAP; PoAu-2
Enough—so be it! Tamenori, *tr. by* Steven D. Carter. WFTW
Enough Time. Stephen Dunn. KS
Enough! Why should a man bemoan. Per Iter Tenebricosum. Oliver St.
　John Gogarty. AnIL; OBMV
Enough words, enough sentences! O real life. Music after Reading.
　Valery Larbaud, *tr. by* Ron Padgett *and* Bill Zavatsky. RHTwFP
Enquiry after Peace. A Fragment. Countess of Winchilsea. PoE
Enrica, 1865. Christina Rossetti. TEP
Enrich My Resignation. Hart Crane. PoA
Ensamples of Our Savior. Robert Southwell. PoEL-2
Enslav'd, the daughters of Albion weep: a trembling lamentation. Visions
　of the Daughters of Albion. Blake. OAEL-2
Enslaved. Claude McKay. BPo
Entailed Farm, The. John Glassco. MoCV; NOBC
Entangled. Jules Supervielle, *tr. fr. French by* James Kirkup. RHTwFP
Entanglement. Francis Sparshott. MoCV
Enter and learn the story of the rulers. Inscriptions at the City of Brass.
　Unknown, tr. fr. Arabic by E. Powys Mathers. *Fr.* The Thousand
　and One Nights. AWP; WaaP, 3 *sts.*
Enter Harlem. Walk with de Mayor of Harlem. David Henderson.
　PoBA
Enter into His gates with thanksgiving. Bible, *O.T. See* Psalms: Psalm C
　("Make a joyful noise. . .").
Enter Patient. W. E. Henley. *Fr.* In Hospital, I. BrPo
Enter the chilly no-man's land of about. The Ghost's Leavetaking.
　Sylvia Plath. NePoEA-2
Enter the dream-house, brothers and sisters, leaving. Newsreel. Cecil
　Day Lewis. MoAB; MoBrPo
Enter the Vampire. Clement Wood. VVA
Entered in the Minutes. Louis MacNeice. LiTB
Entering any unknown lovely mysterious place. Acts of Grace. Steve
　Orlen. NAmP
Entering here, I hope the confetti. Unitarian Easter. Sandra McPherson.
　MAYP
Entering the Body, *sel.* Stephen Berg.
　Survivor, The. NaP
Entering the Gardens of Doom. Sayf al-Rahabi, *tr. fr. Arabic by* Lena
　Jayyusi *and* Samuel Hazo. MAP
Entering the hall, she meets the new wife. The Ejected Wife. *Unknown,*
　tr. by Arthur Waley. OBVE
Entering the publisher's warehouse, a foreign young lady. Anecdote from
　William IV Street. D. J. Enright. OxBC
Enterprise and *Boxer. Unknown.* PAH
Entertained by song and dance here in this wine pavilion. Pleasures of
　Shinbashi. Liu E, *tr. by* Jonathan Chaves. CoBLCP
Entertainment Industry, The. William Langland. *Fr.* The Vision of Piers
　Plowman. NOCV
Entertainment of War, The. Roy Fisher. FaBoMo
Entertainment, or Porch-Verse, at the Marriage of Master Henry Northleigh
　and the Most Witty Mistress Lettice Yard, The. Robert Herrick.
　CaPo
Entertainment to James, *sel.* Thomas Dekker.
　Troynovant ("Troynovant is now no more a city"). ChTr; OBSC
Enthroned above the world although he sit. Immanence. Richard Hovey.
　WGRP

Enthusiast, The. Herman Melville. NAAL-1
Enthusiast, The; or, The Lover of Nature, *sels.* Joseph Warton. EnRP; PoEL-3
  Charms of Nature, The. SeCePo
  "Ye green-robed Dryads, oft at dusky eve " NOEC
Enthusiastic gummed flap, awaiting, An. The Habit of Energy. Diane Ward. LP
Enthusiastically hurting a clouded yellow bud and. A New Cup and Saucer. Gertrude Stein. TTTS
Enticed into rhine-mine-snare; the raging one. Model 3/ Melpomene. Friederike Mayröcker, *tr. by* Beth Bjorklund. CoAuP
Entire country is overrun with private property, The. Gypsy. Josephine Miles. MoP; NoAM
Entire garden of the world, The. Mohammad Taqi Mir, *tr. by* Ahmed Ali. GoT
Entirely. Louis MacNeice. CMoP; LiTB
Entirety dwells here and you, distantly, The. Heloise. Biancamaria Frabotta, *tr. by* Keala Jane Jewell. DMI
Entr'acte. Anna Margolin, *tr. fr. Yiddish by* Marcia Falk. PeBMYV
Entrain airport: New York, Chicago, west. Valediction to My Contemporaries. Horace Gregory. MoAmPo
Entrance. Mihály Ladányi, *tr. fr. Hungarian by* Jascha Kessler. *Fr.* Sketchbook. FOC
Entrance and exit wounds are silvered clean. Recalling War. Robert Graves. CMoP; LiTM; MMA; NoAM; OAEL-2; OBWP; WaP
Entrance Exams. "Cuthbert Bede." FaBoNo
Entrance to Hell, The. Virgil, *into Middle English by.* *Fr.* The Aeneid [*or* Eneados], VI. GoTS
Entrapped inside a submarine. Harry Clifford Canfield. *Fr.* On the Loss of U.S. Submarine S4. FaBoCo; FiBHP
Entreaty. Robert Fitzgerald. OxBSP
Entreaty to the Cloud. Amado Nervo, *tr. fr. Spanish by* Samuel Beckett. MexPo
Entrepreneur, The. David Ray. SoTCo
Entrepreneur chicken shed his tail feathers, surplus, The. Josephine Miles. MoP; NoAM
Entropy. Theodore Spencer. ImOP
Entwined. *Malay Oral Tradition, tr. by* R. J. Wilkinson *and* R. O. Winstedt. WTO
Entwined on the bed in the dark. Two Shapes. Arthur Gregor. TAP
Enueg I. Samuel Beckett. CIP
Enueg II. Samuel Beckett. NoAM
Envelope, The. Maxine W. Kumin. TV
Enviable Isles, The. Herman Melville. AA; FaBoBe
Envies, The. George Bowering. NOBC
"Envious wits, what hath been mine offense." Sir Philip Sidney. *Fr.* Astrophel and Stella, I. PoE; Son
Environment. Lionel Kearns. NOBC
Environs. Larry Eigner. NeAP
Environs of Vanholt II. Charles Spear. ATNZ
Environs of Vanholt I. Charles Spear. ATNZ; PeNZ
Envoi: "Earth puts her colours by." P. H. B. Lyon. BoTP
Envoi: "Fly, white butterflies, out to sea." Swinburne. *See* Fly, white butterflies, out to sea.
Envoi: "Go, dumb-born book." Ezra Pound. *See* Hugh Selwyn Mauberley (Life and Contacts): Envoi (1919).
Envoi: "Go little book, par avion." Richard Tillinghast. MT
Envoi: "God, thou great symmetry." Anna Wickham. MoBrPo
Envoi: "Hear me, whom I betrayed." J. V. Cunningham. VGW
Envoi: "I am the Prince." Charles Causley. FF
Envoi: "I warmed both hands before the fire of Life." D. B. Wyndham Lewis. FiBHP
Envoi: "My country is not a country." Eli W. Mandel. NOBC
Envoi, L': "My towers at last! These rovings end." Herman Melville. AnAmPo; NOBA
Envoi: "Oh, seek me not within a tomb." John G. Neihardt. WGRP
Envoi: "Take of me what is not my own." Kathleen Jessie Raine. NOBE
Envoi: "To my mother, and to my mother's monument." Rosario Ferré, *tr. by the author.* DMH
Envoi: "What has want to give." Kathleen Jessie Raine. WPE
Envoi, L': "Who findeth comfort in the stars and flowers." Thomas Lovell Beddoes. *Fr.* Death's Jest Book. OBNC
Envoi (1919). Ezra Pound. *Fr.* Hugh Selwyn Mauberley (Life and Contacts), XIII. HAP; MoP; UnPo; VGW
  (Envoi: "Go, dumb-born book.") MoAB; MoAmPo; OxBA
Envoi to Poem to the Virgin. Laura Terracina, *tr. fr. Italian by* Muriel Kittel. DMI
Envoy: "Do you remember/ That afternoon." W. E. Henley. BrPo
Envoy: "Go, songs, for ended is our brief, sweet play." Francis Thompson. MoBrPo
Envoy: "Good Night, at last." Robert Duncan. *Fr.* Passages. VGW

Envoy: "If homely virtues draw from me a tune." James Weldon Johnson. TrPWD
Envoy: "Legend of Felix is ended, the toiling of Felix is done, The." Henry van Dyke. *Fr.* The Toiling of Felix. BLPA
Envoy: "On Meall nan Con, the Peak of the Dogs." Alasdair Maclean. PoSH
Envoy: "Sweet World, if you will hear me now." Sarah Morgan Bryan Piatt. AA
Envoy: "They are not long, the weeping and the laughter." Ernest Dowson. *See* They are not long, the weeping and the laughter.
Envoy: "Whose furthest footstep never strayed." Richard Hovey. *Fr.* More Songs from Vagabondia. AA
Envoy, The. Chaucer. *See* Troilus and Criseyde [*or* Criseide]: Go, Little Book ("Go, litel book, go litel myn tragedy").
Envoy of Mr. Cogito, The. Zbigniew Herbert, *tr. fr. Polish by* Bogdana *and* John Carpenter. PwPP
Envy. Charles *and* Mary Lamb. OxBChV
Envy. Adelaide Anne Procter. NOBVV
Envy. Spenser. *Fr.* The Faerie Queene, I, 4. TW
Envy of Poor Lovers, The. Austin Clarke. CIP; CMoP; IPY
Envy the Old. Mark Van Doren. Prf
Envy with heavy heart asked for shrift. William Langland. *Fr.* The Vision of Piers Plowman, Passus V. NAEL-1
Envying the Pelican. Richard Weber. CIP
Eolian [*or* Aeolian] Harp, The. Samuel Taylor Coleridge. EnRP; NAEL-2; NoP; OAEL-2
Eons ago, when the earth was still yeasty. Leopard. Gretchen Kreps. RHPC
Ephelia to Bajazet. Sir George Etherege. APAS
Ephemera. W. B. Yeats. BrPo
Ephemeral. Sándor Weöres, *tr. fr. Hungarian by* Jascha Kessler. FOC
Epi-strauss-ium. Arthur Hugh Clough. NAEL-2
Epic. Patrick Kavanagh. BIrV; CIP; FaBCIP; IPY; NOIV
Epic, The. Tennyson. NAEL-2
Epic of Gilgamesh, The, *sels. Unknown, tr. fr. Babylonian.*
  "Gilgamesh washed his grimy hair, polished his weapons." *Tr. by* E. A. Speiser. Prf
  "Hear me, great ones of Uruk." *Tr. by* N. K. Sandars. DL
  Seduction of Engadu, The. *Tr. by* William Ellery Leonard. ErPo
Epicedium. J. Corson Miller. PAH
Epicedium. Horace L. Traubel. AA
Epicoene; or, The Silent Woman, *sel.* Ben Jonson, *tr. fr. the Latin of by* Jean Bonnefons.
  Still to Be Neat [Still to Be Drest (*or* Dressed)]. *Fr.* I, i. EIL; FF; GBL; HAP; HeIP; JCP; NoP; PrIm; SeCePo; TEP; WeW
  (Clerimont's Song.) InPS; OAEL-1; PoE; PPP; SeCP; SeCV-1; TrGrPo
  (Simplex Munditiis.) AWP; HoPM; NOBE; OBEV
  (Song: "Still to be neat, still to be dressed [*or* drest].") OBS
Epicure, The ("Fill the bowl with rosie wine"). Abraham Cowley. OBS; SeCP
Epicure, The ("Underneath this myrtle shade, The"), *sel.* Abraham Cowley, *after the Greek of* Anacreon. AWP; OBEV
  "Crown me with roses whilest I live." OBVE
Epicure, Dining at Crewe, An. *Unknown.* NTCP
  (Limerick: "Epicure, dining at Crewe, An.") CenHV
  (Waiter, Please.) NBLV
Epicure, Sung by One in the Habit of a Town Gallant, The. Thomas Jordan. *See* Let us drink and be merry. . . .
Epicurean. William James Linton. EBVV
Epicurean Ode, An. John Hall. MeLP; MePo
Epiderm. Michael Dransfield. CBAP
Epidermal Macabre. Theodore Roethke. TW
Epidermis of the Night-Time Growth. Tristan Tzara, *tr. fr. French by* Timothy Baum *and* Michael Benedikt. POS
Epigram: "After some years Bohemian came to this." J. V. Cunningham. VGW
Epigram V: "Against the guide of Truth." *Unknown, tr. fr. Hebrew. Fr.* Duel with Verses over a Great Man. TrJP
Epigram: "All I said was—Alexis is gorgeous." Plato, *tr. fr. Greek by* Peter Jay. PeHV
Epigram: "All through the night my eyes have streamed with rain." Strato, *tr. fr. Greek by* Sydney Oswald. PeHV
Epigram: "And now I, Meleager, am among them." Meleager, *tr. fr. Greek by* Peter Whigham. PeHV
Epigram: "And now you're ready who while she was here." J. V. Cunningham. *See* Five Epigrams: And Now You're Ready Who While She Was Here.
Epigram: "And what is love? Misunderstanding, pain." J. V. Cunningham. CRP; HAP; HoPM; PoA
Epigram: "As honey in wine/ wine, honey." Meleager, *tr. fr. Greek by* Peter Whigham. PeHV
Epigram: "As the body denies the means to look." Pernette Du Guillet, *tr. fr. French by* Joan Keefe *and* Richard Terdiman. PBWP

Epigram: "As Thomas was cudgell'd [*or* cudgel'd] one day by his wife." Swift. FaBoEE

Epigram: "At even, when the hour drew nigh at which we say farewell." Strato, *tr. fr. Greek by* Sydney Oswald. PeHV

Epigram: "At ten a clock, when I the fire rake." Francis Daniel Pastorius. SCAP

Epigram: "At 12 o'clock in the afternoon." Meleager, *tr. fr. Greek by* Sydney Oswald.

Epigram: "Beauty, a silver dew that falls in May." *Unknown.* OBSC

Epigram: "Because I am idolatrous and have besought." Ernest Dowson. ACP; OxBSP

Epigram: "Boy-mad no longer." Rufinus, *tr. fr. Greek by* Alan Marshfield. PeHV

Epigram: "Boys' cocks, Diodore." Strato, *tr. fr. Greek by* Thomas Meyer. PeHV

Epigram: "Boys of Tyre are beautiful, The." Meleager, *tr. fr. Greek by* Peter Whigham. PeHV

Epigram: "Breath of my life, The—no less." Meleager, *tr. fr. Greek by* Peter Whigham. PeHV

Epigram: "Broad and ample he warms himself." *Unknown, tr. fr. Irish by* Thomas Kinsella. NOIV

Epigram: "But yesterday, when from the bath he stept." Strato, *tr. fr. Greek by* Sydney Oswald. PeHV

Epigram: "Cease your labors, lovers of boys." *Unknown. tr. fr. Greek.* PeHV

Epigram: "Charm of my life, my dearest care." Martial, *tr. fr. Latin by* Brian Hill. PeHV

Epigram: "Dark thoughts are my companions. I have wined." J. V. Cunningham. QFR; TW; VGW

Epigram: "Dear, if unsocial privacies obsess me." J. V. Cunningham. VGW

Epigram: "Diodorus is nice, isn't he, Philocles?" Meleager, *tr. fr. Greek by* Peter Whigham. PeHV

Epigram: "Do you not wish to renounce the Devil?" Armand Lanusse, *tr. fr. French by* Langston Hughes. PoNe; TTY

Epigram: "Drink, unhappy lover, drink." Meleager, *tr. fr. Greek by* Peter Whigham. PeHV

Epigram: Dutch, The. George Canning. *See* In matters of commerce. . . .

Epigram: "Enemy of life, decayer of all kind, The." Sir Thomas Wyatt. OxBSP; SiPS

Epigram: "Even if I try not to ogle a boy in the street." Strato, *tr. fr. Greek.* PeHV

Epigram: "Face that should content me wonders well, A." Sir Thomas Wyatt. CTC; EnLoPo; OBSC

Epigram: Fatum Supremum. *Unknown.* OBS

Epigram: "For Hekabé and the women of Ilion." Plato, *tr. fr. Greek by* Peter Jay. PeHV

Epigram III: "Forgive us, son of Amram, be not wroth." *Unknown, tr. fr. Hebrew. Fr.* Duel with Verses over a Great Man. TrJP

Epigram: "Friend [*or* friends] on this scaffold Thomas More lies dead." James Vincent Cunningham. *See* Friend, on This Scaffold Thomas More Lies Dead.

Epigram: "Fruit of all the service that I serve, The." Sir Thomas Wyatt. SiPS

Epigram: "Gathering the bloom of all the fairest boys that be." Strato, *tr. fr. Greek by* Sydney Oswald. PeHV

Epigram: "Give me a boy whose tender skin." Martial, *tr. fr. Latin by* Brian Hill. PeHV

Epigram: "Glad youth had come thy sixteenth year to crown." Ausonius, *tr. fr. Latin.* PeHV

Epigram: Go, Happy Rose. Martial, *tr. fr. Latin by* Brian Hill. PeHV

Epigram: "Gold priests, wooden chalices." *Unknown, tr. fr. Irish by* Thomas Kinsella. NOIV

Epigram: "Golden casket I designed, A." John Swanwick Drennan. BIrV

Epigram: "Golden one is gone from the banquets, The." Hilda Doolittle ("H. D."). PoA

Epigram: "Great woe, fire & war come on me." Skythinos, *tr. fr. Greek by* Thomas Meyer. PeHV

Epigram: "Heat goes deep as cold." *Unknown, tr. fr. Irish by* Thomas Kinsella. NOIV

Epigram: "Here lies my wife. Eternal peace." J. V. Cunningham. NePoAm; NIP; OBAL

Epigram: "Hetero-sex is best for the man of a serious turn of mind." Marcus Argentarius, *tr. by* Fleur Adcock. PeHV

Epigram: "Homer was poor. His scholars live at ease." J. V. Cunningham. VGW

Epigram: "How shall I know if my love lose his youth." Strato, *tr. fr. Greek by* Sydney Oswald. PeHV

Epigram: "How we desire desire! Joy of surcease." J. V. Cunningham. VGW

Epigram: "I am provoked." Strato, *tr. fr. Greek by* W. G. Shepherd. PeHV

Epigram: "I celebrate Rhegion, Italy's tip, licked by." *Unknown, tr. fr. Greek by* Peter Jay. PeHV

Epigram: "I delight in the prime of a boy of twelve." Strato, *tr. fr. Greek by* Thomas Meyer. PeHV

Epigram: "I dined with Demetrius last night." Automedon, *tr. fr. Greek.* PeHV

Epigram: "I don't care for women." *Unknown, tr. fr. Greek.* PeHV

Epigram: "I had gone broke, and got set to come back." J. V. Cunningham. MoAmPo; NePoAm; OxBSP; QFR

Epigram: "I like them pale, fair or honey-skinned." Strato. PeHV

Epigram: "I loved thee beautiful and kind." Robert, Earl Nugent. NOEC

Epigram: "I married in my youth a wife." J. V. Cunningham. RB

Epigram: "I was thirsty." Meleager, *tr. fr. Greek by* Sydney Oswald. PeHV

Epigram: "I who by day am function of the light." J. V. Cunningham. VGW

Epigram: "If men be judged wise." Joseph Solomon Del Medigo. TrJP

Epigram: "If wisdom, as it seems it is." J. V. Cunningham. QFR

Epigram: "If you see someone beautiful." Adaios, *tr. by* Alistair Elliot. PeHV

Epigram: "In whose will is our peace? Thou happiness." J. V. Cunningham. QFR; VGW

Epigram: "It is true that I held Thero fair." Meleager, *tr. fr. Greek by* Peter Whigham. PeHV

Epigram: "Just as he is growing a beard." Flaccus, *tr. fr. Greek. PeHV*

Epigram: "King George, observing with judicious eyes." Joseph Trapp. FaBoCo

Epigram: "King to Oxford sent a troop of horse, The." Sir William Browne. FaBoCo; FaBoEE

Epigram: "Kissing Hippomenes, I crave." Paulos, *tr. fr. Greek by* Andrew Miller. PeHV

Epigram: "Lasses, like nuts at bottom brown." Allan Ramsay. FaBoEE

Epigram: "Life flows to death as rivers to the sea." J. V. Cunningham. VGW

Epigram: "Like when the burning sun doth rise." Strato, *tr. fr. Greek by* Sydney Oswald. PeHV

Epigram: Likeness, The. Martial, *tr. fr. Latin by* Brian Hill. PeHV

Epigram: "Listen, you know the pains of love." Meleager, *tr. fr. Greek by* Peter Whigham. PeHV

Epigram: "Lo! Beauty flashed forth sweetly; from his eyes." Meleager, *tr. fr. Greek by* Sydney Oswald. PeHV

Epigram: "Long hair, endless curls trained by the devoted." Strato, *tr. fr. Greek by* Teddy Hogge. PeHV

Epigram: "Loss of our learning brought darkness, weakness and woe." *Unknown, tr. fr. Greek by* Thomas Kinsella. NOIV

Epigram: "Love brought me quietly in the dreaming night." Meleager, *tr. fr. Greek by* Sydney Oswald. PeHV

Epigram: "Love signed the contract blithe and leal." John Swanwick Drennan. BIrV

Epigram: "Lux my fair falcon, and your fellows all." Sir Thomas Wyatt. AAS; SiPS

Epigram: "Me Polytimus vexes and provokes." Martial, *tr. fr. Latin.* PeHV

Epigram: "Member of the modern great, A." John Cunningham. FaBoEE

Epigram: "Midas, they say, possessed the art of old." "Peter Pindar." NIP

Epigram: "Milo's from home; and, Milo being gone." Martial, *tr. by* Elijah Fenton. OBVE

Epigram: "Most inexplicable the wiles of boys I deem." Rhianus, *tr. fr. Greek by* Sydney Oswald. PeHV

Epigram: "My better half, why turn a peevish scold." Martial, *tr. fr. Latin.* PeHV

Epigram: "My heart still hovering round about you." Robert, Earl Nugent. NOEC

Epigram: "My name is Ebenezer Brown." J. V. Cunningham. RB

Epigram: "My soul, sit thou a patient looker-on." Francis Quarles. NOBE

Epigram: "My soul, thy love is dear: 'twas thought a good." Francis Quarles. *Fr.* Emblems, V, 4. OAEL-1

Epigram: "Naked I came, naked I leave the scene." J. V. Cunningham. *See* Five Epigrams: Epitaph for Someone or Other.

Epigram: "Need from excess—excess from folly growing." Samuel Bishop. NOEC

Epigram: "Nicander, ooh, your leg's got hairs!" Alkaios, *tr. by* Tony Harrison. PeHV

Epigram: "Now art thou fair, Diodorus." Strato, *tr. fr. Greek by* Sydney Oswald. PeHV

Epigram: "O Diodorus, in a storm of spring." *Unknown, tr. fr. Greek by* Sydney Oswald. PeHV

Epigram: On a Slanderer. Martial, *tr. fr. Latin.* PeHV

Epigram: On Bassa. Martial, *tr. fr. Latin.* PeHV

Epigram: On Hedylus. Martial, *tr. fr. Latin.* PeHV

Epigram: On Inclosures. *Unknown.* See 'Tis bad enough in man or woman.

Epigram: "On parent knees, a naked new-born child." Sir William Jones, *after the Sanskrit of* Kalidasa. FaBoEE; OBEV

Epigram: On Sir Francis Drake. *Unknown.* OBS; OBTV

Epigram: On Sir Roger Phillimore. *Unknown.* FaBoCo; NBLV

Epigram: "One boy alone in all the world for me." Meleager, *tr. fr. Greek by* Sydney Oswald. PeHV

Epigram: "Passing the flower-stalls there did I perceive." Strato, *tr. fr. Greek by* Sydney Oswald. PeHV

Epigram: "Perchance some coming after." Strato, *tr. fr. Greek by* Sydney Oswald. PeHV

Epigram: Political Reflection. Howard Nemerov. See No bars are set too close. . . .

Epigram: "Poverty? wealth? seek neither." Kassia, *tr. fr. Greek by* Patrick Diehl. WPOW

Epigram: " 'Prepare to meet the King of Terrors,' cried." Ebenezer Elliott. NOBVV

Epigram: "Quoth Satan to Arnold: 'My worthy good fellow.' " *Unknown.* PAH

Epigram: "Reincarnating Pythagoras, say." Ausonius, *tr. fr. Latin.* PeHV

Epigram: Respice Finem. Francis Quarles. See "My soul, sit thou a patient looker-on."

Epigram: Riddle, A. Martial, *tr. fr. Latin by* Brian Hill. PeHV

Epigram: "Rudely forced to drink tea, Massachusetts, in anger." *Unknown.* PAH

Epigram: "Sighs are my food, drink are my tears." Sir Thomas Wyatt. SiPS

Epigram: "Since first you knew my am'rous smart." Robert, Earl Nugent. NOEC

Epigram: "Since I'm completely drunk." *Unknown, tr. fr. Greek by* Peter Jay. PeHV

Epigram: "Sir, I admit your general [*or* gen'ral] rule." Pope, *also at. to* Matthew Prior *and to* Samuel Taylor Coleridge. FaBoEE; FiBHP; LiTB

Epigram: "Stolen kisses, wary eyes." Strato, *tr. fr. Greek by* Sydney Oswald. PeHV

Epigram: "There was this gym-teacher." Strato, *tr. fr. Greek by* Teddy Hogge. PeHV

Epigram: "This *Humanist* Whom No Beliefs Constrained." J. V. Cunningham. See This *Humanist* Whom No Beliefs Constrained.

Epigram: "This is my curse, Pompous, I pray." J. V. Cunningham. HAP

Epigram: "Those snooty boys in all their purple drag!" Strato, *tr. fr. Greek by* Tony Harrison. PeHV

Epigram II: "Thou fool profane, be silent!" *Unknown, tr. fr. Hebrew. Fr.* Duel with Verses over a Great Man. TrJP

Epigram I: "Thou Guide to doubt, be silent evermore." *Unknown, tr. fr. Hebrew. Fr.* Duel with Verses over a Great Man. TrJP

Epigram: "Thy eyes are sparks, Lycines, god-like made." Strato, *tr. fr. Greek by* Sydney Oswald. PeHV

Epigram: "Thy nags (the leanest things alive)." Matthew Prior. FaBoEE

Epigram: "Time heals not: it extends a sorrow's scope." J. V. Cunningham. VGW

Epigram: "Time was when once upon a time, such toys." Glaukos, *tr. fr. Greek by* Peter Jay. PeHV

Epigram: To Charinus, a Catamite. Martial, *tr. fr. Latin.* PeHV

Epigram: To Dindymus. Martial, *tr. fr. Latin by* Brian Hill. PeHV

Epigram: "To John I ow'd great obligation." Matthew Prior. FaBoCo; FaBoEE; FaFP; OBVE

Epigram: To Labienus. Martial, *tr. fr. Latin.* PeHV

Epigram: To Lygdus. Martial, *tr. fr. Latin.* PeHV

Epigram: To Papilus. Martial, *tr. fr. Latin.* PeHV

Epigram: To Philaenis. Martial, *tr. fr. Latin.* PeHV

Epigram: To Phoebus. Martial, *tr. fr. Latin.* PeHV

Epigram: To Polycharmus. Martial, *tr. fr. Latin.* PeHV

Epigram: "Tom's sickness did his morals mend." Matthew Prior. FaBoEE

Epigram: " 'Twas not so in my time,' surly Grumio exclaims." Samuel Bishop. NOEC

Epigram: "Wealth covers sin—the poor." Kassia, *tr. fr. Greek by* Patrick Diehl. WPOW

Epigram: "Were I a king, I could command content." Edward de Vere, Earl of Oxford. See Were I a king.

Epigram: "What is a communist? One who hath yearnings." Ebenezer Elliott. NOBVV

Epigram IV: "What thought ye to burn, when ye kindled the pyre." *Unknown, tr. fr. Hebrew. Fr.* Duel with Verses over a Great Man. TrJP

Epigram: "When Bibo thought fit from the world to retreat." Matthew Prior. FaBoEE

Epigram: "When Graphicus sat by the baths." Strato, *tr. fr. Greek.* PeHV

Epigram: "When 'mongst the youths you lately came." *Unknown, tr. fr. Greek by* Sydney Oswald. PeHV

Epigram: "When other Ladies to the Shades go down." Pope. See When other fair ones [*or* ladies] to the shades [*or* groves] go down.

Epigram: "When whelmed the altar, priest and creed." Sir William Watson. WGRP

Epigram: "When would-be suicides in purpose fail." Thomas Hood. OBD

Epigram: "While Adam slept, from him his Eve arose." *Unknown.* FaBoEE

Epigram: "Who hath he[a]rd of such[e] cruelty before?" Sir Thomas Wyatt. AAS; SiPS

Epigram: "Why all the racket, you chattering birds?" *Unknown, tr. fr. Greek by* Thomas Meyer. PeHV

Epigram: "Within this mindless vault." J. V. Cunningham. RB; VGW

Epigram: "Woman working hard and wisely, A." Kassia, *tr. fr. Greek by* Patrick Diehl. WPOW

Epigram: "World laid low, and the wind blew like a dust, The." *Unknown, tr. fr. Irish by* Thomas Kinsella. NOIV

Epigram: "Yes, every poet is a fool." Matthew Prior. FaBoEE

Epigram: "You ask me how Contempt who claims to sleep." J. V. Cunningham. ErPo; NePoAm

Epigram: "You beat your pate, and fancy wit will come." Pope. FaBoEE

Epigram: "You were a pretty boy once, Archestratus, and." Philip of Thessalonica, *tr. fr. Greek by* Edith Morgan. PeHV

Epigram: "You wonder why Drab sells her love for gold?" J. V. Cunningham. NePoAm

Epigram Engraved on the Collar of a Dog Given [*or* Which I Gave] to His Royal Highness. Pope. FaBoCo; FaBoEE; FM; InPK; NOEC; NTCP; OxBSP

(Engraved on the Collar of a Dog, Which I Gave to His Royal Highness.) ChTr; LiTB; OxBoLi; SoSe; TTTS

(His Highness's Dog.) RHPC

Epigram for the Dead at Tegea. *Unknown, tr. fr. Greek by* Richmond Lattimore. WaaP

Epigram in a Maid of Honour's Prayer-Book. Pope. FaBoEE

Epigram on a Lawyer's Desiring One of the Tribe to Look with Respect to a Gibbet. Robert Fergusson. OxBS

Epigram on an Academic Visit to the Continent. Richard Porson. See I went to Frankfurt and got drunk.

Epigram on Elphinstone's Translation of Martials' Epigrams. Burns. See O Thou whom poetry abhors.

Epigram on Fasting. Swift. OBVE

Epigram on Florio. John Winstanley. FaBoEE

Epigram on John Bull. Byron. See World Is a Bundle of Hay, The.

Epigram on Milton. Dryden. See Three poets, in three distant ages born.

Epigram on One Who Made Long Epitaphs. Pope. FaBoEE

Epigram on Scolding. Swift. FaBoEE

Epigram on the Feuds between Handel and Bononcini. John Byrom. FaBoEE; NOBL; NOEC

Epigram on the First of April. John Winstanley. NOEC

Epigram on the Play-House at Amsterdam. William Parsons. OBTV

Epigram on the Poor of Boston Being Employed in Paving the Streets, 1774. *Unknown.* PAH

Epigram on the Refusal of the University of Oxford to Subscribe to His Translation of Homer. William Cowper. TW

Epigram on the Year 1390-1. *Unknown.* NIP

Epigram on Two Ladies. Sophia Burrell. ErPo

Epigram on Voltaire. Edward Young. FaBoCo

Epigram on Woman, An. Philip Ayres. FaBoEE

Epigram, to the Household, 1630, An. Ben Jonson. Son

Epigrams, *sel.* Callimachus, *tr. fr. Greek by* A. M. Young.

"Art thou the grave of Charidas? If for Arimmas' son." *Fr.* XV. OBD

Epigrams, *sel.* Rabindranath Tagore.

"Echo always mocks the sound, The." PoA

Epigrams, I-IX. Howard Nemerov. OBAL

Epigrams and Epitaphs, *sel.* C. S. Lewis.

"Save yourself. Run and leave me. I must go back." *Fr.* 6. EBEV

Epigrams must be curt, nor seem. Walter Savage Landor. FaBoEE

Epigrams on Priapus. *Unknown.* ErPo

Epigrams to Ernesto Cardenal in Defense of Claudia, *sel.* Dionne Brand.

"Give up the bitterness." *Fr.* XXXV. PBCV

Epigraph. Blake. See Jerusalem: To the Christians.

Epigraph from *The Judge Is Fury.* J. V. Cunningham. QFR

Epigraphs for Epigones. John Ash. NPo

Epilog: "Like the ears of wheat in a wheat-field growing." Heine. See North Sea, The: Like the stalks of wheat in the fields.

Epilogue: "After our Epilogue this crowd dismisses." Congreve. *Fr.* The Way of the World. NAEL-1

Epilogue: Anemone. Leslie Scalapino. *Fr.* Hmmmm. NPGG

Epilogue: "At the midnight in the silence of the sleep-time." Robert Browning. *See* Asolando: At the midnight in the silence of the sleep-time.

Epilogue: Author to Reader. Henri Coulette. *Fr.* The War of the Secret Agents, XII. NePoEA-2

Epilogue: "Away, for we are ready to a man!" James Elroy Flecker. *Fr.* The Golden Journey to Samarkand. NOBE

Epilogue: "Because the papers meanly ignore me." Zishe Landau, *tr. fr.* Yiddish by Irving Feldman. PeBMYV

Epilogue: "Carol, every violet has." Alfred Noyes. *Fr.* The Flower of Old Japan. MoBrPo

Epilogue: "Giver of bliss and pain, of song and prayer." William Alexander Percy. TrPWD

Epilogue: "Have I spoken too much or not enough of love?" Richard Aldington. BrPo

Epilogue: "He is not dead nor liveth." Dorothy Wellesley. *Fr.* Deserted House. OBMV

Epilogue: "Heaven, which man's generations draws." Francis Thompson. *Fr.* A Judgment in Heaven. MoAB; MoBrPo

Epilogue: "I have crossed an ocean." Grace Nichols. UAS

Epilogue, An: "I have seen flowers come in stony places." John Masefield. FaBoEE; OxBTC

Epilogue: "I thought I had found a swan." Denise Levertov. LLLT

Epilogue: "I too was a little child once." Joseph Eliyia, *tr. fr. Greek by* Rae Dalven. VWA

Epilogue: "If Luther's day expand to Darwin's year." Herman Melville. *Fr.* Clarel. ImOP

Epilogue: "If we shadows have offended." Shakespeare. *Fr.* A Midsummer Night's Dream, V, ii. OBSC

Epilogue: "Like the stalks of wheat in the fields." Heine, *tr. fr. German* by Emma Lazarus. *Fr.* The North Sea. TrJP

Epilogue: "My bibliography has grown." Dallas E. Wiebe. TW

Epilogue: "Nothing now to mark the spot." Rachel Field. *Fr.* A Circus Garland. OBCA

Epilogue: "Now my charms are all o'erthrown." Shakespeare. *Fr.* The Tempest, V, i. CTC

Epilogue: "Now the hungry lion roars." Shakespeare. *See* Midsummer Night's Dream, A: Now the Hungry Lion Roars.

Epilogue: "O chansons foregoing." Ezra Pound. OxBA

Epilogue: " 'O where are you going?' said reader to rider." W. H. Auden. *See* Orators, The: O Where Are You Going? 295

Epilogue: " 'O where are you going?' said reader to rider". Alan Ross. *See* O where are you going.

Epilogue: "Painted autumn overwhelms, The." John Meade Falkner. FaBoPP

Epilogue: "Phoenix on the hot sirocco's breath." H. B. Mallalieu. PoA

Epilogue: "Terence, this is stupid stuff." A. E. Housman. *See* Shropshire Lad, A: Terence, This Is Stupid Stuff.

Epilogue: "That death might not be casual." Burns Singer. FaBoTw

Epilogue: "There I learned how faces fall apart." "Anna Akhmatova," *tr. fr. Russian by* D. M. Thomas. *Fr.* Requiem 1935-1940. AIW

Epilogue: "There is, for me, now, in my life." Éric Clémens. WCI

Epilogue: "There's something in a stupid ass." Byron. Par

Epilogue: "They who have best succeeded on the stage." Dryden. *Fr.* The Conquest of Granada, *Pt.* II. FiP; SeCV-2

Epilogue: "Those blessed structures, plot and rhyme." Robert Lowell. CAPP; HCAP; NAAL-2

Epilogue: "Thus far, with rough and all-unable pen." Shakespeare. *Fr.* King Henry V. CTC

Epilogue: "Time is a thing." Stephen Spender. MoBrPo

Epilogue: "Truly, my Satan, thou art but a dunce." Blake. *Fr.* The Gates of Paradise. HAP; OAEL-2; OBNC; PoE; WeW

Epilogue: "Well, when all is said and done." "Æ." MoBrPo

Epilogue: "What shall we do for Love these days?" Lascelles Abercrombie. *Fr.* Emblems of Love. CH; MoBrPo

Epilogue: "With heart at rest I climbed the citadel's." Baudelaire. *tr. fr. French by* Arthur Symons. AWP

Epilogue: "Years later the girl died." Linda Pastan. KS

Epilogue for a Masque of Purcell. Adrienne Rich. NePoEA; NYBP

Epilogue of the Man of Law's Tale, The. Chaucer. *Fr.* The Canterbury Tales.

    Shipman, The. ACP

Epilogue Spoken by Mrs. Boutell. Dryden. SeCV-2

Epilogue to a Human Drama. Stephen Spender. CMoP

Epilogue to a Poetry Reading. M. K. Joseph. ATNZ; PeNZ

Epilogue to Alun Mabon. John Ceiriog Hughes, *tr. fr. Welsh by* H. Idris Bell. OBWVE

Epilogue to Nathaniel Lee's "Mithridates", *sel.* Dryden.

    "You've seen a pair of youthful lovers die." OBD

Epilogue to Robinson Crusoe. Dan Pagis, *tr. fr. Hebrew by* Warren Bargad *and* Stanley F. Chyet. IP

Epilogue to the Breakfast-Table Series. Oliver Wendell Holmes. *Fr.* The Poet at the Breakfast Table. AA

Epilogue to the Outrider. Dorothy Livesay. CaP

Epilogue to the Satires [*or* 1738] ("Not twice a twelvemonth you appear in print.") Pope. OAEL-1

    Sels.

    "Ask you what provocation I have had?." *Fr.* Dialogue II. OBSV

    (Defence of Satire.) NOEC

    (Power of Ridicule, The.) NOBE

    "Spare then the person, and expose the vice." *Fr.* Dialogue II. OBSV

    "Virtue may choose the high or low degree." *Fr.* Dialogue I. OBSV

    (Triumph of Vice, The.) NOBE; OBSV

Epilogue to "The Sister," *sel.* Goldsmith.

    "Lud! what a group the motley scene discloses!" OBSV

Epilogue to "Tyrannick Love." Dryden. *Fr.* Tyrannic Love. SeCV-2

Epilogue at Wallack's, An. John Elton Wayland. AA

Epiphany. Eileen Shanahan. NeIP

Epiphany. Christopher Smart. *Fr.* Hymns and Spiritual Songs: St. Philip and St. James, 3. NOCV

Epiphany, The. George Strong. GoYe

Epiphany: For the Artist. Elizabeth Sewell. EyDe

Epiphany, 1937. George Seferis, *tr. fr. Greek by* Edmund Keeley *and* Philip Sherrard. VMG

Epipsychidion. Shelley. EnRP

Epipsychidion ("My Song, I fear that thou wilt find but few."). Shelley. EnRP

    Sels.

    "Let us become the overhanging day." OAEL-2

    "Spouse! Sister! Angel! Pilot of the Fate." ChER

    "Thy wisdom speaks in me, and bids me dare." OAEL-2

    "True Love in this differs from gold and clay." OBNC

Episode. Cassiano Nunes, *tr. fr. Spanish by* E. A. Lacey. PeHV

Episode of a Night of May. Arthur Symons. *Fr.* Scènes de la Vie de Bohème. BrPo; OBTV

Episode 17. William Carlos Williams. *Fr.* Paterson. OxBA

Epistemology. Richard Wilbur. CRP; NePoEA; NoAM; NOBA; OxBSP

Epistle, An: "First, last and always dearest, closest, best." A. D. Hope. PoAu-2

Epistle II: To a Socialist in London. Robert Bridges.

Epistle Answering to One That Asked to be Sealed of the Tribe of Ben, An. Ben Jonson. SeCV-1

Epistle Containing the Strange Medical Experience of Karshish, the Arab Physician, An. Robert Browning. NAEL-2

Epistle Dedicatory to Chapman's Translation of the Iliad, The, *sel.* George Chapman.

    Poetry and Learning. OBS

Epistle from a Half-Pay Officer in the Country to His Friend in London, An. Richardson Pack. NOEC

Epistle, from Algiers, to Horace Smith. Thomas Campbell. OBTV

Epistle from Mr. Pope to Dr. Arbuthnot, An. Pope. *See* Epistle to Dr. Arbuthnot.

Epistle from Mrs. Yonge to Her Husband. Lady Mary Wortley Montagu. NAEL-1; NoP

Epistle in Form of a Ballad to His Friends. Villon, *tr. fr. French by* Swinburne. AWP

Epistle of Othea to Hector (A Lytil Bibell of Knyghthod), The, *sel.* Christine de Pisan, *tr. fr. French, ad. by* Joan Keefe.

    "Phoebus, the goddess variant and changeable." PBWP

Epistle to a Desponding Sea-Man. Philip Freneau. MOS

Epistle to a Friend, to Persuade Him to the Wars, An ("Wake, friend, from forth thy lethargy! The drum."), *sel.* Ben Jonson. TEP

    "Whole nature hath been, leavened with madness, swells, The." JCP

Epistle to a Lady, An. Mary Leapor. NOEC

Epistle to a Lady: Of the Characters of Women. Pope. *Fr.* Moral Essays, Epistle II. NAEL-1; NOEC; OAEL-1; OxBoLi, *shorter sel.*

    "Yet Chloe [*or* Cloe] sure was formed without a spot." ErPo; OBSV

    (Chloe.) AWP; NOBE

    "Men, some to bus'ness, some to pleasure take." OBSV

Epistle to a Young Friend. Burns. EBEV

Epistle to Augusta. Byron. EnRP

Epistle to Be Left in the Earth. Archibald MacLeish. CMoP; ImOP; MoAB; MoAmPo; NOBA; TrGrPo

Epistle to Dr. Arbuthnot ("Shut, shut the door, good John."). Pope. InPS; NoP; OAEL-1; PoE; PoEL-3

    Sels.

    (Epistle from Mr. Pope to Dr. Arbuthnot, An.) NOEC

    (To Dr. Arbuthnot, , *abr.*) OxBoLi

    Apologia pro Vita Sua. NOBE

    Atticus ("How did they fume, and stamp, and roar, and chafe"). TW

Atticus ("Peace to all such! but were there one whose fires"). AWP;
　InPK; NoBE; SeCePo
"Bard whom pilf'red pastorals reknown, The." OBSV
Bufo. OBSV
"Let Sporus tremble—"What? That thing of silk."" SCV
　(Sporus.) AWP; ChTr; NOBE; OBSV
"Why did [or do] I write? what sin to me unknown." ChTr, short sel.;
　EBEV; FiP; TOF
Epistle to Elizabeth, Countess of Rutland, sel. Ben Jonson.
　"With you, I know, my offering will find grace." JCP
Epistle to George Keats, sel. Shelley.
　"Should he upon an evening ramble fare." ChER
Epistle to John Guthrie. Sydney Goodsir Smith. OxBS
Epistle to John Hamilton Reynolds ("Dear Reynolds! as last night I lay in
　bed."), sel. Keats. OBNC
　"O that our dreamings all, of sleep or wake." OAEL-2
Epistle to John Lapraik. Burns. EnRP
Epistle to Miss [or Miss Teresa] Blount, on Her Leaving the Town after
　the Coronation. Pope. BoLoP; EBEV; NAEL-1; NOBE; NOEC;
　NoP; OPOP; PoEL-3; PPP
Epistle to Mr. Murray. Byron. FaBoUs
Epistle to My Friend J. B., An. Robert Dodsley. NOEC
Epistle to Robert Lloyd, Esq., An. William Cowper. FiP
Epistle to Robert Nugent, Esq. with a Picture of Doctor Swift in Old Age,
　An, sel. William Dunkin.
　"Hibernia's Helicon is dry." NOEC
Epistle to Sir Richard Temple, sel. Pope.
　Wharton ("Wharton! the scorn and wonder of our days"). AWP
Epistle to Tammus, sel. J. B. Selkirk.
　Border Burn, A. PoSH
Epistle to the Emperor Napoleon (1810). Constance-Marie de Salm-Dyck,
　tr. fr. French by Dorothy Backer. DMF
Epistle to the Gentiles. Alfred Hayes. TrJP
Epistle to the God of Love, The, sel. Christine de Pisan, tr. fr. French by
　Sarah Spence.
　"Adam, David, Samson, Solomon." DMF
Epistle to the President of the Scottish Society of Antiquaries: On Being
　Chosen a Correspondent Member. Alexander Geddes. OxBS
Epistle to the Rapalloan. Archibald MacLeish. PoA
Epistle to the Right Hon. Charles James Fox, An, sel. Thomas Maurice.
　"How cursed that country, how severe its doom." NOEC
Epistle to the Right Honourable William Pulteney, Esq. John Gay.
　OBTV
Epistle Written in the Country to the Right Honourable the Lord Lovelace,
　An, sel. Soame Jenyns.
　"In days, my Lord, when mother Time." OBSV
Epistles, sel. Horace, tr. fr. Latin by Abraham Cowley.
　To Fuscus Arustus. Fr. I, 10. AWP
Epistles to His Friends in Town, sel. John Gilbert Cooper.
　Temper of Aristippus, The. PBBP
Epistles to Mr. Pope, sel. Edward Young.
　"These labouring wits, like paviours, mend our ways." OBSV
Epistolary Briefs to Proclus, sel. José I. de Diego Padró, tr. fr. Spanish
　by Julio Marzán.
　"Friend Proclus, the world isn't a fantasy." Fr. I, II. InW
Epistolary Essay from M. G. to O. B. upon Their Mutual Poems, An.
　Earl of Rochester. APAS
Epistrophe. Imamu Amiri Baraka. PoNe
Epitalamium: "Voice that breathed o'er Eden, The." John Keble.
　NOCV
Epitaph, An: "Come knock your heads against this stone." Blake.
　TEP
Epitaph: "Daniel and Abigail." Miguel de Barrios, tr. fr. Spanish.
　TrJP
Epitaph: "Done to death by slanderous tongues." Shakespeare. Fr. Much
　Ado about Nothing, V, iii. CTC
Epitaph: "Dummer the shepherd sacrific'd." Cotton Mather.
　SCAP
Epitaph, An: "Enough; and leave the rest to fame." Andrew Marvell.
　OBEV
Epitaph: Epitaph on the Lady Mary Villiers, An. Thomas Carew.
　SeCP
Epitaph: "Even such is time." Sir Walter Ralegh. See Even Such Is
　Time.
Epitaph: "Fate to beauty still must give." Claudian, tr. fr. Latin by
　Howard Mumford Jones. AWP
Epitaph: "For this she starred her eyes with salt." Elinor Wylie.
　MoAmPo
Epitaph: "From out the stormy sea unto the shore." Azariah di Rossi, tr.
　fr. Hebrew by A. B. Rhine. TrJP
Epitaph: "Glassblower lies here at rest, A." J. B. Morton. FaBoEE
Epitaph, An: "He worshipped at the altar of Romance." Colin Ellis.
　OxBTC

Epitaph: "Her grieving parents cradled here." Sylvia Townsend Warner.
　MoBrPo
Epitaph: "Here dead lie we because we did not choose." A. E. Housman.
　See Here dead lie we because we did not choose.
Epitaph: "Here—for they could not help but die." Philip Freneau. Fr.
　The Fading Rose. AA
Epitaph, An: "Here lie I, once a witty fair." Samuel Wesley. NOEC
Epitaph I: "Here lies a man, and still no man." Unknown, tr. fr. Hebrew.
　Fr. Duel with Verses over a Great Man. TrJP
Epitaph, An: "Here lies a most beautiful lady." Walter de la Mare.
　LiTB; LiTM; MoAB; MoBrPo; OBEV; RB
Epitaph: "Here lies a simple Jew." Sholom Aleichem, tr. fr. Yiddish by
　Joseph Leftwich. TrJP
Epitaph: "Here lies John Hughes and Sarah Drew." Lady Mary Wortley
　Montagu. FaBoEE
Epitaph, An: "Here lies Nachshon, a man of great renown." Isaac
　Benjacob, tr. fr. Hebrew by Joseph Chotzner. TrJP
Epitaph: "Here lies Sir Tact, a diplomatic fellow." Timothy Steele.
　InPK; NBLV; TW
Epitaph: "Here lies the body of Richard Hind." Francis Jeffrey.
　FaBoEE; OxBoLi
Epitaph: "Here lies the flesh that tried." Louise Driscoll. WGRP
Epitaph: "Here lies the poet Wolker, lover of the world." Jiri Wolker, tr.
　by Karl W. Deutsch. WaaP
Epitaph, An: "Here lieth under this marble ston." Unknown. MeEL
Epitaph: "Here rests his head upon the lap of earth." Thomas Gray. Fr.
　Elegy Written in a Country Churchyard. FaBoPV
Epitaph, An: "His friends he loved. His direst earthly foes." William
　Watson. NOBVV
Epitaph: "Hours before my death." Julio Marzán. InW
Epitaph: "I am old." Christopher Logue. OxBTC
Epitaph: "I am round, round." Oswald de Andrade, tr. fr. Portuguese by
　Jean R. Longland. ATCBP
Epitaph: "I, an unwedded wandering dame." Sylvia Townsend Warner.
　MoBrPo
Epitaph: "I lived in those times. For a thousand years." Robert Desnos,
　tr. fr. French by Kenneth Rexroth. RHTwFP
Epitaph: "I never cared for Life: Life cared for me." Thomas Hardy.
　FaBoEE; FaBoRV
Epitaph: "I, Richard Kent, beneath these stones." Sylvia Townsend
　Warner. MoBrPo
Epitaph, An: "I was, I am not; smiled, that since did weep." Thomas
　Heywood. OxBSP
Epitaph: "If fruits are fed on any beast." John Millington Synge. See If
　fruits are fed on any beast.
Epitaph: "Implacable angel, The/ Has shot his dart." Leone da Modena,
　tr. fr. Hebrew. TrJP
Epitaph: Inscription from Anticyra. Unknown, tr. fr. Greek by Richmond
　Lattimore. WaaP
Epitaph, An: "Interred [or Interr'd] beneath this marble stone." Matthew
　Prior. FaBoEE; NAEL-1; OAEL-1; OBD; OBSV; PoEL-3
Epitaph: Iohannis Sande. Thomas Bastard. FaBoEE
Epitaph: "It was for you that the mountains shook at Sinai." Unknown.
　TrJP
Epitaph: "John Bird, a laborer, lies here." Sylvia T. Warner.
　MoBrPo
Epitaph: "Last year the child died." Olive Senior. PBCV
Epitaph: "Like silver dew are the tears of love." A. E. Coppard.
　OBMV
Epitaph, An: "Like thee I once have stemm'd the sea of life." James
　Beattie. OBEV
Epitaph: "Lovely boy, thou art not dead." Francis Davison. OBSC
Epitaph, An: "Lovely young lady I mourn in my rhymes, A." George
　John Cayley. FiBHP
Epitaph: "Malcolm Lowry." Malcolm Lowry. OBD
Epitaph: "Man who in his life trusts in this world, A." Unknown. TrJP
Epitaph: "Meek Francis lies here, friend, without stop or stay." Matthew
　Prior. FaBoEE
Epitaph: "Mr. Heath-Stubbs as you must understand." John Heath-Stubbs.
　NePoEA; OxBTC
Epitaph, An: "My brother is skull and skeleton now." William Montgomerie.
　OxBS
Epitaph: "My name—my country—what are they to thee." Paulus
　Silentarius. See My name—my country what are they to thee.
Epitaph: "Nor practising virtue nor committing crime." Geoffrey Taylor.
　FaBoEE
Epitaph, An: "O mortal folk you may behold and see." Stephen Hawes.
　See Pastime of Pleasure, The: Epitaph of Graunde [or La Graunde]
　Amoure, The.
Epitaph: "Of many things adulterate." Tristan Corbière, tr. fr. French by
　Joseph T. Shipley. AWP
Epitaph: On Sir Walter Rawleigh at His Execution. Unknown. OBS

Epitaph: "One whom I knew, a student and a poet."   Alex Comfort. MoBrPo; MOS

Epitaph: "Posterity will ne'er survey."   Byron.   *See* Posterity will ne'er survey.

Epitaph: "Roots of mankind are tangled in my hair, The."   Wendy Rose. CDW

Epitaph: "Say that she couldn't forgive."   Anna Margolin, *tr. fr. Yiddish by* Marcia Falk.   PeBMYV

Epitaph: "See here, nice Death, to please his palate."   *At. to.* Pope. FaBoEE

Epitaph: "Serene descent, as a red leaf's descending."   Sara Teasdale. PoA

Epitaph: "She was a high-class bitch and a dandy."   Theodore Spencer. LiTA

Epitaph: "Sir, you should notice me: I am the Man."   Lascelles Abercrombie.   MoBrPo

Epitaph: Snake River.   Lance Henson.   VoR

Epitaph: "Stavro's dead. A truant vine."   Lawrence Durrell.   FaBoCo

Epitaph: "Stone cries from the wall, The."   *Unknown.*   TrJP

Epitaph: "Stop, Christian passer-by!—Stop, child of God."   Samuel Taylor Coleridge.   EnRP; FiP; NAEL-2; NOCV; NoP; OAEL-2

Epitaph: "They hanged him on a clement morning, swung."   Dennis Scott. PBCV

Epitaph: "This is the end of him, here he lies."   Amy Levy.   NOBVV; TrJP

Epitaph, An: "This little vault, this narrow room."   Thomas Carew.   *See* This little vault, this narrow room.

Epitaph: "Thou alive on earth, sweet boy."   Francis Davison.   OBSC

Epitaph: "Time and the World, whose magnitude and weight."   Robert Southey.   OBNC

Epitaph: "Time that bringes all things to light."   Thomas Morton.   SCAP

Epitaph: "Tread softly; bid a solemn music sound."   J. B. Morton. FaBoEE

Epitaph: "Underneath this marble stone."   Abraham Cowley.   *See* Underneath this marble stone.

Epitaph: "Underneath this wooden cross there lies."   Karl Shapiro.   *Fr.* Elegy for a Dead Soldier.   OFD

Epitaph, An: "When I am gone."   Josephine D. Henderson Heard. CBWP-4

Epitaph: "When I put my slate back in the void."   André Frénaud, *tr. fr. French by* Keith Bosley.   RHTwFP

Epitaph: "When I shall be without regret."   J. V. Cunningham.   InPK

Epitaph: "When you perceive these stones are wet."   Sir William Davenant.   ACP

Epitaph: "Wit's perfection, Beauty's wonder."   Francis Davison. OBSC

Epitaph, The: "Write on my grave when I am dead."   Katharine Tynan. WGRP

Epitaph, *sel.*   Marina Tsvetayeva, *tr. fr. Russian.*
"Blow muffled through years of, The."   *Fr.* IV, *tr. by* Elaine Feinstein. OV

Epitaph after Reading Ronsard's Lines from Rabelais.   John Millington Synge.   FaBoEE

Epitaph. Caecil. Boulstr.   Lord Herbert of Cherbury.   SeCP

Epitaph Ending in And, The.   William Stafford.   LCAP; NaP

Epitaph for a Beatnik Poet.   Guy Owen.   CRP

Epitaph for a Bigot.   Dorothy Vena Johnson.   PoNe

Epitaph for a Cat.   Margaret E. Bruner.   PoLF

Epitaph for a Dog.   Samuel Twardowski, *tr. fr. Polish by* Jerzy Peterkiewicz *and* Burns Singer.   OBD

Epitaph for a Funny Fellow.   Morris Bishop.   FPL

Epitaph for a Godly Man's Tomb, An.   Robert Wild.   ChTr; FaBoEE

Epitaph for a Horseman.   Michael Hamburger.   NePoEA-2

Epitaph for a Judge.   Benedict Jeitteles, *tr. fr. Hebrew by* Joseph Chotzner.   TrJP

Epitaph for a Meat-Packer.   Guy Owen.   CRP

Epitaph for a Negro Woman.   Owen Dodson.   PoNe

Epitaph for a Persian Kitten.   Miriam Vedder.   CRH

Epitaph for a Postal Clerk.   X. J. Kennedy.   NIP; PCP

Epitaph for a Reviewer.   Frances Cornford.   OBD

Epitaph for Castlereagh, An.   Byron.   NIP

Epitaph for Cú Chuimne.   *Unknown, tr. fr. Irish by* Thomas Kinsella. NOIV

Epitaph for Erotion.   Martial, *tr. fr. Latin by* James Michie.   FaBoEE

Epitaph for G. B. Shaw.   Max Beerbohm.   FaBoEE

Epitaph for George Moore.   Thomas Hardy.   FaBoEE

Epitaph for James Smith.   Burns.   *See* Lament him, Mauch line husbands a'.

Epitaph for Jean Maillard.   *Unknown, tr. fr. French.*   PeHV

Epitaph for Liberal Poets.   Louis MacNeice.   FaBCIP

Epitaph for Mael Mhuru.   *Unknown.*   NOIV

Epitaph for Mr. Moses Levy.   *Unknown.*   TrJP

Epitaph for My Cat.   Jean Garrigue.   TAP

Epitaph for My Tomb.   Alfonsina Storni, *tr. fr. Spanish by* Perry Higman. LPSS

Epitaph for One Who Would Not Be Buried in Westminster Abbey.   Pope. FaBoEE; OBD

Epitaph for Peter Stuyvesant.   Henricus Selyns.   SCAP

Epitaph for Sir Henry Lee.   *Unknown.*   FaBoEE

Epitaph for Someone or Other.   J. V. Cunningham.   OBAL; SM; VGW

Epitaph for the Poet.   George Barker.   OxBSP

Epitaph for the Race of Man, *sel.*   Edna St. Vincent Millay.
"See where Capella with her golden kids."   *Fr.* VI.   CMoP; MoAB; MoAmPo

Epitaph for the Unknown Soldier.   W. H. Auden.   FaBoCo

Epitaph for William Pitt.   Byron.   FaBoEE

Epitaph in a Churchyard at Thetford, in Norfolk.   *Unknown.*   FaBoUs

Epitaph in Christ Church, Bristol, on Thomas Turner, Twice Master of the Company of Bakers.   Francis Jeffrey.   *See* Like to a baker's oven is the grave.

Epitaph in Form of a Ballad, The.   Villon, *tr. fr. French by* Swinburne. CTC

[Epitaph] In Obitum M.S., [D]G/ Maij [*or* Maii], 1614.   William Browne. EIL; FaBoEE; JCP; NOBE; OBEV; OBS

Epitaph in St. Olave's, Southwark, on Mr. Munday.   *Unknown.* FaBoCo; OxBoLi

Epitaph in Sirmio.   David Morton.   PoLF

Epitaph Intended for Sir Isaac Newton.   Pope.   *See* Nature and Nature's laws lay hid in Night.

Epitaph of Cleonicus.   Theocritus, *tr. fr. Greek by* Charles Stuart Calverley.   FaBoEE

Epitaph of Dionysia.   *Unknown.*   OBEV

Epitaph of Eusthenes, The.   Edward Cracroft Lefroy, *after the Greek of* Theocritus.   *Fr.* Echoes from Theocritus, XXVIII.   AWP

Epitaph of Graunde [*or* La Graunde] Amoure, The.   Stephen Hawes.   *Fr.* The Pastime of Pleasure, 42.   ChTr; EBEV; FaBoRV; OBSC

Epitaph of Hipponax.   Theocritus, *tr. fr. Greek by* Charles Stuart Calverley.   FaBoEE

Epitaph of Maister Win Drowned in the Sea, An.   George Turberville. FaBoEE

Epitaph of Nearchos.   Ammianus, *tr. fr. Greek by* Dudley Fitts.   WeW

Epitaph of Pyramus and Thisbe.   Abraham Cowley.   EnLoPo; FaBoEE

Epitaph of Sir Thomas Gravener [Knight], An.   Sir Thomas Wyatt. OBSC; SiPS

Epitaph on a Child Killed by Procured Abortion.   *Unknown.*   NOEC

Epitaph on a Dentist.   *Unknown. See* Stranger, approach this spot with gravity!

Epitaph on a Dormouse.   *Unknown.*   OxBChV

Epitaph on a Dwarf.   Immanuel Frances, *tr. fr. Hebrew by* Hyam Maccoby.   OBD

Epitaph on a Fir-Tree.   Richard Murphy.   FaBoTw

Epitaph on a Free but Tame Redbreast.   William Cowper.   PBBP

Epitaph on a Great Sleeper.   Sir Aston Cokayne.   FaBoEE

Epitaph on a Hare.   William Cowper.   FiP; FM; HAP; HeIP; NOEC; NoP; PoEL-3

Epitaph on a Jacobite.   Macaulay.   *See* To my true King I offered free from stain.

Epitaph on a Party Girl.   Richard Usborne.   FaBoEE

Epitaph on a Pessimist.   Thomas Hardy.   FaBoEE; FF

Epitaph on a Robin Redbreast, An.   Samuel Rogers.   FaBoEE; FM; PBBP

Epitaph on a Schoolmaster.   Burns.   FaBoCo; FaBoEE

Epitaph on a Soldier.   Joyce Barton.   CN

Epitaph on a Soldier.   Cyril Tourneur.   *Fr.* The Atheist's Tragedy. EIL

Epitaph on a Tyrant.   W. H. Auden.   HeIP; NoAM; OxBSP; RB

Epitaph on a Waiter.   David McCord.   NBLV; NIP; OBAL

Epitaph on a Willing Girl.   *at. to* Thomas Rowlandson.   FaBoEE

Epitaph on a Young Child.   Ivor Gurney.   FaBoEE

Epitaph on a Young Poet Who Died before Having Achieved Success.   Amy Lowell.   OBAL

Epitaph on Achilles.   *Unknown, tr. fr. Greek by* William M. Hardinge. AWP

Epitaph on an Engraver.   Henry David Thoreau.   EyDe

Epitaph on an Infant.   Crinagoras, *tr. fr. Greek by* John William Burgon. AWP

Epitaph on an Irish Priest.   *Unknown.*   FaBoEE

Epitaph on an Unfortunate Artist.   Robert Graves.   FaBoEE; NOBL

Epitaph on Charles I.   James, Marquess of Montrose Graham.   *See* Great, good and just, could I but rate.

Epitaph on Charles II.   Earl of Rochester.   FaBoCo; FiBHP; TrGrPo

Epitaph on Colonel Francis Chartres.   John Arbuthnot.   FaBoEE; OBSV

Epitaph on Dr. Keene.   Thomas Gray.   FaBoEE

Epitaph on Dr. Keene's Wife.   Thomas Gray.   FaBoEE

Epitaph on Elizabeth, L. H. Ben Jonson. EIL; ELP; FaBoEE; HAP; HeIP; NAEL-1; NIP; NoP; OBEV; OBS; PoE; SeCP; SeCV-1
Epitaph on Fop. William Cowper. OBD
Epitaph on G——. Pope. OBD
Epitaph on Himself. Samuel Taylor Coleridge. FaBoEE
Epitaph on Himself. Pope. FaBoEE
Epitaph on His Wife. Dryden. TrGrPo
Epitaph on James Grieve, Laird of Boghead. Burns. TW
Epitaph on James Moore Smythe. Pope. FaBoEE
Epitaph on John Dove. Burns. FaBoCo
Epitaph on John Knott. *Unknown.* ChTr; FaBoEE; OBS; SeCV-1
Epitaph on King Charles I. James Graham Marquess of Montrose. *See* Great, good and just, could I but rate.
Epitaph on Lady Ossory's Bullfinch. Horace Walpole. *Fr.* Epitaphs [*or* Epitaph] on Two Piping-Bullfinches of Lady Ossory's, Buried under a Rose-Bush in Her Garden. ChTr
Epitaph on Laurence Sterne. David Garrick. FaBoEE
Epitaph on M. H., An. Charles Cotton. EBEV; FaBoEE; OPOP
Epitaph on Maria Wentworth. Thomas Carew. PoEL-3
Epitaph on Master Philip Gray, An. Ben Jonson. FaBoEE
Epitaph on Master Vincent Corbett, An. Ben Jonson. JCP
Epitaph on Pegasus, a Limping Gay. "Panormitanus," *tr. fr. Latin.* PeHV
Epitaph on Peter Robinson. Francis Jeffrey. *See* Here lies the preacher, judge and poet, Peter.
Epitaph on Prince Frederick. *Unknown. See* Here lies Fred.
Epitaph on Prince Henry. Hugh Holland. FaBoEE
Epitaph on Robert Southey. Thomas Moore. FaBoCo; FaBoEE
Epitaph on S. P. [Salomon *or* Salathiel Pavy], a Child of Queen Elizabeth's Chapel. Ben Jonson. EIL; HeIP; HoPM; JCP; MePo; Mes; NAEL-1; NoP; OAEL-1; OBD; OBEV; OBS; PoEL-2; PPP; SeCP; SeCV-1; TrGrPo; UnPo
Epitaph on Sir Isaac Newton. Pope. *See* Nature and Nature's laws lay hid in Night.
Epitaph on Sir Philip Sidney. *At. to* Fulke Greville *and to* Sir Edward Dyer. LiTB; OBSC; Prf
Epitaph on Sir Philip Sidney, An. James I, King of England. Son
Epitaph on Sir Philip Sidney. *At. to* Sir Walter Ralegh. SiPS
Epitaph on Sir Thomas Wyatt. Henry Howard, Earl of Surrey. *See* Wyatt Resteth Here.
Epitaph on Sir Walter Pye. John Hoskyns. FaBoEE
Epitaph on the Admirable Dramatic Poet, W. Shakespeare, An. Milton. *See* What needs my Shakespeare for his honoured bones.
Epitaph on the Countess[e] Dowager of Pembroke. William Browne. *See* Underneath this sable hearse.
Epitaph on the Duke of Grafton. Sir Fleetwood Shepherd. FaBoEE
Epitaph on the Earl of Leicester. Sir Walter Ralegh. RB; SiPS
Epitaph on the Earl of Strafford. John Cleveland. FaBoEE; FaBoPV; JCP; MePo; NOBE; OBS; SeCePo; TrGrPo
Epitaph on the Fart in the Parliament House. John Hoskyns. FaBoEE
Epitaph on the Favourite Dog of a Politician. Hilaire Belloc. OBSV
Epitaph on the Lady Mary Villiers. Thomas Carew. CaPo; FaBoEE; NOBE; OBEV; SeCV-1
Epitaph on the Late King of the Sandwich Isles. Winthrop Mackworth Praed. FiBHP
Epitaph on the Marchioness of Winchester, An. Milton. OBS
Epitaph on the Monument of Sir William Dyer at Colmworth, 1641. Lady Catherine Dyer. *Fr.* Sir William Dyer, Knight. BoLoP; EnLoPo
Epitaph on the Politician Himself. Hilaire Belloc. FaBoEE; MoBrPo; NBLV; OBSV
Epitaph on the Secretary to the Muses. Jane Barker. FaBoCo
Epitaph on the Stanton-Harcourt Lovers. Pope. OBD
Epitaph on the Tomb of Sir Edward Giles and His Wife. Robert Herrick. QFR
Epitaph—on the Wife of Dr. Greenwood. Dr. ———Greenwood. FaBoUs
Epitaph on the World. Henry David Thoreau. FF; HeIP
Epitaph on Thomas Clere. Earl of Surrey. AAS; OBWP; SiPS
Epitaph on True, Her Majesty's Dog, An. Matthew Prior. FM
Epitaph on Tuft-Hunter. Thomas Moore. FaBoCo; FaBoEE
Epitaph on Washington. *Unknown.* OHIP
Epitaph on William Hogarth. Samuel Johnson. EBEV
Epitaph on William Jones. *Unknown.* FaBoEE
Epitaph on William Whitehead. *Unknown.* FaBoEE
Epitaph Placed on His Daughter's Tomb. "Mark Twain." PoLF, *ad. by* Robert Richardson
Epitaph to a Dog. Byron. BLPA
Epitaph upon a Child [that Died]. Robert Herrick. *See* Here she lies, a pretty bud.
Epitaph upon a Sober Matron, An. Robert Herrick. CaPo
Epitaph upon a Virgin, An. Robert Herrick. CaPo; FaBoEE; OxBoLi; PoEL-3; SeCV-1
Epitaph upon a Young Married Couple Dead and Buried Together, An. Richard Crashaw. *See* To these whom death again did wed.

Epitaph upon Husband and Wife Who Died and Were Buried Together, An. Richard Crashaw. EBEV; NOBE; OBEV; OBS; TrGrPo
Epitaph upon Mr. Ashton, a Conformable Citizen, An. Richard Crashaw. OBS
Epitaph upon My Dear Brother, Francis Beaumont, An. Sir John Beaumont. JCP
Epitaph upon That Profound and Learned Casuist, the Late Ordinary of Newgate, An. Thomas Brown. OBSV
Epitaph upon the Celebrated Claudy Phillips, Musician, Who Died Very Poor, An. Samuel Johnson. NOEC
Epitaph Upon the Right Honorable Sir Philip Sidney. Fulke Greville *and to* Sir Edward Dyer. *See* Silence augmenteth grief, writing increaseth rage.
Epitaphium Citharistriae. Victor Plarr. EnLoPo; NBLV
Epitaphium Meum. William Bradford. SCAP
Epitaphs. Gabriello Chíabrero, *tr. fr. Italian by* Wordsworth. Sels.
  "Destined to war from very infancy." AWP; PFI
  "Not without heavy grief of heart did he." AWP
  "O flower of all that springs from gentle blood." AWP
  "O thou who movest onward." AWP
  "Pause, courteous spirit!" AWP
  "Perhaps some needful service of the state." AWP
  "There never breathed a man, who, when his life." AWP
  "True is it that Ambrosio Salinero." AWP
  "Weep not, beloved friends!" AWP
Epitaphs, *sel.* Robert Francis.
  "Everyman/ Preacher or lecher, saint or sot." CRP
Epitaphs, *sels.* Gloria A. Maxson. SoTCo
  Baker.
  Golfer.
  Miser.
Epitaphs. Abraham Sutskever, *tr. fr. Yiddish by* Neal Kozodoy. PeBMYV
Epitaphs of the War, 1914–1918 ("A. "I was a Have." B. "I was a Have Not.""), *sels.* Kipling. BrPo; NoP; OBWP
  Batteries Out of Ammunition. MMA
  Beginner, The. FaBoTw
  Bridegroom, The. FaBoEE
  Common Form. FaBoEE; FaBoTw
  Coward, The. FaBoEE; FaBoTw
  Dead Statesman, A. FaBoEE
  Drifter off Tarentum, A. FaBoEE; MMA
  Equality of Sacrifice. FaBoTw
  Refined Man, The. FaBoEE; FaBoTw; MMA
  Son, A. FaBoEE
Epitaphs [*or* Epitaph] on Two Piping-Bullfinches of Lady Ossory's, Buried under a Rose-Bush in Her Garden, *sel.* Horace Walpole. FaBoEE; NOEC
Epitaph on Lady Ossory's Bullfinch. ChTr
Epitaphy of la Graunde Amoure. Stephen Hawes. *See* Pastime of Pleasure, The: Epitaph of Graunde [*or* La Graunde] Amoure, The.
Epithalamia. Thomas Lovell Beddoes. *See* Death's Jest Book: Bridal Song to Amala.
Epithalamion: "Singing, today I married my white girl." Dannie Abse. OBWVE
Epithalamion: "Smile then, children, hand in hand." James Elroy Flecker. BrPo
Epithalamion: "These are the small hours when." Michael Longley. CIP
Epithalamion: "Ye learned sisters which have often times," *sels.* Spenser. AAS; BoLoP; EIL; InPS; NoBE; NoP; OAEL-1; OBEV; OBSC; PoE; PoEL-1; TEP
  "Now al is done; bring home the bride againe." FiP
  "Wake, now my love, awake; for it is time." GBL
  Who Is the Same, Which at My Window Peepes?. NAs
Epithalamion Made at Lincolnes Inne. John Donne. OBS; SeCP
Epithalamion on the Lady Elizabeth and Count Palantine Being Married on St. Valentine's Day, An, *sel.* John Donne.
  "Hail, Bishop Valentine, whose day this is." ChTr; OFD
Epithalamion Teratos. Chapman. *Fr.* Hero and Leander, Fifth Sestiad. EIL
Epithalamium: "Can the lover share his soul." W. J. Turner. OBMV
Epithalamium: "Come, virgin tapers of pure wax." Richard Crashaw. NOCV
Epithalamium: "Crept side by side beyond the thresh." Vassar Miller. NePoEA
Epithalamium: "In the streets the crowds go about their business." Daniel Halpern. MAYP
Epithalamium: "Let mother Earth now deck herself in flowers." Sir Philip Sidney. *Fr.* Arcadia. SiPS
Epithalamium: "So you are married, girl. It makes me sad." Roy McFadden. NeIP

Epithalamium: "This body of my mother, pierced by me." Leo Kennedy. OBCV

Epithalamium: "We have found our peace, and move with a turning globe." Arthur Rex Dugard Fairburn. ATNZ

Epithalamium for Mary Stuart and the Dauphin of France. George Buchanan, *tr. fr. Latin.* GoTS

Epithalamium upon the Marriage of Captain William Bedloe, An. Richard Duke. APAS

Epithalamy to Sir Thomas Southwell and His Lady, An. Robert Herrick. CaPo

Epoch ends, the world is still, The. Matthew Arnold. *Fr.* Bacchanalia; or, The New Age, II. OAEL-2

Epoch of a streetcar drawn by horses, The. Baby Pictures of Famous Dictators. Charles Simic. GeTw; WeW

Epode. Ben Jonson. SeCP; SeCV-1

Epodes, *sels.* Horace, *tr. fr. Latin.*
Counterblast against Garlic, A. *Fr.* III, *tr.* by Roswell Martin Field. NBLV
Country Life. *Fr.* II, *tr.* by Dryden. AWP

Epos. Gyorgy Raba, *tr. fr. Hungarian* by Jascha Kessler. FOC

Epos. Harold Rosenberg. PoA

Eppie Morrie. *Unknown.* ESPB; OxBB

Eppur Si Muove? Robert Hillyer. GoYe

Equality. Armanda Guiducci, *tr. fr. Italian* by Muriel Kittel. DMI

Equality demands no less; history begins with old man crying. Bruce Andrews. *Fr.* Confidence Trick. LP

Equality, Father! Edith Bruck, *tr. fr. Italian* by Anita Barrows. VWA

Equality of Sacrifice. Kipling. *Fr.* Epitaphs of the War, 1914–1918. FaBoTw

Equation. Nizar Qabbani, *tr. fr. Arabic* by Diana Der Hovanessian *and* Lena Jayyusi. MAP

Equation. Sir Herbert Read. BrPo

Equation. Charles Wright. CAPP

Equestrian fell from his horse, An. The Childhood of an Equestrian. Russell Edson. AmPA

Equestrienne. Rachel Lyman Field. *Fr.* A Circus Garland. OBCA

Equilibrists, The. John Crowe Ransom. CMoP; HAP; LiTM; MoAB; MoP; NAAL-2; NIP; NoAM; NOBA; OxBA; PPP; TAP

Equinoctial. István Vas, *tr. fr. Hungarian* by Jascha Kessler. FOC

Equinox, The. DuBose Heyward. PoA

Equipment. Paul Laurence Dunbar. TrPWD

Era. Jaki Seroke. WMBCH

Erased off the face of my earth, all that remains is a white space. House. Diana O Hehir. NPGG

Erce, Erce, Erce, mother of earth. Charms for Unfruitful Land. *Unknown, tr.* by Charles W. Kennedy. AnOE

Erd sould trymbill, the firmament sould schaik, The. Quod Dunbar to Kennedy. William Dunbar. OxBoLi

Ere famous Winthrops bones are laid to rest. Chelmsfords Fate. Benjamin Tompson. SCAP

Ere five score years have run their tedious rounds. A Prophecy. Arthur Lee. PAH

E're I forget the zenith of your love. To My Cosen Mrs. Ellinor Evins. George Alsop. SCAP

Ere I freeze, to sing bravely. Poem of the Frost and Snow. Lewis Morris, *tr.* by Anthony Conran. OBWVE

Ere I had told/ Ten birthdays when among the mountain-slopes. Skating. Wordsworth. *Fr.* The Prelude [or, Growth of a Poet's Mind]: Childhood and School-Time. TOF

Ere last year's moon had left the sky. My Bird. "Fanny Forester." AA

Ere long they come, where that same wicked wight. Spenser. *Fr.* The Faerie Queene: The Cave of Despair. NOBE; OAEL-1

Ere Murfreesboro's thunders rent the air. The Battle of Murfreesboro. Kinahan Cornwallis. PAH

Ere my heart beats too coldly and faintly. The Truants. Walter de la Mare. MoBrPo

Ere on my bed my limbs I lay. The Pains of Sleep. Samuel Taylor Coleridge. EnRP; NAEL-2; OBNC; SeCePo; TEP (Child's Evening Prayer, A.) OxBChV; TrPWD

Ere Sleep Comes Down to Soothe the Weary Eyes. Paul Laurence Dunbar. BANP; CDC; PoNe

Ere space exists, or earth, or sky. The Lord Is King. *Unknown, tr.* by Solomon Solis-Cohen. TrJP

Ere the beard of thistle sails. The Seasons. Thomas Holcroft. NOEC

Ere the steamer bore him Eastward, Sleary was engaged to marry. The Post That Fitted. Kipling. CenHV; OnMSP

Ere yet in Vergil I could scan or spell. "Hic Me, Pater Optime, Fessam Deseris." Lucy Catlin Robinson. AA

Ere yet your footsteps quit the place. Verses Addressed to a Friend, Just Leaving a Favourite Retirement. Samuel Henley. NOEC

Ere You Were Queen of Sheba. Sir Arthur Shipley. FaBoCo

Erector, cherry-/ picker. Haiku and ½. Phyllis Gotlieb. BWV

Eremites, The. Robert Graves. LiTB

Erev Shabbos. Marc Kaminsky. VWA

Erewhile I sang of courtly dame. Homely Rhymes on Bad Times. Samuel Bamford. PF

Ergo Sum. Charles Brasch. ATNZ

Eric. John Barford. PeHV

Erica. Mary Ursula Bethell. ATNZ; PeNZ

Eride, *sel.* Trumbull Stickney.
Now in the Palace Gardens. *Fr.* V. LiTA

Erie Canal, The. William S. Allen. AmFN; AS, *with music;* ILY

Erige Cor Tuum ad Me in Caelum. Hilda Doolittle ("H. D."). CMoP

Erik Satie. J. Bernlef, *tr. fr. Dutch* by Theo Hermans. DuIn

Erinna. Antipater of Sidon, *tr. fr. Greek* by A. J. Butler. AWP

Erith, on the Thames. *Unknown.* FaBoPP; GBP

Erl-King, The. Goethe, *tr. fr. German.* AWP, *tr.* by Sir Walter Scott; OBVE, *tr.* by Sir Walter Scott; WSC, *tr.* by Sir Walter Scott (Invisible King, The.) NU, *tr.* by Robert Bly

Erlinton. *Unknown.* ESPB, A *and* B *vers.;* ESPB

Ermine or blazonry, he knew them not. Andrew. Thomas William Parsons. AA

Ernst was an elephant, a great big fellow. The Four Friends. Alan Alexander Milne. PYC

Eros. Robert Bridges. CMoP; LiTB; NOBE; PoEL-5; QFR

Eros. Emerson. FaBoBe

Eros. Louise Glück. *Fr.* Dedication to Hunger, III. AnAn; GeTw

Eros, blind Father, let me show you the way. Another Lineage. Delmira Agustini, *tr.* by Perry Higman. LPSS

Eros D'Aute. Theodore Wratislaw. GBL

Eros, I wish to guide you, blind Father. Another Breed. Delmira Agustini, *tr.* by Kate Flores. DMH

Eros Out of the Sea. Dilys Bennett Laing. PoA

Eros Possessed. Denis Roche, *tr. fr. French* by Harry Mathews. RHTwFP

Eros, thou yet behold'st me? Shakespeare. *Fr.* Antony and Cleopatra, IV, xiv. EBEV

Eros Turannos. E. A. Robinson. CMoP; GBL; HAP; HeIP; LiTA; LiTM; MoAB; MoAmPo; MoP; NAAL-2; NoAM; NOBA; NoP; OxBA; PoA; PoE; QFR; TAP

Erosion. Jorie Graham. MAYP

Erosion. Edwin John Pratt. CaP

Erosion of rocks blooms, The. The world. Lyn Hejinian. IAT

Erotic Suite, *sels.* José Luis Vega, *tr. fr. Spanish* by Julio Marzán. InW
"My love, like the vast majority."
Poemlove (Fragment).

Erotion. Martial, *tr. fr. Latin* by Kirby Flower Smith. AWP

Erotion. Swinburne. PoEL-5

Erotopaegnia, *sel.* Edoardo Sanguineti, *tr. fr. Italian* by Lawrence R. Smith.
"Grab this mercury, this cold gum, this honey, this sphere." NItP

Errant. John Godfrey. UL

Errantry. Robert Fitzgerald. NYBP

Errata. Charles Simic. NNaP

Errata Slip. Jared Carter. SoTCo

Erris Coast, 1943. Hugh Connell. NeIP

Error Pursued. Helen A. Pinkerton. QFR

Errore. Pier Giorgio Di Cicco. NOBC

Erthe oute of erthe is wonderly wroghte. Earth out of Earth. *Unknown.* MeEL

Erthe Toc of Erthe. *Unknown.* HAP

Erubescent flax curls crisp and dry, The. Smoking Flax. Mary Josephine Benson. CaP

Erudite, solemn/ The pious bird. Rev Owl. A. M. Klein. TrJP

Es fällt ein Stern herunter. Heine, *tr. fr. German* by Richard Garnett. AWP

Es Stehen Unbeweglich. Heine, *tr. fr. German* by James Thomson. AWP; TrJP

Es war einmal. . .No, it's too heavy. Märchenbilder. John Ashbery. KS; LCAP; NOBA

Esau ("Esau,/ Hairy Esau [or Shaggy]"). Leyb Kvitko, *tr. fr. Yiddish.* PeBMYV, *tr.* by Allen Mandelbaum *and* Harold Rabinowitz; VWA, *tr.* by Keith Bosley

Escalator, The. Alex Glasgow. OBET

Escape, An. Abu Nuwas, *tr. fr. Arabic* by E. Powys Mathers. ErPo

Escape. Robert Graves. BrPo; MoBrPo

Escape, The. Ivor Gurney. OxBSP

Escape. Georgia Douglas Johnson. PoBA

Escape, The. Edwin Muir. WaP

Escape. Ilya Rubin, *tr. fr. Russian* by Linda Zisquit. VWA

Escape. Charles Spear. ATNZ

Escape, The. William Stafford. NNaP

Escape, The. Mark Van Doren. MoAmPo
Escape. Elinor Wylie. LiTA; MoAmPo
Escape and Return. Elizabeth Jennings. NePoEA
Escape at Bedtime. Robert Louis Stevenson. TrGrPo
Escape into You, The, *sels.* Marvin Bell.
  Homage to the Runner. CAPP
  Obsessive. SM
Escape me?/ Never. Life in a Love. Robert Browning. OBNC; TrGrPo
Escape to Love, *sel.* Patrick MacDonogh.
  "Alone and Godless, stopped by the sudden edge." BIrV
Escaping a dog, a rooster flaps. Kito, *tr. fr. Japanese by* Hiroaki Sato.
  Fr. Twenty-four Hokku. FCEI
Escaping from the enemy's hand. The Escape. Edwin Muir. WaP
Escaping the world, I became a priest. Ryuko, *tr. by* Lucien Stryk *and*
  Takashi Ikemoto. ZPCJ
Escorted by two policemen, little doubting. Grief. Salvador Díaz Mirón,
  tr. by Samuel Beckett. MexPo
Escorting My Mother Home. Rai San'yo, *tr. fr. Japanese by* Burton
  Watson. FCEI; JLIC-2
Ese!/ Within your will-to-be culture. Pachuco Remembered. Tino
  Villanueva. FIA
Eshu, the God of Fate ("Eshu turns right into wrong"). *Yoruba Oral*
  Tradition, tr. by Ulli Beier. WTO
Eskimo Baby, An. Lucy Diamond. BoTP
Eskimo Chant. *Unknown, tr. fr. Eskimo by* Knud Rasmussen. RFM
Eskimo, explorers state, The. The Immoral Arctic. Morris Bishop.
  FiBHP
Eskimo hunts, The. Al Capone in Alaska. Ishmael Reed. TW
Eskimo Occasion. Judith Rodriguez. CBAP; FaBoWP
Eskimos in Manitoba. Recital. John Updike. OBAL; RR
Esmeralda! Now we rest. Lines Written in Oregon. Vladimir Nabokov.
  NYBP
ESP. Carter Revard. VoR
ESP. Steve Rasnic Tem. BWV
España, Aparta de me Este Caliz, *sel.* César Vallejo, *tr. fr. Spanish.*
  Masses. *Tr. by* Robert Bly. RB
Especially forlorn specimen, An. Dimly Outlined by a Police Artist.
  Charles Simic. PPR
Especially he loves. God Poem. Stanley Moss. VGW; VWA
Especially on hot summer Sumdays. Hot Summer Sunday. A. L.
  Hendricks. PBCV
Especially When the October Wind. Dylan Thomas. LiTB; MoAB;
  MoBrPo; OBWVE; OxBTC
Essay. Bernadette Mayer. UL
Essay. Riekus Waskowsky, *tr. fr. Dutch by* James S. Holmes. DuIn
Essay on Criticism. Pope. FiP; HAP; NAEL-1; OAEL-1; PoEL-3
  Sels.
  "But most by numbers judge a poet's song." *Fr. Pt.* II. FaBoUs;
    HAP; NIP
  (Poetical Numbers.) SeCePo
  "First follow Nature, and your judgment frame." *Fr. Pt.* I. HAP
  "In wit, as nature, what affects our hearts." *Fr. Pt.* II. HAP
  "Little learning is a dangerous thing, A." *Fr. Pt.* II. FPL; HAP;
    HoPM; PoLF; TrGrPo
  (Alps on Alps.) FaFP
  (Little Learning, A.) ChTr; LiTB; NOBE; SeCePo
  "Of all the causes which conspire to blind." *Fr. Pt.* II. NOEC: NoP
  "Some are bewildered in the maze of schools." *Fr. Pt.* I. OBSV
  "Some beauties yet no precepts can declare." *Fr. Pt.* I. HAP
  "Some ne'er advance a judgment of their own." *Fr. Pt.* II. OBSV
  "Such shameless bards we have; and yet 'tis true." *Fr. Pt.* III. OBSV
  "'Tis hard to say, if greater want of skill." *Fr. Pt.* I. FiP; HAP;
    OAEL-1
  "True ease in writing comes from art, not chance." *Fr. Pt.* II. HAP;
    InPK; PrIm; TrGrPo
  (Sound and Sense.) SoSe; UnPo
Essay on Language. Wanda Coleman. BAP
Essay on Lunch. Walker Gibson. NYBP
Essay on Man, An, *sels.* Pope.
  "All are but parts of one stupendous whole." *Fr.* Epistle I. WGRP
  "Awake, my St. John! leave all meaner things." *Fr.* Epistle I.
    NAEL-1; NoP; PoEL-3
  (Wild Garden, The.) PrIm, *fr. ll.* 1–16.
  "Behold the child, by Nature's kindly law." *Fr.* Epistle II. FaBoRV
  "Bliss of man, The (could pride that blessing find)." *Fr.* Epistle I.
    NOEC; NU
  Faith. *Fr.* Epistle III. WGRP
  "Far as creation's ample range extends." *Fr.* I *and* II. FM; ImOP
  "Honor and shame from no condition rise." *Fr.* Epistle IV. TrGrPo
  "Hope humbly then; with trembling pinions soar." *Fr.* Epistle I.
    TrGrPo
  "Know then thyself, presume not God to scan." *Fr.* Epistle II. BLPL,
    ll. 1–18; LiTB, *fr.* II *and* IV; NAEL-1; NOEC, *ll.* 1–18; NoP;
    OAEL-1, *ll.* 1–18; PoEL-3; SeCePo, *ll.* 1–18; TrGrPo, *ll.* 1–18.
  (Know Thyself.) NOBE, *fr. ll.* 1-18.
  (Man.) PrIm, *fr. ll.* 1-18.
  (Paragon of Animals, The.) ACP, *ll.* 1–30.
  (Proper Study of Mankind, The.) FiP, *ll.* 1–30.
  (Riddle of the World.) FaFP, *ll.* 1–18.
Life's Poor Play. *Fr.* Epistle II. SeCePo
"Lo, the poor Indian! whose untutor'd mind." *Fr.* Epistle I. NU
"Look round our world; behold the chain of love." *Fr.* Epistle III.
  OBD
"Nor think, in nature's state they blindly trod." *Fr.* Epistle III.
  OAEL-1
"Placed on this isthmus of a middle state." *Fr.* Epistle II. WeW
Pleasure of Hope, The. *Fr.* Epistle I. ACP
Soul's Calm Sunshine, The. *Fr.* IV. FaBoRV
"What if the foot, ordain'd the dust to tread." *Fr.* Epistle I. FaBoPV
"What would this Man? Now upward will he soar." *Fr.* Epistle I.
  HeIP
"Whate'er the passion—knowledge, fame, or pelf." *Fr.* Epistle II.
  TrGrPo
  (Human Folly.) FiP
Essay on Marriage, *sel.* Anne Finch.
  "O, love, in your sweet name enough." FaBoTw
Essay on Memory, *sel.* Robert David Fitzgerald.
  "Rain in my ears: impatiently there raps." CBAP
Essay on Poetry, *sel.* John Sheffield.
  On Writing for the Stage. FaBoUs
Essay on Psychiatrists, *sels.* Robert Pinsky.
  Dionysus as Psychiatrist. *Fr.* X. HCAP
  Invocation. *Fr.* I. NoAM
  Mad, The. *Fr.* XVIII. NoAM
  Peroration, Concerning Genius. *Fr.* XX. NoAM
  Proposition. *Fr.* III. HCAP; NoAM
  Some Terms. *Fr.* II. HCAP
  Their Patients. *Fr.* XVII. NoAM
  Their Philistinism Considered. *Fr.* XI. NoAM
  Their Seriousness, with Further Comparisons. *Fr.* VI. NoAM
  Their Speech, Compared with Wisdom and Poetry. *Fr.* XIV. NoAM;
    PoA
Essay on the Fleet Riding in the Downes, An. "J. D." CoMu
Essay on Translated Verse, An, *sel.* Earl of Roscommon.
  "Each poet with a different talent writes." FaBoUs
Essay on Woman, An. Mary Leapor. NOEC
Essay upon Satire, An. *At. to* John Sheffield. APAS
Esse. Czeslaw Milosz. TOF
Essence of Existence, The. Jack Kerouac. *Fr.* Mexico City Blues, 182.
  NeAP
Essence of ink, The. Yün Shou-p'ing, *tr. fr. Chinese by* Jonathan Chaves.
  Fr. In My Boat, Painting a Picture. CoBLCP
Essential oils—are wrung. Emily Dickinson. AmPP
Essential poem at the center of things, The. A Primitive like an Orb.
  Wallace Stevens. NOBA
Essentials. Samuel Greenberg. LiTA
Essex Regiment March. George Edward Woodberry. PAH
Essie Parrish in New York. Essie Parrish, *tr. fr. Kashia Pomo Indian by*
  George Quasha. STP
Está Muy Caliente. George Bowering. MoCV
"Established" is a good word, much used in garden books. Time. Mary
  Ursula Bethell. FaBoWP
Estat ai en greu cossirier. Beatriz de Dia, *tr. fr. Provençal by* Paul
  Blackburn. ErPo
Estate, The, *sels.* Charles Brasch.
  "Once more as I gather about me the cloak of the evening." *Fr.* XXII.
    ATNZ
  "Thistle, briar, thorn." *Fr.* XXX. ATNZ
  "What have you seen on the summits, the peaks that plunge their." *Fr.*
    XXIV. PeNZ
Estate and an earldom at seventy-four, An! Earl of Orford. FaBoEE
Estelí/ this mountain town means something. Resurrection. Joy Harjo.
  ER; HATNAP
Estella, Estella, they're cooking up paella. Song in Praise of Paella. C.
  W. V. Wordsworth. FiBHP
Esther [a Young Man's Tragedy], *sels.* Wilfrid Scawen Blunt.
  "He who has once been happy is for aye." OBMV; OBNC; TrGrPo
  (With Esther.) OBEV
I Will Not Tell the Secrets. *Fr.* XLIX. Son
  "When I hear laughter from a tavern door." OBMV; TrGrPo
Esther K. Comes to America: 1931. Jerome Rothenberg. NNaP
Esther's Tomcat. Ted Hughes. OxBC

Esthete in Harlem. Langston Hughes. BANP; BPo
Esthetic of Imitation, An. Donald Finkel. NePoEA
Esthétique du Mal. Wallace Stevens. CMoP; LiTM; NOBA
Esthétique du Mal, *sels.* Wallace Stevens. LiTM
  "He was at Naples writing letters home." CMoP; NOBA
  "How red the rose that is the soldier's wound." CMoP; NOBA; WaP
  (Soldier's Wound, The.) WaaP
  "Life is a bitter aspic. We are not." CMoP
  "Sun, in clownish yellow, but not a clown, The." NOBA
Esthonian Bridal Song. Johann Gottfried von Herder, *tr. fr. German by*
  W. Taylor. AWP
Estimable Mable. Gwendolyn Brooks. FB
Estrich, thou feathered fool and easy prey. Lucasta's Fan, with a
  Looking-Glass in It. Richard Lovelace. CaPo
Estuarial Republic, The. Douglas Dunn. FaBoMo
Estuary, The. Arthur Rex Dugard Fairburn. ATNZ
Estuary. Maruyama Kaoru, *tr. fr. Japanese by* Hiroaki Sato. FCEI
Estuary. Ted Walker. NYBP
Esyllt. Glyn Jones. OBWVE
Et Cetera. Dee Lawrence Walker. GoYe
Et in Arcadia Ego. W. H. Auden. CMoP
Et Incarnatus Est. William Langland. *Fr.* The Vision of Piers Plowman.
  NOBE, *fr.* Passus II (C *text*).
Et Mori Lucrum. John Lancaster Spalding. *Fr.* God and the Soul.
  AA
Et Quid Amabo Nisi Quod Aenigma Est. Stephen Sandy. NYBP
État, *sel.* Anne-Marie Albiach, *tr. fr. French by* Paul Auster.
  "Of the unended in the speed of." PBWP
Etched Away From. Paul Celan, *tr. fr. German by* Michael Hamburger.
  OBVE
Etching. W. E. Henley. *Fr.* In Hospital, XII. BrPo
Etching. Tamura Ryuichi, *tr. fr. Japanese by* Hiroaki Sato. FCEI
Eterna Voluttà, L'. Valery Larbaud, *tr. fr. French by* William Jay Smith.
  CT
Eternal. Agnes Foley Macdonald. CaP
Eternal City, The. A. R. Ammons. CAPP; EyDe; HCAP
Eternal Contour. Florida Watts Smyth. GoYe
Eternal Evening. Sándor Weöres, *tr. fr. Hungarian by* Jascha Kessler.
  FOC
Eternal Father, Strong to Save. William Whiting. FaPoR; MOS; NOCV
Eternal Female groan'd, The! it was heard over all the earth. A Song of
  Liberty. Blake. EnRP
Eternal gates' terrific porter lifted the northern bar. The Secrets of the
  Earth. Blake. *Fr.* The Book of Thel. NOBE
Eternal God, How They're Increased. Cotton Mather. AH
Eternal God, maker of all. The Book. Henry Vaughan. JCP; SeCV-1
Eternal God, our life is but. "Yehoash," *tr. by* Isidore Goldstick. TrJP
Eternal God, Whose Power Upholds, *with music.* Henry Hallam Tweedy.
  AH
Eternal God Whose Searching Eye Doth Scan. Edwin McNeill Poteat.
  TrPWD
Eternal Goodness, The ("O friends! with whom my feet have trod."), *sels.*
  Whittier. AA; OHFP; WGRP
  "And Thou, O Lord! by whom are seen." TrPWD
  "I know not what the future hath." BLRP, *abr.*; NOCV
Eternal Image, The. Ruth Pitter. MoBrPo; OxBTC
Eternal Jew, The. Jacob Cohen, *tr. fr. Hebrew by* I. M. Lask. TrJP
Eternal Justice. Anne Reeve Aldrich. AA
Eternal Kinship, The. Maurice E. Peloubet. GoYe
Eternal Light! Thomas Binney. NOCV; WGRP
Eternal Lord! Eased of a Cumbrous Load. Michelangelo, *tr. fr. Italian by*
  Wordsworth. TrPWD
Eternal Masculine. William Rose Benét. AWP; MoAmPo
Eternal Moment. "Katherine Hale." CaP
Eternal mover, whose diffused glory. Sir Henry Wotton. TrPWD
Eternal Now. Gabriel Preil, *tr. fr. Yiddish by* Grace Schulman.
  PeBMYV
Eternal Power, of earth and air! The Doubter's Prayer. Anne Brontë.
  TrPWD; WGRP
Eternal Return, The. Robert Hillyer. AiP; NYBP
Eternal Road, The, *sel.* Franz Werfel, *tr. fr. German by* Ludwig
  Lewisohn.
  Ye Sorrowers. TrJP
Eternal Ruler of the ceaseless round. John White Chadwick. TrPWD
Eternal Sabbath. Isaac Leibush Peretz, *tr. fr. Yiddish by* Joseph Leftwich.
  TrJP
Eternal spirit/ of dead dried. Black Lotus. Alicia Loy Johnson. NBP
Eternal Spirit of the chainless mind! Sonnet on Chillon. Byron. *Fr.*
  The Prisoner of Chillon. FiP; LiTB; TrGrPo
  (On the Castle of Chillon.) GTBS; GTBS-P
Eternal Spirit, Source of Light. Samuel Davies. AH

Eternal Spirit, you. A Prayer for My Son. Yvor Winters. TrPWD
Eternal Spring, The. Milton. *See* Paradise Lost: Birds their quire apply;
  airs, vernal airs, The.
Eternal Time, that wastest without waste. To Time. "A. W." EiL
Eternal Years, The. Frederick William Faber. PWR
Eternale Footeman's Tale, The. George Moor. BXAP
Eternall and all-working God, which wast. Michael Drayton. *Fr.* Noah's
  Flood. PoEL-2
Eternall Truth, almighty, infinite. Fulke Greville. *Fr.* Caelica, XCVII
  [XCVIII].
  (Sonnet: "Eternall Truth, almighty, infinite.") OBS
Eternities. Norman Mailer. NYBP
Eternities before the first-born day. Mother Night. James Weldon
  Johnson. Son
Eternity ("He who binds [*or* bends] to himself a joy"). Blake. *Fr.*
  Several Questions Answered. AWP; EBEV; FaBoEE; NOBE; NoP;
  OBNC; OxBSP; RB; TrGrPo
Eternity. Emily Dickinson. *See* On this wondrous sea.
Eternity. Eugène Guillevic, *tr. fr. French by* Denise Levertov. RHTwFP
Eternity. Josephine D. Henderson Heard. CBWP-4
Eternity. Robert Herrick. OBD
Eternity, The. Henry Vaughan. *See* I saw eternity the other night.
Eternity encountered on the stair. Chez Madame. Sam Harrison. NeIP
Eternity is like unto a ring. Time and Eternity. Bunyan. WiR
Eternity is passion, girl or boy. Whence Had They Come? W. B. Yeats.
  BoLoP
Eternity of Love Protested. Thomas Carew. MeLP; OBS
Eternity of Nature, The. John Clare. EBEV
Eternity, when I think thee. Quoniam Ego in Flagella Paratus Sum.
  William Habington. ACP
Eternity's Low Voice. Mark Van Doren. EaLo
Eternity's Speech against Time. Fulke Greville. *Fr.* Mustapha: Chorus
  Tertius: Of Time; Eternitie. JCP
Ethan Boldt. Roger Weingarten. AmPA
Ethel in her crimson row boat. Chateaux en Espagne. Henrietta Cordelia
  Ray. CBWP-3
Ethelstan, *sel.* George Darley.
  O'er the Wild Gannet's Bath. ChTr; PoEL-4
Ethereal minstrel! pilgrim of the sky! To a Skylark ("Ethereal minstrel!
  pilgrim of the sky"). Wordsworth. EnRP; PBBP; TrGrPo
  (To the Skylark.) FaFP; GTBS; GTBS-P
Ethick. Robert Bridges. *Fr.* The Testament of Beauty, IV. OxBTC
Ethics. Linda Pastan. InPK
Ethics for Everyman. Roger Woddis. NOBL
Ethics put it well, The. The Magnanimous. Ellen de Young Kay.
  NePoEA
Ethinthus, Queen of Waters. Blake. *Fr.* Europe. ChTr
Ethiopia Saluting the Colors. Walt Whitman. PAH; PoNe
Ethnic Life, The. Daniel Halpern. AmPA
Ethnocide. Howard Fergus. PBCV
Ethnogenesis. Henry Timrod. AmPP; AnAmPo; NOBA; OxBA
Etiquette. W. S. Gilbert. CenHV; FaBoCh; FaBoCo; FiBHP
Eton Boating Song. William Johnson Cory. ELP
Etosion achthos aroures. Robert Bridges. QFR
Etrick Forest is a fair forest[e]. The Outlaw Murray. *Unknown.* ESPB;
  OxBB
Etruscan Notebook, *sels.* Elena Clementelli, *tr. fr. Italian by* Ruth
  Feldman *and* Brian Swann. PBWP
  "Cerveteri road."
  "From gorge to gorge."
  "Net rests on the water's surface, The."
Etruscan Sarcophagus, The. István Vas, *tr. fr. Hungarian by* William Jay
  Smith. MHuP
Etruscan Statue. Esther Raab, *tr. fr. Hebrew by* Bernhard Frank. MHeP
Etruscan Warrior's Head. Helen Rowe Henze. GoYe
Ettrick. Lady John Scott. WPE
Ettrick Forest in November. Sir Walter Scott. *Fr.* Marmion, *introd. to* I.
  FaBoPP
Étude. Joseph Brodsky, *tr. fr. Russian by* Dimitry Pospielovsky *and* Keith
  Bosley. VWA
Etude. Judah Leib Teller, *tr. fr. Yiddish by* Benjamin *and* Barbara
  Harshav. AYP
Étude for Voice and Hand. Gabriel Levin. VWA
Étude Géographique. Stoddard King. AmFN
Étude Réaliste, *sel.* Swinburne. GN
  "Baby's feet, like sea-shells pink, A." *Fr.* I. FaPON; WeW
Euch, are you having your period? Alta. NMM
Euclid. Vachel Lindsay. *Fr.* Poems about the Moon, I. ImOP
Euclid Alone Has Looked on Beauty Bare. Edna St. Vincent Millay.
  CMoP; ImOP; MoAB; MoAmPo; NAAL-2; NoP; Son; TAP
Euclid Avenue. Charles Simic. LCAP

Eudaimon. Kathleen Jessie Raine. PBWP
Eugenio. Hugh Henry Brackenridge *and* Philip Freneau. *Fr.* The Rising Glory of America. AiP
Eugenio Pacelli. Francis Neilson. GoYe
Eugenist, The. Robert Graves. FaBoEE
Eulalie. Poe. Par
Eulogy. Grace Nichols. UAS
Eulogy for Alvin Frost. Audre Lorde. CNA
Eulogy for Hasdai ibn Shaprut. *Unknown, tr. fr. Hebrew by* Israel Abrahams. TrJP
Eulogy for Populations. Ron Welburn. PoBA
Eulogy of the Sagely Virtue of His Imperial Majesty Emperor Shih-tsu, A. Chao Meng-fu, *tr. fr. Chinese by* Jonathan Chaves. CoBLCP
Eulogy on My Own Portrait, A. Yang Shih-ch'i, *tr. fr. Chinese by* Jonathan Chaves. CoBLCP
Eulogy to the Bow and Arrow. *Mongol Oral Tradition, tr. by* C. R. Bawden. WTO
Eumares. Asclepiades, *tr. fr. Greek by* Richard Garnett. AWP
Eumenides, The. Aeschylus, *tr. fr. Greek by* Robert Fagles. NAWM-1
Eumenides at Home, The. James Agate. BXAP
Eunica skornde me, when her I would have sweetly kist. Theocritus, *tr. fr. Greek.* *Fr.* Idylls, XX. OBVE
Eunuch and the unicorn, the. The Primrose Bed. Robert Graves. TEP
Eureka! Alfred Denis Godley. CenHV
Euridice Saved. Linda Gregg. NPGG
Euripides the Athenian. George Seferis, *tr. fr. Greek by* Edmund Keeley *and* Philip Sherrard. VMG
Euro-Squawk. Joan Van Poznak. SoTCo
Europa. William Plomer. MoBS
Europa. Stephen Henry Thayer. AA
Europa. Derek Walcott. AnAn; NoP
Europa,/ your red-haired. For the West. Gary Snyder. NaP
Europa Rides a Black Bull. Antonio Porta, *tr. fr. Italian by* Lawrence R. Smith. NItP
Europe, *sel.* Blake.
  Ethinthus, Queen of Waters. ChTr
Europe, *sels.* Louis Dudek.
  "Commotion of these waves, however strong, cannot disturb, The." OBCV
  "Sea retains such images, The." *Fr.* XCV. OBCV
Europe. Valery Larbaud, *tr. fr. French by* William Jay Smith. CT *Sels.*
  "And you, Italy, one day I knelt." *Fr.* X.
  "At the end of a little sloping street, I recognize." *Fr.* XI.
  "In Colombo or Nagasaki I examine the Baedekers." *Fr.* IV.
  "Midnight at sea like so many other midnights at sea." *Fr.* I.
Europe and America. David Ignatow. AmFN; NNaP; UnPo
Europe lies in ruins: a black headline story. 1945. Sheila Cussons, *tr. by* Jack Cope *and* Uys Krige. PeSA
European Crimes. Charles Churchill. *Fr.* Gotham. NOEC
European food. *Unknown, tr. by* Geoffrey Bownas *and* Anthony Thwaite. PeBJV
European Night, The. Stanislav Vinaver, *tr. fr. Serbo-Croatian, by* Vasa D. Mihailovich. VWA
European Shoe, The. Michael Benedikt. AmPA; TwCP
Eurydice. Linda Gregg. NPGG
Eurydice. Hilda Doolittle ("H. D."). VGW
Eurydice. Sherod Santos. NAmP
Eurymachus's Fancy. Robert Greene. *Fr.* Francesco's Fortunes. OBSC
Eurynome. Eleni Fourtouni, *tr. fr. Greek by the author.* AIW
Eurynome. Jay Macpherson. OBCV
Eurystheus, trembling, called me to the throne. Heracles. Yvor Winters. QFR
Eutaw Springs. Philip Freneau. *See* At Eutaw Springs the valiant died.
Eutawville Lynching, The. Lizelia Augusta Jenkins Moorer. CBWP-3
Euterpe, you must think us common queer. Euterpe; a Symmetric. David McCord. *Fr.* New Chitons for Old Gods. UnS
Euthymiae Raptus; or, The Teares of Peace, *sels.* George Chapman.
  "And, now gives Time, her states description." PoEL-2
  Learning. SeCePo
  Poet Questions Peace, The. JCP
Eutopia. Francis Turner Palgrave. EBVV
Eutychides. E. A. Robinson, *after the Greek of* Lucilius. OBAL
Eutychides is dead, and what is worse. Lucilius, *tr. by* Humbert Wolfe. OBD
Eva Braun. W. D. Snodgrass. *Fr.* The Führer Bunker. CAPP
Eva, I agree to love, among creation, all the creatures! Alfred de Vigny, *tr. fr. French by* Robert Bly. *Fr.* The Shepherd's House. NU
Evacuation of New York by the British. *Unknown.* PAH
Evacuee. Edith Pickthall. CN
Evacuees, The. Freda Laughton. CN

Evadne. Hilda Doolittle ("H. D."). BoWoP
Evan just had the white birch lined up. Fear and Anger in the Mindless Universe. Hayden Carruth. MAYP; NNaP
Evanescence. Harriet Prescott Spofford. AA
Evanescent hue whose pearly gleam, An. An Ideal. Henrietta Cordelia Ray. CBWP-3
Evangelical vicar in want, An. Ronald Arbuthnott Knox. CenHV; OxBoLi
Evangelical vicar in want. Ronald Arbuthnott Knox. CenHV
Evangeline. Longfellow. BeLS, *complete.*
  Sels.
  Embarkation, The. *Fr.* PAH.
  Evangeline in Acadie. AA
  Finding of Gabriel, The. AA
  Lakes of the Atchafalaya, The. PoEL-5
  On the Atchafalaya. AA
  "This is the forest primeval. The murmuring pines and the hemlocks." BeLS
  (Primeval Forest, The.) WBLP
Evangeline. Norma E. Smith. CaP
Evangeline in Acadie. Longfellow. *Fr.* Evangeline. AA
Evangelist, The. Donald Davie. NePoEA
Evangelist St. John my patron was, The. Wordsworth. *Fr.* The Prelude [or, Growth of a Poet's Mind]: Residence at Cambridge. HAP (Newton's Statue.) FaBoRV
Evangelize! Henry Crocker. BLRP
Evanishings. Mary E. Tucker. CBWP-1
Evans Country, The, *sels.* Kingsley Amis.
  Aberdarcy: The Chaucer Road. NOBL
  Aberdarcy: The Main Square. NoAM; NOBL; OxBTC
  Aldport (Mystery Tour). NOBL
  (Terrible Beauty.) ErPo; NePoEA-2
  Brynbwrla. NOBL
  Fforestfawr. NOBL
  Langwell. NOBL; OxBC
  Pendydd. NOBL
Evanthe's niplets are like sard. Niplets. *Unknown, tr. by* Wallace Rice. ErPo
Evaporation Poems. Kathleen Norris. IHMS
Evarra and His Gods. Kipling. MoBrPo
Evasion, An. Douglas Livingstone. PeSA
Evasion. Blanaid Salkeld. NeIP
Evasive souls, of whom the wise lose track. The Imaginative Life. Geoffrey Hill. NoAM
Eve. Arthur J. Bull. UnPo
Eve. Manuel M. Flores, *tr. fr. Spanish by* Samuel Beckett. MexPo
Eve. Jean Follain, *tr. fr. French by* W. S. Merwin. RHTwFP
Eve. David Gascoyne. GTBS-P
Eve. Anne Hébert, *tr. fr. French by* Kathleen Weaver. OV
Eve. Oliver Herford. OBAL
Eve. Ralph Hodgson. BrPo; CH; LiTB; LiTM; MoAB; MoBrPo; OnMSP; TrCP; TrGrPo; UnPo
Eve. Jakov Fichman, *tr. fr. Hebrew by* Robert Friend. VWA
Eve. Milton. *See* Paradise Lost: In bower and field he sought, where any tuft.
Eve. Howard Nemerov. CRP
Eve. Christina Rossetti. CH; FM; GTBS-P; NIP; PoEL-5
Eve, The. Howard Schwartz. VWA
Eve. *Unknown, tr. fr. Irish by* Thomas MacDonagh. BIrV
Eve am I, great Adam's wife. *Unknown.* NOIV
Eve & her envy roving slammed me down. Gislebertus' Eve. John Berryman. LCAP
Eve and the Apple Tree. Itzik Manger, *tr. fr. Yiddish by* Leonard Wolf. PeBMYV
Eve in My Legend. Denis Devlin. IPY
Eve in Reflection. Jay Macpherson. OBCV
Eve is angel, though bone of bone. Waiting for Lilith. Jascha Kessler. VWA
Eve Meets Medusa. Michelene Wandor. AIW
Eve: Night Thoughts. Judson Jerome. SM
Eve of Bunker Hill, The. Clinton Scollard. PAH
Eve of Christmas had arrived, The. A Christmas Ghost. Priscilla Jane Thompson. CBWP-2
Eve of Easter. Bernadette Mayer. UL
Eve of St. Agnes, The. Keats. BeLS; ChER; EnRP; FiP, *abr.*; GoTL; HAP; HoPM; NAEL-2; NIP; NoP; OAEL-2; OBNC; OBNV; PoE; PoEL-4; PoLF; TEP; TrGrPo; WeW
Eve of Saint John, The. Sir Walter Scott. EnRP; PoEL-4
Eve of Saint Mark, The. Keats. CH; EnRP
Eve of Waterloo, The. Byron. *See* Childe Harold's Pilgrimage: There was a sound of revelry by night.

Eve of Waterloo, The. Thomas Hardy. *Fr.* The Dynasts, *pt.* III, Act VI, sc. viii. OAEL-2; OBWP

Eve Penitent. Milton. *See* Paradise Lost: Forsake me not thus, Adam, witness Heav'n.

Eve-Song. Mary Gilmore. CBAP; PoAu-1

Eve Speaks to Adam. Milton. *See* Paradise Lost: With thee conversing, I forget all time.

Eve to Adam. Milton. *See* Paradise Lost: With thee conversing, I forget all time.

Eve, with her basket, was. Eve. Ralph Hodgson. BrPo; CH; LiTB; LiTM; MoAB; MoBrPo; OnMSP; TrCP; TrGrPo; UnPo

Evelyn. Rossiter Johnson. AA

Evelyn. Priscilla Jane Thompson. CBWP-2

Evelyn Hope. Robert Browning. TrGrPo

Evelyn Searching. Denise Panek. GOS

Even. Anne Morrow Lindbergh. AiP

Even a breeze may fail me. Princess Kagami, *tr. fr. Japanese. Fr.* Manyo Shu. Ma

Even a cloud. Even If. Rachel Fishman, *tr. by* Gabriel Preil *and* Howard Schwartz. VWA

Even a flaming fire can be snatched. Empress Jito, *tr. fr. Japanese. Fr.* Manyo Shu. Ma

Even a person free of passion. Saigyo, *tr. fr. Japanese by* Burton Watson. *Fr.* Sixty-four Tanka. FCEI

Even a priceless jewel. Tabito, *tr. fr. Japanese by* Geoffrey Bownas *and* Anthony Thwaite. *Fr.* Manyo Shu. PeBJV

Even a Pyrrhonist. A Lot of Night Music. Anthony Hecht. NIP; OxBC; PPR

Even after Confession. On a Catholic Childhood. Janet Campbell Hall. VoR

Even after my locks. Manzei, *tr. fr. Japanese. Fr.* Manyo Shu. Ma

Even as a child, of sorrow that we give. Pride of Youth. Dante Gabriel Rossetti. *Fr.* The House of Life, XXIV. OBNC

Even as a young man. Once More Fields and Gardens. T'ao Ch'ien, *tr. by* Amy Lowell *and* Florence Ayscough. AWP

Even as children such patients were strange and dreamy. The Schizophrenics. Roy Fuller. AnAn

Even as children they were late sleepers. The Undead. Richard Wilbur. CoAP; OxBC

Even as I Hold You. Alice Walker. MT; WeW

Even as it falls. Gyoko, *tr. by* Steven D. Carter. WFTW

Even as my hand to pen on paper lays. To His Lady, Who Had Vowed Virginity. Walter Davison. OBSC

Even as tender parents lovingly. The Child in the Street. John James Piatt. AA

Even as the day when it is yet at dawning. Canzone: Of His Love, with the Figure of a Sudden Storm. Prinzivalle Doria, *tr. by* Dante Gabriel Rossetti. AWP

Even as the others mock, thou mockest me. Dante, *tr. fr. Italian by* Dante Gabriel Rossetti. *Fr.* La Vita Nuova, VII. AWP

Even as the raven, the crow, and greedy kite. *Unknown.* PBBP

Even as the snow falls to-day. Yakamochi, *tr. fr. Japanese. Fr.* Manyo Shu. Ma

Even as the sun with purple-colour'd face. Venus and Adonis. Shakespeare. BeLS

Even as we kill. On the Birth of My Son, Malcolm Coltrane. Julius Lester. PoBA

Even at its longest. Tameko, *tr. by* Steven D. Carter. WFTW

Even at midnight. Shunzei, *tr. by* Geoffrey Bownas *and* Anthony Thwaite. PeBJV

Even at sea the bodies of the unborn and the dead. The Changes. Robert Pinsky. NPGG

Even at their fairest still I love the less. A Dream of Flowers. Titus Munson Coan. AA

Even beauty must die! That which subdues both gods and mortals. Schiller. OBD

Even before they fall. *Unknown, tr. fr. Japanese by* Burton Watson. *Fr.* Kokin Shu. FCEI

Even During War. Muriel Rukeyser. *Fr.* Letter to the Front, II. TrJP

Even for the wind there was no room. The Way the Bird Sat. Ray A. Young Bear. CDW; VoR

Even from earthly love thy face avert not. Nuru'ddin Abdu 'R-Rahman Jami, *tr. by* E. G. Browne. TOF

Even from the beach I could sense it. Attack of the Crab Monsters. Lawrence Raab. AmPA; NoP

Even from themselves they are a secret. The Close Clan. Mark Van Doren. GoYe

Even gulls appear to feel cold. Natsume Seibi, *tr. fr. Japanese by* Hiroaki Sato. *Fr.* Twenty-seven Hokku. FCEI

Even her heart again a stranger's. Teika, *tr. fr. Japanese by* Hiroaki Sato. *Fr.* Eighty-four Tanka. FCEI

Even I hate. One-Sided Love. Shunzei, *tr. fr. Japanese by* Burton Watson. *Fr.* Thirty Tanka. FCEI

Even I myself cannot see my figure. Song of the Gull. Maruyama Kaoru, *tr. by* Hiroaki Sato. FCEI

Even If. Rachel Fishman, *tr. fr. Yiddish by* Gabriel Preil *and* Howard Schwartz. VWA

Even if I had to sleep alone. Emperor Go-Shirakawa, *tr. fr. Japanese by* Hiroaki Sato. *Fr.* Ryojin Hisho. FCEI

("Hundred days, a hundred nights, A.") PeBJV, *tr. by* Geoffrey Bownas *and* Anthony Thwaite.

Even if I try not to ogle a boy in the street. Strato. PeHV

Even if it were true. Yes, But. James Wright. CAPP

Even if one has. Ryoshun, *tr. by* Steven D. Carter. WFTW

Even if the geraniums are artificial. The Geraniums. Genevieve Taggard. VGW

Even if the song. Another Voice. Paolo Volponi, *tr. by* Lawrence R. Smith. NItP

Even if wars to come sleep small and warm. That Day. Mark Van Doren. WaP

Even if you bore them to the deepest sea. Tsukan, *tr. fr. Japanese. Fr.* Manyo Shu. Ma

Even if you can't shape your life the way you want. As Much as You Can. C. P. Cavafy, *tr. by* Edmund Keeley *and* Philip Sherrard. RB; VMG

Even if you say, "I come." Lady Otomo no Sakanoe, *tr. fr. Japanese. Fr.* Manyo Shu. Ma

Even in a remote place eightfold heaps. Teika, *tr. fr. Japanese by* Hiroaki Sato. *Fr.* A Compendium of Good Tanka. FCEI

Even in a strange land I see. Hasetsukabe Mamaro, *tr. fr. Japanese. Fr.* Manyo Shu. Ma

Even in bed I pose: desire may grow. Carnal Knowledge. Thom Gunn. BoLoP

Even in death they prosper; even in the death. Necropolis. Karl Shapiro. MoAB; PoA

Even in my dreams/ I must no longer meet you. Lady Ise, *tr. by* Etsuko Terasaki *and* Irma Brandeis. BoWoP

Even in my dreams. Keiun, *tr. by* Steven D. Carter. WFTW

Even in my dreams you have denied yourself to me. To Kalon. Ezra Pound. PoA

Even in sleep I see you. The Fire that in the Stone. Tuvia Rübner, *tr. by* Bernhard Frank. MHeP

Even in sleep my eyes are on the elements. An Astronomer's Journal. Jane Shore. PoA

Even in the bluest noonday of July. To Mrs. Will H. Low. Robert Louis Stevenson. NOBVV

Even in the heat. *Unknown, tr. fr. Japanese. Fr.* Manyo Shu. Ma

Even in the moment of our earliest kiss. Edna St. Vincent Millay. VGW

Even in the roaring torrent. *Unknown, tr. fr. Japanese by* Burton Watson. *Fr.* Kokin Shu. FCEI

Even iron can put forth. Almond Blossom. D. H. Lawrence. FaBoPP

Even is come; and from the dark Park, hark. A Nocturnal Sketch. Thomas Hood. FaBoCo; FiBHP

Even jewels that flash. Tabito, *tr. fr. Japanese by* Geoffrey Bownas *and* Anthony Thwaite. *Fr.* Manyo Shu. PeBJV

Even late at night. Winter Moon. Tameshige, *tr. by* Steven D. Carter. WFTW

Even my own heart. Tameko, *tr. by* Steven D. Carter. WFTW

Even my pillow, not knowing, won't talk. Lady Izumi, *tr. fr. Japanese by* Hiroaki Sato. *Fr.* Fifty-one Tanka. FCEI

Even nature gives you no choice. Eeva Kilpi, *tr. by* Aili Jarvenpa. SOP

Even now/ My thought is all of this gold-tinted king's daughter. Black Marigolds. Bilhana, *formerly at. to* Chauras, *tr. by* E. Powys Mathers. AWP; ErPo, *abr.*

Even now. On the Roads of Siberia. H. Leivick. AYP, *tr. by* Benjamin *and* Barbara Harshav; PeBMYV, *tr. by* Cynthia Ozick

Even now I wish that you had been there. Swans Mating. Michael Longley. FaBCIP

Even now she sometimes. Pomegranate. Gail N. Harada. BrSi

Even now the devastation is begun. Goldsmith. *Fr.* The Deserted Village. EBEV

Even now the fragrant darkness of her hair. Terre Promise. Ernest Dowson. NOBVV

Even now there are places where a thought might grow. A Disused Shed in Co. Wexford. Derek Mahon. AnAn; CIP; FaBCIP; FaBoPV; NOIV; OxBC

Even now this landscape is assembling. All Hallows. Louise Glück. AmPA; HCAP; NU

Even on a spring morning. Shepherd in Capri. Nishiwaki Junzaburo, *tr. by* Hiroaki Sato. FCEI

Even on clear nights, lead the most supple children. The Great Bear. John Hollander. LiTM; NePoEA-2; NoAM; NYBP; TwCP

Even on spring days you work the fields. *Unknown, tr. fr. Japanese by* Hiroaki Sato. *Fr.* Manyo Shu. FCEI

Even on the bridge. Kikaku, *tr. fr. Japanese by* Hiroaki Sato. *Fr.* Thirty-three Hokku. FCEI

Even on the Loveliest of Nights. Dov Khomsky, *tr. fr. Hebrew by* Bernhard Frank. MHeP

Even on the plumes. Summer Grasses in the Fields at Dusk. Gyoko, *tr. by* Steven D. Carter. WFTW

Even or odd, of all days in the year. Shakespeare. *Fr.* Romeo and Juliet, I, iii. SCV

Even ordinarily, parting is difficult. Yang Shih-ch'i, *tr. fr. Chinese by* Jonathan Chaves. *Fr.* Inscribed on a Painting of Bamboo Presented to Lec. CoBLCP

Even rocks crack, I tell you. Pride. Dahlia Ravikovich, *tr. by* Chana Bloch. OV

Even So. Dante Gabriel Rossetti. NOBE; NOBVV; OBNC

Even so deep in the jungle they were not safe. The Garden of Ships. Douglas Stewart. CBAP; PoAu-2

Even so distant, I can taste the grief. Deceptions. Philip Larkin. CMoP; ErPo; GTBS-P; NePoEA

" 'Even so' (the exulting Maiden said)." Samuel Taylor Coleridge. *Fr.* The Destiny of Nations. ChER

Even Such Is Time. Sir Walter Ralegh. BLPL; ChTr; EIL; HAP; LiTB; OxBSP; PoRA; RB; SiPS
    (Author's Epitaph, Made By Himself, The.) NAEL-1
    (Conclusion, The: "Even such is time,.") OBEV; WGRP
    (Epitaph: "Even such is time.") CTC; FaBoEE; NOBE; OBSC
    (His Epitaph.) FaBoRV; TrGrPo
    (Verses Made the Night before He Dyed.) AAS

Even swallows seem to have no time. Kikaku, *tr. fr. Japanese by* Hiroaki Sato. *Fr.* Thirty-three Hokku. FCEI

Even that desperate gaiety is gone. There Is No Riot. Martin Carter. PBCV

Even the bad news came slowly and was afraid. Washington Heights, 1959. Michael C. Blumenthal. HCAP

Even the barnacle has certain rights. This Octopus Exploits Women. James Fenton. NoAM

Even the bird calls. Tamekane, *tr. by* Steven D. Carter. WFTW

Even the bluster. Fireflies. Shohaku, *tr. by* Steven D. Carter. WFTW

Even the crows have gone. Singde, *tr. fr. Chinese by* William Schultz. *Fr.* Impressions of a Night's Stay at Shuang-lin Temple, IV. WFTU

Even the day with cherries. Miura Chora, *tr. fr. Japanese by* Hiroaki Sato. *Fr.* Sixteen Hokku. FCEI

Even the dead leaves. Tameie, *tr. by* Steven D. Carter. WFTW

Even the dissident ones speak. America. John Newlove. NOBC

Even the earth between my fingers. Pachacamac. Antonio Cisneros, *tr. by* David Tipton. Per

Even the floating weeds sink. Buson, *tr. fr. Japanese by* Hiroaki Sato. *Fr.* Eighty-seven Hokku. FCEI

Even the frog's voices. Emperor Kogon, *tr. by* Steven D. Carter. WFTW

Even the grains of sand. Lady Kasa, *tr. fr. Japanese by* Geoffrey Bownas *and* Anthony Thwaite. *Fr.* Manyo Shu. PeBJV

Even the hard black. On the Life of Trees. Ernst Jandl, *tr. by* Beth Bjorklund. CoAuP

Even the insects. Autumn. Ietaka, *tr. by* Steven D. Carter. WFTW

Even the little minnows under the bridge. *Unknown, tr. fr. Japanese by* Burton Watson. *Fr.* Kangin Shu. FCEI

Even the liveliest of us had. Another and Another and. Theodore Weiss. DiPo

Even the lone man. Brazil. Tony Harrison. *Fr.* Sentences. OBTV

Even the Mirror Dies. Anja Vammelvuo, *tr. fr. Finnish by* Aili Jarvenpa. SOP

Even the moon. Emperor Go-Shirakawa, *tr. fr. Japanese by* Geoffrey Bownas *and* Anthony Thwaite. *Fr.* Ryojin Hisho. PeBJV

Even the night wind. Empress Eifuku, *tr. by* Steven D. Carter. WFTW

Even the old Nagara Bridge in Naniwa. Lady Ise, *tr. fr. Japanese by* Burton Watson. *Fr.* Kokin Shu. FCEI

Even the pond water. Wisteria in the Rain. Gyoko, *tr. by* Steven D. Carter. WFTW

Even the rising waters. *Unknown, tr. by* Arthur Waley. BoS

Even the sands uncounted of a long. Lady Kasa, *tr. fr. Japanese. Fr.* Manyo Shu. Ma

Even the showers/ fall, then stop. Tonna, *tr. by* Steven D. Carter. WFTW

Even the sky here in Connecticut has it. A Winter without Snow. J. D. McClatchy. FYAP

Even the sky is the colour of copper. Shetland, Hill Dawn. Robin Munro. PoSH

Even the small separations. Separations. Evan Zimroth. ER

Even the soil is withered and saddening. Kito, *tr. fr. Japanese by* Hiroaki Sato. *Fr.* Twenty-four Hokku. FCEI

Even the spring water. The Cutting Edge. Philip Levine. NYBP

Even the stone produces worms tonight. Sterility in Metamorphosis. Adriano Spatola, *tr. by* Lawrence R. Smith. NItP

Even the sun-clouds this morning cannot manage such skirts. Poppies in October. Sylvia Plath. FaBoWP; HCAP; LCAP; NoAM

Even the sun, still warm. August//Fresno 1973. Roberta Spear. AmPA

Even the train is taller than those shacks. Homecoming. John Thompson. MAT

Even the unlived life within us. Like a Beach. Harvey Shapiro. VWA

Even the walls are flowing, even the ceiling. Variation on Heraclitus. Louis MacNeice. MoP; NoAM

Even the wild-ducks skimming. Princess Ki, *tr. fr. Japanese. Fr.* Manyo Shu. Ma

Even the young ones are stooping. *Unknown, tr. by* Hiroaki Sato. FCEI

Even There. Lyn Lifshin. IHMS

Even these stones I placed crudely once. The Little Fire in the Woods. Hayden Carruth. DiL

Even this is movement. Altars and Sacrifice. Jay Wright. FB

Even this late it happens. The Coming of Light. Mark Strand. HCAP

Even This Shall Pass Away. Theodore Tilton. BLPA; WGRP

Even this suburb has overcome Death. Easter. Howard Nemerov. NoP

Even Tho. Grace Nichols. WS

Even though he falls. The Chalk Angel. Dennis Schmitz. NPGG

Even though it's dark. Race. Orkhan Muyassar, *tr. by* Lena Jayyusi *and* Samuel Hazo. MAP

Even though my hands/ are rough from much rice-pounding. *Unknown, tr. by* Kenneth Yasuda. BoWoP

Even to the children/ on the disenchanted shore. The Blade of Grass Sings to the River. Leah Goldberg, *tr. by* Robert Friend. TrJP

Even today this natural barrier commands the Ching-hsiang region. The Red Cliff. Chao Yi, *tr. by* Shirleen S. Wong. WFTU

Even to-day, were I in the city. Nakatomi Yakamori, *tr. fr. Japanese. Fr.* Manyo Shu. Ma

Even tonight and I need to take a walk and clear. Poem about My Rights. June Jordan. GLP; NoAM

Even tonight will pass. Tedium. Giuseppe Ungaretti, *tr. by* Charles Tomlinson. PFI

Even weave of the canvas, The. Painted Passages. Gail N. Harada. BrSi

Even when a man has earned much. Children. Pantiyan Arivutai Nampi, *tr. by* A. K. Ramanujan. PLW

Even when black Saturn. Pari's Green Land, Remembered. Kapilar, *tr. by* A. K. Ramanujan. PLW

Even when I cross those places. Six on the Desert Ways. Otalantaiyar, *tr. by* A. K. Ramanujan. PLW

Even when no thunder sounds. Hitomaro, *tr. fr. Japanese. Fr.* Manyo Shu. Ma

Even while pillowing her lap. Ishikawa Takuboku, *tr. fr. Japanese by* Hiroaki Sato. *Fr.* Forty-seven Tanka in Three Lines. FCEI

Even while the blue light darts into his room. The Blue Light. Tom Dent. UL

Even whilst I watch him I am remembering. To T. A. R. H. Stephen Spender. PeHV

Even with its own ax[e] to grind, sometimes. The Mind, Intractable Thing. Marianne Moore. LiTM; NYBP

Even without that engraved. Rosario, en la Cima. Angela de Hoyos. ER

Even years ago. Written when the Poet Was Seventy-six. Shunzei, *tr. fr. Japanese by* Burton Watson. *Fr.* Thirty Tanka. FCEI

Evenen in the Village. William Barnes. EBVV

Evening/ when you hear a needle, An. A Study in Terror. Tamura Ryuichi, *tr. by* Hiroaki Sato. FCEI

Evening. Richard Aldington. MoBrPo; SeCePo

Evening, An. William Allingham. EnLoPo; NOBVV

Evening. Rose Ausländer, *tr. fr. German by* Beth Bjorklund. CoAuP

Evening. Byron. *Fr.* Don Juan, III. TrGrPo
    (Hesperus the Bringer.) AWP

Evening. John Clare. NOBVV

Evening. Charles Cotton. PoEL-3; WiR

Evening. Emily Dickinson. *See* She sweeps with many-colored brooms.

Evening. Hilda Doolittle ("H. D."). CMoP; FaBoMo; VGW; WPE

Evening. Federico García Lorca, *tr. fr. Spanish by* William Jay Smith. CT

Evening. Wendell Phillips Garrison. *Fr.* Post-Meridian. AA

Evening. John Keble. TrPWD

Evening. King D. Kuka. VoR

Evening. A. Leyeles, *tr. fr. Yiddish by* Benjamin *and* Barbara Harshav. *Fr.* New York. AYP

Evening. Hugh McCrae. PoAu-1

Evening. Itzik Manger, *tr. fr. Yiddish by* Miriam Waddington. VWA

Evening. Mary Matheson. CaP

Evening. W. S. Merwin. NAAL-2

Evening, An. Robert Mezey. NaP

Evening. Thomas Miller. OxBChV

Evening. Khalil Mutran, *tr. fr. Arabic by* Issa Boullata *and* Thomas G. Ezzy. MAP

Evening. Charles Sangster. CaP

Evening. Charles Simic. GeTw

Evening. Edith Sitwell. MoBS

Evening. James Stephens. MoBrPo

Evening. Tristan Tzara, *tr. fr. French*. POS, *tr.* by Charles Simic *and* Michael Benedikt; RHTwFP, *tr.* by Charles Simic *and* Michael Benedikt; VWA, *tr.* by Willis Barnstone *and* Matei Calinescu

Evening. *Unknown.* BoTP

Evening. Victor van Vriesland, *tr. fr. Dutch* by Adrian J. Barnouw. TrJP

Evening. James Wright. NOBA; NYBP; PrIm

Evening! A flight of pigeons in clear sky! The Flute; a Pastoral. José-Maria de Heredia, *tr.* by H. J. C. Grierson. AWP

Evening; an Elegy. Horace Smith. BXAP

Evening, and Maidens. William Barnes. OBEV

Evening—another evening—and the lights flare. Thomas McGrath. *Fr.* Letter to an Imaginary Friend, Part Two, V, 2. NNaP

Evening, as slow thy placid shades descend. William Lisle Bowles. NOEC

Evening at Colonos. Nikos Gatsos, *tr. fr. Greek* by Edmund Keeley *and* Philip Sherrard. *Fr.* Four Songs. VMG

Evening at [*or* on] the Farm. John Townsend Trowbridge. FaPON; GN (Evening on the Farm.) MoShBr

Evening at the Merrills. Hans Lodeizen, *tr. fr. Dutch* by James Brockway. DuIn

Evening before Rain. L. A. G. Strong. OxBTC

Evening Bell. Shotetsu, *tr. fr. Japanese* by Steven D. Carter. WFTW

Evening Bell from a Misty Temple. Wen Cheng-ming, *tr. fr. Chinese* by Jonathan Chaves. CoBLCP

Evening Bell from Misty Temple. Ma Chih-yüan, *tr. fr. Chinese* by Jonathan Chaves. *Fr.* Three Poems to the tune "Lo-mei Feng," 2. CoBLCP

Evening Bread. Jacob Glatstein, *tr. fr. Yiddish*. AYP, *tr.* by Benjamin *and* Barbara Harshav; PeBMYV, *tr.* by Cynthia Ozick. VWA, *tr.* by David G. Roskies *and* Hillel Schwartz.

Evening, The/ enters the house through the roof. Habit. Amiq Hanafi, *tr.* by Mahmood Jamal. PBMUP

Evening has overtaken the parlors. Widow under a New Moon. Kevin Clark. KS

Evening by error. Landscape. Federico García Lorca, *tr. fr. Spanish* by William Jay Smith. *Fr.* Songs of Childhood. CT

Evening by the Sea. Swinburne. FaBoPP

Evening came, a child was missing. Little Bell. Mary E. Tucker. CBWP-1

Evening came, a paw, to the gray hut by the river. Fall Journey. William Stafford. NaP

Evening Closes over Me, The. Manfred Winkler, *tr. fr. Hebrew* by Bernhard Frank. MHeP

Evening clouds suddenly scatter and peaks come into view. Chao Chih-hsin, *tr. fr. Chinese* by James M. Hargett. *Fr.* Miscellaneous Poems on Mountain Travel, II. WFTU

Evening colours her amber breasts. Woman Made of Stars. Earle Thompson. STE

Evening comes. Freeze Tag. Gordon Henry. STE

Evening comes, the fields are still, The. The First-born Star. Matthew Arnold. *Fr.* Bacchanalia; or, The New Age. FaBoRV

Evening comes with an onslaught of wind and rain. Tune: Song of Picking Mulberry ("Evening comes with an onslaught of wind and rain."). Li Ch'ing-chao, *tr.* by Burton Watson. CoBCP

Evening Contemplation. George Washington Doane. AA; AH; BLPA; BLPL; FaBoBe

Evening Dance of the Grey Flies. Patricia K. Page. NOBC

Evening Darkens Over, The. Robert Bridges. CMoP; HAP; NOBVV; PoEL-5

Evening descends: again you leave us. Snow. Salvatore Quasimodo, *tr.* by William Weaver. PFI

Evening downpour: clutching grass blades. Buson, *tr. fr. Japanese* by Hiroaki Sato. *Fr.* Eighty-seven Hokku. FCEI

Evening dusk: crowned with fans. Shiba Sonome, *tr. fr. Japanese* by Hiroaki Sato. *Fr.* Fifteen Hokku. FCEI

Evening dusk: flying in the middle. Kikaku, *tr. fr. Japanese* by Hiroaki Sato. *Fr.* Thirty-three Hokku. FCEI

Evening Ebb. Robinson Jeffers. NoAM

Evening Faces. Keiun, *tr. fr. Japanese* by Steven D. Carter. WFTW

Evening falls on the smoky walls. Ballad of the Londoner. James Elroy Flecker. EnLoPo

Evening falls soon in the hills across the river. The White Eagle. Nan McDonald. PoAu-2

Evening flickers, glows and falters to a halt, The. Poetry's Theme. Faiz Ahmad Faiz, *tr.* by Mahmood Jamal. PBMUP

Evening fog, The. The Night Fog. Kim Hyun-sung, *tr.* by Koh Chang-soo. ACKP

Evening Gleam, The. James Devaney. PoAu-1

Evening has brought its. Witnesses. W. S. Merwin. LCAP

Evening has passed and the moon will soon vanish, The. The Visitor Who Never Came. Nazik al-Mala'ika, *tr.* by Matthew Sorenson *and* Christopher Middleton. MAP

Evening Hawk. Robert Penn Warren. NAAL-2

Evening Hour. Robert Penn Warren. MT

Evening Hymn. William Henry Furness. AA; FaBoBe

Evening Hymn, An. Thomas Ken. OBS; OxBChV

Evening Hymn, *sel.* George Macdonald. "O God, whose daylight leadeth down." TrPWD

Evening Hymn in the Hovels. Francis Lauderdale Adams. OxBS

Evening—I see the bellies of sweetfish. On My Way Home. Onitsura, *tr. fr. Japanese* by Hiroaki Sato. *Fr.* Twenty-three Hokku. FCEI

Evening in Camp. Patricia Ledward. CN; WaP

Evening in November, An. Anne French. ATNZ

Evening in Paradise. Milton. *See* Paradise Lost: Now came still evening on, and twilight gray.

Evening in Summer. Valentin Iremonger. NeIP

Evening in the house. This Evening. Zishe Landau, *tr.* by Irving Feldman. PeBMYV

Evening in the Sanitarium. Louise Bogan. FaBoWP; FYAP; IHMS; TwCP

Evening in the Walls. Jean Wahl, *tr. fr. French* by Charles Guenther. VWA

Evening in the yard. Peyanar, *tr. fr. Tamil* by A. K. Ramanujan. *Fr.* Seven Said by the Foster-Mother, 1. PoA

Evening in Tyringham Valley. Richard Watson Gilder. AA

Evening is clogged with gnats as the light fails. Alceste in the Wilderness. Anthony Hecht. PoA

Evening Is Coming, The. *Unknown.* RAR

Evening is coming, The. Bed-time. Thomas Hood. BoTP

Evening is part of the jig-saw truth of her. Ode in Honour. Francis Scarfe. EAS

Evening is tawny on the old. Gold. Martin Armstrong. BoTP

Evening Jews. Jacob Glatstein, *tr. fr. Yiddish* by Benjamin *and* Barbara Harshav. AYP

Evening Knell, The. John Fletcher. *See* Faithful Shepherdess, The: Priest's Chant, The.

Evening lapses. No pity or pain, the badgered. From Government Buildings. Denis Devlin. IPY

Evening lies along the horizon and gives blood. Yehuda Amichai, *tr.* by Warren Bargad *and* Stanley F. Chyet. IP

Evening Light along the Sound, The. Sherod Santos. NAmP

Evening like that at the bookshelf that is at times, An. At Lake Lietzen; or, The Search for Identity. Gerald Bisinger, *tr.* by Beth Bjorklund. CoAuP

Evening Lull, An. Walt Whitman. NAAL-1

Evening Meal in the Twentieth Century. John Holmes. AiP

Evening mists in the depths of my heart. Princess Shikishi, *tr. fr. Japanese* by Hiroaki Sato. *Fr.* Seventy-eight Tanka. FCEI

Evening moon shines, The. Prince Yuhara, *tr. fr. Japanese*. *Fr.* Manyo Shu. Ma

Evening Motif. Judah Leib Teller, *tr. fr. Yiddish* by Benjamin *and* Barbara Harshav. AYP

Evening Musicale. Phyllis McGinley. OBAL; Son

Evening of Ants, The. Gary Soto. NPGG

Evening of Montale's Death, The. Susan Stewart. NAmP

Evening of My Birthday, The. Yang Shih-ch'i, *tr. fr. Chinese* by Jonathan Chaves. CoBLCP

Evening of Russian Poetry, An. Vladimir Nabokov. NYBP

Evening of the Rose. Anthony Rudolf. VWA

Evening on Calais Beach. Wordsworth. *See* It Is a Beauteous Evening [Calm and Free].

Evening on Howth Head. Eileen Brennan. NeIP

Evening on the Broads. Swinburne. TEP

Evening on the Farm. John Townsend Trowbridge. *See* Evening at [*or* on] the Farm.

Evening on the Potomac. Richard Hovey. AnAmPo

Evening Out, The. Ogden Nash. MoAmPo

Evening outdoors is only a larger lobby. One-Night Expensive Hotel. Ronald G. Everson. NOBC

Evening Prayer. Arthur Fitger, *tr. fr. German* by Jethro Bithell. AWP

Evening Prayer. Jorie Graham. NAmP

Evening Prayer, An. Laura E. Kendall. BLRP

Evening Prayer. Henrietta Cordelia Ray. CBWP-3

Evening Prayer. *Unknown. tr. fr. Hebrew* by Solomon Solis-Cohen. TrJP

Evening Primrose. John Clare. CH; TrGrPo

Evening Prospect. Cheng Chen, *tr. fr. Chinese* by Chang Yin-nan. WFTU

Evening Prospect, An: City Lights. Chiang Shih-ch'üan, *tr. fr. Chinese* by Irving Lo. WFTU

Evening Quatrains. Charles Cotton. *See* Evening.

Evening red and morning gray. *Unknown*. *Fr*. Weather Wisdom. FaBoBe; FaBoUs; OxNR

Evening Refrain. Sherod Santos. MAYP

Evening Revery, An, *sel*. Bryant. "O thou great Movement of the Universe." AA

Evening Scene at Twin Forests. Chin Nung, *tr. fr. Chinese by* Jonathan Chaves. CoBLCP

Evening Shade. John Leland. *See* Day Is Past and Gone, The.

Evening shadow: frogs call out. Hoju, *tr. by* Hiroaki Sato. FCEI

Evening shower, An. Empress Eifuku, *tr. by* Steven D. Carter. WFTW

Evening shower, An. Kikaku, *tr. fr. Japanese by* Hiroaki Sato. *Fr*. Thirty-three Hokku. FCEI

Evening shower has washed, The. Kikaku, *tr. fr. Japanese by* Hiroaki Sato. *Fr*. Thirty-three Hokku. FCEI

Evening Snow. Tamekane, *tr. fr. Japanese by* Steven D. Carter. WFTW

Evening Snow. David Wojahn. NAmP

Evening Song. Cecil Frances Alexander. OHIP

Evening Song. Kenneth Fearing. EAS

Evening Song. John Fletcher. *See* Faithful Shepherdess, The: Priest's Chant, The.

Evening Song. Edith King. BoTP

Evening Song. Sidney Lanier. AnAmPo; UnPo

Evening Song. Jean Toomer. BPo; CDC

Evening Star. George Barker. ErPo

Evening Star. John Clare. *See* Hesperus, the day is gone.

Evening Star, The. *Aborigine Oral Tradition*. *Fr*. Moon-Bone Song [*or* Cycle]. WTO

Evening Star, enemy of lovers, why. Evening Star. George Barker. ErPo

Evening star that in the vaulted skies, The. Verse Written in the Album of Mademoiselle. Pierre Dalcour, *tr. by* Langston Hughes. PoNe; TTY

Evening star that softly sheds, The. The Refracted Lights. Celia Parker Wooley. WGRP

Evening Suit, The. Jean Follain, *tr. fr. French by* W. S. Merwin. RHTwFP

Evening Sun, The. Emily Brontë. CH

Evening sun-beams threw their golden light, The. The Suttee. Thomas Skinner. OBTV

Evening sun shines, The. Emperor Kogon, *tr. by* Steven D. Carter. WFTW

Evening sun sinks. Returning Sails at a Distant Shore. Ma Chih-yüan, *tr. fr. Chinese by* Jonathan Chaves. *Fr*. Three Poems to the tune "Lo-mei Feng," 1. CoBLCP

Evening sunlight, The. Empress Eifuku, *tr. by* Steven D. Carter. WFTW

Evening, the heather, The. Invasion Summer. Laurie Lee. OxBSP

Evening Thought, An. Jupiter Hammon. PoNe

Evening Tide. X. J. Kennedy. TDD

Evening traffic homeward burns. Before Disaster. Yvor Winters. HoPM; QFR

Evening Twilight. Heine, *tr. fr. German by* John Todhunter. *Fr*. The North Sea. AWP

Evening View from P'eng-lai Pavilion. Chu Yi-tsun, *tr. fr. Chinese by* Irving Lo. WFTU

Evening View from the Bell Tower at P'ing-ch'ang. T'ang Hsien-Tsu, *tr. fr. Chinese by* Jonathan Chaves. CoBLCP

Evening voices of cicadas, The. Teika, *tr. fr. Japanese by* Hiroaki Sato. *Fr*. Eighty-four Tanka. FCEI

Evening Walk. Sonja Akesson, *tr. fr. Swedish by* Joanna Bankier. WPOW

Evening Walk, An, *sel*. Wordsworth. "Dear Brook, farewell! To-morrow's noon again." EnRP

Evening Walk in Bengal, An. Reginald Heber. OBTV

Evening Walk in Winter. Mary Ursula Bethell. ATNZ

Evening was in the wood, louring with storm. Haunted. Siegfried Sassoon. CMoP

Evening Wind, The. Bryant. AA

Evening wind: the water strikes. Buson, *tr. fr. Japanese by* Hiroaki Sato. *Fr*. Eighty-seven Hokku. FCEI

Evening windstorm, An. Emperor Fushimi, *tr. by* Steven D. Carter. WFTW

Evening with a Black-and-White Feathered Bird, An. Akhtar-ul-Iman, *tr. fr. Urdu by* Mahmood Jamal. PBMUP

Evening without Angels. Wallace Stevens. VGW

Evenings/ When the house is quiet. Setting the Table. Dorothy Aldis. FaPON

Evening's barefoot monk. Evening. Itzig Manger, *tr. by* Miriam Waddington. VWA

Evenings below my window. Weldon Kees in Mexico, 1965. David Wojahn. MAYP

Evenings ever more willing lapse into my world's evening. Denis Devlin. *Fr*. Memoirs of a Turcoman Diplomat. IPY; NOIV

Evenings I hear. A Plague of Starlings. Robert Hayden. NoAM

Evenings, I lodge with the evening mist. On the Chia-ling River. Wei Yüan, *tr. by* Irving Lo. WFTU

Evening's Love, An, *sels*. Dryden. After the Pangs of a Desperate Lover. *Fr*. II, i. ELP (Love's Fancy.) ErPo

"Calm was the even, and clear [*or* cleer] was the sky." *Fr*. IV, i. FF; SeCV-2

Damon and Celimena. *Fr*. V, i. InvP

"You charm'd me not with that fair face." *Fr*. II, i. SeCV-2

Evenings of beatitude. Hours. Francisco González León, *tr. by* Samuel Beckett. MexPo

Evenings of Ink. Jean Follain, *tr. fr. French by* W. S. Merwin. RHTwFP

Evenings that sometimes forget to light up the stars over Harlem's sky. Harlem Negroes. Berysh Vaynshteyn, *tr. fr. Yiddish by* Benjamin *and* Barbara Harshav. *Fr*. Negroes. AYP

Evenings, When Sparks. Shin Shalom, *tr. fr. Hebrew by* Bernhard Frank. MHeP

Eveningsong. Ramona Wilson. VoR

Eveningsong 2. Ramona Wilson. VoR

Evensong. Carleton Drewry. GoYe

Evensong. C. S. Lewis. TIRV; TrCP

Evensong. Robert Louis Stevenson. TrPWD

Event, The. Rita Dove. NoAM

Event, An. Edward Field. CoAP

Event. Sylvia Plath. NOBA

Event, The. T. Sturge Moore. OBMV

Event worse than the omen, Th'; as his bride. The Death of Eurydice and Orpheus' Journey to Hell. Ovid, *tr. fr. Latin by* George Sandys. *Fr*. Metamorphoses. JCP

Eventual Proteus. Margaret Atwood. MoCV

Ever and ever anon. The Road to the Bow. James David Corrothers. BANP

Ever as We Sailed. Shelley. *Fr*. The Revolt of Islam, XII. SeCePo

Ever been kidnapped. Kidnap Poem. Nikki Giovanni. AmNP; BPo; GOYP; TAP

Ever before my face there went. Vain Finding. Walter de la Mare. BrPo

Ever charming, ever new. John Dyer. *Fr*. Grongar Hill. SeCePo

Ever-dark cypress is alive, The. Ivory. Mario Luzi, *tr. by* I. L. Salomon. PFI

Ever-Fixed Mark, An. Kingsley Amis. ErPo; MoP; NoAM; PeHV

Ever heard Bird. Mellowness and Flight. George Barlow. CNA

Ever let the fancy roam. Keats. *Fr*. Fancy. EnRP; OBEV (Realm of Fancy, The.) GTBS; GTBS-P

Ever myn happe is slack and slo in commyng. Petrarch, *tr. by* Sir Thomas Wyatt. OBVE

Ever Notice How It Is with Women? Margaret Randall. AIW

Ever onward I go! River Messages. Li Hsün, *tr. by* Lois Fusek. ATF

Ever Present. Philip Ayres. OxBSP

Ever rising resentment. Dreaming of the South. Wen T'ing-yün, *tr. by* Lois Fusek. ATF

Ever since boyhood it has been my joy. The Everlasting Mercy. J. C. Squire. BXAP

Ever since heaven and earth were parted. Akahito, *tr. fr. Japanese*. *Fr*. Manyo Shu. Ma

Ever since I dozed off. Komachi, *tr. fr. Japanese by* Burton Watson. *Fr*. Kokin Shu. FCEI

Ever since I realized there was someone callt. No More Love Poems #1. Ntozake Shange. For Colored Girls Who Have Considered Suicide When the Rainbow Is Enuf. BlSi

Ever since my daughters started to walk. The Green Tree. James Reiss. AmPA; DiL

Ever since the day he started. Minaka, *tr. fr. Japanese*. *Fr*. Manyo Shu. Ma

Ever since the great planes were murdered at the end of the gardens. Domus Caedet Arborem. Charlotte Mew. PBWP

Ever since the heart was created. Mohammad Taqi Mir, *tr. by* Ahmed Ali. GoT

Ever since the heavens took a dappled horse. Incongruity of the Age, Satire on a Miser's Horse. Mirza Mohammad Rafi Sauda, *tr. by* Ahmed Ali. GoT

Ever since they'd left the Tennessee ridge. The Event. Rita Dove. NoAM

Ever since T'ien-pao, this silence and desolation. The Man with No Family to Take Leave of. Tu Fu, *tr. by* Burton Watson. CoBCP

Ever Since Uncle John Henry Been Dead. *Unknown*. AS

Ever since your name has entered Hari's ear. Surdas, *tr. by* John Stratton Hawley *and* Mark Juergensmeyer. SSI

Ever ting-a-linging my bedroom clock is ringing. Dawn. Sir John Betjeman. FL

Ever-touring Englishmen, The. *Gond Oral Tradition, tr. by* V. Elwin *and* S. Hivale. WTO

Ever upward like a kite. If We Try. George Sands Johnson. PWR

Ever walked that footpath. A Flower. Mvula Ya Nangolo. WMBCH

Ever Watchful. Ta' Abbata Sharra, tr. fr. Arabic by W. G. Palgrave. AWP

Everett Anderson's Friend. Lucille Clifton. ILY

Evergreen Cemetery. Alfred W. Purdy. MoCV

Evergreen conifers. Spring in Westend. Helga Novak, tr. by Susan L. Cocalis. DMG

Evergreen shadow and the pale magnolia, The. Souls Lake. Robert Fitzgerald. TwCP

Everlasting Arms, The. Bible, O.T. See Psalms: Psalm XCI ("He that dwelleth. . .").

Everlasting Contenders, The. Kenneth Patchen. NaP

Everlasting Forests, The. Dahlia Ravikovich, tr. fr. Hebrew by Chana Bloch. BoWoP

Everlasting Love, The. Annie Johnson Flint. BLRP

Everlasting Mercy, The, sel. John Masefield.
"I opened the window wide and leaned." WGRP

Everlasting Mercy, The. J. C. Squire. BXAP

Everlasting Once, An. Theodore Weiss. AnAn

Everlasting universe of things, The. Mont Blanc. Shelley. EnRP; EnRP; NAEL-2; NIP; NoP; OAEL-2; OBTV; TEP

Everlasting Voices, The. W. B. Yeats. AWP

Everlastings, The. Norman Dubie. GeTw

Every afternoon. The Fire Breather, Mexico City. Jaime Jacinto. BrSi

Every bit of water in the paddies. Boncho, tr. fr. Japanese by Hiroaki Sato. Fr. Twenty-one Hokku. FCEI

Every boatman in. Kyorai, tr. fr. Japanese by Burton Watson. Fr. Twenty Hokku. FCEI

Every bookie. Shake Hands with Your Bets, Friend. Lorenzo Thomas. UL

Every boy knows what it's like. What Every Boy Knows. Antler. GLP

Every branch big with it. Snow in the Suburbs. Thomas Hardy. BoNaP; CMoP; GoJo; MoAB; MoBrPo; OAEL-2; OBMV; OxBTC; PPP

Every Breath. János Pilinszky, tr. fr. Hungarian by William Jay Smith. MHuP

Every Bush New Springing. Unknown. PoEL-2

Every Case. Wislawa Szymborska, tr. fr. Polish by Czeslaw Milosz. PwPP

Every child who has gardening tools. Garden Lore. Juliana Horatia Ewing. OxBChV

Ev-er-y child who has the use. Some Geese. Oliver Herford. Fr. Child's Natural History. FiBHP; NA

Every Christian Born of God. Unknown, tr. fr. German. AH

Every City. David Rokeah, tr. fr. Hebrew by Bernhard Frank. MHeP

Every Day. Ingeborg Bachmann, tr. fr. German. DMG, tr. by Kate Flores; PBWP, tr. by Michael Hamburger

Every Day. Norman MacCaig. OBD

Every Day. Mary Osborn. BoTP

Every day a wilderness—no. Dusting. Rita Dove. HCAP; MAYP

Every day at home I watched the landlord flog his men and bellow. The Victim. Lupenga Mphande. WMBCH

Every day, be with me. The Isle and the Lake, No. 5. Tu Kuo-ch'ing, tr. by Dominic Cheung. IFON

Every day brings a ship. Letters. Emerson. OxBSP

Every-Day Characters, sels. Winthrop Mackworth Praed.
Belle of the Ball-Room, The. EnRP, EnRP; FaBoCo, EnRP.
Portrait of a Lady in the Exhibition of the Royal Academy. NOBL; PoEL-4
Vicar, The. EnRP; OBEV; OBNC; PoEL-4

Every Day Here Is like This. Herman de Coninck, tr. fr. Dutch by James S. Holmes. DuIn

Every day I have to learn more about shame. In Palo Alto. Denis Johnson. NAmP

Every day I meet the horses. Horses at Valley Store. Leslie Marmon Silko. VoR

Every day I receive the Imperial favor. Enclosed with a Letter to My Family. Yang Shih-ch'i, tr. by Jonathan Chaves. CoBLCP

Every day I see from my window. Wild Oats. Norman MacCaig. OxBTC

Every day is as old. As New and as Old. Martin Carter. PBCV

Every day our bodies separate. Marilyn Hacker. AmPA; SM

Every Day Thanksgiving Day. Harriet Prescott Spofford. OHIP

Every Day that I Love You. Teresita Fernández, tr. fr. Spanish by Margaret Randall. AIW

Every day that their sky droops down. Moles. William Stafford. NYBP; RFM

Every day the dark blue sky of brother Van Gogh. The Sensitive Knife. Gerald Stern. DiL

Every day thou might lere. Remember the Day of Judgement. Unknown. MeEL

Every day, throwing my heart down into the valley. Princess Shikishi, tr. fr. Japanese by Hiroaki Sato. Fr. Seventy-eight Tanka. FCEI

Every dusty bar and narrow streak of brilliance. First Notes from One Born and Living in an Abandoned Barn. Pattiann Rogers. NAmP

Every Earthly Creature. John Malcolm Brinnin. LiTA

Every evening a counterfeit minstrel. H. C. Artmann, tr. by Beth Bjorklund. CoAuP

Every evening before the sea departs from Beirut. Sea Desires. Laila al-Saih, tr. by Patricia Alanah Byrne with Salma Khadra Jayyusi. MAP

Every evening, down into the hardweed. Hardweed Path Going. A. R. Ammons. HCAP; UnPo; VGW

Every evening when night retrieves the substance of our longings. Second Telegram ("Every evening when night retrieves the substance of our longings"). Abd al-Aziz al-Maqalih, tr. fr. Arabic by Lena Jayyusi and Christopher Middleton. Fr. Telegrams of Tenderness for Sanaa. MAP

Every farmyard in Nebraska. The Chicken Poem. Don Welch. MOWH

Every game that Harvey plays. Harvey Always Wins. Jack Prelutsky. NTCP

Every hour, every moment. Hilda Doolittle ("H. D."). Fr. Tribute to the Angels. NoAM

Every lady in this land. Mother Goose. OxNR

Every Land Is Exile. Claude Vigée, tr. fr. French by Anthony Rudolf. VWA

Every Life. René Char, tr. fr. French by James Wright. RHTwFP

Every man, even the most doubting Thomas. Ode to the Yorkshire Dales. Cees Buddingh', tr. by Peter Nijmeijer. DuIn

Every Man has his sorrows; yet each still. André Marie de Chénier, tr. fr. French by Arthur Symons. Fr. Elegies, I. AWP

Every morning. Stafford in Kansas. James Baker Hall. BXAP

Every morning at break of day. The Trains. "Seumas O'Sullivan." BoTP

Every morning Father is dead. Where behind the Night Did You Get Lost. Eeva Kilpi, tr. by Aili Jarvenpa. SOP

Every morning I break trail. Changeling VIII. Kristjana Gunnars. NOBC

Every morning I forget how it is. Charles Simic. NNaP

Every morning I get up. To the Tune "A Floating Cloud Crosses Enchanted Mountain." Huang Ho, tr. by Kenneth Rexroth and Ling Chung. AIW; BoWoP

Every morning I went to her charity and learned. To a Red-headed Do-good Waitress. Alan Dugan. CAPP; Son

Every morning, in the dust. A Sparrow in the Dust. Ruth Domino, tr. by Daniel Hoffman and Jerre Mangione. BoWoP

Every morning she'd smear something brown. Man Arrested in Hacking Death Tells Police He Mistook Mother-in-Law for Raccoon. Susan Ludvigson. MAYP; MT

Every morning the prisoner hears. The Prisoner. William Plomer. PeSA

Every night about nine. Whip-poor-will. Donald Hall. BLA

Every night, another customer. At Kresge's Diner in Stonefalls, Arkansas. Edward Hirsch. SM

Every night from eve[n] till morn. To the Nightingale. Sir John Davies. Fr. Hymns of Astraea. OBSC; PBBP; TrGrPo

Every night I sleep. In the Trench. Leon Gellert. PoAu-1

Every night my prayers I say. System. Robert Louis Stevenson. PWR; TEP

Every night the fireflies were our eyes. Fireflies. Faustin Charles. PBCV

Every night when I went to bed. The Lament of the Unmarried Girl. Brian Merriman, tr. fr. Modern Irish by Frank O'Connor. Fr. The Midnight Court. OBVE

Every October millions of little fish come along the shore. Birds and Fishes. Robinson Jeffers. NAAL-2; NoP

Every old man I see. Memory of My Father. Patrick Kavanagh. FaBCIP; InPS; RB

Every one of us saw it. Silence. Alvin Aubert. MT

Every One to His Own Way. John Vance Cheney. AA

Every path a green lady. Four Songs from the Book of Samuel. Eli W. Mandel. MoCV

Every peak is a crater. This is the law of volcanoes. Adrienne Rich. Fr. Twenty-one Love Poems, XI. GLP; NAAL-2; NoAM

Every planet is a small plane. The Plane: Earth. Sun-Ra. PoBA

Every poem is addressed to itself. Interpretations. Jutta Schutting, tr. by Beth Bjorklund. CoAuP

Every promised path ends in the Garden. On the Path. A. L. Strauss, tr. by Robert Friend. VWA

Every restaurant boarded up in softwood. Traveling Light. Alice Fulton. NAmP

Every rose on the little tree. The Little Rose Tree. Rachel Lyman Field. FaPON

Every Second Thought, *sel.* Theodore Weiss.
"Grey and dankish thing, A." DiPo
Every Shuiler Is Christ. Joseph Campbell. TIRV
Every single thing. Saigyo, *tr. by* Geoffrey Bownas *and* Anthony
Thwaite. PeBJV
Every soldier in the streetcar was a relation. Eddy van Vliet, *tr. fr. Dutch
by* James S. Holmes. *Fr.* After the Laws of Good-Bye & Autumn.
DuIn
Every stance seemed crooked. He had. Saint Ras. Anthony McNeill.
PBCV
Every Sunday. *Unknown, tr. by* Geoffrey Bownas *and* Anthony Thwaite.
PeBJV
Every Sunday she prepared the brown oak table. The Poet of the
Mountains. Thomas McCarthy. CIP
Every Thing. Harold Monro. MoBrPo
Every thing, every place is real. Chosha, *tr. by* Lucien Stryk *and* Takashi
Ikemoto. ZPCJ
Every thread of summer is at last unwoven. Puella Parvula. Wallace
Stevens. HCAP; LCAP
Every Thursday morning. The Dustman. Clive Sansom. BoTP
Every Time I Climb a Tree. David McCord. NTCP; PDV; RHPC
Every time I smell Lava soap it is 1948. The Story of Lava. David
Allan Evans. Psk
Every time I take a trip. The Train. Antonio Machado, *tr. by* Perry
Higman. LPSS
Every time I write a letter. Writing Letters. Rodney Bennett. BoTP
Every time the bucks went clattering. Earthy Anecdote. Wallace
Stevens. CMoP; GoJo; RB; RFM
Every time the clock strikes another hour. Fatalities. Diane Ackerman.
BWV
Every time you hear me sing this song. The Railroad Blues. *Unknown.*
AmFP
Every towered city, every street. Exodus from a Renaissance Gallery.
Ellen M. V. Acton. GoYe
Every Town a Home Town. Kaniyan Punkunran, *tr. fr. Tamil by* A. K.
Ramanujan. PLW
Every valley drinks. Winter Rain. Christina Rossetti. BoNaP; WiR
Every word a worm, a fish, an elephant. For My Husband Who Sent Me
Several Rubbings of Ancient Egyptian Stone Tablets. Hsüeh Shao-
hui, *tr. by* Irving Lo. WFTU
Every year at this time. A Typhoon Season. Fei Ma, *tr. by* Dominic
Cheung. IFON
Every year for the last fifty. The Ideal Woman. Cecilia Vicuña, *tr. by*
Anne Twitty. DMH
Every year in June—up here, that's the month for lilacs. What the Light
Was Like. Amy Clampitt. FaBoWP
Every year without knowing it I have passed the day. For the Anniversary
of My Death. W. S. Merwin. CoAP; HCAP; InPK; NAAL-2; NaP;
NOBA
Everybody but Me. Margaret Goss Burroughs. BlSi; FB
Everybody dancin'. Cakewalkman. Sam Abrams. UL
Everybody else, then, going. Exeunt Omnes. Thomas Hardy. QFR
Everybody knew Clifton Cockerell was not half bright. The Beating. T.
R. Hummer. MAYP; MT
Everybody knows her, for they see her every day. Pay Your Debts.
Mrs. Henry Linden. CBWP-4
Everybody likes Suthun Accent. Back home. Suthun Accent. Leonard
Trawick. SoTCo
Everybody loved Chick Lorimer in our town. Gone. Carl Sandburg.
NOBA
Everybody said it was useless. All of Them. Qasim Haddad, *tr. by*
Sharif Elmusa *and* Charles Doria. MAP
Everybody Says. Dorothy Aldis. FaPON; RHPC
Everybody stop and listen to my ditty. Prince of Wales' Marriage.
Unknown. CoMu
Everybody wants to know why I sing the blues. Why I Sing the Blues.
B. B. King. MAT
Everybody went to bat three times. Don Larsen's Perfect Game. Paul
Goodman. ASP
"Everybody Works but Father" as W. S. Gilbert Would Have Written It.
Arthur G. Burgoyne. FiBHP
Everybody's chrysanthemums. Chrysanthemums. Martin Seymour-
Smith. NPo
Everyday/ I think about dying. Survivor. Roger McGough. PoPo
Everyday, Dietrich teaches a mambo class of hillbilly patients. At the
Treatment Center. Jerome Sala. UL
Everyday Things. Jean Ayer. BoTP
Everymaid. John Oxenham. TrCP
Everyman. Siegfried Sassoon. MoBrPo
Everyman. *Unknown.* NAWM-1; OAEL-1; OxBLMV; PoEL-1
Everyman ("I pray you all give your audience.") (*Old English Morality
Play*), *sels. Unknown.* NAEL-1; OAEL-1; PoEL-1

Desertion of Beauty and Strength, The. ACP
"On thee thou must take a long journey." OBD
Everyman/ Preacher or lecher, saint or sot. Robert Francis. *Fr.*
Epitaphs. CRP
Everyman's Library. John Ashbery. NoP
Everyone at Lake Kearney had a nickname. Sway. Louis Simpson.
NoAM
Everyone begins making thunder though taking pigs somewhere. 25th
Dance—Saying Things about Making Gardens—22 March 1964.
Jackson MacLow. LP
Everyone buys his own. Canzonetta. Antonia Pozzi, *tr. by* Brenda
Webster. OV
Everyone can see me standing in the center. Black Hawk in Hiding.
George Keithley. NPGG
Everyone drinks Havdolah wine. Havdolah Wine. Miriam Ulinover, *tr.
by* Seth L. Wolitz. VWA
Everyone else has changed to a flowery robe. Teika, *tr. fr. Japanese by*
Hiroaki Sato. *Fr.* A Compendium of Good Tanka. FCEI
Everyone else sleeping when I step. Elk Camp. Raymond Carver. TSL
Everyone, everyone went away today. Presences. Donald Justice.
CAPP
Everyone everywhere always. No Generation. Rutger Kopland, *tr. by*
Ria Leigh-Loohuizen. DuIn
Everyone gets junk mail, a bill, a notice. Another Letter to Lord Byron.
David R. Slavitt. SM
Everyone grows younger; my thinning hair. Figures of Authority.
Edward Watkins. NYBP
Everyone grumbled. The sky was grey [*or* gray]. Daddy Fell into the
Pond. Alfred Noyes. FaPON; PDV; RHPC
Everyone has only one leg. Great Infirmities. Charles Simic. AnAn
Everyone here has the same idea. Hungry and Waiting. Tom Mandel.
BAP
Everyone in me is a bird. In Celebration of My Uterus. Anne Sexton.
CAPP
Everyone in the World. Joel Dailey. UL
Everyone is gone. Everyone. Blue. Christopher Gilbert. *Fr.* Beginning
by Example. FYAP
Everyone knows he's blind as a bat. The Umpire. Walker Gibson. SD
Everyone Knows the World Is Ending. Alice Fulton. EOEF
Everyone nods with empathy. The Wrong Line. Rachael Beck. SoTCo
Everyone passes under the moon. Meir Wieseltier, *tr. by* Warren Bargad
and Stanley F. Chyet. IP
Everyone Sang. Siegfried Sassoon. BrPo; FaBV; GTBS-P; InvP;
MoBrPo; NAEL-2; NoAM; NOBE; OBEV; OBWP; OxBSP; OxBTC;
TrJP; WaP
Everyone says "It's so long—put it up!" Mikata no Sami, *tr. fr. Japanese
by* Hiroaki Sato. *Fr.* Manyo Shu. FCEI
Everyone says the autumn moon is lovely. Sitting in Meditation at Night,
Facing Hui-shan. Wei Yüan, *tr. by* Irving Lo. WFTU
Everyone suddenly burst out singing. Everyone Sang. Siegfried Sassoon.
BrPo; FaBV; GTBS-P; InvP; MoBrPo; NAEL-2; NoAM; NOBE;
OBEV; OBWP; OxBSP; OxBTC; TrJP; WaP
Everyone thinks I am poisonous. I am not. The Tarantula. Reed
Whittemore. CoAP
Everyone's/ heading in the same direction. Ishikawa Takuboku, *tr. fr.
Japanese by* Hiroaki Sato. *Fr.* Forty-seven Tanka in Three Lines.
FCEI
Everyone's going to ride tomorrow. Gabriel's Blues. Calvin Forbes.
PoA
Everyone's got someone who gave them oranges. Arthur. Tom Paulin.
FaBCIP
Everything but everything. Snapshot. Lajos Kassák, *tr. by* Edwin
Morgan. MHuP
Everything: Eloy, Arizona, 1956. Ai. AmPA; FF
Everything flows. Denise Levertov. *Fr.* Olga Poems. NAAL-2
Everything has a shadow. Poor Shadow. Ilo Orleans. RAR
Everything has been arranged too carefully. The Room. Lawrence Raab.
BLA
Everything has its limit, including sorrow. To Urania. Joseph Brodsky.
BAP
Everything Has Its Reason. Liesl Ujvary, *tr. fr. German by* Beth
Bjorklund. CoAuP
Everything has lasted till today. The Unknown Soldier. Alun Lewis.
MoBrPo
Everything I do is against meaning. Against Meaning. Andrei Codrescu.
UL
Everything in Its Place. Arthur Guiterman. NBLV; OBAL
Everything is/ in order folks. Peter Henisch, *tr. by* Beth Bjorklund.
CoAuP
Everything is blowing, his. Jittoku, Buddhist Mystic—15th Century.
Jane Cooper. ER
Everything is extinguished. Bell-Toll. Pierre Reverdy, *tr. by* Michael
Benedikt. POS

Everything is laughing, singing. It Is a Pleasant Day. *Unknown.* BoTP
Everything is marvelous and beautiful. Kinds of Luck. Abraham Reisen, *tr. by* Leonard Wolf. PeBMYV
Everything Is Normal in Our Courtyard. Claribel Alegría, *tr. fr. Spanish by* Barbara Paschke *and* David Volpendesta. Vol
Everything is, once was not. Life after Death. Richard W. Thomas. PoBA
Everything is only an image. Ernst Schönwiese, *tr. by* Beth Bjorklund. CoAuP
Everything Is Plundered. "Anna Akhmatova," *tr. fr. Russian by* Stanley Kunitz. WPOW
Everything Is Possible. Robert Pack. PPP
Everything Is Round. Gabriela Mistral, *tr. fr. Spanish.* PBWP, *tr. by* D. M. Pettinella
Everything is round. Round. Rachel Boimwall, *tr. by* Gabriel Preil *and* Howard Schwartz. VWA
Everything is sexual at the beach. Concerning Unnatural Nature: An Inverted Form. Hollis Spurgeon Summers. ErPo
Everything Is Swimming. Stevie Smith. FaBoNo
Everything Is Very Simple. Idea Vilariño, *tr. fr. Spanish by* Kate Flores. DMH
Everything Is Wonderful. Jayne Cortez. AIW
Everything lives and nothing is dead. The Fugs. Edward Sanders. PoM
Everything menaces us. Beyond Love. Octavio Paz, *tr. by* Perry Higman. LPSS
Everything passes and vanishes. William Allingham. NOBVV
Everything shall be erased. Villa Sciarra: Rome. Christine Turner Curtis. GoYe
Everything That Acts Is Actual. Denise Levertov. NoAM
Everything that lives has its own proper pride. Proper Pride. D. H. Lawrence. FaBoEE
Everything was as if in a child's drawing. Cuckoo-Clock. Robert Desnos, *tr. by* Michael Benedikt. POS
Everything was bleak then, and. A History of Photography. Albert Goldbarth. MAYP
Everything was wrong; the local slaves wore smiles. Harpers Ferry. Selden Rodman. PoNe
Everything was yellow. The Painters. Judith Hemschemeyer. Psk
Everything We Do. Peter Meinke. GOYP
Everything which projects which curves into space has compacted. Samba. Aimé Césaire, *tr. by* Michael Benedikt. POS
Everything will be forsaken then. Apocrypha. János Pilinszky, *tr. by* Ted Hughes. MHuP
Everything's been different. The Birthday Child. Rose Fyleman. FaPON
Everything's interrelated: the weak. Leit-Motif: Oh Great City of Lima. Mirko Lauer, *tr. by* David Tipton. Per
Everything's still on down the rows of cells of beds with men/ asleep. The Great Escape. Ralph Adamo. MT
Everytime I leave you. Mother. Stephen Vincent. NeAC
Everywhere about is landscape as far as foot can feel. Homage to Paul Delvaux. Ramon Guthrie. PoE
Everywhere, everywhere. Mizuhara Shuoshi, *tr. by* Geoffrey Bownas *and* Anthony Thwaite. PeBJV
Everywhere, everywhere, Christmas tonight! Christmas Everywhere. Phillips Brooks. BLRP; FaFP; OHFP; PWR; WBLP
(Christmas Carol, A: "Everywhere, everywhere, Christmas tonight!") OHIP
Everywhere, everywhere, following me. Camerados. Bayard Taylor. AnAmPo; Par; UnPo
Everywhere fish wheeled and fled. Noah. Wayne Brown. PBCV
Everywhere I hear them whispering. Eulogy. Grace Nichols. UAS
Everywhere Pregnant Women Appear. Eric Nelson. SoTCo
Everywhere the habits of late afternoon are repeated. Simple Rituals. Dyan Sublett. KS
Everywhere things have been taking place. Summer. Douglas Crase. NoP
Everywoman Her Own Theology. Alicia Ostriker. ER
Eve's Advice to the Children of Israel. Joachim Neugroschel. VWA
Eves Apologie. Emilia Lanier. BoWoP
Eve's Birth. Kim Chernin. VWA
Eve's Daughter. Edward Rowland Sill. AnAmPo
Eve's Song in the Garden. Lynn Gottlieb. VWA
Eve's tinted shadows slowly fill the fane. Sir Walter Scott at the Tomb of the Stuarts in St. Peter's. Richard Monckton Milnes. EBVV; OBTV
Evesong. Maureen Duffy. PeHV
Eviction. The. William Allingham. *Fr.* Laurence Bloomfield in Ireland. BIrV; NOIV
Eviction. Elizabeth Brewster. CaP
Eviction. Lucille Clifton. NTCP
Evidence. John Skoyles. NAmP
Evidence at the Witch Trials. James Keir Baxter. OxBC

Evidence Read at the Trial of the Knave of Hearts. "Lewis Carroll." *Fr.* Alice's Adventures in Wonderland, *ch.* 12. FaBoNo; FaFP; GTBS-P; NoBVV; OxBoLi
(Silence in Court.) FaBoCo
Evidently Chicken Town. John Cooper Clarke. FaBoPV
Evil. Arthur Rimbaud, *tr. fr. French by* Robert Lowell. *Fr.* Eighteen-Seventy. OBWP
("Whilst the red spittle of the grape-shot sings.") WaaP, *tr. by* Norman Cameron.
Evil. Rimbaud, *tr. fr. French by* Norman Cameron. WaaP
Evil does not go always. Lines for a Hard Time. Gena Ford. IHMS
Evil Eye, The. John Ciardi. MoBS; NAs
Evil flees the earth. To the Nativity. Fernán Gonzáles de Eslava, *tr. by* Samuel Beckett. MexPo
Evil, if rightly understood. On the Origin of Evil. John Byrom. NOEC
Evil Is No Black Thing. Sarah Webster Fabio. PoBA
Evil Man, An! Richard Beer-Hofmann, *tr. fr. German by* Ludwig Lewisohn. *Fr.* Der Graf von Charolais. TrJP
Evil Nigger Waits for Lightnin.' Amiri Baraka. NOBA
Evil [*or* Evill] spirit, your beauty, haunts me still, An. Michael Drayton. *Fr.* Idea, XX. AAS; EIL; GBL; NOBE; OBSC
Evildoer. Gabriele Wohmann, *tr. fr. German by* Margaret Woodruff. DMG
Ev'n [*or* E'en *or* Even] like two little bank-dividing brooks [*or* brookes]. My Beloved Is Mine, and I Am His; He Feedeth among the Lillies. Francis Quarles. *Fr.* Emblems, V, 3. MeLP; MePo; NOBE; OBEV; OBS; TrGrPo, *abr.*; TrGrPo
(Divine Rapture.) OBEV
Evocation. Amado Nervo, *tr. fr. Spanish by* Samuel Beckett. MexPo
Evolution. John Blight. CBAP
Evolution. Ben King. AnAmPo
Evolution. Peter Porter. OBD
Evolution. Langdon Smith. BeLS; BLPA; FaBoBe; FaFP
Evolution. May Swenson. TrGrPo
Evolution. John Banister Tabb. AA
Evolution. Israel Zangwill. TrJP
Evolution from the Fish. Robert Bly. MoP; NoAM; NOBA
Evolution, though a good thing, has. Bathing with Father. Doug Fetherling. NeAC
Evolutionary Hymn. C. S. Lewis. NOBL
Ewes and lambs, loving the far hillplaces, The. Ad Limina. Joseph Campbell. BIrV
Ewing sweating. Patrick Ewing Takes a Foul Shot. Diane Ackerman. ASP; MAYP
Ex and Squarey. *Unknown.* ChTr; GBP, 1 *st.*
Ex-Basketball Player. John Updike. ASP; InPK; NYBP; SM
Ex-Deputy Sheriff Remembers the Eastern Oklahoma Murderers, An. Jim Barnes. HATNAP
Ex Nihilo. David Gascoyne. *Fr.* Miserere. GTBS-P
Ex Ore Infantium. Francis Thompson. BoTP; FaBV; OHIP; OxBChV
(Child's Prayer, A.) OHIP
Ex-Poet, The. Bill Zavatsky. UL
Ex-Queen among the Astronomers, The. Fleur Adcock. FaBoWP
Ex-Voto. Swinburne. MOS
Exactly. Roberta Metz. TSS
Exactly as if it were in a shed or pen. The Coarse Old Maid. Leyzer Volf, *tr. by* Robert Friend. PeBMYV
Exaggerated lives, phony body postures, overblown gestures. Triplets. Michael Brownstein. UL
Exaltation. Franz Werfel, *tr. fr. German by* Edith Abercrombie Snow. TrJP
Examination, The. Priscilla Jane Thompson. CBWP-2
Examination at the Womb-Door. Ted Hughes. NAEL-2; NAs; OxBC
Examination of Conscience before Going to Sleep. T. Carmi, *tr. fr. Hebrew by* Stephen Mitchell. OBD
Examine the mirror closely, and your face. Sunday, July 14th; a Fine Day at the Baths. Julian Symons. WaP
Example, The. W. H. Davies. MoBrPo; TrGrPo
Example, The. Salvador Díaz Mirón, *tr. fr. Spanish by* Samuel Beckett. MexPo
Exasperated, worn, you conjure a mansion. Desires of Men and Women. John Berryman. LiTM
Excavations. Fleur Adcock. ATNZ
Excavator, explore rock from the great Ice Age. The Cave-Drawing. Vernon Watkins. LiTB
Exceeding sorrow/ Consumeth my sad heart! O Mors! Quam Amara Est Memoria Tua Homini Pacem Habenti in Substantiis Suis. Ernest Dowson. PoBo; OBMV
Exceeding tall, but built so well his height. House-Surgeon. W. E. Henley. *Fr.* In Hospital, XVI. BrPo

Excelente Balade of Charitie, An. Thomas Chatterton. EBEV; EnRP; NOEC; SeCePo

(Excellente Balade of Charity.) LiTB

Excellency of Christ. Giles Fletcher the Younger. *Fr.* Christ's Victory and Triumph: Christ's Victory in Heaven, I. WGRP

Excellent New Ballad, Called the Brawny Bishop's Complaint, An. Arthur Mainwaring. APAS

Excellent New Ballad Called the Prince of Darkness, An. *Unknown.* APAS

Excellent New Ballad Giving a True Account of the Birth and Conception of a Late Famous Poem Called the Female Nine, An. Charles Sackville. APAS

Excellent New Song, An. *Unknown.* OxBSS

Excellent New Song, Being the Intended Speech of a Famous Orator against Peace, An. Swift. APAS

Excellent New Song Called "Mat's Peace, An." Arthur Mainwaring. APAS

Excellent New Song on a Seditious Pamphlet, An. Swift. CoMu

Excellent New Song upon His Grace Our Good Lord Archbishop of Dublin, An. Swift. CoMu

Excellent ritual of oils, of anointing. Sarcophagi. Bernard Spencer. OBD

Excellente Balade of Charity. Thomas Chatterton. *See* Excelente Balade of Charitie, An.

Excelsior. Longfellow. FaPON; FaPoR; NAAL-1; OBCA; OnMSP; PrIm; WBLP

Excelsior. *Unknown.* BXAP

Except for heaven. The Meadow upon the Mercy of Heaven. Hsin Mu, *tr.* by Dominic Cheung. IFON

Except for the fat. Return. John Robert Lee. PBCV

Except for the throng. Basketball Season Begins. Norbert Krapf. TSL

Except I Love. Robert Parry. *Fr.* The Mirror of Knighthood. EIL

Except ourselves, we have no other prayer. Without Ceremony. Vassar Miller. MoAmPo; SM

Except the Lord build the house. Bible, *O.T. Fr.* Psalms, CXXVII. TrJP

Except the Lord, That He for Us Had Been. Henry Ainsworth. AH

Except under the cool shadows of pines. To a Wall of Flame in a Steel Mill, Syracuse, New York, 1969. Larry Levis. DiL; MAYP

Excepting the diner. Poem to Be Read at 3 A.M. Donald Justice. HoPM

Excerpt from a Report to the Galactic Council. Robert Conquest. OxBC

Excerpts from the Modern Tragedy. Sándor Weöres, *tr. fr. Hungarian by* Jascha Kessler. FOC

Exchange, The. Samuel Taylor Coleridge. FiBHP

Exchange. George Rostrevor Hamilton, *after the Greek of* Plato. FaBoEE

Exchange. Dabney Stuart. HoPM

Exchange between the Poet and St. Augustine, An. Petrarch, *tr. fr. Latin by* W. H. Draper. *Fr.* Secretum, I. OxBLMV

Exchange in greed the ungraceful signs. Thrust. The Violent Space. Etheridge Knight. BPo

Exchange of Poems by Tung-yang Stream, An, *sels.* Hsieh Ling-yün, *tr. fr. Chinese by* Burton Watson. CoBCP

"How fetching! Somebody's husband." *Fr.* II.

"How fetching! Somebody's wife." *Fr.* I.

Exchanges. Ernest Dowson. OBMV

Exchanging Glances. William Pitt Root. MAYP

Exciseman, The. Burns. GoTS

Excited pillows torture. Desire. Judah Leib Teller, *tr.* by Benjamin *and* Barbara Harshav. AYP

Excitement. Louise Bennett. PBCV

Exclusive Blue. Robert Francis. CRP

Excommunication, The. Melech Ravitch, *tr. fr. Yiddish by* Miriam Waddington. PeBMYV

Excrement Poem, The. Maxine W. Kumin. CAPP; FaBoWP

Excursion, The. Tu Fu, *tr. fr. Chinese.* AWP, *tr.* by Amy Lowell *and* Florence Ayscough; SD, *tr.* by Amy Lowell *and* Florence Ayscough

Excursion, The. Wordsworth.
Sels.

"Curious child, who dwelt upon a tract, A." *Fr.* IV. WGRP

Despondency Corrected. *Fr.* IV. EnRP

Discourse of the Wanderer, and an Evening Visit to the Lake. *Fr.* IX. EnRP

Prospectus. EnRP; NoP; OAEL-2

Solitary, The. *Fr.* II. EnRP

Wanderer, The. *Fr.* I. EnRP, *abr..*

(Ruined Cottage, The, *diff. version.*) NoP; OAEL-2

Wanderer Recalls the Past, The. *Fr.* I. OBNC

Excursion to the Suburbs, An, *sel.* Tsung Ch'en, *tr. fr. Chinese by* Jonathan Chaves.

"Side by side, we ride out of the city." CoBLCP

Excuse, The. Sir Walter Ralegh. AAS; SiPS

Excuse me if I don't weep. Funeral Song for Mamie Eisenhower. Nellie Wong. BrSi

Excuse of Absence, An. Thomas Carew. CaPo; SeCP

Exeat. Stevie Smith. NAEL-2; NoAM

Execration against Whores, An. John Webster. *Fr.* The White Devil, III, ii. TW

Execration upon Vulcan, An. Ben Jonson. SeCP

Execution. Edward Hirsch. TSL

Execution. James A. Randall, Jr.. BPo

Execution of Alice Holt. *Unknown.* OxBoLi

Execution of Cornelius Vane, The. Sir Herbert Read. BrPo

Execution of Five Pirates for Murder. *Unknown.* OxBSS

Execution of King Charles, The. Andrew Marvell. PoRA

Execution of Luke Hutton, The. *Unknown.* OBET

Execution of Montrose, The. William Edmonstoune Aytoun. OnMSP

Executioners. Berish Weinstein, *tr. fr. Yiddish by* Leonard Wolf. PeBMYV

Executive. Sir John Betjeman. NOBL

Executive's Death, The. Robert Bly. CoAP; NaP

Exeo in a spasm. Enueg I. Samuel Beckett. CIP

Exequies, The. Thomas Stanley. MeLP; OBS

Exequy, The ("Accept, thou shrine of my dead saint"), *sel.* Henry King. GBL; HAP; InvP; JCP; MeLP; NoP; OBS; PoEL-2; PrIm; QFR; SeCePo; SeCP; TEP

(Exequy on [*or* upon] His Wife.) BoLoP; NOBE; OBEV

(Exequy, The: To His Matchless Never to Be Forgotten Friend.) MePo

"Sleep on, my love, in thy cold bed." CH; OBD; TrGrPo

Exequy, An. Peter Porter. NoAM; OxBC

Exequy on [*or* upon] His Wife. Henry King. *See* Exequy, The.

Exequy, The: To His Matchless Never to Be Forgotten Friend. Henry King. *See* Exequy, The.

Exequy: To Peter Allt. Kildare Dobbs. OBCV

Exercise. W. S. Merwin. NOBA

Exercise ("Get loaded"). Pat Nolan. UL

Exercise in a Meadow. Jean Elliot. GoYe

Exercise in Preparation for a Pindaric Ode to Carl Hubbell. Delmore Schwartz. ASP

Exercise ("Just as I stood up"). Pat Nolan. UL

Exert thy voice, sweet harbinger of Spring! To the Nightingale. Countess of Winchilsea. WPE

Exeter Riddle, An. Gavin Ewart. OxBC

Exeunt. Richard Wilbur. BoNaP; HeIP; PoLF; Psk

Exeunt Omnes. Thomas Hardy. QFR

Exhausted now her sighs, and dry her tears. Walter Savage Landor. FaBoEE

Exhausted, the day sinks to sleep. Night. V. A. Zhukovsky, *tr.* by Alan Myers. AAA

Exhaustion. Sa'di Yusuf, *tr. fr. Arabic by* Abdullah al-Udhari. MPAW

Exhortation. Louise Bogan. QFR

Exhortation. Thomas Hastings. AA

Exhortation. János Pilinszky, *tr. fr. Hungarian by* Ted Hughes. MHuP

Exhortation of a Father to His Children, The. Robert Smith. OxBChV

Exhortation: Summer, 1919. Claude McKay. CDC

Exhortation to Learn of Others' Trouble. Earl of Surrey. FaBoEE

Exhortation to Prayer. William Cowper. NOCV

Exhortation to Prayer. Margaret Mercer. AA

Exile. Ernest Dowson. BoLoP; BrPo

Exile. George Rostrevor Hamilton, *after the Greek of* Isidoros of Aigai. FaBoEE

Exile. Amjad Nasir, *tr. fr. Arabic by* May Jayyusi *and* Charles Doria. MAP

Exile, *sel.* "St.-John Perse," *tr. fr. French by* Denis Devlin.

"Syntax of lightning! O pure speech of exile! Far is that other shore where." *Fr.* VII. RHTwFP

Exile. Ray di Palma. IAT

Exile, The. Larry Rubin. GoYe

Exile. Saniyya Salih, *tr. fr. Arabic by* Kamal Boullata. OV

Exile. Dennis Scott. UAS

Exile. Karl Shapiro. *Fr.* Adam and Eve. CRP

Exile. Joseph Stroud. NPGG

Exile. Ellen Bryant Voigt. MAYP

Exile. Jennette Yeatman. GoYe

Exile at Rest, The. John Pierpont. AA

Exile from God. John Hall Wheelock. WGRP

Exile in Nigeria. Ezekiel Mphahlele. PBA

Exile of the Sons of Uisliu, *sels. Unknown, tr. fr. Irish by* Thomas Kinsella. NOIV

"Conchobor, what are you thinking, you."

"Sweet in your sight the fiery stride."

Exile: 2. Rajagopal Parthasarathy. *Fr.* Rough Passage. UAS

Exiled. Edna St. Vincent Millay. MOS; PoRA

Exiled from places of honor about the Throne of Grace. Black Church on Sunday. Joseph M. Mosley, Jr. NBP

Exiled from the Light. Sebastian Salazar Bondy, *tr. fr. Spanish by* Ena Hollis *and* Maureen Ahern. Per

Exiled Heart, The. Maurice Lindsay. OxBS

Exiles. "Æ." BIrV; MoBrPo

Exiles, The. W. H. Auden. OxBTC

Exiles. Constantine P. Cavafy, *tr. fr. Greek by* Edmund Keeley *and* Philip Sherrard. VMG

Exiles. William Hamilton Hayne. AA

Exiles. Patrick O'Connor. TIRV

Exiles, The. Paul Ramsey. *Fr.* Three Epigrams. CRP

Exile's Letter. Li Po, *tr. fr. Chinese by* Ezra Pound. CTC; FaBoMo; OxBA

Exile's Return, The. Robert Lowell. AmPP; OxBA

Exile's Reverie, The. Mary Weston Fordham. CBWP-2

Exile's Reveries, The, *sel.* James Kennedy.
  "Chased from my calling to this hackneyed trade." NOEC

Existential. William Heyen. GeTw

Existentialism. Lloyd Frankenberg. FiBHP

Exit. Wilson Pugsley MacDonald. CaP

Exit. Edwin Arlington Robinson. MoAmPo; OxBSP

Exit from Eden, The. Milton. *See* Paradise Lost:
  So spake our Mother Eve, and Adam heard.

Exit from the Garden of Delights. Aharon Amir, *tr. fr. Hebrew by* Bernhard Frank. MHeP

Exit Line. John Ciardi. WeW

Exit Lines. George Jonas. NeAC

Exit, Pursued by a Bear. Ogden Nash. NYBP

Exit the ribald clown. Colombine. Hugh McCrae. PoAu-1

Exits and Entrances. Naomi Long Madgett. BlSi

Exodus. Carolyn Kizer. AnAn

Exodus. Anita Endrezze Probst. CDW

Exodus. Harvey Shapiro. VWA

Exodus, *sel.* Unknown, *tr. fr. Anglo-Saxon by* Charles W. Kennedy.

Exodus, *sels.* Bible, *O.T.*
  "Let us synge unto the Lorde, for he is become glorious." *Fr.* XV: 1-8, *tr. by* William Tyndale. OBVE
  Lord Is a Man of War, The. *Fr.* XV: 3-10. WaaP
  Parting of the Red Sea, The. AnOE
  Ten Commandments, The. *Fr.* XX: 3-17. WBLP
  Then Sang Moses. *Fr.* XV: 1-18. TrJP
  "Then sang Moses and the children of Israel this song." *Fr.* XV: 1-18. OBWP
  Triumphal Chant. *Fr.* XV: 1-13, 18. TrGrPo

Exodus (August 3, 1492), The. Emma Lazarus. *Fr.* By the Waters of Babylon. WPE

Exodus from a Renaissance Gallery. Ellen M. V. Acton. GoYe

Exodus from Egypt, The. Ezekielos of Alexandria, *tr. fr. Greek by* E. H. Gifford. TrJP

Exodus 1940. Alfred Wolfenstein, *tr. fr. German by* Erna Baber Rosenfeld. VWA

Exodus to Connacht. Fear Dorcha O'Meallain, *tr. fr. Irish by* Thomas Kinsella. FaBoPV; TIRV

Exorcism. Oliver St. John Gogarty. AnIL

Exorcism of the Straight/Man/Demon. Aaron Shurin. GLP

Expanded Want Ad, An. Brad Leithauser. MAYP

Expanded waters gather on the plain, The. The Flood. Ovid, *tr. fr. Latin. Fr.* Metamorphoses: The floods, by nature enemies to land. ChTr

Expanding in the chill. Cold-Weather Love. Ronald G. Everson. MoCV

Expansive puppets percolate self-unction. The Canadian Authors Meet. F. R. Scott. NOBC; OBCV

Expect No Turbulence. Barbara Ferland. PBCV

Expect Nothing. Alice Walker. AmPA; FF

Expectans Expectavi. Charles Hamilton Sorley. FaBoCh; WGRP

Expectant faces brimmed the waiting square. Rome Sunday June 1960. John Hewitt. TIRV

Expectant Father, The. Ai. GeTw

Expectant Mother. Penelope Shuttle. BrRo

Expectation, The. Frederick William Faber. *Fr.* Our Lady's Expectation. ACP

Expectation. Aliza Shenhar, *tr. fr. Hebrew by* Linda Zisquit. VWA

Expectation. Thomas Stanley. OBS

Expectation: Night and Day. Salah Abd al-Sabur, *tr. fr. Arabic by* Diana Der Hovanessian *and* Lena Jayyusi. MAP

Expected Ship, The. John Godfrey Saxe. AnAmPo

Expedition to Wessagusset, The. Longfellow. *Fr.* The Courtship of Miles Standish, PAH. AiP, *st.* 1; BeLS

Expelling Witches. Chiang Shih-ch'üan, *tr. fr. Chinese by* Coy Harmon. WFTU

"Expense of spirit in a waste of shame, The [*or* Th']." Shakespeare. *Fr.* Sonnets, CXXIX. AWP; EBEV; ErPo; GBL; HAP; HeIP; InPS; LiTB; NAEL-1; NIP; NOBE; NoP; OAEL-1; OBEV; OBSC; PoE; PoEL-2; PPP; QFR; SCV; SeCePo; Son; TEP; TrGrPo; UnPo; WeW

Expensive Wife, The. Judah ibn Sabbatai. *Fr.* The Gift of Judah the Woman-Hater. TrJP

Experience, The. Bruce Bennett. SoTCo

Experience. Emerson. FPL; LiTA; PoEL-4; TAP

Experience. Lesbia Harford. CBAP; PoAu-1

Experience. John Boyle O'Reilly. ACP

Experience. Dorothy Parker. NAAL-2

Experience. James Simmons. BIrV

Experience, The. Edward Taylor. *See* Preparatory Meditations before My Approach to the Lord's Supper: Oh, that I always breath'd in such an air.

Experience a table of. Ted Greenwald. IAT

Experience now doth show what God us taught before. On Edward Seymour, Duke of Somerset. *Unknown.* OBSC

Experience that eludes you intrigues you more, The. Season Ticket. Gloria Frym. UL

Experience, though noon auctoritee. The Wife of Bath's Prologue. Chaucer. *Fr.* The Canterbury Tales. NAEL-1; OAEL-1; OxBoLi, *abr.*
  (Prologue to the Wife of Bath's Tale, The.) PoEL-1

"If poor (you say) she drains her husband's purse," *mod. version by* Pope OBSV

"My fifthe housbonde, god his soule blesse!" FiP

Experienced men, inured to city ways. John Gay. *Fr.* Trivia; or, The Art of Walking the Streets of London, II. OAEL-1

Experienced wife, An. A Midwife's Story; Two. Anne Szumigalski. NOBC

Experiences. Christine Busta, *tr. fr. German by* Beth Bjorklund. CoAuP

Experiment results in the transmutation, An. Saturday. Daniel Hoffman. SoTCo

Experiment That Failed, The. John Logan. NU

Expert painter who scrutinizes a marvelous scene is equal to a god, An. On Poetry. Chao Chih-hsin, *tr. by* Irving Lo. WFTU

Expiration, The. John Donne. EiL; MeLP; MePo; OxBSP; SeCP

Explaining to me that my mind. Friends Come. Lucille Clifton. GeTw

Explanation. William Barber. PeHV

Explanation. Hermann Gail, *tr. fr. German by* Beth Bjorklund. CoAuP

Explanation. Geof Hewitt. NeAC

Explanation of America, An, *sels.* Robert Pinsky.
  Serpent Knowledge. NPGG
  Serpent Knowledge. NAAL-2

Explanation of the Grasshopper, An. Vachel Lindsay. FaPON; RAR

Explanations. Lucille Clifton. GeTw

Exploding beyond my very eyes. Peyote Vision. Lew Blockcolski. VoR

Exploding Poem, The. E. G. Hallaman. SoTCo

Exploiter of the shadows. Fox. Clifford Dyment. OxBSP

Exploration. Daniel Hoffman. CoAP

Explorations/ Bronchitis: The Rosario Beach House. Aleida Rodríguez, *tr. fr. Spanish by* Toni Empringham. FIA

Explorers, The. Margaret Atwood. MoCV

Explorers as Seen by the Natives. Doug Fetherling. NOBC

Explorers will come, The. The Explorers. Margaret Atwood. MoCV

Explosion. Delmira Agustini, *tr. fr. Spanish by* Perry Higman. LPSS

Explosion, The. Philip Larkin. EBEV; FaBoMo; HAP; NAEL-2; NoAM; OxBC; RB; SCV; WeW

Expostulation, An. Isaac Bickerstaffe. FaBoCo; FiBHP; NIP

Expostulation and Reply. Wordsworth. EnRP; NAEL-2; OAEL-2

Exposure ("It is December in Wicklow."), *sel.* Seamus Heaney. IPY
  "Rain comes down through the alders." PoPo

Exposure. Wilfred Owen. FaBoMo; InPS; MMA; NoAM; OBWP; RB; WaP

Expounding the Torah. Louis Zukofsky. VWA

Express. William Allingham. NOBVV

Express, The. Stephen Spender. CMoP; GoJo; HeIP; LiTM; MoAB; MoBrPo; MoP; NoAM; TwCP

Express Train. Karl Kraus, *tr. fr. German by* Albert Bloch. TrJP

Expression. Thom Gunn. OxBC

Expression. Isaac Rosenberg. MoBrPo

Expulsion from Paradise. Milton. *See* Paradise Lost:
  Brandish't sword of God before them blaz'd, The.

Expulsion of Hagar, The. Eloise Bibb. CBWP-4

Exquisite stillness! What serenities. Don Juan's Address to the Sunset. Robert Nichols. OBMV

Exquisite torment, dainty Mrs. Hargreaves. Sapphics. D. B. Wyndham Lewis. NOBL

Extasie, The. Abraham Cowley. SeCP

Extasie, The. John Donne. *See* Ecstasy, The.

Extempore Effusion [upon the Death of James Hogg], An. Wordsworth. EBEV; FaBoRV; FiP; NOBE; NoP; OAEL-2; SCV
(Ode: "When first, descending from the moorlands.") NAEL-2; FaBoRV; FiP; NOBE; NoP; OAEL-2; SCV
London, from Hampstead Heath. FaBoPP
Extempore Verses Intended to Allay the Violence of Party-Spirit. John Byrom. See God bless the king! I mean the Faith's Defender.
Extend, there where you venture and come back. Walk on the Moon. N. Scott Momaday. CRP
Extensions of Linear Mobility. Jeanine Hathaway. IHMS
Extermination of the Jews, The. Marvin Bell. CAPP; VWA
Exterminator. Lucien Stryk. CAPP
External Element, The. David McFadden. NeAC
Extinct Birds. Judith Wright. PBWP
Extinct volcanoes are silent. Volcanoes. Bella Akhmadulina, tr. by W. H. Auden. PBWP
Extinction of Plankton. Ono Tozaburo, tr. fr. Japanese by Hiroaki Sato. FCEI
Extinguished are my years of carefree laughter. Pushkin, tr. by Alan Myers. AAA
Extra Inch, The. Siegfried Sassoon. FL
Extra-Inning Ballgame, The. Halvard Johnson. TSL
Extra Joyful Chorus for Those Who Have Read This Far, An. Robert Bly. EAS
Extract. Paul Bowles. PoA
Extract from Addresses to the Academy of Fine Ideas, An. Wallace Stevens. LiTA; LiTM
Extract from Memoirs. Howard Nemerov. OxBC
Extract the quint-essence. Francis Daniel Pastorius. SCAP
Extracts: From the Journal of Elisa Lynch. Maura Stanton. AmPA
Extraordinary patience of things, The! Carmel Point. Robinson Jeffers. NAAL-2; NoAM; NoP
Extraordinary Will. Will Jackett. FaBoUs
Extras. Richard Burton. AA
Extravagant Drunkard's Wish, The. Edward Ward. NOEC
Extreme Unction. Ernest Dowson. ACP; MoBrPo; OAEL-2; OBMV
Extremes. James Whitcomb Riley. FaPON
Extremities. Rae Armantrout. LP
Extrication. A. R. Ammons. CAPP
Exuberant, restless. West Lake. Kenneth O. Hanson. CoAP
Exultation. Hywel ab Owain Gwynedd, tr. fr. Welsh by Gwyn Williams. OBWVE
Exulting in his strength, he seems to dare. Virgil, tr. fr. Latin by Dryden. Fr. The Aeneid [or Eneados], XI. OBVE
Eyam, sel. Anna Seward.
"In scenes paternal, not beheld through years." NOEC
Eyaya-eya./ I recognize/ A bit of song. I Should Be Ashamed. Uvlunuaq. WTO
Eye, The. Robert Herrick. CaPo
Eye, The. Robinson Jeffers. LiTA; LiTM; NoAM; NOBA; OxBA; WaP
Eye. Nishiwaki Junzaburo, tr. fr. Japanese by Geoffrey Bownas and Anthony Thwaite. PeBJV
Eye, The. Allen Tate. LiTA
Eye and Tooth. Robert Lowell. CAPP; NAAL-2
Eye can hardly pick them out, The. At Grass. Philip Larkin. HAP; NePoEA; OxBTC; RB; SD; WeW
Eye closes, An. Inn. Pierre Reverdy, tr. by Eugene Jolas. RHTwFP
Eye, dark, The. Hut Window. Paul Celan, tr. by Joachim Neugroschel. VWA
Eye drags all of winter, The. News Reel. David Ross. GoYe
Eye for an Eye, An. C. M. Donald. GLP
Eye Is More or Less Satisfied with Seeing, The. Allen Curnow. ATNZ
Eye luminous, The. The Offender. Denise Levertov. NePoEA-2
Eye of God. Jim Tollerud. VoR
Eye of Humility, The. Kay Smith. OBCV
Eye of looking back were well, An. Ben Jonson. Fr. Pleasure Reconciled to Virtue. NAEL-1
Eye of potato, thin neck of cabbage. Novena. Mary Swander. KS
Eye of the demon on Albion was turned, The. The Comet. Thomas Lovell Beddoes. FL
Eye of the garden, queen of flowers. To the Rose. Sir John Davies. Fr. Hymns of Astraea. OBSC
Eye of this storm is not quiet, The. To a Gone Era. Irma McClaurin. BlSi
Eye opening is a mouth seeing, The. Eyesight II. Robert Duncan. EAS
Eye standing up eye lying down eye sitting. Making Feet and Hands. Benjamin Péret, tr. by David Gascoyne. EAS; RHTwFP
Eye unacquitted by whatever it holds in allegiance, The. Didactic Piece. Louise Bogan. NoAM
Eye winker. Unknown. OxNR
Eye with the piercing eagle's fire, An. Thaddeus Stevens. Phoebe Cary. PAH

Eyeballs on her behind are like fire, The. The Leopard. Lorenzo Thomas. UL
Eyeglasses circumscribe themselves exactly, The. At the End of the Street of Stars. Pierre Reverdy, tr. by Michael Benedikt. POS
Eyeing the Eyes of One's Mistress. Ebenezer Jones. NOBVV
Eyelashes did their job. The Stillborn (Domesticity # three). Bill Knott. PPR
Eyeless labourer in the night, The. Woman to Man. Judith Wright. CBAP; PoAu-2; WPE
Eyelids glowing, some chill morning, The. Monet: "Les Nymphéas." W. D. Snodgrass. CoAP
Eyelids meet, The. He'll catch a little nap. In the Smoking-Car. Richard Wilbur. LiTM; MoAmPo
Eyelids of eve fall together at last, The. The Eve of Waterloo. Thomas Hardy. Fr. The Dynasts, Pt. III, Act VI, sc. viii. OAEL-2; OBWP (Before Waterloo.) MoAB
Eyes. W. H. Davies. BrPo; FM
Eyes, The. Michel Deguy, tr. fr. French by Clayton Eshleman. RHTwFP
Eyes. Walter de la Mare. BrPo
Eyes. Clarisse Nicoïdski, tr. fr. Judezmo by Stephen Levy. VWA
Eyes:/ shining with rain that poured down. Paul Celan, tr. by Beth Bjorklund. CoAuP
Eyes always open eyes. Eyewash. Niall Montgomery. EAS
Eyes and Tears. Andrew Marvell. MePo
Eyes blinded by three poisons. Ungo, tr. by Lucien Stryk and Takashi Ikemoto. ZPCJ
Eyes, Calm beside Thee (Lady, Could'st Thou Know!). Robert Browning. Son
Eyes closed, you lean on a tree. Wakayama Bokusui, tr. fr. Japanese by Hiroaki Sato. Fr. Forty-four Tanka. FCEI
Eyes do not lie. Remainder. Frederika Blankner. GoYe
Eyes Drawn Up to the Evening Sky. Your Dress. Moyshe-Leyb Halpern, tr. by Benjamin and Barbara Harshav. AYP
Eyes Hide My Love. Samuel Daniel. Fr. Hymen's Triumph. EIL (Secrecy.) OBSC
Eyes like the morning star. The Colorado Trail. Unknown. AS
Eyes, nose, ears, mouth and mind. Yüan Mei, tr. fr. Chinese by Anthony C. Yu. Fr. Life at the Sui Garden, VI. WFTU
Eyes of Dark Sorrow, The. N. M. Rashed, tr. fr. Urdu by Mahmood Jamal. PBMUP
Eyes of Flesh, The. Sandra Hochman. NMM
Eyes of men running, falling, screaming. Unknown. OBWP
Eyes of My Regret, The. Angelina Weld Grimké. CDC
Eyes of Night-Time. Muriel Rukeyser. BoWoP
Eyes of slain stag. In Some Seer's Cloud Car. Christopher Middleton. TwCP
Eyes of the Child Do Not See Me, The. Norman H. Russell. NOVW
Eyes of the pioneer woman are blue, The. The Pioneer Woman—in the North Country. Eunice Tietjens. AmFN
Eyes of twenty centuries, The. Judas Iscariot. Stephen Spender. MoAB; MoBrPo; NIP
Eyes open, I listen to spring. Taigi, tr. fr. Japanese by Hiroaki Sato. Fr. Twenty-nine Hokku. FCEI
Eyes open to a cry of pulleys, The. Love Calls Us to the Things of This World. Richard Wilbur. AmPP; CAPP; CMoP; HAP; HeIP; InPS; MoAmPo; NePoEA; NIP; NoAM; PoE; PoRA; PPP; TAP; TrGrPo; UnPo; VGW
Eyes red, the lips blue, The. The Three Seamstresses. Isaac Leibush Peretz, tr. by Joseph Leftwich. TrJP
Eyes shining without mystery. Pantoum. John Ashbery. SM
Eyes shut tight. Madness. Yoshihara Sachiko, tr. by James Kirkup and Shozo Tokunaga. BoWoP
Eyes So Tristful. Diego de Saldaña, tr. fr. Spanish by Longfellow. AWP
Eyes that drew from me such fervent praise, The. Petrarch, tr. fr. Italian. Fr. Sonnets to Laura: To Laura in Death, XXIV, tr. by Edwin Morgan. NAWM-1
Eyes that glass fear, though fear on furtive foot. A Hare. Walter de la Mare. EBEV
Eyes That Last I Saw in Tears. T. S. Eliot. NOBE
Eyes That Queenly Sit. Elizabeth Daryush. QFR
Eyes that weep for pity of the heart, The. Dante, tr. fr. Italian by Dante Gabriel Rossetti. Fr. La Vita Nuova, XIX. AWP; WGRP, sl. diff. vers.
Eyes, the Blood, The. David Meltzer. PoM; VWA
Eyesight II. Robert Duncan. EAS
Eyes:. . .Medium. All There Is to Know about Adolph Eichmann. Leonard Cohen. InPK
Eyewash. Niall Montgomery. EAS
Eyewitness. Rodney Hall. PoAu-2
Ezek'el saw de wheel. Ezekiel, You and Me. Unknown. AS
Ezekiel. A. N. Stencl, tr. fr. Yiddish by Joseph Leftwich. VWA

Ezekiel, *sels.* Bible, *O.T.*
  Lamentation. *Fr.* XIX: 2-9. TrJP
  Thy Mother Was like a Vine. *Fr.* XIX: 10-14. TrJP
Ezekiel, You and Me. *Unknown.* AS
Ezra Pound. Robert Lowell. MoP; NAAL-2; NoAM; NOBA
Ezra, whom not with eye nor with ear have I ever. Epistle to the
  Rappalloan. Archibald MacLeish. PoA
Ezry. Archibald MacLeish. NOBA

F

F is the fighting Firetruck. Phyllis McGinley. *Fr.* All around the Town.
  FaPON
Fa La La. John Hilton. *See* Madrigal: "My mistress frowns when she
  should play."
Fa, Mi, Fa, Re, La, Mi. *Unknown.* InPK
Fa saw the Forty-second. The Forty-second. *Unknown.* GBP
Fabien Dei Franchi. Oscar Wilde. BrPo
Fabius Lind clings to the flowing mane. Fabius Lind Is Riding the Wind.
  A. Leyeles, *tr. by* Benjamin *and* Barbara Harshav. AYP
Fabius Lind has forgotten his name. Disorder. A. Leyeles, *tr. by*
  Leonard Wolf. PeBMYV
Fabius Lind Is Riding the Wind. A. Leyeles, *tr. fr. Yiddish by* Benjamin
  and Barbara Harshav. AYP
Fabius Lind to Comrade Death. A. Leyeles, *tr. fr. Yiddish by* Benjamin
  and Barbara Harshav. AYP
Fabius Lind to Fabius Lind. A. Leyeles, *tr. fr. Yiddish by* Benjamin *and*
  Barbara Harshav. AYP
Fabius Lind's Days. A. Leyeles, *tr. fr. Yiddish.* AYP, *tr. by* Benjamin
  and Barbara Harshav; PeBMYV, *tr. by* Leonard Wolf
Fabius Lind's Diary, *sels.* A. Leyeles, *tr. fr. Yiddish by* Benjamin *and*
  Barbara Harshav. AYP
  February 15.
  February 4.
  February 1.
  February 7.
  February 17.
  February 10.
  February 23.
  January 30.
  January 28.
Fabius Lind's kingdom. February 17. A. Leyeles, *tr. fr. Yiddish by*
  Benjamin *and* Barbara Harshav. *Fr.* Fabius Lind's Diary. AYP
Fable, The. Gregory O'Brien. *Fr.* Bride of the Disappearing Man.
  ATNZ
Fable, A: "Dingy donkey, formal and unchanged, A." John Hookham
  Frere. FaBoCo
Fable, A: "In Aesop's tales an honest wretch we find." Matthew Prior.
  NoP
Fable: Mountain and the Squirrel, The. Emerson. BeLS; BoTP; FaBoBe;
  GoJo
  (Fable: "Mountain and the Squirrel, The.") AmPP; AnAmPo; BLPL;
    FaBV; FaFP; FaPON; LiTA; NBLV; OBAL; OBCA; OnMSP
Fable: "O the vines were golden, the birds were loud." Frederic Prokosch.
  WaP
Fable: "Once upon a time/ there was a lonely wolf." János Pilinszky, *tr.*
  by Ted Hughes *and* János Csokits. MHuP; OBVE; RB
Fable: "Pity the girl with crystal hair." Joan Aiken. WSC
Fable: "Tale is every time the same, The." Maurice James Craig. NeIP
Fable: "There is an inevitability." Norman Harris. NYBP
Fable: "Under a dung-cake." D. J. Opperman, *tr. by* Jack Cope. PeSA
Fable at the end of April is linear, The. The Modern Fable. Nishiwaki
  Junzaburo, *tr. by* Hiroaki Sato. FCEI
Fable for Critics, A, *sels.* James Russell Lowell.
  Bryant. NOBA; TAP
  Cooper. NOBA; OxBA; TAP
  Hawthorne. AmPP; NOBA; OxBA; TAP
  Holmes. NOBA
  Irving. TAP
  Lowell. AmPP; NOBA; OxBA; TAP
    (On Himself.) AA
  Poe and Longfellow. AmPP; NOBA; OxBA; TAP
    (Poe.) TAP
  "There are truths you Americans need to be told." OBSV
  "There comes Emerson first, whose rich words, every one." NAAL-1
    (Emerson.) AmPP; NOBA; OxBA; TAP
  To His Countrymen. AA
  Whittier. AmPP; NOBA; OxBA
Fable in Two Languages, A, *sel.* Charles W. Pratt.
  Hoity-Toity Oyster, The. SoTCo

Fable Merchant, The. Charles Dobzynski, *tr. fr. French by* Charles
  Guenther. VWA
Fable of Midas, The. Swift. APAS
Fable of the Magnet and the Churn, The. W. S. Gilbert. *Fr.* Patience.
  FaPON; OnMSP
Fable of the Piece of Glass and the Piece of Ice, The. John Hookham
  Frere. OxBChV
Fable of the Speckled Cow. D. J. Opperman, *tr. fr. Afrikaans by* Jack
  Cope, Uys Krige *and* Ruth Miller. PeSA
Fable of the War, A. Howard Nemerov. NePoEA; OBWP
Fabled beast there is that's called Comreigh, A. The Comreigh Critter.
  Gerrit Komrij, *tr. by* Jacob Lowland. DuIn
Fables, *sels.* John Gay.
  Butterfly and the Snail, The. FM
  Lion and the Cub, The. GN
  Turkey and the Ant, The. PBBP
  Wild Boar and the Ram, The. FM; NOEC
Fabric I must keep mended. Rend. Jorie Graham. NAmP
Fabrication of Ancestors. Alan Dugan. CAPP; NoAM
Fabrics swirled in a thousand. Sanetomo, *tr. fr. Japanese by* Burton
  Watson. *Fr.* Twenty-four Tanka. FCEI
Fabulary Satire IV. Daryl Hine. NOBC
Fabullus I will treat you handsomely. Catullus, *tr. by* Richard Lovelace.
  OBVE
Façade, *sels.* Dame Edith Sitwell.
  Hornpipe. FaBoMo; GTBS-P; OAEL-2; SeCePo
  Sir Beelzebub. BoWoP; FaBoWP; HoPM; MoAB; MoBrPo; OxBTC;
    PrIm
    (When Sir Beelzebub.) FaBoMo
  Trio for Two Cats and a Trombone. NAEL-2
  Waltz. RR
Facades for Norma Cole. Michael Palmer. LP
Face, A. Robert Browning. CTC
Face, The. Anthony Euwer. *See* Limeratomy, The: As a Beauty I Am
  Not a Star.
Face. Eugène Guillevic, *tr. fr. French by* Teo Savory. RHTwFP
Face, The. Karoniaktatie. STE
Face. Koh Chang-soo, *tr. fr. Korean by the author.* ACKP
Face, The. Philip Levine. DiL
Face, A. Marianne Moore. OxBSP
Face. Robert Morgan. GeTw
Face, The. Edwin Muir. GTBS-P
Face, The. Shin Dong-jip, *tr. fr. Korean by* Koh Chang-soo. ACKP
Face. Jean Toomer. CDC; NoP
Face-down; odor. Terror. Denise Levertov. PoE
Face drifting away—motley grimace! Farewell in the Basilica. Peter
  Handke, *tr. by* Beth Bjorklund. CoAuP
Face fair as jade! Returning to my Distant Home. Wen T'ing-yün, *tr. by*
  Lois Fusek. ATF
Face grown inward. Eight Poems for August. Lance Henson. NOVW
Face in the Ceiling, The. Stephen Dobyns. BLA
Face in the Mirror, The. Robert Graves. NoP; WeW
Face in the water said, The. Counsel. Naomi Lewis. Mes
Face is quite smooth, The. Goethe's Death Mask. Linda Gregg.
  MAYP
Face Lost in the Wilderness. Fadwa Tuqan, *tr. fr. Arabic by* Patricia
  Alanah Byrne, Salma Khadra Jayyusi, *and* Naomi Shihab Nye. MAP
Face of all the world is changed, I think, The. Elizabeth Barrett
  Browning. *Fr.* Sonnets from the Portuguese, VII. RB
Face of Christ, The. Ch'iao Lin, *tr. fr. Chinese by* Dominic Cheung.
  IFON
Face of Creation, The. Otto Orban, *tr. fr. Hungarian by* Jascha Kessler.
  FOC
Face of Dürer, The. Jon Anderson. NAmP
Face of Helen, The. Christopher Marlowe. *See* Doctor Faustus:
  Was this the face that launched a thousand ships?
Face of Love, The. Ingrid Jonker, *tr. fr. Afrikaans by* Jack Cope. PeSA
Face of Poverty. Lucy Smith. PoNe
Face of the Horse, The. Nikolai Alekseevich Zabolotsky, *tr. fr. Russian
  by* Daniel Weissbort. RB
Face of the landscape is a mask, The. Mask. Stephen Spender. MoAB;
  MoBrPo
Face of the precipice is black with lovers, The. Salvador Dali. David
  Gascoyne. EAS; OxBTC
  (In Defence of Humanism.) FaBoMo
Face of the Waters, The. Robert David Fitzgerald. CBAP; PoAu-2
Face on the floor, The. Hugh D'Arcy. *See* Face upon the floor, The.
Face reigned on the water, A. Two Hands on the Water. Zuhur Dixon,
  tr. by Patricia Alanah Byrne *and* Salma Khadra Jayyusi. MAP
Face that should content me wonders well, A. Sir Thomas Wyatt. CTC;
  EnLoPo; OBSC
Face the Nation. Allen Ginsberg. *Fr.* Wichita Vortex Sutra. NaP
Face, A? There. Between Us. James Merrill. PoE

Face to Face. Adrienne Rich. LiTM; NAAL-2; NoAM; NoP
Face to face and in the face. Ray DiPalma. LP
Face to Face with Reality. John Oxenham. WBLP
Face to face with the sunflower. The Secret Joy. Mary Webb. BoTP
Face up/ they hold her naked body. Ala. Grace Nichols. AIW
Face upon [or on] the Floor, The. Hugh Antoine D'Arcy. BeLS; BLPA; FaBoBe; FaFP; FPL
Face we met yesterday we cannot see again, The. The Face. Shin Dong-jip, tr. by Koh Chang-soo. ACKP
Faced to the island, Mackinnon's boat. Mackinnon's Boat. Charles Tomlinson. AnAn
Faceless pig grunted far away, A. Breyten Breytenbach May Look at the Moon. "Lucebert," tr. by Larry Ten Harmsel. DuIn
Faces. David Chapman Berry. BXAP
Faces. John Ciardi. WeW
Faces, The. Robert Creeley. NoAM
Faces. Walt Whitman. PoEL-5
Faces and Skulls. Jan Carew. PVCV
Faces from a Bestiary. X. J. Kennedy. NePoEA-2
Faces in a door a row of faces. On Parade. Fragano Ledgister. PBCV
Faces in the Street. Henry Lawson. CBAP
Faces may alter, names can't change. Nathaniel Lee to Sir Roger L'Estrange. Nathaniel Lee. FaBoEE
Faces of the children, The. Without Song. Grace Nichols. PBCV
Faces of women long dead, of our family, The. Women Songs. Kadya Molodowsky, tr. by Adrienne Rich. OV
Faces Seen Once. James Dickey. NoAM
Faces surround me that have no smell or color no time. Chain. Audre Lorde. BlSi; ER
Faces that stab the eye are familiar, The. The Thirteenth Telegram ("Faces that stab the eye are familiar"). Abd al-Aziz al-Maqalih, tr. fr. Arabic by Lena Jayyusi and Christopher Middleton. Fr. Telegrams of Tenderness for Sanaa. MAP
Facing a streetlight under batty moths. The Calculation. David Wagoner. NYBP
Facing It. Yusef Komunyakaa. MT
Facing the Chair. "Hugh MacDiarmid." FaBoMo
Facing the New Year. Mark Guy Pearse. BLRP
Facing West from California's Shores. Walt Whitman. MoAmPo; NAAL-1; TAP
Facing Wine with Memories of Lord Ho, sel. Li Po, tr. fr. Chinese by Burton Watson.
  "Wild man of Ssu-ming Mountain." Fr. 1. CoBCP
Facing you, on the wall, across from your bed. Yün Shou-p'ing, tr. fr. Chinese by Jonathan Chaves. Fr. Mourning for Lü Hui-chiu. CoBLCP
Fact. Kenneth Rexroth. OBAL
Fact is, The. Some Me of Beauty. Carolyn M. Rodgers. CNA
Faction du Muet. René Char, tr. fr. French by Thomas Merton. RHTwFP
Faction, that ever dwells. Fulke Greville. Fr. Caelica, XXIX. (Love and Fortune.) OBSC
Factories and trains lose luster. Anthracite. Bartolo Cattafi, tr. by Lawrence R. Smith. NItP
Factory Girl, The. "Bill o' th' Hoylus End." PF
Factory Girl, The. J. A. Phillips. SaC
Factory Girl, The. Unknown. SaC
Factory Girl's Come-All-Ye, The. Unknown. AmFP; OBAL
Factory Hands, The. Polycarp Chimedza. WMBCH
Factory Rainbow, A. Rose Saadi. SaC
Factory Windows Are Always Broken. Vachel Lindsay. FaFP; LiTA; OBCA; OxBSP
Facts. Cecilia Bustamante, tr. fr. Spanish by David Tipton. Per
Facts. "Lewis Carroll." FaBoUs
Facts. W. H. Davies. BrPo
Facts have no eyes. One must. Observation of Facts. Charles Tomlinson. NePoEA-2
Fade in the sound of summer music. Notes for a Movie Script. M. Carl Holman. AmNP; PoBA; PoNe
Faded boy in sallow clothes, A. Emily Dickinson. PoEL-5
Faded Face, The. Thomas Hardy. QFR
Faded Pictures. William Vaughn Moody. AnAmPo
Faded vine flowers. Saito Mokichi, tr. by Geoffrey Bownas and Anthony Thwaite. PeBJV
Fading Beauty. Giovanni Battista Marino, tr. fr. Italian by Samuel Daniel. AWP
Fading Beauty. Unknown. FaBoEE
Fading, desolate: at the autumn coloring. Teika, tr. fr. Japanese by Hiroaki Sato. Fr. Eighty-four Tanka. FCEI
Fading-Leaf and Fallen-Leaf. Richard Garnett. EBVV
Fading mist unveils spring's scene by the jade tower, A. Echoing Heaven's Everlastingness. Niu Chiao, tr. by Lois Fusek. ATF

Fading Rose, The, sel. Philip Freneau.
  "Here—for they could not help but die." AA
Fading, sick, again I hear of war. Wu Wei-yeh, tr. fr. Chinese by Jonathan Chaves. Fr. Country Scene. CoBLCP
Fading Skiff, The. Henrietta Cordelia Ray. CBWP-3
Faerie Fair, The. Florence Harrison. BoTP
Faerie Queene, The, sels. Spenser.
  Address to Venus. Fr. De Rerum Natura, fr. the Latin of Lucretius. AWP
    (Prayer to Venus.) EiL
  "And is there care in heaven? and is there love." Fr. II, 8. NOCV; OAEL-1
    (Guardian Angels.) OBSC
  Artegall and Radigund. Fr. V, 5. OBSC
  "As pilot well expert in perilous wave." Fr. II, 7. OAEL-1
    (Cave of Mammon, The.) PoEL-1
    "At length they came into a larger space." FiP, sts. 21-32.
  "At length nigh to the sea they drew." Fr. V, 2. NoP
  August. Fr. VII, 7. GN
  Autumn. Fr. VII, 7. GN
  "Ay me, how many perils doe unfold." Fr. I, 8. OAEL-1
  Balme. Fr. I, 11. CH
  Behold, O Man. Fr. II, 6. EiL
  Bower of Bliss, The. Fr. II, 12. PoEL-1
    "And in the midst of all, a fountaine stood." CH
    "Eftsoones they heard a most melodious sound." NOBE; OBSC; SCV
    "Thence passing forth, they shortly do arruve." FiP
  Britomart at Isis' Church. Fr. V, 7. PoE
  Cave of Despair, The. Fr. I, 9. OBNV
    "Ere long they come, where that same wicked wight." NOBE; OAEL-1
  Cymochles and Phaedria. Fr. II, 6. OBSC
  Dame Nature. Fr. VII, 7. PoEL-1
  Dance of the Graces, The. Fr. VI, 10. OBSC
    (Dance, The.) TrGrPo
  Despair. Fr. I, 9. SeCePo
  Dragon, The. Fr. I, 11. SeCePo
  Envy. Fr. I, 4. TW
  "Faire knight (quoth he) Hierusalem that is." Fr. I, 10. FaBoPV
  "Faire sir," quoth she, "be not displeasd at all."" Fr. II, 6. MOS
  Fight of the Red Cross Knight and the Heathen Sansjoy, The. Fr. I, 5. FiP
  "From thence into the open fields he fled." Fr. VI, 9. OBSC
  Garden of Adonis, The. Fr. III, 6. NOBE; PoEL-1
    "In that same gardin all the goodly flowres." NOBE
  Garden of Proserpina, The. Fr. II, 7. ChTr
  "Gentle knight was pricking on the plaine, A." Fr. I, 1. EBEV; NAEL-1; OAEL-1
  Happy Isle. Fr. IV, 10. OBSC
  "Hard is the doubt, and difficult to deeme." Fr. IV, 9. OAEL-1
  "He there now does enjoy eternal rest." Fr. I, 9. MOS
    (Sleep after Toil.) ChTr
  Hill of the Graces, The. Fr. VI, 10. NOBE
  House of Ate, The. Fr. IV, 1. OBSC
  House of Richesse, The. Fr. II, 7. CH
  "In such luxurious plentie of all pleasure." Fr. IV, 10. OAEL-1
  "It fortuned (as faire it then befell)." Fr. I, 11. OAEL-1
  Kinds of Trees to Plant. Fr. I, 1. OHIP
  Legend of Britomartis, or of Chastitie, The. Fr. III. NAEL-1, much abr.
    Britomart in the House of Busirane. Fr. III, 11-12. FiP
  Legend of the Knight of the Red Cross, or of Holiness, The. Fr. I, 1-12.
    (Invocation to the Faerie Queene.) FiP
    ("Lo! the man, whose muse whilome did maske.") OAEL-1
  Legend of the Knight of the Red Crosse, or of Holinesse, The. Fr. I, 1-12. NAEL-1; OAEL-1, abr..
    (Invocation to the Faerie Queene.) FiP, induction only.
  "Like as a ship, that through the ocean wyde." Fr. VI, 12. MOS
  "Like as the tide that comes from th' Ocean main." Fr. IV, 3. HoPM
  Mask of Cupid, The. Fr. III, 12. OBSC
    (Masque of Cupid, The.)
    "Noble Mayde, still standing, all this vewd, The." PoEL-1
    "First was Fancy, like a lovely boy, The." NOBE
  Mask of Mutability, The. Fr. VII, 7. OBSC
    (Seasons, The.) GN
  May. Fr. VII, 7. GN
  Mermaids, The. Fr. II, 12. ChTr
  Mutability. Fr. VII, 7 and 8. PoEL-1
  Nature's Reply to Mutability. Fr. VII, 7 and VIII, 1. NOBE
  Nought is on earth more sacred or divine. Fr. V, 7. OAEL-1
  "Now, at the time that was before agreed." Fr. VII, 7. OAEL-1
  "Now strike your sailes, ye jolly mariners." Fr. I, 12 and II, 6. MOS

"O what an endelesse worke have I in hand." *Fr.* IV, 12. MOS

Prince Arthur. *Fr.* I, 7. OBSC

"Redoubted knights, and honorable Dames." *Fr.* III, 9–10. NoP

"Right well I wrote, most mighty soveraine." *Fr.* II *induction.* OAEL-1

Rivers Come to the Hall of Proteus for the Marriage of the Thames and the Medway, The. *Fr.* IV, 2. FaBoPP

"Rugged forhead that with grave foresight, The." *Fr.* IV *proem..* OAEL-1

(Love.) OBSC

Scudamor in the Temple of Venus. *Fr.* IV, 10. PoE

Sea Monsters. *Fr.* II, 12. ChTr

"So as they travelled, the drouping night." *Fr.* IV, 5. OAEL-1

"So forth she comes, and to her coche does clyme." *Fr.* I, 4. NAEL-1; OAEL-1

"So oft as I with state of present time." *Fr.* V *proem.* OAEL-1

"Sudden upriseth from her stately palace." *Fr.* I, 4. PPP

Summer. *Fr.* VII, 7. GN

Temple of Venus, The. *Fr.* IV, 10. EIL

"Then said that royall Pere in sober wise." *Fr.* I, 12. OAEL-1

"Thence forward by that painfull way they pas." *Fr.* I, 10. OAEL-1

"There the most daintie Paradise on ground." *Fr.* II, 12. EBEV

"They sate to meat, and Satyrane his chaunce." *Fr.* III, 9. OAEL-1

"Tho when as chearelesse night ycovered had." *Fr.* III, 12. OAEL-1

"Thus being entered, they behold around." *Fr.* II, 12. OAEL-1

"Well may I weene, faire ladies, all this while." *Fr.* III, 6. OAEL-1

What If Some Little Paine the Passage Have. *Fr.* I, 9. CH

"When I bethinke me on that speech whyleare." *Fr.* VII, 8. OAEL-1

"Whiles someone did chant this lovely lay, The." *Fr.* II, 12. OBVE

(Gather the Rose.) EIL

(Song of Bliss.) FF

"Who now does follow the foule Blatant Beast." *Fr.* VI, 10. OAEL-1

"Who travels by the wearie wandring way." OBD

Winter. *Fr.* VII, 7. GN

Faeries' Song, The. Ben Jonson. *See* Gypsies Metamorphosed, The: Faery Beam upon You, The.

Faery Beam upon You, The. Ben Jonson. *Fr.* The Gypsies Metamorphosed. EBEV; OxBSP; TEP

(Faeries' Song, The.) SeCV-1

(Gipsy Song.) FaBoCh

Faery Song. Keats. *See* Fairy Song.

Faeryland. Robert Pinsky. MAYP

Fafnir and the Knights. Stevie Smith. Mes

Fag-End. Philip O'Connor. EAS

Faggots and their friends now live in Ramrod, The. Larry Mitchell. GLP

Faggots created a rite of cleansing, The. The faggots sit in a circle. Sons and Fathers. Larry Mitchell. GLP

Faggots in Ancient Rome. Juvenal, *tr. fr. Latin.* *Fr.* Satires, II. PeHV

Fagots blazed, the caldron's smoke, The. The Brewing of Soma. Whittier. PoEL-4

Faht's in there? What's in There? *Unknown.* CH

Failing Long Island light, The. Mother and Son. William Heyen. GeTw

Failure, A. C. Day Lewis. NOBE

Failure. Alfred Gong, *tr. fr. German by* Beth Bjorklund. CoAuP

Failure. Kate Tucker Goode. PWR

Failure. Richmond Lattimore. PCP

Failure. Henrietta Cordelia Ray. CBWP-3

Failure and Success. Richard Watson Gilder. PWR

Failures. Arthur W. Upson. WGRP

Fain I Would. *Unknown.* EIL

Fain would I be sleeping, dreaming. The Plaint of the Wife. *Unknown, tr. by* W. R. S. Ralston. AWP

Fain Would I Change That Note. *At. to* Tobias Hume. EIL; ELP; OBS; PoEL-2

(No Other Choice.) EBEV; GBL; NOBE; TrGrPo

Fain would I have a pretty thing. A Proper Song, Entitled: Fain Would I Have a Pretty Thing to Give unto My Lady. *Unknown.* CoMu; EIL; InvP

Fain would I rival thee. To the Eagle. Mary Weston Fordham. CBWP-2

Fain Would I Wed. Thomas Campion. NAEL-1

Faint Echo. Zelda, *tr. fr. Hebrew by* Bernhard Frank. MHeP

Faint, faint and clear. The Wind-swept Wheat. "Madeline Bridges." AA

Faint Falls the Gentle Voice. Henry Timrod. AH

Faint-flushed buds awake within the cup, The. Awakening. Henrietta Cordelia Ray. CBWP-3

Faint Heart. Rufinus Domesticus, *tr. by* F. A. Wright. ErPo

Faint Music. Walter de la Mare. FaBoCh

Faint now in the evening pallor. Silver Jubilee. Llewelyn Wyn Griffith. OBWVE

Faint shines the far moon. The Road. Nikolay Platonovich Ogarev, *tr. by* P. E. Matheson. AWP

Faint stars wake and wonder, The. On the River. William Vaughn Moody. AnAmPo

Faintheart in a Railway Train. Thomas Hardy. CTC; EnLoPo

Faintly as a fisherman's bonfire way in the offing. Princess Shikishi, *tr. fr. Japanese by* Hiroaki Sato. *Fr.* Seventy-eight Tanka. FCEI

Faintly, in the dawn moonlight. Teika, *tr. fr. Japanese by* Hiroaki Sato. *Fr.* A Compendium of Good Tanka. FCEI

Faintly the spring, it seems. Emperor Gotoba, *tr. by* Geoffrey Bownas *and* Anthony Thwaite. PeBJV

Fair am I, mortals, as a stone-carved dream. La Beauté. Baudelaire, *tr. by* Lord Alfred Douglas. AWP

Fair Amazon of Heaven who tookst in hand. To Saint Margaret. Henry Constable. ACP

Fair Amoret is gone astray. A Hue and Cry after Fair Amoret. Congreve. NOEC; OBEV

Fair and bright assembly, A: never strode. Thomas Lovell Beddoes. *Fr.* Death's Jest Book, II, iii. CTC

Fair and Fair. George Peele. *Fr.* The Arraignment of Paris. EIL; OBEV

(Oenone and Paris.) NOBE

(Song of Oenone and Paris.) OBSC

Fair and Unfair. Robert Francis. VGW

Fair Annie ("It's narrow, narrow make your bed"). *Unknown.* ESPB; FaBoBa

Fair Annie ("Learn to mak your bed, Annie"). *Unknown.* OxBB

Fair Annie ("O wha will bake my bridal bread"). *Unknown.* ESPB

Fair Annie ("There livd a lord on yon sea-side"). *Unknown.* ESPB

Fair Annie ("Reivers they stole Fair Annie, The"). *Unknown.* CH

Fair Annie an Sweet Willie. Lord Thomas and Fair Annet. *Unknown.* ESPB

Fair Annie had a costly bower. The Holy Nunnery. *Unknown.* ESPB

Fair Annie of Lochryan. *Unknown.* AS

Fair are the flowers and the children, but their subtle suggestion is fairer. Indirection. Richard Realf. AA

Fair as the night, when all the astral fires. Love Sonnets, VIII. Charles Harpur. PoAu-1

Fair at Windgap, The. Austin Clarke. OxBTC; SeCePo

Fair Beauty Bride, The. *Unknown.* AmFP

Fair below Helvellyn, The. Wordsworth. *Fr.* The Prelude [or, Growth of a Poet's Mind]: Residence in London. FaBoPP

Fair blue sky, A. Breeze and Billow. Albert Durrant Watson. CaP

Fair by inheritance, whom born we see. Of the Nativity of the Lady Rich's Daughter. Henry Constable. OBSC

Fair Caroline, I wonder what. To C. F. H. on Her Christening-Day. Thomas Hardy. NAs

Fair Cassidy. *Unknown, tr. fr. Irish by* Donagh MacDonagh. BIrV

Fair cheek under a merry blue eye, two brows, A. The Beloved. David Roberts, *tr. by* H. Idris Bell. OBWVE

Fair Cloris in a pig-stye lay. A Song to Cloris. Earl of Rochester. ErPo

Fair copy of my Celia's face. To T. H., a Lady Resembling My Mistress. Thomas Carew. CaPo

Fair Cynthia, all the Homage that I may. Thoughts on the Sight of the Moon. Sarah Kemble Knight. SCAP

Fair Cynthia mounted on her sprightly pad. Cynthia on Horseback. Philip Ayres. EnLoPo

Fair daffodils [*or* Faire daffadills], we weep to see. To Daffodils [*or* Daffadills]. Robert Herrick. AWP; BoNaP; CaPo; ELP; FaBoCh; GN; GoJo; GTBS; GTBS-P; InPS; JCP; LiTB; NOBE; NoP; OBEV; OBS; PoEL-3; PoRA; PPP; QFR; SeCP; SeCV-1; TrGrPo; TTTS; UnPo

Fair Damsel from London, The. *Unknown.* AmFP

Fair Danubie is praised for being wide. Rivers. Thomas Storer. EIL; FaBoCh

Fair Days; or, Dawns Deceitful. Robert Herrick. CaPo

Fair England. Helen Gray Cone. AA

Fair Eve knelt close by the guarded gate. The Rose of Eden. Susan K. Phillips. BeLS

Fair Eyes, Ye Mortal Stars Below. Giovanni Battista Guarini, *tr. fr. Italian by* Philip Ayres. PFI

"Fair, fair," cry the ospreys. *Unknown, tr. by* Arthur Waley. BoS

Fair fields, proud Flora's vaunt, why is't you smile. Menaphon's Ditty. Robert Greene. *Fr.* Menaphon. OBSC

Fair flower of fifteen springs, that still. To His Young Mistress. Pierre de Ronsard, *tr. by* Andrew Lang. AWP

Fair Flower of Northumberland, The. *Unknown.* ESPB; OxBB

Fair flower, that dost so comely grow. The Wild Honeysuckle. Philip Freneau. AA; AmPP; AnAmPo; BLPL; LiTA; NAAL-1; NOBA; OxBA; PoEL-4; PoLF; TAP; TrGrPo

Fair, fragile Una, golden-haired. The Enchanted Shell. Henrietta Cordelia Ray. CBWP-3

Fair girl tripping out to meet her love, A. The Power of Interval. Lord De Tabley. NOBVV; OxBSP

Fair Golden Age! When milk was th' onely food. Sir Richard Fanshawe, *after the Italian of* Giovanni Battista Guarini. *Fr.* Il Pastor Fido. OBVE
(Golden Age, The.) OAEL-1; PFI

Fair gull on the water's bank. The Seagull. Siôn Phylip, *tr. by* Joseph P. Clancy. OBWVE

Fair Helen. *Unknown. See* I wish I were where Helen lies.

Fair Hills of Ireland, The. *Unknown, tr. fr. Modern Irish by* Sir Samuel Ferguson. FaBoPP; OBEV

Fair Hope with lucent light in her glad eyes. The Quest of the Ideal. Henrietta Cordelia Ray. CBWP-3

Fair in Frosty May. László Nagy, *tr. fr. Hungarian by* Tony Connor. MHuP

Fair in the Woods, The. Thom Gunn. AnAn

Fair Ines. Thomas Hood. EnRP; OBEV

Fair Iris I love, and hourly I die. Dryden. *Fr.* Amphitryon. AWP
(Mercury's Song [to Phaedra].) OxBSP; PoEL-3; SeCV-2

"Fair is Alexis," I no sooner said. On Alexis. Plato, *tr. by* Thomas Stanley. AWP

Fair is each budding thing the garden shows. The Old-fashioned Garden. John Russell Hayes. AA

Fair is her body, bright her eye. Medieval Norman Song ("Fair is her body, bright her eye"). *Unknown, tr. by* John Addington Symonds. AWP

Fair is my dove, my loved one. Marriage Song. Judah Halevi, *tr. by* Alice Lucas. TrJP

Fair Is My Love. Samuel Daniel. *See* To Delia:
Fair is my love, and cruel as she's fair.

Fair Is My Love. Robert Greene. *Fr.* Perimedes [*or* Perimedes, the Blacksmith]. EiL

Fair Is My Love. *At. to* Shakespeare. *Fr.* The Passionate Pilgrim, VII. EiL

Fair is my love, and cruel as she's fair. Samuel Daniel. *Fr.* To Delia. AAS; NOBE; NoP; OBSC; TEP; TrGrPo
(Beauty, Time and Love.) OBEV
(Fair Is My Love.) LiTB
(Sonnet: "Fair is my love, and cruel as she's fair.") EiL; HoPM

Fair [*or* Faire] is my love that feeds among the lilies. Bartholomew Griffin. *Fr.* Fidessa, More Chaste than Kind, XXXVII. EiL; ErPo; GBL; PoEL-2; TrGrPo

Fair is not my face. A Woman Grows Soon Old. Larin Paraske, *tr. by* Jaakko A. Ahokas. PBWP

Fair is Our Lord's Own City. *Unknown, tr. fr. Irish by* Coslett Quin. TIRV

Fair Is the Rose. *Unknown.* EiL

Fair Is the World. William Morris. FaBoRV
(Autumn on the Upper Thames.) FaBoPP

Fair Is Too Foul an Epithet. Christopher Marlowe. *See* Tamburlaine the Great:
Ah, fair Zenocrate, divine Zenocrate.

Fair Isabel, poor simple Isabel! Isabella; or, The Pot of Basil. Keats. EnRP

Fair Isabel sat in her bower door. Hind Etin. *Unknown.* OxBB

Fair Isabell of Rochroyall. *Unknown.* OxBB

Fair Isle at Sea—thy lovely name. Robert Louis Stevenson. NOBVV

Fair Janet ("If you do love me weel, Willie"). *Unknown.* ESPB

Fair Janet ("Ye maun gang to your father, Janet"). *Unknown.* ESPB; OxBB, *with music*

Fair lady Isabel sits in her bower sewing. Lady Isabel and the Elf-Knight. *Unknown.* ESPB; FaBoBa

Fair lady, will you travel. The Wooing of Etain. *Unknown, tr. by* John Montague. BIrV

Fair lady with the bandaged eye. Ode to Fortune. Fitz-Greene Halleck *and* Joseph Rodman Drake. *Fr.* The Croaker Papers. AA

Fair Lass of Islington, The. *Unknown. See* There was a lass of Islington.

Fair little girl sat under a tree, A. Good Night and Good Morning. Richard Monckton Milnes. BoTP; OxBChV

Fair Lucy was sitting in her own cabin door. Lizie Wan. *Unknown.* AmFP

Fair Lunacy! I see thee, with a crown. Mirthful Lunacy. Thomas Tod Stoddart. *Fr.* The Death-Wake; or, Lunacy. OBNC

Fair Maid and the Sun, The. Arthur O'Shaughnessy. BeLS

Fair Maid by the Shore, The. *Unknown.* AmFP

Fair Maid of Amsterdam, The. *Unknown.* OxBoLi; RB

Fair Maid of the Exchange, The. *At. to* Thomas Heywood.

Fair Maid of the West, The. *Unknown.* CoMu

Fair maid sat in her bower-door, A. The False Lover Won Back. *Unknown*

Fair Maiden. George Peele. *See* Old Wives' [*or* Wife's] Tale, The: Gently Dip.

Fair maiden, fair maiden. Invocation to the Muse. Richard Hughes. MoBrPo

Fair maiden, white and red. A Voice [Speaks] from the Well. George Peele. *Fr.* The Old Wives' [*or* Wife's] Tale. FaBoCh; NOBE; OBSC; OxBoLi

Fair Margaret and Sweet William ("As it fell out in a long summer's day"). *Unknown.* ESPB, A *vers.*; OxBB, *with music.*

Fair Margaret and Sweet William ("Little Marg'et sitting in her high hall door"). *Unknown.* AMFP

Fair Margaret and Sweet William ("Sweet William he would a-wooing ride"). *Unknown.* OBET

Fair Margaret and Sweet William ("Sweet William would a wooing ride"). *Unknown.* ESPB, B *vers.*

Fair Margret was a young ladye. Proud Margret. *Unknown.* OxBB
(Proud Lady Margaret.) ESPB, B *vers.*

Fair Marjorie sat i her bower-door. Young Benjie. *Unknown.* ESPB

Fair Mary of Wallington. *Unknown.* ESPB
(Bonny Earl of Livingston, The.) OxBB

Fair Mary sat at her father's castle gate. Willie of Winsbury. *Unknown.* AmFP

Fair Mildred wide her lattice threw. Mildred's Doves. Henrietta Cordelia Ray. CBWP-3

Fair morn unbars her gates of gold. Dawn's Carol. Henrietta Cordelia Ray. CBWP-3

Fair Morning, The. Jones Very. NOBA

Fair Mother Earth lay on her back last night. Ode to the Spirit of Earth in Autumn. George Meredith. TEP

Fair Musidora starry-eyed. Musidora's Vision. Henrietta Cordelia Ray. CBWP-3

Fair nights beneath the mellow moon. The Maid of Ehrenthal. Henrietta Cordelia Ray. CBWP-3

Fair now is the springtide, now earth lies beholding. The Message of the March Wind. William Morris. OBNC; WiR

Fair, order'd lights (whose motion without noise). The Constellation. Henry Vaughan. SeCV-1

Fair Pamela came to town, The. Pamela in Town. Ellen Mackay Hutchinson Cortissoz. AA

Fair Phoebe and Her Dark-eyed Sailor. *Unknown.* AmFP

Fair Phyllis I saw sitting all alone. *Unknown.* GBL

Fair [*or* Faire] pledges of a fruitful tree. To Blossoms. Robert Herrick. BoNaP; CaPo; GTBS; GTBS-P; JCP; NAEL-1; OBEV; OBS; SeCP; SeCV-1

Fair princess of the spacious air. The Falcon. Richard Lovelace. CaPo; PBBP

Fair rebel to thyself and time. The Revenge. Pierre de Ronsard, *tr. by* Thomas Stanley. AWP

Fair, Rich, and Young. Sir John Harington, *after the Latin of* Martial. EiL; NIP; SeCePo
(Of a Fair Shrew.) FaBoEE

Fair rocks, goodly rivers, sweet woods, when shall I see peace? Echo. Sir Philip Sidney. *Fr.* Arcadia. SiPS

Fair Roslin Chapel, how divine. Roslin and Hawthornden. Henry van Dyke. AA

Fair Salamis, the billow's roar. Sophocles, *tr. fr. Greek by* Winthrop Mackworth Praed. *Fr.* Ajax. AWP

Fair seed-time had my soul, and I grew up. Childhood and School-Time. Wordsworth. *Fr.* The Prelude [*or*, Growth of a Poet's Mind], I. CH; GN; HAP; NOBE; NOBE; NoP; NoP; NU; OBNC; PoE; SCV
(Introduction—Childhood and School-Time.) PoEL-4
(On the Solitary Fells around Hawkshead.) FaBoPP

Fair Sex Avenged by the Fair Sex, or a New Satire on Husbands, The, *sel.* Mlle de———, *tr. fr. French by* Dorothy Backer.
"Thalia, you will remember that recently I made." DMF

Fair shadow, faithless as my sun! The Dream. Sir Edward Sherburne. OxBSP

Fair, shining mountains of my pilgrimage. The Brecon Beacons and the Black Mountains. Henry Vaughan. FaBoPP

Fair ship, that from the Italian shore. Tennyson. *Fr.* In Memoriam A. H. H., IX. PeHV

Fair Singer, The. Andrew Marvell. EnLoPo; MeLP; MePo; NOBE; NoP; PoEL-2

Fair Sou-Chong-Tee, by a shimmering brook. Story of the Flowery Kingdom. James Branch Cabell. OnMSP

Fair stands the wind again. Henley, July 4: 1914-1964. L. E. Sissman. PrIm

Fair star, new-risen to our wondering eyes. Bacchylides. George Meason Whicher. AA

Fair star of evening, splendor of the west. Composed by the Seaside, near Calais, August, 1802. Wordsworth. EnRP; Son

Fair [or Faire] stood the wind for France. Agincourt. Michael Drayton. BeLS; EIL; FaBoBe; FaBoCh; OBEV
   (Ballad of Agincourt, The.) FaPoR; OBNV; PoRA
   (Battle of Agincourt, The.) GN
   (His Ballad of Agincourt.) PoE
   (To the Cambro-Britons and Their Harp, His Ballad of Agincourt.) OBS; OBWP; PrIM

Fair Summer Droops. Thomas Nashe. Fr. Summer's Last Will and Testament. EIL
   (Waning Summer.) OBSC; OxBSP

Fair sun, if you would have me praise your light. Henry Constable. Fr. Diana. OBSC

Fair, sweet and young, receive a prize. Dryden. OBS

Fair Sylvia. Unknown. OBS

Fair, that you may truly know. To Amoret. Edmund Waller. SeCV-1

Fair, the young acacia, thick with leaves. The Young Acacia. Hayyim Nahman Bialik, tr. by Helena Frank. TrJP

Fair these broad meads—these hoary woods are grand. Canadian Boat Song. At. to John Galt and also to "Christopher North." BLPA; CaP; FaBoCh; FaPoR; GoTS; OBEV; OBNC; OxBS

Fair Thou Art. Mordecai ben Isaac, tr. fr. Hebrew by Herbert Loewe. TrJP

Fair-tinted cheeks, clear eyelids drawn. Cimabuella. Bayard Taylor. BXAP

Fair Ursly, in a merry mood. Annibal Cruceius. FaBoEE

Fair Virtue, the Mistress of Philarete ("I wandered out awhile agone."), sels. George Wither.
   Divided Heart, The. TrGrPo
   Hence, Away, You Sirens, also given in Fidelia EIL
   Shall I Wasting in Despair, also given in Fidelia EIL; LiTB; OBS
     (Author's Resolution, The.) AWP; OBEV
     (Lover's Resolution, A.) BoLoP; NOBE
     (Manly Heart, The.) FaBV; GTBS; GTBS-P
     (Sonnet: "Shall I, wasting in despair.") SeCV-1
     (What Care I.) TrGrPo

Fair was the dawn, and but e'en now the skies. Fair Days; or, Dawns Deceitful. Robert Herrick. CaPo

Fair was this yonge wyf, and therwithal. Chaucer. Fr. The Canterbury Tales: The Miller's [or Milleres] Tale. EBEV

Fair were our visions! Oh, they were as grand. In the Land Where We Were Dreaming. Daniel B. Lucas. PAH

Fair witch crept to a young man's side, A. The Witch-Bride. William Allingham. NOBVV

Fair women I saw passing where she passed. Guido Cavalcanti, tr. by Ezra Pound. PFI

Fair Would I Have a Prettie Thing to Give unto My Ladie. Unknown. See Fair would I have a pretty thing.

Fair would I have a pretty thing. Unknown. EIL
   (Fair Would I Have a Prettie Thing to Give unto My Ladie.) CoMu
   (Fair Would I Have a Pretty Thing.) InvP

Faire as unshaded Light; or as the Day. To the Queene, Entertain'd at Night by the Countesse of Anglesey. Sir William Davenant. MeLP; MePo; OBS

Faire Daffadills. Robert Herrick. See Fair Daffadils.

Faire Is My Love. Bartholomew Griffin. Fr. Fidessa, More Chaste than Kind, XXXVII. GBL; PoEL-2
   (My Love.) TrGrPo
   (Sonnet: "Fair is my love that feeds among the lilies.") EIL; ErPo

Faire is my love that feeds among the lilies. See Fair is my love that feeds among the lilies.

Faire knight (quoth he) Hierusalem that is. Spenser. Fr. The Faerie Queene, I, 10. FaBoPV

"Faire sir," quoth she, "be not displeasd at all." Spenser. Fr. The Faerie Queene, II, 6. MOS

Fairest action of our human life, The. Lady Elizabeth Carey. Fr. Mariam, IV. WPE

Fairest day that ever yet has shone, The. The Lost. Jones Very. NOBA; QFR

Fairest flower, all flowers excelling. To a Child Five Years Old. Nathaniel Cotton. OxBChV

Fairest isle, all isles excelling. Song of Venus. Dryden. Fr. King Arthur. OxBoLi; PoEL-3

Fairest Lord Jesus. Unknown, tr. fr. German. WGRP

Fairest of Freedom's Daughters. Jeremiah Eames Rankin. PAH

Fairest of Her Days, The. Unknown. EIL

Fairest of stars, that with your persant light. Balade Simple. John Lydgate. GBL

Fairest thing that shines below. Clad All in White. Abraham Cowley. Fr. The Mistress. SeCV-1

Fairfax, whose name in armes through Europe rings. On the Lord Gen. Fairfax at the Siege of Colchester. Milton. OBS

Fairground. W. H. Auden. NYBP

Fairies, The. William Allingham. AnIL; CH; ChTr; FaBoCh; FaBoPP; FaBV; FaPON; Mes; NOBE; NOBVV; OBEV; OnMSP; OxBChV; PDV; RHPC; WSC
   (Up the Airy Mountain.) FaFP

Fairies. Hilda Conkling. WSC

Fairies. Eleanor Farjeon. RAR

Fairies. Rose Fyleman. FaPON; OxBChV

Fairies, The. Robert Herrick. FaPON; OBS

Fairies, The. Patricia Hubbell. WSC

Fairies, The. Unknown. BoTP

Fairies Are Dancing All Over the World, The. Michael Rumaker. GLP; PeHV

Fairies are taken into the world, The. Scenes of Childhood. Carl Morse. GLP

Fairies Break Their Dances, The. A. E. Housman. OxBSP

Fairies' Farewell, The. Charlotte Brontë. FL

Fairies Feast, The. Charles M. Doughty. CH

Fairies Have Never a Penny to Spend, The. Rose Fyleman. FaPON

Fairies hold a fair, they say, The. The Faerie Fair. Florence Harrison. BoTP

Fairies' Lullaby, The. Shakespeare. See Midsummer Night's Dream, A: You Spotted Snakes [with Double Tongue].

Fairies of the Caldon-Low, The. Mary Howitt. BeLS

Fairweill. Unknown. OxBS

Fairy and the soul proceeded, The. The Magic Car Moved On. Shelley. Fr. Queen Mab, I. GN

Fairy Blessing, The. Shakespeare. See Midsummer Night's Dream, A: Now the Hungry Lion Roars.

Fairy Book, The. Norman Gale. OHIP

Fairy Cobbler, The. A. Neil Lyons. BoTP

Fairy Dances. At. to John Lyly and to Thomas Ravenscroft. See Mayde's Metamorphosis, The: By the Moon ("By the moon we sport and play").

Fairy Dawn. Joseph Rodman Drake. Fr. The Culprit Fay. GN

Fairy Dream, A. Dorothy Graddon. BoTP

Fairy! Fairy! list and mark. The Fay's Crime. Joseph Rodman Drake. Fr. The Culprit Fay. GN

Fairy Feet. Phyllis L. Garlick. BoTP

Fairy Flute, The. Rose Fyleman. BoTP

Fairy Harpers, The. James B. Dollard. CaP

Fairy in Armor, A. Joseph Rodman Drake. Fr. The Culprit Fay. FaPON

Fairy Land, 1. Shakespeare. See Midsummer Night's Dream, A: Over Hill, over Dale.

Fairy Land, 2. Shakespeare. See Midsummer Night's Dream, A: You Spotted Snakes [with Double Tongue].

Fairy Lullaby. Shakespeare. See Midsummer Night's Dream, A: You Spotted Snakes [with Double Tongue].

Fairy Music. Enid Blyton. BoTP

Fairy Palace, The, sel. Michael Drayton. This Palace Standeth in the Air. Mes

Fairy Ring, The. Unknown. BoTP

Fairy Ring, The. Andrew Young. ChTr

Fairy Shoemaker, The. Phyllis L. Garlick. BoTP

Fairy Sleep and Little Bo-Peep, The. Unknown. BoTP

Fairy Song. Keats. FaPON
   (Faery Song.) CH

Fairy Song, A. John Lyly. Fr. Endymion. OBSC

Fairy Song. Winthrop Mackworth Praed. SeCePo

Fairy Song ("Now the hungry lion roars."). Shakespeare. See Midsummer Night's Dream, A: Now the Hungry Lion Roars.

Fairy Song ("Now, until the break of day."). Shakespeare. See Midsummer Night's Dream, A: Now, Until the Break of Day.

Fairy Song ("Over hill, over dale"). Shakespeare. See Midsummer Night's Dream, A: Over Hill, over Dale.

Fairy Song ("You spotted snakes with double tongue."). Shakespeare. See Midsummer Night's Dream, A: You Spotted Snakes [with Double Tongue].

Fairy Song. W. B. Yeats. See Land of Heart's Desire, The: Wind Blows out of the Gates of the Day, The.

Fairy spirits of the breeze. Unwritten Poems. William Winter. AA

Fairy Story. Robert Penn Warren. See Hunt, hunt again.

Fairy Straighttalk. Carl Morse. GLP

Fairy Tale. Gust Gils, *tr. fr. Dutch by* Koos Schuur. DuIn
Fairy Tale. Miroslav Holub, *tr. fr. Czech by* George Theiner. RB
Fairy Tale, A. Kenneth Mackenzie. PoAu-2
Fairy Tales. Itzig Manger, *tr. fr. Yiddish by* Miriam Waddington. VWA
Fairy Temple; or, Oberon's Chapel, The. Robert Herrick. CaPo
Fairy Thorn, The. Sir Samuel Ferguson. CH; OnMSP; OnYI
Fairy Went a-Marketing, A. Rose Fyleman. BoTP; OxBChV
Fairyland. Poe. NAAL-1
Fairyland. Rabindranath Tagore. WSC
Fairy's Reply to Saturn, The. Thomas Hood. *Fr.* The Plea of the Midsummer Fairies. OBNC
Fairy's Wander-Song. Shakespeare. *See* Midsummer Night's Dream, A: Over Hill, over Dale.
Faith. Ada Cambridge. PoAu-1
Faith. William Dean Howells. *See* What Shall it Profit?
Faith. Frances Anne Kemble. FaBoBe
Faith. John Richard Moreland. OHIP
Faith. Ray Palmer. *See* My Faith Looks Up to Thee.
Faith. Pope. *Fr.* An Essay on Man, Epistle III. WGRP
Faith. George Santayana. *See* Sonnets: O world, thou choosest not the better part!
Faith. John Banister Tabb. WGRP
Faith. Lorenzo Thomas. UL
Faith. Victor J. Daley. PoAu-1
Faith. Ella Wheeler Wilcox. BLRP
Faith and Freedom. Wordsworth. *See* It Is Not to Be Thought Of [That the Flood].
"Faith and Practice." John Balaban. GOA
Faith and Sight. Anna M. King. BLRP
Faith and Works. Muriel Spark. OxBSP
Faith-Healer. *Unknown. See* There was a faith-healer of Deal.
Faith Healing. Philip Larkin. NoAM
Faith, Hope and Charity. Juan Gonzalo Rose, *tr. fr. Spanish by* Ena Hollis. Per
Faith, Hope and Love. *Unknown.* BLRP
Faith, I Wish I Were a Leprechaun. Margaret Ritter. FaPON
Faith is a fine invention. Emily Dickinson. AmPP; FaBV; NAAL-1; NOBA; OxBA; TAP
Faith—is the pierless bridge. Emily Dickinson. AmPP
"Faith, master, whither you will." Captain Car; or, Edom o Gordon. *Unknown.* ESPB
Faith on Trial, A, *sel.* George Meredith.
   "Dream is the thought in the ghost, The." WGRP
Faith sees beyond the grave. Faith, Hope and Love. *Unknown.* BLRP
Faith shuts her eyes. Faith. Victor J. Daley. PoAu-1
Faith Trembling. "Madeline Bridges." AA
Faithful, The. Jane Cooper. NePoEA-2; SM
Faithful, The. Michael Waters. KS
Faithful Blackbird. Juan Ramón Jiménez, *tr. fr. Spanish by* Perry Higman. LPSS
Faithful Friend, The. William Cowper. FM
Faithful helm commands the keel, The. At Best. John Boyle O'Reilly. AA
Faithful Lover, The. Robert Pack. NePoEA
Faithful Lovers, The. Jorge Guillén, *tr. fr. Spanish by* Perry Higman. LPSS
Faithful Shepherd, The, *sel.* Giovanni Battista Guarini, *tr. fr. Italian by* Sir Richard Fanshawe.
   Golden Age, The. *Fr.* IV, ix. PFI
Faithful Shepherdess, The, *sels.* John Fletcher.
   Come, Shepherds, Come! *Fr.* I, iii. EIL; ErPo
   God of Sheep, The. *Fr.* V, v.. EIL; FaBoCh
      (To Pan.) TrGrPo
   Priest's Chant, The. *Fr.* II, i. OBS
      (Evening Knell, The.) EIL
      (Evening Song.) GN
      (Folding the Flocks.) CH
   River God, The ("I am this fountain's god"). *Fr.* III, i. TrGrPo
   River-God's Song, The ("Do not fear to put thy feet"). *Fr.* III, i. FaPON; MoShBr
      (Song: "Do not fear to put thy feet.") EIL; OBS
   Satyr's Farewell, The. *Fr.* V, i. OBS
   Satyr's Song. *Fr.* IV, i. OBS
   "Sing his praises that doth keep." *Fr.* I, ii. OBS
      (Hymn to Pan.) NOBE; OBEV
Faithful unto Death. Richard Handfield Titherington. PAH
Faithful watcher sits alone, A. The Watcher. Clara Ann Thompson. CBWP-2
Faithful Wife, The. Barbara L. Greenberg. SM
Faithfully Tinying at Twilight Voice. E. E. Cummings. NYBP
Faithless. Louis Lavater. PoAu-1
Faithless familiars. November. Elizabeth Daryush. QFR

Faithless Nelly Gray. Thomas Hood. BXAP; EnRP; FaBoCo; NA; NOBL
Faithless Sally Brown. Thomas Hood. NOBL; OBNV
   (Sally Brown.) FaBoCo
Faithless Shepherdess, The. *Unknown. See* Unfaithful Shepherdess, The.
Faithless Wife, The. Federico García Lorca, *tr. fr. Spanish.* BoLoP, *tr. by* A. L. Lloyd; ErPo, *tr. by* Robert O'Brien.
Faith's Difficulty. Theodore Maynard. TrPWD
Faith's Vista. Henry Abbey. AA
Faker. Malka Heifetz-Tussman, *tr. fr. Yiddish by* Kathryn Hellerstein. AYP
Faking Boy, The. *Unknown.* RB
Fakir (a religious well known in the East), A. The Fakir. Richard Owen Cambridge. OBTV
Falcon, The. Wilfrid Scawen Blunt. *Fr.* The Love Sonnets of Proteus, II. ACP
Falcon, The. Richard Lovelace. CaPo; PBBP
Falcon, The. Richard Henry Stoddard. AA
Falcon, The. *Unknown. See* Corpus Christi Carol ("Lully, lullay [*or* lulley], lully, lullay [*or* lully]."
Falcon and the Dove, The. Sir Herbert Read. BrPo; FaBoMo
Falcon soars, The. Angelica the Doorkeeper. *Unknown, tr. by* Anne Pennington. RB
Falconer of God, The. William Rose Benét. WGRP
Falconers. Lady Luck. Ann Gottlieb. NMM
Falconry. Anne Wilkinson. MoCV; OBCV
Falcons, The. W. S. Merwin. CAPP
Falkland at Newbury, 1643. Hugh Conway. EBVV
Fall, The. William Barnes. PoEL-4
Fall. Mary Ursula Bethell. ATNZ
Fall, The. Russell Edson. LCAP
Fall, The. Sir Richard Fanshawe, *after the Italian of* Giovanni Battista Guarini. *Fr.* Il Pastor Fido. MePo; OBS
   (Great Favorit Beheaded, A.) OBVE
Fall. Robert Francis. VGW
Fall. Robert Hass. AmPA
Fall, The. Alois Hergouth, *tr. fr. German by* Beth Bjorklund. CoAuP
Fall. Sydney Lea. BLA
Fall, The. Czeslaw Milosz, *tr. fr. Polish by* Czeslaw Milosz *and* Lillian Vallee. OBD
Fall, The. Milton. *See* Paradise Lost: Thus saying, from her husband's hand her hand.
Fall, The. Leonard Nathan. BLA
Fall, The. Earl of Rochester. EnLoPo
Fall. Michael Smith. CIP
Fall and Exile, *sel.* Edmond Jabès, *tr. fr. French by* Rosemarie Waldrop.
   "By the wayside." *Fr.* IV. RHTwFP
Fall and the bees. Where do these evenings take me. In a Park, in Siena, at Twilight. Ory Bernstein, *tr. by* Warren Bargad *and* Stanley F. Chyet. IP
Fall back, all worlds, into the abyss. Feast of the Most Holy Trinity. Aubrey Thomas De Vere. TIRV
Fall breezes/ time to try out the. Kyorai, *tr. fr. Japanese by* Burton Watson. *Fr.* Twenty Hokku. FCEI
Fall chrysanthemums have beautiful colors. T'ao Ch'ien, *tr. fr. Chinese by* Burton Watson. *Fr.* Drinking Wine, VII. CoBCP
Fall Comes in Back-Country Vermont. Robert Penn Warren. NYBP; VGW
Fall days are not entirely free of heat. Sitting at Night on the Moonlit Terrace. Yang Wan-li, *tr. by* Burton Watson. CoBCP
Fall Down. Calvin C. Hernton. CNA; PoBA
Fall eats its leaf from my hand, The: we are friends. Corona. Paul Celan, *tr. by* Joachim Neugroschel. VWA
Fall has come, clear as the eyes of chickens, The. Silence. Robert Bly. NaP
Fall In. Lincoln Kirstein. MoP
Fall in Long Island. Lake Success. Robert Conquest. OxBC
Fall Is Here, The. Mrs. Henry Linden. CBWP-4
Fall Journey. William Stafford. NaP
Fall, Leaves, Fall. Emily Brontë. CH; ELP; FaBoCh; FaBoRV; FaBV; OxBSP; PoEL-5; TrGrPo
Fall 1961. Robert Lowell. OBWP; VGW
Fall of Hyperion, The, *sels.* Keats.
   Dream, A. *Fr.* I. OAEL-2; OBNC
   "Fanatics have their dreams, wherewith they weave." EnRP; OAEL-2; TOF
   "Towards the altar sober-paced I went." *Fr.* I. TOF
Fall of J. W. Beane, The. Oliver Herford. OBAL
Fall of Leaves. Derek S. Savage. PoA
Fall of Maubila, The. Thomas Dunn English. PAH

Fall of Princes, The, *sel.* John Lydgate.
  Letter of Compleynt of Canace, The. *Fr.* I. OxBLMV
Fall of Rain at Miti-Miti, A. Hone Tuwhare. ATNZ
Fall of Richmond, The. Herman Melville. PAH
Fall of Rome, The. W. H. Auden. InPS; MAT; OAEL-2; OxBTC;
  UnPo
Fall of Tecumseh, The. *Unknown*
Fall of the Angels, The. Milton. *See* Paradise Lost: Is this the region,
  this the soil, the clime.
Fall of the City, The, *sel.* Archibald MacLeish.
  Voice of the Studio Announcer. HoPM
Fall of the House of Usher, The, *sel.* Poe.
  Haunted Palace, The. AA; BeLS; CH; ChTr; LiTA; NOBA; OxBA;
  PoEL-4; PrIm; TAP; TrGrPo; WiR; WSC
Fall on, frost! Oemaru, *tr. by* Geoffrey Bownas *and* Anthony Thwaite.
  PeBJV
Fall Practice. Dabney Stuart. SM
Fall rains/ scum collecting on. Masaoka Shiki, *tr. fr. Japanese by* Burton
  Watson. *Fr.* Thirty-nine Haiku. FCEI
Fall, snow, and cease not! Flake by flake. Aubrey Thomas De Vere. *Fr.*
  A Year of Sorrow. ACP
Fall To. Howard Jones. NBP
Fall which twisted love to lust, The. In Praise of Music in Time of
  Pestilence. Daryl Hine. OBCV
Fall winds wail in mulberry branches. Castleside Song. Wang Ch'ang-
  ling, *tr. by* Burton Watson. CoBCP
Fallen, The. Vera Bax. CN
Fallen, The. Duncan Campbell Scott. TrPWD
Fallen as he is, this king of birds still seems. The Dead Eagle. Thomas
  Campbell. EnRP; OBTV
Fallen away now. Prince Munenaga, *tr. by* Steven D. Carter. WFTW
Fallen Elm, The. John Clare. FaBoPV
Fallen flower I see. Moritake, *tr. by* Geoffrey Bownas *and* Anthony
  Thwaite. PeBJV
Fallen flowers rise. Moritake, *tr. by* Harold G. Henderson. SoSe
Fallen from heaven, lies across. River. Ted Hughes. NAEL-2
Fallen? How fallen? States and empires fall. On the Defeat of Henry Clay
  [*or* of a Great Man]. William Wilberforce Lord. AA; PAH
Fallen Leaves. Kathryn Munro Tupper. CaP
Fallen leaves are scattered by evening rain. Regretful Thoughts. Yü
  Hsüan-chi, *tr. by* Geoffrey Waters. BoWoP
Fallen leaves, driven by the wind, invade Po-hsia. Po-hsia. Ku Yen-wu,
  tr. by J. P. Seaton. WFTU
Fallen leaves, fallen leaves. *Unknown, tr. fr. Chinese by* Arthur Waley.
  BoS
Fallen Leaves in a Valley. Sogi, *tr. fr. Japanese by* Steven D. Carter.
  WFTW
Fallen Majesty. W. B. Yeats. PoA
Fallen pile! I ask not what has been thy fate. Netley Abbey. William
  Lisle Bowles. Son
Fallen Star, The. George Darley. OBEV
Fallen Tower of Siloam, The. Robert Graves. WaP
Fallen Tree, The. Patrick Maybin. NeIP
Fallen Tree, The. Andrew Young. BoNaP
Fallen with autumn's falling leaf. On the Death of President Garfield.
  Oliver Wendell Holmes. PAH
Fallen Yew, A. Francis Thompson. BrPo; MoAB; MoBrPo
Fallen Zulu Commander, The. C. M. Van Den Heever, *tr. fr. Afrikaans
  by* Uys Krige *and* Jack Cope. PeSA
Falling. James Dickey. LCAP; MT; NoAM; NYBP
Falling. Bob Kaufman. PoBA
Falling Asleep. Siegfried Sassoon. MoBrPo; OxBTC
Falling Asleep. Ian Serraillier. DuDa
Falling Asleep over the Aeneid. Robert Lowell. MoAmPo; OxBA
Falling Down to Bed. Nila NorthSun. STE
Falling flower, The. Moritake, *tr. by* Babette Deutsch. SoSe
Falling forever. Oche Iron. Peter Blue Cloud. HATNAP
Falling, I caught the curtain. On the Other Side. Czeslaw Milosz, *tr. by*
  Jan Darowski. OBD
Falling ill on a journey, my dreams run round a withered field. Composed
  While Ill. Basho, *tr. fr. Japanese by* Burton Watson. *Fr.* Seventy-
  six Hokku. FCEI
Falling in Love. Jon Anderson. MAYP
Falling in love with a mustache. Uneasy Rider. Diane Wakoski. NIP
Falling Leaves. Ch'iao Lin, *tr. fr. Chinese by* Dominic Cheung. IFON
Falling Leaves. Wu Chia-chi, *tr. fr. Chinese by* Irving Lo. WFTU
Falling leaves/ fall and pile up. Kyotai, *tr. fr. Japanese by* Burton
  Watson. *Fr.* Sixteen Hokku. FCEI
Falling Leaves before the Wind. Shotetsu, *tr. fr. Japanese by* Steven D.
  Carter. WFTW
Falling leaves leave the trees. Poem on Falling Leaves. Liu E, *tr. by*
  Jonathan Chaves. CoBLCP

Falling leaves, making no sound. Issa, *tr. fr. Japanese by* Hiroaki Sato.
  Fr. Forty-four Hokku. FCEI
Falling Moon. Roberta Hill. CDW
Falling of the Snow, The. Raymond Souster. CaP
Falling Out. Helen Chasin. IHMS
Falling separate into the dark. Late at Night. William Stafford. NNaP;
  RFM
Falling Star, The. "Ping Hsin," *tr. fr. Chinese by* Kai-yu Hsu. *Fr.*
  Spring Waters. PBWP
Falling Star, The. Sara Teasdale. MoShBr; OBCA; PDV
Falling Teeth. Shih Jun-chang, *tr. fr. Chinese by* William Shultz.
  WFTU
Fallow Deer at the Lonely House, The. Thomas Hardy. AWP; CH;
  CMoP; OxBSP; RB; TTTS
Fallow Field, The. Julia Caroline Ripley Dorr. AA
Fallow fields, dark pewter sky. Winter Drive. James McAuley. PoA
Falls, The. F. D. Reeve. NYBP
Falls Funeral. John Montague. CIP
Falls of Glomach, The. Andrew Young. OxBS; PoSH
Falltime. Carl Sandburg. PoA
False Achitophel, The. Dryden. *See* Absalom and Achitophel, Pt. I
False beauty who, although in semblance fair. Ballade to His Mistress.
  Villon, *tr. by* Norman Cameron. WeW
False Bride, The. *Unknown.* OBET
False Country of the Zoo. Jean Garrigue. LiTM
False Dawn. Walter de la Mare. FaBoNo
False dreams, all false. Iliad. Humbert Wolfe. MoBrPo
False Enchantment. Jean Starr Untermeyer. MoAmPo
False Favorite's Downfall, The. *Unknown.* APAS
False Fox, The. *Unknown.* ChTr; GBP; PBBP
False Friends-like. William Barnes. NOBVV
False Gallop of Analogies, A. Warham St. Leger. CenHV; FaBoCo;
  FiBHP
False Gods. Walter de la Mare. EaLo
False Heart, The. Hilaire Belloc. FaBoCh; FaBoEE; OxBSP
  (For False Heart.) MoBrPo
False hope which feeds but to destroy, and spill. Mary Sidney Wroth,
  Countess of Montgomery. *Fr.* Urania: Pamphilia to Amphilanthus.
  NAEL-1
False Knight and the Wee Boy, The. *Unknown. See* False Knight upon
  the Road, The.
False Knight upon [*or* on] the Road, The. *Unknown.* AmFP; CH; EnSB;
  ESPB; GBP
  (False Knight and the Wee Boy, The.) FaBoCh; OxBoli; OxBS
False life! a foil and no more. Quickness. Henry Vaughan. ELP;
  MeLP; MePo; NOBE; NOCV; OBS; SeCePo; SeCP; SeCV-1
False Love. At. to John Lilliat. EBEV; OBSC
  (Song: "When love on time and measure makes his ground.") EIL
False Love. Sir Walter Ralegh. *See* Farewell to False Love, A.
False Lover Won Back, The ("Fair maid sat in her bower-door, A").
  Unknown ESPB
False Lover Won Back, The ("Sun shines high on yonder hill, The").
  Unknown. ESPB; OxBB
False Luve, and Hae Ye Played Me This? *Unknown.* GBP
False Nancy. *Unknown.* AmFP
False Security. Sir John Betjeman. CMoP; NoAM; NoP
False Sir John a wooing came. May Colven. *Unknown.* OxBB; TrGrPo
False Though She Be. Congreve. BoLoP; NOBE; OBEV; OxBSP
  (Song: "False though she be to me and love.") EnLoPo
False words of the Buddhists and Taoists, The. Yang Shih-ch'i, *tr. fr.
  Chinese by* Jonathan Chaves. *Fr.* Rhymed Words Sent to My Eldest
  Son. CoBLCP
False world, good night. Since thou hast brought. To the World; a
  Farewell for a Gentlewoman, Virtuous and Noble. Ben Jonson.
  JCP; QFR; SeCP
False World, Thou Liest. Francis Quarles. *See* Emblems: Wilt Thou Set
  Thine Eyes upon That Which Is Not?
False Youth: Autumn: Clothes of the Age. James Dickey. CAPP; MT
Falsehood. William Cartwright. OBEV
Falstaff's Song. Edmund Clarence Stedman. AA
Fame. Robert Browning. SoSe
Fame. Byron. *Fr.* Childe Harold's Pilgrimage, IV. FiP
Fame. Eleanor Hollister Cantus. GoYe
Fame. Emerson. AnAmPo
Fame. Kahlil Gibran, *tr. fr. Arabic by* Adnan Haydar *and* Michael Beard.
  MAP
Fame. Josephine D. Henderson Heard. CBWP-4
Fame. Robert Herrick. FaBoEE
Fame. Charlotte Mew. BrRo; InPK; PBWP
Fame. John Banister Tabb. AA
Fame and Fortune. Michael Drayton. *Fr.* The Legend of Robert, Duke
  of Normandy. OBSC
Fame and Friendship. Austin Dobson. OBEV

Fame is a fickle food. Emily Dickinson. TAP
Fame is a food that dead men eat. Fame and Friendship. Austin Dobson. OBEV
Fame let thy trumpet sound. Joel Barlow. AmPP
Fame, like a wayward girl, will still be coy. Keats. *Fr.* Two Sonnets on Fame, I. EnRP
Fame Makes Us Forward. Robert Herrick. CaPo
Fame, wisdom, love, and power were mine. All Is Vanity, Saith the Preacher. Byron. TrCP
Famed ship *California*, a ship of high renown, The. The Girls around Cape Horn. *Unknown.* AmFP
Fame's pillar here, at last, we set. The Pillar of Fame. Robert Herrick. CaPo; JCP; NIP; SeCP
Familial. Jacques Prévert, *tr. fr. French.* OBD; *tr.* by D. J. Enright; POS, *tr.* by Mark Strand *and* Jean Ballard.
Familiar Epistle, A. Ann Murry. WPE
Familiar Epistle to J. B. Esq., A, *sels.* Robert Lloyd. "Mark yon round parson, fat and sleek." OBSV
Public Schools. NOEC
Familiar Faces, Long Departed. Robert Hillyer. NYBP
Familiar Friends. James S. Tippett. BoTP
Familiar Landscapes. Lawrence Raab. BLA
Familiar Letter to Several Correspondents, A. Oliver Wendell Holmes. FaBoUs
Familiar Lines. *Unknown.* FiBHP
Familiar Music. Bill Berkson. UL
Familiar sound/ of a dog's rough bark, The. Teika, *tr.* by Steven D. Carter. WFTW
Familiar Story. Alan Shapiro. DiPo
Familiar, year by year, to the creaking wain. The Sower. Laurence Binyon. MMA
Families. Thomas Blackburn. OxBSP
Families, when a child is born. On the Birth of His Son. Su Tung-p'o, *tr.* by Arthur Waley. AWP; OBVE; OFD
Family. Hugo Claus, *tr. fr. Dutch by* James S. Holmes. DuIn
Family. Norman MacCaig. FF
Family, A. W. S. Merwin. CAPP
Family. Josephine Miles. FaBoWP; FYAP; GrPl
Family. Tanikawa Shuntaro, *tr. fr. Japanese by* Geoffrey Bownas *and* Anthony Thwaite. PeBJV
Family Album, A. Alter Brody. VWA
Family Album. Lonny Kaneko. BrSi
Family Cat, The. Roy Fuller. OxBC; TEP
Family Court. Ogden Nash. FiBHP
Family 8. Lyn Lifshin. NeAC
Family Evening. Dan Huws. NYBP
Family Fool, The. W. S. Gilbert. *Fr.* Yeoman of the Guard. NBLV
Family Fortunes. C. H. Sisson. OxBC
Family Goldschmitt, The. Henri Coulette. CoAP; FF
Family Grove. Albert Goldbarth. HCAP
Family Jewels. Essex Hemphill. GLP
Family Life. Allan M. Laing. FiBHP
Family Man, A. Maxine W. Kumin. IHMS; TAP
Family Matter, A. Allen Curnow. *Fr.* Trees, Effigies, Moving Objects, VII. PeNZ
Family Name, The. Charles Lamb. Son
Family of crinkled leaves, A. The Fire Tree. "Adunis," *tr.* by Abdullah al-Udhari. MPAW
Family of Eight, The. Abraham Reisen, *tr. fr. Yiddish by* Marcia Falk. VWA
Family Outing—a Celebration. Nicki Jackowska. BrRo
Family Photograph. Gerald Vizenor. VoR
Family Photograph 1939, A. James Keir Baxter. OxBC
Family Pictures. Mervyn Morris. PBCV
Family Portrait. Carlos Drummond de Andrade, *tr. fr. Portuguese by* Elizabeth Bishop. ATCBP
Family portrait not too stale to record, A. Father and Son: 1939. William Plomer. PeSA
Family Portraits. Mary E. Tucker. CBWP-1
Family Prime. Mark Van Doren. VGW
Family Reunion. Louise Erdrich. HATNAP; NoAM
Family Reunion. Maxine W. Kumin. CAPP
Family Reunion. Hollis Spurgeon Summers. GoYe
Family reunion. Nakamura Kusadao, *tr.* by Geoffrey Bownas *and* Anthony Thwaite. PeBJV
Family Romance. Larry Levis. MAYP; NAmP
Family Scene: Mid-Twentieth Century. Linda Pastan. PPR
Family story tells, and it was told true, The. Funnel. Anne Sexton. MoAmPo
Family that has a true follower of the Lord, A. Ravidas, *tr.* by John Stratton Hawley *and* Mark Juergensmeyer. SSI
Family tombs, The. Inscribed on Sun An-chih's "Painting of Pines and Catalpas." Chao Meng-fu, *tr.* by Jonathan Chaves. CoBLCP

Family Trees. Douglas Malloch. OHIP
Family Turn, A. William Stafford. CAPP
Famine once we had. New England's Growth. William Bradford. PAH
Famine Road, The. Eavan Boland. FaBoWP
Famine Song. *Unknown.* WTO
Famine Winter. Hans Vlek, *tr. fr. Dutch by* James S. Holmes. DuIn
Famine Year, The. Lady Wilde. TIRV
Famished end to my tale this night, A. Maghnas O Domhnaill. NOIV
Famous animals. Holiday Inn at Bemidji. Gerald Vizenor. STE
Famous Archer, The. Park Je-chun, *tr. fr. Korean by* Koh Chang-soo. ACKP
Famous Ballad of the Jubilee Cup, The. Sir Arthur Quiller-Couch. NA
Famous Fight at Malago; or, The Englishmen's Victory over the Spaniards, The. *Unknown.* CoMu; OxBSS
Famous Flower of Serving-Men; or, The Lady Turn'd Serving-Man, The. *Unknown.* ESPB; OBET; OxBB
Famous horse, A. *Unknown, tr.* by Geoffrey Bownas *and* Anthony Thwaite. PeBJV
Famous kingdom of the birds, The. Somewhere Is Such a Kingdom. John Crowe Ransom. CMoP; LiTA
Famous Poet. Ted Hughes. LiTM; PoPo
Famous poet Everette, The. The Great Man's Death: An Anecdote. Everette Maddox. MT
Famous Sea-Fight, A. John Looke. CoMu
Famously she descended, her red hair. A Recollection. John Peale Bishop. LiTA; Son
Fan. Walter Lew. BrSi
Fan and the Observatory Dome, The. Shauqi Abi Shaqra, *tr. fr. Arabic by* Abdullah al-Udhari. MPAW
Fan from Korea, A. Chu Yün-ming, *tr. fr. Chinese by* Jonathan Chaves. CoBLCP
Fan-Piece, for Her Imperial Lord. Ezra Pound. MoAB
Fan, the Filly. Wilfrid Thorley. BoTP
Fanaticism? No. Writing is exciting. Baseball and Writing. Marianne Moore. BoWoP
Fanatics have their dreams, wherewith they weave. Keats. *Fr.* The Fall of Hyperion. EnRP; OAEL-2; TOF
Fanciest dive that ever was dove, The. Fancy Dive. Shel Silverstein. ASP
Fancy, The. William Rose Benét. SD
Fancy. Robert Creeley. NOBA
Fancy. Keats. EnRP; OBEV
(Realm of Fancy, The.) GTBS; GTBS-P
Fancy, A. Thomas Lodge. *See* Life and Death of William Longbeard, The: Rose, The.
Fancy, A. Thomas Lodge. *Fr.* Rosalynde; or Euphues' Golden Legacy. EiL; OBSC
(Love's Protestation.) ACP
Fancy. Shakespeare. *See* Merchant of Venice, The: Tell Me Where Is Fancy [or Fancie] Bred.
Fancy. Jonathan Smedley. OxBSP
Fancy, A. *Unknown.* FaBoNo
Fancy, and I, last Evening walkt. To Amoret Gone from Him. Henry Vaughan. EnLoPo; MeLP; OBS; SeCP
Fancy and Imagination. Henrietta Cordelia Ray. CBWP-3
Fancy Dive. Shel Silverstein. ASP
Fancy Dress. Dorothea MacKellar. PoAu-1
Fancy Dress. Siegfried Sassoon. BrPo
Fancy Frigate, The. *Unknown.* OxBSS
Fancy halts my feet at the way-side well, A. The Way-Side Well. Joseph Seamon Cotter, Sr. CDC; PoNe
Fancy (quoth he) farewell, whose badge I long did bear. The Green Knight's Farewell to Fancy. George Gascoigne. OPOP
Fancy, which that I have served long, The. The Restless Heart. Earl of Surrey. SiPS
Fancy's Knell. A. E. Housman. FaBoCh; PoRA
Fand Yields Cuchulain to Emer. *Unknown, tr. fr. Old Irish by* Sean O'Faolain. AnIL
Fane Wald I Luve. *At. to.* Sir John Clerk. OxBS
Fanfare for the Makers, A. Louis MacNeice. NOBE
Fannie ("Fannie has the sweetest foot"). Thomas Bailey Aldrich. AnAmPo; OBAL
Fanning away the heat. A Friend Comes to Visit on a Summer Night. Mo Shih-lung, *tr.* by Jonathan Chaves. CoBLCP
Fanny, *sels.* Fitz-Greene Halleck.
"Fanny was younger once than she is now." CTC
"We owe the ancients something. You have read." OBAL
Fanny Foo-Foo was a Japanese girl. The Japanese Lovers. *Unknown.* BeLS; BLPA
Fanny! If in your arms my soul could slip. Keats to Fanny Brawne. Edgar Lee Masters. PoA

Fanny was younger once than she is now. Fitz-Greene Halleck. *Fr.* Fanny. CTC

Fanny's Removal in 1714. John Winstanley. NOEC

Fantasia. Dorothy Livesay. MoCV; OBCV

Fantasia of a Fallen Gentleman on a Cold Bitter Night on the Embankment. T. E. Hulme. *See* Once, in a finesse of fiddles found I ecstasy.

Fantasies of old age. Merced. Adrienne Rich. NOBA

Fantastic Rock, The. Wu Chen, *tr. fr. Chinese by* Jonathan Chaves. CoBLCP

Fantastic Simile, A. Thomas Lovell Beddoes. Son

Fantasy. Gwendolyn B. Bennett. BlSi; CDC

Fantasy in Purple. Langston Hughes. BANP; CDC

Fantasy of an African Boy. James Berry. PVCV

Fantasy of Little Waters, A. James Scully. NYBP

Fantasy spaceman, The. Star Trek III. Richard Harteis. GLP

Fantasy under the Moon. Emmanuel Boundzekei-Dongala, *tr. fr. French by* Gerald Moore *and* Ulli Beier. TTY

Fantoches. Paul Verlaine, *tr. by* Arthur Symons. AWP; OBMV

Far. Roger Giroux, *tr. fr. French by* Anthony Barnett. RHTwFP

Far/ farther/ and further furthering furthered. Gerhard Rühm, *tr. by* Beth Bjorklund. CoAuP

Far above us where a jay. Morning on the Lièvre. Archibald Lampman. SD

Far and near, and now, from never. Beauty. Isaac Rosenberg. TrJP

Far and wide/ outside St. Vincent. Soufrière. Andrew Salkey. PBCV

Far as creation's ample range extends. Pope. *Fr.* An Essay on Man, I *and* II. FM; ImOP

Far as man can see,/ Comes the rain. Song of the Rain Chant. *Unknown, tr. by* Natalic Curtis. AWP

Far back, in the time of ice. The Ghost Hunter. John Haines. AnAn

Far back when I went zig-zagging. Orion. Adrienne Rich. MoP; NAAL-2; NIP; NoAM; NoP; WPE

Far Brynderwyns heave across the harbour, The. Im Abendrot. K. O. Arvidson. *Fr.* The Four Last Songs of Richard Strauss at Takahe Creek above the Kaipara, III. ATNZ

Far Country, The. Robert Greacen. NeIP

Far court opens for us all July, The. Prothalamion. Maxine W. Kumin. NYBP; TSL

Far Cry after a Close Call, A. Richard Howard. NYBP; UnPo

Far Cry from Africa, A. Derek Walcott. HeIP; MoP; NAEL-2; NoAM; PVCV; TTY; UnPo

Far Cry to Heaven, A. Edith Matilda Thomas. AA; WGRP

Far different dejection once was mine. Crossing the Alps. Wordsworth. *Fr.* The Prelude [or, Growth of a Poet's Mind]: Cambridge and the Alps. OBTV; RB

Far down, down through the city's great gaunt gut. Subway Wind. Claude McKay. PBCV

Far down the Koshu Road. Nishiwaki Junzaburo, *tr. by* Hiroaki Sato. FCEI

Far down the purple wood. The Constant Bridegrooms. Kenneth Patchen. LiTM; NaP

"Far enough down is China," somebody said. Digging for China. Richard Wilbur. GoJo; GrPl; TwCP

Far faint protocols of Katherine's flute, The. Rehearsal. David Fisher. NPGG

Far, far away, beyond a hazy height. October in Tennessee. Walter Malone. AA

Far far away, the Herdboy Star. *Unknown, tr. fr. Chinese by* Burton Watson. *Fr.* Nineteen Old Poems of the Han, X. CoBCP

Far, far down. City Afternoon. Barbara Howes. AmFN

Far far from gusty waves the children's faces. An Elementary School Classroom in a Slum. Stephen Spender. FaBoMo; FF; LiTB; MoAB; MoBrPo; NIP; TrGrPo; TwCP; UnPo

Far far from here. Matthew Arnold. *Fr.* Empedocles on Etna, I, 2. GTBS-P
  (Song of Callicles, The ("Far, far from here").) FiP

Far, far from home they rode on their excursions. Two Englishmen. Douglas Stewart. CBAP

Far, far in the west. Far in the West. Douglas Fraser. PoSH

Far, far out lie the white sails all at rest. An Ocean Musing. Henrietta Cordelia Ray. CBWP-3

Far far the least of all, in want. The Prisoners. Stephen Spender. FaBoMo; MoAB; MoBrPo

Far-Farers, The. Robert Louis Stevenson. BoTP

Far-fetched with tales of other worlds and ways. Home from Abroad. Laurie Lee. OBTV

Far Field, The. Theodore Roethke. NAAL-2; NoAM; NoP; PrIm

Far from a cultural centre he was used. W. H. Auden. *Fr.* Sonnets from China, XIII. CMoP; NoAM

Far from Africa: Four Poems, *sel.* Margaret Danner. AmNP; PoBA
  Garnishing the Aviary. *Fr.* I. BPo

Far from me as the stars, the sea, and the other traditional trappings of poetical mythology. If You Only Knew. Robert Desnos, *tr. by* Michael Benedikt. POS

Far from Our Friends. Jeremy Belknap. AH

Far from our garden at the edge of a gulf. The Gulf. Denise Levertov. NNaP

Far from the Beach. Alda do Espírito Santo, *tr. fr. Portuguese by* Kathleen Weaver. OV

Far from the deep roar of the Aegean main. Plato, *tr. by* Charles Whibley. AWP

Far from the Heart of Culture. W. H. Auden. WaaP

Far from the loud sea beaches. A Visit from the Sea. Robert Louis Stevenson. FM; GN; MOS

Far from the Madding Crowd. Nixon Waterman. BLPA; FaBoBe (Vacation.) WBLP

Far from the parlour have your kitchen plac'd. William King. *Fr.* The Art of Cookery. FaBoUs

Far from the scent of the crocus. That's Life? Alan Bold. FF

Far from the tender tribe of boys remove. Albius Tibullus, *tr. fr. Latin by* John Dart. *Fr.* Odes, I, 4. PeHV

Far from the thronged luxurious town. On Honour. Bernard Mandeville. NOEC

Far from the vulgar haunts of men. On the Same. Roy Campbell. OxBTC

Far from the waves that soothed. The Lonely Shell. Martha Eugenie Perry. CaP

Far from thy dearest self, the scope. To His Mistress in Absence. Tasso, *tr. by* Thomas Stanley. AWP

Far from you I meditate on the riverbank. Meditation on the Lake. Gasper García Laviana, *tr. by* Alejandro Murguía. Vol

Far from your crumpled mountains, plains that vultures ponder. Jamaica. Louis Simpson. PBCV

Far greater numbers have been lost by hopes. Samuel Butler. FaBoEE

'Far I hear the bugle blow.' The Day of Battle. A. E. Housman. *Fr.* A Shropshire Lad, LVI. OHIP; WaaP

Far In a Western Brookland. A. E. Housman. *Fr.* A Shropshire Lad, LII. AWP; PoEL-5

Far in the country of Arden. Cassamen and Dowsabell. Michael Drayton. *Fr.* The Shepherd's Garland, Eclogue VIII (1593 ed.). OBSC

Far in the east, far below. House Song to the East. *Unknown.* TTTS

Far in the grim Northwest beyond the lines. Temagami. Archibald Lampman. OBCV

Far in the Heavens my God retires. The Incomprehensible. Isaac Watts. WGRP

Far in the land of sunny South. A Southern Scene. Priscilla Jane Thompson. CBWP-2

Far in the West. Douglas Fraser. PoSH

Far in the woods my stealthy flute. The Magic Flute. W. D. Snodgrass. NYBP

Far inland/ go my sad thoughts. *Unknown, tr. by* Knud Rasmussen. BoWoP

Far it streches, that big field. *Unknown, tr. by* Arthur Waley. BoS

Far Land, The. John Hall Wheelock. WGRP

Far like a thread. Far. Roger Giroux, *tr. by* Anthony Barnett. RHTwFP

Far moon maketh lovers wise, The. Moonlight. Walter de la Mare. EnLoPo

Far-off/ at the core of space. Swan. D. H. Lawrence. CMoP; PoE

Far off a lonely hound. The Hounds. John Freeman. OBMV; OxBSP

Far-off a young state rises, full of might. Farther. John James Piatt. AA

Far off, above the plain the summer dries. Second Air Force. Randall Jarrell. CMoP; LiTM; NAAL-2; WaP

Far off and furtive, Gopal's in the butter. Surdas, *tr. by* John Stratton Hawley *and* Mark Juergensmeyer. SSI

Far off as the reed-plain of Manu. Lady Kasa, *tr. fr. Japanese. Fr.* Manyo Shu. Ma

Far off at that wayside pool we draw. *Unknown, tr. by* Arthur Waley. BoS

Far off, far off, so faint against the sky. The Old Mountaineer. W. K. Holmes. PoSH

Far off I see the river at Meng Ford. Song of the Breaking of the Willow. *Unknown, tr. by* Burton Watson. CoBCP

Far-off, most secret, and inviolate Rose. The Secret Rose. W. B. Yeats. NAEL-2

Far-off mountain peaks. Issa, *tr. by* Geoffrey Bownas *and* Anthony Thwaite. PeBJV

Far-off mountains hide you from me, The. Absent Lover. *Unknown, tr. by* A. C. Jordan. PBA

Far off the sea is grey and still as the sky. Week-End by the Sea. Edgar Lee Masters. MoAmPo

Far, oh, far is the Mango island. The Constant Cannibal Maiden. Wallace Irwin. AnAmPo; OBAL
Far on its rocky knoll descried. Scenes from Carnac. Matthew Arnold. FaBoPP; OBTV
Far out across Carnarvon bay. The Welsh Sea. James Elroy Flecker. BrPo
Far out at sea. White Horses. Irene F. Pawsey. BoTP
Far out beyond the city's lights, away from din and roar. The Country Store. Unknown. BLPA
Far out in the wilds of Oregon. The Nonpareil's Grave. M. J. McMahon. SD
Far out of sight forever stands the sea. The Slow Pacific Swell. Yvor Winters. HeIP; MOS; NOBA; QFR
Far out, transported by the surgings of the moon. Time of the Sea. Pierre Reverdy, tr. by Michael Benedikt. POS
Far over the misty mountains cold. J. R. R. Tolkien. Fr. The Hobbit. WSC
Far pre-father of feathers, you are flying. The Pterodactyl. Philip José Farmer. BWV
Far Side of Introspection, The. Al Lee. CoAP
Far spread, below. The Story of Vinland. Sidney Lanier. Fr. Psalm of the West. PAH
Far Sweeter than Honey. Abraham Ibn Ezra, tr. fr. Hebrew by Israel Abrahams. TrJP
Far, thundering days, The. Summer Report. Klaus Demus, tr. by Beth Bjorklund. CoAuP
Far to the east I see them in my mind. The Wise Men. Edgar Bowers. NePoEA
Far to the left he saw the huts of men. East Anglian Fen. George Crabbe. Fr. Tales of the Hall. FaBoPP
Far to the south, beyond the blue, there spreads. The Second Asgard. Matthew Arnold. Fr. Balder Dead. FiP
Far Trek. June Brady. RHPC
Far up among the forest-belted mountains. The Desolate Valley. Thomas Pringle. OBTV
Far up the dim twilight fluttered. The Unknown God. "Æ." MoBrPo; WGRP
Far up the lonely mountain-side. A Georgia Volunteer. Mary Ashley Townsend. AA
Far West Once. Robert Penn Warren. BLA
Fara Diddle Dyno. Unknown. ElL; FaBoCh; FaBoCo; FaBoNo
(Madrigal: "Ha ha! ha ha! This world doth pass.") OxBoLi
Faraway hands are folded and folded. The Starry Night. George Starbuck. NYBP
Fare Thee Well. Byron. BLPA; EnRP; FaFP; FPL; OBNC; PoEL-4
Fare Thee Well. Eli Siegel. GOA
Fare thee well, my lovely Dinah, a thousand times adieu. The Holy Ground. Unknown. OxBSS
Fare thee well to Prince's Landing Stage, River Mersey fare thee well. The Leaving of Liverpool. Unknown. OxBSS
Fare Well. Walter de la Mare. GTBS-P; NOBE; OBEV
Fare Ye Well, Lovely Nancy. Unknown. OxBSS
Fare you well, my blue-eyed girl. Blue-eyed Girl. Unknown. AmFP
Fare You Well, My Darling. Unknown. AmFP
Fareweel to a' our Scottish fame. Such a Parcel of Rogues in a Nation. Burns. OxBS
Farewel, dear daughter Sara; now Thou'rt gone. In Saram. John Cotton. SCAP
Farewel to Worldly Joyes, A ("Farewel to unsubstantial joyes"). Anne Killigrew. BoWoP
Farewel ye guilded follies, pleasing troubles. Unknown. MeLP
Farewele! Advent, Christemas is come. Farewell Advent. James Ryman. MeEL
Farewell, A.: "And if I did, what then?" George Gascoigne. See Adventures of Master F. I., The: And if I did, what then?
Farewell, The: "And so, one day when the tide was away out." Pat Wilson. ATNZ
Farewell: "Far from the deep roar of the Aegean main." Plato, tr. by Charles Whibley. AWP
Farewell: "Farewell! Forget our love's declining." Nikolai Alekseyevich Nekrasov, tr. fr. Russian by Alan Myers. AAA
Farewell: " 'Farewell to barn and stack and tree.' " A. E. Housman. See Farewell to Barn and Stack and Tree.
Farewell: "Farewell to the bushy clump close to the river." John Clare. NoP
Farewell, A: "Flow down, cold rivulet, to the sea." Tennyson. FaBoRV
Farewell, The: "Gone, gone—sold and gone." Whittier. AA; AWP; PoNe
Farewell, A: "Good-bye!—no [or nay] do not grieve that it is over." Harriet Monroe. AA; PoA
Farewell, A: "I put thy hand aside, and turn away." "Madeline Bridges." AA

Farewell: "If ever fondest prayer." Byron. See Farewell! If Ever Fondest Prayer.
Farewell: "If I die." Federico García Lorca, tr. fr. Spanish by W. S. Merwin. OBD
Farewell, The: It Was A' for Our Rightfu' King. Burns. EnRP; GoTS; PoEL-4
(Farewell, A: "It was a' for our rightfu' king.") CH; OBEV
Farewell: "It will be hard." Alois Hergouth, tr. by Beth Bjorklund. CoAuP
Farewell: "Juliet, farewell. I would not be forgiven." Wilfrid Scawen Blunt. Fr. The Love Sonnets of Proteus: Farewell to Juliet, XXXIX. TrGrPo
Farewell: "Leave me, my love, it's time to part." Ibrahim Naji, tr. by Issa Boullata and John Heath-Stubbs. MAP
Farewell: "Linden blossomed, the nightingale sang, The." Heine, tr. by John Todhunter. AWP
Farewell: "My boat goes west, yours east." Chao Li-hua, tr. by J. P. Seaton. BoWoP
Farewell, A: "My fairest child, I have no song to give you." Charles Kingsley. BLPA; EBVV; GN; OxBChV
Farewell: "Not soon shall I forget—a sheet." Katharine Tynan. CH
Farewell, A: "Oft have I mused, but now at length I find." Sir Philip Sidney. Fr. Certain Sonnets. TrGrPo
Farewell: "Shores of my native land." Isaac Toussaint L'Ouverture, tr. by Edna Worthley Underwood. TTY
Farewell: "Smell of death was in the air, The." John Press. PoRA
Farewell, A: "Venus, take my votive glass." Matthew Prior. See Venus, take my votive glass.
Farewell: "What happened? My dear, don't cry. The thing." Lörinc Szabó, tr. fr. Hungarian by Edwin Morgan. Fr. Cricket Music. MHuP
Farewell, A: "What is there left to be said?" Arthur Rex Dugard Fairburn. ATNZ; PeNZ
Farewell: "What should I say." Sir Thomas Wyatt. See What should [or shulde] I say[e].
Farewell, A: "While time hustled." James Weigel, Jr. TSM
Farewell, A: "With all my will, but much against my heart." Coventry Patmore. Fr. The Unknown Eros. ACP; BoLoP; EnLoPo; GTBS-P; NOBE; OBEV; OBNC; PoEL-5; TrGrPo
Farewell: "You sang round-dance songs." Liz Sohappy Bahe. CDW
Farewell! A long farewell, to all my greatness! Wolsey's Farewell to His Greatness. Shakespeare and probably John Fletcher. Fr. King Henry VIII, III, ii. OHFP
(Cardinal Wolsey's Farewell.) LiTB
(Farewell to Greatness.) TrGrPo
Farewell, adieu, that courtly life. Haltersick's Song. John Pickering (or Pikerying). Fr. Horestes. OBSC
(Song: "Farewell, adieu, that court-like life!") ElL
Farewell Advent. James Ryman. MeEL
Farewell, all my welfare. Sir Thomas Wyatt. GBL; SiPS
Farewell and adieu to you, Spanish ladies. Spanish Ladies. Unknown. FaBoCh; OxBSS, with music
Farewell and Good. Denis Devlin. IPY
Farewell at the Hour of Parting. Agostinho Neto, tr. fr. Portuguese by Marga Holness. WMBCH
Farewell Ballad of Poppies, A. Eva Brudne. VWA
Farewell, Bristola's dingy piles of brick. Last Verses. Thomas Chatterton. TrGrPo
Farewell!—but whenever you welcome the hour. Long, Long Be My Heart with Such Memories Filled. Thomas Moore. BLPL; FaBoBe
Farewell content. Shakespeare. Fr. Othello, III, iii. TrGrPo
Farewell dear babe, my heart's too much content. In Memory of My Dear Grandchild Elizabeth Bradstreet Who Deceased August, 1665, Being a Year and a Half Old. Anne Bradstreet. NAAL-1; NOCV; SCAP; WPE
Farewell, dear love! Since thou wilt needs be gone. Unknown. ElL; OBSC
Farewell, dear scenes, for ever closed to me. Lines Written upon a Window-Shutter at Weston. William Cowper. NOEC
Farewell fair saint, may not the seas and wind. On His Mistresse Going to Sea. Thomas Cary. OBS
Farewell false friends, farewell ill wine. Farewell to England. Unknown. APAS
Farewell false love, the oracle of lies. A Farewell to False Love. Sir Walter Ralegh. BoLoP; ElL; NAEL-1
(False Love.) OBSC; SiPS
Farewell, farewell! Before our prow. Dover to Munich. Charles Stuart Calverley. NOBL, abr.; OBTV
"Farewell, farewell, my pretty maid." The True Lover's Farewell. Unknown. AS
Farewell—farewell to thee, Araby's daughter! The Peri's Lament for Hinda. Thomas Moore. Fr. Lalla Rookh. OBNC
Farewell for a While. Elizabeth Daryush. QFR

Farewell! for now a stormy morn and dark. Outward Bound. Edward Sydney Tylee. PAH

Farewell! Forget our love's declining. Farewell. Nikolai Alekseyevich Nekrasov, tr. by Alan Myers. AAA

Farewell Frost; or, Welcome the Spring. Robert Herrick. CaPo

Farewell has long been said; I have forgone thee. After a Parting. Alice Meynell. NOBVV

Farewell! If Ever Fondest Prayer. Byron. EnRP
(Farewell.) TrGrPo

Farewell in a Dream. Stephen Spender. MoAB; MoBrPo

Farewell in the Basilica. Peter Handke, tr. fr. German by Beth Bjorklund. CoAuP

Farewell, incomparable element. Hymn to Earth. Elinor Wylie. LiTM; MoAB; MoAmPo

Farewell knives and forks, I'll never wash you again. The Dishwasher. Judith Herzberg, tr. by John Rudge. DuIn

Farewell, Life. Thomas Hood. EnRP

Farewell, love, and all thy laws [or lawes] for ever. Sir Thomas Wyatt. AAS; LiTB; NAEL-1; OAEL-1; SiPS
(Lover Renounceth Love, The.) TrGrPo
(Renancing of Love, A.) GBL; Son

Farewell Mercy, farewell thy piteous grace. John Lydgate. Fr. Court of Sapience. PoEL-1

Farewell, my dearest dear, now I must leave thee. The Seamen and Soldiers' Last Farewell to Their Dearest Jewels. Unknown. OxBSS

Farewell, My Latin Master. Stephen Plaice. NPo

Farewell, my more than fatherland! A Farewell to America. Richard Henry Wilde. AA

Farewell, my tender brother. Think. Beatrice's Last Words. Shelley. Fr. The Cenci. FiP

Farewell, my Youth! for now we needs must part. Ave atque Vale. Rosamund Marriott Watson. NOBE; OAEL-2; OBEV; OBNC

Farewell now, poesy's secret cell, thy ordered grace. Farewell to Hendre Fechan. William Phylip, tr. by H. Idris Bell. OBWVE

Farewell, O Prince, farewell, O sorely tried! Theodor Herzl. Israel Zangwill. TrJP

Farewell of the Attendant Spirit. Milton. See Comus; a Masque Presented at Ludlow Castle: To the ocean now I fly.

Farewell, old friend, we part at last. My Old Straw Hat. Eliza Cook. BrRo

Farewell, Old Year! Old and New. Unknown. BLRP

Farewell, Peace. Unknown. PAH

Farewell Performance. James Merrill. BAP

Farewell, politics, utterly! What can I do? I can not. Arthur Hugh Clough. Fr. Amours de Voyage, Canto III, iii. FaBoPV

Farewell said, cover lowered. Ozaki Hosai, tr. fr. Japanese by Hiroaki Sato. Fr. One Hundred Haiku in Free Form. FCEI

Farewell, sweet boy; complain not of my truth. Fulke Greville. Fr. Caelica, LXXXIV [LXXXV]. FaBoRV; GBL; QFR; Son
(Farewell to Cupid.) OBSC

Farewell, Sweet Dust. Elinor Wylie. LiTA

"Farewell, sweet Jane, for I must go across the flowing sea." Sweet Jane. Unknown. AmFP

Farewell, Sweet Mary. Unknown. AmFP

Farewell Talk with Saiko by a Rainy Window. Rai San'yo, tr. fr. Japanese by Burton Watson. FCEI; JLIC-2

Farewell, the bell upon a ram's neck hung. Corydon's Farewell, on Sailing in the Late Expedition Fleet. Unknown. NOEC

Farewell the reign of cruelty. Sir Thomas Wyatt. SiPS

Farewell This World. Unknown. OxBLMV

Farewell, This World, sel. Unknown. MeEL, abr.
(Cherry Fair, The.) FaBoRV
"This lyfe, I see, is but a cheyre feyre." ChTr

"Farewell! Thou art too dear [or deare] for my possession." Shakespeare. Fr. Sonnets, LXXXVII. EBEV; EiL; GTBS; GTBS-P; InPS; InvP; LiTB; NAEL-1; NOBE; OAEL-1; OBEV; OBSC; PeHV; PoEL-2; QFR; Son; TrGrPo

Farewell; thou busy world, and may. The Retirement. Charles Cotton. Fr. To Mr. Izaak Walton. FaBoPP; OBS

Farewell, thou child of my right hand, and joy. On My First Son [or Sonne]. Ben Jonson. AWP; EBEV; EiL; FaBoEE; FF; HAP; HeIP; HoPM; InPK; InPS; JCP; LiTB; NAEL-1; NIP; NoP; OAEL-1; OBD; OxBSP; PoE; PoEL-2; QFR; RB; SeCP; SeCV-1; TEP; WeW
(On His First Sonne.) OBS
(On My Son.) NOBE

Farewell, Thou Minstrel Harp. Sir Walter Scott. Fr. The Lady of the Lake, VI. OBNC

Farewell thou thing, time-past so known, so dear. His Farewell to Sack. Robert Herrick. CaPo; NAEL-1; SeCP; SeCV-1

Farewell to a Fondling, A. Thomas Churchyard. EiL

Farewell to a Jovial Friend. Gloria Escoffery. PBCV

Farewell to a Southern Melody, A. Huang O, tr. fr. Chinese by Kenneth Rexroth and Ling Chung. BoWoP

Farewell to Agassiz, A. Oliver Wendell Holmes. ImOP

Farewell to Allen University. Josephine D. Henderson Heard. CBWP-4

Farewell to America, A. Richard Henry Wilde. AA

Farewell to an idea. A cabin stands. Wallace Stevens. Fr. The Auroras of Autumn, II. CMoP; HCAP

Farewell to an idea. The mother's face. Wallace Stevens. Fr. The Auroras of Autumn, III. CMoP; HCAP

Farewell to Anactoria. Sappho, tr. fr. Greek by Allen Tate. AWP

Farewell to Arms, A. George Peele. See Polyhymnia: His Golden Lock[e]s [Time Hath to Silver Turned].

Farewell to Barn and Stack and Tree. A. E. Housman. Fr. A Shropshire Lad, VIII. CMoP; MoAB; MoBrPo; SoSe; UnPo

Farewell to Bath. Lady Mary Wortley Montagu. WPE

Farewell, To C. E. G, A. Charles Kingsley. BoTP

Farewell to Cuba. Maria Gowen Brooks. AA

Farewell to Cupid. Fulke Greville. See Caelica:
Farewell, sweet boy; complain not of my truth.

Farewell to Dostoevski. "Hugh MacDiarmid." Fr. A Drunk Man Looks at the Thistle. NAEL-2

Farewell to England. Unknown. APAS

Farewell to English, A, sels. Michael Hartnett.
"Gaelic is the conscience of our leaders." CIP
"Half afraid to break a promise." NOIV

Farewell to Europe. William Pillen. VWA

Farewell to False Love, A. Sir Walter Ralegh. BoLoP; EiL; NAEL-1
(False Love.) OBSC; SiPS

Farewell to Florida. Wallace Stevens. NoAM

Farewell to Folly, sel. Robert Greene.
Maesia's Song. CTC; OBSC; UnPo
(Mind Content, A.) EiL; ViBoPo
(Poor Estate, The.) TrGrPo
(Song: "Sweet are the thoughts that savour of content.") PoEL-2

Farewell to Greatness. Shakespeare and probably John Fletcher. See King Henry VIII: Wolsey's Farewell to His Greatness.

Farewell to Hendre Fechan. William Phylip, tr. fr. Welsh by H. Idris Bell. OBWVE

Farewell to Hiruharama. Haere Ra. James Keir Baxter. PeNZ

Farewell to Ireland. At. to Saint Columcille, tr. by Douglas Hyde. AWP

Farewell to Juliet ("I see you, Juliet, still, with your straw hat"). Wilfrid Scawen Blunt. Fr. The Love Sonnets of Proteus: Farewell to Juliet, XLVII. BoLoP; EnLoPo; OxBTC
"Juliet, farewell. I would not be forgiven." Fr. XXXIX. TrGrPo

Farewell to Kurdistan. Rosemary Tonks. OxBTC

Farewell to Leyden's lonely bound. Mark Akenside. Fr. On Leaving Holland. OBTV

Farewell to Love. John Donne. OAEL-1

Farewell to Love. Michael Drayton. See Idea:
Since there's [or ther's] no help[e], come let us kiss[e] and part.

Farewell to Love. Sir John Suckling. CaPo

Farewell to Malta. Byron. OBTV

Farewell to My Cottage. Samuel Bamford. PF

Farewell to My Mother. "Placido," tr. fr. Spanish by James Weldon Johnson. TTY

Farewell to Nancy. Burns. See Ae Fond Kiss.

Farewell to Narcissus. Robert Horan. NYBP

Farewell to New Zealand. Wynford Vaughan-Thomas. NOBL; OBTV

Farewell to old England for ever. Botany Bay. Unknown. PoAu-1

Farewell to Pari's Hill. Kapilar, tr. fr. Tamil by A. K. Ramanujan. PLW

Farewell to Russia's unwashed features. Mikhail Yurevich Lermontov, tr. by Alan Myers. AAA

Farewell to Sir John Norris and Sir Francis Drake, A. George Peele. OBSC

Farewell to Summer. George Arnold. AA

Farewell to the bushy clump close to the river. John Clare. NoP

Farewell to the Court. Sir Walter Ralegh. OBSC; SiPS
(Like Truthless Dreams.) Son

Farewell to the Court, sel. Earl of Rochester.
"Tired with the noisome follies of the age." TrGrPo

Farewell to the Farm. Robert Louis Stevenson. BoTP; FaPON

Farewell to the Highlands, farewell to the North. My Heart's in the Highlands. Burns. AWP; EnRP; FaFP

Farewell to the world, and to the night farewell. Chikamatsu Monzaemon. See Love Suicides at Sonezaki, The: To this world, farewell.

Farewell to the World of Richard Bishop. Unknown. CoMu

Farewell to Tobacco, A. Charles Lamb. OxBoLi
Farewell to Van Gogh. Charles Tomlinson. CMoP; GTBS-P; PoE
Farewell to Winnipeg. Roy Daniels. OBCV
Farewell, too little and too lately known. To the Memory of Mr. Oldham.
    Dryden. AWP; EBEV; FiP; HAP; HeIP; InPK; InPS; NIP; NOBE;
    NoP; OAEL-1; OBS; PoE; PoEL-3; PPP; Prf; SeCV-2
Farewell, Ungrateful Traitor. Dryden. *Fr. The Spanish Friar [or Fryar]*,
    V, i. BoLoP; ELP; EnLoPo; HAP; LiTB; NOBE
    (Love's Despair.) ACP
    (Song: "Farewell ungrateful[l] traytor [or traitor].") FiP; OBS;
    SeCV-2
Farewell, Unkind! Farewell! to me, no more a father! *Unknown*.
    EnLoPo
Farewell Voyaging World! Conrad Aiken. NYBP
Farewell with a Mischeife. George Gascoigne. AAS
Farewell, ye blooming fields! ye cheerful plains! Michael Bruce. *Fr.*
    Elegy: To Spring. NOEC
Farewells from Paradise. Elizabeth Barrett Browning. OBEV
Farm, The. Donald Hall. LiTM
Farm afternoons, there's much too much blue air. Sonnet of Intimacy.
    Vinícius de Moraes, *tr. by* Elizabeth Bishop. ATCBP
Farm boys wild to couple. The Sheep Child. James Dickey. CAPP;
    HCAP; MoP; MT; NoAM; NOBA; Prf; TAP
Farm-brooks that come down to Rathfarnham. The Loss of Strength.
    Austin Clarke. IPY
Farm Child. R. S. Thomas. BoNaP
Farm Families, *sels*. Lu Yu, *tr. fr. Chinese by* Burton Watson.
    CoBCP
    "It's late, the children come home from school."
    "Snug—the robe sewn from coarse cotton."
Farm Gate. Uys Krige, *tr. fr. Afrikaans by* Uys Krige *and* Jack Cope.
    PeSA
Farm Hands, The. Dilys Bennett Laing. SaC
Farm Implements and Rutabagas in a Landscape. John Ashbery. CoAP;
    SM
Farm near Norman's Lane, The. Olive Mary Finnin. PoAu-2
Farm on the Great Plains, The. William Stafford. HAP; VGW
Farm Picture, A. Walt Whitman. InPS
Farm Wife. John Hanlon Mitchell. CaP
Farm Wife. Ellen Bryant Voigt. MT
Farm Woman: 1942, The. Naomi Mitchison. CN
Farmer, The. "E." CBAP
Farmer, The. A. P. Herbert. CenHV
Farmer, The. Fredegond Shove. MMA
Farmer. Lucien Stryk. CAPP
Farmer, The. *Unknown*. AS
Farmer, The. Ellen Bryant Voigt. BLA; MT
Farmer and the Farmer's Wife, The. P. G. Hiebert. FiBHP;
    NBLV
Farmer and the Shanty Boy, The. *Unknown*. AmFP
Farmer, Dying. Richard Hugo. CAPP
Farmer Goes Beserk. Anne Elder. CBAP
Farmer had a daughter whose beauty ne'er was told, A. The Banks of
    Sweet Dundee. *Unknown*. AmFP
Farmer is busy, so busy, to-day, The. Haymaking. E. M. Adams.
    BoTP
"Farmer, is the harvest ready?" Bread. H. E. Wilkinson. BoTP
Farmer John. John Townsend Trowbridge. PWR
Farmer lived in the north country, A. The Swan Swims So Bonny.
    Unknown. OBET
Farmer of Tilsbury Vale, The. Wordsworth. EBEV
Farmer once planted some little brown seeds, A. A Growing Rhyme. J.
    M. Westrup. BoTP
Farmer ploughs into the ground, The. Seed. Herman Charles Bosman.
    PeSA
Farmer Remembers the Somme, The. Vance Palmer. PoAu-1
Farmer say to de weevil, De. De Ballet of De Boll Weevil. *Unknown*.
    AS
Farmer went trotting on [or upon] his grey mare, A. Mother Goose.
    BoTP; OxNR
Farmer will never be happy again, The. The Farmer. A. P. Herbert.
    CenHV
Farmers. Thomas Lux. LCAP
Farmers. William Alexander Percy. WGRP
Farmer's Boy, The, *sels*. Robert Bloomfield.
    Moonlight. Scattered Clouds. OBNC
    Summer. PBBP
Farmer's Boy, The. *Unknown*. OBET
Farmer's Bride, The. Charlotte Mew. BoLoP; ErPo; FaBoWP; MoAB;
    MoBrPo; OxBTC; TrGrPo; WPE
Farmer's clothes are soaked through and never dried, The. Ise Tayu, *tr.
    by* Kenneth Rexroth *and* Ikuko Atsumi. WPOW
Farmer's Curst Wife, The. *Unknown*. AmFP; ESPB, A *and* B *vers*.

Farmer's eyes are dark, The; he speaks in song. On the Welsh Marches.
    Walter Stone. NYBP
Farmer's goose, who in the stubble, The. The Progress of Poetry. Swift.
    InvP; NOIV
Farmer's plow, The. A Lark along the Road. Tamemasa, *tr. by* Steven
    D. Carter. WFTW
Farmer's Son So Sweet, A. *Unknown*. OBET
Farmer's Thoughts, A. Ch'u Kuang-hsi, *tr. fr. Chinese by* Burton
    Watson. CoBCP
Farmer's Wife, The. Anne Sexton. HoPM; LiTM; NePoEA-2
Farmer's Wife and the Raven, The. John Gay. PBBP
Farmer's wife looked out of the dairy, The. The Rival. Sylvia Townsend
    Warner. MoAB; MoBrPo
Farmhouse lingers, though averse to square, The. A Brook in the City.
    Robert Frost. OxBA
Farmhouse skyline, draped with trees, The. Alan Creighton. CaP
Farmyard, The. A. A. Attwood. BoTP
Farmyard at Chassy. Stephen Dobyns. AnAn
Farolita. Mei-Mei Berssenbrugge. BrSi
Farragut. William Tuckey Meredith. AA; FaBoBe; PAH
Farre have I clambred in my mind. An Hymne in Honour of Those Two
    Despised Virtues, Charitie and Humilitie. Henry More. OBS
Farrell O'Reilly. Oliver St. John Gogarty. OxBTC
Farther. John James Piatt. AA
Farther and farther from the three Pa Roads. On New Year's Eve.
    Ts'uei T'u , *tr. by* Witter Bynner. OFD
Farther east it wouldn't be on the map. Midwest Town. Ruth Delong
    Peterson. AmFN
Farther he went the farther home grew, The. For the Grave of Daniel
    Boone. William Stafford. NoP
Farther in the summer than the birds. Emily Dickinson. *See* Further in
    summer than the birds.
Farther than I have been. The Summit. Kathleen Jessie Raine. *Fr.*
    Beinn Naomh, IV. OxBS
Farther than the west wind I am going. Emigré Jewess. Gabriela
    Mistral, *tr. by* Kate Flores. DMH
Farthest from any war, unique in time. Hollywood. Karl Shapiro.
    LiTM; OxBA
Farthest thunder that I heard, The. Emily Dickinson. NAAL-1
Fascination of What's Difficult, The. W. B. Yeats. BIrV; BrPo;
    NAEL-2; PoEL-5
Fa'se Footrage. *Unknown*. *See* Fause Foodrage.
Fashion. Horace Twiss. BXAP
Fashionable Heart, The. Jack Gilbert. NPGG
Fashions in Dogs. E. B. White. FiBHP
Fast. John Tagliabue. SD
Fast Ball. Jonathan Williams. NeAP
Fast Break. Edward Hirsch. ASP; DiPo; EOEF; TSL
Fast bundled is the firewood. *Unknown, tr. by* Arthur Waley. BoS
Fast express for Gettysburg roared north, The. They Will Look for a Few
    Words. Nancy Byrd Turner. AmFN
Fast falls the snow, O lady mine. To F. C. Mortimer Collins.
    NOBVV
Fast rode the knight. Stephen Crane. *Fr.* War Is Kind, 83.
    NAAL-2
Fasten the chamber! Bluebeard's Closet. Rose Terry Cooke. AA
Faster, faster,/ O Circe, Goddess. The Strayed Reveller. Matthew
    Arnold. OAEL-2
Faster than arrows race the rook and hare. In Honor of My Husband's
    Fiftieth Birthday. Hsüeh Shao-hui, *tr. by* Irving Lo. WFTU
Faster than fairies, faster than witches. From a Railway Carriage. Robert
    Louis Stevenson. BoTP; FaPON; OxBChV; PDV; PYC; RHPC
Fat black bucks in a wine-barrel room. The Congo. Vachel Lindsay.
    CMoP; FaFP; LiTA; MoAB; MoAmPo; NOBA; OxBA; PoNe; PoRA;
    TAP
Fat Blues. Charmaine Crowell. AIW
Fat Boy, The. Mark Vinz. TDD
Fat Boy's Dream, The. Richard McCann. GrPl
Fat Budgie, The. John Lennon. NBLV
Fat cat on the mat, The. Cat. J. R. R. Tolkien. CRH
Fat friar stroking golf balls, The. Walking along the Hudson. Donald
    Petersen. CoAP
Fat-kneed god! Feeder of mangy leopards! You Also, Gaius Valerius
    Catullus. Archibald MacLeish. NoAM; TAP
Fat Lady Travels, The. Cathy Smith-Bowers. KS
Fat Lena's Recipe for Crocodile Soup. Phyllis Janowitz. TDD
Fat Mama at Swenson's. E. Castendyk Briefs. SoTCo
Fat Man in the Mirror, The. Robert Lowell. PoA
Fat Men, The. Cyril Dabydeen. PBCV
Fat men. After Hilary, Age 5. Faye Kicknosway. UL
Fat men go about the streets, The. Ballade of the Poetic Life. J. C.
    Squire. OBMV

Fat, pale proprietor, The. In an Arab Town. Susan Tichy.
MAYP

Fat red barns lean east along Highway 109. Leaving Mendota, 1956.
Lawrence Locke. GrPl

Fat sixty-year-old man woke me, A. "Hello." Birthday. John Ciardi.
NAs

Fat Tuesday. W. S. Di Piero. MAYP

Fata Morgana. Juliane Windhager, tr. fr. German by Beth Bjorklund.
CoAuP

Fatal Dream; or, The Unhappy Favourite, The. Emanuel Collins.
NOEC

Fatal Interview, sel. Edna St. Vincent Millay.
Love Is Not All. Son

Fatal Longing. A. Leyeles, tr. fr. Yiddish by Benjamin and Barbara
Harshav. AYP

Fatal Love. Matthew Prior. FaBoCo; NBLV

Fatal Sisters, The. Thomas Gray, after the Icelandic. EnRP

Fatal Spell, The. Byron. See Childe Harold's Pilgrimage: Oh love! no
habitant of earth thou art.

Fatales Poetae. Henry Parrot. FaBoEE

Fatalities. Diane Ackerman. BWV

Fate. Louis James Block. AA

Fate. W. S. Merwin. KS

Fate. Susan Marr Spalding. AA; BLPA

Fate and the Younger Generation. D. H. Lawrence. OxBoLi

Fate gave the word, the arrow sped. A Mother's Lament for the Death of
Her Son. Burns. HoPM

Fate, I will not ask for wealth or fame. The Higher Good. Theodore
Parker. FaBoBe

Fate in Incognito. Michael Benedikt. OBAL

Fate of Icarus could have been no other, The. Daedalus. Angelos
Sikelianos, tr. by Edmund Keeley and Philip Sherrard. VMG

Fate of John Burgoyne, The. Unknown. PAH

Fate of Narcissus, The. William Warner. Fr. Albion's England.
OBSC

Fate of the Cabbage Rose, The. Wallace Irwin. FiBHP

Fate of the Oak, The. "Barry Cornwall." OHIP

Fate of the Prophets, The. Longfellow. Fr. Christus; a Mystery, I,
Introitus. WGRP

Fate on the left hand, and Death on the right. And Again. Humphrey
Evans. BXAP

Fate struck the hour! Lincoln. Jane L. Hardy. OHIP

Fate to beauty still must give. Claudian, tr. by Howard Mumford Jones.
AWP

Fateful slumber floats and flows, The. For the Briar Rose. William
Morris. NOBVV

Fates of Men (Exeter Book). Unknown, tr. fr. Old English by Charles W.
Kennedy. AnOE

Fates of the Apostles, sel. Cynewulf, tr. fr. Anglo-Saxon by Charles W.
Kennedy.
"Now I pray the man who may love this lay." AnOE

Father. Rose Ausländer, tr. fr. German by Ewald Osers. VWA

Father. Paul Carroll. DiL; NeAP

Father, The. John Donne. Fr. The Litanie. NOCV

Father. Arthur Davison Ficke. TrPWD

Father. Frances Mary Frost. FaPON

Father. Margit Kaffka, tr. fr. Hungarian by Laura Schiff.
PBWP

Father, The. Richmond Lattimore. EyDe

Father. Jean Lipkin. AIW; PeSA

Father. Myra Cohn Livingston. NTCP

Father. Robert Lowell. DiL

Father. John Wheelwright. DiL; UnPo

Father. Paul Zweig. DiL

Father/ I am not equal to the faith required. Confession. Lucille Clifton.
GeTw

Father,/ one day longer on this earth than you. My Father, My Son.
John Malcolm Brinnin. DiL; NYBP

Father/ You are the trunk. Howard Schwartz. VWA

Father, and bard revered! to whom I owe. Dedicatory Sonnet to S. T.
Colerige. Hartley Coleridge. OAEL-2; Son

Father and Child. Gwen Harwood. CBAP; WPE

Father and His Children, The. Unknown. OxBChV

Father and I in the Woods. David McCord. SO

Father and I went down to camp. Yankee Doodle. At. to Edward Bangs
and also Richard Shuckburg. AmFP; FaFP; FaPON
(Yankee's Return from Camp, The.) OPP; OxBoLi; PAH

Father and Mother. X. J. Kennedy. GrPl; RHPC

Father and mother/ patting my head. Unknown, tr. fr. Japanese by
Hiraoki Sato. Fr. Manyo Shu. FCEI

Father and Son. Richard Eberhart. DiL

Father and Son. F. R. Higgins. BIrV; OBMV

Father and Son. David Ignatow. DiL

Father and Son. Stanley Kunitz. CAPP; DiL; MoP; TwCP

Father and Son. Delmore Schwartz. DiL; LiTA

Father and Son: 1939. William Plomer. PeSA

Father at last, A. Nakamura Kusadao, tr. by Geoffrey Bownas and
Anthony Thwaite. PeBJV

Father being the loneliest word in the one language. John Berryman. Fr.
Dream Songs. DiL

Father, between Thy strong hands Thou has bent. Prayer of a Teacher.
Dorothy Littlewort. TrPWD

Father calls me William, sister calls me Will. Jest 'fore Christmas.
Eugene Field. FaBV; FaFP; FaPON; FPL; OHFP; PoLF

Father, chancing to chastise. Harry Graham. Fr. Some Ruthless
Rhymes, IV. CenHV

Father Damien. John Banister Tabb. ACP

Father dead and mother dead. The Female Principle. A. D. Hope.
OxBC

Father Death Blues. Allen Ginsberg. Fr. Don't Grow Old. SM

Father, erect and wise. They Were Pure Gold. Pertti Nieminen, tr. by
Aili Jarvenpa. SOP

Father Father Son and Son. Jon Swan. NYBP

Father, father, where are you going. Little Boy Lost, The ("Father,
father, where are you going?"). Blake. Fr. Songs of Innocence.
EnRP; NoP

Father fell asleep one day. The Dream. Li Nan, tr. by Dominic Cheung.
IFON

Father Fisheye. Peter Balakian. MAYP

Father Grumble. Unknown. AmFP
(Old Man Who Lived in a Wood, The.) MoShBr
(Old Man Who Lived in the Woods, The.) OnUR

Father, Hear the Prayer We Offer. Love Maria Willis. AH

Father heard his children scream. The Stern parent. Harry Graham. Fr.
Some Ruthless Rhymes, I. ChTr

Father, here a temple in Thy name we build. Hymn of Dedication.
Elizabeth E. Scantlebury. BLRP

Father, hold my hand. The White Rose: Sophie Scholl 1921-1943. Erika
Mumford. MOWH

Father, How Wide Thy Glories Shine. Charles Wesley. TrPWD

Father! I bless thy name that I do live. In Him We Live. Jones Very.
OxBA

Father, I expect your eyes. Before the Mountain. Elizabeth Libbey.
AmPA

Father, I have launched my bark. The Pilgrim. Emma C. Embury.
OBCA

Father, I know that all my life. My Times Are in Thy Hand. Anna L.
Waring. PWR

Father, I lift my hands to Thee. Suppliant. Florence Earle Coates.
TrPWD

Father, I loved you as a child, and still. The Mirror. Edgar Bowers.
QFR

Father! I Own Thy Voice. Samuel Wolcott. AH

Father, I scarcely dare to pray. A Last Prayer. Helen Hunt Jackson.
AA; TrPWD

Father, I will not ask for wealth or fame. The Higher Good. Theodore
Parker. AA; FaBoBe

Father in heaven, after each lost day. Petrarch. See Sonnets to Laura: To
Laura in Life.

Father in Heaven! from whom the simplest flower. Felicia Dorothea
Hemans. TrPWD

Father in Heaven! humbly before thee. A Prayer for Peace. Edward
Rowland Sill. TrPWD

Father in heaven, make me wise. A Mother's Prayer. Margaret Elizabeth
Sangster. TrPWD

Father-in-Law. Derek Mahon. FaBCIP

Father in the Railway Buffet. U. A. Fanthorpe. FaBoWP

Father, in Thy Mysterious Presence Kneeling. Samuel Johnson.
AH

Father, in Thy starry tent. Rest in Peace. Wilfred J. Funk. PoLF

Father is hard to live with. Old Storm. David Phillips. NeAC

Father Is Leaving. Viljo Kajava, tr. fr. Finnish by Aili Jarvenpa.
SOP

Father John's bread was made of rye. Rye Bread. William Stanley
Braithwaite. CDC

Father Knows, The. "F. L. H." BLRP

Father, lead me, day by day. A Child's Prayer. Unknown. BLRP

Father Lenin, you understood the moment. James Keir Baxter. Fr.
Autumn Testament, 18. ATNZ

Father Malloy. Edgar Lee Masters. Fr. Spoon River Anthology.
OxBA

Father Mat, sel. Patrick Kavanagh. AnIL; CIP; CMoP; PoE
"In a meadow/ Beside the chapel three boys were playing football."
MoAB

Father Missouri takes his own. Foreclosure. Sterling A. Brown. PoBA; PoNe

Father, Mother, and me. We and They. Kipling. *Fr*. Debits and Credits. NoAM

Father of all! in Death's relentless claim. Oliver Wendell Holmes. TrPWD

Father of all! In every age. The Universal Prayer. Pope. BLPA; FaBoBe; FPL; NoP; WGRP

"Father of lakes!" thy waters bend. Lake Superior. Samuel Griswold Goodrich. AA

Father of Life, with songs of wonder. Margaret L. Woods. *Fr*. The Return. TrPWD

Father of lights! what sunny [*or* sunnie] seed. Cock-crowing. Henry Vaughan. MePo; OAEL-1; PBBP; SeCV-1

Father of love! Evening Prayer. Henrietta Cordelia Ray. CBWP-3

Father of mercies, in Thy Word. O How Sweet Are Thy Words! Anne Steele. BLRP

Father of My Country, The. Diane Wakoski. NoAM; TAP

Father of the Bride. Charles Ghigna. SoTCo

Father of the Man. Elizabeth Mabel Bryan. GoYe

Father of the son, The. *Unknown, tr. by* Geoffrey Bownas *and* Anthony Thwaite. PeBJV

Father of Women, A. Alice Meynell. BrRo; WPE

Father, on the first day on the Hunting Moon. The First Day of the Hunting Moon. Patricia Low. VGW

Father, part of his double interest. John Donne. *Fr*. Holy Sonnets, XVI. JCP; OBS; Son

Father Poem. Joel Oppenheimer. PoM

Father raised words, The. Family. Norman MacCaig. FF

Father. —Say the *confiteor*.—I said it. The Confessor. Giuseppe Gioacchino Belli, *tr. by* Harold Norse. ErPo

Father Short came down the lane. *Unknown*. OxNR

Father, since always now the death to come. Sonnet to My Father. Donald Justice. DiL

Father, sitting on the side of your startled bed. D-Dawn. Margaret McGarvey. GoYe

Father Son and Holy Ghost. Audre Lorde. NoAM; PoBA

Father Takes to the Road and Lets His Hair Down. Alan Chong Lau. BrSi

Father, the visit/ was so unexpected. To My Father. Susannah Fried, *tr. by* Anthony Rudolf. VWA

Father, the world conquered you day by day. Letter. Franco Fortini, *tr. by* Lawrence R. Smith. NItP

Father, the Year Is Fallen. Audre Lorde. PoBA

Father, this year's jinx rides us apart. All My Pretty Ones. Anne Sexton. NAAL-2; NoAM; OPOP

Father, thy hand/ Hath reared. Bryant. *Fr*. A Forest Hymn. TrPWD

Father! Thy wonders do not singly stand. The Spirit Land. Jones Very. HAP

Father, Thy word is past, man shall find grace. Milton. *Fr*. Paradise Lost, *Bk*. III, *ll*. 227–265.
  (Atonement, The.) OBS

Father to Son. Elizabeth Jennings. GOYP

Father to the Man. John Knight. EaLo

Father, unusually tense. Sculpting in the Imperial Presence. Takamura Kotaro, *tr. fr. Japanese by* Hiroaki Sato. *Fr*. A Brief History of Imbecility. FCEI

Father was and aye shall be, The. The Trinity. *Unknown*. ACP

Father was eating partridge and Mother wasn't there. Family. Hugo Claus, *tr. by* James S. Holmes. DuIn

Father, we come not as of old. John W. Chadwick. TrPWD

Father, we thank Thee for the night. A Child's Prayer. *Unknown*. BLRP; BoTP

Father, who designs his babe a priest, The. William Cowper. *Fr*. Tirocinium; or, A Review of Schools. OBSV

Father, Who Mak'st Thy Suff'ring Sons. Arthur Cleveland Coxe. AH

Father, whom I knew well for forty years. The Gardener. John Hall Wheelock. DiL; NYBP

Father, whom I murdered every night but one. Elegy for My Father. Howard Moss. CoAP; DiL; LiTM; NePoEA; VWA

Father! whose hard and cruel law. The Death of Grant. Ambrose Bierce. AA

Father William. "Lewis Carroll." *Fr*. Alice's Adventures in Wonderland, ch. 5. BXAP; FaBoCo; FaBoNo; FaBoPa; FaPON; FiBHP; FPL; GoJo; HoPM; LiTB; NOBL; NOBVV; OxBChV; Par; PDV; PoLF; PoRA; RHPC; TrGrPo; UnPo

Father William. *Unknown*. NA

Father wore an overcoat with a narrow velvet collar. Poem: Alte Zachen. Abba Kovner, *tr. by* Warren Bargad *and* Stanley F. Chyet. IP

Fathered by March, the daffodils are here. Daffodils. Lizette Woodworth Reese. AA

Fatherland, The. James Russell Lowell. GN

Fatherland Song. Björnstjerne Björnson, *tr. fr. Norwegian by* William Ellery Leonard. AWP

Fatherless and motherless. *Unknown*. GBP

Fatherless boy, thirteen, walks and weeps, The. Ballad of the Fatherless Boy. Wang Chiu-ssu, *tr. by* Jonathan Chaves. CoBLCP

Fatherless, 250 people. Verigin, Moving in Alone. John Newlove. NeAC

Fathers, The. Edwin Muir. OxBS

Fathers, The. Benjamin Saltman. VWA

Fathers, The. Siegfried Sassoon. MoP

Fathers brothers uncles. An Act Respecting Indians. Lenore Keeshig-Tobias. GOS

Father's Business, The. Edwin Markham

Father's gone a-flailing. *Unknown*. OxNR

Father's Heart Is Touched, A. Samuel Hoffenstein. FiBHP

Father's Love, The. Mary E. Tucker. CBWP-1

Fathers: naked, you stand for their big faces. This Is a Poem for the Dead. Michael Ryan. AmPA; DiL

Father's Notes of Woe, A. Sir Walter Scott. *Fr*. The Lay of the Last Minstrel, IV. OBNC

Fathers of a Star, The. Zbigniew Herbert, *tr. fr. Polish by* Czeslaw Milosz. PwPP

Fathers of Desire. Herbert Scott. NAmP

Father's Story. Elizabeth Madox Roberts. FaPON

Father's Testament, A. Judah Ibn Tibbon, *tr. fr. Hebrew by* Israel Abrahams. TrJP

Father's voice. William Stafford. RFM

Fathomed at last! Joho, *tr. by* Lucien Stryk *and* Takashi Ikemoto. ZPCJ

Fathomless abyss is human pain, A. To Be. Manuel Gutiérrez Nájera, *tr. by* Samuel Beckett. MexPo

Fathomless Is My Love. Kalola, *tr. fr. Hawaiian by* N. B. Emerson. WTO

Fathoms deep beneath the wave. Song of the Mermaids and Mermen. Sir Walter Scott. *Fr*. The Pirate, *ch*. 16. WSC

Fatigue. Hilaire Belloc. FaBoCo; NBLV; NOBL; OxBTC

Fatigue, regrets. The lights. The Demon Lover. Adrienne Rich. IHMS

Fatigues. Richard Aldington. BrPo

Fatima. Tennyson. GBL; SeCePo; UnPo

Fatness. Alan Ansen. CoAP

Fatted/ on herbs, swollen on crabapples. The Porcupine. Galway Kinnell. NaP; NOBA

Fattened sky, The. The Fifth Hell. Jerome Rothenberg. *Fr*. The Seven Hells of Jigoku Zoshi. NNaP

Fatty, Fatty, Boom-a-latty. *Unknown*. RHPC

Fault, The. Edward Lucie-Smith. NePoEA-2

Fault of the Age, The. Ella Wheeler Wilcox. PWR

Fault/line. Vincent O'Sullivan. ATNZ

Faun, The. Ezra Pound. FaBoCh; FaBoTw

Faun Sees Snow for the First Time, The. Richard Aldington. MoBrPo

Fauna and Flora. Francis Ponge, *tr. fr. French by* Richard Wilbur. RHTwFP

Fauna move about, whereas flora unfold themselves to the eye. Fauna and Flora. Francis Ponge, *tr. by* Richard Wilbur. RHTwFP

Faur Wid I Dee? J. C. Milne. PoSH

Fause Foodrage. *Unknown*. ESPB
  (Fa'se Footrage.) OxBB

Faust. John Ashbery. NoP; TwCP

Faust, *sels*. Goethe, *tr. fr. German*.
  "Chanting sun, as ever, rivals, The." *Fr*. Pt. I, *tr. by* Louis MacNeice. NAWM-2
  Christ Is Arisen. TrCP
  (Easter Chorus.) WGRP, *tr. by* Bayard Taylor.
  "Limits of the sphere of dream, The." *Tr. by* Shelley. WSC
  Lose This Day Loitering. PoLF, *tr. by* John Anster.
  Prologue in Heaven [*or* The Chorus of the Archangels], , 2 *versions Tr. by* Shelley. AWP; OBVE
  Soldier's Song. *Tr. by* Bayard Taylor. AWP
  "Stop playing with your melancholy." *Tr. by* Walter Kaufmann. DL

Faustina hath a spot upon her face. De Naevo in Facie Faustinae. Thomas Bastard. FaBoEE

Faustina hath the fairer face. *Unknown*. OBSC

Faustina, or Rock Roses. Elizabeth Bishop. FaBoMo

Faustine. Swinburne. BeLS; PeHV

Faust's Servant. Roy Fuller. OxBTC

Faustus Triumphant. Thom Gunn. FaBoMo

Favorite Flower, The. Celia Thaxter. AiP

Favorite Grandson Braid. Phillip William George. VoR

Favorite Slave's Story, The. Priscilla Jane Thompson. CBWP-2

Favour. Robert David Fitzgerald. CBAP

Favourite Cat's Dying Soliloquy, A. Anna Seward. FM

Favourite pleasure hath it been with me, A. Wordsworth. *Fr.* The Prelude [or, Growth of a Poet's Mind]: Summer Vacation. EnRP; OAEL-2

Favourite Village, The, *sel.* James Hurdis. "But most of all subdued, or fearful least." PBBP

Fawn in the Snow, The. William Rose Benét. MoAmPo

Fawnia. Robert Greene. *See* Pandosto: Ah Were She Pitiful.

Fawn's Foster-Mother. Robinson Jeffers. MoP; NoAM; NOBA

Fay Wray to the King. Judith Rechter. NMM

Fayned Fancy betweene the Spider and the Gowte, A, *sel.* Thomas Churchyard. Old-Time Service. OBSC

Fay's Crime, The. Joseph Rodman Drake. *Fr.* The Culprit Fay. GN

Fay's Departure, The. Joseph Rodman Drake. *Fr.* The Culprit Fay. GN (First Quest, The.) AA

Fay's Sentence, The. Joseph Rodman Drake. *Fr.* The Culprit Fay. AA; GN

Fear, The. Lascelles Abercrombie. OBMV

Fear. Aldo Camerino, *tr. fr. Italian by* Anita Barrows. VWA

Fear. Gerhard Fritsch, *tr. fr. German by* Beth Bjorklund. CoAuP

Fear, The. Robert Frost. BeLS

Fear. Anna Hajnal, *tr. fr. Hungarian by* Daniel Hoffman. BoWoP; MHuP

Fear, A. Francis Ledwidge. NOIV

Fear. Langdon Elwyn Mitchell. AA

Fear. Thomas Love Peacock. VoR

Fear. Vittoria Aganoor Pompili, *tr. fr. Italian by* Brenda Webster. PBWP

Fear. Pedro Salinas, *tr. fr. Spanish by* Perry Higman. LPSS

Fear. Charles Simic. HCAP

Fear. Dara Wier. MAYP

Fear and Anger in the Mindless Universe. Hayden Carruth. MAYP; NNaP

Fear death?—to feel the fog in my throat. Prospice. Robert Browning. BLPL; DL; FaBV; FiP; LiTB; NAEL-2; OBD; PoLF; PoRA; TrCP; TrGrPo; WGRP

Fear, facing the New Year. Facing the New Year. Mark Guy Pearse. BLRP

Fear falls upon me on the moutain top. The Dog Child. Keaulumoku, *tr. fr. Hawaiian by* M. W. Beckwith. *Fr.* The Kumulipo; a Creation Chant. WTO

Fear is a golden chain around my throat. Motorcycle Racer Thinks of Quitting. Grace Butcher. ASP

Fear Is What Quickens Me. James Wright. CAPP

Fear, jealousy and murder are the same. Gamecock. James Dickey. HoPM; UnPo

Fear Makes the Spectator. Cees Nooteboom, *tr. fr. Dutch by* Peter Nijmeijer. DuIn

Fear me, virgin whosoever. After the Pleasure Party. Herman Melville. PoEL-5

Fear no longer for the lone grey birds. End of the Flower World (A.D. 2300). Stanley Burnshaw. TrJP

Fear No More the Heat o' the Sun. Shakespeare. *Fr.* Cymbeline, IV, ii. AWP; CH; ChTr; EBEV; EiL; ELP; FaFP; FF; GBL; HAP; HeIP; InPS; LiTB; Mes; NAEL-1; NoP; OBD; PoRA; PrIm; QFR; RB; SCV; SoSe; TrGrPo
(Dirge: "Fear no more the heat o' the sun.") OAEL-1
(Dirge for Fidele.) NOBE
(Fidele.) GTBS; GTBS-P; OBEV
(Fidele's Dirge.) FaBoCh; OBSC
(Song: "Fear[e] no more the heat[e] o' the sun.") CTC; FiP; PoE; PoEL-2

Fear not, dear love, that I'll reveal. Secrecy [or Secresie] Protested. Thomas Carew. CaPo; SeCP

Fear not, O little flock! the foe. Battle Hymn. Michael Altenburg, *tr. by* Catherine Winkworth. WGRP

Fear Not, Poor Weary One. Thomas Cogswell Upham. AH

Fear not, shepherds, for I bring. Angel's Song. Charles Causley. OBCP

Fear of Bo-talee, The. N. Scott Momaday. STE

Fear of Death. John Ashbery. FaBoMo; TAP

Fear of Death, The. Elizabeth Jennings. OBD

Fear of Death Confounds Me, The. William Dunbar. *See* I That in heill wes.

Fear of death disturbs me constantly, The. Gabrielle de Coignard, *tr. by* Raymond Oliver. WPOW

Fear of Flying, The. Mona Van Duyn. NMM

Fear of loneliness, the wish, The. The Price. Anne Stevenson. DiPo

Fear of poetry, The, is the/ fear. Reading Time: 1 Minute 26 Seconds. Muriel Rukeyser. PBWP

Fear of the Earth. Alex Comfort. MoBrPo

Fear of the Lord, The. Bible, *O.T. Fr.* Proverbs, I: 7. TrJP

Fear of Trembling, The. John Hollander. NePoEA

Fear. Of you. Loving you. Fear. Pedro Salinas, *tr. by* Perry Higman. LPSS

Fear passes from man to man. Fear. Charles Simic. HCAP

Fear Test: Integrity of Heroes. James Simmons. CIP

Fear the one who has sharp weapons. Song of the Lioness for Her Cub. *Unknown, tr. by* Thomas Hahn. BoWoP

Fear was about me. Hunger. *Unknown.* WTO

Feare not, litle flocke, for it is your fathers good pleasure to give you the kingdome. Bible, *N.T. Fr.* St. Luke, XII: 32-40. OBVE

Fearful Death. *Unknown.* MeEL

Fearful "had the root of the matter," bringing. Courage Means Running. William Empson. LiTB

Fearful night sinks, The. Hymn to the Sun. *Unknown.* TTTS

Fearful of beauty, I always went. The Enamel Girl. Genevieve Taggard. MoAmPo

Fearful the chamber's quiet; the veiled windows. A Development of Idiocy. Ebenezer Jones. OBNC

Fearfull Symmetry. Basil Bunting. PoA

Fearing that Albion should turn his back against the Divine Vision. Blake. *Fr.* Jerusalem. OAEL-2

Fearless, The. Mortimer J. Adler. PoA

Fears, The. Roberto Obregón, *tr. fr. Spanish by* Jack Hirschman. Vol

Fears any one his bride lest she a virgin be not. Reasons for and against Marrying Widows. Henricus Selyns. SCAP

Fears in Solitude. Samuel Taylor Coleridge. EnRP; OBWP

Fears in Solitude, *sels.* Samuel Taylor Coleridge. EnRP; OBWP
Looking Down on Nether Stowey. FaBoPP
O My Mother Isle! FaBoPP
"On the green sheep-track, up the healthy hill." OBNC

Fears of the Eighth Grade. Toi Derricotte. InPS

Fearsome even to action in mind. Hitomaro, *tr. fr. Japanese by* Hiroaki Sato. *Fr.* Manyo Shu. FCEI

Feast, The. Robert Hass. GeTw

Feast. Edna St. Vincent Millay. AnAmPo

Feast, The. David Wagoner. NePoEA-2

Feast and noon grew high, and Sacrifice, The. Milton. *Fr.* Samson Agonistes. EBEV

Feast by the Manzanares. Juan Ruiz de Alarcón, *tr. fr. Spanish by* Samuel Beckett. *Fr.* The Suspicious Truth, I. MexPo

Feast o' Saint [or St.] Stephen, The. Ruth Sawyer. OBCP; OHIP

Feast of Blood, The. Joseph Fawcett. *Fr.* The Art of War. NOEC

"Feast of light! A." Clayfield proclaimed. Clayfield's Daughter Reveals Her Plans. Robert Pack. BLA

Feast of Stephen, The. Anthony Hecht. HAP; KS; NoAM; NoP

Feast of Stephen, The. Kevin Nichols. OBCP

Feast of the Monkeys, The. John Philip Sousa. OBAL

Feast of the Most Holy Trinity. Aubrey Thomas De Vere. TIRV

Feast of the Ram's Horn. Harvey Shapiro. VGW

Feast-Time of the Year, The. *Unknown.* OHIP

Feast's begun, The/ And the wine is done. Water Song. Solomon ibn Gabirol, *tr. by* Israel Abrahams. TrJP

Feasts of Death, Feasts of Love. Stuart Z. Perkoff. NeAP

Feather, The. Vernon Watkins. FaBoTw

Feather for My Cap, A. Ivy O. Eastwick. BoTP

Feather on feather. Snow in Spring. Ivy O. Eastwick. PDV

Feather or Fur. John Becker. FaPON; RHPC

Feather that all, The. Abukbo. Jim Barnes. *Fr.* Four Things Choctaw. HATNAP

"Feathered fowl's in your orchard, father, A." Brown Robin. *Unknown.* ESPB

Feathred songster chaunticleer, The. Bristowe Tragedie: or, The Dethe of Syr Charles Bawdin. Thomas Chatterton. EnRP; OxBB

Feathered Friends. Robert Peters. BXAP

Feathers. Paul Eluard, *tr. fr. French by* Michael Benedikt. POS

Feathers. Leo Vroman, *tr. fr. Dutch.* DuIn

Feathers blacken against the sun. Manifest Destiny. Anita Endrezze-Danielson. CDW

Feathers in a fan, The. Man. Humbert Wolfe. MoBrPo

Feathers of Snow. *Unknown.* GBP

Feathers of the willow, The. Richard Watson Dixon. BoNaP; CH; FaBoCh; GTBS-P; NOBE; OBNC
(Willow.) OBEV

Feathers or Lead? James Broughton. NeAP

Feathers up fast, and steeples; then in clods. The Fountain. Donald Davie. GTBS-P; OxBTC

Feather's Weight, A. G. P. Lathrop. FaBoUs
Featherstone's Doom. Robert Stephen Hawker. OBNC
Feathery forests are blown back, frost rends, The. Winter. John Lyle Donaghy. BIrV
Featureless ghost under the wall cannot jerk out at us, The. Elegy for the Silent Voices and the Joiners of Everything. Kenneth Patchen. NaP
February. John Clare. *Fr*. The Shepherd's [*or* Shepheards] Calendar. NOBE; OBNC
February. John Heath-Stubbs. OBCP
February. W. S. Merwin. NNaP
February. Pier Paolo Pasolini, *tr. fr. Italian by* Lawrence R. Smith. NItP
February. Dorothy Una Ratcliffe. BoTP
February. Henrietta Cordelia Ray. CBWP-3
February. Folgore Da San Gimignano, *tr. fr. Italian by* Dante Gabriel Rossetti. *Fr*. Sonnets of the Months. AWP
February. James Schuyler. NeAP
February. Spenser. *Fr*. The Shepheardes [*or* Shepeards *or* Shepherd's] Calender.
    Oak and the Brere, The. OBSC
February. Leo Vroman, *tr. fr. Dutch by the author and* Peter Nijmeijer. DuIn
February Afternoon. Edward Thomas. NoAM
February dawn spread across the sky. The Grand Finale. István Vas, *tr. by* William Jay Smith. MHuP
February 11, 1977. Frederick Morgan. DiPo
February Evening in New York. Denise Levertov. NoAM
February 15. A. Leyeles, *tr. fr. Yiddish by* Benjamin *and* Barbara Harshav. *Fr*. Fabius Lind's Diary. AYP
February 4. A. Leyeles, *tr. fr. Yiddish by* Benjamin *and* Barbara Harshav. *Fr*. Fabius Lind's Diary. AYP
February Morning. King D. Kuka. VoR
February 1. A. Leyeles, *tr. fr. Yiddish by* Benjamin *and* Barbara Harshav. *Fr*. Fabius Lind's Diary. AYP
February Park. Gerald Vizenor. VoR
February 7. A. Leyeles, *tr. fr. Yiddish by* Benjamin *and* Barbara Harshav. *Fr*. Fabius Lind's Diary. AYP
February 17. A. Leyeles, *tr. fr. Yiddish by* Benjamin *and* Barbara Harshav. *Fr*. Fabius Lind's Diary. AYP
February Sun. Paul Rodenko, *tr. fr. Dutch by* James S. Holmes. DuIn
February 10. A. Leyeles, *tr. fr. Yiddish by* Benjamin *and* Barbara Harshav. *Fr*. Fabius Lind's Diary. AYP
February Thaw. G. J. F. Dutton. PoSH
February; the Boy Breughel. Norman Dubie. LCAP
February 23. A. Leyeles, *tr. fr. Yiddish by* Benjamin *and* Barbara Harshav. *Fr*. Fabius Lind's Diary. AYP
February 22. John Updike. GOA
February Twilight. Sara Teasdale. FaPON; OBCA; PDV; RHPC
February's Forgotten Mitts. Raymond Knister. NOBC
Fecht for Britain? Hoot awa! The Patriot. J. C. Milne. PoSH
Feckless Dinner Party, The. Walter de la Mare. FaBoTw
Fed Drapes. Clark Coolidge. LP
Fedele and Fortunio, *sel*. Anthony Munday.
    I Serve a Mistress. EIL
    (Fedele's Song.) OBSC
    ("I serve a mistress whiter than snow.") HAP
Fedele's Song. Anthony Munday. *See* Fedele and Fortunio: I Serve a Mistress.
Federal Constitution, The. William Milns. PAH
Federal Convention, The. *Unknown*. PAH
Fee, fi, fo, fum. *Unknown*. OxNR
Feed. Raymond Knister. OBCV
Feed/ Upon anticipation as you sow the seed. Harvest Time. Star Powers. GoYe
Feed, silly sheep, although your keeper pineth. William Smith. *Fr*. Chloris, III. Son
Feed the Mexican Back into Her. Cherríe Moraga. GLP
Feede on my flocks securely. To His Flocks. *At. to* Henry Constable *and to* Henry Chettle. FM
Feeding, The. Joel Oppenheimer. NeAP
Feeding a Child. Nuala Ni Dhomhnaill, *tr. fr. Irish by* Michael Hartnett. CIP
Feeding Ducks. Norman MacCaig. OxBS
Feeding Ground. Thomas McCarthy. CIP
Feeding the Fire. Donald Finkel. VWA
Feeding the Lions. Norman Jordan. NBP; PoBA
Feel for your bad fall how could I fail. A Sympathy, a Welcome. John Berryman. GrPl; NYBP
Feel free. To Bobby Seale. Lucille Clifton. CNA; PoBA

Feel how the round world rolls. To an Old Rebel. Lauris Edmond. ATNZ
Feel like a Bird. May Swenson. TrGrPo
Feel of autumn in the tall sky of dusk, A. Hearing Flutes along the Road in the Autumn Night. Fuyutsugu, *tr. by* Burton Watson. JLIC-1
Feel of that leather baby, The. Watching the Jets Lose to Buffalo at Shea. May Swenson. ASP
Feel the edge of the knife. Shoriken. Charles Brasch. ATNZ
Feel the sharpness. The Meeting. Ramona Wilson. VoR
Feeling, The. William Bronk. VGW
Feeling a pain in his breast, when he speaks. Ellas and the Statues. Gülten Akin, *tr. by* Nermin Menemencioglu. PBWP
Feeling and Form. Marilyn Hacker. NoAM
Feeling constricted by the dusty city. In the Second Month of Summer, Taking My Family to the Villages East of the City. Li K'ai-hsien, *tr. by* Jonathan Chaves. CoBLCP
Feeling from the Sea, A. Michael Burkard. NAmP
Feeling Fucked Up. Etheridge Knight. NNaP
Feeling Her End Would Come with Summer's End. Rosalía de Castro, *tr. fr. Spanish by* Kate Flores. DMH
Feeling it with me. Walking on Water. James Dickey. NePoEA-2
Feeling lonely. Hara Sekitei, *tr. by* Geoffrey Bownas *and* Anthony Thwaite. PeBJV
Feeling my face has the terrible shine of fish. Element. P. K. Page. MoCV
Feeling of Time. Giuseppe Ungaretti, *tr. fr. Italian by* Isabella Gardner. PFI
Feeling Regret at the Silk Window. Mao Wen-hsi, *tr. fr. Chinese by* Lois Fusek. ATF
Feeling Sorry for Myself. Lu Yu, *tr. fr. Chinese by* Burton Watson. CoBCP
Feeling That Way Too. Arthur Vogelsang. MAYP
Feeling the icy kick, the endless waves. The Swimming Lesson. Mary Oliver. CAPP
Feeling the urge my mother. Birth. Edith Bruck, *tr. by* Ruth Feldman *and* Brian Swann. BoWoP
Feeling the useless arm. Hospital Observation. Julian Symons. WaP
Feelings about Words. Mary O'Neill. RHPC
Feelings Come As I Pass through Wu-chiang. Wu Wei-yeh, *tr. fr. Chinese by* Jonathan Chaves. CoBLCP
Feelings I don't have I don't have, The. To Women, as Far as I'm Concerned. D. H. Lawrence. InPS; OxBSP; WeW
Feelings in Nature ("Bamboo fishing coat, purple official gown"). Ma Chih-yüan, *tr. fr. Chinese by* Jonathan Chaves. *Fr*. Four Poems to the Tune "Ch'ing-chiang yin", IV. CoBLCP
Feelings in Nature ("In the western village the day grows long"). Ma Chih-yüan, *tr. fr. Chinese by* Jonathan Chaves. *Fr*. Four Poems to the Tune "Ch'ing-chiang yin", II. CoBLCP
Feelings in Nature ("Woodcutter wakes as mountain moon hangs low, The"). Ma Chih-yüan, *tr. fr. Chinese by* Jonathan Chaves. *Fr*. Four Poems to the Tune "Ch'ing-chiang yin", III. CoBLCP
Feelings of a Republican on the Fall of Bonaparte. Shelley. Son
Feelings razed to the ground. Poetry and Politics. Lamberto Pignotti, *tr. by* Lawrence R. Smith. NItP
Feelings Wakened by a Mirror. Po Chü-i, *tr. fr. Chinese by* Burton Watson. CoBCP
Feels. J. C. Milne. PoSH
Fees, The! The fees! The mighty fees! God or Mammon. Alfred Cruickshank. PBCV
Feet. Mary Carolyn Davies. WGRP
Feet. Irene Thompson. BoTP
Feet and faces tingle. Finland. Robert Graves. BrPo
Feet at their loveliest are like two hands. Conceit upon the Feet. William Zaranka. BXAP
Feet covered with mud, the smell of meat on their breath. Making Fun of the Well at the Inn below the Mountain. Chu Yün-ming, *tr. by* Jonathan Chaves. CoBLCP
Feet in fancy gold slippers. The End to Everything. Paul Eluard, *tr. by* Michael Benedikt. POS
"Feet just like ice" say. By Now. Ralph Salisbury. STE
Feet of Judas, The. George Marion McClellan. BANP; PoNe
Feet of Morning, The. Hans Arp, *tr. fr. French by* Michael Benedikt. POS
Feet of morning the feet of noon and the feet of evening, The. The Domestic Stones (fragment). Hans Arp, *tr. by* David Gascoyne. EAS
Feigned Courage. Charles *and* Mary Lamb. GN; OxBChV
Feld, groes or goers, hus, doeg, dung. Returning to Roots of First Feeling. Robert Duncan. PoA
Felicia Ropps. Gelett Burgess. FaPON

Felicia's Café. Medbh McGuckian. FaBCIP
Felicity the healer isn't young. Doctor Frolic. Robert Pinsky. NoAM
Feliks Skrzynecki. Peter Skrzynecki. CBAP
Feline. Ronald Wallace. TDD
Feline Fine. J. Patrick Lewis. TDD
Félire Oengus, *sel.* John Montague.
   Sunset. FaBCIP
Félise. Swinburne. BeLS
Felix Randal. Gerard Manley Hopkins. BrPo; EBEV; EBVV; FaBoMo;
   GTBS-P; HAP; InPS; LiTB; LiTM; MoAB; MoBrPo; MoP; NAEL-2;
   NoAM; NOBE; NoP; OBD; OBEV; OBNC; PoE; PoRA; PrIm; Son;
   SOTW; WeW
Felixstowe; or, The Last of Her Order. Sir John Betjeman. OxBTC
Fell far but the barn (came) up and smacked me. Fed Drapes. Clark
   Coolidge. LP
Fell the edge of the knife. Shoriken. Charles Brasch. PeNZ
Fella from town stopped by the other day, A. How Many Cows? Nyle
   A. Henderson. CowP
Felled Plane Tree, The. Anna Hajnal, *tr. fr. Hungarian by* William Jay
   Smith. BoWoP; MHuP
Feller I Know, A. Mary Austin. AmFN; FaPON
Feller isn't thinkin' mean, A. Out Fishin'. Edgar A. Guest. BLPL;
   PoLF
Fellow poet spoke thus to me, A. With Exultation, As We Can! H.
   Leivick, *tr. by* Benjamin *and* Barbara Harshav. AYP
Fellow Wanderers Gather for the Night in Late Autumn. Cheng Wen-cho,
   tr. fr. Chinese by Kang-i Sun Chang. WFTU
Fellow Workers. "Marie." PF
Fellow, you have no flair for art, I fear. The Sitting Bard. Sir Owen
   Seaman. NOBL
Fellows up in Personnel, The. The Perforated Spirit. Morris Bishop.
   FiBHP
Fellowship. *Unknown.* BLPA
Felo de Se. Thomas Blackburn. OxBTC
Felo de Se. Richard Hughes. OBMV
Felo de Se. Vernon Scannell. OBD
Female. Muhammad al-Ghuzzi, *tr. fr. Arabic by* May Jayyusi *and* John
   Heath-Stubbs. MAP
Female Cabin Boy, The. *Unknown.* OxBSS
Female Dancer. James Camp. Son
Female Frailty, *sel.* Philip Freneau.
   Song of Thyrsis. AA; LiTA
Female Friend, The. Cornelius Whur. FaBoCo
"Female genital, like the blank page anticipating the poem, The."
   Sentience. Sandra McPherson. PoA
Female giants, fauna of women. The Women of Rubens. Wislawa
   Szymborska, *tr. by* Celina Wieniewska. WPOW
Female God, The. Isaac Rosenberg. FaBoTw
Female Husband, Who Had Been Married to Another Female for Twenty-
   one Years, The. *Unknown.* CoMu
Female is fertile, and discipline, The. Praise for Sick Women. Gary
   Snyder. NeAP
Female of the Species, The. Kipling. BLPA; FPL
Female Parricide, The. *Unknown.* APAS
Female Principle, The. A. D. Hope. OxBC
Female Prisoners—Boggo Road. Robin Thurston. UAS
Female Rain. Laura Tohe. STE
Female Sailor, The. *Unknown.* OBET
Female spider/ swept her legends into her palms. Roots of Blue Bells.
   Nia Francisco. HATNAP
Female War Criminal. Evangeline Paterson. CN
Femina. Daphne Marlatt. NOBC
Feminine. H. C. Bunner. AA
Feminism, baby, feminism. Male Rage Poem. Pier Giorgio Di Cicco.
   NOBC
Femme Agée. Lauris Edmond. UAS
Femme et Chatte. Paul Verlaine, *tr. fr. French by* Arthur Symons.
   AWP; OBVE
Fen-chou. T'an Ssu-t'ung, *tr. fr. Chinese by* Timothy C. Wong. WFTU
Fen-Men of Lincolnshire's Holland, The. Michael Drayton. *Fr.*
   Polyolbion, Five and Twentieth Song. FaBoPP
Fence, The. Heather McHugh. GeTw
Fence, A. Carl Sandburg. WeW
Fence beyond fence from breakfast. The Names of the Humble. Les A.
   Murray. CBAP
Fence or an Ambulance, A. Joseph Malins. BLPA
Fence Wire. James Dickey. NYBP; VGW
Fenceposts wear marshmallow hats, The. On a Snowy Day. Dorothy
   Aldis. PDV
Fencing School. John Manifold. CBAP

Fenyeit Freir of Tungland, The. William Dunbar. OxBLMV
Feodosia. Osip Mandelstam, *tr. fr. Russian by* W. S. Merwin *and*
   Clarence Brown. AnAn
Feral Pioneers, The. Ishmael Reed. PoBA; PoNe; UnPo
Ferdinand De Soto lies. The Distant Runners. Mark Van Doren. GOA;
   LiTA; LiTM; MoAmPo
Ferdinando and Elvira; or, The Gentle Pieman. W. S. Gilbert. FaBoCo;
   FaBoNo; FiBHP; NA
Fergus Falling. Galway Kinnell. DiL
Ferishtah's Fancies, *sel.* Robert Browning.
   When I Vexed You. OxBSP
Fern. Ted Hughes. NYBP
Fern Hill. Dylan Thomas. CMoP; FaBoPP; FaBV; FPL; GoJo; GTBS-P;
   HAP; HeIP; InPK; InPS; LiTB; LiTM; MoAB; MoBrPo; MoP;
   NAEL-2; NIP; NoAM; NOBE; NoP; OAEL-2; OBWVE; OxBTC;
   PoE; PoLF; PoRA; PPP; SoSe; TrGrPo; TwCP; WeW
Fernando ("Fernando has a basketball"). Marci Ridlon. NTCP; RHPC
Ferniehirst Castle. Richard Hugo. NoAM
Ferns, The. Gene Baro. RHPC
Ferry, The. George Henry Boker. AA
Ferry Me across the Water. Christina Rossetti. *Fr.* Sing-Song. ChTr;
   GoJo; OxBChV; PDV
   (Ferryman, The.) BoTP
Ferry Ride, *sel.* Selma Robinson.
   Bus Ride. FaPON
Ferry service suspended. *Unknown, tr. by* Burton Watson. FCEI
Ferry window frames a pop-art shovel, The. Debora Sleeping. William
   Logan. MAYP
Ferryman, The. László Nagy, *tr. fr. Hungarian by* George MacBeth.
   MHuP
Ferryman, The. Christina Rossetti. *See* Sing-Song: Ferry Me across the
   Water.
Fertile. Gerrit Komrij, *tr. fr. Dutch by* Jacob Lowland. DuIn
Fertile and rank and rich the coastal rains. Advent. William Everson.
   NeAP; TrCP
Fertile Muck, The. Irving Layton. NoAM; NOBC; OBCV
Fertile Valley of the Nile, The. Eve Merriam. IHMS
Fertilizer plant grinds fish into stink, The. Then the Skin Falls Apart.
   Dara Wier. TV
Fervid breath of our flushed Southern May, The. Evening on the
   Potomac. Richard Hovey. AnAmPo
Festal Board, The. *Unknown.* BLPA
Festal Song. William Pierson Merrill. *See* Rise Up, O Men of God.
Feste Burg Ist Unser Gott, Ein. Martin Luther. *See* Mighty Fortress Is
   Our God, A.
Feste's Song ("Come away, come away, death"). Shakespeare. *See*
   Twelfth Night: Come Away, Come Away, Death.
Feste's Song ("O mistress mine! where are you roaming?"). Shakespeare.
   See Twelfth Night: O [*or* Oh] Mistress Mine [Where Are You
   Roaming?].
Feste's Song ("When that I was and a little tiny boy"). Shakespeare. *See*
   Twelfth Night: When That I Was and a Little Tiny Boy.
Festival, The. Frederic Prokosch. LiTA; WaP
Festival in Fishing Village No. 3. Park Je-chun, *tr. fr. Korean by* Koh
   Chang-soo. ACKP
Festival in Fishing Village No. 19. Park Je-chun, *tr. fr. Korean by* Koh
   Chang-soo. ACKP
Festival in Fishing Village No. 25. Park Je-chun, *tr. fr. Korean by* Koh
   Chang-soo. ACKP
Festival, letting a baby sleep, A. Ozaki Hosai, *tr. fr. Japanese by* Hiroaki
   Sato. *Fr.* One Hundred Haiku in Free Form. FCEI
Festival of the Blind. Ishigaki Rin, *tr. fr. Japanese by* Sato. FCEI
Festival of the Hunter and the Trees. René Char, *tr. fr. French by*
   William Jay Smith. CT
Festival of the Nativity, The. Richard De Ledrede, *tr. fr. Latin by* Robert
   Wyse Jackson. TIRV
Festivals have I seen that were not names. Calais, August 15, 1802.
   Wordsworth. NAs
Festubert: The Old German Line. Edmund Blunden. MMA
Fetch in the holly from the tree. Holly and Mistletoe. Eleanor Farjeon.
   PChr
Fetch me a red flower from that meadow. Speech Warts. Myra Sklarew.
   CRP
Fetchin Water. Claude McKay. PBCV
Fetching Cows. Norman MacCaig. OxBC
Fetching the Wounded. Laurence Binyon. MMA
Fete, A. Larry Eigner. NeAP
Fete confused me, The. Guests played the part of gods. Sigismundo.
   Linda Gregg. AmPA
Fêtes, Fates. John Malcolm Brinnin. LiTA

Feuerzauber. Louis Untermeyer. TrJP

Feuilles d'Automne, *sels.* Victor Hugo, *tr. fr. French by* Francis Thompson.
  Heard on the Mountain. AWP
  Sunset, A. AWP

Fever. Robert Browning. *Fr.* The Dance of Death. FL

Fever, The. Rosemary Dobson. FaBoWP

Fever, A. John Donne. OAEL-1

Fever. Thom Gunn. PeHV

Fever of my song, the vin du pays of my voice, The. Marsyas. Hugo Claus, *tr. by* James S. Holmes. DuIn

Fever 103°. Sylvia Plath. CMoP; FaBoWP; NoAM; NOBA; VGW

Fever Toy, The. Charles Wright. AmPA

Feverish room and that white bed, The. White Heliotrope. Arthur Symons. BoLoP; EBEV

Few are the moonlit nights that I've cared for. Last Stop. George Seferis, *tr. by* Edmund Keeley *and* Philip Sherrard. VMG

Few beds are stonier than one shared by a sleeper. Bed Time. Peter Davison. UnPo

Few days after, A. Death of a Bird. Jon Silkin. NePoEA

Few days ago, A. A Wife Talks to Herself. Stephen Berg. NaP

Few days before I die, A. At the Landing. Maura Stanton. NAmP

Few days before you died, death, A. To a Pope. Pier Paolo Pasolini, *tr. by* James Kirkup. PeHV

Few ever came to help you speak or sell. Peter Dale. *Fr.* The Fragments. NOCV

Few flowery branches are just skimming the low wall, A. Viewing the Plum-Blossoms. Sun Kuang-hsien, *tr. by* Lois Fusek. ATF

Few grains of dust more or less, A. Hunted. Paul Eluard, *tr. by* David Gascoyne. RHTwFP

Few Happy Matches. Isaac Watts. NOEC

Few have seen the King Selkie and few the grand. The Boar of Badenoch and the Sow of Atholl. Naomi Mitchison. PoSH

Few, in the days of early youth. The World I Am Passing Through. Lydia Maria Child. AA

Few leaves fell this afternoon, A. The Course of a Day in a Summer Garden. Peter Handke, *tr. by* Beth Bjorklund. CoAuP

Few light flakes of snow, A. Kyoto: March. Gary Snyder. PPP

Few Lines, A. Jacob Glatstein, *tr. fr. Yiddish by* Benjamin *and* Barbara Harshav. AYP

Few Lines to Fill up a Vacant Page, A. John Danforth. SCAP

Few master a form to be conspicuous in the night. The Firefly. Sandra McPherson. AnAn

Few men in any age have second sight. To a Reviewer Who Admired My Book. John Ciardi. OBAL

Few men of hero-mould. John Bright. Francis Barton Gummere. AA

Few minutes ago, A. To the Cicada. James Wright. KS

Few Muddled Metaphors by Moore-ose Melodist. Tom Hood. *See* Muddled Metaphors.

Few sashay, a few finagle, A. I Knew I'd Sing. Heather McHugh. GeTw

Few Things Can More Inflame. C. Day Lewis. OBMV

Few times back in the early fall, The. Measles. Kaye Starbird. RHPC

Few times only, then away, A. Night Song for a Woman. Alfred W. Purdy. NOBC

Few trembling lines on the palm of my hand, A. A Few Lines. Jacob Glatstein, *tr. by* Benjamin *and* Barbara Harshav. AYP

Few words are best; I wish you well. To Mr. N. C., St. James's Place, London, October 22nd. Pope. OxBSP

Few Words in the Mother Tongue, A. Irena Klepfisz. ER

Fforestfawr. Kingsley Amis. *Fr.* The Evans Country. NOBL

Fhairshon swore a feud. The Massacre of the Macpherson. William Edmonstoune Aytoun. BXAP; CenHV; ChTr; FaBoCo

Fiametta. John Peale Bishop. LiTA

Fiascherino. Charles Tomlinson. NoAM

Fiat Lux. Lloyd Mifflin. AA

Fib Detected, A. Catullus, *tr. fr. Latin by* John Hookham Frere. AWP; OBVE

Fibre shoes tightly woven. *Unknown, tr. by* Arthur Waley. BoS

Fickle Hope. Harrison Smith Morris. AA

Fickle One, The. Pablo Neruda, *tr. fr. Spanish by* Donald D. Walsh. FF

Fickleness of women cannot be fully proved, The. To a Good Friend Who Would Prove the Fickleness of Women with the Example of Queen Anne. Margaretha Susanna von Kuntsch, *tr. by* Susan L. Cocalis *and* Gerlinde Geiger. DMG

Fiction. Charles Sprague. *Fr.* Curiosity. AA

Fiction: A Message. Gavin Ewart. OxBC

Fiction and the Reading Public. Philip Larkin. NOBL; OBSV

Fiction-Makers, The. Anne Stevenson. DiPo

Fiction of relationship, The. New Potatoes. Ken Belford. NeAC

Fiddle, The. Neil Munro. BoTP

Fiddle-de-dee! High June. Catherine A. Morin. BoTP

Fiddle-I-Fee. *Unknown.* AmFP

Fiddlehead, The. David McFadden. NeAC

Fiddler, The. Martin Buber, *tr. fr. German by* Jawaid Awan. VWA

Fiddler and his wife, The. *Unknown.* OxNR

Fiddler of Dooney, The. W. B. Yeats. EBVV; FaBoCh; NBLV

Fiddler settles in, The. Lament for the O'Neills. John Montague. CIP

Fiddler was improvising, The. The Blizzard. Eugene Ware. CowP

Fiddler's Green. John Conolly. OxBSS

Fiddler's Green. Theodore Goodridge Roberts. CaP

Fidele, A. William Collins. EnRP; NOEC
  (Dirge in "Cymbeline.") ELP; Mes; NOBE; SeCePo
  (Fidele.) OBEV

Fidele. Shakespeare. *See* Cymbeline: Fear No More the Heat o' the Sun.

Fidele's Dirge. Shakespeare. *See* Cymbeline: Fear No More the Heat o' the Sun.

Fidelia. George Wither. *See* Fair Virtue, The Mistress of Philarete.

Fidelis. Adelaide Anne Procter. BLPA; FaBoBe

Fidelity. Trumbull Stickney. LiTA

Fidelity. Wordsworth. FM

Fidessa, More Chaste than Kind, *sels.* Bartholomew Griffin.
  Care-Charmer Sleep. *Fr.* XV. AAS; NIP
    (Sleep.) OBSC
  Faire Is My Love. *Fr.* XXXVII. GBL; PoEL-2
    (My Love.) TrGrFo
    (Sonnet: "Fair is my love that feeds among the lilies.") EiL; ErPo
  "Fly [*or* Flye] to her heart; hover about her heart." *Fr.* XXIII. AAS
    (Her Heart.) TrGrPo
  "I have not spent the April of my time." *Fr.* XXXV. AAS
    (Sonnet: "I have not spent the April of my time.") EiL
    (Youth.) OBSC
  "My ladies haire is threeds of beaten gold." *Fr.* XXXIX. AAS

Fie, Fie on Blind Fancy! Robert Greene. *Fr.* Greene's Groatsworth of Wit. EiL
  (Lamilia's Song.) OBSC

Fie, fie upon her! Portrait of Cressida. Shakespeare. *Fr.* Troilus and Cressida, IV, v. TrGrPo

Fie! flattering Fortune, look thou never so fair. Lewis, the Lost Lover. Sir Thomas More. OBSC

Fie [*or* Fye], foolish Earth, think[e] you the heaven wants glory. Fulke Greville. *Fr.* Caelica, XVI. PoEL-1; Son
  (Love's Glory.) OBSC

Fie on Eastern Luxury. Horace. *See* Odes: I, 38. Simplicity.

Fie on Love. James Shirley. OxBSP

Fie, Pleasure, Fie! George Gascoigne. EiL; InvP

"Fie, school of patience, fie, your lesson is." Sir Philip Sidney. *Fr.* Astrophel and Stella, LVI. NAEL-1

Fie upon hearts that burn with mutual fire. Against Fruition. Sir John Suckling. CaPo; ErPo

Field. Susan Griffin. NPGG

Field, The. Jean Valentine. LCAP

Field Ambulance in Retreat. May Sinclair. OBTV

Field and Forest. Randall Jarrell. LCAP; VGW

Field Daisy, The. Jane Taylor. BoTP

Field Day. W. R. Rodgers. BIrV

Field Full of Folk, The. William Langland. *See* Vision of Piers Plowman, The: In a summer [*or* somer] season, when soft[e] was the sun [*or* sunne *or* sonne].

Field-Glasses. Andrew Young. GTBS-P; RB

Field Hospital, The. Paul Muldoon. CIP

Field Hospital, 1945. Andras Fodor, *tr. fr. Hungarian by* Jascha Kessler. FOC

Field-Mouse, The. Enid Blyton. BoTP

Field Mouse, The. "Fiona Macleod." FaPON; MoShBr

Field mouse follows its own shadow, The. Snowfall; a Poem about Spring. James Wright. LCAP; NoAM

Field of Autumn. Laurie Lee. LiTM

Field of Folk, The. William Langland. *See* Vision of Piers Plowman, The: In a summer [*or* somer] season, when soft[e] was the sun [*or* sunne *or* sonne].

Field of Glory, The. E. A. Robinson. AnAmPo; MoAmPo

Field of golden wheat there grows, A. Harvest Song. Richard Dehmel, *tr. by* Ludwig Lewisohn. AWP

Field of Light, A. Theodore Roethke. LiTM; TwCP

Field of Night, The. Miriam Waddington. VWA

Field of Omi in Inami Plain, The. Akahito, *tr. fr. Japanese.* *Fr.* Manyo Shu. Ma

Field of poetry ends here, The. The Dump. Greg Kuzma. PoA

Field of Talavera, The. Thomas Hardy. *Fr.* The Dynasts, *pt.* II, Act IV, sc. iv. CMoP

Field of the Grounded Arms, The. Fitz-Greene Halleck. PoEL-4

Field of Waterloo, The. Thomas Hardy. *Fr.* The Dynasts. FaBoCh (Chorus of the Years.) CMoP ("Yes, the coneys are scared by the thud of hoofs.") WaaP

Field Path. John Clare. OxBSP

Field Poem, A. Laura Valaitis. GOYP

Field Sports. Pope. *See* Windsor Forest: When milder autumn summer's heat succeeds.

Field Sports, *sel.* William Somervile. "When Autumn smiles, all beauteous in decay." FM

Field Work. Doug Cockrell. Psk

Field Work. Seamus Heaney. AnAn; FaBCIP

Fieldmouse, The. Cecil Frances Alexander. OxBChV

Fields, The. W. S. Merwin. CAPP; HCAP

Fields Abroad with Spangled Flowers, The. *Unknown.* ChTr

Fields are black once more, The. Reading in Fall Rain. Robert Bly. GrPl

Fields are chill, The; the sparse rain has stopped. Clearing at Dawn. Li Po, *tr. by* Arthur Waley. AWP

Fields are wrapped in silver snow, The. The Christmas Present. Patricia Hubbell. PDV

Fields from Islington to Marybone, The. Blake. *Fr.* Jerusalem, II, Prologue. ChTr, *4 sts.*; FaBoPV; OBNV (Prelude: "Fields from Islington to Marybone, The.") OBNC

Fields in fog, the low, dull resonance of morning, The. Early Meadow-Rue. Stanley Plumly. LCAP

Fields of Learning. Josephine Miles. NoAM

Fields, Teruko-san, are threshed, Thc. A good. The Hibakusha's Letter (1955). David Mura. BrSi

Fields, the mountains, The. Tonna, *tr. by* Steven D. Carter. WFTW

Fields were silent, and the woodland drear, The. In the Dark. Mary Thacher Higginson. AA

Fields Where We Slept. Muriel Rukeyser. NNaP

Fiend, The. James Dickey. PPP

Fiend/ Saw undelighted all delight, all kind, The. Milton. *Fr.* Paradise Lost, *Bk.* IV, *ll.* 285–357. FaBoPV

Fierce and brooding holocaust of faith, The. Edgar Bowers. *Fr.* Two Poems on the Catholic Bavarians, I. CRP

Fierce Dream, The. Jeffrey Wainwright. DiPo

Fierce is the wind tonight. The Viking Terror. *Unknown, tr. by* Fred Norris Robinson. AnIL

Fierce musical cries of a couple of sparrowhawks hunting on the headland, The. Birds. Robinson Jeffers. InPS; VGW

Fierce Old Trees. Väinö Kirstinä, *tr. fr. Finnish by* Aili Jarvenpa. SOP

Fierce they drove on, impatient to destroy. Homer, *tr. fr. Greek by* Pope. *Fr.* The Iliad, XIII. OBVE

Fierce wrath of Solomon. The Burning of the Temple. Isaac Rosenberg. FaBoMo; TrJP

Fiercely the battle raged and, sad to tel!. Ambrose Bierce. *Fr.* The Devil's Dictionary. OBAL

Fiery earth. To Patrice Lumumba. Roberto Armijo, *tr. by* David Volpendesta. Vol

Fiesolan Idyl, A. Walter Savage Landor. EnRP (Fæsulan Idyl.) SeCePo

Fiesta. Paul Hannigan. PPR

Fife and Drum. Dryden. *Fr.* A Song for St. Cecilia's Day, 1687, 8 *ll.* GN

Fife Tune. John Manifold. CBAP; FaFP; GoJo; InPS; LiTB; LiTM; Mes; NBLV; WaaP; WaP

Fifine at the Fair, *sel.* Robert Browning. "And so I somehow-nohow played." Par

Fifteen Acres, The. James Stephens. BoTP

Fifteen Boys, or Perhaps Even More. Bella Akhmadulina, *tr. fr. Russian by* Daniel Weissbort. WPOW

Fifteen churches lie here. At Dunwich. Anthony Thwaite. MoBS

Fifteen day of July, The. Lord Willoughby. *Unknown.* CoMu

Fifteen Days of Judgment, The. Sebastian Evans. NOBVV

Fifteen foresters in the Braid alow. Johnie Cock. *Unknown.* ESPB

Fifteen Haiku, *sels.* Masaoka Shiki, *tr. fr. Japanese by* Burton Watson. FCEI "Before the/ red blossoms." "I don't know when." "I, who/ hear the drums." "I, who/ listen to a man." "I, who/ plant the pit." "I, who/ think so often of." "If I were to paint." "If you stick the stems."

"Last year in spring." "Sprays of wisteria/ arranged in a vase—/ one cluster." "Sprays of wisteria/ arranged in a vase—/ the blossoms hang down." "Sprays of wisteria, The/ arranged in the vase/ are so short." "These wisterias." "When I look/ at the wisteria blossoms/ I think of long ago." "When I look/ at wisteria blossoms/ I want to get out."

Fifteen Hokku, *sels.* Joso, *tr. fr. Japanese by* Hiroaki Sato. FCEI "Below the boulder where I sit." "Blackening the offing." "Both fields and mountains." "Bottom of loneliness, The." "Colder than the snow." "Dragonfly catches a fly, A." "From my sleeve a katydid." "I run into fireflies." Ill in Bed. "Just seen the bottom of the water." "On the boulder at the bottom." "Thinking I'm after them." Waiting on Basho as He Lay Ill. "White beach: a dog barks." "Wolves' voices harmonize."

Fifteen Hokku, *sels.* Shiba Sonome, *tr. fr. Japanese by* Hiroaki Sato. FCEI "After a wind a firefly." At the Ferry on the Miya River. "Busy, the winter clouds." "Child I carry on my back, The." "Each time they roll in." "Evening dusk: crowned with fans." "Heat's so intense I dry my towel, The." "Ice has vanished—don't be left behind." "Leaves of trees rend, The." "Not content, the violets have dyed." "Robin's call has stumbled on a rock, A." "Rouge vendors come." "So cool: brow laid on the green straw mat." "Spilled from a tree-searing wind." "Violets have withered."

"Fifteen men on the dead man's chest." Derelict. Young E. Allison. BLPA; FaBoBe; FaFP; OnMSP

Fifteen men on the Dead Man's Chest. Pirate Ditty. Robert Louis Stevenson. *Fr.* Treasure Island. NOBVV

Fifteen million/ Dead souls. The Great Escape. Sista Roots. WS

Fifteen Million Plastic Bags. Adrian Mitchell. OBSV; OxBTC

Fifteen or twenty feet below. The Anchorage. Pat Wilson. ATNZ

Fifteen Ships on Georges Banks. *Unknown.* AmFP

Fifteen to Eighteen. Marilyn Hacker. GLP

Fifteen years ago I awoke. Above Machu Picchu, 129 Baker Street, San Francisco. Joseph Stroud. NPGG

Fifteen years ago the edict came: peace with the invader. Border Mountain Moon. Lu Yu, *tr. by* Burton Watson. CoBCP

Fifteen years ago, when soldiers. Graduation Day, 1965. Julio Marzán. InW

Fifteen years in the coal mine. Coal Diggin' Blues. *Unknown.* AmFP

Fifteenth Evening of the First Lunar Month, The. Li Nan, *tr. fr. Chinese by* Dominic Cheung. IFON

Fifteenth of the Eighth Month, The. Kaai Chigetsu, *tr. fr. Japanese by* Hiroaki Sato. *Fr.* Thirteen Hokku. FCEI

15th Raga: For Bela Lugosi. David Meltzer. *Fr.* Ragas. NeAP

Fifteenth Telegram ("Birds that migrated, The"). Abd al-Aziz al-Maqalih, *tr. fr. Arabic by* Lena Jayyusi *and* Christopher Middleton. *Fr.* Telegrams of Tenderness for Sanaa. MAP

5th black law student, The. You've Got to Learn the White Man's Game. Mbembe Milton Smith. ASP

Fifth Choir of Angelicals. Cardinal Newman. *See* Dream of Gerontius, The: Chorus of Angels.

Fifth Day, The. Eeva Kilpi, *tr. fr. Finnish by* Aili Jarvenpa. SOP

Fifth day of the fifth month. Hsü Wei, *tr. fr. Chinese by* Jonathan Chaves. *Fr.* Lotus. CoBLCP

Fifth Day of the First Week, The. Joshua Sylvester. *Fr.* Du Bartas: His Divine Weeks and Works. "Pretty lark, climbing the welkin clear." PBBP

Fifth-Floor Window, The. Lola Ridge. WPE

Fifth from the north wall, The. The Cross of Gold. David Gray. AA

Fifth Hell, The. Jerome Rothenberg. *Fr.* The Seven Hells of Jigoku Zoshi. NNaP

Fifth-month hills. Tsurayuki, *tr. fr. Japanese by* Burton Watson. *Fr.* Kokin Shu. FCEI
Fifth Ode of Horace, The. Horace. *See* Odes: I, 5. "What slender youth bedewed with liquid odours" ("Quis multa gracilis").
Fifth Season, The. Reg Saner. FYAP
Fifth Sense, The. Patricia Beer. MoBS
5th Stanza For Dr. Johnson, Donald Hall, Louis Phillips, and X. J. Kennedy, A. C. L. Grove. SoTCo
Fifties, The. Ira Sadoff. AmPA
Fiftieth Birthday of Agassiz, The. Longfellow. ImOP
Fifty. Kenneth Rexroth. TAP
Fifty Faggots. Edward Thomas. BrPo; MoAB; MoBrPo
50—50. Langston Hughes. NoAM; NOBA; PoE
Fifty-Fifty. Carl Sandburg. ILY
LV. "So oft as I her beauty do behold." Spenser. *Fr.* Amoretti. Son; TrGrPo
LIV. "Of this world's theatre in which we stay." Spenser. *Fr.* Amoretti. NAEL-1; NoP; OAEL-1
Fifty-four years I've entered. Jisso, *tr. by* Lucien Stryk *and* Takashi Ikemoto. ZPCJ
Fifty, not having expected to arrive here. Journey toward Evening. Phyllis McGinley. GoYe; NYBP
50 on 50. Peter Meinke. KS
Fifty-one Tanka, *sels.* Lady Izumi, *tr. fr. Japanese by* Hiroaki Sato. FCEI
  "Aware that your body cannot follow."
  "Breaking off rock azaleas."
  "Dew that formed remains, The."
  "Don't tell people how it was."
  "Down the mountain into the path of darkness."
Elegies For Her Daughter, Ko-Shikibu ("That she may know I love her and miss her").
Elegies for Prince Atsumichi ("Because I do not know where you are").
Elegies for Prince Atsumichi ("Clearly he would notice: in my eyes").
Elegies for Prince Atsumichi ("Dead people come to visit tonight").
Elegies for Prince Atsumichi ("Discard myself—just the thought is bitter").
Elegies for Prince Atsumichi ("I miss your voice as you talked to me").
Elegies for Prince Atsumichi ("I wish I could see you like this snow").
Elegies for Prince Atsumichi ("It would console me to see you").
Elegies for Prince Atsumichi ("No dreams through the night").
Elegies for Prince Atsumichi ("One body, but heart shattered into a thousand pieces").
Elegies for Prince Atsumichi ("Though my heart isn't a summer field").
Elegies for Prince Atsumichi ("You are gone, and I have nothing unhappy to remember").
  "Even my pillow, not knowing, won't talk."
From Prince Atsumichi ("I tell myself not to doubt you").
From Prince Atsumichi ("If I speak of love you'll think I am like everyone else"). LLLT
  "Harbor plovers calling to their friends."
  "Having waited for this one for this."
  "I look around: because charcoal firing warms the air."
  "I want to see and be seen by you."
  "If I should forget you because of this unhappiness."
  "If you'd left me unhappy and hadn't come."
In Reply ("Don't keep your heart from resenting me").
In Reply ("I don't think you are like everyone else").
  "Less troublesome than unforgettable."
Looking at My Grandchildren.
  "Lost in thought—even the firefly from the marsh."
  "Loving you, my heart may shatter."
  "Moon above the clouds doesn't look like the moon, The."
  "No soothing time for someone who thinks of blossoms."
  "No wonder you're grieved this morning."
  "On spring fields there was only snow."
  "Plum fragrance startles me again and again."
  "There's no color called love in this world."
To a Man I Met Only Briefly.
To a Man Who Left Me Early in My Life.
To a Man Who Said, "You've forgotten me."
To a Sage in Harima.
To Someone, when I Was Distressed.
  "Today again, quietly and leisurely I make my ablutions."
  "Tonight, as hail falls on bamboo leaves."
  "Unaware of my black hair in disorder."
  "We retain the flowers in mind as we pass."
  "Which is worse, to love someone far away."
  "Which is worse, to miss someone dead."
  "Which should I think shouldn't exist in this world."

  "You left, the mist lingered by the hedge."
  "You rose with eastern clouds and left."
Fifty-six years, above Buddhas, Patriarchs. Doyu, *tr. by* Lucien Stryk *and* Takashi Ikemoto. ZPCJ
"Fifty stories more to fall." Rhyme of Rain. John Holmes. GrPl
Fifty times the rose has flower'd and faded. On the Jubilee of Queen Victoria. Tennyson. UnPo
Fifty today, old lad? Ode to Me. Kingsley Amis. NAs
Fifty wizards working in the wind. A Poem to Explain Everything about a Certain Day in Vermont. Genevieve Taggard. NYBP
Fifty worlds lie on my table. Plurality of Worlds. Washington Delgado, *tr. by* Maureen Ahern *and* David Tipton. Per
Fifty Years. James Weldon Johnson. BANP
Fig for fickle, A. Walter Scott. Gloria A. Maxson. SoTCo
Fig for Thee, Oh! Death, A. Edward Taylor. NAAL-1
Fig for those by law protected, A! Drinking Song. Burns. *Fr.* The Jolly Beggars. TrGrPo
Fig-tree, a falling woolshed, a filled-in well, A. Mullabinda. David Rowbotham. CBAP; PoAu-2
Fight. *Unknown.* FaFP
Fight at Dajo, The. Alfred E. Wood. PAH
Fight at Sumter, The. *Unknown.* PAH
Fight at [the] San Jacinto, The. John Williamson Palmer. AA; PAH
Fight of Paso del Mar, The. Bayard Taylor. BeLS
Fight of the *Armstrong* Privateer, The. James Jeffrey Roche. PAH
Fight of the Red Cross Knight and the Heathen Sansjoy, The. Spenser. *Fr.* The Faerie Queene, I, 5. FiP
Fight of the Year, The. Robert McGough. OBCP
Fight over the Body of Keitt, The. *Unknown.* PAH
Fight thou with shafts of silver, and o'ercome. Money Gets the Mastery. Robert Herrick. CaPo
Fight was at its hottest, the. Rev. Andrew Brown, over the Hill to Rest. Josephine D. Henderson Heard. CBWP-4
Fight was over, and the battle won, The. An Allegory. Barcroft Henry Boake. CBAP
Fight your little fight, my boy. Don'ts. D. H. Lawrence. LiTB; LiTM; OxBoLi
Fighter, The. Samuel Ellsworth Kiser. BLPA
Fighter. Musaemura Bonus Zimunya. WMBCH
Fighter Learns of Hands, A. Charles Ghigna. TSL
Fighters. René Char, *tr. fr. French by* Thomas Merton. RHTwFP
Fighting Her. David Phillips. NeAC
Fighting McGuire. William Percy French. CenHV
Fighting nature of the intellect, The. Vast Light. Richard Eberhart. CMoP
Fighting Position, A. Sa'di Yusuf, *tr. fr. Arabic by* Abdullah al-Udhari. MPAW
Fighting Race, The. Joseph I. C. Clarke. AA; AnAmPo; BLPA; BLPL; PAH
Fighting South of the Castle. *Unknown, tr. fr. Chinese by* Arthur Waley. AWP; WaaP
Fighting South of the Ramparts. *Unknown, tr. fr. Chinese by* Arthur Waley. OBD
Fights, The. Milton Acorn. MoCV; NOBC
Figmental mannequin, Turk's-head for the trap. To the Eternal Feminine. Tristan Corbière, *tr. by* C. F. MacIntyre. ErPo
Figs. D. H. Lawrence. OAEL-2
Figs from Thistles ("My candle burns at both ends."), *sel.* Edna St. Vincent Millay. FaBV; NoP; PoA
  First Fig. FaFP; FF; FPL; NoAM; PoLF; TAP
Figure. Judah Leib Teller, *tr. fr. Yiddish by* Benjamin *and* Barbara Harshav. AYP
Figure in the Carpet, The. James Camp. TW
Figure of Eight. Louis MacNeice. OxBSP
Figure of Speech. Ernst Jandl, *tr. fr. German by* Beth Bjorklund. CoAuP
Figure who stands on the beach, A. Vincent O'Sullivan. *Fr.* Brother Jonathan, Brother Kafka, 27. PeNZ
Figured Wheel, The. Robert Pinsky. MAYP; NAmP; NoAM; NPGG; PPR
Figurehead, The. Léonie Adams. WPE
Figures, The. Robert Creeley. UnPo
Figures in a Ruined Ballroom. George Hitchcock. VGW
Figures in the fields against the sky! Antonio Machado, *tr. fr. Spanish by* John Dos Passos. *Fr.* Poems. AWP
Figures of Authority. Edward Watkins. NYBP
Figures on the Frieze, The. Alastair Reid. ErPo; NYBP
Filaments of light. In the New Sun. Philip Levine. NNaP

Filbert, The. Robert Southey. FM
File-Hewer's Lamentation, The. Joseph Mather. FaBoPV; NOEC
File into yellow candle light, fair choristers of King's. Sunday Morning, King's Cambridge. Sir John Betjeman. EaLo
Filing-cabinet of human lives, A. Apartment House. Gerald Raftery. AmFN
Filipino Hombre, A. *Unknown.* AS
Fill, fill the goblet full with sack! Song in a Siege. Robert Heath. OBS
Fill High the Bowl. John Keble. NOCV
Fill me the beaker! Garden at Heidelberg. Walter Savage Landor. OBTV
Fill the Bowl, Butler! *Unknown.* MeEL
Fill the bowl with rosie [*or* rosy] wine. Epicure, The ("Fill the bowl with rosie wine"). Abraham Cowley. OBS; SeCP (Today Is Ours.) TrGrPo
Fill up the cups to the full! Picking Fresh Flowers. Huang-fu Sung, *tr. by* Lois Fusek. ATF
Fill Up Those Glasses, Bartender. Jim Bollers. CowP
Fill your dark glasses with water and toast. Rip-off #1: Hippie Capitalism. Geof Hewitt. NeAC
Fille de Joie: Congo. Michael Jackson. ATNZ
Filled out gourd rots, the, The. Motion's Holdings. A. R. Ammons. NoAM
Filling an Order. John Townsend Trowbridge. AnAmPo; OBAL
Filling her compact and delicious body. John Berryman. *Fr.* Dream Songs. BoLoP; CAPP; HAP; HCAP; NoP; OBAL; OPOP; WeW
Filling Station. Elizabeth Bishop. FaBoMo; HAP; HCAP; InPK; NoP; NYBP; WeW
Filling the mind. The Clouds. William Carlos Williams. VGW
Film, A. Albert Goldbarth. MAYP
Film of the Comedian Chaplin, A. Bertolt Brecht, *tr. fr. German by* Michael Hamburger. AnAn
Film Vermouth: Six o'Clock Show. Magda Portal, *tr. fr. Spanish by* Allan Francovich *and* Kathleen Weaver. PBWP
Filth of Your Suspicion, The. Grace Schulman. PeBMYV
Fin de Siècle. Edmund Vance Cooke. BLPA
Fin de Siècle. Newton Mackintosh. NA
Fin God made Buchan flat and gweed. The Lairig. J. C. Milne. PoSH
Final Arrangement, The. Michael Harlow. ATNZ
Final Chorus. Archibald MacLeish. *Fr.* Panic. MoAmPo
Final Chorus, The. Shelley. *See* Hellas: Choruses from "Hellas."
Final Curtain. Roger Woddis. FaBoPa
Final Dance, The. Bernice Zamora. CCP
Final Dirge. *Unknown. See* This ae nighte [*or* ean night], this ae nighte.
Final Exam. Dan Pagis, *tr. fr. Hebrew by* Warren Bargad *and* Stanley F. Chyet. IP
Final Farewell. Tom Clark. UL
Final Hunger, The. Vassar Miller. LiTM
Final Inch, The. Emily Dickinson. *See* 'Twas like a maelstrom, with a notch.
Final Moments, The. Edwin John Pratt. *Fr.* The Titanic. NOBC
Final Mystery, The. Sir Henry Newbolt. WGRP
Final Night, The. Ali Sardar J'afri, *tr. fr. Urdu by* Mahmood Jamal. PBMUP
Final Painting, The. Lee Harwood. EAS
Final Prayer. Enheduanna, *tr. fr. Sumerian by* Aliki *and* Willis Barnstone. BoWoP
Final Prospect, The. Carl L. Stach. KS
Final reply/ to a first conversation. Ilse Tielsch, *tr. by* Beth Bjorklund. CoAuP
Final Soliloquy of the Interior Paramour. Wallace Stevens. HAP; HCAP; LCAP
Final Soliloquy on a Randy Rooster (in a Key of Yellow). Robert Peters. BXAP
Final Struggle, The. Louis James Block. *Fr.* The New World. PAH
Final summer blooms make ready now to fade, The. The Old Park. Afanasi Afanasievich Fet, *tr. by* Alan Myers. AAA
Final Trawl, The. Archie Fisher. OxBSS
Final Word, The. Dom Moraes. NePoEA-2
Finale. Wystan Hugh Auden. *Fr.* Man of La Mancha. AnAn
Finality broods upon the things that pass. A Walk by the Charles. Adrienne Rich. NePoEA; NYBP
Finally. Vittoria Aganoor Pompili, *tr. fr. Italian by* Brenda Webster. PBWP
Finally a free evening. Cinema. Kurt Klinger, *tr. by* Beth Bjorklund. CoAuP
Finally, among the bottles shining. The Lady in the Barbershop. Raphael Rudnik. NYBP

Finally, from your house there is no view. Water Island. Howard Moss. CoAP; NePoEA-2; NYBP; Prf
Finally I have the right to greet creatures whom I do not know. The Musician of Saint-Merry. Guillaume Apollinaire, *tr. by* Roger Shattuck. POS
Finally I heard. In What Manner the Body Is United with the Soule. Jorie Graham. NPGG
Finally I understood Rose's death. Arvo Turtiainen, *tr. fr. Finnish by* Aili Jarvenpa. *Fr.* Ballad of Herman's Rose, V. SOP
Finally retired pensionless. Big Momma. Don L. Lee. BPo; CNA
Finally, to forgo love is to kiss a leaf. Rescue the Dead. David Ignatow. CAPP; PrIm; VGW
Finally toward midnight. Occasional Poem. Peter Handke, *tr. by* Beth Bjorklund. CoAuP
Financial Wisdom. *Unknown.* FaBoUs
Finch-notes and swallow-notes tell the new year. Spring Thoughts. Huang-fu Jan, *tr. by* Witter Bynner. OFD
Finches, The. Thomas William Shapcott. PoAu-2
Finches. Marcia Southwick. PPR
Find. Josephine Miles. NoP; WPE
Finder Found, The. Edwin Muir. PoA
Finders Keepers. Donald Finkel. VWA
Finding a Lucky Number. Gary Soto. MOWH
Finding a Poem. Eve Merriam. RFM
Finding a Teacher. W. S. Merwin. NNaP
Finding a Yiddish Paper on the Riverside Line. Barry Spacks. SM
Finding an Old Newspaper in the Woods. Robert Morgan. WeW
Finding Francesca full of tears, I said. Obituary. Thomas William Parsons. AA
Finding gold A left. Exchange. George Rostrevor Hamilton, *after the Greek of* Plato. FaBoEE
Finding is the first act. Emily Dickinson. NOBA
Finding of Gabriel, The. Longfellow. *Fr.* Evangeline. AA
Finding Serenity. Yüan Mei, *tr. fr. Chinese by* Jonathan Chaves. CoBLCP
Finding the Father. Robert Bly. DiL
Finding the Pistol. Gibbons Ruark. MAT
Finding the Tattooed Lady in the Garden. Pattiann Rogers. MT
Finding Them Lost. Howard Moss. CoAP; NYBP; SM
Finding those beams (which I must ever love). Absence. Sir Philip Sidney. SiPS
Finding You. Virginia Gilbert. IHMS
Fine, a Private Place, A. Diane Ackerman. MAYP
Fine autumn scenery tonight. Passing Seven-Mile Rapids on a Moonlit Night. Li E, *tr. by* Irving Lo. WFTU
Fine Clay. Winifred Shaw. PoAu-1
Fine Day, A. Michael Drayton. *See* Muses' Elysium [*or* Elizium]: Clear [*or* Cleere] had the day been [*or* bin] from the dawn [*or* dawne].
Fine Day for Straw Hats, A. Louis Stimson. PBCV
Fine delight that fathers thought, The; the strong. To R. B. Gerard Manley Hopkins. CMoP; GTBS-P; InvP; OAEL-2
Fine Divine Marquis, The. Gust Gils, *tr. fr. Dutch by* James S. Holmes. DuIn
Fine feelings under blockade! Cargoes just in from Kamschatka! Winter Coming On. Martin Bell, *after the French of* Jules Laforgue. FaBoMo; OBVE; OxBTC
Fine fish to net. Ezra Pound, *after the Chinese.* OBVE
Fine game is grab-bag, a fine game to see, A! Grab-Bag. Helen Hunt Jackson. OBCA
Fine gold is here; yea, heavy yellow gold. The House of Colour. Francis Sherman. CaP
Fine joy brings me great happiness. Beatriz de Dia, *tr. by* Meg Bogin. WT
Fine Knacks for Ladies. *Unknown.* CH; EBEV; ElL; HAP; LiTB; NoP; OBSC; QFR
(Peddler's Song, A.) OAEL-1
Fine, love animals, our childlike. To the Animal Lover. Sándor Rákos, *tr. fr. Hungarian by* Jascha Kessler. *Fr.* Bear Song. FOC
Fine Madam Would-Be, wherefore should you fear. To Fine Lady Would-Be. Ben Jonson. FaBoEE; JCP; NoP; OxBSP
Fine merry franions. Going or Gone. Charles Lamb. BXAP
Fine Old English Gentleman, The. *Unknown.* CH
Fine Old English Gentleman; New Version, The. Charles Dickens. CoMu; FaBoBa; NOBVV; OBSV
Fine rain falls, greening their garden, A. The Visitor. Michael Dennis Browne. OBTV
Fine Work with Pitch and Copper. William Carlos Williams. OxBA
Fine Young Folly. William Habington. *Fr.* The Queen of Aragon. OBS
(Pretty Sport.) NOBE
(Song: "Fine young folly, though you were.") MePo

Finely-spun threads of the script, The. Under a Reading Lamp. Christine Busta, *tr. by* Beth Bjorklund. CoAuP
Fineness of midnight. Midnight. Gabriela Mistral, *tr. by* David Garrison. BoWoP
Finesse be first, whose elegance deplores. Six Poets in Search of a Lawyer. Donald Hall. NYBP
Finest art? Patience merely, The. Sister Mary Appassionata Lectures the Journalism Class. David Citino. SoTCo
Finger, The, *sels.* Felix Pollak. TSM
   "I dream of the finger of the statue." *Fr.* II.
   "I look out of my window at night." *Fr.* I.
   "I may pass through once more next month." *Fr.* III.
Finger, A/ Easily/ Turns the world off. Television. Fei Ma, *tr. by* Dominic Cheung. IFON
Finger Folk. H. M. Tharp. BoTP
Finger of Necessity. Coleman Barks. TW
Finger Play. *Unknown.* BoTP
Finger Play for a Snowy Day, A. *Unknown.* BoTP
Finger-print. Mirko Lauer, *tr. fr. Spanish by* David Tipton. Per
Finger to Finger. Elizabeth Smither. ATNZ
Fingerless nun, The. *Unknown, tr. by* Geoffrey Bownas *and* Anthony Thwaite. PeBJV
Fingernail Sunrise. Vernon Watkins. NYBP
Fingers. Uhuru. Mari Evans. CNA
Fingers aching, nails breaking. Rock Leader. Dave Barthgate. PoSH
Fingers begin to droop, The. Voice. Tamura Ryuichi, *tr. by* Hiroaki Sato. FCEI
Fingers, Fists, Gabriel's Wings. Michael Cleary. TSM
Fingers in the Door. David Holbrook. NePoEA-2
Fingers lie in the lap, The. Year's End. Ellen Bryant Voigt. NoAM
Fingers tremble over the belly. Drawing. James Sherry. LP
Finigan's Wake. *Unknown. See* Finnegan's Wake.
Finis. Waring Cuney. AmNP; BANP
Finis. Walter Savage Landor. *See* Last Fruit Off an Old Tree, The: I Strove with None.
Finish, The. Daniel Hoffman. ASP
Finished at last, he escaped from that hideous. Christ's Descent into Hell. Rainer Maria Rilke, *tr. by* James Wright *and* Sarah Youngblood. Prf
Finished Begging. Ryokan, *tr. fr. Japanese by* Burton Watson. FCEI
Finished Course, The. Saint Joseph of the Studium, *tr. fr. Latin by* John Mason Neale. WGRP
Finistére. Thomas Kinsella. IPY
Finisterre. John Frederick Nims. *See* And yet a kiss (like blubber)'d blur and slip.
Finland. Robert Graves. BrPo
Finland birthed me, the world suckled me. Seas Are My Eyes, Birches My Voice. Tommy Tabermann, *tr. by* Aili Jarvenpa. SOP
Finnegans Wake, *sels.* James Joyce.
   Ballad of Persse O'Reilly, The. FaBoBa; LiTB
   Ondt and the Gracehoper, The. BIrV
Finnegan's Wake. *Unknown.* FaBoBa; NBLV
   (Finigan's Wake.) BLPA
Finnesburn Fragment, The. *Unknown, tr. fr. Anglo-Saxon by* Kevin Crossley-Holland. OBWP
Finnigin to Flannigan. Strickland W. Gillilan. FaBoBe
Finn's Wishes. Desmond O'Grady, *tr. fr. Irish by* the author. CIP
Fir stands sveltely under the moon, A. Onitsura, *tr. fr. Japanese by* Hiroaki Sato. *Fr.* Twenty-three Hokku. FCEI
Fir Tree. Wayne Brown. UAS
Fir-Tree, The. Edith M. Thomas. OHIP
Fir-Tree of Bosnia, The. Dante Gabriel Rossetti. FaBoNo
Fir trees taper into twigs and wear, The. Firewood. John Clare. TrGrPo
Fire. William Carpenter. Psk
Fire, The. Robert Creeley. NOBA
Fire. Fazil Hüsnü Daglarca. CRP
Fire, The. Robert Duncan. *Fr.* Passages. VGW
Fire. Langston Hughes. NOBA
Fire. Kondo Azuma, *tr. fr. Japanese by* Geoffrey Bownas *and* Anthony Thwaite. PeBJV
Fire, The. Sir Walter Scott. OBCP
Fire. Dorothy Wellesley. OBMV
Fire and Brimstone; or, The Destruction of Sodom, *sel.* George Lesley. Lament of the Sodomites. PeHV
Fire and Ice. Robert Frost. AmPP; CMoP; FaBoEE; FaFP; FF; FPL; HeIP; HoPM; InPK; LiTA; LiTM; MoAB; MoAmPo; MoP; NAAL-2; NIP; NoAM; NOBA; OxBA; PPP; PrIm; SoSe; TAP; TrGrPo; TW
Fire and Ice. Michael Pettit. MAYP

Fire at Alexandria, The. Theodore Weiss. NoAM; PoA; TAP
Fire Breather, Mexico City, The. Jaime Jacinto. BrSi
Fire-Bringer, The, *sel.* William Vaughn Moody.
   I Stood within the Heart of God, *with music* AH (Pandora Speaks.) WGRP
Fire Burial. Edgar McInnis. CaP
Fire burns bright on my hearth to-night, The. The Fire Guest. George Alfred Townsend. PWR
Fire Burns Low, The. John Leax. TrCP
Fire darkens, the wood turns black, The. Song for the Sun That Disappeared behind the Rainclouds. *Hottentot Oral Tradition, tr. by* Ulli Beier. TTTS; TTY
Fire-Dragon and the Treasure, The. *Unknown, tr. fr. Anglo-Saxon by* Charles W. Kennedy. *Fr.* Beowulf. AnOE
Fire everywhere, the gentle fire of brushwood. Animas, Las. Mario Luzi, *tr. by* I. L. Salomon. PFI
Fire, fire. Henry Bold. GBL
Fire! Fire! said [*or* says] the town crier. *Unknown.* GBP; OxNR
Fire Guest, The. George Alfred Townsend. PWR
Fire, Hair, Meat and Bone. Fred Johnson. PoBA
Fire I praise was once perduring flame, The. Allen Tate. *Fr.* Sonnets of the Blood, VII. PoA
Fire i' the Flint, The. Lucy Catlin Robinson. AA
Fire in a worldwide darkness, A. Cave Drawings. László Benjámin, *tr. by* Edwin Morgan. MHuP
Fire in leaf and grass, The. Living. Denise Levertov. VGW; WPE
Fire in My Meditation Burned. Henry Ainsworth. AH
Fire in the heavens, and fire along the hills. Christopher John Brennan. *Fr.* The Quest of Silence. CBAP; PoAu-1
Fire in the Hole. Gary Snyder. NAAL-2
Fire in the olive groves throughout the night. Vineta. Charles Spear. PeNZ
Fire in the Snow, The. Vernon Watkins. LiTM
Fire is out, and spent the warmth thereof, The. Dregs. Ernest Dowson. OBMV; SeCePo
Fire Island. Rita Mae Brown. IHMS
Fire Island. May Swenson. PoA; TAP
Fire Island pixie called "Mary," A. *Unknown.* PeHV
Fire-kindled satellite. Napkin and Stone. Vernon Watkins. NYBP
Fire-Logs. Carl Sandburg. AnAmPo
Fire-mist and a planet, A. Each in His Own Tongue. William Herbert Carruth. BLPA; OHFP; WBLP; WGRP
Fire more priceless than diamonds rare. The Father's Love. Mary E. Tucker. CBWP-1
Fire of darkness, battle and desire, The. Beim Schlafengehen. K. O. Arvidson. *Fr.* The Four Last Songs of Richard Strauss at Takahe Creek above the Kaipara. ATNZ
Fire of Drift-wood, The. Longfellow. AmPP; BLPL; NAAL-1; NOBA; NoP; OxBA; TAP
Fire of Frendraught, The. *Unknown.* ESPB; OxBB
Fire of London, The. Dryden. *Fr.* Annus Mirabilis. ChTr
Fire of Meditation burns, The. A Præfatory Poem to the Little Book, Entituled, Christianus per Ignem. Nicholas Noyes. SCAP
Fire of my stomach has forced me, The. Tulsidas, *tr. by* John Stratton Hawley *and* Mark Juergensmeyer. SSI
Fire of our victims, The. The Knell. Muhammad Al-Fituri, *tr. by* Samir M. Zoghby. TTY
Fire of the Fireflies, The. Hung Sheng, *tr. fr. Chinese by* Paul W. Kroll. WFTU
Fire of your anger scalds, The. Shamsuddin Mohammad Vali, *tr. by* Ahmed Ali. GoT
Fire off the bells, ring out wild guns. Another Prince Is Born. Adrian Mitchell. NAs
Fire on the Hills. Robinson Jeffers. CMoP
Fire Place, The. Eli W. Mandel. OBCV
Fire Poem, The. Theodore Enslin. CRP
Fire-Queen. Ruth Fainlight. PoA
Fire rides calmly in the air. At War. Charles Madge. FaBoMo
Fire Seven Times Tried This, The. Shakespeare. *Fr.* The Merchant of Venice, II, ix. CTC
Fire Ship, The. *Unknown.* OxBSS
Fire Side, The; a Pastoral Soliloquy. Isaac Hawkins Browne. *Fr.* The Foundling Hospital for Wit. NOEC
Fire that cancels all that is. Burning Love Letters. Howard Moss. HoPM
Fire that in the Stone, The. Tuvia Rübner, *tr. fr. Hebrew by* Bernhard Frank. MHeP
Fire the Babysitter. David Avidan, *tr. fr. Hebrew by* Warren Bargad *and* Stanley F. Chyet. IP
Fire the heather. Joseph Gordon MacLead. *Fr.* Men of the Rocks. OxBS

Fire: The People. Alfred Corn. *Fr.* A Call in the Midst of the Crowd. MAYP; NAAL-2
Fire threatens, The. Hyena's Song to her Children. *Unknown.* PeSA
Fire to see my wrongs for anger burneth, The. The Wronged Lover. Sir Philip Sidney. *Fr.* Arcadia. SiPS
Fire Tree, The. "Adunis," *tr. fr. Arabic by* Abdullah al-Udhari. MPAW
Fire-Truck, A. Richard Wilbur. AiP
Fire upon the hearth is low, The. In the Firelight. Eugene Field. AA
Fire was first. Genealogy. Donald Finkel. VWA
Fire was furry as a bear, The. Dark Song. Edith Sitwell. CMoP; FaBoTw; PBWP
"Fire, water, woman, are man's ruin!" A Dutch Proverb. Matthew Prior. FaBoEE; NOEC
Fire wings soar into forest depths. Owl Woman. Amber Coverdale Sumrall. GOS
Fire, with well-dried logs supplied, The. The Fire. Sir Walter Scott. OBCP
Firebombing, The. James Dickey. OBWP
Firebowl. Sydney Clouts. VWA
Firebrand. Harry Crosby. EAS
Firebrand from off your altar, Prophet, cast away, The. Message. Hayyim Nahman Bialik, *tr. by* Bernhard Frank. MHeP
Firebreathers at the Café Deux Magots, The. Miller Williams. MT
Fired Pot, The. Anna Wickham. FaBoTw; FaBoWP; OxBTC
Fireflies. Chao Chih-hsin, *tr. fr. Chinese by* Michael S. Duke. WFTU
Fireflies. Faustin Charles. PBCV
Fireflies. Edgar Fawcett. AnAmPo
Fireflies. Carolyn Hall. FaPON
Fireflies. Li Nan, *tr. fr. Chinese by* Dominic Cheung. IFON
Fireflies. "Fiona Macleod." *Fr.* Transcripts from Nature. FM
Fireflies, The, *sel.* Charles Mair.
   "How dreamy-dark it is!" OBCV
Fireflies. Shohaku, *tr. fr. Japanese by* Steven D. Carter. WFTW
Fireflies in the Garden. Robert Frost. RHPC
Fireflies over a Marsh. Tamemasa, *tr. fr. Japanese by* Steven D. Carter. WFTW
Firefly/ fading away pitifully. On the Death of His Younger Sister. Kyorai, *tr. fr. Japanese by* Burton Watson. *Fr.* Twenty Hokku. FCEI
Firefly, The. Sandra McPherson. AnAn
Firefly, The. Ogden Nash. FPL
Firefly. Elizabeth Madox Roberts. GoJo; NTCP; PDV; RAR; TSS
Firefly. George Uba. BrSi
Firefly: a frog opens his mouth a bit. Issa, *tr. fr. Japanese by* Hiroaki Sato. *Fr.* Forty-four Hokku. FCEI
Firefly, airplane, satellite, star. Back Yard, July Night. William Cole. BoNaP
Firefly light. Summer. Ramona Wilson. VoR
Firefly's flame, The. The Firefly. Ogden Nash. FPL
Firelight. E. A. Robinson. NoAM
Firelight. Whittier. *See* Snow-bound; a Winter Idyl:
   Shut in from all the world without.
Firelight and shadows. Look. Charlotte Zolotow. RAR
Firelight flickered on the age-old beams, The. At the Ship. R. P. Lister. FiBHP
Firelight in sunlight, silver-pale. The Marriage of Heaven and Earth. Howard Nemerov. NYBP
Fireman Save My Child. *Unknown. See* No More Booze.
Firemen. Abraham Sutskever, *tr. fr. Yiddish by* Chana Bloch. PeBMYV
Firemen, firemen! Help! X. J. Kennedy. RHPC
Fires. Elizabeth Fleming. BoTP
Fires. William Heyen. MAYP
Fires at Will. René Daumal, *tr. fr. French by* Michael Benedikt. POS
Fires in the dark you build; tall quivering flames. To a Very Wise Man. Siegfried Sassoon. BrPo
Fires lit by the guards, The. Yoshinobu, *tr. by* Geoffrey Bownas *and* Anthony Thwaite. PeBJV
Fires of Driftwood. Isabel Ecclestone MacKay. CaP
Fires of kalpa: have they ever consumed one speck of dust?, The. Impressions. Wen T'ing-shih, *tr. by* Irving Lo. WFTU
Firetail's Nest, The. John Clare. EnRP
Firewood. John Clare. TrGrPo
Fireworks. Babette Deutsch. NYBP; OFD
Fireworks. James Reeves. OnUR
Fireworks. Valerie Worth. NTCP; RR
Firing. Ahmad Nadeem Qasmi, *tr. fr. Urdu by* Mahmood Jamal. PBMUP
Firm as young bones, fine as blown spume, still. Paradigm. Babette Deutsch. TrJP
Firm of Happiness, Limited, The. Norman Cameron. FaBoTw

Firm on the seven Buddhas' cushion. Dogen, *tr. by* Lucien Stryk *and* Takashi Ikemoto. ZPCJ
Firmament Displays on High, The. Barend Toerien, *tr. fr. Afrikaans by* author. PeSA
Firmament, with golden stars adorned, The. Resignation. *Unknown.* OBSC
Firmly set are the rabbit nets. *Unknown, tr. by* Arthur Waley. BoS
Firmly, sweetly,/ refusing. Portrait of a Woman (and a Man). John Figueroa. PBCV
Firmness. Anthony Hecht. OBAL
1st, The. Lucille Clifton. *See* What I remember about that day.
First/ A far thud. Fireworks. Valerie Worth. NTCP; RR
First, The/ tale of Gotham City, the Beggar. The Beggar at the Gate. Ian Wedde. PeNZ
First/ the leaf/ new and shiny. The Chestnuts Are Falling. Lilian Moore. RR
First a flicker of telepathy. Word of Art. Alan Bernheimer. UL
First a monkey, then a man. Dawn of the Space Age. John Ciardi. OBAL
First a sea: soft sand, muds, and marls. What Happened Here Before. Gary Snyder. NNaP; PoM
First a terror of choice, but that was done. I Had a Terror—Since September. Gerald William Barrax. MT
First, after the spots in the Sun. Pasolini. Kevin Killian. BAP
First Aid at 4 A.M. Christopher Bursk. InPK
First American Congress, The. Joel Barlow. PAH
First American Sailors, The. Wallace Rice. PAH
First and foremost I was trying to realize. Steve Benson. IAT
First and Last. Bruce Severy. NOVW
First and Last Man. Ralph McTell. OBET
First and last—the people, dressed up and down. The Departure. Kevin Hart. UAS
First and Second Law. Michael Flanders. FaBoUs
First Anniversary, The. John Donne. *Fr.* An Anatomy of the World. NAEL-1
1st April 1984. Peter Russell. NPo
First, April, she with mellow showers. The Four Sweet Months. Robert Herrick. BoTP; WiR
   (July: The Succession of the Four Sweet Months.) FaPON
First, are you our sort of a person? The Applicant. Sylvia Plath. MAT; NAAL-2; NaP; NMM; NOBA; TwCP
First Aspen, *sel.* Lynn Strongin.
   "Sensuous Latin poet, now I will go off with a thermos, A." IHMS
First, Best Country, The. Goldsmith. *Fr.* The Travel[l]er; or, A Prospect of Society. GN
First Birth, The. Rodney Jones. MAYP; MT
First blossom was the best blossom, The. Apple Blossom. Louis MacNeice. RB
First blow caught me sideways, my jaw, The. The Beating. Ann Stanford. WPE
First blow of October. Now oak leaves shy. Ambition. X. J. Kennedy. BLA
First born of Chaos, who so fair didst come. Hymn: To Light. Abraham Cowley. MeLP; MePo; OBS; SeCV-1
First born of dawn woman, The. A Breeze Swept Through. Luci Tapahonso. GOS
First-born Star, The. Matthew Arnold. *Fr.* Bacchanalia; or, The New Age. FaBoRV
First butterfly. Takahama Kyoshi, *tr. by* Geoffrey Bownas *and* Anthony Thwaite. PeBJV
First came the primrose. A Chanted Calendar. Sydney Thompson Dobell. *Fr.* Balder. BoTP; OBEV
   (Procession of the Flowers, The.) GN
First Canzone of the Convito, The. Dante, *tr. fr. Italian by* Shelley. OBVE
First Carolina Said-Song. A. R. Ammons. OBAL
First Child, Born Out of Breach in Mid-May. Sherod Santos. *Fr.* The Sheltering Ground, I. Son
First childbirth/ her husband feels like. *Unknown, tr. by* Burton Watson. FCEI
First Christmas, The. Emilie Poulsson. OHIP
First Cigarette, The. Joseph Rolnik, *tr. fr. Yiddish by* Irving Feldman. PeBMYV
First clan of autumn, thistleball on a stem. Thistledown. James Merrill. UnPo
First cocks begin clearing the throat of morning, The. A Valley Where I Don't Belong. Marge Piercy. IHMS
First Coffin Poem. David Ignatow. CAPP
First cold front came in, The. Winter's Onset from an Alienated Point of View. Alan Dugan. FF

First cold rain. Basho, *tr.* by Kenneth Koch *and* Harold Henderson. TTTS

First come I. My name is Jowett. Henry Charles Beeching. *Fr.* Balliol Rhymes. CenHV; FaBoCo; FaBoEE; NOBL

First comes love and then comes marriage. Autograph Book/ Prophecy. Anne Halley. NMM

First Communiqué from One Returning from the Zanj Revolt. Abd al-Aziz al-Maqalih, *tr. fr. Arabic by* Lena Jayyusi *and* John Heath-Stubbs. MAP

First Confession. X. J. Kennedy. NePoEA-2; PPP

First cool spell has, The. Burnout in the Overshoot. A. R. Ammons. BLA

First Corinthians, *sels.* Bible, *N.T.*
  "But some one will ask, "How are the dead raised?."" *Fr.* XV: 35-57. DL
  "Now I would remind you, brethren." *Fr.* XV: 1-8. DL
  Though I Speak with the Tongues of Men and Angels. *Fr.* XIII: 1–13. OAEL-1
  (Greatest of These, The, *abr.*) TrGrPo

First Corinthians at the Crossroads. Bruce Dawe. NoAM

First Corncrake. John Hewitt. NeIP

First country to die was normal in the evening, The. The Last War. Kingsley Amis. OBSV; OxBC; SoSe

First cries were, The. Mother Poem. Joel Oppenheimer. PoM

First cut the gourds in slices, and then run. Recipe: Gourds. Nicander. FaBoUs

First Cycle of Love Poems, *sel.* George Barker.
  My Joy, My Jockey, My Gabriel. *Fr.* V. ErPo; MoBrPo

First Date, The. David Avidan, *tr. fr. Hebrew by* Warren Bargad *and* Stanley F. Chyet. *Fr.* Samson, Our Hero, 3. IP

First Day, The. Christina Rossetti. *See* Monna Innominata: I Wish I Could Remember.

First day, The/ I came to in the dark cold trembling. The Creation of the World. Éva Tóth, *tr.* by Laura Schiff. AIW

First Day at Boarding School. Prunella Power. Mes

First day he had gone, The. A Space in the Air. Jon Silkin. NePoEA; TrJP

First day I shot dope, The. Summer Words of [*or* for] a Sistuh [*or* Sister] Addict. Sonia Sanchez. BISi; BPo; TV; UnPo

First day. Jackie and I walking in leaves. Cruel Boys. Gary Soto. MOWH; NPGG

First day of Christmas, The. The Twelve Days of Christmas. *Unknown.* AmFP; FaFP; OxBoLi; OxNR; PChr

First Day of Spring. Robert Long. NAmP

First Day of Spring, The. Pien Kung, *tr. fr. Chinese by* Jonathan Chaves. CoBLCP

First Day of Teaching. Bonaro W. Overstreet. TrPWD

First Day of the Hunting Moon, The. Patricia Low. VGW

First day of this month I saw. Snowdrops. George MacBeth. OBCP

First day of Yole have we in mind, The. Sing We Yule. *Unknown.* MeEL

First day she passed up and down through the Heavens, The. Petrarch, *tr. fr. Italian. Fr.* Sonnets to Laura: To Laura in Death, LXXV, *tr. by* J. M. Synge. OBMV

First day starts, The. "All's changed." Princess Shikishi, *tr. fr. Japanese by* Hiroaki Sato. *Fr.* Seventy-eight Tanka. FCEI

First-Day Thoughts. Whittier. AmPP; NoP; TrCP

First Days. Tuvia Ruebner, *tr. fr. Hebrew by* A. C. Jacobs. VWA

First day's night had come, The. Emily Dickinson. LiTA; LiTM; OxBA; PoE; WPOW

First Death. Donald Justice. MT; SM

First Death in Nova Scotia. Elizabeth Bishop. CoAP; FaBoWP; LCAP; NOBA; NYBP

First Did I Fear. Giles Fletcher the Elder. *Fr.* Lucia, XX. Son

First Dimension of Skunk, The. Ray A. Young Bear. HATNAP

First draw the sea, that portion which between. Instructions to a Painter. Edmund Waller. APAS

First Dream, *sel.* Sister Juana Inés de la Cruz, *tr. fr. Spanish by* Samuel Beckett.
  "But Venus first." BoWoP; MexPo

First drum roll—and he's a coil of air, limbs in all directions, he, The. Acrobatics. Dan Pagis, *tr. by* Warren Bargad *and* Stanley F. Chyet. IP

First Elegy for the Dead in Cyrenaica. Hamish Henderson. OxBS

First enters wearing the neon armour, The. Ten Types of Hospital Visitor. Charles Causley. OxBC

First (entitled to the place). Charles Churchill. *Fr.* The Duellist. OBSV

First Epistle of the First Book of Horace Imitated, The, *sel.* Pope.
  "Well, if a King's a lion, at the least." OBSV

First Epistle of the Second Book of Horace, Imitation of, *sels.* Pope. Ideals of Satire, The. FiP
  "Of little use the man you may suppose." EBEV

First event in his career is, The. Description of an American Billionaire. Hermann Gail, *tr. by* Beth Bjorklund. CoAuP

First Families Move Over! Ogden Nash. FaBoCo

First, feel, then feel, then. Young Soul. Amiri Baraka. BPo; CNA

First few days back at the Indian School, The. Cat or Stomp. Laura Tohe. STE

First Fig. Edna St. Vincent Millay. *Fr.* Figs from Thistles. AiP; FaBoWP; FaFP; FF; FPL; NoAM; PoLF; TAP

First Fight. Then Fiddle. Gwendolyn Brooks. InPK; NIP; PoNe

First Flight. Daniel Hoffman. GrPl

First Flight. Dorothy Wellesley. OBTV

First follow Nature, and your judgment frame. Pope. *Fr.* Essay on Criticism, *pt.* I. HAP

First, for effusions due unto the dead. Upon His Sister-in-Law, Mistress Elizabeth Herrick. Robert Herrick. CaPo

First forget what time it is. Exercise. W. S. Merwin. NOBA

First Forgotten, The. James Keir Baxter. FL

First frost is weeks off, but the prudent man. Discretions of Alcibiades. Robert Pinsky. NPGG

First full moon of overgrown buffalo. America's Wounded Knee. Phillip William George. VoR

First girl I ever kissed was Sally Adams, The. First Kiss. Jonathan Holden. GOYP

First, Goodbye. John Smith. GOYP

First Grade. Phillip William George. VoR

First Grass. H. Leivick, *tr. fr. Yiddish by* Benjamin *and* Barbara Harshav. AYP

First Green Heron. Gary Margolis. ASP

First Grey Hair, The. Mary E. Tucker. CBWP-1

First Grief, The. Felicia Dorothea Hemans. *See* Oh, call my brother back to me.

First halt. They heard within a sugar patch. John Hunter-Duvar. *Fr.* The Emigration of the Fairies. CaP

First having read the book of myths. Diving into the Wreck. Adrienne Rich. CAPP; HCAP; HeIP; InPK; InPS; MoP; MOS; NAAL-2; NIP; NoAM; NOBA; NoP

First hazelnut trundles down from above, The. The Squirrel. Saleem Barakat, *tr. by* Lena Jayyusi *and* Naomi Shihab Nye. MAP

First he drew a strike zone. The Hummer. William Matthews. TDD

First hear the story of Kaspar the rosy-cheeked. Fräulein Reads Instructive Rhymes. Maxine W. Kumin. NYBP; Psk

First horn lifts its arm over the dew-lit grass, The. The House Slave. Rita Dove. NoAM

First Hymn. John Gill. NeAC

First I did take some squills, and fried them all. A Banquet. Sotades, *tr. by* Charles Duke Yonge. FaBoUs

First I locked hands with myself. What a Circus. Alan Dugan. AnAn

First I looked on, after a long time far from home, The. American Change. Allen Ginsberg. HCAP

First I lowered my head. A Woman's Song, about Men. *Unknown, tr. by* Paul-Emile Victor; *English vers. by* Armand Schwerner. OV; STP

First, I need possession of the soil, the dwelling. Ch'ing-ming Nostalgia. Yung Tzu, *tr. by* Dominic Cheung. IFON

First, I put my. The Power of Love He Wants Shih (Everything). Rochelle Owens. NMM

First I saw the white bear, then I saw the black. At the Zoo. Thackeray. NTCP; OxBChV

First I went down to the street. A Ballad of Going Down to the Store. Miron Bialoszewski, *tr. by* Czeslaw Milosz. PwPP

First Ice, The. Shin Dong-jip, *tr. fr. Korean by* Koh Chang-soo. ACKP

First idea was not our own, The. Adam. Wallace Stevens. *Fr.* Notes toward a Supreme Fiction. NOBA

First I'll sing. Later, perhaps, I'll speak. The Condition. T. Carmi, *tr. by* Peter Everwine *and* Shula Starkman. VWA

First illusion, The. Keisen, *tr. by* Lucien Stryk *and* Takashi Ikemoto. ZPCJ

First in a carriage. *Unknown.* OxNR

First in his pride the orient sun's display. Hilaire Belloc. FaBoEE

First in the fight, and first in the arms. Zollicoffer. Henry Lynden Flash. PAH

First in the North. The black sea-tangle beaches. The Mythical Journey. Edwin Muir. NoAM; OxBS

First Invasion of Ireland, The. *Unknown, tr. fr. Irish by* John Montague. BIrV

First It Was Singing. Jon Silkin. NePoEA

First Julep, The. Bliss Carman. AnAmPo

First king was Pharamond, The; after him came. Kings of France. Mary W. Lincoln. BLPA

First Kings, sel. Bible, O.T.
  "And Hiram of Tyre sent his servants unto Solomon." Fr. V: 1-5, 11-14. EyDe

First Kiss. Jonathan Holden. GOYP

First know, my friend, I do not mean. Matthew Green. Fr. The Spleen. NOEC

First lady of the throne room, The. The Restoration of Enheduanna to Her Former Station. Enheduanna. BoWoP

First, last and always dearest, closest, best. Alec Derwent Hope. PoAu-2

First Law of Thermodynamics, The. First and Second Law. Michael Flanders. FaBoUs

First Lawcase, The. Unknown, tr. fr. Irish by John Montague. BIrV

First Lay of Gudrun, The. Unknown, tr. fr. Old Norse by William Morris and Eirikr Magnusson. Fr. The Elder Edda. AWP
  Gudrun Laments over Sigurd. OBVE

First Lesson. Philip Booth. SD; SM; TwCP

First Lessons in Musical Time. Unknown. FaBoUs

First, let me view what noxious nonsense reigns. Richard Savage. Fr. The Authors of the Town. OBSV

First Light. P. J. Kavanagh. NPo

First Light. Thomas Kinsella. BIrV; CMoP; PoE

First light of day in Mississippi. Birthday Poem. Al Young. NPGG

First light of the day, milk-/colored, The. Jacob. Bin Ramke. NAmP

First Love. Charles Stuart Calverley. FiBHP

First Love. Thomas Campion. GBL; OxBoLi

First Love. John Clare. BoLoP; ChTr; EnLoPo; GBL; HAP; NOBVV; NoP

  (I Ne'er Was Struck.) ELP

First Love. Mary Dorcey. BrRo

First Love. Charles Gullans. NePoEA

First Love. Judith Hemschemeyer. Psk

First Love. Kitahara Hakushu, tr. fr. Japanese by Hiroaki Sato. FCEI

First Love. Stanley Kunitz. GOYP

First Love. Carl Lindner. TSL

First Love. Sharon Olds. FYAP

First Love. Robert Polito. PPR

First love/ who played it. Chopin's Minute Waltz. Gerda Mayer. DT

First love is first death. There is no other. The Sequel. Delmore Schwartz. LiTM

First Love Poem, The. Myra Glazer Schotz. VWA

First Maccabees, sels. Bible, Apocrypha.
  Dirge. Fr. II: 8-14. TrJP
  Great Mourning. Fr. I: 25-28. TrJP
  Judas Maccabeus. Fr. III: 1-9. TrJP
  "Then they took whole stones according to the law." Fr. IV: 47-59. OFD

First, make a letter like a monument. The Book of Kells. Padraic Colum. BIrV

First man—you are his child, he is your child, The. Song of the Flood. Unknown. TTTS

First Meditation. Theodore Roethke. Fr. Meditations of an Old Woman. LCAP; NOBA

First Menstruation. Ellen Bass. TV

First Monday Scottsboro Alabama. Tom Weatherly. PoBA

First month of his absence, The. Alun Lewis. LiTM; NAEL-2; OBWP; WaaP

First month of winter: cold air comes. Unknown, tr. fr. Chinese by Burton Watson. Fr. Nineteen Old Poems of the Han, XVII. CoBCP

First morning it flew out of the fog, The. Waders and Swimmers. Stanley Plumly. GeTw

First morning of Three Mile Island: those first disquieting, uncertain, mystifying hours, The. Tar. C. K. Williams. CAPP; GeTw; NAmP

First, my father taught me to read poetry. To Hear My Head Roar. Henry Taylor. MAYP

First-name-only business beggars history, The. Larkin. Gibbons Ruark. DiPo

First News Reel: September 1939. Joan Barton. CN

First Night, A. Peter Kane Dufault. DiPo

First Night at Sea. John Berryman. AnAn

First night, the first night, The. Carol for the Last Christmas Eve. Norman Nicholson. OBCP

First night when I came home, The. Our Goodman. Unknown. AmFP
  (Four Nights' Drunk, The.) AnAmPo; OBAL

First note, simple, The; the second note, distinct. Conrad Aiken. Fr. Preludes for Memnon; or, Preludes to Attitude. LiTA

First Notes from One Born and Living in an Abandoned Barn. Pattiann Rogers. NAmP

First Nowell, The. Unknown. LiTB; PChr

First Ode. Madeleine Des Roches, tr. fr. French by Dorothy Backer. DMF

First of all do you remember the way a bear goes through. Destruction. Joanne Kyger. UL

First of all her name was changed. Dream about Sunsets. Annabelle Hébert. GrPl

First of all it has to be anecdotal; ideas don't exist. The Canadian Prairies View of Literature. David Donnell. NOBC

"First of all, it's all true." The Creation, According to Coyote. Simon J. Ortiz. CDW; HATNAP

First of All My Dreams, The. E. E. Cummings. NYBP; VGW

First of all paint a cage. To Paint the Portrait of a Bird. Jacques Prévert, tr. by Michael Benedikt. POS

First of April, some do say, The. Unknown. BoTP

First of August. A. J. Seymour. PBCV

First of God by whom all grace is spread. Sources of Good Counsel. Peter Idley. OxBChV

First of My Lovers, The. Sydney Carter. OBET

First of summer, lovely sight. Unknown. NOIV

First of the Emigrants, The. Unknown. OxBSS

First of the gods I honor in my prayer is Mother Earth. The Eumenides. Aeschylus, tr. by Robert Fagles. NAWM-1

First of the undecoded messages read: "Popeye sits in thunder," The. Farm Implements and Rutabagas in a Landscape. John Ashbery. CoAP; SM

First One Drew Me, The. Rav Abraham Isaac Kook, tr. fr. Hebrew by Ben Zion Bokser. VWA

First one notices. Tamehide, tr. by Steven D. Carter. WFTW

First one was the gunner's wife and she was dressed in green, The. The Sailors' Wives. Unknown. OxBSS

First or Last. Thomas Hardy. CMoP

First pale shoots, The. On a Picture of Your House. Douglas G. Jones. NOBC

First period, The: the epoch of thought. Six Periods of Creation. Maori Oral Tradition, tr. by Richard Taylor. WTO

First person I loved, The. Coming Out. Jacqueline Lapidus. IHMS

First Philosopher's Song. Aldous Huxley. AWP

First Photos of Flu Virus. Harold Witt. SM

First Poem of the Year. Kishun Ryuki, tr. fr. Japanese by Burton Watson. FCEI

First Position. Mary Mackey. Fr. Arabesque: Five Poems for Women without Children. ER

First Practice. Gary Gildner. AmPA; Psk; TSL; TW

First Praise. William Carlos Williams. VGW

First Pregnancy. Alta. NMM

First Prelude. Francis J. Smith. CRP

First Prelude. Dream in Ohio; the Father. John Logan. Fr. Poem in Progress. LCAP

First Proclamation of Miles Standish, The. Margaret Junkin Preston. PAH

First Psalm, The. Bertolt Brecht, tr. fr. German by Robert Bly. NU

First Quest, The. Joseph Rodman Drake. See Culprit Fay, The: Fay's Departure, The.

First Rain. Robert Creeley. CAPP

First Rain. Tsfrirah Gar, tr. fr. Hebrew by Bernhard Frank. MHeP

First Rain, The. Angelos Sikelianos, tr. fr. Greek by Edmund Keeley and Philip Sherrard. VMG

First Rain: Sent to Magistrate Mo-ch'ing. Sung Hsiang, tr. fr. Chinese by Irving Lo. WFTU

First Rainfall. Alan P. Lightman. BWV

First rape a people. Pan Recipe. John Agard. PBCV

First-Rate Equation, A. Luciano Erba, tr. fr. Italian by Lawrence R. Smith. NItP

First Reader, The. Winfield Townley Scott. PoA

First retainer, The. A Marriage. Robert Creeley. LiTM; NeAP

First Robin, The. Lilian Leveridge. CaP

First rose a low shore pastures green to the water. The Waving of a Hand. W. S. Merwin. CAPP; DiL

First Rule. Maurice Kenny. HATNAP

First, run around in circles. Fat Lena's Recipe for Crocodile Soup. Phyllis Janowitz. TDD

First runner reached us, The. The Finish. Daniel Hoffman. ASP

First Samuel, sels. Bible, O.T.
  Hannah's Song of Thanksgiving. Fr. II: 1–10. AWP
  (Song of Hannah, The.) TrCP, ad. by Michael Drayton.
  Hannah's Thanksgiving. Fr. II: 1–10. BoWoP

First Satire of the Second Book of Horace, The. Pope. OAEL-1; OBSV; PPP; PrIm
   Sels.
   Question of Libel, A. PrIm, *abr.*
   "With all a woman's virtues but the pox." OBSV
First sentence: Her cheap perfume. Seduced by Analogy. Bob Perelman. LP
First September day was blue and warm, The. The Artist on Penmaenmawr. Charles Tennyson Turner. OBNC
1st Series, No. I. James Russell Lowell. *Fr.* The Biglow Papers.
   Letter, A ("Thrash away, you'll hev to rattle"). AmPP; OxBA
   (Mr. Hosea Biglow Speaks.) PAH
1st Series, No. II. James Russell Lowell. *Fr.* The Biglow Papers.
   Letter, A ("This kind o' sogerin' ain't a mite like our October trainin' "). OxBA
1st Series, No. III. James Russell Lowell. *Fr.* The Biglow Papers.
   What Mr. Robinson Thinks. AA; AmPP; PAH
1st Series, No. V. James Russell Lowell. *Fr.* The Biglow Papers.
   Debate in the Sennit, The. PAH
1st Series, No. VII. James Russell Lowell. *Fr.* The Biglow Papers.
   Candidate's Letter, The. AA
First shall the heavens want starry light. A Fancy. Thomas Lodge. *Fr.* Rosalynde; or Euphues' Golden Legacy. EIL; OBSC
   (Love's Protestation.) ACP
First Shaman Song. Gary Snyder. *Fr.* Myths and Texts: Hunting, I. NOBA
First she heard a sound. The Sound. Robert Kelly. PoM
First Shoe, The. Máire Mhac an tSaoi, *tr. fr. Gaelic by* Brendan O Hehir. OV
First shot out of that sling, The. After Goliath. Kingsley Amis. NePoEA-2; NOBL; OxBTC
First shot was fired to Wagnerian music, The. Laocoon. Don Gordon. WaaP
First shower—even a monkey. Basho, *tr. fr. Japanese by* Burton Watson.
   Fr. Seventy-six Hokku. FCEI
First Sight. Philip Larkin. BoNaP; NTCP
First Sight of Her and After. Thomas Hardy. PoEL-5
First sign was your hair, The. I'm Just a Stranger Here, Heaven Is My Home. Carole Gregory Clemmons. PoBA
First silent grass. First Grass. H. Leivick, *tr. by* Benjamin *and* Barbara Harshav. AYP
First Snow. Marie Louise Allen. RAR; RHPC
First Snow. Ted Kooser. GrPl
First Snow-fall, The. James Russell Lowell. AA
First Snow in Alsace. Richard Wilbur. NoP; OBWP
First snow: luckily I find myself residing in my own hut. Basho, *tr. fr. Japanese by* Burton Watson. *Fr.* Seventy-six Hokku. FCEI
First Snow on an Airfield. John Ciardi. PoA
First snow was sleet, The. It swished heavily. Sleet. Norman MacCaig. OBCP
First Snowfall [*or* Snow Fall], The, *sel.* James Russell Lowell. AA; AnAmPo; BLPA; BLPL; FaBoBe; TAP; WBLP
   "Snow had begun in the gloaming, The." FaPON
First Solitude, The, *sels.* Luis de Góngora y Argote, *tr. fr. Spanish by* Edward Meryon Wilson. OBVE
   River Compared to an Oratorical Sentence, The.
   Wedding Feast, The.
   Young Pilgrim Finds Refuge with the Goatherds, The.
First Solo. Walter McDonald. RR
First Song. The. Richard Burton. AA
First Song. Galway Kinnell. CAPP; GoJo; GOYP; GrPl; LiTM; NoP; TwCP
First Song: "Doubt you to whom my Muse these notes intendeth." Sir Philip Sidney. *Fr.* Astrophel and Stella. OBSC
   (To Stella.) EIL
First sorrow of autumn, The. The Seven Sorrows. Ted Hughes. NAEL-2
First spasm became the continuous, The. Recluse. Aldo Camerino, *tr. by* Anita Barrows. VWA
First speaker said, The. "Paper Men to Air Hopes and Fears." Robert Francis. LCAP
First Spring. Duane Niatum. HATNAP
First Spring Day, The. Christina Rossetti. WiR
First Spring Morning. Robert Bridges. BoNaP; BoTP
First stands the lofty Washington. Our Presidents. *Unknown.* BLPA
First star shot up, The. Between Life and Death. Frantisek Gottlieb, *tr. by* Ewald Osers. VWA
First Step, The. C. P. Cavafy, *tr. fr. Greek by* Edmund Keeley *and* Philip Sherrard. Mes

First Step, The. Andrew Bice Saxton. AA
First Steps Up Parnassus. Michael Drayton. *See* My dearly loved friend how oft have we.
First strawberry, The. Original Strawberry. Nancy Willard. LCAP
First, suicide notes should be. Suicide. Alice Walker. FF
First Sun Day of the year. Tonight. Galway Kinnell. *Fr.* The Avenue Bearing the Initial of Christ into the New World. NaP, *fr.* 4.
First Sunday I missed Mass on purpose, The. The Day Zimmer Lost Religion. Paul Zimmer. InPK
First sunlight in the golden bowl of Iowa. With Paul Engle at Fort Madison, 1978. Thomas McCarthy. WCI
First Sunshine. Andreas Okopenko, *tr. fr. German by* Beth Bjorklund. CoAuP
First Telegram ("As I retire, each day, with myself"). Abd al-Aziz al-Maqalih, *tr. fr. Arabic by* Lena Jayyusi *and* Christopher Middleton.
   Fr. Telegrams of Tenderness for Sanaa. MAP
First Test, The. Susan Fromberg Schaeffer. IHMS
First Thanksgiving, The. Jack Prelutsky. NTCP
First Thanksgiving, The. Clinton Scollard. PAH
First Thanksgiving Day, The. Alice Williams Brotherton. OHIP
First Thanksgiving Day. Margaret Junkin Preston. PAH
First Thanksgiving of All. Nancy Byrd Turner. FaPON
First the buffalo. After the War. Gleb Garbovsky, *tr. by* Joseph Langland, Tamas Aczel *and* Laszlo Tikos. BWV
First the falls, then the cave. Behind the Falls. William Stafford. RFM
First the light cracked. Felix Pollak. *Fr.* Tunnel Visions, I. TSM
First, the mandatory poses. Miss Summerfest. Susan Firer. TSL
First the melody, clean and hard. How High the Moon. Lance Jeffers. CNA; PoBA
First the Message Kills. Hans Faverey, *tr. fr. Dutch by* J. M. Coetzee. DuIn
First, the scene endlessly diminishes. Travelling Backward. Gene Baro. NYBP
First the soul of our house left, up the chimney. Tornado. William Stafford. NaP
First the tail begins to stiffen. Cow Pissing. Robert Morgan. GeTw
First, the two men stand pondering. Verona. James Wright. NNaP
First their eyes. Pulling Out. Lyn Lifshin. NeAC
First, then, soliloquies had need be few. On Writing for the Stage. John Sheffield. *Fr.* Essay on Poetry. FaBoUs
First there is the gate from the street, then some flowers inside the wall. Chinese Space. Mei-Mei Berssenbrugge. BAP
First there was a dream not wholly mine. Clouds over Islands. James Seay. MT
First there was a god of night and tempest. From Mythology. Zbigniew Herbert, *tr. by* Czeslaw Milosz. FaBoPV; PwPP
First there was putting hot-water bottles to it. Inevitable. Sir John Betjeman. MoBrPo
First there was the lamb on knocking knees. Dylan Thomas. *Fr.* Altarwise by Owl-Light, III. CMoP
First there were those who died. Living among the Dead. William Matthews. GeTw
First Thesis. Tom Weatherly. *Fr.* Cantos, 7. PoBA
First they cut your wrists and throat. Winter Drought. Michael Ryan. NAmP
First they taught us earth. A Ballad of the Bayonet. Ernest Bryll, *tr. by* Czeslaw Milosz. PwPP
First they were stiff and gaudy. The Magi. George Garrett. MT
First thing I ever knew was funny, The. Laughing Backwards. Jim Hall. GOYP
First thing I saw in the morning, The. Mantova. James Wright. LCAP; NNaP
First thing, I think, is a keen sense, The. Juan Belmonte, Torero. Donald Finkel. NePoEA
First thing that I remember was Carlo tugging away, The. Asleep at the Switch. George Hoey. BeLS
First Thing to Do in a House, The. Anna Wickham. Mes
First Things. Lucienne Desnoues, *tr. fr. French by* Miller Williams. WPOW
First Things First. W. H. Auden. NYBP
First Three, The. Clinton Scollard. PAH
First Time, The. John Newlove. NeAC
First Time, The. Karl Shapiro. ErPo; SM; VGW
First Time: 1950. Honor Moore. GLP
First time ever I saw Johnny Spain was, The. Johnny Spain's White Heifer. Hayden Carruth. MOWH
First Time Ever I Saw Your Face, The. Ewan MacColl. UnAS

First time he kissed me, he but only kissed. Elizabeth Barrett Browning. *Fr.* Sonnets from the Portuguese, XXXVIII. BLPA; BLPL; CTC; FaBoBe

First time I lied to my baby, I told him that it was his face, The. How Lies Grow. Maxine Chernoff. UL

First time I looked seaward, westward. Lone Kauri Road ("First time I looked seaward, westward"). Allen Curnow. *Fr.* Trees, Effigies, Moving Objects, I. ATNZ; PeNZ

First time I met your Pa he took my slip off. Fred Chappell. *Fr.* My Mother Shoots the Breeze. NBLV

First time I visited your parents' house, The. The Old Girl. Gary Lenhart. UL

First time I walked, The. Oranges. Gary Soto. MOWH; NoAM

First time out. Lives. Derek Mahon. FaBCIP

First time that the sun rose on thine oath, The. Elizabeth Barrett Browning. *Fr.* Sonnets from the Portuguese, XXXII. NAEL-2; WPE

First, to the feet, as they bear what you have grown to live in. Praise. William Matthews. AmPA

First Tooth, The. Charles *and* Mary Lamb. OxBChV; RHPC

First travelers to the coves of the Blue Ridge. The Hollow. Robert Morgan. MT

First Travels of Max. John Crowe Ransom. MoAmPo

First truckload, The. Day of the Parade. Alan Chong Lau. BrSi

First Tuesday in the next October. An Auctioneer's Handbill. William Hall. FaBoUs

First Ultraviolet Ballad. Cassiano Ricardo, *tr. fr. Portuguese by* William Jay Smith. CT

First vacation day, A. Jutta Schutting, *tr. by* Beth Bjorklund. CoAuP

First Voyage of John Cabot, The. Hezekiah Butterworth. PAH

First Walk on the Moon. May Swenson. AnAn

First was Eve. Cain's Song. Donald Finkel. VWA

First was Fancy, like a lovely boy, The. Spenser. *Fr.* The Faerie Queene: The Mask of Cupid. NOBE

First wave of a new tide hardly, The. Tides. William Stafford. KS

First we are shown the camp. What a precision. Female War Criminal. Evangeline Paterson. CN

First we burned even. Afterward. Lyn Lifshin. ER

First we have to let forms, colors, sounds sprout. Infinite Millimeter Manifesto. Hans Arp, *tr. by* Michael Benedikt. POS

First weather of spring gathers and slopes, The. Desire. Gary Eddy. KS

First Wedding in the World, The. Joel Rosenberg. VWA

First week the soil was clean, The. Digging for Indians. Gary Gildner. AmPA

First we'll take the red giant who'd beat. So It Shall Be. Moyshe-Leyb Halpern, *tr. by* Benjamin *and* Barbara Harshav *and* Kathryn Helle. AYP

First when Maggie was my care. Whistle o'er the Lave o't. Burns. OxBS

First William the Norman. *Unknown.* OxNR

First Winter. Gail N. Harada. BrSi

First Winter Storm. William Everson. NU

First Woman's Lament. Brenda Chamberlain. *See* Lament: "My man is a bone ringèd with weed."

First words spoken, The. Periods of Adjustment. Shawn Wong. BrSi

First Year, The, *sel.* Edith Jay Scovell.
"Days fail: night broods over afternoon, The." FaBoWP

First you bite your fingernails. American Rhapsody. Kenneth Fearing. MoAmPo

First you close your eyes. A Child Explains Dying. Robert Crum. PPR

First you must blow a bottle round your sleep. Directions for Dreamfishing. Martin Johnston. CBAP

First, you think they are dead. Lobsters in the Window. W. D. Snodgrass. HeIP; NYBP; TAP

First, you will say goodbye. You will turn. First, Goodbye. John Smith. GOYP

Firstborn, The. Gary Soto. NPGG

Firstborn. Charles Wright. DiL

Firstborn Land, The. Ingeborg Bachmann, *tr. fr. German by* Daniel Huws. BoWoP

Firste stok, fader of gentilesse, The. Gentilesse. Chaucer. AWP; NAEL-1; OAEL-1

Firstfruits in 1812. Wallace Rice. PAH

Firstness. Richard Tillinghast. BLA

Firth Park Road: 9:30 A.M. Stanley Cook. NPo

Fisbo, *sel.* Robert Nichols.
"Talking of Ezra Pound and long-dead pantos." OBSV

Fish, The. Elizabeth Bishop. ASP; CAPP; FaBoWP; GoJo; HAP; HeIP; HoPM; InPK; LiTM; MoAB; MoAmPo; MoP; MOS; NAEL-2; NoAM; NOBA; NoP; NU; OPOP; PoE; RB; TrGrPo; WeW

Fish. Arthur Stanley Bourinot. RAR

Fish, The. Rupert Brooke. FM; MOS

Fish, The. Ralph Gustafson. OBCV

Fish. Daniel Halpern. AmPA

Fish. Mary Ann Hoberman. RAR

Fish. Larry Levis. AmPA

Fish, The. Marianne Moore. AmPP; FaBoWP; MoAB; MoAmPo; MoP; MOS; NAAL-2; NoAM; OxBA

Fish, The. Ogden Nash. AnAmPo

Fish, The. Mary Oliver. CAPP

Fish. Joe Rosenblatt. NOBC

Fish. Mario Satz, *tr. fr. Spanish by* Willis Barnstone. VWA

Fish. Takahashi Shinkichi, *tr. fr. Japanese by* Lucien Stryk. NU

Fish. Emily Townsend. NYBP

Fish. W. W. E. Ross. MoCV

Fish, The. L. L. Zeiger. TV

Fish and Bird. Rosemary Brinckman. BoTP

Fish and Chips on the Merry-Go-Round. K. O. Arvidson. ATNZ; PeNZ

Fish Answers, A. Leigh Hunt. *Fr.* The Fish, the Man, and the Spirit. FiBHP; NBLV
(Fish to Man.) MoShBr

Fish are at home, at home among their water plants, The. *Unknown, tr. by* Arthur Waley. BoS

Fish at Mass, The. *Unknown, tr. fr. Latin by* J. F. Webb. BIrV

Fish bones walked the waves off Hatteras. Cottonmouth Country. Louise Glück. CoAP; GeTw

Fish caught in the trap, The. *Unknown, tr. by* Arthur Waley. BoS

Fish Counter at Bonneville, The. William Stafford. AmFN

Fish Crier. Carl Sandburg. AmFN; OxBA

Fish dripping, A. Fish. W. W. E. Ross. MoCV

Fish (fly-replete, in depth of June). Heaven. Rupert Brooke. BrPo; EBEV; HoPM; LiTB; LiTM; MoBrPo; NOBE; PoRA; WGRP

Fish Food. John Wheelwright. LiTA; MOS

Fish in a Painting. Ho Ching-ming, *tr. fr. Chinese by* Jonathan Chaves. CoBLCP

Fish in River: "My house is not quiet, I am not loud." *Unknown, formerly at. to* Cynewulf, *tr. fr. Anglo-Saxon by* Charles W. Kennedy. *Fr.* Riddles (Exeter Book). AnOE

Fish in the minnow-net, The. *Unknown, tr. by* Arthur Waley. BoS

Fish in the Stone, The. Rita Dove. HCAP

Fish in the unruffled lakes. W. H. Auden. BoLoP; CMoP; MoAB; MoBrPo; MoP

Fish leaping. Where the Lilies Were in Flower. Kumattur Kannanar, *tr. by* A. K. Ramanujan. PLW

Fish lives in the brook, The. The Very Nicest Place. *Unknown.* RAR

Fish of the sea couldn't come. How They Brought the Good News by Sea. Norma Farber. PChr

Fish Peddler and Cobbler. Kenneth Rexroth. NNaP

Fish Story. Henry Carlile. ASP

Fish Story. Sharon Olds. TV

Fish-teeming sea. Amergin. *Fr.* Amergin's Songs, III. NOIV

Fish, the Man, and the Spirit, The ("You strange, astonished-looking, angle-faced."), *sel.* Leigh Hunt. ChTr; EnRP; FM; HAP; MOS; NOBL; OBEV; PoEL-4; SeCePo
Fish Answers, A. FiBHP; NBLV
(Fish to Man.) MoShBr

Fish to Man. Leigh Hunt. *See* Fish, the Man, and the Spirit, The: Fish Answers, A.

Fish took a notion, A. Tip-Toe Tail. Dixie Willson. NTCP

Fish Upstairs, The. William Dickey. Psk

Fish wade, The/ through black jade. The Fish. Marianne Moore. AmPP; FaBoWP; MoAB; MoAmPo; MoP; MOS; NoAM; OxBA

Fish, when he's exposed to air, The. The Fish. Ogden Nash. AnAmPo

Fish with the Deep Smile, The. Margaret Wise Brown. PDV

Fisher, The. Roderic Quinn. CBAP; PoAu-1

Fisher Cat, The. Richard Eberhart. GrPl

Fisher, in your bright bark rowing. The Fisherman. *Unknown, tr. by* Anne Higginson Spicer. FaPON

Fisher-lad, A (no higher dares he look). Phineas Fletcher. *Fr.* Piscatorie Eclogues, III. SeCV-1

Fisher Lad of Whitby, The. *Unknown.* OxBSS

Fisher-maids at Shika, The. Kimiko, *tr. fr. Japanese.* *Fr.* Manyo Shu. Ma

Fisherman, The. Abbie Farwell Brown. FaPON

Fisherman, The. Cheng Hsieh, *tr. fr. Chinese by* Jan *and* Yvonne Walls. WFTU

Fisherman, The. Ho Ning, *tr. fr. Chinese by* Lois Fusek. ATF

Fisherman. Honei, *tr. fr. Chinese by* Lucien Stryk *and* Takashi Ikemoto. ZPCJ

Fisherman, The. Leonidas of Tarentum, *tr. fr. Greek by* Andrew Lang. AWP

Fisherman, The. David McCord. PDV
Fisherman, The. Jay Macpherson. Mes; NOBC
Fisherman. Stanley Moss. *See* My father made a synagogue of a boat.
Fisherman. Setcho, *tr. fr. Chinese by* Lucien Stryk *and* Takashi Ikemoto. ZPCJ
Fisherman, The. *Unknown, tr. fr. Portuguese by* Anne Higginson Spicer. FaPON
Fisherman, The. W. B. Yeats. CMoP; HAP; NoAM; SD
Fisherman goes out at dawn, The. The Fisherman. Abbie Farwell Brown.
Fisherman Writes a Letter to the Mermaid, The. Joan Aiken. WSC
Fisherman's Hands, The. Nanine Valen. CRH
Fisherman's Hymn, The. Alexander Wilson. AA
Fisherman's Lyric. Chao Meng-fu, *tr. fr. Chinese by* Jonathan Chaves. CoBLCP
Fisherman's Son. Charles Bruce. CaP
Fisherman's Story, The. Henrietta Cordelia Ray. CBWP-3
Fisherman's swapping a yarn for a yarn, The. The Flower-Boat. Robert Frost. PoA
Fisherman's Wife, The. Amy Lowell. BoWoP
Fishermen. Basil Bunting. PoA
Fishermen. Julio Ortega, *tr. fr. Spanish by* Maureen Ahern *and* David Tipton. Per
Fishermen. Gabriel Preil, *tr. fr. Hebrew.* MeHP, *tr. by* Bernhard Frank; VWA, *tr. by* Betsy Rosenberg.
Fishermen, The. Theocritus, *tr. fr. Greek by* Charles Stuart Calverley. *Fr.* Idylls, XXI. AWP; OBVE
Fishermen among the fireweed, The. By Rail through the Earthly Paradise, Perhaps Bedfordshire. Denise Levertov. NNaP
Fishermen at Ballyshannon. Limbo. Seamus Heaney. CIP; NoAM; OxBC
Fishermen, Drowned beyond the West Coast. Vivian Smith. CBAP
Fishermen return with the stars of the waters [*or* waterstars]. Evening. Tristan Tzara. POS, *tr. by* Charles Simic *and* Michael Benedikt; RHTwFP, *tr. by* Charles Simic *and* Michael Benedikt; VWA, *tr. by* Willis Barnstone *and* Matei Calinescu.
Fishermen say, when your catch is done, The. The Sea Wolf. Violet McDougal. FaPON
Fishermen who go, The. What She Said ("The fishermen who go"). Ammuvanar, *tr. by* A. K. Ramanujan. PLW
Fishermen will relate that in the South. The Lord of the Isle. Stefan George, *tr. by* Ludwig Lewisohn. AWP
Fishermen's faces were seen first. Basho, *tr. fr. Japanese by* Burton Watson. *Fr.* Seventy-six Hokku. FCEI
Fishermen's fires glitter and fade. Staying Overnight on the Banks of Embroidered River. Li K'ai-hsien, *tr. by* Jonathan Chaves. CoBLCP
Fishermen's Song. *Unknown, tr. fr. Maori by* Margaret Orbell. PeNZ
Fisher's Apology, A. *Unknown, tr. fr. Latin by* Arthur Johnstone. GoTS
Fisher's Boy, The. Henry David Thoreau. AA; ChTr; MOS
Fisher's Life, The. *Unknown.* ChTr; GBP
Fishes, The. *Unknown.* GBP
Fishes and the Poet's Hands, The. Frank Yerby. AmNP; PoNe
Fishes' Evening Song. Dahlov Ipcar. RHPC
Fishes' Lamentation, The. *Unknown.* OxBSS
Fishes swim in water clear. *Unknown.* OxNR
Fishing. Solveig Nilsen. TSL
Fishing. Dorothy Wellesley. OBMV
Fishing alone in a frail boat. Walking Out. Betty Adcock. MT
Fishing boats have returned, the! "Ping Hsin," *tr. fr. Chinese by* Julia C. Lin. *Fr.* Three Poems. PBWP
Fishing Boats in Martigues. Roy Campbell. FaBoEE; FaBoPP; OxBSP
Fishing fires far away, The. *Unknown, tr. fr. Japanese.* *Fr.* Manyo Shu. Ma
Fishing Jetty. Ch'ü Ta-chün, *tr. fr. Chinese by* Lynn Struve. WFTU
Fishing on a Lake at Night. Robert Bly. LCAP
Fishing on a wide river from a boat. Supreme Death. Douglas Dunn. FaBoMo
Fishing Pole, The ("A fishing pole's a curious thing"). Mary Carolyn Davies. FaPON
Fishing Season. Val Vallis. PoAu-2
Fishing Song. William Brighty Rands. CenHV
Fishing Song. *Maori Oral Tradition, tr. by* A. Armstrong *and* R. Ngata. WTO
Fishing the Dream. Mike Delp. TSL
Fishing Village. Louis Dudek. *Fr.* Provincetown. MoCV

Fishmarket closed, the fishes gone into flesh, The. Galway Kinnell. *Fr.* The Avenue Bearing the Initial of Christ into the New World. NaP, *fr.* 11.
Fishnet. Robert Lowell. HCAP
Fish's Nightsong. Christian Morgenstern. WeW
Fishvendor, The. William Meredith. SaC
Fisk is/ a/ negroid/ institution. Sharon Scott. JB
Fist Fight. Doug Cockrell. Psk
Fist like the mountain fern half unfurled. Rai San'yo, *tr. fr. Chinese by* Burton Watson. *Fr.* Shortly after I Married, I Had to Go into Mourning, III. FCEI; JLIC-2
Fist, The ("The fist clenched round my heart"). Derek Walcott. LLLT
Fisting, shouting like a petty merchant. Kakua, *tr. by* Lucien Stryk *and* Takashi Ikemoto. ZPCJ
Fit of Rime against Rime, A. Ben Jonson. InvP; MAT; OAEL-1; PoEL-2; SeCP; SeCV-1
   (Fit of Rhyme against Rhyme, A.) TEP
   ("Rhyme, the rack of finest wits.") TEP
Fit Only for Apollo. Francis Beaumont. *See* Masque of the Inner Temple and Gray's Inne, The:
   Shake off your heavy trance!
Fit place to observe the transit of Venus, A. Tahiti. Louis Johnson. PeNZ
Fit theme for song, the sylvan maid. Madam Hickory. Wilbur Larremore. AA
Fitness Center Chant, A. James Koch. SoTCo
Fitting. Alastair Fowler. NPo
Fitz Adam's Story. James Russell Lowell. AmPP
Five a.m., and I've been. Dawn. Lucien Stryk. CAPP
Five Arabic Verses in Praise of Wine. *Unknown, tr. fr. Arabic by* Hartwig Hirschfeld. TrJP
Five Bells. Kenneth Slessor. CBAP; PoAu-2; PoRA; SeCePo
Five Birds Rise. William Hayward. NYBP
Five bolts of hanging silk. Returning from the Seventy-Two Mountains. Hsü Wei, *tr. by* Jonathan Chaves. CoBLCP
Five buds were on the parent tree. Family Portraits. Mary E. Tucker. CBWP-1
Five-Color. Yang Chi, *tr. fr. Chinese by* Jonathan Chaves. CoBLCP
Five-Day Rain, The. Denise Levertov. NeAP
Five Days Old. Francis Webb. PoAu-2
Five Domestic Interiors. Vernon Scannell. OxBC
Five Epigrams, *sels.* James Vincent Cunningham.
   And Now You're Ready Who While She Was Here. OBVE; TW
      (Epigram: "And now you're ready who while she was here.") ErPo
   "Bride loved old words, and found her pleasure marred." OBAL
   Epitaph for Someone or Other. OBAL
      (Epigram: "Naked I came, naked I leave the scene.") VGW
   "Lip was a man who used his head." OBAL
      (Lip.) ErPo
Five Eyes. Walter de la Mare. CRH
Five fearless knights of the first renown. The First American Sailors. Wallace Rice. PAH
Five Feet, The. Ed Sanders. UL
Five feet three inches. After My Fiftieth Birthday. Yu Kuang-chung, *tr. by* Dominic Cheung. IFON
515 Madison Avenue. Rhapsody. Frank O'Hara. NoAM
Five-Fingered Maple, The. Kate Louise Brown. BoTP
Five Flower World Variations. *Unknown, tr. fr. Yaqui Indian by* Jerome Rothenberg. STP
Five for the Grace of Man. Winfield Townley Scott. VGW
5.40. The Bay View. After the office. Aberdarcy: The Chaucer Road. Kingsley Amis. *Fr.* The Evans Country. NOBL
Five Ghost Songs, *sels.* *Ambo Oral Tradition.* TTTS
   "Ah! the roofs."
   "Dove stays in the garden, The."
   "Ghost is gone in rags, The."
   "I have no rattles."
   "See how it circles."
Five gleaming crows. In Air. Peter Clarke. PBA
Five Groups of Verse, *sels.* Charles Reznikoff.
   After I Had Worked All Day. PrIm; VGW
   "He was afraid to go through their grocery store." DiL
   Son with a Future, A. DiL
Five Hens, The. *Unknown.* GBP
   ("There was an old man who lived in Middle Row.") OxNR
Five hours, (and who can do it less in?). The Lady's Dressing Room. Swift. ErPo; NoP; TEP
Five hundred rocks by the river. Lady Fuki, *tr. fr. Japanese.* *Fr.* Manyo Shu. Ma
Five Joys of Mary, The. *Unknown.* MeEL

Five Kernels of Corn. Hezekiah Butterworth. PAH
Five Little Brothers. Ella Wheeler Wilcox. BoTP
Five Little Chickens. *Unknown.* PDV; RAR
  (Chickens, The.) FaPON; MoShBr
Five little monkeys/ Swinging from a tree. The Monkeys and the
  Crocodile. Laura E. Richards. FaPON
Five Little Monsters. Eve Merriam. RAR
Five Little Sisters Walking in a Row. Kate Greenaway. MoShBr
  (Five Sisters.) BoTP
Five Lovesick Poems, *sel.* Gillian Eve Hanscombe.
  "From her grave." *Fr.* IV. AIW
Five Men against the Theme "My Name Is Red Hot. Yo Name Ain
  Doodley Squat." Gwendolyn Brooks. CNA
Five-Minute Orlando Macbeth, The. George MacBeth. NOBL
Five-Minute Water Color. Jules Laforgue, *tr. fr. French by* William Jay
  Smith. CT
Five Minutes after the Air Raid. Miroslav Holub, *tr. fr. Czech by* Ian
  Milner *and* George Theiner. OBD
Five minutes, five minutes more, please! Bedtime. Eleanor Farjeon.
  RAR
Five months after your death, I come like the others. Elegy for a Forest
  Clear-Cut by the Weyerhaeuser Company. David Wagoner. NoAM
Five months have passed. Hair. Yusuf al-Sa'igh, *tr. by* Diana Der
  Hovanessian *with* Salma Khadra Jayyusi. MAP
Five o'clock, grey dawn in February. Father Is Leaving. Viljo Kajava,
  tr. by Aili Jarvenpa. SOP
Five on the Crabs, *sels.* Orampokiyar, *tr. fr. Tamil by* A. K. Ramanujan.
  PLW
  What Her Girl Friend Said to the Foster-Mother ("If you think, mother").
    Fr. 4.
  What Her Girl Friend Said to the Foster-Mother ("In his fields, mother").
    Fr. 5.
  What She Said ("In his fields"). *Fr.* 3.
  What She Said ("In his place, mother,/ field-crabs cut into the pink").
    Fr. 2.
  What She Said ("In his place, mother,/ mud-spattered spotted crabs").
    Fr. 1.
Five on the Riverside Cane, *sels.* Orampokiyar, *tr. fr. Tamil by* A. K.
  Ramanujan. PLW
  What She Said ("Bees, six tiny legs and wings all lovely"). *Fr.* 1.
  What She Said ("Green creepers planted inside the house"). *Fr.* 5.
  What She Said ("Hovering like the heron"). *Fr.* 2.
  What She Said ("In the full river"). *Fr.* 3.
  What She Said ("Like the high fanning tufts on swift horses"). *Fr.* 4.
Five or six years ago I took a wife. A Poem on Returning Home. Chang
  Wen-t'ao, *tr. by* William Schultz. WFTU
Five oxen, grazing in a flowery mead. On a Seal. Plato, *tr. by* Thomas
  Stanley. AWP; FaBoEE
5 Poems. Robert Gray. CBAP
Five Poems about Poetry, *sels.* George Oppen. NNaP
  From Virgil.
  Gesture, The.
Five Poems on Returning to Hangchou, *sels.* Yüan Mei, *tr. fr. Chinese by*
  Jonathan Chaves. CoBLCP
  "Bird in flight parts from the old wood, The."
  "I gaze at this, my hometown."
  "Of all the famous Hangchou sights."
  "Of my flesh and blood, only one remains."
  "One morning I call for a sedan-chair man."
Five Reasons, The. Henry Aldrich. *See* If all be true that I do think.
  V. "Rudely thou wrongst my dear heart's desire." Spenser. *Fr.*
    Amoretti. EIL
Five Sense. Marvin Wyche, Jr.. AmNP
Five Sestinas, *sel.* James Keir Baxter.
  Dark Welcome, The. *Fr.* III. PeNZ
Five Sisters. Kate Greenaway. *See* Five Little Sisters Walking in a Row.
Five soldiers fixed by Mathew Brady's eye. Looking into History.
  Richard Wilbur. VGW
Five Songs. W. H. Auden. *See* Orators, The: O Where Are You Going?
Five Students, the. Thomas Hardy. CMoP; GTBS-P; PoEL-5
Five summer days, five summer nights. The Blue-Fly. Robert Graves.
  CMoP; NAEL-2; NoAM; NYBP
Five Things Sought For— —In the Manner of Han Wo, *sels.* Hsü Pen, *tr.*
  fr. Chinese by Jonathan Chaves. CoBLCP
  "By nature I love to dress my hair."
  "I love the p'i-p'a's music in my heart."
  "Time after time, afraid of the chilly spring weather."
  "Yesterday, as I went down to the bridge at the river."
Five Things White. Edward May. FaBoEE
5:30 A.M. Adrienne Rich. NMM; NOBA
5:32, The. Phyllis McGinley. *Fr.* I Know a Village. NMM; WPE
Five thousand souls are here, and all are bounded. Troopship in the
  Tropics. Alun Lewis. WaP

Five times since July my father. Stopping by Home. David Huddle.
  GOYP
Five Unmistakable Marks, The. David Jones. *Fr.* In Parenthesis, *pt.*
  VII. NAEL-2
  "Across upon this undulated board of verdure chequered bright." NoAm
Five Villanelles, *sel.* Weldon Kees.
  "Crack is moving down the wall, The." *Fr.* I. SM
Five Visions of Captain Cook, *sels.* Kenneth Slessor.
  "Flowers turned to stone! Not all the botany." PoAu-2
  Two Chronometers. SeCePo
Five Voyages of Arnor, The. George Mackay Brown. NePoEA-2
Five Ways to Kill a Man. Edwin Brock. DL
Five Were Foolish. Arthur J. Hodge. AH
Five winter days at Mannheim shall I be. James Boswell. OBTV
Five Words for Joe Dunn on His 22nd Birthday. Jack Spicer. PoM
Five years ago I gouged it after dark. Your Name in Arezzo. James
  Wright. SM
Five years ago we knew such ecstasies. Interim. Frank Ormsby. CIP
Five years have passed [*or* past]; five summers, with the length. Lines
  Composed a Few Miles above Tintern Abbey on Revisiting the Banks
  of the Wye during a Tour, July 13, 1798. Wordsworth. BLPL;
  ChER; EnRP; FaBoPP; FF; FiP; GoTL; HAP; HeIP; InPS; LiTB;
  NAEL-2; NAWM-2; NIP; NoP; OAEL-2; OBNC; PoE; PoEL-4; PPP;
  PrIm; SeCePo; TEP; TrGrPo
Five Years Old. Marie Louise Allen. RAR
Fivesucked the features of my girl by glory. Nicholas Moore. PoA
Fix thy corporeal, and internal eye. Matthew Prior. *Fr.* Solomon on the
  Vanity of the World. FM
Fixer of Midnight. Reuel Denney. OBAL
Fixture, A. Bill Berkson. UL
Fixture, A. May Swenson. NYBP
Flag, The. James Jeffrey Roche. PAH
Flag Goes By, The. Henry Holcomb Bennett. FaBoBe; FaFP; FaPON;
  GN; OHFP; OPP; PWR; WBLP
Flag of a different poem flies, The. Gamble on Red. Pierre Kemp, *tr. by*
  Fred van Leeuwen. DuIn
Flag of the heroes who left us their glory. Union and Liberty. Oliver
  Wendell Holmes. OHIP
Flag on the house you dwelled in the wind blows now and then, The.
  Itamar Ya'oz-kest, *tr. fr. Hebrew by* Bernhard Frank. *Fr.* My
  Father—Is the Root. MHeP
Flagpole Sitter, The. Donald Finkel. CoAP
Flags. Gwendolyn Brooks. AmNP
Flags of all sorts. Things We Dreamt We Died For. Marvin Bell.
  CoAP
Flags of war like storm-birds fly, The. The Battle Autumn of 1862.
  Whittier. PAH
Flake diamond of/ the sea. Larry Eigner. PoM
Flakes of Auspicious Snow Fall Here. Chou Meng-tieh, *tr. fr. Chinese by*
  Dominic Cheung. IFON
Flame, The. Eugène Guillevic, *tr. fr. French by* Teo Savory.
  RHTwFP
Flame and wood and blackened stones like these. Haim Guri, *tr. by*
  Warren Bargad *and* Stanley F. Chyet. IP
Flame burns in the morning, A. Le Chariot. John Wieners. VGW
Flame dances in the stone lamp, A. Memorial in Aachen. Franz Richter,
  tr. by Beth Bjorklund. CoAuP
Flame-flower, day-torch, Mauna Loa. Lines to a Nasturtium. Anne
  Spencer. AmNP; CDC; PoNe
Flame-Heart. Claude McKay. AmNP; BANP; CDC; PoNe
Flame is healed by flame. George Seferis, *tr. fr. Greek by* Edmund
  Keeley *and* Philip Sherrard. *Fr.* Three Secret Poems, I: 7. VMG
Flame of fire mountain. Mount Fuji, Opus 5. Kusano Shimpei, *tr. by*
  Geoffrey Bownas *and* Anthony Thwaite. PeBJV
Flame offered to Ram, The. Tulsidas, *tr. by* John Stratton Hawley *and*
  Mark Juergensmeyer. SSI
Flame out, you glorious skies. The Dead Heroes. Isaac Rosenberg.
  MoBrPo
Flame Point. Jules Supervielle, *tr. fr. French by* Allen Mandelbaum.
  RHTwFP
Flame Tree, The, *sel.* K. O. Arvidson.
  "You might at one time, when you were young perhaps." ATNZ
Flame went flitting through the wood, A. The Scarlet Tanager. Mary
  Augusta Mason. AA
Flames are shooting. Song of the Fire-Charm. *Unknown, tr. by* Frances
  Densmore; *English vers. by* Jerome Rothenberg. STP
Flames rising up, The. Dawn. David Shevin. VWA
Flaming Heart, The. Richard Crashaw. LiTB; NAEL-1; OAEL-1;
  PoEL-2; SeCePo; SeCV-1; TEP
  Sels.
  "Live here, great heart; and love and dy and kill." OBS
  "O Heart! the equal poise of love's both parts." TrGrPo

"O thou undaunted daughter of desires!" HAP
  (Upon the Book and Picture of the Seraphical Saint Teresa.) NOBE; OBEV
Flaming Terrapin, The, *sel.* Roy Campbell.
  "Maternal Earth stirs redly from beneath." *Fr.* I. MoBrPo
Flaming tuba, A. Tuba. Morton Marcus. NAmP
Flamingo, The. Saleem Barakat, *tr. fr. Arabic by* Lena Jayyusi *and* Naomi Shihab Nye. MAP
Flamingo, The. Lewis Gaylord Clark. NA
Flamingo's Dream, A. Aleksander Wat, *tr. fr. Polish by* Czeslaw Milosz. PwPP
Flammonde. E. A. Robinson. AmPP; CMoP; LiTA; LiTM; NoAM
Flanagan got up on a Saturday morning. Lament for Barney Flanagan. James Keir Baxter. ATNZ; NoP
Flanged, all bright colors—red, yellow, blue—the discs. Frisbee. Rolfe Humphries. GrPl
Flannan Isle. W. W. Gibson. CH; PoRA
Flannery O'Connor. Dorothy Walters. IHMS; PoRA
Flap, flap, the captive bird in the cage. The Scholar in the Narrow Street. Tso Ssu, *tr. by* Arthur Waley. AWP
Flap my sole, bim bam! Bim Bam. Dorothy Rosenberg. PoNe
Flapping my flippered feet. Snorkeling in the Caribbean. Alixa Doom. TSL
Flash, The. James Dickey. LCAP
Flash Crimson. Carl Sandburg. MoAmPo
Flash Jack from Gundagai. *Unknown.* PoAu-1
Flash of light across the night, A. Ulric Dahlgren. Kate Brownlee Sherwood. PAH
Flash of lightning, A. Basho, *tr. by* Geoffrey Bownas *and* Anthony Thwaite. PeBJV
Flash of lightning does not satisfy thirst, A. Modern Love Songs. *Unknown, tr. by* B. W. Andrzjewski *and* I. M. Lewis. TTY
Flash Sleep. Robert Frazier. BWV
Flashback. Lois Clark. CN
Flashing light, this ancient mirror. Song of the Ch'in-Dynasty Mirror. Wang Shih-chen, *tr. by* Jonathan Chaves. CoBLCP
Flat on the bank I parted. The Trout. John Montague. FaBCIP; IPY; PoE
Flat on the grey steel bulkhead arch her curves. Pin-up Girl. Louis O. Coxe. WaP
Flat One, A. W. D. Snodgrass. CAPP; LiTM; NePoEA-2; SM
Flat River Girl. *Unknown.* AS
Flattered Flying Fish, The. Emile Victor Rieu. PDV; RHPC; SO
Flaubert in Egypt. Robert Penn Warren. NoAM
Flaubert wanted to write a novel. Style. Howard Nemerov. NoAM
Flaunt of the sunshine I need not your bask. Walt Whitman. *Fr.* Song of Myself, XL. TrGrPo
Flavia's a name a deal too free. *Unknown.* FaBoEE
Flavius, If Your Girl Friend. Catullus, *tr. fr. Latin by* Horace Gregory. ErPo
Flavor of vanilla drifts, A. Dark Romance. Lucha Corpi, *tr. by* Catherine Rodriguez-Nieto. CCP; WPOW
Flavor the speaking of this one. Not to Forget Miss Dickinson. Marshall Schacht. LiTM
Flaw in Paganism, The. Dorothy Parker. NBLV
Flawless His Heart. James Russell Lowell. PAH
Flax. Ivan Bunin, *tr. fr. Russian by* Babette Deutsch *and* Avrahm Yarmolinsky. AWP
Flax-pods unload their pollen. At Taieri Mouth. James Keir Baxter. ATNZ
Flaxen-headed cow-boy, as simple as may be, A. John O'Keefe. NOEC
Flaying of Marsyas, The. Kenneth Rosen. NAmP
Flea, The. John Donne. BLPL; BoLoP; EBEV; FF; FM; HoPM; InPK; InPS; JCP; LiTB; MaT; MePo; NAAL-1; NBLV; NIP; OAEL-1; PoE; SCV; SeCP; SeCV-1; SoSe; TEP; TrGrPo
Flea, The. Roland Young. RHPC
Flea and the Fly, The. *Unknown.* FaPON
  (Fly and a Flea in a Flue, A.) RHPC
Flea flew by a bee, A. The bee. Combinations. Mary Ann Hoberman. *Fr.* Bugs. OBCA
Fleance. Michael Longley. CIP; FaBCIP
Flears, The. John Hollander. AnAn
Fleas. Philip Appleman. SoTCo
Fleas, The. Augustus De Morgan. *See* Great Fleas.
Fleas interest me so much. Pablo Neruda, *tr. by* Elsa Neuberger. TSS
Flea's leap like a wheelbarrow dancing along the kneecaps of old cobblestones, A. Someone's Knocking. Benjamin Péret, *tr. by* Michael Benedikt. POS
Fleas, lice—a horse pisses right by my pillow. Basho, *tr. fr. Japanese by* Burton Watson. *Fr.* Seventy-six Hokku. FCEI
Fleche. Larry Eigner. VGW
Flecking the sun like autumn leaves. Migrants. Sylvia Lynd. CN

Fled are the frosts, and now the fields appear. Farewell Frost; or, Welcome the Spring. Robert Herrick. CaPo
Fled are those times, when, in harmonious strains. Truth in Poetry. George Crabbe. *Fr.* The Village. SeCePo
Fled is the blasted verdure of the fields. James Thomson. *Fr.* The Seasons: Autumn.
Fled is the swiftness of all the white-footed ones. Joseph Auslander. TrJP
Fledgling Bard and the Poetry Society, The. George Reginald Margetson. BANP
Fledglings. Thomas Lake Harris. AA
Fledglings have a language, The. Baby Talk. Anna Bird Stewart. RHPC
Flee from [*or* Fle fro] the press [*or* prees *or* pres] and dwelle with soothfastnesse [*or* sothefastnesse]. Balade de Bon Conseill. Chaucer. TrGrPo
  (Ballad of Good Counsel.) ACP
  (Ballade of Good Counsel.) TrGrPo, *mod. by* Henry van Dyke
  (Truth.) AWP; NAEL-1; NoP; OAEL-1
  (Truth Shall Set You Free.) MeEL
Flee on Your Donkey. Anne Sexton. NYBP
Fleece, The, *sels.* John Dyer.
  "Ah gentle shepherd, thine the lot to tend." *Fr.* I. PoEL-3
  Bedford Level. *Fr.* II. FaBoPP
  English Fog, The. TrGrPo
  Happy Workhouse and the Good Effects of Industry, The. *Fr.* III. NOEC
  How to Shear Sheep. *Fr.* II. FaBoUs
  Wool Trade, The. *Fr.* III. SeCePo
Fleeing from threatened flood, they sailed. The First Invasion of Ireland. *Unknown, tr. by* John Montague. BIrV
Fleet and fair. Gazelles and Unicorn. John Gray. *Fr.* The Long Road. ChTr
Fleet astronomer can bore, The. Vanity [*or* Vanitie]. George Herbert. MePo; NoP; SeCV-1
Fleet at Santiago, The. Charles E. Russell. PAH
Fleet Fighter. Olivia FitzRoy. CN
Fleet ships encountering on the high seas. Good Ships. John Crowe Ransom. WeW
Fleet with flags arrayed, A. A Ballad of the French Fleet. Longfellow. AA; PAH
Fleeting birds may soon in ocean swim, The. To Miss Laetitia Van Lewen. Constantia Grierson. WPE
Fleeting pomps of the world are like the green willow trees, The. Song of Nezahualcoyotl. *Unknown.* DL
Fleeting Too, The. David Rokeah, *tr. fr. Hebrew by* Bernhard Frank. MHeP
Fleggit Bride, The. "Hugh MacDiarmid." OxBS
Flesh. Mary Elizabeth Fullerton. PoAu-1
Flesh. Deborah Levy. AIW
Flesh, The. Murano Shiro, *tr. fr. Japanese by* Geoffrey Bownas *and* Anthony Thwaite. PeBJV
Flesh. Stan Rice. NPGG
Flesh and the Spirit, The. Anne Bradstreet. AmPP; AnAmPo; LiTA; NAAL-1; NOBA; OxBA; SCAP; TAP
Flesh, Celestial Flesh of Woman! Rubén Darío, *tr. fr. Spanish by* Perry Higman. LPSS
Flesh chase night, weather booming and dark. Major Bowes' Diary. Imamu Amiri Baraka. NAAL-2
Flesh Coupon. Jeff Wright. UL
Flesh-Fly and the Bee, The. Coventry Patmore. FaBoEE
Flesh from Flesh. Mal'akhi Bet-Aryeh, *tr. fr. Hebrew by* Bernhard Frank. MHeP
Flesh has a remarkable future. Flesh. Stan Rice. NPGG
Flesh, I Have Knocked at Many a Dusty Door. John Masefield. *Fr.* Sonnets. LiTM
Flesh is sad, alas, The! and all the books are read. Sea-Wind. Stéphane Mallarmé, *tr. by* Arthur Symons. AWP
Flesh of Terror. René Daumal, *tr. fr. French by* Michael Benedikt. POS
Fleshflower. William Pitt Root. GeTw
Fletcher, though some call it thy fault, that wit. Upon the Dramatick Poems of Mr. John Fletcher. William Cartwright. OBS
Fleur de Lys. Rayner Heppenstall. WaP
Fleur has fa'en, The. A Hint o' Snow. William Soutar. PoSH
Flicker, The. Lew Blockcolski. VoR
Flicker flies by. Bend in the River. Simon J. Ortiz. HATNAP
Flicker of blue, A. Kingfisher. Eleanor Farjeon. RR
Flicker with a broken neck, A. On Addy Road. May Swenson. GOYP
Flickering of incessant rain. John Gould Fletcher. *Fr.* Irradiations, II *or* V [VII]. MoAmPo
Flies buzz. Ears Hear. Lucia *and* James L. Hymes, Jr. RAR
Flight. Madison Cawein. AA
Flight, The. John Haines. EAS

Flight. Barbara Howes. NYBP

Flight. Hsin Mu, *tr. fr. Chinese by* Dominic Cheung. IFON

Flight, The. Lloyd Mifflin. AA

Flight, The. Theodore Roethke. *Fr.* The Lost Son. NAAL-2; RB; TrGrPo

Flight. Paul-Jean Toulet, *tr. fr. French by* William Jay Smith. CT

Flight. Harold Vinal. FaPON

Flight. Ruth Whitman. SO

Flight from Famine: A Ballad. Cheng Hsieh, *tr. fr. Chinese by* Jan *and* Yvonne Walls. WFTU

Flight from the Convent, The. Theodore Tilton. AA

Flight in the Desert, The. William Everson. VGW

Flight into Egypt, The. Peter Quennell. LiTB; LiTM

Flight into Egypt, The. W. H. Auden. *Fr.* For the Time Being; a Christmas Oratorio. OxBA

Flight is the bird's value. Aesthetic. Norman Rosten. PoA

Flight of the Arrow, The. Richard Henry Stoddard. AA

Flight of the Birds, The. Edmund Clarence Stedman. GN

Flight of the Bucket, The. Kipling. BXAP

Flight of the Earls, The. Aindrais MacMarcuis. *See* This Night Sees Ireland [*or* Eire] Desolate.

Flight of the Earls, The, 1607, *sel.* Fearghal Og MacWard, *tr. fr. Irish.* "All Ireland's now one vessel's company." BIrV

Flight of the Heart, The. Dora Read Goodale. AA

Flight of the Heart. Louis MacNeice. FaBCIP

Flight of the Roller Coaster. Raymond Souster. NOBC; SO

Flight of the Spirit. Felicia Dorothea Hemans. Son

Flight of the War-Eagle, The. Obadiah Cyrus Auringer. AA

Flight of Youth, The. Richard Henry Stoddard. *See* There Are Gains for All Our Losses.

Flight Plan. Jane Merchant. RHPC

Flight Shot, A. Maurice Thompson. AA

Flight to Italy, *sel.* Cecil Day Lewis. "Winged bull trundles to the wired perimeter, The." OxBTC

Flights. Roger McDonald. CBAP

Fling Out the Banner! George Washington Doane. AH

Fling this useless book away. Written in a Lady's Prayer Book. Earl of Rochester. BoLoP

Fling weh de wash pan, drop de cloes! Excitement. Louise Bennett. PBCV

Flint. Christina Rossetti. *Fr.* Sing-Song. OxBChV; RHPC

Flint Hills, The. Lew Blockcolski. VoR

Flint spark? Lightning? All too late. Gokei, *tr. by* Lucien Stryk *and* Takashi Ikemoto. ZPCJ

Flintlike, her feet struck. Hardcastle Crags. Sylvia Plath. GoYe (Night Walk.) NYBP

Flip, clack! The windscreen wipers clear. Seven Rainy Months. William Plomer. OxBTC

Flip flop/ Flip flap. Fishes' Evening Song. Dahlov Ipcar. RHPC

Flipochinos. Cyn Zarco. UL

Flippantly,/ In the cinemas past sleep. Before Dawn. Horace Hamilton. NYBP

Flirt, The. W. H. Davies. EnLoPo

Flitting, The. John Clare. FaBoPV

Flitting, The. Medbh McGuckian. FaBCIP

Flitting to and fro, by winding paths and sparse fence. Poem on a Sleeping Butterfly. Liu Shih, *tr. by* Irving Lo. WFTU

Float over us, Florence, your banners. History as Decoration. Rosanna Warren. DiPo

Float-rigged strands, The. Saigyo, *tr. fr. Japanese by* Burton Watson. *Fr.* Sixty-four Tanka. FCEI

Float up again. Celan. Asya, *tr. by* Gabriel Preil *and* Howard Schwartz. VWA

Floating. Michael Brownstein. UL

Floating, a floating, A. A Myth. Charles Kingsley. GN

Floating across the lake. Not Thinking of America. Judith Kroll. AmPA

Floating bridge of dreams this spring night, The. Teika, *tr. fr. Japanese by* Hiroaki Sato. *Fr.* Eighty-four Tanka. FCEI

Floating Candles, The. Sydney Lea. MAYP; SM

Floating cloud, A. Myoe, *tr. fr. Japanese by* Burton Watson. *Fr.* Ten Tanka. FCEI

Floating cloud before my eyes, The. Kaya Shirao, *tr. fr. Japanese by* Hiroaki Sato. *Fr.* Twenty-one Hokku. FCEI

Floating clouds, before my eyes. Inscibed on a Painting of Sailboats on the River. Yün Shou-p'ing, *tr. by* Jonathan Chaves. CoBLCP

Floating, face up, on the open. Queer's Song. Richard Howard. *Fr.* Gaiety. ErPo

Floating, floating on misty waves. Fisherman's Lyric. Chao Meng-fu, *tr. by* Jonathan Chaves. CoBLCP

Floating, floating, the river waters. Wang Chiu-ssu, *tr. fr. Chinese by* Jonathan Chaves. *Fr.* After Reading the Poems of Master Han Shan. CoBLCP

Floating, floating, your boat sets sail. Song of the Merchant's Wife. Yang Wei-chen, *tr. by* Jonathan Chaves. CoBLCP

Floating Houses. David Wojahn. SM

Floating Old Man, The. Edward Lear. *See* Limerick: "There was an old man in a boat."

Floating on completely vested time, alacrity. The Shreds of Our Webs. Charles Bernstein. LP

Floating over the roofs and amid clouds, the violin in his hand. Looking at a Chagall Painting. Eli Netser, *tr. by* Bernhard Frank. MHeP

Flock. Lance Henson. VoR

Flock of birds, soaring, twisting, turning, A. Love Is. Ann Darr. GrPl

Flock of crows high from the Northland flies, A. Autumn. Detlev von Liliencron, *tr. by* Ludwig Lewisohn. AWP

Flock of Guinea Hens Seen from a Car, A. Eudora Welty. GrPl; NYBP; PrIm

Flock of gulls, voices swallowed in the dark sea, The. Dark Sea. Maruyama Kaoru, *tr. by* Hiroaki Sato. FCEI

Flock of sheep that leisurely pass by, A. To Sleep. Wordsworth. EnRP; GTBS; GTBS-P; TrGrPo

Flock of winds came winging [*or* flying] from the North, A. The Roaring Frost. Alice Meynell. EBVV; WPE

Flock the egrets in their flight. *Unknown, tr. by* Arthur Waley. BoS

Flocks of birds are singing. *Unknown, tr. fr. Japanese by* Burton Watson. *Fr.* Manyo Shu. FCEI

Flodden Field. *Unknown.* ESPB

Flood, The. Charles G. Bell. GrPl

Flood. Mary Grant Charles. GoYe

Flood, The. John Clare. RB

Flood. James Joyce. MoBrPo

Flood, The. Ewa Lipska, *tr. fr. Polish by* Peter Jay*and* Geri Lipschultz. VWA

Flood. Roger McGough. FF

Flood, The. Lev Mak, *tr. fr. Russian by* Neil Muhlberger *and* Marvin Misemer. VWA

Flood. William Matthews. KS

Flood, The. Ovid, *tr. fr. Latin.* *Fr.* Metamorphoses: The floods, by nature enemies to land. ChTr

Flood, The. Ann Stanford. MOWH

Flood. Judah Leib Teller, *tr. fr. Yiddish by* Benjamin *and* Barbara Harshav. *Fr.* Three Poems of Nightmare. AYP

Flood at the International Writing Program. Bogomil Gjuzel. WCI

Flood didn't save me, The. The Flood. Ewa Lipska, *tr. by* Peter Jay*and* Geri Lipschultz. VWA

Flood of Years, The. Bryant. AA

Flood-tide below me! I see you face to face! Crossing Brooklyn Ferry. Walt Whitman. AmPP; InPS; LiTA; MoP; NAAL-1; NoAM; NOBA; NoP; TAP

Flood-Time on the Marshes. Evaleen Stein. AA

Flood Viewed by the Tourist from Iowa, The. James Whitehead. SM

Flood was down in the Wilga swamps, three feet over the mud, The. How the Fire Queen Crossed the Swamp. Will H. Ogilvie. PoAu-1

Flood Year. Judith Wright. NoAM

Flooded Mind. Norman MacCaig. OxBC

Floods and gales. Et Cetera. Dee Lawrence Walker. GoYe

Floods, by nature enemies to land, The. Ovid, *tr. fr. Latin.* *Fr.* Metamorphoses, I. OBVE, *tr. by* Dryden.

Flood, The. ChTr

Floods Clap Their Hands, The. Bible, *O.T. See* Psalms: Psalm XCVIII ("O sing unto the Lord.").

Floods of men. All the Spirit Powers Went to Their Dancing Place. Gary Snyder. UnPo

Floods of tears well from my deepest heart, The. Immanuel di Roma, *tr. by* J. Chotzner. TrJP

Floods Swell around Me, Angry, Appalling. Zachary Eddy. AH

Floodtide. Askia Muhammad Touré. PoBA; PoNe

Flooer o the Gean. George Campbell Hay. OxBS

Floor. C. K. Williams. GeTw; NAmP

Floor and the Ceiling, The. William Jay Smith. GrPl; OBCA

Floor boards have a sour breath, The. Dust on Spring Street. Louis Grudin. NoP

Floor: Five. Stephen Vincent. *Fr.* Elevator Landscapes. NeAC

Floor Is Dirty, The. Edward Field. NeAP

(Dirty Floor, The.) CoAP

Floor: O. Stephen Vincent. *Fr.* Elevator Landscapes. NeAC

Floorboards creak, The. The New Apartment, Minneapolis. Linda Hogan. ER; HATNAP

Flora. Ray Fraser. NeAC

Floral Invasions. Hsiang Yang, *tr. fr. Chinese by* Dominic Cheung. IFON

Flora's Lamentable Passion ("Flora's in her grove"). *Unknown.* CoMu

Florella; or, The Jealous Lover. *Unknown.* AmFP

Florence. Elizabeth Barrett Browning. *Fr.* Aurora Leigh. FaBoPP

Florence. Walter Savage Landor. SeCePo

Florence, her husband two years overseas. A Wartime Story. Edith Jay Scovell. CN

Florence Vane. Philip Pendleton Cooke. AA; AnAmPo

Florida. Dannie Abse. OxBC

Florida. Elizabeth Bishop. TwCP

Florida. Carl Rakosi. TAP

Florida Road Workers. Langston Hughes. MoAmPo

Floridian Museum of Art, A. Reed Whittemore. EyDe

Florin to the willing guard, A. The Rosy Bosom'd Hours. Coventry Patmore. EnLoPo; NOBVV

Florio, one ev'ning, brisk, and gay. Epigram on Florio. John Winstanley. FaBoEE

Florist was told, cyclamen or azalea, The. Lines to Accompany Flowers for Eve. Carolyn Kizer. BoWoP

Florus, canst thou define that innate spark. To Mr. ———, an Unlettered Poet, on Genius Unimproved. Ann Yearsley. NOEC

Flos Lunae. Ernest Dowson. OBMV

Floss won't save you from an abyss. Emily Dickinson. LiTA

Flour of England, fruit of Spain. Mother Goose. OxNR

Floure and the Leafe, The, *sel.* Chaucer.
   Courtly Scene and a Sudden Storm, A. OxBLMV

Flow at Full Moon. R. A. K. Mason. ATNZ

Flow down, cold rivulet, to the sea. Tennyson. FaBoRV

Flow, flow-he's often near water. Inscribed on a Painting of Bamboo. Wu Chen, *tr. by* Jonathan Chaves. CoBLCP

Flow Gently, Sweet Afton. Burns. AWP; BLPL; FaBoBe; FaFP
   (Afton Water.) BoNaP; FaBoPP; HeIP; NAEL-2
   (Sweet Afton.) EnRP; LiTB; TrGrPo

Flow Not So Fast. John Dowland. QFR

Flow, O My Tears! *Unknown.* EiL

Flow of people looking, A. At the National Gallery. Judith Kazantzis. AIW

Flower. Paul Celan, *tr. fr. German by* Beth Bjorklund. CoAuP

Flower, The. Robert Creeley. CAPP

Flower, A. Carlos José Guadamuz, *tr. fr. Spanish by* David Volpendesta. Vol

Flower, The. George Herbert. AWP; ELP; FaBoRV; JCP; MePo; NAEL-1; NOBE; NOCV; NoP; OBS; PoEL-2; SeCP; SeCV-1

Flower. Ruth Kim Chun-soo, *tr. fr. Korean by* Koh Chang-soo. ACKP

Flower, A. Mvula Ya Nangolo. WMBCH

Flower, The/ my heart. Poem to Be Recited Every 8 Years While Eating Unleavened Tamales. *Unknown, tr. by* Anselm Hollo. STP

Flower!/ When you light the midday with your breath. Sketch of Flower. Ruth Kim Chun-soo, *tr. by* Koh Chang-soo. ACKP

Flower and the Leaf, The, *sel.* Lady of the Arbour.
   "And at the last I cast my mine eye aside." WPE
   ("And as I stood and cast aside mine eye.") PBBP

Flower-Boat, The. Robert Frost. PoA

Flower Chorus. Emerson. BoTP

Flower Ensnarer of Psalms. Rossana Ombres, *tr. fr. Italian by* I. L. Salomon. BoWoP

Flower Farm, The. Greg Pape. NAmP

Flower-fed Buffaloes, The. Vachel Lindsay. AmFN; ChTr; CMoP; FaPON; GoJo; MoAmPo; NOBA; OBCA; PoE; RB; RFM; VGW

Flower Given to My Daughter, A. James Joyce. OBMV; RB

Flower Herding on Mount Monadnock. Galway Kinnell. LCAP; NaP; NoAM; NOBA

Flower in the Crannied Wall. Tennyson. BoNaP; FaBV; FaFP; FaPON; InPK; LiTB; NAEL-2; NIP; TEP; TrGrPo; TSS; WGRP
   (Fragment: "Flower in the crannied wall.") BLPA; FPL

Flower Is Looking, A. Harold Monro. *Fr.* Strange Meetings. MoBrPo

Flower is withered on the stem, The. The Nurse's Lament. Mary Elizabeth Coleridge. NOBVV; OxBSP

Flower Market. Pierre Reverdy, *tr. fr. French by* Kenneth Rexroth. RHTwFP

Flower-Market Quay. Pierre Reverdy, *tr. fr. French by* Michael Benedikt. POS

Flower Master, The. Medbh McGuckian. FaBCIP

Flower of drowsiness. The Menace of the Flower. Alfonso Reyes, *tr. by* Samuel Beckett. MexPo

Flower of Flame, The, *sel.* Robert Nichols.
   "Before I woke I knew her gone." OBMV

Flower of Liberty, The. Oliver Wendell Holmes. OPP

Flower of Mullein, A. Lizette Woodworth Reese. MoAmPo

Flower of Old Japan, The, *sel.* Alfred Noyes.
   "Carol, every violet has." MoBrPo

Flower of the flock. On Sweet Killen Hill. Tom MacIntyre. CIP

Flower of the race, The. Gentlemen. Geoffrey Taylor. FaBoEE

Flower of the shining summer. The Pearly Everlasting. Ernest Fewster. CaP

Flower of This Purple Dye. Shakespeare. *Fr.* A Midsummer Night's Dream, III, ii. CTC

Flower of Virtue is the heart's content, The. Sonnet: Of Virtue. Folgore da San Geminiano, *tr. by* Dante Gabriel Rossetti. AWP

Flower of waves, A. Lady Ise, *tr. by* Etsuko Terasaki *and* Irma Brandeis. BoWoP

Flower of youth, in the ancient frame. Judith. William Young. AA

Flower-Press, The. Penelope Shuttle. AIW

Flower-Rain Terrace, The. Tao-chi, *tr. fr. Chinese by* Jonathan Chaves. CoBLCP

Flower-Seller, The. William Young. *Fr.* Wishmakers' Town. AA

Flower-Seller, The ("The flower-seller's fat"). Eleanor Farjeon. BoTP

Flower Shadows. Mo Shih-lung, *tr. fr. Chinese by* Jonathan Chaves. CoBLCP

Flower, that I hold in my hand. Tuberose. Louis James Block. AA

Flower that smiles to-day, The. Mutability. Shelley. EnRP; NAEL-2; NoP; OBNC; ViBoPo

Flower unblown, A: a book unread. The Year Ahead. Horatio Nelson Powers. WBLP

Flower vase on the general's table, A. The General's Property. Samih al-Qasim, *tr. by* Abdullah al-Udhari. MPAW

Flower Vendor, The. Luis Cabalquinto. BrSi

Flower was offered to me, A. My Pretty Rose Tree. Blake. *Fr.* Songs of Experience. BoLoP; NAEL-2

Flowering Absence, A. John Montague. CIP

Flowering Bars, The. Charles Donnelly. CIP

Flowering Cherry, The. Janet Frame. PeNZ

Flowering Currant. Patrick MacDonogh. ErPo

Flowering herbs of spring, The. Prince Ichihara, *tr. fr. Japanese. Fr.* Manyo Shu. Ma

Flowering Light of the Godhead, The, *sel.* Mechthild von Magdeburg, *tr. fr. German.*
   "Ah dearest Love, for how long." ILwL

Flowering of the Rod, The, *sels.* Hilda Doolittle ("H. D.").
   "Blue-geese, white-geese, you may say." NOBA
   "It is no madness to say." FaBoMo

Flowering plums from the southern passes, fresh and pure. On Virtuous Government—For His Excellency Wang Fu-ssu, Salt Subcontroller of T'ai-chou. Wu Chia-chi, *tr. by* John E. Wills, Jr. WFTU

Flowering sea and the mountains in the moon's waning, The. Epiphany, 1937. George Seferis, *tr. by* Edmund Keeley *and* Philip Sherrard. VMG

Flowering Tree, The. Wang T'ing-hsiang, *tr. fr. Chinese by* Jonathan Chaves. CoBLCP

Flowering Urn, The. Laura Riding. LiTA

Flowering War, The. *Unknown, tr. fr. Aztec Indian by* Jerome Rothenberg. STP

Flowering Without End. Stefan Zweig, *tr. fr. German by* Eden *and* Cedar Paul. *Fr.* Jeremiah. TrJP

Flowers. Harry Behn. FaPON

Flowers. Roo Borson. NOBC

Flowers. Kathleen Fraser. TV

Flowers. Philippe Jaccottet, *tr. fr. French by* Paul Auster. RHTwFP

Flowers, The. Robert Louis Stevenson. FaPON

Flowers. *Gond Oral Tradition, tr. by* V. Elwin *and* S. Hivale. WTO

Flowers and Men ("Flowers achieve their own floweriness and its's a miracle"). D. H. Lawrence. FaBoEE

Flowers Are a Silly Bunch. Arnold Spilka. RHPC

Flowers are blackened with joy. Black Joy. Hans Arp, *tr. by* Michael Benedikt. POS

Flowers are dead, The. Scenery. Ted Joans. PoBA

Flowers' Ball, The. Ben King. AnAmPo

Flowers bloom in abundance, The. Flowers Fill the Palace. Chang Pi, *tr. by* Lois Fusek. ATF

Flowers by the Sea. William Carlos Williams. CMoP; GoJo; MoAB; MoAmPo; NoAM; RB; TAP

Flower's color has passed, The. Teika, *tr. fr. Japanese by* Hiroaki Sato. *Fr.* A Compendium of Good Tanka. FCEI

Flowers colored blue. Flowers. Philippe Jaccottet, *tr. by* Paul Auster. RHTwFP

Flowers did not seem to unfurl from slow bulbs, The. An Easter Garland. Carol Rumens. FaBoWP

Flowers Fill the Palace. Chang Pi, *tr. fr. Chinese by* Lois Fusek. ATF

Flowers Fill the Palace. Wei Ch'eng-pan, *tr. fr. Chinese by* Lois Fusek. ATF

Flowers Fill the Palace. Yin O, *tr. fr. Chinese by* Lois Fusek. ATF

Flowers, flowers,/ They cover the branches like rosy clouds. Thought of Paradise. Wen T'ing-yün, *tr. by* Lois Fusek. ATF

Flowers for Luis Bunuel. Stuart Z. Perkoff. NeAP

Flowers for the Brave. Celia Thaxter. OHIP

Flowers from the earth have arisen, The. Nature's Easter Music. Lucy Larcom. OHIP

Flowers get a darkening brilliance now, The. The Dying Garden. Howard Nemerov. Psk

Flowers hast thou in thyself, and foliage. Sonnet: To His Lady Joan, of Florence. Guido Cavalcanti, *tr. by* Dante Gabriel Rossetti. AWP

Flowers have blossomed in my garden, The. Yakamochi, *tr. fr. Japanese. Fr.* Manyo Shu. Ma

Flowers have fenced-in. The Clearing. Peter Everwine, *after the Nahuatl.* NNaP

Flowers in bud on the trees, The. On the Death of a New Born Child. Mei Yao-Ch'en, *tr. by* Kenneth Rexroth. NaP

Flowers in the Rear Garden, The. Mao Hsi-chen, *tr. fr. Chinese by* Lois Fusek. ATF

Flowers in the Rear Garden, The. Sun Kuang-hsien, *tr. fr. Chinese by* Lois Fusek. ATF

Flowers in the Valley. *Unknown.* OnMSP; OxBoLi

Flowers in the Ward. John Shaw Neilson. CBAP

Flowers left thick at nightfall in the wood, The. In Memoriam (Easter, 1915). Edward Thomas. GTBS-P; NOBE; OBWP; OBWVE; OxBTC

Flowers like a gangster's funeral. Viewing the Body. W. D. Snodgrass. CAPP

Flower's Name, The. Robert Browning. *Fr.* Garden Fancies, I. CTC

Flowers need irrigation, The. Busy. Yüan Mei, *tr. by* Jonathan Chaves. CoBLCP

Flowers nodding gaily, scent in air. A Duet. T. Sturge Moore. OBEV

Flowers of Darkness. Frank Marshall Davis. AmNP; IDB; NoP; PoBA; PoNe

Flowers of Perdita, The. Shakespeare. *See* Winter's Tale, The: Here's flowers for you.

Flowers of Politics, I, The. Michael McClure. NeAP

Flowers of Politics, II, The. Michael McClure. NeAP

Flowers of Sion, *sel.* William Drummond of Hawthornden.
Angels, The. GN
(Nativitie, The.) OBS

Flowers of spring must now. Yakamochi, *tr. fr. Japanese. Fr.* Manyo Shu. Ma

Flowers of the cherry-tree, The. *Unknown, tr. by* Arthur Waley. BoS

Flowers of the field, The. The Hawthorn Hath a Deathly Smell. Walter de la Mare. BrPo

Flowers of the Foothills and Mountain Valleys. Alice Notley. UL

Flowers of the Forest, The. Jane Elliot. CH; FaBoCh; FaBoRV; GoTS; OxBS; WPE
(Lament for Flodden, The.) GTBS; GTBS-P; OBEV

Flowers on the coffee trees, The. Season of Blood. Arnaldo Santos, *tr. by* Michael Wolfers. WMBCH

Flowers Pink with Ebony. Abraham Chalfi, *tr. fr. Hebrew by* Bernhard Frank. MHeP

Flowers sent by the woman arrived too late, The. Birthday. Manfred Winkler, *tr. by* Bernhard Frank. MHeP

Flowers shall hang upon the palls. Death. John Clare. GTBS-P

Flowers shone on the willows, The. Song of the Wine Spring. Wen T'ing-yün, *tr. by* Lois Fusek. ATF

Flowers that blow, The. Okura, *tr. fr. Japanese. Fr.* Manyo Shu. Ma

Flowers that in thy garden rise, The. Sir Henry Newbolt. FaBoTw

Flowers through the window. Nantucket. William Carlos Williams. AnAmPo; HAP; InPS; OxBA; SOTW; TAP; WeW

Flowers turned to stone! Not all the botany. Kenneth Slessor. *Fr.* Five Visions of Captain Cook. PoAu-2

Flowers upon the rosemary spray, The. The Rosemary Spray. Luis de Góngora y Argote, *tr. by* E. Churton. AWP

Flowers upon your lips and hands. Love Poem. Maurice James Craig. NeIP

Flowers will arrive with spring. Yüan Mei, *tr. fr. Chinese by* Anthony C. Yu. *Fr.* Life at the Sui Garden, V. WFTU

Flowery wallpaper: on the window pane painted castle and sunset. A Long Journey. Pentti Saarikoski, *tr. by* Aili Jarvenpa. SOP

Flowing in the spring rain. Buson, *tr. fr. Japanese by* Hiroaki Sato. *Fr.* Eighty-seven Hokku. FCEI

Flowing robe of words you weave, The. The Lethal Thought. Mary Boyd Wagner. GoYe

Flowing Summer, The, *sels.* Charles Bruce. CaP
Attic, The.
Dreaming Trout, The.
Hayfield, The.

Flown Soul, The. George Parsons Lathrop. AA

Flowrets—wreaths—thy banks along. To a Gentleman, Who Desired Proper Materials for a Monody. *Unknown.* NOEC

Fluent in all the languages dead or living. A Balanced Bait in Handy Pellet Form. Allen Curnow. ATNZ

Fluff from his lap robe hangs in a rift. The Train Out. Sydney Lea. MAYP

Fluid. Tristan Tzara, *tr. fr. French by* Timothy Baum. POS

Flukum couldn't stand the strain. 2 Poems for Black Relocation Centers. Etheridge Knight. NNaP

Flung up at the moon. *Unknown, tr. by* Geoffrey Bownas *and* Anthony Thwaite. PeBJV

Flush or Faunus. Elizabeth Barrett Browning. FM

Flush with the pond the lurid furnace burned. The Steam Threshing-Machine. Charles Tennyson Turner. OBNC

Flushed with the hope of high desire. My Hero. Benjamin Brawley. BANP; PoNe

Flute, The. Joseph Russell Taylor. AA

Flute; a Pastoral, The. José-Maria de Heredia, *tr. fr. French by* H. J. C. Grierson. AWP

Flute and Wind in the Hermit's Cell. Khalil Hawi, *tr. fr. Arabic by* Diana Der Hovanessian *and* Sharif Elmusa. MAP

Flute Cried, The. Mahmoud Darwish, *tr. fr. Arabic by* Abdullah al-Udhari. MPAW

Flute Notes from a Reedy Pond. Sylvia Plath. FaBoMo

Flute of Daphnis, The. Edward Cracroft Lefroy, *after the Greek of* Theocritus. *Fr.* Echoes from Theocritus, XXIII. AWP

Flute of May, The. Harry Woodbourne. GoYe

Flute Player. *Gond Oral Tradition, tr. by* V. Elwin *and* S. Hivale. WTO

Flute-Players. Michael Hoyland. NPo

Flute-Priest Song for Rain, *sel.* Amy Lowell.
"Whistle under the water." UnS

Flute Song. Hilda Doolittle ("H. D."). AnAmPo

Flute Song. *Unknown, tr. fr. Hopi Indian by* Natalie Curtis. WTO

Flutesong willow winding weather. World War. Richard Eberhart. WaP

Flutist Diviner. Daisen, *tr. fr. Chinese by* Lucien Stryk *and* Takashi Ikemoto. ZPCJ

Flutter, flutter go the gourd leaves. *Unknown, tr. by* Arthur Waley. BoS

Flutter flutter on clothes and cap, jujube flowers fall. Tune: Sand of Silk-washing Stream ("Flutter flutter on clothes and cap, jujube flowers fall"). Su Tung-p'o, *tr. by* Burton Watson. CoBCP

Fluttering, fluttering. Masaoka Shiki, *tr. fr. Japanese by* Burton Watson. *Fr.* Thirty-nine Haiku. FCEI

Fluttering, kerria roses scatter. Nijiko. Basho, *tr. fr. Japanese by* Burton Watson. *Fr.* Seventy-six Hokku. FCEI

Fluttering Leaves. Rodney Bennett. BoTP

Fluttering red. Poppy. Gerhard Fritsch, *tr. by* Beth Bjorklund. CoAuP

Fluttering spread thy purple pinions. Lines by a Person of Quality. *At. to* Pope, *and to* Swift. NA

Fluttering, twirling in air. Frost on the Ground. Su Shao-lien, *tr. by* Dominic Cheung. IFON

Flux. Richard Eberhart. Psk; VGW

Fly, The. Philip Ayres, *after the Spanish of* Quevedo. OBVE

Fly, The. Blake. *See* Songs of Experience: Little Fly,/ Thy summers play.

Fly, The. Walter de la Mare. OnUR

Fly, The. Barnabe Googe. *See* Once Musing as I Sat.

Fly, The. Miroslav Holub, *tr. fr. Czech by* George Theiner. RB

Fly, The. David Ignatow. PPR

Fly. W. S. Merwin. NNaP

Fly, The. Ogden Nash. FaPON

Fly, The. Karl Shapiro. LiTM; MoP; NIP; NoAM; TW

Fly about a Glass of Burnt Claret, A. Richard Lovelace. CaPo

Fly and a Flea in a Flue, A. *Unknown. See* Flea and the Fly, The.

Fly away, away, swallow. Full Valleys. F. R. Scott. CaP

Fly away! thou heavenly one! On a Dead Babe. James Whitcomb Riley. AnAmPo

Fly Ball. Carol Masters. TSL

Fly Caught in a Cobweb, A. Richard Lovelace. CaPo; SeCP

Fly down, Death: call me. Madboy's Song. Muriel Rukeyser. MoAmPo; TrJP

Fly, envious Time, till thou run out thy race. On Time. Milton. BLPL; LiTB; MePo; OBEV; OBS

Fly fisherman in Wartime. Leonard Bacon. FYAP

Fly-fishing. John Gay. *Fr.* Rural Sports. SD

Fly-flicking cattle-tail, quiet byre. Summer Reflection. Cyril Cusack. TIRV

"Fly, fly, my friends, I have my death wound; fly." Sir Philip Sidney. *Fr.* Astrophel and Stella, XX. OAEL-1; TEP

Fly hence, shadows, that do keep. Dawn. John Ford. *Fr.* The Lover's Melancholy. OBEV, *fr.* V, i.

Fly hence those siren charms of wealth and pow'r. Naboth's Vineyard. John Caryll. APAS
Fly in December. Robert Wallace. NYBP
Fly is brushed off the pale forehead, The. Mistake. Haim Guri, *tr. by* Warren Bargad *and* Stanley F. Chyet. IP
Fly is dying hard, The. Mayday. Ed Roberson. PoBA
Fly, Muse, thy wonted themes, nor longer seek. If Pope Had Written "Break, Break, Break." Sir John Collings Squire. CenHV; FaBoPa ("Break, Break, Break.") BXAP
Fly or beetle on their track, The. The Shepherd Boy. John Clare. NOBVV
Fly Past Alderney. Lois Clark. CN
Fly, Roadster, fly! Song for a Blue Roadster. Rachel Lyman Field. FaPON
Fly That Flew into My Mistress's Eye, A. Thomas Carew. CaPo
Fly, the fly, The. Oh the Toe-Test! Norma Farber. RHPC
Fly [*or* Flye] to her heart; hover about her heart. Bartholomew Griffin. *Fr.* Fidessa, More Chaste than Kind, XXIII. AAS
(Her Heart.) TrGrPo
Fly to the desert, fly with me. Thomas Moore. *Fr.* Lalla Rookh, The Story of the Sultana Nourmahal. BIrV
"Fly to the mountain! Fly!" Conemaugh. Elizabeth Stuart Phelps Ward. PAH
Fly walked on the initial, A. End of a Century. Jean Follain, *tr. by* W. S. Merwin. RHTwFP
Fly, white butterflies, out to sea. White Butterflies. Swinburne. FaPON; PDV
(Envoi: "Fly, white butterflies, out to sea.") GoJo
Flyer's Fall. Wallace Stevens. MoAB
Flyin' Outlaw, The. Curley W. Fletcher. CowP
Flying. Kaye Starbird. PDV
Flying. J. M. Westrup. BoTP; OnUR
Flying. Sa'di Yusuf, *tr. fr. Arabic by* Abdullah al-Udhari. MPAW
Flying at Night. Ted Kooser. InPK
Flying Bells. Yüan Mei, *tr. fr. Chinese by* Jonathan Chaves. CoBLCP
Flying Blossoms. W. H. Davies. BrPo
Flying Cat, The. Naomi Shihab Nye. TDD
Flying Change, The. Henry Taylor. MAYP
The *Flying Cloud. Unknown.* AmFP; OBET; OxBSS
Flying Crooked. Robert Graves. FaBoMo; LiTM; OxBSP; PCP; RB; TwCP
Flying Deeper into the Century. Pier Giorgio Di Cicco. NOBC
Flying Dutchman, The. Jules Laforgue, *tr. fr. French by* William Jay Smith. CT
Flying Dutchman, The. E. A. Robinson. MOS
Flying Dutchman, The. *Unknown.* OxBSS
Flying Fish, The. Jack Cope. PeSA
Flying Fish, The. John Gray. ChTr; NOBVV
"Of the birds that fly in the farthest sea." *Fr.* II. OBNC
Flying-fish loves the salt kiss of brine. My Name. John Wain. PoPo
Flying for ten thousand ages, yet never exhausted. On the Road to An-hsi. Hung Liang-chi, *tr. by* Irving Lo. WFTU
Flying Fox. Thomas W. Shapcott. CBAP
Flying Friendly Skies. Turner Cassity. MT
Flying from the dry pall of the city. The Gray Woods Exploding. Earle Birney. NoAM
Flying Home from Utah. May Swenson. WPE
Flying Horse was in jail. The Urban Experience: Part Two. Lew Blockcolski. VoR
Flying in plane's rib. New York City. George Abbe. GoYe
Flying Inn, The, *sel.* G. K. Chesterson.
Wine and Water. ACP; CenHV; FaBoCo; FiBHP; MoBrPo
Flying Islands of the Night, The, *sel.* James Whitcomb Riley. Dwainie. AA
Flying kite, in the spot in the sky, A. Buson, *tr. fr. Japanese by* Hiroaki Sato. *Fr.* Eighty-seven Hokku. FCEI
Flying Letters. Zerubavel Gilead, *tr. fr. Hebrew by* Dorothea Krook. VWA
Flying loose and easy, where does he go. The Crow. Russell Hoban. TDD
Flying Noises. Thomas Lux. LCAP
Flying sand darkens the air, the moon is a dull yellow. Li K'ai-hsien, *tr. fr. Chinese by* Jonathan Chaves. *Fr.* Songs of the Frontier. CoBLCP
Flying Scrolls, *sels.* Ralph Hodgson. FaBoTw
"Dust thou art, but dust carefully."
"Movement, she explained, would bring poetry to the rich, The."
Flying sea-bird mocked the floating dulse, The. The Sea-Weed. Elisabeth Cavazza Pullen. AA
Flying Snow Rock. Zetsuzo, *tr. fr. Chinese by* Lucien Stryk *and* Takashi Ikemoto. ZPCJ
Flying Tailor, The. James Hogg. BXAP; Par

Flying Wheel, The. Katharine Tynon Hinkson. WGRP
Flying word from here and there, A. The Master. E. A. Robinson. LiTA; LiTM; MoAB; MoAmPo; OHIP
Flyting o' Life and Daith, The. Hamish Henderson. OxBS
Fo' a yeah or mo' on this roof I'se layed. The Signal Fire. Aeschylus, *tr. fr. Greek by* Dallam Simpson. *Fr.* Agamemnon. CTC
Foal. Mary Britton Miller. PDV
Foal, The. William Renton. NOBVV
Foal. Vernon Watkins. OxBTC
Foam Blanches. Anadad Eldan, *tr. fr. Hebrew by* Bernhard Frank. MHeP
Foam fluttered on the sea like birds' wings. Hills of Salt. Dahlia Ravikovich, *tr. by* Chana Bloch. WPOW
Foaming white wave washes over a grave, A. Exultation. Hywel ab Owain Gwynedd, *tr. by* Gwyn Williams. OBWVE
Foamy with clouds like atoie. Get Stuffed. Alurista, *tr. by* Toni Empringham. FIA
Focke-Wulfs. Michael Gottlieb. IAT
Fo'c'sle had gone under the creep, The. The Final Moments. E. J. Pratt. *Fr.* The Titanic. NOBC
Focus. Adrienne Rich. FaBoWP
Fod. *Unknown.* AmFP
Foe at the Gates, The. John Dickson Bruns. PAH
Foetal Song. Joyce Carol Oates. IHMS; NAs
Foetus. Phyllis Haring. PeSA
Fog. Kenneth Patchen. NaP
Fog. Carl Sandburg. AmPP; FaBV; FaFP; FaPON; FPL; HeIP; InPK; MoAB; MoAmPo; NAAL-2; OBCA; PYC; RHPC; SoSe; TAP; TTTS
Fog and snow for New Year's greeting. Rhyming Prophecy for a New Year. Leonard Cooper. FaBoCo
Fog and Town. Ishihara Yoshiro, *tr. fr. Japanese by* Hiroaki Sato. FCEI
Fog at Liang-hsiang. Yüan Mei, *tr. fr. Chinese by* Jonathan Chaves. CoBLCP
Fog comes in with a big sound, The. The Sounding Fog. Susan Nichols Pulsifer. PDV
Fog comes on little cat feet, The. Fog. Carl Sandburg. AmPP; FaBV; FaFP; FaPON; FPL; HeIP; InPK; MoAB; MoAmPo; NAAL-2; OBCA; PYC; RHPC; SoSe; TAP; TTTS
Fog Dream, The. Sandra M. Gilbert. PoA
Fog hanged over the park, the night cold, and, clean. And, Hinges. Ted Greenwald. LP
Fog-Horn. George Herbert Clarke. CaP
Fog obscures the deserted mountain. A Man in Hangchou Spread Word That I Had Died. Ni Tsan, *tr. by* Jonathan Chaves. CoBLCP
Fog of night envelops the flowering trees, The. T'ang Yin, *tr. fr. Chinese by* Jonathan Chaves. *Fr.* Spring—River—Flower—Moon—Night. CoBLCP
Fog over the base: the beams ranging. A Front. Randall Jarrell. OBWP; OxBC; VGW
Fogbound. Roberta Hill Whiteman. ER
Foggy Dew, The. *Unknown.* OBET
Foggy, Foggy Dew, The. *Unknown.* AS; CoMu; ELP; GBP; LiTB; OBET; OxBoLi
Foggy moon, bird-calls in the flowers at dawn. Twenty-first Day of the Seventh Month. Yüan Hung-tao, *tr. by* Jonathan Chaves. CoBLCP
Foghorns ("The foghorns moaned"). Lilian Moore. RHPC
Fogland. Ingeborg Bachmann, *tr. fr. German by* Beth Bjorklund. CoAuP
Foil'd by our fellow-men, depress'd, outworn. Immortality. Matthew Arnold. FiP
Foiled Sleep. "Marie Madelaine," *tr. fr. German by* Ferdinand E. Kappey. PeHV
Fold of my flesh. Sleep Close to Me. Gabriela Mistral, *tr. by* D. M. Pettinella. AIW; PBWP
Folded Flock, The. Wilfrid Meynell. TrPWD
Folded Skyscraper, A, *sel.* William Carlos Williams. Hemmed-in Males. MAT; PoRA
Folding and Unfolding, A. Welton Smith. PoNe
Folding Fan, The. Grey Cohoe. NOVW
Folding its hands. Sokan, *tr. by* Geoffrey Bownas *and* Anthony Thwaite. PeBJV
Folding the Flocks. John Fletcher. *See* Faithful Shepherdess, The: Priest's Chant, The.
Foliage of Vision. James Merrill. VGW
Folk Melody. P. Mustapää, *tr. fr. Finnish by* Aili Jarvenpa. SOP
Folk Museum, The. Medbh McGuckian. CIP
Folk Song, A. *Gond Oral Tradition. See* Old age is come, my head is shaking.
Folk Tune. Esther Raab, *tr. fr. Hebrew by* Robert Friend *and* Shimon Sandbank. VWA
Folk Tune. Richard Wilbur. AmFN
Folk Who Live in Backward Town, The. Mary Ann Hoberman. OBCA; RHPC

Folk who lived in Shakespeare's day, The. Guilielmus Rex. Thomas Bailey Aldrich. AA; AnAmPo

Folk Wisdom. Thomas Kinsella. TwCP

Folklore. Cyril Dabydeen. BrSi

Folks ain't got no right to censuah othah folks about dey habits. Accountability. Paul Laurence Dunbar. PoLF

Folks and Me. Lucile Crites. PWR; WBLP

Folks at home half the time are thinkin' about dirt, The. Soap, the Oppressor. Burges Johnson. PoLF

Folks, I'm telling you. Advice. Langston Hughes. NBLV

Folks in the Northeast Corrida. In Winter. Katharine O'Brien. SoTCo

Folks need a lot of loving in the morning. Need of Loving. Strickland W. Gillilan. BLPA; WBLP

Follies, The. Daniel Mark Epstein. MAYP

Follow. Thomas Campion. *See* Follow Thy Fair Sun [Unhappy Shadow].

Follow a shadow [*or* shaddow], it still flies you. That Women Are but Men's Shadows. Ben Jonson. EiL; OBS

(Shadow, The.) NOBE; OBEV

(Song: That Women Are but Men's Shadows.) OxBSP; SeCP

(Women Men's Shadows.) WBLP

Follow back from the gull's bright arc and the osprey's plunge. Water Ouzel. William H. Matchett. CoAP; NePoEA; NYBP

Follow, follow. Thomas Campion. EnLoPo

Follow my Bangalorey Man. *Unknown.* OxNR

Follow pattern kill Cadogan. Yes, Lord. Bajan Litany. Bruce St. John. PBCV

Follow the Leader. Kathleen Fraser. RHPC

Follow the long snake. Desert River. Patricia Benton. GoYe

Follow the trickroutes. Auras on the Interstates. Gerald Vizenor. STE

Follow Thy Fair Sun [Unhappy Shadow]. Thomas Campion. EiL; ELP; EnLoPo; LiTB; NOBE; NoP; OBSC; PoEL-2; UnPo

(Devotion.) OBEV

(Follow.) CH

(Followe Thy Fair Sonne.) AAS; Prf

Follow Your Saint [Follow with Accents Sweet]. Thomas Campion. AAS; EBEV; EiL; EnLoPo; HAP; OAEL-1; OBSC; PoE; SeCePo; TrGrPo

(Devotion.) NOBE; OBEV

Followe Thy Fair Sonne. Thomas Campion. *See* Follow Thy Fair Sun [Unhappy Shadow].

Followed the bird in the long forest where it cried. In Her Song She Is Alone. Jon Swan. NYBP

Follower. Seamus Heaney. FaBCIP; IPY

Following Deborah's song, long ago. His Mother. Haim Guri, *tr. by* Bernhard Frank. MHeP

Following fantailed shrimp and snowpeas. Chinese Restaurant. Ernest Slyman. SoTCo

Following forbidden streets. The Wraith-Friend. George Barker. OBMV

Following His Rhymes and Answering the Poems of My Friend Next Door, *sel.* Tai Piao-yüan, *tr. fr. Chinese by* Jonathan Chaves. "South of the house, north of the house." *Fr.* VI. CoBLCP

Following the Rhymes of "Autumn Night Song" by Meng Tzu-chou. Yü Chi, *tr. fr. Chinese by* Jonathan Chaves. CoBLCP

Following the Rhymes of Bamboo Branch Songs. Yü Chi, *tr. fr. Chinese by* Jonathan Chaves. CoBLCP

Following the Rhymes of Chiang Hui-shu. Su Tung-p'o, *tr. fr. Chinese by* Burton Watson. CoBCP

Following the Rhymes of Kao Chi-ti's Poem "We Had Planned to Travel to Cloud Cliff." Hsü Pen, *tr. fr. Chinese by* Jonathan Chaves. CoBLCP

Following the Rhymes of Magistrate Liu's Poems, *sel.* Hsü Chung-hsing, *tr. fr. Chinese by* Jonathan Chaves. "Trees are ancient, thick with patterns of moss, The." CoBLCP

Following the Rhymes of Shao-pao Huang's Poem on Being Moved While Visiting the Farmers. Yang Shih-ch'i, *tr. fr. Chinese by* Jonathan Chaves. CoBLCP

Following the Rhymes of the Six Poems "Thinking of the Past at Ku-Su." Ni Tsan, *tr. fr. Chinese by* Jonathan Chaves. CoBLCP

Following the Rhymes of Yang T'ing-ho's Poem "On the Road Back." Li Tung-yang, *tr. fr. Chinese by* Jonathan Chaves. CoBLCP

Following the Rhymes of Yü-chai's Poems on Autumn, *sel.* Ni Tsan, *tr. fr. Chinese by* Jonathan Chaves. "You ask when I will go back home." CoBLCP

Following the wind. Tameko, *tr. by* Steven D. Carter. WFTW

Following the wind and rain. Which Chapter—A Continuation. Wang Jun-hua, *tr. by* Dominic Cheung. IFON

Follows this a narrower bed. Bridal Couch. Donald J. Lloyd. NIP

Folly of Being Comforted, The. W. B. Yeats. AnIL; BrPo; GBL; HeIP; NAEL-2

Fond Affection. *Unknown.* AS

Fond affection, hence, and leave me! Robert Parry. *Fr.* The Mirror of Knighthood. EiL

Fond greeting, hillock there, A. Laoiseach Mac an Bhaird. NOIV

Fond man, Musophilus, that thus dost spend. Poet and Critic. Samuel Daniel. *Fr.* Musophilus; or, Defence of All Learning. OBSC

Fond man, that canst believe her blood. Celia Bleeding, to the Surgeon. Thomas Carew. SeCP

Fond men! whose wretched care the life soon ending. Phineas Fletcher. *Fr.* Brittain's Ida. EiL

Fond woman, which would'st have thy husband die. Jealousy. John Donne. *Fr.* Elegies, I. FF

Fond words have oft been spoken to thee, sleep! To Sleep ("Fond words have oft been spoken to thee, sleep!"). Wordsworth. Son

Fondle me. Marrow of My Bone. Mari E. Evans. BPo

"Fondling," she saith, "since I have hemmed thee here." Shakespeare. *Fr.* Venus and Adonis. OAEL-1

Food. Victor M. Valle, *tr. fr. Spanish by* Toni Empringham. FIA

Food and Drink. Louis Untermeyer. MoAmPo

Food for Fire, Food for Thought. Robert Duncan. NeAP

Food of Love, The. Shakespeare. *Fr.* Twelfth Night, I, i. TrGrPo

Food of the North. D. H. Lawrence. FaBoEE

Food-Rioter Banished, The. William Thom. PF

Fool, The. Padraic Pearse. TIRV

Fool, a fool, A!—I bet a fool i' the forest. A Cold Rendering. *Unknown.* BXAP

Fool, a fool, A! I met a fool i' the forest. Motley's the Only Wear. Shakespeare. *Fr.* As You Like It, II, vii. TrGrPo

Fool and False. *Unknown, tr. fr. Sanskrit by* Arthur Ryder. *Fr.* The Panchatantra. AWP

Fool and the Poet, The. Pope. *See* Epigram: "Sir, I admit your general [*or* gen'ral] rule."

Fool hath said in his heart, The. Psalm XIV ("The fool hath said in his heart. "). Bible, *O.T. Fr.* Psalms. TrJP

Fool much bit by fleas put out the light, A. Richard Lovelace, *after the Greek of* Lucian. FaBoEE

Fool of nature, stood with stupid eyes, The. The Power of Love. Dryden. *Fr.* Cymon and Iphigenia. OBS

Fool Song. Cornel Lengyel. GoYe

Fool, take up thy shaft again. Thomas Stanley. EnLoPo

Fool there was and he made his prayer, A. The Vampire. Kipling. BLPA; BLPL; NOBVV; VVA

Fool there was, and she lowered her pride, A. A Woman's Answer to "The Vampire." Felicia Blake. BLPA

Fool, to put up four crosses at your door. Swift. FaBoEE

Fooled me once and you fooled me bad. All Night Long Fooling Me. *Unknown.* AmFP

Foolish Child. *Unknown, tr. fr. Akan by* J. B. Danquah. PBA

Foolish I, why should I grieve. Of Maids' Inconstancy. Richard Brathwaite. *Fr.* A Strappado for the Devil. EiL

Foolish impatient apricot trees. Vegetable Destiny. Nina Cassian, *tr. by* Michael Impey *and* Brian Swann. PBWP

Foolish little maiden bought a foolish little bonnet, A. What the Choir Sang about the New Bonnet. M. T. Morrison. BLPA

Foolish men who accuse. She Proves the Inconsistency of the Desires and Criticism of Men Who Accuse Women of What They Themselves Cause. Sister Juana Inés de la Cruz, *tr. by* Aliki *and* Willis Barnstone. BoWoP

Foolish prater, what dost thou. The Swallow. Abraham Cowley. EBEV; FM; OBEV; PBBP

Foolish rhythm turns in my idle head, A. A Tune. Arthur Symons. BoLoP; OBNC

Foolish useless man who had done nothing, A. Brummell at Calais. John Glassco. MoCV

Foolish Woman, A. Bible, *O.T. Fr.* Proverbs, IX: 13-18. TrGrPo

Foolishness. Nizar Qabbani, *tr. fr. Arabic by* Diana Der Hovanessian *and* Lena Jayyusi. MAP

Fools. Ben Jonson. *See* Volpone: Fools, They Are the Only Nation.

Fools' Adventure, The, *sel.* Lascelles Abercrombie. Seeker, The. WGRP

Fools Gaze at Painted Courts. Michael Drayton. *Fr.* Polyolbion, Eighteenth Song. ChTr

Fools in Love's College. John Lyly. *See* Mother Bombie: O Cupid! Monarch over Kings.

Fool's Prayer, The ("Royal feast was done, The; the King."), *sel.* Edward Rowland Sill. AA; BeLS; FaBoBe; OHFP; OnMSP; PoLF; WBLP; WGRP

"'Tis not for guilt the onward sweep." TrPWD

Fool's Preferment, A, *sel.* Thomas D'Urfey. I'll Sail upon the Dog-Star. FaBoCh; OxBoLi

Fool's Song. Thomas Holcroft. NOEC

Fools, They Are the Only Nation. Ben Jonson. *Fr.* Volpone, I, ii. InvP
  (Fools.) ElL
  (Nano's Song.) TrGrPo
Foot of death has printed on my chest, The. The Shudder. Donald Hall. NYBP
Foot Race Song. *Unknown, tr. fr. Pima Indian by* Frank Russell. NU; OBVE
Foot slides open, disjointed, The. Achilles' Heel. Herbert Scott. NAmP
Foot Soldiers. John Banister Tabb. OBAL
Foot-wearying mountain. Tsurayuki, *tr. fr. Japanese by* Burton Watson. *Fr.* Kokin Shu. FCEI
Football. F. Scott Fitzgerald. ASP
Football. Walt Mason. ASP; SD
Football and Rowing—an Eclogue. Alfred Denis Godley. CenHV
Football coach coached tennis in the spring, The. In the Spring. Jim Hall. MOWH
Football Game, A. Alice Van Eck. RHPC
Football Song. Sir Walter Scott. SD
Footfall of someone I wait for, The. Buson, *tr. fr. Japanese by* Hiroaki Sato. *Fr.* Eighty-seven Hokku. FCEI
Footnote. Anthony Delius. PeSA
Footnote. Christopher Logue. NPo
Footnote. Norah Smaridge. RAR
Footnote to a Famous Lyric, A. Louise Imogen Guiney. AA
Footnote to a Gray Bird's Pause, A. James Cunningham. JB
Footnote to Enright's "Apocalypse." Martin Bell. FaBoMo
Footnote to John II: 4. R. A. K. Mason. ATNZ; PeNZ
Footnote to Tennyson. Gerald Bullett. FiBHP
Footnote to the Amnesty Report on Torture. Margaret Atwood. NoAM
Footnote to the Lord's Prayer, *sel.* Kay Smith.
  "Heaven which art in Heaven Our Father in Heaven." TrCP
Footnotes to "The Autobiography of Bertrand Russell," *sel.* Mona Van Duyn.
  "This seems, in a world where love must take its chances." *Fr.* II. HAP
Footnotes to the Book of the Setback. Nizar Qabbani, *tr. fr. Arabic by* Abdullah al-Udhari. MPAW
Footpath. Stella Ngatho. WPOW
Footpath would have been enough, A. The Entailed Farm. John Glassco. MoCV; NOBC
Footpaths Cross in the Rice Field. "Lin Ling." *Unknown, tr. by* Kenneth Rexroth *and* Ling Chung. PBWP
Footprints. Hamish Brown. PoSH
Footprints are gone, The. Tameie, *tr. by* Steven D. Carter. WFTW
Footprints of the Heart-of-the-Daybreak, The! Heart-of-the-Daybreak. Eugène Marais, *tr. by* Uys Krige *and* Jack Cope. PeSA
Footprints on the Glacier. W. S. Merwin. MoP; NoAM
Footsteps, The. C. P. Cavafy, *tr. fr. Greek by* Edmund Keeley *and* Philip Sherrard. VMG
Footsteps of a hundred years, The. The Founders of Ohio. William Henry Venable. PAH
Footsteps of Angels. Longfellow. AnAmPo
Footsteps of Spring. Hayyim Nahman Bialik, *tr. fr. Hebrew by* Ruth Nevo. VWA
For a cap and bells our lives we pay. James Russell Lowell. *Fr.* The Vision of Sir Launfal, Prelude to *Pt.* I. AA
  (June Weather.) GN
For a Certain Night. Tachihara Michizo, *tr. fr. Japanese by* Hiroaki Sato. FCEI
For a Child. Fannie Stearns Davis. FaPON
For a Child Born Dead. Elizabeth Jennings. AIW
For a Child Expected. Anne Ridler. LiTM; SeCePo
For a Coming Extinction. W. S. Merwin. HCAP; NNaP; PoE
For a companion. Shiki, *tr. by* Peter Beilenson. TSS
For a Daughter Gone Away. William Stafford. AnAn; SV
For a Daylight Dream. Robert Desnos, *tr. fr. French by* Michael Benedikt. POS
For a Dead Kitten. Sara Henderson Hay. CRH
For a Dead Lady. E. A. Robinson. CMoP; DL; FYAP; HeIP; HoPM; InvP; LiTA; LiTM; MoAB; MoAmPo; MoP; NoAM; NOBA; OxBA; PoEL-5; PoRA
For a dime in the 1930's my father bought a drawstring sack. Passion. Susan Prospere. AnAn
For a Far-out Friend. Gary Snyder. NeAP; PoM
For a Father. Anthony Cronin. FaBoTw
For a Five-Year-Old. Fleur Adcock. ATNZ
For a forehead: Kansas skies. Cosmogony. David Chapman Berry. BXAP
For a Fountain. "Barry Cornwall." OBEV
For a fraction. Caroline beside the Sundial. Kevin Ireland. ATNZ

For a fresh start. Issa, *tr. fr. Japanese by* Nobuyuki Yuasa. *Fr.* Oraga Haru. OFD
For a Friend. Ted Kooser. GOYP
For a Friend. Lyn Lifshin. NeAC
For a Friend. David Steingass. TW
For a God who is laughing like a child. Weightless Now. Giuseppe Ungaretti, *tr. by* Richard Wilbur. PFI
For a good decade. The Drunk in the Furnace. W. S. Merwin. CAPP; LiTM; MAT; MoP; NAAL-2; NePoEA-2; NoAM; NoP; PoE; SM; TwCP
For a Grotto. Mark Akenside. *See* To me, whom in their lays the shepherds call.
For a hollow mind. Ozaki Hosai, *tr. fr. Japanese by* Hiroaki Sato. *Fr.* One Hundred Haiku in Free Form. FCEI
For a Homecoming. Julia Randall. NMM
For a hundred miles the west wind carries the fragrance of millet. Yün Shou-p'ing, *tr. fr. Chinese by* Jonathan Chaves. *Fr.* On the Painting "Joys of Village Life." CoBLCP
For a hundred years. Dream. Emperor Kogon, *tr. by* Steven D. Carter. WFTW
For a Lady I Know. Countee Cullen. *Fr.* Four Epitaphs. AmNP; CDC; PoBA
For a Lamb. Richard Eberhart. CMoP; LiTM; OxBSP; RB
For a living I pick apples. Identity Card. Susan Tichy. MAYP
For a long time. The Pan, the Pot, the Burning Fire I Have in Front of Me. Ishigaki Rin, *tr. by* Hiroaki Sato. FCEI
For a long time at the foot of the stoop. Rosemonde. Guillaume Apollinaire, *tr. by* Michael Benedikt. POS
For a long time I used to get up early. Bird's-Eye View of the Tool and Die Co. John Ashbery. AnAn
For a long time I was bitter. Peire Vidal, *tr. by* Paul Blackburn. Pro
For a long time, I was nailed to the pillory. The Pillory. Renée Vivien, *tr. by* Sandia Belgrade. PeHV
For a long time she listened to the sound. You Had to Know Her. William Hathaway. NAmP
For a long time we've been apart. While It Was Raining. Wen Cheng-ming, *tr. by* Jonathan Chaves. CoBLCP
For a Lost Night. Tachihara Michizo, *tr. fr. Japanese by* Hiroaki Sato. FCEI
For a man that is almost blind. Mock-Medicine. *Unknown.* MeEL
For a Man Who Walked Sideways. Martin Carter. PBCV
For a Masseuse and Prostitute. Kenneth Rexroth. NNaP
For a Memory. Tachihara Michizo, *tr. fr. Japanese by* Hiroaki Sato. FCEI
For a minute, daughter, for an afternoon. The Prevention of Stacy Miller. Peter Miller. MoCV
For a Mocking Voice. Eleanor Farjeon. CH
For a Moment. *Unknown, tr. fr. Burmese by* U Win Pe. PBWP
For a moment I saw a surging river. Impermanence. Lal Ded. BoWoP
For a moment pause. The Mound. Thomas Hardy. OxBTC
For a moment, unaware. For a Moment. *Unknown, tr. by* U Win Pe. PBWP
For a moment we lay in the village of Fushimi. Princess Shikishi, *tr. fr. Japanese by* Hiroaki Sato. *Fr.* Seventy-eight Tanka. FCEI
For a Mouthy Woman. Countee Cullen. OBAL; PoBA
For a Musician. George Wither. *Fr.* Hallelujah; or, Britain's Second Remembrancer. OBS
For a Neighbor Girl. Yü Hsüan-chi. *See* Advice to a Neighbour Girl.
For a Picture Where a Queen Laments over the Tomb of a Slain Knight. Thomas Carew. CaPo
For a piece of the earth. The Earth Cycle Dream. Phillip Yellowhawk Minthorn. STE
For a poem to come to birth. Four Thousand Days and Nights. Tamura Ryuichi, *tr. by* Geoffrey Bownas *and* Anthony Thwaite. PeBJV
For a Poet. Countee Cullen. PoNe; TTY
For a saving grace, we didn't see our dead. The War in the Air. Howard Nemerov. DiPo
For a Second Marriage. James Merrill. NePoEA
  (Upon a Second Marriage.) NoP
For a second the word express appears. Capital. Heather McHugh. MAYP
For a Statue of Chaucer at Woodstock. Mark Akenside. SeCePo
For a Suicide, a Little Early Morning Music. Gibbons Ruark. MT
For A' That and A' That. Shirley Brooks. *See* More Luck to Honest Poverty.
For A' That an' A' That ("bonniest lass that ye meet neist, The"). *At. to* Burns. CoMu
For A' That and A' That ("Is there, for honest poverty"). Burns. EnRP; FaBoBe; FaBoPV; FaFP; FaPoR; LiTB; NAEL-2; OAEL-1; OHFP; TEP; WBLP
  (Man's a Man for A' That, A.) OxBS; TrGrPo
  (Song: For A' That and A' That.) NOEC; OPOP
For A' That and A' That. *Unknown.* BXAP

For a thing done, repentance is no good. Sonnet: He Is Past All Help. Cecco Angiolieri da Siena, *tr. by* Dante Gabriel Rossetti. AWP

For a thousand years, you, African, suffered like a beast. Dawn in the Heart of Africa. Patrice Emery Lumumba. PBA; TTY

For a Very Old Man, on the Death of His Wife. Jane Cooper. NePoEA-2

For a Virgin Lady. Countee Cullen. MoAmPo

For a Voice That Is Singing. Aldo Camerino, *tr. fr. Italian by* Anita Barrows. VWA

For a War Memorial. G. K. Chesterton. MMA

For a while, gentle. Bosho's Old Hut. Kikaku, *tr. fr. Japanese by* Hiroaki Sato. *Fr.* Thirty-three Hokku. FCEI

For a while there we had 25-inch Chinese peasant families. The Not-so-good Earth. Bruce Dawe. CBAP

For a Wife in Jizzen. Douglas Young. OxBS

For a Wine Festival. Vernon Watkins. OxBTC

For a Winnebago Brave. Joseph Bruchac. CDW

For a Woodscolt Miscarried. John William Corrington. MT

For a year he'd collect. The Milkman and His Son. Thomas Lux. PPR

For a year, she walked past my window. Woman through the Window. Marcia Falk. VWA

For a year we lived like troglodytes. Bomb Story (Manchester, 1942). Margery Lea. CN

For a Young Artist. Robert Hayden. NoAM

For aa da scraimin stars at hing. Gallow Hill. William J. Tait. OxBS

For action, I chant out loud, for quiet, I just think. Wu Chen, *tr. fr. Chinese by* Jonathan Chaves. *Fr.* Poems Inscribed on Paintings of Bamboo, 2. CoBLCP

For Adolf Eichmann. Primo Levi, *tr fr Italian.* VWA, *tr. by* Ruth Feldman *and* Brian Swann

For Advanced Seminar Students Only. David Avidan, *tr. fr. Hebrew by* Warren Bargad *and* Stanley F. Chyet. *Fr.* Samson, Our Hero, 6. IP

For Aitana. Rafael Alberti, *tr. fr. Spanish by* Perry Higman. LPSS

For Alan Blanchard. John Oliver Simon. NeAC

For Alissa. Peter Cooley. NAmP

For All. Louise Otto-Peters, *tr. fr. German by* Susan L. Cocalis *and* Gerlinde Geiger. DMG

For All Blasphemers. Stephen Vincent Benét. OxBA

For all I know, I myself. Tsurayuki, *tr. fr. Japanese by* Burton Watson. *Fr.* Kokin Shu. FCEI

For all life's beauties, and their beauteous growth. We Thank Thee. John Oxenham. BLRP

For All Mary Magdalenes. Desanka Maksimovic, *tr. fr. Croatian by* Vasa D. Mihailovich. AIW; WPOW

For All My Grandmothers. Beth Brant. STE

For all, O Lord, my glad thanksgiving this is. Gratitude. Mikhail Yurevich Lermontov, *tr. by* Alan Myers. AAA

For all of us. Laundry and School Epigrams. Bernadette Mayer. UL

For All Sorts and Conditions. Norman Nicholson. EaLo

For all that God in mercy sends. Give Thanks. Helen Isabella Tupper. BLRP

(Thanks for Everything.) WBLP

For all the beauties of the day. Grace at Evening. Edgar A. Guest. TrPWD

For all the gracious gifts in harvests fair. Thanksgiving Day. John Kendrick Bangs. TrPWD

For all the insomniacs in the world. I Need Help. Edward Hirsch. NAmP

For all the saints who from their labors rest. Funeral Hymn. William Walsham Howe. WGRP

For all the ungainly ones, the awkward, silent ones. The Power to Change Geography. Diana O Hehir. NPGG

For all the vision that took fire this night. Burning Bush. Martin Feinstein. TrJP

For all the young and the very lovely. Threnode for Young Soldiers Killed in Action. Juliette de Bairacli-Levy. CN

For all they minimize and abrade away. On a Dead Poet. William Rose Benét. AnAmPo

For all things beautiful, and good, and true. Thanksgiving. John Oxenham. BLRP; WBLP

For All Things Black and Beautiful. Conrad Kent Rivers. CNA

For all those beaten, for the broken heads. Litany for Dictatorships. Stephen Vincent Benét. OxBA

For all Thy ministries. We Thank Thee, Lord. John Oxenham. *Fr.* A Little Te Deum of the Commonplace. WBLP

For All We Have and Are. Kipling. FaPoR

For all! We hear the words resound. For All. Louise Otto-Peters, *tr. by* Susan L. Cocalis *and* Gerlinde Geiger. DMG

For all your days prepare. Preparedness. Edwin Markham. FaFP; MoAmPo

For Allan, Who Wanted to See How I Wrote a Poem. Robert Frost. PChr

For Alva Benson, and for Those Who Have Learned to Speak. Joy Harjo. HATNAP

For Ammonis, Who Died at 29, in 610. C. P. Cavafy, *tr. fr. Greek by* Edmund Keeley *and* Philip Sherrard. VMG

For among My People are found wicked men. As Fowlers Lie in Wait. Bible, *O.T. Fr.* Jeremiah, V: 26-31. TrJP

For Amy Lowell. Countee Cullen. PoA

For an Age of Plastics. Plymouth. Donald Davie. NePoEA-2

For an Amorous Lady. Theodore Roethke. NBLV

For an Amulet. Arthur Rex Dugard Fairburn. ATNZ

For an Autumn Festival, *sel.* Whittier.

Harvest Hymn. OHIP

For an Early Retirement. Donald Hall. TW

For an Emigrant. Randall Jarrell. *See* In that bad year and city of your birth.

For an Epitaph at Fiesole. Walter Savage Landor. FaBoEE; OBNC

For an Eskimo. Annie Charlotte Dalton. CaP

For an Ex-Far East Prisoner of War. Charles Causley. OxBC

For an hour he wonders what the girl could be thinking. The White Skirt. Stephen Dobyns. MAYP

For an Obligate Parasite. Alan Dugan. TW

For an Octogenarian. Brian Turner. UAS

For an officer/ in the old Capital, fox fur. Ezra Pound, *after the Chinese.* OBVE

For Andrew. Fleur Adcock. ATNZ

For Andy Goodman—Michael Schwerner—and James Chaney. Margaret Walker. BPo

For Angela. Zack Gilbert. PoBA

For Angus MacLeod. Iain Crichton Smith. OxBS

For Ann Scott-Moncrieff. Edwin Muir. GTBS-P

For Anna. Irving Layton. NeAC

For Anne. Leonard Cohen. FF

For Anne Gregory. W. B. Yeats. CMoP; CMoP; FaFP; LiTM; NAEL-2; SOTW

For Anne, Who Doesn't Know. Gail Fox. IHMS

For Annie. Poe. AmPP; AnAmPo; BLPL; LiTA; NOBA; OBEV; OxBA

For any golfer of resource. The Crow and the Nighthawk. Watson Kirkconnell. CaP

For Artaud. Michael McClure. NeAP

For at the window of my house. She of the Impudent Face. Bible, *O.T. Fr.* Proverbs, VII: 6-27. TrJP

For August, be your dwelling thirty towers. August. Folgore Da San Gimignano, *tr. fr. Italian by* Dante Gabriel Rossetti. *Fr.* Sonnets of the Months. CTC

For authorities whose hopes. The Paper Nautilus. Marianne Moore. FaBoWP; VGW

For Avi Killed in Lebanon. Mark Osaki. BrSi

For awhile I too was haunted by. Amnesiac. Mark Osaki. BrSi

For awhile today, the rafts almost float side by side. The Orinoco, 1561. Ai. *Fr.* The Gilded Man, I. AnAn

For bards, like these, who neither sing nor say. On His Own Poetry. Charles Churchill. *Fr.* The Prophecy of Famine. NOEC

For being so black. My Father. James Berry. PBCV

For best work. Lorine Niedecker. VGW

For better waters now the little bark. Dante, *tr. fr. Italian by* John Ciardi. *Fr.* Divina Commedia: Purgatorio, I-II. NAWM-1

For Bill. Geof Hewitt. NeAC

For Bill Hawkins, a Black Militant. William J. Harris. PoBA

For Black Poets Who Think of Suicide. Etheridge Knight. CNA; HeIP; InPK; PoBA

For blackmen. Blackmen: Who Make Morning. Angela Jackson. CNA

For Both of Us at Fisk. Sharon Scott. JB

For brave comportment, wit without offence. To His Honoured and Most Ingenious Friend, Master Charles Cotton. Robert Herrick. CaPo

For Bud. Michael S. Harper. PoE

For C. Philip Whalen. NeAP; VGW

For C. K. at His Christening. Daniel Lawrence Kelleher. NeIP

For Cal. James Cunningham. JB

For Carlos Charles Bucillio. Alice Sadongei. HATNAP

For centuries only painters, poets and sculptors. The Aging Actress Sees Herself a Starlet on the Late Show. Miller Williams. MT

For certain he hath seen all perfectness. Dante, *tr. fr. Italian by* Dante Gabriel Rossetti. *Fr.* La Vita Nuova, XVII. AWP

For Ch'iao. Ya Hsien, *tr. fr. Chinese by* Dominic Cheung. IFON

For Christmas Day. Luke Wadding, *tr. by* Thomas Kinsella. TIRV

For Christopher Columbus, *sels.* A. J. Seymour. PBCV

"And so the day beginning." *Fr.* V.

"He dreamed not that the ocean would bear ships." *Fr.* IV.

For Christ's sake let me in. Love's Promises. Alastair Fowler. NPo

"For Christ's sweet sake, I beg an alms." James Russell Lowell. *Fr.* The Vision of Sir Launfal. WGRP, *fr. pt.* II.

For City Spring. Stephen Vincent Benét. BXAP; NBLV

For Colored Girls Who Have Considered Suicide When the Rainbow Is
    Enuf, sels. Ntozake Shange.
    "At 4:30 AM/ she rose." BoWoP
    Dark Phrases. BlSi
    No More Love Poems #1. BlSi
For Communion with God, sel. Thomas Shepherd.
    "Alas, my God, that we should be." TrPWD
For Consciousness. Mervyn Morris. PBCV
For Cora Lightbody, R.N. John Glassco. PoA
For cover—the tall forest. A Landscape Painted on a Fan. Chu Yün-
    ming, tr. by Jonathan Chaves. CoBLCP
For Crethis' store of tales and pleasant chat. Crethis. Callimachus, tr. by
    Richard Garnett. AWP
For D. S. Christine Craig. AIW
For Dan Berrigan. Etheridge Knight. NeAC
For Danny whistling slowly. Feed. Raymond Knister. OBCV
For dateless consummation dateless days. To My Lady. E. S. Miller.
    Son
For David Shapiro. David Lehman. PoA
For dawn, wind. Crow Jane. Imamu Amiri Baraka. PoM
For days and days. For Me from You. Rita Anyiam-St. John. WS
For days I have been walking around. Letter to a Friend in an Unknown
    Place. Anita Barrows. NMM
For days the thought of parting. Mohammad Taqi Mir, tr. by Ahmed Ali.
    GoT
For de Lawd. Lucille Clifton. CNA; PoBA; TAP; TwCP
For dear life some do. Portrait of an Artist. Barbara Howes. IHMS
For death must come, and change, and, though the loss. Immutabilis.
    Alice Learned Bunner. Fr. Vingtaine, II. AA
For dedy liif, my livy deth I wite. Come, Death—My Lady Is Dead.
    At. to Charles, Duc d' Orléans. MeEL
For deep deer-copse beneath Mount Han. Ezra Pound, after the Chinese.
    OBVE
For Deeper Life. Katharine Lee Bates. TrPWD
For Deliverance from a Fever. Anne Bradstreet. NAAL-1
For do but note a wild and wanton herd. The Power of Music.
    Shakespeare. Fr. The Merchant of Venice, V, i. GN
For Don Drummond. Lorna Goodison. PBCV
For Dr. and Mrs. Dresser. Margaret Avison. MoCV
For Drum Hadley. Harold Littlebird. VoR
For Dulcimer and Doubled Voice. Jordan Smith. KS
For E. C. J. Emmett Jarrett. NeAC
For E. J. P. Leonard Cohen. NoP
For E. McC. Ezra Pound. SD
For each ecstatic instant. Emily Dickinson. NAAL-1
"For each man kills the thing he loves"—it's true. Eminent Critic. John
    Frederick Nims. TW
For Each of You. Audre Lorde. CNA
For eating persimmons, too. Masaoka Shiki, tr. fr. Japanese by Burton
    Watson. Fr. Thirty-nine Haiku. FCEI
For Echo is the soul of the voice exerting itself in hollow places. The
    Instruments. Christopher Smart. WiR
For Edward Hicks. David Helwig. NOBC
For Edwin R. Embree. Owen Dodson. CNA
For eight or nine yards I watch. Kaya Shirao, tr. fr. Japanese by Hiroaki
    Sato. Fr. Twenty-one Hokku. FCEI
For eighty-seven years. Muju, tr. by Lucien Stryk and Takashi Ikemoto.
    ZPCJ
For eighty years I've talked of east and west. Kiyo, tr. by Lucien Stryk
    and Takashi Ikemoto. ZPCJ
For Eleanor and Bill Monahan. William Carlos Williams. CRP, abr.;
    VGW
For Elizabeth Bishop. Sandra McPherson. GeTw; MAYP
For Elizabeth Madox Roberts. Janet Lewis. QFR
For Ellen after the Publication of Her Stories. James Whitehead. BLA
For Emily (Dickinson). Maureen Owen. UL
For England when with fav'ring gale. By the Deep Nine. Unknown.
    ChTr
For Erotion's Grave. Martial, tr. fr. Latin by F. A. Wright. OBD
For Esther. Stanley Plumly. LCAP
For Eusi, Ayi Kwei and Gwen Brooks. Keorapetse Kgositsile. PoBA
"For ever and ever." Emperor Meiji, tr. by Geoffrey Bownas and
    Anthony Thwaite. PeBJV
For ever, Fortune, wilt thou prove. James Thomson. GTBS; GTBS-P
For-ever Morning. Laura Riding. LiTA
For every bird there is this last migration. The Death of the Bird. A. D.
    Hope. PoAu-2
For Every Day. Frances Ridley Havergal. Fr. A Teacher's Prayer.
    BLRP
For every evil under the sun. Mother Goose. OxNR
For every parcel I stoop down to seize. The Armful. Robert Frost.
    CMoP; OxBSP

For every year, he grew a new tooth. The Man Who Became Old.
    Alberto Ríos. NoAM
For every year of life we light. A Birthday Poem. James Simmons.
    OxBSP
For everyone. The Swimmer's Moment. Margaret Avison. NOBC
For everything there is a season. Bible, O.T. See Ecclesiastes: To
    Everything There Is a Season.
For Example. Mihály Ladányi, tr. fr. Hungarian by Jascha Kessler.
    FOC
For Exmoor. Jean Ingelow. OBEV
For eyes he waves greentipped. Slug in Woods. Earle Birney. CaP;
    NOBC; OBCV
For Eyes to Bless You. Pamela Mordecai. PVCV
For False Heart. Hilaire Belloc. See I said to Heart, "How goes it?"
For fifteen minutes I stood in front of Chas. A. Stevens. Shopping in
    Chicago. Ed Orr. SoTCo
For fifty years I followed an "overturned cart." Huang Tsung-hsi, tr. fr.
    Chinese by Lynn Struve. Fr. Songs from Living in the Mountains,
    III. WFTU
For fleas, also, the night. Issa, tr. by Geoffrey Bownas and Anthony
    Thwaite. PeBJV
For flowers that bloom about our feet. Spring Prayer. Emerson. BoTP
For Forgiveness. John Donne. See Wilt thou forgive that sin where I
    begun.
For forty-one years I have lived in your borders, America. To America.
    H. Leivick, tr. by Benjamin and Barbara Harshav. AYP
For forty years, for forty-one. This Dim and Ptolemaic Man. John Peale
    Bishop. ImOP; LiTA; LiTM
For forty years I shunned the lust. For a Virgin Lady. Countee Cullen.
    MoAmPo
For Fran. Philip Levine. FF; SM
For Freckle-faced Gerald. Etheridge Knight. BPo; NeAC
For Freda. Margery Smith. CN
For fun I carried mother on my back. Ishikawa Takuboku, tr. fr.
    Japanese by Hiroaki Sato. Fr. Forty-seven Tanka in Three Lines.
    FCEI
For fun the schoolboys crack the ice. Dog with Schoolboys. Jean
    Follain, tr. by Keith Waldrop. RHTwFP
For Gabriel. Laya Firestone. VWA
For gay bard, barren summer. Lament for Lleucu Llwyd. Llywelyn
    Goch ap Meurig Hen, tr. by Joseph P. Clancy. OBWVE
For gear your typewriter and an old rugby boot. Homage to Malcolm
    Lowry. Derek Mahon. FaBCIP
For George Barker at Seventy. David Wright. NPo
For George Santayana. Robert Lowell. CMoP; NAAL-2; VGW
For God, our God is a gallant foe. Ballad for Gloom. Ezra Pound.
    LiTM; MoAmPo
For God While Sleeping. Anne Sexton. NePoEA-2
For God's sake, let me not go mad. Pushkin, tr. by Alan Myers. AAA
For God's sake, let us sit upon the ground. Shakespeare. Fr. King
    Richard II: Let's Talk of Graves. HoPM
For Godsake [or God's sake] hold your tongue, and let me love. The
    Canonization. John Donne. BLPL; EIL; EnLoPo; HAP; JCP; LiTB;
    MePo; NAEL-1; NAWM-1; NIP; NOBE; NoP; OAEL-1; OBS; PoE;
    PoEL-2; PPP; SeCePo; SeCP; SeCV-1; TrGrPo; UnPo
    (Canonisation, The.) SeCePo; TEP
For Good Luck. Juliana Horatia Ewing. FaPON
    (Little Kings and Queens of the May.) BoTP
For goverment, though high, and low, and lower. The Commonwealth of
    the Bees. Shakespeare. Fr. King Henry V. GN
For grief. Exile. Saniyya Salih, tr. by Kamal Boullata. OV
For Guillaume Apollinaire. William Meredith. CoAP
For Gypsy at Minsky's. Garbo Stepping In. Jean Balderston. SoTCo
For H. W. Fuller. Carolyn M. Rodgers. BPo
For Hani, Aged Five, That She Be Better Able to Distinguish a Villain.
    Gene Baro. NYBP
"For he is ishi the last of his tribe." T.V. (1). Anselm Hollo. UL
For he was wounder amiabill. Squire Meldrum at Carrickfergus. Sir
    David Lindsay. Fr. The Historie of Squyer William Meldrum.
    OxBS
For Heather, Entering Kindergarten. Roberta Hill Whiteman. HATNAP;
    NoAM
For Hekabé and the women of Ilion. Plato, tr. by Peter Jay. PeHV
For Her. Mark Strand. GOYP
For her birthday. Susan Wallbank. AIW
For her blood runs in my blood. Rachel. Rachel, tr. by Naomi Nir.
    VWA
For Her Brother. Unknown. See Thousand and One Nights, The:
    Tumadir al-Khansa for Her Brother.
For her gait, if she be walking. William Browne. OBEV
For Her Heart Only. Unknown. EIL
For her they were all in the future. The Ghosts of the Victorians.
    Stephen Plaice. NPo

For here lies Juliet, and her beauty makes. Shakespeare. *Fr.* Romeo and Juliet, V, iii. FaFP
　(Thus with a Kiss I Die.) TrGrPo
　"How oft when men are at the point of death." DL
　(Romeo's Last Words.) FiP
For Hettie. Imamu Amiri Baraka. NeAP; NOBA
For Hidden Mist Pavilion. Yü Hsüan-chi, *tr.* by Geoffrey Waters. BoWoP
For him, it seems, everything was molten. Court-ladies flow in gentle streams. The Laughing Hyena, by Hokusai. D. J. Enright. TwCP
For him who sought his country's good. Washington's Monument. *Unknown.* OHIP; PAH
For his mind, I doe not care. Another Ladyes Exception Present at the Hearing. Ben Jonson. *Fr.* A Celebration of Charis in Ten Lyrick Peeces. SeCP
For His Own Epitaph. Matthew Prior. *See* For My Own Monument.
For his religion it was fit. Samuel Butler. *Fr.* Hudibras, I, 1. OBSV
For His Ring and Watch on the Night Stand. Gladys Cardiff. HATNAP
For His Wife, on Her Birthday. Charles Wesley. NOCV
For Hollis Sigler. Elaine Equi. UL
For Hope. Richard Crashaw. LiTB
　(Answer for Hope.) MeLP
　(M. Crashaw's Answer for Hope.) OBS; SeCV-1
　(On Hope.) MePo; NOBE
For hours I sit here facing the white wall. My Swallows. Gerald Stern. KS
For hours I stood upon the bridge. Loew's Bridge, a Broadway Idyl. Mary E. Tucker. CBWP-1
For hours the princess would not play or sleep. The Yak. Virna Sheard. CaP
For how long known this boundless wash of light. Summer Beach. Frances Cornford. BrRo
For Hoyt Wilhelm. Joel Oppenheimer. ASP
For human nature Hope remains alone. Hope. Theognis, *tr.* by John Hookham Frere. AWP
For I bless the Prince of Peace and pray that all the guns may be nail'd up. Christopher Smart. *Fr.* Jubilate Agno. InPS
For I can snore like a bullhorn. After Making Love We Hear Footsteps. Galway Kinnell. DiL; InPS; NIP; NoAM
For I Dipped [*or* Dipt] into the Future. Tennyson. *Fr.* Locksley Hall. PoLF
　(Prophecy.) WBLP
For I Have Done a Good and Kindly Deed. Franz Werfel, *tr. fr. German* by Edith Abercrombie Snow. TrJP
For I have learned. Wordsworth. *Fr.* Lines Composed a Few Miles above Tintern Abbey [on Revisiting the Banks of the Wye during a Tour, July 13, 1798]. NU
For I have loved [*or* lov'd] the rural walk through lanes. The Sofa. William Cowper. *Fr.* The Task, *Bk.* I. EnRP
　(Rural Sights and Sounds.) NOEC
For I inhabit a wood. Marban, a Hermit Speaks. *Unknown*, *tr.* by Michael Hartnett. BIrV; CIP
For I learn as the years roll onward. Lessons of the Year. *Unknown.* BLRP
For I Will Consider My Cat Jeoffry [*or* Jeoffrey]. Christopher Smart. *Fr.* Jubilate Agno. CTC; FM; HAP; HeIP; NAEL-1; NOEC; NoP; OAEL-1; OBWVE; PoEL-3; PPP; Prf; SCV; TTTS; WeW
　(My Cat Jeoffry.) ChTr; FaBoCh; LiTB; PoF; RB; SeCePo; WiR
　(Of Jeoffry, His Cat.) NU; PrIm
For I will consider my dog Poochkin. Jubilate Canis. Erica Jong. MAYP
For if it's a theme state it. Anne-Marie Albiach, *tr. fr. French* by Keith Waldrop. *Fr.* Enigma, II. RHTwFP
"For if your boone be askeable." Thomas Cromwell. *Unknown.* ESPB
For Innocents' Day. Luke Wadding. NOIV; TIRV
For Inspiration. Michelangelo, *tr.* by Wordsworth. WGRP
　(To the Supreme Being.) AWP; PFI; TrPWD
For Instance. Robert McAlmon. PoA
For instance/ if the sea should break. If Something Should Happen. Lucille Clifton. MAT
For it is the day of the Lord's vengeance. God's Vengeance. Bible, *O.T. Fr.* Isaiah, XXXIV: 8–15. FM
For I've been planted long. "Mine, O Thou Lord of Life, Send My Roots Rain." Lorna Goodison. UAS
For James Baldwin. Kay Boyle. NMM
For James Dean. Frank O'Hara. NeAP; NNaP
For Jan, in Bar Maria. Carolyn Kizer. VGW
For Jane. Charles Bukowski. HoPM
For Jane Myers. Louise Glück. FaBoWP; GeTw
For January I give you vests of skin. January. Folgore Da San Gimignano, *tr. fr. Italian* by Dante Gabriel Rossetti. *Fr.* Sonnets of the Months. PFI
For Jean Vincent d'Abbadie, Baron St -Castin. Alden Nowlan. NOBC

For Jeff. Jon Bowerman. CowP
For Jillian of Berry she dwells on a hill. Jillian of Berry. Beaumont *and* Fletcher. *Fr.* The Knight of the Burning Pestle, IV, v. EIL
　(Another Song.) OBS
For Jim, Easter Eve. Anne Spencer. AmNP; PoNe
For John Berryman. Robert Lowell. NOBA
For John Chappell. Gary Snyder. NNaP
For John Clare. John Ashbery. FYAP
For John Keats, Apostle of Beauty. Countee Cullen. *Fr.* Four Epitaphs. AmNP; CDC; PoBA
For Johnny. John Pudney. OBWP
For Judith. Konrad Bayer, *tr. fr. German* by Beth Bjorklund. CoAuP
For July, in Sierra, by the willow-tree. July. Folgore Da San Gimignano, *tr. fr. Italian* by Dante Gabriel Rossetti. *Fr.* Sonnets of the Months. AWP
For just a moment. Empress Eifuku, *tr.* by Steven D. Carter. WFTW
For Just Men Light Is Sown. Michael Wigglesworth. AH
For K. R. on Her Sixtieth Birthday. Richard Wilbur. NoP
For Kai Snyder. Philip Whalen. PoM
For Kelley. Ken Belford. NeAC
For King, for Robert Kennedy. Robert Hayden. *Fr.* Words in the Mourning Time. CNA
For Kinte. Oliver La Grone. FB
For knighthood is not in the feats of war. The True Knight [*or* True Knighthood]. Stephen Hawes. *Fr.* The Pastime of Pleasure, 27. ACP; OBEV; TrGrPo
For Ku Yen-hsien, A Poem for Him to Give to His Wife. Lu Yün, *tr. fr. Chinese* by Burton Watson. CoBCP
For Kuo Hsiang. Yu Hsuah-chi, *tr. fr. Chinese* by Geoffrey Waters. BoWoP
For lack of food. The Great Figure. Francisco Morales Santos, *tr.* by Juan Felipe Herrera. Vol
For laughing, front teeth. Ozaki Hosai, *tr. fr. Japanese* by Hiroaki Sato. *Fr.* One Hundred Haiku in Free Form. FCEI
For Leon Bismarck Beiderbecke (1903-1931). Michael Horovitz. NPo
For Lerida. David St. John. AmPA; AnAn
For Life I Had Never Cared Greatly. Thomas Hardy. CMoP; LiTM; NoAM
For lighter, whiter skin in just ten days. Brainwashing Dramatized. Don Johnson. PoNe
For Lo! My Jonah How He Slumped. John Wilson. AH
For, lo! the living God doth bare his arm. Democracy. Harriet Monroe. *Fr.* Commemoration Ode. AA
For lo! the sea that fleets about the land. The Dancing Sea. Sir John Davies. *Fr.* Orchestra; or, A Poem[e] of Da[u]ncing. ChTr
For, lo, the winter is past. Bible, *O.T. Fr.* The Song of Solomon, II: 11–12. PDV
　(Lo, the Winter Is Past.) FaPON
For, Lord, the Crowded Cities Be. Rainer Maria Rilke, *tr. fr. German* by Ludwig Lewisohn. AWP; TrJP
For Love. Robert Creeley. NOBA
For Love Has Such a Spirit That If It Is Portrayed It Dies. Charles Bernstein. IAT
For love he offered me his perfect world. Gift to a Jade. Anna Wickham. OxBSP
For love—I would. The Warning. Robert Creeley. NeAP; TAP; VGW
For love no time has she, or inclination. Soame Jenyns. *Fr.* The Modern Fine Lady. OBSV
For love of lovely words, and for the sake. Skerryvore. Robert Louis Stevenson. EyDe
For love of Megan I danced all night. My Autobiography. Ted Berrigan. BAP
For Loves-sake, kisse me once againe. Begging Another, on Colour of Mending the Former. Ben Jonson. *Fr.* A Celebration of Charis in Ten Lyrick Peeces. PoEL-2; SeCP
For Lucas Cranach's Eve. Adelaide Crapsey. QFR
For M. Bruce Williamson. NeIP
For Mack C. Parker. Pauli Murray. PoBA
For Malcolm: After Mecca. Gerald William Barrax. CNA; OFD; PoBA
For Malcolm Who Walks in the Eyes of Our Children. Quincy Troupe. CNA; PoBA
For Malcolm X. Nanina Alba. PoBA
For Malcolm X. Margaret Abigail Walker. BPo; CNA; PoBA; Son
For Malcolm's eyes, when they broke. A Poem for Black Hearts. Imamu Amiri Baraka. IDB; PoBA; PoM; SOTW
For Mama. Deborah Kendrick. TSM
For man to act as if his soul did see. Thomas Traherne. *See* Christian Ethics: Contentment.
For many a year I've watched the ships a-sailing to and fro. The Ships. J. J. Bell. B¬TP
For many blessings I to God upraise. Nature and the Child. John Lancaster Spalding. *Fr.* God and the Soul. AA
For many distant travelers. Acoma. William Oandasan. HATNAP

For many, many days together. Riding Together. William Morris. NOBE; OAEL-2

For many thousand ages. Es Stehen Unbeweglich. Heine, *tr. by* James Thomson. AWP; TrJP

For many unsuccessful years. Against Modesty in Love. Matthew Prior. ErPo

For many years I herded cows. Cows and Logs. Harold Otto. CowP

For Mao Tse-tung; a Meditation on Flies and Kings. Irving Layton. NOBC

For Maria. Cleopatra Mathis. MAYP

For Marianne Moore's Birthday. Kay Boyle. NMM

For Marsha. Angela de Hoyos. ER

For Mary McLeod Bethune. Margaret Abigail Walker. PoNe

For Masturbation. Alan Dugan. CAPP

For Mattie and Eternity. Sterling Plumpp. CNA

For me, for me, two horses wait. The Wizard's Funeral. Richard Watson Dixon. ELP; NOBVV

For Me from You. Rita Anyiam-St. John. WS

For me the jasmine buds unfold. The World Is Mine. Florence Earle Coates. AA

For me, the naked and the nude. The Naked and the Nude. Robert Graves. NYBP; SoSe

For me the night still soughs. After an Eclipse of the Sun. Eugene Heimler, *tr. by* Peter Sherwood *and* Keith Bosley. VWA

For Memories. Nishiwaki Junzaburo, *tr. fr. Japanese by* Hiroaki Sato. FCEI

For mercy, courage, kindness, mirth. Laurence Binyon. BoTP; MoBrPo

For Michael. Valerie Bloom. WS

For Miriam. Marjorie Oludhe Macgoye. WPOW

For modes of faith let graceless Zealots fight. Faith. Pope. *Fr.* An Essay on Man, Epistle III. WGRP

For months/ my books were stacked. February Park. Gerald Vizenor. VoR

For months now you've hated me. Love Letter. David Ray. TW

For more than sixty years he has been blind. War Blinded. Douglas Dunn. DiPo; OBWP

For morn, my dome of blue. A Child's Prayer. Siegfried Sassoon. BoTP

For most of my life, no need to wear specs. Singing, 1977. Roy Fuller. PoPo

For mother-love and father-care. We Thank Thee. *Unknown.* FaPON

For "Mr. Dudley," a Black Spy. James A. Emanuel. BPo

For M.S. Singing *Fruhlingsglaube* in 1945. Frances Cornford. BrRo

For Muh' Dear. Carolyn M. Rodgers. CNA

For Musia's Grandchildren. Irving Layton. NOBC

For My Ancestors. Rolfe Humphries. PoRA

For My Beloved, Combing Her Hair. Yehuda Amichai, *tr. fr. Hebrew by* Bernhard Frank. MHeP

For My Birthday. Yehuda Amichai, *tr. fr. Hebrew by* Bernhard Frank. MHeP

For My Brother and Sister Southwestern Indian Poets. Geary Hobson. STE

For My Brother Jesus. Irving Layton. NoP

For My Brother Who Died before I Was Born. Baron Wormser. GOYP

For My Contemporaries. J. V. Cunningham. CoAP; SM

For My Daughter. Judith Kazantzis. AIW

For My Daughter. Weldon Kees. CoAP; SM

For My Daughter. John Logan. CRP

For My Father. Stephen Berg. DiL

For My Father. Paul Potts. FaBoTw

For My Father. Philip Schultz. DiL

For My Father. Philip Whalen. DiL

For My Funeral. A. E. Housman. CMoP; TrPWD

For My Grandmother. Countee Cullen. *Fr.* Epitaphs. MoAmPo; VGW

For My Grandmother, Bridgid Halpin. Michael Hartnett. BIrV

For My Husband. Ellen Bryant Voigt. NoP

For My Husband Who Sent Me Several Rubbings of Ancient Egyptian Stone Tablets. Hsüeh Shao-hui, *tr. fr. Chinese by* Irving Lo. WFTU

For My Love Rising Early. Ya'ir Hurvits, *tr. fr. Hebrew by* Bernhard Frank. MHeP

For My Lover, Returning to His Wife. Anne Sexton. HCAP; IHMS; NMM; UnPo; WPE

For My Mother. Ellen Bass. TV

For My Mother. Louise Glück. GeTw; UnPo

For My Mother. June Jordan. BoWoP; NMM

For My Mother. Iain Crichton Smith. OxBS

For My Mother. Ellen Bryant Voigt. NIP

For My Mother, Feeling Useless. Paula Rankin. MAYP

For My Mother: Genevieve Jules Creeley. Robert Creeley. PoM

For My Mother's Mother. Judith McDaniel. TV

For My Own Monument. Matthew Prior. OBEV
    (For His Own Epitaph.) FaBoEE

For my part, I never care. Tips Tongueless. Robert Herrick. CaPo

For my part, I'le not meddle with the cause. Homer, *tr. fr. Greek by* George Chapman. *Fr.* Odyssey, XIV. CTC

For My People. Wendy Rose. CDW

For My People. Margaret Abigail Walker. AmNP; CNA; IDB; PoBA; PoNe

For my sins I live in the city of New York. Whitman in Black. Ted Berrigan. UL

For my sister's sake. Hitomaro, *tr. fr. Japanese by* Arthur Waley. *Fr.* Manyo Shu. AWP

For My Son, Noah, Ten Years Old. Robert Bly. CAPP; DiL; InPS

For My Son on the Highways of His Mind. Maxine W. Kumin. MAT

For My Torturer, Lieutenant D—— Leila Djabali, *tr. fr. French by* Anita Barrows. WPOW

For My Twenty-fifth Birthday in Nineteen Forty-one. John Ciardi. WaP

For My Unborn and Wretched Children. Alfred B. Spellman. CNA; PoBA

For My Wife. Julian Symons. WaP

For My Wife: A Poem Written in Sickness. Yüan Mei, *tr. fr. Chinese by* Anthony C. Yu. WFTU

For My Younger Brother Shinkei on the Seventeenth Anniversary of His Death. Kan Sazan, *tr. fr. Chinese by* Burton Watson. JLIC-2

For Natalya Correia. Irving Layton. NeAC

For nations vague as weed. Nothing to Be Said. Philip Larkin. OxBTC

For nearly fifty years I've been a cocky. Now I'm Easy. Eric Bogle. OBET

For New Year, Postumus, ten years ago. A Roman Thank-You Letter. Martial, *tr. by* James Michie. OBCP

For Nicholas, Born in September. Tod Perry. NYBP

For nights on end, I've been pursued by rain and sleet. Crossing Several Mountain Ridges on My Way to P'u-ch'eng from Chiang-shan after a Snowfall. Chiang Shih, *tr. by* Irving Lo. WFTU

For nine months. The Rite. Peter Dale. NAs

For No Clear Reason. Robert Creeley. VGW

For No Good Reason. Peter Redgrove. PoE

For no man wist who was best. The Round Table. Robert Mannyng. ACP

For No One. John Lennon *and* Paul McCartney. WTO

For noble minds, the worst of miseries. Poverty. Theognis, *tr. by* John Hookham Frere. AWP

For Nothing. Andrés Castro Ríos, *tr. fr. Spanish by* Julio Marzán. InW

For Nothing. Gary Snyder. NNaP

For Now. W. S. Merwin. NaP

For now, love thou, I rede, Christ, as I thee tell. Love is Life. Richard Rolle of Hampole. *Fr.* A Song of the Love of Jesus. ACP

For now too nigh/ The archangel stood, and from the other hill. Milton. *Fr.* Paradise Lost, *Bk.* XII, *ll.* 625–649. (Their Banishment.) SeCePo

For, O America, our country!—land. America. Arlo Bates. *Fr.* The Torch-Bearers. AA

For oak and elm have pleasant leaves. Oscar Wilde. *Fr.* The Ballad of Reading Gaol. NoAM

For often my mammy has told. Henry Brooke. *Fr.* Jack the Giant Queller; an Antique History. NOEC

For once he wanted. My Grandfather in Search of Moonshine. George Ella Lyon. GOYP

For once, I hardly noticed what I ate. Runaways Café II. Marilyn Hacker. NoAM

For Once, Then, Something. Robert Frost. NoAM; NOBA

For one brief day, did Queenie stay. Queenie. Mary Weston Fordham. CBWP-2

For one long term, or e'er her trial came. George Canning *and* John Hookham Frere. FaBoCo; FaBoEE
    (Inscription for the Door of the Cell in Newgate Where Mrs. Brownrigg, the 'Prentice-cide, Was Confined Previous to Her Execution.) FaBoEE

For One Moment. David Ignatow. NNaP

For one month afterwards the eye stays true. Departure. Kingsley Amis. NePoEA

For one thing, you can believe it. Contemporary Native American Poetry. Jim Barnes. NOVW

For One Who Died Young. H. R. Hays. EAS

For one who says he feels. Petra von Morstein, *tr. by* Rosemarie Waldrop. BoWoP

For openers, the Federal Government. A How to Change the U.S. Harry Edwards, *arr. in verse by* Walter Lowenfels. NBP; TW

For other beds the priests there used none. Britomart at Isis' Church. Spenser. *Fr.* The Faerie Queene, V, 7. PoE

For Our Lady. Sonia Sanchez. IHMS

For "Our Lady of the Rocks." Dante Gabriel Rossetti. EBEV

For our own private reasons. Reasons. Thomas James. PoA

For Our Soldiers Who Fell in Russia. Franco Fortini, *tr. fr. Italian by* Ruth Feldman. VWA

For Pablo Picasso. Paul Eluard, *tr. fr. French by* Michael Benedikt. POS

For Paddy Mac. Padraic Fallon. CIP

For Patrick, Aetat: LXX. Sir John Betjeman. NAs

For Paul Laurence Dunbar. Countee Cullen. *Fr.* Four Epitaphs. CDC

For physic and farces his equal there scarce is. On Sir John Hill, M. D., Playwright. David Garrick. FaBoCo; FaBoEE; NBLV

For Pity, Pretty Eyes, Surcease. Thomas Lodge. EIL (Armistice.) OBSC

For Poets. Al Young. CNA; PoBA; RFM

For poor brides who were servant girls. Women's Songs ("For poor brides who were servant girls"). Kadya Molodovsky, *tr. by* Irving Feldman. PeBMYV

For printed instructions. No Holes Marred. Suzanne Douglass. RHPC

For prodigal read generous. E. E. Cummings. FaBoEE

For rage and dignity no words compare. A Classical Quatrain. Paul Goodman. VGW

For Randie. Geof Hewitt. NeAC

For reading I can recommend. "Domaine Public." Geoffrey Hill. OxBC

For Real. Jayne Cortez. PoBA

For Rhoda. Delmore Schwartz. *See* Repetitive Heart, The: Calmly We Walk Through This April's Day.

For Richard Chase. Jim Wayne Miller. GOYP

For right is right, since God is God. Right Is Right. Frederick William Faber. WBLP

For Righteousness' Sake. Whittier. PoEL-4

For Robert Frost. Galway Kinnell. NOBA; VGW

For Rosa Yen, Who Lived Here. Greg Pape. AmPA

For Saint John's Day. Luke Wadding. TIRV

For Saint Stephen's Day. Luke Wadding. TIRV

For Sammy Younge. Charlie Cobb. PoBA

For Sapphires. Carolyn M. Rodgers. CNA

For Saturday. Christopher Smart. *Fr.* Hymns for the Amusement of Children, XXXIII. FaBoCh; NOEC; OxBChV (Hymn for Saturday.) OxBChV (Lark's Nest, A.) FaBoCh

For Saundra. Nikki Giovanni. BPo; TTY

For Scholars and Pupils. George Wither. OxBChV

For Scotland's and for freedom's right. Bruce and the Spider. Bernard Barton. BeLS

For seeing, a/ brightness within. A New Light. William Hawkins. MoCV

For seven long years I had declared my passion. The Cywdd to Morvydd. Daffyd ap Gwilym. NOEC

For seven miles by the river hills the dogs and sheep forage. On Hearing that the Port of Shimoda Has Been Opened to the Foreigners. Gessho, *tr. by* Burton Watson. JLIC-2

For seventy-four years. Kokan Shiren, *tr. by* Lucien Stryk *and* Takashi Ikemoto. ZPCJ

For Several Days I Have Not Visited the Garden Pavilion. Wang Chiu-ssu, *tr. fr. Chinese by* Jonathan Chaves. CoBLCP

For several months. P.C. Plod versus the Dale St. Dog Strangler. Roger McGough. MoP

For several weeks I have been reading. Expression. Thom Gunn. OxBC

For Several Years I Have Wanted to Grow a Garden. Chu Yün-ming, *tr. fr. Chinese by* Jonathan Chaves. CoBLCP

For shame, thou everlasting wooer. The Antiplatonick. John Cleveland. MePo; SeCP

For She. Carla Harryman. LP

For Sheridan. Robert Lowell. HCAP

For Shirley. Denise Panek. GOS

For Signs. Thom Gunn. PoE

For six years, having no child. How You Were Born. Sharon Mayer Libera. PPR

For sixty days and upwards. Vicksburg. Paul Hamilton Hayne. AA; PAH

For Sleep, or Death. Ruth Pitter. TrPWD

For Snow. Eleanor Farjeon. CH

For so long/ We looked into mirrors. Us. Julius Lester. PoBA

For so long I sang your praises. Mercenaries. Ahmad Faraz, *tr. by* Mahmood Jamal. PBMUP

For Soldiers. Humphrey Gifford. CH; EIL

For some people the day comes. Che Fece. Il Gran Rifiuto. C. P. Cavafy, *tr. by* Edmund Keeley *and* Philip Sherrard. VMG

For Some Poets. Mae Jackson. PoBA

For some reason I thought you'd be waiting for me. Yosano Akiko, *tr. fr. Japanese by* Hiroaki Sato. *Fr.* Thirty-nine Tanka. FCEI

For some, the sea. Bathing Song. Anne Ridler. NYBP

For some the shuttle leaping in the sun. Rosa Luxembourg. Eileen Duggan. PeNZ

For some time now we have been drawn. Give Us the Right to Vote! Emma Döltz, *tr. by* Susan L. Cocalis *and* Gerlinde Geiger. DMG

For Sonoda Saeko. Wakayama Bokusui, *tr. fr. Japanese by* Hiroaki Sato. *Fr.* Forty-four Tanka. FCEI

For sport my Julia threw a lace. The Silken Snake. Robert Herrick. OxBSP

For Spring. Douglas G. Jones. NOBC

For Starters. Victoria McCabe. CRP

For Steph. Wendy Rose. CDW

For Stephen Dixon. Zack Gilbert. PoBA

For Stephen Drawing Birds. Pattiann Rogers. MAYP

For Steve. Earle Birney. WaP

For such as you, I do believe. The Mother in the House. Hermann Hagedorn. OHIP

For Summer's bloom and Autumn's blight. Josiah Gilbert Holland. *Fr.* Bitter-sweet. TrPWD

For Summer's Here. Ratcliffe Barnett. PoSH

For sunlit hours and visions clear. Gratitude. Clyde McGee. BLRP

For tactical reasons. Goal Consciousness. Erich Fried, *tr. by* Beth Bjorklund. CoAuP

For ten thousand leagues the waves of the Min are encompassed in this view. Climbing to the Very Top of Swallow Rock Once Again, in an Early Morning Rain. Wang Shih-chen, *tr. by* Daniel Bryant. WFTU

For that free Grace bringing us past terrible risks. Minnesota Thanksgiving. John Berryman. GOA

For That He Looked Not upon Her. George Gascoigne. EIL; NoP

For that I never knew you, I only learned to dread you. St. Roach. Muriel Rukeyser. GLP

For that the sonnet no doubt was my own true. Late Sonnet. Hayden Carruth. SM; Son

For the/ Creek Comet. Leaving Oklahoma Again. Barney Bush. NOVW

For the air is purified by prayer which is made aloud. Christopher Smart. *Fr.* Jubilate Agno. Prf

For the Altarpiece of the Roseau Valley Church, Saint Lucia. Derek Walcott. NoP

For the angels who inhabit this town. Locked Doors. Anne Sexton. KS

For the Anniversary of My Death. W. S. Merwin. CoAP; HCAP; InPK; NAAL-2; NaP; NOBA

For the ass whose gristle. Stele. Robert Marteau, *tr. by* Anne Winters. RHTwFP

For the Baptist. William Drummond of Hawthornden. *See* Last and greatest Herald of Heaven's King, The.

For the Bed at Kelmscott. William Morris. *See* Wind's on the wold, The.

For the Bicentenary of Isaac Watts. Norman Nicholson. EaLo

For the Book of Love. Jules Laforgue, *tr. fr. French by* Jethro Bithell. AWP; ErPo

For the Briar Rose. William Morris. NOBVV

For the bumps bangs and scratches of. Auto Mobile. A. R. Ammons. FF; OBAL

For the Candle Light. Angelina Weld Grimké. BlSi; CDC; PoNe

For the Children. Thomas Peacock. VoR

For the Children. Gary Snyder. NoP

For the Children or the Grown-ups? *Unknown.* OBCP

For the Children Who Died in a Smallpox Epidemic. Ryokan, *tr. fr. Japanese by* Hiroaki Sato. FCEI

For the Christian Reader. Anna Owena Hoyers, *tr. fr. German by* Susan L. Cocalis. DMG

For the Coming Year. Peter Everwine. OFD

For the Conjunction of Two Planets. Adrienne Rich. ImOP

For the Courtesan Ch'ing Lin. Wu Tsao, *tr. fr. Chinese by* Kenneth Rexroth *and* Ling Chung. BoWoP; WPOW

For the Crèche. G. K. Chesterton. *Fr.* Songs of Education. FaBoCo

For the Cultural Campaign. Chimedin Jigmed, *tr. fr. Mongol Oral Tradition by* C. R. Bawden. WTO

For the Curious. Yisroel Shtern, *tr. fr. Yiddish by* Robert Friend. PeBMYV

For the days when nothing happens. Thanksgiving. Margaret E. M. Sangster. BLRP

For the Dead. Adrienne Rich. AnAn; NAAL-2

For the Dead Gregorians. Ignacio Ramírez, *tr. fr. Spanish by* Samuel Beckett. MexPo

For the Death of Vince Lombardi. James Dickey. ASP

For the Depressed. Julian Symons. WaP

For the dim regions whence my fathers came. Outcast. Claude McKay. AmNP; PoBA

For the doubling of flowers is the improvement of the gardners talent. Christopher Smart. *Fr.* Jubilate Agno. NOEC

For the dream unfinished. Plain-Chant for America. Katherine Garrison Chapin. OPP

For the Earth God. *Unknown, tr. fr. Dahomean song by* Frances Herskovits. EaLo

For the Eating of Swine. Rodney Jones. MAYP

For the El Paso Weather Bureau. Peter Wild. MAT

For the Examination at Ho-nan-fu: Songs of the Twelve Months, *sel.* Li Ho, *tr. fr. Chinese by* Burton Watson. "Stars rest cold by shoals of cloud." CoBCP

For the Fallen. Laurence Binyon. NOBE; OBEV; OBWP; OxBTC

For the Family of Cuchonnacht O Dalaigh. David O'Bruadair, *tr. fr. Irish by* Thomas Kinsella. NOIV

For the Field. Eric Chock. BrSi

For the First Manned Moon Orbit, *sel.* James Dickey. "So long." AiP

For the first time. A Poem for Positive Thinkers. Barbara Mahone. PoBA

For the first time, on the road north of Tampico. Making a Fist. Naomi Shihab Nye. MAYP

For the first twenty years, since yesterday. The Computation. John Donne. OxBSP

For the Fly-Leaf of a School-Book. Norman Cameron. OxBS

For the Fourth Birthday of My Daughter. George Barker. NAs

For the Gifts of the Spirit. Edward Rowland Sill. TrPWD

For the Girls 'cause They Know. Harold Littlebird. VoR

For the God of Peyote. *Unknown, tr. fr. Huichol Indian by* Jerome Rothenberg. STP

For the Goddess Too Well Known. Elsa Gidlow. PeHV

For the Good of the Pythian Order. Mrs. Henry Linden. CBWP-4

For the Grave of Daniel Boone. William Stafford. NoP

For the Hern and Duck. *Unknown.* PBBP

For the jewel-like dew. Teika, *tr. by* Steven D. Carter. WFTW

For the Lady of a Physicist. Michael Bishop. BWV

For the Lady Olivia Porter; a Present upon a New Year's Day. Sir William Davenant. JCP; MeLP; MePo; OBS

For the Lame. Lucille Clifton. CAPP

For the Land Barons. Gasper García Laviana, *tr. fr. Spanish by* Alejandro Murguía. Vol

For the last time Beowulf uttered his boast. Beowulf and Wiglaf Slay the Dragon. *Unknown, tr. fr. Anglo-Saxon by* Charles W. Kennedy. *Fr.* Beowulf. AnOE

For the Last Time, Fire. Dennis Scott. PVCV; UAS

For the lifting up of mountains. Mountains. Lucy Larcom. WBLP

For the Little Girl Who Asked Why the Kitchen Was So Bright. James Ulmer. TDD

For the Lordes parte is his folke. Bible, *O.T. Fr.* Deuteronomy, XXXII: 9-15. OBVE

For the Lord's Day Evening. Isaac Watts. OxBChV

For the Lost Generation. Galway Kinnell. NePoAm

For the love of God is broader. There's a Wideness. Frederick William Faber. WBLP

For the Magdalene. William Drummond of Hawthornden. PoEL-2

For the man I'd marry I picked a white flower. Alleys. Sandra McPherson. MAYP

For the Margrave of Brandenburg. Ed Ochester. SoTCo

For the Market. Jane Mayhall. TAP

For the Marriage of Faustus and Helen. Hart Crane. InPS; NoAM; NOBA

"Capped arbiter of beauty in this street." *Fr.* III. FaBoMo; LiTM

For the Marsh's Birthday. James Wright. NYBP

For the Master's Use. *Unknown.* BLPA (Watered Lilies, The.) BLRP

For the merry imagination has a secret key. The Merry Imagination. Zelda, *tr. by* Bernhard Frank. MHeP

For the Minority. Robert Peterson. NeAC

For the Moment. Pierre Reverdy, *tr. fr. French by* Ron Padgett. RHTwFP; TTTS

For the Monk San-tsang on His Return to the Western Regions. Li Tung, *tr. fr. Chinese by* Burton Watson. CoBCP

For the Mute. Lucille Clifton. CAPP

For the New Railway Station in Rome. Richard Wilbur. NePoEA

For the New Union Dead in Alabama. Edward Dorn. PoM

For the New Year. Robert Creeley. NaP

For the Nightly Ascent of the Hunter Orion over a Forest Clearing. James Dickey. TwCP

For the one I await the path must have ended. Teika, *tr. fr. Japanese by* Hiroaki Sato. *Fr.* Eighty-four Tanka. FCEI

For the One Who Would Take Man's Life in His Hands. Delmore Schwartz. LiTA; LiTM; MoAB; MoAmPo; VGW; WaP

For the Opening of the William Dinsmore Briggs Room. Yvor Winters. CRP

For the Palace that lies desolate. We Sit Solitary. *Unknown.* TrJP

For the Parents of a Dead Child. Ryokan, *tr. fr. Japanese by* Burton Watson. FCEI

For the Passing of Groucho's Pursuer. John Hollander. *See* Now that high, oft affronted bosom heaves.

"For the pleasures of the many." Variations, Calypso and Fugue on a Theme of Ella Wheeler Wilcox. John Ashbery. LCAP

For the Poet Who Said Poets Are Struck by Lightning Only Two or Three Times. Peter Klappert. NBLV

For the Poor Blind Man. Francisco A. de Icaza, *tr. fr. Spanish by* Samuel Beckett. MexPo

For the Queen Mother. Sir John Betjeman. NAs

For the Rain It Raineth Every Day. Robert Graves. NYBP

For the Rebuilding of a House. Wendell Berry. EyDe

For the Record. Roy Blount, Jr. OBAL

For the Record. George Jonas. MoCV

For the Record. Mihály Ladányi, *tr. fr. Hungarian by* Edwin Morgan. MHuP

For the Record. Adrienne Rich. CAPP; NIP

For the rosebud's break of beauty. Lucy Larcom. *Fr.* A Thanksgiving. TrPWD

For the sake of argument. Do You Know What I Mean? Jack Myers. NAmP

For the second shot. The Zen Archer. James Kirkup. EaLo

For the Sexes the Gates of Paradise ("Mutual forgiveness of each vice"), *sel.* Blake. LiTB; PoEL-4 Epilogue: "Truly my Satan thou art but a dunce." PoE

For the Shadow. Jacques Hamelink, *tr. fr. Dutch by* Paul Vincent. DuIn

For the Sin. *Unknown, tr. fr. Hebrew.* TrJP

For the Sisters of the Hôtel Dieu. A. M. Klein. SoSe

For the Sleepwalkers. Edward Hirsch. FYAP; MAYP

For the Slender Beech and the Sapling Oak. Thomas Love Peacock. *Fr.* Maid Marian. EnRP (Song: "For the tender beech and the sapling oak.") OHIP

For the spiritual musick is as follows. Christopher Smart. *Fr.* Jubilate Agno. NOEC

For the Stranger. Carolyn Forché. MAYP

For the Student Strikers. Richard Wilbur. OxBC

For the Sun Declined, *sel.* Yitzhak Lamdan, *tr. fr. Hebrew by* Simon Halkin. "Where am I, O awesome friend?." TrJP

For the sun that shone at the dawn of spring. A Song of Thanks. Edward Smyth Jones. BANP

For the third time in ten years. Tunes for Bears to Dance To. Ronald Wallace. GOYP

For the Time Being; a Christmas Oratorio, *sels.* W. H. Auden. Flight into Egypt, The. OxBA Fugal-Chorus. LiTM "He is the way." EaLo If on Account of the Political Situation. LiTA; WaP "Led by the light of an unusual star." PChr "Our Father, whose creative Will." TrPWD Well, So That Is That ("Well so that is that. Now we must diomantle the tree."). LiTA; OAEL-2; OBCP (After Christmas.) MoAB; MoBrPo (Flight into Egypt, The.) OxBA

For the time that you return. Sanu Chigami, *tr. fr. Japanese. Fr.* Manyo Shu. Ma

For the Union Dead. Robert Lowell. AmPP; CoAP; FaBoPV; FYAP; HAP; HCAP; HeIP; InPS; LCAP; LiTM; MoP; NAAL-2; NaP; NoAM; NOBA; NoP; OBWP; PoE; SCV; TwCP; UnPo; WeW

For the War-Children. Sylvia Read. CN

For the wealth of pathless forests. A Thanksgiving. Lucy Larcom. OHIP

For the West. Gary Snyder. NaP

For the woman/ African in ancestry. A Freedom Song for the Black Woman. Carole C. Gregory. BlSi

For the Word Is Flesh. Stanley Kunitz. DiL; VGW

For the Yiddish Singers in the Lakewood Hotels of My Childhood. Harvey Shapiro. VWA

For the Young Who Want To. Marge Piercy. Psk

For thee a stead was builded. The Grave. *Unknown.* ACP

For thee I shall not die. I Shall Not Die for Thee. *Unknown, tr. fr. Irish.* AnIL, *tr. by* Douglas Hyde (O Woman, Shapely as the Swan.) BIrV, *tr. by* Padraic Colum; CTC

For thee, O dear dear country! Jerusalem the Golden. Bernard of Cluny, *tr. fr. Latin by* John Mason Neale. *Fr.* De Contemptu Mundi. WGRP, *shorter sel.*

For their son who wears his first *hakama.* Shido, *tr. by* Hiroaki Sato. FCEI

For Them. Michael Brownstein. UL

For them, O God, who only worship Thee. William Wilberforce Lord. *Fr.* Worship. AA

For them, the Arctic is the image, a touch of eternity. For Them. Michael Brownstein. UL

For them the sun shines ever in full might. Life after Death. Pindar, *tr. by* Walter Headlam. EaLo

For there are two heavens, sweet. Two Heavens. Leigh Hunt. GN

For there is hope for a man. South Wind. Nathan Yonathan, *tr. by* Richard Flantz. VWA

For there is hope for a tree. Bible, *O.T. Fr.* Job: Man, that is borne of a woman is of a few dayes, and full of trouble, XIV: 7–17. NAWM-1, *abr.*

For they are dead. Respect for the Dead. Laura Riding. LiTA

For They Shall See God. Luci Shaw. TrCP

For they who fashion songs must live too close to pain. Weltschmerz. Frank Yerby. AmNP

For things immediate. The Bookworm. Sacha Rabinovitch. NPo

For thinking somehow tomorrow will bring something good. Ishikawa Takuboku, *tr. fr. Japanese* by Hiroaki Sato. *Fr.* Forty-seven Tanka in Three Lines. FCEI

For thirty-eight years totally unaware. Ritangen, *tr. by* Lucien Stryk *and* Takashi Ikemoto. ZPCJ

For thirty years the entire world has looked to *lung-men*. Wang P'eng-yün, *tr. fr. Chinese* by Kang-i Sun Chang. *Fr.* Random Thoughts upon Reading History, Hastily Composed. WFTU

For this additional declaration. The Dissenters' Thanksgiving for the Late Declaration. *Unknown.* APAS

For this is not the road against which stand enemy lines. Piyyut for Rosh Hashana. Haim Guri, *tr. by* Ruth Finer Mintz. OFD

For This Is Wisdom. "Laurence Hope." *Fr.* The Teak Forest. PoLF

For this peculiar tint that paints my house. My House. Claude McKay. CDC

"For this same night att [Bucklesfeildberry]." Little Musgrave and Lady Barnard. *Unknown.* ESPB

For this she starred her eyes with salt. Elinor Wylie. MoAmPo

For this the ancient stars were hurled. Evolution. Israel Zangwill. TrJP

For this we were created. Christmas Poem. Vinícius de Moraes, *tr. by* Ashley Brown. ATCBP

For this your mother sweated in the cold. To Jesus on His Birthday. Edna St. Vincent Millay. TrCP; TrGrPo

For those men night was a more bitter day. Odysseus Elytis, *tr. fr. Greek* by Edmund Keeley *and* Philip Sherrard. *Fr.* Heroic and Elegiac Song for the Lost Second Lieute, III. VMG

For those my unbaptized rhymes. His Prayer for Absolution. Robert Herrick. SeCV-1; TrPWD

For those that never know the light. The Children of the Night. E. A. Robinson. OxBA

For Those Who Always Fear the Worst. *Unknown.* NBLV

For those who fell at Thermopylae. The Thermopylae Ode. Simonides, *tr. by* Richmond Lattimore. WaaP

For those who worship Thee there is no death. The Trees of Life. Jones Very. NOBA

For thou art with me here upon the banks. Wordsworth. *Fr.* Lines Composed a Few Miles above Tintern Abbey [on Revisiting the Banks of the Wye during a Tour, July 13, 1798]. Prf

For Though the Eaves [*or* Caves] Were Rabbeted [*or* Rabbited]. Henry David Thoreau. OxBSP; PoEL-4

For though ye be true of your tongue and honestly earn. Good Works. William Langland. *Fr.* The Vision of Piers Plowman. NOCV

For thoughts that curve like winging birds. I Yield Thee Praise. Philip Jerome Cleveland. TrPWD

For three swift days. Gennady Trifonov, *tr. by* Simon Karlinsky. PeHV

For three years, out of key with his time. Ezra Pound. *Fr.* Hugh Selwyn Mauberley. (Life and Contacts), III, i. HAP; MoAmPo; NAAL-2; OxBA; UnPo; VGW

   (E. P. Ode Pour l'Election de Son Sepulchre.) HAP; MoAmPo; MoP; NAAL-2; NoAM; VGW

   (Pour l'Election de Son Sepulchre, I-V.) FaBoMo

For Thus saith The Lord to the men of Judah and Jerusalem. Bible, *O.T. Fr.* Jeremiah, IV: 3-31. OBVE

For to Admire. Kipling. MoBrPo

For to Aske the Waye. *Unknown. Fr.* A Lytell Treatyse for to Lerne Englysshe and Frens. OxBLMV

For Tom Numkena, Hopi/Spokane. Harold Littlebird. VoR

For Tony, Dougal, Mick, Bugs, Nick et Al. Dave Bathgate. PoSH

For too long I've watched the ski boat scan. Why We Always Take Vacations by the Water. Ira Sadoff. BLA

For Travelers Going Sidereal. Robert Frost. OBAL

For treuthe [*or* trewthe] telleth that love [*or* loue] is triacle to abate sinne [*or* of hevene]. William Langland. *Fr.* The Vision of Piers Plowman. OBEV

   (Incarnation, The.) PoEL-1

For Twelfth Day. Luke Wadding. TIRV

For twenty years and more surviving after. Widows. Edgar Lee Masters. MoAmPo

For twenty years I've sought the other. Keso Shogaku, *tr. by* Lucien Stryk *and* Takashi Ikemoto. ZPCJ

For two minutes we gazed at each other. An Encounter. A. Leyeles, *tr. by* Benjamin *and* Barbara Harshav. AYP

For two months the dust of the capital. On First Returning from Taking the Examinations. Wen Cheng-ming, *tr. by* Jonathan Chaves. CoBLCP

For two years he studied with Ammonios Sakkas. From the School of the Renowned Philosopher. Constantine P. Cavafy, *tr. by* Edmund Keeley *and* Philip Sherrard. VMG

For two years I looked forward. Breakfast. Thom Gunn. OxBC

For *Under the Volcano*. Malcolm Lowry. NOBC

For us, born into a still. C. Day Lewis. *Fr.* Overtures to Death, VII. CMoP

For us like any other fugitive. Another Time. W. H. Auden. OxBA

For Us No Night Can Be Happier. Nikolaus Ludwig, Graf von Zinzendorf, *tr. fr. German* by at. to John Gambold. AH

For us, the dead, though young. The Unreturning. Clinton Scollard. PAH

For us their life, their death, are bread. Tristan und Isolt. Gottfried von Strassburg. OBD

For vacant song behold a shining theme! On Some Humming-Birds in a Glass Cage. Charles Tennyson Turner. FM

For Victor Jara. Miller Williams. SM

For Walter Lowenfels. Wendy Rose. CDW

For want I will in woe I plain. Sir Thomas Wyatt. SiPS

For want of a nail. Mother Goose. FaBoBe; OxNR

For wars his life and half a world away. Randall Jarrell. HCAP; OxBC

For We Are Thy People. *Unknown.* TrJP

For we have thought the longer thoughts. Chapter Heading. Ernest Hemingway. PoA

For we the mighty mountain plains have trod. The Sacraments of Nature. Aubrey Thomas De Vere. ACP

For weeks and weeks the autumn world stood still. How One Winter Came in the Lake Region. Wilfred Campbell. CaP; NOBC; OBCV

For weeks before it comes I feel excited, yet when it. Afterthought. Elizabeth Jennings. OBCP

For weeks, now months, the year in burden goes. Ninth Month. Robert Lowell. *Fr.* Marriage, *st.* 11. NAS

For weeks the poem of your body. The Poem Unwritten. Denise Levertov. CAPP

For wha ere had a lealer luve. Brown Adam. *Unknown.* ESPB

For What as Easy. W. H. Auden. NoP

For what is Freedom, but the unfettered use. Samuel Taylor Coleridge. *Fr.* The Destiny of Nations. EnRP

For what mad lover ever died. Samuel Butler. *Fr.* Hudibras. OBD

For what should appear. Last Night. Ilse Aichinger, *tr. by* Beth Bjorklund. CoAuP

For what the world admires I'll wish no more. The Resolve. Mary Lee, Lady Chudleigh. WPE

For what to-morrow shall disclose. Quid Sit Futurum Cras Fuge Quaerere. Matthew Prior. FaBoEE

For what we owe to other days. Exit. E. A. Robinson. MoAmPo; OxBSP

For whatever did it—the cider. A Cure at Porlock. Amy Clampitt. NoAM

For when it dawn'd—they dropp'd their arms. Samuel Taylor Coleridge. *Fr.* The Rime of the Ancient Mariner. UnS

For when they meet, the tensile air. The Paradigm. Allen Tate. NOBA

For Where You Skill. Vincent O'Sullivan. ATNZ

For white plum blossoms. Buson, *tr. fr. Japanese* by Hiroaki Sato. *Fr.* Eighty-seven Hokku. FCEI

For White Skin. Pierre Jean Jouve, *tr. fr. French* by Keith Bosley. RHTwFP

For Who? Mary Weston Fordham. CBWP-2

For who can longer hold? when every Press. John Oldham. *Fr.* Satires [*or* Satyrs] upon the Jesuits. SeCV-2

For whole nights—(don't ask how many). In an Alien Place. Leib Neidus, *tr. by* Ruth Whitman. VWA

For whom do I speak, now. Drifting. Andrew Salkey. PPR

"For Whom the Bell Tolls." Gavin Ewart. WaP

For whom the possessed sea littered, on both shores. Requiem for the Plantagenet Kings. Geoffrey Hill. NAEL-2; NoAM

For why? the gaines doth seldome quitte the charge. George Gascoigne. AAS

For Why the Gains. George Gascoigne. *Fr.* Gascoigne's Memories. Son

For William Edward Burghardt Du Bois on His Eightieth Birthday. Bette Darcie Latimer. PoBA; PoNe

For Wilma. Don Johnson. GOYP

For Windows. Robert Grenier. UL

For Witches. Susan Sutheim. NMM

For Women. Louise Aston, *tr. fr. German* by Susan L. Cocalis. DMG

For X. Louis MacNeice. *See* Trilogy for X: When clerks and navvies fondle.

For years I had not seen such a town. Reunion. Judith Herzberg, *tr. by* Shirley Kaufman. BoWoP

For years I have been a coal miner. A Coal Miner's Goodbye. *Unknown.* AmFP

For years I thought I knew, at the bottom of the dream. The Meeting. Louise Bogan. NoAM; NYBP

For Years I Wallowed. Itzig Manger, *tr. fr. Yiddish by* Leonard Wolf. PeBMYV

For years I've heard. Robin Blaser. NeAP

For years I've lived with Breughel's painting. Proportions. Joseph Stroud. NPGG

For years I've watched the corners for signs. Blues for Benny Kid Paret. Dave Smith. ASP

For years she smiled. The Metamorphosis of Aunt Jemima. William Childress. MAT

For years we endured his insolence. Mask-Maker. Michael Jackson. PeNZ

For You. Carl Sandburg. MoAmPo

For You. James Harvey Spencer. PWR

For you/ I will be a ghetto jew. The Genius. Leonard Cohen. MoCV

For you I have emptied the meaning. Louis Zukofsky. NoAM

For you I have exchanged the lights. Christine Lavant, *tr. by* Beth Bjorklund. CoAuP

For You, Mamá. Cherríe Moraga. GLP

For You, My Son. Horace Gregory. MoAmPo

For You, O Democracy. Walt Whitman. OPP; TrGrPo

For you Time past could not forget. Hymn to Proust. Gavin Ewart. NYBP

For you, who journey to Shiragi. *Unknown, tr. fr. Japanese. Fr.* Manyo Shu. Ma

For your sake, O slave. Lady Ki, *tr. fr. Japanese. Fr.* Manyo Shu. Ma

For Zbigniew Herbert, Summer, 1971, Los Angeles. Larry Levis. FYAP; LCAP

For Zion's Sake. Bible, *O.T. Fr.* Isaiah, LXII: 1–5. TrJP

Forbear, bold youth, all's heaven here. An Answer to Another Persuading a Lady to Marriage. Katherine Philips. HAP; WeW
(To One Persuading a Lady to Marriage.) OBEV

Forbear, fond taper: what thou seek'st, is fire. Francis Quarles. *Fr.* Hieroglyphics of the Life of Man. OBD

Forbear this liquid fire, fly. A Fly about a Glass of Burnt Claret. Richard Lovelace. CaPo

Forbear, thou great good husband, little ant. The Ant. Richard Lovelace. CaPo

Forbearance. Emerson. AA; AnAmPo; GN; LiTA; TAP; TrGrPo; WGRP

Forbearance of kinsmen's wrongs. The Tiger. Kuramakal Ilaveyini, *tr. by* A. K. Ramanujan. PLW

Forbidden, The. Phyllis Haring. PeSA

Forbidding Mourning. John Donne. *See* Valediction, A: Forbidding Mourning.

Force. Edward Rowland Sill. AA; AnAmPo

Force. *Unknown.* FaBoUs

Force. Derek Walcott. OxBC

Force-feeding swans—let me tell. Farmers. Thomas Lux. LCAP

Force of Love, The. Samuel Jones. NOEC

Force That through the Green Fuse Drives the Flower, The. Dylan Thomas. BLPL; CMoP; EBEV; FaBoMo; ImOP; InPS; LiTB; LiTM; MoAB; MoBrPo; MoP; NAEL-2; NoP; OBWVE; OxBTC; PoE; PPP; PrIm; RB; SCV; TEP; UnPo

Forced Feelings, *sel.* Wang Chiu-ssu, *tr. fr. Chinese by* Jonathan Chaves.
"You think I am happy." CoBLCP

Forced March. Miklós Radnóti, *tr. fr. Hungarian by* Emery George. VWA

Forced Music, A. Robert Graves. MoBrPo

Forcing a Way. *Unknown.* NA

Forcing House. Theodore Roethke. CAPP

Ford Madox Ford. Robert Lowell. OxBC; TwCP

Ford o' Kabul River. Kipling. FaBoTw

Fording. Shih Shan-chi, *tr. fr. Chinese by* Dominic Cheung. IFON

Fording a stream I stop. Boncho, *tr. fr. Japanese by* Hiroaki Sato. *Fr.* Twenty-one Hokku. FCEI

Forebears. Monk Gibbon. NeIP

Foreboding, The. Robert Graves. ELP; GBL; PoA

Foreboding sudden of untoward change. By the Conemaugh. Florence Earle Coates. PAH

Forecast. Howard Fergus. PBCV

Forecast. Josephine Miles. NoAM

Foreclosure. Sterling A. Brown. PoBA; PoNe

Forecome and Come. Takahashi Mutsuo, *tr. fr. Japanese by* Hiroaki Sato. *Fr.* Ode in 1,000 Lines. FCEI

Forefather, The. Richard Burton. AA

Forefathers. Edmund Blunden. NOBE; OBEV; OBMV; OxBTC

Foreground, The/ dominated by. Possible Landscape. Alfred Gesswein, *tr. by* Beth Bjorklund. CoAuP

Foreign Affairs. Stanley Kunitz. LiTM; NYBP

Foreign Agents. "Sahir Ludhianvi," *tr. fr. Urdu by* Mahmood Jamal. PBMUP

Foreign Aid. Lionel Kearns. NOBC

Foreign Children. Robert Louis Stevenson. BoTP; GoJo

Foreign Country, A. Natan Zach, *tr. fr. Hebrew by* Laya Firestone. VWA

Foreign Fencers. A. Leyeles, *tr. fr. Yiddish by* Benjamin *and* Barbara Harshav. AYP

Foreign Gate, The, *sel.* Sidney Keyes.
"Moon is a poor woman, The." OBWP

Foreign Land. Washington Delgado, *tr. fr. Spanish by* David Tipton. Per

Foreign Lands. Robert Louis Stevenson. BoTP

Foreign Literature. Thackeray. FaBoNo

Foreign room, slab faces, dusty panes, A. The Rebel General. Chris Wallace-Crabbe. CBAP

Foreign Ruler, A. Walter Savage Landor. OBSV; ViBoPo

Foreign Soil. Dianne Hai-Jew. BrSi

Foreign Woman. Rosario Castellanos, *tr. fr. Spanish by* J. M. Cohen. WPOW

Foreign Woman's Complaint, The. Wen T'ing-yün, *tr. fr. Chinese by* Lois Fusek. ATF

Foreigner. Fleur Adcock. PoPo

Foreigner Comes to Earth on Boston Common, A. Horace Gregory. EaLo

Foreigner Remembered by a Local Man, The. Richard Howard. BAP

Foreigners at the Fair. Fred Emerson Brooks. OBAL

Foreman whacks him hard, The. Any Time, What May Hit You. T. R. Hummer. MAYP

Foreman's Wife, The. Jeff Tagami. BrSi

Forename. surname. Passport. Judah Leib Teller, *tr. fr. Yiddish by* Benjamin *and* Barbara Harshav. *Fr.* Invasion. AYP

Forenoon, The. Christopher Middleton. *Fr.* Herman Moon's Hourbook. NePoEA-2

Forenoon and afternoon and night. Life. Edward Rowland Sill. BLRP

Forenoons. Ernst Jandl, *tr. fr. German by* Beth Bjorklund. CoAuP

Forensic Jocularities. Sir George Rose. OxBoLi

Foreplay of the Alphabet. Darrell Gray. UL

Forepledged. John Lancaster Spalding. AA

Forerunners. Emerson. AA; OBEV; OxBA

Forerunners, The. George Herbert. JCP; MePo; NAEL-1; NoP; TOF

Foreseen for so many years: these evils, this monstrous violence. May–June, 1940. Robinson Jeffers. LiTA; MoAB; MoAmPo; WaP
(Battle.) LiTM

Foreseen in the vision of sages. America. Bayard Taylor. *Fr.* The National Ode, July 4, 1876. AA

Foresight. Lincoln Kirstein. OBWP

Forest. Harriet Gray Blackwell. GoYe

Forest. Jean Garrigue. LiTM; NOBA

Forest and brook-who has gone. Feelings in Nature. Ma Chih-yüan, *tr. fr. Chinese by* Jonathan Chaves. *Fr.* Four Poems to the Tune "Ch'ing-chiang yin," I. CoBLCP

Forest animals walk there. What She Said ("Forest animals walk there"). Kapilar, *tr. by* A. K. Ramanujan. PLW

Forest Birds (A Woman Speaks), *sels.* Chu Yün-ming, *tr. fr. Chinese by* Jonathan Chaves. CoBLCP
"What can I do, I love you so much!" *Fr.* I.
"You and I are like birds in a forest." *Fr.* II.

Forest Hymn, A. Bryant. AA; TAP
"Father, thy hand/ Hath reared," *sel.* TrPWD

Forest Leaves in Autumn, *sel.* John Keble.
November. OBEV
("Red o'er the forest glows the setting sun.") OBNC

Forest nuns, who sheltered us and healed, The. The Krankenhaus of Leutkirch. Richmond Lattimore. NYBP

Forest of Europe. Derek Walcott. PBCV

Forest so much fallen from what she was before, The. Michael Drayton. *Fr.* Polyolbion, Thirteenth Song. SeCePo

Forest Song. Shane Leslie. TIRV

Forest Thoughts. Sir Roger Casement. TIRV

Forest trees stripped in autumn, an ancient Buddhist temple. Autumn, a Visit to the Byodo-in Temple. Gensei, *tr. by* Burton Watson. JLIC-2

Forest was fair and wide, The. Tristrem and the Hunters. *At. to* Thomas of Erceldoune. *Fr.* Sir Tristrem. OxBS

Forest wind blows from a flower-hidden spring, A. The Bridge of Drifted Fragrance. Wu Wen, *tr. fr. Chinese by* Chang Yin-nan. *Fr.* Poems on Yi Garden: Written for Mr. Juan-t'ing, III. WFTU

Forester's Song. A. E. Coppard. FaPON

Forests are branches of a tree lying down. Flying Home from Utah. May Swenson. WPE

Forest's black and dense, The; it grows out of the flatlands. Uri Zvi Greenberg, tr. fr. Yiddish by Leonard Wolf. Fr. In the Kingdom of the Cross. PeBMYV

Forests of Lithuania, The, sel. Donald Davie.
  "But this, so feminine?." OxBTC

Forests were on fire, The. Two Drops. Zbigniew Herbert, tr. by Czeslaw Milosz. RB

Forever. Guillaume Apollinaire, tr. fr. French by Michael Benedikt. POS

"Forever." Charles Stuart Calverley. NOBL; NOBVV

Forever. Raymond Carver. GeTw

Forever/ we'll forge on further and further without ever advancing.
  Forever. Guillaume Apollinaire, tr. by Michael Benedikt. POS

Forever. John Boyle O'Reilly. WGRP

Forever am I conscious, moving here. The Undiscovered Country.
  Thomas Bailey Aldrich. AA

Forever Ambrosia. Christopher Morley. OBAL

Forever Dead. Sappho, tr. fr. Greek by William Ellery Leonard. AWP

Forever in My Dream and in My Morning Thought. Henry David Thoreau. PoEL-4

Forever in the back seat of the car. King over Israel. Dahlia Ravikovich, tr. by Warren Bargad and Stanley F. Chyet. IP

Forever, it comes from the head. Venom. James Dickey. PoA

Forever Mountain. Fred Chappell. BLA

Forever over now, forever, forever gone. The Cameo. Edna St. Vincent Millay. FYAP; LiTA; MoAmPo; UnPo; WPE

Forever the little thud of names, falling. Empty Dwelling Places.
  Kenneth Patchen. PoA

Forever There. Pierre Reverdy, tr. fr. French by Michael Benedikt. POS

Forever; 'tis a single word! "Forever." Charles Stuart Calverley.
  NOBL; NOBVV

Foreword. Jules Laforgue, tr. fr. French by William Jay Smith. CT

Foreword to New Numbers. Christopher Logue. OxBTC

Forge, The. Seamus Heaney. FaBCIP; NAEL-2

Forge me a tool, my Seamus. His Request. Owen Roe O'Sullivan, tr. by Joan Keefe. BIrV

Forget about us. Leave Us Alone. Tadeusz Rozewicz, tr. by Czeslaw Milosz. PwPP

Forget each kindness that you do. A Memory System. Unknown. PWR

Forget everything—everything! Tosu, tr. by Lucien Stryk and Takashi Ikemoto. ZPCJ

Forget everything you have seen. Ernst Schönwiese, tr. by Beth Bjorklund. CoAuP

Forget It. Unknown. PoLF; WBLP

Forget Me Not. Austin Clarke. CIP

Forget Me Not. Bob Kaufman. AmNP

Forget-Me-Not, The. Unknown. BoTP

Forget not, I pray, your Eastland girl. Unknown, tr. fr. Japanese. Fr. Manyo Shu. Ma

Forget Not Yet. Sir Thomas Wyatt. AAS; EIL; HAP; NAEL-1; NoP; OBEV; SiPS
  (Steadfastness.) NOBE; OBSC
  (Supplication, A.) GTBS; GTBS-P

Forget roadside crossings. How to See Deer. Philip Booth. Psk

Forget six counties overhung with smoke. Prologue: The Wanderers.
  William Morris. Fr. The Earthly Paradise. EBVV

Forget the parallel. All Clear. Cecily Pile. CN

Forget the past and live the present hour. Now. Sarah Knowles Bolton.
  PWR

Forget the slander you have heard. Just Forget. Myrtle May Dryden.
  WBLP

Forget the time spent mining the rudiments of praise. Sketch for a Morning in Muncie, Indiana. G. E. Murray. MAYP

Forget Thee? John Moultrie. BLPA; FaBoBe

Forget thine anguish. Meditations. Solomon ibn Gabirol, tr. by Emma Lazarus. TrJP

Forget to mail my letter to my friend Death. Overdue Balance Sheet.
  Thérèse Plantier, tr. by Maxine W. Kumin and Judith Kumin.
  BoWoP

Forget What Did. Philip Larkin. NoAM

Forgetfulness! Josephine D. Henderson Heard. CBWP-4

Forgetfulness. James Russell Lowell. AnAmPo

Forgetfulness. Nicanor Parra, tr. fr. Spanish by Lynn C. Jacox. LPSS

Forgetting. Alfonsina Storni, tr. fr. Spanish by Kate Flores. DMH

Forgetting, I grieve this evening. Princess Shikishi, tr. fr. Japanese by Hiroaki Sato. Fr. Seventy-eight Tanka. FCEI

Forgetting mind, its complications. Kakua, tr. by Lucien Stryk and Takashi Ikemoto. ZPCJ

Forgetting the dark corners. Game of Cards. Ilse Aichinger, tr. by Beth Bjorklund. CoAuP

Forgetting the second cod war. Thinking of Iceland. Tom Paulin.
  FaBCIP

Forgive and Forget. "Totius," tr. fr. Afrikaans by Anthony Delius. PeSA

Forgive me, my God, and overlook my sins. His Illness. Solomon ibn Gabirol, tr. by David Goldstein. TOF

Forgive me, O Lord. Foul Water. Mordecai Temkin, tr. by Jeremy Garber. VWA

Forgive Me, Sire. Norman Cameron. FaBoEE; GTBS-P; OxBS; OxBSP

Forgive me that I pitch your praise too low. Apology for Understatement.
  John Wain. NePoEA-2; OxBTC

Forgive me, you whom they cast in a name. Avraham Shlonsky, tr. by Francis Landy. VWA

Forgive, O Lord, My Little Jokes on Thee. Robert Frost. EaLo; LiTM

Forgive, O Lord, this worldly one. A Prayer for Forgiveness. Aengus the Culdee, tr. by Eoin Neeson. TIRV

Forgive the hours spent listening to radios. Looking at a Dead Wren in My Hand. Robert Bly. NNaP

"Forgive them, for they know not what they do!" Abraham Lincoln.
  Edmund Clarence Stedman. PAH

Forgive Us, O Lord. T. S. Eliot. Fr. Murder in the Cathedral. EaLo

Forgive us, son of Amram, be not wroth. Unknown, tr. fr. Hebrew. Fr. Duel with Verses over a Great Man. TrJP

Forgiven. A. A. Milne. SOP

Forgiven Past, The. Laura Riding. PBWP

Forgiveness. Elizabeth Sewell. EaLo

Forgiveness. Whittier. TrCP

Forgiveness Dream; Man from the Warsaw Ghetto, The. Jean Valentine.
  LCAP

Forgiveness Lane. Martha Gilbert Dickinson Bianchi. AA

Forgivenesses of Sins a Joy Unknown to Angels. Augustus Hillhouse. See Trembling before Thine Awful Throne.

Forgiving My Father. Lucille Clifton. CAPP; GeTw

Forgotten. Malka Heifetz Tussman, tr. fr. Yiddish by Kathryn Hellerstein.
  AYP

Forgotten by the one. Komachi, tr. fr. Japanese by Burton Watson. Fr. Kokin Shu. FCEI

Forgotten City, The. William Carlos Williams. LiTA

Forgotten Dreams. Edward S. Silvera. PoNe

Forgotten Girlhood, sels. Laura Riding. RB
  All the Way Back.
  Around the Corner.
  Children.
  In Laddery Street Herself.
  Into Laddery Street.

Forgotten Island, sel. Radclyffe Hall.
  "As a lamp of fine crystal, wonderfully wrought." PeHV

Forgotten Man, The. Edwin Markham. BLPL; PoLF

Fork. Charles Simic. AmPA; HCAP; LCAP; PCP

Fork of the Road, The. William Renton. NOBVV

Forlorn and glum the couples go. The Houses. Eden Phillpotts.
  OxBTC

Forlorn Saphira, with reclining head. Against Homosexuality. Thomas Gilbert. Fr. View of the Town, A. In an Epistle to a Friend.
  NOEC

Form, The. Bruce Bennett. SoTCo

Form. Heather McHugh. GeTw

Form and Function of the Novel, The. Albert Goldbarth. GeTw

Form decreed of tree and flower, The. Dominica Pentecostes. Aubrey Thomas De Vere. TIRV

Form is the woods: the beast. Jim Harrison. VGW

Form of Boeotia. Odysseus Elytis, tr. fr. Greek by Edmund Keeley and Philip Sherrard. VMG

Form of Epitaph, A. Laurence Whistler. GTBS-P; Mes

Form of Passion, A. David McFadden. NOBC

Form of this "sport" is pain, The. Homage to the Runner. Marvin Bell.
  Fr. The Escape into You. CAPP

Form of Women, A. Robert Creeley. CAPP; NaP

Form of youth without blemish, is not such the form divine, The? Song of My Soul. Ralph Chubb. PeHV

Form Rejection Letter. Philip Dacey. AmPA

Form Was the World. Maurice English. NYBP

Formal Application. Donald W. Baker. FF; SoSe

Formal as a minuet or sonnet. Mystery Story. Howard Nemerov.
  NBLV

Formal exercise for withered fingers, A. Old Fisherman with Guitar.
  George Mackay Brown. OxBC

Formalized/ by middle age. The Song of Bullets. Jessica Hagedorn.
  ER

Formations. William Freedman. VWA

Forme of Prayer, A. Francis Quarles. MePo

Formed long ago, yet made today. Mother Goose. OxNR

Former Barn Lot. Mark Van Doren. FaBV; MoAmPo; PDV

Former Beauties. Thomas Hardy. *Fr.* At Casterbridge Fair, II. NoAM; OBMV; OBNC

"Formerly a Slave." Herman Melville. PoNe; TAP

Formerly I thought of you twice. Four Notions of Love and Marriage. N. Scott Momaday. HATNAP

Forming Child Poems. Simon J. Ortiz. CDW

Forms of Love, The. George Oppen. NNaP

Forms of the Earth at Abiquiu. N. Scott Momaday. CDW

Forsake me not thus, Adam, witness Heav'n. Milton. *Fr.* Paradise Lost, *Bk.* X, *ll.* 914–946.
    (Eve Penitent.) OBS

Forsaken. Zalman Schneour, *tr. fr. Yiddish by* Joseph Leftwich. TrJP

Forsaken, The. Duncan Campbell Scott. CaP; NOBC

Forsaken. *Unknown.* AmFP

Forsaken Bride, The. *Unknown. See* O waly, waly, up the [*or* yon] bank.

Forsaken Garden, A. Swinburne. EBEV; FaBoPP; GTBS-P; LiTB; NOBE; NOBVV; NoP; OAEL-2; OBNC; TEP

Forsaken Maiden's Lament, A. *Unknown. See* He Is Far.

Forsaken Merman, The ("Come, dear children, let us away."), *sel.* Matthew Arnold. BeLS; EBEV; FaBoCh; FaPoR; FiP; GN; MOS; NAEL-2; OBNV
    "Children dear, was it yesterday." BoTP

Forsaken of all comforts but these two. Upone Tabacco. Sir Robert Ayton. OxBS

Forsaken Wife, The. Ts'ao Chih, *tr. fr. Chinese by* Burton Watson. CoBCP

"Forsaking all"—You mean. The Word. Margaret Avison. MoCV

Forsaking the mists. Lady Ise, *tr. by* Geoffrey Bownas *and* Anthony Thwaite. PeBJV

Forsythia. Mary Ellen Solt. BoWoP

Forsythia blossoms gone. Masaoka Shiki, *tr. fr. Japanese by* Burton Watson. *Fr.* Thirty-nine Haiku. FCEI

Fort Bowyer. Charles L. S. Jones. PAH

Fort by the oak trees there, The. The Fort of Rathangan. *At. to* Berchan, *tr. by* Kuno Meyer. CH; ChTr; FaBoCh

Fort Duquesne. Florus B. Plimpton. PAH

Fort McHenry. *Unknown.* PAH

Fort of Ard Ruide, The. *Unknown.* NOIV

Fort of Rathangan, The. *At. to* Berchan, *tr. fr. Old Irish by* Kuno Meyer. CH; ChTr; FaBoCh

Forth from the purple battlements he fared. Sir Eggnogg. Bayard Taylor. BXAP

Forth into the warm darkness faring wide. Wings in the Dark. John Gray. NOBVV

Forth, to the alien gravity. The Launch. Alice Meynell. WPE

Forth to the field of spring. Akahito, *tr. fr. Japanese. Fr.* Manyo Shu. Ma

Forth went the candid man. The Candid Man. Stephen Crane. *Fr.* War Is Kind, IX. MoAmPo

Forthfaring. Winifred Howells. AA

Forties Flick. John Ashbery. NoAM

Fortification of New Ross, The, *sel. Unknown, tr. fr. Norman French.* "I have a whim to speak in verse." NOIV

Fortitude. *Somali Oral Tradition, tr. by* B. W. Andrzejewski *and* I. M. Lewis. WTO

Fortnight before Christmas gypsies were everywhere, A. The Gypsy. Edward Thomas. HeIP; NoAM; NoP

Fortress, The. Anne Sexton. LiTM

Fortress of static, A. Static. Judith Kazantzis. DT

Fortù, Fortù, my beloved one. The Englishman in Italy. Robert Browning. OBTV; PoEL-5

Fortunate,/ Being articulate. Nocturne of the Self-evident Presence. Thomas MacGreevy. BIrV; CIP

Fortunate Fall, The. Alfred Alvarez. VWA

Fortunate Isles, The. Joaquin Miller. WGRP

Fortunate One, The. Harriet Monroe. AA

Fortunate Traveller, The. Derek Walcott. NoAM

Fortunately for you I am resurrected in one piece, or nearly. The Child-Bride. Joyce Carol Oates. GeTw

Fortunatus Nimium. Robert Bridges. BrPo
    (Nimium Fortunatus.) MoAB; MoBrPo

Fortune. Charles Madge. FaBoMo

Fortune. *Unknown.* ACP; HeIP

Fortune. Sir Thomas Wyatt. OBSC; SiPS
    ("Marvaill no more all tho.") AAS

Fortune and Virtue. Thomas Dekker. *Fr.* Old Fortunatus. GoTL; OBSC

Fortune favours the brave, old proverb say. Mr. Cromek to Mr. Stothard. Blake. FaBoEE

Fortune has brought me down—her wonted way. His Children. Hittan of Tayyi, *tr. fr. Arabic by* Sir Charles Lyall. *Fr.* Hamasah. ASP; AWP

Fortune, in power imperious. Of Fortune. Thomas Kyd. *Fr.* Cornelia. EIL

Fortune, Nature, Love. Sir Philip Sidney. PoE

Fortune smiles, cry holy day! [*or* holiday]. Fortune and Virtue. Thomas Dekker. *Fr.* Old Fortunatus. GoTL; OBSC

Fortune Teller, The. Fu'ad Rifqa, *tr. fr. Arabic by* Sargon Boulus *and* Samuel Hazo. MAP

Fortune Welcomed Me at Last. Petronilla Paolini Massimi, *tr. fr. Italian by* Muriel Kittel. *Fr.* Unbind Your Angered Tresses. DMI

Fortunes of Men, The, *sel. Unknown, tr. fr. Anglo-Saxon.* "Another shall hang from the gallows' height." PBBP

Fortunes of War, I Tell You Plain, The. *Unknown.* InPK

Fortune's Treachery. Judah Halevi, *tr. fr. Hebrew by* Solomon Solis-Cohen. TrJP

40 Acres and a Mule. Dick Gallup. UL

Forty Days, *sel.* John Brooks Wheelwright. Second Ascension of Christ, The. NOCV

48 Words for a Woman's Dance Song. Jerome Rothenberg. PoM

Forty-five Years Since the Fall of the Ch'ing Dynasty. Philip Whalen. *See* Summer Palace burnt, the Winter Palace, whatever it was, The.

Forty-four Hokku, *sels.* Issa, *tr. fr. Japanese by* Hiroaki Sato. FCEI
    "Among the fleeing silverfish."
    "Another round of farting."
    "Awakened by a horse's fart, I see a firefly in the air."
    "Awakened by someone gnashing his teeth."
    "Beautiful—the sky."
    "Big cat teases a butterfly, A."
    "Blossom drops, and that, A."
    "Butterfly comes and takes a butterfly, A."
    "By a clump of grass."
    "Cold night: I keep a vigil."
    "Departing wild geese."
    "Door-latch rusted, A."
    "Dragonflies' resting place."
    "Falling leaves, making no sound."
    "Firefly: a frog opens his mouth a bit."
    "Frog keeps still, A."
    "Frog looks at me, A."
    "Frogs play hide-and-seek."
    "From a brat's sleeve."
    "Great sky splendidly darkens, The."
    "Huge firefly, undulating, A."
    "I know, I know it."
    "I let the sparrows play."
    "In the autumn wind a beggar."
    "I've survived, I've survived."
    "Just one mosquito raises a fuss."
    "Kitten twirls around, A."
    "Laconic crow flies by, A."
    "Lending a branch of his antlers."
    "Lying on the ground, I pick young herbs."
    "Mosquito larva plays alone, A."
    "Mountain mist: a horse-dung cleaner."
    "Must be a good day."
    "On a potato leaf, by a dewdrop, a snail."
    "On the heavily loaded bull's head."
    "Pissing and trembling."
    "Shrike call takes a persimmon thief, A."
    "Snow gone, the village fills up."
    "Snowy day: the temple hall's."
    "Sparrow goes in and out of jail, A."
    "Sparrows' friendship breaks up."
    "Through a long night."
    "Wild geese gone, the cove looks cleared."
    "Willow tickles awake, A."

Forty-four Tanka, *sels.* Wakayama Bokusui, *tr. fr. Japanese by* Hiroaki Sato. FCEI
    "Ah, our kiss—may the sea remain as it is."
    "Arm for a pillow, fragrance of hair."
    "At midday when the sea's visible."
    "At times you fall silent."
    "Bird flies away quietly, A."
    "By a window where evening silence falls."
    "By chance I find a strand of your hair."
    "Clouds burn, the sun sets, The."
    "Does its pounding pierce the sun in the sky?."
    "Eyes closed, you lean on a tree."
    For Sonoda Saeko.
    "How long our kiss was!"
    "How lovely! getting drunk faster than I do."

"How many mountains and rivers to cross."
"Huge swells move blue against the winds."
"I drank yesterday, I drink today."
"I weep aloud—may my voice."
"I'm lost in the sea under the shining sun."
"In front of me the sea lies on its side."
"In the dark night it's light."
"In the spring night's fragrant darkness."
"Leaning on the chest of your seasick young mother."
"Lodging the fireflight from a fire."
"Look at the mountain."
"Mountain soars and the sea lies on its side, The."
"Mountaintop: as far as I can see."
"My ship stopped, I've come upon this country."
"My train passes Ono Station."
"Not speaking many words."
On Drinking.
"Parched throat ashen, while sobering up."
"Sadly stars fall; two in love have lain side by side."
"Stars in the great sky fall in confusion."
"Such loneliness! If I could carve in stone."
"Sucked into the hillside darkness."
"Sun's light and the water's light muddy one color, The."
"Thousands of white wings wheel in the morning wind."
"Through the blue, blue moonless night."
"Used to lying together."
"When you smile, the sea becomes fragrant."
"White bird cries in a hushed manner, A."
"White bird—is it not sad?, A."
"Wholly drunk, I see only."
Forty *li* through Chü-yang Pass.   Yang Shih-ch'i, *tr. fr. Chinese by* Jonathan Chaves.   *Fr.* Ten Miscellaneous Poems Written as a Member of the Imperial Retinue.   CoBLCP
49, The.   Nila NorthSun.   GOS
'49 dawn set me high on a roaring yellow tractor, The.   In Kansas. Carter Revard.   HATNAP
"49" Songs, *sels.*   *Unknown, tr. fr. Kiowa Indian.*   STP
  "I don't care if you're married, I'll still get you."
  "If you really love me honey, hey- yah."
  "She said she don't love me anymore because I drink whiskey."
  "You know that I love you, sweetheart, but every time I come around."
49 Stomp, The.   Lew Blockcolski.   VoR
Forty of us looked longingly at the yellow finger.   Drawing a Banana. Myra Schneider.   CN
Forty-second, The.   *Unknown.*   GBP
Forty-seven Tanka in Three Lines, *sels.*   Ishikawa Takuboku, *tr. fr. Japanese by* Hiroaki Sato.   FCEI
  "Act like a wizard."
  "All I'd wanted was to get on a train."
  "As if my thoughts were secretly listened to."
  "By accident I broke a rice bowl."
  "By the eastern sea."
  "Calling out the station name as if singing."
  "Chin buried in the collar of my overcoat."
  "Come to think of it."
  "Coming in front of a mirror store."
  "Cover myself with the quilt."
  "Die for a thing like that?."
  "Even while pillowing her lap."
  "Everyone's/ heading in the same direction."
  "For fun I carried mother on my back."
  "For thinking somehow tomorrow will bring something good."
  "Heart felt/ as if being sucked into a very dark hole."
  "I believe in the coming of a new tomorrow, I say."
  "I get anxious to die, at times."
  "I got out and for about five blocks."
  "I look at my dirty hands."
  "I push the door and step out."
  "I said those words casually."
  "I scolded my child."
  "It rains,/ and the people of my house look depressed."
  "Let down, I stood in the hall."
  "Like a weak-minded scout."
  "Little man I always see on the streetcar, The."
  "Name known, but no relations or kin in this place."
  "No better than the ordinary in talent."
  "Nurse's hand taking my pulse, The."
  "Old letters!/ I was on such familiar terms."
  "On the sand of a sandhill."
  "On the way, a whim, I changed my mind."
  "Parted, I came away and years have passed."
  "Sadness of the lifeless sand."
  "Somehow,/ I feel there are more people than I expect."

"Taking off my gloves, my hands stop."
"That creepy feeling you have."
"That kiss from the past."
"Those days I didn't even notice."
"Though I close my eyes."
"Uneventfully/ and pleasantly I go on putting on weight."
"Useless letter, long, yet to be finished, A."
"Vague sadness, A."
"Water spurting out of a pump, The."
"When was it?."
"Wishing someone would."
Forty Singing Seamen.   Alfred Noyes.   OnMSP
Forty—that's not so old!   Written for the Pavilion of the Drunken Old Man at Ch'u-chou.   Ou-yang Hsiu, *tr. by* Burton Watson. CoBCP
Forty-two years ago (to me if to no one else).   Star-Gazer.   Louis MacNeice.   NAEL-2; NoP
Forty Years Peace.   Arye Sivan, *tr. fr. Hebrew by* Anthony Rudolf *and* Natan Zach.   VWA
Forum Romanum.   István Vas, *tr. fr. Hungarian by* Jascha Kessler. FOC
Forward abrupt.   Night and a Distant Church.   Russell Atkins.   PoBA
Forward! Announce the dust cloud's coming.   The Second Coming. Mohammad Bennis, *tr. by* Sharif Elmusa *and* Charles Doria. MAP
Forward, in disguised laterals, in a broken.   Real Estate.   Lorrie Goldensohn.   NAmP
Forward lay sunlight silver on the sea.   The Waterspout.   William Hart-Smith.   *Fr.* Christopher Columbus.   PoAu-2
Forward rush by the lamp in the gloom, A.   The Contretemps.   Thomas Hardy.   CMoP; LiTM
Forward, sons of the tribe!   Tambourine song for Soldiers Going into Battle.   Hind bint Utba, *tr. by* Bridget Connelly *and* Deirdre Lashgari.   WPOW
"Forward violet thus did I chide, The."   Shakespeare.   *Fr.* Sonnets, XCIX.   OBSC
Forward young woman, Miss Chaos, A.   The Trumpeter.   *Unknown.* CoMu
Forward youth that would appear, The.   An Horatian Ode upon Cromwell's Return from Ireland.   Andrew Marvell.   EBEV; FaBoPV; GTBS; GTBS-P; HAP; InPS; JCP; MePo; NAEL-1; NOBE; NoP; OAEL-1; OBEV; OBS; OBWP; PoEL-2; SeCP; SeCV-1
Fossil.   E. D. Blodgett.   NOBC
Fossil, The.   John Lyle Donaghy.   NeIP
Fossil, The.   Boynton Merrill, Jr.   CRP
Fossil, 1975.   Janet Lewis.   CRP
Fossil Raindrops, The.   Harriet Prescott Spofford.   OBCA
Fossilot, The.   Jane Yolen.   BWV
Fossils, The.   Galway Kinnell.   NYBP
Fossils.   Dan Pagis, *tr. fr. Hebrew by* Bernhard Frank.   MHeP
Fossils, Metal, and the Blue Limit.   Richard Tillinghast.   NAmP
Fo'ty acres jes' fo' me!   Freedom in Mah Soul.   David Wadsworth Cannon, Jr.   PoNe
Foul canker of fair virtuous action.   To Detraction I Present My Poesie. John Marston.   *Fr.* The Scourge of Villainy [*or* Villanie].   OBSC; TW
Foul fa' the breast first treason bred in.   Hobie Noble.   *Unknown.* ESPB; OxBB
Foul Shot.   Edwin A. Hoey.   RHPC
Foul Water.   Mordecai Temkin, *tr. fr. Hebrew by* Jeremy Garber. VWA
Foules Rondel.   Chaucer.   *See* Parlement of Foules, The: Now Welcom[e], Somer [*or* Summer].
Found.   Carol Muske.   AmPA
Found, The.   H. H. ter Balkt, *tr. fr. Dutch by* Scott Rollins.   DuIn
Found a family, build a state.   Fragments of a Lost Gnostic Poem of the Twelfth Century.   Herman Melville.   NOBA; NoP; OxBSP; PoEL-5
Found a hole with a light in it, and saying.   The Little Random Creatures. *Unknown, tr. by* Armand Schwerner.   STP
Found dead a rat—no case could sure be harder.   *Unknown.*   FaBoEE
Found in a Storm.   William Stafford.   RFM
Found in the garden—dead in his beauty.   The Burial of the Linnet. Juliana Horatia Ewing.   OxBChV
Found in the Woods.   Irene F. Pawsey.   BoTP
Found Subjects.   Gerrit Kouwenaar, *tr. fr. Dutch by* Peter Nijmeijer. DuIn
Found while spring-cleaning.   *Unknown, tr. by* Geoffrey Bownas *and* Anthony Thwaite.   PeBJV
Found—Who Lost?   Mary E. Tucker.   CBWP-1
Foundation of American Industry, The.   Donald Hall.   GOA
Foundations.   Leopold Staff, *tr. fr. Polish by* Czeslaw Milosz. PwPP

Founder of the Nation, A. Kevin Ireland. ATNZ
Foundered Tram, The. Harold Monro. BrPo
Founders of Ohio, The. William Henry Venable. PAH
Founding Fathers, Nineteenth-Century Style. Robert Penn Warren. *Fr.* Promises, VIII. NoAM
Foundling, The. Nathan Alterman, *tr. fr. Hebrew by* Bernhard Frank. MHeP
Foundling Hospital for Wit, The, *sels.* Isaac Hawkins Browne.
Fire Side, The; a Pastoral Soliloquy. NOEC
"Thrice happy, who free from ambition and pride."
Fount there is, doth overfling, A. At the Fountain. Marcabrun, *tr. by* Harriet Waters Preston. AWP
Fountain, The. Donald Davie. GTBS-P; OxBTC
Fountain. Elizabeth Jennings. WPE
Fountain, The. James Russell Lowell. AnAmPo; BoTP; OBCA
Fountain, The. "Mustafa," *tr. fr. Arabic by* Dulcie L. Smith. AWP
Fountain, The. A. J. M. Smith. CaP
Fountain, The. Wordsworth. EnRP; GTBS; GTBS-P; SeCePo
Fountain, a Bottle, a Donkey's Ears and Some Books, A. Robert Frost. VGW
Fountain at the Tomb, The. Nicias, *tr. fr. Greek by* Charles Merivale. AWP
Fountain, coolest fountain. Ballad of the Cool Fountain. *Unknown, tr. by* Edwin Honig. BoWoP
Fountain of Fire whom all divide. I Seek Thee in the Heart Alone. Herbert Trench. WGRP
Fountain of forms! Life springs of unique being! Robert Duncan. *Fr.* A Set of Romantic Hymns. DiL
Fountain of tears, river of grief. Christine de Pisan, *tr. by* Joanna Bankier. WPOW
Fountain of Youth, The. Hezekiah Butterworth. PAH
Fountain sheds her flowery spray, The. The Fountain. A. J. M. Smith. CaP
Fountains ("Proud fountains, wave your plumes"). Sir Osbert Sitwell. MoBrPo
Fountains ("This night is pure and clear as thrice refinèd silver"). Sacheverell Sitwell. MoBrPo
Fountains are dry and the roses over, The. The Manor Garden. Sylvia Plath. FaBoWP; LCAP
Fountains mingle with the river, The. Love's Philosophy. Shelley. BLPA; BLPL; BoLoP; EnRP; FaBoBe; FaBV; GTBS; GTBS-P; HoPM; TrGrPo
Fountains that frisk and sprinkle. Ballade Made in the Hot Weather. W. E. Henley. MoBrPo
(Made in the Hot Weather.) GN
Founts of Song, The. "Fiona Macleod." WGRP
Four, The. Geoffrey Grigson. WaP
4 A.M. and still snowing. Elegy for the Other. Cleopatra Mathis. MT
Four Ages of Man, The. W. B. Yeats. TrCP
Four and Eight. ffrida Wolfe. BoTP
Four-and-eighty years are o'er me. The Battle of Monmouth. Thomas Dunn English. PAH
Four and fifty years. Dogen, *tr. by* Lucien Stryk *and* Takashi Ikemoto. ZPCJ
Four and twentieth day of May, The. The Swimming Lady; or, A Wanton Discovery. *Unknown.* ErPo
Four and twenty bonny boys. Sir Hugh; or, The Jew's Daughter. *Unknown.* CH; ESPB, A *and* C *vers.*; FaBoBa (Hugh of Lincoln.) EnSB; OxBB
Four-and-twenty Highland men. Eppie Morrie. *Unknown.* ESPB; OxBB
Four-and-twenty ladies fair. Bonny Baby Livingston. *Unknown.* ESPB
Four and Twenty Merulae. J. Moyr Smith. FaBoNo
Four and twenty noblemen they rode thro Banchory fair. Glenlogie; or, Jean o Bethelnie. *Unknown.* ESPB
Four and twenty nobles sits in the king's ha. Glenlogie; or, Jean o Bethelnie (B *vers.*). *Unknown.* ESPB
Four and twenty tailors. Mother Goose. OxNR (Snail, The.)
Four and twenty white bulls. *Unknown.* GBP
Four arms, two necks, one wreathing. *Unknown.* ElL
Four Attempts at Definition. Ernst Jandl, *tr. fr. German by* Beth Bjorklund. CoAuP
Four be the things I am wiser to know. Inventory. Dorothy Parker. NBLV
Four billion people on this earth. A Great Number. Wislawa Szymborska, *tr. by* Czeslaw Milosz. PwPP
Four Bird Songs. Simon J. Ortiz. HATNAP
Four birds. *Unknown. See* Robin and the wren, The.
Four boards of the coffin lid, The. After Death. Swinburne. NOBVV
Four Brothers. W. S. Di Piero. MAYP

Four Choctaw Songs. Jim Barnes. STE
Four Christmas Carols, *sel. Unknown, tr. fr. Spanish by* Cheli Durán. "How cold the snow." PChr
Four days the earth was rent and torn. Bombardment. Richard Aldington. MMA
Four Dears, The. Ebenezer Elliott. SaC
Four Deer, The. Mary Hoxie Jones. GoYe
Four Directions, The. Emerson Blackhorse Mitchell. NOVW
Four Ducks on a Pond. William Allingham. NOBVV; NOIV
Four Elements in Newfound-land, The. Robert Hayman. *See* Air in Newfounland-land is wholesome, good, The.
Four Epigrams on the Naturalization Bill. John Byrom. NOBL
Four Epitaphs, *sels.* Countee Cullen. AmNP; CDC; PoBA
For a Lady I Know.
For John Keats, Apostle of Beauty.
For My Grandmother. MoAmPo; VGW
For Paul Laurence Dunbar. CDC
Four feet up, under the bruise-blue. Small Woman on Swallow Street. W. S. Merwin. CoAP
Four for Sir John Davies. Theodore Roethke. MoAmPo; NePoAm; NoAM; NOBA
Four Friends, The. A. A. Milne. PYC
Four gallant ships from England came. The Battle of Stonington on the Seaboard of Connecticut. Philip Freneau. PAH
Four gents up and swing Sally Goodin. Sally Goodin. *Unknown.* AmFP
Four Glimpses of Night. Frank Marshall Davis. AmNP; NoP; PoBA; PoNe
Four Glosses, *sels. Unknown.* NOIV
"Bird is calling from the willow, A."
"How lovely it is today!"
"Little bird, The."
"Wall of woodland overlooks me, A."
Four great gates has the city of Damascus. Gates of Damascus. James Elroy Flecker. BrPo
Four great walls have hemmed me in. Four Walls. Blanche Taylor Dickinson. CDC
Four Heads & How to Do Them. John Forbes. CBAP
Four hooves rang out and now are still. Early Waking. Léonie Adams. LiTM
Four horsemen rode out from the heart of the range. The Bushrangers. Edward Harrington. PoAu-1
Four hours the sun his might meridian throne. William Falconer. *Fr.* The Shipwreck, II. MOS
400-Meter Freestyle. Maxine W. Kumin. ASP; SD; SoSe; TSL
4 in 2 goes twice as fast. Crazy Arithmetic. D'Arcy Wentworth Thompson. FaBoCo
Four Irish scholars went. The Little Cat. *Unknown, tr. by* Helen Waddell. CRH
Four Japanese Paintings, *sel.* Arthur Davison Ficke.
Wave Symphony, The. PoA
Four Last Songs of Richard Strauss at Takahe Creek above the Kaipara, The, *sels.* K. O. Arvidson. ATNZ
Beim Schlafengehen. ATNZ
Frühling. *Fr.* I.
Im Abendrot. *Fr.* III.
September. *Fr.* II.
Four-Leaf Clover. Ella Higginson. AA; FaPON
Four-legg'd Elder; or, A Horrible Relation of a Dog and an Elder's Maid, The. Sir John Birkenhead. CoMu
Four-legg'd Quaker, The. *Unknown.* CoMu
Four little children. The Lost Angel. Philip Levine. NOBA
Four Little Foxes. Lew Sarett. FaPON; PDV; RFM; RHPC
Four little girls. Birmingham Sunday. Langston Hughes. PoNe
Four Lyrics for Sibilla Aleramo, *sel.* Dino Campana, *tr. fr. Italian by* L. R. Lind.
"In a moment/ The roses have faded." PFI
Four May Poems. *Unknown. See* Lusty May.
Four May Poems. *Unknown. See* When Flora Had Ourfret the Firth.
Four May Poems: "Be glaid, al ye that luvaris bene." *Unknown.* OxBS
Four May Poems: "Now in this mirthfull tyme of May." *Unknown.* OxBS
Four men stood by the grave of a man. Alexander the Great. *Unknown.* CH
Four miles at a leap, over the dark hollow land. Health. Edward Thomas. SeCePo
Four more days until vacation. Ezra Pound. FL
Four Mountain Wolves. Leslie M. Silko. VoR
Four Nights' Drunk, The. *Unknown. See* First night when I came home, The.
Four Notions of Love and Marriage. N. Scott Momaday. HATNAP

Four o'Clock Flower Blues ("Four o'clock flowers bloom out in the mornin' "). *Unknown.* AmFP

Four of Them, The. Yehuda Karni, *tr. fr. Hebrew by* Jeremy Garbers. VWA

4 Part Geometry Lesson, A. Robin Blaser. NeAP

Four-Paws. Helen Parry Eden. BoTP

Four pelicans went over the house. Pelicans. Robinson Jeffers. FM; MoAmPo

Four Poems for Robin. Gary Snyder. MoP; NNaP; NoAM; NOBA; NoP; SOTW.
Sels.
Autumn Morning in Shokoku-ji, An. HAP; NNaP; NoAM; NOBA; NoP; SOTW; VGW
December at Yase. NoAM
Siwashing It Out Once in Siuslaw Forest. NoAM
Spring Night in Shokoku-ji, A. NNaP; NoAM; NOBA; NoP; SOTW; VGW

Four Poems for the New Year. Charles Wright. AnAn
Sels.
"All day at the window seat."
"How strange it is to awake."
"I have nothing to say about the way the sky tilts."
"I'll tell you I never asked for it."

Four Poems for *The St. Louis Sporting News.* Jack Spicer. PoM

Four Poems from the Sequence "Singing of the Moon." Yang Shen, *tr. fr. Chinese by* Jonathan Chaves. CoBLCP
Sels.
To the Tune "Chieh san ch'eng" ("I love the autumn moon"). *Fr.* III.
To the Tune "Chieh san ch'eng" ("I love the spring moon"). *Fr.* I.
To the Tune "Yu hu-lu" ("I love the summer moon"). *Fr.* II.
To the Tune "Yu hu-lu" ("I love the winter moon"). *Fr.* IV.

Four Poems from the Strontium Age, *sels.* Louis Johnson. ATNZ
Before the Day of Wrath. *Fr.* I.
Haven. *Fr.* IV.
Spring. *Fr.* III.

Four Poems On the Ch'ung-wu Festival, *sels.* Chang Yü, *tr. fr. Chinese by* Jonathan Chaves. CoBLCP
Artemisia Tiger, The.
Hundred-Fold Cord, The.

Four Poems to the Tune "Ch'ing-chiang yin," *sels.* Ma Chih-yüan, *tr. fr. Chinese by* Jonathan Chaves. CoBLCP
Feelings in Nature. *Fr.* I.
Feelings in Nature ("Bamboo fishing coat, purple official gown"). *Fr.* IV.
Feelings in Nature ("In the western village the day grows long"). *Fr.* II.
Feelings in Nature ("Woodcutter wakes as mountain moon hangs low, The"). *Fr.* III.

Four pointes, my will, or I hence departe. A Last Will and Testament. *Unknown.* MeEL

Four Preludes on Playthings of the Wind. Carl Sandburg. CMoP; MoAB; MoAmPo; NOBA

Four Quartets. T. S. Eliot.
Sels.
Burnt Norton. CMoP; LiTM; MoAB; MoAmPo; NAAL-2; PoE
"Words move, music moves." *Fr.* V.UnS
Dry Salvages, The. AiP; LiTB; NoP; OxBA; SeCePo
East Coker. HAP; PPP; VGW
Little Gidding. FaBoMo; FaBoPV; FaBoTw; GTBS-P; MoP; NAEL-2; NAWM-2; NoAM; NOBA; NOBE; OAEL-2; OxBTC; PrIm; TAP
"We shall not cease from exploration." *Fr.* V. ImOP
"Ash on an old man's sleeve." *Fr.* II. FaBoTw

Four Quartz Crystal Clocks. Marianne Moore. AmPP; ImOP; TwCP

Four Questions Addressed to His Excellency, the Prime Minister. James P. Vaughn. AmNP

Four sails of the mill, The. Lubber Breeze. T. Sturge Moore. CH

Four Saints in Three Acts, *sel.* Gertrude Stein.
"Pigeons on the grass alas." TAP

Four Scarlet Berries. Mary Vivian. BoTP

Four-score and seven, so the papers say. The Old Boatman of Death's River. R. Williams Parry, *tr. by* Joseph P. Clancy. OBWVE

Four Seasons, The. Jack Prelutsky. RHPC

Four Seasons. *Unknown. See* Spring is showery, flowery, bowery.

Four seasons fill the measure of the year. The Human Seasons. Keats. EnRP; FaFP; GTBS; GTBS-P; WiR

Four Seasons in the Mountains, The. Chang Yü, *tr. fr. Chinese by*
Sels.
Jonathan Chaves. CoBLCP
Autumn.

Spring.
Summer.
Winter.

Four Seasons of the Year, The. Anne Bradstreet. SCAP

Four Sheets to the Wind and a One-Way Ticket to France. Conrad Kent Rivers. BPo; IDB; PoBA; PoNe
("As a Black child I was a dreamer.") AmNP

Four Songs, *sels.* Nikos Gatsos, *tr. fr. Greek by* Edmund Keeley *and* Philip Sherrard. VMG
Black Sun, The.
Evening at Colonos.
Myrtle Tree, The.
We Who Are Left.

Four Songs from the Book of Samuel. Eli W. Mandel. MoCV

4 squirrels/ are as busy as monks. Maine Vastly Covered with Much Snow. John Tagliabue. InPK

Four Stanzas Written in Anxiety. George Jonas. MoCV

Four stiff-standers. *Unknown.* ChTr; GBP; OxNR, *diff. version*

Four straight brick walls, severely plain. The Quaker Graveyard. S. Weir Mitchell. AA

Four summers ago tar covered a road. Report from K9 Operator Rover on the Motel at Grand Island. William Stafford. SoTCo

Four Sweet Months, The. Robert Herrick. BoTP; WiR
(July: The Succession of the Four Sweet Months.) FaPON

Four Tao philosophers as cedar waxwings. Waxwings. Robert Francis. LCAP; NU

Four Things. Bible, *O.T. Fr.* Proverbs: The Words of Agur, *ll.* 24-28.

Four Things. Henry van Dyke. AA; PoLF
(Four Things to Do.) WBLP

Four things are white, the fifth exceeds the rest. Five Things White. Edward May. FaBoEE

Four Things Choctaw, *sels.* Jim Barnes. HATNAP; STE
Abukbo.
Baii.
Isuba.
Nashoba.

Four Things Make Us Happy Here. Robert Herrick. CaPo

Four Things to Do. Henry van Dyke. *See* Four Things.

IV, 13. Revenge ("Audivere, Lyce"). Horace, *tr. fr. Latin. Fr.* Odes. AWP, *tr. by* Louis Untermeyer.

Four Thousand Days and Nights. Tamura Ryuichi, *tr. fr. Japanese by* Geoffrey Bownas *and* Anthony Thwaite. PeBJV

Four III. E. E. Cummings. FaBoMo; TTTS

Four times the sun had risen and set; and now on the fifth day. The Embarkation. Longfellow. *Fr.* Evangeline. BeLS; PAH

Four Translations from the English of Robert Hershon. Robert Hershon. NeAC

Four trees upon a solitary acre. Emily Dickinson. PoEL-5

Four *Tz'u* from Tun-huang, *sels. Unknown, tr. fr. Chinese by* Burton Watson. CoBCP
Tune: Eternal Longing ("He was a traveler west of the river,/ only he knew how lonely he was"). *Fr.* II.
Tune: Eternal Longing ("He was a traveler west of the river,/ then he took sick, lay an inch away from death"). *Fr.* III.
Tune: Eternal Longing ("He was a traveler west of the river,/ with wealth and eminence rare in this world"). *Fr.* I.
Tune: Magpie on the Branch. *Fr.* IV.

4 Variations On. Gerrit Kouwenaar, *tr. fr. Dutch by* Peter Nijmeijer. DuIn

Four Walls. Blanche Taylor Dickinson. CDC

Four walls, a ceiling, and the baby grows. Baby. Joyce Carol Oates. GeTw

Four-way winds of the world have blown, The. Strike the Blow. *Unknown.* PAH

Four Ways of Dying. Steve Chimombo. WMBCH

Four wet winters and now the dry. Runoff. William Everson. NoAM

Four white heifers with sprawling hooves. The Orotava Road. Basil Bunting. NoAM

Four Winds, The. Charles Henry Lüders. AA

Four Women. Nina Simone. MAT

Four-Word Lines. May Swenson. GLP; WPE

Four years ago,/ in this knot of a village north of the university. The Madwoman of Papine. Abdur-Rahman Slade Hopkinson. PBCV

Four years!—and didst thou stay above. Geist's Grave. Matthew Arnold. FM; NOBVV; TEP

Four years my father fought their war. My Father. Yehuda Amichai, *tr. by* Bernhard Frank. MHeP

Four young men, of a Monday morn. The Prize of the *Margaretta*. Will M. Carleton. PAH

Four Zoas. Blake. *See* Vala; or, The Four Zoas.

Fourpence a Day. *Unknown*. OBET

Fourteen, a sonneteer thy praises sings. A Sonnet upon Sonnets. Burns. Son

14 July 1956. Laurence Lerner. PeSA

Fourteen Men. Mary Gilmore. CBAP

Fourteen months old, she said you were. To a Lady, in a Wartime Queue. Ruth Pitter. CN

1492. Emma Lazarus. WPE

Fourteen small broidered berries on the hem. What the Sonnet Is. Eugene Lee-Hamilton. HoPM; Son

Fourteen Ways of Touching Peter. George MacBeth. CRH

14-Year-Old Convalescent Cat in the Winter, A. Gavin Ewart. OBD; OxBSP

Fourteen years old, learning the alphabet. The Reading Lesson. Richard Murphy. IPY

Fourteenth of July had come, The. La Tricoteuse. George Walter Thornbury. BeLS

Fourth, The. Shel Silverstein. RR

Fourth Act. Robinson Jeffers. LiTA; WaP

Fourth Book of Sibylline Oracles, The, *sel*. "The Jewish Sibyl," *tr. fr. Greek by* Bohn.
There Is a City. TrJP

Fourth Dance Poem. Gerald W. Barrax. PoBA

Fourth day came, but not a breath of air, The. Byron. *Fr.* Don Juan, II. ChER

Fourth Day's Battle, The. Dryden. *Fr.* Annus Mirabilis. OBS

Fourth Eclogue, The. George Wither. *Fr.* The Shephe[a]rd's Hunting. SeCV-1, *abr.*

Fourth, eleventh, ninth, and sixth. The Months of the Year. *Unknown*. FaBoUs

Fourth Floor, Dawn, Up All Night Writing Letters. Allen Ginsberg. CAPP

Fourth month was summer weather, The. *Unknown, tr. by* Arthur Waley. BoS

Fourth Napoleon, *sel*. J. A. R. McKellar.
Love in a Cottage. PoAu-2

Fourth Ode to Persephone. Robert Kelly. *Fr.* The Book of Persephone, 16. PoM

Fourth of July, The. John Pierpont. OPP; PAH

4th of July. William Carlos Williams. PoA

Fourth of July Night. Carl Sandburg. OFD

Fourth Pearl: Temperance, The. Lady Diana Primrose. *Fr.* A Chain of Pearl. WPE

Fourth Poem. Costa Andrade, *tr. fr. Portuguese by* Michael Wolfers. WMBCH

Fourth Song: "Only joy, now here you are." Sir Philip Sidney. *Fr.* Astrophel and Stella. ElL; GBL; HAP; InvP; NAEL-1; NoP; OBSC

Fourth Song the Night Nurse Sang. Robert Duncan. VGW

Fourth Street, San Rafael. Bill Berkson. UL

Fourth watch, the moon sinks, paper window calm. Inscribed on a Painting of Bamboo. T'ang Yin, *tr. by* Jonathan Chaves. CoBLCP

Foweles in The Frith. *Unknown*. *See* Fowls in The Frith.

Fower-an-twenty Heilandmen. *Unknown*. FaBoNo

Fowls [*or* Foweles] in the Frith. *Unknown*. HAP; NAEL-1; OxBSP
(I Live in Great Sorrow.) MeEL

Fowls of heaven, The. James Thomson. *Fr.* The Seasons: Winter. PBBP

Fowre muckle angels wi their trumpets, stalkin. Judgment Day. Robert Garioch, *after the Italian of* Giuseppe Belli. OBVE

Fox. David Campbell. CBAP

Fox. Clifford Dyment. OxBSP

Fox, The. R. Williams Parry, *tr. fr. Welsh by* Gwyn Williams. OBWVE

Fox. Kenneth Rexroth. *Fr.* A Bestiary. NNaP

Fox, The. Marjorie Somers Scheuer. GoYe

Fox, The. *Unknown*. OxNR; PBBP
(Fox Went Out One Frosty Night, The.) BLPA

Fox/ like a tawny rope, The. The Fox. Marjorie Somers Scheuer. GoYe

Fox and crow, their dirty business finished, The. Fabulary Satire IV. Daryl Hine. NOBC

Fox and the cat, as they travell'd one day, The. The Virtuous Fox and the Self-righteous Cat. John Cunningham. OnMSP

Fox and the Crow, The. La Fontaine, *tr. fr. French by* Marianne Moore. OBVE; PPP

Fox and the Goose, The. *Unknown*. OxBLMV

Fox and the Grapes, The. La Fontaine, *tr. fr. French by* Marianne Moore. FM

Fox and the Hare, The. *Unknown*. OBET

Fox at your neck and snakeskin on your feet, A. Leaving Something Behind. David Wagoner. CoAP

Fox came lolloping, lolloping, The. Hunting Song. Donald Finkel. NePoEA
("Fox he came lolloping, lolloping, The.") CoAP; MoBS

Fox came up by Stringer's Pound, The. Midnight. John Masefield. BrPo

Fox Dancing. Suzanne Knowles. RB

Fox flees the farm in a red rogue dazzle. For Hani, Aged Five, That She Be Better Able to Distinguish a Villain. Gene Baro. NYBP

Fox Glove Song. Christina Beer. PeNZ

Fox he came lolloping, lolloping, The. Donald Finkel. *See* Fox came lolloping, lolloping, The.

Fox-Hunters, The. Ebenezer Elliott. TW

Fox is out of breath, The. The Fable. Gregory O'Brien. *Fr.* Bride of the Disappearing Man. ATNZ

Fox is very clever, The. Fox. Kenneth Rexroth. *Fr.* A Bestiary. NNaP

Fox jumped up one winter's night, A. The Fox. *Unknown*. OxNR; PBBP
(Fox Went Out One Frosty Night, The.) BLPA

Fox knew well, that before they tore him, The. John Masefield. *Fr.* Reynard the Fox. OBNV

Fox may steal your hens, sir, A. John Gay. *Fr.* The Beggar's Opera, I, i. NOEC
(Soldier and a Sailor, A.) TEP

Fox of Gascon, though some say of Norman descent, A. The Fox and the Grapes. La Fontaine, *tr. by* Marianne Moore. FM

Fox Went Out One Frosty Night, The. *Unknown*. *See* Fox, The.

Fox Who Watched for the Midnight Sun, The. Norman Dubie. LCAP; MAYP

Fox woman/ dances, string of blue beads. Second Skins—a Peyote Song. Joseph Bruchac. CDW

Foxes, The. Janet Frame. WPE

Foxfire. Nancy Willard. IHMS

Foxglove bells, with lolling tongue, The. Foxgloves. Mary Webb. BoTP

Foxglove by the cottage door, The. Four and Eight. ffrida Wolfe. BoTP

Foxgloves. Mary Webb. BoTP

Foxgloves and Snow. Marion Angus. PoSH

Fox's Counsel, The. Huw Llwyd, *tr. fr. Welsh by* Joseph P. Clancy. OBWVE

Foxtail Pine. Gary Snyder. NaP; NU

Fr. Anselm Williams and Br. Leander Neville. Elizabeth Smither. ATNZ

Fra Bank to Bank, Fra Wood to Wood I Rin. Mark Alexander Boyd. NoP; QFR; Son
(Cupid and Venus.) GoTS; InPK
(Sonet: "Fra bank [*or* banc] to bank [*or* banc], fra wood to wood I rin.") EBEV; OBEV
(Venus and Cupid.) HAP; Prf

Fra Lippo Lippi. Robert Browning. CTC; EBVV; NAEL-2; NoP; OAEL-2; TEP
"I shall paint/ God in the midst." *Sel*. Prf

Fra Pandolf, have you tried to reproduce. Technique. Burnham Eaton. GoYe

Frae great Apollo, poet say. The Poet's Wish; an Ode. Allan Ramsay, *after* Horace. OBVE

Frae nirly, nippin', Eas'lan' breeze. Ille Terrarum. Robert Louis Stevenson. OxBS

Fragile blades of grass. The Builder of Continents. "Ping Hsin," *tr. fr. Chinese by* Kai-yu Hsu. *Fr.* The Stars. WPOW

Fragile splendour of the level sea, The. Mid-Ocean in War-Time. Joyce Kilmer. MOS

Fragment: "At her step the water-hen." Dante Gabriel Rossetti. FM

Fragment, A: "Boy stood on the burning deck, The/ His feet were covered with blisters." *Unknown*. FaBoPa

Fragment: "Breath of life imbued those few dim days, The." Jessie Redmond Fauset. CDC

Fragment: "Cataract, whirling to the precipice, The." John Clare. BoNaP

Fragment, A: "Cold chain of life presseth heavily on me tonight, The." Adah Isaacs Menken. CBWP-1

Fragment: "Encinctured with a twine of leaves." Samuel Taylor Coleridge. *See* Fruit Plucker, The.

Fragment: "Flower in the crannied wall." Tennyson. *See* Flower in the Crannied Wall.

Fragment: "He is an inharmonious note." Sir Roger Casement. TIRV

Fragment, A: "I cannot find my way to Nazareth." Yvor Winters. OBSV

Fragment: "I lived on this earth in an age." Miklós Radnóti, *tr. by* Steven Polgar, Stephen Berg *and* S. J. Martin. VWA

Fragment: "I saw his round mouth's crimson deepen as it fell." Wilfred Owen. OAEL-2

Fragment: "I strayed about the deck, an hour, to-night." Rupert Brooke. BrPo

Fragment, A: "I walked [*or* walk'd] along a stream for pureness rare." Gervase Markham, *at. to* Christopher Marlowe. CTC; OBSC

Fragment: "I would to heaven that I were so much clay." Byron. *Fr.* Don Juan, *on the back of the poet's MS of* I. CTC; FiP; NAEL-2; NOBL; NoP; OAEL-2; OxBSP; PrIm

Fragment: "I'm happiest when most away." Emily Brontë. *See* I'm Happiest When Most Away.

Fragment, A: "In Cloe's chamber, she and I." John Bancks. NOEC

Fragment: "Language has not the power to speak what love indites." John Clare. FaBoEE; OAEL-2; OBNC; OxBSP; PoEL-4

Fragment: "Locke sank into a swoon." W. B. Yeats. NoAM; PrIm

Fragment: "Love's memories haunt my footsteps still." John Clare. NOBVV

Fragment: "Mark you how the peacock's eye." Gerard Manley Hopkins. FM

Fragment: "Mountain summits sleep, glens, cliffs, and caves, The." Alcman. *See* Mountain summits sleep, The: glens, cliffs, and caves.

Fragment 113: "Not honey/ not the plunder of the bee." Hilda Doolittle ("H. D."). NAAL-2

Fragment, A: "Our fancies are but joys all unexprest." Henrietta Cordelia Ray. CBWP-3

Fragment: "Pity, Religion has so seldom found." William Cowper. WGRP

Fragment: Rain. Shelley. ChER

Fragment: "Spruce and limber yellow-hammer, The." Samuel Taylor Coleridge. FM; PBBP

Fragment: "There is a river clear and fair." Catherine Fanshawe. *See* There is a river clear and fair.

Fragment: "There pipes the wood-lark, and the song thrush there." Thomas Gray. FM

Fragment: "Thou strainest through the mountain fern." Robert Louis Stevenson. NOBVV

Fragment: To the Moon. Shelley. *See* Art thou pale for weariness.

Fragment: "Walk with thy fellow-creatures: note the hush." Henry Vaughan. WGRP

Fragment: "What is poetry? Is it a mosaic." Amy Lowell. WGRP

Fragment for the Dark. Elizabeth Jennings. FaBoWP

Fragment from "Clemo Uti—the Water Lilies." Ring Lardner. FiBHP

Fragment from the Elizabethans. W. Bridges-Adams. FaBoCo

Fragment from "The Maladjusted: A Tragedy." Morris Bishop. NBLV

Fragment in Imitation of Wordsworth. Catherine Fanshawe. FaBoNo; FaBoPa

(Fragment: "There is a river clear and fair.") Par

(Fragments.) BXAP

(Imitation of Wordsworth, An.) NA

Fragment of a Character. Thomas Moore. FaBoCo

Fragment of a Greek Tragedy. A. E. Housman. CenHV; FaBoNo; NOBL; Par

Fragment of a Song. "Lewis Carroll." FaBoNo

Fragment of a Song on the Beautiful Wife of Dr. John Overall. *Unknown.* BoLoP

Fragment of a Sonnet. Pierre de Ronsard, *tr. fr. French by* Keats. AWP; OBVE

Fragment of an Agon. T. S. Eliot. LiTB

Fragment of an Anti-Papist Ballad. *Unknown.* CoMu

Fragment of an Ode to Maia Written on May Day, 1818. Keats. EnRP; OAEL-2; OBEV; PoEL-4

Fragment of Death. Villon. *See* Fragment on Death, A.

Fragment of Petronius, A. Petronius Arbiter. *See* Doing, a Filthy Pleasure Is, and Short.

Fragment of Sappho. *Unknown, tr. fr. Greek by* Ambrose Philips. BoLoP

Fragment on Death, A. Villon, *tr. fr. French by* Swinburne. CTC

(Fragment of Death.) AWP

Fragment Reflection I. Doris Turner. JB

Fragment Sixty-eight: "I envy you your chance of death." Hilda Doolittle ("H. D."). NoAM

Fragment, The ("Repeat that, repeat"). Gerard Manley Hopkins. *See* Repeat that, repeat.

Fragment Thirty-six: "I know not what to do." Hilda Doolittle ("H. D."). CMoP; OxBA; VGW

Fragmenta Quintillii Apocalypseôs. Peter Russell. NPo

Fragmenti. Ezra Pound. PoA

Fragments, The, *sel.* Peter Dale.

"Few ever came to help you speak or sell." NOCV

Fragments. Catherine Fanshawe. *See* There is a river clear and fair.

Fragments, *sel.* Michael Jackson.

"Words like branches of deadfall." ATNZ

Fragments. Maruyama Kaoru, *tr. fr. Japanese by* Hiroaki Sato. FCEI

Fragments Intended for the Dramas, *sel.* Thomas Lovell Beddoes.

Beautiful Night, A. ChER

Fragments of a Lost Gnostic Poem of the Twelfth Century. Herman Melville. NOBA; NoP; OxBSP; PoEL-5

Fragments of Ancient Poetry, Collected in the Highlands of Scotland, *sel.* James Macpherson.

"I sit by the mossy fountain; on the top of the hill of winds." NOEC

Fragments on Nature and Life, *sel.* Emerson.

Atom from Atom. ImOP

Fragments were trying to huddle into one, The. Gun Base. Maruyama Kaoru, *tr. by* Hiroaki Sato. FCEI

Fragrance comes from the scent I wear, The. *Unknown, tr. fr. Chinese by* Burton Watson. *Fr.* Tzu Yeh Songs. CoBCP

Fragrance fades from the screens, spring rushes ever on. Speaking of Love. Ku Hsiung, *tr. by* Lois Fusek. ATF

Fragrance of Night, A. Léon-Paul Fargue, *tr. fr. French by* Wallace Stevens. RHTwFP

Fragrance of rice stalks for a hundred *li* on the west wind, The. A Picture of Village Happiness. Yün Shou-p'ing, *tr. by* Irving Lo. WFTU

Fragrance of the red lotus fades, The. Poem to the Tune of "Yi chian mei." Li Ch'ing-chao. WPOW, *tr. by* Marsha Wagner

Fragrances that like a wind disturb. The Islands Where I Was Born. Gloria Rawlinson. ATNZ; PeNZ

Fragrant lotus spread across the banks of the river. Gathering Lotus. Huang-fu Sung, *tr. by* Lois Fusek. ATF

Fragrant prayer upon the air, A. A Poem to Be Said on Hearing the Birds Sing. Biddy Crummy, *tr. by* Douglas Hyde. AWP; WTO

Fragrant the grasses of high Kane-hoa. Anklet Song. *Unknown, tr. by* N. B. Emerson. WTO

Fragrant the Prayer. *Unknown, tr. fr. Irish by* Alice Furlong. TIRV

Fragrant Thy Memories. "Judah," *tr. fr. Hebrew by* Herbert Loewe. TrJP

Frail as the leaves that quiver on the sprays. Homer, *tr. fr. Greek by* Samuel Johnson. *Fr.* The Iliad, VI. OBVE

Frail children of sorrow, dethroned by a hue. Hope. Georgia Douglas Johnson. CDC

Frail frail, lone-growing bamboo. *Unknown, tr. fr. Chinese by* Burton Watson. *Fr.* Nineteen Old Poems of the Han, VIII. CoBCP

Frail, intense passion, A. Revenant. Kathleen Resch. VVA

Frail Life! in which, through mists of human breath. Life and Death. Sir William Davenant. *Fr.* The Christian's Reply to the Philosopher. OBS

Frail scorched grasses are ripped now, The. Drought. Oumar Ba, *tr. by* Kathleen Weaver. PBWP

Frail sound of a tunic trailing, A. Antonio Machado, *tr. fr. Spanish by* John Dos Passos. *Fr.* Poems. AWP

Frail the white rose and frail are. A Flower Given to My Daughter. James Joyce. OBMV; RB

Frail, wistful guardian of the broom. The Sweeper. Agnes Lee. QFR

Frailty. George Herbert. NOCV

Frailty and Hurtfulness of Beauty, The. Earl of Surrey. *See* Brittle beauty [*or* beautie], that nature made so frail[e].

Frailty Is Not My Name. Maureen Ismay. WS

Frailty of Beauty, The. "J. C." *Fr.* Alcilia. EiL

Frailty, Thy Name is Woman. Shakespeare. *See* Hamlet:

O, that this too too solid flesh would melt.

Frame church waits, The. The Rapture Is Coming. Alice Golembiewski Phillips. KS

Frame for the Angels, A, *sel.* Paul Smyth.

"Spring that I was six I found in the woods, The." CRP

Frame within frame, the evolving conversation. Dancers Exercising. Amy Clampitt. NoAM

Framed. Claire Harris. PBCV

Framed in her phoenix fire-screen, Edna Ward. Cottage Street, 1953. Richard Wilbur. CAPP; FaBoMo; HCAP

Framed in the cavernous fire-place sits a boy. An Old Thought. Charles Henry Lüders. AA

Framer of the earth and sky. Saint Ambrose. TrCP

Framework-knitters Lamentation, The. *Unknown.* CoMu

Framework-Knitters Petition, The. C. Briggs. CoMu

France. Wordsworth. *Fr.* The Prelude [*or*, Growth of a Poet's Mind], XI [*X conclusion*]. EnRP; OAEL-2

"O pleasant exercise of hope and joy!" HAP; OBNC

("France leered me forth; the realm that I had crossed.") FaBoPV

(French Revolution, The.) FiP
(Residence in France [Continued].) PoEL-4
One Christmas-Time. RB
To Coleridge in Sicily. OBNC
France; an Ode. Samuel Taylor Coleridge. EnRP
France. Cradle and abstraction. Wildfire. Judit Tóth, *tr. by* Emery George. VWA
France! It is I answering. Republic to Republic. Witter Bynner. PAH
France leered me forth; the realm that I had crossed. Wordsworth. *See* Prelude [or, Growth of a Poet's Mind], The: France.
Francesca di Rimini. Dante, *tr. fr. Italian by* Byron. *Fr.* Divina Commedia: Inferno, V. PFI
Francesco's Fortunes, *sels.* Robert Greene. OBSC
Eurymachus's Fancy.
Penitent Palmer's Ode, The.
Francine's Room. Louise Erdrich. NoAM
Francis Bacon Paints Velázquez's Pope. Wieland Schmied, *tr. fr. German by* Beth Bjorklund. CoAuP
Francis Beaumont's Letter from the Country to Jonson. Francis Beaumont. *See* Mr. Francis Beaumont's Letter to Ben Johnson.
Francisco Coronado rode forth with all his train. Quivíra. Arthur Guiterman. PAH
François am I, heavy my lot. Villon. OBD
Frangipanni. *Unknown.* NA
Frank Albert and Viola Benzena Owens. Ntozake Shange. BlSi
Frank Baker's my name, and a bachelor I am. Starving to Death on a Government Claim. *Unknown.* AmFP; OBAL
(Lane County Bachelor, The.) AS
Frank Courtship, The. George Crabbe. *Fr.* Tales.
Jonas Kindred's Household. OBNC
Frank James, the Roving Gambler. *Unknown.* AmFP
Frank O'Hara. Ted Berrigan. UL
Frank Sinatra. Michael Waters. GeTw
Frank, wilt live handsomely? Trust not too far. Advice to My Best Brother, Colonel Francis Lovelace. Richard Lovelace. CaPo
Frankenstein. Edward Field. FF
Frankenstein Gets His Man. Frank Carr. AmMo
Frankie and Johnny [or Johnnie or Albert]. *Unknown.* AmFP; AS, with music; BeLS; FaFP; FF; NIP; NOBA; OxBoLi; RB; TrGrPo; UnPo
(Josie.) AS
(Sadie.) AS
Frankie Blues. *Unknown.* AS
Frankie Silvers. Frances Silvers. AmFP
Frankie was a good woman. Frankie Blues. *Unknown.* AS
Franklin Hyde. Hilaire Belloc. FaBoUs; NBLV
Franklin James. Edgar Lee Masters. *Fr.* Spoon River Anthology. OBD
Franklin sailed a key-hung kite. Fable. James Facos. NBLV
Franklin's Prologue, The. Chaucer. *Fr.* The Canterbury Tales. NAEL-1; OAEL-1
Franklin's Tale, The. Chaucer. *Fr.* The Canterbury Tales. NAEL-1; OAEL-1
Frankly, I prefer the blue. Sentimental Lines to a Young Man Who Favors Pink Wallpaper While I Personally Lean to the Blue. Margaret Fishback. FiBHP
Franz. Mark Strand. BLA
Franz Kafka had a nightmare. Kafka's Other Metamorphosis. Len Gasparini. NeAC
Franz was./ was Franz? Konrad Bayer, *tr. by* Beth Bjorklund. CoAuP
"Frater Ave atque Vale." Tennyson. ChTr; EBVV; FaBoPP; GTBS-P; GTBS-P; HAP; InPS; NAEL-2; NoP; OBTV; OxBSP
Fraternitas. Confucius, *tr. fr. Chinese by* Ezra Pound. *Fr.* Deer Sing. CTC; OBVE
Fraternity. Anne Reeve Aldrich. AA
Frau Bauman, Frau Schmidt, and Frau Schwartze. Theodore Roethke. CoAP; MoAB; MoP; NAAL-2; NoAM; NOBA; NYBP; SaC; TAP
Fraudulent Days. Michael Benedikt. PoA
Fraudulent perhaps in that they gave. Swans. Lawrence Durrell. MoBrPo; SeCePo
Fraught with stars the dark nights come and go. And Thou, Expectant. Amado Nervo, *tr. by* Samuel Beckett. MexPo
Fräulein Reads Instructive Rhymes. Maxine W. Kumin. NYBP; Psk
Freak is the other, The. Celebrating the Freak. Cynthia MacDonald. Psk
Freaks at Spurgin Road Field, The. Richard Hugo. LCAP; NoAM; SM
Freaks of Fashion. Christina Rossetti. FM
Freckles numberless as stars on my forehead. My Portrait. Moyshe-Leyb Halpern, *tr. by* Joseph Leftwich. TrJP
Fred Apollus at Fava's. Nicholas Moore. ErPo
"Fred, where is north?" West-running Brook. Robert Frost. BLPL; MoAB; MoAmPo; NOBA; NoP
Freddy. Dennis Lee. RHPC

Frederick Douglass. Sam Cornish. PoBA
Frederick Douglass. Paul Laurence Dunbar. PoBA
Frederick Douglass. Robert Hayden. AmNP; CAPP; CNA; GOA; HCAP; IDB; NIP; PoBA; PoNe; Son; TTY
Frederick Douglass: 1817-1895. Langston Hughes. BPo
Frederick the Great/ Accepted quite late. H. F. Cascorbi. SoTCo
Fredericksburg. Thomas Bailey Aldrich. AnAmPo; PAH
Frederiksted, Dusk. Derek Walcott. NoAM
Frédérique, or How I Became a Historian. Herman de Coninck, *tr. fr. Dutch by* James S. Holmes. DuIn
Fredome. John Barbour. *See* Freedom.
Fred's Dead Friend. John Powers. SoTCo
Free America. Joseph Warren. PAH
Free are the Muses, and where freedom is. Breath on the Oat. Joseph Russell Taylor. PAH
Free at las', free at las'. I Thank God I'm Free at Las'. *Unknown.* BPo; TAP
Free Country: July 19, 1979. Giaconda Belli, *tr. fr. Spanish by* Magaly Fernández. VoI
Free evening fades, outside the windows fastened with decorative iron grilles, The. Evening in the Sanitarium. Louise Bogan. FaBoWP; FYAP; IHMS; TwCP
Free Fantasia on Japanese Themes. Amy Lowell. MoAmPo
Free Grace. Charles Wesley. NOCV
Free Harbor. Suad al-Mubarak al-Sabah, *tr. fr. Arabic by* May Jayyusi *and* John Heath-Stubbs. MAP
Free I have my own self-reliance. I Drift in the Wind. Ingrid Jonker, *tr. by* Jack Cope. PeSA; WPOW
Free Intelligence, The. Anna Wickham. OBD
Free Kirk, The. Eighteen-Forty-Three. *Unknown.* FaBoCo
Free Little Bird. *Unknown.* AmFP
Free One, A. W. H. Auden. *See* Watch Any Day.
Free Parliament Litany, A. *Unknown.* OxBoLi
Free Quarters. Jacques Prévert, *tr. fr. French by* Michael Benedikt. POS
Free Silver. *Unknown.* AmFP
Free things are magnets to the moving eye. Birds on a Blighted Tree. Grace Schulman. AnAn
Free thinker! Do you think you are the only thinker. Golden Lines. Gérard de Nerval, *tr. by* Robert Bly. NU
Free Thoughts on Several Eminent Composers. Charles Lamb. FaBoCo; OxBoLi
Free till eventide. Piraeus. Haim Guri, *tr. by* Warren Bargad *and* Stanley F. Chyet. IP
Free Union, *sel.* André Breton, *tr. fr. French by* David Antin. Pos; RHTwFP
"My wife whose hair is a brush fire." TTTS
Free Up de Lan, White Man. Mutabaruka. PBCV
Free woman, A. At last free! The mother of Sumangala, *tr. by* Willis Barnstone. AIW; BoWoP
Freeborn Man. Ewan MacColl. OBET
Freeborn Pindaric never does refuse. A Pindaric on the Grunting of a Hog. Samuel Wesley. NOBL
Freed dove flew to the Rajah's tower, The. The Dove of Dacca. Kipling. GN
Freedom. Joan Agnew. BoTP
Freedom [or Fredome]. John Barbour. *Fr.* The Bruce. FaBoCh; GoTS; OBEV; OxBS; TrGrPo
Freedom. Joel Barlow. OPP
Freedom. Langston Hughes. PoBA
Freedom. Abraham Ibn Ezra, *tr. fr. Hebrew by* Solomon Solis-Cohen. TrJP
Freedom. Sean O Riordain, *tr. fr. Irish by* Coslett Quin. TIRV
Freedom. Adam Zagajewski, *tr. fr. Polish by* Antony Graham. PwPP
Freedom a Come Oh! *Unknown.* PVCV
Freedom; a Poem, Written in Time of Recess from the Rapacious Claws of Bailiffs, *sel.* Andrew Brice.
Poet's Terror at the Bailiffs of Exeter, The. NOEC
Freedom and dignity have reached us. Independence. *Somali Oral Tradition, tr. by* B. W. Andrzejewski *and* I. M. Lewis. WTO
Freedom and Love. Thomas Campbell. GTBS; GTBS-P
Freedom at McNealy's. Priscilla Jane Thompson. CBWP-2
Freedom called them—up they rose. The Gallant Fifty-one. Henry Lynden Flash. PAH
Freedom for the Mind. William Lloyd Garrison. AA; FaBoBe
Freedom I never saw in words. After Bombardment. John Pudney. WaP
Freedom in Mah Soul. David Wadsworth Cannon, Jr. PoNe
Freedom is a dream. Dark Testament. Pauli Murray. AmNP; BlSi
Freedom is a hard-bought thing. Song of the Settlers. Jessamyn West. FaPON

Freedom is more than a word, more than the base coinage. The *Nabara*. C. Day Lewis. OBNV

Freedom, New Hampshire. Galway Kinnell. LCAP; NaP

Freedom of Love. André Breton, *tr. fr. French by* Edouard Roditi. EAS

Freedom of the Hills. Douglas Fraser. PoSH

Freedom of the wholly mad, The. The Phenomenology of Anger. Adrienne Rich. PoE

Freedom Song for the Black Woman, A. Carole C. Gregory. BlSi

Freedom will not come. Freedom. Langston Hughes. PoBA

Freedom won't be sweet for him. Three Dostoievskian Masks. Sándor Rákos, *tr. by* Jascha Kessler. FOC

Freedom's Dawn. Faiz Ahmad Faiz, *tr. fr. Urdu by* Mahmood Jamal. PBMUP

Freedom's first champion in our fettered land! Garrison. Amos Bronson Alcott. AA

Freehand Sketch. Roberto Sosa, *tr. fr. Spanish by* David Volpendesta. VoI

Freely Espousing. James Schuyler. NeAP; NoP

Freely, from a Song Sung by Jewish Women of Yemen. Stephen Levy. VWA

Freely the dead bracken breaks to your stride. Argenteuil County. Peter Dale Scott. MoCV

Freeman, I treat tonight, and treat your friends. The Invitation. Leonard Welsted. NOEC

Freethinkers. Deborah Eibel. VWA

Freeway 280. Lorna Dee Cervantes. NoAM

Freeze Tag. Gordon Henry. STE

Freight Boats. James S. Tippett. FaPON

Freight Train, The. Rowena Bastin Bennett. PDV

Freighter. Bruce Ruddick. CaP

Freighter, gay with rust, The. Jews at Haifa. Randall Jarrell. MoAmPo

Freighting from Wilcox to Globe. *Unknown.* AmFP

Freind! for your epitaphs I'm griev'd. Epigram on One Who Made Long Epitaphs. Pope. FaBoEE

French. Osbert Lancaster. *Fr.* Afternoons with Baedeker. FaBoCo; NOBL

French, 1870-1871, The. *Unknown.* FaBoEE

French and the Spanish Guerrillas, The. Wordsworth. WaaP (Sonnet: French and the Spanish Guerrillas, The.) ChER

French clocks struck two-thirty, and above, The. Under the Arc de Triomphe: October 17. Marilyn Hacker. PoA

French Desire. Keith Abbott. UL

French government, The—or maybe it was the English—placed. Birds in the Night. Luis Cernuda, *tr. by* Erskine Lane. PeHV

French Lisette; a Ballad of Maida Vale. William Plomer. ErPo

French Mood, The. Abo Stoltzenberg, *tr. fr. Yiddish by* Gabriel Preil *and* Howard Schwartz. VWA

French Peasants. Monk Gibbon. NeIP; TIRV

French Revolution, The, *sel.* Blake. Louis XVI. ChER

French Revolution, The. Wordsworth. *See* Prelude [or, Growth of a Poet's Mind], The: France.

French spoken. Sheep Meadow. Samuel Menashe. Mes

Frende, god save you. For to Aske the Waye. *Unknown.* *Fr.* A Lytell Treatyse for to Lerne Englysshe and Frens. OxBLMV

Frenzy. George Crabbe. *Fr.* Sir Eustace Grey. NOBE

Fresco-Sonnets to Christian Sethe. Heine, *tr. fr. German by* John Todhunter. AWP

Frescoes for Mr. Rockefeller's City, *sels.* Archibald MacLeish. UnPo
Burying Ground by the Ties. *Fr.* III. GOA; MoAmPo
Landscape as a Nude. *Fr.* I. AmPP; CMoP

Frescoes that crumble, marbles bullet-scarred. The Fault. Edward Lucie-Smith. NePoEA-2

Fresh Air. Abi Shaqra, Shauqi, *tr. fr. Arabic by* Abdullah al-Udhari. MPAW

Fresh Air. Kenneth Koch. NeAP; NNaP

Fresh Air, The. Harold Monro. CH; ILY

Fresh and fair the morn awaketh. Morn. Josephine D. Henderson Heard. CBWP-4

Fresh Brats. X. J. Kennedy. SoTCo

Fresh bread on the table, pregnant, whole, A. Evening Bread ("Fresh bread on the table"). Jacob Glatstein, *tr. by* David G. Roskies *and* Hillel Schwartz. VWA

Fresh, bright bloom of the daffodils, The. April Fantasie. Ellen Mackay Hutchinson Cortissoz. AA

Fresh day cracks, goat's milkspurt. Six-forty-two Farm Commune Struggle Poem. Jay Leifer. MAT

Fresh Flowers. Wang An-shih, *tr. fr. Chinese by* Burton Watson. CoBCP

Fresh from the dewy hill, the merry year. Blake. EnRP

Fresh I'm cum fra Sandgate Street. A Do Li. *Unknown.* GBP

Fresh in the flush light gleam. The Sorrow of Unicume. Sir Herbert Read. BrPo

Fresh light from a morning sky blocked through clouds. Light. Carol Coates. CaP

Fresh morning gusts have blown away all fear. Sonnet: To a Young Lady Who Sent Me a Laurel Crown. Keats. EnRP

Fresh News from the Past. Marvin Bell. LCAP

Fresh oil pours through your curls. Saul Re-enthroned. Meir Wieseltier, *tr. by* Warren Bargad *and* Stanley F. Chyet. IP

Fresh Paint. Boris Pasternak, *tr. fr. Russian by* Babette Deutsch. TrJP

Fresh palms for the Old Dominion! The Battle of Charlestown. Henry Howard Brownell. PAH

Fresh Spring. Elizabeth Daryush. QFR

Fresh Spring, the Herald. Spenser. *See* Amoretti: LXX. "Fresh Spring, the herald of love's mighty king."

Fresh Start, The. Anna Wickham. ViBoPo

Fresh strewings allow. The Peter-Penny. Robert Herrick. CaPo

Fresh were the breathings of the nightborn gale. Wild Nature. Charles Newton. *Fr.* Stanzas. NOEC

Freshmen. Barry Spacks. NYBP

Fret not thyself because of evildoers. Psalm XXXVII ("Fret not thyself"). Bible, *O.T. Fr.* Psalms.
(Trust in the Lord, 1-7 *paraphrased by* Charles Frederic Sheldon) BLRP

Freud: Dying London, He Recalls the Smoke of His Cigar Beginning to Sing. James Schevill. TAP

Friar, The. Thomas Love Peacock. *Fr.* Maid Marian. SD

Friar and the Nun, The ("The nun walked on her prayer"). *Unknown.* GBP

Friar and the Nun, The ("Ther was a frier of order gray"). *Unknown.* OxBLMV

Friar Complains, A. *Unknown.* MeEL

Friar in the Well, The. *Unknown.* *See* As I Lay Musing ("As I lay musing all alone").

Friar Lubin. Clément Marot, *tr. fr. French by* Longfellow. AWP

Friar of Orders Gray, The. *Unknown.* ACP; NOEC

Friars' Enormities. *Unknown.* MeEL

Friar's Prologue, The. Chaucer. *Fr.* The Canterbury Tales. PoE

Friar's Tale, The. Chaucer. *Fr.* The Canterbury Tales. PoE

Friday. Sir Walter Scott. BoTP

Friday came and the circus was there. The Circus. Elizabeth Madox Roberts. FaPON

Friday Evening. Sean Lucy. CIP

Friday Evening. Julio Marzán. InW

Friday in Berkeley. Untitled I. Ishmael Reed. CNA

Friday Night after Bathing. Stephen Levy. VWA

Friday the Thirteenth. Allen Ginsberg. NNaP

Friday. Wet Dusk. Christopher Logue. OxBTC

Friday, You Look Blue. Alfredo Giuliani, *tr. fr. Italian by* Lawrence R. Smith. NItP

Fridays, when I draw my pension. Betjeman at the Post Office. Stanley J. Sharpless. FaBoCo

Friend!/ Poor, foolish blossom! Beauty. Peter Hille, *tr. by* Jethro Bithell. AWP

Friend. Gwendolyn Brooks. CNA

Friend. Felice Holman. ILY

Friend. Lilian Moore. ILY

Friend, The. Marge Piercy. CAPP; NMM

Friend, A. Marguerite Power. FaBoCo; FaFP

Friend, A. Santob de Carrion. *Fr.* Proverbios Morales. TrJP

Friend, A. W. D. Snodgrass. MAT

Friend. Hone Tuwhare, *tr. fr. Maori by* Kumeroa Ngoingoi Pewhairangi. PeNZ

"Friend/ like someone who gets drunk secretly." What She Said to Her Girl Friend, and What Her Girl Friend Said in Reply. Uruttiran, *tr. by* A. K. Ramanujan. PLW

Friend Advises Me to Stop Drinking, A. Mei Yao Ch'en, *tr. fr. Chinese by* Kenneth Rexroth. HoPM

Friend and Lover. "Madeline Bridges." AA

Friend asks why I swim, A. Janice M. Lynch. *Fr.* Sixty-four Caprices for a Long-Distance Swimmer: Notes on Swimming 100 Miles. TSL, *much abr.*

Friend, because of you I'm filled. *Unknown, tr. by* Meg Bogin. WT

Friend calls us, A. Six Years. Alice Bloch. PeHV

Friend Cato. Anna Wickham. McBrPo

Friend Col and I, both full of whim. David Garrick. FaBoEE

Friend Comes to Visit on a Summer Night, A. Mo Shih-lung, *tr. fr. Chinese by* Jonathan Chaves. CoBLCP

Friend, coming in a friendly wise. If Any Be Pleased to Walk into My Poor Garden. Francis Daniel Pastorius. SCAP

Friend, do you remember the time we went. The Breaking of the Glass. Abdallah al-Tayyib, *tr. by* Salma Khadra Jayyusi *and* Christopher Middleton. MAP

Friend, don't be angry. Mirabai, *tr. by* Willis Barnstone *and* Usha Nilsson. BoWoP

Friend drops me at Indian Cemetary, A. The Hemingway Syndrome. Adrian C. Louis. STE

Friend Hedylus' cloak is a sight to behold. Epigram: On Hedylus. Martial. PeHV

Friend, his seas swell and roar. What She Said. Ammuvanar, *tr. by* A. K. Ramanujan. PLW

Friend, how can I meet my lord? Mirabai, *tr. by* Willis Barnstone *and* Usha Nilsson. BoWoP

Friend, I have watched you down the mountain. A Parting. Wang Wei, *tr. by* Witter Bynner *and* Kiang Kan-Hu. ILY

Friend, if the mute and shrouded dead. Love and Death. Catullus, *tr. by* H. W. Garrod. AWP

Friend, if you had shown consideration. Castelloza, *tr. by* Meg Bogin. WT

Friend, I'm reading your old poems on the north terrace. Loneliness 2. Antonio Cisneros, *tr. by* Maureen Ahern *and* David Tipton. Per

Friend in a tipi in the, A. Two Fawns That Didn't See the Light This Spring. Gary Snyder. HCAP

Friend in the Garden, A. Juliana Horatia Ewing. BoTP; FaPON; OxBChV

Friend, it's your fate to follow love. Drinking Song. Louise Geneviève de Sainctonge, *tr. by* Dorothy Backer. DMF

Friend, listen. What She Said ("Friend, listen"). Ammuvanar, *tr. by* A. K. Ramanujan. PLW

Friend Mussunda. Agostinho Neto, *tr. fr. Portuguese by* Marga Holness. WMBCH

Friend of Humanity and the Knife Grinder, The. George Canning *and* John Hookham Frere. BXAP; FaBoCo; Par (Sapphics.) NOEC

Friend of lovers, the poets' companion, The. Defence of the Moon. Antoni Slonimski, *tr. by* Czeslaw Milosz. PwPP

Friend of mine ever was married to a scold, A. All's Well That Ends Well. *Unknown.* FaFP

Friend of Ronsard, Nashe and Beaumont. On a Birthday. J. M. Synge. ChTr; GBL; OBMV

Friend of the Family, A. Louis Simpson. NNaP

Friend of the Fourth Decade, The. James Merrill. NYBP

Friend of the wise! and teacher of the good! To William Wordsworth. Samuel Taylor Coleridge. EnRP; NAEL-2; OAEL-2

Friend of Two, A. Wilbur Dick Nesbit. PoLF

Friend, on This Scaffold Thomas More Lies Dead. J. V. Cunningham. InPK

(Epigram: "Friend [*or* friends] on this scaffold Thomas More lies dead.") CRP; NePoAM

Friend, on this sunny day, snow sparkling. Letter to Jean-Paul Baudot, at Christmas. Lucien Stryk. CAPP

Friend, Ortho of Syracuse gives thee this charge. Ortho's Epitaph. Theocritus, *tr. by* Charles Stuart Calverley. FaBoEE

Friend Proclus, the world isn't a fantasy. José I. de Diego Padró, *tr. fr. Spanish by* Julio Marzán. *Fr.* Epistolary Briefs to Proclus, I, II. InW

Friend sparrow, do not eat, I pray. Basho, *tr. by* Curtis Hidden Page. AWP

Friend, there be they on whom mishap. Contentment. Charles Stuart Calverley. NOBVV

Friend thinks he knows best, A. The Late Victorian Girl. Bill Manhire. PeNZ

Friend, though thy soul should burn thee, yet be still. The Truth. Archibald Lampman. CaP

Friend, when I think of your delicate feminine face. On the Death of an Acquaintance. Oscar Williams. *Fr.* Variations on a Theme, I. LiTA

Friend Who Just Stands By, The. B. Y. Williams. PoLF

Friend Who Never Came. William Stafford. SM

Friend, whose unnatural early death. David Gascoyne. FaBoTw; TwCP

Friend, with regard to this same hare. To the Rev. Mr. Powell. Christopher Smart. OBWVE

Friend, you are grieved that I should go. Creeds. Karle Wilson Baker. WGRP

Friend, you seem thoughtful. I not wonder much. A Sea Dialogue. Oliver Wendell Holmes. MOS; OBAL

Friendless and faint, with martyred steps and slow. Calvary. E. A. Robinson. MoAmPo; OFD; Son; WGRP

Friendly Address, A. Thomas Hood. PoEL-4

Friendly Beasts, The. *Unknown.* FaPON; ILY; OnMSP; PChr

Friendly Cinnamon Bun, The. Russell Hoban. ILY

Friendly cow all red and white, The. The Cow. Robert Louis Stevenson. BrPo; FaPON; FM; NTCP; OxBChV; PWR

Friendly Game of Football, A. Edward Dyson. CBAP

Friendly Wood, The. Paul Valéry, *tr. fr. French by* William Jay Smith. CT

Friends. John Ashbery. LCAP

Friends. Ray Durem. PoBA

Friends. Mary Goose. STE

Friends. A. E. Housman. SeCePo

Friends. Richard Moore. SM

Friends. Meir Wieseltier, *tr. fr. Hebrew by* Bernhard Frank. MHeP

Friends. W. B. Yeats. MoP; NoAM

Friends,/ The ancient word is dead. Footnotes to the Book of the Setback. Nizar Qabbani, *tr. by* Abdullah al-Udhari. MPAW

Friends,/ you are lucky you can talk. Vidya, *tr. by* Willis Barnstone. BoWoP

Friends admire our many birch trees. These. The Student. Peter Meinke. SoTCo

Friends and loves we have none, nor wealth, nor blest abode. The Seekers. John Masefield. WGRP

Friends are unhappy; their long night. Winter Work. Peter Fallon. CIP

Friends Beyond. Thomas Hardy. EBVV; FaBoRV; GTBS-P; NOBVV; OBEV

Friends Come. Lucille Clifton. GeTw

Friends come and talk. Friends. Meir Wieseltier, *tr. by* Bernhard Frank. MHeP

Friends Departed. Henry Vaughan. *See* They Are All Gone into the World of Light.

Friends forget. I am my own friend for a while. Hide-and-Go-Seek. Jim Simmerman. BLA

Friend's Greeting, A. Edgar Albert Guest. BLPA; BLPL

Friends, I sang as a bird sings. Nightfall. Cassiano Ricardo, *tr. by* Barbara Howes. ATCBP

Friends, my heart is half aweary. The Old Times Were the Best. James Whitcomb Riley. FaFP

Friends of the Muse, to you of right belong. The Strong Heroic Line. Oliver Wendell Holmes. AA

Friends, Romans, countrymen, lend me your ears. Antony's Oration [over Caesar's Body]. Shakespeare. *Fr.* Julius Caesar, III, iii. LiTB; TrGrPo

(Mark Antony Addresses the Mob.) FaPoR

Friends said: about eight o'clock they used to come. Reports of Midsummer Girls. Richmond Lattimore. PCP

Friends surround his bed. A magician. The Death of the Vaudevillian. Mark Sanders. SoTCo

Friends who come to see you, The. Sleep. James Schuyler. GLP

Friends Who Have Failed. Alan Williamson. PPR

Friendship. Hartley Coleridge. *See* When we were idlers with the loitering rills.

Friendship. Dinah Maria Mulock Craik. BLPA

Friendship. Katherine Mansfield. PeHV

Friendship, The. Robert Mezey. NaP

Friendship. Sadi, *tr. fr. Persian by* L. Cranmer-Byng. *Fr.* The Gulistan. AWP

Friendship. Shel Silverstein. ILY; NTCP

Friendship. *Unknown, tr. fr. Aztec Indian by* John Bierhorst. ILY

Friendship. V. A. Zhukovsky, *tr. fr. Russian by* Alan Myers. AAA

Friendship in Perfection. Andrew Michael Ramsay. NOEC

Friendship is constant in all other things. Beauty Is a Witch. Shakespeare. *Fr.* Much Ado about Nothing, II, i. TrGrPo

Friendship is like china. *Unknown.* ILY

Friendship's Mystery; to My Dearest Lucasia. Katherine Philips. PeHV

Frigate Jones, the Pussyfooter ("Frigate Jones was very slow and fat"). Kenneth Burke. OBAL

Frigate Pelican, The. Marianne Moore. InvP

Frigga with Hela. Judy Grahn. UL

Frightened/ by the sound of my own voice. Lawrence Ferlinghetti. *Fr.* A Coney Island of the Mind. TAP

Frightened Flier Goes North, The. Judith Kazantzis. BrRo

Frightened Man, The. Louise Bogan. FaBoWP

Frightened mothers. Demon. Ahmad Faraz, *tr. by* Mahmood Jamal. PBMUP

Frightened Ploughman, The. John Clare. PoEL-4

Frightening. Claudia Lewis. RHPC

Frigid and sweet her parting face. Emily Dickinson. PeHV

Fringed Gentian. Emily Dickinson. *See* God made a little gentian.

Fringed Gentians. Amy Lowell. FaPON

Fringed pink in my garden, The. *Unknown, tr. fr. Japanese. Fr.* Manyo Shu.

Fringes, The. Harris Lenowitz. VWA

Fringilla Melodia, The. Henry Beck Hirst. AA

Fringing cypress forests dim. Sassafras. Samuel Minturn Peck. AA
Frisbee. Rolfe Humphries. GrPl
Frisky Lamb, A. Christina Rossetti. BoTP
Frithiof's Farewell. Esaias Tegnér, *tr. fr. Swedish* by Longfellow. *Fr. Frithiof's Saga.* AWP
Frithiof's Homestead. Esaias Tegnér, *tr. fr. Swedish* by Longfellow. *Fr. Frithiof's Saga.* AWP
Frithiof's Saga, *sels.* Esaias Tegnér, *tr. fr. Swedish* by Longfellow. AWP
   Frithiof's Farewell.
   Frithiof's Homestead.
Fritz. Gerald Stern. AnAn
Frog, The. Hilaire Belloc. FaBoBe; FaBV; FaPON; FiBHP; GoJo; MoShBr; NA; NTCP; OxBChV; RHPC
Frog, The. Carolyn. MoShBr; NBLV; NTCP; RB
Frog, The. Rose Fyleman. BoTP
Frog and a Flea, A. Cynthia Mitchell. RAR
Frog and the Bird, The. Vera Hessey. BoTP
Frog and the Crow, The. *Unknown.* GBP
Frog and the Golden Ball, The. Robert Graves. NoP
Frog and the Mouse, The. ("Frog went walking one day"). *Unknown.* WiR
Frog and the Mouse, The. *Unknown. See* Frog went a-courting, away did ride, huh-huh, A.
Frog Autumn. Sylvia Plath. OxBSP
Frog climbs up a willow, A. Kosai, *tr.* by Hiroaki Sato. FCEI
Frog crawls out and rubs his back, A. Kyohaku, *tr.* by Hiroaki Sato. FCEI
Frog embryos spin, The. Neural Folds. Lucille Day. BWV
Frog emerges with its child on its back, A. Toyo, *tr.* by Hiroaki Sato. FCEI
Frog has legs, The. Kiju, *tr.* by Hiroaki Sato. FCEI
Frog has lifted a fallen blossom, A. Soha, *tr. fr. Japanese* by Hiroaki Sato. FCEI
Frog He Would A-Wooing Go, A. *Unknown.* OxNR, *diff. vers.*; PYC
   (Froggie Went a-Courting.) AmFP
   (Mr. Frog Went a-Courting.) AS, with music
Frog Hunting. Peter Cooley. MAYP
Frog keeps still, A. Issa, *tr. fr. Japanese* by Hiroaki Sato. *Fr.* Forty-four Hokku. FCEI
Frog lay in the step-child's bed, The. The Wooing Frog. James Reeves. SO
Frog looks at me, A. Issa, *tr. fr. Japanese* by Hiroaki Sato. *Fr.* Forty-four Hokku. FCEI
Frog on the Log, The. Ilo Orleans. RAR
Frog Prince, The. Stevie Smith. HAP; Mes
Frog under you, A. The Wife. Denise Levertov. ErPo
Frog went a-courting, away did ride, huh-huh, A. Frog Went a-Courtin'. *Unknown.* BLPA
   (Frog and the Mouse, The.) WiR
Frog went walking one day, A. The Frog and the Mouse. *Unknown.* WiR
Froggie Went a-Courting. *Unknown. See* Frog He Would A-Wooing Go, A.
Frogs croak in moonlight. Chokyusei, *tr.* by Lucien Stryk *and* Takashi Ikemoto. ZPCJ
Frogs Croaking. Masso, *tr. fr. Chinese* by Lucien Stryk *and* Takashi Ikemoto. ZPCJ
Frog's Fate, A. Christina Rossetti. NOBVV
Frogs in rain—as their croaks rise. Sodo, *tr. fr. Japanese* by Hiroaki Sato. FCEI
Frogs jump. Jump or Jiggle. Evelyn Beyer. RAR
Frogs play hide-and-seek. Issa, *tr. fr. Japanese* by Hiroaki Sato. *Fr.* Forty-four Hokku. FCEI
Frogs time out of mind, The. Aesop's Fable of the Frogs. La Fontaine, *tr.* by John Hookham Frere. OBVE
Frolic. "Æ." BoTP; FaPON; MoBrPo
Frolic, A. Robert Herrick. FaBoEE
Frolic. Deborah Levy. DT
Frolic Mariners of Devon, The. William Browne. *Fr.* Britannia's Pastorals, II, Song 3. ChTr
Frolicsome Farmer, The. *Unknown.* CoMu
Frolicsome Parson Outwitted, The. *Unknown.* CoMu
From. Tom Paulin. FaBCIP
From a Book of Hours. Charles Spear. ATNZ
From a branch/ The bird called. The Bird. Max Michelson. TrJP
From a brat's sleeve. Issa, *tr. fr. Japanese* by Hiroaki Sato. *Fr.* Forty-four Hokku. FCEI
From a Brother Dreaming in the Rye. James Cunningham. JB
From a Bus. Malaika Ayo Wangara. NBP
From a Cheerful Alphabet. John Updike. FaBoCo

From a Childhood. Rainer Maria Rilke, *tr. fr. German.* TTTS, *tr.* by M. D. Herter Norton
From a Childhood. Rainer Maria Rilke, *tr. fr. German.* TrJP, *tr.* by C. F. MacIntyre; TTTS, *tr.* by M. D. Herter Norton.
From a church across the street. Ave Maria. Barbara Ferland. PBCV
From a city window, 'way up high. Motor Cars. Rowena Bastin Bennett. FaPON
From a clump of grass. Emperor Kogon, *tr.* by Steven D. Carter. WFTW
From a Connecticut Newspaper. Levi Rockwell. FaBoUs
From a Correct Address in a Suburb of a Major City. Helen Sorrells. WPE
From a distance, I watch. Practical Concerns. William J. Harris. PoBA
From a far-off island whose name I do not know. Coconut. Shimazaki Toson, *tr.* by Geoffrey Bownas *and* Anthony Thwaite. PeBJV
From a high mountain I see how the banks of a river. The Banks of a River. Abraham Sutskever, *tr.* by Ruth Whitman. VWA
From a Lavatory Wall. *Unknown.* FaBoEE
From a Letter to America on a Visit to Sussex: Spring 1942. Frances Cornford. CN
From a Litany. Mark Strand. PPP
From a little seed. Little Things. Eileen Mathias. BoTP
From a London Bookshop. *Unknown.* FaBoUs; NBLV
From a Marriage Broker's Card, 1776. *Unknown.* FaBoUs
From a Milkweed Pod. Robert Frost. KS
   (Pod of the Milkweed.) LiTM
From a Museum Man's Album. John Hewitt. OxBTC
From a New Height. Andrea Zanzotto, *tr. fr. Italian* by Lawrence R. Smith. NItP
From a place I came. Kathleen Jessie Raine. *Fr.* Two Invocations of Death, II. OxBTC
From a Printed Bill, Fixed in the Beak of One in a Group of Five Stuffed Owls in the Shop Window of a Bird Stuffer, at Richmond, Yorkshire. *Unknown.* FaBoUs
From a Railway Carriage. Robert Louis Stevenson. BoTP; FaPON; OxBChV; PDV; PYC; RHPC
From a ruler that's a curse. Charles Cotton. OBSV
From a Survivor. Adrienne Rich. AnAn
From a thousand hills, bird flights have vanished. River Snow. Liu Tsung-yüan, *tr.* by Burton Watson. CoBCP
From a Tobacco Wrapper. *Unknown.* FaBoUs
From a Venetian Sequence. Adèle Naudé. PeSA
From a Very Little Sphinx. Edna St. Vincent Millay. OBAL
From a village up the Hudson. The Dark Girl Dressed in Blue. *Unknown.* BeLS
From a vision red with war I awoke and saw the Prince of Peace. The New Day. Fenton Johnson. BANP
From a Walking Song. Charles Williams. BoTP
From a Window in Princes Street. W. E. Henley. EBVV
From a Woman to a Greedy Lover. Norman Cameron. *Fr.* Three Love Poems, I. FaBoEE
From a wreck of tree in the wash of night. Speak with the Sun. David Campbell. SeCePo
From above my bed. Leaves Making a Sound as They Fall. Shotetsu, *tr.* by Steven D. Carter. WFTW
From across the stream, on the side of the opposite hill. Not Seeing Is Believing. Paul Petrie. TAP
From Age to Age They Gather. Frederick Lucian Hosmer. AH
From all I did and all I said. Hidden Things. Constantine P. Cavafy, *tr.* by Edmund Keeley *and* Philip Sherrard. VMG
From all my lame defeats and oh! much more. The Apologist's Evening Prayer. C. S. Lewis. TrCP
From All Peoples, *sel.* Nathan Alterman, *tr. fr. Hebrew* by Simon Halkin.
   "When our children cried in the shadow of the gallows." TrJP
From all the canals. Midnight. Judah Leib Teller, *tr. fr. Yiddish* by Benjamin *and* Barbara Harshav. *Fr.* Three Poems of Nightmare. AYP
From All These Events. Stephen Spender. LiTB
From almost naught to almost all I flee. On the Calculus. J. V. Cunningham. QFR
From Alpine heights where clad in snow. Ode to the Lake of Geneva. William Parsons. OBTV
From America. James M. Whitfield. BPo
From an Afternoon Caller. Sister Mary Madeleva. CRP
From an Asylum; Kathy Chattle to Her Mother, Ruth Arbeiter. Anne Stevenson. BrRo
From an Inmate Rule Book. Joseph Bruchac. NOVW
From an Irish-Latin Macaronic. Geoffrey Taylor. NeIP
From an island teeming with parrots. Epilogue to Robinson Crusoe. Dan Pagis, *tr.* by Warren Bargad *and* Stanley F. Chyet. IP

From an Old House in America. Adrienne Rich. NNaP
From an old house shaded with macrocarpas. James Keir Baxter. *Fr.*
　Pig Island Letters, II. ATNZ; PeNZ
From an old man. Dusk. Ken Belford. NeAC
From Ancient Fangs. Peter Viereck. LiTA
From anger into the pit of sleep. Wife to Husband. Fleur Adcock.
　ATNZ; PeNZ
From Another Room. Gregory Corso. NeAP
From another world I appear to myself. Make-off. Karin Kiwus, *tr. by*
　Susan L. Cocalis. DMG
From Arranmore the weary miles I've come. Mavrone. Arthur
　Guiterman. BXAP; FiBHP
From back of the box and through the milky window. McLuhan
　Transposed. Suzette Haden Elgin. BWV
From bamboo groves. Yakamochi, *tr. fr. Japanese by* Burton Watson.
　Fr. Manyo Shu. FCEI
From Battle Clamour. Samuele Romanelli, *tr. fr. Hebrew by* Nina Davis
　Salaman. TrJP
From beer you get a beer-belly. Everything Has Its Reason. Liesl
　Ujvary, *tr. by* Beth Bjorklund. CoAuP
From behind the Bars, *sel.* Fadwa Tuqan, *tr. fr. Arabic by* Hatem
　Hossaini.
　From the Diary of—— WPOW
From behind the wall death sends out messages. By the Graveyard,
　Luskentyre. Norman MacCaig. NPo
From Belsen a crate of gold teeth. William Heyen. SM
From bill to breast a snake. Swan. Edward Lowbury. GTBS-P
From Blenheim's clocktower a cheerful bell bangs out. Distilled Water.
　M. K. Joseph. ATNZ; PeNZ
From blue sky birds come. Like the White. Qasim Haddad, *tr. by* Sharif
　Elmusa *and* Charles Doria. MAP
From Braddon's penniless subornation. A New Litany in the Year 1684.
　Unknown. APAS
From breakfast on through all the day. The Land of Nod. Robert Louis
　Stevenson. PWR
From breasts/ Of Africland. Africland. Oliver LaGrone. FB
From breezeway or through front porch screen. The Sheets. Timothy
　Steele. DiPo
From Brooklyn Hill, ours is a doll-size city. Wellington. Louis Johnson.
　ATNZ
From Bulgaria thick, wild cannon pounding rolls. Picture Postcards.
　Miklós Radnóti, *tr. by* Emery George. VWA
From Burton the Anatomist. Maurice James Craig. NeIP
From C. Michael Palmer. BAP
From Calpe's rock, with loss of leg. The Soldier That Has Seen Service.
　Unknown. NOEC
From camp to camp, through the fool womb of time. Shakespeare. *Fr.*
　King Henry V: Now Entertain Conjecture of a Time. FaBoRV
From Carrigskeewaun in Killadoon. Letter to Seamus Heaney. Michael
　Longley. FaBCIP
From cavities of bones. From the Cavities of Bones. Patricia Parker.
　BlSi
From Chekiang I Went to Hsin-an. Hsü Wei, *tr. fr. Chinese by* Jonathan
　Chaves. CoBLCP
From Childhood's Hour. Poe. PoEL-4
　(Alone.) NAAL-1
From Clee to heaven the beacon burns. 1887. A. E. Housman. *Fr.* A
　Shropshire Lad, I. FaPoR; NIP; NOBVV; PrIm; UnPo
From coast to coast. Alpha November Golf Sierra Tango. Tom Clark.
　UL
From Colony to Nation. Irving Layton. NOBC
From Countless Hearts. Gail Brook Burket. AH
From coves below the cliffs of the years. They Say the Butterfly Is the
　Hardest Stroke. Paul Durcan. FaBCIP
From cow-stall to Iowa. To Mr. Hsiao Ch'ien. Lo Fu, *tr. by* Dominic
　Cheung. IFON
From Creature to Ghost. Pauline Hanson. TAP
From dark the striped muscles sprang. "God's First Creature Was Light."
　Winifred Welles. ImOP
From darkness/ I go onto the road/ of darkness. Izumi Shikibu. BoWoP,
　tr. by Willis Barnstone
　("From darkness/ Into the path of darkness.") PBWP, *tr. by* Edwin
　A. Cranston.
From darkness into the path of darkness. To a Sage in Harima. Lady
　Izumi, *tr. fr. Japanese by* Hiroaki Sato. *Fr.* Fifty-one Tanka.
　FCEI
From Darts of Love That Do Such Dole. Christine de Pisan, *tr. fr.*
　French by Naomi Lewis. *Fr.* The Lady, VIII. DMF
From dawn to dark they stood. "Our Left." Francis Orrery Ticknor.
　PAH

From day to day/ The calcium in our cells grows less and less. Leningrad:
　1943. Vera Inber *tr. fr. Russian by* Dorothea Prall Radin *and*
　Alexander Kaun. *Fr.* The Pulkovo Meridian. WaaP
From deep sleep. Nightmare. James A. Emanuel. BPo
From Delphi. Cozette de Charmoy. NPo
From door to door in the land of love. Mohammad Taqi Mir, *tr. by*
　Ahmed Ali. GoT
From Drogheda all along the coast, the irish sea. Back to Dublin. R. A.
　D. Ford. CaP; MoCV
From dusk till dawn the livelong night. Betsy's Battle Flag. Minna
　Irving. OPP; PAH
From early dusk the day was inscrutable. Bread. Mahmoud Darwish, *tr.*
　by Lena Jayyusi *and* Christopher Middleton. MAP
From east and south the holy clan. The Bishop of Rum-ti-Foo. W. S.
　Gilbert. CenHV
From Eastertide to Eastertide. A Ballad of a Nun. John Davidson.
　BeLS; MoBrPo; OnMSP
From Emily Dickinson in Southern California. X. J. Kennedy. NBLV
From endless rains comes autumn's dusk. Wu Wen, *tr. fr. Chinese by*
　Irving Lo. *Fr.* In the Mountains, I. WFTU
From every quarter came the night confounding. Burial at Sea. E. J.
　Pratt. *Fr.* The *Roosevelt and the Antinoe.* CaP
From Exile. Dafydd Benfras, *tr. fr. Welsh by* Anthony Conran.
　OBWVE
From Exile to Exile. Abd-Allah al-Baraduni, *tr. fr. Arabic by* Diana Der
　Hovanessian *and* Sharif Elmusa. MAP
From eyes, from ears. Black Song. Murano Shiro, *tr. by* Geoffrey
　Bownas *and* Anthony Thwaite. PeBJV
From fair Jamaica's fertile plains. "Ada." BlSi
"From fairest creatures we desire increase." Shakespeare. *Fr.* Sonnets, I.
　CTC; LiTB; OBSC; TrGrPo
From Far Away. Delmira Agustini, *tr. fr. Spanish by* D. M. Pettinella.
　PBWP
From Far Away. William Morris. OHIP
From far away. Waking on a Greyhound. Gordon Henry. STE
From far away, from far away. My Letter. Grace Denio Litchfield. AA
From far away we come to you. From Far Away. William Morris.
　OHIP
From Far, from Eve and Morning. A. E. Housman. *Fr.* A Shropshire
　Lad, XXXII. CMoP; HAP; HeIP; MoBrPo; NoP; PoEL-5; PrIm
From Father to Son. Emyr Humphreys. OBWVE
"From fear to fear, successively betrayed." Reflection from Rochester.
　William Empson. PoA
From Feathers to Iron, *sels.* C. Day Lewis.
　Now She Is like the White Tree-Rose. CMoP; FaBoTw; MoBrPo
　Though Bodies Are Apart. NAs
From first light we fear falling. Hotel Fire: New Orleans. Paul Ruffin.
　InPK
From Fortune's frowns and change removed. Old Damon's Pastoral.
　Thomas Lodge. OBSC
From France, desponding and betray'd. On the British Invasion. Philip
　Freneau. PAH
From frozen climes, and endless tracks [*or* tracts] of snow. A Winter-
　Piece. Ambrose Philips. NOEC; OBTV; SeCePo
From gallery-grave and the hunt of a wren-king. W. H. Auden. *Fr.*
　Thanksgiving for a Habitat. EyDe
From garden to garden, ridge to ridge. John Muir. RFM
From Generation to Generation. William Dean Howells. AA
From Generation to Generation. Sir Henry Newbolt. FaBoTw
From ghoulies and ghosties. *Unknown.* OFD; WSC
　(Things That Go Bump in the Night.) NTCP
From giant oaks, that wave their branches dark. Vegetable Loves.
　Erasmus Darwin. *Fr.* The Botanic Garden: The Loves of the Plants.
　SeCePo
From Gloucester Out. Edward Dorn. NOBA; PoM
From gods of other men, fastidious heart. False Gods. Walter de la
　Mare. EaLo
From gorge to gorge. Elena Clementelli, *tr. fr. Italian by* Ruth Feldman
　and Brian Swann. *Fr.* Etruscan Notebook. PBWP
From Government Buildings. Denis Devlin. IPY
From Grant's grave Galena. Old Dubuque. Dave Etter. AmFN
From Greenland to Iceland. *Unknown.* FaFP
From Greenland's Icy Mountains. Reginald Heber. AnAmPo; FaPoR;
　WGRP
From Grenoble. James Elroy Flecker. OBTV
From groves of spice. Sarojini Naidu. FaPON
　(Hindu Cradle Song.) BoTP
From "Growl." David Shevin. SoTCo
From Halifax station a bully there came. Halifax Station. *Unknown.*
　PAH

From harmony, from heavenly [or heav'nly] harmony. A Song for St. Cecilia's Day, 1687. Dryden. AWP; GTBS; GTBS-P; HAP; InPS; LiTB; NAEL-1; OAEL-1; OBEV; OPOP; PoEL-3; PPP; SeCV-2; TEP; TrGrPo; UnS, abr

From Harvest to January. Charles Tennyson Turner. NOBVV

From heart through mind into image. The Past. William Oandasan. STE
    (Words of Tayko mol.) HATNAP

From Heart to Heart. William Channing Gannett. AH
    (Stream of Faith, The.) WGRP

From Heaven High I Come to You. At. to Martin Luther, tr. fr. German. PChr

From Heaven's Gate to Hampstead Heath. The Ballad of Hampstead Heath. James Elroy Flecker. MoBrPo

From heavy dreams fair Helen rose. William and Helen. Sir Walter Scott. EnRP

From her bed's high and odoriferous roome. Homer, tr. fr. Greek by George Chapman. Fr. Odyssey, IV. CTC

From her grave. Gillian Eve Hanscombe. Fr. Five Lovesick Poems, IV. AIW

From her room in Fu-chou tonight. Moonlight Night. Tu Fu, tr. by Burton Watson. CoBCP

From Heraclitus. Alan Dugan. PoA

From here, boulders are pebbles. Looking Down a Hill. A. R. Thompson. PoSH

From here, the quay, one looks above to mark. The Harbour Bridge. Thomas Hardy. NoAM

From here through tunnelled gloom the track. The Railway Junction. Walter de la Mare. OxBTC

From here to there/ To Washington Square. Unknown. OxNR

From Here to There. Rachel Korn, tr. fr. Yiddish by Seymour Mayne and Rivka Augenfeld. VWA

From high antiquity, lofty clouds have gathered at this city wall. T'ung Pass. T'an Ssu-t'ung, tr. by Timothy C. Wong. WFTU

From him rocks/ and trees learned. Cézanne. Rose Ausländer, tr. by Beth Bjorklund. CoAuP

From his brimstone bed at break of day. The Devil's Thoughts. Robert Southey and Samuel Taylor Coleridge. FaBoCo, abr; OBSV; OxBoLi, abr.

From his cradle in the glamourie. Peak and Puke. Walter de la Mare. Mes

From his garden bed our Lord. The Harvesting of the Roses. Menahem ben Jacob. TrJP

From his library in Surrey. Nothing Sacred. Roger Woddis. NOBL

From his own solitude to the world unheeding. Llewelyn Wyn Griffith. Fr. The Barren Tree. OBWVE

From his pouch he took his colors. Longfellow. Fr. The Song of Hiawatha. EyDe

From his shoulder Hiawatha. Hiawatha's Photographing. "Lewis Carroll." BXAP; CenHV; FaBoCo; FaBoPa; FiBHP; NOBL

From his small city Columbus. Voyage. Josephine Miles. LiTM

From his wanderings far to eastward. Longfellow. Fr. The Song of Hiawatha, XXI. GOA

From hollows of a tree. Fable of the Speckled Cow. D. J. Opperman, tr. by Jack Cope, Uys Krige and Ruth Miller. PeSA

From holy flower to holy flower. The Study of a Spider. Lord De Tabley. NOBVV

From Holy, Holy, Holy ones. The Lancashire Puritane. Unknown. CoMu

From honey-dew of milking. Feeding a Child. Nuala Ni Dhomhnaill, tr. by Michael Hartnett. CIP

From house to house he goes. Unknown. BoTP

From immaculate construction to half death. The Man from the Top of the Mind. David Wagoner. NePoEA-2

From inland ledges I had dreamed this bay. At the Battery Sea-Wall. Clifford James Laube. GoYe

From inside the bird a dream hums itself out and turns. These Horses Came. Ray A. Young Bear. CDW

From its dancers circulates among the other/dancers. The Dance. Robert Duncan. NeAP

From its sources which well. Robert Southey. Fr. The Cataract of Lodore. RR

From ivory towers they come. Soul. Austin Black. NBP

From Jerusalem: A First Poem. Gabriel Preil, tr. fr. Hebrew by Robert Friend. VWA

From keel to fighting top, I love. Manila Bay. Arthur Hale. PAH

From lake-caves the tortoise-heads protrude. The Fantastic Rock. Wu Chen, tr. by Jonathan Chaves. CoBLCP

From lake Tung-t'ing we travel west. On the Way to Pa-ling. Yüan Mei, tr. by Jonathan Chaves. CoBLCP

From Le Havre. Charles G. Bell. NePoAm

From learned Florence, long time rich in fame. The Earl of Surrey to Geraldine. Michael Drayton. OBSC

From left to right, she leads the eye. Myth on Mediterranean Beach: Aphrodite as Logos. Robert Penn Warren. HAP; WeW

From Lewis, Monsieur Gérard came. Yankee Doodle's Expedition to Rhode Island. Unknown. PAH

From Life. Lazer Eichenrand, tr. fr. Yiddish by Gabriel Preil and Howard Schwartz. VWA

From life's grim nightmare he is now released. Jacob Epstein. Unknown. FaBoCo

From listening,/ a depth, a well of virtues. Nanak, tr. by John Stratton Hawley and Mark Juergensmeyer. SSI

From listening/ Siddhas, Pirs, Gods, Naths. Nanak, tr. by John Stratton Hawley and Mark Juergensmeyer. SSI

From listening,/ Siva, Brahma, Indra. Nanak, tr. by John Stratton Hawley and Mark Juergensmeyer. SSI

From listening,/ truth, fulfillment, knowledge. Nanak, tr. by John Stratton Hawley and Mark Juergensmeyer. SSI

From Lois in London. Angela McCabe. AmPA

From Lord Wu's Bridge, by Master Sung's Hollow, to Mu-lai Gate. On Hearing That the Market outside the East Gate of the City Has Been Burned Down. Cheng Chen, tr. by William Schultz. WFTU

From low to high doth dissolution climb. Mutability. Wordsworth. Fr. Ecclesiastical Sonnets, III, XXXIV. EBEV; EnRP; HeIP; InPK; LiTB; NOBE; NoP; OAEL-2; OBEV; PoEL-4; PrIm

From Lucy: Holiday Reflections. James Berry. PBCV

From Malay. David Shapiro. UL

From many a field with patriot blood imbrued. Decoration Day. George Hurlbut Barbour. OHIP

From masons laying up brick. Mason's Trick. James Hayford. InPK

From Mathnavi Sehrul Bayaan. Mir Ghulam Hasan, tr. fr. Urdu by Ahmed Ali. GoT

From Matlock Bath's half-timbered station. Matlock Bath. Sir John Betjeman. NYBP

From mental mists to purge a nation's eyes. George Canning and John Hookham Frere. Fr. New Morality. NOEC

From mighty wrongs to petty perfidy. Fame. Byron. Fr. Childe Harold's Pilgrimage, IV. FiP

From Minneapolis and Rio, from Sidney and Hendon South. Evolution. Peter Porter. OBD

From Mitsu Beach. Unknown, tr. fr. Japanese by Geoffrey Bownas and Anthony Thwaite. Fr. Manyo Shu. PeBJV

From Mitsu, dearest shore to me. Unknown, tr. fr. Japanese. Fr. Manyo Shu. Ma

From Mobberley on a bright morning, on a snow-white pure-bred mare. The Wizard of Alderley Edge. Peter Coe. OBET

From moccasins to shoes. First Grade. Phillip William George. VoR

From Molepolole and Morogoro. Reflexions on the Seizure of the Suez, and on a Proposal to Line the Banks of That Canal with Bill. Howard Nemerov. NBLV

From Montauk Point. Walt Whitman. RFM

From moonwater, from mirror mist, a slender porcelain. Gift Hour. Maria Banus, tr. by Willis Barnstone and Matei Calinescu. BoWoP; VWA

From morn to [or till] midnight, all day through. Expectans Expectavi. Charles Hamilton Sorley. FaBoCh; WGRP

From Mount Kamunabi of Mimoro. Unknown, tr. fr. Japanese. Fr. Manyo Shu. Ma

From Mount Nebo. Karl Wolfskehl, tr. fr. German by Erna Baber Rosenfeld. VWA

From My Arm-Chair. Longfellow. BLPA

From my couch I rise, afire. Fire and Ice. Michael Pettit. MAYP

From My Diary, July 1914. Wilfred Owen. FaBoMo; LiTM; MoAB; MoBrPo

From my front wheels the scared rabbits. Iowa, June. Michael Dennis Browne. AmPA

From My High Love. Kenneth Patchen. MoAmPo

From my hill I look down on the freeway and over. All the Way from There to Here. Jack Gilbert. NPGG

From My Lai the Thunder Went West. Richard Ryan. CIP

From My Life I Make a Poem. Eeva-Liisa Manner, tr. fr. Finnish by Aili Jarvenpa. SOP

From my little hut. Keiun, tr. by Steven D. Carter. WFTW

From My Mother's Home. Leah Goldberg. See My Mother's House: My mother's mother died.

From My Mother's House. Leah Goldberg, tr. fr. Hebrew by Bernhard Frank. MHeP

From my mother's sleep I fell into the State. The Death of the Ball Turret Gunner. Randall Jarrell. CAPP; CMoP; FF; HAP; HeIP; HoPM; InPK; LCAP; LiTM; MoAmPo; MT; NAAL-2; NAs; NIP; NoAM;

NOBA; NoP; OBD; OBWP; OxBA; PoE; PPP; PrIm; RB; SoSe; TAP; UnPo; VGW; WaaP; WaP

From my personal album. For Malcolm X. Nanina Alba. PoBA

From My Royzele's Diary. Moyshe-Leyb Halpern, tr. fr. Yiddish by Benjamin and Barbara Harshav and Kathryn Helle. AYP

From My Rural Pen. T. S. Watt. FiBHP

From my sleeve a katydid. Joso, tr. fr. Japanese by Hiroaki Sato. Fr. Fifteen Hokku. FCEI

From My Thought. Daniel Smythe. GoYe

From my wind-blown book I look. Spring. W. R. Rodgers. AnIL

From My Window. Mary Elizabeth Coleridge. OBNC

From My Window. C. K. Williams. CAPP; SV

From my years young in dayes of youth. Epitaphium Meum. William Bradford. SCAP

From Mythology. Zbigniew Herbert, tr. fr. Polish by Czeslaw Milosz. FaBoPV; PwPP

From narrow provinces. The Moose. Elizabeth Bishop. DiPo; FaBoWP; NAAL-2

From near the sea, like Whitman my great predecessor, I call. Ode: Salute to the French Negro Poets. Frank O'Hara. GLP; NeAP; NNaP; PoM; PoNe

From noise of scare-fires rest ye free. The Bellman. Robert Herrick. CaPo; CH; OBS

From now on kill America out of your mind. James Agee. GOA

From now on may it go on falling. Teika, tr. fr. Japanese by Hiroaki Sato. Fr. A Compendium of Good Tanka. FCEI

From now on, the Earth. Test of Earth's gravity. Ferroconcrete sea. Report on the Poem. Otto Orban, tr. by Edwin Morgan. MHuP

From Oberon, in fairy land. Robin Goodfellow. Unknown. FaBoCh

From of old men of genius have been prey to kraken dragons. Inscribed on T'ai-po Shrine, at Colored Stone Jetty. Ch'ü Ta-chün, tr. by Paul W. Kroll. WFTU

From off his pointed head flies Herr Schmidt's hat. End of the World. Jakov van Hoddis, tr. by Edouard Roditi. VWA

From old Fort Walla Walla and the Klickitats. In the Oregon Country. William Stafford. AmFN

From Old Mrs. Mo of Heng Yang: A Letter to My Son, Lo Fu. Yip Wai-lim, tr. fr. Chinese by Dominic Cheung. IFON

From One of Case's Pill-Boxes. John Case. FaBoUs

From One of My Letters. Moyshe-Leyb Halpern, tr. fr. Yiddish by John Hollander. PeBMYV

From one shaft at Cleator Moor. Cleator Moor. Norman Nicholson. FaBoTw

From one shower comes hopes for a bumper harvest. After a Rain. Cha Shen-hsing, tr. by William Schultz. WFTU

From One Who Stays. Amy Lowell. BoWoP

From Orford Ness to Shingle Street. Dawn on the East Coast. Alun Lewis. OBWP

From Our Album. Lawson Fusao Inada. AmPA

From our loves, heat and light are taught to twine. Mutual Love. William Hammond. JCP

From Our Mary to Me. Alice Fulton. PPR

From Our Master. Whittier. See Immortal Love, Forever Full.

From Our Yoke. Jacob Glatstein, tr. fr. Yiddish by Benjamin and Barbara Harshav. AYP

From out a book into my lap. A Withered Rose. "Yehoash," tr. by Isidore Goldstick. TrJP

From out Cologne there came three kings. The Three Kings. Eugene Field. GN

From out my deep, wide-bosomed West. Rejoice. Joaquin Miller. PAH

From out of a wood did a cuckoo fly. The Birds. Unknown. PChr

From out of our/ dwellings have I heard. Desert Stone. Miriam Waddington. VWA

From out of the North-land his leaguer he led. Saint Leger. Clinton Scollard. PAH

From out of the waters it came with a moan. The Beast in Man. George Clutesi. HATNAP

From out the South the genial breezes sigh. The Mother. Unknown, tr. by George Barrow. OHIP

From out the stormy sea unto the shore. Azariah di Rossi, tr. by A. B. Rhine. TrJP

From Outside. Paul Eluard, tr. fr. French by Michael Benedikt. POS

From Outside Comes the Adequate Cause. Giulia Niccolai, tr. fr. Italian by Beverly Allen. DMI

From Paumanok Starting I Fly like a Bird. Walt Whitman. GOA

From peaks in the morning storm. Kyogoku Tamekane, tr. fr. Japanese by Burton Watson. Fr. Twenty-three Tanka. FCEI

From Pent-up Aching Rivers. Walt Whitman. BoLoP; NAAL-1; NOBA

From pitch and catch. Fungo. Stanley Plumly. AmPA

From plains that reel to southward, dim. Heat. Archibald Lampman. CaP; NOBC; OBCV

From plane of light to plane, wings dipping through. Evening Hawk. Robert Penn Warren. NAAL-2

From Plane to Plane. Robert Frost. MoAmPo

From pleasure of the bed. The Chambermaid's Second Song. W. B. Yeats. ErPo

From plum-tree and cherry. Flowering Currant. Patrick MacDonogh. ErPo

From point A a wind is blowing to point B. After the Broken Arm. Ron Padgett. EAS

From Potomac to Merrimac. Edward Everett Hale. PAH

From prehistoric distance, beyond clocks. Street Fight. Harold Monro. FaBoTw

From Pride's embraces and from Fortune's smiles. To a Lady Lately Married. Walter Savage Landor. FL

From Prince Atsumichi ("I tell myself not to doubt you"). Lady Izumi, tr. fr. Japanese by Hiroaki Sato. Fr. Fifty-one Tanka. FCEI

From Prince Atsumichi ("If I speak of love you'll think I am like everyone else"). Lady Izumi, tr. fr. Japanese by Hiroaki Sato. Fr. Fifty-one Tanka. LLLI

From Prison. Todros Ben Judah Abulafia, tr. fr. Hebrew by David Goldstein. TOF

"From public noise and factious strife." To a Young Gentlemen in Love; a Tale. Matthew Prior. TEP

From purling streams and the Elysian scene. Lines Spoken by the Ghost of John Dennis at the Devil Tavern. Thomas Gray. FL

From Rome, for More Public Fountains in New York City. Alan Dugan. Prf

From rude darkness the heroes rose. Passing Chao-ling Again. Tu Fu, tr. by Burton Watson. CoBCP

From Saiga's plain, where we serve. Akahito, tr. fr. Japanese. Fr. Manyo Shu. Ma

From Sand Creek, sel. Simon J. Ortiz.
"At the Salvation Army." STE

From Sand River to Ts'ai Rock, sel. Yang Chi, tr. fr. Chinese by Jonathan Chaves.
"After my illness, so hard to be a traveler." CoBLCP

From Santiago, spurning the morrow. The Destroyer of Destroyers. Wallace Rice. PAH

From Sappho to myself, consider the fate of women. Carolyn Kizer. Fr. Pro Femina, I. NMM

From Scars Where Kestrels Hover. W. H. Auden. FaBoPV
(Missing.) OxBTC

From school to Cam or Isis, and thence home. William Cowper. Fr. The Progress of Error. OBTV

From Sebek's dark waters. Canopic Jar. Rika Lesser. MAYP

From seeing and seeing the seeing has become so exhausted. The Panther. Rainer Maria Rilke, tr. by Robert Bly. NU

From Sex, This Sea. Douglas G. Jones. NOBC

From shadows of rich oaks outpeer. The Pike. Edmund Blunden. LiTM

From shores of Senegal, from Lake Omandaba. O My Swallows! Ernst Toller, tr. by Ashley Dukes. TrJP

From six o'clock I traversed to and fro. Verses to Miss——— J. Wilde. NOEC

From Skye, Early Autumn. M. L. Michal. PoSH

From Soil Somehow the Poet's Word. Kenneth Leslie. OBCV

From some faraway island whose name I do not know. The Coconut. Shimazaki Toson, tr. by Burton Watson. Fr.

From some sweet home, the morning train. The School Girl. William Henry Venable. AA

From something in the trees. For the New Year. Robert Creeley. NaP

From Sorrow Sorrow Yet Is Born. Tennyson. OxBSP

From stainless steel basins of water. The Operation. W. D. Snodgrass. InPK; TAP

From Stirling Castle we had seen. Yarrow Unvisited. Wordsworth. EnRP; GTBS; GTBS-P; PoRA

From Stone to Steel ("From stone to bronze, from bronze to steel"). E. J. Pratt. NoP

From such old boards. "Dangerous Condition": Sign on Inner-City House. Russell Atkins. CNA

From Susquehanna's farthest springs. The Indian Student; or, Force of Nature. Philip Freneau. AnAmPo; OxBA

From Table Isle. Unknown, tr. by Geoffrey Bownas and Anthony Thwaite. PeBJV; TSS

From that blest bed the hero came. Andrew Marvell. Fr. Upon Appleton House, to My Lord Fairfax. JCP

From that first flash when awful Love took flame. Louise Labé, tr. by Willis Barnstone. BoWoP

From that first night. Lady Izumi, tr. by Edwin A. Cranston. PBWP

From that high apple-tree, my love. The Apple Tree. James Keir Baxter. OxBC

From that last acre on oblivion's heap. Edna St. Vincent Millay Exhorts Little Boy Blue. Louis Untermeyer. *Fr.* Mother Goose Up-to-Date. MoAmPo

From that they found most lovely, most abhorred. Beginning. Alden Nowlan. NeAC; NIP; NOBC

From that time in Mexico. Cecilia. Julio Ortega, *tr. by* David Tipton. Per

From the/ Japanese cherries. Airmail Letter. Axel Schulze, *tr. by* Margitt Lehbert. WCI

From the XXIII Summer Olympics, the Poet as Report, *sel.* Joseph C. Fischer.
 Kind of Thanks, A. *Fr.* XVI. TSL

From the acorns on a round tray. Buson, *tr. fr. Japanese by* Hiroaki Sato. *Fr.* Eighty-seven Hokku. FCEI

From the age of the gods. Empress Kogyoku, *tr. fr. Japanese by* Geoffrey Bownas *and* Anthony Thwaite. *Fr.* Manyo Shu. Ma; PeBJV

From the airplane window everything is blue. Vision from the Small Blue Window. Ernesto Cardenal, *tr. by* Francisco X. Alarcón. Vol

From the Antique. Christina Rossetti. EnLoPo

From the Arabic; an Imitation. Shelley. OBEV

From the back it looks like a porch. For Esther. Stanley Plumly. LCAP

From the Ballad of Evil. N. P. van Wyck Louw, *tr. fr. Afrikaans by* Anthony Delius. PeSA

From the bathing machine came a din. Edward Gorey. OBAL

From the bedroom you can see. Return. John Montague. FaBCIP

From the beginning I was a pure man of the land of the gods. Written in the Second Month of 1861 when I Left the Temple and Returned to Lay Life. Tomobayashi Mitsuhira, *tr. by* Burton Watson. JLIC-2

From the beginning you were there. Fear. Gerhard Fritsch, *tr. by* Beth Bjorklund. CoAuP

From the besieged Ardea all in post. The Rape of Lucrece. Shakespeare. BeLS

From the bottom of the furious piling up of appalling dreams. Beyond. Aimé Césaire, *tr. by* Clayton Eshleman *and* Annette Smith. RHTwFP

From the broad sea plain. Emperor Fushimi, *tr. by* Steven D. Carter. WFTW

From the Brothers Grimm to Sister Sexton to Mother Goose; One Transmogrification. David Cummings. BXAP

From the Cadenced Roar of the Waves. Rosalía de Castro, *tr. fr. Spanish by* Kate Flores. DMH

From the *Caledonian Mercury.* Gavin Wilson. FaBoUs

From the Canton of Expectation. Seamus Heaney. CIP

From the cassowary's beak come streaks of light. Morning at Arnheim. William Jay Smith. NePoEA

From the Cavities of Bones. Patricia Parker. BlSi

From the center of the room to the center. Fish. Mario Satz, *tr. by* Willis Barnstone. VWA

From the Chinese. Michael Smith. CIP

From the cliff-top it appeared a place of defeat. The Cave. Arthur Rex Dugard Fairburn. ATNZ; PeNZ

From the cold hands of guards. Letters Come to Prison. Shahid. GLP

"From the colour the nature." Ezra Pound. *Fr.* Cantos, XC. VGW

From the commandant's quarters on Westchester height. Aaron Burr's Wooing. Edmund Clarence Stedman. PAH

From the confusion of estranging years. For Elizabeth Madox Roberts. Janet Lewis. QFR

From the Coptic. Stevie Smith. Mes

From the Corpse Woodpiles, from the Ashes. Robert Hayden. CAPP

From the Crag. Mani Leib, *tr. fr. Yiddish by* David G. Roskies *and* Hillel Schwartz. VWA

From the crevice of a cloudlet. Fellow Workers. "Marie." PF

From the crowded belfry calling. Bega. Marjorie Pickthall. CaP

From the dark mood's control. The Recovery. Edmund Blunden. MoBrPo

From the dark Stygian banks I come. Marvell's Ghost. John Ayloffe. APAS

From the Dark Tower. Countee Cullen. BANP; BPo; CDC; IDB; LiTM; NAAL-2; PoBA; PoNe; Son

From the dark woods that breathe of fallen showers. The Zebras. Roy Campbell. LiTB; MoBrPo; PrIm

From the dark yard by the sheep barn the cock crowed. The Henyard Round. Donald Hall. BLA; PPR; Psk

From the day you retired to this home of three paths. The Retreat of Liu Kuo-pao. Chang Yü, *tr. by* Jonathan Chaves. CoBLCP

From the deep mystery of the past I called her. Evocation. Amado Nervo, *tr. by* Samuel Beckett. MexPo

From the deepest part of a dream the escaped. Doorway to Time in Three Voices. Luis Palés Matos, *tr. by* Rachel Benson. InW

From the Depth of the Abyss. Paul Éluard, *tr. fr. French by* Stephen Spender *and* Frances Cornford. RHTwFP

From the depth of the dreamy decline of the dawn through a notable nimbus of nebulous moonshine. Nephelidia. Swinburne. *Fr.* The Heptalogia. BXAP; FaBoCo; FaBoNo; FaBoPa; HoPM, *first sixteen lines*; NA; Par

From the Depths. Otakar Fischer, *tr. fr. Czech.* VWA

From the Depths. Friederike Mayröcker, *tr. fr. German by* Beth Bjorklund. CoAuP

From the desert I come to thee. Bedouin Song. Bayard Taylor. AA; AnAmPo; FaBoBe

From the Diary of——. Fadwa Tuqan, *tr. fr. Arabic by* Hatem Hossaini. *Fr.* From behind the Bars. WPOW

From the dire monument of thy black room. Calling Lucasta from Her Retirement. Richard Lovelace. CaPo

From the drear wastes of unfulfilled desire. Disappointment. Thomas Stephens Collier. AA

From the dress-box's plashing tis/ Sue paper. The Catch. Richard Wilbur. BLA; DiPo

From the dull confines of the drooping West. His Return to London. Robert Herrick. CaPo; FaBoPP; FF; NAEL-1

From the dunes of your hair—your voice. Echo. Alfred Gong, *tr. by* Beth Bjorklund. CoAuP

From the Dust. Elaine Dallman. VWA

From the Embassy. Robert Graves. PoA

From the field behind our house, a low howling. Back Country. Joyce Carol Oates. Psk

From the firefly. Masaoka Shiki, *tr. fr. Japanese by* Burton Watson. *Fr.* Thirty-nine Haiku. FCEI

From the first cave, the first farm, the first sage. Violence. Robert Lowell. NoAM

From the first cry. First It Was Singing. Jon Silkin. NePoEA

From the Flats. Sidney Lanier. AnAmPo; NOBA; OxBA

From the forests and highlands. Hymn of Pan. Shelley. EnRP; FaBoCh; OBEV; PoEL-4

From the four corners of the earth. Carl Sandburg. *Fr.* The People, Yes, *sec.* 1. CMoP

From the frantic weather into his creaking tomb. His Necessary Darkness. Nancy Sullivan. TAP

From the German of Uhland. James Weldon Johnson. CDC

From the Greek Anthology. Robert Krinagoras, *tr. fr. Greek by* Kenneth Rexroth. SD

From the green woods. West Virginia Handicrafts. Kathleen Spivack. ER

From the Grove Press. Anthony Hecht. OBAL

From the Gulf. Will H. Ogilvie. PoAu-1

From the gurgling of the brook I cannot surmise whether it's the dragon's head or tail. Leaving the Mountains in the Rain from Yellow Dragon Temple. Yi Shun-ting, *tr. by* Timothy C. Wong. WFTU

From the hag [*or* hagg] and hungry [*or* hungrie] goblin. Tom o' Bedlam's Song. *Unknown.* ChTr; InvP; LiTB; Mes; PoEL-2; TrGrPo
 (Loving Mad Tom.) EnSB; HAP; NOBE; WeW
 (Mad Tom's Song.) RB
 (Roaring Mad Tom.) WiR
 (Tom o'Bedlam.) CH, *much abr.*; EBEV; FaBoCh; OAEL-1; OxBoLi; PoRA

From the half/ of the sky. The Approach of the Storm. *Unknown, tr. by* Frances Densmore. OBVE; TTTS

From the Hazel Bough. Earle Birney. HeIP

From the Head. Louis Zukofsky. VWA

From the heart of a flower. Leave It to Me Blues. Joel Oppenheimer. VGW

From the high blue sun:poked wheel of pure dispassion. Kraa. William Pitt Root. SM

From the high deck of Santa Fe's El Capitan. A Siding near Chillicothe. Richmond Lattimore. AmFN

From the high jump of Olympic fame. Babe Didrikson. Grantland Rice. ASP

From the high terrace porch I watch the dawn. On a View of Pasadena from the Hills. Yvor Winters. QFR

From the Highest Camp. Thom Gunn. Son; TwCP

From the hodge porridge. The Farmer's Wife. Anne Sexton. HoPM; LiTM; NePoEA-2

From the hold of this ship. Mediterranean. Israel Pincas, *tr. by* A. C. Jacobs. VWA

From the House of Yemanjá. Audre Lorde. NoAM; NoP

From the icy niche where men placed you. Death Sonnet I. Gabriela Mistral, *tr. by* David Garrison. BoWoP

From the Illinois Shore. Michael Sheridan. NAmP
From the immense hemicycle, from the blue fire of the earth. The Tree of Death. Claude Vigée, tr. by J. R. Le Master and Kenneth L. Beaudoin. VWA
From the Joke Shop. Roy Fuller. OxBC
From the Journals of the Frog Prince. Susan Mitchell. NIP
From the land of refuge. Week-Seek. Jim Tollerud. VoR
From the laurel's fairest bough. The Battle of Valparaiso. Unknown. PAH
From the Liturgy. Juan Gonzalo Rose, tr. fr. Spanish by David Tipton. Per
From the local office, orders flying thicker than comb's teeth. Confiscating Salt. Wang An-shih, tr. by Burton Watson. CoBCP
From the lone shieling of the misty island. The Misty Island. Unknown. PoSH
"From the long fronds." What Her Girl Friend Asked and What She Replied Regarding His Return. Unknown, tr. by A. K. Ramanujan. PLW
From the McMichael's. James McMichael. PPR
From the meat of books I ate with pleasure. I was. Peter Rosei, tr. by Beth Bjorklund. CoAuP
From the Milky Way. Otto Laaber, tr. fr. German by Beth Bjorklund. CoAuP
From the misty shores of midnight, touched with splendors of the moon. Tennyson. Henry van Dyke. AA
From the moment of your birth. God's Little Angel. Patrick J. Murray. TIRV
From the Monkey House and Other Cages: Monkey II. Irena Klepfisz. GLP
From the mountain shades. Birds at a Mountain Home. Emperor Fushimi, tr. by Steven D. Carter. WFTW
From the mountain's base. Dawn Blossoms. Empress Eifuku, tr. by Steven D. Carter. WFTW
From the mountains we come. Warrior Nation Trilogy. Lance Henson. NOVW; VoR
From the mouth of the Harlem Gallery. Lamda. Melvin B. Tolson. PoNe
From the mulberry-rope country of Silla. Lady Otomo no Sakanoe, tr. fr. Japanese by Hiroaki Sato. Fr. Manyo Shu. FCEI
From the North Pole. Benyamin Galai, tr. fr. Hebrew by Bernhard Frank. MHeP
From the North Saskatchewan. Eli Mandel. NOBC
From the north-west a cloud has come up. Prince Sumiya. Mongol Oral Tradition, tr. by C. R. Bawden. WTO
From the Nursery, sels. Jacob Glatstein, tr. fr. Yiddish by Benjamin and Barbara Harshav. AYP
  Boy and a Roll, A.
  Clock and Mommie.
  Night, Be Mood to Me.
From the obscurity of the past, we saw. Nat Turner. Samuel Allen. CNA; FB
From the old slave shack I chose my lady. Trellie. Lance Jeffers. CNA; FB
From the oracular archives and the parchment. Dylan Thomas. Fr. Altarwise by Owl-Light, IX. CMoP
From the Other Shore. William Pitt Root. MAYP
From the other side of the world. To Stanislaw Wyspianski. Katherine Mansfield. ATNZ
From the outer gate. Teika, tr. by Steven D. Carter. WFTW
From the Outside. Mafika Pascal Gwala. WMBCH
From the Pentlands, sel. John Buchan.
  Leap in the Smoke. PoSH
From the pipe pointing the way for me. Ozaki Hosai, tr. fr. Japanese by Hiroaki Sato. Fr. One Hundred Haiku in Free Form. FCEI
From the porch, if they hold to what there is. When Our Voices Broke Off. James Seay. MT
From the porch, in various ways. Boncho, tr. fr. Japanese by Hiroaki Sato. Fr. Twenty-one Hokku. FCEI
From the Prison House. Adrienne Rich. NNaP
From the private ease of Mother's womb. Baby Song. Thom Gunn. Fr. Three Songs. AnAn; NAs; RB
From the Rain Down. Rhina P. Espaillat. GoYe
From the Rain Forest. Desirée Flynn. BrRo
From the ravine pours silent angry darkness. From the Diary of—— Fadwa Tuqan, tr. fr. Arabic by Hatem Hossaini. Fr. From behind the Bars. WPOW
From the Righteous Man Even the Wild Beasts Run Away. David Bromwich. PoA
From the Rio Grande's waters to the icy lakes of Maine. Buena Vista. Albert Pike. PAH
From the Roof. Denise Levertov. NoP

From the Rooftops. Carlo Betocchi, tr. fr. Italian by I. L. Salomon. PFI
From the sad eaves the drip-drop of the rain! Desolate. Sydney Thompson Dobell. OBNC
From the Salt Lake City Airport—82. Joy Harjo. GOS
From the School of the Renowned Philosopher. Constantine P. Cavafy, tr. fr. Greek by Edmund Keeley and Philip Sherrard. VMG
From the sea came a hand. Two Hands. Anne Sexton. CAPP
From the sea of Tsukushi a great wind blows, blackening the sky. The Mongols Are Coming. Rai San'yo, tr. by Burton Watson. JLIC-2
From the slopes of the mountain. Clear Bright. Li Ch'ing-chao, tr. by Kenneth Rexroth. BoWoP
From the small life that loves with tooth and nail. Coventry Patmore. FaBoEE
From the soft dyke-road, crooked and waggon-worn. Haying. John Frederic Herbin. CaP
From the sombre clouds fell slow. Snow Song. Henrietta Cordelia Ray. CBWP-3
From the soul of a man who was homeless. Peace at the Goal. Ella Wheeler Wilcox. PWR
From the Spotted Night. Ray A. Young Bear. HATNAP
From the square. Kay-You-Enn-Aye Radio, Iowa. Michael Augustin, tr. by Margitt Lehbert. WCI
From the starry heav'ns descending. J. R. Newell. BLRP
From the start there's no. Sensai, tr. by Lucien Stryk and Takashi Ikemoto. ZPCJ
From the Suburbs. Louise Glück. Fr. Dedication to Hunger, I. AnAn; GeTw
From the sudden stilling of the mysterious breeze. Passing the Bridge of Immortal Encounter Looking for the Sublime Ascent Temple. Yi Shun-ting, tr. by Timothy C. Wong. WFTU
From the summit he called me. Cat Poem. Bernice Zamora. CCP
From the Sun Itself. Roberta Hill Whiteman. HATNAP
From the sustaining air. Larry Eigner. PoM
From the tattered banana tree after months of waiting. Banana. Charles G. Bell. ErPo
From the tawny light. Everything That Acts Is Actual. Denise Levertov. NoAM
From the thick cover of unknowingness. On the Curve-Edge. Abbie Huston Evans. NYBP
From the thick woods. And You Woods. Shin Dong-jip, tr. by Koh Chang-soo. ACKP
From the thin slats of the Venetian blinds. Underwood. Howard Moss. NePoEA-2; TwCP
From the Threshold to the Sky. Muhammad al-Maghut, tr. fr. Arabic by May Jayyusi and John Heath-Stubbs. MAP
From the time of our old Revolution. That Things Are No Worse, Sire. Helen Hunt Jackson. OHIP
From the time you came into my house. Sad Remembrance. Mei Yao-ch'en, tr. by Burton Watson. CoBCP
From the top of a bridge. The River Is a Piece of Sky. John Ciardi. PDV
From the top of Dragon Gate. Inscribed on My Ink Landscape Painting. Tao-chi, tr. by Joanthan Chaves. CoBLCP
From the tragic-est novels at Mudie's. Dora versus Rose. Austin Dobson. NOBL; PDV
From the Train. Marjorie Wilson. BoTP
From the Travels of Gulliver. Suniti Namjoshi. GLP
From the uttermost part of the earth. I Waste Away. Bible, O.T. Fr. Isaiah, XXIV: 16–20. TrJP
From the veranda I watch the jetsam. Turista. Mark Osaki. BrSi
"From the very beginning." Unknown, tr. by Lucien Stryk and Takashi Ikemoto. ZPCJ
From the very first coming down. The Letter. W. H. Auden. FaBoTw; MoP; NoAM
From the Wave. Thom Gunn. NAEL-2; NoP
From the white campanile a cannonade. Villages. Corrado Govoni, tr. by Felix Stefanile. PFI
From the wilderness remote he breaks. The Red-Man. Frank Prewett. HATNAP
From the wind I get/ the predicate of plants. Saved. Maria Teresa Horta, tr. by Suzette Macedo. PBWP
From the Window Down. Louis O. Coxe. NYBP
From the window I can see the corner of a gutter. The Gutter. Franco Fortini, tr. by Ruth Feldman. VWA
From the window of my grandfather's. Late Gothic. Phyllis Gotlieb. NOBC
From the Window of the Beverly Wilshire Hotel. Michael McClure. EAS
From the window of your sickroom, you look out. Farmyard at Chassy. Stephen Dobyns. AnAn
From the window 28th is slick with rain. Late Conversation. Mark Doty. NAmP

From the winter's grey despair. Ave, Caesar. W. E. Henley. *Fr.* In Hospital, XIV. BrPo

From the Workshop of Brancusi and Giacometti. John Haines. BLA

From the world submerged beneath the ground, in a maze. Man of the Stone City. Mahmoud al-Buraikan, *tr. by* Lena Jayyusi *and* Naomi Shihab Nye. MAP

From the years. Things Kept. William Dickey. NYBP

From Thee to Thee. Solomon ibn Gabirol, *tr. fr. Hebrew by* Israel Abrahams. EaLo; TrJP

From their first dawn, he embraced the night sensations. The Waterfall Song. Duane Niatum. NOVW

From their folded mates they wander far. Black Sheep. Richard Burton. AA

From thence into the open fields he fled. Spenser. *Fr.* The Faerie Queene, VI, 9. OBSC

From these bare trees. Chinese Winter. F. R. Higgins. BIrV

From these sights/ Take one, — that ancient festival, the Fair. Wordsworth. *Fr.* The Prelude [or, Growth of a Poet's Mind]: Residence in London. HAP

From this depth — I came only to draw water. Song of the Brightness of Water. Karol Wojtyla. CRP

From this far, late-come country that still keeps. Gordon Childe. David Martin. PoAu-2

From this high place all things flow. Watershed. Robert Penn Warren. PoA

From this hundred-terraced height. The Centennial Meditation of Columbia. Sidney Lanier. PAH

From this low-lying valley, oh, how sweet. Two Points of View. Lucian B. Watkins. BANP

From this Midland scene — glum slag heaps. George Eliot Country. Amy Clampitt. ER

From this swaying city. Birthday Poem from Venice. Patricia Beer. OxBC

From this time on. Yakamochi, *tr. fr. Japanese.* *Fr.* Manyo Shu. Ma

From this valley they say you are going. Red River Valley. *Unknown.* AS, *with music;* FaBoBe; FaFP

From thorax of storms the voices of verbs. George Barker. *Fr.* Pacific Sonnets, VI [*or* VIII]. LiTM; MOS; WaP

From three dark places Christ came forth this day. Upon Christ's Nativity or Christmas. Rowland Watkyns. OBWVE

From thy fair face I learn, O my loved lord. Michelangelo, *tr. by* John Addington Symonds. PeHV

From thy patient, who while here. Accompanying a Gift ("From thy patient, who while here"). Lizelia Augusta Jenkins Moorer. CBWP-3

From time to time, a butterfly. Chiyojo, *tr. fr. Japanese by* Hiroaki Sato. *Fr.* Seventeen Hokku. FCEI

From Titian's "Bacchanal" in the Prado at Madrid. Thomas Sturge Moore. QFR

From today forward. Tamekane, *tr. by* Steven D. Carter. WFTW

From to-morrow ever. Princess Oku, *tr. fr. Japanese.* *Fr.* Manyo Shu. Ma

From Tomorrow On. *Unknown, tr. fr.* Yiddish *by* Joseph Leftwich. TrJP

From tomorrow, who will visit. Teika, *tr. fr. Japanese by* Hiroaki Sato. *Fr.* A Compendium of Good Tanka. FCEI

From too much love of living. Swinburne. *Fr.* The Garden of Proserpine. OBD

From Travancore to Tripoli. Ballad of the Oedipus Complex. Lawrence Durrell. FaBoCo

From Trollope's Journal. Elizabeth Bishop. FaBoPV; GOA

From troubles of the world. Ducks. Frederick William Harvey. OnUR

From Tuscan came my lady's worthy race. Earl of Surrey. AAS; SiPS

From 22 I see my first 8 weren't. 22 Miles. José Angel Gutiérrez. FIA

From under the flat surface of the planet. Recitation for the Dismantling of a Hydrogen Bomb. Alan Williamson. BAP

From up my own sleeve I came. The Magician. Bin Ramke. MAYP; NAmP

From V. C. (a Gentleman of Verona). Gavin Ewart. OxBC

From Venice Was That Afternoon. Jean Garrigue. LiTA; NOBA

From Villahermosa,/ in Tabasco. Postcard from Mexico, 16.x.1973. Andrew Salkey. PBCV

From Virgil. George Oppen. *Fr.* Five Poems about Poetry. NNaP

From Water-Tower Hill to the brick prison. Point Shirley. Sylvia Plath. NIP; NoP

From what did man fall? The Passion of Christ. Denis Devlin. IPY

From what great sleep. Watts. Alvin Saxon. PoBA

From what proud star I know not, but I found. The Giant Puffball. Edmund Blunden. FaBoTw

From what, sometimes, seems an arbitrary. A Blessing. Mekeel McBride. SM

From Whence Doth This Union Arise? Thomas Baldwin. AH

From where dark clouds of curling smoke arise. Susanna Blamire. *Fr.* Stoklewath; or, The Cumbrian Village. NOEC

From where I live, from windows on four sides. Juniper. Robert Francis. VGW

From where I sit, I see the stars. Midnight. Archibald Lampman. OBCV

From where I stand now. 12 October. Myra Cohn Livingston. NTCP; RHPC

From where I stand the sheep stand still. Sheep. Robert Francis. LCAP

From Which War. Phillip Yellowhawk Minthorn. STE

From Whitehall Stairs, whence oft with distant view. Whitehall Stairs. Aaron Hill. NOEC

From Whitsuntide to Whitsuntide. A Ballad of a Bun. Sir Owen Seaman. CenHV

From Wibbleton to Wobbleton is fifteen miles. *Unknown.* OxNR

From William Tyndale to John Frith. Edgar Bowers. NePoEA; QFR

From winter-sleep. Ladybug's Christmas. Norma Farber. PChr

From withered trees we gather the silkworm floss. P'eng Sun-yü, *tr. fr. Chinese by* Daniel Bryant. *Fr.* North-of-the-River Rhymes, II. WFTU

From Witty Men and Mad. Thomas Randolph. OxBSP

From Wynyard's Gap the livelong day. A Trampwoman's Tragedy. Thomas Hardy. BeLS; NAEL-2; OBNC; OBNV

From year to year I shall return. Among High Hills. William Soutar. PoSH

From yon black clump of wheat that grows. The Lark's Nest. John Clare. PBBP

From yonder gilded minaret. Batuschka. Thomas Bailey Aldrich. AnAmPo

From yonder wood, make blue-eyed Eve proceed. Progress of Evening. Walter Savage Landor. OBNC

From Yorktown on the fourth of May. The Gallant Fighting "Joe." James Stevenson. PAH

From you, Beethoven, Bach, Mozart. Dead Musicians. Siegfried Sassoon. BrPo

"From you I have I been absent in the spring." Shakespeare. *Fr.* Sonnets, XCVIII. AWP; ChTr; EBEV; EiL; LiTB; NAEL-1; NOBE; OBEV; OBSC; TEP

From you, Ianthe, little troubles pass. Walter Savage Landor. *Fr.* Ianthe. OBNC; TrGrPo

(Ianthe.) OBEV

(Ianthe's Troubles.) GBL; NOBE

From you, Rose, I do not like. Rondeau for You. Mário de Andrade, *tr. by* John Nist. TTY

From your eyes I thought. Silences; a Dream of Governments. Jean Valentine. LCAP

From your high bridge wave & wail. Lev Mak, *tr. by* Dan Jaffe. VWA

From Zarkhi's Teachings. Moyshe-Leyb Halpern, *tr. fr.* Yiddish *by* Benjamin *and* Barbara Harshav. *Fr.* Zarkhi on the Sea Shore. AYP

Fronleichnam. D. H. Lawrence. GBL

Front, A. Randall Jarrell. OBWP; OxBC; VGW

Front Lines. Gary Snyder. PoE

Front Page. Abba Kovner, *tr. fr. Hebrew by* Warren Bargad *and* Stanley F. Chyet. IP

Front Porch: A Drama Critic Warns of Clichés. Evan Zimroth. ER

Front Street. Howard Moss. NYBP

Frontier, The. John Hewitt. BIrV

Frontier-guard, A/ I set out in the morning. *Unknown, tr. fr. Japanese.* *Fr.* Manyo Shu. Ma

Frontier-guard when I set out, A. Wakatoneribe Hirotari, *tr. fr. Japanese.* *Fr.* Manyo Shu. Ma

Frontispiece. May Swenson. CoAP; NePoEA; WPE

Frost. Stella Benson. OxBTC

Frost. W. H. Davies. BoNaP

Frost, The. Hannah Flagg Gould. BLPA

Frost. John Hewitt. NeIP

Frost. Edith Matilda Thomas. AA

Frost and snow, frost and snow. Ariel. David Campbell. CBAP; PoAu-2

Frost at Midnight. Samuel Taylor Coleridge. EBEV; EnRP; FiP; HAP; NAEL-2; NAs; NOBE; NoP; OAEL-2; OBNC; PoE; PoEL-4; PPP; PrIm; TOF

Silent Icicles, The, *sel.* FaBoRV

Frost called to water "Halt!" Hard Frost. Andrew Young. BoNaP

Frost has sealed. Tree in December. Melville Cane. MoAmPo

Frost has touched the bamboo grass. Teika, *tr. fr. Japanese by* Hiroaki Sato. *Fr.* A Compendium of Good Tanka. FCEI

Frost hits the *wu-t'ung* by the well, the dry leaves fall. Immortal at the River. Sun Kuang-hsien, *tr. by* Lois Fusek. ATF

Frost in the air and music in the air. The Waits. John Freeman. BoTP

Frost in the Corn, The. Robert McAlmon. AiP

Frost lashed out, The. The Funeral. Itamar Ya'oz-kest, *tr. fr. Hebrew by* Bernhard Frank. *Fr.* Ordeal by Fire. MHeP

Frost-locked all the winter. Spring. Christina Rossetti. OBNC

Frost looked forth, one still, clear night, The. The Frost. Hannah Flagg Gould. BLPA

Frost lustre washes the winter moon. Cold-night Moon—In the Manner of Meng Tung-yeh. Huang Tsung-hsi, *tr. by* Lynn Struve. WFTU

Frost on the Flower. Shakespeare. *Fr.* Romeo and Juliet, IV, v. FaBoRV

Frost on the Ground. Su Shao-lien, *tr. fr. Chinese by* Dominic Cheung. IFON

Frost on your tombstone. Visiting My Wife's Grave. Natsume Seibi, *tr. fr. Japanese by* Hiroaki Sato. *Fr.* Twenty-seven Hokku. FCEI

Frost-packed morning. Ozaki Hosai, *tr. fr. Japanese by* Hiroaki Sato. *Fr.* One Hundred Haiku in Free Form. FCEI

Frost performs its secret ministry, The. Frost at Midnight. Samuel Taylor Coleridge. EBEV; EnRP; FiP; HAP; NAEL-2; NAs; NOBE; NoP; OAEL-2; OBNC; PoE; PoEL-4; PPP; PrIm; TOF

Frost-sad, clouds of white hair. Miscellaneous Poems Written While in Jail. Ch'ien Ch'ien-i, *tr. by* Jonathan Chaves. CoBLCP

Frost shall freeze; fire melt wood. Maxims (Exeter Book). *Unknown, tr. by* Charles W. Kennedy. AnOE

Frost that will not fall from the grebe's wings. Princess Shikishi, *tr. fr. Japanese by* Hiroaki Sato. *Fr.* Seventy-eight Tanka. FCEI

Frost, the Red-nosed, *sel.* Nikolai Alekseyevich Nekrasov, *tr. fr. Russian by* Alan Myers.
 "No storm, but the forest is drumming." AAA

Frosts Are Coming. László Nagy, *tr. fr. Hungarian by* Alan Dixon. MHuP

Frosty Christmas Eve, A. Noel; Christmas Eve, 1913. Robert Bridges. LiTB; NOCV; OBCP; PoEL-5

Frosty Dawn. Rokunyo, *tr. fr. Chinese by* Burton Watson. JLIC-2

Frosty moonlight flows down the stairs. Fellow Wanderers Gather for the Night in Late Autumn. Cheng Wen-cho, *tr. by* Kang-i Sun Chang. WFTU

Frosty Morning, A. William Cowper. *See* Task, The:
 Tis morning; and the sun with ruddy orb.

Frosty Night, A. Robert Graves. CH; MoAB; MoBrPo; MoBS; OxBTC

Frosty, the bite of the autumn air. Blessing the Hounds. Mary Winter. GoYe

Froude informs the Scottish youth. A Hymn on Froude and Kingsley. William Stubbs. CenHV; FaBoEE

Frowardness of the Elect in the Work of Conversion, The. Edward Taylor. SCAP

Frowning, the mountain stronghold stood. The Lost Colors. Elizabeth Stuart Phelps Ward. AA

Frozen Fire. Floris Clark McLaren. CaP

Frozen Girl, The. *Unknown.* AS

Frozen ground is broken, The. In February. P. A. Ropes. BoTP

Frozen Hands. Joseph Bruchac. CDW

Frozen hands and feet come. Love. Kito, *tr. fr. Japanese by* Hiroaki Sato. *Fr.* Twenty-four Hokku. FCEI

Frozen Hero, The. Thomas H. Vance. NYBP

Frozen Jews. Abraham Sutskever, *tr. fr. Yiddish by* Cynthia Ozick. PeBMYV

Frozen Logger, The. *Unknown.* OBAL

Frozen Ocean, The. Viola Meynell. CH

Frozen, rotting, dark leaves. Scene from a Dream. Janet Campbell Hale. STE

Frozen Zone; or, Julia Disdainful, The. Robert Herrick. CaPo

Frugal snail, with forecast of repose, The. The Housekeeper. Vincent Bourne, *tr. by* Charles Lamb. GN; PoLF
 (Snail, The.) MoShBr

Frühling. K. O. Arvidson. *Fr.* The Four Last Songs of Richard Strauss at Takahe Creek above the Kaipara, I. ATNZ

Fruit and Government. Mira Teru Kurka. UL

Fruit breaks on the summer mouth. The Garden. George M. Brady. NeIP

Fruit of all the service that I serve, The. Sir Thomas Wyatt. SiPS

Fruit of Loneliness. May Sarton. PoA

Fruit, of the Earth. Cyril Dabydeen. PVCV

Fruit of the Flower. Countee Cullen. PoLF

Fruit of the orchard is over-ripe, Elaine, The. Lancelot. Arna Bontemps. CDC

Fruit of the Tree, The. David Wagoner. NYBP

Fruit on the trees is aging fast, The. Words to a Song. Agnes Nemes Nagy, *tr. by* Bruce Berlind. BoWoP

Fruit Plucker, The. Samuel Taylor Coleridge. CH
 (Fragment: "Encinctured with a twine of leaves.") OBNC
 (In a Moonlight Wilderness.) FaBoCh

Fruit Rancher, The. Lloyd Roberts. CaP

Fruit that was atop the shelf, The. Till the Sea Runs Dry. *Malay Oral Tradition, tr. by* R. J. Wilkinson. WTO

Fruit-tree's branch by very wealth, The. The Penalty of Virtue. *Unknown, tr. fr. Sanskrit by* Arthur Ryder. *Fr.* The Panchatantra. AWP

Fruit white and lustrous as a pearl. The Lychee. Wang I, *tr. by* Arthur Waley. FaBoCh

Fruitful earth drinks up the rain. All Things Drink. Thomas Stanley, *after the Greek of* Anacreon. AWP

Fruitionless. Ina Coolbrith. AA

Fruits and Vegetables. Umberto Saba, *tr. fr. Italian by* Henry Taylor. PFI

Fruits of Retirement. The. James Camp. SoTCo

Fruits of War, The, *sel.* George Gascoigne.
 "Conference among ourselves we called, A." OBWP

Fruits you give me are more savory than others, The. Marguerite Burnat-Provins, *tr. by* Cassia Borman. BoWoP

Frustration. Elizabeth Daryush. QFR

Frutta di Mare. Geoffrey Scott. ChTr; Mes; OBMV

Fryar was walking in Exeter-Street, A. The Crafty Miss of London; or, The Fryar Well Fitted. *Unknown.* OBSV

Frying Fish. Chan Ch'e, *tr. fr. Chinese by* Dominic Cheung. IFON

Frying Trout While Drunk. Lynn Emanuel. MAYP

Fæsulan Idyl. Walter Savage Landor. *See* Fiesolan Idyl, A.

FTL Addict Fixes, The. Bruce Boston. BWV

Fu-ch'un Mountains in myriad folds. Fishing Jetty. Ch'ü Ta-chün, *tr. by* Lynn Struve. WFTU

Fubsey, let us, you and I. An Inelegant Proposal. William R. Espy. SoTCo

Fuchsia and I seem happy now, The. Cloud Burst. Hubert Witheford. ATNZ

Fuchsia and ragweed and the distant hills. Cushendun. Louis MacNeice. *Fr.* The Closing Album. FaBCIP

Fuchsia Hedges in Connacht. Padraic Colum. TIRV

Fuck I want to be bound by devotion! Tortured. African Sunday. Maureen Owen. UL

Fucking cops are fucking keen, The. Evidently Chicken Town. John Cooper Clarke. FaBoPV

Fucking, I feel at one with the world. Christian Karlson Stead. *Fr.* Clodian Songbook. PeNZ

Fudge Family in Paris, The, *sels.* Thomas Moore.
 "After dreaming some hours of the land of Cockaigne." BIrV
 "At length, my Lord, I have the bliss." OBSV

Fugal-Chorus. W. H. Auden. *Fr.* For the Time Being; a Christmas Oratorio. LiTM

Fugato (Coda). Gad Hollander. VWA

Fugitive, The. Abdul Wahab al-Bayati, *tr. fr. Arabic by* Abdullah al-Udhari. MPAW

Fugitive, The. Alice Meynell. NOCV

Fugitive, The. Priscilla Jane Thompson. CBWP-2

Fugitive Slaves. Jones Very. TAP

Fugitive Slave's Apostrophe to the North Star, The. John Pierpont. AA

Fugitive's Apologue, The. Nanni Balestrini, *tr. fr. Italian by* Lawrence R. Smith. NItP

Fugs, The. Edward Sanders. PoM

Fugue. Shauqi Abi Shaqra, *tr. fr. Arabic by* Sargon Boulus *and* Peter Porter. MAP

Fugue. Constance Carrier. GoYe

Fugue. Howard Nemerov. TAP

Fugue, A. Ellen Bryant Voigt. KS

Fugue of Death. Paul Celan. *See* Black milk of dawn [*or* daybreak] we drink it at dusk [*or* nightfall].

Führer Bunker, The, *sels.* W. D. Snodgrass.
 Dr. Joseph Goebbels.
 "Stand back, make way, you mindless scum." TW
 "Say goodbye to the help, the ranks." CAPP
 Eva Braun. CAPP

Fuimus Fumus. Joshua Sylvester. FaBoEE

Fuji. Cees Nooteboom, *tr. fr. Dutch by* Scott Rollins. DuIn

Fuji alone. Buson, *tr. by* Geoffrey Bownas *and* Anthony Thwaite. PeBJV

Fujiwara no Nakamaro, Governor of Omi, Wrote a Poem on the Two Willows. Yasu, *tr. fr. Chinese by* Surton Watson. JLIC-1

Fujiyama/ is quite a sight, The. Gust Gils. *Fr.* Two Japanese Poems, I. DuIn

Fujiyama—we sell. Tourist Japan. Takenaka Iku, *tr. by* Geoffrey Bownas *and* Anthony Thwaite. PeBJV

Fulfill, O gracious God, to-day. Pentecost. Adelbert Sumpter Coats. TrPWD

Fulfillment. Helene Johnson. CDC; PoNe

Fulfillment. Vassar Miller. NePoEA-2

Fulfillment. William Augustus Muhlenberg. WGRP

Full and True Account of a Horrid and Barbarous Robbery, A, *sel.* John Byrom.
"Dear Martin Folkes, dear scholar, brother, friend." NOBL

Fulle be the year, abundant be the grain. Ezra Pound, *after the Chinese.* OBVE

Full Circle. Maud Sulter. DT

Full Consciousness. Juan Ramón Jiménez, *tr. fr. Spanish by* Robert Bly. NU

Full Cycle. John White Chadwick. PAH

Full days come striding with measured, The. Concerning the Awakening of My Soul. Henriëtte Roland-Holst, *tr. by* Jonathan Crewe. WPOW

Full early in the morning. *Unknown.* BoTP

Full Fathom Five. Arthur Rex Dugard Fairburn. ATNZ; PeNZ

Full Fathom Five. Sylvia Plath. MOS

Full Fathom Five. Shakespeare. *Fr.* The Tempest, I, ii. NAEL-1

Full fathom five thy father lies. June Mercer Langfield. FaBoPa

Full fathom [*or* fadom] five thy father lies. Shakespeare. *Fr.* The Tempest, I, ii. AWP; ChTr; EBEV; EIL; ELP; FaBoCh; HAP; HeIP; HoPM; InPK; InPS; LiTB; MOS; NAEL-1; NoP; OBEV; OxBSP; PoE; PoRA; TEP
(Ariel's Dirge.) GoJo
(Ariel's Song: "Full fathom five thy father lies.") GN; NOBE; OBSC; SeCePo
(Sea Dirge, A.) GTBS; GTBS-P; TrGrPo
(Song: "Full fathom [*or* fadom] five thy father lies.") PoEL-2

Full Heart, The. Robert Nichols. BoNaP

Full House. Terry A. Garey. BWV

Full in her glory, she as Tirzah fair. The Prophet Jeremiah and the Personification of Israel. *At. to* Eleazar Ben Kalir, *tr. by* Nina Davis Salaman. TrJP

Full in the hand, heavy. September Afternoon at Four O'Clock. Marge Piercy. NIP

Full many a dreary hour have I past. To My Brother George. Keats. EnRP

Full many a gem of purest ray serene. A "Prize" Poem. Shirley Brooks. FaBoCo; FaBoNo

"Full many a glorious morning have I seen[e]." Shakespeare. *Fr.* Sonnets, XXXIII. AWP; EBEV; EIL; HAP; LiTB; NoP; OAEL-1; OBSC; PoRA; PPP; SeCePo; Son; TEP; TrGrPo; WeW
(Full Many a Glorious Morning.) FaFP

Full many lift and sing. Negro Poets. Charles Bertram Johnson. BANP

Full many sing to me and thee. The Barren Shore. Coventry Patmore. GBL

Full Moon. Walter de la Mare. BoNaP

Full Moon. Robert Graves. NOBE

Full Moon. Robert Hayden. BPo

Full Moon. Sappho, *tr. fr. Greek by* William Ellery Leonard. AWP

Full Moon, The. Rocco Scotellaro, *tr. fr. Italian by* Lawrence R. Smith. NItP

Full Moon. V. Sackville-West. MoShBr

Full Moon. Elinor Wylie. MoAB; MoAmPo; OPOP; VGW

Full Moon and Little Frieda. Ted Hughes. OxBC; OxBSP

Full Moon at Tierz; before the Storming of Huesca. John Cornford. OBWP

Full moon easterly rising, furious, The. A Love Story. Robert Graves. CMoP; FaBoTw; LiTB; NAEL-2

Full Moon in Malta. Asphodel. BrRo

Full moon is partly hidden by cloud, The. A Fable of the War. Howard Nemerov. NePoEA; OBWP

Full moon is so fierce that I can count the, The. Europa. Derek Walcott. AnAn; NoP

Full moon is the mirror, The. Asadullah Khan Ghalib, *tr. by* Ahmed Ali. GoT

Full moon on the Colosseum, The. Colosseum. Harold Norse. TrJP

Full moon on the night of the seventeenth, A. The Night of the Seventeenth. Li K'ai-hsien, *tr. by* Jonathan Chaves. CoBLCP

Full moon. Our Narragansett gales subside. John Berryman. *Fr.* Dream Songs. CoAP

Full Moon, Rising. Jonathan Holden. GOYP

Full moon rising on the waters of my heart. Evening Song. Jean Toomer. BPo; CDC

Full Moon; Santa Barbara. Sara Teasdale. OBCA

Full moonlit night people. The Net of Moon. Mitchell, *tr. by* Jerome Rothenberg. STP

Full-nelsoned in earth's arms the Crusher sleeps. Last Lines on a Wrestler. X. J. Kennedy. CRP

Full night. The moon has yet to rise. Sodom. Herman Melville. *Fr.* Clarel. AmPP

Full nineteen centuries have passed since then. A Call to Pentecost. Inez M. Tyler. BLRP

Full of courage and promise like the geese gone away. The Prince Enters the Forest. Henri Cole. DiPo

Full of her long white arms and milky skin. The Equilibrists. John Crowe Ransom. CMoP; HAP; LiTM; MoAB; MoP; NAAL-2; NIP; NoAM; NOBA; OxBA; PPP; TAP

Full of oatmeal. Miss Norma Jean Pugh. Mary O'Neill. RHPC

Full of superstition. The New Notebook. Maria Banus, *tr. by* Laura Schiff *and* Dana Beldiman. AIW; PBWP

Full of the Moon. Karla Kuskin. PDV

Full of warning is the solution. Asadullah Khan Ghalib, *tr. by* Ahmed Ali. GoT

Full of years and seasoned like a salt timber. Islandman. Brenda Chamberlain. OBWVE

Full oft doth Mat. with Topaz dine. Earning a Dinner. Matthew Prior. NBLV

Full oft of old the islands changed their name. Epitaph on an Infant. Crinagoras, *tr. by* John William Burgon. AWP

Full often as I rove by path or stile. Wind on the Corn. Charles Tennyson Turner. EBVV

Full, ripe apple, a pear and banana. Rainer Maria Rilke, *tr. fr. German by* Christopher Hawthorne. *Fr.* Sonnets to Orpheus. SOTW

Full sail, reefed sail. Kyorai, *tr. fr. Japanese by* Burton Watson. *Fr.* Twenty Hokku. FCEI

Full summer and at noon; from a waste bed. Noon. "Michael Field." NOBVV

Full Tide. Paraire Henare Tomoana, *tr. fr. Maori by* Margaret Orbell. PeNZ

Full Valleys. Francis Reginald Scott. CaP

Full Vision. Henrietta Cordelia Ray. CBWP-3

Full Well I Know. Hartley Coleridge. Son

Full well I know that she is there. Stanzas in Meditation. Gertrude Stein. PoA

Full well it may be seen. Sir Thomas Wyatt. SiPS

Full well, my gentle sir, I know. To an Artful Theatre Manager. Lorenzo da Ponte, *tr. fr. Italian by* John Mazzinghi. *Fr.* Il Capriccio Dramatico. TrJP

Full Woman, Carnal Apple. Pablo Neruda, *tr. fr. Spanish by* Perry Higman. LPSS

Full year since, I took this eager city, A. An Irishman in Coventry. John Hewitt. BIrV; CIP

Fuller and Warren. *At. to* Moses Whitecotton. AmFP; BeLS

Fulling Cloth for Clothes. Hsieh Hui-lien, *tr. fr. Chinese by* Burton Watson. CoBCP

Fum and Hum, the Two Birds of Royalty. Thomas Moore. OBSV

Fun. Leroy F. Jackson. RAR

Fun with Fishing. Eunice Tietjens. FaPON

Function of Blizzard. Robert Penn Warren. AnAn

Function of Winter, The. Jay Parini. BLA

Function Room, The. Patrice Phillips. MAT

Functional Poem. Mark Halliday. PPR

Fundament Is Shifted, The. Abbie Huston Evans. NYBP

Fundamental Project of Technology, The. Galway Kinnell. BLA; CAPP; SM; SV

Funebrial Reflections. Ogden Nash. *See* Among the Anthropophagi.

Funeral. Murray Bennett. GoYe

Funeral, The. Walter de la Mare. CMoP

Funeral, The. Norman Dubie. InPK; MAYP; NoAM

Funeral, The. Donald Hall. Son

Funeral, The. "M. J.," *tr. fr. Polish by* A. Glanz-Leyeless. TrJP

Funeral. Bert Meyers. PCP

Funeral, A. Yisroel Rabon, *tr. fr. Yiddish by* Robert Friend. PeBMYV

Funeral, The. Stephen Spender. CMoP; MoAB; MoBrPo; NoAM

Funeral, The, *sel.* Sir Richard Steele.
Trim's Song: The Fair Kitchen-Maid. OxBSP

Funeral, The. Itamar Ya'oz-kest, *tr. fr. Hebrew by* Bernhard Frank. *Fr.* Ordeal by Fire. MHeP

Funeral Elegy on the Death of His Very Good Friend, Mr. Michael Drayton. Sir Aston Cokayne. OBS

Funeral Elogy, upon. Mrs. Anne Bradstreet, A. John Norton. SCAP

Funeral gent led us, The. Choosing Coffins. Raymond Souster. MoCV

Funeral Home, The. Robert Mezey. *See* In the Environs of the Funeral Home.

Funeral Hymn. William Walsham Howe. WGRP

Funeral Lament (Kommos) from Epiros. *Unknown, tr. fr. Modern Greek by* Elene Kolb. BoWoP

Funeral March for a Papagallo. Michael Malinowitz. BAP

Funeral March for the Death of the Earth. Jules Laforgue, *tr. fr. French by* William Jay Smith. CT

Funeral Music, *sels.* Geoffrey Hill. NoAM

"My little son, when you could command marvels." *Fr.* VI.

"Not as we are but as we must appear." *Fr.* VIII.

Funeral of Martin Luther King, Jr., The. Nikki Giovanni. AmNP; BPo

Funeral of Napoleon I. Sir John H. Hagarty. CaP

Funeral of Philip Sparrow, The. John Skelton. *Fr.* Phyllyp Sparowe [*or* Philip Sparrow]. ACP, *abr.*

Funeral of Time, The. Henry Beck Hirst. AA

Funeral Oration for a Mouse. Alan Dugan. HAP; NIP; OBD, *st.* 1; PPP

Funeral Plainsong from a Younger Woman to an Older Woman, A. Judy Grahn. GLP

Funeral Poem. Amiri Baraka. CNA

Funeral Procession. Oswald de Andrade, *tr. fr. Portuguese by* Jean R. Longland. ATCBP

Funeral Pyre, The. *Unknown, tr. fr. Anglo-Saxon by* Charles W. Kennedy. *Fr.* Beowulf. AnOE

Funeral Rites of the Rose, The. Robert Herrick. CaPo; OBEV

Funeral Song. John Fletcher *and* Shakespeare. *See* Two Noble Kinsmen, The: The Urns and Odours Bring Away!

Funeral Song. Hayiaku, *tr. fr. Tlingit Indian by* James Koller. STP

Funeral Song. Maruyama Kaoru, *tr. fr. Japanese by* Hiroaki Sato. FCEI

Funeral Song. *Unknown, tr. fr. Sotho by* Dan Kunene *and* Jack Cope. PeSA

Funeral Song for Mamie Eisenhower. Nellie Wong. BrSi

Funeral [*or* Funerall] stone, A. To Laurels. Robert Herrick. CaPo; SeCV-1

Funeral Trains. Ishihara Yoshiro, *tr. fr. Japanese by* Hiroaki Sato. FCEI

Funeral[l], The. John Donne. AWP; BoLoP; EBEV; EnLoPo; HeIP; MeLP; NAEL-1; NAWM-1; NoP; OAEL-1; OBEV; OBS; PoEL-2; PoRA; SeCP; SeCV-1

Funerall Song, A. *Unknown.* CH

Funeral's early, the concert is late, The. 1975. Abraham Sutskever, *tr. fr. Yiddish by* Cynthia Ozick. *Fr.* Poems from a Diary. PeBMYV

Funerary Portraits, *sels.* Rosanna Warren. NOAM
Hunter. *Fr.* II.
Mother. *Fr.* I.
Timarista and Krito. *Fr.* III.

Fungo. Stanley Plumly. AmPA

Funky Football. Ruby C. Saunders. BlSi

Funnel. Anne Sexton. MoAmPo

Funnels, The. Christian Morgenstern, *tr. fr. German by* Geoffrey Grigson. FaBoNo

Funnels In. Bruce Andrews. IAT

Funny. T.V. (2). Anselm Hollo. UL

Funny Fantasies Are Never So Real as Oldstyle. Lawrence Ferlinghetti. *Fr.* A Coney Island of the Mind. ErPo

Funny, how Felicia Ropps. Felicia Ropps. Gelett Burgess. FaPON

Funny Joke, A. Leon Stokesbury. MAYP

Funny Old Man and His Wife, The. *At. to* D'Arcy Wentworth Thompson. OnUR

Funny Rigs of Good and Tender-hearted Masters. *Unknown.* OBET

Funny the Way Different Cars Start. Dorothy W. Baruch. FaPON

Funny thing about a chair, A. The Chair. Theodore Roethke. TDD

Funny you should mention the beach. Was it 1978? Rocks and Deals. Geoffrey Young. UL

Fur in see bi west Spayngne. The Land of Cokaygne. *Unknown.* NOIV

Furies, The. Donald Justice. AnAn

Furious Gun, The. Sir Thomas Wyatt. PoE

Furiously I battle against animals and bottles. Identity of Imagery. Robert Desnos, *tr. by* Michael Benedikt. POS

Furl that Banner, for 'tis weary. The Conquered Banner. Abram Joseph Ryan. AA; AnAmPo; PAH

Furlough in heart and hand, the soldier at last walks. No Furlough. Stephen Stepanchev. WaP

Furnace is of stone and clay, A. The Fire Place. Eli W. Mandel. OBCV

Furnace of Colors, The. Vernon Watkins. NYBP

Furnace tolls the knell of falling steam, The. Elegy Written in a Country Coal-Bin. Christopher Morley. OBAL

Furnished Lives. Jon Silkin. NePoEA-2

Furnished Room, The. James Merrill. NOBA

Furniture. Phyllis Harris. NYBP

Furniture: humble, dependent. Judith Wright. *Fr.* Habitat, IV. CBAP

Furniture-Maker, The. Michael Waters. NAmP

Furniture of the Poem, The. Dennis Saleh. NeAC

Furred magnificence, the precious stones, The. Epiphany: For the Artist. Elizabeth Sewell. EyDe

Furry coat has the bear to wear, A. The Pig's Tail. Norman Ault. BoTP

Furry Home, The. J. M. Westrup. BoTP

Furth on the sey, with this, this dawyng spryngis. Queen Dido Rides Out Hunting. Virgil, *tr. into Middle English by* Gavin Douglas. *Fr.* The Aeneid [*or* Eneados], IV. OxBLMV

Furth on, with this, throuowt the sey we slyde. Aeneas Sees Italy. Virgil, *tr. into Middle English by* Garvin Douglas. *Fr.* The Aeneid [*or* Eneados], III. OxBLMV

Further Advantages of Learning. Kenneth Rexroth. TAP

Further Fables for Our Time, *sel.* James Thurber.
Morals. FaBV

Further in summer than the birds. Emily Dickinson. AmPP; NOBA; NoP; PoE
("Farther in the summer than the birds.") LiTA; PoEL-5; QFR

Further Instructions. Ezra Pound. *See* Lustra:
Come, my songs, let me express our baser passions.

Further Language from Truthful James. Bret Harte. FaBoCo; NOBL
(Truthful James.) CenHV

Further Notice. Philip Whalen. PoM; VGW

Furtive blow, more like, A. There was I. Leda's Version. James Harrison. NIP

Fury against the Moslems at Uhud. Hind bint Utba, *tr. fr. Arabic by* Bridget Connelly *and* Deirdre Lashgari. WPOW

Fury of Aerial Bombardment, The. Richard Eberhart. CMoP; FaBoMo; FF; FYAP; HeIP; HoPM; InPK; LiTA; LiTM; MoP; NIP; NoAM; NoP; OBWP; PrIm; RB; TAP; TwCP; UnPo; VGW; WaP

Fury of Cocks, The. Anne Sexton. CAPP

Fury of Flowers and Worms, The. Anne Sexton. BoWoP

Fury of Hating Eyes, The. Anne Sexton. TW

Fury Said to a Mouse. "Lewis Carroll." *Fr.* Alice's Adventures in Wonderland, *ch.* 3. NoAM; NoP
(Mouse's Tale, The.) FaBoNo

Fury this Friday broke through my wall, The. In Memory of a Friend. George Barker. OxBTC

Fury's Field. Cecil Bodker, *tr. fr. Danish by* Nadia Christensen. PBWP

Fuscus is free, and hath the world at will. In Fuscum. Sir John Davies. FaBoEE

Fuseli! I fancied the floor would tumble down. The Foreigner Remembered by a Local Man. Richard Howard. BAP

Fust Banjo, De. Irwin Russell. *Fr.* Christmas Night in the Quarters. AA; BLPA

Futile Rhetoric No. 1. Park Je-chun, *tr. fr. Korean by* Koh Chang-soo. ACKP

Futile to chide the stinging shower. Perspectives. Dudley Randall. AmNP

Futility. Wilfred Owen. CMoP; FaBoMo; GTBS-P; MMA; MoAB; MoBrPo; NAEL-2; NoAM; NoP; OBWP; RB; SeCePo; TrGrPo

Future, The. George Frederick Cameron. OBCV

Future, The. James Oppenheim. TrJP

Future and the Ancestor, The. Andrée Chedid, *tr. fr. French by* Samuel Hazo *and* Mirène Ghossein. WPOW

Future Generation. Nila NorthSun. STE

Future Generations. Margarete Beutler, *tr. fr. German by* Susan L. Cocalis *and* Gerlinde Geiger. DMG

Future Generations. Abraham Reisen, *tr. fr. Yiddish by* Leonard Wolf. PeBMYV

Future is for tomorrow, The. Anna Gréki, *tr. by* Mildred P. Mortimer. WPOW

Future Work. Fleur Adcock. DiPo

Futurist Aviator Speaks to His Father, Vulcan, The. Filippo Tommaso Marinetti, *tr. fr. Italian by* Felix Stefanile. PFI

Fuzz on the lip of seashells. Recipe for Salt. Barbara Brinson Curiel. ER

Fuzzy fellow without feet, A. Emily Dickinson. TAP

Fuzzy-Wuzzy. Kipling. BrPo; MoBrPo; TrGrPo

Fuzzy Wuzzy. *Unknown.* PYC

Fuzzy Wuzzy, Creepy Crawly. Lillian Schulz. RAR

Fuzzy Wuzzy Was a Bear. *Unknown.* NTCP

Fy let us a to the bridal. The Blythsome Bridal. *At. to* Frances Sempill. GBP

Fye foolish earth. . . *See* Fie foolish earth. . .

Fyftene Joyes of Maryage, The, *sel. Unknown.*
Disposing of a Pregnant Daughter. OxBLMV

G

G. Hilaire Belloc. FiBHP

G ("G, I wrote a poem about your face"). Rutger Kopland, *tr. fr. Dutch by* James S. Holmes. DuIn

G. I. Graves in Tuscany. Richard Hugo. CAPP

G. K. Chesterton. Humbert Wolfe. TrJP
G. K. Chesterton on His Birth. A. E. Housman. FaBoNo; NBLV
G. M. B. Donald Davie. OxBC
G stands for Gnu, whose weapons of defence. Hilaire Belloc. FaBoNo
G. Wilson humbly as before. From the *Caledonian Mercury.* Gavin Wilson. FaBoUs
Gaa-a-Muna, a Mountain Flower. Harold Littlebird. VoR
Gaberlunzie Man, The. *Unknown.* EnSB; GoTS; OxBB, *with music;* OxBS
"Gables are not burning, The." The Finnesburn Fragment. *Unknown, tr. by* Kevin Crossley-Holland. OBWP
Gabriel. Adrienne Rich. VGW
Gabriel, from Hevene-King. The Annunciation. *Unknown.* MeEL
Gabriel Preil, the Grand Duke of New York. The Grand Duke of New York. Dan Pagis, *tr. by* Robert Friend. VWA
Gabrielle, the terrapin, whose tiny eyes. The Terrapin. Elizabeth Smither. PeNZ
Gabriel's Blues. Calvin Forbes. PoA
Gadoshkibos. Diane Burns. STE
Gaelic bard they praise who in fourteen adjectives, A. The Ancient Speech. Kathleen Raine. *Fr.* Eileann Chanaidh. PoSH
Gaelic is the conscience of our leaders. Michael Hartnett. *Fr.* A Farewell to English. CIP
Gaeltacht. Pearse Hutchinson. BIrV
Gaeta from wool and weaving first began. In Gaetam. Thomas Bastard. FaBoEE
Gaffer Gray. Thomas Holcroft. NOEC
Gaggie. Jacob Glatstein, *tr. fr. Yiddish by* Benjamin *and* Barbara Harshav. AYP
Gaiety, *sel.* Richard Howard.
   Queer's Song. ErPo
Gaiety and Good Heart. Otto Orban, *tr. fr. Hungarian by* Edwin Morgan. MHuP
Gaiety of three winds is a game of green, The. White Goat, White Ram. W. S. Merwin. NePoEA
Gaily bedight,/ A gallant knight. Eldorado. Poe. AmPP; AnAmPo; AWP; FaBoBe; FaBoCh; FPL; NOBA; NoP; OxBA; RR; TAP; WiR
Gaily into Ruislip Gardens. Middlesex. Sir John Betjeman. OxBTC
Gaily they grow, the quiet throng. Heather Flowers. Eliseus Williams, *tr. by* Kenneth Hurlstone Jackson. OBWVE
Gain without gladness. Liadain. *Unknown, tr. by* Frank O'Connor. WPOW
Gal, I'm tellin you, I'm tired fo true. The Lament of the Banana Man. Evan Jones. PBCV
Galang dada/ galang gwaan yaw sah. Reggae fi Dada. Linton Kwesi Johnson. PBCV
Galathea, *sel.* John Lyly.
   Cupid's Indictment. EIL
   (Song of Diana's Nymphs, A.) OBSC
Gale in April. Robinson Jeffers. MoAB; MoAmPo
Galente Garden: II. Juan Ramón Jiménez, *tr. by* H. R. Hays. WSC
Galician Winter. Aba Shtoltsenberg, *tr. fr. Yiddish by* Dennis Silk. PeBMYV
Galilee. Perets Markish, *tr. fr. Yiddish by* Leonard Wolf. PeBMYV
Gallant Château. Wallace Stevens. MoAB; MoAmPo
Gallant courtier, A. Tanushi, *tr. fr. Japanese.* Fr. Manyo Shu. Ma
Gallant Fifty-one, The. Henry Lynden Flash. PAH
Gallant Fighting "Joe," The. James Stevenson. PAH
Gallant foeman in the fight, A. Robert E. Lee. Julia Ward Howe. PAH
Gallant frigate, *Amphitrite,* she lay in Plymouth Sound, The. Rounding the Horn. *Unknown.* OxBSS
Gallant laird of Lamington, The. Katharine Jaffray. *Unknown.* ESPB, (B *vers.*)
Gallant Ship, The. Sir Walter Scott. BoTP
Gallant Youth, who may have gained, The. Yarrow Revisited. Wordsworth. EnRP
Gallantly within the Ring. John Hamilton Reynolds. SD
Gallantry. Keith Douglas. NAEL-2; NoAM; OBWP
Gallants attend, and hear a friend. The Battle of the Kegs. Francis Hopkinson. AnAmPo; OBAL
   (British Valor Displayed.) PAH
Galleons in sea-pomp sails. An Armada of Thirty Whales. Daniel Hoffman. NePa
Gallery, The. Andrew Marvell. MeLP; NoP; OBS; PoE
Gallery, The. Tomas Tranströmer, *tr. fr. Swedish by* Samuel Charters. AnAn
Gallery of My Heart. King D. Kuka. VoR
Gallery Shepherds. Patricia Beer. OxBC
Galley, The. Petrarch. *See* Sonnets to Laura: To Laura in Life.
Galley of Count Arnaldos, The. Longfellow. OBEV
Galley-Slave, The. Kipling. BrPo

Galliass, The. Walter de la Mare. FaBoTw
Gallon of, A. Cumulus Clouds. Sheryl L. Nelms. TDD
Gallop apace, you fiery-footed steeds. Shakespeare. *Fr.* Romeo and Juliet, III, ii. GBL
Gallop of Fire, A. Marie E. J. Pitt. PoAu-1
Galloped from the hanged men on the swaying moon. Renderings and Sunderings of Cobbett's "Rural Rides." B. C. Leale. NPo
Galloping around, north and south. T'ang Yin, *tr. fr. Chinese by* Jonathan Chaves. *Fr.* Miscellaneous Feelings. CoBLCP
Galloping away from the pavilion in a great haste. A Toast to the Traveler. Sun Kuang-hsien, *tr. by* Lois Fusek. ATF
Galloping Cat, The. Stevie Smith. BrRo
Galloping collection of boards, The. Somewhere. Robert Creeley. NoAM
Gallow Hill. William J. Tait. OxBS
Gallows, The. Edward Thomas. FM; InPS; LiTB; MoAB; MoBrPo; MoP; NoAM; UnPo
Gallows and Cross. J. E. H. MacDonald. CaP
Gallows in my garden, people say, The. A Ballade of Suicide. G. K. Chesterton. FiBHP; NBLV
Galoshes. Rhoda Warner Bacmeister. NTCP
Galveston with a seawall. Wasn't That a Mighty Storm? *Unknown.* AmFP
Galway. Donagh MacDonagh. NeIP
Galway. Mary Devenport O'Neill. NeIP
Galway called out of sleep. Galway. Donagh MacDonagh. NeIP
Galway is a blackguard place. Clonakilty. *Unknown.* FaBoEE
Galway Races. *Unknown.* OxBoLi; SD
Gamarra is a dainty steed. The "Blood Horse." "Barry Cornwall." GN
Gamble. Linda Hogan. HATNAP
Gamble on Red. Pierre Kemp, *tr. fr. Dutch by* Fred van Leeuwen. DuIn
Gambler, The. *Unknown.* AmFP
Gamblers, The. Anthony Delius. PeSA
Gambler's life I do admire, du-da, du-da. The Gambler. *Unknown.* AmFP
Gambling. Royall Tyler. TAP
Gamboling Man, The. *Unknown.* AS
Game, The. Harold Bond. TSM
Game. Sándor Weöres, *tr. fr. Hungarian by* Jascha Kessler. FOC
Game/ Suppose it's just a game, A. Witold Gombrowicz, *tr. fr. Polish by* Louis Iribarne. *Fr.* The Marriage, Act III. PwPP
Game after Supper. Margaret Atwood. FaBoWP
Game at Salzburg, A. Randall Jarrell. NoAM
Game called kick the can, which used to last about a month, A. We Used to Play. Don Welch. Psk
Game of baseball is not a metaphor, The. Baseball. Gail Mazur. PPR
Game of Cards. Ilse Aichinger, *tr. fr. German by* Beth Bjorklund. CoAuP
Game of Chance, A. Howard Moss. PoA
Game of Chess, A. T. S. Eliot. *Fr.* The Waste Land, II. SCV
Game of Consequences, A. Paul Dehn. ErPo; FiBHP; NOBL
Game of Cricket, The. Hilaire Belloc. FiBHP
Game of Glass, A. Alastair Reid. NePoEA
Game of Life, The. John Godfrey Saxe. BLPA; BLPL
Game out of Hand. Allison Ross. GoYe
Game Resumed. Richmond Lattimore. NYBP
Game was ended and the noise, The. Football. Walt Mason. ASP; SD
Gamecock. James Dickey. HoPM; UnPo
Games. Ory Bernstein, *tr. fr. Hebrew by* Warren Bargad *and* Stanley F. Chyet. IP
Games. Sandra McPherson. LCAP
Games, *sels.* Vasco Popa, *tr. fr. Serbo-Croatian by* Anne Pennington. RB
   Ashes.
   Before Play.
   He.
   Hide-and-Seek.
   Nail, The.
   Rose Thieves, The.
   Seed, The.
Gammer Gurton's Needle, *sel. At. to* William Stevenson *and also to* John Still.
   Back and Side Go Bare, Go Bare. HeIP; InvP; LiTB; NAEL-1
   (Drinking Song.) WiR, , *at. to* John Still.
   (In Praise of Ale.) TrGrPo, , *at. to* John Still.
   (Of Jolly Good Ale and Old.) EIL
   (Song of Ale, A.) OBSC
     Jolly Good Ale and Old. NoP; OBEV; TrGrPo
Gampta, my little grey sister. The Desert Lark. Eugène Marias, *tr. by* Uys Krige *and* Jack Cope. PeSA

Gane were but the winter cauld. Gone Were but the Winter Cold. Allan Cunningham. CH

Gang of labourers on the piled wet timber, A. Morning Work. D. H. Lawrence. MoAB; MoBrPo

Gang wanted to give Oedipus Rex a going away present, The. Oedipus. Josephine Miles. WPE

Ganga. Thomas Blackburn. MoBS

Gangan my lane amang the caulkstane alps. Ice-Flumes Owregie Their Ladies. Douglas Young. SeCePo

Ganges, The. Norman Dubie. LCAP

Gangrel Rymour and the Pairdon of Sanct Anne, The, *sel.* Sydney Goodsir Smith, *after the French of* Tristan Corbiére. "But ae braithless note." OBVE

Gangrene. Philip Levine. VGW

Gangster's Death, The. Ishmael Reed. FoBA

Ganymede. William Plomer. PeHV

Ganymede and Helen. *Unknown, tr. fr. Latin.* PeHV

Gaol Song, The. *Unknown.* GBP

Gap in the Cedar, The. Roy Scheele. Psk; SM

Gar, The. Charles G. Bell. AmFN

Garage in Co. Cork, A. Derek Mahon. DiPo; FaBCIP

Garage Sale. Karl Shapiro. Psk

Garage Sales. Paul Sawyer. SoTCo

Garbage. Eric Tretheway. MOWH

Garbo Stepping In. Jean Balderston. SoTCo

García Lorca. Louis Dudek. MoCV; NOBC

García Lorca: A Photograph of the Granada Cemetery, 1966. Larry Levis. AnAn

Garcia Lorca Murdered in Granada. John Streeter Manifold. CBAP

Garcon! You—you. The Hero of the Commune. Margaret Junkin Preston. AA

Garden, The. Joseph Beaumont. JCP; OBS

Garden, The. George M. Brady. NeIP

Garden, The, *sel.* Abraham Cowley. Great Diocletian. ChTr

Garden, The. William Cowper. *Fr.* The Task, III. EnRP; FaBoRV; NAEL-1; PoE

Garden, The ("You are clear,/ O rose, cut in rock."), *sel.* Hilda Doolittle ("H. D."). LiTA; NoAM

Heat. CMoP; HeIP; InPK; MoAmPo; OxBA; PrIM; TAP; UnPo

Garden, The. Louise Glück. AmPA; NAAL-2; NAEL-2

Garden, The. Susan Griffin. *Fr.* Woman and Nature. NPGG

Garden. Hannu Mäkelä, *tr. fr. Finnish by* Aili Jarvenpa. SOP

Garden, The ("How vainly men themselves amaze"), Andrew Marvell. AWP; BLPL; HAP; InPS; InvP; JCP; LiTB; MeLP; MePo; NAEL-1; NIP; NOBE; NoP; OAEL-1; OBS; PoE; PoEL-2; PoLF; PoRA; PPP; QFR; SeCePo; SeCV-1; TEP; TOF; TrGrPo
(Thoughts in a Garden.) GTBS; GTBS-P; OBEV
"What wondrous life is this I lead!", *sel.* BoNaP; CH; ChTr

Garden, A. Andrew Marvell. *See* Upon Appleton House, to My Lord Fairfax: See how the flowers, as at parade.

Garden, The. Rose Parkwood. WGRP

Garden, The. Ezra Pound. AWP; HeIP; LiTA; MoAB; MoAmPo; NIP; NoP; OxBSP; PPP; SOTW; TwCP

Garden, The. Jacques Prévert, *tr. fr. French by* Michael Benedikt. POS

Garden, The. James Shirley. OBS

Garden, The. Mark Strand. CAPP; GeTw; NoAM

Garden, The. Jones Very. OxBA; TAP

Garden, A. John Wakeman. NPo

Garden, The. Robert Penn Warren. PoA

Garden, The. Oscar Wilde. *See* Impressions: Le Jardin.

Garden, The, *sel.* William Carlos Williams. "It is far to Assisi." CRP; FYAP

Garden: a butterfly, The. Issa, *tr. by* Geoffrey Bownas *and* Anthony Thwaite. PeBJV

Garden and Cradle. Eugene Field. AA

Garden and gardener He made. Thomas Kinsella. TIRV

Garden at Heidelberg. Walter Savage Landor. OBTV

Garden at St. John's, The. May Swenson. NePoEA

Garden beds I wandered by, The. A Conservative. Charlotte Perkins Gilman. AA

Garden Boy, The. Bonisile Joshua Motaung. WMBCH

Garden by the Sea, A. William Morris. *Fr.* The Life and Death of Jason, IV. CH; NOBE; OAEL-2; OBNC; PoEL-5
(Nymph's Song to Hylas, The.) OBEV

Garden called Gethsemane, The. Gethsemane. Kipling. FaBoTw

Garden close from end, The. Asadullah Khan Ghalib, *tr. by* Ahmed Ali. GoT

Garden descends towards the sea, The. H. O. V. de L. Milosz, *tr. by* David Gascoyne. RHTwFP

Garden Fancies, *sels.* Robert Browning.

Flower's Name, The. *Fr.* I. CTC

Sibrandus Schafnaburgensis. *Fr.* II. CTC; EBVV; TEP

Garden flew round with the angel, The. The Pleasures of Merely Circulating. Wallace Stevens. LiTA; MAT; OBAL

Garden Hose, The. Beatrice Janosco. NTCP

Garden in the Sky. Margery Lawrence. CN

Garden is a lovesome thing, God wot!, A. My Garden. Thomas Edward Brown. BLPL; FaBV; InPK; OBEV; PoLF; WBLP; WGRP

Garden is a *lovesome* thing? What rot!, A. My Garden. J. A. Lindon. InPK

Garden is covered in thick shadows of deepest green, The. Pacifying the Western Barbarians. Mao Hsi-chen, *tr. by* Lois Fusek. ATF

Garden is very quiet tonight, The. Dusk Song. William H. A. Moore. BANP

Garden-Lion. "Evelyn Hayes." ChTr

Garden Living. Wu Wei-yeh, *tr. fr. Chinese by* Jonathan Chaves. CoBLCP

Garden Lore. Juliana Horatia Ewing. OxBChV

Garden Moss under Snow. Kaneyoshi, *tr. fr. Japanese by* Steven D. Carter. WFTW

Garden of Abu Mahmoud, The. Naomi Shihab Nye. NAmP

Garden of Adonis, The. Spenser. *Fr.* The Faerie Queene, III, 6. NOBE; PoEL-1
"In that same gardin all the goodly flowres." NOBE

Garden of Amour, The. Guillaume de Lorris *and* Jean de Meun, *tr. fr. French by* Chaucer. *Fr.* The Romance [*or* Romaunt] of the Rose. PoEL-1

Garden of Appleton House, The ("When in the east the morning ray"). Andrew Marvell. *Fr.* Upon Appleton House, to My Lord Fairfax. NOBE

Garden of Cymodoce, The, *sel.* Swinburne. Sark. FaBoPP

Garden of Earthly Delights, The. Charles Simic. NoP

Garden of God, The. "Æ." WGRP

Garden of Love, The. Blake. *Fr.* Songs of Experience. AWP; EnLoPo; EnRP; FaBV; FABV; GBL; HAP; LiTB; MAT; NAEL-2; NoP; PoE; RB; SoSe; TEP; TOF

Garden of mouthings, A. Purple, scarlet-speckled, black. The Beekeeper's Daughter. Sylvia Plath. IHMS

Garden of my soul grows duller, The. The Unfading. "Marie Madelaine," *tr. by* Ferdinand E. Kappey. PeHV

Garden of Proserpina, The. Spenser. *Fr.* The Faerie Queene, II, 7. ChTr

Garden of Proserpine, The, *sels.* Swinburne. AWP; BLPA; BLPL; FaBoRV; FaBV; FaPoR; HAP; LiTB; NOBE; NoP; OBNC; PoEL-5; PoRA; SeCePo; TrGrPo
"From too much love of living." OBD
"Here, where the world is quiet." SCV
Proserpine. ChTr

Garden of Shadow, The. Ernest Dowson. OBNC

Garden of Ships, The. Douglas Stewart. CBAF; PoAu-2

Garden of Shushan! Before the Feast of Shushan. Anne Spencer. BANP; BlSi

Garden of Situations, A. Jack Anderson. PoA

Garden of Song, The. Moses ibn Ezra, *tr. fr. Hebrew by* David Goldstein. TOF

Garden of the Holy Souls, The. Eleanor Hamilton King. *Fr.* Hours of the Passion. ACP

Garden Party, The. Donald Davie. NePoEA

Garden Party. Sir Herbert Read. BrPo

Garden Seat, The. Thomas Hardy. GoJo; HAP; Mes; RB

Garden Song, A. Austin Dobson. BoNaP; OBEV; OBNC

Garden Song, A. Thomas Moore. BoNaP

Garden Song, A. George R. Sims. NOBVV

Garden that recalls the past, A. Saigyo, *tr. fr. Japanese by* Burton Watson. *Fr.* Sixty-four Tanka. FCEI

Garden was, by mesuring, The. The Garden of Amour. Guillaume de Lorris *and* Jean de Meun, *tr. fr. French by* Chaucer. *Fr.* The Romance [*or* Romaunt] of the Rose. PoEL-1

Garden Where There Is No Winter, The. Louis James Block. AA

Garden within was shaded, The. Thisbe. Helen Gray Cone. AA

Garden Year, The. Sara Coleridge. FaBoBe
(Months, The.) OxBChV; RHPC

Gardener, The. Evelyn Eaton. GoYe

Gardener. Emerson. *Fr.* Quatrains. OxBA

Gardener, The. Laurence Housman. TrPWD

Gardener, The. Sidney Keyes. MoAB; MoBrPo

Gardener, The. Louis MacNeice. *Fr.* Novelettes, III. FaBCIP

Gardener, The. Arthur Symons. BoNaP

Gardener, The, *sels.* Rabindranath Tagore. OBMV

In the Dusky Path of a Dream.
　　Yellow Bird Sings, The.
Gardener, The. *Unknown.* ESPB; GBP
Gardener, The. John Hall Wheelock. DiL; NYBP
Gardener, The. Herbert Zand, *tr. fr. German by* Beth Bjorklund. CoAuP
Gardener came running, The. Incident in a Rose Garden. Donald
　　Justice. CRP
Gardener in his old brown hands, The. The Gardener. Arthur Symons.
　　BoNaP
Gardener Janus Catches a Naiad. Edith Sitwell. MoAB; MoBrPo
Gardener stands in his bower-door, The. The Gardener. *Unknown.*
　　ESPB; GBP
Gardener to His God, The. Mona Van Duyn. TrCP; UnPo; WPE
Gardeners. David Ignatow. PCP
Gardeners, The. Christopher Reid. DiPo
Gardener's rule applies to youth and age, The. H. J. Byron. FaBoUs;
　　NBLV
Gardenias. Mark Doty. NAmP
Gardens. Neil Curry. NPo
Gardens Are All My Heart. Eve Triem. GoYe
Gardens, Betrayed, The. Mark Insingel, *tr. fr. Dutch by* James S.
　　Holmes. DuIn
Gardens for the Fire and the Rain. Muhammad al-Asad, *tr. fr. Arabic by*
　　Lena Jayyusi *and* Charles Doria. MAP
Garden's grillwork gate, The. Plainness. Jorge Luis Borges, *tr. by*
　　Norman Thomas Di Giovanni. NYBP
Gardens No Emblems. Donald Davie. LiTM; NePoEA-2; OAEL-2
Gardens of Alcinous, The ("Close to the gates a spacious garden lies").
　　Homer, *tr. fr. Greek by* Pope. *Fr.* Odyssey, VII. OAEL-1; OBVE
Gardens of Alcinous, The ("Without the hall, and close upon the gate").
　　Homer, *tr. fr. Greek by* George Chapman. *Fr.* Odyssey, VII.
　　OAEL-1; OBVE
Gardens of Proserpine, The. Turner Cassity. PoA
Garden's quit with me, The: as yesterday. The Garden. Joseph
　　Beaumont. JCP; OBS
Gare du Midi. W. H. Auden. OxBSP
Garfield's Ride at Chickamauga. Hezekiah Butterworth. PAH
Gargantua, *sel.* Rabelais, *tr. fr. French by* Sir Thomas Urquhart.
　　Inscription above the Entrance to the Abbey of Theleme. FaBoRV
Gargoyle. Thomas Rabbitt. MAYP; MT
Gargoyle. Carl Sandburg. MoP; NoAM; NOBA
Gargoyle. Robert B. Shaw. CRP
Gargoyle spits out a sparrow to a peach tree, A. Onitsura, *tr. fr. Japanese*
　　by Hiroaki Sato. *Fr.* Twenty-three Hokku. TTTS
Garibaldi Hymn, The. Luigi Mercantini, *tr. fr. Italian.* WBLP
Garland and the Girdle, The. Michelangelo, *tr. fr. Italian by* John
　　Addington Symonds. AWP
Garland for a Propagandist. Ted Pauker. NOBL
Garland for a Storyteller. Jessie Farnham. GoYe
Garland for Heliodora, A. Meleager, *tr. fr. Greek by* "Christopher
　　North." AWP
Garland of Precepts, A. Phyllis McGinley. NBLV
Garland of roses, whether you come. Martial, *tr. by* James Michie.
　　FaBoEE
Garland Sunday. Padraic Colum. GoYe
Garlande [*or* Garlands] of Laurell, The, *sels.* John Skelton.
　　To Maystres Jane Blenner-Haiset. AAS
　　To Mistress [*or* Maystres] Isabell Pennell. AAS; InPS; NAs; NOBE;
　　　OBEV; OBSC; OxBoLi; PoEL-1; TrGrPo; TTTS
　　　(In Praise of Isabel Pennell.) CH
　　To Mistress [*or* Maystres] Margaret Hussey. AAS; ACP; EBEV;
　　　EnLoPo; GN; GoJo; HeIP; HoPM; InPS; NOBE; NoP; OAEL-1;
　　　OBEV; OBSC; PoEL-1; PoRA; PPP; SCV; TrGrPo
　　　(Mistress Margaret Hussey.) FaBoCh
　　To Mistress Margaret Tilney. MeEL
　　To Mistress Margery Wentworth. EBEV; EnLoPo; NOBE; OAEL-1;
　　　OBEV; OBSC; TrGrPo
Garlic, The. Bert Meyers. VWA
Garlic like a pearl . . . why? garlic is but garlic. Garwolin—a Town for
　　Ever. Miron Bialoszewski, *tr. by* Czeslaw Milosz. PwPP
Garment is thin, The. Lady Otomo no Sakanoe, *tr. fr. Japanese. Fr.*
　　Manyo Shu. Ma
Garment of Good Ladies, The. Robert Henryson. ACP
Garments of inattention, oh mere items. Teaching Swift to Young Ladies.
　　William Dickey. PoA
Garmont of Gude Ladies, The. Robert Henryson. *See* Wold my guide
　　lady luve me best.
Garnishing the Aviary. Margaret Danner. *Fr.* Far from Africa: Four
　　Poems, I. BPo
Garret, The. Ezra Pound. AnAmPo; SOTW
Garrison. Amos Bronson Alcott. AA

Garrison Town. Emanuel Litvinoff. WaP
Garrisons pent up in a little fort. Sonnet of Brotherhood. R. A. K.
　　Mason. ATNZ; PeNZ
Garrotted Man, The. Barry Goldensohn. NAmP
Garrulous old man who once had owned, The. Under the Casuarina.
　　Elizabeth Riddell. PoAu-2
Garwolin—a Town for Ever. Miron Bialoszewski, *tr. fr. Polish by*
　　Czeslaw Milosz. PwPP
Gary Gotow. George Uba. BrSi
Gas. Jean Day. IAT
Gas and Hot Air. Morris Bishop. OBAL
Gas fire, The. The Persian. Stevie Smith. FaBoWP
Gas from a Burner. James Joyce. TW
Gas Lamp. Willis Barnstone. VWA
Gas-lamps abandoned by the night burn on. Baudelaire in Brussels.
　　Anthony Cronin. BIrV
Gas ring's hoarse exhaling wheeze, The. Twinings Orange Pekoe. Judith
　　Moffett. PoA; SM
Gas Station, The. C. K. Williams. CAPP
Gas was on in the Institute, The. A Shropshire Lad. Sir John Betjeman.
　　MoBS
Gasbags. *Unknown.* NOBL
Gascoigne's Good-Morrow. George Gascoigne. AAS; NOCV
Gascoigne's [*or* Gascoygnes] Good-Night. George Gascoigne. AAS;
　　NOCV
Gascoigne's Lullaby [*or* Lullabie]. George Gascoigne. *See* Sing Lullaby,
　　as women doe.
Gascoigne's Memories, *sels.* George Gascoigne.
　　All Were Too Little. Son
　　And Every Year a World. Son
　　Before Mine Eye. Son
　　For Why the Gains. Son
　　"In haste poste haste, when first my wandring minde." AAS; Son
　　No Haste but Good. Son
　　To Prink Me Up. Son
Gascoigne's Woodmanship. George Gascoigne. AAS; PoEL-1; QFR
Gasholders, russet among fields. Geoffrey Hill. *Fr.* Mercian Hymns,
　　VII. HAP; NoAM; NoP
Gasp, and it was gone!, A. *Unknown, tr. fr. Japanese by* Hiroaki Sato.
　　Fr. Inutsukuba Shu. FCEI
Gassing the woodchucks didn't turn out right. Woodchucks. Maxine W.
　　Kumin. CAPP; HoPM; NIP
Gastrology, *sel.* Archestratus, *tr. fr. Greek by* Isaac D'Israeli.
　　"I write these precepts for immortal Greece." FaBoUs
Gastronomy. Adriaan Morriën, *tr. fr. Dutch by* James S. Holmes. DuIn
Gate, The. Edwin Muir. CMoP; LiTM
Gate at the End of Things, The. *Unknown.* BLPA
Gate of Horn. William Rose Benét. AnAmPo
Gate of Teeth, The. Sándor Weöres, *tr. fr. Hungarian by* Jascha Kessler.
　　FOC
Gate, open. Sanatorium. H. Leivick, *tr. by* Cynthia Ozick. PeBMYV
Gate was open, The; the fence under the aspens, fallen. Mountain Corral.
　　Helen Sorrells. WPE
Gateposts. Medbh McGuckian. FaBCIP
Gates are open on the road, The. The Seekers. Charles Hamilton Sorley.
　　WGRP
Gates clanged and they walked you into jail, The. The Conscientious
　　Objector. Karl Shapiro. OxBA
Gates fly open with a pretty sound, The. Under the Hill. Daryl Hine.
　　MoCV
Gates of Damascus. James Elroy Flecker. BrPo
Gates of Hell, The. Dante, *tr. fr. Italian by* Laurence Binyon. *Fr.*
　　Divina Commedia: Inferno, III. PFI
Gates of Paradise, The, *sel.* Blake.
　　Epilogue: "Truly, my Satan, thou art but a dunce." HAP; OAEL-2;
　　　OBNC; WeW
　　(To the Accuser Who Is the God of This World.) NoP; OxBSP;
　　　TrGrPo
Gate's Open, The. John Blight. CBAP
Gates to England, The. Marjorie Wilson. BoTP
Gateway, The. A. D. Hope. BoLoP; ErPo
Gateway Arch. Cheng Ch'ou-yu, *tr. fr. Chinese by* Dominic Cheung.
　　IFON
Gather all kindreds of this boundless realm. The Poet. Cornelius
　　Mathews. AA
Gather for festival. Hilda Doolittle ("H. D."). *Fr.* Songs from Cyprus,
　　I. MoAmPo
Gather into the mind. First of August. A. J. Seymour. PBCV
Gather me up. Songs of the Priestess. Malka Heifetz-Tussman, *tr. by*
　　Marcia Falk. PeBMYV; VWA

Gather the Rose. Spenser. *See* Faerie Queene, The: Whiles someone did chant this lovely lay, The.

Gather while you may. Rose. Kathleen Raine. WPE

Gather ye bank-notes while ye may. Election Time. *Unknown.* FaBoPa

Gather, ye brave sons of Ukadi Awaka! Moon Song. Chuba Nweke. PBA

Gather Ye Rosebuds. Laurence Fowler. BXAP

Gather ye rosebuds while ye may. To [the] Virgins, to Make Much of Time. Robert Herrick. AWP; BLPA; BoLoP; CaPo; ChTr; ELP; EnLoPo; ErPo; FaBV; FaFP; FF; FPL; GBL; HAP; HeIP; InPK; InPS; JCP; LiTB; NAEL-1; NBLV; NIP; NOBE; NoP; OAEL-1; OBEV; OBS; PoE; PoEL-3; PrIm; QFR; SCV; SeCP; SeCV-1; SoSe; TEP; TrGrPo

(Counsel to Girls.) GTBS; GTBS-P

(To Virgins, to Make Much of Time.) SCV

Gather ye soap-suds while ye may. Counsel to Girls. Archibald Stodart-Walker. *Fr.* The Moxford Book of English Verse. CenHV

Gathered at the River. Denise Levertov. PPR; SV

Gathered in inter-admiration. When the Five Prominent Poets. Josephine Jacobsen. TAP

Gathered under leaded/ skies. Manomin. Phyllis Wolf. STE

Gathering, The. Archie Randolph Ammons. BLA

Gathering, The. E. J. Pratt. *Fr.* Towards the Last Spike. MoCV; OBCV

Gathering, The. Sir Walter Scott. *Fr.* The Lady of the Lake. OBNC

Gathering, The. Herbert B. Swett. PAH

Gathering Cattle in the Deertracks Pasture. Drummond Hadley. CowP

Gathering Leaves. Robert Frost. RB; VGW

Gathering Lotus. Huang-fu Sung, *tr. fr. Chinese* by Lois Fusek. ATF

Gathering Lotus with Singing Girls. Mo Shih-lung, *tr. fr. Chinese* by Jonathan Chaves. CoBLCP

Gathering Mushrooms. Alistair Campbell. ATNZ

Gathering Mushrooms. Paul Muldoon. CIP

Gathering of the People, The. William James Linton. PF

Gathering Song of Donald the Black. Sir Walter Scott. *See* Pibroch of Donuil Dhu.

Gathering Song of Donuil Dhu. Sir Walter Scott. *See* Pibroch of Donuil Dhu.

Gathering Strength. Leo Dangel. MOWH

Gathering the bloom of all the fairest boys that be. Strato, *tr.* by Sydney Oswald. PeHV

Gathering the Bones Together. Gregory Orr. AmPA; GeTw; Psk

Gathering the May rains. Basho, *tr. fr. Japanese* by Burton Watson. *Fr.* Seventy-six Hokku. FCEI

Gathering the Mulberry. Ho Ning, *tr. fr. Chinese* by Lois Fusek. ATF

Gathering the Sparks. Howard Schwartz. VWA

Gathering water-oats. Mizuhara Shuoshi, *tr.* by Geoffrey Bownas and Anthony Thwaite. PeBJV

Gatigwanasti, Ayunini, Suate. Owl and Rooster. Gladys Cardiff. STE

Gatineaus, The. James Wreford Watson. CaP

Gaucelm, three plays of love. Gaucelm Faidit, *tr.* by Paul Blackburn. Pro

Gaudy leaves of autumn, The. *Unknown*, *tr.* by Burton Watson. FCEI

Gauger walked with willing foot, The. A Song of the Road. Robert Louis Stevenson. BrPo

Gauguin. Derek Walcott. NoAM

Gauley Bridge. Muriel Rukeyser. NNaP

Gauley Bridge is a good town for Negroes. George Robinson: Blues. Muriel Rukeyser. NNaP

Gauls Sacrifice, The. C. M. Doughty. *Fr.* The Dawn in Britain. FaBoTw

Gaunt brown walls, The. Interior. William Ernest Henley. *Fr.* In Hospital, III. BrPo

Gaunt in gloom. Nightpiece. James Joyce. PoA

Gaunt in the midst of the prairie. Chicago. John Boyle O'Reilly. PAH

Gaunt kept house with her child for the old man. Montana Fifty Years Ago. J. V. Cunningham. Prf

Gaunt, rueful knight, on raw-boned, shambling hack. Don Quixote. Craven Langstroth Betts. AA

Gaunt thing, The. Babylon Revisited. Imamu Amiri Baraka. BPo; MoP; NoAM; TW

Gautama in the Deer Park at Benares. Kenneth Patchen. NaP

Gave me things I. Swallow the Lake. Clarence Major. PoBA

Gave proof through the night. Poem to My Sister, Ethel Ennis, Who Sang "The Star-spangled Banner" at the Second Inauguration of Richard Milhous Nixon. June Jordan. TAP

Gawain and the Lady of the Castle. *Unknown*, *tr. fr. Middle English by* Brian Stone. *Fr.* Sir Gawain and the Green Knight. EBEV

Gawayn spurred on, and he picked out a path. Sir Gawayn Goes to Receive His Return Blow from the Green Knight. *Unknown*, *tr. fr.*

Middle English by Brian Stone. *Fr.* Sir Gawain and the Green Knight. FaBoPP

Gay, The. "Æ." OBMV

Gay belles of fashion may boast of excelling, The. The Needle. Samuel Woodworth. GN

Gay blade on the gentle hedgerow. Daffodil. Waldo Williams, *tr. by* Gwyn Jones. OBWVE

Gay Boys. James Kirkup. PeHV

Gay citizen, myself, and thoughtful friend. Allen Tate. *Fr.* More Sonnets at Christmas, IV. LiTA; LiTM

Gay Epiphany. James Mitchell. PeHV

Gay, gay, gay, gay. Remember the Day of Judgement. *Unknown.* MeEL

Gay go up and gay go down. The Bells of London. *Unknown.* BoTP; OxNR; PoRA

(London Bells.) ChTr; LiTB; OxBoLi

Gay Goshawk [*or* Goss-Hawk], The. *At. to* Anna Gordon Brown. ESPB, A *and* E *vers.*; GN; OxBB, *with music*; WPE

Gay, guiltless pair. The Winged Worshippers. Charles Sprague. AA

Gay little Girl-of-the-Diving-Tank. At the Carnival. Anne Spencer. BANP; BlSi; CDC; PoNe

Gay Old Hag, The. *Unknown.* BIrV

Gay Psalm from Fort Valley, A. Louie Crew. GLP

Gay Robin Is Seen No More. Robert Bridges. BoTP

Gay the flower,/ Lush its leaves. *Unknown*, *tr. by* Arthur Waley. BoS

Gaze North-east. *Unknown*, *tr. fr. Irish by* John Montague. BIrV

Gaze not on Swans, in whose soft breast. Beauty Extoll'd. *At. to* Henry Noel *and to* William Strode. CuTr; ELP; OBS

(On His Mistress.) PoEL-2

Gaze not on thy beauties pride. Good Counsel [*or* Counsell] to a Young Maid. Thomas Carew. OBS

(Song: Good Counsel to a Young Maid.) CaPo

Gaze not upon my outside, friend. Apple Dumplings. Mary E. Tucker. CBWP-1

Gazelle, The. Yasin Taha Hafiz, *tr. fr. Arabic by* Sharif Elmusa *and* Christopher Middleton. MAP

Gazelle, A. Richard Henry Stoddard. AA

Gazelle Calf, The. D. H. Lawrence. OxBTC; RB

Gazelle-girl/gazelle. King Solomon Vistas. Ian Wedde. ATNZ; PeNZ

Gazelle I send you to the wolves not in the wood they're. Amir Gilboa, *tr. by* Warren Bargad *and* Stanley F. Chyet. IP

Gazelles, The. T. Sturge Moore. BrPo; OBMV

Gazelles and Unicorn. John Gray. *Fr.* The Long Road. ChTr

Gazeteer of Newfoundland. Michael Harrington. CaP

Gazing After the Distant Traveler. Li Hsün, *tr. fr. Chinese by* Lois Fusek. ATF

Gazing after the Distant Traveler. Wei Chuang, *tr. fr. Chinese by* Lois Fusek. ATF

Gazing at Ch'ang-po Mountain. Li K'ai-hsien, *tr. fr. Chinese by* Jonathan Chaves. CoBLCP

Gazing at the hand you squeezed. Lady Heguri, *tr. fr. Japanese.* *Fr.* Manyo Shu. Ma

Gazing at the sky. Ietaka, *tr. by* Steven D. Carter. WFTW

Gazing at them. Saigyo, *tr. fr. Japanese by* Burton Watson. *Fr.* Sixty-four Tanka. FCEI

Gazing west—the isles of paradise. Waiting for the Ferry at Inchon. Liu E, *tr. by* Jonathan Chaves. CoBLCP

Gean Trees, The. Violet Jacob. PoSH

Gebir, *sel.* Walter Savage Landor.

Tamar's Wrestling. *Fr.* I. EnRP

(Shepherd and the Nymph, The.) OBNC

Gee Ho, Dobin. *Unknown.* CoMu

Gee I Like to Think of Dead. E. E. Cummings. HoPM

Gee, Officer Krupke. Stephen Sondheim. OBAL

Gee up, Neddy, to the fair. *Unknown.* OxNR

Geese, The. Jorie Graham. HCAP

Geese fly off, but sometimes they don't take, The. Owning a Dead Man. Marcia Southwick. MAYP

Geese Gone Beyond. Gary Snyder. NoAM

Geese in the pond are drifting, five. Wandsworth Common. David Bromwich. PoA

Gehazi. Kipling. FaBoPV

Geist's Grave. Matthew Arnold. FM; NOBVV; TEP

Gellius, what reason can you give why those ruddy lips of yours. Catullus. PeHV

Gem-like stars, The. Midnight. Henrietta Cordelia Ray. *Fr.* Idyl. CBWP-3

Gem of all isthmuses and isles that lie. Sirmio. Catullus, *tr. by* Charles Stuart Calverley. AWP

Gem of the crimson-colour'd Even. To the Evening Star. Thomas Campbell. GTBS; GTBS-P; OBNC

Gem that gleams at night it may be, A. Tabito, *tr. fr. Japanese by* Hiroaki Sato. *Fr.* Manyo Shu. FCEI

Gemini and Virgo, *sel.* Charles Stuart Calverley. "And, if you asked of him to say." FiBHP

Gemini Elegy. Margaret Gibson. MAYP

Gemini Jones. Willard R. Espy. FaBoUs

Gemlike Flame, The. R. P. Lister. FiBHP

Gems and jewels let them heap. In a Garret. Herman Melville. AnAmPo; OBAL

Gemwood. Marvin Bell. LCAP

Genau'r Glyn, Tywyn, each day from these to Rhys's halls. Ode to Rhys ap Maredudd of Tywyn. Dafydd Nanmor, *tr. by* H. Idris Bell. OBWVE

Gender of a Latin Noun, The. Memorial Lines on the Gender of Latin Substantives. Benjamin Hall Kennedy. FaBoUs

Genealogical Reflection. Ogden Nash. OBAL

Genealogy. Donald Finkel. VWA

Genealogy. Frank Lamont Phillips. AmNP

Genealogy. Eléni Vakaló, *tr. fr. Modern Greek by* Paul Merchant. PBWP

General, The. Siegfried Sassoon. BrPo; CMoP; FaBV; FiBHP; LiTM; MMA; NAEL-2; NOAM; OBWP; OxBoLi; OxBSP; OxBTC; PoE; TW

General Armstrong, The. *Unknown.* PAH

General Communion, A. Alice Meynell. NOCV; WPE

General Custer. Bob McKenty. SoTCo

General dashed along the road, The. The General's Death. Joseph O'Connor. AA

General Description of the West Indian Islands, A, *sels.* John Singleton. PBCV
   "Ah me! How differently th'untutor'd slave." *Fr. bk.* III.
   "But lo! The reaking surface of the vale." *Fr. bk.* II.

General 'eard the firin' on the flank, The. Stellenbosch. Sir Alfred Kipling. OBTV

General Howe's Letter. *Unknown.* PAH

General John. W. S. Gilbert. NA

General Ludd's Triumph. *Unknown.* OBET

General Mule Poems, The, *sel.* Wayne Dodd.
   Of Sitting Bear. KS

General Review of the Sex Situation. Dorothy Parker. NAAL-2

General Robert Smalls. Josephine D. Henderson Heard. CBWP-4

General Secretary's feet whispered over the red carpet, The. Anteroom: Geneva. Denis Devlin. CIP

General Strike 1969. Amelia Rosselli, *tr. fr. Italian by* Lawrence R. Smith. NItP

General Truths. David Avidan, *tr. fr. Hebrew by* Warren Bargad *and* Stanley F. Chyet. *Fr.* Samson, Our Hero, 1. IP

General Vallencey's Waltz. Paul Durcan. FaBCIP

General William Booth Enters into Heaven. Vachel Lindsay. AmPP; CMoP; LiTA; LiTM; MoAB; MoAmPo; NOBA; OxBA; PoA; PoE; TAP; TrGrPo; WGRP

General wonder in our land. *Unknown.* NOIV

Generalities. Robert Conquest. OxBC

General's Death, The. Joseph O'Connor. AA

General's Property, The. Samih al-Qasim, *tr. fr. Arabic by* Abdullah al-Udhari. MPAW

Generation. Rowena Tiempo Torrevillas. WCI

Generation before me departed too soon, The. Generations. Moishe Steingart, *tr. by* Gabriel Preil. VWA

Generation Gap, The. Ruby C. Saunders. BlSi

Generations. Robert Clark. PoAu-2

Generations. István Eörsi, *tr. fr. Hungarian by* William Jay Smith. MHuP

Generations. Judy Dothard Simmons. CNA

Generations. Moishe Steingart, *tr. fr. Yiddish by* Gabriel Preil. VWA

"Generosity of her love provides, The." The Grand Guignols of Love. Michael Benedikt. AmPA

Generous Creed, A. Elizabeth Stuart Phelps Ward. WGRP

Generous man will not deny, The. An Elegy on the Late King of Patagonia. St. John Emile Clavering Hankin. CenHV

Genesis. Buland al-Haidari, *tr. fr. Arabic by* Patricia Alanah Byrne *and* Salma Khadra Jayyusi. MAP

Genesis, *sels.* Caedmon, *tr. fr. Anglo-Saxon.*
   Approach of Pharaoh, The. *Tr. by* C. W. Kennedy. ACP; WaaP
   Noah's Flood. *Tr. by* C. W. Kennedy. AnOE
   "Son of Lamech let a black raven, The." PBBP
   Temptation and Fall of Man, The. *Tr. by* C. W. Kennedy. AnOE

Genesis. Jacob Glatstein, *tr. fr. Yiddish by* Cynthia Ozick. PeBMYV

Genesis. Brian Higgins. FaBoTw

Genesis. Geoffrey Hill. HAP; NePoEA; OAEL-2; OxBC; TOF

Genesis. John Hall Ingham. AA

Genesis. Evan Jones. PBCV

Genesis. Lotte Kramer. VWA

Genesis, *sel.* Delmore Schwartz.
   You Are a Jew! TrJP

Genesis, *sels.* Bible, *O.T.*
   "And God saw that the wickedness of man was great." *Fr.* VI: 5-22. NAWM-1
   "And Joseph was brought down to Egypt." *Fr.* XXXIX-XLVI: 6. NAWM-1
   "And Noah was six hundred years old when the flood of waters." *Fr.* VII: 6-IX: 17. NAWM-1
   And the Lord God planted a garden eastward in Eden. *Fr.* II: 8–22. OAEL-1
   "And the whole earth was of one language, and of one speech." *Fr.* XI: 1-9. EyDe; NAWM-1
   And there came two angels to Sodom at even. *Fr.* XIX: 1–38. HoPM
   "In the beginning God created the heaven and the earth." ImOP, (I: 1-13); NAWM-1, (I-IV).
   "Joseph, being seventeen years old, was feeding the flock with his brethren." *Fr.* XXXVII: 2-35, *abr.*. NAWM-1
   "See, the smell of my sone is as the smell of a feld." *Tr. by* William Tyndale. OBVE

Genesis. Jules Alan Wein. TrJP

Genesis, Exo, Levi, Num, Deutero, Joshua, Judges. Memoria Technica for the Books of the Bible. *Unknown.* FaBoUs

Genesis of Butterflies, The. Victor Hugo, *tr. fr. French by* Andrew Lang. AWP

Geneva. Alastair Reid. NYBP

Genghis Chan: Private Eye. John Yau. BAP

Genia, The. Ann Stanford. WSC

Genial poets, pink-faced. Goodbye to Tolerance. Denise Levertov. NoAM

Genitori. David Ray. TW

Genius, The. Leonard Cohen. MoCV

Genius. R. J. P. Hewison. FaFP

Genius. Philip Levine. NoAM

Genius. Adah Isaacs Menken. CBWP-1

Genius. Louis Saunders Perkins. PeHV

Genius. James Waddington. PF

Genius. Edward Lucas White. AA; WGRP

Genius and Intemperance. John Nicholson. PF

Genius is power. Genius. Adah Isaacs Menken. CBWP-1

Genius Loci. Margaret L. Woods. OBEV

Genius Loci of the Morning. Doug Fetherling. NeAC

Genius of ancient Greece! whose faithful steps. Mark Akenside. *Fr.* The Pleasures of Imagination, I. OBTV

Genius of Burke! forgive the pen seduced. Wordsworth. *Fr.* The Prelude [or, Growth of a Poet's Mind]: Residence in London. FaBoPV

Genius of Culture! thou, whose chaster taste. David Humphreys. *Fr.* A Poem on the Industry of the United States of America. OPP

Genius of Greece! thou livest, though thy domes. William Haygarth. *Fr.* Greece. OBTV

Genji caught a gray bird, fluttering. Journeys. Gary Snyder. NU

Genoa Woman. Dino Campana, *tr. fr. Italian by* Charles Wright. PFI

Gentian weaves her fringes, The. Emily Dickinson. PoRA

Gentilesse. Chaucer. AWP; NAEL-1; OAEL-1

Gentill butler, bell ami. Fill the Bowl, Butler! *Unknown.* MeEL

Gentle agony, A. Spring. Vess Quinlan. CowP

Gentle Alice Brown. W. S. Gilbert. FaBoCo; FiBHP; NA

Gentle analogists rock the surface. Word World. Bob Perelman. LP

Gentle and generous, brave-hearted, kind. The Comfort of the Trees. Richard Watson Gilder. PAH

Gentle and smiling as before. The Wheel. Robert Hayden. BPo

Gentle as a maiden's dream. The Snow Storm. Mary Weston Fordham. CBWP-2

Gentle as Moon on Water. Yona Wallach, *tr. fr. Hebrew by* Warren Bargad *and* Stanley F. Chyet. IP

Gentle as my dead friend's hand. Nakamura Kusadao, *tr. by* Geoffrey Bownas *and* Anthony Thwaite. PeBJV

Gentle at last, and as clean as ever. Grandfather in the Old Men's Home. W. S. Merwin. LiTM; SM

Gentle Check, The. Joseph Beaumont. PBBP

Gentle Craft, The, *sel.* Thomas Deloney.
   Would God That It Were Holiday! EiL

Gentle Echo on Woman, A. Swift. FaBoCo; FiBHP; NBLV; NU

Gentle footsteps on the sand. The Crows. Maria Valli. CBAP

Gentle Ghosts. Simon Rae. NPo

Gentle hands that never weary. Lines to Mother. Rose M. Stein. PWR

Gentle Heart, A: Two. Judith Johnson Sherwin. BoWoP

Gentle hunter. Leopard. *Unknown, tr. fr. Yoruba by* Ulli Beier. *Fr.* Hunter Poems of the Yoruba. RB; WTO

Gentle Jesus Meek and Mild. Charles Wesley. OxBChV
Gentle knight was pricking on the plaine, A. Spenser. *Fr.* The Faerie Queene, I, 1. EBEV; NAEL-1; OAEL-1
Gentle Mary, noble maiden, give us help! Prayer to the Virgin. Saint Columcille, *tr. by* Kuno Meyer *and* John Strachan. TIRV
Gentle Name. Selma Robinson. MoShBr
Gentle Nymphs, Be Not Refusing. William Browne. *Fr.* Britannia's Pastorals, I, Song 3. EIl
Gentle of hand, the Dean of St. Patrick's guided. A Sermon on Swift. Austin Clarke. BIrV; IPY
Gentle Park, A. Moss Herbert. GoYe
Gentle River, Gentle River. *Unknown, tr. fr. Spanish by* Thomas Percy. AWP
Gentle Shepherd, The, *sel.* Allan Ramsay.
  My Peggy [Is a Young Thing]. GN; OxBS
  (Peggy.) OBEV
Gentle slopes are green to remind you, The. The Five Unmistakable Marks. David Jones. *Fr.* In Parenthesis, Pt. VII. NAEL-2
  "Across upon this undulated board of verdure chequered bright." NoAm
Gentle sounds rise up to me. From Mount Nebo. Karl Wolfskehl, *tr. by* Erna Baber Rosenfeld. VWA
Gentle thought there is will often start, A. Dante, *tr. fr. Italian by* Dante Gabriel Rossetti. *Fr.* La Vita Nuova, XXVI. AWP
Gentle Wind, A. Fu Hsüan, *tr. fr. Chinese by* Arthur Waley. AWP
Gentle wind after the rain stirred, A. Rainbow and You. Tachihara Michizo, *tr. by* Hiroaki Sato. FCEI
Gentle winds at Asuka, The. Prince Shiki, *tr. fr. Japanese.* *Fr.* Manyo Shu. Ma
Gentle youth, forbear. Hero Feels the Shaft of Love. Christopher Marlowe. *Fr.* Hero and Leander, First Sestiad. GBL
Gentleman, The. Menahem ben Judah Lonzano, *tr. fr. Hebrew by* A. B. Rhine. TrJP
Gentleman cam oure the sea, A. The Cruel Brother. *Unknown.* ESPB
Gentleman in hunting rode astray, A. The Beggar Woman. William King. NOEC
Gentlemen. Jules Laforgue, *tr. fr. French by* William Jay Smith. CT
Gentlemen. Geoffrey Taylor. FaBoEE
Gentlemen, as we take our seats. The Rehearsal. Horace Gregory. VGW
"Gentlemen, look on this wonder." The Adhesive Autopsy of Walt Whitman. Jonathan Williams. PoM
Gentlemen-Rankers. Kipling. NOBVV
Gentlemen, which of these three vegetables: tomatoes, pumpkins, or squash. A Paragraph Made Up of Seven Sentences Which Have Entered My Memory. Chuck Wachtel. UL
Gentleness of rain was in the wind, The. Fragment: Rain. Shelley. ChER
Gentlest of women, put your weapons by. Lay Your Arms Aside. Pierce Ferriter, *tr. by* Eilean Ni Chuilleanain. BIrV
Gently Dip. George Peele. *Fr.* The Old Wives' [*or* Wife's] Tale. ELP; InPS
  (Fair Maiden.) PoEL-2
  (Song for the Head.) RB
  (Voice from the Well [of Life Speaks to the Maiden], The.) ChTr; NOBE
Gently! Gently! Gently! The Ocean Is like a Wreath. Kuapakaa. WTO
Gently, gently, the wind blows. Kazue Mizumura. TSS
Gently I stir a white feather fan. In the Mountains on a Summer Day. Li Po, *tr. by* Arthur Waley. AWP; SD
Gently I wave the visible world away. The Absinthe-Drinker. Arthur Symons. BrPo; FaBoTw; NOBVV
Gently, Johnny My Jingalo. *Unknown.* OBET
Gently, Lord, oh, gently lead us. In Sorrow. Thomas Hastings. AA
Genuine Poem, Found on a Blackboard in a Bowling Alley in Story City, Iowa. Ted Kooser. ASP
Geo. Ray DiPalma. IAT
Geode, the troll's melon. James Merrill. *Fr.* In Nine Sleep Valley. HCAP
Geographers. Alexander Barclay. *Fr.* The Ship of Fools. ACP
Geographers, The. Karl Shapiro. OxBA
Geography. G. K. Chesterton. *Fr.* Songs of Education. OBSV
Geography, *sels.* Michael Dransfield.
  "In the forest, in unexplored." *Fr.* III. CBAP
  "Sky ceases. There is only." *Fr.* VI. CBAP
Geography. Eleanor Farjeon. FaPON
Geography. Kenneth Koch. NoAM
Geography Lesson. Carol Rumens. FaBoWP

Geography of Music. Kenneth Patchen. UAS
Geometry. Rita Dove. HCAP
Geordie. *Unknown.* AmFP; ESPB, A *and* B *vers.*; FaBoBa; OBET; OxBB, *with music.*
George. Hilaire Belloc. FiBHP
George. Dudley Randall. BPo; NoAM
George I—Star of Brunswick. Thackeray. *Fr.* The Georges. FaBoEE
George II. Thackeray. *Fr.* The Georges. FaBoEE
George III. Byron. *See* Vision of Judgment, The: George the Third.
George III. Robert Lowell. FaBoPV
George III. Thackeray. *Fr.* The Georges. FaBoEE
George III and the Sailor. "Peter Pindar." *Fr.* The Royal Tour, and Weymouth Amusements. NOEC
George III Visits Whitbread's Brewery. "Peter Pindar." *Fr.* Instructions to a Celebrated Laureat. NOEC
George IV. Thackeray. *Fr.* The Georges. FaBoEE
George Allen. *Unknown.* AmFP
George Aloe and the *Sweepstake*, The ("George Alow came from the South"). *Unknown.* ESPB
George-Aloe and the *Sweepstake* too, The. The Sailor's Only Delight. *Unknown.* OxBSS
George and Genevieve. George Hugnet. Gertrude Stein. NoAM
George Burns likes to insist that he always. Of Time and the Line. Charles Bernstein. UL
George Collins came home last Saturday night. Lady Alice. *Unknown.* AmFP
George Crabbe. E. A. Robinson. BLPL; CMoP; LiTA; LiTM; MoAB; MoAmPo; NAAL-2; NOBA; NoP; OxBA; PoEL-5; TAP
George Eliot Country. Amy Clampitt. ER
George-Hector. The Emancipation of George-Hector (a Colored Turtle). Mari E. Evans. AmNP
George Hugnet. Gertrude Stein. NoAM
George Jones. *Unknown.* OxBSS
George Ridler's Oven. *Unknown.* OBET
George Robinson: Blues. Muriel Rukeyser. NNaP
George Sand. Dorothy Parker. FiBHP
"George," she said, "come out of the rain!" The Man in the Rain. Van K. Brock. MT
George Simic. Charles Simic. DiL
George tells the story. The Controls. Harrison Fisher. UL
George the First was always reckoned. The Georges. Walter Savage Landor. ChTr; FaBoCo; FaBoEE; FiBHP; NIP; OBSV (On the Four Georges.) FaBoCo
George the Fourth, the son of Third, the grandson of the Second. Lines on the Succession of the Kings of England (Reversed). *Unknown.* FaBoUs
George, the Regent's, chaste and wise. A Bundle of Truths—A Parody. Alexander Rodger. PF
George the Third. Edmund Clerihew Bentley. *Fr.* Clerihews. FaBoCo; FiBHP; NOBL; OxBoLi
George the Third. Byron. *Fr.* The Vision of Judgment. FiP (George III.) TW, *abr..*
George III said with a smile. *Unknown.* FaBoUs
George the Third's Soliloquy. Philip Freneau. NOBA
George Washington. John Hall Ingham. AA; OHIP; PAH
George Washington. Rosemary *and* Stephen Vincent Benét. FaPON
George Washington. *Unknown.* OHIP
George Washington Goes to a Girlie Movie. Aram Boyajian. NeAC
George Washington, your name is on my lips. Patriotic Poem. Diane Wakoski. OFD; VGW
Georges, The. Walter Savage Landor. ChTr; FaBoCo; FaBoEE; FiBHP; NIP; OBSV
Georges, The, *sels.* Thackeray. FaBoEE
  George I—Star of Brunswick.
  George II.
  George III.
  George IV.
Georgia. Bin Ramke. MT
Georgia. Philippe Soupault, *tr. fr. French.* POS, *tr. by* Michael Benedikt; RHTwFP, *tr. by* Paul Auster.
Georgia Dusk. Jean Toomer. AmNP; BPo; CDC; NAAL-2; NoAM; NoP; PoBA
Georgia Towns. Daniel Whitehead Hicky. AmFN
Georgia Volunteer, A. Mary Ashley Townsend. AA
Georgiad, The, *sels.* Roy Campbell.
  "Hail, mediocrity, beneath whose spell." MoBrPo
  "Next him Jack Squire through his own tear-drops sploshes." OxBTC
Georgian hills above lie shrouded in the night, The. Pushkin, *tr. by* Alan Myers. AAA

Georgian Spring. Roy Campbell. OBSV

Georgics, *sels.* Virgil, *tr. fr. Latin.*
 Care of Bees, The. *Fr.* IV, *tr. by* Dryden. FaBoUs
 "Observe the daily circle of the sun." *Fr.* I, *tr. by* Dryden. FaBoUs
 "What makes a plenteous harvest." *Fr.* I, *tr. by* Dryden. AWP
 We Have Paid Enough Long Since in Our Own Blood. *Tr. by* Richmond Lattimore. WaaP

Georgie Porgie, pudding and pie. Mother Goose. OxNR

Georgie Wedlock. *Unknown.* AmFP

Geraint and Enid. Tennyson. *Fr.* Idylls of the King.
 Enid's Song. FaBoRV

Gerald Massey. William Billington. PF

Gerald the Bitter, with your polished smile. The Widow's Curse.
 Unknown, tr. by Thomas Kinsella. NOIV

Geraldine's Daughter, The. Egan O'Rahilly, *tr. fr. Modern Irish by* James Clarence Mangan. AnIL

"Gerald's here!" my mother called. A Voice in the Garden. Selima Hill. FaBoWP

Geranium, The. Theodore Roethke. CoAP; UnPo; WeW

Geranium, The. Sheridan. BoLoP; ErPo

Geranium, houseleek, laid in oblong beds. John Gray. NOBVV

Geraniums, The. Genevieve Taggard. VGW

Gerarda. Eloise Bibb. CBWP-4

Gereint ab Erbin. *Unknown, tr. fr. Welsh by* Joseph P. Clancy. OBWVE

Germ, The. Ogden Nash. CenHV; MoShBr; RB

German/ Magnus massive. Wintry. Robert Grenier. IAT

German Organ. Antonin Artaud, *tr. fr. French by* Michael Benedikt. POS

German Requiem, A. James Fenton. NAEL-2; NoAM

German Shepherd. Myra Cohn Livingston. RFM

Germanic. Crossing. Anthony Barnett. VWA

Germans in Greek, The. Porson on German Scholarship. Richard Porson. FaBoCo; FaBoEE

Germans live in Germany, The. Home. J. H. Goring. MoShBr

Germinal. "Æ." BlrV; MoBrPo; OBEV; OBMV

Germination. Arlene Stone. VWA

Geron and Histor. Sir Philip Sidney. *Fr.* Arcadia. SiPS

Geronimo. Ernest McGaffey. AA; PAH

Gerontion. T. S. Eliot. AmPP; CMoP; EBEV; GTBS-P; HAP; InPS; LiTA; LiTM; MoP; NAAL-2; NoAM; NOBA; OAEL-2; OxBA; PPP; SeCePo; TAP

Gertie Green made eyes at me. Serve Her Right. John Barford. PeHV

Gertrude and Gulielma, sister-twins. Frederick Goddard Tuckerman. *Fr.* Sonnets, II, xv. HAP; QFR

Gertrude Stein at Snails Bay. Peter Porter. OxBC

Gesse Departing at Early Dusk. Kenko, *tr. fr. Japanese by* Steven D. Carter. WFTW

Gest of Robyn Hode, A. ("It fell upon a Wednesday"). *Unknown.* OxBLMV

Gest of Robyn Hode, A. ("Lythe and listen, gentilmen"). *Unknown.* ESPB; OxBB

Gesture. Donald Finkel. InPK

Gesture, The. Elizabeth Libbey. WeW

Gesture, The. George Oppen. *Fr.* Five Poems about Poetry. NNaP

Gesture by a Lady with an Assumed Name, A. James Wright. LiTM

Gesture of Understanding. Ad Zuiderent, *tr. fr. Dutch by* James S. Holmes. DuIn

Gesture the gesture the gesture the gesture, The. Michael McClure. *Fr.* Hymn to St. Geryon. NeAP

Get a lovely spray of cherry blossoms when you come to me. *Unknown, tr. by* Hiroaki Sato. FCEI

Get a Transfer. *Unknown.* BLPA; WBLP

Get away, they're all gone. Chops Are Flyin. Stanley Crouch. NBP

"Get down, get down, lovin' Henry," she cried. Loving Henry. *Unknown.* AmFP

Get Hence Foule Griefe. Sir Philip Sidney. *Fr.* Arcadia. PoEL-1
 (Contentment.) SiPS

Get into the Boosting Business. *Unknown.* WBLP

Get it right or let it alone. Morals. James Thurber. *Fr.* Further Fables for Our Time. FaBV

Get loaded. Exercise ("Get loaded"). Pat Nolan. UL

Get me that bright moon! Issa, *tr. by* Hiroaki Sato. FCEI

"Get out of my way!" Roosters. Elizabeth Jane Coatsworth. SO

Get ready your money and come to me. *Unknown.* OxNR

Get Somebody Else. Paul Laurence Dunbar. BLRP
 (Too Busy.) WBLP

Get Stuffed. Alurista, *tr. fr. Spanish by* Toni Empringham. FIA

Get the Gasworks. David Ignatow. InPK

"Get the verb right." About Motion Pictures. Ann Darr. GrPl

Get thee a ship well-rigged and tight. In Praise of Fidelia. Mildmay Fane, Earl of Westmorland. OxBSP

Get There If You Can and See the Land. W. H. Auden. InPS

Get to Hell Outa Here. "The Mighty Sparrow." PBCV

Get Up! Joseph Skipsey. InPK; NOBVV; PF

Get Up and Bar the Door. ("It fell about the Martinmas time"). *Unknown.* ESPB; FaBoBa; GoTS; HeIP; NoP; OnMSP; OxBS; PDV; TrGrPo

Get Up and Bar the Door. ("There lived a man at the foot of a hill"). *Unknown.* EnSB

Get Up and Bar the Door. ("The wind it blew from East to West"). *Unknown.* AmFP

Get up at once, now, Margaret May! Eggs for Breakfast. Irene F. Pawsey. BoTP

Get Up, Blues. James A. Emanuel. AmNP; PoBA

Get Up, Get Up. *Unknown.* FiBHP; NTCP

Get up, get up for shame! The blooming morn. Corinna's Going a-Maying. Robert Herrick. BoNaP; CaPo; GN; HAP; InPS; JCP; NAEL-1; NiP; NOBE; NoP; OAEL-1; OBEV; OBS; PoE; PoEL-3; PPP; PrIm; SeCP; SeCV-1; TEP; TrGrPo

Get up, get up, you lazy-head. Get Up, Get Up. *Unknown.* FiBHP; NTCP

Get up, now quickly wipe your eyes. The Piece Worker. Emma Döltz, *tr. by* Susan L. Cocalis *and* Gerlinde Geiger. DMG

"Get up, our Anna dear, from the weary spinning wheel." The Fairy Thorn. Sir Samuel Ferguson. CH; OnMSP; OnYI

"Get up!" the caller calls, "Get up!" Get Up! Joseph Skipsey. InPK; NOBVV; PF

Get up thou lazy lump thou log get up. Lament of a Slug-a-Bed's Wife. Stevie Smith. Mes

Get You Gone. Sir Charles Sedley. ELP

Get Your Body off My Mind. Berta Freistadt. DT

Gethsemane. Arna Bontemps. CDC

Gethsemane. Kipling. FaBoTw

Gettin de Spirit. Una Marson. PBCV

Getting a loan from the bank. Stories from the Res. Nila NorthSun. GOS

Getting a Poem in the Rain. Dick Lourie. NeAC

Getting Across. Carter Revard. VoR

Getting at the Root of the Matter. Henry Taylor. BXAP

Getting Berries. *Unknown, tr. fr. Bella Bella Indian by* Franz Boas. STP

Getting Down to Get Over. June Jordan. PoBA

Getting Drunk with Daughter. Robert Huff. NePoEA-2

Getting Firewood. *Unknown, tr. fr. Bella Bella Indian by* Franz Boas. STP

Getting in the Wood. Gary Snyder. NoAM

Getting Inside the Miracle. Luci Shaw. TrCP

Getting lazy. Masaoka Shiki, *tr. fr. Japanese by* Burton Watson. *Fr.* Thirty-nine Haiku. FCEI

Getting Lost in Nazi Germany. Marvin Bell. VWA

Getting old, I retire to this little mountain district. Late in the Year K'uei-yu. Yü Chi, *tr. by* Jonathan Chaves. CoBLCP

Getting older, I grow more personal. Cry Mercy. Charles Brasch. ATNZ

Getting on Horseback. Yü Chi, *tr. fr. Chinese by* Jonathan Chaves. CoBLCP

Getting Out. Cleopatra Mathis. MAYP

Getting out of bed. *Unknown, tr. by* Geoffrey Bownas *and* Anthony Thwaite. PeBJV

Getting relaxed, getting tense. *Unknown, tr. by* Hiroaki Sato. FCEI

Getting Serious. Gary Soto. NPGG

Getting the Mail. Galway Kinnell. UnPo

Getting Through. James Merrill. NYBP

Getting through with the world. Approach to a City. William Carlos Williams. PoRA

Getting time off from the Buddha. Ozaki Hosai, *tr. fr. Japanese by* Hiroaki Sato. *Fr.* One Hundred Haiku in Free Form. FCEI

Getting to Rome. *Unknown.* NOIV

Getting Up. Stephen Dobyns. MAYP

Getting Up. Lilian McCrea. BoTP

Getting Up Early at Lakeside Pavilion, *sels.* Chiang Shih, *tr. fr. Chinese by* Irving Lo. WFTU
 "Morning light floods my room overlooking the lake."
 "Vapor rises from the water's surface at dawn."

Getting Wise. Marg Yeo. DT

Gettysburg. James Jeffrey Roche. PAH

Gettysburg. Edmund Clarence Stedman. PAH

Gettysburg Ode, The, *sel.* Bayard Taylor.
 Lincoln at Gettysburg. OHIP; PAH

Geve place, ye lovers, here before. *See* Give place, ye lovers, here before.

Ghaists; a Kirk-yard Eclogue, The. Robert Fergusson. OxBS

Ghastly, ghoulish, grinning skull. To a Skull. Joshua Henry Jones. BANP

Ghazal. Philip Dow. NPGG
Ghazel of Unforseen Love. Federico García Lorca, *tr. fr. Spanish by* Perry Higman. LPSS
Ghazal XII. Mirza Ghalib, *tr. fr. Urdu by* W. S. Merwin *and* Aijaz Ahmad. LLLT
Gheluvelt. Robert Bridges. BrPo
Ghetto Lovesong—Migration. Carole Gregory Clemmons. NBP; NMM; PoBA
   (Migration.) PoBA
Ghetto Summer School. Douglas Worth. FF
Ghetto Twilight. Alter Brody. VWA
Ghillies and shepherds are shouting Bravo. Macinnes's Mountain Patrol. Tom Patey. PoSH
Oh, Ghingeli [or Gingilee], my bleeding heart. Moyshe-Leyb Halpern, *tr. fr. Yiddish.* AYP, *tr. by* Benjamin *and* Barbara Harshav *and* Kathryn Helle; TrJP, *tr. by* Joseph Leftwich
Ghost, The, *sel.* Charles Churchill.
   "Pomposo (insolent and loud)." OBSV
Ghost, The. Hilary Corke. NYBP
Ghost, The. W. H. Davies. BrPo
Ghost, The. Walter de la Mare. BrPo; CMoP; ELP; EnLoPo; LiTM; MoAB; MoBrPo; NOBE; OAEL-2; OxBTC
Ghost, The. Robert Lowell, *after the Latin of* Sextus Propertius. PoA
Ghost, The. Heather McHugh. NAmP
Ghost. Christian Morgenstern, *tr. fr. German by* W. D. Snodgrass *and* Lore Segal. WSC
Ghost, The. Fitz-James O'Brien. NOEC
Ghost & Shaman. *Unknown, tr. fr. Bella Bella Indian by* Franz Boas. STP
Ghost Boy. Mark Van Doren. SO
Ghost Dance: August, 1976, The. David Jauss. MOWH
Ghost Dance Songs, *sels. Unknown, tr. fr. Sioux Indian by* James Mooney. STP
   "I'yehe! my children."
   "My children/ when at first I liked the whites."
   "We shall live again."
Ghost-Flowers. Mary Thacher Higginson. AA; WeW
Ghost-grey the fall of night. A Robin. Walter de la Mare. ChTr; CMoP; FaBoRV
Ghost House. Robert Frost. WSC
Ghost Hunter, The. John Haines. AnAn
Ghost in the Martini, The. Anthony Hecht. DiPo; OxBC
Ghost is gone in rags, The. *Ambo Oral Tradition. Fr.* Five Ghost Songs. TTTS
Ghost is someone, A: death has left a hole. The Ghost. Robert Lowell, *after the Latin of* Sextus Propertius. PoA
Ghost Moth, The. Lauris Edmond. ATNZ
Ghost of a Ghost, The. Brad Leithauser. MAYP
Ghost of a little white kitten, The. The Little Cat Angel. Leontine Stanfield. BLPA
Ghost of a mouldy larder is one thing, A: whiskery bread. Corposant. Peter Redgrove. NePoEA-2; OxBTC
Ghost of a wind came over the hill, The. Nancibel. Bliss Carman. AnAmPo
Ghost of an Education, The. James Michie. NYBP
Ghost of another comes to visit and we hold, The. The Dance. Mark Strand. GeTw
Ghost of Ninon would be sorry now, The. Veteran Sirens. Edwin Arlington Robinson. NOBA; QFR; SoSe
Ghost of our blood, I worship You. Adoramus Te, Christe. David O'Bruadair, *tr. by* Thomas Kinsella. NOIV
Ghost of Patroclus, The. Homer, *tr. fr. Greek by* Pope. *Fr.* The Iliad, XXII. PeHV
Ghost of the Cargo Boat, The. Pablo Neruda, *tr. fr. Spanish by* Donald D. Walsh. WSC
Ghost Pet. Horatio Colony. GoYe
Ghost Poem Five. Sister Mary Norbert Körte. IHMS
Ghost Psalms. Márton Kalász, *tr. fr. Hungarian by* Jascha Kessler. FOC
Ghost Story. Robert Pack. MOWH
Ghost Story. Dylan Thomas. OBCP
Ghost, that loved a lady fair, A. The Phantom-Wooer. Thomas Lovell Beddoes. EnRP; NAEL-2; TrGrPo; ViBoPo; WiR
Ghost Voice, *sel.* Roy Fuller.
   "Why do we return? Not in the darkened rooms." OBD
Ghostesses. *Unknown.* ChTr
Ghostly Father, The. Peter Redgrove. MoBS; NePoEA-2
Ghostly Gladness. Richard Rolle of Hampole. HAP
Ghostly Love. Valerie Sinason. DT
Ghostly Story. Milton Acorn. NeAC
Ghostly Tree. Léonie Adams. MoAB; MoAmPo
Ghosts. Harry Behn. RHPC

Ghosts. Elizabeth Jennings. NePoEA-2
Ghosts. Ethna MacCarthy. NeIP
Ghosts. Richard Kendall Munkittrick. AA
Ghosts. Alastair Reid. NYBP
Ghost's Leavetaking, The. Sylvia Plath. NePoEA-2
Ghosts of a Lunatic Asylum. Stephen Vincent Benét. AnAmPo
Ghosts of flowers went sailing, The. Changelings. Mary Potter Thacher Higginson. AA
Ghosts of the Buffaloes, The. Vachel Lindsay. MoAmPo
Ghosts of the Victorians, The. Stephen Plaice. NPo
Ghost's Song, The. *Unknown. See* Wae's me! Wae's me!
Ghosts' Stories. Alastair Reid. NePoEA-2
Ghosts there must be with me in this old house. Solitude. Walter de la Mare. CMoP
Ghosts: they conjure. Translations. Wing Tek Lum. BrSi
Ghosts II. Lauris Edmond. PeNZ
Ghoul, The. Jack Prelutsky. OBCA
Ghoul Care. Ralph Hodgson. MoBrPo
Giant brontosaurus, The. Brontosaurus. Gail Kredenser. RHPC
Giant came to me when I was young, A. The Lost Genius. John James Piatt. AA
Giant Decorative Dahlias. Molly Holden. OxBTC
Giant Has Swallowed the Earth, A. Pattiann Rogers. MT
Giant Killer. George Garrett. CRP
Giant Otters. Jackson Mac Low. LP
Giant-Power from earth's remotest caves, The. Steam Power. Erasmus Darwin. *Fr.* The Botanic Garden: The Economy of Vegetation. NOEC
Giant Puffball, The. Edmund Blunden. FaBoTw
Giant rages in the field, A. Threshing Machine. Wilhelm Szabo, *tr. by* Beth Bjorklund. CoAuP
Giant sparkler,/ Lights of the river. "A 4." Louis Zukofsky. *Fr.* "A" (1–12). VGW
Giant Thunder. James Reeves. BoNaP
Giantess. Baudelaire, *tr. fr. French.* ErPo, *tr. by* Karl Shapiro; OBVE, *tr. by* Roy Campbell.
Giant's Cake, A. Evelina San Garde. BoTP
Giant's Tomb in Georgian Bay. "Katherine Hale." CaP
Giaour, The, *sel.* Byron.
   "But thou, false infidel! shall writhe." VVA
Gibber, The. Theodore Roethke. *Fr.* The Lost Son. NAAL-2
Gibbs, *sel.* Muriel Rukeyser.
   "It was much later in his life he rose." ImOP
Gibraltar. Wilfrid Scawen Blunt. ACP; OBEV
Gibraltar. Richard Chenevix Trench. OBTV
Gid dy/ up gid/ dy up. James Minor. RR
Giddy, I swayed in a Cessna. First Solo. Walter McDonald. RR
Giddy lark reacheth the steepy air, The. The Lark. *Unknown.* PBBP
Gideon at the Well. Geoffrey Hill. NePoEA
"Gie corn to my horse, mither." The Mother's Malison; or, Clyde's Water. *Unknown.* ESPB
Gi'e me a lass with a lump of land. Lass with a Lump of Land. Allan Ramsay. NOEC
Gie the Lass her Fairin'. Burns. CoMu; ErPo
Gife Langour. Lord Darnley. OxBS
Gift. Gerald William Barrax. MT
Gift, The. John Ciardi. LiTM
Gift. Leonard Cohen. SoSe
Gift, The. Robert Creeley. NOBA
Gift. Carol Freeman. *See* Christmas Morning I.
Gift, The. Louise Glück. FaBoWP
Gift. Judith Hemschemeyer. PCP
Gift, The. Mark Jarman. MOWH
Gift, The. Dick Lourie. NeAC
Gift, A. Amy Lowell. AnAmPo
Gift, The. Ed Ochester. Psk
Gift for an Old Official. Hsüan-yeh, *tr. fr. Chinese by* Jonathan D. Spence. WFTU
Gift for the Queen. *Unknown.* OxNR
Gift from Kenya. May Miller. DlSi
Gift from the cold and silent past! The Norsemen. Whittier. PAH
Gift Hour. Maria Banus, *tr. fr. Rumanian by* Willis Barnstone *and* Matei Calinescu. BoWoP; VWA
Gift of a Skull, The. John Skelton. *See* Upon a Dead Man's Head.
Gift of God, The. E. A. Robinson. MoAB; MoAmPo; OxBA
Gift of Gravity, The. Wendell Berry. GeTw
Gift of Great Value, A. Robert Creeley. LCAP; NaP
Gift of Judah the Woman-Hater, The, *sel. Judah ibn Sabbatai.* Expensive Wife, The. TrJP
Gift of Oneself, The. Valery Larbaud, *tr. fr. French.* CT, *tr. by* William Jay Smith; RHTwFP, *tr. by* Ron Padgett *and* Bill Zavatsky.

Gift of Sight. Robert Graves. PCP
Gift of Song, The. Anthony Hecht. NYBP
Gift of Speech, The. Sadi, *tr. fr. Persian by* L. Cranmer-Byng. *Fr.* The
  Gulistan. AWP
Gift of Tongues, The. Robert Morgan. MT
Gift of Water, The. Hamlin Garland. AA
Gift Outright, The. Robert Frost. AiP; AmFN; AmPP; CMoP; GOA;
  LiTM; MoAB; MoAmPo; MoP; NAAL-2; NoAM; NOBA; NoP; OPP;
  OxBA; PPP; WaP
Gift to a Jade. Anna Wickham. OxBSP
Gift to Be Simple, The. Howard Moss. ImOP; Psk; TwCP
Gift with the Wrappings Off. Mary Elizabeth Counselman. RHPC
Gifts. Mary Elizabeth Coleridge. PBWP
Gifts, The. John Heath-Stubbs. OxBC
Gifts. James Thomson ("B. V."). *Fr.* Sunday up the River, XV.
  OBEV
Gifts. Emma Lazarus. TrJP; WGRP
Gifts. Karen Snow. FYAP
Gifts of God, The. George Herbert. *See* When God had first made man.
Gifts of God, The. Jones Very. AA
Gifts of Rain. Seamus Heaney. IPY
Gig at Big Al's. Heather McHugh. GeTw
Gigantic beauty of a stallion, fresh and responsive to my caresses, A. The
  Stallion. Walt Whitman. *Fr.* Song of Myself, XXXII. ASP; PDV
Gigantic flowers, as though. Spring in the Land. Tuvia Rübner, *tr. by*
  Bernhard Frank. MHeP
Gigantic Grandfather. Karl Heinrich Marx. Hans Magnus Enzensberger,
  tr. by Michael Hamburger. FaBoPV
Gil Brenton. *Unknown.* ESPB; OxBB
Gil Morrice. *Unknown.* OxBB
Gil, the Toreador. Charles Henry Webb. AA
Gilbertus Glanvil, whose heart was a hard as an anvil. *Unknown, tr. by*
  Matthew Prior. FaBoEE
Gildas a Latin "History of Britain's Conquest" wrote. Principal British
  Writers. Edward B. Goodwin. FaBoUs
Gilded Boys, The. Felice Picano. PeHV
Gilded Man, The, *sels.* Ai. AnAn
  Barquisimeto, Venezuela, October 27, 1561. *Fr.* II.
  Orinoco, 1561, The. *Fr.* I.
Gilderoy. *Unknown.* OBET
Giles Collin he said to his mother one day. Lady Alice. *Unknown.*
  ESPB, C *vers.*
Giles Collins he said to his old mother. Lady Alice. *Unknown.* ESPB,
  B *vers.*
Giles Corey. *Unknown.* PAH
Giles Corey of the Salem Farms, *sels.* Longfellow. PAH
  Trial, The.
Giles Corey was a wizzard strong. Giles Corey. *Unknown.* PAH
Giles Johnson, Ph.D. Frank Marshall Davis. BPo; PoBA
Gilgamesh washed his grimy hair, polished his weapons. *Unknown, tr. fr.*
  Babylonian by E. A. Speiser. *Fr.* The Epic of Gilgamesh. Prf
Gill Boy. Dennis Schmitz. NPGG
Gill Morice stood in stable-door. Childe Maurice. *Unknown.* ESPB
Gilly Silly Jarter. *Unknown.* OxNR
Gilt and azure hairpin sways back and forth, A. Song of the West Stream.
  Li Hsün, *tr. by* Lois Fusek. ATF
Gimboling. Isabella Gardner. ErPo
Gimel. Stuart Z. Perkoff. VWA
Gimme the ball, Willie is saying. Charge. Christopher Gilbert. MAYP
Gin a body meet a body. Comin' thro' the Rye. Burns. FaFP; LiTB;
  WBLP
Gin a body meet a body. Rigid Body Sings. James Clerk Maxwell.
  FaBoCo; FaBoPa; Par
  (In Memory of Edward Wilson.) BXAP
Gin by Pailfuls. Sir Walter Scott. ChTr
Gin I Were a Doo. *Unknown.* GBP
Gin I were on my milkwhite steed. The Bents and Broom. *Unknown.*
  OxBB
Gin the Goodwife Stint. Basil Bunting. CTC; TW
Gin ye hae'd corneich airth an' time. To His Coy Mistress. Gerry
  Hamill. BXAP
Ginevra. Samuel Rogers. BeLS; PoLF
Ginevra, *sel.* Shelley.
  "She is still, she is cold." ChER
Ginger Bread Mama. Doughtry Long, Jr. BPo; PoBA
Gingerly walked the hare. *Unknown, tr. by* Arthur Waley. BoS
Gingham dog and the calico cat, The. The Duel. Eugene Field. BeLS;
  CenHV; FaBoBe; FaFP; FaPON; FPL; MoShBr; OBAL; OBCA;
  OHFP; OnMSP; PoLF; PoRA; RHPC
Ginkgoes in Fall. Howard Nemerov. HCAP
Giorno dei Morti. D. H. Lawrence. BrPo; FaBoRV; NOBE; SeCePo

Giotto, I have not found. To Giotto. W. Wesley Trimpi. NePoEA
Giotto's Campanile. Guy Butler. PeSA
Giotto's Tower. Longfellow. EyDe
Giovanni da Fiesole on the Sublime; or, Fra Angelico's "Last Judgment."
  Richard Howard. Prf
"Giovinette, Che Fate All'Amore." Lorenzo Da Ponte, *tr. fr. Italian by*
  Natalie MacFarren. *Fr.* Don Giovanni. TrJP
Gipsies. *See also* Gypsies.
Gipsies ("The gipsies seek wide sheltering wood again"). John Clare.
  ChTr
Gipsies ("The snow falls deep"). John Clare. CH; PoEL-4
  (Gipsy Camp, The.) ChTr
  (Gypsies.) NoP; PrIm
Gipsies, The. "Richard Scrace." CaP
Gipsies came to Lord Cassilis' gate, The. Johnny Faa, the Lord of Little
  Egypt. *Unknown.* EnSB
Gipsies lit their fire by the chalk-pit anew, The. The Idlers. Edmund
  Blunden. BoTP; CH
Gipsies seek wide sheltering woods again, The. Gipsies. John Clare.
  ChTr
Gipsy, The. Vali Mohammad Nazir, *tr. fr. Urdu by* Ahmed Ali. GoT
Gipsy Camp, The. John Clare. *See* "The snow falls deep."
Gipsy Girl, The. Ralph Hodgson. MoBrPo
Gipsy Jane. William Brighty Rands. BoTP; FaPON
Gipsy Laddie, The. *Unknown.* FaBoCh; OxBoLi
Gipsy Man. Dorothy King. BoTP
Gipsy-Night. Richard Hughes. OBWVE
Gipsy of the sea. Stormpetrel. Richard Murphy. IPY
Gipsy Queen. John Alexander Chapman. OBEV
Gipsy Song. Ben Jonson. *See* Gypsies Metamorphosed, The: Faery
  Beam upon You, The.
Gipsy Trail, The. Kipling. PoRA
Gipsy's Warning, The. *Unknown.* BeLS
Giraffe, The, *sel. Nikolai* Gumilev, *tr. fr. Russian by* C. M. Bowra.
  "Listen:/ There roams, far away, by the waters of Clead." FaPON
Giraffe, The. Ron Padgett. *Fr.* Three Animals. TTTS
Giraffe. Stanley Plumly. AmPA
Giraffe. William Jay Smith. ILY
Giraffe. *Unknown, tr. fr. Hottentot.* PeSA
Giraffe and the Woman, The. Laura E. Richards. PDV
Giraffe and Tree. Walter James Turner. CH; GrPl
Giraffes Don't Huff. Karla Kuskin. RAR
Girandole. Dorothy Donnelly. NYBP
Gird up thy loins now like a man. Out of the Whirlwind. Bible, *O.T.*
  Fr. Job: Moreover the Lord answered Job, and said, XL: 7–XLI.
  AWP, XXXVIII: 2–XXXIX.
Girl. Dom Moraes. NePoEA-2
Girl, A. Ezra Pound. MoAB; MoAmPo
Girl. *Unknown, tr. fr. Serbian by* Anne Pennington. RB
Girl and Her Fawn, The. Andrew Marvell. BoTP
Girl at the Seaside. Richard Murphy. BIrV
Girl, Boy, Flower, Bicycle. M. K. Joseph. ATNZ; PeNZ
Girl brought me into the house of love, A. A Secret Kept. Judah Al-
  Harizi, *tr. by* Robert Mezey. UnAS
Girl Butterfly Girl. Unsi al-Haj, *tr. fr. Arabic by* Abdullah al-Udhari.
  MPAW
Girl Combs Her Hair, A. Kimiko Hahn. BrSi
Girl comes out of a doorway in the morning, A. Back Street. Arthur
  Rex Dugard Fairburn. *Fr.* Album Leaves. ATNZ; PeNZ
Girl dreamt she was a butterfly, A. Girl Butterfly Girl. Unsi al-Haj, *tr.*
  by Abdullah al-Udhari. MPAW
Girl Friday. Elaine Equi. UL
Girl Friend Describes the Bull Fight, The. Uruttiran, *tr. fr. Tamil by* A.
  K. Ramanujan. PLW
Girl from Ch'ang-kan, The. Cheng Hsieh, *tr. fr. Chinese by* Jonathan
  Chaves. CoBLCP
Girl from Rafah. Samih al-Qasim, *tr. fr. Arabic by* Sharif Elmusa *and*
  Charles Doria. MAP
Girl grows up hidden in far-off rooms, A. In a Boat on a Summer
  Evening. Lu Yu, *tr. by* Burton Watson. CoBCP
Girl Held without Bail. Margaret Abigail Walker. BPo; CNA; PoBA
Girl Help. Janet Lewis. HeIP; InPK; QFR
Girl I Call Alma, The. Linda Gregg. AmPA; AnAn; NPGG
Girl I Left behind Me, The. Thomas Osborne Davis. FaBoBe; FaFP
Girl I Left behind Me, The. ("I'm lonesome since I cross'd the hill").
  Unknown. OBET
Girl I Left behind Me, The. ("My parents raised me tenderly"). *Unknown.*
  AmFP
Girl I Took to the Cocktail Party, The. Trevor Williams. FiBHP
Girl in a grey frock. A Grey Frock. Zinaida Hippius, *tr. by* Temira
  Pachmuss. PBWP

Girl in a Library, A. Randall Jarrell. NAAL-2; NoAM; NOBA; NoP

Girl in a Nightgown. Wallace Stevens. OxBA

Girl in a White Coat. John Malcolm Brinnin. SaC

Girl in a Window, A. James Wright. ErPo

Girl in poor clothes, her skin lustrous as jade, A. A Teahouse at Hoshioka. Liu E, *tr. by* Jonathan Chaves. CoBLCP

Girl in the Hall, The. John Stone. MT

Girl in the lane, The. Mother Goose. OxNR

Girl in the Park, The. Hone Tuwhare. ATNZ

Girl in the sand, The. Nude Kneeling in Sand. John Logan. ErPo

Girl in the tea shop, The. The Tea Shop. Ezra Pound. HeIP

Girl in the Willow Tree, The. Carolyn Maisel. IHMS

Girl in trousers wheeling a red baby, The. Metamorphoses. Roy Fuller. OxBTC

Girl in White. Stephen Dobyns. MAYP

Girl in yellow slacks kept watching me, A. Between You and Me. Samuel Hazo. GOYP

Girl is our hypothetical enemy, you know!, The. Holy Girl. Yoshioka Minoru, *tr. by* Hiroaki Sato. FCEI

Girl is running. Don't tell me, A. Anti-Short Story. Rae Armantrout. IAT

Girl is twirling a parasol, A. Snapshot. John Fuller. NePoEA-2

Girl, nine years of wonder, A. Pasttime. Emilio de Grazia. TSL

Girl of Mt. Hua, The. Han Yü, *tr. fr. Chinese by* Burton Watson. CoBCP

Girl of My Generation. Jacob Glatstein. AYP

Girl of Pompeii, A. Edward Sandford Martin. AA

Girl of the Future, feared of all. A Dresscessional. Carolyn Wells. WBLP

Girl on the stairs listens to her father, A. Tours. C. D. Wright. MT

Girl Powdering Her Neck. Cathy Song. MAYP

Girl, Prince, Lizard. Heather Ross Miller. MT

Girl Talk. Monique Griffiths. WS

Girl tell me de truth. Nothing to Say. Monique Griffiths. WS

Girl thinks if I can only manage, The. Marie Luise Kaschnitz, *tr. fr. German by* Beatrice Cameron. *Fr.* Return to Frankfurt. OV

Girl to Soldier on Leave. Isaac Rosenberg. MMA

Girl today, dreaming, A. Auf dem Wasser zu Singen. Stephen Spender. EnLoPo

Girl, twenty—her black hair, The. Yosano Akiko, *tr. fr. Japanese by* Hiroaki Sato. *Fr.* Thirty-nine Tanka. FCEI

Girl Walking. Charles G. Bell. ErPo

Girl Warrior, The. *Unknown, tr. fr. Spanish by* Angel Flores. DMH

Girl, when rejecting me you never guessed. To a Jilt. Martin Armstrong. FaBoEE

Girl Who Learned to Sing in Crow, The. Paul Mariani. GeTw

Girl Who Loved the Sky, The. Anita Endrezze-Danielson. HATNAP

Girl with Doves. Stephen Gray. PeSA

Girl with Long Dark Hair. Stephen Gray. PeSA

Girl with Pitcher. Ruth Dallas. PeNZ

Girl with the beautiful legs, The. The Tides. Paul Blackburn. PoM

Girl with the Green Skirt. Dana Naone. CDW

Girl with the Jersey, The. Ben King. AnAmPo

Girl working the xerox in the stationery store, The. For Emily (Dickinson). Maureen Owen. UL

Girl Writing Her English Paper, The. Robert Wallace. Psk

Girl, your young loveliness. White Swan. A. Leyeles, *tr. by* Keith Bosley. VWA

Girls. Kenneth Rosen. AmPA

Girls and boys come out to play. *Unknown.* BoTP; PYC

Girls are simply the prettiest things. My Cat and I. Roger McGough. OxBTC

Girls around Cape Horn, The. *Unknown.* AmFP

Girl's back, reflected upside down in the mirror, The. Mediterranean Woman. Kondo Azuma, *tr. by* Geoffrey Bownas *and* Anthony Thwaite. PeBJV

Girls Bathing, Galway 1965. Seamus Heaney. InPS

Girls, brighter than wine, are clothed and naked, The. Night Club. F. R. Scott. NOBC

Girls Can, Too! Lee Bennett Hopkins. RHPC

Girl's far treble, muted to the heat, The. Milkmaid. Laurie Lee. BoLoP; FaBoTw

Girls from Home. Abraham Reisen, *tr. fr. Yiddish.* VWA, *tr. by* Keith Bosley

Girl's Hair, A. Dafydd ab Edmwnd, *tr. fr. Welsh by* Gwyn Williams. OBWVE

Girls have woven themselves into autumn evenings. Girls in Crotona Park. Anna Margolin, *tr. by* Marcia Falk. PeBMYV

Girls in Crotona Park. Anna Margolin, *tr. fr. Yiddish by* Marcia Falk. PeBMYV

Girls in the Plural. Medbh McGuckian. DT

Girls in Their Seasons. Derek Mahon. BoLoP

Girl's Lamentation, The. William Allingham. SeCePo; TIRV

Girls of Llanbadarn, The. Dafydd ap Gwilym, *tr. fr. Welsh.* DiPo, *tr. by* Leslie Norris; OBWVE, *tr. by* Rolfe Humphries.

Girls on mopeds rode to Fécamp parties. The Musical Orchard. Douglas Dunn. FaBoMo

Girls on the Yueh River. Li Po, *tr. fr. Chinese.* ChTr

Girls planting paddy. Raizan, *tr. by* Geoffrey Bownas *and* Anthony Thwaite. PeBJV

Girls scream. School's Out. W. H. Davies. OBMV

Girl's Song. *Unknown, tr. fr. Taitok by* Willard Trask. LLLT

Girls today in society, The. Brush Up Your Shakespeare. Cole Porter. OBAL

Girls, under this tree where you sit observed. Melancholia. Stephen Plaice. NPo

Girls wake, stretch, and pad up to the door, The. Apartment Cats. Thom Gunn. GrPl

Girls Working in Banks. Karl Shapiro. WeW

Girod Street Cemetery: New Orleans. Harry Morris. GoYe

Girt in my guiltless gown, as I sit here and sew. A Woman's Answer. *At. to* Surrey, Earl of. SiPS

Girtonian Funeral, A. *Unknown.* FaBoCo; Par

Gislebertus' Eve. John Berryman. LCAP

Gisli, the Chieftain, *sel.* Isabella Valancy Crawford. Song of the Arrow, The. OBCV

Gist of the Story, The. Salah Abd al-Sabur, *tr. fr. Arabic by* Lena Jayyusi *and* John Heath-Stubbs. MAP

Git Along Down to Town. *Unknown.* AmFP

Git Along, Little Dogies. *Unknown. See* Whoopee-Ti-Yi-Yo.

Gita Govinda, The, *sels.* Jayadeva, *tr. fr. Sanskrit.*
  Hymn to Vishnu. *Tr. by* Sir Edwin Arnold. AWP
  "Sandal and garment of yellow and lotus garlands upon his body of blue." *Tr. by* George Keyt. ErPo

Gitanjali, *sels.* Rabindranath Tagore.
  Day after Day. *Fr.* LXXVI. OBMV
  "Deliverance is not for me in renunciation." *Fr.* LXXIII. WGRP
  "Have you not heard his silent steps?." *Fr.* XLV. WGRP
  "He it is, the innermost one, who awakens my being with his deep hidden touches." *Fr.* LXXII. WGRP
  "Here is thy footstool and there rest thy feet." *Fr.* X. WGRP
  I Have Got My Leave. OBMV
  "I know not from what distant time thou art near coming nearer to meet me.." *Fr.* XLVI. WGRP
  If It Is Not My Portion. *Fr.* LXXIV. OBMV
  "Leave this chanting and singing and telling of beads." *Fr.* XI. WGRP
  On the Slope of the Desolate River. *Fr.* LXIV. OBMV
  Thou Art the Sky. *Fr.* LXVII. OBMV

Giuseppe, da barber, ees greata for "mash." Mia Carlotta. T. A. Daly. NBLV

Giv but to things their tru esteem. Right Apprehension. Thomas Traherne. PoEL-2

Give a man a horse he can ride. Gifts. James Thomson ("B. V."). *Fr.* Sunday up the River, XV. OBEV

Give a man his. Wait for Me. Robert Creeley. NOBA; PPP

Give All to Love. Emerson. AmPP; AnAmPo; AWP; FaFP; FPL; LiTA; NOBA; OBEV; OxBA; PoEL-4; PoLF; TAP; TrGrPo

Give as you would if an angel. How to Give. *Unknown.* BLRP

Give attention to my ditty and I'll not keep you long. My Grandfather's Days. *Unknown.* OBET

Give beauty all her right. Thomas Campion. AAS; OBSC
  (Beauty Is Not Bound.) TrGrPo

Give ear my children to my words. John Rogers' Exhortation to His Children. *Unknown. Fr.* The New England Primer. OBCA

Give Ear, O God, to My Loud Cry. Thomas Prince. AH

Give Ear, O Heavens, to That Which I Declare. Henry Ainsworth. AH

Give ear, O my people, to my law. Psalm LXXVIII ("Give ear, O my people, to my law. "). Bible, *O.T. Fr.* Psalms.
  (Psalm LXXVIII: "There where the deepe did show his sandy flore", *paraphrased by* the Countess of Pembroke) OBVE

Give ear to my prayer, O God. Psalm LV ("Give ear to my prayer. "). Bible, *O.T. Fr.* Psalms. AWP
  (Psalm LV: Exaudi, Deus: "My God most glad to look, most prone to hear," *paraphrased by* the Countess of Pembroke) OBVE, 1-4; WPE
  (Wings.) FaPON, *fr.* 6-7.

Give Ear, Ye Heavens. Bible, *O.T. Fr.* Deuteronomy, XXXII: 1-43. TrJP

Give ear you lusty gallants. A Famous Sea-Fight. John Looke. CoMu

Give God thy heart. Motto for a Sundial. *Unknown.* FaBoEE

Give greatly of your grunts, O pig. Hymn to Joy. Julia Cunningham. PChr

Give her but a least excuse to love me! Song. Robert Browning. *Fr.* Pippa Passes. ViBoPo

Give him the darkest inch your shelf allows. George Crabbe. E. A. Robinson. BLPL; CMoP; LiTA; LiTM; MoAB; MoAmPo; NAAL-2; NOBA; NoP; OxBA; PoEL-5; TAP

Give honor and love for evermore. Peter Cooper. AA

Give Isaac the nymph who no beauty can boast. Sheridan. *Fr.* The Duenna. NOIV

"Give it to him!" The Seventh Round. James Merrill. ASP

Give Lucinda pearl nor stone. To the New Year. Thomas Carew. CaPo

Give me a boy whose tender skin. Martial, *tr.* by Brian Hill. PeHV

Give me a chair. Song of the Poor Man. *Unknown, tr.* by Anselm Hollo. TTY

Give me a color. America. Wendy Rose. CDW

Give me a death like Buddha's. Let me fall. Stanley Moss. SM

"Give me a fillet, Love," quoth I. Love and Life. Julie Mathilde Lippmann. AA

Give me a girle (if one I needs must meet). Women. William Cartwright. ErPo

Give me a good digestion, Lord, and also something to digest. An Ancient Prayer. Thomas H. B. Webb, *after* A Prayer Found in Chester Cathedral. BLPA; FaBoBe

Give me a happy heart and suasive tongue. A Happy Heart. Josephine D. Henderson Heard. CBWP-4

Give Me a Kiss from Those Sweet Lips of Thine. *Unknown.* InvP

Give me a man that is not dull. His Desire. Robert Herrick. OxBSP

Give me a race that is run in a breath. The Hundred-Yard Dash. William Lindsey. AA

Give me a royal niche—it is my due. George III. Thackeray. *Fr.* The Georges. FaBoEE

Give me a spoon of oleo, Ma. Domestic Science. *Unknown.* WBLP

Give me a thrill, says the reader. Fiction and the Reading Public. Philip Larkin. NOBL; OBSV

Give me an apple. The Apple. Tadeusz Rozewicz, *tr.* by Czeslaw Milosz. PwPP

"Give me but two brigades," said Hooker. The Battle of Lookout Mountain. George Henry Boker. PAH

Give me depth. Autumn's Poem. Kim Hyun-sung, *tr.* by Koh Chang-soo. ACKP

Give Me Five. William J. Harris. CNA

Give me, give me Buriano. Bacchus's Opinion of Wine, and Other Beverages. Francesco Redi, *tr. fr. Italian by* Leigh Hunt. *Fr.* Bacchus in Tuscany. AWP; OBVE

Give me, great God! said I, a little farm. Verses Written in the Chiosk at Pera, overlooking Constantinople. Lady Mary Wortley Montagu. OBTV

Give me hunger. At a Window. Carl Sandburg. FaBoBe; TrPWD

Give me, in this inconstant ebb and flow. Seaward Bound. Alice Brown. TrPWD

Give Me Jesus. *Unknown.* BPo

Give Me Leave. "A. W." TrGrPo
  (Petition to Have Her Leave to Die.) OBSC

Give Me My Infant Now. Te-whaka-io-roa, *tr. fr. Maori by* John White. NAs; WTO

Give me, my love, that billing kiss. The Kiss. Thomas Moore. EnLoPo

Give me my robe, put on my crown; I have. Death of Cleopatra. Shakespeare. *Fr.* Antony and Cleopatra, V, ii. FiP
  (Cleopatra's Death.) TrGrPo
  (Immortal Longings.) FaBoRV

Give me my scallop-shell of quiet. The Passionate Man's Pilgrimage. Sir Walter Ralegh. AAS; ChTr; ElL; LiTB; MePo; NOBE; NoP; OBSC; PoE; PoEL-2; PoRA; RB; SeCePo; TrGrPo
  (His Pilgrimage.) OBEV
  (My Pilgrimage.) WGRP
  (Pilgrimage, The.) SiPS

Give me my scallop shell of quiet; let me go. Theme and Variations. W. P. Ker. PoSH

Give Me My Work. George Whetstone. ElL

Give me no more lessons of history. Ecclesiastes. Peter Goldsworthy. UAS

Give Me Not Tears: Despair. Rose Hawthorne Lathrop. AA

Give Me Not Tears: Joy. Rose Hawthorne Lathrop. AA

Give me, O indulgent Fate! The Petition for an Absolute Retreat. Anne Finch, Winchilsea, Countess of. PoEL-3; TrGrPo; WPE

Give me of every language, first my vigorous English. The English Language. William Wetmore Story. GN

Give me of your bark, O Birch-tree! Longfellow. *Fr.* The Song of Hiawatha. Mes
  (Hiawatha's Canoe.) OHIP

Give me one kiss. To Dianeme. Robert Herrick. CaPo; FaBoBe

Give me something to eat. Poor Crow! Mary Mapes Dodge. OBCA

Give me sweet nectar in a kiss. *Unknown.* FaBoEE

Give me that man that dares bestride. His Cavalier. Robert Herrick. CaPo; GoJo

Give me the dance of your boughs, O Tree. Song to a Tree. Edwin Markham. FaPON

Give me the Daulian bird and Locrian Arsinoë. From V. C. (a Gentleman of Verona). Gavin Ewart. OxBC

Give me the hills and wide water. The Hills and the Sea. Wilfred Campbell. CaP

Give me the lowest place: not that I dare. The Lowest Place. Christina Rossetti. NOBVV; TrPWD

Give me the merchants of the Indian mines. Mine Argosy from Alexandria. Christopher Marlowe. *Fr.* The Jew of Malta, I, i. ChTr

Give me the right of way. Irish. Paul Celan, *tr.* by Michael Hamburger. OBVE

Give me the room whose every nook. The Library. Frank Dempster Sherman. AA

"Give me the salt spray in my face." What the Red-haired Bo'sun Said. Charles H. Souter. PoAu-1

Give Me the Splendid Silent Sun. Walt Whitman. AA; BoNaP; FaPON; HAP; MoAmPo; NOBA

Give me the sunlight and the sea. Sunlight and Sea. Alfred Noyes. MOS

Give me the wretched refuse of your teams: pitchers with sore elbows. Amurrika! Philip Appleman. BXAP

Give Me Three Grains of Corn, Mother. Amelia Blandford Edwards. AS, *with music;* BLPA

Give Me Thy Heart. Adelaide Anne Procter. ACP

Give me to die unwitting of the day. Mors Benefica. Edmund Clarence Stedman. AA

Give me truths. Blight. Emerson. NOBA; NoP

Give Me What the Tree Has. Natan Zach, *tr. fr. Hebrew by* Warren Bargad *and* Stanley F. Chyet. IP

Give me white paper! Columbus. Edward Everett Hale. PAH

Give me your hand old Revolutionary. The Centenarian's Story. Walt Whitman. CTC

Give me your pardon, sir. I have done you wrong. Shakespeare. *Fr.* Hamlet, V, ii. DL

Give me your tired, your poor. The Tragic Condition of the Statue of Liberty. Bernadette Mayer. UL

Give money me, take friendship whoso list. Of Money. Barnabe Googe. ElL; FF; NBLV; NoP

Give No White Flower. Brenda Chamberlain. NeIP

Give Not Our Blankets, Tax-Fed Squire. Ebenezer Elliott. *Fr.* The Year of Seeds. Son

Give Our Conscience Light. Aline B. Carter. TrPWD

Give over, now, red roses. Warning of Winter. Mary Ursula Bethell. ATNZ; FaBoWP; PeNZ

Give over seeking bastard joy. Exhortation. Louise Bogan. QFR

Give over to high things the fervent thought. To Lovers of Earth: Fair Warning. Countee Cullen. CDC

Give pardon, blessèd soul, to my bold cries. On the Death of Sir Philip Sidney. Henry Constable. EilL; OBEV; OBSC
  (To Sir Philip Sidney's Soul.) EilL; SeCePo

Give patient eare to sumething I man saye. Admonition to Montgomerie. James I, King of England. GTBS; GTBS-P; OxBS

Give Peace in These Our Days, O Lord. Edmund Grindal. AH

Give Peace, O God, the Nations Cry. John W. Norris. AH

Give place all ye that doth rejoice. Sir Thomas Wyatt. SiPS

Give [*or* Geve] Place, Ye Lovers. Surrey, Earl of. AAS; SiPS
  (Praise of His Love, Wherein He Reproveth Them That Compare Their Ladies with His, A.) EilL

Give place, you ladies, and be gone! A Praise of His Lady. *At. to* John Heywood. EilL; OBEV
  (On the Princess Mary.) OBSC

Give store of days, good Jove, give length of years. Juvenal, *tr. fr. Latin by* Henry Vaughan. *Fr.* Satires, X. OBSV

Give Thanks *or* Thanks for Everything. Helen Isabella Tupper. BLRP

Give thanks for this turn for the better. A Change in Style. Eochadh O'Hussey. NOIV

Give the king thy judgments, O God. Psalm LXXII ("Give the king thy judgments. . ."). Bible, *O.T. Fr.* Psalms.
  (Psalm LXXII: "Looke how the woods, where enterlaced trees", *paraphrased by* the Countess of Pembroke) OBVE

Give the mourning doves any sun. The Ruined Motel. Reginald Gibbons. MAYP

Give the sounds of the curved mated phonographs. Three Found Poems. George Hitchcock. OBAL

Give them my regards when you go to the school reunion. More of a Corpse than a Woman. Muriel Rukeyser. NMM

Give Them the Flowers Now. *Unknown.* WBLP

Give to a little fairy a little mountain. Abode of the Roaming Immortals. Cheng Ch'ou-yu, *tr. by* Dominic Cheung. IFON

Give to me the life I love. The Vagabond. Robert Louis Stevenson. BrPo

Give to the Living. Ida Goldsmith Morris. WBLP

Give to the winds thy fears. Courage. Paul Gerhardt, *tr. by* John Wesley. WGRP

Give unto the Lord, O ye mighty. Psalm XXIX ("Give unto the Lord. . ."). Bible, *O.T. Fr.* Psalms. AWP

Give up the bitterness. Dionne Brand. *Fr.* Epigrams to Ernesto Cardenal in Defense of Claudia, XXXV. PBCV

Give us a good digestion, Lord. *See* Give me a good digestion, Lord.

"Give us a song!" the soldiers cried. The Song of the Camp. Bayard Taylor. AA; AnAmPo; BeLS; GN; WBLP

Give us a virile Christ for these rough days! A Virile Christ. Rex Boundy. WGRP

Give us a watchword for the hour. Evangelize! Henry Crocker. BLRP

Give us a wrack or two, Good Lard. The Wreckers' Prayer. Theodore Goodridge Roberts. OBCV

Give us another poem, he said. Patrick Kavanagh. FaBCIP; IPY

Give Us the Right to Vote! Emma Döltz, *tr. fr. German by* Susan L. Cocalis *and* Gerlinde Geiger. DMG

Give Way. Donald Finkel. NePoEA-2

Give Way! Charlotte Perkins Gilman. WGRP

Give way, an ye be ravished by the sun. To Marygolds. Robert Herrick. NAEL-1

Give way to the man coming at you. Give Way. Donald Finkel. NePoEA-2

Give Way, Ye Gates. Theodore Roethke. CMoP

Giveaway, The. Phyllis McGinley. PoRA

Given Note, The. Seamus Heaney. FaBCIP

Given the morning, its rush of flowers. Machupuchare. What the Mountain Said. Shaking the Dead Bones, Christmas Eve, 1974. Joseph Stroud. NPGG

Giver of bliss and pain, of song and prayer. William Alexander Percy. TrPWD

Giver of Life, The. *Unknown, tr. fr. Dahomean song by* Frances Herskovits. EaLo

Giving and Taking. James Kirkup. EaLo

Giving oneself to the dentist or doctor who is a good one. The Kind of Act Of. Robert Creeley. NeAP

Giving Potatoes. Adrian Mitchell. NBLV; RB

Giving Rabbit to My Cat Bonnie. Anne Stevenson. FaBoWP

Giving Thanks, 4. Bible, *O.T. See* Psalms: Psalm C ("Make a joyful noise. . .").

Giving Up Butterflies. Geraldine Kudaka. BrSi

Giving Up on the Shore. Gabriel Preil, *tr. fr. Hebrew by* Gabriel Levin. VWA

Giving up women is worse than animal laxatives. John Tranter. *Fr.* Crying in Early Infancy, XVIII. NoAM

Giving, while the rain lasts, soft noises. Eaves. Ellis Jones, *tr. by* Anthony Conran. OBWVE

Gizzard and some ruby inner parts, A. Margaret Avison. HAP

Glacier. Norman Nicholson. OBTV

Glad and blithe mote ye be. A Hymn of the Incarnation. *Unknown.* MeEL

Glad at the Cold (1955). Alan Dugan. NoAM

Glad, but not flush'd with gladness. Swinburne. *Fr.* Before the Mirror. OBEV

Glad Christmas comes, and every hearth. December. John Clare. OBCP

Glad Day. Louis Untermeyer. TrJP

Glad Eye, The. Paul Muldoon. NoAM

Glad harvest greets us, The; brave toiler for bread. Song of the Harvest. Henry Stevenson Washburn. OHIP

Glad that I live am I. A Little Song of Life. Lizette Woodworth Reese. FaPON; OBCA

Glad youth had come thy sixteenth year to crown. Ausonius. PeHV

Glade, The. Robert Kelly. *Fr.* The Book of Persephone, 18. PoM

Gladstone. Julian Symons. WaP

Gladstone was still respected. Yeux Glauques. Ezra Pound. *Fr.* Hugh Selwyn Mauberley. (Life and Contacts). MoAmPo

Gladys. Hugo Williams. *Fr.* Calling Your Name in the Zoo. NPo

Glamour of the end attic, the smell of old, The. Perdita. Louis MacNeice. PoA

Glance, A. *Unknown, tr. fr. Irish by* Thomas Kinsella. NOIV

Glance in the mirror reveals, A. Bad Mirror. Hermann Jandl, *tr. by* Beth Bjorklund. CoAuP

Glanced down at Shannon from the sky-way. Irish-American Dignitary. Austin Clarke. BIrV

Glances. William Stafford. SM

Glancing near the hands cutting. Miura Chora, *tr. fr. Japanese by* Hiroaki Sato. *Fr.* Sixteen Hokku. FCEI

Glanmore Sonnets, *sels.* Seamus Heaney.
 "I dreamt we slept in a moss in Donegal." *Fr.* X. NoP
 "This evening the cuckoo and the corncrake." *Fr.* III. IPY
 "Thunderlight on the split logs: big raindrops." *Fr.* VII. IPY
 "Vowels plowed into other: opened ground." *Fr.* I. NoP

Glaring glumly at the sky. *Unknown, tr. by* Geoffrey Bownas *and* Anthony Thwaite. PeBJV

Glasgerion. *Unknown.* ESPB; OxBB

Glasgow Peggie. *Unknown.* ESPB

Glasgow Schoolboys, Running Backwards. Douglas Dunn. OxBC

Glasgow Street. William Montgomerie. OxBS

Glass. Takako Uchino Lento, *tr. fr. Japanese by the author.* BoWoP

Glass. W. S. Merwin. EAS

Glass Blower, The. James Scully. NYBP; TwCP

Glass Bubbles, The. Samuel Greenberg. LiTA

Glass captain who has sailed away, The. Composition in Glass, for. Michael Harlow. ATNZ

Glass covers windows. Covers. Nikki Giovanni. RAR

Glass Dialectic. Howard Nemerov. WaP

Glass Eaters, The. George Jonas. NeAC

Glass falls lower, The. Sad Green. Sylvia Townsend Warner. MoBrPo

Glass has been falling all the afternoon, The. Storm Warnings. Adrienne Rich. AiP; GOYP; NAAL-2; NIP

Glass Hat, The. László Kálnoky, *tr. fr. Hungarian by* Jascha Kessler. FOC

Glass I've wanted to live. Through You. Edwin Honig. TAP

Glass King, The. Eavan Boland. CIP

Glass of Beer, A. James Stephens. CMoP; FaBoCo; FiBHP; InPK; MoP; NBLV; OBMV; OxBS; OxBTC; RB; SeCePo; TW (Righteous Anger.) MoAB; MoBrPo

Glass of Water, The. Wallace Stevens. MoAB; MoAmPo; OxBA; TAP

Glass on the picture from the Bible, The. Darkening Hotel Room. Alfred Corn. MAYP

Glass, out of deep and out of desperate want. Upon Glass: Epigram. Robert Herrick. JCP

Glass Town, The. Alastair Reid. NYBP

Glass was the street. Emily Dickinson. OxBA

Glassblower lies here at rest, A. John Bingham Morton. FaBoEE

Glassed with cold sleep and dazzled by the moon. Train Journey. Judith Wright. PBWP

Glasses are raised, the voices drift into laughter, The. Pub. Julian Symons. LiTB; WaP

Glaucopis. Richard Hughes. OBMV

Glaucous-Gull's Death, The. Daniel James O'Sullivan. NeIP

Glaukos, why is it you and I are honored beyond all men. Sarpedon to Glaukos. Homer, *tr. fr. Greek by* Richard Lattimore. *Fr.* The Iliad, II. WaaP

Glazed day crumbles to its fall, The. Provincetown, Mass. Harvey Shapiro. PoA

Glazier, The. Stéphane Mallarmé, *tr. fr. French.* OBVE, *tr. by* Keith Bosley

Glazunoviana. John Ashbery. LCAP

Gleam ochre. Ladybird. Ingrid Jonker, *tr. by* Jack Cope *and* William Plomer. OV

Gleamed a resplendent star. At Christmas-Tide. Henrietta Cordelia Ray. CBWP-3

Gleaming of gold deceives, The. Last Brightness. Leah Goldberg, *tr. by* Robert Alter. OV

Gleaner, The. Jane Taylor. OxBChV

Gleaners walk toward where the sunlight is, The. Buson, *tr. fr. Japanese by* Hiroaki Sato. *Fr.* Eighty-seven Hokku. FCEI

Glen Lough. Geoffrey Grigson, *tr. fr. Irish by* James Clarence Mangan. FaBoPP; OBTV

Glen of Silence, The. "Hugh MacDiarmid." CMoP

Glen Pean. Denis Rixson. PoSH

Glen Rosa. William Jeffrey. PoSH

Glenaradale. Walter Chalmers Smith. OBEV

Glenarm. John Lyle Donaghy. NeIP

Glenaveril, *sel.* "Owen Meredith." Tears. EBVV

Glencoe. G. K. Chesterton. PoSH

Glencoe. Douglas Stewart. CBAP

Glengormley. Derek Mahon. CIP; FaBCIP

Glenkindie was ance a harper gude. Glasgerion. *Unknown.* ESPB

Glenlogie; or, Jean o Bethelnie. *Unknown.* ESPB

Glenn Miller and I were heroes. Jack Kerouac. *Fr.* Mexico City Blues, 179. NeAP

Glenn Miller's music is a trunk. Carmen Valle, *tr. by* Julio Marzán. InW

Glens, The. John Hewitt. NeIP

Glide Soft, Ye Silver Floods. William Browne. *Fr.* Britannia's Pastorals. EIL, *fr.* II, Song 1.

Glides along midnight, holding up her lamp. Elan. Sándor Weöres, *tr. by* William Jay Smith. MHuP

Glimmers. Jack Marshall. UL

Glimpse, A. Frances Cornford. OBMV

Glimpse. Pearl Cleage Lomax. PoBA

Glimpse, A. Walt Whitman. AmPP; AnAmPo; OxBA; PeHV; PPP

Glimpse of a once-loved face, The. What Do They Say. Gary Snyder. NNaP

Glimpse of an Open Dream. David Avidan, *tr. fr. Hebrew by* Warren Bargad *and* Stanley F. Chyet. IP

Glimpse of the Body Shop, A. Stephen Berg. NaP

Glimpse through an interstice caught, A. A Glimpse. Walt Whitman. AmPP; AnAmPo; OxBA; PeHV; PPP

Glimpsed world, halfway through the film, A. The Malice of Innocence. Denise Levertov. NNaP

Glimpses of Infancy. Priscilla Jane Thompson. CBWP-2

Glint of hoe. Sampu, *tr. by* Geoffrey Bownas *and* Anthony Thwaite. PeBJV

Glion?—Ah, twenty years, it cuts. Obermann Once More. Matthew Arnold. PoEL-5

Glitter of the water and the wake, The. Aberdeen University 1945-49: I. Iain Crichton Smith. UAS

Glittering, adroit, the Sicilian wonder. Death and Empedocles 444 B.C. Horace Gregory. PoA

Glittering Fragments. Hara Tamiki, *tr. fr. Japanese by* Geoffrey Bownas *and* Anthony Thwaite. PeBJV

Glittering, glittering, fireflies in the grass. Tsung Ch'en, *tr. fr. Chinese by* Jonathan Chaves. *Fr.* Miscellaneous Words on the Lake. CoBLCP

Glittering high in the midnight sky the starry rockets soar. Dewey and His Men. Wallace Rice. PAH

Glittering leaves of the rhododendrons, The. Green Symphony. John Gould Fletcher. MoAmPo

Glittering rises in flocks, The. The Approaches. W. S. Merwin. NOBA; Prf

Glittering roofs are still with frost, The; each worn. A January Morning. Archibald Lampman. OBCV

Glittering sky: thirty blows of the staff! Toin, *tr. by* Lucien Stryk *and* Takashi Ikemoto. ZPCJ

Glittering topaz in your glass, The. At a Danse Macabre. Charles Spear. ATNZ; PeNZ

Gloat, glittering talmudist. Talmudist. Stanley Burnshaw. DiPo; VWA

Globe, a paper of the Tories, The. A Suggestion Made by the Posters of the *Globe*. J. E. Thorold Rogers. FaBoEE

Globeflowers on a Riverbank. Tameie, *tr. fr. Japanese by* Steven D. Carter. WFTW

Globetrotter. Washington Delgado, *tr. fr. Spanish by* David Tipton. Per

Gloire de Dijon. D. H. Lawrence. BrPo; CMoP; ELP; EnLoPo; ErPo; GBL; NoAM

Gloom of death is on the raven's wing, The. The Raven. E. A. Robinson, *after* Nicarchus. AWP; FaBoEE; OBAL

Gloom of night had overspread the land, The. The Nativity. Mary Weston Fordham. CBWP-2

Glooms of the live-oaks, beautiful-braided and woven. The Marshes of Glynn. Sidney Lanier. AA; AmPP; AnAmPo; LiTA; NOBA; OxBA; PrIm; WGRP

Gloomy am I, oppressed and sad. The Poet's Arbour in the Birchwood. Edward Williams, *tr. by* Kenneth Hurlstone Jackson. OBWVE

Gloomy and dark art thou, O chief of the mighty Omahas. To the Driving Cloud. Longfellow. ChTr; FaBoRV; PoEL-5

Gloomy Cathedral, A. Paris. Gertrud Kolmar, *tr. by* David Kipp. PBWP

Gloomy cripple with his empty eyes, The. The Cripple. Khalil Khouri, *tr. by* Sharif Elmusa *and* Christopher Middleton. MAP

Gloomy grammarians in golden gowns. Of the Manner of Addressing Clouds. Wallace Stevens. PoA

(On the Manner of Addressing Clouds.) QFR

Gloomy hulls, in armour grim, The. The *Temeraire*. Herman Melville. WaaP

Gloomy night embraced the place. The Shepherds' Hymn. Richard Crashaw. *Fr.* In the Holy Nativity of Our Lord God. NOBE

Gloomy Night of Sadness, The. *Unknown.* AH

Gloomy thought, Ben Bulben, A. The Deserted Mountain. *Unknown, tr. by* John Montague. BIrV

Gloria in Excelsis. *Unknown.* WGRP

"Gloria Patri," The. John Heywood. ACP

Gloriana Dying. Sylvia Townsend Warner. FaBoWP

Glories of Our Blood and State, The. James Shirley. *Fr.* The Contention of Ajax and Ulysses, sc. iii. ChTr; FaBoRV; HAP; InvP; JCP; NoP; OBD; OBS; PoRA; PPP; TrGrPo; WaaP

(Death the Leveller.) BLPL; FaPoR; FF; GTBS; GTBS-P; LiTB; NOBE; OBEV; UnPo

(Dirge: "Glories of our blood and state, The.") ACP; AWP; OAEL-1; PoEL-2

Glories of the world sink down in gloom, The. Sic Transit. Joseph Mary Plunkett. ACP

Glories of the world struck me, made me aria, once, The. John Berryman. *Fr.* Dream Songs. HCAP

Glories, pleasures, pomps, delights, and ease. John Ford. *Fr.* The Broken Heart, V, iii. OBS

Glorious Image of the Maker's Beauty, The. Spenser. *Fr.* Amoretti, LXIV. EBEV; NAEL-1; OAEL-1; Son.

Glorious it is/ to see long-haired winter caribou. *Unknown, tr. fr. Eskimo. Fr.* Song of Caribou, Musk Oxen, Women, and Men Who Would Be Manly. RFM

Glorious sun went blushing to his bed, The. Michael Drayton. *Fr.* Idea's Mirrour, XXV. OBSC

Glorious the day when in arms at Assunpink. Assunpink and Princeton. Thomas Dunn English. PAH

Glorious the sun in mid career. Christopher Smart. *Fr.* A Song to David. FaBoCh

Glorious Things of Thee Are Spoken. John Newton. NOCV; WGRP

Glorious Twelfth, The. Robert Greacen. NeIP

Glorious Victory of Navarino! The. *Unknown.* CoMu

Glorious Virgin, heavenly vision. O Virgin. *Unknown, tr. by* Douglas Hyde. WTO

Glory. D. H. Lawrence. OxBSP

Glory. Marianne Moore. NYBP

Glory. Jacques Prévert, *tr. fr. French by* Michael Benedikt. POS

Glory, The. Edward Thomas. OxBTC; TOF

Glory. Joseph Wise. AH

Glory and Enduring Fame. William Gilmore Simms. Son

Glory and honor and fame and everlasting laudation. Sherman. Richard Watson Gilder. AA

Glory and loveliness have passed away. To Leigh Hunt, Esq. Keats. EnRP; Son

(Dedication: To Leigh Hunt, Esq.) OBNC

Glory be to God for dappled things. Pied Beauty. Gerard Manley Hopkins. AWP; BrPo; CMoP; EaLo; EBVV; FaBoMo; FaFP; GoJo; GTBS-P; HAP; HeIP; HoPM; InPK; InPS; InvP; LiTB; LiTM; MoAB; MoBrPo; MoP; NAEL-2; NoAM; NOBE; NOBVV; NoP; OAEL-2; OBEV; OBMV; OBNC; OxBSP; PoE; PoRA; PPP; PrIm; RB; SCV; SoSe; SOTW; TEP; TrGrPo; TTTS; WeW

Glory be to God on high. The Incarnation. Charles Wesley. NOCV

Glory be to God on high, and on earth peace, good-will towards men. Gloria in Excelsis. *Unknown.* WGRP

Glory Dead. *Unknown.* PBCV

Glory Hallelujah! or, John Brown's Body. *Unknown, at. to* Charles Sprague Hall *and to* Thomas Brigham Bishop. *See* John Brown's body.

Glory is of the sun, too, and the sun of suns. Glory. D. H. Lawrence. OxBSP

Glory of and Grace in the Church Set Out, The. Edward Taylor. *Fr.* God's Determinations. AmPP

Glory of God, The. Bible, O.T. *See* Psalms: Psalm XIX ("The heavens declare the glory of God").

Glory of God in Creation, The. Thomas Moore. OHIP

(Thou Art, O God.) TrPWD

Glory of Hanalei is its heavy rain, The. Alfred Alohikea, *tr. by* S. H. Elbert *and* N. Mahoe. WTO

Glory of Him who moves all things rays forth, The. Dante, *tr. fr. Italian. Fr.* Divina Commedia: Paradiso, I. NAWM-1, *tr. by* John Ciardi.

Glory of Love is brightest when the glory of self is dim, The. The True Apostolate. Ruby T. Weyburn. BLRP

Glory of Nature, The. Frederick Tennyson. OBNC

Glory of soundless heaven, wheel of stars. John Hall Wheelock. NePoAm

Glory of the beauty of the morning, The. The Glory. Edward Thomas. OxBTC; TOF

Glory of the Day Was in Her Face, The. James Weldon Johnson. BANP; CDC; IDB; PoBA

Glory of the great all-mover goes, The. Dante, *tr. fr. Italian by* T. W. Ramsey. *Fr. Divina Commedia*: Paradiso, I. OBD

Glory of Women. Siegfried Sassoon. MMA; NAEL-2; OBWP

Glory to God and to God's Mother chaste. To Dante Alighieri (He Commends the Work of Dante's Life). Giovanni Quirino, *tr. by* Dante Gabriel Rossetti. AWP

Glory to Osiris, the Prince of Everlastingness. He Singeth a Hymn to Osiris, the Lord of Eternity. *Unknown, tr. fr. Egyptian by* Robert Hillyer. *Fr. Book of the Dead.* AWP

Glory to Thee, My God, This Night. Thomas Ken. NOCV

Glory to you, oh pain, sorrow unending! The Grey-eyed King. "Anna Akhmatova," *tr. by* Robert Tracy. PBWP

Glory Trumpeter, The. Derek Walcott. NAEL-2

Glose. Michael Malinowitz. EOEF

Gloss. Padraic Fiacc. CIP

Gloss. David McCord. OBAL

Gloucester Harbor. Elizabeth Stuart Phelps Ward. AA

Gloucester Moors ("Mile behind is Gloucester town, A"), *sel.* William Vaughn Moody. AnAmPo; NOBA; OxBA
  "This earth is not the steadfast place." WGRP

Gloucestershire Wassail. *Unknown.* OBET

Glove, The. Harold Bond. NYBP

Glove, The. Ben Jonson. *Fr. Cynthia's Revels,* IV. EIL; GBL

Glove and Love. Tu Yeh, *tr. fr. Chinese by* Dominic Cheung. IFON

Glove and the Lions, The. Leigh Hunt. BeLS; FaPON; GN; WBLP

Glove Glue. Ken Belford. NeAC

Glow, The. Bill Simpson. CowP

Glow and beauty of the stars, The. Sappho, *tr. by* Willis Barnstone. BoWoP

Glow, little glow-worm, fly of fire. The Glow-Worm. Johnny Mercer. OBAL

Glow of the restaurant is faked, the dream, The. Reality. Raymond Souster. CaP

Glowing, festive, warm, the moon looked down. Thalero. Angelos Sikelianos, *tr. by* Edmund Keeley *and* Philip Sherrard. VMG

Glowing moon, The. Shunzei, *tr. fr. Japanese by* Burton Watson. *Fr. Thirty Tanka.* FCEI

Glowworm. François Dodat, *tr. fr. French by* Bert *and* Odette Meyers. TSS

Glowworm. David McCord. NTCP

Glow-Worm, The. Johnny Mercer. OBAL

Glow-Worm, The. Charlotte Smith. FM

Glowworm in a garden prayed, A. A Very Minor Poet Speaks. Isabel Valle. BLPA

Glow-worm-like the daisies peer. Summer. John Davidson. BoNaP

Glow-Worms. P. A. Ropes. BoTP

Glunk!/ I toss my heels up to my head. Oiseaurie. Margaret Widdemer. BXAP

Glutted, half asleep, browsing in. The Grace of Geldings in Ripe Pastures. Maxine W. Kumin. CAPP

Glutton, The. Robert Graves. CMoP; TW

Glutton [*or* Glutton in the Tavern], The. William Langland. *Fr. The Vision of Piers Plowman.* ACP; PoE

Glutton, The. John Oakman. OxBChV

Glycine's Song. Samuel Taylor Coleridge. *Fr. Zapolya.* CH; OBEV
  (Song: "Sunny shaft did I behold, A.") PBBP

Glyn Cynon Wood. *Unknown, tr. fr. Welsh by* Gwyn Williams. OBWVE

Glyph. *Unknown, tr. fr. Washoe-Paiute Indian by* Mary Austin. LiTA

GN Is Happy. Giulia Niccolai, *tr. fr. Italian by* Beverly Allen. DMI

Gnarled Riverina Gum-Tree, A. Ernest G. Moll. PoAu-2

Gnarly and bent and deaf's a pos.' Zeke. L. A. G. Strong. MoBrPo

Gnat, The. Joseph Beaumont. FM; OBS

Gnat, The ("Gnats are gnumerous"). Eugene Rudzewicz. TDD

Gnawed at by lichens. The Meditation Rock. Mo Shih-lung, *tr. by* Jonathan Chaves. CoBLCP

Gnawing the Breast. Sandra McPherson. LCAP

Gnome. Samuel Beckett. BIrV; OxBSP

Gnome, The. Harry Behn. FaPON; PDV

Gnomes, The. Beth Bentley. SaC

Gnomic Verses, *sels.* Blake.
  Abstinence Sows Sand All Over. EBEV; FaBoEE; FF; GBL; TrGrPo
  Angel That Presided o'er My Birth, The. InPK; NAs; OxBSP; RB; TrGrPo
  Great Things [Are Done] ("Great things are done when men and mountains meet."). OxBSP
  "He has observed the golden rule." TrGrPo
  "Sword sang on the barren heath, The." FaBoEE; TrGrPo
    (Sword and the Sickle, The.) ChTr
  "They said this mystery shall never cease." TrGrPo

Gnostics on Trial. Linda Gregg. NPGG

Gnōthi seautón—and is this the prime. Self-Knowledge. Samuel Taylor Coleridge. SeCePo

Gnu up at the zoo, The. John Hall Wheelock. NYBP

Go and ask Robin to bring the girls over. Vision by Sweetwater. John Crowe Ransom. CMoP; FaBoMo; MoAB; NOBA; OxBA; RB

Go and catch a falling star. John Donne. AWP; EBEV; EIL; ELP; FaBV; FaFP; FPL; HAP; HeIP; InPK; InPS; JCP; LiTB; NAEL-1; NAWM-1; NIP; NOBE; NoP; OBEV; SoSe; TrGrPo
  ("Goe and Catche a falling Starve.") HoPM; MeLP; MePo; PoEL-2; SeCP; SeCV-1

Go and dig my grave both long and narrow. Dig My Grave. *Unknown.* AmFP

Go and lose your way one night. Ahasuerus. Joseph Roth, *tr. by* Erna Baber Rosenfeld. VWA

Go and tell Aunt Nancy. The Old Grey Goose. *Unknown.* ChTr

Go back now; pause to mark. Horizon Thong. George Abbe. GoYe

Go bow thy head in gentle spite. To a Lily. James Matthew Legaré. AA

Go boy, and thy good mistress tell. Macbeth. Horace *and* James Smith. BXAP

"Go break to the needy charity's bread." How Long Shall I Give? *Unknown.* BLRP

Go Bring Me Back My Blue-eyed Boy. *Unknown.* AS

"Go Bring Me," Said the Dying Fair. William Hunter. AH

"Go bring the captive, he shall die." Ortiz. Hezekiah Butterworth. PAH

Go By. Tennyson. *See* Come Not When I Am Dead.

Go call a careful painter, let him show. Of the French Kings Nativity. Benjamin Harris. SCAP

Go! cotton lords and corn lords, go! A Chartist Chorus. Ernest Charles Jones. PF

Go count the stars! Counting. Fenton Johnson. AmNP

Go, daughters of Zion. The Death of Tammuz. Saul Tchernichowsky, *tr. by* L. V. Snowman. TrJP

Go Down Death. James Weldon Johnson. AmNP; DL; PoBA

Go Down, Moses. *Unknown.* AnAmPo; BPo
  (When Israel Was in Egypt's Land.) AH, *with music*; EaLo; NoBA

Go Down, O Sun, Out from the Motu River. Te Aomuhurangi Te Maaka, *tr. fr. Maori by the author.* PeNZ

Go Down, Old Hannah. *Unknown.* AmFP

Go down to Kew in lilac-time, in lilac-time, in lilac-time. The Barrel-Organ. Alfred Noyes. BLPL; BoTP; FaBV; MoBrPo; PoRA

Go, dumb-born book. Envoi (1919). Ezra Pound. *Fr. Hugh Selwyn Mauberley.* (Life and Contacts), XIII. HAP; MoP; UnPo; VGW
  (Envoi: "Go, dumb-born book.") MoAB; MoAmPo; OxBA

Go fetch to me a pint o'wine. The Silver Tassie. Burns. GTBS; GTBS-P; NOBE; OBEV

Go, flaunting Rose! The Aesthete to the Rose. *Unknown.* BXAP

Go Fly a Saucer, *sel.* David McCord. ImOP
  "I've seen one flying saucer. Only when." FaPON

Go For Broke. André Breton, *tr. fr. French by* David Antin. POS

Go, for they call you, Shepherd, from the hill. The Scholar-Gipsy. Matthew Arnold. ChTr; EBEV; EBVV; FaBoPP; FiP; GoTL; HAP; HeIP; NAEL-2; NOBE; NOBVV; NoP; OAEL-2; OBEV; OBNC; PoE; PoEL-5; TEP

Go;—for 'tis Memorial morning. Memorial Day. Clara Ann Thompson. CBWP-2

Go forth and weep. The Death of Tammuz. Saul Tchernichowsky, *tr. by* Mark Elliot Shapiro. VWA

"Go Forward." "A. R. G." BLRP

Go friendly, go lovely, go naked. Jealousy. Stephen Vincent. NeAC

Go from me: I am one of those who fall. Mystic and Cavalier. Lionel Johnson. MoBrPo; SeCePo

Go from me. Yet I feel that I shall stand. Elizabeth Barrett Browning. *Fr. Sonnets from the Portuguese,* VI. BLPL; OBEV; TrGrPo

"Go get me some of your father's gold." Pretty Polly. *Unknown.* AS

Go Get Some Bread. Nicolás Guillén, *tr. fr. Spanish by* Perry Higman. LPSS

Go Get the Axe. *Unknown.* AS

Go, grieving rimes of mine, to that hard stone. Petrarch, *tr. fr. Italian. Fr. Sonnets to Laura*: To Laura in Death, LX, *tr. by* Morris Bishop. NAWM-1

Go, happy rose, and wreathe my dear friend's brow. Go, Happy Rose. Martial, *tr. by* Brian Hill. PeHV

Go, Hart. *Unknown. See* Go, Heart, unto the Lamp of Licht.

Go Heart, Hurt with Adversity. *Unknown.* MeEL; OxBLMV

Go, Heart, unto the Lamp of Licht. *Unknown.* GoTS
  (Go, Hart.) OxBS

Go hert, hurt with adversité. Go Heart, Hurt with Adversity. *Unknown.* MeEL; OxBLMV

Go Home. Janet Reed McFatter. GrPl

Go! hunt the whiter ermine, and present. For the Lady Olivia Porter; a Present upon a New Year's Day. Sir William Davenant. JCP; MeLP; MePo; OBS

Go I must; when I am gone. To His Tomb-Maker. Robert Herrick. SeCV-1

Go Idle Lines. Thomas Watson. *Fr.* The Tears of Fancy. Son

Go, ill-sped book, and whisper to her or. John Berryman. BoLoP

Go inside a stone. Stone. Charles Simic. InPS; NU

Go, let the fatted calf be killed. The Welcome. Abraham Cowley. *Fr.* The Mistress. BoLoP; SeCV-1

Go, let us go my friends, go home. Home. *Zulu Oral Tradition, tr. by* H. Tracey. WTO

Go, litel book, go litel myn tragedy. Go, Little Book ("Go, litel book, go litel myn tragedy"). Chaucer. *Fr.* Troilus and Criseyde [*or* Criseide], V. OAEL-1; ViBoPo
  (Envoy, The.) FiP

Go! little bill, and do me recommende. A Love Letter. *Unknown.* MeEL

Go Little Book. Robert Louis Stevenson. MoBrPo
  (Wishes.) OBEV

Go, Little Book ("Go, litel book, go litel myn tragedy"). Chaucer. *Fr.* Troilus and Criseyde [*or* Criseide], V. OAEL-1; ViBoPo
  (Envoy, The.) FiP

Go little book, par avion. Richard Tillinghast. MT

Go [*or* Goe,] Lovely Rose. Edmund Waller. AWP; BoLoP; CTC; EnLoPo; FF; GTBS; GTBS-P; HAP; HeIP; InPK; NAEL-1; NOBE; OBEV; OPOP; PoE; PoRA; TEP; TrGrPo; UnPo; WeW
  (Song: "Go [*or* Goe] lovely rose.") ELP; GBL; GoJo; JCP; MePo; NIP; NoP; OAEL-1; OBS; PoEL-3; PrIm; SeCP; SeCV-1

Go, loving woodbine, clip with lovely grace. On a Pair of Garters. Sir John Davies. OPOP; SiPS

Go, my songs, seek your praise from the young and from the intolerant. Ité. Ezra Pound. HAP; MoAB; MoAmPo

Go, my songs, to the lonely and the unsatisfied. Commission. Ezra Pound. BoLoP; NIP; OPOP; TwCP

Go naked if you want. Kabir, *tr. by* John Stratton Hawley *and* Mark Juergensmeyer. SSI

Go north any way and sadness clings to the ground. Belfast. Donald Revell. SM

Go not away, dear heart. *Unknown, tr. fr. Japanese. Fr.* Manyo Shu. Ma

Go not, happy day. Tennyson. *Fr.* Maud, *pt.* I, xvii. EBVV

Go not to the hills of Erinn. The Wind on the Hills. Dora Sigerson Shorter. NOBVV

Go not too frequently thy friends to see. Advice to Bores. Abraham Ibn Chasdai, *tr. by* J. Chotzner. TrJP

Go not too near a house of rose. Emily Dickinson. MoAB; MoAmPo; NIP

Go Now, My Song. Andrew Young. ChTr

Go on, brave heros, you whose merits claim. An Ironical Encomium. *Unknown.* APAS

Go on! Go on! A Sermon at Clevedon. T. E. Brown. NOBVV

Go on, high ship, since now, upon the shore. Farewell to Florida. Wallace Stevens. NoAM

Go On, Idea. Ingeborg Bachmann, *tr. fr. German by* Beth Bjorklund. CoAuP

Go on, thou noisy one! Praise of a Train. *Zulu Oral Tradition, tr. by* B. W. Vilakazi. WTO

Go Out. Eileen Mathias. BoTP

Go patter to lubbers and swabs, do ye see. Poor Jack. Charles Dibdin. BeLS

Go, perjured man, and if thou e'er return. Curse, The; a Song. Robert Herrick. CaPo

Go! piteous hart, rased with dedly wo. Unfriendly Fortune. John Skelton. MeEL

Go pretty [*or* prettie] child and bear[e] this flower. To His Saviour, a Child; a Present, by a Child. Robert Herrick. OHIP; SeCP; TrCP
  (Child's Present, A.) OxBChV

Go Right along the Seashore. *Unknown.* PeNZ

Go, Rose, and in her golden hair. To a Rose. Frank Dempster Sherman. AA

Go, rose, my Chloe's bosom grace. Love's Emblem. John Clare. NIP

Go Round. Laura Chester. NPGG

Go, Sad Complaint. Charles d'Orléans. MeEL

Go sad or sweet or riotous with beer. The Old Women. George Mackay Brown. NePoEA-2; OxBS

Go, said old Lyce, senseless lover, go. Lyce. William Walsh. BoLoP

Go seeker, if you will, throughout the land. Burning in the Night. Thomas Clayton Wolfe. AmFN

Go, silly worm, drudge, trudge, and travell. Omnia Somnia. Joshua Sylvester. FaBoEE; OBS
  (Go, Silly Worm.) EIL

Go Sleep, Ma Honey. Edward D. Barker. AA

Go Slow. Langston Hughes. LiTM

Go [*or* Goe], smiling souls [*or* soules], your new-built cages break. To the Infant Martyrs. Richard Crashaw. NAEL-1; NoP; OxBSP; SeCV-1

Go Songs. Francis Thompson. *See* Envoy: "Go, songs, for ended is our brief, sweet play."

Go, songs, for ended is our brief, sweet play. Francis Thompson. MoBrPo
  (Go Songs.) FaBV

Go, Soul [*or* Goe soule], the body's guest. The Lie. Sir Walter Ralegh. AAS; ChTr; CTC; EBEV; FaBoPV; HAP; InvP; LiTB; NAEL-1; NOBE; NoP; OBSC; OPOP; PoEL-2; QFR; RB; SCV; SiPS; TEP; TrGrPo; WGRP
  (Soul's Errand, The.) WGRP

Go soule, go sweetest soule for ever blest. Ariosto, *tr. fr. Italian by* Sir John Harington. *Fr.* Orlando Furioso, XXIX. OBVE

Go, swallow, and tell, now that the summer is dying. Cwmrhydyceirw Elegiacs. Vernon Watkins. PoA

Go Take the World. Jay Macpherson. MoCV; OBCV

Go talk with those who are rumored to be unlike you. For the Student Strikers. Richard Wilbur. OxBC

Go tell at Sparta, traveler passing by. On the Spartan Dead at Thermopylae. Simonides. WeW

Go tell Aunt Rhody [*or* Nancy]. The Old Gray Goose. *Unknown.* AmFP; GBP
  ("Go and tell Aunt Nancy.") ChTr, *sl. diff. vers.*

Go tell him to clear me one acre of ground. The Elfin Knight. *Unknown.* AmFP; WSC

Go tell the king: the daedal. The Last Utterance of the Delphic Oracle. *Unknown, tr. by* Kenneth Rexroth. OBVE

Go tell the Spartans, thou that passest by. Thermopylae. Simonides, *tr. by* William Lisle Bowles. AWP; OBVE; OBWP

Go, Then. Edith Bruck, *tr. fr. Italian by* Anita Barrows. VWA

Go, then, and join the murmuring city's throng! To a Friend. William Lisle Bowles. Son

Go then, my dove, but now no longer mine. Cotton Mather. AiP; SCAP

Go then sweet friend. Go, Then. Edith Bruck, *tr. by* Anita Barrows. VWA

Go thou forth, my book, though late. To His Book. Robert Herrick. CaPo

Go, thou that vainly dost mine eyes invite. Henry King. OxBSP

Go thou thy way, and I go mine. Mizpah. Julia Aldrich Baker. BLPA; FaBoBe

Go Thou to Rome. Shelley. *Fr.* Adonais; an Elegy on the Death of John Keats. ChTr

Go through the gates with closed eyes. Close Your Eyes! Arna Bontemps. AmNP; CDC; FB; PoBA; PoNe

Go Throw Them Out. Moyshe-Leyb Halpern, *tr. fr. Yiddish by* Ruth Whitman. VWA

Go to Bed. *Unknown.* ChTr; GBP; OxNR

Go to bed early wake up with joy. *Unknown.* BoTP

Go to bed first. Go to Bed. *Unknown.* ChTr; GBP; OxNR

Go to bed late. *Unknown.* OxNR

Go to bed, Tom. *Unknown.* OxNR

Go to Old Ireland. *Unknown.* AmFP

Go to sleep, go to sleepy. All the Pretty Little Horses. *Unknown.* AmFP

Go to sleep, my baby. *Unknown, tr. by* Geoffrey Bownas *and* Anthony Thwaite. PeBJV

Go to sleep—though of course you will not. A Goodnight. William Carlos Williams. MoAB; MoAmPo

Go to Sleepy. *Unknown.* AS

"Go to the Ant." Stanley J. Sharpless. NOBL

Go to the Ant [Thou Sluggard]. Bible, *O.T. Fr.* Proverbs, VI: 6-11. FaPON; TrJP
  (Reproof, A.) TrGrPo

Go to the Shine That's on a Tree. Richard Eberhart. UnS

Go to the western gate, Luke Havergal. Luke Havergal. E. A. Robinson. AA; AmPP; AWP; GBL; LiTA; LiTM; MoAB; MoAmPo; NAAL-2; NoAM; NOBA; PoEL-5; QFR; UnPo

Go to where my loved one lives. Mirabai, *tr. by* John Stratton Hawley *and* Mark Juergensmeyer. SSI

Go, Valentine. Robert Southey. Son

Go 'way, fiddle! folks is tired o' hearin' you a-squawkin. Fust Banjo, De. Irwin Russell. *Fr.* Christmas Night in the Quarters. AA; BLPA

Go 'Way f'om Mah Window. *Unknown.* AS

Go 'way from dat window, "My Honey, My Love." Song to the Runaway Slave. *Unknown.* BPo

Go Where Glory Waits Thee. Thomas Moore. OBNC

Go where those others went to the dark boundary. The Envoy of Mr. Cogito. Zbigniew Herbert, *tr. by* Bogdana *and* John Carpenter. PwPP

Go where we will, at ev'ry time and place. Charles Churchill. *Fr.* The Times. PeHV

Go with a perm or a duck tail. How to Dress Like a Femmy Dyke. Jane Barnes. GLP

Go Work in My Vineyard. Frances Ellen Watkins Harper. PWR

Go ye afar. Go teach all nations. Missionary Hymm. James Burke. TIRV

"Go ye into the highways." Compel Them to Come In. Leonard Dodd. BLRP

Go you, O winds that blow from north to south. Alexander Craig. EiL
(To Pandora.) Son

Goal Consciousness. Erich Fried, *tr. fr. German by* Beth Bjorklund. CoAuP

Goat, The. Umberto Saba, *tr. fr. Italian.* PFI, *tr. by* T. G. Bergin; VWA, *tr. by* Anita Barrows
(I have spoken to a goat.) VWA, *tr. by* Anita Barrows

Goat, The. *Unknown.* BLPL; OnUR; PoLF

Goat God, The. Cesare Pavese, *tr. fr. Italian by* William Arrowsmith. AnAn

Goat Paths, The. James Stephens. AWP; CH; GoJo; LiTB; UnPo

Goat was nibbling on a vine, A. The Vine and the Goat. Aesop, *tr. by* William Ellery Leonard. AWP

Goat's-Leaf. Marie de France, *tr. by* Aline Allard. PBWP

Gobbolino, the Witch's Cat. G. C. Westcott. CRH

Goblin, The. Rose Fyleman. BoTP; NTCP

Goblin Feet. John R. R. Tolkien. FaPON

Goblin Goose, The. *Unknown.* FaBoPa

Goblin has a wider mouth, The. How to Tell Goblins from Elves. Monica Shannon. FaPON; RHPC

Goblin lives in our house, in our house, in our house, A. The Goblin. Rose Fyleman. BoTP; NTCP

Goblin marked his monarch well, The. The Fay's Departure. Joseph Rodman Drake. The Culprit Fay. GN
(First Quest, The.) AA

Goblin Market, *sels.* Christina Rossetti. EBEV; NAEL-2; NOBVV; OBNV
"Laughed every goblin." BrRo
Laura and Lizzie Asleep. PeHV
"Morning and evening." BoTP

Goblins on the doorstep. This Is Halloween. Dorothy Brown Thompson. RHPC

Goblin's Song, The. James Telfer. ChTr

God. Gamaliel Bradford. WGRP

God, *sel.* Alexander McLachlan.
"Hail, Thou great mysterious Being!" CaP

God. Harold Monro. *Fr.* Dawn. WGRP

God? Cristoir O'Flynn. TIRV

God. Bob Perelman. IAT

God. Isaac Rosenberg. VWA

God. Boris Slutsky, *tr. fr. Russian by* Dimitry Pospielovsky *and* Keith Bosley. VWA

God. James Cowden Wallace. *See* There is an Eye that never sleeps.

God/ Built a world. Homeless. Malka Heifetz Tussman, *tr. by* Kathryn Hellerstein. AYP

God!/ glad I'm black. Blue Black. Bloke Modisane. PBA

God—/they fear you, they hold you so. Testimony. Carolyn M. Rodgers. BPo

God/ You do not mind if I an unbaptized. Prayer of a Pagan Woman. Cothrai Gogan. TIRV

God, a man at Yale, adopted a monkey. Monkey. Josephine Miles. LiTM

God, A Poem. James Fenton. DiPo; NoAM

God Abandons Antony, The. Constantine P. Cavafy, *tr. fr. Greek by* Edmund Keeley *and* Philip Sherrard. VMG

God above, for man's delight, The. A New Ballade of the Marigolde. William Forrest. CoMu

God almighty's colly cow. The Ladybird. *Unknown.* GBP

God aloft in majesty. God Supreme. Abraham Ibn Ezra, *tr. by* David Goldstein. TOF

God, although this life is but a wraith. Prayer. Louis Untermeyer. WGRP

God and I in space alone. Illusion. Ella Wheeler Wilcox. WGRP

God and Nature. Musa Moris Farhi, *tr. fr. Turkish by the author.* VWA

God and Saint [*or* Sanct] Peter was gangand be the way. How the First Hielandman of God Was Made. *Unknown.* FaBoCo; GBP; OBSV

God and the devil in these letters. The Postman's Bell is Answered Everywhere. Horace Gregory. MoAmPo; NYBP

God and the devil still are wrangling. For a Mouthy Woman. Countee Cullen. OBAL; PoBA

God and the Soul, *sels.* John Lancaster Spalding. AA
At the Ninth Hour.
Et Mori Lucrum.
Nature and the Child.
Starry Host, The.
Void Between, The.

God and Yet a Man, A? *Unknown.* HAP
(Wit Wonders.) MeEL

God! ask me not to record your wonders. Scholfield Huxley. Edgar Lee Masters. *Fr.* Spoon River Anthology. LiTA; TrPWD

God banish from your house. Benediction. Stanley Kunitz. VGW

God be here, God be there. *Unknown.* OxNR

God be in my head. The Knight's Prayer. *Unknown.* BoTP

God Be in My Head. *Unknown. Fr.* Sarum Primer. EaLo
(Hymnus: "God be in my hede.") ChTr; FaBoRV

God be merciful unto us, and bless us. Psalm LXVII ("God be merciful unto us. . ."). Bible, *O.T. Fr.* Psalms.
(Let the Nations Be Glad.) FaPON

God be with you in the Springtime. Through the Year. Julian S. Cutler. BLPA

God Be with You till We Meet Again. Jeremiah Eames Rankin. AH, *with music*

God, bless all little boys who look like Puck. Blessing on Little Boys. Arthur Guiterman. TrPWD

God bless all policemen. Goodbat Nightman. Roger McGough. MoP

God Bless America. John Fuller. OBSV

God Bless Henry. He lived like a rat. John Berryman. *Fr.* Dream Songs. CAPP

God Bless Karl Marx. Charles Hubert Sisson. NPo

God bless our country's emblem. Our Country's Emblem. *Unknown.* WBLP

God bless our dear United States. The People's Prayer. Amos Russel Wells. OPP

God bless our good and gracious King. Impromptu on Charles II. John Wilmot, 2nd Earl of Rochester. FaBoEE; FaBoEE; NBLV; NOBL; OBSV

God bless our meat. *Unknown.* OxNR

God Bless Our Native Land. Frances Ellen Watkins Harper. PWR

God bless the craft of Clanranald. Birlinn Chlann-Raghnaill. Alexander MacDonald, *tr. by* "Hugh MacDiarmid." GoTS

God bless the field and bless the furrow. The Robin's Song. C. Lovat Fraser. BoTP; MoShBr

God bless the King!—I mean the Faith's Defender. Jacobite Toast. John Byrom. FaBoCo; FaBoEE
(Extempore Verses Intended to Allay the Violence of Party-Spirit.) NOBL

"God bless the man who first invented sleep!" Early Rising. John Godfrey Saxe. AnAmPo; BLPL; PoLF

God bless the master of this house. *Unknown.* BoTP; OHIP
(Grace, A.) MoShBr
(Souling Song.) OBET

God bless the master of this house, and all that are therein. The Singers in the Snow. *Unknown.* OHIP

God bless thee and keep thee thro' the coming days. A New Year's Wish. "J. H. S." BLRP

God bless this food, and bless us all. *Unknown.* BLRP

God bless this house from thatch to floor. *Unknown.* OxNR

God Bless You, Dear, To-Day! John Bennett. AA

God braced me with His firm hand. The Tool of Fate. "Yehoash," *tr. by* Isidore Goldstick. TrJP

God breathe a blessing on. Bestiary. A. M. Klein. OBCV

God bring you safe from the death sleep of night. A Donegal Hush Song. Cathal O'Byrne. TIRV

God broke into my house last night. Scapegoat. W. R. Rodgers. CIP

God broke the years to hours and days. As Thy Days So Shall Thy Strength Be. "George Klingle." BLRP

God broke upon this upturned field; trees. Body of a Rook. David Wevill. MoCV

God called the nearest angels who dwell with Him above. The Two Angels. Whittier. AA

God Cares. Helen Annis Casterline. BLRP

God Cares. "Marianne Farningham." BLRP; WBLP
(He Careth.) WBLP

God, consider the soul's need. Death Song for Owain ab Urien. Taliesin, *tr. by* Anthony Conran. OBWVE

God created Cat and asked. *Unknown.* CRH

God decided he was tired. Budgie Finds His Voice. Wendy Cope. FaBoPa

God don't want no coward soldiers. God's Goin' to Set This World on Fire. *Unknown.* AS

God doth dwell in men, from th' blessed seats, A. In Consort to Wednesday, Jan. 1st. 1701. Richard Henchman. SCAP

God dreamed—the suns sprang flaming into space. Creation. Ambrose Bierce. AA

God dwells alone, The. Deserted Shrine. Avner Treinin. VWA, *tr. by* E. A. Levenston

God Everywhere. Abraham ibn Ezra, *tr. fr. Hebrew by* D. E. de L. TrJP

God exists, though he doesn't exist. Phallus. Kazuko Shiraishi, *tr. by* Ikuko Atsumi. BoWoP

God fashioned the ship of the world carefully. Stephen Crane. *Fr.* The Black Riders, VI. MOS

God from His Throne with Piercing Eye. Joseph Steward. AH

God gave His children memory. Roses in December. G. A. Studdert-Kennedy. BLPA

God gave my son in trust to me. My Son. James D. Hughes. BLPA

God, give me speech, in mercy touch my lips. The Unutterable Beauty. G. A. Studdert-Kennedy. TrPWD

God Give to Men ("God give the yellow man"). Arna Bontemps. BANP; BPo; CDC; PoNe

God, Give Us Men! Josiah Gilbert Holland. BLPA; WBLP (Wanted.) TrPWD

God gives them sleep on ground, on straw. Roger Williams. SCAP

God, God, be lenient her first night there. Prayer for a Very New Angel. Violet Alleyn Storey. BLPA

God grant that I may never be. Prayer in April. Sara Henderson Hay. TrPWD

God grant thee thine own wish, and grant thee mine. John Donne. OBVE

God granted, God denies. Frustration. Elizabeth Daryush. QFR

God 'graves His cryptic script with inexorable pen. Palimpsest. Hyman Edelstein. CaP

God Has Mercy [*or* Pity] on Kindergarten Children. Yehuda Amichai, *tr. fr. Hebrew.* IP, *tr. by* Warren Bargad *and* Stanley F. Chyet; VWA, *tr. by* Stephen Mitchell.

God Hasn't Made Room. Mririda n'Ait Attika, *tr. by* Daniel Halpern *and* Paula Paley. PBWP

God hath not promised. What God Hath [*or* Has] Promised! Annie Johnson Flint. BLRP; WBLP

God hath two wings, which The doth ever move. Mercy and Love. Robert Herrick. SeCV-1

God He rejects all prayers that are sleight. Prayers Must Have Poise. Robert Herrick. LiTB

God help who follows his father's craft! The Passing of the Poets. Fearflatha O'Gnive. NOIV

God help who looks upon Enniskillen. A Visit to Enniskillen. Tadhg Dall O'Huiginn. NOIV

God, how I envy you these great oak roots. A Jew Walks in Westminster Abbey. Aubrey Hodes. TrJP

God, How I Hate You. Arthur Graeme West. MMA

"God, how I loathe you!" "Good! Then let me go." Box Step. Bruce Bennett. SoTCo

God! How I Long for You. Kenneth Mackenzie. CBAP

God how is it that we surrender. Nizar Qabbani, *tr. by* Lena Jayyusi *and* W. S. Merwin. MAP

God! how they plague his life, the three damned sisters. The Little Brother. James Reeves. OxBTC

God, I am travelling out to death's sea. Valley of the Shadow. John Galsworthy. OHIP; TrPWD

God I love thee in Thy robe of roses. Zebaoth. Else Lasker-Schüler, *tr. by* Jethro Bithell. TrJP

God, I need a job because I need money. Alan Dugan. CAPP; NoAM

God, I pound and I pound and I pound. The Stone God. Aila Meriluoto, *tr. by* Aili Jarvenpa. SOP

God if he isn't is. Phallic Root. Kazuko Shiraishi, *tr. by* Thomas Fitzsimmons. WPOW

God, if this were enough. If This Were Faith. Robert Louis Stevenson. *Fr.* Songs of Travel. BrPo; OBNC; TrPWD; WGRP

God in the Nation's Life. *Unknown.* BLRP; WBLP

God in Wrath, A. Stephen Crane. *Fr.* The Black Riders, XIX. OxBSP; TAP

God Is. Roland Mathias. CRP

God is a distant, stately lover. Emily Dickinson. SoSe

God is a proposition. Third Enemy Speaks. C. Day Lewis. *Fr.* The Magnetic Mountain, XXI. EaLo

God Is at the Anvil. Lew Sarett. WGRP

God Is Faithful. Frances Ridley Havergal. BLRP

God is great and God is good. *Unknown.* BLRP

God Is in Every Tomorrow. Laura A. Barter Snow. BLRP

God is indeed a jealous God. Emily Dickinson. NOBA

God, is it sinful if I feel. Mary Dixon Thayer. TrPWD

God, Is, Like, Scissors. José Garcia Villa. EaLo

God Is Love. Sir John Bowring. FaBoBe

God is love. Then by inversion. History of Ideas. J. V. Cunningham. NIP

God is never sure He has found. Walking the Wilderness. William Stafford. NaP

God is no botcher, but when God wrought you two. On Botching. John Heywood. FaBoCo; FaBoEE

God Is Not Dumb. James Russell Lowell. *Fr.* Bibliolaters. WGRP

God is older than the sun and moon. Maximus. D. H. Lawrence. TOF

God is our refuge and strength, a very present help in trouble. Psalm XLVI ("God is our refuge and strength. . ."). Bible, *O.T. Fr.* Psalms. AWP
(Though the Earth Be Removed.) TrGrPo

God is praise and glory. Psalm of Battle. *Unknown, tr. fr. Arabic by* E. Powys Mathers. *Fr.* The Thousand and One Nights. AWP

God is shaping the great future of the islands of the sea. The Islands of the Sea. George Edward Woodberry. PAH

God is still glorified. Building in Stone. Sylvia Townsend Warner. MoBrPo

God is the jewel. Kabir, *tr. by* John Stratton Hawley *and* Mark Juergensmeyer. SSI

God is the Most High. Muhammedan Call to Prayer. Bilal, *tr. by* Raoul Abdul. TTY

God is the Old Repair Man. The Old Repair Man. Fenton Johnson. AmNP

God Is Working His Purpose Out. A. C. Ainger. BLRP; FaPoR

God, keep all claw-denned alligators. Prayer for Reptiles. Patricia Hubbell. PDV

God Keep You. "Madeline Bridges." AA

God Knoweth Best. *Unknown.* WBLP
(Your Father Knoweth.) BLRP

God knows/ We have our troubles too. High to Low. Langston Hughes. HCAP

God knows I should have had my fill of song. Castelloza, *tr. by* Meg Bogin. WT

God knows it, I am with you. If to prize. To a Republican Friend, 1848. Matthew Arnold. Son

God knows what beat him down into that deadland. At the Entrance. Douglas Stewart. CBAP

God lay dead in heaven. Stephen Crane. *Fr.* The Black Riders, LXVII. AmPP

God Leads the Way. Cleanthes, *tr. fr. Greek by* C. C. Martindale. EaLo

God let never soe old a man. Old Robin of Portingale. *Unknown.* ESPB

God, listen through my words to the beating of my heart. Margueritte Harmon Bro. TrPWD

God love you. A Poem for the Old Man. John Wieners. NeAP

God love you now, if no one else will ever. Ode for the American Dead in Korea. Thomas McGrath. NePoEA; VGW
(Ode for the American Dead.) AiP

God Lyaeus, Ever Young. John Fletcher. *Fr.* The Tragedy of Valentinian, V, viii. OBEV

God made a little gentian. Emily Dickinson. FaBV
(Fringed Gentian.) AA

God Made a Trance. *Unknown.* OBET

God made a wonderful mother. A Wonderful Mother. Pat O'Reilly. BLPA

God made Him birds in a pleasant humour. The Making of Birds. Katharine Tynan. TIRV

God made my mother on an April day. My Mother. Francis Ledwidge. OHIP; TIRV

God made the bees. Mother Goose. SaC

God Made the Country. William Cowper. *Fr.* The Task, I. FiP; PoEL-3

God made the wicked grocer. The Song against Grocers. G. K. Chesterton. CenHV; FaBoCo

God-Maker, Man, The. Don Marquis. WGRP

God Makes a Path. Roger Williams. PAH; WGRP

God makes not good men wantons, but doth bring. Good Men Afflicted Most. Robert Herrick. LiTB

God makes sech nights all white an' still. The Courtin.' James Russell Lowell. *Fr.* The Biglow Papers: 2d Series, Introduction. AA; AnPP; AnAmPo; BeLS; NOBA; OBAL

God moves in a mysterious way. William Cowper. ELP; FiP

(Light Shining out of Darkness.) EaLo; EBEV; EnRP; FaBoCh; FaFP; FPL; HeIP; LiTB; NOBE; NOCV; NOEC; NoP; PoEL-3; PWR; SeCePo; TOF; TrGrPo; WGRP

God No Longer Speaks. Yankev Fridman, *tr. fr. Yiddish by* Ruth Whitman. PeBMYV

God, O God, whom I have begged. A Poem in Praise of Colum Cille . *At. to* Dallán Forgaill. NOIV

God of Abraham, of Isaac, and of Jacob. *Unknown, tr. fr. Yiddish by* Olga Marx. TrJP

God of all power and might. Cecil Arthur Spring-Rice. *Fr.* In Memoriam, A. C. M. L. TrPWD

God of Bethel Heard Her Cries, The. Richard Allen. AH

God of Galaxies, The. Mark Van Doren. ImOP

God of grave nights. A Chant Out of Doors. Marguerite Wilkinson. TrPWD

God of his goodnes, praysed that he be. *Unknown. Fr.* The Praise of Waterford. NOIV

God of Israel, The. A. Leyeles, *tr. fr. Yiddish by* Benjamin *and* Barbara Harshav. AYP

God of light and blossom. James P. Mousley. GoYe

God of love among the silent flowers, A. The Moment of the Rose. Dunstan Thompson. LiTA

God of Mercy. Kadya Molodovsky, *tr. fr. Yiddish by* Irving Howe. PeBMYV; WPOW

God of Might, God of Right. *Unknown.* TrJP

God of my father discovered at midnight. Oya. Audre Lorde. CNA

God of My Life! Benjamin Colman. AH

God of Our Fathers. Melancthon W. Stryker. AH

God of Our Fathers, Bless This Our Land. John Henry Hopkins, Jr. AH

God of our fathers, known of old. Recessional. Kipling. AWP; BLPA; BLPL; BLRP; BrPo; FaBoPV; FaBV; FaFP; GN; LiTB; MoBrPo; NoAM; NOBE; NOBVV; NoP; OBEV; OBNC; OHFP; PWR; TrGrPo; UnPo; WBLP; WGRP

God of our Fathers, Whose Almighty Hand. Daniel C. Roberts. AH

God of peace! before thee. Hymn of Freedom. Michael J. Barry. TIRV

God of Peace, in Peace Preserve Us, *with music.* Ernst W. Olson. AH

God of Sheep, The. John Fletcher. *Fr.* The Faithful Shepherdess, V, v. EIL; FaBoCh

God of Summer—I have seen. Touring. David Morton. TrPWD

God of the Granite and the Rose! Elizabeth Doten. *Fr.* Reconciliation. TrPWD

God of the Living, The. John Ellerton. WGRP

God of the Nations. Walter Russell Bowie. AH, *with music;* TrPWD

God of the Nations, Near and Far. John Haynes Holmes. AH

God of the Prophets! Bless the Prophets' Sons. Denis Wortman. AH

God of the strong, God of the weak. Richard Watson Gilder. TrPWD
   (God of the Strong, God of the Weak.) AH

God of the vineyard's royal store. The Husbandman. Frances Beatrice Taylor. CaP

God of the World. Israel Najara, *tr. fr. Hebrew by* Israel Abrahams. TrJP

God of the World, Thy Glories Shine. Sewall Sylvester Cutting. AH

God of us who kill our kind! Percy MacKaye. *Fr.* A Prayer of the Peoples. TrPWD, *sts.;* WGRP

God of Visions. Emily Brontë. *See* O thy bright eyes must answer now.

God of War, The. Bertolt Brecht. FaBoPV

God of War, Money Changer of Dead Bodies, The. Aeschylus, *tr. fr. Greek by* Richmond Lattimore. *Fr.* Agamemnon. WaaP

God on high in sovereign might. *Unknown, tr. by* Arthur Waley. BoS

God Once Commanded Us, A. Leah Goldberg, *tr. fr. Hebrew by* Robert Friend. VWA

God only knows what he'd been doing. Painting or sewing? Parish. Norman Dubie. MAYP

God or Mammon. Alfred Cruickshank. PBCV

God Our Father. Frederick William Faber. WGRP

God, Our Lady, *sel.* Concha Michel, *tr. fr. Spanish by* Kate Flores. "Woman, Mother of Man." DMH

God, patient of beginnings. A Prayer for the New Year. Violet Alleyn Storey. TrPWD

God pity all the brave who go. God's Pity. Louise Driscoll. WGRP

God pity the wretched prisoners. In Prison. Ray Riley Smith. PWR

God Poem. Stanley Moss. VGW; VWA

God Prays. Angela Morgan. WGRP

God prosper long our Gracious King. An Ode for the New Year. *At. to* John Gay. OxBoLi

God prosper long our noble king. Chevy Chase. *Unknown.* FaBoBa; GN; OBET
   (Hunting of the Cheviot, The.) ESPB

God Provides. Bible, *N.T. Fr.* St. Matthew, VI: 26-34. BLRP

God Replies. Bible, *O.T. Fr.* Job: Then the Lord Answered ("Who is this that darkeneth counsel by words without knowledge?"). NAWM-1, *abr.*

God rest that Jewy woman. Song for the Clatter-Bones. F. R. Higgins. AnIL; LiTB; OBMV

God rest the soul of Ireland. After the Flight of the Earls. Fearflatha O'Gnive. NOIV

God rest you, merry Innocents. A Carol for Children. Ogden Nash. EaLo

God Rest You [*or* ye] Merry, Gentlemen. Dinah Maria Mulock Craik. FaFP; GN, *sl. diff. vers.;* LiTB

God said—"Let there be light." The Press. Ebenezer Elliott. PF

God said, "Let there be light, and there was light." Mysteries of Life. Mary E. Tucker. CBWP-1

God Save Great Thomas Paine. Joseph Mather. NOEC

God save our gracious King. God Save the King. *At. to.* Henry Carey. WBLP

God Save Our President. Francis DeHaes Janvier. PAH

God Save the Flag. Oliver Wendell Holmes. FaFP; OHFP; OPP

God Save the King. *At. to.* Henry Carey. WBLP

God save the King, that King that sav'd the land. Benjamin Harris. SCAP

God Save the Nation. Theodore Tilton. AA

God Save the People. Ebenezer Elliott. BLPA; EaLo; WBLP

God Save the Plough. Lydia Huntley Sigourney. AnAmPo; OBAL

God save the Rights of Man! Philip Freneau. GOA

God Save the Stock. Charles Spear. ATNZ

God Scatters Beauty. Walter Savage Landor. EnRP
   ("God scatters beauty as he scatters flowers.") FaBoEE

God-seeking. Sir William Watson. WGRP

God Send Easter. Lucille Clifton. CNA

God send the Devil is a gentleman. The Knight Fallen on Evil Days. Elinor Wylie. MoAmPo

God send us a little home. A Prayer for a Little Home. Florence Bone. BLPA; FaBoBe; FaFP

God send us peace, and keep red strife away. At Fredericksburg. John Boyle O'Reilly. PAH

God sends us from I don't know where. Marcabrun, *tr. by* Paul Blackburn. Pro

God sent us wit to banish far. Peace in the World. John Galsworthy. PoLF

God Set Us Here. Nicasius de Sillè, *tr. fr. Dutch.* AH

God sits on the firmament arch. The Creation of Light. Sister Maura. CRP

God Sour the Milk of the Knacking Wench. Alden Nowlan. MoCV

God spoke in a dream. Argument against Metaphor. Gad Hollander. VWA

God spoke once in the dark; dead sound. The Precision. Yvor Winters. EAS

God spoke once that made your girdle fall, The. Daphne. Selden Rodman. PoNe

God strengthen me to bear myself. Who Shall Deliver Me? Christina Rossetti. TOF

God Supreme. Abraham Ibn Ezra, *tr. fr. Hebrew by* David Goldstein. TOF

God Supreme! To Thee We Pray. Penina Moise *and* Edward N. Calisch. AH

God That Doest Wondrously. Moses Ibn Ezra, *tr. fr. Hebrew by* Solomon Solis-Cohen. TrJP

God, that mad'st her well regard her. Dieu Qu'il la Fait. Charles, Duc d' Orléans, *tr. by* Ezra Pound. AWP

God the Architect. Harry Hibbard Kemp. WGRP

God, the Artist. Angela Morgan. BLPA

God, The, is near, and/ difficult to grasp. Patmos. David Gascoyne. OBVE

God the Omniscient. James Cowden Wallace. BLRP

God, thou great symmetry. Anna Wickham. MoBrPo

"God, though [*or* although] this life is but a wraith." Louis Untermeyer. MoAmPo; TrJP; WGRP

God to Be First Served. Robert Herrick. OxBChV

God, to get the clay that stayed me. William Baylebridge. *Fr.* Life's Testament, XIII. PoAu-1

God to Man. *Unknown, tr. fr. Hebrew. Fr.* The Talmud. TrJP

God to Thee We Humbly Bow. George Henry Boker. AH

God, to whom we look up blindly. Bayard Taylor. *Fr.* The Poet's Journal. TrPWD

God told Noah about the rainbow sign. Lining Track. *Unknown.* AmFP

God tried to teach Crow how to talk. Crow's First Lesson. Ted Hughes. MoP; NoAM

God Wants a Man. *Unknown.* BLRP

God wants our best. He in the far-off ages. What Shall We Render. *Unknown.* BLRP

God, we don't like to complain. Caliban in the Coal Mines. Louis Untermeyer. MoAmPo; PDV; TrJP

God, what a day it is to be abroad! Out-of-Doors. Robert Whitaker. TrPWD

God, what a world, if men in street and mart. True Brotherhood. Ella Wheeler Wilcox. WBLP

God, when you thought of a pine tree. God, the Artist. Angela Morgan. BLPA

God who created me. Prayers. Henry Charles Beeching. BoTP; OBEV (Boy's Prayer, A.) GN
(Prayer: "God who created me.") SD

God, who devisedst man who then devised. Prayer for the Age. Myron H. Broomell. TrPWD

God who fled down with a standard yard, The. William Empson. *Fr.* Bacchus. PoA

God who formed the mountains great. All Nature Has a Voice to Tell. James Gilchrist Lawson. BLRP

God who had such heart for us, The. The Cool Gold Wines of Paradise. Robert Farren. SeCePo

God, Who Hath Made the Daisies. E. P. Hood. OHIP

God, who made man out of dust. The Continuing City. Laurence Housman. WGRP

God who mounts the winged winds, The. Homer, *tr. fr. Greek by* Pope. *Fr.* Odyssey, V. OBVE

God, who touchest earth with beauty. A Prayer-Poem. Mary S. Edgar. BLRP

God, Whom Shall I Compare to Thee? Judah Halevi, *tr. fr. Hebrew by* Alice Lucas. TrJP

God whose goodness filleth every clime, The. Jean Racine, *tr. fr. French by* Charles Randolph. *Fr.* Athalie. WGRP

God, whose kindly hand doth sow. Francis Ledwidge. *Fr.* A Dream of Artemis. TrPWD

God, why have you ruined me. Job's Ancient Lament. Owen Dodson. FB

God will have all, or none; serve Him, or fall. Neutrality Loathsome. Robert Herrick. LiTB; NoP

God will never fail us. God Is Faithful. Frances Ridley Havergal. BLRP

God will not let my field lie fallow. The Ploughman. Karle Wilson Baker. WGRP

God wills no man a slave. The man most meek. Washington. James Jeffrey Roche. PAH

God would come, the god would go, The. Man Is God's Nature. Richard Eberhart. EaLo

God, you could grow to love it. Ecclesiastes. Derek Mahon. BIrV; CIP

God, You Have Been Too Good to Me. Charles Wharton Stork. TrPWD; WGRP

Goddamn the Empty Sky. Violeta Parra, *tr. fr. Spanish by* John Felstiner. OV

Goddess, The. Denise Levertov. LiTM; NeAP; NOBA; PoM

Goddess. Judith Johnson Sherwin. BoWoP

Goddess Chiao, The. *Unknown, tr. fr. Chinese by* Burton Watson. CoBCP

Goddess Fortune be praised (on her toothed wheel), The. The Unpredicted. John Heath-Stubbs. BoLoP; OxBC

Goddess of poetry. To the Moon. Yvor Winters. HeIP

Goddess of rhyme, that didst inspire. An Epithalamium upon the Marriage of Captain William Bedloe. Richard Duke. APAS

Goddess of threads gladly. *Unknown, tr. fr. Icelandic by* George Johnston. *Fr.* The Saga of Gisli. OBVE

Goddess of Wisdom Whose Substance Is Desire. Anne Waldman. UL

Goddesse bade the nymphs remove, The. *Unknown, tr. fr. Latin by* Thomas Stanley. *Fr.* The Vigil of Venus. OBVE

Goddis sonne is borne. A Cause for Wonder. *Unknown.* MeEL

Goddwyn, *sel.* Thomas Chatterton.
Ode to Liberty. TrGrPo

Gode sire, pray ich thee. I Am from Ireland. *Unknown.* MeEL

Godfrey Gordon Gustavus Gore. William Brighty Rands. FaPON

Godfrey of Bulloigne; or, The Recoverie of Jerusalem, *sels.* Tasso, *tr. fr. Italian by* Edward Fairfax.
"Joyous birds, hid under greenewood shade, The." *Fr.* XVI. OBVE; PFI
Pluto's Council. OBSC
Prayer Brings Rain, A. OBSC
"Sweet Armida tooke this charge on hand, The." *Fr.* IV. OBVE

Godiva. D. C. Berry. BXAP

Godiva. Tennyson. BeLS

Godlike beneath his grave divinities. The Druid. John Banister Tabb. AA

Godly Casuistry ("The sun had long since in the lap"). Samuel Butler. *Fr.* Hudibras, II, 2. OBS

Godly Dream, A, *sels. Elizabeth Melvill, Lady Culross.* WPE
"I looked down and saw a pit most black."
"Into that pit when I did enter in."
"Then up I rose, and made no more delay."
"This pit is Hell where through thou now must go."
"Weary I was, and thought to sit at rest."

Godly Girzie. Burns. CoMu; ErPo

Godmother. Phyllis B. Morden. RHPC

Godmother. Dorothy Parker. PoRA

Gododdin, The, *sels.* Aneirin, *tr. fr. Welsh.*
"Men went to Catraeth, keen their war-band." *Tr. by* Joseph P. Clancy. OBWVE
"Men went to Gododdin, laughter-loving." *Tr. by* Joseph P. Clancy. OBWP
"To Cattraeth's vale in glitt'ring row." *Tr. by* Thomas Gray. OBVE

Godolphin Horne. Hilaire Belloc. CenHV; FaBoCo

Gods, The. Dennis Lee. NOBC

Gods, The. W. S. Merwin. NaP

Gods. István Vas, *tr. fr. Hungarian by* Donald Davie. MHuP

God's angry man, His crotchety scholar. The Thunderer. Phyllis McGinley. EaLo

Gods are happy, The. The Strayed Reveller to Ulysses. Matthew Arnold. *Fr.* The Strayed Reveller. OBEV

Gods Are Mighty, The. N. P. van Wyck Louw, *tr. fr. Afrikaans by* Jack Cope. PeSA

God's armies of Heaven, with pinions extended. Pro Patria. Adah Isaacs Menken. CBWP-1

Gods, arraigned so often and so often. Gods. István Vas, *tr. by* Donald Davie. MHuP

God's blessings all are uniform. They Are the Same. Priscilla Jane Thompson. CBWP-2

Gods chase/ Round vase. Ode on a Grecian Urn Summarized. Desmond Skirrow. NIP; NOBL

God's child in Christ adopted—Christ my all. My Baptismal Birthday. Samuel Taylor Coleridge. NOCV

God's Controversy with New-England. Michael Wigglesworth. SCAP

God's Dark. John Martin. PoLF

God's Determinations, *sels.* Edward Taylor.
Glory of and Grace in the Church Set Out, The. AmPP
God's Selecting Love in the Decree. PoEL-3
"Infinity, when all things it beheld." AmPP; HAP; NAAL-1; NOBA; OxBA; SCAP
Joy of Church Fellowship Rightly Attended, The. AmPP; NAAL-1; OxBA; SCAP
(In Heaven Soaring Up.) AH, *with music.*
"Peace, peace, my hony [or honey], do not cry." PoEL-3
(Christ's Reply.) NAAL-1
Soul's Groan to Christ for Succo[u]r, The. NAAL-1; PoEL-3

God's Electric Power. Mrs. Henry Linden. CBWP-4

God's Fire upon Children ("God's fire upon cities"). Meir Wieseltier, *tr. fr. Hebrew by* Warren Bargad *and* Stanley F. Chyet. IP

"God's First Creature Was Light." Winifred Welles. ImOP

God's Funeral. Thomas Hardy. WGRP

God's Garden. Richard Burton. WGRP

God's Gifts. Jakov de Haan, *tr. fr. Dutch by* David Soetendorp. VWA

God's Glory. Bible, *O.T. See* Psalms: Psalm XIX ("The heavens declare the glory of God").

God's Goin' to Set This World on Fire. *Unknown.* AS

God's Goin' to Set This World on Fire. *Unknown.* AS

God's Goodness. C. D. Martin. WBLP

God's goose, neck neatly wrung, is being plucked. Function of Blizzard. Robert Penn Warren. AnAn

God's Grandeur. Gerard Manley Hopkins. AWP; BLPL; BrPo; CMoP; EBVV; FaFP; FF; HAP; InPK; InvP; LiTB; LiTM; MoAB; MoBrPo; MoP; NAEL-2; NIP; NoAM; NOBE; NOBVV; NoP; OAEL-2; OBNC; PoE; PPP; PrIm; Son; SoSe; SOTW; TEP; TrCP; TrGrPo; UnPo; WeW

God's Harp. Gustav Falke, *tr. fr. German by* Ludwig Lewisohn. AWP

Gods have heard me, Lyce, The. Revenge ("Audivere, Lyce"). Horace, *tr. fr. Latin.* Fr. Odes, IV, 13. AWP, *tr. by* Louis Untermeyer.

Gods have taken alien shapes upon them, The. The Exiles. "Æ." BIrV; MoBrPo

God's head for a paperweight, A. The Desk. Cid Corman. VGW

Gods i am pent in a cockroach. The Wail of Archy. Don Marquis. *Fr.* Archy and Mehitabel. FiBHP

Gods in Vietnam. Eugene B. Redmond. NBP; PoBA

Gods it is I ask to release me from this watch, The. Agamemnon. Aeschylus, *tr. by* Louis MacNeice. NAWM-1

God's Judgment on a Wicked Bishop. Robert Southey. EnRP; OBNV; OnMSP

God's Language. Ruth Fainlight. VWA

God's Little Angel. Patrick J. Murray. TIRV

God's Little Mountain. Geoffrey Hill. NePoEA

God's Love. *Unknown.* BLRP

God's Mercy. William Langland. *Fr.* The Vision of Piers Plowman. NOCV

God's Mood. Lucille Clifton. CAPP

Gods Must Not Know Us, The. Linda Gregg. NPGG

Gods of Africa regard me, The. Distance. Anthony Delius. PeSA

Gods of the Copybook Headings, The. Kipling. FaPoR; NoAm; OBSV; OHFP; OPOP; OxBTC; TW

Gods of the Earth Beneath, The. Edmund Blunden. BrPo

God's Pity. Louise Driscoll. WGRP

God's Plans. May Riley Smith. BLRP

God's Plans. *Unknown.* BLRP

God's Praises. *Unknown, tr. fr. Irish by* Brendan Kennelly. TIRV

God's Precepts Perfect. Bible, *O.T. Fr.* Psalms: Psalm XIX ("The heavens declare the glory of God"), 7-9. BLRP
  (Glory of God, The.) TrJP
  (God's Glory.) TrGrPo
  (Heavens, The, 1-6) ChTr
  (Heavens Above and the Law Within, The, *Moulton, Modern Reader's Bible*) WGRP
  ("Heavens doe declare, The," *Bay Psalm Book*) SCAP
  (Psalm XIX: "Heavenly frame sets forth the fame, The," *paraphrased by* Sir Philip Sidney) OBVE
  (Psalm XIX: "Spacious firmament on high, The.") WGRP

God's Promises. *Unknown.* BLRP

God's Remembrance. Francis Ledwidge. TIRV

God's rod doth watch while men do sleep; and then. Temptation. Robert Herrick. LiTB

God's Rule. Bible, *O.T. See* Isaiah: Wolf also shall dwell with the lamb, The.

God's Selecting Love in the Decree. Edward Taylor. *Fr.* God's Determinations. PoEL-3

God's spice I was, and pounding was my due. The Martyrdom of Mary, Queen of Scots. Robert Southwell. ACP

God's Sunshine. John Oxenham. WBLP

Gods! The Gods!, The. D. H. Lawrence. CMoP

God's Trails Lead Home. John R. Clements. BLRP

God's Vengeance. Bible, *O.T. Fr.* Isaiah, XXXIV: 8-15. FM

God's Virtue. Barnabe Barnes. *Fr.* A Divine Century of Spiritual Sonnets. NOCV; OBSC
  (Sonnet: "World's bright comforter, whose beamsome light, The.") EiL

God's Ways, Not Our Ways. Henrietta Cordelia Ray. CBWP-3

God's Will. Charles E. Guthrie. BLRP

God's Will. Alice Nevin. BLRP

God's Will for Us. *Unknown.* BLRP; WBLP

God's Will for You and Me. *Unknown. See* Just to be tender, just to be true.

God's will in me. God's Will. Alice Nevin. BLRP

God's Will Is Best. *Unknown.* BLRP

Gods! with what pride I see the titled slave. Charles Churchill. *Fr.* The Author. OBSV

God's World. Mildred Keeling. BLRP

God's World. Edna St. Vincent Millay. BLPL; CMoP; FaBoBe; FaBV; MoAmPo; TrCP

Godspeed. Whittier. Son

Goe and Catche a falling Starre. John Donne. *See* Go and catch a falling star.

Goe, happy Rose, and, enterwove. To the Rose; a Song. Robert Herrick. SeCP
  (To the Rose: Song.) OBS

Goe! hunt the whiter ermine, and present. *See* Go! hunt the whiter ermine and present.

Goe little book, and once a week shake hands. Ad Librum. Samuel Danforth, Jr. SCAP

Goe, Lovely Rose. Edmund Waller. *See* Go, Lovely Rose.

Goe now; and with some daring drugg. Temperance or the Cheap Physitian upon the Translation of Lessius. Richard Crashaw. SeCV-1

Goe, smiling souls, your new-built cages break. *See* Go, smiling souls, your new-built cages break.

Goe soule, the body's guest. *See* Go soul, the body's guest.

Goes through the mud. *Unknown.* OxNR

Goethe in Weimar sleeps, and Greece. Memorial Verses. Matthew Arnold. FiP; NAEL-2; OAEL-2

Goethe said that 'twixt embraces. Not Lotte. Katherine Hoskins. ErPo

Goethe's Blues. Denise Levertov. FaBoWP

Goethe's Death Mask. Linda Gregg. MAYP

Goff; an Heroi-comical Poem, The, *sel.* Thomas Mathison.
  Victory on the Last Green. NOEC

Gofongo, The. Spike Milligan. AmMo

Gogol. Tomas Tranströmer, *tr. fr. Swedish by* Samuel Charters. AnAn

Goin' Back T'morrer. Hamlin Garland. OBAL

Goin' 'cross the Mountain. *Unknown.* AmFP

Goin' down the road, Lawd. Bound No'th Blues. Langston Hughes. AmNP

Goin' down to Cripple Creek, goin' at a run. Cripple Creek. *Unknown.* AmFP

Goin' down to the delta. Mississippi Blues. *Unknown.* AmFP

Goin' Down to Town. *Unknown.* AS

Goin' up State Street, comin' down Main. Take a Whiff on Me. *Unknown.* NOBA

Going. Peter Everwine. NNaP

Going, The. Thomas Hardy. EBEV; ELP; LiTB; NOBE; UnPo

Going. Philip Larkin. CMoP

Going a-Nutting. Edmund Clarence Stedman. GN

Going abruptly into a starry night. Starlight. William Meredith. NePoEA

Going Alone to Spend a Night at the Hsien-Yu Temple. Po Chü-i, *tr. fr. Chinese by* Arthur Waley. Mes

Going alone to the western market. *Unknown, tr. fr. Japanese. Fr.* Manyo Shu. Ma

Going and Staying. Thomas Hardy. CMoP; NoAM

Going Back Again. "Owen Meredith." FiBHP

Going backward. In the Pocket. James Dickey. ASP

Going backward/ All of me and some. In the Pocket. James Dickey. RR

Going Down Hill on a Bicycle. Henry Charles Beeching. OBEV

Going down in. *Unknown, tr. by* Geoffrey Bownas *and* Anthony Thwaite. PeBJV

Going Down the Mountain. Valentin Iremonger. NeIP

Going for Peaches, Fredericksburg, Texas. Naomi Shihab Nye. MT

Going from us at last. The Escape. Mark Van Doren. MoAmPo

Going, Going. Philip Larkin. NoAM

Going Home. Maurice Kenny. STE

Going home by lamplight across Boston Common. A Revivalist in Boston. Adrienne Rich. EaLo

Going Home, 1945, *sel.* L. E. Sissman.
  "My father casts a stone whose ripples ride." DiL

Going Home to Mayo, Winter, 1949. Paul Durcan. CIP

Going In to Dinner. Edward Shanks. OBMV; OxBTC

Going into Breeches. Charles *and* Mary Lamb. OxBChV

Going on six thousand years. After Six Thousand Years. Victor Hugo, *tr. by* Selden Rodman. WaaP

Going On Talking. Gyorgy Raba, *tr. fr. Hungarian by* Jascha Kessler. FOC

Going or Gone. Charles Lamb. BXAP

Going Out to the Country on a Boat Trip. Kao Ch'i, *tr. fr. Chinese by* Jonathan Chaves. CoBLCP

Going Rate, The. Michael Lassell. *Fr.* Times Square Poems. GLP

Going the Rounds; a Sort of Love Poem. Anthony Hecht. BoLoP

Going Through. Bruce P. Woodford. MAT

Going through Changes. Jean Tepperman. NMM

Going To and Fro and Walking Up and Down, *sel.* Charles Reznikoff.
  Autobiography: Hollywood. VWA

Going to Bed. Marchette Chute. PDV

Going to Bed. John Donne. *Fr.* Elegies, XIX. EBEV; LiTB; NAEL-1; PPP

Going—to—her! Emily Dickinson. PeHV

Going to Mass Last Sunday. Donagh MacDonagh. BIrV; NeIP

Going to Moscow. Lauris Edmond. ATNZ

Going to Remake This World. James Welch. CDW

Going to School. Karl Shapiro. TrJP

Going to sleep, I cross my hands on my chest. Death. William Knott. EAS

Going to the desert. Extremities. Rae Armantrout. LP

Going to the Ministry with Chao Tzu-ch'i. Yü Chi, *tr. fr. Chinese by* Jonathan Chaves. CoBLCP

Going to the North. Stanislaw Wygodski, *tr. fr. Polish by* Isaac Komem. VWA

Going to the Shawnee Rodeo. Don Bell. CowP

Going to the Water. Geary Hobson. STE

Going Too Far. Mildred Howells. OnMSP

Going Under of the Evening Land, The. Mekeel McBride. NAmP

Going Up. John Travers Moore. RHPC
Going up for the jump shot. I Try to Turn In My Jock. David Hilton. TSL
Going up the river, or down, their tuneless look. Barges on the Hudson. Babette Deutsch. WPE
Going up through the hill called the vineyard. The Vineyard. W. S. Merwin. NNaP
Going Uptown to Visit Miriam. Victor Hernandez Cruz. FF; MAT
Gol-Darned Wheel, The. *Unknown.* CowP
Golagros and Gawane, *sel. Unknown.*
   "Thai passit in thare pilgramage." OxBS
Gold,/ Silver. *Unknown.* OxNR
Gold. Martin Armstrong. BoTP
Gold. Thomas Hood. WBLP
Gold. Ferenc Juhász, *tr. fr. Hungarian by* David Wevill. MHuP
Gold and all this werdis win. Crucified to the World. *Unknown.* MeEL
Gold and Black. Michael Ondaatje. NoP
Gold-armoured ghost from the Roman road, The. The Youth with Red-gold Hair. Dame Edith Sitwell. FaBoTw
Gold as an infant's humming dream. Long Summer. Laurie Lee. BoNaP
Gold Coast Customs, *sel.* Dame Edith Sitwell.
   "One fantee wave." OBMV
Gold-colored [*or* coloured] skin of my Lebanese friends, The. A Trip to Four or Five Towns. John Logan. CoAP; NNaP
Gold Country, The; Hotel Leger, Mokelumne Hill, Revisited, The. Joseph Stroud. NPGG
Gold earrings, The. Condo Girl. Elaine Equi. UL
Gold Glade. Robert Penn Warren. CRP
Gold! Gold! Gold! Gold! Gold. Thomas Hood. WBLP
"Gold is for the mistress—silver for the maid." Cold Iron. Kipling. OnMSP
Gold Is the Son of Zeus: Neither Moth nor Worm May Gnaw It. "Michael Field." OBMV
Gold I've none, for use or show. Lyric [k] for Legacies. Robert Herrick. FaBoRV; JCP; OBS
Gold Leaves. G. K. Chesterton. OxBTC
Gold locks, and black locks. The Barber's. Walter de la Mare. GoJo
Gold Medal. Philippe Soupault, *tr. fr. French by* Michael Benedikt. POS
Gold mountain men said, The. Chinatown Talking Story. Kitty Tsui. BrSi; ER
Gold of a ripe oat straw, gold of a southwest moon. Falltime. Carl Sandburg. PoA
Gold or iv'ry's not intended ("Non ebur neque aureum"). Horace, *tr. fr. Latin.* Fr. Odes, II, 18. OBVE, *tr. by* Christopher Smart.
Gold priests, wooden chalices. *Unknown, tr. by* Thomas Kinsella. NOIV
Gold, red and green flies. Near Dusk. Joseph Auslander. FaPON
Gold savours well, though it be got. Isabella Whitney. *Fr.* Sweet Nosegay, A, or Pleasant Posy. WPE
Gold-Seekers, The. Hamlin Garland. AA; FaBoBe
Gold Sunday. . .What shall I buy for you? The Sunday before Christmas. Sandor Csoori, *tr. by* Jascha Kessler. FOC
Gold survives the fire that's hot enough. Timer. Tony Harrison. *Fr.* The School of Eloquence. NoAM
Gold tane from the kings harbengers. Robin Hood and Queen Katherine. *Unknown.* ESPB
Gold-tinted Dragon, The. Karla Kuskin. RAR
Gold Tooth Blues. Tennessee Williams. OBAL
Gold Watch. Patrick Kavanagh. InPS
Gold will not buy this voyage. Looking for a Country under Its Original Name. Colleen J. McElroy. BlSi
Gold wings across the sea! The Song of Jehane du Castel Beau. William Morris. *Fr.* Golden Wings. ChTr
Goldbrown upon the sated flood. Flood. James Joyce. MoBrPo
Golden. Francisco A. de Icaza, *tr. fr. Spanish by* Samuel Beckett. MexPo
Golden Age, The. W. H. Auden. *Fr.* Man of La Mancha. AnAn
Golden Age, The. Sir Richard Fanshawe, *after the Italian of* Giovanni Battista Guarini. *See* Il Pastor Fido: Fair Golden Age! When milk was th' onely food.
Golden Age, The. Ernest Francisco Fenollosa. AA
Golden Age, The. Giovanni Battista Guarini, *tr. fr. Italian by* Sir Richard Fanshawe. *Fr.* The Faithful Shepherd, IV, ix. PFI
Golden Age. Mac Hammond. EOEF
Golden Age, The, *sel.* Thomas Heywood.
   Hymn to Diana. EIL
Golden Age, The. Ovid. *See* Metamorphoses: Then sprang up first the golden age, which of itself maintained.
Golden Age, The. Tasso. *See* Aminta: O lovely age of gold!
Golden Age, The. *Unknown.* APAS

Golden Age is come, The. The Newmarket Song. *Unknown.* APAS
Golden age was when the world was young, The. Fulke Greville. *Fr.* Caelica, XLIV. OAEL-1
Golden as your singing-note. Amber Beads. Audrey Alexandra Brown. CaP
Golden Bird, The. Rex Ingamells. PoAu-2
Golden Bough. Elinor Wylie. MoAmPo; PBWP
Golden bracelets and the flags, The. Say It with Music. Philippe Soupault, *tr. by* Eugene Jolas. RHTwFP
Golden bridle of Bellerephon. The Fourth Pearl: Temperance. Lady Diana Primrose. *Fr.* A Chain of Pearl. WPE
Golden Calf. Norman MacCaig. OxBS
Golden Carol, The. *Unknown.* OHIP
Golden casket I designed, A. John Swanwick Drennan. BIrV
Golden cloud slept for her pleasure, A. The Mountain. Mikhail Yurevich Lermontov, *tr. by* Max Eastman. AWP
Golden corn ripens. Green Corn Festival. Merry Harris. GOS
Golden cradle under you, and you young, A. He Meditates on the Life of a Rich Man. Douglas Hyde, *tr. by* Lady Gregory. OBMV
Golden crocus reaches up, The. The Crocus. Walter Crane. RHPC
Golden crow lights on the western huts, The. Approaching Death. Prince Otsu, *tr. by* Burton Watson. JLIC-1
Golden eagle swooped out of the sky, The. Salmon Drowns Eagle. Malcolm Lowry. MoCV; OBCV
Golden Echo, The. Gerard Manley Hopkins. *See* Is there any any, is there none such.
Golden Fantasy. Tamura Ryuichi, *tr. fr. Japanese by* Hiroaki Sato. FCEI
Golden Fleece, The. Oscar Williams. PoA
Golden flie one shew'd to me, A. Upon a Flie. Robert Herrick. FM
Golden flood the weightless seat, The. Spacepoem 3: Off Course. Edwin Morgan. BWV
Golden Gate, The, *sel.* Vikram Seth.
   "Week ago, when I had finished, A." UAS
Golden gift that nature did thee give, The. Earl of Surrey. AAS; SiPS
Golden globe incontinent, The. Midsummer Day in France. Alexander Hume. *Fr.* Of the Day Estivall. FaBoPP
Golden Glove, The. *Unknown.* AmFP
Golden goats with lapis eyes. Panegyric. Harris Lenowitz. VWA
Golden-Green Dawn, A. Abraham Chalfi, *tr. fr. Hebrew by* Bernhard Frank. MHeP
Golden Gullies of the Palmer, The. *Unknown.* PoAu-1
Golden hair that Gulla wears, The. Bought Locks. Martial, *tr. by* Sir John Harington. AWP
Golden head by golden head. Laura and Lizzie Asleep. Christina Rossetti. *Fr.* Goblin Market. PeHV
Golden Hour, The. Thomas Moore. *Fr.* Lalla Rookh. OBNC
Golden Journey to Samarkand, The, *sels.* James Elroy Flecker. FaBoRV
   "And how beguile you? Death has no repose." *Fr.* II. OxBTC
   "Away, for we are ready to a man!" NOBE
   "We who with songs beguile your pilgrimage." BrPo; FaPoR; GoJo; OBMV; Unknown.
Golden Jubilee of Wilberforce. Mrs. Henry Linden. CBWP-4
Golden Lines. Gérard de Nerval, *tr. fr. French by* Robert Bly. NU
Golden Lot, A. Joseph Skipsey. SaC
Golden Mean, The. Earl of Surrey, *after* Horace. OBVE; SiPS
Golden Mile-Stone, The. Longfellow. PoEL-5
Golden mists o'er Cloudland wreathing. Fancy and Imagination. Henrietta Cordelia Ray. CBWP-3
Golden Moonrise. William Stanley Braithwaite. PoBA
Golden New York night. Alternating Nocturne. José Juan Tablada, *tr. by* Samuel Beckett. MexPo
Golden Oldie. Paul Mariani. GeTw
Golden one is gone from the banquets, The. Hilda Doolittle ("H. D."). PoA
Golden pallor of voluptuous light, A. The Mocking Bird. Paul Hamilton Hayne. AmAmPo
Golden Pheasants Flying. Sandor Csoori, *tr. fr. Hungarian by* Daniel Hoffman. MHuP
Golden pheonix swirls across her warmly fragrant skirt, A. Deva-like Barbarian. Niu Chiao, *tr. by* Lois Fusek. ATF
Golden Rod, The. Frank Dempster Sherman. FaPON
Golden Sea-Otter, The. Wakarpa. *Fr.* Kutune Shirka (The Ainu Epic). WTO
Golden Shower, The, *sel.* Roy Campbell.
   "Here, where relumed by changing seasons, burn." OxBTC
Golden Slumbers. Thomas Dekker *and others. Fr.* The Pleasant Comedy of Patient Grissell [*or* Grissel *or* Grissill]. ELP
Golden spider of the sky, The. Solar Myth. Genevieve Taggard. MoAmPo
Golden State. Frank Bidart. DiL; NoAM

Golden sun that brings the day, The. In Praise of the Sun. "A. W." CTC; OBSC

Golden [or Goldyn] Targe, The, sel. William Dunbar. OxBS
   Poet's Dream, The. PBBP; PoEL-1

Golden through the golden morning. The Return. Eleanor Rogers Cox. PAH

Golden trees of England, The. The Jungle Trees. Marjorie Wilson. BoTP

Golden Vanitie, The. Unknown. EnSB

Golden Vanity, The. Unknown. CH; ELP; FaBoCh; OBET; WiR
   (Sweet Trinity (The Golden Vanity), The.) ESPB, B vers.

Golden Voyage; or, The Prosperous Arrival of the James and Mary, The. Unknown. OxBSS

Golden Wedding, The. David Gray. FaBoBe

Golden-wheeled carriage passes the willow embankment, The. Sand of Silk-Washing Stream. Chang Pi, tr. by Lois Fusek. ATF

Golden Wings, sels. William Morris. OBNC
   "Midways of a walled garden." ChTr
   (Ancient Castle, The.) SeCePo
   Song of Jehane du Castel Beau, The. ChTr

Golden, within this golden hive. Danaë. Barbara Howes. WPE

Goldenhair. James Joyce. Fr. Chamber Music, V. BoTP

Goldenrod or Golden-rod is yellow, The. September [Days Are Here]. Helen Hunt Jackson. FaPON; FPL; GoJo; OBCA; PoLF

Goldfinch. John Engels. BLA

Goldfinches, The. Richard Jago. PBBP

Goldfinches. Keats. See I Stood Tiptoe [upon a Little Hill]: Sometimes goldfinches one by one will drop.

Goldfish. Audrey Alexandra Brown. CaP

Goldfish. Harold Monro. BrPo

Goldfish on the Writing Desk. Max Brod, tr. fr. German by Babette Deutsch and Avram Yarmolinsky. TrJP

Goldfish Wife, The. Sandra Hochman. NYBP; UnPo

Goldrush. H. C. ten Berge, tr. fr. Dutch by Wanda Boeke. DuIn

Goldyn Targe, The. William Dunbar. See Right as the stern of day begonth to shine.

Golem, The. Shlomo Reich, tr. fr. French. VWA, tr. by Mira Reich

Golf Links, The. Sarah Norcliffe Cleghorn. FaFP; InPK; PoLF
   (Quatrain ("Golf links lie so near The mill.").) NIP

Golfer. Gloria A. Maxson. Fr. Epitaphs. SoTCo

Golfers. Irving Layton. SD

Golfer's Rubaiyat, The. H. W. Boynton. BXAP

Golgotha. X. J. Kennedy. NYBP

Golgotha Is a Mountain. Arna Bontemps. AmNP; CDC; PoNe

Goliath and David. Louis Untermeyer. TrJP

Goliath was a husky brute. David and Delilah. Clark Stillman. SoTCo

Goliathus goliathus, the one banana. The Zoo. Gilbert Sorrentino. NeAP

Go! little bill, and command me hertely. She Saw Me in Church. Unknown. MeEL

Goll Mac Morna Parts from His Wife. Unknown. NOIV

Gollihar/ Burned the winter grass from his fields. Rahab. Diane Glancy. CRP

Goll's Parting with His Wife. Unknown, tr. fr. Early Modern Irish by Eoin MacNeill. AnIL

Golly, How Truth Will Out. Ogden Nash. LiTA; MoAmPo

Gombeen, The. Joseph Campbell. BIrV

Gondibert, sels. Sir William Davenant.
   "By what bold passion am I rudely led." Fr. I, 3. OBS
   "Of all the Lombards, by their Trophies knowne." Fr. I, i. SeCV-1
   Praise and Prayer. Fr. II, vi. OBEV

Gondola that glides, The. Eugenio Montale, tr. fr. Italian by Dana Gioia. Fr. The Motets, XIII.

Gondoliers, The, sels. W. S. Gilbert.
   Duke of Plaza-Toro, The. FaPON; FiBHP
   Grand Inquisitor's Song, The. OnMSP
   There Lived a King. FiBHP

Gone. Mary Elizabeth Coleridge. OBEV; OBNC

Gone, A. Larry Eigner. NeAP

Gone. David McCord. TDD

Gone. Carl Sandburg. NOBA

Gone. Mary E. Tucker. CBWP-1

Gone. Walter de la Mare. GoJo

Gone are the coloured princes, gone echo, gone laughter. The Ruin. Richard Hughes. OBMV

Gone Are the Days. Norman MacCaig. OxBC

Gone are the days when my heart was young and gay. Old Black Joe. Stephen Collins Foster. FaFP

Gone are the drab monosyllabic days. Tilth. Robert Graves. FaBoEE; OBSV

Gone are the games we played all night. Mahsati, tr. by Deirdre Lashgari. WPOW

Gone are the sensuous stars, and manifold. Chaucer. Benjamin Brawley. BANP

Gone dark now in my insentient time. Solar Eclipse. József Tornai, tr. by Jascha Kessler. FOC

Gone down in the flood, and gone out in the flame! The Sinking of the Merrimac. Lucy Larcom. PAH

Gone—faded out of the story, the sea-faring friend I remember? Pasa Thalassa Thalassa. E. A. Robinson. MOS

Gone, gone—sold and gone. Whittier. AA; AWP; PoNe

Gone, I say, and walk from church. The Truth the Dead Know. Anne Sexton. MoAmPo; NePoEA-2; NoAM; PBWP; TAP

Gone in the Wind. James Clarence Mangan, after the German of Friedrich Rückert. ACP; SeCePo; TIRV

Gone is the city, gone the day. The Right Kind of People. Edwin Markham. BLPA; FPL

Gone is the pain of absence. Asadullah Khan Ghalib, tr. by Ahmed Ali. GoT

Gone Is the Sleepgiver. Penelope Shuttle. BrRo

Gone Is Youth. Salamah, son of Jandal, tr. fr. Arabic by Sir Charles Lyall. Fr. The Mufaddaliyat. AWP

Gone now the baby's nurse. Home after Three Months Away. Robert Lowell. HCAP; NoP

Gone on before me. Tonna, tr. by Steven D. Carter. WFTW

Gone she is a long, long way. Upon a Maid. Robert Herrick. CaPo

Gone the three ancient ladies. Frau Bauman, Frau Schmidt, and Frau Schwartze. Theodore Roethke. CoAP; MoAB; MoP; NAAL-2; NoAM; NOBA; NYBP; SaC; TAP

Gone were but the winter. Spring Quiet. Christina Rossetti. BoNaP; BoTP; CH; GTBS-P; InPS; PoE; PoEL-5; WPE

Gone Were but the Winter Cold. Allan Cunningham. CH

Gone while your tastes were keen to you. For E. McC. Ezra Pound. SD

Gone, with all her sparkling beauty. Gone. Mary E. Tucker. CBWP-1

"Goneys an' gullies an' all o' the birds o' the sea." Sea Change. John Masefield. FaBoTw; MOS; OBMV; RB

Gonna dig my grave both long and narrow. Dig My Grave. Unknown. AmFP

Gonna Lay My Head Down on Some Railroad Line. Unknown. AmFP

Good afternoon, Sir Smasham Uppe! Sir Smasham Uppe. Emile Victor Rieu. RHPC

Good and Bad. James Stephens. MoBrPo

Good and bad and right and wrong. Good and Bad. James Stephens. MoBrPo

Good and Bad Children. Robert Louis Stevenson. Fr. A Child's Garden of Verses. EBVV; FaBoCh; FaFP; OxBChV

Good and Bad Luck. John Milton Hay. See Good Luck and Bad ("Good luck is the gayest of all gay girls").

Good and Bad Wives. Unknown. CoMu

Good and Clever. Elizabeth Wordsworth. OxBTC

Good, and great God, can I not think[e] of thee. To Heaven. Ben Jonson. HAP; JCP; LiTB; NAEL-1; NOCV; OBS; QFR; SeCP; TrPWD; UnPo

Good and great God! How should I fear. No Coming to God without Christ. Robert Herrick. OxBSP

Good Appetite. Mark Van Doren. OxBSP

Good at something, I practiced till I broke. The Standing Broad Jump. Richard Frost. ASP

Good bailiff of my farm, that snug domain. Horace, tr. by John Conington. OBVE

Good Beasts, The. Willis Barnstone. VWA

Good, better, best. Unknown. OxNR

Good Bishop, A. Unknown, tr. fr. German by William Taylor. WGRP

Good Boy, A. Robert Louis Stevenson. PWR

Good Boy, The. Unknown. AS

"Good brother Philip, I have borne you long." Sir Philip Sidney. Fr. Astrophel and Stella, LXXXIII. PBBP

Good-by and Keep Cold. Robert Frost. CMoP

Good-by er Howdy-do. James Whitcomb Riley. CTC

Good-by or Goodbyegood-by to summer! Robin Redbreast. William Allingham. FaBoBe; MoShBr; OxBChV; PBBP

Good-by, my son, good-by. The Wayward Son. Mrs. Henry Linden. CBWP-4

Good-by My Winter Suit. N. M. Bodecker. RHPC

Good-by, sweetheart, our days of bliss. The Parting Lovers. Mrs. Henry Linden. CBWP-4

Good-by, the tears are in my eyes. Villon, tr. by Andrew Lang. AWP

Good-bye. Emerson. AnAmPo; FaFP; LiTA; PWR; TAP; WGRP

Good-bye. Walter de la Mare. NoP

"Good-bye," I said to my conscience. Conscience and Remorse. Paul Laurence Dunbar. AnAmPo

Good-bye, little desk at school, good-bye. Vacation Time. Frank Hutt. BoTP

Good-bye 'Liza Jane. *Unknown. AS, with music*

Good-bye My Fancy! Walt Whitman. FaFP; LiTA; NAAL-1; PrIm; TAP

Good-bye!—no [or nay] do not grieve that it is over. Harriet Monroe. AA; PoA

Good-bye now, and good luck! Enjoy your liberty! Finale. W. H. Auden. *Fr.* Man of La Mancha. AnAn

Good-bye, proud world! I'm going home. Good-bye. Emerson. AnAmPo; FaFP; LiTA; PWR; TAP; WGRP

"Good-bye," said the river, "I'm going downstream." Howard Nemerov. WeW

Good-bye to the Mezzogiorno. W. H. Auden. OxBTC

"Good-bye," you said, and your voice was an echo. Tak for Sidst. Babette Deutsch. PoA

Good Catholic girl, she didn't mind the cleaning. Snow White and the Seven Deadly Sins. R. S. Gwynn. SoTCo

Good children, refuse not these lessons to learn. A Schoolmaster's Admonition. *Unknown.* OxBChV

Good christian Reader judge me not. God's Controversy with New-England. Michael Wigglesworth. SCAP

Good Christians. Robert Herrick. LiTB

Good Christians all attend unto my ditty. A Ballad of the Strange and Wonderful Storm of Hail. *Unknown.* CoMu

Good Christians all, both great and small. The Avondale Mine Disaster. *Unknown.* AmFP

Good Company. Karle Wilson Baker. FaPON; WGRP

Good Company. Henry VIII, King of England. *See* Pastime with good company.

Good Company. *Unknown.* OBET

Good Counsel. James I, King of Scotland. ACP

Good Counsel (Good for good is only fair). *Unknown, tr. fr. Welsh by* Glyn Jones. OBWVE

Good Counsel (Tutor not thyself in science: go to masters for perfection). *Unknown, tr. fr. Turkish by* James Clarence Mangan. NOIV

Good Counsel to a Young Maid ("When you the sunburnt pilgrim see"). Thomas Carew. ErPo; OBS

Good Creatures, Do You Love Your Lives. A. E. Housman. TW

Good dame looked from her cottage, The. The Leak in the Dike. Phoebe Cary. FaFP; FaPON

Good dame Mercy with dame Charite, The. The Seven Deadly Sins. Stephen Hawes. *Fr.* The Pastime of Pleasure. PoEL-1

Good day, good day. In Honour of Christmas. *Unknown.* MeEL

Good day's work I just met someone I can't forget, A. For Pablo Picasso. Paul Eluard, *tr. by* Michael Benedikt. POS

Good day's work, two contracts made, A. Between a Contractor and His Wife. *Unknown.* NOEC

Good Doctor gnashed his way through, The. On to the Source. James Tate. AnAn

Good Dream, The. Denise Levertov. NNaP

Good English Hospitality. Blake. *Fr.* An Island in the Moon. CoMu (Mayors, The.) CH

Good Fairies have trooped off one by one, The. Christenings. Peter Porter. NAs

Good father, I have sent for you because. The Merry Little Maid and Wicked Little Monk. *Unknown.* ErPo

Good flat earth. . . and not so very high, The. Two Mountains Men Have Climbed. Pauline Starkweather. GoYe

Good folk [or folke], for gold or hire [or hyre]. The Crier. Michael Drayton. EiL; InVP (Cryer, The.) PoEL-2

Good folks ever will have their way. The Doctor's Story. Will M. Carleton. BLPA

Good for good is only fair. Good Counsel. *Unknown, tr. by* Glyn Jones. OBWVE

Good for Nothing Man, *sel.* Kenneth Pitchford. Pickup in Tony's Hashhouse. ErPo

Good Frend, *sel.* Hilda Doolittle ("H. D."). "Time has an end, they say." NOBA; VGW

Good Friday. A. J. M. Smith. CaP

Good Friday. Christy Brown. TIRV

Good Friday. John Frederick Nims. TW

Good Friday. Christina Rossetti. OFD; PoEL-5; PoEL-5

Good Friday. *Unknown.* ChTr

Good Friday and the Present Crucifixion. Vincent Buckley. CBAP

Good Friday [or Goodfriday], 1613. Riding Westward. John Donne. InPS; JCP; MeLP; MePo; NAEL-1; NOCV; NoP; OAEL-1; OBS; PoE; PoEL-2; PPP; SeCP; SeCV-1; TEF

Good Friday. Somewhere a death. Good Friday and the Present Crucifixion. Vincent Buckley. CBAP

Good Friday was the day. The Martyr. Herman Melville. PoEL-5; TAP; TrGrPo

Good Gad! who's this? What's this, my son? The Democratic Barber; or, Country Gentleman's Surprise. John Parrish. NOEC

Good God! and can it be that such a nook. The Milking Shed. John Clare. CH

Good God of scholar, simpleton, and sage! Grace. Johnstone G. Patrick. TrPWD

Good God, What a Night That Was. Petronius Arbiter, *tr. fr. Latin by* Kenneth Rexroth. BoLoP; ErPo

Good gray [or grey] guardians of art, The. Museum Piece. Richard Wilbur. CMoP; FaBoMo; InPK; NIP; NoP; TAP

Good Grease. Mary TallMountain. STE

Good Great Man, The. Samuel Taylor Coleridge. PWR

Good grey poet, I'll always remember you. The Entrepreneur. David Ray. SoTCo

Good heaven, I thank thee since it was designed. On Myself. Anne Finch, Countess of Winchilsea. OxBSP; TrGrPo

Good Heaven! this mystery of life explain. Ad Coelum. William Pattison. OxBSP

Good Hours. Robert Frost. AnAmPo

Good house, and ground whereon, A. The Salt Garden. Howard Nemerov. NePoEA

Good house: sparrows delight, A. Congratulations on a New House. Basho, *tr. fr. Japanese by* Burton Watson. *Fr.* Seventy-six Hokku. FCEI

Good Humor Man, The. Phyllis McGinley. MoShBr

Good in graves as heavenly seed are sown, The. The Christmas Reply to the Phylosopher. Sir William Davenant. MeLP

Good is an orchard, the saint saith. Of an Orchard. Katharine Tynan. WGRP

Good Joan, The. Lizette Woodworth Reese. FaPON; MoShBr

Good Junipero, the Padre. Discovery of San Francisco Bay. Richard Edward White. PAH

Good king had three daughters, The. Delgadina. *Unknown, tr. by* Lysander Kemp. DMH

Good King Wenceslas. *Unknown, tr. fr. Latin by* John Mason Neale. OHIP; OnMSP

Good ladies, ye that have your pleasure in exile. The Lady Again Complains. Earl of Surrey. SiPS

Good Lady/ I have corn and beets. A Negro Peddler's Song. Fenton Johnson. AmNP

Good lady, so deeply do I care for you. *Unknown, tr. by* Meg Bogin. WT

Good Lawd Know My Name, De. Frank Lebby Stanton. WBLP

Good Linemen Live in a Closed World. James Whitehead. MT

Good-looking, I'll never stoop for you. Mahsati, *tr. by* Deirdre Lashgari. WPOW

Good Lord, behold this dreadful[l] enemy. The Soul's Groan to Christ for Succo[u]r. Edward Taylor. *Fr.* God's Determinations. NAAL-1; PoEL-3

Good Lord Graeme is to Carlisle gane. Graeme and Bewick. *Unknown.* EnSB

Good Lord Nelson had a swollen gland, The. A Ballad of the Good Lord Nelson. Lawrence Durrell. ErPo; LiTM

"Good lord of the land, will you stay thane." Lord Maxwell's Last Goodnight ("Good Lord of the Land. "). *Unknown.* ESPB, (A *vers.*); OxBB, *with music*

Good Luck and Bad ("Good luck is the gayest of all gay girls"). John Milton Hay, *after the German of* Heine. AnAmPo; FaBoEE; NBLV

Good Man, The. *Unknown, tr. fr. Irish by* Robin Flower. TIRV

Good Man, The. *Unknown, tr. fr. Hebrew. Fr.* The Talmud. TrJP

Good Man in Hell, The. Edwin Muir. MoBrPo; TW

Good man was there [or ther] of religion [or religioun], A. The Poor Parson. Chaucer. *Fr.* The Canterbury Tales: Prologue. ACP; NOCV; WGRP

(Good Parson, The, *mod. by* H.C. Leonard) WGRP ("Parson of a country town was he, The.")

Good Manners. Washington Delgado, *tr. fr. Spanish by* David Tipton. Per

Good master, you and I were born. A Decanter of Madeira, Aged 86, to George Bancroft, Aged 86. Silas Weir Mitchell. AA

Good Medicine. *Unknown.* PWR

Good Memory. Sotero Rivera-Avilés, *tr. fr. Spanish by* Julio Marzán. InW

Good Men Afflicted Most. Robert Herrick. LiTB

Good men and true! in this house who dwell. The Croppy Boy. William B. McBurney. TIRV

Good Moolly Cow, The. Eliza Lee Follen. OBCA

Good Morning. Rose Fyleman. BoTP

Good Morning. Muriel Sipe. RAR

Good morning, Algernon: Good morning, Percy. On Mundane Acquaintances. Hilaire Belloc. FaBoEE; FiBHP; OxBTC

Good Morning America, sel. Carl Sandburg. "Now it's Uncle Sam sitting on top of the world." *Fr.* XIV. OFD

Good morning, daddy! Dream Boogie. Langston Hughes. AmPP; HCAP; RR

Good morning, Father Francis. *Unknown.* OxNR

Good morning, fox of the cave. The Fox's Counsel. Huw Llwyd, *tr. by* Joseph P. Clancy. OBWVE

"Good morning; good morning!" the General said. The General. Siegfried Sassoon. BrPo; CMoP; FaBV; FiBHP; LiTM; MMA; NAEL-2; NOAM; OBWP; OxBoLi; OxBSP; OxBTC; PoE; TW

Good Morning? Heavenly Madam Ping. Fritzi Harmsen van Beek, *tr. fr. Dutch by* Greta Kilburn. DuIn

Good morning, Life—and all. A Greeting. W. H. Davies. MoBrPo

Good morning, Mistress and Master. *Unknown.* OxNR

Good morning to You, Almighty God. Kaddish. Levi Yitzhok, *tr. by* Joseph Leftwich. TrJP

Good morning to you, Lord of the world! Levi Yitzhok, *tr. by* Olga Marx. EaLo

Good-Morrow, The. John Donne. AWP; BoLoP; EBEV; ElL; EnLoPo; FaBoBe; FABV; FF; FPL; HoPM; InPS; InvP; JCP; LiTB; MeLP; MePo; NAEL-1; NAWM-1; NIP; NoP; OAEL-1; OBS; PoE; PoEL-2; PoRA; PPP; SCV; SeCP; SeCV-1; SoSe; TEP; TrGrPo

Good Morrow. Thomas Heywood. *See* Rape of Lucrece, The: Pack, Clouds, Away.

"Good morrow, my lord!" in the sky alone. Sir Lark and King Sun; a Parable. George Macdonald. *Fr.* Adela Cathcart, *ch.* 16. GN

Good morrow to the day so fair. The Mad Maid's Song. Robert Herrick. AWP; CaPo; CH; EnLoPo; OAEL-1; OBEV; SeCV-1; TrGrPo; WiR

Good morrow to thy sable beak. The Blackcock. Joanna Baillie. PBBP

Good morrow to you, Valentine. *Unknown.* OxNR

Good Mr. Peeps or Peps or Pips. The Gospel of Mr. Pepys. Christopher Morley. NBLV

Good Muse, rock me asleep. To His Muse. Nicholas Breton. OBSC

Good Name, A. Shakespeare. *Fr.* Othello, III, iii. FaFP

Good name is better than precious oil, A. "It Is Better. . ." Bible, *O.T. Fr.* Ecclesiastes, VII: 1-9. TrJP

"Good-nature" is thy sterling name. Loveliness. Christopher Smart. *Fr.* Hymns for the Amusement of Children, XIV. NOCV

Good neighbor, tell me why that sound. The Neighbors of Bethlehem. *Unknown.* OHIP

Good Neighbors. May Justus. RAR

Good neighbour, why do you look awry? *Unknown.* TW

Good New Is; the Bad News Is, The. David Ray. SoTCo

Good News Bad News. Keith Abbott. UL

Good News from New England ("Great Jehova's working word effecting wondrously, The."), *sel. At. to* Edward Johnson. SCAP "With hearts revived in conceit, new land and trees they eye." GOA

Good news. It seems he loved them after all. A Song about Major Eatherly. John Wain. OxBTC

Good Night. Ruth Ainsworth. BoTP

Good Night. Joel Dailey. UL

Good Night. Victor Hugo, *tr. fr. French.* BoTP; FaPON

Good-Night, A. Francis Quarles. OBS; TrGrPo

Good night./ Pass the cookies. Things to Say When You Quit Smoking. Laurel Blossom. SoTCo

Good-Night. Edward Thomas. NoP

Good Night and Good Morning. Richard Monckton Milnes. BoTP; OxBChV

Good Night, at last. Robert Duncan. *Fr.* Passages. VGW

Good night, big world. Back to the Ghetto. Jacob Glatstein, *tr. by* Joseph Leftwich. TrJP

Good-night; ensured release. Parta Quies. A. E. Housman. NOBE; TEP

Good night for the fireplace to be, A. The Heat in the Room. Weldon Kees. EAS

Good night, God bless you. *Unknown.* OxNR

Good night! Good night!/ Far flies the light. Good Night. Victor Hugo. BoTP; FaPON

Good Night, Good Night. Dennis Lee. RAR

Good-night! I have to say good-night. Palabras Cariñosas. Thomas Bailey Aldrich. AA

Good night, my table & chairs. Good Night. Joel Dailey. UL

Good night, my two little cloud ladies. For the Girls 'cause They Know. Harold Littlebird. VoR

Good-Night, or Blessing, The. Robert Herrick. CaPo

"Good Night," Says the Owl. Lady Erskine Crum. BoTP

Good night, sweet repose. *Unknown.* OxNR

Good night to the Year Academic. A Grouchy Good Night to the Academic Year. Ted Pauker. NOBL

Good night to thee, Fair Goddess. Sunset Song. *Unknown, tr. by* N. Barnes. WTO

Good night, wide world. Good Night, World. Jacob Glatstein, *tr. by* Benjamin *and* Barbara Harshav. AYP

"Good Night, Willie Lee, I'll See You in the Morning." Alice Walker. WeW

Good Night, World. Jacob Glatstein, *tr. fr. Yiddish by* Benjamin *and* Barbara Harshav. AYP

Good oars, for Arnold's sake. Pax Paganica. Louise Imogen Guiney. AA

Good of the chaplain to enter Lone Bay. Billy in the Darbies. Herman Melville. *Fr.* Billy Budd, Foretopman. HAP; NAAL-1; NAWM-2; NOBA; OxBoLi; PoEL-5

Good Old Body. Christine Donald. AIW

Good Old Days, The. Barbara Fried. NBLV

Good Old Days. Elma Mitchell. PoPo

Good Old Dog, The. Toi Derricotte. InPS

Good old, honest Deacon Brown. Deacon Brown's Conclusion. George Sands Johnson. PWR

Good old Mother Fairie. To Mother Fairie. Alice Cary. OBCA

Good Parson, The. Chaucer. *See* Canterbury Tales, The: Prologue.

Good People. Maura Stanton. NAmP; SM

Good people all attend I pray. The Wreck of the *Royal Charter.* *Unknown.* OxBSS

Good people all come listen to my melancholy tale. George Jones. *Unknown.* OxBSS

Good people all, I pray attend. The New-fashioned Farmer. *Unknown.* OBET

Good people all, of every sort. An Elegy on the Death of a Mad Dog. Goldsmith. *Fr.* The Vicar of Wakefield, *ch.* 17. BeLS; BLPA; FaBoBe; FaBoCh; FaBoCo; FaFP; FPL; GN; NA; NBLV; NOBE; NOEC; NOIV; OBNV; TEP

Good people all, with one accord. An Elegy on That Glory of Her Sex, Mrs. Mary Blaize. Goldsmith. FaBoNo (Elegy on the Glory of Her Sex, Mrs. Mary Blaize, The.) NA (Mrs. Mary Blaize.) FaBoCo

Good people attend now, and I will declare. Man's Amazement. *Unknown.* CoMu

Good people come buy. A New Song of an Orange. *Unknown.* CoMu

Good people do but lend an ear. The Sea Martyrs. *Unknown.* OxBSS

Good people draw near as you pass along. Alphabetical Song on the Corn Law Bill. *Unknown.* OxBoLi

Good people, give attention, a story you shall hear. Lord Delamere. *Unknown.* ESPB

Good people give attention and listen unto me. The Carpet-Weavers' Lament. *Unknown.* OBET

Good people give attention who now around me stand. The Female Sailor. *Unknown.* OBET

Good people, I pray now attend to my muse. The Lord Chancellours Villanies Discovered; or, His Rise and Fall in the Four Last Years. *Unknown.* CoMu

Good people of old England, come listen unto me. On the Late Engagement in Carles Town River. *Unknown.* OxBSS

Good people pay attention and listen to my song. A Great Favourite Song, Entitled The Sailor's Hor npipe. *Unknown.* OxBSS

Good people, what, will you of all be bereft. A Ballad on the Taxes. *At. to* Edward Ward *and to* Henry Hall. OxBoLi (Ballad on the Times, A.) APAS

Good Play, A. Robert Louis Stevenson. FaPON; MoShBr; PWR

Good reader! if you e'er have seen. Nonsense. Thomas Moore. FaBoEE; NA

Good repute is water carried in a sieve. Lalleswari, *tr. by* George Grierson. WPOW

Good Resolution, A. Roy Campbell. OBSV

Good Riddance to Bad Rubbish O at Last. Paul Goodman. TW

Good Samaritan, The. John Henry, Cardinal Newman. OBTV

Good Ship, The. Michael Stephens. UL

Good Ships. John Crowe Ransom. WeW

"Good show!" he said, leaned his head back and laughed. Fleet Fighter. Olivia FitzRoy. CN

Good sir, if you will shew the best of your skill. How to Choose a Wife. *Unknown.* FaBoUs

Good sir, whose powers are these? Shakespeare. *Fr.* Hamlet, IV, i. WaaP

Good sirs, be civil, can one man, d'ye think. Answer of Mr, The Waller's Painter to His Many New Advisers. *Unknown.* APAS

Good Society, A. Pentti Saarikoski, *tr. fr. Finnish by* Aili Jarvenpa. SOP

Good Son Jim. Russell Edson. NAmP

Good Susan, Be as Secret as You Can. *Unknown.* ErPo

Good sword and a trusty hand, A! The Song of the Western Men. Robert Stephen Hawker. EnRP; FaPoR; OBNC

Good Thanksgiving, A. Annie Douglas Green Robinson. PoLF

Good Thing, A. Ray Mathew. CBAP

Good thing about an immaculate conception, The. The Immaculate Conception. Lindsay MacRae. DT

Good Times. Lucille Clifton. AmNP; AmPA; BPo; CNA; FF; GrPl; InPS; PoBA; TAP; TwCP

Good Times and No Bread. Reginald Lockett. CNA

Good toll-gate keeper, kindle a light! Halt and Parley. George Herbert Clarke. CaP

Good Town, The. Edwin Muir. CMoP

Good Tradition, The. *Unknown, tr. fr. Early Modern Irish by* Robin Flower. AnIL

Good Wif was ther of biside Bathe, A. Chaucer. *Fr.* The Canterbury Tales: Prologue. EBEV; InPS

  (Good Wyf was Ther of Bisyde Bathe, A.) TrGrPo

  ("There was a Wife from Bath, a well-appearing," *mod. vers. by* Louis Untermeyer.) TrGrPo

Good Wife, The. Bible, *O.T. See* Proverbs: Who can find a virtuous woman? for her price is far above rubies.

Good Will to Men—Christmas Greetings in Six Languages. Dorothy Brown Thompson. OBCP

Good wine maketh good blood. Logic. *Unknown.* FaBoUs

Good Wish. *Unknown, tr. fr. Gaelic by* Alexander Carmichael. FaBoCh

Good wood. Food for Fire, Food for Thought. Robert Duncan. NeAP

Good Works. William Langland. *Fr.* The Vision of Piers Plowman. NOCV

Good Wyf was Ther of Bisyde Bathe, A. Chaucer. *See* Canterbury Tales, The: Prologue.

Good, your worship, cast your eyes. The Maunding Soldier; or, The Fruits of Warre Is Beggery. Martin Parker. CoMu; WaaP

Goodbat Nightman. Roger McGough. MoP

Goodby Betty, Don't Remember Me. E. E. Cummings. CMoP; PoE

Goodby to spring, goodby to my son. Grieving for Tatsuzo: Today Spring Ended. Rai San'yo, *tr. by* Burton Watson. JLIC-2

Goodbye. Bella Akhmadulina, *tr. fr. Russian by* Barbara Einzig. BoWoP

Goodbye. Chana Bloch. MAYP

Goodbye. William Knott. EAS

Goodbye. Alun Lewis. BoLoP; NAEL-2; OBWP; OxBTC

Goodbye. Sherod Santos. MAYP

Goodbye, The. Myra Sklarew. GOYP

Goodbye/ Until such time as bobolinks do dine. To Janet. Ralph Pomeroy. NYBP

Goodbye, bright creature. In the Cloud of Unknowing. Carol Rumens. DiPo

Goodbye David Tamunoemi West. Margaret Danner. BPo

Goodbye Forever. Lillian Morrison. SoTCo

Goodbye "Hello." Philip Dow. NPGG

Goodbye, lady in Bangor, who sent me. The Correspondence School Instructor Says Goodbye to His Poetry Students. Galway Kinnell. NoAM; NOBA; NoP; TAP

Goodbye, Little Bonny Blue Eyes. *Unknown.* AmFP

Goodbye Nkrumah. Diane DiPrima. NoAM

Goodbye Now, or, Pardon My Gauntlet. Ogden Nash. FiBHP

Goodbye red moon. Moonset, Gloucester, December 1, 1957, 1:58 A.M. Charles Olson. CAPP

Goodbye, Sally. James Simmons. BIrV

Goodbye to Brigid / An Agnus Dei. Padraic Fiacc. CIP

Goodbye to Regal. Daniel Huws. NYBP

Goodbye to Serpents. James Dickey. NYBP

Goodbye to the Poetry of Calcium. James Wright. CAPP

Goodbye to Tolerance. Denise Levertov. NoAM

Goodbye, Winter. Prognosis. Louis MacNeice. CMoP; Mes; NOBE

Goodbye, Zenobia. Saniyya Salih, *tr. fr. Arabic by* Patricia Alanah Byrne, Salma Khadra Jayyusi, *and* Charles Doria. MAP

Goodbyes and griefs come here to join the world. Railway Station. John Hay. WaP

Goodly Child, A. *Unknown.* OxBChV

Goodly host one day was mine, A. Mine Host of "The Golden Apple." Thomas Westwood. GN; OHIP

Goodly number shipped as crew, A. Arion. Pushkin, *tr. by* Alan Myers. AAA

Goodman's Sauce. *Unknown.* FaBoUs

Goodmorning with Light. John Ciardi. WaP

Goodness. Eino Leino, *tr. fr. Finnish by* Aili Jarvenpa. SOP

Goodnight. John Ciardi. OBAL

Goodnight. Stevie Smith. FaBoWP

Goodnight, A. William Carlos Williams. MoAB; MoAmPo

Goodnight Irene. Paul Mariani. BLA

Goodnight to the Season! Winthrop Mackworth Praed. InvP; NOBE; NOBL; OBNC; OxBoLi; PoEL-4

Goods She Can Carry: Canticle of Her Basket Made of Reeds, The. Gibbons Ruark. MAYP

Goodwill, Inc. Dennis Schmitz. AmPA

Goody Blake and Harry Gill, *sel.* Wordsworth.

  "Oh! what's the matter? what's the matter?." Par

Goody Bull and her daughter together fell out. The World Turned Upside Down. *Unknown.* PAH

Goody O'Grumpity. Carol Ryrie Brink. FaPON

Goops they lick their fingers, The. Table Manners. Gelett Burgess. OBCA; RAR; RHPC

Goose. Richard Emil Braun. NoAM

Goose, affected, empty, vain, A. Edward Moore. *Fr.* The Goose and the Swans. PBBP

Goose and the Gander, The. *Unknown.* GBP; RB

Goose and the Swans, The, *sel.* Edward Moore.

  "Goose, affected, empty, vain, A." PBBP

Goose Fish, The. Howard Nemerov. CMoP; HeIP; LiTM; NePoEA; NIP; NoAM; NoP; PoE; SM

Goose Girl, The. Dorothy Roberts. CaP

Goose Pond. Stanley Kunitz. PoA

Goose running along the lane. On the Grass. Miyoshi Tatsuji, *tr. by* Geoffrey Bownas *and* Anthony Thwaite. PeBJV

Goose that laid the golden egg, The. Ars Poetica. X. J. Kennedy. ErPo

Goose that on our Ock's green shore, The. Goodman's Sauce. *Unknown.* FaBoUs

Gooseberries. Stephen Berg. NaP

Gooseberry Fool ("The gooseberry's no doubt an oddity"). Amy Clampitt. NoAM

Goosey, goosey gander,/ Who stands yonder? Betsy Baker. *Unknown.* OxNR

Goosey Goosey Gander—by Various Authors. William Percy French. CenHV

  Kipling's Version.

  Longfellow's Version.

  Macaulay's Version.

  Swineburne's Version.

Goosey, goosey, gander, where shall I wander? Mother Goose. OxNR; PBBP

Gopal has slipped in and stolen my heart, friend. Surdas, *tr. by* John Stratton Hawley *and* Mark Juergensmeyer. SSI

Gorbo, as thou cam'st this way. The Shepheard's Daffodil. Michael Drayton. *Fr.* The Shepherd's Garland, Eclogue IX. ElL

Gordion Knot, The. Thomas Tomkis. *Fr.* Lingua. ElL

Gordon Childe. David Martin. PoAu-2

Gorg, a Detective Story. B. P. Nichol. NOBC

Gorgeous in their beauty. *Unknown, tr. by* Arthur Waley. BoS

Gorgeous Redhead, The. Guillaume Apollinaire, *tr. fr. French by* Michael Benedikt. POS

Gorgeously the *QE2* invaded Grenada. Hardearned Overturned Caribbean Basin Stomp. George Starbuck. BLA

Gorilla at Twenty Nine Years, The. J. D. Reed. NeAC

Gorilla Gorilla. Bruce Dawe. NoAM

Gorilla lay on his back, The. Au Jardin des Plantes. John Wain. NePoEA-2; OxBTC

Goring, The. Sylvia Plath. OBTV

Gormley's Laments, *sel.* Gormley, *tr. fr. Irish by* Joan Keefe.

  "I have loved thirty by three." PBWP

Gosan. Park Je-chun, *tr. fr. Korean by* Koh Chang-soo. ACKP

GoshDarnedIMay. Things Keep Dawning on President Joshua. George Starbuck. SoTCo

Gospel. Kevyn Arthur. PBCV

Gospel According to You, The. *Unknown.* BLRP

Gospel of Labor, The. Henry van Dyke. WBLP; WGRP

Gospel of Mr. Pepys, The. Christopher Morley. NBLV

Gospel of Peace, The. James Jeffrey Roche. PAH

Gosport Tragedy, The. *Unknown.* AmFP

Gossamer threads trail endlessly in the courtyard. Chuang Yü, *tr. by* Shirleen S. Wong. WFTU

Gossip, The. Daniel Halpern. SO

Gossip. Mrs. Henry Linden. CBWP-4

Got a lover, tell you that. *Unknown, tr. by* Paul Blackburn. Pro

Got a peek/ at the moon. Last Night. Oku Onuora. PBCV

Got Dem Blues. *Unknown.* AS

Got entered in the broncs. Chookaloski Mare. Lucky Whipple. CowP

Got me a special place. Martin Luther King. Myra Cohn Livingston. RHPC

Got up and dressed up. Jack Kerouac. *Fr.* Mexico City Blues, 113. NeAP

Got your note today and I'm glad you wrote. A Letter to Peter. Fay Chiang. BrSi

Gotham, *sels.* Charles Churchill. NOEC
    European Crimes.
    Poet as King of Gotham, The.

Gothic columns of petrified motion. M. G. Mainwaring. TOF

Gothic Dusk, The. Frederic Prokosch. PoA

Gothic Gesture, A. Steve Levine. UL

Gothic Landscape. Irving Layton. TrJP

Gothic looks solemn, The. On Oxford. Keats. Par

Gourd Dancer, The. N. Scott Momaday. CDW; STE

Gourd has bitter leaves, The. *Unknown, tr. by* Arthur Waley. BoS

Gourd has still its bitter leaves, The. I Wait My Lord. *Unknown, tr. fr. Chinese by* Helen Waddell. *Fr.* Shi King. AWP

Gourd is overripe, The. Mahuta. Alistair Campbell. ATNZ

Gourd of wine, The. The Servant ("The gourd of wine"). Tachibana Akemi, *tr. fr. Japanese by* Burton Watson. *Fr.* Thirty Tanka. FCEI

Gourmand, The. Harry Graham. FaBoPa

Gourmet's Love-Song, The. P. G. Wodehouse. NOBL

Gout and Wings. Charles Tennyson Turner. NOBVV

Gouty Merchant and the Stranger, The. Horace Smith. BeLS

Government! Tuta Nihoniho, *tr. fr. Maori by* A. Armstrong. WTO

Government governs, The. Leave Everything the Way It Is. Liesl Ujvary, *tr. by* Beth Bjorklund. CoAuP

Government Injunction. Josephine Miles. PoNe

"Government office tower—I can just see the tint of its tiles." Written on Visiting the Shrine of the Minister of the Right Sugawara no Michizane. Rai San'yo, *tr. by* Burton Watson. JLIC-2

Government Pond, The. Yao Nai, *tr. fr. Chinese by* Daniel Bryant. WFTU

Government wine of Peking is sweeter than honey, The. Hsieh Chin, *tr. fr. Chinese by* Jonathan Chaves. *Fr.* Things Experienced upon Withdrawal from Court. CoBLCP

Governor loves to go mapping—round and round, The. Sydney Cove, 1788. Peter Porter. NoAM

Governor of Huai-yang, arm and leg to the rul er, The. In a Provincial Capital Sick in Bed. Hsieh T'iao, *tr. by* Burton Watson. CoBCP

Governor your husband lived so long, The. John Berryman. *Fr.* Homage to Mistress Bradstreet. NOBA

Gowa! Gowa! Crow's Ditty. *Unknown.* GBP

Gowan glitters on the sward, The. The Trysting Bush. Joanna Baillie. WPE

Gowk, The. William Soutar. GoTS

Grab-Bag. Helen Hunt Jackson. OBCA

Grab this mercury, this cold gum, this honey, this sphere. Edoardo Sanguineti, *tr. fr. Italian by* Lawrence R. Smith. *Fr.* Erotopaegnia. NItP

Grace. Emerson. AmPP; NoP; TrPWD

Grace. George Herbert. JCP; SeCV-1

Grace. Johnstone G. Patrick. TrPWD

Grace, A. Thomas Tiplady. TrPWD

Grace, A. *Unknown.* *See* Christmas Carol: "God bless the master of this house."

Grace. Richard Wilbur. LiTA

Grace Abounding. A. R. Ammons. HCAP

Grace after Dinner. Burns. FaBoEE

Grace after Meals. *Unknown, tr. fr. Hebrew by* Alice Lucas. TrJP

Grace and Thanksgiving. Elizabeth Gould. BoTP

Grace at Evening. Edgar A. Guest. TrPWD

Grace at Evening. Edwin McNeill Poteat. TrPWD

Grace at Kirkudbright. Burns. OxBSP

Grace before Meat. Robert Herrick. *See* Here a little child I stand.

Grace before Sleep. Sara Teasdale. TrPWD

Grace comes only after the long study of choice. Traise Yamamoto. BrSi

Grace Darling. *Unknown.* OBET; OxBSS

Grace for a Child. Robert Herrick. AWP; FaPON; InPS; MoShBr; NAEL-1; PoE; TrGrPo

Grace for Children, A. Robert Herrick. OxBChV

Grace for Gardens. Louise Driscoll. TrPWD

Grace for Light. Moira O'Neill. TIRV

Grace full of grace, though in these verses here. Henry Constable. *Fr.* Diana. OBSC

Grace is the focal point. Bar Giamaica, 1959-60. Charles Wright. EOEF

Grace of Animals, The. Richard Harteis. GLP

Grace of Cynthia's Maidenhood, The. Vinnie-Marie D'Ambrosio. IHMS

Grace of Geldings in Ripe Pastures, The. Maxine W. Kumin. CAPP

Grace of the Way, *sel.* Francis Thompson.
    "Now of that vision I, bereaven." MoAB; MoBrPo

Grace of the Word immaculate. Raziel. Iwan Goll, *tr. by* Anthony Rudolf. VWA

Grace that is the health of creatures can only be held in common, The. Healing. Wendell Berry. AnAn

Grace that never can be told. All Needs Met. J. H. Sammis. BLRP

Grace thou source of each perfection. Epiphany. Christopher Smart. *Fr.* Hymns and Spiritual Songs: St. Philip and St. James, 3. NOCV

Grace to Be Said at the Supermarket. Howard Nemerov. SoSe

Graceful Acacia. Walter Savage Landor. PoEL-4

Graceful and sure with youth, the skaters glide. The Skaters. John Williams. SD

Graceful as acorus or lotus flower. Aliter. Confucius, *tr. fr. Chinese by* Ezra Pound. *Fr.* Songs of Ch'en. CTC

Graceful Bastion, The. William Carlos Williams. NYBP

Gracefullest leaper, the dappled fox-cub. Young Reynard. George Meredith. HoPM

Graces of the Holy Ghost, The. *Unknown, tr. fr. Irish by* Douglas Hyde. TIRV

Gracie. Faye Kicknosway. GeTw; NMM

Gracie, 1967. Faye Kicknosway. ER

Graciela. Gary Soto. NoAM

Graciela wouldn't fuck me. De Ambiente. Tatiana de la Tierra. GLP

Gracing the tide-warmth, this seagull. The Seagull. Dafydd ap Gwilym, *tr. by* Glyn Jones. OBWVE

Gracious and gentle widow. Letter to Madame la Marquise de C———. Louise Geneviève de Sainctonge, *tr. by* Dorothy Backer. DMI

Gracious Goodness. Marge Piercy. Psk

Gracious Saviour let me make. Thou Lovest Me. Josephine D. Henderson Heard. CBWP-4

Gracious Saviour, We Adore Thee. Sewall Sylvester Cutting. AH

Gracious Time, The. Shakespeare. *See* Hamlet: Some say that ever 'gainst that season comes.

Gracius and Gay. *Unknown.* SeCePo

Grackle, The ("Grackle's voice is less than mellow."). Ogden Nash. NBLV

Gradatim. Josiah Gilbert Holland. FaFP; OHFP; WGRP

Gradual bud and bloom and seedfall speeded up. July 4th. May Swenson. PoA

Gradually even this disappears. What remains. Of All the Splendor. Ory Bernstein, *tr. by* Warren Bargad *and* Stanley F. Chyet. IP

Graduation Day, 1965. Julio Marzán. InW

Graduation of Pasta, A. Willard R. Espy. SoTCo

Graecinus (well I wot) thou told'st me once. Ovid, *tr. fr. Latin by* Christopher Marlowe. *Fr.* Amores, II, 10. EBEV

Graeme and Bewick. *Unknown.* EnSB

Graf von Charolais, Der, *sel.* Richard Beer-Hofmann, *tr. fr. German by* Ludwig Lewisohn.
    "Evil Man, An!" TrJP

Graffiti. James. NBLV

Graffiti for a Particle Accelerator. Dexter Masters. KS

Graffiti in a University Restroom: "Killing People Is Easier than Writing Poetry." Jim Mitsui. BrSi

Grafted Bud, The. Mary Weston Fordham. CBWP-2

Grafted Tongue, A. John Montague. BIrV; CIP

Graham crackers on the patio. Dreamscape. Roger Zelazny. BWV

Grail, The. Sidney Keyes. FaBoTw

Grain-Barge Wife, The. Wu Chia-chi, *tr. fr. Chinese by* Jonathan Chaves. CoBLCP

Grain Elevator. Abraham Moses Klein. CaP

Grain of Moonlight, A. Asya, *tr. fr. Yiddish by* Gabriel Preil *and* Howard Schwartz. VWA

Grain of Sand, A. Frances Ellen Watkins Harper. PWR

Grains of corn were planted, The. Story of the Corn. K. Fisher. BoTP

Grains of Sand on a Radio. K. Schippers, *tr. fr. Dutch by* Peter Nijmeijer. DuIn

Grains of snow ride down here as bits. Letter from a Black Soldier. Bill Anderson. VGW

Gram died with most of her joints frozen. Angles. Dixie Partridge. TSM

Gramercy, Death, as you've my love to win. Sonnet: He Argues His Case with Death. Cecco Angiolieri da Siena, *tr. by* Dante Gabriel Rossetti. AWP

Grammar, A. Andrei Codrescu. EAS

Grammar commences with a 5-line curse. Palladas, *tr. fr. Greek by* Tony Harrison. OBVE

Grammar Lesson. Linda Pastan. Psk

Grammar-Rules. Sir Philip Sidney. *See* Astrophel and Stella: LXIII. "O grammar-rules, O now your virtues show."

Grammarian's Funeral, A. Robert Browning. NAEL-2; NOBVV; WGRP

Grammer's Shoes. William Barnes. EBVV

Gramophone, The. James Reaney. CaP

Grampa. Dennis Scott. PBCV

Grampaw's Smoking Pipe. Hsiang Yang, *tr. fr. Chinese by* Dominic Cheung. IFON

Gramsci's Ashes. Pier Paolo Pasolini, *tr. fr. Italian by* Lawrence R. Smith. NItP

Gran Mal. Kathryn Rantala. BWV

Granada the Last City. M. K. Joseph. *Fr.* The Tourist in Seat 29. ATNZ

Grand Abacus. John Ashbery. EAS; PoA

Grand advantage—and, if so, A. The Crematorium. Geoffrey Grigson. NPo

Grand attempt some Amazonian dames, A. On a Fortification at Boston Begun by Women. Benjamin Tompson. GOA; PAH; SCAP

Grand Canyon, The. James Merrill. TAP

Grand Chorus of Birds. Aristophanes. *See* Birds, The: Chorus of Birds.

Grand Conversation on Brave Nelson. *Unknown.* OBET

Grand-dad, they say you're old and frail. A Child to His Sick Grandfather. Joanna Baillie. NOEC

Grand dream palace, six windows shut, The. The Dream Palace. Kaiseki, *tr. by* Lucien Stryk *and* Takashi Ikemoto. ZPCJ

Grand Duke of New York, The. Dan Pagis, *tr. fr. Hebrew by* Robert Friend. VWA

Grand Entry, The. Gary Snyder. NoAM

Grand Finale. Irving Layton. NOBC

Grand Finale, The. István Vas, *tr. fr. Hungarian by* William Jay Smith. MHuP

Grand Guignols of Love, The. Michael Benedikt. AmPA

Grand Inquisitor's Song, The. W. S. Gilbert. *Fr.* The Gondoliers. OnMSP

Grand old Duke of York, The. *Unknown.* BoTP

Grand Rapids. Julia A. Moore. OBAL

Grand Ronde Valley, The. Ella Higginson. AA

Grand rough old Martin Luther. The Twins. Robert Browning. Mes

Grandad, I didn't burn it, I. Legacy. Gena Ford. IHMS

Grandchild. Maxine W. Kumin. BLA; ER

Granddaddy longlegs did twilight, The. Ohio Valley Swains. James Wright. NNaP

Granddaughter. Adrienne Rich. *Fr.* Grandmothers. NAAL-2

Grande Jetée. Mary Mackey. AIW

Grande Jetée. Mary Mackey. *Fr.* Arabesque: Five Poems for Women without Children. ER

Grandest writer of late ages, The. Distribution of Honours for Literature. Walter Savage Landor. FaBoEE

Grandeur of Ghosts. Siegfried Sassoon. MoBrPo; OBMV

Grandeur of this earthly round, The. Plato to Theon. Philip Freneau. AA

Grandeza Mexicana, *sel.* Bernardo de Balbuena, *tr. fr. Spanish by* Samuel Beckett.

Immortal Springtime and Its Tokens. MexPo

Grandfa' Grig/ Had a pig. *Unknown.* OxNR

Grandfather. Willis Barnstone. VWA

Grandfather. George Bowering. NOBC

Grandfather. Michael S. Harper. CAPP; GeTw; LCAP; TAP

Grandfather. Lance Henson, *tr. fr. Cheyenne Indian by* Lance Henson. CDW; HATNAP

Grandfather. Derek Mahon. FaBCIP; OxBC

Grandfather. Angus Martin. NPo

Grandfather. Joseph Stroud. NPGG

Grandfather at the Indian Health Clinic. Elizabeth Cook-Lynn. HATNAP

Grandfather Dying. Moishe Kulbak, *tr. fr. Yiddish by* Leonard Wolf. *Fr.* Byelorussia. PeBMYV

Grandfather fulfilled his duty to the grandchildren, The. Death-Charade. Jacob Glatstein, *tr. by* Benjamin *and* Barbara Harshav. AYP

Grandfather has three sparks. Akawense. Phyllis Wolf. STE

Grandfather in the Old Men's Home. W. S. Merwin. LiTM; SM

Grandfather Poem, A. William J. Harris. CNA; PoBA

Grandfather puts down his tea-glass. A Night in Odessa. Louis Simpson. NNaP

Grandfather, sleepless in a room upstairs. John Berryman. *Fr.* The Black Book. VGW

Grandfather, we come to you now. Yahrzeit. Susan Fromberg Schaeffer. VWA

Grandfather wrote from Valley Forge. Prophecy in Flame. Frances Minturn Howard. AmFN

Grandfathers. Michael Castro. VWA

Grandfathers [*or* After a Line by John Peale Bishop], The. Donald Justice. PoCH

Grandfather's boat is out tonight. Grandfather. Angus Martin. NPo

Grandfather's Clock. Henry Clay Work. BLPA; FaFP

Grandfather's Last Letter, A. Norman Dubie. MOWH

Grandfather's Sermon and Michael Smith. E. A. Markham. PBCV

Grandiloquent Goat, The. Carolyn Wells. MoShBr

Grandma and the children left at night. My Polish Grandma. Edward Field. Prf

Grandma Chooses Her Plot at the County Cemetery. Paul Ruffin. GOYP

Grandma Fire. Charles G. Ballard. STE

Grandma sleeps with. Medicine. Alice Walker. NMM

Grandma strides around beaming. The Strikover Rabbi's Wife. Zishe Landau, *tr. by* Irving Feldman. PeBMYV

Grandma told me all about it. The Minuet. Mary Mapes Dodge. OHFP

Grandma we all need partially deaf and busy with weaving listens. I'm Making You Up. "Chrystos." GOS

Grandmamma's Birthday. Hilaire Belloc. FiBHP

Grandma's Advice. *Unknown. See* My grandmother on yonder little green.

Grandma's Bureau. Robert Morgan. EOEF

Grandma's Lost Balance. Sydney Dayre. OBCA

Grandma's Man. James Welch. NoAM

Grandmither, Think Not I Forget. Willa Cather. WPE

Grandmother. Paula Gunn Allen. STE

Grandmother, The. Wendell Berry. MT; SaC

Grandmother. Louise Glück. *Fr.* Dedication to Hunger, II. AnAn; GeTw

Grandmother. Ray A. Young Bear. STE

Grandmother and Child. Ruth Dallas. ATNZ

Grandmother and Grandson. W. S. Merwin. NePoEA-2

Grandmother Came Down to Visit Us, The. Joseph Bruchac. CDW

Grandmother Grace. Ronald Wallace. GOYP; SM

Grandmother, I dreamed of you again. The Visit. Phillip William George. VoR

Grandmother Jackson. David Jackson. OBCP

Grandmother Poems. Marilyn Chin. BrSi

Grandmother, Rocking. Eve Merriam. GrPl; PCP

Grandmother Sleeps. Liz Sohappy Bahe. CDW

Grandmother Watching at Her Window. W. S. Merwin. PrIm; VGW

Grandmothers, The. Mary Oliver. WPE

Grandmothers, *sels.* Adrienne Rich. HCAP; NAAL-2; NoAM

Granddaughter.

Hattie Rice Rich.

Mary Gravely Jones.

Grandmothers Land. William Oandasan. HATNAP

Grandmother's love. Love Necessitates. Eugene B. Redmond. CNA

Grandmother's mother: her age, I guess. Dorothy Q. Oliver Wendell Holmes. AA; NOBA

Grandmother's Old Armchair. *Unknown.* BLPA

Grandmother's Story of Bunker-Hill Battle. O. W. Holmes. PAH

Grandmothers who wring the necks. Classic Ballroom Dances. Charles Simic. GeTw; LCAP

Grandpa and the Uncles. Moishe Kulbak, *tr. fr. Yiddish by* Leonard Wolf. *Fr.* Byelorussia. PeBMYV

Grandpa Bear's Lullaby. Jane Yolen. RHPC

Grandpa Dropped His Glasses. Leroy F. Jackson. RHPC

Grandpa, I saw you die in the Indian hospital at Pawnee. Hartico. Anna Walters. VoR

Grandpapa. Harry Graham. RHPC

Grandparents. Robert Lowell. LiTM

Grandpa's .45. W. M. Ransom. CDW

Grandson, The. James Scully. NYBP

Grandson Is a Hoticeberg, A. Margaret Danner. BlSi; CNA; FB

Granite/ in the hands, waves of the sea. Helsinki. Arvo Turtiainen, *tr. fr. Finnish by* Aili Jarvenpa. *Fr.* Ballad of Herman's Rose. SOP

Granite and Cypress. Robinson Jeffers. AmPP

Granite and Grass. Donald Hall. DiPo

Granite and marble. Homage to Paul Mellon, I. M. Pei, Their Gallery, and Washington City. William Meredith. EyDe

Granite and Steel. Marianne Moore. NYBP

Granite cliff on either shore, A. The Brooklyn Bridge. Edna Dean Proctor. PAH

Granma's Words. Ted D. Palmanteer. STE

Granny/ The children will return. Returning to Granny. Shauqi Abi Shaqra, *tr. by* Abdullah al-Udhari. MPAW

Granny and I with dear Dadu. A Very Odd Fish. D'Arcy Wentworth Thompson. OxBChV

Granny Crack. James Reaney. NOBC

Granpa,/ he was a warrior. Pass It On Grandson. Ted D. Palmanteer. STE

Grant a canoe that shall be swift as a fish! Prayer on Making a Canoe. Unknown, tr. by N. B. Emerson. WTO

Grant at Appomattox. Gertrude Claytor. GoYe

Grant Heaven could once have given us liberty. Predestination and Free Will. Dryden. Fr. The State of Innocence. NOCV

Grant it, Father. Petition. Eleanor Slater. TrPWD

Grant me, dear Lord, the alchemy of toil. Suppliant. Alan Sullivan. CaP

Grant me, indulgent Heaven, a rural seat. The Choice. Nahum Tate. OxBSP

Grant me the great and solemn breath withdrawn. Invocation and Prelude. Stefan George, tr. by Ludwig Lewisohn. AWP

Grant me to share the common, human lot. The Common Lot. Adelbert Sumpter Coats. TrPWD

Grant us the knowledge that we need. Henry van Dyke. Fr. The Builders. TrPWD

Grant Wood's American Landscape. Winfield Townley Scott. GOA

Granted that what we summon is absurd. T. R. Donald Hall. PoA

Granted, we die for good. Table Talk. Wallace Stevens. NoP

Grape Daiquiri. Tina Koyama. BrSi

Grape-gathering. Avraham Shlonsky, tr. fr. Hebrew by I. M. Lask. TrJP

Grape Sherbet. Rita Dove. MOWH

Grapes. Unknown, tr. fr. Greek by Alma Strettell. AWP

Grapes are ripe, the field is plowed, The. Quiet. Giuseppe Ungaretti, tr. by Henry Taylor. PFI

Grapes hang purple. Taste of Purple. Leland B. Jacobs. RHPC

Grapes Making. Léonie Adams. FYAP; UnPo

Grapevine, The. Zoe Kincaid Brockman. GoYe

Graphemic/ hinges/ discourse. St. McC. Charles Bernstein. IAT

Graphemics, sels. Jack Spicer. VGW
"Like a scared rabbit running over and." Fr. 1.
"Love is not mocked whatever use." Fr. 10.
"Walden Pond/ All those noxious gases rising from it." Fr. 7. VGW

Grasping my flying cane, several feet of wood. Drunk, Climbing to the Peak of Iron Tomb on Wei Mountain. Li K'ai-hsien, tr. by Jonathan Chaves. CoBLCP

Grasping with opposite hand the side of his pram. Outside the Supermarket. Roy Fuller. OxBC

Grass, The. George Bowering. MoCV

Grass. Alfred Corn. MAYP

Grass. Carl Sandburg. AWP; BLPL; FaBV; MoAB; MoAmPo; MoP; NAAL-2; NoAM; NOBA; NoP; OBWP; OHFP; OxBA; PoLF; TrGrPo; WaaP

Grass. Mary Morison Webster. PeSA

Grass. Walt Whitman. See Song of Myself: A Child said, What is the grass?

Grass bends, The: blades crack from a wind. Camping Out on Rainy Mountain. Jim Barnes. CDW

Grass caught in willow tells the flood's height. Basil Bunting. Fr. Briggflatts [An Autobiography], IV. FaBoMo

Grass clutches at the dark dirt with finger holds. Grassroots. Carl Sandburg. RFM

Grass comes up tuft by tuft, The. Tuft by Tuft. Remco Campert, tr. by James S. Holmes. DuIn

Grass Fight. Ryokan, tr. fr. Chinese by Burton Watson. JLIC-2

Grass Fingers. Angelina Weld Grimké. CDC

Grass gave way, and suddenly, The. Watercress & Ice. Chase Twichell. MAYP

Grass, Grass. George Bowering. NeAC

Grass-green and aspen-green. Variables of Green. Robert Graves. FaBoEE

Grass hath such a simple faith, The. Grass. Mary Morison Webster. PeSA

Grass high under apple trees. Passing an Orchard by Train. Robert Bly. CAPP

Grass hung wet on Rydal banks, The. With Wordsworth at Rydal. James Thomas Fields. AA

Grass hut fenced with hibiscus is by a winding stream, A. Song of a Dandy. Sun Kuang-hsien, tr. by Lois Fusek. ATF

Grass Is a Reasonable Colour, The. John Newlove. NeAC

Grass is half-covered with snow, The. Snowfall in the Afternoon. Robert Bly. EAS; NOBA

Grass is very green, my friend, The. A Unison. William Carlos Williams. NOBA

Grass of fifty Aprils hath waved green, The. On the Proposal to Erect a Monument in England to Lord Byron. Emma Lazarus. AA

Grass of Kasuga Moor. Unknown, tr. fr. Japanese by Geoffrey Bownas and Anthony Thwaite. Fr. Kokin Shu. PeBJV

Grass of levity. An Inscription. Unknown. ElL

Grass of love would load, The. Princess Hirokawa, tr. fr. Japanese by Geoffrey Bownas and Anthony Thwaite. Fr. Manyo Shu. PeBJV

Grass on the Cliff. Robinson Jeffers. Fr. The Trumpet, V. PoA

Grass on the Mountain, The. Unknown, tr. fr. Paiute Indian by Mary Austin. AmFN; AWP; FaPON; GOA

Grass people bow, The. To Turn Back. John Haines. BoNaP

Grass resurrects to mask, to strangle. The Distant Fury of Battle. Geoffrey Hill. NoP

Grass shakes, The. Growing Dark. James Schuyler. GLP

Grass shines in the wind. Peter Rosei, tr. by Beth Bjorklund. CoAuP

Grass singed and low. Chickory. Zerubavel Gal'ed. TrJP

Grass Snake and Fish. Gyula Illyés, tr. fr. Hungarian by Charles Tomlinson. MHuP

Grass so deep you can no longer see the little old cottage. Abandoned Garden. Kikuchi Gozan, tr. by Burton Watson. JLIC-2

Grass that is under me now, The. The Dying Lover. Richard Henry Stoddard. AnAmPo

Grass Widows. Robert B. Shaw. CRP

Grasse-Hopper, The. Richard Lovelace. See Oh thou that swing'st upon the waving beard.

Grasse: The Olive Trees. Richard Wilbur. NAAL-2; NoAM; NOBA; NYBP

Grasses and trees, The. Yasuhide, tr. by Geoffrey Bownas and Anthony Thwaite. PeBJV

Grasses and trees, When. Keiun, tr. by Steven D. Carter. WFTW

Grasses are clothed, The. Divine Abundance. Unknown. BLRP

Grasses are light brown, The. September. Joanne Kyger. UL

Grasses of spring remain hidden from view, The. Viewing the Plum-Blossoms. Ho Ning, tr. by Lois Fusek. ATF

Grasses on Chin-ling's shores lie still in the evening sun. Song of the River City. Ou-yang Chiung, tr. by Lois Fusek. ATF

Grasshopper, The. Abraham Cowley, after the Greek of Anacreon. AWP; FM; OAEL-1; OBVE; SeCV-1; WiR

Grasshopper, The. Richard Lovelace. CaPo; EBEV; FaBoPV; JCP; NAEL-1; NOBE; NoP; OAEL-1; OBEV; OBS; PPP; SeCePo; SeCV-1

Grasshopper, The. David McCord. GrPl

Grasshopper, The. Thomas Stanley, after the Greek of Anacreon. OBVE

Grasshopper, A. Richard Wilbur. HAP; HoPM; WeW

Grasshopper copters whir. Airport in the Grass. X. J. Kennedy. RR

Grasshopper Green. Nancy Dingman Watson. BoTP; FaPON; RAR

Grasshopper, the grasshopper, The. An Explanation of the Grasshopper. Vachel Lindsay. FaPON; RAR

Grasshopper thrice-happy! who. The Grasshopper. Thomas Stanley, after the Greek of Anacreon. OBVE

Grasshopper Wings. Unknown, tr. fr. Chinese by Burton Watson. CoBCP

Grasshopper, your fairy [or tiny] song. Earth ("Grasshopper, your fairy song"). John Hall Wheelock. LiTA; MoAmPo

Grasshoppers/ Chirping in the sleeves. Kawai Chigetsu-ni, tr. by Kenneth Rexroth and Ikuko Atsumi. WPOW

Grasshoppers. John Clare. TTTS

Grasshoppers beware. The Cropdusting. William Zaranka. BXAP

Grasshoppers four a-fiddling went. Rilloby-Rill. Sir Henry Newbolt. BXAP

Grasshopper's Song, The. H. N. Nachman, tr. fr. Hebrew by Jessie Sampter. FaPON

Grassroots. Carl Sandburg. RFM

Grassy road with few passersby, A. Passing the Retreat of Hsü Ching-po. Wu Chia-chi, tr. by John E. Wills, Jr. WFTU

Gratiana Dancing [or Dauncing] and Singing. Richard Lovelace. CaPo; JCP; MeLP; MePo; OBEV, 2 sts.; OBS; SeCV-1, 2 sts.

Gratitude. William Cornish. See Pleasure It Is.

Gratitude. Louise Glück. FaBoWP; HeIP

Gratitude. Mikhail Yurevich Lermontov, tr. fr. Russian by Alan Myers. AAA

Gratitude. Annette Lynch. FF

Gratitude. Clyde McGee. BLRP

Gratitude. Christopher Smart. Fr. Hymns for the Amusement of Children, XXII. NOEC

Gratitude to Mother Earth, sailing through night and day. Prayer for the Great Family. Gary Snyder. HAP; OFD

Gratulatory to Mr., A Ben. Johnson for His Adopting of Him to Be His Son. Thomas Randolph. JCP; OBS

Grave, The, sels. Robert Blair.
"Oft in the lone church-yard at night I've seen." OBD

"Tell us! ye dead! Will none of you in pity." OBD

"While some affect the sun, and some the shade." EnRP

("Whilst some affect the sun, and some the shade.") NOEC

Grave, The. John Lyle Donaghy. NeIP

Grave, A. Marianne Moore. CMoP; FaBoWP; HAP; HeIP; LiTA; MoP; MOS; NAAL-2; NoAM; NOBA; PoE; TAP; UnPo; WeW; WPE

Grave, The. Saul Tchernichowsky. *See* There are many like him here.

Grave, The. *Unknown*. ("For thee a stead was builded"). ACP

Grave, The. *Unknown*. ("When the turf is thy tower"). ChTr

Grave and dignified manners. *Unknown, tr. by* Arthur Waley. BoS

Grave and the Rose, The. Victor Hugo, *tr. fr. French by* Andrew Lang. AWP

Grave at Cassino. Noah Stern, *tr. fr. Hebrew by* Harold Schimmel. VWA

Grave but ends the struggle!—Follows then, The. The Triumph. William Gilmore Simms. Son

Grave charge in Mayfair bathroom case. Headline History. William Plomer. FaBoCo

Grave for New York, A. "Adunis," *tr. fr. Arabic by* Lena Jayyusi *and* Alan Brownjohn. MAP

Grave grows inward in, The. The Fears. Roberto Obregón, *tr. by* Jack Hirschman. Vol

Grave House of Commons, by hook or by crook, The. A Ballad, November 1680, Made upon Casting the Bill against the Duke of York. *Unknown*. APAS

Grave in Hollywood Cemetery, Richmond, A. Margaret Junkin Preston. AA

Grave in Ukraine, A. Saul Tchernichowsky, *tr. fr. Hebrew by* L. V. Snowman TrJP

Grave of Hipponax, The. Edward Cracroft Lefroy, *after the Greek of* Theocritus. *Fr.* Echoes from Theocritus, XXX. AWP

Grave of Keats, The. Shelley. *See* Adonais; an Elegy on the Death of John Keats: Go Thou to Rome.

Grave of King Arthur, The. Thomas, the Younger Warton. EnRP

Grave of Li Po, The. Huang Ching-jen, *tr. fr. Chinese by* Daniel Bryant. WFTU

Grave of Love, The. Thomas Love Peacock. CH; OxBSP

Grave of Rury, The. Thomas Rolleston. AnIL

Grave of Shelley, The. Oscar Wilde. OBTV

Grave physician, used to write for fees, A. Upon the Author of the "Satire against Wit." Sir Charles Sedley. APAS

Grave said to the Rose, The. The Grave and the Rose. Victor Hugo, *tr. by* Andrew Lang. AWP

Grave-Tree, The. Bliss Carman. CaP

Grave wise man that had a great rich lady, A. Of an Heroical Answer of a Great Roman Lady to Her Husband. Sir John Harington. BoLoP; ErPo

Grave-Yard, The. Jones Very. NOBA

Gravedigger, The. Bliss Carman. BoNaP

Gravelly Run. A. R. Ammons. CoAP; NAAL-2; NoAM; PoA; Prf

Graven Thoughts. Sir Philip Sidney. *Fr.* Arcadia. SiPS

Graves. Orkhan Muyassar, *tr. fr. Arabic by* Lena Jayyusi *and* Samuel Hazo. MAP

Graves Are Made to Waltz On. Peter Viereck. PoA

Graves as Exercises. Elizabeth Smither. ATNZ

Graves at Elkhorn. Richard Hugo. UnPo

Grave's Cherub, The. Sydney Clouts. PeSA

Graves grow deeper, The. The Dead. Mark Strand. HeIP

Graves of a Household, The. Felicia Dorothea Hemans. FaPoR; WBLP; WPE

Graves the rain makes wet and sleek, The. *Unknown, tr. fr. Welsh by* Gwyn Jones. *Fr.* The Stanzas of the Graves. OBWVE

Graves! Where in dust are laid our dearest hopes! Vigilantius, or a Servant of the Lord Found Ready. Cotton Mather. SCAP

Gravestone, The. Abd al-Karim Kassid, *tr. fr. Arabic by* Lena Jayyusi *and* Anthony Thwaite. MAP

Gravestones. Vernon Watkins. TEP

Graveyard, The. Hayyim Nahman Bialik, *tr. fr. Hebrew by* Bertha Beinkinstadt. TrJP

Graveyard. Robert Peter Tristram Coffin. AmFN

Graveyard, The. Jane Cooper. NePoEA-2

Graveyard, The. *Unknown, tr. fr. Chinese by* Burton Watson. CoBCP

Graveyard by the Sea. Thomas Lux. AnAn; LCAP; NAmP

Graveyard by the Sea, The, *sel.* Paul Valéry, *tr. fr. French by* C. Day Lewis.
"To an impervious nothingness they're thinned." OBD

Graveyard in Norfolk. Sylvia Townsend Warner, *tr. fr. Greek by* Edmund Keeley *and* Philip Sherrard. OBD

Graveyard in Queens, A. John Montague. IPY

Graveyard Rabbit, The. Frank Lebby Stanton. AA

Graveyard, The—who makes his home in that yard. The Graveyard. *Unknown, tr. by* Burton Watson. CoBCP

Gravida. Pierre Jean Jouve, *tr. fr. French by* David Gascoyne. RHTwFP

Gravity. John Frederick Nims. BLA

Gray and dingy house in Meudon. House in Meudon. Margarita Aliger, *tr. by* Elaine Feinstein. VWA

Gray as a dove, toward evening, my grandfather came from the pasture. Grandfather Dying. Moishe Kulbak, *tr. fr. Yiddish by* Leonard Wolf. *Fr.* Byelorussia. PeBMYV

Gray [*or* Grey] as a mouse. Oliphaunt. J. R. R. Tolkien. AmMo; RHPC

Gray-blue shadows lift. Starlight Scope Myopia. Yusef Komunyakaa. MAYP

Gray boulder stands there like a drunken sentry, A. Tree and Boulder. Yün Shou-p'ing, *tr. by* Irving Lo. WFTU

Gray brick, ash, hand-bent railings, steps so big. Cumberland Station. Dave Smith. HCAP; MAYP

Gray cows, The. March. Ilse Aichinger, *tr. by* Beth Bjorklund. CoAuP

Gray despair. The Old Mare. Elizabeth Jane Coatsworth. MoAmPo

Gray Eyes. Tess Gallagher. NAmP

Gray Folk, The. Edith Nesbit. NOBVV

Gray fur collars on a steel limb. Golgotha. X. J. Kennedy. NYBP

Gray Glove. Roo Borson. NOBC

Gray [*or* Grey] Goose and Gander. *Unknown*. GBP; OxBoLi; OxNR

Gray gray of frosty grasses, insects chirp-chirping. Village Night. Po Chü-i, *tr. by* Burton Watson. CoBCP

Gray *or* Grey haunted eyes, absent-mindedly glaring. The Face in the Mirror. Robert Graves. NoP; WeW

Gray heron flies past, A. Splitting Wood Near Morris, Oklahoma on Robbie and Lesa McMurtry's Farm. Lance Henson. HATNAP

Gray Hills Taught Me Patience, The. Allen Eastman Cross. AH

Gray Light, The. A. Leyeles, *tr. fr. Yiddish by* Benjamin *and* Barbara Harshav. AYP

Gray maidservant lets me in, A. Matinees. James Merrill. HCAP; NOBA; Prf

Gray Mare, The. *Unknown*. AmFP

Gray mist wolf. Four Mountain Wolves. Leslie Silko. VoR

Gray Nights. Ernest Dowson. Son

Gray old Owl could scarce believe his eyes, The. The Last Violet. Oliver Herford. OHIP

Gray on gray post, this silent little bird. The Spotted Flycatcher. Walter de la Mare. OxBSP

Gray owl sing fum de chimbly top, De. A Plantation Ditty. Frank Lebby Stanton. AA

Gray sea and the long black land, The. Meeting at Night. Robert Browning. AWP; BoLoP; ELP; FaBV; FF; FiP; GBL; HeIP; InPS; InvP; MOS; NAEL-2; NOBE; OBEV; OBNC; PoRA; SCV; SeCePo; SoSe; TrGrPo; UnPo; WeW

Gray Silk Twisting. Patrick Lane. NeAC

Gray smoke rose from the morning ground. Actual Vision of Morning's Extrusion. Alan Dugan. PPP

Gray Squirrel, The. Humbert Wolfe. GoJo; MoBrPo

Gray steel, cloud-shadow-stained. Watch the Lights Fade. Robinson Jeffers. CMoP; NOBA

Gray Swan, The. Alice Cary. BeLS; GN

Gray swept the angry waves. How the *Cumberland* Went Down. Silas Weir Mitchell. PAH

Gray Thrums. Clara Doty Bates. OBCA

Gray tide flows and flounders in the rocks, The. At Sainte-Marguerite. Trumbull Stickney. LiTA; OxBA

Gray tiled roof, A. Seeds of Lead. Amir Gilboa. VWA, *tr. by* Stephen Mitchell

Gray waves rock against the gray skyline, The. When Nature Hath Betrayed the Heart That Loved Her. Sophie Jewett. AA

Gray Weather. Robinson Jeffers. CMoP

Gray whale/ Now that we are sending you to the end. For a Coming Extinction. W. S. Merwin. HCAP; NNaP; PoE

Gray Woods Exploding, The. Earle Birney. NoAM

Grazing Locomotives. Archibald MacLeish. AnAmPo

Greasin' the Miles. Nick Johnson. CowP

Greasy oysters on friday nights. Cycles, Cycles. Suzanne Berger Rioff. NMM

Greasy sky-line where the grey, A. The Sailor. Goodridge MacDonald. CaP

Greasy Spoon Blues. Len Gasparini. NeAC

Great, A. E. E. Cummings. NYBP

Great A, little a. Mother Goose. OxNR

Great A was alarmed at B's bad behaviour. Alphabet. *Unknown*. FaBoUs; OxNR

Great Adventure, The. *Unknown*. *See* Over the mountains.

Great Alexander sailing was from his true course turned. The Speaking Tree. Muriel Rukeyser. VGW

Great All in All, that art my rest, my home. Francis Quarles. *Fr.* Emblems, IV, 3. TrPWD

Great Amazon of God behold your bread. For Mary McLeod Bethune. Margaret Abigail Walker. PoNe

Great and glorious thing it is, A. Arithmetic on the Frontier. Kipling. OBWP

Great and Strong. Miroslav Holub, *tr. fr. Czech by* George Theiner. RB

Great Annelid Worm, A. Bruce Hawkins. BWV

Great Artist Reconsiders the Homeric Simile, The. John Tranter. NoAM

Great Auk's Ghost, The. Ralph Hodgson. MoShBr; RHPC

Great-Aunt Francesca. Joe-Anne McLaughlin. PPR

Great-Aunt Rebecca. Elizabeth Brewster. NOBC

Great Bacchus: From the Greek. Matthew Prior. FaBoCo

Great Bear, The. John Hollander. LiTM; NePoEA-2; NoAM; NYBP; TwCP

Great Bear Lake Meditations, The, *sels.* J. Michael Yates.
  "Again and again I go away from you." HoPM
  "I persist in a little fabric between me and the world." NOBC
  "*Legend*: The god in the sun made two men." HoPM
  "Wolves say to the dogs, The." HoPM

Great beasts rumble and sway, The. Under the Shawl. Rose Drachler. VWA

Great Bell Roland, The. Theodore Tilton. PAH

Great big dog. The Tale of a Dog and a Bee. *Unknown.* BoTP

Great bird landed here, A. Heptonstall Old Church. Ted Hughes. InPS

Great Bird of Love over the Kingdom, The. Paul Zimmer. BLA

Great birth will come after ages, A. The Song of the Woman. *Unknown,* *tr. fr. Old Irish by* Kuno Meyer. *Fr.* The Voyage of Bran. TIRV

Great black hill, The. Pari's Hill Is Partial to Dancers. Kapilar, *tr. by* A. K. Ramanujan. PLW

Great blue ceremony of the air, The. Mary and the Bramble. Lascelles Abercrombie. OBMV

Great Blue Heron, The. Carolyn Kizer. CoAP; NePoEA-2; WPE

Great Book, The. Jean-Paul de Dadelsen, *tr. fr. French by* Anselm Hollo. RHTwFP

Great Breath, The. "Æ." MoBrPo; OBEV; OBMV; WGRP

Great bright leaves have fallen, The. Before a Funeral. Lauris Edmond. ATNZ

Great Britain Through the Ice: Or, Premature Patriotism. Charles Tennyson Turner. Son

Great Brown Owl, The. Jane Euphemia Browne. OxBChV

Great Central Railway, Sheffield Victoria to Banbury. Sir John Betjeman. NYBP

Great Citadels whereon the Gold Sun Falls. John Berryman. *Fr.* Sonnets, IX. Son

Great cry, A, went up from the stockyards and slaughterhouses. The Delicate, Plummeting Bodies. Stephen Dobyns. FYAP

Great cup tumbled, ringing like a bell, The. The Grail. Sidney Keyes. FaBoTw

Great Dark, The. Martin Carter. PVCV

Great, dark wings, passing my roof over. An Old Story Is Retold. John Hollander. BAP

Great Day, The. W. B. Yeats. BIrV; CMoP; FF; OxBSP

Great Days of the Poet, The. Robert Desnos, *tr. fr. French by* Michael Benedikt. POS

Great Despair of the London Whigs, The. *Unknown.* APAS

Great dignity had T'ai-jên. *Unknown, tr. by* Arthur Waley. BoS

Great Diocletian. Abraham Cowley. *Fr.* The Garden. ChTr

Great dream stinks like a whale gone aground, The. Why the Soup Tastes like the Daily News. Marge Piercy. MAT

Great Duke of Wellington, The. Edmund Clerihew Bentley. *Fr.* Clerihews. CenHV

Great earth itself, The. Hitomaro, *tr. fr. Japanese. Fr.* Manyo Shu. Ma

Great-enough both accepts and subdues. Phenomena. Robinson Jeffers. NOBA; OxBA

Great Escape, The. Ralph Adamo. MT

Great Escape, The. Sista Roots. WS

Great Farewells, The. Amanda Benjamin Hall. GoYe

Great Farter, The. Nakasuk, *tr. fr. Eskimo by* Jerome Rothenberg. STP

"Great father Alighier, if from the skies." To Dante. Vittorio Alfieri, *tr. by* Lorna De' Lucchi. AWP

Great Favorit Beheaded, A. Sir Richard Fanshawe, *after the Italian of* Giovanni Battista Guarini. *See* Il Pastor Fido: Fall, The.

Great Favourite Song, Entitled The Sailor's Hornpipe, A. *Unknown.* OxBSS

Great Fear, The. Piera Oppezzo, *tr. fr. Italian by* Muriel Kittel. DMI

Great Figure, The. Francisco Morales Santos, *tr. fr. Spanish by* Juan Felipe Herrera. Vol

Great Figure, The. William Carlos Williams. AiP; InPK; MoP; NoAM; QFR; TTTS

Great Fire, The. Dryden. *Fr.* Annus Mirabilis. FiP

Great fish's eyes never shut, The. Rosario Castellanos, *tr. by* Willis Barnstone. BoWoP

Great Fleas. Augustus De Morgan. BXAP
  (Fleas, The.) FaBoCo

Great folks are of a finer mould. Epigram on Scolding. Swift. FaBoEE

Great fool, The. Work Song. Raymond Mazisi Kunene, *tr. by* D. K. Rycroft. WTO

Great Fortune is an hungry thing. Aeschylus, *tr. fr. Greek by* Gilbert Murray. *Fr.* Agamemnon. AWP

Great Fountains, The. Anne Hébert, *tr. fr. French by* Willis Barnstone. BoWoP

Great Freight, The. Ingeborg Bachmann, *tr. fr. German by* Bill Crisman. PBWP

Great Friend. Henry David Thoreau. PoEL-4

Great friend and servant of the good. Ben Jonson. *Fr.* Pleasure Reconciled to Virtue. NAEL-1

Great Frost, The. John Gay. *Fr.* Trivia; or, The Art of Walking the Streets of London. SeCePo

Great furred noses nuzzling at haybales. Elk at Black Fork Canyon. Tom Sleigh. PPR

Great Garret, or 100 Wheels, The. James McMichael. AmPA

Great Gawd, I'm Feelin' Bad. *Unknown.* AS

Great God accept our gratitude. Doxology. Josephine D. Henderson Heard. CBWP-4

Great God, attend while Zion sings. Isaac Watts. AmFP

Great God, How Frail a Thing Is Man. Mather Byles. AH

Great God, how short's mans time; each minute speaks. Meditations for July 19, 1666. Philip Pain. SCAP

Great God, I Ask Thee for No Meaner Pelf. Henry David Thoreau. NOBA; TrPWD

Great God, let all my tuneful pow'rs. Ottiwell Heginbothom. AmFP

Great God of Nations, now to Thee. Hymn of Gratitude. *Unknown.* BLRP

Great God Pan, The. Elizabeth Barrett Browning. *See* Musical Instrument, A.

Great God Paused among Men. Daniel Berrigan. MAT

Great God, Preserver of All Things. Francis Daniel Pastorius. AH

Great God, the Followers of Thy Son. Henry Ware, Jr. AH

Great God, Thou giver of all good. *Unknown.* BLRP

Great God, Thy Works. Mather Byles. AH

Great Goddesse to whose throne in Cynthian fires. The Shadow of Night. George Chapman. PoEL-2

Great gold apples of night, The. People. D. H. Lawrence. BrPo

Great, good and just, could I but rate. His Metrical Vow. James, Marquess of Montrose Graham. OxBS
  (Epitaph on Charles I.) NOBE
  (Epitaph on King Charles I.) OBS
  (Lines on the Execution of King Charles I.) GoTS

Great-Grandfather. Freda Downie. FaBoWP

Great-grandmother talks by the hour to me. Irish Grandmother. Katherine Edelman. AmFN

Great-great Grandma, Don't Sleep in Your Treehouse Tonight. X. J. Kennedy. GrPl

Great grief came over me. Aleqaajik. WTO

Great Guest Comes In, The. Edwin Markham. WBLP

Great heart, who taught thee so to dye? Epitaph: On Sir Walter Rawleigh at His Execution. *Unknown.* OBS

Great-hearted Christ, importunate and mild. Chad Walsh. *Fr.* The Psalm of Christ. TrCP

Great House, The. Edwin Muir. EyDe

Great Hunger, The. Patrick Kavanagh. FaBCIP
  Sels.
  "April, and no one able to calculate." IPY
  "Clay is the word and clay is the flesh." *Fr.* I. IPY; NoAM; OxBTC
  "He gave himself another year." BIrV
  "Health and wealth and love he too dreamed of in May." MoAB
  "Maguire is not afraid of death, the Church will light him a candle." CIP
  "Poor Paddy Maguire, a fourteen-hour day." IPY

Great-in-counsels made her this reply, The. Ulysses Leaves the Nymph Calypso. Homer, *tr. fr. Greek by* George Chapman. *Fr.* Odyssey, V. JCP

Great Infirmities. Charles Simic. AnAn

Great Insohreckshan, Di. Linton Kwesi Johnson. FaBoPV

Great is Caesar: He has conquered Seven Kingdoms. Fugal-Chorus. W. H. Auden. *Fr.* For the Time Being; a Christmas Oratorio. LiTM

Great is my envy of you, earth, in your greed. Petrarch, *tr. fr. Italian.* *Fr.* Sonnets to Laura: To Laura in Death, XXXII, *tr. by* Edwin Morgan. NAWM-1

Great is the folly of a feeble brain. Joseph Hall. *Fr.* Virgidemiarum, I, Satire VII. EBEV

Great is the sun, and wide [*or* wise] he goes. Summer Sun. Robert Louis Stevenson. MoBrPo; PWR

Great is thy worke in Wildernesse, Oh man.   Mr. Eliot Pastor of the Church of Christ at Roxbury.   Edward Johnson.   SCAP

Great Jack of Lent, clad in a robe of air.   A Copy of Non Sequitors.   *Unknown*.   FaBoNo

Great Jehovah speaks to us, The.   The Names and Order of the Books of the Old Testament.   Thomas Russell.   BLPA

Great Jehova's working word effecting wondrously, The.   Good News from New-England.   Edward Johnson.   SCAP

Great king.   Harvest of War.   Kappiyarrukkappiyanar, *tr. by* A. K. Ramanujan.   PLW

Great King.   Tuini Ngawai, *tr. fr. Maori by* Margaret Orbell.   PeNZ

Great king, the sovereign [*or* sov'raigne] ruler of this land.   To His Late Majesty Concerning the True Form of English Poetry.   Sir John Beaumont.   JCP; OBS

"Great lady, were you Helen long ago?"   Helen—Old.   Isabel Ecclestone MacKay.   CaP

Great Lakes of Canada, The.   Gordon Perry.   FaBoUs

Great Land, The.   William Rose Benét.   OPP

Great Lord of All, Whose Work of Love.   Jacob Duché.   AH

Great love goes mad to be spoken: you went out.   Preserves.   Jack Butler.   MT

Great love may seem like none at all.   Sent in Parting.   Tu Mu, *tr. by* Burton Watson.   CoBCP

Great Lover, The.   Rupert Brooke.   BrPo; FaFP; FPL; HoPM; LiTB; LiTM; MoBrPo; PoRA; TrGrPo; WaP

Great [*or* Greate] Macedon, that out of Persia chased, The.   In Praise of Wyatt's Psalms.   Henry Howard, Earl of Surrey.   AAS; SiPS   (Greate Macedon that out of Persy chased, The.)   AAS

Great Magicians, The.   C. Day Lewis.   EaLo

Great Man, A.   Goldsmith.   NA

Great Man, The.   Eunice Tietjens.   WGRP

Great man from time past had no fixed abode, The.   Weeping for the Priest Gempin.   Emperor Saga, *tr. by* Burton Watson.   JLIC-1

Great Man's Death: An Anecdote, The.   Everette Maddox.   MT

Great many gentlemen take great delight, A.   Bold Reynard the Fox.   *Unknown*.   OBET

Great master! Boyish, sympathetic man!   To John Keats.   Amy Lowell.   Son

Great masters of the common-place, The.   Staff-Nurse: Old Style.   W. E. Henley.   *Fr.* In Hospital, VIII.   BrPo

Great melech lies waking over Judah, The.   Saul.   Else Lasker-Schüler, *tr. by* Joachim Neugroschel.   VWA

Great Men Have Been among Us.   Wordsworth.   EnRP; FaBoPV; PoEL-4; Son   (England, 1802, III.)   OBEV

Great Merchant, Dives Pragmaticus, Cries His Wares, The, *sel.*   Thomas Newbery.   "What lack you, sir? What seek you? What will you buy?."   OxBChV

Great moment in *Blade Runner* where Roy.   Final Farewell.   Tom Clark.   UL

Great Moth, The.   Robert Gittings.   OxBTC

Great Mourning.   Bible, Apocrypha.   *Fr.* First Maccabees, I: 25-28.   TrJP

Great Nature clothes the soul, which is but thin.   The Soul's Garment.   Margaret Cavendish, Duchess of Newcastle.   SeCePo; WPE

Great nature she doth clothe the soul within.   Soul and Body.   Margaret Cavendish, Duchess of Newcastle.   OxBSP

Great Nebula in Andromeda, The.   Hugh Seidman.   AmPA

Great Number, A.   Wislawa Szymborska, *tr. fr. Polish by* Czeslaw Milosz.   PwPP

Great one, austere.   Prayer before Work.   May Sarton.   SaC

Great Overdog, The,/ That heavenly beast.   Canis Major.   Robert Frost.   *Fr.* A Sky Pair.   MoAB; MoAmPo

Great Pacific railway, The.   The Railroad Cars Are Coming.   *Unknown*.   AmFN, *with music;* AS, *with music;* FaPON

Great Painter! to thy soul aglow with thought.   Raphael.   Henrietta Cordelia Ray.   CBWP-3

Great Palaces of Versailles, The.   Rita Dove.   NAmP; NoAM

Great Panjandrum Himself, The.   Samuel Foote.   FaBoCh; FaBoCo; MoShBr; Par; PoLF

Great Pelides, stretch'd along the shore.   The Ghost of Patroclus.   Homer, *tr. fr. Greek by* Pope.   *Fr.* The Iliad, XXII.   PeHV

Great philosopher did choke, A.   Samuel Butler.   FaBoEE

Great Physician, The.   Sadi, *tr. fr. Persian by* Sir Edwin Arnold.   *Fr.* The Bustan.   AWP

Great Poems, The.   Greg Kuzma.   KS

Great poets are not in the language but in business, The.   Poetry Paper.   Andrei Codrescu.   EAS

Great poisoned drum, The.   Myotan, *tr. by* Lucien Stryk *and* Takashi Ikemoto.   ZPCJ

Great pompous ague, and vapid arguments.   On Fatherish Men.   Amelia Rosselli, *tr. by* Muriel Kittel.   DMI

Great Potter works no private favors, The.   Spirit Expounds.   T'ao Ch'ien, *tr. fr. Chinese by* Burton Watson.   *Fr.* Substance, Shadow, and Spirit.   CoBCP

Great Pretenderer, The.   Pat Nolan.   UL

Great Prince of heaven, begotten of that King.   To God the Son.   Henry Constable.   OBSC

Great princes have great playthings.   Playthings.   William Cowper.   WaaP

Great Rain of the South, The.   Pablo Neruda, *tr. fr. Spanish by* Perry Higman.   LPSS

Great River, The.   Henry Van Dyke.   TrPWD

Great Sad One, The.   Uri Zvi Greenberg, *tr. fr. Hebrew by* Robert Mezey *and* Ben Zion Gold.   VWA

Great St. Bernard, The.   Samuel Rogers.   OBTV

Great Santa Barbara Oil Disaster OR, The.   Conyus.   AmPA

Great Sassacus fled from the eastern shores.   Death Song.   Alonzo Lewis.   PAH

Great Scarf of Birds, The.   John Updike.   NYBP

Great Sea.   Charles Brasch.   ATNZ

Great Sea, The.   Uvavnuk.   *Unknown, tr. by* Knud Rasmussen.   NU

Great sea-roads to England, The.   The Gates to England.   Marjorie Wilson.   BoTP

Great Silkie of Sule Skerry, The.   *Unknown*.   ChTr; ESPB; FaBoBa; FaBoCh; GBP; MAT; MOS   (Grey Selchie of Sule Skerry, The.)   OxBB

Great Sir, having just had the good luck to catch.   Copy of an Intercepted Despatch from His Excellency Don Strepitoso Diabolo.   Thomas Moore.   OBSV

Great sir, our poor hearts were ready to burst.   The Humble Address.   *Unknown*.   APAS

Great sky hazy with scents of plum blossoms, The.   Teika, *tr. fr. Japanese by* Hiroaki Sato.   *Fr.* Eighty-four Tanka.   FCEI

Great sky splendidly darkens, The.   Issa, *tr. fr. Japanese by* Hiroaki Sato.   *Fr.* Forty-four Hokku.   FCEI

Great Society, The.   Robert Bly.   NoAM

Great soul, thou sittest with me in my room.   To the Spirit of Keats.   James Russell Lowell.   Son

Great soul, to all brave souls akin.   The Star.   Marion Couthouy Smith.   PAH

Great South Land, The, *sel.*   Rex Ingamells.   "They made impudent inspection of our coast."   CBAP

Great Sovereign of the earth and sea.   Europa.   Stephen Henry Thayer.   AA

Great Spaces.   Howard Moss.   TwCP

Great Spirit of the speeding spheres.   John Haynes Holmes.   TrPWD

Great Spirits Now on Earth.   Keats.   Son   (Addressed to Haydon.)   EnRP; OBNC

Great star has fallen into my lap, A.   Reconciliation.   Else Lasker-Schüler, *tr. by* Robert Alter.   PBWP

Great Statue of the General Du Puy, The.   Wallace Stevens.   *Fr.* Notes toward a Supreme Fiction.   LiTA

Great, still shape, alone, A.   Ireland.   John James Piatt.   AA

Great stone hearth has gone, The.   Fire.   Dorothy Wellesley.   OBMV

Great streets of silence led away.   Emily Dickinson.   NOCV

Great Summons, The.   Ch'ü Yüan, *tr. fr. Chinese by* Arthur Waley.   AWP

Great sun has changed itself into a pumpkin moon, The.   Goodbye.   Sherod Santos.   MAYP

Great Swamp Fight, The.   Caroline Hazard.   PAH

Great swart cheek and the gleam of tears, A.   The Washer-Woman.   Otto Leland Bohanan.   BANP

Great tempest on the Plain of Ler, A.   *Unknown*.   NOIV

Great Things ("Great things are done when men and mountains meet.").   Blake.   *Fr.* Gnomic Verses.   OxBSP

Great Things.   Thomas Hardy.   GTBS-P; NOBE

Great Things Have Happened.   Alden Nowlan.   GOYP

Great thoughts in crude, unshapely verse set forth.   On Reading.   Thomas Bailey Aldrich.   AA

Great thrushes have not appeared this year, The.   The Unremarkable Year.   Roy Fuller.   OxBC

Great tiger, The.   Folk Tune.   Esther Raab, *tr. by* Robert Friend *and* Shimon Sandbank.   VWA

Great Time, A.   William Henry Davies.   LiTB; MoBrPo

Great *Titanic*.   *Unknown*.   AmFP

Great Tom.   Richard Corbet.   OxBoLi

"Great Unaffected Vampires and the Moon."   Stevie Smith.   NoAM

Great Uncle Joe.   Apology.   Duane Niatum.   HATNAP

Great unequal conflict past, The.   Occasioned by General Washington's Arrival in Philadelphia, on His Way to His Residence in Virginia.   Philip Freneau.   PAH

Great Venus, Queene [or Queen] of Beautie [or Beauty] and of grace. Address to Venus. Lucretius, tr. fr. Latin by Spenser. Fr. De Rerum Natura (On the Nature of Things), The Faerie Queene, IV, 10. AWP

Great Victory, The. R. V. Gilbert. BLRP

Great Vocabulary. Dale A. Schreiber. SoTCo

Great Wager, The. G. A. Studdert-Kennedy. TrCP

Great Wagon, The. Tontainan Ilantiraiyan, tr. fr. Tamil by A. K. Ramanujan. PLW

Great Wall, The. Lucebert, tr. fr. Dutch by James S. Holmes. DuIn

Great Wanagan Creek Flood, The. Bill Lowman. CowP

Great War, The. Vernon Scannell. OBWP

Great Way of the Man, The. Norman H. Russell. NOVW

Great Way—simple as it is, The. Speaking My Mind. Chung-ch'ang T'ung, tr. by Burton Watson. CoBCP

Great Wheel, The. "Hugh MacDiarmid." OxBS

Great white lilies in the grass, The. Pallor. Agnes Mary Frances Robinson. NOBVV

Great, wide, beautiful, wonderful World. The Wonderful World. William Brighty Rands. FaPON
(Child's World, The.) OHIP
(World, The.) BoTP; OxBChV

Great without pomp, without ambition brave. Tribute to Washington. Unknown. OHIP

Great woe, fire & war come on me. Skythinos, tr. by Thomas Meyer. PeHV

Great you call Demosthenes. Self-Portrait. Moses Mendelssohn. TrJP

Greate Macedon that out of Persy chased, The. Earl of Surrey. See Great Macedon . . . .

Greater Cats, The. Victoria Mary Sackville-West. OBMV

Greater Friendship Baptist Church, The. Carole C. Gregory. BlSi

Greater, he called them, than Homer or Chaucer. The Men of Sudbury. Carlos Baker. GOA

Greater Love. Wilfred Owen. BrPo; CMoP; EnLoPo; FaBoMo; FaBoRV; FaFP; GTBS-P; LiTB; LiTM; MoAB; MoBrPo; MoP; NoAM; WaaP; WaP

Greater than memory of Achilles or Ulysses. The Wallabout Martyrs. Walt Whitman. GOA

Greater Trial, The. Countess of Winchilsea. TrGrPo

Greatest bore is boredom, The. Unknown. CenHV

Greatest in many things, in some the least. On a Distinguished Politician. J. E. Thorold Rogers. FaBoEE

Greatest of These, The. Bible, N.T. See First Corinthians: Though I Speak with the Tongues of Men and Angels.

Greatest of virtues is humility. Against Women's Fashions. John Lydgate. ACP

Greatest Person in the Universe, The. Daniel L. Marsh. BLRP

Greatest saints and sinners have been made, The. Samuel Butler. FaBoEE

Greatest self-made man in the world today, The. Our Noble Booker T. Washington. Mrs. Henry Linden. CBWP-4

Greatgrandma's bending to pluck some vegetable. Recipe. Albert Goldbarth. VWA

Greatly shining,/ The autumn moon floats in the thin sky. Wind and Silver. Amy Lowell. BoWoP; HeIP; MoAmPo

Greatness. Unknown. OBS

Grecian Kindness. Earl of Rochester. OxBSP

Grecian Muse, to earth who bore, The. California. Thomas Lake Morris. AA

Greece, sels. William Haygarth. OBTV
"Genius of Greece! thou livest, though thy domes."
"Mournful is the remembrance which awakes."

Greece. Derek Walcott. AnAn

Greece was; Greece is no more. The "White City." Richard Watson Gilder. PAH

Greed. Unknown. OxNR
(Four birds.) ChTr
(Robin, Wren, Martin, Swallow.) GBP

Greedy hawk with sudden sight of lure, The. Unknown. PBBP

Greedy Jane. Unknown. OxBChV

Greedy Little Pig, The. Irene F. Pawsey. BoTP

Greedy Richard. Jane Taylor. OxBChV

Greedy Seasons. Eileen Myles. UL

Greedy the People, The. E. E. Cummings. SoSe

Greedy Tom. Unknown. OxNR

Greek Antiquities: First Floor. Lauris Edmond. UAS

Greek Archipelagoes. Patrick Leigh-Fermor. OBTV

Greek Architecture. Herman Melville. NoP

Greek Epigram. Ezra Pound. MoAB; MoAmPo

Greek Room, The. James W. Thompson. BPo

Greek ship, A/ Sails on the sea. The Couple. Sandra Hochman. NYBP

"Greek Tragedy" of course is the sort of thing. Their Philistinism Considered. Robert Pinsky. Fr. Essay on Psychiatrists, XI. NoAM

Greeks, The. Tom Clark. PoA

Greeks Are Blinding Polyphemus, The. Gyorgy Raba, tr. fr. Hungarian by Jascha Kessler. FOC

Greeks' chieftains, all irked with the war, The. Virgil, tr. fr. Latin, tr. by the 5th Earl of Surrey. Fr. The Aeneid [or Eneados], II. OAEL-1

Greeks were wrong who said our eyes have rays, The. Lamarck Elaborated. Richard Wilbur. NePoEA

Green. Walter de la Mare. FaBoNo

Green. D. H. Lawrence. GBL; MoBrPo; PoA

Green Afternoon, The. Henry Rago. VGW

Green and growing thorn-tree, A. Forgive and Forget. "Totius," tr. by Anthony Delius. PeSA

Green and silent spot, amid the hills, A. Fears in Solitude. Samuel Taylor Coleridge. EnRP; OBWP

Green and the Black, The. Anthony Bailey. NYBP

Green and Yellow. Unknown. OBET

Green Apples. Dudley Randall. FB

Green Apples. Ruth Stone. InPS

Green are the tussocks of the marsh-grass springing. Yellow. Kenton Kilmer. GoYe

Green arsenic smeared on an egg-white cloth. L'Art, 1910. Ezra Pound. HeIP; OxBA

Green as a seedling the one lane shines. City Traffic. Eve Merriam. PDV

Green Autumn Stubble, The. Unknown, tr. fr. Irish by Patrick Browne. WTO

Green Banana Leaves. Yün Shou-p'ing, tr. fr. Chinese by Jonathan Chaves. CoBLCP

Green be the turf above thee. On the Death of Joseph Rodman Drake. Fitz-Greene Halleck. AA; AnAmPo; BLPA; PAH; PoEL-4

Green Bed, The. Unknown. AmFP

Green blood fresh pulsing through the trees. April and Dying. Anne Reeve Aldrich. AA

Green-blue ground; The. On Gay Wallpaper. William Carlos Williams. MoAB; MoAmPo; TAP

Green, blue, yellow, and red. The One. Patrick Kavanagh. MoBrPo; TIRV

Green bottle, a gray pipe, a very stiff and moral-looking tablecloth, A. Biography of a Still Life. Charles Edward Eaton. KS

Green boughs bow down low when the dragonfly appears at the turning in the footpath. Suicided by Night. Robert Desnos, tr. by Michael Benedikt. POS

Green Breeks. Douglas Dunn. FaBoPV

Green Briar Shore, The. Unknown. AmFP

Green Broom. Unknown. See There was an old man and he lived in a wood.

Green bubbles—new brewed wine. A Question Addressed to Liu Shih-chiu. Po Chü-i, tr. by Burton Watson. CoBCP

Green Buddhas/ On the fruit stand. Watermelons. Charles Simic. OBAL

Green Candles. Humbert Wolfe. MoBrPo; RHPC; SO

Green catalpa tree has turned, The. April Inventory. W. D. Snodgrass. CAPP; CoAP; HAP; LiTM; NePoEA; NoAM; NoP; TAP; TwCP

Green cheese, yellow laces. Unknown. OxNR

Green Coconuts: Rio. Lawrence Durrell. OBTV

Green Corn Festival. Merry Harris. GOS

Green cornfield. Onitsura, tr. by Geoffrey Bownas and Anthony Thwaite. PeBJV

Green Cornfield, A. Christina Rossetti. BoTP

Green creepers planted inside the house. What She Said ("Green creepers planted inside the house"). Orampokiyar, tr. fr. Tamil by A. K. Ramanujan. Fr. Five on the Riverside Cane, 5. PLW

Green Dryad's Plea, The. Thomas Hood. Fr. The Plea of the Midsummer Fairies. OBNC

Green elm with the one great bough of gold, The. October. Edward Thomas. NoAM

Green Enravishment of Human Life. Sister Juana Inés de la Cruz, tr. fr. Spanish. MexPo, tr. by Samuel Beckett; WPOW, tr. by Samuel Beckett and Octavio Paz

Green Eye, The. James Merrill. PoA

Green eye—and a red—in the dark, A. The Train. Mary Elizabeth Coleridge. BoTP

Green Eye of the Yellow God, The. J. Milton Hayes. BLPA

Green-eyed Care. Old Cat Care. Richard Hughes. OBMV

Green Family, The. Colleen Thibaudeau. NOBC

Green Figs at Table. James Keir Baxter. ATNZ

Green flag—wineshop by the river, A. The Tavernkeeper. Cheng Hsieh, tr. by Jan W. Walls. WFTU

Green Frog at Roadstead, Wisconsin. James Schevill. TAP

Green garden of growing weeds, A. Playing with Fire. James Simmons. CIP

Green-Gown, The. *Unknown.* CoMu

Green grape, and you refused me. Brief Autumnal. *Unknown, tr. by* Dudley Fitts. WeW

Green Grass. *Unknown.* CH; GBP; OxBoLi; OxNR

Green Grass Growing All Around, The. *Unknown.* MoShBr

Green grass is bowing, The. The Wind in the Grass. Siegfried Emerson. BoTP

Green, Green, and Green Again. Conrad Aiken. *Fr.* And in the Human Heart, XXVIII. Son

Green, Green Is El Aghir. Norman Cameron. MoBS; OBWP; OxBTC (El Aghir.) FaBoTw

Green green, river bank grasses. *Unknown, tr. fr. Chinese by* Burton Watson. *Fr.* Nineteen Old Poems of the Han, II. CoBCP

Green green the cypress on the ridge. *Unknown, tr. fr. Chinese by* Burton Watson. *Fr.* Nineteen Old Poems of the Han, III. CoBCP

Green, green the pine trees on the hill. Pine Pavilion Hill. Chu Yi-tsun, *tr. fr. Chinese by* Irving Lo. *Fr.* Quatrains on Yung-chia, I. WFTU

Green, green, the young herbs are green in the snowy field. Raizan, *tr. fr. Japanese by* Hiroaki Sato. *Fr.* Thirteen Hokku. FCEI

Green grew the reeds and pale they were. Symbols. Vance Thompson. AA

Green Grow the Rashes, O. Burns. CoMu, *diff. vers.*; CTC; EnRP; ErPo, *diff. vers.*; FaFP; LiTB; NAEL-2, *diff. vers.*; NoP; OAEL-1; PPP; SeCePo
(Green Grows the Rashes.) GBP, *diff. vers.*
(Song: Green Grow the Rashes.) AWP

Green Grow the Rushes O. *Unknown. See* I'll sing you one.

Green Groweth the Holly. *Unknown.* OxBLMV

Green Grows the Rashes. Burns. *See* Green Grow the Rashes, O.

Green Hammock, White Magnolia Tree. Ruth Gilbert. PeNZ

Green Hills of Africa, The. Roy Fuller. NoP; OBTV

Green hills sloping from the nothern wall. Seeing a Friend Off. Li Po, *tr. by* Burton Watson. CoBCP

Green Horse, The. Bin Ramke. MAYP

Green-house is my summer seat, The. The Faithful Friend. William Cowper. FM

Green, humped, wrinkled hills: with such a look, The. The Green Hills of Africa. Roy Fuller. NoP; OBTV

Green I love you green. Sleepwalkers' Ballad. Federico García Lorca, *tr. by* John Frederick Nims. WeW

Green, I Rewrite. Eddy van Vliet, *tr. fr. Dutch by* James S. Holmes. DuIn

Green Ice. Vivienne Finch. BrRo

Green is go. Yellow. David McCord. RHPC

Green is the color of everything. One West Coast. Al Young. NPGG

Green is the night, green kindled and apparelled. The Candle, a Saint. Wallace Stevens. PoRA

Green Island. William Logan. MAYP

Green Isle of Lovers, The. Robert Charles Sands. AA

Green Jade Plum Trees in Spring. Ou-yang Hsiu, *tr. fr. Chinese by* Kenneth Rexroth. NaP

Green Knight's Farewell to Fancy, The. George Gascoigne. OPOP

Green Lady, The. Charlotte Druitt Cole. BoTP

Green lady, green lady, come doon for thy tea. *Unknown.* GBP

Green lamp flares on the table, The. This Life. Rita Dove. AmPA

Green lawn/ a picket fence. Alice Walker. *Fr.* Once. BlSi; PoBA

Green Leaf that will outlast the winter. Louis Zukofsky. VGW

"Green leaves, what are you doing." The Five-Fingered Maple. Kate Louise Brown. BoTP

Green Light. Kenneth Fearing. PoE; VGW

Green light floods the city square, The. Sunken Evening [in Trafalgar Square]. Laurie Lee. LiTM; NYBP

Green light—go. "At the Corner of Muck and Myer." Paul Violi. UL

Green light trailed through the park at dusk, A. The Evening of Montale's Death. Susan Stewart. NAmP

Green Linnet, The. Wordsworth. EnRP; GTBS; GTBS-P; PBBP

Green little vaulter in the sunny grass. To the Grasshopper and the Cricket. Leigh Hunt. EnRP; GN; OBNC; Son

Green Lowland of Pianos, A. Jerzy Harasymowicz, *tr. fr. Polish by* Czeslaw Milosz. PwPP

Green Martyrs. Richard Murphy. *Fr.* The Battle of Aughrim. NOIV

Green mistletoe! Winter. Walter de la Mare. ChTr; OAEL-2; OBMV

Green Mossy Banks of the Lee, The. *Unknown.* OBET

Green mothering of moss knits shadow and light, The. Rain Forest. Dave Smith. HCAP; MT

Green mountain and I are old acquaintances, The. Written on the Wall of the Flying Cloud Cave in Kweichow. Sung Hsiang, *tr. by* Irving Lo. WFTU

Green Mountain Boy. Florida Watts Smyth. GoYe

Green Mountain Boys, The. Bryant. PAH

Green mwold on zummer bars do show. Tokens. William Barnes. PoEL-4

Green peaches and red apricots!, The. The Taoist Nun. Mao Hsi-chen, *tr. by* Lois Fusek. ATF

Green Place, A. William Jay Smith. GrPl

Green plant on shipboard, changing. A Pot Of Earth. Jules Supervielle, *tr. by* Denise Levertov. RHTwFP

Green Plumes of Royal Palms. LeRoy V. Brant. AH

Green Rain. Dorothy Livesay. NOBC

Green Rain. Mary Webb. BoNaP; CH; FaPON

Green Red Brown and White. May Swenson. VGW

Green Refrain, A. Avraham Huss, *tr. fr. Hebrew by* Mark Elliott Shapiro. VWA

Green Revolutions. Barbara Guest. FaBoWP

Green Riders. Rachel Field. TSS

Green River. Bryant. AnAmPo; NOBA; OxBA

Green River, The. Lord Alfred Bruce Douglas. OBEV

Green Roads, The. Edward Thomas. FaBoPP; NoAM

Green rushes with red shoots. Plucking the Rushes. *Unknown.* BoLoP; Mes; OBVE

Green rustlings, more-than-regal charities. Royal Palm. Hart Crane. CMoP; MoAB; MoAmPo; MoP; NoAM; NoP; TrGrPo

Green-shadowed people sit, or walk in rings. Spring. Philip Larkin. MoBrPo

Green Shepherd, The. Louis Simpson. NePoEA; NYBP

Green shingles of rest homes unfold revealing, The. The United States Prepare for the Permanent Revolution. George Hitchcock. EAS

Green shutters, shut your shutters! Windyridge. Sir John Betjeman. *Fr.* Beside the Seaside. OxBTC

Green Slates. Thomas Hardy. FaBoPP

Green Sleeves ("Green sleeves and tartan ties"). *Unknown.* GBP

Green Snake, when I hung you round my neck. To the Snake. Denise Levertov. AmPP; LiTM; NePoEA-2; NMM; PoA

Green Song. Philip Booth. BoNaP

Green Spring. Ryokan, *tr. fr. Chinese by* Burton Watson. FCEI; JLIC-2

Green Spring receiveth. The Great Summons. Ch'ü Yüan, *tr. by* Arthur Waley. AWP

Green spring, start of the second month. Green Spring. Ryokan, *tr. by* Burton Watson. FCEI; JLIC-2

Green star Sirius. Winter Dawn. D. H. Lawrence. BrPo

Green Stems. Margaret Wise Brown. RHPC

Green Stream, A. Wang Wei, *tr. fr. Chinese by* Witter Bynner *and* Kiang Kang-hu. SD

Green stream full of life. Dark Stream. Ingrid Jonker, *tr. by* Jake Cope *and* William Plomer. OV

Green Sussex. Tennyson. *Fr.* Prologue to General Hamley. FaBoPP

Green Symphony. John Gould Fletcher. MoAmPo

Green Things Growing. Dinah Maria Mulock Craik. FaFP; GN; OHIP

Green Tomatoes. Dennis Trudell. KS

Green Train, The. E. V. Rieu. SO

Green Tree, The. James Reiss. AmPA; DiL

Green trees form shade, the path is covered with moss. Recording My Happiness upon Returning Home. Wen Cheng-ming, *tr. by* Jonathan Chaves. CoBLCP

Green Valley. Dorothy Vena Johnson. PoNe

Green Valley, The. Sylvia Townsend Warner. MoBrPo

Green water of the Fen flows on and on, The. Spirit of the Yellow River. Sun Kuang-hsien, *tr. by* Lois Fusek. ATF

Green water reflects scales of bright red. A Miscellany on the Garden of Autumn Clouds: Peach-Blossom Pond. Sung Wan, *tr. by* Yin-nan Chang. WFTU

Green Willow, The. *Unknown.* OBSC
(Complaint of a Lover Forsaken of His Love, The.) CoMu

Green Willow, Green Willow. *Unknown.* AmFP

Green willow's quiet, A. Chiyojo, *tr. fr. Japanese by* Hiroaki Sato. *Fr.* Seventeen Hokku. FCEI

Greenback Dollar, The. *Unknown.* AmFP

Greener Grass. Frank Steele. Psk

Greene's Farewell to Folly, *sel.* Robert Greene.
"Sweet are the thoughts that savour of content." PoEL-2

Greene's Groatsworth of Wit, *sels.* Robert Greene.
Fie, Fie on Blind Fancy! EIL
(Lamilia's Song.) OBSC
Palinode, A. OBSC

Greene's Mourning Garment, *sels.* Robert Greene.
Hexametra Alexis in Laudem Rosamundi. EIL; GBL; PoEL-2
Shepherd's Wife's Song, The. EIL; HAP; OBSC

Greene's Vision, *sel.* Robert Greene.
Description of Sir Geoffrey Chaucer, The. CTC; OBSC
(Sir Geoffrey Chaucer.) FaBoCh

Greenest jade for a clothes-pounding stone. Ch'ing-yang Ford. *Unknown, tr. by* Burton Watson. CoBCP

Greenest of grass in the long meadow grows, The.   June.   Jane G. Stewart.   BoTP
Greenham Women.   Wendy Poussard.   AIW
Greenhouse in October, The.   Peter Levi.   PoPo
Greenland Fossil an Icy Poet.   H. C. ten Berge, tr. fr. Dutch by Theo Hermans.   DuIn
Greenland Men, The.   Unknown.   OxBSS
Greenland Voyage; or, The Whale Fisher's Delight, The.   Unknown. OxBSS
Greenland Whale, The.   Unknown.   See 'Twas in the year of forty-nine.
Greenland Whale Fishery, The ("I cannot stay all on the shore").   Unknown. OxBSS
Greenland Whale Fishery, The ("One thousand eight hundred and twenty-four").   Unknown.   AmFP
Greenland Whale Fishery, The ("We may no longer stay on shore"). Unknown.   OBET
Greenland Winter, A.   Lucy Diamond.   BoTP
Greenness.   Angelina Weld Grimké.   CDC
Greens.   David Ray.   SM; VGW
Greens.   Unknown.   AS
Greens and fruit the color of the loveliest.   Fruits and Vegetables. Umberto Saba, tr. by Henry Taylor.   PFI
Greensleeves.   Unknown.   TTTS
Greenwich Observatory.   Sidney Keyes.   MoAB; MoBrPo
Greenwood.   Richard Jackson.   KS
Greenwood fawn at the hidden brook, The.   Song for the Greenwood Fawn.   I. L. Salomon.   GoYe
Greeting, A.   William Henry Davies.   MoBrPo
Greeting.   Henrietta Cordelia Ray.   CBWP-3
Greeting from a Distance.   Hans Sahl, tr. fr. German by Erna Baber Rosenfeld.   VWA
Greeting from England.   Unknown.   PAH
Greeting of the Roses, The.   Hamlin Garland.   AA
Greeting to Queen Elizabeth, the Rare White Heron of Single Flight, A. Wiremu Kingi Kerekere, tr. fr. Maori by Wiremu Kingi Kerekere. PeNZ
Greg Hoffman.   Mel Glenn.   RR
Gregory Griggs, Gregory Griggs.   Unknown.   OxNR
Grenada.   Mikhail Arkadyevich Svetlov, tr. fr. Russian by Alexander Kaun.   WaaP
Grenadier.   A. E. Housman.   OBMV; OBWP
Grenadier, The.   Unknown.   GBP; OxNR
Grendel.   Unknown, tr. fr. Anglo-Saxon by Burton Raffel.   Fr. Beowulf. NU
Grene groweth the holy.   Love Ever Green.   Henry VIII, King of England.   MeEL
Gresford Disaster, The.   Unknown.   GBP; OBET
Gretel in Darkness.   Louise Glück.   AmPA; NoAM
Grevus is my sorow.   Unkindness Has Killed Me.   Unknown.   MeEL
Grew in Hades.   Creation.   Maori Oral Tradition, tr. by Richard Taylor. WTO
Grey and dankish thing, A.   Theodore Weiss.   Fr. Every Second Thought.   DiPo
Grey and Green.   Arthur Symons.   Fr. At Dieppe.   FaBoPP
Grey as a guinea-fowl is the rain.   Two Kitchen Songs.   Dame Edith Sitwell.   CMoP
Grey beards wag, the bald heads nod, The.   Miniature.   Eden Phillpotts. OxBSP
Grey brick upon brick.   Dublin.   Louis MacNeice.   Fr. The Closing Album.   CIP; FaBoPP; OBTV; OxBTC
Grey Brother.   U. M. Montgomery.   BoTP
Grey Cock, or, Saw You My Father?, The.   Unknown.   ELP; ESPB; FaBoBa; OBET
Grey countries and grim empires pass away.   Morning in the North-west. Arthur Stringer.   CaP
Grey dust runs on the ground like a mouse, The.   Dust.   P. A. Ropes. BoTP
Grey Eye Weeping, A.   Egan O'Rahilly, tr. fr. Irish by Frank O'Conner. AnIL; FaBoPV; OBMV
Grey-eyed King, The.   "Anna Akhmatova," tr. fr. Russian by Robert Tracy.   PBWP
Grey flies, fragile, slender-winged and slender-legged.   Evening Dance of the Grey Flies.   Patricia K. Page.   NOBC
Grey friar, The.   Cloisters.   Anthony Barnett.   VWA
Grey Frock, A.   Zinaida Hippius, tr. fr. Russian by Temira Pachmuss. PBWP
Grey Funnel Line, The.   Cyril Tawney.   OBET
Grey Galloway.   Thomas S. Cairncross.   PoSH
Grey girl who had not been singing stopped, The.   New Year's Eve. John Berryman.   LiTM
Grey goat grazed on the hill, The.   Grey Brother.   U. M. Montgomery. BoTP

Grey-green stretch of sandy grass, The.   Grey and Green.   Arthur Symons.   Fr. At Dieppe.   FaBoPP; NOBVV
Grey Hair, The.   Judah Halevi, tr. fr. Hebrew by J. Chotzner.   TrJP
Grey hills of that country fall away, The.   Cadaver Politic.   Tom Paulin. FaBCIP
"Grey Horse Troop," The.   Robert William Chambers.   PAH
Grey in the sky and blue against the trees.   Journey.   Sam Harrison. NeIP
Grey is the color of time.   Morning Song.   Charlotte DeClue. STE
Grey Linnet, The.   James McCarroll.   CaP
Grey, low ceiling, sough of sea wind along forest.   The Lairdless Place. Kate Rennie Archer.   GoYe
Grey October.   "Critics, The."   OBET
Grey Ones, The.   Louis MacNeice.   CMoP
Grey psychopath in her season, The.   Cat.   Joe Rosenblatt.   NOBC
Grey pussy-willows.   Slumber in Spring.   Elizabeth Gould.   BoTP
Grey [or Gray] sea and the long black land, The.   Meeting at Night. Robert Browning.   AWP; BoLoP; ELP; FaBV; FF; FiP; GBL; HeIP; InPS; InVP; MOS; NOBE; NOBVV; OBEV; OBNC; OPOP; OxBSP; PoRA; SCV; SeCePo; SoSe; TrGrPo; UnPo; WeW
Grey Selchie of Sule Skerry, The.   Unknown.   See Great Silkie of Sule Skerry, The.
Grey sky, grey city-smoke.   9th July, 1932.   Mary Ursula Bethell. PeNZ
Grey the sky, and growing dimmer.   Twilight.   Louisa S. Guggenberger. NOBVV
Grey was the morn, all things were grey.   A Bit of Colour.   Horace Smith.   BoTP
Grey water tanks in grey mist.   Bayonne Turnpike to Tuscarora.   Allen Ginsberg.   NNaP
Grey winter hath gone like a wearisome guest.   September in Australia. Henry Clarence Kendall.   PoAu-1
Grey Wolf, The.   Arthur Symons.   BrPo; FaBoTw
Grey Woman.   Gladys Cardiff.   CDW
Greyer than the tide below, the tower.   Homage to Jack Yeats.   Thomas MacGreevy.   OBMV
Greyhound, The.   Saleem Barakat, tr. fr. Arabic by Lena Jayyusi and Naomi Shihab Nye.   MAP
Greyhound should be headed like a snake, A.   The Properties of a Good Greyhound.   Dame Juliana Berners.   RB
Greyish bird, A.   The Mockingbird of Mockingbirds.   Denise Levertov. ER
Greyish yellow is the color of the dust.   Meir Wieseltier, tr. by Warren Bargad and Stanley F. Chyet.   IP
Greyport Legend, A.   Bret Harte.   AnAmPo; GN; MOS
Grey's River Roundup.   Howard Norskog.   CowP
Grief.   Gerrit Achterberg, tr. fr. Dutch by James Brockway.   DuIn
Grief.   Wendell Berry.   GeTw; MT
Grief.   Elizabeth Barrett Browning.   FPL; HeIP; InPK; NOBVV; OBEV; OBNC; PoLF; TrGrPo; WPE
Grief.   Salvador Díaz Mirón, tr. fr. Spanish by Samuel Beckett.   MexPo
Grief.   Unknown, tr. fr. Welsh by Aneirin Talfan Davies.   OBWVE
Grief/ o grief.   Alarum.   Urszula Koziol, tr. by Czeslaw Milosz.   PwPP; WPOW
Grief and God.   Stephen Phillips.   WGRP
Grief fills the room up of my absent child.   Shakespeare.   Fr. King John, III, iv.   OBD
Grief for her absent master in her wrought.   The Dog.   Frederick William Faber.   FM
Grief hath been known to turn the young head gray.   The Young Gray Head.   Caroline Anne Bowles Southey.   BeLS
Grief, I deny.   Grief.   Gerrit Achterberg, tr. by James Brockway. DuIn
Grief of a Girl's Heart, The.   Unknown.   See Donal Og.
Grief of Love, The.   Unknown, tr. fr. Arabic by Wilfrid Scawen Blunt. AWP
Grief Plucked Me Out of Sleep.   Jill King.   PeSA
Grief Streams Down My Chest.   Lance Jeffers.   PoBA
Griefs of Women, The.   David R. Slavitt.   BXAP
Griesly Wife, The.   John Manifold.   MoBrPo; MoBS
Grievance, A.   James Kenneth Stephen.   BXAP; FaBoPa; Par
Grievance I.   Tu Yeh, tr. fr. Chinese by Dominic Cheung.   IFON
Grieve Not, Dear Love.   John Digby.   OxBSP
Grieve Not for Beauty ("Grieve not for the invisible, transported brow"). Witter Bynner.   PoA
Grieve Not, Ladies.   Anna Hempstead Branch.   FaFP
Grieved for Buonaparté.   Wordsworth.   See I grieved for Buonaparté.
Grieving for Tatsuzo: Today Spring Ended.   Rai San'yo, tr. fr. Chinese by Burton Watson.   JLIC-2
Grieving for the Student Abe.   Michizane, tr. fr. Chinese by Burton Watson.   JLIC-1

Grieving heart can't be rolled up like a mat, A. A Piece of Rush Matting. Sung Wan, *tr. fr. Chinese* by William Schultz. *Fr.* Songs Composed in Prison, I. WFTU

Grievous folly shames my sixtieth year, A. Hafiz, *tr. fr. Persian* by Richard Le Gallienne. *Fr.* Odes, IV. AWP

"Grill me some bones," said the Cobbler. At the Keyhole. Walter de la Mare. MoAB; MoBrPo

Grim Deirdre sought the stony fist, her grief. Love. Thomas Kinsella. FaBCIP

Grim monarch! see, deprived of vital breath. To a Lady on the Death of Her Husband. Phillis Wheatley. TAP

Grimsby Fisherman, The. *Unknown.* OxBSS

Grimsby Lads, The. John Conolly *and* Bill Meek. OxBSS

Grinder, who serenely grindest. Lines on Hearing the Organ. Charles Stuart Calverley. CenHV; FaBoCo; FiBHP; NOBL

Grinders; or, The Saddle on the Right Horse, The. *Unknown.* GBP

Grinding Vibrato. Jayne Cortez. BlSi

Grinding yoke from Israel's neck he tore, The. Eulogy for Hasdai ibn Shaprut. *Unknown, tr.* by Israel Abrahams. TrJP

Grinning, the foreman asked them for a vote. In the Jury Room. Hodding Carter. MAT

Gripped by the Dread. Jacques Dupin, *tr. fr. French* by Paul Auster. RHTwFP

Griselda's dead, and so's her patience. Patient Griselda. Chaucer. *Fr.* The Canterbury Tales: The Clerk's Tale. PoRA

Grizzel Grimme. *Unknown.* FaBoEE

Grizzly. Bret Harte. AA; AnAmPo

Grizzly Bear. Mary Austin. FaPON; GoJo; OnUR; PDV

Grizzly Bear is huge and wild, The. Infant Innocence. A. E. Housman. CenHV; ChTr; FaBoCh; FaBoCo; FaBoNo; FaFP; LiTB; NOBL; OxBoLi

Groans of nature in this nether world, The. William Cowper. *Fr.* The Task, VI. NoP

"Grob! Grob," goes the raven peering from his rift. Cypress Grove. Austin Clarke. IPY

Grocery had provided him with, The. Dialog outside the Lakeside Grocery. Ishmael Reed. UL

Groggy fighter on his knees, The. Athletes. Walker Gibson. SD

Groined by deep glens and walled along the west. The Glens. John Hewitt. NeIP

Groins, for his fleshly burglary of late. Upon Groins: Epigram. Robert Herrick. CaPo

Grongar Hill ("Silent nymph, with curious eye!"), *sels.* John Dyer. *Fr.* Looking Back. ChTr; EnRP; FaBoPP; GoTL; NOEC; NoP; OBWVE; PoEL-3

    "Ever charming, ever new." SeCePo

    "O may I with myself agree." TrGrPo

Groom's Lament, The. Robert Peterson. NeAC

Groping along the tunnel, step by step. The Rear-Guard. Siegfried Sassoon. MoBrPo; NAEL-2; NoAM; OBWP; WaP

Groping back to bed after a piss. Sad Steps. Philip Larkin. NoAM; NoP

"Gross, Coarse, Hideous" (Police Description of My Pictures). D. H. Lawrence. FaBoEE

Gross innocent. Pablo Neruda, *tr. fr. Spanish.* *Fr.* Elephant. TTTS

Gross sun squats above, The. Dom Moraes. NePoEA-2

Grotesque. Amy Lowell. BoWoP

Grotesque Love-Letter, A. *Unknown.* MeEL

Grotesque, the line of trees, pronged. Outside. Phyllis Beauvais. IHMS

Grotesques, *sels.* Robert Graves. CMoP

    "Dr. Newman with the crooked pince-nez."

    "Sir John addressed the Snake-god in his temple."

Grotesques, *sel.* Don Marquis.

    "Was it fancy, sweet nurse." FiBHP

Grotto, The. Ray Fraser. NeAC

Grotto, The. Francis Scarfe. PoA

Grotto, The. Clark Stillman. SoTCo

Grouchy Good Night to the Academic Year, A. Ted Pauker. NOBL

Ground beneath my feet is cracked, The. Day Twenty-three. Victor Coleman. NOBC

Ground Birds in Open Country. Stanley Plumly. NAmP

Ground for the Floor. *Unknown.* OBET

Groundhog, The. Richard Eberhart. CMoP; FaBoMo; FaFP; LiTA; LiTM; MoAB; MoAmPo; MoP; NIP; NoAM; NoP; NU; TAP; UnPo; WaP

Groundhog, The. Luci Shaw. TrCP

Ground Hog Day. Lilian Moore. RHPC

Ground Hog Lock. Gerald Stern. AnAn

Groundhog is, at best, a simple soul, The. The Groundhog. Luci Shaw. TrCP

Ground Hog sleeps. Ground Hog Day. Lilian Moore. RHPC

Groundhog we dumped in the woods, The. Middle Age. Paula Rankin. MAYP; MT

Ground is white with snow, The. Resolution. Ted Berrigan. OFD

Ground-Squirrel Song. *Navajo Indian Oral Tradition.* TTTS

Ground-Swell, The. E. J. Pratt. CaP

Ground-Thumping Song. *Unknown, tr. fr. Chinese* by Burton Watson. CoBCP

Group of jolly cowboys, discussing plans at ease, A. When the Work's All Done This Fall. *Unknown.* AS

Group of Musings, A, *sels.* Henrietta Cordelia Ray. CBWP-3

    Noonday Thought.

    Starlight Thought.

    Sunrise Thought.

    Sunset Thought.

Group of Officials, A, *sel.* Yang Shih-ch'i, *tr. fr. Chinese* by Jonathan Chaves.

    "Beyond the temple, a hidden cliff." CoBLCP

Group of professional, A. The Physics of Ochun. Victor Hernandez Cruz. UL

Grove, The. Edwin Muir. LiTM

Grove and Building. Edgar Bowers. NePoEA

Grove beyond the Barley, The. Alden Nowlan. MoCV

Grover Cleveland. Joel Benton. PAH

Groves are down, The. Gary Snyder. *Fr.* Myths and Texts: Logging, XIV. NaP

Groves of Blarney, The. Richard Alfred Millikin. FaBoPP; OxBoLi

Groves of Eden, vanished now so long, The. Pope. *Fr.* Windsor Forest. OAEL-1

Groves were God's first temples, The. A Forest Hymn. Bryant. AA; TAP

Grow old along with me! Robert Browning. *Fr.* Rabbi Ben Ezra. BLPL; FaBV; FaFP; FiP; NAEL-2; OBNC; TEP; WGRP

Grow weary if you will, let me be sad. Lesbia. Richard Aldington. PoLF

Growing Dark. James Schuyler. GLP

Growing gray by a gate. Ten Groschen. Aaron Zeitlin, *tr.* by Robert Friend. PeBMYV

Growing in Grace. Jack R. Clemo. NOCV

Growing Old. Matthew Arnold. FaFP; FiP; NAEL-2; NOBVV; OAEL-2; PoEL-5

Growing Old. Douglas Fraser. PoSH

Growing Old. Rose Henderson. RHPC

Growing Old. *Unknown, tr. fr. Irish* by Frank O'Connor. ErPo

Growing Old [*or* Growing Older]. Rollin J. Wells. BLPA; WBLP

Growing old. Byron. *Fr.* Don Juan, I. NOBE; SCV

Growing Rhyme, A. J. M. Westrup. BoTP

Growing River, The. Rodney Bennett. BoTP

Growing Smiles. *Unknown.* PoLF

Growing Together. Joyce Carol Oates. IHMS

Growing Up. Harry Behn. PDV; RHPC

Growing Up. U. A. Fanthorpe. AIW

Growing Up. Linda Gregg. NPGG

Growing Up. Tanikawa Shuntaro, *tr. fr. Japanese* by Geoffrey Bownas *and* Anthony Thwaite. PeBJV

Growltiger's Last Stand. T. S. Eliot. FaBoCh; OBCA

Grown and Flown. Christina Rossetti. NOBVV

Grown Old and Full of Years. Tsfrirah Gar, *tr. fr. Hebrew* by Bernhard Frank. MHeP

Grown old in love from seven till seven times seven. Blake. FaBoEE; OAEL-2

Grown over with straggly saw grass. Sanetomo, *tr. fr. Japanese* by Burton Watson. *Fr.* Twenty-four Tanka. FCEI

Grown sick of war, and war's alarms. On the British King's Speech. Philip Freneau. PAH

Grown-up. Edna St. Vincent Millay. NoAM

Grown up under the sun. The Axes Rust. Jan G. Elburg, *tr.* by Koos Schuur. DuIn

Growth can sit there from. Regenesis. Ron Welburn. NBP

Growth of Heptarchy we trace, The. Edward B. Goodwin. *Fr.* English History in Rhyme, or a Rhyming Epitome of the History of England, from B.C. 55 to A.D. 1872. FaBoUs

Growth of Love, The, *sels.* Robert Bridges.

    "Man that sees by chance his picture, made, A." *Fr.* XXXIX. NoAM

    My Lady Pleases Me. *Fr.* XXX. Son

    O Weary Pilgrims. *Fr.* XXIII. MoAB; MoBrPo

    "They that in play can do the thing they would." *Fr.* I. NoAM

    Whole World Now, The. *Fr.* III. Son

Gr-r-r—there go, my heart's abhorrence!　Soliloquy of the Spanish Cloister.　Robert Browning.　FaBoCo; InPK; LiTB; NAEL-2; NIP; NOBL; NOBVV; NoP; OAEL-2; TEP; TOF; TrGrPo; TW

Grudges mend and wear and turn in winter.　Household.　Laura Jensen.　LCAP

Gruesome.　Roger McGough.　AmMo

Gruesome ghoul, the grisly ghoul, The.　The Ghoul.　Jack Prelutsky.　OBCA

Grumble Family, The.　*Unknown*.　PWR; WBLP

Grunion.　Myra Cohn Livingston.　RFM

Grunion.　Wendy Rose.　CDW

Gryll/ Had his fill.　Gryll's State.　Roy Blount, Jr..　OBAL

Gryll Grange, *sel*.　Thomas Love Peacock.
　　Love and Age.　NOBVV; OBEV; OBNC

Gryll's State.　Roy Blount, Jr.　OBAL

Guadalajara Hospital.　Ai.　MAYP

Guadalupe, W.I.　Nicolás Guillén, *tr. fr. Spanish by* Anselm Hollo.　TTY

Guard.　Michael C. Martin.　WaP

Guard, 8, The.　Lyn Hejinian.　LP

Guard at the Binh Thuy Bridge, The.　John Balaban.　FYAP

Guard has a right to despair, The.　He stands by God.　In Galleries.　Randall Jarrell.　EyDe

Guard of the Sepulcher, A.　Edwin Markham.　WGRP

Guarded Wound, The.　Adelaide Crapsey.　WPE

Guardian Angel, The.　Michael Guttenbrunner, *tr. fr. German by* Beth Bjorklund.　CoAuP

Guardian Angel, The.　Amable Tastu, *tr. fr. French by* Beth Archer.　DMF

Guardian Angels.　Spenser.　*See* Faerie Queene, The: And is there care in heaven? and is there love.

Guardians, The.　Geoffrey Hill.　NePoEA-2; NoP

Guarding the doors of the Hispanic Society.　The Spanish Lions.　Phyllis McGinley.　NYBP

Guards arrive in carts, The.　The Final Arrangement.　Michael Harlow.　ATNZ

Guards of the Heart, *sel*.　Joe Ross.
　　"Years, bring little pain, yet they add, The."　*Fr*. I, ii.　BAP

Guatemala, with your *huipil*.　*Guatemalan Huipil*.　Rafael Sosa, *tr. by* Magaly Fernández.　Vol

Guatemalan *Huipil*.　Rafael Sosa, *tr. fr. Spanish by* Magaly Fernández.　Vol

Gubbinal.　Wallace Stevens.　NAAL-2; SOTW

Gude and Godlie Ballatis, The, *sel*.　*Unknown*.
　　Till Christ ("Till Christ, quhome I am haldin for to lufe").　OxBS

Gude Lord Graeme is to Carlisle gane.　The Bewick and the Graeme.　*Unknown*.　OxBB

Gude Lord Scroop's to the huntin gane.　Hughie Grame.　*Unknown*.　ESPB

Gude Wallace.　*Unknown*.　ESPB

Gudrun Laments over Sigurd.　*Unknown, tr. fr. Old Norse by* William Morris *and* Eirikr Magnusson.　*Fr*. The Elder Edda: The First Lay of Gudrun.　OBVE

Gudrun of old days.　The First Lay of Gudrun.　*Unknown, tr. fr. Old Norse by* William Morris *and* Eirikr Magnusson.　*Fr*. The Elder Edda.　AWP

Gudveig.　Francis Berry.　OBTV

Guerdon, The.　John James Piatt.　AA

Guerrilla.　Cosmo Pieterse.　WMBCH

Guerrillas.　Roger McTair.　PBCV

Guerrilla, The.　*Unknown, tr. by* Philippa Rumsey.　WMBCH

Guerrilla Handbook, A.　Imamu Amiri Baraka.　PoBA

Guerrilla Promise.　Mvula Ya Nangolo.　WMBCH

Guerrilla's Goodbye, A.　Javier Heraud, *tr. fr. Spanish by* Maureen Ahern.　Per

Guerrilla's Word, A.　Javier Heraud, *tr. fr. Spanish by* Maureen Ahern.　Per

Guess Who.　Fred Chappell.　NBLV

Guess Who!　Sista Roots.　WS

Guess who is this creature.　A Song to the Wind.　Taliesin, *tr. by* A. P. Graves.　FaBoCh

Guessed you but how I loved you, watched your smile.　To W. J. M. "G. G."　PeHV

Guessing.　*Unknown, tr. fr. Burmese by* U Win Pe.　PBWP

Guest.　D. J. Enright.　Mes; OxBC

Guest, The.　Harriet McEwen Kimball.　AA

Guest.　E. A. Lacey.　PeHV

Guest, The.　*Unknown. See* Yet if his majesty, our sovereign [*or* sovereign] Lord.

Guest, a guest, A/ And white his horse.　*Unknown, tr. by* Arthur Waley.　BoS

Guest Arrives, A.　Tu Fu, *tr. fr. Chinese by* Burton Watson.　CoBCP

Guest leaves; the window gleams in the twilight, A.　Written on the Wall of Ku Tzu-p'eng's Studio.　Cheng Hsiao-hsü, *tr. by* Irving Lo.　WFTU

Guests, The.　Franco Fortini, *tr. fr. Italian by* Lawrence R. Smith.　NItP

Guests are taking their seats, The.　*Unknown, tr. by* Arthur Waley.　BoS

Gui d'Ussel, because of you I'm quite distraught.　Marie de Ventadour, *tr. by* Meg Bogin.　WT

Gui d'Ussel, it disturbs me.　Dialogue.　Marie de Ventadour, *tr. by* Joan M. Ferrante.　DMF

Guid day now, bonnie Robin.　Robin Redbreast's Testament.　*Unknown*.　GBP

Guid-Mornin to Your Majesty!　Burns.　*Fr*. A Dream.　NAs

Guide and Friend.　*Unknown*.　BLRP

Guide Me, O Thou Great Jehovah.　William Williams.　OBWVE
　　(Christian Pilgrim's Hymn, The.)　WGRP
　　(Divine Hand, The.)　BLRP

Guide to Familiar American Incest, A, *sel*.　Dennis Saleh.
　　Inventing a Family.　NeAC

Guide to Jerusalem.　Dennis Silk.　VWA

Guide to Patrons, A.　Alattur Killar, *tr. fr. Tamil by* A. K. Ramanujan.　PLW

Guide to Perfection, A.　Kevin Ireland.　ATNZ

Guide to the Ruins.　Howard Nemerov.　EyDe

Guide to the Symphony.　Weldon Kees.　VGW

Guided by/ The tightening, sighing wind.　Night Flute.　Fei Ma, *tr. by* Dominic Cheung.　IFON

Guided Missiles Experimental Range.　Robert Conquest.　OxBC

Guides ask for silence, and have.　Waitomo.　Kendrick Smithyman.　ATNZ

Guides urged us, praised us up to the Lion Gate, its.　Remembering Mykenai.　Alfred Corn.　SM

Guido, I wish that you and Lapo and I.　Dante, *tr. by* Kenneth Koch.　RB; TTTS

Guido, I would that Lapo, thou, and I.　Sonnet: To Guido Cavalcanti.　Dante, *tr. by* Shelley.　AWP
　　(Sonnet: Dante Alighieri to Guido Cavalcanti.)　OBVE
　　(To Guido Cavalcanti.)　PFI

Guilielmus Rex.　Thomas Bailey Aldrich.　AA; AnAmPo

Guillaume Apollinaire/ Didn't care.　Margaret Blaker.　SoTCo

Guillotine is the masterpiece of plastic art, The.　The Head.　Blaise Cendrars, *tr. by* Ron Padgett.　RHTwFP

Guilt.　Lorenzo Thomas.　UL

Guilt and Sorrow, *sel*.　Wordsworth.
　　Salisbury Plain and Stonehenge.　FaBoPP

Guilt, Desire and Love.　James Baldwin.　GLP

Guilt unavowed is guilt in its extreme.　Error Pursued.　H. A. Pinkerton.　QFR

Guilty Even if I Were Innocent.　Buland al-Haidari, *tr. fr. Arabic by* Abdullah al-Udhari.　MPAW

Guilty Man.　Uuno Kailas, *tr. fr. Finnish by* Aili Jarvenpa.　SOP

"Guilty or Not Guilty?"　*Unknown*.　BeLS; BLPA

Guinea.　Jacques Roumain, *tr. fr. French by* Langston Hughes.　TTY

Guinea Corn.　*Unknown*.　PBCV

Guinea-Pig, The.　*Unknown*.　NA

Guise and disguise, the mirroring and masquerades.　Venice Revisited.　Amy Clampitt.　ER

Guita Bruner.　Pablo Guevara, *tr. fr. Spanish by* Maureen Ahern *and* David Tipton.　Per

Guitar.　Federico García Lorca, *tr. fr. Spanish by* Keith Waldrop.　InPK

Guitar.　David St. John.　MAYP

Guitar, The/ makes dreams cry.　The Six Strings.　Federico García Lorca, *tr. by* Donald Hall.　RB

Guitarist Tunes Up, The.　Frances Cornford.　SoSe

Gulbeyaz.　Byron.　*Fr*. Don Juan, V.　PoEL-4

Gulf, The.　Denise Levertov.　NNaP

Gulf, The.　Derek Walcott.　NoP

Gulf Stream.　"Susan Coolidge."　AA

Gulfs of blue air, two lochs like spectacles.　High Up on Suilven.　Norman MacCaig.　PoSH

Gulistan, The, *sels*.　Sadi, *tr. fr. Persian*.
　　Alas!　*Tr. by* L. Cranmer-Byng.　AWP
　　Courage.　*Tr. by* Sir Edwin Arnold.　AWP
　　Friendship.　*Tr. by* L. Cranmer-Byng.　AWP
　　Gift of Speech, The.　*Tr. by* L. Cranmer-Byng.　AWP
　　He Hath No Parallel.　*Tr. by* L. Cranmer-Byng.　AWP
　　Help.　*Tr. by* Sir Edwin Arnold.　AWP
　　Hyacinths to Feed Thy Soul.　BLPA; BLPL; FaBoBe
　　Love's Last Resource.　*Tr. by* L. Cranmer-Byng.　AWP
　　Mesnevi.　*Tr. by* L. Cranmer-Byng.　AWP
　　On the Deception of Appearances.　*Tr. by* L. Cranmer-Byng.　AWP

Sooth-Sayer, The. *Tr. by* Sir Edwin Arnold. AWP
Take the Crust. *Tr. by* L. Cranmer-Byng. AWP
Wealth. *Tr. by* Sir Edwin Arnold. AWP
Gull-haunted,/ the windblown shore of Susaki. Sanetomo, *tr. fr. Japanese by* Burton Watson. *Fr.* Twenty-four Tanka. FCEI
Gull is whispering to the anchor's ear, A. Sad Parting. Maruyama Kaoru, *tr. by* Hiroaki Sato. FCEI
Gull, it is said, The. Nakasuk. WTO
Gull Lake set in the rolling prairie. At Gull Lake; August, 1810. Duncan Campbell Scott. NOBC; OBCV
Gull, up close, A. Seagulls. John Updike. Psk
Gullfish. Tom Weatherly. *Fr.* Cantos, 4. PoBA
Gulling Sonnets, The, *sels.* Sir John Davies. Son
    "As when the bright cerulean firmament."
    "Hardness of her heart and truth of mine, The."
    "Into the middle temple of my heart."
    "Lover, under burthen of his mistress' love, The." EIL
    "Mine eye, mine ear, my will, my wit, my heart."
    "My case is this."
    "Sacred muse that first made love divine, The."
    To His Good Friend, Sir Anthony Cooke.
    "To love, My Lord, I do knight's service owe."
    "What eagle can behold her sunbright eye."
Gulliver. Sylvia Plath. NOBA
Gulliver by then perceived. Himalaya Days. Gyorgy Raba, *tr. by* Jascha Kessler. FOC
Gulls. William Carlos Williams. NoP; OxBA
Gulls and Dreams. Lionel Stevenson. CaP
Gulls in an äery morrice. W. E. Henley. PBBP
Gulls sprinted for harbour. Underwater Pieces. Kendrick Smithyman. ATNZ
Gulping air, two of them. Why Don't They Go Back to Transylvania? Robert Peters. VVA
Gum, oats and syrup. Levant. Lawrence Durrell. OBTV
Gumble. Michael Dugan. RHPC
Gun, The. Stephen Dobyns. AnAn
Gun Base. Maruyama Kaoru, *tr. fr. Japanese by* Hiroaki Sato. FCEI
Gun Emplacement. Maruyama Kaoru, *tr. fr. Japanese by* Geoffrey Bownas *and* Anthony Thwaite. PeBJV
Gun explodes them, The. The Sprinters. Lee Murchison. SD
Gun full swing the swimmer catapults and cracks, The. 400-Meter Freestyle. Maxine W. Kumin. ASP; SD; SoSe; TSL
Gun, glinting, deep snow, A. Ozaki Hosai, *tr. fr. Japanese by* Hiroaki Sato. *Fr.* One Hundred Haiku in Free Form. FCEI
Gun-metal is somehow cool even in this heat. On Duty. Frederick D'Aguiar. PBCV
Gun Teams. Gilbert Frankau. OxBTC
Gun, the trap, the axe are borne, The. Revenge of the Hunted. Robert Arthur Douglas Ford. MoCV
Gunclick/ hopesfears/ lovehate. Las' Rights. Brian Meeks. PBCV
Gunfighter, The. Alistair Campbell. ATNZ
Gunga. Rachel Field. *Fr.* A Circus Garland. OBCA
Gunga Din. Kipling. BrPo; EBVV; FaFP; FPL; LiTB; MoBrPo; OBTV; OnMSP
Gunnar's Howe above the House at Lithend. William Morris. OBTV
Gunner. Randall Jarrell. OFD
Gunner, The. Francis Webb. CBAP
Gunpowder Plot, The. *Unknown.* FaBoUs
Gunpowder Plot Day. *Unknown.* FaBoPV; OxNR
Guns. Sa'di Yusuf, *tr. fr. Arabic by* Abdullah al-Udhari. MPAW
Guns are hushed, The. On every field once flowing. The Rear Guard. Irene Fowler Brown. PAH
Guns blazing. *Unknown, tr. by* Geoffrey Bownas *and* Anthony Thwaite. PeBJV
Guns in the Grass, The. Thomas Frost. PAH
Guns know what is what, but underneath, The. Memories of a Lost War. Louis Simpson. OBWP; VGW
Guns roar at dawn, The. Guns. Sa'di Yusuf, *tr. by* Abdullah al-Udhari. MPAW
Guns spell money's ultimate reason, The. Ultima Ratio Regum. Stephen Spender. CMoP; FaFP; LiTB; LiTM; OAEL-2; OBWP; SeCePo; WaaP; WaP
Gunslinger, *sel.* Edward Dorn.
    Idle Visitation, An. NOBA
Gup, Scot! John Skelton. OxBoLi
Gurgling waters foam and play, The. On the rapids of the St. Lawrence. Henrietta Cordelia Ray. CBWP-3
Guru is the stepping stone, The. Nanak, *tr. by* John Stratton Hawley *and* Mark Juergensmeyer. SSI
Gus the Greek is a short-order cook. Greasy Spoon Blues. Len Gasparini. NeAC

Gus: The Theatre Cat. T. S. Eliot. CenHV; OBCA; OxBTC
Gustavo said. What the Rooster Does before Mounting. Cyn Zarco. BrSi; UL
Gusts of the sun race on the approaching sea. Of Thomas Traherne and the Pebble Outside. Sydney Clouts. VWA
Gusty and raw was the morning, a fog hung over the seas. The Fight of Paso del Mar. Bayard Taylor. BeLS
Gut eats all day, and lechers all the night. On Gut. Ben Jonson. JCP; NoP
Guthlac, *sel.* Cynewulf, *tr. fr. Anglo-Saxon.*
    Death of Saint Guthlac. ACP
Gutter, The. Franco Fortini, *tr. fr. Italian by* Ruth Feldman. VWA
Guttural Muse, The. Seamus Heaney. NOIV; NoP
"Guv!" means "Sir!" and "Luv!" On Listening to a Bus Conductor. Anne Bloch. Mes
Guvener B. is a sensible man. What Mr. Robinson Thinks. James Russell Lowell. *Fr.* The Biglow Papers: 1st Series, No. III. AA; AmPP; PAH
Guy. Emerson. NOBA
Guy asked me, The. Ever Notice How It Is with Women? Margaret Randall. AIW
Guy Fawkes '58. Fiona Kidman. PeNZ
Guy Mannering, *sels.* Sir Walter Scott.
    Nativity Chant, The. ChTr; FaBoCh; NAs
    Twist Ye, Twine Ye! Even So. *Fr. ch.* 4. EnRP
    Wasted, Weary, Wherefore Stay. *Fr. ch.* 27. EnRP
Guyana not Ghana. Marc Matthews. PBCV
Guys and Dolls. Frank Loesser. OBAL
Guys of the Volye, *sels.* Berysh Vaynshteyn, *tr. fr. Yiddish by* Benjamin *and* Barbara Harshav. AYP
    "Chilly walls with sharp steel hooks."
    Dogs of Dawn.
Gwan! Gwan! Cry the Fish Hawks. *Unknown, tr. fr. Chinese by* Burton Watson. CoBCP
G'way an' quit dat noise, Miss Lucy. When Malindy Sings. Paul Laurence Dunbar. PoBA; PoNe
Gwendoline. Bayard Taylor. BXAP
Gwine find a beauty shop. Kinky Hair Blues. Una Marson. PBCV
Gwine to Run All Night; or, De Camptown Races. Stephen Collins Foster. *See* Camptown Races, The.
Gwladys Rhys. W. J. Gruffydd, *tr. fr. Welsh by* Myrddin Lloyd. OBWVE
Gyang ower by Rothiemurchus whan the snaw lies thick. Rothiemurchus. Colin Lamont. PoSH
Gyges' ring they bear about them still, A. Lovers How They Come and Part. Robert Herrick. GBL; OxBoLi; OxBSP; PoEL-3
Gymnasiad, The, or Boxing Match, *sel.* Paul Whitehead.
    "As when two monarchs of the brindled breed." NOEC
Gymnasts, The. Irving Feldman. ASP
Gypsies. John Clare. *See* Snow falls deep.
Gypsies. Rachel Field. BoTP
Gypsies. John Langhorne. *Fr.* The Country Justice. NOEC
Gypsies. Alden Nowlan. NeAC
Gypsies came to our good lord's gate, The. The Gypsy Laddie. *Unknown.* ESPB, A *vers.*; HAP
Gypsies came to our Lord's yett, The. Johny Faa. *Unknown.* OxBB
Gypsies carry sacks of walnuts out of the groves, The. Coleridge Crossing the Plain of Jars; 1833. Norman Dubie. LCAP
Gypsies in the Wood. *Unknown.* BoTP; OxBoLi; OxBSP; OxNR
Gypsies Metamorphosed, The, *sels.* Ben Jonson.
    All Your Fortunes We Can Tell Ye. ChTr
    Faery Beam upon You, The. EBEV; OxBSP; TEP
    (Faeries' Song, The.) SeCV-1
    (Gipsy Song.) FaBoCh
    "To the old, long life and treasure." OxBSP
Gypsies [or Gipsies] they came to my Lord Cassilis' yett [or gate], The. The Gypsy Laddie. *Unknown.* ESPB, B *vers.*; FaBoBa
    (Johnny Faa, the Lord of Little Egypt.) EnSB
Gypsy. Josephine Miles. MoP; NoAM
Gypsy, The. Edward Thomas. HeIP; NoAM; NoP
Gypsy Bible, The. Julian Tuwim, *tr. fr. Polish by* Isaac Komem. VWA
Gypsy Countess, The. *Unknown.* OBET
Gypsy Davy, The. *Unknown.* AmFP; AS, *with music.*
Gypsy Laddie, The ("Gypsies came to our good lord's gate, The"). *Unknown.* ESPB, A *vers.*; HAP
Gypsy Laddie, The ("Gypsies they came to my lord Cassilis' yett, The"). *Unknown.* ESPB, B *vers.*; FaBoBa
Gypsy-race my pity rarely move, The. Gypsies. John Langhorne. *Fr.* The Country Justice. NOEC
Gyres, The. W. B. Yeats. GTBS-P; HAP; NoAM

Gyre's Galax. Norman Henry Pritchard II. PoBA
Gyroscope. Howard Nemerov. NoAM

H

H. O. V. de L. Milosz, *tr. fr. French by* David Gascoyne. RHTwFP
H. Baptisme. George Herbert. *See* Since, Lord, to thee.
H. M. S. *Glory* at Sidney. Charles Causley. OBTV
H. M. S. *Hero.* Michael Roberts. OxBTC
H. M. S. Pinafore, *sels. W. S. Gilbert.*
  Englishman, The. NOBL
  Sir Josephs's Song. LiTB
H-óran ó a vee-ó. A Complaint about Exile. Mairi MacLeod, *tr. by* Joan Keefe. PBWP
H. Rap Brown. Henry Blakely. CNA
H was an indigent Hen. Bruce Porter. NA
H——y P——tt. *Unknown.* CoMu
Ha! are there wood-ghosts in this solitude. La Belle Sauvage. John Hunter-Duvar. *Fr.* De Roberval. OBCV
Ha ha ha! This world doth pass. Fara Diddle Dyno. *Unknown.* EiL; FaBoCh; FaBoCo; FaBoNo
  (Madrigal: "Ha ha! ha ha! This world doth pass.") OxBoLi
Ha! Original Sin. Ogden Nash. FaBoCo; NBLV
Ha! sir, I have seen you sniffing and snoozling. The Faun. Ezra Pound. FaBoCh; FaBoTw
Ha' we lost the goodliest fere o' all. Ballad of the Goodly Fere. Ezra Pound. CMoP; LiTA; LiTM; MoAB; MoAmPo; MoBS; OFD; PoRA; TrCP; TrGrPo
Ha! whare ye gaun, ye crowlin' ferlie! To a Louse [on Seeing One on a Lady's Bonnet at Church]. Burns. BLPA; EnRP; FaFP; InvP; LiTB; NAEL-2; NOEC; OxBS; PrIm
Haarlem Heights. Arthur Guiterman. PAH
Habakkuk. Edouard Roditi. VWA
Habeas Corpus. Helen Hunt Jackson. AA; WGRP
Habeas Corpus Blues, The. NYBP
Habit. Amiq Hanafi, *tr. fr. Urdu by* Mahmood Jamal. PBMUP
Habit of Energy, The. Diane Ward. LP
Habit of Perfection, The. Gerard Manley Hopkins. ACP; BrPo; LiTB; MoAB; MoBrPo; MoP; NoAM; NoP; OBEV; OBMV; PoRA; RB; TrGrPo; UnS, *st.* 1.
Habitat, *sels.* Judith Wright. CBAP
  "Charity lotteries for dream houses, The." *Fr.* VI.
  "Furniture: humble, dependent." *Fr.* IV.
Habitation. Margaret Atwood. BoWoP; FaBoWP
Habits of the Hippopotamus. Arthur Guiterman. FaBV; FiBHP; OBCA; OnUR; RHPC
Habitué. Helen Frith Stickney. GoYe
¿Habla Usted Español? James Reiss. AmPA
Hack and Hew. Bliss Carman. CaP
Had Cowley ne'er spoke, Killigrew ne'er writ. Sir John Denham. FaBoEE
Had everyone Suum. To the Archbishop of Tuam. *Unknown.* FaBoEE
Had Gadyaa Kid, a Kid. *Unknown, tr. fr. Hebrew.* TrJP
"Had he and I but met." The Man He Killed. Thomas Hardy. BrPo; CMoP; DL; FaFP; FF; HAP; HeIP; LiTB; LiTM; MoAB; MoBrPo; NIP; OBWP; RB; WaaP; WeW
Had he been at home, he would have slept. Prince Shotoku, *tr. fr. Japanese. Fr.* Manyo Shu. Ma
Had I an inn at Bethlehem. Lineage. Robert Farren. TIRV
Had I been mindful of my high descent. Hadewijch, *tr. by* Frans van Rosevelt. PBWP
Had I but plenty of money, money enough and to spare. Up at a Villa—Down in the City. Robert Browning. FaBoPP; GTBS-P; INPS; NOBE; OBTV; PoRA; PPP
Had I but strength enough, and time. Charles Robinson. BXAP
Had I but the torrent's might. The Death of Hoel. Thomas Gray. NOEC
Had I concealed my love. Elinor Wylie. BLPL
Had I expected this? Teika, *tr. fr. Japanese by* Hiroaki Sato. *Fr.* A Compendium of Good Tanka. FCEI
Had I foreknown my sweet lord's coming. *Unknown, tr. fr. Japanese. Fr.* Manyo Shu. Ma
Had I heard my father mention. Never in My Life. Walter McDonald. MT
Had I lived till now. Poem for the Year Twenty Twenty. Al Lee. AmPA
Had I my wish I would distend my guts. The Extravagant Drunkard's Wish. Edward Ward. NOEC

Had I not cradled you in my arms. Pocahontas to Her English Husband, John Rolfe. Paula Gunn Allen. STE
Had I not seen him by a swerve of eye. Heron in Swamp. Frances Minturn Howard. GoYe
Had I the Choice. Walt Whitman. SoSe
Had I the heavens' embroidered cloths. Aedh Wishes for the Cloths of Heaven. W. B. Yeats. MoBrPo; NoAM; OBEV
  (He Wishes for the Cloths of Heaven.) CMoP; NOBVV; SOTW
Had I the power/ To cast a bell. A Bell. Clinton Scollard. AA
Had I the power. The Queen's Song. James Elroy Flecker. BrPo
Had I the wings of a bird. Thoughts. Maggie Pogue Johnson. CBWP-4
Had Lucan hid the truth to please the time. To the Translator of Lucan's Pharsalia (1614). Sir Walter Raleigh. SiPS
Had me a cat, the cat pleased me. Fiddle-I-Fee. *Unknown.* AmFP
Had mournful Ovid been to Brent condemned. William Diaper. *Fr.* Brent; a Poem to Thomas Palmer Esq. OBSV
Had my soul tottered off to sleep. Wondrous the Merge. James Richard Broughton. GLP
Had not there been the man. Wakamiya Ayumaro, *tr. fr. Japanese. Fr.* Manyo Shu. Ma
Had one sharp pebble skinned the toes. Accidents. Alfred Dorn. SoTCo
Had Sacharissa liv'd when Mortals made. At Penshurst [Another]. Edmund Waller. OAEL-1; SeCV-1
Had she come all the way for this. The Haystack in the Floods. William Morris. BeLS; EBEV; EBVV; HAP; NAEL-2; NoP; OAEL-2; OBNC; OBNV; PoEL-5; PoRA; WeW
Had Sorrow Ever Fitter Place. Samuel Daniel. *Fr.* Hymen's Triumph. EiL
  (Sorrow.) OBSC
Had the Marquis de Sade but been born. The Fine Divine Marquis. Gust Gils, *tr. by* James S. Holmes. DuIn
Had there been falsehood in my breast. Emily Brontë. NOBVV
Had there been peace there never had been riven. Drummond Allison. FaBoTw
Had this effulgence disappeared. Composed upon an Evening of Extraordinary Splendour and Beauty. Wordsworth. EnRP; OAEL-2
"Had we a king," said Wallace then. Gude Wallace. *Unknown.* ESPB
Had we but world enough, and time. To His Coy Mistress. Andrew Marvell. AWP; BoLoP; EBEV; ELP; EnLoPo; ErPo; FaBV; FaFP; FF; FPL; GBL; HAP; HeIP; HoPM; InPK; InPS; InvP; JCP; LiTB; MAT; MeLP; MePo; NAEL-1; NIP; NOBE; NoP; OAEL-1; OBD; OBEV; OBS; OPOP; PoE; PoEL-2; PoLF; PoRA; PPP; PrIm; SCV; SeCePo; SeCP
Had we but world enough, and time. To His Coy Mistress. Stanley J. Sharpless. BXAP
Had we but world enough, and time. To His Importunate Mistress. Peter De Vries. NBLV
Had we foreknown. Princess Nukada, *tr. fr. Japanese. Fr.* Manyo Shu. Ma
Had We Two Met. Walter Savage Landor. FaBoEE; OxBSP
Hadad, *sel.* James Abraham Hillhouse.
  Demon-Lover, The. AA
Hades and Euclid. Harry Martinson, *tr. fr. Swedish by* Robert Bly. BWV
Hadn't heard of the atom bomb. The Seals in Penobscot Bay. Daniel Hoffman. TwCP
Hadrian's Address to His Soul When Dying. Emperor Hadrian, *tr. fr. Latin by* Byron. OBVE
"Ah! gentle, fleeting, wav'ring sprite," *sel.* OBD
Hadrian's Lane. Ray DiPalma. LP
Hae ye ivver been at Elsdon? At Elsdon. George Chatt. FaBoPP
Hae ye smelt the tang o heather. Wine o Living. Matt Marshall. PoSH
Haemorrhage. Padraic Fiacc. CIP
Haere Ra. James Keir Baxter. PeNZ
Hag, The ("The hag is astride"). Robert Herrick. CaPo; FaBoCh; WiR; WSC
Hag and the Slavies, The. Jean de la Fontaine, *tr. fr. French by* Edward Marsh. AWP; OBVE
Hag is astride, The. The Hag. Robert Herrick. CaPo; FaBoCh; WiR; WSC
Hag of Beare, The. *Unknown, tr. fr. Irish.* BIrV, *tr. by* John Montague; NOIV, *tr. by* Thomas Kinsella; OBVE, *tr. by* Lady August Gregory; PBWP, *tr. by* John Montague
Hag-ridden. Robert Graves. BIrV

Hagar. Francis Lauderdale Adams. OxBS
Hagar. Elisabeth Eybers, *tr. fr. Afrikaans by the author*. PeSA
Hagar and Ishmael. Else Lasker-Schüler, *tr. fr. German*. BoWoP, *tr. by* Rosemarie Waldrop; VWA, *tr. by* Joachim Neugroschel.
Hagar Leaves Abraham's House. Itzig Manger, *tr. fr. Yiddish by* Leonard Wolf. PeBMYV
Hagar to Ishmael. Deborah Eibel. VWA
Haggadah. Abraham M. Klein. TrJP
Hai. Stuart Z. Perkoff. VWA
Hai! daughter of the Thundercloud. Dance-Song of the Lightning. *Unknown*. PeSA
Haidée. Byron. *Fr.* Don Juan, IV. SeCePo
Haidée and Don Juan. Byron. *Fr.* Don Juan, II. OBNC
Haifa. Dovid Knut, *tr. fr. Russian by* Daniel Weissbort. VWA
Haiku: "Above her sash." Iida Dakotsu, *tr. by* Geoffrey Bownas *and* Anthony Thwaite. PeBJV
Haiku: "Above the treetops." Masaoka Shiki, *tr. fr. Japanese by* Burton Watson. *Fr.* Thirty-nine Haiku. FCEI
Haiku: "Accent back home, The." *Unknown*, *tr. by* Geoffrey Bownas *and* Anthony Thwaite. PeBJV
Haiku: After I'm Dead. Masaoka Shiki, *tr. fr. Japanese by* Burton Watson. *Fr.* Thirty-nine Haiku. FCEI
Haiku: "After scolding my wife." Ozaki Hosai, *tr. fr. Japanese by* Hiroaki Sato. *Fr.* One Hundred Haiku in Free Form. FCEI
Haiku: "Again and again." Masaoka Shiki, *tr. by* Geoffrey Bownas *and* Anthony Thwaite. PeBJV
Haiku: "Against the broad sky." Takahama Kyoshi, *tr. by* Geoffrey Bownas *and* Anthony Thwaite. PeBJV
Haiku: "Airing books." Masaoka Shiki, *tr. fr. Japanese by* Burton Watson. *Fr.* Thirty-nine Haiku. FCEI
Haiku: "All its advertisements." *Unknown*, *tr. by* Geoffrey Bownas *and* Anthony Thwaite. PeBJV
Haiku: "Already dawn, before the Buddha's altar." Ozaki Hosai, *tr. fr. Japanese by* Hiroaki Sato. *Fr.* One Hundred Haiku in Free Form. FCEI
Haiku: "Already winter." Nakamura Kusadao, *tr. by* Geoffrey Bownas *and* Anthony Thwaite. PeBJV
Haiku: "Althea nodding all day, it has darkened." Ozaki Hosai, *tr. fr. Japanese by* Hiroaki Sato. *Fr.* One Hundred Haiku in Free Form. FCEI
Haiku: "Always someone resting there." Masaoka Shiki, *tr. fr. Japanese by* Burton Watson. *Fr.* Thirty-nine Haiku. FCEI
Haiku: "Ants stopped coming." Ozaki Hosai, *tr. fr. Japanese by* Hiroaki Sato. *Fr.* One Hundred Haiku in Free Form. FCEI
Haiku: "As bad as a dyer's." *Unknown*, *tr. by* Geoffrey Bownas *and* Anthony Thwaite. PeBJV
Haiku: "As if the first time." Ernst David, *tr. by* Beth Bjorklund. CoAuP
Haiku: "As the bat flies." Masaoka Shiki, *tr. by* Geoffrey Bownas *and* Anthony Thwaite. PeBJV
Haiku: "At the shouts and cheers." *Unknown*, *tr. by* Geoffrey Bownas *and* Anthony Thwaite. PeBJV
Haiku: "August heat." Gerald Vizenor. VoR
Haiku: "Autumn storm dying, The." Hara Sekitei, *tr. by* Geoffrey Bownas *and* Anthony Thwaite. PeBJV
Haiku: "Autumn wind:/ Everything I see." Takahama Kyoshi, *tr. by* Geoffrey Bownas *and* Anthony Thwaite. PeBJV
Haiku: "Autumn wind:/ Eyes distended." Watanabe Suiha, *tr. by* Geoffrey Bownas *and* Anthony Thwaite. PeBJV
Haiku: "Autumn wind—/ I open out." Kato Shuson, *tr. by* Geoffrey Bownas *and* Anthony Thwaite. PeBJV
Haiku: "Autumn's bright moon." Kaga no Chiyo, *tr. by* R. H. Blyth. PBWP
Haiku: "Before the/ red blossoms." Masaoka Shiki, *tr. fr. Japanese by* Burton Watson. *Fr.* Fifteen Haiku. FCEI
Haiku: "Big pine's darkening, The." Ozaki Hosai, *tr. fr. Japanese by* Hiroaki Sato. *Fr.* One Hundred Haiku in Free Form. FCEI
Haiku: "Biting hard pears, arguing." Ozaki Hosai, *tr. fr. Japanese by* Hiroaki Sato. *Fr.* One Hundred Haiku in Free Form. FCEI
Haiku: "Blowing the evening sun." Ozaki Hosai, *tr. fr. Japanese by* Hiroaki Sato. *Fr.* One Hundred Haiku in Free Form. FCEI
Haiku: "Bright moonlight." Kawabata Bosha, *tr. by* Geoffrey Bownas *and* Anthony Thwaite. PeBJV
Haiku: "Carp pennant, The." *Unknown*, *tr. by* Geoffrey Bownas *and* Anthony Thwaite. PeBJV
Haiku: "Carrying fresh water with both hands." Ozaki Hosai, *tr. fr. Japanese by* Hiroaki Sato. *Fr.* One Hundred Haiku in Free Form. FCEI
Haiku: "Carved into Buddha's form." Ozaki Hosai, *tr. fr. Japanese by* Hiroaki Sato. *Fr.* One Hundred Haiku in Free Form. FCEI

Haiku: "Children are shouting." Ozaki Hosai, *tr. fr. Japanese by* Hiroaki Sato. *Fr.* One Hundred Haiku in Free Form. FCEI
Haiku: "Chrysanthemums have all withered." Ozaki Hosai, *tr. fr. Japanese by* Hiroaki Sato. *Fr.* One Hundred Haiku in Free Form. FCEI
Haiku: "Cicadas shrieking." Matsumoto Takashi, *tr. by* Geoffrey Bownas *and* Anthony Thwaite. PeBJV
Haiku: "Cigarette is dead, The." Ozaki Hosai, *tr. fr. Japanese by* Hiroaki Sato. *Fr.* One Hundred Haiku in Free Form. FCEI
Haiku: "Clipped the nails, the fingers." Ozaki Hosai, *tr. fr. Japanese by* Hiroaki Sato. *Fr.* One Hundred Haiku in Free Form. FCEI
Haiku: "Clods of earth." Naito Meisetsu, *tr. by* Geoffrey Bownas *and* Anthony Thwaite. PeBJV
Haiku: "Clog with a broken thong." Masaoka Shiki, *tr. fr. Japanese by* Burton Watson. *Fr.* Thirty-nine Haiku. FCEI
Haiku: "Cold spring day." Kawahigashi Hekigoto, *tr. by* Geoffrey Bownas *and* Anthony Thwaite. PeBJV
Haiku: "Country road—/ boys whacking at a snake." Masaoka Shiki, *tr. fr. Japanese by* Burton Watson. *Fr.* Thirty-nine Haiku. FCEI
Haiku: "Cricket singing, A." Masaoka Shiki, *tr. fr. Japanese by* Burton Watson. *Fr.* Thirty-nine Haiku. FCEI
Haiku: "Crickets/ in the corner of the garden." Masaoka Shiki, *tr. fr. Japanese by* Burton Watson. *Fr.* Thirty-nine Haiku. FCEI
Haiku: "Crow wordlessly flew away, A." Ozaki Hosai, *tr. fr. Japanese by* Hiroaki Sato. *Fr.* One Hundred Haiku in Free Form. FCEI
Haiku: "Daily routine." Masaoka Shiki, *tr. fr. Japanese by* Burton Watson. *Fr.* Thirty-nine Haiku. FCEI
Haiku: "Daybreak, big waves, the clear sky." Ozaki Hosai, *tr. fr. Japanese by* Hiroaki Sato. *Fr.* One Hundred Haiku in Free Form. FCEI
Haiku: "Dead fly husk." Ishida Hakyo, *tr. by* Geoffrey Bownas *and* Anthony Thwaite. PeBJV
Haiku: "Dead squid, A." Masaoka Shiki, *tr. fr. Japanese by* Burton Watson. *Fr.* Thirty-nine Haiku. FCEI
Haiku: "Dew of the rouge-flower, The." Kaga no Chiyo, *tr. by* R. H. Blyth. PBWP
Haiku: "Doll as well, A." *Unknown*, *tr. by* Geoffrey Bownas *and* Anthony Thwaite. PeBJV
Haiku: "Dragging across." Iida Dakotsu, *tr. by* Geoffrey Bownas *and* Anthony Thwaite. PeBJV
Haiku: "Driving huge bulls up the hill." Ozaki Hosai, *tr. fr. Japanese by* Hiroaki Sato. *Fr.* One Hundred Haiku in Free Form. FCEI
Haiku: "Early morning road, a dog, An." Ozaki Hosai, *tr. fr. Japanese by* Hiroaki Sato. *Fr.* One Hundred Haiku in Free Form. FCEI
Haiku: "Early winter." Naito Meisetsu, *tr. by* Geoffrey Bownas *and* Anthony Thwaite. PeBJV
Haiku: "Eastern guard tower." Etheridge Knight. BPo; MoP; NeAC; SM; TAP
Haiku: "Emptying the boat, they all climbed up." Ozaki Hosai, *tr. fr. Japanese by* Hiroaki Sato. *Fr.* One Hundred Haiku in Free Form. FCEI
Haiku: "European food." *Unknown*, *tr. by* Geoffrey Bownas *and* Anthony Thwaite. PeBJV
Haiku: "Every Sunday." *Unknown*, *tr. by* Geoffrey Bownas *and* Anthony Thwaite. PeBJV
Haiku: "Everywhere, everywhere." Mizuhara Shuoshi, *tr. by* Geoffrey Bownas *and* Anthony Thwaite. PeBJV
Haiku: "Fall rains/ scum collecting on." Masaoka Shiki, *tr. fr. Japanese by* Burton Watson. *Fr.* Thirty-nine Haiku. FCEI
Haiku: "Fallen flowers rise." Moritake, *tr. by* Harold G. Henderson. SoSe
Haiku: "Falling flower, The." Moritake, *tr. by* Babette Deutsch. SoSe
Haiku: "Family reunion." Nakamura Kusadao, *tr. by* Geoffrey Bownas *and* Anthony Thwaite. PeBJV
Haiku: "Famous horse, A." *Unknown*, *tr. by* Geoffrey Bownas *and* Anthony Thwaite. PeBJV
Haiku: "Farewell said, cover lowered." Ozaki Hosai, *tr. fr. Japanese by* Hiroaki Sato. *Fr.* One Hundred Haiku in Free Form. FCEI
Haiku: "Father at last, A." Nakamura Kusadao, *tr. by* Geoffrey Bownas *and* Anthony Thwaite. PeBJV
Haiku: "Father of the son, The." *Unknown*, *tr. by* Geoffrey Bownas *and* Anthony Thwaite. PeBJV
Haiku: "Feeling lonely." Hara Sekitei, *tr. by* Geoffrey Bownas *and* Anthony Thwaite. PeBJV
Haiku: "Festival, letting a baby sleep, A." Ozaki Hosai, *tr. fr. Japanese by* Hiroaki Sato. *Fr.* One Hundred Haiku in Free Form. FCEI
Haiku: "First butterfly." Takahama Kyoshi, *tr. by* Geoffrey Bownas *and* Anthony Thwaite. PeBJV
Haiku: "Fluttering, fluttering." Masaoka Shiki, *tr. fr. Japanese by* Burton Watson. *Fr.* Thirty-nine Haiku. FCEI

Haiku: "Lonely sound—/ simmering in the firepit." Masaoka Shiki, tr. fr. Japanese by Burton Watson. Fr. Thirty-nine Haiku. FCEI

Haiku: "Long night/ when the waterfall." Masaoka Shiki, tr. fr. Japanese by Burton Watson. Fr. Thirty-nine Haiku. FCEI

Haiku: "Looking through." Masaoka Shiki, tr. by Geoffrey Bownas and Anthony Thwaite. PeBJV

Haiku: "Lord Buddha's yellow flowers, The." Ozaki Hosai, tr. fr. Japanese by Hiroaki Sato. Fr. One Hundred Haiku in Free Form. FCEI

Haiku: "Losing in Love." Unknown, tr. by Geoffrey Bownas and Anthony Thwaite. PeBJV

Haiku: "Making her doll." Unknown, tr. by Geoffrey Bownas and Anthony Thwaite. PeBJV

Haiku: "Masked by the pines." Unknown, tr. by Geoffrey Bownas and Anthony Thwaite. PeBJV

Haiku: "Medicine-fetcher, The." Unknown, tr. by Geoffrey Bownas and Anthony Thwaite. PeBJV

Haiku: "Moonlit night I return." Ozaki Hosai, tr. fr. Japanese by Hiroaki Sato. Fr. One Hundred Haiku in Free Form. FCEI

Haiku: "Morning fog/ one man's got a fire going." Masaoka Shiki, tr. fr. Japanese by Burton Watson. Fr. Thirty-nine Haiku. FCEI

Haiku: "Morning-glories' white continues to bloom." Ozaki Hosai, tr. fr. Japanese by Hiroaki Sato. Fr. One Hundred Haiku in Free Form. FCEI

Haiku: "Mountain water, trickly." Ozaki Hosai, tr. fr. Japanese by Hiroaki Sato. Fr. One Hundred Haiku in Free Form. FCEI

Haiku: "No by torchlight, The." Kawahigashi Hekigoto, tr. by Geoffrey Bownas and Anthony Thwaite. PeBJV

Haiku: "Noisy cricket, The." Watanabe Suiha, tr. by Geoffrey Bownas and Anthony Thwaite. PeBJV

Haiku: "Nothing there but." Kawabata Bosha, tr. by Geoffrey Bownas and Anthony Thwaite. PeBJV

Haiku: "Now she's borne her brat." Unknown, tr. by Geoffrey Bownas and Anthony Thwaite. PeBJV

Haiku: "Now she's got a baby." Unknown, tr. by Geoffrey Bownas and Anthony Thwaite. PeBJV

Haiku: "Off the beaten track." Ernst David, tr. by Beth Bjorklund. CoAuP

Haiku: "On a warm roof, working." Ozaki Hosai, tr. fr. Japanese by Hiroaki Sato. Fr. One Hundred Haiku in Free Form. FCEI

Haiku: "On an onion tuft." Matsumoto Takashi, tr. by Geoffrey Bownas and Anthony Thwaite. PeBJV

Haiku: "On far hills." Takahama Kyoshi, tr. by Geoffrey Bownas and Anthony Thwaite. PeBJV

Haiku: "On scattered hailstones." Hara Sekitei, tr. by Geoffrey Bownas and Anthony Thwaite. PeBJV

Haiku: "On the pilgrimage to Ise." Unknown, tr. by Geoffrey Bownas and Anthony Thwaite. PeBJV

Haiku: "On the snow." Kawabata Bosha, tr. by Geoffrey Bownas and Anthony Thwaite. PeBJV

Haiku: "On the stolen." Takahama Kyoshi, tr. by Geoffrey Bownas and Anthony Thwaite. PeBJV

Haiku: "On the straw roof grass grows." Ozaki Hosai, tr. fr. Japanese by Hiroaki Sato. Fr. One Hundred Haiku in Free Form. FCEI

Haiku: "One or two, immersed in darkness." Ozaki Hosai, tr. fr. Japanese by Hiroaki Sato. Fr. One Hundred Haiku in Free Form. FCEI

Haiku: "Outlandish names." Unknown, tr. by Geoffrey Bownas and Anthony Thwaite. PeBJV

Haiku: "Pear blossoms." Mizuhara Shuoshi, tr. by Geoffrey Bownas and Anthony Thwaite. PeBJV

Haiku: "Peeling pears/ sweet juice drips." Masaoka Shiki, tr. fr. Japanese by Burton Watson. Fr. Thirty-nine Haiku. FCEI

Haiku: "People going home." Masaoka Shiki, tr. fr. Japanese by Burton Watson. Fr. Thirty-nine Haiku. FCEI

Haiku: "Pillow hard as stone!" Kawabata Bosha, tr. by Geoffrey Bownas and Anthony Thwaite. PeBJV

Haiku: "Pine cone, as it is, A." Ozaki Hosai, tr. fr. Japanese by Hiroaki Sato. Fr. One Hundred Haiku in Free Form. FCEI

Haiku: "Pomegranate opened its mouth, A." Ozaki Hosai, tr. fr. Japanese by Hiroaki Sato. Fr. One Hundred Haiku in Free Form. FCEI

Haiku: "Praying mantis drops with a thud, A." Ozaki Hosai, tr. fr. Japanese by Hiroaki Sato. Fr. One Hundred Haiku in Free Form. FCEI

Haiku: "Prevailing west wind." Ernst David, tr. by Beth Bjorklund. CoAuP

Haiku: "Purple so deep, A." Masaoka Shiki, tr. fr. Japanese by Burton Watson. Fr. Thirty-nine Haiku. FCEI

Haiku: "Ran and caught up, in the wind." Ozaki Hosai, tr. fr. Japanese by Hiroaki Sato. Fr. One Hundred Haiku in Free Form. FCEI

Haiku: "Reed-warbler, The." Mizuhara Shuoshi, tr. by Geoffrey Bownas and Anthony Thwaite. PeBJV

Haiku: "Rejecting a slanderous mind." Ozaki Hosai, tr. fr. Japanese by Hiroaki Sato. Fr. One Hundred Haiku in Free Form. FCEI

Haiku: "Right under the big sky." Ozaki Hosai, tr. fr. Japanese by Hiroaki Sato. Fr. One Hundred Haiku in Free Form. FCEI

Haiku: "Sad and forlorn: the shrike." Kato Shuson, tr. by Geoffrey Bownas and Anthony Thwaite. PeBJV

Haiku: "Sea becomes light, a window is open, The." Ozaki Hosai, tr. fr. Japanese by Hiroaki Sato. Fr. One Hundred Haiku in Free Form. FCEI

Haiku: Seasons in Santa Fe. Gerald Vizenor. HATNAP

Haiku: "Sheltering from rain." Unknown, tr. by Geoffrey Bownas and Anthony Thwaite. PeBJV

Haiku: "Shuttlecock:/ Smooth as oil." Takahama Kyoshi, tr. by Geoffrey Bownas and Anthony Thwaite. PeBJV

Haiku: "Sick-room window." Ishida Hakyo, tr. by Geoffrey Bownas and Anthony Thwaite. PeBJV

Haiku: "Single set of footsteps coming, A." Ozaki Hosai, tr. fr. Japanese by Hiroaki Sato. Fr. One Hundred Haiku in Free Form. FCEI

Haiku: "Sketching from life." Masaoka Shiki, tr. fr. Japanese by Burton Watson. Fr. Thirty-nine Haiku. FCEI

Haiku: "Sky blazing/ as I go down the gravel path." Masaoka Shiki, tr. fr. Japanese by Burton Watson. Fr. Thirty-nine Haiku. FCEI

Haiku: "Sky is high, The." Takahama Kyoshi, tr. by Geoffrey Bownas and Anthony Thwaite. PeBJV

Haiku: "Small rural newspaper, The." Ozaki Hosai, tr. fr. Japanese by Hiroaki Sato. Fr. One Hundred Haiku in Free Form. FCEI

Haiku: "Snake falls, A." Masaoka Shiki, tr. by Geoffrey Bownas and Anthony Thwaite. PeBJV

Haiku: "Snake fled, The." Takahama Kyoshi, tr. by Geoffrey Bownas and Anthony Thwaite. PeBJV

Haiku: "Snake-gourd in bloom." Masaoka Shiki, tr. by Geoffrey Bownas and Anthony Thwaite. PeBJV

Haiku: "Snake, killed, A." Ozaki Hosai, tr. fr. Japanese by Hiroaki Sato. Fr. One Hundred Haiku in Free Form. FCEI

Haiku: "Snap, the thong broke." Ozaki Hosai, tr. fr. Japanese by Hiroaki Sato. Fr. One Hundred Haiku in Free Form. FCEI

Haiku: "Snow fades into the river, The." Ozaki Hosai, tr. fr. Japanese by Hiroaki Sato. Fr. One Hundred Haiku in Free Form. FCEI

Haiku: "Snow has cleared, The." Ozaki Hosai, tr. fr. Japanese by Hiroaki Sato. Fr. One Hundred Haiku in Free Form. FCEI

Haiku: "Snowy sky turns into a single crow, The." Ozaki Hosai, tr. fr. Japanese by Hiroaki Sato. Fr. One Hundred Haiku in Free Form. FCEI

Haiku: "So few the cicadas." Masaoka Shiki, tr. by Geoffrey Bownas and Anthony Thwaite. PeBJV

Haiku: "So hard to fall for." Unknown, tr. by Geoffrey Bownas and Anthony Thwaite. PeBJV

Haiku: "Solitary crow/ upward over the summit." Ernst David, tr. by Beth Bjorklund. CoAuP

Haiku: "Soon to die." Masaoka Shiki, tr. by Geoffrey Bownas and Anthony Thwaite. PeBJV

Haiku: "Sound of the florist's scissors, The." Ozaki Hosai, tr. fr. Japanese by Hiroaki Sato. Fr. One Hundred Haiku in Free Form. FCEI

Haiku: "Sparrows all at once are gone, The." Ozaki Hosai, tr. fr. Japanese by Hiroaki Sato. Fr. One Hundred Haiku in Free Form. FCEI

Haiku: "Sparrows scurrying." Ishida Hakyo, tr. by Geoffrey Bownas and Anthony Thwaite. PeBJV

Haiku: "Splashing hot water over my navel." Ozaki Hosai, tr. fr. Japanese by Hiroaki Sato. Fr. One Hundred Haiku in Free Form. FCEI

Haiku: "Sprays of wisteria, The/ arranged in the vase/ are so short." Masaoka Shiki, tr. fr. Japanese by Burton Watson. Fr. Fifteen Haiku. FCEI

Haiku: "Sprays of wisteria/ arranged in a vase—/ one cluster." Masaoka Shiki, tr. fr. Japanese by Burton Watson. Fr. Fifteen Haiku. FCEI

Haiku: "Sprays of wisteria/ arranged in a vase—/ the blossoms hang down." Masaoka Shiki, tr. fr. Japanese by Burton Watson. Fr. Fifteen Haiku. FCEI

Haiku: "Spring rain." Kaga no Chiyo, tr. by R. H. Blyth. PBWP

Haiku: "Stars above the peaks." Mizuhara Shuoshi, tr. by Geoffrey Bownas and Anthony Thwaite. PeBJV

Haiku: "Stepping on a tendril." Hara Sekitei, tr. by Geoffrey Bownas and Anthony Thwaite. PeBJV

Haiku: "Sticking out my head from." Kato Shuson, tr. by Geoffrey Bownas and Anthony Thwaite. PeBJV

Haiku: "Stray cat, A." Masaoka Shiki, tr. fr. Japanese by Burton Watson. Fr. Thirty-nine Haiku. FCEI

Haiku: "Strewn out in the smog." Ernst David, *tr.* by Beth Bjorklund. CoAuP

Haiku: "Summer grass/ way in the distance." Masaoka Shiki, *tr. fr. Japanese by* Burton Watson. *Fr.* Thirty-nine Haiku. FCEI

Haiku: "Summer storm/ all the sheets of blank paper." Masaoka Shiki, *tr. fr. Japanese by* Burton Watson. *Fr.* Thirty-nine Haiku. FCEI

Haiku: "Supper eaten, still blessed." Ozaki Hosai, *tr. fr. Japanese by* Hiroaki Sato. *Fr.* One Hundred Haiku in Free Form. FCEI

Haiku: "Their many children each reading." Ozaki Hosai, *tr. fr. Japanese by* Hiroaki Sato. *Fr.* One Hundred Haiku in Free Form. FCEI

Haiku: "There it was, my face." Ozaki Hosai, *tr. fr. Japanese by* Hiroaki Sato. *Fr.* One Hundred Haiku in Free Form. FCEI

Haiku: "These are the mornings and evenings." Ozaki Hosai, *tr. fr. Japanese by* Hiroaki Sato. *Fr.* One Hundred Haiku in Free Form. FCEI

Haiku: "These wisterias." Masaoka Shiki, *tr. fr. Japanese by* Burton Watson. *Fr.* Fifteen Haiku. FCEI

Haiku: "They've cut down the willow." Masaoka Shiki, *tr. fr. Japanese by* Burton Watson. *Fr.* Thirty-nine Haiku. FCEI

Haiku: "Thinking about something." Ozaki Hosai, *tr. fr. Japanese by* Hiroaki Sato. *Fr.* One Hundred Haiku in Free Form. FCEI

Haiku: "This year/ I took sick with the peonies." Masaoka Shiki, *tr. fr. Japanese by* Burton Watson. *Fr.* Thirty-nine Haiku. FCEI

Haiku: "To one of the ears." Ozaki Hosai, *tr. fr. Japanese by* Hiroaki Sato. *Fr.* One Hundred Haiku in Free Form. FCEI

Haiku: "Tram-car full, The." *Unknown, tr.* by Geoffrey Bownas *and* Anthony Thwaite. PeBJV

Haiku: "Traveller in bed, The." *Unknown, tr.* by Geoffrey Bownas *and* Anthony Thwaite. PeBJV

Haiku: "Twilight cicadas." Masaoka Shiki, *tr. fr. Japanese by* Burton Watson. *Fr.* Thirty-nine Haiku. FCEI

Haiku: "Udders dripping." Iida Dakotsu, *tr.* by Geoffrey Bownas *and* Anthony Thwaite. PeBJV

Haiku: "Unable to put thread through a needle." Ozaki Hosai, *tr. fr. Japanese by* Hiroaki Sato. *Fr.* One Hundred Haiku in Free Form. FCEI

Haiku: "Undergraduates/ By and large shabby." Nakamura Kusadao, *tr.* by Geoffrey Bownas *and* Anthony Thwaite. PeBJV

Haiku: "Waiting for his turn." *Unknown, tr.* by Geoffrey Bownas *and* Anthony Thwaite. PeBJV

Haiku: "Walking down to eat my meal." Ozaki Hosai, *tr. fr. Japanese by* Hiroaki Sato. *Fr.* One Hundred Haiku in Free Form. FCEI

Haiku: "Walking home at night." Ernst David, *tr.* by Beth Bjorklund. CoAuP

Haiku: "Wallet gone completely empty." Ozaki Hosai, *tr. fr. Japanese by* Hiroaki Sato. *Fr.* One Hundred Haiku in Free Form. FCEI

Haiku: "Warm and snug." Hara Sekitei, *tr.* by Geoffrey Bownas *and* Anthony Thwaite. PeBJV

Haiku: "Wasting in summer." Kawabata Bosha, *tr.* by Geoffrey Bownas *and* Anthony Thwaite. PeBJV

Haiku: "Waves on the ebb." Watanabe Suiha, *tr.* by Geoffrey Bownas *and* Anthony Thwaite. PeBJV

Haiku: "We drained the pond." Ozaki Hosai, *tr. fr. Japanese by* Hiroaki Sato. *Fr.* One Hundred Haiku in Free Form. FCEI

Haiku: "Wears dirty clogs." Ozaki Hosai, *tr. fr. Japanese by* Hiroaki Sato. *Fr.* One Hundred Haiku in Free Form. FCEI

Haiku: "When I look/ at the wisteria blossoms/ I think of long ago." Masaoka Shiki, *tr. fr. Japanese by* Burton Watson. *Fr.* Fifteen Haiku. FCEI

Haiku: "When I look/ at wisteria blossoms/ I want to get out." Masaoka Shiki, *tr. fr. Japanese by* Burton Watson. *Fr.* Fifteen Haiku. FCEI

Haiku: "When she wails." *Unknown, tr.* by Geoffrey Bownas *and* Anthony Thwaite. PeBJV

Haiku: "Where the autumn sun shines, on a stone." Ozaki Hosai, *tr. fr. Japanese by* Hiroaki Sato. *Fr.* One Hundred Haiku in Free Form. FCEI

Haiku: "Where the castle stood." Masaoka Shiki, *tr. fr. Japanese by* Burton Watson. *Fr.* Thirty-nine Haiku. FCEI

Haiku: "While she ties her sash." *Unknown, tr.* by Geoffrey Bownas *and* Anthony Thwaite. PeBJV

Haiku: "Wild geese flying." Watanabe Suiha, *tr.* by Geoffrey Bownas *and* Anthony Thwaite. PeBJV

Haiku: "Wind blows grey, The." Naito Meisetsu, *tr.* by Geoffrey Bownas *and* Anthony Thwaite. PeBJV

Haiku: "Winter fly, The." *Unknown, tr.* by Geoffrey Bownas *and* Anthony Thwaite. PeBJV

Haiku: "With a face saying I caught something." Ozaki Hosai, *tr. fr. Japanese by* Hiroaki Sato. *Fr.* One Hundred Haiku in Free Form. FCEI

Haiku: "Woman in dark glasses, A." Ozaki Hosai, *tr. fr. Japanese by* Hiroaki Sato. *Fr.* One Hundred Haiku in Free Form. FCEI

Haiku: "Woman in the newspaper, The." Ozaki Hosai, *tr. fr. Japanese by* Hiroaki Sato. *Fr.* One Hundred Haiku in Free Form. FCEI

Haiku: "Wonderful breasts, here's a mosquito." Ozaki Hosai, *tr. fr. Japanese by* Hiroaki Sato. *Fr.* One Hundred Haiku in Free Form. FCEI

Haiku: Written when Sick in Bed ("I keep on asking"). Masaoka Shiki, *tr. fr. Japanese by* Burton Watson. *Fr.* Thirty-nine Haiku. FCEI

Haiku: Written when Sick in Bed ("I'm trying to sleep"). Masaoka Shiki, *tr. fr. Japanese by* Burton Watson. *Fr.* Thirty-nine Haiku. FCEI

Haiku Ambulance. Richard Brautigan. InPK

Haiku and ½. Phyllis Gotlieb. BWV

Haiku monkey's, The. Shokusanjin, *tr.* by Geoffrey Bownas *and* Anthony Thwaite. PeBJV

Haiku of a Day. José Juan Tablada, *tr. fr. Spanish by* Samuel Beckett. MexPo

Haiku of the Flowerpot. José Juan Tablada, *tr. fr. Spanish by* Samuel Beckett. MexPo

Hail, aged God who lookest on thy Father. He Prayeth for Ink and Palette That He May Write. *Unknown, tr. fr. Egyptian by* Robert Hillyer. *Fr.* Book of the Dead. AWP

Hail and beware the dead who will talk life until you are blue. A Newly Discovered "Homeric" Hymn. Charles Olson. MoP; NeAP; NoAM; PoM

Hail, beauteous Dian, queen of shades. Hymn to Diana. Thomas Heywood. *Fr.* The Golden Age. ElL

Hail, beauteous stranger of the grove [*or* wood]! To the Cuckoo. Michael Bruce, *revised by* John Logan. OBEV
(Ode: To the Cuckoo.) NOEC; PBBP

Hail, Bishop Valentine, whose day this is. John Donne. *Fr.* An Epithalamion on the Lady Elizabeth and Count Palantine Being Married on St. Valentine's Day. ChTr; OFD

Hail, blessed Virgin, full of heavenly grace. On the Infancy of Our Saviour. Francis Quarles. OBS; SeCePo

Hail, Columbia. Joseph Hopkinson. AA; AnAmPo; FaBoBe; FaFP; OPP; PAH

Hail, Comly and Clene. *Unknown.* *Fr.* The Second Shepherd's Play. NAs
(Haylle, Comly and Clene.) OBEV; OxBoli
(Shepherds at Bethlehem, The.) ChTr

Hail, Dionysos. Dudley Randall. BPo

Hail, ever-pleasing Solitude! Hymn on Solitude. James Thomson. NOEC

Hail falls on the ocean, the night falls: "Have someone turn on the cowbeacons! Max Jacob, *tr.* by Jerome Rothenberg. RHTwFP

Hail, fathers, hail! Flute Song. *Unknown, tr.* by Natalie Curtis. WTO

Hail Flag of the Union! Hail Flag of the free! Stars and Stripes. Mary Weston Fordham. CBWP-2

Hail, Freedom! thy bright crest. New National Hymn. Francis Marion Crawford. PAH

Hail, glorious day which miracles adorn. On Christmas Day. Earl of Orrery. TIRV

Hail, great Apollo! guide my feeble pen. The British Lyon Roused. Stephen Tilden. TIRV

Hail, guest! We ask not what thou art. America Greets an Alien. John Montgomery. OPP

Hail! Hail! Hail! A Dance Chant. *Unknown, tr.* by E. S. Parker. WGRP

Hail, happy bride, for thou art truly blest! On the Death of Mrs. Bowes. Lady Mary Wortley Montagu. BoWoP

Hail, happy Britain, Freedom's blest retreat. "Prophecy." Gulian Verplanck. PAH

Hail, happy day, when, smiling like the morn. To the Right Honourable William, Earl of Dartmouth. Phillis Wheatley. AmPP

Hail, happy lot of the laborious man. Poverty, in Imitation of Milton. Samuel Jones. NOEC

Hail, happy saint, on thine immortal throne. On the Death of the Rev. Mr. George Whitefield. Phillis Wheatley. NAAL-1

Hail happy William, thou art strangely great. A Panegyric. *Unknown.* APAS

Hail! Ho!/ Sail! Ho! A Sea-Song from the Shore. James Whitcomb Riley. BoTP

Hail, Holy Land. Thomas Tillam. GOA; SCAP

Hail, holy Lead!—of human feuds the great. Ambrose Bierce. *Fr.* The Devil's Dictionary. OBAL

Hail, Holy Light. Milton. *See* Paradise Lost: Hail holy light, ofspring [*or* offspring] of Heav'n first born.

Hail holy light, ofspring [*or* offspring] of Heav'n first born. Milton. *Fr.* Paradise Lost, *Bk.* III, *ll.* 1–55. OAEL-1; SCV; TOF
(Hail, Holy Light.) FiP

(Holy Light.) NOBE

(Light.) LiTB; OBEV; OBS

Hail! King I thee call. A Lyric from a Play. *Unknown.* MeEL

Hail! lovely flower, first honour of the year. On a Daffodil, the First Flower the Author Had Seen That Year. Samuel Johnson. FL

Hail, mediocrity, beneath whose spell. Roy Campbell. *Fr.* The Georgiad. MoBrPo

Hail mer-/ry, tricky, and clandestine. Ode to Pornography. Jack Anderson. PoA

Hail, mildly pleasing solitude. Hymn on Solitude. James Thomson. NOEC

Hail, Muse! et caetera.—We left Juan sleeping. Byron. *Fr.* Don Juan, III. OAEL-2

Hail! muse of my Lancastria fair. Elijah Ridings. *Fr.* The Isles of Britain. PF

Hail native language, that by sinews weak. Milton. *Fr.* At a Vacation Exercise [in the College]. JCP; OBS

Hail, O most worthy in all the world! *Unknown, tr. fr. Anglo-Saxon by* Charles W. Kennedy. *Fr.* Christ 1: Advent Lyrics, IX. AnOE

Hail, Oh Hail to the King. Beatrice Quickenden. AH

Hail, old patrician trees, so great and good! Of Solitude. Abraham Cowley. OBS

Hail Our Incarnate God! William Duke. AH

Hail, pious days! thou most propitious time. On the Sentence Passed by the House of Lords on Dr. Sacheverell. *Unknown.* APAS

Hail, Queen of Heaven. *Unknown.* OxBSP

Hail, Sabbath! day of mercy, peace, and rest! Ebenezer Elliott. *Fr.* The Village Patriarch, III. PF

Hail sacred shades! cool, leavy house! Upon the Priory Grove, His Usual Retirement. Henry Vaughan. FaBoPP

Hail[e], sister springs! Saint Mary Magdalene; or, The Weeper. Richard Crashaw. MeLP; MePo; OAEL-1; OBEV; SeCP; SeCV-1

Hail sons of generous valor. To the Defenders of New Orleans. Joseph Rodman Drake. PAH

Hail Sovereign Queen of secrets, who hast power. John Fletcher *and* Shakespeare. *Fr.* The Two Noble Kinsmen, V, i. PoEL-2

Hail [*or* Haile *or* Hale] sterne superne! Hail in eterne. Ballad of Our Lady. William Dunbar. ACP

(Ane Ballat of Our Lady.) OxBS

(Hymn to Mary.) MeEL

Hail, Sympathy! thy soft idea brings. William Lisle Bowles. Byron. *Fr.* English Bards and Scotch Reviewers. OBNC

Hail! the Glorious Golden City. Felix Adler. AH, *with music;* WGRP

Hail then ye daring few! who proudly soar. The Air Balloon. Henry James Pye. *Fr.* Aerophorion. NOEC

Hail, thou Great God in thy Boat. He Embarketh in the Boat of Ra. *Unknown, tr. fr. Egyptian by* Robert Hillyer. *Fr.* Book of the Dead. AWP

Hail, Thou great mysterious Being! Alexander McLachlan. *Fr.* God. CaP

Hail thou most sacred venerable thing! Hymn to Darkness. John Norris. MePo; OBS

Hail thou, my native soil! thou blessed plot. The Frolic Mariners of Devon. William Browne. *Fr.* Britannia's Pastorals, II, Song 3. ChTr

Hail, thou who shinest from the moon. He Establisheth His Triumph. *Unknown, tr. fr. Egyptian by* Robert Hillyer. *Fr.* Book of the Dead. AWP

Hail to Hobson! Hail to Hobson! hail to all the valiant set! The Men of the *Merrimac.* Clinton Scollard. PAH

Hail to the Brightness of Zion's Glad Morning. Thomas Hastings. AH

(Latter Day, The.) AA

Hail to the Chief Who in Triumph Advances. Sir Walter Scott. *Fr.* The Lady of the Lake, II. EnRP; PoEL-4

Hail to the Joyous Day. Royall Tyler. AH

Hail to the land whereon we tread. New England. James Gates Percival. AA

Hail to the Queen. *Unknown.* AH

Hail to the Sabbath Day. Stephen Greenleaf Bulfinch. AH

Hail to the sage divine of Milan's plains! On Hearing That Torture Was Suppressed throughout the Austrian Dominions. John Codrington Bampfylde. Son

Hail to thee, beautiful, mighty, and golden! Deirdre's Song at Sunrise. Sister Maura. CaP

Hail to thee, blithe computer! On National Data Banks. Louis Phillips. SoTCo

Hail to Thee, Blithe Owl. Ring Lardner. OBAL

Hail to thee, blithe roadster! To a Bicycle. *Unknown.* BXAP

Hail to thee, blithe Spirit! To a Skylark. Shelley. EnRP; FaBoBe; FaBV; FaFP; FaPON; FPL; GN; GTBS; GTBS-P; HAP; InPS; InvP;

LiTB; NAEL-2; NoP; OAEL-2; OBEV; OBNC; OHFP; PBBP; PoLF; TEP; TrGrPo

(Ode to a Skylark.) NOBE

Hail to thee, gallant foe. Cervera. Bertrand Shadwell. PAH

Hail to thee thou holy Babe. Christmas Hymn. *Unknown, tr. by* Douglas Hyde. TIRV

Hail to you, green hymn, that in superb. To an Araucaria. Salvador Díaz Mirón, *tr. by* Samuel Beckett. MexPo

Hail, Tranquil Hour of Closing Day. Leonard Bacon. AH

Hail Wedded Love! Jay Macpherson. MoCV

Hail wedded love, mysterious law, true source. Milton. *Fr.* Paradise Lost, *Bk.* IV, *ll.* 750–775.

(Their Wedded Love.) SeCePo

(Wedded Love.) OBS

Haile from the dead, or from eternity. Lines on a Purple Cap Received as a Present from My Brother. George Alsop. SCAP

Haile great Redeemer, man, and God, all haile. A Hymne to Our Saviour on the Crosse. George Chapman. PoEL-2

Haile, sister springs. *See* Hail, sister springs.

Haill! Quene of Heven and steren of blis. A Little Hymn to Mary. *Unknown.* MeEL

Haill warld waited, The. Problems. Alexander Scott. FF

Hailstones falling like sharp blue sky chips. Crazy Horse Monument. Peter Blue Cloud. HATNAP

Hain't no use to weep, hain't no use to moan. Down in the Lonesome Garden. *Unknown.* BPo

Hair. Yusuf al-Sa'igh, *tr. fr. Arabic by* Diana Der Hovanessian *with* Salma Khadra Jayyusi. MAP

Hair. Remy de Gourmont, *tr. fr. French by* Jethro Bithell. AWP; ErPo

Hair. Maxine Silverman. VWA

Hair, The. May Swenson. *Fr.* Poet to Tiger. GLP

Hair—/ silver-gray. Face. Jean Toomer. CDC; NoP

Hair-bowed Rose, deep in lush grass of the river. Profile of Rose. Glyn Jones. OBWVE

Hair—braided chestnut. Portrait in Georgia. Jean Toomer. NoP

Hair, five feet long. Yosano Akiko, *tr. fr. Japanese by* Hiroaki Sato. *Fr.* Thirty-nine Tanka. FCEI

Hair grown and face pale. Basho, *tr. fr. Japanese by* Burton Watson. *Fr.* Seventy-six Hokku. FCEI

Hair is heaven's water flowing eerily over us. Hair Poem. William Knott. EAS

Hair is the top of a person. The Top and the Tip. Charlotte Zolotow. RAR

Hair long, cheekbones high. Three Dreams. James Michie. NePoEA-2

Hair ornament of the sun, The. Mitsuhashi Takajo, *tr. by* Kenneth Rexroth *and* Ikuko Atsumi. BoWoP

Hair Poem. William Knott. EAS

Hair splayed on the pillow. I think: a Kyoto comb's the thing. Biting Through. Traise Yamamoto. BrSi

Hair-Tonic Bottle, The. Ben King. OBAL

Hair washed,/ she wrings it out. *Unknown, tr. by* Burton Watson. FCEI

Hairband, homespun, opera-hat, afghan. Motley. Peter Davison. NBLV

Haircut. Sue May. DT

Haircut. Karl Shapiro. TwCP

Hairdo and ornaments all the latest fashion. Beginning of Spring—A Stroll with My Wife. Hsü Chün-ch'ien, *tr. by* Burton Watson. CoBCP

Hairline Fracture, A. Amy Clampitt. NoAM

Hairnet covered her head, A. For All My Grandmothers. Beth Brant. STE

Hairs in My Nose, The. Aram Boyajian. NeAC

Hairy Dog, The. Herbert Asquith. FaPON; PDV; RHPC

Hairy Toe, The. *Unknown.* PYC

Hairy was here. News from the Cabin. May Swenson. NYBP

Haiti: Skin Diving. Jane Shore. ASP

Haitian Suite. Gregory Orr. MAYP

Haka: Hinemotu. Te Aomuhurangi Te Maaka. PeNZ

Haka: The Blossoming. Pita Sharples, *tr. fr. Maori by* Pita Sharples. PeNZ

Haka: The Feathered Albatross. Muru Walters, *tr. fr. Maori by the author.* PeNZ

Halcyon, *sel.* Hilda Doolittle ("H. D."). "I'm not here." MoAmPo

Halcyon Days. Jim Barnes. CDW

Halcyon Days. Walt Whitman. OxBA

Halcyon's Nest, The. Giles Fletcher the Younger. *Fr.* Christ's Victory and Triumph: Christ's Triumph after Death, IV. FaBoPP

Half. Hawley Truax. NYBP

Half/ way/ in the dark. Without Tears for the Roses. Nanni Balestrini, *tr. by* Lawrence R. Smith. NItP

Half a bar, half a bar. The Village Choir. *Unknown.* FaBoPa

Half a dozen white loves lie. The Loaves. Ronald G. Everson. TDD

Half a league, half a league. The Charge of the Light Brigade. Tennyson. BeLS; BLPA; FaBoBe; FaBV; FaFP; FaPON; FaPoR; FPL; GN; HoPM; NAEL-2; NIP; NOBVV; OBWP; OHFP; PrIm; TEP; WBLP

Half a mile from the shining sea. A Song of Degrees. W. P. Ker. PoSH

Half afraid to break a promise. Michael Hartnett. *Fr.* A Farewell to English. NOIV

Half an Hour. C. P. Cavafy, *tr. fr. Greek by* Edmund Keeley *and* Philip Sherrard. VMG

Half asleep,/ chanting a No play. *Unknown, tr. by* Burton Watson. FCEI

Half asleep. Fishing the Dream. Mike Delp. TSL

Half-asleep in the shade of the trees. Cricket Match. David Cram. SoTCo

Half awake in my Sunday nap. Three Green Windows. Anne Sexton. NYBP

Half-bent Man. Richard Eberhart. NYBP

Half Black, Half Blacker. Sterling Plumpp. PoBA

Half-blown Rose, The. Samuel Daniel. *See* To Delia: Look, Delia, how we esteem the half-blown rose.

Half-Breed Girl, The. Duncan Campbell Scott. CaP

Half-bridge over nothingness. Northhanger Ridge. Charles Wright. HCAP

Half close your eyelids, loosen your hair. Aedh Thinks of Those Who Have Spoken Evil of His Beloved. W. B. Yeats. NoAM
  (He Thinks of Those Who Have Spoken Evil of His Beloved.) CTC; NOBVV

"Half-cracked" to Higginson, living. "I Am in Danger—Sir." Adrienne Rich. HCAP; NOBA

Half-door, hall door. Purgatory. W. B. Yeats. CMoP

Half doun the hill, whaur fa's the linn. The Gowk. William Soutar. GoTS

Half-drying rocks in shades of gray. Bog. Leen Volwerk. PoSH

Half-heard. Christopher Koch. PoAu-2

Half-hidden by trees, the sheer roof of the barn. The Barn. Stephen Spender. CMoP

Half-hidden in a graveyard. The Stranger. Walter de la Mare. BrPo; OxBTC

Half Holiday. Olive Enoch. BoTP

Half-holiday for the burial, A. Of course, they punish. Black Spring. Robert Lowell. NaP

Half in slumber, half awake, gently aglow. White Jade Bitter Melon. Yu Kuang-chung, *tr. by* Dominic Cheung. IFON

Half in the dim light from the hall. To———. William Stanley Braithwaite. PoBA

Half in the Family, Half Out. Po Chü-i, *tr. fr. Chinese by* Burton Watson. CoBCP

Half-Light. Jean Percival Waddell. CaP

Half-Mast. Lloyd Mifflin. PAH

Half Moon. Federico García Lorca, *tr. fr. Spanish by* W. S. Merwin. RFM

Half-moons of her calves eclipse, The. Notes on a Girl. Peter Kane Dufault. ErPo

Half my friends are dead. Sea Canes. Derek Walcott. HeIP

Half my life has passed me by. The Waters, Indeed, Are to the Palate, Bitter. Hubert Witheford. ATNZ

Half of a clasping of the hands. Half. Hawley Truax. NYBP

Half of death. In Prague. Paul Celan, *tr. by* Joachim Neugroschel. VWA

Half of his/ body hung in. Spirits. Victor Hernandez Cruz. PoBA; WSC

Half of Life. Friedrich Hölderlin, *tr. fr. German by* James Blair Leishman. ChTr; OBVE

Half of me is beautiful. Lilith. Ruth Feldman. VWA

Half of my life is gone, and I have let. Mezzo Cammin. Longfellow. FPL; NAAL-1; NoP; PoE; TAP

Half of our borders, rivers and mountains were gone. In the Home of the Scholar Wu Su-chiang. Wu Tsao, *tr. by* Kenneth Rexroth *and* Ling Chung. BoWoP; WPOW

Half-Open Window at Midnight, A. Munir Niazi, *tr. fr. Urdu by* Mahmood Jamal. PBMUP

Half Past Four, October. Anna Hajnal, *tr. fr. Hungarian by* Daniel Hoffman. BoWoP; MHuP

Half past four one April morning. One Morning. Jan Hanlo, *tr. by* James S. Holmes. DuIn

Half past nine—high time for supper. In Praise of Cocoa, Cupid's Nightcap. Stanley J. Sharpless. ErPo; FiBHP; NBLV

Half-past three in the morning! Louise on the Door-Step. Charles MacKay. EBVV

Half past twelve. Time's gone by quickly. Since Nine O'Clock. C. P. Cavafy, *tr. by* Edmund Keeley *and* Philip Sherrard. VMG

Half remembering, yet not remembering, just waked up from a dream. Song on Being Too Lazy to Get Up. Shao Yung, *tr. by* Burton Watson. CoBCP

Half seeing and half smelling a scrap. Existential. William Heyen. GeTw

Half-shut doors through which we heard that music, The. Multitudes Turn in Darkness. Conrad Aiken. PoA

Half Sigh. *Unknown, tr. by* Miriam Koshland. PBA

Half spirit, the older. The Jest. Austin Clarke. BIrV

Half squatter, half tenant (no rent). Manuelzinho. Elizabeth Bishop. FaBoWP; NYBP

Half the face illumined. A Half-Open Window at Midnight. Munir Niazi, *tr. by* Mahmood Jamal. PBMUP

Half the time they munched the grass, and all the time they lay. Cows. James Reeves. NTCP

Half the year has hot nights, like this. Elegies for the Hot Season. Sandra McPherson. AmPA

Half then all our chickens. Great-Aunt Francesca. Joe-Anne McLaughlin. PPR

Half-Tide Ledge. R. P. Blackmur. MOS

Half Way. Robert Desnos, *tr. fr. French by* Michael Benedikt. POS

Half-way across the racing river. Midstream. D. J. Enright. OxBC

Half-way, for One Commandment Broken. A. E. Housman. OxBSP; PeHV

Half-Way Pause, A. Dante Gabriel Rossetti. NOBVV

Half-world's width divides us, The; where she sits. Divided. David Gray. AA

Half yet remains unsung, but narrower bound. Milton. *Fr.* Paradise Lost, *Bk.* VII, *ll.* 21–39. FaBoPV

Halfglimpses of the sea. Clearings. Blaise Cendrars, *tr. by* John Dos Passos. RHTwFP

Halfway. Maxine W. Kumin. GoYe

Halfway across a bridge one night. The Swerve. William Stafford. SM

Halfway Down. A. A. Milne. FaPON; RAR; SO

Halfway through Illinois on the radio. Jackpot. Jorie Graham. KS

Halfwit. Basil Dowling. ATNZ

Halibut Cove Harvest. Kenneth Leslie. CaP; NOBC

Halieutica, *sels.* William Diaper, *after the Greek of* Oppian.
  "Lamprey, glowing with uncommon fires, The." OBVE
  "Shelly crawlers each returning year, The." FM
  "Strange the formation of the eely race." OBVE
  (Eels and Tortoises.) NOEC
  "When pleasing heat, and fragrant blooms inspire." BXAP
  "When they in throngs a safe retirement seek." OBVE

Halifax Station. *Unknown.* PAH

Hall of Ifor Hael, The. Evan Evans, *tr. fr. Welsh by* Gwyn Williams. OBWVE

Hall of Ocean Life. John Hollander. PoA

Hallaj's corpse was burnt and when the flame. Faridu'ddin Attar, *tr. fr. Persian by* Afkham Darbandi *and* Dick Davis. *Fr.* The Conference of the Birds. TOF

Hallelujah! A. E. Housman. FiBHP
  (On the Death of a Female Officer of the Salvation Army.) FaBoNo

Hallelujah./ Praise the Lord, O my soul. Bible, *O.T.* Psalms, CXLVI. TrJP

Hallelujah, hallelujah, Catherine. Carol to Catherine. Sister Juana Inés de la Cruz, *tr. by* Kate Flores. DMH

Hallelujah, I'm a Bum. *Unknown.* AS, *with music*
  (Hallelujah, Bum Again.) GBP
  "Oh why don't you work," *sel.* SaC, *abr.*

Hallelujah; or, Britain's Second Remembrancer, *sels.* George Wither.
  For a Musician. OBS
  Hymn L: Rocking Hymn, A. SeCV-1
  (Rocking Hymn, A.) OxBChV
  Hymne I: Generall Invitation to Praise God, A. SeCV-1

Hallelujah! Praise the Lord. Edwin Francis Hatfield. AH

"Hallelujah!" was the only observation. Hallelujah! A. E. Housman. FaBoNo; FiBHP
  (On the Death of a Female Officer of the Salvation Army.) FaBoNo

Hallo My Fancy. William Cleland. CH; OxBoLi

Hallow days o Yule are come, The. The Wife of Usher's Well. *Unknown.* ESPB

Hallow-Fair. Robert Fergusson. OxBS

Hallow the threshold, crown the posts anew! On the Queen's Return from the Low Countries. William Cartwright. MePo; OBEV

Hallowed be the Ordainer of/ the world! A Little Prayer. Paul Goodman. LiTA

Hallowed be the Sabbaoth.   Epitaph in St. Olave's, Southwark, on Mr. Munday.   *Unknown.*   FaBoCo; OxBoLi
Hallowed Ground.   Thomas Campbell.   BLPA
Hallowe'en.   Harry Behn.   FaPON; PDV
Hallowe'en.   Eleanor Farjeon.   Mes
Halloween.   Myra Cohn Livingston.   OFD
Hallowe'en.   Lizelia Augusta Jenkins Moorer.   CBWP-3
Hallowe'en 1971.   Michael Dennis Browne.   AmPA
Halloween Witches.   Felice Holman.   WSC
Hallowing of Hell, The, *sel.*   Robin Morgan.
   "And blessed be the women who get you through."   GLP
Hallway whispers still echo.   I Know, You'd Rather Be Dead.   Edward L. Hooper.   TSM
Halo.   Ralph Nixon Currey.   PeSA
Halsted Street Car.   Carl Sandburg.   NAAL-2
Halt, A.   Zbigniew Herbert, *tr. fr. Polish by* Czeslaw Milosz.   PwPP
Halt and Parley.   George Herbert Clarke.   CaP
Halt! Shoulder arms! Recover! As you were!   Sonnet to Britain.   William Edmonstoune Aytoun.   FaBoCo
Halted against the shade of a last hill.   Spring Offensive.   Wilfred Owen.   BrPo; GTBS-P; LiTB
Haltersick's Song.   John Pickering (or Pikerying),.   *Fr. Horestes.*   OBSC
   (Song: "Farewell, adieu, that court-like life!")   EiL
Hamadryad, The.   Walter Savage Landor.   *Fr. The Hellenics.*   EnRP
Hamasah, *sel.*   Hittan of Tayyi, *tr. fr. Arabic by* Sir Charles Lyall.   His Children.   ASP; AWP
Hamatraya.   Emerson.   AmPP; HeIP; MAT; NOBA; NoP; OxBA; PoEl-4; PrIm; TAP
Hambone and the Heart, The.   Dame Edith Sitwell.   OBMV
Hame came our goodman.   Our Goodman.   *Unknown.*   ESPB
Hame, Hame, Hame.   Allan Cunningham.   CH; OBEV
   (Loyalty.)   GN, *abr.*
Hameed.   Salah Niyazi, *tr. fr. Arabic by* Lena Jayyusi *and* Charles Doria.   MAP
Hamelin Town's in Brunswick.   The Pied Piper of Hamelin.   Robert Browning.   BeLS; BLPL; FaBoBe; FaBoCh; FaFP; GN; OBNV; OxBChV
Hamilton Greene.   Edgar Lee Masters.   *Fr. Spoon River Anthology.*   MoP; NoAM; OxBA
Hamlen Brook.   Richard Wilbur.   BLA; CAPP
Hamlet.   Abdul Wahab al-Bayati, *tr. fr. Arabic by* Abdullah al-Udhari.   MPAW
"Hamlet."   Emmett Jarrett.   NeAC
Hamlet.   Shakespeare.   NAWM-1
   Sels.
   And Will He Not Come Again.   *Fr. IV, v.*   PoEL-2
      (Ophelia's Songs, 2 ("And will he not come again").)   TrGrPo
   "Angels and ministers of grace defend us!"   *Fr. I, iv.*   EBEV
   "Give me your pardon, sir. I have done you wrong."   *Fr. V, ii.*   DL
   "Good sir, whose powers are these?."   *Fr. IV, v.*   WaaP
   "How all occasions do inform against me."   *Fr. IV, iv.*   HoPM
   How Should I Your True Love Know.   *Fr. IV, v.*   EBEV; EnLoPo; LiTB; Mes; PoRA; QFR
      (Ophelia's Songs, 1 ("How should I your true love know").)   ChTr; GBL; OBSC; TrGrPo
      (Song: "How should I your true love know.")   CH
   "I am dead, Horatio. Wretched queen, adieu!"   *Fr. V, ii.*   FaBoRV
      (Death of Hamlet.)   FiP
   "I am thy father's spirit."   *Fr. I, v.*   OBD
   "It faded on the crowing of the cock."   *Fr. I, i.*   TOF
   "O, that this too too solid flesh would melt."   *Fr. I, i.*   SCV
      (Frailty, Thy Name is Woman.)   TrGrPo
   Polonius' Advice to Laertes.   *Fr. I, iii.*   OHFP
      (Polonius to Laertes.)   GN
      (This Above All.)   TrGrPo
      (To Thine Own Self Be True.)   FaFP; LiTB
   "Rugged Pyrrhus, he whose sable arm, The."   *Fr. II, ii.*   Par
   "Some say that ever 'gainst that season comes."   *Fr. I, i.*   OFD; PChr
      (Bird of Dawning, The.)   FaBoRV
      (Christmas.)   ChTr
      (Gracious Time, The.)   GN
   "There is a willow grows aslant a brook."   *Fr. V, i.*   RB
      (Ophelia's Death.)   ChTr
   "To be, or not to be, that is the question."   *Fr. III, i.*   FaFP; FF; FiP; HoPM; LiTB; OBD; TrGrPo
      (Hamlet's Soliloquy.)   WBLP
      (Soliloquy from "Hamlet.")   OHFP
   Tomorrow Is Saint Valentine's Day.   EnLoPo; OFD
      (Saint Valentine's Day.)   CH; LiTB
      (Song: "Tomorrow is Saint Valentine's Day.")   FaPON; NTCP

   "What ceremony else?."   *Fr. V, i.*   EBEV
   "What man dost thou dig it for?."   *Fr. V, i.*   DL
Hamlet.   Stanley J. Sharpless.   BXAP; NBLV
Hamlet in Russia, A Soliloquy.   Boris Pasternak, *tr. fr. Russian by* Robert Lowell.   FaBoPV
Hamlet was shown at our cinema.   The Village Cinema.   Stanislaw Grochowiak, *tr. by* Czeslaw Milosz.   PwPP
Hamletism.   Antoni Slonimski, *tr. fr. Polish by* Peter Dale Scott *and* Czeslaw Milosz.   PwPP
Hamlet's Soliloquy.   Shakespeare.   *See* Hamlet: To be, or not to be, that is the question.
Hamlet's Soliloquy Imitated.   Richard Jago.   BXAP; FaBoCo; FaBoPa
Hammam Name, The.   James Elroy Flecker.   BrPo; PeHV
Hammer, A.   Eugène Guillevic, *tr. fr. French by* Denise Levertov.   RHTwFP
Hammer, The,/ struck my nail.   Almanac.   May Swenson.   NYBP
Hammer and Anvil.   Samuel Valentine Cole.   PoLF
Hammer Falls, Is Falling, The.   Marianne Boruch.   PPR
Hammer keeps a-ring-in' on somebody's coffin, The.   Way Over in the New Buryin' Groun.'   *Unknown.*   AS
Hammer Man.   *Unknown.*   AS
Hammer, Ring.   *Unknown.*   AmFP
Hammers, The.   Ralph Hodgson.   GoJo; MoBrPo; NOBE; OxBTC
Hammers and Anvil, The.   John Clifford.   *See* Last eve I paused beside the blacksmith's door.
Hammerstroke and.   The Murdered Girl Is Found on a Bridge.   Jane Hayman.   NYBP
Hammock.   Horiguchi Daigaku, *tr. fr. Japanese by* Geoffrey Bownas *and* Anthony Thwaite.   PeBJV
Hampstead; the Horse Chestnut Trees.   Thom Gunn.   NoP
Hampton Court.   Pope.   *See* Rape of the Lock, The: Close by those meads, for ever crowned with flow'rs.
Hamra Night.   Sa'di Yusuf, *tr. fr. Arabic by* Abdullah al-Udhari.   MPAW
Hamsters.   Marci Ridlon.   RAR
Hamtramck: The Polish Women.   Toi Derricotte.   InPS
Ha'nacker Mill.   Hilaire Belloc.   FaPoR; MoBrPo; OxBTC; RB
Hand, The.   Brian Fawcett.   NOBC
Hand, The.   Howard Moss.   TAP
Hand.   Edouard Roditi.   EAS
Hand, The.   R. S. Thomas.   NOCV; OxBC
Hand, A/ to the light.   Night Meeting.   Gyorgy Raba, *tr. by* Jascha Kessler.   FOC
Hand a shade of moonlight on the pillow, The.   Non Ti Fidar.   Louis Zukofsky.   VGW
Hand and Foot, The.   Jones Very.   OxBA; PoEL-4; QFR; TAP
Hand at Callow Hill Farm, The.   Charles Tomlinson.   NePoEA-2
Hand-clapping Rhyme.   *Unknown.*   NTCP
Hand Etc.   Gerrit Kouwenaar, *tr. fr. Dutch by* Peter Nijmeijer.   DuIn
Hand, Eye.   Patricia Hampl.   NAmP
Hand goes up, The.   Country Greeting.   Frank Steele.   Psk
Hand in hand they dance in a row.   The Clothes-Line.   Charlotte Druitt Cole.   BoTP
Hand Is a Cake, The.   Hagiwara Sakutaro, *tr. fr. Japanese by* Sato.   FCEI
Hand-Jive.   Sandie Castle.   UL
Hand-Mirror, A.   Walt Whitman.   NAAL-1; OxBA; TW
Hand of art here torpid lies, The.   Epitaph on William Hogarth.   Samuel Johnson.   EBEV
Hand of Lincoln, The.   Edmund Clarence Stedman.   AA; AnAmPo; OHIP
Hand of Music, The.   N. M. Rashed, *tr. fr. Urdu by* Mahmood Jamal.   PBMUP
Hand of Snapshots, A, *sels.*   Louis MacNeice.   FaBCIP
   Left-Behind, The.
   Once-in-Passing, The.
Hand of Solo, A.   Thomas Kinsella.   CIP; NOIV
Hand of the copper boy pours tea.   Café Tableau.   May Swenson.   ErPo
Hand on the Prophet, God.   Birth (al-Maulid).   Muhammad al-Mahdi al-Majdhoub, *tr. by* Salma Khadra Jayyusi *and* Charles Doria.   MAP
Hand over hand we inch.   Our grips.   The Properties of Breath.   Jean Hanff Korelitz.   NPo
Hand-Shadows.   Jarold Ramsey.   NIP
Hand tells the bowstring, The.   Japanese Archery.   Aleksander Wat, *tr. by* Richard Lourie.   NIP
Hand that aches for the pitchfork heft, The.   Work.   Robert Penn Warren.   *Fr.* Boy's Will, Joyful Labor without Pay, and Harvest Home.   SaC
"Hand that rocks the cradle, The"—but there is no such hand.   The Modern Baby.   William Croswell Doane.   BLPA
Hand That Rocks the Cradle Is the Hand That Rules the World, The.   William Ross Wallace.   BLPL; FaFP; PoLF; WBLP

Hand that rounded Peter's dome, The. Emerson. *Fr.* The Problem. EyDe

Hand That Signed the Paper Felled a City, The. Dylan Thomas. MoAB; MoBrPo; MoP; NoAM; NOBE; NoP; OBWP; RB; SeCePo; TrGrPo; WaP

Hand that swept the sounding lyre, The. On a Dead Poet. Frances Sargent Osgood. AA

Hand trembling towards hand; the amazing. Sonnet Reversed. Rupert Brooke. NOBL

Handbook of Versification. Gilbert Sorrentino. PoA

Handcart Song, The. *Unknown.* AmFP

Handful came to Seicheprey, A. Seicheprey. *Unknown.* PAH

Handful here, that once was Mary's earth, The. Her Epitaph. Thomas William Parsons. AA

Handful of Ashes. Ilya Rubin, *tr. fr. Russian by* Linda Zisquit. VWA

Handful of Dust, A. James Oppenheim. TrJP

Handful of old men walking down the village street, A. Memorial Day. Theodosia Garrison. OHIP

Handicapped Children Swimming. Michael Dennis Browne. TSL

Handing back the baby. *Unknown, tr. by* Geoffrey Bownas *and* Anthony Thwaite. PeBJV

Handkerchief still lying there, A. Ozaki Hosai, *tr. fr. Japanese by* Hiroaki Sato. *Fr.* One Hundred Haiku in Free Form. FCEI

Handle a large kingdom with as gentle a touch. Tao Te Ching. Lao Tzu, *tr. by* Witter Bynner. OBD

Handling Sin, *sel.* Robert Mannyng. Dancers of Colbek, The. PoE

Handloom, The. Judith Rodriguez. FaBoWP

Handmaid of Religion, The. Edgell Rickword. OBSV

Hands. Donald Finkel. CoAP; MAT

Hands. Alex Glasgow. OBET

Hands, The. Tony Harrison. FaBoTw

Hands. Robinson Jeffers. GOA

Hands, The. Denise Levertov. NeAP; PoM

Hands. Donna Masini. ER

Hands. Anne Stevenson. BLA

Hands and lit faces eddy to a line. The Night Journey. Rupert Brooke. BrPo

Hands are being plated, The; they'll be brass. Clock without Hands. John Frederick Nims. PoA

Hands clenched under my shawl. "Anna Akhmatova," *tr. fr. Russian by* Robert Tracy. PBWP

Hands folded like napkins in my lap. Robert Peterson. NeAC

Hands must touch and handle many things, The. The New Man. Jones Very. NOBA

Hands of beggars peddle cigarets, The. Cante Hondo. Ellen de Young Kay. NePoEA

Hands of the lighted city clock, The. Twelve. Jacob Glatstein, *tr. by* Benjamin *and* Barbara Harshav. AYP

Hands of the queen are smeared with grease, The. The Breasts of the Queen Are Turned out of Wood. Stanislaw Grochowiak, *tr. by* Czeslaw Milosz. PwPP

Hands released, I twirl the letter-board. Tenneimyo, *tr. by* Lucien Stryk *and* Takashi Ikemoto. ZPCJ

Hands that eased my mother's labor drew, The. Rhyme for the Child as a Wet Dog. Judith Johnson Sherwin. TAP

Hands Up. Anthony Rudolf. VWA

Hands upon hands. Pleading Voices. Shalom Katav, *tr. by* Yoffee Berkovitz. VWA

Hands were not made for hitting. A Fighter Learns of Hands. Charles Ghigna. TSL

Hands were yours, the arms were yours, The. Mark Strand. *Fr.* Elegy for My Father. DiL; GeTw; HCAP; LCAP

(Empty Body, The.) UnPo

Handsel Ring, The. George Houghton. AA

Handsome face drinking water, A. Meeting Etsujin. Boncho, *tr. fr. Japanese by* Hiroaki Sato. *Fr.* Twenty-one Hokku. FCEI

Handsome friend, charming and kind. Beatrice, Countess de Die, *tr. by* Meg Bogin. WPOW

Handsome? I hardly know. Her profile's fine. A Countrywoman of Mine. Elaine Goodale Eastman. AA

Handsome one, white-black checkered son of the water. The Muscovy Drake. E. A. S. Lesoro, *tr. by* Dan Kunene *and* Jack Cope. PeSA

Handsome young airman lay dying, A. The Dying Airman. *Unknown.* AS, *with music;* FaBoNo; FaFP; OxBoLi; RB

Handwriting on the Wall, The. Knowles Shaw. BLPA

Handwriting on the Wall. *Unknown.* AmFP

Handy dandy. *Unknown.* OxNR

Hang a small bugle cap on, as big as a crown. The Beau's Receipt for a Lady's Dress. *Unknown.* CoMu

Hang at my hand as I write now. Verses for a First Birthday. George Barker. MoAB; MoBrPo

Hang-Glider's Daughter, The. Marilyn Hacker. MAYP

Hang it all, Ezra Pound, there is only the one sestina! Donald Hall. NePoEA

Hang it all, Robert Browning. Ezra Pound. *Fr.* Cantos, II. AmPP; HAP; MoAB; MoAmPo; NoAM; NOBA; OxBA; PoA

Hang Me, O Hang Me, and I'll Be Dead and Gone. *Unknown.* AmFP

Hang out our banners on the outward walls. Shakespeare. *Fr.* Macbeth, V, v. EBEV

Hang out your cloth, and let the trumpet sound. The Character of a Trimmer. *Unknown.* APAS

Hang sorrow, cast away care. *Unknown.* OBS

Hang thee, vile North Easter. Another Ode to the North-East Wind. *Unknown.* Par

Hang to Your Grit! Louis E. Thayer. WBLP

Hang Up the Baby's Stocking! *Unknown.* OBCP

Hang up those dull and envious fools. In the Person of Womankind (In Defense of Their Inconstancy). Ben Jonson. NAEL-1

(Another. In Defence of Their Inconstancie.) SeCP

Hang up your weaponed wit. J. V. Cunningham. QFR

Hang your serious songs. Sipsop's Song. Blake. *Fr.* An Island in the Moon. FaBoNo

Hanged Man, The. John Oliver Simon. BWV

Hanged man, please grow wild and luminous. To Her Dead Mate: Montana, 1966. Elizabeth Libbey. AmPA

Hanging, A. Frank Mkalawile Chipasula. WMBCH

Hanging, The. J. E. H. MacDonald. OBCV

Hanging/ out under the bridge. Getting Across. Carter Revard. VoR

Hanging Burley. Jim Wayne Miller. MT

Hanging Fire. Audre Lorde. ER; NIP; NoAM; NoP

Hanging from fresh trees. Lemons, Lemons. Al Young. HeIP

Hanging from the beam. The Portent. Herman Melville. AmPP; AnAmPo; InPK; NAAL-1; NOBA; NoP; OBWP; OxBA; PoE; PoEL-5; PrIm; TAP; WiR

Hanging from the branches of a green/ willow tree. Lady Ise, *tr. by* Willis Barnstone. BoWoP

Hanging Johnny. *Unknown.* GBP

Hanging Man, The. Sylvia Plath. HCAP

Hanging of Sam Archer, The. *Unknown.* AmFP

Hanging of the Crane, The, *sel.* Longfellow. New Household, A. GN

Hanging on the wall, an iron face watches me. The Mask. Irma McClaurin. BlSi

Hanging on the walls. Gallery of My Heart. King D. Kuka. VoR

Hanging Out the Linen Clothes. *Unknown.* AS

Hangman. Ai. AmPA

Hangman, hangman, slack on the line. *Unknown. See* Maid Freed from the Gallows, The.

Hangman's Love Song, The. Stanley Moss. VGW

Hangman's Tree. Lillian Zellhoefer White. AmFN

Hangover Cure. Alexis, *tr. fr. Greek.* FaBoUs

Hangover Cure. Amphis, *tr. fr. Greek.* FaBoUs

Hangover Cure. Nicochares, *tr. fr. Greek.* FaBoUs

Hangover Mass. X. J. Kennedy. DiPo

Hangs./ whipped/ blood. Biography. Amiri Baraka. TAP

Hank. Stephen Tapscott. PPR

Hankering after Truth, A. Veronica Williams. WS

Hannah Bantry. *Unknown.* OxNR

Hannah Binding Shoes. Lucy Larcom. GN

Hannah's Song of Thanksgiving. Bible, *O.T. Fr.* First Samuel, II: 1–10. AWP

(Song of Hannah, The.) TrCP, *ad. by* Michael Drayton.

Hannah's Thanksgiving. Bible, *O.T. Fr.* First Samuel, II: 1–10. BoWoP

Hannelore will thus be my wife. Andreas Okopenko, *tr. fr. German by* Beth Bjorklund. *Fr.* Bachelors and Language. CoAuP

Hannibal ("Produce the urn that Hannibal contains"). Juvenal, *tr. fr. Latin by* William Gifford. *Fr.* Satires, X. OBVE

Hannibal ("Put Hannibal i' th' scale"). Juvenal, *tr. fr. Latin by* Henry Vaughan. *Fr.* Satires, X. OBVE

Hannibal ("Throw Hannibal on the scales, how many pounds"). Juvenal, *tr. fr. Latin by* Robert Lowell. *Fr.* Satires, X. OBVE

Hans Breitmann's Party [*or* Barty]. Charles Godfrey Leland. AnAmPo; CenHV; FaBoCo; NOBL; OBAL

Hans, there are moments when the whole mind. James Merrill. CAPP

Hans Verhagen & Son. Hans Verhagen, *tr. fr. Dutch by* James S. Holmes. DuIn

Hansel and Gretel. Anne Sexton. InPS

Hansel, Gretel and Ruby Redlips. Anita Endrezze-Danielson. HATNAP

Hanukah. Jakov de Haan, *tr. fr. Dutch by* David Soetendorp. VWA

Hap. Thomas Hardy. AWP; CMoP; EaLo; EBVV; MoBrPo; NAEL-2; NIP; NoAM; NoP; OAEL-2; PPP; Son; TEP

Happen you will rise. For the Lame. Lucille Clifton. CAPP

Happened like this: it was hot as hell. The Death of the Craneman. Alfred Hayes. LiTA; WaP

Happening at Sordid Creek. Peter Porter. NoAM

Happening on Aegina. John Logan. CAPP

Happier, I would surely be. The Unfortunate Male. Kalonymos ben Kalonymos, *tr. fr. Hebrew by* J. Chotzner. *Fr.* The Touchstone. TrJP

Happiest Day, the Happiest Hour, The. Poe. AmPP; LiTA; OxBA

Happiest Heart, The. John Vance Cheney. AA; WGRP

Happily Ever After, from the Story of the Same Name. Janet Dubé. DT

Happiness. William Dickey. Psk

Happiness. Louise Glück. MAYP

Happiness. Hermann Jandl, *tr. fr. German by* Beth Bjorklund. CoAuP

Happiness. Priscilla Leonard. BLPA

Happiness. Carl Sandburg. AnAmPo; OxBA

Happiness amidst Troubles. Immanuel di Roma, *tr. fr. Italian by* J. Chotzner. TrJP

Happiness doesn't have any songs. Pain. Edith Södergran, *tr. by* Samuel Charters. WPOW

Happiness Found, *sel.* Augustus Montague Toplady. "Lord, it is not Life to live." TrPWD

Happiness is like a crystal. Happiness. Priscilla Leonard. BLPA

Happiness Is the Art of Being Broken. Bruce Dawe. NoAM

Happiness Is When. Tachibana Akemi, *tr. fr. Japanese by* Burton Watson. *Fr.* Thirty Tanka. FCEI

Happiness Makes Up in Height for What It Lacks in Length. Robert Frost. MoAB; MoAmPo

Happiness of 6 A.M. Harvey Shapiro. NYBP

Happy. Alastair Fowler. NPo

Happy about Being Old. Yüan Mei, *tr. fr. Chinese by* Jonathan Chaves. CoBLCP

Happy are men who yet before they are killed. Insensibility. Wilfred Owen. CMoP; FaBoTw; InPS; LiTB; LiTM; MMA; MoAB; OBWP; OxBTC; WaP

Happy are they and charmed in life. Memorial: On the Slain at Chickamauga. Herman Melville. AA

Happy Are Those Who Have Died. Charles Péguy, *tr. fr. French by* Jessie Degen *and* Richard Eberhart. WaaP

Happy are you, whom Quantock overlooks. William Diaper. *Fr.* Brent; a Poem to Thomas Palmer Esq. NOEC; OBSV

Happy Army, The. Peter Bland. ATNZ

Happy band on the hill slope, A. The Battle of Waun Gaseg. Llywelyn ab y Moel, *tr. by* H. Idris Bell. OBWVE

Happy Bird, The. John Clare. PBBP

Happy Birthday. Frank Bidart. HCAP

Happy Britannia. James Thomson. *Fr.* The Seasons: Summer. FaBoPP; SeCePo

Happy Child, A. Kate Greenaway. BoTP

Happy choristers of air. A Pastoral[l] Hymn[e]. John Hall. MeLP; OBS; TrPWD

Happy Christmas, A. Frances Ridley Havergal. BLRP

Happy Countryman, The. Nicholas Breton. *See* Passionate Shepherd, The: Merry Country Lad, The.

Happy Day (or Independence Day). James Cunningham. JB

Happy Day Will Soon Appear, The. *Unknown.* AH

Happy He. *Unknown.* EIL

Happy he whose eyes have view'd. Boethius, *tr. fr. Latin by* Samuel Johnson. *Fr.* The Consolation of Philosophy, III, 12. OBVE

Happy Heart, The. Thomas Dekker *and others.* *See* Pleasant Comedy of Patient Grissell [*or* Grissel *or* Grissill], The: Art thou poor, yet hast thou golden slumbers?

Happy Heart, A. Josephine D. Henderson Heard. CBWP-4

Happy Hen, The. James Agee. ErPo

Happy Husbandman; or, Country Innocence, The. *Unknown.* CoMu

Happy insect, what can be. The Grasshopper. Abraham Cowley, *after the Greek of* Anacreon. AWP; FM; OAEL-1; OBVE; SeCV-1; WiR

Happy [*or* Happie] is he that from all business clear. The Praises of a Country Life. Ben Jonson. OBVE; SeCP

Happy Is the Country Life. *Unknown.* OBS

Happy Is the Man. Bible, *O.T.* *Fr.* Proverbs, III: 13-18. TrJP

Happy Is the Man. Bible, *O.T.* *See* Psalms: Psalm I ("Blessed is the man. . .").

Happy is the man who loves the woods and waters. Beatus Vir. Richard Le Gallienne. OHIP

Happy is the man whom Thou hast set apart. "Yehoash," *tr. by* Isidore Goldstick. TrJP

Happy Isle. Spenser. *Fr.* The Faerie Queene, IV, 10. OBSC

Happy Life, The. Martial, *tr. by* Earl of Surrey. NOBE; OBVE; SiPS

Happy Life, The. Sir Henry Wotton. *See* How happy is he born and taught.

Happy Life of a Country Parson, The. Pope. BXAP

Happy Man, A. Carphyllides, *tr. fr. Greek by* E. A. Robinson. AWP

Happy moments tell me, pray. The Birth of Time. Josephine D. Henderson Heard. CBWP-4

Happy Myrtillo. Henry Carey. SeCePo

Happy New Year, A, *sels.* W. H. Auden. OBSV
   "Colonel from Cheltenham stopped everyone, A."
   "Cry went through me like a stab of a knife, A."
   "Doctors attended behind each chair."
   "In corduroy trousers and seedy black coats."
   "On a lorry the centre of a gaping crowd."

Happy New Year, Anyway. Joanna Cole. NTCP

Happy Nightingale, The. *Unknown.* OxBChV

Happy Pair, The, *sel.* Sir Charles Sedley. Marriage and Money. OBSV

Happy Pair, A. Priscilla Jane Thompson. CBWP-2

Happy people die whole, they are all dissolved in a moment. Post Mortem. Robinson Jeffers. MoAmPo; TrGrPo

Happy road that brought me here, The. Shankill. Eileen Shanahan. NeIP

Happy, Saviour, Would I Be. Edwin H. Nevin. AH

Happy Song-sparrow, that on woodland side. The Fringilla Melodia. Henry Beck Hirst. AA

Happy Swain, The. Ambrose Philips. EnLoPo

Happy that first white age! when wee. Boethius, *tr. fr. Latin by* Henry Vaughan. *Fr.* The Consolation of Philosophy, II, 5. OBVE

Happy that this is another. Where We Could Go. Gary Soto. NAmP

Happy the dead! Consolation in War. Lewis Mumford. NYBP

Happy the feeling from the bosom thrown. Sonnet: To———. Wordsworth. ChER

Happy the Man. Horace. *See* Odes: III, 29. "Descended of an ancient line" ("Tyrrhena regum progenies").

Happy the man, who free as air. The Widower. Royall Tyler. OBAL

Happy the man, who his whole time doth bound. The Old Man of Verona. Claudian, *tr. by* Abraham Cowley. AWP; OBVE

Happy the man who in his pot contains. The Suet Dumpling. *Unknown.* BXAP

Happy the man who, safe on shore. The Hurricane. Philip Freneau. MOS; TAP

Happy the man, who void of cares and strife. The Splendid Shilling. John Phillips. BXAP; NOEC; OAEL-1; Par

Happy the man whose wish and care. Ode on [*or* to] Solitude. Pope. AWP; FiP; FL; HeIP; InVP; NAEL-1; PoRA; Prf; TEP (Quiet Life, The.) GTBS; GTBS-P (Solitude.) FaFP; TrGrPo

Happy the nations of the moral North! Donna Julia. Byron. *Fr.* Don Juan, I. PoEL-4

Happy the savage of those early times. European Crimes. Charles Churchill. *Fr.* Gotham. NOEC

Happy the wild birds that can soar. Unfair to Men. *Unknown, tr. by* Gwyn Jones. OBWVE

Happy the young man who disregards. The Voyage. Charles Hubert Sisson. NPo

Happy they who die for the earth which also dies. Happy Are Those Who Have Died. Charles Péguy, *tr. by* Jessie Degen *and* Richard Eberhart. WaaP

Happy those early days [*or* dayes]! when I. The Retreat[e]. Henry Vaughan. AWP; BLPL; FF; GTBS; GTBS-P; HAP; HeIP; InPK; InPS; InVP; JCP; LiTB; MeLP; MePo; NAEL-1; NIP; NOBE; NOCV; NoP; OAEL-1; OBEV; OBS; OBWVE; PoE; PoEL-2; PoRA; PPP; SeCePo; SeCP; SeCV-1; TOF; TrGrPo

Happy Thought. Robert Louis Stevenson. BoTP; FaBoBe; OxBChV; PWR; RAR; RHPC

Happy, thrice happy times in silver age! Desiderium. Phineas Fletcher. *Fr.* The Purple Island, I. OBS

Happy to have these fish! The Catch. Raymond Carver. ASP

Happy Too Much. Boethius, *tr. fr. Latin by* Elizabeth I, Queen of England. *Fr.* The Consolation of Philosophy, II. CTC

Happy Tree, The. Gerald Gould. WGRP

Happy trifles, can ye bear. Sent to Miss Bell H——, with a Pair of Buckles. John Cunningham. FaBoUs

Happy View, A. C. Day Lewis. CMoP

Happy Warrior, The. Sir Herbert Read. MMA

Happy Warrior, The. Wordsworth. *See* Who is the happy warrior?

Happy Were He. Earl of Essex. EIL; OxBSP (Content.) OBSC

Happy whitethroat on the sweeing bough, The. The Happy Bird. John Clare. PBBP

Happy who like Ulysses, or that lord. Heureux Qui, comme Ulysse, A Fait un Beau Voyage. Joachim Du Bellay, *tr. by* G. K. Chesterton. AWP

Happy Winter, Steamy Tub. Karen Gundersheimer. RAR

Happy Workhouse and the Good Effects of Industry, The. John Dyer. *Fr.* The Fleece, III. NOEC

Happy ye leaves when as those lily [*or* lilly] hands. Spencer. *Fr.* Amoretti, I. EBEV; NAEL-1; OAEL-1; PoE; Son

Happy Youth, that shalt possesse. To My Cousin (C.R.) Marrying My Lady (A.). Thomas Carew. SeCP

Happy's the man whose pleasant labours with the lark. The Ploughman, in Imitation of Milton. Samuel Jones. NOEC

Harald, the Agnostic Ale-loving Old Shepherd Enemy of the Whisky-drinking Ploughmen and Harvesters, Walks over the Sabbath Hill to the Shearing. George Mackay Brown. NePoEA-2

Harangue on the Death of Hayyim Nahman Bialik. César Tiempo, *tr. fr. Spanish by* Donald Devenish Walsh. TrJP

Harbach 1944. János Pilinszky, *tr. fr. Hungarian by* Jascha Kessler. FOC

Harbingers are come, The. See, see their mark. The Forerunners. George Herbert. JCP; MePo; NAEL-1; NoP; TOF

Harbor, The. John Engels. KS

Harbor. Nancy Price. IHMS

Harbor, The. Carl Sandburg. TAP

Harbor at Seattle, The. Robert Hass. NPGG; SV

Harbor Dawn, The. Hart Crane. *Fr.* The Bridge: Powhatan's Daughter. AmPP; CMoP; FaBV; GOA; LiTM; MoAB; MoAmPo; NoAM; NOBA; OxBA; PrIm; TrGrPo

Harbor is old, I can't wait any longer, The. George Seferis, *tr. fr. Greek by* Edmund Keeley *and* Philip Sherrard. *Fr.* Mythistorima, IX. VMG

Harbor of Illusion, The. Charles Bernstein. UL

Harbor plovers calling to their friends. Lady Izumi, *tr. fr. Japanese by* Hiroaki Sato. *Fr.* Fifty-one Tanka. FCEI

Harbour. Edward Kamau Brathwaite. PBCV

Harbour, The. Winifred M. Letts. TIRV

Harbour Bridge, The. Thomas Hardy. NoAM

Harbour roars out, The. Creide's Lament for Cael. *Unknown.* NOIV

Hard aport! Now close to shore sail! Adrian Block's Song. Edward Everett Hale. PAH

Hard as hurdle arms, with a broth of goldish flue. Harry Ploughman. Gerard Manley Hopkins. FaBoMo

Hard brown bug, maybe a beetle, A. He Faces the Second Winter. Philip Levine. *Fr.* Sierra Kid. PoA

Hard, but you can polish it. Donald Justice. *Fr.* Things. CRP (Stone.) TDD

Hard by the Indian lodges, where the bush. The Corn Husker. Pauline Johnson. CaP

Hard by the lilied Nile I saw. A Crocodile. Thomas Lovell Beddoes. *Fr.* The Last Man. FM; NOBVV; OBTV; RB

Hard by the tall elms and a wooded hill. The Old Rustic Mill. George Sands Johnson. PWR

Hard captains of industry, The. Still Century. Tom Paulin. FaBCIP

Hard Country. Philip Booth. CoAP

Hard Daddy. Langston Hughes. BANP

Hard Frost. Andrew Young. BoNaP

Hard frosts march together. Frosts Are Coming. László Nagy, *tr. by* Alan Dixon. MHuP

Hard Heart of Mine. Henry Alline. AH

Hard helmets and high boots. Daredevil. Kirby Congdon. PeHV

Hard is my fate, thus to want bread. Between an Unemployed Artist and His Wife. *Unknown.* NOEC

Hard is the doubt, and difficult to deeme. Spenser. *Fr.* The Faerie Queene, IV, 9. OAEL-1

Hard is the stone, but harder still. The Image-Maker. Oliver St. John Gogarty. OBEV; OBMV; PoRA

Hard it is, very hard. The Choice of the Cross. Dorothy L. Sayers. *Fr.* The Devil to Pay. TrCP

Hard it was for this garden soil. Sheikh Ibrahim Zauq, *tr. fr. Urdu by* Ahmed Ali. GoT

Hard Journey, A. Yes. Hayden Carruth. VGW

Hard knowledge to come by. The Music of the Spheres. Marvin Bell. PoA

Hard Listener, The. William Carlos Williams. OxBSP

Hard Lovers, The. George Dillon. PoA

Hard Questions. Margaret Tsuda. RFM

Hard Rock was "known not to take no shit." Hard Rock Returns to Prison from the Hospital for the Criminal Insane. Etheridge Knight. InPS; MoP; NIP; NNaP; TAP; UnPo

Hard sand breaks, The. Hermes of the Ways. Hilda Doolittle ("H. D."). LiTA; WPE

Hard shape to describe—not circular, not square, A. A Playful Poem on a Chicken Egg. Hsieh Chin, *tr. by* Jonathan Chaves. CoBLCP

Hard stones! Hard stones! The Convict Song. Alfred Cruickshank. PBCV

Hard Strain in a Delicate Place. Janet Sylvester. MAYP

Hard Structure of the World, The. Richard Eberhart. NoAM

Hard Summer, The. Medbh McGuckian. FaBCIP

Hard Times. John Ashbery. NoAM

Hard Times. *Unknown.* AmFP

Hard tin bird was my lover, A. Weathercock. Elizabeth Jennings. NePoEA

Hard to Bear. Tudor Jenks. OBCA

Hard to pronounce and play, the OBOE. Oboe. Laurence McKinney. NBLV

Hard was thy fate in all the scenes of life. William Roscoe. OBD

Hard-working Miner, The. *Unknown.* AmFP, 2 *vers.*

Hardcastle Crags. Sylvia Plath. GoYe

Hardearned Overturned Caribbean Basin Stomp. George Starbuck. BLA

Harden now thy tyred hart with more then flinty rage. Thomas Campion. AAS; OBVE

Harder lesson, to learn continence, A. Cymochles and Phaedria. Spenser. *Fr.* The Faerie Queene, II, 6. OBSC

Harder Task, The. *Unknown.* BLRP

Harder time is coming, A. The Respite. Ingeborg Bachmann, *tr. by* Michael Hamburger. WPOW

Hardest work I ever did, The. Bile Them Cabbage Down. *Unknown.* AmFP

Hardly a Man Is Now Alive. Ring Lardner. OBAL

Hardly spring, with ice. Chiyo, *tr. fr. Japanese by* David Ray. BoWoP

Hardness of her heart and truth of mine, The. Sir John Davies. *Fr.* The Gulling Sonnets. Son

Hardness Scale, The. Joyce Peseroff. LLLT; PPR

Hardon ("Get One Today"). Ian Wedde. PeNZ

Hardship of Accounting, The. Robert Frost. FaBoCh; FaBoCo; FaFP; OBAL

Hardweed Path Going. A. R. Ammons. HCAP; UnPo; VGW

Hardy Perennial. Richard Eberhart. GOYP

Hardy's Plymouth. Geoffrey Grigson. FaBoPP

Hare, A. Walter de la Mare. EBEV

Hare. Molly Holden. TEP

Hare, The. C. H. Sisson. NPo

Hare and the Pig, The. L. J. Bridgman. RHPC

Hare and the Tortoise, The. Ian Serraillier. SO

Hare-hunting. William Somervile. *Fr.* The Chase. NOEC

Hare in the Moon, The. Ryokan, *tr. fr. Japanese by* Geoffrey Bownas *and* Anthony Thwaite. PeBJV

Hare in the Snow, The. Gloria Rawlinson. ATNZ

Hare in Winter. Marge Piercy. NeAC

Hare, Mr. Hare. *Unknown, tr. by* Geoffrey Bownas *and* Anthony Thwaite. PeBJV

Hare-skin sky. A distinct. By Day. Paul Celan, *tr. by* Joachim Neugroschel. AnAn

Hare we had run over, The. Interruption to a Journey. Norman MacCaig. RB

Hares at Play. John Clare. RB

Hares on the Mountain. *Unknown.* ErPo; OBET

Hares on their forms at dusk were not so still. Robin Hyde. *Fr.* The Houses, IV. PeNZ

Hari has fashioned an offering of lights. Surdas, *tr. by* John Stratton Hawley *and* Mark Juergensmeyer. SSI

Hari helps his people. Mirabai, *tr. by* Willis Barnstone *and* Usha Nilsson. BoWoP

Hari, look at me a while. Mirabai, *tr. by* Willis Barnstone *and* Usha Nilsson. BoWoP

Hark. John Webster. *See* Duchess of Malfi, The: Hark, Now Everything Is Still.

Hark! / What booming. Arcana Sylvarum. Charles De Kay. AA

Hark! ah, the nightingale. Philomela. Matthew Arnold. OAEL-2; OBEV; PBBP; PPP; UnPo

Hark, All Ye Lovely Saints. *Unknown.* OAEL-1

Hark, All You Ladies. Thomas Campion. ElL ("Harke, al you ladies that do sleep.") AAS; EBEV; PoEL-2 (Proserpina.) OBSC

Hark, and Hear My Trumpet Sounding. *Unknown.* AH

Hark at the lips of this pink whorl of shell. Frank Dempster Sherman. AA

Hark! do I hear again the roar. Columbus Dying. Edna Dean Proctor. PAH

Hark! even here, into the chambers of the Palace. Naga Okimaro, *tr. fr. Japanese. Fr.* Manyo Shu. Ma

Hark! from the tombs a doleful sound. Plenary. *Unknown.* AmFP

Hark! from yon covert, where those tow'ring oaks. Hare-hunting. William Somervile. *Fr.* The Chase. NOEC

Hark! from yon high grey Downs the tremulous musical sheep bells. Above the Medway. A. J. Munby. *Fr.* The Vales of the Medway. FaBoPP

Hark, happy lovers, hark! A Kiss. William Drummond of Hawthornden. EIL

Hark, hark! Hark! Hibiscus and Salvia Flowers. D. H. Lawrence. FaBoPV

Hark, hark!/ Bow-wow./ The watch-dogs bark. Shakespeare. *Fr.* The Tempest. SoSe

Hark! hark! down the century's long reaching slope. Yorktown Centennial Lyric. Paul Hamilton Hayne. PAH

Hark! hark! that pig—that pig! the hideous note. Ode to a Pig while His Nose Was Being Bored. Robert Southey. NOBL

Hark, hark, the dogs do bark. Mother Goose. OxNR (Beggars Are Coming to Town, The.) OBP

Hark! Hark! the Lark. Shakespeare. *Fr.* Cymbeline, II, iii. AWP; BoTP; CH; ChTr; FaBoCh; FaBV; FaFP; FaPON; HeIP; LiTB; NIP; NoP; PrIm; TrGrPo

(Aubade: "Hark! hark! the lark at heaven's gate sings.") OBEV

(Morning Song, A.) GN

(Song: "Hark! hark! the lark at heaven's gate sings.") EIL; FiP

(Song to Imogen.) OBSC

Hark! Hark! with Harps of Gold. Edwin Hubbell Chapin. AH

Hark, how chimes the Passing Bell. The Passing Bell. James Shirley. ACP

Hark how the lyrick choristers o' th' wood. To Clarastella on St. Valentines Day Morning. Robert Heath. OBS

Hark how the mower Damon sung. Damon the Mower. Andrew Marvell. JCP; NAEL-1; OAEL-1

Hark, how the Passing Bell. Upon a Passing Bell. Thomas Washbourne. FaBoRV

Hark, I hear the bells of Westgate. Westgate-on-Sea. Sir John Betjeman. OxBoLi

Hark I hear the cannons roar. A Carrouse to the Emperor, the Royal Pole, and the Much-wronged Duke of Lorrain. *Unknown.* CoMu

Hark! I hear the tramp of thousands. The Reveille. Bret Harte. GN; OHIP; PAH

Hark! in the still night. Who goes there? Sixteen Dead Men. Dora Sigerson Shorter. ACP

Hark! My Beloved! Bible, *O.T. Fr.* The Song of Solomon, II: 8-13. TrJP

("Voice of my darling, The.") BoWoP, 8–14, *ad. by* Willis Barnstone.

Hark, my Flora! Love doth call us. A Song of Dalliance. William Cartwright. ErPo; JCP

Hark, Now Everything Is Still. John Webster. *Fr.* The Duchess of Malfi, IV, ii. EIL; HAP; NoP; OBD; QFR; SeCePo

(Hark.) CH

(Hearke, Now Every Thing Is Still.) OBS

(Shrouding of the Duchess of Malfi, The.) NOBE; OBEV

Hark! O hark, you guilty trees. Orpheus to Woods. Richard Lovelace. CaPo

Hark! one saith: "Proclaim!" All Flesh Is Grass. Bible, *O.T. Fr.* Isaiah, XL: 6–8. TrJP

Hark, reader! wilt be learn'd i' th' wars? To My Truly Valiant, Learned Friend, Who in His Book Resolved the Art Gladiatory into the Mathematics. Richard Lovelace. CaPo; PoEL-3

Hark! she is call'd, the parting houre is come. On the Glorious Assumption of Our Blessed Lady. Richard Crashaw. OBS

Hark, the bells are ringing. *Unknown, tr. fr. Japanese. Fr.* Manyo Shu. Ma

Hark, the bonny Christchurch bells! Christchurch Bells. *Unknown.* OBET

Hark! the cock crows, and yon bright star. The New Year. Charles Cotton. GoTL; OBS

Hark! the flow of the four rivers. Farewells from Paradise. Elizabeth Barrett Browning. OBEV

Hark! the herald angels sing/ timidly. Dean Inge. Humbert Wolfe. FaBoEE

(On Dean Inge.) ChTr

Hark! the Mavis. Burns. *See* Ca' the Yowes.

Hark! the tiny cowslip bell. Spring Has Come. *Unknown.* BoTP

Hark! the Vesper Hymn Is Stealing. Thomas Moore. EnRP

Hark! They cry! I hear by that. Yolp, Yolp, Yolp, Yolp. *Unknown.* EIL

Hark! 'tis freedom that calls, come, patriots, awake! *Unknown.* PAH

Hark! 'Tis the Saviour of Mankind. John Murray. AH

Hark! 'tis the twanging horn o'er yonder bridge. The Winter Evening. William Cowper. *Fr.* The Task, IV. SeCePo (Post-Boy, The.) FiP

Hark! 'tis the voice of the mountain. The Battle of Eutaw. William Gilmore Simms. PAH

Hark to the rumble of the earthquake god! Ruaumoko—the Earthquake God. Mohi Turei, *tr. by* A. Armstrong. WTO

Hark to the story of Willie the Weeper. Willy the Weeper. *Unknown.* GBP

Hark to the thrush gurgling in yonder tree! The Thrush. Alfred Austin. TEP

Hark to the whimper of the sea-gull. The Sea-Gull. Ogden Nash. FaFP; FPL; MOS

Hark, ye sighing sons of sorrow. The Mouldering Vine. *Unknown.* AmFP

Hark! Young Democracy from sleep. Bernard O'Dowd. *Fr.* Young Democracy. PoAu-1

Harke, al you ladies that do sleep. Thomas Campion. *See* Hark, All You Ladies.

Harlackenden, among these men of note Christ hath thee seated. Among These Troopes of Christs Souldiers, Came. Mr. Roger Harlackenden. Edward Johnson. SCAP

Harlem. Jean Brierre, *tr. fr. French by* John F. Matheus. TTY

Harlem ("Here on the edge of hell"). Langston Hughes. PPP

Harlem ("What happens to a dream deferred"). Langston Hughes. *Fr.* Lenox Avenue Mural. Aip; AmNP; AmPP; GLP; HCAP; HeIP; HoPM; InPS; NoP; PoNe

(Dream Deferred.) FF; LiTM; PoBA; PPP; SoSe

Harlem—a Negro Ghetto. Berysh Vaynshteyn, *tr. fr. Yiddish by* Benjamin *and* Barbara Harshav *and* Kathryn Helle. AYP

Harlem at Night. Rose Ausländer, *tr. fr. German by* Beth Bjorklund. CoAuP

Harlem Dancer, The. Claude McKay. BANP; BPo; FF; NoAM; Son; TAP

Harlem dud. For "Mr. Dudley," a Black Spy. James A. Emanuel. BPo

Harlem Freeze Frame. Lebert Bethune. PoBA

Harlem Gallery, *sels.* Melvin Beaunearus Tolson.

Birth of John Henry, The. BPo; TTY

Sea-Turtle and the Shark, The. PoBA

Harlem Gallery: From the Inside. Larry Neal. BPo

Harlem in January. Julia Fields. CNA

Harlem is vicious. Return of the Native. Amiri Baraka. BPo

Harlem, Montana; Just Off the Reservation. James Welch. CDW; HATNAP; NOVW; STE

Harlem Negroes. Berysh Vaynshteyn, *tr. fr. Yiddish by* Benjamin *and* Barbara Harshav. *Fr.* Negroes. AYP

Harlem Riot, 1943. Pauli Murray. PoBA

Harlem Shadows. Claude McKay. AmPP; BANP; PoNe

Harlem Sounds: Hallelujah Corner. William Browne. AmNP

Harlem Sweeties. Langston Hughes. LiTM; NoP; PoNe; TTY

Harlequin of Dreams, The. Sidney Lanier. AA

Harlot, The. Hamish Brown. PoSH

Harlot's Catch. Robert Nichols. ErPo; FaBoTw

Harlot's House, The. Oscar Wilde. EBVV; MoBrPo; NAEL-2; NoAM

Harmonica Man. P. Wolny. PCP

Harmonics. William Vaughn Moody. AnAmPo

Harmonie du Soir. Baudelaire, *tr. fr. French by* Lord Alfred Douglas. AWP

Harmoniums. Kathryn Rantala. BWV

Harmony is the passion of my ignorance. Predilections. Alfredo Giuliani, *tr. by* Lawrence R. Smith. NItP

Harnessed and zipped on a bright. Hazard's Optimism. William Meredith. ASP

Harnet and the Bittle, a Wiltshire Tale, The ("A harnet zet in a hollur tree"). John Yonge Akerman. ChTr

Haro! Haro! The Appeal to Harold. H. C. Bunner. AA

Harold the Dauntless, *sel.* Sir Walter Scott.

Tis Merry in Greenwood. FaPON; OHIP

Harold the Valiant. Mary Elizabeth DeWitt Stebbins. AA

Harold's Song: Rosabelle. Sir Walter Scott. *See* Lay of the Last Minstrel, The: Rosabelle.

Haroun Al-Rachid for Heart's-Life. *Unknown, tr. fr. Arabic by* E. Powys Mathers. *Fr.* The Thousand and One Nights. AWP

Haroun, the Caliph, through the sunlit street. Power. Thomas Stephens Collier. AA

Haroun's Favorite Song. *Unknown, tr. fr. Arabic by* E. Powys Mathers. *Fr.* The Thousand and One Nights. AWP

Harp, The. Bruce Weigl. MAYP

Harp of David, The. Jacob Cohen, *tr. fr. Hebrew by* Sholom J. Kahn. TrJP

Harp of David, The. "Yehoash," tr. fr. Yiddish by Alter Brody. TrJP

Harp of Sorrow, The. Ethel Clifford. WGRP

Harp of the North, farewell! The hills grow dark. Farewell, Thou Minstrel Harp. Sir Walter Scott. Fr. The Lady of the Lake, VI. OBNC

Harp of the North! that mouldering long hast hung. The Chase. Sir Walter Scott. Fr. The Lady of the Lake, I. EnRP

Harp of Wild and Dream-like Strain. Emily Brontë. Mes

Harp Song. Lu Yu, tr. fr. Chinese by Burton Watson. CoBCP

Harp Song of the Dane Women. Kipling. Fr. Puck of Pook's Hill. HAP; OBNC; PoRA; SeCePo

Harp That Once through Tara's Halls, The. Thomas Moore. ACP; AnIL; BLPL; EnRP; FaPoR; GN; NAEL-2; PoLF

Harpalus' Complaint of Phillida's Love. Unknown. OBSC

Harper, The. Unknown, tr. fr. Early Modern Irish by Frank O'Connor. AnIL

Harpers Ferry. Selden Rodman. PoNe

Harpkin. Unknown. GBP

Harps Hung Up in Babylon. Arthur Colton. AnAmPo; WGRP

Harried/ earth is swept, The. The Wind Increases. William Carlos Williams. NAAL-2

Harried we were, and spent. The Waradgery Tribe. Mary Gilmore. PoAu-1

Harriet. Audre Lorde. BlSi

Harriet. Robert Lowell. NoP

Harriet Beecher Stowe. Paul Laurence Dunbar. BPo

Harriet Simper Has Her Day. John Trumbull. Fr. The Progress of Dulness. AmPP

Harriet there was always somebody calling us crazy. Harriet. Audre Lorde. BlSi

Harriet Tubman. Margaret Abigail Walker. PoNe

Harrowing of Hell, The. Unknown. ACP

Harry Parry. Unknown. GBP; OxNR

Harry Pearce. David Campbell. PoAu-2

Harry Ploughman. Gerard Manley Hopkins. FaBoMo

Harry, whose tuneful and well-measured song. To Mr. H. Lawes on His Airs. Milton. AWP; NoP
(Sonnet: To Mr. H. Lawes, on His Aires.) OBS

Harsh bray and hollow, The. Two Kitchen Songs. Dame Edith Sitwell. CMoP

Harsh Climate. Charles Simic. LCAP

Harsh cry the crows. The Solitary. Friedrich Wilhelm Nietzsche, tr. by Ludwig Lewisohn. AWP

Hart Crane. Julian Symons. PoA

Hart he loves the high wood, The. Mother Goose. FaBoCh; GBP; OxNR

Hart-Leap Well. Wordsworth. BeLS

Hart Loves the High Wood, The. Unknown. RB

Hartico. Anna Walters. VoR

Hartlaub Gull, The. H. C. ten Berge, tr. fr. Dutch by Greta Kilburn. DuIn

Hart's Castle. Gawin Douglas. Fr. King Hart. PoEL-1

Harvest, The. Shafiq al-kamali, tr. fr. Arabic by Sargon Boulus. MAP

Harvest, The. Yusuf al-Khal, tr. fr. Arabic by Abdullah al-Udhari. MPAW

Harvest. Mary Désirée Anderson. CN

Harvest. Ellen Mackay Hutchinson Cortissoz. AA

Harvest, The. Alice C. Henderson. BoTP

Harvest. M. M. Hutchinson. BoTP

Harvest. Philip Levine. AnAn

Harvest. Thomas Nashe. Fr. Summer's Last Will and Testament. OBSC

Harvest. Gene Shuford. GoYe

Harvest and Consecration. Elizabeth Jennings. NePoEA-2

Harvest Bow, The. Seamus Heaney. FaBCIP; NoAM

Harvest Dawn Is Near, The. George Burgess. AH

Harvest Home. Henry Alford. WGRP

Harvest Home. Dryden. Fr. King Arthur. PrIm
(Song: "Your hay it is mow'd, and your corn is reap'd.") SeCV-2

Harvest Home. Arthur Guiterman. RHPC

Harvest-Home. Theocritus, tr. fr. Greek by Charles Stuart Calverley. Fr. Idylls, VII. AWP

Harvest Hymn. Whittier. Fr. For an Autumn Festival. OHIP

Harvest Month. Natan Zach, tr. fr. Hebrew by Warren Bargad and Stanley F. Chyet. IP

Harvest Moon, The. Longfellow. GN

Harvest moon:/ On the bamboo mat. Kikaku, tr. fr. Japanese by Geoffrey Bownas and Anthony Thwaite. PeBJV

Harvest moon. Ransetsu, tr. fr. Japanese by Geoffrey Bownas and Anthony Thwaite. PeBJV

Harvest of the Sea. Máire Mhac an tSaoi. PBWP

Harvest of War. Kappiyarrukkappiyanar, tr. fr. Tamil by A. K. Ramanujan. PLW

Harvest Poem. David Fisher. NPGG

Harvest Song. Joseph Campbell. OFD

Harvest Song. Richard Dehmel, tr. fr. German by Ludwig Lewisohn. AWP

Harvest Song. Ludwig Heinrich Christoph Hölty, tr. fr. German by Charles T. Brooks. AWP

Harvest Song. Jean Toomer. NoP

Harvest Song. Unknown. BoTP; OxNR

Harvest Time. Star Powers. GoYe

Harvest Time. G. A. Watermeyer, tr. fr. Afrikaans by Guy Butler, Uys Krige and Jack Cope. PeSA

Harvest to Seduce, A. Melville Cane. NYBP

Harvestcall. Niyi Osundare. UAS

Harvester's Song. George Peele. Fr. The Old Wives' [or Wife's] Tale. TrGrPo
"Lo! here we come a-reaping, a-reaping," 4 ll.

Harvesting of the Roses, The. Menahem ben Jacob, tr. fr. Hebrew. TrJP

Harvesting Wheat for the Public Share. Li Chü, tr. fr. Chinese by Kenneth Rexroth and Ling Chung. BoWoP; OV; PBWP

Harvey Always Wins. Jack Prelutsky. NTCP

Has a gold tooth, sits long hours. Black Bourgeoisie. Amiri Baraka. BPo

Has any one seen my fair. Cressid. Nora Perry. AA

Has Any One Supposed It Lucky to Be Born? Walt Whitman. Fr. Song of Myself, VII. NAs

Has anybody seen my Mopser? The Bandog. Walter de la Mare. BrPo

Has anybody seen my mouse? Missing. A. A. Milne. MoShBr; PDV

Has anyone come again, sad heart? Loneliness. Faiz Ahmad Faiz, tr. by Mahmood Jamal. PBMUP

Has auld Kilmarnock seen the dell? Tam Samson's Elegy. Burns. PoEL-4

Has dawn come so soon? Emperor Fushimi, tr. fr. Japanese by Steven D. Carter. WFTW

Has frost left last night. Sunlight Shining of Red Leaves. Masayori, tr. by Steven D. Carter. WFTW

Has he tempered the viol's wood. Ezra Pound. Fr. Cantos, LXXXII. HAP

Has it flown away. Shunzei, tr. fr. Japanese by Geoffrey Bownas and Anthony Thwaite. PeBJV

Has it grown so late? Tonna, tr. fr. Japanese by Steven D. Carter. WFTW

Has just crawled across. A Great Annelid Worm. Bruce Hawkins. BWV

Has not altered. Spenser's Ireland. Marianne Moore. FaBoWP; LiTA; LiTM; NoAM; NOBA; OxBA; TAP

Has not the night been as a drunken rose. The Drunken Rose. Amarou, tr. by E. Powys Mathers. AWP

Has only books. A Room. Sa'di Yusuf, tr. by Abdullah al-Udhari. MPAW

"Has the Marquis La Fayette." A New Song. Joseph Stansbury. PAH

Has the same carriage. Perspective. Pierre Reverdy, tr. by David Gascoyne. RHTwFP

Has there any old fellow got mixed with the boys? The Boys. Oliver Wendell Holmes. WBLP

Has thrust his nose under every board. Ego. Robert Siegel. GeTw; PoA

Hasbrouck and the Rose. H. Phelps Putnam. OxBA

Haschish, The. Whittier. AnAmPo; OBAL

Hasidic Jew from Sadagora. Rose Ausländer, tr. fr. German by Ewald Osers. VWA

Hasidim Dance. Nelly Sachs, tr. fr. German by Keith Bosley. VWA

Hassan, sels. James Elroy Flecker.
Hassan's Serenade. Fr. I, ii. OBEV
War Song of the Saracens. Fr. III, iii. FaBV; MoBrPo

Hassan's Serenade. James Elroy Flecker. Fr. Hassan, I, ii. OBEV

Hast thou a charm to stay the morning-star. Hymn before Sunrise, in the Vale of Chamouni. Samuel Taylor Coleridge. EnRP; WGRP

Hast thou a cunning instrument of play. Preparation. Thomas Edward Brown. OBEV

Hast thou a lamp, a little lamp. The Lamp. Sarah Pratt McLean Greene. AA

Hast Thou Given the Horse Strength. Bible, O.T. Fr. Job: Then the Lord Answered ("Who is this that darkeneth counsel by words without knowledge?"), XXXIX: 19–25. ChTr
(Horse, The.) FaPON, abr.; TrGrPo

Hast Thou Heard It, O My Brother. Theodore Chickering Williams. AH

Hast Thou Heard the Nightingale? Richard Watson Gilder. AA

Hast thou named all the birds without a gun? Forbearance. Emerson. AA; AnAmPo; GN; LiTA; TAP; TrGrPo; WGRP

Hast thou no mercy, wind, that thou should'st tear from me. The Mother's Lament. Mary E. Tucker. CBWP-1
Hast Thou Not Seen an Aged Rifted Tower. Hartley Coleridge. EnRP
"Hast thou ony greencloth." Robin Hood's End. *Unknown.* GoTL
Hast thou seen reversed the prophet's miracle. Frederick Goddard Tuckerman. *Fr.* Sonnets, IV, x. NOBA
"Hast thou seen that lordly castle." The Castle by the Sea. Ludwig Uhland, *tr. by* Longfellow. AWP
Hast thou seen the down i' th' air. A Song to a Lute. Sir John Suckling. CaPo; TrGrPo
(Song: "Hast thou seen the down i' th' air.") EnLoPo
Hast thou then survived. Wordsworth. *Fr.* Address to My Infant Daughter. Par
Haste, haste my verses with your sharpened teeth. Unto the Breach. Andrea Poliziano, *tr. by* John Addington Symonds. PeHV
Haste thee, nymph, and bring with thee. Milton. *Fr.* L'Allegro. GN
(Mirth, with Thee I Mean to Live.) FaBV
Haste to the mighty ocean. August. Henrietta Cordelia Ray. CBWP-3
Haste to the Wedding. Alex Comfort. ErPo
Hasten hither, little book. Company in Loneliness. *Unknown.* NOIV
Hasten on your childhood to the hour when white. Pablo Picasso, *tr. by* David Gascoyne. EAS
Hastening on, the wanderer strode. The Wanderer. "Yehoash," *tr. by* Isidore Goldstick. TrJP
Hasty and inexperienced creatures of the moment. Interruption. C. P. Cavafy, *tr. by* Edmund Keeley *and* Philip Sherrard. VMG
Hasty Pudding, The. Joel Barlow. AmPP; NOBA, *abr.;* OBAL, *abr.;* OxBA, *Sec. 1;* TAP
Hat Bar. Mildred Weston. FiBHP
Hatch, The. Norma Faber. SO
Hatched in a rasping darkness of dry sand. Letter IV. William Empson. LiTB
Hate! Pavel Grigoryevich Antokolsky, *tr. fr. Russian by* Babette Deutsch. TrJP
Hate. James Stephens. MoAB; MoBrPo
Hate, be a faithful prop, and find. Hate! Pavel Grigoryevich Antokolsky, *tr. by* Babette Deutsch. TrJP
Hate is only one of many responses. Frank O'Hara. NeAP; SOTW
Hate Mail. Steve Kowit. UL
Hate me or love, I care not, as I pass. The Unicorn. Ruth Pitter. MoBrPo
Hate only will I love. Love and Hate. *Unknown, tr. by* Frank O'Connor. TW
Hate-Song, A. Shelley. EnLoPo
Hate the Idle Pleasures. Shakespeare. *See* King Richard III: Now is the winter of our discontent.
Hated dog sits, The. In Memory of the Moon (A Killing). Charlotte DeClue. STE
Hateful Old Age, *sel. Unknown, tr. fr. Welsh by* Gwyn Jones. "Before my back was bent I was eloquent." OBWVE
Hatefully Poetry My Love. André Frénaud, *tr. fr. French by* Serge Gavronsky. RHTwFP
Hater he came and sat by a ditch, A. A Hate-Song. Shelley. EnLoPo
Hath any loved you well, down there. Marie de France, *tr. fr. French by* Arthur O'Shaughnessy. *Fr.* Chartivel. EnLoPo; WPOW
(Song from "Chartivel.") AWP
Hath God, who freely gave you his own Son. To the Rev'd Mr. Jno. Sparhawk on the Birth of his Son. Samuel Sewall. SCAP
Hath not the dark stream closed above thy head. The Tears of the Poplars. Edith M. Thomas. AA
Hath not the morning dawned with added light? Ethnogenesis. Henry Timrod. AmPP; AnAmPo; NOBA; OxBA
Hath the rude laugh of Boreas frighted thee. To a Mayflower. William E. Marshall. CaP
Hatikvah—a Song of Hope. Naphtali Herz Imber, *tr. fr. Hebrew by* Henry Snowman. TrJP
Hatred. Gwendolyn B. Bennett. AmNP; BANP; BlSi; CDC; PoBA
Hatred and greed and pride shall die. He Shall Speak Peace. Thomas Curtis Clark. WBLP
Hatred and vengeance, my eternal portion. Lines Written during a Period of Insanity. William Cowper. *Fr.* The Task. EBEV; FaBoRV; FiP; HAP; NOEC; NoP; OAEL-1; OPOP; PPP; Prf; TW
(Lines Written under the Influence of Delirium.) PoEL-3
Hatred, more powerful than love, unites us. A Litany of Hate. Renée Vivien, *tr. by* Beth Archer. DMF
Hatred of Distant Places. Ku Hsiung, *tr. fr. Chinese by* Lois Fusek. ATF
Hatred of Distant Places. Wen T'ing-yün, *tr. fr. Chinese by* Lois Fusek. ATF

Hatred of Men with Black Hair. Robert Bly. NaP; TW
Hats off!/ Along the street there comes. The Flag Goes By. Henry Holcomb Bennett. FaBoBe; FaFP; FaPON; GN; OHFP; OPP; PWR; WBLP
Hatshepsut, old girl, old friend. Sister Pharaoh. Ruth Whitman. MAT
Hattage. A. P. Herbert. FiBHP
Hatteras Calling. Conrad Aiken. BoNaP; NOBA; TAP
Hatters, The. Nan McDonald. PoAu-2
Hattie Rice Rich. Adrienne Rich. *Fr.* Grandmothers. NAAL-2
Hauf-Roads up Schiehallion. Donald Campbell. PoSH
Haughty eagle bird, of birds the best, The. My Love Is Past. Thomas Watson. PBBP
Haughty lion, from his burning sand, A. The Lion and the Wave. William Allingham. FM
Haughty Snail-King, The. Vachel Lindsay. SO
Haul all together! Cheerily Man. *Unknown.* RR
Haul Away, My Rosy. *Unknown.* AmFP
Haul up the flag, you mourners. Elegy for Two Banjos. Karl Shapiro. LiTA; TrJP; WaP
Hauled up from the field by obscure. The Victors. Anthony McNeill. PBCV
Hauling over Wolf Creek Pass in Winter. Walter McDonald. MT
Haunched like a faun, he hooed. Metamorphosis. Sylvia Plath. PoA
Haunt him, Mona! Haunt him, demon sister! The Brother-in-Law. Larry Rubin. MT; TW
Haunted. Siegfried Sassoon. CMoP
Haunted by an offshore wind. The Cartographers. Heather Allen. KS
Haunted Country. Robinson Jeffers. OxBA
Haunted House, The ("Some dreams we have are nothing else but dreams."), *sels.* Thomas Hood. EBEV
"Centipede along the threshold crept, The." WiR
"O, very gloomy is the House of Woe." SeCePo
Haunted House. Valerie Worth. WSC
Haunted Houses. Longfellow. PWR
Haunted Oak, The. Paul Laurence Dunbar. BANP; UnPo
Haunted Oven, The. X. J. Kennedy. WSC
Haunted Palace, The. Poe. *Fr.* The Fall of the House of Usher. AA; AnAmPo; BeLS; CH; ChTr; LiTA; NOBA; OxBA; PoEL-4; PrIm; TAP; TrGrPo; WiR; WSC
Haunter, The. Thomas Hardy. NOBE; QFR
Haunting, The. Irving Layton. NeAC
Haunts me the lugubrious shape. Half-bent Man. Richard Eberhart. NYBP
Haunts of the Halcyon, The. Charles Henry Lüders. AA
Havana Blues. Henry Carlile. SM
Havana businessman sent me a cigar wrapped in a goldleaf, A. Literary Manners II. Max Jacob, *tr. by* Jerome Rothenberg. RHTwFP
Havana Dreams. Langston Hughes. PoNe
Havdala. Amir Gilboa, *tr. fr. Hebrew by* Warren Bargad *and* Stanley F. Chyet. IP
Havdolah. Susan Litwack. VWA
Havdolah Wine. Miriam Ulinover, *tr. fr. Yiddish by* Seth L. Wolitz. VWA
Have a house. I Have a House. Doris Mühringer, *tr. by* Beth Bjorklund. CoAuP
Have-at a Venture. *Unknown.* CoMu; ErPo
Have broken more treaties. The United States of America We. Sam Abrams. UL
Have Courage, My Boy, to Say No! L. M. Hilton. WTO
Have done with care, my hearts! aboard amain. A Farewell to Sir John Norris and Sir Francis Drake. George Peele. OBSC
Have done, you men and women all! The Animals in the Ark. *Unknown. Fr.* The Deluge. ChTr; GBP
Have fair fallen, O fair, fair have fallen, so dear. Henry Purcell. Gerard Manley Hopkins. TEP
Have Faith. Edward Carpenter. WGRP
Have Gentlemen perhaps forgotten this? A Poet Speaks from the Visitors' Gallery. Archibald MacLeish. NYBP
Have, have ye no regard, all ye. His Saviour's Words, Going to the Cross. Robert Herrick. NOCV
Have Head, Have Tail. Nellie Wong. ER
Have I a hundred years since or. John Landless Leads the Caravan. Iwan Goll, *tr. by* William Carlos Williams. TrJP
Have I a wife? Bedam I have! The Brewer's Man. L. A. G. Strong. FaBoCo; FiBHP
Have I Found Her? *Unknown.* EiL
Have I no weapon-word for thee—some message brief and fierce? To the Pending Year. Walt Whitman. OxBSP
Have I nocht made ane honest shift. Sir David Lindsay. *Fr.* Ane Satire [*or* Satyre] of the Three [*or* Thrie] Estaitis. GoTS

Have I not blessed thee? Then go forth; nor fear. To His Book. Robert Herrick. CaPo

Have I not forgotten you! To a Man Who Said, "You've forgotten me." Lady Izumi, *tr. fr. Japanese by* Hiroaki Sato. *Fr.* Fifty-one Tanka. FCEI

Have I spent all my life turning. Simon and the Tarantula. James Wright. AnAn; NNaP

Have I spoken too much or not enough of love? Richard Aldington. BrPo

Have I the heart to wander on the earth. George Santayana. *Fr.* Sonnets. AnAmPo

Have I the power to bid the frost not melt. To Barba. Edward May. FaBoEE

Have I, this moment, led thee from the beach. Walter Savage Landor. GBL

Have I told you the name of a lady? Have You Seen the Lady? John Philip Sousa. OBAL

Have learned to burn my hands with fire. Breaking Ground in Me. Tom Kryss. NeAC

Have mercy, Lord, on me. Lord, Have Mercy. Nahum Tate. TIRV

Have No Fear! Eileen Duggan. ATNZ

Have No Mercy. Aimé Césaire, *tr. fr. French by* Clayton Eshleman and Annette Smith. RHTwFP

Have no self-pity now for loneliness. The Fallen. Vera Bax. CN

Have patience; it is fit that in this wise. Sorrow. George Santayana. WGRP

Have pity, God, on one you cast down here. Wilderness. Ilyas Farhat, *tr. by* Salma Khadra Jayyusi *and* John Heath-Stubbs. MAP

Have pity on us, Power just and severe. John Hall Wheelock, *after* St. Theresa of Avila. EaLo; NePoAm

Have pity, pity, friends, have pity on me. Epistle in Form of a Ballad to His Friends. Villon, *tr. by* Swinburne. AWP

Have the poets left a single spot for a patch to be sewn? Antar, *tr. by* A. J. Arberry. *Fr.* The Mu'allaqat. TTY

Have the spring mists. Tsurayuki, *tr. fr. Japanese by* Burton Watson. *Fr.* Kokin Shu. FCEI

Have thou no other gods but me. The Ten Commandments. *Unknown.* FaBoUs; OxBChV

Have ye beheld (with much delight). Upon the Nipples of Julia's Breast. Robert Herrick. CaPo; ErPo; NAEL-1

Have ye heard of our hunting, o'er mountain and glen. The Hunters of Men. Whittier. AnAmPo

Have ye seen the morning sky. The Happy Swain. Ambrose Philips. EnLoPo

Have ye seen the would-be-not-humble dandy. The Road to Zoagli. Max Beerbohm. FaBoNo

Have you a gold cup. The Question. Robert Duncan. NeAP

Have you any gooseberry wine. Mazilla and Mazura. *Unknown.* ChTr

Have you any work for a tinker, Mistris. *Unknown.* OBS

Have You Been at Carrick? *Unknown, tr. fr. Irish by* Edward Walsh. BIrV

Have you been at sea on a windy day. A Windy Day. Winifred Howard. FaPON

Have you been to that country where the gold. Mignon. Goethe, *tr. fr. German by* Robert Bly. *Fr.* Wilhelm Meister's Apprenticeship, *Bk.* I *ch.* 1. NU
("Knowest thou the land where bloom the lemon trees.") AWP, *tr. by* James Elroy Flecker.

Have you come to the Red Sea place in your life. At the Place of the Sea. Annie Johnson Flint. BLPA
(Red Sea Place in Your Life, The.) BLRP

Have you dug the spill. Harlem Sweeties. Langston Hughes. LiTM; NoP; PoNe; TTY

Have you ever heard of lynching in the great United States? Lynching. Lizelia Augusta Jenkins Moorer. CBWP-3

Have you ever heard of the Sugar-Plum Tree? The Sugar-Plum Tree. Eugene Field. FaFP; NBLV; OxBChV

Have you ever heard that a tailor was ill? The Tailor. Joseph Leftwich. TrJP

Have you ever heard the wind go "Yooooo?" The Night Wind. Eugene Field. FaPON

Have you ever saddled your horse. Early Morning Roundup. Owen Barton. CowP

Have you ever sat by the railroad track. Empties Coming Back. Angelo de Ponciano. BLPA

Have You Ever Seen? *Unknown.* RHPC

Have you ever seen the moon. Have You Seen It. Lula Lowe Weeden. CDC

Have you ever smelled summer? That Was Summer. Marci Ridlon. NTCP

Have you forgotten yet? Aftermath. Siegfried Sassoon. BrPo; MoBrPo; TrJP; WaP

Have you gazed on naked grandeur, where there's nothing else to gaze on. The Call of the Wild. Robert W. Service. CaP

Have you got a brook in your little heart. Emily Dickinson. FaBV

Have you had a kindness shown? Pass It On. Henry Burton. BLRP; PWR

Have you heard, my friend, the slander that the Negro has to face? Immortality. Lizelia Augusta Jenkins Moorer. CBWP-3

Have You Heard of Artemisia? Heather McPherson. PeNZ

Have you heard of one Humpty Dumpty. The Ballad of Persse O'Reilly. James Joyce. *Fr.* Finnegans Wake. FaBoBa; LiTB

Have you heard of our fighting Twenty-first. The Dash for the Colors. Frederick G. Webb. BeLS

Have you heard of the dreadful fate. The Ashtabula Disaster. Julia A. Moore. OBAL

Have you heard of the manly turning taken. The Day of Inverlochy. Iain Lom. GoTS

Have you heard of the quaint people. Strawberries in November. Shaw Neilson. PoAu-1

Have you heard of the terrible family They. They Say. Ella Wheeler Wilcox. WBLP

Have you heard of the wonderful one-hoss shay. Deacon's Masterpiece, The; or, The Wonderful "One-Hoss Shay." Oliver Wendell Holmes. *Fr.* The Autocrat of the Breakfast Table, *ch.* 11. AmPP; FaFP; FPL; LiTA; MoShBr; NOBA; OBAL; OBCA; OHFP; OxBA; PoLF; PoRA; TAP; WBLP
(Wonderful "One-Hoss Shay," The.) BeLS; FaBoBe

Have you heard the blinking toad. The Song of the Toad. John Burroughs. FaPON

Have you heard the story that gossips tell. John Burns of Gettysburg. Bret Harte. AnAmPo; OHIP; PAH

Have you heard the tale of the aloe plant. The Aloe Plant. Henry Harbaugh. BLPA

Have you heard? The troubles. Sulpicia, *tr. by* Aliki *and* Willis Barnstone. BoWoP

Have you listened for the things I have left out? Unsaid. A. R. Ammons. NOBA

Have you listened still on a desert hill. Range Cow in Winter. Vern Mortensen. CowP

Have you lived long, sir, in these parts? An Interview. K. W. Grandsen. OxBTC

Have You Lost Faith? *Unknown.* WBLP

Have you never seen. Bring the Wine! Li Po, *tr. by* Burton Watson. CoBCP

Have you no weathervane? Straws. Elizabeth J. Coatsworth. AmFN

Have you not fallen asleep to strong men's rowing. The Rowers. Laura Benét. GoYe

Have you not heard his silent steps? Rabindranath Tagore. *Fr.* Gitanjali, XLV. WGRP

Have you not heard the poets tell. The Ballad of Baby Bell. Thomas Bailey Aldrich. AnAmPo

Have you not in a chimney seen. A Description of Maidenhead. Earl of Rochester. NOBL

Have you not noted, in some family. The Birth-Bond. Dante Gabriel Rossetti. *Fr.* The House of Life, XV. Son

Have you noticed. Angels. Anne Szumigalski. Mes; NOBC

Have you noticed the docile appeal. Letter from a State Hospital. Frank Mundorf. GoYe

Have you noticed the little shadow? Les Jours Gigantesques/The Titanic Days. Kathleen Fraser. NPGG

Have you observ'd the wench in the street. *Unknown.* OBS

Have you seen a woman. A Mirror for Autumn. "Adunis," *tr. by* Abdullah al-Udhari. MPAW

Have you seen an apple orchard in the spring? An Apple Orchard in the Spring. William Martin. GN; PWR

Have you seen but a bright lily grow. Ben Jonson. *Fr.* The Devil Is an Ass. FaBoCh
(So Sweet Is She.) GN
(So White, So Soft, So Sweet.) TrGrPo

Have you seen, in fields of snow. Frozen Jews. Abraham Sutskever, *tr. by* Cynthia Ozick. PeBMYV

Have You Seen It. Lula Lowe Weeden. CDC

Have you seen me at all. Before the Thaw. John Gill. NeAC

Have you seen the daikon of Mihara. Daikon Song. Rai Kyohei, *tr. by* Burton Watson. JLIC-2

Have you seen the Hidebehind? The Hidebehind. Michael Rosen. AmMo

Have You Seen the Lady? John Philip Sousa. OBAL

Have you seen the listening snake? The Vines. John Gray. NOBVV

Have you seen walking through the village. Ollie McGee. Edgar Lee Masters. OBD

Have you sometimes, calm, silent let your tread aspirant rise. Heard on the Mountain. Victor Hugo, tr. fr. French by Francis Thompson. Fr. Feuilles d'Automne. AWP

Have you the Giesbach seen? a fall. Arthur Hugh Clough. Fr. Mari Magno. OBTV

Have you time for a story. Charity Overcoming Envy. Marianne Moore. NYBP

Haven. Donald Jeffrey Hayes. AmNP; PoNe

Haven. Louis Johnson. Fr. Four Poems from the Strontium Age, IV. ATNZ

Haven and Last Refuge of My Pain, The. Michelangelo, tr. fr. Italian by George Santayana. AWP; PFI

Haven't been to one in almost three years. Powwow 79, Durango. Paula Gunn Allen. STE

Haven't I danced the big dance. The New Platform Dances. Jack A. Mapanje. WMBCH

Haven't I said that part of having intercourse. Leslie Scalapino. Fr. Hmmmm. NPGG

Haven't you slept, sad guard. Conversation at the Bend in the Road. Buland al-Haidari, tr. by Abdullah al-Udhari. MPAW

Having a Coke with You. Frank O'Hara. GLP

Having a fine new suit. Apologue. Tony Connor. BoLoP

Having a Wonderful Time. D. B. Wyndham Lewis. FiBHP

Having attained success in business. Robert Whitmore. Frank Marshall Davis. BPo; NoP; PoBA; PoNe

Having avantbiographed the world. En Passant. Andrei Codrescu. UL

Having been raised in the fine mimetic. Orb. Maxine W. Kumin. KS

Having been tenant long to a rich lord. Redemption. George Herbert. Fr. The Temple. EaLo; FF; HAP; InPK; InPS; JCP; LiTB; MeLP; MePo; NAEL-1; NOBE; NOCV; NoP; OBS; PoE; SCV; SeCP; SeCV-1; Son; SoSe; TEP; TrCP; WeW

Having changed my tangled hair into Shimada style. Yosano Akiko, tr. fr. Japanese by Hiroaki Sato. Fr. Thirty-nine Tanka. FCEI

Having Climbed to the Topmost Peak of the Incense-Burner Mountain. Po Chü-i, tr. fr. Chinese by Arthur Waley. SD

Having come to this place. This Place in the Ways. Muriel Rukeyser. AiP

Having committed the heart to love. Asadullah Khan Ghalib, tr. by Ahmed Ali. GoT

Having confused me. A Voice from the Roses. Maxine W. Kumin. NMM

Having crossed the threshold. The Threshold. Fu'ad Rifqa, tr. by Sargon Boulus and Samuel Hazo. MAP

Having crowded once onto the threshold of mortality. Divinities. W. S. Merwin. PoA

Having Drowned. Bernice Zamora. CCP

Having Eaten Breakfast. D. C. Berry. BXAP

Having eaten fish. Natsume Seibi, tr. fr. Japanese by Hiroaki Sato. Fr. Twenty-seven Hokku. FCEI

Having fallen down the manhole. Rick De Travaille. Lewis Turco. Fr. Bordello. SM

Having Followed the Sound of Rain into the Mountain but Found No Rain. Lo Fu, tr. fr. Chinese by Dominic Cheung. IFON

Having found the Way. After Going Astray in the Underbrush. Ernst David, tr. by Beth Bjorklund. CoAuP

"Having heard the defense and the prosecution." The Decision. Camille Bélot, tr. fr. French by Beth Archer. Fr. The Unwed Mother. DMF

Having heard the instruction. One Modern Poet. Carl Sandburg. OBAL

"Having her under me," the man said, "in bed, and remembering." Leslie Scalapino. Fr. Hmmmm. NPGG

Having hooded my face with hair. The Sibyl's Song. Michele Roberts. BrRo

Having inherited a vigorous mind. My Descendants. W. B. Yeats. Fr. Meditations in Time of Civil War, IV. LiTB

Having interred [or interr'd] her infant-birth. An Ode, upon a Question Moved, Whether Love Should Continue Forever? Herbert of Cherbury. JCP; MeLP; MePo; NOBE; OBS; SeCP

Having invented a new Holocaust. U. S. 1946 King's X. Robert Frost. NIP

Having known war and peace. Turning Fifty. Judith Wright. NAs

Having learned to play the guitar. On Learning to Play the Guitar. Ray Fraser. NeAC

Having left hard [or solid] ground behind. The Insular Celts. Ciaran Carson. BIrV; CIP

Having left us, which of us does she care for? Looking at My Grandchildren. Lady Izumi, tr. fr. Japanese by Hiroaki Sato. Fr. Fifty-one Tanka. FCEI

Having little kids around, they say, is truly bliss. Did You? William Cole. RHPC

Having lived a Coney Island life. A Coney Island Life. James L. Weil. AmFN

Having lost my leather purse. My Son. Ruth Stone. WPE

Having Lost My Sons, I Confront the Wreckage of the Moon: Christmas, 1960. James Wright. CoAP; HCAP; NAAL-2

Having met you as in a dream. Unknown, tr. fr. Japanese. Fr. Manyo Shu. Ma

Having no father anymore, having got up. The Homecoming of Emma Lazarus. Galway Kinnell. NaP

Having passed by the carton of Camembert cheese. Sleepless Nights. Benjamin Péret, tr. by Michael Benedikt. POS

Having planted a plantain. Basho, tr. fr. Japanese by Burton Watson. Fr. Seventy-six Hokku. FCEI

Having put yourself on the way. Spirits, Dancing. Arthur Gregor. NYBP; VGW

Having Read Books. Heather McHugh. GeTw

Having Replaced Love with Food and Drink. Diane Wakoski. NAs

Having scrubbed away the gray sweat. Old Michael. George M. Brady. NeIP

Having seen Hari's face, our eyes are opened wide. Surdas, tr. by John Stratton Hawley and Mark Juergensmeyer. SSI

Having seen your smile. Yakamochi, tr. fr. Japanese. Fr. Manyo Shu. Ma

Having so rich a treasury, so fine a hoard. The Daisy. Marya Zaturenska. GrPl; MoAmPo

Having split up the chaparral. The Wide Land. A. R. Ammons. TwCP

Having taken her slowly by surprise. A Pause for Breath. Ted Hughes. NYBP

"Having this day my horse, my hand, my lance." Sir Philip Sidney. Fr. Astrophel and Stella, XLI. HAP; NAEL-1; OBSC; PoE; Son

Having to Love Something Else, The. Russell Edson. AnAn

Having used every subterfuge. A Renewal. James Merrill. OxBSP; SM

Having waited a long time. Spring Worm I. Tu Yeh, tr. by Dominic Cheung. IFON

Having waited for this one for this. Lady Izumi, tr. fr. Japanese by Hiroaki Sato. Fr. Fifty-one Tanka. FCEI

Having washed the gravestone. Ozaki Hosai, tr. fr. Japanese by Hiroaki Sato. Fr. One Hundred Haiku in Free Form. FCEI

Having written several poems which I will not publish. Baedeker for Metaphysicians. Brian Higgins. FaBoTw

Haw Lantern, The. Seamus Heaney. NoAM

Hawaii Dantesca. Charles Wright. HCAP; LCAP

Hawk, The. George Mackay Brown. RB

Hawk. Aaro Hellaakoski, tr. fr. Finnish by Aili Jarvenpa. SOP

Hawk, The. Raymond Knister. OBCV

Hawk. Brian Turner. UAS

Hawk, The. W. B. Yeats. PoA

Hawk and Snake. Leslie Silko. VoR

Hawk Is a Woman. Hildegarde Flanner. WPE

Hawk Nailed to a Barn Door. Peter Blue Cloud. VoR

Hawk Roosting. Ted Hughes. CMoP; GTBS-P; HAP; HeIP; LiTM; NePoEA-2; OxBTC; PPP; TwCP; UnPo

Hawk with heavy-lidded eyes, The. The Last Summer. Vivian Smith. PoAu-2

Hawking. Michael Drayton. Fr. Polyolbion, Twentieth Song. SD

Hawking. Keiun, tr. fr. Japanese by Steven D. Carter. WFTW

Hawking. Shotetsu, tr. fr. Japanese by Steven D. Carter. WFTW

Hawking for the Partridge. Thomas Ravenscroft. OxBoLi

Hawk's Eyes. Yvor Winters. PoA

Hawk's Way. Ted Olson. HoPM

Hawktree. Dave Smith. HCAP

Haworth Churchyard, sel. Matthew Arnold. "Where, behind Keighley, the road." FaBoPP

Hawser tied against a stiff north wind, The. Mooring at Night. T'an Ssu-t'ung, tr. by Timothy C. Wong. WFTU

Hawthorn, The. Unknown. ChTr; GBP

Hawthorn Hath a Deathly Smell, The. Walter de la Mare. BrPo

Hawthorn Hedge, The. Judith Wright. PoAu-2; WPE

Hawthorn morning moving, The. Renewal by Her Element. Denis Devlin. CIP

Hawthorne. Amos Bronson Alcott. AA

Hawthorne. Longfellow. PoEL-5

Hawthorne. James Russell Lowell. Fr. A Fable for Critics. AmPP; NOBA; OxBA; TAP

Hawthorne Garland, A. Richard Harter Fogle. NIP; OBAL

Hay Appeareth, The. Bible, O.T. Fr. Proverbs, XXVII: 25. FaPON

Hay Fever. A. D. Hope. NoAM

Hay for the Horses. Gary Snyder. CAPP; GrPl; NaP

Hay Harvest. Patrick Reginald Chalmers. BoTP

Hay has long been built into the stack, The. From Harvest to January. Charles Tennyson Turner. NOBVV

Hay, hay, by this day. The Scholar Complains. *Unknown.* MeEL

Hay Hotel, The. Oliver St. John Gogarty. BIrV

Hay is for horses. *Unknown.* OxNR

Hay-Making Song: Miyazaki Prefecture. *Unknown, tr. fr. Japanese by* Hiroaki Sato. FCEI

Hay Scuttle. Robert Morgan. MAYP

Hay-Time. C. M. Lowe. BoTP

Hay-Time; or, The Constant Lovers. A Pastoral. Josiah Relph. NOEC

Hayeswater Boat, The, *sel.* Matthew Arnold.
Hayeswater. FaBoPP

Hayfield, The. Charles Bruce. *Fr.* The Flowing Summer. CaP

Haying. Jorie Graham. KS

Haying. John Frederic Herbin. CaP

Hayle holy-land wherein our holy lord. Upon the First Sight of New England, June 29, 1638. Thomas Tillam. GOA; SCAP (Hail, Holy Land.) AH

Haylle, Comly and Clene. *Unknown.* *See* Second Shepherd's Play, The: Hail, Comly and Clene.

Haymakers, Rakers. Thomas Dekker. *Fr.* The Sun's Darling. ELP

Haymaking. E. M. Adams. BoTP

Haymaking. A. P. Graves. BoTP

Haymaking. Edward Thomas. BrPo; MoAB; MoBrPo; SeCePo

Haymaking. William Carlos Williams. *Fr.* Pictures from Brueghel, VI. NOAM

Hayseed. *Unknown.* AS

Haystack in the Floods, The. William Morris. BeLS; EBEV; EBVV; HAP; NAEL-2; NoP; OAEL-2; OBNC; OBNV; PoEL-5; PoRA; WeW

Haytime. Irene F. Pawsey. BoTP

Hazardous Occupations. Carl Sandburg. SaC

Hazard's friend Elliot is homosexual. Wholesome. William Meredith. TAP

Hazard's Optimism. William Meredith. ASP

Haze. Henry David Thoreau. *See* Week on the Concord and Merrimack Rivers, A: Woof of the Sun (Ethereal Gauze).

Haze, char, and the weather of All Souls'. In the Elegy Season. Richard Wilbur. InPK; MoAB; NePoEA; NYBP

Haze is spreading, The. Spring Dawn. Ietaka, *tr. by* Steven D. Carter. WFTW

Hazel Stick for Catherine Ann, A. Seamus Heaney. FaBCIP; NoAM

Haziness is the blackness of pines. Kikaku, *tr. fr. Japanese by* Hiroaki Sato. *Fr.* Thirty-three Hokku. FCEI

Hazlitt Sups. Katharine Day Little. GoYe

Hazy moon has detached itself, The. Natsume Seibi, *tr. fr. Japanese by* Hiroaki Sato. *Fr.* Twenty-seven Hokku. FCEI

He. John Ashbery. SOTW

He. Lawrence Ferlinghetti. NeAP; PoM

He. Stanley Kunitz. VGW

He. Vasco Popa, *tr. fr. Serbo-Croatian by* Anne Pennington. *Fr.* Games. RB

He. Paul Rodenko, *tr. fr. Dutch by* Ramón E. du Pré. DuIn

He/ and she, A. A Pair. May Swenson. RFM

He/ From the world out there. Present Winter. Murano Shiro, *tr. by* Geoffrey Bownas *and* Anthony Thwaite. PeBJV

He Abjures Love. Thomas Hardy. OBNC

He accepts the circle, speech and so. Anne-Marie Albiach, *tr. by* Keith Waldrop. BoWoP

He adored the desk, its brown-oak inlaid with ebony. Geoffrey Hill. *Fr.* Mercian Hymns, X. HAP; NoAM; NoP

He: Age Doesn't Matter When You're Both in Love. Julia Alvarez. *Fr.* 33. Son

He all that time among the sewers of Troy. Troy. Edwin Muir. CMoP

He always comes on market days. The Balloon Man. Rose Fyleman. BoTP

He always has something to grumble about. A Chip on His Shoulder. *Unknown.* BLPA; WBLP

He always took me to visit the squadron. Two Memorial Poems. David Avidan, *tr. by* Warren Bargad *and* Stanley F. Chyet. IP

He always was one for a jeer and a jest. Epitaph for a Funny Fellow. Morris Bishop. FPL

He and his, unwashed all winter. The Native. W. S. Merwin. NePoEA-2; PoRA

He and I. End of a Course. I. A. Richards. CRP

He and She. Sir Edwin Arnold. BLPA

He and She. Eugene Fitch Ware. PoLF

He Approacheth the Hall of Judgment. *Unknown, tr. fr. Egyptian by* Robert Hillyer. *Fr.* Book of the Dead. AWP

He as O, A. E. E. Cummings. InPS

He ascended from a lonely crag in winter. On the Death of Karl Barth. Jack R. Clemo. NOCV

He Asked about the Quality. C. P. Cavafy, *tr. fr. Greek by* Edmund Keeley *and* Philip Sherrard. PeHV

He Asked Them What Did They Know & They Told Him. *Unknown, tr. fr. Seneca Indian by* Jerome Rothenberg *and* Richard Johnny John. STP

He Asketh Absolution of God. *Unknown, tr. fr. Egyptian by* Robert Hillyer. *Fr.* Book of the Dead. AWP

He ate and drank the precious words. Emily Dickinson. AA

He awoke this morning from a strange dream. Chief Leschi of the Nisqually. Duane Niatum. CDW; STE

He bare him [*or* hym] up, he bare him [*or* hym] down. The Corpus Christi Carol. *Unknown.* ACP; HAP; MeEL; OxBLMV

He behind the straight plough stands. Ploughman at the Plough. Louis Golding. OHIP

He Biddeth Osiris to Arise from the Dead. *Unknown, tr. fr. Egyptian by* Robert Hillyer. *Fr.* Book of the Dead. AWP

He bought an old ship's lifeboat. A Fine Day for Straw Hats. Louis Stimson. PBCV

He breaks through the curve and dies. But the body in the green. The Wind Blows on the Border. Antonio Porta, *tr. by* Lawrence R. Smith. NItP

He breathes into my earpiece late at night. The Obscene Caller. Cheri Fein. TW

He broke past the corners. Sharp-Shin. David Wagoner. BLA

He brought a Grecian queen, whose youth and freshness. Portrait of Helen. Shakespeare. *Fr.* Troilus and Cressida, II, ii *and* IV, i. TrGrPo

He brought a light so she could see. Strains of Sight. Robert Duncan. CMoP; PoE

He brought a lily white. To his Mother. John Banister Tabb. *Fr.* The Child. AA

He brought a team from Inversnaid. The Man from Inversnaid. Robert Fuller Murray. SD

He brought peace to myriad lands. *Unknown, tr. by* Arthur Waley. BoS

He built a house, time laid it in the dust. His Monument. Sarah Knowles Bolton. PWR

He built a mud-wall'd hovel, where he kept. George Crabbe. *Fr.* The Borough: Peter Grimes. SaC

He built himself a house. Fairy Tale. Miroslav Holub, *tr. by* George Theiner. RB

He built right on the top of the land. Where She Was Not Born. Yvonne. CNA

He by no means flies straight at petunia. The Bee and the Petunia. Katherine Hoskins. ErPo

He called a conquered land his own. Wolfe Tone. Austin Clarke. CIP

He calleth to me out of Seir, Watchman, what of the night? Watchman, What of the Night? Bible, *O.T. Fr.* Isaiah, XXI: 11–15. AWP

He calls you in his wedding coat. The Wedding Coat. Harriet Rose. BrRo

He came,/ striding. Paul Bunyan. Arthur Stanley Bourinot. *Fr.* A Legend of Paul Bunyan. AmFN; FaPON

He came, a youth, singing in the dawn. Paul Laurence Dunbar. James David Corrothers. BANP; PoNe

He came all so still. Ancient Christmas Carol. *Unknown.* OHIP; PChr

He came and took me by the hand. The Mystery. Ralph Hodgson. CH; MoAB; MoBrPo; WGRP

He came apart in the open. Martin's Blues. Michael S. Harper. CNA; HCAP; PoBA

He came at midnight, his legs cut off. War's End. Dahlia Ravikovich, *tr. by* Warren Bargad *and* Stanley F. Chyet. IP

He came back. Dry River Bed. Andrew Salkey. PBCV

He came back and shot. He shot him. When he came. Incident. Imamu Amiri Baraka. NoAM

He came down the old road. Ghost Boy. Mark Van Doren. SO

He came from hills to comfortable plains. The Mountaineer. Robert Nathan. TrJP

He came from Malta; and Eumelus says. A Maltese Dog. Tymnes, *tr. by* Edmund Blunden. FaBoCh; FaBoEE; OBD

He came from where he started. The Tramp. Ben King. AnAmPo

He came in silvern armor, trimmed with black. Gwendolyn B. Bennett. AmNP; CDC; PoBA; PoNe

He came to a strange and unknown place. From Mathnavi Sehrul Bayaan. Mir Ghulam Hasan, *tr. by* Ahmed Ali. GoT

He came to his love's window at the dead of the night. The Little Drummer. *Unknown.* AmFP

He came to my desk with a quivering lip. A New Leaf. Kathleen Wheeler. BLRP; WBLP

He came to us. The Deposition of the Burden. Tadeusz Rozewicz, *tr. by* Czeslaw Milosz. PwPP

He came to us every other summer. The Missionary Visits Our Church in Scranton. Jay Parini. MAYP

He Came to Visit Me. Martin Seymour-Smith. FaBoTw
He Came Too Late. Elizabeth Bogart. AA
He can hear the owl's flight in daylight. Blind Man. Michael Hamburger. NePoEA-2
He can only drink tea now, screwed and filed. Pink Slip at Tool & Dye. Dave Smith. NoAM
He. Can't exactly be named. Anatomy of a Supper. Gábor Görgey, tr. by Jascha Kessler. FOC
He can't remain forever underwater. The Diver. Ben Howard. SM
He cared about us children. Shoemaker Nikke. Arvo Turtiainen, tr. by Aili Jarvenpa. SOP
He Careth. "Marianne Farningham." See God Cares.
He carries a scythe, but he's young. A Man Walking through Clachtoll. Norman MacCaig. NPo
He carries shadows in his face like caves. On the Apparition of Oneself. William Burford. PoA
He cast his net at morn where fishers toiled. Failure. Kate Tucker Goode. PWR
He caught his chisel, hastened to his bench. The Death of Azron. Alice Wellington Rollins. AA
He ceased; and Satan stayed not to reply. Milton. Fr. Paradise Lost, Bk. II, ll. 1010–1055.
(Satan ("He ceased; and Satan stayed not to reply").) SeCePo
He chants a boy-chant. The Grace of Cynthia's Maidenhood. Vinnie-Marie D'Ambrosio. IHMS
He Charges Her to Lay Aside Her Weapons. Pierce Ferriter, tr. fr. Late Middle Irish by Earl of Longford. AnIL
"He chases shadows," sneered the British tars. The First Voyage of John Cabot. Hezekiah Butterworth. PAH
He clasps the crag with crooked hands. The Eagle. Tennyson. BoTP; CH; FaBoCh; FaPON; FF; FiP; FM; GN; GoJo; GTBS-P; HeIP; InPK; NAEL-2; NOBVV; NoP; NTCP; OAEL-2; OxBSP; PBBP; PDV; PrIM; Prlm; RHPC; SeCePo; TrGrPo; UnPo; WiR
He climbed to the top. Fergus Falling. Galway Kinnell. DiL
He climbed to the treetop. Columns. Meir Wieseltier, tr. by Warren Bargad and Stanley F. Chyet. IP
He climbed up the peak. High Brow. Robert Fitch. SD
He climbs the stair. Waterchew! Gregory Corso. VGW
He Comes Among. George Barker. OBMV
He comes down to the shadow. Heron. Ted Walker. NYBP
He comes from afar. Air Traveler. Lillian Morrison. RHPC
He comes from the house as lightning flickers in the sky. Love and Music. Gond Oral Tradition, tr. by V. Elwin and S. Hivale. WTO
He comes from the north. Unknown, tr. fr. Sioux Indian by James Koller. Fr. Sioux Metamorphoses. STP
He comes gusting out of the house. Spring Storm. Jim Wayne Miller. GOYP
He comes in solemn state. Unknown, tr. by Arthur Waley. BoS
He comes in the night! He comes in the night! Santa Claus. Unknown. BoTP
He Comes Not To-night. Josephine D. Henderson Heard. CBWP-4
He comes running. A Poem about a Wolf Maybe Two Wolves. Unknown, tr. by Jerome Rothenberg and Richard Johnny John. STP
He comes, the happy warrior. Sinfonia Eroica. Alice Archer James. AA
He comes, the old one, his shabby cap askew. Old Man with a Mowing Machine. May Carleton Lord. GoYe
He comes, the pest and terror of the yard. Summer. Robert Bloomfield. Fr. The Farmer's Boy. PBBP
He comes through the door. The Assassin's Fatal Error. Lawrence Raab. AmPA
He comes unknown and heard and stands there. Man into a Churchyard. Bernard Gutteridge. EAS
He comes with herald clouds of dust. Superior Nonsense Verses. Unknown. NA
He comes with western winds, with evening's wandering airs. Emily Brontë. Fr. The Prisoner. ELP
He Cometh. Judah Halevi, tr. fr. Hebrew by Emma Lazarus. TrJP
He Cometh Forth into the Day. Unknown, tr. fr. Egyptian by Robert Hillyer. Fr. Book of the Dead. AWP
He cometh, O bliss! He Cometh. Judah Halevi, tr. by Emma Lazarus. TrJP
He Commandeth a Fair Wind. Unknown, tr. fr. Egyptian by Robert Hillyer. Fr. Book of the Dead. AWP
He cooked cornbread. Ned Christie. Robert J. Conley. STE
He could have come to tell us. Never Give a Bum an Even Break. James Welch. NoAM
He Could Have Found His Way. Kathleen Dalziel. PoAu-1
He could help us out. Tennis in the City. F. R. Higgins. ASP
He could hit a blade of grass with his spear. A Skilful Spearman! Unknown, tr. fr. Hawaiian. WTO

He could not die when trees were green. The Dying Child. John Clare. EnRP; TrGrPo
He could not fall so far. Somnambulist. John Russell Hervey. ATNZ
He could see the little lake. The Lake. James Stephens. MoBrPo
He could sing sweetly on a string. Orpheus. Elizabeth Madox Roberts. MoAmPo
He could trimble. Oui Papa. Delano Abdul Malik de Coteau. PBCV
He couldn't hear their roar. Drowned Sailor. Neufville Shaw. CaP
He couldn't use his driver any better on the tee. A Lesson from Golf. Edgar Albert Guest. ASP
He Cracked a Word. Allen Curnow. ATNZ
He cradled his head in those hands. Morning. Alberto Ríos. MAYP
He cranes his neck against the dawning sky. Three Poets at Yuyama. Unknown, tr. by Hiroaki Sato. FCEI
He crawls along the mountain walls. On the Heights. Lucius Harwood Foote. AA
He crawls to the edge of the foaming creek. Meeting the Mountains. Gary Snyder. NoAM
He cried aloud to God: "The men below." Genius. Edward Lucas White. AA; WGRP
He crouches, and buries his face on his knees,/ And hides in the dark of his hair. The Last of His Tribe. Henry Clarence Kendall. CBAP; PoAu-1
He cut a sappy sucker from the muckle rodden-tree. The Whistle. Charles Murray. GoTS; OxBS
He cuts down the lakes so they appear straight. He. John Ashbery. SOTW
He debated whether. Arthur Ridgewood, M.D. Frank Marshall Davis. BPo
He deemed his task a solemn one. Priest and Pagan. Albert Durrant Watson. CaP
He deemed it best to let them all disrobe. The Rape of Mensola. Boccaccio, tr. fr. Italian by Joseph Tusiani. Fr. Nymphs of Fiesole. PFI
He Defendeth His Heart against the Destroyer. Unknown, tr. fr. Egyptian by Robert Hillyer. Fr. Book of the Dead. AWP
He did not come/ A gnostic. Incarnation Poem. John Leax. TrCP
He did not come of a long line of stone-cutters. The Man Who Went Absent from the Native Literature. Anthony Cronin. CIP
He did not come to woo U Nu. Just Dropped In. William Cole. FiBHP; GoJo
He Did Not Know. Harry Hibbard Kemp. WGRP
He did not wear his scarlet coat. Oscar Wilde. Fr. The Ballad of Reading Gaol. BeLS; BrPo; MoBrPo; NoAM; NOBE; NOBVV; OAEL-2; OBMV; OBNC; OBNV
He did not wear his swallow tail. The Gourmand. Harry Graham. FaBoPa
He didn't know, King Kleomenis, he didn't dare. In Sparta. C. P. Cavafy, tr. by Edmund Keeley and Philip Sherrard. VMG
He didn't know much music. The Mocking-Bird. Frank Lebby Stanton. AA
"He Didn't Oughter." A. P. Herbert. FiBHP
He "Digesteth Harde Yron." Marianne Moore. CMoP; NoAM
He dines alone surrounded by reflections. Witch Doctor. Robert Hayden. AmNP; MAT; NoAM
He disagrees with Simone de Beauvoir. His Plans for Old Age. William Meredith. TAP
He disappeared in the dead of winter. In Memory of W. B. Yeats. W. H. Auden. CMoP; FaFP; HAP; HeIP; HoPM; LiTB; LiTM; MoAB; MoBrPo; MoP; NAEL-2; NIP; NoAM; NOBE; OAEL-2; OPOP; OxBTC; PoE; PPP; PrIm; TrGrPo; UnPo; WeW
He discovers himself on an old airfield. The Old Pilot. Donald Hall. LCAP
He divides the hours into casts of the shadows. The Angel with the Sun Dial (Cathedral at Chartres). Christine Busta, tr. by Beth Bjorklund. CoAuP
He does not come, but I wait. Teika, tr. fr. Japanese by Hiroaki Sato. Fr. Eighty-four Tanka. FCEI
He does not hear the struck string. Music God. Mark Van Doren. UnS
He does not lounge with the old men. For William Edward Burghardt Dubois on His Eightieth Birthday. Bette Darcie Latimer. PoNe
He does not think that I haunt here nightly. The Haunter. Thomas Hardy. NOBE; QFR
He doesn't know when it was that the last door closed. After Some Day of Decision. Reed Whittemore. NePoEA
He doesn't like it, of course. His Body. Sandra McPherson. AmPA; GeTw
He doesn't remember his name and we've never been able to give him one. Vampyr. Stephen Spera. VVA
He doesn't seem. Kyorai, tr. fr. Japanese by Burton Watson. Fr. Twenty Hokku. FCEI

He doeth well who doeth good. Best of All. *Unknown.* WBLP

He Done His Level Best. "Mark Twain." AiP

He drank enough. D. H. Lawrence. *Fr.* Snake. RR

He draws the long threads. Harlem at Night. Rose Ausländer, *tr. by* Beth Bjorklund. CoAuP

He dreamed first. Adam's Dying. Ridgely Torrence. FYAP

He dreamed not that the ocean would bear ships. A. J. Seymour. *Fr.* For Christopher Columbus, IV. PBCV

He dreamed of lovely women as he slept. Undergraduate. Merrill Moore. ErPo

He dreamed of overturned Gothic cathedrals. Mother. Julian Przybos, *tr. by* Czeslaw Milosz. PwPP

He dreamt that he saw the buffalant. A Quadrupedremian Song. Thomas Hood. AmMo; FaBoNo

He drew a circle that shut me out. Outwitted. Edwin Markham. BLPA; FPL; MoAmPo

He drew hundreds of women. Beauty and Sadness. Cathy Song. MAYP; NoAM

He drives onto the grassy shoulder and unfastens. Earth Walk. William Meredith. MAT

He drops his line east of a plank bridge. Inscribed on a Painting "Fishing in the Snow on a Wintry River." Ching An, *tr. by* Irving Lo. WFTU

He drowsed and was aware of silence heaped. The Death-Bed. Siegfried Sassoon. LiTM; MMA

He dumped her in the wheelbarrow. Wheelbarrow. Eleanor Farjeon. FiBHP

He dwelt among "Apartments let." Jacob. Phoebe Cary. OBAL

He Embarketh in the Boat of Ra. *Unknown, tr. fr. Egyptian by* Robert Hillyer. *Fr.* Book of the Dead. AWP

He ended, and they both descend the hill. Milton. *Fr.* Paradise Lost, *Bk.* XII, *ll.* 606–649. NAWM-1 (Adam Fallen.) NOCV

He ended; and thus Adam last replied. Milton. *Fr.* Paradise Lost, *Bk.* XII, *ll.* 552–649. HeIP (Retreat from Paradise, The.) PoEL-3

He ended, nor the Argicide refus'd. Homer, *tr. fr. Greek by* William Cowper. *Fr.* Odyssey, V. OBVE

He entered with the authority of politeness. The Southerner. Karl Shapiro. NYBP; PoNe

He Entereth the House of the Goddess Hathor. *Unknown, tr. fr. Egyptian by* Robert Hillyer. *Fr.* Book of the Dead. AWP

He enters, and they on the edge of a chair. In the Study. Thomas Hardy. *Fr.* Satires of Circumstance, VIII. BrPo

He escaped under the river. One Day When It Was Night Out. Robert Desnos, *tr. by* Michael Benedikt. POS

He Establisheth His Triumph. *Unknown, tr. fr. Egyptian by* Robert Hillyer. *Fr.* Book of the Dead. AWP

He ever acted well by man or woman. George IV. Thackeray. *Fr.* Georges, The. FaBoEE

He expects the old names to return. Mail Call. John Bensko. MAYP

He Faces the Second Winter. Philip Levine. *Fr.* Sierra Kid. PoA

He fails who climbs to power and place. Failure and Success. Richard Watson Gilder. PWR

He fears the tiger standing in his way. The Drunkard. Philip Levine. NePoEA-2

He fed them generously who were his flocks. W. D. Snodgrass. Son

He feels small as he awakens. The Awakening. Robert Creeley. NeAP

He Fell among Thieves. Sir Henry Newbolt. EBVV; FaPoR; OBEV; OBWP; OnMSP; OxBTC

He fell from the roof. News. Louis Dudek. *Fr.* Provincetown. MoCV

He fell off the wheel of souls. DOA in Dulse. Diane Burns. STE

He felt the web of light tearing, the rainbow. Webern's Mountain. Fred Chappell. BLA

He felt the wild beast in him betweenwhiles. George Meredith. *Fr.* Modern Love, IX. NOBVV

He finished his speech in a/ gruesome way. Introducing a Madman. Keith Waldrop. TW

He first deceased; she for a little tried. Upon the Death of Sir Albert Morton's Wife. Sir Henry Wotton. BoLoP; EnLoPo; FaBoEE; NOP; OBD; OBEV; OBS; SeCP; TrGrPo; WeW

He floats down the Seine. Body Fished from the Seine. Gregory Corso. SM

He followed his own mind. *Unknown, tr. by* James Koller. STP

He followed me up and he followed me down. Lady Isabel and the Elf Knight (Pretty Polly). *Unknown.* AmFP

He for whom I wait. Teika, *tr. by* Geoffrey Bownas *and* Anthony Thwaite. PeBJV

He found a formula for drawing comic rabbits. Epitaph on an Unfortunate Artist. Robert Graves. FaBoEE; NOBL

He found a Woman in the cave. Thalaba and the Magic Thread. Robert Southey. SeCePo

He found her by the ocean's moaning verge. George Meredith. *Fr.* Modern Love, XLIX. NoP; OAEL-2

He from the wind-bitten North with ship and companions descended. A Drifter off Tarentum. Kipling. *Fr.* Epitaphs of the War, 1914–1918. FaBoEE; MMA

He fumbles at your soul. Emily Dickinson. NAAL-1; NOCV

He gathered cherry-stones, and carved them quaintly. An Art Master. John Boyle O'Reilly. AA

He gave himself another year. Patrick Kavanagh. *Fr.* The Great Hunger. BIrV

He gave his card. How many times have I. Contact. Dorothy Livesay. CaP

He gave his strength and his loveliness for his country. On a Soldier Killed in the Great War. R. Williams Parry, *tr. by* H. Idris Bell. OBWVE

He gave silver shoes to the rabbit. Blake Leads a Walk on the Milky Way. Nancy Willard. OBCA

He gave the solid rail a hateful kick. The Egg and the Machine. Robert Frost. MoAmPo

He gave us all a good-bye cheerily. Messmates. Sir Henry Newbolt. CH; EBVV

He gazed at her with his whole soul. Dark Eyes at Forest Hills. I. L. Martin. SD

He gets mostly dead sage and thornbush. Prospero on the Mountain Gathering Wood. Jack Gilbert. NPGG

He Giveth More. Annie Johnson Flint. BLRP; WBLP

He goes, his horse as his shield. Kikaku, *tr. fr. Japanese by* Hiroaki Sato. *Fr.* Thirty-three Hokku. FCEI

He goes regularly to the taverna. The Twenty-fifth Year of His Life. C. P. Cavafy, *tr. by* Edmund Keeley *and* Philip Sherrard. PeHV

He goes through his lands. *Unknown, tr. by* Arthur Waley. BoS

He goes up the staircase. *Unknown, tr. by* Burton Watson. FCEI

He got his friends to agree to shoot him standing against a stone wall. David Ignatow. *Fr.* Leaving the Door Open. CAPP

He grew old between the fires of Troy. Euripides the Athenian. George Seferis, *tr. by* Edmund Keeley *and* Philip Sherrard. VMG

He grew where waves ride nine feet high. In Memoriam: Roy Campbell. Ralph Nixon Currey. PeSA

He had a big workshop. It was part of the world. My Father. Pablo Guevara, *tr. by* David Tipton. Per

He had a many-coloured glance like flowers. Edward James. *Fr.* Carmina Amico. PeHV

He had a stroke of luck. No Chance Operations. James Sherry. LP

He had been coming a very long time. For Malcolm Who Walks in the Eyes of Our Children. Quincy Troupe. CNA; PoBA

He had been long t'wards Mathematicks. Portrait of Sidrophel. Samuel Butler. *Fr.* Hudibras, II, 3. PoEL-3

He had done for her all that a man could. I Will Write. Robert Graves. PCP

He had driven half the night. Hay for the Horses. Gary Snyder. CAPP; GrPl; NaP

He had got, finally. A Poem for Speculative Hipsters. Imamu Amiri Baraka. NoAM; NOBA

He had in his hand a red plant. Meeting by the Gjulika Meadow. Geoffrey Grigson. WaP

He had lived in Spain. The Garden of Abu Mahmoud. Naomi Shihab Nye. NAmP

He had need of a way. Being Somebody. Edwin Honig. TAP

He had no friend. About to Die. *Gond Oral Tradition, tr. by* V. Elwin *and* S. Hivale. WTO

He had no royal palace. A Christmas Verse. "Kay." BoTP

He had not reckoned on a visitor. Death Was a Woman. Sydney King Russell. GoYe

He "Had Not Where to Lay His Head." Frances Ellen Watkins Harper. PWR

He had played for his lordship's levee. The Child-Musician. Austin Dobson. GN

He had red hair. A Boy Thirteen. Jeff Irish. DL

He Had Served Eighty Masters. Lesbia Harford. PoAu-1

He had smiled at us. Maximus, to Gloucester, Letter 19. Charles Olson. *Fr.* The Maximus Poems. CMoP

He had studied in private years ago. Artichoke. Henry Taylor. MAYP; MT

He had this idea about the hill. Jill, Afterwards. Philip Dacey. MOWH; SM

He had to be brown and in heat, soft men. Tarzan Once More. Rutger Kopland, *tr. by* Ria Leigh-Loohuizen. DuIn

He hadn't been right. Whitley at Three O'Clock. Jeff Worley. GOYP

He halted in the wind, and—what was that. A Boundless Moment. Robert Frost. NAAL-2

He hands/ down the gift. The Gift. Robert Creeley. NOBA

He hangs between his wings outspread. The Eagle. Andrew Young. PoSH

He has annihilated the enemies! War Song. *Zulu Oral Tradition, tr. by* D. K. Rycroft. WTO

He has built himself a cottage in the wood. A Cottage in the Wood. Russell Edson. LCAP

He has come back at last, the boy with the inky fingers. Self-Congratulatory Ode on Mr. Auden's Election to the Professorship of Poetry at Oxford. Ronald Mason. FaBoPa

He has come to report himself. The Missing Person. Donald Justice. CAPP; NYBP

He has conned the lesson now. Fairy Song. Winthrop Mackworth Praed. SeCePo

He has gone. Last Journey. Enrique Gonzáles Martínez, *tr. by* Samuel Beckett. MexPo

He has gone into the forest. Journey to the Interior. William Jay Smith. DiPo

He has hanged himself—the Sun. November. F. W. Harvey. OxBTC

He has held. Perevin Muruvalar, *tr. by* A. K. Ramanujan. PLW

He has never heard of tides. German Shepherd. Myra Cohn Livingston. RFM

He has not even seen you, he. War Baby. Pamela Holmes. CN

He has not woo'd, but he has lost his heart. A Country Dance. Charles Tennyson Turner. NOBVV

He has observed the golden rule. Blake. *Fr.* Gnomic Verses. TrGrPo

He has only to pass by a tree moodily walking head down. The Fiend. James Dickey. PPP

He has opened all his parcels. The Hippopotamus's Birthday. Emile Victor Rieu. Mes

He has solved it—Life's wonderful problem. Laurels and Immortelles. *Unknown.* BLPA

He has sprouted; he has burgeoned. Inanna's Song. *Unknown, tr. by* Diane Wolkstein *and* Samuel Noah Kramer. LLLT

He has the sign. Portrait of Malcolm X. Etheridge Knight. CNA; PoBA

He has time. Sleep, Leopard, Sleep. David Avidan, *tr. by* Bernhard Frank. MHeP

He hasn't gone to work. The Poem Circling Hamtramck, Michigan All Night in Search of You. Philip Levine. NNaP

He Hath Need of Rest. Josephine D. Henderson Heard. CBWP-4

He Hath No Parallel. Sadi, *tr. fr. Persian by* L. Cranmer-Byng. *Fr.* The Gulistan. AWP

He hath no place to rest his head. Judaeus Errans. Louis Golding. TrJP

He heard, and dreamed the night-wind on. Muse-haunted. Hugh McCrae. PoAu-1

He Hears the Bugle at Killarney. Tennyson. *See* Princess, The: Splendor Falls [on Castle Walls], The.

He Hears the Cry of the Sedge. W. B. Yeats. OxBTC; RB

He hears the summer at a distance. Vanishing Point. Peter Cooley. AmPA

He held her as she wavered. The Bicycle. David Wojahn. NAmP

He Held Radical Light. A. R. Ammons. CAPP; PoE

He Hides within the Lily. William Channing Gannett. AH
(Consider the Lilies.) WGRP

He hie fie finger. The Man. Robert Creeley. OBAL

He hoes the grain under a midday sun. Pitying the Farmer. Li Shen, *tr. by* Burton Watson. CoBCP

He Hola. Keri Hulme. PeNZ

He Holdeth Fast to the Memory of His Identity. *Unknown, tr. fr. Egyptian by* Robert Hillyer. *Fr.* Book of the Dead. AWP

He imagines her. The Modes of Vallejo Street, San Diego, Los Angeles, 3. Hugh Seidman. UnPo

He invented a rainbow but lightning struck it. Bushed. Earle Birney. MoCV; NoAM; NOBC; NoP; OBCV

He is a bad sleeper and it is a joy to me. A Bad Sleeper. Paul Verlaine, *tr. by* François Pirou. PeHV

He is a heart. *Unknown, tr. by* Myles Dillon. AnIL

He is a man for whom words. The Vice-President of the Universe. Don Welch. SoTCo

He is a path, if any be misled. Excellency of Christ. Giles Fletcher the Younger. *Fr.* Christ's Victory and Triumph: Christ's Victory in Heaven, I. WGRP

He is a sterling nobleman. The Man of the Time. Edwin Waugh. PF

He is a tower unleaning. But how will he not break. Vaunting Oak. John Crowe Ransom. OxBA; VGW

He is always right. The Interrogator. Elizabeth Jennings. WPE

He is an eagle's head smaller than I. He. Paul Rodenko, *tr. by* Ramón E. du Pré. DuIn

He is an Englishman! The Englishman. W. S. Gilbert. *Fr.* H. M. S. Pinafore. NOBL

He is an inharmonious note. Sir Roger Casement. TIRV

He is an utter failure as a devil. A Devil. Zbigniew Herbert, *tr. by* Czeslaw Milosz. RB

He is as portly. The Rhinoceros. Herman de Coninck, *tr. by* Theo Hermans. DuIn

He is beautiful and still. He May Be a Photograph of Himself. Tina Reid. AIW

He is coming, Adzed-Head. *Unknown.* NOIV

He is coming back. Invalided Home. Frances Bellerby. CN

He is coming, my long-desired lord. The River of Heaven. *Unknown. Fr.* Manyo Shu. AWP

He is daily with us, loving, loving, loving. "Daily with You." Annie Johnson Flint. BLRP

He is dead, the beautiful youth. Killed at the Ford. Longfellow. OHIP

He Is Declared True of Word. *Unknown, tr. fr. Egyptian by* Robert Hillyer. *Fr.* Book of the Dead. AWP

He Is Far. *Unknown.* OAEL-1
(Forsaken Maiden's Lament, A.) SeCePo

He is firm and strong. Oriki Erinle. *Unknown, tr. by* Ulli Beier. PBA; TTY

He is from those mountains. What She Said ("He is from those mountains"). Kapilar, *tr. by* A. K. Ramanujan. PLW

He is galloping his horse past the Chi-lu Mountain. Pacifying the Western Barbarians. Sun Kuang-hsien, *tr. by* Lois Fusek. ATF

He is gone on the mountain. Coronach. Sir Walter Scott. *Fr.* Lady of the Lake, III. CH; EnRP; GTBS; GTBS-P; OHIP; TrGrPo; WiR

He is in the canals behind your forehead. Soda Water with a Boyhood Friend. August Kleinzahler. BAP

He Is like the Lotus. *Unknown, tr. fr. Egyptian by* Robert Hillyer. *Fr.* Book of the Dead. AWP; EaLo
(Death as a Lotus Flower.) TTY, *tr. by* Ulli Beier.

He Is like the Serpent Saka. *Unknown, tr. fr. Egyptian by* Robert Hillyer. *Fr.* Book of the Dead. AWP

He is made one with Nature. Shelley. *Fr.* Adonais; an Elegy on the Death of John Keats. WGRP

He is making love with his wife on the roof. The Roof of the World. Michael Dennis Browne. AmPA

He is more than a hero. Sappho, *tr. by* Mary Barnard. PBWP

He is murdered upright in the day. Vaticide. Myron O'Higgins. IDB; PoBA

He Is My Countryman. Antoni Slonimski, *tr. fr. Polish by* Frances Notley. TrJP

He is my love/ my sweet nutgrove. *Unknown, tr. by* Michael Hartnett. BIrV

He is no friend who in thine hour of pride. Friendship. Sadi, *tr. fr. Persian by* L. Cranmer-Byng. *Fr.* The Gulistan. AWP

He is not a brother to me. The Brother. Semion Yakovlevich Nadson, *tr. by* H. Badanes. TrJP

He Is Not Dead. James Whitcomb Riley. *See* I cannot say, and I will not say.

He is not dead nor liveth. Dorothy Wellesley. *Fr.* Deserted House. OBMV

He is not ded that somtyme hath a fall. Sir Thomas Wyatt. AAS; OBVE

He is not here, the old sun. No Possum, No Sop, No Taters. Wallace Stevens. HCAP; OxBA; TAP; VGW

He is not John, the gardener. A Friend in the Garden. Juliana Horatia Ewing. BoTP; FaPON; OxBChV

He is not the wise man, who comes. The Imbecile. Donald Finkel. NePoEA-2

He is old, two weeks to eighty. Blue Sparks in Dark Closets. Richard Snyder. Psk

He is older than the naval side of British history. Chief Petty Officer. Charles Causley. OxBTC

He is one of the prophets come back. He. Lawrence Ferlinghetti. NeAP; PoM

He is only beautiful. Aborigine. Hugo Williams. OBTV

He is patient. Obatala, the Creator. *Yoruba Oral Tradition, tr. by* Ulli Beier. WTO

He is running like a wasp. Pole Vault. Murano Shiro, *tr. by* Satoru Sato *and* Constance Urdang. SD

He is rust/ in moonlight. Coyote Fragments. Lance Henson. HATNAP

He is Shaka the unshakable. Shaka, King of the Zulus. *Unknown, tr. by* A. C. Jordan. PBA; TTY

He is sherrier. The Thinnest Shadow. John Ashbery. TTTS

He is sleeping, soundly sleeping. A "Departed Friend." Julia A. Moore. FiBHP

He is so small, he does not know. Six Weeks Old. Christopher Morley. RHPC

He is stark mad, who ever says. The Broken Heart. John Donne. EBEV

He is that fallen lance that lies as hurled. A Soldier. Robert Frost. OFD; OPP; WaaP; WaP

He Is the Lonely Greateness. Madeleine Caron Rock. CH

He is the oldest grandfather. The Memory Sire. Barney Bush. HATNAP

He is the pond's old father, its brain. The Snapper. William Heyen. AmPA; MAYP; PCP

He is the primal rock. Gray, wise, and old. Nation. Mendel Naigreshel, *tr. by* Joachim Neugroschel. VWA

He is the victim whom the lean predict. Die Bauernhochzeit. Kendrick Smithyman. ATNZ

He is the way. W. H. Auden. *Fr.* For the Time Being; a Christmas Oratorio. EaLo

He is thinking of everyone. Age. Robert Creeley. PPR

He is to weet a melancholy carle. A Portrait. Keats. BXAP

He is very busy with his looking. Young Heroes. Gwendolyn Brooks. BPo

He is walking in the road. Conceited Man. *Gond Oral Tradition, tr. by* V. Elwin *and* S. Hivale. WTO

He is wasted now. Dylan, Who Is Dead. Samuel Allen. PoBA

He isn't all Indian. Our Hired Man (And His Daughter, Too). Monica Shannon. FaPON

He it is, the innermost one, who awakens my being with his deep hidden touches. Rabindranath Tagore. *Fr.* Gitanjali, LXXII. WGRP

He Jests at Scars [That Never Felt a Wound]. Shakespeare. *Fr.* Romeo and Juliet, II, ii. LiTB (Living Juliet, The.) TrGrPo, II, i.

He jumped me while I was asleep. Assailant. John Raven. BPo

He jumped, seeing an island like a hand. Hart Crane. Julian Symons. PoA

He keeps the valley like this with his heart. Prospero without His Magic. Jack Gilbert. NPGG

He keeps tossing her. Atalanta. Jan Kemp. ATNZ

He Kept On Burning, *sels.* Ai. AnAn
  Buchenwald, 1945. *Fr.* II.
  Peru, 1955. *Fr.* III.
  Spain, 1929. *Fr.* I.

He kidded himself for so long. We the Revolutionaries; or, This America. Moyshe-Leyb Halpern, *tr. by* Benjamin *and* Barbara Harshav. AYP

He [*or* When he] killed the noble Mudjokivis. The Modern Hiawatha. George A. Strong. *Fr.* The Song of Milkanwatha. FaBoCo; FaBoPa; FaFP; FaPON; FiBHP; MoShBr; NA; Par; RHPC (Hiawatha Revisited.) BXAP

He Kindleth a Fire. *Unknown, tr. fr. Egyptian by* Robert Hillyer. *Fr.* Book of the Dead. AWP

He knelt beside her pillow, in the dead watch of the night. Asleep. William Winter. AA

He knelt, the Savior knelt and prayed. The Agony in the Garden. Felicia Dorothea Hemans. TrCP

He Knew on Earth. Unsi al-Haj, *tr. fr. Arabic by* Sargon Boulus *and* Alistair Elliot. MAP

He knew what I wanted. O Dirty Bird Yr Gizzard's Too Big & Full of Sand. James Koller. PoM

"He Knoweth Not That the Dead Are Thine." Mary Elizabeth Coleridge. OBNC

He Knoweth the Souls of the West. *Unknown, tr. fr. Egyptian by* Robert Hillyer. *Fr.* Book of the Dead. AWP

He knows he must explain this. The Modes of Vallejo Street, San Diego, Los Angeles, 9. Hugh Seidman. UnPo

He knows it, he has a. Celebration. Sybren Polet, *tr. by* James S. Holmes. DuIn

He knows not bit nor bridle, his nostrils are flaming. The Neighing North. Annie Charlotte Dalton. CaP

He larved ond he larved on he merd such a nauses. The Ondt and the Gracehoper. James Joyce. *Fr.* Finnegans Wake. BIrV

He lay, and those who watched him were amazed. The Sprig of Lime. Robert Nichols. GTBS-P

He lay in the middle of the world, and twitcht. John Berryman. *Fr.* Dream Songs. HCAP; NoP; PoE

He lay in's armour; as if that had been. A Soldier's Death. Cyril Tourneur. *Fr.* The Atheist's Tragedy. SeCePo

He lay on the bed, thinking. The Man on the Bed. Debora Greger. MAYP

He lay on the floor covered in shit. 999 Call. Elizabeth Bartlett. FaBoWP

He Leadeth Me. Joseph Henry Gilmore. AH, *with music;* BLRP; WBLP; WGRP

He leads us on. Through the Maze. *Unknown.* BLRP

He Leads Us Still. Arthur Guiterman. OHIP

He leaned. Treaty-Trip from Shulus Reservation. Patrick Lane. NeAC

He leans forward in his chair. The Gesture. Elizabeth Libbey. WeW

He leant at the door. The Unfrocked Priest. Joseph Campbell. AnIL

He learns by groping if there's hair or there isn't. *Unknown, tr. by* Hiroaki Sato. FCEI

He left his pants upon a chair. The Mistake. Theodore Roethke. *Fr.* Three Epigrams, 2. NBLV

He left the kitchen. Dory Miller. Sam Cornish. CNA

He left the office where he'd been given. He Asked about the Quality. C. P. Cavafy, *tr. by* Edmund Keeley *and* Philip Sherrard. PeHV

He Let the House Be. Max Hölzer, *tr. fr. German by* Beth Bjorklund. CoAuP

He lies/ Beside me. On Death and Love. Janet Campbell Hale. VoR

He lies low in the levelled sand. At the Grave of Walker. Joaquin Miller. AA; AnAmPo

He lies unloosened of his white clothes. Tanabe Sakimaro, *tr. fr. Japanese. Fr.* Manyo Shu. Ma

He lies upon his bed. Archibald MacLeish. *Fr.* Einstein. ImOP

He lifted up, among the actuaries. So Long? Stevens. John Berryman. *Fr.* Dream Songs. HAP; HCAP; NOBA

He lifts the heavy tube. The Elk Uncovers the Heavens. John Bensko. MT

He lights a lamp at such an awkward spot. *Unknown, tr. fr. Japanese by* Hiroaki Sato. *Fr.* Inutsukuba Shu. FCEI

He Liked the Dead. Malcolm Lowry. OxBTC

He listened at the porch that day. A Year's Spinning. Elizabeth Barrett Browning. NAEL-2

He lists them. Yahrzeit. Dan Jaffe. VWA

He lived amid the floricultural attractions. The Garden Boy. Bonisile Joshua Motaung. WMBCH

He Lived amidst th' Untrodden Ways. Hartley Coleridge. FaBoCo; Par (On Wordsworth.) FaBoPa; FiBHP (Wordsworth Unvisited.) NOBL

He lived at Dingle Bank—he did. Dingle Bank. Edward Lear. FaBoNo

He lived in a cave by the seas. Double Ballade of Primitive Man. Andrew Lang *and* Edward Burnett Tylor. CenHV

He lives among a dog. The Child. Donald Hall. NePoEA-2

He lives in the outer land. Blood Marksman and Kureldei the Marksman. *Tatar (Turkic) Oral Tradition, tr. fr. German and Russian versions by* Norman Cohn. WTO

He lives in the sky. The Eagle above Us. Santiago Altamirano, *tr. by* Anselm Hollo. STP

He Lives Long Who Lives Well. Thomas Randolph. WBLP

He lives on edge throughout his days. Hare. Molly Holden. TEP

He lives, who last night flopped from a log. Burning. Galway Kinnell. CoAP

He liveth long who liveth well. Length of Days. Horatius Bonar. PWR

He longs/ He strokes with words the place of longing. I Remember Having Loved. Hasan Abdallah, *tr. by* Lena Jayyusi *and* Christopher Middleton. MAP

He looked about six or seven, only much too thin. The Forgiveness Dream; Man from the Warsaw Ghetto. Jean Valentine. LCAP

He looked for her and found her. He Knew Joy on Earth. Unsi al-Haj, *tr. by* Sargon Boulus *and* Alistair Elliot. MAP

He looks back over the last metaphor. The Great Artist Reconsiders the Homeric Simile. John Tranter. NoAM

He looks down to watch the river twist. Gargoyle. Thomas Rabbitt. MAYP; MT

He looks like a fat little old man. Dead Seal. Alfred W. Purdy. MoCV; MoP

He looks up the high walls. Dead Poet in the Mountains. Michael Guttenbrunner, *tr. by* Beth Bjorklund. CoAuP

He look't and saw what numbers numberless. The Parthians. Milton. *Fr.* Paradise Regained, *Bk.* III, *ll.* 310–343. OBS

He loved her, having felt his love begin. The Contrast. Helen Gray Cone. AA

He loved his cabin: there. Salt Water Story. Richard Hugo. NAAL-2; NoAM; NoP

He loved the brook's soft sound. The Peasant Poet. John Clare. OAEL-2; OBNC; WGRP

He loved three things in life. "Anna Akhmatova," *tr. fr. Russian by* Barbara Einzig. BoWoP

He Loves and He Rides Away. Sydney Thompson Dobell. OBNC

He loves it when the lawyer shouts. Watching TV, the Elk Bones Up on Metaphysics. John Bensko. MT

He loves me. *Unknown.* OxNR

He loves not well whose love is bold. My Queen. William Winter. AA

He lying spilt like water from a bowl. Alison Boodson. ErPo

He made no history, even. Elegy for a Countryman. Padraic Fallon. NeIP

He made no promise. Chikako, *tr. by* Steven D. Carter. WFTW

He made no promise. Empress Eifuku, *tr. by* Steven D. Carter. WFTW

He Made Us Free. Maurice Francis Egan. AA

He Maketh Himself One with Osiris. *Unknown, tr. fr. Egyptian by* Robert Hillyer. *Fr.* Book of the Dead. AWP

He Maketh Himself One with the God Ra. *Unknown, tr. fr. Egyptian by* Robert Hillyer. *Fr.* Book of the Dead.

He Maketh Himself One with the Only God, Whose Limbs Are the Many Gods. *Unknown, tr. fr. Egyptian by* Robert Hillyer. *Fr.* Book of the Dead. AWP

He-man, the sea-man, The. Pickup in Tony's Hashhouse. Kenneth Pitchford. *Fr.* Good for Nothing Man. ErPo

He May Be a Photograph of Himself. Tina Reid. AIW

He may be six kinds of a liar. Loyalty. Berton Braley. BLPA

He Meditates on the Life of a Rich Man. Douglas Hyde, *tr. fr. Irish by* Lady Gregory. OBMV

He met a lady. From the Hazel Bough. Earle Birney. HeIP

He Met Her at the Green Horse. Peter Levi. NePoEA-2

He might have won the highest guerdon that heaven to earth can give. Saturninus. Katherine Eleanor Conway. AA

He mightn't have had wherewith to buy. Last Mathematician. Hyman Edelstein. CaP

He motions me over with a question. Kidnaper. Tess Gallagher. AmPA

(Kidnapper.) AnAn

He moved among blocked facades. Yiddish Poet. A. C. Jacobs. VWA

He moves as the season permits. Nomad's Utopia. Antonio Porta, *tr. by* Lawrence R. Smith. NItP

He moves his quiet shadow. Ozaki Hosai, *tr. fr. Japanese by* Hiroaki Sato. *Fr.* One Hundred Haiku in Free Form. FCEI

He muscled in on my turf. Creature. Sándor Rákos, *tr. by* Daniel Hoffman. MHuP

He must be hardly twenty-two. And yet. The Next Table. Constantine P. Cavafy, *tr. by* John Mavrogordato. PeHV

He must be heading. Tameshige, *tr. by* Steven D. Carter. WFTW

He never acted well by man or woman. George IV. Thackeray. *Fr.* The Georges. FaBoEE

He Never Did That to Me. Noel Coward. NBLV

He Never Expected Much. Thomas Hardy. NAEL-2; NAs; NoAM; OxBTC; SCV

He never felt twice the same about the flecked river. This Solitude of Cataracts. Wallace Stevens. LCAP

He never lives to tell. Calenture. Alastair Reid. NYBP; PrIm

He never made the dive—not while I watched. The Springboard. Louis MacNeice. PoA

He never spoke a word to me. Simon the Cyrenian Speaks. Countee Cullen. AmNP; BPo; HAP; MoAmPo; TrCP; TTY

He nods his head, leads a floating life. Written in Jest: On "The Old Man Who Rolled with the Punch." Wu Wei-yeh, *tr. by* Irving Lo. WFTU

He nothing common did or mean. King Charles on [*or* upon] the Scaffold. Andrew Marvell. *Fr.* An Horatian Ode upon Cromwell's Return from Ireland. ChTr; FaBoRV

He, of his gentleness. In the Wilderness. Robert Graves. CH; EaLo; MoAB; MoBrPo; SeCePo

He once did love with fond affection. Forsaken. *Unknown.* AmFP

He only knew of death what all men may. The Death of the Beloved. Rainer Maria Rilke, *tr. by* J. B. Leishman. OBD

He opened the car door. There was a low rumble. The Meeting. Nicki Jackowska. BrRo

He opens his eyes with a cry of delight. A Child's Christmas Day. *Unknown.* OBCP

He Overcometh the Serpent of Evil in the Name of Ra. *Unknown, tr. fr. Egyptian by* Robert Hillyer. *Fr.* Book of the Dead. AWP

He Paid Me Seven. *Unknown.* BPo

He painted the mountain over and over again. Dearest Reader. Michael Palmer. NPGG

He passes the inn. Tamekane, *tr. by* Steven D. Carter. WFTW

He paused on the sill of a door ajar. The Newcomer's Wife. Thomas Hardy. BoLoP; OxBTC

He Perceives His Rashness in Love, but Has No Choice. Guido Guinicelli, *tr. fr. Italian by* Dante Gabriel Rossetti. AWP

He picks up what he thinks is/ a road map. My Father; October 1942. William Stafford. CAPP; DiL; NaP

He placed the medicine. Wrong Kind of Love. Ray A. Young Bear. NOVW

He places his hand on her head as a hand placed against pain. Rain. Haim Guri, *tr. by* Mark Elliott Shapiro. VWA

He planked down sixpence and he took his drink. Henry Turnbull. W. W. Gibson. FaBoTw

He played by the river when he was young. Washington. Nancy Byrd Turner. FaPON; RHPC

He pledged himself to live with poetry until old age. Sung Hsiang, *tr. fr. Chinese by* Irving Lo. *Fr.* Upon Reading the Works of Tu Fu. WFTU

He plodded away through drifts of ice. Susan Howe. IAT

He Praises Her Hair. *Unknown, tr. fr. Late Middle Irish by* Earl of Longford. AnIL

He Praises His Wife When She Has Left Him. *Unknown, tr. fr. Late Middle Irish by* Robin Flower. AnIL

He Praises the Trees. *Unknown, tr. fr. Irish by* Robin Skelton. BIrV

He prayed for patience; Care and Sorrow came. His Answer. Clara Ann Thompson. BlSi; CBWP-2

He Prayeth Best. Samuel Taylor Coleridge. *Fr.* The Rime of the Ancient Mariner. FaPON

(He Prayeth Well.) BoTP, *sl. longer sel..*

He Prayeth for Ink and Palette That He May Write. *Unknown, tr. fr. Egyptian by* Robert Hillyer. *Fr.* Book of the Dead. AWP

He Prayeth Well. Samuel Taylor Coleridge. *See* Rime of the Ancient Mariner, The: He Prayeth Best.

He preached upon "Breadth" till it argued him narrow. Emily Dickinson. AmPP; NAWM-2; NOCV

He preaches to the crowd that power is lent. Vox Populi. Dryden. *Fr.* The Medal [*or* Medall]. NOBE

"Almighty crowd, thou shorten'st all dispute." OBS

He preferr'd Hanover to England. George I—Star of Brunswick. Thackeray. *Fr.* The Georges. FaBoEE

He pushed back the eastern borders three thousand miles. Song of History: Peter the Great. Sakuma Shozan, *tr. by* Burton Watson. JLIC-2

He pushes behind the words. Waiting. Robert Creeley. VGW

He put away his tiny pipe. Spring Cricket. Frances Rodman. FaPON

He put his acorn helmet on. A Fairy in Armor. Joseph Rodman Drake. *Fr.* The Culprit Fay. FaPON

(Elfin Knight, An). BoTP

He Puts Me to Rest. David Ignatow. VGW

He quickly arms him for the field. Pigwiggin Arms Himself. Michael Drayton. *Fr.* Nymphidia. MoShBr

(Arming of Pigwiggen, The.) GN

He quickly steps over the air. Hurdler. Grace Butcher. ASP

He Raise a Poor Lazarus. *Unknown.* AH

He raised his sword. Happily Ever After, from the Story of the Same Name. Janet Dubé. DT

He ran the course and as he ran he grew. Innocence. Thom Gunn. LiTM; NePoEA-2

He raped her. Ripped the filaments from her skull. The Head-Rape. D. M. Thomas. BWV

He reaches Weymouthtreads the Esplanade. The Royal Tour. "Peter Pindar." OxBoLi

He realized that night how much he was in their power. The Movies. Jack Gilbert. NPGG

He remembered the street he walked along. The Literary Man Observes a Window to the Sky. Kevin Ireland. ATNZ

He Remembers Forgotten Beauty. W. B. Yeats. CTC; LLLT

(Michael Robartes Remembers Forgotten Beauty.) BrPo

He Remembers How He Didn't Understand What Lieutenant Dawson Meant. James Whitehead. MT

He remembers more than twenty years ago. The Literary Exile. Kevin Ireland. ATNZ

He replied to his own question, and with the unmannered. A Meditation on John Constable. Charles Tomlinson. NePoEA-2

He Resigns. John Berryman. OxBSP; SM; WeW

He Resolves to Say No More. Thomas Hardy. TEP

He rested in the cool, that traveller. The African Tramp. Geoffrey Haresnape. PeSA

He Revisits Cambridge. Tennyson. *See* In Memoriam A. H. H.: I past [*or* passed] beside the reverend walls.

He rides about the ranks, and strives t'inspire. Richard III's Speech. Sir John Beaumont. *Fr.* Bosworth Field. JCP

He rides at their head. The College Colonel. Herman Melville. AA; OBWP

He rises and begins to round. The Lark Ascending. George Meredith. PBBP; WiR

He riseth up early in the morning. The Mighty Hunter. J. B. Worley. PoLF

He roars in the swamp. The Alligator. Beatrice Ravenel. WPE

He rode forth armed: breast-plate and crest. A Romance. Chester Kallman. PoA

He rode into town upon a wild-eyed mountain horse. Yellowjacket. Peter Blue Cloud. HATNAP

He rode through bitter mountains. Love and the Mountains. Antonio Machado, *tr. by* Perry Higman. LPSS

He rose at dawn and, fired with hope. The Sailor Boy. Tennyson. MOS

He rose up on his dying bed. Hope. Langston Hughes. OBAL

He rubbed his eyes and wound the silver horn. Little Boy Blue. John Crowe Ransom. LiTM

He runs before the wise men: He. He. Stanley Kunitz. VGW

He Runs into an Old Acquaintance. Alden Nowlan. GOYP

He Said. Jean Valentine. TAP

He said:/ "Let's stay here." Party Piece. Brian Patten. BoLoP

He said God who gave the wound would give the cure. Christian Karlson Stead. *Fr.* Quesada, VII. ATNZ

He said, "Good-night, my heart is light." Premonition. Richard Hovey. AnAmPo

He said he had been a soldier. Dorothy Wordsworth. SaC

He said he was tired and sore all day. Uncle Mells and the Witches' Tree. Elizabeth Madox Roberts. WSC

He said he would be back and we'd drink wine together. Waiting for Icarus. Muriel Rukeyser. NNaP

He said, I want to be wrapped. Warrior Dreams. Ray A. Young Bear. NOVW

He Said: "If in His Image I Was Made." Trumbull Stickney. LiTA

He said: The road you are going will lead you to Hate. The Road to Hate. Patrick Kavanagh. TW

He said to them, Look at this: you see. The Tall Wind. K. O. Arvidson. ATNZ; PeNZ

He said, unreal the buffalo is standing. Unreal the Buffalo Is Standing. *Unknown.* GOA

He sang an old song. The Kilkenny Boy. Eileen Shanahan. NeIP

He sang into the genius of the microphone. The Idea of Mick Jagger at a Concert. Jerry Harp. SoTCo

He sang of joy: whate'er he knew of sadness. A Hero. Florence Earle Coates. OHIP

He sang of life, serenely sweet. The Poet. Paul Laurence Dunbar. BPo

He sang one song and died—no more but that. The Singer of One Song. Henry Augustin Beers. AA

He sang the airs of olden times. The Blind Psalmist. Elizabeth Clementine Kinney. AA

He sat alone upon an ash-heap by. Love. Nicholas Moore. ErPo

He sat at the Algonquin, smoking a cigar. At the Algonquin. Howard Moss. Psk

He sat at the dinner table. Just like a Man. *Unknown.* BoTP

He sat by a fire of seven-fold heat. The Refiner's Fire. *Unknown.* BLRP

He sat in a wheeled chair, waiting for dark. Disabled. Wilfred Owen. BrPo; CMoP; FF; InPS; LiTM; MMA; MoP; NAEL-2; NIP; NoAM; OBWVE; OxBTC; WaP

He sat in his cell staring. The Baboon. Rhydwen Williams, *tr.* by R. Gerallt Jones. OBWVE

He sat upon the rolling deck. Sailor. Langston Hughes. PoA

He saw, abandoned to the sand. The Trail beside the River Platte. William Heyen. GOA

He saw beneath the bughouse wall. Solo for Bent Spoon. Donald Finkel. NePoEA-2

He saw her from the bottom of the stairs. Home Burial. Robert Frost. NAAL-2; PrIm; TAP

He saw in every palm-leaf something new. On the Flesh of Christ. John William Corrington. MT

He saw it clearly and clairvoyant bright. Blueprint. D. B. Steinman. GoYe

He saw the portrait of his enemy, offered. The Enemy's Portrait. Thomas Hardy. EyDe; TW

He says/ that I am like a rock. Agreement. Kishwar Naheed, *tr.* by Mahmood Jamal. PBMUP

He says he doesn't feel like working today. My Erotic Double. John Ashbery. LCAP; PoE

He says *My reign is in peace,* so slays. A Foreign Ruler. Walter Savage Landor. OBSV; ViBoPo

He says no with his head. The Dunce. Jacques Prévert, *tr.* by Lawrence Ferlinghetti. RHTwFP

He says that woman speaks with nature. Susan Griffin. *Fr.* Woman and Nature. NPGG

He says the waves in the ship's wake. Leaving Forever. Denise Levertov. InPK

He says what and what I have to do—to be—to live. No Say. Millie Murray. WS

He says when he comes in a bar. Meeting My Best Friend from the Eighth Grade. Gary Gildner. ASP; SM

He scanned it, staggered, dropped the loop. Emily Dickinson. OBD; PoEL-5

He scans the world with calm and fearless eyes. The New Negro. James Edward McCall. CDC

He scarce had ceas't when the superior Fiend. Milton. *Fr.* Paradise Lost, *Bk.* I, *ll.* 283–313. (Satan and the Fallen Angels.) LiTB; OBS (Satan ("He scarce had ceas't when the superior Fiend").) SeCePo

He scattered tarantulas over the roads. The Devil in Texas. *Unknown.* NBLV; RB

He scorned his land, his tongue denied. Dic Siôn Dafydd. Thomas Jacob Thomas, *tr.* by H. Idris Bell. OBWVE

He scribbles some in prose and verse. Dilettante, The: A Modern Type. Paul Laurence Dunbar. AnAmPo

He seemed to know the harbour. The Shark. Edwin John Pratt. NOBC

He Sees His Beloved. James I, King of Scotland. *Fr.* The Kingis Quair. GoTS; PoEL-1

He sees the gentle stir of birth. If Birth Persists. Matthew Arnold. *Fr.* Resignation. FaBoRV

He sees the rosy apples cling like flowers to the bough. The Fruit Rancher. Lloyd Roberts. CaP

He sees them pass. Once. Eric N. Batterham. CH

He Sees Through Stone. Etheridge Knight. MT; NBP; NNaP; PoBA

He seized me round the waist and kissed my throat. Charleston in the 1860s. Adrienne Rich. CoAP; NAAL-2

He sells them puce-painted T-shirts. Attitudes and Beliefs. Anne Stevenson. ER

He served his God so faithfully and well. On a Puritan. Hilaire Belloc. FaBoEE

He served his master well from youth to age. Old Stephen. Charles Tennyson-Turner. EBVV

He set out and kept hunting. The Hunter. Frank O'Hara. NNaP

He set out snares. Poultry. Diana Der Hovanessian. GrPl

He shall not hear the bittern cry. Lament for Thomas MacDonagh. Francis Ledwidge. BIrV (Thomas MacDonagh.) NOIV

He Shall Speak Peace. Thomas Curtis Clark. WBLP

He Shall Speak Peace unto the Nations. Lila V. Walters. WBLP

He:: She./ Here :: There. /. Alienation & Alliteration. Sybren Polet, *tr.* by Peter Nijmeijer. DuIn

He showed me hights I never saw. Emily Dickinson. PoE

He shuddered briefly and stared down the long valley. The Return of Robinson Jeffers. Robert Hass. AmPA; AnAn

He shudders . . . feeling on the shaven spot. Electrocution. Lola Ridge. WPE

He Singeth a Hymn to Osiris, the Lord of Eternity. *Unknown, tr. fr. Egyptian* by Robert Hillyer. *Fr.* Book of the Dead. AWP

He Singeth in the Underworld. *Unknown, tr. fr. Egyptian* by Robert Hillyer. *Fr.* Book of the Dead. AWP

He sipped at a weak hock and seltzer. The Arrest of Oscar Wilde at the Cadogan Hotel. Sir John Betjeman. CMoP; EBEV; InvP; MoBrPo; MoP; MoP; NoAM; NoP; OxBTC

He sits/ among his drums. A Portrait of Rudy. James Cunningham. CNA

He sits above the clang and dust of Time. The Sovereign Poet. Sir William Watson. WGRP

He sits and begs; he gives a paw. Chums. Arthur Guiterman. RAR

He sits at the bar in the Alhambra. Simple. Naomi Long Madgett. FB; PoBA

He Sits Down on the Floor of a School for the Retarded. Alden Nowlan. GOYP

He sits in front of the bright, blazing grate. The Old Freedman. Priscilla Jane Thompson. CBWP-2

He sits in silence on his porch at night. An Old Habitant. Frank Oliver Call. CaP

He sits in the corner. Corner. Amal Dunqul, *tr.* by Sharif Elmusa *and* Thomas G. Ezzy. MAP

He sits over the glimmering coal. The Old Age Pensioner. Joseph Campbell. AnIL

He sits there, staring into the keyboard. The Recital. Lloyd Schwartz. PPR

He sleeps at last—a hero of his race. A Dead Soldier. George Edgar Montgomery. AA

He sleeps on the top of a mast. The Unbeliever. Elizabeth Bishop. LiTA; NAAL-2; NoAM

He sleeps undreaming; all his world. On a Child Asleep in a Tube Shelter. Sheila Shannon. CN

He slew the noble Mudjekeewis. What Hiawatha Probably Did. *Unknown.* NBLV

He slid out of the skin, leaving it. Summer. Diane Wakoski. VGW

He slowed once. On the Tomb of Kalamachius, the Jogger. Elliot Richman. TSL

He slumbers well and has a right to slumber. The Poet to the Sleeping Saki. Goethe, *tr.* by John Weiss. PeHV

He Smelt the Smell of Death within the Marrow. Louis Johnson. ATNZ

He sniffs the autumn air. Shaman/Bear. Anita Endrezze-Danielson. NOVW

He snuggles his fingers. After Winter. Sterling A. Brown. PoBA; PoNe

He spake, to whom I, answ'ring, thus replied. Homer, *tr. fr. Greek by* William Cowper. *Fr.* Odyssey, XI. OBD

He speaks not well who doth his time deplore. The Heroic Age. Richard Watson Gilder. AA; OHIP

He speaks to me of other things. Differences. Kath McKay. DT

He spoke of undying love. The Talker. Benjamin Appel. TrJP

He spoke while sitting on what seemed to be. Memory II. George Seferis, *tr. by* Edmund Keeley *and* Philip Sherrard. VMG

He Sports by Himself. Susan Miles. BXAP

He stands in the door. Dried Fruit. Philip Dow. BXAP

He stands with his forefeet on the drum. Two Performing Elephants. D. H. Lawrence. RB

He stared at ruin. Ruin stared straight back. John Berryman. *Fr.* Dream Songs. CAPP; HCAP

He stares upward at a monstrous face. The Pieta. Rhenish, 14th C., The Cloisters. Mona Van Duyn. Prf

He startles awake. His eyes are full of white light. The Hermit Wakes to Bird Sounds. Maxine W. Kumin. GrPl; Psk

He stayed, and was imprisoned in possession. W. H. Auden. *Fr.* Sonnets from China, IV. CMoP

He Steals Furs. Anna Swirszczynska, *tr. fr. Polish by* Magnus Jan Krynski *and* Robert A. Maguire. PwPP

He Stepped inside my Door. Eeva Kilpi, *tr. fr. Finnish by* Aili Jarvenpa. SOP

He steps down from the dark train, blinking; stares. Ten Days Leave. W. D. Snodgrass. MoAmPo; Psk; UnPo

He steps out from the others. Passion of Ravensbrück. János Pilinszky, *tr. by* Ted Hughes. MHuP

  (Passion According to Ravensbrüek, The.) FOC, *tr. by* Jascha Kessler

He still believes by middle-age. The Traveler. Duane Niatum. HATNAP

He stood, a worn-out City clerk. Peace. Charles Stuart Calverley. EBVV

  (Peace: A Study.) NOBVV

He stood alone within the spacious square. James Thomson ("B. V."). *Fr.* The City of Dreadful Night, IV. NOBVV; WiR

He stood among a crowd at Drumahair [*or* Dromahair]. The Man Who Dreamed of Faeryland. W. B. Yeats. CMoP; NAEL-2; NoAM; NoP

He stood and call'd/ His legions, angel forms, who lay intranced. Milton. *Fr.* Paradise Lost, *Bk.* I, *ll.* 300–304.

  (Satan's Legions and the Beech Leaves of the Casentino.) FaBoPP

He stood, and heard the steeple. Eight o'Clock. A. E. Housman. BrPo; CMoP; InPK; MoAB; MoBrPo; MoP; NoAM; NoP; OxBSP; PoE; SoSe; TrGrPo

He stood before my heart's closed door. The Refiner's Gold. Frances Ellen Watkins Harper. PWR

He stood before the Sanhedrim. Religion and Doctrine. John Milton Hay. WGRP

He stood on his head by the wild seashore. His Mother-in-Law. Walter Parke. FiBHP

He stood upon the coast of County Clare. St Enda. Laurence Lerner. PeSA

He stoops above the clumsy snare. The Snare. Patrick MacDonogh. NeIP

He stoops down eating sunflowers. Healing Song. Michael S. Harper. CAPP

He stopped on the irreproachable sidewalk. Elysee. Larry Eigner. VGW

He stretched me thin; he puffed me fat. Life. Clark Stillman. SoTCo

He strides across the grassy corn. The Scarecrow. Andrew Young. FaBoTw

He strings the separate nor near you. Drawing on Kreisler. James Sherry. LP

He strode along the chapel aisle. Sabbath Reflection. Denis Wrafter. NeIP

He studies very late. Glowworm. François Dodat, *tr. by* Bert *and* Odette Meyers. TSS

He stumbled all morning through the market. Below Mount T'ui K'oy, Home of the Gods, Todos Santos Cuchumatán, Guatemalan Highlands. Joseph Stroud. NPGG

He stumbles silver-haired among his bees. The Veteran. Edmund Blunden. BrPo

He swims and I swim and not only the lakes in our. GN Is Happy. Giulia Niccolai, *tr. by* Beverly Allen. DMI

He swings down like the flourish of a pen. Skier. Robert Francis. RFM; SD; TSL

He switched on the electric light and laughed. Intimate Supper. Peter Redgrove. FaBoMo; OxBC

He takes the long review of things. To a Certain Most Certainly Certain Critic. David McCord. OBAL

He talked of Delhi brothels half the night. Long Tom. W. W. Gibson. OxBTC

He talks and talks. Like Ripples on the Water. *Gond Oral Tradition, tr. by* V. Elwin *and* S. Hivale. WTO

He taught Math at the Ecole Centrale. Salomon. Pierre Morhange, *tr. by* Edouard Roditi. VWA

He tells many bad things. Young Training. Lawrence McGaugh. PoBA

He tells me in Bangkok he's robbed. Baby Villon. Philip Levine. CoAP; NaP

He tells you when you've got on too much lipstick. The Perfect Husband. Ogden Nash. FaBoUs

He that but once too nearly hears. The Music of Forefended Spheres. Coventry Patmore. *Fr.* The Victories of Love, I, ii. FaBoRV

He that can trace a ship making her way. The Heart Is Deep. Roger Wolcott. SCAP

He that dwelleth in the secret place of the most High. Psalm XCI ("He that dwelleth. . ."). Bible, *O.T. Fr.* Psalms. AWP

  (Everlasting Arms, The, *Moulton, Modern Reader's Bible*) WGRP

  (Mighty Fortress, A.) TrGrPo

He that for fear his Master did deny. To St. Peter and St. Paul. Henry Constable. Son

He that from dust of worldly tumults flies. Of True Liberty. Sir John Beaumont. OBS

He that had come that morning. Ballad of John Cable and Three Gentlemen. W. S. Merwin. CoAP; NePoEA; NOBA

He that has grown to wisdom hurries not. Sonnet: Of Moderation and Tolerance. Guido Guinicelli, *tr. by* Dante Gabriel Rossetti. AWP

He that has sail'd upon the dark blue sea. Byron. *Fr.* Childe Harold's Pilgrimage, II. MOS

He that has seen a great oak dry and dead. Joachim Du Bellay, *tr. fr. French by* Spenser. *Fr.* Ruins of Rome. FaBoPP

He That Hath No Mistress. *Unknown.* GBL; OxBSP

He that hath such acuteness, and such wit. On Mr. Francis Beaumont (Then Newly Dead.) Richard Corbet. OBS

He that intends to take a wife. The Wife-Hater. *Unknown.* CoMu

He that is by Mooni now. Mooni. Henry Clarence Kendall. OBEV

He that is down needs fear no fall. Bunyan. *Fr.* The Pilgrim's Progress. EBEV

  (Enough!) BLRP

  (Shepherd Boy Sings [in the Valley of Humiliation], The.) EaLo; GN; NOBE; OBEV; WGRP

  (Shepherd Boy's Song, The.) BoTP

  (Song of the Shepherd Boy.) OxBSP

  (Song of the Shepherd in the Valley of Humiliation, The.) OBS

He that is in the battle slain. Fight. *Unknown.* FaFP

He That Is Slow to Anger. Bible, *O.T. Fr.* Proverbs, XVI: 32. FaPON

He that is weary, let him sit. Employment ("He that is weary, let him sit.") George Herbert. JCP; OBS; SeCP; TEP

He that lies at the stock. *Unknown.* OxNR

  (Rock, Ball, Fiddle.) CH; OxBoLi

He That Loves. Sir Philip Sidney. ErPo

He That Loves a Rosy Cheek. Heinrich von Rugge, *tr. fr. German by* Jethro Bithell. AWP

He that loves and fears to try. He That Loves. Sir Philip Sidney. ErPo

He That Ne'er Learns His ABC. *Unknown.* GBP

He That Never Read a Line. *Unknown, tr. fr. Old Irish by* Robin Flower. AnIL

He that of such a height hath built his mind. To the Lady Margaret, Countess of Cumberland. Samuel Daniel. OBSC

He that only rules by terror. The Captain. Tennyson. MOS

He that owns wealth, in mountain, wold, or waste. Wealth. Sadi, *tr. fr. Persian by* Sir Edwin Arnold. *Fr.* The Gulistan. AWP

He That Regards the Precious Things of Earth. Moses Ibn Ezra, *tr. fr. Hebrew by* Solomon Solis-Cohen. *Fr.* The World's Illusion. TrJP

He that to God's law doth cling. Freedom. Abraham Ibn Ezra, *tr. by* Solomon Solis-Cohen. TrJP

He that will be a lover in every wise. Three Things Jeame Lacks. *Unknown.* MeEL

He that will court a wench that is coy. *Unknown.* ErPo

He that will give good words to thee, will flatter. Shakespeare. *Fr.* Coriolanus, I, i. FaBoPV

He that will not love must be. Not to Love. Robert Herrick. CaPo

He that would live for aye. *Unknown.* FaBoUs

He that would the daughter win. *Unknown.* FaBoUs

He that would thrive must rise at five. *Unknown.* FaBoUs; OxNR

He the Beloved, *sel.* Qorratu'l-Ayn, *tr. fr. Farsi by* Deirdre Lashgari. "Cupbearer, O victorious Falcon, come!" WPOW

He, the indiscreet agent. Doves. Joachim Neugroschel. VWA

He there now does enjoy eternal rest. Spenser. *Fr.* The Faerie Queene, I, 9. MOS (Sleep after Toil.) ChTr

He Thinks of His Past Greatness When a Part of the Constellations of Heaven. W. B. Yeats. PoEL-5

He Thinks of Those Who Have Spoken Evil of His Beloved. W. B. Yeats. *See* Half close your eyelids, loosen your hair.

He thinks when we die we'll go to China. Heaven. Cathy Song. NoAM

He thought he kept the universe alone. The Most of It. Robert Frost. HAP; NAAL-2; NoP; NU; TOF; WeW

He thought he saw a buffalo [*or* a banker's clerk *or* an elephant]. The Mad Gardener's Song. "Lewis Carroll." *Fr.* Sylvie and Bruno. BLPL; FaBoCo; FaBoNo; FiBHP, 6 *sts.*; NA; OnUR, 4 *sts.*; OxBChV; WiR

He thought to quell the stubborn hearts of oak. Buonaparte. Tennyson. Son

He threw a tantrum, tossed a fit. Andujar in the Pique of His Career. Bob McKenty. SoTCo

He threw the shroud about his head. John Donne's Statue. John Peale Bishop. EyDe

He thrust his joy against the weight of the sea. The Surfer. Judith Wright. RR; WPE

He ties him to a breezy tree. Issa, *tr. by* Hiroaki Sato. FCEI

He tips his boy baby's hand in an icy. Three Sonnets for Iva. Marilyn Hacker. GLP

He Told His Life Story to Mrs Courtly. Stevie Smith. NBLV (Autumn.) FaBoWP

He told the barmaid he had things to do. Dodona's Oaks Were Still. Patrick MacDonogh. NeIP

He told the crowd "The devils." John Logan. *Fr.* A Short Life of the Hermit. CRP

He too has an eternal part to play. The Historical Judas. Howard Nemerov. NoP

He too must with me wash his body, though. An Anniversary of Death. John Wieners. PoM

He took a thousand islands and he didn't lose a man. Dewey in Manila Bay. R. V. Risley. PAH

He Took Her. Tom Masson. OBAL

He took her fancy when he came. What He Took. *Unknown.* CoMu

He took her one day. A Fine, a Private Place. Diane Ackerman. MAYP

He took the quaint cup in unpractised hands. Poor Fool. Evan V. Shute. CaP

He took three big gulps. Big Man. Mason Jordan Mason. PoNe

He tossed a life preserver to the young castaway in '55. Otto Orban, *tr. by* Jascha Kessler. FOC

He touches, and the wheel of time goes round. Hurdy-Gurdy Man in Winter. Vernon Watkins. NYBP

He travels after a winter sun. Tilly. James Joyce. RB

He Tries out the Concords Gently. "Eduard Bagritsky," *tr. fr. Russian by* C. M. Bowra. TrJP

He tunes his lyre within his lowly dwelling. The Lowly Bard. "Fanny Forester." PF

He turned his field into a meeting-place. W. H. Auden. *Fr.* In Time of War, VIII. SCV

He turns comedy into tragedy. What's Next. Tawfiq Sayigh, *tr. by* Abdullah al-Udhari. MPAW

He turns to you, measly immortal page. Page. Sandra McPherson. PoA

He Understands the Great Cruelty of Death. Petrarch. *See* Sonnets to Laura: To Laura in Death.

He unto whom thou art so partial. Post-Obits and the Poets. Martial, *tr. by* Byron. AWP; FaBoEE; OBVE

He used me today. The Gardener. Evelyn Eaton. GoYe

He used to come here till he donned gold braid. To a Tyrant. Joseph Brodsky, *tr. by* Alan Myers. VWA

He used to dream of things he'd do. The Dreamer. Thomas Nunan. WBLP

He usually managed to be there when. Because He Liked to Be at Home. Kenneth Patchen. NaP

He waited for me at the gate-screen, heigh-ho! *Unknown, tr. by* Arthur Waley. BoS

He waits perpetually crouched, teeth. Mean Rufus Throw-Down. David Smith. TDD

He wakens from the clover rick. The Sun-Witch to the Sun. George Howe. NYBP

He wakes; speak to him. Shakespeare. *Fr.* King Lear, IV, vii. SCV "How does my royal lord? How fares your Majesty?" Prf

He walked through the woods. The Walk. W. W. Eustace Ross. SD

He walked up and down the street 'till the shoes fell off his feet. Tramp, Tramp, Tramp, Keep on a-Tramping. *Unknown.* AS

He Walketh by Day. *Unknown, tr. fr. Egyptian by* Robert Hillyer. *Fr.* Book of the Dead. AWP

He walks still upright from the root. The Hewel, or Woodpecker. Andrew Marvell. *Fr.* Upon Appleton House, to My Lord Fairfax. ChTr

He walks, the enchanter, on his sea of glass. Antichrist. Edwin Muir. EaLo

He walks with shopping basket, and an air. Halfwit. Basil Dowling. ATNZ

He waltzes into the lane. Makin' Jump Shots. Michael S. Harper. ASP; PoE

He wants and doesn't want to roast them. *Unknown, tr. by* Hiroaki Sato. FCEI

He wants to be. Self-Portrait. Robert Creeley. NoAM

He Was. Richard Wilbur. SaC

He was a big two-fisted brute. Bucko-Mate. Samuel Schierloh. GoYe

He was a druggist. The storefront building. The Shriving. Jared Carter. MOWH

He was a farmer, he didn't think much of towns. Stephen Vincent Benét. *Fr.* John Brown's Body. AiP

He was a fine young man. The first day he was born. Odysseus Elytis, *tr. fr. Greek by* Edmund Keeley *and* Philip Sherrard. *Fr.* Heroic and Elegiac Song for the Lost Second Lieute, VI. VMG

He was a good boy. Uncle's First Rabbit. Lorna Dee Cervantes. CCP; NoAM

He was a good man. Wake Cry. Waring Cuney. BANP

He was a man as hot as whiskey. Andrew Jackson. Martha Keller. AmFN

He was a mighty hunter in his youth. The White Cat of Trenarren. Alfred Leslie Rowse. OxBTC

He was a rat, and she was a rat. What Became of Them? *Unknown.* BoTP; OBCA; OxBChV

He was a reprobate I grant. The Deceased. Keith Douglas. FaBoTw

He was a selfish shellfish. Idyll. Stoddard King. NBLV

He was a singer caroling in dark. Countee Cullen. Eugene T. Maleska. PoNe

He was a traveler west of the river,/ only he knew how lonely he was. Tune: Eternal Longing. *Unknown, tr. fr. Chinese by* Burton Watson. *Fr.* Four *Tz'u* from Tun-huang, II. CoBCP

He was a traveler west of the river,/ then he took sick, lay an inch away from death. Tune: Eternal Longing. *Unknown, tr. fr. Chinese by* Burton Watson. *Fr.* Four *Tz'u* from Tun-huang, III. CoBCP

He was a traveler west of the river,/ with wealth and eminence rare in this world. Tune: Eternal Longing. *Unknown, tr. fr. Chinese by* Burton Watson. *Fr.* Four *Tz'u* from Tun-huang, I. CoBCP

He was a young god. Genesis. Evan Jones. PBCV

He was afraid of naked thought. Golden Fantasy. Tamura Ryuichi, *tr. by* Hiroaki Sato. FCEI

He was afraid to go through their grocery store. Charles Reznikoff. *Fr.* Five Groups of Verse. DiL

He was Aijö, born alone. Aijö's Song. Eino Leino, *tr. by* Aili Jarvenpa. SOP

He Was Always Nursing Some Human Wound of His. Giancarlo Marmori, *tr. fr. Italian by* Lawrence R. Smith. NItP

He was an old wolf, no teeth, his tail all but bare. *Unknown, tr. fr. Sioux Indian by* James Koller. *Fr.* Sioux Metamorphoses. STP

He was as loyal as them all—and more. Peeping Tom. Francis Hope. ErPo

He was as old as old could be. Danny Murphy. James Stephens. BoTP; OnUR

He was at Naples writing letters home. Wallace Stevens. *Fr.* Esthétique du Mal. CMoP; NOBA

He was born in Alabama. Of De Witt Williams on His Way to Lincoln Cemetery. Gwendolyn Brooks. *Fr.* A Street in Bronzeville. CAPP; NoAM; NOBA

He was born in Deutschland, as you would suspect. The Progress of Faust. Karl Shapiro. MoAB; NYBP

He was found by the Bureau of Statistics to be. The Unknown Citizen. W. H. Auden. FF; HeIP; InPK; LiTA; LiTM; MoAB; NBLV; NIP; NOBL; NYBP; OBSV; PoRA; SoSe; UnPo

He was, he tells his grandson, a grandson. The Numbering at Bethlehem. Albert Goldbarth. NAmP

He was impoverished, possessing a full island. Castaway. John Nerber. PoA

He was in logick a great critic. The Metaphysical Sectarian. Samuel Butler. *Fr.* Hudibras, I, 1. MeLP

(Hudibras, the Presbyterian Knight, *abr.*) OxBoLi

(Portrait of Hudibras.) PoEL-3

(Presbyterian Knight and Independent Squire, *abr.*) OBS

(Sir Hudibras, His Passing Worth.) FaBoCo

He was in love with Truth and knew her near. Walt Whitman. Harrison Smith Morris. AA

He was just a young aviator. Lindbergh. *Unknown.* AmFP

He was just back. Vietnam. Clarence Major. PoBA

He was like the Lord drunk. Alcoholic. F. D. Reeve. NYBP

He was lying dead on a stone. Victim No. 48. Mahmoud Darwish, *tr. by* Abdullah al-Udhari. MPAW

He was no good. Somewhere. Black Jess. Peter Kane Dufault. NYBP

He was no longer my father. The Mirror. Paul Muldoon, *tr. by* Michael Davitt. CIP

He was not able to read or write. The Gardener. Louis MacNeice. *Fr.* Novelettes, III. FaBCIP

He was not bad, as emperors go, not really. Two Pieces for Suetonius. Robert Penn Warren. NOBA

He was not only friend and my lover. Second Woman's Lament. Brenda Chamberlain. NeIP

He was older and. Passage. John M. Roderick. GOYP

He was once a tiny, helpless thing. Aaron Nicholas, Almost Ten. Janet Campbell Hale. VoR

He was reading late, at Richard's, down in Maine. Henry's Understanding. John Berryman. CAPP; MoP; NoAM; NOBA

He was really her favorite. In Spite of His Dangling Pronoun. Lyn Lifshin. IHMS

He was sitting there on a stone. Elderberry Flute Song. Peter Blue Cloud. STE

He was six years old, just six that day. A Little Boy's Vain Regret. Edith Matilda Thomas. AA

He was sixty [years old]. Still teaching. Lessons in Parsing. Rashid Husain. MAP, *tr. by* Lena Jayyusi *and* Peter Porter; MPAW, *tr. by* Abdullah al-Udhari

He was so handsome and gracious, and also a good swimmer. The Lord. Erika Mitterer, *tr. by* Beth Bjorklund. CoAuP

He was standing on the edge of us. We Never Know. Yusef Komunyakaa. MT

He was still Uncle. The Empress Brand Trim: Ruby Reminisces. Sherley Anne Williams. BlSi

He was such a curious lover of shells. Full Fathom Five. Arthur Rex Dugard Fairburn. ATNZ; PeNZ

He Was the Best of All. Hans Lodeizen, *tr. fr. Dutch by* James S. Holmes. DuIn

He was the best postilion. The Postilion Has Been Struck by Lightning. Patricia Beer. OxBC

He was the doctor up to Combe. Coroner's Jury. L. A. G. Strong. OxBTC

He was the first always: Fortune. Envy. Adelaide Anne Procter. NOBVV

He was the first man amongst the dead. In the Valley of Death. Amiq Hanafi, *tr. by* Mahmood Jamal. PBMUP

He was the last. Truly the last. The Butterfly. Pavel Friedmann, *tr. by* Dennis Silk

He was the slave of Ambition. The Mills of the Gods. *Unknown.* BLPA; FPL

He was the uncle who when he was young. I Would Visit Him in the Corner. Alberto Rios. NAmP

He was the youngest son of a strange brood. Otto. Theodore Roethke. DiL

He was their servant (some say he was blind). W. H. Auden. *Fr.* Sonnets from China, VII. CMoP

He was there/ Old Man Coyote. Medicine-Tail, *tr. by* W. S. Merwin. STP

He was, through boyhood's storm and shower. G. K. Chesterton. FiBHP

He was warned aginst the *womern.* On a Splendid Match. James Whitcomb Riley. AnAmPo

He washes his horse. Masaoka Shiki, *tr. by* Geoffrey Bownas *and* Anthony Thwaite. PeBJV

He wasn't handsome or young or even clever, but oh. On Don Juan del Norte, Not Don Juan Tenorio del Sur. Alan Dugan. ErPo

He watched the stars and noted birds in flight. W. H. Auden. *Fr.* Sonnets from China, VI. CMoP

He watched with all his organs of concern. W. H. Auden. PoA

He wears a beard to let us see that he is pure within. Sanctimony. *Malay Oral Tradition, tr. by* R. J. Wilkinson. WTO

He welcomes us still. His Welcome. Auvaiyar, *tr. by* A. K. Ramanujan. PLW

He went down to the field of a morning. The Second Year. Marion Montgomery. KS

He went inside the café where they used to sit together. Lovely White Flowers. Constantine P. Cavafy, *tr. by* Edmund Keeley *and* Philip Sherrard. OBD

He went into a grey day. For One Who Died Young. H. R. Hays. EAS

He went into his harvest barn. The Farmer. "E." CBAP

He went off; didn't say when he'd be back. Holiday's End. Haim Guri, *tr. by* Warren Bargad *and* Stanley F. Chyet. IP

He went out to their glorious. The Summons. James Laughlin. LiTA

He went there. Poem of the Conscripted Warrior. "Rui Nogar," *tr. by* Dorothy Guedes *and* Philippa Rumsey. TTY

He went to fix the awning. Fixer of Midnight. Reuel Denney. OBAL

He went to the wood and caught it. *Unknown.* GBP; OxNR

He went with another. Gabriela Mistral, *tr. by* Muriel Kittel. AIW

He whittled scallops for a hardy thatch. The Thatcher. Brendan Kennelly. CIP

He who ascends to mountain-tops shall find. The Isolation of Genius. Byron. WBLP

He who becomes his contrary. Shekhina and the Kiddushim. Edouard Roditi. VWA

He who began from brick and lime. In Obitum Ben. Jons. Mildmay Fane, Earl of Westmorland. OxBSP

He who burns the sere weeds. *Unknown, tr. fr. Japanese. Fr.* Manyo Shu. Ma

He Who Calls Himself Leader. Moyshe-Leyb Halpern, *tr. fr. Yiddish by* Benjamin *and* Barbara Harshav *and* Kathryn Helle. AYP

He who could win the girl I love. A Girl's Hair. Dafydd ab Edmwnd, *tr. by* Gwyn Williams. OBWVE

He who crosses a park in great and flourishing Havana. Central Park *Some People (3 P.M.).* Nancy Morejón, *tr. by* Sylvia Carranza. PBWP

He who died at Azan sends. After Death in Arabia. Sir Edwin Arnold. WGRP

He who dreads arrival and speeds in the night. The Journey. Dan Pagis, *tr. by* Bernhard Frank. MHeP

He who has borne my golden fall. The Tree Celebrates the River. Leah Goldberg, *tr. by* Bernhard Frank. MHeP

He Who Has Lost All. David Diop, *tr. fr. French by* Anne Atik. TTY

He who has lost soul's liberty. Soul's Liberty. Anna Wickham. MoBrPo; OxBSP

He who has no hands. Orator. Emerson. *Fr.* Quatrains. OxBA

He who has no house and no home to return to. Continually. Herbert Zand, *tr. by* Beth Bjorklund. CoAuP

He who has once been happy is for aye. Wilfrid Scawen Blunt. *Fr.* Esther [a Young Man's Tragedy]. OBMV; OBNC; TrGrPo (With Esther.) OBEV

He who has rolled his pants up to his knee. Crossing a Creek. Herbert Clark Johnson. PoNe

He who has toiled and bought for himself books. Proverbs. Samuel Ha-Nagid, *tr. by* Israel Abrahams. TrJP

He who hath led will lead. Guide and Friend. *Unknown.* BLRP

He who in his youth. Wordsworth. *Fr.* The Prelude [or, Growth of a Poet's Mind]: Books. TOF

He who is my master. The "Word" of a Watch-Dog. Sandag, Mongol Oral Tradition, *tr. by* C. R. Bawden. WTO

He Who Knows ("He who knows not and knows not that he knows not"). *Unknown, tr. fr. Arabic.* BLPA

He who knows not what thing is Paradise. Angelo Poliziano, *tr. fr. Italian. Fr.* Three Ballate, II. AWP, *tr. by* John Addington Symonds

He who mounts the Heavenly Dragon has the following of myriad souls. Upon Leaving the Capital: A Farewell to My Several Friends. K'ang Yu-wei, *tr. by* Irving Lo. WFTU

He, who navigated with success. Death of a Young Son by Drowning. Margaret Atwood. BoWoP; NIP; NOBC

He who offends a woman. Machiavelli, *tr. by* J. R. Hale. PFI

He, who once was my brother, is dead by his own hand. Justice Is Reason Enough. Diane Wakoski. AmPA

He who plants a tree. Plant a Tree. Lucy Larcom. OHFP; WBLP

He who saved Ankoma Oh nature. Prelude to Akwasidae. *Unknown, tr. by* Halim El-Dabh. TTY

He who sits from day to day. On a Certain Occasion for the Year 1790. William Cowper. NOCV

He who stole my virginity/ is the same man. Silabhattarika, *tr. by* W. S. Merwin *and* J. Moussaieff Masson. WPOW

He who tears his heart out of his breast at night reaches for the rose. Paul Celan, *tr. by* Beth Bjorklund. CoAuP

He who would acclaim Cleanness in becoming style. *Unknown, tr. fr. Middle English by* Brian Stone. *Fr.* Cleanness. NOCV

He who would echo Horace' lays. Horace. John Osborne Sargent. AA

He who writ this, not without pains and thought. Prologue. Dryden. *Fr.* Secret Love; or, The Maiden Queen. SeCV-2
He Whose Hand and Eye Are Gentle. *Unknown, tr. fr. Welsh by* Kenneth Hurlstone Jackson. OBWVE
He will be shot. He is a guilty man. Guilty Man. Uuno Kailas, *tr. by* Aili Jarvenpa. SOP
He Will Give Them Back. "George Klingle." BLRP
He will go over and tell the king. Over the Wall: Berlin, May 1975. C. H. Sisson. OBTV; OxBC
He will have turned. Old Story. Lance Henson. VoR
He will insist on. The Bath. Joel Oppenheimer. NeAP
He will silently plan for thee. God's Plans. *Unknown.* BLRP
He will sit at the bare table, reading a dictionary. Time of Waiting. Geoffrey Dutton. CBAP
He will watch the hawk with an indifferent eye. Icarus. Stephen Spender. MoP; PrIm
(Discovered in Mid-Ocean.) MoBrPo
He Wishes for the Cloths of Heaven. W. B. Yeats. *See* Had I the heavens' embroidered clothes.
He with body waged a fight. The Four Ages of Man. W. B. Yeats. TrCP
He woke at five and, unable. Physical Universe. Louis Simpson. CAPP; InPS
He woke from slumber rubbing his eyes. Memories of the Village School. Al-Tijani Yusuf Bashir, *tr. by* Issa Boullata *and* John Heath-Stubbs. MAP
He wonders if he ought to wash his clothes. *Unknown, tr. by* Hiroaki Sato. FCEI
He wore old Oregon on his chest. Prefontaine. Charles Ghigna. ASP
He works/ stone to. Rock Painting. Carroll Arnett. VoR
He worshipped at the altar of Romance. Colin Ellis. OxBTC
He would/ in the case of a divorce. Tove Ditlevsen, *tr. fr. Danish by* Ann Freeman. *Fr.* Divorce, I. OV
He would burn his books and gladly die. An Aged Writer. Roy McFadden. NeIP
He would declare and could himself believe. Never Again Would Birds' Song Be the Same. Robert Frost. FYAP; HAP; InPK; NIP; NoAM; NoP; Son; VGW
He would drink by himself. Casualty. Seamus Heaney. FaBoPV; IPY; NAEL-2; PoE
He Would Have His Lady Sing. Digby Mackworth Dolben. EBEV
He would not lie uncovered. Burial of the Dog. Susan Musgrave. NoAM
He Would Not Stay for Me; and Who Can Wonder? A. E. Housman. PeHV
He writes from the provinces: It is. Reply to the Provinces. Galway Kinnell. NYBP
He wrote them all down, the missing. That Night. John Welch. NPo
He wrote upon his heart. Donald Jeffrey Hayes. CDC
He wrought at one great work for years. A Ballad of Heaven. John Davidson. BeLS
He yelled at me in Greek. John Berryman. *Fr.* Dream Songs. FYAP
Head, The. Blaise Cendrars, *tr. fr. French by* Ron Padgett. RHTwFP
Head, The. Padraic Fallon. CIP
Head, A. James Schuyler. PoM
Head and Bottle. Edward Thomas. BrPo
Head/ The eye distinct, The. The Invasion. Pierre Reverdy, *tr. by* John Ashbery. POS
Head and the feet keep warm, The. *Unknown.* FaBoUs
Head and the Heart, The. John Godfrey Saxe. AnAmPo
Head bumper. *Unknown.* OxNR
Head Couples. William H. Matchett. NYBP
Head in a cloud Moses stands. Moses. Sydney Tremayne. OxBS
Head Is a Paltry Matter, The. Pier Giorgio Di Cicco. NOBC
Head is stately, calm, and wise, The. The Head and the Heart. John Godfrey Saxe. AnAmPo
Head Itself. Laura Riding. PoA
Head-lice make merry on my head. Emperor Go-Shirakawa, *tr. fr. Japanese by* Hiroaki Sato. *Fr.* Ryojin Hisho. FCEI
Head of cheese raised by wolves, A. The Wild Cheese. James Tate. PPR
Head of Medusa. Marya Zaturenska. MoAmPo
Head of the congregation here stands at the head, The. The Poem on the Jews. Avot Yeshurun, *tr. by* Harold Schimmel. VWA
Head or Tail, A—which does he lack? The Hippo. Theodore Roethke. VGW
Head poking from a vermilion tower, all eight directions cramped. After Getting Drunk, I Scribble Songs and Poems. Lu Yu, *tr. by* Burton Watson. CoBCP
Head pressed against the shoulder, thirty times, The. Tape Mark. Nanni Balestrini, *tr. by* Lawrence R. Smith. NItP

Head pure, sinless quite of brain or soul, A. Burns. FaBoEE
Head-Rape, The. D. M. Thomas. BWV
Head Table Wives. Bonnie Jacobson. SoTCo
Head the ship for England! Homeward Bound. William Allingham. FaBoBe
Head tilts back, like a heavy leaf, the eyes sew shut, The. Infant. Diana O Hehir. NPGG
Headboard to Headboards, A. László Nagy, *tr. fr. Hungarian by* Jascha Kessler. FOC
Heading for cloud-mantled mountains, I press on to the other side. Singde, *tr. by* William Schultz. WFTU
Heading for Eugene. Lorenza Schmidt. FIA
Headland. Brewster Ghiselin. PoA
Headlands, 2365. John Oliver Simon. BWV
Headless bird flew back, The. Codex Minor. Rachel Hadas. EOEF
Headless Phantoms, The. *Unknown, tr. fr. Early Modern Irish by* Eoin MacNeill. AnIL
Headless squirrel, some blood, A. A Day Begins. Denise Levertov. NaP
Headless, without an arm, a figure leans. On a Cast from an Antique. George Pellew. AA
Headline History. William Plomer. FaBoCo
Headlong Hall, *sel.* Thomas Love Peacock.
In His Last Binn Sir Peter Lies. EnRP
Headmaster of a national school, The. Politik. Tom Paulin. FaBCIP
Headrock. Brian Coffey. CIP
Heads, impenetrable, The. Oxen: Ploughing at Fiesole. Charles Tomlinson. OxBTC
Heads in the Women's Ward. Philip Larkin. OBD
Heads leaning out beyond the line have all fallen now, The. Show for the Eyes. Pierre Reverdy, *tr. by* Michael Benedikt. POS
Heads of strong old age are beautiful, The. Promise of Peace. Robinson Jeffers. LiTA; LiTM; MoAB; MoAmPo
Headstone, like a petrified congregation, The. In the Old Jewish Cemetery, Prague, 1970. Edward Lowbury. VWA
Headstones are thin, The; the trees are thick. The Cows near the Graveyard. Howard Nelson. NU
Headwaters of the Lung River. Hsü Ts'an, *tr. fr. Chinese by* Pao Chia-lin. WFTU
Heal Me, My God. Judah Halevi, *tr. fr. Hebrew by* David Goldstein. TOF
Healed of My Hurt. Herman Melville. AmPP
Healer, The. Charles Simic. AnAn
Healing. Wendell Berry. AnAn
Healing. Abraham Reisen, *tr. fr. Yiddish by* Joseph Leftwich. TrJP
Healing of the Leper, The. Vernon Watkins. FaBoTw
Healing Song. Michael S. Harper. CAPP
Healing Song. *Unknown, tr. by* Frances Densmore. OBVE
Health. Margo Lockwood. PPR
Health, A. Edward Coote Pinkney. AA; AnAmPo
Health. Edward Thomas. SeCePo
Health and Fitness. J. B. Morton. FaBoCo
Health and wealth and love he too dreamed of in May. Patrick Kavanagh. *Fr.* The Great Hunger. MoAB
Health at the Ford, A. Robert Cameron Rogers. AA; FaBoBe
Health Counsel. Sir John Harington. FaBoUs
Health Food. *Unknown.* FaBoUs
Health from the lover of the country, me. To Fuscus Arustus. Horace, *tr. fr. Latin by* Abraham Cowley. *Fr.* Epistles, I, 10. AWP
Health! I seek thee; dost thou love. Robert Bloomfield. *Fr.* Shooter's Hill. OBNC
Health is the first good lent to men. Four Things Make Us Happy Here. Robert Herrick. CaPo
Health of Body Dependent on Soul. Jones Very. WGRP
Health to great Gloucester—from a man unknown. Charles Churchill. OBSV
(Dedication to the Sermons, The.) QFR
Health to the Maxwels' veteran Chief! To Terraughty, on His Birth-Day. Burns. NAs
Health to the Tackers, A. *Unknown.* APAS
Health unto His Majesty, A. Jeremy Savile. ChTr
Healthy Spot, A. W. H. Auden. AiP
Heap cassia, sandal-buds and stripes. Robert Browning. *Fr.* Paracelsus. OBEV
Heap high the farmer's wintry hoard. The Corn-Song. Whittier. GN; OHIP
Heap of Rags, The. W. H. Davies. BrPo
Heaps on Heaps. Matthew Concanen. *Fr.* A Match at Football. SD
Hear/ sister Chile. Chile. Roberto Vargas, *tr. by* Alejandro Murguía. Vol

Hear and Be Stunned. Jacob Glatstein, *tr. fr. Yiddish by* Benjamin *and* Barbara Harshav. AYP

Hear! hear! Lilian's Song. George Darley. OBNC

Hear, Hear, O Ye Nations. Frederick Lucian Hosmer. AH

"Hear how a baai a taak." Two Cultures. David Dabydeen. UAS

Hear how selection was the efficient cause. Darwin on Species. *Unknown.* FaBoUs

Hear, Lord, hear. The Leper Cleansed. John Collop. TrGrPo

Hear me/ don't you hear me. Tambourine. James Cunningham. JB

Hear me as if thy eares had palate, Jack. An Ode in the Praise of Sack. *Unknown.* OBS

Hear me, great ones of Uruk. *Unknown, tr. fr. Babylonian by* N. K. Sandars. *Fr.* The Epic of Gilgamesh. DL

Hear me [*or* Heare mee], O God! A Hymn to God the Father. Ben Jonson. MePo; NoP; OBS; SeCP; SeCV-1; TrCP; TrPWD

Hear me, whom I betrayed. J. V. Cunningham. VGW

Hear me! ye firm and uncorrupted few. The Death of the Factory Child. John Critchley Prince. PF

Hear me, ye smokeless skies and grass-green earth. Charles Mair. *Fr.* The Last Bison. NOBC

Hear Me Yet. *Unknown.* ElL

Hear my voice, birds of war! Ojibwa War Songs. *Unknown, tr. by* H. H. Schoolcraft. AWP

Hear my voice in glad thanksgiving. Thanksgiving. N. M. Yazykov, *tr. by* Alan Myers. AAA

Hear, nature, hear; dear goddess, hear! Lear's Curse on Goneril. Shakespeare. *Fr.* King Lear, I, iv. TW

Hear now a curious dream I dreamed last night. My Dream. Christina Rossetti. BrRo

Hear now, O Soul, the last command of all. The Final Mystery. Sir Henry Newbolt. WGRP

Hear Now the Fable of the Missing Link. Judith Moffett. BLA

Hear now this fairy legend of old Greece. James Russell Lowell. *Fr.* Rhœcus. AA

Hear, O Israel!/ Will you never tire of repeating in your prayers. Hear, O Israel! André Spire, *tr. by* Stanley Burnshaw. TrJP; VWA

Hear, O Israel! Adah Isaacs Menken. CBWP-1

Hear, O Israel. Shema Yisrael. *Unknown.* TrJP

Hear, O Israel! André Spire, *tr. fr. French by* Stanley Burnshaw. TrJP; VWA

Hear, O Israel! and plead my cause against the ungodly nation. Hear, O Israel! Adah Isaacs Menken. CBWP-1

Hear, O Israel, Jehovah, the Lord our God is one. Israel. Israel Zangwill. TrJP

Hear, O Israel, the commandments of life. The Path of Wisdom. Bible, Apocrypha. *Fr.* Baruch, III: 9–IV: 4. TrJP

Hear, O Lord, my loud cry. The Serenity of Faith. Bible, *O.T. Fr.* Psalms: Psalm XXVII ("The Lord is my light. . ."), 7-14. BLRP

Hear one voice. Spring in the Woods. Marguerite Clerbout, *tr. by* Kathleen Weaver. OV

Hear, sweet spirit, hear the spell. A Voice Sings. Samuel Taylor Coleridge. *Fr.* Remorse. CH

Hear the dreary, dreary rain. Voices of the Rain. Henrietta Cordelia Ray. CBWP-3

Hear the fluter with his flute. The Amateur Flute. *Unknown.* BXAP; Par

Hear the legend of the Admen. The Legend of the Admen. Everett W. Lord. BLPA

Hear the sledges with the bells. The Bells. Poe. AA; AnAmPo; FaFP; FaPON, *st.* 1; FPL; GN; LiTA; OBAL; OBCA; OHFP; PoLF; RR; TAP; WBLP

Hear the sound. Listen. Charles Patterson. NBP

Hear the Voice of the Bard! Blake. *Fr.* Songs of Experience. EBEV; ELP; NAEL-2; NAWM-2; NOBE; NU; PoE; RB
  (Bard, The.) WGRP
  (Hear the Voice.) OBEV
  (Introduction: "Hear the voice of the bard!") EnRP; HAP; InPS; NOEC; NoP; OAEL-2; PoEL-4; TEP
  (Poet's Voice, The.) ChTr

Hear the Word of the Lord. Bible, *O.T. Fr.* Isaiah, I: 10–23. TrJP

Hear the word that Jesus spake. A Lost Word of Jesus. Henry Van Dyke. TrCP; WGRP

Hear this and tremble, all. Upon My Lord Chief Justice's Election of My Lady Anne Wentworth for His Mistress. Thomas Carew. CaPo

Hear through the morning drums and trumpets sounding. Jackson at New Orleans. Wallace Rice. PAH

Hear what Claudius suffered: When his wife knew he was asleep. Juvenal, *tr. fr. Latin by* Hubert Creekmore. *Fr.* Satires, VI. ErPo

Hear, ye children, the instruction of a father. The Legacy. Bible, *O.T. Fr.* Proverbs, IV: 13. TrJP

Hear, Ye Ladies [That Despise]. John Fletcher. *Fr.* The Tragedy of Valentinian. ElL; ELP; NOBE; OBEV
  (Mighty Love.) TrGrPo
  (Song: "Heare ye Ladies that despise.") PoEL-2

Hear ye not the gloomy yelling. Madness. Robert Browning. *Fr.* The Dance of Death. FL

Hear, ye virgins, and I'll teach. To Virgins. Robert Herrick. CaPo

. . . heard him gladly. Waldere I. *Unknown, tr. by* Charles W. Kennedy. AnOE

Heard in a Violent Ward. Theodore Roethke. HCAP

Heard in the Cougate. Robert Garioch. OxBTC

Heard on the Mountain. Victor Hugo, *tr. fr. French by* Francis Thompson. *Fr.* Feuilles d'Automne. AWP

Heard ye eer of the silly blind harper. The Lochmaben Harper. *Unknown.* ESPB; OxBB, *with music*

Heard ye how the bold McClellan Took Manassas. How McClellan Took Manassas. *Unknown.* PAH

Heard ye o' the tree o' France. The Tree of Liberty. Burns. FaBoPV

Heard ye that thrilling word. Dirge for Ashby. Margaret Junkin Preston. PAH

Heard ye the thunder of battle. Trafalgar. Francis Turner Palgrave. BeLS; FaBoBe

Heare, ye ladies that despise. *See* Hear, ye ladies that despise.

Hearing. W. S. Merwin. NoAM

Hearing a Flute at Broken Bridge. Yün Shou-p'ing, *tr. fr. Chinese by* Jonathan Chaves. CoBLCP

Hearing a Flute on the River Chi. Wen Cheng-ming, *tr. fr. Chinese by* Jonathan Chaves. CoBLCP

Hearing a Song from My Boat. Chang Yü, *tr. fr. Chinese by* Jonathan Chaves. CoBLCP

Hearing a sound that may be thy return. Hildegarde Flanner. *Fr.* Sonnets in Quaker Language, VI. WPE

Hearing Flutes along the Road in the Autumn Night. Fuyutsugu, *tr. fr. Chinese by* Burton Watson. JLIC-1

Hearing how tourists, dazed with reverence. Aldport (Mystery Tour). Kingsley Amis. *Fr.* The Evans Country. NOBL
  (Terrible Beauty.) ErPo; NePoEA-2

Hearing I ask from the holy races. Voluspo. *Unknown, tr. fr. Old Norse by* Henry Adams Bellows. *Fr.* The Elder Edda. AWP

Hearing James Brown at the Café des Nattes. Richard A. Long. AmNP

Hearing Loom and Shuttle. Yü Chi, *tr. fr. Chinese by* Jonathan Chaves. CoBLCP

Hearing Men Shout at Night on MacDougal Street. Robert Bly. InPS

Hearing of Harvests Rotting in the Valleys. W. H. Auden. MoAB; MoBrPo
  (Paysage Moralisé.) LiTB; OAEL-2; UnPo

Hearing of the Earthquake in Kyoto. Rai San'yo, *tr. fr. Chinese by* Burton Watson. JLIC-2

Hearing of the End of the War. Richard Tillinghast. MAYP

Hearing of you, I never lost a brother. Stepping Outside. Tess Gallagher. AmPA

Hearing one saga, we enact the next. Remembering the 'Thirties. Donald Davie. FaBoPV; NePoEA; OxBTC

Hearing our voices raised. Looking On. Anthony Thwaite. NePoEA-2

Hearing Russian Spoken. Donald Davie. GTBS-P; NePoEA-2

Hearing Steps. Charles Simic. HCAP

Hearing that on Sunday I would leave. The Emerald. James Merrill. *Fr.* Up and Down. CAPP

Hearing the Cuckoo on the Nineteenth Day of the Third Month. Huang Tsung-hsi, *tr. fr. Chinese by* Lynn Struve. WFTU

Hearing the Snow. Kido, *tr. fr. Chinese by* Lucien Stryk *and* Takashi Ikemoto. ZPCJ

Hearing the thunder-clap. Kawabata Bosha, *tr. by* Geoffrey Bownas *and* Anthony Thwaite. PeBJV

Hearing the Wind at Night. May Swenson. BoNaP

Hearing your words, and not a word among them. Edna St. Vincent Millay. CMoP; MoP; NoAM; VGW

Heark how she laughs aloud. Lucasta Laughing. Richard Lovelace. PoEL-3

Hearke, Now Every Thing Is Still. John Webster. *See* Duchess of Malfi, The: Hark, Now Everything Is Still.

Hearken all ye, 'tis the feast o' Saint Stephen. The Feast o' Saint [*or* St.] Stephen. Ruth Sawyer. OBCP; OHIP

Hearken, Lady Betty, hearken. Christopher Anstey. *Fr.* The New Bath Guide. NOEC

Hearken?—now the hermit bee. The Quiet Enemy. Walter De la Mare. BrPo

Hearken the stirring story. The Fall of Maubila. Thomas Dunn English. PAH

Hearken, thou craggy ocean pyramid! To Ailsa Rock. Keats. EnRP;
    OBNC
    (Sonnet to Ailsa Rock.) MOS
Hearken to me, gentlemen. King Estmere. *Unknown.* ESPB; OBNV;
    OxBB
Hears not my Phillis how the birds. Sir Charles Sedley. EnLoPo;
    SeCV-2
Hearse comes up the road, The. Twelve Minutes. J. C. Hall. OBD
Hearse Song, The. *Unknown.* AS, A *and* B *vers., with music*; OxBoLi;
    RB
Hearse was the oven of the crematory, The. The Funeral. "M. J.," *tr.
    by* A. Glanz-Leyeless. TrJP
Hears't thou, my soul, what serious things. Dies Irae. Thomas of
    Celano, *tr. by* Richard Crashaw. AWP; TIRV
    (Day of Judgment, The.) OBVE
Heart. Richard Adler *and* Jerry Ross. *Fr.* Damn Yankees. ASP
Heart. Guillaume Appollinaire. *See* My heart like an upside down flame.
Heart, The. Stephen Crane. *See* Black Riders, The: In the Desert.
Heart, The. David Ignatow. VWA
Heart, The. Donald Justice. MT
Heart, The. Harvey Shapiro. HoPM
Heart, The. Jakov Steinberg, *tr. fr. Hebrew by* Harry H. Fein. TrJP
Heart, The, *sels.* Francis Thompson.
    "Heart you hold too small and local thing, The." OBMV
    "O nothing in this corporal earth of man." OBMV
    (All's Vast.) MoAB; MoBrPo
    (Correlated Greatness.) GTBS-P
Heart aches. Breathless. Wilfred Noyce. OBTV
Heart and Mind. Dame Edith Sitwell. OxBTC; TwCP
Heart and service to you proffer'd, The. Sir Thomas Wyatt. SiPS
Heart asks pleasure—first, The. Emily Dickinson. AmPP; CMoP;
    MoAB; MoAmPo; NAAL-1; NOBA; NoP; OxBA; PPP; PrIM;
    TrGrPo; WPE
Heart! But this grand world rolls onward through the shadows of the years.
    Alexander Anderson. *Fr.* A Song of Labour. PF
Heart cold in the breast with terror, grieving. Lament for Llywelyn ap
    Gruffudd. Gruffudd ab yr Ynad Coch, *tr. by* Joseph P. Clancy.
    OBWVE
Heart, Crown, and Mirror, *sels.* Guillaume Apollinaire, *tr. fr. French by*
    Roger Shattuck.
    "In this mirror I am enclosed." TTTS
    "Kings who have died." TTTS
    "My heart like an upside down flame." TTTS
    (Heart.) POS
Heart Exchange. Sir Philip Sidney. *See* Arcadia: My True Love Hath
    My Heart [and I Have His].
Heart felt/ as if being sucked into a very dark hole. Ishikawa Takuboku,
    tr. fr. Japanese by Hiroaki Sato. *Fr.* Forty-seven Tanka in Three
    Lines. FCEI
Heart Flies Up, Erratic as a Kite, The. Delmore Schwartz. PoA
Heart free, hand free. Sic Vita. William Stanley Braithwaite. BANP
Heart Has Its Reasons, The. Felice Picano. PeHV
Heart has learnt, The. Asadullah Khan Ghalib, *tr. by* Ahmed Ali. GoT
Heart has like a mirror, The. Mohammad Taqi Mir, *tr. by* Ahmed Ali.
    GoT
Heart has need of some deceit, The. Only the Polished Skeleton.
    Countee Cullen. PrIm; VGW
Heart has powerful wings;—take me by the hand, The. Caterina Bon
    Brenzoni, *tr. fr. Italian by* Muriel Kittel. *Fr.* The Heavens. DMI
Heart-Hungry. Josephine D. Henderson Heard. CBWP-4
Heart, I thought, The. Asadullah Khan Ghalib, *tr. by* Ahmed Ali. GoT
Heart is a snail, The. Catalogue. Hilde Domin, *tr. by* Tudor Morris.
    VWA
Heart Is Deep, The. Roger Wolcott. SCAP
Heart, knowing, The. What He Said. Allur Nanmullai, *tr. by* A. K.
    Ramanujan. PLW
Heart leaps with the pride of their story, The. The Fleet at Santiago.
    Charles E. Russell. PAH
Heart, let us this once reason together. Heart. Donald Justice. MT
Heart made full of thought, A. Maghnas O Domhnaill. NOIV
Heart must always come again to home. The Heart's Wild Geese. Henry
    Treece. WaP
Heart ("My heart like an upside down flame"). Guillaume Apollinaire.
    See Heart, Crown, and Mirror: In this mirror I am enclosed.
Heart, my heart, what will you do? Flight of the Heart. Louis
    MacNeice. FaBCIP
Heart of a Girl Is a Wonderful Thing, The. *Unknown.* BLPA
Heart of a Woman, The. Georgia Douglas Johnson. BANP; BlSi; CDC;
    PoLF; PoNe
Heart of All the Scene, The. Emerson. *Fr.* Woodnotes I ("When the
    pine tosses its cones"). AA

Heart of Autumn. Robert Penn Warren. MT
Heart of cold. Bones of cold. Scalp of cold. Adrienne Rich. *Fr.*
    Contradictions: Tracking Poems, 2. ER
Heart of Herakles, The. Kenneth Rexroth. *Fr.* The Lights in the Sky are
    Stars. NU
Heart of man is encumbered, The. A Child's Christmas without Jean
    Cocteau. David Fisher. NPGG
Heart of Midlothian, The, *sel.* Sir Walter Scott.
    Proud Maisie ("Proud Maisie is in the wood"). *Fr. ch.* 38. CH; ChTr;
    EnRP; FaBoCh; FF; GoTS; OAEL-2; OBEV; OxBS; PBBP; PoEL-4;
    SeCePo; TEP; TrGrPo; UnPo
    (Madge Wildfire Sings.) OBNC
    (Madge Wildfire's Death Song.) HAP
    (Madge Wildfire's Song.) NOBE
    (Pride of Youth, The.) GTBS; GTBS-P
Heart of Oak. David Garrick. NOEC; OxBoLi
Heart of Oak. Charles Henry Lüders. AA
Heart of Ruin. Arun Kolatkar. UAS
Heart of the Backlog. Robert Penn Warren. MT
Heart of the church is broken, The. Bombed Church. Elizabeth
    Berridge. CN
Heart-of-the-Daybreak. Eugène Marais, *tr. fr. Afrikaans by* Uys Krige
    and Jack Cope. PeSA
Heart of the heartless world. Huesca. John Cornford. BoLoP
    (To Margot Heinemann.) OBWP; OxBTC
Heart of the Tree, The. H. C. Bunner. OHFP; OHIP
Heart of the Woods. Wesley Curtright. PoNe
Heart of the World, The. Rabbi Nahman of Bratzlav, *tr. fr. Yiddish by*
    Joseph Leftwich. TrJP
Heart of Thomas Hardy, The. Sir John Betjeman. TW
Heart on the Hill, The. Petrarch. *Fr.* Sonnets to Laura: To Laura in
    Life, CCV, *tr. by* C. B. Cayley. AWP
Heart oppress'd with desperate thought. Sir Thomas Wyatt. SiPS
Heart soars up like a bird, The. The Flight of the Heart. Dora Read
    Goodale. AA
Heart Specialist. Elias Lieberman. ImOP
Heart-summoned. Jesse Stuart. GoYe
Heart that seeks something, The. Ozaki Hosai, *tr. fr. Japanese by* Hiroaki
    Sato. *Fr.* One Hundred Haiku in Free Form. FCEI
Heart that yearns for fame never dies, A. Wu Wen, *tr. fr. Chinese by*
    Irving Lo. *Fr.* Starting Out on a Journey in a Windstorm, II. WFTU
Heart that's been broken, A. Maureen Owen. LLLT
Heart to heart! In a Silence. Richard Hovey. AnAmPo
Heart turned to ashes. Singde, *tr. fr. Chinese by* William Schultz. *Fr.*
    Impressions of a Night's Stay at Shuang-lin Temple, II. WFTU
Heart was always the enemy, The. Mohammad Taqi Mir, *tr. by* Ahmed
    Ali. GoT
Heart was filled to flowing, The. Mohammad Taqi Mir, *tr. by* Ahmed
    Ali. GoT
Heart, we will forget him! Emily Dickinson. AA; LLLT
Heart Will Have Its Way, The. Israel Efrat, *tr. fr. Hebrew by* Bernhard
    Frank. MHeP
Heart you hold too small and local thing, The. Francis Thompson. *Fr.*
    The Heart. OBMV
Heartbreak. Pierre Reverdy, *tr. fr. French by* Michael Benedikt. POS
Heartbreak Camp. Roy Campbell. OxBTC
Heartfelt Pity. Ben-Zion Tomer, *tr. fr. Hebrew by* Bernhard Frank. *Fr.*
    Song Sequence. MHeP
Hearth. Peggy Bacon. FaPON
Hearth and Home. Stoddard King. OBAL
Hearth of Urien, The. Llywarch the Aged, *tr. fr. Welsh by* William
    Barnes. ChTr
Hearthstone. Harold Monro. OBMV
Heartiest congratulations to Emma Slade this autumn. News of Old Girls.
    Elizabeth Baines. NPo
Heartland. Jim Barnes. HATNAP
Heartland. Paul Engle. WCI
Hearts, The. Robert Pinsky. BAP
Heart's Abysses, The. Walter Savage Landor. FaBoEE; OBSV
Hearts are pumping, The—feel!—the air. Air Shaft. Ian Healy. *Fr.*
    Poems from the Coalfields, I. PoAu-2
Heart's Content. *Unknown.* PoLF
Hearts-Ease. Walter Savage Landor. EnRP
Heart's Ease. Mary E. Tucker. CBWP-1
Heart's Haven. Dante Gabriel Rossetti. *Fr.* The House of Life, XXII.
    Son
Hearts, like doors, will ope with ease. *Unknown.* OxNR
Heart's Location, The. Peter Meinke. GOYP
Heart's Music. At. to Thomas Campion. AAS; OBEV
Heart's Needle, *sels.* W. D. Snodgrass.
    Child of My Winter Born. *Fr.* I. MoAmPo

"Easter has come around." *Fr.* VI. CAPP; NePoEA

"Here in the scuffled dust." *Fr.* VII. NePoEA

"I thumped on you the best I could." *Fr.* VIII. NePoEA; NoAM

"Late April and you are three; today." *Fr.* II. NePoEA

"No one can tell you why." *Fr.* IV. NePoEA

"Vicious winter finally yields, The." *Fr.* X. NePoEA; SM

Heart's Proof, The. James Buckham. BLRP; WBLP

Heart's Summer, The. Epes Sargent. AA

Hearts that are great beat never loud. A Thought. Abram Joseph Ryan. PWR

Heart's Wild Geese, The. Henry Treece. WaP

Heartstring. Blessed wood. Copacetic Mingus. Yusef Komunyakaa. MAYP

Heat. Hilda Doolittle ("H. D."). *Fr.* The Garden. CMoP; HeIP; InPK; MoAmPo; OxBA; PrIM; TAP; UnPo

Heat. Archibald Lampman. CaP; NOBC; OBCV

Heat. Kenneth Mackenzie. CBAP; PoAu-2

Heat and cold, twilight and dawn succeed each other so swiftly. Spring River. Po Chü-i, *tr.* by Burton Watson. CoBCP

Heat and Sweat. Mongane Wally Serote. WMBCH

Heat goes deep as cold. *Unknown, tr.* by Thomas Kinsella. NOIV

Heat haze: a bug I don't know. Suburb. Buson, *tr. fr. Japanese* by Hiroaki Sato. *Fr.* Eighty-seven Hokku. FCEI

Heat in the Room, The. Weldon Kees. EAS

Heat is past that did me fret, The. A Farewell to a Fondling. Thomas Churchyard. EIL

Heat Lightning. Robert Penn Warren. MT

Heat-lightning streak. Gerard Manley Basho. InPK

Heat of the night bears down, sleep easily broken. Saigon. Narushima Ryuhoku, *tr.* by Burton Watson. JLIC-2

Heat-sensitive. Agency. Andrew Joron. BWV

Heat Spell in Venice. Leah Goldberg, *tr. fr. Hebrew* by Bernhard Frank. MHeP

Heat uncovers the window and attic-fan, The. Looking for My Old Indian Grandmother in the Summer Heat of 1980. Diane Glancy. STE

Heathen Are Come into Thine Inheritance, The. Bible, O.T. *See* Psalms: Psalm LXXIX ("O God, the heathen are come into Thine inheritance").

Heathen Chinee, The. Bret Harte. *See* Which I wish to remark.

Heathen Hymn, A, *sel.* Sir Lewis Morris.

"I praise Thee not, with impious pride." TrPWD

Heathen Pass-ee, The. Arthur Clement Hilton. CenHV; FaBoCo; NOBL

Heather Flowers. Eliseus Williams, *tr. fr. Welsh* by Kenneth Hurlstone Jackson. OBWVE

Heather was blooming, the meadows were mawn, The. Hunting Song. Burns. PBBP

Heat's on, dead wind shoots up, The. John Garfield. Nicholas Christopher. MAYP

Heat's on the hooker, The. Translations from the English. George Starbuck. VGW

Heat's so intense I dry my towel, The. Shiba Sonome, *tr. fr. Japanese* by Hiroaki Sato. *Fr.* Fifteen Hokku. FCEI

Heave at the windlass!—Heave O, cheerly, men! Windlass Song. William Allingham. GN

Heave Away ("Heave away, heave away! I'd rather court a yellow gal"). *Unknown.* AS

Heave Away, My Johnny. *Unknown.* OxBSS

Heaven. Martha Gilbert Dickinson Bianchi. AA

Heaven. Rupert Brooke. BrPo; EBEV; HoPM; LiTB; LiTM; MoBrPo; NOBE; PoRA; WGRP

Heaven. Michael Dennis Browne. SoTCo

Heaven. George Herbert. SeCP; TrCP; TrGrPo; TTTS

Heaven. Langston Hughes. *See* Heaven, Heaven, Heaven Is the Place.

Heaven. Philip Levine. LCAP; NaP

Heaven. Milton. *See* Paradise Lost: No sooner had th' Almighty ceas't, but all.

Heaven. Howard Moss. BLA

Heaven. Cathy Song. NoAM

Heaven. Gary Soto. NPGG

Heaven. *Unknown.* PoLF

Heaven. Isaac Watts. *See* There is a land of pure delight.

Heaven above is softer blue. Possession. *Unknown.* BLRP

Heaven and earth. Hitomaro, *tr. fr. Japanese* by Geoffrey Bownas *and* Anthony Thwaite. *Fr.* Manyo Shu. PeBJV

Heaven and Earth. James I, King of England. *See* Sonnet: "Azured [*or* Azur'd] vault, the crystal circles bright, The."

Heaven and earth, and all that hear me plain. A Protest. Sir Thomas Wyatt. OBSC; SiPS

Heaven and earth go on forever, never ceasing. Substance Addresses Shadow. T'ao Ch'ien, *tr. fr. Chinese* by Burton Watson. *Fr.* Substance, Shadow, and Spirit. CoBCP

Heaven and Hell. Pablo Guevara, *tr. fr. Spanish* by Maureen Ahern *and* David Tipton. Per

Heaven and Hell. Nalungiaq, *tr. fr. Eskimo* by Edward Field. DL; STP

Heaven and Hell. Willie Nelson. InPK

Heaven and Hell. James Kenneth Stephen. CenHV

Heaven and Hell. Francis Thompson. OxBSP

Heaven bade the dark bird. *Unknown, tr.* by Arthur Waley. BoS

Heaven Can't Wait. Robert N. Feinstein. SoTCo

Heaven expands, autumn arcs high, the night still long. Following the Rhymes of "Autumn Night Song" by Meng Tzu-chou. Yü Chi, *tr.* by Jonathan Chaves. CoBLCP

Heaven, from thy endless goodness, send prosperous life. This Royal Infant. Shakespeare *and probably* John Fletcher. *Fr.* King Henry VIII, V, iv. NAs

Heaven-Haven. Gerard Manley Hopkins, *tr. fr. Hebrew.* ACP; BrPo; HeIP; MoAB; MoBrPo; MoP; MOS; NoAM; NOBE; NOCV; OBEV; OBNC; OxBSP; RB; SoSe; SOTW; TOF; TrGrPo

Heaven, Heaven, Heaven Is the Place. Langston Hughes. AH

(Heaven.) NOBA

"Heaven in Ordinarie." Daniel Wolff. SM

Heaven Is Here. John G. Adams. AH

Heaven is mirrored, Love, deep in thine eyes. Aidenn. Katrina Trask. AA

Heaven is not reached [*or* gained] at [*or* by] a single bound. Gradatim. Josiah Gilbert Holland. FaFP; OHFP; WGRP

Heaven is open every day. The Way to Heaven. Charles Goodrich Whiting. AA

Heaven is what I cannot reach. Emily Dickinson. NOCV

Heaven made a high hill. *Unknown, tr.* by Arthur Waley. BoS

Heaven, O Lord, I Cannot Lose. Edna Dean Proctor. AA

Heaven of Animals, The. James Dickey. CAPP; CoAP; HeIP; LiTM; MT; NAAL-2; NoAM; NOBA; PoE; TAP

Heaven shall forgive you bridge at dawn. Ballade d'une Grande Dame. G. K. Chesterton. OxBoLi

Heaven, the earth, and all the liquid mayne, The. Virgil, *tr. fr. Latin* by Sir Walter Ralegh. *Fr.* The Aeneid [*or* Eneados], VI. OBVE

Heaven, unmoved, weeps on forever. Sunday Piece. Jules Laforgue, *tr.* by William Jay Smith. CT

Heaven which art in Heaven Our Father in Heaven. Kay Smith. *Fr.* Footnote to the Lord's Prayer. TrCP

Heaven, which man's generations draws. Francis Thompson. *Fr.* A Judgment in Heaven. MoAB; MoBrPo

Heaven Will Protect the Working-Girl, *sel.* Edgar Smith. FaFP

"You may tempt the upper classes." FiBHP

Heavenly Aeroplane, The. *Unknown.* NOCV

Heavenly Archer, bend thy bow. Dust to Dust. Walter de la Mare. TrPWD

Heavenly City, The. Stevie Smith. FaBoTw

Heavenly Eloquence. Samuel Daniel. *See* Musophilus; or, Defence of All Learning: English Poetry.

Heavenly Evil, holy One. Hymn to Evil. Louis Ginsberg. PoA

Heavenly Father, bless this food. *Unknown.* BLRP

"Heavenly Father," take to thee. Emily Dickinson. PoEL-5

Heavenly fields of Paradise, The. Heine, *tr. fr. German* by Alistair Elliot. *Fr.* Zum Lazarus. OBD

Heavenly Foreigner, The, *sel.* Denis Devlin.

"Spires, firm on their monster feet rose light and thin, The." CIP

Heavenly Jerusalem, of the Earth. Leah Goldberg, *tr. fr. Hebrew* by Robert Friend. VWA

Heavenly Stranger, The. Ada Blenkhorn. BLRP

Heavenly Vision. William Billings. AmFP

Heavens, The. Bible, O.T. *See* Psalms: Psalm XIX ("The heavens declare the glory of God").

Heavens, The, *sel.* Caterina Bon Brenzoni, *tr. fr. Italian* by Muriel Kittel. "Heart has powerful wings;—take me by the hand, The." DMI

Heavens Above and the Law Within, The. Bible, O.T. *See* Psalms: Psalm XIX ("The heavens declare the glory of God").

Heavens Are Our Riddle, The. Herbert Bates. AA

Heavens bright lamp, shine forth some of thy light. George Alsop. SCAP

Heavens declare the glory of God, The. Bible, O.T. *Fr.* Psalms: Psalm XIX. AWP; FaPON, 1-4; NAWM-1; OBVE, *tr.* by Miles Coverdale; WBLP

God's Precepts Perfect, 7-9. BLRP

(Glory of God, The.) TrJP

(God's Glory.) TrGrPo

(Heavens, The, 1-6.) ChTr

(Heavens Above and the Law Within, The, *Moulton, Modern Reader's Bible.*) WGRP

("Heavens doe declare, The," *Bay Psalm Book.*) SCAP

(Psalm XIX: "Heavenly frame sets forth the fame, The," *paraphrased by* Sir Philip Sidney.) OBVE

(Psalm XIX: "Spacious firmament on high, The.") WGRP

Heavens Do Declare, The. *Unknown.* AH

Heavens doe declare, The. Bible, *O.T. See* Psalms: Psalm XIX ("The heavens declare the glory of God").

Heavens doe declare/ The majesty of God, The. *Unknown. Fr.* The Bay Psalm Book. SCAP

Heavens first in tune I'll set, The. Love Sets Order in the Elements. Thomas Nabbes. *Fr.* Microcosmus. UnS

Heaven's Immortal. Ho Ning, *tr. fr. Chinese* by Lois Fusek. ATF

Heaven's Immortal. Huang-fu Sung, *tr. fr. Chinese* by Lois Fusek. ATF

Heaven's Immortal. Wei Chuang, *tr. fr. Chinese* by Lois Fusek. ATF

Heaven's Magnificence. William Augustus Muhlenberg. AA

Heaven's mercy shines, wonders and glorys meet. The Mercies of the Year. John Danforth. SCAP

Heavens, ocean, and all earth, rejoice! Sedulius Scottus, *tr. fr. Latin. Fr.* The Defeat of the Norsemen. NOIV

Heaven's power is infinite; earth, air, and sea. Ovid, *tr. fr. Latin* by Dryden. *Fr.* Metamorphoses: Philemon and Baucis. OAEL-1

Heavens revolve both night and day, The. Asadullah Khan Ghalib, *tr.* by Ahmed Ali. GoT

Heavens themselves, the planets and this center, The. Shakespeare. *Fr.* Troilus and Cressida, I, iii. ImOP

Heaven's Wanderer in Heaven, for Tu Fu. Park Je-chun, *tr. fr. Korean* by Koh Chang-soo. ACKP

Heavens! what a goodly prospect spreads around. Happy Britannia. James Thomson. *Fr.* The Seasons: Summer. FaBoPP; SeCePo (Britannia.) FaBoPP

Heaviest Cross of All, The. Katherine Eleanor Conway. AA

Heaving Roses of the Hedge Are Stirred, The. Richard Watson Dixon. CH

(Winter Will Follow.) GTBS-P

Heaving the Lead Line. *Unknown.* AmFP

Heavy and dull, the motionless clouds. Motionless Clouds. T'ao Ch'ien, *tr.* by Burton Watson. CoBCP

Heavy bear who goes with me, The. Delmore Schwartz. *Fr.* The Repetitive Heart. LiTA; LiTM; NoAM; NOBA; TAP; TrJP; TwCP; UnPo

Heavy breathing fills all my chamber. August 24, 1963—1:00 A.M.— Omaha. Donna Whitewing. NOVW

Heavy cart rumbles, A. Shoha, *tr.* by Geoffrey Bownas *and* Anthony Thwaite. PeBJV

Heavy Clouds Passing before the Sun. Jean Day. IAT

Heavy feeling, A. The Fifth Day. Eeva Kilpi, *tr.* by Aili Jarvenpa. SOP

Heavy glacier and the terrifying Alps, The. Long Lines. Paul Goodman. VGW

(Long Lines: Youth and Age.) PeHV

Heavy hangs the raindrop. The Two Children. Emily Brontë. PoEL-5

Heavy-hearted. Judah al-Harizi, *tr. fr. Hebrew.* TrJP

Heavy, heavy, hangs my head. The Sad Child's Song. Mark Van Doren. SO

Heavy Heavy Heavy. John Malcolm Brinnin. NYBP

Heavy, heavy, heavy, hand and heart. Tenebrae. Denise Levertov. NoP

Heavy heavy lies over our head. Game out of Hand. Allison Ross. GoYe

Heavy mist, A. A muffled sea. Atheling Grange; or, The Apotheosis of Lotte Nussbaum. William Plomer. OBNV

Heavy mists have crept away, The. Mark. Ernest McGaffey. AA

Heavy rain crumbles a wall of my house, A. Night Rain: A Wall Collapses. Yang Shih-ch'i, *tr.* by Jonathan Chaves. CoBLCP

Heavy smells of Spring, The. Jack. Louis Golding. TrJP

Heavy snow./ On the nineteenth of the month. Somewhat in the Kingdom of His Majesty, No. 2. Yang Tse, *tr.* by Dominic Cheung. IFON

Heavy sounds are over-sweet, The. City-Storm. Harold Monro. MoBrPo

Heavy umbrellas, The. Crocus Night. James Schuyler. PoM

Heavy with child. In My Name. Grace Nichols. AIW

Heavy with salt, and warm. The Equinox. DuBose Heyward. PoA

Heavyweight champ of Seattle, The. *Unknown.* OBAL

Hebe. James Russell Lowell. AA

Hebrew Letters in the Trees. J. Rutherford Willems. VWA

Hebrew Melodies, *sel.* Heine, *tr. fr. German* by Charles Godfrey Leland.

By the Waters of Babylon. TrJP

Hebrew nation did not write it, The. Blake. OAEL-2

Hebrew of Your Poets, Zion, The. Charles Reznikoff. VGW; VWA

Hebrew Script. Tali Loewenthal. VWA

Hebrew Sibyl, The. Ruth Fainlight. VWA

Hebrews. James Oppenheim. TrJP

Hecatompathia; or, Passionate Century of Love, *sels.* Thomas Watson.

Come, Gentle Death! EIL

Here Lieth Love. EIL

(Love's Grave.) OBSC

"Some that reporte great Alexanders life." AAS

"Speake gentle heart, where is thy dwelling place?." AAS

Time. FaBoRV; OBSC

Hector. Valentin Iremonger. CIP; NeIP

Hector Protector was dressed all in green. Mother Goose. MoShBr; OxNR

Hector, the captain bronzed, from simple fight. Geoffrey Scott. *Fr.* The Skaian Gate. OBMV

He'd become completely degraded. His erotic tendencies. Days of 1896. Constantine P. Cavafy, *tr.* by Edmund Keeley *and* Philip Sherrard. PeHV

He'd been sitting in the café since ten-thirty. Two Young Men, 23 to 24 Years Old. Constantine P. Cavafy, *tr.* by Edmund Keeley *and* Philip Sherrard. PeHV

He'd found some lumber from an old fence rotting. Boy with a Hammer. Russell Hoban. PCP

He'd had enough of lying in the furze. The Ghostly Father. Peter Redgrove. MoBS; NePoEA-2

He'd Nothing but His Violin. Mary Kyle Dallas. AA, *abr.*

He'd play, after the bawdy songs and blues. When de Saints Go Ma'chin' Home. Sterling A. Brown. AmNP

He'd rent the horse and it sounding like it had asthma. The Horse. Faye Kicknosway. GeTw

Hedge/ the leaning tower, The. Decorations. Nishiwaki Junzaburo, *tr.* by Hiroaki Sato. FCEI

Hedge before me, one behind, A. *Unknown, tr.* by Flann O'Brien. BIrV

Hedge Life. James Dickey. LCAP

Hedge of trees surrounds me, A. The Scribe. *Unknown, tr.* by Kuno Meyer. AnIL

Hedge Schoolmaster, A. Padraic Fallon. CIP

Hedge-Sparrows and House-Sparrows. Roy Fuller. AnAn

Hedgehog, The. J. J. Bell. RHPC

Hedgehog, The. Edith King. BoTP

Hedgehog. Paul Muldoon. BIrV; NoAM

Hedgehog and His Coat, The. Elizabeth Fleming. BoTP

Hedgehog is a little beast, The. The Hedgehog. Edith King. BoTP

Hedgehog sleeps beneath the hedge, The. The Hedgehog. J. J. Bell. RHPC

Hedgerows are wiser than I, The. Easter Thought. Leo Cox. CaP

Hedges are dazed as cock-crow, heaps of leaves, The. Departure in Middle Age. Roland Mathias. CRP; OBWVE

Hedges Freaked with Snow. Robert Graves. OxBTC

Heed the old oracles. The Undersong. Emerson. *Fr.* Woodnotes II ("As sunbeams stream through liberal space"). AA

Heedless o' My Love. William Barnes. GBL

Heedless of the spray from the steaming waves. Beach Rainbow. Takahashi Shinkichi, *tr.* by Geoffrey Bownas *and* Anthony Thwaite. PeBJV

Heedless she strayed from note to note. The Waiting Chords. Stephen Henry Thayer. AA

Heemi. Hone Tuwhare. PeNZ

Heidi men call me when their homes I visit. Song of the Seeress. *Unknown, tr.* by Paul B. Taylor *and* W. H. Auden. NAWM-1

Heifer Clambers Up, A. Gary Snyder. NOBA

Heigh ho! daisies and buttercups. Maternity. Jean Ingelow. *Fr.* Songs of Seven. OHIP

Heigh ho! my heart is low. *Unknown.* OxNR

Heigh-ho on a Winter Afternoon. Donald Davie. NePoEA-2; OxBTC

Heigh-ho, what shall a shepheard doe. James Shirley. *Fr.* The Triumph of Beautie Song. PePo

Heigh in the hevynnis figure circulere. The Kingis Quair, *abr.* James I, King of Scotland. OxBS

Heigh, Po is brave. *Unknown, tr.* by Arthur Waley. BoS

Heigh, the green coat. *Unknown, tr.* by Arthur Waley. BoS

Heigho! the lark and the owl! Shelley. *Fr.* Charles the First, sc. V. PBBP

Height of the Ridiculous, The. Oliver Wendell Holmes. AA; FaFP; FiBHP; FPL; MoShBr; OBAL; OBCA

Heimkehr, Die, *sels.* Heine, *tr. fr. German* by Ezra Pound. AWP

"Mutilated choir boys, The."

"Tell me where thy lovely love is."

"This delightful young man."

Heine's mother was a monster. A Century Piece for Poor Heine. John Logan. NNaP

Heinrich Heine. Ludwig Lewisohn. TrJP

Heir of Linne, The. *Unknown.* ESPB, B *vers.*

Heir of Shakespeare, shepherds and cavaliers. To the Gentile Poet. Mani Leib, *tr. by* John Hollander. PeBMYV
Heir to the office of a man not dead. A Miltonic Sonnet for Mr. Johnson on His Refusal of Peter Hurd's Official Portrait. Richard Wilbur. TW
Heirloom. Leonard Cohen. NOBC
Heirloom. A. M. Klein. NIP; NOBC; OBCV; TrJP
Hektor to Andromache. Homer, *tr. fr. Greek by* Richmond Lattimore. *Fr.* The Iliad, VI. WaaP
Hélas! Oscar Wilde. BrPo; MoBrPo; NAEL-2; Son; TEP; TIRV
Helbatrawss, The. Kingsley Amis. NOBL
Held between wars. Käthe Kollwitz. Muriel Rukeyser. NMM
Hele helele the King is a great king. Offering to the Storm. Aimé Césaire, *tr. by* Michael Benedikt. POS
Heledd and Inge, when the torches are red. In Berlin, August 1945: Lehrte Bahnhof. Alun Llywelyn-Williams, *tr. by* Joseph P. Clancy. OBWVE
Helen. "Susan Coolidge." AA
Helen. Hilda Doolittle ("H. D."). AnAmPo; BoWoP; FaBoWP; LiTM; MoAmPo; NAAL-2; NoAM; NOBA; NoP; TAP; TW
Helen. Odysseus Elytis, *tr. fr. Greek by* Edmund Keeley *and* Philip Sherrard. VMG
Helen. James Harrison. NBLV
Helen. Christopher Marlowe. *See* Doctor Faustus: Was this the face that launched a thousand ships?
Helen. George Seferis. VMG
Helen. Edward A. U. Valentine. AA
Helen. Paul Valéry, *tr. fr. French.* CT, *tr. by* William Jay Smith; OBVE, *tr. by* Robert Lowell.
Helen Grown Old. Janet Lewis. QFR
Helen, had I known yesterday. Release. D. H. Lawrence. CMoP
Helen Hunt Jackson. Ina Coolbrith. AA
Helen in Egypt, *sels.* Hilda Doolittle ("H. D.").
"Alas, my brothers." NOBA
"Another shout from the wharves." NOBA
Helen in Hollywood. Judy Grahn. ER
Helen Keller. Edmund Clarence Stedman. AA
Helen like the Rose. Evan Lloyd. *Fr.* The Powers of the Pen. OBWVE
Helen of Kirconnell. *Unknown.* AWP; CH; ELP; GoTS; LiTB; OBEV
Helen of Troy. Christopher Marlowe. *See* Doctor Faustus: Was this the face that launched a thousand ships?
Helen—Old. Isabel Ecclestone MacKay. CaP
Helen, the Sad Queen. Paul Valéry, *tr. fr. French by* Joseph T. Shipley. AWP
Helen, thy beauty is to me. To Helen. Poe. AA; AmPP; AnAmPo; AWP; BoLoP; CH; ChTr; FaBoBe; FaBV; FaFP; FL; FPL; GBL; HAP; HeIP; HoPM; InPS; InvP; LiTA; NAAL-1; NIP; NOBA; NOBE; NoP; OBEV; OxBA; PoE; PoEL-4; PoLF; PoRA; PrIm; PrIM; TAP; TrGrPo; WeW
Helen Todd: My Birthname. Sandra McPherson. NAmP
Helena and Hermia. Shakespeare. *Fr.* A Midsummer Night's Dream, III, ii. GN
Helena Embarks for Palestine. Cynewulf, *tr. fr. Anglo-Saxon by* Charles W. Kennedy. *Fr.* Elene. AnOE
Helen's Lamentation. Homer, *tr. fr. Greek by* Congreve. *Fr.* The Iliad, XXIV. OBVE
Helen's lips, as drifting dust. Consolation. Arthur Guiterman. BXAP
Heliodore. John Daniel Logan. CaP
Heliogabalus. John Hollander. NBLV; OBAL
Heliotrope. Harry Thurston Peck. AA
Hell ("At once with him they rose"). Milton. *Fr.* Paradise Lost, *Bk.* II, *ll.* 475–628.
Hell. *Unknown, tr. fr. Gaelic by* Douglas Hyde. WTO
Hell and Heaven. *Unknown.* OxBoLi
Hell-bound Train, The. *Unknown.* BeLS; BLPA
Hell freezing over. To keep sane. Mandelstam. David Young. AmPA
Hell Gate. A. E. Housman. NoAM; UnPo
Hell in Texas. *Unknown.* BLPA; CowP, *diff. vers.*
Hell is a city much like London. Shelley. *Fr.* Peter Bell the Third. OBD; OBSV
Hell is a red barn on a hill. The Curse. Robert Francis. TW
"Hell" said the Devil, as it might have been. Reborn. Kingsley Amis. OxBC
Hell, Well, Heaven. Mongane Wally Serote. WMBCH
Hell whose rains and cold appal. Hell. *Unknown, tr. by* Douglas Hyde. WTO
Hellas, *sel.* Shelley.
Choruses from "Hellas."
"Life may change, but it may fly not." *Fr.* 1. EnRP
"Darkness has dawned in the east." *Fr.* 3. EnRP

"World's great age begins anew, The." *Fr.* 4. EnRP; FiP; HeIP; NAEL-2; PoE; TEP
(Chorus from "Hellas.") AWP
(Chorus: "World's great age begins anew, The.") EBEV; HAP; NOBE; NoP; OAEL-2; PoEL-4
(Final Chorus, The.) SeCePo
(Hellas.) ChTr; OBEV
(New World, A.) TrGrPo
"Worlds on worlds are rolling ever." EnRP; NoP; TEP
(Chorus: "Worlds on worlds are rolling ever.") NAEL–2
(Worlds on Worlds.) HeIP
Hellenics, The, *sels.* Walter Savage Landor.
Hamadryad, The. EnRP
Iphigeneia and Agamemnon. BeLS
(Iphigenia.) EnRP
On the Hellenics. EnRP
Ternissa! You Are Fled. PoEL-4
(On Ternissa's Death.) ELP
(Ternissa.) NOBE; OBNC
Hello. John Berryman. NAs
Hello. Gregory Corso. PoM
Hello. Naomi Shihab Nye. MT
Hello. Benjamin Péret, *tr. fr. French by* Michael Benedikt. POS
Hello dar, Miss Melerlee! Miss Melerlee. John Wesley Holloway. BANP; PoNe
Hello, Girls, *with music. Unknown.* AS
Hello, Hello. William Matthews. PCP
"Hello, hello, hello, sir." Jump-Rope Rhyme. *Unknown.* NTCP
Hello There. Brian S. Salome. BXAP
Hello there, Biscuit! You're a better-looking broad. Hello. John Berryman. NAs
Hello there, Walt! To Walt Whitman. Tom MacInnes. CaP
Hello Up There. Marge Piercy. NBLV
Hell's Pavement. John Masefield. BrPo
Hellvellyn. Sir Walter Scott. FM; TEP
Helmet, The. Philip Levine. LCAP
Helmet and rifle, pack and overcoat. The Battle. Louis Simpson. InPS; OBWP; PVCV
Helmets; a Fragment, The. Thomas Penrose. NOEC
Helmsman, The. Hilda Doolittle ("H. D."). CMoP; OxBA
Heloise. Biancamaria Frabotta, *tr. fr. Italian by* Keala Jane Jewell. DMI
Help! X. J. Kennedy. RHPC
Help. Sadi, *tr. fr. Persian by* Sir Edwin Arnold. *Fr.* The Gulistan. AWP
Help. Whittier. Son
Help[e] me! help[e] me! now I call. To His Mistresses. Robert Herrick. CaPo; ErPo; SeCP
Help! Help! Trouble at the Farm. Ivy O. Eastwick. BoTP
Help, Lord, because the Godly Man, *with music.* Francis Rous. AH
Help me now. Emmett Jarrett. NeAC
Help me to help your life. Letter to P. Robert Friend. NYBP
Help me to hold the Vision Undefiled. The Scribe's Prayer. Arthur Guiterman. TrPWD
Help Me to Seek. Sir Thomas Wyatt. FF; InvP
("Helpe me to seke for I lost it there.") AAS
(Rondeau.) SiPS
Help Thy Servant. Andrew Broaddus. AH
Help Wanted. Franklin Waldheim. BLPA
Helpe me to seke for I lost it there. Sir Thomas Wyatt. *See* Help Me to Seek.
Helpless am I indeed. "Laborers Together with God." Lucy Alice Perkins. BLRP
Helsinki. Arvo Turtiainen, *tr. fr. Finnish by* Aili Jarvenpa. *Fr.* Ballad of Herman's Rose. SOP
Hem and Haw. Bliss Carman. AnAmPo
Hem of His Garment, The. Anna Elizabeth Hamilton. TrPWD
Hemingway House in Key West, The. Philip Schultz. MAYP
Hemingway Syndrome, The. Adrian C. Louis. STE
Hemlock in the Furrows. Adah Isaacs Menken. CBWP-1
Hemlocks slumped, The. Bonus. A. R. Ammons. HCAP
Hemmed-in Males. William Carlos Williams. *Fr.* A Folded Skyscraper. MAT; PoRA
Hemorrhage, The. Stanley Kunitz. WaP
Hemp, The. Stephen Vincent Benét. FL
Hems gathered up, sash not yet tied. *Unknown, tr. fr. Chinese by* Burton Watson. *Fr.* Tzu Yeh Songs. CoBCP
Hen, The. Lord Alfred Bruce Douglas. RHPC
Hen. Paul Eluard, *tr. fr. French by* Michael Benedikt. POS
Hen, The. Oliver Herford. NA
Hen, The. Christian Morgenstern, *tr. fr. German by* W. D. Snodgrass *and* Lore Segal. RB

Hen and Cock. *Unknown*. GBP

Hen and the Carp, The. Ian Serraillier. OnUR

Hen and the Oriole, The. Don Marquis. *Fr.* Archy and Mehitabel. FiBHP

Hen: Cock, cock, I have la-a-a-yd. Hen and Cock. *Unknown*. GBP

Hen-eagle broods, sick, A. What He Said to His Heart, Arguing against Further Ambition and Travel. Ilankiranar, *tr. by* A. K. Ramanujan. PLW

Hen Flower, The. Galway Kinnell. NNaP

Hen is a ferocious fowl, The. The Hen. Lord Alfred Bruce Douglas. RHPC

Hen It Is a Noble Beast, The. William McGonagall. NBLV

Hen, one who could have brought more geese, a female, a wild one, dead, A. The Wings of a Wild Goose. Chrystos. GLP

Hen remarked to the mooley cow, The. Art. *Unknown*. BLPA; NBLV

Hen under Bay-Tree. Ruth Pitter. OxBTC

Hen Woman. Thomas Kinsella. CIP; IPY

Hence all you vain delights. Melancholy. John Fletcher. *Fr.* The Nice Valor. GTBS; GTBS-P; OBEV
  (O Sweetest Melancholy.) TrGrPo
  (Passionate Man's Song, The.) OBS
  (Song: "Hence all you vaine delights.") PoEL-2

Hence, Away, You Sirens. George Wither. *Fr.* Fair Virtue, the Mistress of Philarete. EIL

Hence Cupid! with your cheating toys. Against Love. Katherine Philips. BoWoP; WPE

Hence, heart, with her that must depart. A Bequest of His Heart. Alexander Scott. OBEV

Hence, hence, profane; soft silence let us have. A Dirge upon the Death of the Right Valiant Lord, Bernard Stuart. Robert Herrick. SeCV-1

Hence, hence unhallowed ears and hearts more hard. The Argument of Democritus Platonissans, or the Infinitie of Worlds. Henry More. SeCV-2

Hence, loath'd vulgarity. Fashion. Horace Twiss. BXAP

Hence, loathèd Melancholy. L'Allegro. Milton. AWP; FaFP; FiP; GTBS; GTBS-P; HAP; HoPM; InPS; JCP; LiTB; NAEL-1; NoP; OAEL-1; OBEV; OBS; PoE; PPP; SeCePo; TEP; TrGrPo

Hence These Rimes. Bert Leston Taylor. FiBHP

Hence, vain deluding joys. Il Penseroso. Milton. AWP; FiP; GTBS; GTBS-P; HAP; HoPM; InPS; JCP; LiTB; NAEL-1; NoP; OAEL-1; OBEV; OBS; PoE; PPP; TEP; TrGrPo

Hence ye prophane; I hate ye all. Horace. *See* Odes: III, 1. "Tread back—and back, the lewd and lay!" ("Odi profanum vulgus").

Henceforth, from the Mind. Louise Bogan. LiTA; QFR; WPE

Henceforth I will not set my love. Sir Arthur Gorges. GBL

Henchman, The. Whittier. OBEV

Hendecasyllabics. Swinburne. FaBoRV

Hendecasyllabics. Tennyson. EBEV; FaBoCo; NOBL

Hengest Cyning. Jorge Luis Borges, *tr. fr. Spanish by* Norman Thomas di Giovanni. NYBP

Henley, July 4: 1914-1964. L. E. Sissman. PrIm

Henri Rousseau Style, The. Lauris Edmond. ATNZ

Henri was suited to appraise the arts. A Portrait of Henri III. Théodore Agrippa d' Aubigné, *tr. fr. French*. *Fr.* Tragiques, Les. PeHV

Henry Adams. W. H. Auden. OBAL

Henry and King Pedro, clasping. The Death of Don Pedro. *Unknown*, *tr. by* John Gibson Lockhart. AWP

Henry and Mary. Robert Graves. BrPo; GoJo; ILY; MoShBr; SO

Henry before Agincourt: October 25, 1415. John Lydgate. CH

Henry C. Calhoun. Edgar Lee Masters. *Fr.* Spoon River Anthology. LiTA; LiTM

Henry David Thoreau/ Rhymed his name with Burrow. Peg Russell. SoTCo

Henry VIII. *Unknown*. FaBoUs

Henry V before Agincourt. Shakespeare. *Fr.* King Henry V, IV, iii. FaPoR
  (St. Crispin's Day.) FF

Henry V's Conquest of France. *Unknown*. *See* As our king lay musing on his bed.

Henry got me with child. Amanda Barker. Edgar Lee Masters. *Fr.* Spoon River Anthology. NoAM

Henry hates the world. What the world to Henry. John Berryman. *Fr.* Dream Songs. NaP

Henry Hudson's Quest. Burton Egbert Stevenson. PAH

Henry in Ireland to Bill underground. An Elegy for W. C. W., the Lovely Man. John Berryman. *Fr.* Dream Songs. NoP

Henry James. Robert Louis Stevenson. OBNC

Henry James/ Only liked dames. Martha H. Freedman. SoTCo

Henry James/ (Whatever his other claims). Jacobean. Clifton Fadiman. FiBHP

Henry James at Newport. Weldon Kees. PoA

Henry K. Sawyer. *Unknown*. AmFP

Henry King, Who Chewed Bits of String, and Was Early Cut Off in Dreadful Agonies. Hilaire Belloc. CenHV; FaBoNo; FaBoUs; NBLV

Henry Martyn. *Unknown*. ESPB

Henry My Son. *Unknown*. OBET

Henry Purcell. Gerard Manley Hopkins. TEP

Henry sats in de bar and was odd. John Berryman. *Fr.* Dream Songs. HCAP

Henry Turnbull. W. W. Gibson. FaBoTw

Henry Ward Beecher. Charles Henry Phelps. AA

Henry was a young king. Henry and Mary. Robert Graves. GoJo; ILY; SO
  (Henry Was a Worthy King.) BrPo; MoShBr

Henry was every morning fed. The Boy and the Snake. Charles *and* Mary Lamb. OxBChV

Henry's Confession. John Berryman. *Fr.* Dream Songs. LCAP; MoP; NAAL-2; NoAM; PoE; TwCP

Henry's Lament. Samuel Daniel. *Fr.* The Complaint of Rosamond. OBSC

Henry's mind grew blacker the more he thought. John Berryman. *Fr.* Dream Songs. FaBoMo; NOBA

Henry's pelt was put on sundry walls. John Berryman. *Fr.* Dream Songs. MoP; NoAM

Henry's Secret. Dorothy Kilner. OxBChV

Henry's Understanding. John Berryman. CAPP; MoP; NoAM; NOBA

Hens, The. Elizabeth Madox Roberts. GoJo; OBCA; PDV

Hen's Nest. John Clare. PBBP; Son

Henyard Round, The. Donald Hall. BLA; PPR; Psk

Hep-Cat Chung, 'ware my town. Confucius, *tr. fr. Chinese by* Ezra Pound. *Fr.* Songs of Cheng. CTC

Heptalogia, The, *sels.* Swinburne.
  Higher Pantheism in a Nutshell, The. BXAP; FaBoNo; NA; Par
    John Jones. NA
    (At the Piano.) FaBoNo
  Nephelidia. BXAP; FaBoCo; FaBoNo; FaBoPa; HoPM, *first sixteen lines*; NA; Par
  Sonnet for a Picture. BXAP; FaBoNo; OAEL-2

Heptonstall Old Church. Ted Hughes. InPS

Her/ strong/ white/ legs. Romp. Dave Etter. WeW

Her, a Statue. Thomas Tod Stoddart. OBNC

Her Accident. Thomas Hood. *Fr.* Miss Kilmansegg and Her Precious Leg. EBVV

Her aged hands are worn with works of love. To One Being Old. Langdon Elwyn Mitchell. AA

Her angel looked upon God's face. The Eternal Image. Ruth Pitter. MoBrPo; OxBTC

Her Answer. John Bennett. AA; BLPA

Her Application to Elysium. Kathleen Norris. IHMS

Her Apron through the Trees. Roger Weingarten. AmPA

Her arms across her breast she laid. The Beggar Maid. Tennyson. BeLS; BoTP; OnMSP

Her arms are gravelled at the undertow. Airport. Martin Johnston. CBAP

Her arms have the beauty. What He Said. Orerulavanar, *tr. by* A. K. Ramanujan. PLW

Her arms pinned back, impaled against the night. Jacob and the Angel. Stephen Mitchell. VWA

Her beauty/ is like Atlantis. The Old Woman. Anna Swirszczynska, *tr. by* Czeslaw Milosz. PwPP

Her body dances in my dream, and my body. A Foreign Country. Natan Zach, *tr. by* Laya Firestone. VWA

Her body is not so white as. Queen-Ann's-Lace. William Carlos Williams. AmPP; BLPL; MoAB; MoAmPo; NAAL-2; NoAM; NOBA; NoP; PrIm; TAP

Her boredom took her away. So simple. Ella Mi Fu Rapita! Gavin Ewart. NoAM

Her breast is cold; her hands how faint and wan! Virtue. Walter de la Mare. MMA

Her breast is fit for pearls. Emily Dickinson. PeHV

Her breasts stormed out in front of her. Shipwreck. Adriaan Morriën, *tr. by* Ria Leigh-Loohuizen. DuIn

Her Careful Distinct Sex Whose Sharp Lips Comb. E. E. Cummings. ErPo

Her casement like a watchful eye. Balder's Wife. Alice Cary. AA

Her chair drawn to the door. The Laundress. Thomas Kinsella. IPY

Her chariot ready straight is made. The Queen's Chariot. Michael Drayton. *Fr.* Nymphidia. OBS

Her chaunging lookes no colour longe can holde. Seneca, *tr. fr. Latin by* John Studley. *Fr.* Medea, IV. OBVE

Her cheeks were white, her eyes were wild. The Sea. W. H. Davies. FaBoTw

Her Christening. Thomas Hood. *Fr.* Miss Kilmansegg and Her Precious Leg. NOBVV

Her cloudlike hair tumbles free. Thoughts of Paradise. Wei Chuang, *tr. by* Lois Fusek. ATF

Her Commendation. Francis Davison. OBSC

Her cruel hands go in and out. A Maiden and Her Hair. W. H. Davies. BrPo

Her Dairy. Peter Newell. NA

Her Dancing Days. Anna Adams. BrRo

Her day out from the workhouse-ward, she stands. The Ice. W. W. Gibson. OxBTC

Her Dead Brother. Robert Lowell. NePoEA

Her Death. Thomas Hood. *Fr.* Miss Kilmansegg and Her Precious Leg. NOBVV

Her Dilemma. Thomas Hardy. BrPo; NOBVV

Her dimpled cheeks are pale. A Southern Girl. Samuel Minturn Peck. AA

Her drunken eye led to the ruin. Mohammad Taqi Mir, *tr. by* Ahmed Ali. GoT

Her Dwarf. George P. Elliott. MAT

Her Education. Thomas Hood. *Fr.* Miss Kilmansegg and Her Precious Leg. EBVV

Her Elegy. *Unknown, tr. fr. Papago Indian.* BoWoP, *tr. by* Ruth Underhill; STP, *tr. by* Armand Schwerner.

Her Epitaph. Thomas William Parsons. AA

Her eyebrows are like willows. Song of the Fisherman. Wei Ch'eng-pan, *tr. by* Lois Fusek. ATF

Her Eyes. John Crowe Ransom. LiTM; OBAL

Her Eyes. E. A. Robinson. AnAmPo

Her eyes are bright as sparkling stars. Mine. Mary E. Tucker. CBWP-1

Her eyes are velvet, soft and fine. My Poker Girl. Tom Masson. OBAL

Her Eyes Are Wild. Wordsworth. NAs

Her eyes be like the violets. Anne. Lizette Woodworth Reese. AA

Her eyes? Dark pools of deepest shade. Portrait. George Leonard Allen. CDC

Her eyes had the blue of desperate days. Hart Crane. AnAn

Her eyes in sleep. *Unknown, tr. by* W. S. Merwin *and* J. Moussaieff Masson. UnAS

Her eyes lined with kohl. What Her Girl Friend Said ("Her eyes lined with kohl"). Peyanar, *tr. fr. Tamil by* A. K. Ramanujan. *Fr.* Nine on Happy Reunion, 9. PLW

Her eyes long hollowed out to pits of shadow. The Worshiper. Vassar Miller. NePoEA-2

Her eyes the glow-worm lend thee. The Night-Piece, to Julia. Robert Herrick. CaPo; CH; ELP; InvP; JCP; LiTB; NAEL-1; NoP; OAEL-1; OBEV; OBS; PoE; PoEL-3; PoRA; SeCP; SeCV-1; TEP (On a Dark Road.) BoTP

Her eyes were gentle; her voice was for soft singing. An Old Woman Remembers. Sterling A. Brown. CNA; PoBA

Her face has made my life most proud and glad. Of His Lady's Face. Jacopo da Lentino, *tr. by* Dante Gabriel Rossetti. PFI (Sonnet: Of His Lady's Face.) AWP

Her face her tongue her wit. *At. to* Sir Arthur Gorges. GBL

Her face thins almost. Each Day. Sister Maura. CRP

Her face was in a bed of hair. Emily Dickinson. NU

Her face was like sad things: was like the lights. A Stranger. Lionel Johnson. NOBVV

Her Fairness, Wedded to a Star. Edward J. O'Brien. FaBoBe

Her father is sick. He dozes most afternoons. Anastasia McLaughlin. Tom Paulin. FaBCIP

Her father loved me; oft invited me. Shakespeare. *Fr.* Othello, I, iii. EBEV; SCV

Her feet beneath her petticoat. The Bride. Sir John Suckling. *Fr.* A Ballad [*or* Ballade] upon a Wedding. TrGrPo

Her fingers. Frigga with Hela. Judy Grahn. UL

Her fingers float in the vacant air. Festival in Fishing Village No. 25. Park Je-chun, *tr. by* Koh Chang-soo. ACKP

Her fingers on the girl's bare neck, light. Timarista and Krito. Rosanna Warren. *Fr.* Funerary Portraits, III. NOAM

Her fingers shame the ivory keys. Amy Wentworth. Whittier. AnAmPo; BeLS

Her flowers were exclusive blue. Exclusive Blue. Robert Francis. CRP

Her Garden. Freda Downie. FaBoWP

Her gentle limbs did she undress. Christabel and Geraldine. Samuel Taylor Coleridge. *Fr.* Christabel, *Pt.* I. PeHV

Her Going. Shirley Kaufman. PCP

Her gold embroidered silken skirts softly rustle. Echoing Heaven's Everlastingness. Ku Hsiung, *tr. by* Lois Fusek. ATF

Her grieving heart is about to break. Pure Serene Music. Sun Kuang-hsien, *tr. by* Lois Fusek. ATF

Her grieving parents cradled here. Sylvia Townsend Warner. MoBrPo

Her Hair. Sir Robert Chester. *Fr.* Love's Martyr. EIL

Her hair curled in at the nape of her neck. Doric. Anghelos Sikelianos. VMG, *tr. by* Edmund Keeley *and* Philip Sherrard.

Her hair the net of golden wire. So Fast Entangled. *Unknown.* TrGrPo

Her hair upgathered thus behind the neck. Doric. Anghelos Sikelianos, *tr. by* Edmund Keeley *and* Philip Sherrard. ErPo

Her hair was a waving bronze and her eyes. Disappointment. John Boyle O'Reilly. ACP

Her hair was tawny with gold, her eyes with purple were dark. A Court Lady. Elizabeth Barrett Browning. BeLS

Her hand a goblet bore for him. The Two. Hugo von Hofmannsthal, *tr. by* Ludwig Lewisohn. AWP

Her hand in my hand. Dunce Song 6. Mark Van Doren. DuDa

Her hand in my hand. Suddenly. Yusuf al-Sa'igh, *tr. by* Diana Der Hovanessian *with* Salma Khadra Jayyusi. MAP

Her hand that holds. Jesus Drum. Pearl Cleage Lomax. CNA

Her hands are cold; her face is white. Under the Violets. Oliver Wendell Holmes. *Fr.* The Professor at the Breakfast Table. AA

Her health is good. She owns to forty-one. Occupation: Housewife. Phyllis McGinley. *Fr.* I Know a Village. WPE

Her Heards Be Thousand Fishes. Spenser. *Fr.* Colin Clout's Come Home Again. FPo

Her Heart. Bartholomew Griffin. *See* Fidessa, More Chaste than Kind: Fly [*or* Flye] to her heart; hover about her heart.

Her heart is like her garden. My Mother's Garden. Alice E. Allen. BLPA; BLPL; FaBoBe

Her Horoscope. Mary Ashley Townsend. AA

Her house is become like a man dishonored. Dirge. Bible, Apocrypha. *Fr.* First Maccabees, II: 8-14. TrJP

Her Husband. Ted Hughes. OxBC

Her husband is gone towards Naniwa. Tajihi Yanushi, *tr. fr. Japanese.* *Fr.* Manyo Shu. Ma

Her imaginary playmate was a grown-up. Cinderella. Randall Jarrell. LCAP; NAAL-2

Her Irish maids could never spoon out mush. Mary Winslow. Robert Lowell. PPP

Her iron beats. Domestic Scene. Michael Hartnett. BIrV

Her Kind. Anne Sexton. CAPP; CoAP; FF; HCAP; HeIP; LiTM; PPP; TAP; TwCP; WPOW

Her kiss on the mirror. A Hidden Message. Kevin Ireland. ATNZ

Her leggings could burn. Of Three Friendly Warnings This Is the Third. *Unknown, tr. by* Jerome Rothenberg *and* Richard Johnny John. STP

Her Letter. Bret Harte. AnAmPo; PoLF

Her life is in the marble! yet a fall. Her, a Statue. Thomas Tod Stoddart. OBNC

Her Lips Are Copper Wire. Jean Toomer. NoAM

Her lips blue from tasting, her eyes so blue. Among Blackberries. Michael Waters. GeTw

Her lips they are redder than coral. *Unknown.* FaBoCo

Her lips were so near. In Explanation. Walter Learned. AA

Her little face is like a walnut shell. Visitor. W. E. Henley. *Fr.* In Hospital, XX. BrPo

Her little hot room looked over the bay. Sanary. Katherine Mansfield. ATNZ

Her long with ardent look his eye pursu'd. Milton. *Fr.* Paradise Lost, *Bk.* IX, *ll.* 397–470. UnPo

Her Longing. Theodore Roethke. NAAL-2; NU

Her love is true I know. True Love. Waring Cuney. CDC

Her lute hangs shadowed in the apple-tree. A Sea-Spell. Dante Gabriel Rossetti. WSC

Her make-up is perfect, her face is a bright flower. Apricot Garden in Blossom. Yin O, *tr. by* Lois Fusek. ATF

Her Man Described by Her Owne Dictamen. Ben Jonson. *Fr.* A Celebration of Charis in Ten Lyrick Peeces. SeCP

Her Merriment. W. H. Davies. EnLoPo

Her Mother. Alice Cary. OHIP

Her mother died when she was young. Kemp Owyne. Alice Cary. EnSB; ESPB; OHIP

Her mother's old and can't help herself. Keno. Dara Wier. MAYP

Her Mouth. Richard Aldington. BrPo

Her Mouth an O. The Poetess Ko Ogimi. Helen Chasin. NMM

Her mouth is a crushed flower. Her Mouth. Richard Aldington. BrPo

Her mouth is as fragrant as a vine. Cleopatra. Swinburne. BeLS

Her Music. Martha Gilbert Dickinson Bianchi. AA

Her name is at my tongue whene'er I speak. Ever Present. Philip Ayres. OxBSP

Her Name Is Helen. Beth Brant. GLP

Her Name like the Hours. Gloria Evans Davies. OBWVE

Her name was Ate, mother of debate. The House of Ate. Spenser. *Fr.* The Faerie Queene, IV, 1. OBSC

Her name was Cissie. Cissie. Lotte Kramer. CN

Her name was Marian Claribel Lee. The Ballad of Sir Brian and the Three Wishes. Newman Levy. FiBHP

Her Oak. Malka Heifetz-Tussman, *tr. fr. Yiddish by* Kathryn Hellerstein. AYP

Her old age/ is waiting for her. Night Prayers. Dinah Livingstone. DT

Her own son the mother called. The Boy Changed into a Stag Cries Out at the Gate of Secrets. Ferenc Juhász, *tr. by* Kenneth McRobbie. MHuP

Her Passing. William Drummond of Hawthornden. *See* Beauty [*or* Beautie], and the life, The.

Her patience is infinite. The Problems of a Writing Teacher. David Ray. NePoEA-2

Her Picture. Ellen Mackay Hutchinson Cortissoz. AA

Her Polka Dots. Peter Newell. NA

Her Praises. Anthony Scoloker. EIL

Her Precious Leg. Thomas Hood. *Fr.* Miss Kilmansegg and Her Precious Leg. NOBVV

Her pretty feet. Upon Her Feet. Robert Herrick. CaPo; OxBSP; PoE

Her Rambling. Thomas Lodge. *Fr.* The Life and Death of William Longbeard. OBSC

Her red cloth is like the lightning. Red Beauty. *Unknown, tr. by* V. Elwin *and* S. Hivale. WTO

Her red pump tapping, her ankle-length gown slit at the knee. Mrs. Applebaum's Sunday Dance Class. Philip Schultz. MAYP

Her refusal to accept a room of solitude. Pieces. Duane Niatum. HATNAP

Her Reply. Sir Walter Ralegh. *See* If all the world and love were young.

Her ringlets glistened like the gold of morn. A Picture. Henrietta Cordelia Ray. CBWP-3

Her Rival for Aziza. *Unknown, tr. fr. Arabic by* E. Powys Mathers. *Fr.* The Thousand and One Nights. AWP

Her robe, willow tinted, is stitched with a gold phoenix. Heaven's Immortal. Ho Ning, *tr. by* Lois Fusek. ATF

Her sad brows are the green of a far mountain. A Southern Song. Mao Hsi-chen, *tr. by* Lois Fusek. ATF

Her sails are spread and colours flying. The Emigrant Ship. Henry Dalton. PVCV

Her scarf *à la* Bardot. Twice Shy. Seamus Heaney. TwCP

Her seas and mountains made. The Weaving of the Wing. Ralph Hodgson. BrPo

Her Second Husband Hears Her Story. Thomas Hardy. OBD

Her sense of humor has no gold stop. Telephonist. Janet Frame. WPE

Her Seventeenth Winter. John Leax. CRP

Her Shadow. Elisabeth Cavazza Pullen. AA

Her shadow races with slanting moonbeams. Written for My Neighbor. Shen Yüeh, *tr. by* Burton Watson. CoBCP

Her sheer silken skirt is the color of the autumn waves. Deva-like Barbarian. Wei Ch'eng-pan, *tr. by* Lois Fusek. ATF

Her shining black hair is swept high. The Taoist Nun. Niu Chiao, *tr. by* Lois Fusek. ATF

Her shoes could burn. Of Three Friendly Warnings This Is the First. *Unknown, tr. by* Jerome Rothenberg *and* Richard Johnny John. STP

Her shoes could burn. Of Three Friendly Warnings This Is the Second. *Unknown, tr. by* Jerome Rothenberg *and* Richard Johnny John. STP

Her sight is short, she comes quite near. Jenny Wren. W. H. Davies. MoBrPo

Her Sister. Moira O'Neill. AIW; OxBTC

Her Sleep. Jill Hoffman. TV

Her sleeping head with its great gelid mass. Perseus. Robert Hayden. NoAM

Her soft plump shoulders. What Her Girl Friend Said to Him. Ammuvanar, *tr. by* A. K. Ramanujan. PLW

Her Son. Ebba M. Leaf. PWR

Her soul is a select district. Paysage Choisi. Francis Sparshott. MoCV

Her spirit hiding among skin and bones. Beside a Deathbed. Vassar Miller. MT

Her stiffening captor lies in wait. Mercedes, Her Aloneness. Colette Inez. IHMS

Her Story. Naomi Long Madgett. IHMS; PoBA

Her Strong Enchantments Failing. A. E. Housman. FaBoTw; MAT; NOBE; NOBVV; OAEL-2; OPOP

Her suffering ended with the day. A Death-Bed. James Aldrich. AA

Her summer *kimono*. Matsumoto Takashi, *tr. by* Geoffrey Bownas *and* Anthony Thwaite. PeBJV

Her sweet weight on my heart a night. Emily Dickinson. PeHV

Her tears fell in two reddening streams. Deep Gratitude. Niu Chiao, *tr. by* Lois Fusek. ATF

Her thin puny little body. Clinic Day. Jo Barnes. BrRo

Her Time. Theodore Roethke. NAAL-2

Her touch heals. Sarah: Cherokee Doctor. Wendy Rose. STE

Her Triumph. Ben Jonson. OPOP

Her Triumph. Ben Jonson. *See* Celebration of Charis in Ten Lyrick Peeces, A: Triumph of Charis, The.

Her True Body. Jerred Metz. VWA

Her upswept hair is like a thick green cloud. Spring in the Phoenix Tower. Ou-yang Chiung, *tr. by* Lois Fusek. ATF

Her veil was artificial flowers and leaves. Christopher Marlowe. *Fr.* Hero and Leander, First Sestiad. HoPM

Her Voice. Barney Bush. HATNAP

Her Voice Could Not Be Softer. Austin Clarke. NOIV

Her voice did quiver as we parted. On Fanny Godwin. Shelley. ChER; OBNC

Her voice enters the room. Felix Pollak. *Fr.* Tunnel Visions, II. TSM

Her voice is like some angel picking at the door. Alan Brunton. PeNZ

Her Voice Is the Tidying of a House. Gregory O'Brien. ATNZ

Her voice was like the song of birds. A Child. Richard Watson Gilder. AA

Her ways were gentle while a babe. Elizabeth Oakes Smith. *Fr.* The Sinless Child. AA

Her Whole Life Is an Epigram. Blake. FaBoEE; InPK; OAEL-2

Her Words from the Corner. Ory Bernstein, *tr. fr. Hebrew by* Warren Bargad *and* Stanley F. Chyet. IP

Her wraithful turnings and her soft answers head me off. Soft Answers. Robert Bagg. FF

Her young employers, having got in late. A Summer Morning. Richard Wilbur. FaBoMo; NBLV

Her-zie. Stevie Smith. Mes

Hera, Hung from the Sky. Carolyn Kizer. NMM; WPE

Heracles. Yvor Winters. QFR

Heraclitus. William Johnson Cory, *paraphrased fr. the Greek of* Callimachus. AWP; EBVV; FaBoEE; FaPoR; NOBE; OBEV; OBNC; OxBSP; PeHV; PoRA; SeCePo

Heralded into a belly swelling bladder bloating banquet. On Meeting the Clergy of the Holy Catholic Church in Osaka. Joy Kogawa. BrSi

Heralds of Christ. Laura S. Copenhaver. AH

Herb-Leech, The. Joseph Campbell. AnIL

Herbert Glerbett. Jack Prelutsky. RHPC

Herbert Street Revisited. John Montague. CIP; FaBCIP; IPY

Herbert White. Frank Bidart. AmPA

Herbs in the Attic. Marilyn Nelson Waniek. MAYP

Hercules Furens, *sel.* Seneca, *tr. fr. Latin by* Jasper Heywood. "Let oken club now strike, and poast of might." *Fr.* IV. OBVE

Hercules Musarum. Robert Kelly. BAP

Hercules Oetaeus, *sel.* Seneca, *tr. fr. Latin by* John Studley. "Let other mount aloft, let other sore." *Fr.* II. OBVE

Herd, The. Frances Cornford. FM

Herd Boy, The. Lu Yu, *tr. fr. Chinese by* Arthur Waley. ChTr

Herdboy returns, none too early, The. Yang Shih-ch'i, *tr. fr. Chinese by* Jonathan Chaves. *Fr.* A Painting of Water Buffaloes. CoBLCP

Herdmen, The. William Byrd. *See* What pleasure have great princes.

Herds, The. W. S. Merwin. NaP; NYBP

Herdsman. Michael Pettit. MAYP

Herdsmen, The. Theocritus, *tr. fr. Greek by* Charles Stuart Calverley. *Fr.* Idylls, IV. AWP

Here. Marvin Bell. AmPA

Here. Paul Celan, *tr. fr. German by* Beth Bjorklund. CoAuP

Here. Robert Creeley. NOBA

Here. Philip Larkin. CMoP; PoE

Here. Eeva-Liisa Manner, *tr. fr. Finnish by* Aili Jarvenpa. SOP

Here. Bob Orr. PeNZ

Here. R. S. Thomas. GTBS-P; RB

Here. Hat Bar. Mildred Weston. FiBHP

Here/ High on the hill. Song of the Hill. Edith Lodge. GoYe

Here/ I sing th green branch. At Pakiri Beach. David Mitchell. PeNZ

Here/ With my beer/ I sit. Beer. George Arnold. AA; OBAL

Here a little child I stand. Grace for a Child. Robert Herrick. AWP; FaPON; InPS; MoShBr; NAEL-1; PoE; TrGrPo

(Another Grace for a Child.) GoJo; HeIP; InvP; OBS; OxBChV; SeCV-1

(Child's Grace, A.) BOTP; EaLo; FaBoCh; OBEV

(Grace before Meat.) ChTr

Here a pretty baby lies. Robert Herrick. OBEV

("Upon a Child.") OBS; SeCV-1; TrGrPo

Here, a sheer hulk, lies poor Tom Bowling. Poor Tom. Charles Dibdin. NOEC; OxBoLi

Here a solemn fast we keep[e]. An Epitaph upon a Virgin. Robert Herrick. CaPo; FaBoEE; OxBoLi; PoEL-3; SeCV-1

Here a wandering seaweed. Anti-Nostalgia. Henryk Grynberg, *tr. by* Isaac Komem. VWA

Here, above/ cracks in the buildings are filled with battered moonlight. The Man-Moth. Elizabeth Bishop. CAPP; LiTA; LiTM; MAT; MoAB; MoAmPo; MoP; NoAM; NOBA; PPP

Here again, another useless sign of the floating world. Teika, *tr. fr. Japanese by* Hiroaki Sato. *Fr.* Eighty-four Tanka. FCEI

Here again, blossoms falling. Late spring. Onitsura, *tr. fr. Japanese by* Hiroaki Sato. *Fr.* Twenty-three Hokku. FCEI

Here again (she said) is March the third. March the 3rd. Edward Thomas. NAs

Here, all star-paven at our Lady's well. A Heretic's Pilgrimage. Eva Gore-Booth. TIRV

Here All We See. Walter de la Mare. RAR

Here am I, little jumping Joan. Mother Goose. NTCP; OxNR

Here am I now cast down. Ex Nihilo. David Gascoyne. *Fr.* Miserere. GTBS-P

Here am I, sitting in a German inn. James Boswell. OBTV

Here among long-discarded cassocks. Diary of a Church Mouse. Sir John Betjeman. OxBTC

Here and Now. Catherine Cater. AmNP; PoNe

Here and Now. Philip Levine. PoA; VWA

Here and There. Ralph Meredith. Mes

Here and there frogs croak. Kikaku, *tr. by* Hiroaki Sato. FCEI

Here and there in the searing beam. Deer among Cattle. James Dickey. CAPP

Here are/ blue teapot. Components. Roger McDonald. CBAP

Here are cakes for thy body. The Other World. *Unknown, tr. fr. Egyptian by* Robert Hillyer. *Fr.* Book of the Dead. AWP; OBD

Here are fine gifts, children. Sappho, *tr. by* Willis Barnstone. BoWoP

"Here are flowers soluble in the eyes." Deceptions. René Daumal, *tr. by* Michael Benedikt. POS

Here are no signs of festival. African Christmas. John Press. OBCP

Here are old trees, tall oaks, and gnarled pines. The Antiquity of Freedom. Bryant. AA

Here are Paolo and Francesca. An Illustration to Dante. Fleur Adcock. ATNZ

Here are sweet peas, on tiptoe for a flight. Sweet Peas. Keats. *Fr.* I Stood Tiptoe [upon a Little Hill]. GN

Here are the lady's knives and forks. *Unknown.* OxNR

Here are the Schubert *Lieder.* Now begin. For M.S. Singing *Fruhlingsglaube* in 1945. Frances Cornford. BrRo

Here Are Told the Misfortunes of Women. Christine de Pisan, *tr. fr. French by* Sarah Spence. *Fr.* The Book of Fortune's Changes. DMF

Here are two pictures from my father's head. Wounds. Michael Longley. FaBCIP; FaBoPV; OBD

Here are weeds about his mouth. Wide Empty Landscape with a Death in the Foreground. N. Scott Momaday. CDW

Here as I sit by the Jumna bank. Studies at Delhi, 1876. Sir Alfred Comyn Lyall. OBTV

Here, as in a painting, yellow noon burns [*or* noon burns yellow]. Natalya Yevgenevna Gorbanyevskaya, *tr. by* Daniel Weissbort. BoWoP; PBWP

Here, at last, is the fever. A Day in My Union Suit. Michael Pettit. MAYP

Here at right of the entrance this bronze head. A Bronze Head. W. B. Yeats. LiTB

Here, at the airport, waiting. At the Airport. John Malcolm Brinnin. MoAB

Here at the center of the turning year. New Year. Stephen Spender. AWP

Here at the country inn. The Forefather. Richard Burton. AA

Here at the river neck. *Unknown, tr. fr. Japanese. Fr.* Manyo Shu. Ma

Here at the roots of the mountains. Rapids at Night. Duncan Campbell Scott. CaP

Here at the row of shacks on the hunting ground. *Unknown, tr. by* Hiroaki Sato. FCEI

Here at the seashore they use the clouds over & over. Rhode Island. William Meredith. NoP

Here at the Vespasian-Carlton, it's just one. Boom! Howard Nemerov. LiTM; NBLV; NIP

Here at the wayside station, as many a morning. The Wayside Station. Edwin Muir. FaBoTw

Here at this sudden age of mine. An Autumn Walk. Witter Bynner. GoYe

Here at Woodlands, Moriah. Salmon Courage. Marlene Philip. PVCV

Here Awa', There Awa'. *Unknown.* OBS

Here be rural graces, sylvan places. Wild Cherry Tree. Edmund Blunden. BrPo

Here beside dwelleth. The Magician and the Baron's Daughter. *Unknown.* MeEL

Here between lunch and teatime, and days and hours between. Lines to Dr. Ditmars. Kenneth Allan Robinson. ImOP

Here bring your purple and gold. Flowers for the Brave. Celia Thaxter. OHIP

Here busy and yet innocent lyes dead. On the Death of a Monkey. Thomas Heyrick. FM; MePo

Here, but Unable to Answer. Richard Hugo. CAPP; DiL

Here by the grey north sea. A Northern Vigil. Bliss Carman. OBEV

Here by the moorway you returned. Your Last Drive. Thomas Hardy. OBNC

Here, by the shore, we go out each morning. Diving for Pearls. Traise Yamamoto. BrSi

Here, Caelia, for thy sake I part. To the Mutable Fair. Edmund Waller. SeCP

Here, Charmian, take my bracelets. Cleopatra. W. W. Story. AA

Here Cleita sleeps. You ask her life and race? The Monument of Cleita. Edward Cracroft Lefroy, *after the Greek of* Theocritus. *Fr.* Echoes from Theocritus, XXIX. AWP

Here clove the keels of centuries ago. The Salt Flats. Sir Charles G. D. Roberts. CaP

Here come I to my own again. The Prodigal Son. Kipling. *Fr.* Kim. NoAM

Here come real stars to fill the upper skies. Fireflies in the Garden. Robert Frost. OxBSP; RHPC

Here come the hounds, ting-a-ling. *Unknown, tr. by* Arthur Waley. BoS

Here come the line-gang pioneering by. The Line-Gang. Robert Frost. OxBSP

Here comes a girl so damned shapely. Girl Walking. Charles G. Bell. ErPo

Here comes a lady who would like to be murdered. The Crazy Lady. Kurt Klinger, *tr. by* Beth Bjorklund. CoAuP

Here Comes a Lusty Wooer. *Unknown.* CH; OxNR

Here comes another, bumping over the sage. Tumbleweed. David Wagoner. BoNaP

Here comes Kate Summers who, for gold. The Bird of Paradise. W. H. Davies. BrPo

Here comes my lady with her little baby. *Unknown.* OxNR

Here comes Old Man Adkins with a battle-ax. Coal Loadin' Blues. *Unknown.* AmFP

Here comes the elephant. The Elephant. Herbert Asquith. BoTP

Here comes the Marshal. The Proclamation. Longfellow. *Fr.* John Endicott. PAH

Here comes the powdered milk I drank. Spring Snow. William Matthews. AnAn

Here comes the shadow not looking where it is going. Sire. W. S. Merwin. CoAP; NaP; VGW

Here continueth to rot. Epitaph on Colonel Francis Chartres. John Arbuthnot. FaBoEE

(Colonel Chartres.) OBSV

Here costive many minutes did I strain. Privy-Love for My Landlady. George Farewell. NOEC

Here cursing swearing Burton lies. Burns. FaBoEE

Here dead lie we because we did not choose. A. E. Housman. FaBoEE; FPL; NoP; OAEL-2; PoLF

(Epitaph.) NOBVV

Here deare Iöas lies. Iöas' Epitaph. William Drummond of Hawthornden. PoEL-2

Here Delia's buried at fourscore. Hildebrand Jacob. FaBoEE

Here did sway the eltrot flow'rs. Times o' Year. William Barnes. BoNaP

Here do I put my name for to betraye. *Unknown.* FaBoUs

Here dock and tare. In the Grave No Flower. Edna St. Vincent Millay. NAAL-2

Here doth Dionysia lie. Epitaph of Dionysia. *Unknown.* OBEV

Here down my wearied limbs I'll lay. On Himself. Robert Herrick. CaPo

Here enter not vile bigots, hypocrites. Inscription above the Entrance to the Abbey of Theleme. Rabelais, *tr. fr. French by* Sir Thomas Urquhart. *Fr.* Gargantua. FaBoRV

Here even experts can. Ragoût Fin de Siècle (with Reference to Certain Cafés). Erich Kästner, *tr. by* Walter Kaufman. ErPo; PeHV

Here, ever since you went abroad. What News. Walter Savage Landor. BoLoP

Here every soldier. The Hotel. Shauqi Abi Shaqra, *tr. by* Abdullah al-Udhari. MPAW

Here falls no light of sun nor stars. Richard Hovey. *Fr.* Taliesin. AA

Here, far from all the pomp ambition seeks. Sonnet upon a Swedish Cottage. Sir John Carr. OBTV

Here, five feet deep, lies on his back. On the Astrologer and Almanac Maker, John Partridge. Swift. FaBoEE

Here Followeth the Songe of the Death of Mr. Thewlis. *Unknown.* CoMu

Here Follow[e]s Some Verses upon the Burning of Our House. Anne Bradstreet. *See* In silent night, when rest I took.

Here for a little we pause. Benicasim. Sylvia Townsend Warner. OBWP

Here—for they could not help but die. Philip Freneau. *Fr.* The Fading Rose. AA

Here 40 years ago on moonless nights. Between Talcy and Mer. Carole Oles. BLA

Here, from laborious art, proud towns, ye rose! On Catania and Syracuse Swallowed Up by an Earthquake, from the Italian of Filicaja. Anna Seward. Son

Here from the brow of the hill I look. The Old Mill. Thomas Dunn English. AA

Here from the start, from our first of days, look. The Tally Stick. Jarold Ramsey. NIP

Here further up the mountain slope. The Birthplace. Robert Frost. EyDe; OFD

Here goes a poor old chimney sweeper. The Chimney Sweeper. *Unknown.* AmFP

Here halt we our march, and pitch our tent. The Green Mountain Boys. Bryant. PAH

Here has my salient faith annealed me. Key West. Hart Crane. CMoP

Here Have I Been These One and Twenty Years. Arthur Hugh Clough. NAs

Here have I seen the king, when great affairs. Sir John Denham. *Fr.* Cooper's Hill. PoE

Here, here are our enjoyments done. Lucasia, Rosania and Orinda Parting at a Fountain, July 1663. Katherine Philips. PeHV

Here, here I live with what my board. His Content in the Country. Robert Herrick. CaPo; SeCV-1; TEP

Here, here, oh here Eurydice. Orpheus to Beasts. Richard Lovelace. CaPo

Here hold this glove (this milk-white cheveril glove). Richard Barnfield. *Fr.* Sonnets, XIV. PeHV

Here, houses close their sleepy window eyes. Arizona Village. Robert Stiles Davieau. AmFN

Here I Am. Abraham Sutskever, *tr. fr. Yiddish.* PeBMYV, *tr.* by Chana Bloch; TrJP, *tr.* by Joseph Leftwich.

Here I am. Friend Mussunda. Agostinho Neto, *tr.* by Marga Holness. WMBCH

Here I am. Navaho Sings. Nan Benally. GOS

Here I am,/ Novice of many years. Two Roads, Etc. Dorothy Walters. IHMS

Here I am again. From Delphi. Cozette de Charmoy. NPo

Here I am, an industry without chimneys. The Perfection of Dentistry. Marvin Bell. AmPA; CoAP

Here I am, an old man in a dry month. Gerontion. T. S. Eliot. AmPP; CMoP; EBEV; GTBS-P; HAP; InPS; LiTA; LiTM; MoP; NAAL-2; NoAM; NOBA; OAEL-2; OxBA; PPP; SeCePo; TAP

Here I am, full-grown, flourishing. Here I Am. Abraham Sutskever, *tr.* by Chana Bloch. PeBMYV

Here I am on this ledge again. Dance Script with Electric Ballerina. Alice Fulton. KS

Here I am once more. Do you remember. Postcards from Kodai. Kevin Crossley-Holland. OBTV

Here I am, seated, with all my words. Silence Concerning an Ancient Stone. Rosario Castellanos, *tr.* by George D. Schade. PBWP

Here I am, sprouted to my full height. Here I Am. Abraham Sutskever, *tr.* by Joseph Leftwich. TrJP

Here I am, still standing at the crossroads. The Land of Metamorphoses. René Daumal, *tr.* by Michael Benedikt. POS

Here I am turning your words. Lenin. Mihály Ladányi, *tr.* by Edwin Morgan. MHuP

Here I am whole, I know. Herdsman. Michael Pettit. MAYP

Here I am with my rabbits. *Unknown.* OxNR

Here I bend my young head and am still. Izi Kharik, *tr.* by Leonard Wolf. PeBMYV

Here I come creeping, creeping everywhere. The Voice of the Grass. *At.* to Sarah Roberts Boyle. AA

Here I come creeping, creeping everywhere. The Song of the Grass. *At.* to Leigh Hunt. BoTP

Here I Have Never Been. Jacob Glatstein, *tr. fr. Yiddish by* Benjamin and Barbara Harshav. AYP

Here I lie asleep. The Absence. Denise Levertov. NaP

Here I lie at rest: Alfonsina says. Epitaph for My Tomb. Alfonsina Storni, *tr.* by Perry Higman. LPSS

Here I lie at the chancel door. On Elizabeth Ireland. *Unknown.* FaBoEE

Here I lie for the last time. Epitaph on an Irish Priest. *Unknown.* FaBoEE

Here I ligg, Sydney Slugabed Godless Smith. Sydney Goodsir Smith. *Fr.* Under the Eildon Tree, Elegy V. OxBS

Here I myself might likewise die. Poetry Perpetuates the Poet. Robert Herrick. FaBoEE

Here I sit. Bad Morning. Langston Hughes. OBAL

Here I slept with my face turned. Prospect Beach. Lou Lipsitz. VGW

Here I stand. Ask the Mountains. Phil George. NOVW

Here I stand. The Climber Surveys His Mountain. Hugh Ouston. PoSH

Here I stand/ Humble, with outstretched arms. Hymn to the Air Spirit. *Unknown.* WTO

Here I thought I was. *Unknown, tr. fr. Japanese by* Burton Watson. *Fr.* Manyo Shu. FCEI

Here in a beautiful dell where the river runs. Akahito, *tr. fr. Japanese.* *Fr.* Manyo Shu. FCEI

Here in a distant place I hold my tongue. Egan O Rahilly. *Unknown, tr.* by James Stephens. EBEV; OBMV; SeCePo

Here, in a field. In a Field. Robert Pack. MAT; NePoEA-2

Here in a quiet and dusty room they lie. The Seed Shop. Muriel Stuart. BoNaP; GoTS

Here, in huge cauldrons, the rough mass they stow. The Iron Industry in Birmingham. Richard Jago. *Fr.* Edge-Hill; or, The Rural Prospect Delineated and Moralised. NOEC

Here in Katmandu. Donald Justice. *See* We have climbed the mountain.

Here, in late spring, the summer is on us already. Hot Afternoons Have Been in West 15th Street. Paul Blackburn. VGW

Here in my curving hands I cup. This Quiet Dust. John Hall Wheelock. MoAmPo

Here in my hands a small cold-chisel. The Little Chisel. N. P. van Wyck Louw, *tr.* by Jack Cope *and* Uys Krige. PeSA

Here in my head, the home that is left for you. Burning the Letters. Randall Jarrell. MoAB; MoAmPo

Here, in my rude log cabin. The Battle of New Orleans. Thomas Dunn English. PAH

Here in my vaster pools, as white as snow or milk. Lincolnshire's Holland Speaks of Her Waterfowl. Michael Drayton. *Fr.* Polyolbion, Five and Twentieth Song. FaBoPP

Here in Nantucket does the tiny soul. Phenomenal Survivals of Death in Nantucket. Louise Glück. AmPA; SM

Here in Netanya. Meir Wieseltier, *tr. fr. Hebrew by* Warren Bargad *and* Stanley F. Chyet. IP

Here in our aging district the wood pigeon lives with us. All Morning. Theodore Roethke. NaP

Here in our cloud we talk. Quiet Town. William Stafford. MAT

Here, in the/ book. The Book of Mysteries. Anthony Barnett. VWA

Here in the capital I wonder. Tabito, *tr. fr. Japanese.* *Fr.* Manyo Shu. Ma

Here in the cool and book-infested den. Ulysses' Library. David Daiches. PoA

Here in the country's heart. The Country Faith. Norman Gale. BoTP; OBEV; WGRP

Here in the dark, O heart. Second Best. Rupert Brooke. MoBrPo

Here in the dark what ghostly figures press! In Tesla's Laboratory. Robert Underwood Johnson. AA

Here in the green scooped valley I walk to and fro. The Green Valley. Sylvia Townsend Warner. MoBrPo

Here, in the hidden palm of the Pajaro Valley. Stonehouse. Jeff Tagami. BrSi

Here, in the hollow caverns of the rocks. The Wily Fox. Edward Davies, *tr.* by Joseph P. Clancy. OBWVE

Here in the midnight, where the dark mainland and island. Night Hymns on Lake Nipigon. Duncan Campbell Scott. OBCV

Here, in the most Unchristian basement. The Men's Room in the College Chapel. W. D. Snodgrass. MoAmPo; PPP

Here in the newspaper—the wreck of the East Bound. The It's Here In. Russell Atkins. AmNP; PoBA

Here in the night are the seven wonders of the world. The Spaces inside Sleep. Robert Desnos, *tr.* by Michael Benedikt. POS

Here, in the night, I'm staring. Dino Campana and the Bear. Edward Hirsch. MAYP

Here in the pine shade is the nest of night. Night and the Pines. Duncan Campbell Scott. OBCV

Here, in the sand, where someone laid him down. Cruciform. Winifred Welles. NYBP

Here in the scuffled dust. W. D. Snodgrass. *Fr.* Heart's Needle, VII. NePoEA

Here in the self is all that men can know. John Masefield. *Fr.* Lollingdon Downs. AWP

Here in the uplands. Scotland. Sir Alexander Gray. GoTS; OxBS

Here, in the withered arbor, like the arrested wind. Statue and Birds. Louise Bogan. EyDe; MoAB; MoAmPo

Here in their health and youth they're sitting down. Schoolgirl on Speech-Day in the Open Air. Iain Crichton Smith. NePoEA-2

Here in this bleak city of Rochester. Sestina d'Inverno. Anthony Hecht. NoAM; NoP

Here in this car is surcease from a thousand dead. Surcease. Patrick Lane. NeAC

Here in this carload. Written in Pencil in the Sealed Railway-Car. Dan Pagis, *tr. by* Stephen Mitchell. OBD

Here in this dim, dull, double-bedded room. Children: Private Ward. W. E. Henley. *Fr.* In Hospital, XVIII. BrPo

Here in this foreground of sunny Italian fields. Two Figures on Canvas. Gerald William Barrax. MT

Here in this great house in the barrack square. The Hambone and the Heart. Edith Sitwell. OBMV

Here, in This Little Bay. Coventry Patmore. *Fr.* The Unknown Eros. BoNaP

    (Magna Est Veritas.) GTBS-P; HAP; NOBE; NOBVV; OBEV; OBNC; OxBSP

    (Truth.) TrGrPo

Here in this narrow room there is no light. Prothalamium. A. J. M. Smith. CaP

Here in this room where first we met. As She Feared It Would Be. Lilla Cabot Perry. *Fr.* Meeting after Long Absence, I. AA

Here in this sequestered close. A Garden Song. Austin Dobson. BoNaP; OBEV; OBNC

Here in this world/ I won't live. Lady Izumi, *tr. by* Willis Barnstone. BoWoP

Here in veins of metal and glass. The Dead Sea. Henryk Grynberg, *tr. by* Isaac Komem. VWA

Here is a beetle as black as my hat. E. S. Goodwill. BXAP

Here is a child who is leaning over a paper. The Mirror. John N. Morris. PoA

Here is a coast; here is a harbor. Arrival at Santos. Elizabeth Bishop. FaBoWP; OxBC

Here is a cup left empty in their. Broken Home. William Stafford. NNaP

Here is a family so little famous. Photograph in a Stockholm Newspaper for March 13, 1910. Don Coles. NOBC

Here is a famous world. There Is No Place to Hide. Gwendolyn MacEwen. *Fr.* The T. E. Lawrence Poems. NOBC

Here is a fat animal, a bear. Self-Portrait, as a Bear. Donald Hall. SO

Here is a fountain of Christ's blood. Our Saviour's Love. *Unknown.* OBET

Here is a hole full of men shouting. Excavations. Fleur Adcock. ATNZ

Here is a house with a pointed door. A Little Finger Game. E. J. Falconer. BoTP

Here is a man dreaming. Windows. João Cabral de Melo Neto, *tr. by* Jean Valentine. ATCBP

Here is a merry song; if that you please to buy it. A Net for a Night Raven. *Unknown.* OxBSS

Here is a place that is no place. Madhouse. Calvin C. Hernton. IDB; PoNe

    (Patient: Rockland County Sanitarium, The.) PoBA

Here is a poem for the two of us to play. The Newly Pressed Suit. Roger McGough. MoP

Here is a rarity. Know Thyself. Kenneth Burke. OBAL

Here is a room with heavy-footed chairs. The Nature of an Action. Thom Gunn. NePoEA

Here Is a Song. John Peck. AH

Here is a symbol in which. Rock and Hawk. Robinson Jeffers. NoAM; NOBA; OxBA

Here Is a Toast That I Want to Drink. Walter Lathrop. PoLF

Here is a world my poetry cannot reach. Mirror Fantasy. Koh Chang-soo, *tr. by the author.* ACKP

Here is a world which slowed the hands of time. Okefenokee Swamp. Daniel Whitehead Hicky. AmFN

Here is another poem in a picture. Untitled. Daryl Hine. NoAM

Here is cruel Psamtek, see. The Story of Cruel Psamtek. *Unknown.* NA

Here is dominion for peace. Country Reverie. Carol Coates. CaP

Here is fresh matter, poet. Church and State. W. B. Yeats. CMoP

Here is Israel. Pictures at an Exhibition. Nathan Rosenbaum. GoYe

Here is Joe Blow the poet. On Being Asked for a Peace Poem. Howard Nemerov. OxBC

Here is Klito's little shack. Kenneth Rexroth, *after the Greek of* Leonidas. NNaP

Here is my foot, so small it cannot walk. In Jail. Juan Antonio Corretjer, *tr. by* Julio Marzán. InW

Here is no peace, although the air has fainted. Innocent Landscape. Elinor Wylie. OxBA

Here is no shadow but cloudshadow and nightshadow. Hide in the Heart. Lloyd Frankenberg. LiTA

Here Is No Southern Island. László Nagy, *tr. fr. Hungarian by* Jascha Kessler. FOC

Here is the ancient floor. The Self-Unseeing. Thomas Hardy. EBEV; HAP; MoBrPo; NOBE; NOBVV; OBNC; PrIm; RB; WeW

Here is the church. Claritas. James Camp. SoTCo

Here is the church, and here is the steeple. *Unknown.* OxNR

Here is the crab tree. The Crab Tree. Oliver St. John Gogarty. AnIL

Here is the Dog. Since time began. The Dog. Oliver Herford. FaBV

Here is the fern's frond, unfurling a gesture. Fern. Ted Hughes. NYBP

Here is the foreign cliff and the fabled sea. On a Picture by Michele Da Verona, of Arion as a Boy Riding upon a Dolphin. Anne Ridler. PoA

Here is the key to the writing desk. Resignation. Wilhelm Szabo, *tr. by* Beth Bjorklund. CoAuP

Here is the long-bided hour: the labor of years is accomplished. Work. Pushkin, *tr. by* Babette Deutsch *and* Avrahm Yarmolinsky. AWP

Here is the passing of an uneventful hour. The Age of the Street. Anthony Howell. NPo

Here is the perfect vision: in the dawn. First Flight. Dorothy Wellesley. OBTV

Here is the place. Looking for Maimonides: Tiberias. Shirley Kaufman. VWA

Here is the place; right over the hill. Telling the Bees. Whittier. AnAmPo; AWP; BLPL; NOBA; TAP

Here is the salt in the shaker. Hand, Eye. Patricia Hampl. NAmP

Here is the scene: She follows him. Dying at the Edge of Death. Hameed Said, *tr. by* Diana Der Hovanessian *and* Lena Jayyusi. MAP

Here is the shadow of truth for only the shadow is true. A Way to Love God. Robert Penn Warren. NAAL-2

Here is the soundless cypress on the lawn. The Nightingale near the House. Harold Monro. MoBrPo

Here is the story. Freddy. Dennis Lee. RHPC

Here is the stream again under the rainbow. Tchicaya U Tam'si, *tr. fr. French by* E. S. Yntema. *Fr.* Debout. PBA

Here Is the Tale. Anthony C. Deane. NA

    (Jack and Jill—as Kipling Might Have Written It.) CenHV; FaBoPa

Here is the tale of Carrousel. The Ballad of a Barber. Aubrey Beardsley. NOBVV

Here is the train! The Holiday Train. Irene Thompson. BoTP

Here is the train to Glasgow. The Train to Glasgow. Wilma Horsburgh. OnUR

Here is the water by which. Azumabito, *tr. fr. Japanese.* *Fr.* Manyo Shu. Ma

Here is the way the white man's heaven felt. On a Picture by Pippin, Called "The Den." Selden Rodman. PoNe

Here is the yoke, with arrow and share near by. The Laborer. José-Maria de Heredia, *tr. by* Wilfrid Thorley. AWP

Here is this transport. Scrawled in Pencil in a Sealed Railway Car. Dan Pagis, *tr. by* Anthony Rudolf. VWA

Here is thy footstool and there rest thy feet. Rabindranath Tagore. *Fr.* Gitanjali, X. WGRP

Here it begins, the day we shall not forget. Bidean Nam Bian. A. M. Dobson. PoSH

Here it comes! Frightening. Claudia Lewis. RHPC

Here it's harvest. Dust. Love. Jorie Graham. NPGG

Here its like that. Blue Tanganyika. Lebert Bethune. PoBA

Here, it's the West. The Imperial Hotel. Nakano Shigeharu, *tr. by* Geoffrey Bownas *and* Anthony Thwaite. PeBJV

Here Jack and Tom are paired with Moll and Meg. George Meredith. *Fr.* Modern Love, XVIII. InvP; PoEL-5

Here Keats and Shelley heard. Piazza di Spagna. Willard M. Grimes. GoYe

Here lapped in hallowed slumber Saon lies. Saon of Acanthus. Callimachus, *tr. by* John Addington Symonds. AWP

Here lay a fair fat land. Culbin Sands. Andrew Young. GTBS-P; OxBS; OxBTC

Here let me rest me feet! Reverie of a Mum. Nancy Keesing. CBAP

Here let my Lord hang up his conquering lance. The Celestial City. Giles Fletcher the Younger. *Fr.* Christ's Victory and Triumph: Christ's Triumph after Death, IV. OBS

Here let the brows be bared. At the Tomb of Washington. Clinton Scollard. OHIP

Here lie Ciardi's pearly bones. Elegy Just in Case. John Ciardi. TwCP

Here lie I, Martin Elginbrodde. *At. to* George Macdonald. FaBoEE; WGRP

(At Aberdeen.) FaBoCo

Here lie I, once a witty fair. Samuel Wesley. NOEC

Here lie I, Timon. Timon's Epitaph. Shakespeare. *Fr.* Timon of Athens, V, iv. AWP

Here lie my old bones: my vexation now ends. Messenger Mounsey. FaBoEE

Here lie the banes o' Tammy Messer. Tammy Messer. *Unknown.* FaBoEE

Here lie the bones of Elizabeth Charlotte. *Unknown. See* Here lies the body of Elizabeth Charlotte.

Here lie the relics of a martyred knight. On Sir John Fenwick. Henry Hall. APAS

Here lie two poor lovers, who had the mishap. Pope. *Fr.* Three Epitaphs on John Hewet and Sarah Drew, III. FaBoEE

(Epitaph on the Stanton-Harcourt Lovers.) OBD

Here lie Willie Michie's [*or* M——hie's] banes. Epitaph on a Schoolmaster. Burns. FaBoCo; FaBoEE

(On a Schoolmaster in Cleish Parish, Fifeshire.) OBD

Here Lies. Stevie Smith. PoA

Here lies/ A bully. Tombstone. Lucia M. *and* James L. Hymes, Jr.. RHPC

Here lies a bard, Hipponax—honored name! The Grave of Hipponax. Edward Cracroft Lefroy, *after the Greek of* Theocritus. *Fr.* Echoes from Theocritus, XXX. AWP

Here lies a bard, let epitaphs be true. My Epitaph. H. J. Daniel. FaBoEE

Here lies a clerk who half his life had spent. The Volunteer. Herbert Asquith. MMA; OBWP; OxBTC

Here lies a Doctor of Divinity. Richard Porson. FaBoEE

(On a Doctor of Divinity.) FaBoCo

Here lies a dog: may every dog that dies. Epitaph on the Favourite Dog of a Politician. Hilaire Belloc. OBSV

Here lies a great and mighty king. The King's Epitaph. John Wilmot, 2nd Earl of Rochester. SeCePo

Here lies a great sleeper, as everybody knows. Epitaph on a Great Sleeper. Sir Aston Cokayne. FaBoEE

Here lies a Lady. John Crowe Ransom, *tr. fr. German.* AWP; CMoP; HAP; InvP; LiTM; MoAB; MoAmPo; MoP; NAAL-2; NoAM; PoRA; RB; TAP; VGW

Here lies a little bird. On a Little Bird. Martin Armstrong. CH

Here lies a man. And here, a girl. They live. Memorial. Robert Pinsky. HCAP; SM

Here lies a man, and still no man. *Unknown, tr. fr. Hebrew. Fr.* Duel with Verses over a Great Man. TrJP

Here lies a man who was killed by lightning. At Great Torrington, Devon. *Unknown.* FaBoCo; FaBoEE

Here lies a most beautiful lady. Walter de la Mare. LiTB; LiTM; MoAB; MoBrPo; OBEV; RB

Here lies a peer. Epitaph on the Duke of Grafton. Sir Fleetwood Shepherd. FaBoEE

Here lies a piece of Christ; a star in dust. An Epitaph for a Godly Man's Tomb. Robert Wild. ChTr; FaBoEE

Here lies a poet—where's the great surprise! "Z. Z." FaBoEE

Here lies a poet who would not write. Here Lies. Stevie Smith. PoA

Here lies a poor woman who always was tired. *Unknown.* FaBoEE

Here Lies a Prisoner. Charlotte Mew. MoBrPo

Here lies a shoe-maker whose knife and hammer. At His Father's Grave. John Ormond. FaBoTw; OBD; OBWVE

Here lies a simple Jew. Sholom Aleichem, *tr. by* Joseph Leftwich. TrJP

Here lies Boghead among the dead. Epitaph on James Grieve, Laird of Boghead. Burns. TW

Here lies Bogus, beatnik bard. Epitaph for a Beatnik Poet. Guy Owen. CRP

Here lies, but seven years old, our little maid. Afraid. Walter de la Mare. WeW

Here lies David Garrick, describe me who can. David Garrick. Goldsmith. *Fr.* Retaliation. NOEC

Here lies Dr. Keene, the good Bishop of Chester. Epitaph on Dr. Keene. Thomas Gray. FaBoEE

Here lies Factotum Ned at last. Fragment of a Character. Thomas Moore. FaBoCo

Here lies Fred. On Prince Frederick. *Unknown.* FaBoCo; FaBoEE; NOBL

(Epitaph on Prince Frederick.) OxBoLi

Here lies free from blood and slaughter. In Memory of Captain Underwood Who Was Drowned. *Unknown.* FaBoEE

Here lies Hersh Itsi's son: on his unseeing. Inscribed on a Tombstone. Mani Leib, *tr. by* John Hollander. PeBMYV

Here lies Hilaire Belloc, who. Hilaire Belloc. Humbert Wolfe. FaBoEE

Here lies I, no wonder I'm dead. *Unknown.* FaBoEE

Here lies in death, who living always lied. On Ryñeveld, an Unpopular Dutch Judge. *Unknown.* FaBoEE

Here lies intombed/ Beneath these bricks. Epitaph on a Willing Girl. *At. to* Thomas Rowlandson. FaBoEE

Here lies John Bun. John Bun. *Unknown.* FaBoCo; NBLV

Here lies John Hughes and Sarah Drew. Lady Mary Wortley Montagu. FaBoEE

Here lies John Knott. Epitaph on John Knott. *Unknown.* ChTr; FaBoEE; OBS; SeCV-1

Here lies John Trot, the friend of all mankind. Blake. FaBoEE

Here lies Johnny Pidgeon. Epitaph on John Dove. Burns. FaBoCo

Here lies Jonson [*or* lyes Johnson] with the rest. Upon Ben Jonson. Robert Herrick. CaPo; FaBoEE; NoP; OBS; SeCV-1

Here lies Judge A——, he's done with legal tort. Epitaph for a Judge. Benedict Jeitteles, *tr. by* Joseph Chotzner. TrJP

Here lies Landor. Walter Savage Landor. FaBoEE

Here lies Lord Coningsby—be civil. Lord Coningsby's Epitaph. Pope. FaBoEE

Here lies magnanimous Humility. Upon the Tomb of the Most Reverend Mr. John Cotton. Benjamin Woodbridge. SCAP

Here lies Mary, the wife of John Ford. At Potterne, Wiltshire. *Unknown.* FaBoCo

Here lies Mistress Keene the Bishop of Chester. Epitaph on Dr. Keene's Wife. Thomas Gray. FaBoEE

Here lies Mr. Chesterton. G. K. Chesterton. Humbert Wolfe. TrJP

Here lies my dear wife, a sad slattern and a shrew. *Unknown.* FaBoEE

Here lies my poor wife, much lamented. *Unknown.* FaBoEE

Here lies my poor wife, without bed or blanket. *Unknown.* FaBoEE

Here lies my wife. At Leeds. *Unknown.* FaBoCo

Here lies my wife. Susannah Prout. Walter de la Mare. FaBoEE

Here lies my wife. Eternal peace. J. V. Cunningham. NePoAm; NIP; OBAL

Here lies my wife: here let her lie! Epitaph on His Wife. Dryden. TrGrPo

Here lies Nachshon, a man of great renown. Isaac Benjacob, *tr. by* Joseph Chotzner. TrJP

Here lies New Critic who would fox us. J. V. Cunningham. *Fr.* Three Epigrams. MoAmPo; OBAL

Here lies Nolly Goldsmith, for shortness call'd Noll. On Oliver Goldsmith. David Garrick. FaBoEE

Here lies old Forty-five Per Cent. Old Forty-five Per Cent. *Unknown.* FaBoEE

Here lies old Hobson, Death hath broke his girt. On the University Carrier (Who Sickn'd in the Time of His Vacancy). Milton. EBEV; FaBoCh; FaBoEE; MePo; PrIm; SaC

Here lies our good Edmund, whose genius was such. Goldsmith. *Fr.* Retaliation. FaBoEE; FaBoPV

(Edmund Burke.) InvP; NOEC

Here lies our Sovereign Lord the King. Epitaph on Charles II. Earl of Rochester. FaBoCo; FiBHP; TrGrPo

Here lies Piron, a complete nullibiety. My Epitaph. Alexis Piron. OBD

Here lies Piron—a man of no position. Alexis Piron, *tr. fr. French.* FaBoEE

Here lies poor Burton. A Brewer. *Unknown.* FaBoCo

Here lies poor Johnson. Reader! have a care. Doctor Johnson. Soame Jenyns. FaBoEE; OBSV

Here lies resting, out of breath. Little Elegy. X. J. Kennedy. CoAP; GoJo; HoPM

Here lies Sir John Plumpudding of the Grange. *Unknown.* FaBoEE

Here lies Sir Tact, a diplomatic fellow. Timothy Steele. InPK; NBLV; TW

Here lies that poet, buried in the night. On a Poet. Henry Parrot. FaBoEE

Here lies the author of the "Apparition." An Author's Epitaph, Written by Himself. Abel Evans. FaBoEE

Here lies the best and worst of fate. On the Duke of Buckingham. James Shirley. FaBoEE

Here lies the body of Andrew Gear. Andrew Gear of Sunderland. *Unknown.* FaBoCo

Here lies the body of Daniel Saul. *Unknown.* FaBoEE

Here lies the body of Edith Bone. On Myself. Edith Bone. FaBoEE

Here lies the body of Elizabeth Charlotte. On an Aberdeen Favourite. *Unknown.* FaBoPP

("Here lie the bones of Elizabeth Charlotte.") FaBoEE

Here lies the body of Richard Hind. Francis Jeffrey. FaBoEE; OxBoLi

(On Richard Hind.) FaBoCo

Here lies the body of Sir John Guise. *Unknown.* FaBoEE

Here lies the body of this world. Epitaph on the World. Henry David Thoreau. FF; HeIP

Here lies the body of W. W. On William Wilson, Tailor. *Unknown*. FaBoEE

Here lies the body of William Jones. Epitaph on William Jones. *Unknown*. FaBoEE

Here lies the corpse of Doctor Chard. *Unknown*. FaBoEE

Here lies the corpse of William Prynne. On William Prynne. Samuel Butler. FaBoEE

Here lies the Devil—ask no other name. On a Lord. Samuel Taylor Coleridge. FaBoCo; FiBHP

Here lies the flesh that tried. Louise Driscoll. WGRP

Here lies the good old knight Sir Harry. Epitaph for Sir Henry Lee. *Unknown*. FaBoEE

Here lies the great. False marble, where? *Unknown*. FaBoEE

Here lies, the Lord have mercy upon her. Upon One of the Maids of Honour to Queen Elizabeth. John Hoskyns. FaBoEE

Here lies the man that madly slain. John Hoskyns. FaBoEE

Here lies the man who in life. On a Contentious Companion. John Hoskyns. FaBoEE

Here lies the man who stripp'd Sin bare. Ebenezer Elliott. FaBoEE

Here lies the noble warrior that never blunted sword. Epitaph on the Earl of Leicester. Sir Walter Ralegh. RB; SiPS

Here lies the poet Wolker, lover of the world. Jiri Wolker, *tr. by* Karl W. Deutsch. WaaP

Here lies the preacher, judge, and poet, Peter. On Peter Robinson. Francis Jeffrey. FaBoCo; FaBoEE; NBLV
(Epitaph on Peter Robinson.) OxBoLi

Here lies the purple sleeping and here lie. To a Dead Actress. Luis de Sandoval y Zapata, *tr. by* Samuel Beckett. MexPo

Here lies the Reverend Jonathan Doe. On the Reverend Jonathan Doe. *Unknown*. ChTr; FaBoEE

Here lies the street of the three balls. To an Avenue Sport. Helen Johnson Collins. PoNe

Here lies Thomas Logge—a Rascally Dogge. Thomas Logge. Walter de la Mare. FaBoEE

Here lies to each her parent's ruth. On My First Daughter. Ben Jonson. EBEV; FaBoEE; HoPM; InPS; JCP; NAEL-1; NOBE; NoP; OBS; PoE; SeCP; SeCV-1; TEP

Here lies what had not birth, nor shape, nor frame. Epitaph on James Moore Smythe. Pope. FaBoEE

Here lies, whom hound did ne'er pursue. Epitaph on a Hare. William Cowper. FiP; FM; HAP; HeIP; NOEC; NoP; PoEL-3

Here lies Will Smith—and, what's something rarish. On Will Smith. *Unknown*. FaBoCo

Here lies wise and valiant dust. Epitaph on the Earl of Strafford. John Cleveland. FaBoEE; FaBoPV; JCP; MePo; NOBE; OBS; SeCePo; TrGrPo

Here lies with Death auld Grizzel Grimme. Grizzel Grimme. *Unknown*. FaBoEE

Here lies, within his tomb, so calm. On the Clerk of a Country Parish. William Shenstone. FaBoEE

Here lies wrapped up in forty thousand towels. On Queen Caroline's Deathbed. Pope. TW

Here lies wrapped up tight in sod. Epitaph for a Postal Clerk. X. J. Kennedy. NIP; PCP

Here lieth John Cruker, a maker of bellows. The Bellows Maker of Oxford. John Hoskyns. FaBoEE

Here Lieth Love. Thomas Watson. *Fr.* Hecatompathia; or, Passionate Century of Love. EIL
(Love's Grave.) OBSC

Here lieth one, who did most truly prove. On the Oxford Carrier. Milton. NA

"Here lieth One whose name was writ on water!" On Keats. Shelley. FaBoEE

Here lieth the worthy warrior/ Who never bloodied sword. On the Earl of Leicester. *Unknown*. FaBoEE

Here lieth Thom Nick's body. Upon a Fool. John Hoskyns. FaBoEE

Here lieth under this marble ston. *Unknown*. MeEL

Here lith the fresshe flowr of Plantagenet. On the Death of Elizabeth, Queen of Henry VII, and Mother of Henry VIII. *Unknown*. FaBoRV

Here lived the soul enchanted. Poe's Cottage at Fordham. John Henry Boner. AA

Here lives a man, who, by relation. Written over a Gate. John Sheffield. NIP

Here Lives the Jewish People, *sel.* H. Leivick, *tr. fr. Yiddish by* Benjamin *and* Barbara Harshav.
"Towering life of the towering city, The." AYP

Here living and the stone. Duomo, Milan. Raymond Henri. *Fr.* View of the Cathedral. EyDe

Here Lockyer lyes interred, enough his Name. Advertising Epitaph: On One Lockyer, Inventor of a Patent Medicine. *Unknown*. FaBoUs

Here, Lord, Retired, I Bow in Prayer. Matthew Bolles. AH

Here luxury's the common lot. The light. Grasse: The Olive Trees. Richard Wilbur. NAAL-2; NoAM; NOBA; NYBP

Here lyeth he, who was born and cried. On One That Lived Ingloriously. John Hoskyns, *after the Greek of* Simonides. FaBoEE

Here 'mid these leafy walls. Woodland Worship. Ethelwyn Wetherald. CaP

Here, mower, take my shiners bright. The Recruiting Sergeant. *Unknown*. OBET

Here must wee rest; and where else should wee rest? A Serious and a Curious Night-Meditation. Thomas Traherne. SeCP

Here my chameleon muse herself doth change. To His Good Friend, Sir Anthony Cooke. Sir John Davies. *Fr.* The Gulling Sonnets.

Here my meat is, clean and dressed. Epitaph for a Meat-Packer. Guy Owen. CRP

Here Nature holds as in a hollowed hand. The Skylark's Nest. R. H. Long. PoAu-1

Here, newness is all. Or almost all. And like. Day Begins at Governor's Square Mall. Leon Stokesbury. MAYP; MT

Here not the flags, the rhythmic. Neutrality. Sidney Keyes. MoAB; MoBrPo

Here now once more I lie. Tenth Reunion. Edward Steese. GoYe

Here, O lily-white lady mine. The Handsel Ring. George Houghton. AA

Here, O my Lord, I see Thee face to face. Horatius Bonar. *Fr.* This Do in Remembrance of Me. TrPWD

Here often, when a child, I lay reclined. Tennyson. FaBoPP

Here, on the dormant, serrated sides. Fuji. Cees Nooteboom, *tr. by* Scott Rollins. DuIn

Here on the earth's brink. The Fiddler. Martin Buber, *tr. by* Jawaid Awan. VWA

Here on the edge of hell. Harlem. Langston Hughes. PPP
(Puzzled.) UnPo

Here on the heich hill. Stanes. Duncan Glen. PoSH

Here on the hill where my wife and I live. My Wife and I. Saibara, *tr. by* Hiroaki Sato. FCEI

Here on the mellow hill. Autumn Scene. Basil Dowling. BoNaP

Here on this hill hay-making is over. Hay-Making Song: Miyazaki Prefecture. *Unknown, tr. by* Hiroaki Sato. FCEI

Here on this open, ancient book. Diary of a Raccoon. Gertrude Ryder Bennett. GoYe

Here once did sound sweet words, a-spoke. The Vield Path. William Barnes. NOBVV

Here once the evenings sobbed. The Pear-Tree. Iwan Goll, *tr. by* Babette Deutsch *and* Avram Yarmolinsky. TrJP

Here one day, gone the next. Watch for the Ice. Brian Turner. UAS

Here, or not many feet from hence. Certain True Woords Spoken Concerning One Benet Corbett after Her Death. Richard Corbett. SeCP

Here Pause: The Poet Claims at Least This Praise. Wordsworth. EnRP

Here penned within the human fold. The Human Fold. Edwin Muir. LiTM

Here, people buy. Chinatown. Chiang Hsun, *tr. by* Dominic Cheung. IFON

Here ploughshares rot and farmers. Garrison Town. Emanuel Litvinoff. WaP

Here, reader, turn your weeping eyes. The Orator's Epitaph. Lord Brougham. NBLV

Here redbuds like momentary trees. Locus. Robert Hayden. FYAP

Here rests his head upon the lap of earth. Thomas Gray. *Fr.* Elegy Written in a Country Churchyard. FaBoPV

Here Reynolds is laid, and to tell you my mind. Sir Joshua Reynolds. Goldsmith. *Fr.* Retaliation. FaBoEE; NOEC; OBD; SeCePo

Here [*or* How] richly, with ridiculous display. Epitaph on the Politician Himself. Hilaire Belloc. FaBoEE; MoBrPo; NBLV; OBSV
(On a Politician.) TW

Here room and kingly silence keep. By the Pacific Ocean. Joaquin Miller. AA

Here, said the spirit. Science Fiction. Nancy Willard. BLA

Here shadowe lie. Lady Tanfield. TOF

Here she lies, a pretty bud. Upon a Child That Died. Robert Herrick. CaPo; CH; InPK; NoP; OBEV; SeCV-1
(Epitaph Upon a Child that Died.) OBD; OBEV

Here she lies (in bed of spice). Upon a Maid. Robert Herrick. CaPo; ChTr; FaBoCh; FaBoEE; OxBoLi

Here She Stands. Jean-Joseph Rabéarivelo, *tr. fr. French by* Miriam Koshland. PBA

Here She Was Wont to Go. Ben Jonson. *Fr.* The Sad Shepherd. OxBSP
(Aeglamour's Lament.) CH
Here shift the scene, to represent. Swift. *Fr.* Verses on the Death of Doctor Swift [D.S.P.D., Occasioned by Reading a Maxim in Rochefoucauld]. OBD
Here should my wonder dwell, and here my praise. Sir John Denham. *Fr.* Cooper's Hill. NAEL-1
Here sit a shepherd and a shepherdess. The Green Shepherd. Louis Simpson. NePoEA; NYBP
Here sits the Lord Mayor. Mother Goose. OxNR
Here, six years old, by Destiny's crime. Epitaph for Erotion. Martial, *tr. by* James Michie. FaBoEE
Here sleeps at length poor Col, and without screaming. Epitaph on Himself. Samuel Taylor Coleridge. FaBoEE
Here something stubborn comes. Seed Leaves. Richard Wilbur. BoNaP
Here sparrows build upon the trees. My Early Home. John Clare. BoTP; PoLF
Here stand I, for whores as great. *Unknown.* FaBoEE
Here stands a good old apple tree. Apple Wassail. *Unknown.* OBET
Here stood a lofty church—there is a steeple. Pleasant Delusion of a Sumpteous Citty. Sarah Kemble Knight. SCAP
Here stood Hypocrisy, in sober brown. Timothy Dwight. *Fr.* The Triumph of Infidelity. NOCV
(Smooth Divine, The.) AA; WGRP
Here take my picture; though I bid farewell. His Picture. John Donne. *Fr.* Elegies, V. MePo
(Elegie V: His Picture.) MeLP; OBS
Here tame boys fly down the long light of halls. To a Visiting Poet in a College Dormitory. Carolyn Kizer. PoA
Here—that means here, where the cherry blossom wants to be. Here. Paul Celan, *tr. by* Beth Bjorklund. CoAuP
Here the boat set me down, and I wait. Queen of the River. Elizabeth Nannestad. ATNZ; PeNZ
Here the crow starves, here the patient stag. Rannoch, by Glencoe. T. S. Eliot. *Fr.* Landscapes, IV. FaBoPP; NAEL-2; PoSH; RB
Here the delicate dance of silence. Woodtown Manor. John Montague. IPY
Here the eye is inevitably cast. Sakhara. R. A. D. Ford. NOBC
Here the foot prints stop. After Twenty Years. Fadwa Tuquan. PBWP
Here the Frailest Leaves of Me. Walt Whitman. NAAL-1
Here the hangman stops his cart. The Carpenter's Son. A. E. Housman. *Fr.* A Shropshire Lad, XLVII. MoAB; MoBrPo
Here the hills are earth's bones. Asian Desert. Dorothy Wellesley. OBMV
Here the horse-mushrooms make a fairy ring. The Fairy Ring. Andrew Young. ChTr
Here the human past is dim and feeble and alien to us. Haunted Country. Robinson Jeffers. OxBA
Here the jack-hammer jabs into the ocean. Colloquy in Black Rock. Robert Lowell. CAPP; MoAB; MoAmPo; NAAL-2
Here the Messiah lives. Encounter in Safed. Moshe Yungman, *tr. by* Gabriel Preil *and* Howard Schwartz. VWA
Here the oceans twain have waited. Panama. J. J. Roche. PAH
Here the round begins again. A Traveller. J. R. Rowland. CBAP
Here the rude clamour of the sportsman's joy. James Thomson. *Fr.* The Seasons: Autumn. PBBP
Here, then, I come. *Unknown, tr. by* Arthur Waley. BoS
Here then my lists of works. To My Friends. Konstantin Nikolayevich Batyushkov, *tr. by* Alan Myers. AAA
Here, then, we stand, on the Canadian shore. John Hunter-Duvar. *Fr.* De Roberval. CaP
Here they are. The soft eyes open. The Heaven of Animals. James Dickey. CAPP; CoAP; HeIP; LiTM; MT; NAAL-2; NoAM; NOBA; PoE; TAP
Here they are. Think of it. Women Open Cautiously. Deborah Lee. BrSi
Here they come. The Trash Men. Charles Bukowski. NoP
Here they gallop pak, pak. *Unknown, tr. by* Arthur Waley. BoS
Here they lie mottled to the ground unseen. Partidges. John Masefield. OxBTC
Here they went with smock and crook. Forefathers. Edmund Blunden. NOBE; OBEV; OBMV; OxBTC
Here they were all running, running past my heart. Golden Pheasants Flying. Sandor Csoori, *tr. by* Daniel Hoffman. MHuP
Here those of us who really understand. Manhattan. Osbert Lancaster. *Fr.* Afternoons with Baedeker. NOBL
Here through our little world of outward sense. Eternal Moment. "Katherine Hale." CaP
Here time unfastens knot and strap. Glen Rosa. William Jeffrey. PoSH

Here to the leisured side of life. The Lamplighter. "Seumas O'Sullivan." BIrV
Here today. Death. Jeffrey Miller. UL
Here Together Met. Louis Johnson. ATNZ; PeNZ
Here, too, like in Jerusalem. The Jews. Mieczyslaw Jastrun, *tr. by* Isaac Komem. VWA
Here too there are guys like the guys of the Volye. Mangin Street. Berysh Vaynshteyn, *tr. fr. Yiddish by* Benjamin *and* Barbara Harshav. *Fr.* New York Everywhere. AYP
Here tradesmen, 'tis plain, at no roguery stop. London Adulterations. *Unknown.* OBET
Here under leafy bowers. Under Leafy Bowers. Judah al-Harizi. TrJP
Here under the radiant rays of the sun. Facing the Chair. "Hugh MacDiarmid." FaBoMo
Here used to be. The Worship of Cromm Cruaich. *Unknown, tr. fr. Old Irish by* Kuno Meyer. *Fr.* The Voyage of Bran. TIRV
Here war is harmless like a monument. W. H. Auden. *Fr.* Sonnets from China, XII. OBWP
Here was raised. The Plain of Adoration. *Unknown, tr. by* John Montague. BIrV
Here was the sound of water falling only. The Owl. Robert Penn Warren. MoAmPo
Here, watching T.V. Hunting the Dugong. Gladys Cardiff. HATNAP
Here We Are. Raquel Jodorowsky, *tr. fr. Spanish by* Kate Flores. DMH
Here we are all, by day; by night we are hurled. Dreams. Robert Herrick. CaPo; HAP; NAEL-1; OxBSP
Here we are assembled on the bank. Waiting for the Pakeha. Alistair Campbell. ATNZ
"Here we are at the river" I said to no one. The Gift. Dick Lourie. NeAC
Here we are gathering duckweed. *Unknown, tr. by* Arthur Waley. BoS
Here we are, if you have any more. Thomas Middleton. *Fr.* The Changeling, V, iii. PoEL-2
Here we are, picking the first fern-shoots. Song of the Bowmen of Shu. Ezra Pound, *after the Chinese.* OBVE
Here we bring new water. A New Year Carol. *Unknown.* BoTP; CH; OxBoLi
(New Year, The.) OBCP
(New Year's Water.) GBP; OFD
Here we broached the Christmas barrel. The House of Hospitalities. Thomas Hardy. RB
Here we can observe the superior mirages. Traveller's Guide to Antarctica. Adrien Stoutenburg. NYBP
Here we come a-caroling. *Unknown.* FaPON
Here We Come a-Haying. Eunice Close. BoTP
Here We Come a-Piping. *Unknown.* BoTP; CH
Here we come a-wassailing. Wassail Song. *Unknown.* PChr
Here we come again, again, and here we come again! The Children's Carol. Eleanor Farjeon. PChr; RHPC
Here we go a-walking, so softly, so softly. From a Walking Song. Charles Williams. BoTP
Here we go around this ring. Marriage. *Unknown.* AmFP
Here we go dancing jingo-ring. *Unknown. See* Here we go to the jingo ring.
Here we go round ring by ring. *Unknown.* OxNR
Here we go the jingo-ring. The Merry-ma-Tanzie. *Unknown.* GBP ("Here we go dancing jingo-ring.") OxNR
Here we go up, up, up. *Unknown.* BoTP
Here we halt our march, and pitch our tent. The Green Mountain Boys. Bryant. PAH
Here we have the sea of children; here. Geography Lesson. Carol Rumens. FaBoWP
Here we have thirst. An Egyptian Pulled Glass Bottle in the Shape of a Fish. Marianne Moore. PBWP
Here We March All Around in a Ring. *Unknown.* AmFP
Here we sit (every other one) bored. Head Table Wives. Bonnie Jacobson. SoTCo
Here we stan' on the Constitution, by thunder! The Debate in the Sennit. James Russell Lowell. *Fr.* The Biglow Papers: 1st Series, No. V. PAH
Here We Were Born. Marcelino dos Santos, *tr. fr. Portuguese by* Margaret Dickinson. WMBCH
Here We Will Stay. Tawfiq Zayyad, *tr. fr. Arabic by* Sharif Elmusa *and* Charles Doria. MAP
Here were planes. But everything else was gone. Wendling. Coman Leavenworth. *Fr.* Norfolk Memorials, III. LiTA
Here, west of winter, lies the ample flower. Prayer for This Day. Hildegarde Flanner. TrPWD
Here Where Coltrane Is. Michael S. Harper. CAPP; CNA; PoBA
Here, where fecundity of Babel frames. Babylon and Sion (Goa and Lisbon). Luis de Camões, *tr. by* Richard Garnett. AWP

Here where I watch the dew. Hymn to Dispel Hatred at Midnight. Yvor Winters. TW

Here, where men's eyes were empty and as bright. Ghosts of a Lunatic Asylum. Stephen Vincent Benét. AnAmPo

Here, where my father lies under the ornamental plum. Churchyard of St. Mary Magdalene, Old Milton. John Heath-Stubbs. NePoEA

Here where no increase is. Supplication. Josephine Johnson. TrPWD

Here where our Lord once laid his head. Upon the Holy Sepulchre. Richard Crashaw. FaBoEE

Here, where [or when] precipitate Spring with one light bound. A Fiesolan Idyl. Walter Savage Landor. EnRP (Fæsulan Idyl.) SeCePo

Here, where relumed by changing seasons, burn. Roy Campbell. Fr. The Golden Shower. OxBTC

Here where stands the Palace of Yoshinu. Akahito, tr. fr. Japanese. Fr. Manyo Shu. Ma

Here, where summer slips. The Red and the Green. Anne Wilkinson. MoCV

Here, where the baby paddles in the gutter. Lean Street. G. S. Fraser. OxBS

Here, where the breath of the scented-gorse floats through the sun-stained air. Breton Afternoon. Ernest Dowson. OBNC

Here where the fields lie lonely and untended. A Deserted Home. Sidney Royse Lysaght. CH

Here where the lonely glance blows over stone and aloe. Form of Boeotia. Odysseus Elytis, tr. by Edmund Keeley and Philip Sherrard. VMG

Here where the meadows gave ease to tired feet. On One Dying in a Convent. Stephen Lucius Gwynn. TIRV

Here, where the night is clear as sea-water. Lament for a Sailor. Paul Dehn. WaP

Here where the parrots come down. Thomas and Charlie. Peter Wild. AmPA

Here, where the red man swept the leaves away. Frederick Goddard Tuckerman. Fr. Sonnets, IV, ix. NOBA; TAP

Here where the river is slender and small. The Dipper. Phoebe Hesketh. PoSH

Here, where the taut wave hangs. Life's Circumnavigators. W. R. Rodgers. GTBS-P

Here where the wild ducks. Taniha Ome, tr. fr. Japanese. Fr. Manyo Shu. Ma

Here where the wind is always north-north-east. New England. E. A. Robinson. GOA; HeIP; MoAB; MoAmPo; NAAL-2; NOBA; NoP; OxBA; TAP

Here where the wind skins Drumochter. Drumochter. Anne B. Murray. PoSH

Here, where the world is quiet. Swinburne. Fr. The Garden of Proserpine. AWP; BLPA; BLPL; FaBoRV; FaBV; FaPoR; HAP; HeIP; LiTB; NAEL-2; NOBE; NOBVV; NoP; OBNC; PoE; PoEL-5; PoRA; SCV; SeCePo; TrGrPo

Here, where Vespasian's legions struck the sands. Embarcation. Thomas Hardy. BrPo; OBWP

Here where we are, wrapped in the afternoon. Obligations. Jane Cooper. NePoEA-2

Here where you left me alone. Letter from Slough Pond. Isabella Gardner. CAPP

Here within these confines. Redeemer. Kizito Z. Muchemwa. WMBCH

Here X. lies dead, but God's forgiving. J. E. Thorold Rogers. FaBoEE

Here, yes, I am here. Tristesse d'animal. Lauris Edmond. ATNZ

Here you are. The Well-intentioned Question. Wendy Rose. STE

Here you get alarmed at the confusion. Lamberto Pignotti, tr. fr. Italian by Lawrence R. Smith. Fr. Reductions. NItP

Here! You sons of the men. English Thornton. Edgar Lee Masters. Fr. Spoon River Anthology. OxBA

Hereabouts the signs are good. Midsummer. Thomas Kinsella. IPY

Heredity. Thomas Bailey Aldrich. AA

Heredity. Arthur Guiterman. OBAL

Heredity. Thomas Hardy. CTC; EBEV; ImOP; RB

Heredity. Tony Harrison. Fr. The School of Eloquence. NAEL-2; NoAM

Heredity. William Dean Howells. AnAmPo

Here're recorded my birth and marriage. Chronicle of Lima. Antonio Cisneros, tr. by Maureen Ahern and David Tipton. Per

Here's A, B, and C. A Learned Song. Unknown. Fr. Mother Goose's Melody. FaBoUs

Here's a dying invalid. Ozaki Hosai, tr. fr. Japanese by Hiroaki Sato. Fr. One Hundred Haiku in Free Form. FCEI

"Here's a fine bag of meat." Bags of Meat. Thomas Hardy. FM; RB

Here's a good rule of thumb. Reflection on Ingenuity. Ogden Nash. RB

Here's a guessing story. What Is It? H. E. Wilkinson. BoTP

Here's a hand to the boy who has courage. Our Heroes. Phoebe Cary. BLPA

Here's a health to the blacksmith, the best of all fellows. The Blacksmith's Song. Unknown. GBP

Here's a health to the Tackers, my boys. A Health to the Tackers. Unknown. APAS

Here's a health unto His Majesty. A Health unto His Majesty. Jeremy Savile. ChTr

Here's a hotel where even the stairs. Hot Springs. Earle Birney. OxBC

Here's a large one for the lady. The Broom Squire's Song. Unknown. OxNR

Here's a little mouse and. Four III. E. E. Cummings. FaBoMo; TTTS

Here's a man who falls hard asleep. Man Asleep in a Child's Bed. Thomas Lux. AnAn

Here's a mellow cup of tea, golden tea! Barry Pain. Fr. The Poets at Tea, VII. Par

Here's a poor widow from Babylon. Unknown. OxNR

Here's a song. Season Song. Unknown, tr. by Flann O'Brien. RB (Scel Lem Duib.) BIrV

Here's a song of praise for a beautiful world. The Beautiful World. W. Lomax Childress. OHIP

Here's a toast to the snail! The Snail. Giuseppe Giusti, tr. by Nigel Dennis. PFI

Here's a Woman Lived to an Extreme Old Age. "Zelda," tr. fr. Hebrew by Bernhard Frank. MHeP

Here's an example from/ A butterfly. The Example. W. H. Davies. MoBrPo; TrGrPo

Here's an old lady, almost ninety-one. Two Old Ladies. Siegfried Sassoon. OxBTC

Here's Cooper, who's written six volumes to show. Cooper. James Russell Lowell. Fr. A Fable for Critics. NOBA; OxBA; TAP

Here's Finiky Hawkes. Unknown. OxNR

Here's flowers for you. Shakespeare. Fr. The Winter's Tale, IV, iii. GBL
(Flowers of Perdita, The.) FiP
Some Flowers o' the Spring. ChTr

Here's fourteen pills for thirteen pence. From One of Case's Pill-Boxes. John Case. FaBoUs

Here's good wind, here's sweet wind. Song of the Full Catch. Constance Lindsay Skinner. CaP

Here's one in whom Nature feared—faint at such vying. Cardinal Bembo's Epitaph on Raphael. Thomas Hardy, after Pietro Bembo. EyDe; FaBoEE

Here's shade and comfort by this towering tree. Christmas 1942. Eric Irvin. PoAu-2

Here's something folk tales tell. Remember Haiti, Cuba, Vietnam. Andrew Salkey. PBCV

Here's string o' wild geese. Unknown. PBBP

Here's Sulky Sue. Mother Goose. OxNR

Here's the garden she walked across. The Flower's Name. Robert Browning. Fr. Garden Fancies, I. CTC

Here's the mould of a musical bird long passed from light. In a Museum. Thomas Hardy. UnS

Here's the spot. Look around you. Above on the height. Caldwell of Springfield. Bret Harte. PAH

Here's the Tender Coming. Unknown. GBP
(Press-Gang, The.) ChTr

Here's the woman who will make all womankind crystal clear! Another Complaint of Lord Pierrot. Jules Laforgue, tr. by William Jay Smith. CT

Here's to the best of the good. Cowboy's Toast. Dick Gibford. CowP

Here's to the blood, in his mettle and pride. The Cock of the Game. Unknown. OBET

Here's to the Grimsby lads out at the trawling. The Grimsby Lads. John Conolly and Bill Meek. OxBSS

Here's to the maiden of bashful fifteen. Drinking Song. Sheridan. Fr. The School for Scandal. NOIV
(Here's to the Maiden.) ELP
(Song: "Here's to the maiden [or maid] of bashful fifteen.") NOEC; OxBoLi; PoRA

Here's to the man who invented stairs. Stairs. Oliver Herford. FiBHP

Here's to the men who lose! To the Men Who Lose. George L. Scarborough. BLPA

Here's to the poor widow from Babylon. Unknown. BoTP

Here's to the Red of it. A Toast to the Flag. John Jay Daly. OPP; PoLF

Here's to thee, old apple tree. Unknown. OxNR

Here's to your eyes. Toast. Frank Horne. BANP; PoNe

Here's two or three jolly boys. Unknown. OxNR

Here's what I think. The Clock. Felice Holman. GrPl

Here's witts extraction morall and divine. One Presenting a Rare Book to Madame Hull. John Saffin. SCAP

Here's yr young married. Voices. David Michell. UAS

Heretic, The. Bliss Carman. WGRP

Heretics All. Hilaire Belloc. ACP

Heretic's Pilgrimage, A. Eva Gore-Booth. TIRV

Heretic's Tragedy, The. Robert Browning. OAEL-2

Hereto I come to view a voiceless ghost. After a Journey. Thomas Hardy. CMoP; EBEV; ELP; EnLoPo; FaBoPP; GBL; GTBS-P; OBNC; OxBTC; PoE; PoEL-5

Heretse! Baboon. Unknown. PeSA

Hereux Qui, comme Ulysse, A Fait un Beau Voyage. Joachim Du Bellay, tr. fr. French by G. K. Chesterton. Fr. Regrets, XXXI. AWP

Herezsometobaccozhere. We Got Everything We Needed Here and Aint It Something. Unknown, tr. by Jerome Rothenberg and Richard Johnny John. STP

Heriot's Ford. Kipling. PoRA

Heritage. Gwendolyn B. Bennett. AmNP; BANP; BlSi; PoBA

Heritage. Countee Cullen. AmNP; BANP; BPo; FaBV, abr.; HeIP; MoAmPo; NAAL-2; NoAM; NoP; PoBA; TTY

Heritage. Mary Gilmore. CBAP

Heritage. Augustus Young. CIP

Heritage of hopes and fears, An. The Soul. Madison Cawein. AA

Herm whose length measured degrees of heat, The. William Empson. Fr. Bacchus. PoA

Herman Altman. Edgar Lee Masters. Fr. Spoon River Anthology. OxBA

Herman Melville. Conrad Aiken. NoAM; NOBA; TAP

Herman Melville. W. H. Auden. LiTA; OxBA

Herman Moon's Hourbook, sels. Christopher Middleton. NePoEA-2
Abasis.
Ant Sun, The.
Forenoon, The.
Ode on Contemplating Clapham Junction.
Pointed Boots.
Waterloo Bridge.

Hermaphrodite fairy of Kew, A. Unknown. PeHV

Hermaphrodite's Song, The. Lorna Mitchell. BrRo

Hermaphroditus. Swinburne. TEP

Hermaphroditus, a delight, a. Ovid, Meet a Metamorphodite. Jonathan Williams. PoM

Hermes came to me in a dream. I said. Sappho, tr. fr. Greek by Willis Barnstone. BoWoP

Hermes, god/ of crossed sticks. Prayer to Hermes. Robert Creeley. PoM

Hermes, lord of the dead, look down and guard the fathers' power. The Libation Bearers. Aeschylus, tr. by Robert Fagles. NAWM-1

Hermes of the Ways. Hilda Doolittle ("H. D."). LiTA; WPE

Hermetic Bird. Philip Lamantia. VGW

Hermetic Workmen. René Char, tr. fr. French by William Jay Smith. CT

Hermit, The. Eloise Bibb. CBWP-4

Hermit, The. Robert Bly. CAPP

Hermit, The. W. H. Davies. BrPo; MoBrPo

Hermit, The. Hsü Pên, tr. fr. Chinese by Henry H. Hart. RFM

Hermit and the Soul, The. Henrietta Cordelia Ray. CBWP-3

Hermit Cackleberry Brown, on Human Vanity, The. Jonathan Williams. OBAL; PoM

Hermit Feng's Residence on the Lake. Hsü Pen, tr. fr. Chinese by Jonathan Chaves. CoBLCP

Hermit Has a Visitor, The. Maxine W. Kumin. BoWoP

Hermit Hoar. Samuel Johnson. NBLV

Hermit in his cave beside the sea, The. The Hermit and the Soul. Henrietta Cordelia Ray. CBWP-3

Hermit Li's Herb Garden Retreat at T'ung-ch'uan. Hsü Pen, tr. fr. Chinese by Jonathan Chaves. CoBLCP

Hermit Marbán, The. Unknown. NOIV

Hermit Picks Berries, The. Maxine W. Kumin. RFM

Hermit Wakes to Bird Sounds, The. Maxine W. Kumin. GrPl; Psk

Hermit's Song, A ("My heart stirs quietly now to think"). Unknown, tr. fr. Irish by James Simmons. BIrV

Hermit's Song, The. Unknown. See I wish, O Son of the Living God.

Hern flew east, the hern flew west, The. See Heron flew east, the heron flew west, The.

Hernando De Soto. Rosemary and Stephen Vincent Benét. NBLV

Herndon. Silas Weir Mitchell. PAH

Hero, A. Florence Earle Coates. OHIP

Hero, The. Robert Graves. PCP

Hero, The. Marianne Moore. Fr. Part of a Novel, Part of a Poem, Part of a Play. CMoP; NOBA; OxBA; PoA

Hero, The. Siegfried Sassoon. OBWP

Hero, The. Roger Woddis. FaBoPa

Hero and Leander, sels. Thomas Hood. EnRP
Death of Leander, The.
Scylla's Lament.

Hero and Leander, sels. Christopher Marlowe (First and Second Sestiads), completed by George Chapman. AAS (First and Second Sestiads); NoP (First and Second Sestiads); OBSC (First and Second Sestiads)
"Amorous Leander, beautiful and young." Marlowe, fr. First Sestiad. PeHV
Amorous Neptune. Marlowe, fr. Second Sestiad. NOBE
"And now the sun that through the horizon peeps." Marlowe, fr. Second Sestiad. OAEL-1
Bridal Song. Chapman, fr. Fifth Sestiad. NOBE; OBEV
"By this, Leander, being near the land." Marlowe, fr. Second Sestiad. EBEV; ErPo
Epithalamion Teratos. Chapman, fr. Fifth Sestiad. EIL
"Her veil was artificial flowers and leaves." Marlowe, fr. First Sestiad. HoPM
Hero Feels the Shaft of Love. Marlowe, fr. First Sestiad. GBL
It Lies Not in Our Power to Love or Hate. Marlowe, fr. First Sestiad. TrGrPo
(Who Ever Loved, That Loved Not at First Sight?.) BLPL; FaFP; LiTB
"Leander to the envious light." Chapman, fr. Third Sestiad argument.. OAEL-1
Love at First Sight. Marlowe, fr. First Sestiad. NOBE
"New light gives new directions, fortunes new." Chapman, fr. Third Sestiad. OAEL-1
"Now from Leander's place she rose, and found." Chapman, fr. Fourth Sestiad. EBEV
"On Hellespont, guilty of true love's blood." Marlowe, fr. First Sestiad. OAEL-1; PoE; PoEL-2; SeCePo; TEP
Repentance. Chapman, fr. Third Sestiad. OBSC
"So on she goes, and in her idle flight." Marlowe, fr. Second Sestiad. PoE
Wedding of Alcmane and Mya, The. Chapman, fr. Fifth Sestiad. OBSC

Hero and Leander. Joseph S. Newman. FiBHP

Hero does everything nicely and well, The. About the Hero. Mihály Ladányi, tr. by Edwin Morgan. MHuP

Hero Entombed I. Peter Quennell. LiTB

Hero Feels the Shaft of Love. Christopher Marlowe. Fr. Hero and Leander, First Sestiad. GBL

Hero first thought it, The. Truth. "Æ." AnIL; MoBrPo

Hero of Bridgewater, The. Charles L. S. Jones. PAH

Hero of the Commune, The. Margaret Junkin Preston. AA

Hero who to Smyrna bay, The. Letter from Smyrna to His Sisters at Crux-Easton, 1733. Thomas Lisle. OBTV

Herod. A. Leyeles, tr. fr. Yiddish by Benjamin and Barbara Harshav. AYP

Heroes. Robert Creeley. NOBA; NoP; PPP

Heroes, The. Louis Simpson. OBWP

Heroes. Walt Whitman. Fr. Song of Myself, XXXIII and XXXV. AA

Heroes, and kings! your distance keep. Epitaph for One Who Would Not Be Buried in Westminster Abbey. Pope. FaBoEE; OBD

Heroes never tire. General Truths. David Avidan, tr. fr. Hebrew by Warren Bargad and Stanley F. Chyet. Fr. Samson, Our Hero, 1. IP

Heroes paused upon the plain, The. The Byrnies. Thom Gunn. MoP; NePoEA-2; NoAM; OxBTC

Heroes screamed from my fingertips. Bard. Gavin Bantock. FaBoTw

Heroic Age, The. Richard Watson Gilder. AA; OHIP

Heroic and Elegiac Song for the Lost Second Lieutenant of the Albanian Campaign, sels. Odysseus Elytis, tr. fr. Greek by Edmund Keeley and Philip Sherrard. VMG
"For those men night was a more bitter day." Fr. III.
"He was a fine young man. The first day he was born." Fr. VI.
"In the distance crystal bells ring out." Fr. XIII.
"Now that his fatherland has darkened on earth." Fr. VIII.
"Now with a still wind in his quiet hair." Fr. IV.
"Sun, bronze voice, and holy etesian wind." Fr. X.
"There where the sun first dwelt." Fr. I.

Heroic Vengeance. Milton. Fr. Samson Agonistes. OBS

Heroides, sel. Ovid, tr. fr. Latin by George Turberville.
"To Paris that was once her owne though now it be not so." OBVE

Heroique Stanzas, Consecrated to the Glorious Memory of His Most Serene and Renowned Highnesse, Oliver, Late Lord Protector of This Common-Wealth. Dryden. SeCV-2

Heroisms. "Marie." PF

Heron. Philip Booth. NePoEA; Psk

Heron, The. John Lyle Donaghy. NeIP
Heron. Stanley Plumly. AmPA
Heron, The. Theodore Roethke. PDV; RFM
Heron, The. *Unknown. See* Heron flew east, the heron flew west, The.
Heron. Ted Walker. NYBP
Heron, The. Vernon Watkins. GTBS-P; TwCP; UnPo
Heron [*or* Hern] flew east, the heron [*or* hern] flew west, The. The Corpus Christi Carol, The ("Heron flew east, the heron flew west. *Unknown.* GBP
  (Heron, The.) EnSB
  (Knight in the Bower, The.) ChTr
Heron in Swamp. Frances Minturn Howard. GoYe
Heron is harsh with despair. Brenda Chamberlain. NeIP
Heron stalks, The. Sunset at Twin Lake. Anita Endrezze-Danielson. HATNAP
Heron Standing in a River, A. Shotetsu, *tr. fr. Japanese by* Steven D. Carter. WFTW
Heron stands in water where the swamp, The. The Heron. Theodore Roethke. PDV; RFM
Heron Weather. Douglas Crase. NoP
Herons. Robin Blaser. NeAP
Herons, The. Francis Ledwidge. ACP
Hero's Portion. John Montague. NOIV
Herr Bruckner often wandered into church. Lives of the Great Composers. Dana Gioia. EOEF
Herrick's Julia. Helen Smith Bevington. BXAP
Herring. Kenneth Rexroth. *Fr.* A Bestiary. HoPM
Herring and ling! The Red Herring. *Unknown.* FaBoNo
Herring is prolific, The. Herring. Kenneth Rexroth. *Fr.* A Bestiary. HoPM
Herring loves the merry moonlight, The. Sir Walter Scott. *Fr.* The Antiquary, 40. FaBoCh, 1 *st.*
Herring-run was over, The. The long days. The Hayfield. Charles Bruce. *Fr.* The Flowing Summer. CaP
Herring Weir, The. Sir Charles G. D. Roberts. *Fr.* Songs of the Common Day. NOBC
Herrings. Swift. *Fr.* Verses for Fruitwomen.
Herself ("Herself listening to herself, having no name"). John Holmes. HoPM
Hersilia. William Johnson Cory. NOBVV
Hertha. Swinburne. OAEL-2
Hertza. Benjamin Fondane, *tr. fr. French by* Matei Calinescu *and* Willis Barnstone. VWA
Hervé Riel. Robert Browning. BeLS; FaBoBe; GN; MOS; OnMSP
He's a fool that marries at Yule. A Scottish Proverb. *Unknown.* FaBoUs
He's a little dog, with a stubby tail, and a moth-eaten coat of tan. Bum. W. Dayton Wedgefarth. BLPA
He's a little man with a corporation who can say. The Beak. Elizabeth Smither. ATNZ
He's an old grey horse, with his head bowed sadly. The Old Whim Horse. Edward Dyson. CBAP
He's Coming. Mark Van Doren. FaBV
He's dead/ the dog won't have to. Death. William Carlos Williams. NAAL-2; OxBA; VGW
He's Doing Natural Life. Conyus. PoBA
He's gone, and all our plans. To His Love. Ivor Gurney. MMA; NAEL-2; OBWP
He's gone, and Fate admits of no return. Epitaph on the Secretary to the Muses. Jane Barker. FaBoCo
He's Gone Away. *Unknown.* AS
He's gone, I am now sad and lonely. My Johnny. *Unknown.* OBET
He's gone to bed at last, that flaring, glaring. My Stearine Candles. James Henry. NOBVV
He's helping me now—this moment. This Moment. Annie Johnson Flint. BLRP
He's lean/ He's clean. Dry Rock Number. Tina Reid. AIW
He's lost him completely. And he now tries to find. In Despair. C. P. Cavafy, *tr. by* Edmund Keeley *and* Philip Sherrard. PeHV
He's my poor relation and despite everything. To the Memory of a Pre-Incaic Wiseman. Mirko Lauer, *tr. by* David Tipton. Per
He's neither Chinese. A Buddhist Priest. Ho Xuan Huong, *tr. by* Nguyen Ngoc Bich *and* Burton Raffel. PBWP
He's no Apollo Belvedere. Babe Ruth. Damon Runyon. ASP
He's not from some country. What She Said about Her Unfaithful, Estranged Husband. Netumpalliyattan, *tr. by* A. K. Ramanujan. PLW
He's nothing much but fur. A Kitten. Eleanor Farjeon. CRH

He's on my front porch rapping. The Businessman of Alicante. Philip Levine. NaP
He's one of the hard talkers. To a Friend Shot on a Mexican Bus. Daniel Halpern. NAmP
He's out stuck in a bird's craw. Gary Snyder. *Fr.* Myths and Texts: Burning, IV. NaP
He's still among us. Elegy for a Man Who Died and Died. Mamdouh Udwan, *tr. by* May Jayyusi *and* Naomi Shihab Nye. MAP
He's still young—; thirty, but looks younger. Self-Portrait. Frank Bidart. HCAP
He's struttin' sho ernuff. De Drum Majah. Ray Garfield Dandridge. BANP
He's the man—we all recognize. Man Asleep in the Desert. Thomas Lux. LCAP
He's the man who climbs his barn. Man in the Moon. Linda Hogan. HATNAP
He's the reaper, the buyer, the keeper of grand houses. Caravati's Salvage: Richmond, Virginia. Dave Smith. KS
He's very odd, standing on yellow sand. Clown, and All the Sea behind Him. Vincent O'Sullivan. ATNZ
He's walked each path beneath the pines. A Little Landscape by Yen Wen-kuei. Yü Chi, *tr. by* Jonathan Chaves. CoBLCP
Hesiod, 1908. Alexander Mair. GoTS
Hesitant door chain, The. Into Blackness Softly. Mari E. Evans. PoBA
Hesitating Ode. Miklós Radnóti, *tr. fr. Hungarian by* Steven Polgar, Stephen Berg *and* S. J. Marks. LLLT
Hesperia. Swinburne. OBNC
Hesperides, The. Tennyson. OAEL-2
Hesperos, you bring home all the bright dawn disperses. Sappho, *tr. by* Willis Barnstone. BoWoP
Hesperus. John Clare. EBVV; FaBoRV; GTBS-P; NOBVV; OAEL-2
Hesperus' Hymn[e] to Cynthia. Ben Jonson. *See* Cynthia's Revels: Hymn to Diana.
Hesperus' Song. Ben Jonson. *See* Cynthia's Revels: Hymn to Diana.
Hesperus the Bringer. Byron. *See* Don Juan: Evening.
Hesperus! the day is gone. Hesperus. John Clare. EBVV; FaBoRV; GTBS-P; NOBVV; OAEL-2
  (Evening Star, The.) ChTr
Hester. Charles Lamb. EnRP; GTBS; GTBS-P; OBEV
Hester MacDonagh. Jeannette Slocomb Edwards. GoYe
Hetero-sex is best for the man of a serious turn of mind. Marcus Argentarius, *tr. by* Fleur Adcock. PeHV
Heterosexuals can get AIDS too. An Alarming New Development. Ron Schreiber. GLP
"Heureux Qui comme Ulysse." John Manifold. WaaP; WaP
Heureux Qui, comme Ulysse, A Fait un Beau Voyage. Joachim Du Bellay, *tr. fr. French by* G. K. Chesterton. *Fr.* Regrets, XXXI. AWP
Hev ye seen owt o' maw bonnie lad. Maw Bonnie Lad. *Unknown.* GBP
Heve hes Cock Robin. Mother Goose. *See* Who killed Cock [*or* poor] Robin?
Hewel, or Woodpecker, The. Andrew Marvell. *Fr.* Upon Appleton House, to My Lord Fairfax. ChTr
Hex on the Mexican X, A. David McCord. FiBHP
Hexameter and Pentameter. *Unknown.* ChTr; FaBoNo
Hexametra Alexis in Laudem Rosamundi. Robert Greene. *Fr.* Greene's Mourning Garment. ElL; GBL; PoEL-2
Hey Betty Martin. *Unknown.* AS
Hey, boys, joint ahead. Track-lining Song. *Unknown.* AmFP
Hey brother, why do you want me to talk? Kabir, *tr. by* John Stratton Hawley *and* Mark Juergensmeyer. SSI
Hey, Bug! Lilian Moore. RHPC
Hey, crazy!/ when you know I have a husband. *Unknown, tr. fr. Japanese by* Burton Watson. *Fr.* Kangin Shu. FCEI
Hey Derry Derry. Thomas Dekker. *See* Shoemaker's Holiday, The: Drinking Song.
Hey diddle diddle/ And hey diddle dan! Mother Goose. OxNR
Hey [*or* Sing hey], diddle, diddle,/ The cat and the fiddle. Mother Goose. FaBoBe; FaFP; HoPM; OxBoLi; OxNR
Hey diddle diddle/ The physicists fiddle. Paul Dehn. *Fr.* Rhymes for a Modern Nursery. FiBHP
Hey diddle diddle, the cat and the fiddle,/ Bombers come with the moon. Maturity. J. Elgar Owen. WaP
Hey diddle dinkety, poppety, pet. Mother Goose. OxNR
  (Merchants of London, The.) GBP
Hey diddle, dinkety, poppety pet. *Unknown.* BoTP
Hey diddle dout,/ My candle's out. *Unknown.* OxNR
Hey ding a ding. *Unknown.* OxNR
Hey, dorolot, dorolot! *Unknown.* OxNR
"Hey, down a down!" did Dian sing. A Nymph's Disdain of Love. *Unknown.* EiL

Hey Father Death, I'm flying home. Father Death Blues. Allen
Ginsberg. *Fr.* Don't Grow Old. SM
Hey girl, how long you been here? Motown/ Smokey Robinson. Jessica
Hagedorn. BrSi; UL
Hey! hey! by this day! The Unhappy Schoolboy. *Unknown.* OxBChV
Hey, hey, hey, hey/ I will have the whetstone. I Will Have the
Whetstone. *Unknown.* FaBoNo; GBP
Hey-ho-day! me no care a dammee! Negro Song at Cornwall. *Unknown.*
PBCV
Hey-ho, he is splendid! *Unknown, tr. by* Arthur Waley. BoS
Hey-ho Knave; a Catch. *Unknown.* GBP
Hey-How for Hallowe'en. *Unknown.* FaBoCh
(Witches, The.) ChTr
Hey, Joe! Cigarette! Cioccolat'! Cigarette for the Bambino. Gavin
Ewart. WaP
Hey, Johnnie Cope, are ye wauking yet? Johnnie Cope. Adam Skirving.
OxBS
Hey, laddie, hark, to the merry, merry lark. The Sky-Lark's Song. John
Bennett. *Fr.* Master Sky-Lark. AA
Hey let's fight that shaman, let's fight that ghost first & then that shaman.
Ghost & Shaman. *Unknown, tr. by* Franz Boas. STP
Hey, little yellow boy. From a Bus. Malaika Ayo Wangara. NBP
Hey love bird, crying cuckoo. Mirabai, *tr. by* John Stratton Hawley *and*
Mark Juergensmeyer. SSI
Hey, my kitten, my kitten. Mother Goose. OxNR
Hey! My Pony! Eleanor Farjeon. FaPON
Hey Nonny No! *Unknown.* CH; ChTr; EBEV; EIL; OBEV; TrGrPo
(Round, A.) FaBoCh
Hey! now, now, now. Welcome! Our Messiah. *Unknown.* MeEL
Hey! [*or* Hay!] now [*or* nou] the day dawis [*or* daunss]. The Night Is
Near [*or* Neir] Gone. Alexander Montgomerie. GoTS; OBEV;
OxBS
(Hey! Now the Day Dawns.) CH
Hey Qazi. Kabir, *tr. by* John Stratton Hawley *and* Mark Juergensmeyer.
SSI
Hey Robin. Joseph Skipsey. EBVV
Hey, sidewalk pacers. Just for One Day. Lillian Morrison. RHPC
Hey, smoke a cigarette. The Rainy Season. Wu Sheng, *tr. by* Dominic
Cheung. IFON
Hey there poleece. Poem to a Nigger Cop. Bobb Hamilton. TTY
Hey! who's pulverized the sky! Snow Song. Zalman Shne'ur, *tr. by*
Bernhard Frank. MHeP
Hey, women, spotted with typhus and riddled with rakes of fingers. Perets
Markish, *tr. by* Leonard Wolf. PeBMYV
Hey, Wully Wine. *Unknown.* CH
Hey, young bride! Teasing Song. Princess Magogo, *tr. by* D. K.
Rycroft. WTO
Hi! Walter de la Mare. OBD
Hi De Buckras Hi! Grace Nichols. AIW
Hi-Fashion Girl. Elaine Equi. UL
Hi, Jimmis, nagah, matty man, you deh 'pon um again. Deh 'Pon Um
Again. Michael McTurk. PBCV
Hi, mawning Susie, how yuh is? yuh get de small-pox yet? Lizzie
Discourses on the Small-Pox. Edward Cordle. PBCV
Hi there. My name is George. Notes on the Peanut. June Jordan.
NoAM
Hi thi, Jenny, lyev thi loom. Coaxin'. Joseph Ramsbottom. PF
Hi! we shout with voice ecstatic. Roundel in the Rain. *Unknown.*
FiBHP
Hialmar Speaks to the Raven. Charles Leconte de Lisle, *tr. fr. French by*
James Elroy Flecker. AWP
Hiatus. Margaret Avison. HAP
Hiawatha Revisited. George A. Strong. *See* Song of Milkanwatha, The:
Modern Hiawatha, The.
Hiawatha's Brothers. Longfellow. *Fr.* The Song of Hiawatha. BoTP
Hiawatha's Canoe. Longfellow. *See* Song of Hiawatha, The:
Give me of your bark, O Birch-tree!
Hiawatha's Childhood. Longfellow. *Fr.* The Song of Hiawatha, III.
FaPON; OHFP; WBLP
("At the door on summer evenings.") BoTP
("Downward through the evening twilight.") FaBV
Hiawatha's Photographing. "Lewis Carroll." BXAP; CenHV; FaBoCo;
FaBoPa; FiBHP; NOBL
Hiawatha's Wooing. Longfellow. *Fr.* The Song of Hiawatha, X. BeLS
Hibakusha's Letter (1955), The. David Mura. BrSi
Hibernia. Stuart Howard-Jones. NOBL
Hibernia's Helicon is dry. William Dunkin. *Fr.* An Epistle to Robert
Nugent, Esq. with a Picture of Doctor Swift in Old Age. NOEC
Hibiscus and Salvia Flowers. D. H. Lawrence. FaBoPV
Hibiscus come to tiny bloom, The. The Magnolia Flower. Wei Ch'eng-
pan, *tr. by* Lois Fusek. ATF

Hibiscus on the Sleeping Shores. Wallace Stevens. InPS
Hibou et Minou allèrent à la mer. Le Hibou et la Poussiquette. Francis
Steegmuller. NYBP
Hic, Hoc, the Carrion Crow. *Unknown.* OxBoLi
Hic Jacet. Louise Chandler Moulton. AA
Hic jacet Tom Shorthose. *Unknown.* FaBoEE
Hic liber ad me pertinet. Robert Barclay. FaBoUs
Hic liber est meus. To the Borrower of This Book. Samuel Showell, Jr.
FaBoUs
"Hic Me, Pater Optime, Fessam Deseris." Lucy Catlin Robinson. AA
Hic Vir, Hic Est. Charles Stuart Calverley. OxBoLi
Hicche-Hykeres Tale, The. W. F. N. Watson. BXAP
Hick-a-more, Hack-a-more. Mother Goose. OxNR
Hickenthrift and Hickenloop. X. J. Kennedy. WSC
Hickety, pickety. *Unknown.* BoTP
Hickety pickety i sillickety [*or* i-silicity]. *Unknown.* GBP; OxNR
Hickety, pickety, my black hen. Mother Goose. *See* Higgledy, piggledy,
my black hen.
Hickory, dickory, dock. Mother Goose. FaBoBe; FaFP; OxNR
Hickup, hickup, go away. Charm: Hiccups. *Unknown.* FaBoUs
Hid by the august foliage and fruit. To a Chameleon. Marianne Moore.
GoYe
Hid in a maze of quaintly-fashioned things. A Wedgewood Bowl.
Frances Beatrice Taylor. CaP
Hid near a lily-spangled stream. Balthasar. Charles Spear. ATNZ
Hidden Bow. Mordecai Temkin, *tr. fr. Hebrew by* Jeremy Garber.
VWA
Hidden entrance to an overgrown path. Raymondsville. Christine Busta,
tr. by Beth Bjorklund. CoAuP
Hidden Essence. Henrietta Cordelia Ray. CBWP-3
Hidden Flame. Dryden. *See* Secret Love; or, The Maiden Queen:
I feed a flame within, which so torments me.
Hidden immortal. Near a Waterfall at Ryumon. Lady Ise, *tr. by* Etsuko
Terasaki *and* Irma Brandeis. BoWoP
Hidden in the library at dusk. Point of Origin. Dan Pagis, *tr. by*
Bernhard Frank. MHeP
Hidden in water plants, a frog. Ryusui, *tr. by* Hiroaki Sato. FCEI
Hidden in wonder and snow, or sudden with summer. Laurentian Shield.
F. R. Scott. NOBC; OBCV
Hidden Justice. Gerald Stern. KS
Hidden Line, The. Joseph Addison Alexander. BLPA
Hidden lovers' woes. His Own True Wife. Wolfram von Eschenbach,
tr. by Jethro Bithell. AWP
Hidden Message, A. Kevin Ireland. ATNZ
Hidden monastery garden, poppies, drowsy noontime, The. Siege. Dan
Pagis, *tr. by* Warren Bargad *and* Stanley F. Chyet. IP
Hidden Name. Victor Segalen, *tr. fr. French by* Nathaniel Tarn.
RHTwFP
Hidden People and the Star People, The. *Unknown, tr. fr. Osage Indian
by* Barbara Tedlock. *Fr.* Ceremony of Sending. STP
Hidden Reason. Margot Jordan. WS
Hidden strength, A. Chastity. Milton. *Fr.* Comus; a Masque Presented
at Ludlow Castle. OBS
Hidden Things. Constantine P. Cavafy, *tr. fr. Greek by* Edmund Keeley
and Philip Sherrard. VMG
Hidden Weaver, The. Odell Shepard. WGRP
Hide-and-Go-Seek. Jim Simmerman. BLA
Hide and Seek. Phyllis Drayson. BoTP
Hide and Seek. Robert Graves. NTCP
Hide-and-Seek. Vasco Popa, *tr. fr. Serbo-Croatian by* Anne Pennington.
Fr. Games. RB
Hide and Seek. A. B. Shiffrin. RAR
Hide and Seek. Penelope Shuttle. NPo
Hide-and-Seek Shadow. Margaret Hillert. RAR
Hide in the Heart. Lloyd Frankenberg. LiTA
Hide not, hide not. The Rousing Canoe Song. Hermia Harris Fraser.
CaP
Hide not thy love and myne shal bee. Pure Simple Love. Aurelian
Townshend. SeCP
Hide not thy talent in the earth. The One Talent. William Cutler. PWR
Hide of My Mother, The. Edward Dorn. NeAP
Hide this one night thy crescent, kindly Moon. To the Moon. Pierre de
Ronsard, *tr. by* Andrew Lang. AWP
Hide Thou Me. *Unknown.* AmFP
Hidebehind, The. Michael Rosen. AmMo
Hides. Berysh Vaynshteyn, *tr. fr. Yiddish by* Benjamin *and* Barbara
Harshav. AYP
Hidesong. Aig Higo. TTY
Hiding. Dorothy Aldis. FaPON
Hiding in the/ cucumber garden. Vidya, *tr. by* W. S. Merwin *and* J.
Moussaieff Masson. WPOW

Hiding Our Love. Carolyn Kizer. UnAS
Hiding Place. Richard Armour. NIP
Hiding tuft, a green-barked yew-tree, A. The Hermit's Song. *Unknown, tr. by* Frank O'Connor. KiLC
Hie Away, Hie Away. Sir Walter Scott. *Fr.* Waverley, 12. EnRP; MoShBr
Hie, hie, says Anthony. Mother Goose. OxNR
Hie prudence, and wirking mervelous, The. The Preiching of the Swallow. Robert Henryson. OxBS
Hie to the market, Jenny come trot. *Unknown.* OxNR
Hie upon Hielands [*or* High up on highland*or* High upon Highlands]. Bonnie [*or* Bonny] George [*or* James] Campbell. *Unknown.* AmFP; CH; ELP; EnRP; ESPB; FaBoBa; GBP; GoTS; NoP; OxBB, *with music;* OxBoli
("O it's up in the Highlands.") ESPB
Hiems. Shakespeare. *See* Love's Labour's Lost: When Icicles Hang by the Wall.
Hierarchie of the Blessed Angles, sel. Thomas Heywood.
"I sought thee round about, O thou my God!" WGRP
Hieroglyph. Paul Auster. VWA
Hieroglyphics of the Life of Man, sel. Francis Quarles.
"Forbear, fond taper: what thou seek'st, is fire." OBD
Hierusalem, my happy [*or* happie] home. *Unknown.* NOBE; OBD; PoEL-2; TOF
(New Jerusalem, The.) OBEV
Higgledy-piggledy/ Andrea Doria. Last Words. John Hollander. OBAL
Higgledy-piggledy/ Anna Karenina. The Russian Soul II. John Hollander. NBLV
Higgledy-piggledy/ Archangel Raphael. Paradise Lost, Book V: An Epitome. Anthony Hecht. NBLV
Higgledy-piggledy,/ Benjamin Harrison. Historical Reflections. John Hollander. OBAL
Higgledy-piggledy/ Franklin D. Roosevelt. Danish Wit. John Hollander. NBLV
Higgledy, piggledy/ Gloria Vanderbilt. Poor Kid. William Cole. OBAL
Higgledy-piggledy/ Heliogabalus. Heliogabalus. John Hollander. NBLV; OBAL
Higgledy-piggledy/ John Simon Guggenheim. No Foundation. John Hollander. OBAL
Higgledy-piggledy/ Josephine Bonaparte. Appearance and Reality. John Hollander. OBAL
Higgledy-piggledy/ Ludwig van Beethoven. E. William Seaman. WeW
Higgledy-piggledy/ Mme. de Maintenon. Firmness. Anthony Hecht. OBAL
Higgledy-piggledy/ President Jefferson. Twilight's Last Gleaming. Arthur W. Monks. NIP; OFD
Higgledy-piggledy/ Ralph Waldo Emerson. From the Grove Press. Anthony Hecht. OBAL
Higgledy-piggledy/ Thomas Stearns Eliot. Vice. Anthony Hecht. OBAL
Higgledy-Piggledy here we lie. Charade. *Unknown.* OxNR
Higgledy, piggledy, my black hen. Mother Goose. FaBoBe; PBBP
(Hickety, pickety, my black hen.) OxNR
Higglety, Pigglety, Pop! Samuel Goodrich. OxNR; RAR; RHPC
High above hate I dwell. Sanctuary. Louise Imogen Guiney. AA
High above Suilven an eagle soars. Assynt. Alan Gilchrist. PoSH
High adventure. Maps. Dorothy Brown Thompson. RHPC
High amid/ gothic rocks the altar stands. Sub Specie Aeternitatis. Robert Hayden. AmPP
High and solemn mountains guard Riouppéroux. Riouppéroux. James Elroy Flecker. OBEV; OBTV
High bare field, brown from the plough, and borne, A. The Potato Harvest. Sir Charles G. D. Roberts. CaP; NOBC
High blow tousled all the yachts, A. September: Last Day at the Beach. Richard Tillinghast. GOYP
High Bridge above the Tagus River at Toledo, The. William Carlos Williams. CTC
High Brow. Robert Fitch. SD
High-coiffed the muse in green brocade. Remark. Charles Spear. PeNZ
High-cool/2. James Cunningham. JB
High Country Weather. James Keir Baxter. ATNZ
High diddle ding, did you hear the bells ring? *Unknown. See* High ding a ding. . . .
High ding a ding, and ho ding a ding. The Parliament Soldiers. *Unknown.* GBP
("High diddle ding, did you hear the bells ring?") OxNR
High Diver. Robert Francis. NePoAm; SD
High Fidelity. Thom Gunn. PoA
High Flight. John Gillespie Magee, Jr. FaFP; FaPON
High Germany. Edward Shanks. OBMV
High Germany. *Unknown.* OBET; WaaP

High grew the snow beneath the low-hung sky. The Axe of the Pioneer. Isabella Valancy Crawford. CaP
High heaven had a firm charge. *Unknown, tr. by* Arthur Waley. BoS
High Heels. Ron Padgett. UL
High, high and far away. Buzzard. Michael Daugherty. PoSH
High, high in the branches. The Ferns. Gene Baro. RHPC
High Hills, The. Ivor Gurney. FaBoPP
High in the afternoon the dove. Kendrick Smithyman. *Fr.* Considerations. ATNZ
High in the breathless hall the minstrel sate. Song at the Feast of Brougham Castle. Wordsworth. EnRP
High in the esteem of He. Hind and Her Mother. "Al-Akhtal al-Saghir," *tr. by* Issa Boullata *and* Thomas G. Ezzy. MAP
High in the pine-tree. *Unknown.* BoTP
High in the sanctuary. Ishikawa Toshitari, *tr. fr. Japanese. Fr.* Manyo Shu. Ma
High in the woodland, on the mountain-side. The Ant-Heap. A. C. Benson. EBVV
High Island. Richard Murphy. CIP; NOIV
High Jumper. Don Welch. TSL
High June. Catherine A. Morin. BoTP
High-loping Cowboy, The. Curley W. Fletcher. AiP
High-lying, sea-blown stretches of green turf. The Beds of Fleur-de-Lys. Charlotte Perkins Gilman. AA
High Midnight was garlanding her head, The. Moonlight. Jacques Tahureau, *tr. by* Andrew Lang. AWP
High noon. Water Glass. Jutta Schutting, *tr. by* Beth Bjorklund. CoAuP
High o'er his moldering castle walls. A Voice from the Invisible World. Goethe, *tr. by* James Clarence Mangan. AWP
High o'er the Hills. William Walker. AH
High on a mountain's highest ridge. Wordsworth. *Fr.* The Thorn. Par
High on a ridge of tiles. Maurice James Craig. NeIP
High on a slope in New Guinea. The Man in the Dead Machine. Donald Hall. CAPP
High on a throne of royal state, which far. Milton. *Fr.* Paradise Lost, *Bk.* II, *ll.* 1–42. NIP; OAEL-1, *ll.* 1–309.
High on Ben Alder on wintery night. Night Expedition from Ben Alder Cottage. Roger A. Redfern. PoSH
High on his figured couch beyond the waves. Theseus and Ariadne. Robert Graves. HAP
High on his stockroom ladder like a dunce. Playboy. Richard Wilbur. FF; MoP; NIP; NoAM; NOBA; NoP; WeW
High on Rodborough. The Ballad of Rodborough Common. Jenny Joseph. NPo
High on the dove-cot. Doves. E. J. Falconer. BoTP
High on the Hog. Julia Fields. CNA
High on the mountain of sunrise where standeth the Temple of Sebek. He Knoweth the Souls of the West. *Unknown, tr. fr. Egyptian by* Robert Hillyer. *Fr.* Book of the Dead. AWP
High on the peak of Mikasa. Akahito, *tr. fr. Japanese by* Geoffrey Bownas *and* Anthony Thwaite. *Fr.* Manyo Shu. PeBJV
High on the wall that holds Jerusalem. G. K. Chesterton. OBTV
High over Mecca Allah's prophet's corpse. Dissatisfaction with Metaphysics. William Empson. CMoP
High overhead. Thomas Edward Brown. NOBVV
High pink wall; plaster in map shapes peeling, A. Blue Arm. Bernard Spencer. NoAM
High-placed above me the branches quiver. The Lost. *Malay Oral Tradition, tr. by* R. J. Wilkinson *and* R. O. Winstedt. WTO
High Poetic Circles. Gavin Ewart. NPo
High poetry and low. Wallace Stevens. PoA
High poets are gone, The. For the Family of Cuchonnacht O Dalaigh. David O'Bruadair, *tr. by* Thomas Kinsella. NOIV
High-priced jeans, the new car, The—she got what. A Teen-Ager. W. D. Snodgrass. TW
High Priest, The. *Unknown, tr. fr. Hebrew by* Arthur Davis. TrJP
High Priests of telescopes and cyclotrons, The. Ode to Terminus. W. H. Auden. HAP
High Renaissance. George Starbuck. NBLV; OBAL
High rise the pole-banners. *Unknown, tr. by* Arthur Waley. BoS
High-speed metal snake switches its tail, A. The Chief of the West, Darkling. David Knight. MoCV
High-spirited friend. The Noble Balm. Ben Jonson. OBEV
High spurt the waters of that fountain. *Unknown, tr. by* Arthur Waley. BoS
High Stick. Billy Collins. ASP
High stretched upon the swinging yard. Disguises. Thomas Edward Brown. WGRP
High Summer. Ebenezer Jones. NOBVV
High Summer on the Mountains. Idris Davies. OxBTC

High summer's sheen upon all things. The Web. Theodore Weiss. CoAP

High the vanes of Shrewsbury gleam. The Welsh Marches. A. E. Housman. FaBoTw

High Tide. Jean Starr Untermeyer. MoAmPo

High Tide at Gettysburg, The. Will Henry Thompson. AA; AnAmPo; BeLS; BLPA; FaBoBe; PAH

High Tide on the Coast of Lincolnshire (1571), The. Jean Ingelow. BeLS; EBVV; FaBoPP; GN; Mes, abr.; OnMSP

High to Low. Langston Hughes. HCAP

High-toned Old Christian Woman, A. Wallace Stevens. CMoP; MoP; NAAL-2; NoAM; NOBA; PPP; TAP

High-toned Old Fascist Gentleman, A. William Zaranka. BXAP

High towered the palace and its massive pile. Palace of the Gnomes. Maria Gowen Brooks. Fr. Zophiël. AA

High towers the grass where once we'd meet and wander. Parting. Malay Oral Tradition, tr. by R. J. Wilkinson and R. O. Winstedt. WTO

High trees grieve like the sea's water, The. In Wicklow. Rhoda Coghill. NeIP

High up above/ the surface of the water. Irises in a Marsh. Tamemasa, tr. by Steven D. Carter. WFTW

High up among the mountains, through a lovely grove of cedars. Bears. Arthur Guiterman. PoRA

High up, birches have a homely aspect. Stopping by Shadows. Robin Fulton. PoSH

High up, I/ see deer circle. On Foinaven. Donald G. Saunders. PoSH

High up in the courts of heaven today. A Little Dog-Angel. Norah M. Holland. PoLF

High Up on Suilven. Norman MacCaig. PoSH

High upon the hillside where the shadows play. Skippets, the Bad One. Christine E. Bradley. BoTP

High walls and huge the body may confine. Freedom for the Mind. William Lloyd Garrison. AA; FaBoBe

High walls. . . of stones. Aran Islands. Irving Layton. NeAC

High waves of wind. New York Landscapes. J. L. Teller, tr. by Benjamin and Barbara Harshav. AYP

High waves that come riding across the sea. Raimbaut de Vaqueiras, tr. by Paul Blackburn. Pro

High Wheat Country. Elijah L. Jacobs. AmFN

High Wind, The. Unknown. See Arthur O'Bower has broken his bands.

High Wind at the Battery. Ralph Pomeroy. NYBP

High wind. . . They turn their backs to it, and push. Glasgow Schoolboys, Running Backwards. Douglas Dunn. OxBC

High Windows. Philip Larkin. FaBoMo; NAEL-2; NoAM

High Wonders. Naomi Marks. BXAP

High-yellow of my heart, with breasts like tangerines. The Peasant Declares His Love. Emile Roumer, tr. by John Peale Bishop. ErPo; TTY

Higher. Unknown. FiBHP

Higher/ clarion calls of form. My Jacobean Fatigues. Miron Bialoszewski, tr. by Czeslaw Milosz. PwPP

Higher Catechism, The. Sam Walter Foss. WGRP

Higher Empiricism, The. Francis C. Golffing. PoA

Higher Good, The. Theodore Parker. AA; FaBoBe

Higher Love. Jeff Wright. UL

Higher Pantheism, The. Tennyson. WGRP

Higher Pantheism in a Nutshell, The. Swinburne. Fr. The Heptalogia. BXAP; FaBoNo; NA; Par

Higher than a house,/ Higher than a tree. Mother Goose. OxNR

Higher than gull's nests, higher than children go. Rock Climbing. Jane Cooper. NMM

Higher than heaven they sit. The Hope of the World. Sir William Watson. WGRP

Highest Divinity. Unknown, tr. fr. Hebrew by Israel Zangwill. TrJP

Highest of Immortals bright. Indra, the Supreme God. Unknown, tr. fr. Sanskrit by Romesh Dutt. Fr. Vedic Hymns. AWP

Highland Cattle, sel. Dinah Maria Mulock Craik. "Down the wintry mountain." GN

Highland Glen near Loch Ericht, A. Arthur Hugh Clough. See Bothie of Tober-na-Vuolich, The: There is a stream, I name not its name.

Highland Harry Back Again. At. to Burns. EBEV

Highland Loves. Rennie McOwan. PoSH

Highland Mary. Burns. AWP; EnRP; GTBS; GTBS-P; OBEV; TrGrPo; WBLP

Highland Mary. Mary Weston Fordham. CBWP-2

Highland Region. Victor Price. PoSH

Highland Shooting Lodge. Maurice Lindsay. PoSH

Highland Tinker, The. Unknown. CoMu

Highlandmen hae a' come down, The. The Lady of Arngosk. Unknown. ESPB

Highlands of Hudson! ye saw them pass. The Storming of Stony Point. Arthur Guiterman. PAH

Highly Renowned. Gusai and others, tr. fr. Japanese by Hiroaki Sato. FCEI

Highty, tighty, paradighty, clothed [all] in green. Unknown. ChTr; OxNR

Highway, The. William Channing Gannett. WGRP

Highway, The. W. S. Merwin. PoA

Highway, The. Sir Philip Sidney. See Astrophel and Stella, LXXXIV.

Highway ended, The. 7 Years from Somewhere. Philip Levine. AnAn

Highway forever draws away, The. Lily. Rosanna Warren. MAYP

Highway of Shinanu, The. Unknown. Fr. Manyo Shu. Ma

Highway Patrol Stops Me, Going Too Slow. Robert Peterson. NeAC

"Highway, since you my chief Parnassus be." Sir Philip Sidney. Fr. Astrophel and Stella, LXXXIV. EIL; OBSC

(Highway, The.) LiTB; OBEV

Highway Single Sun. Tristan Tzara, tr. fr. French by Charles Simic and Michael Benedikt. POS

Highway to Glory Song. W. H. Auden. Fr. Man of La Mancha. AnAn

Highway to Shinano, The. Unknown, tr. fr. Japanese by Geoffrey Bownas and Anthony Thwaite. Fr. Manyo Shu. PeBJV

Highwayman, The. Alfred Noyes. BeLS; FaBV; FaFP; FaPON, abr.; FPL; OBNV; OHFP; PoLF

Highwaymen, The. John Gay. Fr. The Beggar's Opera, II, i. WiR

Hike, The. Neil Weiss. SD

Hiking. Joseph Bruchac. CDW

Hiking a levee through the salt marsh. Wings and Seeds. Sandra McPherson. GeTw

Hiking Up Hieizan with Alam Lau/Buddha's Birthday 1974. Garrett Kaoru Hongo. BrSi

Hilaire Belloc. Humbert Wolfe. FaBoEE

Hilas, o Hilas, why sit we mute. Chloris and Hilas. Made to a Saraban. Edmund Waller. SeCV-1

Hill, The. Rupert Brooke. MoBrPo; OxBTC; Son

Hill, The. Robert Creeley. CRP

Hill, A. Anthony Hecht. CoAP; NYBP

Hill, The. Horace Holley. WGRP

Hill, The. Edgar Lee Masters. Fr. Spoon River Anthology. CMoP; FYAP; LiTA; LiTM; NoAM; NOBA; OxBA; TAP

Hill above the Mine, The. Malcolm Cowley. SaC

Hill asleep, The. Wakayama Bokusui, tr. by Geoffrey Bownas and Anthony Thwaite. PeBJV

Hill-billy, hill-billy come to buy. Pedlar. Confucius, tr. fr. Chinese by Ezra Pound. Fr. Wei Wind. CTC; OBVE

Hill Burns, The. Nan Shepherd. PoSH

Hill Farmer Speaks, The. R. S. Thomas. GTBS-P; OBWVE

Hill field: under the moon. Naito Meisetsu, tr. by Geoffrey Bownas and Anthony Thwaite. PeBJV

Hill Love. James Macmillan. PoSH

Hill of Beans, A. Rita Dove. BLA

Hill of Intrusion, The. William Sydney Graham. NePoEA

"Hill of Jews," says one. Montjuich. Philip Levine. AnAn

Hill of secluded Hatsuse, The. Unknown. Fr. Manyo Shu. Ma

Hill of the Graces, The. Spenser. Fr. The Faerie Queene, VI, 10. NOBE

Hill of Zion yields, The. Mount Zion. Unknown. AmFP

Hill People. Harriet Gray Blackwell. AmFN

Hill Summit, The. Dante Gabriel Rossetti. Fr. The House of Life, LXX. NoP

Hill, the Frenzy, The. Alain Delahaye, tr. fr. French by Anthony Barnett. RHTwFP

Hill Wife, The ("One ought not to have to care."), sels. Robert Frost. CMoP; HAP; InPS; LiTM; NoP

House Fear. VGW; WSC

Impulse, The. HoPM

Loneliness. VGW

Hill you may say is a hill; take a hill, A. Object Lesson. Paul Henderson. ATNZ

Hillcrest. E. A. Robinson. MoAB; OxBA

Hillman Looks Back, The. Rennie McOwan. PoSH

Hills, The. Frances Cornford. MoBrPo

Hills. Robin Munro. PoSH

Hills afloat across the water are. Lamentation on Ninety-Mile Beach. Barry Mitcalfe. PeNZ

Hills and rivers of the lowland country, The. A Protest in the Sixth Year of Ch'ien Fu. Ts'ao Sung, tr. by Arthur Waley. FaBV

Hills and the Sea, The. Wilfred Campbell. CaP

Hills are calling me from care and reason, The. Bright Abandon. Tessa Sweazy Webb. GoYe

Hills are stark, their outlines hard with frost, The. Aviemore. Janet Waller. PoSH

Hills are white, but not with snow, The. An Orchard at Avignon. Agnes Mary Frances Robinson. NOBVV; OBTV

Hills are wroth, The; the stones have scored you bitterly. To a Young Girl Leaving the Hill Country. Arna Bontemps. CDC

Hills Brothers Coffee. Luci Tapahonso. STE

Hills, I told them; and water, and the clear air, The. Instead of an Interview. Fleur Adcock. OBTV

Hills in emerald robes of richest dye, The. Among the Berkshire Hills. Henrietta Cordelia Ray. CBWP-3

Hills in the fog, under an ash blue sky, The. November Morning Near Abingdon. Valery Larbaud, tr. by Ron Padgett and Bill Zavatsky. RHTwFP

Hills moved. I watched their shadows. Beetle on the Shasta Daylight. Shirley Kaufman. NYBP; WPE

Hills of God, The. A. A. Buist. PoSH

Hills of God, Break Forth in Singing. John Wright Buckham. AH

Hills of Pomeroy, The. Ewart Milne. NeIP

Hills of Rest, The. Albert Bigelow Paine. WGRP

Hills of Salt. Dahlia Ravikovich, tr. fr. Hebrew by Chana Bloch. WPOW

Hills of Sewanee, The. George Marion McClellan. BANP

Hills of the Middle Distance. Archie Mitchell. PoSH

Hills of Tsa la gi, The. Robert J. Conley. STE

Hills of Zion, The. The Four of Them. Yehuda Karni. VWA, tr. by Jeremy Garbers

Hills picking up the/ moonlight like. Nina Cassian, tr. by Stavros Deligiorgis. BoWoP

Hills step off into whiteness, The. Sheep in Fog. Sylvia Plath. FaBoWP; HCAP; LCAP; NaP

Hills stirring under their woven, The. Goethe's Blues. Denise Levertov. FaBoWP

Hills turn hugely in their sleep, The. Robert Hillyer. Fr. Prothalamion. MoAmPo

Hills yet hills, and still the yellow town, The. Naples Again. Arthur Freeman. NYBP

Hillside. Alexander Craig. PoAu-2

Hillside Pause. Catharine Morris Wright. GoYe

Hillside Thaw, A. Robert Frost. CMoP

Hillstones pebbles and boulders. Mountain Sculpture. James Will. PoSH

Hilltop, The. Richard Hugo. CAPP

Hilo, Hanakahi, rain rustling lehua. Unknown, tr. by S. H. Elbert and N. Mahoe. WTO

Him that I love I wish to be. Even. Anne Morrow Lindbergh. AiP

Himalaya Days. Gyorgy Raba, tr. fr. Hungarian by Jascha Kessler. FOC

Himalayan Balsam. Anne Stevenson. FaBoWP

Himself, sel. Edwin John Ellis.
   "At Golgotha I stood alone." OBMV

"Himself on the Wood there," says one. Cross Talk. Cyril Cusack. TIRV

Hind and Her Mother. "Al-Akhtal al-Saghir," tr. fr. Arabic by Issa Boullata and Thomas G. Ezzy. MAP

Hind and the Panther, The, sels. Dryden.
   "But gratious [or gracious] God, how well dost thou provide." Fr. I. TrPWD
   (Church's Testimony, The.) ACP
   Catholic Church, The. Fr. II. OBS
   Church of England, The. Fr. I. OBS
   Conversion. Fr. III. ACP
   (Worldly Vanity.) FiP
   "Dame, said the Panther, times are mended well." Fr. II. PoEL-3
   King James II. Fr. III. ACP
   "Milk white Hind, immortal and unchang'd, A." Fr. I. SeCV-2
   (Churches of Rome and of England, The, much abr.) ACP
   "One evening, while the cooler shade she sought." Fr. I. PoEL-3
   "Portly prince, and goodly to the sight, A." Fr. III. OBSV
   Presbyterians, The. Fr. I. OBS
   Private Judgement Condemned. Fr. I. OBS
   (Confessio Fidei.) NOBE
   (Prayer, A: "What weight of ancient witness can prevail.") FiP
   "To this the Panther, with a scornful smile." Fr. III. SeCV-2

Hind Etin. Unknown. ESPB, A and B vers.; OxBB

Hind Horn. Unknown. AmFP; ESPB, A and B vers.

Hind, knocked sprawling by my shot, The. Death of a Hind. Alasdair Maclean. PoSH

Hindoo: He Doesn't Hurt a Fly or a Spider Either, The. A. K. Ramanujan. OxBC

Hinds of Kerry, The. William S. Wabnitz. GoYe

Hindu Cradle Song. Sarojini Naidu. See Cradle Song: "From groves of spice."

Hinky Dinky, Parlee-Voo. Unknown. AS

Hint at the hilltop of the moon, A. Teika, tr. fr. Japanese by Hiroaki Sato. Fr. Eighty-four Tanka. FCEI

Hint for the Incomplete Angler. Kendrick Smithyman. ATNZ; PeNZ

Hint from Voiture. William Shenstone. EnLoPo

Hint o' Snow, A. William Soutar. PoSH

Hinted Wish, A. Martial, tr. fr. Latin by Francis Lewis. AWP

Hints on Pronunciation for Foreigners. Unknown. FaBoUs

Hinty, minty, cuty, corn. Counting-out Rhymes. Unknown. FaPON

Hinx! minx!/ The old witch winks! Unknown. MAT; OxNR

Hippo, The. Theodore Roethke. VGW

Hippodromania; or, Whiffs from the Pipe, sel. Adam Lindsay Gordon. "Rest, and be thankful! On the verge." CBAP

Hippolytus, sels. Euripides, tr. fr. Greek. NAWM-1, tr. by Rex Warner
   No More, O My Spirit. Tr. by Hilda Doolittle ("H. D."). AWP
   O for the Wings of a Dove. Tr. by Gilbert Murray. AWP

Hippopotamothalamion. John Hall Wheelock. FiBHP; FYAP

Hippopotamus, The. Hilaire Belloc. CenHV; FaBoNo; FiBHP; InPK

Hippopotamus. Joanna Cole. NTCP

Hippopotamus, The. T. S. Eliot. AWP; HoPM; LiTB; NAEL-2; OBMV; VGW

Hippopotamus, The. Oliver Herford. NA

Hippopotamus, The. Ogden Nash. FaBV; OnUR

Hippopotamus, The. Jack Prelutsky. RHPC

Hippopotamus had a bride, a. Hippopotamothalamion. John Hall Wheelock. FiBHP; FYAP

Hippopotamus is strong, The. Habits of the Hippopotamus. Arthur Guiterman. FaBV; FiBHP; OBCA; OnUR; RHPC

Hippopotamus's Birthday, The. Emile Victor Rieu. Mes

Hipporhinostricow. Spike Milligan. AmMo

Hipsaw! my deaa! you no do like a-me! Unknown. Fr. Dancing Songs, I. PBCV

Hir bowgy cheekes been as softe as clay. A Description of His Ugly Lady. Thomas Hoccleve. MeEL

Hiraeth. Unknown, tr. fr. Welsh by Aneirin Talfan Davies. OBWVE

Hiraeth in N.W.3. Wynford Vaughan-Thomas. NOBL

"Hiram, I think the sump is backing up." Mending Sump. Kenneth Koch. BXAP; HeIP; InPK; MoP; NeAP; NoAM; NoAM

Hired Man's Way, The. John Kendrick Bangs. OBCA

Hireling's wages to the priest are paid, A. Poet vs. Parson. Ebenezer Elliott. Son

Hiroona, sels. Horatio Nelson Huggins. PBCV
   "But mark you well the words I say."
   "Clear transparent sea with light, The."

Hiroshige. Mark Perlberg. NYBP

Hiroshima. Mary Beadnell. CN

Hiroshima Bomb, The. Roberto Roversi, tr. fr. Italian by Lawrence R. Smith. NItP

Hiroshima Exit. Joy Kogawa. BrSi

His/ name was. A Marriage. Anthony Barnett. VWA

His Age, Dedicated to His Peculiar Friend, Master John Wickes, under the Name of Posthumus. Robert Herrick. CaPo; SeCP

His age drawn out behind him to be watched. Old Man. Elizabeth Jennings. NePoEA-2

His Answer. Clara Ann Thompson. BlSi; CBWP-2

His Answer to "Her Letter." Bret Harte. AnAmPo

His Are the Thousand Sparkling Rills. Cecil Alexander. TIRV

His armies love massacre. A King's Double Nature. Kakkai Patiniyar Naccellaiyar, tr. by A. K. Ramanujan. PLW

His art is eccentricity, his aim. Pitcher. Robert Francis. NePoAm; OxBSP; SD; SoSe; WeW

His artificial feet calumped in holy rhythm. Deacon Morgan. Naomi Long Madgett. BlSi

His baby cry. The Birth of Shaka. Mbuyiseni Oswald Mtshali. WMBCH

His Ballad of Agincourt. Michael Drayton. See Fair stood the wind for France.

His Banner over Me. Gerald Massey. WGRP

His bark/ The daring mariner shall urge far o'er. Prophecy. Luigi Pulci, tr. fr. Italian. Fr. Morgante Maggiore, II. PAH

His bed is like his death. Genesis. Buland al-Haidari, tr. by Patricia Alanah Byrne and Salma Khadra Jayyusi. MAP

His being gone is a gift to my people. Wulf and Eadwacer. Unknown, tr. by Willis Barnstone and Elene Kolb. BoWoP

His Being Was in Her Alone. Sir Philip Sidney. ELP

His bicycle stood at the window-sill. A Constable Calls. Seamus Heaney. FaBoPV; IPY; NOIV

His blood is on us. In Memory of Izziddin al-Qalaq. Ahmad Dahbur, tr. by Lena Jayyusi and Charles Doria. MAP

His blood on my arm is warm as a bird. Prayer for Messiah. Leonard Cohen. OBCV
His Body. Sandra McPherson. AmPA; GeTw
His body doubled. On the Swag. R. A. K. Mason. ATNZ; PeNZ
His body is smashed. The Crucifix. Sir Herbert Read. BrPo
His body lies interred within this mould. Epitaph on a Soldier. Cyril Tourneur. Fr. The Atheist's Tragedy. ElL
His body lies upon the shore. Richard Somers. Barrett Eastman. AA
His Books. Robert Southey. See My Days among the Dead Are Past.
His breath smelled when he spoke. In the Woman Arms of the Ground. Alberto Rios. NAmP
His broad-brimmed hat pushed back with careless air. Vaquero. Joaquin Miller. AA
His brother after dinner. Uncle Bull-Boy. June Jordan. PoBA
His brother said that pain was what he knew. Traction: November 22, 1963. Howard Moss. AmFN
His brow spreads large and placid, and his eye. The "Chief." W. E. Henley. Fr. In Hospital, XV. BrPo
His Camel. Alqamah, tr. fr. Arabic by Sir Charles Lyall. Fr. The Mufaddaliyat. AWP
His car was worth a thousand pounds and more. One Poet Visits Another. W. H. Davies. TW
His care-free swagger was a fine invention. W. H. Auden. Fr. Sonnets from China, V. CMoP
His case inspires interest. A Man of Words. John Ashbery. PoA
His Cavalier. Robert Herrick. CaPo; GoJo
His chair at the table, empty. Killed in Action. Juliette de Bairacli-Levy. CN
His Charge to Julia at His Death. Robert Herrick. SeCV-1
His cherished woods are mute. The stream glides down. At Chappaqua. Joel Benton. AA
His Children. Hittan of Tayyi, tr. fr. Arabic by Sir Charles Lyall. Fr. Hamasah. ASP; AWP
His chosen comrades thought at school. What Then? W. B. Yeats. CMoP
His clumsy body is a golden fruit. Deaf-Mute in the Pear Tree. P. K. Page. NoAM; PoE
His coat threadbare like a wolf pack. Gogol. Tomas Tranströmer, tr. by Samuel Charters. AnAn
His cock is big and red when I am there. Paul Goodman. PeHV
His coffin, lined top, sides, and back. The Dragons. Gerrit Komrij, tr. by Jacob Lowland. DuIn
His comb was redder than the fine coral. Chaucer. Fr. The Canterbury Tales: The Nun's Priest's Tale. PBBP
His compassionate face, slightly wan. On the Street. C. P. Cavafy, tr. by Rae Dalven. BoLoP
His Content in the Country. Robert Herrick. CaPo; SeCV-1; TEP
His corpse owre a' the city lies. The Dead Liebknecht. "Hugh MacDiarmid," after the German of Rudolf Leonhard. FaBoPV; OBVE
His daughter Charlotte said to Mr. Brontë. Sampler from Haworth. Frances Minturn Howard. WPE
His delicate fingers, moving among the roses. The Utopia of Lord Mayor Howard. Randolph Stow. PoAu-2
His Desire. Robert Herrick. OxBSP
His desires, growing. Black Man's Feast. Sarah Webster Fabio. PoBA; PoNe
His Discourse with Cupid. Ben Jonson. Fr. A Celebration of Charis in Ten Lyrick Peeces. SeCP
His dogs would follow him. They are pure. Hunter. Rosanna Warren. Fr. Funerary Portraits, II. NOAM
His Dream of the Sky-Land: A Farewell Poem, sel. Li Po, tr. fr. Chinese by Shigeyoshi Obata.
"Seafarers tell of the Eastern Isle of Bliss, The." WSC
His dreams are ranged with the mountains of Etsu. Monk from Etsu Returning to a Hermitage. Enkei, tr. by Lucien Stryk and Takashi Ikemoto. ZPCJ
His echoing axe the settler swung. The Settler. Alfred Billings Street. AA; FaBoBe; PAH
His eight children and their mother. The Death of the Shoemaker. Ahmad Dahbur, tr. by Lena Jayyusi and Charles Doria. MAP
His Ejaculation to God. Robert Herrick. SeCV-1
His Epitaph. Sir Walter Ralegh. See Even Such Is Time.
His Excellency General Washington. Phillis Wheatley. See Celestial choir! enthron'd in realms of light.
His Excuse for Loving. Ben Jonson. Fr. A Celebration of Charis in Ten Lyrick Peeces. JCP; PoEL-2; QFR; SeCP; SeCV-1
His eyes are green and his nose is brown. The King of the Hobbledygoblins. Laura E. Richards. OBCA
His eyes are quickened so with grief. Lost Love. Robert Graves. AWP; CH; FaBoCh; Mes; MoAB; MoBrPo; NoP

His Face. Florence Earle Coates. OHIP
His face is gone golden with the dusk. A Death in the Family. Bill Manhire. ATNZ
His face is smooth as sculptured faces are. Plastic Airman. Wrenne Jarman. CN
His face is streaked with prepared tears. The Clown. Janet Frame. ATNZ; PeNZ
His face is truly of the Roman mould. A Character. Charlotte Fiske Bates. AA
His face was blue, on his fingers. Mourning and Melancholia. Alfred Alvarez. VWA
His face was the oddest that ever was seen. The Strange Man. Unknown. FaPON
His falchion flashed along the Nile. The Exile at Rest. John Pierpont. AA
His fame stole his real name. Abd-Allah al-Baraduni, tr. fr. Arabic by Diana Der Hovanessian and Sharif Elmusa. Fr. A Rose from al-Mutanabbi's Blood. MAP
His family roots are in the mountains. The Prosperous Villager. Li K'ai-hsien, tr. by Jonathan Chaves. CoBLCP
His Farewell to His Unkind and Unconstant Mistress. Francis Davison. ElL; OBSC
His Farewell to Sack. Robert Herrick. CaPo; NAEL-1; SeCP; SeCV-1
His father gave him a box of truisms. The Truisms. Louis MacNeice. FaBCIP; NOBE; OBSV
His father said: Marry her. She's had a hard life. The Chosen—Kalgoorlie, 1894. Fay Zwicky. VWA
His Father's Hands. Thomas Kinsella. FaBCIP; PoE
His feet were shod with music and had wings. Milton. Lloyd Mifflin. AA
His finger resembled. The Accident. Len Gasparini. NeAC
His fingers wake, and flutter; up the bed. Conscious. Wilfred Owen. MMA
His first day they asked. Arbeit Macht Frei. Dennis Schmitz. AnAn; NPGG
His flaggy wings when forth he did display. The Dragon. Spenser. Fr. The Faerie Queene, I, 11. SeCePo
His flesh/ fish underwater. The Death of the Epileptic Poet Yesenin. Aram Boyajian. NeAC
His footprints have failed us. Dead in the Sierras. Joaquin Miller. AA
His fourscore years and five. Whittier. Margaret E. Sangster. AA
His frailty discrete, the rodent turns, looks. Buteo Regalis. N. Scott Momaday. NOVW
His friend the light is already cutting. On an Infant. Gyula Illyés, tr. by Jascha Kessler. FOC
His friend the watchman was still awake. A Leave-Taking. Arno Holz, tr. by Jethro Bithell. AWP
His friends he loved. His direst earthly foes. William Watson. NOBVV
His friends went off and left Him dead. The Resurrection. Jonathan Henderson Brooks. AmNP; CDC; PoNe
His fur resembles waves. Lynx. Ben Howard. GrPl
His furs of lamb's wool so glossy! Unknown, tr. by Arthur Waley. BoS
His gentle heart shows through. Manong Benny. Virginia Cerenio. BrSi
His Gift and Mine. Unknown. BLRP
His gimpy leg was testimony to/ some other surgeon's art. Old Doc. Mark Vinz. Psk
His Golden Lock[e]s [Time Hath to Silver Turned]. George Peele. Fr. Polyhymnia. ElL; FaBoRV; HeIP; NoP
(Farewell to Arms, A.) NOBE; OBEV; OBWP; PoRA
(Old Knight, The.) ChTr; OBSC; TrGrPo
(Sonnet, A: "His golden locks time hath to silver turned.") ELP; InPS; PoEL-2
His Grace! impossible! what dead! A Satirical Elegy on the Death of a Late Famous General. Swift. FF; HoPM; NBLV; NoP; OBSV; PoE; PoEL-3
His Grace of Marlborough, legends say. Tradition of Conquest. Sarah Morgan Bryan Piatt. AA
His Grange, or Private Wealth. Robert Herrick. CaPo; FM; GoJo; SeCV-1
His green eyes on the homestead of another man. The Snake. Andrew Suknaski. NOBC
His hair was yellow and long. A Tale of Last Stands. Fred Red Cloud. NOVW
His haire was blacke and in small curls did twine. Giles Fletcher the Younger. Fr. Christ's Victory and Triumph: Christ's Victory on Earth, II. SeCV-1
His Half-Breed Wife. Doris Seale. GOS
His hand came out of the east. Homer, tr. fr. Greek by Christopher Logue. Fr. The Iliad, XVI. OBVE

His Hand Shall Cover Us. Isaac ben Samuel of Dampière, *tr. fr. Hebrew* by Nina Davis Salaman. TrJP

His hands were talented for intricate transactions. With a Posthumous Medal. John Malcolm Brinnin. SaC

His hat and sword went along with him, she did not. Song of Ho Mantzu. Sun Kuang-hsien, *tr.* by Lois Fusek. ATF

His hat is rammed on. Near the School for Handicapped Children. Thomas W. Shapcott. CBAP

His hatbrim's full Copernican ellipse. The Portrait of Prince Henry. Sydney Clouts. VWA

His head like a fist rooted in his abdomen. The Agents. Robert Conquest. EAS

His head split in four parts. Promenade. David Ignatow. TrJP

His headstone said. The Funeral of Martin Luther King, Jr. Nikki Giovanni. AmNP; BPo

His heart swells. Peyanar, *tr. fr. Tamil* by A. K. Ramanujan. *Fr.* Seven Said by the Foster-Mother, 3. PLW

His heart, to me, was a place of palaces and pinnacles and shining towers. I Have Been through the Gates. Charlotte Mew. MoAB; MoBrPo; TrGrPo

His heart was light, and all the living day. Canadian Farmer. Genevieve Bartole. CaP

His Helplessness. John Berryman. *Fr.* Dream Songs. NoP

His Highness's Dog. Pope. *See* I am his Highness' dog of Kew.

His Hill. Kapilar, *tr. fr. Tamil* by A. K. Ramanujan. PLW

His home is on the heights; to him. The Poet. Edwin Markham. WGRP

His Hope or Sheet-Anchor. Robert Herrick. CaPo

His hottest love and most delight. The Happy Hen. James Agee. ErPo

His house is a haven where fingers dare. Heart Specialist. Elias Lieberman. ImOP

His Illness. Solomon ibn Gabirol, *tr. fr. Hebrew* by David Goldstein. TOF

His Immortality. Thomas Hardy. CMoP

His iron-frame, long deem'd so ably plann'd. Watt's Improvements to the Steam Engine. Thomas Baker. *Fr.* The Steam Engine; or, The Power of the Flame. FaBoUS

His is the body laid to rest in grave-site West. The Hunter: 20,000 A.D. Andrew Joron. BWV

His job was. Branches Back Into. Ken Belford. NeAC

His kiss a bristling. Against Winter. Elaine Feinstein. VWA

His Lachrimae or Mirth, Turn'd to Mourning. Robert Herrick. SeCV-1

His Lady's Cruelty. Sir Philip Sidney. *See* Astrophel and Stella: XXXI. "With how sad steps, O [*or* Oh] Moon, thou climb'st the skies!"

His Lady's Death. Pierre de Ronsard, *tr. fr. French* by Andrew Lang. AWP

His Lady's Eyes. Fulke Greville. *See* Caelica: You little stars that live in skies.

His Lady's Hand. Sir Thomas Wyatt. *See* O Goodly Hand.

His Lady's Might. Philippe Desportes. *See* Those eyes that [*or* which] set my fancy on a fire.

His Lady's Tomb. Pierre de Ronsard, *tr. fr. French* by Andrew Lang. AWP

His lamp, his bow, and quiver laid aside. Cupid Turned Plowman. Moschus, *tr.* by Matthew Prior. AWP
  (Cupid a Plowman.) OBVE

His landlocked dreams were rainbow-tides that ran. Old Voyager. Walter Blackstock. GoYe

His last days linger in that low attic. The Old Jockey. F. R. Higgins. OBMV; OxBTC

His Late Wife's Wedding-Ring. George Crabbe. *See* Ring so worn, as you behold, The.

His Legs Ran About. Ted Hughes. LLLT

His Letanie, to the Holy Spirit. Robert Herrick. *See* His Litany to the Holy Spirit.

His life is a mere. His Life. Gábor Devecseri, *tr.* by Robert Graves. MHuP

His life is in the body of the living. The Soul and Body of John Brown. Muriel Rukeyser. MoAmPo

His Litany to the Holy Spirit. Robert Herrick. BLPL; ELP; JCP; PoLF; QFR; SeCePo; TEP

His locks were wild, and wild his eye. Taking Long Views. May Kendall. CenHV

His logic unperturbed, exacting new. Metaphysician. Robert Fitzgerald. PoA

His lordship's steed. Riding. William Allingham. OxBChV

His loss known. *Unknown, tr.* by Geoffrey Bownas *and* Anthony Thwaite. PeBJV

His Lunch Bucket. Doug Cockrell. Psk

His lungs heaving all day in a sulphur mist. Black Money. Tess Gallagher. GeTw

His *magnum opus*. *Unknown, tr.* by Geoffrey Bownas *and* Anthony Thwaite. PeBJV

His Majesty. Theron Brown. AA

His mansion in the pool. Emily Dickinson. OBAL

His Metrical Prayer. James Graham, Marquess of Montrose. *See* Let them bestow on ev'ry airth a limb.

His Metrical Vow. James Graham, Marquess of Montrose. OxBS

His Monument. Sarah Knowles Bolton. PWR

His most kind sister all his secrets knew. Repentance. Chapman. *Fr.* Hero and Leander, Third Sestiad. OBSC

His Mother. Haim Guri, *tr. fr. Hebrew*. IP, *tr.* by Warren Bargad *and* Stanley F. Chyet; MHeP, *tr.* by Bernhard Frank.

His Mother in Her Hood of Blue. Lizette Woodworth Reese. OHIP

His Mother-in-Law. Walter Parke. FiBHP

His mother loved him. All the world of man. His Mother's Love. Noah Stern, *tr.* by Harold Schimmel. VWA

His Mother's Joy. John White Chadwick. AA

His Mother's Love. Noah Stern, *tr. fr. Hebrew* by Harold Schimmel. VWA

His Mother's Service to Our Lady. Villon, *tr. fr. French* by Dante Gabriel Rossetti. AWP; CTC

His Mother's Wedding Ring. George Crabbe. *See* Ring so worn, as you behold, The.

His naked skin clothed in the torrid mist. The Serf. Roy Campbell. GTBS-P; LiTB; MoBrPo; OBMV

His name is/ Rubin. Rubin. Charles Cooper. PoBA

His name is Jason, he's. Stud. Michael Lassell. *Fr.* Times Square Poems. GLP

His name it is Pedro-Pablo-Ignacio-Juan-/ Francesco García y Gabaldon. A Feller I Know. Mary Austin. AmFN; FaPON

His name, they told me afterwards, was Able. In Memory of My Uncle Timothy. Alastair Reid. NePoEA-2

His name was/ Mohammed Sceab. In Memoriam. Giuseppe Ungaretti, *tr.* by Henry Taylor. PFI

His name was Chance, Jack Chance, he said. Ballad of a Strange Thing. H. Phelps Putnam. OxBA

His native sea-washed isle. Sea-Distances. Alfred Noyes. MOS

His Necessary Darkness. Nancy Sullivan. TAP

His nose is short and scrubby. My Dog. Marchette Chute. FaPON; PDV

His Own Epitaph. Robert Herrick. CaPo

His Own Epitaph, When He Was Sick. John Hoskyns. FaBoEE

His own face. *Unknown, tr.* by Geoffrey Bownas *and* Anthony Thwaite. PeBJV

His Own True Wife. Wolfram von Eschenbach, *tr. fr. German* by Jethro Bithell. AWP

His pads furring the scarp's rime. The Snow-Leopard. Randall Jarrell. CAPP; LiTM; TwCP

His paintings grew darker every year. The Artist. Stanley Kunitz. CAPP

His palms spotless. What She Said to Him, after Meeting His Concubine. Cakalacanar, *tr.* by A. K. Ramanujan. PLW

His paper propped against the electric toaster. Daniel at Breakfast. Phyllis McGinley. OBSV

His Parting from Her. John Donne. *Fr.* Elegies, XII. EBEV
  (Elegie: His Parting from Her.) OBS

His pendulous body tolled. A Hanging. Frank Mkalawile Chipasula. WMBCH

His Petition to Queen Anne of Denmark (1618). Sir Walter Ralegh. SiPS

His Picture. John Donne. *Fr.* Elegies, V. MePo
  (Elegie V: His Picture.) MeLP; OBS

His Pilgrimage. Sir Walter Ralegh. *See* Give me my scallop-shell of quiet.

His place, as he sat and as he thought, was not. A Quiet Normal Life. Wallace Stevens. LCAP; NAAL-2; NoAM

His place is before, not in, the National Gallery. London Pavement Artist. James Schevill. TAP

His Plans for Old Age. William Meredith. TAP

His plumage is dun. Jailbird. Vernon Scannell. OxBC

His poems, yellow, torn and fading. Langston Hughes. Lew Blockcolski. VoR

His Poetry His Pillar. Robert Herrick. CaPo; JCP; QFR
  (His Poetrie His Pillar.) OBS; SeCP

His pole and paddle have been with him a long time. Chang Yü, *tr. fr. Chinese* by Jonathan Chaves. *Fr.* Paintings. CoBLCP

"His policy," do you say? Mr. Johnson's Policy of Reconstruction. Charles Graham Halpine. PAH

His Prayer for Absolution. Robert Herrick. SeCV-1; TrPWD

His Prayer to Ben Jonson [*or* Johnson]. Robert Herrick. CaPo; JCP; NAEL-1; NoP; OBS; OxBoLi; OxBSP; SeCV-1; TrGrPo

His Presence Came Like Sunrise. Ralph Spaulding Cushman. BLRP
His pride/ Had cast him out from Heaven, with all his host. Milton. *Fr.* Paradise Lost, *Bk.* I, *ll.* 36–75.
  (Satan ("His pride/ Had cast him out from Heaven, with all his host").) TrGrPo
His Quest. Lewis Frank Tooker. AA
His rags glint in the sun. Beggar. Murano Shiro, *tr. by* Geoffrey Bownas *and* Anthony Thwaite. PeBJV
His Relative Confides in Professor Sigmund Freud. Judd Teller, *tr. fr. Yiddish by* Grace Schulman. PeBMYV
His Remedie for Love. Michael Drayton. *Fr.* Idea. AAS
His Request. Owen Roe O'Sullivan, *tr. fr. Irish by* Joan Keefe. BIrV
His Request to Julia. Robert Herrick. CaPo; OBS
His Return to London. Robert Herrick. CaPo; FaBoPP; FF; NAEL-1
His Reward. Sir Thomas Wyatt. *See* With Serving Still.
His role is to invert the fairy tale. Psychiatrist. Peter De Vries. OBAL
His Running My Running. Robert Francis. ASP
His Sailing from Julia. Robert Herrick. PoEL-3
His savings spent. Father of the Bride. Charles Ghigna. SoTCo
His Saviour's Words, Going to the Cross. Robert Herrick. NOCV
His shadow monstrous on the palace wall. Oedipus. Thomas Blackburn. FaBoTw
His Shield. Marianne Moore. LiTM
His shoulder did I hold. Any Saint. Francis Thompson. MoBrPo
His sister named Lucy O'Finner. "Lewis Carroll." FaBoNo
His sleepless nights are battlefields of madness. Foreign Fencers. A. Leyeles, *tr. by* Benjamin *and* Barbara Harshav. AYP
His Son. Callimachus, *tr. fr. Greek by* G. B. Grundy. AWP
His soul extracted from the public sink. The Scurrilous Scribe. Philip Freneau. AA
His soul stretched tight across the skies. T. S. Eliot. *Fr.* Preludes (I-IV). HeIP; LiTA; NoP; OBMV; PPP; SeCePo; SOTW; TwCP; UnPo; VGW; WeW
His soul to God! on a battle-psalm! Albert Sidney Johnston. Francis Orrery Ticknor. PAH
His Sovereignty. Kalonymos ben Moses of Lucca, *tr. by* Nina Davis Salaman. TrJP
His sovereignty is o'er my gathered throng. His Sovereignty. Kalonymos ben Moses of Lucca, *tr. by* Nina Davis Salaman. TrJP
His speckled pastures dipped to meet the beach. Biography. Charles Bruce. CaP
His speculation he regretted. I Want a Tenant; a Satire. John O'Keefe. NOEC
His spirit in smoke ascended to high heaven. The Lynching. Claude McKay. BANP; IDB; PoBA
His Statement of the Case. James Herbert Morse. AA
His stature was not very tall. The Description of Sir Geoffrey Chaucer. Robert Greene. *Fr.* Greene's Vision. CTC; OBSC
  (Sir Geoffrey Chaucer.) FaBoCh
His sullen kinsmen, by the winter sea. Santa Claus. Dom Moraes. NoAM
His sun went down in the morning. Our Ernest. "Elmo." PWR
His Swans. Geoffrey Grigson. FaBoRV
His tail fell off, but the frog. Bunsoku, *tr. by* Hiroaki Sato. FCEI
His team of darkies pull well. *Unknown, tr. by* Arthur Waley. BoS
His Tears to Thamesis. Robert Herrick. FaBoPP
His teeth are white as curds. The Arrow of Desire. *Gond Oral Tradition, tr. by* V. Elwin *and* S. Hivale. WTO
His theme/ over and over. Williams: An Essay. Denise Levertov. InPS
His Throne Is with the Outcast. James Russell Lowell. TrCP
His tongue was touched with sacred fire. Henry Ward Beecher. Charles Henry Phelps. AA
His triumphs of a moment done. On the Departure of the British from Charleston. Philip Freneau. PAH
His trousers are wind. Song to a Lover. *Unknown, tr. by* Willis Barnstone. BoWoP
His tundra'd mind sprouts leaflets. Senile. Pat Folk. PCP
His Uncle came on Franklin Hyde. Franklin Hyde. Hilaire Belloc. FaBoUs; NBLV
His was the first corpse I had ever seen. My Wicked Uncle. Derek Mahon. FaBCIP; OxBC
His watch is wicked, going up. What We Call Living. Heather McHugh. NAmP
His way in farming all men knew. At Marshfield. William Cleaver Wilkinson. *Fr.* Webster; an Ode. AA
His ways are strange: sometimes. Mohammad Taqi Mir, *tr. by* Ahmed Ali. GoT
His Welcome. Auvaiyar, *tr. fr. Tamil by* A. K. Ramanujan. PLW
His well shaped ears were chestnut brown and they. The Huckster's Horse. Julia Hurd Strong. GoYe

His wheel of logic whirled and spun all day. The Philosopher. Edward Rowland Sill. AnAmPo
His whiskers didn't come, his mustache is gone. A Mustacheless Bard. J. Gordon Coogler. OBAL
His Wife. Shirley Kaufman. LCAP
His Wife. Rachel, *tr. fr. Hebrew by* Sholom J. Kahn. WPOW
His wild heart beats with painful sobs. The Happy Warrior. Sir Herbert Read. MMA
His Will Be Done. Annie Johnson Flint. BLRP
His Winding-Sheet. Robert Herrick. CaPo; OBEV
His window is over the factory flume. Widow Brown's Christmas. John Townsend Trowbridge. BeLS
His Wisdom. Nicholas Breton. *See* I would thou wert not fair, or I were wise.
His words were magic and his heart was true. Uncle Ananias. E. A. Robinson. MoAmPo; NIP
His work is done, his toil is o'er. Faithful unto Death. Richard Handfield Titherington. PAH
Hiss, hiss—the north wind blows. Commiserating with the Poor. Li K'ai-hsien, *tr. by* Jonathan Chaves. CoBLCP
Hist, but a word, fair and soft! Master Hugues of Saxe-Gotha. Robert Browning. OAEL-2
Hist Whist. E. E. Cummings. OFD; RHPC; SO
Histoire. Harry Mathews. BAP
Historical Judas, The. Howard Nemerov. NoP
Historical Materialism. Cees Buddingh', *tr. fr. Dutch by* James S. Holmes. DuIn
Historical Museum, Manitoulin Island. Lisel Mueller. PoA
Historical Poem. *Unknown. See* Charles II.
Historical Reflections. John Hollander. OBAL
Historie of Squyer William Meldrum, The, *sel.* Sir David Lindsay. Squire Meldrum at Carrickfergus. OxBS
Historiography. Lorenzo Thomas. UL
History. G. K. Chesterton. *Fr.* Songs of Education. OBSV
History. Robert Fitzgerald. FYAP
History. Robert Francis. LCAP
History. Jorie Graham. NPGG
History. Arthur Gregor. TAP
History. Art Lange. UL
History. D. H. Lawrence. BrPo
History. James Liddy, *tr. fr. Irish.* CIP
History. Myra Cohn Livingston. RHPC
History. Robert Lowell. CAPP; HCAP; TAP
History. Bob Perelman. IAT
History among the Rocks. Robert Penn Warren. *Fr.* Kentucky Mountain Farm. GOA; MoAmPo
History and Abstraction. Thomas Lux. AmPA
History as Decoration. Rosanna Warren. DiPo
History Classes. Tony Harrison. *Fr.* The School of Eloquence. NoAM
History during Nocturnal Snowfall. Robert Penn Warren. DiPo
History has to live with what was here. History. Robert Lowell. CAPP; HCAP; TAP
History Lesson, A. Miroslav Holub, *tr. fr. Czech by* George Theiner. RB
History Lesson. Mark Van Doren. NYBP
History Lessons. Seamus Deane. CIP
History: Madness. Stan Rice. NPGG
History Makers. George Campbell. PVCV
History mistory. Realpolitik. Blossom S. Kirschenbaum. SoTCo
History of a Literary Movement. Howard Nemerov. NePoEA; PoE
History of blacklife is put down in the motions, The. Sound of Afroamerican History Chapt I, The. S. E. Anderson. PoBA
History of Civilization, A. Albert Goldbarth. HCAP; MAYP
History of Education. David McCord. OBAL
History of Golf—Sort Of, A. Thomas L. Hirsch. ASP
History of Ideas. J. V. Cunningham. NIP
History of Insipids, The. John Freke. APAS
History of Lesbianism, A. Judy Grahn. GLP; PeHV
History of Lit: A Communication. István Vas, *tr. fr. Hungarian by* Jascha Kessler. FOC
History of Love, A. William Carlos Williams. VGW
History of My Heart. Robert Pinsky. NAmP; NPGG
History of my self, The. The Great Fear. Piera Oppezzo, *tr. by* Muriel Kittel. DMI
History of Peru. Washington Delgado, *tr. fr. Spanish by* David Tipton. Per
History of Photography, A. Albert Goldbarth. MAYP
History of the Flood, The. John Heath-Stubbs. MoBS; OxBTC
History of the Human Body/ Winfield's Infield Hit/ The Lassitude of the Infinite, The. Elinor Nauen. UL

History of the Revolution. Pentti Saarikoski, *tr. fr. Finnish by* Aili Jarvenpa. SOP
History of the World, The. Roger Weingarten. NAmP
History of Truth, The. W. H. Auden. FaBoMo
History of World Languages. Dennis Joseph Enright. OxBC
History she (Zelda) said stops here. Inside History. Angela McCabe. AmPA
History Teacher in the Warsaw Ghetto Rising. Evangeline Paterson. CN
History, the angel, was stirred. Northern Ireland: Two Comments. Seamus Deane. CIP
History to the historian. History. Robert Francis. LCAP
Hist? Through the corridor's echoes. Clinical. William Ernest Henley. *Fr.* In Hospital, XI. BrPo
Hit!/ Smash/ Guts. Insanity. Gaston Dubois. ASP
Hit me! Jab me! Third Degree. Langston Hughes. BPo
Hit wes upon a Scere-thorsday that vre loverd aros. Judas. *Unknown.* ESPB
Hitch Haiku, *sels.* Gary Snyder. LCAP
    "After weeks of watching the roof leak." InPK
They Didn't Hire Him. SM
Hitchcock Blue. Lucie Brock-Broido. EOEF
Hitchhiker, The. Ai. GeTw
Hitchhiker. Jack Marshall. NYBP
Hitchhikers, The. Diane Wakoski. NoAM
Hitching into Frisco. Thom Gunn. *Fr.* Three Songs. AnAn
Hither thou com'st: the busy [*or* busie] wind all night. The Bird. Henry Vaughan. FM; OBEV; PoE; PoEL-2; SeCV-1
Hither We Come, Our Dearest Lord. Enoch W. Freeman. AH
Hither, where tangled thickets of the acacia. The Babiaantje. F. T. Prince. MoBrPo
Hitherto and Henceforth. Annie Johnson Flint. BLRP
Hitherto Hath the Lord Helped. *Unknown.* BLRP
Hitherto the Lord hath helped us. Hitherto and Henceforth. Annie Johnson Flint. BLRP
Hitler courts in bombed Berlin. "The Ballad of Helmut Franze." Jerome Sala. UL
Hitler, frothy-mouth, wooden-head. *Unknown, tr. by* Barry Mitcalfe. WTO
Hitler Spring. Eugenio Montale, *tr. fr. Italian by* William Arrowsmith. AnAn
Hitomaro. Anzai Hitoshi, *tr. fr. Japanese by* Hiroaki Sato. FCEI
Hit's a mighty fur ways up de Far'well Lane. My Honey, My Love. Joel Chandler Harris. *Fr.* Uncle Remus and His Friends. AA; FaBoBe
Hits and Runs. Carl Sandburg. ASP; SD
Hittites, The. Roy Fuller. OxBSP
Hitty Pitty within the wall. *Unknown.* OxNR
Hmmmm, *sels.* Leslie Scalapino. NPGG
    "As Rimbaud said, I thought today sitting in the library."
Epilogue: Anemone.
    "Haven't I said that part of having intercourse."
    "Having her under me," the man said, "in bed, and remembering.""
    "How can I help myself, as one woman said to me about wanting."
    "How was I to know that the woman, seated next to me on the bus."
Seeing the Scenery.
    "So I decided watching an old woman like her, who could rise so easily."
    "We put our heads into the window of a car which was passing."
    "Woman who had been dressed by someone, in the same way that, A."
Ho. Al Young. NPGG
Ho, a song by the fire! Dartmouth Winter-Song. Richard Hovey. AA
Ho, all you cats in all the street. Cat's Meat. Harold Monro. OBMV
Ho, boys, ho! for California, O! The Banks of Sacramento. *Unknown.* AS
Ho! brother [*or* broder] Teague, dost hear de decree. Lilli Burlero [*or* Lilliburlero]. Thomas, Lord Wharton. APAS; NOIV; OxBoLi
    (New Song, A.) CoMu
Ho, Brother Teig. *Unknown.* GBP
Ho! City of the gay! The Return of Napoleon from St. Helena. Lydia Huntley Sigourney. AA
Ho! Cupid calls, come Lovers, come. Cupids Call. James Shirley. ErPo
Ho, Everyone That Thirsteth. A. E. Housman. OAEL-2
Ho, for taxis green or blue. Taxis. Rachel Lyman Field. FaPON
Ho! for the blades of Harden! The Blades of Harden. Will H. Ogilvie. *Fr.* Whaup o' the Reed. GoTS
Ho, for the Pirate Don Durk of Dowdee! The Pirate Don Durk of Dowdee. Mildred Plew Meigs. OnUR; PDV
Ho, giant! This is I! The Bean-Stalk. Edna St. Vincent Millay. WSC
Ho! he exclaim'd, King George of England standeth in judgement! The Absolvers. Robert Southey. *Fr.* A Vision of Judgement. EnRP

Ho, ho, my servants and officers! *Unknown, tr. by* Arthur Waley. BoS
Ho! Ho! The fine fellow. Camden Magpie. Hugh McCrae. PoAu-1
Ho, Moeris! Whether on the way so fast? Lycidas and Moeris. Virgil, *tr. fr. Latin by* Dryden. *Fr.* Eclogues, IX. AWP
Ho! Persephone brings flowers, to them. The Old Men. Irving Feldman. TwCP
Ho! pony. Down the lonely road. Army Correspondent's Last Ride. George Alfred Townsend. AA
"Ho!" quod the knight, "Good sir, namore of this." The Nun's Priest's Prologue. Chaucer. *Fr.* The Canterbury Tales. OAEL-1
    ("Stop!" cried the knight. "No more of this good sir!") NAWM-1
"Ho, Rose!" quoth the stout Miles Standish. The First Proclamation of Miles Standish. Margaret Junkin Preston. PAH
"Ho, sailor of the sea!" "How's My Boy?" Sydney Thompson Dobell. CH; GN; OHIP
"Ho, there! Fisherman, hold your hand!" The Second Mate. Fitz-James O'Brien. AA
"Ho! why dost thou shiver and shake." Gaffer Gray. Thomas Holcroft. NOEC
Ho, woodsmen of the mountain-side! A Cry to Arms. Henry Timrod. PAH
Ho! Ye Sun, Moon, Stars, all ye that move in the heavens. The Child Is Introduced to the Cosmos at Birth. *Unknown, tr. by* Alice Fletcher. AnAmPo
    (Ho! Ye Sun, Moon, Stars.) PrIM
Hob Gobbling's Song. James Russell Lowell. OBCA
Hob, shoe, hob; hob, shoe, hob. *Unknown.* OxNR
Hob the Elf. Norman M. Johnson. BoTP
Hob upon a Holiday ("Hob yawned three times and rubbed his eyes"). *Unknown.* NOEC
Hobbes clearly proves that every creature. Swift. *Fr.* On Poetry; a Rhapsody. HAP; SCV
    (Critics.) SeCePo
Hobbit, The, *sel.* J. R. R. Tolkien.
    "Far over the misty mountains cold." WSC
Hobie Noble. *Unknown.* ESPB; OxBB
Höbinger. Elfriede Gerstl, *tr. fr. German by* Beth Bjorklund. CoAuP
Hobnelia seated in a dreary Vale. Thursday; or, The Spell. John Gay. *Fr.* The Shepherd's Week. PoEL-3
    "Last May-day fair I search'd to find a snail." FaBoUs
    "When first the year, I heard the cuckoo sing." PBBP
Hoboes in, The. Things of the Spirit. Mason Jordan Mason. PoNe
Hobson and His Men (Hobson went toward death and hell). Robert Loveman. PAH
Hobthrush, The. *Unknown.* GBP
Hoc Cygno Vinces. Henry Hawkins. ACP
Hoc Est Corpus. Alex Comfort. LiTB; LiTM
Hoccleve Remembers His Madness. Thomas Hoccleve. *Fr.* The Complaint. CoBLMV
Hock-Cart, or Harvest Home, The. Robert Herrick. CaPo; EBEV; FaBoPV; JCP; NAEL-1; OBS; SeCP; SeCV-1
Hockey. Scott Blaine. ASP
Hockey Poem, The. Robert Bly. TSL
Hocus Pocus. Eat with Care. *Unknown.* FaBoUs
Hoddley, poddley, puddle and fogs. *Unknown.* FaBoNo; OxNR
Hoddy doddy. *Unknown.* OxNR
Hog at the Manger. Norma Farber. PChr
Hog butcher for the world. Chicago. Carl Sandburg. AiP; AmPP; AnAmPo; BLPL; CMoP; FaBV; LiTM; MoAB; MoAmPo; MoP; NAAL-2; NoAM; NOBA; NoP; OxBA; PoA; TAP; UnPo; VGW
Hog-calling Competition. Morris Bishop. RHPC
Hog Drovers. *Unknown.* AmFP
Hog-Eye. *Unknown.* AS
Hog-Eye Man, The. *Unknown.* AS
Hog Meat. Daniel Webster Davis. BANP
Hogan. Archie Washburn. NOVW
Hogger on his death-bed lay, A. The Dying Hogger. *Unknown.* AS
Hoggie dead, A! a hoggie dead! a hoggie dead! *Unknown.* PBBP
Hognose snake is mostly sham, The. Slither Tither. Irene Warsaw. SoTCo
Hogwash. Robert Francis. LCAP
Hogyn. *Unknown.* GBP
Hohenlinden. Thomas Campbell. BeLS; CH; ChTr; EnRP; FaBoCh; FaBoRV; FaPoR; GN; GTBS; GTBS-P; NOBE; OBNC; OBWP; OnMSP; WaaP; WBLP
Hoise up the sail, cried they who understand. A Sea-Voyage from Tenby to Bristol. Katherine Philips. WPE
Hoist up and I could lean over, A. The Bull Moses. Ted Hughes. NoP
Hoity-Toity Oyster, The. Charles W. Pratt. *Fr.* A Fable in Two Languages. SoTCo

"Hoka hey, Lakotas," Sioux warriors used to shout. Of Sitting Bear. Wayne Dodd. *Fr.* The General Mule Poems. KS

Hokey, pokey, whisky, thum. *Unknown.* OxNR

Hokku: In the Falling Snow. Richard Wright. *Fr.* Hokku Poems. IDB

Hokku Poems, *sel.* Richard Wright. AmNP; PoBA
  Hokku: In the Falling Snow. IDB

Hold, are you mad? you damn'd confounded dog. Epilogue. Dryden. *Fr.* Tyrannic Love. SeCV-2

Hold back, as less from friends. If There's Nothing out the Windows Look at Books. Lyn Hejinian. LP

Hold back thy hours. Bridal Song ("Hold back thy hours"). Francis Beaumont *and* Fletcher. *Fr.* The Maid's Tragedy, I, ii. EIL; ErPo; TrGrPo

Hold fast to dreams. Dreams. Langston Hughes. RHPC

Hold Fast Your Dreams. Louise Driscoll. BLPA; FaBoBe; FaPON; FPL

Hold, furious youth—better thy heat assuage. The Best Time for Conception. Claude Quillet, *tr. fr. Latin by* George Sewell. *Fr.* Callipaedia; or, The Art of Getting Beautiful Children. FaBoUs

Hold hard, Ned! Lift me down once more, and lay me in the shade. The Sick Stockrider. Adam Lindsay Gordon. CBAP; PoAu-1

Hold her softly, not for long. At a Child's Baptism. Vassar Miller. GoJo

Hold, hold it tight. Song for a Girl on Her First Menstruation. *Unknown, tr. by* Joe Prentuo. BoWoP; OV

Hold, hold your hand, hold; mercy, mercy, spare. A Sonnet on Sir William Alexander's Harsh Verses after the English Fashion. James I, King of England. Son

Hold it up sternly—see this it sends back, (who is it? is it you?). A Hand-Mirror. Walt Whitman. NAAL-1; OxBA; TW

Hold my hand; soon we'll be rounding the cape. Letter IV. Angelos Sikelianos, *tr. by* Edmund Keeley *and* Philip Sherrard. VMG

Hold my rooster, hold my hen. Precious Things. *Unknown.* TTY

Hold! pale death, at the poor man's shack and the pasha's palace. Horace, *tr. fr. Latin, by* James Michie. *Fr.* Odes: I, 4. "Hold! pale death, at the poor man's shack and the pasha's palace." OBD

Hold suffering on a tight leash. Desert. Agnes Gergely, *tr. by* Emery George. VWA

"Hold the horse's head" the farmer said. The Horse's Head. Brendan Kennelly. CIP

Hold the Wind. *Unknown.* GBP

Hold the Wind. Villon. OBD

Hold them now, Earth, now hand of man cannot. The Last Survivor's Speech. *Unknown, tr. fr. Anglo-Saxon by* Alfred David. *Fr.* Beowulf. NAEL-1

Hold-up. Louis MacNeice. FaBCIP

Hold up your hands. *Unknown.* OxNR

"Hold your hand, Lord Judge," she says. The Maid Freed from the Gallows. *Unknown.* ESPB

Holding a child's hand intently. Ozaki Hosai, *tr. fr. Japanese by* Hiroaki Sato. *Fr.* One Hundred Haiku in Free Form. FCEI

Holding a picture up to the wall. Sketch. Robert Farnsworth. GOYP

Holding a Raccoon's Jaw. Gjertrud Schnackenberg. PPR

Holding black whips. Thoughts of Chairman Mao. David Young. AmPA

Holding Hands. Lenore M. Link. FaPON; MoShBr; NTCP; RAR; RHPC

Holding herself as if she had. A Drunken Satyr from Newton County Tells How He Met Daphne. Michael Burns. SoTCo

Holding its huge life open to the sky. To My Friends. Stephen Berg. NaP; NYBP

Holding the arm of his helper, the blind. The Visitor. Gibbons Ruark. MT

Holding the Mirror Up to Nature. Howard Nemerov. PoA

Holding the naked body I had bought. A Bought Embrace. G. S. Fraser. WaP

Holding the Sky. William Stafford. RFM

Holding the Thought of Love. Bernadette Mayer. BAP

Hole in the Floor, A. Richard Wilbur. NOBA; SoSe

Hole in the Sea, The. Marvin Bell. NYBP

Hole Seen, The. May Swenson. SoTCo

Hole, Where Once in Passion We Swam. Dave Smith. NoAM

Holes, The. Stephen Berg. NaP; NYBP

Holes in my arms. For Real. Jayne Cortez. PoBA

Holes in the floor of the barn loft, The. Hay Scuttle. Robert Morgan. MAYP

Holiday, The. Thomas Frank Bignold. OBTV

Holiday. H. Leivick, *tr. fr. Yiddish by* Benjamin *and* Barbara Harshav. *Fr.* Remembrances. AYP

Holiday, A. Lizette Woodworth Reese. AA

Holiday-Afternoon Rhapsody. Imre Csanádi, *tr. fr. Hungarian by* Edwin Morgan. MHuP

Holiday at Hampton Court. John Davidson. EBVV

Holiday Girls. Vicki Raymond. UAS

Holiday in Reality. Wallace Stevens. OxBA

Holiday Inn at Bemidji. Gerald Vizenor. STE

Holiday Piece. Denis Glover. ATNZ

Holiday Task, A. Gilbert Abbott à Beckett. NA

Holiday Train, The. Irene Thompson. BoTP

Holidays. Eva Mylonas, *tr. fr. Modern Greek by* Kimon Friar. BoWoP

Holiday's End. Haim Guri, *tr. fr. Hebrew by* Warren Bargad *and* Stanley F. Chyet. IP

Holiness[e] on the head. Aaron. George Herbert. MeLP; MePo; OAEL-1; OBS

Holland, that scarce deserves the name of land. Andrew Marvell. *Fr.* The Character of Holland. ChTr; OBSV; OBTV

Hollandaise. Sharon Bryan. MAYP

Hollin, Green Hollin. *Unknown.* GBP

Hollis laughed. Johnna at the Windmill. Diane Glancy. CRP

Holloe Menn, The. Harrison Everard. BXAP

Hollow, The. Robert Morgan. MT

Hollow Echo. Fazil Hüsnü Daglarca. CRP

Hollow eyes of shock remain, The. Two Years Later. John Wieners. PoM

Hollow Flute, The. Avner Strauss. VWA

Hollow Land, The, *sel.* William Morris.
  "Christ keep the Hollow Land." ChTr
  (Song: "Christ keep the Hollow Land.") PoEL-5

Hollow Men, The. T. S. Eliot. InPS; LiTA; LiTM; MoAB; MoAmPo; NAAL-2; OAEL-2; OBMV

Hollow of Light. Hans Andreus, *tr. fr. Dutch by* James S. Holmes. DuIn

Hollow Thesaurus, The. Roger McDonald. CBAP

Hollow Tree, A. Robert Bly. NNaP

Hollow winds begin to blow, The. Signs of Rain. Edward Jenner. BLPA; BoNaP; FaBoUs

Holly, The. Walter de la Mare. CMoP

Holly against Ivy, *sels. Unknown.* MeEL
  "Nay! nay! Ivy."
  "Holy bereth beris."

Holly and Ivy, *sels. Unknown.* MeEL
  "Nay! Ivy, Nay!"
  "Holy stond in the hall."

Holly and Ivy a great party. Carol in Praise of the Holly and Ivy. *Unknown.* OHIP

Holly and Mistletoe. Eleanor Farjeon. PChr

Holly and the Ivy, The ("The holly and the ivy,/ When they are both full grown"). *Unknown.* CH; ChTr; ELP; GBP; OBET; OFD; PChr

Holly Beareth Berries, *sel. Unknown.* PBBP, *abr.*
  "Nay!, nay, Ivy."

Holly Beareth Berries. *Unknown. See* Holly against Ivy.

Holly Tree, The. Robert Southey. EnRP

Hollyhock, A. Frank Dempster Sherman. AA

Hollyhocks, The. Craven Langstroth Betts. AA

Hollyhocks are ten feet tall, The. Wet Summer. May Williams Ward. GoYe

Holly's up, the house is all bright, The. The Christmas Tree. Peter Cornelius. PChr

Hollywood. Karl Shapiro. LiTM; OxBA

Holmes. James Russell Lowell. *Fr.* A Fable for Critics. NOBA

Holocaust. Myra Sklarew. CRP

Holocaust 1944. Anne Ranasinghe. VWA

Holocaust, pentecost: what heaped heartbreak. My Grandfather's Church Goes Up. Fred Chappell. SM

Holstein cows parked. Black and White. Tom Schmidt. NeAC

Holstenwall. Sidney Keyes. FaBoTw

Holston lolls like a tongue here, its banks, The. Sex. Charles Wright. PPR

Holy. George Campbell. PBCV

Holy angels, in envy I cast no sigh. Gaspara Stampa, *tr. fr. Italian by* J. Vitiello. BoWoP

Holy Baptisme. George Herbert. PoEL-2

Holy be the white head of a Negro. Holy. George Campbell. PBCV

Holy bereth beris. *Unknown. Fr.* Holly against Ivy. MeEL

Holy Bible, Book Divine. John Burton. BLRP; WBLP

Holy boy, The. Children of Love. Harold Monro. MoBrPo

Holy City, The. Frederic Edward Weatherly. BLRP; WBLP

Holy Cross. Sir Shane Leslie. TIRV

Holy Cross. *Unknown.* ACP

Holy Fair, The. Burns. EnRP; OBSV

Holy Family. Muriel Rukeyser. MoAmPo
Holy Family. Katharine Tynan. TIRV
Holy Father, Great Creator. Alexander V. Griswold. AH
Holy Ghost, The. John Donne. *Fr.* The Litanie. NOCV
Holy Girl. Yoshioka Minoru, *tr. fr. Japanese by* Hiroaki Sato. FCEI
Holy God, We Praise Thy Name. Clarence A. Walworth. AH
Holy Grail, The, *sel.* Jack Spicer.
  Book of Gawain, The. PoM
Holy Grail, The. Tennyson. *Fr.* Idylls of the King.
  Percivale's Quest. OAEL-2
Holy Ground, The. *Unknown.* OxBSS
Holy Hill, A. "Æ." AWP
Holy, Holy, Holy. Reginald Heber. OHIP
"Holy, holy, holy!" the choir chants sweet and low. An Opening Service.
  Clara Ann Thompson. CBWP-2
Holy Innocents, The. Robert Lowell. InvP; MoAB; MoAmPo; NePoEA;
  OBCP; OxBC
Holy is the Closed Temple. *Unknown, tr. by* Arthur Waley. BoS
Holy Is the Desire to Proclaim the Existence of God. Meir Wieseltier, *tr.
  fr. Hebrew by* Warren Bargad *and* Stanley F. Chyet. IP
Holy Jesus, Thou art born. Victoria Saffelle Johnson. TrPWD
Holy Land of Walsingham, The. *See* As You [*or* Ye] Came from the
  Holy Land of Walsingham.
Holy Light. Milton. *See* Paradise Lost: Hail holy light, ofspring [*or*
  offspring] of Heav'n first born.
Holy Longing, The. Goethe, *tr. fr. German by* Robert Bly. NU
Holy man, ungird your gabardeen. Rest. Roots. Seymour Mayne.
  NOBC
Holy men. Freethinkers. Deborah Eibel. VWA
Holy Nativity of Our Lord God, The. Richard Crashaw. *See* Come we
  shepherds whose blest sight.
Holy Night. Nathaniel Anketell Benson. CaP
Holy Night. Lucille Clifton. GeTw
Holy Night. Yrjö Jylhä, *tr. fr. Finnish by* Aili Jarvenpa. SOP
Holy Nunnery, The. *Unknown.* ESPB
Holy of England! since my light is short. On First Entering Westminster
  Abbey. Louise Imogen Guiney. AA
Holy of Holies, The. G. K. Chesterton. WGRP
Holy of holies—a hill-top chapel. Bridestones. Ted Hughes. AnAn
Holy Office, The. James Joyce. FaBoTw; NoAM; OxBTC
Holy Ones, the Young Ones, The. Chayyim Zeldis. TrJP
Holy Order. J. B. Boothroyd. FiBHP
Holy Poet, I have heard. John Hall Wheelock. *Fr.* Thanks from Earth to
  Heaven. TrPWD
Holy Rood, The, *sel.* John Davies of Hereford.
  Although We Do Not All the Good We Love. Son
Holy-Rood come forth and shield. The Old Wives Prayer. Robert
  Herrick. SeCV-1
Holy Rose, The. Vyacheslav Ivanov, *tr. fr. Russian by* Babette Deutsch
  and Avrahm Yarmolinsky. AWP
Holy Satyr. Hilda Doolittle ("H. D."). MoAmPo
Holy Scripture, Writ Divine. From a London Bookshop. *Unknown.*
  FaBoUs; NBLV
Holy Song of the Holy Grocer, The. H. Leivick, *tr. fr. Yiddish by*
  Benjamin *and* Barbara Harshav. AYP
Holy Sonnets, *sels.* John Donne.
  "As due by many titles I resign[e]." *Fr.* II. JCP; MePo; OBS
  "At the round earths imagined corners, blow." *Fr.* VII. BLPL; EaLo;
    EBEV; FaBoRV; HAP; HeIP; InPS; JCP; LiTB; MeLP; MePo;
    NAEL-1; NAWM-1; NOBE; NoP; OAEL-1; OBD; OBS; PoE;
    PoEL-2; PPP; QFR; SeCP; SeCV-1; Son; TEP; TOF
    (Blow Your Trumpets.) ChTr
  "Batter my heart, three person'd God; for you." *Fr.* XIV. BLPL;
    EaLo; EBEV; FaFP; FF; HAP; HeIP; HoPM; InPK; InPS; JCP; LiTB;
    MeLP; MePo; NAEL-1; NIP; NOBE; NoP; OAEL-1; OBS; PoE;
    PoEL-2; PPP; PrIm; SeCePo; SeCP; SeCV-1; Son; SoSe; TEP; TOF;
    TrCP; TrGrPo; TrPWD
  "Death be not proud, though some have called thee." *Fr.* X. ChTr;
    DL; ElL; FaBoRV; FaBV; FaFP; FF; FPL; HAP; HeIP; InPK; InPS;
    InvP; JCP; LiTB; MeLP; MePo; NAEL-1; NAWM-1; NIP; NOBE;
    NoP; OAEL-1; OBD; OBS; PoE; PoEL-2; PoRA; PPP; PrIm; SCV;
    SeCP; SeCV-1; TEP; TrCP; TrGrPo; WeW
    (Death.) OBEV
  "Father, part of his double interest." *Fr.* XVI. JCP; OBS; Son
  "I am a little world made cunningly." *Fr.* V. NAEL-1; NIP; NoP;
    OBS; PoE; SeCP; Son; TEP
  "If faithful soules be alike glorifi'd." *Fr.* VIII. OBS
  "If poisonous [*or* poysonous] mineral[l]s, and if that tree." *Fr.* IX.
    EBEV; JCP; LiTB; MePo; NAEL-1; NoP; OAEL-1; OBS; PoEL-2;
    PPP; SeCP; Son; UnPo
  "O might those sighes and teares returne againe." *Fr.* III. OBS

  "Oh my black[e] soule! now thou art summoned." *Fr.* IV. EBEV;
    JCP; OAEL-1; OBS; Son; TEP; TOF
  "Oh, to vex me, contraries [*or* contraryes] meet in one." *Fr.* XIX.
    OAEL-1; PoEL-2; Son
    (Devout Fits.) SeCePo
  "Show me dear[e] Christ, thy spouse, so bright and clear." *Fr.* XVIII.
    MeLP; NAEL-1; NoP; OBS; PoE; Son
  "Since she whom I lov'd hath paid [*or* payd] her last debt." *Fr.* XVII.
    JCP; MePo; NAEL-1; Son
  "Spit in my face you Jew[e]s, and pierce my side." *Fr.* IX. JCP;
    OBS; Son; TOF
  "This is my play's [*or* playes] last scene, here heavens appoint." *Fr.*
    VI. EBEV; JCP; MeLP; MePo; OBS; SeCP; Son; TEP
  "Thou hast made me, and shall thy work[e] decay?." *Fr.* I. EBEV;
    MeLP; NAEL-1; NOBE; NOCV; NoP; OBS; PoEL-2; SeCP; Son;
    TEP
  "What if this present were the world's last night?." *Fr.* XIII. EBEV;
    HeIP; InPS; JCP; LiTB; MeLP; NAEL-1; NOCV; OBS; PoE; Son;
    TEP
  "Why are we[e] by all creatures waited on?." *Fr.* XII. JCP; NOCV;
    OBS; PoE; PoEL-2; TrCP
  "Wilt thou love God, as he thee! then digest." *Fr.* XV. JCP; OBS;
    TrCP
Holy Spirit, Faithful Guide. Marcus Morris Wells. AH
Holy Spirit, Lord of light. Hymn to the Holy Spirit. Stephen Langton.
  TrCP
Holy Spirit, Truth Divine. Samuel Longfellow. AH
Holy Spring. Dylan Thomas. WaP
Holy stond in the hall [*or* halle]. Holly and Ivy. *Unknown.* MeEL
  (Nay, Ivy, Nay.) CH
Holy store is abandoned, The. The Holy Song of the Holy Grocer. H.
  Leivick, *tr. by* Benjamin *and* Barbara Harshav. AYP
Holy Supper is kept, indeed, The. James Russell Lowell. *Fr.* The
  Vision of Sir Launfal, *pt.* II. OnMSP
Holy Thursday. Charles Wright. AnAn; GeTw
Holy Thursday ("Is this a holy thing to see"). Blake. *Fr.* Songs of
  Experience. EnRP; FF; InPS; NAEL-2; NOEC; NoP; OAEL-2;
  TEP
Holy Thursday (" 'Twas on a Holy Thursday, their innocent faces clean").
  Blake. *Fr.* Songs of Innocence. CH; EnRP; InPS; NAEL-2;
  NAWM-2; NOBE; NOEC; NoP; OAEL-2; OFD; PoE; SCV; TEP;
  TrCP
Holy Tide, The. Frederick Tennyson. OBEV
Holy Transportations, *sel.* Charles Fitz-Geffry.
  Take Frankincense, O God. ChTr
Holy virtue of living, the soul's delight, The. A Hymn of Form. Gordon
  Bottomley. BrPo
Holy Was Demeter Walking th' Corn Furrow. Edward Sanders. PoM
Holy water come and bring. The Spell. Robert Herrick. CaPo; WSC
Holy Well, The ("As it fell out on a holiday"). *Unknown.* OBET
Holy Well, The ("As it fell out one May morning"). *Unknown.* FaBoCh;
  GBP; NOCV
Holy Willie's Prayer. Burns. EBEV; GoTS; NOEC; OBSV; OxBS; PoE;
  PoEL-4; PPP; TW
Holyhead, Sept. 25th, 1727. Swift. BIrV
Homage. Gilbert Highet. *See* Homage to Ezra Pound.
Homage. Gustave Kahn, *tr. fr. French by* Jethro Bithell. TrJP
Homage. R. J. Schoeck. GoYe
Homage. Dezsö Tandori, *tr. fr. Hungarian by* Daniel Hoffman. MHuP
Homage and Lament for Ezra Pound in Captivity. Robert Duncan.
  NOBA
Homage of War. Bruce Williamson. NeIP
Homage to a Government. Philip Larkin. EBEV; FaBoPV; NoAM
Homage to Arthur Waley. Weldon Kees. NaP
Homage to Chagall. Duane Niatum. CDW
Homage to David Smith. John Haines. LCAP
Homage to Diana. Sir Walter Ralegh. *See* Praised be Diana's fair and
  harmless light.
Homage to Elvis, Homage to the Fathers. Bruce Weigl. MAYP
Homage to Ezra Pound. Gilbert Highet. Par
Homage to Guillaume Apollinaire. Blaise Cendrars, *tr. fr. French by*
  Anselm Hollo. RHTwFP
Homage to Hart Crane. Peter Balakian. MAYP
Homage to Hieronymus Bosch. Thomas MacGreevy. BIrV; EAS
Homage to Jack Yeats. Thomas MacGreevy. OBMV
Homage to John Millington Synge. Mairtin O Direain, *tr. fr. Irish by*
  Thomas Kinsella. NOIV
Homage to Life. Jules Supervielle, *tr. fr. French by* Kenneth Rexroth.
  RHTwFP
Homage to Malcolm Lowry. Derek Mahon. FaBCIP

Homage to Mallarmé, *sel.* Daniel Mark Epstein.
   Barrel Organ, The. DiPo
Homage to Marcel Proust. Thomas MacGreevy. CIP
Homage to Mistress Bradstreet, *sels.* John Berryman.
   "Governor your husband lived so long, The." NOBA
   "I trundle the bodies, on the iron bars." NOBA
   "O all your ages at the mercy of my loves." NOBA
   "So squeezed, wince you I scream? I love you & hate." FF
   "Winters close, springs open, no child stirs, The." NAAL-2; NAs
Homage to My Hips. Lucille Clifton. CAPP
Homage to Paul Cézanne, *sel.* Charles Wright. NAAL-2
   "Dead are a cadmium blue, The." HCAP
Homage to Paul Delvaux. Ramon Guthrie. PoE
Homage to Paul Mellon, I. M. Pei, Their Gallery, and Washington City.
   William Meredith. EyDe
Homage to René Magritte. George Melly. EAS
Homage to Robert Bresson. Jon Anderson. MAYP
Homage to Sextus Propertius, *sels.* Ezra Pound.
   Elegy VII. ErPo; InvP; VGW
   "Now if ever it is time to cleanse Helicon." VGW
   "Shades of Callimachus, Coan ghosts of Philetas." CMoP; HAP;
      MoAB; NOBA; OBVE; OxBA
   "When, when, and whenever death closes our eyelids." MoAB;
      OBMV; PoA
   "Who, who will be the next man to entrust his girl to a friend?."
      FaBoMo
Homage to Texas. Robert Graves. LiTB
Homage to the British Museum. William Empson. CMoP; FaBoMo;
   LiTM; MoAB; MoBrPo; PoE
Homage to the Carracci. Tom Disch. PoA
Homage to the Empress of the Blues. Robert Hayden. CNA; HCAP;
   LCAP; PoBA; PoNe
Homage to the New World. Michael S. Harper. LCAP
Homage to the Philosopher. Babette Deutsch. ImOP; TrJP
Homage to the Runner. Marvin Bell. *Fr.* The Escape into You.
   CAPP
Homage to thee, O Ra, at thy tremendous rising! The Dead Man Ariseth
   and Singeth a Hymn to the Sun. *Unknown, tr. fr. Egyptian by* Robert
   Hillyer. *Fr.* Book of the Dead. AWP
Homage to William Cowper. Donald Davie. NePoEA
Homage to Wren. Louis MacNeice. EyDe
Home, The. Susan Axelrod. NMM
Home, *parody, sels.* H. C. Bunner.
   "Home, Sweet Home." ("As sea-foam blown of the winds, as blossom of
      brine that is drifted"). CenHV; OBAL
   "Home, Sweet Home." ("Brown o' San Juan"). OBAL
   "Home, Sweet Home." ("Mid pleasures and palaces though we may
      roam"). OBAL
Home. Sam Cornish. CNA
Home. Matilda C. Edwards. PWR
Home. Karen Gershon. CN
Home. J. H. Goring. MoShBr
Home. Edgar A. Guest. BLPA; BLPL; FaBoBe; OBAL; OHFP;
   PWR
Home. W. E. Henley. GN; MoBrPo; MOS; PoLF
Home. Jean Jaszi. RAR
Home. Vincent O'Sullivan. PeNZ
Home. Miki Rofu, *tr. fr. Japanese by* Geoffrey Bownas *and* Anthony
   Thwaite. PeBJV
Home. Sipho Sepamla. WMBCH
Home, The. Rabindranath Tagore. GoJo
Home. *Unknown. Zulu Oral Tradition, tr. by* H. Tracey. WTO
Home. John Witte. NIP
Home/ oh/ home. Africa. Lucille Clifton. CNA
Home/ where my/ ground. Home. Sam Cornish. CNA
Home after Three Months Away. Robert Lowell. HCAP; NoP
Home alone/ my mother off cherry-viewing. Masaoka Shiki, *tr. fr.
   Japanese by* Burton Watson. *Fr.* Thirty-nine Haiku. FCEI
Home Alone These Last Hours of the Afternoon, Dusk Now, the Sabbath
   Setting In, I Sit Back, and These Words Start Welling Up in Me.
   Stephen Levy. VWA
Home and Mother. Hettye Rayburn Ramsey. PWR
Home at Last. G. K. Chesterton. WGRP
Home! at the word, what blissful visions rise. Home, Sweet Home, with
   Variations. H. C. Bunner. CenHV; OBAL
Home-bound ship stood out to sea, The. The Mystery of Cro-a-tàn.
   Margaret Junkin Preston. PAH
Home Burial ("He saw her from the bottom of the stairs."), *sel.* Robert
   Frost. NAAL-2; PrIm; TAP
   "You could sit there with the stains on your shoes." OBD

Home-coming. Léonie Adams. MoAmPo
Home-Coming. Albert Ehrenstein, *tr. fr. German by* Babette Deutsch *and*
   Avram Yarmolinsky. TrJP
Home for Thanksgiving. W. S. Merwin. NoAM
Home from Abroad. Laurie Lee. OBTV
Home from Guatemala, back at the Waldorf. Arrival at the Waldorf.
   Wallace Stevens. HCAP
Home from his journey Farmer John. Farmer John. John Townsend
   Trowbridge. PWR
Home from his morning task the swain retreats. Summer. James
   Thomson. *Fr.* The Seasons: Summer. FM
Home from Praying. Joseph Rolnik, *tr. fr. Yiddish by* Irving Feldman.
   PeBMYV
Home from the observatory. Stella. Charles Henry Crandall. AA
Home from work. *Unknown, tr. by* Burton Watson. FCEI
Home Greeting, A. Priscilla Jane Thompson. CBWP-2
Home Ground, *sels.* Charles Brasch. PeNZ
   "Before the light of evening can go out." *Fr.* XIII.
   "I tramp my streets into recognition." *Fr.* III.
   "In drab derelict marsh near the madhouse." *Fr.* XXV.
Home, home from the horizon far and clear. At Night. Alice Meynell.
   CH
Home, home—where's my baby's home? Anne Hutchinson's Exile.
   Edward Everett Hale. PAH
Home is more than just four walls. Hearth and Home. Stoddard King.
   OBAL
Home is mysterious: a place to die, a place to breed. Destinations.
   Josephine Jacobsen. WPE
Home Is So Sad. Philip Larkin. InPK; OxBSP
Home Is Where There Is One to Love Us. Charles Swain. BLPA;
   BLPL; FaBoBe
Home Leave. Barbara Howes. TwCP
Home Life. Pat Nolan. UL
Home Movies. Carter Revard. VoR
Home No More Home to Me. Robert Louis Stevenson. CH
Home of Aphrodite, The. Euripides, *tr. fr. Greek by* Gilbert Murray.
   Fr. Bacchae. AWP
Home of the Percys' high-born race. Alnwick Castle. Fitz-Greene
   Halleck. AA; AnAmPo
Home of the Soul. Ellen M. Huntington Gates. BLRP
Home on the Range, A. *Unknown.* FaBoBe
Home Revisited: Midnight. John Ciardi. NYBP
Home-Sickness. Justinus Kerner, *tr. fr. German by* James Clarence
   Mangan. AWP
Home-Sickness. Hedwig Lachmann, *tr. fr. German by* Jethro Bithell.
   TrJP
Home Song. Longfellow. GN
Home, Sweet Home. John Howard Payne. *Fr.* Clari, the Maid of Milan.
   AA; AnAmPo; BLPA; FaBoBe; FaFP; WBLP
Home Sweet Home with Variations, *parody.* H. C. Bunner. BXAP;
   CenHV; OBAL
   Sels.
   "As sea-foam blown of the winds, as blossom of brine that is drifted."
      CenHV; OBAL
   "Brown o' San Juan." OBAL
   "Mid pleasures and palaces though we may roam." OBAL
Home They Brought Her Warrior Dead. Tennyson. *Fr.* The Princess,
   Pt. V. TrGrPo
H(ome), thou return'st from Thames, whose Naiads long. An Ode on the
   Popular Superstitions of the Highlands of Scotland. William Collins.
   EnRP; NOEC; OAEL-1
Home Thoughts. Denis Glover. PeNZ
Home Thoughts from Abroad. Robert Browning. AWP; BoNaP; BoTP;
   EBVV; FaBoBe; FaBV; FaFP; FaPON; FaPoR; FiP; FPL; GN; HeIP;
   LiTB; NAEL-2; NOBE; NOBVV; NoP; OBEV; OBNC; OBTV; PoLF;
   PoRA; PrIm; TEP; TrGrPo
Home Thoughts from Abroad. *Unknown.* Par
Home-Thoughts from France. Isaac Rosenberg. MMA
Home Thoughts, from the Sea. Robert Browning. NAEL-2
Home without a Bible. Charles D. Meigs. WBLP
Home without a Cat, A. "Mark Twain." CRH
Home! You're Where It's Warm Inside. Jack Prelutsky. RHPC
Homecoming, The. James Keir Baxter. ATNZ
Homecoming. Hayyim Nahman Bialik, *tr. fr. Hebrew by* Bernhard Frank.
   MHeP
Homecoming. Bruce Dawe. CBAP
Homecoming, The. Gerrit Komrij, *tr. fr. Dutch by* Jacob Lowland.
   DuIn
Homecoming. Robert Lowell. CAPP
Homecoming. Anna Margolin, *tr. fr. Yiddish.* VWA, *tr. by* Keith
   Bosley

Homecoming. Sonia Sanchez. PoBA
Homecoming. Dennis Scott. PBCV
Homecoming. Michael Sheridan. NAmP
Homecoming. John Thompson. MAT
Homecoming. Peter Viereck. CoAP
Homecoming—Massachusetts. John Ciardi. NYBP
Homecoming of Emma Lazarus, The. Galway Kinnell. NaP
Homecoming Singer, The. Jay Wright. PoBA
Homeland, The. Hugh Reginald Haweis. BLRP
Homeless. Louis Aragon, tr. fr. French by Joachim Neugroschel. POS
Homeless. Malka Heifetz Tussman, tr. fr. Yiddish by Kathryn Hellerstein. AYP
Homeless!/ The Living Bread. Despised and Rejected. Katharine Lee Bates. TrCP
Homely Advice to the Unemployed. Samuel Laycock. PF
Homely Meats. John Davies of Hereford. See Scourge of Folly, The: Author Loving These Homely Meats, The.
Homely Rhymes on Bad Times. Samuel Bamford. PF
Homeowners unite. The Firebombing. James Dickey. OBWP
Homer. Albert Ehrenstein, tr. fr. German by Babette Deutsch and Avram Yarmolinsky. TrJP
Homer Mitchell Place, The. John Engels. SM
Homer was poor. His scholars live at ease. James Vincent Cunningham. VGW
Homeric Hymns, sels. Unknown, tr. fr. Greek by Shelley.
   Hymn to Athena. AWP
   Hymn to Castor and Pollux. AWP
   Hymn to Earth the Mother of All. AWP
   Hymn to Mercury, abr OBVE
   Hymn to Selene. AWP
Homer's grace is unparalleled; it is Homer's! Isaiah and Homer. A. Leyeles, tr. by John Hollander. PeBMYV
Home's not merely four square walls. Home Is Where There Is One to Love Us. Charles Swain. BLPA; BLPL; FaBoBe
Homes of England, The. Felicia Dorothea Hemans. FaPoR; WPE
Home's the place we head for in our sleep. Indian Boarding School: The Runaways. Louise Erdrich. HATNAP; NoAM
Homes were built, houses, shops. Batlonim. Yankev Fridman, tr. by Ruth Whitman. PeBMYV
Homes where children live exude a pleasant rumpledness. Where Children Live. Naomi Shihab Nye. MAYP
Homesick. Else Lasker-Schüler, tr. fr. German by Michael Hamburger. PBWP
Homesick? and yet your country walks. To Henry Vaughan. Arthur James Marshall Smith. OBCV
Homesick Blues. Langston Hughes. CDC; MoAmPo
Homesickness. Else Lasker-Schüler. See Homesick.
Homestead—Winter Morning. Mary Ballard Duryee. GoYe
Hometown. Luis Cabalquinto. BrSi
Hometown. Sam Cornish. PPR
Hometown Piece for Messrs. Alston and Reese. Marianne Moore. OBAL
Homeward Bound. William Allingham. FaBoBe
Homeward Bound, sels. Heine, tr. fr. German.
   And When I Lamented. Tr. by Emma Lazarus. TrJP
   Dearest Friend, Thou Art in Love. Tr. by Emma Lazarus. TrJP
   Du bist wie eine Blume. AWP, tr. by Kate Freiligrath Kroeker.
   ("Thou Seemest Like a flower.") TrJP, tr. by Emma Lazarus.
   I, a Most Wretched Atlas. Tr. by Emma Lazarus. TrJP
   Mortal, Sneer Not at the Devil. Tr. by Emma Lazarus. TrJP
   Thou Hast Diamonds. Tr. by Emma Lazarus. TrJP
Homeward Bound. Ezekiel Mphahlele. WMBCH
Homeward Bound. Unknown. OxBSS
Homeward Bound. George Edward Woodberry. Fr. Wild Eden, XXV. AA
Homeward Journey, The. Leonard Aaronson. TrJP
Homework. Allen Ginsberg. NoAM
Homework. Russell Hoban. RHPC
Homework. Jane Yolen. RHPC
Homework sits on top of Sunday, squashing Sunday flat. Homework. Russell Hoban. RHPC
Homing. Arna Bontemps. CDC
Homing, The. John Jerome Rooney. AA
Homing Pigeons. Ted Walker. NYBP
Hommes à Femme. Karin Kiwus, tr. fr. German by Susan L. Cocalis. DMG
Homo Factus Est. Digby Mackworth Dolben. TrPWD
Homo Sapiens. Earl of Rochester. See Satire [or Satyr] against [Reason and] Mankind, A.
Homosexuality. Frank O'Hara. PeHV; PoA; TAP
Homunculus et la Belle Étoile. Wallace Stevens. MoAB; MoAmPo

Honest Abe Lincoln. Max Shulman. OBAL
Honest Deacon, The ("An honest man was Deacon Ray"). Isaac Hinton Brown. PWR
Honest regular work Dick Daring gave up. A Shining Night or Dick Daring, the Poacher. Unknown. CoMu
Honest Stradivari made me. The Violin's Complaint. William Roscoe Thayer. AA
Honest, Wouldn't You? Unknown. WBLP
Honestly I wish I were dead! Sappho, tr. by Willis Barnstone. BoWoP
Honesty. Sir Thomas Wyatt. See Throughout the World, If It Were Sought.
Honesty at a Fire. Sir John Collings Squire. FiBHP
Honey/ When de man. Sister Lou. Sterling A. Brown. AmNP; PoBA; PoNe
Honey. James Wright. KS
Honey Bear. Elizabeth Lang. BoTP
Honey Bee, The. Don Marquis. FPL
Honey bee is sad and cross, The. The Honey Bee. Don Marquis. FPL
Honey combs did not produce that year, The. Theme and Variations. Ingeborg Bachmann, tr. by Beth Bjorklund. CoAuP
Honey Dripping from the Comb. James Whitcomb Riley. AA
Honey-flowers to the honey-comb. Chimes. Dante Gabriel Rossetti. OBNC
Honey-hued beauty, you are. Black Lady in an Afro Hairdo Cheers for Cassius. R. Ernest Holmes. ASP
Honey Lamb, The. Jonathan Williams. PoM
Honey-Mead: "I am valued by men, fetched from afar." Unknown, formerly at. to Cynewulf, tr. fr. Anglo-Saxon by Charles W. Kennedy. Fr. Riddles (Exeter Book). AnOE
Honey Moon. Kathleen Leland Baker. NBLV
Honey people murder mercy U.S.A. In Memoriam: Martin Luther King, Jr. June Jordan. PoBA
Honey, pepper, leaf-green limes. Jamaica Market. Agnes Maxwell-Hall. TTY
Honey, see dat jay-bird dah. Settin' on de Fence. Unknown. WBLP
Honey, Take a Whiff on Me. Unknown. OxBoLi
Honey, trus' der Lawd a bit, an' doan fohgit to smile! Trus' an' Smile. B. Y. Williams. BLRP
Honeyed by time. The Wooden Chamber. Anne Hébert, tr. by Birgit Swenson. WPOW
Honeymoon. Samuel L. Albert. GoYe
Honeystain/ the rhetoricians of blackness. The Anti-Semanticist. Everett Hoagland. BPo
Honeysuckle (Chevrefoil). Marie de France, tr. by Patricia Terry. BoWoP
Honeysuckle, nightshade. Poem for L. C. Peter Klappert. AmPA
"Honeysuckle Was the Saddest Odor of All, I Think." Thadious M. Davis. BlSi
Honeysuckle Yellow. Pierre Kemp, tr. fr. Dutch by Fred van Leeuwen. DuIn
Hongo Store 29 Miles Volcano Hilo, Hawaii, The. Garrett Kaoru Hongo. MAYP; MOWH
Honi. Dan Pagis, tr. fr. Hebrew by Warren Bargad and Stanley F. Chyet. IP
Honi Soit Qui Mal Y Pense. Ian Young. PeHV
Honor a going thing, goldfinch, corporation, tree. Mechanism. A. R. Ammons. HAP
Honor and shame from no condition rise. Pope. Fr. An Essay on Man, Epistle IV. TrGrPo
Honor and truth and manhood. Things That Endure. Ted Olson. WBLP
Honor in chief, our oath is to uphold. Chorus Primus: Wise Counsellors. Fulke Greville. Fr. Mustapha. OBS
Honor of God and man is not on, The. Trees Once Walked and Stood. Joshua Tan Pai, tr. by Yishai Tobin. VWA
Honor to those who in the life they lead. Thermopylae. C. P. Cavafy, tr. by Edmund Keeley and Philip Sherrard. VMG
Honorable the City Clerk, The: Dear Sir. Letter to the City Clerk. Frederick Adams Wright. FaFP
Honour. Abraham Cowley. BoLoP
Honour Dishonoured. Wilfrid Scawen Blunt. OBMV
Honour is flashed off exploit, so we say. In Honour of St. Alphonsus Rodriguez. Gerard Manley Hopkins. EBEV
Honour is so sublime perfection. To the Countesse of Bedford. John Donne. MeLP
Honour of Bristol, The. At. to Laurence Price. OxBSS
Honour thy parents; but good manners call. God to Be First Served. Robert Herrick. OxBChV
Honour with Age. Walter Kennedy. OxBS

Honourable Entertainment Given to the Queen's Majesty in Progress at Elvetham, 1591, The. Nicholas Breton *and others.*
Sels.
Phillida and Coridon. Nicholas Breton. OBEV; TTTS
(Pastoral, A.) TrGrPo
(Phyllida and Corydon.) ElL; SeCePo
(Ploughman's Song, The.) NOBE; OBSC
With Fragrant Flowers We Strew the Way. Thomas Watson. ElL
(Ditty of the Six Virgins, The.) OBSC
Honoured I lived e'erwhile with honoured men. Honour Dishonoured. Wilfrid Scawen Blunt. OBMV
Honours that the people give always, The. The Thespians at Thermopylae. Norman Cameron. GTBS-P
Hoo, Suffolk. *Unknown.* GBP
Hooded Crow, The. Rennie McOwan. PoSH
Hooded in angry mist, the sun goes down. Herbert Asquith. *Fr.* Nightfall. OBD
Hoofer, The. A. K. Redwing. VoR
Hook. Floyd Skloot. ASP
Hook for Leviathan, A. Norman Cameron
Hook shot kisses the rim and, A. Fast Break. Edward Hirsch. ASP; DiPo; EOEF; TSL
Hooker's Across! George Henry Boker. PAH
Hoop, a rolling O, oh those have power, A. Ode on Zero. Phoebe Pettingell. PoA
Hoopoe. George Darley. *See* Nepenthe: Solitary wayfarer!
Hoopoe Bird, The. Saleem Barakat, *tr. fr. Arabic by* Lena Jayyusi *and* Naomi Shihab Nye. MAP
Hoosen Johnny. *Unknown.* AS; FaPON
Hootali Ajignat. William Dickey. BLA
Hooter wakes me up to face the day again, The. Unaccompanied. Harvey Andrews. OBET
Hop-Garden, The, *sels.* Christopher Smart.
Hops along the Medway. FaBoPP
How to Cure Hops and Prepare Them for Sale. FaBoUs
Hop hop, thump thump. Stevie Smith. *Fr.* The Dedicated Dancing Bull and the Water Maid. WPE
Hop-poles stand in cones, The. The Midnight Skaters. Edmund Blunden. FaBoTw; GoJo; GTBS-P; MoBrPo; NOBE; OBD
Hop, Skip, and Jump. Gary Snyder. LCAP
Hope. William Lisle Bowles. EnRP
Hope. Emily Brontë. NoP
Hope, *sel.* William Cowper.
"Though clasp'd and cradled in his nurse's arms." PoEL-3
Hope. Sir Richard Fanshawe, *after the Italian of* Giovanni Battista Guarini. *Fr.* Il Pastor Fido. OBS
Hope. Josephine D. Henderson Heard. CBWP-4
Hope. George Herbert. PoEL-2; WeW
Hope. William Dean Howells. AA; MOS
Hope ("He rose up on his dying bed"). Langston Hughes. OBAL
Hope ("Sometimes when I'm lonely"). Langston Hughes. ILY; OBAL; OBCA
Hope. Randall Jarrell. MoAB; MoAmPo
Hope. Georgia Douglas Johnson. CDC
Hope. Frank O'Connor, *tr. fr. Irish by* the author. CIP; KiLC
Hope. F. D. Reeve. PoA
Hope. Tom Sleigh. PPR
Hope. Edith Södergran, *tr. by* Jaakko A. Ahokas. PBWP
Hope. Phillips Stewart. CaP
Hope. Theognis, *tr. fr. Greek by* John Hookham Frere. AWP
Hope. Clara Ann Thompson. CBWP-2
Hope. Mary E. Tucker. CBWP-1
Hope and Despair. Lascelles Abercrombie. OBMV
Hope and Faith. Isaac Leibush Peretz, *tr. fr. Yiddish by* Henry Goodman. TrJP
Hope and Fear. Swinburne. FaBoBe
Hope and Joy. Christina Rossetti. OxBChV
Hope Deferred. Clara Ann Thompson. CBWP-2
Hope Evermore and Believe. Arthur Hugh Clough. WGRP
Hope humbly then; with trembling pinions soar. Pope. *Fr.* An Essay on Man, Epistle I. TrGrPo
Hope I dreamed of was a dream, The. Mirage. Christina Rossetti. BoLoP; LLLT; PoRA
Hope is a crushed stalk. Dark Testament. Pauli Murray. AmNP
Hope is like a harebell trembling from its birth. Comparisons. Christina Rossetti. OxBChV
Hope is the thing with feathers. Emily Dickinson. AmPP; BLPL; MoAB; MoAmPo; MoShBr; NOBA; OxBA; TAP
"Hope" is the Thing with Whiskers. David Shevin. SoTCo
Hope, is this thy hand. Fickle Hope. Harrison Smith Morris. AA

Hope, like the hyaena [*or* hyena], coming to be old. Henry Constable. *Fr.* Diana. EnLoPo; OBSC; Son
Hope! Not distant is the Springtime. Hope and Faith. Isaac Leibush Peretz, *tr. by* Henry Goodman. TrJP
Hope of the World, The. Sir William Watson. WGRP
Hope springs eternal in the human breast. The Pleasure of Hope. Pope. *Fr.* An Essay on Man, Epistle I. ACP
Hope Thou in God. Josephine D. Henderson Heard. CBWP-4
Hope! Thou vain, delusive maiden. Hope. Josephine D. Henderson Heard. CBWP-4
Hope was but a timid friend. Hope. Emily Brontë. NoP
Hope we not in this life only. Not in Vain. *Unknown.* BLRP
Hope, whose weak being ruined is. Against Hope. Abraham Cowley. *Fr.* The Mistress. LiTB; MeLP; OBS; SeCV-1
(On Hope.) MePo; NOBE
Hope ye, my verses, that posterity. Joachim Du Bellay, *tr. fr. French by* Spenser. *Fr.* Ruins of Rome. PoE
Hopeless Desire Soon Withers and Dies. "A. W." OBSC
Hopeless, this weakness of mine. Domination as Another Form of Weakness. David Avidan, *tr. by* Bernhard Frank. MHeP
Hopelessly handcuffed to a mysterious butterfly. A Lost Mohican Visits Hell's Kitchen. A. K. Redwing. VoR
Hopes are pedaled along the rioting tarmac. The Factory Hands. Polycarp Chimedza. WMBCH
Hopes grimly banished from the heart. Exiles. William Hamilton Hayne. AA
Hope's Okay. A. R. Ammons. HCAP
Hoping all the time. *Unknown, tr. fr. Japanese by* Arthur Waley. *Fr.* Kokin Shu. AWP
Hoping my face shows the pleasure I felt, I'm. Tone. Rae Armantrout. IAT
Hoping this night my true love to see. *Unknown.* FaBoUs
Hopping frog, A. Zempo, *tr. by* Hiroaki Sato. FCEI
Hopping frog—is a cat chasing you. Suiyu, *tr. by* Hiroaki Sato. FCEI
Hoppity. A. A. Milne. FaBV; NTCP
Hoppy. Reginald Gibbons. DiPo
Hops. Boris Pasternak, *tr. fr. Russian by* Jon Stallworthy *and* Peter France. BoLoP; TTTS
Hops along the Medway. Christopher Smart. *Fr.* The Hop-Garden. FaBoPP
Hop't She. *Unknown.* GBP; PBBP
Hora Christi. Alice Brown. TrPWD; WGRP
Horace. John Osborne Sargent. AA
Horace, Book V, Ode III. Charles Larcom Graves. CenHV
Horace Kephart. Robert Morgan. MAYP
Horae Canonicae, *sels.* Donald Davie. CRP
Compline.
Prime.
Horae Canonicae, *sels.* W. H. Auden.
Lauds. TrCP
Prime. CMoP; PoE
Sext. SaC
Vespers. FaBoMo
Horas Tempestatis Quoque Enumero: The Sundial. John Hollander. NePoEA
Horat. Ode 29. Book 3. Horace. *See* Odes: III, 29. "Descended of an ancient line" ("Tyrrhena regum progenies").
Horatian Epode to the Duchess of Malfi. Allen Tate. FaBoMo
Horatian Ode. Joseph Warren Beach. PoA
Horatian Ode upon Cromwell's Return from Ireland, An ("Forward youth that would appear, The."). Andrew Marvell. EBEV; GTBS; GTBS-P; HAP; InPS; JCP; MePo; NOBE; NoP; OAEL-1; OBEV; OBS; OBWP; PoEL-2; SeCP; SeCV-1
Sels.
King Charles on [*or* upon] the Scaffold. ChTr; FaBoRV
"Where, twining subtile fears with hope." OBD
Horatian Variation. Leonard Bacon. NYBP
Horatians, The. W. H. Auden. NYBP
Horatio, of ideal courage vain. Feigned Courage. Charles *and* Mary Lamb. GN; OxBChV
Horatius at the Bridge. Macaulay. *Fr.* Lays of Ancient Rome. BeLS; FaBoCh; FaFP; FaPoR; OBNV, *abr.;* OBWP; OHFP, *abr.;* PoLF
Horch, horch, die Bell am Backdoor ringt! Morning Song. Kurt M. Stein. FiBHP
Hordes of women wept for me. Memories. Horiguchi Daigaku, *tr. by* Geoffrey Bownas *and* Anthony Thwaite. PeBJV
Horeb's mountain top of old. Mountain Tops. Lizelia Augusta Jenkins Moorer. CBWP-3
Horestes, *sel.* John Pickering (or Pikerying).
Haltersick's Song. OBSC
(Song: "Farewell, adieu, that court-like life!") ElL

Horizon. Philippe Soupault, *tr. fr. French by* Rosmarie Waldrop. POS; RHTwFP

Horizon Is Definitely Speaking, The. Diana Chang. BrSi

Horizon lowers, The. Departure. Pierre Reverdy, *tr. by* Michael Benedikt. POS

Horizon Thong. George Abbe. GoYe

Horizon without Landscape. Tom Lowenstein. VWA

Horizons. Kim Hyun-sung, *tr. fr. Korean by* Koh Chang-soo. ACKP

Horizontal in a deckchair on the bleak ward [*or* Horizontal on a deckchair in the Ward]. Ezra Pound. Robert Lowell. MoP; NAAL-2; NoAM; NOBA

Horizontal on amber air, three boughs of green. Lost. Stephen Spender. PoPo

Horizontal World. Thomas Saunders. CaP

Horn, The. Léonie Adams. MoAB; MoAmPo

Horn. Sydney Lea. KS

Horn, The. James Reaney. OBCV

Horn, The. James Reeves. SO

Horn and Hardart is closing. Samurai and Hustlers. Joe Johnson. CNA

Horn Blow, The. Jeff Tagami. BrSi

Horn for weapon, and wool for shield. The Zodiac Song. John Ruskin. NOBVV

Horn: "Time was when I was weapon and warrior." *Unknown, formerly at. to* Cynewulf, *tr. fr. Anglo-Saxon by* Charles W. Kennedy. *Fr.* Riddles (Exeter Book). AnOE

Horned Lizard. Charles Molesworth. GrPl

Horned Snake, The. Louis Oliver. HATNAP

Hornet. Anne Sexton. AnAn

Hornet flies into my room, A. Summer Haloed. Sandor Csoori, *tr. by* Jascha Kessler. FOC

Hornets occasionally build their nests near roads. Homer, *tr. fr. Greek by* Christopher Logue. *Fr.* The Iliad, XVI. OBVE

Hornless hart carries off the harem, The. The Royal Stag. "Hugh MacDiarmid." FaBoMo

Hornpipe. Dame Edith Sitwell. *Fr.* Façade. FaBoMo; GTBS-P; OAEL-2; SeCePo

Horns [*or* Hornes] to bulls wise Nature lends. Beauty. Thomas Stanley, *after the Greek of* Anacreon. AWP; OBVE

Horny-Goloch, The. *Unknown*. AmMo; FaBoCh

Horribeloved Klaubautermann. Klabauterwife's Letter. Christian Morgenstern, *tr. by* W. D. Snodgrass *and* Lore Segal. WSC

Horrible crime was committed, A. Pearl Bryan. *Unknown*. AmFP

Horrible Decree, The, *sel.* Charles Wesley.
"Sinners, abhor the Fiend." NOCV

Horrible Things. Roy Fuller. OnUR

Horrid Voice of Science, The. Vachel Lindsay. PoA

Horror. Peter Baum, *tr. fr. German by* Jethro Bithell. AWP

Horror. Henry Treece. EAS

Horror Comic. Robert Conquest. OxBTC

Horror Movie. Howard Moss. NePoEA-2

Horror Story. Hans Andreus, *tr. fr. Dutch by* James S. Holmes. DuIn

Horror Story Written for the Cover of a Matchbook, A. Chuck Wachtel. UL

Horse, The. José María Eguren, *tr. fr. Spanish by* Cheli Durán. WSC

Horse. Louise Glück. AnAn; MAYP

Horse, The. Faye Kicknosway. GeTw

Horse, The. Philip Levine. CoAP

Horse, The. Francis Ponge, *tr. fr. French by* Beth Archer. NU

Horse. Kenneth Rexroth. *Fr.* A Bestiary. NNaP

Horse, The. Naomi Royde-Smith. CenHV; FaBoCo; FiBHP

Horse, The. Bible, *O.T. See* Job: Then the Lord Answered ("Who is this that darkeneth counsel by words without knowledge?").

Horse, a liberator, The. Description of a Plaza, a Monument and Allegories in Bronze. Antonio Cisneros, *tr. by* David Tipton. Per

Horse almost in the room, The. Delight. J. Bernlef, *tr. by* James S. Holmes. DuIn

Horse and a flea and three blind mice, A. Whoops! *Unknown*. FaFP; NTCP; RHPC

Horse and hattock. The Witch's Broomstick Spell. *Unknown*. ChTr; GBP

Horse and His Rider, The. Joanna Baillie. NOEC

Horse and mule live thirty years, The. Liquor and Longevity. *Unknown*. FPL

Horse & Rider. Wey Robinson. BXAP; SD

Horse and Riot. Ishihara Yoshiro, *tr. fr. Japanese by* Hiroaki Sato. FCEI

Horse and the Mule, The. John Huddlestone Wynne. OxBChV

Horse and the Whip, The. Eliezer Steinbarg, *tr. fr. Yiddish by* Curt Leviant. VWA

Horse beneath me seemed, The. The Ride. Richard Wilbur. BLA; PPR

Horse Boyle was called Horse Boyle because of his brother Mule. Dresden. Ciaran Carson. CIP

Horse breaks glass, A. Horses. Myra von Riedemann. OBCV

Horse can't walk while kicking, A. Horse Sense. *Unknown*. BLPA; PWR; WBLP

Horse Chestnut. Gary Miranda. SM

Horse-Chestnut Time. Kaye Starbird. PDV

Horse Chestnut Tree, The. Richard Eberhart. CMoP; LiTM; MoAB; MoAmPo; NePoAm

Horse Did Not Come Back, The. Erumai Veliyanar, *tr. fr. Tamil by* A. K. Ramanujan. PLW

Horse farts, A. *Unknown, tr. by* Geoffrey Bownas *and* Anthony Thwaite. PeBJV

Horse he sits on is saddleless, The. Young Horseman. Lajos Kassák, *tr. by* Edwin Morgan. MHuP

Horse, huge. Inviolable. Daniel Hoffman. GrPl

Horse I am, whom bit, A. The Trojan Horse. William Drummond of Hawthornden. EyDe

Horse in the Drugstore, The. Tess Gallagher. AmPA; AnAn

Horse is loose, The. Ojibe Kurome. *Fr.* Manyo Shu. PeBJV

Horse is Lorca's word, fierce as wind. Weed. Robert Hass. MAYP

Horse Named Bill, The. *Unknown*. AS

Horse: not one less than twenty. Isuba. Jim Barnes. *Fr.* Four Things Choctaw. HATNAP

Horse of Death, The. Leo Vroman. DuIn

Horse Sense. *Unknown*. BLPA; PWR; WBLP

Horse Show, The. William Carlos Williams. CMoP; NOBA; TAP; VGW

Horse that carried Miss Kilmansegg, The. Her Accident. Thomas Hood. *Fr.* Miss Kilmansegg and Her Precious Leg. EBVV

Horse Thief, The. William Rose Benét. MoAmPo; OnMSP

Horse Trader's Song, The. *Unknown*. AmFP

Horse-Watering Hole, The. Yang Wei-chen, *tr. fr. Chinese by* Jonathan Chaves. CoBLCP

Horse Weebles. Edward Kamau Brathwaite. PBCV

Horseback. Carolyn Kizer. ASP

Horseman, The. Walter de la Mare. GoJo; RHPC

Horseman at the Roadside, The. Yang Wei-chen, *tr. fr. Chinese by* Jonathan Chaves. CoBLCP

Horseman on the Skyline, The. Henry Lawson. CBAP

Horsemen, The. Gene Baro. NePoEA-2

Horses, The. Ted Hughes. NoAM

Horses. Murilo Mendes, *tr. fr. Portuguese by* W. S. Merwin. ATCBP

Horses, The ("Barely a twelvemonth after"). Edwin Muir. CMoP; HAP; HeIP; MoBrPo; MoP; NoAM; NOBE; NoP; OAEL-2; OxBTC; PoE; RB; TEP; WeW

Horses. Melech Ravitch, *tr. fr. Yiddish by* Seymour Levitan. PeBMYV

Horses. Myra von Riedemann. OBCV

Horses. Gwyn Thomas, *tr. fr. Welsh by* Joseph P. Clancy. OBWVE

Horses. Dorothy Wellesley. OBMV; OxBTC

Horses Aboard. Thomas Hardy. FM

Horses and Men in the Rain. Carl Sandburg. PoLF

Horses at Valley Store. Leslie Silko. VoR

Horses Chawin' Hay. Hamlin Garland. OBAL

Horses gallop over the vast plain. Horses. Murilo Mendes, *tr. by* W. S. Merwin. ATCBP

Horses Graze. Gwendolyn Brooks. CNA

Horses in front of me. Merry-go-round. Mark Van Doren. SO

Horses in horsecloths stand in a row. Horses Aboard. Thomas Hardy. FM

Horses in Snow. Roberta Hill Whiteman. NoAM

Horses Neighing at the Foot of the Mountain. Mahmoud Darwish, *tr. fr. Arabic by* Abdullah al-Udhari. MPAW

Horses of Achilles, The. Constantine P. Cavafy, *tr. fr. Greek by* Edmund Keeley *and* Philip Sherrard. OBD

Horses of Marini, The. Tania Van Zyl. PeSA

Horses of the sea, The. Christina Rossetti. *Fr.* Sing-Song. FaPON; GoJo; NTCP

Horses of the sea, The; remember. On a Horse Carved in Wood. Donald Hall. EyDe

Horses on the Camargue. Roy Campbell. GTBS-P; OBTV; PeSA; SeCePo

Horses out of their brains bored all, The. Flying Noises. Thomas Lux. LCAP

Horses, the pigs, The. Familiar Friends. James S. Tippett. BoTP

Horses were ready, the rails were down, The. Where the Pelican Builds. Mary Hannay Foott. PoAu-1

Horseshoe, The. James Tate. NAmP

Horsey Gap. *Unknown*. FaBoPP; GBP

Hos Ego Versiculos. Francis Quarles. *Fr.* Argalus and Parthenia. OBS, *See also* Man's Mortality *sl. diff. vers. at. to* Simor. Wastell, *fr.* Microbiblion.

Hosanna. Heidi Pataki, *tr. fr. German by* Beth Bjorklund. CoAuP

Hosanna. Thomas Traherne. PoEL-2; SeCV-2

Hosanna—musick is divine. Psalm CXLVII: "Praise ye the Lord." Christopher Smart. NOCV

Hosanna to Christ. Isaac Watts. NOCV

Hose and Iron. Greg Kuzma. MAT

Hospital, The. Patrick Kavanagh. BIrV; CIP; FaBCIP

Hospital. Geoffrey C. Millard. PeSA

Hospital. Karl Shapiro. VGW

Hospital/Poem. Sonia Sanchez. BPo; PoBA

Hospital Barge at Cérisy. Wilfred Owen. OBTV; RB

Hospital Breakfast: With Grace After. John Frederick Nims. BLA

Hospital Evening. Gwen Harwood. FaBoWP

Hospital for Defectives. Thomas Blackburn. GTBS-P; OxBTC

Hospital for sick and needy Jews, A. The New Jewish Hospital at Hamburg. Heine, *tr. by* Charles Godfrey Leland. TrJP

Hospital Kangaroos, The. Peter Kocan. UAS

Hospital Observation. Julian Symons. WaP

Hospital Prison Ship, The. Philip Freneau. *Fr.* The British Prison Ship, III. AmPP

Hospital—Retrospections, The. Kenneth Mackenzie. CBAP

Hospital Songs, *sel.* Jack Dann. "When we invent a machine to read." BWV

Hospital Waiting-Room, The. W. H. Davies. BrPo

Hospital Window, The. James Dickey. CAPP; DiL; HCAP; MT; NoAM

Hospitality in Ancient Ireland. *Unknown, tr. fr. Irish by* Kuno Meyer. OnYI; TIRV

Hoss, The. James Whitcomb Riley. AnAmPo

Host is riding from Knocknarea, The. The Hosting of the Sidhe. W. B. Yeats. NoAM

Host of printed letters I can offer, A. To Whom This May concern. Leo Vroman, *tr. by the author and* Peter Nijmeijer. DuIn

Host of the Air, The. W. B. Yeats. BrPo; CH

Hostess' Daughter, The. Ludwig Uhland, *tr. fr. German by* Margarete Münsterberg. AWP

Hostess of the Ferry Inn, The. Gwerfyl Mechain, *tr. fr. Welsh by* H. Idris Bell. OBWVE

Hostile picture which stays with me, The. The Walls of Urbino. Paolo Volponi, *tr. by* Lawrence R. Smith. NItP

Hosting of the Sidhe, The. W. B. Yeats. NoAM

Hosts, The. George M. Brady. NeIP

Hot Afternoons Have Been in West 15th Street. Paul Blackburn. VGW

Hot Bath in an Old Hotel. Paula Rankin. MT

Hot cross buns! Hot-cross Buns!/ One a penny, two a penny. Mother Goose. BoTP; OxNR

Hot cross buns, hot cross buns/ One a penny poker. *Unknown.* OxNR

Hot Day at the Races. Tom Raworth. EAS

Hot Dog Poem, The. Jane Barnes. GLP

Hot Evening, A. Sa'di Yusuf, *tr. fr. Arabic by* Lena Jayyusi *and* Naomi Shihab Nye. MAP

Hot Flame of My Grief, The. Moses ibn Ezra, *tr. fr. Hebrew by* Solomon Solis-Cohen. FaBWP

Hot horn hand in my face is all. My Mother Shoots the Breeze. Fred Chappell. MT

Hot in June a narrow winged. A Nameless One. Margaret Avison. HeIP; NOBC

Hot is the sun, so hot the birds complain. Ali Dabir, *tr. by* Ahmed Ali. GoT

Hot Line. Louella Dunann. RHPC

Hot mice feeding in red, The. Paul Klee. John Haines. LCAP

Hot midsummer night on Water Street, A. Hot Night on Water Street. Louis Simpson. CAPP; TwCP

Hot night makes us keep our bedroom window open, The. "To Speak of Woe That Is in Marriage." Robert Lowell. CAPP; MoP; NAAL-2; NoAM

Hot night of the ramparts. Embrace the Blade. Joyce Mansour, *tr. by* Carol Cosman. PBWV

Hot Night on Water Street. Louis Simpson. CAPP; TwCP

Hot nights I slept with you, The. For Maria. Cleopatra Mathis. MAYP

Hot Pease Man, The. Mother Goose. OxNR

Hot-spit-and-damn of unchartable cargo flashes past. Red Letters. Mekeel McBride. NAmP

Hot Springs. Earle Birney. OxBC

Hot Stuff. Edward Botwood. PAH

Hot Summer Sunday. A. L. Hendricks. PBCV

Hot sun [*or* sunne], cool[e] fire, tempered with sweet air[e]. Bethsabe's Song. George Peele. *Fr.* David and Bethsabe, sc. i. GBL; NOBE; NoP; OBSC; OxBoLi; OxBSP; PoEL-2; RB; TEP (Bethsabe Bathing.) ElL; TrGrPo

Hot sun. Lizards frolic. Election 1960. James Keir Baxter. ATNZ

Hot through Troy's ruin Menelaus broke. Menelaus and Helen. Rupert Brooke. SeCePo

Hot wind sweeps over the vegetable patches. The Drought. Cheng Min, *tr. by* Kai-yu Hsu. OV

Hotel, The. Shauqi Abi Shaqra, *tr. fr. Arabic by* Abdullah al-Udhari. MPAW

Hotel. Guillaume Apollinaire, *tr. fr. French by* Michael Benedikt. POS

Hotel. Adam Wazyk, *tr. fr. Polish.* VWA, *tr. by* Isaac Komem

Hotel Brown Poems, The. John Ash. NPo

Hotel Continental. William Jay Smith. WaP

Hotel de l'Univers et Portugal. James Merrill. MoAB; NePoEA-2; PoA

Hotel Fire: New Orleans. Paul Ruffin. InPK

Hotel in Paris. Dennis Trudell. PoA

Hotel Paradiso e Commerciale. John Malcolm Brinnin. NYBP; TwCP

Hotel Sierra. David St. John. MAYP

Hôtel Transylvanie. Frank O'Hara. NeAP; PoM

Hotels are quieter this year: the merest, The. At Large in the Eighties. Louis Johnson. ATNZ

Hottentot, The. Thomas Pringle. OBTV

Houdini. Eli W. Mandel. NOBC

Hound, The. Robert Francis. SoSe

Hound, The. Sidney Lanier. *Fr.* The Jaquerie. AA

Hound/ Could never be called refined. The Angry Poet. Frank O'Connor. CIP

Hound of Heaven, The. Francis Thompson. ACP; BLPL; BrPo; FaBV; FaFP; GoTL; LiTB; LiTM; MoAB; MoBrPo; NAEL-2; OBMV; PoEL-5; SeCePo; TrGrPo; WGRP

Hound was cuffed, the hound was kicked, The. The Hound. Sidney Lanier. *Fr.* The Jaquerie. AA

Hounded Lovers, The. William Carlos Williams. NYBP; TrGrPo

Hounded slave that flags in the race, leans by the fence, The. The Wounded Person. Walt Whitman. *Fr.* Song of Myself, XXXIII. PoNe

Hounds, The. John Freeman. OBMV; OxBSP

Hounds are all out, and the morning does peep, The. The Huntsman's Rouse. Henry Carey. SeCePo

Hound's Nest for a Parafen. James Sherry. LP

Hounds of Spring, The. Swinburne. *See* Atalanta in Calydon: When the Hounds of Spring [Are on Winter's Traces].

Hounds of the Soul, The. Louis Ginsberg. TrJP

Hounds sleep well, The. It is not they who stir the fox. With Hands like Leaves. James Still. GrPl

Hour, The. Uri Zvi Greenberg, *tr. fr. Hebrew by* Robert Mezey *and* Ben Zion Gold. VWA

Hour, The. Vivian Virtue. PVCV

Hour after hour the cards were fairly shuffled. Whist. Eugene Fitch Ware. PoLF

Hour at last come round, The. The Dying Gaul. Desmond O'Grady. BIrV

Hour before sunrise, An. Marichi. Kenneth Rexroth. PPR

Hour cannot be more quiet and dark, The. Listening to Red Maples on an Empty Mountain. Lan Ling, *tr. by* Dominic Cheung. IFON

"Hour gets later, the times get worse, The." Preliminary Poem. John Heath-Stubbs. OxBC

Hour-Glass, The. Robert Herrick. CaPo

Hour Glass, The ("Consider this small dust, here in the glass"). Ben Jonson. BLPL; LiTB

Hour-glass whispers to the lion's roar, The. Our Bias. W. H. Auden. MoP; NoP

Hour-hand and the minute-hand upon a polished dial, The. The Speed Track. "Peter." BoTP

Hour has grown late, The. Love in the Night. Emperor Hanazono, *tr. by* Steven D. Carter. WFTW

Hour has grown late, The. Wild Goose Lingering on an Inlet. Shinkei, *tr. by* Steven D. Carter. WFTW

Hour is dark. The river comes to its end, The. Mary Ursula Bethell. *Fr.* By the River Ashley, VI. ATNZ; PeNZ

"Hour is late, The," the shepherds said. The Shepherd Left Behind. Mildred Plew Meigs. TrCP

Hour is very weary, as before sleep, The. The Hour. Uri Zvi Greenberg, *tr. by* Robert Mezey *and* Ben Zion Gold. VWA

Hour of Death, The. Felicia Dorothea Hemans. OBNC

Hour of Magic, The. W. H. Davies. MoBrPo

Hour of Peaceful Rest, The. William Bingham Tappan. AA (There Is an Hour of Peaceful Rest.) AH

Hour of Sleep, The. Robert Ellis, *tr. fr. Welsh by* H. Idris Bell.
   OBWVE
Hour ten he rose, ten-sworded, every finger. Timoshenko. Sidney
   Keyes. OBWP
Hour told by the owl and the moon, The. Lament for Better or Worse.
   Gene Baro. NePoEA-2
Hour was: a child's legs, The. Jerusalem and the Hour. Rashid Husain,
   tr. by Lena Jayyusi *and* Peter Porter. MAP
Hour was on us, The; where the man? Lincoln. John Vance Cheney.
   OHIP
Hour when the moon mists over. Dawn. Philippe Jaccottet, *tr. by* W. S.
   Merwin. RHTwFP
Hour with Thee, An. Sir Walter Scott. BoLoP
Hourglass, The. Russell Edson. AnAn
Hourglass [*or* The Houre-Glasse], The ("Do but consider this small dust").
   Ben Jonson. EnLoPo; NIP; OAEL-1; SeCP
Hours, The. John Peale Bishop. OxBA
Hours, The. Christopher Pearse Cranch. PWR
Hours, The. Norman Dubie. GeTw
Hours. Francisco González León, *tr. fr. Spanish by* Samuel Beckett.
   MexPo
Hours, The. Paul Ramsey. CRP
Hours, The. Susan Tichy. MAYP
Hours after fate had brot us 2gether in. She Employed the Familiar "Tu"
   Form. Doug Fetherling. NeAC
Hours and hours go by, traffic flows. The Them Decade. Terence
   Winch. UL
Hours are viewless angels, The. The Hours. Christopher Pearse Cranch.
   PWR
Hours before dawn we were woken by the quake. William Empson.
   FaBoMo; FaBoTw; LiTB; OxBTC
Hours before my death. Julio Marzán. InW
Hours before my death. Epitaph. Julio Marzán. InW
Hour's Glory, The. Henrietta Cordelia Ray. CBWP-3
Hours I spent with thee, dear heart, The. The Rosary. Robert Cameron
   Rogers. AA; FaBoBe; WBLP
Hour's Late, The. Abba Kovner, *tr. fr. Hebrew by* Warren Bargad *and*
   Stanley F. Chyet. IP
Hours of a Bridge, The. W. S. Merwin. LCAP
Hours of rest are over, The. To-Day. Lessie M. Drown. PWR
Hours of Sleep. *Unknown.* NBLV
Hours of Sleepy Night, The. Thomas Campion. *Fr.* The Mountebank's
   Mask. ElL
   (Dismissal.) OBSC
Hours of the Day, The, *sel.* Richard Kenney.
   In Retrospect. Son
Hours of the Passion, *sel.* Eleanor Hamilton King.
   Garden of the Holy Souls, The. ACP
Hours of the Passion, The. *Unknown.* MeEL
Hours of the Passion, *sel.* William of Shoreham.
   "At Prime Jesus was y-led." ACP
Hours of the spring night are not many, The. Michizane, *tr. fr. Japanese
   by* Burton Watson. *Fr.* Kokin Shu. FCEI
Hours of the spring night are not many, The. Rainy Night. Michizane,
   tr. by Burton Watson. JLIC-1
Hours Rise Up, The. E. E. Cummings. OxBA
   (Impression.) MoAmPo
House. Gerrit Achterberg, *tr. fr. Dutch by* James Brockway. DuIn
House, A. Sandra Agard. WS
House, The. George Bowering. NOBC
House. Robert Browning. NAEL-2
House, The. Murray Edmond. *Fr.* Poems of the End Wall. ATNZ; PeNZ
House, The. Uuno Kailas, *tr. fr. Finnish by* Aili Jarvenpa. SOP
House, The. Philip Levine. CAPP
House, The. Paula Nelson. GoYe
House. Diana O Hehir. NPGG
House, A. Steve Orlen. BLA; NAmP
House. Saibara, *tr. fr. Japanese by* Hiroaki Sato. FCEI
House, The. Tania Van Zyl. PeSA
House, The. William Carlos Williams. VGW
House across the Way, The. Ralph Hodgson. FaBoTw
House/ in which I live, The. Not Provable. Ilse Tielsch, *tr. by* Beth
   Bjorklund. CoAuP
House and hollow; village and valley-side. Winter Encounters. Charles
   Tomlinson. LiTM
House and Home. Joseph Beaumont. OBS
House and homeland they buy, selling dreams. Business. Mihály
   Ladányi, *tr. fr. Hungarian by* Jascha Kessler. *Fr.* Sketchbook.
   FOC
House and Land. Allen Curnow. ATNZ; PeNZ
House Beautiful, The. Robert Louis Stevenson. NOBE

House Blessing, A. William Cartwright. *See* Ordinary, The: Saint
   Francis and Saint Benedight.
House Blessing. Arthur Guiterman. TrPWD
House-Builders, The. Kamala Das. PBWP
House, by right, The. The Will. Sipho Sepamla. WMBCH
House by the Side of the Road, The. Sam Walter Foss. AnAmPo;
   BLPA; BLPL; FaBoBe; FaFP; OHFP; WBLP; WGRP
House Carpenter, The. *Unknown. See* I have just come from the salt,
   salt sea.
House Cat, The. Annette Wynne. RAR
House dawned, The. Reconciliation. David Rosenmann-Taub, *tr. by*
   Charles Guenther. VWA
House Divided, A. Michael Ondaatje. MoCV
House Fear. Robert Frost. *Fr.* The Hill Wife. VGW; WSC
House. For Sale. Leonard Clark. RHPC
House for Sale. André Frénaud, *tr. fr. French by* Keith Bosley.
   RHTwFP
House full, a hole full, A. *Unknown.* OxNR
House full of loud noises, A. A House. Sandra Agard. WS
House full, yard full. *Unknown.* NTCP
House Guest. Elizabeth Bishop. NYBP; TAP
House had gone to bring again, The. The Need of Being Versed in
   Country Things. Robert Frost. NoAM; NoBA; OxBA; UnPo
House I Go to in My Dream, The. George Barker. OnUR
House, I still inhabit you. House. Gerrit Achterberg, *tr. by* James
   Brockway. DuIn
House in Broad Street, red brick, with nine rooms, The. The Things.
   Conrad Aiken. HAP; WeW
House in Denver. Thomas Hornsby Ferril. AmFN
House in Meudon. Margarita Aliger, *tr. fr. Russian by* Elaine Feinstein.
   VWA
House in St. Petersburg. Stanley Burnshaw. VWA
House in Taos, A. Langston Hughes. CDC
House in the Fields. Shotetsu, *tr. fr. Japanese by* Steven D. Carter.
   WFTW
House in the Green Well, The. John Hall Wheelock. MoAmPo
House in the Heart, The. Naomi Shihab Nye. NAmP
House in the Wood, The. Randall Jarrell. LCAP
House inside still looks like a house, The. Moving. Frank Steele.
   GOYP; MOWH
House is a cote for doves, The. Miguel Hernández, *tr. by* Perry Higman.
   LPSS
House Is an Enigma. Laura Jensen. LCAP
House is closed, The. Alfred Kolleritsch, *tr. by* Beth Bjorklund.
   CoAuP
House is crammed: tier beyond tier they grin, The. "Blighters."
   Siegfried Sassoon. CMoP; FaBoTw; MMA; MoP; NoAM; OxBSP
House Is Empty, The. Yona Wallach, *tr. fr. Hebrew by* Warren Bargad
   and Stanley F. Chyet. IP
House is filled, The. The last heartthrob. Near the Ocean. Robert
   Lowell. NOBA
House is inhabited by squirrels, The. The Abandoned House. Patricia
   Hubbell. WSC
House is large, its kitchen vast, The. Ravidas, *tr. by* John Stratton
   Hawley *and* Mark Juergensmeyer. SSI
House Is Old, The. Ron Schreiber. GLP
House is so quiet now, The. The Vacuum. Howard Nemerov.
   NePoEA; NIP; RB
House is yours, The. The House. William Carlos Williams. VGW
House leaks and leans, The. The Ancestors. John Peale Bishop.
   PoA
House lies vacant now, forbear to knock, The. Miser. Gordon LeClaire.
   CaP
House-Mates. Leon Gellert. CBAP
House Mouse, The. Jack Prelutsky. RAR
House my earthly parent left, The. The Cottage. Jones Very. OxBA
House Next Door, The. Douglas Dunn. OxBC
House o' the Mirror, The. Helen Adam. MAT; NMM
House of Ate, The. Spenser. *Fr.* The Faerie Queene, IV, 1. OBSC
House of Broughton Street, The. Mary Ann Larkin. AiP
House of Christmas, The. G. K. Chesterton. MoBrPo
House of Colour, The. Francis Sherman. CaP
House of Desire, The. Sherley Anne Williams. AIW; BISi
House of Falling Leaves, The. W. S. Braithwaite. PoLF; PoNe
House of five fires, you never raised me. In the Longhouse, Oneida
   Museum. Roberta Hill Whiteman. NoAM; STE
House of God, The. A. D. Hope. OxBC
House of God is due to be converted, The. Development. D. J. Enright.
   OxBSP
House of Hospitalities, The. Thomas Hardy. RB
House of Life, The, *sels.* Dante Gabriel Rossetti.
   Ardour and Memory. *Fr.* LXIV. OAEL-2

Autumn Idleness. *Fr.* LXIX. GBL; OAEL-2
Barren Spring. *Fr.* LXXXIII. EBVV; NoP; OAEL-2; OBNC; PoEL-5
Birth-Bond, The. *Fr.* XV. Son
Body's Beauty. *Fr.* LXXVIII. OAEL-2; Son; TrGrPo
(Lilith.) PoEL-5
Bridal Birth. *Fr.* II. Son
Choice, The. *Fr.* LXXIII. GTBS-P; OBEV
Heart's Haven. *Fr.* XXII. Son
Hill Summit, The. *Fr.* LXX. NoP
Inclusiveness. *Fr.* LXIII. NAEL-2
Kiss, The. *Fr.* VI. NOBVV; Son
Life-in-Love. *Fr.* XXXVI. HAP
Lost on Both Sides. *Fr.* XCI. NoP; SeCePo
Love Enthroned. *Fr.* I. OBNC
Lovesight. *Fr.* IV. EBVV; GTBS-P; NAEL-2; OBNC; TrGrPo
Mid-Rapture. *Fr.* XXVI. BLPL; FaBoBe
Nuptial Sleep. *Fr.* VI. EBVV; NAEL-2; NOBVV
One Hope, The. *Fr.* CI. NAEL-2; OAEL-2
Pride of Youth. *Fr.* XXIV. OBNC
Severed Selves. *Fr.* XL. BoLoP
Silent Noon. *Fr.* XIX. HAP; NAEL-2; NoP; OBNC; PoEL-5; TrGrPo; UnAS
Sonnet, A [*or* The: "Sonnet is a moment's monument"]. *Fr. introd.* HeIP; NAEL-2; NoP; Son
Soul's Beauty. *Fr.* LXXVIII. OBEV
Superscription, A. *Fr.* XCVII. EBVV; GTBS-P; NAEL-2; NoP; OAEL-2; OBNC; PoEL-5; SeCePo
Willowwood ("And now love sang: but his was such a song"). *Fr.* L. NAEL-2; OAEL-2
Willowwood ("I sat with love upon a woodside well"). *Fr.* XLIX. NAEL-2; OAEL-2; PoEL-5
Willowwood ("O ye, all ye that walk in Willowwood"). *Fr.* LI. NAEL-2; OAEL-2
Willowwood ("So sang he: and as meeting rose and rose"). *Fr.* LII. NAEL-2; OAEL-2
Without Her. *Fr.* LIII. GBL; OBNC; PoEL-5; Son
House of Lords, The. William Schwenck Gilbert. *Fr.* Iolanthe. NAEL-2; TrGrPo
House of Madam Juju, The. Kanai Mieko, *tr. fr. Japanese by* Christopher Drake. BoWoP
House of Mercy, A. Stevie Smith. FaBoWP
House of Night, The, *sels.* Philip Freneau.
"By some sad means, when reason holds no sway." PoEL-4
Death's Epitaph. AA, *br. sel.*
"Trembling I write my dream, and recollect." NAAL-1, *much abr.*
House of Red Leaves, The. Liu E, *tr. fr. Chinese by* Jonathan Chaves. CoBLCP
House of Richesse, The. Spenser. *Fr.* The Faerie Queene, II, 7. CH
House of sleepers, A—I, alone unblest. Insomnia. Edith Matilda Thomas. AA
House of the Living. Claude Vigée, *tr. fr. French by* Henry Braun
House of the Mouse, The. Lucy Sprague Mitchell. NTCP
House of the Trees, The. Ethelwyn Wetherald. CaP
House of Wisdom, The. Bible, *O.T. Fr.* Proverbs, IX: 1-6. TrGrPo
House on a Cliff. Louis MacNeice. NOIV
House on Buder Street, The. Gary Gildner. TAP
House on 15th S.W., The. Richard Hugo. CAPP
House on fire, A! We stumbled over the snow. Houses Burning; Quebec. Patrick Anderson. NOBC
House on the Hill, The. E. A. Robinson. AA; FaPON; GoJo; MoAmPo; NAEL-2; PrIm; TrGrPo
House on the River. Ad Zuiderent, *tr. fr. Dutch by* James S. Holmes. DuIn
House Plants. David McFadden. NOBC
House ringed round with trees and in the trees, A. Asylum. John Freeman. OBMV
House silent. In the Old House. Joan Aiken. WSC
House Slave, The. Rita Dove. NoAM
House-Slave, The. Mervyn Morris. PBCV
House-snake dwells here still, The. The Closed World. Denise Levertov. NoP
House Song to the East. *Unknown, tr. fr. Navajo Indian.* TTTS
House-Surgeon. William Ernest Henley. *Fr.* In Hospital, XVI. BrPo
House That Jack Built, The. Mother Goose. BoTP; FaBoBe; OxBoLi; OxNR
House That Jack Built, The ("This is the house that Jack built"). *Unknown.* FaBoBe
House That Jack Built, The ("This is the knife with a handle of horn"). *Unknown.* NBLV; OxBoLi
House That Was, The. Laurence Binyon. MoBrPo
House-Top, The. Herman Melville. LiTA; NAAL-1; NOBA; Prf

House wall that I must climb down to get to you, A. Blundering. Jutta Schutting, *tr. by* Beth Bjorklund. CoAuP
House was empty and, The. Music in an Empty House. Hugh Sykes Davies. EAS
House was in the mountains, The. Pavilion. Bill Manhire. ATNZ
House Was Quiet and the World Was Calm, The. Wallace Stevens. AiP; HAP; NoP; VGW
House was shaken by a rising wind, The. Brainstorm. Howard Nemerov. HAP; SM
House was still—the room was still, The. Charlotte Brontë. NOBVV
House where I was born, The. The Doves. Katharine Tynan. AWP
House where the long embankments are old, A. On a Winter Day Drinking Wine at a Friend's House in the Country. I Nagashiro, *tr. by* Burton Watson. JLIC-1
House with antipodes, A. Shadow. Sybren Polet, *tr. by* James S. Holmes. DuIn
House, with blind unhappy face, The. The Gray Folk. Edith Nesbit. NOBVV
House with coarse stuccoed, The. The House. Tania Van Zyl. PeSA
House with Nobody in It, The. Joyce Kilmer. BLPA; BLPL
House with Two Doors. Enrique Gonzáles Martínez, *tr. fr. Spanish by* Samuel Beckett. MexPo
House, you are done. Consecration of the House. Wolfe Seymour Fairbridge. PoAu-2
Housebreaker types/ that's the kind. *Unknown, tr. by* Burton Watson. FCEI
Household. Laura Jensen. LCAP
Household of Eight. Abraham Reisen, *tr. fr. Yiddish by* Nathan Halper. PeBMYV
Household of Ruth, The. Mrs. Henry Linden. CBWP-4
Household Remedies. *Unknown.* OBET
Housekeeper, The. Vincent Bourne, *tr. fr. Latin by* Charles Lamb. GN; PoLF
Houseless Downs, The. George Ferebe. *Fr.* The Shepherds' Song, Sung before Queen Anne, on the Wiltshire Downs, 11 June 1613. FaBoPP
Houseplant. Felicity Napier. BrRo
Houses. Aileen Fisher. NTCP
Houses, The, *sels.* Robin Hyde.
  "Adolicus; that's a creeper rug, its small." *Fr.* III. ATNZ; PeNZ
  "Hares on their forms at dusk were not so still." *Fr.* IV. PeNZ
  "None of it true; for Christ's sake, spill the ink." *Fr.* V. ATNZ; PeNZ
  "Old nursery chair; its legs, cut down, are broken." *Fr.* I. ATNZ
Houses. Donald Justice. EyDe
Houses. Dan Pagis, *tr. fr. Hebrew by* Warren Bargad *and* Stanley F. Chyet. IP
Houses, The. Eden Phillpotts. OxBTC
Houses, an embassy, the hospital. Days of 1964. James Merrill. CoAP; HCAP; NAAL-2; PoE
Houses, and again willows. A Topic for a Painting. Natsume Seibi, *tr. fr. Japanese by* Hiroaki Sato. *Fr.* Twenty-seven Hokku. FCEI
Houses and rooms are full of perfumes. Walt Whitman. *Fr.* Song of Myself, II. TrGrPo; UnPo
Houses are crowding the town. Ozaki Hosai, *tr. fr. Japanese by* Hiroaki Sato. *Fr.* One Hundred Haiku in Free Form. FCEI
Houses are faces. Houses. Aileen Fisher. NTCP
Houses are haunted, The. Disillusionment of Ten o'Clock. Wallace Stevens. AnAmPo; CMoP; FF; InPS; InPS; NAAL-2; NoAM; OxBA; RB; SOTW; TTTS
Houses are swaying, swimming in gray light. Homecoming. Anna Margolin. VWA, *tr. by* Keith Bosley
Houses Burning; Quebec. Patrick Anderson. NOBC
Houses, churches, mixed together. A Description of London. John Bancks. NOEC
Houses die, and will not die, The. Heartland. Jim Barnes. HATNAP
"Houses I dreamed and drew alive come now," he said. Architect. Louise Townsend Nicholl. EyDe
Houses of Corr an Chait are cold, The. Seamas Dall Mac Cuarta, *tr. by* Thomas Kinsella. NOIV
Houses of Emily Dickinson, The. Larry Rubin. NIP
Houses, Past and Present. Eli Bachar, *tr. fr. Hebrew by* Jeremy Garber. VWA
Houses pick like hens into the landscape, The. Countryside in France. Hans Andreus. DuIn
Houses Were Left Full of Smoke, The. Leonel Rugama, *tr. fr. Spanish by* Alejandro Murguía. Vol
Housesnake's made her nest in the woodshed, A. This Cold Nothing Else. Dara Wier. MAYP
Housewife, The. Catherine Cate Coblentz. BLRP; TrPWD
Housewife. Josephine Miles. PCP
Housewife. Susan Fromberg Schaeffer. IHMS

Housewife. Anne Sexton. NMM
Housewifery. Edward Taylor. *See* Huswifery.
Housewife's Lament, The ("I used to have fine buckles"). *Unknown, tr. fr. Italian by* Muriel Kittel. DMI
Housewife's Lament, The ("One day as I was walking"). *Unknown.* MAT
Housewife's Letter: To Mary. Anne Halley. NMM
Housework. Amanda Berenguer, *tr. fr. Spanish by* Priscilla Joslin. WPOW
Housing Shortage. Naomi Replansky. NMM
Housing Starts. Peter Davison. EyDe
Houston Street. Lisa Vice. ER
Hoverer, The. Margit Szécsi, *tr. fr. Hungarian by* Jascha Kessler. FOC
Hovering and huge, dark, formless sway, The. The Virgin Mary. Edgar Bowers. NePoEA; QFR
Hovering like the heron. What She Said. Orampokiyar, *tr. fr. Tamil by* A. K. Ramanujan. *Fr.* Five on the Riverside Cane, 2. PLW
How. S. J. Marks. NYBP
How? Abraham Sutskever, *tr. fr. Yiddish.* PeBMYV, *tr. by* Chana Bloch; VWA, *tr. by* Ruth Whitman.
How a Girl Got Her Chinese Name. Nellie Wong. WPOW
How a Girl Was Too Reckless of Grammar [by Far]. Guy Wetmore Carryl. AnAmPo; FiBHP; OBAL
How a Guitar Can Lie on a Chair. K. Schippers, *tr. fr. Dutch by* Peter Nijmeijer. DuIn
How a Puppy Grows. Leroy F. Jackson. RAR
How all occasions do inform against me. Shakespeare. *Fr.* Hamlet, IV, iv. HoPM
How am I hitched. Suffering. Albert Ehrenstein, *tr. by* Babette Deutsch. TrJP
How Amiable Are Thy Tabernacles! Bryant. *See* Dedication: "Thou, whose unmeasured temple stands."
How amiable are thy tabernacles, O Lord of hosts! Psalm LXXXIV ("How amiable are thy tabernacles. . .") Bible, *O.T. Fr.* Psalms. FaPON; TrJP
   (Psalm LXXXIV: "How lovely are thy dwellings fair!," *paraphrased by* Milton.) TrPWD
   How Lovely Are Thy Tabernacles. *Fr.* 1-5. TrJP
   Sparrow, The. *Fr.* 3. FaPON
How and with what will you fill. How? Abraham Sutskever, *tr. by* Ruth Whitman. VWA
How Annandale Went Out. E. A. Robinson. MoAB; MoAmPo; NoAM; NoAm; NOBA
How are our Spirituall Gamesters slipt away? Elegy upon the Death of That Holy Man of God Mr. John Allen. Edward Taylor. PoEL-3
How are songs begot and bred? Songs. Richard Henry Stoddard. AA
How are the Mighty Fallen. Bible, *O.T. See* Second Samuel: Beauty of Israel is slain [*or* slaine] upon thy high places, The.
How are thy servants blest, O Lord! Joseph Addison. TrPWD
How Are You, Dear World, This Morning? Horace Logo Traubel. TrJP
How Are You, Sanitary? Bret Harte. AnAmPo
How are you so smooth-faced. Girl. *Unknown, tr. by* Anne Pennington. RB
How, as a spider's web is spun. To Jessie's Dancing Feet. William De Lancey Ellwanger. AA
How awesome/ the imperial command. *Unknown. Fr.* Manyo Shu. FCEI
"How bare! How all the lion-desert lies." Macrinus against Trees. "Michael Field." WPE
How Beastly the Bourgeois Is. D. H. Lawrence. ChTr; LiTM; NAEL-2; OBSV; TW
How beautiful and calm how crimson pale. The Spirit Craft. Charles G. Ballard. VoR
How beautiful is genius when combined. Sacred Poetry. John Wilson. WBLP
How beautiful is night! Night. Robert Southey. GN
How beautiful is the rain! Rain in Summer. Longfellow. BoTP; GN
How beautiful it was, that one bright day. Hawthorne. Longfellow. PoEL-5
How beautiful the Earth is still. Anticipation. Emily Brontë. OBNC
How beautiful their feet. Martin Farquhar Tupper. *Fr.* The Train of Religion. FaBoCo
How beautiful this hill of fern swells on! Stanzas from "Child Harold." John Clare. *Fr.* Child Harold. OBNC
   (In Epping Forest.) FaBoPP
How beautiful this immortal spirit. The Guardian Angel. Amable Tastu, *tr. by* Beth Archer. DMF
How beautiful to live as thou didst live! Tennyson. Florence Earle Coates. AA
How Beautiful upon the Mountains. Bible, *O.T. Fr.* Isaiah, LII: 7–10. TrJP
How Beautiful You Are: 3. Elaine Edelman. IHMS

How, beyond all foresight. Against Portraits. Charles Tomlinson. PoPo
How Big Was Alexander? Elijah Jones. BLPA
How bitter for these border men! Call to Arms. Tso Yen-nien, *tr. by* Burton Watson. CoBCP
How blessed is he, who leads a country life. To My Honour'd Kinsman, John Driden, of Chesterton. Dryden. OBS
How blest art thou, canst love the countrey, Wroth. To Sir Robert Wroth. Ben Jonson. SeCV-1
How blest is he, who for his country dies. To the Earl of Oxford, Late Lord Treasurer. Swift, *after the Latin of* Horace. OBVE
How blest was the created state. The Fall. Earl of Rochester. EnLoPo
How blest would be Ïerne's isle. Written in Ireland. Mary Alcock. NOEC; OBTV
How blurred and misty are the pines in the evening! Written in the Mountains. Wang Ts'ai-wei, *tr. by* Pao Chia-lin. WFTU
How brave a ladybug must be! Raindrops. Aileen Fisher. RAR
How brave the peasant who lives beside the lake. Hsü Chung-hsing, *tr. fr. Chinese by* Jonathan Chaves. *Fr.* Song of Catching Tigers. CoBLCP
"How brent is your brow, my Lady Elspat!" Lady Elspat. *Unknown.* ESPB
How bright on the blue. The Kite. Harry Behn. FaPON
How busie are the sonnes of men? Roger Williams. GOA; SCAP
How calm, how beautiful, comes on. The Golden Hour. Thomas Moore. *Fr.* Lalla Rookh. OBNC
How calmly cows move to the milking sheds. The Herd. Frances Cornford. FM
"How came that blood on thy coat-lap?" The Dead Brother. *Unknown.* EnSB
How can a girl with such a big belly be so desirable? Mrs. Loewinsohn &c. Ron Loewinsohn. NeAP
How can I begin to thank. Life of T. S. Eliot. Michael Frayn. FaBoPa
How can I call out? How can I shout? At Night. Bella Akhmadulina, *tr. by* Daniel Halpern *and* Albert Todd. BoWoP
How can I care whether you sigh for me. Song: How Can I Care? Robert Graves. GBL
How can I climb the Mount of Purgatory? Cato. C. H. Sisson. NOCV
How can I forget?—spring hazes lost. Teika, *tr. fr. Japanese by* Hiroaki Sato. *Fr.* Eighty-four Tanka. FCEI
How can I give thee up, my child, my dearest, earliest born. Wail of the Divorced. Mary E. Tucker. CBWP-1
How can I help myself, as one woman said to me about wanting. Leslie Scalapino. *Fr.* Hmmmm. NPGG
How Can I Keep My Maidenhead. Burns. ErPo
How can I look at my unhappiness. The Displacement. Hubert Witheford. ATNZ
How can I regret my life. The Signal. David Ignatow. NNaP
How Can I See You, Love. David Vogel, *tr. fr. Hebrew by* A. C. Jacobs. VWA
How can I sing light-souled and fancy-free. Lorenzo de' Medici, *tr. fr. Italian by* John Addington Symonds. *Fr.* Two Lyrics, II. AWP
How Can I Smile? Florence B. Hodgdon. BLRP
How can I sustain. Private Pain in Time of Trouble. Kathleen Spivack. AmPA
How can I tell what I've seen? Kakua, *tr. by* Lucien Stryk *and* Takashi Ikemoto. ZPCJ
How can I tell you. How. S. J. Marks. NYBP
How can I, that girl standing there. Politics. W. B. Yeats. CMoP; FF; HeIP; InPS; OxBTC; PoE; SCV
"How can I then return in happy plight." Shakespeare. *Fr.* Sonnets, XXVIII. OBSC
How can I think what thoughts. Candle, Lamp & Firefly. Tess Gallagher. NAmP
How can I turn this wheel that turns my life. The Wheel. Edwin Muir. NoAM
How can I, who cannot control. Blind Steersmen. Francis Ernest Kobina Parkes. PBA
How can it be. Tamesuke, *tr. by* Steven D. Carter. WFTW
How can it be. Dancer. Roy Scheele. GOYP
How can it be that I forget. Recollection. Anne Reeve Aldrich. AA
How Can Man Die Better. Tyrtaeus, *tr. fr. Greek by* T. F. Higham. WaaP
How can one e'er be sure. Lady Horikawa, *tr. fr. Japanese by* Curtis Hidden Page. *Fr.* Hyaku-Nin-Isshu. AWP
How can one make an absence flower. A Flowering Absence. John Montague. CIP
How can one tell what Love may be about. Psychoanalysis. Gavin Ewart. NYBP
How can our minds and bodies be. Grace before Sleep. Sara Teasdale. TrPWD
How can that tree but withered be. Song. *Unknown.* ElL

How can the tree but waste and wither away. No Pleasure without Some
    Pain. Lord Thomas Vaux. ElL
    (Death in Life.) OBSC
How can they write or paint. Observations in a Cornish Teashop.
    Kenneth Rexroth. OBAL
How can we find? how can we rest? Thoughts on the Shape of the Human
    Body. Rupert Brooke. BrPo
How can we justify a life. For Tony, Dougal, Mick, Bugs, Nick et Al.
    Dave Bathgate. PoSH
"How can you, friend?" the Swedish say. How Do You Do? H. Bedford
    Jones. WBLP
How can you hear a scream in this huge city. Pride of Cities. Akhtar-ul-
    Iman, tr. by Mahmood Jamal. PBMUP
How can you know, or understand, our loss. Navajo Signs. Winifred
    Fields Walters. NOVW
How can you live, how exist. The Likeness. Arthur Gregor. VGW
How can you look at the Neva. "Anna Akhmatova." AnAn, tr. by
    Stanley Kunitz with Max Hayward; BoWoP, tr. by Stanley Kunitz and
    Max Hayward
How can you plead that you have no wraps? Unknown, tr. by Arthur
    Waley. BoS
"How can you say you have no bedclothes?" Unknown, tr. by Arthur
    Waley. BoS
How can you set to the table a-dining? The Lost Baby. Unknown.
    AmFP
How can your playful ways, my love. Mirza Mohammad Rafi Sauda, tr.
    by Ahmed Ali. GoT
How changed is here each spot man makes or fills! Matthew Arnold. Fr.
    Thyrsis. FaBoPP; FiP; Mes; NAEL-2; NOBE; NoP; OBEV;
    OBNC
How cold are thy baths, Apollo! Jugurtha. Longfellow. AA
How cold the snow. Unknown, tr. fr. Spanish by Cheli Durán. Fr. Four
    Christmas Carols. PChr
How coldly the moon stands above the garden. There'll Be No Better.
    Gerda Mayer. DT
How Come the Truck-Loads? Judith Rodriguez. FaBoWP
How come to town she was, tied bright and prim. On a Photograph of
    My Mother at Seventeen. Miller Williams. MT
How comely glisten the rounded cheeks. Fatness. Alan Ansen.
    CoAP
How comes that blood all over thy shirt? Edward. Unknown.
    HoPM
How comest thou, O flower so fair. The Snowdrop. Mary Weston
    Fordham. CBWP-2
How comforting. The Day They Cleaned Up the Border El Salvador,
    February, 1981. Wendy Rose. HATNAP
How compare either of this grim twain? Thomas Hardy and A. E.
    Housman. Max Beerbohm. NBLV
How cool beneath this stone the soft moss lies. Epitaph for a Negro
    Woman. Owen Dodson. PoNe
How cool it feels. Basho, tr. by Kenneth Koch and Harold Henderson.
    TTTS
How could her dim eyes. Recollection. Duane Big Eagle. STE
How could I have possibly said. Winter Evening. Anzai Hitoshi, tr. by
    Hiroaki Sato. FCEI
How could I love you more? Richard Aldington. BrPo
How could I possibly have lived until today. Princess Shikishi, tr. fr.
    Japanese by Hiroaki Sato. Fr. Seventy-eight Tanka. FCEI
How could nothing turn so gold? Message at Sunset for Bishop Berkeley.
    Heather McHugh. GeTw
How could one struggle for freedom. Asadullah Khan Ghalib, tr. by
    Ahmed Ali. GoT
How could they think women a recreation? Don Giovanni on His Way to
    Hell II ("How could they think women a recreation?"). Jack Gilbert.
    NPGG
How Could We, Beforehand, Live in Quiet. Nikolai Stepanovich
    Gumilev, tr. fr. Russian by Jeannette Eyre. WaaP
How could you be so happy, now some thousand years. Note to Wang
    Wei. John Berryman. NYBP
How could you dream mere body's eloquence. A Prophecy. Christopher
    Levenson. ErPo
How could you not keep them. Old Clothes. Phil Hey. GOYP
How Crazy Are Those Who Love You So Much. Kishwar Naheed, tr. fr.
    Urdu by Mahmood Jamal. PBMUP
How cursed that country, how severe its doom. Thomas Maurice. Fr.
    An Epistle to the Right Hon. Charles James Fox. NOEC
How Cyrus Laid the Cable. John Godfrey Saxe. AnAmPo; PAH
How daur ye ca' me "Howlet-face." Burns. FaBoEE
How dear to my heart are the grand politicians. The Old Hokum
    Buncombe. Robert E. Sherwood. NBLV
How dear to my [or this or the] heart are the scenes of my childhood.
    The Old Oaken Bucket. Samuel Woodworth. AnAmPo; BLPA;

FaBoBe; FaFP; FaPON; FPL; WBLP
    (Bucket, The.) AA
How dear to my heart is the old village drugstore. The Hair-Tonic Bottle.
    Ben King. OBAL
How dear to my heart was the old-fashioned hurler. The Old-fashioned
    Pitcher. George E. Phair. SoSe
How Death Came. Unknown, tr. fr. Hottentot by W. H. I. Bleek. PeSA;
    TTY
How Death Comes. Unknown. MeEL
How deep is his duplicity who in a flash. High Diver. Robert Francis.
    NePoAm; SD
How Delicately. Joyce Carol Oates. EOEF
How delicious is the winning. Freedom and Love. Thomas Campbell.
    GTBS; GTBS-P
How delightful, at sunset, to loosen the boat! The Excursion. Tu Fu.
    AWP, tr. by Amy Lowell and Florence Ayscough; SD, tr. by Amy
    Lowell and Florence Ayscough
How delightful to meet Mr. Hodgson! Lines to Ralph Hodgson, Esqre.
    T. S. Eliot. NBLV; OBAL
How delightful to see. Sheep Shearing. Unknown. OBET
How desolate! Solitude. Thomas Traherne. OBS
How did a great Red-tailed Hawk. The Dead by the Side of the Road.
    Gary Snyder. HAP; InPS
How did a timid seedling ever. An Accident. Wu Sheng, tr. by Dominic
    Cheung. IFON
How did he die/ O if I told you. The Gangster's Death. Ishmael Reed.
    PoBA
How Did He Get Here? H. Leivick, tr. fr. Yiddish by Ruth Whitman.
    VWA
How did it come ungathered all the sheaved throng, The. Failure.
    Richmond Lattimore. PCP
How did it happen that we quarreled? Words! Words! Jessie Redmond
    Fauset. CDC
How did it know where I was standing? Kitten. Judith Herzberg, tr. by
    the author. DuIn
How Did It Seem to Sylvia? Gjertrud Schnackenberg. SM
How did she come here, what it was new and sparkling. Deir El Bahari:
    Temple of Hatshepsut. D. J. Enright. OBTV
How did she leave the world? with what contempt? Ben Jonson. Fr. An
    Elegy on the Lady Jane Paulet. OBD
How did the party go in Portman Square? Juliet. Hilaire Belloc.
    BoLoP; EnLoPo
How did they fume, and stamp, and roar, and chafe. Atticus. Pope.
    Fr. The Epistle to Dr. Arbuthnot. TW
How did they kill my grandmother? How They Killed My Grandmother.
    Boris Slutsky, tr. by Daniel Weissbort. VWA
How did you come to me, my sweet? To a Child Who Inquires. Olga
    Petrova. BLPA
How Did You Die? Edmund Vance Cooke. BLPA; OHFP; PWR
How did you feel, you libertarians. Jacob Godbey. Edgar Lee Masters.
    Fr. Spoon River Anthology. LiTA
"How did you know her?" Story from Russian Author. Peter Redgrove.
    NePoEA-2
How Different! Ebenezer Elliott. EBEV
How dishonest the sun. Seeing through the Sun. Linda Hogan. ER;
    HATNAP
How distinct is Matokata, the Target Bay. "Toneri." Fr. Manyo Shu.
    Ma
How do I enter the silence of stones. Mona Sa'udi, tr. by Kamal
    Boullata. WPOW
How do I feel. Second Nature. Diana Chang. BrSi
How do I feel about Hong Kong? The Kowloon-Canton Railway. Yu
    Kuang-chung, tr. by Dominic Cheung. IFON
How do I love thee? Let me count the ways. Elizabeth Barrett Browning.
    Fr. Sonnets from the Portuguese, XLIII. BoLoP; CTC; EBVV;
    FaBoBe; FaBV; FaFP; FF; FPL; HeIP; HoPM; InPK; LiTB; NAEL-2;
    NIP; NoP; PoE; PoLF; PoRA; Son; TEP; TrGrPo; UnPo;
    WPE
How do robins build their nests? What Robin Told. George Cooper.
    FaPON
How do they do it, the ones who make love. Sex without Love. Sharon
    Olds. MAYP; NIP; TSL
How do we know, by the bank-high river. The Last Lap. Kipling.
    OxBTC
How Do You Do? H. Bedford Jones. WBLP
How do you do? Sure You Can Ask Me a Personal Question. Diane
    Burns. STE
How Do You Do? Unknown. See Misty-Moisty Was the Morn.
How do you know it is time to bloom. Creative Force. Maude Miner
    Hadden. GoYe
How do you know that the pilgrim track. The Year's Awakening.
    Thomas Hardy. CMoP; OxBTC

How do you like to go up in a swing. The Swing. Robert Louis Stevenson. FaBoBe; FaFP; GoJo; NTCP; PDV; TEP

How do you like what you have. Gertrude Stein. *Fr.* Portraits and Repetition. AiP

How do you make bread talk, this old treasure all wrapped. Bread Is Born. Anne Hébert, *tr. by* Maxine W. Kumin. BoWoP

How do you manage to be in Chu-lin? *Unknown, tr. by* Arthur Waley. BoS

How do you recognize death? Minor Elegy. Henriqueta Lisboa, *tr. by* Willis Barnstone *and* Nelson Cerqueira. BoWoP

How Do You Shape an Axe Handle? Gary Snyder. NoAM

How Do You Spell "Missile"?: Preliminary Instructions in the Nuclear Age. George Uba. BrSi

How does a person get to be a capable liar? Golly, How Truth Will Out. Ogden Nash. LiTA; MoAmPo

How does it happen, tell me. Judge Somers. Edgar Lee Masters. *Fr.* Spoon River Anthology. FaBoEE; OBSV

How does it help me if, with flawless art. Louise Labé, *tr. by* Raymond Oliver. WPOW

How does it know. The Seed. Aileen Fisher. OnUR

How does it look, the yellow patch. Song of the Yellow Patch. H. Leivick, *tr. fr. Yiddish by* Benjamin *and* Barbara Harshav. *Fr.* Poems of the Yellow Patch. AYP

How does my royal lord? How fares your Majesty? Shakespeare. *Fr.* King Lear: He wakes; speak to him. Prf

How does one cut an axe-handle. *Unknown, tr. by* Arthur Waley. BoS

How does one get outside. Dear Miss. Herman Gladwin. PeNZ

"How does the water/ Come down at Lodore?" The Cataract of Lodore. Robert Southey. GN; OxBChV; TEP; WBLP

How does your little toe. Meetings and Absences. Roy Fuller. OnUR

How dost thou wear and weary out thy days. Samuel Daniel. *Fr.* The Tragedie of Philotas. OBSC

How doth the city sit solitary, that was full of people! The Misery of Jerusalem. Bible, *O.T.* Lamentations, I. AWP

How Doth the Little Busy Bee. Isaac Watts. FaPON; HoPM

How doth the little crocodile. "Lewis Carroll." *Fr.* Alice's Adventures in Wonderland, *ch.* 2. FaBoCh; FaBoCo; FaBoEE; FaBoNo; FaFP; FaPON; MoShBr; NBLV; NOBL; NOBVV; Par; RB; TTTS (Crocodile, The.) HoPM; RHPC; TrGrPo

How dreamy-dark it is! Charles Mair. *Fr.* The Fireflies. OBCV

How dull and how insensible a beast. An Essay upon Satire. *At. to* John Sheffield. APAS

How Dumb Is He? Claudia Nabors. SoTCo

How Each Thing Save the Lover in Spring Reviveth to Pleasure. Earl of Surrey. *See* When Windsor walls sustain'd my wearied arm.

How easily my heart falls back into habits. It's All in Your Head. Marilyn Nelson Waniek. KS

How easily the ripe grain. The Widow. W. S. Merwin. NYBP; UnPo; VGW

How easy it is here. The Beauty of Dawn. Felix Mnthali. WMBCH

How easy 'tis to sail with wind and tide! The Medal Reversed. Elkanah Settle. APAS

How empty seems the town now you are gone! From One Who Stays. Amy Lowell. BoWoP

How erring oft the judgment in its hate. The English Fog. John Dyer. *Fr.* The Fleece. TrGrPo

How everything gets tamed. Mountain, Fire, Thornbush. Harvey Shapiro. VGW

How Everything Happens. May Swenson. HAP; RFM

How fades that native breath. Sweets That Die. Langdon Elwyn Mitchell. AA

How fair a flower is sown. Coventry Patmore. FaBoEE

How fair is youth that flies so fast! Then be happy, ye who may. Triumph of Bacchus and Ariadne. Lorenzo de' Medici, *tr. fr. Italian by* Richard Aldington. *Fr.* Carnival Songs. CTC

How far are they deceived who hope in vain. Ephelia to Bajazet. Sir George Etherege. APAS

How far, if you're hale and hearty. Olympic Event. Lois Leurgans. SoTCo

How Far Is It Called to the Grave? *Unknown.* BLPA

How Far Is It to Bethlehem? Frances Chesterton. BoTP; PChr

"How far is it to Bethlehem Town?" How Far to Bethlehem? Madeleine Sweeny Miller. BLPA; FPL

How far is it to peace, the piper sighed. Our Lady Peace. Mark Van Doren. WaP

"How far is St. Helena from a little child at play?" A St. Helena Lullaby. Kipling. EBEV; FaBoCh; OBMV; PoEL-5

How far shall I go with our lunch maid? To Kaji Island. *Unknown, tr. by* Hiroaki Sato. FCEI

How far shall I go with our lunch maid? To the Barrier Mount. *Unknown, tr. by* Hiroaki Sato. FCEI

How Far to Bethlehem? Madeleine Sweeny Miller. BLPA; FPL

"How fared you when you mortal were?" After. Ralph Hodgson. MoBrPo

How fashionably sad my early poems are! About My Poems. Donald Justice. PoA

How feels the guiltless dreamer, who. Memory. Edward Coate Pinkney. AnAmPo

How fell sage Helen? through a swain like thee. A Countryman's Wooing. Theocritus, *tr. by* Charles Stuart Calverley. ErPo

How felt the land in every part. Washington's Vow. Whittier. OHIP

How fetching! Somebody's husband. Hsieh Ling-yün, *tr. fr. Chinese by* Burton Watson. *Fr.* An Exchange of Poems by Tung-yang Stream, II. CoBCP

How fetching! somebody's wife. Hsieh Ling-yün, *tr. fr. Chinese by* Burton Watson. *Fr.* An Exchange of Poems by Tung-yang Stream, I. CoBCP

How fever'd is the man who cannot look. Keats. *Fr.* Two Sonnets on Fame, II. EnRP

How few of us are left, how few! *Unknown, tr. by* Arthur Waley. BoS

"How few," the Muse in plaintive accents cries. Erasmus Darwin. *Fr.* The Temple of Nature; or, The Origin of Society, IV. FM

How fierce in its loyalties the beat of the heart. Coronary Thrombosis. William Price Turner. OxBS

How fierce was I when I did see. Upon Julia Washing Herself in the River. Robert Herrick. CaPo

How Fine N'est-ce Pas. Gust Gils, *tr. fr. Dutch by* James S. Holmes. DuIn

How Firm a Foundation. "K.," *perhaps* Robert Keene, *sometimes at. to* George Keith. WGRP

How first we met do you still remember? Brussels and Oxford. William Hurrell Mallock. EBVV

How Five and Twenty Shillings Were Expended in a Week. *Unknown.* OBET

How fleet is air! how many things have breath. William King. *Fr.* Mully of Mountown. FM

How fond are men of rule and place. The Lion and the Cub. John Gay. *Fr.* Fables. GN

How foolish men on expeditions go! On Riding to See Dean Swift in the Mist of the Morning. Pope *and* Thomas Parnell. FaBoEE

How foolishly I loved. Poema Morale. Charles Gullans. NePoEA

How forlorn. Wakayama Bokusui, *tr. by* Geoffrey Bownas *and* Anthony Thwaite. PeBJV

How fortunate he is! *Unknown. Fr.* Manyo Shu. Ma

How fresh, O Lord, how sweet and clean. The Flower. George Herbert. AWP; ELP; FaBoRV; JCP; MePo; NAEL-1; NOBE; NOCV; NoP; OBS; PoEL-2; SeCP; SeCV-1

How full of joy were the days of youth. Vali Mohammad Nazir, *tr. by* Ahmed Ali. GoT

How funny you are today New York. Steps. Frank O'Hara. CAPP

How gently sings my soul and whets its wings. Laurence Dakin. *Fr.* Tancred, III, i. CaP

How glad I am that I was bound apprentice. For Patrick, Aetat: LXX. Sir John Betjeman. NAs

How gladdening would be this falling snow. Empress Komyo. *Fr.* Manyo Shu. Ma

How Glorious Are the Morning Stars. Benjamin Keach. AH

How Glorious Is Thy Name. Bible, *O.T. See* Psalms: Psalm VIII ("O Lord our Lord, how excellent is thy name. . .").

How glows each patriot bosom that boasts a Yankee heart. The *United States* and *Macedonian. Unknown.* PAH

How God speeds the tax-bribed plough. Drone *v.* Worker. Ebenezer Elliott. FaBoPV; OBSV

How Goes the Night? *Unknown, tr. fr. Chinese by* Helen Waddell. *Fr.* Shi King. AWP

How good to leave everything! Departure. Erika Mitterer, *tr. by* Beth Bjorklund. CoAuP

How goodly are thy tents, O Jacob [*or* the tentes of Jacob]. Balaam's Blessing. Bible, *O.T. Fr.* Numbers. OBVE; TrGrPo

How Goodly Is Thy House, *with music.* Henry S. Jacobs. AH

How Grand and How Bright. *Unknown.* GBP

How Great My Grief. Thomas Hardy. BrPo

How Great unto the Living Seem the Dead! Charles Heavysege. CaP (Dead, The.) NOBC

How happy a thing were a wedding. On Marriage. Thomas Flatman. FaBoUs; FiBHP; NOBL (Bachelor's Song, The.) EnLoPo

How happy I can be with my love away! The Absence. Sylvia Townsend Warner. MoBrPo

How happy in his low degree. Country Life. Horace, *tr. fr. Latin by* Dryden. *Fr.* Epodes, II. AWP

How happy is he born and taught. The Character of a Happy Life. Sir Henry Wotton. EiL; GTBS; GTBS-P; LiTB; NOBE; OBEV; OBS; TrGrPo

(Happy Life, The.) WGRP

How happy is the blameless vestal's lot! The Vestal. Pope. *Fr.* Eloisa to Abelard. ACP

How happy is the little stone. Emily Dickinson. RB

How Happy the Man. *Unknown.* OBET

How happy to be a fish. Fish and Bird. Rosemary Brinckman. BoTP

How happy uncle us'd to be. Uncle an' Aunt. William Barnes. NOBVV

How hard for unaccustomed feet. In the Time of Trouble. Leslie Savage Clark. TrPWD

How hard is my fortune. The Convict of Clonmel. *Unknown.* AnIL; SD, *tr. by* Jeremiah Joseph Callanan

How hard it is for the river here to re-enter. Wanting a Child. Jorie Graham. MAYP

How hard it is, we say. Clothes Maketh the Man. Theodore Weiss. NoAM

How hard the years dies: no frost yet. Intercession in Late October. Robert Graves. MoAB

How hath the oppressor ceased! Downfall of the Tyrant. Bible, *O.T. Fr.* Isaiah, XIV:4–19. TrGrPo

How have I bin religious? what strange good. To Fletcher Reviv'd. Richard Lovelace. OBS

How have I laboured? Ortus. Ezra Pound. LiTA

How he advanced, with a white fillet twisted. The Lyre Player. Stefan George, *tr. by* Carol North Valhope *and* Ernst Morowitz. PeHV

How he found his life long ago. How Just One Poor Man Lives. Alonzo Gonzales Mó, *tr. by* Allan F. Burns. STP

How He Saved St. Michael's. Mary A. P. Stansbury. BLPA

How He Saw Her. Ben Jonson. *Fr.* A Celebration of Charis in Ten Lyrick Peeces. QFR; SeCP; SeCV-1

How he survived them they could never understand. The Jew Wrecked in the German Cell. W. H. Auden. WaP

(Diaspora, The.) LiTA

How he thought. Drop the Wires. Hugh Seidman. AmPA

How headlights sugar. Starbirth. Albert Goldbarth. BWV

How helpless my heart! Komachi, *tr. by* Geoffrey Bownas *and* Anthony Thwaite. PeBJV

How Her Teeth Were Pulled. *Unknown, tr. fr. Paiute Indian by* Jarold Ramsey. STP

How High the Moon. Lance Jeffers. CNA; PoBA

How high Thou art! our songs can own. The Mediator. Elizabeth Barrett Browning. TrPWD

How history repeats itself. Can't. Harriet Prescott Spofford. PAH

How Hong Kong Was Destroyed. Dahlia Ravikovitch, *tr. fr. Hebrew.* IP, *tr. by* Warren Bargad *and* Stanley F. Chyet; MHeP, *tr. by* Bernhard Frank; OV, *tr. by* Chana Bloch.

"How, how," he said. "Friend Chang," I said. The Chinese Nightingale. Vachel Lindsay. MoAmPo

How I Brought the Good News from Aix to Ghent (or Vice Versa). R. J. Yeatman *and* W. C. Sellar. BXAP; FaBoPa; FiBHP; OnMSP

How I Came to Be a Graduate Student. Wendy Rose. STE

How I Came to Have a Man's Name. Emma Lee Warrior. HATNAP

How I doe love thee, Beaumont, and thy Muse. To Francis Beaumont. Ben Jonson. OBS

How I forsook/ Elias and Pisa after, and betook. Sir Richard Fanshawe, *after the Italian of* Giovanni Battista Guarini. *Fr.* Il Pastor Fido. AWP

How I go courting a charming beauty bright. Charming Beauty Bright. *Unknown.* AmFP

How I Got Ovah. Carolyn M. Rodgers. CNA

How I Learned English. Gregory Djanikian. MOWH

How I loved him. Courtship. Diana O Hehir. NPGG

How I loved those old movies. Old Movies. John Cotton. FF

How I regret it now. Udobe Ushimaro. *Fr.* Manyo Shu. Ma

How I think of it! *Unknown, tr. fr. Japanese by* Burton Watson. *Fr.* Kokin Shu. FCEI

How I waste and waste away. Yakamochi. *Fr.* Manyo Shu. Ma

How I wish I. The Value of pi. *Unknown.* FaBoUs

How I wish I had known/ beforehand of this journey. *Unknown, tr. by* Kenneth Yasuda. BoWoP

How I wish I were able to say what I think. Gertrude Stein. *Fr.* Stanzas in Meditation. PBWP

How I wish the Argo had never reached the land. Medea. Euripides, *tr. by* Rex Warner. NAWM-1

How ill doth he deserve a Lovers name. Eternity of Love Protested. Thomas Carew. MeLP; OBS

How impotent a deity am I! Sir Samuel Garth. *Fr.* The Dispensary. OBSV

How in Heaven's name did Columbus get over. Columbus. Arthur Hugh Clough. AmFN

How Infinite Are Thy Ways. William Force Stead. *See* Uriel: I thought the night without a sound was falling.

How innocent their lives look. Photos of a Salt Mine. Patricia K. Page. NoAM; NOBC

How intimate was the earth in days gone by. The Earth. David Gwenallt Jones, *tr. by* Dyfnallt Morgan. OBWVE

How is it all gonna turn out. "Haida Charlie," *tr. by* James Koller *after* John Swanton. STP

How is it I can eat bread here and cut meat. Evening Meal in the Twentieth Century. John Holmes. AiP

How is it now? Questions [2]. Donald Hall. FF

How is it proved? The Great Wager. G. A. Studdert-Kennedy. TrCP

How is it, Salma, that when you are near me. Salma. Ilyas Farhat, *tr. by* Salma Khadra Jayyusi *and* John Heath-Stubbs. MAP

How is it that I am so careless here. Meditation 62. Philip Pain. NOBA

How is it with another woman? An Attempt at Jealousy. Marina Tsvetayeva, *tr. by* Robert Perelman *and* Aleksandar Petrov. WPOW

"How is she?" I asked. Lily, Lois & Flaubert; the Site of Loss. Kathleen Fraser. NPGG

How Is the Gold Become Dim. Bible, *O.T. Fr.* Lamentations. ChTr

How Is the Night? *Unknown, tr. fr. Chinese by* Burton Watson. CoBCP

How it chirrups, the mulberry-finch! *Unknown, tr. by* Arthur Waley. BoS

How it feels to be touching. We Become New. Marge Piercy. TAP

How it goes. Severance. Kit Robinson. IAT

How It Is. Uri Zvi Greenberg, *tr. fr. Hebrew by* Robert Mezey *and* Ben Zion Gold. VWA

How It Is. Maxine W. Kumin. CAPP; NoAM

How it is possible to wake this empty. The House in the Heart. Naomi Shihab Nye. NAmP

How it responds with its heart. For a Voice That Is Singing. Aldo Camerino, *tr. by* Anita Barrows. VWA

How It Seemed to Him Away from Home. James Whitehead. BLA

How It Strikes a Contemporary. Robert Browning. CTC; FaBoPV; GTBS-P; OAEL-2

How it tapered, the bamboo rod. *Unknown, tr. by* Arthur Waley. BoS

How it was in that place, how light hung in a bright pool. Wolfpen Creek. James Still. MT

How It's Done. Alvin Aubert. MT

How Jack Found That Beans May Go Back on a Chap. Guy Wetmore Carryl. HoPM

How joyous his neigh! Song of the Horse. *Unknown, tr. by* Natalie Curtis. AWP

How Just One Poor Man Lives. Alonzo Gonzales Mó, *tr. fr. Mayan by* Allan F. Burns. STP

How kind, how secretly, the sun. The Garden. Robert Penn Warren. PoA

How large unto the tiny fly. The Fly. Walter de la Mare. OnUR

How! Liberty of Conscience! that's a change. Dr. Wild's Ghost. *Unknown.* APAS

How Lies Grow. Maxine Chernoff. UL

How life and death in Thee. To Our Blessed Lord upon the Choice of His Sepulchre. Richard Crashaw. ACP

(Upon Our Saviour's Tomb Wherein Never Man Was Laid.) OAEL-1

How lightly we. A Visiting Card. Gregory O'Brien. ATNZ

How like a marriage is the season of clouds. Cloud Country. James Merrill. NePoEA

"How like a winter hath my absence been[e]." Shakespeare. *Fr.* Sonnets, XCVII. AWP; EiL; EnLoPo; EyDe; GTBS; GTBS-P; NAEL-1; NOBE; OAEL-1; OBEV; OBSC; PoRA; Son; TEP; TrGrPo

How like an angel came I down. Wonder. Thomas Traherne. CH; HAP; LiTB; NAEL-1; NoP; PoE; SeCePo; SeCP; SeCV-2; TOF; TrGrPo

How like the leper, with his own sad cry. The Buoy-Bell. Charles Tennyson Turner. Son

How Lillies Came White. Robert Herrick. CaPo

How little I have really cared about nature: I always. Neighbors. A. R. Ammons. CAPP

How loneliness spreads from me. Here. Eeva-Liisa Manner, *tr. by* Aili Jarvenpa. SOP

How lonely, the light of the moon. Saigyo, *tr. fr. Japanese by* Burton Watson. *Fr.* Sixty-four Tanka. FCEI

How long/ can man gaze at his own whirling center? Dizziness. Shin Dong-jip, *tr. by* Koh Chang-soo. ACKP

How long ago Hector took off his plume. Parting in Wartime. Frances Cornford. FaBoWP; NIP

How long ago she planted the hawthorn hedge. The Hawthorn Hedge. Judith Wright. PoAu-2; WPE

How long ago we dreamed. Carol of the Three Kings. W. S. Merwin. PChr
How long, dear Savior, O how long. Isaac Watts. AmFP
How long, how long must I regret? The Lost Tribe. Ruth Pitter. WPOW
How long, how long within this world will you remain. Mirza Mohammad Rafi Sauda, tr. by Ahmed Ali. GoT
How Long I Sailed. Hartley Coleridge. Son
How long it seems since that mild April night. Seaward. Celia Thaxter. AA
How long I've loved thee, and how well. Love's Wisdom. Margaret Deland. AA
How Long, Jehovah? Henry Ainsworth. AH
How long must we two hide the burning gaze. United. Paulus Silentiarius, tr. by W. H. D. Rouse. AWP
How long, O lion, hast thou fleshless lain? The Lion's Skeleton. Charles Tennyson Turner. FM; NOBVV
How long, O sister, how long. The Bells at Midnight. Thomas Bailey Aldrich. PAH
How long our kiss was! Wakayama Bokusui, tr. fr. Japanese by Hiroaki Sato. Fr. Forty-four Tanka. FCEI
"How long shall fortune faile me now." The Earl of Westmoreland. Unknown. ESPB
How long shall I endure without reply. The Medal of John Bays; a Satire against Folly and Knavery. Thomas Shadwell. APAS
How Long Shall I Give? Unknown. BLRP
How long shall you and I be bound. Water Whirligigs. D. J. Opperman, tr. by Jack Cope and Uys Krige. PeSA
How long she waited for her executioner! Head of Medusa. Marya Zaturenska. MoAmPo
How long since I've spent a whole night. Love Song to a Stranger. Joan Baez. UAS
How long the stars. Nansen, tr. by Lucien Stryk and Takashi Ikemoto. ZPCJ
How long this giant hugged and spanned. Windmill on the Cape. William Vincent Sieller. GoYe
How Long This Night Is. Unknown. See Merry It Is.
How long this way: that everywhere. Red Sea. James Agee. Fr. Two Songs on the Economy of Abundance. MoAmPo
How long we sit in front of them. Careers. Marjorie Welish. UL
How Long Will I Stand. Moyshe-Leyb Halpern, tr. fr. Yiddish by Benjamin and Barbara Harshav. AYP
How long will it last? Lady Horikawa, tr. fr. Japanese by Kenneth Rexroth and Ikuko Atsumi. WPOW
How long will you remain a boy? Meditation. Carl Rakosi. VWA
How long wilt thou forget me O Lord. Psalm XIII ("How long wilt thou forget me O Lord. . ."). Bible, O.T. Fr. Psalms.
(Psalm XIII: "How long, O Lord, shall I forgotten be?" paraphrased by Sir Philip Sidney.) OBVE
How long, young men, unsoldiered, disregarding. A Call to Action. Callinus, tr. by T. F. Higham. WaaP
How Looks the Night? Gerard Manley Hopkins. OxBSP
How lost is the little fox at the borders of night. Night of Wind. Frances Mary Frost. FaPON
How lovely are the tombs of the dead nymphs. Panope. Dame Edith Sitwell. MoAB; MoBrPo
How lovely are thy dwellings fair! Psalm LXXXIV. Milton. TrPWD
How Lovely Are Thy Tabernacles. Bible, O.T. Fr. Psalms: Psalm LXXXIV ("How amiable are thy tabernacles. . ."), 1-5. TrJP
How lovely! getting drunk faster than I do. Wakayama Bokusui, tr. fr. Japanese by Hiroaki Sato. Fr. Forty-four Tanka. FCEI
How lovely is the heaven of this night. A Beautiful Night. Thomas Lovell Beddoes. ChER
How lovely is the sound of oars at night. Boats at Night. Edward Shanks. CH
How lovely it is today! Unknown. Fr. Four Glosses. NOIV
How lovely it was, after the official fright. The Phenomenon. Karl Shapiro. CMoP; NYBP
How Low Is the Lowing Herd. Walt Kelly. FiBHP
How lush, how loose, the uninhibited squash is. Squash in Blossom. Robert Francis. FYAP
How McClellan Took Manassas. Unknown. PAH
How McDougal Topped the Score. Thomas E. Spencer. PoAu-1
How many a time have I. Swimming. Byron. Fr. The Two Foscari. GN
How many autumns have I passed. Teika, tr. fr. Japanese by Hiroaki Sato. Fr. Eighty-four Tanka. FCEI
How many autumns? unable to soothe myself. Raizan, tr. fr. Japanese by Hiroaki Sato. Fr. Thirteen Hokku. FCEI
How Many Bards Gild the Lapses of Time! Keats. EnRP
How many blessed groups this hour are bending. Sabbath Sonnet. Felicia Dorothea Hemans. Son

How many bullets does it take. Death in Yorkville. Langston Hughes. PoBA
How many buttons are missing today! Nobody Knows but Mother. Mary Morrison. BLPA
How Many Cows? Nyle A. Henderson. CowP
How many dawns, chill from his rippling rest. To Brooklyn Bridge. Hart Crane. Fr. The Bridge. AiP; AmPP; BLPL; CMoP; EyDe; HAP; HeIP; InPS; LiTA; LiTM; MoAB; MoAmPo; NoAM; NOBA; NoP; OxBA; PoE; PrIm; TAP; WeW
(Proem: To Brooklyn Bridge.) AmFP; AmPP; CMoP; HeIP; NoAm; NoP; TAP; WeW
How many days do they live on the branch. Falling Leaves. Wu Chia-chi, tr. by Irving Lo. WFTU
How many days has my baby to play? Mother Goose. OxNR
How Many Days Has My Baby to Play? Unknown. BoTP
How many days of spring rain. Rainy Season. Kan Sazan, tr. by Burton Watson. JLIC-2
How Many Devils Can Dance on the Point. D. J. Enright. AnAn
How many doors will this man open. Death. Roy Fuller. NoAM
How many evenings in the arbor by the river. Li Ch'ing-chao, tr. by Eugene Eoyang. BoWoP
How many faults you might accuse me of. Elinor Wylie. NAAL-2
How many fires. George Reavey. EAS
How Many Heavens. Dame Edith Sitwell. TrCP
How many humble hearts have dipped. To a Post-Office Inkwell. Christopher Morley. PoLF
How many kalpa have elapsed. Face. Koh Chang-soo, tr. by the author. ACKP
How many kinds of meetings, Lord. Meetings. János Pilinszky, tr. by William Jay Smith. MHuP
How many lives, made beautiful and sweet. Giotto's Tower. Longfellow. EyDe
How many men are killed by power, by power. Sejanus. Juvenal, tr. fr. Latin by Robert Lowell. Fr. Satires, X. OBVE
How many miles to Babylon [or Barley-Bridge]? Mother Goose. BoTP; FaBoCh; GBP; MoShBr; OxBoLi; OxBSP; OxNR
How many moments must (amazing each). E. E. Cummings. PoA
How many mountains and rivers to cross. Wakayama Bokusui, tr. fr. Japanese by Hiroaki Sato. Fr. Forty-four Tanka. FCEI
How Many New Years Have Grown Old. Unknown. EiL
How Many Nights. Galway Kinnell. CAPP; MAT; NaP
How many nights have you wakened. Kanemasa, tr. by Geoffrey Bownas and Anthony Thwaite. PeBJV
How many now are left. Gift for an Old Official. Hsüan-yeh, tr. by Jonathan D. Spence. WFTU
How many paltry, foolish, painted things. Michael Drayton. Fr. Idea, VI. AAS; EnLoPo; GBL; HAP; HeIP; NAEL-1; NIP; NoP; OAEL-1; OBSC; PrIm; TEP
(Sonnet: "How many paltry. . .") EiL
How Many Poems Were Lost ("How many poems were forever lost"). Abba Kovner, tr. fr. Hebrew by Warren Bargad and Stanley F. Chyet. IP
How many scenes, O sun. Ode to the Sun. Eloise Bibb. CBWP-4
How many skies does the earth hold? Ourobouros. Jorge Plescoff, tr. by Yishai Tobin. VWA
How many strive to force a way. Forcing a Way. Unknown. NA
How Many Temptations I Pass Through. Patrizia Cavalli, tr. fr. Italian by Muriel Kittel. DMI
How many thousand of my poorest subjects. The Cares of Majesty. Shakespeare. Fr. King Henry IV, Pt. II, III, i. LiTB
(O Gentle Sleep.) FaBoRV
(Soliloquy on Sleep.) FiP
How many times. Tamekane, tr. by Steven D. Carter. WFTW
How Many Times? Thomas Lovell Beddoes. See Torrismond: How many times do I love thee, dear?
How many times, Death. O All Down within the Pretty Meadow. Kenneth Patchen. HAP; WeW
How many times do I love thee, dear? Thomas Lovell Beddoes. Fr. Torrismond, Sc. iii. LiTB; PoEL-4; TrGrPo
(How Many Times?) ELP
(How Many Times Do I Love Thee, Dear?.) EnRP
How many times now. Night at the End of the Year. Tamemasa, tr. by Steven D. Carter. WFTW
How many times these low feet staggered. Emily Dickinson. AmPP; HAP; NAAL-1; PoEL-5; WeW
How many ways can you bring me ten? Making Tens. M. M. Hutchinson. BoTP
How Many Ways ("How many ways, how many times"). John Masefield. Fr. Sonnets. LiTB; WGRP
How many wise men and heroes. To the Tune "The River Is Red." Ch'iu Chin, tr. by Kenneth Rexroth and Ling Chung. AiP; BoWoP; PBWP

How Marigolds Came Yellow. Robert Herrick. ChTr; TTTS
How marvelous a fellow. *Unknown. Fr.* Manyo Shu. FCEI
How memory cuts away the years. Autumn. Jean Starr Untermeyer. MoAmPo
How Metaphor Can Save Your Life. Myra Sklarew. CRP
How mighty a wizard. Z Is for Zoroaster. Eleanor Farjeon. WSC
How mobile is the bed on these. Rain. Vladimir Nabokov. GrPl
How monarchs die is easily explained. On a Royal Demise. Thomas Hood. FiBHP
How Morning Glories Could Bloom at Dusk. Jorie Graham. NPGG
How mournful seems, in broken dreams. Not Lost, but Gone Before. Caroline Elizabeth Norton. BLRP; WBLP
How much are they deceived who vainly strive. Love and Jealousy. William Walsh. BoLoP
How much better it seems now. The Next Poem. Dana Gioia. DiPo
How Much Christian. Jacob Glatstein, *tr. fr. Yiddish by* Benjamin *and* Barbara Harshav. AYP
How Much Earth. Philip Levine. NNaP
How much had happened on the earth. Mohammad Taqi Mir, *tr. by* Ahmed Ali. GoT
How much has the light thickened outside the window, under the green bough? Wang Kuo-wei, *tr. by* Irving Lo. WFTU
How much I should like to begin. At the Edge. Denise Levertov. NAAL-2
How much living have you done? The Poet Speaks. Georgia Douglas Johnson. AmNP
How much longer. Peter Turrini, *tr. by* Beth Bjorklund. CoAuP
How Much Longer? Robert Mezey. OBWP
How Much Longer Will I Be Able to Inhabit the Divine Sepulcher. John Ashbery. NeAP; PoM
How much mystery this atom bears in the universe. Tormented Mystic. Al-Tijani Yusuf Bashir, *tr. by* Matthew Sorenson *and* Patricia Alanah Byrne. MAP
How much of me is sandwiches radio beer? Lonesome in the Country. Al Young. MAT; NPGG
How much, preventing God, how much I owe. Grace. Emerson. AmPP; NoP; TrPWD
How much too eloquent are the songs we sing. Ellery Street. David Ferry. PPR
How much wood would a woodchuck chuck? If a Woodchuck Would Chuck. *Unknown.* FaPON
How must you be now, old woman. Words to Remind Me of Grandmother. Andrés Castro Ríos, *tr. by* Julio Marzán. InW
How mutable is every thing that here. Meditation 29. Philip Pain. *Fr.* Meditations for July 26, 1666. NOBA
How My Father Died. Nissim Ezekiel. VWA
How named is the god. Hitomaro. *Fr.* Manyo Shu. Ma
How near me came the hand of Death. A Widow's Hymn. George Wither. OBEV
How nice it is to eat! Beautiful Meals. T. Sturge Moore. BoTP
How nice to be a local swan. Sitting Pretty. Margaret Fishback. PoLF
How No Age Is Content with His Own Estate. Earl of Surrey. *See* Laid in My Quiet Bed [in Study as I Were].
How no shoe fit them. My Mother's Feet. Stanley Plumly. GeTw
How noteless men, and Pleiads, stand. Emily Dickinson. PoE
How now, spirit! whither wander you? Shakespeare. *Fr.* A Midsummer Night's Dream. GN
How odd/ Of God. The Chosen People. W. N. Ewer. FaBoEE
How Oft Has the Banshee Cried. Thomas Moore. AWP
How Oft Have I My Dere and Cruell Foo. Petrarch, *tr. fr. Italian by* Sir Thomas Wyatt. AAS; PFI
How oft I dream of childhood days, of tricks we used to play. Rosie Nell. *Unknown.* AS
How oft I prayed to hold her in my arms. Faint Heart. Rufinus Domesticus, *tr. by* F. A. Wright. ErPo
How Oft in Schoolboy Days. Frederick Goddard Tuckerman. Son
How oft when men are at the point of death. Shakespeare. *Fr.* Romeo and Juliet: For here lies Juliet, and her beauty makes. DL
(Romeo's Last Words.) FiP
"How oft, when thou, my music, music play'st." Shakespeare. *Fr.* Sonnets, CXXVIII. EIL; NAEL-1; PoE
How often does a man need to see a woman? The Word Made Flesh. W. J. Turner. OBMV
How often have I started out. Inspiration. Robert W. Service. WeW
How often have my tears. In Allusion to the French Song. Richard Lovelace. CaPo
How often I have said. Life Encompassed. Donald Davie. PoPo
How often in the years that close. A Meditation. Herman Melville. GOA
How often should we think of this, that we. Meditations for August 1, 1666. Philip Pain. SCAP
How often, when life's summer day. Walter Savage Landor. FaBoEE

How Old Are You? H. S. Fritsch. PoLF
How Old Brown Took Harper's Ferry. Edmund Clarence Stedman. OnMSP; PAH; PoNe
How Old Is My Heart. Christopher John Brennan. *Fr.* The Wanderer. PoAu-1
How old may Phillis *or* Phyllis be, you ask. Phillis's *or* Phyllis's Age. Matthew Prior. EnLoPo; FaBoEE
(Phyllis's Age.) FaBoEE
How old was Mary out of whom you cast. *Unknown.* MoAB; MoBrPo
How old were you when the Medes broke through? Political Customs. Roberto Roversi, *tr. by* Lawrence R. Smith. NItP
How on Solemn Fields of Space. Elizabeth Daryush. NOCV
How one loves. October Thoughts. Jean Follain, *tr. by* W. S. Merwin. RHTwFP
How One Winter Came in the Lake Region. Wilfred Campbell. CaP; NOBC; OBCV
How our child carries them piggyback. Issa, *tr. by* Hiroaki Sato. FCEI
How our good king does Papists hate. Satire on Old Rowley. *Unknown.* APAS
How Paddy Stole the Rope. *Unknown.* BLPA
How perfect they are without your help. Them. Hugo Williams. *Fr.* Calling Your Name in the Zoo. NPo
How perfectly/ the gramophone remembers. A Shoeshine for Louis Armstrong. Peter Goldsworthy. UAS
How pitiful is her sleep. In Memory of Kathleen. Kenneth Patchen. MoAmPo
How placid, how divinely sweet. Meandering Wye. Robert Bloomfield. *Fr.* The Banks of Wye. OBNC
How placidly shine/ The river, the spring, and the sun. Rosalía de Castro, *tr. fr. Galician by* Benjamin M. Woodbridge, Jr. PBWP
How plainly one may see. Hitomaro. *Fr.* Manyo Shu. Ma
How Pleasant Is This Flowery Plain. *Unknown.* OBS
How pleasant it is that always. Florence Smith. BLPA
How Pleasant It Is to Have Money. Arthur Hugh Clough. *See* Spectator ab Extra: As I Sat at the Café.
How Pleasant to Know Mr. Lear. Edward Lear. ChTr; EBEV; FaBoCo; FiBHP; HAP; NOBE; NOBL; NOBVV; NoP; WeW
(By Way of Preface.) NBLV
(Self-Portrait of the Laureate of Nonsense.) FaBoCh
How pleased within my native bowers. Song: The Landscape. William Shenstone. SeCePo
How poor, how rich, how abject, how august. Edward Young. *Fr.* Night Thoughts, Night I. OAEL-1
How Potchikoo Got Old. Louise Erdrich. *Fr.* Old Man Potchikoo. HATNAP
How prone we are to sin, how sweet were made. And Forgive Us Our Trespasses. Aphra Behn. EBEV
"How Quick You Are!" *Unknown, tr. fr. Chinese by* Burton Watson. CoBCP
How quiet and how still to-day old Bethel's corners 'round. The Day after Conference. Josephine D. Henderson Heard. CBWP-4
How quiet is the morning in the hills! Morning in the Hills. Bliss Carman. NOBC
How quietly in ruined state. Aix-La-Chappelle, 1945. Edgar Bowers. NePoEA
How rare to be born a human being! Gary Snyder. *Fr.* Myths and Texts: Hunting, XVI. NaP
How red the rose that is the soldier's wound. Wallace Stevens. *Fr.* Esthétique du Mal. CMoP; NOBA; WaP
(Soldier's Wound, The.) WaaP
How rewarding to know Mr. Smith. Mr. Smith. William Jay Smith. FiBHP
How rich and pleasing thou, my Julia, art. To Julia. Robert Herrick. CaPo
How rich, O Lord! how fresh thy visits are. Unprofitablenes. Henry Vaughan. SeCV-1
How rich we were, to know them, exiles. Priest Lake. William Stafford. PoA
How richly, with ridiculous display. *See* Here richly, with ridiculous display.
How Roses Came Red. Robert Herrick. CaPo; ChTr; SoSe
How sad it must be. A Poem for My Father. Sonia Sanchez. BPo; IHMS
How sad the note of that funereal drum. On the Death of Commodore Oliver H. Perry. John Gardiner Calkins Brainard. PAH
How sad we sing no more in harmony. The Dead. Gloria A. Maxson. *Fr.* Two Guitars. TSM
How safe, methinks, and strong, behind. After Floods on the Wharfe. Andrew Marvell. *Fr.* Upon Appleton House, to My Lord Fairfax. FaBoPP
How say that by law we may torture and chase. She's Free! Frances Ellen Watkins Harper. AIW; BlSi; Son

How see you Echo? When she calls I see. Echo. Viscountess Grey of Fallodon. CH

How seldom, friend, a good, great man inherits. The Good Great Man. Samuel Taylor Coleridge. PWR

"How shall I a habit break?" A Builder's Lesson. John Boyle O'Reilly. PoLF; PWR

How shall I address Thee, O God? how shall I praise Thee? *Unknown, tr. fr. Hindustani.* Fr. Nanak and the Sikhs. WGRP

"How shall I be a poet?" Poeta Fit, Non Nascitur. "Lewis Carroll." FaBoNo; OBSV

How shall I begin my song. Songs for the Four Parts of the Night. Owl Woman (Juana Manwell), *tr. by* Frances Densmore. PBWP

How shall I behold the face. Milton. *Fr.* Paradise Lost, *Bk.* IX, *ll.* 1080–1098. TOF

How shall I forsake wisdom? In Praise of Wisdom. Solomon ibn Gabirol, *tr. by* Solomon Solis-Cohen. TrJP

How shall I guard my soul so that it be. The Song of Love. Rainer Maria Rilke, *tr. by* Ludwig Lewisohn. AWP

How shall I know if my love lose his youth. Strato, *tr. by* Sydney Oswald. PeHV

How shall I name you, immortal, mild, proud shadows? W. B. Yeats. NU

How shall I plead my cause, when you, my judge. Cleopatra and Antony. Dryden. *Fr.* All for Love. FiP

How shall I report. The Commendations of Mistress Jane Scrope. John Skelton. *Fr.* Phyllyp Sparowe [*or* Philip Sparrow]. OBSC

How shall I speak of doom, and ours in special. Tales from a Family Album. Donald Justice. NePoEA-2

How shall I still mankind's good will retrieve. August, Graf von Platen. *Fr.* Sonnets to Karl Theodore German, XXII. PeHV

How shall I tell the torments of that hour. The Author Consults a Critic and Sells His Manuscript. Francis Hawling. *Fr.* The Signal; or, A Satire against Modesty. NOEC

How shall the river learn. Max Schmitt in a Single Scull. Richmond Lattimore. AiP; EyDe

How shall the wine be drunk, or the woman known? A Voice from under the Table. Richard Wilbur. AmPP; HAP; NePoEA; NOBA

How shall we adorn. Angle of Geese. N. Scott Momaday. CDW; HATNAP; NOVW; QFR

How Shall We Honor Them? *Unknown.* OPP

How shall we know it is the last good-by? The Last Good-by. Louise Chandler Moulton. AA

How shall we please this age? If in a song. To Nysus. Sir Charles Sedley. FaBoEE; OBSV

How shall we praise the magnificence of the dead. Tetélestai. Conrad Aiken. LiTA; LiTM; MoAB; MoAmPo; PrIm

How Shall We Rise to Greet the Dawn? Sir Osbert Sitwell. WGRP

How shall we speak of Canada. W. L. M. K. F. R. Scott. NOBC

How shall we tell an angel. Angels. Gertrude Hall. AA

How shall your name go down in history. To Youth. Josephine D. Henderson Heard. CBWP-4

How shalt thou bear the Cross that now. The Eternal Years. Frederick William Faber. PWR

How she labors without end. To Be Born Male. Adela Zamudio, *tr. by* Robert L. Smith *and* Judith Candullo. DMH

How She Resolved to Act. Merrill Moore. MoAmPo

How should I act, I demanded to know (to get something). Friday, You Look Blue. Alfredo Giuliani, *tr. by* Lawrence R. Smith. NItP

How Should I Be So Pleasant. Sir Thomas Wyatt. SiPS
(Betrayal.) OBSC

How should I describe you—eternal. Koala. Alan Ross. OBTV

How should I direct my steps to her now? A Woman. Sa'di Yusuf, *tr. by* Lena Jayyusi *and* Naomi Shihab Nye. MAP

How should I love my best? Herbert of Cherbury. PoEL-2; SeCP

How should I praise thee, Lord! how should my rymes. The Temper. George Herbert. MePo; NOCV; NoP; OBS; PoEL-2

How should I your true love know. An Old Song Ended. Dante Gabriel Rossetti. BoLoP; EBVV

How Should I Your True Love Know. Shakespeare. *Fr.* Hamlet, IV, v. EBEV; EnLoPo; LiTB; Mes; PoRA; QFR.
(Ophelia's Songs, 1 ("How should I your true love know").) ChTr; GBL; OBSC; TrGrPo
(Song: "How should I your true love know.") CH

How should the world be luckier if this house. Upon a House Shaken by the Land Agitation. W. B. Yeats. CMoP

How sick I get. Father. Paul Carroll. DiL; NeAP

How silent comes the water round that bend. Minnows. Keats. *Fr.* I Stood Tiptoe [upon a Little Hill]. GN

How silently the years have sped away. To My Dead Brother. Clara Ann Thompson. CBWP-2

How silly that soldier is pointing his gun at the wood. Russians. Keith Douglas. OxBTC

How silly were those sages heretofore. Samuel Butler. *Fr.* Satire upon the Licentious Age of Charles II. NOBL

How simply violent things. From a Letter to America on a Visit to Sussex: Spring 1942. Frances Cornford. CN

How Singular. Tom Hood. FaBoNo

How singular some old words are! Singular Singulars, Peculiar Plurals. Willard R. Espy. FaBoUs

How Sleep the Brave. William Collins. GN; NOBE; OBEV
(Ode: "How sleep the brave, who sink to rest.") ELP
(Ode Written in 1746.) GTBS; GTBS-P; TrGrPo
(Ode Written in the Beginning of the Year 1746.) AWP; EnRP; HAP; HeIP; NAEL-1; NOEC; NoP; OxBSP; PoE; PoEL-3

How sleep the brave who sink to rest. On a Watchman Asleep at Midnight. James Thomas Fields. CenHV

How slight a thing may set one's fancy drifting. Honey Dripping from the Comb. James Whitcomb Riley. AA

How slow they are awakening, these trees. Plain Fare. Daryl Hine. CoAP

How slowly glide the hours by, the minutes hours seem. The Drunkard's Wife. Mary E. Tucker. CBWP-1

How slowly learns the child at school. Citizenship; Form 8889512, Sub-Section Q. Gilbert Keith Chesterton. OxBoLi

How slowly time crawls for me. On My Two-Hundredth Birthday. Jacob Glatstein, *tr. by* Benjamin *and* Barbara Harshav *and* Kathryn Helle. AYP

How small a tooth hath mined the season's heart! Frost. Edith Matilda Thomas. AA

How Small Is Man. John Stuart Blackie. PoSH

How smooth that lake expands its ample breast! Anne Radcliffe. WPE

How soft a caterpillar steps. Emily Dickinson. TSS

How Soon. Gyula Illyés, *tr. fr. Hungarian by* William Jay Smith. MHuP

How soon doth man decay! Mortification. George Herbert. MePo; SeCP

How Soon Hath Time [the Subtle Thief of Youth]. Milton. FF; HeIP; InPS; LiTB; NAEL-1; NAs; PoE; SeCePo; Son

How soon you take quite naturally. How Soon. Gyula Illyés, *tr. by* William Jay Smith. MHuP

How sorely the rain besets me! Naga Okimaro. *Fr.* Manyo Shu. Ma

How splendid he was! *Unknown, tr. by* Arthur Waley. BoS

How splendid in the morning glows. Hassan's Serenade. James Elroy Flecker. *Fr.* Hassan, I, ii. OBEV

How spoke the king, in his crucial hour victorious? King of the Belgians. Marion Couthouy Smith. PAH

How stands the glass around? Why, Soldiers, Why? *at. to* James Wolfe. OBET
(How Stands the Glass Around?) PAH

How startling to find the portraits of the gods. Roy Fuller. *Fr.* Mythological Sonnets, XVI. ErPo; Son

How stately stand yon pines upon the hill. Spring to Winter. George Crabbe. *Fr.* The Ancient Mansion. ChTr
(In Suffolk.) FaBoPP

How still he stands as mists begin to move. The Guard at the Binh Thuy Bridge. John Balaban. FYAP

How still, how happy! These [*or* Those] are words. Emily Brontë. NOBVV; OBNC

How still it is here in the woods. Solitude. Archibald Lampman. BoNaP; OBCV

How still the day is, and the air how bright! By the Wood. Robert Nichols. MMA

How Still the Hawk. Charles Tomlinson. LiTM

How still the room is! But a while ago. In Death. Mary Emily Bradley. AA

How straight it flew, how long it flew. Seaside Golf. Sir John Betjeman. SD

How strange at night [*or* it is] to wake. Night and Sleep. Coventry Patmore. EBVV
(Shadow of Night, The.) CH

How strange is Love; I am not one. The Gourmet's Love-Song. P. G. Wodehouse. NOBL

How Strange It Is. Claudia Lewis. RHPC

How strange it is to awake. Charles Wright. *Fr.* Four Poems for the New Year. AnAn

How strange it seems! These Hebrews in their graves. The Jewish Cemetery at Newport. Longfellow. AmPP; HAP; HeIP; HoPM; NOBA; NoP; OxBA; TAP

How strange the pride of many Irishmen! The New Style. David O'Bruadair, *tr. by* John Montague. BIrV

How strange to awake in a city. Hearing Men Shout at Night on MacDougal Street. Robert Bly. InPS

How strange to think of giving up all ambition! Watering the Horse. Robert Bly. CAPP; NaP

How strangely blind is prejudice, the Negro's greatest foe! Prejudice. Lizelia Augusta Jenkins Moorer. CBWP-3
How strangely this sun reminds me of my love! Stephen Spender. PeHV
How struts my love my cavalier. Cock-a-Hoop. Isabella Gardner. WPE
How subtle-secret is your smile! Did you love none then? Nay, I know. Oscar Wilde. Fr. The Sphinx. MoBrPo
"How sweet and lovely dost thou make the shame." Shakespeare. Fr. Sonnets, XCV. TrGrPo
How sweet and silent is the place. A Communion Hymn. Alice Freeman Palmer. TrPWD
How sweet, how sweet will be the night. How Sweet the Night. Rachael Bates. CN
How sweet I roam'd from field to field. Blake. CH; ChER; ChTr; EnLoPo; EnRP; FL; LiTB; NAEL-2; NOEC; NoP; OAEL-2; OBNC; PoEL-4; SeCePo; TrGrPo
(Prince of Love, The.) NOBE
How Sweet Is the Language of Love. Oliver Holden. AH
How sweet is the shepherd's sweet lot! The Shepherd. Blake. Fr. Songs of Innocence. BoTP; EnRP
How sweet it is, at first approach of morn. Oliver Goldsmith, the Younger. Fr. The Rising Village. OBCV
How sweet the answer Echo makes. Echo. Thomas Moore. ELP (Echoes.) GTBS; GTBS-P
How sweet the chime of the Sabbath bells! Creeds of the Bells. George W. Bungay. PWR
How sweet the harmonies of afternoon. Blackbird. Tennyson. FM; PBBP
How Sweet the Moonlight Sleeps. Shakespeare. Fr. The Merchant of Venice, V, i. FaBoRV; TrGrPo
(Moonlight.) OHFP
How Sweet the Name of Jesus Sounds. John Newton. NOCV. (Name of Jesus, The.) NOEC
"Jesus, my Shepherd, Husband, Friend," sel. TrPWD
How Sweet the Night. Rachael Bates. CN
How sweet the silent backward tracings! Memories. Walt Whitman. PCP
How sweet the tuneful bells' responsive peal! William Lisle Bowles. OBTV
(Bells of Ostend, The.) EnRP
(Sonnet: At Ostend.) NOEC
How Sweet Thy Precious Gift of Rest. Menahem ben Makhir of Ratisbon, tr. fr. Hebrew by Herbert Loewe. TrJP
How sweet, to see the dells so shady. An Englishman with an Atlas; or, America the Unpronounceable. Morris Bishop. GOA
How sweet to wear a shape of snow. Duck in Central Park. Frances Higginson Savage. GoYe
How sweet, when weary, dropping on a bank. Summer. John Clare. BoNaP
How sweetly did the moments glide. The Cottager's Complaint, on the Intended Bill for Enclosing Sutton-Coldfield. John Freeth. NOEC; OBET
How sweetly doth My Master sound! My Master! The Odour. George Herbert. OBS
How sweetly on the wood-girt town. Pentucket. Whittier. PAH
How sweetly sings this stream. Laurence Dakin. Fr. Pyramus and Thisbe, III, iii. CaP
How swift along the winding way. Upon Boys Diverting Themselves in the River. Thomas Foxton. OxBChV
How swift is the coming of old age! Praising Spectacles. Yüan Mei, tr. by Anthony C. Yu. WFTU
How tenderly the evening creeps between. Evening. Hugh McCrae. PoAu-1
How terrible their trust, the little leaves. April, 1942. Mark Van Doren. WaP
How that vast heaven intitled First is rolled. William, of Hawthornden Drummond. EIL
How the blithe lark runs up the golden stair. The Skylark. Frederick Tennyson. GN
How the Bulls Were Begotten, sel. Unknown, tr. fr. Irish by Thomas Kinsella.
Two Bulls, The. NOIV
How the cloth-plant spreads. Unknown, tr. by Arthur Waley. BoS
How the Cumberland Went Down. Silas Weir Mitchell. PAH
How the Days Passed. Who. Natan Zach, tr. fr. Hebrew by Warren Bargad and Stanley F. Chyet. IP
How the days went. Now That I Am Forever with Child. Audre Lorde. PoBA
How the Death of a City Is Never More than the Sum of the Deaths of Those Who Inhabit Its Spaces. Victor Coleman. NOBC
How the Doughty Duke of Albany like a Coward Knight Ran Away Shamefully, sel. John Skelton.
"O ye wretched Scots." OBSV

How the earth burns! Each pebble underfoot. The Oasis of Sidi Khaled. Wilfrid Scawen Blunt. OBTV
How the elements solidify! Event. Sylvia Plath. NOBA
How the Fire Queen Crossed the Swamp. Will H. Ogilvie. PoAu-1
How the First Hielandman of God Was Made. Unknown. FaBoCo; GBP; OBSV
How the four seasons march in succession. Rhyme-Prose on the Small Hills. Yakatsugu, tr. by Burton Watson. JLIC-1
How the frail, shimmering hollyhocks. The List. Carl Dennis. KS
How the Great Guest Came. Edwin Markham. BeLS; BLPA; BLPL
How the Hen Sold Her Eggs to the Stingy Priest. Nancy Willard. LCAP
How the Invalids Make Love. Susan Feldman. AmPA
How the Joy of It Was Used Up Long Ago. Linda Gregg. NPGG
How the Lover Perisheth in His Delight, As the Fly in the Fire. Petrarch, tr. by Sir Thomas Wyatt. Fr. Sonnets to Laura. Son
How the majestic stellar lights of Heav'n. Compensation. Henrietta Cordelia Ray. CBWP-3
How the mountains talked together. A Farewell to Agassiz. Oliver Wendell Holmes. ImOP
How the old mountains drip with sunset. Emily Dickinson. RB
How the quails bicker. Unknown, tr. by Arthur Waley. BoS
How the red road stretched before us, mile on mile. Independence. Nancy Cato. PoAu-2; WPE
How the river cools your blood is something you can't. Autobiography, Chapter XVII: Floating the Big Piney. Jim Barnes. HATNAP
How the splendour of these veils and of this dress. Phaedra. Osip Mandelstam, tr. by James Greene. OBVE
How the wanton hunter tamed. Asadullah Khan Ghalib, tr. by Ahmed Ali. GoT
How the waters closed above him. Emily Dickinson. DL; PoEL-5
How the wind howls this morn. The End of May. William Morris. NOBVV
How the winds are all composure. St. Philip and St. James. Christopher Smart. Fr. Hymns and Spiritual Songs, XIII. NOCV; NOEC
How the Women Will Stop War. Aristophanes, tr. fr. Greek by B. B. Rogers. Fr. Lysistrata. WaaP
How these old hills flow down. The Rock of This Odd Coincidence. Penelope Scambly Schott. KS
How they are provided for upon the earth. Beginners. Walt Whitman. AA
How They Bite. Unknown. SD
How They Brought the Good News by Sea. Norma Farber. PChr
How They Brought the Good News from Ghent to Aix. Robert Browning. BeLS; BLPL; FaBoBe; FaFP; FaPoR; GN; HoPM; NAEL-2
How they came into the world. A History of Lesbianism. Judy Grahn. GLP; PeHV
How they glimmer in the dark. The Eyes of Dark Sorrow. N. M. Rashed, tr. by Mahmood Jamal. PBMUP
How They Killed My Grandmother. Boris Slutsky, tr. fr. Russian by Daniel Weissbort. VWA
How They Made the Golem. John Robert Colombo. MoCV
How they sting! Myoe, tr. fr. Japanese by Burton Watson. Fr. Ten Tanka. FCEI
How thin and sharp is the moon tonight. Winter Moon. Langston Hughes. RHPC
How Things Fall. Donald Finkel. VWA
How Things Work. Gary Soto. NoAM
How this woman came by the courage, how she got. John Berryman. Fr. Dream Songs. TAP
How this year of years do I best see. May Trees in a Storm. Geoffrey Grigson. GBL
How those loose rocks got piled up here like this. 18,000 Feet. Ed Roberson. PoNe
How Time Consumeth All Earthly Things. Thomas Proctor. See Ay me, ay me, I sigh to see the scythe afield.
How time reverses. For My Contemporaries. J. V. Cunningham. CoAP; SM
How Times Have Changed! Merle Collins. WS
How to Be Happy. Unknown. BLPA
How to Be Old. May Swenson. ER; MAT; UnPo
How to behold what cannot be held? Giovanni da Fiesole on the Sublime; or, Fra Angelico's "Last Judgment." Richard Howard. Prf
How to Build a Ha-ha. William Mason. Fr. The English Garden. FaBoUs
How to Catch Trout. Thomas Barker. Fr. The Art of Angling. FaBoUs
How to Catch Wasps. John Philips. Fr. Cyder. FaBoUs
How to Change the U.S.A. Harry Edwards, arr. in verse by Walter Lowenfels. NBP; TW
How to Choose a Horse. Unknown. FaBoUs
How to Choose a Wife. Unknown. FaBoUs
How to Conceive Boys. Claude Quillet, tr. fr. Latin by George Sewell. Fr. Callipaedia; or, The Art of Getting Beautiful Children. FaBoUs

How to Cure Hops and Prepare Them for Sale. Christopher Smart. *Fr.* The Hop-Garden. FaBoUs

How to Dress Like a Femmy Dyke. Jane Barnes. GLP

How to Dress like a Scary Dyke. Jane Barnes. GLP

How to Eat Alone. Daniel Halpern. MAYP

How to explain that on the day. Irreconcilables. Arthur Gregor. NYBP

How to Exterminate Rats. James Grainger. *Fr.* The Sugar Cane. FaBoUs

How to Fertilize Soil. James Grainger. *See* Sugar Cane, The: Compost.

How to Fertilize Soil. John Scott. *Fr.* Amoebaean Eclogues, II. FaBoUs

How to Find Love in an Instant. Michael Lassell. *Fr.* Times Square Poems. GLP

How to Get Grizzly Spirit. *Unknown, tr. fr. Tlingit Indian by* James Koller. STP

How to Get On in Society. John Betjeman. NOBL; OBSV; OxBTC

How to Get There. Bonnie Nims. RHPC

How to Get There. Frank O'Hara. NoP

How to Get to Canada. Ted Berrigan. UL

How to Give. *Unknown.* BLRP

How to Grow Cucumbers. William Cowper. *Fr.* The Task, III. FaBoUs

How to Keep Accounts. *Unknown.* FaBoUs

How to keep—is there any any, is there none such. The Leaden Echo and the Golden Echo. Gerard Manley Hopkins. BrPo; CMoP; FaFP; GTBS-P; LiTB; LiTM; MoAB; MoBrPo; NOBVV; OBMV; OBNC; SOTW

How to Kill. Keith Douglas. FaBoMo; NOBE; RB

How to Like It. Stephen Dobyns. BLA

How to Meditate. Jack Kerouac. PoM

How to Murder Your Best Friend. Diana O Hehir. NPGG

How to Paint a Perfect Christmas. Miroslav Holub, *tr. fr. Czech by* George Theiner *and* Ian Milner. OBCP

How to Reach the Moon. Marsha Pomerantz. VWA

How to Read Me. Walter Savage Landor. NOBVV

How to remember you correctly when I'm not sure you're dead. To an Old San Francisco Poet. Keith Abbott. UL

How to See Deer. Philip Booth. Psk

How to Shear Sheep. John Dyer. *Fr.* The Fleece, II. FaBoUs

How to Sign. Laurie Stroblas. TSM

How to speak of it. Tabito. *Fr.* Manyo Shu. PeBJV

How to Start a War. Phyllis McGinley. OBSV

How to Survive Nuclear War. Maxine W. Kumin. PPR

How to Take Off Your Clothes at the Picnic. Bill Manhire. ATNZ

How to tell. Kyorai, *tr. fr. Japanese by* Burton Watson. *Fr.* Twenty Hokku. FCEI

How to Tell Goblins from Elves. Monica Shannon. FaPON; RHPC

How to Tell Juan Don from Another. Gardner E. Lewis. FiBHP

How To Tell the Wild Animals. Carolyn Wells. FaFP; FaPON; FiBHP; NBLV

How to th' ascent of that steep savage hill. Milton. *Fr.* Paradise Lost, *Bk.* IV, *ll.* 172–201. (Satan Journey's to the Garden of Eden.) ChTr

How to the invisible. Elementary Cosmogony. Charles Simic. NNaP

How to the Singer Comes the Song? Richard Watson Gilder. WGRP

How to Treat Elves. Morris Bishop. FiBHP; OBAL; OBCA

How to Walk in a Crowd. Robert Hershon. FF

How to Watch Your Brother Die. Michael Lassell. GLP

How to weave your web of medicinal flesh into words. Big Fine Woman from Ruleville. Jayne Cortez. ER

How to win her. A Serious Poem. Ernest Walsh. ErPo

How to Write a Letter. Elizabeth Turner. MoShBr; OxBChV

How to Write a Poem about the Sky. Leslie Silko. NoP

How truly now I understand. *Unknown. Fr.* Manyo Shu. Ma

How Tuesday Began. Kathleen Fraser. NYBP

How ugly—take a good look at a man who acts wise. Tabito. *Fr.* Manyo Shu. FCEI

How unhappy (though unmarried) is an uncle who, bereft. Horace, Book V, Ode III. Charles Larcom Graves. CenHV

How unpleasant to meet Mr. Eliot. Lines for Cuscuscaraway and Mirza Murad Ali Beg. T. S. Eliot. FiBHP; NBLV; OBAL

How vainly men themselves amaze. The Garden. Andrew Marvell. AWP; BLPL; HAP; InPS; InvP; JCP; LiTB; MeLP; MePo; NAEL-1; NIP; NOBE; NoP; OAEL-1; OBS; PoE; PoEL-2; PoLF; PoRA; PPP; QFR; SeCePo; SeCP; SeCV-1; TEP; TOF; TrGrPo (Thoughts in a Garden.) GTBS; GTBS-P; OBEV

How very modern once they were. The Modernists. Tom MacInnes. CaP

How very quiet things can be. Just Three. William Wise. RAR

How very sad it is to think. Poor Brother. *Unknown.* NA

How Violets Came Blue. Robert Herrick. CaPo; TTTS

How warm this woodland wild recess! Recollections of Love. Samuel Taylor Coleridge. ChER; NAEL-2

How was I to know that the woman, seated next to me on the bus. Leslie Scalapino. *Fr.* Hmmmm. NPGG

How was the weather on that day? Letter to Sigmund Freud. Judah Leib Teller, *tr. fr. Yiddish by* Benjamin *and* Barbara Harshav. *Fr.* Psychoanalysis. AYP

How was this I did not see. The Faded Face. Thomas Hardy. QFR

How was thy mother a lioness. Lamentation. Bible, *O.T. Fr.* Ezekiel, XIX: 2-9. TrJP

How We Beat the Favourite. Adam Lindsay Gordon. CBAP

How We Became a Nation. Harriet Prescott Spofford. PAH

How We Burned the *Philadelphia*. Barrett Eastman. PAH

How we desire desire! Joy of surcease. James Vincent Cunningham. VGW

How we envy their not caring. The Card-Players. David Ray. VGW

How We Heard the Name. Alan Dugan. CoAP; NoAM

How well (dear Brother) art thou called Stone? To My Reverend Dear Brother, M. Samuel Stone. John Cotton. SCAP

How well for the birds that can rise in their flight. *Unknown, tr. by* Frank O'Connor. WTO

How well her name an army doth present. Ana(Mary-Army)gram. George Herbert. OAEL-1

How well I know him, old soldier in blue. The Ancestor. Dave Smith. SM

How well I know that fountain. Song of the Soul That Knows God by Faith. Saint John of the Cross, *tr. by* Seamus Heaney. TIRV

How well I know what I mean to do. By the Fire-Side. Robert Browning. EBVV; OAEL-2

How well I remember those days of danger. The Road to Pengya. Tu Fu, *tr. by* Rewi Alley *and* Edward Field. Prf

How well my eyes remember the dim path! Elegy: Summer-House on the Mound. Robert Bridges. GoTL

How well you served me above ground. Spirit's Song. Louise Bogan. NYBP

How well your black coat fits! *Unknown, tr. by* Arthur Waley. BoS

How were the temples of the three gods built? Vigil at Dawn. Gábor Garai, *tr. by* Daniel Hoffman. MHuP

How when one entered a cottage. The Answer. John Montague. CIP; TIRV

"How will he hear the bell at school." Mutterings over the Crib of a Deaf Child. James Wright. LCAP

How will I think of you. December 21st. Jean Valentine. LCAP

How will it go, crumbling earthquake, towering inferno, juggernaut, volcano, smashup. A New Reality Is Better Than a New Movie! Imamu Amiri Baraka. NoAM

How Will You Call Me, Brother. Mari E. Evans. BISi

How will you cross the autumn mountain alone? Princess Oku, *tr. by* Willis Barnstone. BoWoP

How will you fill your goblet? How? Abraham Sutskever, *tr. by* Chana Bloch. PeBMYV

How will you manage. Princess Daihaku. *Fr.* Manyo Shu. AWP

How will you your Christmas keep? Keeping Christmas. Eleanor Farjeon. OBCP

How winsome are the lilies of my garland. Yakamochi. *Fr.* Manyo Shu. Ma

How wisely Nature did decree. Eyes and Tears. Andrew Marvell. MePo

How wonderful you were, so pious and holy. Sabbath. Jakov de Haan, *tr. by* David Soetendorp. VWA

How would it all end? Both Earth and Heaven. Huda Namani, *tr. by* Lena Jayyusi *and* John Heath-Stubbs. MAP

How would it be if I came in the night. Vengeance. Mazisi Kunene. WMBCH

How would it be if you took yourself off. Landscape with Tractor. Henry Taylor. MAYP; PPR

How you became a poet's a mystery! Heredity. Tony Harrison. *Fr.* The School of Eloquence. NAEL-2; NoAM

How you dazzle my mind, panarchaic grandeur. Rebecca. Joseph Eliyia, *tr. by* Rae Dalven. VWA

How You Get Born. Erica Jong. UnPo

How you go along all day. Strange. Kirby Doyle. NeAP

How you make free. *Unknown, tr. by* Arthur Waley. BoS

How You Were Born. Sharon Mayer Libera. PPR

How young I was. Old Age. *Gond Oral Tradition, tr. by* V. Elwin *and* S. Hivale. WTO

Howard slapped the man next to him on the shoulder. Coming of Age in "The Movement." Wendy Rose. ER

Howard's Way. Richard Howard. PPR

"How'd I solve de Negro Problum?" Uncle Rube on the Race Problem. Clara Ann Thompson. CBWP-2

Howdy, Honey, Howdy! Paul Laurence Dunbar. PoLF

However dry and windless. Bamboo. William Plomer. PeSA

However gracefully/ the spare leaves of the fig tree. Casa d'Amunt.
Alastair Reid. NePoEA

However it came, this great house has gone done. The Great House.
Edwin Muir. EyDe

However long I wait for him. *Unknown.* *Fr.* Manyo Shu. Ma

However loud I call to the man. *Unknown.* *Fr.* Manyo Shu. Ma

However much I beat him. *Unknown.* *Fr.* Manyo Shu. Ma

However much I praise, you do not listen. Second Rose Motif. Cecília
Meireles, *tr.* by James Merrill. ATCBP

However the battle is ended. An Inspiration. Ella Wheeler Wilcox.
AnAmPo; WGRP
(Only One Way.) PWR

However we wrangled with Britain awhile. Literary Importation. Philip
Freneau. TAP

However wide creation is. All That Is Needed. János Pilinszky, *tr.* by
William Jay Smith. MHuP

Howie gave sentence of slaughter. The Desertion of the Women and
Seals. George Mackay Brown. OxBC

Howl. Allen Ginsberg. AmPP; CAPP; GLP; InPS; NaP; NeAP; NoAM;
NoP; PoM; SOTW; TAP

Howl, *sels.* Allen Ginsberg. AmPP; PoM
  "I saw the best minds of my generation destroyed by madness." *Fr.* I.
    MoP; NaP; NIP; NoAM; NoP; SOTW, *abr.*, *fr.* *ll.* 1-30; TAP
  "What sphinx of cement and aluminum bashed open their skulls." *Fr.*
    II. NeAP; SOTW, *abr.*; TAP

Howl, howl, howl! O! you are men of stones. Shakespeare. *Fr.* King
Lear, V, iii. OBD

Howling of Wolves, The. Ted Hughes. OxBTC

Howling storm is brewing, A. The Storm. Heine, *tr.* by Louis
Untermeyer. AWP

Howrah Bridge. James Keir Baxter. ATNZ

"How's My Boy?" Sydney Thompson Dobell. CH; GN; OHIP

"How's your father?" came the whisper. Conversational. *Unknown.*
FiBHP

Hozo Pass. Basho, *tr.* *fr.* *Japanese* by Burton Watson. *Fr.* Seventy-six
Hokku. FCEI

Hsi. Lady Wang Wei, *tr.* *fr.* *Chinese* by Burton Watson.
CoBCP

Hsi-li Echoed My Poems, and I Respond to Him, *sel.* Yang Shih-ch'i, *tr.*
fr. *Chinese* by Jonathan Chaves.
  "Not sobered up from my muddy Kao-yang drunk." CoBLCP

Hsi Shih received the favor of Wu. Following the Rhymes of the Six
Poems "Thinking of the Past at Ku-Su." Ni Tsan, *tr.* by Jonathan
Chaves. CoBLCP

Hsiu-chou. T'ang Hsien-Tsu, *tr.* *fr.* *Chinese* by Jonathan Chaves.
CoBLCP

Hsün-yang on the Yangtze, seeing off a guest at night. Song of the Lute.
Po Chü-i, *tr.* by Burton Watson. CoBCP

Hub for the Universe, A. Walt Whitman. *Fr.* Song of Myself, XLVIII.
FaFP

Hubbard is dead, the old plumber. Elegy for Alfred Hubbard. Tony
Connor. SoSe

Hubert's Museum. Louis Simpson. OxBC

Huc omnes pariter. Boethius, *tr.* *fr.* *Latin* by John Walton. *Fr.* The
Consolation of Philosophy, III, 2. OBLMV

Huck Finn at Ninety, Dying in a Chicago Boarding House Room. James
Schevill. TAP

Huckleberry, Gooseberry, Raspberry Pie. Clyde Watson. RHPC

Hucksters haggle in the mart, The. For a War Memorial. G. K.
Chesterton. MMA

Huckster's Horse, The. Julia Hurd Strong. GoYe

Hudibras, *sels.* Samuel Butler.
  Argument, The. *Fr.* I, 1. EBEV; NAEL-1; OAEL-1; SeCV-2
  "Egyptians say, the sun has twice, The." *Fr.* II, 3. ImOP
  "For his religion it was fit." *Fr.* I, 1. OBSV
  "For what mad lover ever died." OBD
  Godly Casuistry ("The sun had long since in the lap"). *Fr.* II, 2.
    OBS
  Hudibras the Sectarian ("Besides he was a shrewd Philosopher"). *Fr. 1.*
    SeCePo
  "In mathematic[k]s he was greater." *Fr.* I, 1. ImOP; NOBL
  Independent Squire ("A squire he had whose name was Ralph"). *Fr.* I,
    1. NOBE
  Metaphysical Sectarian, The ("He was in logick a great critic").
    MeLP, I, 1.
  (Hudibras, the Presbyterian Knight, *abr.*) OxBoLi
  (Portrait of Hudibras.) PoEL-3
  (Presbyterian Knight and Independent Squire, *abr.*) OBS
  (Sir Hudibras, His Passing Worth.) FaBoCo

Portrait of Sidrophel. *Fr.* II, 3. PoEL-3

Presbyterian Church Government ("Synods are whelps of the
Inquisition"). *Fr.* I, 3. OBS

"Question then, to state it first, The." *Fr.* I, 3. NOBL

"Quoth he, My faith as adamantine." *Fr.* II, 1. OBSV

"Quoth he, to bid me not to love." *Fr.* II, 1. NOBL

Sidrophel, the Rosicrucian Conjurer ("This said, he turned about his
steed"). *Fr.* II, 3. OxBoLi

"Some were for setting up a king." *Fr.* III, 2. EBEV

"There is a tall long-sided dame." *Fr.* II, 1. OBSV

"This place (quoth she) they say's enchanted." *Fr.* II, 1. NOBL

"What makes a knave a child of God." *Fr.* III, 1. NOBL;
OBSV

"When civil fury first grew high." *Fr.* I, 1. EBEV; SeCV-2
(Presbyterian Knight.) PWR
("When civil dudgeon first grew high.") OAEL-1

Hudibras and Milton Reconciled. William Somervile. NOEC

Hudibras, the Presbyterian Knight. Samuel Butler. *See* Hudibras:
Metaphysical Sectarian, The ("He was in logick a great critic").

Hudibras the Sectarian ("Besides he was a shrewd Philosopher"). Samuel
Butler. *Fr.* Hudibras, I, 1. SeCePo

Hudney, Sutej IX, X, XI, 7, 9, 25, 58, 60, 61, 64. Index. Paul Violi.
EOEF

Hudson burns in the white shine of a March sun, The. On the Hudson.
A. Leyeles, *tr.* by Benjamin *and* Barbara Harshav. AYP

Hue and Cry after Blood and Murder, A. *Unknown.* APAS

Hue and Cry after Fair Amoret, A. Congreve. NOEC; OBEV

Hue of nightfall, The. Evening Bell. Shotetsu, *tr.* by Steven D. Carter.
WFTW

Hue quam precipiti. Boethius, *tr.* *fr.* *Latin* by John Walton. *Fr.* The
Consolation of Philosophy, I, 2. OBLMV

Huesca. John Cornford. BoLoP

Huey. Etheridge Knight. NNaP

Huff the talbot and our cat Tib. The Wars of the Roses. *Unknown.*
GBP

Huffy Henry hid the day. John Berryman. *Fr.* Dream Songs. CAPP;
HCAP; NAAL-2; NoP; PoE

Hug, The. Tess Gallagher. NAmP

Hug me closer, closer, mother. Little Bessie. *Unknown.* AmFP

Hug o' War. Shel Silverstein. NTCP; RHPC

Huge and alert, irascible yet strong. A Toast to Our Native Land.
Robert Bridges. OPP; PAH

Huge commentators grace my learned shelves. James Bramston. *Fr.* The
Man of Taste. FaBoCo

Huge doll of my body, The. My Life. Mark Strand. NoAM

Huge firefly, undulating, A. Issa, *tr.* *fr.* *Japanese* by Hiroaki Sato. *Fr.*
Forty-four Hokku. FCEI

Huge fish, bold and noble, A. Fish in a Painting. Ho Ching-ming, *tr.* by
Jonathan Chaves. CoBLCP

Huge gate and its heavy doors, A. Buson, *tr.* *fr.* *Japanese* by Hiroaki
Sato. *Fr.* Eighty-seven Hokku. FCEI

Huge-headed oak. He Praises the Trees. *Unknown, tr.* by Robin Skelton.
BIrV

Huge hippopotamus hasn't a hair, The. The Hippopotamus. Jack
Prelutsky. RHPC

Huge Leviathan, The. Spenser. *Fr.* Visions of the World's Vanity.
ChTr

Huge mammalian rocks in front of the lawn, The. With Stephen in
Maine. Stanley Plumly. BLA; NAmP

Huge shoe mounts up from the horizon, A. The Wounded Breakfast.
Russell Edson. LCAP

Huge snowflakes dancing down. *Unknown, tr.* by Geoffrey Bownas *and*
Anthony Thwaite. PeBJV

Huge swells move blue against the winds. Wakayama Bokusui, *tr.* *fr.*
Japanese by Hiroaki Sato. *Fr.* Forty-four Tanka. FCEI

Huge upon the hazy plain. Grazing Locomotives. Archibald MacLeish.
AnAmPo

Huge, viewless, ocean into which we cast. To Silence. Thomas Lovell
Beddoes. Son

Huge wound in my head began to heal, The. The Wound. Thom Gunn.
NePoEA

Hugging my breasts I lightly kick. Yosano Akiko, *tr.* *fr.* *Japanese* by
Hiroaki Sato. *Fr.* Thirty-nine Tanka. FCEI

Hugging the Jukebox. Naomi Shihab Nye. MAYP

Hugging the Shore. Mary E. Tucker. CBWP-1

Hugh Maguire. Eochy O'Hussey, *tr.* *fr.* *Late Middle Irish* by Frank
O'Connor. AnIL

Hugh of Lincoln. *Unknown.* *See* Four and twenty bonny boys.

Hugh Selwyn Mauberley. (Life and Contacts). Ezra Pound. AmPP;
CMoP, *complete with* Mauberly; InPS; LiTA; LiTM, *complete with*
Mauberly; NoAM, *complete with* Mauberly; NOBA, *complete with*

Mauberly; NoP, *complete with* Mauberly; TAP, *complete with* Mauberly.

Sels.

"Age demanded an image, The." *Fr.* II. HAP; MoAmPo; VGW

"Beneath the sagging roof." *Fr.* X. MoAmPo

Brennhaum. *Fr.* I. MoAmPo

Envoi (1919). *Fr.* XIII. HAP; MoP; UnPo; VGW

(Envoi: "Go, dumb-born book.") MoAB; MoAmPo; OxBA

"For three years, out of key with his time." *Fr.* III. HAP; MoAmPo; NAAL-2; OxBA; UnPo; VGW

(E. P. Ode Pour l'Election de Son Sepulchre.) HAP; MoAmPo; MoP; NAAL-2; NoAM; VGW

(Pour l'Election de Son Sepulchre, I-V.) FaBoMo

Mr. Nixon. *Fr.* I. MoAmPo

"Siena Mi Fe'; Disfecemi Maremma." *Fr.* I. MoAmPo

"Tea-rose tea-gown, etc., The." *Fr.* III. MoAmPo; NOBE

"There died a myriad." *Fr.* V. FF; MoAmPo; NOBE; PoE; WaaP

"These fought in any case." *Fr.* IV. FF; HeIP; MoAmPo; NOBE; OBWP; PoE; VGW; WaaP

Yeux Glaques. *Fr.* I. MoAmPo

Hugh Spencer's Feats in France. *Unknown.* ESPB

Hughie at the Inn. Elinor Wylie. NYBP; WPE

Hughie Graham ("Our lords are to the mountains gane"). *Unknown.* OxBB, *with music.*

Hughie Grame ("As it befell upon one time"). *Unknown.* ESPB

Hughley Steeple. A. E. Housman. *Fr.* A Shropshire Lad, LXI. FaBoPP

"Hullo!" Sam Walter Foss. CenHV

Hull's Surrender. *Unknown.* PAH

Humaine Cares. Nathaniel Wanley. OBS

Human Abstract, The. Blake. *Fr.* Songs of Experience. EnRP; NAEL-2; NOEC; OAEL-2; PoE; PoEL-4; PPP

Human Animal, The. Jane Mayhall. TAP

Human being consists of a superimposition, The. Fires at Will. René Daumal, *tr. by* Michael Benedikt. POS

Human beings/ there you are in the night mist. The Poem of A. Cathy Bernheim, *tr. by* Mary Ann Caws. DMF

Human beings in this world are the same. The Coffee-House Philosopher. Giuseppe Gioacchino Belli, *tr. by* Harold Norse. PFI

Human Clay, The. Ilya Abu Madi, *tr. fr. Arabic by* Issa Boullata *and* Naomi Shihab Nye. MAP

Human contours are so easily lost, The. The Human Form Divine. Kathleen Jessie Raine. WPE

Human Debasement; a Fragment. Edward Rushton. NOEC

Human face becoming locked insect face. Richard Hunt's Arachne. Robert Hayden. FB

Human Fold, The. Edwin Muir. LiTM

Human Folly. Pope. *See* Essay on Man, An: Whate'er the passion— knowledge, fame, or pelf.

Human Form Divine, The. Kathleen Jessie Raine. WPE

Human Geography. Gloria Fuertes, *tr. fr. Spanish by* Willis Barnstone. BoWoP

Human Greatness. Edwin Barclay. PBA

Human Happiness. Dryden. *Fr.* The Indian Emperor, IV, i. FiP

Human Image, The, *sel.* Blake.

London ("There souls of men are bought and sold"). ChTr

Human Life. Matthew Prior. FaBoEE

Human Life, *sels.* Samuel Rogers.

Another and the Same. OBNC

Man's Going Hence. OBNC

Human Life; on the Denial of Immortality. Samuel Taylor Coleridge. ChER

Human Mind, The. Ai Shih-te, *tr. fr. Chinese by* William C. White. TrJP

Human parent chases a crow away, A. Onitsura, *tr. by* Hiroaki Sato. FCEI

Human Plan, The. Charles Henry Crandall. AA

Human Qualities. Dahlia Ravikovich, *tr. fr. Hebrew by* Warren Bargad *and* Stanley F. Chyet. IP

Human race is going to the cemetery, The. Etel Adnan. *Fr.* The Beirut-Hell Express. WPOW

Human race, on its little ball, The. The Isolation of Two Milliard Light Years. Tanikawa Shuntaro, *tr. by* Geoffrey Bownas *and* Anthony Thwaite. PeBJV

Human Races, The. Richard Percival Lister. FiBHP

Human Relations. Emmett Jarrett. NeAC

Human Relations, *sel.* Antonio Porta, *tr. fr. Italian by* Lawrence R. Smith.

"Walking becomes unbearable, another year." NItP

Human Relations. C. H. Sisson. TW

Human Remains. Bruce Boston. BWV

Human Seasons, The. Keats. EnRP; FaFP; GTBS; GTBS-P; WiR

Human Soul. René Maran, *tr. fr. French by* Mercer Cook. TTY

Human Species, The. Raymond Queneau, *tr. fr. French by* Teo Savory. RHTwFP

Human Things. Howard Nemerov. BoNaP

Human Touch, The. Spencer Michael Free. BLPA; FaBoBe

Human Tragedy, The, *sel.* Alfred Austin.

"When with staid mothers' milk and sunshine warmed." FaBoCo

Human Use of Human Beings, The. Sybren Polet, *tr. fr. Dutch by* Peter Nijmeijer. DuIn

Human Wisdom. Washington Delgado, *tr. fr. Spanish by* David Tipton. Per

Humane Conditions, The. Stanislaw Baranczak, *tr. fr. Polish by* Magnus Jan Krynski *and* Robert A. Maguire. PwPP

Humanities Lecture. William Stafford. NNaP; NoAM

Humble Address, The. *Unknown.* APAS

Humble Administrator's Garden, The. Vikram Seth. UAS

Humble-Bee, The. Emerson. AA; AnAmPo; FaPON; FM; GN; NOBA; OxBA

Humble Beginnings. Thomas Lovell Beddoes. NOBVV

Humble Heart, A. Alfred Norris. PWR

Humble Petition of Bruar Water to the Noble Duke of Athole, The, *sel.* Burns.

"Sober laverock, warbling wild, The." PBBP

Humble springs of stately Plimouth Beach, The. Upon the Springs Issuing out from the Foot of Plimouth Beach. Samuel Sewall. SCAP

Humble Wish; off Porto-Sancto, March 29, 1779, An, *sels.* Edward Thompson.

"I never yet arraigned the will of heaven." OBTV

I've served my country nine and twenty years. NOEC

Humbly. Ramón López Velarde, *tr. fr. Spanish by* Samuel Beckett. MexPo

Humbly I Confess That I Am Mortal. Elio Pagliarani, *tr. fr. Italian by* Lawrence R. Smith. NItP

Humbly resolving to pray that God. Sleeping on Fists. Alberto Ríos. DiL

Humility. Marie Luise Kaschnitz, *tr. fr. German by* Michael Hamburger. WPOW

Hummer, The. William Matthews. TDD

Humming bee purrs softly o'er his flower, The. The Cricket. Frederick Goddard Tuckerman. FM; NOBA; QFR

Humming My Verse, in My Leisure, beneath Blossoming Cassia Trees. Yün Shou-p'ing, *tr. fr. Chinese by* Irving Lo. WFTU

Hummingbird, The. Michael Flanders. RHPC

Hummingbird, The. Harry Hibbard Kemp. FaPON

Humming-Bird. D. H. Lawrence. CMoP; InPS; LiTB; LiTM; NoAM; RB; SeCePo

Hummingbird. Harold Littlebird. VoR

Hummingbird. Marge Piercy. GeTw

Humming-Bird, The. Mary E. Tucker. CBWP-1

Hummingbird, he has no song, The. The Hummingbird. Michael Flanders. RHPC

Humming Birds. Betty Sage. RAR

Humor me no longer, Sancho; faithful squire, all that is past. Don Quixote's Farewell. W. H. Auden. *Fr.* Man of La Mancha. AnAn

Humorless, hundreds of trunks gray in the blue expanse. Leafless Trees, Chickahominy Swamp. Dave Smith. MAYP

Humorous Lovers, The, *sel.* William Cavendish, Duke of Newcastle.

"We'll, placed in Love's triumphant chariot high." OxBSP

Humorous Verse. Abu Dolama, *tr. fr. Arabic by* Raoul Abdul. TTY

Humour Out of Breath, *sel.* John Day.

Ditty, A. EIL

Humours of the King's Bench Prison, a Ballad, The. Leonard Howard. NOEC

Hump, The. Kipling. *Fr.* Just-So Stories. OxBChV

Humphrey Hardfeature's Descriptions of Cast-Iron Inventions. *Unknown.* OBET

Humps are lumps. Lumps. Judith Thurman. RHPC

Humpty Dumpty sat on a wall. Mother Goose. FaBoBe; OxBoLi; OxNR

Humpty Dumpty's Poem. "Lewis Carroll." *See* Through the Looking-Glass: In winter, when the fields are white.

Humpty Dumpty's Recitation. "Lewis Carroll." *See* Through the Looking-Glass: In winter, when the fields are white.

Humpty Dumpty's Song. "Lewis Carroll." *See* Through the Looking-Glass: In winter, when the fields are white.

Hunan, Hubei, Taishan, Taiwan. The Sword of Li Ling. Lo Ch'ing, *tr. by* Dominic Cheung. IFON

Hunchback, The. John Peale Bishop. PoA

Hunchback and the Dwarf, The. Marutanilanakanar, *tr. fr. Tamil by* A. K. Ramanujan. PLW
Hunchback in the Park, The. Dylan Thomas. EBEV; FaBoTw; MoAB; MoBrPo; NAEL-2; NoAM; NoP; PrIm; TwCP
Hunchback on the corner, with gum and shoelaces, The. Pursuit. Robert Penn Warren. HAP; LiTA; MoAmPo; TwCP
Hunchback Woman. The Hunchback and the Dwarf. Marutanilanakanar, *tr. by* A. K. Ramanujan. PLW
Hunchbacked/ by his heart. The Life. Philip Dow. AmPA
Hunchbacked and corrected. Ken Belford. NeAC
Hunchèd camels of the night, The. An Arab Love-Song. Francis Thompson. AWP; MoAB; MoBrPo
Hunder pipers canna blaw, A. Calvinist Sang. Alexander Scott. OxBS
Hundred ballads I have written, A. Christine de Pisan, *tr. by* Joan M. Ferrante. DMF
Hundred beauties are present, A. Asadullah Khan Ghalib, *tr. by* Ahmed Ali. GoT
Hundred buffalo, A. Bone Yard. Jim Barnes. CDW
Hundred days, a hundred nights, A. Emperor Go-Shirakawa. *See* Ryojin Hisho: Even if I had to sleep alone.
Hundred-Fold Cord, The. Chang Yü, *tr. fr. Chinese by* Jonathan Chaves. *Fr.* Four Poems On the Ch'ung-wu Festival. CoBLCP
Hundred-gated City! thou. Hundred-gated Thebes. George Darley. *Fr.* Nepenthe. NOBE
Hundred griefs are like a hundred arrows, A. Night at an Inn: Written in the Style of Meng Chiao. Chiang Shih, *tr. by* Irving Lo. WFTU
Hundred mares, all white, A! their manes. The Mares of the Camargue. Frédéric Mistral, *tr. fr. Provençal by* George Meredith. *Fr.* Mirèio. AWP
Hundred men shouting at once, helping to rattle the oars, A. Blue Rapids. Lu Yu, *tr. by* Burton Watson. CoBCP
Hundred rivers day and night flow on, The. Beginning to Autumn: A Poem to Send to Tzu-yu. Su Tung-p'o, *tr. by* Burton Watson. CoBCP
Hundred ruddy peach-moons ring the grass, A. Under the September Peach. Robert Wallace. Son
Hundred-sunned Phenix. George Darley. *See* Nepenthe: O Blest Unfabled Incense Tree.
Hundred thousand li of journey, how many dangers?, A. For the Monk San-tsang on His Return to the Western Regions. Li Tung, *tr. by* Burton Watson. CoBCP
Hundred thousand Northmen, A. Wait for the Wagon. *Unknown.* PAH
Hundred thousand welcomes, thou Body of the Lord, A. *Unknown, tr. by* Douglas Hyde. WTO
Hundred Ways of Playing Solitaire, A, *sel.* Belle Randall. Mabel Woo. CRP
Hundred-Yard Dash, The. William Lindsey. AA
Hundred-year old flies sit. Quietude. Mihály Ladányi, *tr. by* Jascha Kessler. FOC
Hundred Years Ago, A. *Unknown.* AS
Hundred years ago this morn, A. Gerald Massey. *Fr.* Robin Burns. PF
Hundred Years from Now, A. Mary A. Ford. BLPA
Hundred years from now, dear heart, A. In a Rose Garden. John Bennett. BLPA; FaBoBB
Hundred years have passed and gone, A. Centenary's Day. Marcus Garvey. PBCV
Hundred years is a very long time, A. A Hundred Years Ago. *Unknown.* AS
Hundreds of migrating hawks are roosting in the hedgerows. Driving into Enid. Michael Van Walleghen. FYAP
Hundreds of stars in the pretty sky. Only One Mother. George Cooper. OHIP
(Only One.) AA
(Our Mother.) BoTP; FaPON
Hundreth Good Poyntes of Husbandry, A, *sel.* Thomas Tusser. "When harvest is done all thing placed and set." FaBoUs
Hung be the heavens with black, yield day to night. A King Is Dead. Shakespeare. *Fr.* King Henry VI, Pt. I, I, i. ChTr
Hung between thief and thief. Improperia. Francis Sparshott. MoCV
Hung from a stone branch of city wall. Beware the Months of Fire. Patrick Lane. NeAC
Hung low with clouds. Emperor Kogon, *tr. by* Steven D. Carter. WFTW
Hunga a twis man tripe. Pressure Drop. Oku Onuora. PBCV
Hunger. Laurence Binyon. OxBTC
Hunger. Jeannie Ebner, *tr. fr. German by* Beth Bjorklund. CoAuP
Hunger. Rimbaud, *tr. fr. French by* Edgell Rickword. AWP
Hunger. Samik, *tr. fr. Eskimo by* Edward Field. STP
Hunger. Charles Simic. NNaP
Hunger. Gaspara Stampa, *tr. fr. Italian by* Brenda Webster. WPOW
Hunger. Ruth Stone. InPS

Hunger. *Unknown, tr. fr. Eskimo.* WTO
Hunger. *Unknown, tr. by* Ulli Beier. PBA; TTY
Hunger, and sultry heat, and nipping blast. The French and the Spanish Guerrillas. Wordsworth. WaaP
(Sonnet: French and the Spanish Guerrillas, The.) ChER
Hunger and Thirst. John Peale Bishop. PoA
Hunger crawls into you. Hunger in New York City. Simon J. Ortiz. MAYP
Hunger Fell upon Us, A. Jacob Glatstein, *tr. fr. Yiddish by* Benjamin *and* Barbara Harshav *and* Kathryn Helle. AYP
Hunger in New York City. Simon J. Ortiz. MAYP
Hunger is beating me. *Yoruba Oral Tradition, tr. by* Ulli Beier *and* B. Gbadamosi. WTO
Hunger makes a person climb up to the ceiling. Hunger. *Unknown, tr. by* Ulli Beier. PBA; TTY
Hunger makes a person lie down. *Yoruba Oral Tradition, tr. by* Ulli Beier. WTO
Hungering on the gray plain of its birth. A Lion Named Passion. John Hollander. NePoEA-2; NoAM
Hungry and thirsty we break these stones in the heat of the sun. The Roadmenders' Song. *Gond Oral Tradition, tr. by* V. Elwin *and* S. Hivale. WTO
Hungry and Waiting. Tom Mandel. BAP
Hungry Black Child, The. Adam David Miller. PoBA
Hungry Crow, The. Ch'en Wei-sung, *tr. fr. Chinese by* Madeline Chu. WFTU
Hungry Dead, The. Jim Wayne Miller. MT
Hungry Grass, The. Donagh MacDonagh. BIrV; NeIP
Hungry man looks into the restaurant, A. Propaganda Art. Väinö Kirstinä, *tr. by* Aili Jarvenpa. SOP
"Hungry winter, this winter." To Hell with It. Frank O'Hara. NeAP
Hunk, The. Judson Jerome. SoTCo
Hunt. Melvin Walker La Follette. NePoEA
Hunt, The. Pope. *Fr.* Windsor Forest. NIP
Hunt, The. Harriet Prescott Spofford. AA
Hunt, The. *Unknown.* CoMu
Hunt, hunt again. If you do not find it, you. Treasure Hunt. Robert Penn Warren. NoP
(Fairy Story.) NYBP
Hunt in the Black Forest, A. Randall Jarrell. CoAP; LCAP
Hunt Is Up, The. *Unknown.* CH; GBP
Hunt is up, the hunt is up, The. The Song of the Hunt. John Bennett. *Fr.* Master Sky-Lark. AA
Hunt not, fish not, shoot not. Bishop Blomfield's First Charge to His Clergy. *At. to* Sydney Goodsir Smith. FaBoEE
Hunt was up, the hunt was up, The. The Capture of Edwin Alonzo Boyd. Peter Miller. MoCV
Hunted. Paul Éluard, *tr. fr. French by* David Gascoyne. RHTwFP
Hunted City, The, *sel.* Kenneth Patchen.
"Little hill climbs up to the village and puts its green hands, The." NaP
Hunter, The. Ogden Nash. SD
Hunter, The. Frank O'Hara. NNaP
Hunter, The. Raymond Souster. NOBC
Hunter. Rosanna Warren. *Fr.* Funerary Portraits, II. NOAM
Hunter crouches in his blind, The. The Hunter. Ogden Nash. SD
Hunter of the Prairies, The. Bryant. AA
Hunter Once, Now an Ascetic, A. Marippittiyar, *tr. fr. Tamil by* A. K. Ramanujan. PLW
Hunter Poems of the Yoruba, *sels. Unknown, tr. fr. Yoruba by* Ulli Beier. RB
Baboon.
Blue Cuckoo.
Buffalo.
Chicken.
Colobus Monkey.
Elephant.
Hyena.
Kob Antelope.
Leopard.
Red Monkey.
Hunter Radiation Center: Halloween. Alice Mattison. PPR
Hunter Trials. Sir John Betjeman. FiBHP
Hunter: 20,000 A.D, The. Andrew Joron. BWV
Hunters are back from beating the winter's face, The. The Woman Thing. Audre Lorde. BiSi; NMM
Hunters in the Snow, The. William Carlos Williams. *Fr.* Pictures from Brueghel, III. LCAP
Hunters in the Snow: Brueghel. Joseph Langland. LiTM; NePoEA
Hunter's Moon. Stephen Sandy. NYBP
Hunter's Morning. Harold Littlebird. STE

Hunters of Kentucky; or, Half Horse and Half Alligator, The. Samuel Woodworth. AS; FAH

Hunters of Men, The. Whittier. AnAmPo

Hunters of the Deer, The. Dale Zieroth. NOBC

Hunter's Prayer. *Unknown, tr. fr. Hottentot.* PeSA

Hunter's Song, The. "Barry Cornwall." GN

Hunter's Song. Mvula Ya Nangolo. WMBCH

Hunters went out with guns, The. Good Grease. Mary TallMountain. STE

Hunting, The. Thomas Lux. PPR

Hunting. Jack Sheedy. ASP

Hunting. Gary Snyder. *Fr. Myths and Texts.*
  "All beaded with dew." *Fr.* VII. NaP
  "Birds in a whirl, drift to the rooftops." *Fr.* III. NaP
  First Shaman Song. *Fr.* I. NOBA
  "How rare to be born a human being!" *Fr.* XVI. NaP
  "Out the Greywolf valley." *Fr.* XII. NaP
  "Swallow-shell that eases birth, The." *Fr.* IV. NaP
  This Poem Is for Bear. *Fr.* VI. NoBA; NU
    ("Bear down under the cliff, A.") HCAP; NaP
  This Poem is for Deer. *Fr.* VIII. NaP; NOBA
    ("Missed a last shot.") NoBA; NU

Hunting. Yehoash, *tr. fr. Yiddish by* Isidore Goldstick. TrJP

Hunting Civil War Relics at Nimblewilt Creek. James Dickey. GOA

Hunting for Blueberries. Thomas James. AmPA

Hunting for Grouse. Roseann Lloyd. TSL

Hunting horn upon the plain, A. The Mystery of the Three Horns. Jules Laforgue, *tr. by* William Jay Smith. CT

Hunting Horns. Guillaume Apollinaire, *tr. fr. French by* Paul Blackburn. RHTwFP

Hunting in the Ordos, the Pheasants and Hares Were Many. Hsüan-yeh, *tr. fr. Chinese by* Jonathan D. Spence. WFTU

Hunting my cat along the evening brook. Night Heron. Frances Mary Frost. RHPC

Hunting of Cupid, The, *sels.* George Peele.
  Song of Coridon and Melampus. OBSC
  What Thing Is Love. EiL; ELP; NOBE; SeCePo
  (Love.) EiL; ELP; NOBE; OBSC; SeCePo

Hunting of the Cheviot, The. *Unknown. See* God prosper long our noble king.

Hunting of the Gods, The. *Unknown.* OxBoLi

Hunting of the Hare, The. Margaret Lucas, Duchess of Newcastle. FM

Hunting of the Snark, The, *sel.* "Lewis Carroll." FaBoNo; FiBHP, *much abr.;* NA, *much abr.;* OBNC; OBNV; OnMSP; PoEL-5
  Baker's Tale, The. EBEV; NAEL-2

Hunting of Whales, The. Jacques Prévert, *tr. fr. French by* Michael Benedikt. POS

Hunting Season. Mykie Silz Reidy. TSL

Hunting season. Long Hair. Gary Snyder. NOBA

Hunting Song. Burns. PBBP

Hunting Song. Henry Fielding. *Fr.* Don Quixote in England. OxBoLi

Hunting Song. Donald Finkel. NePoEA

Hunting Song. Sir Walter Scott. *Fr.* The Lay of the Last Minstrel. EnRP; GN; GTBS; GTBS-P; TrGrPo; WiR

Hunting-Song. *Unknown, tr. fr. Navajo Indian by* Natalie Curtis. AWP

Hunting Song. Paul Whitehead. *Fr.* Apollo and Daphne. OxBoLi

Hunting the Dugong. Gladys Cardiff. HATNAP

Hunting them, a man must sweat, bear. The Lilies. Wendell Berry. GeTw

Hunting tribes of air and earth, The. Man the Enemy of Man. Sir Walter Scott. *Fr.* Rokeby, III. WBLP

Huntington sleeps in a house six feet long. Southern Pacific. Carl Sandburg. AnAmPo

Huntress, The. José Joaquín Pesado, *tr. fr. Spanish by* Samuel Beckett. MexPo

Huntsman's Rouse, The. Henry Carey. SeCePo

Huntsmen, The. Walter de la Mare. CenHV; RAR

Hurdler. Grace Butcher. ASP

Hurdy-Gurdy Man, The. Elizabeth Fleming. BoTP

Hurdy-Gurdy Man in Winter. Vernon Watkins. NYBP

Hurl down the nerve-gnarled body hurtling head. The Final Hunger. Vassar Miller. LiTM

Hurled back, defeated, like a child I sought. Earthborn. Peter McArthur. CaP

Hurly, hurly, roon the table. *Unknown. Fr.* Two Graces. FaBoCh

Hurlygush. Maurice Lindsay. OxBS

Huron, The. Ruth Herschberger. WPE

The Huron Carol. Jesse Edgar Middleton. *See* Jesous Ahatonhia.

Hurrah! for a day with the farmer. A Day at the Farm. "L. J." BoTP

Hurrah for revolution and more cannon-shot! The Great Day. W. B. Yeats. BIrV; CMoP; FF; OxBSP

Hurrah for the choice of the nation! Lincoln and Liberty. *Unknown.* AS

Hurrah for the Lachlan. The Shearer's Song. *Unknown.* PoAu-1

Hurrah for Trees! László Nagy, *tr. fr. Hungarian by* Jascha Kessler. FOC

Hurrah, Hurrah. Remco Campert, *tr. fr. Dutch by* Greta Kilburn. DuIn

Hurrah! to them who do nothing. Non-Commitment. Chinua Achebe. UAS

Hurrahing in Harvest. Gerard Manley Hopkins. BoNaP; BrPo; ChTr; CMoP; FaBoPP; InvP; MoAB; MoBrPo; NAEL-2; PoE; TOF

Hurricane, The. Hart Crane. CMoP; MoAB; MoAmPo; OxBA; TrCP

Hurricane, The. Philip Freneau. MOS; TAP

Hurricane, The. Luis Palés Matos, *tr. fr. Spanish by* Alida Malkus. FaPON

Hurrier, The. Harold Monro. MoBrPo

Hurry of the Spirits, in a Fever and Nervous Disorders, The. Isaac Watts. NOEC

Hurry On, My Weary Soul. *Unknown.* AH

"Hurry!" said the leaves. A Summer Shower. *Unknown.* BoTP

Hurry the baby as fast as you can. Making a Man. Nixon Waterman. BLPA

Hurry, worry, unwary. Old Amusement Park. Marianne Moore. NYBP

Hurrying Away from the Earth. Robert Bly. NaP; PoA

Hurrying Brook, The. Edmund Blunden. BoNaP

Hurrying, hurrying, we've downed our cups of wine. Setting Out from Hiroshima, Saying Goodby to My Father. Rai San'yo, *tr. by* Burton Watson. FCEI; JLIC-2

Hurrying to catch my Comet. Naturally the Foundation Will Bear Your Expenses. Philip Larkin. FaBoPV

Hurt./ U worried abt a. To All Sisters. Sonia Sanchez. PoBA

Hurt?/ Who me? On Hurt. Meiling Jin. WS

Hurt Hawks. Robinson Jeffers. AmPP; CMoP; FYAP; LiTA; LiTM; MoAB; MoAmPo; MoP; NAAL-2; NoAM; NOBA; NoP; OxBA; PrIm; RB; TAP; UnPo

Hurt is red, The. It is a sore with a big, big eye. Have Head, Have Tail. Nellie Wong. ER

Hurt No Living Thing. Christina Rossetti. *Fr.* Sing-Song. FaPON; FM; PDV; RHPC; TSS

Hurt of Love, The. George Macdonald. TrCP

Hurt people crawl as if they. These Days. William Stafford. NNaP

Husband and Heathen. Sam Walter Foss. OBAL

Husband and wife we loved each other then. The Old Man's Song, about His Wife. *Unknown, tr. by* Armand Schwerner. STP

Husband of Poverty, The, *sel.* Henry Neville Maughan.
  "There was a Knight of Bethlehem." BoTP

Husband, put down Spinoza, Pericles. Put Off Constricting Day. Mary Stanley. PeNZ

Husbandman, The. Frances Beatrice Taylor. CaP

Husbandman and Serving-Man, The. *Unknown.* OBET

Husbandry, *sel.* Sir Anthony Fitzherbert.
  Memorial Verses for Travellers. FaBoUs

Husbandry. William Hammond. JCP

Husbands and Wives. Miriam Hershenson. NTCP

Husband's Lament, The. Brian Merriman, *tr. fr. Modern Irish by* Frank O'Connor. *Fr.* The Midnight Court. OBVE

Husband's Message, The. *Unknown, tr. fr. Anglo-Saxon by* Charles W. Kennedy. AnOE

Husband's Return, The. Priscilla Jane Thompson. CBWP-2

Hush. Mani Leib, *tr. fr. Yiddish by* Marie Syrkin. PeBMYV

Hush. David St. John. DiL; LCAP; MAYP

Hush-a-ba birdie [*or* burdie], croon, croon. *Unknown.* GBP; OxNR

Hush-a-baa, baby/ Dinna mak' a din. *Unknown.* OxNR

Hush-a-by, baby/ Your name is so lovely. Italian Lullaby. *Unknown.* FaPON

Hush-a-bye a baa lamb. *Unknown.* OxNR

Hush-a-bye, baby/ The beggar shan't have 'ee. *Unknown.* OxNR

Hush-a-bye, baby, on the tree-top. Mother Goose. OxNR

Hush-a-bye, baby, they're gone to milk. *Unknown.* OxNR

Hush and Baloo. *Unknown.* GBP

Hush and hush—no sound be heard. Hush. Mani Leib, *tr. by* Marie Syrkin. PeBMYV

Hush dove the summer. Miriam Waddington. CaP

Hush Honey. Ruby C. Saunders. BlSi

Hush, hush. Now We Are Sick. J. B. Morton. *Fr.* When We Were Very Silly. FaBoPa

Hush, Hush. Mani Leib, *tr. fr. Yiddish by* Joseph Leftwich. TrJP

Hush, hush,/ Nobody cares! Now We Are Sick. J. B. Morton. FaBoPa

Hush, hush, do not speak. Hush, Hush. Mani Leib, *tr. by* Joseph Leftwich. TrJP

Hush, hush, little baby. Evening. *Unknown.* BoTP

Hush is over all the teeming lists, A. Frederick Douglass. Paul Laurence Dunbar. PoBA

Hush, little baby, don't say a word. *Unknown.* OxNR

Hush! lullaby, my baby, nor mix thy tears with mine. The Mother's Lullaby. John Clare. NAs

Hush, lullay. Léonie Adams. MoAB; MoAmPo

Hush, my baby, do not cry. *Unknown.* OxNR

Hush! my dear, lie still and slumber. A Cradle Hymn. Isaac Watts. OBEV; OxBChV; PoEL-3

Hush! not a whisper! Oars, be still! The Coracle Fishers. Robert Bloomfield. *Fr.* The Banks of Wye. OBNC

Hush! oh ye billows. Joseph Sheridan Le Fanu. *Fr.* Beatrice. TIRV

Hush, Suzanne! The Mouse in the Wainscot. Ian Serraillier. PDV

Hush thee, my babby. *Unknown.* OxNR

Hush Thee, Princeling. Anna Elizabeth Bennett. AH

Hush up, baby,/ Don't say a word. The Mocking Bird. *Unknown.* AmFP

Hush ye, hush ye! honey, darlin.' Clara Ann Thompson. CBWP-2

Hush! Yo' mouth. Hush Honey. Ruby C. Saunders. BlSi

Hushaby,/ Don't you cry. All the Pretty Little Horses. *Unknown.* AmFP; OxBoLi; TTTS

Hushabye My Darling. Clyde Watson. RAR

Hush'd Be the Camps To-Day. Walt Whitman. OHIP

Hushed are the pigeons cooing low. The Christmas Silence. Margaret Deland. OHIP

Hushed by the Hands of Sleep. Angelina Weld Grimké. CDC

Hushed to inaudible sound the deepening rain. The Lyre-Bird. Roland Robinson. PoAu-2

Hushie ba, burdie beeton. *Unknown.* OxNR

Hushing of the Wye, The. Tennyson. *See* In Memoriam A. H. H.: Danube to the Severn gave, The.

Hustle and Grin. *Unknown.* WBLP

Hustler, The. *Unknown.* TW

Hustlers. Dennis Cooper. UL

Huswifery. Edward Taylor. EaLo; FaBV; LiTA; NAAL-1; NIP; NOBA; NOBE; NoP; OxBA; SaC; SCAP; TAP

Hut. G. J. F. Dutton. PoSH

Hut in the bush of bark or rusty tin, The. The Hatters. Nan McDonald. PoAu-2

Hut near Desolated Pines. Alistair Campbell. ATNZ

Hut: Thinking of a Friend. Gensei, *tr. fr. Chinese* by Burton Watson. JLIC-2

Hut Window. Paul Celan, *tr. fr. German* by Joachim Neugroschel. VWA

Huts at Esquimaux, The. Norman Dubie. MOWH

Huts that stand like plaited baskets. Village and Factory. Alexander Ilyich Bezymensky, *tr.* by Babette Deutsch. TrJP

Huxley Hall. Sir John Betjeman. OBSV

Huzza for our liberty, boys. Terrapin War. *Unknown.* PAH

Huzza! Hodgson, we are going. The Lisbon Packet. Byron. NBLV

Huzza, my Jo Bunkers! no taxes we'll pay. A Radical Song of 1786. St. John Honeywood. PAH

Hwaet! A dream came to me. The Dream of the Rood. *Unknown, tr.* by Michael Alexander. NOCV

Hy-Brasail—the Isle of the Blest. Gerald Griffin. *See* On the ocean that hollows the rocks where ye dwell.

Hyacinth. Louise Glück. NoAM

Hyacinths to Feed Thy Soul. Sadi, *tr. fr. Persian. Fr.* The Gulistan. BLPA; BLPL; FaBoBe

Hyaenas [or Hyenas], The. Kipling. NAEL-2; OBSV

Hyaku-Nin-Isshu, sels. *Unknown, tr. fr. Japanese* by Curtis Hidden Page. AWP

"Day will soon be gone, The." Fujiwara no Michinobu.

"How can one e'er be sure." Lady Horikawa.

"I would that even now." Princess Shoku.

"Like a great rock, far out at sea." Lady Sanuki.

Hyd, Absalon, thy gilte tresses clear. Chaucer. *Fr.* The Legend of Good Women: Prologue. HAP

(Balade: "Hide [*or* Hyd], Absalon, thy gilte tresses clere.") AWP; ChTr; EBEV; FiP; GBL; NOBE; OAEL-1; OBEV

(Lady without Paragon, A.) MeEL

Hyder Iddle. *Unknown.* NA; OxNR

Hye Nonny Nonny Noe. *Unknown.* FaBoCo; NOBL

Hyena. Carol Muske. AmPA

Hyena. *Unknown, tr. fr. Hurutsche* by George Economou. TTY

Hyena. *Unknown.* PeSA

Hyena. *Unknown, tr. fr. Yoruba* by Ulli Beier. *Fr.* Hunter Poems of the Yoruba. RB

Hyena's Song to her Children. *Unknown, tr. fr. Hottentot.* PeSA

Hygienist, in your dental chair. Ode to a Dental Hygienist. Earnest Albert Hooton. FiBHP

Hyla Brook. Robert Frost. BoNaP

Hylas. Sextus Propertius, *tr. fr. Latin* by F. A. Wright. *Fr.* Elegies, I, 20. AWP

Hylas, the world's perceptual scene. Equation. Sir Herbert Read. BrPo

Hymen, sel. *Hilda Doolittle ("H. D.").*

"Never more will the wind." CTC; TrGrPo

Hymenaei, sel. Ben Jonson.

Angel Describes Truth, An. OBS

Hymeneal, sel. Catullus, *tr. fr. Latin* by James Michie.

"Unmuzzle the broad joke." PeHV

Hymeneal Song on the Nuptials of the Lady Anne Wentworth and the Lord Lovelace, An. Thomas Carew. CaPo

Hymeneall Dialogue, An. Thomas Carew. SeCP

Hymen's Triumph, sels. Samuel Daniel.

Constancy. OBSC

Early Love. ErPo

Eyes Hide My Love. EIL

(Secrecy.) OBSC

Had Sorrow Ever Fitter Place. EIL

(Sorrow.) OBSC

Love Is a Sickness. ELP; NOBE; OBEV; PoEL-2

(Love.) EIL; OBSC

Hymettus' bees are out on filmy wing. The Sunflower to the Sun. Mary Elizabeth DeWitt Stebbins. AA

Hymmnn. Allen Ginsberg. NOBA

Hymn: After Reading "Lead, Kindly Light." Paul Laurence Dunbar. TrPWD

Hymn: "And many voices marshalled in one hymn." Thomas Lovell Beddoes. NOBVV

Hymn: "By the rude bridge that arched the flood." Emerson. *See* By the rude bridge that arched the flood.

Hymn: "Church's Restoration, The." Sir John Betjeman. FaBoPa

Hymn: "Dear Lord, Whose serving-maiden." Josephine Preston Peabody. TrPWD

Hymn: "Drop, drop, slow tears." Phineas Fletcher. EIL; OBS; OxBSP

Hymn: "Eternal Ruler of the ceaseless round." John White Chadwick. TrPWD

Hymn: "Father, we come not as of old." John W. Chadwick. TrPWD

Hymn: "For Summer's bloom and Autumn's blight." Josiah Gilbert Holland. *Fr.* Bitter-sweet. TrPWD

Hymn: "Framer of the earth and sky." Saint Ambrose, *tr. fr. Latin.* TrCP

Hymn: "God of the strong, God of the weak." Richard Watson Gilder. TrPWD

Hymn: "Great Spirit of the speeding spheres." John Haynes Holmes. TrPWD

Hymn: "Hush! oh ye billows." Joseph Sheridan Le Fanu. *Fr.* Beatrice. TIRV

Hymn, A: "Hymn of glory let us sing, A." The Venerable Bede, *tr. fr. Latin* by Elizabeth Charles. WGRP

Hymn: "Lord, by whose breath all souls and seeds are living." Andrew Young. EaLo

Hymn: "Lord, when the wise men came from far[r]." Sidney Godolphin. HAP; JCP; MeLP; MePo; NOCV; OBS

Hymn: "Lord, with glowing heart I'd praise thee." Francis Scott Key. TrPWD

Hymn, A: "Lord, within thy fold I be." Priscilla Jane Thompson. CBWP-2

Hymn: "Mighty fortress is our God, A." Martin Luther. *See* Mighty Fortress Is Our God, A.

Hymn: "My God, I love thee, not because." Saint Francis Xavier, *tr. fr. Latin.* WGRP

Hymn: "New every morning is thy love." John Keble. *See* New every morning.

Hymn: "Now the day is over." Sabine Baring-Gould. OxBChV

Hymn: "Now we must praise heaven-kingdom's Guardian." Caedmon, *tr. by* D. K. Fry. TrCP

Hymn: "O Christ, the glorious Crown." Philip Howard. ACP

Hymn [*or* Prayer], A: "O God of Earth and altar." G. K. Chesterton. TrPWD; WGRP

Hymn: "O thou who camest from above." Charles Wesley. SeCePo; TrPWD

Hymn[e]: "Queen[e] and huntress, chaste, and fair." Ben Jonson. *See* Cynthia's Revels: Hymn to Diana.

Hymn L: Rocking Hymn, A. George Wither. *Fr.* Hallelujah; or, Britain's Second Remembrancer. SeCV-1

Hymn: "Room! room! make room for the bouncing belly." Ben Jonson. *See* Pleasure Reconciled to Virtue: Hymn to Comus.

Hymn: "Since without Thee we do no good." Elizabeth Barrett Browning. TrPWD

Hymn: "Sing, my tongue, the Saviour's glory." Saint Thomas Aquinas. WGRP

Hymn: "Some sort of fire leaped out of the dirty and poor and merciless city." Otto Orban, *tr.* by Emery George. VWA

Hymn: "Thou God of all, whose presence dwells." John Haynes Holmes. TrPWD

Hymn: "Thou hidden love of God, whose height." John Wesley. NOEC

Hymn: To Light. Abraham Cowley. MeLP; MePo; OBS; SeCV-1

Hymn: "When storms arise." Paul Laurence Dunbar. TrPWD

Hymn: "Where is this stupendous stranger." Christopher Smart. *See* Hymns and Spiritual Songs: Nativity of Our Lord and Saviour Jesus Christ, The.

Hymn: "Where should I seat you, where." Márton Kalász, *tr.* by Jascha Kessler. FOC

Hymn: "Wilt Thou forgive that sin where I begun." John Donne. *See* Wilt Thou forgive that sin where I begun.

Hymn: "Words of hymns abruptly plod, The." Louise Townsend Nicholl. EaLo

Hymn about a Spoonful of Soup, A. Jozef Wittlin, *tr. fr. Polish* by Isaac Komem. VWA

Hymn before Sunrise, in the Vale of Chamouni. Samuel Taylor Coleridge. EnRP; WGRP

Hymn for Atonement Day. Judah Halevi, *tr. fr. Hebrew* by Solomon Solis-Cohen. TrJP

Hymn for Canada, A. Albert Durrant Watson. CaP

Hymn for Christmas. Felicia Dorothea Hemans. GN

Hymn for Christmas Day, A. John Byrom. NOCV; PoEL-3

Hymn for Easter Morn. John Mason Neale. TrCP

Hymn for Lanie Poo, *sel. Amiri Baraka.*
  Each Morning. IDB; PoBA

Hymn for Pentecost. James Clarence Mangan. TIRV

Hymn for St. John's Eve. *Unknown, tr. fr. Latin* by Dryden. AWP

Hymn for Saturday. Christopher Smart. *See* Hymns for the Amusement of Children: For Saturday.

Hymn for the Close of the Week. Peter Abelard, *tr. fr. Latin.* TrCP

Hymn for the Dedication of a Church. Andrews Norton. AA

Hymn for the Eve of the New Year. Abraham Gerondi, *tr. fr. Hebrew* by Solomon Solis-Cohen. TrJP

Hymn from the French of Lamartine, *sel.* Whittier.
  "O Thou who bidst the torrent flow." TrPWD

Hymn in Adoration of the Blessed Sacrament. Richard Crashaw. *See* With all the powers my poor heart hath.

Hymn in Columbus Circle. Stephen Vincent Benét. OBAL

Hymn of Apollo. Shelley. EnRP; OAEL-2
  (Song of Apollo.) NAEL-2

Hymn of Dedication. Elizabeth E. Scantlebury. BLRP

Hymn of Form, A. Gordon Bottomley. BrPo

Hymn of Freedom. Michael J. Barry. TIRV

Hymn of glory let us sing, A. The Venerable Bede, *tr.* by Elizabeth Charles. WGRP

Hymn of Gratitude. *Unknown.* BLRP

Hymn of Heavenly Beauty, An, *sel.* Spenser.
  "But whoso may, thrice happy man him hold." WGRP

Hymn of Pan. Shelley. EnRP; FaBoCh; OBEV; PoEL-4

Hymn of Saint Thomas in Adoration of the Blessed Sacrament, The. Richard Crashaw. OBS

Hymn of Sivaite Puritans. *Unknown.* WGRP

Hymn of Thanksgiving, A. Wilbur D. Nesbit. OHIP

Hymn of the Earth. William Ellery Channing. AA

Hymn of the Incarnation, A. *Unknown.* MeEL

Hymn of the Moravian Nuns of Bethlehem. Longfellow. PAH

Hymn[e] of the Nativity. Richard Crashaw. *See* Come we shepherds, whose blest sight.

Hymn of the Sea, A. Bryant. MOS

Hymn of the West. Edmund Clarence Stedman. PAH

Hymn of the World Without. Bible, *O.T. See* Psalms: Psalm CIV ("Bless the Lord, O my soul. . .").

Hymn of Touch, A. Gordon Bottomley. BrPo

Hymn of Trust. Oliver Wendell Holmes. *See* Professor at the Breakfast Table, The: O Love Divine, That Stooped to Share.

Hymn of Trust, A. Nettie M. Sargent. BLRP

Hymn of Unity. *Unknown, tr. fr. Hebrew* by H. M. Adler. TrJP

Hymn of Victory: Thutmose III. Amon-Re, *tr. fr. Egyptian* by James Henry Breasted. WaaP

Hymn of Weeping. Amittai ben Shefatiah, *tr. fr. Hebrew* by Nina Davis Salaman. TrJP

Hymn on Froude and Kingsley, A. William Stubbs. CenHV; FaBoEE

Hymn on Solitude. James Thomson. NOEC

Hymn on the Morning of Christ's Nativity [*or* On the Morning of Christ's Nativity]. Milton. *Fr.* On the Morning of Christ's Nativity. FiP; NAEL-1; NOBE; OBEV

Hymn [*or* Hymne] on the Nativity [*or* Nativitie] of My Saviour, A. Ben Jonson. SeCV-1; TrCP

Hymn on the Omnipresence, An. John Byrom. TrPWD

Hymn on the Seasons, A. James Thomson. *Fr.* The Seasons. EnRP

Hymn Sung at the Completion of the Concord Monument. Emerson. *See* By the rude bridge that arched the flood.

Hymn to Adversity. Thomas Gray. EnRP; GTBS; GTBS-P

Hymn to Amen Ra, the Sun God. *Unknown, tr. fr. Egyptian* by Frank Lloyd Griffith. WGRP

Hymn to Athena. *Unknown, tr. fr. Greek* by Shelley. *Fr.* Homeric Hymns. AWP

Hymn to Bacchus, A. Robert Herrick. JCP

Hymn to Castor and Pollux. *Unknown, tr. fr. Greek* by Shelley. *Fr.* Homeric Hymns. AWP

Hymn [*or* Hymne] to Christ, at the Author's Last Going into Germany, A, *sel.* John Donne. EBEV; JCP; LiTB; MeLP; MePo; OBS; SeCV-1
  Dark Churches. FaBoRV

Hymn to Colour. George Meredith. OBNC

Hymn to Comus. Ben Jonson. *Fr.* Pleasure Reconciled to Virtue. OAEL-1, *complete.*
  (Hymn: "Room! room! make room for the bouncing belly.") NAEL-1
  (Hymn to Comus.) ElL; SeCePo
  (Hymn to the Belly.) SeCePo

Hymn to Contentment, A. Thomas Parnell. NOEC

Hymn to Cynthia. Ben Jonson. *See* Cynthia's Revels: Hymn to Diana.

Hymn to Darkness. John Norris. MePo; OBS

Hymn to Diana. Catullus, *tr. fr. Latin* by Richard Claverhouse Jebb. AWP

Hymn to Diana. Thomas Heywood. *Fr.* The Golden Age. ElL

Hymn to Diana. Ben Jonson. *Fr.* Cynthia's Revels, V, vi. AWP; CH; ChTr; ElL; GTBS; GTBS-P; HAP; HeIP; NOBE; NoP; OAEL-1; OBEV; OBS; PoRA; QFR; SeCP; TrGrPo; WiR
  (Hesperus' Hymn[e] to Cynthia.) JCP; SeCV-1
  (Hesperus' Song.) GN
  (Hymn: "Queen and huntress, chaste, and fair.") InPS
  (Hymn to Cynthia.) PoE; PrIm; SeCePo
  (Hymne, The: "Queene and huntress, chaste, and faire.") PoEL-2

Hymn to Dispel Hatred at Midnight. Yvor Winters. TW

Hymn to Earth. Elinor Wylie. LiTM; MoAB; MoAmPo

Hymn to Earth the Mother of All. *Unknown, tr. fr. Greek* by Shelley. *Fr.* Homeric Hymns. AWP

Hymn to Evil. Louis Ginsberg. PoA

Hymn to God in Time of Stress, A. Max Eastman. TrPWD

Hymn[e] to God My God, In My Sickness[e]. John Donne. ChTr; EBEV; HeIP; InPS; MeLP; MePo; NAEL-1; NIP; NoP; OAEL-1; OBD; OBS; PoE; PoEL-2; PPP; SeCP; SeCV-1; TOF; TrPWD

Hymn to God the Father , A. John Donne. AWP; EaLo; EBEV; HAP; InPK; JCP; LiTB; MeLP; MePo; NAEL-1; NOBE; OAEL-1; OBS; PoEL-2; PoRA; SCV; SeCP; SeCV-1; TOF; TrGrPo; TrPWD; ViBoPo; WGRP

Hymn to God the Father, A. Ben Jonson. MePo; NoP; OBS; SeCP; SeCV-1; TrCP; TrPWD

Hymn to Her Unknown. Walter James Turner. OBMV

Hymn to Intellectual Beauty. Shelley. BLPL; EnRP; HAP; HeIP; NAEL-2; NoP; OAEL-2; OBNC; PoE; TOF

Hymn to Jesus, A. Richard of Caistre. MeEL

Hymn to Joy. Julia Cunningham. PChr

Hymn to Love. Lascelles Abercrombie. *Fr.* Emblems of Love. OBEV

Hymn to Marduk, *sels. Unknown, tr. fr. Assyrian.* WGRP
  "O Marduk, lord of countries, terrible one."
  "O Mighty, powerful, strong one of Ashur."

Hymn to Mary, A. William Dunbar. *See* Hail sterne superne! Hail in eterne.

Hymn to Mercury. *Unknown, tr. fr. Greek* by Shelley. *Fr.* Homeric Hymns. OBVE

Hymn to Moloch. Ralph Hodgson. OxBTC

Hymn to My God in a Night of My Late Sicknesse, A. Sir Henry Wotton. MeLP; MePo; OBS

Hymn to Night. Melville Cane. MoAmPo

Hymn to Night, A. Max Michelson. TrJP

Hymn to Pan. John Fletcher. *See* Faithful Shepherdess, The: Sing his praises that doth keep.

Hymn to Pan. Keats. *Fr.* Endymion [a Poetic Romance], I. ChER; PoEL-4

Hymn to Priapus. D. H. Lawrence. CMoP; MoAB; OBMV; PoE

Hymn to Proserpine. Swinburne. EBVV; NAEL-2; OAEL-2; OBNC; PoEL-5; TEP

Hymn to Proust. Gavin Ewart. NYBP

Hymn to St. Geryon, *sel.* Michael McClure.
  "Gesture the gesture the gesture the gesture, The." NeAP
Hymn to Saint Teresa. Richard Crashaw. *See* Love, Thou art absolute, sole Lord.
Hymn to Science. Mark Akenside. PoEL-3
Hymn to Selene. *Unknown, tr. fr. Greek by* Shelley. *Fr.* Homeric Hymns. AWP
Hymn to the Air Spirit. *Unknown, tr. fr. Eskimo.* WTO
Hymn to the Belly. Ben Jonson. *See* Pleasure Reconciled to Virtue: Hymn to Comus.
Hymn to the Creator. John Clare. NOBVV
Hymm to the Cross. *Unknown. See* Steadfast Cross, among all other.
Hymn to the Evening, An. Phillis Wheatley. WPE
Hymn to the Fallen. *Unknown, tr. fr. Chinese by* Arthur Waley. OBWP
Hymn to the Holy Spirit. Stephen Langton. TrCP
Hymn to the Morning, An. Phillis Wheatley. TAP
Hymn to the Name and Honour [*or* Honor] of the Admirable Saint[e] T[h]eresa, A. Richard Crashaw. JCP; NOBE; NOP; OBEV; OBS; PoEL-2; SeCV-1, *abr.*
  Sels.
  "Love, thou are absolute sole lord." HAP
  "Thou art love's victim; and must die." OBD
Hymn to the Night. Longfellow. AA; BLPL; NOBA; OxBA; PWR; TAP; TrGrPo
Hymn to the Spirit of Nature. Shelley. *See* Prometheus Unbound: Life of Life.
Hymn to the Sun, The. Akhenaton, *tr. fr. Egyptian by* J. E. Manchip White. TTY
Hymn to the Sun. C. M. Doughty. *Fr.* The Dawn in Britain. FaBoTw
Hymn to the Sun. William Alexander Percy. TrPWD
Hymn to the Sun. Michael Roberts. FaBoCh; OxBTC
Hymn to the Sun. *Unknown.* TTTS
Hymn to the Sunrise. *Unknown.* NA
Hymn to the Supreme Being on Recovery from a Dangerous Fit of Illness, *sel.* Christopher Smart.
  "But, O immortals! What had I to plead." NOEC
Hymn to the Thousand Islands. Henrietta Cordelia Ray. CBWP-3
Hymn to the Virgin. Sir Walter Scott. *Fr.* The Lady of the Lake, III. EnRP
Hymn to the Virgin Mary. Conor O'Riordan, *tr. fr. Irish by* Eleanor Hull. TIRV
Hymn to the West. Edmund Clarence Stedman. *See* O Thou, whose glorious orbs on high.
Hymn to the Winds. Joachim Du Bellay, *tr. fr. French by* Andrew Lang. AWP
Hymn to the Women of the Middle Class. Ursula Krechel, *tr. fr. German by* Susan L. Cocalis. DMG
Hymn to These Newly Abbreviated States. John Updike. SoTCo
Hymn to Tirumal (Visnu). Kirantaiyar, *tr. fr. Tamil by* A. K. Ramanujan. PLW
Hymn to Tsui-Xgoa. *Unknown, tr. fr. Hottentot.* PeSA
Hymn to Venus, The. *Unknown, formerly at. to* Homer, *tr. fr. Greek by* Congreve.
  Sels.
  "Among the springs which flow from Ida's head." OBVE
  "But when the golden-thron'd Aurora made." OBVE
Hymn to Vishnu. Jayadeva, *tr. fr. Sanskrit by* Sir Edwin Arnold. *Fr.* The Gita Govinda. AWP
Hymn to Zeus. Aeschylus, *tr. fr. Greek by* Gilbert Murray. *Fr.* Agamemnon. WGRP
Hymn to Zeus. Cleanthes, *tr. fr. Greek by* Edward Hayes Plumptre. WGRP
Hymn Tunes, The. Edward Lucie-Smith. PVCV
Hymn Written after Jeremiah Preached to Me in a Dream. Owen Dodson. AmNP
Hymn Written for the Two Hundredth Anniversary of the Old South Church, Beverly, Massachusetts. Lucy Larcom. OHIP
Hymn Written in Windsor Forest, A. Pope. *See* All hail, once pleasing, once in spiring shade.
Hymnal. Harold Vinal. TrPWD
Hymne, The: "Queene and huntress, chaste, and faire." Ben Jonson. *See* Hymn, The: Queen and huntress. . .
Hymne I: Generall Invitation to Praise God, A. George Wither. *Fr.* Hallelujah; or, Britain's Second Remembrancer. SeCV-1
Hymne in Honour of Beautie, An, *sel.* Spenser.
  Beauty. OBSC
Hymne in Honour of Those Two Despised Virtues, Charitie and Humilitie, An. Henry More. OBS
Hymn[e] in Praise [*or* Prayse] of Neptune, A. Thomas Campion. BoNaP; MOS; NOBE; OBEV; OBSC; WiR

Hymne of the Ascension, An. William, of Hawthornden Drummond. OBS
Hymne of the Nativity, An. Richard Crashaw. *See* Hymn of the Nativity.
Hymne to Christ, at the Author's Last Going into Germany, A. John Donne. *See* Hymn to Christ. . .
Hymne to God My God, in My Sicknesse. John Donne. *See* Hymn to God. . .
Hymne to Our Saviour on the Crosse, A. George Chapman. PoEL-2
Hymns and Spiritual Songs. Christopher Smart.
  Sels.
  Ascension of Our Lord Jesus Christ. *Fr.* XIV. NOCV
  Epiphany. *Fr.* III. NOCV
  Nativity of Our Lord and Saviour Jesus Christ, The. *Fr.* XXXII. EBEV; HAP; NOBE; NOCV; PoEL-3
    (Christmas Day, *sts.* 6–9) ChTr; OBCP
    (Hymn.) NAs; NOEC
  St. Philip and St. James. *Fr.* XIII. NOCV; NOEC
Hymns for the Amusement of Children. Christopher Smart.
  Sels.
  Elegance. *Fr.* XIII. NOCV
  For Saturday. *Fr.* XXXIII. FaBoCh; NOEC; OxBChV
    (Hymn for Saturday.) OxBChV
    (Lark's Nest, A.) FaBoCh
  Gratitude. *Fr.* XXII. NOEC
  Long-Suffering of God. *Fr.* XXIX. NOCV
  Loveliness. *Fr.* XIV. NOCV
  Mirth. *Fr.* XXV. OxBChV
  Moderation. *Fr.* IX. NOCV
  Mutual Subjection. *Fr.* XXVI. NOCV
  Taste. *Fr.* XV. NOCV
Hymns of Astraea, *sels.* Sir John Davies.
  Of Astraea. TrGrPo
  To the Nightingale. OBSC; PBBP; TrGrPo
  To the Rose. OBSC
  To the Spring. EIL
Hymns of the Marshes, *sel.* Sidney Lanier.
  Sunrise. AA; PoEL-5
Hymns to Our Lady of Chartres, *sel.* Geoffrey Hill.
  "Eia, with handbells, jews' harps, risible." DiPo
Hymns to the Night, *sel.* "Novalis," *prose poem version, tr. fr. German by* Robert Bly.
  Second Hymn to the Night, The. NU
Hymn's Triumph, *sel.* Samuel Daniel.
  Had Sorrow Ever Fitter Place. EIL
    (Sorrow.) OBSC
Hymnus: "God be in my hede." *Unknown. See* Sarum Primer: God Be in My Head.
Hymnus in Noctem. George Chapman. *Fr.* The Shadow of Night. PoEL-2
Hynde Horn. *Unknown.* GN
Hypatia, *sel.* Elizabeth Tollet.
  "What cruel laws depress the female kind." NOEC
Hyperbole! Can't you arise. Prose for Des Esseintes. Donald Davie, *after the French of* Stéphane Mallarmé. OBVE
Hyperboreans, The. Tom Paulin. FaBCIP
Hyperion; a Fragment, *sels.* Keats. EnRP; OAEL-2
  Bruised Titans, The. OBNC
  "Deep in the shady sadness of a vale." *Fr.* I. ChER; FiP; PoEL-4
    (Saturn.) OBNC; TrGrPo
  Hyperion and Saturn. *Fr.* II. SeCePo
  Recollection of the Stone Circle near Keswick, A. *Fr.* II. FaBoPP
Hyperion and Saturn. Keats. *Fr.* Hyperion; a Fragment, II. SeCePo
Hypochondriacus. Charles Lamb. BXAP
Hypocrisy will serve as well. Samuel Butler. FaBoEE
Hypocrite, The. John Caryll. APAS
Hypocrite, The. Kalonymos ben Kalonymos, *tr. fr. Hebrew by* J. Chotzner. *Fr.* The Touchstone. TrJP
Hypocrite Auteur. Archibald MacLeish. AmPP
Hypocrite is strange of race, A. The Hypocrite. Kalonymos ben Kalonymos, *tr. fr. Hebrew by* J. Chotzner. *Fr.* The Touchstone. TrJP
Hypocrite Swift. Louise Bogan. PoA
Hypocrite Women. Denise Levertov. CAPP; MAT; NMM; PoM
Hypocrites shed tears. On Watching Politicians Perform at Martin Luther King's Funeral. Etheridge Knight. NNaP
Hypsithilla, ask me over. An Invitation to an Invitation. Catullus, *tr. by* Gardner E. Lewis. ErPo

Hysteria. Chu Shu-chen, *tr. fr. Chinese by* Kenneth Rexroth. NaP

I

I. E. E. Cummings. NYBP
"I." Louis Golding. TrJP
I. Eino Leino, *tr. fr. Finnish by* Aili Jarvenpa. SOP
I/ am going to rise. Vive Noir! Mari E. Evans. IHMS; PoBA
I,/ at one time. The Self-Hatred of Don L. Lee. Don L. Lee. BPo
I/ Have Arrived. Status Symbol. Mari E. Evans. IDB
I/ is the total black, being spoken. Coal. Audre Lorde. BlSi; NoP; PoBA
I/ love/ you so. Chocolate Chocolate. Arnold Adoff. RHPC
I/ never/ guessed any. I. E. E. Cummings. NYBP
I/ never liked/ white folks. Alice Walker. *Fr.* Once. PoBA
I/ no, it was Caligula, fat. Sparrows. Remco Campert, *tr. by* John Scott *and* Graham Martin. DuIn
I. . ./One. . ./ I smelt the weird Atlantic. Finistére. Thomas Kinsella. IPY
I/ want you/ to listen. Kenneth Patchen. *Fr.* The Journal of Albion Moonlight. NaP
I/ was five/ when/ mom and dad got married. Black Sketches. Don L. Lee. NeAC
I/ will/ remember/ with my breath. Night Practice. May Swenson. RR
I,——A. B. do declare. Tax Return. *Unknown.* FaBoUs
I, a blue wolf. The "Word" of a Wolf Encircled by the Hunt. Sandag, *tr. by* C. R. Bawden. WTO
I, a boat with a bony keel. A Dentist's Window. James Keir Baxter. OxBC
I, a dear child to my father. Isonokami Otomaro. *Fr.* Manyo Shu. Ma
I, a Most Wretched Atlas. Heine, *tr. fr. German by* Emma Lazarus. *Fr.* Homeward Bound. TrJP
I, a princess, king-descended, decked with jewels, gilded, drest. A Royal Princess. Christina Rossetti. BrRo
I, a slave, chained to an oar of poem. Stoic. Lawrence Durrell. NYBP
I a tender young maid have been courted by many. My Thing Is My Own. *Unknown.* CoMu
I, a wanderer north of Tu-ling. Parting from the Courtier Sung. Yin Shih, *tr. by* Burton Watson. CoBCP
I abandoned hope next to a clockwork. The Beginnings of the Fugitive. Louis Aragon, *tr. by* Joachim Neugroschel. POS
I abdicate my daily self that bled. Vita Nuova. Stanley Kunitz. VGW
I abhor the slimy kiss. Kisses Loathesome. Robert Herrick. CaPo; OxBSP
I abide and abide and better abide. Sir Thomas Wyatt. BoLoP; EnLoPo; SiPS
I Accompanied My Mother on a Visit to the Itsukushima Shrine. Rai San'yo, *tr. fr. Chinese by* Burton Watson. JLIC-2
I Accompanied My Uncle Shumpo on an Outing to Lake Biwa. Rai San'yo, *tr. fr. Chinese by* Burton Watson. FCEI; JLIC-2
I accompanied the Castilian. Max Hölzer, *tr. by* Beth Bjorklund. CoAuP
I add one further word to you, a question rather. Henri Michaux, *tr. fr. French by* Richard Ellmann. *Fr.* I Am Writing to You from a Far-Off Country, IV. RHTwFP
I admire the driven, those who rise from choice. Cinema at the Lighthouse. Henri Coulette. *Fr.* The War of the Secret Agents, VI. NePoEA-2
I admire the quixotic display of your paramountcy. On His Royal Blindness Paramount Chief Kwangala. Jack A. Mapanje. WMBCH
I advise rest; the farmhouse. To a Print of Queen Victoria. James Keir Baxter. OxBC
I advocate a semi-revolution. A Semi-Revolution. Robert Frost. LiTM
I agree;/ you said when you heard the sound. Firing. Ahmad Nadeem Qasmi, *tr. by* Mahmood Jamal. PBMUP
I ain't gonna tell no body. 34 Blues. Charlie Patton. FaBoPV
I aint, ner don't p'tend to be. My Philosofy. James Whitcomb Riley. AnAmPo
I ain't never been to heaven but Ah been told. Swing Low, Sweet Chariot. *Unknown.* GBP
I ain't superstitious. Superstitions. Maggie Pogue Johnson. CBWP-4
I almost caught the bentwood chair. Urban Ode. Sandra McPherson. MAYP
I almost know you now. You are your name. Eight Lines for a Script Girl. George Jonas. NeAC
I almost ruined the stew and where. The Pigs for Circe in May. Joanne Kyger. PoM
I, Alphonso, live and learn. Alphonso of Castile. Emerson. NOBA

I always choose the plainest food. In Praise of Water-Gruel. Matthew Green. *Fr.* The Spleen. FaBoUs
I always crane my neck to see more of the giraffe. The Silver Mouth. Shauqi Abi Shaqra, *tr. by* Abdullah al-Udhari. MPAW
I always knew/ you were singing! Throat Song: The Whirling Earth. Wendy Rose. HATNAP
I always like summer. Knoxville, Tennessee. Nikki Giovanni. AmNP; BlSi; BPo; CNA; PoBA; SO
I always liked to go to bed. A Song for My Mother—Her Stories. Anna Hempstead Branch. OHIP
I always loved this solitary hill. L' Infinito. Giacomo Leopardi, *tr. by* Lorna De' Lucchi. AWP
I always loved to call my lady Rose. *Unknown.* EiL
I always say I won't go back to the mountains. Sourdough Mountain Lookout. Philip Whalen. NeAP; PoM
I always see, I don't know why. The Knowledgeable Child. L. A. G. Strong. OBMV
I always shout when Grandma comes. Afternoon with Grandmother. Barbara A. Huff. FaPON
I always take one you don't expect. Photograph. Sue May. DT
I always talk of living in the mountains. For Several Years I Have Wanted to Grow a Garden. Chu Yün-ming, *tr. by* Jonathan Chaves. CoBLCP
I always think of a coffin's quiet. A Poem for a Poet. Audre Lorde. NMM
"I always think that when I see you you." Estimable Mable. Gwendolyn Brooks. FB
I always thought. Here I Have Never Been. Jacob Glatstein, *tr. by* Benjamin *and* Barbara Harshav. AYP
I always wake up. As Though It Had Never Been. Sándor Weöres, *tr. by* Jascha Kessler. FOC
I always wanted a red balloon. Tragedy. Jill Spargur. BLPA
I always was afraid of Somes's Pond. Atavism. Elinor Wylie. PoA
I always wondered why. The Answer. Chuck Wachtel. UL
I always write with a mask upon my face. The Mask. Valery Larbaud, *tr. by* Ron Padgett *and* Bill Zavatsky. RHTwFP
I Am. John Clare. EBEV; EBVV; EnRP; GTBS-P; HAP; InvP; LiTB; NAEL-2; NOBE; NOBVV; NoP; OAEL-2; OBNC; PoEL-4; Prf; PrIm; TOF; TrGrPo
I Am. Hilda Conkling. FaPON
I Am. Bill Kushner. UL
I Am. Mani Leib, *tr. fr. Yiddish by* John Hollander. PeBMYV
I am/ look/ ing at. You Too? Me Too—Why Not? Soda Pop. Robert Hollander. NIP
I am a babe of royalty. Royal Education. Winthrop Mackworth Praed. OBSV
I am a bard of no regard. Burns. *Fr.* The Jolly Beggars. PoE
I Am a Black Woman. Mari E. Evans. CNA; NMM
I am a bonded highwayman, Cole Younger is my name. Cole Younger. *Unknown.* AmFP
I Am a Book I neither Wrote nor Read. Delmore Schwartz. TAP
I am a boy. A Young David: Birmingham. Helen Morgan Brooks. PoNe
I am a broken-hearted milkman, in grief I'm arrayed. Polly Perkins. *Unknown.* ELP; OxBoLi
I am a bunch of red roses. Love Song. *Unknown, tr. by* Reza Baraheni *and* Zahra-Soltan Shokoohtaezeh. BoWoP
I am a camel in all the sand. Camel. Alan Brownjohn. RHPC
I am a child/ of six generations here. The Sequence of Generations. Hayim Be'er, *tr. by* Stephen Mitchell. VWA
I am a circus dancer. The Circus Dancer. Celia Dropkin. PeBMYV *tr. by* Grace Schulman, VWA, *tr. by* Howard Schwartz
I am a composite being of all the people of America. I Am the Flag. Lawrence M. Jones. OPP
I Am a Cowboy in the Boat of Ra. Ishmael Reed. NBP; NoP; PoBA; PrIm
I am a crazy woman with a painted face. I Light Your Streets. Meridel LeSueur. ER
I am a dangerous beast at this moment. Prelude for a Flower. Ruth Kim Chun-soo, *tr. by* Koh Chang-soo. ACKP
I am a dispossessed Ontario wood. Silverthorn Bush. Robert Finch. NOBC
I am a doorway of few words. The Doorway. Lin Huan-ch'ang, *tr. by* Dominic Cheung. IFON
I am a downright Country-man, both faithful (aye) and true. The Downright Country-Man; or, The Faithful Dairy Maid. *Unknown.* CoMu
I am a faire maide, if my glasse doe not flatter. The Wooing Maid. Martin Parker. CoMu
I am a feather on the bright sky. The Delight Song of Tsoai-Talee. N. Scott Momaday. CDW; GrPl; InPK; STE

I am a frightful monster. Be a Monster. Roy Fuller. AmMo
I am a frog. The Frog Prince. Stevie Smith. HAP; Mes
I am a gentleman in a dustcoat trying. Piazza Piece. John Crowe
  Ransom. AnAmPo; BoLoP; ErPo; HeIP; MoAB; MoAmPo; MoP;
  NAAL-2; NoAM; NOBA; NoP; OPOP; OxBA; Son; SoSe; TAP;
  TrGrPo
I Am a Guitar. Viljo Kajava, tr. fr. Finnish by Aili Jarvenpa. SOP
I am a hand weaver to my trade. The Weaver and the Factory Maid.
  Unknown. OBET
I Am a Horse. Hans Arp, tr. fr. French. FaBoNo, tr. by Harriet Watts;
  POS, tr. by Michael Benedikt
I Am a Hunchback. Robert Louis Stevenson. OxBSP
I Am a Jew. David Martin. VWA
I am a jolly soldier. Bunker's Hill, or the Soldier's Lamentation. John
  Freeth. NOEC
I am a jolly young fellow. The Jolly Driver. Unknown. CoMu
I am a jovial collier lad, as blithe as blithe can be. Down in a Coal Mine.
  J. B. Geoghegan. AmFP
I am a jovial marriner, our calling is well known. The Jovial Marriner;
  or, The Sea-Man's Renown. John Playford. CoMu
I am a kind of farthing dip. A Portrait. Robert Louis Stevenson.
  SeCePo
I Am a King. I. Z. Rimon, tr. fr. Hebrew by Shlomo Vinner and Howard
  Schwartz. VWA
I am a king's daughter, you a king's wife. A Letter to Her Mother.
  Eristi-Aya, tr. by Willis Barnstone. BoWoP
I am a lady. Small Sad Song. Alastair Reid. NYBP
I am a lamp, a lamp that is out. She Warns Him. Frances Cornford.
  EnLoPo
I Am a Leaf. Yehuda Amichai, tr. fr. Hebrew by Shlomo Vinner and
  Howard Schwartz. VWA
I am a lioness. 'Aisha bint Ahmad al-Qurtubiyya, tr. by Elene Margot
  Kolb. WPOW
I am a little girl with my pants pulled down around my ankles. Pants.
  Lisa Vice. GLP
I am a little orphan girl. An Orphan Girl. Mrs. Henry Linden.
  CBWP-4
I am a little world made cunningly. John Donne. Fr. Holy Sonnets, V.
  NAEL-1; NIP; NoP; OBS; PoE; SeCP; Son; TEP
I Am a Live Man. Yehuda Amichai, tr. fr. Hebrew by Warren Bargad
  and Stanley F.Chyet. IP
I am a lone, unfathered chick. Orphan Born. Robert Jones Burdette.
  OBAL
I am a man before the mast, I plough the trackless sea. The Common
  Sailor. Unknown. OxBSS
I am a man defeated in his loins. Beggar to Burgher. Arthur Rex
  Dugard Fairburn. PeNZ
I am a man now. Here. R. S. Thomas. GTBS-P; RB
I am a man of Chiang-nan. Wang T'ing-hsiang, tr. fr. Chinese by
  Jonathan Chaves. Fr. Songs of Chiang-nan. CoBLCP
I am a man of few beliefs. Thespian in Jerusalem. Myra Glazer Schotz.
  VWA
I am a man of war and might. A Soldier. Sir John Suckling. PoE;
  SeCV-1
I am a man with no ambitions. The Advantages of Learning. Martial, tr.
  by Kenneth Rexroth. ErPo
I am a man without childhood. Drowning. Jacques Roubaud, tr. by
  Robert Kelly. RHTwFP
I am a miner. The light burns blue. Nick and the Candlestick. Sylvia
  Plath. CAPP; CoAP; LCAP; PBWP
I am a most superior person. Henry Charles Beeching. Fr. Balliol
  Rhymes. CenHV
I am a native of the land of Erin. A Convict's Lament on the Death of
  Captain Logan. Unknown. PoAu-1
I Am a Negro. Muhammad al-Fituri, tr. fr. Arabic by Halim El-Dabh.
  TTY
I am a nobleman of vast estate. The Well of Baln. Ursula K. Le Guin.
  BWV
I Am a Parcel of Vain Strivings Tied. Henry David Thoreau. NOBA;
  NoP; PoEL-4; TAP
  (Sic Vita.) AmPP; AnAmPo; OxBA
I am a peevish student, I. Melancholia. Unknown. NA
I am a poet. Combat. Clementina Suárez, tr. by Magaly Fernández.
  Vol
I am a poor lad and my fortune is bad. Limbo. Unknown. OBET
I am a poor old man, come listen to my song. When This Old Hat Was
  New. Unknown. OBET
I am a poor prisoner condemned to die. The Execution of Luke Hutton.
  Unknown. OBET
I am a poor wayfaring stranger. Poor Wayfaring Stranger. Unknown.
  AmFP

I am a pretty wench. Unknown. OxNR
I am a reaper whose muscles set at sundown. All my oats are cradled.
  Harvest Song. Jean Toomer. NoP
I am a rich widow, I live all alone. The Rich Widow. Unknown.
  AmFP
I am a river. No More. Carl Clark. JB
I am a roving gambler, I've gambled all around. The Roving Gambler.
  Unknown. AS
I am a roving shanty boy, love to sing and dance. The Roving Shanty
  Boy. Unknown. AmFP
I am a roving traveler and go from town to town. The Gamboling Man.
  Unknown. AS
I am a sailor stout and bold. The Rambling Sailor. Unknown. OxBSS
I am a sea-shell flung. Frutta di Mare. Geoffrey Scott. ChTr; Mes;
  OBMV
I am a senseless thing, with a hey, with a hey. A New Ballad, to an Old
  Tune, Called, I Am the Duke of Norfolk, etc. Unknown. APAS
I am a sincere man. José Martí, tr. fr. Spanish by Seymour Resnick. Fr.
  Simple Verses. TTY
I am a sinful man of men. The Joyce's Repentance. Unknown, tr. by
  Douglas Hyde. TIRV
I am a skinny girl. The Skinny Girl. Anne Hébert, tr. by Willis
  Barnstone. BoWoP
I am a sleeping body. Ark Apprehensive. Jay Macpherson. Fr. The
  Ark. NOBC
I am a soldier blithe and gay. The Rambling Soldier. Unknown. OBET
I am a soul in the world: in. The Invention of Comics. Amiri Baraka.
  AmNP; CRP; LiTM; PoBA
I am a spring. The Well. T. E. Brown. NOBVV
I am a stag: of seven tines. The Alphabet Calendar of Amergin.
  Unknown, tr. by Robert Graves. BIrV
I am a stranger. The Jewish Woman. Gertrud Kolmar, tr. by Henry A.
  Smith. VWA
I am a stranger in the land. Death. Unknown. BLPA; FPL
I am a sundial, and I make a botch. On a Sundial. Hilaire Belloc.
  FaBoEE
I am a sundial. Ordinary words. Hilaire Belloc. FaBoEE
I am a sundial, turned the wrong way round. Hilaire Belloc. FaBoEE
I am a thief. Listen. Jessica Hagedorn. WPOW
I am a trombone. By the chinaberry tree. New Orleans. Hayden Carruth.
  AmFN
I am a very mature person. A Decision. Edith Södergran, tr. by Jaakko
  O. Ahokas. PBWP
I am a very old pussy. An Old Cat's Confessions. Christopher Pearse
  Cranch. OBCA
I am a very personable man. A New Shakespeare. Andrew Lang.
  CenHV
I Am a Victim of Telephone. Allen Ginsberg. NBLV
I am a wandering, bitter shade. What's in a Name? Helen F. More.
  PAH
I am a weaver by my trade. Wil the Merry Weaver, and Charity the
  Chamber-Maid; or, A Brisk Encounter between a Youngman and His
  Love. Unknown. CoMu
I am a white falcon, hurrah! The Falcon. Richard Henry Stoddard. AA
I am a widow, robed in black, alone. Christine de Pisan, tr. by Willis
  Barnstone. BoWoP
I am a wild and wicked youth. The Rambling Boy. Unknown. OBET
I Am a Woman, sel. Akhtar Amiri, tr. fr. Farsi by Fereshte Mahamadi.
  "My home is the mountain." WPOW
I am a woman and I'm angry. One Angry Woman. Veronica Williams.
  WS
I am a woman and my poems. The Practice of Magical Evocation.
  Diane di Prima. PoM
I am a wonder. I vary my voice. Riddle: Jay: Higora. Unknown.
  PBBP
I am a word in a foreign language. Finches. Marcia Southwick. PPR
I am a young dairy maid, buxom and tight. The Buxom Young Dairy
  Maid. Unknown. OBET
I am a young executive. No cuffs than mine are cleaner. Executive. Sir
  John Betjeman. NOBL
I am a young girl. Unknown, tr. by Carol Cosman. PBWP
I am a young girl, gay. Unknown, tr. by Willis Barnstone. BoWoP
I am a young jolly brisk sailor. Tarpauling Jacket. Unknown. OxBoLi
I am a youthful lady, my troubles they are great. A New Song Called the
  Victory. Unknown. OxBSS
  (Victory.) CoMu
I am adrift in a desert where too much sun. Desert Shipwreck. Barbara
  Leslie Jordan. GoYe
I am afraid. Unknown. WSC
I am afraid I may be Ilia. Fear. Anna Hajnal, tr. by Daniel Hoffman.
  BoWoP; MHuP

I am afraid of being crushed in the pincers. Sometimes. Greg Kuzma. Psk

I am afraid to. Nizar Qabbani, *tr. by* Diana Der Hovanessian *and* Lena Jayyusi. MAP

I am afraid to begin this poem. For My Mother. Ellen Bass. TV

I am afraid to own a body. Emily Dickinson. LiTA

I am afraid to think about my death. No Coward's Song. James Elroy Flecker. OxBSP

I am alert to these letters in extraordinary numbers. Bordering Manuscript. James Applewhite. PoA

I am alive at night. Moon Song, Woman Song. Anne Sexton. PPP

I am alive—I guess. Emily Dickinson. NOBA

I am all bent to glean the golden ore. To His Lady Selvaggia Vergiolesi; Likening His Love to a Search for Gold. Cino da Pistoia, *tr. by* Dante Gabriel Rossetti. AWP; PFI

I am all things. Some Magic. James Koller. PoM

I Am Almost Asleep. Eldon Grier. MoCV

I am already quite scarce. For years. The Last Ones. Dan Pagis, *tr. by* Stephen Mitchell. VWA

I am always aware of my mother. Mother. Nagase Kiyoko, *tr. by* Kenneth Rexroth *and* Ikuko Atsumi. AIW; BoWoP

I am Ambassador of Otherwhere. From the Embassy. Robert Graves. PoA

I am among those ways of harsh sweetness. A Walk. Pierre Jean Jouve, *tr. by* Keith Bosley. RHTwFP

I am an American. Elias Lieberman. FaPON; OPP; PoLF

I Am an Ancient Mariner. *Unknown.* OxBSS

I am an ancient reluctant conscript. Old Timers. Carl Sandburg. NoAM

I am an April Woman. April Woman. Salma Khadra Jayyusi, *tr. by the author and* Charles Doria. MAP

"I am an owl of orders gray." The Song of the Owl. Richard Kendall Munkittrick. OBCA

I am an unadventurous man. De Gustibus. St. John Emile Clavering Hankin. CenHV

"I am an urn of anger," cried the bull. The Bull. Freda Laughton. NeIP

I am Andrew Cecil Bradley. Cecil Arthur Spring-Rice. *Fr.* Balliol Rhymes. CenHV

I am anxious after praise. Egoism. W. Craddle. FiBHP

I am approaching. Past dry. Loot. Thom Gunn. ErPo; NePoEA-2

"I am as brown as brown can be." The Brown Girl. *Unknown.* ELP; ESPB (A *and* B *vers.*); OBET (Bonny Brown Girl, The.) OxBB

I Am as Happy as a Queen on Her Throne. Mrs. Henry Linden. CBWP-4

I am as I am and so will I be. Sir Thomas Wyatt. SiPS

I am ashamed before the earth. Therefore I Must Tell the Truth. Torlino, *tr. by* Washington Matthews. STP

I am asleep, dreaming a terrible dream, so I awake. Light. Frank Bidart. *Fr.* Elegy, IV. HCAP

I am assembled here, at ease. September. K. O. Arvidson. *Fr.* The Four Last Songs of Richard Strauss at Takahe Creek above the Kaipara, II. ATNZ

I am at a loss on this very street. At a Loss. Moshe Dor, *tr. by* Bernhard Frank. MHeP

I am at Deep Well where the spirit-trees. Roland Robinson. *Fr.* Deep Well. CBAP

I am at my post. *Unknown. Fr.* Manyo Shu. Ma

I am back from up the country—very sorry that I went. Up the Country. Henry Lawson. CBAP

I am become a frightful bloody murtherer. Fragment from the Elizabethans. W. Bridges-Adams. FaBoCo

I am become a shell of delicate alleys. Airliner. Francis Webb. CBAP

I am becoming a god! Everything Is Possible. Robert Pack. PPP

I am becoming one. A Poem of Towers. James Wright. CAPP

I Am Being Dragged by Red Dolphins. István Kormos, *tr. fr. Hungarian by* Edwin Morgan. MHuP

I am black and I have seen black hands. I Have Seen Black Hands. Richard Wright. PoBA

I am bleeding. The Song of the Woman with Her Parts Coming Out. Susan Griffin. GLP

I am blessed with my location. The Lost Pictures. Hollis Spurgeon Summers. HoPM

I am blessing two, not one. The Time of Creation Has Come. *Yoruba Oral Tradition, tr. by* Ulli Beier. WTO

I am blood of your ancient blood, bone of your fragile bone. To the Jews in Poland. Jozef Wittlin, *tr. by* Isaac Komem. VWA

I am Branson; Nature's laws. Henry Charles Beeching *and* John Bowyer Nichols. *Fr.* Balliol Rhymes. FaBoEE

I am bright with the wonder of you. Brightness. Denis Glover. PeNZ

I am broken by the tumult of the years. Old Joyce. Sean Jennett. NeIP

"I am busy," said the sea. Day. Cecil Arthur Spring-Rice. BoTP

I am but a little girl. String of Pearls. Katri Vala, *tr. by* Aili Jarvenpa. SOP

I am but a little woman. Kivkarjuk. WTO

I am, by fate, slave to your will. To My More Than Meritorious Wife. Earl of Rochester. OxBSP

I am called by name of man. *Unknown.* GBP

I am called Chyldhod [*or* Childhoud] in play is all my mynde [*or* mind]. *Fr.* Pageant Verses. Sir Thomas More. AAS; Mes

I am carrying your grin. Diary of Days for Adjoa. Jackie Kay. DT

I am caught in the new power. Custer Must Have Learned to Dance. Elizabeth Woody. STE

I am caught up in her. Woman. Jane Chambers. IHMS

I am certain. Vietnam. Ahmad Faraz, *tr. by* Mahmood Jamal. PBMUP

I am Charlotte. I don't say hello. Charlotte, Her Book. Elizabeth Bartlett. FaBoWP

I Am Cherry Alive. Delmore Schwartz. RHPC; TTTS

I am climbing. *Unknown, tr. by* W. S. Merwin. STP

I am coal! Black Cry. José Craveirinha, *tr. by* Eduardo Mondlane. WMBCH

I am cold and alone. The Boy Fishing. Edith Jay Scovell. FaBoWP

I am come into my garden, my sister, my spouse. Bible, *O.T. Fr.* The Song of Solomon, V. OBVE; TOF

I am come to make thy tomb. John Webster. *Fr.* The Duchess of Malfi, IV, ii. ChTr

I Am Coming to You. Jacob Glatstein, *tr. fr. Yiddish by* Benjamin *and* Barbara Harshav. AYP

I am concerned because my mind. Ballade to My Psychoanalyst. Kenneth Lillington. FiBHP

I am content. The Fossil. Boynton Merrill, Jr. CRP

I am content, I do not care. Careless Content. John Byrom. NOEC

I am Count Orlo come to day farewell. Orlo's Valediction. Jon Manchip White. NePoEA

I Am Crying from Thirst. Alonzo Lopez. NOVW

I am dangerous. Scissor-Man. George MacBeth. FaBoMo

I am dead, Horatio. Wretched queen, adieu! Shakespeare. *Fr.* Hamlet, V, ii. FaBoRV (Death of Hamlet.) FiP

I Am Disquieted When I See Many Hills. Hyam Plutzik. VGW

I am dressed in my old grey running suit. The Work-out. Geoffrey Movius. MAT

I am driving; it is dusk; Minnesota. Driving toward the Lac Qui Parle River. Robert Bly. LCAP; NaP; NoP

I am drunk of the pot. I, Lessimus, of Salt Lake City. Robert Peters. BXAP

I am dying, Egypt, dying. Antony to Cleopatra. William Haines Lytle. AA; BeLS (Antony and Cleopatra.) BLPA

I am dying, Egypt, dying. Death of Antony. Shakespeare. *Fr.* Antony and Cleopatra, IV, xv. FiP

I am dying, Egypt, dying, so float me down the Nile. Tallulah at the Schubert. Bruce Berger. SoTCo

I am ebbing—but not like the sea. The Hag of Béara. *Unknown.* NOIV

I am enamored, and yet not so much. Sonnet: He Will Not Be Too Deeply in Love. Cecco Angiolieri da Siena, *tr. by* Dante Gabriel Rossetti. AWP

I am entrenched. Winter. Samuel Menashe. GrPl

I am Eve, great Adam's wife. Eve. *Unknown, tr. by* Thomas MacDonagh. BIrV

I am expatriate. Retired Lion by the Clothesline in the Cold Attic. Laura Jensen. AnAn

I Am Fashion's Toy. Mary E. Tucker. CBWP-1

I am featly-tripping Lee. Henry Charles Beeching. *Fr.* Balliol Rhymes. CenHV; FaBoEE

I am fevered with the sunset. The Sea Gypsy. Richard Hovey. AnAmPo; FaPON; PDV

I am filled with joy. Dead Man's Song, Dreamed by One Who Is Alive. Paulinaoq. WTO

I am filled with the sorrow of all things seen. Euridice Saved. Linda Gregg. NPGG

I am fish. Fish. Emily Townsend. NYBP

I am fixed in waiting. Sagimusume: The White Heron Maiden. Jonny Kyoko Sullivan. WPOW

I am fourteen. Hanging Fire. Audre Lorde. ER; NIP; NoAM; NoP

I am François to my great dismay. Villon, *tr. by* David Lunde. SoTCo

I Am from Ireland. *Unknown. See* I am of Ireland.

I am full of grief, and the tear runs from my eye. Five Arabic Verses in Praise of Wine. *Unknown, tr. by* Hartwig Hirschfeld. TrJP

I am furious with myself. Elsa Tió, *tr. by* Willis Barnstone. BoWoP

I am gai. I am poet. I dvell. Vers Nonsensiques. George Du Maurier. NA

"I am Gaspar. I have brought frankincense." The Three Kings. Rubén Darío, tr. by Lysander Kemp. PChr

I Am Getting a Mountain View. Floyd Skloot. SoTCo

I am glad daylong for the gift of song. Rhapsody. William Stanley Braithwaite. AmNP; BANP

I am glad of that other life. The Dark. William Heyen. EyDe

I am going blind. Perhaps. Lucille Clifton. CAPP; GeTw

I am going to be there where her body was when it was. My Mother's College. Sharon Olds. ER

I am going to bring back Solomon. Get to Hell Outa Here. "The Mighty Sparrow." PBCV

I am going to gather the dodder. Unknown, tr. by Arthur Waley. BoS

I am going to market. Marketing. E. J. Falconer. BoTP

I Am Going to Sleep [Suicide Poem]. Alfonsina Storni, tr. fr. Spanish. BoWoPo, tr. by Aliki and Willis Barnstone. DMH, tr. by Kate Flores.

I Am Goya. Andrei Voznesensky. OBWP

I am greeting you, Mayor of Lagos. Mayor of Lagos. Yoruba Oral Tradition, tr. by Ulli Beier. WTO

I Am Growing Old. George Sands Johnson. PWR

I Am Ham Melanite. William Millett. GoYe

I am hands. In Laddery Street Herself. Laura Riding. Fr. Forgotten Girlhood. RB

I Am He That Aches with Love. Walt Whitman. LLT

I Am He That Walks with the Tender and Growing Night. Walt Whitman. Fr. Song of Myself: I am the poet of the Body and I am the poet of the Soul. ChTr

"I am he who bursts the guarded gate." Boast of Masopha. Z. D. Mangoaela. PeSA

I am hearing the shape of the rain. In the Mountain Tent. James Dickey. CAPP; MT

I Am Here. Robert Mezey. VWA

I am here again/ pox marks have obscured my dimples. I Would Be a Painter Most of All. Len Chandler. NBP

I am here, I have traversed the Tomb. He Cometh Forth into the Day. Unknown, tr. fr. Egyptian by Robert Hillyer. Fr. Book of the Dead. AWP

I am here only. Ayohu Kanogisdi. Carroll Arnett. STE

I am here with my beautiful bountiful downy womanful child. At a Summer Hotel. Isabella Gardner. GrPl

I am Hermes. I stand in the crossroads by a windy. Anyte, tr. by Willis Barnstone. BoWoP

I am his Highness' dog at Kew. Epigram Engraved on the Collar of a Dog Given [or Which I Gave] to His Royal Highness. Pope. FaBoCo; FaBoEE; FM; InPK; NOEC; NTCP; OxBSP
(Engraved on the Collar of a Dog, Which I Gave to His Royal Highness.) ChTr; LiTB; OxBoLi; SoSe; TTTS
(His Highness's Dog.) RHPC

I am holding this turquoise. The Serenity in Stones. Simon J. Ortiz. CDW

I am Huxley, blond and merry. John Bowyer Buchanan Nichols. Fr. Balliol Rhymes. CenHV

I am immortal! I know it! I feel it! Dryad Song. Margaret Witter Fuller. WGRP

I am in a desert. Bushed. Barry McKinnon. NOBC

"I Am in Danger—Sir." Adrienne Rich. HCAP; NOBA

I am in great misery tonight. Suibne Geilt. NOIV

I am in Heaven. The Plains of Heaven. Lorrie Goldensohn. NAmP

I am in Hong Kong. How Hong Kong Was Destroyed. Dahlia Ravikovich, tr. by Chana Bloch. OV

I am in love, but am not so in love. Cecco Angiolieri da Siena, tr. by Felix Stefanile. PFI

I am in love with the laughing sickness. Zizi's Lament. Gregory Corso. NeAP; VGW

I am in my Eskimo-hunting-song mood. Eskimo Occasion. Judith Rodriguez. CBAP; FaBoWP

I am in prison for trying to swindle the/ Keepsake Corporation. The Keepsake Corporation. David Fisher. NPGG

I am in the castle, my younger brother is beyond. The Other Side of the Valley. Unknown, tr. by Burton Watson. CoBCP

I am in the old room across from the synagogue. The Old Room. W. S. Merwin. NYBP

I am in the tub with my body. To My Body. Nancy Sullivan. TAP

I am inside someone. An Agony. As Now. Amiri Baraka. AmPP; BPo; LiTM; NAAL-2; PoE; PPP

I am interested in the logic of secrets, how it has always moved me. La Reproduction Interdite/ Not to Be Reproduced. Kathleen Fraser. NPGG

I Am Ireland. Padraic Pearse, tr. fr. Irish by Lady Gregory. OBMV

I am Jesu that cum to fight. Undo Your Heart. Unknown. MeEL

I am leading a quiet life. Autobiography. Sonja Akesson, tr. by Ingrid Claréus. BoWoP

I Am like a Book. David Rokeah, tr. fr. Hebrew by Robert Mezey. VWA

I am like a field/ waiting. Like a Field Waiting. Raquel Chalfi, tr. by Myra Glazer Schotz. VWA

I am like a flag unfurled in space. Presaging. Rainer Maria Rilke, tr. by Jessie Lemont. AWP; TrJP

I am like a foolish elk. Into the Silence of the Forest. Eeva-Liisa Manner, tr. by Aili Jarvenpa. SOP

I am like a jackfruit on the tree. The Jackfruit. Ho Xuan Huong, tr. by Nguyen Ngoc Bich. PBWP

I Am like a Rose. D. H. Lawrence. OxBSP

I am like the bread you will break. The Same Voice, Still. Yves Bonnefoy, tr. by Paul Auster. RHTwFP

"I am like the last apple." Last Apple. Malka Heifetz-Tussman, tr. by Marcia Falk. PeBMYV

I Am Listening: A Lyric of Roots. Anita Valerio. GOS

I am living more alone now than I did. The Last Chapter. Walter de la Mare. CMoP; MoBrPo

I Am Lonely. "George Eliot." Fr. The Spanish Gypsy. GN

I am lonely. Poem for Some Black Women. Carolyn M. Rodgers. BlSi

I am looking for a past. The Journey. David Ignatow. Psk

I am looking rather seedy now while holding down my claim. The Little Old Sod Shanty [on My Claim]. Unknown. AS

I am lost in hot fits. Air. Amiri Baraka. SOTW

"I am Lot's pillar, caught in turning." Columns and Caryatids. Carolyn Kizer. WPE

I am luminous with age. Rites of Ancient Ripening. Meridel LeSueur. ER

I am lying face up on a raft. Dream. David Ignatow. VWA

I am made to sow the thistle for wheat, the nettle for a nourishing dainty. The Price of Experience. Blake. Fr. Vala; or The Four Zoas. EnRP; Prf
(Night II (Enion's Lament).) PoE

I am making/ a wind come here. Unknown, tr. by W. S. Merwin. STP

I am making soup. Recipe: Sausage. Axionicus. FaBoUs

I Am Mama Bear. Nedine Davis. TSM

I am Mani Leyb, whose name is sung. I Am. Mani Leib, tr. by John Hollander. PeBMYV

I Am Married to Myself. Melinda Goodman. ER

I am merry,/ Pretty, pleasing. Unknown, tr. by Muriel Kittel. DMF

I am Miss Stein. Gertrude Stein at Snails Bay. Peter Porter. OxBC

I am monarch of all I survey. Verses Supposed to Be Written by Alexander Selkirk during His Solitary Abode on the Island of Juan Fernandez. William Cowper. FPL; NOEC; PoEL-3; PoLF
(Alexander Selkirk.) FiP
(Solitude of Alexander Selkirk, The.) GTBS; GTBS-P; LiTB

I am my ancient self. The Pilgrim. Richard Wightman. WGRP

I Am My Beloved's. Bible, O.T. Fr. The Song of Solomon, VII: 11–14. TrJP
("I am my lover's and he desires me.") BoWoP, ad. by Willis Barnstone.

I Am My Beloved's, and His Desire Is towards Me. Francis Quarles. See Emblems: Like to the Arctic Needle.

I am my lover's and he desires me. Bible, O.T. See Song of Solomon, The: I Am My Beloved's.

I am my own. As I Am My Father's. Rose Drachler. VWA

I am my prison. Conundrum. Carl Clark. JB

I am myself at last; now I achieve. I Am like a Rose. D. H. Lawrence. OxBSP

I am nailing them up to the cathedral door. Everywoman Her Own Theology. Alicia Ostriker. ER

I Am New York City. Jayne Cortez. BoWoP

I am no brazen face to hale the Lord. Rabbi Yom-Tob of Mayence Petitions His God. A. M. Klein. TrJP

I am no shepherd of a child's surmises. Montana Pastoral. J. V. Cunningham. MAT; MoAmPo; PrIm; VGW

I Am No Subject unto Fate. Unknown. OBS

I am nobody/ A red sinking autumn sun. Hokku Poems. Richard Wright. AmNP; PoBA

I am not/ alone. Getting Wise. Marg Yeo. DT

I Am Not a Bug. Gabriele Wohmann, tr. fr. German by Susan L. Cocalis. DMG

I Am Not a Camera. W. H. Auden. EyDe

I Am Not a Conspiracy Everything Is Not Paranoid. Susan Musgrave. NoAM

I am not a flower of song. Ghazal XII. Mirza Ghalib, tr. by W. S. Merwin and Aijaz Ahmad. LLLT

I am not a handsome man. Eclipse. Ed Roberson. PoNe
I Am Not a Honey-Hearted Child. Leyzer Volf, tr. fr. Yiddish by Robert Friend. PeBMYV
I am not a metaphor or symbol. The Distant Drum. Calvin C. Hernton. FF; TTY
I am not a painter, I am a poet. Why I Am Not a Painter. Frank O'Hara. CAPP; HCAP; MoP; NeAP; NoAM; NOBA; PoE; PoM
I am not blind. For Steph. Wendy Rose. CDW
I am not bred and born New Englander. Late Comer. Fanny de Groot Hastings. GoYe
I am not concerned at all with the golden age of those pines. Beyond Time. Mieczyslaw Jastrun. PwPP
I am not dazzled by my muse's features. The Muse. E. A. Baratynsky, tr. by Alan Myers. AAA
I am not gay by your definition. Explanation. William Barber. PeHV
I am not going to invite you. Blond. Joseph de Roche. HeIP
I am not, I am not but in your earth. The Mother. Hugo Claus, tr. by James S. Holmes. DuIn
I am not in. There's Nobody. Idea Vilariño, tr. by Kate Flores. DMH
I am not looking for your jugular. The Threat. Andrei Codrescu. UL
I am not Mahomet. E. C. Bentley. Fr. Clerihews. NOBL
I am not moved to love thee, my Lord God. Miguel de Guevara, tr. by Samuel Beckett. MexPo
I Am Not One of Those Who Left the Land. "Anna Akhmatova," tr. fr. Russian by Stanley Kunitz with Max Hayward. AnAn
I am not one who much or oft delight. Personal Talk. Wordsworth. EnRP; NOBE
I am not poor, but I am proud. Thought. Emerson. AmPP
I am not resigned to the shutting away of loving hearts. Dirge without Music. Edna St. Vincent Millay. CMoP; DL; LiTA; TrGrPo
I am not some country which you can destroy. Bangladesh. Kaifi A'Zmi, tr. by Mahmood Jamal. PBMUP
I am not sure I would always fight for my life. What Would You Fight For? D. H. Lawrence. OxBSP
I am not sure if I knew the truth. Youth. "Laurence Hope." WeW
I am not surprised. On a Clear Day I Can See Forever. Alex Kuo. BrSi
I Am Not That Woman. Kishwar Naheed, tr. fr. Urdu by Mahmood Jamal. PBMUP
I am not the first one infatuated with the glorious maiden. The Phoenix. Ilya Abu Madi, tr. by Issa Boullata and Naomi Shihab Nye. MAP
I Am Not the Woman I Am. Diane Glancy. GOS
I am not treacherous, callous, jealous, superstitious. A Face. Marianne Moore. OxBSP
I am not what I was yesterday. The Butterfly. Alice Archer James. AA
I am not yet born; O hear me. Prayer before Birth. Louis MacNeice. FaBCIP; GTBS-P; LiTB; NAs; TIRV; TwCP
I am not you. Africa's Plea. Roland Tombekai Dempster. TTY
I am not your God. African Easter. Abioseh Nicol. PBA
"I Am Not Yours." Sara Teasdale. VGW
I am now so weary with waiting. Gaspara Stampa, tr. by Harold M. Priest. WPOW
I am of Ireland. The Irish Dancer. Unknown. AnIL; FaBoCh; GBP; NOBE; OBEV; SeCePo
   (I Am from Ireland.) HAP; MeEL
   (Ich Am of Irlonde.) PoEL-1
   (Icham of Irlaunde.) HAP
"I Am of Ireland." W. B. Yeats. CMoP; LiTB
I am of little worth and poor, apart. Song of Loneliness. Judah Halevi, tr. by Nina Davis Salaman. TrJP
I am of Shropshire, my shins be sharp. A Shropshire Lad. Unknown. ChTr
I Am of the Earth. Anna Walters. VoR
I am of this world. Unknown. Fr. Manyo Shu. PeBJV
I am of this world. On the Death of Emperor Tenji. Unknown, tr. by Geoffrey Bownas and Anthony Thwaite. BoWoP
I am off down the road. Goblin Feet. J. R. R. Tolkien. FaPON
I am Ojistoh, I am she, the wife. Ojistoh. Pauline E. Johnson. NOBC
I am old. Christopher Logue. OxBTC
I am old and blind! Milton's Prayer for [or of] Patience. Elizabeth Lloyd Howell. AA; WGRP
I am on a journey. Unknown. Fr. Manyo Shu. PeBJV
I am on my way running. Song for a Young Girl's Puberty Ceremony. Unknown, tr. by Frances Densmore. OV
I am one of a band of outlaws, Cole Younger is my name. Cole Younger. Unknown. BeLS
I am one of passion's asses. The Girls of Llanbadarn. Dafydd ap Gwilym, tr. by Rolfe Humphries. OBWVE
I am one of those troubled hearts. Human Soul. René Maran, tr. by Mercer Cook. TTY

I am, outside. Incredible panic rules. John Berryman. Fr. Dream Songs. CAPP
I Am Panting. Anna Swirszczynska, tr. fr. Polish by Czeslaw Milosz. PwPP
I am peopled by women. A Folding and Unfolding. Welton Smith. PoNe
I am picking wild grapes last year. The Winemaker's Beat-étude. Alfred W. Purdy. MoCV
I am poor and old and blind. Belisarius. Longfellow. PoEL-5; WiR
I am poor brother Lippo, by your leave! Fra Lippo Lippi. Robert Browning. CTC; EBVV; NAEL-2; NoP; OAEL-2; TEP
I am poor, I don't bring you. Without Offerings. Jacob Glatstein, tr. by Benjamin and Barbara Harshav. AYP
I am proud of your soft, brown eyes. David Ignatow. Fr. Sunlight: A Sequence for My Daughter. CAPP
I am provoked. Strato, tr. by W. G. Shepherd. PeHV
I am purely evil. Song of the Bomber. Ethel Mannin. CN
I am Queen Anne, of whom 'tis said. Queen Anne. Unknown. ChTr
I am quite mad and you are wholly sane. Mad Woman. Suad al-Mubarak al-Sabah, tr. by May Jayyusi and John Heath-Stubbs. MAP
I am quite sure he thinks that I am God. Bishop Doane on His Dog. George Washington Doane. BLPA; FaBoBe
I Am Raftery ("I am Raftery, hesitant and confused"). Derek Mahon. OxBC
I Am Raftery [or Raferty]. Anthony Raftery, tr. fr. Modern Irish. AnIL, tr. by James Stephens; AWP, tr. by Douglas Hyde; SeCePo, tr. by Douglas Hyde
I am Raifteiri, the poet, full of courage and love. Anthony Raftery, tr. by Thomas Kinsella. NOIV
I am rather tall and stately. Unknown. Fr. Balliol Rhymes. FaBoEE; NOBL
I am reading. The Distant Orgasm. James Tate. AmPA
I am reading Li Po. The T.V. is on. Growing Up. Linda Gregg. NPGG
I am remembering in the long ago. The Dream of the Rood. Unknown. ACP
I am reminded, by the tan man who wings. The Elevator Man Adheres to Form. Margaret Danner. PoBA; PoNe
I am reminded of the vestment. I'm Not Here/ Never Was. Constanta Buzea, tr. by Stavros Deligiorgis. BoWoP
I am riding on a limited express, one of the crack trains of the nation. Limited. Carl Sandburg. HAP; MoAB; MoAMPo; OxBA
I Am Rose. Gertrude Stein. OBCA; RHPC; TrJP
I am round, round. Oswald de Andrade, tr. by Jean R. Longland. ATCBP
I am Scheherazade. Scheherazade. Barbara Burford. DT
I am scorned by patterns which hold. Moon at Three A.M. Lance Henson. CDW
I am sick body and soul. The wife of Kuramochi. Fr. Manyo Shu. Ma
I am sick today. Labour Pains. Yosano Akiko, tr. by Kenneth Rexroth and Ikuko Atsumi. AIW
I am silver and exact. I have no preconceptions. Mirror. Sylvia Plath. FaBoWP; HAP; NYBP
I Am Singing the Cold Rain. Lance Henson, tr. fr. Cheyenne Indian by the author. HATNAP; STP
I am sitting. The Muddy Puddle. Dennis Lee. RHPC
I am sitting across the table. Sunday at the State Hospital. David Ignatow. CAPP
I Am Sitting Here. Yehuda Amichai, tr. fr. Hebrew by Ruth Nevo. VWA
I am sitting here. The Poor Girl's Meditation. Unknown, tr. by Padraic Colum. BIrV; OBMV
I am sitting in a strange room listening. Baby-Sitting. Gillian Clarke. FaBoWP
I am sitting in Mike's Place trying to figure out. One Thousand Fearful Words for Fidel Castro. Lawrence Ferlinghetti. VGW
I am sitting in the black chair. Sunday Afternoon. Carol Jane Bangs. NIP
I am sitting sad and lonely. Lines to Florence. Mary Weston Fordham. CBWP-2
I am slow as the world. I am very patient. Three Women. Sylvia Plath. NAs
I am slowly dying, water evaporating. George Bowering. Fr. Summer Solstice. NOBC
I am smoking Camels and crying. The Clouds. Arthur Vogelsang. MAYP
I am so fragile this morning. The U. S. Coast and Geodetic Survey Ship Pioneer. Robert Hershon. NeAC
I Am So Glad and Very. E. E. Cummings. CMoP
I Am So Good. Sibilla Aleramo, tr. fr. Italian by Muriel Kittel. DMI
I am so little and grey. The Prayer of the Mouse. Carmen Bernos de Gasztold. PDV

I am so old a king that I remember. The Old King. John Heath-Stubbs. NePoEA

I am so out of love through poverty. Sonnet: Of Why He Would Be a Scullion. Cecco Angiolieri da Siena, *tr. by* Dante Gabriel Rossetti. AWP; PFI

I am so passing rich in poverty. Sonnet: He Jests Concerning His Poverty. Bartolomeo di Sant' Angelo, *tr. by* Dante Gabriel Rossetti. AWP

I am so tired and weary. Supplication. Joseph Seamon Cotter, Jr. BANP; CDC; PoNe

I am sorry to speak of death again. Poetics against the Angel of Death. Phyllis Webb. MoCV; NOBC

I am soul in the world: in. The Invention of Comics. Amiri Baraka. LiTM

I am spending this evening with you. Another Spring, Another Year. Anja Vammelvuo, *tr. by* Aili Jarvenpa. SOP

I am standing on the threshold of eternity at last. On the Threshold. *Unknown.* BLPA

I am standing upon the seashore. The Ship. *Unknown.* PoLF

I am still bitter about the last place we stayed. Codicil. Ruth Stone. BoWoP

I am still hurt, Plin. A Letter for Allhallows. Peter Kane Dufault. NYBP

I Am Stone of Many Colors. Tauhindauli. STE

I am strange here and often I am still trying. Evening. W. S. Merwin. NAAL-2

I Am Suibne the wanderer. Suibne Geilt. NOIV

I am surprised to find today. The Professor Waking. James Tate. FF

I am surprised to see. Letter Written on a Ferry while Crossing Long Island Sound. Anne Sexton. CoAP; NAAL-2; NYBP; TwCP

I am taking part in a great experiment. Sacred Objects. Louis Simpson. CAPP

I Am Taliesin. I Sing Perfect Metre. *Unknown, tr. fr. Welsh by* Ifor Williams. OBWVE

I am Te-ngau-reka-a-tu. Taiaha Haka Poem. Apirana Taylor. PeNZ

I am telling you now a number of half-conditioned ideas. Sunday Evening. Barbara Guest. NeAP

I am telling you this. Blue Ruth: America. Michael S. Harper. PoBA

I am ten and a half and my father. Goodnight Irene. Paul Mariani. BLA

I am ten and no one I love has died. Deborah Lee. Yvonne. CNA

I am Tex Ritter. I am not Eldridge Cleaver. The Skyjacker. Stan Rice. NPGG

I am that Dido which thou here do'st see. Decimus Magnus Ausonius, *tr. by* Sir Walter Ralegh. OBVE

I am that man who with a luminous look. Brevities. Siegfried Sassoon. PoLF

I am that man with helmet made of thorn. For an Ex-Far East Prisoner of War. Charles Causley. OxBC

I am that serpent-haunted cave. The Pythoness. Kathleen Jessie Raine. MoBrPo

I am that which began. Hertha. Swinburne. OAEL-2

I am that woman whose works are good. Sovereign Queen. Padeshah Khatun, *tr. by* Deirdre Lashgari. WPOW

I am the American heartbreak. American Heartbreak. Langston Hughes. AmPP; BPo; LiTM

I am the ancient Apple-Queen. Pomona. William Morris. NOBVV; WiR

I Am the Autumn. Itzik Manger, *tr. fr. Yiddish by* Joseph Leftwich. TrJP

I Am the Beginning. Isaiah Shembe, *tr. fr. Zulu by* G. C. Oosthuizen. WTO

I am the binge you need. Tango. Elena Jordana, *tr. by* William M. Davis. DMH

I am the bird of the wayside. Christine Ama Ata Aidoo. PBWP

I am the black centipede, the rusher with a black nose. Praises of the Train. Demetrius Segooa. PeSA

I Am the Blood. Isaac Rosenberg. MoBrPo

I am the blue! I come from the lower world. Helen. Paul Valéry, *tr. by* Robert Lowell. OBVE

I am the boy perched in the high. Haitian Suite. Gregory Orr. MAYP

I am the captain of my soul. Probably. Keith Preston. NBLV

I Am the Cat. Leila Usher. BLPA

I am the cat of cats. I am. The Cat of Cats. William Brighty Rands. OxBChV; RHPC

(Kitty: What She Thinks of Herself.) MoShBr

I am the cat that walks by himself. Kipling. CRH

I am the chaunt-rann of a Singer. The Poet. Padraic Fiacc. CIP; NeIP

I am the child of the Yangtse running. Child of the World. Edna L. S. Barker. GoYe

I am the child of the Yei-ie. Yei-ie's Child. Charles C. Long. NOVW

I am the crazy woman. Birthright. Geraldine Kudaka. BrSi

I am the dancer of the wood. The Spirit of the Birch. Arthur Ketchum. OHIP

I am the darker brother. I, Too, Sing America. Langston Hughes. PoLF

I am the Dean, and this is Mrs. Liddell. *Unknown. Fr.* Balliol Rhymes. FaBoEE

I am the Dean of Christ Church, Sir. Cecil Arthur Spring-Rice. *Fr.* Balliol Rhymes. CenHV; FaBoCo; FaBoEE; NOBL

I Am the Door. Richard Crashaw. NAEL-1

I am the dragon's daughter. The Song of the Dragon's Daughter. Ursula K. Le Guin. BWV

I Am the Duke of Norfolk. *Unknown.* GBP

I am the fair one of the palace field. The Olive. *Unknown, tr. by* Grace Warwick. PFI

I am the family face. Heredity. Thomas Hardy. CTC; EBEV; ImOP; RB

I am the farmer, stripped of love. The Hill Farmer Speaks. R. S. Thomas. GTBS-P; OBWVE

I Am the Flag. Lawrence M. Jones. OPP

I am the flute of Daphnis. On this wall. The Flute of Daphnis. Edward Cracroft Lefroy, *after the Greek of* Theocritus. *Fr.* Echoes from Theocritus, XXIII. AWP

I am the ghost of Shadwell Stair. Shadwell Stair. Wilfred Owen. FaBoTw

I am the Gilly of Christ. Joseph Campbell. AnIL; TIRV

I am the god of things that burrow and creep. The Gods of the Earth Beneath. Edmund Blunden. BrPo

I am the great Professor Jowett. *Unknown.* FiBHP

I Am the Great Sun. Charles Causley. TOF

I am the Kiwi bird. The Kiwi Bird. Nina Cassian, *tr. by* Laura Schiff. OV

"I am the landscape," he said. Zeroing In. Denise Levertov. ER

I am the leaf that fell—from the top. Chronique Scandaleuse. Richard Augustine Chima. WMBCH

I am the least. The Mite. Boynton Merrill, Jr. CRP

I am the lip parched with thirst. Asadullah Khan Ghalib, *tr. by* Ahmed Ali. GoT

I Am the Little Irish Boy. Henry David Thoreau. NAs

I am the little man who smokes and smokes. John Berryman. *Fr.* Dream Songs. WeW

I am the little New Year, ho, ho! The New Year. *Unknown.* BoTP

I Am the Lord. Alexander Mack, *tr. fr. German by* Sheema Z. Buehne. AH

I am the Lord of Light, the self-begotten Youth. He Maketh Himself One with the God Ra. *Unknown, tr. fr. Egyptian by* Robert Hillyer. *Fr.* Book of the Dead. AWP

I am the magical mouse. The Magical Mouse. Kenneth Patchen. SO

I am the man that hath seen affliction. Affliction. Bible, *O.T. Fr.* Lamentations, III: 1–15. TrJP

I am the month when roses. June. Mary Weston Fordham. CBWP-2

I am the mother of sorrows. The Paradox. Paul Laurence Dunbar. PoBA

I Am the Mountainy Singer. Joseph Campbell. AnIL; MoBrPo

I am the Muse who sung alway. Solution. Emerson. OBAL

I am the nor'west air nosing among the pines. Time. Allen Curnow. ATNZ

I am the old one here. Desert Tortoise. Byrd Baylor. RHPC

I Am the One. Thomas Hardy. OxBTC

I am the one in your dreams. The Dark Lord of Savaiki. Alistair Campbell. ATNZ

I am the one who looks the other way. The Bystander. Rosemary Dobson. CBAP; Mes

I am the one whom ringdoves see. I Am the One. Thomas Hardy. OxBTC

I am the one whose thought. Death. William Bell Scott. NOBVV

I Am the Only Being Whose Doom. Emily Brontë. MAT; TW

I am the only me I am. Me I Am! Jack Prelutsky. RHPC

I Am the People, the Mob. Carl Sandburg. AmPP; OxBA; TAP

I Am the Poet Davies, William. W. H. Davies. OxBSP

I am the poet of the Body and I am the poet of the Soul. Walt Whitman. *Fr.* Song of Myself, XXI. WeW

I Am He That Walks with the Tender and Growing Night. ChTr

I am the poet who waits. Foreplay of the Alphabet. Darrell Gray. UL

I am the Prince. Charles Causley. FF

I am the Prince in the Field. He Maketh Himself One with Osiris. *Unknown, tr. fr. Egyptian by* Robert Hillyer. *Fr.* Book of the Dead. AWP

I am the pure lotus. He Is like the Lotus. *Unknown, tr. fr. Egyptian by* Robert Hillyer. *Fr.* Book of the Dead. AWP; EaLo

(Death as a Lotus Flower.) TTY, *tr. by* Ulli Beier

I am the pure, the true of word, triumphant. He Defendeth His Heart against the Destroyer. *Unknown, tr. fr. Egyptian* by Robert Hillyer. *Fr.* Book of the Dead. AWP

I am the pure traveler. He Entereth the House of the Goddess Hathor. *Unknown, tr. fr. Egyptian* by Robert Hillyer. *Fr.* Book of the Dead. AWP

I am the reality of things that seem. Poetry. Ella Heath. WGRP

I am the rooftree and the keel. Tapestry Trees. William Morris. BoNaP; FaPON; OHIP

I Am the Rose of Sharon. Bible, *O.T. See* Song of Solomon, The: I am the rose of Sharon, and the lily of the valleys.

I am the ruined queen. Dido: Swarming. Kathleen Spivack. PoA

I am the serpent, fat with years. He Is like the Serpent Saka. *Unknown, tr. fr. Egyptian* by Robert Hillyer. *Fr.* Book of the Dead. AWP

I am the seventh son of the son. Malcolm X—an Autobiography. Larry Neal. AmNP; BPo

I am the shadow in the shadow of the wicker. Home Revisited: Midnight. John Ciardi. NYBP

I am the sister of him. Little. Dorothy Aldis. FaPON; NTCP

I am the smoke king. The Song of the Smoke. W. E. B. DuBois. PoBA; UnPo

I am the sorrow in the wheat fields. Ellen Bass. NMM

I am the spirit astir. Autochthon. Sir Charles G. D. Roberts. CaP

I am the spirit of the morning sea. Richard Watson Gilder. AA

I am the stage, impassive, mute and cold. Nature. Alfred de Vigny, *tr. by* Margaret Jourdain. AWP

I am the terrour of the sea. On the Crocodile. Thomas Heyrick. FM

I am the tomb of Crethon; here you read. The Tomb of Crethon. Leonidas of Tarentum, *tr. by* John Hermann Merivale. AWP

I am the toy-maker; I have brought from the town. The Toy-Maker. Padraic Colum. SaC

I Am the Train of Sadness. Nizar Qabbani, *tr. fr. Arabic* by Abdullah al-Udhari. MPAW

I am the true vine, and my Father is the husbandman. Bible, *N.T. Fr.* St. John, XV: 1-18. OBVE

I am the trumpet blown by time. The Trumpet. Ilya Grigoryevich Ehrenburg, *tr. by* Y. Hornstein. TrJP

I am the Turquoise Woman's son. The War God's Horse Song. *Unknown.* LiTA, *tr. by* Dane Coolidge *and* Mary Roberts Coolidge; RB, *tr. by* Louis Watchman; TTTS

I am the unicorn and bow my head. The Lady and the Unicorn. May Sarton. ER

I Am the Very Model [*or* Pattern] of a Modern Major-General. W. S. Gilbert. *Fr.* The Pirates of Penzance. NBLV; NOBL; NOP (Modern Major-General, The.) NBLV

I am the Virgin; from this granite ledge. The Wayside Virgin. Langdon Elwyn Mitchell. AA

"I Am the Way." Alice Meynell. ACP; NOBVV; OBMV; OxBSP

I am the wind which breathes upon the sea. The Mystery. *At. to* Amergin, *tr. by* Douglas Hyde. TIRV

I am the woman-drawer. The Song of the Woman-Drawer. Mary Gilmore. PoAu-1

I am the woman of sweaty language, the belly. Faye Kicknosway. *Fr.* Night Braid. ER

I am the woman of the principal fountain. Shaman. María Sabina, *tr. by* Henry Munn. WPOW

I am the woman who sits by the river. Let Us Gather at the River. Marge Piercy. GeTw

I am thinking of tents and tentage, tents through the ages. Thinking of Tents. Reed Whittemore. TAP

I am 32 years old. Writ on the Eve of My 32nd Birthday. Gregory Corso. NAs

I am this fountain's god. The River God ("I am this fountain's god"). John Fletcher. *Fr.* The Faithful Shepherdess, III, i. TrGrPo

I am throwing hard again. In My Meanest Daydream. Gary Gildner. ASP; TSL

I am thy father's spirit. Shakespeare. *Fr.* Hamlet, I, v. OBD

I am thy fugitive, thy votary. To the Lord Love. "Michael Field." OBMV

I am Thy grass, O Lord! Trust. Lizette Woodworth Reese. AA

I am tired of being the child, the maiden aunt. Untitled. Ellen Bass. PPR

I am tired of cursing the Bishop. Crazy Jane on the Mountain. W. B. Yeats. CMoP

I am tired of planning and toiling. The Cry of the Dreamer. John Boyle O'Reilly. BLPA

I am tired of the tundra of the mind. The Technology of Inspiration. Lynn Emanuel. SoTCo

"I am tired of this barn!" said the colt. The Barn. Elizabeth J. Coatsworth. OBCP

I am tired of work; I am tired of building up somebody else's civilization. Tired. Fenton Johnson. BANP; IDB; PoBA; PoLF; PoNe; TTY

I am to follow her. There is much grace. George Meredith. *Fr.* Modern Love, XLII. NAEL-2; NOBVV

I am to my honey what marijuana is. Skirt Dance. Ishmael Reed. FF; UL

I Am Told. Victor Segalen, *tr. fr. French* by Nathaniel Tarn. RHTwFP

I Am Too Near. Wislawa Szymborska, *tr. fr. Polish* by Czeslaw Milosz. BoWoP; PBWP; PwPP

I am too near, too clear a thing for you. A Flower of Mullein. Lizette Woodworth Reese. MoAmPo

I am too young to grow a beard. Street Song. Thom Gunn. HeIP; NoP; OxBC

I am trying/ to learn to walk again. Walk. Frank Horne. BPo

I am trying to decide to go swimming. The Wind Is Blowing West. Joseph Ceravolo. TTTS

I am trying to imagine. Re-forming the Crystal. Adrienne Rich. TAP

I am trying to pry open your casket. Dear Reader. James Tate. EAS

I am 25 years old. My Poem. Nikki Giovanni. AmNP; BPo; PoBA

I am two fools, I know. The Triple Fool. John Donne. GBL

I am type of singleness. Artemis. Dulcie Deamer. PoAu-1

"I am unable," yonder beggar cries. A Lame Beggar. John Donne. FF

I am unhappy that I am not God. He Puts Me to Rest. David Ignatow. VGW

I am unjust, but I can strive for justice. Why I Voted the Socialist Ticket. Vachel Lindsay. MoAmPo

I am unleafed. October. Judah Leib Teller, *tr. by* Benjamin *and* Barbara Harshav. AYP

I am up tonight in the pinnacles bold. The Old Night Hawk. Bruce Kiskaddon. CowP

I am valued by men, fetched from afar. Honey-Mead: "I am valued by men, fetched from afar." *Unknown, formerly at. to* Cynewulf, *tr. fr. Anglo-Saxon* by Charles W. Kennedy. *Fr.* Riddles (Exeter Book). AnOE

I am very fond of the little ribs of women. Vincent McHugh. *Fr.* Talking to Myself. ErPo

I am waiting for my case to come up. Lawrence Ferlinghetti. *Fr.* Oral Messages. AiP; CAPP; GOA

I am waiting for the dawning. Waiting for the Dawning. *Unknown.* BLRP

I am walking a trail. Intimidations of an Autobiography. James Tate. NoAM

I am walking and I. Ray A. Young Bear. STP

I am walking rapidly through striations of light and dark. I Dream I'm the Death of Orpheus. Adrienne Rich. NMM

I am Walt Disney of the Kingdom of Satan. Another Catalogue Item. David Avidan, *tr. fr. Hebrew* by Warren Bargad *and* Stanley F. Chyet. *Fr.* Traveling in the City, 12. IP

I am warm. The Promise. Johari M. Kunjufu. BlSi

I am wearing absent-minded red. Spots of Blood. Phyllis Webb. NOBC

I am Weary, Mother. Mary E. Tucker. CBWP-1

I am weary of lying within the chase. Ballade de Marguerite. *Unknown, tr. by* Oscar Wilde. AWP

I Am Weary of Straying. Sarah E. York. AH

I am weary of the Garden. Said the Rose. George Henry Miles. BLPA

I am weary of these times and their dull burden. Quid Restat. Lucius Beebe. RFM

I am weaving a song of waters. Gwendolyn B. Bennett. BlSi

I Am What You Make Me ("I am whatever you make me, nothing more"). Franklin K. Lane. OPP

I am who the trail took. Exploration. Daniel Hoffman. CoAP

I am willowy boughs. I Am. Hilda Conkling. FaPON

I am wind on sea. Amergin. *Fr.* Amergin's Songs, II. NOIV

"I Am with Thee." Ernest Bourner Allen. BLRP

I Am with Those. Ingrid Jonker, *tr. fr. Afrikaans* by Jack Cope *and* William Plomer. BoWoP

I Am with You. Lajos Kassák, *tr. fr. Hungarian* by Edwin Morgan. MHuP

I am within as white as snow. *Unknown.* ChTr; GBP

I am wondering how I could have changed her blood. Marlow and Nancy. Sandra McPherson. AmPA

I Am Writing to You from a Far-Off Country, *sels.* Henri Michaux, *tr. fr. French by* Richard Ellmann. RHTwFP

"Dawn is grey here, she went on to tell him, The. It was not always like this." *Fr.* III.

"Education regarding chills is not well handled in this country, The." *Fr.* XII.

"I add one further word to you, a question rather." *Fr.* IV.

"I am writing to you from the end of the world." *Fr.* V.

"She writes to him again." *Fr.* XI.

"There are constantly, she told him further, lions in the village." *Fr.* VII.

"We have here, she said, only one sun in the month, and for only a little while." *Fr.* I.

"We women here all live with tightened throats." *Fr.* VI.

"When you walk in the country, she further confided to him." *Fr.* II.

I am writing to you in answer to your letter. The Connection. Daniil Kharms, *tr. by* George Gibian. FaBoNo

I am yesterday, to-day and to-morrow. He Walketh by Day. *Unknown, tr. fr. Egyptian by* Robert Hillyer. *Fr.* Book of the Dead. AWP

I am—yet what I am none cares or knows. I Am. John Clare. EBEV; EBVV; EnRP; GTBS-P; HAP; InvP; LiTB; NAEL-2; NOBE; NOBVV; NoP; OAEL-2; OBNC; PoEL-4; Prf; PrIm; TOF; TrGrPo (Written in Northampton County Asylum.) OBEV

I am your big trimmer. The Big Trimmer. Ronald P. Tanaka. BrSi

I Am Your Loaf, Lord. David Ross. GoYe

I am your mother, your mother's mother. Jalal ed-Din Rumi, *tr. by* Elizabeth Daryush. OBVE

I am your noble savage. First and Last Man. Ralph McTell. OBET

I am your son, white man! Mulatto. Langston Hughes. NAAL-2

I am yours, you are mine. Frau Ava, *tr. by* Willis Barnstone. BoWoP

I amna' fou' sae muckle as tired—deid dune. Sic Transit Gloria Scotia. "Hugh MacDiarmid." CMoP

I an I Alone; or Goliath. Michael Smith. PBCV

I, an unwedded wandering dame. Sylvia Townsend Warner. MoBrPo

I and my cousin Wildair met. Praise-God Barebones. Ellen Mackay Hutchinson Cortissoz. AA

I and my shadow open the door. On a Snowy Night. Koh Chang-soo, *tr. by the author.* ACKP

I and my sisters three. Victorian Song. John Chipman Farrar. GoYe

I and my white Pangur. The Monk and His Pet Cat. *Unknown.* CH

I and myself swore enmity. Alack. Interior. J. C. Squire. OxBSP

I and Pangur Bán, my cat. Pangur Bán. *Unknown, tr. by* Robin Flower. AnIL; CRH; FaBoCh; RB

I and the other intruders. Of Objects Considered as Fortresses in a Baleful Place. Hyam Plutzik. VGW

I and the poet Isaac Raboy. Neighbors. Joseph Rolnik, *tr. fr. Yiddish by* Irving Feldman. *Fr.* Poets. PeBMYV

I and You. Moyshe-Leyb Halpern, *tr. fr. Yiddish by* Benjamin *and* Barbara Harshav. AYP

I, Angelo, obese, black-garmented. Angelo Orders His Dinner. Bayard Taylor. AnAmPo; BXAP; Par

I appear like a bird from nowhere. Below Hekla. Selima Hill. FaBoWP

I approach with such. Something. Robert Creeley. NaP

I argue/ that where the body is concerned. Saddle and Cell. The Three Marias, *tr. by* Helen R. Lane. BoWoP

I arise above the clouds. The Airman's Breastplate. Oliver St. John Gogarty. TIRV

I arise and see. Emperor Hanazono, *tr. by* Steven D. Carter. WFTW

I arise from dreams of thee. The Indian Serenade. Shelley. AWP; BLPL; EnRP; HoPM; LiTB; OBEV; TrGrPo; TTTS (Indian Girl's Song, The.) NAEL-2 (Lines to an Indian Air.) FaBoBe; FiP; GTBS; GTBS-P

I arise today. Saint Patrick's Breastplate; or, The Deer's Cry. *At. to* Saint Patrick. TIRV, *tr. by* Kuno Meyer; WGRP (Deer's Cry, The.) AnIL, *tr. by tr. by* Whitley Stokes, John Strachan, *and* Kuno Meyer

I, Arnor the red poet, made. The Five Voyages of Arnor. George Mackay Brown. NePoEA-2

I arose early and stepped outside. February Morning. King D. Kuka. VoR

I arose swiftly that night, for I heard a knock at my door. The Future. James Oppenheim. TrJP

I arrive/ in the unbearable heat. Song for My Father. Jessica Hagedorn. BrSi; ER

I arrive/ Langston. Do Nothing till You Hear from Me. David Henderson. CNA; PoBA

I Arrive in a Small Boat, Alone. Susan Ludvigson. KS

I arrive where an unknown earth is under my feet. Landfall. *Maori Oral Tradition, tr. by* A. S. Thomson. WTO

I arrived on a hill whose top was covered with meadows. In the Hill Country. Max Jacob, *tr. by* John Ashbery. RHTwFP

I ascended to heaven again last week. The Monk of Montaudon, *tr. by* Paul Blackburn. Pro

I ask:/ How much is five. Dialogue. Erika Mitterer, *tr. by* Beth Bjorklund. CoAuP

I ask a mountain woman for a light. Brewing Tea at Moon Pond. Chang Yü, *tr. fr. Chinese by* Jonathan Chaves. *Fr.* Seven Poems on Living in the Mountains: Seeing Off. CoBLCP

I ask but one thing of you, only one. To a Friend. Amy Lowell. FPL; PoLF

I ask but right: let her that caught me late. Ovid, *tr. fr. Latin by* Christopher Marlowe. *Fr.* Amores, I, 3. EBEV

I ask for the strength to follow through my life. Time of Day. Selden Rodman. PoA

I ask good things that I detest. Robert Louis Stevenson. TrPWD

I ask if she is all right. She is clearly not. The Piss Artist. W. G. Shepherd. NPo

I Ask My Teachers. Sister Mary Madeleva. *Fr.* Concerning Death. CRP

I ask no kind return of love. Fanny Greville. *Fr.* A Prayer for Indifference. OBEV

I ask not how thy suffering came. Fraternity. Anne Reeve Aldrich. AA

I ask the muse about this drifting. The Muse's Answer. Gibbons Ruark. MT

I ask thy aid, O potent rum! Resentments Composed because of the Clamor of Town Topers Outside My Apartment. Sarah Kemble Knight. AiP; SCAP

I ask, who will buy a poem? Mahon O'Heffernan, *tr. by* Thomas Kinsella. NOIV (Who Will Buy a Poem?) AnIL, *tr. by* Kenneth Jackson

I ask You not for victory. The Prizefighter's Prayer. Menotti Vincent Caprani. TIRV

I ask you this. Langston Hughes. CDC; EaLo

I asked a thief to steal me a peach. Blake. NAEL-2; NoP; OBNC; PoE (Angel, The.) LiTB

I asked an aged man, a man of cares. What Is Time? James Marsden. PWR

I asked for just a crumb of bread. More than We Ask. Faith Wells. BLRP

I asked for peace. Requests. Digby Mackworth Dolben. TrPWD

I asked her, "Is Aladdin's lamp." The Sorceress. Vachel Lindsay. PDV; WSC

I asked her why she didn't. Girl with Long Dark Hair. Stephen Gray. PeSA

I asked if I got sick and died, would you. A Question. J. M. Synge. MoBrPo; NOIV; OBMV; OxBTC

I asked if I should pray. Mohini Chatterjee. W. B. Yeats. NoAM

I asked my dear friend, Orator Prigg. Orator Prigg. Blake. OBSV

I Asked My Mother ("I asked my mother for fifty cents"). *Unknown.* FaFP; MoShBr; OxBoLi; RHPC

I asked no other thing. Emily Dickinson. NOBA; OxBA

I asked of Echo, t'other day. Echo. John Godfrey Saxe. AnAmPo

I asked professors who teach the meaning of life to tell me what is happiness. Happiness. Carl Sandburg. AnAmPo; OxBA

I asked the grave-digger, "Do you have." Ahmad al-Mushari al-Udwani, *tr. fr. Arabic by* Hilary Kilpatrick *and* Charles Doria. *Fr.* Personal Reflections. MAP

I asked the headless snake. Christine Lavant, *tr. fr. German by* Beth Bjorklund. CoAuP

I asked the heaven of stars. Night Song at Amalfi. Sara Teasdale. MoAmPo

I asked the holly, "What is your life if?" Trees. Ted Hughes. NYBP

I Asked the Little Boy Who Cannot See. *Unknown.* OnUR

I asked the Master for a motto sweet. God's Will. Charles E. Guthrie. BLRP

I asked thee oft what poets thou hast read. Upon the Same (Detractor). Robert Herrick. CaPo

I asked you one day who posted. Economics Lesson. Rocco Scotellaro, *tr. by* Paul Vangelisti. PFI

I at my window sit, and see. Autumn ("I at my window sit, and see.") *Unknown.* NOEC

I ate my fill of army bread. The Air Sentry. Patrick Barrington. CenHV

I ate pancakes one night in a Pancake House. The Player Piano. Randall Jarrell. MT; NAAL-2

I attach no importance to life. The Spectral Attitudes. André Breton, *tr. by* David Gascoyne. EAS

I attend her palanquin a hundred miles. Rai San'yo, *tr. fr. Chinese by* Burton Watson. *Fr.* Mount Yoshino, I. JLIC-2

I attended the burial of all my rosy feelings. Transaction. A. R. Ammons. HCAP; PoA

I, Attila. Sister. Jerzy Harasymowicz, *tr. by* Czeslaw Milosz. PwPP

I await his coming. Guessing. *Unknown, tr. by* U Win Pe. PBWP

I Awake Crying on My Birthday. K'uang Chou-yi, *tr. fr. Chinese by* Irving Lo. WFTU

I awake from sleep. Kenko, *tr. fr. Japanese by* Steven D. Carter. WFTW

I awakened to dryness and the ferns were dead. The Tragedy of Leaves. Charles Bukowski. HoPM

I awoke from sleep. Ietaka, *tr. by* Steven D. Carter. WFTW

I awoke hot, startled in daylight, calling. Mother. Philip Dow. NPGG

I awoke in profuse sweat, arms aching. Hag-ridden. Robert Graves. BIrV

I awoke in the Midsummer not-to-call night, in the white and the walk of the morning. Moonrise. Gerard Manley Hopkins. FaBoPP; MoAB; MoBrPo; NOBVV; RB; SeCePo

I awoke only to hear the dull clobbing of the wind. Night Shore. Barry O. Higgs. PeSA

I awoke with a pain in my head. November 1967. Paul Durcan. FaBCIP

I Awoke with the Room Cold. Marge Piercy. NeAC

I banked the five in the side. Kelly. Robert Hershon. NeAC

I bargained with life for a penny. My Wage. Jessie Belle Rittenhouse. BLPA

I bathe and step out of the Spring. Yosano Akiko, tr. fr. Japanese by Hiroaki Sato. Fr. Thirty-nine Tanka. FCEI

I bathe in orchid water. The Lord among the Clouds. Unknown, tr. fr. Chinese by Burton Watson. Fr. Nine Songs. CoBCP

I bear an unseen burden constantly. The Burden of Love. "Owen Innsley." AA

I bear, in sign of love. Francis Andrewes. Fr. Shepherdess' Valentine. OFD

I been 'buked an' I been scorned. Hell and Heaven. Unknown. OxBoLi

I been ridin' fer cattle the most of my life. The High-loping Cowboy. Curley W. Fletcher. AiP

I been scarred and battered. Still Here. Langston Hughes. BPo

I been t'inkin' 'bout de preachah; whut he said de othah night. Philosophy. Paul Laurence Dunbar. BPo

I before E. Unknown. FaBoUs

I beg God's grace, guardian of the parish. In Praise of Tenby. Unknown, tr. by Joseph P. Clancy. OBWVE

I beg of you, Chung Tzu. Unknown, tr. fr. Chinese by Arthur Waley. BoS

I beg the pardon of these flowers. With Lilacs. Charles Henry Crandall. AA

I began in Ohio. Stages on a Journey Westward. James Wright. LCAP; NaP

I began this fall by watching a thin red squirrel. Pick and Poke. Gerald Stern. AnAn

I began to play my music and the raven stopped in mid-flight. The Lament of Orpheus. István Kormos, tr. by Edwin Morgan. MHuP

I began with everything. Speaking of Loss. Lucille Clifton. CAPP

I begin through the grass once again to be bound to the Lord. Reconciliation. "Æ." OBMV; TrCP

I begin with the hills. This House. Ray A. Young Bear. CDW

I beheld, and lo a great multitude, which no man could number. Heavenly Vision. William Billings. AmFP

I beheld her, on a Day. How He Saw Her. Ben Jonson. Fr. A Celebration of Charis in Ten Lyrick Peeces. QFR; SeCP; SeCV-1

I, Being Born a Woman and Distressed. Edna St. Vincent Millay. BoLoP; NIP; NoP; OPOP
(Sonnet: "I, being born a woman and distressed.") ErPo

I Believe. J. B. Lawrence. BLRP

I Believe. Saul Tchernichowsky, tr. fr. Hebrew by Reginald V. Feldman. TrJP

I believe a leaf of grass is no less than the journey-work of the stars. Walt Whitman. Fr. Song of Myself, XXXI. PDV

I believe if I should die. Creed. Mary Ashley Townsend. BLPA; FaBoBe

I believe in human kindness. A Creed. Norman Macleod. WGRP

I believe in the brook as it wanders. Nature's Creed. Unknown. OHIP

I believe in the coming of a new tomorrow, I say. Ishikawa Takuboku, tr. fr. Japanese by Hiroaki Sato. Fr. Forty-seven Tanka in Three Lines. FCEI

I believe in the flesh and the appetites. Walt Whitman. Fr. Song of Myself, XXIV. Prf

I believe in the increasing of life: whatever. The Escape. Ivor Gurney. OxBSP

I believe in the ultimate justice of Fate. Credo. Georgia Douglas Johnson. PoBA

I believe in this stalled magnificence. The Snowbound City. John Haines. EAS

I believe in you my soul. Walt Whitman. Fr. Song of Myself, V. Prf Swiftly Arose. TrCP

I believe the earth/ exists. Credo. Denise Levertov. Fr. Mass for the Day of St. Thomas Didymus. AIW

I believe the yellow flowers think with me. Alice Notley. UL

I believed:/ a tree when kissed. Love. Tymoteusz Karpowicz, tr. by Czeslaw Milosz. PwPP

I bend over an old hollow cottonwood stump. A Hollow Tree. Robert Bly. NNaP

I Bended unto Me. Thomas Edward Brown. NOBVV; NTCP

I Bent to Touch a Damp Cloth to Your Mouth. Sherod Santos. Fr. The Sheltering Ground, IV. Son

I bent unto the ground. The Voice of God. James Stephens. WGRP

I, Bertold Brecht, came out of the black forests. Of Poor B.B. Bertolt Brecht, tr. by Michael Hamburger. RB

I beseech God's favour, faultless your gift. Petition for Reconciliation. Cynddelw Brydydd Mawr, tr. by Joseph P. Clancy. OBWVE

I bespeak words. Clere Parsons. FaBoTw

"I bet I can hold my breath." One-Upmanship. Miriam Chaikin. NTCP

I bind the Soul that fathered me. The Hanging. J. E. H. MacDonald. OBCV

I bind unto myself to-day. St. Patrick's Breastplate. At. to Saint Patrick, tr. by Frances Alexander. FaBoCh

I blame Myrtis. Korinna, tr. fr. Greek by John Dillion. PBWP

"I bleed by the black stream." Haemorrhage. Padraic Fiacc. CIP

I bless [e] Thee, Lord, because I grow. Paradise. George Herbert. OAEL-1; SeCP; TrGrPo

I Bless Thee, Lord, for Sorrows Sent. Samuel Johnson. AH

I Bless This Man. Pindar, tr. fr. Greek by Richmond Lattimore. Fr. Nemean Odes. SD

I block out the midday brightness with a screen depicting dark woods. Impromptu on a Hangover. P'i Jih-hsiu, tr. by Burton Watson. CoBCP

I Blow My Pipes. Hugh McCrae. PoAu-1

I born/ from/ a force. Motto Vision 1971. Delano Abdul Malik de Coteau. PBCV

I bought a shop on Dizengoff. Buying a Shop on Dizengoff. Erez Biton, tr. by Judith Katz. VWA

I break off a branch, and prod my lazy donkey. A Trip to a Mountain Village. Li K'ai-hsien, tr. by Jonathan Chaves. CoBLCP

I Break the Sky. Owen Dodson. PoBA

I breathe, sweet Gib, the temperate air of Wrest. To my Friend G.N., from Wrest. Thomas Carew. CaPo

I breathed upon the aluminum microphone-stand a body's length away. Thus Crosslegged on Round Pillow Sat in Space. Allen Ginsberg. NNaP

I bring fresh showers for the thirsting flowers. The Cloud. Shelley. BLPL; ChER; EnRP; FaPON; GN; ImOP, abr.; LiTB; NAEL-2; NoP; OHFP; PoEL-4; PWR; TrGrPo

I bring myself back from the streets that open like long. Home for Thanksgiving. W. S. Merwin. NoAM

I bring ye love. Question. What will love do? Upon Love, by Way of Question and Answer. Robert Herrick. CaPo

I bring you. Big Dog. Anselm Hollo. UL

I bring you a goat. Hroswitha von Gandersheim, tr. fr. Latin by Patrick Diehl. Fr. Paphnutius. WPOW

I bring you news. Unknown. NOIV

I bring you now these flowers. Elegy for Maria Alves. Joaquim Cardozo, tr. by Elizabeth Bishop. ATCBP

I bring you now this tiny piece of seaweed which once mingled. Idée Fixe. Robert Desnos, tr. by Michael Benedikt. POS

I bring you with reverent hands. A Poet to His Beloved. W. B. Yeats. BrPo

I brocht my love a cherry. Auld Sang. William Soutar. OxBS

I broil shrimp and play with my illness. Miura Chora, tr. fr. Japanese by Hiroaki Sato. Fr. Sixteen Hokku. FCEI

I broke a glass, got bloodstains on the sheet. Eight Days in April. Marilyn Hacker. ER

I broke one day a slender stem. A Spray of Honeysuckle. Mary Emily Bradley. AA

I brought my great carriage that thunders. Unknown, tr. by Arthur Waley. BoS

I brought my life this far. Anniversary. Odysseus Elytis, tr. by Edmund Keeley and Philip Sherrard. VMG

I brought my love. Beloved. Iyamide Hazeley. WS

I brought with me from home a bundle of clothes. Two Trunks. Kuan Kuan, tr. by Dominic Cheung. IFON

I brush the spider webs from the dismantled sky. Housework. Amanda Berenguer, tr. by Priscilla Joslin. WPOW

I built a house in the middle of the ocean. Earth-Ocean. Guillaume Apollinaire. POS, Michael Benedikt
(Ocean of Earth.) POS, Roger Shattuck

I built a hut in a little wood. My Hut. Eileen Mathias. BoTP

I Built My Hut. T'ao Yuan-ming. See Two Drinking Songs: I built my hut near where people live.

I built my hut in a place where people live. T'ao Ch'ien, tr. fr. Chinese by Burton Watson. Fr. Drinking Wine, V. CoBCP

I built my hut near where people live. T'ao Yuan-ming. Fr. Two Drinking Songs, 1. NU
(I Built My Hut.) AWP, tr. by Arthur Waley.

I built on the sand. Foundations. Leopold Staff, tr. by Czeslaw Milosz. PwPP

I buried a skunk in the garden. Dead Skunk. Richard Eberhart. BLA

I buried Mama in her wedding dress. She Didn't Even Wave. Ai. MAYP

I buried you deeper last night. To a Persistent Phantom. Frank Horne. AmNP; BANP; CDC

I Burn for England with a Living Flame. Gervase Stewart. WaaP (Poem: "I burn for England with a living flame.") WaP

I burn in the darkness. Ceremony. Jack Dann. BWV

I burn no incense, hang no wreath. Votive Song. Edward Coate Pinkney. AA; AnAmPo

I burn your letters. Arson. Peter Goldsworthy. UAS

I burne, and cruell you, in vaine. To My Mistris, I Burning in Love. Thomas Carew. SeCP

I Burned My Candle at Both Ends. Samuel Hoffenstein. FiBHP

I burned my life that I might find. The Alchemist. Louise Bogan. AWP; LLLT; MoAmPo

I buy scallions and go home through leafless trees. Buson, *tr. fr. Japanese by* Hiroaki Sato. *Fr.* Eighty-seven Hokku. FCEI

I Call and I Call ("I call, I call. Who do ye call?"). Robert Herrick. ChTr

I call the land of Ireland. Amergin. *Fr.* Amergin's Songs, I. NOIV

I call up words that he may write them down. Demands of the Muse. Vernon Watkins. PoA

I call you with honest words. Bláthmac Mac Con Brettan. *Fr.* A Poem to Mary. NOIV

I called at your. From an Afternoon Caller. Sister Mary Madeleva. CRP

I called him to come in. Evening. James Wright. NOBA; NYBP; PrIm

I called one day—on Eden's strand. From Emily Dickinson in Southern California. X. J. Kennedy. NBLV

I called out of mine affliction. Jonah's Prayer. Bible, *O.T. Fr.* Jonah, II: 3–11. TrJP

I called over friends. Summer Moon. Tamemasa, *tr. by* Steven D. Carter. WFTW

I called to the wind. Kyorai, *tr. by* Harry Behn. WSC

I called today, Peter, and you were away. The Thermal Stair. W. S. Graham. FaBoMo

I came/ in the blinding sweep. To Mother. Frank Horne. *Fr.* Letters [*or Notes*] Found near a Suicide. BPo

I came/ heavy with child in the fierce sun. Waiheke 1972—Rocky Bay. Christina Beer. PeNZ

I Came a-Riding. Reinmar von Zweter, *tr. fr.* German by Jethro Bithell. AWP

I came, a scooped out woman. Desert March. Gerda Norvig. VWA

I came across her browsing on a slope. Cow Dance. Bruce Beaver. PoAu-2

I came as a question. The Harvest. Shafiq al-kamali, *tr. by* Sargon Boulus. MAP

I came as a shadow. Nocturne Varial. Lewis Alexander. PoBA; PoNe

I came back at last to my own house. The Substitute for Time. John Koethe. EOEF

I came back to where we killed the deer. Ben Alder 1963-1977. Des Hannigan. PoSH

I came before the water. Mussel Hunter at Rock Harbor. Sylvia Plath. NYBP

I came from England into France. The Journey into France. *Unknown.* CoMu; FaBoBa; OBTV

I Came from Ethiopia. A. Leyeles, *tr. fr.* Yiddish by Benjamin and Barbara Harshav. AYP

I came from Salem City. Unknown. AmFP

I came from somewhere. Poem of the Future Citizen. José Craveirinha, *tr. by* Dorothy Guedes *and* Philippa Rumsey. TTY

I came here with a young girl. The Cemetery at Academy, California. Philip Levine. NaP; NYBP

I came home and found a lion in my living room. The Lion for Real. Allen Ginsberg. GLP; HCAP; RB

I came, I saw, and was undone. The Thraldome. Abraham Cowley. *Fr.* The Mistress. SeCV-1

I came into oxygen. Martha Nelson Speaks. George Bogin. MOWH

I came into the City and none knew me. An Upper Chamber. Frances Bannerman. OBEV

I came one day upon a cream-painted wooden house. At Evans Street. Janet Frame. ATNZ

I came out a winner. O Realm Bejewelled. Forugh Farrokhzad, *tr. by* Jascha Kessler *and* Amin Banani. WPOW

I came out of the hospital like a woman. Adrienne Rich. *Fr.* Contradictions: Tracking Poems, 11. ER

I came then to the city of my brethren. The Shore of Life. Robert Fitzgerald. VGW

I came to a field. Charles Simic. NNaP

I came to a great door. The Beast. Theodore Roethke. SO

I came to pay you a visit, but you were sad and I empty-handed. Manfred Winkler, *tr. by* Bernhard Frank. MHeP

I came to the crowded Inn of Earth. The Inn of Earth. Sara Teasdale. LiTA

I Came to the New World Empty-handed. Hildegarde Hoyt Swift. AmFN

I came to this spring field to pick violets. Akahito. *Fr.* Manyo Shu. FCEI

I came to you. Africa and the Caribbean. Jennifer Brown, *tr. by* Laura Schiff. AIW

I came to you with a greeting. Morning Song. A. A. Fet, *tr. by* Max Eastman. AWP

I came too late to the hills: they were swept bare. The Wilderness. Kathleen Jessie Raine. BoWoP; PoSH; WPE

I came upon a child of God. Woodstock. Joni Mitchell. NIP

I came upon them by a strip of sea. The Net Menders. Brian Vrepont. PoAu-2

I can afford to discriminate. The Discriminator. Vernon Scannell. OxBC

I can almost see. On the Rouge. Raymond Souster. NOBC

I Can Be a Tiger. Mildred Leigh Anderson. RAR

I can bear/ not seeing you. Lady Kasa. *Fr.* Manyo Shu. FCEI

I can change my-/ self more easily. Margaret Atwood. NeAC

I can catch the man. *Unknown, tr. fr. Chippewa Indian by* Frances Densmore. *Fr.* Love Charm Songs. OV

I can clear a beach or swimming pool without. Stereo. Don L. Lee. AmNP

I can feel the tug. Punishment. Seamus Heaney. FaBoPV; InPS; NAEL-2; NoAM; NoP

I Can Fly. Felice Holman. NTCP; RHPC

I can get through a doorway without any key. The Wind. James Reeves. RHPC

I can give myself to her. Yosano Akiko, *tr. by* Kenneth Rexroth *and* Ikuko Atsumi. WPOW

I can hear myslf, my voice that is, in the. Blue Book 42. Steve Benson. IAT

I can hear the wind whistling. 40 Acres and a Mule. Dick Gallup. UL

I can hear you making. Rain. Hone Tuwhare. ATNZ

I can imagine, in some otherworld. Humming-Bird. D. H. Lawrence. CMoP; InPS; LiTB; LiTM; NoAM; RB; SeCePo

I can imagine someone who found. California Hills in August. Dana Gioia. DiPo; InPK

I can indeed afford a pause of peace. The Asbestos-suited Man in Hell. Gordon Challis. ATNZ

I can love both fair and brown. The Indifferent. John Donne. BoLoP; NAEL-1; NAWM-1; SeCV-1; TEP

I can make out the rigging of a schooner. North Haven. Elizabeth Bishop. CAPP; HCAP

"I" Can Never Be a Great Man, An. Stephen Spender. OBMV

I Can No Longer Laugh with Real Joy. Anna Malfaiera, *tr. fr. Italian by* Muriel Kittel. DMI

I can no longer plead for love. Asadullah Khan Ghalib, *tr. by* Ahmed Ali. GoT

I can not. Self Portrait I. Tove Ditlevsen, *tr. by* Ann Freeman. OV

I can not do it alone. Jesus and I. Dan Crawford. BLRP

I can only say I have waited for you. Time of Waiting in Amsterdam. Ingrid Jonker, *tr. by* Jack Cope *and* William Plomer. BoWoP; OV

I can preserve your letters, not your love. Ceremony. Vassar Miller. NePoEA

I can rarely see anyone without fighting him. Others prefer the internal. My Occupations. Henri Michaux, *tr. by* Richard Ellman. RHTwFP

I can remember. I can remember. The Boy Actor. Noel Coward. OxBTC

I can remember it as if it were only yesterday. Ars Poetica. Cees Buddingh', *tr. by* James Brockway. DuIn

I can remember looking cross-lots from. House in Denver. Thomas Hornsby Ferril. AmFN

I can remember our sorrow, I can remember our laughter. Memory. Helen Hoyt. PoLF

I can ride the wildest bronco in the wild and woolly West. The Gol-Darned Wheel. *Unknown.* CowP

I can see a picture. Pictures. F. Ann Elliott. BoTP

I can see by your eyes. Juanita, Wife of Manuelito. Simon J. Ortiz. MAYP

I can see him now. My Grandfather Was a Quantum Physicist. Duane Big Eagle. STE

I can see my self years back at Sunion. Adrienne Rich. *Fr.* Twenty-one Love Poems, VIII. GLP

I can see outside the gold wings without birds. The Clear Air of October. Robert Bly. NaP

I can shake the wild hay, and wet seed sticks to my hand. Stalks of Wild Hay. H. L. Davis. PoA

I can sing of myself a true song. *Unknown, tr. fr. Anglo-Saxon by* L. Iddings. *Fr.* The Seafarer, Pt. I. PoRA

I carry it on my keychain, which itself. The Ring. Diane Wakoski. PoA

"I carry my death within me." My Death. A. J. M. Smith. OBCV

I carry the ground-hog along by the tail. The Hunter. Raymond Souster. NOBC

I carry three passengers on a nightly journey. The Trip. Emmett Jarrett. NeAC

I carry you in a glass jar. The Doll. Gregory Orr. AmPA

I carry your heart with me (I carry it in). E. E. Cummings. TAP; UnAS

I carve my first head. Then I carve another. Hallowe'en 1971. Michael Dennis Browne. AmPA

I cast from me the medications. Loneliness. Franz Werfel, tr. by Edith Abercrombie Snow. TrJP

I catch myself drifting. Harbor. Nancy Price. IHMS

I catch the movement of his lips. Marina Tsvetayeva, tr. fr. Russian by Paul Schmidt. Fr. The Daughter of Jairus, V. BoWoP

I Catcha da Plenty of Feesh. Unknown. AS

I Caught a Fish ("I caught a little fish one day"). Bertram Murray. OnUR

I caught a tremendous fish. The Fish. Elizabeth Bishop. ASP; CAPP; FaBoWP; GoJo; HAP; HeIP; HoPM; InPK; LiTM; MoAB; MoAmPo; MoP; MOS; NAAL-2; NoAM; NOBA; NoP; NU; OPOP; PoE; RB; TrGrPo; WeW

I caught the American bull. Buffalo. Henry Dumas. PoBA

I caught this morning morning's minion. The Windhover. Gerard Manley Hopkins. ACP; BrPo; CMoP; EaLo; EBVV; GTBS-P; HAP; InPK; InPS; InVP; InvP; LiTB; LiTM; MoAB; MoBrPo; MoP; NAEL-2; NoAM; NOBE; NOBVV; NoP; OAEL-2; OBNC; PBBP; PoE; PoEL-5; PoRA; PPP; PrIm; RB; SCV; TEP; TOF; UnPo; WeW

I caught you grazing on my knee. To a Flea in a Glass of Water. Desmond A. Greig. PeSA

I cease not from desire till my desire. Hafiz, tr. fr. Persian by Gertrude Lowthian Bell. Fr. Odes, IX. AWP

I celebrate myself, and sing myself. Walt Whitman. Fr. Song of Myself, I. AA; NAWM-2; NoAM; NoP; PoE (Myself.) BLPL; FaBoBe

I celebrate Rhegion, Italy's tip, licked by. Unknown, tr. by Peter Jay. PeHV

I celebrate the personality of Jack! Jack and Jill. Charles Battell Loomis. BXAP

I certainly have lost something. Kenneth Koch. Fr. Days and Nights, V. NoAM

I chanced to see one day. Mohammad Taqi Mir, tr. by Ahmed Ali. GoT

I chanced upon a new book yesterday. To Edward Fitzgerald. Robert Browning. NAEL-2; OxBSP; TW

I chanced upon an early walk to spy. The Orchard and the Heath. George Meredith. OBNC

I, Chang P'ing-tzu, had traversed the Nine Wilds and seen their wonders. The Bones of Chuang Tzu. Chang Heng, tr. by Arthur Waley. AWP

I change, and so do women too. Written on a Looking-Glass. Unknown. FaBoEE

I changed a grown man's clothes on a stripped ward. In a Building Named for a Governor. Christopher L. Dornin. CRP

I charge you, lady young and fair. He Charges Her to Lay Aside Her Weapons. Pierce Ferriter, tr. by Earl of Longford. AnIL

I charge you, O winds of the West, O. Mathilde Blind. Fr. Love in Exile. TrJP

I charm thy life. Kehama's Curse. Robert Southey. Fr. The Curse of Kehama. OBNC

I chastise the bones of an old villain of a thousand years ago. Rai San'yo, tr. fr. Chinese by Burton Watson. Fr. Random Thoughts on the Writing of History, II. JLIC-2

I checked/ three thousand haiku. Masaoka Shiki, tr. fr. Japanese by Burton Watson. Fr. Thirty-nine Haiku. FCEI

I cherished you, my darling. Lady Otomo no Sakanoe. Fr. Manyo Shu. Ma

I Ching tells me t'ai, the sign of peace, The. Winter in Jerusalem. James Keir Baxter. ATNZ

I choose not to walk among ghosts. Antigone VI. Herbert Martin. PoBA

I chopped down the house that you had been saving to live in next summer. Variations on a Theme by William Carlos Williams. Kenneth Koch. BXAP; CAPP; FF; NBLV; NIP; NoAM; NoP; PoM

I chose the blonde from the chemist's, thirty-six. Happening at Sordid Creek. Peter Porter. NoAM

I chose the road myself, I know it now precisely. Rondeau of My Life's Walk. A. Leyeles, tr. by Benjamin and Barbara Harshav. AYP

I circled on leather paws. The Return. Theodore Roethke. PoA

I clasp in the hot pit and bed. Memorial Couplets for the Dying Ego. George Barker. EBEV

"I climb a lofty hill and gaze toward the distant sea." Viewing the Sea from the Li-shuo Pavilion. Wang Shih-chen, tr. by Daniel Bryant. WFTU

I Climb That Barren Ridge. Unknown, tr. fr. Chinese by Burton Watson. CoBCP

I climb that wooded hill. Unknown, tr. fr. Chinese by Arthur Waley. BoS

I climb the Barra half-hill. View. Robin Munro. PoSH

I climb the black rock mountain. Where Mountain Lion Lay [or Laid] Down with Deer. Leslie Marmon Silko. STE; VoR; WPOW

I climb the hill: from end to end. Tennyson. Fr. In Memoriam A. H. H., C. PoEL-5

I climb the tower of Ste. Anne des Monts. The Bell of Ste. Anne Des Monts. Leo Cox. CaP

I climb those northern hills. Unknown, tr. fr. Chinese by Arthur Waley. BoS

I climb to the tower-top and lean upon broken stone. I See Phantoms of Hatred and of the Heart's Fullness and of the Coming Emptiness. W. B. Yeats. Fr. Meditations in Time of Civil War, VII. LiTB

I climb'd a hill, whose Summit crown'd with wood. An Essay on the Fleet Riding in the Downes. "J. D." CoMu

I climb'd [or climbed] the dark brow of the mighty Hellvellyn. Hellvellyn. Sir Walter Scott. FM; TEP

I climbed a [or the] hill as light fell short. The Song of Honour. Ralph Hodgson. LiTB; MoBrPo

I climbed down to the stream and looked back. To Raise a Chimney. Gary Young. MOWH

I climbed into the chinaberry. The Evening of Ants. Gary Soto. NPGG

I climbed the dark brow of the mighty Hellvellyn. See I climb'd the dark brow of the mighty Hellvellyn.

I climbed the hill as light fell short. The Song of Honor [or Honour]. Ralph Hodgson. LiTB; MoBrPo

I climbed the stair in Antwerp church. Antwerp and Bruges. Dante Gabriel Rossetti. OBTV

I climbed through woods in the hour-before-dawn dark. The Horses. Ted Hughes. NoAM

I climbed towards you on a ray of moonlight. Fantasy under the Moon. Emmanuel Boundzekei-Dongala, tr. by Gerald Moore and Ulli Beier. TTY

I cling and swing. The Fifteen Acres. James Stephens. BoTP

I clipped and the brown petals. Boundaries. Roberta Spear. MAYP

I close my eyes, the world recedes. Kiss ("I close my eyes, the world recedes"). Tanikawa Shuntaro, tr. by Hiroaki Sato. FCEI

I close the book in my hands. Chang Yü, tr. fr. Chinese by Jonathan Chaves. Fr. Paintings. CoBLCP

I closed my book to listen. Church Bells. Clara Ann Thompson. CBWP-2

I closed my ears with stinging bugs. Elegy for a Puritan Conscience. Alan Dugan. CAPP; SM

I closed my eyes. Phantoms. Ben-Zion Tomer, tr. by Bernhard Frank. MHeP

I closed my eyes as I sat in the jet. Day Flight. Jack Davis. CBAP

I Closed My Eyes To-Day and Saw. William Force Stead. OBMV

I Closed My Shutters Fast Last Night. Georgia Douglas Johnson. PoNe

I come/ from a long line. My Elbow Ancestry. Larry Mollin. NeAC

I come/ to the White Painted Woman. Puberty Rite Dance Song (Traditional). Unknown, tr. by Willis Barnstone. BoWoP

I come alone. To surprise you. Visit. James Welch. AmPA

I come among the peoples like a shadow. Hunger. Laurence Binyon. OxBTC

I come back to the cottage in. Only Years. Kenneth Rexroth. TAP

I come back to the geography of it. Maximus, to Gloucester, Letter 27. Charles Olson. Fr. The Maximus Poems. NOBA; PoE

I come dis night to sing an' pray. Oh, Yes! Oh, Yes! Wait 'til I Git on My Robe. Unknown. BoAN-2

I come from a wet land. For My Brother and Sister Southwestern Indian Poets. Geary Hobson. STE

I come from Alabama. Oh! [or O] Susanna. Stephen Collins Foster. AnAmPo; FaFP; OBAL

I come from Bohem, yet no news I bring. John Taylor. Fr. Taylor's Travels from London to Prague. OBTV

I come from far away. I have forgotten my country. Foreign Woman. Rosario Castellanos, tr. by J. M. Cohen. WPOW

I come from haunts of coot and hern. The Brook. Tennyson. Fr. Brook, The; an Idyl. BoNaP; BoTP; FaBV; FaPON; GN; GoJo (Brook's Song, The.) FaBoBe; FaFP

I come from nothing, but from where. A Song of Derivations. Alice Meynell. WGRP

I come from Salem County. Cowboy Song. Charles Causley. NePoEA; PoRA

I come from the city of Boston. Boston. John Collins Bossidy; *also at. to* Samuel C. Bushnell. FaBoCo; FaBoEE; NBLV; OBAL; OxBoLi. *See also* And this is good old Boston.

I come from the nigger yard of yesterday. Martin Carter. *Fr.* I Come from the Nigger Yard. PBCV

I come home from you through the early light of spring. Adrienne Rich. *Fr.* Twenty-one Love Poems, IV. BoWoP; GLP

I come more softly than a bird. Snow. Mary Austin. *Fr.* Rhyming Riddles. BoNaP; GrPl

I come of a mighty race. Hebrews. James Oppenheim. TrJP

I come out of a California orange grove. Smudging. Diane Wakoski. AmPA; PrIm

I come to Bury Caesar. Sydney Justin Harris. PoA

I Come to Supplicate. Simeon ben Isaac ben Abun of Mainz, *tr. fr. Hebrew* by Nina Davis Salaman. TrJP

I come to the bench in front of the loom. The Weaver. Giovanni Pascoli, *tr. by* E. J. Scovell. PFI

I come to the depths of stillness between heaven and earth to hear. It Is the Silence. Ya'akov Beser, *tr. by* Bernhard Frank. MHeP

I come to thee, O God long since forgot. Before the Statue of Apollo. Saul Tchernichowsky, *tr. by* L. V. Snowman. TrJP

I come to work as well as play. The March Wind. *Unknown.* RHPC

I come to you, Vulcan, to give back the laugh. The Futurist Aviator Speaks to His Father, Vulcan. Filippo Tommaso Marinetti, *tr. by* Felix Stefanile. PFI

I come to you with the vertigoes of the source. Yvonne Caroutch, *tr. fr. French by* David Cloutier. BoWoP

I command that the world be conquered. The Story of the World. Moyshe-Leyb Halpern, *tr. by* Benjamin *and* Barbara Harshav *and* Kathryn Helle. AYP

I confront you, oh life without sheaves. Time. Juana de Ibarbourou, *tr. by* Perry Higman. LPSS

I Conquer the World with Words. Nizar Qabbani, *tr. fr. Arabic by* Diana Der Hovanessian *and* Lena Jayyusi. MAP

I, Conscience, know this Mother-Wit me it taught. The Age of Reason. William Langland. *Fr.* The Vision of Piers Plowman. NOCV

I Consider the Tree. Martin Buber, *tr. fr. German by* Howard Schwartz. VWA

I cough and am still alone. Ozaki Hosai, *tr. fr. Japanese by* Hiroaki Sato. *Fr.* One Hundred Haiku in Free Form. FCEI

I could always rely on the continuity. The Servant in Literature. Marjorie Welish. UL

I could bring you jewels—had I a mind to. Emily Dickinson. TAP

I could divide a leaf. Propositions. Phyllis Webb. MoCV

I could do nothing: nothing. Do you. The Child Taken from the Mother. Minnie Bruce Pratt. GLP

I could draw its map by heart. Amor Loci. W. H. Auden. NOCV

I could have a job, but am too lazy to choose it. Lazy Man's Song. Po Chü-i, *tr. by* Arthur Waley. OBVE

I could have painted pictures like that youth's. Pictor Ignotus. Robert Browning. CTC; TEP

I could have said makes love. Behind That Wall My Roommate Fucks His Girl. Geof Hewitt. NeAC

I could have stemmed misfortune's tide. The Wife. Anna Peyre Dinnies. AA

I could have wept and howled. Song of the Unloved. *Unknown, tr. by* Jack Cope *and* Dan Kunene. PeSA

I could have written, "I left." Writing. Anne French. ATNZ

I could kill you right now. Lobo. Charles Lillard. NOBC

I could look at. Joy. Robert Creeley. PPP

I could love her with a love so warm. The World Is a Mighty Ogre. Fenton Johnson. AmNP

I could never dance until I met Rose at a party where. The Truth Made Breakfast. Jeffrey Miller. UL

I could not choose but gaze; a fascination. Shelley. *Fr.* The Revolt of Islam, I. ChER

I could not dig: I dared not rob. A Dead Statesman. Kipling. *Fr.* Epitaphs of the War, 1914–1918. FaBoEE; NBLV

I could not eat much. Strangely Insane. Michael Burkard. NAmP

I could not, ever and anon, forbear. The Solitary. Wordsworth. *Fr.* The Excursion, II. EnRP

I could not hope/ to touch the sky. Sappho, *tr. fr. Greek by* Willis Barnstone. BoWoP

I could not look on Death, which being known. The Coward. Kipling. *Fr.* Epitaphs of the War, 1914–1918. FaBoEE; FaBoTw

I could not name a single blessing. Neither Shadow of Turning. Jack R. Clemo. NOCV

I could not save the heart. Mohammad Taqi Mir, *tr. by* Ahmed Ali. GoT

I could not see You with my eyes. Sight and Insight. Eleanor Slater. TrPWD

I could not sleep/ For the sea was so smooth. Walrus Hunting. Aua. WTO

I could not sleep for thinking of the sky. John Masefield. *Fr.* Lollingdon Downs, V. LiTM

I Could Not though I Would. George Gascoigne. PoEL-1

I could replace. Earth Psalm. Denise Levertov. PPP

I could resign that eye of blue. To Cloe. Martial, *tr. by* Thomas Moore. AWP; NBLV

I could say. Hilda Doolittle ("H. D."). *Fr.* Sigil, XIII. AnAn

I could say it's the happiest period of my life. The Ongoing Story. John Ashbery. HCAP

I could say that. Where Late the Sweet Birds Sang. William D. Crago. TSM

I could take the Harlem night. Juke Box Love Song. Langston Hughes. GrPl; IDB; PoBA; TTTS

I could wish to be dead! The Tragic Mary Queen of Scots, II. "Michael Field." OBMV

I couldn't make him stay! Paying Homage at the Golden Gate. Sun Kuang-hsien, *tr. by* Lois Fusek. ATF

I couldn't touch a stop and turn a screw. Thirty Bob a Week. John Davidson. EBEV; EBVV; FaBoPV; FaBoTw; FaFP; LiTB; NOBE; NOBVV; OAEL-2; OBNC; OxBS; OxBTC

I couldn't wait. My childhood angered me. The Wise Child. Edward Lucie-Smith. PBCV

I count black-lipped. Come Back Blues. Michael S. Harper. PoBA

I count my blessings. Sheep. Rochelle Kraut. UL

I Count My Time by Times That I Meet Thee. Richard Watson Gilder. AA

I, country-born an' bred, know where to find. Spring. James Russell Lowell. *Fr.* The Biglow Papers: 2d Series, No. VI.

I cover all my faults. Ash. Kim Hyun-sung, *tr. by* Koh Chang-soo. ACKP

I crave an ampler, worthier sphere. Anno 1829. Heine, *tr. by* Charles Stuart Calverley. AWP; OBVE

I crave, dear Lord. Ike Walton's Prayer. James Whitcomb Riley. AA

I craved for flash of eye and sword. Dreams. Israel Zangwill. TrJP

I crawl up the couch leg feeling. Whose Scene? Ruth Stone. BoWoP

I crept at night out through the moonlit garden. Intimate Melodies. Leyb Naydus, *tr. by* Naomi Wolf. PeBMYV

I cried unto God with my voice, even unto God with my voice. Psalm LXXVII ("I cried unto God with my voice. "). Bible, *O.T. Fr.* Psalms. AWP

"Waters saw thee, O God, The." *Fr.* 16-19. MOS

I crisscross my feelings with a view. Anne Waldman. UL

I cross a stream, cross another stream. Seeking out Hermit Hu. Kao Ch'i, *tr. by* Jonathan Chaves. CoBLCP

I cross'd pynot [*or* crossed the pynot], an't' pynot cross'd me. Against the Magpie. *Unknown.* GBP; PBBP

I crossed over the county line. Crossing the County Line. Elizabeth Randall-Mills. GoYe

I crossed the spring mountains. Tsurayuki, *tr. fr. Chinese by* Geoffrey Bownas *and* Anthony Thwaite. PeBJV

I crouch over my radio. Speech. Henry Taylor. MAT; NBLV

I cry I cry. No Categories! Stevie Smith. NoP

I, Cry, Love! Love! Theodore Roethke. LCAP

I cry out war to those who spend their utmost. Stormy Nights. Robert Louis Stevenson. BrPo

I Cry to You as I Pass Your Windows. Christopher John Brennan. *Fr.* The Wanderer. PoAu-1

I cry your mercy—pity—love!—aye, love! To Fanny. Keats. BoLoP; EBEV; EnRP; PPP; Son; TrGrPo

I curse my bearing, childhood, youth. J. M. Synge. FaBoEE

I cut in two/ A long November night. Hwang Chin-i, *tr. by* Peter H. Lee. PBWP

I cut the deck. A Valentine for Ben Franklin Who Drives a Truck in California. Diane Wakoski. NoAM

I dance on all the mountains. This Poem is for Deer. Gary Snyder. *Fr.* Myths and Texts: Hunting, VIII. NaP; NOBA

("Missed a last shot.") NoBA; NU

I dance on your paper. Jack o' the Inkpot. Algernon Blackwood. BoTP

I Danced before I Had Two Feet. Max Dunn. PoAu-2

I danced in the morning. Lord of the Dance. Sydney Carter. OBET

I Danced to the Rumble of the Drum. Elevena Burbank. AiP

I dare not ask a kiss. To Electra. Robert Herrick. BLPL; CaPo; HoPM; OBEV; OBS; SeCV-1

I Dare Not Pray to Thee. Maurice Baring. TrPWD

I dare not think that thou art by, to stand. Infinity. Philip Henry Savage. AA

I daresay that's the custom in your church. Bagman O'Reilly's Curse. Les A. Murray. TW

I, dark in light, exposed. Milton. *Fr.* Samson Agonistes: The Blindness of Samson, 5 *ll.*. TrGrPo

I dedicate this poem. Daughters. Astra. BrRo

I Dedicate to You. Jutta Schutting, *tr. fr. German by* Beth Bjorklund. CoAuP

I delight in the prime of a boy of twelve. Strato, *tr. by* Thomas Meyer. PeHV

I delight in this naethingness. De Profundis. "Hugh MacDiarmid." SeCePo

I deliver the jewel. Lady Otomo no Sakanoe. *Fr.* Manyo Shu. Ma

"I delivered." *Unknown, tr. fr. Japanese by* Geoffrey Bownas *and* Anthony Thwaite. PeBJV

I demand a thatched house. The Poet's Request. *Unknown, tr. by* John Montague. BIrV

I descended in the evening to the fountain. Saul's Song of Love. Saul Tchernichowsky, *tr. by* Robert Friend. VWA

I desire that my body be. When I Am Dead. George MacBeth. OxBTC

I desired to talk. The Political Prisoner. Mazisi Kunene. WMBCH

I despise my friends more than you. To an Enemy. Maxwell Bodenheim. TrJP

I detected the memory of her voice as it alit and perched. Route. Philippe Soupault, *tr. by* Michael Benedikt. POS

I did but look and love awhile. The Enchantment. Thomas Otway. OBEV

I did but prompt the age to quit their clogs. On the Detraction Which Followed upon My Writing Certain Treatises. Milton. FaBoPV; NoP

(On the same.) Son

I did not cry at all. Song of the Captured Woman. James Devaney. PoAu-1

I did not fall from the sky. The Women of Dan Dance with Swords in Their Hands to Mark the Time When They Were Warriors. Audre Lorde. ER; NAAL-2; NoAM

I did not grow up among paintings. Nostalgia. Bin Ramke. MT

I did not know she'd take it so. Under the Mistletoe. Countee Cullen. PChr

I Did Not Know the Truth of Growing Trees. Delmore Schwartz. LiTM

I did not know where you kept your heart. A "Case of Assault." Lydia Stephanou. BoWoP, *tr. by* Kimon Friar

I did not know why I liked it, all the waiting. Softball Dreams. Karen Kevorkian. ASP

I did not know you. Celan. Anthony Barnett. VWA

I did not live until this time. To My Excellent Lucasia, on Our Friendship. Katherine Philips. MeLP; OBS; PeHV; WPE; WPOW

I Did Not Lose My Heart in Summer's Even. A. E. Housman. LiTM

I did not meet her. Tangi. Hone Tuwhare. ATNZ

I did not see the frigate Constitution. Resurrection. Richard Palmer Blackmur. PoA

I did not think that I should find them there. The Clerks. E. A. Robinson. AA; AnAmPo; MoAB; MoAmPo; NAAL-2; PoEL-5

I did not want to be old Mr. Uncle Dog; the Poet at 9. Robert Sward. CoAP; PrIm; VGW

I did not want to grow, but quick-fingered memories. The Tower. Dan Pagis, *tr. by* Stephen Mitchell. VWA

I did see the moth go up. Mohammad Taqi Mir, *tr. by* Ahmed Ali. GoT

I didn't believe. The Bridge. Leopold Staff, *tr. by* Czeslaw Milosz. PwPP

I didn't even make. I've Never Written a Baseball Poem. Elisavietta Ritchie. ASP

I Didn't Find Light by Accident. Hayyim Nahman Bialik, *tr. fr. Hebrew by* Ruth Nevo. VWA

I didn't get much sleep last night. Underwear. Lawrence Ferlinghetti. OBAL

I didn't give her a goodbye kiss. Grandmother Grace. Ronald Wallace. GOYP; SM

I Didn't Know My Soul. Avraham Ben-Yitzhak, *tr. fr. Hebrew by* A. C. Jacobs. VWA

I didn't know where the temple was. Visiting the Temple of Accumulated Fragrance. Wang Wei, *tr. by* Burton Watson. CoBCP

I didn't make you know how glad I was. A Servant to Servants. Robert Frost. CMoP; NAAL-2

I didn't mean/ to recall the past. Sanetomo, *tr. fr. Japanese by* Burton Watson. *Fr.* Twenty-four Tanka. FCEI

I didn't take/ a good look at him. *Unknown, tr. fr. Japanese. Fr.* Manyo Shu. FCEI

I didnt thing I'd. I Was Surprised to Find Myself Out Here & Acting like a Crow. *Unknown, tr. by* Jerome Rothenberg *and* Johnny John. STP

I didn't want this, not. Marina Tsvetayeva, *tr. fr. Russian by* Elaine Feinstein *and* Angela Livingstone. *Fr.* Poem of the End. OBVE

I die/ If I but spy. Upon Julia. Ernest Radford. BXAP

I die a strange death. . . Life does not kill me. The Ineffable. Delmira Agustini, *tr. by* Kate Flores. DMH

I die, and yet not dies in me. Dhu 'L-nun, *tr. fr. Persian by* A. J. Arberry. TOF

I Die because I Do Not Die. St. Theresa of Avila, *tr. fr. Spanish by* E. Allison Peers. TOF

I die; but when the grave shall press. Emily Brontë. TEP

I die for Your holy word without regret. Antonio Enriquez Gomez. TrJP

I died as mineral and became a plant. Jalal ed-Din Rumi, *tr. by* R. A. Nicholson. TOF

I died at the first blow and was buried. *See* I died with the first blow. . .

I died for beauty—but was scarce. Emily Dickinson. AnAmPo; AWP; BLPL; BoWoP; FaFP; LiTA; LiTM; MoAB; MoAmPo; NAAL-2; NAWM-2; NOBA; NoP

I died; they wrapped me in a shroud. A Dream of Death. "Owen Innsley." AA

I Died True. Beaumont *and* Fletcher. *See* The Maid's Tragedy: Aspatia's Song.

I died with [or at] the first blow and was buried. Autobiography. Dan Pagis. IP, *tr. by* Warren Bargad *and* Stanley F. Chyet; MHep, *tr. by* Bernard Frank; VWA, *tr. by* Robert Friend

I dig in the soft earth all. The Negatives. Philip Levine. NePoEA-2

I diligently concoct my elixir in a crucible of Himalayan bamboo. Wen T'ing-shih, *tr. fr. Chinese by* Timothy C. Wong. *Fr.* Miscellaneous Verses on Living in the Mountains, I. WFTU

I dined with a friend in the East, one day. The Sunbeam. *Unknown.* NA

I dined with Demetrius last night. Automedon. PeHV

I dip with my hands. Tsurayuki, *tr. fr. Japanese by* Burton Watson. *Fr.* Kokin Shu. FCEI

I disapprove even of eloquent/ Myrtis. Korinna, *tr. fr. Greek by* Richmond Lattimore. WPOW

I discover you in bits and pieces. Odette Aslan, *tr. by* Carol Cosman. OV

I Discuss the Past and Not the Present, *sel.* Chin Nung, *tr. fr. Chinese by* Jonathan Chaves.
"Who bought a mountain and became a hermit there?." CoBLCP

I do affirm that thou hast saved the race. Delay. C. F. Bates. AA

I do be thinking God must laugh. Boys. Winifred M. Letts. TIRV

I Do But Ask That You Be Always Fair. Edna St. Vincent Millay. Son

I do confess, in many a sigh. Lying. Thomas Moore. FiBHP

I do confess thou'rt smooth and fair. To His Forsaken Mistress. Sir Robert Ayton. ElL; ErPo; OBEV; OBS; SeCePo

(Inconstancy Reproved.) GBL

I Do Love My Charlie So. Zelda Sayre Fitzgerald. AiP

I do not ask for love, ah! no. Lethe. Georgia Douglas Johnson. CDC

I do not ask—for you are fair. The Complaisant Swain. Ovid, *tr. fr. Latin by* F. A. Wright. *Fr.* Amores, III, 14. AWP

I do not ask, Oh Lord, that life may be. Per Pacem ad Lucem. Adelaide Anne Procter. TrPWD

I do not ask that God will keep all storms away. The All-sufficient Christ. Bernice W. Lubke. BLRP

I Do Not Ask Thee, Lord. *Unknown.* BLRP

I do not ask Thee, Lord, for outward sign. Jesus Himself. Henry Burton. BLRP

I do not ask Thee straightway to appear. Supplication. Edith Lovejoy Pierce. TrPWD

I do not believe that Heaven and Hell are in different places. No Discharge. Arthur Waley. OBD

I do not believe this room. A Game of Glass. Alastair Reid. NePoEA

I do not cherish memories. Sign on My Door Jamb. Agnes Gergely, *tr. by* Thomas Land. MHuP

I do not complain. Teika, *tr. fr. Japanese by* Steven D. Carter. WFTW

I do not count the hours I spend. Waldeinsamkeit. Emerson. NOBA; WGRP

I do not dream of Sussex downs. Home Thoughts. Denis Glover. PeNZ

I do not fear to lay my body down. Exile from God. John Hall Wheelock. WGRP

I do not fear to tread the path that those I love long since have trod. My Creed. Jeanette Leonard Gilder. WGRP

I do not feel the peace of the saints. A Bird in the Hand. Vassar Miller. CRP

I do not go, my dear, to storm. On Going to the Wars. Earle Birney. WaP

I do not grudge them: Lord, I do not grudge. The Mother. Padraic Pearse. TIRV

I do not hear the words. The Bone Step-Women. Brenda Marie Osbey. ER

I do not know/ In what strange far off earth. Holocaust 1944. Anne Ranasinghe. VWA

I don't know what the Bible says.　As Long as You're Happy.　Jack Myers.　NAmP

I don't know what you think you're doing.　To an Adolescent Weeping Willow.　Marvin Bell.　DiL

I don't know when.　Masaoka Shiki, tr. fr. Japanese by Burton Watson.　Fr. Fifteen Haiku.　FCEI

I don't know whether the gray deer knows.　The Deer.　Asya, tr. by Gabriel Preil and Howard Schwartz.　VWA

I don't know who it is.　The Lovely Étan.　Unknown.　NOIV

I don't know who they are.　The Pointed People.　Rachel Field.　FaPON; WSC

I don't know why the horned lizard wants to live.　Justification of the Horned Lizard.　Pattiann Rogers.　NAmP

I don't know why you tell me I'm drunk.　Toxaoci, tr. by James Koller.　STP

I Don't Let the Girls Worry My Mind.　Unknown.　AmFP

I don't like Agnes Snaggletooth.　Agnes Snaggletooth.　X. J. Kennedy.　ILY

I Don't Like Beetles.　Rose Fyleman.　OxBChV

I Don't Like No Railroad Man.　Unknown.　AS, with music

"I don't like the look of little Fan, mother."　Little Fan.　James Reeves.　Mes; SO

I Don't Like You.　Kit Wright.　OnUR

I don't look back: God knows the fruitless efforts.　We See Jesus.　Annie Johnson Flint.　BLRP

I don't mind eels.　The Eel.　Ogden Nash.　FaBV; FaPON; NTCP

I don't much recommend IH 35 for scenic vistas.　Charley's Green Guide.　Michael Holstein.　SoTCo

I don't operate often. When I do.　John Berryman.　Fr. Dream Songs.　NaP

I don't pretend to drink.　A Welcome for Etheridge.　James Cunningham.　JB

I Don't Remember Anything of Then.　Frank O'Hara.　Fr. Ode to Michael Goldberg's Birth and Other Births.　NAs; NeAP

I don't remember exactly when Budberg died.　A Magic Mountain.　Czeslaw Milosz, tr. by Lillian Vallee.　AnAn

I don't remember the name of the story.　The Mystery of the Caves.　Michael Waters.　GeTw; MAYP

I don't see.　A Witness.　Helga Osswald, tr. by Susan L. Cocalis.　DMG

I don't see my mother dancing.　Legacy.　Márton Kalász, tr. by Jascha Kessler.　FOC; MHuP

I don't see you these days.　In This Shanty Shebeen without You.　Richard Augustine Chima.　WMBCH

I don't sleep. All night.　Mirabai, tr. fr. Hindi by Willis Barnstone and Usha Nilsson.　BoWoP

I don't take things as they come, you weren't.　Poème Antipoème.　Elio Pagliarani, tr. by Lawrence R. Smith.　NItP

I don't think I'm being manipulated.　That Act.　Tanikawa Shuntaro, tr. by Hiroaki Sato.　FCEI

I don't think it important.　The Beast Section.　Welton Smith.　PoBA

I don't think that I believe in "gay life."　Sonnet No. 22.　Mark Ameen.　GLP

I don't think you are like everyone else.　In Reply Lady Izumi, tr. fr. Japanese by Hiroaki Sato.　Fr. Fifty-one Tanka.　FCEI

I don't trust my impressions.　Alfred Kolleritsch, tr. by Beth Bjorklund.　CoAuP

I don't understand by what perversity.　A Shelf Is a Ledge.　Gregory Orr.　BLA

I don't understand it myself.　Too Lazy to Write Poetry.　Chu Yün-ming, tr. by Jonathan Chaves.　CoBLCP

I Don't Want Any More Visitors.　Ingrid Jonker, tr. fr. Afrikaans by Ingrid Jonker.　PeSA

I Don't Want to Be a Gambler.　Unknown.　AS

I don't want to be a nun.　Unknown, tr. fr. Spanish by Willis Barnstone.　BoWoP

I don't want to be sheltered here.　For the Yiddish Singers in the Lakewood Hotels of My Childhood.　Harvey Shapiro.　VWA

I don't want to boast.　Vindication.　Daniil Kharms, tr. by George Gibian.　FaBoNo

I don't want to come, yet suddenly I'm here.　Delirium: Jesting at Illness.　Yüan Mei, tr. by J. P. Seaton.　WFTU

I don't want to hear you beg.　Isn't It Funny?　Essex Hemphill.　GLP

I don't want to pay down the last penny of my soul.　Osip Mandelstam, tr. by W. S. Merwin and Clarence Brown.　AnAn

I Don't Want to See Black But.　Amir Gilboa, tr. fr. Hebrew by Bernhard Frank.　MHeP

"I don't want to take a beautiful bud," said the god.　Yosano Akiko, tr. fr. Japanese by Hiroaki Sato.　Fr. Thirty-nine Tanka.　FCEI

I don't want your greenback dollar.　The Greenback Dollar.　Unknown.　AmFP

I Doubt a Lovely Thing Is Dead.　Neil Tracy.　CaP

I doubt if ten men in all Tilbury Town.　E. A. Robinson.　Fr. Captain Craig.　PoEL-5

I doubt if the wind in your boots.　Stiles.　John Pudney.　NYBP

I doubt if you knew.　The Rescue.　John Logan.　CoAP; NYBP

I doubt not God is good, well meaning, kind.　Yet Do I Marvel.　Countee Cullen.　AmNP; BANP; BPo; CDC; FF; IDB; NAAL-2; NoAM; PoBA; PoNe; Son; TAP; TTY

I doubt that you remember her—except.　Secrets.　Robert Pack.　MOWH

I drag a boat over the ocean.　Lal Ded, tr. fr. Kashmiri by Willis Barnstone.　BoWoP

I drag my hope along with my bag of nails.　The Phantom Skin.　René Daumal, tr. by Michael Benedikt.　POS

I drag my shirt across the floor.　Eager Street.　Kendra Kopelke.　AiP

I dragged my feet through desert gloom.　The Prophet.　Pushkin, tr. by Babette Deutsch.　WGRP

I drank at every vine.　Feast.　Edna St. Vincent Millay.　AnAmPo

I drank cool water from the fountain.　The Raisin.　James Wright.　TAP

I drank firmly.　His Father's Hands.　Thomas Kinsella.　FaBCIP; PoE

I drank up two glasses of hot tea and milk.　Tuesday.　Zishe Landau, tr. by Ruth Whitman.　VWA

I drank yesterday, I drink today.　Wakayama Bokusui, tr. fr. Japanese by Hiroaki Sato.　Fr. Forty-four Tanka.　FCEI

I draw a deep breath.　Remembering.　Akjartoq.　WTO

I draw the breath of Old Japan.　The Professor in Nirvana.　Osman Edwards.　Fr. Residential Rhymes, IV.　OBTV

I dreaded that first robin, so.　Emily Dickinson.　AmPP; HAP; MoAmPo; NAAL-1

I Dream.　Jacques Roubaud, tr. fr. French by Robert Kelly.　RHTwFP

I Dream a World.　Langston Hughes.　AmNP

I dream I am flying above the city.　The Question.　David Ignatow.　CAPP

I Dream I'm the Death of Orpheus.　Adrienne Rich.　NMM

I dream my love goes riding out.　Song for a Dancer.　Kenneth Rexroth.　TAP

I dream now of green places.　In the Third Year of War.　Henry Treece.　WaP

I dream of a headless man.　Green Martyrs.　Richard Murphy.　Fr. The Battle of Aughrim.　NOIV

I dream of a red-rose tree.　Women and Roses.　Robert Browning.　NAEL-2

I dream of a vase of humble and simple clay.　The Vase.　Gabriela Mistral, tr. by Perry Higman.　LPSS

I dream of Jeanie with the light brown hair.　Jeanie with the Light Brown Hair.　Stephen Collins Foster.　AnAmPo; FaFP

I dream of journeys repeatedly.　The Far Field.　Theodore Roethke.　NAAL-2; NoAM; NoP; PrIm

I dream of Serenity.　I'm a Dreamer.　Kattie M. Cumbo.　BlSi

I dream of the birth of the child.　Creation of the Child.　Susan Litwack.　VWA

I dream of the finger of the statue.　Felix Pollak.　Fr. The Finger, II.　TSM

I Dream You.　Jules Supervielle, tr. fr. French by James Kirkup.　RHTwFP

I dream'd I walk'd in raptures high.　Thomas Baker.　Fr. The Steam Engine; or, The Power of the Flame.　BXAP

I dream'd that I walk'd in Italy.　Going Back Again.　"Owen Meredith."　FiBHP

(Check to Song.)　FaBoCo

I dream'd this mortal part of mine.　See I dreamed this mortal part of mine.

I dream'd we both were in bed.　See I dreamed we both were in bed.

I dreamed a dream: I dreamt that I espied.　Arthur Hugh Clough.　NOBVV

I dreamed a dream last night, when all was still.　Reality.　Angela Morgan.　WGRP

I dreamed a dream next Tuesday week.　My Dream.　Unknown.　NA

I dreamed [or dreamt] a dream the other night.　Lowlands.　Unknown.　ChTr; OxBoLi

I dreamed a dream the other night, when everything was still.　Prospecting Dream.　Unknown.　AmFP

I dreamed a dreary dream this night.　The Braes of Yarrow.　Unknown.　ESPB; OxBB

I dreamed all my fortitude screamed.　Letter across Doubt and Distance.　M. Carl Holman.　AmNP; PoNe

I dreamed I called you on the telephone.　For the Dead.　Adrienne Rich.　AnAn; NAAL-2

I dreamed I held/ A sword against my flesh.　Lady Kasa, tr. fr. Japanese by Kenneth Rexroth.　BoWoP; WPOW

I dreamed I lay in a little gray boat.　Waking.　Katharine Pyle.　OBCA

I Dreamed I Moved among the Elysian Fields.　Edna St. Vincent Millay.　NoP

I dreamed I saw a little brook. A Vision of Children. Thomas Ashe. EBVV

I dreamed I saw Joe Hill last night. Joe Hill. Alfred Hayes. UnPo

I dreamed I stood upon a little hill. Two Loves. Lord Alfred Bruce Douglas. PeHV

I dreamed I was a barber; and there went. The Barber. John Gray. NOBVV

I dreamed I was a cave-boy. The Cave-Boy. Laura Elizabeth Richards. FaPON

I dreamed I was digging a grave. Immortality. Ai. MAYP

I dreamed I was holding. Lady Kasa, tr. fr. Japanese. Fr. Manyo Shu. Ma

I dreamed it rose. Black Buoy. Robert H. Davis. HATNAP

I Dreamed Last Night of My True Love. Unknown. AS

I dreamed of a shark following us two. Sharks. Dick Lourie. NeAC

I dreamed of an island where I was the governor. Sancho Panza's Dream. W. H. Auden. Fr. Man of La Mancha. AnAn

I dreamed of him last night, I saw his face. The Dead Poet. Lord Alfred Bruce Douglas. PeHV

I dreamed of Ted Williams. Dream of a Baseball Star. Gregory Corso. SD; VGW

I dreamed of war-heroes, of wounded war-heroes. The Heroes. Louis Simpson. OBWP

I dreamed that/ the gentiles [or goyim] crucified Mozart. Mozart. Jacob Glatstein. PeBMYV, tr. by Cynthia Ozick; VWA, tr. by Ruth Whitman

I dreamed [or dream'd] that, as I wandered by the way. The Question. Shelley. CH; EnRP; FiP; OBEV (Dream of the Unknown, The.) GTBS; GTBS-P

I dreamed that, buried in my fellow clay. Dream, The ("I dreamed that buried in my fellow clay.") Unknown. NOEC

I Dreamed That I Was Old. Stanley Kunitz. GOYP

I dreamed that I was thrown from a crag. Francisco de Terrazas, tr. by Samuel Beckett. MexPo

I Dreamed That in a City Dark as Paris. Louis Simpson. CoAP; NePoEA

I dreamed that one had died in a strange place. A Dream of Death. W. B. Yeats. GBL

I dreamed that someone's coming. Someone like No One Else. Forugh Farrokhzad, tr. by Deirdre Lashgari. WPOW

I dreamed the setting sun would rise no more. Parting. To——— Robert Frost. AnAmPo

I dreamed there was an Emperor Antony. Cleopatra's Lament. Shakespeare. Fr. Antony and Cleopatra, V, ii. UnPo

I dreamed there would be spring no more. Tennyson. Fr. In Memoriam A. H. H., LXIX. NOBE

I dreamed [or dream'd] this mortal part of mine. The Vine. Robert Herrick. CaPo; ErPo; NAEL-2; NoP

I dreamed two spirits came—one dusk as night. The Two Spirits. James Benjamin Kenyon. AA

I dreamed [or dream'd] we both were in bed. The Vision to Electra. Robert Herrick. SeCP

I dreamed you were my child, and I had come. The Dream. Paul Petrie. TAP

I dreamt/ I clasped a sword. Lady Kasa, tr. fr. Japanese. Fr. Manyo Shu. FCEI

I Dreamt a Dream. Arthur Hugh Clough. Fr. Dipsychus, pt. I, sc. v. NAEL-2

I dreamt a dream the other night. Lowlands. Unknown. ChTr; OxBoLi

I dreamt a dream! what can it mean? The Angel. Blake. Fr. Songs of Experience. CH; EnRP; LiTB

I dreamt about you last night. Dream. Unknown, tr. by Armand Schwerner. STP

I dreamt her sensual proportions. The Death of Venus. Robert Creeley. NOBA

I dreamt I came to a kind inn. A Kind Inn. George Dillon. GoYe

I dreamt I climbed to a high, high plain. The Pitcher. Yüan Chen, tr. by Arthur Waley. AWP

I dreamt I dwelt in marble halls. The Palace of humbug. "Lewis Carroll." FaBoNo

I dreamt I saw great Venus by me stand. A Dream of Venus. Bion, tr. by Leigh Hunt. AWP

I dreamt. I saw three ladies in a tree. The Three Ladies. Robert Creeley. NeAP

I dreamt I was a fugitive. The Fugitive. Abdul Wahab al-Bayati, tr. by Abdullah al-Udhari. MPAW

I dreamt it! such a funny thing. What the Prince of I Dreamt. Henry Cholmondeley-Pennell. NA

I dreamt last night. For No Clear Reason. Robert Creeley. VGW

I dreamt last night. The Fierce Dream. Jeffrey Wainwright. DiPo

I dreamt last night of you, John-John. John-John. Thomas MacDonagh. AWP

I dreamt (no "dream" awake—a dream indeed). In Sleep. Alice Meynell. BrRo

I dreamt of a great sword. Lady Kasa, tr. fr. Japanese. Fr. Manyo Shu. PeBJV

I Dreamt of Saichi and Woke with a Feeling of Uneasiness. Ryokan, tr. fr. Chinese by Burton Watson. JLIC-2

I dreamt of the old house. To My Sister. Olga Berggolts. BoWoP, tr. by Daniel Weissbort

I dreamt one night—it was a horrid dream. Out of the Frying Pan into the Fire. James Henry. NOBVV

I dreamt that I was God Himself. Ezra Pound, after the German of Heine. FaBoEE

I dreamt that the goyim. . See I dreamed that the gentiles crucified Mozart.

I dreamt we slept in a moss in Donegal. Seamus Heaney. Fr. Glanmore Sonnets, X. NoP

I Dreamt You Went. Berta Freistadt. DT

I dressed my father in his little clothes. The Boat. Robert Pack. CoAP; DiL; NePoEA-2; SM

I Drift in the Wind. Ingrid Jonker, tr. fr. Afrikaans by Jack Cope. PeSA; WPOW

I drink a lot of skimmed milk. The Confessions of Gerrit. Gerrit Henry. BAP

I drink champagne early in the morning. Cordon Negro. Essex Hemphill. GLP

I Drink the Wine of Your Dreams. Pertti Nieminen, tr. fr. Finnish by Aili Jarvenpa. SOP

I drink to your glory my god. The Scorner. Felix TchiKaya U'Tamsi, tr. by Gerald Moore and Ulli Beier. TTY

I drink water and my stomach bulges. Kito, tr. fr. Japanese by Hiroaki Sato. Fr. Twenty-four Hokku. FCEI

I drive my carriage from the Upper East Gate. Unknown, tr. fr. Chinese by Burton Watson. Fr. Nineteen Old Poems of the Han, XIII. CoBCP

I drive through zero. Old Man Sweeping. George Barlow. NAmP

I dropped my pen;—and listened to the wind. Sonnet: Composed while the Author Was Engaged in Writing a Tract Occasioned by the Convention of Cintra. Wordsworth. ChER

I dropped my sail and dried my dropping seines. Mass at Dawn. Roy Campbell. PeSA

I Drove through This Old World This Afternoon. Clark Coolidge. LP

I drove to Little Hunger promontory. Little Hunger. Richard Murphy. BIrV

I drove up to the graveyard, which. The Soul Longs to Return Whence It Came. Richard Eberhart. CMoP

I dug a grave under an oak-tree. Amy Lowell. Fr. Dreams in War Time. BoWoP

I dug and dug amongst the snow. Christina Rossetti. FaBoEE

I dug, beneath the cypress shade. The Grave of Love. Thomas Love Peacock. CH; OxBSP (Beneath the Cypress Shade.) EnRP

I dug in with all the spirit of spring. Knowing. Mary Coghill. BrRo

I dusted the bed. Unknown, tr. fr. Japanese Fr. Manyo Shu. FCEI

I dwell/ In a dark small cell. The Genia. Ann Stanford. WSC

I dwell alone—I dwell alone, alone. Autumn. Christina Rossetti. BrRo

I dwell apart. The Hermit. Hsü Pên, tr. by Henry H. Hart. RFM

I dwell in a lonely house I know. Ghost House. Robert Frost. WSC

I dwell in Grace's court. Content and Rich. Robert Southwell. OBSC

I dwell in possibility. Emily Dickinson. NAWM-2; NIP; NoAM; NOBA; OxBA

I dwell in this leaky Western castle. Dowager. John Montague. AnAn; IPY

I dwell on the misty steppe. The "Word" of an Antelope Caught in a Trap. Sandag, Mongol Oral Tradition, tr. by C. R. Bawden. WTO

I dwelt alone. Eulalie. Poe. Par

I dwelt in a city enchanted. The City of Prague. William Jeffery Prowse. CenHV

I eagerly await your miniature, wish the artist would hurry. Letter to My Wife. Keidrych Rhys. WaP

I eat my cereal with a sliced peach. Getting a Poem in the Rain. Dick Lourie. NeAC

I eat my food. Unknown, tr. fr. Japanese. Fr. Manyo Shu. FCEI

I eat my peas with honey. Unknown. CenHV; NTCP; OnUR; RHPC (Peas.) FaBoUs; FaPON

I eat plastic. RDA (Recommended Daily Addictions). Julia Older. SoTCo

I eat what I wish. Cat's Menu. Richard Shaw. CRH; RHPC

I edged back against the night. High Tide. Jean Starr Untermeyer. MoAmPo

I embrace these shoulders and I look. Étude. Joseph Brodsky, tr. by Dimitry Pospielovsky and Keith Bosley. VWA

I embraced the summer dawn. Dawn. Rimbaud, *tr. fr. French by* Enid Rhodes Peschal. *Fr.* Illuminations. SOTW; TTTS

I employ the blind mandolin player. A Music. Wendell Berry. VGW

I empty myself of the names of others. I empty my pockets. The Remains. Mark Strand. NYBP; PPP

I enact my being here. The Work. Robert Duncan. *Fr.* Dante Études. CAPP

I encountered the crowd returning from amusements. Resolution of Dependence. George Barker. FaBoTw; LiTB; LiTM

I enter and find I stand. George Barker. *Fr.* At Thurgarton Church. PoPo

I Enter by the Darkened Door. Jenny King. BXAP

I enter, jingling hindu temple bells, deodorant ears. Blessing a Bride and Groom; a Wedding Night Poem. Robert Peters. BXAP

I entered into unknowning. Stanzas Concerning an Ecstasy Experienced in High Contemplation. Saint John of the Cross, *tr. by* K. Kavanaugh *and* O. Rodrigues. TOF

I entered it before I understood it. Spring at Nant Dywelan. Bobi Jones, *tr. by* Joseph P. Clancy. OBWVE

I entered my parlor one bright summer morn. The Humming-Bird. Mary E. Tucker. CBWP-1

I entered with a torch before me. Fleance. Michael Longley. CIP; FaBCIP

I entrust my all to you, Aurelius. Catullus. PeHV

I envy e'en the fly its gleams of joy. Written in Prison. John Clare. OAEL-2

I Envy Not Endymion. William Alexander, Earl of Stirling. *Fr.* Aurora, XXIX. Son
(Sonnet: "I envy not Endymion now no more.") EIL

I envy not in any moods. Tennyson. *Fr.* In Memoriam A. H. H., XXVII. LiTB; OBNC; PeHV

I envy you your chance of death. Hilda Doolittle. NoAM

I escorted my mother's brother. *Unknown, tr. fr. Chinese by* Arthur Waley. BoS

I, even I, am he who knoweth the roads. De Aegypto. Ezra Pound. VGW

I even I know the Eastern Gate of Heaven. He Knoweth the Souls of the East. *Unknown, tr. fr. Egyptian by* Robert Hillyer. *Fr.* Book of the Dead. AWP

I exchange eyes with the Mad Queen. Vision. Harry Crosby. EAS

I exist that I may say. Document. Tuvia Ruebner, *tr. by* Harold Schimmel. VWA

I Expect You Think This Huge Dark Coat. C. M. Donald. GLP

I Expected My Skin and My Blood to Ripen. Wendy Rose. NOVW; WPOW

I expected Sydney women. Surprise Surprise. Rachel McAlpine. ATNZ

I expected this face but did not predict it. Elijah Speaking. Doug Fetherling. NOBC

I face the yellow flowers. A Painting of Chrysanthemums in the Boneless Style of Hsü Ch'ung-ssu. Yün Shou-p'ing, *tr. by* Jonathan Chaves. CoBLCP

I faced the star maker, the candy butcher. Mystic Moment. James Tate. NAmP

I failed to draw a map and you followed it perfectly. Lens. Michael Palmer. LP

I Fancy That I'm Standing Guard. Haim Guri, *tr. fr. Hebrew by* Bernhard Frank. MHeP

I fasted for some forty days on bread and buttermilk. The Pilgrim. W. B. Yeats. RB

I fasted three canonical hours. The Maiden's Plight. Brian Merriman, *tr. fr. Modern Irish by* Frank O'Connor. *Fr.* The Midnight Court. BIrV

I Fasten Down the Day. Bert Schierbeek, *tr. fr. Dutch by* Charles McGeehan. DuIn

I fear, I fear the rarity. Death by Rarity. Marguerite Young. LiTA

I fear no earthly powers. On Himself. Robert Herrick. CaPo

I Fear No Power a Woman Wields. Ernest McGaffey. AA

I fear that appearances are worshipped throughout France. The Rat and the Elephant. La Fontaine, *tr. by* Marianne Moore. OBVE

I fear that I shall never make. Poet-Tree. Earle Birney. OxBC

I fear the fragrance of a full cup. Sent to Liang-fen. Singde, *tr. fr. Chinese by* Julie Landau. WFTU

I fear thy kisses, gentle maiden. Shelley. GTBS; GTBS-P

I fear to be gainsaid. A Maiden's Lament. Pernette Du Guillet, *tr. fr. French by* Dorothy Backer. *Fr.* The Triumph of the Muses over Love. DMF

I fear to love thee, Sweet, because. To Olivia. Francis Thompson. MoBrPo

I fear you letters. The Aleph Bet. Fay Lipshitz. VWA

I feared your wrath Eurynome. Eurynome. Eleni Fourtouni, *tr. fr. Greek by the author.* AIW

I fed this dove. Doves. Jutta Schutting, *tr. by* Beth Bjorklund. CoAuP

I feed a flame within, which so torments me. Dryden. *Fr.* Secret Love; or, The Maiden Queen. AWP
(Hidden Flame.) OBEV

I Feel. Elizabeth Jennings. PoPo

I feel a breath from other planets blowing. Rapture. Stefan George, *tr. by* Ludwig Lewisohn. AWP

I feel a newer life in every gale. May. James Gates Percival. BoTP

I feel a poem in my heart to-night. Embryo. Mary Ashley Townsend. AA

I feel an apparition. Wallace Stevens, *after the French of* Jean Le Roy. OBVE

I Feel Empty. Yona Wallach, *tr. fr. Hebrew by* Warren Bargad *and* Stanley F. Chyet. IP

I Feel I Am. John Clare. OAEL-2; SeCePo
(Sonnet: "I feel I am;—I only know I am.") NOBVV

I feel I am alone tonight. The City a Wrecked Ship. Amal Dunqul, *tr. by* Sharif Elmusa *and* Thomas G. Ezzy. MAP

I feel I could be turned to ice. I Feel. Elizabeth Jennings. PoPo

I feel I know what you have worked through, you. For John Berryman. Robert Lowell. NOBA

I feel I'd like to be alone. Testament. Mikhail Yurevich Lermontov, *tr. by* Alan Myers. AAA

I feel it when the game is done. Footnote to Tennyson. Gerald Bullett. FiBHP

I feel my face being bitten by the tides. The Knowledge That Comes through Experience. Jane Cooper. NMM

I feel my heart melting. Dusk. Gabriela Mistral, *tr. by* David Garrison. BoWoP

I feel my limbs. Samih al-Qasim, *tr. fr. Arabic by* Sharif Elmusa *and* Naomi Shihab Nye. *Fr.* After the Apocalypse. MAP

I feel, O Laudanum, thy power divine. In Praise of Laudanum. William Harrison. NOEC

I feel one tit. Dawn. Eileen Myles. UL

I feel remorse for all that time has done. Love's Remorse. Edwin Muir. OxBTC

I feel ridiculous. Put Down. Léon Damas, *tr. by* Seth L. Wolitz. TTY

I feel someone dying of an illness. Taigi, *tr. fr. Japanese by* Hiroaki Sato. *Fr.* Twenty-nine Hokku. FCEI

I Feel Sorry for the Garden. Forugh Farrokhzad, *tr. fr. Persian by* Deirdre Lashgari. OV

I feel that in the days gone by. In Days Gone By. Ida M. Mills. BoTP

I feel the breath of the summer night. A Summer Night. Elizabeth Stoddard. AA

I feel the cold this night for Aodh. Mag Uidhir's Winter Campaign. Eochadh O'Hussey. NOIV

I feel the spring far off, far off. Spring in War-Time. Sara Teasdale. OHIP

I feel the stubborn humming. Swift Floods. Kata Szidónia Petröczi, *tr. by* Laura Schiff. WPOW

I feel your steps in the hall. Karin Boye, *tr. fr. Swedish by* Nadia Christensen. *Fr.* A Dedication. PBWP

I fell asleep, and had a dream. An Unromantic Awakening. Priscilla Jane Thompson. CBWP-2

I fell asleep in the daytime. Recording a Dream. Yang Shih-ch'i, *tr. by* Jonathan Chaves. CoBLCP

I fell down. Three Ways to Screw Up on Your Way to The Doings Three Ways. *Unknown, tr. by* Jerome Rothenberg *and* Richard Johnny John. STP

I fell from one once. Judy Cole. Horse Chestnut. Gary Miranda. SM

I fell in the battle of Ashdod. Since Then. Yehuda Amichai, *tr. by* Shlomo Vinner *and* Howard Schwartz. VWA

I felt a cleavage [*or* cleaving] in my mind. Emily Dickinson. NOBA; OxBA

I felt a funeral, in my brain. Emily Dickinson. AmPP; AnAmPo; BoWoP; CMoP; LiTA; NAAL-1; NOBA; NoP; OxBA; PBWP; PoE; PoEL-5; PoRA; SCV; TAP

I felt a spirit of love begin to stir. Dante, *tr. fr. Italian by* Dante Gabriel Rossetti. *Fr.* La Vita Nuova, XV. AWP

I felt for the button. The Return: Intensive Care. Sydney Lea. NAmP

I felt my heart beat like an engine high in the air. Depression. Robert Bly. NaP

I felt no pain when they cut it off. Child with Six Fingers. Carol Muske. AmPA

I felt no tremor and I caught no sounds. The White Dust. W. W. Gibson. MoBrPo

I felt such love for you. A Poem for My Wet Nurse. Cheng Hsieh, *tr. by* Jonathan Chaves. CoBLCP

I felt the lurch and halt of her heart. Lightning. D. H. Lawrence. CMoP; MoAB; MoBrPo

I felt the wind soft from the land of souls. Elizabeth Barrett Browning. *Fr.* Aurora Leigh. OBTV

I felt the wind soft from the land of souls. Olives and Mountains. Elizabeth Barrett Browning. *Fr.* Aurora Leigh, VII. FaBoPP
I felt the world a-spinning on its nave. The Last Journey. John Davidson. *Fr.* The Testament of John Davidson. GoTS
"Oh, long before the bere was steeped for malt." PoSH
I felt thy touch divine, rapt Poesy. Sonnet to Poesy. James Waddington. PF
I fight a battle every day. The Fighter. Samuel Ellsworth Kiser. BLPA
I Fight Back. Lillian Allen. PBCV
I Fights Mit Sigel! Grant P. Robinson. BLPA
I figured/ anything anybody. Mrs. Sadie Grindstaff, Weaver and Factotum. Jonathan Williams. OBAL
I fill this cup to one made up. A Health. Edward Coote Pinkney. AA; AnAmPo
I finally found a way of using the tree. The Beckett Kit. Linda Gregg. AmPA
I find him in the garden. Staked tomato-plants are what. Early Discoveries. David Malouf. CBAP
I find my love fishing. *Unknown, tr. by* Boris de Rachewiltz; *English vers. by* Ezra Pound and Noel Stock. BoWoP; PBWP
I find [*or* fynde] no peace and all my war[r] is done. Petrarch, *tr. fr. Italian by* Sir Thomas Wyatt. *Fr.* Sonnets to Laura: To Laura in Life, CIV. AAS; LiTB; OAEL-1; OBVE; SiPS (Description of the Contrarious Passions in a Lover.) FF; Son; TrGrPo
I first heard it scrabbling crablike by the window. Spring Snow. Chugan Engetsu, *tr. by* Burton Watson. JLIC-2
I first remember you in Paris, blaze. Memoir. Honor Moore. GLP
I first saw my face in a dream. Yagi Jukichi, *tr. by* Geoffrey Bownas *and* Anthony Thwaite. PeBJV
I first see the spring light. Miura Chora, *tr. fr. Japanese by* Hiroaki Sato. *Fr.* Sixteen Hokku. FCEI
I first tasted under Apollo's lips. Evadne. Hilda Doolittle. BoWoP
I first would have him understand. On His Garden Book. Francis Daniel Pastorius. SCAP
I fish until the clouds turn blue. Shifting Colors. Robert Lowell. HCAP
I fixe mine eye on thine, and there. Witchcraft by a Picture. John Donne. EyDe
I fled Him, down the nights and down the days. The Hound of Heaven. Francis Thompson. ACP; BLPL; BrPo; FaBV; FaFP; LiTB; LiTM; MoAB; MoBrPo; NAEL-2; OBMV; PoEL-5; SeCePo; TrGrPo; WGRP
I flee the city, temples, and each place. Louise Labé, *tr. by* Willis Barnstone. BoWoP
I flew my kite. Kite. David McCord. PDV
I flew past Theising's Drug Store. Skating in Pleasant Hill, Ohio. Kathleen Iddings. ASP
I float/ On the wind. Tamaki of a Hundred Lovers. Hirini Melbourne. PeNZ
I floated on a cloud one day. Cloud Fantasy. Henrietta Cordelia Ray. CBWP-3
I flung my soul to the air like a falcon flying. The Falconer of God. William Rose Benét. WGRP
I flung open all six windows on the moon. Bassui, *tr. by* Lucien Stryk *and* Takashi Ikemoto. ZPCJ
I follow from my window down. From the Window Down. Louis O. Coxe. NYBP
I follow the deer through shadows. Deer Hunt, Salt Lake Valley. Helen Handley. GrPI
I follow the scent of a woman. Dancing the Shout to the True Gospel; or, The Song Movement Sisters Don't Want Me to Sing. Rita Mae Brown. NMM; PeHV
I Followed a Path. Patricia Parker. BlSi
I followed her to the station, with her suitcase in my hand. Love in Vain. Robert Johnson. UnPo
I followed, o splendid season. A Poem to Show the Trouble That Befell Him When He Was at Sea. Thomas Prys, *tr. by* Gwyn Williams. OBTV; OBWVE
I followed the narrow cliffside trail half way up the mountain. The Deer Lay Down Their Bones. Robinson Jeffers. NoAM
I followed where they led. His Throne Is with the Outcast. James Russell Lowell. TrCP
I forget everything. I forget faces. The Keeper. William Carpenter. Psk
I forget my lips are rouged. Chiyojo, *tr. fr. Japanese by* Hiroaki Sato. *Fr.* Seventeen Hokku. FCEI
I forgive you, Lima, for having bred me. Nata Natal. Juan Gonzalo Rose, *tr. by* Ena Hollis. Per
I forgotten who. Bumi. Imamu Amiri Baraka. PoBA
I fought that war. The Classics Revisited. Mirko Lauer, *tr. by* David Tipton. Per
I found a/ hummingbird. The Container. Cid Corman. VGW
I found a/ weed. Reflective. A. R. Ammons. HCAP

I found a ball of grass among the hay. Mouse's Nest. John Clare. ChTr; InPK; LiTB; NAEL-2; RB
I found a dimpled spider, fat and white. Design. Robert Frost. BLPL; CMoP; HeIP; InPK; InPS; MoP; NAAL-2; NIP; NoAM; NOBA; NoP; PPP; PrIm; Son; SoSe; TAP
I found a garden of thyme and thrift. The Perfect Garden. Winifred Robertson. PoSH
I Found a Horseshoe. *Unknown.* AS
I found a house at Florence on the hill. Florence. Elizabeth Barrett Browning. *Fr.* Aurora Leigh. FaBoPP
I found a little beetle, so that Beetle was his name. Forgiven. A. A. Milne. SOP
I found a little brown purse. Found in the Woods. Irene F. Pawsey. BoTP
I found a little fairy flute. Fairy Music. Enid Blyton. BoTP
I found a pigeon's skull on the machair. Perfect. "Hugh MacDiarmid." RB
I found a yellow flower in the grass. A Summer Sanctuary. John Hall Ingham. AA
I found another baby scorpion today. Playing House. Jack Gilbert. NPGG
I found at daybreak yester morn. Medieval Norman Song. *Unknown, tr. by* John Addington Symonds. AWP
I Found Her Out There. Thomas Hardy. CH; CMoP; NoAM; NOBE; OAEL-2; PoE; PoEL-5
I found him in the guard-room at the Base. Lamentations. Siegfried Sassoon. OBSV
I found his wool face, I went away. Reading Walt Whitman. Calvin Forbes. PoBA
I found in Innisfail the fair. Alfrid's Itinerary through Ireland. *Unknown, tr. by* James Clarence Mangan. OBTV; TIRV
I found in Munster, unfettered of any. *Unknown, tr. fr. Middle Irish by* James Clarence Mangan. *Fr.* Prince Alfrid's Itinerary. BIrV
I Found It. Fadwa Tuqan, *tr. fr. Arabic by* Patricia Alanah Byrne *and* Salma Khadra Jayyusi. MAP
I found it in a legendary land. On Discovering a Butterfly. Vladimir Nabokov. NYBP
I found it in the bottom drawer. The Manual. Larry Rubin. MT
I found lodging. Tsurayuki, *tr. fr. Japanese by* Burton Watson. *Fr.* Kokin Shu. FCEI
I found myself in this house. Siege. Sargon Boulus, *tr. by* Sargon Boulus *and* Alistair Elliot. MAP
I found myself one day. The Hatch. Norma Faber. SO
I found myself one day all, all alone. Angelo Poliziano, *tr. fr. Italian by* John Addington Symonds. *Fr.* Three Ballate, I. AWP
I found myself one day all, all alone. Three Ballate, I. Angelo Poliziano, *tr. by* John Addington Symonds. AWP
I found myself, young girls, while it was May. Dance Song. Angelo Poliziano, *tr. by* John Heath-Stubbs. AWP
I found that ivory image there. Crazy Jane Grown Old Looks at the Dancers. W. B. Yeats. CMoP; EBEV
I found the colour of your. At Castor Bay. Sam Hunt. PeNZ
I found the phrase [*or* words] to every thought. Emily Dickinson. AA; AmPP
"I found the place last winter." Eric's voice. The Dreaming Trout. Charles Bruce. *Fr.* The Flowing Summer. CaP
I found the preserves in the cellar. Preserves. Michael Waters. GeTw
I found Thee in my heart, O Lord. Edward Dowden. *Fr.* New Hymns for Solitude. TrPWD
I found them here when I came. We Call Them Greasers. Gloria Anzaldúa. GLP
I found them there today. Mementos, II ("I found them there today."). William DeWitt Snodgrass. NePoEA-2
I found this jawbone at the sea's edge. Relic. Ted Hughes. NAEL-2
I found this photograph. Returning to the Town Where We Used to Live. Susan Musgrave. NOBC
I found this salamander. Samuel. Bobbi Katz. RHPC
I found you in a newspaper. Idea of a Swimmer. Jean-Richard Bloch, *tr. by* "S. P." TrJP
I found your body, a little purse. Trapped Mouse. Julia Cunningham. TSS
I found your Horace with the writing in it. On First Looking into Loeb's Horace. Lawrence Durrell. FaBoMo; LiTM
I, François Villon, ta'en at last. Would I Be Shrived? John D. Swain. BLPA
I, from my chamber window, mark. Autumn Thoughts. Mary E. Tucker. CBWP-1
I from my window looked at early dawning. Bereft. Josephine D. Henderson Heard. CBWP-4
I from the first was the bankside willow. For My Younger Brother Shinkei on the Seventeenth Anniversary of His Death. Kan Sazan, *tr. by* Burton Watson. JLIC-2

I fynde no peace and all my warr is done. *See* I find no peace and all my war is done.

I galloped on a scarlet filly. Absalom. Zerubavel Gilead, *tr. by* Dorothea Krook. VWA

I gat your letter, winsome Willie. To William Simpson, Ochiltree. Burns. OxBS

I gather shells and pebbles. Kamatari. *Fr.* Manyo Shu. Ma

I gather thyme upon the sunny hills. Immalee. Christina Rossetti. BoNaP

I gathered mosses in Easedale. Dorothy Wordsworth. SaC

I Gave Her Cakes; I Gave Her Ale. Cakes and Ale. *Unknown.* FaFP

I gave my life to learning how to live. Postscript. Sandra Hochman. NMM

I gave my musk scent to her white *kosode. Unknown,* tr. by Hiroaki Sato. FCEI

I gave myself to him. Emily Dickinson. FaBV

I gave myself to Love Divine. Saint Theresa of Avila, *tr. by* E. Allison Peers. OxBS

I gave to Hope a watch of mine: but he. Hope. George Herbert. PoEL-2; WeW

I Gaze across the Distant Hills. William Williams, *tr. fr. Welsh by* H. Idris Bell. OBWVE

I gaze at this, my hometown. Yüan Mei, *tr. fr. Chinese by* Jonathan Chaves. *Fr.* Five Poems on Returning to Hangchou. CoBLCP

I gaze at you. The Tattooed Man. Robert Hayden. CAPP; NoAM

I gaze upon a city. Thomas Hood. OBTV

I gaze upon the beauty of the stars. The Beauty of the Stars. Moses Ibn Ezra, *tr. by* Solomon Solis-Cohen. TrJP

I gaze, where August's sunbeam falls. Newark Abbey. Thomas Love Peacock. NOBE; OBNC

I gaze with grief upon our generation. A Thought. Mikhail Yurevich Lermontov, *tr. by* Max Eastman. AWP

I gazed, and lo! Afar and near. Battle of Somerset. Cornelius C. Cullen. PAH

I gazed through the darkness, one very dark night. The Light in the Window. C. L. Erickson. PWR

I gazed upon the glorious sky. June. Bryant. AA

I gently touched her hand: she gave. I Pressed Her Rebel Lips. *Unknown.* BoLoP; ErPo

I get anxious to die, at times. Ishikawa Takuboku, *tr. fr. Japanese by* Hiroaki Sato. *Fr.* Forty-seven Tanka in Three Lines. FCEI

I get called sir. Don't Call Me Sir Call Me Strong. Kitty Tsui. ER

I get my degree. Lawd, Dese Colored Chillum. Ruby C. Saunders. BlSi

I get so drunk, I could be called the Earl of Dissipation! Chin Nung, *tr. fr. Chinese by* Jonathan Chaves. *Fr.* Thirty Poems of Longing for People. CoBLCP

I get up. I am sick of/ Rouging my cheeks. Morning. Chu Shu-chen, *tr. by* Kenneth Rexroth. OxBS

I give and bequeath. Extraordinary Will. Will Jackett. FaBoUs

I give my word on it. There is no way. Still and All. Burns Singer. NePoEA-2; OxBS

I give rest to clear words. A Dawn of Jaffa Pigeons. Eli Bachar, *tr. by* Jeremy Garber. VWA

I give thee thanks, Adonai! My Soul in the Bundle of Life. *Unknown, tr. fr. French by* E. Margaret Rowley. *Fr.* The Dead Sea Scrolls. TrJP

I give Thee thanks, my King. Mael Isu O Brolchain. NOIV

I Give up Trying to Learn to Play the Lute. Michizane, *tr. fr. Chinese by* Burton Watson. JLIC-1

I give you a house of snow. The Dove of New Snow. Vachel Lindsay. MoAmPo

I Give You Back. Joy Harjo. HATNAP

I give you horses for your games in May. May. Folgore Da San Gimignano, *tr. fr. Italian by* Dante Gabriel Rossetti. *Fr.* Sonnets of the Months. PFI

I give you meadow-lands in April, fair. April. Folgore Da San Gimignano, *tr. fr. Italian by* Dante Gabriel Rossetti. *Fr.* Sonnets of the Months. PFI

I give you now Professor Twist. The Purist. Ogden Nash. FiBHP; GoJo; MoAmPo; MoShBr; NBLV; OBCA

I Give You Thanks My God. Bernard Dadié, *tr. fr. French by* Donatus Ibe Nwoga. TTY

I give you the end of a golden string. To the Christians. Blake. *Fr.* Jerusalem, IV, Prologue. EnRP; WGRP (Epigraph.)

I give you this Bible and more to take. Inscription on the Flyleaf of a Bible. Dannie Abse. TrJP

I glance from humble toil and see. Kitchen Window. James Edward Hervey MacDonald. CaP

I go/ through Sunday's tunnel, hushed and deep. How to Get There. Bonnie Nims. RHPC

I go/ towards the trumpets of light. Tammuz. Nathan Alterman, *tr. by* Robert Friend. VWA

I go along the high banks of the Ju. *Unknown, tr. by* Arthur Waley. BoS

I go around to the back of the grave. Ozaki Hosai, *tr. fr. Japanese by* Hiroaki Sato. *Fr.* One Hundred Haiku in Free Form. FCEI

I go back again. Hawk and Snake. Leslie Marmon Silko. VoR

I go back ways to hurl rooftops. In My Mind. Norman MacCaig. OxBC

I Go by Road. Catulle Mendès, *tr. fr. French by* Alice Meynell. AWP; TrJP

I go by taper of cornstalk. All Hallows Eve. Kathryn Stripling Byer. KS

I go digging for clams once every two or three years. Clamming. Reed Whittemore. NYBP; TAP

I go down to Dupont Street. Chinatown Chant. Tom MacInnes. CaP

I Go Dreaming Roads in My Youth. Luis Omar Salinas. AiP

I go in. A It's. Kit Robinson. UL

I go in under foliage. In Rain. Wendell Berry. GeTw

I go north, up to the mountains. You Were Still the Sun's There. Sandor Csoori, *tr. by* Jascha Kessler. FOC

I go on, and the clear water meets me again. Chiyojo, *tr. fr. Japanese by* Hiroaki Sato. *Fr.* Seventeen Hokku. FCEI

I go on loving him. Lady Kasa. *Fr.* Manyo Shu. FCEI

I go one step forward. Student. Cheng Min, *tr. by* Kenneth Rexroth *and* Ling Chung. PBWP

I go out at the northern gate. *Unknown, tr. by* Arthur Waley. BoS

I go out of darkness/ Onto a road of darkness. Izumi Shikibu, *tr. by* Kenneth Rexroth. WPOW

I go out to totem street. Knock on Wood. Henry Dumas. CNA; PoBA

I go separately. Santa Fe Trail. Barbara Guest. NeAP; PoM

I go through hollyhocks. A Las Trampas U.S. Charles Tomlinson. TwCP

I go to bed late these days. On Approaching Fifty. István Vas, *tr. by* William Jay Smith. MHuP

I go to concert, party, ball. My Rival. Kipling. OxBTC

I go to knit two clans together. The Wedding of the Clans. Aubrey Thomas De Vere. AnIL

I go to put a letter. Stone Age. Pat Nolan. UL

I go to say goodbye to the Cailleach. The Wild Dog Rose. John Montague. BIrV; CIP; IPY; PoE

I go to school. Why Do You Want to Suffer Less. David Fisher. NPGG

I go to school in the morning. Embroidery. Catherine Nomura Crystal. AiP

I go to school with my daughters wearing a dress. Sex Films. Vivienne Joseph. ATNZ

I go to the toilet. It's My Fault. Robert Fox. SoTCo

I go to the Turkish shop, buy a bun. The Turkish Bakery. *Unknown, tr. by* Peter H. Lee. PBWP

I go to work. Workday. Linda Hogan. HATNAP

I got a brown baby. Brown Baby Blues. Una Marson. PVCV

I got a friend named Percy. Percy/ 68. Glenn Myles. NBP

I got a gal and she loves me. Cripple Creek. *Unknown.* AmFP

I Got a Gal at the Head of the Holler. *Unknown.* AS

I Got a Home in Dat Rock. *Unknown.* BPo

I got a letter from an old acquaintance in New York. Hate Mail. Steve Kowit. UL

I Got a Letter from Jesus. *Unknown.* AS

I got a one-eyed wife, a headless child. Guess Who. Fred Chappell. NBLV

I got a valentine from Timmy. Valentine. Shel Silverstein. RHPC

I got his name and phone. On Finding Out that the One You Slept with the Night Before Was Murdered the Next Day. Chuck Ortleb. GLP

I got married on the great lawn. I Am Married to Myself. Melinda Goodman. ER

I got me flowers to straw [*or* strew *or* strow] Thy [*or* the] way. Easter ("I got me flowers to straw Thy Way"). George Herbert. BoTP; CH; FaBoCh; NAEL-1; NOBE; OBEV; OBS; OHIP; TrGrPo

I got one good look. Coon Song. A. R. Ammons. MoP; NOBA

I got out and for about five blocks. Ishikawa Takuboku, *tr. fr. Japanese by* Hiroaki Sato. *Fr.* Forty-seven Tanka in Three Lines. FCEI

I got pocketed behind 7X-3824. Ambition. Morris Bishop. AmFN

I got so I could take his name. Emily Dickinson. CMoP

I Got the Blues. *Unknown.* TTY

I got this job. For Hollis Sigler. Elaine Equi. UL

I got those little white schoolhouse blues. Little White Schoolhouse Blues. Florence Becker Lennon. PoNe

I got to Kansas City on a Frid'y. Kansas City. Oscar Hammerstein II. OBAL

I got up in the night. The Riverman. Elizabeth Bishop. NYBP

I got up this morning and meant to be good. The Wrong Start. Marchette Chute. RHPC

I gotta/ buy me a new. Après le Bain. William Carlos Williams. OBAL

I grant indeed that fields and flocks have charms. Rural Life. George Crabbe. *Fr.* The Village. NOBE

I greet my love with wine and gladsome lay. Sabbath, My Love. Judah Halevi, *tr. by* Solomon Solis-Cohen. TrJP

I greet thee, my Redeemer sure. Salutation to Jesus Christ. John Calvin. WGRP

I greet you, son, with joy and winter rue. Muse in Late November. Jonathan Henderson Brooks. PoNe

I grew/ for you. The Strong Bond. Juana de Ibarbourou, *tr. by* Linda Scheer. PBWP

I grew out of a vicious, viscous swamp. A Reed. Osip Mandelstam *tr. by* James Greene. VWA

I grew up bent over. Prodigy. Charles Simic. GeTw

I grieve and dare not show my discontent. On Monsieur's Departure. Elizabeth I, Queen of England. NAEL-1; WPE

I grieve for my second daughter. Written on Seeing the Flowers, and Remembering My Daughter. Kao Ch'i. DL

I grieve in my frenzy for the heart. Mohammad Taqi Mir, *tr. by* Ahmed Ali. GoT

I grieve to think of you alone. Prescience. Donald Jeffrey Hayes. PoNe

I grieved for Buonaparté, with a vain. Wordsworth. EnRP (1801.) Son

I grow. Survivor. Judy Dothard Simmons. CNA

I grow a white rose. José Martí, *tr. fr. Spanish by* Seymour Resnick. *Fr.* Simple Verses. TTY

I grow accustomed to a new disguise. Journal. John Ciardi. PoA

I grow old under an intensity. Mirror. James Merrill. CoAP; NePoEA-2; SM

I grow together everywhere. Mandelstam. Richard Burns. VWA

I guess because it was Key West. Meeting the Reincarnation Analyst. Gary Gildner. AmPA

I guess it is ever green. Evergreen Cemetery. Alfred W. Purdy. MoCV

I guess it will come suddenly. And every. Amir Gilboa, *tr. by* Warren Bargad *and* Stanley F. Chyet. IP

I guess it's too late to live on the farm. Essay. Bernadette Mayer. UL

I guess there is a garden named. The Mirror Perilous. Alan Dugan. LiTM; TwCP

I Guess Work the Time Up, *sel.* Bruce Andrews. "Apart/ meant —licking stick good golly. If." IAT

I guess you love me now. Songs of Divorce. Jane Green, *tr. by* Frances Densmore. WPOW

I. H. B. William Winter. AA

I had/ a dream of women, dark. A Dream of Women. Carolyn Maisel. IHMS

I had a beginning but shall have no end. Stone Angel. Anne Ridler. EaLo

I had a bicycle called "Splendid." Arthur Waley. Mes

I Had a Black Man. *Unknown.* OxBoLi

I had a cat and the cat pleased me. *Unknown.* OxNR

I had a chair at every hearth. The Lamentation of the Old Pensioner. W. B. Yeats. HAP; lnPK; NoAM; TW; WeW

I had a dog/ Whose name was Buff. *Unknown.* OxNR

I had a dog and his name was Blue. Old Blue. *Unknown.* SD

I had a dog like a love. Penny Trumpet. Raphael Rudnik. MAT; NYBP

I had a donkey, that was all right. The Donkey. Theodore Roethke. GrPl; OBCA; RAR

I Had a Dove [and the Sweet Dove Died], *sel.* Keats. CH; FM Song: "I had a dove, and the sweet dove died." FaPON; PBBP

I had a dream. A wondrous thing. Spring and Death. Gerard Manley Hopkins. BrPo

I had a dream one winter's night. A Dream. Maggie Pogue Johnson. CBWP-4

I had a dream three walls stood up wherein a raven bird. Anger's Freeing Power. Stevie Smith. OxBC

I had a dream, which was not all a dream. Darkness. Byron. EnRP; LiTB; NAEL-2; OAEL-2; OPOP; PoE; PoEL-4; TEP

I had a duck and the young duck died. Archibald Stodart-Walker. FM

I Had a Duck-billed Platypus. Patrick Barrington. CenHV; FiBHP

I had a feeling in my neck. Mumps. Elizabeth Madox Roberts. FaPON

I Had a Future. Patrick Kavanagh. BIrV; NoAM

I had a good teacher. Education. Don L. Lee. AmNP

I had a great big flower pot. The Terracotta Flower Pot. Jenny Morris. SoTCo

I Had a Hippopotamus, *sel.* Patrick Barrington. "I had a hippopotamus; I loved him as a friend." CenHV; ILY

I had a little bird. The Orphan's Song. Sydney Thompson Dobell. CH; ELP; OBNC

I had a little chamber in the house. Elizabeth Barrett Browning. *Fr.* Aurora Leigh. FaBoPP

I had a little cow. *Unknown.* OxNR

I had a little dog and his name was Blue Bell. *Unknown.* OxNR

I had a little hen, the prettiest ever seen. *Unknown.* BoTP

I had a little hobby-horse. *Unknown.* BoTP

I had a little hobby horse, it was well shod. Mother Goose. OxNR

I had a little horse, his name was Dappled Grey. *Unknown.* OxNR

I had a little husband. *Unknown.* BoTP; FaFP; OxNR

I had a little moppet. Mother Goose. OxNR

I had a little nag. *Unknown.* OxNR

I had a little nut tree. A Nut Tree. *Unknown.* TTTS

I had a little nut-tree, nothing would it bear. Mother Goose. BoTP; CH; GBP; MoShBr; OxBoLi; OxNR

I Had a Little Pig. *Unknown.* RHPC

I had a little pony. Mother Goose. BoTP; OxNR

I had a little sorrow. The Penitent. Edna St. Vincent Millay. AnAmPo

I had a Mother who read to me. The Reading Mother. Strickland W. Gillilan. BLPA

I had a place outside, a place I wanted to find again. Toward the Other. Alain Veinstein, *tr. by* Rosmarie Waldrop. RHTwFP

I had a silver penny. Nursery Rhyme of Innocence and Experience. Charles Causley. GoJo

I Had a Terror—Since September. Gerald William Barrax. MT

"I had a true love but she left me." The Quaker's Wooing. *Unknown.* AS

I had a vision when the night was late. The Vision of Sin. Tennyson. OAEL-2

I had about as much chance, Mother. The Fish. L. L. Zeiger. TV

I had always been told. The Crippler. Danny Siegel. VWA

I had ambition, by which sin. Ambition. W. H. Davies. MoBrPo; TrGrPo

I had an uncle named Sol. Nobody Loses All the Time. E. E. Cummings. CMoP; DL; FaBoCo; FF; LiTM; NAAL-2; NBLV; NOBA; RB; TwCP

I had an uncle once who kept a rock in his pocket. I've Got a Home in That Rock. Raymond R. Patterson. FF; PoBA; PoNe

I had as lief be embraced by the porter at the hotel. Two Figures in Dense Violet Light. Wallace Stevens. MoAB; MoAmPo

I had awakened early. Second Ode to Persephone. Robert Kelly. *Fr.* The Book of Persephone. PoM

I had become callous like most. On the Death of Lisa Lyman. Della Burt. BlSi

I had been hungry, all the years. Emily Dickinson. LiTA; LiTM; MoAmPo

I had been sitting for days. Long Distance. Dana Naone. CDW

I had been thinking about love, how hard. All That We Try to Do. Steve Orlen. PPR

I had been waiting. First Menstruation. Ellen Bass. TV

I Had But Fifty Cents. *Unknown.* BeLS; BLPA; NBLV

I had but one illusion—a pleasant fancy. Our Lives Are Rivers. Luis G. Urbina, *tr. by* Samuel Beckett. MexPo

I had come prepared to answer questions. At the Gate in the Middle of My Life. Linda Gregg. NAmP

I had come to the edge of the water. Seamus Heaney. *Fr.* Station Island, VII. FaBCIP

I had come to the house, in a cave of trees. Medusa. Louise Bogan. AWP; BoWoP; HoPM; MoAB; MoAmPo; NoAM; NoP; WPE

I had eight birds hatcht in one nest. In Reference to Her Children, 23 June, 1656. Anne Bradstreet. BoWoP; TAP

I had expected. To Stephen Spender. Timothy Corsellis. WaP

I had for my winter evening walk. Good Hours. Robert Frost. AnAmPo

I had forgotten how to pray. When I Had Need of Him. Samuel Ellsworth Kiser. BLRP

I had four brothers over the sea. The Tokens of Love. *Unknown.* GBP

I had gone broke, and got set to come back. J. V. Cunningham. *Fr.* Three Epigrams. NePoAm; OxBSP; QFR (Epigram: "I had gone broke.") MoAmPo

I had gone broke, and got set to come back. James Vincent Cunningham. *Fr.* Three Epigrams. MoAmPo

I had heard/ before, of an. Mr. Brodsky. Charles Tomlinson. MoP; NoAM; OxBC

I had long known the diverse tastes of the wood. Gift of Sight. Robert Graves. PCP

I had lost myself. Tameie, *tr. by* Steven D. Carter. WFTW

I had my birth where stars were born. My Birth. Minot Judson Savage. AA; WGRP

I had my papers, but I was running. Dark in the Reich of the Blond. William Heyen. MAYP

I had never guessed. Teika, *tr. by* Steven D. Carter. WFTW

I had never heard of the whiteness. David Schloss. PoA

I had no desire for life. Writing My Feelings. Yüan Mei, *tr.* by Jonathan Chaves. CoBLCP

I had no God but these. Christ and the Pagan. John Banister Tabb. TrCP

I had no mother. Eve's Song in the Garden. Lynn Gottlieb. VWA

I had no thought of violets of late. Alice Dunbar Moore Nelson. BANP; BlSi; CDC; PoBA; PoNe; Son

I had no time to hate, because. Emily Dickinson. FPL; PoLF

I had no voice. Lilith's Child. Edward Francisco. DL

I had no wish to be stone-hearted. Perplexity. Ibrahim Tuqan, *tr.* by Christopher Tingley *and* John Heath-Stubbs. MAP

I had not been there before where the vagina opens. The First Birth. Rodney Jones. MAYP; MT

I had not fastened my sash over my gown. Tzu Yeh, *tr.* by Kenneth Rexroth *and* Ling Chung. WPOW

I had not minded walls. Emily Dickinson. AWP

I had not thought to have unlockt my lips. Temperance and Virginity. Milton. *Fr.* Comus; a Masque Presented at Ludlow Castle. OBS

I Had Occasion to Tell a Visitor about an Old Trip I Took. Lu Yu, *tr. fr. Chinese by* Burton Watson. CoBCP

I had often, cowled in the slumberous heavy air. Dürer; Innsbruck, 1495. "Ern Malley." CBAP

I had over-prepared the event. Villanelle: The Psychological Hour. Ezra Pound. CTC; NAAL-2

I had seen, as dawn was breaking. La Nuit Blanche. Kipling. MoBrPo

I had soaked the old house. Zimmer and His Turtle Sink the House. Paul Zimmer. Psk

I had the invitation of the king. This Our Life. Harold Monro. Mes

"I had this dream." My Dream. Lew Blockcolski. VoR

I had thought of putting an/ altar. Isabella Maria Brown. PoNe

I had thought of the bear in his lair as fiercely free. Part of the Darkness. Isabella Gardner. CAPP

I had three friends. Three Friends. *Unknown, tr.* by Ulli Beier. BoWoP; PBA

I Had to Be Secret. Mark Van Doren. SO

I had to kick their law into their teeth in order to save them. Negro Hero. Gwendolyn Brooks. CAPP

I had to laugh. Montana Wives. Gwendolen Haste. AmFN

I had two pigeons bright and gay. *Unknown.* OxNR; PBBP

I had walked life's way with an easy tread. I Met the Master. *Unknown.* BLRP; PoLF

I had walked since dawn and lay down to rest on a bare hillside. Vulture. Robinson Jeffers. NAAL-2; NoAM; NOBA; NoP

I had wanted a daughter. Mothers of Sons. Lesley Saunders. BrRo

I had watched the ascension and decline of the moon. W. J. Turner. *Fr.* The Seven Days of the Sun. OBMV

I had written him a letter which I had, for want of better. Clancy of the Overflow. Andrew Barton Paterson. PoAu-1

I had written to Aunt Maud. Waste. Harry Graham. FaBoCo (Aunt Maud.) MoShBr

I hae seen great anes and sat in great ha's. My Ain Fireside. Elizabeth Hamilton. FaBoBe

I hailed me a woman from the street. My Madonna. Robert W. Service. BLPA

I hailed the bus and I went for a ride. Bus Ride. Selma Robinson. *Fr.* Ferry Ride. FaPON

I handed her my silver. The Lady and the Gypsy. Vernon Scannell. Mes

I handed my teacher a poem. Silence Is Nearer to Truth. Margot Jordan. WS

I hang by my heels from the sky. Hera, Hung from the Sky. Carolyn Kizer. NMM; WPE

I happened once upon a time. James Hatley. *Unknown.* ESPB

I happened to come to the foot of a pine tree. In Reply to Questions. T'ai-shang, *tr.* by Burton Watson. CoBCP

I hardly know how to speak to you now. Cambridge Elegy. Sharon Olds. BLA

I hardly recognize that autumn has entered my mirror. Boudoir Feeling. Hsü Ts'an, *tr.* by Irving Lo. WFTU

I hardly suppose I know anybody who wouldn't rather be a success than a failure. Kindly Unhitch That Star, Buddy. Ogden Nash. LiTA

I hate and love. Why? You may ask but. Odi et Amo. Catullus. CTC, *tr.* by Ezra Pound

("I hate and love; wouldst thou the reason know?") OBVE, *tr.* by Richard Lovelace

("I love and hate. Ah! never ask why so!") OBVE, *tr.* by Walter Savage Landor

I hate being stuck up here, glaciated, hard all over. To a Maori Figure Cast in Bronze outside the Chief Post Office, Auckland. Hone Tuwhare. ATNZ

I Hate Harry. Miriam Chaikin. RHPC

I Hate Mosquitoes. Shu Wei, *tr. fr. Chinese by* Barry L. Gartell. WFTU

"I hate my verses, every line, every word." Love the Wild Swan. Robinson Jeffers. MoAB; MoAmPo; NoAM; Son; TW

I Hate Poetry. Julia Vinograd. AIW

"I hate successful people," you declare. What's Hard. Laurence Lerner. NePoEA-2

I hate that drum's discordant sound. John Scott of Amwell. NIP; NOEC; TW

I hate the dreadful hollow behind the little wood. Tennyson. *Fr.* Maud, I, i. FaBoPV

I hate the man who builds his name. The Poet and the Rose. John Gay. TEP

I hate these phrases: Of power absolute. Joshua Sylvester, *after the French of* Guy du Faur de Pibrac. FaBoEE

I hate to spend the night. Thanks Just the Same. *Unknown.* PoLF

I hated thee, fallen tyrant! I did groan. Feelings of a Republican on the Fall of Bonaparte. Shelley. Son

"I hates to think of dyin'," says the skipper to the mate. The Worried Skipper. Wallace Irwin. BLPA

I Haue [*or* Have] a Yong Suster. *Unknown.* *See* I Have a Young Sister.

I Have a Big Favour to Ask You, Brothers. Zishe Landau, *tr. fr. Yiddish by* Ruth Whitman. VWA

I Have a Blue Piano. Else Lasker-Schüler, *tr. fr. German by* Ralph Manheim. TrJP

I have a bookcase, which is what. Shake, Mulleary, and Go-ethe. H. C. Bunner. FiBHP

I have a bottle and a pen. Thoughts from a Bottle. Carl Clark. JB

I have a bowl of paper whites. Window Ledge in the Atom Age. E. B. White. NBLV; OBAL

I have a boy of five years old. Anecdote for Fathers. Wordsworth. EnRP

I have a dog. My Doggie. C. Nurton. BoTP

I have a dog of Blenheim birth. My Dog Dash. John Ruskin. FM

I have a dream bone. The Hollow Flute. Avner Strauss. VWA

I have a fairy by my side. My Fairy. "Lewis Carroll." FaBoNo

I have a feeling that my boat. Oceans. Juan Ramón Jiménez, *tr.* by Robert Bly. NU

"I have a few remarks," he smiled." William Matthews. SoTCo

I have a fifth of therapy. Interview with Doctor Drink. James Vincent Cunningham. OxBSP; TW; VGW

I Have a Friend. Anne Spencer. CDC

I have a friend. My Friend. Samuel Allen. FB

I have a friend. Secret Talk. Eve Merriam. ILY

I have a friend, once "Hey war buddy!" Village Hairdresser. Anzai Hitoshi, *tr.* by Hiroaki Sato. FCEI

I have a friend, she says. The Cross-eyed Lover. Donald Finkel. Prf

I have a friend who would give a price for those long fingers all of one length. Snakes, Mongooses, Snake-Charmers and the Like. Marianne Moore. CMoP

I have a garden here, shaped. Letter from an Institution: III. Michael Ryan. AmPA

I have a garden of my own. A Garden Song. Thomas Moore. BoNaP

I Have a Gentle Cock [*or* Gentil Cok]. *Unknown.* MeEL; NOBE; NoP; PBBP; SeCePo

I have a golden ball. A Rune of Riches. Florence Converse. BoTP

I have a grief. Agitato ma Non Troppo. John Crowe Ransom. OxBA

I Have a House. Doris Mühringer, *tr. fr. German by* Beth Bjorklund. CoAuP

I have a jolly shilling, a lovely jolly shilling. The Jolly Shilling. *Unknown.* OBET

I have a life that did not become. Easter Morning. A. R. Ammons. HCAP; NAAL-2; NoAM; NoP

I have a lion, a furry faced lion. The Animal House. Sandy Brechin. Mes

I have a little budgie. The Fat Budgie. John Lennon. NBLV

I have a little home amidst the city's din. The Complacent Cliff-Dweller. Margaret Fishback. PoLF

I have a little house. My Little House. J. M. Westrup. BoTP

I have a little inward light, which still. The Inward Light. Henry Septimus Sutton. WGRP

I have a little kinsman. The Discoverer. Edmund Clarence Stedman. AA; AnAmPo

I have a little shadow that goes in and out with me. My Shadow. Robert Louis Stevenson. FaBoBe; FaBV; FaPON; OnUR; OxBChV; PDV; PWR; TEP

I have a little sister, they call her Peep-Peep. Mother Goose. BoTP; OxNR

I have a little windmill on my head. Sliding Trombone. Georges Ribemont-Dessaignes, *tr.* by David Gascoyne. EAS

I have a mackintosh shiny brown. Chestnut Buds. Evelyn M. Williams. BoTP

I have a mistress, for perfections rare. A Devout Lover. Thomas Randolph. HoPM; OBEV

I have a need not to encounter myself anymore and to forget about everything. Forever There. Pierre Reverdy, *tr.* by Michael Benedikt. POS

I Have a New Garden. *Unknown.* MeEL
(Pear-Tree, The.) GBP

I have a new umbrella. My New Umbrella. M. M. Hutchinson. BoTP

I have a picture in my room in which. Intaglio. Henri Coulette. NePoEA

I have a place to come to. My Place. David Ignatow. CAPP

I have a pretty little flow'r. Francis Daniel Pastorius. SCAP

I have a proved, unerring Guide. The Unerring Guide. Anna Shipton. BLRP

I have a purple dragon. My Dragon. X. J. Kennedy. RAR

I Have a Rendezvous with Death. Alan Seeger. AiP; BLPA; DL; FaBV; FaFP; OHFP; WaP
(Rendezvous, The.) FaPoR; WGRP

I Have a Rendezvous with Life. Countee Cullen. CDC

I have a river in my mind. Six o'Clock. Owen Dodson. PoNe

I Have a Roof. Ada Jackson. TrPWD

I have a room whereinto no one enters. Memory. Christina Rossetti. OBNC

I have a secret place to go. Keziah. Gwendolyn Brooks. RAR; RHPC

"I have a ship in the North Countrie." The Sweet Trinity; or, The Golden Vanity. *Unknown.* OBET

I have a sister, little sister, living in Chung-li. Tu Fu, *tr. fr. Chinese by* Burton Watson. *Fr.* Seven Songs Written During the Ch'ien-yüan Era, 4. CoBCP

I have a smiling face, she said. The Mask. Elizabeth Barrett Browning. OBNC

I have a story fit to tell. The Strong Swimmer. William Rose Benét. PoNe

I have a stove. And Even, Even If They Take Away the Stove. Miron Bialoszewski, *tr. by* Czeslaw Milosz. PwPP

I have a suit, blessings upon it. Describing a Suit. Hafiz Ibrahim, *tr. by* Christopher Tingley *and* Christopher Middleton. MAP

I have a terrible fear of being an animal. César Vallejo, *tr. by* Robert Bly. EAS

I have a tree, a graft of love. Arbor Amoris. Villon, *tr. by* Andrew Lang. AWP

I have a vision. High Heels. Ron Padgett. UL

I have a walking stick. Ryokan, *tr. by* Burton Watson. JLIC-2

I have a whim to speak in verse. *Unknown, tr. fr. Norman French. Fr.* The Fortification of New Ross. NOIV

I have a white cat whose name is Moon. Moon. William Jay Smith. CRH; PDV

I have a white dog. My Dog, Spot. Rodney Bennett. BoTP

I Have a Wild Desire to Die. Herbert Zand, *tr. fr. German by* Beth Bjorklund. CoAuP

I have a young love. The Sailor. Sylvia Townsend Warner. OBMV

I Have a Young Sister. *Unknown.* CH; MeEL; NAEL-1; NoP; OAEL-1
(I Haue [*or* Have] a Yong Suster.) InPS; PoEL-1
("I have a young suster.") EBEV

I have achieved. That which the lonely man. The Seeker. Lascelles Abercrombie. *Fr.* The Fools' Adventure. WGRP

I have all/ my mother's habits. Mother's Habits. Nikki Giovanni. BlSi

I have all these parts stuffed in/ me. Past. Arnold Adoff. TDD

I have allowed myself. For Masturbation. Alan Dugan. CAPP

I have already come to the verge of. An Unborn Child. Derek Mahon. FaBCIP

I have always aspired to a more spacious form. Ars Poetica? Czeslaw Milosz, *tr. by* Lillian Vallee. AnAn

I Have Always Been. Elizabeth McKim. ER

I have always been a communist. Communism. Franco Fortini, *tr. by* Lawrence R. Smith. NItP

I have always been sorry. To the Tune "Glittering Sword Hilts." Liu Yü Hsi, *tr. by* Kenneth Rexroth. UnAS

I Have Always Found It So. Birdie Bell. BLRP

I Have Always Heard of These Old Men. *Unknown.* AmFP

I have always known. The Way It Is. Gloria C. Oden. CNA; IHMS

I have always laughed. Voice. Ron Padgett. UL

I always loved the word *guitar*. Guitar. David St. John. MAYP

I Have an Orchard. Christopher Marlowe. *Fr.* The Tragedy of Dido, IV, v. ChTr

I have an ox but its tail is missing. Shitago, *tr. by* Burton Watson. FCEI
(Song of the Tailless Ox.) JLIC-1

I have an uncle I don't like. Manners. Mariana Griswold Van Rensselaer. FaPON; RHPC

I have answers to all of your questions. Michael Palmer. UL

I Have Approached. Alan Paton. PeSA

I have assumed a conscious sociability. Garden Party. Sir Herbert Read. BrPo

I have awakened from the unknowing to the knowing. For William Edward Burghardt Du Bois on His Eightieth Birthday. Bette Darcie Latimer. PoBA; PoNe

I have baptized thee Withy, because of thy slender limbs. To———? Richard Dehmel, *tr. by* Jethro Bithell. AWP

I have beaten him often, head and heel. Poète Manqué. Ernest Sandeen. CRP

I have beaten my sword into an axe. Wu Chia-chi, *tr. fr. Chinese by* John E. Willis, Jr.. *Fr.* Miscellaneous Poems, II. WFTU

I have become without desire. Twoborn. Rokwaho. STE

I have been/ Three separate times, in war. James Harold Manning. *Fr.* What Is Truth?. CaP

I have been a/ way so long. Homecoming. Sonia Sanchez. PoBA

I have been a censor for fifteen months. Censorship. Arthur Waley. OxBTC; WaP

I Have Been a Foster. *Unknown.* EBEV; FaBoRV; GBP; OxBSP

I have been a movie fan. He Never Did That to Me. Noel Coward. NBLV

I have been abus'd of late. The Scolding Wives Vindication; or, An Answer to the Cuckold's Complaint. *Unknown.* CoMu

I have been bent no less. Time's Mirror. Peyton Houston. *Fr.* Sonnet Variations, LXXVII. Son

I have been cherish'd and forgiven. Hartley Coleridge. PoEL-4

I have been cruel to a fat pigeon. Fly. W. S. Merwin. NNaP

I have been dreaming all a summer day. Dreams. Victor James Daley. PoAu-1

I have been figuring that in a way. The Time Is Today. John Chipman Farrar. GoYe

I have been here before. Sudden Light. Dante Gabriel Rossetti. BoLoP; CTC; ELP; FPL; NOBE; NOBVV; NoP; OAEL-2; OBNC; OPOP; PoLF; TrGrPo
(Song IV: Sudden Light.) CTC

I have been here. Dispersed in meditation. Agnosco Veteris Vestigia Flammae. J. V. Cunningham. QFR; VGW

I have been here for a half hour. The Library. Aidan Carl Mathews. CIP

I have been in a marine aquarium and I have seen. The Marine Aquarium. Louis Dudek. *Fr.* Atlantis. MoCV

I Have Been in Great Distress. Countess de Die Beatrice, *tr. fr. Provençal by* Muriel Kittel. DMF

I have been in heavy thought. Beatrice, Countess de Die, *tr. by* Paul Blackburn. Pro

"I have been in the hills all day." Levavi Oculos. Marion Campbell. PoSH

I have been my arm. Margo Taft. NMM

I have been one acquainted with the night. Acquainted with the Night. Robert Frost. ChTr; CMoP; FPL; HAP; LiTM; MoAmPo; MoP; NoAM; NOBA; PDV; PoE; PoLF; PPP; Son; SoSe; TAP; TwCP; VGW; WeW

I have been profligate of happiness. To Olive. Lord Alfred Bruce Douglas. OBEV

I have been seeing his face everywhere, the face of a former lover. The Lover. Robert Duncan. PeHV

I have been so great a lover. The Great Lover. Rupert Brooke. BrPo; FaFP; FPL; HoPM; LiTB; LiTM; MoBrPo; PoRA; TrGrPo; WaP

I have been taken, have been bound. The Wheat. *Unknown, tr. by* Grace Warwick. PFI

I have been there. On Looking at an Old Climbing Photograph. Douglas Fraser. PoSH

I have been there again, and seen the backs. Again. Jon Stallworthy. OxBC

I Have Been through the Gates. Charlotte Mew. MoAB; MoBrPo; TrGrPo

I have been treading on leaves all day until I am autumn-tired. A Leaf-Treader. Robert Frost. MoAmPo

I have been up and down the town. Hunger. Ruth Stone. InPS

I have been walking today. Furnished Lives. Jon Silkin. NePoEA-2

I have been warned. It is more than thirty years since I wrote. But I Am Growing Old and Indolent. Robinson Jeffers. NOBA; TAP

I have been wondering. A Letter. Anthony Hecht. NYBP; OxBC

I have been young, and now am not too old. Report on Experience. Edmund Blunden. FaBoTw; GTBS-P; NOBE; OBMV; OBWP

"I have beene all day looking after." The Witches' Song. Ben Jonson. CH

I have believed too long in one thing. March Weather. Jon Swan. NYBP

I have borne the anguish of love, which ask me not to describe. Hafiz, *tr. fr. Persian by* John Hindley. *Fr.* Odes, XI. AWP

I Have Bowed before the Sun. Anna Walters. WPOW

I have brothers, younger brothers in a place far away. Tu Fu, *tr. fr. Chinese by* Burton Watson. *Fr.* Seven Songs Written During the Ch'ien-yüan Era, 3. CoBCP

I have brought berries on a grape-leaf. Keepsake from Quinault. Dorothy Alyea. GoYe

I have burned ten thousand volumes. On the Day of Washing the Buddha in the Year *Ting-wei*. T'ang Hsien-Tsu, *tr. by* Jonathan Chaves. CoBLCP

I have but one story. Summer Is Gone. *Unknown, tr. by* Sean O'Faolain. AnIL

I have carried for five years. The Return. Jon Silkin. NePoEA-2

I have carried it with me each day: that morning I took. A Morning. Mark Strand. GeTw; HCAP

I have carried my pillow to the windowsill. Summer near the River. Carolyn Kizer. CoAP; VGW

I have carried my word in you like a flame. A Voice. Yves Bonnefoy, *tr. by* Paul Auster. RHTwFP

I have cast off the world. After Entering Religious Life. Saigyo, *tr. fr. Japanese by* Burton Watson. *Fr.* Sixty-four Tanka. FCEI

I have climbed into silence trying for clear air. Recuerdo. Paula Gunn Allen. STE

I have come back again. The Return of the Native. Harley Matthews. PoAu-2

I have come down to the garden. At the Place of the Roman Baths. "Richard Scrace." CaP

I have come far enough. A Form of Women. Robert Creeley. CAPP; NaP

I have come far to have found nothing. Cid Corman. *Fr.* Three Tiny Songs. VGW

I have come on the River of Yellow Flowers. A Green Stream. Wang Wei, *tr. by* Witter Bynner *and* Kiang Kang-hu. SD

I have come to catch birds. The Bird Catcher. *Unknown, tr. by* Ulli Beier. TTY

I have come to rely. Birds and Roses Are Birds and Roses. William Heyen. GeTw

I have come to the borders of sleep. Lights Out. Edward Thomas. BrPo; Mes; MMA; NOBE; OBD

I Have Come to the Conclusion. Nelle Fertig. FF

I have come to where the world drops off. Visit to a Hospital. Jean Valentine Chace. GoYe

I have come to you, Babi Yar. Babi Yar. Lev Ozerov, *tr. by* Daniel Weissbort. VWA

I have come upon the visage again. Wood Floor Dreams. Lance Henson. VoR

I have continued to seek her. The Constant Lover. Louis Simpson. NYBP

I have courage and hardihood. Besieged. Zalman Schneour, *tr. by* Joseph Leftwich. TrJP

I have crossed an ocean. Grace Nichols. UAS

I have crossed the bridges of Cé. C. Louis Aragon, *tr. by* William Jay Smith. CT

I Have Cut an Eagle. James Koller. PoM

I have desired to go. Heaven-Haven. Gerard Manley Hopkins. ACP; BrPo; HeIP; MoAB; MoBrPo; MoP; MOS; NoAM; NOBE; NOCV; OBEV; OBNC; OxBSP; RB; SoSe; SOTW; TOF; TrGrPo

I have determined that my dear lord's name. *Unknown. Fr.* Manyo Shu. Ma

I have discovered a country. Connais-Tu le Pays? Richard Shelton. NYBP

I have discovered finally to-day. The Silent Pool. Harold Monro. BrPo

I have discovered that most of. January Morning. William Carlos Williams. InPS; SOTW

I have dispensed with reasoning. Of Reason and Discovery. Don Mattera. WMBCH

I have done all I could. The Tree and the Lady. Thomas Hardy. MoAB; MoBrPo

I have done it again. Lady Lazarus. Sylvia Plath. CAPP; FaBoWP; HCAP; MAT; MoP; NAAL-2; NaP; NIP; NoAM; NOBA; NoP; PrIm; TAP; VGW

I have done one braver thing. The Undertaking. John Donne. MePo; NAEL-1; NOBE

I have done the deed—Didst thou not hear a noise? Shakespeare. *Fr.* Macbeth, II, ii. EBEV
(Macbeth Does Murder Sleep.) FiP

I Have Dreamed of You So Much. Robert Desnos, *tr. fr. French by* Paul Auster. RHTwFP

I have dreamt it again: standing suddenly still. Wormwood. Thomas Kinsella. CIP; FaBCIP

I have drifted in silence. Imitations Based on the American. Frank Polite. BXAP

I have drunk ale from the Country of the Young. He Thinks of His Past Greatness When a Part of the Constellations of Heaven. W. B. Yeats. PoEL-5

I have eaten/ the plums. This Is Just to Say. William Carlos Williams. FF; GoJo; HoPM; InPK; InPS; NAAL-2; NIP; NoAM; NOBA; NoP; RHPC; SOTW; TAP

I have eaten the city. Manhattan. H. R. Hays. EAS

I have escaped from the two acre rolled garden. If It Would All Please Hurry. James Tate. MAYP

I have fallen in love with American names. American Names. Stephen Vincent Benét. AmFN; GOA; OBAL; OPP; OxBA

I have fastened everything within a black cloak. The Assignation. Juana de Ibarbourou, *tr. by* Brian Swann. PBWP

I have fathered. Father Poem. Joel Oppenheimer. PoM

I have felt it as they've said. Larry Eigner. PoM

"I have finished another year," said God. New Year's Eve. Thomas Hardy. MoBrPo; NoAM

I Have Folded My Sorrows. Bob Kaufman. AmNP; PoBA

I have followed you model. Ode to a Model. Vladimir Nabokov. OBAL

I have forgotten you as one forgets at dawning. Words. Helen Morgan Brooks. PoNe

I have forsaken. Ito Sachio, *tr. by* Geoffrey Bownas *and* Anthony Thwaite. PeBJV

I have forsworn it while I life. The Wake at the Well. *Unknown.* GBP

I Have Fought the Good Fight. Jared Bell Waterbury. AH

I have found out a gift for my Erin. A Pastoral Ballad by John Bull. Thomas Moore. BIrV; OBSV

I have found violets. April hath come on. April. Nathaniel Parker Willis. AnAmPo

I have friends. Cheryl Thomas. ILY

I have gathered luss/ At the wane of the moon. The Herb-Leech. Joseph Campbell. AnIL

I have gone back in boyish wonderment. Return. Sterling Allen Brown. CDC

I have gone far from my beloved ones. Jerusalem the Dismembered. Uri Zvi Greenberg, *tr. fr. Hebrew by* Charles A. Cowen. *Fr.* Jerusalem. TrJP

I have gone out, a possessed witch. Her Kind. Anne Sexton. CAPP; CoAP; FF; HCAP; HeIP; LiTM; PPP; TAP; TwCP; WPOW

I have gone past all those times when the poets. In Memory of Leopardi. James Wright. NaP

I have got a new-born sister. Choosing a Name. Charles *and* Mary Lamb. OxBChV

I Have Got My Leave. Rabindranath Tagore. *Fr.* Gitanjali. OBMV

I Have Got to Stop Loving You. Ai. GeTw

I have great need that the Saint grant help. Cynewulf, *tr. fr. Anglo-Saxon by* Charles W. Kennedy. *Fr.* Juliana. AnOE

I have grown old. Shotetsu, *tr. by* Steven D. Carter. WFTW

I have grown old and dull, and out of date. War Widow. Margaret Hamilton Noël-Paton. CN

I have grown past hate and bitterness. Nationality. Mary Gilmore. CBAP; PoAu-1; WTO

I have grown used to the retreat of seasons. Lady Anne Bathing. Anthony Delius. PeSA

I have had not one word from her. Sappho, *tr. by* Mary Barnard. PeHV

I have had playmates, I have had companions. The Old Familiar Faces. Charles Lamb. AWP; BLPA; EnRP; FaBoBe; FaBoRV; FaFP; FaPoR; FPL; GTBS; GTBS-P; NOBE; OBEV; RB; ViBoPo

I have had to learn the simplest things. Maximus, to Himself. Charles Olson. *Fr.* The Maximus Poems. CAPP; CMoP; CMOP; NeAP; NOBA; PoE; PoM; VGW

I Have Had to Learn to Live with My Face. Diane Wakoski. ER

I have had to stop answering yes and no. Diseases of the Moon. Doug Fetherling. NeAC

I have heard/ He does not bestow horses for poems. A Miserly Patron. *Unknown, tr. by* Myles Dillon. AnIL

I Have Heard. *Unknown.* FiBHP

I have heard a mother bird. Welcome to Spring. Irene Thompson. BoTP

I have heard about the Indian. Preface to Dying. Gyorgy Raba, *tr. by* Jascha Kessler. FOC

I have heard ingenuous Indians say. Roger Williams. SCAP

I have heard of fish. The Sun. Anne Sexton. NYBP; PBWP

I have heard of this destruction. The Letter. Charles Reznikoff. VWA

I have heard some jealous women say. Romantic. George Garrett. HoPM

I have heard talk of bold Robin Hood. Robin Hood's Golden Prize. *Unknown.* ESPB

I have heard tell somewhere. The Old Dog in the Ruins of the Graves at Arles. James Wright. NNaP

I have heard that hysterical women say. Lapis Lazuli. W. B. Yeats. CMoP; FaBoMo; FaBoTw; FF; HeIP; InPS; LiTB; LiTM; MAT; MoP; NAEL-2; NAWM-2; NoAM; NOBE; NoP; OAEL-2; TEP

I have heard the pigeons of the Seven Woods. In the Seven Woods. W. B. Yeats. CMoP; NoAM
I have heard the stirring chorus. I Have Heard. *Unknown.* FiBHP
I Have Heard Them Knock. Michael Hartnett. NOIV
I have heard your voice floating, royal and real. To Dinah Washington. Etheridge Knight. PoBA
I have helped to kill. Self-Judgment. Berta Lask, *tr. by* Susan L. Cocalis *and* Gerlinde Geiger. DMG
I have hopped, when properly wound up. The Tin Frog. Russell Hoban. RHPC; TSS
I have humped my bluey in all the States. My Old Black Billy. Edward Harrington. PoAu-1
I have imagined all this. The Sleeping. Lynn Emanuel. AiP; MAYP
I have in my hand here a brown bottle. The Bottle. Al Levine. GrPl
I have it in my heart to serve God so. Of His Lady in Heaven. Jacopo da Lentino, *tr. by* Dante Gabriel Rossetti. AWP; PFI
I have just come down from my father. The Hospital Window. James Dickey. CAPP; DiL; HCAP; MT; NoAM
"I have just come from the salt, salt sea." The House Carpenter. *Unknown.* AS
I have just flown 1100 miles from Australia. Christchurch, N. Z. Earle Birney. OxBC
I have just seen a most beautiful thing. The Black Finger. Angelina Weld Grimké. AmNP; PoBA
I have killed the moth flying around. Moth-Terror. Benjamin De Casseres. TrJP
I have known it from the beginning. Aristophanes' Symposium. Rita Mae Brown. IHMS
I have known nights rain-washed and crystal-clear. Wisdom. Frank Yerby. AmNP
I have known one bound to a bed by wrist and ankle. The Choice. Hilary Corke. NYBP
I have known the inexorable sadness of pencils. Dolor. Theodore Roethke. AmPP; CMoP; HCAP; HeIP; HoPM; LiTM; MoP; NoAM; OxBSP; PoA
I have known the silence of the stars and of the sea. Silence. Edgar Lee Masters. MoAmPo
I have known the strange nurses of Kindness. But I Do Not Need Kindness. Gregory Corso. NeAP
I have known them, known them all. Gentlemen. Jules Laforgue, *tr. by* William Jay Smith. CT
I Have Labored Sore. *Unknown.* WeW
I have lain in the sun. Fortunatus Nimium. Robert Bridges. BrPo (Nimium Fortunatus.) MoAB; MoBrPo
I have learned not to worry about love. New Face. Alice Walker. AIW
I have learned sloppiness from an old sow. For the Eating of Swine. Rodney Jones. MAYP
I have led a good life, full of peace and quiet. The Good Boy. *Unknown.* AS
I have led her home, my love, my only friend. Tennyson. *Fr.* Maud, I, xviii. ChER; EBVV; ELP; FiP; NAEL-2; NOBVV; PoEL-5
I have left you four flies. To the Spider in the Crevice behind the Toilet Door. Janet Sutherland. DT
I have let all my balloons aloose. Breaking Out. A. R. Ammons. CAPP
I Have Lighted the Candles, Mary. Kenneth Patchen. TrCP
I Have Lived and I Have Loved. *Unknown.* TTTS
I have lived in important places, times. Epic. Patrick Kavanagh. BIrV; CIP; FaBCIP; IPY; NOIV
I Have Lived Long Enough. Shakespeare. *Fr.* Macbeth, V, iii. TrGrPo
I have lived long enough, having seen one thing, that love hath an end. Hymn to Proserpine. Swinburne. EBVV; NAEL-2; OAEL-2; OBNC; PoEL-5; TEP
I have lived my life. Momoyo. *Fr.* Manyo Shu. Ma
I Have Lived This Way for Years and Do Not Wish to Change. Michael C. Blumenthal. HCAP
I have lived with Christ. After Golgotha. Jabra Ibrahim Jabra, *tr. by* Abdullah al-Udhari. MPAW
I have looked at this photograph. Rescue. Dabney Stuart. NYBP
I have looked through the pine-trees. .303. Keith Douglas. FL
I have lost a true man's mettle. Hitomaro. *Fr.* Manyo Shu. Ma
I have lost, and lately, these. Upon the Loss [e] of His Mistresses. Robert Herrick. CaPo; NAEL-1; PoE; SeCV-1
I have lost her, I know. Mother. Daniel Lawrence Kelleher. NeIP
I Have Lost My Shoes. Constantino Suasnavar, *tr. fr. Spanish by* Muna Lee. FaPON
I Have Loved England. Alice Duer Miller. *Fr.* The White Cliffs. BLPL; PoLF
I Have Loved Flowers. Robert Bridges. GoJo; MoAB; MoBrPo
I have loved large cities, capitals of the world. The Master City. Rose J. Orente. GoYe

I have loved thirty by three. Gormley, *tr. fr. Irish by* Joan Keefe. *Fr.* Gormley's Laments. PBWP
I have made a pledge. Kenko, *tr. by* Steven D. Carter. WFTW
I have made a sirventes against the city of Toulouse. Sirventes. Paul Blackburn. NeAP; PoM
I have made a sirventes in which no word is missing. Bertrans de Born, *tr. by* Paul Blackburn. Pro
I have made tales in verse, but this man made. The Waggon-Maker. John Masefield. EBEV
I have marked, as on the heather now I strayed. As on the Heather. Reinmar von Hagenau, *tr. by* Jethro Bithell. AWP
I have met them at close of day. Easter, 1916. W. B. Yeats. BrPo; CMoP; FaBoMo; FaBoPV; FaPoR; HAP; HeIP; InPS; LiTM; MoAB; MoP; NAEL-2; NAWM-2; NIP; NoAM; NOBE; NOIV; NoP; OAEL-2; OBWP; OxBTC; PoE; PPP
I have mislaid the torment and the fear. Success. William Empson. OxBTC
I have moved to Dublin to have it out with you. John Berryman. *Fr.* Dream Songs. MoP; NoAM
I have my heart on my fist. The Tomb of the Kings. Anne Hébert, *tr. by* Kathleen Weaver. PBWP
I have my piety too, which could. An Epitaph on Master Vincent Corbett. Ben Jonson. JCP
I have never been on the cloudy slopes of Olympus. The Valley of Men. Uri Zvi Greenberg. VWA, *tr. by* Robert Mezey *and* Ben Zion Gold
I Have Never Forgotten You. André Frénaud, *tr. fr. French by* Kenneth Rexroth. RHTwFP
I have never seen him, this invisible member of the panel, this thirteenth juror. The People vs. the People. Kenneth Fearing. MoAmPo
I have never seen the place where I was born. Birthplace. Tahereh Saffarzadeh, *tr. by* Deirdre Lashgari. AIW; WPOW
I have never seen volcanoes. Emily Dickinson. PoEL-5
I have no ale. The Muse. W. H. Davies. BrPo
I have no answer to the blank inequity. Mama's Promise. Marilyn Nelson Waniek. ER
I have no case to bring against socialism. Confession of Faith. Imre Csanádi, *tr. by* Edwin Morgan. MHuP
I have no darkened cape. Dominatrix. Clifford Young. VVA
I have no desire to live, but I am afraid of death. Ts'ai Yen, *tr. fr. Chinese by* Kenneth Rexroth *and* Ling Chung. *Fr.* Eighteen Verses Sung to a Tatar Reed Whistle, XI. WPOW
I have no dog, but it must be. My Dog. John Kendrick Bangs. BLPA; BLPL; FaBoBe
I have no embroidered headband. Sappho, *tr. fr. Greek by* Willis Barnstone. BoWoP
I have no illusions. Visibility. Maura Stanton. NAmP
I have no mind to bow to the Buddha, peer into the heart. Natsume Soseki, *tr. fr. Chinese by* Burton Watson. JLIC-2
I have no more a golden store. The Merry Jovial Beggar. Peter Casey, *tr. by* Douglas Hyde. TIRV; WTO
I have no name. Infant Joy. Blake. *Fr.* Songs of Innocence. FaPON; GoJo; NAEL-2; NAs; OxBSP; PoLF; TEP
I have no news of the animals. The Animals. Charles Simic. GeTw
I Have No Pain. *Unknown.* FaBoCo
I have no rattles. *Ambo Oral Tradition.* *Fr.* Five Ghost Songs. TTTS
I Have No Seed to Scatter through the World. Patrizia Cavalli, *tr. fr. Italian by* Muriel Kittel. DMI
I Have No Strength for Mine. Joanne Kyger. PoM
I have no vessel, I receive. Ozaki Hosai, *tr. fr. Japanese by* Hiroaki Sato. *Fr.* One Hundred Haiku in Free Form. FCEI
I have no wife. To the Old Masters. Wing Tek Lum. BrSi
I have no wit, no words, no tears. A Better Resurrection. Christina Rossetti. NOBVV; TrPWD
I have not been as Joshua when he fought. Three Helpers in Battle. Mary Elizabeth Coleridge. EaLo
I have not ever seen my father's grave. Father Son and Holy Ghost. Audre Lorde. NoAM; PoBA
I Have Not Lingered in European Monasteries. Leonard Cohen. NOBC
I have not loved the world, nor the world me. The Poet and the World. Byron. *Fr.* Childe Harold's Pilgrimage, III. SeCePo
I have not met her for so long. Prince Kadobe. *Fr.* Manyo Shu. Ma
I have not seen your writing. The Letter. Patricia Beer. OxBC
I have not so much emulated the birds that musically sing. To Soar in Freedom and in Fullness of Power. Walt Whitman. RFM
I have not spent the April of my time. Bartholomew Griffin. *Fr.* Fidessa, More Chaste than Kind, XXXV. AAS (Sonnet: "I have not spent the April of my time.") EiL (Youth.) OBSC
I have not told my garden yet. Emily Dickinson. AnAmPo (Secret, The.) AA
I have not used my darkness well. Squall. Stanley Moss. CoAP

I have not written my poem. The Experiment That Failed. John Logan. NU

I have nothing new to ask of you. Another Year Come. W. S. Merwin. NYBP; OFD; PCP

I have nothing to give you, but my anger. A Love Poem for My Country. Frank Mkalawile Chipasula. WMBCH

I have nothing to say about the war. Yehuda Amichai, *tr. fr.* Hebrew by Warren Bargod *and* Stanley F. Chyet. *Fr.* Songs of the Land of Zion Jerusalem, 4. IP

I have nothing to say about the way the sky tilts. Charles Wright. *Fr.* Four Poems for the New Year. AnAn; CAPP

I have nothing to say about this garden. Unexpected Visit. Fleur Adcock. ATNZ

I have often sung of the snow. Shining Thing. Gabriel Preil, *tr. by* Bernhard Frank. MHeP

I have outlived most things and people round me. Prince P. A. Vyazemsky, *tr. by* Alan Myers. AAA

I have pined for the sight of the sea for years. The Beautiful Sea. Mary E. Tucker. CBWP-1

I have poured my dreams in the pot's dim womb. Peter Titheradge. *Fr.* Teatime Variations: after W. B. Yeats. FaBoPa

I have praised many loved ones in my song. Mother. Theresa Helburn. FaPON; OHIP

I have prepared my sister's tongue. The Joy of Cooking. Elaine Magarrell. SoTCo

I have properly spoken. A Poem for Anton Schmidt. William Pillen. VWA

I have read, in some old marvellous tale. The Beleaguered City. Longfellow. AnAmPo

I have read my name on a rock. In the Arab Maghreb. Badr Shakir al-Sayyab, *tr. by* Lena Jayyusi *and* Christopher Middleton. MAP

I Have Recently Edited My Unworthy Poems, *sel.* Chin Nung, *tr. fr.* Chinese by Jonathan Chaves.
   "In the silences between peals of the bell." CoBLCP

I have risen from your body. The Onion. John Thompson. NOBC

I have robbed the garrulous streets. For the Goddess Too Well Known. Elsa Gidlow. PeHV

I have said that the soul is not more than the body. A Hub for the Universe. Walt Whitman. *Fr.* Song of Myself, XLVIII. FaFP

I have seen a court, and a dozen courts. A Christmas Revel. Dafydd Bach ap Madog Wladaidd. OBMV

I have seen a gum-tree. Flesh. Mary Elizabeth Fullerton. PoAu-1

I have seen a lovely thing. Blight. Arna Bontemps. BANP; CDC

I have seen, at the beginning of day. The Lady Clothed in Flame. Dante, *tr. fr.* Italian by C. H. Sisson. *Fr.* Divina Commedia: Purgatorio, III. PFI

I Have Seen Black Hands. Richard Wright. PoBA

I have seen bus depots. Reflecting on the Aging-Process. Robert Peters. BXAP

I have seen come on. Death. John Stone. MT

I have seen flowers come in stony places. John Masefield. FaBoEE; OxBTC

I have seen her, wonderful! This Version of Love. Dorothy Hewett. CBAP

I have seen mannequins. W. J. Turner. *Fr.* The Seven Days of the Sun. OBMV

I have seen my ghost broken. To Conquer Variety. Hart Crane. AnAn

I have seen, O desolate one, the voice has its tower. Bell Tower. Léonie Adams. MoAB; MoAmPo

I have seen old ships sail like swans asleep. The Old Ships. James Elroy Flecker. BrPo; CH; FaBoRV; MoBrPo; MOS; OBMV; PoRA

I have seen tall chimneys without smoke. Drought. Frederick E. Laight. OBCV
   (Soliloquy.) CaP

I have seen the Birds of Paradise. The Birds of Paradise. John Peale Bishop. GoJo

I have seen the flame. It is everywhere. The Flame. Eugène Guillevic, *tr. by* Teo Savory. RHTwFP

I have seen the light coming up over the town, like ash. Overture to Strangers. Phyllis Haring. PeSA

I have seen the poets of the West. That Poem. Juan Sáez Burgos, *tr. by* Julio Marzán. InW

I Have Seen the Robins Fall. Louis Dudek. CaP

I have seen the sea in many moods. The Sea. Ken Noyle. MOS

I have seen the smallest minds of my generation. Problem in Social Geometry—the Inverted Square! Ray Durem. NBP; PoBA

I have seen the soft light flicker. Message from Ohanapecosh Glacier. W. M. Ransom. CDW

I have seen the white horsemen riding to hell. Apocalypse and Resurrection. John Clifford Bayliss. EAS

I have seen the young Negroes and Puerto Ricans. A Documentary on Airplane Glue. David Henderson. MAT

I have seen them at many hours. Moths. Julia Fields. *Fr.* Poems: Birmingham 1962–1964. PoBA; PoNe

I have seen you suffer in the midst of winters. Harlem. Jean Brierre, *tr. by* John F. Matheus. TTY

I have seen your feet gilded by morning. Metamorphoses of M. John Peale Bishop. ErPo

I Have Set My Heart So High. *Unknown.* OAEL-1

I have set out to follow the day. The Cry of Generations. Mordechai Husid, *tr. by* Seymour Mayne *and* Rivka Augenfeld. VWA

I have settled down. Sleepless on a Summer Night. Umberto Saba. VWA, *tr. by* Keith Bosley

I have seven measures of white thread. Summer Spinning. Saibara, *tr. by* Hiroaki Sato. FCEI

I have snapped off my burning. Maui. Meg Campbell. PeNZ

"I have so many women" he said inside her. Splitting the Infinite. Yona Wallach, *tr. by* Warren Bargod *and* Stanley F. Chyet. IP

I have so much faith in you. I believe. To Trust. Antonia Pozzi, *tr. by* Lynne Lawner. PBWP

I Have Some Friends before Me Gone. *Unknown.* AH

I have something for you to laugh at, Cato. Catullus, *tr. by* James Michie. PeHV

I have sought long with steadfastness. Sir Thomas Wyatt. SiPS

I have sought the elusive aroma. Barbecue Service. James Applewhite. MT

I have sown beside all waters in my day. A Black Man Talks of Reaping. Arna Bontemps. AmNP; BANP; BPo; CDC; FB; IDB; PoBA; PoNe

I have sown upon the fields. The Idle Flowers. Robert Bridges. BoNaP; ChTr

I have spent a restless and sleepless night. Dawn. Juana de Ibarbourou, *tr. by* Perry Higman. LPSS

I have spoken with [*or* to] a goat. The Goat. Umberto Saba. PFI, *tr. by* T. G. Bergin; VWA, *tr. by* Anita Barrows
   (I have spoken to a goat.) VWA, *tr. by* Anita Barrows

I have spot-resistant trousers. Summer Song. W. W. Watt. FiBHP

I have strolled the long groves of the classics and canons. Rhyme-Prose on the Idle Life. P'an Yüeh, *tr. by* Burton Watson. CoBCP

I have struggled all day with a thought like a wild noble horse. Wild Horse. Elder Olson. GrPl

I have studied the tight curls on the back of your neck. Movement Song. Audre Lorde. CNA

I have sworn ten thousand times. Kenneth Rexroth, *after the Greek of* Palladas. NNaP

I Have Taken a Thrush. Vincent O'Sullivan. ATNZ

I have taken that vow. The Red-haired Man's Wife. James Stephens. MoBrPo

I have taken the woman of beauty. The Bear's Song. *Unknown, tr. by* Constance Lindsay Skinner. *Fr.* Three Songs from the Haida. AWP

I have talked to you, talked. Mirabai, *tr. by* John Stratton Hawley *and* Mark Juergensmeyer. SSI

I have ten little fingers. Ten Fingers. *Unknown.* RAR

I have that sure enclitic to my act. Hart Crane. AnAn

I have the greatest fun at night. The Quilt. Mary Effie Lee Newsome. CDC

I have the obit of my lady dere. The Whole Treasure of All Wordly Bliss. Charles, Duc d' Orléans. OxBLMV

I Have the Right. Ana Blandiana, *tr. fr.* Rumanian by Laura Schiff. OV

I have this deal of death about my hands. Blood. Ray Bremser. NeAP

I have this to say, if I can say it. Before Sentence Is Passed. Richard Palmer Blackmur. LiTA

I have thought long this wild wet night that brought no rest. A Sleepless Night. Egan O'Rahilly, *tr. by* Frank O'Connor. AnIL

I have thought of beaches, fields. Bundles. Carl Sandburg. MoAmPo

I Have Three Daughters. Ruth Stone. InPS; NMM

I have thrown wide my window. Midnight. Michael Roberts. OBMV

I have to get in. Maine. Elinor Nauen. UL

I have to jump up. Wide Awake. Myra Cohn Livingston. RAR

I have to live with myself, and so. Myself. Edgar A. Guest. BLPA; BLPL

I have to live with myself, and so. Myself. Waring. PWR

I have to take my little brother. Lil' Bro.' Karama Fufuka. RHPC

I have told you. Tenth Symphony. John Ashbery. NOBA

I have tossed hours upon the tides of fever. Bout with Burning. Vassar Miller. LiTM; MoAmPo; MT; NePoEA

I have touched the furrows of centuries. Cachikel Woman. Vidaluz Meneses, *tr. by* David Volpendesta. Vol

I have traveled, I have traveled. The Consumptive. Priscilla Jane Thompson. CBWP-2

I have travelled sometime up and down our coast. Gazeteer of Newfoundland. Michael Harrington. CaP

I have tried to shift the stars. The Juniper Moon Pulls at My Bones. Earle Thompson. HATNAP

I have trod this path a hundred times. The Miracle. Emerson. FM

I have turned the newspaper boy into a diver. Dear Norman. Carol Ann Duffy. NPo

I have turned to the landscape because men disappoint me. The Ram's Horn. John Hewitt. BIrV

I Have Twelve Oxen. *Unknown*. ChTr; GBP
(Twelve Oxen, The.) CH

I have two friends—two glorious friends—two better could not be. The Two Friends. Charles Godfrey Leland. AA

I have two sparrows white as snow. Michael Drayton. *Fr*. Muses' Elysium [*or* Elizium]: The Second Nimphall. PBBP

"I have two wives." Mohammed Ibrahim Speaks. Martha Beidler. FF

I have waited on my lord. *Unknown*. *Fr*. Manyo Shu. Ma

I have walked a great while over the snow. The Witch. Mary Elizabeth Coleridge. BrRo; WPE

I have wanted other things more than lovers. Monody to the Sound of Zithers. Kay Boyle. PoA

I have watched you. Saying Goodbye. Suzanne Juhasz. IHMS

I have watched you dancing. Theme Brown Girl. Elton Hill. NBP

I have watched you grow. Soweto. Sipho Sepamla. WMBCH

I have watched your fingers drum. The Hand. Howard Moss. TAP

I have wept with the spring storm. After the Persian. Louise Bogan. PoA

I have wished a bird would fly away. A Minor Bird. Robert Frost. CMoP

I have wished you dead and myself dead. Years. Alicia Ostriker. ER

I have with fishing-rod and line. The Wounded Hawk. Herbert Edward Palmer. FaBoTw

I have wrapped my dreams in a silken cloth. For a Poet. Countee Cullen. PoNe; TTY

I have wrought these words together out of a wryed existence. The Wife's Complaint. *Unknown*, *tr. by* Michael Alexander. BoLoP

I have xeroxed my navel. Certified Copy. Ann Deagon. NIP

I have your lewd letter received. Skelton Laureate, Defender, against Lusty Garnesche, Well-beseen Christopher, Challenger. John Skelton. TW

I haven't sung your praise. To My Country. "Rahel", *tr. by* Diane Mintz. PBWP

I hear/ he won't give horses for poems. An Insult. *Unknown*. NOIV

I hear a sudden cry of pain! The Snare. James Stephens. BoTP; CH; CMoP; PDV

I Hear a Voice. H. Leivick, *tr. fr. Yiddish by* David G. Roskies. VWA

I hear a whistling. Emmett Till. James A. Emanuel. CNA; NIP; PoBA

I hear again the tread of war go thundering through the land. Albert Sidney Johnston. Kate Brownlee Sherwood. PAH

I Hear America Griping. Morris Bishop. AmFN

I Hear America Singing. Walt Whitman. AiP, *ll*. 1-9; AmFN; AnAmPo; AWP; FaBoBe; FaBV; FaFP; FaPON; FF; FPL; HAP; LiTA; MoAmPo; OPP; PDV; SaC; TrGrPo; WeW

I hear an army charging up the land. James Joyce. *Fr*. Chamber Music, XXXVI. MoP

I hear and behold God in every object, yet understand God not in the least. Walt Whitman. *Fr*. Song of Myself, XLVIII. WGRP

I Hear and See Not Strips of Cloth Alone. Walt Whitman. WaaP

I hear eating. Night Fun. Judith Viorst. RAR

I hear enormous noises in the night. March Winds. Cecil Francis Lloyd. CaP

I hear ghosts of grouse. Opening Day. Bruce Severy. NOVW

I hear her voice like. Her Voice. Barney Bush. HATNAP

I hear in my heart, I hear in its ominous pulses. The Wild Ride. Louise Imogen Guiney. AA

I hear it in the wind. Autumn Dusk. Empress Eifuku, *tr. by* Steven D. Carter. WFTW

I Hear It Said. Barbara Young. BLPA

I Hear It Was Charged against Me. Walt Whitman. LiTA; MoAmPo; PPP

I hear leaves drinking rain. The Rain. W. H. Davies. BoTP; OxBTC

I hear many voices. To Adhiambo. Gabriel Okara. PBA

I hear my mother whose hips have/ broadened. Violets for Mother. Lonny Kaneko. BrSi

I hear some say, this man is not in love. Michael Drayton. *Fr*. Idea, XXIV. TrGrPo

I Hear Something Falling. Natan Zach, *tr. fr. Hebrew by* Warren Bargad *and* Stanley F. Chyet. IP

I hear that Andromeda. Sappho, *tr. fr. Greek by* Mary Barnard. PBWP

I hear that the peonies are magnificent. To Hsü Shih-t'ing. Hsü Wei, *tr. by* Jonathan Chaves. CoBLCP

I hear that you have burned ten thousand of your poems. Twenty-eight Characters Sent to Tung-ts'un. Cheng Hsieh, *tr. by* Jonathan Chaves. CoBLCP

I hear the beat. The Talking Drums. Kojo Gyinaye Kyei. PBA

I hear the bell striking. Lady Kasa. *Fr*. Manyo Shu. FCEI

I hear the doctor's loud success. Waiting for the Doctor. Colette Inez. IHMS

I hear the halting footsteps of a lass. Harlem Shadows. Claude McKay. AmPP; BANP; PoNe

I hear the man downstairs slapping the hell out of his stupid wife again. The.38. Ted Joans. WeW

I hear the noise about thy keel. Tennyson. *Fr*. In Memoriam A. H. H., X. EBVV

I hear the robins singing in the rain. On a Gloomy Easter. Alice Freeman Palmer. OHIP

I hear the shadowy horses, their long manes a-shake. Michael Robartes Bids His Beloved Be at Peace. W. B. Yeats. BrPo; MoP; NoAM

I hear the sound of affliction. They are weeping. How It Is. Uri Zvi Greenberg, *tr. by* Robert Mezey *and* Ben Zion Gold. VWA

I hear the twang of the mid-string. Empress Kogyoku. *Fr*. Manyo Shu. Ma

I hear them. the crickets. Owl. Rokwaho. STE

I hear voices praising Tshombe, and the Portuguese. Hatred of Men with Black Hair. Robert Bly. NaP; TW

I hear you call. The Call of the River Nun. Gabriel Okara. PBA

I hear you, little bird. Joy of the Morning. Edwin Markham. AA; FaPON

I Hear You've Let Go. Rosario Ferre, *tr. fr. Spanish by* Willis Barnstone. BoWoP

I heard a/ couple of fleas. Archy, the Cockroach, Speaks. Don Marquis. *Fr*. Certain Maxims of Archy. FaPON

I heard a bird at dawn. The Rivals. James Stephens. BoTP; FaPON; InvP; OBEV; OBMV

I Heard a Bird Sing. Oliver Herford. NTCP; PDV; PoLF; RHPC

I heard a brooklet gushing. Whither? Wilhelm Müller, *tr. by* Longfellow. AWP

I heard a clash, and a cry. Middle Ages. Siegfried Sassoon. SO

I heard a cow low, a bonnie cow low. *Unknown*. *Fr*. The Queen of Elfan's [*or* Elfland's] Nourice [*or* Nourrice]. ESPB; FaBoCh

I heard a fly buzz—when I died. Emily Dickinson. AmPP; AnAmPo; BoWoP; CMoP; DL; FF; HAP; HoPM; InPK; LiTA; LiTM; MoAB; MoAmPo; MoP; NAAL-1; NAWM-2; NoAM; NOBA; NoP; OBD; OxBA; PoE; PoRA; PPP; SCV; SOTW; TAP; TOF; WeW

I heard a horseman. The Horseman. Walter de la Mare. GoJo; RHPC

I Heard a Linnet Courting. Robert Bridges. BrPo; LiTB; LiTM; OBMV
(Linnet, The.) OBEV

I heard a man and his wife. A Man and His Wife. Peter Redgrove *and* Penelope Shuttle. PoPo

I heard a mouse. The Mouse. Elizabeth Jane Coatsworth. BoTP; FaPON; MoShBr; OBCA

I Heard a Noise and Wishèd for a Sight. *Unknown*. EBEV; HAP; InvP
(Shadow, A.) EIL
(Shadow and Substance.) OAEL-1

I Heard a Soldier. Herbert Trench. CH

I heard a thousand blended notes. Lines Written in Early Spring. Wordsworth. EnRP; FPL; GTBS; GTBS-P; NAEL-2; OAEL-2; PoLF
(Written in Early Spring.) GTBS; GTBS-P

I heard a voice at evening softly say. Day by Day. Julia Harris May. BLRP

I heard a voice that cried, "Make way for those who died!" The March. J. C. Squire. OHIP

I heard a woman's voice that wailed. In Ruin Reconciled. Aubrey Thomas De Vere. BIrV

I heard a wood thrush in the dusk. Wood Song. Sara Teasdale. AnAmPo

I heard an ancient sound: a cock that crew. Daybreak. Frances Cornford. FM

I heard an angel speak last night. A Curse for a Nation. Elizabeth Barrett Browning. WPE; WPOW

I heard an ignorant crow call, "Life is now." Old Snapshot. Ronald G. Everson. MoCV

I heard an old farm-wife. The Son. Ridgely Torrence. InvP

I heard an owl at midday. Como lo Siento. Lorna Dee Cervantes. NoAM

I heard from a decent man the other day. On Hearing It Has Been Ordered in the Chapterhouse of Ireland That the Friars Make No More Songs or Verses. Padraigin Haicead, *tr. by* Thomas Kinsella. NOIV

"I heard him fall. He's lying." The Secret. Lonny Kaneko. BrSi

I heard how, to the beat of some quick tune. The Dancer. Sadi, *tr. fr. Persian by* Sir Edwin Arnold. *Fr*. The Bustan. AWP

I Heard Immanuel Singing. Vachel Lindsay. HAP

I heard in the night the pigeons. No Child. Padraic Colum. OBMV

I heard my love was going to Yang-chou. *Unknown*, *tr. fr. Chinese by* Arthur Waley. *Fr*. Tzu Yeh Songs. BoWoP

I heard my loved published in church. The False Bride. *Unknown.*
OBET
I heard no sound where I stood. The Sleeping House. Tennyson. *Fr.*
Maud, *Pt.* I, xiv. OBNC
I heard of gold at Sutter's Mill. When I Went Off to Prospect.
Unknown. AmFP
I Heard of Master Kan's Illness but Couldn't Get There in Time. ("I heard
of the illness, raced a thousand miles"). Rai San'yo, *tr. fr. Chinese
by* Burton Watson. JLIC-2
I heard one who said: "Verily." Cassandra. E. A. Robinson. CMoP;
LiTA; LiTM; NoAM; OxBA
I heard, or seemed to hear, the chiding Sea. Sea-Shore. Emerson.
LiTA; MOS; OxBA
I heard that you were. Lady Ishikawa. *Fr.* Manyo Shu. Ma
I heard the bells of Bethlehem ring. The Birds of Bethlehem. Richard
Watson Gilder. AA
I heard the bells on Christmas Day. Christmas Bells. Longfellow. AH,
with music; AnAmPo; BLRP; FaFP; FaPON; OBCP; PChr, *st.* 1;
WBLP
I heard the carping [*or* herde a carpyng] of a clerk. Robyn and
Gandeleyn. *Unknown.* EnSB; ESPB; OxBB
(Robin and Gandelyn.) EnSB
I heard the crude gin sobbing. Those Makheta Nights. Frank Mkalawile
Chipasula. WMBCH
I heard the dogs howl in the moonlight night. A [*or* The] Dream.
William Allingham. BIrV; NOBVV
I heard the farm cocks crowing loud, and faint, and thin. Daybreak in a
Garden. Siegfried Sassoon. BoTP
I heard the front door. After a Death. Gregory Orr. AnAn; GeTw
I heard the happy lark exult. Inst., Ult., and Prox. Sir A. P. Herbert.
FaBoUs
I heard the Indian Agent say. The Old Man's Lazy. Peter Blue Cloud.
HATNAP
I heard the old, old men say. The Old Men Admiring Themselves in the
Water. W. B. Yeats. CMoP; FaBoCh; GoJo; PCP
I Heard the Old Song. B. W. Vilakazi, *tr. fr. Zulu.* PeSA
I heard the Poor Old Woman say. Lament for the Poets: 1916. Francis
Ledwidge. AWP
I heard the sea murmur in my ears. One Goes with Me along the Shore.
Manfred Winkler, *tr. by* Mary Zilzer. VWA
I heard the sighing of the reeds. In Ireland: By the Pool at the Third
Rosses. Arthur Symons. FaBoPP; OBNC
I heard the snap of the trap from the hot-water-cupboard. The Mouse.
Louis Johnson. ATNZ
I heard the snowflakes whisper in the still dark night. Snowflakes. Ruth
M. Arthur. BoTP
I heard the songs. The Songs. *Unknown, tr. by* K. Kennedy. WTO
I heard the sound of his name sung. Titicaca. Cees Nooteboom, *tr. by*
Scott Rollins. DuIn
I heard the trailing garments of the Night. Hymn to the Night.
Longfellow. AA; BLPL; NOBA; OxBA; PWR; TAP; TrGrPo;
I heard the wild beasts in the wood complain. Mundus Morosus.
Frederick William Faber. ACP
I heard the wild geese flying. Wild Geese. Elinor Chipp. FaPON
I heard the wind coming. Hearing the Wind at Night. May Swenson.
BoNaP
I heard them in their sadness say. Dust. "Æ." WGRP
I heard this "fucking beautiful." Poetry Reading. Eileen Myles.
UL
I heard this morning. Summer 1970. Lindiwe Mabuza. WPOW
I heard two workers say, "This chaos/ Will soon be ended." Idiom of the
Hero. Wallace Stevens. OxBA
I Heard You Solemn-sweet Pipes of the Organ. Walt Whitman.
OxBA
I heare the whistling plough-man all day long. On the Plough-Man.
Francis Quarles. OBS
"I heeard da ole folks talkin' in our house da other night." Why Adam
Sinned. Alex Rogers. BANP
I Held a Shelley Manuscript. Gregory Corso. VGW
I held Europe in my hand. Yonder. Richard Eberhart. GOA
I Held His Name. Alberto Ríos. NoAM
I Held It Truth. Tennyson. *Fr.* In Memoriam A. H. H., I. HeIP;
LiTB; NoP; OBNC
I held my breath for years. The Ghost. Heather McHugh. NAmP
I held on her neck. Doe. Philip Dow. NPGG
I held you. Eventual Proteus. Margaret Atwood. MoCV
I helped a little lame dog. My Little Dog. Pearl Forbes MacEwen.
BoTP
I herde a carpyng of a clerk. *See* I heard the carping of a clerk.
I herde the lover sighing wondir sore. The Lady Resists the Lover's
Pleas. *At. to* Alain Chartier, *French tr. at. to* Sir Richard Ros. *Fr.*
La Belle Dame sans Mercy. OxBLMV

I hereby swear that to uphold your house. Elinor Wylie. *Fr.* One
Person, XVI. LiTA; MoAB; NAAL-2; OxBA; Son
(Sonnet from "One Person.") LiTA; MoAmPo
I, Hermes, have been set up. Anyte, *tr. by* Kenneth Rexroth. OBVE
I hesitate to write about the spring. The Faithful Lover. Robert Pack.
NePoEA
I hid my love when young till I. Secret Love. John Clare. FaBV;
OBNC; PoE; PoEL-4; TrGrPo
(Song: "I hid my love when young while I.) NOBVV; OAEL-2; RB
I hid the peppermint. I Had to Be Secret. Mark Van Doren. SO
I Hid You. Miklós Radnóti, *tr. fr. Hungarian by* Steven Polgar, Stephen
Berg *and* S. J. Marks. LLLT; UnAS; VWA
I hide my grief thoughout the weary days. To Richard, My Son. Vera
Bax. CN
I hired a carpenter. The Death King. Anne Sexton, *tr. by* Jeffrey Fiskin
and Erik Vestville. AnAn
I hit my wife and went out and saw. The Winter Moon. Tagaki Kyozo,
tr. by James Kirkup *and* Nakamo Michio. LLLT
I hoard a little spring of secret tears. On Shooting a Swallow in Early
Youth. Charles Tennyson Turner. FM; NOBVV
I Hoed and Trenched and Weeded. A. E. Housman. *Fr.* A Shropshire
Lad, LXIII. LiTM; MoBrPo; TrGrPo; TrGrPo
I hold a dog, my skin. Ozaki Hosai, *tr. fr. Japanese by* Hiroaki Sato.
Fr. One Hundred Haiku in Free Form. FCEI
I hold a letter in my hand. A Poem for the Meeting of the American
Medical Association. Oliver Wendell Holmes. PoEL-5
I hold a newspaper, reading. Fish. Takahashi Shinkichi, *tr. by* Lucien
Stryk. NU
I hold a rattlesnake in my hand, gently. Victory Drive, near Fort
Benning, Georgia. Bin Ramke. MT
I hold him, verily, of mean emprise. He Perceives His Rashness in Love,
but Has No Choice. Guido Guinicelli, *tr. by* Dante Gabriel Rossetti.
AWP
I hold in my hands. Look Closely. Morton Marcus. FF
I hold it good—as who shall hold it bad? Columbia's Agony. "Orpheus
C. Kerr." OBAL
I hold it true that thoughts are things. Secret Thoughts. Ella Wheeler
Wilcox. PWR
I hold my honey and I store my bread. My Dreams, My Works, Must
Wait Till after Hell. Gwendolyn Brooks. NoP
I hold that Christian grace abounds. My Creed. Alice Cary. WGRP
I hold that when a person dies. A Creed. John Masefield. WGRP
I hold the glass door wide. Visiting. Tony Beyer. ATNZ
I hold your love up as a lantern. The blackness of night. The Clover
Flower. Ali Abdallah Khalifa, *tr. by* Lena Jayyusi *and* Alistair Elliot.
MAP
I Honour You in Dread. Ramón López Velarde, *tr. fr. Spanish by* Samuel
Beckett. MexPo
I Hope and Fear. Thomas Lodge. *Fr.* Phyllis, XXXV. Son
I hope he doesn't see me walking past his bed. Letter. Alexander
Bergman. TrJP
I Hope I Don't Have You Next Semester, But. Edwin S. Godsey.
HoPM
I Hope, I Fear. William Alexander, Earl of Stirling. *Fr.* Aurora,
LXVIII. Son
I hope the old Romans. Ancient History. Arthur Guiterman. OBCA
I hope when I am dead that I shall lie. Oblivion. Jessie Redmond
Fauset, *fr. the French of* Massillon Coicou. BANP; PoNe
I hope you'll forgive the black paint. I Have Lived This Way for Years
and Do Not Wish to Change. Michael C. Blumenthal. HCAP
I hug myself and again it's hard to breathe. Raizan, *tr. fr. Japanese by*
Hiroaki Sato. *Fr.* Thirteen Hokku. FCEI
I hung my verses in the wind. The Test. Emerson. AA; OBAL
I hung you there, moccasins of worn buckskin. The Moccasins of an Old
Man. Ramona Carden. NOVW
I hunt. Photographer. Philip Booth. EyDe
I, I should sing as wretchedly. My Language. Ida Hahn-Hahn, *tr. by*
Susan L. Cocalis. DMG
I identify, tonight, with certain insects. The Powder of Sympathy. James
Tate. AnAn
I idle stand that I may find employ. The Idler. Jones Very. AA
I idolize you with litanies. Hertha Kräftner, *tr. fr. German by* Beth
Bjorklund. *Fr.* Litanies. CoAuP
I imagine Druids timeless, so lacking. Druid Stones at Kensaleyre.
Richard Hugo. AnAn
I imagine him still with heavy brow. Beethoven's Death Mask. Stephen
Spender. OxBTC
I imagine myself/ a mouth. Fruit, of the Earth. Cyril Dabydeen. PVCV
I imagine the time of our meeting. Forms of the Earth at Abiquiu. N.
Scott Momaday. CDW
I imagine the womb as a honeycomb. Ian Wedde. *Fr.* Losing the
Straight Way, III. ATNZ

I imagine this [or the] midnight moment's forest. The Thought-Fox. Ted Hughes. FaBoMo; HeIP; InPs; MoP; NePoEA-2; NoAM; NoP; NYBP; SCV

I imagine us dancing, a Mexican ballroom somewhere. Catch. Ethna McKiernan. TSL

I imagine where God has never been. Peter Levi. TOF

I imagined the bombs and fighters. Air Raid. Peter Wild. Psk

I, in My Intricate Image. Dylan Thomas. EAS; LiTB

I indulge myself. The Thin Man. Donald Justice. SM

I inherited forty acres from my father. Cooney Potter. Edgar Lee Masters. Fr. Spoon River Anthology. SaC

I inherited naive open-heartedness. February 7. A. Leyeles, tr. fr. Yiddish by Benjamin and Barbara Harshav. Fr. Fabius Lind's Diary. AYP

"I instinctively/ reject." On Rainy Shadows. Ernst Jandl, tr. by Beth Bjorklund. CoAuP

I intended an ode. Urceus Exit. Austin Dobson. Fr. Rose-Leaves. OBEV

I invite you, child, to dance. You come. I bow my blond head. Song for a Dance. Abraham Sutskever, tr. by Ruth Whitman. VWA

I is the ghost of Stevey Fizzlegig. The Ghost. Fitz-James O'Brien. NOEC

I jes' don' know ef de kohn'll grow. Good Lawd Know My Name, De. Frank Lebby Stanton. WBLP

I Jocky Bell o'Braikenbrow lyes under this stane. On Jocky Bell. Unknown. FaBoEE

I joy/ You joy. Conjugation. Patricia Hubbell. ILY

I joy not in no earthly bliss. The Quiet Mind. Unknown. OBSC

I joy to see how, in your drawen work. Spencer, Fr. Amoretti, LXXI. PoE

I jump on one leg for joy. Fresh Air. Abi Shaqra, Shauqi, tr. by Abdullah al-Udhari. MPAW

I jump with terror seeing him. Modes of Pleasure. Thom Gunn. PeHV; PPP

I just came by the prison door. Pray Remember the Poor. Christopher Smart. NOEC

I just had to start a conversation. Unknown, tr. fr. Japanese by Burton Watson. Fr. Kangin Shu. FCEI

I just said I didn't know. Parachutes, My Love, Could Carry Us Higher. Barbara Guest. NeAP

I just turned a pan. Another Day. Isabella Maria Brown. PoNe

I Just Walk Around, Around, Around. Moishe Kulbak, tr. fr. Yiddish by Ruth Whitman. VWA

I keep dreaming I'm dead. Qaqatcguk, tr. by James Koller. STP

I keep feeling all space as my image. Sanders Russell. EAS

I keep him waiting, tuck in the curtains. Planning the Perfect Evening. Rita Dove. MAYP

I keep my parents in a garden. Eden Is a Zoo. Margaret Atwood. WPE

I keep on asking. Written when Sick in Bed. Masaoka Shiki, tr. by Burton Watson. Fr. Thirty-nine Haiku. FCEI

I keep pushing this. The Prophets. Richard Shelton. NYBP

I keep running around. Unknown, tr. by Jerome Rothenberg. STP

I keep the custom of the Ferry. The Hostess of the Ferry Inn. Gwerfyl Mechain, tr. by H. Idris Bell. OBWVE

I keep the heart engaged, the heart. Asadullah Khan Ghalib, tr. by Ahmed Ali. GoT

I Keep Three Wishes Ready. Annette Wynne. PDV

I Keep to Myself Such Measures. Robert Creeley. NoAM

I keep watch alone. Paddy House. Shotetsu, tr. by Steven D. Carter. WFTW

I kenning through astronomy divine. VIII. Edward Taylor. Fr. Preparatory Meditations before My Approach to the Lord's Supper. AmPP; LiTA; NAAL-1; NOBA; NoP; OxBA; PoEL-3; SCAP; TAP

I kept my answers small and kept them near. Answers. Elizabeth Jennings. NePoEA; OxBSP; OxBTC

I kept the house on the corner of Linden and Pineapple Streets. Birdie McReynolds. Samuel Hoffenstein. BXAP; NBLV

I killed a fly. The Fly. David Ignatow. PPR

I killed them, but they would not die. The Immortals. Isaac Rosenberg. FaBoTw; MMA; TrJP

I kiss the notorious fly. Death of the Lord of the Flies. Lucebert, tr. by Larry Ten Harmsel. DuIn

I kissed a kiss in youth. Scintilla. William Stanley Braithwaite. AmNP; BANP; CDC

I kissed them in fancy as I came. Two Lips. Thomas Hardy. BoLoP

I Kissed You. Unknown. BLPA

I kneel down to peer into a culvert. Kneeling Down to Look into a Culvert. Robert Bly. NoAM

I kneel not now to pray that Thou. Harry Hibbard Kemp. WGRP

I kneel on the warm earth. Leaving Knee-prints in the Warm Earth. Cheng Wen-tao. WCI

I knew a boy who took long walks. Stalky Jack. William Brighty Rands. BoTP

I Knew a Boy with Hair like Gold. Melvin Walker La Follette. NePoEA-2

I Knew a Cappadocian. A. E. Housman. FiBHP

I knew a man who like us awoke alone. The American Poet—"But Since It Came to Good. . ." William Hathaway. UL

I knew a man who used to say. The Statesman. Hilaire Belloc. NOBE

I knew a most superior camper. The Bunyip and the Whistling Kettle. John Manifold. LiTB; PoAu-2; WaP

I knew a simple soldier boy. Suicide in [the] Trenches. Siegfried Sassoon. BrPo; MMA

I knew a tiny sandpiper. A Certain Sandpiper. X. J. Kennedy. TDD

I Knew a Woman [Lovely in Her Bones]. Theodore Roethke. AmPP; BoLoP; CAPP; ErPo; HAP; HeIP; HoPM; InPK; LiTM; MAT; MoAmPo; MoP; NAAL-2; NIP; NoAM; NOBA; NoP; PoE; PrIm; SM; SoSe; TAP; TwCP; UnPo

(Poem.) TrGrPo

I knew an old lady. Antique Shop. Carl Carmer. FaPON

I knew Ibrahim. The Deserted Well. Yusuf al-Khal, tr. by Sargon Boulus and Naomi Shihab Nye. MAP

I Knew I'd Sing. Heather McHugh. GeTw

I knew it was coming. Early Autumn. Keiun, tr. by Steven D. Carter. WFTW

I knew like a song your vows weren't strong. Mahsati, tr. by Deirdre Lashgari. AIW; WPOW

I knew not 'twas so dire a crime. Last Words. Emily Brontë. WPE

I knew the dignity of the words. My Grandfather's Funeral. James Applewhite. MT

I knew the man. I see him, as he stands. Lincoln. George Henry Boker. OHIP

I knew too that through them I knew too that he was through, I knew. A Valentine to Sherwood Anderson. Gertrude Stein. NoAM

I knew when I said. Nizar Qabbani, tr. by Lena Jayyusi and W. S. Merwin. MAP

I knew you forever and you were always old. Some Foreign Letters. Anne Sexton. MoAmPo

I knock again and try the key. A Pagan Reinvokes the Twenty-third Psalm. Robert Wolf. TrPWD

I Knocked My Head against the Wall. Anna Swirszczynska, tr. fr. Polish by Czeslaw Milosz. PwPP

I know/ how fascinated we are with clarity. Salah Fa'iq, tr. by Patricia Alanah Byrne and Salma Khadra Jayyusi. MAP

"I know/ how you must feel!" Saigyo. tr. fr. Japanese by Burton Watson. Fr. Sixty-four Tanka. FCEI

I know/ I saw/ a spooky witch. October Magic. Myra Cohn Livingston. PDV

I know/ Not these my hands. Amaze. Adelaide Crapsey. QFR

I know/ that when a grumbling old woman. Superstition. Minji Karibo. WPOW

I know/ what you're thinking. ESP. Steve Rasnic Tem. BWV

I know a bank where the wild thyme blows. A Violet Bank. Shakespeare. Fr. A Midsummer Night's Dream, II, i. FaPON ("I know a place whereon the wild thyme blows.") BoNaP (Where the Wild Thyme Blows.) TrGrPo

I know a dog called Isaac. Three Dogs. E. C. Brereton. BoTP

I know a flower of beauty rare. The Lay of the Captive Count. Goethe, tr. by James Clarence Mangan. AWP

I Know a Flower So Fair and Fine. Nicolai Frederik Severin Grundtvig, tr. fr. Norwegian by Olav Lee. AH

I know a funny litle man. Mr. Nobody. Unknown. BOTP; FaPON

I know a garden with three strange gates. The Last Gate. Stella Mead. BoTP

I know a girl. The Canal Bank. James Stephens. GrPl

I know a green grass path that leaves the field. The Green River. Lord Alfred Bruce Douglas. OBEV

I know a Jew fish crier down on Maxwell Street. Fish Crier. Carl Sandburg. AmFN; OxBA

I Know a Lady. Joyce Carol Thomas. CNA

I know a little butterfly with tiny golden wings. The Butterfly. Margaret Rose. BoTP

I know a little cupboard. The Cupboard. Walter de la Mare. FaPON; NTCP

I know a little garden-close. A Garden by the Sea. William Morris. Fr. The Life and Death of Jason, IV. CH; NOBE; OAEL-2; OBNC; PoEL-5 (Nymph's Song to Hylas, The.) OBEV

I know a little language of my cat, tho Dante says. Robert Duncan. Fr. Dante. PoM (Little Language, A.) NoAM

I know a little man both ept and ert. Gloss. David McCord. OBAL

I know a little what it is like, once here at high tide. Seaweeds. Sandra McPherson. AmPA; PoA

I Know a Man. Robert Creeley. CAPP; InPS; MAT; NOBA; OxBSP; PoM; PPP

I Know a Name! *Unknown.* BLRP

I know a place/ that's oh, so green. A Boy's Place. Rose Burgunder. PDV

I know a place all fennel-green and fine. A Green Place. William Jay Smith. GrPl

I know a place, in the ivy on a tree. The Bird's Nest. John Drinkwater. PDV

I know a place that holds the Sky. The Upside-Down World. Hamish Hendry. BoTP

I know a place where the sun is like gold. Four-Leaf Clover. Ella Higginson. AA; FaPON

I know a place whereon the wild thyme blows. Shakespeare. *See* Midsummer Night's Dream, A: Violet Bank, A.

I know a pool where nightshade preens. Crazed. Walter de la Mare. OxBSP

I know a retired dentist who only paints mountains. Mountains. W. H. Auden. FaBoPV

I know a shiftless, lazy lout. Precedented. Marcy S. Powell. SoTCo

I know a solemn secret to keep between ourselves. The Elfin People Fill the Tubes. Winifred M. Letts. BoTP

I know a soul that is steeped in sin. I Know a Name! *Unknown.* BLRP

I know a space where Love delights to dream. A Sacred Grove. Edward Cracroft Lefroy, *after the Greek of* Theocritus. *Fr.* Echoes from Theocritus, XXIV. AWP

I know a story, fairer, dimmer, sadder. My Babes in the Wood. Sarah Morgan Bryan Piatt. AA

I know a town tormented by the sea. Galway. Mary Devenport O'Neill. NeIP

I Know a Village, *sels.* Phyllis McGinley.
   5:32, The. NMM; WPE
   Occupation: Housewife. WPE

I know a wasted place high in the Alps. Edgar Bowers. *Fr.* Two Poems on the Catholic Bavarians, 2. CRP

I know a way. The Song in the Dell. Charles Edward Carryl. AA

I know a young lady's high-piled ashen hair. His Helplessness. John Berryman. *Fr.* Dream Songs. NoP

I know all. He Asked Them What Did They Know & They Told Him. *Unknown, tr. by* Jerome Rothenberg *and* Richard Johnny John. STP

I know, although when looks meet. Crazy Jane and Jack the Journeyman. W. B. Yeats. CMoP

I know an ice handler who wears a flannel shirt. Ice Handler. Carl Sandburg. OxBA

I know and I don't know what I am. Kaai Chigetsu, *tr. fr. Japanese by* Hiroaki Sato. *Fr.* Thirteen Hokku. FCEI

I know, as my life grows older. Whatever Is—Is Best. Ella Wheeler Wilcox. BLPA; PWR

I know, blue modest violets. Violets. Kate Louise. BoTP

I know but will not tell. Alan Dugan. CAPP; DiL

I Know de Moonlight. *Unknown.* BPo

I know four winds with names like some strange tune. Weather Words. David McCord. ImOP

I know him;/ He'll give no horse for a poem. *Unknown, tr. by* Vivian Mercier. BIrV

I know him, February's thrush. The Thrush in February. George Meredith. OBNC

I know him now, not now to know demanding. Nunc Scio, Quid Sit Amor. L. A. MacKay. OBCV

I know how people get treated when they die. Andeyek, *tr. by* James Koller. STP

I know I am/ The Negro Problem. Dinner Guest: Me. Langston Hughes. BPo

I know I change. Daguerreotype Taken in Old Age. Margaret Atwood. BoWoP; NoAM

I know I have the best of time and space. Walt Whitman. *Fr.* Song of Myself, XLVI. NoAM

I know, I know it. Issa, *tr. fr. Japanese by* Hiroaki Sato. *Fr.* Forty-four Hokku. FCEI

I know, I know what song the. Adaption—Year 2000. Edward Wellen. BWV

I know I look the kind of dolt. To a Junior Waiter. A. P. Herbert. FiBHP

I know I'm more alone than ever. Entering the Gardens of Doom. Sayf al-Rahabi, *tr. by* Lena Jayyusi *and* Samuel Hazo. MAP

I Know I'm Not Sufficiently Obscure. Ray Durem. BPo; PoBA

I Know Inside. Yüan Mei, *tr. fr. Chinese by* Jonathan Chaves. CoBLCP

I know it is my sin which locks thine ears. Church Lock and Key. George Herbert. OxBSP

I know it must be winter (though I sleep). Winter Sleep. Edith M. Thomas. AA

I know lots of men who are in love. I Never Even Suggested It. Ogden Nash. FiBHP; FPL; LiTA; PoLF

I know monks masturbate at night. The Earnest Liberal's Lament. Ernest Hemingway. OBAL; OBSV

I Know Moonlight. *Unknown.* AS

I Know Moonrise. *Unknown.* UnPo

I know my body's of so frail a kind. Man. Sir John Davies. *Fr.* Nosce Teipsum. EiL
   (I Know Myself a Man.) ChTr

"I know my soul hath power to know all things." OBEV

I Know My Soul. Claude McKay. BPo

I know my soul hath power to know all things. Sir John Davies. *Fr.* Nosce Teipsum: Man. OBEV

I Know Myself a Man. Sir John Davies. *See* Nosce Teipsum: Man.

I know not by what methods rare. Eliza M. Hickock. BLRP

I know not from what distant time thou art ever coming nearer to meet me. Rabindranath Tagore. *Fr.* Gitanjali, XLVI. WGRP

I know not how it falls on me. Emily Brontë. NOBVV

I know not how it may be with others. Old Furniture. Thomas Hardy. OxBTC

I know not how to speak to thee, girl (damselle?). Reed Whittemore. AmFN

I know not if among rocks. The Chimera. Dino Campana, *tr. by* William Weaver. PFI

I know not if from uncreated spheres. Buonarroti Michelangelo, *tr. fr. Italian by* George Santayana. *Fr.* Three Poems, I. AWP; PFI

I know not of my forefathers. Lost. Bruce Ignacio. NOVW

I know not of what we ponder'd. Companions. Charles Stuart Calverley. FaBoCo; NA; NOBL

I know not that the men of old. The Men of Old. Richard Monckton Milnes. OBEV

I know not what is in the well, mother! The Well. Manuel de la Parra, *tr. by* Samuel Beckett. MexPo

I know not what spell is o'er me. Lorelei. Heine. TrJP, *tr. by* Emma Lazarus
   (Loreley, The.) WSC, *tr. by* Aaron Kramer

I know not what the future hath. Whittier. *Fr.* The Eternal Goodness. BLRP, *abr.*; NOCV

I know not what to do. Hilda Doolittle. ("H. D.") CMoP; OxBA; VGW

I know not what will befall me: God hangs a mist o'er my eyes. Mary Gardiner Brainard. *Fr.* Not Knowing. AA; PWR

I know not when this tiresome man. The Sundowner. Shaw Neilson. CBAP; PoAu-1

I Know Not Where the Road Will Lead. Evelyn Atwater Cummins. AH

I Know Not Whether I Am Proud. Walter Savage Landor. EnRP

I know not who thou art, oh lovely one! To the Lady in the Chemisette with Black Buttons. Nathaniel Parker Willis. OBAL

I know not why my soul is rack'd [*or* racked]. Changed. Charles Stuart Calverley. FiBHP; NoBVV

I know not why or whence he came. The Deserter. Joseph Seamon Cotter, Jr. CDC

I Know Nothing of the Sleep Which Tames You. Giancarlo Marmori, *tr. fr. Italian by* Lawrence R. Smith. NItP

I know now. I Thought It Was Tangiers I Wanted. Langston Hughes. PoNe

I know some lonely houses off the road. Emily Dickinson. MoAB; MoAmPo; OxBA; PoRA; SO; WSC

I Know Something Good about You. Louis C. Shimon. BLPA

I know that all beneath the moon decays. William Drummond of Hawthornden. JCP; Son

I know that any weed can tell. Louis Ginsberg. TrJP

I know that face! Daphne. Bliss Carman. OBCV

I know that He exists. Emily Dickinson. AmPP

I know that his eyes look into mine. Assurance. Josephine D. Henderson Heard. CBWP-4

I Know That I Am a Great Sinner. Swami Purohit. OBMV

I Know That I Must Die Soon. Else Lasker-Schüler, *tr. fr. German by* Ralph Manheim. TrJP

I know that I shall meet my fate. An Irish Airman Foresees His Death. W. B. Yeats. FaBoCh; FaBoMo; GoJo; GTBS-P; HeIP; HoPM; LiTM; MMA; MoAB; MoBrPo; MoP; NoAM; NOAM; NOBE; NoP; OBD; OBMV; OBWP; PPP; SCV; TrGrPo; WaaP; WaP; WeW

I know that if thou please thou canst provide. George Wither. *Fr.* Brittan's Remembrancer. SeCV-1

I know that in this world no one needs me. Six Lines. Aaron Zeitlin, *tr. by* Robert Friend. PeBMYV

I know that life is Jason. The Golden Fleece. Oscar Williams. PoA

I know that mind. ESP. Carter Revard. VoR

I know that my Redeemer liveth—but out of the depths of time. The Redeemer. "Fiona Macleod." WGRP

I know that the sun rising. Pindar's Revenge. Edward Sanders. PoM
I know that this my crying, like the crying. Night. Hayyim Nahman Bialik, *tr.* by Maurice Samuel. AWP
I know that what our neighbours call *longueurs*. Byron. *Fr.* Don Juan, II. OBSV
I know the barn where they got you. For a Woodscolt Miscarried. John William Corrington. MT
I know the bottom, she says. I know it with my great tap root. Elm. Sylvia Plath. NoAM; NOBA; NoP
  (Elm Speaks, The.) NYBP
I know the colour rose, and it is lovely. Pathology of Colours. Dannie Abse. NoAM
I know the footsteps of the sparrow. Ozaki Hosai, *tr. fr. Japanese by* Hiroaki Sato. *Fr.* One Hundred Haiku in Free Form. FCEI
I know the gun. The Foreman's Wife. Jeff Tagami. BrSi
I know the hedge in Briar Lane. I Must Away. May Sarson. BoTP
I know the injured pride of sleep. Night and Morning. Austin Clarke. AnIL; CIP; IPY; MoAB; NeIP
I know the night is near at hand. Vespers. S. Weir Mitchell. WGRP
I know the [*or a*] thing that's most uncommon. On a Certain Lady at Court. Pope. NOBE; NOEC; OBEV; OxBSP; TrGrPo
I know the reputation/ of the idle ways. Lady Kii, *tr. by* Kenneth Rexroth *and* Ikuko Atsumi. WPOW
I know the ships that pass by day. The Lights. J. J. Bell. BoTP
I know the sky will fall one day. Child's Song. Gerald Gould. BoTP
I know the truth——give up all other truths! Marina Tsvetayeva, *tr. by* Elaine Feinstein *and* Angela Livingstone. OBD
I know the ways [*or* wayes] of learning: both the head. The Pearl. George Herbert. EBEV; HAP; JCP; MePo; NOCV; OAEL-1; PoEL-2; SeCP
  (Pearl, the. Matth. 13.) SeCV-1
I know thee. My name is Tom. Archaic Song of Dr. Tom the Shaman. *Unknown, tr. by* Jerome Rothenberg. STP
I know there are some fools that care. The Deformed Mistress. Sir John Suckling. BXAP; ErPo
I know there is a worm in the human heart. John Clare. Jon Anderson. AmPA
I know there is someone. Poem to Be Read and Sung. César Vallejo, *tr. by* James Wright *and* Robert Bly. EAS
I Know Things. Adèle Davide. Mes
I know this body but a sink of folly. The Tragedy of Charles Duke of Byron. George Chapman. OBD
I know thou art a senseless thing. The Old Crib. Mary E. Tucker. CBWP-1
I know two things about the horse. The Horse. Naomi Royde-Smith. CenHV; FaBoCo; FiBHP
I know two women. The Wife. Robert Creeley. VGW
I know very well, goddess, she is not beautiful. Calypso's Island. Archibald MacLeish. MoAB; NoP
I know very well what I'd rather be. Rathers. Mary Austin. FaPON
I know well this body of mine. Yakamochi. *Fr.* Manyo Shu. Ma
I know what I feel like. Changing. Mary Ann Hoberman. RHPC
I know what my heart is like. Ebb. Edna St. Vincent Millay. AnAmPo
I know what the caged bird feels, alas! Sympathy. Paul Laurence Dunbar. AmNP; CDC; IDB; PoBA; PoNe
I know where I belong. Wonders. Lorenzo Thomas. UL
I Know Where I'm Going. *Unknown.* ELP; GBP; MoShBr; OBET; WTO
I know why, getting up in the cold dawn. To a Daughter with Artistic Talent. Peter Meinke. Psk
"I know, within my mouth, for bashful fear." Love's Despair. Richard Lynche. *Fr.* Diella, XIII. EIL
I know you: solitary griefs. The Precept of Silence. Lionel Johnson. MoBrPo
I know you'd do anything for me. Adjustments. H. N. Beckerman. TSM
I Know, You'd Rather Be Dead. Edward L. Hooper. TSM
I knowed a man, which he lived in Jones. Thar's More in the Man than Thar Is in the Land. Sidney Lanier. NOBA
I Korinna am here to sing the courage. Korinna, *tr. by* Willis Barnstone. BoWoP
I lack the braver mind. Confession of Faith. Elinor Wylie. MoAmPo
I laid me down upon a bank. Blake. EnLoPo; GBL
I laid my haffet on Elfer Hill. Elfer Hill. *Unknown, tr. by* Robert Jamieson. AWP
I Lais, once an arrow. Kenneth Rexroth, *after the Greek of* Sekundos. NNaP
I laks yo' kin' of lovin'. Long Gone. Sterling A. Brown. BANP; BPo; CDC
I lang hae thought, my youthfu' friend. Epistle to a Young Friend. Burns. EBEV
  (Letter to a Young Friend.) OHFP

I lately lost a preposition. The Naughty Preposition. Morris Bishop. FiBHP; NBLV; NYBP
I lately saw, what now I sing. The Sparrow and Diamond. Matthew Green. FM; PBBP
I laugh and sing, but cannot tell. To Lucasta. Richard Lovelace. OBS
I laugh at each dull bore, taste's parasite. Fresco-Sonnets to Christian Sethe. Heine, *tr. by* John Todhunter. AWP
I laughed at the lovers I passed. Terenure. Blanaid Salkeld. NeIP
I Laughed When the Painter, Caroline. Angus Martin. NPo
I laved my hands. Lost for a Rose's Sake. *Unknown, tr. by* Andrew Lang. AWP
I lay among the ferns. Among the Ferns. Edward Carpenter. WGRP
I lay and speculated on the impact of a bullet. Terror. Thomas O'Brien. NeIP
I lay at the edge of a well. The Underground Stream. James Dickey. NOBA
I lay dear treasure for you. The Pack. Frank Prewett. HATNAP
I lay down with my love and there was song. Armorial. Ralph Gustafson. MoCV
I lay i' the bosom of the sun. Palabras Grandiosas. Bayard Taylor. AnAmPo; OBAL
I lay in my coffin under the sod. Post Mortem. Arthur Munby. NOBVV
I lay in my tent at mid-day. The Crossing at Fredericksburg. George Henry Boker. PAH
I lay in silence, dead. A woman came. Another Way. Ambrose Bierce. AA
I lay in the Holy Cross. Reginald Pugh, The Man Who Came from the Army. Emma Lee Warrior. HATNAP
I lay my hand. Tribal Cemetery. Janet Campbell Hale. NOVW
I lay on Delos of the Cyclades. The Ship. Lloyd Mifflin. AA
I lay quietly listening to some musical rabbi. Night Poem in an Abandoned Music Room. William Pillen. VWA
I lay, rumpled like a lizard in the sun. Cattle Sale. Philip Salom. UAS
I lay waiting. Bog Queen. Seamus Heaney. AnAn; NoAM
I lay with my heart under me. Cicada. Adrien Stoutenburg. NYBP; RFM
I leaf through the flat plains. Poem from "The Revolution." Ilya Rubin, *tr. by* Linda Zisquit. VWA
I lean on a lighthouse rock. Girl at the Seaside. Richard Murphy. BIrV
I leaned out of window, I smelt the white clover. Seven Times Three— Love. Jean Ingelow. *Fr.* Songs of Seven. PoLF
I leant [*or* leaned] upon a coppice gate. The Darkling Thrush. Thomas Hardy. BrPo; CMoP; EBVV; FaFP; FPL; HAP; InPS; LiTB; LiTM; MoAB; MoBrPo; MoP; NAEL-2; NeIP; NoAM; NOBE; NOBVV; NoP; OAEL-2; OBEV; OBNC; PBBP; PoE; PPP; RB; SoSe; TEP; TOF; TrGrPo; UnPo; WaP
I learn, as the years roll onward. Life's Lessons. *Unknown.* BLRP; FPL; PoLF
I learn you were hurt my sweet and hurt again. Clotho. Hilaire Kirkland. *Fr.* Clotho, Lachesis, Atropos, I. PeNZ
I learned in my credulous youth. Why, Some of My Best Friends Are Women. Phyllis McGinley. NMM
I learned to be honest. A Question of Climate. Audre Lorde. NoAM
I learned two things. Riding Lesson. Henry Taylor. ASP; NBLV
I learnt the collects and the catechism. Elizabeth Barrett Browning. *Fr.* Aurora Leigh. TEP
I leave behind me the elm-shadowed square. Outward Bound. Thomas Bailey Aldrich. AA
I leave Mortality, and things below. The Extasie. Abraham Cowley. SeCP
I leave my father and mother behind. Hasetsukabe Hitomaro. *Fr.* Manyo Shu. Ma
I leave my heart in the doorway. Thank You for the Valentine. Diane Wakoski. HoPM
I Leave Myself. Tadeusz Nowak, *tr. fr. Polish by* Czeslaw Milosz. PwPP
I leave the ferry-boat at the river-bank. Someone Burning Firewood. Shin Dong-jip, *tr. by* Koh Chang-soo. ACKP
I leave the paper doors open. Ozaki Hosai, *tr. fr. Japanese by* Hiroaki Sato. *Fr.* One Hundred Haiku in Free Form. FCEI
I leave their fields. The Long Night Home. Charles F. Gordon. NBP
I Leave This at Your Ear. William Sydney Graham. OPOP
I Leave Tonight from Euston. *Unknown.* PoSH
I leave with unreverted eye the towers. Florence. Walter Savage Landor. SeCePo
I leave you in your garden. To Yvor Winters, 1955. Thom Gunn. GTBS-P
I Left. Tuvia Ruebner, *tr. fr. Hebrew by* Betsy Rosenberg. VWA
I left my hills. Izumi Shikibu, *tr. by* Willis Barnstone. BoWoP

I left my prayers and the kneeling pilgrims. Fair Cassidy. *Unknown.* BIrV, *tr. by* Donagh MacDonagh

I left my temporary home and set off. I Left. Tuvia Ruebner, *tr. by* Betsy Rosenberg. VWA

I left old Lake Chemo a long way behind me. Lake Chemo. James Wilton Rowe. AmFP

I left parts of myself everywhere. St. Thomas Aquinas. Charles Simic. BAP

I left the capital. Noin, *tr. by* Geoffrey Bownas *and* Anthony Thwaite. PeBJV

I left the farm I loved. I went. Exile. George Rostrevor Hamilton, *after the Greek of* Isidoros of Aigai. FaBoEE

I left thee with a courage high. J. C. Squire. *Fr.* My Father's Cot. BXAP

I left Warnemünde and Germany with a sense of little ease. Denmark. Humbert Wolfe. OBTV

I, Lessimus, of Salt Lake City. Robert Peters. BXAP

I let a stranger. Ernst Nowak, *tr. by* Beth Bjorklund. CoAuP

I let roots pull foot tendons. Contest. Susan Bright. TSL

I let the incense grow cold. Li Ch'ing-chao, *tr. by* Kenneth Rexroth. BoWoP

I let the sparrows play. Issa, *tr. fr. Japanese by* Hiroaki Sato. *Fr.* Forty-four Hokku. FCEI

I lie beneath my patchwork blanket at the southern window. Rising from Sleep. Wang Chiu-ssu, *tr. by* Jonathan Chaves. CoBLCP

I lie down, I get up. Taigi, *tr. fr. Japanese by* Hiroaki Sato. *Fr.* Twenty-nine Hokku. FCEI

I lie down with God, and may God lie down with me. *Unknown, tr. by* Eleanor Hull. TIRV

I lie down with Thee, O Jesus. Night Prayer. *Unknown, tr. by* Douglas Hyde. TIRV

I lie for a long time on my left side and my right side. Dead Color. Charles Wright. HCAP; LCAP

I lie here beside you. Mount Gilboa. Malka Heifetz-Tussman, *tr. by* Marcia Falk. PBWP

I lie in darkness, as the dead shades gather. Matangi Hauroa, *tr. by* Barry Mitcalfe. WTO

I lie in the hay. Swallow Tails. Tom Robinson. FaPON

I lie on my side. Matauwhi Bay V. Amanda Eason. DT

I Lie on the Chilled Stones of the Great Wall. Stephen Shu Ning Liu. BrSi

I lie under the crust of the night singing. Pregnant Woman. Ingrid Jonker. OV, *tr. by* Jack Cope *and* William Plomer; PeSA, *tr. by* Jack Cope *and* Uys Krige

I lie under your hand—a cur. Dog. Ingrid Jonker, *tr. by* Jack Cope *and* William Plomer. PBWP

I lie upon my bed and hear and see. The Largest Life. Archibald Lampman. CaP

I lie with you. Your arms. Lying, with You. Ernst Jandl, *tr. by* Beth Bjorklund. CoAuP

I lift my eyes, but I cannot see. A Seeker in the Night. Florence Earle Coates. TrPWD

I Lift My Eyes Up to the Hills. Cotton Mather. AH

I lift my head from lowly bed. Moschatel. Daniel James O'Sullivan. NeIP

I Lift My Heart to Thee. Thomas Sternhold. AH

I lift my songs. Battle Song. Macuilxochitl. WPOW, *tr. by* Catherine Rodriquez-Nieto

I lift the Lord on high. Père Lalement. Marjorie Pickthall. CaP; NOBC; OBCV

I lift these hands with iron fetters banded. South Carolina to the States of the North. Paul Hamilton Hayne. PAH

I lift this sumach-bough with crimson flare. Torch-Light in Autumn. John James Piatt. AA

I lifted her hair strand by strand. Teika, *tr. fr. Japanese by* Hiroaki Sato. *Fr.* Eighty-four Tanka. FCEI

I lifted my eyes to the sky. Twilight Thoughts in Israel. Melech Ravitch, *tr. by* Seymour Levitan. VWA

I light the lamp. Gyodai, *tr. by* Geoffrey Bownas *and* Anthony Thwaite. PeBJV

I Light Your Streets. Meridel LeSueur. ER

I like/ the feel of your pulsating fibers. Yuri Kageyama. BrSi

I like a church; I like a cowl. The Problem. Emerson. AA; AmPP; AnAmPo; AWP; LiTA; NAAL-1; NOBA; NoP; OxBA; TAP; WGRP

I like a look of agony. Emily Dickinson. InPS; NAAL-1; NoP; OxBSP; PoE; TAP

I like bars close to home and home run down. The Hilltop. Richard Hugo. CAPP

I like blowing bubbles, and swinging on a swing. Things I Like. Marjorie H. Greenfield. BoTP

I like coffee, I like tea. *Unknown.* FaFP

I like fun—and I like jokes. Thoughts on a Pore Joke. James Whitcomb Riley. AnAmPo

I like gayety and horsing around. Monk of Montaudon, *tr. by* Paul Blackburn. Pro

I Like Housecleaning. Dorothy Brown Thompson. FaPON

I like it back here. Ars Poetica. Charles Wright. AnAn

I like it here just fine. Girl Held without Bail. Margaret Abigail Walker. BPo; CNA; PoBA

I Like It When It's Mizzly. Aileen Fisher. PDV

I Like Little Pussy. Jane Taylor. FaBoBe
(I Love Little Pussy.) FaPON; OxNR

I like movies because. Why I Like Movies. Patricia Jones. BlSi

I Like My Body When It Is With Your Body. E. E. Cummings. *Fr.* Sonnets—Actualities. BoLoP; ErPo; LLLT; Son; VGW

I like my fingers. Mark's Fingers. Mary O'Neill. RHPC

I like not lady-slippers. Tiger-Lilies. Thomas Bailey Aldrich. GN

I like not tears in tune, nor will [*or do*] I prize. On the Memory of Mr. Edward King, Drowned in the Irish Seas. John Cleveland. OAEL-1; OBS; SeCP
(Upon the Death of Mr. King Drowned in the Irish Seas.) HAP

I like people. Trombone Solo. Stoddard King. NBLV

I like rust on a nail. And the Same Words. David Ignatow. NNaP

I like the fall. The Mist and All. Dixie Willson. FaPON

I like the hunting of the hare. The Old Squire. Wilfrid Scawen Blunt. FaPoR; OBEV; SD

I like the man who faces what he must. The Inevitable. Sarah Knowles Bolton. AA; WGRP

I like the story of the circus waif. The Road. Herbert Morris. DiPo

I like the streets of New York City, where I was born. Autobiography: Hollywood. Charles Reznikoff. *Fr.* Going To and Fro and Walking Up and Down. VWA

I like the town on rainy nights. Rainy Nights. Irene Thompson. BoTP; RHPC

I like the way, in winter, cars. The Short Days. John Updike. AnAmPo

I like the way my little harp makes trees. Weeping and Wailing. Gerald Stern. CAPP

I like the wind. Wind Secrets. Diane Wakoski. AmPA

I like them delicately boiled. Poème de Terre; or, Love Song to a Potato. Jack Little. SoTCo

I Like Them Fluffy. A. P. Herbert. NBLV

I like them pale, fair or honey-skinned. Strato. PeHV

I like to crawl around the house after my brother's wife. *Unknown, tr. by* James Koller. STP

I like to drink a bitter tea. To a Lady. Stanislaw Grochowiak, *tr. by* Czeslaw Milosz. PwPP

I like to find. Pleasures. Denise Levertov. CAPP; NeAP; NoAM; NOBA; PoE

I like to fish. The Big One. Luis Cabalquinto. BrSi

I like to ride in a tramcar. Travelling. Dorothy Graddon. BoTP

I like to ride in my uncle's plane. Flying. Kaye Starbird. PDV

I like to see/ The spotted clown. The Clown. Dorothy Aldis. PDV

I like to see a thing I know. New Sights. *Unknown.* BoTP

I like to see a thunder storm. Elizabeth Jane Coatsworth. PDV

I like to see it lap the miles. Emily Dickinson. BoWoP; FaBV; FaPON; InPK; LiTA; LiTM; MoAB; MoAmPo; MoShBr; NAAL-1; NAWM-2; NoAM; NOBA; OBAL; OBCA; OxBA; PDV; PrIm; SoSe
(Railway Train, The.) AnAmPo

I like to see you lean back in your chair. To Don at Salaam. Gwendolyn Brooks. CAPP

I Like to Sing Also. John Updike. FiBHP

I like to think. Snowdrops. Mary Vivian. BoTP

I like to think (and/ the sooner the better!). All Watched Over by Machines of Loving Grace. Richard Brautigan. MAT

I Like to Think of Harriet Tubman. Susan Griffin. NMM

I like to think one day. To This Hill Again. James Macmillan. PoSH

I like to think that ours will be more than just another story. Wishful Thinking. Michael C. Blumenthal. HCAP

I like to toss him up and down. My Cats. Stevie Smith. FaBoNo

I like to walk/ And hear the black crows talk. Crows. David McCord. MoAmPo; PDV; RFM

I like to watch the ants at work. Ants. Mary Ann Hoberman. RAR

I like working near a door. I like to have my work-bench close by. Monologue. Hone Tuwhare. PeNZ

I like wrestling with Herbie because. Wrestling. Kathleen Fraser. RHPC

I like you, Mrs. Fry! I like your name! A Friendly Address. Thomas Hood. PoEL-4

I like your muse because she's gay and witty. W. H. Auden. *Fr.* Letter to Lord Byron. NOBL

I like your spirit full of loving. Nine Reasons Why. Deborah Levy. DT

I liked him as he did not look for an ideal object. Czeslaw Milosz, *tr. fr. Polish by the author*. *Fr*. Bobo's Metamorphosis, V. PwPP

I liked to sit. Kinaxixi. Agostinho Neto, *tr. by* Marga Holness. WMBCH

I liked your poems "Michael," "We Are Seven." Dear Wordsworth. William Hathaway. UL

I likes a woman. Preference. Langston Hughes. HCAP; NOBA

I likes my gray. Little Book 107. Hannah Weiner. IAT

I linger, knowing you are eager (having seen). Eurydice. Linda Gregg. NPGG

I 'listed at home for a lancer. Lancer. A. E. Housman. MoBrPo; OBWP

I listen, and the mountain lakes. Maybe Alone on My Bike. William Stafford. NYBP

I listen for him through the rain. At Daybreak. Siegfried Sassoon. PeHV

I listen for the sounds of cannon, cries. On Lookout Mountain. Robert Hayden. OBET

I listen to a waterfall. Yün Shou-p'ing, *tr. fr. Chinese by* Jonathan Chaves. *Fr*. On the Painting "Mist over Ten Thousand Mountains." CoBLCP

I listen to my parent's language. When Father Came Home for Lunch. Jim Mitsui. BrSi

I listen to the wind. Falling Leaves before the Wind. Shotetsu, *tr. by* Steven D. Carter. WFTW

I listen to this. Look Back. Carroll Arnett. STE

I listened, there was not a sound to hear. Full Moon; Santa Barbara. Sara Teasdale. OBCA

I listened to the Phantom by Ontario's shore. The Poet. Walt Whitman. *Fr*. By Blue Ontario's Shore, *sec*. IX–XVII. MoAmPo

I lit a fire, the blue sky having abandoned me. To Live Here. Paul Eluard, *tr. by* Michael Benedikt. POS

I live a life of almost total idleness. To My Now Distant But Once Much Loved Friend, Mr. Michael White. Christopher Logue. NPo

I live among the grasses. The Field-Mouse. Enid Blyton. BoTP

I live among the Pigmies and the Cranes. Pigmies and Cranes. Walter Savage Landor. NOBVV

I live but in the present,—where art thou? Today. Jones Very. TAP

I live, but not in myself. Stanzas of the Soul that Suffers with Longing to See God. Saint John of the Cross, *tr. by* K. Kavanaugh *and* O. Rodrigues. TOF

I live for those who love me. What I Live For. George Linnaeus Banks. BLPA; FaBoBe; WBLP

(My Aim.) WBLP

(Why Do I Live?) PWR

I live here: "Wessex" is my name. A Popular Personage at Home. Thomas Hardy. FM

I live, I die, I burn myself and drown. Louise Labé, *tr. by* Willis Barnstone. BoWoP

I live in a room named East. Suddenly. Robin Blaser. PoM

I live in a stone house high in the mountains. Tequila. Elizabeth Spires. MAYP

I live in a town. Family Jewels. Essex Hemphill. GLP

I live in an orchard. Confetti of bruised petals. Postcard from the Garden. Marge Piercy. NoAM

I Live in Cuba. Lourdes Casal, *tr. fr. Spanish by* Margaret Randall. AIW

I Live in Great Sorrow. *Unknown*. *See* Fowls [*or* Foweles] in the Frith.

I Live in Helsinki. Pentti Saarikoski, *tr. fr. Finnish by* Aili Jarvenpa. SOP

I live in the town. The Town Child. Irene Thompson. BoTP

I live in the twilight of my vices. A Prayer for Rivers. Keith Wilson. GOYP

I live in this house, walls being plastered. Keep Me Still, for I Do Not Want to Dream. Larry Eigner. NeAP

I live invisible (in my whole sky). Too Bright a Day. Norman MacCaig. GTBS-P

I live my father's old age. My Father. Abraham Chalfi. VWA, *tr. by* Shlomo Vinner *and* Howard Schwartz

I live my life in growing orbits. Rainer Maria Rilke, *tr. by* Robert Bly. NU

I Live Not Where I Love. *Unknown*. OBET

I live now in an ancient book. Haim Guri, *tr. by* Warren Bargad *and* Stanley F. Chyet. IP

I live on the water. Winding Up. Derek Walcott. NoAM

I live on this depraved and lonely cliff. Vittoria da Colonna, *tr. by* Willis Barnstone. BoWoP

I live where darkness/ is not. Mukta Bai, *tr. by* Willis Barnstone. BoWoP

I live without inhabiting/ Myself. Saint John of the Cross, *tr. fr. Spanish by* Roy Campbell. *Fr*. Coplas about the Soul Which Suffers with Impatience to See God. OBVE

I live, yet no true life I know. I Die because I Do Not Die. St. Theresa of Avila, *tr. by* E. Allison Peers. TOF

I lived a life without love, and saw the being. The Mirage. Oscar Williams. LiTM

I lived alone as happy as Larry. The Husband's Lament. Brian Merriman, *tr. fr. Modern Irish by* Frank O'Connor. *Fr*. The Midnight Court. OBVE

I lived among a people. Rumors of the Turning Wheel. Anne Halley. PPR

I lived among great houses. The Statesman's Holiday. W. B. Yeats. CMoP; OxBTC

I lived at a time when. No Denying. Mihály Ladányi, *tr. by* Jascha Kessler. FOC

I lived here nearly 5 years before I could. Chicago Poem. Lew Welch. NeAP; PoM

I lived in a wood for a number of years. Ground for the Floor. *Unknown*. OBET

I lived in the first century of world wars. Muriel Rukeyser. UnPo

I lived in those times. For a thousand years. Robert Desnos, *tr. by* Kenneth Rexroth. RHTwFP

I lived inside a machine. On Being a Householder. Alan Dugan. NoAM

I lived my days apart. A Mystic as Soldier. Siegfried Sassoon. WGRP

I lived on this earth in an age. Miklós Radnóti, *tr. by* Steven Polgar, Stephen Berg *and* S. J. Martin. VWA

I Lived the Beloved home. Odysseus Elytis, *tr. fr. Greek by* Edmund Keeley *and* Philip Sherrard. VMG

I lived with Mr. Punch, they said my name was Judy. Variations. Randall Jarrell. VGW

I loathe, abhor, detest, despise. Dried Apple Pies. *Unknown*. BLPA

I loathe [*or* lothe] that I did love. The Aged Lover Renounceth Love. Lord Thomas Vaux. EIL; OAEL-1; PoEL-1

(Image of Death, The.) OBSC

I loed you for yir kindness. The Deean Tractorman, Clear. Edith Anne Robertson. OxBS

I loitered weeping with my bride for gladness. James Agee. *Fr*. Lyrics. MoAmPo

I long for nothing more. György Petri, *tr. by* William Jay Smith. MHuP

I long for you. Chikako, *tr. by* Steven D. Carter. WFTW

I long not now, a little while at least. Protest. Countee Cullen. CDC

I long to talke with some old lover's ghost. Love's Deity [*or* Deitie]. John Donne. AWP; EIL; GBL; LiTB; MePo; SeCePo; SeCP; SeCV-1

I longed for you. My Grandchild-Generation. Jacob Glatstein, *tr. by* Benjamin *and* Barbara Harshav. AYP

I look across the table and think. Incident. Norman MacCaig. FF

I look along the valley of my gun. The Possibility That Has Been Overlooked Is the Future. Michael Hartnett. NOIV

"I look and smell," Aunt Sponge declared, "as lovely as a rose!" Aunt Sponge and Aunt Spiker. Roald Dahl. RHPC

I look around: because charcoal firing warms the air. Lady Izumi, *tr. fr. Japanese by* Hiroaki Sato. *Fr*. Fifty-one Tanka. FCEI

I look around: humans like green stalks. Buson, *tr. fr. Japanese by* Hiroaki Sato. *Fr*. Eighty-seven Hokku. FCEI

I look at my dirty hands. Ishikawa Takuboku, *tr. fr. Japanese by* Hiroaki Sato. *Fr*. Forty-seven Tanka in Three Lines. FCEI

I look at the comb, look at the water, look at what has fallen. Washing My Hair. Tadaomi, *tr. by* Burton Watson. JLIC-1

I look at the crisp golden-threaded hair. Canzone: His Portrait of His Lady, Angiola of Verona. Fazio degli Uberti, *tr. by* Dante Gabriel Rossetti. AWP

I look at the evening sky. Ozaki Hosai, *tr. fr. Japanese by* Hiroaki Sato. *Fr*. One Hundred Haiku in Free Form. FCEI

I look at the light. Ryota, *tr. by* Geoffrey Bownas *and* Anthony Thwaite. PeBJV

I look at the naked woman. Married. Moyshe-Leyb Halpern, *tr. by* Benjamin *and* Barbara Harshav. AYP

I look at the swaling sunset. In Trouble and Shame. D. H. Lawrence. OBMV

I look at the water and reeds. The Present. Franco Fortini, *tr. by* Lawrence R. Smith. NItP

I Look at Your Land. Aila Meriluoto, *tr. fr. Finnish by* Aili Jarvenpa. SOP

I look back at the shore. Ozaki Hosai, *tr. fr. Japanese by* Hiroaki Sato. *Fr*. One Hundred Haiku in Free Form. FCEI

I look down the mountainside. Just below my window. In a Mountain Cabin in Norway. Robert Bly. RFM

I look far to the end of the haze. Princess Shikishi, *tr. fr. Japanese by* Hiroaki Sato. *Fr*. Seventy-eight Tanka. FCEI

I look for an explanation. Complaint. Alistair Paterson. *Fr*. Incantations for Warriors, XXII. PeNZ

I look for the way. Poetics. A. R. Ammons. NoP

I look in that one kind of dwindled. And in this. Album—A Runthru. Clark Coolidge. LP

I Look into My Glass. Thomas Hardy. BrPo; EBEV; FaBoTw; HAP; NAEL-2; NOBE; NOBVV; NoP; OxBSP; PrIm; SCV; WeW

I look into the eyes of the child. The Eyes of the Child Do Not See Me. Norman H. Russell. NOVW

I look into the henyard. The Darkling Chicken. Robert Peters. BXAP

I look on kingship in high pines. Exile. Jennette Yeatman. GoYe

I look onto an alley here. A Day for Anne Frank. C. K. Williams. GeTw

I look out at the white sleet covering the still streets. Sleet Storm on the Merritt Parkway. Robert Bly. NOBA

I look out of my window at night. Felix Pollak. Fr. The Finger, I. TSM

I look out today. Ietaka, tr. by Steven D. Carter. WFTW

I Look Outside. Paavo Haavikko, tr. fr. Finnish by Aili Jarvenpa. SOP

I look to Thee in ev'ry need. The Christian Life. Samuel Longfellow. WGRP

I Look Up to the Sky. Samuel Ha-Nagid, tr. fr. Hebrew by David Goldstein. TOF

I look upon the world—and she resembles a garden. The End of Man Is Death. Moses Ibn Ezra, tr. by Solomon Solis-Cohen. TrJP

I look upon thy happy face. To a Child. George Edgar Montgomery. AA

I look. You look. Over. R. S. Thomas. FF

I looked across and beyond the churned-up lake. A Dream. Hugh Connell. NeIP

I looked and I saw. Who but the Lord? Langston Hughes. BPo

I Looked and Saw History Caught. Alfred B. Spellman. NBP

I looked at that face, dumbfounded. Esse. Czeslaw Milosz. TOF

I looked down and saw a pit most black. Elizabeth Melvill, Lady Culross. Fr. A Godly Dream. WPE

I looked far back into other years, and lo, in bright array. Mary, Queen of Scots. Henry Glassford Bell. BeLS; BLPA; FaBoBe

I Looked for a Sounding-Board. Henriëtte Roland-Holst, tr. fr. Dutch by Jonathan Crewe. WPOW

I looked for that which is not, nor can be. A Pause of Thought. Christina Rossetti. NOBE; OBNC

I looked from the stair-well. Karamazov. Ben Belitt. DiL

I looked in my heart while the wild swans went over. Wild Swans. Edna St. Vincent Millay. CMoP; MoAmPo; PBWP; UnPo

I looked in the first glass. The Three Mirrors. Edwin Muir. NoAM

I Looked in the Mirror. Beatrice Schenk De Regniers. PDV

I looked into a lake and saw a forest. Playmates. Lillian Everts. GoYe

I looked into my body. X-Ray. Leonora Speyer. ImOP

I looked like Abraham Lincoln. Elliott Hawkins. Edgar Lee Masters. Fr. Spoon River Anthology. OxBA

I looked on that prophetic land. Presences Perfected. Siegfried Sassoon. MoBrPo

I looked one night, and there Semiramis. A Look into the Gulf. Edwin Markham. AA

I looked outside. Pools of water. Amir Gilboa, tr. by Warren Bargad and Stanley F. Chyet. IP

I looked over Jordan and [or an'] what did I see. Swing Low, Sweet Chariot. Unknown. AmFN; FaPON; UnPo

I looked over my shoulder. Gathering Strength. Leo Dangel. MOWH

I looked to find a man who walked with God. Enoch. Jones Very. HAP

I looked to find Spring's early flowers. The Lament of the Flowers. Jones Very. AnAmPo; NOBA; OxBA

I Looked Up from My Writing. Thomas Hardy. MMA; NoAM

I looked upon the earth: it was a floor. Our Lady in the Middle Ages. Frederick William Faber. ACP

I, Lord, of All Mortals! Malay Oral Tradition, tr. by R. O. Winstedt. WTO

I lose my head, but not your madness from my brain. Nawab Mirza Khan Dagh, tr. by Ahmed Ali. GoT

I lost it—what did I lose. What Did I Lose? Sun Yü-tang. Mes

I lost my mare in Lincoln Lane. Unknown. OxNR

I lost my pardner, what'll I do? Skip to My Lou. Unknown. AmFP

I lost my soul in a fit of temper. Lost, One Soul. Sandy McIntosh. AIW

I lost my temper twice today. To My Four-Year-Old Daughter. Gail Todd. TV

I lost my way. Narihira, tr. fr. Japanese by Burton Watson. Fr. Kokin Shu. FCEI

I lost the love, of heaven above. A Vision. John Clare. ChTr; EBVV; FaBoRV; GTBS-P; NAEL-2; NOBVV; OAEL-2; OBNC; OPOP; PoE; PPP

   (I Lost the Love of Heaven.) ELP

I Lov'd Thee Once. Sir Robert Ayton. OBS

I Love. Samuel Chimsoro. WMBCH

I Love. Stevie Smith. FaBoCo

I Love a Flower. At. to. Thomas Philipps. MeEL

I Love a Hill. Ralph Hodgson. BrPo

I love Adam. He is brave of heart. Eve. Jakov Fichman, tr. by Robert Friend. VWA

I Love All Beauteous Things. Robert Bridges. BoTP; BrPo; CMoP; EBEV; TrCP

I love all shining things. Shining Things. Elizabeth Gould. BoTP

I love and fear him. Lady Kasa, tr. by Kenneth Rexroth. BoWoP

I love and hate. Ah! never ask why so! Catullus. See Odi et Amo.

I love, and he loves me again. A Nymph's Secret. Ben Jonson. OBEV

I love and worship thee in that thy ways. Madonna Natura. "Fiona Macleod." WGRP

I love at early morn from new-mown swath. Summer Images. John Clare. ChTr; OBNC

I love bars and taverns. Bars. Nicolás Guillén, tr. by Perry Higman. LPSS

I love breasts, hard. Breasts. Charles Simic. NNaP

I Love But Thee. Heine, tr. fr. German by Louis Untermeyer. AWP

I love contemplating—apart. Napoleon and the British Sailor. Thomas Campbell. BeLS

I love crows. Crows. William Witherup. PCP

I love him not; but shew no reason can. Antipathy. Rowland Watkyns, after the Latin of Martial. FaBoEE

I love him wisely if I love him well. John Gambril Nicholson. Fr. A Chaplet of Southernwood. PeHV

"I love, I love and whom love ye?" I Love a Flower. At. to. Thomas Philipps. MeEL

I love it, I love it! and who shall dare. The Old Arm-Chair. Eliza Cook. AnAmPo; BrRo; InPK; WBLP

I Love Little Pussy. Jane Taylor. See I Like Little Pussy.

I love, loved, and so doth she. Sir Thomas Wyatt. SiPS

I love more than ever my solitary life. Reply to Her Daughter, IV. Madeleine Des Roches, tr. by Dorothy Backer. DMF

I Love Mountains. Ho Shao-chi, tr. fr. Chinese by J. D. Schmidt. WFTU

I Love My Country. Francisco Carrillo, tr. fr. Spanish by Maureen Ahern and David Tipton. Per

I love my God, but with no love of mine. Adoration. Mme Guyon. WGRP

I Love My Jean. Burns. See Of A' the Airts [the Wind Can Blaw].

I Love My Jesus Quite Alone. At. to Johannes Kelpius, tr. fr. German by Christopher Witt. AH

I love my little son, and yet when he was ill. The Two Parents. "Hugh MacDiarmid." FaBoTw; OxBTC

I Love My Love. Helen Adam. NeAP; NMM; WPOW

I Love My Love in the Morning. Gerald Griffin. ACP

I love my love with a v. Gertrude Stein. Fr. Before the Flowers of Friendship Faded Faded. PeHV

I Love My Master. Nancy Morejón, tr. fr. Spanish by Kathleen Weaver. AIW

I love my native land with such perverse affection! Native Land. M. Y. Lermontov, tr. by Alan Myers. AAA

I love my prairies, they are mine. My Prairies. Hamlin Garland. FaPON

I love my sad God. My Wander-Brother. Jacob Glatstein, tr. by Benjamin and Barbara Harshav. AYP

I love my work and my children. God. Ovid in the Third Reich. Geoffrey Hill. FaBoMo; NoAM; PoPo

I love noodles. Give me oodles. Oodles of Noodles. Lucia Hymes Lucia and James L. Hymes, Jr. RHPC

I love not thy perfections. When I hear. Depreciating Her Beauty. Wilfrid Scawen Blunt. Fr. The Love Sonnets of Proteus, VI. OBMV

I love Octopussy, his arms are so long. The Octopussycat. Kenyon Cox. FaPON

I love old gardens best. A Charleston Garden. Henry Bellamann. PoLF

I love sixpence, jolly little sixpence. Mother Goose. OxNR

I Love Somebody. Unknown. AmFP

I love sweets. Ellen West. Frank Bidart. NAAL-2; PPR

I love the autumn moon. To the Tune "Chieh san ch'eng." Yang Shen, tr. fr. Chinese by Jonathan Chaves. Fr. Four Poems from the Sequence "Singing of the Moon," III. CoBLCP

I love the dark race of poets. Luminous Night. Louis Simpson. CAPP

I love the days of long ago. My Africa. Michael Dei-Anang. PBA

I love the English country scene. I Love. Stevie Smith. FaBoCo

I love the evenings, passionless and fair, I love the evens. A Sunset. Victor Hugo, tr. fr. French by Francis Thompson. Fr. Feuilles d'Automne. AWP

I love the fitful gust that shakes. Autumn. John Clare. BoTP

I love the languor of your sensual lips.   Renée Vivien, *tr.* by Beth Archer. DMF

I love the lazy Southern spring.   The First Julep.   Bliss Carman. AnAmPo

I love the little winding lanes.   Lanes in Summer.   Malcolm Hemphrey. BoTP

I Love the Lord.   *Unknown.*   AH

I love the memory of the days that walked.   The Days and the Giants. Unsi al-Haj, *tr.* by Abdullah al-Udhari.   MPAW

I Love the Night.   Matilda Caroline Edwards.   PWR

I love the old melodious lays.   Whittier.   AA; AnAmPo; NoP; OxBA; TAP

I love the p'i-p'a's music in my heart.   Hsü Pen, *tr. fr. Chinese by* Jonathan Chaves.   *Fr.* Five Things Sought For——In the Manner of Han Wo.   CoBLCP

I love the rite of Luther's congregation.   Fyodor Ivanovich Tyutchev, *tr.* by Alan Myers.   AAA

I love the sea.   The Sea at Evening.   Christopher Laird.   PBCV

I love the serenity of living in the woods.   Wang Chiu-ssu, *tr. fr. Chinese* by Jonathan Chaves.   *Fr.* Living in the Woods.   CoBLCP

I love the silent majority.   I Love.   Samuel Chimsoro.   WMBCH

I love the sound of the horn in the deep, dim woodland.   The Sound of the Horn.   Alfred de Vigny, *tr.* by Wilfred Thorley.   AWP

I love the spring moon.   To the Tune, "Chieh san ch'eng" ("I love the spring moon").   Yang Shen, *tr. fr. Chinese by* Jonathan Chaves.   *Fr.* Four Poems from the Sequence "Singing of the Moon", I.   CoBLCP

I love the stillness you leave behind you.   What I Have to Tell You, Until Next Time.   David Avidan, *tr.* by Warren Bargad *and* Stanley F. Chyet.   IP

I love the stream flowing endlessly.   Robert Bly Finds Something in New Jersey.   Carol Poster.   BXAP

I love the summer moon.   To the Tune "Yu hu-lu" ("I love the summer moon").   Yang Shen, *tr. fr. Chinese* by Jonathan Chaves.   *Fr.* Four Poems from the Sequence "Singing of the Moon", II.   CoBLCP

I love the winter moon.   To the Tune "Yu hu-lu" ("I love the winter moon").   Yang Shen, *tr. fr. Chinese* by Jonathan Chaves.   *Fr.* Four Poems from the Sequence "Singing of the Moon", IV.   CoBLCP

I Love the Woods.   Leib Neidus, *tr. fr. Yiddish* by Keith Bosley.   VWA

I love the word.   Yes.   Brendan Kennelly.   CIP

I Love Thee.   Josephine D. Henderson Heard.   CBWP-4

I love thee, Betty.   *Unknown.*   OxNR

I love thee now; thy beauties move me yet.   To His Mistress, Dead and Darkly Return'd.   Roger Johnson.   VVA

I love thee when thy swelling buds appear.   The Tree.   Jones Very.   GN; OHIP

I love these gardens, all their show.   The Gardeners.   Christopher Reid. DiPo

I love this boy, not for his beauty only.   F. W. Soodley.   PeHV

I love this byre.   Shadows are kindly here.   The Innkeeper's Wife.   Clive Sansom.   OBCP

I Love This Sunlight Cold.   Amir Gilboa, *tr. fr. Hebrew by* Warren Bargad *and* Stanley F. Chyet.   IP

I Love Thy Kingdom, Lord.   Timothy Dwight.   AH
(Love to the Church.)   AA

I love to go out in late September.   Blackberry Eating.   Galway Kinnell. InPK

I love to hear a lobster laugh.   Fun.   Leroy F. Jackson.   RAR

I love to hear the little bird.   The Bird.   Samuel Hoffenstein.   FiBHP

I love to hear thine earnest voice.   To an Insect.   Oliver Wendell Holmes. AnAmPo

I love to listen to men in bars.   Frank Sinatra.   Michael Waters.   GeTw

I love to rise in a summer morn.   The Schoolboy.   Blake.   *Fr.* Songs of Experience.   BoNaP; CH; FaBoCh

I love to see boards lying on the ground in early spring.   Old Boards. Robert Bly.   NaP

I love to see the little stars.   The Oneness of the Philosopher with Nature. G. K. Chesterton.   FaBoNo

I love to see the old heath's withered brake.   Emmonsail's Heath in Winter.   John Clare.   PoEL-4

I love to see those loving and beloved.   Lonely Love.   Edmund Blunden. OxBTC

I love to see, when leaves depart.   Autumn.   Roy Campbell.   GTBS-P; MoBrPo; OBMV; OxBTC

I Love to Steal Awhile Away.   Phoebe Hinsdale Brown.   AH
(Private Devotion.)   AA

I love to think of things I hate.   The Complete Misanthropist.   Morris Bishop.   FiBHP; FPL; TW

I love to wander through the woodlands hoary.   October.   S. W. Whitman.   BoTP

I love watching the water.   Trinket.   Marvin Bell.   AnAn

I Love What Is Not.   Manfred Winkler, *tr. fr. Hebrew by* Mary Zilzer. VWA

I love wine but have no wine to drink.   On Hearing That San-p'ing's Newly Brewed Chrysanthemum Wine Is Ready to Drink.   Pien Kung, *tr.* by Jonathan Chaves.   CoBLCP

I Love You.   Ilyas Abu Shabaku, *tr. fr. Arabic by* Adnan Haydar *and* Michael Beard.   MAP

I Love You.   *Unknown.*   RHPC

I Love You.   Ella Wheeler Wilcox.   BLPA; FaBoBe; FPL

I love you.   Notes.   Cecilia Bustamante, *tr.* by David Tipton.   Per

I love you,/ Not only for what you are.   Love.   *At. to.* Roy Croft. BLPA; FaBoBe

"I love you."   Hilda Doolittle ("H. D.").   *Fr.* Sigil, XIX.   AnAn

I love you/ do not forget me.   Lady Kasa.   *Fr.* Manyo Shu.   FCEI

I love you,/ it's utterly hopeless.   Lady Kasa.   *Fr.* Manyo Shu.   FCEI

I love you.   Equation.   Nizar Qabbani, *tr.* by Diana Der Hovanessian *and* Lena Jayyusi.   MAP

I love you and the rosebush.   Armando Uribe, *tr.* by Miller Williams. HoPM

I love you, because in my thousand and one nights.   Love without Love. Luis Lloréns Torres.   InW, *tr.* by Julio Marzán

I love you better than I love my race.   Charles Mair.   *Fr.* Tecumseh. NOBC

I love you first because your face is fair.   V-Letter.   Karl Shapiro. NoAM; TrJP; WaP
(Love Letter.)   NYBP

I love you for your brownness.   To a Dark Girl.   Gwendolyn B. Bennett. BANP; BlSi; CDC; PoBA

I love you ginger bread mama.   Ginger Bread Mama.   Doughtry Long, Jr. BPo; PoBA

I love you, great new Titan!   Soldier: Twentieth Century.   Isaac Rosenberg.   MMA

"I love you, Horowitz," he said, and blew his nose.   Love in Brooklyn. John Wakeman.   SoSe

I love you, I like you.   Love.   William Jay Smith.   RHPC

I Love You It's True.   Carole Stewart.   WS

I love you more than human heart can bear.   I Love You.   Ilyas Abu Shabaku, *tr.* by Adnan Haydar *and* Michael Beard.   MAP

"I love you, Mother," said little John.   Which Loved Best?   "Joy Allison."   WBLP
(Which Loved Her Best?)   OHIP

I love you, Mrs. Acorn. Would your husband mind.   Song (October 1969).   Kath Fraser.   AIW; PeHV

I love you, my plain pine box.   First Coffin Poem.   David Ignatow. CAPP

I love you, not because I love the guillotine.   Ode to Freedom.   Aaron Zeitlin, *tr.* by Keith Bosley.   VWA

I love you, rotten.   Medlars and Sorb-Apples.   D. H. Lawrence.   NoAM; OAEL-2

I love you so much.   Chimera.   Mary Ann Henn.   SoTCo

I love you—Titan lover.   Girl to Soldier on Leave.   Isaac Rosenberg. MMA

I love you well, my steel-white dagger.   Dagger.   Mikhail Yurevich Lermontov, *tr.* by Max Eastman.   AWP

"I love you," you said between two mouthfuls of pudding.   A Considered Reply to a Child.   Jonathan Price.   BoLoP

I love your eyebrows, said one.   You Must Have Been a Sensational Baby.   Harold Norse.   GLP

I love your hands.   Your Hands.   Angelina Weld Grimké.   CDC; PoBA

I love your lips when they're wet with wine.   I Love You.   Ella Wheeler Wilcox.   BLPA; FaBoBe; FPL

I loved/ secretly.   *Unknown, tr. fr. Latin by* Willis Barnstone.   *Fr.* Carmina Burana.   BoWoP

I loved a child of this countrie.   *Unknown.*   GBL; PBWP

I Loved a Lass.   George Wither.   CH; NOBE; OBEV
(Love Sonnet, A.)   EiL; FaBoPP; GBL; OBS

I loved booze.   Clifton.   Joan Larkin.   GLP

I Loved Everything in the World.   Sandro Penna, *tr. fr. Italian by* W. S. Di Piero.   PFI

I loved her like the leaves.   Hitomaro.   *Fr.* Manyo Shu.   PeBJV

I loved her softness, her warm human smell.   The Lion's Bride.   Gwen Harwood.   BoWoP

I loved him not; and yet, now he is gone.   The Maid's Lament.   Walter Savage Landor.   *Fr.* The Citation and Examination of William Shakespeare.   OBEV; OBNC

I loved him three storms ere he loved me again.   Love's Flight.   Else Lasker-Schüler, *tr.* by Jethro Bithell.   TrJP

I loved my friend.   Langston Hughes.   iLY; NTCP

I loved my lord, my black-haired lord, my young love.   The Magnet. Ruth Stone.   MoAmPo

I loved my love from green of spring.   Grown and Flown.   Christina Rossetti.   NOBVV

I loved my native city, as you do, as everyone does.   Sketch for a Memoir.   Adam Wazyk, *tr.* by Czeslaw Milosz.   PwPP

I loved swimming until it became a nightmare for. Medals and Money: A Re-evaluation. Barbara Lamblin. ASP

I loved the light of course. Memories of Italy (Broken Sestina). John Ash. BAP; NPo

I Loved Thee. Robert, Earl Nugent. *See* I loved thee beautiful and kind.

I Loved Thee, Atthis, in the Long Ago. Bliss Carman. CaP

I loved thee beautiful and kind. Robert, Earl Nugent. NOEC
    (I Loved Thee.) FiBHP

I loved thee long and dearly. Florence Vane. Philip Pendleton Cooke. AA; AnAmPo

I loved thee once, I'll love no more. On A Woman's Inconstancy. Sir Robert Ayton. EiL
    (To an Inconstant One.) OBEV; QFR

I loved thee, though I told thee not. The Secret. John Clare. GBL

I loved to talk of home. Pacific Epitaphs. Dudley Randall. MoP

I loved you. Disposition No. 1. Shafiq al-Kamali, *tr. by* Sargon Boulus *and* Christopher Middleton. MAP

I Loved You Once. Pushkin, *tr. fr. Russian.* AmNP, *tr. by* Dudley Randall
    ("I loved you; even now I may confess.") BoLoP, *tr. by* Reginald Mainwaring Hewitt
    ("I loved you once: of love, perhaps, an ember.") AAA, *tr. by* Alan Myers

I loved you, so I drew these tides of men into my hands. A To S. Thomas Edward Lawrence. PeHV

I. M. H. Maurice Baring. ACP

I made a loaf of bread. The White Bird. Roy McFadden. NeIP

I made a pilgrimage to find the God. Revelation. Edwin Markham. WGRP

I made a posy [*or* posie], while the day ran by. Life. George Herbert. FaBoRV; JCP; LiTB; MeLP; MePo; NoP; OBS; SeCP; SeCV-1

I made a song and placed it far, near God. Fugato (Coda). Gad Hollander. VWA

I made a song for my dear love's delight. A Song's Worth. Susan Marr Spalding. AA

I made a way through fire and big winds. Boring Days. Aba Shtoltsenberg, *tr. by* Dennis Silk. PeBMYV

I made another garden, yea. Arthur O'Shaughnessy. OBEV

I made god upon god. Hilda Doolittle ("H. D."). *Fr.* Pygmalion. WGRP

I made hay while the sun shone. The Last Laugh. Sir John Betjeman. PoPo

I made her wet, and myself. *Unknown, tr. by* Sato. FCEI

I made my fire of little sticks. Little Sticks. Eric Rolls. PoAu-2

I made my song a coat. A Coat. W. B. Yeats. CMoP; LiTM; NAEL-2; NoAM; OxBSP; PoEL-5

I made peanut butter sandwiches. The Runaway. Bobbi Katz. RHPC

I made the cross myself whose weight. A Little Parable. Anne Reeve Aldrich. AA

I made the Muses sick. The Death of the Gods; an Ode Written in Imitation of Pindar. L. Ker. NOEC

I made up my mind for to change my way. The Trail to Mexico. *Unknown.* AmFP

I, Maister Andro Kennedy. The Testament of Mr. Andro Kennedy. William Dunbar. OxBS

I make a pact with you, Walt Whitman. A Pact. Ezra Pound. AmPP; AnAmPo; LiTA; MoP; NAAL-2; NoAM; NOBA; OxBA; TAP

I make a pillow of a rock-root on Mount Kamo. Hitomaro. *Fr.* Manyo Shu. FCEI

I make a simple assertion. Working with Tools. A. R. Ammons. CAPP

I make a trip to each clock in the apartment. Two Mornings and Two Evenings. Elizabeth Bishop. PoA

I make all the poetic pauses. Dana Naone. CDW

I make free with old albums. At the Wailing Wall. Aidan Carl Mathews. CIP

I make man's ancient food. Bread. Nancy Keesing. PoAu-2

I make myself wake early. Waking, the Love Poem Sighs. Jim Hall. GOYP

I Make Poems, Gentlemen! Gloria Fuertes, *tr. fr. Spanish by* Kate Flores. DMH

I make this dirge for you Miss Mary Binning I miss you. *Unknown, tr. by* Armand Schwerner. BoWoP

I make this song about me full sadly. The Wife's Lament. *Unknown.* WPE
    ("I make this song sadly about myself.") BoWoP, *tr. by* Willis Barnstone *and* Elene Kolb
    ("I sing of myself, a sorrowful woman.") PBWP, *tr. by* Kemp Malone
    ("Song I sing of sorrow unceasing, A.") AnOE, *tr. by* Charles W. Kennedy

I make you sightsee the sheer walls. To an Alcoholic. Sandra McPherson. MAYP

I march'd three miles through scorching sand. On a Curate's Complaint of Hard Day. Swift. TIRV

I marked all kindred powers the heart finds fair. Love Enthroned. Dante Gabriel Rossetti. *Fr.* The House of Life, I. OBNC

I marked the slow withdrawal of the year. In Memorabilia Mortis. Francis Sherman. CaP

I married a man of the Croydon class. Nervous Prostration. Anna Wickham. AIW; FaBoWP; TW

I Married in My Youth a Wife. J. V. Cunningham. *Fr.* Three Epigrams. MoAmPo; RB; TW

I marry'd a wife of late. Keep a Good Tongue in Your Head. Martin Parker. CoMu

I marvel not Bassanio was so bold. Portia. Oscar Wilde. BrPo

I marvell'd why a simple child. Only Seven. Henry S. Leigh. BXAP

I, Maximus of Gloucester, to You ("By ear, she sd"). Charles Olson. *Fr.* The Maximus Poems, NeAP.

I, Maximus of Gloucester, to You ("Off-shore, by islands hidden in the blood"). Charles Olson. *Fr.* The Maximus Poems. LiTM; NoAM; NOBA; PoM

I may be dead to-morrow, uncaressed. For the Book of Love. Jules Laforgue, *tr. by* Jethro Bithell. AWP; ErPo

I may be silent, but. Silent, But. Tsuboi Shigeji, *tr. by* Geoffrey Bownas *and* Anthony Thwaite. PeBJV

I may be smelly and I may be old. The River God. Stevie Smith. BrRo; FaBoNo; FaBoTw; FaBoWP; PBWP

I may even be. Power and Light. James Dickey. NAAL-2

I May, I Might, I Must. Marianne Moore. FaBoWP; FF; OBAL; OxBSP

I may not touch the hand I saw. A Separation. William Johnson Cory. OBNC

I may pass through once more next month. Felix Pollak. *Fr.* The Finger, III. TSM

I May Reap. Patrick Kavanagh. TIRV

I may well once more. Tamehide, *tr. by* Steven D. Carter. WFTW

I mean/ if I didn't know. Discovering. Sharon Scott. JB

I mean/ the fiddleheads have forced their babies. May 10th. Maxine W. Kumin. BoNaP; NYBP; RFM

I mean, I'm a no shoes hillbilly an' home. Gracie. Faye Kicknosway. GeTw; NMM

I mean to mark the Midway Day. Mezzo Cammin. Judith Moffett. SM

I measure every grief I meet. Emily Dickinson. MoAB; MoAmPo

I measured myself by the wall in the garden. Day Dreams, or Ten Years Old. Margaret Johnson. BLPA

I meditate long. She. Manfred Winkler. VWA, *tr. by* Mary Zilzer

I meditate upon a swallow's flight. Coole Park, 1929. W. B. Yeats. OAEL-2; OBMV

I meet you in an evil time. An Eclogue for Christmas. Louis MacNeice. FaBoMo; NoAM; OBMV

I member we went to the hospital that day. The Killing of the Birds. Shirley Williams. BoWoP

I mend the fyre and beikit me about. Robert Henryson. *Fr.* The Testament of Cresseid. EBEV; PoE

I met a cracksman coming down the Strand. Theodore Martin. *Fr.* The Thieves' Anthology. FaBoPa

I met a friend yesterday. Civilized. Ahmad Nadeem Qasmi, *tr. by* Mahmood Jamal. PBMUP

I met a girl from Derrygarve. A New Song. Seamus Heaney. CIP; FaBoTw

I met a guy I used to know, who said. Ozymandias II. Howard Nemerov. Son

I met a lady/ on a lazy street. From the Hazel Bough. Earle Birney. NIP

i met a little elf man, once. The Little Elf. John Kendrick Bangs. AA; FaBoBe; NTCP; OBCA; RAR
    (Little Elfman, The.) OnUR; OBMV; PDV

I met a little woman. The Toad. Elizabeth Jane Coatsworth. RAR

I Met a Man. Hughes Mearns. *See* As I was going up the stair.

I met a man as I went walking. Puppy and I. A. A. Milne. BoTP; FaPON; OnUR; PDV; PYC

I met a man in an onion bed. The Man in the Onion Bed. John Ciardi. SO

I met a man in South Street, tall. Cutty Sark. Hart Crane. *Fr.* The Bridge, III. FaBoMo

I met a man mowing. Hay Harvest. Patrick Reginald Chalmers. BoTP

I met a man with a triple-chin. The Man Who Sang the Sillies. John Ciardi. OBCA

I met a rat under a bridge. And we sat there in the mud. The Rat's Legs. Russell Edson. NAmP

I met a seer. The Book of Wisdom. Stephen Crane. *Fr.* The Black Riders, XXXVI. HoPM; MoAmPo

I met a strange woman. C Is for Charms. Eleanor Farjeon. WSC

I met a toad. Warty Bliggens, the Toad. Don Marquis. *Fr.* Archy and Mehitabel. FiBHP

I met a traveler [*or* traveller] from an antique land. Ozymandias [*or* Ozymandias of Egypt *or* Sonnet: Ozymandias]. Shelley. AWP; BeLS; CH; DL; EnRP; FaBoBe; FaBoCh; FaBoRV; FaFP; FaPoR; FF; FiP; FPL; GTBS; GTBS-P; HAP; HeIP; HoPM; InPK; InPS; NAEL-2; NIP; NOBE; NoP; OAEL-2; OBNC; PoE; PoLF; PoRA; PrIM; RB; SCV; Son; SoSe; TEP; TrGrPo; WeW

I met a traveller from an antique land. Ozymandias Revisited. Morris Bishop. BXAP; NBLV

I met an elf-man in the woods. How to Treat Elves. Morris Bishop. FiBHP; OBAL; OBCA

I met an honest man today. Alien. William Price Turner. OxBS

I met ayont the cairney. Empty Vessel. "Hugh MacDiarmid." FaBoTw; NoP; OxBS

I Met by Chance. Heine, *tr. fr. German by* John Todhunter. AWP

I met Death—he was a sportsman—on Cole's/ Island. Cole's Island. Charles Olson. *Fr.* The Maximus Poems. PoM

I met God in the morning. His Presence Came Like Sunrise. Ralph Spaulding Cushman. BLRP

I met her as a blossom on a stem. The Dream. Theodore Roethke. LLLT; NoP; NYBP; UnPo

I Met Her in the Garden Where the Praties Grow. *Unknown.* AS

I met her on the first of August. Nessa. Paul Durcan. FaBCIP

I met him again, he was trudging along. I Fights Mit Sigel! Grant P. Robinson. BLPA

I met Louisa in the shade. Louisa. Wordsworth. EnRP; GBL

I met Musette/ In the water-closet. Vague Lyric by G. M. Max Beerbohm. FaBoEE

I Met My Solitude. Naomi Replansky. BrRo

I met Poetry, an old prostitute walking. Moral Story II. David Wright. PeSA

I met the Bishop on the road. Crazy Jane Talks with the Bishop. W. B. Yeats. BoLoP; CMoP; EBEV; ErPo; InPK; MoP; NAEL-2; NoAM; NoP; OAEL-2; PoE; PPP; TOF

I met the Love-Talker one eve in the glen. The Love-Talker. "Ethna Carbery." CH; WPE

I Met the Master. *Unknown.* BLRP; PoLF

I Met This Guy Who Died. Gregory Corso. NAs; Psk

I met this lovely scene once before, on horseback. Gazing at Ch'ang-po Mountain. Li K'ai-hsien, *tr. by* Jonathan Chaves. CoBLCP

I met with a country lass. Thankful Country Lass, The; or, The Jolly Batchelor Kindly Entertained. *Unknown.* CoMu

I met with a jovial girl. Roaring Lad and the Ranting Lass, The; or, A Merry Couple Madly Met. *Unknown.* CoMu

I met with the girls coming from afar off. Love-Song of the Water Carriers. *Unknown.* PeSA

I met you on the way. Adam. Celia Dropkin, *tr. by* Grace Schulman. PeBMYV

I mid the hills was born. Harold the Valiant. Mary Elizabeth DeWitt Stebbins. AA

I might have resented. Being Sad. Orban Veli Kanik, *tr. by* Talat Sait Halman. LLLT

I might not, if I could. Lines by a Medium. *Unknown.* NA

"I might—unhappy word—oh me, I might." Sir Philip Sidney. *Fr.* Astrophel and Stella, XXXIII. OAEL-1; OBSC

I mind as 'ow the night afore that show. The Chances. Wilfred Owen. MMA; OxBTC

I mind once on a forenoon in early summer sitting. Language As Inevitable Metaphor. Idea As Inevitable Figment. Hayden Carruth. BLA

I mind, when I dream at nicht. The Gean Trees. Violet Jacob. PoSH

I Minded God. Henry Ainsworth. AH

I mingle with the young and gay. I Smile, but Oh! My Heart Is Breaking. Mary E. Tucker. CBWP-1

I mingle with your bones. The One Lost. Isaac Rosenberg. MoBrPo

I miss the peace and quiet of Chicago. Poem after Apollinaire. Ira Sadoff. AmPA

I miss the sun. Especially this winter. Turner's Sunrise. Helen Smith Bevington. EyDe

I miss your voice as you talked to me. Elegies for Prince Atsumichi. Lady Izumi, *tr. fr. Japanese by* Hiroaki Sato. *Fr.* Fifty-one Tanka. FCEI

I missed him when the sun began to bend. Lost and Found. George Macdonald. WGRP

I Missed His Book, I Read His Name. John Updike. OBAL

I missed you at services last night. Kol Nidre. Sharon A. Stern. TSM

I mistook a warbler for a sparrow. Buson, *tr. fr. Japanese by* Hiroaki Sato. *Fr.* Eighty-seven Hokku. FCEI

I mock myself: another year and I'm still unable to return. Mocking Myself. Ku Yen-wu, *tr. by* J. P. Seaton. WFTU

I mock thee not, though I by thee am mocked. To Flaxman. Blake. FaBoEE; OxBoLi

I move among my pots and pans. Trimming the Sails. Vassar Miller. NMM

I move back by shortcut. The World. Vern Rutsala. Psk

I move on feeling and have learned to distrust those who don't. Poem of Angela Yvonne Davis. Nikki Giovanni. PoBA

I move the curtain back. After I Have Voted. Laura Jensen. AmPA

I Move the Meeting Be Adjourned. Nicanor Parra, *tr. fr. Spanish by* Miller Williams. *Fr.* Manifesto. HoPM

I Move to Random Consolations. William Heyen. AmPA

I Moved in My House. Gillian Hanscombe *and* Suniti Namjoshi. DT

I moved, to keep the moon. On Aesthetics, More or Less. Peter Kane Dufault. NYBP

I moved to the window to wait for somebody. A Suicide. Tom Kryss. NeAC

I Mun Be Married a Sunday. Nicholas Udall. *Fr.* Ralph Roister Doister. EIL

I Muriel stood at the altar-table. Don Baty, the Draft Register. Muriel Rukeyser. NNaP

I Muse Not. Francis Davison. TW

I mused/ Up and down, up and down, the terraced streets. Elizabeth Barrett Browning. *Fr.* Aurora Leigh. OBTV

I must/ Not trust. Anacreontic. Robert Herrick. CaPo

I Must Away. H. M. Sarson. BoTP

I must be dreaming through the days. Experience. Lesbia Harford. CBAP; PoAu-1

"I must be going, no longer staying." The Grey Cock. *Unknown.* ELP; OBET

I must be mad, or very tired. Meeting-House Hill. Amy Lowell. MoAmPo; OxBA; PoRA

I must build it. Beginning. Kurt Klinger, *tr. by* Beth Bjorklund. CoAuP

I must complain, yet doe enjoy my love. Thomas Campion. AAS

I must confess that often I'm. *Time* like an Ever-rolling Stream. P. G. Wodehouse. FiBHP

I must depart, but like to his last breath. Parted Souls. Lord Herbert of Cherbury. SeCP

I must depart now. Yukihira, *tr. by* Geoffrey Bownas *and* Anthony Thwaite. PeBJV

I must explain why it is that at night, in my own house. Still Life. Reed Whittemore. CoAP

I must go back to winter. Two Decisions. Vernon Watkins. OxBTC

I must go down to the seas again, to the lonely sea and the sky. Sea Fever. John Masefield. FaBoBe; FaBV; FaPON; FaPoR; FPL; MoAB; MoBrPo; MOS; OBTV; OHFP; OxBTC; PDV; PoLF; TrGrPo

I must go down to the seas again, where the billows romp and reel. Sea-Chill. Arthur Guiterman. BXAP; FaBoPa; MOS

I must go. I must gather my few things. Listening to Her. Natan Zach, *tr. by* Laya Firestone. VWA

"I must go now, goodbye," said the god of night. Yosano Akiko, *tr. fr. Japanese by* Hiroaki Sato. *Fr.* Thirty-nine Tanka. FCEI

I Must Go Walk the Wood So Wild. *Unknown.* MeEL (Wood So Wild, The.) WiR

I must grope as I pick. Mitsune, *tr. by* Geoffrey Bownas *and* Anthony Thwaite. PeBJV

I must have passed the crest a while ago. The Long Hill. Sara Teasdale. LiTA; MoAmPo

I must, I will have gin!—that skillet take. Strip Me Naked, or Royal Gin for Ever; a Picture. *Unknown.* NOEC

I must lie down with them all soon and sleep. Thomas Kinsella. *Fr.* Nightwalker. BIrV

I must not gaze at them although. The Barrier. Claude McKay. BANP

I must not grieve my love, whose eyes would read. Samuel Daniel. *Fr.* To Delia. OBEV ("Sonnet: "I must not grieve my love, whose eyes would read."") EIL

I must not think of thee; and, tired yet strong. Renouncement. Alice Meynell. BoLoP; MoBrPo; NOBE; OBEV; OBMV; OBNC; Son; WPE

I must once again. Absalom. Yona Wallach, *tr. by* Warren Bargad *and* Stanley F. Chyet. IP

I must possess you utterly. Possession. Richard Aldington. MoBrPo

I must remember. Spreading Wings on Wind. Simon J. Ortiz. HATNAP

I must remember to dismiss. Nature Study, after Dufy. Helen Smith Bevington. NYBP

I must tell you. The Grass. George Bowering. MoCV

I must tell you. Young Sycamore. William Carlos Williams. TAP

I must travel again. A New Journey. Javier Heraud, *tr. by* Maureen Ahern. Per

I must wait for a stranger to knock on my door. David Ignatow. NNaP

I mustn't ask about him. Tune: Drunk among the Flowers. Mao Wen-hsi, *tr. by* Burton Watson. CoBCP

I, my dear, was born to-day. On My Birthday, July 21. Matthew Prior. OBEV

I myself and Pangur Bán. Pangur Bán. *Unknown.* NOIV

I myself saw furious with blood. Aeneas at Washington. Allen Tate. FYAP; LiTA; NoAM; NOBA; OxBA

I nail Picasso's girl with a mirror. Notes from an Analyst's Couch. Anita Endrezze Probst. CDW

I, named by the tribe, am no rabbi. Axioms. Gad Hollander. VWA

I neatly paint spring water on the porcelain pot. Landscape in a Pot. Lo Ch'ing, *tr. by* Dominic Cheung. IFON

I Need Help. Edward Hirsch. NAmP

I Need No Gravestone. Bertolt Brecht, *tr. fr. German by* Michael Hamburger. OBD

I Need No Sky. Witter Bynner. EaLo

I Need Not Go. Thomas Hardy. NOBE; OBEV; OxBTC

I need not shout my faith. Thrice eloquent. Silence. Charles Hanson Towne. WGRP

I need not your needles. *Unknown.* OxNR

I need only fall asleep/ to return. Ana Blandiana, *tr. fr. Rumanian by* Stavros Deligiorgis. BoWoP

I need so much the quiet of your love. At Nightfall. Charles Hanson Towne. BLPA; FaBoBe

I need something easy. Honey Moon. Kathleen Leland Baker. NBLV

I needed somewhere with a flirt of grace. George MacBeth. *Fr.* The Renewal. PoPo

I ne'er could any lustre see. Sheridan. *Fr.* The Duenna, I, ii. NOEC

I ne'er was struck before that hour. First Love. John Clare. BoLoP; ChTr; EnLoPo; GBL; HAP; NOBVV; NoP
(I Ne'er Was Struck.) ELP

I neither trim the sail nor tend the mast. Shu Wei, *tr. fr. Chinese by* Barry L. Gartell. *Fr.* Composed on a Moonlit Night Outing on Ancient West, II. WFTU

I never asked for more than thou hast given. G. Lowes Dickinson. PeHV

I never asked you to be perfect—did I? The Imperfect Lover. Siegfried Sassoon. BrPo

I never barked when out of season. On a Dog of Lord Eglinton's. Burns. OxBSP

I never believed that in my broken life. Ts'ai Yen, *tr. fr. Chinese by* Kenneth Rexroth *and* Ling Chung. *Fr.* Eighteen Verses Sung to a Tatar Reed Whistle, XIII. BoWoP; WPOW

I never bought a young gazelle. 'Twas Ever Thus. *Unknown.* BXAP

I never build a song by night or day. My Comrade. Edwin Markham. AA

I never cared for Life: Life cared for me. Thomas Hardy. FaBoEE; FaBoRV

I never cast a flower away. Partings. Maria Jane Jewsbury. OxBChV

"I never could stand you too long." There Are So Many Fatherless Children Around. John Wieners. PPR

I never crossed your threshold with a grief. The Closed Door. Theodosia Pickering Garrison. BLPA

I never did on cleft Parnassus dream. Prologue to the First Satire. Persius, *tr. fr. Latin by* Dryden. *Fr.* Satires. AWP

"I never drank of Aganippe well." Sir Philip Sidney. *Fr.* Astrophel and Stella, LXXIV. HeIP; NAEL-1; OBSC; Son

I Never Even Suggested It. Ogden Nash. FiBHP; FPL; LiTA; PoLF

I never feared the darkness as a child. The Black-out. Mary Désirée Anderson. CN

I never felt so much. A Birthday. Edwin Muir. NAs

I never gave a lock of hair away. Elizabeth Barrett Browning. *Fr.* Sonnets from the Portuguese, XVIII. EBVV; HAP

I never had a happier time. One Saturday. "Marian Douglas." AA

I Never Had a Piece of Toast. James Payn. CenHV; FaBoPa

I never had you nor, I suppose. Half an Hour. Constantine P. Cavafy, *tr. by* Edmund Keeley *and* Philip Sherrard. VMG

I never have got the bearings quite. The Flag. James Jeffrey Roche. PAH

I never hear the word "escape." Emily Dickinson. CMoP; NOBA

I never imagined I. Images for a Painter. David Wright. NPo

I never knew happiness. Mohammad Taqi Mir, *tr. by* Ahmed Ali. GoT

I never knew him well. Elegy for John Wilborg. Sylvester Pollet. SoTCo

I never knew the earth had so much gold. Feuerzauber. Louis Untermeyer. TrJP

I never know. When All the World Is Full of Snow. N. M. Bodecker. RHPC

I never learned the names. Santa Caterina. Myra Glazer Schotz. VWA

I never let you come to the games. I never. Basketball. Stephen Vincent. NeAC

I never look upon the sea. Aunt Zillah Speaks. Herbert Edward Palmer. FaBoTw

I never lost as much but twice. Emily Dickinson. BLPL; MoAB; MoAmPo; NAAL-1; NoAM; NOBA; NoP; TAP

I never loved a dear gazelle. Tèma con Variazióni. "Lewis Carroll." FaBoNo

I never minded having such old parents. Late Child. Robert Pinsky. *Fr.* Three on Luck. AnAn

I never played for you. You'd have thrown. For the Death of Vince Lombardi. James Dickey. ASP

I never plucked—a bumblebee. *Unknown.* WeW

I never quite saw fairy-folk. Very Nearly. Queenie Scott-Hopper. FaPON

I never read of any enforceable regulation. Because Sometimes You Can't Always Be So. Kenneth Patchen. NaP

I never really felt the cold, never. Never Really. Stanislaw Baranczak, *tr. by* Magnus Jan Krynski *and* Robert A. Maguire. PwPP

I never reared a young gazelle. 'Twas Ever Thus. Henry S. Leigh. FaBoCo; FaBoPa

I never said I loved you, John. "No, Thank You, John." Christina Rossetti. NAEL-2; TEP

I never saw a moor. Emily Dickinson. AA; FaFP; FaPON; FPL; GN; HeIP; LiTA; LiTM; MoAB; MoAmPo; PoLF; TAP; TrGrPo; WGRP

I never saw a purple cow. The Purple Cow. Gelett Burgess. FaBoCo; FaBoNo; FaFP; FaPON; FiBHP; FPL; GrPl; NA; NBLV; NTCP; OBAL; OBCA; PDV; PoLF; RHPC (Nonsense Quatrains.) CenHV

I never saw a wild thing. Self-Pity. D. H. Lawrence. OxBTC; RB

I never saw more frogs. One of the Many Days. Norman MacCaig. PoSH

I never saw that stone tablet. The Death of Moses. Margit Szécsi, *tr. by* Laura Schiff. OV

I never saw you madam, lay [*or* sawe my Ladye] laye apart. Earl of Surrey. AAS; SiPS (Complaint That His Ladie After She Knew of His Love Kept Her Face Alway Hidden from Him.) PoEL-1 (Cornet, The.) OBSC

I never see the colored boats of night. The Age of Sheen. Dorothy Hughes. NYBP

I never see the red rose crown the year. John Masefield. *Fr.* Sonnets. GoYe

I never set my two eyes on a head was so fine as your head. A Translation from Walter von der Vogelweide. Walther von der Vogelweide, *tr. by* J. M. Synge. MoBrPo

I Never Shall Love the Snow Again. Robert Bridges. BrPo; CH; CMoP; FaBV

I never thought for a moment. Emily Dickinson, Bismarck and the Roadrunner's Inquiry. Ray A. Young Bear. HATNAP

I never thought that my love would leave me. Love Is Teasing. *Unknown.* OBET

I never told you. What They Do to You in Distant Places. Marvin Bell. Psk

I never wander where the bord'ring reeds. Fly-fishing. John Gay. *Fr.* Rural Sports. SD

I never wanted to be a star. On Earth. Forugh Farrokhzad, *tr. by* Girdhard Tikku. BoWoP

I never wholly feel that summer is high. High Summer. Ebenezer Jones. NOBVV

I never will complain of my dear husband, Mrs. Henn. "He Didn't Oughter." A. P. Herbert. FiBHP

I never yet arraigned the will of heaven. Edward Thompson. *Fr.* An Humble Wish; off Porto-Sancto, March 29, 1779. OBTV

I newly had your little house erected. To My Lady Rogers, the Authors Wives Mother, How Doctor Sherwood Commended Her House in Bathe. Sir John Harington. EyDe

I no longer care, keeping close my silence. The Chain. Christine Craig. AIW

I No Longer Know the Night. Odysseus Elytis, *tr. fr. Greek by* Edmund Keeley *and* Philip Sherrard. VMG

I no longer want to go away toward those vast bowls of evening. Love Again. Pierre Reverdy, *tr. by* John Ashbery. POS; RHTwFP

I, now at Carthage. He, shot dead at Rome. *Vale* from Carthage. Peter Viereck. LiTM; MoAmPo

I now had only to retrace. Charlotte Brontë. NOBVV

I now mean to be serious;—it is time. Lady Adeline Amundeville. Byron. *Fr.* Don Juan, XIII. PoEL-4

I now solicit not the Muses nine. William Woty. *Fr.* A Mock Invocation to Genius. NOEC

I now think[e], Love is rather deaf[e], then blind. My Picture Left in
  Scotland. Ben Jonson. MePo; NAEL-1; PoEL-2; QFR; SeCP;
  SeCV-1
I now will throw myself down. A Dialogue. David Ignatow. NNaP
I nursed it in my bosom while it lived. Memory. Christina Rossetti.
  OBNC
I objurgate the centipede. The Centipede. Ogden Nash. FaPON
I, Oedipus, the club-foot, made to stumble. Oedipus. Edwin Muir.
  CMoP
I of my Spenser quite bereft. Book-Lender's Lament. Unknown.
  FaBoUs
I offer my back to the silken net. An Allegory. David Ignatow. VGW
I offer myself to each as his reward. The Gift of Oneself. Valery
  Larbaud, tr. by Ron Padgett and Bill Zavatsky. RHTwFP
I offer myself to everyone as his reward. The Gift of Oneself. Valery
  Larbaud, tr. by William Jay Smith. CT
I offer you the chance to forgive your wounds. Song from the Maker of
  Totems. Duane Niatum. STE
I offer you the golden flagon. Offering Wine. Yü Wu-ling, tr. by Burton
  Watson. CoBCP
I oft stand in the snow at dawn. Don Marquis. Fr. To a Lost
  Sweetheart. FiBHP
I often dream of Auschwitz now. Dreams of Auschwitz. Boris Slutsky,
  tr. by Daniel Weissbort. VWA
I often have been told. The Constitution and the Guerrière. Unknown.
  PAH
I often read the writings of the sages. Words from the Goblet of Wisdom.
  Yüan Mei, tr. by Jonathan Chaves. CoBLCP
I often sit and wish that I. A Kite. Unknown. RAR
I often think how once we used in summer fields to play. The Little
  Factory Girl to a More Fortunate Playmate. Unknown. SaC
I often wake up as though after my death. You Usually Come in the
  Morning. György Petri, tr. by William Jay Smith. MHuP
I often wander on the beach. The Old Swimmer. Christopher Morley.
  SD
I Often Want to Let My Lines Go. Leib Neidus, tr. fr. Yiddish by Ruth
  Whitman. VWA
I often wish I were a King. If I Were King. A. A. Milne. OnUR
I often wonder as the fairy-story. The Lucky Marriage. Thomas
  Blackburn. GTBS-P
I often wonder how it is. My Playmate. Mary I. Osborn. BoTP
I, Okura, must excuse myself now. Okura, tr. by Hiroaki Sato. Fr.
  Manyo Shu. FCEI
I, Okura, will leave now. Okura. Fr. Manyo Shu. Ma
"I on my horse, and Love on me, doth try." Sir Philip Sidney. Fr.
  Astrophel and Stella, XLIX. NAEL-1; NoP; OAEL-1; PoE
I on the sunny side of Three Rivers. For Ku Yen-hsien, A Poem for Him
  to Give to His Wife. Lu Yün, tr. by Burton Watson. CoBCP
I once believed a single line. For E. J. P. Leonard Cohen. NoP
I once broke evening bread with the brown-faced, white-smiled Prince of
  Siam. Words of Oblivion and Peace. Gabriel Preil, tr. by Robert
  Friend. VWA
I once conjectur'd that those tygers hard. Seaconk or Rehoboths Fate.
  Benjamin Tompson. SCAP
I Once Did a Bamboo Painting for Somebody. Hsü Wei, tr. fr. Chinese
  by Jonathan Chaves. CoBLCP
I once did an hour-long TV show reading. Osip Mandelshtam. Irving
  Layton. NeAC
I once did court a damsel most beautiful and bright. A Lover's Lament.
  Unknown. AmFP
I once had a sweet little doll, dears. The Lost Doll. Charles Kingsley.
  Fr. The Water Babies. FaPON; MoShBr
  (Little Doll, The.) OxBChV
I once had money and a friend. Money and a Friend. Unknown. BLPA
I once heard the survivors. Don Marquis. Fr. Certain Maxims of Archy.
  NBLV
I once hit clothespins. Clothespins. Stuart Dybek. ASP
I once knew a fellow named Arthur McBride. Arthur McBride. GBP;
  OBET
I once knew a lass and I oft heard her tell. So I Let Her Go. Unknown.
  AmFP
I once knew a little girl, a charming beauty bright. The Rejected Lover.
  Unknown. AmFP
I Once Knew a Man. Lucille Clifton. CAPP; GeTw
I once knowed an ole Sexion Boss but he done been laid low. The Old
  Section Boss. Unknown. BPo
I once lov'd a boy, and a bonny, bonny boy. Unknown. WTO
I Once Loved a Young Man. Unknown. AmFP
I once loved a young man as dear as my life. I'm Going to Georgia.
  Unknown. AmFP
I once may see when yeares shall wreck my wrong. Samuel Daniel. Fr.
  To Delia. AAS

I once spent an evening in a village. The Man Upright. Thomas
  MacDonagh. BIrV
I once thought that snowflakes were feathers. Snowflakes. Marchette
  Chute. PDV
I once was a bold fellow and went with a team. The Carter. Unknown.
  OBET
I Once Was a Maid. Burns. Fr. The Jolly Beggars, OxBoLi. EnRP,
  sl. diff. vers.; PoEL-4
I once was a Pirate what sailed the 'igh seas. Cat Morgan Introduces
  Himself. T. S. Eliot. NOBL
I once was a seaman stout and bold. Jolly Soldier. Unknown. AmFP;
  OFD
I once was happy, when, while yet a child. Charlotte Smith. Fr. Beachy
  Head. WPE
I once was in service. Rosemary Lane. Unknown. OBET
I once wrote a letter as follows. The Invoice. Robert Creeley.
  VGW
I, only accountant, from the height of this corner room surrounded by an.
  "St.-John Perse," tr. fr. French by Denis Devlin. Fr. Snows, IV.
  RHTwFP
I Only Am Escaped Alone to Tell Thee. Howard Nemerov. CoAP;
  HeIP; NoAM
I only have a measly ant. October Arriving. Charles Simic. BLA
I, only I, am best at being worst, Lord. Surdas, tr. by John Stratton
  Hawley and Mark Juergensmeyer. SSI
I only knew one poet in my life. How It Strikes a Contemporary. Robert
  Browning. CTC; FaBoPV; GTBS-P; OAEL-2
I only know that I was there. Ante-natal Dream. Patrick Kavanagh.
  NAs
I open my eyes. A Factory Rainbow. Rose Saadi. SaC
I open the door and walk in. Pop. David McFadden. NeAC
I open the phone book, and look for my adolescence. Equation. Charles
  Wright. CAPP
I open the pine door. Sanetomo, tr. fr. Japanese by Burton Watson. Fr.
  Twenty-four Tanka. FCEI
I open the scrolls of Babylon. Babylon, O Babylon. Pablo Guevara, tr.
  by David Tipton. Per
I opened and read. The Crow's Letter. Saijo Yaso, tr. by Geoffrey
  Bownas and Anthony Thwaite. PeBJV
I opened my door to this nutty witch. I've been suicidal. After Reading
  Sylvia Plath. Alta. IHMS
I opened the window wide and leaned. John Masefield. Fr. The
  Everlasting Mercy. WGRP
I ordered this, this clean wood box. The Arrival of the Bee Box. Sylvia
  Plath. FaBoMo; FaBoWP; HCAP; NaP
I ought to feel ashamed. Eva Braun. W. D. Snodgrass. Fr. The Führer
  Bunker. CAPP
I Ought to Weep. Unknown. MeEL
I Ovid poet of my wantonnesse. Ovid, tr. fr. Latin by Christopher
  Marlowe. Fr. Amores, II, 1. OBVE
I owe him for pictures. Buck. Michael S. S. Harper. CAPP
I owe nothing to winter. My Winter Past. Eldon Grier. NOBC
I owe you an apology. A Question of Form and Content. Jon
  Stallworthy. OxBC
I own John Graydon's place. John Graydon. Wilson Pugsley
  MacDonald. CaP
I pace back and forth in my room, rest my knee on the. Tale about a
  Flower. György Somlyó, tr. by Daniel Hoffman. MHuP
I pace the sounding sea-beach and behold. Milton. Longfellow. AA;
  AmPP; AWP; NoP; TAP; TrGrPo
I paced alone on the road across the field. The Home. Rabindranath
  Tagore. GoJo
I Paint What I See. E. B. White. NBLV; NYBP
I painted her a gushing thing. Disillusioned. "Lewis Carroll." CenHV
  (My Fancy.) FaBoCo
I painted my eyes with black antimony. Love Song. Unknown, tr. by H.
  Gaden. BoWoP
I painted on the roof of a skyscraper. People Who Must. Carl Sandburg.
  PDV
I painted rouge on my lips. Lover of Love. Hagiwara Sakutaro, tr. by
  Hiroaki Sato. FCEI
I painted the mailbox. That was fun. Painting the Gate. May Swenson.
  WeW
I paints and paints. Shirley Brooks. CenHV
I park the car because I'm happy. Now. Christopher Gilbert. MAYP
I park the car half in the ditch and switch off and sit. Stealing Trout.
  Ted Hughes. NYBP
I parted from my life last night. On the Death of His Wife. Muireadach
  O'Dalaigh, tr. by Frank O'Connor. BIrV; CIP
I passed a tomb among green shades. Her Rival for Aziza. Unknown, tr.
  fr. Arabic by E. Powys Mathers. Fr. The Thousand and One Nights.
  AWP

I passed along the water's edge below the humid trees. The [or An] Indian upon God. W. B. Yeats. MoBrPo; WGRP

I passed by a garden, a little Dutch garden. A Little Dutch Garden. Harriet Whitney Durbin. AA

I passed by the beach. Akahito, tr. by Kenneth Rexroth. HoPM

I passed by the house of the young man who loves me. Unknown, tr. by J. E. Manchip White. TTY

I passed the window and saw their lovely flash of wings. Regret for the Mourning Doves Who Failed to Mate. Bruce Weigl. NAmP

I past [or passed] beside the reverend walls. Tennyson. Fr. In Memoriam A. H. H., LXXXVII. EBVV
(He Revisits Cambridge.) FaBoPP

I pause not now to speak of Raleigh's dreams. John Smith's Approach to Jamestown. James Barron Hope. PAH

I paused in a garden alley of cypress and rose, resembling Paradise. Last Things. Kathleen Jessie Raine. NYBP

I paused last eve beside of a blacksmith's door. John Clifford. See Last eve I passed beside of a blacksmith's door.

I peeled bits of straw and I got switches too. John Clare. NAEL-2
(Bits of Straw.) WiR

I peeped through the window. Unknown. OxNR

I peer adown a shining group. Tribute. Eloise Bibb. CBWP-4

I peer into quietness. Taigi, tr. fr. Japanese by Hiroaki Sato. Fr. Twenty-nine Hokku. FCEI

I perched for rest, and imagined. Seamus Heaney. Fr. Sweeney Astray, 23. PPR

I persist in a little fabric between me and the world. J. Michael Yates. Fr. The Great Bear Lake Meditations. NOBC

I pick up your scroll of poems, read in front of the lamp. Aboard a Boat, Reading Yüan Chen's Poems. Po Chü-i, tr. by Burton Watson. CoBCP

I picked fresh mint. My Garden. Norah Hussey. BoTP

I Picked Up Your Cast Away Hide. Mary Moran. GOS

I picture her there in the quaint old room. Dreaming in the Trenches. William Gordon McCabe. AA

I pitched my day's leazings in Crimmercrock Lane. The Dark-eyed Gentleman. Thomas Hardy. MoAB; MoBrPo; NBLV; UnPo

I pity those rice stalks. Komachi, tr. fr. Japanese by Burton Watson. Fr. Kokin Shu. FCEI

I place myself at the edge of thy Grace. Unknown, tr. by Douglas Hyde. WTO

I place these numbed wrists to the pane. Nightmare Begins Responsibility. Michael S. Harper. CAPP; DiL; GeTw; HCAP; LCAP; TAP

I placed a jar in Tennessee. Anecdote of the Jar. Wallace Stevens. AmPP; CMoP; HCAP; HeIP; HoPM; InPK; LiTA; MoAB; MoAmPo; MoP; NAAL-2; NAWM-2; NIP; NoAM; NOBA; NoP; OxBA; OxBSP; PoA; PPP; PrIm; SOTW; TAP; UnPo

I placed my dream in a boat. Cecília Meireles, tr. by Eloah F. Giacomelli. WPOW

I planned to get drunk to ease my sadness. Yang Chi, tr. fr. Chinese by Jonathan Chaves. Fr. Living in a Riverside Village—Miscellaneous Impressions. CoBLCP

I planned to have a border of lavender. Paul Goodman. GLP; VGW

I plant corn four years. Corn-Planter. Maurice Kenny. NOVW; STE

I planted beans at the foot of the southern mountain. Returning to My Home in the Country. T'ao Ch'ien, tr. by Burton Watson. CoBCP

I planted rice before Spring Festival. Su Tung-p'o, tr. fr. Chinese by Burton Watson. Fr. Eastern Slope. CoBCP

I planted this tree. Trees. Jutta Schutting, tr. by Beth Bjorklund. CoAuP

"I play a spade.—Such strange new faces." Arrivals at a Watering-Place. Winthrop Mackworth Praed. NOBL

"I play for seasons, not eternities!" George Meredith. Fr. Modern Love, XIII. OBNC

I play it cool. Motto. Langston Hughes. PoBA; PoNe

I play pool. I aim toward the faces. Games. Sandra McPherson. LCAP

I play the Masonic Funeral March. Birmingham. Julia Fields. Fr. Poems: Birmingham 1962–1964. PoBA; PoNe

I play your furies back to me at night. High Fidelity. Thom Gunn. PoA

I played a game of baseball, I belong to Casey's Nine. Slide, Kelly, Slide. John W. Kelly. FaFP

I played I was two polar bears. The Bear Hunt. Margaret Widdemer. FaPON

I Played on the Grass with Mary. Ernest Walsh. ErPo

I played with you 'mid cowslips blowing. Love and Age. Thomas Love Peacock. Fr. Gryll Grange. NOBVV; OBEV; OBNC

I pledge allegiance to the old. Double Agent. Heather McHugh. AnAn

I pledge myself through thick and thin. Tory Pledges. Thomas Moore. FaBoCo; OBSV

I pluck heng-herbs at the Chin-ling riverside. Wang T'ing-hsiang, tr. fr. Chinese by Jonathan Chaves. Fr. Songs of Chiang-nan. CoBLCP

I pluck, I pluck and throw away spring grasses. Raizan, tr. fr. Japanese by Hiroaki Sato. Fr. Thirteen Hokku. FCEI

I pluck my gray hair. Basho, tr. fr. Japanese by Burton Watson. Fr. Seventy-six Hokku. FCEI

I plucked a throstle from the throat of God. The Thrush. Timothy Corsellis. WaaP; WaP

I plucked my soul out of its secret place. I Know My Soul. Claude McKay. BPo

I plucked pink blossoms from mine apple-tree. An Apple Gathering. Christina Rossetti. NAEL-2; OBNC

I ply with all the cunning of my art. The Craftsman. Marcus B. Christian. PoNe

I polish your skin. It is that of a woman. A Song in Praise of a Favourite Humming-Top. Hone Tuwhare. PeNZ

I ponder how He died, despairing once. Before an Old Painting of the Crucifixion. N. Scott Momaday. QFR

I pound the rice. Unknown. Fr. Manyo Shu. PeBJV

I pour out wine in a libation to the river god. Meeting My Fellow Countryman, Yü Wu-chung. Yang Chi, tr. by Jonathan Chaves. CoBLCP

I poured water in the basin. Onitsura, tr. fr. Japanese by Hiroaki Sato. Fr. Twenty-three Hokku. FCEI

I praise a patron high-hearted in strife. In Praise of Owain Gwynedd. Cynddelw Brydydd Mawr, tr. by Joseph P. Clancy. OBWVE

I praise a snakeskin or a stone. Snakeskin and Stone. Keith Douglas. NePoEA

I praise God's mankind in an old woman. Lines: I Praise God's Mankind in an Old Woman. Wilfred Watson. NOBC

I praise him not; it were too late. Ode Recited at the Harvard Commemoration. James Russell Lowell. AiP

I praise Saint Everyman, his house and home. Here Together Met. Louis Johnson. ATNZ; PeNZ

I praise sky. Praise. Dinah Livingstone. AIW

I praise the disk of the rising sun. Vidya, tr. fr. Sanskrit by Daniel H. H. Ingalls. Fr. The Sun. PBWP; WPOW

I praise the Frenchman, his remark was shrewd. William Cowper. Fr. Retirement. BLPA

I praise Thee not, with impious pride. Sir Lewis Morris. Fr. A Heathen Hymn. TrPWD

I praise you, Autumn, season of ripe gold. Autumn. A. Leyeles, tr. by Benjamin and Barbara Harshav. AYP

I pray attend unto this Jest. The Fair Maid of the West. Unknown. CoMu

I pray for memory. Turtle. Robert Lowell. LCAP

I pray from the heart a prayerbook. Amir Gilboa, tr. by Warren Bargad and Stanley F. Chyet. IP

I Pray from the Heart a Psalter. Amir Gilboa, tr. fr. Hebrew by Bernhard Frank. MHeP

I pray! My little body and whole span. Supplication of the Black Aberdeen. Kipling. BLPA

I pray not for the joy that knows. Marion Franklin Ham. TrPWD

"I pray," said Rolfe, "a word." Ungar and Rolfe. Herman Melville. Fr. Clarel. OxBA

I pray that the great world's flowering stay as it is. The Gardener to His God. Mona Van Duyn. TrCP; UnPo; WPE

I pray the Lord my soul to take. Ogden Nash. Fr. One from One Leaves Two. NBLV

I pray the prayer the Easterners do. Salaam Alaikum. Unknown. PoLF

I pray, Dante, shouldst thou meet with Love. To Dante Alighieri: He Mistrusts the Love of Lapo Gianni. Guido Cavalcanti, tr. by Dante Gabriel Rossetti. AWP

I pray the Nymph Penaeis stay, I chase not as a fo. Ovid, tr. fr. Latin by Arthur Golding. Fr. Metamorphoses, I. OBVE

I pray Thee O Lord. Julian Tuwim, tr. by Wanda Dynowska. TrJP

I pray you all give [or gyve] your audience [or audyence]. Everyman. Unknown. NAWM-1; OAEL-1; OxBLMV; PoEL-1

I pray you, be not wroth. Unknown. Fr. Vox Populi, Vox Dei. FaBoPV

I pray you, Christ, to change my heart. Christ's Bounty. Unknown, tr. by Brendan Kennelly. TIRV

I pray you, do not idly tempt me. Disillusion. E. A. Baratynsky, tr. by Alan Myers. AAA

I pray you, forgive me in the stillness of your shoes swollen on these sands. Haim Gouri, tr. by Warren Bargad and Stanley F. Chyet. IP

I pray you, let us roam no more. Thomas Moore. Fr. Odes to Nea. OBNC

I pray you, what's asleep? As the Day Breaks. Ernest McGaffey. AA

I prayed for riches, and achieved success. Answered Prayers. Ella Wheeler Wilcox. PWR

I prefer to sit all day. The One Song. Mark Strand. CAPP
I prefer ugliness. Clean Men. Stanislaw Grochowiak, *tr. by* Czeslaw Milosz. PwPP
I press [*or* presse] not to the quire, nor dare I greet. To My Worthy Friend Master George Sands [*or* Sandys], on His Translation of the Psalms. Thomas Carew. CaPo; JCP; MeLP; MePo; OBS; SeCV-1
I press pen to paper like a pistol to the temple. Amir Gilboa, *tr. by* Warren Bargad *and* Stanley F. Chyet. IP
I Pressed Her Rebel Lips. *Unknown.* BoLoP; ErPo
I prithee send me back my heart. *At. to* Henry Hughes Suckling *and also to* Sir John Suckling. JCP
I Promise Nothing. A. E. Housman. PPP
I promise to make you more alive than you've ever been. Ordeal. Nina Cassian, *tr. by* Michael Impey *and* Brian Swann. PBWP
I promise you by the harsh funeral. Burns Singer. *Fr.* Sonnets for a Dying Man, XLVIII. NePoEA-2
I promise you these days and an understanding. Tourist Death. Archibald MacLeish. NAAL-2
I promised: a thousand poems. Spring Worm II. Tu Yeh, *tr. by* Dominic Cheung. IFON
I promised once if I got hold of. Written in a Copy of Swift's Poems, for Wayne Burns. James Wright. NOBA
I promised Sylvia to be true. John Wilmot, 2nd Earl of Rochester. SeCePo
I promised to take your picture. The Photograph. Barbara Drake. ASP
I propose to you. The Statue. Robert Creeley. LCAP
I protest my isolation. Waiting Inside. David Ignatow. CAPP
I prove a theorem and the house expands. Geometry. Rita Dove. HCAP
I provide my past with you, the most. Antonville. Peter Seaton. LP
I puff my breast out, my neck swells. The Weathercock: "I puff my breast out, my neck swells." *Unknown, formerly at. to* Cynewulf, *tr. fr. Anglo-Saxon by* Geoffrey Grigson. *Fr.* Riddles (Exeter Book). RB
I pull out of the depths of the earth. Etnairis Rivera, *tr. by* Julio Marzán. InW
I pulled on a creeper. Masaoka Shiki, *tr. fr. Japanese by* Burton Watson. *Fr.* Thirty-nine Haiku. FCEI
I pumped the iron handle and watched the water. My Father Washes His Hands. Fred Chappell. MT
I purged my sins in a blaze of kisses. The Visit. "Badawi al-Jabal," *tr. by* Matthew Sorenson *and* John Heath-Stubbs. MAP
I push the door and step out. Ishikawa Takuboku, *tr. fr. Japanese by* Hiroaki Sato. *Fr.* Forty-seven Tanka in Three Lines. FCEI
I put aside a story. Kaya Shirao, *tr. fr. Japanese by* Hiroaki Sato. *Fr.* Twenty-one Hokku. FCEI
I put away my book, chin in hand, alone. Rai San'yo, *tr. fr. Chinese by* Burton Watson. *Fr.* Landscape Vignettes, II. JLIC-2
I put good rice in water. *Unknown. Fr.* Manyo Shu. FCEI
I put in for a five-day leave. Michizane, *tr. fr. Japanese by* Burton Watson. *Fr.* Kokin Shu. FCEI
(On Vacation: Poem to Record My Thoughts.) JLIC-1
I put my father in his cradle. Re-education. Sybren Polet, *tr. by* André Lefevere. DuIn
I put my hand upon her toe. Gently, Johnny My Jingalo. *Unknown.* OBET
I put my hat upon my head. A 5th Stanza For Dr. Johnson, Donald Hall, Louis Phillips, and X. J. Kennedy. C. L. Grove. SoTCo
I put my hat upon my head. A Second Stanza for Dr. Johnson. Donald Hall. FiBHP
I put my hat upon my head. Samuel Johnson. NOBL
I put my hat upon my head, *parody.* F. A. V. Madden. BXAP
I put my hat upon my head, *parody.* Ian Sainsbury. BXAP
I put my hat upon my head, *parody.* Zan Stirling. BXAP
I put my hat upon my head, *parody.* Peter Veale. BXAP; NBLV
I put my soul in the palm of your hand. My Soul in the Palm of Your Hand. Levi Ben-Amittai, *tr. by* Bernhard Frank. MHeP
I put on a clean shirt. Song of Agony. Gouveia de Lemos, *tr. by* Margaret Dickinson. WMBCH
I put on my new suit, the wind and fire. My Burned Suit. Ilyas Farhat, *tr. by* Salma Khadra Jayyusi *and* John Heath-Stubbs. MAP
I put out my hands before me, into the dark. In the Dark. Amir Gilboa, *tr. by* Bernhard Frank. MHeP
I Put the Tip of the Pen to the Paper. Amir Gilboa, *tr. fr. Hebrew by* Bernhard Frank. MHeP
I put thy hand aside, and turn away. "Madeline Bridges." AA
I quarreled with kings till the Sabbath. Song of the Sabbath. Kadya Molodowsky, *tr. by* Jean Valentine. PBWP; WPOW
I quarreled with my brother. The Quarrel. Eleanor Farjeon. FaPON
I quickly removed. The White Motor. André du Bouchet, *tr. by* Paul Auster. RHTwFP
I Quite Like Men. Fran Landesman. DT

"I quite realized," said Columbus. E. C. Bentley. *Fr.* Clerihews. FiBHP
I raced west away from the dawn. Thaba Bosio. S. D. R. Sutu, *tr. by* Dan Kunene *and* Jack Cope. PeSA
I rage, I melt, I burn. John Gay. *Fr.* Acis and Galatea. NAEL-1
I, Rainey Betha, 22. Plaint. Charles Henri Ford. EAS
I raise my cup and invite. Moon, Flowers, Man. Su Tung-p'o, *tr. by* Kenneth Rexroth. NaP
I raise my hands. Sketch of Hands. Koh Chang-soo, *tr. by the author.* ACKP
I raise my hands, and the clear water. Chiyojo, *tr. fr. Japanese by* Hiroaki Sato. *Fr.* Seventeen Hokku. FCEI
I raise my winecup to the flowers. To the Tune "Stopping My Horse to Listen." Yang Shen, *tr. by* Jonathan Chaves. CoBLCP
I raise the blind and sit by the window. December Morning. Fleur Adcock. ATNZ
I raise the curtains and go out. Alone. Chu Shu-chen, *tr. by* Kenneth Rexroth. BoWoP
I Raised a Great Hullabaloo. *Unknown.* PDV; RHPC
I ran for a catch. Coulson Kernahan. CenHV
I ran from the prison house but they captured me. The Prison House. Alan Paton. PeSA
I ran into the afterlife. Once, Driving West of Billings, Montana. Susan Mitchell. NAmP
I ran onto Mehitabel again. The Old Trouper. Don Marquis. *Fr.* Archy and Mehitabel. FaBoCo
I ran out in the morning, when the air was clean and new. Autumn Morning at Cambridge. Frances Cornford. PoRA
I ran to the church. Journey Back to Christmas. Gwen Dunn. OBCP
I ran until lips tripped over. Escape. Ilya Rubin, *tr. by* Linda Zisquit. VWA
I ran up and grabbed your arm, the way a man. At the Washing of My Son. David Ray. DiL
I ran upon life unknowing, without or science or art. Tennyson. FaBoEE
I rank fifth in a list. Again. Lipogram. Sacha Rabinovitch. NPo
I reach from pain. Reuben, Reuben. Michael S. Harper. GeTw; PoE
I reach the marble-streeted town. The Marble-streeted Town. Thomas Hardy. FaBoPP
I reached that waterhole, its mud designed. Roland Robinson. *Fr.* The Wanderer. CBAP
I reached the highest place in Spoon River. Henry C. Calhoun. Edgar Lee Masters. *Fr.* Spoon River Anthology. LiTA; LiTM
I Read a Tight-fisted Poem Once. Nancy Woods. RFM
I read about the Blaskets and Dunquin. J. M. Synge. FaBoEE
I read books beside Ox Tail River. Cheng Chen, *tr. fr. Chinese by* William Schultz. *Fr.* Reading beside Ox Tail River, I. WFTU
I read how Quixote in his random ride. Parable. Richard Wilbur. OxBSP
I read in the *New York Times.* Not the Arms Race. Sam Abrams. UL
I read it in the restroom, in pink nail polish. I'm Sorry, Your Mother Is Crazy, & I'm a Chinese Shiksa. Deborah Lee. BrSi
I read last night of the Grand Review. A Second Review of the Grand Army. Bret Harte. PAH
I read last night with many pauses. Troy. Robin Flower. SeCePo
I read my sentence steadily. Emily Dickinson. QFR
I read of a thousand killed. A Thousand Killed. Bernard Spencer. OBWP
I read or write, I teach or wonder what is truth. Apologia pro Vita Sua. Sedulius Scottus, *tr. by* Helen Waddell. BIrV
I read somewhere that a swan, snow-white. The Watch of a Swan. Sarah Morgan Bryan Piatt. AA
I read the marble-lettered name. A Grave in Hollywood Cemetery, Richmond. Margaret Junkin Preston. AA
I read the word shack. Shack. Murray Edmond. ATNZ
I read verses about Poland. Verses about Poland. Adam Zagajewski, *tr. by* Antony Graham. PwPP
I read with varying degrees. Edna St. Vincent Millay. *Fr.* Journal. ImOP
I read your testimony and I thought. John Beecher. *Fr.* To Alexander Meiklejohn. GOA
I reade in ancient times of yore. The Map of Mock-Begger Hall. *Unknown.* CoMu
I really can't write poetry. A Discussion of Poetry to Demonstrate to the Students the Coming of a New Age. Cheng Chen, *tr. by* William Schultz. WFTU
"I really take it very kind." Domestic Asides; or, Truth in Parentheses. Thomas Hood. EnRP
I really thought that drinking here would. Knocking Around. John Ashbery. NoAM
I reason, earth is short. Emily Dickinson. TAP

I recall/ that when I held the Leghorn. Terribilis Est Locus Iste. John Engels. AnAn
I recall a small, young boy. Written at the Graveside. Yüan Mei, *tr. by* Anthony C. Yu. WFTU
I recall, before the banks. By the Bridge. Ted Walker. NYBP
I recall: beside some rivulet, lonely shepherds arrange their fires. Perets Markish, *tr. by* Leonard Wolf. PeBMYV
I recall everything, but more than all. Double Sonnet. Anthony Hecht. SM; Son
I recall that former splendid party. Early Summer, Paying a Second Visit to the Kankantei of the Kansho-in in the Toei. Rokunyo, *tr. by* Burton Watson. JLIC-2
I recall that time when once I lived. Nazca Pottery. Javier Sologuren, *tr. by* Maureen Ahern *and* David Tipton. Per
I reckon it was in the early Fifties. Progress. George Ella Lyon. MOWH
I Reckon—When I Count at All. Emily Dickinson. MoAmPo; NIP
I reclaim the moment, call the madness madness. Emanations. Hameed Said, *tr. by* Lena Jayyusi *and* Naomi Shihab Nye. MAP
I recognize the quiet and the charm. Dutch Interior. May Sarton. SM
I recognized him by his skips and hops. Pan and the Cherries. Paul Fort, *tr. by* Jethro Bithell. AWP
I recollect a nurse call'd Ann. A Terrible Infant. Frederick Locker-Lampson. FiBHP
I recollect in early life. My First Love. Harry Graham. FiBHP
I recover now the time I drove. Art McCooey. Patrick Kavanagh. CIP; FaBCIP
I regretted the arrival of my death. What Profit? Immanuel di Roma, *tr. by* J. Chotzner. TrJP
I release a turtle. Ozaki Hosai, *tr. fr. Japanese by* Hiroaki Sato. Fr. One Hundred Haiku in Free Form. FCEI
I release you, my beautiful and terrible. I Give You Back. Joy Harjo. HATNAP
I Remember ("I remember/ watching the women."). Rita Anyiam–St. John. WS
I Remember. Thomas Hood. *See* I remember, I remember.
I Remember ("I remember/ January,/ 1968"). Mae Jackson. CNA; PoBA
I Remember. Liu E, *tr. fr. Chinese by* Jonathan Chaves. CoBLCP
I Remember. Ricardo Sánchez, *tr. fr. Spanish by* Toni Empringham. FIA
I Remember. Stevie Smith. BoLoP; BoWoP; FaBoWP; InPK; OxBC
I remember/ you weaving your beautiful rug. Rug of Woven Magic. Nan Benally. GOS
I remember. Pablo Guevara, *tr. fr. Spanish by* Maureen Ahern *and* David Tipton. Fr. Civil Marriage. Per
I remember a dim evening in Kishinyov. A Woman from the Book of Genesis. Dovid Knut, *tr. by* John Glad. VWA
I remember a far tall island. The Child's Return. Phyllis Allfrey. PBCV
I remember a house where all were good. In the Valley of the Elwy. Gerard Manley Hopkins. NOBVV; NOCV; TOF
I remember a strong old man. I Remember. Ricardo Sánchez, *tr. by* Toni Empringham. FIA
I remember at times. Scholar II. Seamus Deane. CIP; NOIV
I remember coming up. Breath. Reginald Gibbons. MAYP
I remember distinctly the tired tumult of my urges. Journey to a Parallel. Bruce McM. Wright. PoNe
I remember ever so long. *Unknown. Fr.* Manyo Shu. Ma
I Remember Galileo. Gerald Stern. FYAP
I remember gestures of infants. To Drink. Gabriela Mistral, *tr. by* Gunda Kaiser. NU
I remember God as an eccentric millionaire. Quite Apart from the Holy Ghost. Adrian Mitchell. OBSV
I remember, gracious, graceful moon. To the Moon. Giacomo Leopardi, *tr. by* Kenneth Koch. TTTS
I Remember Having Loved. Hasan Abdallah, *tr. fr. Arabic by* Lena Jayyusi *and* Christopher Middleton. MAP
I remember hiding in the hall closet. Light under the Door. Marilyn Nelson Waniek. MAYP
I remember how. How Times Have Changed! Merle Collins. WS
I remember how I came here. Winter Evening Poem. Laura Jensen. LCAP
I remember how, long ago, I found. Crystals like Blood. "Hugh MacDiarmid." HAP; NoP; RB
I Remember How She Sang. Rob Penny. CNA; PoBA
I remember how we stood. The Last Corn Shock. Glenn Ward Dresbach. FaPON
I remember, I burn brushwood. Teika, *tr. fr. Japanese by* Hiroaki Sato. *Fr.* A Compendium of Good Tanka. FCEI
I Remember, I Remember. Thomas Hood. BLPA; ELP; EnRP; FaBoBe; FaBV; FaFP; FaPON; FaPoR; FPL; LiTB; NOBE; PoEL-4

(Past and Present.) GTBS; GTBS-P
(I Remember.) CH
I Remember, I Remember. Philip Larkin. FaBoPP; NOBL
I remember in October. Dispossessed. Janice Gould. GOS
I remember it well; 'twas a morn dull and gray. Macdonald's Raid. Paul Hamilton Hayne. PAH
I remember long veils of green rain. Green Rain. Dorothy Livesay. NOBC
I remember Longwood. Blind Adolphus. Angela McCabe. AmPA
I remember my father, slight. Subterfuge. Vassar Miller. TSM
I remember my mother, the day that we met. For the Crèche. G. K. Chesterton. *Fr.* Songs of Education. FaBoCo
I remember my mother's Aunt Rebecca. Great-Aunt Rebecca. Elizabeth Brewster. NOBC
I remember myself waiting. Prehistory. David Avidan, *tr. by* Warren Bargad *and* Stanley F. Chyet. IP
I remember now how first I knew what death was. Original Sin. Alexander Kinnan Laing. NYBP
I remember partly. Southwest Passage. Dudley Fitts. PoA
I remember reading as a boy, Giotto. The Perfect Symbol. Louis Johnson. ATNZ
I remember rising one night. Letter No. 18. Dennis Brutus. WMBCH
I remember rooms that have had their part. Rooms. Charlotte Mew. PBWP
I remember striding through the August twilight. Calling on Peadar O'Donnell at Dungloe. John Hewitt. CIP
I remember that before. Flying Letters. Zerubavel Gilead, *tr. by* Dorothea Krook. VWA
I remember that year, under the blossoms. Tune: Lotus-leaf Cup. Wei Chuang, *tr. by* Burton Watson. CoBCP
I remember the boy, pink hand. Economics. Alvin Aubert. MT
I remember the Chillicothe ball players grappling the Rock. Hits and Runs. Carl Sandburg. ASP; SD
I remember the day/ Mama called me in from. Rice and Rose Bowl Blues. Diane Mei Lin Mark. BrSi
I remember the day I arrived. Doubting. Louis Simpson. NNaP
I remember the day when we first met among the flowers. Offering Congratulations to the Enlightened Reign. Ou-yang Chiung, *tr. by* Lois Fusek. ATF
I remember the dread with which I at a quarter past four. False Security. Sir John Betjeman. CMoP; NoAM; NoP
I remember the evening. The Swarming Bees. James Laughlin. VGW
I remember the feel of a hammer. Robert Winner. DiL
I remember the forehead born. Uncle. Philip Levine. NNaP
I remember the Indian Hospital. Birthplace. Duane Big Eagle. STE
I remember the neckcurls, limp and damp as tendrils. Elegy for Jane. Theodore Roethke. AmPP; CAPP; CoAP; FF; HAP; HCAP; InPK; InPS; LiTM; MoAB; MoAmPo; NoP; PoE; TAP; TwCP; WeW
I remember the night. Somebody Call. Carolyn M. Rodgers. JB
I remember the Roman Emperor, one of the cruellest of them. Exeat. Stevie Smith. NAEL-2; NoAM
I remember the room I had as a child. The muslin of the. Little Poem. Max Jacob, *tr. by* William Jay Smith. CT
I Remember the Room Was Filled with Light. Judith Hemschemeyer. SM
I remember the time. A Little Girl's Dream World. Della Burt. BlSi
I remember them, man and wife, in their little car. Couple. Walter Stone. NYBP
I remember, they sent. Corpse-bearing. Thomas Ashe. EBVV; NOBVV
I remember those years when we shared the joy of love. To the Tune "Heavenly Immortal." Yang Shen, *tr. by* Jonathan Chaves. CoBLCP
I remember today a Quebec roadside, the crucifix. The Crucifix. Daniel Berrigan. CRP
I remember waking. Flashback. Lois Clark. CN
I remember we had a straw mat. Straw Mat. Fu'ad Rifqa, *tr. by* Abdullah al-Udhari. MPAW
I remember Wednesday was the day. Two Lean Cats. Myron O'Higgins. PoBA; PoNe
I remember when a Sunday friend and I. Letter to My Mother. Anita Skeen. IHMS
I remember when he took me on a trip to this place. Chin Nung, *tr. fr. Chinese by* Jonathan Chaves. *Fr.* On Twisting River Is the Old Home of My Father. CoBLCP
I remember when I was at Entsu-ji. Ryokan, *tr. by* Burton Watson. JLIC-2
I remember when I was young. Long Winter Night. Ryokan, *tr. by* Burton Watson. FCEI; JLIC-2
I remember when the unicorns. The Days of the Unicorns. Phyllis Webb. NOBC

I remember when we first fled the rebels. Song of P'eng-ya. Tu Fu, *tr.* by Burton Watson. CoBCP

I remember when we made our first promises of love. I Remember. Liu E, *tr.* by Jonathan Chaves. CoBLCP

I remember when you shared my insomnia. The Broken Lampstand. Wu Wei-yeh, *tr.* by Jonathan Chaves. CoBLCP

I remember you at the bathroom mirror. The Magician. Gary Miranda. SM

I remember you in young peaches like jade. Elegy for the Wife of a Friend. Yü Hsüan-chi, *tr.* by Geoffrey Waters. BoWoP

I remember, you tell me, a daughter, a love, as high as my kneecap. Shore. Diana O Hehir. NPGG

I remember. (at what hour of the day). The Agonizing Memory. Pierre Louÿs, *tr. fr. French.* Fr. Chansons de Bilitis. PeHV

I renounce the blindness of the magazines. A Prayer to Escape from the Market Place. James Wright. NaP

I rescue a needle from the ashes. Ozaki Hosai, *tr. fr. Japanese by* Hiroaki Sato. *Fr.* One Hundred Haiku in Free Form. FCEI

I reside at Table Mountain and my name is Truthful James. The Society upon the Stanislaus. Bret Harte. AA; AnAmPo; BeLS; OBAL (Plain Language from Truthful James.) FaBoCo

I resign! Song of Resignation. Yehuda Amichai, *tr.* by Assia Gutmann. NYBP

I Resigned Myself to Being Here. John Giorno. UL

I retrace your path in my bare feet. Letter from a Wife. S. Carolyn Reese. PoNe

I return from my second T'ien-t'ai trip. On the Twenty-First Day of the Fifth Month, I Reached Home. Yüan Mei, *tr.* by Jonathan Chaves. CoBLCP

I return the bitterness. Transformation. Lewis Alexander. CDC; PoNe

I Return unto Zion. Bible, *O.T. Fr.* Zechariah, VIII: 3-5. TrJP

I returned, and saw under the sun. Bible, *O.T. Fr.* Ecclesiastes, IX: 11-12. Prf

I returned to a long strand. North. Seamus Heaney. InPS

I returned yet again to look time in the eye the Seventies the old garden. The Face of Creation. Otto Orban, *tr.* by Jascha Kessler. FOC

I, Richard Kent, beneath these stones. Sylvia Townsend Warner. MoBrPo

I Ride an Old Paint. *Unknown.* AmFP; AS, *with music*

I ride home, I gallop. *Unknown, tr.* by Arthur Waley. BoS

I ride through a dark, dark land by night. Ichabod! The Glory Has Departed. Ludwig Uhland, *tr.* by James Clarence Mangan. AWP

I ride through Queens. An Invitation to Madison County. Jay Wright. PoBA

I rise at 2 a.m. these mornings, to. The Feral Pioneers. Ishmael Reed. PoBA; PoNe; UnPo

I rise in the dawn, and I kneel and blow. The Song of the Old Mother. W. B. Yeats. MoBrPo

"I rise on Sugar-loaf Mountain." Molasses River. Richard Kendall Munkittrick. OBCA

I rise up. Giaconda Belli, *tr. fr. Spanish by* Angel Flores. *Fr.* Song To the New Day. DMH

I rise up from rest. Morning Prayer. Aua. WTO

I roamed the woods today and seemed to hear. A Fear. Francis Ledwidge. NOIV

I rob my breast to reach those altitudes. Hart Crane. AnAn

I rode one evening with Count Maddalo. Shelley. *Fr.* Julian and Maddalo. OAEL-2, *abr.*; OBTV

I Rode Southern, I Rode L & N. *Unknown.* AmFP

I rode till I reached the House of Wealth. Rest Only in the Grave. James Clarence Mangan. BIrV

I rode to church last Sunday. My Love She Passed Me By. *Unknown.* AmFP

I Rode with My Darling. Stevie Smith. BrRo

I rose at night, and visited. The Unborn. Thomas Hardy. CMoP

I rose betimes to go I knew not where. The Poor Man's Province. John Wright. NOEC

I rub my head and find a turtle shell. The Neo-Classical Urn. Robert Lowell. NAAL-2

I run/ I run because. The Jogger from Schönbrunn. Hermann Jandl, *tr.* by Beth Bjorklund. CoAuP

I run into fireflies. Joso, *tr. fr. Japanese by* Hiroaki Sato. *Fr.* Fifteen Hokku. FCEI

I run my hand across your forehead. Eugenio Montale, *tr. fr. Italian. Fr.* The Motets, XII. Dana Gioia

I rush to the newspapers. The News & the Weather. Rika Lesser. MAYP

I rush to the office when I'm in the city. Staying Overnight at T'ien-ning Ch'an Temple. Chang Yü, *tr.* by Jonathan Chaves. CoBLCP

I rush to your dwelling. Pursuit. Julian Tuwim, *tr.* by Watson Kirkconnell. TrJP

I said:/ Now will the poets sing. Scottsboro, Too, Is Worth Its Song. Countee Cullen. PoBA

I said, Ah! what shall I write? A, a, a, Domine Deus. David Jones. FaBoTw; NOCV

I said, I like our bodies clean. Friday Night after Bathing. Stephen Levy. VWA

I said, "I will find God," and forth, I went. Seeking God. Edward Dowden. WGRP

I said: "I will take heed to my ways." Psalm XXXIX. Bible, *O.T. Fr.* Psalms.
(Lord, Make Me to Know Mine End.) TrJP

I said I would have my fling. The Price He Paid. Ella Wheeler Wilcox. WBLP

I said I wouldn't fly again. William Empson. *Fr.* Autumn on Nan-Yueh. PoPo

I said I'd get her a towel and ran. Girls. Kenneth Rosen. AmPA

I said, in drunken pride of youth and you. Challenge. Sterling A. Brown. CDC

I said, "Let me walk in the fields." Obedience. George Macdonald. BLRP; WGRP

I said: "My heart, now let us sing a song." A Wedding Song. John White Chadwick. AA

I said, "No!" to my parents and left the house. The Dance. Morton Marcus. NAmP

"I," said the duck, "I call it fun." Who Likes the Rain? Clara Doty Bates. BoTP

I said: "The moon is obviously a boat." Nocturnal Landscape. Malcolm Cowley. PoA

I said the word "spatial," and in it. Space Fiction. Norman MacCaig. TEP

I said—Then, dearest, since 'tis so. The Last Ride Together. Robert Browning. BoLoP; FiP; LiTB; NAEL-2; OBEV; PoEL-5; UnPo

I Said, This Misery Must End. Christopher Brennan. *Fr.* Pauca Mea. PoAu-1

I said those words casually. Ishikawa Takuboku, *tr. fr. Japanese by* Hiroaki Sato. *Fr.* Forty-seven Tanka in Three Lines. FCEI

I said to Death: "Supposing it were true." Dancing Partners. Philip Child. CaP

I said to Heart, "How goes it?" Heart replied. The False Heart. Hilaire Belloc. FaBoCh; FaBoEE; OxBSP
(For False Heart.) MoBrPo

I said to heaven that glowed above. Hafiz, *tr. fr. Persian by* Emerson. *Fr.* Odes, XII. AWP

I said to her tears: "I am fallible and hungry." Plea. John Ciardi. OxBSP

I Said to Love. Thomas Hardy. GBL

I said to my baby. Same in Blues. Langston Hughes. *Fr.* Lenox Avenue Mural. InPS

I Said to My Heart. Charles Mordaunt, Earl of Peterborough. NOEC

I Said to Poetry. Alice Walker. AIW

I said to Sorrow's awful storm. The Soul's Defiance. Lavinia Stoddard. AA

I said to the stream, Be still, and it was still. Miracles. Julia Randall. CRP

I said, "Why should a pyramid." The Innovator. Stephen Vincent Benét. EyDe

I said: "Within the garden trimly bordered." Inspiration. E. V. Knox. CenHV

I sail over the ocean blue. I Catcha da Plenty of Feesh. *Unknown.* AS

I sailed in my dreams to the Land of Night. Fantasy. Gwendolyn B. Bennett. BlSi; CDC

I sailed, in the days of my youth. Ulysses. Umberto Saba, *tr.* by Henry Taylor. PFI

I sailed through many waters. Autobiography. Patricia Beer. PoPo

I salute from a distance of six steps away. Poem-Object. André Breton, *tr.* by Michael Benedikt. PoS

I salute God, asylum's gift. Poem on His Death-Bed. Cynddelw Brydydd Mawr, *tr.* by Joseph P. Clancy. OBWVE

I salute the most high lord. The Poet's Loves. Hywel ab Owain Gwynedd, *tr.* by Gwyn Williams. OBWVE

I salute you birds who break into and disperse the formations of. To Scream. Aimé Césaire, *tr.* by Michael Benedikt. POS

I sang as one. The Conflict. C. Day Lewis. LiTB; LiTM; MoAB; MoBrPo; NoP

I sang the songs of red revenge. Homer. Albert Ehrenstein, *tr.* by Babette Deutsch *and* Avram Yarmolinsky. TrJP

I sat all morning in the college sick bay. Mid-Term Break. Seamus Heaney. InPS; NIP; NoP

I sat alone at my window. Retrospect. Josephine D. Henderson Heard. CBWP-4

I sat alone with my conscience. Conscience. Charles William Stubbs. BLPA

I sat at my loom in silence. The Weaver. *Unknown.* BLRP

I sat before my glass one day. The Other Side of a Mirror. Mary Elizabeth Coleridge. BoWoP

I sat behind the glowing grate, fresh heaped. A Meditation on Rhode Island Coal. Bryant. TAP

I sat beside the glassy evening sea. The Departure. William Vaughn Moody. AnAmPo

I sat beside the red stock route. Harry Pearce. David Campbell. PoAu-2

I sat by a stream in a. Classic. A. R. Ammons. NOBA

I sat by the granite pillar, and sunlight fell. Commemoration. Sir Henry Newbolt. FaBoTw

I sat here this morning, detached, summoning up, I think. The Deviator. Bertram J. Warr. OBCV

I sat in my chamber yesternight. Robert Graves. FL

I sat in the cold limbs of a tree. The Man in the Tree. Mark Strand. EAS

I sat in the door of our cottage. An Autumn Day. Clara Ann Thompson. CBWP-2

I sat in the school of sorrow. The School of Sorrow. Harold Hamilton. BLRP

I sat me down upon a green bank-side. Bronx. Joseph Rodman Drake. AnAmPo

I sat next to the Duchess at tea. *Unknown.* SoSe

I sat on chushioned otter-skin. The Madness of King Goll. W. B. Yeats. NAEL-2

I sat on the Dogana's steps. Ezra Pound. *Fr.* Cantos, III. TAP

I sat wi' my love, and I drank wi' my love. *Unknown.* GBP

I sat with her, and spoke right goldenly. The Lady of Life. Thomas Michael Kettle. ACP

I sat with John Brown. That night moonlight framed. Narrative. Russell Atkins. PoBA

I sat with love upon a woodside well. Willowwood. Dante Gabriel Rossetti. *Fr.* The House of Life, XLIX. NAEL-2; OAEL-2; PoEL-5

I saw/ a cook a specialist. To the Heart. Tadeusz Rozewicz, *tr. by* Czeslaw Milosz. PwPP

I saw a bee, I saw a flower. The Bee-Orchis. Andrew Young. ChTr

I Saw a Broken Town. Mabel Esther Allan. CN

I saw a brown squirrel to-day in the wood. Mr. Squirrel. V. M. Julian. BoTP

I Saw a Chapel All of Gold. Blake. EnRP; LiTB

I saw a cottage in the sky. Friends. John Ashbery. LCAP

I saw a dead man's finer part. His Immortality. Thomas Hardy. CMoP

I saw a donkey. The Donkey. *Unknown.* RHPC

I saw a doo flee our the dam. *Unknown.* GBP

I saw a fair maiden. A Lullaby of the Nativity. *Unknown.* MeEL (Lullay My Liking). ELP

I saw a famous man eating soup. Soup. Carl Sandburg. NOBA; NOBE; OBCA

I Saw a Fish-Pond All on Fire. *Unknown.* ChTr; GBP; NOBL; OxNR

I saw a fly within a bead. The Amber Bead. Robert Herrick. CaPo; ChTr

(Trapped Fly, A.) WiR

I saw a frieze on whitest marble drawn. Ecstasy. W. J. Turner. CH

I saw a gardener with a watering can. The Progress of Poetry. "Christopher Caudwell." OxBTC

I saw a gnome. The Gnome. Harry Behn. FaPON; PDV

I saw a hare jump across a ditch. The Hare. C. H. Sisson. NPo

I saw a hawk devour a screaming bird. Hawk Is a Woman. Hildegarde Flanner. WPE

I saw a herd of the wild red deer. Caenlochan. Helen B. Cruickshank. PoSH

I saw a holly sprig brought from a hurst. A Vision of the World's Instability. Richard Verstegan. EIL

I saw a hunchback climb over a hill. The Hunchback. John Peale Bishop. PoA

I Saw a Jolly Hunter. Charles Causley. OnUR; PYC

I Saw a Little Girl I Hate. Arnold Spilka. RHPC

I saw a little snail. Little Snail. Hilda Conkling. FaPON

I saw a little tailor sitting stitch, stitch, stitching. Tailor. Eleanor Farjeon. OxBChV

I saw a maiden, fairest of the fair. Charity. Henrietta Cordelia Ray. CBWP-3

I saw a man. Man. Mieczyslaw Jastrun, *tr. by* Czeslaw Milosz. PwPP

I saw a man, by some accounted wise. Erastus Wolcott Ellsworth. *Fr.* What Is the Use? AA

I saw a man pursuing the horizon. Stephen Crane. *Fr.* The Black Riders, XXIV. AmPP; FF; HoPM; LiTA; LiTM; MAT; MoAmPo; NOBA

I saw a man standing. Gate of Horn. William Rose Benét. AnAmPo

I saw a mesa. Leaving Port Authority for the St. Regis Rezz. Wendy Rose. HATNAP

I saw a Monk of Charlemaine. The Monk. Blake. *Fr.* Jerusalem, III, Prologue. EnRP

I saw a mouth jeering. Gargoyle. Carl Sandburg. MoP; NoAM; NOBA

I saw a pale tree, the leafless boughs—but two. Ecstasy. Hélène Swarth, *tr. by* Jonathan Crewe. WPOW

I Saw a Peacock with a Fiery Tail. *Unknown.* CH; ChTr; FaBoCh; GBP; ImOP; OxBoLi; OxBSP; OxNR; RB

I saw a people rise before the sun. Yom Kippur. Israel Zangwill. TrJP

I Saw a Phoenix in the Wood Alone. *Fr.* Sonnets to Laura: Songs. AWP, *tr. by* Spenser; Ch Tr, *tr. by* Helen Lee Peabody.

I saw a picture once by Angelo. An Unpraised Picture. Richard Burton. AA

I Saw a Professional Juggler by the Roadside and Presented Him with This Poem. Kung Tzu-chen, *tr. fr. Chinese by* Shirleen S. Wong. *Fr.* Miscellaneous Poems of the Year *Chi-hai*, XIX. WFTU

I saw a proud, mysterious cat. The Mysterious Cat. Vachel Lindsay. ChTr; FaPON; GoJo; OBCA

I saw a robin. All on a Christmas Morning. Elizabeth J. Coatsworth. ILY

I saw a sailor once. Metamorphosis. Jane Yolen. BWV

I saw a shadow on the ground. The Sky. Elizabeth Madox Roberts. MoAmPo

I saw a ship a-sailing. Mother Goose. FaBoBe; MoShBr; NTCP; OxNR

I saw a ship a-sailing. Romance. Gabriel Setoun. BoTP

I Saw a Ship A-Sailing. *Unknown.* BoTP

I saw a ship a-sailing, a-sailing, a-sailing. An Old Song Re-sung. John Masefield. LiTB

I saw a ship of martial build. The Berg. Herman Melville. AmPP; LiTA; NOBA; NoP; PoEL-5; TAP

I saw a silvery creature scurrying. Riddle 29: The Moon and the Sun. *Unknown, tr. by* Burton Raffel. GoJo

I saw a slowly stepping train. God's Funeral. Thomas Hardy. WGRP

I saw a snail. Little Snail. Hilda Conkling. FaPON

I Saw a Stable. Mary Elizabeth Coleridge. OBCP; OxBSP; PChr

I saw a star slide down the sky. The Falling Star. Sara Teasdale. MoShBr; OBCA; PDV

I saw a staring virgin stand. Two Songs from a Play. W. B. Yeats. *Fr.* The Resurrection, I. CMoP; FaBoTw; HAP; LiTB; NOBE; NoP; OAEL-2; PoE; PPP; PrIm

I saw a stately lady. The Stately Lady. Flora Sandstrom. BoTP

I saw a swete semly syght. The Virgin's Lullaby. *Unknown.* OxBLMV

I saw a tiny pebble fall. What Price. Lulu Minerva Schultz. GoYe

I saw a trap passing by like shadow. Lady Suro. Park Je-chun, *tr. by* Koh Chang-soo. ACKP

I saw a trash-pit, filled and topped with earth. Where Lie All the Slain. Harry Morris. CRP

I saw a tree that was greater than all the others. Edith Södergran, *tr. by* Jaakko A. Ahokas. PBWP

I saw a vision yesternight. To the State of Love; or, The Senses' Festival. John Cleveland. MePo

I saw a vulture in the sky. Life and Death. W. J. Turner. FaBoTw

I saw a young snake glide. Snake. Theodore Roethke. NOBA; NYBP; RFM

I saw about her spotless wrist. Upon a Black Twist, Rounding the Arm of the Countess of Carlisle. Robert Herrick. CaPo

I saw an aged beggar in my walk. The Old Cumberland Beggar. Wordsworth. EnRP; LaA

I saw an old black man walk down the road. Black Soul of the Land. Lance Jeffers. FB

I saw, and trembled for the day. A Warning. Coventry Patmore. EnLoPo

I Saw as a Child. Zindzi Mandela. WMBCH

I saw between a shadow and a bough. The Ungathered Apples. James Wright. ErPo

I saw bleak Arrogance, with brows of brass. Arrogance. Walter de la Mare. OxBSP

I saw by looking in his eyes. The Wandering Jew. E. A. Robinson. QFR

I saw cold thunder in the grass. Herons. Robin Blaser. NeAP

I saw dawn creep across the sky. A Summer Morning. Rachel Field. PDV

I saw each soul as light, each single body. Night of Souls. Ann Stanford. WPE

I saw Esau sawing wood. *Unknown.* FaBoNo

I Saw Eternity. Louise Bogan. LiTA

"I saw Eternity the other night." The Experience. Bruce Bennett. SoTCo

I saw eternity the other night. The World. Henry Vaughan. AWP; EBEV; FaBV; GoTL; HAP; HeIP; JCP; LiTB; MePo; NAEL-1; NOBE; NOCV; OAEL-1; OBS; PoEL-2; PPP; SeCP; SeCV-1; TEP; TrCP; TrGrPo; WGRP
  (Eternity, The.) OBEV
  (Vision, A.) ImOP

I saw fair[e] Chloris walk alone. On Chloris Walking in the Snow in the Snow. William Strode. ELP; JCP; OAEL-1
  (Chloris in the Snow.) NOBE; OBEV
  (On a Gentlewoman Walking in the Snow.) OBS; OxBSP

I saw five birds all in a cage. *Unknown.* GBP

I Saw from the Beach. Thomas Moore. OBNC

I saw God! Do you doubt it? What Thomas an Buile Said in a Pub. James Stephens. MoAB; MoBrPo; MoP; PoRA; TrGrPo; WGRP
  (What Tomas Said in a Pub.) CMoP; NoAM

I Saw God Wash the World. William Leroy Stidger. BLPA

I saw her amid the dunghill debris. Tinker's Wife. Patrick Kavanagh. CIP; InPS; MoP; NoAM

I saw her first abreast the Boston Light. The *William P. Frye.* Jeanne Robert Foster. PAH

I saw her first in gleams. The Spirit's Odyssey. M. Krishnamurti. InPK

I saw her once, briefly. It Was Your Song. Steve Kowit. UL

I saw her once, one little while, and then no more. And Then No More. Friedrich Rückert, *tr. by* James Clarence Mangan. BIrV; BLPA

I saw her plucking cowslips. The Witch. Percy H. Ilott. BoTP

I saw her scan her sacred scroll. Alma Mater's Roll. Edward Everett Hale. AA

I saw him a squat man with red hair. Off Brighton Pier. Alan Ross. OBWP

I saw him beat the surges under him. Shakespeare. *Fr.* The Tempest, II, i. MOS

I saw him brought into Emergency. Empty Holds a Question. Pat Folk. GOYP

I saw him dead, a leaden slumber lyes [*or* lies]. Andrew Marvell. *Fr.* A Poem upon the Death of Oliver Cromwell. JCP; OBS
  (Cromwell Dead.) ChTr

I saw him forging link by link his chain. The Slave. Jones Very. TAP

I saw him in the Airstrip Gardens. Betjeman, 1984. Charles Causley. FaBoCo; NOBL; OxBTC

I saw him lying there—my father—with eyes. The Addict. Larry Rubin. GoYe

I saw him once before. The Last Leaf. Oliver Wendell Holmes. AA; AmPP; AnAmPo; FaBoBe; FaPON; NAAL-1; PoLF; PWR; WBLP

I saw him to the last, the grey. Painting of My Father. Padraic Fallon. NOIV

I saw Him with flesh all bespred—He came from East. The Coming of Christ. *Unknown.* ACP

I saw him yesterday. The Quarrel. Josephine D. Henderson Heard. CBWP-4

I saw his round mouth's crimson deepen as it fell. Wilfred Owen. OAEL-2

I saw in dream a dapper mannikin. Im Traum sah ich ein Männchen klein und putzig. Heine, *tr. by* Sir Theodore Martin. AWP

I Saw in Louisiana a Live-Oak Growing. Walt Whitman. AiP; AWP; InPK; InPS; LiTA; MAT; NAAL-1; NIP; NoAM; NOBA; NoP; OxBA; PrIm

I saw it all, Polly, how when you had call'd for sop. Poor Poll. Robert Bridges. EBEV; OxBoLi; OxBTC

I saw it in an empty window. In an Empty Window. Ray Fraser. NeAC

I saw it light the cactus sky. Back Again from Yucca Flats. Reeve Spencer Kelley. AmFN

I saw it, the mystical beast in the shadows. The Mystical Beast in the Shadows. Richard Eberhart. BLA

I saw magic on a green country road. Michael Hartnett. BIrV

I Saw My Darling. Frederick Morgan. UnPo

I saw my daughter. When I Came to Israel. Bert Meyers. VWA

I saw my face. Jew. Pierre Morhange, *tr. by* Edouard Roditi. VWA

I saw my grandmother grow weak. First Death. Donald Justice. MT; SM

I Saw My Lady Weep. *Unknown.* EIL; ELP; EnLoPo; LiTB; OBSC; TrGrPo
  (My Lady's Tears.) EBEV; NOBE; OBEV

I Saw My Life as Whitest Flame. Christopher Brennan. *Fr.* Towards the Source. PoAu-1

I saw my love, younger than primroses. In a Wood. E. J. Scovell. GBL

I saw myself leaving. Reflections. Carl Gardner. PoBA

I saw new worlds beneath the water lie. On Leaping over the Moon. Thomas Traherne. LiTB; Mes; NAEL-1; SeCV-2

I saw no way—the heavens were stitched. Emily Dickinson. BoWoP

I saw old Autumn in the misty morn. Autumn. Thomas Hood. BLPL; LiTB; OBEV
  (Ode: Autumn.) OAEL-2; OBNC; PoEL-4; UnPo

I saw old Duchesses with their young loves. Vanity. Anna Wickham. FaBoTw

I saw on earth another light. The Light from Within. Jones Very. WGRP

I saw on the slant hill a putrid lamb. For a Lamb. Richard Eberhart. CMoP; LiTM; OxBSP; RB

I saw on the snow. Merry Christmas. Aileen Fisher. RHPC

I saw one hung upon a cross. Gallows and Cross. J. E. H. MacDonald. CaP

I saw one of them who sat on the hat of another. I Saw Several of Them. Jacques Prévert, *tr. by* Mark Strand *and* Jean Ballard. POS

I saw, one sultry night above a swamp. Fireflies. Edgar Fawcett. AnAmPo

I saw our singer again I liked him as much as ever Monday mornings. Animal Song. Alfredo Giuliani, *tr. by* Lawrence R. Smith. NItP

I saw red evening through the rain. Robert Louis Stevenson. NOBVV

I Saw Several of Them. Jacques Prévert, *tr. fr. French by* Mark Strand *and* Jean Ballard. POS

I saw that country in a dream. Wilderness Theme. Ian Mudie. PoAu-2

I saw that thieves had burgled as they do. Ilyas Farhat, *tr. by* Salma Khadra Jayyusi *and* John Heath-Stubbs. MAP

I saw the beauty of my love. Shamsuddin Mohammad Vali, *tr. by* Ahmed Ali. GoT

I saw the best minds of my generation. Squeal. Louis Simpson. BXAP; FiBHP; Par; UnPo

I saw the best minds of my generation destroyed by madness, starving hysterical naked. Allen Ginsberg. *Fr.* Howl, I. AmPP; CAPP; GLP; InPS; MoP; NaP; NeAP; NIP; NoAM; NoP; PoM; SOTW; TAP

I saw the best mutts of my germination destroyed by badness. From "Growl." David Shevin. SoTCo

I saw the bird that can the sun endure. Joachim Du Bellay, *tr. fr. French by* Spenser. *Fr.* Visions, VII. Son

I Saw the Bird That Dares Behold the Sun. Joachim Du Bellay, *tr. fr. French by* Spenser. Son

I saw the black trees leaning. Trees and Evening Sky. N. Scott Momaday. CDW

I saw the bodies of earth's men. The Navigators. W. J. Turner. OBMV

I saw the constellated matin choir. Edmund Clarence Stedman. AA

I saw the curl of his waving lash. Reflections of a Proud Pedestrian. Oliver Wendell Holmes. AnAmPo

I saw the dark clouds burst. Mirabai, *tr. by* John Stratton Hawley *and* Mark Juergensmeyer. SSI

I saw the day lean o'er the world's sharp edge. Sunset. Ella Wheeler Wilcox. AnAmPo

I saw the dead/ dying a second time. The Pulverized Screen. Edmond Jabès, *tr. by* Anthony Rudolf. VWA

I saw the Devil walking down the lane. The Devil's Bag. James Stephens. WSC

I saw the early morning mist. The Dead Horse. Cecília Meireles, *tr. by* James Merrill. ATCBP

I saw the farmer plough the field. Harvest. M. M. Hutchinson. BoTP

I saw the first pear. Orchard. Hilda Doolittle ("H. D."). CMoP; LiTA; LiTM; MoAmPo; OxBA

I saw the garden where my aunt had died. The Entertainment of War. Roy Fisher. FaBoMo

I saw the ghostesses. Ghostesses. *Unknown.* ChTr

I saw the holes the Sherman tank. The Houses Were Left Full of Smoke. Leonel Rugama, *tr. by* Alejandro Murguía. Vol

I saw the islands in a ring all round me. Letter to Pearse Hutchinson. Eiléan Ni Chuilleanáin. FaBoWP

I saw the Master of the Sun. He stood. The Sun God. Aubrey Thomas De Vere. ACP

I saw the midlands. Kisses in the Train. D. H. Lawrence. MoAB; MoBrPo

I saw the moon/ One windy night. Flying. J. M. Westrup. BoTP; OnUR

I saw the moon, so broad and bright. Donnybrook. James Stephens. TIRV

I Saw the Object ("I saw the object of my pining thought"). Thomas Watson. *Fr.* The Tears of Fancy. EIL; Son

I saw the old Chinese men standing. Some Painful Butterflies Pass Through. Tess Gallagher. MAYP

I saw the old god of war stand in a bog between chasm and rockface. The God of War. Bertolt Brecht. FaBoPV

I saw the peril of the marsh. The Onlooker. Wade Wellman. VVA

I saw the ramparts of my native land. Sonnet: Death Warnings. Francisco de Quevedo y Villegas, *tr. by* John Masefield. AWP

I saw the reflection in the mirror. Drunken Americans. John Ashbery. HCAP

I saw the roofs of Elfin Town. Elfin Town. Rachel Field. WSC

I saw the salt. Ode to Salt. Pablo Neruda, *tr. by* Robert Bly. NU

I saw the shapes that stood upon the clouds. London Nightfall. John Gould Fletcher. MoAmPo

I saw the shepherd fold the sheep. The Folded Flock. Wilfrid Meynell. TrPWD

I saw the silver morning mist. The Dead Horse. Cecília Meireles, *tr. by* James Merrill. PBWP

I saw the sky descending, black and white. Where the Rainbow Ends. Robert Lowell. HCAP; MoAB; MoAmPo; NePoEA; TrGrPo

I saw the snake again at dusk. Close to Home. Frank Steele. MOWH

I saw the spiders marching through the air. Mr. Edwards and the Spider. Robert Lowell. CAPP; CMoP; CoAP; FaBoMo; HeIP; InPS; LiTM; MoAB; NAAL-2; NePoEA; NOBA; NoP; SM; SoSe; TwCP

I saw the spires of Oxford. The Spires of Oxford. Winifred M. Letts. FaFP; OHFP; OnYI; PoLF; PoRA; WGRP

I saw the spot where our first parents dwelt. The Garden. Jones Very. OxBA; TAP

I Saw the Sun at Midnight, Rising Red. Joseph Mary Plunkett. TIRV

I saw the sun set in clouds. Emperor Tenji. *Fr.* Manyo Shu. FCEI

I saw the throng, so deeply separate. A General Communion. Alice Meynell. NOCV; WPE

I saw the twinkle of white feet. Hebe. James Russell Lowell. AA

I saw the two starlings. The Manoeuvre. William Carlos Williams. PCP

I Saw the Vision of Armies. Walt Whitman. WaaP

I Saw the Wind Today. Padraic Colum. GoJo (Wind, The.) PDV

I saw them at games every. Seven Mexican Children. Tom Schmidt. NeAC

I saw them chase the gipsies. The Gipsies. "Richard Scrace." CaP

I Saw Them Lynch. Carol Freeman. NMM; PoBA

I saw these dreamers of dreams go by. The Gold-Seekers. Hamlin Garland. AA; FaBoBe

I saw this house. Prince Odai. *Fr.* Manyo Shu. Ma

I saw this much from the window. The Gap in the Cedar. Roy Scheele. Psk; SM

I Saw Three Ships. Kevyn Arthur. PBCV

I Saw Three Ships. *Unknown. See* As I Sat under a Sycamore Tree.

I saw three ships come sailing by. Mother Goose. OxNR

I Saw Three Ships Come Sailing In. *Unknown.* BLPA

I saw three ships go sailing by. The North Ship. Philip Larkin. RB

I saw three withered women limp across. The Private Meeting Place. James Wright. NYBP

I saw thy beauty in its high estate. To a Magnolia Flower in the Garden of the Armenian Convent at Venice. Silas Weir Mitchell. AA

I saw—twas in a dream, the other night. Montefiore. Ambrose Bierce. AA

I saw two hares in the corn. The Dance. Gareth Alban Davies, *tr. by* Gwyn Jones. OBWVE

I saw two trees embracing. All That Time. May Swenson. FF

I saw where in the shroud did lurk. On an Infant Dying as Soon as Born. Charles Lamb. GTBS; GTBS-P; OBEV

I saw with open eyes. Stupidity Street. Ralph Hodgson. BrPo; CH; LiTM; MoAB; MoBrPo; OBD; OxBTC; PDV

I saw you/ peeking out thru the flower pots. As the World Turns. Larry Mollin. NeAC

I saw you/ on my walk last. Glimpse. Pearl Cleage Lomax. PoBA

I saw you/ I saw you in the distance in front of the wall. That Memory. Pierre Reverdy, *tr. by* John Ashbery. POS

I saw you die. Murdered Little Bird. *Unknown.* FiBHP

I saw you in Houston, waiting for the verdict. On Visiting the M. D. Anderson. Salma Khadra Jayyusi, *tr. by the author and* Charles Doria. MAP

I saw you once, Medusa; we were alone. The Muse as Medusa. May Sarton. ER

"I saw you take his kiss!" "'Tis true." The Kiss. Coventry Patmore. *Fr.* The Angel in the House, II, viii. BoLoP; EnLoPo; FiBHP; NOBVV

I saw you toss the kites on high. The Wind. Robert Louis Stevenson. BoTP; GN

I saw you walking. At Long Last. Lindsay Patterson. CNA

I saw your manager fight. He was. Elegy for Lyn James. Leslie Norris. OBWVE

I sawe a mayd sitte on a bank. The Carelesse Nurse Mayd. Thomas Hood. FaBoNo

I Say. Malka Heifetz-Tussman, *tr. fr. Yiddish by* Marcia Falk. VWA

I say hello to the sunshine. Alan Brunton. PeNZ

I Say I'll Seek Her. Thomas Hardy. QFR

I say it under the rose. Thalia. Thomas Bailey Aldrich. AA

I say no more for Clavering. Clavering. E. A. Robinson. OxBA

I say now, Fernando, that on that day. Hibiscus on the Sleeping Shores. Wallace Stevens. InPS

"I say, stranger." Between the Walls of the Valley. Elisabeth Peck. AmFN

I say the women don't sleep right. Explanation. Geof Hewitt. NeAC

I say things to myself. Phraseology. Jayne Cortez. BlSi

I say this evening we'll all get drunk. Suction's Anthem. Blake. *Fr.* An Island in the Moon. FaBoNo

I Say to Myself. Moyshe-Leyb Halpern, *tr. fr. Yiddish by* Leonard Wolf. PeBMYV

I say to the Almighty. I Say. Malka Heifetz-Tussman, *tr. by* Marcia Falk. VWA

I say to the lead. Poem without a Title. Charles Simic. NNaP

I say to thee, do thou repeat. The Kingdom of God. Richard Chenevix Trench. WBLP

I, says the buzzard. From Virgil. George Oppen. *Fr.* Five Poems about Poetry. NNaP

I scarce believe [*or* beleeve] my love to be so pure. Love's Growth. John Donne. JCP; MePo; NoP; SeCV-1

I scarcely think. The Zoo. Humbert Wolfe. MoShBr

I Scattered My Sighs to the Wind. Hayyim Nahman Bailik, *tr. fr. Hebrew by* Naomi Nir. VWA

I schal yow tel wyth hert and mode. The Philosopher's Stone. *Unknown.* OxBLMV

I scissor the stem of the red carnation. Salome. Ai. NoAM

I scolded my child. Ishikawa Takuboku, *tr. fr. Japanese by* Hiroaki Sato. *Fr.* Forty-seven Tanka in Three Lines. FCEI

I scorn the doubts and cares that hurt. A Garden Song. George R. Sims. NOBVV

I scream/ You scream. *Unknown.* FaBoNo

I Scream You Scream. Don McKay. NOBC

I scuff/ my feet along. Sulk. Felice Holman. RHPC

I Search Again for a Word Today. Faiz Ahmad Faiz, *tr. fr. Urdu by* Mahmood Jamal. PBMUP

I search the room with all my mind. Officers' Mess (1916). Harold Monro. BrPo

I search the treetops, low-hung branches, for a trace of pink. Palace Song. Wang Chien, *tr. by* Burton Watson. CoBCP

I see a beautiful gigantic swimmer swimming naked through the eddies of the sea. The Beautiful Swimmer. Walt Whitman. PeHV

I see a farmer walking by himself. The Farmer. Fredegond Shove. MMA

I see a girl climbing the mountain. The Pilgrim. Brendan Kennelly. TIRV

I see a man who is dull. An Ancient Song of a Woman of Fez. *Unknown, tr. by* Willis Barnstone. AIW; BoWoP

I see a tiny fluttering form. The Southern Snow-Bird. William Hamilton Hayne. AA

I see a woman/ I see my wife. Tanikawa Shuntaro, *tr. fr. Japanese by* Hiroaki Sato. *Fr.* Two Portraits, D. FCEI

I see a woman/ it's a woman who was my lover. Tanikawa Shuntaro, *tr. fr. Japanese by* Hiroaki Sato. *Fr.* Two Portraits, C. FCEI

I see a world torn apart. Why? Richard Augustine Chima. WMBCH

I see another world when I look in the mirror. Parrot. Park Je-chun, *tr. by* Koh Chang-soo. ACKP

I see around me here. The Wanderer Recalls the Past. Wordsworth. *Fr.* The Excursion, I. OBNC

I see as through a skylight in my brain. Persephone. Michael Longley. FaBCIP

I see at last our great Lamorna Cove. Lamorna Cove. W. H. Davies. BrPo

I see before me now a traveling army halting. Bivouac on a Mountain Side. Walt Whitman. AA; AiP; ChTr; OxBA; PoLF

I see before me the gladiator lie. The Dying Gladiator. Byron. *Fr.* Childe Harold's Pilgrimage, IV. NOBE

I see bodies in the morning kneel. Shirley Kaufman. BoWoP

I See Cleopatra. Nurunnessa Choudhury, *tr. fr. Bengali by the author and* Paul Joseph Thompson. AIW

I see her against the pearl sky of Dublin. My Mother's Sister. C. Day Lewis. OxBTC

I see her in my sleep, my red, terrible girl. Sylvia Plath. *Fr.* Three Women. TV

I see her on a beach. Penelope. Janet Dubé. DT

I see her on a lonely forest track. The Maroon Girl. Walter Adolphe Roberts. PVCV

I see her seventeen. Arizona Highways. James Welch. CDW; NoAM

I see her stand with arms a-kimbo. Hersilia. William Johnson Cory. NOBVV

I see her still, unsteadily riding the edge. My Grandmother Washes Her Feet. Fred Chappell. MT

I see her yet, that dark-eyed one. A Memory. Adah Isaacs Menken. CBWP-1

"I see 'herrin'. "—I hear the glad cry. With the Herring Fishers. "Hugh MacDiarmid." LiTM

I see him old, trapped in a burly house. A Pauper. Allen Tate. LiTM

I See His Blood upon the Rose. Joseph Mary Plunkett. OnYI; PoLF; TIRV; WGRP

I see in his last preached and printed booke. On John Donne's Book of Poems. John Marriot. CH

I see it. Song for the Dead, III. *Unknown, tr. by* Frances S. Herskovits. TTY

I see I've come a pilgrimage. I didn't. The *Weepers Tower* in Amsterdam. Paul Goodman. VGW

I See My Girl. Sharon Olds. BLA

I see my mother waving—her unfussed, smiling. Distances. Katherine Gallagher. AIW

I See My Plaint. *At.* to John Harington. EIL

I see no bird arise. My Sun-killed Tree. Marguerite Harris. GoYe

I see no equivalents. The Poet at Night-Fall. Glenway Wescott. PoA

I see no leader among the crowd. The Long Poem. Yusuf al-Khal, tr. by Abdullah al-Udhari. MPAW

I See Phantoms of Hatred and of the Heart's Fullness and of the Coming Emptiness. W. B. Yeats. *Fr.* Meditations in Time of Civil War, VII. LiTB

I see rain falling and the leaves. For George Barker at Seventy. David Wright. NPo

I see that chance hath chosen me. Sir Thomas Wyatt. SiPS

I see that there it is on the beach. Memorial Service for the Invasion Beach Where the Vacation in the Flesh Is Over. Alan Dugan. TwCP

I see that wreath which doth the wearer arm. To My Dead Friend Ben: Johnson. Henry King. SeCP

I see that you're a poetry lover, sweet Diane. Sweet Diane. George Barlow. CNA

I See the Boys of Summer. Dylan Thomas. LiTB

I see the children running out of school. The Poet Laments the Coming of Old Age. Edith Sitwell. NAEL-2; NoAM

I see the clear weather darken. Raimon Jordan, *tr. by* Paul Blackburn. Pro

I see the cloud-born squadrons of the gale. A Storm in the Distance. Paul Hamilton Hayne. AA

I see the dawn e'en now begin to peer. *Unknown, tr. fr. Italian. Fr.* Popular Songs of Tuscany, *tr. by* John Addington Symonds. AWP

I see the golden hunter go. Bliss Carman. *Fr.* Songs of the Sea-Children, LIV. OBCV

I see the horses and the sad streets. The Eye. Allen Tate. LiTA

I see the map of summer, lying still. Movies for the Home. Howard Moss. NePoEA-2; NYBP

I See the Moon. *Unknown.* GBP, *diff. version*; NTCP; OxNR; PYC; RAR

I see the mosquito kneeling on the soft underside of my arm, kneeling. The Mosquito. Rodney Jones. MAYP; MT

I see the shadow of a warbler. Kito, *tr. fr. Japanese by* Hiroaki Sato. *Fr.* Twenty-four Hokku. FCEI

I see the sparrow bones folded in their thin shoes. The Fathers. Benjamin Saltman. VWA

I see the star-lights quiver. The Flight from the Convent. Theodore Tilton. AA

I see the thighs of a man and a woman. Tears. Ruth Kim Chun-soo, *tr. by* Koh Chang-soo. ACKP

I see the thin bell-ringer standing at corners. The Jew at Christmas Eve. Karl Shapiro. VGW

I see the Usk, and know my blood. The Storm. Henry Vaughan. FaBoPP

I see the young bride move among. George Barker. *Fr.* The True Confession of George Barker. ErPo

I see thee pine like her in golden story. Coleridge. Theodore Watts-Dunton. Son

I see thee still! thou art not dead. A Remembrance. Willis Gaylord Clarke. AA

I see them/ Puerto Ricans. You're Nothing but a Spanish Colored Kid. Felipe Luciano. PoBA

I see them coming up the road. A Happy Pair. Priscilla Jane Thompson. CBWP-2

I see them, crowd on crowd they walk the earth. The Dead. Jones Very. AA; AnAmPo; HAP; NOBA; OxBA; TAP

I see them working in old rectories. The Country Clergy. R. S. Thomas. GTBS-P; OxBTC

I see these ancestors of ours. Triptych. Frank A. Collymore. PBCV

I see they worked you over. What you in for? Coming of Age in the County Jail. Carter Revard. VoR

I see trees breaking off their branches. Khairi Mansour, *tr. fr. Arabic by* Lena Jayyusi. *Fr.* Nightwatch. MAP

I See Trees Falling. Sirkka Turkka, *tr. fr. Finnish by* Aili Jarvenpa. SOP

I see why the touched needle scents about. Mysteries Revealed after Death. John Reynolds. *Fr.* Death's Vision. NOEC

I see you. Letters from Kazuko (Kyoto, Japan—Summer 1980). Alan Chong Lau. BrSi

I see you, a child. The Album. C. Day Lewis. EnLoPo; OxBTC

I see you displaced, condensed, within my dream. Dream. Josephine Miles. PoA

I see you in her bed. The Lovemaker. Robert Mezey. NePoEA-2

I see you in the silver. Arctic Tern in a Museum. Effie Lee Newsome. PoNe

I see you, Juliet, still, with your straw hat. Farewell to Juliet. Wilfrid Scawen Blunt. *Fr.* The Love Sonnets of Proteus: Farewell to Juliet, XLVII. BoLoP; EnLoPo; OxBTC

I see you now. Mountain Drive. Cothrai Gogan. TIRV

I see you, prisoner of Dzeleka. Song of a Prison Guard. Lupenga Mphande. WMBCH

I see you sitting. Matmiya. Mary TallMountain. HATNAP

I see you with my inner eye. Greeting from a Distance. Hans Sahl, *tr. by* Erna Baber Rosenfeld. VWA

I see'd her in de springtime. She Hugged Me and Kissed Me. *Unknown.* BPo

I seek mercy/ for the women stoned. For All Mary Magdalenes. Desanka Maksimovic, *tr. by* Vasa D. Mihailovich. AIW; WPOW

I Seek Thee in the Heart Alone. Herbert Trench. WGRP

I seen a dunce of a poet once, a-writin' a little book. Gelett Burgess. *Fr.* The Protest of the Illiterate. FiBHP

I seen Ol' Edgar Martin a-ridin' by jus now. Ol' Edgar Martin. Carlos Ashley. CowP

I sell myths not poems. With each poem goes a little myth. De Rerum Natura. Andrei Codrescu. UL

I send a garland to my love. The Lover's Posy. Rufinus Domesticus, *tr. by* W. H. D. Rouse. AWP

I send a message, my worthy chief. A Message to a Loved One Dead. Josephine D. Henderson Heard. CBWP-4

I send a rose with a card for myself. My Regrets. Michael Andre. UL

I send, I send here my supremest kiss. His Tears to Thamesis. Robert Herrick. FaBoPP

I send my poisoned candies through the mail. End of the Affair. Geoffrey Grigson. GBL

I send thee a shell from the ocean beach. With a Nantucket Shell. Charles Henry Webb. AA

I send thee myrrh, not that thou mayest be. Not of Itself but Thee. *Unknown, tr. by* Richard Garnett. AWP

I send these along. Prince Munenaga, *tr. by* Steven D. Carter. WFTW

I send you here a wreath of blossoms blown. Roses. Pierre de Ronsard, *tr. by* Andrew Lang. AWP

I send your own words back. Lines to a Friend in Trouble. W. S. Di Piero. MAYP

I sent a letter to my love. George Barker. *Fr.* The True Confession of George Barker. FaBoTw

I sent for Radcliffe; was so ill. The Remedy Worse than the Disease. Matthew Prior. FaBoEE; TrGrPo

I sent my Collie to the wash. Gelett Burgess. CenHV

I sent my love two roses,—one. The White Flag. John Milton Hay. AnAmPo

I sent my mother copies of my poems in print. Poems. Gary Gildner. Psk

I sent you this bluebird of the name of Joe. Happiness. William Dickey. Psk

I Serve a Mistress. Anthony Munday. *Fr.* Fedele and Fortunio. EIL (Fedele's Song.) OBSC
("I serve a mistress whiter than snow.") HAP

I Served in a Great Cause. Horace L. Traubel. AA

I Set Aside. Mary Morison Webster. PeSA

I set forth hopeful—cotton-blossom Lal. Lalleswari, *tr. by* George Grierson. WPOW

I set my heart to sing of leaves. Anticipation. Lord De Tabley. ELP

I set sail. When I Am with You. Ghazi al-Gosaibi, *tr. by* Sharif Elmusa *and* Charles Doria. MAP

I shake my hair in the wind of morning. Triumph of Love. John Hall Wheelock. MoAmPo

I shake my robe—and mists disperse, leaving clear autumn sky. Hsü Chung-hsing, *tr. fr. Chinese by* Jonathan Chaves. *Fr.* At Dawn, Climbing the Heavenly Pillar Peak of Myst. CoBLCP

"I shall arise." For centuries. Resurgam. *Unknown.* WGRP

I shall be capricious, I shall have a whim. A Man's Woman. Mary Carolyn Davies. PoLF

"I shall be careful to say nothing at all." How She Resolved to Act. Merrill Moore. MoAmPo

I Shall Be Married on Monday Morning. *Unknown.* ErPo

I shall be quite content. Growing Old. Douglas Fraser. PoSH

I Shall Be Watching. János Pilinszky, *tr. fr. Hungarian by* William Jay Smith. MHuP

I shall begin by learning to throw. Formal Application. Donald W. Baker. FF; SoSe

I shall come back to die. In This Dark House. Edward Davison. OBMV

I shall come this way again. Auf Wiedersehen. Donald Jeffrey Hayes. CDC

I shall cry God to give me a broken foot. Flash Crimson. Carl Sandburg. MoAmPo

I shall dance, I shall have hope. Dance Hymn. Isaiah Shembe. WTO, *tr. by* B. G. M. Sundkler

I shall dance tonight. Celebration. Alonzo Lopez. ILY

I shall die, but that is all that I shall do for Death. Conscientious Objector. Edna St. Vincent Millay. WPOW

I Shall Empty My Head like Jam. Meir Wieseltier, *tr. fr. Hebrew by* Bernhard Frank. MHeP

"I shall forget," I said. Akinoosa Obitomaro. *Fr.* Manyo Shu. PeBJV

I Shall Forget You Presently, My Dear. Edna St. Vincent Millay. TAP

I shall gather myself into myself again. The Crystal Gazer. Sara Teasdale. MoAmPo

I shall give you five words for your birthday. Five Words for Joe Dunn on His 22nd Birthday. Jack Spicer. PoM

I shall go among red faces and virile voices. Cattle Show. "Hugh MacDiarmid." FaBoMo; GoTS; HAP; MoBrPo; OBMV; OxBTC

I shall go as my father went. The Tenancy. Mary Gilmore. CBAP; PoAu-1

I Shall Go Back. Edna St. Vincent Millay. MoAmPo; UnPo

I shall go out when the light comes in. Death at Daybreak. Anne Reeve Aldrich. AA

I shall go to Mamre's oaks. Abraham. Eisig Silberschlag. VWA

I shall hate you. Hatred. Gwendolyn B. Bennett. AmNP; BANP; BlSi; CDC; PoBA

I shall knock three times at the door. Ali al-Sharqawi, *tr. fr. Arabic by* Lena Jayyusi *and* Naomi Shihab Nye. *Fr.* Psalm 23 to the Singer's Nectar. MAP

I shall know why—when time is over. Emily Dickinson. NOCV

I Shall Laugh Purely. Robinson Jeffers. LiTA; LiTM; WaP

I shall leave tonight from Euston. I Leave Tonight from Euston. *Unknown.* PoSH

I shall lie hidden in a hut. Prophecy. Elinor Wylie. BLPL; BoWoP; FaBoWP; PrIm; VGW

I shall make a new song now. Guillaume de Poitiers, *tr. by* Paul Blackburn. Pro

I shall make a song like your hair. Secret. Gwendolyn B. Bennett. BlSi; CDC

I shall make a vers about/ nothing. Guillaume de Poitiers, *tr. by* Paul Blackburn. Pro

I shall make it simple so you understand. Simple Poem. Anthony Thwaite. DiPo

I shall never forget you, Broadway. Broadway. Carl Sandburg. AiP

I shall never get you put together entirely. The Colossus. Sylvia Plath. CAPP; FaBoWP; HCAP; LiTM; NePoEA-2; NoAM; NOBA; NoP; TAP

I Shall Never Go On Bragging. Moyshe-Leyb Halpern, *tr. fr. Yiddish by* Benjamin *and* Barbara Harshav. AYP

I Shall Not Care. Sara Teasdale. MoAmPo; TrGrPo; UnPo

I Shall Not Die for Thee. *Unknown, tr. fr. Modern Irish by* Douglas Hyde. AnIL

I shall not forget. Teika, *tr. by* Steven D. Carter. WFTW

I shall not linger in that draughty square. French. Osbert Lancaster. *Fr.* Afternoons with Baedeker. FaBoCo; NOBL

I Shall Not Pass Again This Way ("The bread that bringeth strength I want to give"). *Unknown.* BLRP; WBLP

I Shall Not Pass This Way Again ("Through this toilsome world, alas!"). *Unknown.* BLPA; FPL

I Shall Not Pass This Way Again. Eva Rose York. FaFP; OHFP; WBLP

I shall not regard my swelled head as a sign of real glory. Aimé Césaire, *tr. fr. French by* Emile Snyders. *Fr.* Return to My Native Land. TTY

I Shall Not Want: In Deserts Wild. Charles F. Deems. AH

I shall not wonder more, then. Change. Raymond Knister. CaP; OBCV

I shall note first/ the ones I loved. The Chronicler. Alexander Bergman. TrJP

I shall paint/ God in the midst. Robert Browning. *Fr.* Fra Lippo Lippi. Prf

I Shall Remember. Jacob Glatstein, *tr. fr. Yiddish by* Benjamin *and* Barbara Harshav. AYP

I shall say, Lord, "Is it music, is it morning." Resurgam. Marjorie Pickthall. OBCV; TrCP

I shall say what inordinate love is. Inordinate Love. *Unknown.* EBEV; MeEL; OxBSP

I shall see justice done. Witch. Patricia Beer. OxBC

I shall slough my self as a snake its skin. "I." Louis Golding. TrJP

I Shall Take You in Rough Weather. Frank Prewett. HATNAP

I shall take you, wild as a frost. Wild Song. Judah Leib Teller, *tr. by* Benjamin *and* Barbara Harshav. AYP

I shall think of nothing more now. Lady Abe. *Fr.* Manyo Shu. Ma

I Shall Transport Myself. Jacob Glatstein, *tr. fr. Yiddish by* Benjamin *and* Barbara Harshav. AYP

I shall walk down the road. Death. Maxwell Bodenheim. TrJP

I Shall Weep. Peretz Hirshbein, *tr. fr. Yiddish by* Joseph Leftwich. TrJP

I shall write of the old men I knew. In These Dissenting Times. Alice Walker. InPS; PoBA

I shave my face, comb my hair. Getting Serious. Gary Soto. NPGG

I shaved my head, became a monk. Bothered by Something. Ryokan, *tr. by* Burton Watson. JLIC-2

I shipped, d'ye see, in a Revenue sloop. The Darned Mounseer. W. S. Gilbert. *Fr.* Ruddigore. NOBL

I shipped on board of a Liverpool liner. Sally Brown. *Unknown.* AmFP

I shiver, Spirit fierce and bold. At the Grave of Burns. Wordsworth. EnRP

I shoot the hippopotamus. The Hippopotamus. Hilaire Belloc. CenHV; FaBoNo; FiBHP; InPK

I shop in the streets of my hometown with/ my family. Bruce Beaver. *Fr.* Letters to Live Poets, II. CBAP

I shot a golf ball into the air. The Ball and the Club. Forbes Lindsay. SD

I shot a rocket in the air. Enough. Tom Masson. OBAL

I shot an arrow into the air. A Shot at Random. D. B. Lewis. FaBoCo; FaFP; FiBHP

I shot an arrow into the air. The Arrow and the Song. Longfellow. AA; AnAmPo; FaFP; PWR

I shot my friend to save my country's life. The Body Politic. Donald Hall. NePoEA

I shot pool in a bar last night. Burning Out. Robert Long. NAmP

I Should Be Ashamed. Uvlunuaq, *tr. fr. Eskimo.* WTO

I should have been too glad, I see. Emily Dickinson. NOCV

I should have cut my life. Eviction. Elizabeth Brewster. CaP

I should have seen the sign: "Fresh paint." Fresh Paint. Boris Pasternak, *tr. by* Babette Deutsch. TrJP

I should have thought. At Baia. Hilda Doolittle ("H. D."). LiTA; NAAL-2; NOBA

I should like a great lake of ale. I Should Like to Have a Great Pool of Ale. At. to St. Bridget, *tr. by* Kenneth Jackson. AnIL

I should like on this divine October afternoon. Aching. Alfonsina Storni, *tr. by* Kate Flores. DMH

"I should like," said the vase from the china-store. The Toys Talk of the World. Katharine Pyle. OBCA

"I should like to buy you a birthday present," said Billy to Betsy Jane. Betsy Jane's Sixth Birthday. Alfred Noyes. ILY

I should like to creep. A Mona Lisa. Angelina Weld Grimké. BlSi; CDC

I Should Like to Have a Great Pool of Ale. At. to St. Bridget, *tr. fr. Middle Irish by* Kenneth Jackson. AnIL

I should like to rise and go. Travel. Robert Louis Stevenson. BrPo; FaBoCh; FaPON; MoShBr

I should like to see that country's tiled bedrooms. Keeping Their World Large. Marianne Moore. WaP

I should not presume to express any view. Triangular Legs. A. P. Herbert. NBLV

I should pray but my soul is stopt. At the Ocean's Verge. Ralph Gustafson. OBCV

I should quit this craft. James Weigel, Jr.. *Fr.* Testaments, XXVI. TSM

I should speak. In This Wind. Mirkka Rekola, *tr. by* Aili Jarvenpa. SOP

I should write him and him. Letters. Remco Campert, *tr. by* James S. Holmes. DuIn

I shout my words above the blowing wind. I Sing America Now! Jesse Stuart. AmFN

I shouted day and night. Let Zulu Be Heard. Isaiah Shembe, *tr. by* G. C. Oosthuizen. WTO
I shudder thinking. The Cold Irish Earth. Knute Skinner. InPK
I shut the door but can't sit down. Relaxing in the Evening in My Study. Yang Wan-li, *tr. by* Burton Watson. CoBCP
I shut the door, hoping to drive off sorrow. Written for My Own Amusement. Wang An-shih, *tr. by* Burton Watson. CoBCP
I shut the door on the racket. Shoe Shop. Barton Sutter. SM; SoSe
I sieze the sphery harp. I strike the strings. Enitharmon Revives with Los. Blake. *Fr.* Vala; or The Four Zoas, The Four Zoas. OBNC (Enitharmon's Song.) ChTr
I sigh for the heavenly country. The Heavenly City. Stevie Smith. FaBoTw
I sike al when I singe. The Crucifixion. *Unknown.* MeEL
I sing a song of sixpence, and of rye. Anthony C. Deane. NOBL
I sing a song reluctantly. Beatrice, Countess de Die, *tr. fr. Provençal by* Carol Cosman *and* Howard Bloch. PBWP
I sing a theme deserving praise. The Manchester Ship Canal. *Unknown.* OBET
I sing a woeful ditty. A Ballad Called the Haymarket Hectors. *Unknown.* APAS
I Sing America Now! Jesse Stuart. AmFN
I Sing an Old Song. Oscar Williams. LiTM
I sing Europe, its railways and its theaters. My Muse. Valery Larbaud, *tr. by* Ron Padgett *and* Bill Zavatsky. RHTwFP
I Sing for the Animals. *Oral Tradition, tr. fr. Teton Sioux Indian.* TTTS
I sing her worth and praises hy [*or* high]. A Description. Herbert of Cherbury. OPOP; SeCP
I Sing No New Songs. Frank Marshall Davis. PoBA; PoNe
I sing no song. I spin instead. Spider. Norma Farber. PChr
I sing not of the draper's praise, nor yet of William Wood. An Excellent New Song upon His Grace Our Good Lord Archbishop of Dublin. Swift. CoMu
I sing of a hero, unsung, unrecorded. Crispus Attucks McCoy. Sterling A. Brown. BPo
I Sing of a Maiden. *Unknown.* CABA; CH; EBEV; ELP; FaBoCh; FF; InPK; InPS; LiTB; MeEL; NAEL-1; NOBE; NOCV; NoP; OAEL-1; OxBLMV; PoE; PoEL-1; SCV; TOF; TrGrPo. *See also* I Syng of a Mayden.
  (Carol: "I sing of a maiden.") OBEV; OxBoCh
  (I sing of a mayden.) HAP
  (Maiden Makeles, The.) ChTr
  (Maiden that is Makeless, A.) OFD
  (Two Carols to Our Lady.) ACP
I sing of a woman and summer. Canto Cantare Cantavi Cantatum. Rita Mae Brown. PeHV
I sing of autumn and the falling fruit. Ship of Death. D. H. Lawrence. MoAB; MoBrPo
I sing of brooks, of blossom[e]s, birds, and bowers. The Argument of His Book. Robert Herrick. AWP; CaPo; EBEV; HAP; HeIP; InVP; InVP; JCP; NAEL-1; NoP; OAEL-1; OBS; PoE; PoEL-3; PoRA; SeCePo; SeCP; SeCV-1; TEP; TEP; TrGrPo; TTTS; ViBoPo
I sing of George Augustus Chadd. The Ballad of Private Chadd. A. A. Milne. CenHV
I sing of great hotels and a man. In the foyer. The Strand Hotel, Rosslare. James Liddy. CIP
I sing of myself, a sorrowful woman. Wife's Lament. *Unknown, tr. by* Kemp Malone. PBWP; PoE
I Sing of Olaf Glad and Big. E. E. Cummings. HeIP; LiTM; MoP; NAAL-2; NoAM; NOBA; NoP; OBSV; OBWP; VGW
  (I Sing of Olaf.) LiTA; WaP
I Sing of Shine. Etheridge Knight. BPo
I sing of slum scabs on city faces. Today. M. A. Walker. FB
I sing of sweepers, frequent in thy streets. The Sweepers. William Whitehead. NOEC
I sing of the Good Samaritan. The Song of the Good Samaritan. Vernon Watkins. LiTM
I sing of Tony Caesar, a big league arbiter of unimpeachable repute. Decline and Fall of a Roman Umpire. Ogden Nash. SD
I sing of warfare. Virgil, *tr. by* Robert Fitzgerald. NAWM-1
I sing th' adventures of mine worthy wights. Thomas Morton. SCAP
I sing the birth was born [*or* borne] tonight. A Hymn [*or* Hymne] on the Nativity [*or* Nativitie] of My Saviour. Ben Jonson. SeCV-1; TrCP
I Sing the Body Electric, *sels.* Walt Whitman. CTC
  "O my body! I dare not desert the likes of you in other men and women, nor the likes of the parts of you." ErPo
  "This is the female form." ErPo
I sing the furious battles of the spheres. Ad Johannuelem Leporem, Lepidissimum, Carmen Heroicum. *Unknown.* FaBoNo
I sing the glorious Power with azure eyes. Hymn to Athena. *Unknown, tr. fr. Greek by* Shelley. *Fr.* Homeric Hymns. AWP

I sing the heat that is like a newborn babe, desperate heat. To the Health of the Serpent. René Char, *tr. by* Jackson Mathews. RHTwFP
I sing the hymn of the conquered, who fell in the battle of life. Io Victis! William Wetmore Story. AA; WGRP
I sing the Man, by Heav'ns peculiar grace. A Poem on Elijahs Translation. Benjamin Colman. SCAP
I sing the Name which none can say. To the Name above Every Name, the Name of Jesus, a Hymn. Richard Crashaw. SeCV-1
I sing the praise of honored wars. Soldier's Song. *Unknown.* WiR
I sing the simplest flower. Karl Shapiro. *Fr.* Six Religious Lyrics, I. CMoP
I sing the tree is a heron. Merce of Egypt. Charles Olson. NoP
I sing the uplift and the up-welling. Jehovah. Israel Zangwill. WGRP
I Sing to Myself. Alma Villanueva. CCP
I sing *tree*, making green. Last Night's Dream. Denise Levertov. NoAM
I sink into a rare luminous blindness. Blindness. Delmira Agustini, *tr. by* D. M. Pettinella. PBWP
I sink my hands into the earth. Prayer for the Soul of My Country. Otto René Castillo, *tr. by* Wilfredo Castaño. VoI
I sit alone late at night. An Extra Joyful Chorus for Those Who Have Read This Far. Robert Bly. EAS
I sit alone on a rock by the stream. Autumn. Chang Yü, *tr. fr. Chinese by* Jonathan Chaves. *Fr.* Four Seasons in the Mountains. CoBLCP
I Sit and Look Out. Walt Whitman. AnAmPo; NAAL-1; OxBA; TAP
I Sit and Sew. Alice Dunbar Nelson. BlSi; CDC; WPOW
I Sit and Wait for Beauty. Mae V. Cowdery. BlSi
I sit at a gold table with my girl. At the Altar. Robert Lowell. *Fr.* Between the Porch and the Altar, IV. InPK
I sit at the top of the tree. Crow Resting. Edward Pygge. BXAP; FaBoPa
I sit beneath the throne of Allah! I, Lord, of All Mortals! *Malay Oral Tradition, tr. by* R. O. Winstedt. WTO
I sit beside my old ship, the timbers rotting. The Old Jason, the Argonaut. Denis Glover. PeNZ
I sit beside my peaceful hearth. The Due of the Dead. Thackeray. OBWP
I sit beside old retired Italians. Park. David Ignatow. Psk
I sit by the mossy fountain; on the top of the hill of winds. James Macpherson. *Fr.* Fragments of Ancient Poetry, Collected in the Highlands of Scotland. NOEC
I sit by the window, reading a book. With a Book at Twilight. Jakov Steinberg. VWA, *tr. by* Mark Elliott Shapiro
I sit clumsy in my flesh, my legs. The Cigarette Poem. Faye Kicknosway. IHMS
I sit down at a table and open a book of poems. Library. Louis Jenkins. NU
I sit down beside my brass lamp. Peeling Pippins. Mary TallMountain. HATNAP
I sit down on the floor of a school for the retarded. He Sits Down on the Floor of a School for the Retarded. Alden Nowlan. GOYP
I sit for my portrait on the veranda. Portrait. Brenda Marie Osbey. MT
I Sit Here. Kumeroa Ngoingoi Pewhairangi, *tr. fr. Maori by* the author. PeNZ
I sit here long, the lamp burns dim. Green Banana Leaves. Yün Shou-p'ing, *tr. by* Jonathan Chaves. CoBLCP
I sit here with affection for the lingering Year. The Year *Hsin-hai* (1551), New Year's Eve. Wen Cheng-ming, *tr. by* Jonathan Chaves. CoBLCP
I sit here with the wind is in my hair. To Helen of Troy (N.Y.). Peter Viereck. WeW
I sit high on this bridge in Laventille. The Spoiler's Return. Derek Walcott. PBCV
I sit idly here. Chikako, *tr. by* Steven D. Carter. WFTW
I sit in a huge auditorium. The Return. Dennis Saleh. NeAC
I sit in an office at 244 Madison Avenue. Spring Comes to Murray Hill. Ogden Nash. FiBHP
I sit in another house whose character is. The House Is Old. Ron Schreiber. GLP
I sit in one of the dives. September 1, 1939. W. H. Auden. CMoP; LiTA; MoAB; MoBrPo; OxBA; PoE; PrIm; WaP
I sit in the dusk. I am all alone. Tableau at Twilight. Ogden Nash. FiBHP
I sit in the top of the wood, my eyes closed. Hawk Roosting. Ted Hughes. CMoP; GTBS-P; HAP; HeIP; LiTM; NePoEA-2; OxBTC; PPP; TwCP; UnPo
I sit musing, ten minutes from the Jap. A Letter for Marian. Thomas McGrath. VGW
I sit on a hard bench in the park. Spot-Check at Fifty. Vernon Scannell. NAs
I sit on a sunstruck wall. Eternal Evening. Sándor Weöres, *tr. by* Jascha Kessler. FOC

I sit on the back platform of the train. The Train Butcher. Thomas Hornsby Ferril. GoYe
I sit on the edge. The Piano. Frank Daley. NOBC
I sit on the ground. Place-of-Many-Swans. Charlotte DeClue. STE
I sit on the surge called ten stories tall. The Seesaw. Oscar Williams. LiTA
I sit pie-eyed all afternoon. Suburban Garden a Nature Reserve. W. G. Shepherd. NPo
I sit thinking of a rowing-boat I saw. The Waiting-Room. Robin Fulton. PoA
I sit waiting for one of two kinds of miracle. Incanto. Stan Rice. NPGG
I Sit with My Dolls. Unknown, tr. fr. Yiddish by Joseph Leftwich. TrJP
I sit with my toes in the brook. Unknown. FaBoNo
I sit with my wine—there's no singing or dancing. Drinking. Chu Yün-ming, tr. by Jonathan Chaves. CoBLCP
I sit within my room and joy to find. The Presence. Jones Very. HAP
I sleep alone; throughout the night. Kaai Chigetsu, tr. fr. Japanese by Hiroaki Sato. Fr. Thirteen Hokku. FCEI
I Sleep, but My Heart Waketh. Bible, O.T. Fr. The Song of Solomon, V: 2-16; VI: 1-3. TrJP
("I sleep but my heart is awake.") BoWoP, ad. by Willis Barnstone, 2–18.
I sleep in your arms. In Your Arms. Miklós Radnóti, tr. by Steven Polgar and Stephen Berg and S. J. Marks. VWA
I Sleep to the Patter of the Rain. Tuomas Anhava, tr. fr. Finnish by Aili Jarvenpa. SOP
I sleep with thee, and wake with thee. To Mary: I Sleep with Thee, and Wake with Thee. John Clare. GBL
(To Mary.) EnLoPo
I slept and dreamed that life was Beauty. Duty. Ellen S. Hooper. BLPA
I slept under rhododendron. Gary Snyder. Fr. Four Poems for Robin. MoP; NNaP; NOBA; NoP; SOTW
(Siwashing It Out Once in Siuslaw Forest.) NoAM
I slip a boiled egg out of its shell. Ozaki Hosai, tr. fr. Japanese by Hiroaki Sato. Fr. One Hundred Haiku in Free Form. FCEI
I slip and I slide. Icy. Rhoda Warner Bacmeister. RAR
I slipped my cap into the cage. Free Quarters. Jacques Prévert, tr. by Michael Benedikt. POS
I slump in the bucket seat. Twink Drives Back, in a Bad Mood, from a Party in Massachusetts. George Amabile. NYBP
I smashed a hot dog into her face. The Hot Dog Poem. Jane Barnes. GLP
I smell lavender in trays late nights when I. Curfew. Bee Bee Tan. ER
I smell the smell. Unknown, tr. fr. Japanese by Geoffrey Bownas and Anthony Thwaite. Fr. Kokin Shu. PeBJV
I Smile, but Oh! My Heart Is Breaking. Mary E. Tucker. CBWP-1
I So Liked Spring. Charlotte Mew. OxBTC
I sometimes feel a cold love burning. Guerrilla. Cosmo Pieterse. WMBCH
I sometimes hold it half a sin. Tennyson. Fr. In Memoriam A. H. H., V. TOF
I sometimes think I'd like to be. The Best of All. Margaret G. Rhodes. BoTP
I sometimes think I'd rather crow. To Be or Not to Be. Unknown. FaBoCo; FaFP; MoShBr; RHPC
I Sometimes Think of the Lamb. Gerald Stern. BLA
I sometimes think that I shall never view. Déjà, Indeed. John Updike. SoTCo
I sought a theme and sought for it in vain. The Circus Animals' Desertion. W. B. Yeats. CMoP; FaBoMo; FaBoTw; LiTB; MAT; MoP; NAEL-2; NAWM-2; NIP; NiP; NoAM; NOBE; NOIV; NoP; OAEL-2; OxBTC; PrIm; TEP
I Sought All Over the World. John Tagliabue. Psk
I sought his love in sun and stars. The Search. Thomas Curtis Clark. WGRP
I sought, I found, she asked me what I would. Rachel Speght. Fr. A Dream. WPE
I sought my death, and found it in the womb. Written the Night Before He Was Beheaded. Chidiock Tichborne. OBD
I sought of bishop and priest and judges. On Christians, Mercy Will Fall. Unknown, tr. by D. Myrddin Lloyd. OBWVE
I sought on earth a garden of delight. George Santayana. Fr. Sonnets. AnAmPo
I sought thee round about, O thou my God! Thomas Heywood. Fr. Hierarchie of the Blessed Angels. WGRP
I Sought with Eager Hand. Allan Dowling. ErPo

I sowed the seeds of love. The Seeds of Love. At. to Mrs. Fleetwood Habergham. FaBoCh; GBP, longer version; OBET; OxBoLi, sl. diff.; WiR
(I Sowed the Seeds of Love.) ELP
I span and Eve span. Eve-Song. Mary Gilmore. CBAP; PoAu-1
I spat up streams of crimson blood. Natsume Soseki, tr. by Burton Watson. JLIC-2
I speak for Erin. The Muse of Amergin. Unknown, tr. by John Montague. BIrV
I Speak, I Say, I Talk. Arnold L. Shapiro. GrPl
I speak now of printers and bookmen. Printers. Denis Glover. PeNZ
I speak of that great house. Beyond the Hunting Woods. Donald Justice. NePoEA; NYBP
I speak of that lady I heard last night. The Lady's Complaint. John Heath-Stubbs. TwCP
I speak of the history of the world. Plain Song Talk. Richard Eberhart. PoA
I speak of walls and chains; of the vials. Terms of Appointment. Arthur Rex Dugard Fairburn. PeNZ
I speak this poem now with grave and level voice. Immortal Autumn. Archibald MacLeish. CMoP; LiTA; MoAB; MoAmPo; NAAL-2; TrGrPo
I speak to him. Shotetsu, tr. by Steven D. Carter. WFTW
I spent a nicht amang the cognoscenti. I Was Fair Beat. Robert Garioch. OxBTC
I spent a night turning in bed. The Whip. Robert Creeley. EOEF; MoP; NaP; NeAP; PoE; PoM
I spent my afternoon like my morning and that was good. 1,000 Illustrations and a Complete Concordance. Michael Andre. UL
I spied a bear/ On the drifting floe. Bear Hunting. Aua. WTO
I spied a very small brown duck. Duck-chasing. Galway Kinnell. TwCP; VGW
I spied John Mouldy in his cellar. John Mouldy. Walter de la Mare. OxBChV; RB
I splashed water on my face. Scholar I. Seamus Deane. NOIV
I spoiled the day. A Wasted Day. Frances Cornford. MoBrPo
I spoke—he said—to the wall, I spoke to the rafters, I shouted "Yes." Augmentation of the Unknown. Yannis Ritsos, tr. by Kimon Friar and Kostas Myrsiades. AnAn
I Spoke the Words of the World. Hans Andreus, tr. fr. Dutch by Johanna H. Prins. DuIn
I spoke with a tangle-haired forester from Saskatchewan. A Summing Up. Gabriel Preil, tr. by Jeremy Garber. VWA
I spoke without caring. Investigation. Julia Vinograd. IHMS
I sport with you. Lord of the River. Unknown, tr. fr. Chinese by Burton Watson. Fr. Nine Songs. CoBCP
I sprang to the rollocks and Jorrocks and me. How I Brought the Good News from Aix to Ghent (or Vice Versa). R. J. Yeatman and W. C. Sellar. BXAP; FaBoPa; FiBHP; OnMSP
I sprang to the stirrup, and Joris, and he. How They Brought the Good News from Ghent to Aix. Robert Browning. BeLS; BLPL; FaBoBe; FaFP; FaPoR; GN; HoPM; NAEL-2
I Spread Out unto Thee My Hands. Henry Ainsworth. AH
I Spy. N. E. Hussey. BoTP
I staid the night for shelter at a farm. See I Stayed. . .
I stand amid the roar. Poe. Fr. A Dream within a Dream. ChTr
I stand and gaze at the tomb. Tanabe Sakimaro. Fr. Manyo Shu. Ma
I stand and listen, head bowed. Self-employed. David Ignatow. NNaP
I stand and watch the rain. Rain and the Tyrants. Jules Supervielle, tr. by David Gascoyne. RHTwFP
I stand as on some mighty eagle's beak. From Montauk Point. Walt Whitman. RFM
I stand before the window that opens. Street Kid. Duane Niatum. STE
I stand before your cage to make my sketch. Artist and Ape. Gordden Link. GoYe
I stand beside the sea and cast. Caught. Gaston Dubois. ASP
I stand by the gate. My Country. Zindzi Mandela. AIW
I stand here every afternoon. The Balloon Man. E. Herbert. BoTP
I stand here in the sight of everyone a man full of sense. The Pretty Redhead. Guillaume Apollinaire, tr. by James Wright. RHTwFP
I stand high in the belfry tower. On the Tower. Annette von Droste-Hülshoff, tr. by James Edward Tobin. PBWP; WPOW
I stand in a looking glass. Island. Ishigaki Rin, tr. by Hiroaki Sato. FCEI
I stand in front of the tree. Pre-Positions. Jose Isaacson, tr. by Yishai Tobin. VWA
I stand in moonlight. The Borning Room. Michael S. Harper. CAPP
I stand in my door and look over the low fields of Drynam. The Widow of Drynam. Patrick MacDonogh. NeIP
I stand in the dark light in the dark street. Birthplace Revisited. Gregory Corso. NeAP; PoM; VGW
I stand in the hall upstairs. Closed Doors. Marie Thorson. PWR

I stand in the late sun. The Reply. Philip Levine. PoA

I Stand in the Midday. Rokhl Korn, *tr. fr. Yiddish by* Seymour Levitan. PeBMYV

I stand in the rain. Chuangtzu Poem No. 6. Park Je-chun, *tr. by* Koh Chang-soo. ACKP

I stand on slenderness all fresh and fair. A Cut Flower. Karl Shapiro. BoNaP; HAP; WeW

I stand on the deck of a small boat as rain sends bright daggers. The Island of Rhum. Roy Ferguson. PoSH

I stand on the first step under the torn mouths of hours. Patience Is When You Stop Waiting. C. K. Williams. CAPP

I stand on the mark beside the shore. The Runaway Slave at Pilgrim's Point. Elizabeth Barrett Browning. BrRo; PoNe

I stand on the porch. Exchanging Glances. William Pitt Root. MAYP

I stand on the tower's high balcony. On the Tower. Annette von Droste-Hülshoff, *tr. by* Ruth Angress. DMG

I stand there slapping a house. The Apprentice Painter. Jack Myers. AmPA

I stand to-day on this historic ground. The National Cemetery, Beaufort, South Carolina. Josephine D. Henderson Heard. CBWP-4

I stand upon a hill and see. A Map of the City. Thom Gunn. NAEL-2; PoE

I stand upon my miracle hill. Miracle Hill. Emerson Blackhorse Mitchell. NOVW

I stand upon the summit of my life. Thalatta! Thalatta! Joseph Brownlee Brown. AA

I stand upon the threshold of two years. Backward—Forward. *Unknown.* BLRP

I stand within the stony, arid town. The City Tree. Isabella Valancy Crawford. CaP

I stand within the willowing shadows of Memp-ch-ton. On Hearing the Marsh Bird's Water Cry. Duane Niatum. CDW

I star in the loam. Deadsong. Don Domanski. NOBC

I stared at the printed words. Printed Words. Liz Sohappy Bahe. CDW

I start awake at night afraid of death. Sonnet 21. Paul Goodman. VGW

I start out for a walk at last after weeks at the desk. After Long Busyness. Robert Bly. CAPP; PoA

I started early, took my dog. Emily Dickinson. AmPP; HAP; InPK; LiTM; MOS; NAAL-1; PoEL-5; WeW
   (By the Sea.) LiTA

I started on the trail of June twenty-third. The Lone Star Trail. *Unknown.* AS

I started out towards evening. Burning Ship. Jaroslav Seifert, *tr. by* Jeffrey Fiskin *and* Erik Vestville. AnAn

I started picking up the stones. Apologia pro Vita Sua. A. R. Ammons. CAPP; HCAP; NOBA

I stay;/ But it isn't as if. An Empty Threat. Robert Frost. RFM

I stay clear. I Have No Strength for Mine. Joanne Kyger. PoM

I stayed [*or* staid] the night for shelter at a farm. The Witch of Coös. Robert Frost. *Fr.* Two Witches. InPS; LiTM; MoAB; MoP; NoAM; NOBA; PoE

I stepped from plank to plank. Emily Dickinson. CMoP; NOBA; NOCV; OxBSP

I stick my tongue in you. Gray Silk Twisting. Patrick Lane. NeAC

I still get the urge. Girl Friday. Elaine Equi. UL

I still have a sister in Guang Dung. The Landlord's Wife. Marilyn Chin. BrSi

I still have this vertical pain under my left shoulder blade. Song for a Little Bit of Breath. Marvin Bell. BLA

I still remember Conch-Shell Slope, west of the River Tzu. Hsieh Chin, *tr. fr. Chinese by* Jonathan Chaves. *Fr.* In Grief, Lamenting for My Elder Brother Ts'ang-ch. CoBLCP

I still remember our first games. Letter to a Sister Who Lives in a Distant Country. Daisy Zamora, *tr. by* Barbara Paschke. Vol

I still remember the time at the mountain hut. A Painting of Yams. Yün Shou-p'ing, *tr. by* Jonathan Chaves. CoBLCP

I stirred wet sand and gathered myself. Seamus Heaney. *Fr.* Sweeney Redivivus. NoAM

I Stole Brass. *Unknown.* ChTr

I stole the prince and I brought him here. The Grand Inquisitor's Song. W. S. Gilbert. *Fr.* The Gondoliers. OnMSP

I stole through the dungeons, while everyone slept. Alternative Endings to an Unwritten Ballad. Paul Dehn. FiBHP

I stood among the wanting many. Just Making It. Richard W. Thomas. PoNe

I stood and leant upon the mast. The Voyage. Heine, *tr. by* John Todhunter. AWP

I stood and watched him dig one hole all day. Robert Frost's Left-leaning *Trespassers Will Be Shot* Sign. William Zaranka. BXAP

I stood aside to let the cows. Man and Cows. Andrew Young. EBEV

I stood at eve, as the sun went down, by a grave where a woman lies. 'Ostler Joe. George R. Sims. BeLS; BLPA

"I stood at the back of the shop, my dear." At the Draper's. Thomas Hardy. *Fr.* Satires of Circumstance, XII. BrPo; MoAB; MoBrPo; OBD

I stood beside a hill. February Twilight. Sara Teasdale. FaPON; OBCA; PDV; RHPC

I stood between them. Near Anahorish. Seamus Heaney. PPR

I stood between two mirrors when you died. William Jay Smith. NePoEA

I stood by Honor and the Dean. Sahara. Coventry Patmore. *Fr.* The Angel in the House. EBVV

I stood by the bars at evening. By the Pasture Bars. George Sands Johnson. PWR

I stood in a meadow. Green Valley. Dorothy Vena Johnson. PoNe

I stood in front of City Lights. City Lights: I Took That Picture. Steve Albert. PPR

I Stood in Jerusalem. Zelda, *tr. fr. Hebrew by* Marcia Falk. VWA

I stood in the gloom of a spacious room. Awake, My Lute! C. S. Lewis. CenHV; FaBoNo

I Stood in the Maytime Meadows. *Unknown.* TTTS

I stood in the ride, and the glamour. My Woodcock. Patrick Reginald Chalmers. CenHV

I stood in the shelter of a great tree. Tumbleweed. Ramona Carden. NOVW

I stood in Venice on the Bridge of Sighs. Byron. *Fr.* Childe Harold's Pilgrimage, IV. EnRP, *abr.;* OBTV, *abr..*
   (On the Bridge of Sighs.) FaBoPP, 4 *sts.*

I Stood on a Tower in the Wet. Tennyson. OxBSP

I stood on Brocken's sovereign height, and saw. Lines Written in the Album at Elbingerode, in the Hartz Forest. Samuel Taylor Coleridge. OBTV

I stood on the bridge at midnight. *Unknown.* FaFP

I stood still and was a tree amid the wood. The Tree. Ezra Pound. CMoP

I Stood Tiptoe [upon a Little Hill], *sels.* Keats. EnRP; FaPON
   Minnows. GN
   "Sometimes goldfinches one by one will drop." PBBP
   (Goldfinches.) GN
   Sweet Peas. GN

I stood today on a mound of clay. Created Clay. Maimee Lee Brown. PWR

I Stood upon a High Place. Stephen Crane. *Fr.* The Black Riders, IX. LiTA

I stood watching the great hulk of desire. Coming Back. Linda Gregg. NPGG

I stood with three comrades in Parliament Square. Armistice Day. Charles Causley. NAEL-2; OBWP

I stood within the City disinterred. At Pompeii. Shelley. *Fr.* Ode to Naples. FaBoPP

I stood within the cypress gloom. Implora Pace. Charles Lotin Hildreth. AA

I Stood within the Heart of God. William Vaughn Moody. *Fr.* The Fire-Bringer. AH
   (Pandora Speaks.) WGRP

I stoop to gather a seabird's feather. The Feather. Vernon Watkins. FaBoTw

I stooped to the silent Earth and lifted a handful of her dust. A Handful of Dust. James Oppenheim. TrJP

I stop for a short rest at the wine seller's west of the city. Leaving the City. Liu K'o-chuang, *tr. by* Burton Watson. CoBCP

I stop my boat on the pure Ssu. Mooring My Boat on the Ssu River and Watching the Moon. Wen Cheng-ming, *tr. by* Jonathan Chaves. CoBLCP

I Stopped along the Road to Look at the Old House of Lord Minamoto. Michizane, *tr. fr. Chinese by* Burton Watson. JLIC-1

I stopped deep. African in Louisiana. Kojo Gyinaye Kyei. PBA

I stopped in a sidestreet surplus shop, just south of Yorkville. The Cot. Grover Amen. NYBP

I stopped over at a motel on E3. The Gallery. Tomas Tranströmer, *tr. by* Samuel Charters. AnAn

I stopped to pick up the bagel. The Bagel. David Ignatow. CAPP; FF; TwCP

I strayed about the deck, an hour, to-night. Rupert Brooke. BrPo

I strayed, all alone, where the Autumn. A Rose in October. James Whitcomb Riley. OBAL

I strayed along the strand with mussels strewn. Along the Strand. Alfred Mombert, *tr. by* Jethro Bithell. TrJP

I stretch out flat to the horizon. Before They Made Things Be Alive They Spoke. Lucario Cuevish, *tr. by* Jerome Rothenberg. STP

I string shells. Shells. Lorna Dee Cervantes. CCP

I Stroll. Peter Redgrove. NePoEA-2

I strolled across/ An open field. The Waking. Theodore Roethke. RFM; TTS

I strolled beside the shining sea. The Cumberbunce. Paul West. NA

I strove with all, for all were worth my strife. Epitaph for G. B. Shaw. Max Beerbohm. FaBoEE

I Strove with None. Walter Savage Landor. *Fr.* The Last Fruit Off an Old Tree. ChTr; EnRP; FaPoR; NOBE; OBNC
  (Dying Speech of an Old Philosopher.) FaBoEE; GTBS-P; HeIP; NOBVV; NoP
  (End, The.) SeCePo
  (Finis.) OBEV
  (On His Seventy-fifth Birthday.) AWP; BLPL; EBEV; LiTB; OAEL-2; TrGrPo

I struck for what I deemed the right. After the Battle. George Sylvester Viereck. GoYe

I struck out at its legs and arms. Demons. Aimé Césaire, *tr.* by Michael Benedikt. POS

I struck the board, and cried [or cry'd] : No more. The Collar. George Herbert. AWP; BLPL; EaLo; EBEV; HAP; HeIP; InPS; JCP; LiTB; MeLP; MePo; NAEL-2; NOBE; NOCV; NoP; OAEL-1; OBS; OBWVE; PoE; PoEL-2; PoRA; PPP; SCV; SeCePo; SeCP; SeCV-1; TEP; TOF; TrGrPo; WeW

I struck tomorrow square in the face. Hidesong. Aig Higo. TTY

I studied my tables over and over. A Mortifying Mistake. Anna Maria Pratt. AA

I study out a dark similitude. The Swan. Theodore Roethke. VGW

I study the lives on a leaf: the little. The Minimal. Theodore Roethke. HCAP; MoP; NoAM; NOBA; RB; TSS

I Substitute for the Dead Lecturer. Amiri Baraka. NAAL-2; NOBA; PoE

I suck deep in air come from Provence to here. Peire Vidal, *tr.* by Paul Blackburn. Pro

I suddenly saw I was wrang when I felt. Deep-Sea Fishing. "Hugh MacDiarmid." SeCePo

I suffer, being ruled by poetry and books. Self-Ridicule. Yüan Mei, *tr.* by Anthony C. Yu. WFTU

I suffer enough, now it would all be the same. Teika, *tr. fr. Japanese by* Hiroaki Sato. *Fr.* A Compendium of Good Tanka. FCEI

I suffered so much from printer's errors. The Author's Epitaph. *Unknown.* FiBHP

I summon something. The Day Glo Question of Identity. Jeffrey Miller. UL

I summon the landslide. Thirst. Jacques Dupin, *tr.* by Auster. RHTwFP

I summon to the winding ancient stair. A Dialogue of Self and Soul. W. B. Yeats. CMoP; FaBoMo; LiTB; LiTM; MoBrPo; NAEL-2; NoAM; PoE

I sundry see, for beauty's gloss. That He Findeth Others as Fair, but Not So Faithful as His Friend. George Turberville. EIL

I supped where bloomed the red rose. Supper. Walter De la Mare. NYBP

I suppose it's because we're on foot I'm reminded. Kyran's Christening. Alden Nowlan. NeAC

I suspect. Blue Stones. Larry Levis. DiL

I suspect he knew that trunks are metaphors. Houdini. Eli W. Mandel. NOBC

I swam the Huron of love, and am not ashamed. The Huron. Ruth Herschberger. WPE

I swear by what the sages spoke. Crazy Bill to the Bishop. Robert Peters. BXAP

I swear I ain't done what Richard. Say Hello to John. Sherley Anne Williams. BISi

I swear I don't even remember her name. Forgetfulness. Nicanor Parra, *tr.* by Lynn C. Jacox. LPSS

I sweep the street and lift me hat. The Old Man at the Crossing. Strong. OBMV

I swept and ended up not sweeping. Taigi, *tr. fr. Japanese by* Hiroaki Sato. *Fr.* Twenty-nine Hokku. FCEI

I swing up on the sideboard of the old car. Almost Grown. Ai. MAYP

I switch on the light. Crickets tick. Sleep in the Heat. Laura Jensen. AmPA; AnAn

I swore I would go back. O Lyric Love. Winfield Townley Scott. VGW

I swore to stab the sonnet with my pen. Karl Shapiro. *Fr.* White-haired Lover. PoA

I swung and swung at empty air. The Abominable Baseball Bat. X. J. Kennedy. WSC

I syng of a mayden that is makeles. I Sing of a Maiden. *Unknown.* CH; EBEV; ELP; FaBoCh; FF; InPS; LiTB; MeEL; NOBE; NOCV; NoP; OAEL-1; OxBLMV; PoEL-1; SCV; TrGrPo. *See also* I Sing of a Maiden.

I tackle my father so hard. Touch Football. Jack Driscoll. TSL

I take as my theme, "The Independent Woman." Carolyn Kizer. *Fr.* Pro Femina, II. MAT; NMM

I take down the old guitar from the wall. The Old Guitar. John Hollander. DiPo

I take four devils with me when I ride. Gervase Stewart. WaP

I take him down upon the beach. Son and Surf. Julia Hurd Strong. GoYe

I? Take immortality? Were it offered. Imitation of Intimations. Timoshenko Aslanides. UAS

I take it he doesn't think at all. The Pike. John Bruce. SD

I take it you already know. Hints on Pronunciation for Foreigners. *Unknown.* FaBoUs

I take my chaperon to the play. The Chaperon. H. C. Bunner. AA; AnAmPo

I take my old clothes out of the cupboard and deck. My Best Clothes. Eli Netser. MHeP, *tr.* by Bernhard Frank

I take my son outside. What I Tell Him. Simon J. Ortiz. CDW

I take off my shirt, I show you. Taking Off My Clothes. Carolyn Forché. AmPA; AnAn; NoAM

I take the dogs into. La Bagarède. Galway Kinnell. NYBP

I take the twist-about, empty street. The Rendezvous. Bernard Spencer. GTBS-P

I Take Thee Life. Margot Ruddock. OBMV

I take their hands. They. R. S. Thomas. OxBTC

I take you by the hand. Your eyes. Goodbye to Brigid / An Agnus Dei. Padraic Fiacc. CIP

I take you looking at the statue. The Statue. Kenneth Allott. EAS

I takes and paints. Poem by a Perfectly Furious Academician. Shirley Brooks. FiBHP; NOBVV

I takes up for my colored men. The Generation Gap. Ruby C. Saunders. BISi

I talk and no one listens. Doubt. Pat Nolan. UL

I talk through my mouth with many tongues. Riddle: Nightingale. *Unknown.* PBBP

I talk to my inner lover, and I say, why such rush? The Radiance. Kabir, *tr.* by Robert Bly. LLLT

I talked one midnight with the jolly ghost. All in a Garden Green. W. E. Henley. OBMV

I Talked to a Frenchman. Adam Zagajewski, *tr. fr. Polish by* Antony Graham. PwPP

I talked to old Lem. Old Lem. Sterling A. Brown. BPo; FB; IDB; PoBA; PoNe; TTY

I tangled with. Extrication. A. R. Ammons. CAPP

I tarry in days shaped like the high staired street. A Birthday Memorial to Seventh Street. Audre Lorde. CNA

I taste a draught beer never brewed. Emily's Haunted Housman. David Cummings. BXAP

I taste a liquor never brewed. Emily Dickinson. AmPP; CMoP; FaBV; FF; HeIP; LiTA; LiTM; MoAmPo; NAAL-1; NoAM; NOBA; NoP; OxBA; PoEL-5; SoSe; TAP; WPE

I taught myself to live simply and wisely. "Anna Akhmatova," *tr.* by Richard McKane. PBWP

I teach-a bird an' I blow-a da ring. The Educated Love Bird. Peter Newell. FiBHP

I teach how we cheat the young. A 4 Part Geometry Lesson. Robin Blaser. NeAP

I tell him how it used to be in Paguate. Harold Littlebird. *Fr.* After the Pow-Wow. STE

I tell my secret? No indeed, not I. Winter: My Secret. Christina Rossetti. BrRo; NAEL-2; NOBVV; TEP

I tell myself not to doubt you. From Prince Atsumichi. Lady Izumi, *tr. fr. Japanese by* Hiroaki Sato. *Fr.* Fifty-one Tanka. FCEI

I Tell of Another Young Death. César Tiempo, *tr. fr. Spanish by* Donald Devenish Walsh. TrJP

I tell Therese. Therese. Alden Nowlan. NeAC

I tell words that talk in trees, this hill. Pot Shot. Padraic Fallon. CIP

I tell ye, Sue, it ain't no use! Goin' Back T'morrer. Hamlin Garland. OBAL

I tell yeh whut! The chankin'. Horses Chawin' Hay. Hamlin Garland. OBAL

I tell you, hopeless grief is passionless. Grief. Elizabeth Barrett Browning. FPL; HeIP; InPK; NOBVV; OBEV; OBNC; PoLF; TrGrPo; WPE

I tell you how dat hypocrite do. That Hypocrite. *Unknown.* BPo

I tell you, Lesbia, life is love. Catullus to Lesbia. James Reeves. ErPo

I tell you that I see her still. I Only Am Escaped Alone to Tell Thee. Howard Nemerov. CoAP; HeIP; NoAM

I term tobacco that which is ear. Who Is It. Benjamin Péret, *tr.* by Michael Benedikt. POS

I tethered my horse beside the plum blossoms. From Chekiang I Went to Hsin-an. Hsü Wei, *tr.* by Jonathan Chaves. CoBLCP

I Thank God I'm Free at Las'. *Unknown.* BPo; TAP

I thank the, Lord so dere, that wold vowchsayf. *Unknown. Fr.* Noah. PoE

I thank thee and I praise thee, O thou radiant grace. Thanksgiving. "Yehoash," *tr.* by Isidore Goldstick. TrJP

I Thank Thee, Lord. *Unknown.* BLRP; WBLP

I thank you, dear blessed mother. Mother's Birthday. Lydia Wagenlander. PWR

I thank you for the many steps. Dear Mother. Ebba M. Leaf. PWR

I Thank You God for Most This Amazing. E. E. Cummings. EaLo; MoAB; TAP

(I Thank You God.) TrCP

I that had found the way so smooth. The Return. Jessie Fauset. CDC

I that in heill wes [*or* health was] and gladnes[s]. Lament for the Makaris. William Dunbar. ACP; ChTr; EBEV; GoTS; HAP; NoP; OxBS

(Fear of Death Confounds Me, The.) MeEL

(Lament for the Makers.) OAEL-1; OBEV; PoEL-1

(Timor Mortis Conturbat Me.) FaBoRV; NOBE, *abr.*

I that lived ever about you. English Girl. *Unknown, tr.* by E. Powys Mathers. OBMV

I that whilom lived secure. A Testament. *Unknown.* OBSC

I, the bosun's mate, John Reading. Death of the Bosun's Mate. Louis Johnson. PeNZ

I' the how-dumb-deid o' the cauld hairst nicht. The Eemis-Stane. "Hugh MacDiarmid." NAEL-2

I, the old woman of Beare. The Old Woman of Beare Regrets Lost Youth. *Unknown, tr.* by Frank O'Connor. AnIL; OBMV

I the People. Alice Notley. UL

I, the poet William Yeats. To Be Carved on a Stone at Thoor Ballylee. W. B. Yeats. FaBoEE; NoAM; NoP

I, therefore, will begin. Soul of the age! Ben Jonson. *Fr.* To the Memory of My Beloved Master William Shakespeare [and What He Hath Left Us]. NOBE

I Think. James Schuyler. TTTS

I think a lot about it. Around the Rough and Rugged Rocks the Ragged Rascal Rudely Ran. John Ashbery. InPS

I think a time will come when you will understand. For My Father. Paul Potts. FaBoTw

I Think about the Dead Woman in a Poem. Marie-Francoise Prager, *tr. fr. French* by Carl Hermy. DMF

I think about you & it's like having spirits come down on me. Yuwaku, *tr.* by James Koller. STP

I think all this is somewhere in myself. The Room. W. S. Merwin. NaP; NOBA

I think and think again:—What thinks the goose. The Difference. Guido Gozzano, *tr.* by Carol L. Golino. PFI

I think at a distance I hear a loud voice. The Missionary. Mrs. Henry Linden. CBWP-4

I think between my cradle-bars. Ballade of Faith. Tom MacInnes. CaP

I Think Continually of Those Who Were Truly Great. Stephen Spender. ChTr; CMoP; EaLo; HAP; HeIP; LiTB; LiTM; MoAB; MoBrPo; NOBE; NoP; OAEL-2; OxBTC; PoRA; TrGrPo; WaP

I think flowers can see. Thoughts of a Little Girl. María Enriqueta, *tr.* by Emma Gutiérrez Suárez. FaPON

I think God sang when He had made. The Star. Beatrice Redpath. CaP

I think he sits at that strange table. At It. R. S. Thomas. OxBC

I think I am becoming. Interior Monologue 666. Tom Marshall. NOBC

I think I could turn and live with animals. Walt Whitman. *Fr.* Song of Myself, XXXII. HAP; NU; PDV; TrGrPo; WeW; WGRP

(Animals.) FaFP

I think I grow tensions. The Flower. Robert Creeley. CAPP

I think I have no other home than this. Old Memories of Earth. R. A. K. Mason. ATNZ; PeNZ

I think I heard the belle. The Old Lady's Lament for Her Youth. Villon, *tr.* by Robert Lowell. BoLoP

I Think I Know No Finer Things than Dogs. Hally Carrington Brent. BLPA

I think I like it here, I mean I think. Somewhere on the Coast of Maine. Robert Long. NAmP

I think I remember this moorland. We Have Been Here Before. Morris Bishop. FiBHP; NYBP

I think I see her sitting bowed and black. Oriflamme. Jessie Redmond Fauset. BANP; BlSi; PoBA

I Think I See Him There. Waring Cuney. CDC

I think I shall end by not feeling lonesome. Street Cries. Marjorie Welish. EOEF

I Think I Should Have Loved You Presently. Edna St. Vincent Millay. NAAL-2

I think I sing that little song. Union Man. Albert Morgan. AmFP

I think I smell smoke. Il Janitoro. George Ade. OBAL

I think I understand today how she could come to love it best. Ravel and Unravel. Jorie Graham. BLA

"I think I want some pies this morning." Greedy Richard. Jane Taylor. OxBChV

I think if I lay dying in some land. The Harbour. Winifred M. Letts. TIRV

I think if I should cross the room. The Room's Width. Elizabeth Stuart Phelps Ward. AA

I think if you had loved me when I wanted. Success. Rupert Brooke. OxBTC

I think I'll die. Masaoka Shiki, *tr. fr. Japanese* by Burton Watson. *Fr.* Thirty-nine Haiku. FCEI

I think I'll get a paper. Nerves. "Sagittarius." OxBTC

I think I'll wash my testicles with care. *Unknown, tr.* by Hiroaki Sato. FCEI

I think in fours. Thought. Fazil Hüsnü Daglarca. CRP

I think it better that in times like these. On Being Asked for a War Poem. W. B. Yeats. NIP; OBWP

I think it is a funny thing. Humming Birds. Betty Sage. RAR

I think it is all light at the end; I think it is air. The Quilt. Larry Levis. MAYP

I think it is in Virginia, that place. Low Fields and Light. W. S. Merwin. LCAP

I think it is over, over. In Harbor. Paul Hamilton Hayne. AA; AnAmPo

I think it quite a charming myth. Monkeys. Frank A. Collymore. PBCV

I think it's very funny. How a Puppy Grows. Leroy F. Jackson. RAR

I think it's worth it today. Souster. Ray Fraser. NeAC

I think mice. Mice. Rose Fyleman. BoTP; FaPON; NTCP; PDV; RAR; RHPC

I think now of latitudes solitary, Asian, and velvet. In a Valley of this Restless Mind. Ewart Milne. NeIP

I think of a flower that no eye has ever seen. Beauty. Laurence Binyon. MoBrPo

I think of all the galloping. Johnny's Team. Eugene Field. PWR

I think of all the things at school. Johnny's Hist'ry Lesson. Nixon Waterman. FPL; PoLF

I think of Amundsen, enormously bit. On the Eyes of an SS Officer. Richard Wilbur. CAPP

I think of corner shots, the ball. Day and Night Handball. Stephen Dunn. AmPA

I think of flowers and birds. Miura Chora, *tr. fr. Japanese* by Hiroaki Sato. *Fr.* Sixteen Hokku. FCEI

I think of God. The Hairs in My Nose. Aram Boyajian. NeAC

I think of him/ Who lives south of the big sea. *Unknown, tr.* by Wai-lim Yip. BoWoP

I Think of Housman Who Said the Poem Is a Morbid Secretion, like a Pearl. Judith Kroll. UnPo

I think of Issa, a man of few words. Night Journal. Charles Wright. BLA

I think of my name, Julia Grahm. Waiting for Winter. George Keithley. NPGG

I think of my wife, and I think of Lot. Marriage Couplet. William Cole. OBAL

I Think of Oblivion. Yehuda Amichai, *tr. fr. Hebrew* by Ruth Nevo. VWA

I think of the Celts as rather a whining lady. The Celts. Stevie Smith. NoP

I think of the sea changing and changing. Marina. O. B. Hardison, Jr. AiP; CRP

I think of the tribes: the women prized for fatness. The Tribes. Roy Fuller. LiTM

I think of the unknowing art my watching made. Voyeur. John Edward Hardy. ErPo

I think of things like the shadow of a branch. The Shadow of a Branch. Edith Marcombe Shiffert. WPE

I Think of Those. Paul Henderson. ATNZ

I think of when she comes. Shen Yüeh, *tr. fr. Chinese* by Burton Watson. *Fr.* Six Poems on Remembering. CoBCP

I think of when she sits. Shen Yüeh, *tr. fr. Chinese* by Burton Watson. *Fr.* Six Poems on Remembering. CoBCP

I think of when she sleeps. Shen Yüeh, *tr. fr. Chinese* by Burton Watson. *Fr.* Six Poems on Remembering. CoBCP

I think, old bone, the world's not with us much. To William Wordsworth from Virginia. Julia Randall. NMM; WPE

I think she sleeps: it must be sleep, when low. George Meredith. *Fr.* Modern Love, XV. NAEL-2

I think some saint of Eirinn wandering far. Fuchsia Hedges in Connacht. Padraic Colum. TIRV

I think sometimes. Blue Waves. David St. John. MAYP

I Think Table. Linda Pastan. ER
I think that I am drawing to an end. Barry Pain. *Fr.* The Poets at Tea, II. Par
I think that I live in a street. For the Record. George Jonas. MoCV
I think that I shall never make. In a Garden. Donald Campbell Babcock
I think that I shall never see/ A billboard. Song of the Open Road. Ogden Nash. AnAmPo; FaBoCo; FPL; OBAL
I think that I shall never see/ a poem. Fleas. Philip Appleman. SoTCo
I think that I shall never see/ A poem. Trees. Joyce Kilmer. BLPA; FaBoBe; FaFP; FaPON; FPL; OHFP; WBLP; WGRP
I think that I shall never ski. Winter Trees. Conrad Diekmann. SD
I think that I shall never view. Teresa's Red Adidas. Paul B. Janeczko. TDD
I think that is some faery spirit strewed. The Salesman. Robert Mezey. NePoEA
I think that look of Christ might seem to say. The Meaning of the Look. Elizabeth Barrett Browning. TrCP
I think that man hath made no beauteous thing. To Melody. George Leonard Allen. CDC
I think that night's our balance. Suite to Fathers. Jim Harrison. AmPA; DiL
I think that the root of the wind is water. Emily Dickinson. RB
I think that we retain of our dead friends. Remembrance. John Henry Boner. AA
I think the dead are tender. Shall we kiss? She. Theodore Roethke. BoLoP; ErPo; NIP
I think the dead lie hungry in the dark. The Hungry Dead. Jim Wayne Miller. MT
I think the gentle soul of him. Ilicet. Theodosia Pickering Garrison. PoLF
I think the loathed minutes one by one. Moments. Ivor Gurney. OxBSP
I think the May rains. Onitsura, *tr. fr. Japanese by* Hiroaki Sato. *Fr.* Twenty-three Hokku. FCEI
I Think the New Teacher's a Queer. Perry Brass. PeHV
I think the thing you call Renown. Winthrop Mackworth Praed. *Fr.* The Chaunt of the Brazen Head. OBSV
I think, therefore I am, said a man whose mother quickly. The Philosophers. Russell Edson. NAmP
I think they had no pattern. Beside the Line of Elephants. Edna Becker. RHPC
"I think," thought Sam Butler. English Liberal. Geoffrey Taylor. FaBoEE
I think today. Runaway. William Wise. RAR
I think when Judas' mother heard. Judas Iscariot. Countee Cullen. PoLF
I think you're bashful. The First Date. David Avidan, *tr. fr. Hebrew by* Warren Bargad *and* Stanley F. Chyet. *Fr.* Samson, Our Hero, 3. IP
I thirst, but not as once I did. My Soul Thirsts for God. William Cowper. TrCP
I thirst for God, to Him my soul aspires. The Living God. Abraham Ibn Ezra, *tr. by* Alice Lucas. TrJP
I thirst for violins, as drunkards thirst. Ideal and Reality. Joseph Campbell. BIrV
I thought a life of solitude was in the cards. Love's Will. Lewis Warsh. UL
I thought he was dumb. Tortoise Shout. D. H. Lawrence. LiTM; NAEL-2
I thought I had found a swan. Denise Levertov. LLLT
I thought I saw a turnoff for Word Processing. Passing the Corporate Forest. Michael McFee. SoTCo
I thought I saw an angel flying low. Nocturne at Bethesda. Arna Bontemps. AmNP; BANP; CDC; PoNe
I thought I saw buffalo. *Unknown, tr. fr.* Sioux Indian by James Koller. *Fr.* Sioux Metamorphoses. STP
I thought I was growing wings. Seeing for a Moment. Denise Levertov. CAPP
I thought I was so tough. Tamer and Hawk. Thom Gunn. FaBoTw; NePoEA
I thought I woke: the midnight sun. Paul Goodman. PoA
I thought I would wear it. *Unknown. Fr.* Manyo Shu. Ma
I thought I'd win the spelling bee. Banananananananana. William Cole. RHPC
I thought if only I could marry. Unfair to Women. *Unknown, tr. by* Gwyn Jones. OBWVE
I thought it made me look more "working class." Turns. Tony Harrison. *Fr.* The School of Eloquence. NAEL-2; NoAM
I thought it was mist. Tamehide, *tr. by* Steven D. Carter. WFTW
I Thought It Was Tangiers I Wanted. Langston Hughes. PoNe
I thought it would last my time. Going, Going. Philip Larkin. NoAM
I Thought Myself to be Guest. Gerhard Fritsch, *tr. fr. German by* Beth Bjorklund. CoAuP

I thought of cards along the mantelpiece. December Fragments. Richmond Lattimore. PChr
I thought of Chatterton, the marvellous Boy. We Poets in Our Youth. Wordsworth. *Fr.* Resolution and Independence. FaBoRV
I thought of the delicate things he had said. The Boy and the Dream. Anna Wickham. AIW
I thought of Thee, my partner and my guide. Wordsworth. *Fr.* The River Duddon, XXXIV. FaBoRV
    (After-Thought.) EnRP; OBNC; SeCePo
    (To the River Duddon: After-Thought.) FaBoPP
    (Valediction to the River Duddon.) NOBE
    (Valedictory Sonnet to the River Duddon.) OBEV
I thought once how Theocritus had sung. Elizabeth Barrett Browning. *Fr.* Sonnets from the Portuguese, I. EBVV; GBL; NOBE; NoP; OBEV; OBNC; WPE
I thought Silver must have snaked logs. Silver. A. R. Ammons. NoP
I thought that I knew all there was to know. Small, Smaller. Russell Hoban. TDD; TSS
I thought that Love had been a boy. *Unknown.* EnLoPo
I thought the dawn would flush to sudden glory. Mountain Vigil. Douglas Fraser. PoSH
I thought the earth. Sleeping in the Forest. Mary Oliver. CAPP; InPS; NU
I thought the night without a sound was falling. William Force Stead. *Fr.* Uriel. TrPWD
    (How Infinite Are Thy Ways.) OBMV
I thought there could be. Princess Hirokawa. *Fr.* Manyo Shu. Ma
I Thought There Were Limits. Douglas G. Jones. MoCV
I thought this morning of my yellowed Juliette cap. The Moon Pond. Medbh McGuckian. FaBCIP
I thought to die that night in the solitude. The Edge. Lola Ridge. OnYI
I thought to make. Masaoka Shiki, *tr. by* Geoffrey Bownas *and* Anthony Thwaite. PeBJV
I Thought to Spend My Time. Claribel Alegría, *tr. fr. Spanish by* Darwin J. Flakoll. DMH
I thought you always knew it well. One Way of Looking at It. Arthur Munby. NOBVV
I thought you loved me. *Zulu Oral Tradition, tr. by* H. Tracey. WTO
"I thought you loved me." "No, it was only fun." In the Orchard. Muriel Stuart. ErPo; FF; OxBTC
I thought you were good. Divorce Song. *Unknown, tr. by* Carl Cary. STP
I threw a penny in the air. *Unknown.* CenHV
I threw the inside of my gizzard out, splashing. Zimmer Drunk and Alone, Dreaming of Old Football Games. Paul Zimmer. MAT
I thrive on youth and joy. Beatrice, Countess de Die, *tr. by* Meg Bogin. WT
I, through all chances that are given to mortals. To Ausonius. Paulinus of Nola, *tr. by* Helen Waddell. PeHV
I throw off all the ceremony. Yom Kippur. Eric Chaet. VWA
I throw open the door. April Fourth. Robert Mezey. NaP
I throw things away. Old Bibles. Marilyn Nelson Waniek. MAYP
I thumped on you the best I could. W. D. Snodgrass. *Fr.* Heart's Needle, VIII. NePoEA; NoAM
I, thy humble subject. Ama-no-Inukai Okamaro. *Fr.* Manyo Shu. Ma
I, thy servant, full of sighs, cry unto thee. Penitential Psalm. *Unknown.* WGRP
I-Tie-All-My-People-Together. Michelle Cliff. ER
I tink I hear my brudder say. Stars Begin to Fall. *Unknown.* AA
I to My Perils. A. E. Housman. ViBoPo; WeW
I to the hills lift up mine eyes. Bible, *O.T. See* Psalms: Psalm CXXI ("I will lift up mine eyes unto the hills").
I to the hills lift up mine eyes. *Unknown. Fr.* The Bay Psalm Book. OBCA
I to the Hills Will Lift Mine Eyes. Francis Rous. AH
I to the Lord from My Distress. *Unknown.* AH
I Told Jesus. Sterling Plumpp. PoBA
I told my son. Saul's Progress. Harvey Shapiro. DiL
I told myself in singing words. As It Was. Lilla Cabot Perry. *Fr.* Meeting after Long Absence, II. AA
I told the Sun that I was glad. The Sun. John Drinkwater. FaPON; NTCP
I told the water god on my hill to let the snow fall. Emperor Temmu. *Fr.* Manyo Shu. FCEI
I tongue-lashed wind and rain. Daio, *tr. by* Lucien Stryk *and* Takashi Ikemoto. ZPCJ
I, Too. Langston Hughes. AmNP; CDC; FF; HCAP; HeIP; OPP
I too/ grew up the same way. Observing Children. Saigyo, *tr. fr. Japanese by* Burton Watson. *Fr.* Sixty-four Tanka. FCEI
I too am a continent. Woman Undiscovered. Gertrud Kolmar, *tr. by* Henry A. Smith. DMG

I Too beneath Your Moon, Almighty Sex. Edna St. Vincent Millay. NAAL-2

I, too, dislike it: there are things that are important beyond all this fiddle. Poetry. Marianne Moore. AmPP; BLPL; BoWoP; CMoP; FaBoWP; FF; HAP; HeIP; LiTA; LiTM; MoAB; MoAmPo; MoP; NAAL-2; NIP; NoAM; NOBA; NoP; OxBA; PoE; TAP; UnPo; ViBoPo

I, too, have plucked a stalk of grass. Ronald Johnson. *Fr.* Letters to Walt Whitman, V. VGW

I, too, in my day. *Unknown, tr. by* Geoffrey Bownas *and* Anthony Thwaite. PeBJV

I, Too, Know What I Am Not. Bob Kaufman. NBP

I, too, once spouted yards of poetry, and rushed. Shadow Shadow. Roger Weingarten. NAmP

I, too, saw God through mud. Apologia pro Poemate Meo. Wilfred Owen. FaBoRV; LiTM; MoAB; MoBrPo; NAEL-2

I, too, sing America. I, Too. Langston Hughes. AmNP; CDC; FF; HCAP; HeIP; OPP

(I, Too, Sing America.) IDB; PoBA; PoLF; PoNe

I too was a little child once. Joseph Eliyia, *tr. by* Rae Dalven. VWA

I too was born out of a lion's mouth. Let Heroes Account to Love. Alan Dugan. NoAM

I too when I die do not wish. Poem for Dr. Spock. Ed Ochester. SoTCo

I took/ a coney island of the mind. Clickety-Clack. Paul Blackburn

I took a day to search for God. Vestigia. Bliss Carman. CaP; WGRP

I took a piece of plastic clay. Sculpture. *Unknown.* BLPL; PoLF

I took a piece of the rare cloth of Ch'i. A Present from the Emperor's New Concubine. Lady Pan, *tr. by* Kenneth Rexroth. BoWoP

I took away three pictures. Sandhill People. Carl Sandburg. CMoP

I took leave of my beloved one evening: how I wish. At Taliq, *tr. fr. Arabic by* A. R. Nykl. PeHV

I took money and bought flowering trees. Planting Flowers on the Eastern Embankment. Po Chü-i, *tr. by* Arthur Waley. BoNaP

I took my girl to a fancy ball. I Had But Fifty Cents. *Unknown.* BeLS; BLPA; NBLV

I took my girlfriend to your last poetry reading. Short Order. Charles Bukowski. HoPM

I took my heart in my hand. Twice. Christina Rossetti. GBL; NOBE; OBEV; OBNC; TOF; TrCP; ViBoPo

I took my oath I would inquire. The Inquest. W. H. Davies. GTBS-P; NOBE; OxBTC; RB

I took off down the town's disaster route. Soliloquy in a Motel. Walker Gibson. GrPl

I took one small breath to lift her. The Minyan. Jack Myers. VWA

I took the last. What Came to Me. Jane Kenyon. PPR

I took up the burden of life anew. To My Mother. Mary Weston Fordham. CBWP-2

I tossed my friend a wreath of roses, wet. Gifts. Mary Elizabeth Coleridge. PBWP

I touch and recollect. Tiresias' Lament. Ellen de Young Kay. NePoEA

I touch jig-saw fragments. A. L. Hendricks. *Fr.* D'Où Venons Nous? Que Sommes Nous? Où Allons No. PBCV

I touch you in the night, whose gift was you. The Science of the Night. Stanley Kunitz. MoAmPo; TwCP

I touch your face. Poems of Night. Galway Kinnell. NaP

I touched a shining mote of sand. Philip Child. CaP

I touched the flesh with my eyes. Fish. Joe Rosenblatt. NOBC

I touched the nothingness of air once. I Read a Tight-fisted Poem Once. Nancy Woods. RFM

I traced the Circus whose grey stones incline. In the Old Theatre, Fiesole. Thomas Hardy. OBTV

I tramp my streets into recognition. Charles Brasch. *Fr.* Home Ground, III. PeNZ

I Travel Day and Night. Su Tung-p'o, *tr. fr. Chinese by* Burton Watson. CoBCP

I travel far in a little boat. Traveling by Boat at Shun-ch'ang. Hsü Chung-hsing, *tr. by* Jonathan Chaves. CoBLCP

I travel in a train. I Am a Horse. Hans Arp, *tr. by* Harriet Watts. FaBoNo

I travel on thousands of trains. I Am the Train of Sadness. Nizar Qabbani, *tr. by* Abdullah al-Udhari. MPAW

I traveld thro' a land of men. The Mental Traveller. Blake. EnRP; NAEL-2; OAEL-2; OPOP; PoE; PoEL-4

I Traveled [*or* travell'd] among Unknown Men. Wordsworth. *Fr.* Lucy. AWP; EnRP; FaBV; GTBS; GTBS-P; OBNC

I traveled [*or* travell'd] on, seeing the hill, where lay. The Pilgrimage. George Herbert. ChTr; FaBoRV; NAEL-1

I traveled to the ocean. Prayer to the Pacific. Leslie Silko. CDW; NoP; VoR

I Traveled with Them. "Mustafa," *tr. fr. Arabic by* J. B. Trend. AWP

I travelled in the Arab homeland. The Ruler and the Sparrow. Nizar Qabbani, *tr. by* Abdullah al-Udhari. MPAW

I travelled on, seeing the hill, where lay. The Pilgrimage. George Herbert. PoE

I travelled the land from Leap to Corbally. The Volatile Kerryman. Owen Roe O'Sullivan, *tr. by* Sean O'Riada. BIrV

I traversed a dominion. Mute Opinion. Thomas Hardy. CMoP

I tread the dark and my steps are silent. Brightness as a Poignant Light. David Ignatow. DiL

I tried/ to live like others. Successful Attempt. Hermann Jandl, *tr. by* Beth Bjorklund. CoAuP

I tried but I could not remember my dream. The Hills of Pomeroy. Ewart Milne. NeIP

I tried each thing, only some were immortal and free. As One Put Drunk into the Packet-Boat. John Ashbery. HAP; HCAP

I Tried to Exchange Two Painting for Some Grain But Failed. Hsü Wei, *tr. fr. Chinese by* Jonathan Chaves. CoBLCP

I tried to live by bread alone. Satisfied. Edgar Cooper Mason. BLRP

I tried to live small. Housing Shortage. Naomi Replansky. NMM

I tried to tell her. Offspring. Naomi Long Madgett. FB

I tripped along a narrow way. Forthfaring. Winifred Howells. AA

I trow that gude ending. Bruce Consults His Men. John Barbour. *Fr.* The Bruce. GoTS

I trundle the bodies, on the iron bars. John Berryman. *Fr.* Homage to Mistress Bradstreet. NOBA

I trust I have not wasted breath. Tennyson. *Fr.* In Memoriam A. H. H., CXX. ImOP; SeCePo

I Try in Poetic Fashion. Lucebert, *tr. fr. Dutch by* James S. Holmes. DuIn

I try the dead lighter. Lighter. Sargon Boulus, *tr. by* Sargon Boulus *and* Alistair Elliot. MAP

I try to call him back. Boncho, *tr. fr. Japanese by* Hiroaki Sato. *Fr.* Twenty-one Hokku. FCEI

I try to hold your face in my mind's million eyes. A Bride's Hours. Jean Valentine. FaBoWP

I try to knead and spin, but my life is low the while. In Leinster. Louise Imogen Guiney. AA

I Try to Turn In My Jock. David Hilton. TSL

I turn and gaze far. Empress Yamato-hime. *Fr.* Manyo Shu. Ma

I turn my steps where the lonely road. In Dark Hour. Seumas MacManus. WGRP

I turn on all the lights. My Mother Tries to Visit Me in the Dead of Night. Diane Wakoski. TV

I turn the carriage, yoke and set off. *Unknown, tr. fr. Chinese by* Burton Watson. *Fr.* Nineteen Old Poems of the Han, XI. CoBCP

I turn the lea-green down. Ploughman. Patrick Kavanagh. TIRV

I turn the page and read. At the British Museum. Richard Aldington. MoBrPo

I turn to look: cold in the evening dusk, mountain cherries. Raizan, *tr. fr. Japanese by* Hiroaki Sato. *Fr.* Thirteen Hokku. FCEI

I turn to look: everything behind me. Miura Chora, *tr. fr. Japanese by* Hiroaki Sato. *Fr.* Sixteen Hokku. FCEI

I turn to you. To the Divine Neighbor. Judah Leib Teller, *tr. by* Gabriel Preil *and* Howard Schwartz. VWA

I turn you out of doors. Alain Chartier, *tr. fr. French by* Edward Lucie-Smith. BoLoP

I turned and gave my strength to woman. Two Generations. L. A. G. Strong. OBMV

I turned aside into the trees, among the shadows. In the Garden of the Turkish Consulate. Pinhas Sadeh, *tr. by* Harris Lenowitz. VWA

I turned my back when in the pot they tossed. Walthena. Elisabeth Peck. AmFN

I turned to speak to God. Not All There. Robert Frost. FaBoCo

I twitch and jerk on my nerves' piano-wire. The Internal Saboteur. Martin Seymour-Smith. NPo

I, Ulysses, refuse to learn the songs. The Island of the Sirens. Timoshenko Aslanides. UAS

I understand Death's contract. A Scream. Muhammad al-Faituri, *tr. by* Sargon Boulus *and* Peter Porter. MAP

I understand the large hearts of heroes. Heroes. Walt Whitman. *Fr.* Song of Myself, XXXIII *and* XXXV. AA

I understand you well enough, John Donne. A Letter to John Donne. C. H. Sisson. NOCV

I understood the rest too well. Understanding. Sara Teasdale. AnAmPo

I unfolded my fear. Passion without a Name. Lucha Corpi. CCP

I upon the first creation. Gratitude. Christopher Smart. *Fr.* Hymns for the Amusement of Children, XXII. NOEC

I use no colors, just number threes. Drawing Wildflowers. Jorie Graham. NPGG

I used to be a drill man. Drill Man Blues. George Sizemore. AmFP; WTO

I used to be a monk, but gave it over. Saul's Death: Two Sestinas. Joe W. Haldeman. BWV

I used to be sure but I've forgotten how to count. Beginning to End. Carla Harryman. LP

I used to believe I wouldn't live past 16. Fan. Walter Lew. BrSi

I used to dream militant. Revolutionary Dreams. Nikki Giovanni. CNA

I used to dream of Chuang Tzu. A Painting of the Butterfly Dream by the Master Artist Li Tsai. Chu Yün-ming, tr. by Jonathan Chaves. CoBLCP

I used to fall. My Heart Belongs to Daddy. Cole Porter. OBAL

I used to fall in love with pop stars. True Life Romance. Lindsay MacRae. DT

I used to have an old grey horse. Goin' Down to Town. Unknown. AS

I used to have fine buckles. The Housewife's Lament. Unknown, tr. by Muriel Kittel. DMI

I used to lie on my back, imagining. Childhood. Maura Stanton. MAYP; SM

I used to look at with disgust. Falling Down to Bed. Nila NorthSun. STE

I Used to Love My Garden. C. P Sawyer. FaBoCo

I used to love to lie awake past bedtime. Rechargeable Dry Cell Poem. Jim Wayne Miller. GOYP

I used to make fun of you when you were a little girl & poor. Song for the Richest Woman in Wrangell. Guxnawu, tr. by James Koller. STP

I used to pray in furnished rooms. Evidence. John Skoyles. NAmP

I used to prefer them and now I'm one of them. Older Men. Alfred Corn. GLP

I used to scratch medals, when I was a lad. Ambition. Joachim Ringelnatz, tr. by Christopher Middleton. OBD

I used to see her in the door. Paul. James Wright. NePoEA

I used to tell you, "Frances, we grow old." Kenneth Rexroth, after the Latin of Ausonius. NNaP

I used to think. Enough Time. Stephen Dunn. KS

I Used to Think. Chirlane McCray. AIW

I Used to Think in Lines That Were Irregular to the Right. Roger Zelazny. BWV

I used to think that grown-up people chose. Childhood. Frances Cornford. FaBoWP; OxBSP; OxBTC

I used to walk on solid gr'und. To a Sea Eagle. "Hugh MacDiarmid." MoBrPo

I used to walk the morning stream. Walk. Brian Merriman, tr. fr. Modern Irish by Brendan Behan. Fr. The Midnight Court. BIrV

I Used to Watch You, Sleeping. Kathleen Jessie Raine. Fr. My Mother's Birthday. NAs

I used to watch your wrists in class. Schools and Schoolmasters. Hilene Flanzbaum. PPR

I usta wonder who i'd be. Adulthood. Nikki Giovanni. NMM

I usually hate crows. Basho, tr. fr. Japanese by Burton Watson. Fr. Seventy-six Hokku. FCEI

I verse a settler's tale of olden times. Charles Harpur. Fr. The Creek of the Four Graves. CBAP

I Vision God. Unknown. TTY

I visit once again. Pushkin, tr. by Alan Myers. AAA

I Vow to Thee, My Country. Cecil Arthur Spring-Rice. BoTP

I vow'd unvarying faith; and she. Coventry Patmore. Fr. The Angel in the House, II, xi. NoBVV (Constancy Rewarded.) OxBSP

I wage not any feud with death. Tennyson. Fr. In Memoriam A. H. H., LXXXII. LiTB

I wait and watch: before my eyes. The Waiting. Whittier. WGRP

I wait, dear child, for you to come. You'll Never Know. Ruby Marion Wray. PWR

I wait for her who restores my fingertips. Song of Expectancy. George Hitchcock. EAS

I wait for his foot fall. Earth Trembles Waiting. Blanche Shoemaker Wagstaff. PoLF

I Wait My Lord. Unknown, tr. fr. Chinese by Helen Waddell. Fr. Shi King. AWP

I wait to tangle fear around my hand. Night along the Mackinac Bridge. Roberta Hill. CDW; STE

I wait, with those that rest. Ark to Noah. Jay Macpherson. Fr. The Ark. NOBC; PoA

I waited and I. Princess Nukada. Fr. Manyo Shu. PeBJV

I waited and worked/ To win myself leisure. Koheleth. Louis Untermeyer. TrJP

I Waited for Chuang Hsüan-yüan. Mo Shih-lung, tr. fr. Chinese by Jonathan Chaves. CoBLCP

I waited for the train at Coventry. Godiva. Tennyson. BeLS

I waited for you in my hut, I did. Hut: Thinking of a Friend. Gensei, tr. by Burton Watson. JLIC-2

I waited full two hours, or more. The Tryst. Mary E. Tucker. CBWP-1

I waited in the little sunny room. Eve's Daughter. Edward Rowland Sill. AnAmPo

I wake, but before I know it it is done. Aging. Randall Jarrell. PoA

I wake despondent. Morning. Tove Ditlevsen, tr. by Nadia Christensen. PBWP

I wake from a nap, light clouds. Waking from a Nap. Ni Tsan, tr. by Jonathan Chaves. CoBLCP

I wake from my dawn pillow. Frosty Dawn. Rokunyo, tr. by Burton Watson. JLIC-2

I wake in a dark flat. Afterlives. Derek Mahon. CIP

I wake in the morning early. Singing-Time. Rose Fyleman. RAR

I wake in the night. Middle of the Way. Galway Kinnell. NU

I Wake, My Friend, I. Faye Kicknosway. IHMS

I Wake Thinking of Myself as a Man. Susan Griffin. GLP

I wake to find myself lying in an open field. Robert Bly Says Something Too. Henry Taylor. BXAP

I wake to see the morning. Morning and Myself. Nia Francisco. STE

I wake to sleep, and take my waking slow. The Waking. Theodore Roethke. AmPP; CAPP; CoAP; CRP; HAP; HCAP; HeIP; InPK; InPS; LiTM; MoAmPo; MoP; NAAL-2; NIP; NoAM; NOBA; NoP; OPOP; PPP; PrIm; SM; SoSe; TAP; TwCP; WeW

I wake to the sound of rain. Felix Pollak. Fr. Tunnel Visions, III. TSM

I wake up first and with a sense of. Genius Loci of the Morning. Doug Fetherling. NeAC

I wake up in the bed my grandmother died in. Stove. Philip Booth. FYAP

I wake up in the middle of the night. Finger-print. Mirko Lauer, tr. by David Tipton. Per

I wake up in your bed. I know I have been dreaming. Adrienne Rich. Fr. Twenty-one Love Poems, II. GLP; NAAL-2; NoAM; UnAS

I wake up my car. Morning Bird Songs. Tomas Tranströmer, tr. by Robert Bly. InPS

I waked; the sun was in the sky. On Waking from a Dreamless Sleep. Annie Fields. AA

I wakened my thoughts from slumber. The Sources of My Being. Moses Ibn Ezra, tr. by David Goldstein. TOF

I wakened on my hot, hard bed. The Watch. Frances Cornford. HeIP; InPK; MoBrPo; OxBTC; RR

I wakened, still a child. The Life Ahead. Philip Levine. NoAM

I Walk ("I walk/ in a garden of cool embers"). Philippe Jaccottet, tr. fr. French by Paul Auster. RHTwFP

I walk a road—an ancient, trodden way. Another While. Morris Jacob Rosenfeld. TrJP

I Walk Along. Moyshe-Leyb Halpern, tr. fr. Yiddish by John Hollander. PeBMYV

I walk along the bustling streets. Girls from Home. Abraham Reisen. VWA, tr. by Keith Bosley

I walk among men with tall bones. Clouds on the Sea. Ruth Dallas. Fr. Letter to a Chinese Poet, IV. PeNZ

I walk among my great-grandfather's trees. Letter from Thurlby Domain. Charles Brasch. ATNZ

I walk and I wonder. Spring. Isaac Rosenberg. TrJP

I walk at dawn across the hollow hills. Poem. Ruthven Todd. EAS

I walk back. Getting the Mail. Galway Kinnell. UnPo

I walk behind you, hand. Days of 1956. Robin Magowan. EAS

I walk [or walked] beside the prisoners to the road. A Camp in the Prussian Forest. Randall Jarrell. CMoP; MoAmPo; OBWP; OxBC

I walk down a long. A Poem for Museum Goers. John Wieners. NeAP

I walk down the garden paths. Patterns. Amy Lowell. AWP; BoWoP; DL; FaFP; FPL; LiTA; MoAmPo; OnMSP; OxBA; TrGrPo

I walk down the narrow. The Man in the Mirror. Mark Strand. NYBP

I walk downhill, slow. Roll Call: A Land of Old Folk and Children. Isaac J. Black. CNA

I walk in loneliness through the greenwood. Unknown, tr. by Willis Barnstone. BoWoP

I walk in nature still alone. Great Friend. Henry David Thoreau. PoEL-4

I walk in the old street. Louis Zukofsky. VGW

I walk into your house, a friend. A Friend. W. D. Snodgrass. MAT

I walk naked under my clothes like anyone else. Dramatic Monologue in the Speaker's Own Voice. Vassar Miller. TSM

I walk on grass as soft as wool. An Old Woman Laments in Spring-Time. Dame Edith Sitwell. ViBoPo

I walk on the waste-ground for no good reason. For No Good Reason. Peter Redgrove. PoE

I walk on two legs. Cynthia Ozick. VWA

I walk out alone into the darkness. Mikhail Yurevich Lermontov, tr. by Alan Myers. AAA

I walk over a moistened bridge. Ozaki Hosai, tr. fr. Japanese by Hiroaki Sato. Fr. One Hundred Haiku in Free Form. FCEI

I walk the dusty ways of life. The Troubadour of God. Charles Wharton Stork. WGRP

I walk the purple carpet into your eye. Inside Out. Diane Wakoski. CoAP; NYBP

I walk through a field of heads. Amassing Knowledge. Mark Rich. SoTCo

I walk through the long schoolroom questioning. Among School Children. W. B. Yeats. AnIL; BLPL; CMoP; GTBS-P; HAP; InPS; LiTB; LiTM; MoAB; MoBrPo; MoP; NAEL-2; NAWM-2; NIP; NoAM; NOBE; NoP; OAEL-2; OAEL-2; OxBTC; PoE; PPP; PrIm; TrGrPo; WeW

I walk today, the pain of childbirth in each step. Rosario Murillo, *tr. by* Barbara Paschke. Vol

I walk upon the rocky shore. My Mother. Josephine Rice Creelman. OHIP

I walk'd in the lonesome evening. William Allingham. EnLoPo

I walked a mile with Pleasure. Along the Road. Robert Browning Hamilton. BLPA; BLPL

I walked about the garden in the evening. Soothsayer. Mary Ursula Bethell. ATNZ

I walked abroad in [*or* on] a snowy day. Soft Snow. Blake. FF; SoSe; TEP

I walked all the way from East St. Louis. East St. Louis Blues. *Unknown.* AmFP

I walked [*or* walk'd] along a stream for pureness rare. Gervase Markham, *at. to* Christopher Marlowe. CTC; OBSC

I walked along the winding road. The Prisoner. Charles Spear. ATNZ

I walked beside the evening sea. Ebb and Flow. George William Curtis. AA

I walked beside the stone. My Grandmother's Burial Ground. Elizabeth Cook-Lynn. HATNAP

I walked entranced/ Through a land of Morn. A Vision of Connaught in the Thirteenth Century. James Clarence Mangan. AnIL; NOIV

I walked especially to the Brown Deer Grill. Sidonie. Jack Collom. UL

I walked in a desert. Stephen Crane. *Fr.* The Black Riders, XLII. NAAL-2

I walked in loamy Wessex lanes, afar. The Pity of It. Thomas Hardy. CMoP; LiTM; WaP

I walked into a loge in the Teatro Melisso. Pound at Spoleto. Lawrence Ferlinghetti. PoM

I walked on the banks of the tincan banana dock. Sunflower Sutra. Allen Ginsberg. AmPP; CoAP; HCAP; InPS; MAT; NAAL-2; NeAP; NOBA

I walked on the edge of the churchyard, my shoes hurt my. At the Pauwels. Diane Glancy. CRP

I walked over the grave of Henry James. Richard Eberhart. VGW

I walked past you. We Were Suntanned Gods. Pentti Saaritsa, *tr. by* Aili Jarvenpa. SOP

I Walked [*or* Walkt] the Other Day to Spend My Hour. Henry Vaughan. JCP; MePo; OBS

I walked through Ballinderry in the spring-time. Lament for the Death of Thomas Davis. Sir Samuel Ferguson. BIrV; NOIV

I walked through the woodland meadows. The Bird with a Broken Wing. Hezekiah Butterworth. WBLP

I walked, when love was gone. A Breath of Air. James Wright. NOBA

I walked where in their talking graves. At the British War Cemetery, Bayeux. Charles Causley. NAEL-2; OBWP; OxBC

I walked with a flower. Earth, Sky. Sydney Clouts. PeSA

I walked with my shadow. Hide-and-Seek Shadow. Margaret Hillert. RAR

I walked with you as far as the graineries beside the gates. Songs for a Three-String Guitar. Léopold Sédar-Senghor, *tr. by* Miriam Koshland. PBA

I walked with you this eleventh in the coppice. November Poppies. Hilary Corke. NYBP

I wallow in the tavernas and brothels of Beirut. In the Tavernas. Constantine P. Cavafy, *tr. by* Edmund Keeley *and* Philip Sherrard. AnAn

I wander aimless, to and fro. Aimless. Louis Palagyi, *tr. by* Watson Kirkconnell. TrJP

I wander all night in my vision. The Sleepers. Walt Whitman. AmPP; NAAL-2

I wander by the edge. He Hears the Cry of the Sedge. W. B. Yeats. OxBTC; RB

I wander down on Clinton street south of Polk. Clinton South of Polk. Carl Sandburg. AmFN

I wander through a crowd of women. At Piccadilly Circus. Vivian de Sola Pinto. OBMV

I wander through [*or* thro'] each chartered [*or* charter'd] street. London. Blake. *Fr.* Songs of Experience. AWP; ChER; ChTr; EnRP;

FaBoPP; FaBoPV; FF; HAP; HeIP; InPK; InPS; LiTB; MAT; Mes; NAEL-2; NAWM-2; NIP; NOBE; NOEC; NoP; OAEL-2; OBNC; PoE; PoEL-4; PrIm; RB; SCV; SeCePo; TEP; UnPo; WeW

I wandered forth at night alone. Lament over the Ruins of the Abbey of Teach Molaga. *Unknown, tr. by* James Clarence Mangan. NOIV

I wandered in a suburb of the north. James Thomson ("B. V."). *Fr.* The City of Dreadful Night, XVIII. NOBVV

I Wandered Lonely as a Cloud. Wordsworth. BoNaP; EnRP; FaBoPP; InPK; InPS; NAEL-2; NoP; OAEL-2; PoRA; TEP; TTTS; UnPo; ViBoPo

(Daffodils, The.) BLPA; FaBoBe; FaBV; FaFP; FaPON; FiP; FPL; GN; GoJo; GTBS; GTBS-P; LiTB; NOBE; OBEV; OBNC; OHFP; PWR; SCV; TrGrPo; WBLP

I wandered up an autumn loaning. The Hills of God. A. A. Buist. PoSH

I wandered up to Beaucourt; I took the river track. Beaucourt Revisited. A. P. Herbert. MMA

I wandering went/ Among the haunts and dwellings of mankind. Shelley. *Fr.* Prometheus Unbound, III. FiP

I want/ a love to hold. Defense Rests. Vassar Miller. MoAmPo

I want a good lover. What Do You Want? John Newlove. NOBC

I want a hero: an uncommon want. Byron. *Fr.* Don Juan, I. EnRP; NAEL-2, *abr.;* NoP; OAEL-2, *abr.;* PoE, *abr..*

I want a strike where we all go out. Strike. Gioconda Belli, *tr. by* David Volpendesta. Vol

I Want a Tenant; a Satire. John O'Keefe. NOEC

I want an egg for Easter. An Egg for Easter. Irene F. Pawsey. BoTP

I want and don't want to cut it down. *Unknown, tr. by* Hiroaki Sato. FCEI

I want and don't want to slash him. *Unknown, tr. by* Hiroaki Sato. FCEI

I want free life and I want fresh air. Lasca. Frank Desprez. BeLS; BLPA; FaBoBe

I Want God's Heab'n to Be Mine. *Unknown.* BoAN-2

I want him to have another living summer. A 14-Year-Old Convalescent Cat in the Winter. Gavin Ewart. OBD; OxBSP

I want it to be clear for us. On My Stand. Sharon Scott. JB

I want my dance. Yanette Delétang-Tardif, *tr. by* Martha Collins. DMF

I want my funeral to include this detour. Detour. Michael Longley. CIP

I want no paradise only to be. The Kiwi Bird in the Kiwi Tree. Charles Bernstein. UL

I want nothing but your fire-side now. Hearthstone. Harold Monro. OBMV

I want only to forget. Teika, *tr. by* Steven D. Carter. WFTW

I want something suited to my special needs. Needs. A. R. Ammons. NIP; OBAL

I want the New Year's opening days. A Prayer for the New Year. *Unknown.* BLRP

I want the world to see me. Waves of Pleasure. "Miraji," *tr. by* Mahmood Jamal. PBMUP

I want things. On the Corner. Kit Robinson. IAT

I want to be. The Last of the Fire Kings. Derek Mahon. FaBCIP; FaBoPV

I want to be a wag and not a jerk. Purple Goatee. George Starbuck. SoTCo

I want to be a white horse! Three Presidents. Robert Bly. LCAP

I want to be buried in an anonymous crater inside the moon. Unholy Missions. Bob Kaufman. CNA; TTY

I want to be in a garden with my love. *Unknown, tr. by* Willis Barnstone. BoWoP

I Want to Be, Mother. *Unknown, tr. fr. Spanish by* Kate Flores. DMH

I want to be near this mild unforgiving man. Father. Paul Zweig. DiL

"I want to be new," said the duckling. The New Duckling. Alfred Noyes. BoTP; FaPON

I want to be with my love in a garden. *Unknown, tr. by* Willis Barnstone. BoWoP

I want to become a great night bird. The Great Bird of Love over the Kingdom. Paul Zimmer. BLA

I want to clear my head. Bent Branches. Amjad Nasir, *tr. by* May Jayyusi *and* Charles Doria. MAP

"I want to die"—at times I think. Natsume Seibi, *tr. fr. Japanese by* Hiroaki Sato. *Fr.* Twenty-seven Hokku. FCEI

I Want to Die While You Love Me. Georgia Douglas Johnson. AmNP; BANP; BlSi; CDC

I want to die with the dying day. When the Day Comes. Manuel Gutiérrez Nájera, *tr. by* Samuel Beckett. MexPo

I want to drown in good-salt water. Miss Millay Says Something Too. Samuel Hoffenstein. BXAP; NBLV

"I want to fight you," he said in a Belfast accent. Experience. James Simmons. BIrV

I want to flee to the frozen north when cliques who prattle. Faggots in Ancient Rome. Juvenal, *tr. fr. Latin*. *Fr.* Satires, II. PeHV

I want to flood you with unrest. Sappho to Eranna. Rainer Maria Rilke, *tr. by* Edward Snow. UnAS

I want to forget my manners. Hope. Edith Södergran, *tr. by* Jaakko A. Ahokas. PBWP

"I want to get away somewhere and re-read Proust." Problems of a Journalist. Weldon Kees. NaP

I want to give you a spoonful of hot soup. A Hymn about a Spoonful of Soup. Jozef Wittlin, *tr. by* Isaac Komem. VWA

I want to go aboard my ship, and sail and sail away. The Dream Ship. W. K. Holmes. BoTP

I want to go on. First Prelude. Francis J. Smith. CRP

I want to Go to Keta. Kobena Eyi Acquah. UAS

I Want to Know. John Drinkwater. FaPON

I want to know today. Sargon Boulus, *tr. by* Sargon Boulus *and* Alistair Elliot. MAP

I want to know why when I'm late. I Want to Know. John Drinkwater. FaPON

I want to lament the princess who was killed. In Memory, 1978. Judith Kazantzis. AIW; BrRo

I want to live again. To Speak I Know Not Where. Angèle Vannier, *tr. by* Barbara Johnson. DMF

I want to look at what happened. Ofay-Watcher Looks Back. Mongane Wally Serote. WMBCH

I want to make half-a-sirventes upon two kings. Bertrans de Born, *tr. by* Paul Blackburn. Pro

I want to praise bodies. To Praise. Ellen Bass. ER

I want to remember the fallen palm. Oblivion. Ellis Ayitey Komey. PBA

I Want to Say Your Name. Léopold Sédar Senghor, *tr. fr. French by* Kenneth Koch. TTTS

I want to see and be seen by you. Lady Izumi, *tr. fr. Japanese by* Hiroaki Sato. *Fr.* Fifty-one Tanka. FCEI

I want to see here. Augusto Ngangula. Costa Andrade, *tr. by* Michael Wolfers. WMBCH

I want to see him. Lady Ise, *tr. fr. Japanese by* Burton Watson. *Fr.* Kokin Shu. FCEI

I want to see it face to face. Nothing. Charles Simic. NNaP

I want to see the slim palm trees. Heritage. Gwendolyn B. Bennett. AmNP; BANP; BlSi; PoBA

I want to sleep. Masaoka Shiki, *tr. by* Geoffrey Bownas *and* Anthony Thwaite. PeBJV

I want to speak to you while I can. I Am Here. Robert Mezey. VWA

I want to tell you how the light bends down. Evening Snow. David Wojahn. NAmP

I want to travel the common road. The Common Road. Silas H. Perkins. BLPA; FaBoBe

I want to understand the steep thing. Climbing You. Erica Jong. PoA

I Want to Write a Jewish Poem. Gary Pacernick. VWA

I want to write a poem. Noises. Fred Johnson. CNA

I want two geraniums. Javier Heraud, *tr. fr. Spanish by* Maureen Ahern. *Fr.* Earth Poems. Per

I Want You. Arthur L. Gillom. BLPA; FaBoBe

I want you in the warm. Siren Song. Marg Yeo. DT

I want you to come rushing in the rain. Yang Mu, *tr. by* Dominic Cheung. IFON

I want you to come rushing in the wind. Yang Mu, *tr. by* Dominic Cheung. IFON

I want you to see me in it. The White Dress. Roberta Spear. MAYP

I want you when the shades of eve are falling. I Want You. Arthur L. Gillom. BLPA; FaBoBe •

I wanta say just gotta say something. Beautiful Black Men. Nikki Giovanni. BPo; NMM

I wanted a rib sandwich. Rib Sandwich. William J. Harris. CNA

I wanted my name. A Poem for Ed "Whitey" Ford. Jonathan Holden. MAYP

I wanted so ably. The World. Robert Creeley. MoP; NaP; NoP

I wanted so to see you. Unknown, *tr. fr. Japanese by* Burton Watson. *Fr.* Kangin Shu. FCEI

I wanted the gold, and I sought it. The Spell of the Yukon. Robert W. Service. BLPA; BLPL; FaBoBe; FaFP

I wanted this morning to bring you a gift of roses. The Roses of Sa'adi. Marceline Desbordes-Valmore, *tr. by* Barbara Howes. BoWoP

I wanted to be a nature poet. "Honeysuckle Was the Saddest Odor of All, I Think." Thadious M. Davis. BlSi

I wanted to be sure to reach you. To the Harbormaster. Frank O'Hara. CoAP; CRP; MOS; NAAL-2; PoM

I wanted to bring you this Jap iris. For C. Philip Whalen. NeAP; VGW

I wanted to drive back the clouds, with these hands sweep clear the evil stars. In Prison. Rai Mikisaburo, *tr. by* Burton Watson. JLIC-2

I wanted to harness and go. Baroness Mu Impeded in Her Wish to Help Famine Victims in Wei. Confucius, *tr. fr. Chinese by* Ezra Pound. *Fr.* Yung Wind. CTC

I wanted to know about love. Bearded Lady. Bernice Zamora. CCP

I wanted to know my mother when she sat. Leroy. Amiri Baraka. BPo; PoBA

I wanted to see you,/ thighs showing. Leila Miccolis, *tr. fr. Portuguese by* Willis Barnstone *and* Nelson Cerqueira. BoWoP

I wanted to spare you this, the lying alone. Cool Nights of October. David Wojahn. NAmP

I wanted to take a walk. Walking Past Paul Blackburn's Apt. on 7th St. Diane Wakoski. TAP

I wanted to write. For Saundra. Nikki Giovanni. BPo; TTY

I wanted to write the lips of sleepers. Amir Gilboa, *tr. by* Warren Bargad *and* Stanley F. Chyet. IP

I wanted to write you a letter. Letter from a Contract Worker. Antonio Jacinto, *tr. by* Margaret Dickinson. WMBCH

I wanted without delay to give order to the world, so I put first my boxes. Ruler. Gyula Illyés, *tr. by* William Jay Smith. MHuP

I wanted you, nameless woman of the South. Southern Cross. Hart Crane. *Fr.* The Bridge. NAAL-2

I wanted you when skies were red. Unanswered. Martha Gilbert Dickinson Bianchi. AA

I ward off lance-sharp tongues and lips of steel. Written in Prison. Ch'ien Ch'ien-yi, *tr. by* Irving Lo. WFTU

I warmed both hands before the fire of Life. D. B. Wyndham Lewis. FiBHP

I warn, like the one drop of rain. The Voice of the Void. George Parsons Lathrop. AA

"I warn ye all, ye gay ladies." Child Waters. *Unknown.* ESPB, A *and* B *vers.*; FaBoBa; OBET; OxBB

I warned the parents, you know. Father to the Man. John Knight. EaLo

I was a bachelor, I lived by myself. The Weaver. *Unknown.* AS

I was a bathing beauty in "The American Venus." Bubbles. Bill Berkson. UL

I was a boy when I heard three red words a thousand Frenchmen. Threes. Carl Sandburg. AnAmPo; CMoP; OxBA; PoLF

I was a cat two lives ago. Encolpius. Thom Gunn. *Fr.* Three Songs. AnAn

I was a child and overwhelmed: Mozart. The Corner Knot. Robert Graves. NYBP

I was a girl waiting by the roadside for my boyfriend to come. The Elwha River. Gary Snyder. NoAM

I was a high-born gentleman. Gypsy Davy. *Unknown.* AS

I was a humble clerk. The African Trader's Complaint. Dennis C. Osadebay. PBA

I was a joke at dinners; aye, any would-be wit. Revenge to Come. Sextus Propertius, *tr. fr. Latin by* Kirby Flower Smith. *Fr.* Elegies, III, 25. AWP

I was a lady of high renown. Jamie Douglas. *Unknown.* ESPB (Lord Douglas) OxBB

I was a leather skinned harridan. Granny Crack. James Reaney. NOBC

I was a lover of turkey and holly. Anne Wilkinson. OBCV

I was a mere boy in a stone-cutter's shop. Abraham. Delmore Schwartz. VWA

I was a peasant girl from Germany. Elsa Wertman. Edgar Lee Masters. *Fr.* Spoon River Anthology. MoP; NoAM; OxBA

I was a quack, and there are men who say. Advertising Epitaph: On a Quack. *Unknown.* FaBoUs

I was a Roman soldier in my prime. A Guard of the Sepulcher. Edwin Markham. WGRP

I was a scout and messenger. A shell. War and Peace. Barry Goldensohn. WGRP

I Was a Skinny Tomboy Kid. Alma Villanueva. CCP

"I Was a Stranger and Ye Took Me In." Mary E. Tucker. CBWP-1

I was a stricken deer, that left the herd. The Garden. William Cowper. *Fr.* The Task, III. EnRP; FaBoRV; NAEL-1 (Stricken Deer, The.) FiP

I was a woman always liked spangles. Sleep, Madame, Sleep. Annemarie Ewing. NePoAm

I was a young maid truly. The Sandgate Girl's Lamentation. *Unknown.* CoMu; ELP

I was all night at this. Putting On My Shoes I Hear the Floor Cry Out beneath Me. Michael Heffernan. BXAP

I was alone once, waiting. For the Marsh's Birthday. James Wright. NYBP

I was already. Three Shades of Light on the Windowsill. Susan Griffin. NPGG

I was altered in the placenta. The Dead Poet. Alfred W. Purdy. NOBC

I was always called in early for dinner. Don't Forget. Stephen Berg. PoA

I was always fascinated. Mother, May I? Alma Villanueva. CCP; WPOW

I was angry with my cow. The Cry of the Child. William Zaranka. BXAP

I was angry with my friend. A Poison Tree. Blake. *Fr.* Songs of Experience. AWP; EnRP; FaFP; HAP; HoPM; LiTB; NAEL-2; NoP; PoEL-4; PPP; RB; SCV; SoSe; TrGrPo; TW; WeW

I was asking for something specific and perfect for my city. Mannahatta. Walt Whitman. AA; EyDe; GOA; MoAmPo

I was bat seven year alld. *See* I was but seven. . .

I was beautiful when we came into Egypt. Sarai. Joseph Sherman. VWA

I Was Before I Was. Dan Pagis, *tr. fr. Hebrew by* Warren Bargad *and* Stanley F. Chyet. IP

I was blind and deaf. Fighter. Musaemura Bonus Zimunya. WMBCH

I was born alive. Amarillo. Alan Bernheimer. IAT

I Was Born at a Place of Pines. Geoffrey Lehmann. *Fr.* Ross's Poems. CBAP

I was born conscious, I can't remember. Rino's Song. Lynne Lawner. IHMS

I was born far from a river. Islandish. A. Leyeles, *tr. by* Benjamin *and* Barbara Harshav. AYP

I was born in a beggar family. Tulsidas, *tr. fr. Hindi by* John Stratton Hawley *and* Mark Juergensmeyer. SSI

I was born in a flimsy nest. Shades of Origin. Sebastian Salazar Bondy, *tr. by* David Tipton. Per

I was born in a small hospital in Tokyo. Mama says. Liv Ullmann. *Fr.* Changing. TV

I was born in a time of peace. Ts'ai Yen, *tr. fr. Chinese by* Kenneth Rexroth *and* Ling Chung. *Fr.* Eighteen Verses Sung to a Tatar Reed Whistle, I. BoWoP; PBWP; WPOW

I was born in Belfast between the mountain and the gantries. Carrickfergus. Louis MacNeice. AnIL; FaBCIP; FaBoPP; NAEL-2; NoAM; NOIV

I was born in Boston, a city you all know well. The Boston Burglar. *Unknown.* AmFP

I was born in Bristol, and it is possible. Family Fortunes. C. H. Sisson. OxBC

I was born in Illinois. My Fathers Came from Kentucky. Vachel Lindsay. AmFN

I was born in the city. Greener Grass. Frank Steele. Psk

I was born in the Congo. Ego Tripping. Nikki Giovanni. MoP; Psk

I was born in the month of the bull. Brooding Likeness. Louise Glück. MAYP

I was born in Utah, many long years have come and gone. Open Range. Melvin L. Whipple. CowP

I was born not too long ago. Interview with myself. Mascha Kaléko, *tr. by* Susan L. Cocalis. DMG

I was born on Double Creek, on a forty-acre hill. On Double Creek. James Still. MT

I was born on the prairie. Prairie Birth. Grace Stone Coates. OPP

I was born the year of the gray pennies. 1943. Sandra McPherson. FaBoWP

I was born there. A Revolt in Verse. Bogdan Czaykowski, *tr. by* Czeslaw Milosz. PwPP

I Was Born upon Thy Bank, River. Henry David Thoreau. PoEL-4

I was born with a divine jewel. Ikuzanchu, *tr. fr. Chinese by* Lucien Stryk *and* Takashi Ikemoto. ZPCJ

I was born with a song in my tongue. Ars. Marina Tsvetayeva, *tr. by* Willis Barnstone *and* Edward Brown. BoWoP

I was broke and out of a job in the city of London. Paddy, Get Back. *Unknown.* AmFP

I was brought up in a rampart. The Stolen Fifer. Padraic Fiacc. NeIP

I was brought up in a small town in the Mohave Desert. After Tsang Chih. Alice Notley. UL

I was brought up in Sheffield, all of a high degree. The Sheffield 'Prentice. *Unknown.* AmFP

I was buried near this dyke. Blake. FaBoEE

I was burning incense, paying respects to my mother. The Night of the First Full Moon. Li K'ai-hsien, *tr. by* Jonathan Chaves. CoBLCP

"I was but [*or* bat] seven year auld [*or* alld]." The Laily Worm and the Machrel of the Sea. *Unknown.* ChTr; ESPB; InvP; OxBB; PoEL-1

I was carried to a font. Dithyramb in Retrospect. Peter Hopegood. PoAu-2

I was certain that lute and calligraphy would help my studies. Michizane, *tr. fr. Japanese by* Burton Watson. *Fr.* Kokin Shu. FCEI (I Give Up Trying to Learn to Play the Lute.) JLIC-1

I was combing some long hair coming out of a tree. In the Forest. Russell Edson. LCAP

I was conceived in the summer of Nineteen Eighteen. True Confessional. Lawrence Ferlinghetti. NAs

I was cut in two. The Married Man. Robert Phillips. GeTw

I was dead and I wanted peace. A Grammar. Andrei Codrescu. EAS

I was descending from the mountains of sleep. Afternoon Sleep. Robert Bly. NaP

I was directed by my grandfather. Direction. Alonzo Lopez. NOVW

I was drawn to look at an apartment. The Empty Apartment. Aaron Zeitlin, *tr. by* Ruth Whitman. VWA

I was easy, a somnambulist, as I climbed. On Pali Lookout. Stephen Shu Ning Liu. BrSi

I was eighteen when I came in these gates. Words from Hell. David Helwig. NOBC

I Was Fair Beat. Robert Garioch. OxBTC

I was far forward on the plain, the burning swamp. The Little Girl with Bands on Her Teeth. Genevieve Taggard. VGW

I was feeling all this magic. A Feeling from the Sea. Michael Burkard. NAmP

I was fightin' this Model T through the Oklahoma clay. Going to the Shawnee Rodeo. Don Bell. CowP

I was fishing in the abandoned reservoir. Quinnapoxet. Stanley Kunitz. AnAn; DiL

I was 5 years old. New York City—1935. Gregory Corso. Psk

I was floating through a cross section. Genghis Chan: Private Eye. John Yau. BAP

I was foretold that on a certain day. Sonnet XX. Louise Labé. BoWoP, *tr. by* Willis Barnstone
(Sonnet: "Seer foretold that I would love one day, A.") PBWP, *tr. by* Joan Keefe *and* Richard Terdiman.

I was foretold, your rebell [*or* rebel] sex. A Deposition from Love. Thomas Carew. CaPo; MeLP; OBS

I was frightened, for a wind. The Secret. James Stephens. WSC

I was gentle and peaceful. Awakening. Lil Milagro Ramírez, *tr. by* Barbara Paschke. Vol

I was going along a dusty highroad. Mountain Talk. A. R. Ammons. HCAP

I was going thru the big earth. A Song about a Dead Person—or Was It a Mole? *Unknown, tr. by* Jerome Rothenberg *and* Richard Johnny John. STP

I was going thru the big smoke. Another Song about That Same Dead Person or Mole—Whichever it Was. *Unknown, tr. by* Jerome Rothenberg *and* Richard Johnny John. STP

I was going to say something. Ancestor. Thomas Kinsella. BIrV; FaBCIP; NOIV; PoE

I was, I am not; smiled, that since did weep. Thomas Heywood. OxBSP

I was ill, lying on my bed of old papers. The Secret Garden. Rita Dove. NoAM

I was in paradise the other day. The Monk of Montaudon, *tr. by* Paul Blackburn. Pro

I was in the army of the Zanj. First Communiqué from One Returning from the Zanj Revolt. Abd al-Aziz al-Maqalih, *tr. by* Lena Jayyusi *and* John Heath-Stubbs. MAP

I was in the beginning. I. Eino Leino, *tr. by* Aili Jarvenpa. SOP

I was in the lane and saw the car pass. A and B. C. H. Sisson. OxBC

I was invested in mother-earth, the crypt of roots. Geoffrey Hill. *Fr.* Mercian Hymns, IV. NoAM

I was just beginning to feel in the mood. An Old Husband Suspects Adultery. Gavin Ewart. NoAM

I was led into captivity by the bitch business. Money. C. H. Sisson. OxBSP

I was looking for the powerful spring grass, how powerful. Sixty-Six Poems for a Blackfoot Bundle. *Unknown, tr. by* Jerome Rothenberg. STP

I was looking through my dictionary. Dictionary Black. Sista Roots. WS

I Was Made Erect and Lone. Henry David Thoreau. PoEL-4

I was myself blown. For My People. Wendy Rose. CDW

I was never the light lad. The Spawn of Slums. James W. Thompson. BPo

I was never the one to spot him walking. Blueberry Man. David Bergman. GLP

I was never there. A Young Deer/Dust. Hemda Roth, *tr. by* Myra Glazer Schotz. VWA

I was not born to Helicon, nor dare. A Gratulatory to Mr. Ben Johnson for His Adopting of Him to Be His Son. Thomas Randolph. JCP; OBS

I was not deaf, do not think I was deaf. Caliban's Song. Jane Yolen. BWV

I was not sorrowful, I could not weep. Spleen. Ernest Dowson. BrPo; MoBrPo; NOBVV

I was not to know. *Unknown. Fr.* Manyo Shu. PeBJV

I was not train'd in Academic bowers. Written at Cambridge. Charles Lamb. EnRP

I was of delicate mind. I stepped aside for my needs. The Refined Man. Kipling. *Fr.* Epitaphs of the War, 1914–1918. FaBoEE; FaBoTw; MMA

I was on a white coast once. Canticle. David Shapiro. TTTS

I was on the drive in eighty. Silver Jack. John P. Jones. CowP

I was one of those who sees something cross the moon. During the War. Marvin Bell. CAPP

I was out in my kayak. Spring Fiord. *Unknown, tr. by* Armand Schwerner. STP

I was out in the country one beautiful night. The Widow's Old Broom. *Unknown.* AmFP

I was out walking an' a-ramblin' one day. The Wild Rippling Water. *Unknown.* FaBoBa

I was passing through the village of mottled bamboo. Woman Tung. Wu Chia-chi, *tr. by* Jonathan Chaves. CoBLCP

I was playing golf that day. *Unknown.* FiBHP

I was playing with my hoop along the road. The Turn of the Road. James Stephens. SO; WSC

I was plucking liquorice, liquorice. *Unknown, tr. fr. Chinese by* Arthur Waley. BoS

I was pretty once, I say it judiciously. Femme Agée. Lauris Edmond. UAS

I was pulling Veronica out of the lawn when this hornet came. A. R. Ammons. *Fr.* Sphere, 115-120. NoAM

I was raised up in Louisville, a town you all knew well. Frank James, the Roving Gambler. *Unknown.* AmFP

I Was Received in an Early Audience at Heaven-Gate. Yang Shih-ch'i, *tr. fr. Chinese by* Jonathan Chaves. CoBLCP

I was round and small like a pearl. *Unknown.* GBP

I was roused this morning in May. The Horse of Death. Leo Vroman. DuIn

I was run over by the truth one day. To Whom It May Concern. Adrian Mitchell. OBWP

I was running back when I heard him call. Ballad for the Unknown Soldier. Allan Taylor. OBET

I was seeing, as the police. Conception. Sandra McPherson. NAmP

"I was seized by the terror of turning into a rabbit." Dialogue with Herz. Antonio Porta, *tr. by* Lawrence R. Smith. NItP

I was sent in to see her. Tear. Thomas Kinsella. IPY; NOIV

I was setting out from my house. The Dragonfly-Mother. Denise Levertov. InPS

I was seventy-seven, come August. The Little Old Lady in Lavender Silk. Dorothy Parker. NBLV; NIP

I was sick. Jesus Was Crucified or: It Must Be Deep. Carolyn M. Rodgers. BlSi; PoBA

I Was Sick and in Prison. Jones Very. NOBA

I Was Sitting in McSorley's. E. E. Cummings. NoAM

I was sitting in my study. Papa's Letter. *Unknown.* WeW

I was sitting in the sitting room. Gruesome. Roger McGough. AmMo

I was sixteen years of age. Song Ballet. *Unknown.* AmFP

I was sleeping. A Translation From. Fred Levinson. AmPA

I Was Sleeping Where the Black Oaks Move. Louise Erdrich. HATNAP

I was sleepless, I was awake all night. Sleepless. Al-Khansa, *tr. by* Willis Barnstone. BoWoP

I was smoking a cigarette. The Duet. Ella Wheeler Wilcox. AnAmPo

I was so chill, and overworn, and sad. Anna Wickham. MoBrPo

I was so sick last night I. Morning After. Langston Hughes. MoP; NAAL-2; NBLV; NoAM

I was somewhere in a dream just a while ago. Chuang Yü, *tr. fr. Chinese by* Shirleen S. Wong. WFTU

I was spawned from the glacier. The Iceberg. Sir Charles G. D. Roberts. CaP

I was standing in a crap game doing no harm, Baby! You've Been a Good Old Wagon, but You've Done Broke Down. Ben Harney. OBAL

I was stung by a man-of-war. The Lesson. Larry Rubin. GoYe

I was sung to you. A Lament to My Mother. Guy C. Z. Mhone. WMBCH

I Was Surprised to Find Myself Out Here & Acting like a Crow. *Unknown, tr. fr. Seneca Indian by* Jerome Rothenberg *and* Johnny John. STP

I was taken there as a child. Señor Excellent. Daniel Halpern. NAmP

I was takin' off my bonnet. Darwinism in the Kitchen. *Unknown.* FiBHP; NBLV

I Was That Woman. Debjani Chatterjee. WS

I was the chief of the race—he had stricken my father dead. The Voyage of Maeldune. Tennyson. PoEL-5

I was the choice of many old men when I was young. The Old Wife. Rolly Kent. FF

I was the clumsy child. Apples. Michael Waters. GeTw

I was the father. The Settlers. Judith Hemschemeyer. SO

I was the first fruits of the battle of Missionary Ridge. Knowlt Hoheimer. Edgar Lee Masters. *Fr.* Spoon River Anthology. OxBA

I was the first made woman. I first wept. Lilith. Allen Grossman. VWA

I was the last passenger of the day. The Bus. Leonard Cohen. HeIP

I was the Moor Moraima. A Lovely Young Moor. *Unknown, tr. by* Willis Barnstone. BoWoP

I was the only child of Frances Harris of Virginia. Hamilton Greene. Edgar Lee Masters. *Fr.* Spoon River Anthology. MoP; NoAM; OxBA

I was the only girl under the stairs. The Big House. Paul Muldoon. NoAM

I was the patriarch of the shining land. John Sutter. Yvor Winters. MoAmPo; MoP; NoAM; NOBA; QFR

I was the second of three children. Medium Poem. Eileen Myles. UL

I was the staunchest of our fleet. The Derelict. Kipling. BrPo; NoAM

I was there. A Yearning. Arapera Hineira Blank, *tr. by the author.* PeNZ

I was there. Whispers, for two voices. Sandor Csoori, *tr. by* Alan Dixon. MHuP

I was there and I remember the brown brocade. In Memory of V. R. Lang. Mac Hammond. PoA

"I was thinking, Mother, of that poor old horse." Reserved. Walter de la Mare. GTBS-P

I was thinking of a son. Menstruation at Forty. Anne Sexton. CAPP

I was thirsty. Meleager, *tr. by* Sydney Oswald. PeHV

I was three-ish. The Right Arm. Paul Muldoon. NoAM

I was thy neighbour once, thou rugged pile! Elegiac Stanzas Suggested by a Picture of Peele Castle, in a Storm [Painted by Sir George Beaumont]. Wordsworth. ChER; EnRP; FaBoPP; GTBS; GTBS-P; NAEL-2; NoP; OAEL-2; OBNC; PoE

I was tired of being a woman. Consorting with Angels. Anne Sexton. NMM

I was trying/ to find a light bulb. Light Bulbs and Bananas. Hal J. Daniel III. SoTCo

I was twelve when my father gave me this .22. Merle Bascom's .22. Donald Hall. TSL

I was upon the high and blessed mound. Sonnet: Of the Grave of Selvaggia, on the Monte della Sambuca. Cino da Pistoia, *tr. by* Dante Gabriel Rossetti. AWP

I was walking a mile. Tennyson. *Fr.* Maud, pt. I, ix. EBVV

I was walking along, reciting the Lord's Prayer. The Orange Tree. Ellen Pearce. IHMS

I was walking along the Sea of Galilee. Walking along the Sea of Galilee. Dovid Knut, *tr. by* John Glad. VWA

I was walking down by the old/ Santee. Second Carolina Said-Song. A. R. Ammons. OBAL

I was walking downtown. The Man in Black. Mark Strand. EAS

I was walking in a government warehouse. Fifteen Million Plastic Bags. Adrian Mitchell. OBSV; OxBTC

I was walking in the park in spring. To Archangel. Jan Hanlo, *tr. by* James S. Holmes. DuIn

I was warned about this book. About This Book. Mechthild of Magdeburg, *tr. by* Susan L. Cocalis. DMG

I Was Washing Outside in the Darkness. Osip Mandelstam, *tr. fr. Russian by* W. S. Merwin *and* Clarence Brown. FaBoPV

"I was with Grant," the stranger said. The Aged Stranger. Bret Harte. AA; AmFN; AnAmPo

I was working in a factory. I'd seen "Blow Up" and a mini skirt. Words in Works in Russian. Stephen Rodefer. IAT

I was wrapped in black. Us. Anne Sexton. CAPP

I was wrong, quite wrong. Soliloquy II. Richard Aldington. BrPo; MMA

I was yesterday in Ben Dorain and in her precincts. Last Leave of the Hills. Duncan Ban MacIntyre. GoTS

I was young/ when I foreswore. A Deposition by John Wilmot. Vincent McHugh. ErPo

I was young./ A hundred yards off. Wheel Turning on the Hub of the Sun. William Pitt Root. MAYP

I wash my face in water. *Unknown.* See I washed my face in water.

I wash my hands several times a day. Proportion Poetry. Majken Johansson, *tr. by* Joanna Bankier. OV

I washed my face in water. I washed my face in water. *Unknown.* ChTr; GBP

("I wash my face in water.") GBP

I wasn't getting anywhere. Impressionist. Heather McHugh. MAYP

I wasn't good. Growing Up. U. A. Fanthorpe. AIW

I wasn't thinking of snow-hunger. Making a Season. Nicki Jackowska. DT

I Waste Away. Bible, *O.T. Fr.* Isaiah, XXIV: 16–20. TrJP

I waste my teeming age. I do not know. Abishag. Jacob Fichman.
 TrJP, *tr. by* Robert Friend; VWA, *tr. by* Sholom J. Kahn
I watch, across the loch. Above Inverkirkaig. Norman MacCraig.
 PoSH
I Watch, and Long Have Watched. Wordsworth. Son
I watch her fingers where they prance. Enigma. Hugh McCrae.
 PoAu-1
I watch her in the corner there. Arachne. Rose Terry Cooke. AA
I watch the battle in the orange-grove. The Rout of San Romano. Jon
 Manchip White. NePoEA
I watch the calligraphy of shadows. Philodendron. Helen Armstead
 Johnson. AmNP
I watch the curious hastened trait of twilight. Sadness, Glass, Theory.
 Roy Fuller. WaP
I watch the dung-cart stumble by. In December. Andrew Young.
 SeCePo
I watch the farmers in their fields. Farmers. William Alexander Percy.
 WGRP
I watch the hands which once beat iron. The Cataloguing. Simon Rae.
 NPo
I watch the happier people of the house. Neurasthenia. Agnes Mary
 Frances Robinson. NOBVV
I watch the Indians dancing to help the young corn at Taos pueblo. New
 Mexican Mountain. Robinson Jeffers. GOA; InPS; MoP; NoAM
I watch the leaves that flutter in the wind. Leaves at My Window. John
 James Piatt. AA
I watch the orderly stack the day's dead. Guadalajara Hospital. Ai.
 MAYP
I watch the roses float. Stephen Vincent. NeAC
I watch them on the drill field, the awkward and the grave. The Drill.
 Harry Brown. WaaP
I watch you. Watching You. Simon J. Ortiz. HATNAP
I watch you packing the past. Gentle Ghosts. Simon Rae. NPo
I watch your daughter two years old. Hands. Donna Masini. ER
I watched a laughing cloud. Evening. King D. Kuka. VoR
I watched a man in a cafe fold a slice of bread. In a Cafe. Richard
 Brautigan. PCP
I watched an armory combing its bronze bricks. Frank O'Hara. NoP
I watched him as he entered. Shipmates. Merle Collins. WS
I watched last night the rising moon, upon a foreign strand. The Moon
 behind the Hill. *Unknown.* WTO
I watched old squatting chimpanzee: he traced. Sporting Acquaintances.
 Siegfried Sassoon. OxBTC
I watched the hills drink the last color of light. Thought's End. Léonie
 Adams. MoAB; MoAmPo
I watched the new moon fly. The Golden Bird. Rex Ingamells.
 PoAu-2
I watched the seeds come down this afternoon. At a Country Hotel.
 Howard Nemerov. PoRA
I watched the woman in the room. Between Love and Death. Frank
 Stanford. MT
I watched thee when the foe was at our side. Love and Death. Byron.
 EBEV; NOBE
I watched them from the window, thy children at their play. Thoughts of
 Home. Arthur Hugh Clough. FL
I watched them once, at dusk, on television, run. Salmon. Jorie
 Graham. MAYP
I watched them playing there upon the sand. The Castle. Sidney
 Alexander. PoNe
I watched them tearing a building down. Which Are You? *Unknown.*
 FPL; PoLF
I watched two. Last May. Carroll Arnett. STE
I watches me climb. First Flight. Daniel Hoffman. GrPl
I watcht as the flung screen door. The Envies. George Bowering.
 NOBC
I watered my horse at the Long Wall caves. Susan Ch'en Lin, *tr. by*
 Burton Watson. CoBCP
I wear a cobra's black bonnet. Godiva. D. C. Berry. BXAP
I wear a pair of old slippers. Shalamouses. Moyshe-Leyb Halpern, *tr. by*
 Benjamin *and* Barbara Harshav. AYP
I wear a warning bloodcoat. Elba. Gerrit Kouwenaar, *tr. by* Peter
 Nijmeijer. DuIn
I weave the night, I cross the weft with stars. In the Flight of the Blue
 Heron: To Montezuma. Anita Endrezze Probst. CDW
I Weep ("I weep/ Not as the young do noisily"). Angelina Weld Grimké.
 CDC
I weep aloud—may my voice. Wakayama Bokusui, *tr. fr. Japanese by*
 Hiroaki Sato. *Fr.* Forty-four Tanka. FCEI
I weep, but with no bitterness I weep. Souvenir. Alfred de Musset, *tr.*
 by George Santayana. AWP
I weep for my loved one. Song of Despair. Rangiaho, *tr. by* Barry
 Mitcalfe. WTO

I weep those dead lips, white and dry. Linen Bands. Vance Thompson.
 AA
I weigh 486 lbs on Jupiter. A Letter to Ron Silliman on the Back of a
 Map of the Solar System. Dennis Schmitz. LCAP
I welcome the anonymity of the middle years. Bruce Beaver. *Fr.* Letters
 to Live Poets, XIX. CBAP
I welcomed the Spring in romantic Chungking. Lyric to Spring. Joseph
 W. Stilwell. OBAL
I well remember how some threescore years. Very Old Man. James
 Henry. NOBVV
I well remember, Sauda. Mirza Mohammad Rafi Sauda, *tr. by* Ahmed
 Ali. GoT
I Wende to Dede. *Unknown.* *See* I Went to Death.
I went a-riding, a-riding. Texas. Amy Lowell. AmFN
I went a roaming, maidens, one bright day. Angelo Poliziano, *tr. fr.*
 Italian by John Addington Symonds. *Fr.* Three Ballate, III. AWP
I went a-sailing with my deer. A Tail of the See. Elizabeth T. Corbett.
 OBCA
I went across the pasture lot. The Cornfield. Elizabeth Madox Roberts.
 GoJo
I went away. Rafael Alberti, *tr. fr. Spanish by* Mark Strand. *Fr.*
 Metamorphosis of the Carnation. AnAn
I went away last August. Eat-It-All Elaine. Kaye Starbird. PDV;
 RHPC
I went back there this morning and alone. Return to Solitude. Ad
 Zuiderent, *tr. by* James S. Holmes. DuIn
I went by the Druid stone. The Shadow on the Stone. Thomas Hardy.
 QFR
I went down by Cascadilla. Cascadilla Falls. A. R. Ammons. NIP;
 NOBA
I went down dock the other day. Looking for a Ship. Harry Aisthorpe.
 OxBSS
I Went Down into the Desert to Meet Elijah. Vachel Lindsay. WGRP
I went down to malcolmland. Half Black, Half Blacker. Sterling
 Plumpp. PoBA
I went down to Saint James this morning. St. James Infirmary.
 Unknown. AmFP
I Went Down to the Depot. *Unknown.* AS
I went down to the river. Life Is Fine. Langston Hughes. NBLV
I went down to the river, poor boy. Bow Down Your Head and Cry.
 Unknown. WTO
I went for a walk over the dunes again this morning. Corsons Inlet. A.
 R. Ammons. CoAP; MoP; NAAL-2; NoAM; NOBA; NoP; PoE; PPP
I went into a public-'ouse to get a pint o' beer. Tommy. Kipling.
 BrPo; EBEV; FaBV; FaPoR; MoBrPo; NoP; OBWP; OxBTC
I went into my garden to gather some herbs. Bertha Jacobs, *tr. by*
 Jonathan Crewe. WPOW
I went into my grandmother's garden/ And there I found a farden.
 Unknown. OxNR
I went into my grandmother's garden,/ And there I found a farthing.
 Unknown. OxNR
I went into my mother as. To the Unborn and Waiting Children. Lucille
 Clifton. InPK
I went into the country. *Unknown, tr. fr. Chinese by* Arthur Waley. BoS
I Went into the Maverick Bar. Gary Snyder. CAPP; HCAP; MAT;
 NAAL-2; PoE
I went into the stable, to see what I could see. Old Wichet. *Unknown.*
 GBP
I went into town one night. One Red Rose. Ernie Fanning. CowP
I went my Sunday mornings round. John Clare. NOBVV
I went on Friday afternoons. Au Tombeau de Mon Père. Ronald
 McCuaig. PoAu-2
I went one night. Travelogue. Ernst Jandl, *tr. by* Beth Bjorklund.
 CoAuP
I went out alone to gather rocks. Prostration. David Semah, *tr. by*
 Yoffee Berkovitz. VWA
I went out at daybreak and stood on Primrose Hill. Birds Waking. W.
 S. Merwin. NOBA
I Went Out into That Welcome Cold. Amir Gilboa, *tr. fr. Hebrew by*
 Bernhard Frank. MHeP
I Went Out into the Garden. Moses ibn Ezra, *tr. fr. Hebrew by* Solomon
 Solis-Cohen. TrJP
I went out on a frosty morning. Ice Cold. Sean O Riordain, *tr. by*
 Thomas Kinsella. NOIV
I went out only once with my bow last year. Hunter's Morning. Harold
 Littlebird. STE
I went out seeking love. More Stanzas Applied to Spiritual Things. Saint
 John of the Cross, *tr. by* K. Kavanaugh *and* O. Rodrigues. TOF
I went out to the city streets. The Hero. Roger Woddis. FaBoPa
I went out to the hazel wood. The Song of Wandering Aengus. W. B.
 Yeats. BrPo; CH; CMoP; FaBoCh; GoJo; MAT; MoAB; MoBrPo;
 PoEL-5; PoRA; SOTW; TTTS; UnAs; WSC

I went to a foreign land to work for money. Sure a Poor Man. *Unknown, tr. by* M. K. Pukui *and* A. L. Korn. WTO

"I went to a mausoleum today, and found." Lineage. Frank Bidart. *Fr.* Elegy, V. HCAP

I went to a party. The Rose on My Cake. Karla Kuskin. ILY

I went to bat for the Lady Chatte. A Lass in Wonderland. Francis Reginald. MoCV

I went to ch'ch, 'tother night. Sister Johnson's Speech. Maggie Pogue Johnson. CBWP-4

I went to court last night. Puck Goes to Court. Fenton Johnson. CDC

I Went to Death. *Unknown.* FaBoRV (I Wende to Dede.) HAP

I went to dig a grave for Love. Love's Change. Anne Reeve Aldrich. AA

I went to Frankfort, and got drunk. Porson's Visit to the Continent. Richard Porson. FaBoCo; FaBoEE (Epigram on an Academic Visit to the Continent.) OxBoLi

I Went to Gold Mountain to Visit a Ch'an Master. Mo Shih-lung, *tr. fr. Chinese by* Jonathan Chaves. CoBLCP

I went to heaven. Emily Dickinson. FaBV

I went to her who loveth me no more. Arthur William Edgar O'Shaughnessy. OBNC

I went to ma daddy. Hard Daddy. Langston Hughes. BANP

I went to market and bought me a cat. An Old Rhyme. *Unknown.* BoTP

I went to Noke. *Unknown.* GBP; OxNR

I went to play with Billy. He. What Johnny Told Me. John Ciardi. ILY

I went to San Francisco. Trip: San Francisco. Langston Hughes. AmFN

I went to school. Class of 19——. Frederick Dec. PCP

I Went to See Irving Babbitt. Richard Eberhart. OBAL

I went to Strasbourg, where I got drunk. On a German Tour. Richard Porson. FiBHP

I went to the animal fair. Animal Fair. *Unknown.* AS, *with music;* BLPA; FaBoBe; FPL; MoShBr; NTCP; RHPC

I went to the coffeehouse. Cup and Rose. Nizar Qabbani, *tr. by* Diana Der Hovanessian *and* Lena Jayyusi. MAP

I went to the dances at Chandlerville. Lucinda Matlock. Edgar Lee Masters. *Fr.* Spoon River Anthology. CMoP; FaBV; FF; HAP; LiTA; LiTM; MoAmPo; MoP; NoAM; NOBA; OxBA

I went to the eastern hills. *Unknown, tr. fr. Chinese by* Arthur Waley. BoS

I went to the fields with the leisure I got. The Frightened Ploughman. John Clare. PoEL-4

I went to the Garden of Love. The Garden of Love. Blake. *Fr.* Songs of Experience. AWP; EnLoPo; EnRP; FaBV; GBL; HAP; LiTB; MAT; NAEL-2; NoP; PoE; RB; SoSe; TEP; TOF

I went to the Hotel Broog. A Difference of Zoos. Gregory Corso. VGW

I went to the park. The Balloon. Karla Kuskin. PDV

I went to the toad that lies under the wall. *Unknown.* OxNR

I went to the valley. Lucille Clifton. CNA

I went to the wood of flowers. The Wood of Flowers. James Stephens. BoTP; PDV

I went to turn the grass once after one. The Tuft of Flowers. Robert Frost. AWP; GoYe; LiTA; MoAB; MoAmPo; NAAL-2; OxBA

I went to worship in a house of God. Prayer in a Country Church. Ruth B. Van Dusen. TrPWD

I went tunneling into the earth. The Tunnel. Russell Edson. NAmP

I went up one pair of stairs. Just Like Me. *Unknown.* BoTP

I went up to Moses and said to him. Moses. Amir Gilboa, *tr. by* Stephen Mitchell. VWA

I went up to the light of truth as if into a chariot. To Truth. *Unknown, tr. fr. Greek by* J. Rendel Harris. *Fr.* Solomon, XXXVIII. WGRP

I went uptown last Saturday night. Blue Monday. *Unknown.* AmFP

I went visiting Miss Melinda. Strawberry Jam. May Justus. FaPON

I went walking (said the girl). Septentrion. René Char, *tr. by* Thomas Merton. RHTwFP

I Wept as I Lay Dreaming. Heine, *tr. fr. German by* John Todhunter. AWP

I whispered, "I am too young." Brown Penny. W. B. Yeats. BoLoP; CMoP; ELP; FaBoCh; LLLT

I, who/ hear the drums. Masaoka Shiki, *tr. fr. Japanese by* Burton Watson. *Fr.* Fifteen Haiku. FCEI

I, who/ listen to a man. Masaoka Shiki, *tr. fr. Japanese by* Burton Watson. *Fr.* Fifteen Haiku. FCEI

I, who/ plant the pit. Masaoka Shiki, *tr. fr. Japanese by* Burton Watson. *Fr.* Fifteen Haiku. FCEI

I, who/ think so often of. Masaoka Shiki, *tr. fr. Japanese by* Burton Watson. *Fr.* Fifteen Haiku. FCEI

I, who a decade past had lived recluse. A Lawn-Tennisonian Idyll. *Unknown.* FaBoPa

I who am dead a thousand years/ And wrote this sweet archaic song. To a Poet a Thousand Years Hence. James Elroy Flecker. ChTr; FaBoRV; MoBrPo; PoRA

I who am dead a thousand years/ And wrote this crabbed post-classic screed. To a Poet a Thousand Years Hence. John Heath-Stubbs. OxBC

I who am nothing, and this tissue. Hoc Est Corpus. Alex Comfort. LiTB; LiTM

I who am street-known am also street knowing. Investigator. Miriam Waddington. CaP

I who by day am function of the light. James Vincent Cunningham. VGW

I, who cut off my sorrows. Akazome Emon, *tr. fr. Japanese by* Kenneth Rexroth *and* Ikuko Atsumi. BoWoP; WPOW

I who employ a poet's tongue. Timid Lover. Countee Cullen. BANP

I who have bred only daughters. Woman into Man. Susan Wallbank. AIW

I who have counted me for a strong man. *Unknown, tr. fr. Japanese. Fr.* Manyo Shu. Ma

I who have favour'd many, come to be. To the Most Learned, Wise, and Arch-Antiquary, M. John Selden. Robert Herrick. SeCV-1

I who have not sown. I May Reap. Patrick Kavanagh. TIRV

I who was driven mad and cast out. The Hebrew Sibyl. Ruth Fainlight. VWA

I whom you touched am other things beside. Atropos. Hilaire Kirkland. *Fr.* Clotho, Lachesis, Atropos, III. PeNZ

I will accomplish that and this. In After Days. George Frederick Cameron. CaP

I will admit freely that it hurt. Small Talk in a Garden. O. B. Hardison, Jr. CRP

I will always love you. Frank O'Hara. LLLT

I will always miss the feeling. Poem for Viet Nam. Ray A. Young Bear. STE

I will arise and drive now. By Yon Bonny Banks or Thereabout. Vonna Adrian. SoTCo

I will arise and go now, and go to Innisfree. The Lake Isle of Innisfree. W. B. Yeats. BrPo; CMoP; FaBoPP; FaBV; FaFP; FaPON; FaPoR; FPL; HeIP; InPK; InPS; LiTM; MoAB; MoBrPo; MoP; NAEL-2; NoAM; NOBE; NoP; OBEV; OxBTC; PoE; PoRA; PrIm; TEP; TrGrPo; WeW

I will arise and go now, and go to Inverness. The Cockney of the North. Harry Graham. CenHV

I will arise, and leave these haggard realms. The Prodigal Son. Arthur Symons. BrPo

I will attempt the Capel track. Ante Mortem. Syd Scroggie. PoSH

I Will Be. E. E. Cummings. VGW

I will be a lion. Wild Beasts. Evaleen Stein. RAR

I will be exacting before the closing. Song of the Closing Service. Aliza Shenhar, *tr. by* Linda Zisquit. VWA

I will be in Ostia. Ostia Will Receive You. Friederike Mayröcker, *tr. by* Beth Bjorklund. CoAuP

I will be patient while my Lord. Cinderella. Ruby C. Saunders. BlSi

I will be the gladdest thing. Afternoon on a Hill. Edna St. Vincent Millay. AnAmPo; BoTP; FaPON; GrPl; NTCP; OBCA; OxBA; PDV; TTTS

I will be your mouth now, to do your singing. A Funeral Plainsong from a Younger Woman to an Older Woman. Judy Grahn. GLP

I will begin to delineate the green family. The Green Family. Colleen Thibaudeau. NOBC

I Will Believe. William H. Roberts. BLRP

I Will Bow and Be Simple. *Unknown.* EaLo

I will build my fire today. A Charm for Lighting the Fire. *Unknown, tr. by* Thomas Kinsella. NOIV

I will call you. My Friend the Wind. King D. Kuka. VoR

I will carry my coat and not put on my belt. *Unknown, tr. fr. Chinese by* Arthur Waley. *Fr.* Tzu Yeh Songs. BoWoP

I will carry you across. In Me. Yankev-Yitskhok Segal, *tr. by* Grace Schulman. PeBMYV

I will come to him. Women's Songs. Kadya Molodovsky, *tr. by* Irving Feldman. PeBMYV

I will consider the outnumbering dead. Merlin. Geoffrey Hill. InPK

I will die after years of loafing, without having finished these poems. Before Death. Alfonso Quijada Urías, *tr. by* Barbara Paschke. VoI

I will die in Miami in the sun. Variations on a Text by Vallejo. Donald Justice. CAPP; NoAM

I will drink in remembrance of the whiteness of mountains. To Drink to Friends. André Frénaud, *tr. by* Keith Bosley. RHTwFP

I will drink to your health, sweet Amy. To Amy. J. Gordon. OBAL

I will enjoy thee now, my Celia, come. A Rapture. Thomas Carew. CaPo; ErPo; JCP; NAEL-1; OAEL-1; SeCP

I Will Enter. Grace Nichols. UAS

I will found a habitation by the water. Unearthing. Betsy Rosenberg. VWA

I Will Give My Love an Apple without E'er a Core. Unknown. RB

I Will Go Away. Zvi Shargel, tr. fr. Yiddish by Gabriel Preil and Howard Schwartz. VWA

I Will Go Back to the Great Sweet Mother. Swinburne. Fr. The Triumph of Time. NAEL-2
(Sea, The.) TrGrPo

I will go down to the sea again. Sea Song. Norah M. Holland. CaP

I Will Go into the Ghetto. Charles Reznikoff. VGW

I will go out and hear the strain. Macquarie Place. Robert David Fitzgerald. PoAu-2

I Will Go with My Father a-Ploughing. Joseph Campbell. AnIL; FaPON; OFD

I will go with the first air of morning. Fishing. Dorothy Wellesley. OBMV

I will grieve alone. In Response to a Rumor That the Oldest Whorehouse in Wheeling, West Virginia, Has Been Condemned. James Wright. CAPP; CoAP; NNaP; NoAM; TW

I will haunt these States. A Vow. Allen Ginsberg. OBWP

I will have all my beds blown up, not stuft. Ben Jonson. Fr. The Alchemist, II, i. EBEV

I Will Have the Whetstone. Unknown. FaBoNo; GBP

I will have to accept women. This Form of Life Needs Sex. Allen Ginsberg. NNaP

I will hold beauty as a shield against despair. Beauty as a Shield. Elsie Robinson. BLPA

I will install windows in my dream. Windows. Mordechai Husid, tr. by Seymour Mayne and Rivka Augenfeld. VWA

I Will Keep Christmas. P. A. Ropes. BoTP

I will keep the fire of hope ever burning on the altar of my soul. Realization. Ananda Acharya. WGRP

I will lay down my silk robe. The Good Old Dog. Toi Derricotte. InPS

I will lift up mine eyes unto the hills. Psalm CXXI. Bible, O.T. Fr. Psalms. AWP; FaPON
("I to the hills lift up mine eyes," Bay Psalm Book.) OBCA
(Pilgrim's Song, The, Moulton, Modern Reader's Bible.) WGRP
(Song of Trust, A.) TrGrPo

I Will Live and Survive. Irina Ratushinskaya, tr. fr. Russian by David McDuff. AIW

I will live in Ringsend. Ringsend. Oliver St. John Gogarty. AnIL; OBMV; OxBTC

I Will Look Up. Josephine D. Henderson Heard. CBWP-4

I will look with detachment. On Being Head of the English Department. Pinkie Gordon Lane. BlSi

I will make known the eagle's nature. The Nature of the Eagle. Unknown, tr. fr. Middle English. Fr. The Bestiary. PBBP

I will make love. Unknown, tr. fr. Spanish by Willis Barnstone. BoWoP

I will make you brooches and toys for your delight. Romance. Robert Louis Stevenson. BLPL; BrPo; EBVV; GoTS; MoBrPo; OBEV; TrGrPo
(My Valentine.) FaPON; GrPl; OFD
(Song of a Traveller, The.) BoTP

I will name wilderness the castle which you were. True Name. Yves Bonnefoy, tr. by Galway Kinnell. RHTwFP

"I will never eate nor drinke," Robin Hood said. Robin Hood's Death. Unknown. ESPB

I will no longer kiss. On Himself. Robert Herrick. CaPo

I will not be inhabited. The Turtle's Belly. Ellen Pearce. IHMS

I will not call death darkness' daughter. Death. E. A. Baratynsky, tr. by Alan Myers. AAA

I will not climb these heights again. Saint Colm-Cille and the Cairn of Farewell. John Irvine. TIRV

I will not comb my morning hair. Unknown, tr. fr. Japanese. Fr. Manyo Shu. Ma

I will not die for you. Unknown, tr. by Thomas Kinsella. NOIV

I will not doubt, though all my ships at sea. Faith. Ella Wheeler Wilcox. BLRP

I will not from to-day. Imamatsuribe Yosofu, tr. fr. Japanese. Fr. Manyo Shu. Ma

I will not have you think me less. A Jewish Poet Counsels a King. Santob de Carrion, tr. fr. Spanish. Fr. Consejos y Documentos al Rey Dom Pedro. TrJP

I Will Not Let Thee Go. Robert Bridges. BeLS; BLPL; CMoP; EnLoPo; FaBoBe; OBNC

I will not play at tug o' war. Hug o' War. Shel Silverstein. NTCP; RHPC

I will not say to you, "This is the Way; walk in it." To My Son. Unknown. PoLF

I Will Not Tell the Secrets. Wilfrid Scawen Blunt. Fr. Esther [a Young Man's Tragedy], XLIX. Son

I will not toy with it nor bend an inch. The White City. Claude McKay. BPo; NoAM; TAP; TW

I will now address myself to the problem of writing. A Week of Doodle. Reed Whittemore. NePoEA

I will pluck from my tree a cherry-blossom wand. The Cherry-Blossom Wand. Anna Wickham. MoBrPo

I will praise Christopher Smart. To Christopher Smart. Joseph Stroud. NPGG

I will praise thee, O Lord, with my whole heart. Psalm IX. Bible, O.T. Fr. Psalms.
(I Will Sing Praise.) FaPON

I Will Put Chaos into Fourteen Lines. Edna St. Vincent Millay. Son

"I will put upon you the Telephone Curse," said the witch. The Witch of East Seventy-second Street. Morris Bishop. NYBP

I will reach into the grab-bag of unconscious things. Private Pantomime. Ruth Stone. PoA

I will read a few of these to see if they exist. The Theory of the Flower. Michael Palmer. NPGG

I will remember you on Bloom Street. Bloom Street. Angela McCabe. AmPA

I will return and look on Matsushima once again. Teika, tr. fr. Japanese by Hiroaki Sato. Fr. A Compendium of Good Tanka. FCEI

I will rise. Wine Bowl. Hilda Doolittle ("H. D."). NoP

I will rise, I will go from the places that are dark with passion and plain. Seaward. George Edward Woodberry. Fr. Wild Eden, XLI. AA

I will show you a way. Assimilation. Eeva-Liisa Manner, tr. by Aili Jarvenpa. SOP

I will sing a song,/ A song that is strong. My Breath. Orpingalik, tr. by K. Rasmussen. WTO

I will sing a song of battle. The Song of Chess. At. to Abraham ibn Ezra, tr. by Nina Davis Salaman. TrJP

I will sing, if ye will hearken. The Laird o' Logie. Unknown. CH; ESPB

I will sing no more songs! O'Bruadair. David O'Bruadair, tr. by James Stephens. BIrV

I Will Sing Praise. Bible, O.T. See Psalms: Psalm IX ("I will praise thee, O Lord. . .").

I will sing unto the Lord, for he hath triumphed gloriously. Triumphal Chant. Bible, O.T. Fr. Exodus, XV: 1-13, 18. TrGrPo

I will sing unto the Lord, for He is highly exalted. Then Sang Moses. Bible, O.T. Fr. Exodus, XV: 1-18. TrJP

I will sing you a song of that beautiful land. Home of the Soul. Ellen M. Huntington Gates. BLRP

I will sleep. December. Ron Padgett. EAS

I will speak about women of letters, for I'm in the racket. Carolyn Kizer. Fr. Pro Femina, III. CAPP; MAT; NMM

I will start. Strategy for a Marathon. Marnie Mueller. ASP

I will strike down wooden houses; I will burn aluminum. Prophecy. Donald Hall. BAP

I will take nails. Eclipse. Tomaz Salamun, tr. by Michael Scammel and Veno Taufer. VWA

I will take warning. Unknown, tr. by Arthur Waley. BoS

I will teach you my townspeople. Tract. William Carlos Williams. BLPL; DL; FF; LiTA; LiTM; MoAB; MoAmPo; MoP; NoAM; NOBA; TAP; TrGrPo; TwCP; VGW

I will teach you to become American, my students. Notes for a Lecture. David Ignatow. NNaP

I will tell a true tale of myself. Seafarer. Unknown, tr. by Kemp Malone. PoE

I will tell you of a fellow. Common Bill. Unknown. AS

I will tell you of a gallant soldier. The Soldier's Wooing. Unknown. AmFP

I will think of you, love. Unknown. Fr. Manyo Shu. Ma

I will track you down the years. Quest. Naomi Long Madgett. BPo

I will tread the sharpness of the. Hitomaro. Fr. Manyo Shu. Ma

I will visit/ Unknown woman. Spirit Song. Unknown. WTO

I will wait for the harvest. The Harvest. Yusuf al-Khal, tr. by Abdullah al-Udhari. MPAW

I will walk with a lover of wisdom. Little Elegy. Denis Devlin. NOIV

I Will Write. Robert Graves. PCP

I Will Write Songs against You. Charles Reznikoff. VGW

I will write you a letter. I Think. James Schuyler. TTTS

I will write you a poem instead of bringing rice. Paying a Sick-call to Yao Ts'un-tao in the Rain. Shen Chou, tr. by Jonathan Chaves. CoBLCP

I, Willie Wastle. Unknown. OxNR

I wish a cricket in a wicker boat. A Japanese Birthday Wish. Thomas Burnett Swann. GoYe

I wish all the/ mandragona. Blue Funk. Joel Oppenheimer. NeAP

I wish, God, for some end I do not will. Elizabeth Jennings. *Fr.* The Sonnets of Michelangelo, LXXV. TOF

I wish, how I wish that I had a little house. The Shiny Little House. Nancy M. Hayes. BoTP

I wish I could lend a coat. Akahito. *Fr.* Manyo Shu. AWP

I Wish I Could Meet the Man That Knows. John Ciardi. RHPC

I Wish I Could Remember. Christina Rossetti. *Fr.* Monna Innominata. Son

(First Day, The.) BLPL; BoLoP; FaBoBe; GBL

I wish I could rest my mind. Be Still Heart. Nilene O. A. Foxworth. AIW

I wish I could see you like this snow. Elegies for Prince Atsumichi. Lady Izumi, *tr. fr. Japanese by* Hiroaki Sato. *Fr.* Fifty-one Tanka. FCEI

I wish I could tell. Tamesuke, *tr. by* Steven D. Carter. WFTW

I wish I could walk deep into a field. Why. Michael Ryan. PPR

I wish I had a boat. Tenth Telegram. Abd al-Aziz al-Maqalih, *tr. fr. Arabic by* Lena Jayyusi *and* Christopher Middleton. *Fr.* Telegrams of Tenderness for Sanaa. MAP

I wish I had a man any man. Chiaroscuro. Carole Bergé. ErPo

I wish I had a pony. *Unknown. Fr.* Manyo Shu. FCEI

I wish I had an aeroplane. A Penny Wish. Irene Thompson. BoTP

I wish I had been born beside a river. The Upper Canadian. James Reaney. NOBC

I wish I had the leisure. Mononobe Komaro. *Fr.* Manyo Shu. Ma

I wish I had the voice of Homer. Cancer's a Funny Thing. John Burdon Sanderson Haldane. OxBTC

I wish I knew geography—for what would tell me why. Lines on a Mysterious Occurrence. Alfred Denis Godley. CenHV

I wish I lived in a caravan. The Pedlar's Caravan. William Brighty Rands. BoTP; OxBChV

I wish I loved the human race. Wishes of an Elderly Man. Sir Walter Alexander Raleigh. CenHV; FaBoCh; FaBoCo; FaBoEE; FiBHP; FPL; NBLV; NOBL

I wish I owned a Dior dress. Reflections at Dawn. Phyllis McGinley. FiBHP; NBLV; NOBL

I Wish I Was a Grown Up Man. Maggie Pogue Johnson. CBWP-4

I Wish I Was a Little Bird. *Unknown.* AS

I Wish I Was a Mole in the Ground. *Unknown.* AmFP

I Wish I Was by That Dim Lake. Thomas Moore. PoEL-4

I wish I was in de land ob cotton. Dixie. Daniel Decatur Emmett. AnAmPo; FaFP; FaPON; TrGrPo

I Wish I Was Single Again. *See* I Wish I Were Single Again.

I wish I was where I would be. John Clare. NOBVV

I wish I were a/ Elephantiaphus. *Unknown. See* I Wish I Were ("I wish I were a/ Elephantiaphus.").

I wish I were an Emperor. Wishes. F. Rogers. BoTP

I wish I were close. Akahito, *tr. by* Kenneth Rexroth. HoPM; UnAS

I Wish I Were ("I wish I were a/ Elephantiaphus."). *Unknown.* FaBoNo; FaFP; OxBoLi

I Wish I Were [*or* Was] Single Again. *Unknown.* AmFP, 2 *versions*; AS

(Single Girl, The.) AmFP

I wish I were the little key. A Child's Wish. Abram Joseph Ryan. AA

I wish I were where Helen lies. Helen of Kirconnell. *Unknown.* AWP; CH; ELP; GoTS; LiTB; OBEV

(Fair Helen.) FaFP; GTBS; GTBS-P

I Wish, I Wish. *Unknown.* OBET

I Wish My Tongue Were a Quiver. L. A. MacKay. *Fr.* The Ill-tempered Lover. CaP; OBCV; TW

I wish not Thasos rich in mines. Mimnermus Incert. Walter Savage Landor. PoEL-4

I wish not to lie here. Iona; the Graves of the Kings. Robinson Jeffers. PrIm

I wish, O son of the Living God. The Wish of Manchin of Liath. *Unknown, tr. by* Kenneth Jackson. AnIL

(Hermit's Song, The.) TIRV, *tr. by* Kuno Meyer

I wish something slow and gentle and good. Trinity. Pattiann Rogers. NAmP

I wish sometimes, although a worthlesse thing. Giles Fletcher the Elder. *Fr.* Licia, XII. AAS

I wish that I could get in line. They Don't Speak English in Paris. Ogden Nash. OBAL

I wish that I could have my wish to-night. Shakespeare. Henry Ames Blood. AA

I wish that my room had a floor. Gelett Burgess. FiBHP; InvP; OBCA

I wish that there were some wonderful place. The Land of Beginning Again. Louisa Fletcher. BLPA

I wish that when you died last May. May and Death. Robert Browning. FaBoRV; NOBE

I wish the rent. Little Lyric (of Great Importance). Langston Hughes. NBLV; OBAL

I wish there were a man going to my home. Otomobe Fushimaro. *Fr.* Manyo Shu. Ma

I wish there were a touch of these boats about my life. Boat Poem. Bernard Spencer. FaBoTw; OxBTC

I wish they would hurry up their trip to Mars. A Projection. Reed Whittemore. AiP; NePoEA

I wish to be given beautiful things this Christmas. Six Things for Christmas. John May, *tr. by* Arthur Waley. Mes

"I wish to buy a dog," she said. On Buying a Dog. Edgar Klauber. NTCP

I wish to go away and live. Asadullah Khan Ghalib, *tr. by* Ahmed Ali. GoT

I wish to God my child was born. *Unknown.* AmFP

I wish to make a positive statement. Peace. George Jonas. NeAC

I wish to make my sermon brief. Praise of Little Women. Juan Ruiz, Archpriest of Hita, *tr. by* Longfellow. AWP

I wish to paint my eyes. *Unknown, tr. by* Willis Barnstone. BoWoP; UnAS

I wish to submit a memorial expressing my feelings. Submitting a Memorial Requesting Permission to Return Home and Care for My Parents. Yang Chi, *tr. by* Jonathan Chaves. CoBLCP

I wish you for your birthday as you are. Moving In. Karl Shapiro. NAs

I Wish You Had Warned Me ("I wish you had put a red light on."). Veronica Williams. WS

I wish you triumphs that are yours already. For Marianne Moore's Birthday. Kay Boyle. NMM

I wish you were a pleasant wren. Child's Talk in April. Christina Rossetti. GN

I wish you were not flying, and I wish. For a Homecoming. Julia Randall. NMM

I wish you would come. Izumi Shikibu, *tr. by* Willis Barnstone. BoWoP

I wish you'd been a Bryon. Sane, Plain, and Tedious to Know. Jenny Morris. SoTCo

I wish you'd speak to Mary, Nurse. The Game of Cricket. Hilaire Belloc. FiBHP

I wish your breast was made of glass. The Lover's Lament. *Unknown.* AS

I wished you awake for the bird song. Bird Song. Betsy Rosenberg. VWA

I wist not what to wish, yet sure thought I. Anne Bradstreet. *Fr.* Contemplations. PBWP

I with the morning's love have oft made sport. Sunrise on the Sea. Shakespeare. *Fr.* A Midsummer Night's Dream, III, ii. ChTr

I with uncovered head. James Russell Lowell. *Fr.* Ode Recited at the Harvard Commemoration, VIII *and* XII. OHIP

I, with whose colors [*or* colours] Myra dressed [*or* dress'd] her head. Fulke Greville. *Fr.* Caelica, XXII. GBL; HAP; InvP; QFR

(Myra.) EIL; NOBE; OBEV; OBSC

(To Myra.) LiTB

i without dot, An. Studium Generale. Alfred Gong, *tr. by* Beth Bjorklund. CoAuP

I woke/ Just about daybreak and fell back. Poems to a Brown Cricket. James Wright. NaP; NYBP

I woke before the day, when the night bird. Thomas Iron-Eyes. Marnie Walsh. WPOW

I woke before the morning, I was happy. A Good Boy. Robert Louis Stevenson. PWR

I woke by first light in a wood. Donald Justice. NePoEA

I woke this morning and sunlight. Spider Dream. Elaine Hall. GOS

I Woke Up. Revenge. A. Poulin, Jr.. TW

I woke up at night and my language was gone. Nothingness. Aharon Amir. VWA

I woke up this mornin'. Sylvester's Dying Bed. Langston Hughes. NoAM; UnPo

I woke up this mornin'. Empty Bed Blues. Bessie Smith. OBAL; UnPo

I woke up this mornin' with the blues all round my bed. I Got the Blues. *Unknown.* TTY

I woke with this marble head in my hands. George Seferis, *tr. fr. Greek by* Edmund Keeley *and* Philip Sherrard. *Fr.* Mythistorima, III. VMG

I wold fain be a clarke. The Scholar Complains. *Unknown.* MeEL

(Schoolboy's Lament, The.) OxBLMV

I wolde witen of sum wis wight. The World an Illusion. *Unknown.* MeEL

I, Woman. Irma McClaurin. BlSi

I won a noble fame. Sir Marmaduke's Musings. Theodore Tilton. AA

I Wonder. Jeannie Kirby. BoTP

I wonder about/ the brother. Come On Home. Sharon Scott. JB

I wonder about the trees. The Sound of Trees. Robert Frost. NoAM

(Sound of the Trees, The.) OxBA

I Wonder as I Wander. *Unknown, arr. by* Jacob Niles. EaLo; PChr
I wonder as into bed I creep. Sweet Dreams. Ogden Nash. OnUR
I wonder, by my troth, what thou and I. The Good-Morrow. John
     Donne. AWP; BoLoP; EBEV; EiL; EnLoPo; FaBoBe; FaBV; FF;
     FPL; HoPM; InPS; InvP; JCP; LiTB; MeLP; MePo; NAEL-1;
     NAWM-1; NIP; NoP; OAEL-1; OBS; PoE; PoEL-2; PoRA; PPP;
     SCV; SeCP; SeCV-1; SoSe; TEP; TrGrPo
I wonder, dear, if you had been. A Conjecture. Charles Francis
     Richardson. AA
I wonder do you feel to-day. Two in the Campagna. Robert Browning.
     EBEV; EBVV; ELP; GTBS-P; NAEL-2; NOBE; NOBVV; NoP;
     OAEL-2; OBNC; PoE; PoEL-5; SeCePo; TOF; TrGrPo
I wonder how many old men last winter. The Minneapolis Poem. James
     Wright. FYAP; NoAM; UnPo
I Wonder How My Home Is. *Unknown, tr. fr. Tewa Indian by* H. J.
     Spinden. WTO
I wonder how the organist. The Organist. George W. Stevens. BLPA
I wonder if all muses are assigned a poet to keep. Think Small. Elaine
     Equi. UL
I wonder if Christ had a little black dog. The Little Black Dog.
     Elizabeth Gardner Reynolds. PoLF
I wonder if his appetite was good? Byron. *Fr.* Don Juan, V. OAEL-2
I wonder if in that far isle. Braddan Vicarage. Thomas Edward Brown.
     FaBoPP
I wonder if the elephant. Pete at the Zoo. Gwendolyn Brooks. ILY;
     PDV
I wonder if the old cow died or not. The Question. W. W. Gibson.
     MMA
I wonder if the sap is stirring yet. The First Spring Day. Christina
     Rossetti. WiR
I wonder if they sleep better here. Graveyard by the Sea. Thomas Lux.
     AnAn; LCAP; NAmP
I wonder if, when Galatea woke. A Question. Edna Livingston. GoYe
I wonder: is there no way for us to meet again. Wallada, *tr. by* A. R.
     Nykl. PBWP
I Wonder, Love. Pedro Salinas, *tr. fr. Spanish by* Perry Higman. LPSS
I wonder poet, can you take it. The Muse to an Unknown Poet. Paul
     Potts. FaBoTw
I wonder, since we are both travelling out. The Travelling Out. Lucile
     Adler. IHMS; NYBP
I wonder sometimes if the soldiers lying. Song for the Heroes. Alex
     Comfort. MoBrPo
I wonder what day of the week. An Untimely Thought. Thomas Bailey
     Aldrich. PWR
I wonder what eagle did to him. Gaxe, *tr. by* James Koller. STP
I Wonder What It Feels Like to Be Drowned? Robert Graves. BrPo;
     MoBrPo
I wonder what kind of night is this night? Night of the First Full Moon.
     Liang Ch'i-ch'ao, *tr. by* Cecile Chu-chin Sun. WFTU
I wonder what my kite can see. The Kite. Pearl Forbes MacEwen.
     BoTP
I wonder what the clover thinks. A Song of Clover. Helen Hunt
     Jackson. GN
I wonder what to mean by sanctuary, if a real or. Triphammer Bridge.
     A. R. Ammons. NAAL-2; NOBA
I wonder where it could of went to. Legend. John Van Alstyn Weaver.
     AmFN
I wonder whether the Girls are mad. William Bond. Blake. OxBB
I wonder why. Tom Poole. NBP
I wonder why I am living at this time. The Revenant. Robert Siegel.
     GeTw
I wonder why the grass is green. I Wonder. Jeannie Kirby. BoTP
I Wondered ("I wondered/ if in my sleep I could find that place."). Rita
     Anyiam–St. John. WS
I wondered if the others felt. The Search Party. William Matthews.
     GeTw
I wondered why the covers felt so cold. Night Snow. Po Chü-i, *tr. by*
     Burton Watson. CoBCP
I won't be my father's Jack. Mother Goose. OxNR
"I won't go with you. I want to stay with Grandpa!" My Last Afternoon
     with Uncle Devereux Winslow. Robert Lowell. NAAL-2; NoP;
     VGW
I won't let you go, this spring evening turns dark. Yosano Akiko, *tr. fr.*
     Japanese by Hiroaki Sato. *Fr.* Thirty-nine Tanka. FCEI
I work all day, and get half drunk at night. Philip Larkin. OPOP; SoSe
I work all day long for you, until the sun go down. *Unknown.* WTO
I work and I remember. I conceive. That's All. Lawrence Joseph.
     EOEF
I work for a newspaper. Not Allowed to Write. Gloria Fuertes, *tr. by*
     Robert L. Smith *and* Judith Candullo. DMH
I work in a foreign country. Foreign Land. Washington Delgado, *tr. by*
     David Tipton. Per

I work nights at the University Bookshop. Thoughts of Jack Kerouac–&
     Other Things. Peter Olds. ATNZ; PeNZ
I work or play, as I think best. Emancipation. *Unknown.* BLPA; FPL
I work to music on the radio. The Campus. David Posner. NYBP
I Worship Thee, O Holy Ghost. William F. Warren. AH
I worshipped, when my veins were fresh. William Baylebridge. *Fr.*
     Life's Testament, VI. PoAu-1
I wot full well that beauty cannot last. To His Friend, Promising That
     Though Her Beauty Fade, Yet His Love Shall Last. George
     Turberville. OBSC
     (To His Friend.) CTC
I would adore doing it over. A Plan to Live My Life Again. Diana O
     Hehir. NPGG
I would ask of you, my darling. Will You Love Me When I'm Old?
     Unknown. BLPA; BLPL; FaBoBe
I Would Be a Painter Most of All. Len Chandler. NBP
I would be dismal with all the fine pearls of the crown of a king. To a
     Blue Flower. John Shaw Neilson. PoAu-1
I would be married, but I'd have no wife. On Marriage. Richard
     Crashaw. FaBoEE
I would be ready, Lord. Ready. Margaret Junkin Preston. PWR
I would be true, for there are those who trust me. My Creed. Howard
     Arnold Walter. FaFP; PoLF; WBLP
I would be wandering in distant fields. In Bondage. Claude McKay.
     PoBA
I would conceal it, yet. Kanemori, *tr. by* Geoffrey Bownas *and* Anthony
     Thwaite. PeBJV
I would despise myself if I had the strength for it. The Cost of
     Pretending. Peter Davison. TW
I would go around biting my nails. Salvador Villanueva, *tr. by* Julio
     Marzán. InW
I would go round and round. Lonely Monday. J. Patrick Lewis. ILY
I would have been surprised, but I had seen him. The Messenger. Grace
     Schulman. AnAn
I would have gone; God bade me stay. Weary in Well-doing. Christina
     Rossetti. SeCePo; TrPWD
I would I had been island-born. A Ballade of Islands. Lucy Catlin
     Robinson. AA
I would I had something to do—or to think! All in the Downs. Tom
     Hood. CenHV
I would I had thrust my hands of flesh. Edmund Pollard. Edgar Lee
     Masters. *Fr.* Spoon River Anthology. ErPo
I Would I Might Forget That I Am I. George Santayana. AWP
I would I were a bird so free. *Unknown, tr. by* John Addington Symonds.
     Fr. Popular Songs of Tuscany. AWP
I Would I Were Actaeon. *At. to* ———Bewe. EiL
     (Actaeon.) OBSC
I would, if I could. Mother Goose. OxNR
I would immortalize these nymphs: so bright. L'Après-Midi d'un Faune.
     Stéphane Mallarmé, *tr. by* Aldous Huxley. AWP
I would in rich and golden coloured raine. Thomas Lodge. *Fr.* Phyllis,
     XXXIV *after the French of* Pierre de Ronsard. AAS
I would lie low—the ground on which men tread. The Earth. Jones
     Very. AnAmPo; OxBA
I would like/ to love my enemies. Peter Turrini, *tr. by* Beth Bjorklund.
     CoAuP
I would like/ to make. Oh—Yeah! Sharon Scott. JB
I would like all things to be free of me. Proof. Brendan Kennelly.
     CIP
I would like it if people knew this song. Guillaume de Poitiers, *tr. fr.*
     Provençal by Paul Blackburn. Pro
I would like my last poem thus. My Last Poem. Manuel Bandeira, *tr.*
     by Elizabeth Bishop. ATCBP
I would like my love to die. Samuel Beckett. BIrV; CIP; NOIV
I would like to be as mobile as my mind. Evaporation Poems. Kathleen
     Norris. IHMS
I would like to be that elderly Chinese gentleman. Dreaming in the
     Shanghai Restaurant. D. J. Enright. OBTV
I would like to bury. The Fury of Hating Eyes. Anne Sexton. TW
I would like to dive. The Diver. W. W. E. Ross. NOBC; OBCV
I would like to give you. Unposted Birthday Card. Norman MacCaig.
     NAs
I would like to have a quiet place. My Penultimate Speech at a Meeting
     of Some People of Good Will. J. Monika Walther, *tr. by* Susan L.
     Cocalis. DMG
I would like to remind/ the management. The Music Crept by Us.
     Leonard Cohen. FF
I would like to scream but there is no one to hear. Setting/ Slow Drag.
     Carolyn M. Rodgers. JB
I would like to sleep with deer. A Moral Poem Freely Accepted from
     Sappho. James Wright. CAPP
I would like to think. Art. Hjalmar Flax, *tr. by* Julio Marzán. InW

I would like to watch you sleeping. Variation on the Word *Sleep*.
Margaret Atwood. NIP; NOBC
I Would Like You for a Comrade. Edward Abbott Parry. OxBChV
I would live all my life in nonchalance and insouciance. Introspective
Reflection. Ogden Nash. NBLV
I would live for a day and a night. The Song-Maker. Anna Wickham.
MoBrPo
I would make a vessel, ship, a boat. Calvary. Padraig De Brun, *tr. by*
Máire Mhac an tSaoi. TIRV
I would make my way without a thought of you. *Unknown, tr. fr.
Japanese*. *Fr.* Manyo Shu. Ma
I would not alter thy cold eyes. Flos Lunae. Ernest Dowson. OBMV
I would not ask Thee that my days. A Humble Heart. Alfred Norris.
PWR
(Prayer for Faith.) BLRP
I would not be a servingman to carry the cloke-bag still. Merrythought's
Song. Beaumont *and* Fletcher. *Fr.* The Knight of the Burning
Pestle, IV, i. OBS
I would not be the moon, the sickly thing. In Dispraise of the Moon.
Mary Elizabeth Coleridge. BoNaP; CH
I would not feign a single sigh. John Clare. GBL
I would not have a god come in. Mastery. Sara Teasdale. WGRP
I Would Not Live Alway. William Augustus Muhlenberg. AA, *with
music*; AH, *with music*
I would not marry a blacksmith. Soldier Boy for Me. *Unknown*.
AmFP
I would not paint—a picture. Emily Dickinson. NAAL-1; NOBA
I would not tell them why I had smashed the window. "In This House,
There Shall Be No Idols." Carolyn M. Rodgers. JB
I would not want, I think, a higher intelligence, one. Erosion. Jorie
Graham. MAYP
I would not write a lament for you. Salt. Anne Hartigan. CIP
I would prefer to live quietly in silks. Running through Sleep. Kathleen
Norris. IHMS
I would quickly reach my loved one's dwelling. Hitomaro. *Fr.* Manyo
Shu. Ma
I would rather be myself. Written at the Po-Shan Monastery. Hsin Ch'i-
chi, *tr. by* Irving Y. Lo. ILY
I would rather ruffle leaves. Summer Lightning. T. Sturge Moore.
BrPo
I Would Rather Run Back. Sandor Csoori, *tr. fr. Hungarian by* Alan
Dixon. MHuP
I would revive you with a swallow's nest. To My Grandmother. Medbh
McGuckian. FaBCIP
I would rid myself of an old way of life. Diogenes. Arthur Rex Dugard
Fairburn. PeNZ
I would set all things whatsoever front to back. Wyndham Lewis. *Fr.*
One-Way Song. CTC
I would show you this. Love Expresses with Candle as a Metaphor.
Tamemasa, *tr. by* Steven D. Carter. WFTW
I would tell a marvelous vision. The Dream of the Cross. *Unknown, tr.
by* Sally Purcell. EBEV
I would that all men my hard case would know. Behold the Deeds! H.
C. Bunner. NBLV
I would that even now. Princess Shoku, *tr. fr. Japanese by* Curtis Hidden
Page. *Fr.* Hyaku-Nin-Isshu. AWP
I would that folk forgot me quite. Tess's Lament. Thomas Hardy.
FaBoTw; TEP
I would that we were, my beloved, white birds on the foam of the sea.
The White Birds. W. B. Yeats. UnAS
I would the gift I offer here. Whittier. *Fr.* Songs of Labor. OxBA
I would thou wert not fair, or I were wise. Nicholas Breton. *Fr.* The
Strange Fortunes of Two Excellent Princes. EIL; InvP
(His Wisdom.) OBSC
I would to heaven that I were so much clay. Byron. *Fr.* Don Juan, *on
the back of the poet's MS of Canto* I. CTC; FiP; NAEL-2; NOBL;
NoP; OAEL-2; OxBSP; PrIm
I would unto my fair restore. Of Joan's Youth. Louise Imogen Guiney.
AA
I Would Visit Him in the Corner. Alberto Rios. NAmP
I would worry less if she sang. If She Sang. Gerald William Barrax.
CNA
I would worship if I could. Great Spaces. Howard Moss. TwCP
I Wouldn't. John Ciardi. TDD
I wouldn't coax the plant if I were you. Woman with Flower. Naomi
Long Madgett. AmNP; FB
I wouldn't have seen her. First Green Heron. Gary Margolis. ASP
I wouldn't marry a bachelor. Old Maid's Song. *Unknown*. AmFP
I wouldn't much object, if I were black. A Negro Cemetery Next to a
White One. Howard Nemerov. OxBSP
I wouldn't question the kisses you may offer. For Nothing. Andrés
Castro Ríos, *tr. by* Julio Marzán. InW

I wouldn't say night with fog. Fog and Town. Ishihara Yoshiro, *tr. by*
Hiroaki Sato. FCEI
I write about a silly ass. Hero and Leander. Joseph S. Newman.
FiBHP
I write because not to write is a breach of faith. Beth Brant. *Fr.* A
Simple Act (Story Two: My House). ER
I write characters in lamplight. Yüan Mei, *tr. fr. Chinese by* Jonathan
Chaves. *Fr.* Miscellaneous Poems on Growing Old. CoBLCP
I write, Honora, on the sparkling sand! Elegy Written at the Sea-Side,
and Addressed to Miss Honoria Sneyd. Anna Seward. PeHV
I write in praise of the solitary act. Against Coupling. Fleur Adcock.
ATNZ
I write in the sand. Ishikawa Takuboku, *tr. by* Geoffrey Bownas *and*
Anthony Thwaite. PeBJV
I write my name as one. An Autograph. Whittier. AA
I write of Jam, a subject stiff. On Jam. Hilaire Belloc. NBLV
I Write Only to Relieve My Inner Grief. Vittoria da Colonna, *tr. fr.
Italian by* Muriel Kittel. DMI
I Write Poems. Gloria Fuertes, *tr. fr. Spanish by* Philip Levine. WPOW
I write these precepts for immortal Greece. Archestratus, *tr. fr. Greek by*
Isaac D'Israeli. *Fr.* Gastrology. FaBoUs
I write this poem. For Musia's Grandchildren. Irving Layton. NOBC
I write to make you suffer. Anne-Marie Kegels, *tr. by* Willis Barnstone.
BoWoP
I write what I have to write. The Prevaricator. Shirley Vogler Meister.
SoTCo
I write you to protest the line. Opening Letter to Manufacturers of
Bathroom Wallpaper. Katharine O'Brien. SoTCo
I wrote a song shining as glass. P. Mustapää, *tr. by* Aili Jarvenpa.
SOP
I wrote some lines once on a time. The Height of the Ridiculous. Oliver
Wendell Holmes. AA; FaFP; FiBHP; FPL; MoShBr; OBAL; OBCA
I wrote the postcard to you and went out. Getting Through. James
Merrill. NYBP
I wrung my hands under my dark veil. "Anna Akhmatova," *tr. by* Max
Hayward *and* Stanley Kunitz. BoLoP
I yearn to be more than I am. More. Yrjö Jylhä, *tr. by* Aili Jarvenpa.
SOP
I years had been from home. Emily Dickinson. BLPL; NOBA; OxBA;
PoRA
I Yield Thee Praise. Philip Jerome Cleveland. TrPWD
I you assure. To Mistress Margaret Tilney. John Skelton. *Fr.* The
Garlande [*or* Garlands] of Laurell. MeEL
Ia Drang Valley. Yusef Komunyakaa. MT
Iago Prytherch his name, though, be it allowed. A Peasant. R. S.
Thomas. OBWVE
Iambes VIII. André Marie de Chénier, *tr. fr. French by* Tom Paulin.
FaBoPV
Iambic Feet Considered as Honorable Scars. William Meredith. OxBSP;
PoA
Iambicum Trimetrum. Spenser. BoLoP; EBEV; EIL; OBEV; OPoP;
PoEL-1
(Iambica.) OxBoLi
Ianthe, *sels.* Walter Savage Landor.
Absence. EnRP
Do You Remember Me?. EnRP
("Do you remember me? or are you proud?") OBNC
(Ianthe's Question.) OBEV
"From you, Ianthe, little troubles pass." OBNC; TrGrPo
(Ianthe.) OBEV
(Ianthe's Troubles.) GBL; NOBE
"Ianthe! you resolve [*or* are called] to cross the sea!" OBNC
(Absence.) EnRP
"Mild is the parting year, and sweet." EnLoPo; TEP
(Autumn.) TrGrPo
"My hopes retire; my wishes as before." GBL; OBNC
"Past ruin'd Ilion Helen lives." CTC; ELP; EnLoPo; EnRP; GBL;
HAP; HeIP; NoP; OBNC; PoRA; TrGrPo; WeW
(Ianthe.) LiTB; PoEL-4
(Passed Ruin'd Ilion.) AWP
(To Ianthe.) NOBE
(Verse: "Past ruin'd Ilion. .") OBEV
"Proud word you never spoke, but you will speak." EnLoPo; GBL;
OBEV
Remain, Ah Not in Youth Alone. HAP; OBNC
"Thou hast not rais'd, Ianthe, such desire." GBL
Well I Remember [How You Smiled]. HAP; OBNC; TrGrPo
(Ianthe.) HAP; OBNC; TrGrPo
"When Helen first saw wrinkles in her face." EnLoPo
"Ye walls! sole witnesses of happy sighs." EnLoPo
Ibant Obscuræ. Thomas Edward Brown. OBNC
Ibby Damsel. *Unknown*. AmFP

Iberian! palter no more! To Spain—a Last Word. Edith M. Thomas. PAH
Ibikunle! the Lord of his Quarters. Praise of Ibikunle. Yoruba Oral Tradition, *tr. by* B. Awe. WTO
Ibn Battuta. Dick Davis. NPo
Icarian Is the Sea. Hans Tentije, *tr. fr. Dutch by* Scott Rollins. DuIn
Icarus. Ronald Botrall. GTBS-P
Icarus. Valentin Iremonger. BIrV; CIP; NeIP
Icarus. Harry Lyman Koopman. AA
Icarus. Stephen Spender. MoP; PrIm
Icarus. *Unknown. See* Love winged my hopes and taught me how to fly.
Icarus. Jane Yolen. BWV
Ice. Ai. FYAP
Ice. David Bottoms. BLA
Ice, The. W. W. Gibson. OxBTC
Ice. Sir Charles G. D. Roberts. BoNaP; OBCV; RHPC
Ice. Stephen Spender. FaBoMo; GTBS-P; SeCePo
Ice age is here, The. Attention. Adrienne Rich. TAP
Ice built, ice bound, and ice bounded. Alaska. Joaquin Miller. PAH
Ice Cold. Sean O Riordain, *tr. fr. Irish by* Thomas Kinsella. NOIV
Ice Cream. Peter Wild. Psk
Ice-Cream Man, The. Rachel Field. FaPON
Ice-Cream Wars, The. John Ashbery. CAPP; PoA
Ice, Eden. Paul Celan, *tr. fr. German by* Michael Hamburger. OBD
Ice-Fishing. Denise Pendleton. ASP
Ice-Floes, The. E. J. Pratt. CaP
Ice flow cut this valley, The. The Ice Has Spoken. Denis Rixson. PoSH
Ice-Flumes Owregie Their Ladies. Douglas Young. SeCePo
Ice Handler. Carl Sandburg. OxBA
Ice has been cracking all day. Spring. Michael Hogan. InPK
Ice Has Spoken, The. Denis Rixson. PoSH
Ice has vanished—don't be left behind. Shiba Sonome, *tr. fr. Japanese by* Hiroaki Sato. *Fr.* Fifteen Hokku. FCEI
Ice honed by wind. Tracking the Siuslaw Man. Jim Barnes. HATNAP
Ice, Ice. Gerald Stern. AnAn
Ice in the school-room, listen. A Schooling. Seamus Deane. CIP
Ice is smooth, smooth, smooth, The. Hockey. Scott Blaine. ASP
Ice Man, Magic, Bird and McAdoo. Take Who Takes You. Fred Gardner. ASP
Ice on my laid-out sleeve still frozen, The. Teika, *tr. fr. Japanese by* Hiroaki Sato. *Fr.* A Compendium of Good Tanka. FCEI
Ice over time. David Shapiro. UL
Ice River. David Baker. SM
Ice-Skaters. Elder Olson. SD
Ice Skin, The. James Dickey. NYBP
Ice tinkled in glasses. Blues and Bitterness. Lerone Bennett, Jr. FF; PoBA
Ice wedged fast. Saigyo, *tr. fr. Japanese by* Burton Watson. *Fr.* Sixty-four Tanka. FCEI
Iceball, The. William Hathaway. NAmP
Iceberg, The. Sir Charles G. D. Roberts. CaP
Iced with a vanilla. A Meeting of Cultures. Donald Davie. OBTV; OxBC
Icehouse in Summer, The. Howard Nemerov. MoP; NoAM
Icehouse keeper, The. *Unknown, tr. by* Burton Watson. FCEI
Iceland First Seen. William Morris. OBTV
Iceman, The. Gordon Challis. ATNZ; PeNZ
Ich Am of Irlonde. *Unknown. See* I am of Ireland.
Ich sterbe. . .Life ebbs with an easy flow. The End of a War. Sir Herbert Read. OBMV; WaP
Ich Weiss Nicht Was Soll es Bedeuten. Heine, *tr. fr. German by* Alexander Macmillan. AWP
"Ich wünscht', ich wäre ein Vöglein." The Bird. Louis Simpson. NePoEA-2
Ichabod. Whittier. AA; AnAmPo; LiTA; NAAL-1; NOBA; OxBA; PAH; PoEL-4; TAP
Ichabod! The Glory Has Departed. Ludwig Uhland, *tr. fr. German by* James Clarence Mangan. AWP
Icham of Irlaunde. *Unknown. See* I am of Ireland.
Ichot a burde in boure bryht. Blow, Northern Wind. *Unknown.* GBL; OBEV
(Love for a Beautiful Lady.) MeEL
Ichthycide. Joe Rosenblatt. NOBC
Ichthyology. Gerrit Achterberg, *tr. fr. Dutch by* James S. Holmes. DuIn
Icicles. Robert Pinsky. BLA; SM
Icicles upon the pane, The. February. Henrietta Cordelia Ray. CBWP-3
Icily. René Daumal, *tr. fr. French by* Michael Benedikt. POS
Ickle ockle, blue bockle. *Unknown.* OxNR
Icon. Fleur Adcock. ATNZ
Icon. Mark Osaki. BrSi

Icons. Miriam Waddington. NOBC
Icos. Charles Tomlinson. GTBS-P
Icosasphere, The. Marianne Moore. ImOP
Icy. Rhoda Warner Bacmeister. RAR
Icy, empty dawn cracks in the fields, The. Pacifists. George Woodcock. NOBC
Icy evil that struck his father down, The. El-Hajj Malik El-Shabazz. Robert Hayden. CNA; PoBA
Icy scar in the afterglow sends off the setting sun, An. The Moon on the Night of the Third of the Month. Chiang Ch'un-lin, *tr. by* Irving Lo. WFTU
Icy sky, snow-blanketed earth, the wind like a tiger. Sixteen Songs of the Capital: Chicken Feather Shop. Chiang Shih-ch'üan, *tr. by* Irving Lo. WFTU
I'd a dream to-night. Mater Dolorosa. William Barnes. CH; NOBE; OBEV
I'd almost know, the nights I snuck in late. Fifteen to Eighteen. Marilyn Hacker. GLP
I'd already lost my hair. Now my sun. The Corn. Daniel David Moses. HATNAP
I'd arrived the previous night from the country. The Wonder Castle. Gyula Illyés, *tr. by* Kenneth McRobbie. MHuP
I'd be encouraged if I liked what I compose. *Unknown, tr. by* Meg Bogin. WT
I'd been on duty from two till four. Stand-to: Good Friday Morning. Siegfried Sassoon. FaBoTw
I'd build a house with windows. Skycoast. Samuel Hazo. GrPl
I'd Choose to Be a Daisy. *Unknown.* BoTP
I'd draw all this into a fine element,—a color. The Rug. Michael McClure. NeAP
I'd fill up the house with guests this minute. A Revel. Donagh MacDonagh. NeIP
I'd have liked it to have been so. Sadness of the Bare Copula. Dezsö Tandori, *tr. by* Kenneth McRobbie. MHuP
I'd Have You, Quoth He. *Unknown.* ErPo; FF
I'd Leave. Andrew Lang. FaPON
I'd like a different dog. Dogs and Weather. Winifred Welles. FaPON
I'd like a little/ Of that nourishing victual. *Unknown.* FaFP
I'd like to/ pull. The Intelligent Sheepman and the New Cars. William Carlos Williams. OBAL
I'd Like to Be a Lighthouse. Rachel Field. PDV; RAR
I'd like to be a Lombard for Lombarda. Lombarda, *tr. by* Meg Bogin. WT
I'd like to be called a traveler. Basho, *tr. fr. Japanese by* Burton Watson. *Fr.* Seventy-six Hokku. FCEI
I'd like to be the sort of friend that you have been to me. A Friend's Greeting. Edgar Albert Guest. BLPA; BLPL
I'd like to have a word. The Book of Lies. James Tate. SM
I'd like to hear a sermon done. S.P.C.A. Sermon. Stuart Hemsley. FiBHP
I'd like to live with you. Marina Tsvetayeva, *tr. by* Paul Schmidt. BoWoP
I'd Like to Mark Myself. Milton Acorn. NeAC
I'd like to open the door. On the Anniversary of Basho's Death I Visited His Grave in Kiso. Kaai Chigetsu, *tr. fr. Japanese by* Hiroaki Sato. *Fr.* Thirteen Hokku. FCEI
I'd like to peddle toy balloons. The Balloon Seller. Elizabeth Fleming. BoTP
I'd like to run like a rabbit in hops. Rabbit. Tom Robinson. FaPON
I'd like to see you as in a clear mirror. *Unknown. Fr.* Manyo Shu. FCEI
I'd like to speak to you cracked crystal crying like a dog. Where Are You. Benjamin Péret, *tr. by* Michael Benedikt. POS
I'd like to wrestle free. Durable Material. Hans Vlek, *tr. by* James S. Holmes. DuIn
I'd look back and see the coffee mornings. A Hankering after Truth. Veronica Williams. WS
I'd Love to Be a Fairy's Child. Robert Graves. BoTP; FaPON; PDV
I'd love to give a party. A Wish. Elizabeth Gould. BoTP
I'd love to take a camel trek. Double Occupancy—Sahara Style. Ned Pastor. SoTCo
I'd make a bed for you. Labasheedy (the Silken Bed). Nuala Ni Dhomhnaill, *tr. by* The Author. CIP
I'd mend them but there's not half a sheet of paper in my bag. Torn Windows, No Paper. Keijo Shurin, *tr. by* Burton Watson. FCEI
I'd much rather sit there in the sun. Ruth Krauss. RHPC; SO
I'd never dare to walk across. The Invisible Bridge. Gelett Burgess. NA
I'd oft heard tell of this Sledburn fair. Sledburn Fair. *Unknown.* CH
I'd often seen before. The Sheaf. Andrew Young. ChTr
"I'd rather be loved, and love, than be Shakespeare." Portrait: My Wife. John Holmes. UAS

I'd rather have fingers than toes. On Digital Extremities. Gelett Burgess. FaPON

I'd rather have habits than clothes. Gelett Burgess. NA

I'd rather have the thought of you. Choice. Angela Morgan. PoLF

I'd rather listen to a flute. Samuel Hoffenstein. FiBHP

I'd run about/ on the desert. Her Elegy. *Unknown, tr. by* Armand Schwerner. BoWoP, *tr. by* Ruth Underhill; STP

I'd sit inside the abandoned shack all morning. About a Year After He Got Married He Would Sit Alone in an Abandoned Shack in a Cotton Field Enjoying Himself. James Whitehead. MT

I'd smoke in the freezer. Shoplifters. Maura Stanton. MAYP

I'd walk her home after work. New York, Summer. Jack Gilbert. NPGG

I'd Want Her Eyes to Fill with Wonder. Kenneth Patchen. LLLT

I'd wave the gnats away and try. Crew Practice on Lake Bled, in Jugoslavia. James Scully. NYBP

I'd weave a wreath for those who fought. Through Fire in Mobile Bay. *Unknown.* PAH

I'd wed you without herds, without money, or rich array. Cashel of Munster. *At. to.* William English, *tr. by* Sir Samuel Ferguson. BIrV; GBL; OBEV

Idaho. *Unknown.* GBP

Idbury bells are ringing. Country Thought. Sylvia Townsend Warner. MoBrPo

Idea, *sels.* Michael Drayton.
   "As other men, so I myself do muse." *Fr.* IX. JCP; Son
   "Calling to my mind [*or* minde] since first my love begun." *Fr.* LI. NOBE; OBSC; PoEL-2
   "Deare [*or* Dear], why should you command [*or* commaund] me to my rest." *Fr.* XXXVII. AAS; NOBE; OBSC; PoEL-2; Son
   (Night and Day.) LiTB
   (Sonnet: "Dear [*or* Deere], why should you command me to my rest.") EIL
   "Evil [*or* Evill] spirit, your beauty, haunts me still, An." *Fr.* XX. AAS; EIL; GBL; NOBE; OBSC
   His Remedie for Love. AAS
   "How many paltry, foolish, painted things." *Fr.* VI. AAS; EnLoPo; GBL; HAP; NAEL-1; NIP; NoP; OAEL-1; OBSC; PrIm; TEP
   (Sonnet: "How many paltry. .") EIL
   "I hear some say, this man is not in love." *Fr.* XXIV. TrGrPo
   "If he, from heaven that filched the living fire." *Fr.* XIV. AAS; NoP; TEP
   "Into these loves, who but for passion looks." *Fr. introd. sonnet.* NoP
   (To the Reader of These Sonnets.) AAS; NAEL-1; Son
   Like an Adventurous Seafarer Am I. *Fr.* I. Son
   Methinks I See Some Crooked Mimic Jeer. *Fr.* XXXI. Son
   "Nothing but no and I, and I and no." *Fr.* V. GBL; PoEL-2
   "Since there's [*or* ther's] no help[e], come let us kiss[e] and part." *Fr.* LXI. AAS; AWP; BoLoP; EnLoPo; GBL; HAP; HeIP; InPS; JCP; NAEL-1; NOBE; NoP; OAEL-1; OBSC; PoEL-2; PrIm; SeCePo; Son; SoSe; TEP; TrGrPo
   (Farewell to Love.) BLPL
   (Love's Farewell.) GTBS; GTBS-P
   (Parting, The.) LiTB; OBEV; SCV
   (Sonnet: "Since there's no help. . .") EIL
   "Stay, speedy time; behold, before thou pass." *Fr.* XVII (*also given as VII in* Idea's Mirrour). OBSC
   "There's nothing grieves me, but that age should haste." AAS, VIII; OAEL-1, VIII.
   "To nothing fitter can I thee compare." *Fr.* X. EIL; OBSC; Son; TrGrPo
   "Truce, gentle love, a parley now I crave." *Fr.* LXIII. NoP
   "When first I ended, then I first begun." *Fr.* LXII (*also given as L in* Idea's Mirrour). TrGrPo
   "Whilst thus my pen strives to eternize thee." *Fr.* XLIV. AAS; OBSC; Son
   "Why should your fair eyes with such sovereign grace." *Fr.* XLIII. OBSC
   "Witlesse gallant, a young wench that woo'd, A." *Fr.* XXI. AAS
   "You are [*or* You're] not alone when you are still alone." *Fr.* XI. PoEL-2; TrGrPo

Idea of a Swimmer. Jean-Richard Bloch, *tr. fr. French by* "S. P." TrJP

Idea of Ancestry, The. Etheridge Knight. BPo; CNA; NIP; NNaP; PoBA; SV

Idea of Detroit, The. Jim Gustafson. UL

Idea of Entropy at Maenporth Beach, The. Peter Redgrove. FaBoMo

Idea of justice may be precious, An. Frank O'Hara. NeAP

Idea of Mick Jagger at a Concert, The. Jerry Harp. SoTCo

Idea of Order at Key West, The. Wallace Stevens. CMoP; FF; HAP; HCAP; HeIP; MoAB; MoAmPo; MoP; MOS; NAAL-2; NAWM-2; NIP; NIP; NoAM; NOBA; NoP; OxBA; PoE; PPP; PrIm; TAP

Idea of San Francisco, The. Jim Gustafson. UL

Idea of Trust, The. Thom Gunn. Psk

Ideal. Padraic Pearse, *tr. fr. Modern Irish by* Thomas MacDonagh. AWP

Ideal, An. Henrietta Cordelia Ray. CBWP-3

Ideal, The. Francis Saltus Saltus. AA

Ideal and Reality. Joseph Campbell. BIrV

Ideal Angels. John Robert Colombo. MoCV

Ideal Husband to His Wife, The. Sam Walter Foss. AnAmPo

Ideal Woman, The. Cecilia Vicuña, *tr. fr. Spanish by* Anne Twitty. DMH

Idealism. Ronald Arbuthnott Knox. FaBoCo; NBLV

Ideals of Satire, The. Pope. *Fr.* First Epistle of the Second Book of Horace, Imitation of. FiP

Ideas. James Merrill. PPR

Idea's Mirrour, *sels.* Michael Drayton.
   "Black pitchy night, companion of my woe." *Fr.* XLV. OBSC
   "Glorious sun went blushing to his bed, The." *Fr.* XXV. OBSC
   "If chaste and pure devotion of my youth." *Fr.* XXXVIII. OBSC
   "My fair, look from those turrets of thine eyes." *Fr.* XXXIV. OBSC
   "My heart, imprisoned in a hopeless isle." *Fr.* XXII. OBSC
   "Read here (sweet maid) the story of my woe." *Fr.* I. OBSC
   "Stay speedy time; behold, before thou pass." *Fr.* VII (*also given as XVII in* Idea). OBSC
   "When first I ended, then I first begun." *Fr.* L (*also given as LXII in* Idea). TrGrPo

Ideas move and move the thinker. Lyn Hejinian. IAT

Idée Fixe. Robert Desnos, *tr. fr. French by* Michael Benedikt. POS

Identification in Belfast (I.R.A. Bombing). Robert Lowell. OxBC

Identities. Al Young. NPGG

Identity. Thomas Bailey Aldrich. AA

Identity. Robert Friend. VWA

Identity. Elizabeth Jennings. NePoEA

Identity Card. Susan Tichy. MAYP

Identity, known or unknown, survives. Indecision. Helen Pinkerton. QFR

Identity of Imagery. Robert Desnos, *tr. fr. French by* Michael Benedikt. POS

Ideological Contradictions in Washing a Dish. Kyra Galván, *tr. fr. Spanish by* Kate Flores. DMH

Ides of March, The. Constantine P. Cavafy, *tr. fr. Greek by* Edmund Keeley *and* Philip Sherrard. VMG

Idiom of the Hero. Wallace Stevens. OxBA

Idiot, The. John Ashbery. *Fr.* Two Sonnets. VGW

Idiot, The. Adèle Naudé. PeSA

Idiot, The. Dudley Randall. BPo

Idiot. Allen Tate. FaBoMo; LiTA

Idiot, The. Keith Wilson. Psk

Idiot Boy, The. Wordsworth. OBNV

Idiot greens the meadows with his eyes, The. Idiot. Allen Tate. FaBoMo; LiTA

"Idle as trout in light Colonel Jones." The Famine Road. Eavan Boland. FaBoWP

Idle Charon. Eugene Lee-Hamilton. NOBVV

Idle dayseye, the laborious wheel, The. O. Richard Wilbur. LiTA

Idle Droning. Po Chü-i, *tr. fr. Chinese by* Burton Watson. CoBCP

Idle Flowers, The. Robert Bridges. BoNaP; ChTr

Idle Fyno. *Unknown.* ChTr; PoEL-2

Idle Life I Lead, The. Robert Bridges. LiTM

Idle poet, here and there, An. The Revelation. Coventry Patmore. *Fr.* The Angel in the House, I, viii. OxBSP
   ("Idle poet, here and there, An.") EnLoPo; GBL; GTBS-P; HAP; OBNC
   (Revelation, The.) OxBSP

Idle Thoughts. Lu Yu, *tr. fr. Chinese by* Burton Watson. CoBCP

Idle Visitation, An. *Fr.* Gunslinger. NOBA

Idle Words. Walter Savage Landor. OBSV

Idleness. Weir Mitchell. AA

Idler, The ("Idler holds that rose as always rose, An"). Elizabeth Jennings. NePoEA

Idler, The. Jones Very. AA

Idler with a wand for a walking stick, An. Batyushkov. Osip Mandelstam, *tr. by* W. S. Merwin *and* Clarence Brown. OBVE

Idlers, The. Edmund Blunden. BoTP; CH

Idleset: "Ill's the airt o the Word the day." Thurso Berwick. OxBS

Idling. István Vas, *tr. fr. Hungarian by* Jascha Kessler. FOC

Idling pivot of the frigate bird, The. Man o' War Bird. Derek Walcott. TTY

Idly she yawned, and threw her heavy hair. George Moore. ErPo

Idol in the Porch, The. José Juan Tablada, *tr. fr. Spanish by* Samuel Beckett. MexPo

Idolatry. Arna Bontemps. AmNP; PoNe

Idols. Richard Burton. TrPWD

Idyl: "And my young sweetheart sat at board with me." Alfred Mombert, *tr. by* Ludwig Lewisohn. AWP

Idyl, An: Come Down, O Maid. Tennyson. *See* Princess, The: Come Down, O Maid, [from Yonder Mountain Height].

Idyl: Sunrise. Henrietta Cordelia Ray. BlSi

Idyl: Sunset. Henrietta Cordelia Ray. BlSi

Idyl in Idleness, An. Robert Pack. NePoEA

Idyl of Spring, An. Henrietta Cordelia Ray. CBWP-3

Idyl, *sels.* Henrietta Cordelia Ray. CBWP-3
  Midnight.
  Noontide.
  Sunrise.
    (Idyl: Sunrise.) BlSi
  Sunset.
    (Idyl: Sunset.) BlSi

Idyll: "Adam and Eve, without serpent." Kendrick Smithyman. ATNZ

Idyll: "At noon the sun puffed up, outsize." Francis Webb. PoAu-2

Idyll: "He was a selfish shellfish." Stoddard King. NBLV

Idyll: "Hermit hoar, in solemn cell." Samuel Johnson. *See* Hermit Hoar.

Idyll: "Within a quad of aging brick." John Updike. ASP

Idyll of the Rose. Ausonius, *tr. fr. Latin by* John Addington Symonds. AWP

Idylls, *sels.* Theocritus, *tr. fr. Greek.*
  "Amorous shepherd lov'd a charming boy, An." *Fr.* XXIII, *tr. by* Thomas Creech. PeHV
  "And so an easier life our Cyclops drew." *Fr.* XI. OBVE, *tr. by* Elizabeth Barrett Browning.
    (Cyclops, The.) AWP
  Death of Daphnis, The. *Fr.* I, *tr. by* Charles Stuart Calverley. AWP
  Enchantment, The. *Fr.* II, *tr. by* Thomas Creech. CTC; OBVE
  "Eunica skornde me, when her I would have sweetly kist." *Fr.* XX. OBVE
  Fishermen, The. *Fr.* XXI, *tr. by* Charles Stuart Calverley. AWP; OBVE
  Harvest-Home. *Fr.* VII, *tr. by* Charles Stuart Calverley. AWP
  Herdsmen, The. *Fr.* IV, *tr. by* Charles Stuart Calverley. AWP
  Incantations, The. *Tr. by* Charles Stuart Calverley. AWP
  "Shepheard Paris bore the Spartan bride, The." *Fr.* XXVII, *tr. by* Dryden. OBVE
  "Wine, friend, and truth, the proverb says, agree." *Fr.* XXVI, *tr. by* Thomas Creech. PeHV

Idylls of the King. Geoffrey Hill. *Fr.* An Apology for the Revival of Christian Architecture in England, 11. FaBoRV; NoAM; PoE

Idylls of the King, *sels.* Tennyson.
  Balin and Balan.
    Vivien's Song ("But now the wholesome music of the wood"). OAEL-2
  Coming of Arthur, The.
    Merlin's Riddling. FaBoRV
  Geraint and Enid.
    Enid's Song. FaBoRV
  Holy Grail, The.
    Percivale's Quest. OAEL-2
  Lancelot and Elaine.
    Song of Love and Death, The. OBNC
  Last Tournament, The.
    "As the crest of some slow-arching wave." FaBoPP
    Tristram's Song. FaBoRV
  Merlin and Vivien.
    In Love, If Love Be Love. PoEL-5; TrGrPo
      (All in All.) LiTB
      (Vivien's Song.) OBNC
  Passing of Arthur, The. NAEL-2; OBNC
    (Morte d'Arthur, *incorporated in the* Idylls *with changes, as* The Passing of Arthur) DL; FiP; OAEL-2
    "And answer made King Arthur, breathing hard." EBEV
    "But now farewell. I am going a long way."" FaBoRV
    Prayer ("Pray for my soul. More things are wrought by prayer"). WGRP
  Pelleas and Ettarre. NAEL-2
    "Rose, but one, none other rose had I, A." PoEL-5

Iesu. George Herbert. *See* Jesu is in my heart. . .

Iesu, swete son dere! Our Lady's Song. *Unknown.* OBEV

If. Franklin P. Adams. OBAL

If. John Kendrick Bangs. OBCA

If. Mortimer Collins. FiBHP; Par

If. Rebecca Foresman. WBLP

If. Haim Gouri, *tr. fr. Hebrew by* Warren Bargad *and* Stanley F. Chyet. IP

If. Anselm Hollo. UL

If. William Dean Howells. AA

If. Kipling. BLPA; FaBoBe; FaFP; FaPoR; FPL; OHFP; OxBChV; OxBTC; PWR; WBLP

If. Patrick Lane. NOBC

If. P. A. Ropes. BoTP

If. Alice Todd. BoTP

If. *Unknown.* NA

If/ ice shall melt. If Ice. W. W. Eustace Ross. NOBC; OBCX

If a calving cow. What Her Mother Said. *Unknown, tr. by* A. K. Ramanujan. PLW

If a child of my clan should die. A King's Last Words. Ceraman Kanaikkal Irumporai, *tr. by* A. K. Ramanujan. PLW

If a clear fountain still keeping a sad course. The Duke's Song. Mary Sidney Wroth, Countess of Montgomery. *Fr.* Urania. WPE

If a cuckoo comes into the village. A Theory. Charles Simic, *tr. by* Jeffrey Fiskin *and* Erik Vestville. AnAn

If a custom-tailored vet. Cole Porter. *Fr.* Always True to You in My Fashion. NBLV

If a flame has fallen among the cedars. If. Haim Gouri, *tr. by* Warren Bargad *and* Stanley F. Chyet. IP

If a good man were ever housed in Hell. The Good Man in Hell. Edwin Muir. MoBrPo; TW

If a Maid Be Fair. Laura Goodman Salverson. CaP

If a man who turnips cries. The Turnip Vendor. Mother Goose. OxNR

If a man with a shovel came down the road. The Diggers. W. S. Merwin. EAS

If a man would be a soldier, he'd expect, of course, to fight. A Little Rhyme and a Little Reason. Henry Anstadt. BLRP

If a man's drunk from morning on. Kari Sober. Kapilar, *tr. by* A. K. Ramanujan. PLW

If a monkey drives a car. Poems We Can Understand. Paul Hoover. EOEF

If a person conceives an opinion. Poeta Loquitur. Swinburne. OAEL-2

If a seed is there. *Unknown, tr. fr. Japanese by* Burton Watson. *Fr.* Kokin Shu. FCEI

If a small, homely woman. Hommes à Femme. Karin Kiwus, *tr. by* Susan L. Cocalis. DMG

If a task is once begun. Always Finish. *Unknown.* BLPA; FaBoBe; WBLP

If a woman. Mathematics for the Women's Movement. Sigrid Weigel, *tr. by* Susan L. Cocalis. DMG

If a Woodchuck Would Chuck. *Unknown.* FaPON

"If, after attaining Buddhahood, anyone in my land." Gary Snyder. *Fr.* Myths and Texts: Burning, X. NaP

If after kirk ye bide a wee. An Angel Unawares. *Unknown.* BLRP

If after rude and boisterous seas. The Plaudite, or End of Life. Robert Herrick. CaPo

If again in the spring. Seeing the Plum Blossoms by the River. Lady Ise, *tr. by* Etsuko Terasaki *and* Irma Brandeis. BoWoP

If Ah evah git to glory, an' Ah hop to mek it thoo. Black Mammies. John Wesley Holloway. BANP

If all a top physicist knows. After Reading a Child's Guide to Modern Physics. W. H. Auden. NYBP

If all be true that I do think. Henry Aldrich. FaBoEE; FF
  (Catch, A.) InvP; OBS; OxBSP
  (Five Reason, The.) FaBoCo

If all my days were summer, could I know. Revelation. Warren F. Cook. BLRP

If all of me is still there. Plenty-hawk, *tr. by* W. S. Merwin. STP

If all the answer's to be the Sinai sort. Golden Calf. Norman MacCaig. OxBS

If all the calendar's events. If I Were May. Carlos Rigby, *tr. by* Jack Hirschman. Vol

If all the good people were clever. Good and Clever. Elizabeth Wordsworth. OxBTC

If all the harm that women have done. A Thought. James Kenneth Stephen. FiBHP

If all the land were apple-pie. If. *Unknown.* NA

If All the Pens That Ever Poets Held. Christopher Marlowe. *Fr.* Tamburlaine the Great, *Pt.* I, Act V, sc. ii. ChTr
  (Beauty.) TrGrPo

If all the seas were one sea. Mother Goose. BOTP; OnUR; OxNR

If all the ships I have at sea. My Ships. Ella Wheeler Wilcox. PoLF

If All the Skies Were Sunshine. Henry Van Dyke. WBLP; WGRP

If all the trees in all the woods were men. Cacoëthes Scribendi. Oliver Wendell Holmes. AA; NBLV

If all the Voices of Men. Horace Logo Traubel. AA

If all the world and love were young. The Nymph's Reply to the Shepherd. Sir Walter Ralegh. CTC; EIL; FF; HAP; HeIP; HoPM; InPK; InPS; LiTB; NAEL-1; NBLV; NIP; NOBE; NoP; PoE; PPP; RB; SeCePo; SiPS; TrGrPo; WeW
  (Answer to Marlowe.) OAEL-1; OBSC
  (Her Reply.) BoLoP; OBEV
  (Nimphs Reply to the Sheepheard, The.) AAS
  (Nymph's Reply to the Passionate Shepherd.) FaBoPa

If all the world were apple-pie. Mother Goose. FaFP

If All the World Were [or Was] Paper. *Unknown.* FaBoCo; FaBoNo; GBP; NTCP; OxNR; PYC; TTTS

If along the highroad. *Unknown. tr. by* Arthur Waley. BoS

If amorous faith, a heart of guileless ways. Signs of Love. Petrarch, *tr. fr. Italian. Fr.* Sonnets to Laura: To Laura in Life, CLXXXVIII, *tr. by* C. B. Cayley. AWP

If an audience could be arranged. Nizar Qabbani, *tr. fr. Arabic by* Diana Der Hovanessian *and* Lena Jayyusi. *Fr.* Notes on the Book of Defeat. MAP

If an eagle be imprisoned. America. Henry Dumas. PoBA

If an unkind word appears. On File. John Kendrick Bangs. WBLP

If angels sung a Savior's birth. *At. to* John Stephenson. AmFP

If, antique hateful bird. The Raven. Adrienne Rich. NePoEA-2

If any ask why there's no great She-Poet. Dedication of the Cook. Anna Wickham. MoBrPo

If Any Be Pleased to Walk into My Poor Garden. Francis Daniel Pastorius. SCAP

If any flower that here is grown. Inscription in a Garden. George Gascoigne. OBSC; TrGrPo

If any God should say. Rebirth. Kipling. OBNC

If any have a stone to shy. The Pebble. Elinor Wylie. MoAmPo

If any little word of mine. The Little Word. *Unknown.* PWR

If any man would know the very cause. He Is Out of Heart with His Time. Guerzo di Montecanti, *tr. by* Dante Gabriel Rossetti. AWP

If any mourn us in the workshop, say. Batteries Out of Ammunition. Kipling. *Fr.* Epitaphs of the War, 1914–1918. MMA

If any question why we died. Common Form. Kipling. *Fr.* Epitaphs of the War, 1914–1918. FaBoEE; FaBoTw

If any wench Venus's girdle wear. John Gay. *Fr.* The Beggar's Opera, I, i. PoEL-3

If anybody comes to I. On Dr. Lettsom. *Unknown.* FaBoEE

If anyone asks. Tameuji, *tr. by* Steven D. Carter. WFTW

If anyone has fun. Notes on a Track Meet. David McCord. SD

If anyone long for a musical song. The Wanton Trick. *Unknown.* CoMu

If art and industry should doe as much. New English Canaan; Prologue. Thomas Morton. SCAP

If as a flowre doth spread and die. Employment ("If as a flowre doth spread and die."). George Herbert. SeCV-1

If, as Plato called them, shadows. Boethius at Cavalzero. John Macoubrie. CRP

If, as well may happen. Read Me, Please! Robert Graves. NYBP

If asked the day that this man dies. At a Loss. James L. Weil. GoYe

If at forty you met yourself. Sonnet Manqué. Sándor Weöres, *tr. by* Jascha Kessler. FOC

If at my death you do not believe. Asadullah Khan Ghalib, *tr. by* Ahmed Ali. GoT

If at your coming princes disappear. Comets and Princes. Samuel Johnson. FaBoEE

If aught can teach us aught, Affliction's looks. Affliction. Sir John Davies. *Fr.* Nosce Teipsum. NOBE; OBSC

If aught I may have said or done. An Evening Prayer. Laura E. Kendall. BLRP

If aught [or ought] of oaten stop, or pastoral song. Ode to Evening. William Collins. AWP; EBEV; EnRP; FaBoBe; GTBS; GTBS-P; HAP; LiTB; NAEL-1; NOBE; NOEC; NoP; OAEL-1; OBEV; PoE; PoEL-3; PPP; SeCePo; TrGrPo; ViBoPo

(To Evening.) GTBS; GTBS-P

If aught that stumbles in my speech. Abstemia. Gelett Burgess. NA

If babies could speak they'd tell mother or nurse. Bringing Up Babies. Roy Fuller. RHPC

If bees stay at home. *Unknown. Fr.* Weather Wisdom [or Weather Wise]. OxNR

If, before being earth, the thought of sound. Anticipation. Joseph Tusiani. GoYe

If Bethlehem were here today. Christmas Morning. Elizabeth Madox Roberts. MoAmPo; PChr

If Birds That neither Sow nor Reap. Roger Williams. AH

If Birth Persists. Matthew Arnold. *Fr.* Resignation. FaBoRV

If birthdays happened once a week. Birthdays. Mary Ann Hoberman. RAR

If Blood Is Black Then Spirit Neglects My Unborn Son. Conrad Kent Rivers. PoBA

If blossoms could blossom. To Be Sung. Peter Viereck. FaBV

If but some vengeful god would call to me. Hap. Thomas Hardy. AWP; CMoP; EaLo; EBVV; MoBrPo; NAEL-2; NIP; NoAM; NoP; OAEL-2; PPP; Son; TEP

If by chance someone asks. Teika, *tr. fr. Japanese by* Hiroaki Sato. *Fr.* A Compendium of Good Tanka. FCEI

If by dull rhymes our English must be chained. On the Sonnet. Keats. NIP; NoP; OAEL-2

If by Eternity. Riekus Waskowsky, *tr. fr. Dutch by* André Lefevere. DuIn

If by his torturing, savage foes untraced. The Captive Escaped in the Wilds of America. Addressed to the Honorable Mrs. O'Neill. Charlotte Smith. Son

If by your art, my dearest father, you have. Shakespeare. *Fr.* The Tempest, I, ii. MOS

"If Candlemas be fine and clear." At Candlemas. Charles Causley. OBCP

If Candlemas Day be fair and bright. *Unknown.* FaBoUs

If care do cause men cry, why do not I complain. Earl of Surrey. SiPS

If caste was what the Creator had in mind. Kabir, *tr. by* John Stratton Hawley *and* Mark Juergensmeyer. SSI

If chance assign'd. Sir Thomas Wyatt. SiPS

If chaste and pure devotion of my youth. Michael Drayton. *Fr.* Idea's Mirrour, XXXVIII. OBSC

If come into this world again I must. Dew on a Dusty Heart. Jean Starr Untermeyer. MoAmPo

If "compression is the first grace of style." To a Snail. Marianne Moore. CMoP; FaBoMo; FaBoWP; NAAL-2

If Cynthia Be a Queen. Sir Walter Ralegh. SiPS

If Dante mourns, there wheresoe'er he be. To One Who Had Censured His Public Exposition of Dante. Boccaccio, *tr. fr. Italian by* Dante Gabriel Rossetti. *Fr.* Sonnets. AWP

If dead, we cease to be; if total gloom. Human Life; on the Denial of Immortality. Samuel Taylor Coleridge. ChER

If deare Anthea, my hard fate it be. To Anthea. Robert Herrick. OBS

If Death and Liberty. Severe Figures. Charles Simic. KS

If Doughty Deeds ("If daughty deeds my lady pleases."). Robert Graham. GoTS; GTBS; GTBS-P; OBEV

If down his throat a man should choose. An Unsuspected Fact. Edward Cannon. NA

If dreams could dream, beyond the canon of landscapes. Psyche's Dream. Ann Lauterbach. BAP; EOEF

If, dumb too long, the drooping Muse hath stayed. To the Earl of Warwick, on the Death of Mr. Addison. Thomas Tickell. NOEC

If earthward you could wing your flight. England Expects? Sir Owen Seaman. NOBL

If Easter Be Not True. Henry H. Barstow. BLRP

If echoes from the fitful past. Abstrosophy. Gelett Burgess. CenHV; NA

If e'er in thy sight I found favour, Apollo. The Poet's Prayer. *Unknown.* OBSV

If even now/ in the midst of rejection. Empress Eifuku, *tr. by* Steven D. Carter. WFTW

If ever a garden was a Gethsemane. For Jim, Easter Eve. Anne Spencer. AmNP; PoNe

If ever against this easy blue and silver. Interruption. Robert Graves. LiTB; LiTM

If ever chance or choice thy footsteps lead. The Flying Tailor. James Hogg. BXAP; Par

If Ever Hapless Woman Had a Cause. Countess of Pembroke. WPE

If ever happiness hath lodg'd with man. Consummate Happiness. Wordsworth. *Fr.* The Prelude [or, Growth of a Poet's Mind]: Summer Vacation. OBNC

If ever I had dreamed of my dead name. Sonnet to My Friend, with an Identity Disc. Wilfred Owen. PeHV

If Ever I Marry, I'll Marry a Maid. *Unknown.* EIL

If ever I should condescend to prose. Poetical Commandments. Byron. *Fr.* Don Juan, I. FiP; OxBoLi

(Poet's Credo.) SeCePo

If ever man might him avaunt. Sir Thomas Wyatt. SiPS

If ever mercy move you murder me. To the Mercy Killers. Dudley Randall. DL

If ever round our domicile you chance to be a-wandering. "Everybody Works but Father" as W. S. Gilbert Would Have Written It. Arthur G. Burgoyne. FiBHP

If ever sad and lonely Mir. Mohammad Taqi Mir, *tr. by* Ahmed Ali. GoT

If ever Sorrow spoke from soul that loves. Henry Constable. *Fr.* Diana. EIL

If ever there lived a Yankee lad. Darius Green and His Flying-Machine. John Townsend Trowbridge. AnAmPo; BeLS; BLPL; FaBoBe; MoShBr; OBAL; OBCA; OxBChV; PoLF

If ever there were a time for her. The Emeritus. Leonard Nathan. MOWH

If ever two were one, then surely we. To My Dear and Loving Husband. Anne Bradstreet. AmPP; AnAmPo; BLPL; BoWoP; FF; HAP; HeIP; NAAL-1; NIP; NOBA; NOCV; OPOP; OxBA; OxBSP; PoE; PoEL-3; PoLF; PrIm; SCAP; TAP; WeW; WPE

If ever you go to Dolgelley. The Dolgelley Hotel. Thomas Hughes. CenHV; FaBoCo

If Ever You Go to Dublin Town. Patrick Kavanagh. AnIL; CMoP; InPS; IPY

If ever you go to the North Countree. Edenhall. "Susan Coolidge." OBCA

If ever you should follow. Belden Hollow. Leslie Nelson Jennings. GoYe

If ever you should go by chance. How To Tell the Wild Animals. Carolyn Wells. FaFP; FaPON; FiBHP; NBLV

If ever your spirits are damp, low. A Drinking Song. *Unknown.* FaBoUs

If every good boy deserves favor, and all cows eat grass. Syllogism. Bin Ramke. KS

If Everything Happens That Can't Be Done. E. E. Cummings. SoSe; WeW

If everywhere in the street. Song: "If everywhere in the street." Denis Glover. *Fr.* Sings Harry, II. PeNZ
(Sings Harry to an Old Guitar.) ATNZ

If external action is effete. The Past Is the Present. Marianne Moore. NAAL-2

If faithful soules be alike glorifi'd. John Donne. *Fr.* Holy Sonnets, VIII. OBS

If fancy [*or* fansy] would favor. Sir Thomas Wyatt. AAS; SiPS

If Fathers Knew but How to Leave. *Unknown.* EIL

If fictive music fails your lyre, confess. What's Good for the Soul Is Good for Sales. Richard Wilbur. NBLV

If flowers want to grow. The City. David Ignatow. PCP

If from the height of that celestial sphere. To Shakespeare. Frances Anne Kemble. Son

If from the public way you turn your steps. Michael. Wordsworth. EnRP; GoTL; NAEL-2; OAEL-2

If fruits are fed on any beast. Epitaph after Reading Ronsard's Lines from Rabelais. J. M. Synge. FaBoEE
(Epitaph: "If fruits are fed on any beast.") OBD

If girls were as charming after the fact as before it. Andante, ma Non Assai. Rufinus Domesticus, *tr. by* Dudley Fitts. ErPo

If glassware were really glassware. Drinking Song. Louis Aragon, *tr. by* Michael Benedikt. POS

If God Exists. Ewa Lipska, *tr. fr. Polish by* Peter Jay *and* Geri Lipshultz. VWA

If God kept a terrarium. W. J. Turner. *Fr.* The Seven Days of the Sun. OBMV

If Gravity Were Like Weather. Bruce Boston. BWV

If Gray Had Had to Write His Elegy in the Cemetery of Spoon River Instead of in That of Stoke Poges. J. C. Squire. BXAP; FaBoPa

If grief come early. First or Last. Thomas Hardy. CMoP

If grief for grief can touch thee. Emily Brontë. EnLoPo; OBNC

If Hamlet would betray. Midrash on Hamlet. Francis Landy. VWA

If He be truly Christ. Second Seeing. Louis Golding. WGRP

If he chanced to spit, it was whole basketsful of goldfinches. Shrovetide's Countenance. Rabelais, *tr. by* Sir Thomas Urquhart. FaBoNo

If he could solve the riddle. Sphinx. Robert Hayden. HCAP

If he does not look at her face. The Circumcision. Linda Zisquit. VWA

If he found a little liquor. Auvaiyar, *tr. by* A. K. Ramanujan. PLW

If he, from heaven that filched the living fire. Michael Drayton. *Fr.* Idea, XIV. AAS; NoP; TEP

If he has been so careful. Painting a Madonna. Rosanna Warren. KS

If He Let Us Go Now. Shirley Williams. BoWoP

If he that erst the form so lively drew. Earl of Surrey. SiPS

If health and strength permit thee, don't refuse. Choosing a Wet-Nurse. M. Saint-Marthe, *tr. fr. French. Fr.* Paedotrophiae; or, The Art of Bringing Up Children. FaBoUs

If heaven were to do again. The Peaceful Shepherd. Robert Frost. *Fr.* A Sky Pair. MoAB; MoAmPo

If heav'n the grateful liberty would give. The Choice. John Pomfret. NOEC

If here and now be but a timely span. Here and Now. Catherine Cater. AmNP; PoNe

If homely virtues draw from me a tune. James Weldon Johnson. TrPWD

If hope grew on a bush. Hope and Joy. Christina Rossetti. OxBChV

If hungry, Lord, I need bread. In Harbor. Lizette Woodworth Reese. TrPWD

If I/ Could go. Wouldn't You? John Ciardi. RAR

If I am left behind and long for you. *Unknown. Fr.* Manyo Shu. FCEI

If I am proud, you surely know. Called Proud. Walter Savage Landor. GBL

If I am the forlorn chrysanthemum awaiting execution. The Chrysanthemum and the Sword. Tu Yeh, *tr. by* Dominic Cheung. IFON

If I Am Too Brown or Too White for You. Wendy Rose. HATNAP

If I bring back. For My Unborn and Wretched Children. Alfred B. Spellman. CNA; PoBA

If I But Knew. Amy E. Leigh. AA

If I buy a horse. *Unknown. Fr.* Manyo Shu. FCEI

If I can do some good today. My Daily Prayer. Grenville Kleiser. BLRP

If I can find this place near-abandoned. Jersey Bait Shack. Peter Balakian. MAYP

If I can stop one heart from breaking. Emily Dickinson. AH, *with music;* FPL; OHFP; PoLF; PWR, *with music*

If I can't twist my thread with yours. Teika, *tr. fr. Japanese by* Hiroaki Sato. *Fr.* A Compendium of Good Tanka. FCEI

If I come, surprising her. *Unknown. Fr.* Manyo Shu. Ma

If I come to her. *Unknown. Fr.* Manyo Shu. Ma

If I consider/ My body like the fields. Lady Ise, *tr. by* Donald Keene. WPOW

If I could be a gipsy-boy. The Caravan. Madeleine Nightingale. BoTP

If I could believe that death. Gaspara Stampa, *tr. by* Lynne Lawner. PBWP

If I could chop wood. Karate. Stanley Plumly. ASP

If I could climb the garden wall. There. Rodney Bennett. BoTP

If I could do this, I would. Terms. Lorrie Goldensohn. NAmP

If I could drive steel like John Henry. Drivin' Steel. *Unknown.* AS

If I could fetch you all the poets. This Fugitive Beauty. Eli Netser, *tr. by* Bernhard Frank. MHeP

If I could get within this changing I. John Masefield. *Fr.* Sonnets. WGRP

If I could go on kissing your honeyed eyes. Catullus. PeHV

If I could have/ Two things in one. Moriturus. Edna St. Vincent Millay. LiTA

If I could have lived another year. Franklin James. Edgar Lee Masters. *Fr.* Spoon River Anthology. OBD

If I could have my way. Tameyo, *tr. by* Steven D. Carter. WFTW

If I could hide in the woods. O, Beautiful They Move. William Pillen. VWA

If I could I surely would. Pharoah's Army Got Drownded. *Unknown.* AS

If I could, I'd write. Housewife's Letter: To Mary. Anne Halley. NMM

If I could know that here about. Evelyn. Rossiter Johnson. AA

If I could linger on his lovely chest. Louise Labé, *tr. by* Aliki *and* Willis Barnstone. BoWoP

If I could live to God for just one day. Just One Day. Susan E. Gammons. PWR

If I Could Meet God. Dennis Schmitz. NPGG

If I Could Only Live at the Pitch That Is near Madness. Richard Eberhart. FF; LiTM; MAT; MoAB

If I could raise rivers, I'd raise them. Douglas Crase. *Fr.* The Revisionist. NAAL-2

If I could reach you now, in any way. Letter to a Mute. Thomas James. AmPA

If I could rise and see my father young. Gil Orlovitz. *Fr.* Art of the Sonnet. DiL

If I could see a little fish. On the Bridge. Kate Greenaway. RHPC

If I could see the capital. Tabito. *Fr.* Manyo Shu. Ma

If I Could Shut the Gate against My Thoughts. *Unknown.* EIL; NOCV

If I could start my life again. The Child's Dream. Susan Ludvigson. MAYP

If I could teach you how to fly. The Question. Dennis Lee. ILY

If I could tell you. Impasse. Langston Hughes. LiTM

If I could track you down to have you taste. Patterns. Roberta Hill Whiteman. HATNAP

If I Could Walk Out into the Cold Country. Elizabeth Brewster. NOBC

If I could wish. Wish. Dorothy Brown Thompson. RAR

If I deny my kinship to a man. A Gentle Park. Moss Herbert. GoYe

If I describe my house. The House. George Bowering. NOBC

If I did come of set intent. To Archinus. Callimachus, *tr. by* F. A. Wright. AWP

If I die. Farewell. Federico García Lorca, *tr. by* W. S. Merwin. OBD

If I Die a Railroad Man, *with music. Unknown.* AS

If I die, don't take me to the cemetery. Life-Hook. Juana de Ibarbourou, *tr. by* Marti Moody. AIW; WPOW

If I die here in a strange land. Song of a Man about to Die in a Strange Land. *Unknown, tr. by* Mary Austin. DL

If I die or something happens to us. Tourists on Paros. Michael Ryan. NAmP

If I don't drive around the park. Observation. Dorothy Parker. *Fr.* Some Beautiful Letters. FiBHP

If I don't go out I'll only mope. Out and Back on the Fifteenth Night of the First Month. Mei Yao-ch'en, *tr. by* Burton Watson. CoBCP

If I don't take anything to the party I'll feel bad. *Unknown, tr. by* James Koller. STP

If I drink water while this doth last. Thomas Love Peacock. *Fr.* Crotchet Castle. NBLV

If I drop the clock it shatters. Chebutykin. Dick Davis. NPo

If I eat one more piece of pie, I'll die! Pie Problem. Shel Silverstein. RHPC

If I enjoy myself in this world. Tabito. *Fr.* Manyo Shu. FCEI

If I entreat this lady that all grace. Sonnet: To a Friend Who Does Not Pity His Love. Guido Cavalcanti, *tr.* by Dante Gabriel Rossetti. AWP

If I Ever Grow Old: Grim and Gleeful Resolutions. Elinor Nauen. UL

If I Felt Less. Morris Wintchevsky, *tr. fr. Yiddish by* Joseph Leftwich. TrJP

If I Forget Thee. Emanuel Litvinoff. TrJP; VWA

If I forget thee not, New York. A Curse. Irving Feldman. TW

If I found the iron kettle. Choosing a Death. Alberta Turner. LCAP

If I freely may discover. Ben Jonson. *Fr.* The Poetaster, II, ii. EIL

If I get a horse, my beloved. *Unknown. Fr.* Manyo Shu. Ma

If I go/ when she's not expecting me. *Unknown. Fr.* Manyo Shu. FCEI

If I had a child how old would it be. Yearly Regret. Kikaku, *tr. fr. Japanese by* Hiroaki Sato. *Fr.* Thirty-three Hokku. FCEI

If I had a donkey that wouldn't go. *Unknown.* OxNR

If I had a hundred dollars to spend. The Animal Store. Rachel Lyman Field. PDV

If I had a little wife. *Unknown.* OxNR

If I had a son! A little child. Barren. Rachel, *tr. by* L. V. Snowman. TrJP

If I had a trunk like a big elephant. If. John Kendrick Bangs. OBCA

If I had [*or* I'd] as much money as I could spend. Mother Goose. FaFP; OxNR

If I Had but Two Little Wings. Samuel Taylor Coleridge. BoTP; CH; OHIP

If I had chosen thee, thou shouldst have been. As to His Choice of Her. Wilfrid Scawen Blunt. *Fr.* The Love Sonnets of Proteus, VIII. Son

If I had eyeballs up my asshole I could watch. The Flaying of Marsyas. Kenneth Rosen. NAmP

If I had known. *Unknown, tr. fr. Japanese by* Geoffrey Bownas *and* Anthony Thwaite. *Fr.* Kokin Shu. PeBJV

If I Had Known. Mary Carolyn Davies. BLPA

If I had known in the morning. Our Own. Margaret E. M. Sangster. BLPA

If I had known what trouble you were bearing. If I Had Known. Mary Carolyn Davies. BLPA

If I had lightly given at the first. A Lodging for the Night. Elinor Wylie. ErPo

If I had never known your face at all. Sir William Watson. *Fr.* Sonnets to Miranda, VIII. FaBoBe

If I had peace to sit and sing. The Singer. Anna Wickham. MoBrPo

If I had thought thou couldst have died. To Mary. Charles Wolfe. OBEV

If I had to guess, I'd say. 1805 Gratiot. Richard Hugo. PPR

If I had to tell what the world is for me. Czeslaw Milosz, *tr. fr. Polish by the author and* Peter Dale Scott. *Fr.* Throughout Our Lands, III. PwPP

If I had wit for to indite. A Secret. *Unknown.* OBSC

If I had won my Wendy. Luck. Evan V. Shute. CaP

If I hated you, I would give you my hate. Silent Love. Gabriela Mistral, *tr. by* Perry Higman. LPSS

If I have any taste, it is hardly. Hunger. Rimbaud, *tr. by* Edgell Rickword. AWP

If I have complained I hope I have done with it. The Gods. W. S. Merwin. NaP

If I have faltered more or less. The Celestial Surgeon. Robert Louis Stevenson. BrPo; EBVV; MoBrPo; TrGrPo; TrPWD; WGRP

If I have given you delight. The Appeal. Kipling. OBD

If I Have Lifted Up Mine Eyes to Admire. Amos Niven Wilder. TrPWD

If I Have Made, My Lady, Intricate. E. E. Cummings. CMoP; FaBV; NOBA; PoRA

If I have run my course and seek the pearls. The Marathon Runner. Fenton Johnson. CDC

If I have since done evil in my life. The Sinner-Saint. Wilfrid Scawen Blunt. ACP

If I have wounded any soul to-day. My Evening Prayer. Charles H. Gabriel. BLPA; FaBoBe

"If I hold my breath and do not speak." Ganga. Thomas Blackburn. MoBS

If I hope that Death is a pass. From Skye, Early Autumn. M. L. Michal. PoSH

If I knew you and you knew me. At Church Next Sunday. *Unknown.* BLRP

If I knew you and you knew me. To Know All Is to Forgive All. Nixon Waterman. BLPA

If I lay on that beach with you. Adrienne Rich. *Fr.* Twenty-one Love Poems, XV. GLP

If I lay waste and wither up with doubt. What Shall it Profit? William Dean Howells. AA

(Faith.) WGRP

If I leave all for thee, wilt thou exchange. Elizabeth Barrett Browning. *Fr.* Sonnets from the Portuguese, XXXV. Son

If I leave her and go away. *Unknown. Fr.* Manyo Shu. FCEI

If I Leave Here Alive. Solomon Mahaka. WMBCH

If I leave you behind. *Unknown. Fr.* Manyo Shu. Ma

If I left this place. Prince Munenaga, *tr.* by Steven D. Carter. WFTW

If I, like Solomon. O to Be a Dragon. Marianne Moore. CTC; GoYe

If I live [*or* grow] to be old, for I find I go down. The Old Man's Wish. Walter Pope. CoMu; OBS

If I Lost My Little Cat. *Unknown.* CRH

If I Love You. Frank Prewett. HATNAP

If I make it over the pass. Hauling over Wolf Creek Pass in Winter. Walter McDonald. MT

If I make the lashes dark. Before the World Was Made. W. B. Yeats. GTBS-P

If I make up this leaf. Two Pictures of a Leaf. Marvin Bell. LCAP

If I Might Be an Ox. *Unknown.* RB

If I might only love my God and die! If Only. Christina Rossetti. TrCP

If I must go, let it be easy, slow. Improvisation on an Old Theme. Dorothy Livesay. CaP

If I must, I'll have to pick them haphazardly. Teika, *tr. fr. Japanese by* Hiroaki Sato. *Fr.* A Compendium of Good Tanka. FCEI

If I must of my senses lose. Theodore Roethke. TwCP

If I Only Was the Fellow. Will S. Adkin. BLPA

If I owned all of Alba. Saint Columcille. NOIV

If I pour petrol on a white child's face. A Poem in Black and White. Mongane Wally Serote. WMBCH

If I profane with my unworthiest hand. Shakespeare. *Fr.* Romeo and Juliet, I, v. Son; SoSe

If I ransom my injuries. On the Sidelines. Lillian Morrison. TSM

If I really, really trust Him. A Question. *Unknown.* BLRP

If I rest for a moment near The Equestrian. Music. Frank O'Hara. NoP

If I revel. Tabito. *Fr.* Manyo Shu. PeBJV

If I Ride This Train. Joe Johnson. PoBA

If I said, "Little wives." The Wives. Donald Hall. CoAP

If I say I grieve. Autumn Evening. Shotetsu, *tr.* by Steven D. Carter. WFTW

If I say to you "Come, Ponto, want some meat?" My Dog Ponto. Edgar Lee Masters. FM

If I seek your advice, pretty friend Alamanda. Alamanda, *tr. by* Meg Bogin. WT

If I sent my forlorn love. Lady Otomo no Sakanoe. *Fr.* Manyo Shu. Ma

If I shall ever win the home in heaven. Daniel Gray. Josiah Gilbert Holland. AA

If I should die. Emily Dickinson. MoAB

If I Should Die. Ben King. *See* If I Should Die Tonight.

If I should die and leave you here a while. Turn Again to Life. Mary Lee Hall. BLPL; PoLF

If I Should Die before I Wake. Robert Mezey. *See* Accidents will happen—still in time.

If I should die, think only this of me. The Soldier. Rupert Brooke. *Fr.* 1914, V. BrPo; FaBV; FaFP; FaPoR; FF; FPL; HeIP; LiTB; LiTM; MoBrPo; NAEL-2; NIP; NOBE; OBEV; OBWP; OxBTC; PoA; PoLF; PoRA; Son; TEP; TrGrPo; WaP

If I Should Die To-Night. Charles Walter Brown. PWR

If I Should Die Tonight. Ben King. BLPL; FiBHP; PoLF

(If I Should Die.) AnAmPo; NBLV; OBAL

If I Should Die Tonight. Arabella Eugenia Smith. BLPA

If I Should Ever by Chance. Edward Thomas. FaBoCh; GoJo; MoAB; MoBrPo; MoShBr; OBMV; OBWVE; OxBChV

If I should ever need to reach your heart. Understanding. Pauline E. Soroka. PoLF

If I should forget you because of this unhappiness. Lady Izumi, *tr. fr. Japanese by* Hiroaki Sato. *Fr.* Fifty-one Tanka. FCEI

If I should go away. Postscript for Gweno. Alun Lewis. BoLoP; GTBS-P

If I should go before the rest of you. Joyce: By Herself and Her Friends. Joyce Grenfell. OBD

If I should now forget, or not remember thee. To Spencer. George Turberville. OBTV

If I should pass the tomb of Jonah. Losers. Carl Sandburg. CMoP; MoAB; MoAmPo; NoAM; TrGrPo

If I should pray this lady pitiless. Guido Cavalcanti, *tr. by* Ezra Pound. PFI

If I should round the corner quickly. The Mythos of Samuel Huntsman. Hyam Plutzik. LiTM

If I Should Sleep with a Lady Called Death. E. E. Cummings. BoLoP; VGW

If I should touch her she would shriek and weeping. Secretary. Ted Hughes. ErPo

If I should treat my lady with aplomb. Ballad of Fat Margot. Augustus Young. CIP

If I shouldn't be alive. Emily Dickinson. FM

If I sing because I must. Signature. Hannah Kahn. IHMS

If I speak always of the dead. Salah Fa'iq, tr. by Patricia Alanah Byrne and Salma Khadra Jayyusi. MAP

If I speak of love you'll think I am like everyone else. From Prince Atsumichi. Lady Izumi, tr. fr. Japanese by Hiroaki Sato. Fr. Fifty-one Tanka. LLLT

If I Stand in My Window. Lucille Clifton. BPo; CAPP

If I stay quiet, I am always praying. The Scholar's Wife. Susan Mernit. VWA

If I take an acorn. If. Alice Todd. BoTP

If I tell you that the sun in the woods. "Poetry Ought to Have a Practical Purpose." Paul Eluard, tr. by Michael Benedikt. POS

If I think of a horse wandering about sleeplessly. Night. Robert Bly. NaP

If I told you corner of Grey. Northern Building Society Office Showing Police Headquarters, Auckland. Riemke Ensing. ATNZ

If I wanted to be satisfied. Peter Turrini, tr. by Beth Bjorklund. CoAuP

If I Went Away. Desmond O'Grady, tr. fr. Irish. CIP

If I were a cassowary. Impromptu. Samuel Wilberforce. CenHV; FaBoNo; NBLV

If I were a chipmunk. No Escape. Harriet L. Delafield. GoYe

If I were a cinnamon peeler. The Cinnamon Peeler. Michael Ondaatje. NOBC

If I were a cloud in heaven. Lise. Rose Terry Cooke. AA

If I were a man, in what a wealth of moon. Woman! Juana de Ibarbourou, tr. by Kate Flores. DMH

If I were a mouse. The Furry Home. J. M. Westrup. BoTP

If I Were a Pig. Elizabeth Fleming. BoTP

If I were a tree. Open House. Aileen Fisher. RAR

If I Were an Apple. Unknown. BoTP

If I Were Bigger Than Anyone. Ruth Harnden. RAR

If I were called in. Water. Philip Larkin. FaBoMo; OxBSP

If I Were Dead. Coventry Patmore. Fr. The Unknown Eros. ACP

If I were doing my laundry I'd wash my dirty Iran. Homework. Allen Ginsberg. NoAM

If I were fierce, and bald, and short of breath. Base Details. Siegfried Sassoon. FF; HelP; MMA; MoBrPo; OxBSP; SoSe

If I were fire, I'd burn the world away. Sonnet: Of All He Would Do. Cecco Angiolieri da Siena, tr. by Dante Gabriel Rossetti. AWP; PFI

If I were French, I'd write. Breasts. Maxine Chernoff. UL

If I were hanged on the highest hill. Mother o' Mine. Kipling. Fr. The Light That Failed. FaFP; WBLP

If I were in a fairy tale. The Duck. Edith King. BoTP

If I Were King. A. A. Milne. OnUR

If I Were King. Joseph Huntly McCarthy, par. fr. the French of Villon. FaFP; PoLF

If I were less the man, I might have kept. Samuel A. DeWitt. Fr. Two Sonnets for a Lost Love, II. GoYe

If I were Lord of Tartary. Tartary. Walter de la Mare. OxBChV

If I Were Loved, as I Desire to Be. Tennyson. Son

If I Were May. Carlos Rigby, tr. fr. Spanish by Jack Hirschman. Vol

If I were oh, so very small. If. P. A. Ropes. BoTP

If I Were Old. Will H. Ogilvie. PoSH

If I were rich what would I do? Why Tomas Cam Was Grumpy. James Stephens. CMoP

If I were stone dead and buried under. Felo de Se. Richard Hughes. OBMV

If I were the kind of man I want. Broads. David R. Slavitt. BXAP

If I were the Prime Minister of Britain. I Don't Like You. Kit Wright. OnUR

If I Were Tickled by the Rub of Love. Dylan Thomas. FF

If I were to paint. Masaoka Shiki, tr. fr. Japanese by Burton Watson. Fr. Fifteen Haiku. FCEI

If I were to see. Grandmother. Ray A. Young Bear. STE

If I Were to Tell of Our Labours, Our Hard Lodging. Aeschylus, tr. fr. Greek by Louis MacNeice. Fr. Agamemnon. WaaP

If I were very sure. The Coup de Grace. Edward Rowland Sill. AA; PPP

If I were well-to-do. Birthday. D. H. Lawrence. NAs

If I when my wife is sleeping. Danse Russe. William Carlos Williams. CMoP; PPP

("If when my wife is sleeping.") NOBA; NoP; TAP

If I with her could only join. For the Lady of a Physicist. Michael Bishop. BWV

If Ice. W. W. Eustace Ross. NOBC; OBCV

If I'd as much money/ As I could tell. Unknown. OxNR

If I'd known/ it was old age calling. Unknown, tr. fr. Japanese by Burton Watson. Fr. Kokin Shu. FCEI

If I'd known you were coming, love. Unknown. Fr. Manyo Shu. FCEI

If ("If all the land were apple-pie"). Unknown. NA

If "ifs" and "ands." Proverb. Unknown. FaBoBe

If I'm not mistaken. Final Exam. Dan Pagis, tr. by Warren Bargad and Stanley F. Chyet. IP

If I'm not too quiet. Tea for Two. Pat Nolan. UL

If, in an odd angle of the hutment. Eighth Air Force. Randall Jarrell. CAPP; FF; MoP; NoAM; NOBA; NoP; OBWP; SM

If in Beginning Twilight. E. E. Cummings. NYBP

If in his study he hath so much care. Antiquary. John Donne. EBEV; FF

If in some far-off, future day. Epitaph for a Cat. Margaret E. Bruner. PoLF

If in that secret place. Barter. Margaret Widdemer. WGRP

If in that Syrian garden, ages slain. Easter Hymn. A. E. Housman. EaLo; EBEV; MoAB; OFD

If in the latter. Epitaph for Liberal Poets. Louis MacNeice. FaBCIP

If, in the month of dark December. Written after Swimming from Sestos to Abydos. Byron. MOS; NAEL-2; NBLV; NoP; OBTV

If in the scent of violets there came. A Tea-shop. Ruth Dallas. ATNZ

If, in the silent mind of One all-pure. In Utrumque Paratus. Matthew Arnold. OBNC; PoEL-5

If in the World There Be More Woe. Sir Thomas Wyatt. ElL; SiPS
(Disdain.) TrGrPo
(Treizane.) OBSC

If in two thousand years a stumbling boy. Scrolls. Lotte Kramer. CN

If, in well-bred society, ('hear! hear!'). Nathaniel Parker Willis. Fr. Lady Jane, The; a Humorous Novel in Rhyme. OBAL

If injured monarchs may their cause explore. A Dialogue between King William and the Late King James on the Banks of the Boyne. Charles Blount. APAS

If it/ Were lighter touch. The Guarded Wound. Adelaide Crapsey. WPE

If it ain't simply this, what is it? Keep Talking. Philip Levine. WeW

If It All Went Up in Smoke. George Oppen. VWA

If It Be Destined. Petrarch, tr. fr. Italian by Edward Fitzgerald. Fr. Sonnets to Laura: To Laura in Life, XI. AWP

If It Be True. Esther Johnson. OxBSP

If it can't be out on the hill somewhere. Grandma Chooses Her Plot at the County Cemetery. Paul Ruffin. GOYP

If it could be wrapped. Unknown, tr. by Geoffrey Bownas and Anthony Thwaite. PeBJV

If it feels at all like going up in smoke—the fire. To Rise, So Suddenly. Robin Behn. KS

If it form the one landscape that looks as bad. Quicksands. William Zaranka. BXAP

If it form the one landscape that we, the inconstant ones. In Praise of Limestone. W. H. Auden. CMoP; FaBoPV; FYAP; HAP; MoAB; MoP; NAEL-2; NoAM; NoP; OAEL-2; PPP

If It Is Not My Portion. Rabindranath Tagore. Fr. Gitanjali, LXXIV. OBMV

If it is only for the taking off. In Praise of Clothes. Erica Jong. MAYP

If it is true that we no longer seek. The Fear of Trembling. John Hollander. NePoEA

If it is you, there/ in the light boat on the pond. Lady Ise, tr. by Etsuko Terasaki and Irma Brandeis. BoWoP

If it must be; if it must be, O God! David Gray. Fr. In the Shadows. OxBS

If it rains. Sokan, tr. by Geoffrey Bownas and Anthony Thwaite. PeBJV

If it rains. What Her Girl Friend Said, Consoling Her when She Was Distressed by the Town's Gossip. Uloccanar, tr. by A. K. Ramanujan. PLW

If it were death to love. Lady Kasa. Fr. Manyo Shu. Ma

If it were done when 'tis done, then 'twere well. Shakespeare. Fr. Macbeth, I, vii. UnPo
(Vaulting Ambition.) FiP

If it were not for the voice. Nakatsukasa, tr. fr. Japanese by Arthur Waley. Fr. Shui Shu. AWP

If it were real/ Perhaps I'd understand it. Komachi, tr. by Rob Swigart. WPOW

If it were set anywhere else but so. Head Itself. Laura Riding. PoA

If It Would All Please Hurry. James Tate. MAYP

If Italy is a boot. Italian Woman. Diane Wakoski. GrPl

If It's Ever Spring Again. Thomas Hardy. OxBTC

If it's rice-grain, say it's rice-grain. The Lover's Prayer. *Malay Oral Tradition, tr. by* R. J. Wilkinson *and* R. O. Winstedt. WTO

If it's well styled. *Unknown, tr. by* Geoffrey Bownas *and* Anthony Thwaite. PeBJV

If, Jerusalem, I Ever Should Forget Thee. Heine, *tr. fr. German by* Margaret Armour. TrJP

If Jesus Christ is a man. The Song of a Heathen. Richard Watson Gilder. AA; AnAmPo; WGRP

If Justice Moved. Bettie M. Sellers. KS; TW

If life be time that here is spent. Of the Loss of Time. John Hoskyns. FaBoEE

If life is love, blessed be it! Explosion. Delmira Agustini, *tr. by* Perry Higman. LPSS

If life were never bitter. If. Mortimer Collins. FiBHP; Par

If Life's a Lousy Picture, Why Not Leave before the End. Roger McGough. OxBTC

If little mice have birthdays. Birthday Cake. Aileen Fisher. PDV

If livelihood by knowledge were endowed. Mesnevi. Yusuf Sa'di, *tr. fr. Persian by* L. Cranmer-Byng. *Fr.* The Gulistan. AWP

If looks could kill. Sumo Wrestlers. James Kirkup. OBTV

If, Lord, Thy Love for Me Is Strong. St. Theresa of Avila, *tr. fr. Spanish by* Arthur Symons. AWP; PBWP

If love be life, I long to die. Dispraise of Love, and Lovers' Follies. "A. W." EIL; OBSC; TrGrPo

If love could be bought. *Unknown, tr. fr. Japanese by* Burton Watson. *Fr.* Kokin Shu. FCEI

If Love, for Love of Long Time Had. John Heywood. EIL

If love is what would make one offer himself. Coming and Going. Louis Johnson. ATNZ

If love were what the rose is. A Match. Swinburne. ELP; NOBVV

If Luther's day expand to Darwin's year. Herman Melville. *Fr.* Clarel. ImOP

If man has forgotten tenderness, yet it remains. War Casualty in April. Frances Bellerby. CN

If Mary came would Mary. A Penitent Considers Another Coming of Mary. Gwendolyn Brooks. NoAM; PChr

If Mary goes far out to sea. Stately Verse. *Unknown.* FaPON

If me want for go in a Ebo. *Unknown. Fr.* Work-Songs, II. PBCV

If meat the gods give, I the steam. Steam in Sacrifice. Robert Herrick. CaPo

If medals were ordained for drinks. To a Boon Companion. Oliver St. John Gogarty. OBMV

If men be judged wise. Joseph Solomon Del Medigo. TrJP

If mine eyes can speak to do hearty errand. Sapphics. Sir Philip Sidney. *Fr.* Arcadia. SiPS

If music [*or* musique] and sweet poetry [*or* poetrie] agree. To His Friend Master R.L., In Praise of Music and Poetry. Richard Barnfield. AAS; EIL; Son; UnS

If Music be the food of love, play on. The Food of Love. Shakespeare. *Fr.* Twelfth Night, I, i. TrGrPo

If my appearance pleases you. Lady. Jules Laforgue, *tr. by* William Jay Smith. CT

If my best wines mislike thy taste. Quits. Thomas Bailey Aldrich. AA

If My Bones Must Be Handed Over. Milán Füst, *tr. fr. Hungarian by* Edwin Morgan. MHuP

If, My Darling. Philip Larkin. EBEV; LiTM

If my fat/ was too much for me. Invitation. Grace Nichols. AIW

If my garden oak spares one bare ledge. Creed. Anne Spencer. CDC

If My Hands Were Mute. Manfred Winkler, *tr. fr. Hebrew by* Mary Zilzer. VWA

If my imprisonment has no end. From Prison. Todros Ben Judah Abulafia, *tr. by* David Goldstein. TOF

If my legs cannot move. Lillian Morrison. TSM

If My Life Could Be Simple. Caroline Griffin. DT

If my mirror talks itself blind. Snowsong. Reinhard Priessnitz, *tr. by* Beth Bjorklund. CoAuP

If my mother had never been the protected child. House in St. Petersburg. Stanley Burnshaw. VWA

If my nipples were to drip milk. Sappho, *tr. by* Willis Barnstone. BoWoP

If my recent love-labours. *Unknown. Fr.* Manyo Shu. PeBJV

If, my religion safe, I durst embrace. To Sir Henrie Savile upon His Translation of Tacitus. Ben Jonson. OBS; SeCV-1

If my torch goes out it will be dark. Search. Claribel Alegría, *tr. by* Aliki *and* Willis Barnstone. BoWoP

If my vain soul needs blows and bitter losses. Ella Wheeler Wilcox. *Fr.* The Christian's New-Year Prayer. TrPWD

If my works are not visibly engraved. First Ode. Madeleine Des Roches, *tr. by* Dorothy Backer. DMF

If Nancy Hanks/ Came back as a ghost. Nancy Hanks. Rosemary *and* Stephen Vincent Benét. FaBV; FaPON; NTCP

If nature prompts you, or if friends persuade. William Whitehead. *Fr.* A Charge to the Poets. OBSV

If Nature says to you. The Daily Grind. Fenton Johnson. AmNP

If need be, I'd follow you. *Unknown. Fr.* Manyo Shu. Ma

If neither brass, nor marble, can withstand. The Power of Time. Swift. FaBoEE

(Shall I Repine.) OxBSP

If night takes the form of a whale and. Isabel Fraire, *tr. by* Thomas Hoeksema. BoWoP

If nine times you your bridegroom kiss. The Tithe: To The Bride. Robert Herrick. CaPo

If no love is, O God, what fele I so. Chaucer. *Fr.* Troilus and Criseyde [*or* Criseide], I. FF; OAEL-1 (Song of Troylus, The.) AWP

If No One Ever Marries Me. Laurence Alma-Tadema. OxBChV; RHPC

If no one sees you, friend. Poem about Your Face. Nathan Alterman, *tr. by* Ruth Nevo. VWA

If none be true I in the world today. The Gospel According to You. *Unknown.* BLRP

If Not. H. A. C. Evans. FaBoPa

If not for the bamboos. Joben, *tr. by* Steven D. Carter. WFTW

If not so my children. Abutsu, *tr. by* Steven D. Carter. WFTW

If now thou seest me a wreck, worn out and minished of sight. Old Age. Al-Aswad, Son of Ya'fur, *tr. fr. Arabic by* Sir Charles Lyall. *Fr.* The Mufaddaliyat. AWP

If, O Maecenas, versed in lore antique. Horace, *tr. by* Sir Theodore Martin. OBVE

If of a beetle you'd make game. "Oh That My Love Were in My Arms." *Malay Oral Tradition, tr. by* R. J. Wilkinson *and* R. O. Winstedt. WTO

If of thy mortal goods thou art bereft. Hyacinths to Feed Thy Soul. Yusuf Sa'di, *tr. fr. Persian. Fr.* The Gulistan. BLPA; BLPL; FaBoBe

If on Account of the Political Situation. W. H. Auden. *Fr.* For the Time Being; a Christmas Oratorio. LiTA; WaP

If on the Book itself we cast our view. The Scriptures. Dryden. *Fr.* Religio Laici. OBS

If Once You Have Slept on an Island. Rachel Lyman Field. RHPC

If one can die of love. Lady Kasa. *Fr.* Manyo Shu. FCEI

If one could have that little head of hers. A Face. Robert Browning. CTC

If one could only die for something. To Die for Something. József Tornai, *tr. by* William Jay Smith. MHuP

If one did not climb the T'ai Mountain tall. Climbing T'ai Mountain. Yüan Mei, *tr. by* Anthony C. Yu. WFTU

If One Had a Blue Vase and a Clock in an Old Wooden Cabinet. Hertha Kräftner, *tr. fr. German by* Beth Bjorklund. CoAuP

If one has the eye this world. Mohammad Taqi Mir, *tr. by* Ahmed Ali. GoT

If one is not used. Kenko, *tr. by* Steven D. Carter. WFTW

If one must live in the world. Ryoshun, *tr. by* Steven D. Carter. WFTW

If one revolves a vine-enamored thumb. Images for the Gospel of Christ. Paul Ramsey. CRP

If one should bring me this report. Of One Dead. Tennyson. *Fr.* In Memoriam A. H. H., XIV. EBVV, *abr.;* OAEL-2, *abr.*

If one should tell them what's clearly seen. Crumbs or the Loaf. Robinson Jeffers. CMoP

If Only. Christina Rossetti. TrCP

If only/ The heart had a lid. Swahili Love Song. *Unknown, tr. by* Jan Knappert. LLLT

If only I could pretend to be a bow woven with rattan. *Unknown, tr. by* Hiroaki Sato. FCEI

If only I could send you one small slice. Letter from the Vieux Carre. Ethel Green Russell. GoYe

If only I could write you a summer-poem. Let the Wind Recite. Yang Mu, *tr. by* Dominic Cheung. IFON

If only I had my phantom to send to you. Teika, *tr. fr. Japanese by* Hiroaki Sato. *Fr.* Forty-four Tanka. FCEI

If only I had time. *Unknown. Fr.* Manyo Shu. FCEI

If only Mr. Roosevelt. E. C. Bentley. *Fr.* Clerihews. CenHV

If only my body. Lady Ise, *tr. fr. Japanese by* Burton Watson. *Fr.* Kokin Shu. FCEI

If only my heart were an unwavering rock. The Bridge. Katri Vala, *tr. by* Aili Jarvenpa. SOP

If only my heart were as it is normally. The Fifteenth of the Eighth Month. Kaai Chigetsu, *tr. fr. Japanese by* Hiroaki Sato. *Fr.* Thirteen Hokku. FCEI

If only once the chariot of the Morn. The Glory of Nature. Frederick Tennyson. OBNC

If only sleep would come, as it has come. One Night. Umberto Saba, *tr. by* Felix Stefanile. PFI

If only the phantom would stop reappearing! Faust. John Ashbery. NoP; TwCP

If only the sun were shining tonight. Egret. André Breton, tr. by Michael Benedikt. POS

If only the world. Tonna, tr. by Steven D. Carter. WFTW

If only the world. Sanetomo, tr. fr. Japanese by Burton Watson. Fr. Twenty-four Tanka. FCEI

If only there were. Saigyo, tr. fr. Japanese by Burton Watson. Fr. Sixty-four Tanka. FCEI

If only they hadn't shown that cruel mercy. A Skull Changed to Glass. Stephen Spender, tr. by Jeffrey Fiskin and Erik Vestville. AnAn

If only those scraps from Aleppo, from Qumran. I Saw Three Ships. Kevyn Arthur. PBCV

If only, when one heard. Unknown, tr. fr. Japanese by Arthur Waley. Fr. Kokin Shu. AWP

If only you'd seen if only you'd seen. The Voice of My White City. Abba Kovner, tr. by Warren Bargad and Stanley F. Chyet. IP

If orange chiffon sadness. Orange Chiffon. Jayne Cortez. BlSi

If origin had lived in these birds. Daybreak. Phillip Yellowhawk Minthorn. STE

If Orpheus voyce had force to breathe such musickes love. Sir Philip Sidney. Fr. Astrophel and Stella. PoEL-1

If ought of oaten stop, or pastoral song. See If aught of oaten stop, or pastoral song.

If Our Dogs Outlived Us. Debra Hines. MOWH

If our love too. Tameshige, tr. by Steven D. Carter. WFTW

If our love were not. Our Love. Xavier Villaurrutia, tr. by Perry Higman. LPSS

If out of a dire suspicion. Wet Hair: If Now His Mother Should Come. Robert Penn Warren. Fr. Penological Study: Southern Exposure, III. NoAM

If parting be decreed for the two of us. Parting. Judah Halevi, tr. by Nina Salaman. AWP; TrJP

If people came to know where my king's palace is, it would vanish into air. Fairyland. Rabindranath Tagore. WSC

If people in this neighborhood get sick. Ballad of the Neighborhood Shaman. Kao Ch'i, tr. by Jonathan Chaves. CoBLCP

If Pigs Could Fly. James Reeves. OnUR

If Pliny, Lord High Treasurer of all. Painture. Richard Lovelace. CaPo

If poisonous [or poysonous] mineral[l]s, and if that tree. John Donne. Fr. Holy Sonnets, IX. EBEV; JCP; LiTB; MePo; NAEL-1; NoP; OAEL-1; OBS; PoEL-2; PPP; SeCP; Son; UnPo

If poor (you say) she drains her husband's purse. Chaucer. Fr. The Canterbury Tales: The Wife of Bath's Prologue. OBSV

If Pope Had Written "Break, Break, Break . . ." J. C. Squire. CenHV; FaBoPa
("Break, Break, Break.") BXAP

If Porcelain, Then Only the Kind. Stanislaw Baranczak, tr. fr. Polish by Frank Kujawinski. PwPP

If poysonous mineralls, and if that tree. See If poisonous minerals, and if that tree.

If pure is the heart why should it not. Mohammad Taqi Mir, tr. by Ahmed Ali. GoT

If questioning could make us wise. Because She Would Ask Me Why I Loved Her. Christopher John Brennan. CBAP

If raisins grew on you from head to toe. Two Gardens. Yona Wallach, tr. by Warren Bargad and Stanley F. Chyet. IP

If recollecting were forgetting. Emily Dickinson. AA

If rightly tuneful bards decide. Amoret. Mark Akenside. OBEV

If Rome so great, and in her wisest age. To Edward Allen (Alleyne). Ben Jonson. OBS

If sadly thinking, with spirits sinking. The Deserter's Lamentation. John Philpot Curran. FaBoRV; SeCePo

If St. Paul be fair and clear. Unknown. FaBoUs

If she asks why the sun. To Jann, in Her Absence. C. J. Driver. PeSA

If she be made of white and red. Shakespeare. Fr. Love's Labour's Lost, I, ii. CTC

If she could only break the glass. The Mirror Poems. Toi Derricotte. ER

If She Sang. Gerald William Barrax. CNA

If she should die (as well suspect we may). Upon Thought Castara May Die. William Habington. Fr. Castara, Pt. I. ACP

If sleep and death be truly one. Tennyson. Fr. In Memoriam A. H. H., XLIII. OBNC

If sloth or negligence the task forbear. Tartar. Solyman Brown. Fr. Dentologia; a Poem on the Diseases of the Teeth and Their Proper Remedies. FaBoUs

If snow falls on the far field. Mother's Song. Unknown, tr. by Willis Barnstone. BoWoP

If so be a toad be laid. A Charme, or an Allay for Love. Robert Herrick. FaBoCh; FaBoUs

If so it hap, This of-spring of my care. Samuel Daniel. Fr. To Delia. AAS

If So the Man You Are, sels. D. B. Wyndham Lewis. OBSV
"Am I too dangerous, that no man can let."
"I'm no He-man you know, I'm not a He."
"You now solicit a few enemy thrusts."

If some boy were to come to me by night. Guest. E. A. Lacey. PeHV

If someone insults you. Autant En Emporte le Vent. Marguerite de Navarre, tr. by Aline Allard. PBWP

If someone said, Escape. Longface Mahoney Discusses Heaven. Horace Gregory. VGW

If someone says you're too short. Apothegms and Counsels. Colette Inez. EOEF

If Someone, Something, somehow (as Man dreams). A Musical Critic Anticipates Eternity. Siegfried Sassoon. UnS

If someone was walking across. A Confession. Robert Mezey. AmPA; NaP

If something should go wrong. Birth. Eddy van Vliet, tr. by Peter Nijmeijer. DuIn

If Something Should Happen. Lucille Clifton. MAT

If sometimes strangeness seems on me to fall. The New House. Joseph Easton McDougall. CaP

If Spirits Walk. Sophie Jewett. AA

If Still They Live. Edith Matilda Thomas. Fr. The Inverted Torch. AA

If strange things happen where she is. On Portents. Robert Graves. FaBoMo

If Suddenly a Clod of Earth. Harold Monro. Fr. Strange Meetings. MoBrPo

If suddenly, wonderfully, glittering among the leaves. The Daily Manna. Sara Henderson Hay. GoYe

If sunlight fell like snowflakes. Sunflakes. Frank Asch. NTCP

If taken in hand, autumn frost. Basho, tr. fr. Japanese by Burton Watson. Fr. Seventy-six Hokku. FCEI

If that my hand, like yours, dear George, were skilled. To G. H. B. James Bayard Taylor. Son

If the air is absent. Under the Trapeze. Ernst David, tr. by Beth Bjorklund. CoAuP

If the Birds Knew. John Ashbery. PoA

If the Black Frog Will Not Ring. Ed Roberson. PoBA

If the blues would let me. Miss Blues'es Child. Langston Hughes. TTTS

If the butterfly courted the bee. Topsy-turvy World. William Brighty Rands. OxBChV

If the Cardinals Were like Us. Sandra McPherson. AnAn

If the day looks kinder gloomy. Just Try This. Unknown. WBLP

If the deep wood is haunted, it is I. Nocturne. Robert Hillyer. FYAP; UnAs

If the devices fail pens. Alan Davies. Fr. Name. LP

If the doorkeeper denies. On the Journey to Your Heart. Heidi Pataki, tr. by Beth Bjorklund. CoAuP

If the Drink. R. A. K. Mason. ATNZ

If the driver is good. The Great Wagon. Tontaiman Ilantiraiyan, tr. by A. K. Ramanujan. PLW

"If the dull substance of my flesh were thought." Shakespeare. Fr. Sonnets, XLIV. Son

If the earth won't yield me gold. The Digger for Gold. Abraham Chalfi, tr. by Bernhard Frank. MHeP

If the fat butcher thinks he slays. Mutton. Unknown. BXAP

If the First of July be rainy weather. Unknown. FaBoUs

If the gods of heaven and earth. Lady Kasa. Fr. Manyo Shu. Ma
("If the gods/ of heaven and earth.") FCEI, tr. by Burton Watson.

If the great outside system—species and stars—proceeds. Across Space and Time. Charles Olson. PoM

If the heart of a man is deprest [or depressed] with cares. John Gay. Fr. The Beggar's Opera, II, ii. ELP; EnLoPo; HeIP; NAEL-1 (Would You Have a Young Virgin?.) TEP

If the hill overlooking our city has always been known. Vespers. W. H. Auden. Fr. Horae Canonicae. FaBoMo

If the lady hath any loveliness, let it die. Blackberry Winter. John Crowe Ransom. OxBA; PoRA

If the loved one had not made. Asadullah Khan Ghalib, tr. by Ahmed Ali. GoT

If the maiden coughs immediately after. J. H. Thomas. BXAP

"If the mist comes down, just sit still." Weather Rhymes. Hamish Brown. PoSH

If the moon shines/ On the black pines. What Night Would It Be? John Ciardi. PDV

If the oak is out before the ash. Unknown. Fr. Weather Wisdom. OxNR

If the ocean was milk. Unknown. ILY

If the Owl Calls Again. John Haines. BoNaP; CoAP; HeIP; LCAP; NU

If the quick spirits in your eye. Persuasions to Enjoy. Thomas Carew. CaPo; MePo; NOBE; OBEV; SeCP; SeCV-1
(Persuasions to Joy; a Song.) OBEV
(Song: Persuasions [or Persuasions] to Enjoy.) CaPo; NAEL-1; SeCP
If the red slayer think he slays. Brahma. Emerson. AA; AmPP; AWP; EaLo; HAP; LiTA; NOBA; NoP; OBEV; OxBA; PoE; PoRA; TAP; TrGrPo; UnPo; WGRP
If the robin sings in the bush. Unknown. PBBP
If the scorn of your bright eyne. Shakespeare. Fr. As You Like It, IV, iii. CTC
If the sons of company directors and judges' private daughters. Palaces of Gold. Leon Rosselson. OBET
If the speed is open. A Piano. Gertrude Stein. Fr. Tender Buttons. PBWP
If the spray-bead gem be won. Joseph Rodman Drake. Fr. The Culprit Fay. GN
If the Stars Should Fall. Samuel Allen. IDB; PoBA
If the table was empty before. Silent Movies. Pedro Juan Pietri. InW
If the thunder rolls for a while. Hitomaro. Fr. Manyo Shu. Ma
If the time ever came. Poem for Ben Barney. Leslie Silko. CDW; VoR
If the true guru is gracious. Nanak, tr. by John Stratton Hawley and Mark Juergensmeyer. SSI
If the twenty-fourth of August be fair and clear. Unknown. FaBoUs
If the unfortunate fate engulfing me. Farewell to My Mother. "Placido," tr. by James Weldon Johnson. TTY
If the wild bowler thinks he bowls. Brahma. Andrew Lang. BXAP; CenHV; FaBoCo; NOBL
If the woman in the purple petticoat. Give No White Flower. Brenda Chamberlain. NeIP
If the Word "Exists." Aleksander Wat, tr. fr. Polish by Czeslaw Milosz. PwPP
If the year is meditating a suitable gift. Request to a Year. Judith Wright. CBAP; FaBoWP; NoAM
If There Are Any Heavens [My Mother Will (All by Herself) Have]. E. E. Cummings. MoAB; MoAmPo; NAAL-2
If there be a law that allows. Unknown. Fr. Manyo Shu. Ma
If there be a power of sweetness, let it lie. Blackberry Winter. John Crowe Ransom. AnAmPo; OxBA; PoRA
If there be any lover in the world, O Moslems, 'tis I. Jalal ed-Din Rumi, tr. by R. A. Nicholson. TOF
If there be graveyards in the heart. God Bless You, Dear, To-Day! John Bennett. AA
If There Be Sorrow. Mari E. Evans. PoNe
If there exists a hell—the case is clear. To Sir Toby. Philip Freneau. NAAL-1; NoP; TAP
If There Had Anywhere Appeared. Richard Chenevix Trench. TrFWD
If there had been one bird, if there had been. Deserted Beach. Ruth Dallas. ATNZ
If there is a man white as marble. Metaphor as Degeneration. Wallace Stevens. LCAP
If there is an outside out there. On Finding the Tree of Life. Alan Dugan. CAPP
If there is no change in the ocean. No Change in Me. Unknown. AmFP
If there is someone above. Double-face, tr. by W. S. Merwin after Robert Lowie. STP
If there must be a god in the house, must be. Less and Less Human, O Savage Spirit. Wallace Stevens. VGW
If there was a broken whispering by night. Parting at Dawn. John Crowe Ransom. AnAmPo
If there was a house with three girls in it. It Used to Be. Ciaran Carson. CIP
If there was a sequel to the life. Comfort for the Sick Child. Gregory O'Brien. ATNZ
If there was only a road there. The Blue West. Dahlia Ravikovich, tr. by Chana Bloch. PBWP
If there were an open way. On One Condition. Charles Madge. EAS
If there were dreams to sell. Dream-Pedlary. Thomas Lovell Beddoes. BoTP; CH; EnRP; FaBoBe; HAP; LiTB; NOBE; OBEV; OBNC; PoEL-4; TrGrPo; WiR
If there were no past, but specious present only. Speculative Evening. Marguerite Young. LiTA
If there were no such thing. Narihira, tr. fr. Japanese by Burton Watson. Fr. Kokin Shu. FCEI
If there were, oh! an Hellespont of cream. The Author Loving These Homely Meats. John Davies of Hereford. Fr. The Scourge of Folly. EIL; FaBoNo; Son
(Buttered Pippin-Pies.) ChTr
(Homely Meats.) FaBoCh
If there's a fox, he said, I'll whistle the beggar. Mahony's Mountain. Douglas Stewart. PoAu-2; SeCePo

If there's a wind, we get it. Lobster Cove Shindig. Lillian Morrison. BoNaP
If there's no wick within the lamp. And Tomorrow Wend Our Ways. Malay Oral Tradition, tr. by R. J. Wilkinson and R. O. Winstedt. WTO
If There's Nothing out the Windows Look at Books. Lyn Hejinian. LP
If they ask, who here doth lie. Epitaph on Sir Walter Pye. John Hoskyns. FaBoEE
If they had cursed the man. A Part-Sequence for Change. Robert Duncan. VGW
If They Honoured Me, Giving Me Their Gifts. "Michael Field." OBMV
If they knew my heart. The Last Words. Alma Villanueva. CCP
If they made any noise in forming. Sinkholes. Janet Reed McFatter. GrPl
If they massacre me. Flesh. Deborah Levy. AIW
If they really lived. Ernst Schönwiese, tr. by Beth Bjorklund. CoAuP
If they say my furred cloak. Chanson. Pernette du Guillet, tr. by Joan Keefe and Richard Terdiman. PBWP
If They Spoke. Mark Van Doren. ImOP
If they true bailiffs be, who for the law maintaining. On Mercenary and Unjust Bailiffs. Henricus Selyns. SCAP
If they wanted freedom. Eeva-Liisa Manner, tr. tr. Finnish by Jaakko A. Ahokas. Fr. Cambrian, V. PBWP
If this air were to speak to you. Your Air of My Air. Hugo Margenat, tr. by Julio Marzán. InW
If This Be All. Anne ("Acton Bell") Brontë. TrPWD
If this be love, to draw [or drawe] a weary [or wearie] breath. Samuel Daniel. Fr. To Delia. AAS; GBL; OBSC; TrGrPo
If this brain's over-tempered. I've Tasted My Blood. Milton Acorn. MoCV; NOBC
If this bright lily. A Song at Easter. Charles Hanson Towne. BLRP
If this country were a sea (that is solid rock). Pennines in April. Ted Hughes. PPP
If this divine quiet. Calm. Aldo Camerino, tr. by Anita Barrows. VWA
If this is peace, this dead and leaden thing. Dead Fires. Jessie Redmond Fauset. BANP; PoNe
If this life-saving rock should fail. On Middleton Edge. Andrew Young. SD
If this little world to-night. Oliver Herford. Fr. The Bashful Earthquake. AA
If this our little life is but a day. A Sonnet to Heavenly Beauty. Joachim du Bellay, tr. by Andrew Lang. AWP; CTC
If this town should tumble down. Audrey Beecham. CN
If this uncertain age in which we dwell. The Lesson for Today. Robert Frost. LiTA; LiTM; WaP
If this was our battle, if these were our ends. To a President. Witter Bynner. OBAL
If This Were Faith. Robert Louis Stevenson. Fr. Songs of Travel. BrPo; OBNC; TrPWD; WGRP
If this world's friends might see but once. The Seed Growing Secretly. Henry Vaughan. SeCV-1
If thou a reason dost desire to know. To Cynthia, on Her Embraces. Sir Francis Kynaston. GBL
If thou art sleeping, maiden. Gil Vicente, tr. by Longfellow. AWP; CTC
If thou beest he; but O how fall'n! how chang'd. Milton. Fr. Paradise Lost, Bk. I, ll. 84-124. SCV
If thou be'st ice, I do admire. The Miracle. Sir John Suckling. CaPo
If thou canst wake with me, forget to eate. John Ford. Fr. The Lover's Melancholy, IV, ii. PoEL-2
If thou didst feed on western plains of yore. To a Goose [or Gosse]. Robert Southey. BXAP; FM; NOBL; Son
If thou dislik'st the piece thou light'st on first. To the Sour[e] Reader. Robert Herrick. NBLV; NoP; SeCP
If thou hast squander'd years to grave a gem. A Charge. Herbert Trench. OBEV
If thou in surety safe wilt sit. Look or You Leap. Jasper Heywood. EIL
(Lookers-On, The.) ACP
If Thou Indeed Derive Thy Light from Heaven. Wordsworth. EnRP; TrCP
If thou must love me, let it be for nought. Elizabeth Barrett Browning. Fr. Sonnets from the Portuguese, XIV. CTC; FaFP; HeIP; InPS; LiTB; OBEV; OBNC; TrGrPo
If thou of fortune be bereft. Not by Bread Alone. Unknown, tr. by James Terry White. PoLF
If thou serve a lord of prise. A Warning to Those Who Serve Lords. Unknown. MeEL
If thou shouldst ever come by choice or chance. Ginevra. Samuel Rogers. BeLS; PoLF
If Thou Shouldst Return. Clara Ann Thompson. CBWP-2

"If thou survive my well-contented day." Shakespeare. *Fr.* Sonnets, XXXII. EIL; OBSC
 (Post Mortem.) GTBS; GTBS-P
If thou wert lying cold and still and white. Reconciliation. Caroline Atherton Briggs Mason. AA
If thou wilt come and dwell with me at home. Daphnis to Ganymede. Richard Barnfield. *Fr.* The Affectionate Shepherd. EIL
If thou wilt ease thine heart. Thomas Lovell Beddoes. *Fr.* Death's Jest Book, II. EnRP
 (Dirge: "If Thou wilt ease Thine heart.") LiTB; OBNC; PoEL-4
 (Wolfram's Dirge.) NOBE; OBEV
If Thou Wilt Hear. John Grave. AH
If thou wilt love me, thou shalt be my boy. Richard Barnfield. *Fr.* The Affectionate Shepherd. PBBP
If thou wilt mighty be, flee from the rage. Sir Thomas Wyatt. SiPS
If thou wouldest roses scent. Francis Daniel Pastorius. SCAP
If Thou Wouldst Know. Hayyim Nahman Bialik, *tr. fr. Hebrew by* Harry H. Fein. TrJP
If thou wouldst learne, not knowing how, to pray. A Forme of Prayer. Francis Quarles. MePo
If thou would'st view fair Melrose aright. Melrose Abbey. Sir Walter Scott. *Fr.* The Lay of the Last Minstrel, II. FaBoPP; SeCePo
 (Sir William of Deloraine at the Wizard's Tomb.) OBNC
If through my perjured lips Thy voice may speak. A Prayer for a Preacher. Edward Shillito. TrPWD
If thy sad heart, pining for human love. Sarah Helen Whitman. *Fr.* Sonnets from the Series Relating to Edgar Allan Poe, VI. AA
"If thy wife is small bend down to her and." Ian Wedde. *Fr.* Earthly: Sonnets for Carlos, 9. ATNZ; PeNZ
If tied, it would slip off. Mikata Shami. *Fr.* Manyo Shu. Ma
If time and space, as sages say. T. S. Eliot. FL
If tired of trees I seek again mankind. The Vantage Point. Robert Frost. OxBA
If to be absent were to be. To Lucasta, [on] Going beyond the Seas. Richard Lovelace. CaPo; GTBS; GTBS-P; LiTB; MeLP; MOS; OBEV; OBS; SeCP; SeCV-1
If to demands of others I agree. Resolving Doubts. William Dickey. ErPo
If to Die. Myrtle Romilu. BLRP
If to the Pump Room in the morn we go. *Unknown. Fr.* The Diseases of Bath; a Satire. NOEC
If to your twilight land of dream. In Memoriam—Leo: A Yellow Cat. Margaret Sherwood. BLPA
If (touched by love's own secret) we, like homing. E. E. Cummings. PoA
If 'Trane had only seen. Poem No. 21. Doughtry Long. CNA
If trees were tall and grasses short. By the Babe Unborn. G. K. Chesterton. NAs
If true that notion, which but few contest. *Unknown.* FaBoEE
If 'twere not for the dignity inborn. Henry F. Lott. PF
If two groups of writers run into each other. Literary Manners I. Max Jacob, *tr. by* Jerome Rothenberg. RHTwFP
If waker care, if sodayne pale coulor. Sir Thomas Wyatt. AAS
If we are truly free, and live in a free country. Turning Away from Lies. Robert Bly. LCAP
If we, as we are, are dust, and dust, as it will, rises. Snow. Charles Wright. CAPP; LCAP
If We Believed in God. Jessie Wiseman Gibbs. BLRP
If We Cannot Live People as People. Charles Lynch. CNA; PoBA
If we could be taken alone together in a driverless. The Possible Salvation of Continuous Motion. Pattiann Rogers. MT
If we could get the hang of it entirely. Entirely. Louis MacNeice. CMoP; LiTB
If we could know the mystery. Our Task. Henrietta Cordelia Ray. CBWP-3
If we could miss a ship every day. Le Touquet. Mark Jarman. BLA
If we could push ajar the gates of life. God's Plans. May Riley Smith. BLRP
If We Didn't Have Birthdays. "Dr. Seuss." RHPC
If We Didn't Have to Eat, *sel.* Nixon Waterman. OBAL
 "Life would be an easy matter." FiBHP
If we dreamed that we loved her aforetime. To San Francisco. S. J. Alexander. PAH
If we gave unto the living as we lavish on the dead. Give to the Living. Ida Goldsmith Morris. WBLP
If we had been given names to love. Bird-Window-Flying. Tess Gallagher. NAmP
If we had dope for an excuse, or love. In Memory of My First Chapatis. Diane DiPrima. PoM
If we hate the rush hour subways. One Year to Life on the Grand Central Shuttle. Audre Lorde. CNA
If We Knew. May Riley Smith. BLPA

If We Must Die. Claude McKay. AmNP; AmPP; BANP; BPo; FaBV; IDB; MoP; NoAM; PBCV; PoBA; PoNe; PPP; Son; TTY; UnPo
If we must part. A Valediction. Ernest Dowson. BoLoP
If we shadows have offended. Shakespeare. *Fr.* A Midsummer Night's Dream, V, ii. OBSC
If we shall live, we live. Meeting. Christina Rossetti. GBL; Mes
If we stayed with each other long enough. The River Again and Again. Linda Gregg. NPGG
If We Try. George Sands Johnson. PWR
If we were a generation that was led astray. Among the Grieving One Should Speak Softly. Helena Anhava, *tr. by* Aili Jarvenpa. SOP
"If we were fucking." Lit. Crit. Christopher Logue. NPo
If we've loved them, it's what we want, and sometimes. Meeting the Dead. Alicia Ostriker. ER
If what began (look far and wide) will end. John Frederick Nims. PoA
If what I find I do not love. Resignation. Santob de Carrion, *tr. by* George Ticknor. TrJP
If what you want is jobs. Revolutionary Letter #19. Diane DiPrima. IHMS
If when Don Cupid's dart. Love's Offence. Sir John Suckling. CaPo
If When I Die. William Fowler. EIL
If, when I kneel to pray. Charles Francis Richardson. AA
If when my wife is sleeping. Danse Russe. William Carlos Williams. CMoP; InPS; NOBA; NoP; PoE; PPP; TAP
If when the sun at noone displayes. A Beautifull Mistress. Thomas Carew. OBS
If when the wind blows. Daniel Webster's Horses. Elizabeth J. Coatsworth. AmFN; MoAmPo; OBCA
If when they brought the good news. Gospel. Kevyn Arthur. PBCV
If, when you walk around the Cape's sand flats. To White South Africa. Cosmo Pieterse. WMBCH
If, whittler and dumper, gross carver. The Arc Inside and Out. A. R. Ammons. NoP
If wisdom, as it seems it is. J. V. Cunningham. QFR
If wisdom's height is only disenchantment. A Word to the Wise. Caroline Duer. AA
If wishes were horses. Mother Goose. FaBoBe; OxNR
If Wishing for the Mystic Joys of Love. Thomas Chatterton. OxBSP
If wit or honesty cou'd save. An Epitaph on True, Her Majesty's Dog. Matthew Prior. FM
If with complaint the pain might be express'd. Sir Thomas Wyatt. SiPS
If with light head erect I sing. Henry David Thoreau. *Fr.* Inspiration. AA; BLPL; FaBoBe; WGRP, *abr.*
If with pleasure you are viewing any work a man is doing. Do It Now. Berton Braley. BLPA; FaFP; WBLP
If within the cruel Southland you have chanced to take a ride. Jim Crow Cars. Lizelia Augusta Jenkins Moorer. CBWP-3
If Women Could Be Fair. Edward de Vere, Earl of Oxford. EIL
 (Renunciation, A.) GTBS; GTBS-P
If words were nothing but signs. Tristan Tzara, *tr. by* Michael Benedikt. POS
If ye fear to be affrighted. A Charm. Robert Herrick. ChTr
If ye will with Mab find grace. The Fairies. Robert Herrick. FaPON; OBS
If yet I have not all thy love. Lovers' Infiniteness [e]. John Donne. EIL; LiTB; MeLP; OBS; PoEL-2; SeCP; SeCV-1
If yet there be a few that take delight. Nahum Tate. *Fr.* The Loyal General. SeCV-2
If yo' brother done you wrong. You Fight On. *Unknown.* AS
If You. Robert Creeley. MoP; NeAP; NOBA; SM
If you are/ in Spain. Drowning in Spain. Tom Schmidt. NeAC
If you are a delicate man. A Warning. Alexander Nicolson. PoSH
If you are a fashion editor or a photographer or work. Noelle. Hugo Williams. *Fr.* Calling Your Name in the Zoo. NPo
If you are a gentleman. *Unknown.* OxNR
If you are a revolutionary. The Reactionary Poet. Ishmael Reed. CNA
If you are involved in a fantasy relationship with someone. The Bells Are Ringing for Me and Chagall. Terence Winch. UL
If you are merry sing away. Mirth. Christopher Smart. *Fr.* Hymns for the Amusement of Children, XXV. OxBChV
If you are on the Gloomy Line. Get a Transfer. *Unknown.* BLPA; WBLP
If you are one of the truly elect. Theodotos. C. P. Cavafy, *tr. by* Edmund Keeley *and* Philip Sherrard. VMG
If you are still alive when you read this. Goodbye. William Knott. EAS
If you are tempted to reveal. Three Gates. Beth Day, *after the Arabian.* BLPA
If you are true to your name. Narihira, *tr. by* Geoffrey Bownas *and* Anthony Thwaite. PeBJV

If you arrive in the land of the wind, the bottom of the sea. You Will See Far. Väinö Kirstinä, *tr. by* Aili Jarvenpa. SOP

If you ask for the cause of our national flaws. Eureka! Alfred Denis Godley. CenHV

If you ask me how it is. Why My Hair Is Not Gray. Picirantaiyar, *tr. by* A. K. Ramanujan. PLW

If you ask me whence the story. Goosey Goosey Gander—by Various Authors (Longfellow's Version). William Percy French. CenHV

If You Ask Me Who I Am. Armando Guebuza, *tr. fr. Portuguese by* Margaret Dickinson. WMBCH

If You Black Get Back. Cheryl Clarke. AIW

If You But Knew. *Unknown.* BLPA; FaBoBe

If You Can Hear My Hooves. Harold Littlebird. STE; VoR

If you can keep your head when all about you. If. Kipling. BLPA; FaBoBe; FaFP; FaPoR; FPL; OHFP; OxBChV; OxBTC; PWR; WBLP

If you cannot on the ocean. Your Mission. Ellen M. Huntington Gates. BLPA; BLRP

If you can't be a pine on the top of the hill. Be the Best of Whatever You Are. Douglas Malloch. BLPA

If You Can't Eat You Got To. E. E. Cummings. CMoP; PrIm

If you can't trim your sails to suit the weather. If Not. H. A. C. Evans. FaBoPa

If You Come. Lucie Delarue-Mardrus, *tr. fr. French by* Barbara Johnson. DMF

If you come as softly. Memorial I. Audre Lorde. AIW

If you come at all. Yourself and Myself. *Unknown, tr. by* Thomas Kinsella. NOIV

If You Come Back. Jack Cope. PeSA

If You Come Softly. Audre Lorde. AmNP

If you complain your flames are hot. To Her Lover's Complaint. Jane Barker. OxBSP

If you could be small. Karla Kuskin. *Fr.* Square as a House. TSS

If you could bring her glories back! Babylon. Ralph Hodgson. BrPo

If you could crowd them into forty lines! Limitations. Siegfried Sassoon. MoBrPo

If you could see, fair brother, how dead beat. Prolonged Sonnet: When the Troops Were Returning from Milan [*or* When The Troops Were Returning from Milan]. Niccolò degli Albizzi, *tr. by* Dante Gabriel Rossetti. AWP; OBVE; PFI; WaaP

If you could see me die. Song of the Negro on the Ferry. José Craveirinha, *tr. by* Chris Searle. WMBCH

If you desire to paralyze. The Better Way. Walter Leaf. FaBoCo

If you do love, as well as I. The Thought. Herbert of Cherbury. InvP

"If you do love me weel, Willie." Fair Janet. *Unknown.* ESPB

If you do not come, must I sleep alone. Teika, *tr. fr. Japanese by* Hiroaki Sato. *Fr.* A Compendium of Good Tanka. FCEI

If you do not shake the bottle. On Tomato Ketchup. *Unknown.* FaBoUs; NBLV

If you don't come to the mountains in autumn. Staying Overnight at Blue Cloud Temple. Mo Shih-lung, *tr. by* Jonathan Chaves. CoBLCP

If you don't know how, why pretend? To the Tune "Red Embroidered Shoes." Huang Ö, *tr. by* Kenneth Rexroth *and* Ling Chung. PBWP; WPOW

If you don't like my apples. *Unknown.* GBP; OxBoLi

If You Don't Stay Bitter for Too Long. Charles Mungoshi. WMBCH

If you draw a bow, draw a strong one. Tu Fu, *tr. fr. Chinese by* Burton Watson. *Fr.* On the Border, First Series, 6. CoBCP

If you drink the milk of the black cow, Gopal. Surdas, *tr. by* John Stratton Hawley *and* Mark Juergensmeyer. SSI

If you evah go to Houston. Midnight Special. *Unknown.* AS

If you ever, ever, ever meet a grizzly bear. Grizzly Bear. Mary Austin. FaPON; GoJo; OnUR; PDV

If you find a paddling pool. The Paddling Pool. E. M. Adams. BoTP

If you for orders, and a gown design. John Oldham. *Fr.* A Satyr Address'd to a Friend That Is About to Leave the University, and Come Abroad in the World. OBS

"If you're so out of love with happiness." OBSV

If you give me your attention, I will tell you what I am. The Disagreeable Man. W. S. Gilbert. FiBHP

If you go a-picnicking and throw your scraps about. Picnics. *Unknown.* BoTP

If you go away,/ why should I adorn myself? *Unknown, tr. by* Kenneth Yasuda. BoWoP

If You Had Known. Thomas Hardy. FaBoRV; GBL

If You Happy Would Be. Abraham Fernández. AH

If You Have a Friend. *Unknown.* FaFP
    (Say It Now.) BLPA; WBLP
    (Speak Out.) PWR

If you have a thing to do. Do It Right. Samuel O. Buckner. WBLP

If you have a word of cheer. Tell Her So. Mrs. Henry Linden. CBWP-4

If you have a word of cheer. Tell Him So. J. A. Egerton. PWR

If You Have an Enemy. John Skoyles. NAmP

If you have ever, like me. Please Excuse Typing. John Basil Boothroyd. FiBHP

If you have forgotten water-lilies floating. Water-Lilies. Sara Teasdale. MoAmPo

If you have formed a circle to go into. To God. Blake. OAEL-2

If you have lost the radio beam, then guide yourself by the sun or the stars. Any Man's Advice to His Son. Kenneth Fearing. CMoP

If you have no time. Izumi Shikibu, *tr. by* Willis Barnstone. BoWoP

If you have revisited the town, thin Shade. To a Shade. W. B. Yeats. AnIL; LiTB; NAEL-2; PoEL-5

If You Have to Scream, Please Do It Quietly. Stanisław Barańczak, *tr. fr. Polish by* Frank Kujawinski. PwPP

If you have yourself come to God. Mohammad Taqi Mir, *tr. by* Ahmed Ali. GoT

If you haven't made noise enough to warn him, singing, shouting. Meeting a Bear. David Wagoner. HAP

If you hear a kind word spoken. Tell Him So. *Unknown.* BLPA; BLPL; WBLP

If you hear rustling in the straw. David Philips. BXAP

If you hold a blue rock to your ear. Why Stone Does Not Sing by Itself. Anita Endrezze-Danielson. STE

If You Imagine. Raymond Queneau, *tr. fr. French by* Michael Benedikt. RHTwFP

If you iron tonic need. Dietary Advice. *Unknown.* FaBoUs

If you killed a helpless being, O cruel one. Sheikh Ibrahim Zauq, *tr. by* Ahmed Ali. GoT

If you knew how mulish, reluctant. Mulish. Hans Andreus, *tr. by* James Brockway. DuIn

If you lack, makers of Buddhas. Omiwa Okimori. *Fr.* Manyo Shu. Ma

If you let them squeeze in the line. The Rude. Mark McCloskey. SoTCo

If you like to visit the garden, go. Mohammad Taqi Mir, *tr. by* Ahmed Ali. GoT

If you live along with all the other people. Worm Either Way. D. H. Lawrence. NoAM

If you look out from some high, high window. Sweet Loving Friendship. Peter Bellamy. OBET

If you love God, take your mirror between your hands and look. Mahmud Djellaladin Pasha, *tr. by* E. Powys Mathers. ErPo

If you love me. Izumi Shikibu, *tr. by* Willis Barnstone. BoWoP

If you love me, as I love you. Samuel Hoffenstein. FiBHP

If you mean to keep this appointment. Instructions for Elijah. Myra Sklarew. CRP

If you may their mother, had e'er been at sea. Sir George Dallas. *Fr.* India Guide, The; or, Journal of a Voyage to the East Indies in 1780. OBTV

If you never do anything for anyone else. The Immoral Proposition. Robert Creeley. LiTM; NeAP; PoM

If you, O Aynabo, my fleet and fiery horse. Battle Pledge. *Somali Oral Tradition, tr. by* M. Laurence. WTO

If You Only Knew. Robert Desnos, *tr. fr. French by* Michael Benedikt. POS

If you plant grain. A Robin's Poem. Nikki Giovanni. AmNP

If you ponder it,/ no obstacle blocks your path. Nanak, *tr. by* John Stratton Hawley *and* Mark Juergensmeyer. SSI

If you ponder it,/ there is mindfulness, wisdom of mind. Nanak, *tr. by* John Stratton Hawley *and* Mark Juergensmeyer. SSI

If you ponder it,/ you find the door of deliverance. Nanak, *tr. by* John Stratton Hawley *and* Mark Juergensmeyer. SSI

"If you raise canary birds," my grandfather said to me. Summer Nights. James Tate. AnAn; NAmP

If you really care for me. *Unknown, tr. by* Willis Barnstone. BoWoP

If you really love me honey, hey- yah. *Unknown, tr. fr. Kiowa Indian.* *Fr.* "49" Songs. STP

If You Saw a Negro Lady. June Jordan. IHMS; NMM

If You See a Fairy Ring. *Unknown.* BoTP

If you see a tall fellow ahead of a [*or* the] crowd. Forget It. *Unknown.* PoLF; WBLP

If you see my mother, partner, tell her pray for me. Mack Maze. WTO

If you see someone beautiful. Adaios, *tr. by* Alistair Elliot. PeHV

If You See This Man. Thomas Lux. AmPA

If you set out in this world. The Seventh. Attila József, *tr. by* John Batki. RB

If you should bid me make a choice. The Windmill. E. V. Lucas. BoTP

If you should find my bones after thousands of years. Self Portrait. Esther Raab, *tr. by* Bernhard Frank. MHeP

If you should go before me, dear, walk slowly. Walk Slowly. Adelaide Love. BLPA

If you should meet a crocodile. *Unknown.* OnUR; PDV

If you should see a man. The Truth. Ted Joans. AmNP; TTY
(Voice in the Crowd.) AmFP

If you should seek my footprints you would find. The Inflammable Man.
Gordon Challis. ATNZ

If you smoke a cigarette. A Cigarette. *Mongol Oral Tradition, tr. by* C.
R. Bawden. WTO

If you so heed your mother. *Unknown. Fr.* Manyo Shu. Ma

If you stay to school dinners. *Unknown.* WTO

If you stick the stems. Masaoka Shiki, *tr. fr. Japanese by* Burton Watson.
Fr. Fifteen Haiku. FCEI

If you stop caressing me. My True Memory. Asya, *tr. by* Gabriel Preil
and Howard Schwartz. VWA

If you strike. Genuine Poem, Found on a Blackboard in a Bowling Alley
in Story City, Iowa. Ted Kooser. ASP

If you strike a thorn or rose. Keep a-Goin.' Frank Lebby Stanton.
FaFP; OHFP; PWR; WBLP

If you take the moon in your hands. Hilda Doolittle ("H. D."). *Fr.*
Sigil, XI. AnAn; FaBoWP
(Moon in Your Hands, The.) BoWoP; NYBP

If you tenderly love me. *Unknown, tr. by* Arthur Waley. BoS

If you, that have grown old, were the first dead. The New Faces. W. B.
Yeats. GTBS-P

If You Think Kindly of Me. *Unknown, tr. fr. Chinese by* Burton Watson.
CoBCP

If you think, mother. What Her Girl Friend Said to the Foster-Mother ("If
you think, mother"). Orampokiyar, *tr. fr. Tamil by* A. K.
Ramanujan. *Fr.* Five on the Crabs, 4. PLW

If you think you are beaten, you are. The Victor. C. W. Longenecker.
PWR

If you think you are beaten, you are. Thinking. Walter D. Wintle.
WBLP
(Man Who Thinks He Can, The.) PoLF; SoSe

If you wait, he won't come. Landscape. Ishigaki Rin, *tr. by* Hiroaki
Sato. FCEI

If you wake at midnight, and hear a horse's feet. A Smuggler's Song.
Kipling. *Fr.* Puck of Pook's Hill. OxBChV

If you walked past the lot on any good Sunday. The Wrecker Driver
Foresees Your Death. David Baker. MAYP

If you wander far enough. Oh No. Robert Creeley. HeIP; InPK; NaP;
SM

If you want my apartment, sleep in it. Rent. Jane Cooper. ER; FYAP;
TAP

If you want to find the sergeant. The Old Battalion. *Unknown.* OBET

If you want to go to heaven. The Blood-strained Banders. *Unknown.*
AmFP

If You Want to Go to Heben. *Unknown.* GBP

If you want to have the kind of a church. It Isn't the Church—It's You.
Unknown. BLPA; WBLP

If You Want to Know Me. Noémia da Sousa, *tr. fr. Portuguese by*
Margaret Dickenson. AIW; WMBCH

If you want to know what we are. Buck Up. Felicia Lamport. SoTCo

If you want to know where the privates were. Where They Were.
Unknown. AS

If you want to live in the country. The Power of Maples. Gerald Stern.
NU

If you want to live in the kind of a town. It Isn't the Town, It's You. R.
W. Glover. BLPA

If you want to psychoanalyze this high-/ minded form. A Poem Not about
a Zebra. Pamela White Hadas. BLA

If you want to speak. Listen to Me. Kishwar Naheed, *tr. by* Mahmood
Jamal. PBMUP

If you were a Chinese born in America, who would you believe. A
Chinaman's Chance. Marilyn Chin. BrSi

If you were an Eskimo baby. An Eskimo Baby. Lucy Diamond.
BoTP

If you were an owl. That's What We'd Do. Mary Mapes Dodge.
OBCA

If you were busy being kind. If. Rebecca Foresman. WBLP

If you were coming in the Fall. Emily Dickinson. AmPP; NOBA;
OxBA; PoRA

If you were exchanged in the cradle and/ your real mother died. A Story
That Could Be True. William Stafford. GOYP; NTCP

If you were going to get a pet. If You. Robert Creeley. MoP; NeAP;
NoAM; NOBA; SM

If you were just in keeping our pact of love. Wallada, *tr. by* A. R. Nykl.
PBWP

If you were only one inch tall, you'd ride a worm to school. One Inch
Tall. Shel Silverstein. OBCA

If you were queen of bloaters. A Catch. Tom Hood. CenHV

If you were twenty-seven. Heaven. Philip Levine. LCAP; NaP

If you will come on such a day. The Gardener. Sidney Keyes. MoAB;
MoBrPo

If you will tell me why the fen. I May, I Might, I Must. Marianne
Moore. FaBoWP; FF; OBAL; OxBSP

If you wish to live for ever. *Unknown.* FaBoUs

If you wish to pull a cork. Lilliputian's Beer Song. Septimus Winner.
OBAL

If you won't hug she, never. Reggae Blue Sweater. Caroline Knox.
SoTCo

If you would happy company win. Titmouse. Walter de la Mare.
BrPo

If you would know the love which I you bear. Sir John Davies. *Fr.*
Sonnets to Philomel. NePoEA; SiPS

If you would learn. The Antiquary. Joseph Campbell. OxBTC

If you would only stop to count your blessings. Count Your Blessings.
Mrs. Henry Linden. CBWP-4

If you your lips would keep from slips. Our Lips and Ears. *Unknown.*
BLPA; WBLP

If you'd died I would've cut off my hair. *Unknown, tr. by* James Koller
after John Swanton. STP

If you'd have me go on loving you. Ezra Pound. *Fr.* Impressions of
François-Marie Arouet (de Voltaire). MoAB

If you'd left me unhappy and hadn't come. Lady Izumi, *tr. fr. Japanese
by* Hiroaki Sato. *Fr.* Fifty-one Tanka. FCEI

If you'll listen a while, I'll sing you a song. Jim Fisk. *Unknown.* AS

If you'll listen for a moment, I will tell you now, my friends. What We
Teach at Claflin. Lizelia Augusta Jenkins Moorer. CBWP-3

If your child tastes salty. If. Anselm Hollo. UL

If You're Anxious for to Shine in the High Aesthetic [*or* Esthetic] Line.
W. S. Gilbert. *Fr.* Patience. NAEL-2, *with add. verse;* NBLV
(Aesthete, The.) EBVV
(Bunthorne's Song.) FiBHP; LiTB; OAEL-2
(Song: "If you're anxious for to shine. . .") NBLV

If You're Ever Going to Love Me. *Unknown.* BLPA

If You're My Friend for Life. Jan Kemp. ATNZ

If you're not home, where. Numbers, Letters. Amiri Baraka. BPo;
NOBA

If you're off to Philadelphia in the morning. Philadelphia. Kipling.
OBTV

If you're so out of love with happiness. John Oldham. *Fr.* A Satyr
Address'd to a Friend That Is About to Leave the University, and
Come Abroad in the World: If you for orders, and a gown design.
OBSV

If you've ever been in a car. Stun. James Schuyler. MAT

If you've ever been one. Misnomer. Eve Merriam. RHPC

If you've got a job to do. Do It Now! *Unknown.* BLPA; FaFP;
WBLP

Ifa divination was performed for Tiger. Tiger. *Yoruba Oral Tradition,
tr. by* B. King. WTO

Ifa speaks in parables. *Yoruba Oral Tradition, tr. by* J. A. Adediji.
WTO

Ifor Hael's hall, poorly it looks. The Hall of Ifor Hael. Evan Evans, *tr.
by* Gwyn Williams. OBWVE

Ignorance of Death. William Empson. CMoP; LiTM; NoAM; OBD

Ignorance of the Wise. Iftiqar Arif, *tr. fr. Urdu by* Mahmood Jamal.
PBMUP

Ignorant dawn of W. B. Yeats, The. We Love You the Way You Are.
David McFadden. NeAC

Ignorant, in the sense. Death of an Irishwoman. Michael Hartnett.
CIP

Ignorant men, who disclaim. Sister Juana Inés de la Cruz, *tr. fr. Spanish
by* Judith Thurman. *Fr.* A Satirical Romance. PBWP

Ignotum per Ignotius, or a Furious Hodge-Podge of Nonsense; a Pindaric.
Unknown. NOEC

Ignu. Allen Ginsberg. NaP

IHaveNoTimefor. Last Straw. George Starbuck. SoTCo

Ijajee's Story. Charlotte DeClue. STE

Ike Walton's Prayer. James Whitcomb Riley. AA

Ikhnaton's Night. Agnes Nemes Nagy, *tr. fr. Hungarian by* Laura Schiff.
OV

Ikons of the Dead, The. George Barker. NPo

Il Insonio Insonado, *sel.* Nathaniel Whiting.
Office of Poetry, The. OBS

Il Janitoro. George Ade. OBAL

Il Pastor Fido, *sels.* Sir Richard Fanshawe, *after the Italian of* Giovanni
Battista Guarini.
"Fair Golden Age! When milk was th' onely food." OBVE
(Golden Age, The.) OAEL-1
Fall, The. MePo; OBS
(Great Favorit Beheaded, A.) OBVE
Hope. OBS
"How I forsook/ Elias and Pisa after, and betook." AWP
"Learn women all from this housewifery." OBVE
Ode on His Majesty's Proclamation. NOBE

(Ode, upon Occasion of His Majesties Proclamation in the Year 1630, An.) MePo; OBS
Of Beauty. BoLoP
  (Beauty.) GBL
  (Nymph's Song.) OxBSP
"Our beauty is to us that which to men." OBVE
Rose, A. OBEV; OBS; PoEL-2; SeCePo
  (Rose of Life, The.) AWP
"Well may that kisse be sweet that's giv'n t' a sleek." OBVE
Il Penseroso. Milton. AWP; FiP; GTBS; GTBS-P; HAP; HoPM; InPS; JCP; LiTB; NAEL-1; NoP; OAEL-1; OBEV; OBS; PoE; PPP; TEP; TrGrPo
"Sweet bird that shunn'st the noise of folly," sel. CH
Il Piccolo Rifiuto. Louis MacNeice. CMoP
Il Pleut Doucement sur la Ville. Paul Verlaine, tr. fr. French by Ernest Dowson. AWP; BrPo
Ile gaze no more on her bewitching face. Song: Murdring Beautie. Thomas Carew. SeCP
Ile give thee leave my love, in beauties field. William Alexander, Earl of Stirling. Fr. Aurora, XXVI. OxBS
Ile sooth his plots: and strow my hate with smiles. George Chapman. Fr. Bussy d'Ambois, IV, ii. PoEL-2
I'le tell you a tale of my love and I. The Shepheard and the Milkmaid. Unknown. CoMu
Ilex Tree, The. Agnes Lee. PoA
Iliad. Michael Casey. SoTCo
Iliad, The, sels. Homer, tr. fr. Greek.
  Achilles Shows Himself in the Battle by the Ships. Fr. XVIII, tr. by George Chapman. OBS
  Achilles to Lycaon. Fr. XXI, tr. by Richmond Lattimore. WaaP
  "Achilles with wild fury in his heart." Fr. XXIII, tr. by Robert Fitzgerald. OBWP
  "Ajax the swift swerv'd never from the side." Fr. XIII, tr. by William Cowper. OBVE
  "All grave old men, and souldiers they had bene, but for age." Fr. III, tr. by George Chapman. OBVE
  "And as in winter time when Jove his cold-sharpe javelines throwes." Fr. XII, tr. by George Chapman. OBVE
  "And as when with the West-wind's flawes the sea thrusts up her waves." Fr. IV, tr. by George Chapman. OBVE
  "And now was Paris come/ From his high towres." Fr. VI, tr. by George Chapman. OBVE
  "And when they came together in one place." Fr. IV, tr. by Tennyson. OBVE
  Andromache's Lamentation. Fr. XXIV, tr. by Congreve. OBVE
  "As when an architect some palace wall." Fr. XVI, tr. by William Cowper. OBVE
  "As when devouring flames some forest seize." Fr. II, tr. by William Cowper. OBVE
  "As when of frequent bees." Fr. II, tr. by George Chapman. OBVE
  "As when the winds, ascending by degrees." Fr. IV, tr. by Pope. OBVE
  "At her departure his disdain return'd." Fr. I, tr. by Dryden. OBVE
  "At this th' impatient hero sowrly smil'd." Fr. I, tr. by Dryden. OBVE
  "Big with great purposes and proud, they sat." Fr. VIII, tr. by William Cowper. OBVE
  "But ere sterne conflict mixt both strengths, faire Paris stept before." Fr. III, tr. by George Chapman. OBVE
  "But now, no longer deaf to honour's call." Fr. VI, tr. by Pope. OBVE
  Death of Hector, The. Fr. XXII, tr. by George Chapman. OBS
  "Embodied close, the lab'ring Grecian train." Fr. V, tr. by Pope. OBVE
  "Fierce they drove on, impatient to destroy." Fr. XIII, tr. by Pope. OBVE
  "Frail as the leaves that quiver on the sprays." Fr. VI, tr. by Samuel Johnson. OBVE
  Ghost of Patroclus, The. Fr. XXII, tr. by Pope. PeHV
  Hektor to Andromache. Fr. VI, tr. by Richmond Lattimore. WaaP
  Helen's Lamentation. Fr. XXIV, tr. by Congreve. OBVE
  "His hand came out of the east." Fr. XVI, tr. by Christopher Logue. OBVE
  "Hornets occasionally build their nests near roads." Fr. XVI, tr. by Christopher Logue. OBVE
  Like leaves on trees the race of man is found. Fr. VI, tr. by Pope. OBVE
  "Meanwhile the troops beneath Patroclus' care." Fr. XVI, tr. by Pope. OBVE

  "Nor lingered Paris in the lofty house." Fr. VI, tr. by Tennyson. OBVE
  "Nor long the trench or lofty walls oppose." Fr. XII, tr. by Pope. OBVE
  "Now front to front the hostile armies stand." Fr. III, tr. by Pope. OBVE
  "Now side by side, with like unweary'd care." Fr. XIII, tr. by Pope. OBVE
  "Now when the solemn rites of pray'r were past." Fr. I, tr. by Dryden. OBVE
  "Now, when twelve days complete had run their race." Fr. I, tr. by Dryden. OBVE
  "Oileus by his brother's side stood close." Fr. XIII, tr. by George Chapman. OBVE
  Parting of Hector and Andromache, The. Tr. by William B. Smith and Walter Miller.
  Patroclus' Body Saved. Fr. XVII, tr. by E. R. Dodds. WaaP
  Priam and Achilles. Fr. XXIV, tr. by George Chapman. OBS
  Sarpedon to Glaukos. Fr. II, tr. by Richard Lattimore. WaaP
  Sarpedon's Speech. Fr. II, tr. by George Chapman. OBS
  "So saying, light-foot Iris passed away." Fr. XVIII, tr. by Tennyson. OBVE
  "Son of Enops, Thestor next he smote, The." Fr. XVI, tr. by William Cowper. OBVE
  "Their ardour kindless all the Grecian pow'rs." Fr. XII, tr. by Pope. OBVE
  "Their ground they stil made good." Fr. V, tr. by George Chapman. OBVE
  "Then first he form'd th' immense and solid shield." Fr. XVIII, tr. by Pope. OBVE
  "Then rising in his rage above the shores." Fr. XXI, tr. by Pope. OBVE
  "There sate the seniors of the Trojan Race." Fr. III, tr. by Pope. OBVE
  "This said, he reacht to take his sonne." Fr. VI, tr. by George Chapman. OBVE
  "Thus at the panting dove a falcon flies." Fr. XXII, tr. by Pope. OBVE
  "Thus to Glaucus spake/ Divine Sarpedon." Fr. XII, tr. by Sir John Denham. OBVE
  Trojans Outside the Walls, The. Fr. VIII, tr. by George Chapman. OBVE
  "Troops exulting sate in order round, The." Fr. VIII, tr. by Pope. OBVE
  "Unweary'd watch their list'ning leaders keep, Th'." Fr. X, tr. by Pope. OBVE
  "Why boast we, Glaucus! our extended reign." Fr. XII, tr. by Pope. OBVE
  "Why dost thou so explore." Fr. VI, tr. by George Chapman. OBVE
  "Wrath of Peleus son, O muse, resound, The." Fr. Invocation, tr. by Dryden. OBVE
Iliad. Humbert Wolfe. MoBrPo
Ilicet. Theodosia Pickering Garrison. PoLF
Ilicet. Swinburne. NOBVV
Ilkla Moor. Unknown. FaBoPP
I'll/ break/ you. Figure of Speech. Ernst Jandl, tr. by Beth Bjorklund. CoAuP
I'll act out a weird dream. Marie-Francoise Prager, tr. by Willis Barnstone and Elene Kolb. BoWoP
Ill-advised, in these parts, to shout. The Dam, Glen Garry. Robert Symmens. PoSH
I'll always dress in black and rave. Christine de Pisan, tr. by Willis Barnstone. BoWoP
Ill at ease, I returned to my old dwelling. Encountering Fire Again in the Fifth Month. Huang Tsung-hsi, tr. by Lynn Struve. WFTU
I'll be an amulet, I'll be good news. Haim Guri, tr. by Warren Bargad and Stanley F. Chyet. IP
I'll be an otter, and I'll let you swim. River-Mates. Padraic Colum. AWP
I'll be brief. On Time. Lindolf Bell, tr. by William Jay Smith. CT
I'll Be Fourteen Next Sunday. Unknown. AmFP
I'll be going home today. Bunky Boy Bunky Boy Who's My Little Bunky Boy. Larry Mollin. NeAC
I'll be the strongest amid you. The Strongest. "Yehoash," tr. by Marie Syrkin. TrJP
I'll believe then that you are dead. Then I'll Believe. B. W. Vilakazi, tr. by Jack Cope. PeSA
I'll build a house of arrogance. Haven. Donald Jeffrey Hayes. AmNP; PoNe
Ill busi'd man! why should'st thou take such care. My Midnight Meditation. Henry King. MePo; OBS
I'll buy you a tartan bonnet. Unknown. OxNR

I'll call thy frown a headsman, passing grim. To My Lady. George Henry Boker. *Fr.* Sonnets. AA

I'll call you Bedford, Ed. That's what you called me. Last Words to James Wright. Richard Hugo. KS

I'll carry you off. Fragment of an Agon. T. S. Eliot. LiTB

I'll come to thee in all those shapes. To Electra. Robert Herrick. CaPo

I'll descend mid other men. Freedom. Sean O Riordain, *tr. by* Coslett Quin. TIRV

I'll do what the raids suggest. A Boy. John Ashbery. DiL; NeAP

I'll eat when I'm hungry, I'll drink when I'm dry. Rye Whisky. *Unknown.* OxBoLi

I'll faint no more beneath the burden. Submission. Clara Ann Thompson. CBWP-2

Ill fares the land, to hastening ills a prey. Goldsmith. *Fr.* The Deserted Village. OBSV

I'll find me a spruce. Christmas Tree. Aileen Fisher. PDV

I'll Find My Self-Belief. Jacob Glatstein, *tr. fr. Yiddish by* Ruth Whitman. VWA

I'll Follow Thee. Clara Ann Thompson. CBWP-2

I'll frame, my Heliodora! a garland for thy hair. A Garland for Heliodora. Meleager, *tr. by* "Christopher North." AWP

I'll get up soon, and leave my bed unmade. The Widower in the Country. Les A. Murray. DiPo

"I'll give to you a paper of pins." Paper of Pins. *Unknown.* AmFP

I'll go among the dead to see my friend. An Afternoon at the Beach. Edgar Bowers. MT

I'll go into the bedroom silently and lie down between the bridegroom and the bride. Love Poem on Theme by Whitman. Allen Ginsberg. CAPP; NaP

I'll go, said I, to the woods and hills. The Apostate. A. E. Coppard. OBMV

I'll go up on the mountain top. Liza Jane. *Unknown.* AS

I'll grab hold of a butt of dream. Amir Gilboa, *tr. by* Warren Bargad *and* Stanley F. Chyet. IP

I'll greet the sun once more. Once More. Forugh Farrokhzad, *tr. by* Jascha Kessler *and* Amin Banani. BoWoP

I'll Have a Collier for My Sweetheart. William Oliver. WTO

I'll have you by the short and curly hair. Catullus, *tr. by* James Michie. PeHV

Ill in Bed. Joso, *tr. fr. Japanese by* Hiroaki Sato. *Fr.* Fifteen Hokku. FCEI

I'll keep your shirt white. Death Song ("I'll keep your shirt white"). *Unknown, tr. by* Reza Baraheni *and* Zahra-Soltan Shokoohtaezeh. BoWoP

Ill lay he long, upon this last return. John Berryman. *Fr.* Dream Songs. TAP

I'll lay you five hundred pounds. The Broomfield Hill. *Unknown.* AmFP

I'll leave my shadow. Testament. Sebastian Salazar Bondy, *tr. by* David Tipton. Per

I'll let my villages stand. Self-Made. Ilse Aichinger, *tr. by* Beth Bjorklund. CoAuP

I'll lick these screwfaced torches all night long. Fat Tuesday. W. S. Di Piero. MAYP

I'll make a fire tonight. Basho, *tr. fr. Japanese by* Burton Watson. *Fr.* Seventy-six Hokku. FCEI

I'll make a straw house. Loving My Grandchild. Kaai Chigetsu, *tr. fr. Japanese by* Hiroaki Sato. *Fr.* Thirteen Hokku. FCEI

I'll make a tune for dancing, gay and. *Unknown, tr. by* Paul Blackburn. Pro

I'll make a vers while I'm asleep here. Guillaume de Poitiers, *tr. by* Paul Blackburn. Pro

I'll Marry Not at All. *Unknown.* AmFP

Ill Met by Zenith. Ogden Nash. NYBP

I'll Never Love Thee More. James, Marquess of Montrose Graham. *See* My dear and only love, I pray.

"I'll never reach forty," my mother would say. She'd Say. Frank Davey. NOBC

I'll Never Use Tobacco. *Unknown.* FaBoUs

I'll not die of love. *Unknown. Fr.* Manyo Shu. FCEI

I'll not forget/ I swear. The Cliffs at Manzanilla. Jan Carew. PBCV

I'll not forget the warm blue night when my bold girl. A Thing Remembered. *Unknown, tr. by* E. Powys Mathers. ErPo

I'll not touch wood nor, fingers crossed. Favour. Robert David Fitzgerald. CBAP

I'll not weep that thou art going to leave me. Emily Brontë. WPE

Ill Omens. Thomas Moore. PoEL-4

I'll prop her, I swear, ankle, butt and chin. The Nude on the Bathroom Wall. Gena Ford. IHMS

I'll put on my boots and I'll blow the man down. Blow the Man Down. *Unknown.* OxBSS, *vers.* II, *with music*

("Come all you young fellows who follow the sea.") OxBSS, *vers.* I, *with music*

I'll Reinvent the Rose for You. Louis Aragon, *tr. fr. French by* Michael Benedikt. POS

I'll rest me in this sheltered bower. The Arbour. Anne Brontë. EBVV

I'll rush upon you. Guerrilla Promise. Mvula Ya Nangolo. WMBCH

I'll Sail upon the Dog-Star. Thomas D'Urfey. *Fr.* A Fool's Preferment. FaBoCh; OxBoLi

Ill sat to be with the calm, The. Essentials. Samuel Greenberg. LiTA

I'll shoot a little bird for little brother. *Unknown, tr. by* James Koller *after* John Swanton. STP

I'll sing of heroes, and of kings. Love. Abraham Cowley, *after the Greek of* Anacreon. AWP; OBVE

I'll sing you a good old song. The Fine Old English Gentleman. *Unknown.* CH

I'll sing you a new ballad, and I'll warrant it first-rate. The Fine Old English Gentleman; New Version. Charles Dickens. CoMu; FaBoBa; NOBVV; OBSV

I'll sing you a one-O. *See* I'll sing you one-O.

I'll sing you a song. A Bar on the Piccola Marina. Noel Coward. NBLV

I'll sing you a song/ and it'll be a sad one. Sioux Indians. *Unknown.* AmFP

I'll sing you a song/ Nine verses long. *Unknown.* OxNR

I'll sing you a song/ The days are long. *Unknown.* OxNR

I'll sing you a song about two true lovers. William Taylor. *Unknown.* OBET

I'll sing you a song of Peace and Love. Whack Fol the Diddle. Peadar Kearney. FiBHP

I'll sing you a song of the world and its ways. Six Feet of Earth. *Unknown.* BLPA

I'll sing you a true song of Billy the Kid. Billy the Kid. *Unknown.* FaBoBe

I'll sing you [a] one-O [or twelve O]. Carol of the Numbers. *Unknown.* AmFP

(Dilly Song, The.) GBP; OBET

(Green Grow the Rushes O.) OxBoLi

I'll sit down again, Steve, with your shy ghost. For Steve. Earle Birney. WaP

I'll still walk with the rain open and dreaming. With the Rain. Amir Gilboa, *tr. by* Warren Bargad *and* Stanley F. Chyet. IP

I'll teach my sons. My Sons. Ron Loewinsohn. NeAP

"I'll tell—being past all praying for." On the Death-Bed. Thomas Hardy. *Fr.* Satires of Circumstance, XIII. BrPo

I'll tell my own daddy. *Unknown.* OxNR

I'll tell everything I can. "Lewis Carroll." *Fr.* Through the Looking-Glass, *ch.* 8. InVP; Par

(A-Sitting on a Gate.) PoRA

(Aged, Aged Man, The.) BXAP; FaBoPa; OxBChV

(Ways and Means.) FiBHP; NA

(White Knight's Ballad, The.) FaBoNo; HAP

(White Knight's Song, The.) FaBoCh; FaBoCo; InPS; NAEL-2; NOAM; NOBE; NOBL; NoP; OAEL-2

I'll tell you/ in my own way. Marcabrun, *tr. by* Paul Blackburn. Pro

I'll tell you a sad, sad story. The Dude Wrangler. Gail Gardner. CowP

I'll tell you a story/ About Jack a Nory. Mother Goose. OxNR

I'll tell you a story, a story anon. King John and the Bishop. *Unknown.* ESPB

I'll tell you everything, I give you my word! "Shatnes" or Uncleanliness. Eliezer Steinbarg, *tr. by* Seth L. Wolitz. VWA

I'll tell you how the sun rose. Emily Dickinson. AmPP; FaBV; MoShBr; PDV; PoEL-5; TAP

I'll tell you I never asked for it. Charles Wright. *Fr.* Four Poems for the New Year. AnAn

I'll tell you of a come-lye young lady fair. Fair Phoebe and Her Dark-eyed Sailor. *Unknown.* AmFP

I'll tell you of a wild Colloina boy. The Wild Colloina Boy. *Unknown.* AmFP

I'll tell you the story of Jimmy Jet. Jimmy Jet and His TV Set. Shel Silverstein. OBCA; RHPC

I'll Tell You What a Flapper Is. Anne Hobson Freeman. GrPl

I'll tell you what I heard that day. Upon the Hill before Centreville. George Henry Boker. PAH

I'll tell you what is real. The Storyteller. Ree Young. MOWH

Ill-tempered Lover, The, *sel. L. A. MacKay.*
I Wish My Tongue Were a Quiver. CaP; OBCV; TW

I'll test my power. Song of the Man Who Succeeded. *Unknown, tr. by* Jerome Rothenberg *from* Frances Densmore. STP

I'll think of thee, mine own, dear one. To a Loved One. Mary Weston Fordham. CBWP-2

I'll Twine White Violets. Meleager, *tr. fr. Greek by* Goldwin Smith. NIP

I'll untie my sash brocaded with a wheel design. Brocaded Sash. *Unknown, tr. by* Hiroaki Sato. FCEI

"I'll wager, I'll wager, I'll wager with you." The Broomfield Hill. *Unknown.* ESPB

I'll wait until I've circled. The Trees along the River. Luci Tapahonso. GOS

I'll wake you and shake you. To the Laggards. Joseph Bovshover, *tr. by* Joseph Bovshover. TrJP

I'll Wear Me a Cotton Dress. *Unknown.* BPo

Ill Wind, The. Jay Macpherson. MoCV

I'll write a poem, then sink to dreams. Count William's Escapade. Guillaume de Poitiers, *tr. by* Hubert Creekmore. ErPo

I'll write, because I'll give. To Critics. Robert Herrick. CaPo

I'll write no more of love, but now repent. On Himself. Robert Herrick. CaPo

I'll write no more verses—plague take 'em! Those Flapjacks of Brown's. Bert Leston Taylor. OBAL

Illa iuventus, that is so nise. Fearful Death. *Unknown.* MeEL

Ille Terrarum. Robert Louis Stevenson. OxBS

Illegal Operation, The. Patrick Conrad, *tr. fr. Dutch by* Peter Nijmeijer. DuIn

Illegitimate Things. William Carlos Williams. MoAB; MoAmPo; RR

Illi Morituri. Mary Morison Webster. PeSA

Illicit. D. H. Lawrence. *See* In front of the sombre mountains.

Illiterate, The. William Meredith. NoP

Ills of all the human race, The. Misunderstood. Lizelia Augusta Jenkins Moorer. CBWP-3

Ill's the airt o the Word the day. Idleset: "Ill's the airt o the Word the day." Thurso Berwick. OxBS

Illumination, The. Stanley Kunitz. TAP

Illumination. Jeffrey Wainwright. DiPo

Illumination. Simone Weil, *tr. fr. French by* Carol Cosman. OV

Illumination for Victories in Mexico. "Grace Greenwood." PAH

Illuminations. Leah Goldberg, *tr. fr. Hebrew by* Robert Alter. OV

Illuminations, *sels.* Rimbaud, *tr. fr. French.*
After the Flood. *Tr. by* Enid Rhodes Peschal. SOTW
Chercheuses de Poux, Les. *Tr. by* T. Sturge Moore. AWP
Dawn. *Tr. by* Enid Rhodes Peschal. SOTW
Lice Seekers, The. *Tr. by* Kenneth Koch *and* George Guy. SOTW

Illusion. Ella Wheeler Wilcox. WGRP

Illusions, The: they fit like an iron lung, and. Memorandum/ The Accountant's Notebook. Kathleen Norris. OBAL

Illustration. John Ashbery. NAAL-2

Illustration, The/ is nothing to you without the application. To a Steam Roller. Marianne Moore. BoWoP; CMoP; FaBoMo; MoAB; MoAmPo; OxBA; VGW

Illustration—a Footnote, The. Denise Levertov. PoA

Illustration to Dante, An. Fleur Adcock. ATNZ

Illustrious Ancestors. Denise Levertov. AmPP; MoP; NAAL-2; NOBA; VGW

Illustrious Holland! hard would be his lot. Byron. *Fr.* English Bards and Scotch Reviewers. OBSV

Illustrious monarch of Iberia's soil. Columbus to Ferdinand. Philip Freneau. OBCA; PAH

Illustrious One, in whom death is the vagrom wound. Singing Death. Stan Rice. FYAP

Illyrian woodlands, echoing falls. To E.L., on His Travels in Greece. Tennyson. SeCePo

Illyria's hair fell down. The Oracular Portcullis. James Reaney. ErPo

I'm a broken-hearted Gardener, and don't know what to do. The Broken-hearted Gardener. *Unknown.* ChTr; GBP

I'm a decent boy just landed. No Irish Need Apply. *Unknown.* WTO

I'm a Dreamer. Kattie M. Cumbo. BlSi

I'm a fashionable beau, just turn'd out the newest go. The Dandy O. *Unknown.* CoMu

I'm a Flower, *abr.* Nishiyama Soin, *tr. fr. Japanese by* Sato. FCEI

I'm a freeborn man of the travelling people. Freeborn Man. Ewan MacColl. OBET

I'm a gay tra, la, la. Swiss Air. Bret Harte. NA

I'm a grandchild of the gods. The Complaint of New Amsterdam. Jacob Steendam. PAH

I'm a gwine to tell you bout de comin' ob de Saviour. In Dat Great Gittin'-up Mornin.' *Unknown.* AA

I'm a heartbroken raftsman, from Greenville I came. Jack Haggerty. *Unknown.* AmFP

I'm a-layin' around, just spendin' muh time. The Strawberry Roan. Curley W. Fletcher. CowP

I'm a lean dog, a keen dog, a wild dog, and lone. Lone Dog. Irene Rutherford McLeod. FaPON; PDV; RHPC

I'm a little butterfly. *Unknown.* OxNR

I'm a little Hindoo. *Unknown.* FaFP

I'm a mad immortal between heaven and earth. To the Tune "Nan-hsiang-tz." Shen Chou, *tr. by* Jonathan Chaves. CoBLCP

I'm a peevish old man with a penny-whistle. Beggar's Serenade. John Heath-Stubbs. BoLoP; ErPo

I'm a pig, I'm a seagull. The Animals. Stephen Berg. NaP

I'm a poor cotton weaver as many one knows. The Poor Cotton Weaver. *Unknown.* OBET

I'm a poor little girl. The Wagoner's Lad. *Unknown.* AmFP

I'm a poor lonesome cowboy. Poor Lonesome Cowboy. *Unknown.* AS

I'm a poor working man, and I own it. A Labourer's Song. James Dawson. PF

I'm a pretty little thing. The Field Daisy. Jane Taylor. BoTP

I'm a prize for a captain to fall on. An Excellent New Song. *Unknown.* OxBSS

I'm a rambling wretch of poverty, from Tip'ry town I came. The Son of a Gambolier. *Unknown.* AS

I'm a rarem tarem fisherman that sails from Grimsby town. The Grimsby Fisherman. *Unknown.* OxBSS

I'm a riddle in nine syllables. Metaphors. Sylvia Plath. HeIP; InPK; SoSe

I'm a Roman Jew and I've been Roman. A Roman Roman. Crescenzo del Monte, *tr. by* Barbara Garvin. VWA

I'm a Soldier in the Army of the Lord. *Unknown.* AmFP

I'm a stable cat, a working cat. The Stable Cat. Leslie Norris. PChr

I'm a strange contradiction; I'm new, and I'm old. Hannah More. GN

I'm a stranger in your city, my name is Paddy Flynn. Portland County Jail. *Unknown.* AS

I'm a tiger in the rain. Sad Day in Berlin. Sarah Kirsch, *tr. by* Gerda Mayer. PBWP

I'm a Westmeath solicitor long lost in Peking, long, lost, and forgotten. General Vallencey's Waltz. Paul Durcan. FaBCIP

I'm a young lad, Jack Rollins by name. Blooming Sally. *Unknown.* OBET

Im Abendrot. K. O. Arvidson. *Fr.* The Four Last Songs of Richard Strauss at Takahe Creek above the Kaipara, III. ATNZ

I'm about to go shopping. James Schuyler. TTTS

I'm Agoing to Lay Down My Sword. *Unknown.* AH

I'm all alone in this world, she said. 50—50. Langston Hughes. NoAM; NOBA; PoE

I'm Alone in the Evening. Michael Rosen. RHPC

I'm always/ most surprised. Justice. Petra von Morstein, *tr. by* Rosemarie Waldrop. BoWoP

I'm always scared. Aren't/ you. Public Television. Eileen Myles. BAP

I'm always told to hurry up. Going to Bed. Marchette Chute. PDV

I'm an Old Cowhand. Johnny Mercer. OBAL

"I'm annoyed by a nerd." Accent Schmaccent. J. F. O'Connor. SoTCo

I'm as free a little bird as I can be. Free Little Bird. *Unknown.* AmFP

I'm ashamed of my thoughts. *Unknown.* NOIV

I'm ashamed, with this set of discordant bones. Delighted that Jippo Has Come to See Me in My Illness. Rai San'yo, *tr. by* Burton Watson. FCEI; JLIC-2

I'm at a table with Canadians. First Night at Sea. John Berryman. AnAn

I'm at one with this, this only. Daibai, *tr. by* Lucien Stryk *and* Takashi Ikemoto. ZPCJ

I'm Black and Blue. Heine, *tr. fr. German by* John Todhunter. AWP

"I'm bored. My cape, please." Stavrogin's Farewell. János Pilinszky, *tr. fr. Hungarian by* Jascha Kessler. *Fr.* Three Poems. FOC

I'm buried beneath the layered debris. Note. Meir Wieseltier, *tr. by* Warren Bargad *and* Stanley F. Chyet. IP

I'm but a festering lump. Ejo, *tr. by* Lucien Stryk *and* Takashi Ikemoto. ZPCJ

I'm by myself. Up in the Pine. Nancy Dingman Watson. RHPC

I'm called by the name of a man. *Unknown.* OxNR; PBBP

I'm Captain Jinks of the Horse Marines. Captain Jinks. *Unknown.* BLPA; FaFP

I'm careful of the words I say. Be Careful. *Unknown.* NBLV

I'm ceded—I've stopped being theirs. Emily Dickinson. WPOW

I'm colored with the color of dusk, oh *rana.* Mirabai, *tr. by* John Stratton Hawley *and* Mark Juergensmeyer. SSI

I'm comfortable here, on 50 mg. of Librium. Chelsea. Robert Long. NAmP

"I'm corrupt," he said to me in the French. The Corrupt Man in the French Pub. Brian Higgins. OxBTC

I'm cross with god who has wrecked this generation. John Berryman. *Fr.* Dream Songs. FaBoMo

I'm dead—/ dead of bad company. Kabir, *tr. by* John Stratton Hawley *and* Mark Juergensmeyer. SSI

I'm determined to be an old maid. I'll Marry Not at All. *Unknown.* AmFP

I'm Doing Fine. Margot Schroeder, *tr. fr. German by* Susan L. Cocalis.
DMG
I'm driving a car in Tel Aviv. End of the Trip. David Avidan, *tr. fr.*
Hebrew by Warren Bargad *and* Stanley F. Chyet. *Fr.* Traveling in
the City, 19. IP
I'm driving my car back to you filled. The Furniture of the Poem.
Dennis Saleh. NeAC
I'm eating alone lately. Things of Late. David Phillips. NeAC
I'm eight years older than Artaud when he died. Surrealism in the Middle
Ages. Philip Lamantia. UL
I'm far frae my hame, an' I'm weary aftenwhiles. My Ain Countree.
Mary Lee Demarest. WGRP
I'm fine, thanks. Interview. Gábor Görgey, *tr. by* Jascha Kessler.
FOC; MHuP
I'm folding up my little dreams. My Little Dreams. Georgia Douglas
Johnson. BANP; BISi; CDC; PoNe
I'm for it, as the last leaves shred. The Function of Winter. Jay Parini.
BLA
I'm full of everything I do not want. Sonnet: Of the 20th of June 1291.
Cecco Angiolieri da Siena, *tr. by* Dante Gabriel Rossetti. AWP
I'm getting old and feeble and I cannot work no more. The Old Miner's
Refrain. *Unknown.* AS
I'm getting older. Narihira, *tr. fr. Japanese by* Burton Watson. *Fr.*
Kokin Shu. FCEI
I'm Getting Out and Going Some 30 Kilometers towards the Coast.
Antonio Cisneros, *tr. fr. Spanish by* Maureen Ahern *and* David
Tipton. Per
I'm getting used to not understanding. At the Protestant Museum. Hugh
Maxton. CIP
I'm giving a party to-morrow at three. My Party. Queenie Scott-Hopper.
BoTP
I'm Glad. *Unknown.* RHPC
I'm glad I am living this morning. God's World. Mildred Keeling.
BLRP
I'm glad our house is a little house. Song for a Little House.
Christopher Morley. BoTP; FaPON
I'm glad that I am born to die. Shout for Joy. *Unknown.* AmFP
I'm glad the sky is painted blue. I'm Glad. *Unknown.* RHPC
I'm goin' away for to stay a little while. He's Gone Away. *Unknown.*
AS
I'm goin' out West, down on the Rio Grande. Alice B. *Unknown.*
AS
I'm goin' to whoop you, Sammy Taylor. A Domestic Storm. Priscilla
Jane Thompson. CBWP-2
I'm going/ to put down. April Fool. Joan Drew Ritchings. SoTCo
"I'm going down," she said, tying her yellow scarf. Going down the
Mountain. Valentin Iremonger. NeIP
(Descending.) EnLoPo
I'm going out to clean the pasture spring. The Pasture. Robert Frost.
BLPL; CMoP; FaPON; GoJo; MoAB; MoAmPo; MoShBr; NAAL-2;
NOBA; OxBA; PDV; PoE; TTTS
I'm going out to cut the Gordian knot. The Grotto. Clark Stillman.
SoTCo
I'm going to be just like you, Ma. A Dance for Ma Rainey. Al Young.
NBP
I'm going to break out. Carmen Valle, *tr. by* Julio Marzán. InW
I'm going to bring you something. Conversations in Mayan. Alonzo
Gonzales Mó, *tr. by* Allan F. Burns. STP
I'm going to California. Bina Mossman, *tr. by* S. H. Elbert *and* N.
Mahoe. WTO
I'm Going to Georgia. *Unknown.* AmFP
I'm going to make a town boys,. good enough? Guillaume de Poitiers, *tr.*
by Paul Blackburn. Pro
I'm Going to Plant a Heart on the Earth. Rosario Murillo, *tr. fr. Spanish*
by Barbara Paschke. Vol
I'm Going to Rocky Island. *Unknown.* AmFP
I'm Going to Sleep. Alfonsina Storni, *tr. fr. Spanish by* Perry Higman.
LPSS
I'm going to the North on the left rail. Going to the North. Stanislaw
Wygodski, *tr. by* Isaac Komem. VWA
I'm going to write a novel, hey. John Updike. FiBHP
I'm go'n' to lay down my sword and shield. Ain' Go'n' to Study War No
Mo'. *Unknown.* AS
I'm gonna die & won't see you all any more. Tsakak, *tr. by* James Koller
after John Swanton. STP
I'm gonna marry my brother's wife. *Unknown, tr. by* James Koller *after*
John Swanton. STP
I'm gonna walk to the graveyard. Young Gal's Blues. Langston Hughes.
NAAL-2
I'm grateful, really grateful. Sulpicia, *tr. by* John Dillon. PBWP
I'm growin auld, I'm growin' cauld. The Spell o' the Hills. Douglas
Fraser. PoSH

"I'm growing old, I've sixty years." Carcassonne. Gustave Nadaud, *tr.*
by John R. Thompson. BLPA; FaBoBe
I'm Happiest When Most Away. Emily Brontë. NAEL-2; SeCePo
(Fragment: "I'm happiest when most away.") Mes
I'm happy, Kerouac, your madman Allen's. Malest Cornifici Tuo Catullo.
Allen Ginsberg. NeAP
I'm having an affair with Hamlet. "Hamlet." Emmett Jarrett.
NeAC
I'm Here. Theodore Roethke. *Fr.* Meditations of an Old Woman.
CoAP; NYBP
I'm here an not here. Me head's. From Lucy: Holiday Reflections.
James Berry. PBCV
I'm here, on the dark porch, restyled in my mother's chair. Sitting at
Night on the Front Porch. Charles Wright. LCAP
I'm hiding, I'm hiding. Hiding. Dorothy Aldis. FaPON
I'm Honest Abe. Honest Abe Lincoln. Max Shulman. OBAL
I'm Hungry! Jack Prelutsky. RHPC
I'm hungry, oh so hungry. The Birds on the School Windowsill. Evelyn
Dainty. BoTP
I'm hurting a lot today. The Japanese Consulate. Frank Polite. UL
I'm in a large movie theater. I go to the john. Dream with Fred Astaire.
Bill Berkson. UL
I'm in a small Mexican town outside. Carravagio. Janet Hamill. UL
I'm in Hong Kong. How Hong Kong Was Destroyed. Dahlia
Ravikovich. IP, *tr. by* Warren Bargad *and* Stanley F. Chyet; MHeP,
tr. by Bernhard Frank
I'm in trouble. Bubble Gum. Nina Payne. RHPC
I'm jilted, forsaken, outwitted. The Jilted Nymph. Thomas Campbell.
EnLoPo
I'm Just a Stranger Here, Heaven Is My Home. Carole Gregory
Clemmons. PoBA
"I'm King of the cabbages green." Old King Cabbage. Richard Kendall
Munkittrick. OBCA
I'm king of the road! I gather. His Majesty. Theron Brown. AA
I'm like a skiff on the ocean tost. John Gay. EnLoPo
I'm living in a cave. *Unknown, tr. by* Jerome Rothenberg. STP
I'm lonesome since I crossed the hill. The Girl I Left behind Me.
Unknown. OBET
I'm looking for a single flea, midnight. Ozaki Hosai, *tr. fr. Japanese by*
Hiroaki Sato. *Fr.* One Hundred Haiku in Free Form. FCEI
I'm looking mighty seedy while holding down my claim. Little Old Sod
Shanty. *Unknown.* AmFP; AS, *with music*
I'm lost in the sea under the shining sun. Wakayama Bokusui, *tr. fr.*
Japanese by Hiroaki Sato. *Fr.* Forty-four Tanka. FCEI
I'm made in sport by Nature. On an Indian Tomineois, the Least of
Birds. Thomas Heyrick. FM
I'm makin' a road. Florida Road Workers. Langston Hughes.
MoAmPo
I'm Making You Up. "Chrystos." GOS
"I'm Mark's alone!" you swore. Given cause to doubt you.
Contemplation. John Frederick Nims. InPK
I'm melted down into a black ooze. In a Remote Cloister Bordering the
Empyrean. Joel Sloman. VGW
I'm middle-aged. Political Activist Living Alone. Pat Arrowsmith.
AIW; BrRo
I'm mighty glad to see you, Mrs. Curtis. The Transparent Man.
Anthony Hecht. BLA; FYAP
I'm more afraid of those I love than dying. A Letter Catches Up with Me.
Eric Chaet. VWA
I'm mortified and yet delighted. *Unknown, tr. by* Hiroaki Sato. FCEI
"I'm much in love, but look at me." Princess Shikishi, *tr. fr. Japanese by*
Hiroaki Sato. *Fr.* Seventy-eight Tanka. FCEI
I'm neither sound. Asadullah Khan Ghalib, *tr. by* Ahmed Ali. GoT
I'm no Alice. Pool. Wanda Barford. Mes
I'm no He-man you know, I'm not a He. D. B. Wyndham Lewis. *Fr.* If
So the Man You Are. OBSV
I'm no longer the bitter girl. Love Which Frees. Gloria Fuertes, *tr. by*
Philip Levine. WPOW
I'm no reformer; for I see more light. Optimism. Ella Wheeler Wilcox.
PWR
I'm nobody! Who are you? Emily Dickinson. AmPP; AnAmPo;
BoWoP; NBLV; NOBA; OBCA; OxBSP; PDV; RHPC; SO; TAP;
WPE
I'm Not a Man. Harold Norse. GLP
I'm not about to lay off the real muse. Angel with Horn. Margit Szécsi,
tr. by Jascha Kessler. FOC
I'm not alone. Interior. Joseph Milbauer, *tr. by* Edouard Roditi. VWA
I'm not depressed, as I walk along this street. The People in These
Houses. Jack Matthews. KS
I'm not diminished. A Question of Energy. Amber Coverdale Sumrall.
TSM
I'm not here. Hilda Doolittle ("H. D."). *Fr.* Halcyon. MoAmPo

I'm Not Here/ Never Was. Constanta Buzea, *tr. fr. Rumanian by* Stavros Deligiorgis. BoWoP

I'm not interested in the poverty. I Go Dreaming Roads in My Youth. Luis Omar Salinas. AiP

I'm Not Really Lazy. Arnold Spilka. RHPC

I'm Not Rich. Joseph Rolnik, *tr. fr. Yiddish by* Keith Bosley. VWA

I'm not some lovable rime-spook. School of Poetry. Lucebert, *tr. by* James S. Holmes. DuIn

I'm not sure there will be walls. Portrait by Alice Neel. Aaron Kramer. EyDe

I'm not without you. The Place of O. Ray A. Young Bear. VoR

I'm now arriv'd the soul desired port. Edmund Davie 1682; Annagram. Benjamin Tompson. SCAP

"I'm of no use," said a little brown seed. The Little Brown Seed. Harriett Mulford Lothrop. PWR

I'm off in search of the immortals! The Taoist Nun. Hsüeh Chao-yün, *tr. by* Lois Fusek. ATF

"I'm off to Kuwana Town," old Pussy said. *Unknown, tr. by* Geoffrey Bownas *and* Anthony Thwaite. PeBJV

"I'm old." Old Botany Bay. Mary Gilmore. PoAu-1

I'm old and you're going away. Sending Tzu-lung Off to a Post in Chi-chou. Lu Yu, *tr. by* Burton Watson. CoBCP

I'm Older than You, Please Listen. Arthur Rex Dugard Fairburn. ATNZ; PeNZ

I'm on his mind. *Unknown, tr. fr. Japanese by* Burton Watson. *Fr.* Kangin Shu. FCEI

I'm on My Way to Canaan. *Unknown.* AH

I'm on my way to Leutamirsk, the train is leaving soon. The Cat Merchant. Yisroel Rabon, *tr. by* Robert Friend. PeBMYV

I'm Only a Broken-down Miner. *Unknown.* AmFP

I'm only a consumer, and it really doesn't matter. Cheer for the Consumer. Nixon Waterman. OBAL

I'm only a merchant of time. The Fable Merchant. Charles Dobzynski, *tr. by* Charles Guenther. VWA

I'm only a poor little mouse, ma'am. The Mouse. Laura E. Richards. OBCA

I'm out of town and visiting old friends. How It Seemed to Him Away from Home. James Whitehead. BLA

I'm out to find the new, the modern school. The Fledgling Bard and the Poetry Society. George Reginald Margetson. BANP

I'm practically broke and homeless. To Have Taken the Trouble. C. P. Cavafy, *tr. by* Edmund Keeley *and* Philip Sherrard. VMG

"I'm pregnant," I wrote to her in delight. 1974. Marilyn Hacker. GLP

I'm quiet as an old leather belt lapped snakewise. Quiet. Brian Swann. AmPA

I'm quite the opposite of my clever master. Faust's Servant. Roy Fuller. OxBTC

I'm Really Not Lazy. Arnold Spilka. RHPC

I'm red pepper in a shaker. Sugar in the Cane. Tennessee Williams. OBAL

"I'm rich,"/ said/ Irish. Eternities. Norman Mailer. NYBP

I'm riding in a train. I Am a Horse. Hans Arp. FaBoNo, *tr. by* Harriet Watts; POS, *tr. by* Michael Benedikt

I'm running from myself down this percolating highway. Percolating Highway. Michael Castro. VWA

I'm running on the bridge. Jonathan. Yona Wallach, *tr. by* Warren Bargad *and* Stanley F. Chyet. IP

I'm rushing to an important meeting. A Moment at the Louvre. Dan Pagis, *tr. by* Bernhard Frank. MHeP

I'm Sad. Forugh Farrokhzad, *tr. fr. Persian by* Reza Baraheni. BoWoP

I'm Sad and I'm Lonely. *Unknown.* AS

I'm shouting/ I'm singing. Spring. Karla Kuskin. PDV; RHPC

I'm sick of love; O let me lie. To Sycamores. Robert Herrick. CaPo

I'm sick of you hypocrites babbling about gods! The Sanctimonious Poets. Friedrich Hölderlin, *tr. by* Robert Bly. NU

I'm sitting alone by the fire. Her Letter. Bret Harte. AnAmPo; PoLF

I'm sitting by the hearthstone now. Twilight Musings. Mary Weston Fordham. CBWP-2

I'm Smith of Stoke, aged sixty-odd. Epitaph on a Pessimist. Thomas Hardy. FaBoEE; FF

I'm Sneaky Bill, I'm terrible mean and vicious. Sneaky Bill. William Cole. RHPC

I'm so sorry for old Adam. Old Adam. *Unknown.* AS

I'm so sorry I got happy too late. Now Look What Happened. Molly Peacock. MAYP

I'm Soaked Through with You. Rachel Korn, *tr. fr. Yiddish by* Ruth Whitman. VWA

I'm sorry but we can't go to the immersions tonight. The Ganges. Norman Dubie. LCAP

I'm sorry to say my dear wife is a dreamer. Be Off! Stevie Smith. OxBC

I'm sound asleep, when a knock at the gate wakes me. Recording My Happiness. Wang Chiu-ssu, *tr. by* Jonathan Chaves. CoBLCP

I'm speaking again. Speaking. Michael Ryan. AmPA

I'm speeding west somewhere in the top of Ohio or Indiana. Drive Imagining. Arthur Vogelsang. MAYP

I'm straddling the top tier, my wet shirt clinging. Hanging Burley. Jim Wayne Miller. MT

I'm sure every word that you say is absurd. A Woman's Reason. Gelett Burgess. FaBoNo

I'm sure if I were a woman I should hate. Sonnet: Equality of the Sexes. Gavin Ewart. Son

I'm swinging through a department store of the future. Hi-Fashion Girl. Elaine Equi. UL

I'm Taking Off. Barbro Backberger, *tr. fr. Swedish by* Joanna Bankier. OV

I'm taught P-l-o-u-g-h. O-U-G-H. Charles Battell Loomis. NBLV

I'm telling you. Móir Hatching. Nuala Ni Dhomhnaill, *tr. by* Joan Keefe. OV

I'm Thankful That My Life Doth Not Deceive. Henry David Thoreau. PoEL-4

I'm thankful that the sun and moon. Gasbags. *Unknown.* NOBL

I'm that distinguished twice-born hero. The Death of Digenes Akritas. John Heath-Stubbs. NePoEA

I'm the best that ever done it. Times-Square-Shoeshine-Composition. Maya Angelou. RR

I'm the bloke that's trained to sit behind the public stamp machines. A Song of the GPO. Gerry Hamill. NOBL

I'm the goose that lays golden eggs. Rodomontade in the Menagerie. Eve Merriam. SoTCo

I'm the great Sir William Anson. *Unknown. Fr.* Balliol Rhymes. FaBoEE

I'm the Kilfenora teaboy. The Kilfenora Teaboy. Paul Durcan. FaBCIP

I'm the king of the castle. King of the Castle. *Unknown.* OxNR

I'm the pert little pimpernel. Pimpernel. Charlotte Druitt Cole. BoTP

I'm the snow on mountains. *Unknown, tr. by* Reza Baraheni *and* Zahra-Soltan Shokoohtaezeh. *Fr.* Death Songs. BoWoP

"I'm the sort of girl." Nausicäa. Irving Layton. ErPo

I'm the sub-average male *Time* reader. The Sub-average *Time* Reader. Ernest Wittenberg. FiBHP

I'm thinking about you. What else can I say? Postcard. Margaret Atwood. NoAM

I'm thinking of sweeping. Ozaki Hosai, *tr. fr. Japanese by* Hiroaki Sato. *Fr.* One Hundred Haiku in Free Form. FCEI

I'm Thinking of You. Margot Schroeder, *tr. fr. German by* Susan L. Cocalis. DMG

I'm thirty years old. Paris by Night. Gustave Kahn, *tr. by* Edouard Roditi. VWA

I'm three I'm balancing. This Is My Death-Dream. Ralph Salisbury. STE

I'm Through with You. *Unknown.* WTO

"I'm tired of children!"—to anyone who says that. Basho, *tr. by* Hiroaki Sato. FCEI

I'm tired of Love: I'm still more tired of Rhyme. Fatigue. Hilaire Belloc. FaBoCo; NBLV; NOBL; OxBTC

I'm tired of murdering children. (End) of Summer (1966). William Knott. EAS

I'm tired of symbols, of laws divine. To My Generation. Benyamin Galai, *tr. by* Jacob Sonntag. TrJP

I'm tired of trying to think. Existentialism. Lloyd Frankenberg. FiBHP

I'm tired of words. The clearer—the madder still. February 10. A. Leyeles, *tr. by* Benjamin *and* Barbara Harshav. *Fr.* Fabius Lind's Diary. AYP

I'm told you raised your hand against yourself. On the Suicide of the Refugee W. B. Bertolt Brecht, *tr. by* John Willett. OBD

Im Traum sah ich ein Männchen klein und putzig. Heine, *tr. fr. German by* Sir Theodore Martin. AWP

I'm travellin' down the Castlereagh, and I'm a station-hand. A Bushman's Song. Andrew Barton Paterson. PoAu-1

I'm trav'ling to my grave. The Traveler. *Unknown.* AmFP

I'm trying to sleep. Written when Sick in Bed. Masaoka Shiki, *tr. fr. Japanese by* Burton Watson. *Fr.* Thirty-nine Haiku. FCEI

I'm twenty-seven years. Kokuin, *tr. by* Lucien Stryk *and* Takashi Ikemoto. ZPCJ

I'm undecided, Samson said to the columns. For Advanced Seminar Students Only. David Avidan, *tr. fr. Hebrew by* Warren Bargad *and* Stanley F. Chyet. IP

I'm up against the wall. The Wall. William Hawkins. MoCV

I'm upset you are upset. Jill. Ronald David Laing. WeW

"I'm very drowsy," said the Bear. Hard to Bear. Tudor Jenks. OBCA

I'm very good friends with both our cats. The Two Cats. Elizabeth J. Coatsworth. ILY; TDD

I'm walking a side street. Sometimes, at Thirty-Six. Roger Weingarten. NAmP

I'm wanton—no I've stopped that. Complaynt. Anne Waldman. UL

I'm war. Remember me? Achtung! Achtung! Mary Hacker. CN

I'm wearin' [or wearing] awa', John [or Jean]. The Land o' the Leal. Carolina Oliphant, Baroness Nairne. GTBS; GTBS-P; OBEV; OxBS; WBLP; WGRP

I'm weary o' the rose as o' my brain. The Great Wheel. "Hugh MacDiarmid." OxBS

I'm weary of towns, it seems a'most a pity. Tired of Towns. Andrew Lang. EBVV

I'm wife; I've finished that. Emily Dickinson. CMoP

I'm wild and woolly. Cowboy. Unknown. ChTr

I'm willing to go along quite a way. Petit Salon des Indépendants. Cees Buddingh', tr. by James S. Holmes. DuIn

I'm woken up. Central Heating System. Stephen Spender. GrPl

I'm writing just after an encounter. Whatever You Say Say Nothing. Seamus Heaney. OBWP; OxBC

I'm yours, dearest, as are the winter towns. Marceline, to Her Husband. Elizabeth Libbey. AmPA

Image, The. Roy Fuller. GTBS-P; OxBTC

Image, The. Richard Hughes. OBMV

Image. Anna de Noailles, tr. fr. French by Carol Cosman. PBWP

Image. T. E. Hulme. InPK; OxBTC

Image, The. Tamura Ryuichi, tr. fr. Japanese by Hiroaki Sato. FCEI

Image, The/ the peawnees. The Pride. John Newlove. MoCV; NOBC

Image comes, An. Laser. A. R. Ammons. CAPP; NAAL-2; NoAM; NOBA

Image comes down to live as fact, and turns. The Shadowgraphs. Richmond Lattimore. NYBP

Image dance of change, An. Siegfried Sassoon. MoBrPo

Image in a Mirror. Mae Winkler Goodman. GoYe

Image in the bulb-ringed mirror. Mask. Elizabeth Cox. GoYe

Image in the Mirror. Peggy Susberry Kenner. JB

Image-Maker, The. Oliver St. John Gogarty. OBEV; OBMV; PoRA

Image-Nation (the Poesis). Robin Blaser. PoM

Image-Nation 13 (the Telephone). Robin Blaser. PoM

Image-Nation 3. Robin Blaser. PoM

Image o' God, The. Joe Corrie. OxBS

Image of City. Lance Henson. VoR

Image of Death, The. Lord Thomas Vaux. See I loathe that I did love.

Image of earth, The. The Year of Winter. Tauhindauli. STE

Image of God, The. Francesco de Aldana, tr. fr. Spanish by Longfellow. WGRP

Image of Irelande, The, sel. John Derricke. "No table there is spread." OBTV

Image of Leda, An. Frank O'Hara. HCAP

Image of Lethe, An. The Coming of War; Actaeon. Ezra Pound. CMoP; PoA; PoE

Image the images the great games therefore the locked. The Book of Job and a Draft of a Poem to Praise the Paths of the Living. George Oppen. NNaP

Imageries of dreams reveal a gracious age. The Age of a Dream. Lionel Johnson. OBMV

Images. Richard Aldington. MoBrPo; PoA

Images. Merle Collins. WS

Images, sels. Anna Hajnal, tr. fr. Hungarian by Jascha Kessler. FOC
Cast Rose.
Dead Girl.
Yellow.

Images. Valery Larbaud, tr. fr. French by William Jay Smith. CT

Images. Kathleen Raine. NYBP

Images. Richard Schaukal, tr. fr. German by Ludwig Lewisohn. AWP

Images break upon a sad day, The. Gladstone. Julian Symons. WaP

Images drip down my back like sweat. On the Morning of the Third Night above Nisqually. W. M. Ransom. CDW; NU

Images flicker across the stage. Visual Conspiracy. Fyna Dowe. WS

Images for a Painter. David Wright. NPo

Images for the Gospel of Christ. Paul Ramsey. CRP

Images from the Midwest. Georgi Belev. WCI

Images leap with him from branch to branch. A Poet at Twenty. Donald Hall. EAS

Images of Angels. Patricia K. Page. MoCV; NoAM

Images of beauty and of destruction. Sgoran Dhu. Nan Shepherd. PoSH

Images of J—— assail him. The Bus Trip. Joel Oppenheimer. NeAP

Images! Venerable as Druidical trees. George Barker. Fr. In Memory of David Archer. FaBoMo

Imaginary Elegies, I-IV. Jack Spicer. NeAP

Imaginary Iceberg, The. Elizabeth Bishop. FaBoWP; LiTM; MoAB; MoAmPo

Imaginary man, go. Here is your passport. Instructions for Crossing the Border. Dan Pagis, tr. by Stephen Mitchell. VWA

Imaginary Sonnets, sel. Eugene Lee-Hamilton. Luther to a Bluebottle Fly. Son

Imaginary Translation. Marilyn Hacker. DiPo

Imagination. John Davidson. Fr. New Year's Eve. MoBrPo

Imagination. Shakespeare. See Midsummer Night's Dream, A: Lunatic, the Lover, and the Poet, The.

Imagination and Taste, How Impaired and Restored. Wordsworth. Fr. The Prelude [or, Growth of a Poet's Mind], XII and XIII [XI and XII]. PoE; PoEL-4, XII abr.; TOF

Imagination, How Impaired and Restored. Fr. XII and XIII. OBNC Oh! Mystery of Man. Fr. XII. FiP

Imagination as Nihilo frothed like salt foam, like waves breaking. Mom's Homecooked Trees. Michael Stephens. UL

Imagination, How Impaired and Restored. Wordsworth. Fr. The Prelude [or, Growth of a Poet's Mind]: Imagination and Taste, How Impaired and Restored, XII and XIII. OBNC

Imagination ("Imagination—here the power so called"). Wordsworth. Fr. The Prelude [or, Growth of a Poet's Mind]: Cambridge and the Alps. FiP

Imagination of Necessity, The. Andrei Codrescu. EAS

Imagination of the Retina, The. S. R. Compton. BWV

Imaginative Life, The. Geoffrey Hill. NoAM

Imagine. Remco Campert, tr. fr. Dutch by Greta Kilburn. DuIn

Imagine: A Town. Daphne Marlatt. Fr. Steveston. NOBC

"Imagine being the first to say: surveillance." Inventors. Michael C. Blumenthal. DiPo; NoAM

Imagine father that you had a brother were. Landscape with Next of Kin. Olga Broumas. BoWoP

Imagine Grass. Knute Skinner. SM

Imagine it, a Sophocles complete. The Fire at Alexandria. Theodore Weiss. NoAM; PoA; TAP

Imagine lamenting our longing, no. Yona Wallach, tr. by Leonore Gordon. VWA

Imagine observing ones fear. Lyn Hejinian. UL

Imagine that any mind ever thought a red geranium! Red Geranium and Godly Mignonette. D. H. Lawrence. GTBS-P; NoAM

Imagine that July morning: Cape Henry and Virginia. The Tempest. William Jay Smith. MoAmPo

Imagine the South. George Woodcock. MoCV; NOBC

Imagine them as they were first conceived. Images of Angels. Patricia K. Page. MoCV; NoAM

Imagine what Mrs. Haessler would say. Dance of the Abakweta. Margaret Danner. PoNe

Imagined Description of Myself, in Another Scene, An. Ory Bernstein, tr. fr. Hebrew by Warren Bargad and Stanley F. Chyet. IP

Imagining How It Would Be to Be Dead. Richard Eberhart. LiTA

Imbecile, The. Donald Finkel. NePoEA-2

(Im)C-A-T(mo). E. E. Cummings. HAP

Imitated from the Persian. Robert Southey. See Lord! Who Art Merciful as Well as Just.

Imitating the Old Poems. Pao Chao, tr. fr. Chinese by Burton Watson. CoBCP

Imitation of Chaucer. Pope. FaBoPa; Par

Imitation of Intimations. Timoshenko Aslanides. UAS

Imitation of Joy. Salvatore Quasimodo, tr. fr. Italian by Jack Bevan. PFI

Imitation of Julia A. Moore. "Mark Twain." OBAL

Imitation of Martial, Book II Ep, An 105. "Captain H—" NOEC

Imitation of Spenser. Keats. EnRP; FL

Imitation of Walt Whitman. James Kenneth Stephen. See Clear cool note of the cuckoo which has ousted the legitimate nest-holder, The.

Imitation of Water. João Cabral de Melo Neto, tr. fr. Portuguese by Ashley Brown. ATCBP

Imitation of Wordsworth, An. Catherine Fanshawe. See There is a river clean and fair.

Imitations Based on the American. Frank Polite. BXAP

Imitations of Horace. Pope. See First Epistle of the Second Book of Horace [Imitated].

Immaculate Conception, The. Lindsay MacRae. DT

Immalee. Christina Rossetti. BoNaP

Immanence. Richard Hovey. WGRP

Immanent. Walter de la Mare. PoA

Immeasurable haze. To the Holy Spirit. Yvor Winters. MoAmPo; QFR; VGW

Immeasurable sadness! Sadness. Tennyson. FaBoEE

Immense and Red. Jacques Prévert, tr. fr. French by William Jay Smith. CT

Immense hope, and forbearance, The. Spring Day. John Ashbery. NOBA

Immense pale houses! The sunshine and the snow. American Scenes (1904). Donald Justice. MT

Immensity. Mabel Esther Allan. CN

Immensity [or Immensitie] cloistered [or cloysterd] in thy dear [or deare] womb [or wombe]. Nativity [or Nativitie]. John Donne. Fr. La Corona. OBS; Son

Immersed in night, my senses sharpen, hear. Porch. Alden Nowlan. NeAC

Immigrants. Robert Frost. GOA

Immigrants. Nancy Byrd Turner. AmFN

Immigration Act of 1924, The. Laureen Mar. BrSi

Immigration Law. Margaret Randall. ER

Immigration, women in industry, aged. Picture Collection. Marjorie Welish. UL

Immobile. A. Leyeles, tr. fr. Yiddish by Benjamin and Barbara Harshav. AYP

Immoderate Death that wouldst not once confer. On the Death of the Lord Treasurer. Unknown. FaBoEE

Immoderate use turns to restraint. Measures. Jackson MacLow. LP

Immolation. Robert Farren. TIRV

Immoral Arctic, The. Morris Bishop. FiBHP

Immoral Proposition, The. Robert Creeley. LiTM; NeAP; PoM

Immorality, An. Ezra Pound. CMoP; GoJo; GrPl; LiTM; MoAB; MoAmPo; NOBA; OBAL

Immortal, The. Blake. Fr. The Book of Los, ch. 2. LiTB

Immortal, The. Marjorie Pickthall. CaP

Immortal. Sara Teasdale. WGRP

Immortal. Mark Van Doren. MoAmPo

Immortal Aphrodite, on your patterned throne. Sappho, tr. by Josephine Balmer. AIW

Immortal at the River. Chang Pi, tr. fr. Chinese by Lois Fusek. ATF

Immortal at the River. Ho Ning, tr. fr. Chinese by Lois Fusek. ATF

Immortal at the River. Ku Hsiung, tr. fr. Chinese by Lois Fusek. ATF

Immortal at the River. Li Hsün, tr. fr. Chinese by Lois Fusek. ATF

Immortal at the River. Lu Ch'ien-i, tr. fr. Chinese by Lois Fusek. ATF

Immortal at the River. Mao Hsi-chen, tr. fr. Chinese by Lois Fusek. ATF

Immortal at the River. Mao Wen-hsi, tr. fr. Chinese by Lois Fusek. ATF

Immortal at the River. Niu Hsi-chi, tr. fr. Chinese by Lois Fusek. ATF

Immortal at the River. Sun Kuang-hsien, tr. fr. Chinese by Lois Fusek. ATF

Immortal at the River. Yen Hsüan, tr. fr. Chinese by Lois Fusek. ATF

Immortal at the River. Yin O, tr. fr. Chinese by Lois Fusek. ATF

Immortal Autumn. Archibald MacLeish. CMoP; LiTA; MoAB; MoAmPo; NAAL-2; TrGrPo

Immortal clothing I put on. The Transfiguration. Robert Herrick. CaPo

Immortal Flowers. Wallace Rice. AA

Immortal glories in my mind revive. Joseph Addison. Fr. A Letter from Italy [to the Right Honourable Charles Lord Halifax]. OBTV

Immortal Hate. Milton. See Paradise Lost: There the companions of his fall, o'erwhelmed.

Immortal heat, O let thy greater flame. Love ("Immortal heat, O let thy greater flame"). George Herbert. Fr. The Temple. Son

Immortal Imogen, crowned queen above. The Two Swans. Thomas Hood. CH

Immortal is an ample word. Emily Dickinson. NOCV

Immortal Israel. Judah Halevi, tr. fr. Hebrew by Solomon Solis-Cohen. TrJP

Immortal Longings. Shakespeare. See Antony and Cleopatra: Death of Cleopatra.

Immortal[l] love, autho[u]r of this great frame. Love. George Herbert. HoPM; SeCV-1; Son

Immortal Love, Forever Full. Whittier. AH, with music

Immortal Mind, The. Byron. WGRP

Immortal Newton never spoke. On Mr. Nash's Present of His Own Picture at Full Length. Earl of Chesterfield. NOEC

Immortal Part, The. A. E. Housman. Fr. A Shropshire Lad, XLIII. MoBrPo; UnPo

Immortal spirit hath no bars, The. Dawn. Frederick George Scott. CaP

Immortal Springtime and Its Tokens. Bernardo de Balbuena, tr. fr. Spanish by Samuel Beckett. Fr. Grandeza Mexicana. MexPo

Immortal stood frozen amidst, The. The Immortal. Blake. Fr. The Book of Los, ch. 2. LiTB

Immortal with his bamboo cane, The. The Cane of Ch'iung Bamboo. Hsü Chung-hsing, tr. by Jonathan Chaves. CoBLCP

Immortality. "Æ." AWP; OBMV; TIRV; WGRP

Immortality. Ai. MAYP

Immortality. Matthew Arnold. FiP

Immortality. "Badawi al-Jabal," tr. fr. Arabic by Matthew Sorenson and John Heath-Stubbs. MAP

Immortality. Richard Henry Dana. AA; WGRP

Immortality. Samuel Greenberg. LiTA

Immortality. Arthur Sherburne Hardy. AA

Immortality. Frank Horne. BANP

Immortality. Joseph Jefferson. BLPA

Immortality. "Nicolai Maksimovich Minsky," tr. fr. Russian by Babette Deutsch. TrJP

Immortality. Susan Langstaff Mitchell. TIRV

Immortality. Lizelia Augusta Jenkins Moorer. CBWP-3

Immortality. Lizette Woodworth Reese. AA

Immortality. Sir Philip Sidney. See Song: Who Hath His Fancy [or Fancie] Pleased.

Immortality. Bible, O.T. See Job: Man, that is borne of a woman is of a few dayes, and full of trouble.

Immortall love, authour of this great frame. See Immortal love, author of this great frame.

Immortals, The. Isaac Rosenberg. FaBoTw; MMA; TrJP

Immortals come and assemble, The. Inscribed on a Wall Painting of Assembled Immortals. Chao Meng-fu, tr. by Jonathan Chaves. CoBLCP

Immunity. Carol Muske. BLA

Immutabilis. Alice Learned Bunner. Fr. Vingtaine, II. AA

Imogene. Eloise Bibb. CBWP-4

Impartial Inspection, The. Unknown. APAS

Impartial Law enrolled a name, The. My Name and I. Robert Graves. Mes; NoAM; NYBP

Impasse. Langston Hughes. LiTM

Impatient all the foggy day for night. Fever. Thom Gunn. PeHV

Impatient as we were for all of them to join us. The Bungalows. John Ashbery. CoAP

Impatient with cripples, foreigners, children. Il Piccolo Rifiuto. Louis MacNeice. CMoP

Impatient with Desire. George Granville. OxBSP

Impatient with the enigmatic, Al Capone. Suite for Celery and Blind Date. Philip Dow. BXAP

Impenitentia Ultima. Ernest Dowson. BrPo

Imperator Victus. Hart Crane. OxBA

Imperceptively the world became haunted by her white dress. The White Dress. Marya Zaturenska. MoAmPo

Impercipient, The. Thomas Hardy. EBVV; NAEL-2; PrIm; TrGrPo; WGRP

Imperfect Enjoyment, The. Earl of Rochester. BoLoP; ErPo

Imperfect enough once for all at thirty. Last Things, Black Pines at 4 a.m. Robert Lowell. NOBA

Imperfect Lover, The. Siegfried Sassoon. BrPo

Imperfect Sestina. Phyllis Webb. NOBC

Imperfect Times. Washington Delgado, tr. fr. Spanish by Maureen Ahern and David Tipton. Per

Imperfections Is the Summit. Yves Bonnefoy, tr. fr. French by Anthony Rudolf. RHTwFP

Imperial. Arthur Rex Dugard Fairburn. Fr. Album Leaves. ATNZ

Imperial Adam. A. D. Hope. CBAP; ErPo; HAP; NIP; NoAM; NoP

Imperial boy had fallen in his pride, The. My Fatherland. William Cranston Lawton. AA

Imperial City of fairest Nara, The. Ono Oyu. Fr. Manyo Shu. Ma

Imperial consort of the fairy king, The. The Wild Duck's Nest. Wordsworth. FM
(Sonnet: Wild Duck's Nest, The.) ChER

Imperial Hotel, The. Nakano Shigeharu, tr. fr. Japanese by Geoffrey Bownas and Anthony Thwaite. PeBJV

Imperial Thumbprint. Tom Weatherly. PoBA

Imperialists in Retirement. Edward Lucie-Smith. PVCV

Imperious Muse, your arrows ever strike. Japanese Beetles. X. J. Kennedy. OBAL

Imperiously ringing, "Νὰ τὰ ποῦμε." Chimes for Yahya. James Merrill. AnAn

Impermanence. Lal Ded, tr. fr. Kashmiri. BoWoP

Impersonal the aim. Night of Battle. Yvor Winters. PoA

Impetuous Samuel. Harry Graham. NA

Impiety, sel. Helene Magaret.
"Lord, I have not time to pray." TrPWD

Implacable angel, The/ Has shot his dart. Leone da Modena. TrJP

Implacable, unmerciful, fulfilled. Eric. John Barford. PeHV

Implicated generations made, The. Celtic Cross. Norman MacCaig. OxBS

Implora Pace. Charles Lotin Hildreth. AA

Imploring Mecca. Be-Bop Boys. Langston Hughes. OBAL

Imponderable the dinosaur. Cape Hatteras. Hart Crane. Fr. The Bridge, IV. InPS; MoAB; MoAmPo
"Nasal whine of power whips a new universe." MoAB
(Power.) MoAmPo

Importance of Mirrors, The. Helga Sandburg. IHMS
Important! Liesl Ujvary, tr. fr. German by Beth Bjorklund. CoAuP
"Important is the nation's health." The Double Standard. Franklin P. Adams. OBAL
Important Matters. Charles Mungoshi. WMBCH
Important thing is not, The. Is. Patrick Kavanagh. FaBoTw
Importer, An. Robert Frost. FaBoCo
Impossibilities to His Friend. Robert Herrick. OxBSP
Impossible, The. Abd al-Wahhab al-Bayyati, tr. fr. Arabic by Salma Khadra Jayyusi and Christopher Middleton. MAP
Impossible, The. Jules Laforgue, tr. fr. French by William Jay Smith. CT
Impossible outside you want always the other. A continual. Live Acts. Charles Bernstein. UL
Impossible Pictures, The. Tom Paulin. CIP
Impossible to call a lamb a lambkin. Gone Are the Days. Norman MacCaig. OxBC
Impossible to Trust Women. Unknown. MeEL
Imposture, The, sels. James Shirley.
  O Fly My Soul. Fr. II, ii. OBS
    (Song of Nuns, A.) ACP
  Piping Peace. ACP; NOBE
    (Song: "You virgins that did late despair.") PoEL-2
Impotence. Marvin Bell. AmPA
Imprecation against Foes and Sorcerers, An. Unknown, tr. fr. Sanskrit by A. A. MacDonnell. WSC
Impression. René Altmann, tr. fr. German by Beth Bjorklund. CoAuP
Impression. E. E. Cummings. See Hours Rise Up, The.
Impression de Nuit; London. Lord Alfred Douglas. OBEV
Impression du Matin. Oscar Wilde. BrPo; EBVV; MoBrPo; NAEL-2; NoAM
Impression of Early Summer, An. Hagiwara Sakutaro, tr. fr. Japanese by Hiroaki Sato. FCEI
Impression which this seal shall make, The. Sent to a Lady, with a Seal. Robert Lloyd. FaBoUs
Impressionist. Heather McHugh. MAYP
Impressions. Wen T'ing-shih, tr. fr. Chinese by Irving Lo. WFTU
Impressions, sels. Oscar Wilde.
  Le Jardin. SeCePo
    (Garden, The.) PoRA
  "Sea is flecked with bars of grey, The." MOS
    (Les Silhouettes.) BrPo; EBVV
Impressions at the Vulture Peak. Chou Meng-tieh, tr. fr. Chinese by Dominic Cheung. IFON
Impressions of a Night's Stay at Shuang-lin Temple, sels. Singde, tr. fr. Chinese by William Schultz. WFTU
  "After the leaves have quivered and fallen." Fr. III.
  "Even the crows have gone." Fr. IV.
  "Heart turned to ashes." Fr. II.
Impressions of François-Marie Arouet (de Voltaire), sel. Ezra Pound.
  "If you'd have me go on loving you." MoAB
Impressions of My Father, sel. Marcia Lee Masters.
  Country Ways. Fr. I. GoYe
Impressions of My Village. Wu Sheng, tr. fr. Chinese by Dominic Cheung. IFON
Impressions of the Countryside. Ito Togai, tr. fr. Chinese by Burton Watson. JLIC-2
Impressions of Things Encountered, sel. Shu Wei, tr. fr. Chinese by Barry L. Gartell.
  "My, my! My, oh my!" WFTU
Imprimis—My departed shade I trust. Mira's Will. Mary Leapor. NOEC
Imprimis, there's a table blotted. An Inventory of the Furniture of a Collegian's Chamber. John Winstanley. OBSV
Imprisoned, The. Robert Fitzgerald. TwCP
Imprisoned Soul, The. Walt Whitman. See At the last, tenderly.
Imprisoned winds slumber within their caves, Th'. On the Dark, Still, Dry, Warm Weather Occasionally Happening in the Winter Months. Gilbert White. NOEC
Impromptu. Benjamin Franklin. See Jack, eating rotten cheese, did say.
Impromptu. Thomas Gray. See Old and abandoned by each venal friend.
Impromptu. Márton Kalász, tr. fr. Hungarian by Jascha Kessler. FOC
Impromptu. Samuel Wilberforce. CenHV; FaBoNo; NBLV
Impromptu. Wu Wei-yeh, tr. fr. Chinese by Jonathan Chaves. CoBLCP
Impromptu Heart. Dan Pagis, tr. fr. Hebrew by Bernhard Frank. MHeP
Impromptu Inspirations, sels. Yang Wei-chen, tr. fr. Chinese by Jonathan Chaves. CoBLCP
  "This morning the air is fine for Ch'ing-ming." Fr. II.
  "Willow catkins, white as cotton." Fr. I.
Impromptu; Late Spring at Pan-shan. Wang An-shih, tr. fr. Chinese by Burton Watson. CoBCP

Impromptu on a Hangover. P'i Jih-hsiu, tr. fr. Chinese by Burton Watson. CoBCP
Impromptu on Charles II. Earl of Rochester. ChTr; FaBoEE; FaBoEE; NBLV; NOBL; OBSV
Impromptu Poem in Yün-chien. Zekkai Chushin, tr. fr. Japanese by Burton Watson. FCEI
Impromptu Poems, sels. Li K'ai-hsien, tr. fr. Chinese by Jonathan Chaves. CoBLCP
  "All morning long I correct my books."
  "Beside the river—waterbirds, in the river—fish."
  "In my house is my book collection, filled with book-worms."
  "Sitting by the riverside with a torn net."
  "To drink, no fine wines, to eat, no fish."
  "Write in a lively style, as fish swim in the water."
Improperia. Francis Sparshott. MoCV
Improved Binoculars, The. Irving Layton. NOBC
Improved Farm Land. Carl Sandburg. RFM
Improvisation of the Dead Boy. Mário de Andrade, tr. fr. Portuguese by Richard Eberhart. ATCBP
Improvisation on an Old Theme. Dorothy Livesay. CaP
Improvisations, sels. Chu Yün-ming, tr. fr. Chinese by Jonathan Chaves. CoBLCP
  "No robe, no sleeves, my hair uncombed." Fr. II.
  "Old man Chih-shan has a head of white hair." Fr. I.
  "Unruly hair, bare feet—busily studying books." Fr. III.
Improvisations: Light and Snow, sel. Conrad Aiken.
  "When I was a boy, and saw bright rows of icicles." BoNaP
Improvisations on Aesop. Anthony Hecht. OBAL
Improvised on Horseback to Say Good-bye to Those Who Are Seeing Me Off, sel. Wen Cheng-ming, tr. fr. Chinese by Jonathan Chaves.
  "Beneath the Shrine of the Three Loyal Ones." CoBLCP
Improvised while Living in the Outskirts of the Capital. Taikyoku Zosu, tr. fr. Japanese by Burton Watson. FCEI
Impulse, The. Robert Frost. Fr. The Hill Wife. HoPM
Impulses of memory. Turtledoves. Jacob Glatstein, tr. by Benjamin and Barbara Harshav. AYP
In a bald skull sits our friend in a helmet. Adrienne Rich. Fr. Contradictions: Tracking Poems, 22. ER
In a Bar near Shibuya Station, Tokyo. Paul Engle. AmFN
In a basement just off Saint-Michel. 104 Boulevard Saint-Germain. Kenneth Pitchford. NYBP
In a Bath Teashop. Sir John Betjeman. EnLoPo
In a Boat on a Summer Evening. Lu Yu, tr. fr. Chinese by Burton Watson. CoBCP
In a Boat on the Cha River. Chang Yü, tr. fr. Chinese by Jonathan Chaves. CoBLCP
In a Book-Box I Found the Lost Manuscript of a Poem. Chang Yü, tr. fr. Chinese by Jonathan Chaves. CoBLCP
In a book the life of the turtle dove. The Nature of the Turtle Dove. Unknown, tr. fr. Middle English. Fr. The Bestiary. PBBP
In a borrowed field they dig in their feet. Women's Tug of War at Lough Arrow. Tess Gallagher. ASP; MAYP
In a bowl to sea went wise men three. The Wise Men of Gotham. Thomas Love Peacock. Fr. Nightmare Abbey, ch. 11. BXAP; FaBoNo
  (Men of Gotham, The.) CH
  (Seamen Three.) WiR
  (Three Men of Gotham.) FaBoCh; OBEV
In a branch of a willow hid. To a Caty-did. Philip Freneau. AA; TAP
In a bright little bar that was carefully waxed. Scheveningen, Off Season. Valery Larbaud, tr. by William Jay Smith. CT
In a Building Named for a Governor. Christopher L. Dornin. CRP
In a Cafe. Richard Brautigan. PCP
In a Café. Rosemary Dobson. CBAP
In a cafe under a lazy fan. Country Nun. Geoff Page. CBAP
In a Cathedral City. Thomas Hardy. EnLoPo; FaBoPP
In a cavern, in a canyon. Paul Dehn. Fr. Rhymes for a Modern Nursery. FiBHP
In a cavern [or cabin], in a canyon. Oh, My Darling Clementine. At. to Percy Montross. AnAmPo; FaBoBe; FaFP
  (Clementine.) AmFP; OBAL
In a certain sense, they are not serious. Their Seriousness, with Further Comparisons. Robert Pinsky. Fr. Essay on Psychiatrists, VI. NoAM
In a chain reaction. Atomic Pantoum. Peter Meinke. SM
In a channel. Saigyo, tr. fr. Japanese by Burton Watson. Fr. Sixty-four Tanka. FCEI
In a chariot of light from the regions of day. Liberty Tree. Thomas Paine. OPP; PAH
In a Child's Album. Wordsworth. See To a Child.
In a Chinese window. Elephants from the Sea. Ian Young. NeAC

In a Christian Churchyard. James Thomson. NOBVV

In a Churchyard. Richard Wilbur. HeIP

In a city, Trieste or Udine. The Day of My Death. Pier Paolo Pasolini, tr. by Lawrence R. Smith. NItP

In a climate where. Intuition. Anthony Delius. PeSA

In a coffee house at 3 am. My Son and I. Philip Levine. DiL

In a coign of the cliff between lowland and highland. A Forsaken Garden. Swinburne. EBEV; FaBoPP; GTBS-P; LiTB; NOBE; NOBVV; NoP; OAEL-2; OBNC; TEP

In a cold glade sacred to nothing. Tales Told of the Fathers. John Hollander. DiL

In a cool curving world he lies. The Fish. Rupert Brooke. FM; MOS

In a Copy of Browning. Bliss Carman. AnAmPo

In a Copy of Omar Khayyám. James Russell Lowell. AA

In a corner. Dissember. Charles Shaw. GoYe

In a corner of blue sky. Daily Wages. Amrita Pritam, tr. by the author and Charles Brasch. PBWP

In a Corner of Eden. Peter Levi. NePoEA-2

In a cottage embosom'd within a deep shade. Blue Ey'd Mary. Unknown. CoMu

In a cottage in Fife. Two Comical Folk. Mother Goose. OxNR

In a cottage on a moor. Leawood Hall. Ernest Charles Jones. PF

In a Country Church. R. S. Thomas. FaBoMo; TOF

In a Country Museum. Patricia Beer. FaBoWP

In a creek in Muko Bay. Unknown. Fr. Manyo Shu. PeBJV

In a dark, dark wood, there was a dark, dark house. The Dark House. Unknown. NTCP

In a Dark Time. Theodore Roethke. CAPP; EaLo; HAP; HeIP; MAT; MoAmPo; MoP; NAAL-2; NoAM; NOBA; NoP; NYBP; PoE; PPP; TAP

In a days-and-nights ghetto. In a Ghetto. Jacob Glatstein, tr. by Ruth Whitman. VWA

In a dear little home of tarpaulin and boards. No Thoroughfare. Ruth Holmes. BoTP

In a Desert Town. Lionel Stevenson. AmFN

In a dingy kitchen/ Facing a Ghetto backyard. Lamentations. Alter Brody. TrJP; VWA

In a Double Rainbow. Harold Littlebird. VoR

In a Dream. David Ignatow. PoA

In a dream he fled the house. Coleridge. Medbh McGuckian. CIP

"In a dream I never exactly dreamed." Another Life. Frank Bidart. HCAP

In a dream I open the door. The Fat Boy's Dream. Richard McCann. GrPl

In a dream I returned to the river of bees. The River of Bees. W. S. Merwin. HeIP; LCAP

In a Dream, I Visited a Place Called the Monastery of Heavenly Music. Ku T'ai-ch'ing, tr. fr. Chinese by Irving Lo. WFTU

In a Dream Ship's Hold. Suzanne Bernhardt. VWA

In a dream: ten years of shadowy events. I Awake Crying on My Birthday. K'uang Chou-yi, tr. by Irving Lo. WFTU

In a Drear-nighted December. Keats. CH; ELP; EnRP; NOBE; TEP (Stanzas: "In a drear-nighted December.") ChER; OBEV; OBNC

In a dull and metric month. Song for February. Tom Paulin. FaBCIP

In a factory building there are wheels and gearings. Our Father's Hand. Annie Johnson Flint. BLRP

In a far-away northern county in the placid pastoral region. The Ox-Tamer. Walt Whitman. RB

In a far off hamlet near the sea. Uranne. Mary Weston Fordham. CBWP-2

In a fashionable suburb of Santa Barbara. In Montecito. Randall Jarrell. CoAP; MAT; NoP; NYBP; VGW

In a few moments. The Death of a Negro Poet. Conrad Kent Rivers. BPo

In a Field. Robert Pack. MAT; NePoEA-2

In a field. Keeping Things Whole. Mark Strand. CoAP; HCAP; HeIP; LCAP; PPP; TAP

In a field of swaying grain. Death Seed. Ricarda Huch, tr. by Susan C. Strong. PBWP

In a field with scentless winter trees. Kaya Shirao, tr. fr. Japanese by Hiroaki Sato. Fr. Twenty-one Hokku. FCEI

In a fisherman's hut crickets mingle. Basho, tr. fr. Japanese by Burton Watson. Fr. Seventy-six Hokku. FCEI

In a flash of lightning, sixty years. Ryokan, tr. by Burton Watson. JLIC-2

In a frosty sunset. Winter: East Anglia. Edmund Blunden. OxBTC

In a Garden. Elizabeth Jennings. NOCV

In a garden shady this holy lady. Song for St. Cecilia's Day. W. H. Auden. FaBoTw; TwCP

In a garden where the whitethorn spreads her leaves. Alba Innominata. Unknown, tr. by Ezra Pound. AWP

In a Garret. Elizabeth Akers Allen. AA

In a Garret. Herman Melville. AnAmPo; OBAL

In a gay jar upon his shoulder. The Amphora. Fyodor Sologub, tr. by Babette Deutsch and Avrahm Yarmolinsky. AWP

In a Ghetto. Jacob Glatstein, tr. fr. Yiddish by Ruth Whitman. VWA

In a glass room. Tale of the Assyrian Statue. Mahmoud al-Buraikan, tr. by Lena Jayyusi and Naomi Shihab Nye. MAP

In a Glass-Window for Inconstancy. Lord Herbert of Cherbury. OxBSP; SeCP

In a glorius garden grene. The Lily-White Rose. Unknown. MeEL

In a golden cage, the parrots announce the coming dawn. The Beautiful Lady Yü. Li Hsün, tr. by Lois Fusek. ATF

In a Gondola, sel. Robert Browning.
    "Moth's kiss, first, The!" BoLoP; GBL; OBEV
    (Song: "Moth's kiss, first, The!") BoLoP; GBL; TrGrPo

In a goodly night, as in my bede I laye. Waking Alone. Unknown. MeEL

In a gorge titanic. Ula Masondo's Dream. William Plomer. MoBS

In a grass hut lodged at the end of the narrow lane. In the Year with the Cyclical Sign Mou-shen. T'ao Ch'ien, tr. by Burton Watson. CoBCP

In a Grave-Yard. William Stanley Braithwaite. PoBA

In a green place lanced through. The Blue Heron. Theodore Goodridge Roberts. CaP; NOBC; OBCV

In a grove most rich of shade. Sir Philip Sidney. Fr. Astrophel and Stella. OBSC; SiPS

In a hailstorm. Saigyo, tr. fr. Japanese by Burton Watson. Fr. Sixty-four Tanka. FCEI

In a harbour grene aslepe whereas I lay. See In a herber green. . .

In a Hard Intellectual Light. Richard Eberhart. CMoP; LiTM

In a heavy bowl two pears. Sadness and Still Life. Bin Ramke. MAYP

In a herber [or a harbour or an arbour] green [or grene], asleep [or aslepe] whereas [or where as or where] I lay. Robert Wever. Fr. Lusty Juventus.
    (In an Arbour Green.) ELP
    (In Youth Is Pleasure.) ChTr; NOBE; OBEV
    (Of Youth He Singeth.) EIL
    (Youth.) OBSC

In a hidden bay. Emperor Fushimi, tr. by Steven D. Carter. WFTW

In a hidden spot on the northern mountain. Yün Shou-p'ing, tr. fr. Chinese by Jonathan Chaves. Fr. On the Day of the Mid-Autumn Festival of the Year. CoBLCP

In a high-fashion journal for queers. Unknown. PeHV

In a hole of the heel of an old brown stocking. Stocking Fairy. Winifred Welles. FaPON

In a hotel in Tashkent. Political Relations. Audre Lorde. GLP

In a Hotel Writing-Room. John Cowper Powys. OxBTC

In a Hundred Years. At. to Elizabeth Doten. BLPA

In a hut of mud and fire. Gautama in the Deer Park at Benares. Kenneth Patchen. NaP

In a Large Greek Colony, 200 B.C. C. P. Cavafy, tr. fr. Greek by Edmund Keeley and Philip Sherrard. VMG

In a little house I pictures suspended, it is not a fix'd house. My Picture-Gallery. Walt Whitman. NAAL-1

In a little house on Western Hill, undisturbed by crowd or clamor. A Tz'u-yün Poem Written in Response: Tiger Hill. Liu Shih, tr. by Irving Lo. WFTU

In a lodge by the river, far removed from affairs of men. Spring Dawn by the River. Emperor Saga, tr. by Burton Watson. JLIC-1

In a lonely, frozen park. Sentimental Conversations. Paul Verlaine, tr. by Lloyd Alexander. WSC

In a Lonely Place. Stephen Crane. AnAmPo

In a loose robe of tinsel forth [or tynsell foorth] she came. Corinna Bathes. George Chapman. Fr. Ovid's Banquet of Sense. OBSC

In a lovely garden, filled with fair and blooming flowers. The Mission of the Flowers. Frances E. W. Harper. BlSi

In a Lovely Garden Walking. Ludwig Uhland, tr. fr. German by George MacDonald. AWP

In a maiden-time professed. Thomas Middleton. Fr. The Witch. OxBSP

In a marsh lake. The White Egret. Kenneth Rosen. NAmP

In a meadow/ Beside the chapel three boys were playing football. Patrick Kavanagh. Fr. Father Mat. AnIL; CIP; CMoP; MoAB; PoE

In a Meadow. John Swinnerton Phillimore. OBEV

In a mean abode in [or on] the Shankill Road. The Ballad of William Bloat. Unknown. NOBL
    (Belfast Linen.) WTO

In a Minor Key. Judah Leib Teller, tr. fr. Yiddish by Benjamin and Barbara Harshav. AYP

In a Mirror. Marcia Stubbs. MAT
In a mirror of bronze. To the Fortuneteller Hsüeh T'ieh-yai. Hsieh Chin, *tr. by* Jonathan Chaves. CoBLCP
In a moment/ The roses have faded. Dino Campana, *tr. fr. Italian by* L. R. Lind. *Fr.* Four Lyrics for Sibilla Aleramo. PFI
In a Moonlight Wilderness. Samuel Taylor Coleridge. *See* Encinctured with a twine of leaves.
In a more hostile view, the psychiatrists. Dionysus as Psychiatrist. Robert Pinsky. *Fr.* Essay on Psychiatrists, X. HCAP
In a Motion. Laura Chester. NPGG
In a motorboat in dark water. Poets. Bozhidar Bozhilov, *tr. by* Cornelia Bozhilova. WCI
In a Mountain Cabin in Norway. Robert Bly. RFM
In a mountain stream. Tsuneyori, *tr. by* Steven D. Carter. WFTW
In a mountain village. Saigyo, *tr. fr. Japanese by* Burton Watson. *Fr.* Sixty-four Tanka. FCEI
In a muddy creek. *Unknown, tr. by* Geoffrey Bownas *and* Anthony Thwaite. PeBJV
In a Museum. Thomas Hardy. UnS
In a Museum Cabinet. May Swenson. WSC
In a museum, I ask. Tutankhamen. William Dickey. Psk
In a Museum in the Capital. William Stafford. LCAP
In a Music-Hall. John Davidson. EBVV
In a nation of one hundred fine, mob-hearted, lynching, relenting, repenting millions. Bryan, Bryan, Bryan, Bryan. Vachel Lindsay. CMoP; LiTA; OxBA; OxBoLi
In a neighborhood of tinkling jade. Ballad of the Deserted Mansion. Kao Ch'i, *tr. by* Jonathan Chaves. CoBLCP
In a net of mist the moon depends on the wood. Spring Song. George Brandon Saul. GoYe
In a new house greeting the first of the year. New House. Rai San'yo, *tr. by* Burton Watson. FCEI; JLIC-2
In a night hour this is how the things are written. And now night. Amir Gilboa, *tr. by* Warren Bargad *and* Stanley F. Chyet. IP
In a nook. In May. J. M. Synge. MoBrPo
In a one-button gray wool sweater. Harmonica Man. P. Wolny. PCP
In a Park, in Siena, at Twilight. Ory Bernstein, *tr. fr. Hebrew by* Warren Bargad *and* Stanley F. Chyet. IP
In a Parlor Containing a Table. Galway Kinnell. NBLV; OxBSP
In a patch of sky. Teika, *tr. by* Steven D. Carter. WFTW
In a place I came to live. Poems from Iowa City. Asher Reich, *tr. by* Vivian Eden. WCI
In a place of worhip I know, they made a strange mosaic. The Wall. Ludvik Askenazy. VWA
In a poem two otherwise separate things are brought together. Austrian Poem 1979/80. Peter Handke, *tr. by* Beth Bjorklund. CoAuP
In a pond of silence a turtle. Ozaki Hosai, *tr. fr. Japanese by* Hiroaki Sato. *Fr.* One Hundred Haiku in Free Form. FCEI
In a Prominent Bar in Secaucus [One Day]. X. J. Kennedy. AiP; FYAP; HoPM; NBLV; NIP; OBAL; PPP
In a Provincial Capital Sick in Bed. Hsieh T'iao, *tr. fr. Chinese by* Burton Watson. CoBCP
In a Quarter. Léon-Paul Fargue, *tr. fr. French by* Wallace Stevens. RHTwFP
In a quiet water'd land, a land of roses. The Dead at Clonmacnois [*or* Clonmacnoise]. Angus O'Gillan, *tr. by* Thomas William Rolleston. AnIL; FaBoPP; OBEV; OBMV
In a Railway Compartment. John Fuller. NePoEA-2
In a rape field sparrows. Basho, *tr. fr. Japanese by* Burton Watson. *Fr.* Seventy-six Hokku. FCEI
In a real city, from a real house. The Noodle-Vendor's Flute. D. J. Enright. NoP
In a red winter hat blue. Self-Portrait. William Carlos Williams. *Fr.* Pictures from Brueghel, I. LCAP
In a Remote Cloister Bordering the Empyrean. Joel Sloman. VGW
In a Remote Korean Village. Koh Chang-soo, *tr. fr. Korean by the author*. ACKP
In a Roman tram, where the famous Roman mob. The Thief. Stanley Kunitz. MoAmPo; VGW
In a room of black enamel, gold. A Marriage. Michael Jackson. ATNZ
In a room on a shelf away from everything else. I Held His Name. Alberto Ríos. NoAM
In a room on the seventh floor. Guilty Even if I Were Innocent. Buland al-Haidari, *tr. by* Abdullah al-Udhari. MPAW
In a Rose Garden. John Bennett. BLPA; FaBoBe
In a rundown tenement. The Healer. Charles Simic. AnAn
In a salt ring of moonlight. Moorings. Norman MacCaig. OxBTC
In a scented wood. The Night. Helen Leuty. BoTP
In a Season of Unemployment. Margaret Avison. MoCV; NOBC
In a sense. Life. Artie Gold. NOBC

In a sharp wind trying to part. Ozaki Hosai, *tr. fr. Japanese by* Hiroaki Sato. *Fr.* One Hundred Haiku in Free Form. FCEI
In a shoe box stuffed in an old nylon stocking. The Meadow Mouse. Theodore Roethke. HeIP; NaP; NIP; RB
In a Shoreham Garden. Laurence Lerner. NePoEA-2
In a shower, black chopped wood. Boncho, *tr. fr. Japanese by* Hiroaki Sato. *Fr.* Twenty-one Hokku. FCEI
In a shuttered room I roast. Dylan Thomas. OBTV
In a sick shade of spruce, moss-webbed, rock-fed. As It Looked Then. E. A. Robinson. CMoP
In a Silence. Richard Hovey. AnAmPo
In a silent room surrounded by sand I sleep. Miranda in Reno. Nicholas Christopher. BAP
In a single night. Ishikawa Takuboku, *tr. by* Geoffrey Bownas *and* Anthony Thwaite. PeBJV
In a small bitterness of wind. Young Argonauts. Sheila Wingfield. SD
In a Small Country. Uuno Kailas, *tr. fr. Finnish by* Aili Jarvenpa. SOP
In a small theodolite of paper. Soluble Noughts and Crosses; or, California, Here I Come. Roger Roughton. EAS
In a small wheelbarrow. A Cathedral. Stanislav Vinaver, *tr. by* Vasa D. Mihailovich. VWA
In a snug little cot lived a fat little mouse. The Country Mouse and the City Mouse. OxBChV
In a snug little court as I stood t'other day. The Pleasing Constraint. Aristaenetus, *tr. by* Richard Brinsley Sheridan *and* Nathaniel Brassey Halhed. ErPo
In a solitude of the sea. The Convergence of the Twain (Lines on the Loss of the *Titanic*). Thomas Hardy. BrPo; FaBoTW; HeIP; InPK; InPS; LiTB; LiTM; MoAB; MoBrPo; MoP; MOS; NAEL-2; NIP; NoAm; NoP; OAEL-2; OxBTC; PrIm; TEP
In a Southern garden Lucinda sits. The Bones of Incontention. Robert David Cohen. NYBP
In a spathe of silence. The Messenger. Frances Horovitz. BrRo
In a "Speakeasy"—the Flower Girl. Moyshe-Leyb Halpern, *tr. fr. Yiddish by* Benjamin *and* Barbara Harshav. AYP
In a splendid sheath. Burial. Hone Tuwhare. ATNZ
In a spongelike landscape. The Corpse of a Cat. Hagiwara Sakutaro, *tr. by* Hiroaki Sato. FCEI
In a Spring Still Not Written Of. Robert Wallace. BoNaP
In a stable of boats I lie still. The Lifeguard. James Dickey. ASP; NoP; NYBP
In a stately hall at Brentford, when the English June was green. The Last Meeting of Pocahontas and the Great Captain. Margaret Junkin Preston. PAH
In a Station of the Metro. Ezra Pound. AmPP; HAP; HeIP; InPK; MoAB; MoAmPo; MoP; NAAL-2; NIP; NoAm; NOAM; NOBA; NoP; OxBA; PoE; TAP; UnPo; VGW; WeW
In a still room at hush of dawn. The Eavesdropper. Bliss Carman. AnAmPo
In a summer [*or* somer] season, when soft[e] was the sun [*or* sunne *or* sonne]. William Langland. *Fr.* The Vision of Piers Plowman. (Field Full of Folk, The.) PoE
(Field of Folk, The.) PoEL-1
(On Malverne Hilles, the Place of Piers Plowman's Vision.) FaBoPP
(Prologue: "In a summer season, when soft was the sun", , *mod. by* J. B. Trapp (B *text*)) EBVV; OAEL-1
In a tabernacle of a toure [*or* tower]. Quia Amore Langueo. *Unknown.* ACP; MeEL
In a tangled, scented hollow. Sleep. Lewis Frank Tooker. AA
In a temple at Kioto in far-away Japan. The Three Wise Monkeys. Florence Boyce Davis. WBLP
In a throng,/ A festival company. Wordsworth. *Fr.* The Prelude [*or*, Growth of a Poet's Mind]: Summer Vacation. EBEV
In a Time of Pestilence. Thomas Nashe. *See* Summer's Last Will and Testament: Adieu, Farewell, Earth's Bliss[e].
In a Time of Sickness. Orpingalik, *tr. fr. Eskimo by* Edward Field. STP
In a Town Garden. Donald Mattam. FiBHP
In a town with a name as beautiful. Dogknotting in Quezaltenango. Vincent O'Sullivan. PeNZ
In a Township of Asia Minor. C. P. Cavafy, *tr. fr. Greek by* Edmund Keeley *and* Philip Sherrard. VMG
In a Train. Robert Bly. CAPP; NaP; TTTS
In a U-Haul North of Damascus. David Bottoms. FYAP; MAYP; MT
In a valley in Switzerland a brass band marches. Switzerland. Anthony Thwaite. OBTV
In a valley of this restles mind. Quia Amore Langueo. *Unknown.* OBEV
In a Valley of this Restless Mind. Ewart Milne. NeIP
In a valley of this restless mind. Quia Amore Langueo ("In a valley [*or* the vale *or* the vaile] of this restless mind [*or* restles mind]"). *Unknown, tr. by* Helen Gardner. NOBE; NOCV; OBEV; PoEL-1

In a Warm Bath. Carl Rakosi. TAP
In a water pail, nodding at each other. Buson, *tr. fr. Japanese by* Hiroaki Sato. *Fr.* Eighty-seven Hokku. FCEI
In a wee cot hoose far across the muir. Kate Dalrymple. *Unknown.* GBP
In a week of perpetual rain. The Tray. Thomas Cole. NePoAm
In a weird, forlorn voice. The President Slumming. James Tate. OBAL
In a while, all the rooms will be sealed. Departure of '82. Sa'di Yusuf, *tr. by* Lena Jayyusi *and* Naomi Shihab Nye. MAP
In a while they rose and went out aimlessly riding. Merlin Enthralled. Richard Wilbur. CMoP; NePoEA; NYBP
In a white gully among fungus red. Native Born. Eve Langley. PoAu-2; WPE
In a wide garden peonies open amply. Kaai Chigetsu, *tr. fr. Japanese by* Hiroaki Sato. *Fr.* Thirteen Hokku. FCEI
In a wild moraine of forgotten books. The Old School List. James Kenneth Stephen. CenHV
In a Wine Cellar. Victor James Daley. PoAu-1
In a winter-seared forest. Teika, *tr. fr. Japanese by* Hiroaki Sato. *Fr.* A Compendium of Good Tanka. FCEI
In a Wood. Thomas Hardy. OBNC
In a Wood. Edith Jay Scovell. GBL
In a Wood Clearing. Wilson Pugsley MacDonald. CaP
In a wood they call the Rouge Bouquet. Rouge Bouquet. Joyce Kilmer. PAH
In a wooden room, surrounded by lights and/ Faces. The Killing. George MacBeth. FaBoMo
In a world of orange serenity. The Lacemaker (Vermeer). Anne Marx. GoYe
In a year the nightingales were said to be so loud. The Kingfisher. Amy Clampitt. HCAP; SM
In Adam's fall/ We sinned all. *Unknown. Fr.* The New England Primer. OBCA
(ABC, An.) GBP
In Adoration of Love. Takamura Kotaro, *tr. fr. Japanese by* Hiroaki Sato. FCEI
In advance, much deconstruction and rebuilding. Angling. David Gullette. PPR
In Aesop's tales an honest wretch we find. Matthew Prior. NoP
In After Days. George Frederick Cameron. CaP
In After Days. Austin Dobson. OBEV
In after times when strength or courage fail. Buffel's Kop. Roy Campbell. PeSA
In Age. William Lisle Bowles. *Fr.* Milton: On the Busts of Milton, in Youth and Age. Son
In agreement/ (between two suicide attempts). Positive. Otto Laaber, *tr. by* Beth Bjorklund. CoAuP
In Agrigentum, earlier in Olympia. Empedocles on Etna. Herbert B. Mallalieu. PoA
In Agypt's land contaygious to the Nile. Pharao's Daughter. Michael Moran. BIrV
In Air. Peter Clarke. PBA
In Akishino/ is it raining. Saigyo, *tr. fr. Japanese by* Burton Watson. *Fr.* Sixty-four Tanka. FCEI
In Akishino is it raining on the villages. Teika, *tr. fr. Japanese by* Hiroaki Sato. *Fr.* A Compendium of Good Tanka. FCEI
In Aku Aku is there double. Oh, Noa, Noa! William Cole. NBLV
In all directions, forever, silence swarms. Apotheosis. Jules Laforgue, *tr. by* William Jay Smith. CT
In all humanity, we crave. The Commons' Petition to Charles II. Earl of Rochester. FaBoCo
In all my Emma's beauties blest. Translation of a South American Ode. Goldsmith. NOIV
In all my short, happy life, I've never. I've Never Been Lost. Itsik Fefer, *tr. by* John Hollander. PeBMYV
In all of earth and heaven. Sogen, *tr. by* Lucien Stryk *and* Takashi Ikemoto. ZPCJ
In All the Argosy of Your Bright Hair. Dunstan Thompson. WaP
In all the cathedrals of Europe. The Laughing Angel: Reims. Liz Socolow. PPR
In All the Days of My Childhood. Russell Edson. AmPA
In all the Eastern hemisphere. The Fall of J. W. Beane. Oliver Herford. OBAL
In all the good Greek of Plato. Survey of Literature. John Crowe Ransom. FaBoCh; LiTA; NBLV; OBAL; TAP; TwCP; VGW
In All the Magic of Christmas-Tide. John Jacob Niles. AH
In all the old paintings. Annunciation. Kay Smith. NIP
In all the strange and candid portraits. Loren Eiseley's Time Passages. Robert Frazier. BWV

In all the tongues of all the lands unborn. To Siva, the Unmaker. Ursula K. Le Guin. BWV
In All These Acts. William Everson. NoP
In all these rotten shops, in all this broken furniture. The Dancing. Gerald Stern. DiL
In all those stories the hero. Heroes. Robert Creeley. NOBA; NoP; PPP
IN) all those who got. E. E. Cummings. FaBoEE
In all those years at work I must have seen. Prostate Operation. Robert Pinsky. *Fr.* Three on Luck. AnAn
In all thy humors, whether grave or mellow. Temperament. Martial, *tr. by* Joseph Addison. AWP
In all-under-heaven where our sovereign. Hitomaro. *Fr.* Manyo Shu. FCEI
In all weathers? If imagination permit. World without End. Charles Brasch. ATNZ
In all your transparent pretence, in your painted hair and lips. A Woman Who Suddenly Entered the Room. Mieczyslaw Jastrun, *tr. by* Czeslaw Milosz. PwPP
In Allusion to the French Song. Richard Lovelace. CaPo
In America. Michael Sheridan. NAmP
"In America," began. The Student. Marianne Moore. NAAL-2; TwCP
In Amsterdam there dwelt a maid. The Fair Maid of Amsterdam. *Unknown.* OxBoLi; RB
In an Abandoned Garden. Nishiwaki Junzaburo, *tr. fr. Japanese by* Hiroaki Sato. FCEI
In an Age of Fops and Toys. Emerson. *Fr.* Voluntaries, III. FPL; LiTA; PoLF
In an Album. James Russell Lowell. AnAmPo; OBAL
In an Alien Place. Leib Neidus, *tr. fr. Yiddish by* Ruth Whitman. VWA
In an Arab Town. Susan Tichy. MAYP
In an Arbour Green. Robert Wever. *See* Lusty Juventus:
   In a herber [*or* a harbour *or* an arbour] green [*or* grene], asleep [*or* aslepe] whereas [*or* where as *or* where] I lay.
In an Artist's Studio. Christina Rossetti. NAEL-2; NoP
In an elegy for a musician. An Elegy for Bob Marley. William Matthews. MAYP
In an Empty Window. Ray Fraser. NeAC
In an envelope marked. Personal. Langston Hughes. AmNP; NOBA; PoNe
In an evening shower ducks walk around. Kikaku, *tr. fr. Japanese by* Hiroaki Sato. *Fr.* Thirty-three Hokku. FCEI
In an exciting world of love-bites, nipple-nipping. The Lovesleep. Gavin Ewart. OxBC
In an hour of great light. Darkness. Bartolo Cattafi, *tr. by* Lawrence R. Smith. NItP
In an Indian ditch lies. The World's Last Unnamed Poem. A. K. Redwing. VoR
In an instant, by instinct, I apprehended. An Act. Kenneth Rosen. AmPA
In an invisible dress, the breeze. The Breeze. Li Nan, *tr. by* Dominic Cheung. IFON
In an Iridescent Time. Ruth Stone. MoAmPo
In an oak there liv'd an owl. The Owl in the Oak. *Unknown.* FaBoNo ("There was an owl lived in an oak.") OxNR
In an ocean, 'way out yonder. The Dinkey-Bird. Eugene Field. AA; AmMo; NA
In an old and ashen island. Sappho's Tomb. Arthur Stringer. CaP
In an old, dark house. Fly in December. Robert Wallace. NYBP
In an Old House. Spencer Brown. NYBP
In an Old Orchard. Peter Kane Dufault. NYBP
In an old pond a frog. Buson, *tr. fr. Japanese by* Hiroaki Sato. *Fr.* Eighty-seven Hokku. FCEI
In an old pond a sandal lies sunken. Buson, *tr. fr. Japanese by* Hiroaki Sato. *Fr.* Eighty-seven Hokku. FCEI
In an old worn-out basin. Ugly Things. Teresita Fernández, *tr. by* Margaret Randall. AIW
In an orchard a little fountain flows. Song of the Ill-Married. *Unknown, tr. by* Patricia Terry. BoWoP
(Weaving Song.) DMF
In an unlit hospital. Resurrection. Sa'di Yusuf, *tr. by* Abdullah al-Udhari. MPAW
In an upper room at midnight. The Love Feast. W. H. Auden. ErPo
In ancient days there lived a Turk. Kafoozalum. *Unknown.* BeLS; BLPA
In Ancient December. Alice Notley. UL
In ancient Egypt. The Fertile Valley of the Nile. Eve Merriam. IHMS
In ancient times, as story tells. Baucis and Philemon; Imitated from the Eighth Book of Ovid. Swift. GN; GoTL; NOEC; OAEL-1
In ancient times e'er peace with lenient smile. Danebury. *Unknown.* PeHV

In ancient times, no matter where. Little Britain. *Unknown.* NOEC
In ancient times—'twas no great loss. On a Nomination to the Legion of Honour. *Unknown.* FaBoEE
In ancient times when an officer had to say goodbye. Pacifying the Western Barbarians. Wen T'ing-yün, *tr. by* Lois Fusek. ATF
In and Out, *sel.* L. E. Sissman. NYBP
  Severance of Connections, 1946. TwCP
In and out among the narrow little ways of the town. Good Friday. Christy Brown. TIRV
In and Out [Severence of Connections, 1946]. L. E. Sissman. NYBP; TwCP
In and out the bushes, up the ivy. The Chipmunk's Day. Randall Jarrell. OBCA; RHPC
  (Chipmunk, The.) RR
  (Chipmunk's Song, The.) PDV
In anguish we uplift. War Song. John Davidson. OBNC
In Answer to Your Query. Naomi Lazard. NBLV
In Antarctica drooping their little shoulders. The View from Here. William Stafford. RFM
In any element, you are scot-free. Have No Fear! Eileen Duggan. ATNZ
In Apia Bay. Sir Charles G. D. Roberts. PAH
In Aprell and in May. Besse Bunting. *Unknown.* MeEL
In April. Ethelwyn Wetherald. CaP
In April/ Come he will. The Cuckoo. *Unknown.* BoTP
In April around Easter the streams grow clear. Marcabrun, *tr. by* Paul Blackburn. Pro
In April one seldom feels cheerful. Waste Land Limericks. Wendy Cope. FaBoWP
In April [*or* Aprill], the koocoo can sing her song by rote. The Koocoo. *Unknown.* GBP; TTTS
In April we will pierce his body. Letters to a Stranger. Thomas James. AmPA
In Aprile at the hicht of noon. On Seein an Aik-Tree Sprent Wi Galls. Robert Garioch. OxBS
In Arabia's book of fable. Princess Sabbath. Heine, *tr. by* Charles Godfrey Leland. TrJP
In Arcadia. Lawrence Durrell. MoBrPo
In Arden. Charles Tomlinson. OxBC
In Armorik, that called is Britaine [*or* Britayne]. The Franklin's Tale. Chaucer. *Fr.* The Canterbury Tales. NAEL-1; OAEL-1
In Assisi. Michael C. Blumenthal. MAYP
In Auchtermuchty there dwelt ane man. The Wife of Auchtermuchty. *Unknown.* GoTS
In August. William Dean Howells. GN
In August the steamy saliva of the streets of the sea. Movie within a Movie. Denis Johnson. MAmP
In August we carried the old horsehair mattress. Green Apples. Ruth Stone. InPS
In August, when the air of love was peeled. Bible Story. Charles Causley. TOF
In August, when the days are hot. August Heat. *Unknown.* RAR
In Autumn. Jon Anderson. AmPA
In autumn a dove looks as if loneliness. Kaai Chigetsu, *tr. fr. Japanese by* Hiroaki Sato. *Fr.* Thirteen Hokku. FCEI
In autumn a friend. Autumn in Gaol. Tsuboi Shigeji, *tr. by* Geoffrey Bownas *and* Anthony Thwaite. PeBJV
In autumn down the beechwood path. Beech Leaves. James Reeves. OnUR
In autumn, the bats. The Bat. Roberta Spear. AmPA; MAYP
In autumn when the woods are red. Robert Louis Stevenson. NOBVV
In Autumpne, whan the sonne in vyrgyne. The Bowge of Courte. John Skelton. AAS
In awful ruins Ætna thunders nigh. *Unknown, tr. by* Sir Walter Scott. FL
In Back of the Real. Allen Ginsberg. AmPP; HeIP
In Ball's Market after surfing till noon. The Supremes. Mark Jarman. NAmP
In Baltimore there lived a boy. The Boy Who Laughed at Santa Claus. Ogden Nash. CenHV
In Barracks. Siegfried Sassoon. FaBoTw
In bars 21 and 23 of the Aria to his "Goldberg Variations." Words Most Often Mispronouncd in Poetry. Alex Kuo. UL
In battle-line of sombre gray. Spirit of the. Tudor Jenks. AA; PAH
In battledress, yes, I was there. That dramatic great wartime eruption. On First Looking into Michael Grant's *Cities of Vesuvius.* Gavin Ewart. OBTV
In Beauty May I Walk. *Unknown, tr. fr. Navajo Indian by* Jerome K. Rothenberg. RB
In bed/ with my friend's young brother. A Sugar-Candy Bird. Ian Young. NeAC

In bed./ My hand on Mark's bare chest. At Rochdale. Ian Young. NeAC
In bed, dull man? Upon My Lord Brohall's Wedding. Sir John Suckling. CaPo
In bed I muse on Tenier's boors. The Bench of Boors. Herman Melville. AnAmPo; NAAL-1; OBAL
In bed I toss and turn in the night's deep watches. Autumn Night. Michizane, *tr. by* Burton Watson. JLIC-1
In bed we laugh, in bed we cry. Translation of Lines by Benserade. Samuel Johnson, *after the French of* Isaac Benserade. FaBoEE
In bed with the stranger who had picked him up. A Bride. Harry Fainlight. BoLoP
In Belgrade, the windows of the tourist. Endurance. Carolyn Forché. NAmP; SV
In Berlin, August 1945: Lehrte Bahnhof. Alun Llywelyn-Williams, *tr. fr. Welsh by* Joseph P. Clancy. OBWVE
In Bertram's Garden. Donald Justice. BoLoP; ErPo; MT; NePoEA; VGW
In Beverley town a maid did dwell. The Beverley Maid and the Tinker. *Unknown.* CoMu
In Black Chasms. Leslie Norris. WSC
In black core of night, it explodes. African Dream. Bob Kaufman. AmNP; PoBA
In Blackwater Woods. Mary Oliver. CAPP
In Blanco County. Russell T. Fowler. NOBC
In Bloemfontein. Alan Ross. BoLoP
In blows the loitering air of spring. Spring Air. Gene Derwood. FaFP
In Blue. D. C. Berry. BXAP
In Bohemia. Arthur Symons. BrPo
In Bondage. Claude McKay. PoBA
In Boston, Mass. Nuala's Fiddle. Tomas O Canainn. NPo
In bower and field he sought, where any tuft. Milton. *Fr.* Paradise Lost, *bk.* IX, *ll.* 417–492. TEP
  (Eve.) OBS, *fr. ll.* 417–466.
In bowler hats and Sunday suits. Orange March. Richard Murphy. *Fr.* The Battle of Aughrim. NOIV
In boxes lined with faded satin. Pawnshop Window. R. H. Grenville. GoYe
In boyhood once I rated. Sabbath. Jacob Glatstein, *tr. by* Cynthia Ozick. PeBMYV
In Breughel's great picture, The Kermess. The Dance. William Carlos Williams. AmPP; CMoP; GoJo; GrPl; HAP; HeIP; InPK; LiTM; MoP; NAAL-2; NIP; NoAM; NoAm; NOBA; NoP; OxBA; PoE; PrIm; SoSe; TAP; WeW
In bright morning sunlight, the horse appears pink. The Triangular Field. Stephen Dobyns. MAYP
In bright sunlight and gentle breeze. Soil and Flower. Hsiang Yang, *tr. by* Dominic Cheung. IFON
In Britain's isles, as Heylyn notes. Matthew Prior. *Fr.* Alma; or, The Progress of the Mind. NOEC
In broad daylight. Lament for Kepa Anaha Ehau. Arapeta Awatere, *tr. by the author.* PeNZ
In Broad Street building (on a winter night). The Gouty Merchant and the Stranger. Horace Smith. BeLS
In Bruges town is many a street. Incident at Bruges. Wordsworth. OBTV
In Bruton Town there lived a farmer. Bruton Town. *Unknown.* EnSB
"In Buckinghamshire hedgerows." The Icosasphere. Marianne Moore. ImOP
In building houses, I'm content with few. Yüan Mei, *tr. fr. Chinese by* Anthony C. Yu. *Fr.* Life at the Sui Garden, IV. WFTU
In building the great sanctuary. Kose Natemaro. *Fr.* Manyo Shu. Ma
In Cabin'd Ships at Sea. Walt Whitman. MOS
In California. Donald Davie. NoAM
In California/ ankle-high animals occupy the tablelands. Report from California. Lois Moyles. NYBP
In calling it "sage." Tabito. *Fr.* Manyo Shu. PeBJV
In calm and cool and silence, once again. First-Day Thoughts. Whittier. AmPP; NoP; TrCP
In calm fellowship they sleep. In a Grave-Yard. William Stanley Braithwaite. PoBA
In came her sister. Lady Maisry. *Unknown.* ESPB, A *and* B *vers.*; OBET; OxBB, *with music*
In came the herring, the king of the sea. The Fishes' Lamentation. *Unknown.* OxBSS
In canary grass insects. Ethan Boldt. Roger Weingarten. AmPA
In candent ire the solar splendor flames. Aestivation [an Unpublished Poem, by My Late Latin Tutor]. Oliver Wendell Holmes. *Fr.* The Autocrat of the Breakfast Table, *ch.* 11. NA; NOBL; OBAL
  (Intramural Aestivation, or Summer in Town, by a Teacher of Latin.) ChTr; FaBoNo

In Carmel Bay the people say. Abalone. *Unknown.* AS
In Carpenter's Woods. Gerald Stern. CAPP
In Carrowdore Churchyard. Derek Mahon. CIP; FaBCIP
In caves with a single purpose. Fish and Chips on the Merry-Go-Round. K. O. Arvidson. ATNZ; PeNZ
In Celebration. Ellen Bass. NMM
In Celebration. Mark Strand. NoAM
In Celebration of a Child's Future. Issa, *tr. fr. Japanese by* Hiroaki Sato. FCEI
In Celebration of My Uterus. Anne Sexton. CAPP
In Celia's face a question did arise. Lips and Eyes. Giovanni Battista Marino, *tr. by* Thomas Carew. OBVE; OxBSP; PFI
In Cemeteries. D. J. Enright. OxBC
In Central Park. Moyshe-Leyb Halpern, *tr. fr. Yiddish.* AYP, *tr. by* Benjamin *and* Barbara Harshav; PeBMYV, *tr. by* John Hollander.
In Chagall's Village. Rose Ausländer, *tr. fr. German by* Ewald Osers. VWA
In Chapman's day poets had to write about Gods. On First Looking into Chapman's Homer II. Peter Peterson. BXAP
In chariot like an hibiscus flower at his side. Confucius, *tr. fr. Chinese by* Ezra Pound. *Fr.* Songs of Cheng. CTC
In Chekhov's Three Sisters, everyone. Suffocation. Linda Pastan. BLA
In Cherbourg Roads the pirate lay. The Eagle and Vulture. Thomas Buchanan Read. PAH
In Chester town there lived. A Brisk Young Widow. *Unknown.* OBET
In Childbed. Thomas Hardy. NAs
In childhood, I played with a wooden sword. The Lone Swordsman. Lo Ch'ing, *tr. by* Dominic Cheung. IFON
In childhood you think. Thanksgiving. John N. Morris. OFD
In childhood's sunny day my heart was taught to love. To Whittier. Josephine D. Henderson Heard. CBWP-4
In childhood's unsuspicious hours. Epicurean. William James Linton. EBVV
In China,/ even the peasants. Lost Sister. Cathy Song. NoAM
In China they have ghost chairs. Once and Future. Diana Chang. BrSi
In Chota Nagpur and Bengal. Tree Marriage. William Meredith. GLP
In Christ Church, Bristol, on Thomas Turner, Twice Master of the Company of Bakers. Francis Jeffrey. *See* Like to a baker's oven is the grave.
In Christ there is no East or [*or* nor] West. All One in Christ. John Oxenham. BLRP
In Chu hai, dead machine guns lie frozen in the sun. Chrome Babies Eating Chocolate Snowmen in the Moonlight. A. K. Redwing. VoR
In Church. Thomas Hardy. *Fr.* Satires of Circumstance, II. BrPo; InPK; MoAB; MoBrPo; SCV
"In churches," said the Pardoner, "when I preach." Chaucer. *See* Canterbury Tales, The: Pardoner's Prologue, The.
In cinemas we sought. Sing, Brothers, Sing! W. R. Rodgers. MoAB; MoBrPo
In Cipres springes [*or* Cyprus springs] (wheras [*or* whereas] dame Venus dwelt). Earl of Surrey. AAS; SiPS
In Clarke County, the story goes, the family name. Virginia Reel. Charles Wright. AnAn
In Cloe's chamber, she and I. John Bancks. NOEC
In Clonmel Parish Churchyard. Sarah Morgan Bryan Piatt. AA
In Cnidus born, the consort I became. By Heraclides. *Unknown, tr. by* William Cowper. OBVE
In cold gray. A Song Sung. Federico García Lorca, *tr. fr. Spanish by* William Jay Smith. *Fr.* Songs of Childhood. CT
In Cold Hell, in Thicket. Charles Olson. PoM
In cold rain at Kao-yu. Mooring at Night at Kao-yu. Wang Shih-chen, *tr. by* Jonathan Chaves. CoBLCP
In Cold Storm Light. Leslie Silko. NoAM; NoP; VoR
In college once I climbed the tree. Sickle Pears. Owen Dodson. AmNP
In Colombo or Nagasaki I examine the Baedekers. Valery Larbaud, *tr. fr. French by* William Jay Smith. *Fr.* Europe, IV. CT
In Come de Animuls Two by Two. *Unknown.* GBP
In comes the captain's daughter, the captain of the yeos. The Boys of Wexford. *Unknown.* ELP
In coming down to Manchester to gain my liberty. The Soldier's Farewell to Manchester. *Unknown.* CoMu
In coming to the feast I found. The Horn. Léonie Adams. MoAB; MoAmPo
In Commendation of George Gascoigne's Steel Glass. Sir Walter Ralegh. SiPS
In Commendation of Music. William Strode. ELP; OBEV
In Commissioner Street. The Work Song. Sipho Sepamla. WMBCH
In companies or lone. The Knitters. Padraic Colum. SaC

In concord then they set up hasty ways. Freighter. Bruce Ruddick. CaP
In Consort to Wednesday, Jan. 1st. 1701. Richard Henchman. SCAP
In Cool, Green Haunts. Mahlon Leonard Fisher. WeW
In Cordoba the Caliph's Gardens. Cordoba. Asher Mendelssohn. VWA
In corduroy trousers and seedy black coats. W. H. Auden. *Fr.* A Happy New Year. OBSV
In Corfu (I was not there). An Olive Tree in Corfu. Christine Busta, *tr. by* Beth Bjorklund. CoAuP
In countries where no birds are alive. For Edwin R. Embree. Owen Dodson. CNA
In Country Sleep. Dylan Thomas. LiTB
In court to serve decked with fresh array. The Courtier's Life. Sir Thomas Wyatt. FaBoEE
In Crete the old orange trees are cut back until they are stumps. The Cemetery of Orange Trees in Crete. Gerald Stern. CAPP
In Crisis. Lawrence Durrell. LiTM
In crystal towers [*or* towns] and turrets richly set. Content. Geffrey Whitney. ElL
(Song: "In crystal towers and turrets richly set.") ACP
In danger the holothurian splits itself in two. Autonomy. Wislawa Szymborska, *tr. by* Czeslaw Milosz. PwPP
In Dante's Whirlwind. Gyula Illyés, *tr. fr. Hungarian by* Jascha Kessler. FOC
In Dark Hour. Seumas MacManus. WGRP
In dark sockets. Jars. Paul Raboff. VWA
In darkness I sought lodging at a mountain monastery. Passing the Night at the Monastery of Eternal Peace. Hung Sheng, *tr. by* Paul W. Kroll. WFTU
In Dat Great Gittin'-up Mornin'. *Unknown.* AA
In dawn's early glow. Tameie, *tr. by* Steven D. Carter. WFTW
In dawn's first light. Chikako, *tr. by* Steven D. Carter. WFTW
In daylight, even. The Countershadow. Philip Booth. NYBP
In Days Gone By. Hera Katene-Horvath. PeNZ
In Days Gone By. Ida M. Mills. BoTP
In days, my Lord, when mother Time. Soame Jenyns. *Fr.* An Epistle Written in the Country to the Right Honourable the Lord Lovelace. OBSV
In days of old,/ So I've been told. The Feast of the Monkeys. John Philip Sousa. OBAL
In days of old, a woman emulating Tyrtheus. The Deliverance of Argos. Adelaïde-Gillette Dufresnoy, *tr. by* Dorothy Backer. DMF
In days of old, those far off times. The Toad. Robert S. Oliver. RHPC
In dazzling/ utter darkness. A Dream. Sándor Weöres, *tr. by* Jascha Kessler. FOC
In de dead of night I sometimes. The Old Cabin. Paul Laurence Dunbar. PoLF
In de Lord, in de Lord. My Soul's Been Anchored in de Lord. *Unknown.* BoAN-2
In de Vinter Time. *Unknown.* AS
In dead of winter imprisoned within. Royal Pearl. Irena Klepfisz. ER
In Deadly Fear. Blake. *Fr.* Jerusalem. SeCePo
In Dear Detail, by Ideal Light. William Stafford. NaP
In Death. Mary Emily Bradley. AA
In death I know well enough all things end in emptiness. To Show My Sons. Lu Yu, *tr. by* Burton Watson. CoBCP
In death the dead remember their spirit. Funeral Poem. Amiri Baraka. CNA
In Death's Field. Al-Khansa, *tr. fr. Arabic by* Willis Barnstone. BoWoP
In Debtor's Yard the stones are hard. Oscar Wilde. *Fr.* The Ballad of Reading Gaol. NOBVV
In December. Andrew Young. SeCePo
In December, when the days draw to be short. Little John Nobody. *Unknown.* OxBoLi
In deep Siberian mines retain. Message to Siberia. Pushkin. AAA, *tr. by* Alan Myers; AWP, *tr. by* Max Eastman; TTY, *tr. by* Max Eastman
In Defence of Humanism. David Gascoyne. *See* Face of the precipice is black with lovers, The.
In Defense of Black Poets. Conrad Kent Rivers. BPo
In Defense of Felons. Robert Mezey. NePoEA
In Defense of Metaphysics. Charles Tomlinson. MoBrPo
In Defense of Satire. Sir Carr Scroope. APAS
In Defense of Superficiality. Elder Olson. NYBP
In deference to the cloud parade. The Cloud Parade. Laura Jensen. LCAP
In Defiance to the Dutch. *Unknown.* APAS
In degenerate times, people love extravagance. To Ch'eng Fei-t'ao. Wu Chia-chi, *tr. by* Jonathan Chaves. CoBLCP
In Despair. Constantine P. Cavafy, *tr. fr. Greek by* Edmund Keeley *and* Philip Sherrard. PeHV

In despair at not being able to rival the creations of God. Hymn to Her Unknown. W. J. Turner. OBMV
In Dessexshire as It Befel. *Unknown.* GBP
In dim green depths rot ingot-laden ships. Sunken Gold. Eugene Lee-Hamilton. NOBVV
In Discreet Splendor. A. L. Strauss, *tr. fr. Hebrew by* Robert Friend. VWA
In Disguise. Joseph Rolnik, *tr. fr. Yiddish by* Keith Bosley. VWA
In Dispraise of the Moon. Mary Elizabeth Coleridge. BoNaP; CH
In distress, in the dark. Holy Is the Desire to Proclaim the Existence of God. Meir Wieseltier, *tr. by* Warren Bargad *and* Stanley F. Chyet. IP
In Distrust of Merits. Marianne Moore. EaLo; LiTA; LiTM; MoAB; MoAmPo; NAAL-2; OBWP; OxBA; TrGrPo; WaaP; WaP
In Dives' Dive. Robert Frost. VGW
In dog-days plowmen quit their toil. The Swimmer. John Crowe Ransom. SD
In Domrèmy a maid. The Maid of Arc. Gordon Bottomley. GoTL
In drab derelict marsh near the madhouse. Charles Brasch. *Fr.* Home Ground, XXV. PeNZ
In dream I saw two Jews that met by chance. Moses and Jesus. Israel Zangwill. TrJP
In Dream: The Privacy of Sequence. Ray A. Young Bear. CDW
In dream the waterfall. The Practice of Absence. Robert Friend. VWA
In dreams a dark château. The Dark Château. Walter de la Mare. BrPo
In dreams my life came toward me. American Dreams. Louis Simpson. CAPP
In Dreamy Swoon. George Darley. *Fr.* Nepenthe. OBNC
In Dresden, in the square one day. The Violinist. Archibald Lampman. CaP
In Dublin's fair city, where the girls are so pretty. Cockles and Mussels. *Unknown.* ELP
In due course of course you will [all] be issued with. Unarmed Combat. Henry Reed. *Fr.* Lessons of the War. HeIP; LiTB
In Due Season. W. H. Auden. Prf
In due season the amphibious crocodile. Amphibious Crocodile. John Crowe Ransom. OBAL
In Dulci Jubilo. *Unknown, tr. fr. German by* John Wedderburn. ChTr
In each mans heart that doth begin. Loves World. Sir John Suckling. SeCV-1
In each world they may put us. Do Not Die. W. S. Merwin. CAPP
In Earliest Spring. William Dean Howells. *See* Tossing his mane of snows in wildest eddies and tangles.
In early days/ If kings were made by men. Human Debasement; a Fragment. Edward Rushton. NOEC
In early morning twilight, raw and chill. The Eviction. William Allingham. *Fr.* Laurence Bloomfield in Ireland. BIrV; NOIV
In Early Spring, While at the Temple at Bamboo Ravine Mountain. Doji, *tr. fr. Chinese by* Burton Watson. JLIC-1
In Early Years. Yüan Mei, *tr. fr. Chinese by* Anthony C. Yu. WFTU
In early youth's unclouded scene. Thirty-eight. Charlotte Smith. WPOW
In Earthen Vessels. Whittier. BLRP
In eastern village and western village. Silkworm Song of Torchlit Fields. Kao Ch'i, *tr. by* Jonathan Chaves. CoBLCP
In Egypt. Paul Celan, *tr. fr. German by* Joachim Neugroschel. VWA
In Egypt they worshiped me. I Am the Cat. Leila Usher. BLPA
In Egypt's sandy silence, all alone. On a Stupendous Leg of Granite, Discovered Standing by Itself in the Deserts of Egypt, with the Inscription Inserted Below. Horace Smith. PrIm
In eighteen hundred and eighty nine. Obituary. Conrad Aiken. OBAL
In 1876/ The Cooper & Bailey Great London Circus. The Cooper & Bailey Great London Circus. Robert Hershon. MAT
In 1861, George Hew sailed in a rowboat. The Network. Arthur Sze. AiP
In eighty-eight, ere I was born. Sir Francis Drake; or, Eighty-eight. *Unknown.* GBP; OxBSS
In elder times an ancient custom 'twas. Swearing. Henry Fitzsimon. ACP
In elderis dayis, as Esope can declair. The Taill of the Foxe, That Begylit the Wolf, in the Schadow of the Mone. Robert Henryson. OxBS
In encampments. What the Servants Said to Him, as He Returned Home. Maturaittamilkkuttan Katuvan Mallanar, *tr. by* A. K. Ramanujan. PLW
In endless caravans had men. Mohammad Taqi Mir, *tr. by* Ahmed Ali. GoT
In England from the train you see. From the Train. Marjorie Wilson. BoTP
In England now I hear the window shake. At Home the Green Remains. John Figueroa. PBCV

In England rivers all are males. On the American Rivers. James Smith. FaBoUs
In English the poetics became meubles—furniture. A Later Note on Letter 15. Charles Olson. *Fr.* The Maximus Poems. CAPP
In enterprise of martial kind. The Duke of Plaza-Toro. W. S. Gilbert. *Fr.* The Gondoliers. FaPON; FiBHP
In Epping Forest. John Clare. *See* Child Harold: Stanzas from "Child Harold."
In Eternum ("In eternum I was ons determined."). Sir Thomas Wyatt. AAS; NOBE; SiPS
In ethics class so many years ago. Ethics. Linda Pastan. InPK
In Europe, you can't move without going down into history. In the Yukon. Ralph Gustafson. MoCV
In Evening Air. Theodore Roethke. CAPP; NYBP; TAP
In every dream thy lovely features rise. William Barnes. BoLoP
In every household. Emperor Hanazono, *tr. by* Steven D. Carter. WFTW
In every leaf that crowns the plain. Faith. John Richard Moreland. OHIP
In every old lady I chance to meet. Old Ladies. Will Allen Dromgoole. WeW
In every part of every living thing. Lake Superior. Lorine Niedecker. FaBoWP
In every place ye may well see. What Women Are Not. *Unknown.* MeEL
In every second back yard. Among Old Houses. Ruth Dallas. ATNZ
In every seed to breathe the flower. Faith. WGRP
In every street and bylane. Mohammad Taqi Mir, *tr. by* Ahmed Ali. GoT
In every trembling bud and bloom. An Easter Canticle. Charles Hanson Towne. OHIP; TrPWD
In evil hour did Pope's declining age. On the Edition of Mr. Pope's Works with a Commentary and Notes. Thomas Edwards. TW
In evrich mart that stands on British ground. The School-Mistress. William Shenstone. NOEC
In ev'ry race, in ev'ry clime. Lines to a Graduate. Lizelia Augusta Jenkins Moorer. CBWP-3
In ev'ry thought, in ev'ry wish I own. Joseph Howe. *Fr.* Acadia. CaP
In ev'ry town where Thamis rolls his tide. The Alley; an Imitation of Spenser. Pope. NOEC
In Explanation. Walter Learned. AA
In Extremis. Margaret Fishback. FiBHP
In fact, what change? The chimney of the spine. In Retrospect. Richard Kenney. *Fr.* The Hours of the Day. Son
In Faguell, a fayre countré. The Knight of Curtesy. *Unknown.* OxBLMV
In fair Worcester City and in Worcestershire. The Gosport Tragedy. *Unknown.* AmFP
In faith, good Histor, long is your delay. Geron and Histor. Sir Philip Sidney. *Fr.* Arcadia. SiPS
"In faith, I do[e] not love thee with mine eyes." Shakespeare. *Fr.* Sonnets, CXLI. PoEL-2; TrGrPo
In faith I wot not what to say. Sir Thomas Wyatt. SiPS
In faith methinks it is no right. Resignation. Sir Thomas Wyatt. OBSC
"In faith, Squier, thou hast thee wel yquit." The Introduction to the Franklin's Prologue. Chaucer. *Fr.* The Canterbury Tales. NAEL-1
In faith thou shalt haue mine. Robin Hood Rescuing Three Squires. *Unknown.* ESPB, A *and* B *vers.*
  (Robin Hood and the Three Squires.) EnSB
In fall when we went the roads. Fear Dara Wier. MAYP
In fallow college days, Tom Harland. The Ballad of Lager Bier. Edmund Clarence Stedman. OBAL
In far-off England, years ago. Destiny. Eloise Bibb. CBWP-4
In Fargo, North Dakota, a man. To Flood Stage Again. James Wright. NOBA; Prf
In fashion as a snow-white rose, lay then. The Saints in Glory. Dante, *tr. fr. Italian by* Henry F. Cary. *Fr.* Divina Commedia: Paradiso, XXXI. WGRP
In Favor of One's Time. Frank O'Hara. NeAP; PoA
In fear of the rich mouth. The Frightened Man. Louise Bogan. FaBoWP
In February. P. A. Ropes. BoTP
In February I give you gallant sport. February. Folgore Da San Gimignano, *tr. fr. Italian by* Dante Gabriel Rossetti. *Fr.* Sonnets of the Months. AWP
In February there are days. When. Dorothy Aldis. RHPC
In feeling I was but a child. One Year Ago. Adah Isaacs Menken. CBWP-1
In fellowship Religion has its founts. George Meredith. *Fr.* The Test of Manhood. WGRP

In Fen-shui there once lived a woodsman. A Ballad of the Righteous Tiger. Sung Wan, *tr. by* William Schultz. WFTU
In Festubert. Edmund Blunden. OBMV
In Fields of Summer. Galway Kinnell. BoNaP; RFM; VGW
In Fine, Transparent Words. David Vogel, *tr. fr. Hebrew by* A. C. Jacobs. VWA
In Fire. H. Leivick, *tr. fr. Yiddish by* Benjamin *and* Barbara Harshav. AYP
In fire, on are the heat. Tirumal. Katuvan Ilaveyinanar, *tr. by* A. K. Ramanujan. PLW
In fire-script. Thou Shalt Not. Malka Heifetz-Tussman, *tr. by* Marcia Falk. VWA
In First People's sky there is no moon. Raven/Moon. Anita Endrezze Probst. VoR
In Flanders Fields. Hugo Claus, *tr. fr. Dutch by* Theo Hermans. DuIn
In Flanders Fields. John McCrae. BLPA; CaP; FaBV; FaFP; FaPoR; FPL; NOBC; OBCV; OBWP; OHFP; OPP; WBLP
In Flanders Fields the cannons boom. Another Reply to "In Flanders Fields." J. A Armstrong. BLPA
In Flanders Now. Edna Jaques. CaP
In Flaundres [*or* Flandres] whylom [*or* whilom] was a companye [*or* compaignye]. The Pardoner's Tale. Chaucer. *Fr.* The Canterbury Tales. FiP; HAP; NAEL-1; NoP; OAEL-1; PoE; PoEL-1
  ("It's of three rioters I have to tell," *mod. vers. by* Nevill Coghill) SCV
  ("There was a company of young folk living," *mod. vers. by* Theodore Morrison) NAWM-1
  Death and the Three Revellers. OBNV
  "But, sires o word forgat I in my tale." EBEV
  "This olde man gan looke in his visage." OBD
In Flavia's eyes is every grace. On Miss Eleanor Ambrose, a Celebrated Beauty in Dublin. Philip Dormer Stanhope, 4th Earl of Chesterfield. FaBoEE
In flight in escape. Nelly Sachs, *tr. by* Arthur Wensinger. BoWoP
In flood those running waters. *Unknown, tr. by* Arthur Waley. BoS
In flowed at once a gay embroidered race. A Young Traveller Is Presented to the Goddess Dulness. Pope. *Fr.* The Dunciad, IV. NOEC
In flowing garments. The Guardian Angel. Michael Guttenbrunner, *tr. by* Beth Bjorklund. CoAuP
In fond delusion once I left thy side. A Sonnet to My Mother. Heine, *tr. by* Emma Lazarus. TrJP
In Fond du Lac, Bronxville, Butte, Chicago. Last Year's Discussion: The Nobel Russian. Phyllis McGinley. FaBoEE
In forgiving mood, this sultry July afternoon. Goodbye to Regal. Daniel Huws. NYBP
In form and feature, face and limb. The Twins. Henry Sambrooke Leigh. CenHV; FaPON; RHPC
In form most people look to Sung and Yuan models. Rai San'yo, *tr. fr. Chinese by* Burton Watson. *Fr.* Twenty-seven Quatrains Discussing Poetry, XXVI. JLIC-2
In former days my father and mother. Cuckoo: "In former days my father and mother." *Unknown, formerly at. to* Cynewulf, *tr. fr. Anglo-Saxon by* Charles W. Kennedy. *Fr.* Riddles (Exeter Book). AnOE
In former days we'd both agree. Bhartrihari, *tr. fr. Sanskrit by* John Brough. BoLoP
In former times. *Unknown, tr. by* Geoffrey Bownas *and* Anthony Thwaite. PeBJV
In former times, when Israel's ancient creed. Absolute and Abitofhell. Ronald Arbuthnott Knox. CenHV; FaBoCo
In former years I passed this city. Sha-ch'eng, "Sand City." Yang Shih-ch'i, *tr. by* Jonathan Chaves. CoBLCP
In fragrant Dixie's arms. Church Burning: Mississippi. James A. Emanuel. PoBA; PoNe
In Francum. Sir John Davies. FaBoEE
In Freedom's War, of "Thirty Years" and more. Enfant perdu. Heine, *tr. by* Lord Houghton. AWP
In Freiburg Station. Rupert Brooke. OBTV
In Fresno it is 1923, and your shy father. Lost Fan, Hotel Californian, Fresno, 1923. Larry Levis. AnAn
In from the night. Answer Me. Adah Isaacs Menken. CBWP-1
In Front of a Japanese Photograph. John Peck. SM
In front of a police box I picked up a dead leaf. Beautiful Dead Leaf. Takamura Kotaro, *tr. by* Hiroaki Sato. FCEI
In Front of a Poster of Garibaldi. Stanley Moss. DiL
In front of Hua-yang cave, autumns pass like sleet. Drinking at the Cave Mouth. Tsung Ch'en, *tr. by* Jonathan Chaves. CoBLCP
In front of me, the palings of a fence. For Signs. Thom Gunn. PoE
In front of me the sea lies on its side. Wakayama Bokusui, *tr. fr. Japanese by* Hiroaki Sato. *Fr.* Forty-four Tanka. FCEI
In front of my eyes. Chikako, *tr. by* Steven D. Carter. WFTW

In front of my horse's head, I see Red Heart Station. Red Heart Station. Yang Shih-ch'i, *tr. by* Jonathan Chaves. CoBLCP
In front of our mouths, wherever we swim. Goldfish on the Writing Desk. Max Brod, *tr. by* Babette Deutsch *and* Avram Yarmolinsky. TrJP
In front of the City Hotel in Kumasi. A Rock Thrown into the Water Does Not Fear the Cold. Audre Lorde. NAAL-2
In Front of the Landscape. Thomas Hardy. OBNC
In front of the mighty washing machine. The Small Lady. Stevie Smith. TEP
In front of the ox, he raises his head to hoe. A Song of Crows Gleaning the Grain. Cha Shen-hsing, *tr. by* William Schultz. WFTU
In front of the sombre mountains. On the Balcony. D. H. Lawrence. BrPo; GBL
  (Illicit.) PoA
In front of the stove the dog, brown, is sleeping. Age. Tomioka Taeko, *tr. by* Hiroaki Sato. FCEI
In front of you I go. I Am with You. Lajos Kassák, *tr. by* Edwin Morgan. MHuP
In front the horse's rump bright as a lantern. Sleighride. Patrick Anderson. CaP; OBCV
In full glare [*or* flare] of sunlight I came here, man-tall but thin. The Roundhouse Voices. Dave Smith. GeTw; MAYP; MT; NoAM
In Fur. William Stafford. RFM
In Fury and Terror. The Storm. Elizabeth Jane Coatsworth. OBCA
In Fuscum. Sir John Davies. FaBoEE
In Gaetam. Thomas Bastard. FaBoEE
In Galilee. Mary Frances Butts. AA
In galleons, on war-horses, with their lances. Our House. Marco Martos, *tr. by* David Tipton. Per
In Galleries. Randall Jarrell. EyDe
In gayer hours, when high my fancy ran. Richard Savage. *Fr.* The Bastard. NOEC; OBSV
In Genesis, the world was made. Old Testament Contents. *Unknown.* BLPA
In Genoa the superb O'Connell dies. The Dead Tribune. Denis Florence MacCarthy. ACP
In Glasgow, in 'Eighty-four. In a Music-Hall. John Davidson. EBVV
In Glencullen. J. M. Synge. FM; OBMV
In go-cart so tiny. Kate Greenaway. FaPON
In God's Eternity. Hosea Ballou I. AH
In God's name let me begin. Argula's Answer. Argula von Grumbach, *tr. fr. German by* Susan L. Cocalis. *Fr.* An Answer in Verse for Someone Studying in Ingolst. DMG
In going to my naked bed, as one that would have slept. Amantium Irae Amoris Redintegratio. Richard Edwards. EIL; OBEV; OBSC
In gold sandals. Sappho, *tr. by* Willis Barnstone. BoWoP
In Golden Gate Park That Day. Lawrence Ferlinghetti. *Fr.* A Coney Island of the Mind. RB
In Golden Smock, Walking. Jan Kemp. ATNZ
In golden winters one misses them most. California Dead. G. E. Murray. MAYP
In good King Charles's golden days. The Vicar of Bray. *Unknown.* FaBoPV; GBP; NOBE; NOBL; OBSV; OxBoLi
  (In Good King Charles's Golden Days.) InvP
In Good King Charles's Golden Days. *Unknown. See* Vicar of Bray, The.
In good old Stalin's early days. Garland for a Propagandist. Ted Pauker. NOBL
In Gosport of late a young damsel dia dwell. The Gosport Tragedy. *Unknown.* AmFP
  (Pretty Polly.) AmFP
In Goya's Greatest Scenes. Lawrence Ferlinghetti. *Fr.* A Coney Island of the Mind. FF; HeIP; LiTM; NeAP; NoAM; PoM; TAP
In graves where drips the winter rain. The Song of the Graves. *Unknown, tr. fr. Welsh by* Ernest Rhys. *Fr.* The Black Book of Carmarthen. OBMV
In gray rain, October or November. An Oregon Story. Janice Gould. GOS
In grey April when the bud rounded. The Flute of May. Harry Woodbourne. GoYe
In grey-haired Celia's withered arms. A Paraphrase from the French. Matthew Prior. OxBoLi
In Grief, Lamenting for My Elder Brother Ts'ang-ch, *sel.* Hsieh Chin, *tr. fr. Chinese by* Jonathan Chaves.
  "I still remember Conch-Shell Slope, west of the River Tzu." CoBLCP
In grimy winter dusk. Stop. Richard Wilbur. LCAP
In groves of green trees. Black Students. Julia Fields. NBP
In Hades. Anna Callender Brackett. AA

In haist ga thy thee to sum hoill.　John Rolland.　*Fr.* The Seven Seages. OxBS

In Hampton Beach, the airs of March were bland.　The Attack.　Thomas Buchanan Read.　PAH

In Hans' old mill his three black cats.　Five Eyes.　Walter de la Mare. CRH

In Harbor.　Paul Hamilton Hayne.　AA; AnAmPo

In Harbor.　Lizette Woodworth Reese.　TrPWD

In hard/ country.　Hard Country.　Philip Booth.　CoAP

In Hardwood Groves.　Robert Frost.　HAP

In Harmony with Kao "The Second" Ch'i's Poem "On Hearing a P'i-p'a Played Next Door."　Hsü Pen, *tr. fr. Chinese by* Jonathan Chaves. CoBLCP

In Harry's Discounts Men & Boys.　Hunting.　Jack Sheedy.　ASP

In Hässelby.　Evening Walk.　Sonja Akesson, *tr. by* Joanna Bankier. WPOW

In haste poste haste, when first my wandring minde.　George Gascoigne. *Fr.* Gascoigne's Memories.　AAS; Son

In Hatchobori.　Basho, *tr. fr. Japanese by* Burton Watson.　*Fr.* Seventy-six Hokku.　FCEI

In Havana in 1948 I ate fried dog.　Salts and Oils.　Philip Levine.　BLA

In health, they do abuse.　*Unknown.*　FaBoUs

In hearts like thine ne'er may I hold a place.　Answer to — — —'s Professions of Affection.　Byron.　OxBSP

In Heaven/ Some little blades of grass.　The Blades of Grass.　Stephen Crane.　*Fr.* The Black Riders, XVIII.　MoAmPo

In Heaven a spirit doth dwell.　Israfel.　Poe.　AA; AmPP; AWP; BLPL; LiTA; NAAL-1; NOBA; OxBA; PoE; PoEL-4; TAP

In heaven and earth, no ground to plant my single staff.　Sesson Yubai, *tr. by* Burton Watson.　FCEI

In heaven-high musings and many.　The Strength of Fate.　Euripides, *tr. fr. Greek by* A. E. Housman.　*Fr.* Alcestis.　AWP

In heaven soaring up, I dropped an ear.　The Joy of Church Fellowship Rightly Attended.　Edward Taylor.　*Fr.* God's Determinations. AmPP; NAAL-1; OxBA; SCAP
　(In Heaven Soaring Up.)　AH, *with music.*

In heaven, too.　Heard in a Violent Ward.　Theodore Roethke.　HCAP

In Heavenly Realms of Hellas Dwelt.　E. E. Cummings.　NOBA; OBSV

In Heavy Mind.　James Agee.　MoAmPo

In Hebrew "In the beginning."　From the Head.　Louis Zukofsky.　VWA

In Hell.　Mark Jarman.　BLA

In her body's perfect sweet.　Isabel.　Richard Hovey.　AnAmPo

In her boudoir, the young lady—unacquainted with grief.　*Unknown, tr. by* Arthur Waley.　OBVE

In her first passion woman loves her lover.　Byron.　*Fr.* Don Juan, I. ErPo

In her gnarled sleep it/ begins.　The Cherry Tree.　Thom Gunn.　GLP; Psk

In her hand the knife, brisk, brilliant as moon-claw.　Cleaning a Fish. Dave Smith.　NoAM

In her hands she holds.　The Man She Called Honey, and Married. Alberto Ríos.　MAYP

In Her Only Way.　Robert Graves.　OxBSP

In her ornate tower by bright moonlight always she thinks of him.　Tune: Deva-like Barbarian.　Wen T'ing-yün, *tr. by* Burton Watson. CoBCP

In her own isle's remotest grove.　The Temple of Venus.　Soame Jenyns. NOEC

In Her Praise.　Robert Graves.　BIrV

In her room at the prow of the house.　The Writer.　Richard Wilbur. CAPP; HCAP; NoAM; OxBC

In her room on an autumn night, her thoughts are lonely.　Willow Branches.　Ku Hsiung, *tr. by* Lois Fusek.　ATF

In her sleep, as dawn began to break.　The Mother of Dante.　Angelos Sikelianos, *tr. by* Edmund Keeley *and* Philip Sherrard.　VMG

In Her Song She Is Alone.　Jon Swan.　NYBP

In hermit's robe, clean and simple.　Ch'ien Ch'ien-i, *tr. fr. Chinese by* Jonathan Chaves.　*Fr.* Miscellaneous Feelings at West Lake. CoBLCP

In High Places.　Harriet Monroe.　PoA

In high school we danced the lindy white-style.　Sonja Henie Sonnet. Edward Field.　ASP

In High Spirits.　Ryokan, *tr. fr. Chinese by* Burton Watson.　JLIC-2

"In highest way of heaven the Sun did ride."　Sir Philip Sidney.　*Fr.* Astrophel and Stella, XXII.　OBSC; Son

In Him.　James Vila Blake.　WGRP

In Him.　Annie Johnson Flint.　BLRP

In him inexplicably mixed appeared.　Byron.　*Fr.* Lara.　OAEL-2

In Him We Live.　Jones Very.　OxBA

In his chamber, weak and dying.　A Strike among the Poets.　*Unknown.* FaBoCo; FiBHP

In his country.　What She Said to Her Girl Friend　Kapilar, *tr. by* A. K. Ramanujan.　PLW

In his country of cool seas, they say.　What She Said.　Ceyti Valluvan Peruncattan, *tr. by* A. K. Ramanujan.　PLW

In his dream Jacob was in a wilderness.　Jacob.　Charles Reznikoff. VWA

In his father's face flying.　Icarus.　Ronald Botrall.　GTBS-P

In his fields.　What She Said ("In his fields").　Orampokiyar, *tr. fr. Tamil by* A. K. Ramanujan.　*Fr.* Five on the Crabs, 3.　PLW

In his fields, mother.　What Her Girl Friend Said to the Foster-Mother ("In his fields, mother").　Orampokiyar, *tr. fr. Tamil by* A. K. Ramanujan.　*Fr.* Five on the Crabs, 4.　PLW

In his final World Series, Pete Rose.　The Last Baseball Samurai.　Tom Clark.　ASP

In his grief.　While at Prayer.　Abba Kovner, *tr. by* Warren Bargad *and* Stanley F. Chyet.　IP

In His Last Binn Sir Peter Lies.　Thomas Love Peacock.　*Fr.* Headlong Hall.　EnRP

In his low-ceilinged oaken room.　The Silent Room.　Kingsley Amis. OxBC

In his malodorous brain what slugs and mire.　God.　Isaac Rosenberg. VWA

In his own image the Creator made.　On Man.　Walter Savage Landor. OBNC

In his place, mother,/ mud-spattered spotted crabs.　What She Said ("In his place, mother,/ mud-spattered spotted crabs").　Orampokiyar, *tr. fr. Tamil by* A. K. Ramanujan.　*Fr.* Five on the Crabs, 1.　PLW

In his place, mother,/ field-crabs cut into the pink.　What She Said ("In his place, mother,/ field-crabs cut into the pink").　Orampokiyar, *tr. fr. Tamil by* A. K. Ramanujan.　*Fr.* Five on the Crabs, 2.　PLW

In his portrait of Carlyle, Whistler builds.　After Whistler.　Stanley Plumly.　AnAn; NAmP

In his sea lit.　The Double Play.　Robert Wallace.　SD

In his sockets there were eyeballs full of thirst.　Self-Portrait at Thirty. Miklós Veress, *tr. by* Richard Wilbur.　MHuP

In his tall senatorial.　The Drum; the Narrative of the Demon of Tedworth. Dame Edith Sitwell.　FaBoTw

In His Utter Wretchedness.　John Audelay.　MeEL

In his well-known History of the Revolution, Trotsky tells.　History of the Revolution.　Pentti Saarikoski, *tr. by* Aili Jarvenpa.　SOP

In holly hedges starving birds.　Christmas Eve.　John Davidson.　OHIP

In honnour of this heghe fest, of custume yere by yere.　A Lover's New Year's Gift.　John Lydgate.　PoEL-1

In Honor of My Husband's Fiftieth Birthday.　Hsüeh Shao-hui, *tr. fr. Chinese by* Irving Lo.　WFTU

In Honour of Christmas.　*Unknown.*　MeEL

In Honour of St. Alphonsus Rodriguez.　Gerard Manley Hopkins. EBEV

In Honour of St. David's Day.　*Unknown.*　OBWVE

In Honour of Taffy Topaz.　Christopher Morley.　CRH

In honour of the dumb the blind the deaf.　Paul Éluard, *tr. fr. French by* Samuel Beckett.　*Fr.* Second Nature, V.　RHTwFP

In Horse Latitudes.　Katha Pollitt.　PPR

In Hospital.　James Elroy Flecker.　OxBTC

In Hospital, *sels.*　W. E. Henley.
　After.　*Fr.* VI.　BrPo
　Anterotics.　*Fr.* XXVI.　BrPo
　Apparition.　*Fr.* XXV.　BrPo; TrGrPo
　Ave, Caesar.　*Fr.* XIV.　BrPo
　Before.　*Fr.* IV.　BrPo; MoBrPo
　Casualty.　*Fr.* XIII.　BrPo
　"Chief, The."　*Fr.* XV.　BrPo
　Children: Private Ward.　*Fr.* XVIII.　BrPo
　Clinical.　*Fr.* XI.　BrPo
　Discharged.　*Fr.* XXVIII.　BrPo
　Enter Patient.　*Fr.* I.　BrPo
　Etching.　*Fr.* XII.　BrPo
　House-Surgeon.　*Fr.* XVI.　BrPo
　Interior.　*Fr.* III.　BrPo
　Interlude: "O, the fun, the fun and frolic."　*Fr.* XVII.　BrPo
　Lady-Probationer.　*Fr.* IX.　BrPo
　Music ("Down the quiet eve").　*Fr.* XXIII.　BrPo
　Nocturn: "At the barren heart of midnight."　*Fr.* XXVII.　BrPo
　Operation.　*Fr.* V.　BrPo
　Pastoral: "It's the Spring."　*Fr.* XXII.　BrPo
　Romance.　*Fr.* XXI.　BrPo; PAH
　Scrubber.　*Fr.* XIX.　BrPo
　Staff-Nurse: New Style.　*Fr.* X.　BrPo
　Staff-Nurse: Old Style.　*Fr.* VIII.　BrPo
　Suicide.　*Fr.* XXIV.
　Vigil.　*Fr.* VII.　BrPo

Visitor. *Fr.* XX. BrPo
Waiting. *Fr.* II. NAEL-2; NOBVV
In Hospital: Poona, I. Alun Lewis. OBWVE; SeCePo
In hot career or ranging far and wide. The Huntress. José Joaquín
Pesado, *tr. by* Samuel Beckett. MexPo
In Hungarian. Gábor Garai, *tr. fr. Hungarian by* Edwin Morgan. MHuP
In hushed silence come the hollow echoes. Watching a Game of Chess:
Second Series. Ch'ien Ch'ien-yi, *tr. by* Irving Lo. WFTU
In Illness, Dismissing My Singing Girl. Ssu-k'ung Shu, *tr. fr. Chinese by*
Burton Watson. CoBCP
In Imitation of Anacreon. Matthew Prior. FaBoEE
In Imitation of Ancient-Style Poetry, *sel.* Singde, *tr. fr. Chinese by*
William Schultz.
"North wind blowing through the barren willows, The." *Fr.* XL.
WFTU
In Imitation of Sun Kuang-hsien's Style. Hsiang Hung-tso, *tr. fr. Chinese*
by Irving Lo. WFTU
In Imitation of "The King of Huai-nan." Pao Chao, *tr. fr. Chinese by*
Burton Watson. CoBCP
In Immemoriam. "Cuthbert Bede." NA
In Impressions of Hawk Feathers Willow Leaves Shadow. Elizabeth
Woody. STE
In India. Karl Shapiro. NYBP
In India, Deeply Moved. Mokurai, *tr. fr. Chinese by* Burton Watson.
JLIC-2
In India lives a bird that is unique. Faridu'ddin Attar, *tr. fr. Persian by*
Afkham Darbandi *and* Dick Davis. *Fr.* The Conference of the Birds.
TOF
In Innocence. J. V. Cunningham. OxBSP
In innocence I said. In Innocence. J. V. Cunningham. OxBSP
In innocence the lines of our palms. To Bear Bryant, Somewhere on That
Taller Tower. Don Welch. TSL
In Ionia whence sprang old poets' fame. Phoebe on Latmus. Michael
Drayton. *Fr.* Endimion and Phoebe. OBSC
In Ireland, *sel.* Arthur Symons.
By the Pool at the Third Rosses. *Fr.* II. FaBoPP; OBNC
In Ireland: By the Pool at the Third Rosses. Arthur Symons. FaBoPP;
OBNC
In Ireland, in Ireland. Frederick Morgan. BLA
In Italy, where this sort of thing can occur. A Hill. Anthony Hecht.
CoAP; NYBP
In its absence it has become beautiful. The Glove. Harold Bond.
NYBP
In its going down, the moon. Robert Hoggra. LLLT; LLLT; MoCV
In its tenth year we realize. Bring the War Home. William Matthews.
GeTw
In Jail. Juan Antonio Corretjer, *tr. fr. Spanish by* Julio Marzán. InW
In January. Lorna Dee Cervantes. CCP
In January/ it's so nice. January. Maurice Sendak. RAR
In January, 1962. Ted Kooser. Psk
In Japanese,/ two characters combine. Definitions of the Word *Gout*.
Tina Koyama. BrSi
In jealously of cause and pride of plan. Autonomous. Mark Van Doren.
LiTA
In Jersey City where I did dwell. The Butcher Boy. *Unknown.* AmFP
In Jerusalem Are Women. Arye Sivan, *tr. fr. Hebrew by* David Shevin.
VWA
In Josef Koudelka's photograph, untitled & with no date. Sensationalism.
Larry Levis. MAYP; NAmP
In Judgment of the Leaf. Kenneth Patchen. UnAS; VGW
In July month, ae bonny morn. My Winsome Dear. Robert Fergusson.
Fr. Leith Races. SeCePo; VGW
In july of 19 somethin. With All Deliberate Speed. Don L. Lee. JB
In jumping and tumbling. Tumbling. *Unknown.* OxBChV
In June. Ruth Kim Chun-soo, *tr. fr. Korean by* Koh Chang-soo. ACKP
In June, amid the golden fields. The Groundhog. Richard Eberhart.
CMoP; FaBoMo; FaFP; LiTA; LiTM; MoAB; MoAmPo; MoP; NIP;
NoAM; NoP; NU; TAP; UnPo; WaP
In June and Gentle Oven. Anne Wilkinson. MoCV; NOBC
In June I give you a close-wooded fell. June. Folgore Da San
Gimignano, *tr. fr. Italian by* Dante Gabriel Rossetti. *Fr.* Sonnets of
the Months. AWP
In June the bush we call. The Victors. Denise Levertov. NoP
In just-/ spring when the world is mud. E. E. Cummings. *Fr.* Chansons
Innocentes, I. AmPP; FaBV; FaPON; HeIP; MoAB; MoAmPo;
MoShBr; NAAL-2; NIP; NoP; PrIm; SoSe; WeW
(In Just-.) InPK
In just an instant mist and cloud. Inscribed on "Drunk in the Autumn
Woods." Tao-chi, *tr. by* Jonathan Chaves. CoBLCP
In just the same way. Empress Eifuku, *tr. by* Steven D. Carter. WFTW
In Kansas. Carter Revard. HATNAP

In Katsushika of the grebes. *Unknown. Fr.* Manyo Shu. FCEI
In Kensington Gardens. Arthur Symons. EnLoPo
In Kerem Abraham. Tabernacle of Peace. Hayim Be'er, *tr. by* Stephen
Mitchell. VWA
In Kerry. John Millington Synge. FaBoPP; GBL; MoBrPo
In kirtle of myrtle the goose girl goes. The Goose Girl. Dorothy
Roberts. CaP
In Köln, a town of monks and bones. Cologne. Samuel Taylor
Coleridge. FaBoEE; NBLV; OBTV; TW
In Korets, my city in Volhynia. Korets Landscape. Yankev-Yitskhok
Segal, *tr. by* Grace Schulman. PeBMYV
In kraals of slanting shade the herd. Buffalo. Charles Eglington. PeSA
In labour when. Blessed Event. Ada Jackson. CN
In Ladbroke Square the light on waxen branches. Pictures in a Gallery
Undersea. Christian Karlson Stead. ATNZ
In Laddery Street Herself. Laura Riding. *Fr.* Forgotten Girlhood. RB
In Lady Lusher's drawing-room, where float the strains of Brahms. The
Martyred Democrat. C. J. Dennis. CBAP
In Lamplight, Watching My Wife Preparing a Flower, *sels.* Ch'ien
Ch'ien-i, *tr. fr. Chinese by* Jonathan Chaves. CoBLCP
"Clusters of cold-weather blossoms."
"Narcissus and chrysanthemum."
In lamplight, I open your book, and start to weep. Lamenting for Kao
Ch'ing-ch'iu, Chi-ti. Chang Yü, *tr. by* Jonathan Chaves.
CoBLCP
In Lantana Street's mid-morning. At the Nature-Strip. Judith Rodriguez.
CBAP
In Larch Wood. Larch Wood Secrets. Ivy O. Eastwick. BoTP
In last week's *New York Times* I read. Veterans Day, 1981. Carole
Oles. PPR
In Late Spring of the Year *Keng-hsü*, *sels.* Yüan Mei, *tr. fr. Chinese by*
Jonathan Chaves. CoBLCP
"Old house from my childhood, The."
"Once again to see West Lake!"
"Peonies below the stairs, The."
In late spring, the orioles are flying round the steps. Sand of Silk-
Washing Stream. Mao Hsi-chen, *tr. by* Lois Fusek. ATF
In late sun, the beauty of river and hill. Chüeh-chü. Tu Fu, *tr. by*
Burton Watson. CoBCP
In late winter/ I sometimes glimpse bits of steam. The Bear. Galway
Kinnell. CAPP; CoAP; InPS; NNaP; RFM; TAP; VGW
In late years returning to my old school. After a Long Time in the
Provinces, I Returned to My Old School in My Late Years. Umberto
Saba, *tr. by* Burton Watson. JLIC-1
In leaf after leaf we seem to hear the sighing of the wind. Wu Chen, *tr.*
fr. Chinese by Jonathan Chaves. *Fr.* Poems Inscribed on Paintings of.
Bamboo, I. CoBLCP
In Leinster. Louise Imogen Guiney. AA
In Lesbos long ago the moon would rise. Sappho Lives Again. Renée
Vivien, *tr. by* Beth Archer. DMF
In Librum. Sir John Davies. FaBoEE
In Lidda, in Ramla, in the Galilee. Here We Will Stay. Tawfiq Zayyad,
tr. by Sharif Elmusa *and* Charles Doria. MAP
In Lieu. Louis MacNeice. CMoP
In Lieu of a Preface to *The Great Commonwealth Book*. K'ang Yu-wei,
tr. fr. Chinese by Irving Lo. WFTU
In life I had a fear of death. Asadullah Khan Ghalib, *tr. by* Ahmed Ali.
GoT
In life I stroll the capital city. Poem in the Form of a Coffin-Puller's
Song. Miu Hsi, *tr. by* Burton Watson. CoBCP
In life I was the town drunkard. Chase Henry. Edgar Lee Masters.
OBD
In Life's Stable. Kadya Molodovsky, *tr. fr. Yiddish by* Ruth Whitman.
VWA
In lily ponds, the plump colorful buds. What the Concubine Said When
She Heard the Wife Complain about the Concubine's Wiles.
Villakaviralinar, *tr. by* A. K. Ramanujan. PLW
In Lincolnshire, a village full of tongues. On Looking at Stubbs's
Anatomy of the Horse. Edward Lucie-Smith. NePoEA-2
In Lithuania, on the Neman. The Little House in Lithuania. Samuel
Marshak, *tr. by* Daniel Weissbort. VWA
In Little Hands. Mani Leib, *tr. fr. Yiddish by* Keith Bosley. VWA
In Little Rock the people bear. The Chicago "Defender" Sends a Man to
Little Rock. Gwendolyn Brooks. AmNP; PoBA
In Loch Lene. Sunset. John Montague. *Fr.* Félire Oengus. FaBCIP
In Lombardy. Donald Revell. SM
In London at Bessborough Gardens. Conrad. Antoni Slonimski, *tr. by*
Isaac Komem. VWA
In London city was Bicham born. Young Beichan. *Unknown.* ESPB;
FaBoBa

In London City where I once did dwell, there's where I got my learning. Barbara Allen. *Unknown.* BeLS
  (Barbra Allen.) AS, *with music.*
In London here the streets are grey, an' grey the sky above. Irish Skies. Winifred M. Letts. TIRV
In London I never know what to be at. Country and Town. Charles Morris. NOEC
In London, September, 1802. Wordsworth. *See* Written in London, September, 1802.
In London there I was bent. London Lickpenny. *Unknown.* CoMu; FaBoPP; OBSV
  (London Lackpenny.) ChTr
In London was young Beichan born. Young Beichan and Susie Pye. *Unknown.* OnMSP
In loneliness and distance how faint the lights. On a Fall Night. Levi Ben-Amittai, *tr. by* Bernhard Frank. MHeP
In loneliness or grief, I treasure yet my friendship with Ben A'an   In Praise of Ben Avon. Brenda G. Macrow. PoSH
In lonely watches night by night. Requiescant. Frederick George Scott. OHIP
In looking o'er the prospects. The Prospect of the Future. Mrs. Henry Linden. CBWP-4
In loopy links the canker crawls. Indifference. *Unknown.* NA
In Lord Carpenter's Country. Barry O. Higgs. PeSA
In Los Angeles/ while the mountains cleared of smog. Tongue-tied in Black and White. Michael S. Harper. HCAP
In Louisiana. Albert Bigelow Paine. AA; AmFN
In Love. David Wevill. MoCV
In Love, at Stonehenge. Coventry Patmore. *Fr.* The Angel in the House. FaBoPP
In Love for Long. Edwin Muir. BoLoP; LiTM; MoBrPo
In Love, If Love Be Love. Tennyson. *Fr.* Idylls of the King: Merlin and Vivien. PoEL-5; TrGrPo
  (All in All.) LiTB
  (Vivien's Song.) OBNC
In love they wore themselves in a green embrace. Adolescence. Patricia K. Page. CaP; OBCV
In love to be sure what disasters we meet. The Lover's Arithmetic. *Unknown.* OxBoLi
In Love with the Bears. Greg Kuzma. NYBP
In love's rubber armor I come to you. Love Sonnet. John Updike. Son
In loving, each one hath free choice. Isabella Whitney. *Fr.* Sweet Nosegay, A, or Pleasant Posy. WPE
In lowly dale, fast by a river's side. James Thomson. *Fr.* The Castle of Indolence, I. EnRP; NOEC
  (Land of Indolence, The.) SeCePo
In lungs fresh like honeycomb. Indian. Laura Jensen. AmPA
In Lythe Strathdon. Charles Murray. PoSH
In Magic Words. Merrill Moore. Son
In Maidstone Gaol, I am lamenting. Farewell to the World of Richard Bishop. *Unknown.* CoMu
In man, ambition is the common'st thing. Ambition. Robert Herrick. CaPo
In Manchester there are a thousand puddles. Watch Your Step—I'm Drenched. Adrian Mitchell. RB
In many forms we try. The Bohemian Hymn. Emerson. WGRP
In marble walls [*or* halls] as white as milk. Mother Goose. ChTr; GBP; OxNR; TSS
In March. Philip Martin. PoAu-2
In March and April, thereabout. Alison. *Unknown.* HAP
In March birds couple, a new birth. *At. to* Henry Vaughan *and* Thomas Stanley, *fr. the Welsh of* Aneirin. FaBoEE; FaBoRV
  (Leaves Come Again, The.) FaBoEE
In March I dreamed of mud. From the Journals of the Frog Prince. Susan Mitchell. NIP
In March I give you plenteous fisheries. March. Folgore Da San Gimignano, *tr. fr. Italian by* Dante Gabriel Rossetti. *Fr.* Sonnets of the Months. AWP
In March, kites bite the wind. Paper Dragons. Susan Alton Schmeltz. RHPC
In March the seed. Mater Dei. Padraic Fallon. NOCV
In March, the small river. Love Poem: The Dispossessed. T. R. Hummer. MAYP
In Marion, the honey locust trees are falling. Two Poems about President Harding. James Wright. CoAP; MoP
"In martial sports I had my cunning tried." Sir Philip Sidney. *Fr.* Astrophel and Stella, LIII. NAEL-1
In mathematic[k]s he was greater. Samuel Butler. *Fr.* Hudibras, I, 1. ImOP; NOBL
In matters of commerce the fault of the Dutch. A Political Despatch. George Canning. FaBoCo

  (Dutch, The.) OBTV
  (Epigram: Dutch, The.) OxBoLi
In May. Blue Tropic. Luis Cabalquinto. BrSi
In May. John Millington Synge. MoBrPo
In May. *Unknown.* BoTP
In May, approaching the city, I. The Ritualists. William Carlos Williams. NYBP
In May I go a-walking. In May. *Unknown.* BoTP
In May or else in September. To Pass the Time. Benjamin Péret, *tr. by* Michael Benedikt. POS
In May rain, the smoke from the seaweed. Teika, *tr. fr. Japanese by* Hiroaki Sato. *Fr.* A Compendium of Good Tanka. FCEI
In May rains the water, the waves. Teika, *tr. fr. Japanese by* Hiroaki Sato. *Fr.* Eighty-four Tanka. FCEI
In May, when sea-winds pierced our solitudes. The Rhodora [On Being Asked Whence Is the Flower]. Emerson. AA; AmPP; AnAmPo; AWP; BoNaP; FaBV; FaFP; GN; HeIP; LiTA; NAAL-1; NOBA; NoP; OHFP; OxBA; PoE; PWR; TAP; TrGrPo
In Me. Yankev-Yitskhok Segal, *tr. fr. Yiddish by* Grace Schulman. PeBMYV
In me is death, in you my life. Michelangelo. OBD
In Me, Past, Present, Future Meet. Siegfried Sassoon. OBEV; OxBSP
In me there is a vast and lonely place. Zora Cross. *Fr.* Love Sonnets, XLIX. CBAP
In melancholic fancy. Hallo My Fancy. William Cleland. CH; OxBoLi
In mellowy orchards, rich and ripe. The Snitterjipe. James Reeves. AmMo
In Memorabilia Mortis. Francis Sherman. CaP
In Memorial. J. Gordon Coogler. OBAL
In Memoriam. "Max Adeler." FaBoCo
In Memoriam. Tom Disch. BAP
In Memoriam. Dave Gingell. PoSH
In Memoriam. W. J. Gruffydd, *tr. fr. Welsh by* R. Gerallt Jones. OBWVE
In Memoriam. Michael Longley. FaBCIP
In Memoriam. Padraig de Brun. WTO
In Memoriam. Giuseppe Ungaretti, *tr. fr. Italian by* Henry Taylor. PFI
In Memoriam I. Franco Fortini, *tr. fr. Italian by* Ruth Feldman. VWA
In Memoriam, II. Richard Weber. *See* Suddenly she slapped me, hard across the face.
In Memoriam, A. C. M. L., *sel.* Cecil Arthur Spring-Rice. "God of all power and might." TrPWD
In Memoriam: A. C., R.J.O., K.S. Sir John Betjeman. NYBP
In Memoriam A. H. H. Tennyson. EBVV, *abr.*; OAEL-2, *abr.* *Sels.*
  "Again at Christmas did we weave." *Fr.* LXXVIII. PChr
  "And, star and system rolling past." *Fr.* Epilogue. ImOP
  "As sometimes in a dead man's face." *Fr.* LXXIV. LiTB
  Be Near Me. *Fr.* L. ELP; HAP; HeIP; LiTB; NOCV; NoP; PoEL-5; SCV
  "By night we linger'd [*or* lingered] on the lawn." *Fr.* XCV. HAP; NoP; OBNC; PoEL-5; TOF
  Calm Is the Morn. *Fr.* XI. ChTr; EBEV; ELP; FaBoRV; FiP; HeIP; LiTB; NOBE; NoP; OBNC; PoEL-5; TrGrPo
  (Lincolnshire Wolds and Lincolnshire Sea.) FaBoPP
  "Contemplate all this work of Time." *Fr.* CXVIII. FF
  "Danube to the Severn gave, The." *Fr.* XIX. FF; GTBS-P; NoP
  (Hushing of the Wye, The.) FaBoPP
  "Dark house, by which once more I stand." *Fr.* VII. EBEV; GTBS-P; HAP; HeIP; NOBE; NoP; OBD; OBNC; PeHV; PoEL-5; SCV; UnPo
  (Dark House.) LiTB
  "Do we indeed desire the dead." *Fr.* LI. OBD
  "Doors, where my heart was used to beat." *Fr.* CXIX. NoP; OBNC; PoEL-5; SCV
  "Fair ship, that from the Italian shore." *Fr.* IX. PeHV
  "I cannot see the features right." *Fr.* LXX. LiTB; PoEL-5
  "I climb the hill: from end to end." *Fr.* C. PoEL-5
  "I dreamed there would be spring no more." *Fr.* LXIX. NOBE
  "I envy not in any moods." *Fr.* XXVII. LiTB; OBNC; PeHV
  "I hear the noise about thy keel." *Fr.* X. EBVV
  I Held It Truth. *Fr.* I. HeIP; LiTB; NoP; OBNC
  "I past [*or* passed] beside the reverend walls." *Fr.* LXXXVII. EBVV
  (He Revisits Cambridge.) FaBoPP
  "I sometimes hold it half a sin." *Fr.* V. TOF
  "I trust I have not wasted breath." *Fr.* CXX. ImOP; SeCePo
  "I wage not any feud with death." *Fr.* LXXXII. LiTB
  "If sleep and death be truly one." *Fr.* XLIII. OBNC
  "Love is and was my lord and king." *Fr.* CXXVI. NOBE; NOCV; OBEV; OBNC
  (My Lord and King.) ChTr
  "My own dim life should teach me this." *Fr.* XXXIV. SeCePo

"Now fades the last long streak of snow." *Fr.* CXV. FaBoRV; GTBS-P; NOBE; OBNC

"O living will that shalt endure." *Fr.* CXXXI. FaBoBe

(Prayer, The: "O living will that shalt endure.") WGRP

"O sorrow, cruel fellowship." *Fr.* III. HAP

Of One Dead. *Fr.* XIV.

"Oh yet We Trust." *Fr.* LIV. EaLo; LiTB; NoP; OBNC; TrGrPo

(Larger Hope, The.) WGRP

"Old warder of these buried bones." *Fr.* XXXIX. PoEL-5

"Old yew, which graspest at the stones." *Fr.* II. ELP; GTBS-P; NOBE; NoP; OBNC; PoEL-5; UnPo

"On that last night before we went." *Fr.* CIII. PoEL-5

"One writes, that 'other friends remain.'" *Fr.* VI. PoEL-5

"Path by which we twain did go, The." *Fr.* XXII. SCV

"Peace; come away: the song of woe." *Fr.* LVII. EBVV

Ring Out, Wild Bells. *Fr.* CVI. BLPL; EBVV; FaFP; FaPON, 2 *sts.*; FaPoR; FiP, 7 *sts.*; LiTB; OFD; TrGrPo; WiR, 7 *sts., incl. 2 sts. fr.* CV.

(Ring Out the Old, Ring In the New.) WBLP

"Risest thou thus, dim dawn, again." *Fr.* LXXII. OBNC; PoEL-5

"Sad Hesper o'er the buried sun." *Fr.* CXXI. NoP

"So careful of the type?" but no." *Fr.* LVI. FF; HAP; NoP; OBNC; TOF

Strong Son of God. *Fr.* Proem. EaLo; HAP; LiTB; NAWM-2; TrCP; TrGrPo; TrPWD; WGRP

"Sweet after showers, ambrosial air." *Fr.* LXXXVI. EBVV

"Tears of the widower, when he sees." *Fr.* XIII. PeHV

"That which we dare invoke to bless." *Fr.* CXXIV. NOCV; TOF; WGRP

There Rolls the Deep. *Fr.* CXXIII. FaBoRV; HAP; NOBE; SeCePo

"Thou comest, much wept for: such a breeze." *Fr.* XVII. EBVV

"Thy voice is on the rolling air." *Fr.* CXXX. HeIP; NoP; PeHV

"Till now the doubtful dusk reveal'd." *Fr.* XCV. GTBS-P

"Time draws near the birth of Christ, The." *Fr.* XXVIII. FaBoRV; NOCV; PChr

"'Tis well, 'tis something; we may stand." *Fr.* XVIII. EBVV

"To-night the Winds Begin." *Fr.* XV. GTBS-P; LiTB; NOBE; OBNC; PoEL-5

"Unwatch'd [*or* unwatched], the garden bough shall sway." *Fr.* CI. ELP; GTBS-P; OBNC; PoEL-5; SCV

(Somersby, Lincolnshire; after Leaving the Refectory.) FaBoPP

"We leave the well-beloved place." *Fr.* CII. PoEL-5

"What words are these have fallen from me." *Fr.* XVI. EBEV

"When Lazarus left his charnel-cave." *Fr.* XXXI. TOF

"When on my bed the moonlight falls." *Fr.* LXVII. NoP; SeCePo

"When rosy plumelets tuft the larch." *Fr.* XCI. OBNC

"Wild bird, whose warble, liquid sweet." *Fr.* LXXXVIII. NoP; PBBP

"Wish, that of the living whole, The." *Fr.* LV. HAP, LV; NoP, LV; OBNC, LV; TOF, LV.

"Witch-elms that counterchange the floor." *Fr.* LXXXIX. OBNC

"With such compelling cause to grieve." *Fr.* XXIX. EBVV

"With trembling fingers did we weave." *Fr.* XXX. EBVV

"You say, but with no touch of scorn." *Fr.* XCVI. NOCV

(Doubt.) WGRP

In Memoriam. Alphonse Campbell Fordham. Mary Weston Fordham. CBWP-2

In Memoriam (Easter, 1915). Edward Thomas. GTBS-P; NOBE; OBWP; OBWVE; OxBTC

In Memoriam: Ernst Toller. W. H. Auden. NYBP

In Memoriam F. A. S. Robert Louis Stevenson. BrPo

In Memoriam Francis Ledwidge. Seamus Heaney. CIP; FaBCIP; NoAM

In Memoriam Frederick Douglass. Eloise Bibb. CBWP-4

In Memoriam Frederick Douglass. Henrietta Cordelia Ray. CBWP-3

In Memoriam I, Elizabeth at Twenty. Richard Weber. ErPo

In Memoriam II. Franco Fortini, *tr. fr. Italian by* Ruth Feldman. VWA

In Memoriam; Ingvald Bjorndal and His Comrade. Malcolm Lowry. OBCV

In Memoriam James Joyce, *sels.* "Hugh MacDiarmid."

In the Fall. InPS

"It was Landor who first said." FaBoPV

We Must Look at the Harebell. NAEL-2

In Memoriam John Coltrane. Michael Stillman. InPK; RR

In Memoriam: John Davidson. Ronald Campbell Macfie. GoTS

In Memoriam—Leo: A Yellow Cat. Margaret Sherwood. BLPA

In Memoriam M. Tambimuttu. Derek Stanford. NPo

In Memoriam: Martin Luther King, Jr. June Jordan. PoBA

In Memoriam of E. B. Clark. Lizelia Augusta Jenkins Moorer. CBWP-3

In Memoriam Paul Celan. Gad Hollander. VWA

In Memoriam Paul Laurence Dunbar. Henrietta Cordelia Ray. CBWP-3

In Memoriam: Roy Campbell. Ralph Nixon Currey. PeSA

In Memoriam S. L. Akintola. David Knight. MoCV

In Memoriam S.C.W., V.C. Charles Hamilton Sorley. MMA

In Memoriam. Susan Eugenia Bennett. Mary Weston Fordham. CBWP-2

In Memory, *sel.* Lionel Johnson.

"Ah! fair face gone from sight." OBNC; PoEL-5

In Memory. Katha Pollitt. MAYP

In Memory, 1978. Judith Kazantzis. AIW; BrRo

In Memory of a Friend. George Barker. OxBTC

In Memory of Ann Jones. Dylan Thomas. *See* After the Funeral.

In Memory of Arthur Clement Williams. Eloise Bibb. CBWP-4

In Memory of Arthur Winslow. Robert Lowell. TwCP

In Memory of Arthur Winslow, *sel.* Robert Lowell.

Death from Cancer. TwCP

In Memory of Basil, Marquess of Dufferin and Ava. Sir John Betjeman. OBWP

In Memory of Bryan Lathrop. Edgar Lee Masters. PoA

In Memory of Captain Underwood Who Was Drowned. *Unknown.* FaBoEE

In Memory of David Archer, *sel.* George Barker.

"Images! Venerable as Druidical trees." FaBoMo

In Memory of Edward Wilson. James Clerk Maxwell. *See* Gin a body meet a body.

In Memory of Eva Gore-Booth and Con Markiewicz. W. B. Yeats. FaBoPV; MoAB; NoAM; OAEL-2; OBMV; OxBTC

In Memory of Francois Rabelais. Yunna Moritz, *tr. fr. Russian by* Elaine Feinstein. VWA

In Memory of General Grant. Henry Abbey. AA

In Memory of George Whitby, Architect. Sir John Betjeman. EyDe

In Memory of Izziddin al-Qalaq. Ahmad Dahbur, *tr. fr. Arabic by* Lena Jayyusi *and* Charles Doria. MAP

In Memory of James M. Rathel. Josephine D. Henderson Heard. CBWP-4

In Memory of Jane Fraser [*or* Frazer]. Geoffrey Hill. MoP; NAEL-2; NePoEA; NoAM; OxBTC

In Memory of John Lothrop Motley. Bryant. AA

In Memory of Kathleen. Kenneth Patchen. MoAmPo

In Memory of Leopardi. James Wright. NaP

In Memory of Major Robert Gregory. W. B. Yeats. AnIL; EBEV; OAEL-2

In memory of me, when I am long departed. To Natalia Nikolaevna Pushkina. Prince P. A. Vyazemsky, *tr. by* Alan Myers. AAA

In Memory of My Arab Grandmother. Evelyn Arcad Zerbe. WPOW

In Memory of My Dear Grandmother [Anne Bradstreet]. Anne Bradstreet. BoWoP; NAAL-1; TrCP

In Memory of My Dear Grandchild Elizabeth Bradstreet Who Deceased August, 1665, Being a Year and a Half Old. Anne Bradstreet. NAAL-1; NOCV; SCAP; WPE

In Memory of My Father. James Agee. DiL

In Memory of My Feelings. Frank O'Hara. NAAL-2; NeAP; PoM

In Memory of My First Chapatis. Diane DiPrima. PoM

In Memory of My Forever-Gone Nineteenth Year. Tu Yeh, *tr. fr. Chinese by* Dominic Cheung. IFON

In Memory of My Mother (I do not think of you lying in the wet clay). Patrick Kavanagh. BIrV; CIP; FaBCIP; MoP; NoAM

In Memory of My Mother (You will have the road gate open, the front door ajar). Patrick Kavanagh. BIrV

In Memory of My Uncle Timothy. Alastair Reid. NePoEA-2

In Memory of Radio. Amiri Baraka. NAAL-2; NeAP; NoP; PoM

In Memory of Reinhold Koehler. Wieland Schmied, *tr. fr. German by* Beth Bjorklund. CoAuP

In Memory of Sigmund Freud. W. H. Auden. HAP; LiTB; NoAM; OAEL-2; OxBA

In Memory of the Circus Ship *Euzkera*. Walker Gibson. FiBHP

In Memory of the Moon (A Killing). Charlotte DeClue. STE

In Memory of the Unknown Poet, Robert Boardman Vaughn. Donald Justice. CAPP; DiPo; NoAM

In Memory of the Utah Stars. William Matthews. GeTw; MAYP; Psk

In Memory of Those Murdered in the Dublin Massacre. Paul Durcan. FaBCIP

In Memory of V. R. Lang. Mac Hammond. PoA

In Memory of W. B. Yeats ("He disappeared in the dead of winter."). W. H. Auden. CMoP; FaFP; HAP; HeIP; HoPM; LiTB; LiTM; MoAB; MoBrPo; NoAM; NOBE; OAEL-2; OxBTC; PPP; PrIm; TrGrPo; UnPo; WeW

"Earth, receive an honoured guest," *sel.* ChTr; FaBoRV; FaBoTw, 4 *sts.;* Mes

In Memory of W. H. Auden. David R. Slavitt. SM

In Memory of Walter Savage Landor. Swinburne. PoEL-5

In Memphis—in Tennessee. On the Birth of a Black/Baby/Boy. Etheridge Knight. DiL

In Mem'ry's fairest court a shrine is set. To Laura. Henrietta Cordelia Ray. CBWP-3

In Men Whom Men Condemn as Ill. Joaquin Miller. *Fr.* Byron. PoLF

In Mercy, Lord, Incline Thine Ear. Isaac M. Wise. AH

In Merioneth, over the sad moor. Dead. Lionel Johnson. BrPo; OBNC; PoEL-5

In merry old England, it once was a rule. On the New Laureate. *Unknown.* FaBoCo

In merry Scotland, in merry Scotland. Henry Martyn. *Unknown.* ESPB

In mery May, quhen medis springis. Prologue to the Avowis of Alexander. John Barbour. *Fr.* The Buik of Alexander. OxBS

In Mexico. Evaleen Stein. AA

In mid-river we join the ancient force. Baptism. Dale Zieroth. NOBC

In middle life when the skin slackens. Ambulando. Charles Brasch. ATNZ; PeNZ

In midnight sleep of many a face of anguish. Old War-Dreams. Walt Whitman. AnAmPo; OxBSP

In midst of this city celestial. The Celestial City. Giles Fletcher the Younger. *Fr.* Christ's Victory and Triumph: Christ's Triumph after Death, IV. NOBE

In midst of woods or pleasant grove. Blackbird, The ("In midst of woods or pleasant grove"). *Unknown.* EIL

In Mike's Diner the other day. Meanwhile. Joel Dailey. UL

In Mind. Denise Levertov. NMM

In minds pure glasse when I my selfe behold. William Drummond of Hawthornden. OBS

In mine own monument I lie. Richard Lovelace. OxBSP

In Missing. Ray A. Young Bear. CDW

In Mississippi/ balloons of hunger. No New Music. Stanley Crouch. PoBA

In Missoula, Montana, where the townsfolk water. Pendant Watch. Madeline DeFrees. NMM

In mists and rains, the day. Basho, *tr. fr. Japanese by* Burton Watson. *Fr.* Seventy-six Hokku. FCEI

In Modern Dress. Craig Raine. NoAM

In mole-blue indolence the sun. The Jungle. Alun Lewis. OBWVE

In Montecito. Randall Jarrell. CoAP; MAT; NoP; NYBP; VGW

In moonlight, we would enjoy these flowers together. Looking at Chrysanthemums. Chang Yü, *tr. fr. Chinese by* Jonathan Chaves. *Fr.* Seven Poems on Living in the Mountains: Seeing Off. CoBLCP

In Morfudd's Arms. Dafydd ap Gwilym, *tr. fr. Welsh by* Rolfe Humphries. OBWVE

In Mornigan's park there is a deer. *Unknown.* GBP (Riddle: "In Mornigan's park there is a deer.") ChTr

In morning dew, dirty and cool. Basho, *tr. fr. Japanese by* Burton Watson. *Fr.* Seventy-six Hokku. FCEI

In morning light my damson show'd [*or* showed]. The Plum Tree by the House. Oliver St. John Gogarty. OBEV; PoRA

In morning's first light. Emperor Fushimi, *tr. by* Steven D. Carter. WFTW

In Mosa's Time. Roberta Hill Whiteman. ER

In moss-prankt dells which the sunbeams flatter. Lovers, and a Reflection. Charles Stuart Calverley. FaBoCo; FaBoPa; NA

In most cases. Who Makes the Journey. Cathy Song. BrSi

In most things I did as my father had done. George II. Thackeray. *Fr.* The Georges. FaBoEE

In mothers womb thy fingers did me mak. A Thankful Acknowledgment of God's Providence. John Cotton. SCAP

In Mountjoy jail one Monday morning. Kevin Barry: Died for Ireland, 1st November, 1920. *Unknown.* FaBoBa

In Mourning for the Summer. Tachihara Michizo, *tr. fr. Japanese by* Sato. FCEI

In mourning for your second son. Consoling Wu Te-cheng on the Death of His Son. Shen Chou, *tr. by* Jonathan Chaves. CoBLCP

In moving-slow he has no peer. The Sloth. Theodore Roethke. AnAmPo; FiBHP; NePoAm; OBAL; OBCA; RHPC

In Mr. Po's ten chapters of Lo-yang poems. On Lo-tien's Poem on the Three Friends of the Northern Window. Michizane, *tr. by* Burton Watson. JLIC-1

In Murasaki's time. Tale of Genji. Hugh Seidman. AmPA

In musty light, in the thin brown air. In the Basement of the Goodwill Store. Ted Kooser. GOYP

In Mutual Time. Steven Lavoie. UL

In my backyard. Lightning Bugs. Ernest Slyman. SoTCo

In my bamboo rainhat, I avoid tree branches dripping with dew. Mountain Rain. Ho Shao-chi, *tr. by* J. D. Schmidt. WFTU

In my bath. Yosano Akiko, *tr. by* Sanford Goldstein *and* Seishi Shinoda. OV

In my bed at night. Bible, *O.T. See* Song of Solomon, The: On My Bed I Sought Him.

In my bed your body is an island. I Arrive in a Small Boat, Alone. Susan Ludvigson. KS

In my begging bowl. Ryokan, *tr. by* Geoffrey Bownas *and* Anthony Thwaite. PeBJV

In my beginning is my end. In succession. East Coker. T. S. Eliot. *Fr.* Four Quartets. HAP; PPP; VGW

In my birthplace, the garden and the hedges. Teika, *tr. fr. Japanese by* Hiroaki Sato. *Fr.* Eighty-four Tanka. FCEI

In My Boat, Painting a Picture, *sel.* Yün Shou-p'ing, *tr. fr. Chinese by* Jonathan Chaves. "Essence of ink, The." CoBLCP

In my boat that goes. Saigyo Hoshi, *tr. by* Arthur Waley. AWP

In my cave lives a solitary rat. Chez-Nous. Albert Gordon Austin. PoAu-2

In my childhood trees were green. Autobiography. Louis MacNeice. FaBCIP; NOIV; RB

In my country, made for testing catapults and snares. Jubilant Poem. Roque Dalton, *tr. by* Barbara Paschke *and* David Volpendesta. Vol

In my country, sir. A Collective Shot. Jaime Suárez Quemain, *tr. by* Wilfredo Castaño. Vol

In My Craft or Sullen Art. Dylan Thomas. BoLoP; CMoP; GTBS-P; HAP; HeIP; InvP; LiTM; MAT; MoP; NIP; NoAM; NoP; PoE; WeW

In my dream by Henry James there is a sentence. My Dreams by Henry James. Michael Ryan. SV

In my dream I embraced. With the Thin Girl. György Petri, *tr. by* William Jay Smith. MHuP

In my dream said a plum-blossom. Tabito. *Fr.* Manyo Shu. Ma

In my dream the brooding child. The Child. George Keithley. NPGG

In my dreams. Desire. Mary Mackey. ER

In My Dreams. Stevie Smith. FaBoWP

In my dreams I hear my tribe. Then and Now. Kath Walker. IHMS

In My Dreams I Searched for You. *Gond Oral Tradition, tr. by* V. Elwin *and* S. Hivale. WTO

In my dry cell. The Riven Quarry. Gloria C. Oden. PoBA

In My Eye. Martin Seymour-Smith. NPo

In my family there are two famous paintings. I Tried to Exchange Two Painting for Some Grain But Failed. Hsü Wei, *tr. by* Jonathan Chaves. CoBLCP

In My Father's House, *sel.* Bruce Smith. Address. Son

In My Father's House. *Unknown.* AS

In my father's house are many cobwebs. Portrait of the Artist as an Old Man. Michael Dransfield. CBAP

In my fingers the world can be grasped. Seismograph. Ephraim Auerbach, *tr. by* Howard Schwartz. VWA

In My First Hard Springtime. James Welch. AmPA; CDW

In my garden. Emperor Meiji, *tr. by* Geoffrey Bownas *and* Anthony Thwaite. PeBJV

In My Garden. *Unknown.* BoTP

In my garden. Yakamochi. *Fr.* Manyo Shu. FCEI

In my garden fall the plum-blossoms. Tabito. *Fr.* Manyo Shu. Ma

In my garden grows a tree. The Apple Rhyme. Madeleine Nightingale. BoTP

In my grandmother's house there was always chicken soup. A Story about Chicken Soup. Louis Simpson. LCAP; NNaP; PoE; TAP

In my grass hut. Shunzei, *tr. fr. Japanese by* Burton Watson. *Fr.* Thirty Tanka. FCEI

In my heart among the clouds of fog. Black Veins. Hans Arp, *tr. by* Michael Benedikt. POS

In my heart washed by darkness. Today. Jung Han-mo, *tr. by* Koh Chang-soo. ACKP

In my heart's depth. Akazome Emon, *tr. by* Kenneth Rexroth *and* Ikuko Atsumi. WPOW

In my house is my book collection, filled with book-worms. Li K'ai-hsien, *tr. fr. Chinese by* Jonathan Chaves. *Fr.* Impromptu Poems. CoBLCP

In my hut, square light cast. Basho, *tr. fr. Japanese by* Burton Watson. *Fr.* Seventy-six Hokku. FCEI

In my kindergarten class. Kindergarten. Ron Rogers. NOVW

In my land there are no distinctions. Poem for the Young White Man Who Asked Me How I, an Intelligent, Well-read Person, Could Believe in the War between Races. Lorna Dee Cervantes. CCP; WPOW

In my left pocket a Chickasaw hand. The Truth Is. Linda Hogan. HATNAP

In My Lifetime. James Welch. CDW; STE

In my little garden. In My Garden. *Unknown.* BoTP

In My Meanest Daydream. Gary Gildner. ASP; TSL

In my memory you flare. Gerrit Achterberg, *tr. by* James Brockway. DuIn

In My Mind. Norman MacCaig. OxBC

In my morning bed. Yakamochi. *Fr.* Manyo Shu. FCEI, *tr. by* Hiroaki Sato; Ma

In my mountain hamlet. Muneyuki, *tr. by* Geoffrey Bownas *and* Anthony Thwaite. PeBJV

In my mountain home. Tonna, *tr. by* Steven D. Carter. WFTW

In My Name. Grace Nichols. AIW

In my native home. Ietaka, *tr. by* Steven D. Carter. WFTW

In my own shire, if I was sad. A. E. Housman. *Fr.* A Shropshire Lad, XLI. BrPo

In my own twentieth century. Natalya Gorbanyevskaya, *tr. fr. Russian by* Daniel Weissbort. PBWP

In my rudyard-kipling-simple years I read. The Thrifty Elephant. John Holmes. NYBP

In my season as red as the red-breasted. The Reality of Autumn. Duane Niatum. HATNAP

In my shanks. Reb Hanina. Paul Raboff. VWA

In my sleep I was fain of their fellowship, fain. Sunrise. Sidney Lanier. *Fr.* Hymns of the Marshes. AA; PoEL-5

In my sleeve the colored ball worth a thousand in gold. Temari. Ryokan, *tr. by* Burton Watson. JLIC-2

In my stone eyes I see. What Riddle Asked the Sphinx. Archibald MacLeish. HoPM

In My Thirtieth Year. Archibald MacLeish. *See* And I have come upon this place.

In My Time, at Your Place. Yehuda Amichai, *tr. fr. Hebrew by* Warren Bargad *and* Stanley F.Chyet. IP

In my village, another year has gone floating by. Sitting by Myself. K'ang Hai, *tr. by* Jonathan Chaves. CoBLCP

In my ward. Twenty of My Sons. Anna Swirszczynska, *tr. by* Magnus Jan Krynski *and* Robert A. Maguire. PwPP

In my young days I drank a/ Lot of wine. A Friend Advises Me to Stop Drinking. Mei Yao Ch'en, *tr. by* Kenneth Rexroth. HoPM

In my younger years. Dreams. Nikki Giovanni. CNA; PoBA

In my youth. Opposition. Kaneko Mitsuharu, *tr. by* Geoffrey Bownas *and* Anthony Thwaite. PeBJV

In my youth the growls. Tennyson. FaBoEE

In my youth's summer I did sing of one. The Wandering Outlaw. Byron. *Fr.* Childe Harold's Pilgrimage, III. FiP

In Mysterious Ways. Faye Kicknosway. GeTw

In Nagasaki Bay, southwest where sky and water meet. Dutch Ship. Rai San'yo, *tr. by* Burton Watson. JLIC-2

In Nakedness. Marnie Pomeroy. ErPo

"In nature apt to like when I did see." Sir Philip Sidney. *Fr.* Astrophel and Stella, XVI. NAEL-1

In Nature There Is neither Right nor Left nor Wrong. Randall Jarrell. OxBC

In "nature" there's no choice. Beyond the End. Denise Levertov. NeAP; VGW

In Neglect. Robert Frost. OxBSP; VGW

In New Ross. Valentin Iremonger. NeIP

In New South Wales, as I plainly see. William Forster. *Fr.* The Devil and the Governor. CBAP; PoAu-1

In newspapers, all see. Emperor Meiji, *tr. by* Geoffrey Bownas *and* Anthony Thwaite. PeBJV

In night, when colors [*or* colours] all to black[e] are cast. Fulke Greville. *Fr.* Caelica, C. AAS; OAEL-1; QFR; Son

In Nine Sleep Valley, *sel.* James Merrill.

"Geode, the troll's melon." HCAP

In 1915 my grandfather's. Grandfather. Michael S. Harper. CAPP; GeTw; LCAP; TAP

In 1958 in Kansas. Why We Sometimes Paint by Numbers. Colleen J. McElroy. ER

In 1945, when the keepers cried kaput. The Gift. John Ciardi. LiTM

In 1943 Althea was a welder. Of Althea and Flaxie. Cheryl Clarke. GLP

In 1943/ my father. Post-War. Libby Houston. CN

In nineteen hundred and twenty-two. Mr. Vachel Lindsay Discovers Radio. Samuel Hoffenstein. BXAP

In nineteen hundred they preferred. Upper Family. Maxwell Bodenheim. OBAL

In 1910 a royal princess. English. Osbert Lancaster. *Fr.* Afternoons with Baedeker. FaBoCo; NOBL

In 1939 the skylark had nothing to say to me. The Ninth of July. John Hollander. CoAP

In 1933 my parents won in a raffle. A Man of Action. Charles B. Stetler. GOYP

In nineteen years, we have parted, and met. To Hsiao Shih-ying. Hsieh Chin, *tr. by* Jonathan Chaves. CoBLCP

In no country. No Offence. D. J. Enright. OxBTC

In No Strange Land. Francis Thompson. *See* O world invisible, we view thee.

In North Great George's Street. "Seumas O'Sullivan." BIrV

In North Ward they do many strange dances. Juan Chi, *tr. fr. Chinese by* Burton Watson. *Fr.* Singing of Thoughts. CoBCP

In northern climes where furious tempests blow. Daniel Defoe. *Fr.* The Diet of Poland, A Satire. OBTV

In Northern seas there roams a fish called a K'un. The P'eng That Was a K'un. *At. to* Chuang Tzu, *tr. by* Robert Graves. AmMo

In Norway land there lived a maid. The Grey Selchie of Sule Skerry. *Unknown.* OxBB

In Nottamun Town not a soul would look up. Nottamun Town. *Unknown.* FaBoNo; OxBoLi

In Nottingham county there lives at Swan Green. Byron. FL

In Nottingham there lives a jolly tanner. Robin Hood and the Tanner. *Unknown.* ESPB

In November. Anne Reeve Aldrich. AA

In November. Archibald Lampman. NOBC; OBCV

In November, in the days to remember the dead. St. Malachy. Thomas Merton. VGW

In No. 64 Von Tempsky has his picture up. Von Tempsky's Dance. Murray Edmond. PeNZ

In numbers, and but these few. An Ode on the Birth of Our Saviour. Robert Herrick. GN

In Nunhead Cemetery. Charlotte Mew. FaBoWP

In O-Yashima, the dominion under heaven. Tanabe Sakimaro. *Fr.* Manyo Shu. Ma

In obedience to the imperial command. Yakamochi. *Fr.* Manyo Shu. Ma

In Obitum Ben. Jons. Mildmay Fane, Earl of Westmorland. OxBSP

In Obitum Promi. Henry Parrot. FaBoCo

In Obtuse Angle's Study. Blake. *Fr.* An Island in the Moon. FaBoNo

In Ocean's wide domains. The Witnesses. Longfellow. GOA

In October. Michael Hamburger. NePoEA

In October. October. Maurice Sendak. RHPC

In October at midnight in the olive groves. Thoughts from Abroad. Patrick Maybin. NeIP

In October marching, taking the sweet air. Towards Lillers. Ivor Gurney. NAEL-2

In October of the year. Ox Cart Man. Donald Hall. CAPP; FYAP; InPS; LCAP

In October the pregnant woman walked by the river. In October. Michael Hamburger. NePoEA

In Ohio. James Wright. NNaP

In Ohio, where these things happen. The Breathers. James Reiss. AmPA

In Oklahoma. Life Is Motion. Wallace Stevens. SD

In Oklahoma an old man died, long ago. Elf Night. Ron Rogers. STE

In old age affection thins. Old Age. Jacob Glatstein, *tr. by* Cynthia Ozick. PeBMYV

In Old Buda, a street almost as wide as a square. Brazilian Rain Forest. Gyula Illyés, *tr. by* William Jay Smith. MHuP

In old commercial Boston down on Milk Street. Gas Lamp. Willis Barnstone. VWA

In old Kentuck in de arternoon. Clare de Kitchen. *Unknown.* BLPA

In One Battle. Amiri Baraka. BPo

In one breath you have consumed. Mohammad Taqi Mir, *tr. by* Ahmed Ali. GoT

In one corner agile incest. Max Ernst. Paul Eluard, *tr. by* Robert Bly. POS

In 100% surefire arsenic. Shake'nbake Ballad. Peter Van Toorn. NOBC

In one morning burned to the ground—the old estate. I Stopped along the Road to Look at the Old House of Lord Minamoto. Michizane, *tr. by* Burton Watson. JLIC-1

In one of these excursions, travelling then/ Through Wales on foot. The Climb to Snowdon. Wordsworth. *Fr.* The Prelude [*or*, Growth of a Poet's Mind]: Conclusion ("It was a close, warm, breezeless summer night"). FaBoRV

(Snowdon Sunrise, The.) FaBoPP

In one of Watteau's pencil sketches. Nude. Daniel Halpern. MAYP

In One Place. Robert Wallace. Psk

In one place, flying clubs. Hsü Wei, *tr. fr. Chinese by* Jonathan Chaves. *Fr.* Inscribed on Paintings for the People of Hangchow. CoBLCP

In one room of the house. The Eve. Howard Schwartz. VWA

In one week we dismantled. Cutting Beetle-Blighted Ponderosa Pine. Jonathan Holden. KS

In only thee, my timid, fleet gazelle. The Timid Gazelle. Kasmuneh. TrJP

In open country the September fields. Harvest. M. D. Anderson. CN

In Orangeburg My Brothers Did. Alfred B. Spellman. BPo; PoBA

In Orbit. Henry Taylor. BXAP

In orchard under the hawthorne. Vergier. *Unknown, tr. by* Ezra Pound. GBL
In Order To. Kenneth Patchen. NaP
In order to perfect all readers. Wall, Cave, and Pillar Statements, after Asôka. Alan Dugan. CoAP
In Order to Say It. Idea Vilariño, *tr. fr. Spanish by* Kate Flores. DMH
In order to wake the living, who sleep. Old Liu's Dawn. Chan Ch'e, *tr. by* Dominic Cheung. IFON
In Orknay. William Fowler. GoTS; OxBS
In other men we faults can spy. The Turkey and the Ant. John Gay. *Fr.* Fables. PBBP
In our cabin we eat breaded oysters and fries. Marriage. Raymond Carver. GeTw
In our content, before the autumn came. Elinor Wylie. *Fr.* One Person, XII. NAAL-2
In our Country, in our Country. The Merry Hay-Makers; [or, Pleasant Pastime between the Young-Men and Maids, in the Pleasant Meadows]. *Unknown.* CoMu
In our Durham County I am sorry for to say. The Durham Lock-out. *Unknown.* CoMu
In our fields, fallow and burdened, in grass and furrow. Christopher Fry. *Fr.* The Boy with a Cart. LiTB
In our house every floor was a wailing wall. My Guardian Angel Stein. Philip Schultz. InPS; KS; MAYP
In Our Manner of Speaking. Kendrick Smithyman. ATNZ
In our old shipwrecked days there was an hour. George Meredith. *Fr.* Modern Love, XVI. BoLoP; NOBVV (Love Dies.) SeCePo
In Our Time. Michael Roberts. WaP
In our town, people live in rows. The Fired Pot. Anna Wickham. FaBoTw; FaBoWP; OxBTC
In Oxford City. *Unknown.* OBET
In Oxford there lived a merchant by trade. The Crafty Farmer. *Unknown.* AmFP; ESPB
In Paco town and in Paco tower. The Ballad of Paco Town. Clinton Scollard. PAH
In pain she bore the son who her embrace. Moses Ibn Ezra, *tr. by* Solomon Solis-Cohen. TrJP
In painting bamboo, the spirit must be transmitted. A Painting of Bamboo by Ni Yün-lin. Yang Chi, *tr. by* Jonathan Chaves. CoBLCP
In pairs/ as if to illustrate their sisterhood. For the Sisters of the Hôtel Dieu. Abraham Moses Klein. SoSe
In Palo Alto. Denis Johnson. NAmP
In Pandora's Box, a silence of almost. The Time Machine. Jon Anderson. AnAn; NAmP
In Panelled Rooms. Ruth Herschberger. LiTA
In paper case. Epitaph on a Dormouse. *Unknown.* OxBChV
In Paradise. Arlo Bates. AA
In paradise the work week is fixed at thirty hours. Report from Paradise. Zbigniew Herbert, *tr. by* Czeslaw Milosz. OBD
In Parenthesis, *sels.* David Jones.
  "And the place of their waiting a long burrow." FaBoMo
  "And to Private Ball it came." OBWVE
  "But sweet sister death has gone debauched today and stalks." OBWP
  "But why is Father Larkin talking to the dead?." PoE
  Five Unmistakable Marks, The. *Fr. pt.* VII. NAEL-2
    "Across upon this undulated board of verdure chequered bright," *sel.* NoAm
  King Pellam's Launde. *Fr.* IV. OAEL-2
    "So thus he sorrowed till it was day," *sel.* NoAM
    "You can hear the silence of it." FaBoMo
In Parliament Square. The Statue. Edith Roseveare. Mes
In part these nightly terrors to dispel. Moonlight. Scattered Clouds. Robert Bloomfield. *Fr.* The Farmer's Boy. OBNC
In parts, through prospects scattered far and near. Birmingham and Wolverhampton. James Woodhouse. *Fr.* The Life and Lucubrations of Crispinus Scriblerus. NOEC
In paschall feast, the end of ancient rite. Of the Blessed Sacrament of the Altar. Robert Southwell. OBEV
In Passing. Gerald Jonas. GrPl; TDD
In pasture where the leaf and wood. The Quest. James Wright. NYBP
In "pastures green"? Not always; sometimes He. He Leadeth Me. *Unknown.* BLRP
In Paths Untrodden. Walt Whitman. NOBA; OxBA
In Patterdale. Wordsworth. *Fr.* The Prelude [or, Growth of a Poet's Mind]: Childhood and School-Time. FaBoRV
In Peblis town sum tyme, as I heard tell. *At. to* John Reid of Stobo. *Fr.* The Thre Prestis of Peblis. OxBS
In Pennsylvania; it's sort of like losing. Another Night on the Porch Swing. Cathleen Quirk. NMM
In Perfect Time. Dinah Livingstone. DT

In Perspective. Robert Graves. OxBSP
In Peterborough Churchyard. Paulus Silentiarius, *tr. fr. Greek.* FaBoEE; NOBL
In petticoat of green. Of Phyllis. William Drummond of Hawthornden. EIL; GN (Phyllis.) GN
In Piam Memoriam. Geoffrey Hill. NePoEA-2; OxBC
In Pilgrim Life Our Rest. Edwin Sandys. AH
In Pilsen. Five Minutes after the Air Raid. Miroslav Holub, *tr. by* Ian Milner *and* George Theiner. OBD
In pious times ere [*or* e'r] priestcraft did begin. Dryden. *Fr.* Absalom and Achitophel, Pt. I. FaBoPV; HAP; NoP; OAEL-1; PoE; SeCV-2
In Piranesi's rarer prints. Prelusive. Herman Melville. *Fr.* Clarel. AmPP
In pity for man's darkening thought. Two Songs from a Play. W. B. Yeats. *Fr.* The Resurrection, II. CMoP; FaBoTw; HAP; LiTB; NOBE; NoP; OAEL-2; PPP; PrIm
In place of melodies, I offer you nothing. My Book. Louise Ackermann, *tr. by* Beth Archer. DMF
In placid hours well-pleased we dream. Art. Herman Melville. AmPP; NAAL-1; NOBA
In Plague Time. Thomas Nashe. *See* Summer's Last Will and Testament: Adieu, Farewell, Earth's Bliss[e].
In Pleasant Lands Have Fallen the Lines. James Flint. AH
In Populated. Lucille Clifton. GeTw
In Portugal, 1912. Alice Meynell. NOCV
In Postures That Call. Oscar Williams. WaP
In Prague. Paul Celan, *tr. fr. German by* Joachim Neugroschel. VWA
In Prague, a rabbi, name of Pelf. The Rabbi. Christian Morgenstern, *tr. by* W. D. Snodgrass *and* Lore Segal. OBD
In Praise of a Beggar's Life. "A. W." EIL; TrGrPo (Song in Praise of a Beggar's Life, A.) OBSC
In Praise of a Contented Mind. *Unknown.* NAEL-1
In Praise of a Cremation Ground. Kataiyan Kannanar, *tr. fr. Tamil by* A. K. Ramanujan. PLW
In Praise of a Girl. Huw Morus, *tr. fr. Welsh by* Gwyn Williams. OBWVE
In Praise of Aed. *Unknown, tr. fr. Old Irish by* Robin Flower. AnIL
In Praise of Ale. *At. to* Thomas Bonham. OBS (Pipe and Can II.) OBEV ("When as the chill charocco blows.") OBEV ("When that the chill charocco blows.") FaBoCh
In Praise of Ale. *At. to* William Stevenson *and also to* John Still. *See* Gammer Gurton's Needle: Back and Side Go Bare, Go Bare.
In Praise of Antonioni. Stephen Holden. NYBP
In Praise of Ben Avon. Brenda G. Macrow. PoSH
In Praise of Beverly. Steve Orlen. MAYP
In Praise of Clothes. Erica Jong. MAYP
In Praise of Cocoa, Cupid's Nightcap. Stanley J. Sharpless. ErPo; FiBHP; NBLV
In Praise of Fidelia. Mildmay Fane, Earl of Westmorland. OxBSP
In Praise of His Daphnis. Sir John Wotton. EIL
In Praise of His Lady. Matthew Grove. *Fr.* Pelops and Hippodamia. EIL
In Praise of His Love. Sir John Wotton. EIL
In Praise of His Loving and Best-beloved Fawnia. Robert Greene. *See* Pandosto: Ah Were She Pitiful.
In Praise of Isabel Pennell. John Skelton. *See* Garlande [*or* Garlands] of Laurell, The: To Mistress [*or* Maystres] Isabell Pennell.
In Praise of Ivy. *Unknown.* MeEL
In Praise of Laudanum. William Harrison. NOEC
In Praise of Limestone. W. H. Auden. CMoP; FaBoPV; FYAP; HAP; MoAB; MoP; NAEL-2; NoAM; NoP; OAEL-2; PPP
In Praise of Llamas. Arthur Guiterman. FiBHP
In Praise of Mary. *Unknown.* MeEL
In Praise of Merit. Mao Wen-hsi, *tr. fr. Chinese by* Lois Fusek. ATF
In Praise of Music in Time of Pestilence. Daryl Hine. OBCV
In Praise of Old Women. Marya Fiamengo. WPOW
In Praise of Owain Gwynedd. Cynddelw Brydydd Mawr, *tr. fr. Welsh by* Joseph P. Clancy. OBWVE
In Praise of Seafaring Men, in Hopes [*or* hope] of Good Fortune. *Unknown, also at. to* Sir Richard Grenville. OBTV; OxBSS
In Praise of Tenby. *Unknown, tr. fr. Welsh by* Joseph P. Clancy. OBWVE; OxBSS
In Praise of the Lowest Line. János Pilinszky, *tr. fr. Hungarian by* Jascha Kessler. FOC
In Praise of the Male Sex, As Seen by Certain Females. Christiana Mariana von Ziegler, *tr. fr. German by* Susan L. Cocalis *and* Gerlinde Geiger. DMG
In Praise of the Sun. "A. W." CTC; OBSC
In Praise of Three Young Men. Lochlann Og O Dalaigh. NOIV

In Praise of Virginity. Hroswitha, *tr. fr. Latin* by John Dillon. PBWP

In Praise of Water-Gruel. Matthew Green. *Fr.* The Spleen. FaBoUs

In Praise of Wisdom. Solomon ibn Gabirol, *tr. fr. Hebrew* by Solomon Solis-Cohen. TrJP

In Praise of Wyatt's Psalms. Earl of Surrey. AAS; SiPS

In pride of May. *Unknown.* OBSC

In Prison. Rai Mikisaburo, *tr. fr. Chinese* by Burton Watson. JLIC-2

In Prison. Ray Riley Smith. PWR

In Procession. Robert Graves. TwCP

In Progress. Christina Rossetti. BoWoP; NAEL-2; WPE

In Prospect Street, outside the Splendid Bar. Sweeney to Mrs. Porter in the Spring. L. E. Sissman. NYBP

In protest/ against government policies. Peter Henisch, *tr.* by Beth Bjorklund. CoAuP

In Puerto Rico in 1939 my mother has leaned. Gardenias. Mark Doty. NAmP

In Puna's fragrant glades. Puna's Fragrant Glades. Princess Lili'u-o-ka-lani, *tr.* by S. H. Elbert *and* N. Mahoe. WTO

In purest song one plays the constant fool. Infirmity. Theodore Roethke. CoAP; NAAL-2; NYBP

In Puritan New England a year had passed away. The First Thanksgiving Day. Alice Williams Brotherton. OHIP

In Pusseyville, where pussies live. Cats and Dogs. Howard Moss. OBAL

In Queen Victoria's early days. The New Vicar of Bray. Colin Ellis. NOBL

In quietness and confidence. A Hymn of Trust. Nettie M. Sargent. BLRP

In Railway Halls. Stephen Spender. FaBoMo

In Rain. Wendell Berry. GeTw

In Rainy September. Robert Bly. CAPP

In Rama. George Alfred Townsend. AA

In re Solomon Warshawer. A. M. Klein. MoCV

In Reading Gaol by Reading Town. Oscar Wilde. *Fr.* The Ballad of Reading Gaol. FaFP; LiTB

In red wool jacket and earflaps. The Week-End Indian. Anita Endrezze Probst. VoR

In Reference to Her Children, 23 June, 1656. Anne Bradstreet. BoWoP; TAP

In Reply ("Don't keep your heart from resenting me"). Lady Izumi, *tr. fr. Japanese* by Hiroaki Sato. *Fr.* Fifty-one Tanka. FCEI

In Reply ("I don't think you are like everyone else"). Lady Izumi, *tr. fr. Japanese* by Hiroaki Sato. *Fr.* Fifty-one Tanka. FCEI

In Reply to Questions. T'ai-shang, *tr. fr. Chinese* by Burton Watson. CoBCP

In Reply When Lesser Officials of Chung-tu Brought a Pot of Wine and Two Fish to My Inn as Gifts. Li Po, *tr. fr. Chinese* by Burton Watson. CoBCP

In Respect of the Elderly. Thomas Peacock. VoR

In Respectful Memory of Mr. Yarker, *sel.* John Close. "And have we lost another friend?" FaBoCo

In Response to a Rumor That the Oldest Whorehouse in Wheeling, West Virginia, Has Been Condemned. James Wright. CAPP; CoAP; NNaP; NoAM; TW

In Response to Executive Order 9066: All Americans of Japanese Descent Must Report to Relocation Centers. Dwight Okita. BrSi

In restaurants we argue. They Eat Out. Margaret Atwood. NeAC; NoAM; NoP

In Retrospect. Maya Angelou. UnAS

In Retrospect. Richard Kenney. *Fr.* The Hours of the Day. Son

In revel and carousing. Theodosia Burr: The Wrecker's Story. John Williamson Palmer. PAH

In Richard's days, when lost his pastur'd plain. The Country Justice. John Langhorne. LaA

In right I have no power to live. The Soul's Bitter Cry. *Unknown.* WGRP

In Romney Marsh. John Davidson. EBVV; FaBoPP; GoTS; OxBTC

In rosy-fingered dawn they go. Jersey Cattle. Ralph Nixon Currey. OxBTC

In round round rooms of our wanderings. Hiroshima Exit. Joy Kogawa. BrSi

In Ruin Reconciled. Aubrey Thomas De Vere. BIrV

In ruling well what guerdon? Life runs low. The Two Old Kings. John Byrne Leicester Warren, 3rd Baron De Tabley. OBEV

In sable weeds the beaux and belles appear. The Mourners. Bevil Higgons. APAS

In sad and ashy weeds I sigh. Elegy on the Death of Her Husband. Anne Howard. WPE

In sad dissolution rust quotations. Dissolution. Jacob Glatstein, *tr. by* Benjamin *and* Barbara Harshav. AYP

In sad revery. Tameko, *tr.* by Steven D. Carter. WFTW

In Saginaw, in Saginaw. The Saginaw Song. Theodore Roethke. NBLV; RB

In Sakurada quarters, dawn breaking, scrambling into his clothes. New Year's Day. Rai San'yo, *tr.* by Burton Watson. JLIC-2

In Salem. Lucille Clifton. AmPA

In Salem seasick spindrift drifts or skips. Salem. Robert Lowell. AiP; NePoEA; Son

In San Francisco, spring was not a season. Letter from Vermont. Ellen Bryant Voigt. AnAn

In San Jose Costa Rica where I now live. Song of Wandering Times. Rosario Murillo, *tr.* by Magaly Fernández. Vol

In San Juan I wonder how my home is. I Wonder How My Home Is. *Unknown, tr.* by H. J. Spinden. WTO

In Santa Croce. Franco Fortini, *tr. fr. Italian* by Lawrence R. Smith. NItP

In Santa Maria del Popolo. Thom Gunn. CMoP; FaBoMo; GTBS-P; NePoEA-2; OxBC; PoE; QFR

In Saram. John Cotton. SCAP

In Saturday Market, there's eggs a-plenty. Saturday Market. Charlotte Mew. *Fr.* Saturday Market. FaPON

In Saturn's reign, at Nature's early birth. Juvenal, *tr. fr. Latin* by Dryden. *Fr.* Satires, VI. OAEL-1; OBSV; OBVE

In Scarlet town, where I was born [*or* bound]. Barbara Allen. *Unknown.* FaFP

    (Barbara Allen's Cruelty.) OBEV

    (Bonny Barbara Allan.) TrGrPo

In scenes paternal, not beheld through years. Anna Seward. *Fr.* Eyam. NOEC

In schomer, when the leves spryng. Robin Hood and the Potter. *Unknown.* ESPB

In School-Days. Whittier. AA; AnAmPo; BLPA; FaBoBe; FaPON; FPL; OBCA; OxBChV

In school I was taught the names. Columbus Day. Jimmie Durham. HATNAP

In Scorching Time. Alex Stevens. KS

In Scotia so fair, 'tis a custom they say. To Lydia, with a Coloured Egg, on Easter Monday. John Jones. FaBoUs

In Scotland there was a babie born. Hind Horn. *Unknown.* ESPB

In Scotland town where I was borned. Hind Horn. *Unknown.* AmFP

In Scotland, where the porridge grows. Of the Stalking of the Stag. Sir Owen Seaman. CenHV

In sea-cold Lyonesse. Sunk Lyonesse. Walter de la Mare. FaBoCh; LiTM

In screit place, this hindir nicht. The Man of Valour to His Fair Lady. William Dunbar. MeEL

In secret/ be quiet say nothing. Pablo Picasso, *tr.* by David Gascoyne. EAS

In secret place where once I stood. The Flesh and the Spirit. Anne Bradstreet. AmPP; AnAmPo; LiTA; NAAL-1; NOBA; OxBA; SCAP; TAP

In seed time learn, in harvest teach, in winter enjoy. Blake. *Fr.* The Marriage of Heaven and Hell. FF

    (Proverbs of Hell.) NAEL-2

In semi-darkness embers glimmer. By the Fireside. A. A. Fet, *tr.* by Alan Myers. AAA

In sensuous coil. Kings. *Unknown, tr. fr. Sanskrit* by Arthur Ryder. *Fr.* The Panchatantra. AWP

In Sepia. Jon Anderson. NAmP; PoA

In September by San Ubaldo more coyotes were seen. Ecology. Ernesto Cardenal, *tr.* by Alejandro Murguía. Vol

In 728, Longing for His Deceased Wife. Tabito. *Fr.* Manyo Shu. FCEI

In seventeen hundred and forty-four. The Kilruddery Hunt. Thomas Mozeen. BIrV

In seventeen hundred and seventy-five. The Bombardment of Bristol. *Unknown.* PAH

In Shadow. Hart Crane. NOBA

In shadowy calm the boat. Hope. Phillips Stewart. CaP

In Shaka's days we lived well. Those Were the Days. *Zulu Oral Tradition, tr.* by H. Tracey. WTO

In shantung suits we whites are cool. The Devil-Dancers. William Plomer. PeSA

In shaping the snow into blossoms. "Ping Hsin," *tr. fr. Chinese* by Kai-yu Hsu. *Fr.* Spring Waters. BoWoP; WPOW

In shards the sylvan vases lie. The Ravaged Villa. Herman Melville. CTC; NOBA; PoEL-5

In Sherwood lived stout Robin Hood. *Unknown.* OBSC

In shining groups, each stem a pearly ray. Ghost-Flowers. Mary Thacher Higginson. AA; WeW

In Siberia's wastes. Siberia. James Clarence Mangan. BIrV; NOBVV; NOIV

In Sickness Written Soon after the Author's Coming to Live in Ireland, upon the Queen's Death, October 1714. Swift. NOEC

In signe of favor stedfast still. To His Darrest Freind. John Steward of Baldynnis. OxBS

In silence. Echo of Mandela. Zindzi Mandela. WMBCH

In silence I lie. Buddha's Death Day: February 15, 1815. Issa, *tr. fr. Japanese by* Nobuyuki Yuasa. *Fr.* Oraga Haru. OFD

In silence I must take my seat. Table Rules for Little Folk[s]. *Unknown.* FaBoUs; OxBChV

In silence the heart raves. It utters words. True Love. Robert Penn Warren. BLA

In silent gaze the tuneful choir among. Stanzas to Mr. Bentley. Thomas Gray. NoP

In silent horror o'er the desert-waste. Persian Eclogue the Second. William Collins. FL

In silent night, when rest I took. Some Verses upon the Burning of Our House, July 10th, 1666. Anne Bradstreet. NOBA; TAP
(Here Follow[e]s Some Verses upon the Burning of Our House.) AIP; BoWoP; NAAL-1; NoP; SCAP
(Upon the Burning of Our House, July 10th, 1666.) AnAmPo; OxBA; WPE

In silk robes so spotless. *Unknown, tr. by* Arthur Waley. BoS

In simmer, whan aa sorts foregether. Embro to the Ploy. Robert Garioch. OxBS

In sixteen hundred and sixty-six. *Unknown.* FaBoUs

In 62 the Starving Seabirds Reached the Center of Lima. Antonio Cisneros, *tr. fr. Spanish by* Ena Hollis *and* David Tipton. Per

In skins of the young lamb. *Unknown, tr. by* Arthur Waley. BoS

In Sleep. Richard Burton. AA

In Sleep. Alice Meynell. BrRo

In sleep when an old man's body is no longer aware of its boundaries. A Journey through the Moonlight. Russell Edson. LCAP

In Sligo the country was soft; there were turkeys. Sligo and Mayo. Louis MacNeice. FaBoPP

In slow procession, one by one, silently. From Far Away. Delmira Agustini, *tr. by* D. M. Pettinella. PBWP

In slumbers of midnight the sailor-boy lay. The Mariner's Dream. William Dimond. BeLS

In small backyards old men's long underwear. The Patricians. Douglas Dunn. OxBC

In small green cup an acorn grew. The Acorn. *Unknown.* BoTP

In Snow. H. Leivick, *tr. fr. Yiddish by* Benjamin *and* Barbara Harshav. AYP

In snow veined with his blood and the white bruise. Snow Owl. Dave Smith. AnAn

In so far as we are filled. Asadullah Khan Ghalib, *tr. by* Ahmed Ali. GoT

In sober mornings, doe [*or* do] not thou reherse [*or* rehearse]. When He Would Have His Verses Read. Robert Herrick. CaPo; NOBE; OBS; SeCV-1

In Sobieski's Shield. Edwin Morgan. BWV

In Solitary Confinement, Sea Point Police Cells. C. J. Driver. PeSA

In some far field my true-love lies. Epitaph on a Soldier. Joyce Barton. CN

In some far-off. Saigyo, *tr. fr. Japanese by* Burton Watson. *Fr.* Sixty-four Tanka. FCEI

In some recumbent, poised lagoon. The Axeltree. Gene Van Troyer. BWV

In Some Seer's Cloud Car. Christopher Middleton. TwCP

In some unused lagoon, some nameless bay. The Dismantled Ship. Walt Whitman. AmPP; MOS; NoP; OxBA

In some versions of the universe the stars. Stars. Howard Moss. AnAn

In Some Way or Other the Lord Will Provide. Mrs. M. A. W Cook. AH

In somer when the shawes be sheyne. May in the Green-Wood. *Unknown.* OBEV

In somer, when the shawes be sheyne. Robin Hood and the Monk. *Unknown.* ESPB; FaBoBa; OBNV, *abr.*

In something you have written in school, you say. Serpent Knowledge. Robert Pinsky. *Fr.* An Explanation of America. NPGG

In Sorrow. Thomas Hastings. AA

In sour seasons, in diff-/icult wind. Dislike of Tasks. Richmond Lattimore. SaC

In South Oregon the Klamath play. The Woyi. Lew Blockcolski. VoR

In Spain, where the courtly Castilian hidalgo twangs lightly. Carmen. Newman Levy. FiBHP

In Spanish he whispers there is no time left. The Visitor. Carolyn Forché. FYAP

In Sparkhill buried lies that man of mark. Local Note. Arthur Guiterman. NBLV

In Sparta. C. P. Cavafy, *tr. fr. Greek by* Edmund Keeley *and* Philip Sherrard. VMG

In Spite. Malka Heifetz Tussman, *tr. fr. Yiddish by* Kathryn Hellerstein. AYP

In spite of all the learned have said. The Indian Burying Ground. Philip Freneau. AA; AmPP; AnAmPo; HAP; HeIP; LiTA; NAAL-1; NOBA; NoP; OBD, *abr.*; OxBA; PoEL-4; PoLF; TAP

In spite of all the solemn-hearted fools. The Joy of Love. Allan Dowling. ErPo

In Spite of All This Much Needed Thunder. Zack Gilbert. PoNe

In Spite of His Dangling Pronoun. Lyn Lifshin. IHMS

In spite of ice, in spite of snow. On Observing a Large Red-Streak Apple. Philip Freneau. NAAL-1

In spite of love. Family Pictures. Mervyn Morris. PBCV

In spite of Rice, in spite of Wheat. Epigram on the Poor of Boston Being Employed in Paving the Streets, 1774. *Unknown.* PAH

In spite of sun. Everything Is Normal in Our Courtyard. Claribel Alegría, *tr. by* Barbara Paschke *and* David Volpendesta. Vol

In spite of what the quarrymen said. Clearsightedness. Andrew Salkey. PBCV

In spots/ it is warm enough. Ken Belford. NeAC

In spring and fall there are many fine days. Moving House ("In spring and fall there are many days"). T'ao Ch'ien, *tr. by* Burton Watson. CoBCP

In spring I came to the Chao-yang, now spring comes again. Manifold Little Hills. Wei Chuang, *tr. by* Lois Fusek. ATF

In Spring I look gay. *Unknown.* BoTP; OxNR

In spring if there are dogs they will bark. Ballade of Sayings. W. S. Merwin. NNaP

In Spring of the Year *Ping-shen, sels.* Ch'ien Ch'ien-i, *tr. fr. Chinese by* Jonathan Chaves.
"Pavilions of dance, terraces of song." CoBLCP
"Willow catkins beyond the garden wait for evening tides." CoBLCP

In spring they croak. Onitsura, *tr. fr. Japanese by* Hiroaki Sato. *Fr.* Twenty-three Hokku. FCEI

In spring too, what first stands out is Mount Otowa. Princess Shikishi, *tr. fr. Japanese by* Hiroaki Sato. *Fr.* Seventy-eight Tanka. FCEI

In spring when everything. Desire. Isaac de Botton, *tr. by* Stephen Levy. VWA

In spring when maple buds are red. Daylight Saving Time. Phyllis McGinley. RHPC

In Springtime. Samuel Taylor Coleridge. *See* All nature seems at work.

In Springtime. Kipling. BrPo

In springtime/ when the plum trees bloom. Tsurayuki, *tr. fr. Japanese by* Burton Watson. *Fr.* Kokin Shu. FCEI

In Staffordshire I was born. The Posy of Thyme. *Unknown.* OBET

In State, *sel.* Forceythe Willson.
"O Keeper of the Sacred Key." AA

In stature, the Manlet was dwarfish. The Manlet. "Lewis Carroll." BXAP; Par
(Little Man That Had a Little Gun, The.) FaBoNo

In stone settlements when the moon is stone. Peter Levi. EBEV; TOF

In streets, among the rocks of time and weather. The Mountains. Louis Dudek. CaP

In streets east, streets west, they expound the Buddhist canon. The Girl of Mt. Hua. Han Yü, *tr. by* Burton Watson. CoBCP

In Such a Night. Shakespeare. *See* Merchant of Venice, The.

In such a night, when every louder wind. A Nocturnal Reverie. Countess of Winchilsea. EBEV; GoTL; NAEL-1; NOEC; NoP; PBWP; PoE; PoEL-3; SeCePo; WPE

In such an armor he may rise and raid. Bronzeville Man with a Belt in the Back. Gwendolyn Brooks. IDB; PoBA

In such luxurious plentie of all pleasure. Spenser. *Fr.* The Faerie Queene, IV, 10. OAEL-1

In Suffolk. George Crabbe. *See* How stately stand yon pines upon the hill.

In summer elms are made for me. Dilemma of the Elm. Genevieve Taggard. MoAmPo

In summer I am very glad. Playgrounds. L. Alma Tadema. BoTP

In Summer, in the open air. Summer Sabbath. Jessie E. Sampter. TrJP

In summer this town is full of rebels. The Cannery. Lucien Stryk. CAPP

In summer time, when leaves grew green and birds were singing. King Edward the Fourth and a Tanner of Tamworth. *Unknown.* ESPB

In summer time, when leaves grow green/ Down a down a down. Robin Hood and the Tinker. *Unknown.* ESPB

In summer time when leaves grow green/ And birds sit on the tree. Under the Greenwood Tree. *Unknown.* GBP

In summer time, when leaves grow green and flowers are fresh and gay. Robin Hood and the Curtal Friar. *Unknown.* ESPB

In summer time, when leaves grow green, when they doe grow both green and long. The Noble Fisherman; or, Robin Hood's Preferment. *Unknown.* ESPB

In summer, when the days were long. Summer Days. Wathen Mark Wilks Call. EBVV
In summer, when the grass is thick, if mother has the time. The Fairy Book. Norman Gale. OHIP
In summer when the hills are blond. January. Geoffrey Dutton. PoAu-2
In summer when the woods are green. In the Fair Forest. *Unknown.* BoTP
In summer's heat, and mid-time of the day. Corinnae Concubitus. Ovid, *tr. fr. Latin by* Christopher Marlowe. *Fr.* Amores. EBEV; GBL; OBVE
(Elegy: "In summer's heat and mid-time of the day.") BoLoP
In summer's mellow midnight. The Night Wind. Emily Brontë. ChER; ChTr; EBVV; NAEL-2; TEP
In summertime it was a paradise. The Seaside: In and Out of the Season. Charles Tennyson Turner. Son
In summertime on Bredon. Bredon Hill. A. E. Housman. *Fr.* A Shropshire Lad, XXI. BrPo; EBVV; FaBoPP; MoAB; MoBrPo; NAEL-2; SoSe
In sun and snow slumbers. Photo at the Bridge. Dan Pagis, *tr. by* Warren Bargad *and* Stanley F. Chyet. IP
In sunburnt parks where Sundays lie. Cobb Would Have Caught It. Robert Fitzgerald. GrPl; HAP; InvP; SD; TwCP; WeW
In sunlight on the Avenue. Galway Kinnell. *Fr.* The Avenue Bearing the Initial of Christ into the New World. LiTM
In sunlight raindrops look like dew. Battle of Similes. *Malay Oral Tradition, tr. by* R. J. Wilkinson *and* R. O. Winstedt. WTO
In Sylvia Plath Country. Erica Jong. IHMS
In t' other hundred, o'er yon swarthy moor. The Country Curate. Henry Taylor. NOEC
In taking of my lonely walk on a cold and wintry day. The Collier Lad's Lament. *Unknown.* OBET
In talking. To a Lady Holding the Floor. Mildred Weston. FiBHP
In Tall Grass. Carl Sandburg. PoA
In T'ang China Longing for Home. Bensho, *tr. fr. Chinese by* Burton Watson. JLIC-1
In tangled wreaths, in clustered gleaming stars. Yellow Jessamine. Constance Fenimore Woolson. AA
In Taurus was the sun and flowery Spring. Ganymede and Helen. *Unknown.* PeHV
In tears to her mother poor Harriet came. The Disappointment. Jane Taylor. FaBoUs
In Teesdale. Andrew Young. FaBoPP; OxBSP
In temporary pain. The New God. Witter Bynner. *Fr.* The New World. WGRP
In Temptation. Charles Wesley. *See* Jesus, Lover of My Soul.
In ten thousand pine trees. A Painting of People Strolling through a Pine Forest. Hsü Wei, *tr. by* Jonathan Chaves. CoBLCP
In tender May when the sweet laugh of Christ. The Puritan. Karl Shapiro. MoAmPo
In Tenebris, *sels.* Thomas Hardy. LiTB; NOBE; NoP; PrIm; SeCePo
"There have been times when I well might have passed and the ending have come." *Fr.* III. OAEL-2
"When the clouds' swoln bosoms echo back the shouts of the many and strong." *Fr.* II. BrPo; CMoP; LiTM; NoAM; OxBTC
"Wintertime nighs." *Fr.* I. NoAM; OAEL-2
In Tennessee. Ted Kooser. SoTCo
In Tennessee once the [heart of the] campfire glowed. Youthful Picnic Long Ago: Sad Ballad on Box. Robert Penn Warren. BLA
(Recollection Long Ago: Sad Music.) SV
In Tennessee, The dogwood tree. Tennessee. Francis Brooks. *Fr.* Intaglios. AA
In terms of some green myth, sailing or drowning. Sailing or Drowning. Allen Curnow. ATNZ
In terror the aches. Shechem. David Shevin. VWA
In Tesla's Laboratory. Robert Underwood Johnson. AA
In Texas Grass. Quincy Troupe. PoBA
In Thankfull Remembrance for My Dear Husband's Safe Arrivall Sept. 3, 1662. Anne Bradstreet. TrPWD
In that ago when being was believing. The History of Truth. W. H. Auden. FaBoMo
In that ancient time—in eternity. Words Spoken by Pasternak during a Bombing. Bella Akhmadulina, *tr. by* Jean Valentine *and* Olga Carlisle. BoWoP
In that awful hour when I'm on my deathbed. Repentance. Brendan Behan, *tr. by* Ulick O'Conner. TIRV
In that bad year and city of your birth. To the New World. Randall Jarrell. CAPP
(For an Emigrant.) OxBA
In that country of thresholds we move like vandals. Papermill Graveyard. Ben Belitt. NYBP

In that country the animals. The Animals in That Country. Margaret Atwood. NoAM; NoP
In that dark world the only light. Tick Picking in the Quetico. Don Johnson. MAYP
In that day I had hoped for a pair of boots to guard my feet on the terrible trek. My Head on My Shoulders. Jeremy Ingalls. GoYe
In that desolate land and lone. The Revenge of Rain-in-the-Face. Longfellow. PAH
In that fair land where slope and plain. The Maiden of the Smile. Alfred Austin. TEP
In that hotel my life. The Illumination. Stanley Kunitz. TAP
In that I have so greatly failed thee, Lord. So Little and So Much. John Oxenham. BLRP
In that land all is and nothing's ought. Neither Here nor There. W. R. Rodgers. LiTB; LiTM; MoAB; MoBrPo
In that little ugly hut. *Unknown. Fr.* Manyo Shu. FCEI
In that lost Caucasian garden. The Naming of the Beasts. Francis Sparshott. NIP; NOBC
In that most wretched hovel. *Unknown. Fr.* Manyo Shu. Ma
In that November off Tehuantepec. Sea Surface Full of Clouds. Wallace Stevens. AmPP; CMoP; MoAB; MoAmPo; MOS; VGW
In that, O Queen of queens, thy birth was free. To Our Blessed Lady. Henry Constable. ACP; OBSC
In that photograph of the child and her mother there is a side space. Silence. Susan Griffin. *Fr.* Woman and Nature. NPGG
In that Poussin the clouds are like golden tea. Poussin. Louis MacNeice. EyDe
In that proud party, which her so goodley graceth. Spenser. *Fr.* Amoretti, XIII. Son
In that rapacious littoral now slaked by sea. Shore Birds. Vi Gale. GoYe
In that same gardin all the goodly flowres. Spenser. *Fr.* The Faerie Queene: The Garden of Adonis. NOBE
In that so sudden summer storm they tried. Summer Storm. Louis Simpson. ErPo; OxBC
In that soft mid-land where the breezes bear. Rodney's Ride. *Unknown.* PAH
In that strident summer of battle. Hone Tuwhare. ATNZ
In that town were hard spaces. Town I Left. Helen Sorrells. IHMS
In that tribe the priests are chosen. Finders Keepers. Donald Finkel. VWA
In the/ In the Quarter. Cultural Exchange. Langston Hughes. PoNe
In the Absence of Bliss. Maxine W. Kumin. NoAM
In the absence of the great wine-drinkers the world. Asadullah Khan Ghalib, *tr. by* Ahmed Ali. GoT
In the afternoon on the thirteenth. Crazy Movie. Gregorio Barrios, *tr. by* Toni Empringham. FIA
In the afternoon sun. Beams. Audre Lorde. NoAM
In the Aging City. Fadwa Tuqan, *tr. fr. Arabic by* Patricia Alanah Byrne, Salma Khadra Jayyusi, *and* Naomi Shihab Nye. MAP
In the air that limps between seashells. A Hot Evening. Sa'di Yusuf, *tr. by* Lena Jayyusi *and* Naomi Shihab Nye. MAP
In the air there are no coral-/ Reefs or ambergris. Duncan Campbell Scott
In the Akitsu Dale of Yoshinu. Akahito. *Fr.* Manyo Shu. Ma
In the alley. Snow Print Two: Hieroglyphics. B. J. Ebensen. TSS
In the almost sweet autumn veiled by mallow. Maneuvers. Nelo Risi, *tr. by* Lawrence R. Smith. NItP
In the America of the dream. Lonesome Dream. Lisel Mueller. CoAP
In the American Tree. Kit Robinson. IAT
In the Amorite City. Haim Guri, *tr. fr. Hebrew by* Warren Bargad *and* Stanley F. Chyet. IP
In the *Analects* Confucius says. Portoncini dei Morti. Daniel Halpern. MAYP
In the Ancient Manner. Chao Meng-fu, *tr. fr. Chinese by* Jonathan Chaves. CoBLCP
In the antique forest dreary. Rhyme of the Antique Forest. Henrietta Cordelia Ray. CBWP-3
In the April Rain. Mary Anderson. BoTP
In the Arab House. Al-Munsif al-Wahaybi, *tr. fr. Arabic by* Salma Khadra Jayyusi *and* Naomi Shihab Nye. MAP
In the Arab Maghreb. Badr Shakir al-Sayyab, *tr. fr. Arabic by* Lena Jayyusi *and* Christopher Middleton. MAP
In the Arc of Your Mallet. Jalal ed-Din Rumi, *tr. fr. Persian by* John Moyne *and* Coleman Barks. UnAS
In the Army. Fujita Koshiro, *tr. fr. Chinese by* Burton Watson. JLIC-2
In the attention it pays to each detail. Love. Kelly Cherry. CRP
In the Attic. Donald Justice. SM
In the attic, at night, a poor man sits. Moishe Kulbak, *tr. fr. Yiddish by* Leonard Wolf. *Fr.* Songs of a Poor Man. PeBMYV
In the autumn dusk a woman. Buson, *tr. fr. Japanese by* Hiroaki Sato. *Fr.* Eighty-seven Hokku. FCEI

In the autumn paddies, the roof mats for the makeshift. Teika, *tr. fr. Japanese by* Hiroaki Sato. *Fr.* A Compendium of Good Tanka. FCEI

In the autumn wind a beggar. Issa, *tr. fr. Japanese by* Hiroaki Sato. *Fr.* Forty-four Hokku. FCEI

In the Aztec design God crowds. Ultimate Problems. William Stafford. NU

In the back bedroom, laughing when you pull. First Time: 1950. Honor Moore. GLP

In the back streets of a starport city. The Star Drifter Grounded. Bruce Boston. BWV

In the Backs. Frances Cornford. BrRo

In the Backs. James Kenneth Stephen. NOBVV

In the bad old days a bewigged old Squire. Wigs and Beards. Robert Graves. NOBL

In the Badlands. David Wagoner. UnPo

In the Baggage Room at Greyhound. Allen Ginsberg. NaP; NoP

In the barn the tenant cock. Morning. John Cunningham. NOEC

In the Barrio. Alurista, *tr. fr. Spanish by* Toni Empringham. FIA

In the basement my mother tended. Translations. P. Y. Ikeda. BrSi

In the Basement of the Goodwill Store. Ted Kooser. GOYP

In the Bavarian steeple, on the hour. The Spire. Ellen B. Voigt. NoAM

In the Bay. Arthur Symons. *Fr.* Amorix Exsul, III. OBNC; PBBP

In the bay of Matsuho of Awaji Island. Kasa no Kanamura. *Fr.* Manyo Shu. FCEI

In the Bay of Naniwa. *Unknown. Fr.* Manyo Shu. PeBJV

In the Bayou. Don Marquis. AmFN

In the Bazaars of Hyderabad. Sarojini Naidu. FaPON

In the Beach House. Anne Sexton. PPP

In the beautiful woman. *Unknown, tr. by* Geoffrey Bownas *and* Anthony Thwaite. PeBJV

In the beer-garden with its drowsy ivy-leaves. We Just Sit About Quietly. Mihály Ladányi, *tr. by* Edwin Morgan. MHuP

In the Beginning. Rachel Fishman, *tr. fr. Yiddish by* Gabriel Levin. VWA

In the Beginning. Harriet Monroe. AA

In the Beginning. Jenny Lind Porter. GoYe

In the Beginning. Valerie Sinason. BrRo

In the Beginning. Sándor Weöres, *tr. fr. Hungarian by* Jascha Kessler. FOC

In the beginning. Testament. Lucille Clifton. GeTw

In the beginning, at every step, he turned. The Sickness of Adam. Karl Shapiro. *Fr.* Adam and Eve. CRP; MoAB

In the beginning God created the heaven and the earth. Bible, *O.T. Fr.* Genesis. ImOP, I: 1-13; NAWM-1, I-IV.

In the beginning, God, the great schoolmaster. The Autograph on the Soul. Adah Isaacs Menken. CBWP-1

In the beginning he merely marked. West Coast Indian. George Clutesi. HATNAP

In the beginning, I really did not know what was happening. In Memory of My Forever-Gone Nineteenth Year. Tu Yeh, *tr. by* Dominic Cheung. IFON

In the beginning I stood by the window. Windows in Providence. Aliki Barnstone. BoWoP

In the Beginning My Mother Screeched. Ya'akov Beser, *tr. fr. Hebrew by* Bernhard Frank. MHeP

In the beginning was the desert. The Desert. Al-Munsif al-Wahaybi, *tr. by* Salma Khadra Jayyusi *and* Naomi Shihab Nye. MAP

In the beginning there were transports. Genesis. Jules Alan Wein. TrJP

In the Beginning Was a Word. Robert Graves. PoA

In the Beginning Was the. Lee Murchison. SD

In the beginning was the air. Memory Air. Charles Dobzynski, *tr. by* Anita Barrows. VWA

In the Beginning Was the Bird. Henry Treece. LiTB; WaP

In the beginning was the tune. A. Leyeles, *tr. by* Benjamin *and* Barbara Harshav. AYP

In the beginning was the Word. The Word. Bible, *N.T. Fr.* St. John, I: 1-5. TrGrPo

In the beginning, when green came on the pasture. In the Beginning. Jenny Lind Porter. GoYe

In the bell toll of a clang. Salt. Ruth Stone. NMM

In the bend of your mouth soft murder. Lion. May Swenson. LiTM; SoSe

In the big room my father stands. Petrified Minute. Zoltán Zelk, *tr. by* Barbara Howes. MHuP

In the bird scream and whistle. Natalya Gorbanevskaya, *tr. by* Daniel Weissbort. OV

In the Bistro. Gwen Harwood. FaBoWP

In the black forest. Song of the Trees of the Black Forest. Edmond Jabès, *tr. by* Anthony Rudolf. VWA

In the black winter morning. Bereft. Thomas Hardy. BoLoP; NoAM

In the blackness. Narihira, *tr. by* Geoffrey Bownas *and* Anthony Thwaite. PeBJV

In the blasts of wind. Autumn Wind. Akera Kanko, *tr. by* Burton Watson. FCEI

In the bleak mid-winter. Christina Rossetti. InPS; NOBVV

In the blizzard. From the Spotted Night. Ray A. Young Bear. HATNAP

In the Blood. Gerald Costanzo. SoTCo

In the blood-stained warmth of sties. Celebration of the Nadir. János Pilinszky, *tr. by* William Jay Smith. MHuP

In the blossom-land Japan. An Old Song. "Yehoash," *tr. by* Marie Syrkin. AWP

In the bloud of Adam death was taken. Charm: Bleeding. *Unknown.* FaBoUs

In the blue distance. Nelly Sachs, *tr. by* Ruth *and* Matthew Mead. BoWoP; OV

In the blue eye of the medievalist there is a cart in the road. Another November. Stanley Plumly. AnAn; LCAP

In the blue-green shadows. On a Landscape by Myself. Yün Shou-p'ing, *tr. by* Jonathan Chaves. CoBLCP

In the blue hubbub of the same-through-wealth sky. Geography. Kenneth Koch. NoAM

In the blue night. Pine Tree Tops. Gary Snyder. NOBA; Prf

In the bluebell forest. Bluebells. Olive Enoch. BoTP

In the blurring low-blood-pressure. The Judgment. Kathleen Spivack. BoWoP

In the book of the iron angels there is nothing. Of the Beloved Caravan. Conny Hannes Meyer, *tr. by* Herbert Kuhner. VWA

In the *Boston Sunday Herald* just three lines. To an American Poet Just Dead. Richard Wilbur. HCAP; NBLV; NoP

In the bowl of buildings alias the back yard. Milk at the Bottom of the Sea. Oscar Williams. LiTA

In the bramble bush shelley slowly eats a lark's heart. Hot Day at the Races. Tom Raworth. EAS

In the Breeze. Boris Pasternak, *tr. fr. Russian by* C. M. Bowra. TrJP

In the bright bay of your morning, O God. Claire Goll, *tr. by* Babette Deutsch *and* Avram Yarmolinsky. TrJP

In the bright broad Swiss glare I stand listening. Recessional. Thomas MacGreevy. CIP

In the broad dawn sky. Ietaka, *tr. by* Steven D. Carter. WFTW

In the broken light, in owl weather. Colloquy. Weldon Kees. NaP; NYBP

In the brothel. Matsumoto Takashi, *tr. by* Geoffrey Bownas *and* Anthony Thwaite. PeBJV

In the brushwood field of Ina. Ina Field. Kagura, *tr. by* Hiroaki Sato. FCEI

In the burned-/ out highway. Beer Bottle. Ted Kooser. SM

In the Cabinet. Shlomo Vinner, *tr. by* Laya Firestone *and* Howard Schwartz. VWA

In the cafe, the chandelier hangs from the ceiling. Spain, 1929. Ai. *Fr.* He Kept On Burning, I. AnAn

In the Cage. Robert Lowell. FF; NOBA; SM; Son

In the California autumnal scene. Autumn in California. Charles West. SoTCo

In the calm of the autumn river, mist rises on the Hsiang. Immortal at the River. Chang Pi, *tr. by* Lois Fusek. ATF

In the candlelight in my hand. Buson, *tr. fr. Japanese by* Hiroaki Sato. *Fr.* Eighty-seven Hokku. FCEI

In the cantina. At the Cantina. Gary Soto. MAYP

In the Canyon of Echo, there's a railroad begun. Echo Canyon. *Unknown.* AmFP

In the capital. Kenko, *tr. by* Steven D. Carter. WFTW

In the capital for a short stay. Tune: Full River Red. Ch'iu Chin, *tr. by* Pao Chia-lin. WFTU

In the capital is the one I love, like. Narihira, *tr. by* Geoffrey Bownas *and* Anthony Thwaite. PeBJV

In the Carolinas. Wallace Stevens. VGW

In the Case of Lobsters. Petra von Morstein, *tr. fr. German by* Rosemarie Waldrop. BoWoP

In the casket a corpse of wicker. The Cry That Kills the Senses: Meditation after a Nightmare. Susan Tichy. ER

In the Cathedral. Patricia Beer. OxBC

In the Cathedral Close. Edward Dowden. EBVV

In the cathedral the acolytes are praying. The Habeas Corpus Blues. Conrad Aiken. NYBP

In the cave with a long-ago flare. Painters. Muriel Rukeyser. EyDe

In the cedar canoe gliding and paddling. Geese Gone Beyond. Gary Snyder. NoAM

In the Cellars. Jiri Gold, *tr. fr. Czech by* Jaroslav Kotan *and* Daniel Weissbort. VWA

In the Cemetery. Thomas Hardy. *Fr.* Satires of Circumstance, VI. BrPo; InPK; Son

In the cemetery of childhood. Cemetery of Childhood. Joaquim Cardozo, *tr. by* Elizabeth Bishop. ATCBP

In the cemetery of Lodz. Mother. Julian Tuwim, *tr. by* Isaac Komem. VWA

In the censer the coals are high. Final Prayer. Enheduanna, *tr. by* Aliki *and* Willis Barnstone. BoWoP

In the center of the earth. *Unknown, tr. fr. Chippewa Indian by* Frances Densmore. *Fr.* Love Charm Songs. OV

In the centre of the poster, Napoleon. A Poster of Our Dazzling Victory at Saarbrucken. Arthur Rimbaud, *tr. fr. French by* Robert Lowell. *Fr.* Eighteen-Seventy. FaBoPV; OBWP

In the Chagall Village. Rose Ausländer, *tr. fr. German by* Beth Bjorklund. CoAuP

In the chaos of the autumn sun. The Smell of Old Newspapers Is Always Stronger after Sleeping in the Sun. Mike Lowery. Psk

In the cheap room. Episode. Cassiano Nunes, *tr. by* E. A. Lacey. PeHV

In the Cheviots. Maurice Lindsay. PoSH

In the *chih-yüan* period, the being *hsin-mao.* Poem of Prefectural Judge Yang T'ien-jui. Chao Meng-fu, *tr. by* Jonathan Chaves. CoBLCP

In the Children's Hospital. "Hugh MacDiarmid." NAEL-2; NoP

In the child's homework. *Unknown, tr. by* Geoffrey Bownas *and* Anthony Thwaite. PeBJV

In the chill of night. Spring Moon in Lingering Cold. Shotetsu, *tr. by* Steven D. Carter. WFTW

In the Ch'ing-ming festival. 1970s. Liu K'o-hsiang, *tr. by* Dominic Cheung. IFON

In the chorus of memories a blessing in disguise. Declension. Stephen Sandy. PoA

In the Churchyard. Eleanor Ross Taylor. UnPo

In the Churchyard at Cambridge. Longfellow. AmPP; PoEL-5; TAP

In the City. Israel Zangwill. WGRP

In the city/ We anticipated its coming abruptly, the shivering. Early Snow. Lo Fu, *tr. by* Dominic Cheung. IFON

In the City of Bogotá. Greg Pape. MAYP

In the city of Marseilles, there lived a beautiful lady. The Lowly Peasant. *Unknown, tr. by* Rina Benmayor. PBWP

In the city of St. Francis they have taken down the statue of St. Francis. Afterwards, They Shall Dance. Bob Kaufman. PoNe; TwCP; VGW

In the City of Slaughter, *sel.* Hayyim Nahman Bialik, *tr. fr. Hebrew by* Bernhard Frank.
  "Come with me to the City of Slaughter, come, enter its courtyards." MHeP

In the City of Wu, I Obtained a Record of Names from the Civil Service Examinations. Kung Tzu-chen, *tr. fr. Chinese by* Shirleen S. Wong. WFTU

In the clear light that confuses everything. The Laurel Tree. Louis Simpson. NNaP

In the clear world. Blue Specks. Nurunnessa Choudhury, *tr. by the author and* Paul Joseph Thompson. AIW

In the clearing stands. Missionaries in the Jungle. Linda Piper. BISi

In the cliff over the frog pond. The Fossils. Galway Kinnell. NYBP

In the close covert of a grove. The Geranium. Sheridan. BoLoP; ErPo

In the Cloud of Unknowing. Carol Rumens. DiPo

In the coal-pit, or the factory. A Golden Lot. Joseph Skipsey. SaC

In the cock-crowing land of Azuma. Mushimaro. *Fr.* Manyo Shu. Ma

In the coiled shell sounds Ocean's distant roar. The Tutelage. Robert Mowry Bell. AA

In the cold, cold parlor. First Death in Nova Scotia. Elizabeth Bishop. CoAP; FaBoWP; LCAP; NOBA; NYBP

In the cold forbidding capital. *Unknown, tr. by* Burton Watson. FCEI

In the cold October night-time. The Boatman's Song. Thomas Hardy. *Fr.* The Dynasts, *Pt.* I, Act V, sc. vii. WaaP

In the cold shed sharpening saws. Sixth-Month Song in the Foothills. Gary Snyder. HCAP

In the cold winds, leaves are cleared from the trees. Princess Shikishi, *tr. fr. Japanese by* Hiroaki Sato. *Fr.* Seventy-eight Tanka. FCEI

In the cool evening, the good provider plucked. A Plum. Mani Leib, *tr. by* John Hollander. PeBMYV
  ("In the cool evening the master.") VWA, *tr. by* David G. Roskies *and* Hillel Schwartz

In the cool, impersonal room. The Egoist Dead. Elizabeth Brewster. CaP

In the cool waters of the river. Woman. Valente Malangatana, *tr. by* Dorothy Guedes *and* Philippa Rumsey. PBA; TTY

In the copper marsh. Heron. Philip Booth. NePoEA; Psk

In the corner. Science/Fiction. Adrianne Marcus. BWV

In the corner a violet jug the bells the folds of paper. Pablo Picasso, *tr. by* David Gascoyne. EAS

In the corner the fire made a place. Two Women. Tania Van Zyl. PeSA

In the Counselor's Waiting Room. Bettie M. Sellers. InPK

In the country that was a time. That Time, That Country. Susan Donnelly. PPR

In the county of Essex there lived a squire. The Wandering Shepherdess. *Unknown.* OBET

In the County Tyrone, in [*or* near] the town of Dungannon. The Old [*or* Ould] Orange Flute. *Unknown.* FaBoBa; GBP; OxBoLi; WTO

In the Course of Time. Natan Zach, *tr. fr. Hebrew by* Warren Bargad *and* Stanley F. Chyet. IP

In the court of examinations. Spring Vista from the Tower of Illuminated Distance. Li Meng-yang, *tr. by* Jonathan Chaves. CoBLCP

In the Courtyard. Miriam Ulinover, *tr. fr. Yiddish by* Seth L. Wolitz. VWA

In the courtyard where young Lajcsi, limping. More Powerful than the Sea. Zoltán Zelk, *tr. by* Barbara Howes. MHuP

In the cowslip's peeps I lie. Clock-a-Clay. John Clare. EBEV; EBVV; FaPON; LiTB; NAEL-2; OAEL-2; OBNC; PoEL-4 (Clock-o'-Clay.) TrGrPo

In the cream gilded cabin of his steam yacht. Mr. Nixon. Ezra Pound. *Fr.* Hugh Selwyn Mauberley. (Life and Contacts). MoAmPo

In the crimson of the morning, in the whiteness of the noon. The Coming of His Feet. Lyman W. Allen. BLPA

In the cross field. Out West. Gary Snyder. NNaP

In the Cross of Christ I Glory. Sir John Bowring. WGRP

In the crowd at the station. Ishikawa Takuboku, *tr. by* Geoffrey Bownas *and* Anthony Thwaite. PeBJV

In the crowd's multitudinous mind. Crucifixion. Eva Gore Booth. WGRP

In the curdled afterglow of night. Scott-Moncrieff's Beowulf. Charles Spear. ATNZ

In the custom of the Jews. The Unveiling. Suzanne Bernhardt. VWA

In the daily space. Daily Space. João Cabral de Melo Neto, *tr. by* W. S. Merwin. ATCBP

In the daisied lap of summer. The Season's Lovers. Miriam Waddington. MoCV; OBCV

In the Dark. Frances Louisa Bushnell. AA

In the Dark. Amir Gilboa, *tr. fr. Hebrew by* Bernhard Frank. MHeP

In the Dark. Mary Thacher Higginson. AA

In the Dark. Sophie Jewett. TrPWD

In the dark. The Black Jewel. W. S. Merwin. CAPP

In the dark/ each sits alone. Train. Ken Smith. EAS

In the dark aisles of Bruckner's symphonies. Bruckner. James Camp. MAT

In the dark and narrow street. When the Night and Morning Meet. Dora Greenwell. EBVV

In the dark at first, we see things in their sleep. Girandole. Dorothy Donnelly. NYBP

In the dark beneath the earth. Dead Waters. Manuel Gutiérrez Nájera, *tr. by* Samuel Beckett. MexPo

In the dark church of music. Vivaldi. Delmore Schwartz. NYBP

In the dark garden at night. Kaya Shirao, *tr. fr. Japanese by* Hiroaki Sato. *Fr.* Twenty-one Hokku. FCEI

In the dark Naomi. A Horror Story Written for the Cover of a Matchbook. Chuck Wachtel. UL

In the dark night it's light. Wakayama Bokusui, *tr. fr. Japanese by* Hiroaki Sato. *Fr.* Forty-four Tanka. FCEI

In the Dark None Dainty. Robert Herrick. CaPo

In the dark womb where I began. C. L. M. John Masefield. LiTM; MoBrPo; OxBTC

In the dreaming church. Rufus Prays. L. A. G. Strong. MoBrPo

In the darkness. Aspiring Poet. Koh Chang-soo, *tr. by the author.* ACKP

In the darkness/ of the house of the white brother. Indian School. Norman H. Russell. MAT

In the darkness deep. The Song of the Turnkey. Harry Bache Smith. AA

In the darkness east of Chicago. A Valedictory to Standard Oil of Indiana. David Wagoner. NYBP

In the darkness of the well. Ozaki Hosai, *tr. fr. Japanese by* Hiroaki Sato. *Fr.* One Hundred Haiku in Free Form. FCEI

In the dating bar, the potted ferns lean down. A History of Civilization. Albert Goldbarth. HCAP; MAYP

In the Dawn. Odell Shepard. WGRP

In the dawn-dirty light, in the biggest snow of the year. Roe Deer. Ted Hughes. NoAM

In the dawn twilight. Night Train. Hagiwara Sakutaro, *tr. by* Hiroaki Sato. FCEI

In the days before the high tide. A Sea Song. Digby Mackworth Dolben. EBVV

In the days of Caesar Augustus. Christmas Day; the Family Sitting. John Meade Falkner. NOCV; OxBTC

In the days of my season of salad. A Song of Renunciation. Sir Owen Seaman. CenHV

In the Days of Old Rameses. *Unknown.* AS

In the Days of Rin-Tin-Tin. Daniel Hoffman. SM

In the days of the Prince's glory. The Palace of Prince Ma. Yang Shih-ch'i, *tr. fr. Chinese by* Jonathan Chaves. *Fr.* Three Poems on Ch'ang-sha. CoBLCP

In the days that tried our fathers. The Rejected "National Hymns." "Orpheus C. Kerr." OBAL

In the days when everyone said. Meantime. Heather McHugh. GeTw

In the days when my wife lived. Hitomaro. *Fr.* Manyo Shu. Ma

In the dead hour of night. The Silent Night. Mrs. Henry Linden. CBWP-4

In the Dead of the Night. Norman Dubie. AmPA

In the dead of winter, crossing the mountain pass. Moon over the Mountain Pass. Hsü Ts'an, *tr. by* Pao Chia-lin. WFTU

In the dead park a bench sprawls drunkenly. End of the Season on a Stormy Day—Oban. Iain Crichton Smith. NePoEA-2

In the Dean's porch a nest of clay. In the Cathedral Close. Edward Dowden. EBVV

In the Deep Channel. William Stafford. NaP; RB

In the Deep Museum. Anne Sexton. MoAmPo; Prf

In the deep shadow of the porch. Bind-Weed. "Susan Coolidge." GN

In the depths of night. Plum Blossoms Late at Night. Shinkei, *tr. by* Steven D. Carter. WFTW

In the depths of the Greyhound Terminal. In the Baggage Room at Greyhound. Allen Ginsberg. NaP; NoP

In the depths of the parasol I see the marvelous prostitutes. A Man and Woman Absolutely White. André Breton, *tr. by* David Antin. POS

In the Desert. Stephen Crane. *Fr.* The Black Riders, III. FaBoEE; LiTM; NOBA; OxBSP; TAP

(Heart, The.) HoPM; MoAmPo; TW

In the desert of Itabira. Travelling in the Family. Carlos Drummond de Andrade, *tr. by* Elizabeth Bishop. ATCBP

In the deserted, moon-blanch'd street. A Summer Night. Matthew Arnold. SeCePo

In the deserted village, sunken down. The Deserted Village. "Robin Hyde." ATNZ; PeNZ; WPE

In the desolate depths of a perilous place. The Bogeyman. Jack Prelutsky. RHPC

In the desolate painted hall, swallows fly in the beams. Song of the Jade Tower in Spring. Wei Ch'eng-pan, *tr. by* Lois Fusek. ATF

In the desolated alleys near Saint Paul's. Love among the Ruins of London. Muriel Grainger. CN

In the dew dripping. Prince Otsu. *Fr.* Manyo Shu. PeBJV

In the Dials. W. E. Henley. BrPo

In the dim light, red and red. First Love. Kitahara Hakushu, *tr. by* Hiroaki Sato. FCEI

In the dimness of the night, summer night. Lachesis Net. P. Mustapää, *tr. by* Aili Jarvenpa. SOP

In the distance. Afterword. Nishiwaki Junzaburo, *tr. by* Hiroaki Sato. FCEI

In the distance. Sparrow Flock. Ono Tozaburo, *tr. by* Hiroaki Sato. FCEI

In the distance crystal bells ring out. Odysseus Elytis, *tr. fr. Greek by* Edmund Keeley *and* Philip Sherrard. *Fr.* Heroic and Elegiac Song for the Lost Second Lieute, XIII. VMG

In the distillation process, what can be. Sub Rosa. Susan Prospere. AnAn

In the Distress upon Me. Henry Ainsworth. AH

In the Dock. Walter de la Mare. LiTM

In the Dome Car of the "Canadian." Sid Marty. NOBC

In the dome of my sires as the clear moonbeam falls. Newstead Abbey. Byron. ChER

In the Dordogne. John Peale Bishop. OBWP; VGW

In the downhill of life, when I find I'm declining. Tomorrow. John Collins. GTBS; GTBS-P

In the Downtown Tombs of long long ago. Partial Luetic History of an Individual at Risk. J. M. Regan. GLP

In the dragoon's ride from out the north. A Bold Dragoon. *Unknown.* OBET

In the dream I enter the house. Bone-Flower Elegy. Robert Hayden. NoAM

In the dream, in the charmed dream we are flying. The Eye of Humility. Kay Smith. OBCV

In the dream of the northern poets. The Advance Guard. John Hay. AnAmPo

In the drifting rain the cows in the yard are as black. Milking before Dawn. Ruth Dallas. PeNZ

In the drinking-well. Aunt Eliza. Harry Graham. ChTr; FaFP; NA

In the dripping dew of the foot-wearying mountain. Prince Otsu. *Fr.* Manyo Shu. FCEI

In the drunken city. City of San Salvador. Tirso Canales, *tr. by* Juan Felipe Herrera. VoI

In the Dry Riverbed. Zelda, *tr. fr. Hebrew by* Marcia Falk. VWA

In the Due Honor of the Author Master Robert Norton. John Smith. SCAP

In the dungeon-crypts, idly did I stray. Emily Brontë. *Fr.* The Prisoner. NOBVV

In the dusk of the evening. Old Mountain Road. Charles Simic. FYAP

In the dusk the path. Izumi Shikibu, *tr. by* Kenneth Rexroth. WPOW

In the dusky light. Tamenori, *tr. by* Steven D. Carter. WFTW

In the Dusky Path of a Dream. Rabindranath Tagore. *Fr.* The Gardener. OBMV

In the ear of an anchor, a gull croaks. Sorrow of Parting. Maruyama Kaoru, *tr. by* Geoffrey Bownas *and* Anthony Thwaite. PeBJV

In the early evening, as now, a man is bending. Louise Glück. HCAP

In the early morning. Linda Pastan. TV

In the early morning/ when the light and the sea smell come stumbling in. In Solitary Confinement, Sea Point Police Cells. C. J. Driver. PeSA

In the earnest path of duty. Charlotte Forten. BlSi

In the earth—the earth—thou shalt be laid. Warning and Reply. Emily Brontë. WPE

In the East, in the East is my heart. My Heart Is in the East. Judah Halevi. TrJP

In the Egypt of my night. Locusts of Silence. Seymour Mayne. VWA

In the Egyptian Museum. Janet Lewis. NYBP; QFR

In the elbow of a macaroni. A Blue Jeaned Rock Queen in Search of Happiness on a Blind Thursday at 1/3 Speed and Crying. A. K. Redwing. VoR

In the Elegy Season. Richard Wilbur. InPK; MoAB; NePoEA; NYBP

In the Emptied Rest Home. Bella Akhmadulina, *tr. fr. Russian by* Jean Valentine *and* Olga Carlisle. BoWoP

In the empty center of the cyclone. Christine Lavant, *tr. by* Beth Bjorklund. CoAuP

In the empty lot—a place. The Wild. Wendell Berry. VGW

In the Empty Street Every Shutter Is Bolted. Tuvia Rübner, *tr. fr. Hebrew by* Bernhard Frank. MHeP

In the encyclopedia. Fact. Kenneth Rexroth. OBAL

In the End. Peter Everwine, *after* Natan Sach. NNaP

In the end. Narihira, *tr. fr. Japanese by* Burton Watson. *Fr.* Kokin Shu. FCEI

In the end darkness drowned Zenobia. Goodbye, Zenobia. Saniyya Salih, *tr. by* Patricia Alanah Byrne, Salma Khadra Jayyusi, *and* Charles Doria. MAP

In the end God alone knows. To the Hunter. Sándor Rákos, *tr. fr. Hungarian by* Jascha Kessler. *Fr.* Bear Song. FOC

In the end I find. Narihira, *tr. fr. Japanese by* Burton Watson. *Fr.* Kokin Shu. FCEI

In the End of Days. Bible, *O.T. Fr.* Isaiah, II: 2–4. TrJP

In the End-of-Summer Light. Yisroel-Yankev Schwartz, *tr. fr. Yiddish by* Seymour Levitan. PeBMYV

In the end of the sabbath, as it began to dawn toward the first day of the week. Bible, *N.T. Fr.* St. Matthew, XXVIII. NAWM-1

In the end you are tired of those places. Locations. Jim Harrison. AmPA

In the end you are weary of this ancient world. Zone. Guillaume Apollinaire. RHTwFP, *tr. by* Samuel Beckett; SOTW, *tr. by* Ron Padgett

In the Environs of the Funeral Home. Robert Mezey. NePoEA

(Funeral Home, The.) LiTM

In the Evening. C. P. Cavafy, *tr. fr. Greek by* Edmund Keeley *and* Philip Sherrard. AnAn; VMG

In the Evening. Thomas Hardy. ImOP

In the Evening. Countess Lara, *tr. fr. Italian by* Muriel Kittel. DMI

In the evening. At Sunset. Ivy O. Eastwick. BoTP

In the evening. A Green Lowland of Pianos. Jerzy Harasymowicz, *tr. by* Czeslaw Milosz. PwPP

In the evening/ haze darkening on the hills. Another Night in the Ruins. Galway Kinnell. CoAP

In the evening. Beggars and Kings. W. S. Merwin. AnAn

In the evening. Tajihi. *Fr.* Manyo Shu. PeBJV

In the evening I gaze out from atop a high tower. On the Road to Tang Lake. P'eng Sun-yü, *tr. by* William H. Nienhauser, Jr. WFTU

In the evening I would sit. Edna St. Vincent Millay. *Fr.* Journal. SaC

In the evening land, a woman. The Going Under of the Evening Land. Mekeel McBride. NAmP

In the evening light. Ietaka, *tr. by* Steven D. Carter. WFTW

In the evening my thoughts go toward the end of the clouds. Teika, *tr. fr. Japanese* by Hiroaki Sato. *Fr.* A Compendium of Good Tanka. FCEI

In the evening sky, swallows. The Vision of the Blessed Gabriele. Penelope Shuttle. NPo

In the evening the dusk. The Poet Is Dead. William Everson. NoAM; NoP

In the evening there is a snail. Talking to the Mule. Laura Jensen. AmPA

In the evening there were flocks of nighthawks. September 2. Wendell Berry. PoA

In the evening they bore the stranger into the death chamber. En Route. Georg Trakl, *tr.* by Joachim Neugroschel. AnAn

In the Evening, Walking in the Western Fields. Chang Yü, *tr. fr. Chinese* by Jonathan Chaves. CoBLCP

In the evening, when the world knew he was dead. In the Evening. Thomas Hardy. ImOP

In the evenings they listen to the same. The Intruder. Frank Stanford. MT

In the eye of my heart, I can see her. For Marsha. Angela de Hoyos. ER

In the eye of seafaring man. The Winds of Change. Charles G. Ballard. VoR

In the Eyes of a Screech Owl. Ono Tozaburo, *tr. fr. Japanese* by Sato. FCEI

In the Eyes of the Gods. André Breton, *tr. fr. French* by Michael Benedikt. POS

In the fair fields of suburban. Decks. Robert Phillips. GeTw

In the Fair Forest. *Unknown.* BoTP

In the Fall. "Hugh MacDiarmid." *Fr.* In Memoriam James Joyce. InPS

"Let the only consistency." FaBoMo

In the fall, I believe again in poetry. Still. Aila Meriluoto, *tr.* by Jaakko A. Ahokas. PBWP

In the fall-out of daisies on the rockland. Absent Daughter. Barend Toerien, *tr.* by the author. PeSA

In the Falling Deer's Mouth. Michael Levien. PoRA

In the falling snow. Hokku: In the Falling Snow. Richard Wright. *Fr.* Hokku Poems. IDB

In the family drinking well. Sister Nell. *Unknown.* FaPON

In the far corner. The Blackbird. Humbert Wolfe. BoTP; FaPON; GoJo; GrPl; RHPC

In the far realm of our Lord. Yakamochi, *tr.* by Geoffrey Bownas *and* Anthony Thwaite. *Fr.* Manyo Shu. PeBJV

In the Far Years. Wilson Pugsley MacDonald. CaP

In the few warm weeks. A Christmas Message. Gavin Ewart. FaBoMo

In the Field. Phyllis Janik. IHMS

In the Field. Jung Han-mo, *tr. fr. Korean* by Koh Chang-soo. ACKP

In the Field. Richard Wilbur. NAAL-2; NYBP

In the field I've roped off, thinking to pick spring herbs. Akahito. *Fr.* Manyo Shu. FCEI

In the Fields. Charlotte Mew. BoNaP; MoAB; MoBrPo

In the Fields of My Father's Youth. W. H. Oliver. ATNZ

In the fields of spring. *Unknown.* ILY

In the fields, the silos open their mouths. Hangman. Ai. AmPA

In the fierce peak of the day it's quietly they wade. The Beach Women. Robert Pinsky. PPR

In the fire, a telegraph pole. Hara Tamiki, *tr.* by Geoffrey Bownas *and* Anthony Thwaite. PeBJV

In the Firelight. Eugene Field. AA

In the First Cave. Seymour Mayne. VWA

In the first days, in the forgotten calendars. Imperial. Arthur Rex Dugard Fairburn. *Fr.* Album Leaves. ATNZ

In the first dream she is the enemy. The Other Woman. Jane Shore. PPR

In the First House. Joseph Joel Keith. GoYe

In the First Place of My Life. Ray A. Young Bear. STE

In the first rank of these did Zimri stand. Dryden. *Fr.* Absalom and Achitophel, Pt. I. HAP

   (Zimri ("In the first rank of These did Zimri stand.").) SeCePo

In the first ruder age, when love was wild. Love's Force. Thomas Carew. CaPo

In the first season. I Picked Up Your Cast Away Hide. Mary Moran. GOS

In the first spring winds, my branches grow new green. Willow Branches. Niu Chiao, *tr.* by Lois Fusek. ATF

In the first sunbath. Death of a Dove. Nurunnessa Choudhury, *tr.* by the *author and* Paul Joseph Thompson. AIW

In the first taxi he was alone, tra-la. The Taxis. Louis MacNeice. FaBCIP; OxBTC

In the first year of freedom's second dawn. George III. Byron. *Fr.* The Vision of Judgment. TW

In the first year of the last disgrace. News of the World II. George Barker. FaBoTw; LiTB

In the 5 a.m. dusk. Dionne Brand. *Fr.* Military Occupations. PBCV

In the flash of that explosion. Wedding Day at Nagasaki. Rodney Hall. CBAP

In the Fleeting Hand of Time. Gregory Corso. NAs

In the Flight of the Blue Heron: To Montezuma. Anita Endrezze Probst. CDW

In the Flowering Season. Michael Roberts. FaBoTw

In the Flux. Fadwa Tuqan, *tr. fr. Arabic* by Patricia Alanah Byrne, Salma Khadra Jayyusi, *and* Charles Doria. MAP

In the footsteps of the walking air. Kenneth Patchen. EAS

In the Ford plant. The Foundation of American Industry. Donald Hall. GOA

In the Forest. George Bowering. NOBC

In the Forest. Russell Edson. LCAP

In the Forest. Pinhas Sadeh, *tr. fr. Hebrew* by Harris Lenowitz. VWA

In the forest hearing. The World Has Many Places Many Ways. Norman H. Russell. NOVW

In the forest, in unexplored. Michael Dransfield. *Fr.* Geography, III. CBAP

In the Forest of Noyous Heaviness. Charles d'Orléans. OxBLMV

In the Forest of Your Eyes. Arlindo Barbeitos, *tr. fr. Portuguese* by Donald Burness. WMBCH

In the former world. Abutsu the Nun, *tr.* by Steven D. Carter. WFTW

In the fragile fireland. Trip. Reinhard Priessnitz, *tr.* by Beth Bjorklund. CoAuP

In the full river. What She Said ("In the full river"). Orampokiyar, *tr. fr. Tamil* by A. K. Ramanujan. *Fr.* Five on the Riverside Cane, 3. PLW

In the furrows of the world. Nation. Charlie Cobb. PoBA

In the Garden. Tom Schmidt. NeAC

In the Garden. *Unknown.* SoSe

In the Garden at Swainston. Tennyson. OBEV; OBNC

In the garden, blooming white, camellias. Monk Kudo Asked Me, "What's Your Haikai Eye Like?" Onitsura, *tr. fr. Japanese* by Hiroaki Sato. *Fr.* Twenty-three Hokku. FCEI

In the garden by the street. Stealing. Ono Tozaburo, *tr.* by Hiroaki Sato. FCEI

In the Garden City Café with its murals on the wall. Huxley Hall. Sir John Betjeman. OBSV

In the garden is a peach-tree. *Unknown, tr.* by Arthur Waley. BoS

In the Garden of Eden, planted by God. Trees. Bliss Carman. OHIP

In the garden of spring. Yakamochi. *Fr.* Manyo Shu. Ma

In the Garden of the Lord. Helen Keller. WGRP

In the Garden of the Turkish Consulate. Pinhas Sadeh, *tr. fr. Hebrew* by Harris Lenowitz. VWA

In the garden on a summer night. Brazen Image. Anne Hartigan. CIP

In the Garden Palace. *Unknown. Fr.* Manyo Shu. Ma

In the garden. Summer's end. Evening. On a bench. Verses Written on Sand. Melech Ravitch, *tr.* by Seymour Mayne *and* Rivka Augenfeld. VWA

In the garden there strayed. In the Garden. *Unknown.* SoSe

In the garden where no one comes. Princess Shikishi, *tr. fr. Japanese* by Hiroaki Sato. *Fr.* Seventy-eight Tanka. FCEI

In the garret under the sloping eaves. Wedding Gift. Minna Irving. BLPA

In the gathering dew. Lady Sagami, *tr.* by Willis Barnstone. BoWoP

In the gathering gloom they lie. Terror. "Yehoash," *tr.* by Isidore Goldstick. TrJP

In the Ghetto. Hugo Sonnenschein, *tr. fr. German* by Edouard Roditi. VWA

In the ghetto of my mouth. The Golem. Shlomo Reich, *tr.* by Mira Reich. VWA

In the Giant's Castle. Ruth Dallas. PeNZ

In the girdered dark. A Drink of Milk. John Montague. FaBCIP

In the glassed-in jazz club acres above. Night above the Town. Thomas Lux. NAmP

In the Gloaming. James C. Bayles. NA

In the Gloaming. Charles Stuart Calverley. BXAP; NOBL

In the Gloaming ("In the gloaming, oh my darling"). Meta Orred. FaFP

In the gloaming to be roaming. In the Gloaming. Charles Stuart Calverley. BXAP; NOBL

In the gloom of dusk. Tamehide, *tr.* by Steven D. Carter. WFTW

In the gloom of whiteness. Snow. Edward Thomas. FaBoTw

In the gloomy ocean bed. The *Kearsarge.* James Jeffrey Roche. AA; PAH

In the glorious age of the Emperor, a god. Yakamochi. *Fr.* Manyo Shu. Ma

In the Glorious Epiphanie of Our Lord God. Richard Crashaw. PoEL-2
In the Gold Mines. B. W. Vilakazi. TTY
In the golden air, the risky autumn. Piazzas. Barbara Guest. NeAP
In the Golden Land. Moyshe-Leyb Halpern, *tr. fr. Yiddish by* Benjamin *and* Barbara Harshav *and* Kathryn Helle. AYP
In the golden twilight the rain. The Terrace in the Snow. Su Tung-p'o, *tr. by* Kenneth Rexroth. NaP
In the Grass. Annette von Droste-Hülshoff, *tr. fr. German by* James Edward Tobin. PBWP
In the Grass. Hamlin Garland. AA
In the grass hut no one to help me up. Death Bed Poem. Jakusho, *tr. by* Burton Watson. JLIC-1
In the Grave No Flower. Edna St. Vincent Millay. NAAL-2
In the Graveyard. Macdonald Clarke. PWR
In the great gardens, after bright spring rain. Edith Sitwell. *Fr.* The Sleeping Beauty. OxBTC
(Innocent Spring, The.) NOBE
In the Great House, and in the House of Fire. He Holdeth Fast to the Memory of His Identity. *Unknown, tr. fr. Egyptian by* Robert Hillyer. *Fr.* Book of the Dead. AWP
In the great night my heart will go out. Owl Woman's Death Song. *Unknown, tr. by* Ruth Underhill. BoWoP
In the great place the great house is gone from. Slave Quarters. James Dickey. NYBP
In the great ship, full-oared. Empress Otomaro. *Fr.* Manyo Shu. Ma
In the great wind, in the sky. Ozaki Hosai, *tr. fr. Japanese by* Hiroaki Sato. *Fr.* One Hundred Haiku in Free Form. FCEI
In the great world—which, being interpreted. Byron. *Fr.* Don Juan, XI. OxBoLi
In the green hedge tall and thick. June in Wiltshire. Geoffrey Grigson. WaP
In the green light of water, like the day. The Swans. Edith Sitwell. CMoP; WPE
In the greenest of our valleys. The Haunted Palace. Poe. *Fr.* The Fall of the House of Usher. AA; AnAmPo; BeLS; CH; ChTr; LiTA; NOBA; OxBA; PoEL-4; PrIm; TAP; TrGrPo; WiR; WSC
In the greenhouse lives a wren. *Unknown.* OxNR
In the Greenwood, *sel.* Desmond O'Grady, *tr. fr. Irish by the author.* "My darling, my love." *Fr.* I. CIP
In the grey evening. The Garden Hose. Beatrice Janosco. NTCP
In the grey wastes of dread. Horses on the Camargue. Roy Campbell. GTBS-P; OBTV; PeSA; SeCePo
In the grime-ridden sunlight in the downtown Wimpy bar. In Memory of Those Murdered in the Dublin Massacre. Paul Durcan. FaBCIP
In the groined alcoves of an ancient tower. The Second Volume. Robert Mowry Bell. AA
In the grotto at the end of the alley. The Portrait's All Feet. Rocco Scotellaro, *tr. by* Lawrence R. Smith. NItP
In the groves of Africa from their natural wonder. An African Elegy. Robert Duncan. NoAM
In the grownups' stories for the young. The Wolf. Unsi al-Haj, *tr. by* Sargon Boulus *and* Alistair Elliot. MAP
In the gun muzzle a crow had nested. Fragments. Maruyama Kaoru, *tr. by* Hiroaki Sato. FCEI
In the half-empty City Hall. October. Julio Ortega, *tr. by* David Tipton. Per
In the Hamlet. Abraham Sutskever, *tr. fr. Yiddish by* Chana Bloch. PeBMYV
In the harbor of Askalon. Light of Judea. Claude Vigée. VWA
In the harbour, in the island, in the Spanish Seas. Trade Winds. John Masefield. FaBoCh; OBMV
In the Harlem ghetto, in such exile. Harlem—a Negro Ghetto. Berysh Vaynshteyn, *tr. by* Benjamin *and* Barbara Harshav *and* Kathryn Helle. AYP
In the hazy night. Emperor Fushimi, *tr. by* Steven D. Carter. WFTW
In the heart of the Hills of Life, I know. My Springs. Sidney Lanier. UnPo
In the heart of the hills the rain unabated. *Malay Oral Tradition, tr. by* R. J. Wilkinson *and* R. O. Winstedt. WTO
In the heart of the Indian territory of Oklahoma. Go For Broke. André Breton, *tr. by* David Antin. POS
In the heat haze a fox. Boncho, *tr. fr. Japanese by* Hiroaki Sato. *Fr.* Twenty-one Hokku. FCEI
In the heat-locked room. As a Child Seeing a Cardinal. John Gill. NeAC
In the heat of the day a funnel cloud. For the El Paso Weather Bureau. Peter Wild. NeAC
In the Heat of the Morning. Anne Szumigalski. FaBoWP
In the heights of heaven is the throne of your dwelling. Sanctification. Joseph Ibn Abithur, *tr. by* David Goldstein. TOF
In the Henry James Country. William Abrahams. WaP

In the heraldry of moral rearmament. A Pigeon. Hugo Claus, *tr. by* Theo Hermans. DuIn
In the heydays of 'forty-five. For George Santayana. Robert Lowell. CMoP; NAAL-2; VGW
In the high jungle where Assam meets Tibet. Moschus Moschiferus. Alec Derwent Hope. CBAP; GrPl
In the high seat, before-dawn dark. Why Log Truck Drivers Rise Earlier than Students of Zen. Gary Snyder. NNaP; SOTW
In the Highlands. Robert Louis Stevenson. BrPo; FaBoCh; FaBV; GoTS; OBEV; OxBS; PoSH
In the Hill Country. Max Jacob, *tr. fr. French by* John Ashbery. RHTwFP
In the hills of Nara. Sena Gyomon. *Fr.* Manyo Shu. Ma
In the Holy Nativity of Our Lord God ("Come we shepheards whose blest sight."). Richard Crashaw. PoEL-2; SeCV-1
Sels.
(Hymn[e] of the Nativity, An.) HAP; MeLP; MePo; OBS
(Holy Nativity, The.) WGRP
Shepherds' Hymn, The ("Gloomy night embraced the place"). NOBE
Shepherd's Hymn, The ("We saw Thee in Thy balmy nest"). ACP; TrGrPo, 3 *sts.*
(Verses from the Shepherd's Hymn.) OBEV
In the Home of the Scholar Wu Su-chiang. Wu Tsao, *tr. fr. Chinese by* Kenneth Rexroth *and* Ling Chung. BoWoP; WPOW
In the Horse Carriage. Hagiwara Sakutaro, *tr. fr. Japanese by* Hiroaki Sato. FCEI
In the Hospital. Arthur Guiterman. WGRP
In the Hospital. Laura Jensen. AmPA
In the Hospital of the Holy Physician. Nancy Willard. IHMS
In the hot valley of the never was. The Last Campaign. Geoffrey Lehmann. PoAu-2
In the hottest time, when all is still and windless. *Unknown, tr. fr. Chinese by* Burton Watson. *Fr.* Tzu Yeh Songs. CoBCP
In the hour of death, after this life's whim. Dominus Illuminatio Mea. Richard Doddridge Blackmore. OBEV
In the hour [*or* houre] of my distress [*or* distresse]. His Litany to the Holy Spirit. Robert Herrick. BLPL; ELP; JCP; PoLF; QFR; SeCePo; TEP
(His Letanie, to the Holy Spirit.) OBS; SeCV-1
(Litany to the Holy Spirit.) OBEV
In the Hours of Darkness. James Flexner. FaPON
In the House at Midnight. Tsfrirah Gar, *tr. fr. Hebrew by* Bernhard Frank. MHeP
In the house of red leaves are the most beautiful dances. The House of Red Leaves. Liu E, *tr. by* Jonathan Chaves. CoBLCP
In the House of the Dying. Jane Cooper. NMM
In the house of the hangman. The Hangman's Love Song. Stanley Moss. VGW
In the House of the Judge. Dave Smith. MAYP
In the house with the tortoise chair. Poem to Ease Birth. *Unknown, tr. by* Anselm Hollo. BoWoP; STP
In the huge, rectangular room, the ceiling. My Mother, Who Came from China, Where She Never Saw Snow. Laureen Mar. WPOW
In the huge, wide-open, sleeping eye of the mountain. The Bear. Ted Hughes. FaBoMo
In the human cities, never again to. Despisals. Muriel Rukeyser, *tr. by* Edmund Keeley. AnAn; NMM; Prf
In the hungry kitchen. Kitchen Poem. Francis Scarfe. EAS
In the Huon Valley. James McAuley. CBAP
In the ideal American. In Ancient December. Alice Notley. UL
In the Inner City. Lucille Clifton. CNA; HeIP
In the inside of the letter *a* there sprouts a finger placed on lips. And on the Very First Day. Benjamin Péret, *tr. by* Michael Benedikt. POS
In the interests of economy. Icon. Fleur Adcock. ATNZ
In the interim, how the children should be educated. Allen Curnow. *Fr.* A Small Room with Large Windows, III. PeNZ
In the Interstices. Ruth Stone. ErPo
In the Isle of Dogs. John Davidson. OBNC
In the Jury Room. Hodding Carter. MAT
In the Kamunabi Mountains. *Unknown. Fr.* Manyo Shu. Ma
In the Kifah Street, near the Fadl Mosque. A Woman. Yasin Taha Hafiz, *tr. by* Sharif Elmusa *and* Christopher Middleton. MAP
In the Kingdom of the Cross, *sel.* Uri Zvi Greenberg, *tr. fr. Yiddish by* Leonard Wolf.
"Forest's black and dense, The; it grows out of the flatlands." PeBMYV
In the kitchen/ making dishes with a brush. A Plea to My Sister. James Cunningham. JB
In the kitchen of the old house, late. In the Old House. Donald Hall. NePoEA-2

In the laboratory waiting room. Through a Glass Eye, Lightly. Carolyn Kizer. BoWoP

In the Ladies' Room at the Bus Terminal. William Zaranka. BXAP

In the Lake of Omi. *Unknown, tr. fr. Japanese by* Geoffrey Bownas *and* Anthony Thwaite. *Fr.* Manyo Shu. PeBJV

In the lamplight falling. Night. Peter Everwine. NNaP

In the land of Azuma. Mushimaro. *Fr.* Manyo Shu. FCEI, *tr. by* Hiroaki Sato; PeBJV, *tr. by* Geoffrey Bownas *and* Anthony Thwaite.

In the land of dwarfs. Forugh Farrokhzad, *tr. by* Girdhard Tikku. BoWoP

In the land of God. Cecil County. Ron Welburn. PoBA

In the land of Koshi. Yakamochi. *Fr.* Manyo Shu. Ma

In the land of Tao-chou. The People of Tao-chou. Po Chü-i, *tr. by* Arthur Waley. ChTr

In the land of turkeys in turkey weather. Dance of the Macabre Mice. Wallace Stevens. CMoP; NOBA; OxBA

In the land of Yamato. Emperor Jomei, *tr. by* Geoffrey Bownas *and* Anthony Thwaite. *Fr.* Manyo Shu. PeBJV

In the land where our Sovereign rules. Yotsuna. *Fr.* Manyo Shu. Ma

In the Land Where We Were Dreaming. Daniel B. Lucas. PAH

In the land where white clouds hover. *Unknown. Fr.* Manyo Shu. Ma

In the last bar on the way to your wild game. Nine Charms against the Hunter. David Wagoner. ASP; TW

In the last days. Apocalypse. Francis Ernest Kobina Parkes. PBA

In the Last Few Moments Came the Old German Cleaning Woman. Jane Cooper. SM

In the Last Flicker of the Sinking Sun. Peretz Markish, *tr. fr. Yiddish by* Keith Bosley. VWA

In the last minutes he said more to her. Seamus Heaney. *Fr.* Clearances, VII. CIP

In the last storm, when hawks. The Epitaph Ending in And. William Stafford. LCAP; NaP

In the late winter. The Bear. Galway Kinnell. TAP

In the leafy tree-tops. Yakamochi. *Fr.* Manyo Shu. Ma

In the lethargy which follows the machinations. Amelia Rosselli, *tr. fr. Italian by* Lawrence R. Smith. *Fr.* Martial Variations. NItP

In the Library. Elizabeth Brewster. OBCV

In the Library. Michael Patrick Hearn. NTCP

In the Library. Ed Ochester. Psk

In the licorice fields at Pontefract. The Licorice Fields at Pontefract. Sir John Betjeman. CMoP

In the life we live [*or* lead] together every paradise is lost. Against Botticelli. Robert Hass. AmPA; NPGG

In the light of dawn. Yoshimoto, *tr. by* Steven D. Carter. WFTW

In the light of the moon. Hayim Be'er, *tr. by* Stephen Mitchell. VWA

In the lips' flare. Bridges and Tunnels. Beth Bentley. EyDe

In the little weeds. Saigyo, *tr. fr. Japanese by* Burton Watson. *Fr.* Sixty-four Tanka. FCEI

In the Local Museum. Walter de la Mare. HAP

In the loneliness of my heart. Lady Kasa. *Fr.* Manyo Shu. Ma

In the lonesome latter years. The Promissory Note. Bayard Taylor. AnAmPo; BXAP; Par

In the long journey out of the self. Journey to the Interior. Theodore Roethke. LCAP; NYBP; VGW

In the long night. Sermon on the Mount. Jeff Wright. UL

In the long run for both of us. North/South. Paul Mariani. BLA

In the long run we must fix our compass. Respected, Feared, and Somehow Loved. Marjorie Welish. BAP

In the long, sleepless watches of the night. The Cross of Snow. Longfellow. HeIP; NOBA; OxBA; TAP

In the Longhouse, Oneida Museum. Roberta Hill Whiteman. NoAM; STE

In the Lord put I my trust. Psalm XI ("In the Lord put I my trust. . . ."). Bible, *O.T. Fr.* Psalms.

  (Psalm XI: "Since I do trust Jehova still," *paraphrased by* Sir Philip Sidney) OBVE

In the loud waking world I come and go. Nihil Humani Alienum. Titus Munson Coan. AA

In the love of home and country and the flag of Uncle Sam. Loyalty to the Flag. Lizelia Augusta Jenkins Moorer. CBWP-3

In the Loveless Landscape of my Solitude. Hugues C. Pernath, *tr. fr. Dutch by* Paul Vincent. DuIn

In the Loverly Half-Light. André Breton, *tr. fr. French by* Michael Benedikt. POS

In the low house, whose thick lights. Lady Day. Padraic Fallon. NeIP

In the lowlands is the goat's-peach. *Unknown, tr. by* Arthur Waley. BoS

In the lure of the spring scene, she hates his being away. Sand of Silk-Washing Stream. Ku Hsiung, *tr. by* Lois Fusek. ATF

In the Luxembourg Gardens. Thomas McCarthy. WCI

In the Lybian desert I. Modo and Alciphron. Sylvia Townsend Warner. MoBrPo

In the Madison Zoo. Roberta Hill. CDW

In the Madness of Love. Gary Soto. NPGG

In the magnolia's ever. In the Park. Eugenio Montale, *tr. by* James Merrill. PFI

In the mandrill. The Mandrill. Conrad Aiken. RHPC

In the manger of course were cows and the Child Himself. Pig. Anthony Hecht. OxBC

In the Manner of G. S. George Seferis, *tr. fr. Greek by* Edmund Keeley *and* Philip Sherrard. VMG

In the mantle of dawn dreamy boats. Fishermen. Julio Ortega, *tr. by* Maureen Ahern *and* David Tipton. Per

In the maple-sugar bush. March. Elizabeth Jane Coatsworth. PDV; RHPC

In the Marble Quarry. James Dickey. AmFN; NoP

In the market, in the cloister—only God I saw. Baba Kuhi of Shiraz, *tr. by* R. A. Nicholson. TOF

In the marketplace they are piling the dry sticks. Witch Burning. Sylvia Plath. CAPP

In the mass is the one. The One. Ida Procter. CN

In the Matter of Two Men. James David Corrothers. BANP

In the Meadow There's a Dead Deer. *Unknown, tr. fr. Chinese by* Burton Watson. CoBCP

In the merry month of May. Phillida and Coridon. Nicholas Breton. *Fr.* The Honourable Entertainment Given to the Queen's Majesty in Progress at Elvetham, 1591. OBEV; TTTS

  (Pastoral, A.) TrGrPo

  (Phyllida and Corydon.) EIL; SeCePo

  (Ploughman's Song, The.) NOBE; OBSC

In the merry month of May. The Sound of the Drum. *Unknown.* OBET

In the merry month of May from my home I started. The Rocky Road to Dublin. *Unknown.* FaBoBa

In the middle of a plain. Basho, *tr. fr. Japanese by* Burton Watson. *Fr.* Seventy-six Hokku. FCEI

In the Middle of August. Edward Hirsch. MAYP

In the Middle of Life. Tadeusz Rozewicz, *tr. fr. Polish by* Czeslaw Milosz. PwPP

In the middle of noisy children. Voice of my Brothers. Pentti Saaritsa, *tr. fr. Finnish by* Aili Jarvenpa. SOP

In the middle of our times. Middle. Jimmie Durham. HATNAP

In the middle of the harbour. Derek Walcott. *Fr.* A Sea-Chantey. TTY

In the middle of the night. In Childbed. Thomas Hardy. NAs

In the middle of the night he started up. Silver Wedding. Ralph Hodgson. OxBTC; TrGrPo

In the middle of the night in the next room. The Cell of Himself. Arthur Freeman. TwCP

In the Middle of the Road. Carlos Drummond de Andrade, *tr. fr. Portuguese by* Elizabeth Bishop. ATCBP

In the Middle of the Road. Jacob Glatstein, *tr. fr. Yiddish by* Benjamin *and* Barbara Harshav. AYP

In the middle of the sea. *Unknown, tr. by* Jerome Rothenberg. STP

In the middle of the sea lies an island. Minotaur. Robert Fisher. AmMo

In the midmost of ocean. The Sea. Lloyd Frankenberg. MOS

In the midst of love. Emperor Fushimi, *tr. by* Steven D. Carter. WFTW

In the midst of my garden. The Palm Tree. Abd-ar-Rahman I, *tr. by* J. B. Trend. AWP

In the midst of the crowd, together with a dancing child. Saltimbanques. Pierre Reverdy, *tr. by* William Jay Smith. CT

In the midst of the valley is motherwort. *Unknown, tr. by* Arthur Waley. BoS

In the midst of words your wordless image. The Heart. Harvey Shapiro. HoPM

In the Mirror. Elizabeth Fleming. BoTP; OnUR

In the mirror it's plain to see. Bald. Bill Zavatsky. UL

In the mist something's visible. Onitsura, *tr. fr. Japanese by* Hiroaki Sato. *Fr.* Twenty-three Hokku. FCEI

In the mist, the flowering nutmeg is beautiful. Joy at Renewal. Mao Wen-hsi, *tr. by* Lois Fusek. ATF

In the month of Beaver. Ts'eekkaayah. Mary TallMountain. STE

In the month of February. *Unknown.* BoTP

In the Month of Green Fire. Sophie Himmell. GoYe

In the month of the long decline of roses. Hendecasyllabics. Swinburne. FaBoRV

In the Moonlight. Thomas Hardy. *Fr.* Satires of Circumstance, XV. BrPo; NoAM

In the moonlight. Anecdote of the Prince of Peacocks. Wallace Stevens. SOTW

In the Morgue. Israel Zangwill. TrJP

In the Morning. Jayne Cortez. BlSi

In the Morning. Paul Laurence Dunbar. BPo

In the Morning. Siv Cedering Fox. TDD
In the Morning. Jacob Glatstein, tr. fr. Yiddish by Benjamin and Barbara Harshav. AYP
In the morning he steps out. The Crier. Philip Kahclamet, tr. by Dell Hymes. STP
In the morning I am alone in the icy room. The Mountain. Shirley Kaufman. TV
In the morning I didn't know. Comfortable Strangers. Terence Winch. UL
In the Morning I Look for You. Solomon Ibn Gabirol, tr. fr. Hebrew by David Goldstein. TOF
In the Morning I Will Pray. William Henry Furness. AH
In the morning in the blue snow. Annual Gaiety. Wallace Stevens. MoAB; MoAmPo
In the morning light a line. The Morning Light. Louis Simpson. NNaP
In the morning mist. Yoshimoto, tr. by Steven D. Carter. WFTW
In the morning rain. Rainy Morning. Sotero Rivera-Avilés, tr. by Julio Marzan. InW
In the morning the city. City [San Francisco]. Langston Hughes. AmFN; PDV; RHPC
In the morning the hawk and the sun flew up together. Night and the Child. Judith Wright. SeCePo
In the morning the shadow of the old city falls. Shadow of the Old City. Yehuda Amichai, tr. by Shirley Kaufman. VWA
In the morning they build embankments against floods. Wu Chia-chi, tr. fr. Chinese by Jonathan Chaves. Fr. Returning to the Alluvial Fields. CoBLCP
In the morning, very early. Barefoot Days. Rachel Lyman Field. FaPON
In the Motel. X. J. Kennedy. RHPC
In the mountain stream. Tameyo, tr. by Steven D. Carter. WFTW
In the mountain sunset the graveyard. Ozaki Hosai, tr. fr. Japanese by Hiroaki Sato. Fr. One Hundred Haiku in Free Form. FCEI
In the Mountain Tent. James Dickey. CAPP; MT
In the mountain where you are unworshiped. Inanna and Ebih. Enheduanna, tr. by Aliki and Willis Barnstone. BoWoP
In the Mountains, sel. Wu Wen, tr. fr. Chinese by Irving Lo. "From endless rains comes autumn's dusk." Fr. I. WFTU
In the mountains o' the west. The Maid o' the West. John Clare. OAEL-2
In the Mountains on a Summer Day. Li Po, tr. fr. Chinese by Arthur Waley. AWP; SD
In the Mountains, Parting from Master Ning. Kao Ch'i, tr. fr. Chinese by Jonathan Chaves. CoBLCP
In the mountain's shadow. Ryokan, tr. by Burton Watson. FCEI
In the Mourning Time. Robert Hayden. BPo
In the mud of the Cambrian main. A Ballade of Evolution. Grant Allen. EBVV
In the Museum. Isabella Gardner. CAPP; NYBP
In the Museum Art School at night the men. Life Study. Steve Orlen. MAYP
In the Museum of Man. A Pre-Columbian Sculpture. Adam Wazyk, tr. by Czeslaw Milosz. PwPP
In the Music. Robert Currie. TDD
In the mustardseed sun. Poem on His Birthday. Dylan Thomas. NAs
In the Naked Bed, in Plato's Cave. Delmore Schwartz. LiTA; LiTM; MoAB; MoAmPo; NoAM; NOBA; PoA; VGW
In the name of Allah, the Merciful the Compassionate! Love Charm. Malay Oral Tradition, tr. by R. O. Winstedt. WTO
In the name of God, the merciful, the compassionate! Of Iron Am I. Malay Oral Tradition, tr. by W. W. Skeat. WTO
In the name of our dear brothers dead. A Marching Litany to Our Martyrs. Jack A. Mapanje. WMBCH
In the name of the Father full of virtue. Exodus to Connacht. Fear Dorcha O'Meallain, tr. by Thomas Kinsella. FaBoPV; TIRV
In the name of those washing others' clothes. Act. Roque Dalton, tr. by Jack Hirschman. VoI
In the nativity of time. Love Made in the First Age: To Chloris. Richard Lovelace. CaPo; JCP; NAEL-1; OAEL-1; SeCP
In the negro gardens negro birds. To Eliza, Duchess of Dorset. Joseph Deericks Bennett. LiTA
In the Neolithic Age. Kipling. NOBVV
In the network, in the ruin. Trope Market. Jackson MacLow. LP
In the new city of marble and bright stone. The Unknown Soldier. Conrad Aiken. Fr. The Soldier, II. WaaP; WaP
In the new season. Guillaume de Poitiers, tr. by Paul Blackburn. Pro
In the New Sun. Philip Levine. NNaP
In the next century. The Beak of the Dove. Juan Gonzalo Rose, tr. by David Tipton. Per
In the night. The Peaks. Stephen Crane. Fr. War Is Kind, XVIII. AA; WGRP

In the Night. Elizabeth Jennings. NePoEA; NYBP
In the Night. Elizabeth Madox Roberts. WSC
In the Night. James Stephens. OBMV
In the Night. Unknown. NA; NBLV
In the night/ Gray, heavy clouds muffled the valleys. The Peaks. Stephen Crane. Fr. War Is Kind, XVIII. AA; WGRP
In the Night Birds Fell. Abraham Chalfi, tr. fr. Hebrew by Bernhard Frank. MHeP
In the night I get up and walk. Skylights. Tess Gallagher. MAYP
In the Night of the Full Moon. Carl Busse, tr. fr. German by Jethro Bithell. AWP
In the night the agile mole. The Unfortunate Mole. Mary Kennedy. GoYe
In the night the man could hear the wind walking. Harvest. Gene Shuford. GoYe
In the night there was a murder in the street. Of Autumn. Veronica Porumbacu, tr. by Willis Barnstone and Matei Calinescu. BoWoP; VWA
In the north the cloud flower blossoms. The Cloud-Flower Lullaby. Unknown, tr. by H. J. Spinden. WTO
In the northern hemisphere. Kangaroo. D. H. Lawrence. EBEV; InPS; OBTV; OxBTC
In the northwestern pond there is a dragon-ox. Hsü Wei, tr. fr. Chinese by Jonathan Chaves. Fr. Songs of Yen-ching. CoBLCP
In the numb, numberless days. The Burning. N. Scott Momaday. HATNAP
In the Nuptial Chamber. Thomas Hardy. Fr. Satires of Circumstance, X. BrPo; InPK
In the nuptial room there was a black, cosmic cold. Wedding. Maria Banus, tr. by Laura Schiff. OV
In the Ocean. Patricia Goedicke. TSL; TV
In the ocean there's a very sad turtle. Jack Kerouac. Fr. Mexico City Blues, 229. PoM
In the old back streets o' Pimlico. The Rambling Sailor. Charlotte Mew. PoRA
In the Old Churchyard at Fredericksburg. Frederick Wadsworth Loring. AA
In the Old City. Yehuda Amichai, tr. fr. Hebrew by Laya Firestone and Howard Schwartz. VWA
In the Old City. Jacob Fichman, tr. fr. Hebrew by Sholom J. Kahn. TrJP
In the old colony days, in Plymouth the land of the Pilgrims. The Courtship of Miles Standish. Longfellow. BeLS
In the old days (a custom laid aside). Abraham Davenport. Whittier. AmPP; NoP
In the old days back when. Death Crown. Robert Morgan. MT
In the old days I had no wine to drink. Poem in the Form of a Coffin-Puller's Song. T'ao Ch'ien, tr. by Burton Watson. CoBCP
In the old days I had too much respect for nature. I put myself in front of. Intervention. Henri Michaux, tr. by Richard Ellmann. RHTwFP
In the old days with married women's stockings. The Libertine. Louis MacNeice. MoP; NoAM
In the old deep sing-song of the sea. Old Deep Sing-Song. Carl Sandburg. RR
In the Old Guerilla War. Linda Pastan. TW
In the Old House. Joan Aiken. WSC
In the Old House. Donald Hall. NePoEA-2
In the old Jewish Cemetery, Prague, 1970. Edward Lowbury. VWA
In the old man's eyes. Takahama Kyoshi, tr. by Geoffrey Bownas and Anthony Thwaite. PeBJV
In the old neighborhood, each funeral parlor. "Teach Us to Number Our Days." Rita Dove. NoAM
In the old, old days when the West was young. The Texas Ranger. Margie B. Boswell. AiP
In the "Old South." Whittier. AA
In the old stone pool. Basho, tr. by Cid Corman. InPK
In the Old Theatre, Fiesole. Thomas Hardy. OBTV
In the old time, by the forks of the Santiam. A Kalapuya Prophecy. Unknown, tr. by Jarold Ramsey. STP
In the old time women's cunts had teeth in them. How Her Teeth Were Pulled. Unknown, tr. by Jarold Ramsey. STP
In the old village, no house without a persimmon tree. Basho, tr. fr. Japanese by Burton Watson. Fr. Seventy-six Hokku. FCEI
In the olive darkness of the sally-trees. The Bull. Judith Wright. GrPl; PoAu-2
In the one cool room of the house. Developing a Wife. Andrew Taylor. CBAP
In the one light on. First Aid at 4 A.M. Christopher Bursk. InPK
In the one-two domestic goose one-two one-two step. Henry Beissel. Fr. New Wings for Icarus. MoCV

In the only free. In the Ladies' Room at the Bus Terminal. William Zaranka. BXAP
In the open-faced river. Giving Up on the Shore. Gabriel Preil, *tr. by* Gabriel Levin. VWA
In the Open Fields. Hugo Sonnenschein, *tr. fr. German by* Edouard Roditi. VWA
In the Operating Room. Alden Nowlan. NOBC
In the Orchard. Ibsen, *tr. fr. Norwegian by* Sir Edmund Gosse. AWP
In the Orchard. James Stephens. SO; WSC
In the Orchard. Muriel Stuart. ErPo; FF; OxBTC
In the Orchard. Swinburne. BoLoP
In the Oregon Country. William Stafford. AmFN
In the original liturgy. The Book of Juniper. Tom Paulin. FaBCIP
In the Orpheum Building. Kit Robinson. UL
In the outer suburbs the coalmen race their carts. The Coalmen. László Nagy, *tr. by* Tony Connor. MHuP
In the Outhouse. Mitsuye Yamada. *Fr.* Camp Notes. WPOW
In the outlying districts where we know something. Everyman's Library. John Ashbery. NoP
In the oval mirror. Reflection. Iain Crichton Smith. PoPo
In the paddy grow the weeds. *Unknown, tr. by* Geoffrey Bownas *and* Anthony Thwaite. PeBJV
In the painkilling cold that wrapped. Snow. David Wevill. MoCV
In the painting. Up against the Wall. D. C. Berry. BXAP
In the palace and beyond. Yakamochi. *Fr.* Manyo Shu. FCEI
In the pale summertime, when far above you. Of Swimming in Lakes and Rivers. Bertolt Brecht, *tr. by* H. R. Hays. SD
In the pallid soughing of the dawn. Bucolic Funeral. Justo Sierra, *tr. by* Samuel Beckett. MexPo
In the palm. A Guerrilla Handbook. Imamu Amiri Baraka. PoBA
In the Pantry. "Hugh MacDiarmid." NoAM
In the pantry the dear dense cheeses. O Cheese. Donald Hall. DiPo
In the Paralelo a one-legged. Entered in the Minutes. Louis MacNeice. LiTB
In the Park. Gwen Harwood. CBAP
In the Park. Eugenio Montale, *tr. fr. Italian by* James Merrill. PFI
In the parlour of the shanty where the lives have all gone wrong. Will Yer Write It Down for Me? Henry Lawson. CBAP
In the past/ —just as now—/ there were a million women. A Million. Yonathan Ratosh, *tr. by* Bernhard Frank. MHeP
In the Past. Trumbull Stickney. AnAmPo; NOBA; OxBA
In the past I always passed away. My Children's-Children's Past. Jacob Glatstein, *tr. by* Benjamin *and* Barbara Harshav. AYP
In the past too, hearts have separated from hearts. Teika, *tr. fr. Japanese by* Hiroaki Sato. *Fr.* Eighty-four Tanka. FCEI
In the path of the late sun. Kyogoku Tamekane, *tr. fr. Japanese by* Burton Watson. *Fr.* Twenty-three Tanka. FCEI
In the Pauper's Turnip-Field. Herman Melville. OxBSP; PoEL-5
In the pause. Wallflower to a Moonbeam. Louis Untermeyer. BXAP
In the Pea Patch. Maxine W. Kumin. CAPP
In the pear orchard someone stands. Buson, *tr. fr. Japanese by* Hiroaki Sato. *Fr.* Eighty-seven Hokku. FCEI
In the Person of Woman Kind. Ben Jonson. NAEL-1; NIP; SeCV-1
(Another. In Defence of Their Inconstancie.) SeCP
In the "phoenix ranks" I was granted the Purple Robe. Selling My Official Robe. Yang Chi, *tr. by* Jonathan Chaves. CoBLCP
In the photograph he stands alone. Chinese Camp, Kamloops (circa 1883). Andrew Suknaski. NOBC
In the photograph you and I sit together. Family Scene: Mid-Twentieth Century. Linda Pastan. PPR
In the Picture. Thomas M. Disch. BWV
In the picture the people stroll and stroll all day. Public Holiday: Paris. Joyce Horner. GoYe
In the pinch of time, facing. Victorian Grandmother. Margo Lockwood. Psk
In the Pines. *Unknown.* AmFP
In the pines, a storm. Tameko, *tr. by* Steven D. Carter. WFTW
"In the Pink." Siegfried Sassoon. CMoP
In the place where. Judy Grahn. *Fr.* Edward the Dyke and Other Poems. PeHV
In the placid summer midnight. Street Scene. W. E. Henley. BoTP
In the Plaza We Walk. Nephtalí De León. FIA
In the pleasant pastime of temple viewing. Manners. Edith Marcombe Shiffert. WPE
In the Pocket. James Dickey. ASP; RR
In the policeman's arms. *Unknown, tr. by* Geoffrey Bownas *and* Anthony Thwaite. PeBJV
In the pond in the park. Water Picture. May Swenson. BoNaP

In the Poppy Field. James Stephens. PoRA
In the Port. Berish Weinstein, *tr. fr. Yiddish by* Leonard Wolf. PeBMYV
In the presence of thistles. The Thistle. Jerzy Harasymowicz, *tr. by* Czeslaw Milosz. PwPP
In the Prison Pen. Herman Melville. PoEL-5; TAP
In the profoundest depths the wind breaks every bell. Maturity. Tristan Tzara, *tr. by* Michael Benedikt. POS
In the Proscenium. Gene Derwood. LiTA
In the Public Garden. Marianne Moore. NOBA
In the Public Gardens. Sir John Betjeman. NYBP
In the purple light, heavy with redwood, the slopes drop seaward. Apology for Bad Dreams. Robinson Jeffers. AmPP; LiTA; MoAB; MoAmPo; NOBA; OxBA
In the pushcart market, on Sunday. Galway Kinnell. *Fr.* The Avenue Bearing the Initial of Christ into the New World. NaP, 6.
In the quarter of the Negroes. Cultural Exchange. Langston Hughes. BPo; PoBA; PoNe
In the Queen's Room. Norman Cameron. *Fr.* Three Love Poems, II. OxBTC
In the quiet before cockcrow when the cricket's. Dear Men and Women. John Hall Wheelock. NYBP; Prf
In the quiet house, on a morning of snow. The Christmas Tree. Frederick Morgan. BLA
In the quiet time. Ghostly Love. Valerie Sinason. DT
In the quiet waters. Fafnir and the Knights. Stevie Smith. Mes
In the rain/ I came. To Sing in the Darkness. Doris Mühringer, *tr. by* Beth Bjorklund. CoAuP
In the rain that has passed by. Lost City. Ingrid Jonker, *tr. by* Jack Cope *and* Ruth Miller. PeSA
In the rain, the naked old father is dancing, he will get wet. Natural History. Robert Penn Warren. FF; NAAL-2
In the rains of winter the pa children. The Dark Welcome. James Keir Baxter. *Fr.* Five Sestinas, III. ATNZ; PeNZ
In the rain's push and the wind's hand. From My Thought. Daniel Smythe. GoYe
In the rat race he won by a whisker. Lifelines. Gavin Ewart. EAS
In the reading room in the New York Public Library. Reading Room, The New York Public Library. Richard Eberhart. GOYP
In the realm of action the sound is pure force. Nanak, *tr. by* John Stratton Hawley *and* Mark Juergensmeyer. SSI
In the realm of wisdom, wisdom reigns. Nanak, *tr. by* John Stratton Hawley *and* Mark Juergensmeyer. SSI
In the reign of/ that far-off ancestor too. Yakamochi. *Fr.* Manyo Shu. FCEI
In the remote age of the gods. Yakamochi. *Fr.* Manyo Shu. Ma
In the Restaurant. Thomas Hardy. *Fr.* Satires of Circumstance, XI. BrPo; MoAB; MoBrPo
In the ring of high hills. Feodosia. Osip Mandelstam, *tr. by* W. S. Merwin *and* Clarence Brown. AnAn
In the Ringwood. Thomas Kinsella. CMoP; FaBCIP
In the riprap. Mussels. Mary Oliver. NU
In the river of Matsura. Tabito. *Fr.* Manyo Shu. Ma
In the river rapids. Globeflowers on a Riverbank. Tameie, *tr. by* Steven D. Carter. WFTW
In the rockbound pool. Sanetomo, *tr. fr. Japanese by* Burton Watson. *Fr.* Twenty-four Tanka. FCEI
In the Room. James Thomson ("B. V."). NOBVV
In the Room of the Bride-Elect. Thomas Hardy. *Fr.* Satires of Circumstance, IV. BrPo; InPK
In the Root Cellar. Maxine W. Kumin. FaBoWP
In the rude age when scyence was not so rife. Earl of Surrey. AAS
(Another Tribute to Wyatt.) SiPS
In the Rue Monsieur le Prince. Song for "Buvez les Vins du Postillion"— Advt. Jean Garrigue. TAP
In the Rut. Hamish Brown. PoSH
In the Sack of the Wind. Abraham Sutskever, *tr. fr. Yiddish by* Chana Bloch. PeBMYV
In the sad spirit. To the Unknown Light. Edward Shanks. TrPWD
In the salon of Madame des Ricochets. World. André Breton, *tr. by* Michael Benedikt. POS
In the sample room. Butterfly. Tsuboi Shigeji, *tr. by* Geoffrey Bownas *and* Anthony Thwaite. PeBJV
In the sand I grew, by the rocky sea-wall. The Husband's Message. *Unknown, tr. by* Charles W. Kennedy. AnOE
In the scented bud of the morning—O. The Daisies. James Stephens. AWP
In the schools of Arizona. Put Your Mother on the Ceiling. Greg Pape. NAmP

In the scramble to get away. Udobe Ushimaro. *Fr.* Manyo Shu. PeBJV

In the sea at Ashkelon stand the amphoras of Rome. Decline of an Empire. Dan Pagis, *tr. by* Warren Bargad *and* Stanley F. Chyet. IP

In the sea, Biscayne, there prinks. Homunculus et la Belle Étoile. Wallace Stevens. MoAB; MoAmPo

In the sea of Iwami. Hitomaro. *Fr.* Manyo Shu. Ma

In the Sea of Tears. Naomi Replansky. BrRo

In the sea-port of Saint Malo 'twas a smiling morn in May. Jacques Cartier. Thomas D'Arcy McGee. CaP

In the Season When the World's in Leaf and Flower. Compiuta Donzella, *tr. fr. Italian by* Muriel Kittel. DMI

In the Second Month of Summer, Taking My Family to the Villages East of the City. Li K'ai-hsien, *tr. fr. Chinese by* Jonathan Chaves. CoBLCP

In the second scene she has to strip. Man Watching His Wife in a Play. Elizabeth Smither. ATNZ

In the Secret House. Christopher Middleton. FaBoMo

In the sedge beyond Chalco. The Flowering War. *Unknown, tr. by* Jerome Rothenberg. STP

In the Selkirks. Duncan Campbell Scott. CaP

In the Seminole darkness of your singing eyes. Poem to a Redskin. Wendy Rose. CDW

In the Seraglio. David R. Slavitt. ErPo; PeHV

In the Servants' Quarters. Thomas Hardy. MoAB; MoBrPo

In the service of/ My mighty Lord. Yakamochi. *Fr.* Manyo Shu. PeBJV

In the setting sun even its shadow. Kaya Shirao, *tr. fr. Japanese by* Hiroaki Sato. Twenty-one Hokku. FCEI

In the setting sunlight. Yoshimoto, *tr. by* Steven D. Carter. WFTW

In the Seven Woods. W. B. Yeats. CMoP; NoAM

In the seventh month the fire ebbs. *Unknown, tr. by* Arthur Waley. BoS

In the shabby train no seat is vacant. The Refugees. Randall Jarrell. MoAB; MoAmPo

In the shade of a remote mountain. Saigyo, *tr. fr. Japanese by* Burton Watson. *Fr.* Sixty-four Tanka. FCEI

In the shadow of Old South Church the turn of spring is. A Foreigner Comes to Earth on Boston Common. Horace Gregory. EaLo

In the Shadow of the Valley of Death. Abu al-Qasim al-Shabbi. DL

In the Shadows, *sel.* David Gray.

"If it must be; if it must be, O God!" OxBS

In the Shadows of Early Sunlight. Robert Wallace. TDD

In the shafts of sleep. Somnia. Alfred Gong, *tr. by* Beth Bjorklund. CoAuP

In the shaking of the sieve, the refuse. The Test of Men. Bible, Apocrypha. *Fr.* Ecclesiasticus, XXXVI: 5-8. TrJP

In the shape of this night, in the still fall of snow, Father. At the New Year. Kenneth Patchen. LiTM

In the Shire of Phestos hard by Cnossus dwelt of yore. Ovid, *tr. fr. Latin by* Arthur Golding. *Fr.* Metamorphoses, IX. PeHV

In the shoppes. Gemwood. Marvin Bell. LCAP

In the shower not ten minutes ago and blind from the vinegar rinse. Under the Umbrella of Blood. William Pitt Root. GeTw

In the Shreve High football stadium. Autumn Begins in Martins Ferry, Ohio. James Wright. CAPP; HCAP; InPK; InPS; NaP; NoAM; TSL

In the shut drawer, even now, they rave and grieve. Packet of Letters. Louise Bogan. GrPl; PCP

In the Silence. Stephany Fuller. BPo

In the Silence of Endless Night. N. M. Rashed, *tr. fr. Urdu by* Mahmood Jamal. PBMUP

In the silence that falls on my spirit. My Father's Voice in Prayer. May Hastings Nottage. BLRP

In the silence that prolongs the span. Black Jackets. Thom Gunn. HeIP; NAEL-2; TwCP

In the silences between peals of the bell. Chin Nung, *tr. fr. Chinese by* Jonathan Chaves. *Fr.* I Have Recently Edited My Unworthy Poems. CoBLCP

In the Silent Night. Isaac Leibush Peretz, *tr. fr. Yiddish by* Joseph Leftwich. TrJP

In the Silks. Diane Ackerman. MAYP

In the six-acre field. Lost. Millen Brand. NYBP

In the sixth month all is bustle. *Unknown, tr. by* Arthur Waley. BoS

In the sixth month, deep in the mountains. Summer. Chang Yü, *tr. fr. Chinese by* Jonathan Chaves. *Fr.* The Four Seasons in the Mountains. CoBLCP

In the sky. Hameed. Salah Niyazi, *tr. by* Lena Jayyusi *and* Charles Doria. MAP

In the sky. How Strange It Is. Claudia Lewis. RHPC

In the sky above the skylarks. Hozo Pass. Basho, *tr. fr. Japanese by* Burton Watson. *Fr.* Seventy-six Hokku. FCEI

In the sky, not a sliver of cloud. On the Night of the Sixteenth of the Eighth Month. Liu E, *tr. by* Jonathan Chaves. CoBLCP

In the sky of men the bread of stars seemed to me shadowy and hardened. Fighters. René Char, *tr. by* Thomas Merton. RHTwFP

In the sky there is a moon and stars. Proportion. Amy Lowell. BoWoP

In the sleet too, the heron. Kikaku, *tr. fr. Japanese by* Hiroaki Sato. *Fr.* Thirty-three Hokku. FCEI

In the Slums. George Campbell. PBCV

In the small beauty of the forest. George Oppen. NNaP

In the small New England places. Graveyard. Robert Peter Tristram Coffin. AmFN

In the Smoking-Car. Richard Wilbur. LiTM; MoAmPo

In the smoky outhouses of the court of love. In the Queen's Room. Norman Cameron. *Fr.* Three Love Poems, II. OxBTC

In the Snack-Bar. Edwin Morgan. FF

In the Snake Park. William Plomer. NYBP; OxBTC

In the snow. Ishikawa Takuboku, *tr. by* Geoffrey Bownas *and* Anthony Thwaite. PeBJV

In the snow piled. Kyogoku Tamekane, *tr. fr. Japanese by* Burton Watson. *Fr.* Twenty-three Tanka. FCEI

In the snow piled up. Tamekane, *tr. by* Steven D. Carter. WFTW

In the Snowfall. Gwerfyl Mechain, *tr. fr. Welsh by* Willis Barnstone. BoWoP

In the soft armchair sprawls the boy unmoving. The Limits of Physics. Dan Pagis, *tr. by* Warren Bargad *and* Stanley F. Chyet. IP

In the solitude after midnight. Reliance. Chang Ts'o, *tr. by* Dominic Cheung. IFON

In the sorrow and the terror of the nations. The Mother. Nettie Palmer. PoAu-1

In the Soul Hour. Robert Mezey. AmPA; NaP

In the south. Autumn's Fragrance. Kim Hyun-sung, *tr. by* Koh Chang-soo. ACKP

In the South be drooping trees. Confucius, *tr. fr. Chinese by* Ezra Pound. *Fr.* Chou and the South. CTC

In the South be drooping trees. Chou and the South. *Unknown, tr. fr. Chinese by* Ezra Pound. *Fr.* Shi King. CTC

In the south is a tree with drooping boughs. *Unknown, tr. by* Arthur Waley. BoS

In the south is an upturning tree. *Unknown, tr. by* Arthur Waley. BoS

In the south, sleeping against. Legacy. Amiri Baraka. MoP; NoAM; NOBA; PoBA

In the south there are lucky fish. *Unknown, tr. by* Arthur Waley. BoS

In the South there is a saying. Why Are Daddies So Mean? Jane Chambers. GLP

In the southern land many birds sing. The South. Wang Chien, *tr. by* Arthur Waley. AWP

In the southern village the boy who minds the ox. The Herd Boy. Lu Yu, *tr. by* Arthur Waley. ChTr

In the space between school & supper. Skating after School. Barbara Crooker. TSL

In the space of time. Ashkelon. Anthony Rudolf. VWA

In the spaces between the stars still water dances. David Ignatow. *Fr.* Leaving the Door Open. CAPP

In the spreading haze. A Lark. Tonna, *tr. by* Steven D. Carter. WFTW

In the Spring. William Barnes. GBL

In the Spring. Jim Hall. MOWH

In the Spring. Meleager, *tr. fr. Greek by* Andrew Lang. AWP

In the Spring. Tennyson. *Fr.* Locksley Hall. BoNaP

In the spring, by the big shuck-pile. Burning the Cat. W. S. Merwin. NIP

In the spring dusk I find our next-door painter. Yosano Akiko, *tr. fr. Japanese by* Hiroaki Sato. *Fr.* Thirty-nine Tanka. FCEI

In the spring haze. *Unknown, tr. fr. Japanese by* Geoffrey Bownas *and* Anthony Thwaite. *Fr.* Kokin Shu. PeBJV

In the spring meadow. *Unknown.* *Fr.* Manyo Shu. PeBJV

In the spring night's fragrant darkness. Wakayama Bokusui, *tr. fr. Japanese by* Hiroaki Sato. *Fr.* Forty-four Tanka. FCEI

In the Spring, on the trees. Fluttering Leaves. Rodney Bennett. BoTP

In the spring woods, how good it is to see. Aspects of the World like Coral Reefs. William Bronk. VGW

In the squadron you will be replaced. One of Our Aircraft Failed to Return. Patricia M. Saunders. CN

In the square of a lighted window. Observation of a Bee. Leah Goldberg, *tr. by* Stephen Mitchell. WPOW

In the Stadsmuzeum at Bruges, there is a picture by Gerard David. Coming Events. John Montague. FaBCIP

In the stagnant pride of an outworn race. Santiago. Thomas A. Janvier. PAH

In the state of old Kentucky. The Death of Samuel Adams. *Unknown.* AmFP

In the State of "Old Palmetto," from the town of Eutawville. The Eutawville Lynching. Lizelia Augusta Jenkins Moorer. CBWP-3
In the States. Robert Louis Stevenson. AiP; BrPo
In the steamy, stuffy Midlands, 'neath an English summer sky. Switzerland. Alfred Denis Godley. OBTV
In the still air the music lies unheard. The Master's Touch. Horatius Bonar. TrPWD
In the still-blistering late afternoon. The Farmer. Ellen Bryant Voigt. BLA; MT
In the still morning when you move. Tropics. Ellen Bryant Voigt. SM
In the Still, Star-lit Night. Elizabeth Stoddard. AA
In the stillness. Expectant Mother. Penelope Shuttle. BrRo
In the strange city of life. Nostalgia. Walter de la Mare. LiTM
In the strange house. The Messenger. Jean Valentine. LCAP
In the Stravinsky book by Lillian Libman. Reading in the Night. Roy Fuller. OxBC
In the Street. John Shaw Neilson. CBAP
In the streetcar conductor's uniform. Portrait: The Freedom Fighter. George Jonas. NeAC; NOBC
In the streets the crowds go about their business. Daniel Halpern. MAYP
In the Study. Thomas Hardy. Fr. Satires of Circumstance, VIII. BrPo
In the stump of the old tree, where the heart has rotted out. Hugh Sykes Davies. EAS
In the stupors before sleep. It Is for the Waking Man to Tell His Dreams. John Ciardi. BLA
In the Suburbs. Louis Simpson. CAPP; MAT
In the Subway ("Rush hour"). A. Leyeles, tr. fr. Yiddish by Benjamin and Barbara Harshav. Fr. New York. AYP
In the Subway ("Wall, A"). A. Leyeles, tr. fr. Yiddish by Benjamin and Barbara Harshav. Fr. New York. AYP
In the Subway ("Walled-in"). A. Leyeles, tr. fr. Yiddish by Benjamin and Barbara Harshav. Fr. New York. AYP
In the summer heat and fever crackling. The Boy; or, Son of Rip-off. Malcolm Glass. BXAP
In the summer I live so. Winter Saint. A. R. Ammons. TW
In the summer months on every crossing to Piraeus. Watching for Dolphins. David Constantine. OBTV
In the summer of 1945. Thinking of Constantin Brancusi. Wieland Schmied, tr. by Beth Bjorklund. CoAuP
In the summer of the first year of Chia-yu (A.D. 1056). The Cicada. Ou-yang Hsiu, tr. by Arthur Waley. AWP
In the Summer We Eat. Zhenya Gay. RAR
In the summer we rode in the clay country. Elements. Arthur Rex Dugard Fairburn. ATNZ
In the sun, counting the money. Ozaki Hosai, tr. fr. Japanese by Hiroaki Sato. Fr. One Hundred Haiku in Free Form. FCEI
In the sunny orchard closes. In the Orchard. Ibsen, tr. by Sir Edmund Gosse. AWP
In the supermercado the music. A Supermarket in Guadalajara, Mexico. Denise Levertov. RR
In the surround of snow-touched mountains. A Circle Begins. Harold Littlebird. STE
In the swamp a wild hog. The Bengal Tiger. Michael Spence. SoTCo
In the swamp in secluded recesses. Walt Whitman. Fr. Memories of President Lincoln: When Lilacs Last in the Dooryard Bloom'd. RFM
In the sweet shire of Cardigan. Simon Lee. Wordsworth. EnRP; NAEL-2
(Simon Lee the Old Huntsman.) GTBS; GTBS-P
In the Tail of the Scorpion. Genevieve Taggard. VGW
In the tall quiet pines of Washington. For Tom Numkena, Hopi/Spokane. Harold Littlebird. VoR
In the Tank. Thom Gunn. NoAM
In the Tavern. Moishe Kulbak, tr. fr. Yiddish by Leonard Wolf. PeBMYV
In the Tavern. Zishe Landau, tr. fr. Yiddish by Irving Feldman. PeBMYV
In the Tavernas. C. P. Cavafy, tr. fr. Greek by Edmund Keeley and Philip Sherrard. AnAn
In the ten-acre field. Unknown, tr. by Arthur Waley. BoS
In the Tent, Elche. Bill Manhire. ATNZ
In the Tenth Month of the Year Jen-tzu, sel. Yün Shou-p'ing, tr. fr. Chinese by Jonathan Chaves. "Scorpion's tails, silver hooks." CoBLCP
In the thatched cottage I have settled, lingering long. The Thatched Cottage. Hung Sheng, tr. by Paul W. Kroll. WFTU
In the Theatre. Dannie Abse. NoAM
In the thick grasses. Tonna, tr. by Steven D. Carter. WFTW
In the thick rain, the ink-splash rain. Sailing in the Rain. Hsiang Yang, tr. by Dominic Cheung. IFON

In the third-class seat sat the journeying boy. Midnight on the Great Western. Thomas Hardy. CH; NOBE
In the third day of May. The Boy and the Mantle. Unknown. ESPB; OxBB
In the third decade of March. Where Art Is a Midwife. Tom Paulin. FaBCIP
In the third month, a sudden flow of blood. The Vow. Anthony Hecht. InPK; NePoEA; Prf
In the third winter of the war. A Jew's Calendar. Karen Gershon. CN
In the Third Year of War. Henry Treece. WaP
In the tides of the warm south wind it lay. Verazzano. Hezekiah Butterworth. PAH
In the time of old sin without sadness. Variations on [or of] an Air: After [Algernon Charles] Swinburne. G. K. Chesterton. FaBoPa; NOBL; Par
In the Time of Revolution, sels. Julius Lester. PoBA
  "It cannot be/ reasoned with." Fr. V.
  "One needs a lyric poet in these." Fr. IV.
  "One needs a lyric poet in this." Fr. VI.
In the Time of Trouble. Leslie Savage Clark. TrPWD
In the time of wild roses. Bab-Lock-Hythe. Laurence Binyon. SD
In the time when herbs and flowers. Fulke Greville. Fr. Caelica, LXXVI.
  (Caelica and Philocell.) OBSC
In the time when swan and swan. Waratah. Roland Robinson. PoAu-2
In the tiny village. What She Said. Vayilanrevan, tr. by A. K. Ramanujan. PLW
In the top and front of a bus, eager to meet his fate. Figure of Eight. Louis MacNeice. OxBSP
In the Touch of This Bosom There Worketh a Spell. Samuel Taylor Coleridge. Fr. Christabel, pt. I. RB
In the Town. Unknown, tr. fr. French by Eleanor Farjeon. OBCP; PChr
In the town of Athy one Jeremy Lanigan. Lanigan's Ball. Unknown. OxBoLi
In the town of Odessa. Dvonya. Louis Simpson. NNaP; NOBA
In the Train. Itzig Manger, tr. fr. Yiddish by Leonard Wolf. PeBMYV
In the Train. James Thomson ("B. V."). Fr. Sunday at Hampstead. BoTP; OBEV
In the tranquil sun of spring. Yakamochi. Fr. Manyo Shu. Ma
In the Tree House at Night. James Dickey. NoP
In the tree-searing wind. Kikaku, tr. fr. Japanese by Hiroaki Sato. Fr. Thirty-three Hokku. FCEI
In the Tree-Top. Lucy Larcom. OBCA
In the Trench. Leon Gellert. PoAu-1
In the Trenches. Richard Aldington. MMA
In the "Trocadero." Max Hölzer, tr. fr. German by Beth Bjorklund. CoAuP
In the tunnel/ Light is haloed. The Dark Scent of Prayer. Rose Drachler. VWA
In the tunnel of woods, as the road. Last Things. William Meredith. NoAM
In the Turkish Ward. Peter Balakian. MAYP
In the turn of the world. Sacheverell Sitwell. Fr. The Turn of the World. PoPo
In the Twentieth Century of My Trespass on Earth. Galway Kinnell. Fr. The Dead Shall Be Raised Incorruptible, 4. TW
In the twenty-eight houses of the sky: the starry shuttle which has never woven silk. Bad Craftsmen. Victor Segalen, tr. by Nathaniel Tarn. RHTwFP
In the Twilight. James Russell Lowell. AA
In the twilight. Unknown. Fr. Manyo Shu. FCEI
In the twilight darkness. "Oyakeme." Fr. Manyo Shu. Ma
In the 2 A.M. Club, a working man's bar. Robert Peterson. NeAC
In the Uji, the river of eighty clans of officials. Hitomaro. Fr. Manyo Shu. FCEI
In the unnavigable dusk, when. Owl. Peter Kane Dufault. NYBP
In the vacant lot behind the hospital. Night Blooming Flowers. Katha Pollitt. MAYP
In the vacant lots. Song of Degrees. Paul Auster. VWA
In the vale [or vaile] of restless mind. Quia Amore Langueo. Unknown, tr. by Helen Gardner. NOBE; NOCV; PoEL-1
In the Valley. Priscilla Jane Thompson. CBWP-2
In the valley: ever-rumple of brook. Landscape with Mountain. Sándor Weöres, tr. by Peter Redgrove. MHuP
In the Valley of Cauteretz. Tennyson. BoLoP; NAEL-2; NOBE
In the Valley of Death. Amiq Hanafi, tr. fr. Urdu by Mahmood Jamal. PBMUP
In the Valley of the Elwy. Gerard Manley Hopkins. NOBVV; NOCV; TOF
In the valley of the Pegnitz, where across broad meadowlands. Nuremberg. Longfellow. AmPP

In the valley shade. Chikako, *tr. by* Steven D. Carter. WFTW
In the Van Gogh Room. Traise Yamamoto. BrSi
In the vastness. Secret Society of Failures. Lucha Corpi. CCP
In the veins of glass. Alchemy. Saqi Farooqi, *tr. by* Mahmood Jamal. PBMUP
In the very earliest time. Magic Words. *Unknown.* NU; STP
In the vestibule behind the church I saw the parson. Parson's Pleasure. Barry O. Higgs. PeSA
In the village. Ryokan, *tr. by* Geoffrey Bownas *and* Anthony Thwaite. PeBJV
In the village churchyard she lies. In the Churchyard at Cambridge. Longfellow. AmPP; PoEL-5; TAP
In the village it must be a clear night with the light of a red. The Everlastings. Norman Dubie. GeTw
In the village of the dead. First Shaman Song. Gary Snyder. *Fr.* Myths and Texts: Hunting, I. NOBA
In the village there is a crying child. Upper Garrison Farm: A Ballad a Lament for a Woman Killed by the Soldiery. Shih Jun-chang, *tr. by* William Shultz. WFTU
In the violet country. Dont Tell Bad Dreams Says Tita's Mother. John Oliver Simon. NeAC
In the visions of sailors. Between Rivers and Seas. Lance Henson. VoR
In the Waiting Room. Elizabeth Bishop. FaBoWP; HeIP; InPS; LCAP; NAAL-2; NoAM; NOBA; PoE; Prf
In the waiting room of the railway. The Hen. Christian Morgenstern, *tr. by* W. D. Snodgrass *and* Lore Segal. RB
In the waking night. The Cage. David Gascoyne. EAS
In the Ward. Robert Lowell. NAAL-2; PPR
In the warm wind by the Ch'ang Gate, dry catkins fall. Willow Branches. Sun Kuang-hsien, *tr. by* Lois Fusek. ATF
In the wave-bright Naniwa Bay. *Unknown. Fr.* Manyo Shu. Ma
In the waves rolling in. Taigi, *tr. fr. Japanese by* Hiroaki Sato. *Fr.* Twenty-nine Hokku. FCEI
In the way we made the world from a boat. Anti-Memoirs. Simon Schuchat. UL
In the Week When Christmas Comes. Eleanor Farjeon. PChr; PDV
In the West/ circles a wheel. Wandering Chorus. B. Alquit, *tr. by* Howard Schwartz. VWA
In the western village the day grows long. Feelings in Nature. Ma Chih-yüan, *tr. fr. Chinese by* Jonathan Chaves. *Fr.* Four Poems to the Tune "Ch'ing-chiang yin," II. CoBLCP
In the Wet Shadows. Ramón López Velarde, *tr. fr. Spanish by* Samuel Beckett. MexPo
In the White Giant's Thigh. Dylan Thomas. LiTB
In the white moonlight, where the willow waves. The Graveyard Rabbit. Frank Lebby Stanton. AA
In the white of noon-day's brightness the city seems blotted out. In the Old City. Jacob Fichman, *tr. by* Sholom J. Kahn. TrJP
In the white-washed medical-smelling milkhouse. My Grandmother Washes Her Vessels. Fred Chappell. MT
In the whole village. *Unknown, tr. by* Geoffrey Bownas *and* Anthony Thwaite. PeBJV
In the whole wide world. Empress Eifuku, *tr. by* Steven D. Carter. WFTW
In the wicker fish-trap by the bridge. *Unknown, tr. by* Arthur Waley. BoS
In the Wide Awe and Wisdom of the Night. Sir Charles G. D. Roberts. CaP
In the wild October night-time, when the wind raved round the land. The Night of Trafalgar. Thomas Hardy. *Fr.* The Dynasts, *pt.* I, Act V, sc. vii. ChTr; FaBoCh; MoBrPo; MOS; OBMV (Trafalgar.) CH
In the Wilderness. Robert Graves. CH; EaLo; MoAB; MoBrPo; SeCePo
In the Wilderness. Edith Lovejoy Pierce. TrPWD
In the wilds there is a dead doe. *Unknown, tr. by* Arthur Waley. BoS
In the wind and rain rising from my inkpot. Inscription for a Painting. Yün Shou-p'ing, *tr. by* Irving Lo. WFTU
In the wind that ripples over them. Last Scene in the First Act. Marge Piercy. NoAM
In the windmill of evening. The Windmill of Evening. Shlomo Reich. VWA, *tr. by* Mira Reich
In the window of a grange. Fulke Greville. *Fr.* Caelica, LXXIV. OBSC (Love and Honour.)
In the wineskins of full-blown sheets. The Night Works. Antonin Artaud, *tr. by* Michael Benedikt. POS
In the Winter Dark. Dan Gerber. KS
In the winter dusk. Surveillances. Tom Paulin. CIP
In the winter lamp. Iida Dakotsu, *tr. by* Geoffrey Bownas *and* Anthony Thwaite. PeBJV
In the Winter of My Thirty-eighth Year. W. S. Merwin. NOBA

In the winter the rabbits match their pelts to the earth. White Season. Frances Mary Frost. FaPON
In the winter time we go. White Fields. James Stephens. BoNaP; FaPON; MoShBr
In the wintertime. Toe'osh; a Laguna Coyote Story. Leslie Silko. CDW; NoAM; STE; VoR
In the wintertime my father wears a hat. Clock on Hancock Street. June Jordan. FaBoWP
In the Woman Arms of the Ground. Alberto Rios. NAmP
In the wondrous light of a pair of brown eyes. Admiration. Josephine D. Henderson Heard. CBWP-4
In the Wood. Eileen Mathias. BoTP
In the Woods. Dorothy Baker. BoTP
In the Woods. Frederick George Scott. CaP
In the woods behind the city they saw a parachute snagged high. Instant Coffee. John Yau. UL
In the woods I came on an old friend fishing. Finding a Teacher. W. S. Merwin. NNaP
In the woodyard were green and dry. The Rick of Green Wood. Edward Dorn. NeAP; PoM
In the Workhouse. George R. Sims. *See* It is Christmas Day in the workhouse.
In the world are millions and millions of men, and each man. Angel and Stone. Howard Nemerov. NYBP
In the world which He has created. Hymmnn. Allen Ginsberg. NOBA
In the World's Heart. Blaise Cendrars, *tr. fr. French by* Anselm Hollo. RHTwFP
In the worst inn's worst room, with mat half-hung. The Duke of Buckingham. Pope. *Fr.* Moral Essays, Epistle III. NOBE (Death of Buckingham, The.) FiP
In the wracks of Walsingham. A Lament for the Priory of Walsingham. *Unknown.* FaBoPP; GBP (Lament for Our Lady's Shrine at Walsingham, A.) PoEL-2 (Wreck of Walsingham, The.) ACP Bitter was it, O to view, *sel.* ChTr
In the wrath of the lips that assail us. Stigmata. Charles Warren Stoddard. TrPWD
In the yard choking. Without Names. Jeff Tagami. BrSi
In the Year *Chi-hai*. Tai Piao-yüan, *tr. fr. Chinese by* Jonathan Chaves. CoBLCP
In the Year 4 after Father. Aila Meriluoto, *tr. fr. Finnish by* Aili Jarvenpa. SOP
In the Year 1945 an Original Child Was Born. Thomas Merton. *Fr.* Original Child Bomb. NAs
In the year 1910—and I give the date without uncertainty. Versos de Montalgo. *Unknown, pr. tr. by* Frank J. Dobie. AS
In the year ninety-eight, when our troubles were great. The Cow Ate the Piper. *Unknown.* GBP
In the year of one thousand seven hundred and ninety eight. Dunlavin Green. *Unknown.* FaBoBa
In the year of the blizzard. Chief. Michael S. S. Harper. PPR
In the year *tan-o*. Rhyme-Prose on the Owl. Chia Yi, *tr. by* Burton Watson. CoBCP
In the Year 200 B.C. C. P. Cavafy, *tr. fr. Greek by* Edmund Keeley *and* Philip Sherrard. VMG
In the Year with the Cyclical Sign Mou-shen. T'ao Ch'ien, *tr. fr. Chinese by* Burton Watson. CoBCP
In the years of her age the most beautiful. Petrarch, *tr. fr. Italian by* J. M. Synge. *Fr.* Sonnets to Laura: To Laura in Death. OBMV
In the years that pass through. Waking at Dusk from a Nap. William Matthews. AnAn
In the Yukon. Ralph Gustafson. MoCV
In the zero of the night, in the lipping hour. The Approach to Thebes. Stanley Kunitz. PoA
In the zócalo. Three Portraits. George Hitchcock. VGW
In the Zoo. Solomon Mahaka. WMBCH
In thee, thou valiant man of Persia. The Overreacher. Christopher Marlowe. *Fr.* Tamburlaine the Great, *Pt.* I, Act I. NIP
In their congealed light. Through Binoculars. Charles Tomlinson. OAEL-2
In their own way, by their own lights. Meditations for a Savage Child. Adrienne Rich. LCAP
In their ragged regimentals. Carmen Bellicosum. Guy Humphreys McMaster. AA; GN; PAH
In their religion they are so unev'n. Daniel Defoe. *Fr.* The True-born Englishman, II. OBSV
In their seasons. Tameko, *tr. by* Steven D. Carter. WFTW
In their small, queer houses. Ant-Hills. "Marian Douglas." OBCA
In them days/ they won't hardly no way to know if. First Carolina Said-Song. A. R. Ammons. OBAL

In these all-white courtyards where the south wind blows. The Mad Pomegranate Tree. Odysseus Elytis, *tr. by* Edmund Keeley *and* Philip Sherrard. VMG

In these ambiguous photos, their faces gaze. A Nisei Picnic. David Mura. BrSi

In these cold evenings, when the rain. Fear of the Earth. Alex Comfort. MoBrPo

In these dark rooms where I live out empty days. The Windows. C. P. Cavafy, *tr. by* Edmund Keeley *and* Philip Sherrard. VMG

In these days, every mother's son or daughter. In These Days. Ebenezer Elliott. Son

In these days of indigestion. Some Little Bug. Roy Atwell. PoLF

In these deep solitudes and awful cells. Eloïsa to Abelard. Pope. NAEL-1; PoEL-3; TEP

In These Dissenting Times. Alice Walker. InPS; PoBA

In These Exhausting Lowlands. Eddy van Vliet, *tr. fr. Dutch by* Peter Nijmeijer. DuIn

In these few years. Mother's Voice. Robert Creeley. CAPP; NIP

In These Houses of Swift Easy Women. Brenda Marie Osbey. ER; MT

In these miraculous Catalan streets, yellow. Survivors. Elaine Feinstein. VWA

In these ohias light depends. Above the Falls at Waimea. Don Johnson. MAYP

In things a moderation keep. Moderation. Robert Herrick. FaBoEE

In 'thirty-nine, in Poland. Children's Crusade 1939. Bertolt Brecht, *tr. by* Michael Hamburger. MoBS

In this age of decadence people love antiques. Collecting Antiques. Cheng Hsieh, *tr. by* Jonathan Chaves. CoBLCP

In this air. One of the Regiment. Douglas Le Pan. CaP

In this beloved marble view. On the Bust of Helen by Canova. Byron. EyDe

In this blue light. San Sepolcro. Jorie Graham. AnAn; HCAP

In this book I see your face and in your face. Frontispiece. May Swenson. CoAP; NePoEA; WPE

In this buff-gray cliff. Sandstone. Anne Marriott. CaP

In this café Durruti. The Midget. Philip Levine. NaP

In This City. Salvatore Quasimodo, *tr. fr. Italian by* Allen Mandelbaum. PFI

In this city how many masters are clouds. Amsterdam. Jean Garrigue. TAP

In this cold monument lies one. An Epitaph on M. H. Charles Cotton. EBEV; FaBoEE; OPOP

In this cold room. Samuel Hearne in Wintertime. John Newlove. NOBC

In this competition. No Dialects Please. Merle Collins. WS

In this cool corner where dark stars of ivy. Destroying Angel. Hilary Corke. NYBP

In this country I planted not one seed. Sailing from the United States. Stanley Moss. VGW

In this country lightning quickens stone. Mineral Kingdom. Jacques Dupin, *tr. by* Paul Auster. RHTwFP

In this country there is neither measure nor balance. Two Campers in Cloud Country. Sylvia Plath. NYBP

In This Dark House. Edward Davison. OBMV

In this dark place I am still with God. Simon Judson. Lewis Turco. *Fr.* Bordello. SM

In This Deep Darkness ("In this deep heavy darkness"). Natan Zach, *tr. fr. Hebrew by* Peter Everwine *and* Shula Starkman. VWA

In this desolation. The Soldier. Uys Krige, *tr. by the author.* PeSA

In this distant outpost. Yakamochi. *Fr.* Manyo Shu. FCEI

In this factory, here the axe-grinders. University Curriculum. William Price Turner. OxBS

In this falling of seasons. Burning against the Wind. Judith Minty. GeTw

In this glass palace are flowers in golden baskets. The Lovers. Conrad Aiken. NYBP

In this green month when resurrected flowers. Memorial Wreath. Dudley Randall. CNA; IDB; PoBA; PoNe

In this heat. Kyorai, *tr. fr. Japanese by* Burton Watson. *Fr.* Twenty Hokku. FCEI

In this high pasturage, the Blunden time. The Archaeological Picnic. Sir John Betjeman. EnLoPo

In this house, she said, in this high second storey. Under. J. C. Squire. FaBoTw

"In This House, There Shall Be No Idols." Carolyn M. Rodgers. JB

In this imperfect, gloomy scene. The Female Friend. Cornelius Whur. FaBoCo

In this kind of weather. Changes around the Bay. Michael Palmer. NPGG

In this kind of wind. Almost Dancing. Jim Simmerman. MOWH

In this little urn[e] is laid. Upon Prue, His Maid. Robert Herrick. JCP; NAEL-1; NoP; SeCV-1
(Upon Prew, His Maid.) CaPo; SeCV-1

In this lone, open glade I lie. Lines Written in Kensington Gardens. Matthew Arnold. FaBoPP; NAEL-2; NIP

In this long summer wilderness. What He Said in the Desert. Otalantaiyar, *tr. by* A. K. Ramanujan. PLW

In This Manner. Nanni Balestrini, *tr. fr. Italian by* Lawrence R. Smith. NItP

In this meadow starred with spring. Morning Glory. Siegfried Sassoon. TrCP

In this merry morn of May. Medieval Norman Song. *Unknown, tr. by* John Addington Symonds. AWP

In this mirror I am enclosed. Guillaume Apollinaire, *tr. fr. French by* Roger Shattuck. *Fr.* Heart, Crown, and Mirror. TTTS (Heart.) POS

In this mountain village. Tamesuke, *tr. by* Steven D. Carter. WFTW

In this my green world. What There Is. Kenneth Patchen. LLLT

In this nation. Of Being Numerous #24. George Oppen. *Fr.* Of Being Numerous. GOA

In this our English coast much blessed blood is shed. A Song of Four Priests Who Suffered Death at Lancaster. *Unknown.* ACP

In this parable of vengeance. The Impossible Pictures. Tom Paulin. CIP

In this place they make small gardens bloom. And after a Long While. Ory Bernstein, *tr. by* Warren Bargad *and* Stanley F. Chyet. IP

In this place years ago. At the Door of the Native Studies Director. Robert H. Davis. HATNAP

In this quiet town, it is odd to discover. In New Ross. Valentin Iremonger. NeIP

In This River. Valentin Iremonger. NeIP

In this road that I must take. Journey. Roy Daniells. MoCV

In this room, holding hands. All Day We've Longed for Night. Sarah Webster Fabio. BlSi

In This Shanty Shebeen without You. Richard Augustine Chima. WMBCH

In this small character is sent. Upon a Braid of Hair in a Heart. Henry King. EnLoPo

In this small fort, besieged with snow. Lines Written on a Window at The Leasowes. William Shenstone. OxBSP

In this small sideroom a lovely. Not for Sale. Hans Vlek, *tr. by* James S. Holmes. DuIn

In this squalid, dirty dooryard. The Pear Tree. Edna St. Vincent Millay. MoAmPo

In this stoned and. Definition of Nature. Eugene B. Redmond. PoBA

In This Strange Labyrinth How Shall I Turn? Mary Sidney Wroth, Countess of Montgomery. *Fr.* A Crown of Sonnets Dedicated to Love. NAEL-1

In this sweet book, the treasury of wit. To His Lady. Sir John Davies. SiPS

In this the hour of new reckonings! This Hour. Oliver La Grone. PoNe

In this Theayter they has plays. An Old Woman, Outside the Abbey Theater. L. A. G. Strong. FiBHP; MoBrPo

In this time of rain and thunder. What He Said. Peyanar, *tr. fr. Tamil by* A. K. Ramanujan. *Fr.* Nine on Happy Reunion, 1. PLW

In this town, in the blurred and snowy dawn. Geneva. Alastair Reid. NYBP

In this very special, final Mod Squad episode. TV Blooper Spotter. Jack Skelley. UL

In this vintage season, when the skies are full of movement. I Didn't Know My Soul. Avraham Ben-Yitzhak, *tr. by* A. C. Jacobs. VWA

In this way the day slipped. Expectation: Night and Day. Salah Abd al-Sabur, *tr. by* Diana Der Hovanessian *and* Lena Jayyusi. MAP

In This Wind. Mirkka Rekola, *tr. fr. Finnish by* Aili Jarvenpa. SOP

In this woman the earth speaks. Earth and Fire. Wendell Berry. CNA

In this world. Narihira, *tr. fr. Japanese by* Burton Watson. *Fr.* Kokin Shu. FCEI

In this world. Flannery O'Connor. Dorothy Walters. IHMS; PoRA

In this world. Shunzei, *tr. fr. Japanese by* Burton Watson. *Fr.* Thirty Tanka. FCEI

In this world. Tsurayuki, *tr. fr. Japanese by* Burton Watson. *Fr.* Kokin Shu. FCEI

In this world. *Unknown, tr. fr. Japanese by* Burton Watson. *Fr.* Kokin Shu. FCEI

In this world is there. *Unknown, tr. fr. Japanese by* Geoffrey Bownas *and* Anthony Thwaite. *Fr.* Kokin Shu. PeBJV

In this world of ours. Tonna, *tr. by* Steven D. Carter. WFTW

In this world of poison corn. Crow. Kenneth Rosen. NAmP

In this world (the Isle of Dreams). The White Island; or, The Place of the Blest [*or* Blessed]. Robert Herrick. ChTr; JCP; NoP; OAEL-1; OBS; TOF; WiR

In this worlds raging sea. Regrat. William Drummond of Hawthornden. PoEL-2

In th'olde dayes of the King [*or* Kyng] Arthour. The Wife of Bath's Tale. Chaucer. *Fr.* The Canterbury Tales. NAEL-1; OAEL-1

In Thorney Moor Woods in Nottinghamshire. The Nottinghamshire Poacher. *Unknown.* OBET

In Those Days. Iain Crichton Smith. NPo

In those days/ When civilization kicked us in the face. The Vultures. David Diop, *tr. by* Ulli Beier. PBA; TTY

In those old days which poets say were golden. Beer. Charles Stuart Calverley. BXAP; CenHV; FaBoCo

In those painful days, we knew. Yesterday's Illusion *or* Remembering the Thirties. Alun Llywelyn-Williams, *tr. by* R. Gerallt Jones. OBWVE

In those twelve days let us be glad. The New Dial. *Unknown.* OBET

In those years when our sense, desire and wit. Fulke Greville. *Fr.* Caelica, XCVI. NOCV

In thy coach of state. A Crowned Poet. Anne Reeve Aldrich. AA

In Thy garden, in Thy garden, though the rain. The Garden of the Holy Souls. Eleanor Hamilton King. *Fr.* Hours of the Passion. ACP

In tight pants, tight skirts. The Young Ones, Flip Side. James A. Emanuel. PCP

In till this tyme that I of tell. Macbeth. Andrew of Wyntoun. OxBS

In Time. Robert Graves. FaBoEE

In Time. Kathleen Jessie Raine. WPE

In time. When the Storms Come. Lupenga Mphande. WMBCH

In time a message back, like this, to say. Ian Wedde. *Fr.* Earthly: Sonnets for Carlos, 18. ATNZ

In time all undertakings are made good. In Time. Robert Graves. FaBoEE

In Time like Air. May Sarton. NYBP

In Time like Glass. W. J. Turner. MoBrPo; OBMV

In Time of Crisis. Raymond R. Patterson. *See* You Are the Brave.

In Time of Gold. Hilda Doolittle ("H. D."). PoA

In Time of Grief. Lizette Woodworth Reese. AA

In Time of Need. William Stafford. UnPo

In Time of Need. Katharine Tynan. TrPWD

In Time of Pestilence. Thomas Nashe. *See* Summer's Last Will and Testament: Adieu, Farewell, Earth's Bliss[e].

In Time of "The Breaking of Nations." Thomas Hardy. BoLoP; CMoP; EBEV; HAP; LiTB; LiTM; MMA; MoAB; MoBrPo; MoP; NAEL-2; NoAM; NOBE; NoP; OAEL-2; OBEV; OBWP; PPP; QFR; RB; WeW

In Time of War, *sels.* W. H. Auden.
And the Age Ended. *Fr.* XII. Son
"He turned his field into a meeting-place." *Fr.* VIII. SCV
"Some of our dead are famous, but they would not care." GLP
They Wondered Why. *Fr.* II. Son

In time of yore when shepherds dwelt. Olden Love-making. Nicholas Breton. OBSC

In time [*or* tyme] the strong and stately [*or* statelie] turrets fall. Giles Fletcher the Elder. *Fr.* Licia, XXVIII. AAS; EBEV; NIP (Time.) OBSC

In time to come, if such a crime should be. Horace. *See* Odes: III, 29. "Descended of an ancient line" ("Tyrrhena regum progenies").

In time we rode that trail. Thanksgiving at Snake Butte. James Welch. AiP; STE

In time we see that silver drops. Doralicia's Song. Robert Greene. *Fr.* Arbasto. OBSC

In Time's concatenation and/ Carnal conventicle. Robert Penn Warren. *Fr.* Mortmain, I. NOBA; Prf (After Night Flight.) DiL

In times like these, when widows, orphans weep. To a Friend in Love during the Riots. William Parsons. NOEC

In times o'ergrown with rust and ignorance. Priestcraft and Private Judgement. Dryden. *Fr.* Religio Laici. OBS

In times when princes canceled nature's law. Tarquin and Tullia. Arthur Mainwaring. APAS

In times yet to come. Prince Munenaga, *tr. by* Steven D. Carter. WFTW

In to thir dirk and drublie dayis. Meditatioun in Wyntir. William Dunbar. OxBS; SeCePo

In today's expensive atmosphere. Poems Are Cheap. Amiq Hanafi, *tr. by* Mahmood Jamal. PBMUP

In Tolouse or Ankara, in Hungary or Scotland. All. Antoni Slonimski, *tr. by* Wanda Dynowska. TrJP

In tombs of gold and lapis lazuli. Oil and Blood. W. B. Yeats. VVA

In Tommy Morton's byre. Birth. Craig Raine. *Fr.* Anno Domini. NAs

In tottering row, like shadows, silently. By the Sea. Richard Watson Dixon. OBNC

In town, in the foodshop, men are making sandwiches. Big Sheep Knocks You About. Sharon Bryan. MAYP

In Tribute. Vernal House. CaP

In tropical climes there are certain times of day. Mad Dogs and Englishmen. Noel Coward. CenHV; FiBHP; NBLV; NOBL; OBTV

In troth, I do myself persuade. Love Enthroned. Richard Lovelace. CaPo

In Trouble and Shame. D. H. Lawrence. OBMV

In truth how glorious was the High Priest. The High Priest. *Unknown,* *tr. by* Arthur Davis. TrJP

In truth, O Love, with what a boyish kind. Sir Philip Sidney. *Fr.* Astrophel and Stella. EiL; InvP; PoE

In Tuaim Inbhir here I find. The Ivy Crest. *Unknown, tr. by* Robin Flower. AnIL

In Tupelo, Mississippi. The Tupelo Destruction. *Unknown.* AmFP

In Two Fields. Waldo Williams, *tr. fr. Welsh by* Gwyn Jones. OBWVE

In tyme the strong and statelie turrets. *See* In time the strong and stately turrets.

In Uganda an Early King. Alice Walker. InPS

In unexperienced infancy. Shadows in the Water. Thomas Traherne. HAP; LiTB; MePo; NoP; OAEL-1; OBS; PoEL-2; SeCP

In unplowed Maine he sought the lumberers' gang. Emerson. *Fr.* Woodnotes I. TAP

In us and into us and ours. For Eusi, Ayi Kwei and Gwen Brooks. Keorapetse Kgositsile. PoBA

In using there are always two. Song of the Fucked Duck. Marge Piercy. BoWoP; NMM

In Utrumque Paratus. Matthew Arnold. OBNC; PoEL-5

In utter chaos no sooner were you born. Lamenting for My Late Daughter. Wu Wei-yeh, *tr. by* Jonathan Chaves. CoBLCP

In vacant corners, on the hamlet waste. How to Fertilize Soil. John Scott. *Fr.* Amoebaean Eclogues, II. FaBoUs

In Vain. Rose Terry Cooke. AA

In Vain. Adah Isaacs Menken. CBWP-1

In Vain. Jacques Prévert, *tr. fr. French by* Teo Savory. POS

In vain/ They shook their garments. Irony of God. Eva Warner. TRCP

In vain, dear Madam, yes, in vain you strive. An Epistle to a Lady. Mary Leapor. NOEC

In vain did Heav'n its miracles produce. A Poem on England's Happiness. *Unknown.* APAS

In Vain Earth Decks Herself. Moses Ibn Ezra, *tr. fr. Hebrew by* Solomon Solis-Cohen. *Fr.* The World's Illusion. TrJP

In vain her veins incised—jagged boulders. Spokane Falls. Phillip William George. VoR

In vain, in vain, my love, to the river bank you go. Khwaja Mir Dard, *tr. by* Ahmed Ali. GoT

In vain! In vain! My pleading all in vain! Arria to Poetus. Mary E. Tucker. CBWP-1

In vain, in vain—the all-composing hour. The Triumph of Dullness [*or* Dulness]. Pope. *Fr.* The Dunciad, IV. EBEV; FaBoPV; FiP; NOBE; NOEC; NoP; SCV (Reign of Chaos, The.) FiP

In Vain, Mine Eyes. Sir Philip Sidney. *Fr.* Arcadia. SiPS

In vain, poor nymph, to please our youthful sight. An Elegy, to an Old Beauty. Thomas Parnell. NOEC

In vain to me the smiling mornings shine. Sonnet on the Death of Mr. Richard West. Thomas Gray. EnRP; NOEC; NoP; OBD; PeHV; PoE; PoEL-3; SeCePo (On the Death of Mr. Richard West.) NOBE; Son; TrGrPo

In vain we call old notions fudge. International Copyright. James Russell Lowell. AA

In vain you search in the dust. Milan August 1943. Salvatore Quasimodo, *tr. by* Jack Bevan. PFI

In vain your bangles cast. Abiku. Wole Soyinka. PBA

In vaine faire sorceresse, thy eyes speake charmes. To a Wanton. William Habington. SeCP

In valleys green and still. A. E. Housman. BrPo; FaBoTw; OAEL-2; SCV

In Vienna there are ten young girls. Little Viennese Waltz. Federico García Lorca, *tr. by* William B. Logan. SOTW

In Vietnam. Militerotics. Chuck Ortleb. GLP

In villages from which their childhoods came. The City. W. H. Auden. *Fr.* The Quest. Son

In Vinculis, *sel.* Wilfrid Scawen Blunt.
Deeds That Might Have Been, The. TrGrPo

In vine-trailing Iwami's sea. Hitomaro. *Fr.* Manyo Shu. FCEI

In Virgyne the sweltrie sun gan sheene. An Excelente Balade of Charitie. Thomas Chatterton. EBEV; EnRP; NOEC; SeCePo (Excellente Balade of Charity.) LiTB

In Vistas of Stone. Abo Stoltzenberg, *tr. fr. Yiddish by* Gabriel Preil *and* Howard Schwartz. VWA

In Wakefield there lives a jolly pinder. The Jolly Pinder of Wakefield. *Unknown.* ESPB

In waking hours. Komachi, *tr. fr. Japanese by* Burton Watson. *Fr.* Kokin Shu. FCEI

In War. Gladys M. Haines. CN

In War. Mason Jordan Mason. PoNe

In warm war-sun they erupt. Mules. Ted Walker. NYBP

In Waste Places. James Stephens. MoAB; MoBrPo

In water-heavy nights behind grandmother's porch. Adolescence—I. Rita Dove. NoAM

In water nothing is mean. The fugitive. Patience. Elaine Feinstein. BrRo; FaBoWP

In Weather. Robert Hass. AmPA; GeTw

In Wee-John-Boo the bellies of bloodhounds. Orange Jews. Ted Berrigan *and* Ron Padgett. EAS

In western skies. Sunset. Henrietta Cordelia Ray. *Fr.* Idyl. BlSi; CBWP-3

In Westminster Abbey. Sir John Betjeman. CMoP; FaBoCo; InPK; NBLV; NIP; NoAM; NOBL; OAEL-2; OBSV; TOF

In Westminster not long ago. The Ratcatcher's Daughter. *Unknown.* ChTr; GBP; OxBoLi

In wet green midspring, midnight and the wind. Mrs. Walpurga. Muriel Rukeyser. NMM

In wet May, in the months of change. An Exequy. Peter Porter. NoAM; OxBC

In what a silence princes pass away. On the Death of a Prince; a Meditation. Thomas Philipott. JCP

In what a strange bewilderment do we. Morn. Helen Hunt Jackson. AA

In what estate so ever I be. Timor Mortis. *Unknown.* FF; NoP ("In what state that ever I be.") PBBP

In what finite tendon dost thou rise? Spirituality. Samuel Greenberg. LiTA

In what heaven or hell. Once More O Ye Etc. Michael Reck. PPR

In what house, the jade flute that sends these dark notes drifting. Spring Night in Lo-Yang—Hearing a Flute. Li Po, *tr. by* Burton Watson. CoBCP; TTTS

In What Manner the Body Is United with the Soule. Jorie Graham. NPGG

In What Manner the Soule Is United to the Body. Sir John Davies. *Fr.* Nosce Teipsum. LiTB; PoEL-2 (Soul and Body, The.) CTC; NoBE; OBSC

In what order or what degree. Be True to Your Condition in Life. John Audelay. MeEL

In what place in years to come. Sitting Alone in the Courtyard. Yü Chi, *tr. by* Jonathan Chaves. CoBLCP

In what state that ever I be. *Unknown. See* Timor Mortis.

In what torn ship soever I embark. A Hymn[e] to Christ, at the Author's Last Going into Germany. John Donne. EBEV; LiTB; MeLP; MePo; NAEL-1; OBS; SeCV-1

In where the smoke runs black against the snow. Spring Offensive, 1941. Maurice Biggs. PoAu-2

In Which She Satisfies a Fear with the Rhetoric of Tears. Sister Juana Inés de la Cruz, *tr. by* Aliki *and* Willis Barnstone. BoWoP

In whitest hour of pain the iron air. Prayer in Time of War. Henry Treece. WaP

In whose will is our peace? Thou happiness. James Vincent Cunningham. QFR; VGW

In Wicklow. Rhoda Coghill. NeIP

In wild flight. *Unknown, tr. fr. Sioux Indian by* James Koller. *Fr.* Sioux Metamorphoses. STP

In wildest woods, on treetop shelves. The Darkling Elves. Jack Prelutsky. RHPC

In willow shade. Saigyo, *tr. fr. Japanese by* Burton Watson. *Fr.* Sixty-four Tanka. FCEI

In Windsor Castle. Earl of Surrey. *See* So cruel [*or* cruell *or* crewell] prison how could betide [*or* howe coulde betyde], alas.

In Winter. William Dunbar. OxBLMV

In Winter. Katharine O'Brien. SoTCo

In Winter. Michael Ryan. MAYP

In Winter. Arthur Symons. BrPo

In Winter. Robert Wallace. BoNaP

In winter I get up at night. Bed in Summer. Robert Louis Stevenson. GoJo; NBLV; OxBChV

In winter in my room. Emily Dickinson. AmPP; ErPo; LiTA; MoP; NAAL-1; NoAM; NOBA; OxBA

In Winter in the Woods Alone. Robert Frost. HeIP

In winter my beloved is. Fogland. Ingeborg Bachmann, *tr. by* Beth Bjorklund. CoAuP

In winter, the house of Gaggie the bear-trainer is warm. Gaggie. Jacob Glatstein, *tr. by* Benjamin *and* Barbara Harshav. AYP

In winter-time we go. White Fields. James Stephens. BoTP

In winter twilight on a side street. Ghostly Story. Milton Acorn. NeAC

In winter two kinds of fields on the hills. Prosser. Raymond Carver. GeTw

In winter, when it's cold out. Baseball Note. Franklin P. Adams. SD

In winter, when the fields are white. "Lewis Carroll." *Fr.* Through the Looking-Glass, *ch.* 6. EBEV; NOBVV (Humpty Dumpty's Poem.) Mes (Humpty Dumpty's Recitation.) ChTr; FaBoCo; FaBoNo; FiBHP (Humpty Dumpty's Song.) GTBS-P; OnMSP; OxBChV; OxBoLi

In winter when the nights are long. The Beggar Wind. Mary Austin. BoNaP

In winter when the rain rain'd cauld. Tak' Your Auld Cloak about Ye. *Unknown.* OxBS

In Winter's Dusk. Dovid Hofshteyn, *tr. fr. Yiddish by* Robert Friend. *Fr.* On Winter Evenings; 1912. PeBMYV

In winter's just return, when Boreas gan his reign. Earl of Surrey. AAS; SiPS

In wintertime I have such fun. Quoits. Mary Effie Lee Newsome. CDC

In Wintry Midnight, o'er a Stormy Main. Petrarch, *tr. fr. Italian by* William Barnes. ChTr

In wiser days, my darling rosebud, blown. To My Daughter Betty. Thomas Michael Kettle. TIRV

In wishing nothing we enjoy still most. Human Happiness. Dryden. *Fr.* The Indian Emperor, IV, i. FiP

In wit, as nature, what affects our hearts. Pope. *Fr.* Essay on Criticism, *pt.* II. HAP

In wizened old terminal birth. Back Always. Clark Coolidge. UL

In wonted walkes. Sir Philip Sidney. PoEL-1

In woods still winter bare. Shadbush. Christina Rainsford. GoYe

In Worcester, Massachusetts. In the Waiting Room. Elizabeth Bishop. FaBoWP; HeIP; InPS; LCAP; NAAL-2; NoAM; NOBA; PoE; Prf

In Word and Will I am a friend to you. On Himself. William Oldys. FaBoEE

In wrath and grief away the Paynims fly. *Unknown, tr. fr. Old French by* Dorothy L. Sayers. *Fr.* The Song of Roland. OBWP

In Xanadu did Kubla Khan. Kubla Khan; or, A Vision in a Dream. Samuel Taylor Coleridge. AWP; CH; ChER; ChTr; ELP; EnRP; EyDe; FaBoBe; FaBoCh; FaBV; FaFP; FF; FiP; FPL; GN; GoJo; HAP; HeIP; HoPM; InPK; InPS; InvP; LiTB; MAT; NAEL-2; NAWM-2; NIP; NOBE; NoP; OAEL-2; OBEV; OBNC; OPOP; PoE; PoEL-4; PoRA; PrIm; SCV; SoSe; TEP; TOF

In Yad Vashem, where all vows are renewed. Hands Up. Anthony Rudolf. VWA

In Yamashiro, near Koma. Yamashiro. Saibara, *tr. by* Hiroaki Sato. FCEI

In Yatano Field the reeds have turned color. Teika, *tr. fr. Japanese by* Hiroaki Sato. *Fr.* A Compendium of Good Tanka. FCEI

In yellow meadows I take no delight. Sir Thomas Browne. FaBoEE

In Yellow Towns. Léon-Paul Fargue, *tr. fr. French by* Lydia Davis. RHTwFP

In yon heavens. Mountain Haze. Keiun, *tr. by* Steven D. Carter. WFTW

In yonder grave a Druid lies. Ode Occasioned by the Death of Mr. Thomson. William Collins. NOEC; PoE (Ode on the Death of [Mr.] Thomson.) NAEL-1; SeCePo

In yonder marble hero's shade. Italian. Osbert Lancaster. *Fr.* Afternoons with Baedeker. FaBoCo

In yonder old cathedral. The Two Coffins. Eugene Field. AnAmPo

In younger years I stayed away from the world. On Being Assigned as Military Adviser to the Garrison Army. T'ao Ch'ien, *tr. by* Burton Watson. CoBCP

In Your Arms. Miklós Radnóti, *tr. by* Steven Polgar *and* Stephen Berg *and* S. J. Marks. VWA

In Your Arrogance. Lynne Lawner. ErPo

In Your Bad Dream. Richard Hugo. LCAP

In your ears my song. You Laughed and Laughed and Laughed. Gabriel Okara. PBA

In your hesitant moments, remember Cornford and Fox. They Live. Randall Swingler. WaP

In your lamb's wool and cuffs of leopard's fur. *Unknown, tr. by* Arthur Waley. BoS

In your lamb's wool sauntering. *Unknown, tr. by* Arthur Waley. BoS

In your next letter I wish you'd say. Letter to N. Y. Elizabeth Bishop. CAPP; NoP; TwCP

In your presence I rediscovered my name. Your Presence. David Diop, *tr. by* Ulli Beier. PBA

In your quest or request God is remote. Huda Na mani, *tr. by* Lena Jayyusi *and* Samuel Hazo. MAP

In your quiet hand I touch. The Survivors. Miriam Waddington. VWA

In your watercolor, Nely Silvínová. Robert Mezey. *Fr.* Theresienstadt Poems. NaP; VWA

In your words. Lazer Eichenrand, *tr. by* Gabriel Preil *and* Howard Schwartz. VWA
In Your Young Dream. Richard Hugo. InPK
In Youth. William Lisle Bowles. *Fr.* Milton: On the Busts of Milton, in Youth and Age. Son
In Youth. Evaleen Stein. AA
In youth from rock to rock I went. To the Daisy. Wordsworth. EnRP
In youth, gay scenes attract our eyes. The Vanity of Existence. Philip Freneau. AmPP
In youth I couldn't sing to the common tune. Returning to My Home in the Country. T'ao Ch'ien, *tr. by* Burton Watson. CoBCP
In youth I loved the adventurous race. To Match the Prince of Lang-yeh's Poem in the Old Style. Wang Seng-ta, *tr. by* Burton Watson. CoBCP
In youth I served my time. Retirement. *Unknown, tr. by* Frank O'Connor. ErPo
In Youth Is Pleasure. Robert Wever. *See* Lusty Juventus: In a herber [*or* a harbour *or* an arbour] green [*or* grene], asleep [*or* aslepe] whereas [*or* where as *or* where] I lay.
In youth, it was a way I had. Indian Summer. Dorothy Parker. NIP
In youth we dream of death. Hardy Perennial. Richard Eberhart. GOYP
In youth's spring, it was my lot. The Lake. Poe. NAAL-1
In Yüeh Viewing the Past. Li Po, *tr. fr. Chinese by* Burton Watson. CoBCP
In zummer, leate at evenen tide. The Rwose in the Dark. William Barnes. NOBVV
In zummertide, I took my road. Sheep in the Sheade. William Barnes. FM
Ina Field. Kagura, *tr. fr. Japanese by* Hiroaki Sato. FCEI
Ina, 1979. Bea Medicine. GOS
Inability to Depict an Eagle. Richard Eberhart. GOA
Inadvertently I passed the border of her teeth. The Tongue. Zbigniew Herbert, *tr. by* Czeslaw Milosz. PwPP
Inanimate are rocks, desks, bubble, The. Lyn Hejinian. IAT
Inanna and An. Enheduanna, *tr. fr. Sumerian; ad. by* Aliki *and* Willis Barnstone. BoWoP
Inanna and Ebih. Enheduanna, *tr. fr. Sumerian; ad. by* Aliki *and* Willis Barnstone. BoWoP
Inanna and Enlil. Enheduanna, *tr. fr. Sumerian; ad. by* Aliki *and* Willis Barnstone. BoWoP
Inanna and Ishkur. Enheduanna, *tr. fr. Sumerian; ad. by* W. W. Hallo *and* J. J. A. van Dijk. BoWoP
Inanna and the Anunna. Enheduanna, *tr. fr. Sumerian; ad. by* Aliki *and* Willis Barnstone. BoWoP
Inanna and the City of Uruk. Enheduanna, *tr. fr. Sumerian; ad. by* Aliki *and* Willis Barnstone. BoWoP
Inanna and the Divine Essences. Enheduanna, *tr. fr. Sumerian; ad. by* Aliki *and* Willis Barnstone. BoWoP
Inanna Exalted, *sel.* Enheduanna, *tr. fr. Sumerian by* Anne Draffkorn Kilmer *based on a text by* W. W. Hallo *and* J. J. A. van Dijk.
"O lady of all truths bright light going forth." WPOW
Inanna's Song. *Unknown, tr. fr. Sumerian by* Diane Wolkstein *and* Samuel Noah Kramer. LLLT
Inapprehensiveness. Robert Browning. NOBVV
Inaudible move day and night. Silence. John Lancaster Spalding. AA
Incandescence. Lucille Clifton. GeTw
Incantation. Alistair Paterson. *Fr.* Incantations for Warriors, V. PeNZ
Incantation to Get Rid of a Sometime Friend. Emanuel DiPasquale. TW
Incantation to Oedipus. Dryden. *Fr.* Oedipus, III, i. OFD; WSC (Spell, A.) WiR
Incantations. The. Theocritus, *tr. fr. Greek by* Charles Stuart Calverley. *Fr.* Idylls. AWP
Incantations for Warriors, *sels.* Alistair Paterson. PeNZ
Complaint. *Fr.* XXII.
Incantation. *Fr.* V.
Incanto. Stan Rice. NPGG
Incarnate for our marriage you appeared. The Marriage. Yvor Winters. QFR
Incarnate Love. Wilbur Fisk Tillett. BLRP
Incarnatio Est Maximum Donum Dei. William Alabaster. MePo
Incarnation, The. William Langland. *Fr.* The Vision of Piers Plowman. OBEV; PoEL-1
Incarnation, The. William Langland. *See* Vision of Piers Plowman, The: For trewthe telleth that loue is triacle of hevene.
Incarnation, The. Charles Wesley. NOCV
Incarnation and Passion, The. Henry Vaughan. TrCP
Incarnation Poem. John Leax. TrCP
Incendiary. Vernon Scannell. OxBC
Incense, and flesh of swine, and this year's grain. III, 23. To Phidyle ("Caelo supinas si tuleris"). Horace, *tr. fr. Latin by* Austin Dobson. *Fr.* Odes. AWP

Incense of Belsen is stench in the nostrils of heaven. Eichmann. Audrey Beecham. CN
Incense of the Lucky Virgin. Robert Hayden. AmPP
Incentive/ born in ancient. On Riots. Cy Leslie. NBP
Incessantly/ A wild gazelle. The Gazelle. Yasin Taha Hafiz, *tr. by* Sharif Elmusa *and* Christopher Middleton. MAP
Incey Wincey Spider. *Unknown.* PYC
Inchcape Rock, The. Robert Southey. BeLS; ChTr; FaBoBe; GN; OBNV
Incident. Fleur Adcock. ATNZ
Incident. Amiri Baraka. NoAM
Incident. Countee Cullen. BPo; CDC; FF; IDB; NAAL-2; NoAM; NTCP; OBCA; PoBA; PoNe; SoSe; VGW
Incident. Karl Kopp. GOYP
Incident, An. Douglas Le Pan. MoCV
Incident. Muhammad al-Faituri, *tr. fr. Arabic by* Sargon Boulus *and* Peter Porter. MAP
Incident. Norman MacCaig. FF
Incident. Felix Pollak. TSM
Incident at Bruges. Wordsworth. OBTV
Incident at Imuris. Alberto Rios. UL
Incident Characteristic of a Favourite Dog. Wordsworth. FM
Incident here and there, An. Hilda Doolittle ("H. D."). *Fr.* The Walls Do Not Fall. NAAL-2; OBWP
Incident in a Rose Garden. Donald Justice. CRP
Incident in the Early Life of Ebenezer Jones, Poet, 1828, An. Sir John Betjeman. CMoP; MoP; NoAM
Incident of the French Camp. Robert Browning. BeLS; FaPoR; GN; OBWP; TrGrPo
Incident on a Front Not Far from Castel di Sangro. Harry Brown. NYBP
Incident on a Journey. Thom Gunn. NePoEA
Incidental Pieces to a Walk. James Cunningham. JB
Incidents in Playfair House. Nicholas Moore. ErPo
Incidents in the Life of My Uncle Arly. Edward Lear. FaBoNo; FPL; MoShBr; NA; OAEL-2; OxBoLi; TrGrPo
Incipit Vita Nova. William Morton Payne. AA
Inclination. Aimé Césaire, *tr. fr. French by* Michael Benedikt. POS
Incline Thine ear, O God. Therefore, We Thank Thee, God. Reuben Grossman, *tr. by* L. V. Snowman. TrJP
Inclusiveness. Dante Gabriel Rossetti. *Fr.* The House of Life, LXIII. NAEL-2
Incognita. Austin Dobson. CenHV; EBVV
Incognita of Raphael. William Allen Butler. AA
Incomparable treasure, heart's blood spilt. The Poetry of Gerard Manley Hopkins. Monk Gibbon. TIRV
Incompatibility. Luciano Erba, *tr. fr. Italian by* Lawrence R. Smith. NItP
Incompleteness. Henrietta Cordelia Ray. CBWP-3
Incomprehensible, The. Isaac Watts. WGRP
Inconclusive Evening, An. Frances Bellerby. FaBoTw
Incongruity of the Age, Satire on a Miser's Horse. Mirza Mohammad Rafi Sauda, *tr. fr. Urdu by* Ahmed Ali. GoT
Inconstancy Reproved. Sir Robert Ayton. *See* I loved thee once; I'll love thee no more.
Inconstancy's the Greatest of Sins. Lord Herbert of Cherbury. OxBSP
Inconvenience, An. John Raven. BPo; CRP
Incorrigible, brash. Dandelions. Louis MacNeice. *Fr.* Nature Notes. FaBCIP
Incorrigible Music, An. Allen Curnow. ATNZ
Incorrigible, ruthless. The Sea. Louis MacNeice. *Fr.* Nature Notes. FaBCIP
Incorrigible, uncommitted. Cats. Louis MacNeice. *Fr.* Nature Notes. FaBCIP
Incorrigible, unmusical. Corncrakes. Louis MacNeice. *Fr.* Nature Notes. FaBCIP
Increasing moonlight drifts across my bed, The. Fredericksburg. Thomas Bailey Aldrich. AnAmPo; PAH
Increasingly/ it crumbles away. Situation. Alois Vogel, *tr. by* Beth Bjorklund. CoAuP
Incrusted in his island home that lies beyond the sea. The Neutral British Gentleman. "Orpheus C. Kerr." OBAL
Incurable Love, The. José Luis Quesada, *tr. fr. Spanish by* Jack Hirschman. Vol
Indecision. Helen Pinkerton. QFR
Indeed I must confess. Platonic[k] Love. Abraham Cowley. *Fr.* The Mistress. NoP; SeCV-1
Indeed Indeed, I Cannot Tell. Henry David Thoreau. TW
Indeed indeed it is growing very sultry. The Cubical Domes. David Gascoyne. EAS
Indeed, it will soon be over, I shall be done. Intimations of Mortality. Stanley Kunitz. MoAmPo

Indeed profound. The more sacred. The more inscrutable. The More. Eli Netser, *tr. by* Bernhard Frank. MHeP

Indeed, Sir Peter, I could wish, I own. On Clergymen Preaching Politics. John Byrom. SeCePo

Indeed, this world is flat: as for the other, nonsense. The Cigarette. Jules Laforgue, *tr. by* William Jay Smith. CT

Indeed, who cares. On a Sixth Floor. A. Leyeles, *tr. by* Benjamin *and* Barbara Harshav. AYP

Indelible lust (for you). From Malay. David Shapiro. UL

Indelicate is he who loathes. Epidermal Macabre. Theodore Roethke. TW

Independance ("Independance wid a vengeance"). Louise Bennett. PBCV

Independence. Nancy Cato. PoAu-2; WPE

Independence. Adebayo Faleti, *tr. fr. Yoruba by* Bakare Gbadamosi *and* Ulli Beier. PBA

Independence. Guy Mason. CaP

Independence. *Somali Oral Tradition, tr. by* B. W. Andrzejewski *and* I. M. Lewis. WTO

Independence Bell—July 4, 1776. *Unknown.* BLPA; FaBoBe; FPL; OPP

Independence Day. Wendell Berry. OFD

Independence Day. William Jay Smith. TwCP

Independence Day. Royall Tyler. PAH

Independence Twenty-One ("Independence tun Big-Smady!"). Louise Bennett. PBCV

Independent, The. Phyllis McGinley. FaBoEE

Independent Squire ("A squire he had whose name was Ralph"). Samuel Butler. *Fr.* Hudibras, I, 1. NOBE

Index, *sel.* Hugues C. Pernath, *tr. fr. Dutch by* James S. Holmes. "This is a request, a realization." *Fr.* 31. DuIn

Index. Paul Violi. EOEF

India. Florence Earle Coates. AA

India. W. J. Turner. MoBrPo; PDV

India Guide, The; or, Journal of a Voyage to the East Indies in 1780, *sels.* Sir George Dallas. "If you my dear mother, had e'er been at sea." OBTV Miss Emily Brittle Sails for India. NOEC

Indian. Laura Jensen. AmPA

Indian America. Mah-do-ge Tohee. STE

Indian at the Burial-Place of His Fathers, An. Bryant. HeIP

Indian Blood. Mary TallMountain. STE

Indian Boarding School: The Runaways. Louise Erdrich. HATNAP; NoAM

Indian Burying Ground, The. Philip Freneau. AA; AmPP; AnAmPo; HAP; LiTA; NAAL-1; NOBA; NoP; OBD, *abr.;* OxBA; PoELF-4; PoLF

Indian Camp. Janet Reed McFatter. GrPl

Indian Cave Jerry Ramsey Found, The. William Stafford. NoAM

Indian chief who, fam'd of yore, The. The Prophecy of King Tammany. Philip Freneau. GOA

Indian Convert, The. Philip Freneau. TAP

Indian Dance. Frederick Niven. CaP

Indian Education. Adrian C. Louis. STE

Indian Elephant, The. C. J. Kaberry. FiBHP

Indian Emperor, The, *sels.* Dryden. Ah, Fading Joy. *Fr.* IV, iii. ChTr; FiP (Song: "Ah fading joy, how quickly art thou past!") NoP Human Happiness. *Fr.* IV, i. FiP

Indian Girl's Song, The. Shelley. *See* I arise from dreams of thee.

Indian Guys at the Bar. Simon J. Ortiz. STE

Indian Hunter, The. Eliza Cook. BLPA

Indian Lass, The. *Unknown.* OBET

Indian Love Letter. Soge Track. NOVW

Indian Love Song. Lew Blockcolski. VoR

Indian Macho. Louis Oliver. STE

Indian Maid, The; Demararie, Oct. 27, 1781. Edward Thompson. NOEC; OBTV

Indian Names. Lydia Huntley Sigourney. AmFN; FaPON; GOA; OBCA; PAH; PoLF

Indian Night Tableau. Hyman Edelstein. CaP

Indian Princess, The. The Pet Deer. James Tate. EAS

Indian Queen, The, *sel.* Sir Robert Howard *and* John Dryden. "Poor mortals that are clogged with earth below." TEP

Indian Reservation: Caughnawaga. A. M. Klein. LiTM; NOBC; NoP; OBCV

Indian Rock, Bainbridge Island, Washington. Duane Niatum. CDW

Indian School. Norman H. Russell. MAT

Indian Serenade, The. Shelley. AWP; BLPL; EnRP; HoPM; LiTB; OBEV; TrGrPo; TTTS

Indian Singing in 20th Century America. Gail Tremblay. HATNAP

Indian Song: Survival. Leslie Silko. CDW; VoR

Indian Student; or, Force of Nature, The. Philip Freneau. AnAmPo; OxBA

Indian Summer. Nicolae Breban, *tr. fr. Rumanian by* Malinda Cox. WCI

Indian Summer. Wilfred Campbell. CaP; NOBC; OBCV

Indian Summer. Emily Dickinson. *See* These are the days when birds come back.

Indian Summer. Edward Hirsch. NAmP

Indian Summer. Barbara Howes. IHMS

Indian Summer. Mani Leib, *tr. fr. Yiddish by* John Hollander. PeBMYV

Indian Summer. Susanna-Strickland Moodie. CaP

Indian Summer. Dorothy Parker. NIP

Indian Summer. John Banister Tabb. AA

Indian Summer. Leo Vroman, *tr. fr. Dutch by* James S. Holmes. DuIn

Indian Summer at Land's End. Stanley Kunitz. CAPP

Indian Summer Day on the Prairie, An. Vachel Lindsay. RFM

Indian Summer: Montana, 1956. W. M. Ransom. CDW

Indian upon God, The [*or* An]. W. B. Yeats. MoBrPo; WGRP

Indian war was over, The. The Captive's Hymn. Edna Dean Proctor. PAH

Indian weed [now] withered quite, The. Religious Use of [Taking] Tobacco. *Unknown, at. to* Robert Wisdome. EIL; OBS (Pipe and Can, I ("The Indian weed withered quite").) OBEV

Indian, who lived at Muskingum, remote, An. The Indian Convert. Philip Freneau. TAP

Indian Women Are Listening; to the Nuke Devils, The. Wendy Rose. GOS

Indians. John Fandel. AmFN; NYBP

Indians. Charles Sprague. GN

Indians at the Guthrie. Gerald Vizenor. STE; VoR

Indian's Bride, The. Edward Coate Pinkney. AnAmPo

Indians Come Down from Mixco, The. Miguel Angel Asturias, *tr. fr. Spanish by* Donald Devenish Walsh. FaPON

Indians count of men as dogs, The. Roger Williams. SCAP

Indian's Grave, The. George J. Mountain. CaP

Indians have mostly gone, The. Like Ghosts of Eagles. Robert Francis. GOA; LCAP

Indians prize not English gold, The. Roger Williams. SCAP

Indians stole fair Annie, The. Fair Annie. *Unknown.* CH; ESPB, A, B *and* E *vers.;* FaBoBa; OxBB

Indian's Welcome to the Pilgrim Fathers, The. Lydia Huntley Sigourney. AA

Indifference. G. A. Studdert-Kennedy. TrCP

Indifference. "Harry Graham." NBLV

Indifference, The. Sir Charles Sedley. SeCV-2

Indifference. *Unknown.* NA

Indifferent, The. John Donne. BoLoP; NAEL-1; NAWM-1; SeCV-1; TEP

Indigestion of the Vampire, The. W. S. Merwin. NaP

Indignant at the fumbling wits, the obscure spite. Paudeen. W. B. Yeats. HAP; OxBSP; PoEL-5

Indignation Dinner, An. James David Corrothers. BANP; PoNe

Indigo against ocher, Atlantic. Acadian Lane. David St. John. SM

Indigo Eater, The. Lucebert, *tr. fr. Dutch by* Scott Rollins. DuIn

Indigo Glass in the Grass, The. Wallace Stevens. PoA

Indigo, magenta, color of ghee. Whitebeard on Videotape. James Merrill. NoP

Indirection. Richard Realf. AA

Individualist Speaks, The. Louis MacNeice. OBMV

Indolence. Robert Bridges. BrPo

Indolence. Vernon Watkins. FaBoTw

Indolent Gardener, The. Mary Kennedy. BoNaP

Indoors. George Johnston. PoA

Indoors, I am official custodian of our museum. Outdoor Anniversary with Maria. Penelope Shuttle. NPo

Indoors the tang of a tiny oil lamp. Outdoors. House on a Cliff. Louis MacNeice. NOIV

Indra, the Supreme God. *Unknown, tr. fr. Sanskrit by* Romesh Dutt. *Fr.* Vedic Hymns. AWP

Induction, The. Milton. *See* Paradise Lost: Of man's first disobedience, and the fruit.

Induction to "A Mirror for Magistrates." Thomas Sackville, *fr.* A Mirror [*or* Mirour] for Magistrates. AAS; OBSC (Complaint of Henry Duke of Buckingham, The.) PoEL-1 *Sels.* Midnight ("Midnight was come, when every vital thing"). CH Shield of War, The. Troy. SeCePo Winter ("The wrathful winter, 'proaching on apace").

Indulgent Nature on each kind bestows. On Dr. Evans Cutting Down a Row of Trees. *Unknown.* FaBoEE

Industrial Evils. Joseph Cottle. *Fr.* Malvern Hills. NOEC

Industrial Landscape. Giancarlo Majorino, *tr. fr. Italian by* Lawrence R. Smith. NItP

Industrial Size. Jeff Wright. UL

Industrious, unfatigued in faction's cause. The Character of a Certain Whig. William Shippen. APAS

Inebriety. George Crabbe. BXAP

Ineffable, The. Delmira Agustini, *tr. fr. Spanish by* Kate Flores. DMH

Ineffable Dou, The. Sydney Goodsir Smith. OxBS

Inelegant Proposal, An. William R. Espy. SoTCo

Inert in his chair. Drugged. Walter de la Mare. BrPo

Inertia. Kirti Chaudhari, *tr. by* Leonard Nathan. WPOW

Inertia. Vivienne Finch. BrRo

Inevitable. Sir John Betjeman. MoBrPo

Inevitable, The. Sarah Knowles Bolton. AA; WGRP

Inevitable, of course. Very old now, she. Elegy for Delina. Albert Rowe. CRH

Inexhaustible. Israel Zangwill. TrJP

Inexorable. William Drummond of Hawthornden. *See* Madrigal.

Inextinguishable Blaze. Charles Wesley. *See* Hymn: "O thou who camest from above."

Infallibility. Thomas Stephens Collier. AA

Infancy. Carlos Drummond de Andrade, *tr. fr. Portuguese by* Elizabeth Bishop. ATCBP

Infant. Diana O Hehir. NPGG

Infant Diseases and Their Treatment. M. Saint-Marthe, *tr. fr. French. Fr.* Paedotrophiae; or, The Art of Bringing Up Children. FaBoUs

Infant Innocence. A. E. Housman. CenHV; ChTr; FaBoCH; FaBoCo; FaBoNo; FaFP; LiTB; NOBL; OxBoLi

Infant Joy. Blake. *Fr.* Songs of Innocence. FaPON; GoJo; NAEL-2; NAs; OxBSP; PoLF; TEP

Infant she played in the shadow. Anne and the Peacock. Noel Welch. FF

Infant Song. Charles Causley. NAs; OxBC

Infant Sorrow. Blake. *Fr.* Songs of Experience. InPS; NAEL-2; NAs; OBNC; OxBSP; PoEL-4; RB

Infants of Summer. Lennox Raphael. NBP

Infelice. Stevie Smith. FaBoWP

Infelix. Adah Isaacs Menken. CBWP-1

Inferno. Dante, *tr. fr. Italian. Fr.* Divina Commedia. NAWM-1, *tr. by* John Ciardi.

    "And now we walked along the solid mire." *Fr.* XV. OBVE

    Francesca of Rimini. *Fr.* V. PFI

    Gates of Hell, The. *Fr.* III. PFI

    "Like fire-flies that the peasant on the hill." *Fr.* XXVI. Prf

    "Now the hard margin bears us on, while steam." PeHV

    Pier delle Vigne. *Fr.* XII. HoPM

    "Through me you enter the city of lament." *Fr.* III. OBD

    Ugolino. *Fr.* XXXII-XXXIII. AnAn; FaBoPV; PFI

Infida's Song. Robert Greene. *Fr.* Never Too Late. OBSC

Infidel Reclaimed, The. Edward Young. *Fr.* Night Thoughts, Night VII. NOEC

Infidelity. Olga Berggolts, *tr. fr. Russian by* Daniel Weissbort. BoWoP

Infidelity. Louis Untermeyer. TrJP

Infinite. Giacomo Leopardi, *tr. fr. Italian by* William Jay Smith. CT; PFI

Infinite, The. John Boyle O'Reilly. TIRV

Infinite consanguinity it bears. Hart Crane. *Fr.* Voyages (I–VI), III. OxBA

Infinite Debt, The. Rachael Bates. CN

Infinite grief! amazing woe! Look on Him Whom They Pierced, and Mourn. Isaac Watts. NOCV

Infinite Millimeter Manifesto. Hans Arp, *tr. fr. French by* Michael Benedikt. POS

Infinite power essenciall, The. Mary, Queen of Heaven. *Unknown.* MeEL

Infinite Power, eternal Lord. The Comparison and Complaint. Isaac Watts. TrPWD

"Infinite," The. Word horrible! at feud. Legem Tuam Dilexi. Coventry Patmore. *Fr.* The Unknown Eros, X. PoEL-5

Infinite Truth and Might! whose love. Thy Name We Bless and Magnify. John Power. BLRP

Infinite weariness comes into the faces of the old tenements, An. Ghetto Twilight. Alter Brody. VWA

Infinito, L.' Giacomo Leopardi, *tr. fr. Italian by* Lorna De' Lucchi. AWP

Infinity. Philip Henry Savage. AA

Infinity. Walt Whitman. *Fr.* Song of Myself, XLIV–XLV. AA

Infinity Effect at the Hôtel Soubise. Alfred Corn. EOEF

Infinity, when all things it beheld. Edward Taylor. *Fr.* God's Determinations. AmPP; HAP; NAAL-1; NOBA; OxBA; SCAP

Infir Taris. *Unknown.* ChTr; OxNR

Infirm and aged, doth he sit. The Old Year. Priscilla Jane Thompson. CBWP-2

Infirmity. Theodore Roethke. CoAP; NAAL-2; NYBP

Inflammable Man, The. Gordon Challis. ATNZ

Inflammable Woman, The. James Keir Baxter. OxBC

Inflatable Globe, The. Theodore Spencer. LiTA; WaP

Inflation. Charles O. Hartman. PoA

Inflictis. Archibald Stodart-Walker. *Fr.* The Moxford Book of English Verse. CenHV

Influence. Sarah Knowles Bolton. PWR

Influence of Local Attachment, The, *sel.* Richard Polwhele.

    Visit to the Author's Paternal Seat, A. NOEC

Influence of Natural Objects. Wordsworth. *Fr.* The Prelude [or, Growth of a Poet's Mind]: Childhood and School-Time. AWP

Influence of Time on Grief. William Lisle Bowles. *See* O Time! who know'st a lenient hand to lay.

Informer, art thou in the tree. On the Meetings of the Scotch Covenanters. *Unknown.* FaBoEE

Informing Spirit, The. Emerson. AWP

Infusorial earthmounds of the Upper Amazon, The. Lost Explorer. Edmund Pennant. GoYe

Ingenious insect, but of ruthless mold. To the Spider. Thomas Russell. Son

Ingenious Little Old Man, The. John Bennett. FaPON

Inglorious friend! most confident I am. Sonnet to a Clam. John Godfrey Saxe. AnAmPo

Ingmar Bergman's "Seventh Seal." Robert Duncan. CAPP; PoE

Ingoldsby Legends, The, *sels.* "Thomas Ingoldsby."

    Cynotaph, The. FM

    Not a Sous Had He Got, *sel.* FaBoCo

    Jackdaw of Rheims, The. FaBoCo; OBNV; OnMSP

Ingots of silver. Tachibana Akemi, *tr. fr. Japanese by* Burton Watson. *Fr.* Thirty Tanka. FCEI

Ingrateful [I] Beauty Threatened. Thomas Carew. CaPo; InvP; MeLP; OBEV; OBS; SeCP; SeCV-1

Ingratitude. Francis Thynne. PBBP

Ingratitude, how deadly is the smart. Anna Seward. NOEC

Ingrown. James Berry. PBCV

Inhabitants of Old Jerusalem, The. The Popish Plot. Dryden. *Fr.* Absalom and Achitophel, Pt. I. ACP

Inhabited Emptiness, An. Jiri Gold, *tr. fr. Czech by* Jaroslav Kotan *and* Daniel Weissbort. VWA

Inheritance, The. Maureen Hawkins. WS

Inheritance. Mary Potter Thacher Higginson. AA

Inheritance, The. Sami Mahdi, *tr. fr. Arabic by* May Jayyusi. MAP

Inheritance. Kendrick Smithyman. ATNZ

Inheritance. *Unknown, tr. fr. Irish by* Frank O'Connor. TW

Inheritors, The. Gary Geddes. NOBC

Inheritors, The. Dorothy Livesay. CaP

Inhibition. Fahmida Riaz, *tr. fr. Urdu by* Mahmood Jamal. PBMUP

Inhuman, The. Eugenio Montale, *tr. fr. Italian by* G. Singh. OBD

Inhuman Henry. A. E. Housman. FiBHP; NBLV

Inimitably quick. Static Autumn. Yvor Winters. PoA

Inis Fal. Egan O'Rahilly, *tr. fr. Irish by* James Stephens. BIrV; OBMV

Inishkeel Parish Church. Tom Paulin. FaBCIP

Initial. Arthur Boyars. NePoEA-2

Initiate, The. W. S. Merwin. NNaP

Initiation. Jayne Cortez. PoBA

Initiation. Rainer Maria Rilke, *tr. fr. German by* C. F. MacIntyre. TrJP

Initiation, The. Brian Turner. ATNZ

Initiation at Firawa. Michael Jackson. ATNZ

Injian Ocean sets an' smiles, The. For to Admire. Kipling. MoBrPo

Injured Maple. Ronald G. Everson. NOBC

Injustice. Lucie Delarue-Mardrus, *tr. fr. French by* Barbara Johnson. DMF

Injustice of the Courts. Lizelia Augusta Jenkins Moorer. CBWP-3

Ink bottles and pens. Flute and Wind in the Hermit's Cell. Khalil Hawi, *tr. by* Diana Der Hovanessian *and* Sharif Elmusa. MAP

Ink runs from the corners of my mouth. Eating Poetry. Mark Strand. CAPP; GrPl; MAT; MoP; NoAM; PPP; TAP

Inkstone Inscription for the Blind Scholar Ho Yung-kuang, An. Chin Nung, *tr. fr. Chinese by* Jonathan Chaves. CoBLCP

Inland,/ far inland go my thoughts. Song of the Rejected Woman. Kibkarjuk, *tr. by* Knud Rasmussen; *into English by* Tom Lowenstein. WPOW

Inland City. John Crowe Ransom. CMoP

Inland Lighthouse, The. James McMichael. AmPA

Inland, within a hollow Vale, I stood. Near Dover, September 1802. Wordsworth. EnRP

    (Sonnet september, 1802.) ChER

Inlet of Okura is echoing, The. Hitomaro. *Fr.* Manyo Shu. Ma

Inmost sense, The. Jacob Glatstein, *tr. by* Cynthia Ozick. PeBMYV

Inn. Pierre Reverdy, *tr. fr. French by* Eugene Jolas. RHTwFP

Inn of Earth, The. Sara Teasdale. LiTA

Inn That Missed Its Chance, The. Amos Russel Wells. TrCP

Inn towers impressively on the bank of the ancient river, The. To the Innkeeper at Five Rivers, Sun Pen. Chang Yü, *tr. by* Jonathan Chaves. CoBLCP

Innate Helium. Robert Frost. ImOP

Inner Brother. Stephen Stepanchev. WaP

Inner-City Lullaby. Russell Atkins. CNA

Inner deep of the sea has an interstice, The. Interstice in the Deep. Israel Efrat, *tr. by* Bernhard Frank. MHeP

Inner Ear. T. R. Hummer. MT

Inner greet. Greenberg said it. Columbus. Muriel Rukeyser. GOA

Inner Light, The. F. W. H. Myers. *Fr.* Saint Paul. WGRP

Inner Part, The. Louis Simpson. PBCV

Inner Realm, The. Priscilla Jane Thompson. CBWP-2

Inner Source, The. Andrei Codrescu. UL

Inner Temple Masque, The, *sel.* William Browne.
    Sirens' Song, The. NOBE; OBEV
    (Song of the Sirens.) EIL
    (Song of the Syrens.) ChTr; OBS
    (Syrens' Song, The.) GBL

Inner Tube. Michael Ondaatje. NoAM

Inner Vision, The. Wordsworth. *See* Most Sweet It Is with Unuplifted Eyes.

Innery. Reinhard Priessnitz, *tr. fr. German by* Beth Bjorklund. CoAuP

Inniskeen Road: July Evening. Patrick Kavanagh. CIP; FaBCIP; IPY; MoP; NoAM; NoP

Innkeeper's Wife, The. Clive Sansom. OBCP

Innocence, The. Robert Creeley. NeAP

Innocence. Thom Gunn. LiTM; NePoEA-2

Innocence. Patrick Kavanagh. FaBCIP; RB

Innocence. Anne Spencer. CDC

Innocence of her, The. The Innocent Breasts. Joel Oppenheimer. PoM

Innocent, The. Gene Derwood. WaP

Innocent Breasts, The. Joel Oppenheimer. PoM

Innocent Country-Maid's Delight; or, A Description of the Lives of the Lasses of London, The. *Unknown.* CoMu

Innocent decision: to enjoy. Triple Feature. Denise Levertov. FF; NoP

Innocent eyes not ours. All Things Wait upon Thee. Christina Rossetti. GN

Innocent Ill, The. Abraham Cowley. OPOP

Innocent Landscape. Elinor Wylie. OxBA

Innocent Play. Isaac Watts. NOEC

Innocent spirits, bright, immaculate ghosts. From Generation to Generation. William Dean Howells. AA

Innocent Spring, The. Edith Sitwell. *See* Sleeping Beauty, The: In the great gardens, after bright spring rain.

Innocent, sweet Day is dead, The. Night and Day. Sidney Lanier. AA

Innocent X/ is said to have. Francis Bacon Paints Velázquez's Pope. Wieland Schmied, *tr. by* Beth Bjorklund. CoAuP

Innocently a frog squats. Senka, *tr. by* Hiroaki Sato. FCEI

Innocents, The. Jay Macpherson. OBCV

Innocent's Song. Charles Causley. GTBS-P; OBCP

Innominatus. Sir Walter Scott. *See* Lay of the Last Minstrel, The

Innovator, The. Stephen Vincent Benét. EyDe

Innumerable Beauties, thou white haire. Herbert of Cherbury. PoEL-2

Innumerable Christ, The. "Hugh MacDiarmid." EaLo; EBEV; NoP; OxBS

Innumerable worlds! We dream of them. Contemplation of the Heavens. Bill Manhire. PeNZ

Inordinate Love. *Unknown.* EBEV; MeEL

Inquest, The. W. H. Davies. GTBS-P; NOBE; OxBTC; RB

Inquietude. Pauli Murray. BISi

Inquiring about the Health of Li Te-hua, *sel.* Hsü Chung-hsing, *tr. fr. Chinese by* Jonathan Chaves.
    "Who would have thought that a disease of the ordinary world." CoBLCP

Inquisitors, The. Robinson Jeffers. MoAmPo

Inrush of children, An. Epigraphs for Epigones. John Ash. NPo

Insanity. Gaston Dubois. ASP

Insatiable Priest, The. Matthew Prior. OxBSP

Inscape. Susan Litwack. VWA

Inscibed on a Painting of Sailboats on the River. Yün Shou-p'ing, *tr. fr. Chinese by* Jonathan Chaves. CoBLCP

Inscribed in Melrose Abbey. *Unknown.* FaBoEE; FaBoRV

Inscribed on a Landscape by Mi Yüan-hui. Chao Meng-fu, *tr. fr. Chinese by* Jonathan Chaves. CoBLCP

Inscribed on a Lichen-Covered Wall in My Hut, *sel.* Chin Nung, *tr. fr. Chinese by* Jonathan Chaves.
    "Three lines of "clerk script" calligraphy." CoBLCP

Inscribed on a Painting. Hsü Wei, *tr. fr. Chinese by* Jonathan Chaves. CoBLCP

Inscribed on a Painting. Ni Tsan, *tr. fr. Chinese by* Jonathan Chaves. CoBLCP

Inscribed on a Painting ("At the country inn, thousands of peach trees"). T'ang Yin, *tr. fr. Chinese by* Jonathan Chaves. CoBLCP

Inscribed on a Painting ("On the mountain, old trees, still green in autumn"). T'ang Yin, *tr. fr. Chinese by* Jonathan Chaves. CoBLCP

Inscribed on a Painting ("Places I go, leaning on my bramble cane, The"). T'ang Yin, *tr. fr. Chinese by* Jonathan Chaves. CoBLCP

Inscribed on a Painting ("Thatched hut among the pines, door open near a cliff"). T'ang Yin, *tr. fr. Chinese by* Jonathan Chaves. CoBLCP

Inscribed on a Painting. Tao-chi, *tr. fr. Chinese by* Jonathan Chaves. CoBLCP

Inscribed on a Painting. Ts'ao Chen-chi, *tr. fr. Chinese by* William H. Nienhauser, Jr. WFTU

Inscribed on a Painting. Yü Chi, *tr. fr. Chinese by* Jonathan Chaves. CoBLCP

Inscribed on a Painting ("Magic mists twirl around the sky"). Yün Shou-p'ing, *tr. fr. Chinese by* Jonathan Chaves. CoBLCP

Inscribed on a Painting ("Who needs a raft that can invade the stars?"). Yün Shou-p'ing, *tr. fr. Chinese by* Jonathan Chaves. CoBLCP

Inscribed on a Painting by Myself. Ni Tsan, *tr. fr. Chinese by* Jonathan Chaves. CoBLCP

Inscribed on a Painting by Shih-ku, *sel.* Yün Shou-p'ing, *tr. fr. Chinese by* Jonathan Chaves.
    "Through the windy valley." CoBLCP

Inscribed on a Painting: Cultivating Leisure, *sel.* Wen Cheng-ming, *tr. fr. Chinese by* Jonathan Chaves.
    "Volumes of books, tea and incense." CoBLCP

Inscribed on a Painting "Fishing in the Snow on a Wintry River." Ching An, *tr. fr. Chinese by* Irving Lo. WFTU

Inscribed on a Painting of a Fisherman. T'ang Yin, *tr. fr. Chinese by* Jonathan Chaves. CoBLCP

Inscribed on a Painting of a Wu-t'ung Tree by Myself. Tao-chi, *tr. fr. Chinese by* Jonathan Chaves. CoBLCP

Inscribed on a Painting of Bamboo. T'ang Yin, *tr. fr. Chinese by* Jonathan Chaves. CoBLCP

Inscribed on a Painting of Bamboo. Wu Chen, *tr. fr. Chinese by* Jonathan Chaves. CoBLCP

Inscribed on a Painting of Bamboo Presented to Lec, *sel.* Yang Shih-ch'i, *tr. fr. Chinese by* Jonathan Chaves.
    "Even ordinarily, parting is difficult." CoBLCP

Inscribed on a Painting of Dragons by Ch'en So-weng. Hsieh Chin, *tr. fr. Chinese by* Jonathan Chaves. CoBLCP

Inscribed on a Plantain Leaf to Show to a Certain Person. Liu Ling-hsien, *tr. fr. Chinese by* Burton Watson. CoBCP

Inscribed on a Snowscape. Yün Shou-p'ing, *tr. fr. Chinese by* Jonathan Chaves. CoBLCP

Inscribed on a Tombstone. Mani Leib, *tr. fr. Yiddish by* John Hollander. PeBMYV

Inscribed on a Wall Painting of Assembled Immortals. Chao Meng-fu, *tr. fr. Chinese by* Jonathan Chaves. CoBLCP

Inscribed on an Album Leaf Painted by Dr. Lin. Pien Kung, *tr. fr. Chinese by* Jonathan Chaves. CoBLCP

Inscribed on "Drunk in the Autumn Woods." Tao-chi, *tr. fr. Chinese by* Jonathan Chaves. CoBLCP

Inscribed on Landscapes I Painted Myself. Rai San'yo, *tr. fr. Chinese by* Burton Watson. JLIC-2

Inscribed on My Ink Landscape Painting. Tao-chi, *tr. fr. Chinese by* Joanthan Chaves. CoBLCP

Inscribed on My Large Landscape Hanging Scroll "Listening to a Waterfall." Tao-chi, *tr. fr. Chinese by* Jonathan Chaves. CoBLCP

Inscribed on My Little Painting of Plum Blossom and Bamboo. Tao-chi, *tr. fr. Chinese by* Jonathan Chaves. CoBLCP

Inscribed on Paintings for the People of Hangchow, *sels.* Hsü Wei, *tr. fr. Chinese by* Jonathan Chaves. CoBLCP
    "In one place, flying clubs."
    "Puppets which perform before the curtains, The."

Inscribed on Sun An-chih's "Painting of Pines and Catalpas." Chao Meng-fu, *tr. fr. Chinese by* Jonathan Chaves. CoBLCP

Inscribed on T'ai-po Shrine, at Colored Stone Jetty. Ch'ü Ta-chün, *tr. fr. Chinese by* Paul W. Kroll. WFTU

Inscribed on the Painting "Meaning of a Poem by Wang Wei." Li Tung-yang, *tr. fr. Chinese by* Jonathan Chaves. CoBLCP

Inscribed on the Painting "River in Autumn." Ni Tsan, *tr. fr. Chinese by* Jonathan Chaves. CoBLCP

Inscribed on the Painting "Solitary Crane." Yü Chi, *tr. fr. Chinese by* Jonathan Chaves. CoBLCP

Inscribed on the Painting "Spring Dawn at Peach Blossom Spring" by Scholar Shang Te-fu. Chao Meng-fu, *tr. fr. Chinese by* Jonathan Chaves. CoBLCP

Inscribed on the Painting "Stabbing a Tiger" by Chao Tzu-ang. Yang Shih-ch'i, *tr. fr. Chinese by* Jonathan Chaves. CoBLCP

Inscribed on the Wall at the Temple of the Auspicious Talisman. Tao-chi, *tr. fr. Chinese by* Jonathan Chaves. CoBLCP

Inscribed on the Wall of a Rice Cake Shop. Chin Nung, *tr. fr. Chinese by* Jonathan Chaves. CoBLCP

Inscriptio. Pope. OxBSP

Inscription: "Eagle, stooping from yon snow-blown peaks, The." Whittier. GOA

Inscription: "For one long term, or e'er her trial came." George Canning *and* John Hookham Frere. FaBoCo; FaBoEE

(Inscription for the Door of the Cell in Newgate Where Mrs. Brownrigg, the 'Prentice-cide, Was Confined Previous to Her Execution.) Par

Inscription, An: Grass of levity. *Unknown.* EiL

Inscription: "He wrote upon his heart." Donald Jeffrey Hayes. CDC

Inscription: "Whoe'er thou art whose path in summer lies." Mark Akenside. NOEC

Inscription above the Entrance to the Abbey of Theleme. Rabelais, *tr. fr. French by* Sir Thomas Urquhart. *Fr.* Gargantua. FaBoRV

Inscription at Mount Vernon. *Unknown.* OHIP

Inscription by the Sea, An. E. A. Robinson, *after* Glaucus. AWP; ChTr; FaBoEE

Inscription for a Graveyard. Yvor Winters. CRP

Inscription for a Grotto. Mark Akenside. NOEC; PoEL-3

Inscription for a Headstone. Austin Clarke. BIrV; CIP

Inscription for a Mirror in a Deserted Dwelling. William Rose Benét. MoAmPo

Inscription for a Painting, An: "A Forest in the Frost." Yün Shou-p'ing, *tr. fr. Chinese by* Irving Lo. WFTU

Inscription for a Portrait of Dante. Boccaccio, *tr. fr. Italian by* Dante Gabriel Rossetti. *Fr.* Sonnets. AWP

Inscription for a Wayside Spring. Frances Cornford. BrRo

Inscription for an Old Bed. William Morris. OBEV; WiR

Inscription for Arthur Rackham's Rip Van Winkle. James Elroy Flecker. BrPo

Inscription for Marye's Heights, Fredericksburg. Herman Melville. UnPo

Inscription for My Evergreen Pavilion. Ch'en Pao-shen, *tr. fr. Chinese by* Yi-yu Cho Woo. WFTU

Inscription for the Door of the Cell in Newgate Where Mrs. Brownrigg, the 'Prentice-cide, Was Confined Previous to Her Execution. George Canning *and* John Hookham Frere. *See* For one long term, or e'er her trial came.

Inscription for the Entrance to a Wood. Bryant. AmPP; OxBA; TAP

Inscription for the Sign of *The Jolly Barber*, with a Razor in One Hand, and a Pot of Beer in the Other, *sel.* Swift.
"Roam not from pole to pole, but enter here." FaBoUs

Inscription for the Tank. James Wright. TwCP

Inscription in a Garden. George Gascoigne. OBSC; TrGrPo

Inscription on a Chemise. *Unknown, tr. fr. Arabic by* E. Powys Mathers. *Fr.* The Thousand and One Nights. ErPo

Inscription on the Flyleaf of a Bible. Dannie Abse. TrJP

Inscription on the Monument of a Newfoundland Dog. Byron. TEP

Inscription on the Tombe of the Lady Mary Wentworth, The. Thomas Carew. *See* And here the precious dust is laid.

Inscription, An: "Over the sheer rocks over the gorges." Stanislav Vinaver, *tr. by* Vasa D. Mihailovich. VWA

Inscriptions at the City of Brass. *Unknown, tr. fr. Arabic by* E. Powys Mathers. *Fr.* The Thousand and One Nights. AWP; WaaP, 3 *sts.*

Inscriptions on Greek tombstones intrigued him. Ronald Wyn. Robert Bagg. TwCP

Inscrutable Cat. Leyb Kvitko, *tr. fr. Yiddish by* Allen Mandelbaum *and* Harold Rabinowitz. PeBMYV

Insect Eyes. Ruth Kim Chun-soo, *tr. fr. Korean by* Koh Chang-soo. ACKP

Insect Heads. Robert Bly. CAPP

Insect Kitchen, The. Nicki Jackowska. BrRo

Insect or blossom? Fragile, fairy thing. The Mariposa Lily. Ina Coolbrith. AA

Insect spills its notes, An. Miura Chora, *tr. fr. Japanese by* Hiroaki Sato. *Fr.* Sixteen Hokku. FCEI

Insect voice has separated, An. Sitting Quietly at Night. Kito, *tr. fr. Japanese by* Hiroaki Sato. *Fr.* Twenty-four Hokku. FCEI

Insects. Isidor Schneider. TrJP

Insects, The. Nancy Willard. LCAP

Insects have a speculative gaze, The. Not Machines. Peter Redgrove. NPo

Insects near a Hut in the Fields. Masayori, *tr. fr. Japanese by* Steven D. Carter. WFTW

Insensibility. Wilfred Owen. CMoP; FaBoTw; InPS; LiTB; LiTM; MMA; MoAB; OBWP; OxBTC; WaP

Inseparable. Philip Bourke Marston. BoLoP

Inseparable from the fire. Coda. William Carlos Williams. NOBA

Insert, The. R. L. Barth. InPK

Inside a cave in a narrow canyon near Tassajara. Hands. Robinson Jeffers. GOA

Inside and Out. Robert Phillips. GeTw

Inside, beneath the desert sky, beneath the radar. San Xavier Du Bac/ for Jon. Jorie Graham. NAmP

Inside Diameter. Clarence Major. UL

Inside every widow. Portrait of a Widow. Avner Strauss. VWA

Inside God's Eye. Pattiann Rogers. NAmP

Inside History. Angela McCabe. AmPA

Inside I could hear. Star Motel. Bill Berkson. UL

Inside, it is bare but dimly alive. Thomas Kinsella. *Fr.* The Messenger. CIP

Inside its zig-zag lines the little camp is asleep. The Magazine Fort, Phoenix Park, Dublin. William Wilkins. SeCePo

Inside my father's close. My Father's Close. *Unknown, tr. by* Dante Gabriel Rossetti. AWP

Inside of a whirlpool, The. Warning. John Ciardi. PDV

Inside of King's College Chapel, Cambridge. Wordsworth. *Fr.* Ecclesiastical Sonnets, *pt.* III, XLIII. EnRP; OBNC

Inside or out, the key is pain. It holds. Hospital. Karl Shapiro. VGW

Inside Out. Diane Wakoski. CoAP; NYBP

Inside the brain they are holding a mass funeral for the dead brain cells. The Brain Cells. Donald Hall. TAP

Inside the Cave. Geoffrey Grigson. FaBoPP

Inside the child. Night Watch. Margo Magid. NMM

Inside the coconut is Katerina's baby. A Coconut for Katerina. Sandra McPherson. LCAP

Inside the fog that encloses the trees. Trees Lose Parts of Themselves Inside a Circle of Fog. Francis Ponge, *tr. by* Robert Bly. NU

Inside the light of a three-way lamp. The Fire Burns Low. John Leax. TrCP

Inside the nighttime of the storm. The Enormous Hand. Jorge de Lima, *tr. by* June Jordan. ATCBP

Inside the processing complex. Industrial Size. Jeff Wright. UL

Inside the River. James Dickey. PoA

Inside the skull the wakeful brain. The Camera Obscura. John Addington Symonds. NOBVV

Inside the tower not a broken tower two. Image-Nation (the Poesis). Robin Blaser. PoM

Inside the Tulip. George Bowering. MoCV

Inside the veins there are navies setting forth. Waking from Sleep. Robert Bly. CAPP; EAS; NOBA; NoP

Inside this clay jug there are canyons and pine mountains. The Clay Jug. Kabir. NU

Inside this shell. What Is Lived. Carmen Valle. *tr. by* Julio Marzán. InW

Insight. Mary Goose. STE

Insights. Catherine Davis. NePoEA; QFR

Insincere Wish Addressed to a Beggar, An. Mary Elizabeth Coleridge. NOBVV

Insistently through sleep—a tide of voices. The Harbor Dawn. Hart Crane. *Fr.* The Bridge: Powhatan's Daughter. AmPP; CMoP; FaBV; GOA; LiTM; MoAB; MoAmPo; NoAM; NOBA; OxBA; PrIm; TrGrPo

Insomnia. Elizabeth Bishop. LLLT

Insomnia. Ethna MacCarthy. NeIP

Insomnia. John Banister Tabb. TrPWD

Insomnia. Edith Matilda Thomas. AA

Insomnia, *sel.* Marina Tsvetayeva, *tr. fr. Russian by* Elaine Feinstein *and* Angela Livingston.
"Black as the centre of an eye, the centre, a blackness." PBWP

Insomnia I. Howard Nemerov. DiPo

Insomnia the Gem of the Ocean. John Updike. NBLV

Insomniac Poem. Ron Loewinsohn. NeAP

Insomniac Sleeps Well for Once and, The. Hayden Carruth. NNaP

Insomniacs, The. Adrienne Rich. NYBP

Insomuch, Bassa, as I never saw. On Bassa. Martial. PeHV

Inspection. Wilfred Owen. WaP

Inspection, The. Frederick B. Watt. CaP

Inspector Hsü Claims He Has Found the Secret of Youth. T'ang Hsien-Tsu, *tr. fr. Chinese by* Jonathan Chaves. CoBLCP
Inspiration. Mary Elizabeth Fullerton. PoAu-1
Inspiration. W. W. Gibson. WGRP
Inspiration. Samuel Johnson. *See* Life of Ages, Richly Poured.
Inspiration. E. V. Knox. CenHV
Inspiration, The. James Montgomery. *Fr.* The West Indies. PAH
Inspiration. Robert W. Service. WeW
Inspiration. John Banister Tabb. WGRP
Inspiration ("Whate'er we leave to God, God does."), *sel.* Henry David Thoreau. AA; AmPP; AnAmPo; BLPL; FaBoBe; NOBA; OxBA
"If with light head erect I sing." WGRP, *abr.*
Inspiration. *Unknown, tr. fr. Greek by* J. Rendel Harris. *Fr.* Solomon, VI. WGRP
Inspiration, An. Ella Wheeler Wilcox. AnAmPo; WGRP
Inspirations. William James Dawson. WGRP
Inspire our sons to seek their man-shadows. If We Cannot Live People as People. Charles Lynch. CNA; PoBA
Inst., Ult., and Prox. A. P. Herbert. FaBoUs
Instability. Henrietta Cordelia Ray. CBWP-3
Instalment, The, *sel.* Edward Young.
"Since Brunswick's smile has authoris'd my muse." FaBoCo
Instamatic. Edwin Morgan. FF
Instamatic The Moon February 1973. Edwin Morgan. BWV
Instans Tyrannus. Robert Browning. EBEV
Instant acts. Turning On Daytime TV. Alex Kuo. UL
Instant Coffee. John Yau. UL
Instead of a Journey. Michael Hamburger. NYBP
Instead of an Autobiography. László Kálnoky, *tr. fr. Hungarian by* Edwin Morgan. MHuP
Instead of an Interview. Fleur Adcock. OBTV
Instead of cabbage, acorns boil to-morrow. Hangover Cure. Nicochares. FaBoUs
Instead of Incense (Blessed Lord) if wee. Nathaniel Wanley. *Fr.* Royal [*or* Royall] Presents. TrPWD
Instead of Neat Inclosures. Robert Herrick. *Fr.* An Ode of the Birth of Our Saviour. ChTr
Instead of oil love feeds. Mohammad Taqi Mir, *tr. by* Ahmed Ali. GoT
Instead of wasting thoughts on unavailing things. Tabito. *Fr.* Manyo Shu. Ma
Instead of you, I choose the blood. The Unwanted. Mary Gordon. IHMS
Instinct of Self-Preservation, The. Nanni Balestrini, *tr. fr. Italian by* Lawrence R. Smith. NItP
Instinctively, unwittingly. Janet Lewis. QFR
Institutions. Janet Fox. BWV
Instructed in love. Ingeborg Bachmann, *tr. fr. German by* Daniel Huws. *Fr.* Songs in Flight. WPOW
Instructed to speak of God with emphasis. Memorial to a Missionary. Keith Sinclair. ATNZ; PeNZ
Instruction. Conrad Hilberry. ASP
Instruction from Bly. Cynthia MacDonald. ER; NMM
Instruction in the Art. Philip Booth. SD
Instruction Manual, The. John Ashbery. HAP; InPS; MoP; NeAP; NoAM; NOBA; PoM; SOTW; WeW
Instruction sore long time I bore. Charles Kingsley. CenHV
Instructions. Anita Skeen. IHMS
Instructions for Crossing the Border. Dan Pagis, *tr. fr. Hebrew by* Stephen Mitchell. VWA
Instructions for Elijah. Myra Sklarew. CRP
Instructions for Fishing the Eel. Dennis Schmitz. AnAn
Instructions for the Messiah. Myra Sklarew. VWA
Instructions for the Waitress. Yehuda Amichai, *tr. fr. Hebrew by* Warren Bargad *and* Stanley F. Chyet. IP
Instructions of King Cormac, The, *sel. Unknown, tr. fr. Irish by* Kuno Meyer.
"O Cormac, grandson of Conn," said Carbery." BIrV
Instructions to a Celebrated Laureat, *sel.* "Peter Pindar."
George III Visits Whitbread's Brewery. NOEC
Instructions to a Painter. Edmund Waller. APAS
Instructions to a Princess. Ishmael Reed. CNA; PoBA
Instructions to the Double. Tess Gallagher. FaBoWP
Instructor said, The. Theme for English B. Langston Hughes. HCAP; MoP; NIP; NoAM; NOBA; NoP
Instrument, The. Kathleen Jessie Raine. PoA
Instruments, The. Christopher Smart. WiR
Insular Celts, The. Ciaran Carson. BIrV; CIP
Insult, The. Robert Layzer. NePoEA
Insult, An. *Unknown.* NOIV
Insult before Gift-Giving. Frank Bolton, *tr. fr. Tsimshian Indian by* Armand Schwerner. STP

Insulted. Priscilla Jane Thompson. CBWP-2
Insusceptibles, The. Adrienne Rich. HeIP; SM; Son
Intaglio. Henri Coulette. NePoEA
Intaglios, *sels.* Francis Brooke. AA
On the Plains.
Tennesee.
Integrity. Adrienne Rich. CAPP
Intellect of man is forced to choose, The. The Choice. W. B. Yeats. CMoP; NoAM; OxBSP; OxBTC
Intellectual, The. Karl Shapiro. CMoP
Intellectuals, The. Dudley Randall. PoBA
Intelligence unconcerned. Asadullah Khan Ghalib, *tr. by* Ahmed Ali. GoT
Intelligent Sheepman and the New Cars, The. William Carlos Williams. OBAL
Intendant Yao Shan Has Requested Six Poems on Living in the Mountains, The, *sel.* Yang Shih-ch'i, *tr. fr. Chinese by* Jonathan Chaves. White Stone Slope. CoBLCP
Intended for Sir Isaac Newton. Pope. *See* Nature and Nature's laws lay hid in Night.
Intense and terrible beauty, how has our race with the frail naked nerves. Gale in April. Robinson Jeffers. MoAB; MoAmPo
Intense Landscape, The. Alain Delahaye, *tr. fr. French by* Paul Auster. RHTwFP
Inter, mitzy, titzy, tool. *Unknown.* OxNR
Intercession in Late October. Robert Graves. MoAB
Intercessors. Austin Clarke. CMoP
Interests of a black man in a cellar, The. Black Tambourine. Hart Crane. InPK; InPS; NoAM; OxBA; OxBSP; PPP; TAP
Interface. Gloria Anzaldúa. GLP
Interference. Scott Keyes. SoTCo
Interim. Clarissa Scott Delany. CDC; PoNe
Interim. Frank Ormsby. CIP
Interim Balance. Alois Hergouth, *tr. fr. German by* Beth Bjorklund. CoAuP
Interior. H. C. Artmann, *tr. fr. German by* Beth Bjorklund. CoAuP
Interior. Padraic Colum. MoBrPo
Interior. William Ernest Henley. *Fr.* In Hospital, III. BrPo
Interior. Joseph Milbauer, *tr. fr. French by* Edouard Roditi. VWA
Interior. Sir John Collings Squire. OxBSP
Interior at Petworth: From Turner. Rosanna Warren. NoAM
Interior Landscape. Gloria Fuertes, *tr. fr. Spanish by* Willis Barnstone. BoWoP
Interior Monologue 666. Tom Marshall. NOBC
Interior of the Arizona Indian museum, The. The Meanings in the Pattern. Judy Grahn. UL
Interior Patio. Sebastian S. Bondy, *tr. fr. Spanish by* David Tipton. Per
Interior with Mme. Vuillard and Son. Kathleen Fraser. NPGG
Interlinked is truth to duty, have you had the precious thought. Duty, or Truth at Work. Lizelia Augusta Jenkins Moorer. CBWP-3
Interlude, An. John Peale Bishop. LiTA
Interlude, An. Robert Duncan. CMoP
Interlude. Walter Savage Landor. GTBS-P
Interlude. Edith Sitwell. MoAB; MoBrPo
Interlude. Welton Smith. PoBA
Interlude: "O, the fun, the fun and frolic." William Ernest Henley. *Fr.* In Hospital, XVII. BrPo
Interlude of Joy. George Seferis, *tr. fr. Greek by* Edmund Keeley *and* Philip Sherrard. VMG
Interlude: The Casement. Christopher John Brennan. PoAu-1
Intermission Greetings at the Paris Opera—1898. David R. Slavitt. SoTCo
Internal Cerberus, whose griping fangs. Conscience. Sir Edward Sherburne. ACP
Internal Firesides. Mathilde Blind. FM
Internal Migration: On Being on Tour. Alan Dugan. NoAM
Internal Saboteur, The. Martin Seymour-Smith. NPo
International Brigade Arrives at Madrid, The. Pablo Neruda, *tr. fr. Spanish by* Angel Flores. WaaP
International Brigade Dead. Thomas O'Brien. NeIP
International Chainpoem. *Unknown.* EAS
International Conference. Colin Ellis. FaBoEE
International Copyright. James Russell Lowell. AA
International Episode, An. Caroline Duer. AA; PAH
International Hymn. George Huntington. PoLF
International Ski-Flying Championship, Obersdorf. Elisavietta Ritchie. ASP
Internus. Sándor Weöres, *tr. fr. Hungarian by* Edwin Morgan. MHuP
Interpretations. Jutta Schutting, *tr. fr. German by* Beth Bjorklund. CoAuP

Interpreters, The. Swinburne. PoEL-5
Interracial. Georgia Douglas Johnson. PoNe; TTY
Interred [or Interr'd] beneath this marble stone. Matthew Prior. FaBoEE; NAEL-1; OAEL-1; OBD; OBSV; PoEL-3
Interrogation. Qasim Haddad, tr. fr. Arabic by Lena Jayyusi and Christopher Middleton. MAP
Interrogation, The. Edwin Muir. CMoP; LiTB; SeCePo
Interrogation. Sándor Rákos, tr. fr. Hungarian by Daniel Hoffman. MHuP
Interrogator, The. Elizabeth Jennings. WPE
Interrupted Reproof, The. Priscilla Jane Thompson. CBWP-2
Interruption. Constantine P. Cavafy, tr. fr. Greek by Edmund Keeley and Philip Sherrard. VMG
Interruption. Robert Graves. LiTB; LiTM
Interruption to a Journey. Norman MacCaig. RB
Interstice in the Deep. Israel Efrat, tr. fr. Hebrew by Bernhard Frank. MHeP
Interval. Joseph Auslander. FYAP
Interval with Fire. Dorothy Livesay. CaP
Intervention. Henri Michaux, tr. fr. French by Richard Ellmann. RHTwFP
Interview, sel. Gábor Görgey, tr. fr. Hungarian by Jascha Kessler. FOC
   "I'm fine, thanks." MHuP
Interview, An. K. W. Grandsen. OxBTC
Interview. Sara Henderson Hay. OBCA
Interview near Florence, An. Samuel Rogers. Fr. Italy. OBNC
Interview with a Tourist. Margaret Atwood. IHMS
Interview with a Winner. Donald Finkle. ASP
Interview with Doctor Drink. J. V. Cunningham. OxBSP; TW; VGW
Interview with myself. Mascha Kaléko, tr. fr. German by Susan L. Cocalis. DMG
Intery, mintery, cutery corn. Mother Goose. OxNR
Intil the pit-mirk nicht we northwart sail. Arctic Convoy. J. K. Annand. OxBS
Intimacy. Al Young. NPGG
Intimate Associations. Baudelaire, tr. fr. French by Robert Bly. NU
Intimate Earth, The. Pamela Kircher. KS
Intimate Melodies. Leyb Naydus, tr. fr. Yiddish by Naomi Wolf. PeBMYV
Intimate Parnassus. Patrick Kavanagh. MoBrPo
Intimate Supper. Peter Redgrove. FaBoMo; OxBC
Intimates. D. H. Lawrence. BoLoP; NBLV; OxBSP
Intimations. Alma Johanna Koenig, tr. fr. German by Edouard Roditi. VWA
Intimations kill me, The. Unknown, tr. by Paul Blackburn. Pro
Intimations of Immortality. Wordsworth. See Ode: Intimations of Immortality from Recollections of Early Childhood: Our birth is but a sleep and a forgetting.
Intimations of Mortality. Stanley Kunitz. MoAmPo
Intimations of Sublimity. Wordsworth. Fr. The Prelude [or, Growth of a Poet's Mind]: School-Time. OBNC
Intimidations of an Autobiography. James Tate. NoAM
Into a bistro on the Boulevard St. Michel. A Film of the Comedian Chaplin. Bertolt Brecht, tr. by Michael Hamburger. AnAn
Into a forest. Otsuji, tr. fr. Japanese by Harry Behn. WSC
Into a little close of mine I went. Lorenzo de' Medici, tr. fr. Italian by John Addington Symonds. Fr. Two Lyrics, I. AWP
Into a sweet May morning. John of Hazelgreen. Unknown. ESPB
Into a ward of the whitewashed walls. Somebody's Darling. Marie La Coste. BLPA; UnPo; WBLP
Into a world where children shriek like suns. On a Child Who Lived One Minute. X. J. Kennedy. HoPM; NYBP
Into azure cloudland searching. To My Distant Beloved. Alois Jeitteles, tr. by the Reverend Dr. Troutbeck. TrJP
Into Battle. Julian Grenfell. FaPoR; MMA; OBEV; OBMV; OBWP; OxBTC; WaaP
Into Blackness Softly. Mari E. Evans. PoBA
Into Fish. Sheryl L. Nelms. GOYP
Into Hell's cave stepped a new guest. Arrival in Hell. Ricarda Huch, tr. by Susan C. Strong. PBWP
Into her mother's bedroom to wash the ballooning body. Jessie Mitchell's Mother. Gwendolyn Brooks. BoWoP; NAs; NMM
Into his rosy chamber stepped the Sun. At Sunset. Henrietta Cordelia Ray. CBWP-3
Into Laddery Street. Laura Riding. Fr. Forgotten Girlhood. RB
Into my empty head there come. Morning Swim. Maxine W. Kumin. CAPP; SM; WPE
Into my eyes he loving looked. The Mirror. Judah Halevi, tr. by Emma Lazarus. TrJP

Into My Heart [an Air That Kills]. A. E. Housman. Fr. A Shropshire Lad, XL. ChTr; CMoP; EBEV; LiTB; LiTM; Mes; MoAB; MoBrPo; NoAM; NoBE; NOBVV; OAEL-2; OxBTC (Yon Far Country.) SeCePo
Into our empty room. Their Party, Our House. Jon Swan. NYBP
Into Slumbers. John Fletcher. See Tragedy of Valentinian, The: Care-charming Sleep [Thou Easer of All Woes].
Into Snowy Night. Hannu Mäkelä, tr. fr. Finnish by Aili Jarvenpa. SOP
Into Suburbia between eight and nine. Three-handed Fugue. Phyllis Gotlieb. NOBC
Into that pit. Burning Shit at An Khe. Bruce Weigl. MAYP
Into that pit when I did enter in. Elizabeth Melvill, Lady Culross. Fr. A Godly Dream. WPE
Into the bit-flaked sugar-snow. Maple Feast. Frances Mary Frost. RHPC
Into the blinding sun. Nicholas Virgilio. InPK
Into the blue river hills. Sunset from Omaha Hotel Window. Carl Sandburg. AiP
Into the Book. Martin Grossman. VWA
Into the bosom of the one great sea. The Unity of God. Panatattu. WGRP
Into the caverns of the sea. Joy Enough. Barrett Eastman. AA
Into the crucible of life. Onwardness. Doris Hedges. CaP
Into the Dark. Paul Monette. AmPA
Into the darkness of an old well. Buson, tr. fr. Japanese by Hiroaki Sato. Fr. Eighty-seven Hokku. FCEI
Into the Depths. Adah Isaacs Menken. CBWP-1
Into the Devil tavern. The Three Troopers. George Walter Thornbury. BeLS
Into the dusk and snow. A Traveller. Unknown. WGRP
Into the endless dark. City Lights. Rachel Lyman Field. FaPON; PDV; RHPC
Into the furnace let me go alone. Baptism. Claude McKay. PBCV; PoNe
Into the Glacier. John Haines. CoAP
Into the inmost temple thus I came. The Temple of Venus. Spenser. Fr. The Faerie Queene, IV, 10. EIL
Into the Known. Tess Gallagher. AnAn
Into the lonely park all frozen fast. Colloque Sentimental. Paul Verlaine, tr. by Ernest Dowson. BrPo (Sentimental Conversation.) WSC, tr. by Lloyd Alexander
Into the middle temple of my heart. Sir John Davies. Fr. The Gulling Sonnets. Son
Into the moonlit midnight. The Aardvark. Christopher Logue. NPo
Into the night. The Inland Lighthouse. James McMichael. AmPA
Into the Noiseless Country. Thomas William Parsons. AA
Into the pool of silence our tears made. The Ancient Couple on Lu Mountain. Mark Van Doren. VGW
Into the quiet of this room. The Room. William Soutar. EBEV
Into the Rivers. Paul Celan, tr. fr. German by Beth Bjorklund. CoAuP
Into the sacral cavity can fit the skull of a deer. O'Keeffe Retrospective. May Swenson. ER
Into the scented woods we'll go. Green Rain. Mary Webb. BoNaP; CH; FaPON
Into the shadow Kunai-mai-pa Mo. Kunai-mai-pa Mo. Ethel Anderson. PoAu-2
Into the Silence of the Forest. Eeva-Liisa Manner, tr. fr. Finnish by Aili Jarvenpa. SOP
Into the Silent Land! Song of the Silent Land. Johann Gaudenz von Salis-Seewis, tr. by Longfellow. AWP
Into the silent places. The Old Year and the New. Annie Johnson Flint. BLRP
Into the silver night. Revelation. Sir Edmund W. Gosse. OBEV
Into the skies, one summer's day. The Thought. William Brighty Rands. OBEV
Into the slain tons of needles. By Canoe through the Fir Forest. James Dickey. NYBP
Into the street the Piper stept. Robert Browning. Fr. The Pied Piper of Hamelin. BoTP
Into the sunshine. The Fountain. James Russell Lowell. AnAmPo; BoTP; OBCA
Into the thick of the fight he went, pallid and sick and wan. Wheeler at Santiago. James Lindsay Gordon. PAH
Into the town of Conemaugh. The Man Who Rode to Conemaugh. John Eliot Bowen. PAH
Into the Tree. Czeslaw Milosz, tr. fr. Polish by Robert Hass. AnAn
Into the west of the waters on the living ocean's foam. Homeward Bound. George Edward Woodberry. Fr. Wild Eden, XXV. AA
Into the Wind. Barbara J. Petoskey. TSL

Into the woods my master went. A Ballad of Trees and the Master. Sidney Lanier. AA; AnAmPo; FPL; LiTA; NOBA; OxBA; PoEL-5; PoLF; WGRP
(Into the Woods My Master went.) AH

Into these loves, who but for passion looks. Michael Drayton. *Fr.* Idea, *introd. sonnet.* NoP
(To the Reader of These Sonnets.) AAS; NAEL-1; Son

Into thir dirk and drublie dayis. In Winter. William Dunbar. OxBLMV

Into thir inmost bower. Milton. *Fr.* Paradise Lost, *Bk.* IV. FF, *ll.* 738–757; TOF, *ll.* 738–775.

Into what fictive worlds can imagination. The Horatians. W. H. Auden. NYBP

Into whose ear the deeds are spoken. The only. History. Jorie Graham. NPGG

Into your arms I came. To the Anxious Mother. Valente Malangatana, *tr.* by Dorothy Guedes *and* Philippa Rumsey. PBA

Intolerable woman, where's the name. The Vampire. Arthur Symons. VVA

Intolerably sad, profound. Before the Anæsthetic; or, A Real Fright. Sir John Betjeman. SeCePo

Intoxicated by absence, oh no longer. Sète. Max Hölzer, *tr.* by Beth Bjorklund. CoAuP

Intra-Political. Margaret Avison. MoCV

Intramural Aestivation, or Summer in Town, by a Teacher of Latin. Oliver Wendell Holmes. *See* Autocrat of the Breakfast Table, The: Aestivation [an Unpublished Poem, by My Late Latin Tutor].

Intrepid Ricardo, The. E. C. Bentley. *Fr.* Clerihews. CenHV

Introducing a Madman. Keith Waldrop. TW

Introduction: "Clear transparent sea with light, The." Horatio Nelson Huggins. *Fr.* Hiroona. PBCV

Introduction, The: "Did I my lines intend for public[k] view." Countess of Winchilsea. NAEL-1; WPOW

Introduction: "Hear the voice of the bard!" Blake. *See* Songs of Experience: Hear the Voice of the Bard!

Introduction: "I bespeak words." Clere Parsons. FaBoTw

Introduction, An: "I don't know politics but I know the names." Kamala Das. WPOW

Introduction: " 'I have a few remarks,' he smiled." William Matthews. SoTCo

Introduction: "Romance, who loves to nod and sing." Poe. *See* Romance, who loves to nod and sing.

Introduction: "Should you ask me, whence these stories." Longfellow. *Fr.* The Song of Hiawatha. NOBA; PoE

Introduction, The: "They were introduced in a grave glade." Louis MacNeice. FaBCIP

Introduction: "To be a writer and write things." John Ashbery. CAPP

Introduction and Anecdotes. "Peter Pindar." *Fr.* Bozzy and Piozzi. PoEL-3

Introduction—Childhood and School-Time. Wordsworth. *See* Prelude [or, Growth of a Poet's Mind], The: Childhood and School-Time.

Introduction of a refrain, The. 'Twixt Cup and Lip. Mark Hollis. FiBHP; NBLV

Introduction of the Shopping Cart. Gerald Costanzo. MAYP

Introduction to a Prayer. Fritzi Harmsen van Beek, *tr.* by Claire Nicolas White. DuIn

Introduction to a Pub in Limerick. Knute Skinner. SoTCo

Introduction to Dogs, An. Ogden Nash. MoShBr

Introduction to Some Poems, An. William Stafford. CAPP

Introduction to "Songs of Innocence." Blake. *See* Songs of Innocence: Piping Down the Valleys Wild.

Introduction to the Franklin's Prologue, The. Chaucer. *Fr.* The Canterbury Tales. NAEL-1

Introduction to the Man of Law's Prologue, The. Chaucer. *Fr.* The Canterbury Tales. FiP

Introduction to the Pardoner's Prologue, The. Chaucer. *Fr.* The Canterbury Tales. NAEL-1; NoP

Introductions, or, What's in a Name, *sels.* Bonnie Jacobson. SoTCo
"Ah, Miss Barton."
"Earl and Lady Chatham, The."

Introit. Padraic Fiacc. CIP

Introspective Reflection. Ogden Nash. NBLV

Introversion. Evelyn Underhill. WGRP

Intruder. Susan Feldman. AmPA

Intruder, The. Carolyn Kizer. BoWoP; ER; InPK; NePoEA-2

Intruder, The. James Reeves. OnUR; PDV

Intruder, The. Frank Stanford. MT

Intrusion. Denise Levertov. CAPP

Intuition. Anthony Delius. PeSA

Intuitive guilt and the sun's harsh light. On the Seventh Anniversary of the Death of My Father. Robert Pack. NePoEA

Inuit and Seal. Rosanne Wasserman. BAP

Inundation, The. Howard Sergeant. EAS

Inutsukuba Shu, *sels. Unknown, tr. fr. Japanese by* Hiroaki Sato. FCEI
"Dammit, they get pulled up all the time."
"Down the ass-tuft the dew drips, drips."
"Gasp, and it was gone!, A."
"He lights a lamp at such an awkward spot."
"It's so hot it makes him squat."
"Looks as if about to snatch the blossoms."
"Robe of haze is wet at its hem, A."
"They sucked me to their satisfaction."
"Too beautiful for me, but I have to cleave in."
"Wind, blow, and don't blow!"

Invalided Home. Frances Bellerby. CN

Invalid's Song. Harata Tangikuku, *tr. fr. Maori by* Margaret Orbell. PeNZ

Invariably when wine redeems the sight. The Wine Menagerie. Hart Crane. NoAM; NOBA; OxBA; VGW

Invasion. "Adunis," *tr. fr. Arabic by* Abdullah al-Udhari. MPAW

Invasion. Ellen Duggan. PeNZ

Invasion, The. Pierre Reverdy, *tr. fr. French by* John Ashbery. POS; RHTwFP

Invasion, *sel.* Judah Leib Teller, *tr. fr. Yiddish by* Benjamin *and* Barbara Harshav.
Passport. AYP

Invasion Exercise on the Poultry Farm. Sir John Betjeman. NOBL

Invasion from Dutchland is all the discourse, An. All Shams. *Unknown.* APAS

Invasion Spring. Ruth Tomalin. CN

Invasion Summer. Laurie Lee. OxBSP

Invective against Ibis, *sel.* Ovid, *tr. fr. Latin by* Thomas Underdowne.
"While Thracians shal with arrowes war, Iaziges with bowe." OBVE

"Invent" and "father" are said at the forehead. How to Sign. Laurie Stroblas. TSM

Invent it now. Your own place. Your Own Place. Edward Lucie-Smith. PBCV

Invented a Person. Lenore G. Marshall. GoYe

Inventing a Family. Dennis Saleh. *Fr.* A Guide to Familiar American Incest. NeAC

Inventing a story with grass. A Birth. James Dickey. NOBA

Invention, The. Paul Éluard, *tr. fr. French by* Samuel Beckett. RHTwFP

Invention begs from door to door in the indescribable darkness. Kissing Natalia. Eldon Grier. NOBC

Invention of Comics, The. Amiri Baraka. AmNP; CRP; LiTM; PoBA

Invention of Fire, The. Andrew Taylor. CBAP

Invention of New Jersey, The. Jack Anderson. TW

Invention of the Telephone, The. Peter Klappert. AmPA

Invention of White People, The. Leslie Silko. STP

Invention of Zero, The. Constance Urdang. VWA

Inventor of the geodesic domes. Air. Philip Dow. BXAP

Inventors. Michael C. Blumenthal. DiPo; NoAM

Inventor's Wife, The. E. R. Corbett. PoLF

Inventory. Otto Laaber, *tr. fr. German by* Beth Bjorklund. CoAuP

Inventory. Mihály Ladányi, *tr. fr. Hungarian by* Edwin Morgan. MHuP

Inventory. Dorothy Parker. NBLV

Inventory. Frank Stanford. MT

Inventory, in Answer to the Usual Mandate Sent by a Surveyor of the Taxes, Requiring a Return of the Number of Horses, Servants, Carriages, etc., Kept, The. Burns FaBoUs

Inventory of the Furniture of a Collegian's Chamber, An. John Winstanley. OBSV

Inverey cam doun Deeside, whistlin and playin. The Baron of Brackley. *Unknown.* ESPB, A *and* B *vers.*
(Baron of Braikley, The.) OxBB

Inversnaid. Gerard Manley Hopkins. ACP; BLPL; BrPo; CMoP; FaBoPP; GTBS-P; LiTB; LiTM; MoAB; MoBrPo; NoAM; OAEL-2; PoRA; PoSH; RB; RR; UnPo

Inverted Torch, The, *sels.* Edith Matilda Thomas. AA
If Still They Live.
Tell Me.
When in the First Great Hour.
Will It Be So?.

Investigation. Julia Vinograd. IHMS

Investigator. Miriam Waddington. CaP

Investment, The. Robert Frost. CMoP; OxBA

Investor's Soliloquy. Kenneth Ward. FaFP; FPL

Inviolable. Daniel Hoffman. GrPl

Invisible, The. Richard Watson Gilder. WGRP

Invisible Bridge, The. Gelett Burgess. NA

Invisible hand, An. Sierra. Alfonsina Storni, *tr. by* Rachel Benson. PBWP

Invisible History. Walta Borawski. GLP

Invisible, indivisible Spirit. Hilda Doolittle ("H. D."). *Fr.* Tribute to the Angels. BoWoP

Invisible King, The. Goethe. *See* O who rides by night thru' the worldland so wild?

Invisible Landscape. Charles Wright. LCAP

Invisible machines of war, The. Facts. Cecilia Bustamante, *tr. by* David Tipton. Per

Invisible Playmate, The. Margaret Widdemer. FaPON

Invisible Trumpets Blowing. E. J. Pratt. *Fr.* Brébeuf and His Brethren. CaP

Invisible Woman, The. Robin Morgan. IHMS; NMM

Invisible Work. Margaret Gibson. MT

Invitation. Harry Behn. FaPON

Invitation, The. Robert Herrick. CaPo

Invitation. Solomon ibn Gabirol, *tr. fr. Hebrew by* Israel Zangwill. TrJP

Invitation, The. Charles Kingsley. NOBVV

Invitation. Kadya Molodovsky, *tr. fr. Yiddish by* Irving Feldman. PeBMYV

Invitation. Grace Nichols. AIW

Invitation, The. Goronwy Owen, *tr. fr. Welsh by* George Borrow. OBWVE

Invitation, The. Shelley. GTBS; GTBS-P; OBEV

Invitation. *Malay Oral Tradition, tr. by* R. J. Wilkinson *and* R. O. Winstedt. WTO

Invitation, The. Leonard Welsted. NOEC

Invitation Standing. Paul Blackburn. VGW

Invitation to a Dance. Susan Wallbank. AIW

Invitation to a Spirit. *Malay Oral Tradition, tr. by* W. W. Skeat. WTO

Invitation to an Invitation, An. Catullus, *tr. fr. Latin by* Gardner E. Lewis. ErPo

Invitation to Dalliance. *Unknown.* FaBoEE

Invitation to Eternity. John Clare. PoEL-4

(Invite to Eternity.) NAEL-2; NOBVV; OAEL-2; OBNC

Invitation to Hsiao Ch'u-shih. Po Chü-i, *tr. by* Arthur Waley. OBVE

Invitation, to Jane, The. Shelley. *See* Best and brightest, come away.

Invitation to Juno. William Empson. CMoP; FaBoMo

Invitation to Lubberland, An. *Unknown.* FaBoNo; GBP

Invitation to Madison County, An. Jay Wright. PoBA

Invitation to Mary. Mairtin O Direain, *tr. fr. Irish by* the author. TIRV

Invitation to the Bee. Charlotte Smith. OxBChV

Invitation to the Dance. Apollinaris, *tr. fr. Latin by* Howard Mumford Jones. AWP

Invitation (To the Night and All Other Things Dark). Ronda Davis. JB

Invite to Eternity. John Clare. *See* Invitation to Eternity.

Invited guests in silent order sat, Th'. Animal Magnetism; the Pseudo-Philosopher Baffled. Laurence Hynes Halloran. NOEC

Invites His Nymph to His Cottage. Philip Ayres. EnLoPo

Invites Poets and Historians to Write in Cynthia's Praise. Philip Ayres. Son

Inviting a Friend to Supper. Ben Jonson, *after Martial.* AWP; JCP; LiTB; NOBE; NoP; OAEL-1; OBS; OxBoLi; PoEL-2; PPP; SeCP; SeCV-1

Invocation, An: "Almighty God, who fillest the recesses of the heavens." Bishop Patrick. NOIV

Invocation: "American muse, whose strong and diverse heart." Stephen Vincent Benét. *Fr.* John Brown's Body. AmFN; OPP

Invocation: "Appear, O Mother, was the perpetual cry." Wilfred Watson. MoCV

Invocation: "As pools beneath stone arches take." John Drinkwater. PoA

Invocation: "Come down from heaven to meet me when my breath." Siegfried Sassoon. MoBrPo

Invocation: "Come, lovely Muse, desert for me." Samuel Hoffenstein. BXAP

Invocation: "Dolphin plunge, fountain play." Louis MacNeice. SO

Invocation: "Earth, ocean, air, belovèd brotherhood!" Shelley. *Fr.* Alastor; or, The Spirit of Solitude. FiP

Invocation: "Empty my heart, Lord, of daily vices." Theodore Spencer. TrPWD

Invocation: "Good morning to you, Lord of the world!" Levi Yitzhok, *tr. by* Olga Marx. EaLo

Invocation: "Great-hearted Christ, importunate and mild." Chad Walsh. *Fr.* The Psalm of Christ. TrCP

Invocation: "Land earth-root." Nakasuk. WTO

Invocation: "Of man's first disobedience, and the fruit." Milton. *See* Paradise Lost: Of man's first disobedience, and the fruit.

Invocation, An: "Last night my soul departed." Muireadhach Albanach O Dalaigh. NOIV

Invocation: "Let me be buried in the rain." Helene Johnson. AmNP; BANP; PoNe

Invocation: "Maidens young and virgins tender." Horace. *See* Odes: I, 21. To Apollo and Diana ("Dianam tenerae dicite virgines").

Invocation, An: "My claw is tired of scribing!" Saint Columcille. NOIV

Invocation: "O mother-maid! O maiden-mother free!" Chaucer. *Fr.* The Canterbury Tales: The Prologue of the Prioress's Tale.

Invocation: "O Thou whose equal purpose runs." Wendell Phillips Stafford. TrPWD

Invocation: "Rarely, rarely, comest thou." Shelley. *See* Rarely, Rarely, Comest Thou.

Invocation: "Senator Smoot (Republican, Ut.)." Ogden Nash. OBAL

Invocation: "Silent, about-to-be-parted-from house." Denise Levertov. PoA

Invocation: "Ten bloody years with this quill lying." Valentin Iremonger. BIrV

Invocation: "There is no balm on earth." Gilbert Thomas. TrPWD

Invocation: "Thou, whose endearing hand once laid in sooth." Edmund Clarence Stedman. AA

Invocation, An: "To God, the everlasting, who abides." John Addington Symonds. WGRP

Invocation: "Truth, be more precious to me than the eyes." Max Eastman. WGRP

Invocation: Two Invocations of the Virgin, I. Chaucer. *Fr.* The Canterbury Tales: The Prologue to the Second Nun's Tale. ACP

Invocation, *sel.* Samuel Hoffenstein.
  "Come, live with me and be my love." NBLV

Invocation. Robert Pinsky. *Fr.* Essay on Psychiatrists, I. NoAM

Invocation, An, *sel.* John Addington Symonds.
  "O God, unknown, invisible, secure." TrPWD

Invocation. William Drummond of Hawthornden. *See* Phoebus, Arise.

Invocation and Prelude. Stefan George, *tr. fr. German by* Ludwig Lewisohn. AWP

Invocation and Proposition. Carlos de Sigüenza y Góngora, *tr. fr. Spanish by* Samuel Beckett. *Fr.* Eastern Evangelic Planet. MexPo

Invocation before the Rice Harvest. *Malay Oral Tradition, tr. by* R. O. Winstedt. WTO

Invocation for a Storm. *Unknown, tr. fr. Hawaiian.* WTO

Invocation of Comus, The. Milton. *See* Comus; a Masque Presented at Ludlow Castle: Star that bids the shepherd fold, The.

Invocation of Death. Kathleen Jessie Raine. *See* Two Invocations of Death: Death, I repent.

Invocation of Peace, *sel.* "Fiona Macleod."
  "Deep peace, pure white of the moon to you." BoTP

Invocation of Silence. Richard Flecknoe. OxBSP

Invocation to Rain in Summer. William Cox Bennett. GN

Invocation to Saint Bride. John Irvine. TIRV

Invocation to Sappho. Elsa Gidlow. IHMS

Invocation to the Faerie Queene. Spenser. *See* Faerie Queene, The: Legend of the Knight of the Red Cross, or of Holiness, The.

Invocation to the Mummy. Antonin Artaud, *tr. fr. French by* Michael Benedikt. POS

Invocation to the Muse. Richard Hughes. MoBrPo

Invocation to the Muse. Henrietta Cordelia Ray. CBWP-3

Invocation to the Social Muse. Archibald MacLeish. LiTM

Invocation to Urania. Milton. *See* Paradise Lost: Descend from Heav'n Urania, by that name.

Invocation to Youth. Laurence Binyon. OBEV

Invoice, The. Robert Creeley. VGW

Involuntarily. Hanny Michaelis, *tr. fr. Dutch by* Manfred Wolf. DuIn

Inward Conversation. Baudelaire, *tr. fr. French.* InPK

Inward Light, The. Henry Septimus Sutton. WGRP

Inward Morning, The. Henry David Thoreau. AmPP; NoP

Inwards. Yehudah Offen, *tr. fr. Hebrew by* Bernhard Frank. MHeP

Io dwelt within the breathing-space of immensity. Chant to Io. Tiwai Paraone, *tr. by* A. Alpers. WTO

Io! Paeàn! Io! sing. Charles Lamb. *Fr.* The Triumph of the Whale. ImOP

Io Victis! William Wetmore Story. AA; WGRP

Iöas' Epitaph. William Drummond of Hawthornden. PoEL-2

Iolanthe, *sels.* William Schwenck Gilbert.
  Contemplative Sentry, The. FiBHP
  House of Lords, The. NAEL-2; TrGrPo
  Nightmare. NOBL; NoP; OxBoLi; PoRA
    (Chancellor's Nightmare, The.) FaBoNo

Iona. Arthur Cleveland Coxe. AA

Iona; the Graves of the Kings. Robinson Jeffers. PrIm

Ionian Islands, The, *sel.* Richard Monckton Milnes.
  Corfou. OBTV

Ionic. Constantine P. Cavafy, *tr. fr. Greek by* Edmund Keeley *and* Philip Sherrard. VMG

Iowa. Michael Dennis Browne. NYBP
Iowa City under the Sky of the Mayflower. Eduardo Espina-Villafan, *tr. fr. Spanish by* Judy Berry. WCI
Iowa, June. Michael Dennis Browne. AmPA
Iowa Land. Marvin Bell. SaC
Iowa Recollected in Tranquility. Peter Jay. WCI
Iowa River runs in winter backwards, The. Of Time and River. Affonso Romano de Sant'Anna. WCI
Ipecacuanha. George Canning. ChTr; FaBoNo
Iphigeneia, when she heard her doom. Iphigeneia and Agamemnon. Walter Savage Landor. *Fr.* The Hellenics. BeLS
(Iphigenia.) EnRP
Iphigenia [*or* Iphigeneia] in Aulis. Euripides, *tr. fr. Greek. Sels.*
 Aftermath, The. *Tr. by* Richmond Lattimore. WaaP
 "And Pergamos,/ City of the Phrygians." AWP, *tr. by* Hilda Doolittle ("H. D."); OBVE, *tr. by* Hilda Doolittle ("H. D.").
Iphione. Thomas Caulfield Irwin. EnLoPo
Ipsa Quae. Nicholas Breton. *See* On a hill there grows a flower.
Ipsey Wipsey spider. *Unknown.* OxNR
IpsofactopaperAnswerallquesti. Headrock. Brian Coffey. CIP
Iram indeed is gone with all his rose. Omar Khayyám, *tr. fr. Persian by* Edward Fitzgerald. *Fr.* The Rubáiyát of Omar Khayyám of Naishápúr. OBVE
Ire. R. S. Thomas. OxBSP
Ireland. John Hewitt. CIP; FaBoPP
Ireland. Walter Savage Landor. *See* Ireland Never Was Contented.
Ireland. John James Piatt. AA
Ireland. Richard Ryan. CIP
Ireland. Dora Sigerson Shorter. OBEV; TIRV
Ireland. Francis Stuart. NeIP
Ireland. Egan Swift. FaBoPV
Ireland Lake. Robert Hershon. NeAC
Ireland Never Was Contented. Walter Savage Landor. FaBoCo; FaBoEE; OxBoLi; OxBSP
(Ireland.) GTBS-P
Ireland 1977. Paul Durcan. FaBCIP
Ireland 1972. Paul Durcan. FaBCIP
Ireland Weeping. William Livingston, *tr. fr. Gaelic.* GoTS
Ireland with Emily. Sir John Betjeman. GTBS-P; OxBTC
Iris. David St. John. LCAP
Iris. William Carlos Williams. InPS; LCAP; WeW
Iris, lilac, lily, milk. Lalique. Hal Porter. PoAu-2
Iris looks exactly like the one in the water, The. Basho, *tr. fr. Japanese by* Burton Watson. *Fr.* Seventy-six Hokku. FCEI
Irises. Padraic Colum. BoNaP
Irises in a Marsh. Tamemasa, *tr. fr. Japanese by* Steven D. Carter. WFTW
Irish. Paul Celan, *tr. fr. German by* Michael Hamburger. OBVE
Irish Airman Foresees His Death, An. W. B. Yeats. FaBoCh; FaBoMo; GoJo; GTBS-P; HeIP; HoPM; LiTM; MMA; MoAB; MoBrPo; MoP; NoAM; NOBE; NoP; OBD; OBMV; OBWP; PPP; SCV; TrGrPo; WaaP; WaP; WeW
Irish-American Dignitary. Austin Clarke. BIrV
Irish Antiquities. Thomas Moore. FaBoEE
Irish Childhood in England: 1951, An. Eavan Boland. CIP
Irish Cliffs of Moher, The. Wallace Stevens. DiL; LCAP; NOBA; TOF; VGW
Irish Dancer, The. *Unknown.* AnIL; FaBoCh; GBP; NOBE; OBEV; SeCePo
Irish faults are not so very new, The. Written on the Sense of Isolation in Contemporary Ireland. Robert Greacen. NeIP
Irish Grandmother. Katherine Edelman. AmFN
The Irish Harper and His Dog. Thomas Campbell. CH
Irish have the thickest ankles in the world, The. John Berryman. *Fr.* Dream Songs. TAP
Irish Hotel. David Wevill. NYBP
Irish lady can say, that to-day is every day, The. Cézanne. Gertrude Stein. TAP
Irish Lake, An. W. R. Rodgers. BIrV
Irish Lamentation, An. Goethe, *tr. fr. German by* James Clarence Mangan. AWP
Irish Lords. Charles H. Souter. PoAu-1
Irish Marriage Night, An. Brian Merriman, *tr. fr. Modern Irish by* Frank O'Connor. *Fr.* The Midnight Court. BIrV
Irish Music. Larry Levis. MAYP
Irish Peasant to His Mistress, The. Thomas Moore. ACP; TIRV
An Irish Picture. J. Stanyan Bigg. NOBVV
Irish Reaper's Harvest Hymn. John Keegan. TIRV
Irish Schoolmaster, The. Thomas Hood. BXAP

Irish Schoolmaster, The. James A. Sidney. FiBHP
Irish Skies. Winifred M. Letts. TIRV
Irish Song (Rosie O'Grady). Noel Coward. NBLV
Irish Wake Song. Richard O'Connell. SoTCo
Irish Wild-flower, An. Sarah Morgan Bryan Piatt. AA
Irishman in Coventry, An. John Hewitt. BIrV; CIP
Iron. Walter de la Mare. NOBL
Iron autumn. Iida Dakotsu, *tr. by* Geoffrey Bownas *and* Anthony Thwaite. PeBJV
Iron bells toll, The. Van Gogh. David Mitchell. PeNZ
Iron bludgeon at Po-lang on that day of yore, The. Visiting the Temple of Chang Tzu-fang. Chu Yi-tsun, *tr. by* Irving Lo. WFTU
Iron Eyes. Terence Winch. UL
Iron flower of the prophet's angry message, The. The Word. Gustave Kahn, *tr. by* Edouard Roditi. VWA
Iron Gate, The, *sel.* Oliver Wendell Holmes.
 "As on the gauzy wings of fancy flying." AA
Iron Heaven. Betti Alver, *tr. by* Willis Barnstone *and* Felix Oinas. BoWoP
Iron horse draweth nigh, with its smoke nostrils high, The. The Utah Iron Horse. *Unknown.* AmFP
Iron Industry in Birmingham, The. Richard Jago. *Fr.* Edge-Hill; or, The Rural Prospect Delineated and Moralised. NOEC
Iron Landscapes (and the Statue of Liberty). Thom Gunn. FaBoPV; OBTV
Iron Lung, The. Stanley Plumly. AmPA; GeTw; LCAP
Iron queen of uncreations. The Gardens of Proserpine. Turner Cassity. PoA
Iron scallops border the path, barely. Earliest Spring. Denise Levertov. LCAP
Iron, sulphur, steam: the wastes. Saratoga Ending. Weldon Kees. NaP
Iron thing coming from Pompi, from the round-house. The Train. *Unknown, tr. by* D. F. van der Merwe. TTY
Iron will's demanded of. Rijunkyoku, *tr. by* Lucien Stryk *and* Takashi Ikemoto. ZPCJ
Ironic: LL.D. William Stanley Braithwaite. BANP
Ironical Encomium, An. *Unknown.* APAS
Irony. Louis Untermeyer. TrJP
Irony of God. Eva Warner. TrCP
Irradiations, *sels.* John Gould Fletcher. MoAmPo
 "Flickering of incessant rain." *Fr.* II *or* V [VII].
 "Morning is clean and blue and the wind blows up the clouds, The." *Fr.* V [XXII].
 "O seeded grass, you army of little men." *Fr.* IV *or* IX [XV].
 "Over the roof-tops race the shadows of clouds." *Fr.* I *or* III [V].
 "Trees, like great jade elephants, The." *Fr.* III *or* VII [X]. MoAmPo
Irrational. Philip Lamantia. UL
Irreconcilables. Arthur Gregor. NYBP
Irredeemably Buried. Hanny Michaelis, *tr. fr. Dutch by* Marjolijn de Jager. DuIn
Irreproachably Atzesivano. The Suicide of Atzesivano Disciple of Buddha. Angelos Sikelianos, *tr. by* Edmund Keeley *and* Philip Sherrard. VMG
Irresistible bacilli are at work, The. With the Most Susceptible Element, the Mind, Already Turned under the Toxic Action. Walter Benton. WaP
Irresponsible citizen. Abelardo Sanchez Leon, *tr. by* David Tipton. Per
Irresponsive silence of the land, The. Christina Rossetti. *Fr.* The Thread of Life. NOBE; OBNC
(Aloof.) OBEV, I; TrGrPo, I.
Irrevocable. Mary Wright Plummer. WGRP
Irrigation. Susan Tichy. MAYP
Irritable Song. Russell Atkins. AmNP
Irving. James Russell Lowell. *Fr.* A Fable for Critics. TAP
Is. Patrick Kavanagh. FaBoTw
Is/ red beans. Energy. Victor Hernandez Cruz. PoBA
Is a caterpillar ticklish? Only My Opinion. Monica Shannon. FaPON; RAR
I's a little Alabama Coon. Little Alabama Coon. Hattie Starr. AA
Is a little wind. Four Bird Songs. Simon J. Ortiz. HATNAP
Is a memory, like the uncertain touch past noon. Memory. Kitahara Hakushu, *tr. by* Hiroaki Sato. FCEI
Is a monstrance. The Moon Is the Number 18. Charles Olson. CMoP; PoE
Is a short string of beautiful. My Past. Dennis Cooper. GLP; UL
Is a son born into this world of woe? Charles Churchill. *Fr.* The Times. OBSV
Is all this sorrow? I don't know. Yehuda Amichai, *tr. fr. Hebrew by* Warren Bargad *and* Stanley F. Chyet. *Fr.* Laments on the War Dead, 6. IP

Is an enchanted thing. The Mind Is an Enchanting Thing. Marianne Moore. CMoP; HeIP; InPK; InvP; MoAB; MoAmPo; NAAL-2; OxBA; PoE; PPP; WPOW

Is anything central? The One Thing That Can Save America. John Ashbery. AiP; NoAM; NOBA

Is by admitting. The Way Things Work. Jorie Graham. NPGG

Is even more fun than going to San Sebastian, Irún, Hendaye. Having a Coke with You. Frank O'Hara. GLP

Is gazing at the moon again. The Selenologist. Bill Manhire. PeNZ

Is God invisible? This very room. Adele Greeff. GoYe

I's gonna shine. Unknown. WTO

Is he here? Is he here? Unknown. Fr. Manyo Shu. FCEI

Is he in the shoals. A Heron Standing in a River. Shotetsu, tr. by Steven D. Carter. WFTW

Is heaven a place where pearly streams. What Is Heaven? Philip James Bailey. PWR

Is is a legend already: a wide wide stubble. Victory Bonfire. Ruth Pitter. CN

Is it a dream. For My Husband. Ellen Bryant Voigt. NoP

Is it a happiness? On a Birth. Geoffrey Grigson. NAs

Is It a Month. J. M. Synge. BIrV

Is it a shower of rain? Saigyo, tr. by Geoffrey Bownas and Anthony Thwaite. PeBJV

Is It a Sin to Love Thee? Unknown. BLPA

Is it always so bleak a sight? Sanetomo, tr. fr. Japanese by Burton Watson. Fr. Twenty-four Tanka. FCEI

Is it an idle fantasy. The Mist Maiden. Henrietta Cordelia Ray. CBWP-3

Is it any better in Heaven, my friend Ford. To Ford Madox Ford in Heaven. William Carlos Williams. AmP; NOBA

Is it bad to have come here. Gallant Château. Wallace Stevens. MoAB; MoAmPo

Is it because autumn dew has collected. Teika, tr. fr. Japanese by Hiroaki Sato. Fr. A Compendium of Good Tanka. FCEI

Is It Because I Am Black? Joseph Seamon Cotter, Jr. BANP

Is It Because of Some Dear Grace. Louis Golding. TrJP

Is it because our mighty Sovereign stays. Yakamochi. Fr. Manyo Shu. Ma

Is it because that lad is dead. Vision. Frank Sidgwick. MMA

Is it children we are killing now? My God. Victor Hugo. Fr. A Recollection of the Night of the Fourth. OBD

Is it enough? I'm Here. Theodore Roethke. Fr. Meditations of an Old Woman. CoAP; NYBP

Is it enough to think to-day. Memorial Day. Annette Wynne. OHIP

Is it for long you deign to visit my seclusion. To the Muse ("Is it for long you deign to visit my seclusion"). Afanasi Afanasievich Fet, tr. by Alan Myers. AAA

Is it illusion? or does there a spirit from perfecter ages. Arthur Hugh Clough. Fr. Amours de Voyage. EBEV

(Spirit from Perfecter Ages.) OBNC

Is it ironical, a fool enigma. Dartmoor: Sunset at Chagford. T. E. Brown. NOBVV

Is it just like picking a lock. The Bomb Disposal. Ciaran Carson. CIP

Is it my clothes, my way of walking. Disembarking at Quebec. Margaret Atwood. PoE

Is it naught? Is it naught. Cuba. Edmund Clarence Stedman. PAH

Is it no dream that I am he. Walter Savage Landor. GBL

Is it not fine to fling against loaded dice. Hughie at the Inn. Elinor Wylie. NYBP; WPE

Is it not strange that men can die. Reflection. W. J. Turner. OBMV

Is it not sure a deadly pain. Unknown. EnLoPo

Is it not sweet to die? for, what is death. Death Sweet. Thomas Lovell Beddoes. NOBVV

Is it not time now. Emperor Go-Komatsu, tr. fr. Japanese by Steven D. Carter. WFTW

Is It Not You, Lord! Padraig De Brun. TIRV

"Is It Nothing to You?" May Probyn. OBEV

Is it poetry I'm after those moments when. Vocation. Carol Rumens. DiPo

Is It Possible? Sir Thomas Wyatt. ELP; GBL; NoP; SiPS

(Varium et Mutabile.) OBSC; QFR

Is it raining. Mary, can you see? Wildflowers. Richard Howard. NoAM

Is It Really Worth the While? Unknown. BLPA

Is It Right to Move to the Country? Giovanni Giudici, tr. fr. Italian by Lawrence R. Smith. NItP

Is it serious, or funny. B. Larry Eigner. NeAP

Is it that summer and winter. Hitomaro. Fr. Manyo Shu. Ma

Is it the horn that, on this holy day. Ebenezer Elliott. Fr. The Village Patriarch, IV. PF

Is it the petals falling from the rose? The Dance of the Daughters of Herodias. Arthur Symons. BrPo

Is it the wind of the dawn that I hear. Duet. Tennyson. Fr. Becket. GBL

Is it the wind, the many-tongued, the weird. The Draft Riot. Charles De Kay. PAH

Is it thy wil, thy Image should keepe open. Shakespeare. Fr. Sonnets, LXI. PoEL-2

Is it time now to go away? Death of a Vermont Farm Woman. Barbara Howes. MoAmPo; SM

Is it too much to ask that I should be. Toleration. John Barford. PeHV

Is It True? Sarah Williams. BLPA

Is it true that black birds infinitely dispersed. To Krishna Haunting the Hills. Andal, tr. by Willis Barnstone. BoWoP

Is it Ulysses that approaches from the east. The World as Meditation. Wallace Stevens. HeIP; LCAP; MoAB; NIP; PPP

Is It Well-Lighted, Papa? James Bertram. SM

Is It Wise? Stevie Smith. NAEL-2

Is it worth while, dear, now. Long Plighted. Thomas Hardy. NOBVV

Is it you? Are you there. Poem Wondering If I'm Pregnant. Kathleen Fraser. IHMS; NMM

Is John Smith within? Mother Goose. OxNR

Is Life itself but many ways of thought. Substitution. Anne Spencer. BlSi; CDC

Is life soiled? Life. Shin Dong-jip, tr. by Koh Chang-soo. ACKP

Is Life Worth Living? Alfred Austin. FaPoR; PWR

Is made up of reservoirs. The Hard Structure of the World. Richard Eberhart. NoAM

Is melting an old frost moon. Dawn's Rose. Ted Hughes. Fr. Crow. PoE

Is memory most of miseries miserable. Memory. Dante Gabriel Rossetti. OxBSP

Is My Team Ploughing [or Plowing]. A. E. Housman. Fr. A Shropshire Lad, XXVII. CMoP; EBVV; LiTM; MoAB; MoBrPo; NoAM; NoP; OBD; OBEV; TrGrPo

Is no one awake yet this cold cold winter morn? Who Can Tell When He Is Awake. James Tate. MAYP

Is not man's greatest heart's desire. Omnia Vanitas. Dugald Buchanan. GoTS

Is not the picture strangely like? On Seeing a Pigeon Make Love. Leigh Hunt. FM

Is not this hearth, where goats now feed? The Hearth of Urien. Llywarch the Aged, tr. by William Barnes. ChTr

Is pariah art possible? Can that animal ataraxia. A Meditation. János Pilinszky, tr. by Jascha Kessler. FOC

Is, perhaps, the face of Christ. The Face of Dürer. Jon Anderson. NAmP

Is seacoast fog, is starfish caught. New England Is New England Is New England. Brenda Heloise Green. GoYe

Is she dead? Confessional. Frank Bidart. GLP

"Is she fitting for your wife, Billy boy, Billy Boy." Billy Boy. Unknown. OBET

Is she not beautiful? reposing there. N. T. Carrington. Fr. On Seeing a Fine Frigate at Anchor in a Bay off Mount Edgecumbe. FaBoPP

"Is she sound asleep?" Unknown, tr. by Geoffrey Bownas and Anthony Thwaite. Mes; PeBJV

Is shut/ 22 hours a day and all day Sunday. The Pitt-Rivers Museum, Oxford. James Fenton. FaBoMo

"Is Sin, then, fair?" The Sting of Death. Frederick George Scott. OBCV

Is someone who, walking into a department store. A Briton. Herman de Coninck, tr. by Theo Hermans. DuIn

Is something like the rest. The Politics of Rich Painters. Amiri Baraka. VGW

Is that an attitude for a flower, to stand. Hyacinth. Louise Glück. NoAM

Is that dance slowing in the mind of man. Four for Sir John Davies. Theodore Roethke. MoAmPo; NoAM; NOBE

Is that foolish youth still sawing. Ancient Autumn. Charles Simic. BLA

Is that the person I once loved. Natsume Seibi, tr. fr. Japanese by Hiroaki Sato. Fr. Twenty-seven Hokku. FCEI

"Is that the Three-and-Twentieth, Strabo mine." The Legion. Robert Graves. BrPo

Is that you sistah Harris? An Afternoon Gossip. Priscilla Jane Thompson. CBWP-2

Is the ball very stupid ma mignonne? At the Ball! Charles Henry Webb. OBAL

Is the clock wound up, is it wound? The Insect Kitchen. Nicki Jackowska. BrRo

Is the eternal voice, Coltrane is. Orishas. Larry Neal. NBP

Is the fish ready? You're a tedious while.　Dialogue between a Squeamish
　Cotting Mechanic and His Sluttish Wife, in the Kitchen.　Edward
　Ward.　*Fr.* Nuptial Dialogues.　NOEC
Is the flood growing to whelm us?　Rains.　Anna Hajnal, *tr. by* Jascha
　Kessler.　FOC
Is the hour that late?　Emperor Fushimi, *tr. fr. Japanese by* Steven D.
　Carter.　WFTW
Is the kitchen tap still dripping?　Guest.　D. J. Enright.　Mes; OxBC
Is the live branch better than the dead?　Woodcutter's Hut.　Zotan, *tr. by*
　Lucien Stryk *and* Takashi Ikemoto.　ZPCJ
Is the mind the glass of the body?　The Trees, and What They Raise.
　Lorrie Goldensohn.　NAmP
Is the Moon Tired?　Christina Rossetti.　BoTP
Is the noise of grief in the palace over the river.　A Mother in Egypt.
　Marjorie Pickthall.　CaP
Is the Prince of Omi a fisherman?　Prince Omi.　*Fr. Manyo Shu.*　Ma
Is the struggle and strife.　Let the Rest of the World Go By.　J. Keirn
　Brennan.　UnPo
Is the total black, being spoken.　Coal.　Audre Lorde.　BlSi; CNA;
　NoAM; NoP; PoBA
Is the university of hunger the wide waste.　University of Hunger.　Martin
　Carter.　PBCW
Is the way o'ercast with shadows?　Jesus Understands.　*Unknown.*
　BLRP
Is there a cause why we should wake the dead?　The Yew-Tree.　Vernon
　Watkins.　EaLo; LiTB
Is there a great green commonwealth of Thought.　John Masefield.　*Fr.*
　Sonnets.　LiTM; MoBrPo
Is There a Voice.　Philip Appleman.　BXAP
Is there an imagination that sits enthroned.　Wallace Stevens.　*Fr.* The
　Auroras of Autumn, VII.　CMoP; HCAP
Is there another poetry than the poetry of celebration?　C. K. Stead.　*Fr.*
　Quesada, III.　ATNZ
Is there any reason why a poem shouldn't.　Functional Poem.　Mark
　Halliday.　PPR
"Is there anybody there?" said the traveller.　The Listeners.　Walter de la
　Mare.　AWP; BLPL; BrPo; CMoP; FaFP; FaPON; HAP; HeIP;
　HoPM; InPK; InvP; LiTB; LiTM; MoAB; MoBrPo; MoP; NoAM;
　NOBE; NoP; OBEV; OBMV; OnMSP; PoRA; SoSe; TrGrPo; WeW;
　WSC
Is there anything as I can do ashore for you.　A Valediction (Liverpool
　Docks).　John Masefield.　OBMV
Is there anything I can do.　The Key to Everything.　May Swenson.
　IHMS; NePoEA
Is there anything in Spring so fair.　Apple Blossoms.　Henry Adams
　Parker.　BoTP
Is there ever a new beginning when every.　Marriage.　Elaine Feinstein.
　AIW
Is there, for honest poverty.　For A' That and A' That ("Is there, for
　honest poverty").　Burns.　EnRP; FaBoBe; FaBoPV; FaFP; FaPoR;
　LiTB; NAEL-2; OAEL-1; OHFP; TEP; WBLP
　(Man's a Man for A' That, A.)　OxBS; TrGrPo
　(Song: For A' That and A' That.)　NOEC; OPOP
Is there never a man in all Scotland.　Johnie Armstrong.　*Unknown.*
　ESPB
Is There No Balm in Christian Lands?　*Unknown.*　AH
Is there no middle earth?　Vampire.　Jean Pedrick.　VVA
Is there no secret place on the face of the earth.　The Moneyless Men.
　Henry T. Stanton.　BLPA
Is there no vision in a lovely place?　William Montgomerie.　*Fr.* Kinfauns
　Castle.　OxBS
Is there not one spark of pity for five poor unhappy men.　Execution of
　Five Pirates for Murder.　*Unknown.*　OxBSS
Is there nothing to be said about the cockroach which is kind?　Cockroach.
　Mary Ann Hoberman.　*Fr.* Bugs.　OBCA
Is there ony room at your head, Saunders?　*Unknown.*　*Fr.* Clerk
　Saunders.　OBD
Is there still any shadow there, on the rainwet window of the coffee pot.
　Memo.　Kenneth Fearing.　CMoP; PoE
Is this a fast, to keep.　To Keep a True Lent.　Robert Herrick.　TrCP
　(True Lent, A.)　OFD; OHIP
Is this a holy thing to see.　Holy Thursday ("Is this a holy thing to see").
　Blake.　*Fr.* Songs of Experience.　EnRP; FF; InPS; NAEL-2; NOEC;
　NoP; OAEL-2; TEP
Is This Africa.　Roland Tombekai Dempster.　PBA
Is This All That Remains of Love?　Yusuf al-Sa'igh, *tr. fr. Arabic by*
　Diana Der Hovanessian *with* Salma Khadra Jayyusi.　MAP
Is this dancing sunlight.　Symphony.　Frank Horne.　AmNP
Is this her in golden smock, walking?　In Golden Smock, Walking.　Jan
　Kemp.　ATNZ

Is this man turning angel as he stares.　The Messengers.　Thom Gunn.
　PoA
Is this really the failure. .　Masaccio's Expulsion.　Jorie Graham.　AnAn
Is this stuff poetry? It's what birds sing in cages.　Longing for the Birds of
　Solomon.　Joseph L. Baird.　TSM
Is this the movie in which James Mason.　A Gothic Gesture.　Steve
　Levine.　UL
Is this the object.　Judith Kroll.　AmPA; SM
Is this the price of beauty! Fairest, thou.　Charleston.　Richard Watson
　Gilder.　PAH
Is this the region, this the soil, the clime.　Milton.　*Fr. Paradise Lost, Bk.*
　I, *ll.* 242–270.　TEP
　(Fall of the Angels, The.)　FiP, *ll.* 242–363.
　(Satan as Rebel-Liberator.)　FF, *ll.* 242–255.
"Is this the road that climbs above and bends."　The Chalk-Pit.　Edward
　Thomas.　BrPo
Is this the Seine?　An Ode to Spring in the Metropolis.　Sir Owen
　Seaman.　FiBHP
Is this the self I thought I knew, within.　Reflections.　Vivian Smith.
　CBAP
Is This the Time to Sound Retreat?　*Unknown.*　BLRP
Is this the ultimate exile no man born.　Ultimate Exile IV.　Ralph Nixon
　Currey.　PeSA
Is this the way my Father.　Matin Hymn.　Josephine D. Henderson
　Heard.　CBWP-4
Is this where idealism ends.　Guerillas.　Roger McTair.　PVCV
Is this your special light.　Six Nations Museum Onchiota, New York—
　January.　Wendy Rose.　HATNAP
Is thy face like my mother's, my fair child!　Byron.　*Fr. Childe Harold's
　Pilgrimage, III.*　ChER, 15 *sts.;* EnRP; OAEL-2, *abr.*
Is thy sun obscured to-day.　My Grace Is Sufficient.　Josephine D.
　Henderson Heard.　CBWP-4
Is to love, this—to nurse a name.　Rhoda Coghill.　NeIP
Is true Freedom but to break.　Stanzas on Freedom.　James Russell
　Lowell.　GN
"Is water nigh?"　The Gift of Water.　Hamlin Garland.　AA
Is what you first see, stepping off the train.　Welcome to Hiroshima.
　Mary Jo Salter.　DiPo
Is without world.　The Howling of Wolves.　Ted Hughes.　OxBTC
Is Wolly's wife now dead and gone?　A Jacobite Scot in Satire on
　England's Unparalleled Loss.　*Unknown.*　APAS
Is yo eye so empty.　Signals.　Jewel C. Latimore.　PoBA
Is your crop of millet.　What Her Friend Said to Her, before the Rains.
　Kapilar, *tr. by* A. K. Ramanujan.　PLW
Is your place a small place?　Your Place.　John Oxenham.　BLRP
Isaac.　Stanley Burnshaw.　VWA
Isaac.　Amir Gilboa, *tr. fr. Hebrew by* Howard Schwartz.　VWA
Isaac.　Haim Guri, *tr. fr. Hebrew by* Naomi Tauber *and* Howard
　Schwartz.　VWA
Isaac.　Barry Holtz.　VWA
Isaac.　A. C. Jacobs.　VWA
Isaac and Archibald.　E. A. Robinson.　OxBA
Isaac and Esau.　Rose Drachler.　VWA
Isaac Leybush Peretz.　Moyshe-Leyb Halpern, *tr. fr. Yiddish by* Kathryn
　Hellerstein.　VWA
Isabel.　Richard Hovey.　AnAmPo
Isabel met an enormous bear.　Adventures of Isabel.　Ogden Nash.
　CenHV; MoAmPo; MoShBr; NTCP; OBAL; OBCA; OnMSP; OnUR;
　PDV; RHPC
Isabella; or, The Morning, *sel.*　Sir Charles Hanbury Williams.
　"Monkey, lap-dog, parrot, and her Grace, The."　NOEC
Isabella; or, The Pot of Basil.　Keats.　EnRP
Isabella spits at Spain.　Bourbons.　Walter Savage Landor.　OBSV
Isabelle.　James Hogg.　BXAP; Par
Isaiah, *sels.*　Bible, *O.T.*
　All Flesh Is Grass.　*Fr.* XL: 6–8.　TrJP
　"Comfort ye, comfort ye my people."　*Fr.* XL: 1–11.　EaLo; OBVE,
　　(1-8); TrJP, (1-5).
　Downfall of the Tyrant.　*Fr.* XIV:4–19.　TrGrPo
　For Zion's Sake.　*Fr.* LXII: 1–5.　TrJP
　God's Vengeance.　*Fr.* XXXIV: 8–15.　FM
　Hear the Word of the Lord.　*Fr.* I: 10–23.　TrJP
　How Beautiful upon the Mountains.　*Fr.* LII: 7–10.　TrJP
　I Waste Away.　*Fr.* XXIV: 16–20.　TrJP
　In the End of Days.　*Fr.* II: 2–4.　TrJP
　Israel, My Servant.　*Fr.* XLI: 8–16.　TrJP
　Let Me Sing of My Well-beloved.　*Fr.* V.　TrJP
　Messiah, The.　*Fr.* VII: 14–25.　AWP
　My Thoughts Are Not Your Thoughts.　*Fr.* LV: 8–13.　TrJP
　Rod of Jesse, The.　*Fr.* XI: 1–11.　AWP; OBVE; TrJP
　Song of the Harlot.　*Fr.* XXIII: 16.　TrJP

Song of The Suffering Servant, The. *Fr.* LII: 13-LIII: 12. NAWM-1

Vision of the Day of Judgment. *Fr.* LXIII, Moulton, Modern Reader's Bible. WGRP

Watchman, What of the Night?. *Fr.* XXI: 11–15. AWP

Whom Shall One Teach. *Fr.* XXVIII: 9–13. TrJP

"Wildernesse and the solitarie place shall be glad for them, The." *Fr.* XXX. OBVE

"Wolf also shall dwell with the lamb, The." *Fr.* XI: 6–9. PDV (God's Rule.) FM
    (Peaceable Kingdom.) FaPON

Isaiah and Homer. A. Leyeles, *tr. fr. Yiddish by* John Hollander. PeBMYV

Iscah. Howard Schwartz. VWA

I'se been upon de karpet. Old Maid's Soliloquy. Maggie Pogue Johnson. CBWP-4

I'se got a gal in the Sourwood Mountain. Sourwood Mountain. *Unknown.* AmFP

I'se wild Nigger Bill. Wild Negro Bill. *Unknown.* BPo

Ishi. Bert Schierbeek, *tr. fr. Dutch by* Charles McGeehan. DuIn

Ishmael. Gabriel Levin. VWA

Ishmael. Herbert Edward Palmer. OBEV

Ishtar. Judith Wright. NoAM

Isidor. Louis Simpson. NNaP

Isis and the Animals: I. Hugo Claus, *tr. fr. Dutch by* Theo Hermans. DuIn

Isis Wanderer. Kathleen Jessie Raine. OxBS

Island, The. James Dickey. SM

Island. Langston Hughes. HCAP

Island, The. Sean Jennett. NeIP; SeCePo

Island, The. Edwin Muir. OAEL-2

Island. Ishigaki Rin, *tr. fr. Japanese by* Hiroaki Sato. FCEI

Island, An. Shawn Wong. BrSi

Island, The. George Woodcock. MoCV

Island and the Cattle, The. Nicholas Moore. EAS

Island Funeral. Frank Stanford. MT

Island in the Evening, The. Fairfield Porter. PoA

Island in the Moon, An, *sels.* Blake.
    Good English Hospitality. CoMu
    (Mayors, The.) CH
    In Obtuse Angle's Study. FaBoNo
    Sipsop's Song. FaBoNo
    Suction's Anthem. FaBoNo
    "When old corruption first begun." RB
    (Quid the Cynic's Song.) FaBoNo

Island of Mull. *Unknown, fr. the Gaelic of* Douglas Macphail. PoSH

Island of Rhum, The. Roy Ferguson. PoSH

Island of Shadow. Nostalgie d'Automne. Leslie Daiken. NeIP

Island of the Sirens, The. Timoshenko Aslanides. UAS

Island of the Three Marias. Alberto Ríos. NoAM

Island of Yorrick, The. N. M. Bodecker. WSC

Island off the main, An. Tycoon, Poet, Saint. Abdur-Rahman Slade Hopkinson. PVCV

Island Quarry. Hart Crane. PPP

Island that had flowered to the sun, The. The Coming of Dusk upon a Village in Haiti. Henry Rago. HoPM

Island was a word he woke upon, The. Settler. Stewart Lindh. PoA

Island Waters. Tony Beyer. PeNZ

Island where all is elucidated, An. Utopia. Wislawa Szymborska, *tr. by* Czeslaw Milosz. PwPP

Islanders, Inlanders. Michael Mott. PoA

Islandish. A. Leyeles, *tr. fr. Yiddish by* Benjamin *and* Barbara Harshav. AYP

Islandman. Brenda Chamberlain. OBWVE

Islands, The, *sel.* Charles Brasch.
    "Always, in these islands, meeting and parting." *Fr.* II. ATNZ

Islands, The. Hilda Doolittle ("H. D."). MoAmPo

Islands, The. Randall Jarrell. EAS

Islands and peninsulas, continents and capes. Geography. Eleanor Farjeon. FaPON

Islands and the mountains in the day, The. Shelley. *Fr.* The Revolt of Islam, III. ChER

Islands are green. Alaskan Fragments June 1981—Summer Solstice. Wendy Rose. HATNAP

Islands are places. Shore Thing. Bernhard Hillila. SoTCo

Islands move inward. The Name of Our Country. Dennis Schmitz. AmPA

Islands of the Sea, The. George Edward Woodberry. PAH

Island's Prince, of frame more than celestial, The. The All-seeing Intellect. Phineas Fletcher. *Fr.* The Purple Island, VI. JCP

Island's strange, it seems to me, The. Long Island. Marcy S. Powell. SoTCo

Islands Where I Was Born, The. Gloria Rawlinson. ATNZ; PeNZ

Islands which whisper to the ambitious, The. At Epidaurus. Lawrence Durrell. LiTB; OBTV

Isle and the Lake, No. 5, The. Tu Kuo-ch'ing, *tr. fr. Chinese by* Dominic Cheung. IFON

Isle of a summer sea. Cuba. Harvey Rice. PAH

Isle of Man, The. *Unknown.* GBP

Isle of Man Shore, The. *Unknown.* AmFP

Isle of Portland, The. A. E. Housman. *Fr.* A Shropshire Lad, LIX. MoBrPo

Isle of Streams; or, the Jamaica Hermit, The, *sels.* William Hosack. PBCV
    "Blazing noon, fierce, unrelenting noon!, The."
    "But hark! The sharp beat of the Afric drum."

Isle of the Long Ago, The. Benjamin Franklin Taylor. FaFP; WBLP

Isled in the midnight air. The Moth. Walter de la Mare. BrPo

Isles of Britain, The, *sel.* Elijah Ridings.
    "Hail! muse of my Lancastria fair." PF

Isles of Greece, The. Byron. *Fr.* Don Juan, III. AWP; ChTr; FaPoR; FiP; LiTB; NOBE; OBEV; OBTV

Isles of Greece, The. Demetrios Capetanakis. GTBS-P

Islet the Dachs. George Meredith. FM

Isn't it foolish to dash off outside. Footnote. Norah Smaridge. RAR

Isn't It Funny? Essex Hemphill. GLP

Isn't it strange. A Bag of Tools. R. L. Sharpe. BLPA

Isn't it strange some people make. Some People. Rachel Field. FaPON; NTCP; PDV; RHPC

Isn't it wonderful, when you think. Wonderful. Julian S. Cutler. PWR

Isn't making love. This. Anne Stevenson. ER

Isn't she soft and still? Captive. Marion Strobel. ErPo

"Isn't the violet a dear little flower? And the daisy, too." The Lay Preacher Ponders. Idris Davies. OxBTC

Isolation. Arthur Symons. OxBSP

Isolation of Genius, The. Byron. WBLP

Isolation of Two Milliard Light Years, The. Tanikawa Shuntaro, *tr. fr. Japanese by* Geoffrey Bownas *and* Anthony Thwaite. PeBJV

Isolation: To Marguerite. Matthew Arnold. *Fr.* Switzerland, IV. EBVV; TEP

Isolda/ naked blood spelling-book. Birth. Cecilia Bustamante, *tr. by* David Tipton. Per

Israel. Israel Zangwill. TrJP

Israel Freyer's Bid for Gold. Edmund Clarence Stedman. PAH

Israel in ancient days. Old-Testament Gospel. William Cowper. TrCP

Israel, My Servant. Bible, *O.T.* *Fr.* Isaiah, XLI: 8–16. TrJP

Israeli Navy, The. Marvin Bell. VWA

Israel's Duration. Judah Halevi, *tr. fr. Hebrew by* Nina Davis Salaman. TrJP

Israfel. Poe. AA; AmPP; AWP; BLPL; LiTA; NAAL-1; NOBA; OxBA; PoE; PoEL-4; TAP

Issa's little daughter, Sato-jo. Immunity. Carol Muske. BLA

Issue of great Jove, draw near you Muses nine, The. The Garden. Nicholas Grimald. OAEL-1

Issues from the hand of God, the simple soul. Animula. T. S. Eliot. CRP; LiTB; NAs

Issues of the Fall. Sydney Lea. SM

Is't here the fairies haunt the place. On a Nook Called Fairyland. Henrietta Cordelia Ray. CBWP-3

Istanbul. 21 March. I woke today. The Thousand and Second Night. James Merrill. NYBP

Isuba. Jim Barnes. *Fr.* Four Things Choctaw. HATNAP

Isuzu River. Rai San'yo, *tr. fr. Chinese by* Burton Watson. JLIC-2

Isuzu River—/ like a mirror left behind. Tameie, *tr. fr. Japanese by* Steven D. Carter. WFTW

It. Hermann Jandl, *tr. fr. German by* Beth Bjorklund. CoAuP

It. Howard Moss. BLA

It. Gary Snyder. LCAP

It Ain't Blues That Blows an Ill Wind. Colleen J. McElroy. ER

It ain't gonna rain, it ain't gonna snow. Ain't Gonna Rain. *Unknown.* AS

It Ain't Neccessarily So. Ira Gershwin. OBAL

It ain't no use to grumble and complain. Rain. James Whitcomb Riley. BoNaP

It ain't the failures he may meet. The Quitter. *Unknown.* BLPA; WBLP

It ain't the guns nor armament. Co-operation. J. Mason Knox. BLPA

It all began. Loss. Alex Kuo. BrSi

It all began so easy. Christina. Louis MacNeice. BoLoP

It All Comes Together Outside the Restroom in Hogansville. James Seay. MT

It all happened so fast. Fenya was in the straight chair. Norman Dubie. AmPA

It all happens in a moment, telephone-still. Death of the Trackstar. William Meissner. TSL

It all seems like today: he returns. A Veteran of the Great War. John Bensko. MAYP

It all wears out. I keep telling myself this, but. Down by the Station, Early in the Morning. John Ashbery. HCAP

It always comes, and when it comes they know. Women in Love. Donald Justice. SM

It Always Seems. A. M. Sayers. BXAP

It appeared inside our classroom. The Creature in the Classroom. Jack Prelutsky. RHPC

It appears to be the pampas. The Man in the Dream Is Death. Lynne Butler. IHMS

It asked for bread and butter first. The Perfect Child. Adrian Porter. NBLV

It Autumnne was, and on our hemispheare. William, of Hawthornden Drummond. OBS

It avoids the large receptacles. Vulnerability. Bartolo Cattafi, tr. by Lawrence R. Smith. NItP

It baffles the foreigner like an idiom. Drug Store. Karl Shapiro. CMoP; OxBA; TwCP

It befell at Martynmas. Captain Car; or, Edom o Gordon. Unknown. ESPB

It began/ reasonably enough. The Man Who Owned Cars. Elliot Fried. GOYP

It began as a joke: she did not like to leave the house. Another Poem about the Madness of Women. Tom Wayman. NOBC

It began here, on the horned road. Your Voice. Michael Burkard. NAmP

It began in her pram. The Renaming. Valerie Sinason. BrRo

It begins again, the nocturnal pulse. The Assassination. Donald Justice. CAPP

It begins quietly. The Deviation. Louise Glück. Fr. Dedication to Hunger, IV. AnAn; GeTw

It begins with an easy voice saying. Nightmare. Lyall Wilkes. OBD

It begins with my dog, now dead, who all his long life. The Retrieval System. Maxine W. Kumin. FaBoWP; WeW

It bends far over Yell'ham Plain. The Comet at Yell'ham. Thomas Hardy. CMoP; GBL

It breaks the heart, don't ask. Ni Tsan, tr. fr. Chinese by Jonathan Chaves. Fr. Two Poems to the Tune "Jen-yüeh yüan." CoBLCP

It brims in the white cistern; flows. A Meditation upon the Toothache. Laurence Lerner. NePoEA-2

It burns in the void. The World. Kathleen Jessie Raine. OxBTC

It cam from Pizzeria. Around the World. Gary Lenhart. UL

It came/ Out of the blackness of the spaces between galaxies. The Second Coming. Carl Clark. JB

It came as a stray dog and still is. Ozaki Hosai, tr. fr. Japanese by Hiroaki Sato. Fr. One Hundred Haiku in Free Form. FCEI

It came today to visit. The Visitor. Jack Prelutsky. AmMo

It Came upon the Midnight Clear. Edmund Hamilton Sears. AH, with music; FaPON

(Angels' Song, The.) PWR

(Peace on Earth.) FaFP

It came upon the noontide air. Bishop James A. Shorter. Josephine D. Henderson Heard. CBWP-4

It can be beautiful this sitting by oneself all alone except for the world. Moon Watching by Lake Chapala. Al Young. NPGG

It can be so tedious, a bore. Moods of Rain. Vernon Scannell. BoNaP

It cannot be/ reasoned with. Julius Lester. Fr. In the Time of Revolution, V. PoBA

It cannot be that He who made. Reincarnation. David Banks Sickels. AA

It cannot be that men who are the seed. Our First Century. George Edward Woodberry. PAH

It cannot come. Balboa, the Entertainer. Amiri Baraka. NoAM

It can't be the passing of time that casts. Rip. James Wright. NaP

It chanced his lips did meet her forehead cool. George Meredith. Fr. Modern Love, VI. NOBVV

It chanced to be our washing day. Oliver Wendell Holmes. Fr. The September Gale. FiBHP

It comes about that the drifting of these curtains. The Curtains in the House of the Metaphysician. Wallace Stevens. PoA

It comes back. Deceased. Cid Corman. PCP; VGW

"It comes back to me." An Apple Fell in the Night and a Wagon Stopped. James McMichael. PPR

It Comes during Sleep. Philip Dow. NPGG

It Comes from Deep Caverns. René Daumal, tr. fr. French by Michael Benedikt. POS

It comes, the blast of death! that sudden glare. The Simoom. Martin Farquhar Tupper. OBTV

It comes to me more and more. The Love of the Father. Unknown. BLRP

It comes to this. Revelations. David Meltzer. NeAP

It comes to this, in plain words. Victory. Eileen Duggan. ATNZ

It comes with the force of a body blow. Clair de Lune. Jules Laforgue, tr. by William Jay Smith. CT

It consisted of 8 to 10 pages of short essays. Her Application to Elysium. Kathleen Norris. IHMS

It Could Be. Alfonsina Storni, tr. fr. Spanish by Kate Flores. DMH

It could be a clip, it could be a comb. Obsessive. Marvin Bell. Fr. The Escape into You. LCAP; SM

It could be a jaw-bone. Viking Dublin; Trial Pieces. Seamus Heaney. IPY

It could be tomorrow. Iowa City under the Sky of the Mayflower. Eduardo Espina-Villafan, tr. by Judy Berry. WCI

It could have happened. Every Case. Wislawa Szymborska, tr. by Czeslaw Milosz. PwPP

It could only be seen/ when he closed his eyes. Hebrew Script. Tali Loewenthal. VWA

It Couldn't Be Done. Edgar Albert Guest. BLPA; FaBoBe; FaFP; FPL; WBLP

It crawled away from 'neath my feet. That Hill. Blanche Taylor Dickinson. CDC

It Did. Robert Lowell. NoAM

It did not last; the Devil howling Ho. J. C. Squire. FaBoCo; FaBoEE

It did not seem important at the time. As It Was. John Mander. Mes

It didn't require great character at all. The Power of Taste. Zbigniew Herbert, tr. by John Carpenter and Bogdana Carpenter. AnAn

It didn't seem like history. Seemed, more. The Painted Bridge. Eleanor Ross Taylor. PPR

It diffuses daylight. One Moment's Mirror. Paul Eluard, tr. by Michael Benedikt. POS

It does, it does, I have seen it. America Bleeds. Angelo Lewis. PoBA

It does not happen. That love, removes. Audubon, Drafted. Amiri Baraka. PPP; TTY

It does not worry me that this verse has three stresses. The Eumenides at Home. James Agate. BXAP

It doesn't always do to let a mug know everything. Charlie Piecan. L. Murray and F. Leigh. OxBoLi

It doesn't breathe. My Nose. Dorothy Aldis. RHPC

It Doesn't Count. István Vas, tr. fr. Hungarian by Edwin Morgan. MHuP

It doesn't do to do much talking. Not Much Talking. Unknown. PWR

It doesn't look like a finger it looks like a feather of broken glass. Hugh Sykes Davies. EAS

It doesn't show. Old Map of Barnstable County. Brendan Galvin. KS

It doesn't surprise me. The Amphibians. Mirko Lauer, tr. by David Tipton. Per

It don't seem hordly right, John. Jonathan to John. James Russell Lowell. Fr. The Biglow Papers: 2d Series, No. II. PAH

It droops towards death; yet look, sooner or later the leaf. In Dante's Whirlwind. Gyula Illyés, tr. by Jascha Kessler. FOC

It dropped so low—in my regard. Emily Dickinson. CMoP; HAP; InPK; OxBA; OxBSP

It embarrasses. Personal Poem. Ingrid Wendt. NMM

It faces west, and round the back and sides. Domicilium. Thomas Hardy. FaBoPP; FL

It faded on the crowing of the cock. Shakespeare. Fr. Hamlet, I, i. TOF

It falles me here to write of Chastity. The Legend of Britomartis, or of Chastitie. Spenser. Fr. The Faerie Queene, III. NAEL-1, much abr.

Britomart in the House of Busirane. Fr. III, 11–12. FiP

It feels good as it is without the giant. Wallace Stevens. Fr. Notes toward a Supreme Fiction. NOBA

It feels like a bear eating me. Divorce. Adam Koehn. AiP

It fell about the Lammbmass tide. Bonny Lizie Baillie. Unknown. ESPB

It fell about [or and about or upon] the Lammas tide. The Battle of Otterburn [or Otterbourne]. Unknown. ESPB; GoTS; OnMSP; OxBB. See also Yt fell abowght the Lamasse tyde. ("It fell upon the Lammas tide.") FaBoCh

It fell about the Lammas time. Lord Livingston. Unknown. ESPB; OxBB

It fell about the Martinmas[s] time. Edom o' Gordon. Unknown. OxBB

(Captain Car.) ESPB; FaBoBa

It fell about the Martinmas time. Get Up and Bar the Door. Unknown. ESPB; FaBoBa; GoTS; HeIP; NoP; OnMSP; OxBS; PDV; TrGrPo

It fell about the Martinmas tyde. Jamie Telfer of [or in] the Fair Dodhead. Unknown. ESPB; OxBB

It fell ageyns the next nyght. The Fox and the Goose. *Unknown.* OxBLMV

It fell in the ancient periods. Uriel. Emerson. LiTA; NAAL-1; NOBA; OxBA

It Fell in the City. Eve Merriam. RAR

It fell on a day, and a bonnie simmer [*or* bonny summer] day. The Bonnie House o' Airlie. *Unknown.* ESPB; OBEV; OxBS

It Fell on a Summer's Day. Thomas Campion. ErPo; HAP; WeW

It fell upon a bonny simmer day. The Bonnie House o' Airlie. *Unknown.* OxBB

It Fell upon a Holy Eve. Spenser. *Fr.* The Shepheardes [*or* Shepeards *or* Shepherd's] Calender: August. InvP
(Roundelay, A: "It fell upon a holy eve.") EIL

It fell upon a Wednesday. A Gest of Robyn Hode. *Unknown.* OxBLMV

It fell upon a Wodensday [*or* Wednesday]. Brown Robyn's [*or* Robin's] Confession. *Unknown.* ACP; CH; ESPB; GBP

It fell upon the Lammas tide. *Unknown. See* It fell about the Lammas tide.

It fell upon the Lammas time. Young Ronald. *Unknown.* ESPB

It fell upon us like a crushing woe. Colonel Ellsworth. Richard Henry Stoddard. PAH

It fell when I was sleeping. In my dream. The Land-Mine. George MacBeth. OBWP

It felt like the zero in brook ice. The Funeral. Norman Dubie. InPK; MAYP; NoAM

It flashes you at the AAUP bazaar. Cursing the First Book. John Woods. SoTCo

It flows through old hushed Egypt and its sands. The Nile. Leigh Hunt. EBEV; EnRP; NOBE; OBNC

It follows me. Lac Courte Orielles; 1936. Phyllis Wolf. STE

It follows now you are to prove. Ben Jonson. *Fr.* Pleasure Reconciled to Virtue. NAEL-1

It fortuned (as faire it then befell). Spenser. *Fr.* The Faerie Queene, I, 11. OAEL-1

It gets awful lonely. Lonely. Bloke Modisane. PBA

It gets dark and I get scared. Feeling That Way Too. Arthur Vogelsang. MAYP

It gets run over by a van. Your Dog Dies. Raymond Carver. GeTw

It glimmers like a wakeful lake in the dusk narrowing room. The Mirror. Isaac Rosenberg. NoAM

It goes fwunkety. The Washing Machine. Jeffrey Davies. PCP

It goes on being Alexandria still. Just walk a bit. Exiles. C. P. Cavafy, *tr. by* Edmund Keeley *and* Philip Sherrard. VMG

It grows dark, it seems. *Unknown, tr. fr. Japanese by* Geoffrey Bownas *and* Anthony Thwaite. *Fr.* Kokin Shu. PeBJV

It had been badly shot. Widgeon. Seamus Heaney. FaBCIP

It had to be a big book to be a whale. Publishing 2001. Bob Rosenthal. UL

It hain't no use to grumble and complane [*or* complain]. James Whitcomb Riley. *Fr.* Wet-Weather Talk. AnAmPo
("Rain frogs.") BoNap

It hangs from heaven to earth. Tapestry. Charles Simic. LCAP

It happen sometimes; a pair of eyes a profile. Almost Love. Magaly Sánchez, *tr. by* Margaret Randall. AIW

It happened/ in a second. Where Is Justice? Eliezer Steinbarg, *tr. by* Seth L. Wolitz. VWA

It Happened Before. Wrenne Jarman. CN

It happened before my eyes. Love's Fool. Margit Szécsi, *tr. by* Kenneth McRobbie. MHuP

It happened in Jacksboro in the year of 'seventy-three. The Buffalo Skinners. *Unknown.* AmFP

It happened, it happened all on a Saturday night. Johnny Dyers. *Unknown.* AmFP

It happened not far away. Clonfeacle. Paul Muldoon. CIP

It happened on a Sunday. Camp. Patrick Anderson. OBCV

It happened once, before the duller. Green Slates. Thomas Hardy. FaBoPP

It happened once upon a time. James Hatley. *Unknown.* ESPB

It happened to be on one certain day. The Wreck of the *Rambler*. *Unknown.* OxBSS

It happens lonely—no one. The Moment. William Stafford. NNaP

It happens sometimes when the children play. Children's Games. Abraham Reisen, *tr. by* Leonard Wolf. PeBMYV

It happens through the blond window, the trees. Ascension. Denis Devlin. BIrV

It happens. Will it go on? Paralytic. Sylvia Plath. FaBoWP

It happens with me that I become out. Out and In Again. Malka Heifetz-Tussman, *tr. by* Kathryn Hellerstein. AYP

It has a head like a cat, feet like a cat. *Unknown.* NTCP

It has all/ come back today. From Gloucester Out. Edward Dorn. NOBA; PoM

It has been a long time now. Marriage and Midsummer's Night. Linda Gregg. NAmP; NPGG

It has been a month since I gave up shaving. House Plants. David McFadden. NOBC

It has been days, and still this wind. A State of Fever. Sa'di Yusuf, *tr. by* Lena Jayyusi *and* Naomi Shihab Nye. MAP

It has been hours in these rooms. E. W. Mandel. *Fr.* Minotaur Poems. OBCV, I.

It has been many years. Biographical Note. Gabriel Preil, *tr. by* Howard Schwartz. VWA

It has happened before that death came after breakfast. Enemy Action. N. K. Cruikshank. CN

It has happened suddenly. Je Suis une Table. Donald Hall. EAS; NePoEA

It has no wings. Loneliness and July Ninth. Claribel Alegría, *tr. by* Aliki *and* Willis Barnstone. BoWoP

It has not been given me to have a friend. Friend Who Never Came. William Stafford. SM

It has rained. Wet. Yusuf al-Sa'igh, *tr. by* Diana Der Hovanessian *with* Salma Khadra Jayyusi. MAP

It has to be the end of the day. Surf-casting. W. S. Merwin. NOBA

It hath been said of old that plays are feasts. To the Reader of Master William Davenant's Play, The Wits. Thomas Carew. CaPo

It Is a Beauteous Evening [Calm and Free]. Wordsworth. AWP; BLPL; ChTr; EnRP; FaBoPV; FaBoRV; FiP; HeIP; LiTB; NAEL-2; NiP; NoP; OAEL-2; OBTV; PoEL-4; PoLF; PPP; SeCePo; Son; TEP (Evening on Calais Beach.) OBEV; TrGrPo

It is a bright house. Bright House. Fukao Sumako, *tr. by* Kenneth Rexroth *and* Ikuko Atsumi. UnAS

It is a clearing deep in a forest: overhanging boughs. Johnson's Cabinet Watched by Ants. Robert Bly. MoP; NOBA

It is a clever pushbutton you have, Juan Trippe. What Bright Pushbutton? Samuel Allen. PoNe

It is a cold and snowy night. The main street is deserted. Driving to Town Late to Mail a Letter. Robert Bly. BoNaP; CAPP; HeIP; InPK; NaP; VGW

It is a cramped little state with no foreign policy. Shame. Richard Wilbur. FaBoMo; OxBC

It is a deep, late hour, late for everything. Late Hour. A. Leyeles, *tr. by* Benjamin *and* Barbara Harshav. AYP

It is a funny thing, but true. Folks and Me. Lucile Crites. PWR; WBLP

It is a God-damned lie to say that these. Another Epitaph on an Army of Mercenaries. "Hugh MacDiarmid." InPK; MoP; NAEL-2; NIP; NoAM; OBWP; RB

It is a green globe like a vegetable light bulb. Avocado. John Logan. CAPP

It is a kind of shadow. The Umbrella. Ann Stanford. NYBP

It is a land with neither night nor day. Cobwebs. Christina Rossetti. NAEL-2

It Is a Lie. John Fowles. AnAn

It is a lost road into the air. An Airstrip in Essex, 1960. Donald Hall. LCAP; LiTM

"It is a month, and isna mair." The White Fisher. *Unknown.* ESPB

It is a new America. Brown River, Smile. Jean Toomer. *Fr.* The Blue Meridian. AmNP; PoBA

It is a pilgrim coming from the East. The Pilgrim from the East. Gustave Kahn, *tr. by* Jethro Bithell. TrJP

It Is a Pleasant Day. *Unknown.* BoTP

It is a red motionless sea. From the Rooftops. Carlo Betocchi, *tr. by* I. L. Salomon. PFI

It is a simple ritual. My Brother. Patricia Parker. GLP

It is a solemn evening, golden-clear. The After-Glow. Mathilde Blind. OBNC

It is a squad car idling. Lust. William Matthews. PCP

It is a sultry day; the sun has drunk. Summer Wind. Bryant. PoEL-4

It is a test you have to pass. Essie Parrish in New York. Essie Parrish, *tr. by* George Quasha. STP

It is a theatre floating through the clouds. Wallace Stevens. *Fr.* The Auroras of Autumn, VI. CMoP; HCAP

It is a thought breaking the granite heart. On the Death of Her Body. James Keir Baxter. ATNZ; PeNZ

It is a tide pool, shallow, water coming in. Looking into a Tide Pool. Robert Bly. CAPP; MAT

It is a time of hunger. Personal Song. Arnatkoak. WTO

It is a very curious fact. Lines for a Worthy Person Who Has Drifted by Accident into a Chelsea Revel. Sir A. P. Herbert. NOBL

It is a warm grey afternoon in August. Out of Control; the Quarry. Christopher Dewdney. NOBC

It is a water hand, this right one. Look to the Back of the Hand. Judith Minty. PoA

It is a willow when summer is over. Willow Poem. William Carlos Williams. NAAL-2

It is a winter night. Fever and chill. A Winter's Tale. Robert Patrick Dana. NYBP

It is a winter's tale. A Winter's Tale. Dylan Thomas. CMoP; LiTB

It is a wonder foam is so beautiful. Spray. D. H. Lawrence. BoNaP

It is a year of good harvest. Harvesting Wheat for the Public Share. Li Chü, tr. by Kenneth Rexroth and Ling Chung. BoWoP; OV; PBWP

It is all a rhythm. The Rhythm. Robert Creeley. LiTM

It is all blood and breaking. She Understands Me. Lucille Clifton. CAPP

It is all falling away, the days fall faster now. Descending. Robert Pack. NePoEA-2

It is all one in Venus' wanton school. John Lyly. SeCePo

It is all right. All they do. To the Muse. James Wright. NAAL-2; NNaP; NoP

It is almost the end of spring. Pure Serene Music. Mao Hsi-chen, tr. by Lois Fusek. ATF

It is almost the hour of dawn. The Unfortunate Woman. Ho Ning, tr. by Lois Fusek. ATF

It is almost too simple. Hut. G. J. F. Dutton. PoSH

It is always a temptation to an armed and agile nation. Dane-Geld. Kipling. OxBTC

It is always night here. Star & Garter Theater. Dennis Schmitz. LCAP; NPGG

It is always so: the declining. Returning from Harvest. Vernon Watkins. NYBP

It is always someone else. Destiny of the Poet. Claude Vigée, tr. by Anthony Rudolf. VWA

It is an ancestral castle. Life in the Castle. Anne Hébert, tr. by Aliki and Willis Barnstone. BoWoP

It is an ancient custom. An Ancient Custom. Anatoly Steiger, tr. by John Glad. VWA

It is an ancient Mariner. The Ancient Mariner: The Wedding Guest's Version of the Affair from His Point of View. Unknown. FaBoPa

It is an ancient Mariner. The Rime of the Ancient Mariner. Samuel Taylor Coleridge. BeLS; CH; ChER; EBEV; EnRP; FaBoBe; FaBoCh; FaBV; FaFP; FiP; HAP; HeIP; HoPM; InPS; LiTB; MOS; NAEL-2; NOBE; NoP; OAEL-2; OBEV; OBNC; OBNV; PoE; PoEL-4; PrIm; TEP; TrGrPo

It is an auncient waggonere. The Rime of the Auncient Waggonere. William Maginn. BXAP

It is an honorable thought. Emily Dickinson. NOCV

It is an old established hotel. The Latest Hotel Guest Walks over Particles That Revolve in Seven Other Dimensions Controlling Latti. Ruth Stone. BAP

It is an old stove. Stove. Ken Belford. NeAC

It is as if the birds have segregated you. The Hoopoe Bird. Saleem Barakat, tr. by Lena Jayyusi and Naomi Shihab Nye. MAP

It is as if they are ashamed. The Elephants Dying. Michael C. Blumenthal. NoAM

It is as if you're lugging a commode. On Your Back. Gerrit Komrij, tr. by Jacob Lowland. DuIn

It is as true as strange, else trial feigns. John Davies of Hereford. ElL

It Is at Moments after I Have Dreamed. E. E. Cummings. OxBA

It is at morning, twilight they expire. After Midnight. Charles Vildrac, tr. by Jethro Bithell. AWP

It is beautiful to have chosen. Homage to Life. Jules Supervielle, tr. by Kenneth Rexroth. RHTwFP

It Is Becoming Now to Declare My Allegiance. C. Day Lewis. LiTM

It is best to turn on the set. Violence on Television. Louis Jenkins. NU

It is better. Abandoning Your Car in a Snowstorm: Rosslyn, Virginia. Michael C. Blumenthal. NoAM

"It Is Better. . ." Bible, O.T. Fr. Ecclesiastes, VII: 1-9. TrJP

It is better now that time. Initiation at Firawa. Michael Jackson. ATNZ

It is better this year. If the Birds Knew. John Ashbery. PoA

It Is Better to Be Together. Ruth Miller. PeSA

It is blue-butterfly day here in spring. Blue-Butterfly Day. Robert Frost. RFM

It is by means/ of poetry. Words Read in a Poem in a Dream. Jascha Kessler. FOC

It is Christmas Day in the workhouse, and the cold, bare walls are bright. Christmas Day in the Workhouse. George R. Sims. BeLS; BLPA (In the Workhouse.) OBCP

It is Christmas in the mansion. Christmas in the Heart. Unknown. OHIP

It is cold here. The Moths. W. S. Merwin. HeIP

It is cold, the snow is deep. Poor North. Mark Strand. AnAn

It is cold without flesh, without bones. Dead in Wars and in Revolutions. Mary Devenport O'Neill. NeIP

It is colder now. Epistle to Be Left in the Earth. Archibald MacLeish. CMoP; ImOP; MoAB; MoAmPo; NOBA; TrGrPo

It is common knowledge to every schoolboy and even. Portrait of the Artist as a Prematurely Old Man. Ogden Nash. BLPL; FaFP; InPS; LiTA; LiTM

It is conceivable that when one dies. Momentariness. Stefan Brecht. BAP

It is consummation, a mad rape. Pitch Seven. Hamish Brown. PoSH

It is dangerous for a woman to defy the gods. Letter to My Sister. Anne Spencer. AmNP; BISi; PoBA; PoNe

It Is Dangerous to Read Newspapers. Margaret Atwood. HeIP; OBWP

It is dangerous to stand in early fall. Having Read Books. Heather McHugh. GeTw

It is dark. The Last Bus. Mark Strand. TwCP

It is dark and lonesome here. The Lover. Richard Henry Stoddard. AA

It is dark, now, and grave. Melting Pot. Michael Echeruo. TTY

It is dark up here on the heights. Le Sacré-Coeur. Charlotte Mew. OBTV

It is December in Wicklow. Exposure. Seamus Heaney. IPY

It is decided, dear Theramenes. Phaedra. Jean Racine, tr. by Kenneth Muir. NAWM-2

It is deep summer. Far out. There. Robert Mezey. NaP

It Is Difficult Now to Speak of Poetry. George Oppen. Fr. Of Being Numerous. NNaP

It is difficult to imagine how vulnerable they are. The Birds. David Posner. NYBP

It is difficult to meet with so exquisite a beauty. Lotus Leaf Cup. Wei Chuang, tr. by Lois Fusek. ATF

It is disastrous to be a wounded deer. Hello. Gregory Corso. PoM

It is done! Laus Deo! Whittier. AmPP; PAH

It is done by us all, as God disposes, from. The Excrement Poem. Maxine W. Kumin. CAPP; FaBoWP

It is dusk/ On the bridle path. Memory. Joseph Stroud. NPGG

It is early dawn. The city forty miles away draws airplanes. Written Forty Miles South of a Spreading City. Robert Bly. NNaP

It is early, yet. The Grand Canyon. James Merrill. TAP

It is easier to forgive an enemy than to forgive a friend. Blake. Fr. Jerusalem, IV. OAEL-2

It is easily forgotten, year to. Memorial Day. Michael Anania. NoAM

It is easy enough to be pleasant. Worth While. Ella Wheeler Wilcox. BLPA; FPL

It is easy enough to love flowers but these. Giant Decorative Dahlias. Molly Holden. OxBTC

It is easy to be young. (Everybody is). How to Be Old. May Swenson. ER; MAT; UnPo

It Is Enough. Philip Appleman. BXAP

It is enough for me. Old Man Told Me. Lance Henson. VoR

It is enough for me to. The Bridge. Khalil Hawi, tr. by Diana Der Hovanessian and Lena Jayyusi. MAP

It is enough that you visit the earth. Riverbed for Damien. Gregory O'Brien. ATNZ

It is enough; time presses, we are thrifty. It Is Enough. Philip Appleman. BXAP

It is equal to living in a tragic land. Dry Loaf. Wallace Stevens. NOBA; OxBA; PoRA

It is essential I remember. Man White, Brown Girl and All That Jazz. Gloria C. Oden. PoBA

It is evening. One bat dances. A Soul. Randall Jarrell. CMoP

It is far from just between us. Unknown. NOIV

It is far to Assisi. William Carlos Williams. Fr. The Garden. CRP (Mental Hospital Garden, The.) FYAP

It Is Finished. Barney Bush. STE

It is finished. The enormous dust-cloud over Europe. Armistice. Paul Dehn. OxBTC

It is fitting that you be here. On Seeing Two Brown Boys in a Catholic Church. Frank Horne. BANP; CDC; PoBA; PoNe; TTY

It Is Five Years Now. Gyula Illyés, tr. fr. Hungarian by William Jay Smith. MHuP

It is folly for any man in the world. The Praises of God. Unknown, tr. by Kenneth Jackson. AnIL

It is foolish for Rubens to show her. Susanna and the Elders. Jack Gilbert. NPGG

It Is for the Waking Man to Tell His Dreams. John Ciardi. BLA

It is for us/ to praise the Lord of all. The Kingdom of God. Rab. TrJP

It is for you, my mother fair. For You. James Harvey Spencer. PWR

It is four in the afternoon. Time still for a poem. Public Journal. Phyllis McGinley. NBLV

It is friday. We have come. Forgiving My Father. Lucille Clifton. CAPP; GeTw

It is from the ideas of you that you emerge. Correspondences. Robert Duncan. PoM

It is from the lips from the lip blowing flying songy. Sonsito. Victor Hernandez Cruz. RR

It is fun to ride the horse. Horse. Kenneth Rexroth. *Fr.* A Bestiary. NNaP

It is going to be a splendid summer. Future Work. Fleur Adcock. DiPo

It is good sometimes to grasp our helplessness. The Flood. Charles G. Bell. GrPl

It is good to be out on the road, and going one knows not where. Tewkesbury Road. John Masefield. BoTP

It is good to see the sunshine ebb on distant hills. The Spirit of the Cairngorms. Axel Firsoff. PoSH

It is good to strive against wind and rain. A Mood. Amélie Rives. AA

It is half-past nine on a July night. Letter to Ben, 1972. Paul Durcan. FaBCIP

It is hanging/ in the edge of sunshine. *Unknown, tr. fr. Chippewa Indian by Frances Densmore. Fr.* Poems for the Game of Silence. STP

It is hard. Being a Giant. Robert Mezey. GrPl

It is hard going to the door. The Door. Robert Creeley. NaP; NeAP; NoAM; PoM; VGW

It is hard, inland. In Winter. Robert Wallace. BoNaP

It is hard to beat a good meal. Thomas Kinsella. *Fr.* A Technical Supplement. CIP

It Is Hard to Catch Trout. Piuvkaq, *tr. fr. Eskimo.* WTO

It is hard to kill the never-born. The Monster. David Lunde. BWV

It is hard to remember parents at their loving. Train Song. Fiona Kidman. PeNZ

It is hardly sensuous, but having. How to Take Off Your Clothes at the Picnic. Bill Manhire. ATNZ

It Is Her Cousin's Death. Gail Fox. NOBC

It is hot today, dry enough for cutting grain. August from My Desk. Roland Flint. AmFN

It is I, America, calling! A Call to Arms. Mary Raymond Shipman Andrews. PAH

It is I that am under sorrow at this time. Another Song. William Ross. GoTS

It is impossible to find anything good. Flood. Mary Grant Charles. GoYe

It is in captivity. The Bull. William Carlos Williams. LiTM; NoP; TwCP

It is in the rock, but not in the stone. *Unknown.* ChTr

It Is in Winter That We Dream of Spring. Robert Burns Wilson. AA

It is increasingly less difficult to get up. Alfred Kolleritsch, *tr. by* Beth Bjorklund. CoAuP

It is indecent by any standard. Having Drowned. Bernice Zamora. CCP

It is Isis the mystery. Don Juan. D. H. Lawrence. PoA

It is June, it is June. Andraitx—Pomegranate Flowers. D. H. Lawrence. NoP

It is late afternoon. The Caves. Janice Gould. GOS

It is late at night and still I am losing. In Dives' Dive. Robert Frost. VGW

It is late in the day of the world. Latter Day Lysistrata. Lauris Edmond. PeNZ

It is late in the year. Night in the House by the River. Tu Fu, *tr. by* Kenneth Rexroth. NaP

It is late last night the dog was speaking of you. Donal Og. *Unknown, tr. by* Lady Augusta Gregory. RB

(Grief of a Girl's Heart, The.) ChTr

It is Leviathan, mountain and world. History. Robert Fitzgerald. FYAP

It is like riding Death and not dying. Sometimes Heaven Is a Mean Machine. William Pitt Root. MAYP

It is like the plot of an ol/ novel. Instructions to a Princess. Ishmael Reed. CNA; PoBA

It is likely enough that lions and scorpions. Ante Mortem. Robinson Jeffers. MoAmPo

It is little I repair to the matches of the Southron folk. At Lord's. Francis Thompson. EBVV; OxBSP

It is lonely by the red window with no one to talk to. The Beautiful Lady Yü. Sun Kuang-hsien, *tr. by* Lois Fusek. ATF

It is lonely in the tasseled curtains, the mats are chill. Sand of Silk-Washing Stream. Yen Hsüan, *tr. by* Lois Fusek. ATF

It is lonely within the green tower. Song of the Wine-Spring. Li Hsün, *tr. by* Lois Fusek. ATF

It is made to be rolled down. A Poem like a Grenade. John Haines. EAS

It Is March ("It is March and black dust falls out of the books"). W. S. Merwin. NaP

It is midnight. Poem at Thirty. Sonia Sanchez. BlSi; BPo; CNA; NMM; PoBA

It is midnight. The Mailman. Mark Strand. CAPP

It is midnite. The room is blue. Death Songs. L. V. Mack. PoBA

It Is Mine, This Country Wide. *Unknown.* GOA

It is miserable. Líadan and Cuirithir. *Unknown.* NOIV

It is Monday morning. The Goldfish Wife. Sandra Hochman. NYBP; UnPo

It is morning darling look the sun. Aubade: N.Y.C. Robert Wallace. HoPM

It is morning, Senlin says, and in the morning. Conrad Aiken. *Fr.* Senlin; a Biography. LiTM, II, ii.

("It is morning, Senlin says, and in the morning.") LiTM; NoAM (Morning Song.) CMoP; MoAB; TrGrPo

(Morning Song of Senlin.) LiTA; MoAmPo; OxBA

"It is most true that eyes are formed to serve." Sir Philip Sidney. *Fr.* Astrophel and Stella, V. NAEL-1; OAEL-1; OBSC; Son

It is much like ocean the way it opens. Open Country. Richard Hugo. LCAP

It is myself. To a Dog Injured in the Street. William Carlos Williams. LCAP; LiTM; MoAB

It Is Near Toussaints'. Ivor Gurney. OBD

It Is Nearly Summer. Bill Manhire. ATNZ

It is neither the horror of the white sunset nor the sickly dawn. Declamatory Poem. Max Jacob, *tr. by* Michael Brownstein. RHTwFP

It is never enough to know what you want. "The Wish to Be Believed." Mona Van Duyn. PoA

It is New Year's Day. Best Loved of Africa. Margaret Danner. PoBA; PoNe

It is night again. Tzu Yeh, *tr. by* Kenneth Rexroth *and* Ling Chung. WPOW

It is night and the barbarians have not come. Poem Beginning with a Line by Cavafy. Derek Mahon. FaBCIP

It is night like a red rag. A Moment of War. Laurie Lee. OBWP

It is 1939. Album. Lucille Clifton. ER

It is no flaming lustre made of light. The Celestial City. Giles Fletcher the Younger. *Fr.* Christ's Victory and Triumph: Christ's Triumph after Death, IV. OBD

It is no idle fabulous tale, nor is it fayned newes. Newes from Virginia. Richard Rich. PAH

It is no longer one whose noise. Mohammad Taqi Mir, *tr. by* Ahmed Ali. GoT

It is no madness to say. Hilda Doolittle ("H. D."). *Fr.* The Flowering of the Rod. FaBoMo

It is no vulgar nature I have wived. George Meredith. *Fr.* Modern Love, XXXV. NAEL-2

It is noble country where we dwell. Our Country. Henry David Thoreau. GOA

It Is Not Always May. Longfellow. PWR

It is not anything he says. Kavin Agash. Richard Hovey. AnAmPo

It is not bad. Let them play. The Bloody Sire. Robinson Jeffers. CMoP; LiTM; PoA

It Is Not Beauty I Demand. George Darley. NAEL-2; OAEL-2

(Loveliness of Love, The.) GTBS; GTBS-P

(Song, A: "It is not beauty I demand.") OBNC

It is not, Celia, in our power. To a Lady Asking Him How Long He Would Love Her. Sir George Etherege. OBEV

It is not cosy to live. From the Chinese. Michael Smith. CIP

It is not death, that sometime in a sigh. Thomas Hood. OBNC; ViBoPo

It is not easy. Tove Ditlevsen, *tr. fr. Danish by* Ann Freeman. *Fr.* Divorce, III. OV

It is not easy to achieve a thing. Asadullah Khan Ghalib, *tr. by* Ahmed Ali. GoT

It is not easy to be less than lovers. For M. Bruce Williamson. NeIP

It is not enough. The Prophet's Warning or Shoot to Kill. Ebon Dooley. PoBA

It is not enough to drink. "When the Wild Goose Finds Food He Calls His Comrades" *I Ching.* Jan Kemp. PeNZ

It is not far to my place. Visit. A. R. Ammons. CoAP; GrPl; TwCP

It is not four years ago. Proffered Love Rejected. Sir John Suckling. ErPo

It Is Not Growing Like a Tree. Ben Jonson. *Fr.* To the Immortal[l] Memory [or Memorie] and Friendship of That Noble Pair[e], Sir Lucius Cary and Sir Henry Morrison. ChTr; HeIP; LiTB

(Noble Nature, The.) GN; GTBS; GTBS-P

(Oak and Lily.) TrGrPo

(Part of an Ode, A.) OBEV

It is not—I swear it by every fiery omen to be seen these nights. Readings, Forecasts, Personal Guidance. Kenneth Fearing. MoAmPo

It is not in the books. The Three Movements. Donald Hall. NePoEA-2

It Is Not, Lord, the Sound of Many Words. Henry Lok. *Fr.* Sundry Christian Passions Contained in Two Hundred. Son

It is not mine to run, with eager feet. Not Mine. Julia Caroline Ripley Dorr. PWR

It is not right for you to know, so do not ask, Leuconoe. I, 13. Ad Leuconoen. Horace, *tr. fr. Latin. Fr.* Odes. AWP, *tr. by* F. P. Adams.

It is not so much the image of the man. Photograph of Haymaker, 1890. Molly Holden. OxBTC

It Is Not So with Me. Blake. *Fr.* Vala; or The Four Zoas, The Four Zoas. SeCePo

It is not that I love you less. The Selfe Banished. Edmund Waller. MePo; OBS

It is not the earth that I worship. Earth Song. Thomas Peacock. VoR

It is not the fear of death. André's Request to Washington. *Unknown.* PAH

It is not the foreignness *per se* of heroes. Why the British Girls Give In So Easily. Nicholas Moore. WaP

It is not the moon, I tell you. Mock Orange. Louise Glück. MAYP; NoAM

It is not the sea. Poem near the sea. *Unknown.* WMBCH

It is not the weight of the jewel or plate. The Perfect Gift. Edmund Vance Cooke. PChr

It is not the wolf. Pigs. Andrea Hollander Budy. KS

It is not the young whom we find feeding the pigeons. The Pigeon-Feeders in Battery Park. Julia Cooley Altrocchi. GoYe

It Is Not to Be Thought Of [That the Flood]. Wordsworth. EnRP; FiP (England, 1802 ("It is not to be thought of").) NOBE; OBEV (Faith and Freedom.) GN, 4 *ll.* (We Must Be Free or Die.) FaPoR

It is not vertue, wisdom, valour, wit. Woman. Milton. *Fr.* Samson Agonistes. OBS

It is not what they built. It is what they knocked down. A German Requiem. James Fenton. NAEL-2; NoAM

It is nothing to me, the beauty said. Nothing and Something. Frances Ellen Watkins Harper. PWR

It is now my brave boys we are clear of the sea. The Antarctic Muse. Thomas Perry. OBTV

It is of a fearless Irishman a story I will tell. Brennan on the Moor. *Unknown.* AmFP ("It's of a famous highwayman a story I will tell.") GBP ("It's of a fearless highwayman a story now I'll tell.") FaBoBa

It is of a fine frigate, dare not mention her name. The Fancy Frigate. *Unknown.* OxBSS

It is of a flash packet, she's a packet of fame. The *Dreadnought.* *Unknown.* OxBSS

It is, of course, the wrong house. The Houses of Emily Dickinson. Larry Rubin. NIP

It is on the sea and under the waves of the sea. Cycle. Sean Jennett. WaP

It is only thanks to your good looks. A Woman Talks to Her Thigh. Anna Swirszczynska, *tr. by* Czeslaw Milosz. PwPP

It is our hand. Patience of a People. Frederick Bryant, Jr. CNA

It is past midnight in a thick fog when sirens. Street Fire. Daniel Halpern. AmPA

It is people at the edge who say. Sayings from the Northern Ice. William Stafford. NU

It is plain now what you are. Your head has dropped. Carrion. Harold Monro. *Fr.* Youth in Arms, IV. MMA

It is portentous, and a thing of state. Abraham Lincoln Walks at Midnight. Vachel Lindsay. AmFN; AmPP; CMoP; FaBV; FaFP; FaPON; GOA; LiTA; MoAmPo; NOBA; OFD; OHFP; OHIP; OxBA; PAH; TAP; VGW

It is possible to state. Behaviorally. Anselm Hollo. UL

It is quite natural to be. Elephant. Alan Brownjohn. OnUR

It is rather strange to be speaking, but I know you are there. A Voice at a Seance. Anthony Hecht. AnAn

It is reported. Sharks in Shallow Water. Fred Levinson. AmPA

It is rough. Poem about a Seashell. Ranice Henderson Crosby. NMM

It is said in the ancient writings. Tulsidas, *tr. by* John Stratton Hawley *and* Mark Juergensmeyer. SSI

It is said that many a king in troubled Europe. Rulers: Philadelphia. Fenton Johnson. AmFN; PoNe

It is said that that western land is of Earth the best. The Land Called Scotia. St. Donatus. NOIV

It is said there are those who can never be sane. Bill. Peter Kocan. CBAP

It is sayde full ryfe. *Unknown. Fr.* Shepherd's Play (Townley cycle). FaBoUs

It is senseless for any man. Praise of God. *Unknown.* NOIV

It is she alone that matters. Bouquet of Belle Scavoir. Wallace Stevens. MoAB; MoAmPo

It is snowing heavily again. Between Us. Stephen Berg. NaP

It Is So Long Since My Heart Has Been with Yours. E. E. Cummings. UnAS

It is so much easier to forget than to have been Mr. Whittier. Mr. Whittier. Winfield Townley Scott. VGW

It is so peaceful on the ceiling! Sleeping on the Ceiling. Elizabeth Bishop. TTTS

It is so quiet. It is 1957. Sharks, Caloosahatchee River. Greg Pape. MAYP

It is so small a thing. Matthew Arnold. *Fr.* Empedocles on Etna, I, 2. OBEV

It is so still in the house. The Mother's Song. *Unknown, tr. by* Peter Freuchen. OBCP; WTO

It is some school, brick, green, a sleepy hill. An Officer's Prison Camp Seen from a Troop Train. Randall Jarrell. WaP

It is sometime since I have been. The Hill. Robert Creeley. CRP

It is spring in the mountains. Written on the Wall at Chang's Hermitage. Tu Fu, *tr. by* Kenneth Rexroth. HoPM; NaP

It is strange to think of the Annas, the Vronskys, the Pierres, all the Tolstoyan lot wiped out. Fate and the Younger Generation. D. H. Lawrence. OxBoLi

It is strange we trust each other. Why Doubt God's Word? Albert Benjamin Simpson. BLRP

"It is such a beautiful day I had to write you a letter." Thoughts of a Young Girl. John Ashbery. TAP; VGW

It is summer, city summer. Chicago, Summer Past. Richard Snyder. Psk

It is taking a long time. Sestina for My Dead in the First Snow. John Engels. AnAn

It is talked the warld all over. Sheath and Knife. *Unknown.* ESPB

It is ten years, now, since we rowed to Children's Island. The Babysitters. Sylvia Plath. NoP

It is ten years since I have seen these shirts. The Shirt Poem. Gerald Stern. CAPP

It is terrible, I admit that. All for Nothing. Lörinc Szabó, *tr. by* Edwin Morgan. MHuP

It is the association after all. A Way of Looking. Elizabeth Jennings. NePoEA

It is the bare and leafless Tree. Holy Cross. Shane Leslie. TIRV

It is the best, erely and late. Be True to Your Condition in Life. John Audelay. MeEL

It is the best thing. Pregnancy. Sandra McPherson. BoWoP; NMM

It is the bittern's solemn cry. Solitude. Frederick Peterson. AA

It is the black night, the crimson clock. The Clock. Mauro Moto, *tr. by* Mark Strand. ATCBP

It is the bottomless swoon of never forgetting. Earthsleep. Fred Chappell. KS

It is the box from which no jack will spring. The Funeral. Donald Hall. Son

It is the breezes. Empress Eifuku, *tr. by* Steven D. Carter. WFTW

It is the cause, it is the cause, my soul. Shakespeare. *Fr.* Othello, V, ii. EBEV (Othello and Desdemona.) FiP

It is the clay that makes the earth stick to his spade. In Nunhead Cemetery. Charlotte Mew. FaBoWP

It is the counterpoise that minds. Noble Love. Richard Flecknoe. ACP

It is the day of all the year. *Unknown.* OxNR

It is the endless dance of the dead. Quincy Troupe. PoBA

It is the evening hour. To Mary: It Is the Evening Hour. John Clare. BoLoP; ChTr; GBL; Mes (Mary.) EnLoPo

It is the first mild day of March. To My Sister. Wordsworth. EnRP; OAEL-2 (Change in the Year, A.) BoTP

It is the football season once more. Autumn. Vernon Scannell. OxBTC

It is the gentle poet's art. Iron. Walter de la Mare. NOBL

It is the Harvest Moon! On gilded vanes. The Harvest Moon. Longfellow. GN

It Is the Hush of Night. Byron. *Fr.* Childe Harold's Pilgrimage, III. LiTB Lake Leman ("Clear, placid Leman! thy contrasted lake"). OBNC, *sl. diff. sel.*

It is the lake within the lake that drowns. My Lady the Lake. Peter Davidson. WeW

It is the last of the ninth, two down, bases loaded. The Lady Pitcher. Cynthia MacDonald. Psk

It is the man, himself. Aleph. Stuart Z. Perkoff. VWA

It is the memory of the peacock and the muses. Letter to R. Willard Maas. WaP

It is the middle of October. The First Dimension of Skunk. Ray A. Young Bear. HATNAP

It is the miller's daughter. The Miller's Daughter. Tennyson. OBEV; TrGrPo

It is the morning of our love. An Aspect of Love, Alive in the Ice and Fire. Gwendolyn Brooks. BPo; CAPP; TAP

It is the nature of man that puzzles me. The Nature of Man. Charles Hubert Sisson. FaBoTw

It is the Negro's tragedy I feel. The Negro's Tragedy. Claude McKay. BPo

It is the old story: complaints about the moon. The Story. Mark Strand. AnAn

It is the orange flower on dark-flushed stem. The Cactuses. Hubert Witheford. ATNZ

It is the pain, it is the pain, endures. William Empson. CMoP; EnLoPo; MoP; NoAM; OAEL-2; PoE

It is the picnic with Ruth in the spring. The Picnic. John Logan. NePoEA-2

It is the same infrequent star. The Star of Calvary. Nathaniel Hawthorne. AA

It is the sea's edge lubbers love. Sailing, Sailing. Gray Burr. NYBP

It Is the Season. Josephine Jacobsen. TAP

It is the season of the sweet wild rose. George Meredith. *Fr.* Modern Love, XLV. GBL; PoEL-5

It is the selfsame thing. Asadullah Khan Ghalib, *tr. by* Ahmed Ali. GoT

It Is The Silence. Ya'akov Beser, *tr. fr. Hebrew by* Bernhard Frank. MHeP

It is the silver seeking salvation. The Plight. James W. Thompson. BPo

It is the sinking of things. Rain. James Wright. NaP

It is the sinners' dust-tongued bell claps me to churches. Dylan Thomas. OxBTC

It is the snow-gum silently. The Snow-Gum. Douglas Stewart. PoAu-2

It is the spot I came to seek. An Indian at the Burial-Place of His Fathers. Bryant. HeIP

It Is the Stars That Govern Us. Michael Magee. PoA

It is the thirty-first of March. Peter Bell. John Hamilton Reynolds. OBNC; Par

It is the time of rain and snow. Lady Izumi, *tr. by* Kenneth Rexroth. WPOW

It is the way of a pleasant path. Green Frog at Roadstead, Wisconsin. James Schevill. TAP

It is the white of faces from which the sunburn has been suddenly scared away. Driftwood from a Ship. Galway Kinnell. AnAn

It is the white plum tree. 'Tis the White Plum Tree. John Shaw Neilson. PoAu-1

It is the year's end, the winds are blasting, and I. December 30th. Ivor Gurney. NAEL-2

It is their way to find the surface. Poem by the Charles River. Robin Blaser. NeAP

It is this deep blankness is the real thing strange. Let It Go. William Empson. FaBoMo; OPOP; OxBSP; OxBTC

It is this rainy afternoon that reaches me. This Afternoon. Juan Sáez Burgos, *tr. by* Julio Marzán. InW

It Is This Way with Men. C. K. Williams. CAPP

It is three o'clock in the morning. Trials of a Tourist. Anne Tibble. FaBoCo; NBLV

It is time for the others to come. The Magus. James Dickey. NAs

It is time to be old. Terminus. Emerson. AA; AmPP; AWP; FPL; NOBA; OxBA; PoEL-4; PoLF; TAP

It is time to open the great door. Fluid. Tristan Tzara, *tr. by* Timothy Baum. POS

It is time to put a stop once for all. Say It with Vegetables. Paul Snoek, *tr. by* Alasdair Mackinnon. DuIn

It is time to recompose the face. Peter Porter. *Fr.* Returning. PoPo

It is to a goodly child well fitting. A Goodly Child. *Unknown.* OxBChV

It is to my own as if the man made them a gift. Eadwacer. *Unknown, tr. by* Kemp Malone. PBWP

It is told, in Buddhi-theosophic schools. Transcendentalism. *Unknown.* NA

It is tomorrow now. Morning Star. Thomas Hornsby Ferril. VGW

It Is Too Late. Longfellow. *Fr.* Morituri Salutamas. BLPL; PoLF (Too Late?.) WBLP

It is too late for suicide. Apologia Pro Vita. June Siegel. SoTCo

It is too late for the word. Too Late. Rachel Korn, *tr. by* Seymour Mayne *and* Rivka Augenfeld. VWA

It is true—/ I've always loved. Alice Walker. *Fr.* Once. NMM; PoBA

It is true, Martin Heidegger, as you have written. The Envelope. Maxine W. Kumin. TV

It is true, modern life is complicated. For the Market. Jane Mayhall. TAP

It is true, that even in the best-run state. The Murder of William Remington. Howard Nemerov. CMoP; CoAP

It is true that I held Thero fair. Meleager, *tr. by* Peter Whigham. PeHV

It is true that, older than man and ages to oulast him. Gray Weather. Robinson Jeffers. CMoP

It is 12:20 in New York a Friday. The Day Lady Died. Frank O'Hara. CAPP; HCAP; MoP; NAAL-2; NeAP; NoAM; NOBA; NoP; PoE; PoM; SOTW

It is twenty years. The Piper. W. S. Merwin. NAAL-2

It is very aggravating. The Truth about Horace. Eugene Field. AnAmPo

It is very early now, no light yet, nor. La Brea. Richard Kenney. DiPo

It is warm at the silk window. The Beautiful Spring Scene. Ho Ning, *tr. by* Lois Fusek. ATF

It is warm within the mandarin duck curtains. Offering Deep Affection. Ku Hsiung, *tr. by* Lois Fusek. ATF

It is well for small birds that can rise up on high. *Unknown, tr. by* Thomas Kinsella. NOIV

It is what he does not know. On a Squirrel Crossing the Road in Autumn, in New England. Richard Eberhart. HeIP; LiTM; PoCH; Psk

It is what we both knew in the sunlight of a restaurant's garden. The Circus Ringmaster's Apology to God. Norman Dubie. MAYP

It is whatever day, whatever time it is. Sunday Morning. Wayne Moreland. PoBA

It is when I hear Mozart. Deafness. Richard Ryan. BIrV

It is when I work on the old Volvo. Thoreau. Rodney Jones. MAYP

It is windy today. A wall of wind crashes against. Cloudy Day. Jimmy Santiago Baca. InPS

It is winter and the new year. The New Year. Mark Strand. *Fr.* Elegy for My Father. UnPo

It Is Winter, I Know. Merrill Moore. MoAmPo

It is winter in California, and outside. California Winter. Karl Shapiro. AiP

It is worthless to write a line. Bernard de Ventadour, *tr. by* Paul Blackburn. Pro

It is written in the skyline of the city. Pact. Kenneth Fearing. CMoP

It is written that a hurricane holds the power. An Antipastoral Memory of One Summer. Dave Smith. MAYP; MT

It is you. An Elegy for Hölderlin. Fu'ad Rifqa, *tr. by* Abdullah al-Udhari. MPAW

It is your last day and hour and you are alone. Who. Edwin Honig. TAP

It is yourself you seek. Man Alone. Louise Bogan. NYBP

"It isn't a game for girls." Reaching Yellow River. Roberta Hill Whiteman. HATNAP

It isn't between him and me. It's between me and me. Story in Poetic Form: The Androgyne. Marguerite Grépon, *tr. by* Barbara Johnson. DMF

It isn't in my bones. Politics. Marco Martos, *tr. by* David Tipton. Per

It isn't pleasant. The Inhuman. Eugenio Montale, *tr. by* G. Singh. OBD

It isn't proper, I guess you know. Read This with Gestures. John Ciardi. RHPC

It isn't raining rain to me. April Rain. Robert Loveman. BoTP; TrJP (Rain Song.) WBLP

It isn't that the threat of the bomb is great. Cocoon. Ishigaki Rin, *tr. by* Ayusawa Takako. WPOW

It isn't that we are deprived of a bright moon. Rain on the Night of the Full Moon. Hsü Ts'an, *tr. by* Irving Lo. WFTU

It Isn't the Church—It's You. *Unknown.* BLPA; WBLP

It Isn't the Cough. *Unknown.* FaFP

It isn't the thing you do, dear. At Sunset. Margaret Elizabeth Munson Sangster. PWR (Sin of Omission, The.) BLPA

It Isn't the Town, It's You. R. W. Glover. BLPA

It isn't winter that brings it. Earth. Margaret Atwood. PoE

It keeps eternal whisperings around. On the Sea. Keats. EnRP; FF; LiTB; NoP; OAEL-2; TEP; TrGrPo (Sonnet: On the Sea.) MOS (Sonnet on the Sea.) SeCePo

It Keeps Going On. Benjamin Péret, *tr. fr. French by* Michael Benedikt. POS

It later befell in the years that followed. The Fire-Dragon and the Treasure. *Unknown, tr. fr. Anglo-Saxon by* Charles W. Kennedy. *Fr.* Beowulf. AnOE

It lay, dark in the corner of the field. Suicide Pond. Kathy McLaughlin. PoA

It lies around us like a cloud. The Other World. Harriet Beecher Stowe. AA; WGRP

It Lies Not in Our Power to Love or Hate. Christopher Marlowe. *Fr.* Hero and Leander, First Sestiad. TrGrPo (Who Ever Loved, That Loved Not at First Sight?.) BLPL; FaFP; LiTB

It lies not on the sunlit hill. The White Peace. "Fiona Macleod." FaBoBe

It little profits that an idle king. Ulysses. Tennyson. AWP; EBEV; FaPoR; FF; FiP; FPL; HAP; HeIP; HoPM; InPK; InPS; LiTB; MOS; NAEL-2; NAWM-2; NIP; NOBE; NOBVV; NoP; OAEL-2; PoE; PoRA; PPP; PrIm; SCV; SeCePo; SoSe; TEP; TrGrPo; UnPo; WeW

It looked extremely rocky for the Mudville nine that day. Casey at the Bat. Ernest Lawrence Thayer. AnAmPo; BeLS; BLPA; FaBoBe; FaFP; FPL; PoRA

It looks a piece of golden, broken glass. Onion Skin in Barn. Kenneth Slade Alling. NePoAm

It looks like any building. The Library. Barbara A. Huff. FaPON; RHPC

It looks like the streets are flowing sweetly in the night. Los Angeles Nocturne. Xavier Villaurrutia, *tr.* by Perry Higman. LPSS

It matters little where I was born. What Does It Matter? Noah Barker. PWR

It matters not, O breeze. Mohammad Taqi Mir, *tr.* by Ahmed Ali. GoT

It May Be. Alfonsina Storni, *tr. fr. Spanish* by Mark I. Smith. OV

It may be a sin to sit in the room. A Conversation with Mr. Yao. Sung Chang-kyung. WCI

It may be good, like it who list. Sir Thomas Wyatt. FaBoPV; SiPS

It may be these things never did occur. Kinnereth. Rachel, *tr.* by A. M. Klein. TrJP

It may be 'tis observ'd, I want relations. George Wither. *Fr.* The Tired Petitioner. SeCV-1

It may be we are in the last days. Time. Amy Clampitt. NIP

It may happen again—this much. The Flight. John Haines. EAS

It may have been the pride in me for aught. The Corridor. E. A. Robinson. AnAmPo

It may indeed be phantasy, when I. To Nature. Samuel Taylor Coleridge. OAEL-2

It May Not Always Be So. E. E. Cummings. *Fr.* Sonnets—Unrealities. BoLoP; FaBV

It may spare me the folly. Constructive Criticism. May Richstone. SoTCo

It means, perhaps, not very much. Of Time and Us. David R. Bunch. BWV

It midnights, not a moon is out. The Midnightmouse. Christian Morgenstern, *tr. by* W. D. Snodgrass *and* Lore Segal. RB

It Might Be a Lump of Amber. Walter de la Mare. FaBoNo

It might be any night. These Days. Andrew Motion. DiPo

It might be anywhere. A Lighthouse in Maine. Derek Mahon. FaBCIP; OBTV

It might be true. Boone. Susan Mitchell. NAmP

It mounts at sea, a concave wall. From the Wave. Thom Gunn. NAEL-2; NoP

It must be hunky dory on Venus. The synapse. Jeremy. Jeffrey Miller. UL

It must be so—Plato, thou reason'st well. Cato's Soliloquy. Joseph Addison. *Fr.* Cato, V, i. WBLP

It must be something. To the Field Goal Kicker in a Slump. Linda Pastan. ASP

It must have been a night like this one. Indian Summer. Edward Hirsch. NAmP

It must have been a year. Fire, Hair, Meat and Bone. Fred Johnson. PoBA

It must have been for one of us, my own. Not Thou but I. Philip Bourke Marston. BLPA; BLPL

It must have been one o'clock at night. To Remain. Constantine P. Cavafy, *tr.* by John Mavrogordato. ErPo

It must have been one or one-thirty. To Remain. Constantine P. Cavafy, *tr.* by Nikos Stangos *and* Stephen Spender. BoLoP

It must've been a dream. Out in the Woods. Carroll Arnett. NOVW

It never occurred to me, never. The Meeting. Howard Moss. GOYP; NYBP

It nods and curtseys and recovers. A. E. Housman. *Fr.* A Shropshire Lad, XVI. NOBVV

It occurs to me now. The Lesson. Charles Simic. HCAP

It often happens that we despise a thing. Brief Discourse: That Woman's Excellence Surpasses Man's. Marie de Romieu, *tr.* by Dorothy Backer. DMF

It ofttimes has been told, that the British seamen bold. The *Constitution* and the *Guerriére*. *Unknown.* AmFP

It once might have been, once only. Youth and Art. Robert Browning. CTC; NAEL-2; NOBVV

It ought to be impossible to be mistaken. An Incorrigible Music. Allen Curnow. ATNZ

It ought to come in April. Wearing of the Green. Aileen Fisher. RHPC

"It Out-Herods Herod. Pray You, Avoid It." Anthony Hecht. CoAP; NiP; NoAM; NOBA; OxBC

It Pays. Arnold Bennett. *See* Limerick: "There was a young man of Montrose."

It pulses like a skin, at dusk. By the Sluice. Anthony Thwaite. PoPo

It quickned next a toyful Ape, and so. John Donne. *Fr.* The Progress[e] of the Soul[e]. PoEL-2

It raindrops on the cold. Introit. Padraic Fiacc. CIP

It rained in my sleep. September. Linda Pastan. Psk

It rained quite a lot, that spring. You woke in the morning. Metropolitan Nightmare. Stephen Vincent Benét. ImOP; NYBP

It rained toward day. The morning came sad and white. Colder Fire. Robert Penn Warren. *Fr.* To a Little Girl, One Year Old, in a Ruined Fortress. LiTM

It Rains ("It rains, and nothing stirs within the fence"). Edward Thomas. OxBTC; PoE

It rains,/ and the people of my house look depressed. Ishikawa Takuboku, *tr. fr. Japanese by* Hiroaki Sato. *Fr.* Forty-seven Tanka in Three Lines. FCEI

It rains, it rains in merry Lincoln. Little Sir Hugh. *Unknown.* OBET

It Rains on Friday. Sung Chang-kyung. WCI

It reaches to Gold Fish Dike. Blue Mud Shoal. Yang Shih-ch'i, *tr. fr. Chinese by* Jonathan Chaves. *Fr.* Ten Scenes at the Hsiao Family Stone Ridge. CoBLCP

It Really Must Be Nice. E. E. Cummings. AnAmPo

"It relaxes me," he said. Six Reasons for Drinking. Vernon Scannell. OxBC

"It rests me to be among beautiful women." Tame Cat. Ezra Pound. OBAL

It rises over the lake, the farms. The Kite. Mark Strand. NYBP

It Rolls On. Morris Bishop. ImOP

It rose dark as a stack of peat. Suilven. Andrew Young. OxBS

It said "Come home, here is an end, a goal." Woodrow Wilson. Robinson Jeffers. FaBoPV

It said welcome. The Second Coming. John William Corrington. HoPM

It sat between my husband and my children. Seele im Raum. Randall Jarrell. LCAP

It Says. Jon Silkin. VWA

It seconds the crickets of the province. The Rocking Chair. Abraham Moses Klein. CaP; HeIP; NoP

It seemed as if voices were raised. The Dead. Salvatore Quasimodo, *tr.* by Jack Bevan. PFI

It seemed corrival of the world's great prime. A Fallen Yew. Francis Thompson. BrPo; MoAB; MoBrPo

It seemed that out of the battle I escaped. Strange Meeting. Wilfred Owen. BrPo; CMoP; FaBoMo; FaBoRV; GTBS-P; HeIP; HoPM; LiTB; MMA; MoAB; MoBrPo; MoP; NAEL-2; NoAM; NOBE; NoP; OAEL-2; OBWP; PoE; RB; SCV; TrGrPo; WaaP; WaP

It seemed to be but chance, yet who shall say. May 30, 1893. John Kendrick Bangs. AA

It seems a certain time ago: a-maybe. One Time. Douglas Livingstone. PeSA

It seems a day. Nutting. Wordsworth. EnRP; NAEL-2; NU; OAEL-2; RB

It seems, before sleep, something has been dishonest. Each Day Does That. Jon Anderson. NAmP

It seems disrespectful to Villon to put it so, but. Old Theme. W. R. Moses. KS

It seems high time/ I challenged you to song-contest! A Dispute between Women. *Unknown*, *tr.* by Tom Lowenstein. STP

It seems I have no tears left. They should have fallen. Tears. Edward Thomas. GTBS-P; LiTB; NAEL-2

It seems like a dream. An Autumn Morning. *Unknown.* BoTP

It seems like a dream—that sweet wooing of old. Bachelor Hall. Eugene Field. BLPA; FPL

It seems like the same thing all over again. Coming Home from Camp. Lonny Kaneko. BrSi

It seems me speaking all the lonely time. Soliloquy: South Africa. Arthur Nortje. WMBCH

It seems no work of man's creative hand. Pedra. John William Burgon. BLPA

It seems now far off and foolish, a memory. Lot Later. Howard Nemerov. HoPM

It seems so simple now, that life of thine. Washington. Geraldine Meyrich. OHIP

It seems so strange that I once loved you so. Twenty Years After. Evan V. Shute. CaP

It Seems That God Bestowed Somehow. Amanda Benjamin Hall. AH

It seems that I hear that beauty who. Lament of the Lovely Helmet-Dealer. Villon, *tr. by* Hubert Creekmore. ErPo

It seems the breeze has quarreled with. Nawab Mirza Khan Dagh, *tr. by* Ahmed Ali. GoT

It seems the sea, that scourge of ages. To Vyazemsky. Pushkin, *tr. by* Alan Myers. AAA

It seems they never complete these things. The Classical Style. Michael Palmer. NPGG

It seems to me I'd like to go. Far from the Madding Crowd. Nixon Waterman. BLPA; FaBoBe
(Vacation.) WBLP

It seems to me I'm watching over walls. Haim Guri, *tr. by* Warren Bargad *and* Stanley F. Chyet. IP

"It seems to me," said Booker T. Booker T. and W. E. B. Dudley Randall. MoP; NoAM

It seems too enormous just for a man to be. The Highway. W. S. Merwin. PoA

It seems wrong that out of this bird. A Blackbird Singing. R. S. Thomas. OBWVE

It semes white and is red. The Sacrament of the Altar. *Unknown*. MeEL

It settles softly on your things. The Dust. Gertrude Hall. AA

It shall be said [*or* sayd] I died [*or* dy'de] for Coelia. William Percy. *Fr.* Coelia, XIX. ElL

It shines in the garden. The Garden. Mark Strand. CAPP; GeTw; NoAM

It should be brief; if lengthy, it will steep. A Model Sermon. *Unknown*. FaBoUs

It sifts from leaden sieves. Emily Dickinson. SoSe

It singeth low in every heart. The Abiding Love. John White Chadwick. BLPA; FaBoBe
(Auld Lang Syne.) WGRP

It sings to me in sunshine. Segovia and Madrid. Rose Terry Cooke. AA

It sleeps among the thousand hills. The Unnamed Lake. Frederick George Scott. CaP; NOBC

It sleeps by day! Lucky Lion! *Zulu Oral Tradition, tr. by* H. Tracey. WTO

It Smashes Barricades. Anna Swirszczynska, *tr. fr. Polish by* Magnus Jan Krynski *and* Robert A. Maguire. PwPP

It smiles to see me. Lethargy. Donald Justice. CRP

It snowed yesterday. Akahito. *Fr.* Manyo Shu. Ma

It snows in Chagall's village in March. Snow That Falls on Chagall's Village. Ruth Kim Chun-soo, *tr. by* Koh Chang-soo. ACKP

It snows on this place. Wednesday at North Hatley. Ralph Gustafson. NOBC

It so happens I am sick of being a man. Walking Around. Pablo Neruda, *tr. by* Robert Bly. EAS

It sometimes happens. Curse of the Cat Woman. Edward Field. WeW

It soothes the savage doubts. Apocalypse. D. J. Enright. OBSV

It sounded as if the streets were running. Emily Dickinson. NAAL-1; OxBSP; PBWP
(Storm.) AnAmPo

It sounds as if it's raining/ finally. The Unmarked Ceiling. Mary Michaels. DT

It sounds unconvincing to say "When I was young." In the Winter of My Thirty-eighth Year. W. S. Merwin. NOBA

It speaks in voices varying with the wind. Africa. Adèle Naudé. PeSA

It spreads, the campaign—carried on. Glory. Marianne Moore. NYBP

It squeaks, it creaks. The Tyrolean Elephant. Hans Arp, *tr. by* Michael Benedikt. POS

It stands alone. The Sheiling. Edward Thomas. PoSH

It started with an alto horn. Jazz. Frank London Brown. PoNe

It started with her shape on the map. Highland Region. Victor Price. PoSH

It starts: a white girl in a dark house. Alternatives. Kingsley Amis. OxBC

It starts in the small hours. An interlude. James Merrill. *Fr.* Mirabell: Books of Number. NoAM

It starts out. The Light Year. John Ridland. OFD

It starts, somehow, in the hot damp. Barn Fire. Thomas Lux. LCAP; NAmP

It stepped into my room. Elegy and Flame. Horace Gregory. FYAP

It stops the town we come through. Troop Train. Karl Shapiro. OxBA; WaaP; WaP

It storms in Amherst five days. Winter Bouquet. Lewis Turco. EOEF

It struck me every day. Emily Dickinson. PPP

It swings upon the leafless tree. The Snow-filled Nest. Rose Terry Cooke. OBCA

It takes a fast car. Lost Parents. Lawrence Ferlinghetti. PoM

It takes a heap o' children to make a home that's true. Edgar A. Guest Considers "The Good Old Woman Who Lived in a Shoe" and the Good Old Truths Simultaneously. Louis Untermeyer. *Fr.* Mother Goose Up-to-Date. NIP
(Edgar A. Guest Considers "The Old Woman Who Lived in a Shoe" and the Good Old Verities at the Same Time.) FiBHP; OBAL
(Edgar A. Guest Syndicates the Old Woman Who Lived in a Shoe.) MoAmPo

It takes a heap o' livin' in a house t' make it home. Home. Edgar A. Guest. BLPA; BLPL; FaBoBe; OBAL; OHFP; PWR

It takes a little courage. The Only Way to Win. *Unknown*. WBLP

It takes a long time to hear what the sands. The Bones. W. S. Merwin. LiTM; NePoEA-2

It takes at least a billion years. Sorrow. Shin Dong-jip, *tr. by* Koh Chang-soo. ACKP

It takes much art. La Carte. Justin Richardson. FiBHP

It takes so long to sit in the balcony and wait for sweet. A Rose and a Baby Ruth. Shelby Stephenson. SoTCo

It takes time, and there are setbacks. A Difficult Adjustment. Lauris Edmond. FaBoWP

It takes time to make. Time to Myself. Paulette Jiles. NOBC

It thinks, permanent address, states, stands apart, exits. Mimesis. Barrett Watten. LP

It took generations to mature. Liberace. Jonathan Holden. MAYP

It took place in a world. The Rabbit in the Moon. Ryokan, *tr. by* Burton Watson. FCEI

It took the sea a thousand years. Erosion. E. J. Pratt. CaP

It Took TV to Civilize Our Village. Richard Moore. *Fr.* Word from the Hills, XXXIV. Son

It took 27 years to write this poem. Ruth. Colleen J. McElroy. BlSi

It trembled off the keys,—a parting kiss. Her Music. Martha Gilbert Dickinson Bianchi. AA

It tried to get from out the cage. The Cage. James Stephens. OxBTC

It troubled me as once I was. Emily Dickinson. ImOP

It turns out/ You can kill them. Redwings. James Wright. NNaP

It turns the corner. Arc. Tom Clark. UL

It Used to Be. Ciaran Carson. CIP

It used to be only Sunday afternoons. Watching Football on TV. Howard Nemerov. ASP

It wants to be somewhere else. Looking at Henry Moore's Elephant Skull Etchings in Jerusalem during the War. Shirley Kaufman. LCAP

It wants to reveal itself as progress. Alfred Kolleritsch, *tr. by* Beth Bjorklund. CoAuP

It Was. Roger Giroux, *tr. fr. French by* Paul Auster. RHTwFP

It was a bad sign I was born under. The Judas Goat. Susan Musgrave. NIP; NOBC

It was a beautiful and silent day. Wordsworth. *Fr.* The Prelude [or, Growth of a Poet's Mind]: Residence in France. OBTV

It Was a Beauty That I Saw. Ben Jonson. *Fr.* The New Inn. OBS
(Lovel's Song.) TrGrPo

It was a bleak November morning. The *Jervis Bay*. *Unknown*. OxBSS

It was a blue fly with wings of pomegranate gold. Blue Fly. Joaquim Maria Machado de Assis, *tr. by* Frances Ellen Bruckland. TTY

It was a Borgia-pot, he told me. The Curiosity-Shop. Peter Redgrove. OxBC

It was a bowl of roses. A Bowl of Roses. W. E. Henley. MoBrPo

It was a bright and cheerful afternoon. Summer and Winter. Shelley. BoNaP

It was a bright day and all the trees were still. Silence. W. J. Turner. MoBrPo

It was a chill November eve and on the busy town. Saved. *Unknown*. FaBoUs

It was a chilly winter's night. A Winter Night. William Barnes. ChTr; FaBoRV; NOBE; OBNC

It was a clear. A Little Boy. Ruth Kim Chun-soo, *tr. by* Koh Chang-soo. ACKP

It was a cough that carried her off. *Unknown*. FaBoNo

It was a damp mild day of clinging mists that we met. Meeting at a Salesyard. John Ennis. CIP

It was a dare that made us break. Cruelty. T. R. Hummer. MAYP

It was a dark, dank, dreadful night. The Malfeasance. Alan Bold. AmMo

It was a day of turning when you came. The Turning. Philip Murray. NePoAm

It was a dim October day. Thomas Caulfield Irwin. *Fr.* Swift. BIrV

It was a dismal, and a fearful night. Abraham Cowley. *Fr.* On the Death of Mr. William Hervey [*or* Harvey]. EBEV; FaBoRV; NOBE; OBEV; OBS; SeCP; SeCV-1

It was a distant winter. On the edge of the flatlands. On Guard. Meir Wieseltier, *tr.* by Warren Bargad *and* Stanley F. Chyet. IP

It was a draper eminent. The Seraph and the Snob. May Kendall. CenHV

It was a dreary day in Padua. Countess Laura. George Henry Boker. BeLS

It was a dreary morning when the chaise. Residence at Cambridge. Wordsworth. *Fr.* The Prelude [*or*, Growth of a Poet's Mind], III. FaBoPP; HAP; ImOP

"Evangelist St. John my patron was, The." HAP (Newton's Statue.) FaBoRV

"Caverns there were within my mind, which sun." FaBoPP Newton. ImOP

It was a feather of paint. An Urban Guerrilla. Allen Curnow. *Fr.* Moro Assassinato, II. PeNZ

It was a foreign ship that sailed. Newcomers. Abraham Reisen, *tr.* by Keith Bosley. VWA

It was a friar of orders gray [*or* grey]. The Friar of Orders Gray. *Unknown.* ACP; NOEC

It Was a Funky Deal. Etheridge Knight. BPo; PoBA

It was a gallant sailor man. The Two Anchors. Richard Henry Stoddard. BeLS

It Was a Gentle Air. Rubén Darío, *tr. fr. Spanish by* Perry Higman. LPSS

It Was a Goodly Co. E. E. Cummings. LiTA; LiTM; WaP

It was a graveyard scene. The crescent moon. "Great Unaffected Vampires and the Moon." Stevie Smith. NoAM

It was a great pleasure. Spitting on Ira Rosenblatt. Robert Hershon. NeAC

It was a grey day. Tom Thomson. Arthur Stanley Bourinot. CaP

It was a hand. God looked at it. The Hand. R. S. Thomas. NOCV; OxBC

It was a hard thing to undo this knot. Gerard Manley Hopkins. NOBVV (At a Welsh Waterfall.) FaBoPP

It was a heartfelt game, when it began. Portrait. Judith Wright. OxBSP

It was a heat to melt the mountains in. Loch Ossian. Syd Scroggie. PoSH

It was a house of female habitation. A House of Mercy. Stevie Smith. FaBoWP

It was a kind and northern face. Praise for an Urn. Hart Crane. AWP; CMoP; HAP; LiTM; MoAB; MoAmPo; NoAM; NOBA; OxBA; PPP; WeW

It was a Knight in Scotland borne. The Fair Flower of Northumberland. *Unknown.* ESPB; OxBB

It was a lady of the north she lov'd a gentleman. Room for a Jovial Tinker; Old Brass to Mend. *Unknown.* CoMu; OxBB

It was a late afternoon in a cowtown saloon. Murph and McClop. *Unknown.* CowP

It was a little captive cat. The Singing Cat. Stevie Smith. CRH; OxBTC

It was a long time ago. As I Grew Older. Langston Hughes. AmPP; BANP

It Was a Long Time Before. Leslie Silko. NoAM

It Was a Lording's Daughter. *At. to* Shakespeare. *Fr.* The Passionate Pilgrim. EiL

It Was a Lover and His Lass. Shakespeare. *Fr.* As You Like It, V, iii. AWP; CH; EiL; ELP; GBL; GTBS; GTBS-P; HeIP; InPS; LiTB; NAEL-1, *fr.* V, iii; NAEL-1; NOBE; NoP; OBEV; RB; TTTS (Country Song.) TrGrPo (Pages' Song, The.) OBSC; SeCePo (Song: "It was a lover and his lass.") CTC; FiP

It was a maid of brenten arse. A Maid of Brenten Arse. *Unknown.* GBP

It was a Maine lobster town. Water. Robert Lowell. CMoP; HeIP; LCAP; NOBA; NoP; PoE; SM

It was a mighty monarch's child. Mir träumte von einem Königskind. Heine, *tr.* by Richard Garnett. AWP

It was a mile of greenest grass. The Occasional Yarrow. Stevie Smith. FaBoNo

It was a miniature country once. Japan. Anthony Hecht. LiTM

It was a miracle he glimpsed an owl sway. The Owl in the Rearview Mirror. Duane Niatum. NOVW

It was a mischievous wind that pushed him; a murderous gust that jarred young Jan from the scaffold. Monument. A. M. Sullivan. GoYe

It was a mother and a maid. The Milk White Doe. *Unknown, tr.* by Andrew Lang. AWP

It was a night in winter. Clive Sansom. *Fr.* The Witnesses. PChr

It was a night of early spring. Wisdom. Sara Teasdale. AnAmPo; MoAmPo

It was a noble Roman. On Fort Sumter. *Unknown.* PAH

It was a noble Roman. Where There's a Will There's a Way. John Godfrey Saxe. AnAmPo

It was a poor man's marble. On the Sixth Floor. Bartolo Cattafi, *tr.* by Lawrence R. Smith. NItP

It was a puritanicall ladd. Off a Puritane. *Unknown.* CoMu

It was a question of whether it couldn't. It. Howard Moss. BLA

It was a railway passenger. Striking. Charles Stuart Calverley. CenHV

It was a rainbow impossibly. Prisms. Philip Dacey. Psk

It was a rich merchant man. The Merchant and the Fidler's Wife. *Unknown.* CoMu; OxBB

It was a river said one day. The Clever River. Eliezer Shteynbarg, *tr.* by Leonard Wolf. PeBMYV

It was a robber's daughter, and her name was Alice Brown. Gentle Alice Brown. W. S. Gilbert. FaBoCo; FiBHP; NA

It was a sergeant old and gray. Picciola. Robert Henry Newell. AA

It Was a Special Treat. Luci Tapahonso. STE

It was a still autumnal day. We Walked among the Whispering Pines. John Henry Boner. AA

It was a summer evening. Sentences While Remembering Hiraethog. T. Glynne Davies, *tr.* by R. Gerallt Jones. OBWVE

It was a summer [*or* summer's] evening. The Battle of Blenheim. Robert Southey. BeLS; EnRP; FaBoPV; FaBV; FaPoR; FPL; GN; OBNC; OBWP; PoLF; TrGrPo; WBLP (After Blenheim.) GTBS; GTBS-P

It was a summer's night, a close warm night. Wordsworth. *Fr.* The Prelude [*or*, Growth of a Poet's Mind]: Conclusion ("It was a close, warm, breezeless summer night"). PoEL-4

It was a tall young oysterman lived by the river-side. The Ballad of the Oysterman. Oliver Wendell Holmes. AnAmPo; FaPP; MOS; MoShBr

It was a tortoise aspiring to fly. Improvisations on Aesop. Anthony Hecht. OBAL

It was a tree that neither of us. The Maidenhair Tree. Neil Curry. NPo

It was a violent time. Wheels, racks, and fires. A Mirror for Poets. Thom Gunn. LiTM; NePoEA

It was a wasp, or an imprudent bee. The Wasp. Daryl Hine. NYBP

It was a way of punishing the house, setting it a blaze. Interior at Petworth: From Turner. Rosanna Warren. NoAM

It was a wondrous realm beguiled. Alfred Domett. *Fr.* Ranolf and Amohia, Canto I, iii. OBTV

It was a wooded lakeside, away up. A Spurt of Literary Criticism. W. R. Moses. SoTCo

It was a worthy Lord of Lorn. *See* It was the worthy Lord of Lorn.

It was about the deep of night. A Ballad of Christmas. Walter de la Mare. OBCP

It was about the Martinmas time. Barbara Allan. *Unknown.* EnSB

It was [in and] about the merry month of May. Sir John Graeme *and* Barbara Allan. *Unknown.* OxBoLi (Barbara Allan.) ENSB (Bonny Barbara Allen [*or* Allan].) AWP; BoLop; CH; HeIP; LiTB; NoP; ESPB, A *and* B *vers*.); OxBB, *with music*.

It was after vespers one evening. Low Church. Stanley J. Sharpless. NBLV

It was afternoon, and my brother split. A Burial, Green. Marcia Southwick. MAYP

It was all different; that, at least, seemed sure. Mutability. William D. Snodgrass. DiPo

It was all like a childhood picture. Cuckoo. Robert Desnos, *tr.* by Armand Schwerner. RHTwFP

It was all the clods at once become. Earth Dweller. William Stafford. LCAP

It Was All Very Tidy. Robert Graves. OxBTC; RB

It was almost easy to say goodby. The Soldiers Returning. Richard Shelton. GOYP

It was already late autumn. Paying Homage at the Golden Gate. Niu Hsi-chi, *tr.* by Lois Fusek. ATF

It was always. Hose and Iron. Greg Kuzma. MAT

It Was an April Morning. Wordsworth. FaBoPP

It was an English ladye bright. Song of Albert Graeme. Sir Walter Scott. *Fr.* The Lay of the Last Minstrel, VI. EnRP

It was an evening in November. The Pig. *Unknown.* FaBoEE

It was an hill placed in an open plain. The Dance of the Graces. Spenser. *Fr.* The Faerie Queene, VI, 10. OBSC (Dance, The.) TrGrPo

It was an international rage. Royston Ellis. *Fr.* The Cherry Boy, 6. PeHV

It was an old, old, old, old lady. One, Two, Three. H. C. Bunner. FaPON; PoLF

It was as if. Spring Song. Peter Fallon. CIP

It was as if I were widely awake. Après un Rêve. Martin Seymour-Smith. NPo

It was as if the devil of evil had got. García Lorca. Louis Dudek. MoCV; NOBC

It was at a pow wow. Future Generation. Nila NorthSun. STE

It was at dinner as they sat. The Laird of Wariston. *Unknown.* ESPB

It was at night; I saw my father lie. My Father's Death. Ugo Foscolo, *tr. by* Lorna de' Lucchi. PFI

It was at the very date to which we have come. An Anniversary. Thomas Hardy. OxBTC

It was awful long ago. The Anxious Farmer. Burges Johnson. BoNaP

It was before spoken things. It Was. Roger Giroux, *tr. by* Paul Auster. RHTwFP

It Was Beginning Winter. Theodore Roethke. *Fr.* The Lost Son. NAAL-2

It was better when we were. For My Mother. Louise Glück. GeTw; UnPo

It was between the night and day. Evening by the Sea. Swinburne. FaBoPP

It was but a little thing. The Peace-Offering. Thomas Hardy. OxBSP

It was but until yesterday. Mohammad Taqi Mir, *tr. by* Ahmed Ali. GoT

It was but yesterday, my love, thy little heart beat high. Lament of Anastasius. William Bourne Oliver Peabody. AA

It was by these men's valor that wide-lawned Tegea. Epigram for the Dead at Tegea. *Unknown, tr. by* Richmond Lattimore. WaaP

It was Captain Pierce of the *Lion* who strode the streets of London. The First Thanksgiving. Clinton Scollard. PAH

It was cause for laughter of a special brand. The Fish. Ralph Gustafson. OBCV

It was Christmas Eve in the year fourteen. Under the Snow. Robert Collyer. AA

It was cold, and all they gave him to wear. Back in the States. Louis Stimson. PBCV

It was cold then in the cautious hours. Curtain. Lance Henson. VoR

It was dark. Thinking in the Dark. Amiq Hanafi, *tr. by* Mahmood Jamal. PBMUP

It was dark and frosty, pain congealed into ice. Deportation. "M. B.", *tr. by* A. Glanz-Leyeless. TrJP

It was December. Even There. Lyn Lifshin. IHMS

It was distant, as usual, drops still on the windowpane. A Poem Too Late. Natan Zach, *tr. by* Warren Bargad *and* Stanley F. Chyet. IP

It was down in old Joe's barroom. Those Gambler's Blues. *Unknown.* AS

It was Earl Haldan's daughter. Charles Kingsley. GN

It was early, early in the spring. The Croppy Boy. *Unknown.* AmFP; AnIL; FaBoBa; NOIV; OxBoLi

It was early, early one mornin'. Stagolee. *Unknown.* TTY

It was early in the month of cold December. On Board the *Leicester Castle*. *Unknown.* OxBSS

It was early in the season, the fall of 'sixty-three. Michigan-I-O. *Unknown.* AmFP

It was early last December. The Drunkard and the Pig. *Unknown.* OBAL

It was early Monday morning Willie Leonard arose. Willie Leonard; or, The Lake of Cold Finn. *Unknown.* AmFP

It was early morning. Isaac. Amir Gilboa, *tr. by* Howard Schwartz. VWA

It was early Sunday mornin. Stagolee. *Unknown.* MAT

It was early Sunday morning, in the year of sixty-four. *Kearsarge* and *Alabama*. *Unknown.* PAH

It was Easter as I walked in the public gardens. 1929. W. H. Auden. SOTW

It was easy enough. Circe. Hilda Doolittle ("H. D."). PoRA

It was easy then to catch. A Record. Gyula Illyés, *tr. by* William Jay Smith. MHuP

It was far in the night and the bairnies grat. Gerry Hamill. BXAP

It was far in the sameness of the wood. The Demiurge's Laugh. Robert Frost. OxBA

It was fifty years ago. The Fiftieth Birthday of Agassiz. Longfellow. ImOP

It was for you, my slave. Lady Ki. *Fr.* Manyo Shu. PeBJV

It was for you that the mountains shook at Sinai. *Unknown.* TrJP

It was frosty winter season. Philomela's Second Ode. Robert Greene. *Fr.* Philomela, the Lady Fitzwater's Nightingale. OBSC

It Was Gentle. Hedva Harkavi, *tr. fr.* Hebrew *by* Tova Weizman. VWA

It was good for the virgin mary. Poem for Unwed Mothers. Nikki Giovanni. OBAL

It was his story. It would always be his story. In Memory of the Unknown Poet, Robert Boardman Vaughn. Donald Justice. CAPP; DiPo; NoAM

It was hurry and scurry at Monmouth town. Molly Pitcher. Kate Brownlee Sherwood. PAH

It was I who did command. Lady Fujiwara. *Fr.* Manyo Shu. Ma

It was impossible for one to read. Holy Was Demeter Walking th' Corn Furrow. Edward Sanders. PoM

It was in a dream. Rather than Cry. Ishikawa Takuboku, *tr. by* Geoffrey Bownas *and* Anthony Thwaite. PeBJV

It was in Abomey that I felt. Dahomey. Audre Lorde. NAAL-2

It was in an empty lot. How I Learned English. Gregory Djanikian. MOWH

It was in and about the Martinmas time. Bonny Barbara Allan. *Unknown.* AWP; BoLoP; CH; ESPB; HeIP; InPK; LiTB; NAEL-1; NoP; OxBB
(Sir John Graeme and Barbara Allan.) OxBoli

It was in autumn that I met. A Picture. Dora Greenwell. EBVV

It was in '58, the year they moved out. Basket Catch. Bart Schneider. TSL

It was in October, a favorite season. Elegy for a Nature Poet. Howard Nemerov. BoNaP; HoPM

It was in October the woe began. The Fire of Frendraught. *Unknown.* ESPB

It was in search of you they lost. Mohammad Taqi Mir, *tr. by* Ahmed Ali. GoT

It was in the calm resurrection after the rain. Resurrection after the Rain. Alfredo Giuliani, *tr. by* Lawrence R. Smith. NItP

It was in the city of Expert. The Oxford Girl; or, Expert Town. *Unknown.* AmFP

It was in the fields. The trees grew still. Jeanne d'Arc. Louise Glück. GeTw

It was in the lovely month of May. The Troubled Soldier. *Unknown.* AS

It was in the merry month of May. The Trail to Mexico. *Unknown.* AS

It was in the month of January the hills. Month of January. Frankie Armstrong. BrRo

It was in the years 39. Hans Verhagen & Son. Hans Verhagen, *tr. by* James S. Holmes. DuIn

It was in winter. Steeples, spires. The Fortunate Traveller. Derek Walcott. NoAM

It was intill a pleasant time. Earl Mar's Daughter. *Unknown.* GN
(Earl of Mar's Daughter, The.) CH; ESPB

It was June, and I was twenty. When I Was Twenty. Bliss Carman. AnAmPo

It was June fifteenth in nineteen eighty-four. The Great Wanagan Creek Flood. Bill Lowman. CowP

It was just before the last fierce charge, two soldiers drew a-rein. The Last Fierce Charge. *Unknown.* AmFP

It was just one night. *Unknown, tr. fr. Japanese by* Burton Watson. *Fr.* Kangin Shu. FCEI

It was King Wên that laboured. *Unknown, tr. by* Arthur Waley. BoS

It was Landor who first said. "Hugh MacDiarmid." *Fr.* In Memoriam James Joyce. FaBoPV

It was last Monday morning as I have heard them say. Lancashire Lads. *Unknown.* CoMu

It was last year. Fox Glove Song. Christina Beer. PeNZ

It was late afternoon in the Woody Saloon. Saturday Night in Woody. Jesse Smith. CowP

It was late in the night when the Squire came home. The Gipsy Laddie. *Unknown.* FaBoCh; OxBoLi

It was late last night when my lord come home. The Gypsy Davy. *Unknown.* AmFP

It was late last Saturday evening. Blow the Candle Out. *Unknown.* FaBoBa

It was late, we. Man and Wife. Mitchell Goodman. VGW

It was laughing time, and the tall giraffe. Laughing Time. William Jay Smith. FaPON

It was less than two thousand we numbered. With Corse at Allatoona. Samuel H. M. Byers. PAH

It was like a church to me. The Moor. R. S. Thomas. OBWVE

It was like silver, like an ending. Testimonies. Yehuda Amichai, *tr. by* Warren Bargad *and* Stanley F.Chyet. IP

It was lonely in the zero dark, Admetus. Alcestis. Isabel Williams Verry. GoYe

It was long ago. Chikako, *tr. by* Steven D. Carter. WFTW

It was long ago. Dream. Shotetsu, *tr. by* Steven D. Carter. WFTW

It was love that built the mountains. The Work of Love. Margaret E. Sangster. BLRP

It was Mama who was partial. Emma. Yvonne. CNA
(Premonition (in a Voice My Mother Called "Not Your Own").) TV
It was many and many a year ago. A Poe-'em of Passion. Charles
Fletcher Lummis. BXAP
It was many and many a year ago. Andrew M'Crie. Robert Fuller
Murray. CenHV; FaBoCo
It was many and many a year ago. Annabel Lee. Poe. AA; AiP;
AmPP; AnAmPo; AWP; BeLS; BLPA; CH; DL; FaFP; FaPON; FPL;
HelP; LiTA; NAAL-1; NOBA; NoP; OBCA; OnMSP; OPOP; OxBA;
PrIm; TAP; TrGrPo; WBLP
It was many and many a year ago. Samuel Brown. Phoebe Cary.
OBAL
It Was Miss Scarlet with the Candlestick in the Billiard Room. Bernadette
Mayer. UL
It was much later in his life he rose. Muriel Rukeyser. *Fr.* Gibbs.
ImOP
It was Murupaenga who brought me here. Slave Girl's Song. *Unknown,*
tr. by Margaret Orbell. PeNZ
It was my bridal night I remember. I Remember. Stevie Smith.
BoLoP; BoWoP; FaBoWP; InPK; OxBC
It Was My Choice. Sir Thomas Wyatt. QFR; SiPS
It was my father forced him into the desert. Isaac. A. C. Jacobs. VWA
It was my first/ time in Kula. Kula. a Homecoming. Diane Mei Lin
Mark. BrSi
It was my thirtieth year to heaven. Poem in October. Dylan Thomas.
LiTB; NAEL-2; NAs; NoAM; PoA; PoRA; PrIm; RB; SeCePo; SoSe
It was my war, though it ended. First News Reel: September 1939. Joan
Barton. CN
It was near evening, the room was cold. The Oath. Allen Tate.
FaBoMo; LiTM; OxBA; VGW
It was near Lorient, the sun shone brightly and we used to go for walks.
Literature and Poetry. Max Jacob, *tr. by* John Ashbery. RHTwFP
It was nearly morning when the giant. The Reason for Skylarks.
Kenneth Patchen. NaP
It was night-time! God, the Father Good. What the Devil Said. James
Stephens. CMoP
It was 1945, and it was May. When I Was Conceived. Michael Ryan.
MAYP; NAmP
It was no costume jewellery I sent. With a Gift of Rings. Robert
Graves. GBL
It was not a very formal affair but. A Chinese Banquet. Kitty Tsui.
GLP
It was not death, for I stood up. Emily Dickinson. NAAL-1; NOBA;
NoP
It was not death to me. The Kiss of God. G. A. Studdert-Kennedy.
BLRP
It was not dying: everybody died. Losses. Randall Jarrell. HCAP;
LCAP; LiTM; OxBA; PoA; TAP; UnPo; WaP
It Was Not Fate. William H. A. Moore. BANP
It Was Not in the Winter. Thomas Hood. ELP, *longer vers.*
(It Was the Time of Roses.) CH
(Time of Roses.) OBEV
It was not like your great and gracious ways. Departure. Coventry
Patmore. *Fr.* The Unknown Eros, I, viii. ACP; NOBE; OBEV;
OBNC; SeCePo
It was not long e're he perceiv'd the skies. Michael Drayton. *Fr.* The
Moone-Calfe. PoEL-2
It was not meant for human eyes. The Combat. Edwin Muir. CMoP;
LiTB; Mes; MoBrPo; NOBE
It was not our duty to question but to guard. Bread and a Pension. Louis
Johnson. ATNZ; PeNZ
It was not so much the gossip that attracted me. Mess Sergeant. Garry
Geddes. UAS
It was not that I could not see her. Narihira, *tr. by* Geoffrey Bownas *and*
Anthony Thwaite. PeBJV
It was not that you said I thought you knew. Colloquial. Rupert Brooke.
BrPo
It was not the wind—the oil is gone. Michizane, *tr. fr. Japanese by*
Burton Watson. FCEI
(Lamp Goes Out, The.) JLIC-1
It was not yet dawn. The Night of My Return. Philippe Thoby-Marcelin,
tr. by William Jay Smith. CT
It Was Not You. André Spire, *tr. fr. French by* Jethro Bithell. TrJP
It was nothing but a rose I gave her. A Sigh. Harriet Prescott Spofford.
AA
It was on a cold winter's night. When Poor Mary Came Wandering
Home. *Unknown.* AS
It was on a May, on a midsummer's day. Sir Hugh; or, The Jew's
Daughter. *Unknown.* AmFP; ESPB
It was on a Wednesday night, the moon was shining bright. Jesse James.
Unknown. AS; BeLS; FaBoBe; UnPo; WiR

It was on an evning sae saft and sae clear. The Broom of Cowdenknows.
Unknown. ESPB
It was on one Monday morning,/ All in the month of May. Lisbon.
Unknown. AmFP
It was on one Monday morning just about one o'clock. The *Titanic*.
Unknown. AmFP
It was on the seventeenth, by break of day. The Battle of Bunker Hill.
Unknown. PAH
It was on the twenty-first day of December. Ella Speed. *Unknown.*
AmFP
It was once suggested by Brecht. After Brecht. D. J. Enright. AnAn
It was one afternoon when I was young. The Tale the Hermit Told.
Alastair Reid. NePoEA-2
It was one strange and rainy. Horror Story. Hans Andreus, *tr. by* James
S. Holmes. DuIn
It was one summer's morning on the fourteenth day of May. The Mower.
Unknown. CoMu
It was one Sunday morning of June the eighth day. Henry K. Sawyer.
Unknown. AmFP
It was only a small place and they had cheered us too much. St. Aubin
d'Aubigne. Paul Dehn. OBWP
It was only important. The Moss of His Skin. Anne Sexton. CoAP;
IHMS; SM
It was only the clinging touch. The Child. George Edward Woodberry.
Fr. Wild Eden, XXX. AA
It was only two fields away from the house. In Memoriam I, Elizabeth at
Twenty. Richard Weber. ErPo
It was over Target Berlin the flak shot up our plane. World War II.
Edward Field. GLP
It was Pablo who saw him most clearly. Write, Do Write. Marilyn
Chin. BrSi
It was plain to see the sense of being a woman. The Inflammable
Woman. James Keir Baxter. OxBC
It was planted early. Boundary. A. L. Hendricks. PBCV
It was pleasant and delightful on one midsummer's morn. Pleasant and
Delightful. *Unknown.* OBET, *with music;* OxBSS, *with music*
It was pneumonia. Lament of the Virtues and Verses on Account of the
Death of Don Guido. Antonio Machado, *tr. by* Charles Tomlinson
and Henry Gifford. OBVE
It was Private Blair, of the regulars, before dread El Caney. Private Blair
of the Regulars. Clinton Scollard. PAH
It was proper for them, awaking in ordered houses. Apology. Anthony
Cronin. CIP
It was quite a day at Melrose. All the folks had come to town there.
Coronation Day at Melrose. Peter Bladen. PoAu-2
It was raining in winter. Ruth Kim Chun-soo, *tr. fr. Korean by* Koh
Chang-soo. *Fr.* The Song of Choyong, I. ACKP
It was roses, roses, all the way. The Patriot. Robert Browning. TrGrPo
It was running down to the great Atlantic. The Stream. Lula Lowe
Weeden. CDC
It was said at the/ flirting creekwater's birth. To an Imaginary Father.
Wendy Rose. CDW
It was said by the Reverend. Not a Thing of Paint or Feathers. Joseph
Bruchac. NOVW
It was said that/ Should you want tea. Drinking Tea. Chang Ts'o, *tr. by*
Dominic Cheung. IFON
It was seven years then. Rachel's Lament. Linda Zisquit. VWA
It was shattered. The Battle of Maldon. *Unknown, tr. by* Kevin
Crossley-Holland. OBWP
It was six men of Indostan. The Blind Men and the Elephant. John
Godfrey Saxe. BLPA; BoTP; FaBoBe; FPL; OBCA; OnMSP; OnUR;
WBLP
It was so so cold she let in the wind. *Unknown, tr. by* Hiroaki Sato.
FCEI
It was something to see that their white was different. Holiday in Reality.
Wallace Stevens. OxBA
It was something you did not know. An Air by Sammartini. Louis
Dudek. OBCV
It was such a bright morning. Beautiful Sunday. "Jake Falstaff."
BoNaP
It was sudden. The Sea Fog. Josephine Jacobsen. NYBP
It was Sunday morning, I had the *New York Times*. First Love. Sharon
Olds. FYAP
It was supposed to be Arts & Crafts for a week. At the Smithville
Methodist Church. Stephen Dunn. BLA
It was taken a long time ago. The Verdict. Norman Cameron. SeCePo
It was taken some time ago. This Is a Photograph of Me. Margaret
Atwood. NoAM; NoP
It was that fierce contested field when Chickamauga lay. Thomas at
Chickamauga. Kate Brownlee Sherwood. PAH

It was the anonymity I noticed first. Zero Population Growth. Lauris Edmond. *Fr.* Two Birth Poems, II. ATNZ

It was the arrival of the kings. The Adoration of the Magi. Christopher Pilling. OBCP

It was the beginning of me. Look at My Face, a Collage. Carolyn M. Rodgers. JB

It was the busy hour of 4. Spring Arithmetic. *Unknown.* FiBHP

It was the calm and silent night! A Christmas Hymn. Alfred Domett. GN; WGRP

It was the charming month of May. Chloe. Burns. GN

It was the cooling hour, just when the rounded. Haidée and Don Juan. Byron. *Fr.* Don Juan, II. OBNC

It was the day before July 14. Phantom of the Clouds. Guillaume Apollinaire, *tr. by* Roger Shattuck. POS

It was the departure, the sun was risen. Farewell Voyaging World! Conrad Aiken. NYBP

It was the dingiest bird. Robin Redbreast. Stanley Kunitz. Prf

It was the enshrouded pier, la cathédrale engloutie, which. To See the Minstrels. Sue Roe. NPo

It was the frog in the well. The Marriage of the Frog and the Mouse. *Unknown.* EBEV

It was the fruit on high. Soul's Kiss. Samuel Greenberg. LiTA

It was the garden of the golden apples. The Long Garden. Patrick Kavanagh. FaBCIP; IPY

It was the hole for looking in. It All Comes Together Outside the Restroom in Hogansville. James Seay. MT

It was the hour of noon, when thus the Son. Milton. *Fr.* Paradise Regained, *Bk.* II, *ll.* 260-389. EBEV

It Was the Last of the Parades. Louis Simpson. NYBP

It was the light that first caught his eye. The Light. Gregory O'Brien. *Fr.* Bride of the Disappearing Man. ATNZ

It Was the Lovely Moon. John Freeman. BoNaP

It was the man from Ironbark who struck the Sydney town. The Man from Ironbark. A. B. Paterson. PoAu-1

It was the middle of the night. Franz. Mark Strand. BLA

It was the morning of that blessed day. Petrarch, *tr. fr. Italian. Fr.* Sonnets to Laura: To Laura in Life, III, *tr. by* Joseph Auslander. NAWM-1

It was the morning of the first of May. *Unknown, tr. fr. Italian by* John Addington Symonds. *Fr.* Popular Songs of Tuscany. AWP

It was the night of love. Khwaja Haider Ali Atish, *tr. by* Ahmed Ali. GoT

It was the rainbow gave thee birth. The Kingfisher. W. H. Davies. NOBE; OBEV; OBWVE

It was the schooner *Hesperus.* The Wreck of the Hesperus,. Longfellow. AnAmPo; BeLS; BLPA; FaBoBe; FaFP; FPL; GN; MOS; OBCA; OBNV; PAH; WBLP

It was the season, when through all the land. Birds of Killingworth, The (The Poet's Tale). Longfellow. *Fr.* Tales of a Wayside Inn, *pt.* I. OnMSP; OxBS

"Do you ne'er think what wondrous beings these?" WBLP, 2 *sts.*

It was the sixth dawn. Still the *Fiat Lux. Eve.* Manuel M. Flores, *tr. by* Samuel Beckett. MexPo

It was the *Stately Southerner*, that carried the Stripes and Stars. The *Stately Southerner. Unknown.* AmFP

It was the *Stately Southerner* that earned the stripes and stars. *Unknown. See* 'Tis of a gallant yankee ship that flew the stripes and stars.

It was the Sung Dynasty. Dream. Norman Dubie. NAmP

It Was the Time. Joachim Du Bellay, *tr. fr. French by* Spenser. Son

It Was the Time of Roses. Thomas Hood. *See* It Was Not in the Winter.

It was the time when, granted from the gods. Virgil, *tr. fr. Latin by* Earl of Surrey. *Fr.* The Aeneid [*or* Eneados], II. NAEL-1

It was the time when lilies blow. Lady Clare. Tennyson. BeLS; FaPON; OnMSP

It was the time, when rest, soft sliding downe. Joachim Du Bellay, *tr. fr. French by* Spenser. *Fr.* Visions, I. AWP; Son

It was the very noon of night: the stars above the fold. The Story of the Shepherd. *Unknown.* OHIP

It was the virgin Zennora, who dwelt. John Heath-Stubbs. *Fr.* Artorius. EBEV

It was the west wind caught her up, as. The Ring Of. Charles Olson. NOBA; VGW

It was the wild midnight. The Death of Leonidas. George Croly. BeLS

It was the wind. Autumn Evening. George Anthony. EAS

It was the winter wild[e]. Hymn on the Morning of Christ's Nativity [*or* On the Morning of Christ's Nativity]. Milton. *Fr.* On the Morning of Christ's Nativity. FiP; NAEL-1; NOBE; OBEV

It was the [*or* a] worthy Lord of Lorn [*or* Learne]. The Lord of Lorn and the False [*or* Fals] Steward, *with music. Unknown.* ESPB; OxBB

It was the year the Icondic. Ballad of the Icondic. John Ciardi. OBAL

It was then night: the sound[e] and quiet sleep [*or* slepe]. Virgil, *tr. fr. Latin by* the Earl of Surrey. *Fr.* The Aeneid [*or* Eneados], IV. OAEL-1; PoEL-1

It was there, but I said it couldn't be true in daylight. Nightmare of Mouse. Robert Penn Warren. SO

It was there, early Sunday. Seeing My Name in TV Guide. Gerald Costanzo. SoTCo

It was they who called you. Black Thread. Bartolo Cattafi, *tr. by* Lawrence R. Smith. NItP

It was this way. Rumoresque Senum Severiorum. Marcus Argentarius, *tr. by* Dudley Fitts. ErPo

It was Thomas Macdonough, as gallant a sailor. The Battle of Plattsburg Bay. Clinton Scollard. PAH

It was three slim does and a ten-tined buck in the bracken lay. The Revenge of Hamish. Sidney Lanier. PoEL-5

It was through a mucous membrane, a kind of mouth. Lion, Leopard, Lady. Douglas Le Pan. OBCV

It was Tiny's habit. Sketches of Harlem. David Henderson. PoNe

It was told that/ When the monk awoke. The Legend of Tea. Chang Ts'o, *tr. by* Dominic Cheung. IFON

It was too lonely for her there. The Impulse. Robert Frost. *Fr.* The Hill Wife. HoPM

It was touching when I started. Aunt Nerissa's Muffin. Wallace Irwin. FiBHP

It was upon a Cristemesse night. The Dancers of Colbek. Robert Mannyng. *Fr.* Handling Sin. PoE

It was upon a Lammas night. The Rigs o' Barley. Burns. LiTB (Corn Rigs Are Bonnie.) ErPo; OxBS (Song: "It was upon a Lammas night.") BoLoP

It was upon a Shere Thorsday that oure Loverd aras. Judas. *Unknown.* PoE

It was upon the twilight of that day. Samuel Daniel. *Fr.* The Civil Wars, VIII. OBWP

It was very early in the spring. The Croppy Boy. *Unknown.* AnIL

It was very late at an empty table. Ballad of an Empty Table. Tom Kryss. NeAC

It was very pleasant. A Certain Peace. Nikki Giovanni. CNA

It was water I was trying to think of all the time. Appoggiatura. Donald Jeffrey Hayes. AmNP; PoBA; PoNe

It was when I said. On the Road Home. Wallace Stevens. NU

It was when my songs became quiet. How I Came to Be a Graduate Student. Wendy Rose. STE

It was, when scarce had rang the morning bells. An Almanack for the Year of Our Lord, 1657. Samuel Bradstreet. SCAP

It was when the words on the covers of books. The Complete Introductory Lectures on Poetry. Bernadette Mayer. UL

It was when weather was Arabian I went. Allegory of the Adolescent and the Adult. George Barker. LiTB

It was where the wooden bridge. Dora Markus. Eugenio Montale, *tr. by* Alfred Corn. PFI

It was wild. Assassination. Don L. Lee. AmNP; FF; NeAC; OFD; PoBA

It was winter. The woman wearing scarves of rain. Once upon a Time. Mekeel McBride. KS

"It Was Wrong to Do This" Said the Angel. Stephen Crane. *Fr.* The Black Riders, LIV. LiTA

It was years ago, at the end of Deborah's Song. His Mother. Haim Guri, *tr. by* Warren Bargad *and* Stanley F. Chyet. IP

It was you:/ I could have crawled. Watching Salmon Jump. Simon J. Ortiz. CDW

It was you, Atthis, who said. Sappho, *tr. by* Mary Barnard. PeHV

It was you that black nite. Witchcraft Woman. Nora Naranjo-Morse. GOS

It was your mother wanted you. The Son. R. S. Thomas. NAs

It was your smell that, for a day after, I carried with me. The Anniversary. William Dickey. GOYP

It Was Your Song. Steve Kowit. UL

It was your vision of the pilot. Adrienne Rich. *Fr.* Twenty-one Love Poems, XIV. GLP

It wasn't by chance that Marpessa preferred Idas over Apollo. Marpessa's Choice. Yannis Ritsos, *tr. by* Edmund Keeley. AnAn

It wasn't Ernest; it wasn't Scott. Song for the Squeeze-Box. Theodore Roethke. NBLV; NePoAm

It wasn't in my time, or so I suppose. Responses to Montale. Brian Turner. PeNZ

It wasn't our battalion, but we lay alongside it. Sergeant-Major Money. Robert Graves. MMA; OBWP

It wasn't that she didn't recognize him in the light from the hearth. Penelope's Despair. Yannis Ritsos, *tr. by* Edmund Keeley. AnAn

It wasn't the daffodils so much. Daffodils. Michael Heffernan. SM

It went many years. The Lockless Door. Robert Frost. NOBA; WSC

It were best to sleep. November 1956. Evan Jones. PBCV

It were my soul's desire. The Soul's Desire. *Unknown, tr. by* Eleanor Hull. TIRV

It wes in November an' aw nivor will forget. The Oakey Street Evictions. Thomas Armstrong. OBET

It wes upon a Scere Thorsday that oure Lord aros. Judas Sells His Lord. *Unknown.* MeEL

It will be all the same in a hundred years. In a Hundred Years. *At. to* Elizabeth Doten. BLPA

It will be as it is in this life, the same room. Strophes. O. V. de L. Milosz, *tr. by* Ezra Pound. RHTwFP

It will be hard. Alois Hergouth, *tr. by* Beth Bjorklund. CoAuP

It will be in the form of an old man. I Want to Write a Jewish Poem. Gary Pacernick. VWA

It will be looked for, book, when some but see. To My Book. Ben Jonson. NAEL-1; SeCV-1

It will be strange. When the Vacation Is Over for Good. Mark Strand. NYBP

It will happen in the summer. Terminal Vision. Diana O Hehir. NPGG

It will not always be like this. A Day in Autumn. R. S. Thomas. BoNaP

It will not hurt me when I am old. Moonlight. Sara Teasdale. GOYP; VGW

It will not resemble the sea. The New Poem. Charles Wright. CAPP; GeTw; HCAP

It will not shine again. Emily Brontë. NOBVV

It Will Pour. A. Leyeles, *tr. fr. Yiddish by* Benjamin *and* Barbara Harshav. AYP

It will rain tonight. New Life. Joseph E. Kariuki. TTY

"It would be/ a mercy if." Phone Call to Rutherford. Paul Blackburn. PoM

It would be at the end. The End of the Street. John Haines. LCAP

It Would Be Easy. Peter Ackroyd. NPo

It would be nice to simply melt away. Leavings. Gerard Benson. BXAP

It would be painful to interfere. Memo. Charles G. Ballard. VoR

It would be too easy. Interim Balance. Alois Hergouth, *tr. by* Beth Bjorklund. CoAuP

It would be very pleasant to die with a wolf woman. Yoldugu, *tr. by* James Koller. STP

It would be wrong for us. It is not right. Sappho, *tr. by* Willis Barnstone. BoWoP

It would console me to see you. Elegies for Prince Atsumichi ("It would console me to see you"). Lady Izumi, *tr. fr. Japanese by* Hiroaki Sato. *Fr.* Fifty-one Tanka. FCEI

It would never be morning, always evening. Memory of Brother Michael. Patrick Kavanagh. FaBCIP; MoAB

It would seem that I thought. Looking at Old Note-Books. C. H. Sisson. NPo

It wouldn't be so bad if he. In Extremis. Margaret Fishback. FiBHP

It wouldn't have lasted long anyway. In the Evening. Constantine P. Cavafy, *tr. by* Edmund Keeley *and* Philip Sherrard. AnAn; VMG

It wound through strange scarred hills, down cañons lone. The Old Santa Fe Trail. Richard Burton. PAH

It woz in April nineteen eighty-wan. Great Insohreckshan, Di. Linton Kwesi Johnson. FaBoPV

It wuz one day, I believe in May, when old Si Hubbard to me did say. Si Hubbard. *Unknown.* AS

Ita. Yolanda Ulloa, *tr. fr. Spanish by* Margaret Randall. AIW

Italia, Io Ti Saluto. Christina Rossetti. OBTV; WPE

Italia! Oh Italia! thou who hast. Italy. Vincenzo da Filicaia, *tr. by* Byron. AWP; PFI

Italian. Osbert Lancaster. *Fr.* Afternoons with Baedeker. FaBoCo

Italian in England, The. Robert Browning. FaBoPV; OBNV

Italian Lullaby. *Unknown.* FaPON

Italian soldier shook my hand, The. George Orwell. OBWP

Italian Woman. Diane Wakoski. GrPl

Italy. Byron. *Fr.* Beppo; a Venetian Story. SeCePo

    (Italy versus England.) NOBE

Italy. Vincenzo da Filicaia, *tr. fr. Italian by* Byron. AWP; PFI

Italy, *sels.* Samuel Rogers. OBNC

    Byron Recollected at Bologna.

    Interview near Florence, An.

Italy of the South. Robert Browning. *See* De Gustibus: What I love best in all the world.

Italy versus England. Byron. *See* Beppo; a Venetian Story: Italy.

Itanami. *Unknown.* PBCV

Itchin, when I behold thy banks again. To the River Itchin, near Winton. William Lisle Bowles. OAEL-2

Ité. Ezra Pound. HAP; MoAB; MoAmPo

Item. E. E. Cummings. MoAB; MoAmPo

Items riddle space. Cloud Spots. Steven Lavoie. UL

Iter Boreale. Robert Wild. APAS

Iter Supremum. Arthur Sherburne Hardy. AA

Ithaca. Katharyn Machan Aal. ER

Ithaca last night, Syracuse at noon, Cedar Rapids tonight. Seeing Auden Off. Philip Booth. PoA

Ithaca: The Palace at Four A.M., *sel.* Richard Howard. Last Words. DiPo

Ithaka. Constantine P. Cavafy, *tr. fr. Greek by* Edmund Keeley *and* Philip Sherrard. VMG

'Ithin the woodlands, flow'ry gleaded. My Orcha'd in Linden Lea. William Barnes. EBVV; NOBVV

Ithocles, *sel.* John Addington Symonds. "That night, when storms were spent and tranquil heaven." PeHV

Itinerant astrologers of no great wealth. Professionals. Turner Cassity. MT

Itinerant trade is the business of petty men. Wu Chia-chi, *tr. fr. Chinese by* John E. Wills, Jr.. *Fr.* On the Ninth Day of the Month, Thinking of Ch'eng, II. WFTU

It'll be a long time again before my friends. Peire Vidal, *tr. by* Paul Blackburn. Pro

It's/ snowing defective. Self-Pity Is a Kind of Lying, Too. James Schuyler. PoM

It's A. Kit Robinson. UL

It's a bit like saying there's little to burn, now that. Narcissus Pseudonarcissus. Elio Pagliarani, *tr. by* Lawrence R. Smith. NItP

It's a box of furniture in a right angle. Where He Hangs His Hat. Deborah Lee. BrSi

It's a brisk young butcher, as I have heard 'em say. Leicester Chambermaid. *Unknown.* CoMu

It's a debatable land. The winds are variable. Helen Smith Bevington. *Fr.* Report from the Carolinas. AmFN

It's a Different Story When You're Going into the Wind. David McFadden. NeAC

It's a dull poem. Steve Jonas. PeHV

"It's a '49," Rhinehardt said, and slammed. Making Money: Drought Year in Minkler, California. Gary Soto. NoAM

It's a Gay Old World. *Unknown.* FaFP

It's a good thing Dad deserted Mom. How I Came to Have a Man's Name. Emma Lee Warrior. HATNAP

"It's a good way to live and." Sky Diving. Ishmael Reed. UL

It's a grand thing when you're old, love. Life's Golden Sunset. Mrs. Henry Linden. CBWP-4

It's a great deal better to lose than win. After Reading Certain Books. Mary Elizabeth Coleridge. EaLo

It's a hell/ creeping back into. Back into the Garden. Sarah Webster Fabio. BlSi

It's a late starting dawn that breathes my vision. Late Starting Dawn. Richard Brautigan. PCP

It's a long hot walk up Fathead Mountain you know. Hiking Up Hieizan with Alam Lau/Buddha's Birthday 1974. Garrett Kaoru Hongo. BrSi

It's a long walk in the dark. John's Song. Joan Aiken. DuDa

It's a madman, I said. Dream. Nana Issaia, *tr. by* Helle Tzalopoulou Barnstone. BoWoP

It's a mighty hard row that my poor hands has hoed. Pastures of Plenty. Woody Guthrie. WTO

It's a Queer Time. Robert Graves. MoAB; MoBrPo

It's a question of bright stars. Dogwood Blossoms. Peter Blue Cloud. STE

It's a real rock. Wobbly Rock. Lew Welch. PoM

It's a rheumatic world if you ever stop to listen. What Happens in Shakzpeare. Alan Brunton. PeNZ

It's a rum. "And Now." John Basil Boothroyd. FiBHP

It's a sitting-pretty, windy-city kind of a place. Tonight in Chicago. *Unknown.* AmFN

It's a south wind that drives you back. Hardon ("Get One Today"). Ian Wedde. PeNZ

It's a strange country. As a Man Walks. Louis Simpson. CAPP

It's a strange courage. El Hombre. William Carlos Williams. CMoP; LiTA

It's a strange courage. Nuances of a Theme by Williams. Wallace Stevens. LiTA

It's a sunny pleasant anchorage, is Kingdom Come. Port of Many Ships. John Masefield. MOS; OBMV

It's a Terrible Thing! Everett Hoagland. BPo

It's a very odd thing. Miss T. Walter de la Mare. CenHV; FaBoBe; GoJo; GrPl; MoShBr; NTCP; OnUR; PDV

It's a warm wind, the west wind, full of birds' cries. The West Wind. John Masefield. FaFP; FPL; LiTB; LiTM; MoAB; MoBrPo

It's a white nest! A Small Bird's Nest Made of White Reed Fiber. Robert Bly. NNaP

"It's a Whole World, the Body. A Whole World!"—Swami Satchidandanda. David Young. FF

It's a Woman's World. Eavan Boland. CIP

It's about/ the ball,/ the bat,/ and the mitt. Analysis of Baseball. May Swenson. ASP

It's after one. Last Statement. Vladimir Mayakovsky, tr. by Tom Paulin. FaBoPV

It's all a blur of speed. Suspension. Constance E. Studer. TSM

It's all a trick, quite easy when you know it. W. W. Skeat. FaBoCo; FiBHP

It's all dust like the quicksand. Mohammad Taqi Mir, tr. by Ahmed Ali. GoT

It's all familiar. A Dream. Bella Akhmadulina, tr. by Jean Valentine and Olga Carlisle. BoWoP

It's all in/the sound. A song. William Carlos Williams. PCP

It's All in Your Head. Marilyn Nelson Waniek. KS

It's all right, together with me tonight. Love Song. Pattiann Rogers. NAmP

It's All the Same. Thadious M. Davis. BlSi

It's all very well for preachin'.' The Pledge at Spunky Point. John Hay. OBAL

It's All Very Well Now. Virginia Graham. CN

It's all very well to dream of a dove that saves. Birdwatchers of America. Anthony Hecht. HoPM; NoAM; NOBA; PPP

It's all very well to write reviews. Lasca. Frank Desprez. BeLS; BLPA; FaBoBe

It's almost stopped, just the way the bow stalls. The Breaking. Zsuzsa Beney, tr. fr. Hungarian by Jascha Kessler. Fr. A Broken Glass. FOC

It's Already Autumn. Elio Pagliarani. PCP

It's Always. Marcelin Pleynet, tr. fr. French by Serge Gavronsky. RHTwFP

It's always been nineteen something for me. 2000. Dave Smith. BLA

It's always there, like the drone. Exchange. Dabney Stuart. HoPM

It's an old box camera. Camera. Ted Kooser. Psk

It's an old story. Ahmad Faraz, tr. by Mahmood Jamal. PBMUP

It's an ordinary evening. Tabula Rasa? Luciano Erba, tr. by Lawrence R. Smith. NItP

It's an owercome sooth for age an' youth. Robert Louis Stevenson. NOBVV

It's as if you thought your body. Tulsidas, tr. by John Stratton Hawley and Mark Juergensmeyer. SSI

It's autumn in the country I remember. Mnemosyne. Trumbull Stickney. LiTA; NOBA; OxBA

It's awf'lly bad luck on Diana. Hunter Trials. Sir John Betjeman. FiBHP

It's bad luck with a coughing baby. John Tranter. Fr. Crying in Early Infancy. CBAP

It's beautiful here. Rural. Erich Fried, tr. by Beth Bjorklund. CoAuP

It's been a long time. The Jews of Brisk. Judd Teller, tr. by Grace Schulman. PeBMYV

It's been going on a long time. A Way of Life. Howard Nemerov. NIP

It's been like fixing a clock, jamming the wheels. Making Up for a Soul. David Wagoner. VGW

It's been raining for days. Ozaki Hosai, tr. fr. Japanese by Hiroaki Sato. Fr. One Hundred Haiku in Free Form. FCEI

It's been so long since I headed for East Mountain. Thinking of East Mountain. Li Po, tr. by Burton Watson. CoBCP; TTTS

It's been suggested there's another sex. Preannual Poem. Yona Wallach, tr. by Warren Bargad and Stanley F. Chyet. IP

It's been this way for some time. New Jersey Turnpike. Richard Cumbie. NBLV

It's best to be best. Best? Siv Widerberg, tr. by Verne Moberg. NTCP

It's better not to ask, not to deny. Nurse's Song. M. K. Joseph. ATNZ

"It's better to be on the safe side," my father used to say. The Safe Side. Norman Nicholson. PoPo

It's between Ourselves. Michel Deguy, tr. fr. French by Anthony Rudolf. RHTwFP

It's bright the icy foam as it flows. From Exile. Dafydd Benfras, tr. by Anthony Conran. OBWVE

It's Christmas Day. I did not get. Otto. Gwendolyn Brooks. PChr; PDV

It's clear by now I'll never like. A Birthday Gift. Stephen Dunn. BLA

It's clear, Trojan cried out to Greek. Why They Waged War. John Peale Bishop. NYBP

It's clear, you run wild with my message. All the answers. Two Words. Peter Seaton. LP

It's cold at last and cautious winds creep. Grandfather at the Indian Health Clinic. Elizabeth Cook-Lynn. HATNAP

It's cold, cold, cold. Before the Bath. Corinna Marsh. RAR

It's cold on Lakeside Road. Things That Happen Where There Aren't Any People. William Stafford. CAPP

It's Comforting. Judy Dothard Simmons. CNA

It's coming/ you feel it. It. Hermann Jandl, tr. by Beth Bjorklund. CoAuP

It's common to say of bad acting, or family photos like these. Family Grove. Albert Goldbarth. HCAP

It's cozy to be a poet in a bed, on a copse, knoll, in a room. Wilderness Sacred Wilderness. Philip Lamantia. UL

It's crazy to think one could describe them. Invocation. Robert Pinsky. Fr. Essay on Psychiatrists, I. NoAM

Its Curtains. Ted Joans. PoBA

It's dangerous to walk. Good Manners. Washington Delgado, tr. by David Tipton. Per

It's dark around the earth mortar. Miura Chora, tr. fr. Japanese by Hiroaki Sato. Fr. Sixteen Hokku. FCEI

Its dark green—what if it should be unable to resist. Teika, tr. fr. Japanese by Hiroaki Sato. Fr. A Compendium of Good Tanka. FCEI

It's dark in this wood, soft mocker. Praise to the End! Theodore Roethke. InPS

It's dark on purpose. Visiting the Oracle. Lawrence Raab. AmPA

It's dark out, Jack. All the Roary Night. Kenneth Patchen. LiTM

It's day one of the end. The Eighties Becoming. Bob Rosenthal. UL

Its days are over now; no farmyard airs. The Traction Engine. W. H. Auden. FL

It's difficult to say what it all meant. Jack, Afterwards. Philip Dacey. SM

It's doing your job the best you can. Success! Berton Braley. WBLP

It's easy to talk of the patience of Job. Humph! Job hed nothin' to try him! The Inventor's Wife. E. R. Corbett. PoLF

Its echoes. Haunted House. Valerie Worth. WSC

Its edges foamed with amethyst and rose. The Great Breath. "Æ." MoBrPo; OBEV; OBMV; WGRP

It's Eleven O'Clock. Nancy Chambers. RAR

It's fifty miles to Sittingen's Rocks. Prince Robert. Unknown. AmFP; ESPB, (A and B vers.); OxBB

It's fifty-one springtimes since she was a bride. Dancing at Whitsun. Austin John Marshall. OBET

Its flames sputter cleanly. When Oakwood Burns. Kim Hyun-sung, tr. by Koh Chang-soo. ACKP

Its former green is blue and thin. The Garden Seat. Thomas Hardy. GoJo; HAP; Mes; RB

It's four long years since I reached this land. Lousy Miner. Unknown. AmFP

It's full of the moon. Full of the Moon. Karla Kuskin. PDV

It's fun to clean house. I Like Housecleaning. Dorothy Brown Thompson. FaPON

It's fun turning somersaults. Somersaults. Jack Prelutsky. RAR

It's funny that smells and sounds return. Scrapbooks. Nikki Giovanni. CNA

Its gaze filled my abyss, its gaze melted. Pain. Enrique Gonzáles Martínez, tr. by Samuel Beckett. MexPo

It's getting late. I see you, just. To Friends. Franco Fortini, tr. by Lawrence R. Smith. NItP

It's Going Out. Heine, tr. fr. German by Alistair Elliot. OBD

It's going to be a thick night tonight. Officers' Mess. Gavin Ewart. OxBTC

It's going to come out all right—do you know? Caboose Thoughts. Carl Sandburg. CMoP

It's going to rain. The Watchers. Paul Blackburn. NYBP

It's good, it's good not to shield the heart this way. Perets Markish, tr. by Leonard Wolf. PeBMYV

It's good to be mad and to know that my long hyacynthine hair. Fragmenta Quintillii Apocalypseôs. Peter Russell. NPo

It's Great When You Get In. Eugene O'Neill. ASP

It's guys like Emerson that always fuck it up. Novembers or Straight Life. Maureen Owen. UL

It's hair and dress, framing old portrait faces. Eternal Contour. Florida Watts Smyth. GoYe

It's Halloween. Jack Prelutsky. NTCP

It's hard to be clever these nights. Moscow Night, End of December 1934. A. Leyeles, tr. by Benjamin and Barbara Harshav. AYP

It's hard to know if you're alive or dead. It's a Queer Time. Robert Graves. MoAB; MoBrPo

It's hard to see but think of a sea. Louis Zukofsky. VGW

It's hard to tell what bird it is. After Frost. Brian Patten. EBEV

It's hard when folks can't find th'work. The Dalesman's Litany. Unknown. OBET

Its hectares of white. Glacier. Norman Nicholson. OBTV

It's Here in The. Russell Atkins. AmNP; PoBA

It's here we took him alive. As he fought well we offered him some office. Mongol Libation. Victor Segalen, *tr.* by Nathaniel Tarn. RHTwFP

It's holiday night. Riding Westward. Harvey Shapiro. VWA

It's ice that burns, it is frozen fire. Defining Love. Francisco de Quevedo, *tr.* by Perry Higman. LPSS

It's in the Egg. Joe Rosenblatt. NOBC

It's in the Name. Kitty Tsui. BrSi

It's in the perilous boughs of the tree. Childhood's Retreat. Robert Duncan. NoAM

It's in Your Face. *Unknown.* PoLF

It's I've got a ship in the north country. The Golden Vanity. *Unknown.* ELP

It's just a clay puppet, but how it can dance! Ravidas, *tr.* by John Stratton Hawley *and* Mark Juergensmeyer. SSI

It's just no use. Execution. James A. Randall, Jr. BPo

It's kind of you to let me have my hat. Hattage. Sir Alan Patrick Herbert. FiBHP

It's Lamkin was a mason good. Lamkin. *Unknown.* ESPB; FaBoBa; OxBB

It's late afternoon and already dark. Michael. Michael Sheridan. NAmP

It's late in the evening. Bedraggled. The Patriarch Jacob Meets Rachel. Itzig Manger, *tr.* by Leonard Wolf. PeBMYV

It's late, the children come home from school. Lu Yu, *tr. fr. Chinese by* Burton Watson. *Fr.* Farm Families. CoBCP

It's late when I try to sleep, resting. The Voyages. Gregory Orr. BLA

It's like a story. Alive or Not. Alfred W. Purdy. NOBC

It's like him, of course. On Board Ship. Constantine P. Cavafy, *tr.* by Edmund Keeley *and* Philip Sherrard. AnAn

It's like in the art galleries. Where I Hang My Hat. Dick Gallup. UL

It's like the riddle Tolstoy. Slow Dance. David St. John. AmPA; AnAn; LCAP

It's like violence done to the atmosphere. Swans in Flight. Miroslav Holub, *tr.* by Ewald Osers. FaBoPV

It's little I care what path I take. Departure. Edna St. Vincent Millay. MoAmPo

It's me/ bathed and ashy. Me, in Kulu Se and Karma. Carolyn M. Rodgers. PoBA

It's merely idleness to believe. Asadullah Khan Ghalib, *tr.* by Ahmed Ali. GoT

Its metal top refused my father's twisting. The Soup Jar. Dabney Stuart. MT

It's midnight in a drizzling fog. North of Santa Monica. Carter Revard. VoR

It's Midsummer Day. Haytime. Irene F. Pawsey. BoTP

It's morning and the line has formed. A Cow of Our Time. Tom Disch. EOEF

It's mournful to tell you a story so sad. The Loss of the *Evelyn Marie.* *Unknown.* OxBSS

It's My Fault. Robert Fox. SoTCo

It's my lunch hour, so I go. A Step Away from Them. Frank O'Hara. HCAP; InPS; NAAL-2; VGW

Its Name Is Known. Daniel Lawrence Kelleher. NeIP

"It's narrow, narrow, make your bed." Fair Annie. *Unknown.* ESPB; FaBoBa

It's Nation Time. Imamu Amiri Baraka. NoP

It's nice that though you are casual about me. Sulpicia, *tr.* by Aliki *and* Willis Barnstone. BoWoP

It's 1962 March 28th. Things I Didn't Know I Loved. Nazim Hikmet, *tr.* by Randy Blasing *and* Mutlu Konuk. LLLT

It's no go the merry-go-round, [*or* merrygoround], it's no go the rickshaw. Bagpipe Music. Louis MacNeice. CMoP; GTBS-P; LiTB; LiTM; MoP; NAEL-2; NBLV; NOBE; NOBL; NoP; OAEL-2; OBSV; OxBTC; RB; SeCePo

It's no good/ being an actor. Ian Young. NeAC

It's No Good! D. H. Lawrence. InPS

It's no joke at all, I'm not that sort of poet. The Confession. Wen Yi-tuo. ChTr

It's No Use Raising a Shout. W. H. Auden. OBMV

It's no use, the Christian thinks of himself first. One Thing to Take, Another to Keep. Crescenzo del Monte, *tr.* by Barbara Garvin. VWA

It's not a bit windy. Toadstools. Elizabeth Fleming. BoTP

It's not adultery, the lawyers say. Stop, Science—Stop! Sir Alan Patrick Herbert. FiBHP

It's not as if we never played at cards. Playing at Cards. Belle Randall. CRP

It's not celestial music it's the girl in the bathroom singing. Ode on Celestial Music. Brian Patten. OxBTC

It's not easy to live in the mountains. Living in the Mountains ("It's not easy to live in the mountains"). Sen of Kyuho, *tr.* by Lucien Stryk *and* Takashi Ikemoto. ZPCJ

It's not enough to be a simple nurse. Professional Individual. Tom · Riley. SoTCo

It's not hard to forget what they ate. Place on a Grave. Frank Stanford. MT

It's not my world, I grant, but I made it. Ride. Josephine Miles. FaBoWP

It's not of May this impure air. Gramsci's Ashes. Pier Paolo Pasolini, *tr.* by Lawrence R. Smith. NItP

It's not that you're not wise. A Political Animal. Bruce Bennett. SoTCo

It's not the case, though some might wish it so. Orchard Trees, January. Richard Wilbur. BLA

It's not true that death is a lump like this, or a blow. Death; She Was Always Here. Yona Wallach, *tr.* by Leonore Gordon. VWA

It's November. The Song of This House. Stephen Vincent. NeAC

It's O! but aw ken well. A, U, Hinny Burd. *Unknown.* GBP

It's of a blind beggar, and he lost his sight. The Blind Beggar. *Unknown.* AmFP

It's of a brisk young butcher, as I have heard them say. The Leicester Chambermaid. *Unknown.* CoMu; OBET

It's of a crafty miller and he. The Miller and His Sons. *Unknown.* OBET

It's of a famous [*or* fearless] highwayman a story I will [*or* now I'll] tell. Brennan on the Moor. *Unknown.* FaBoBa; GBP

It's of a little shepherdess who was keeping of her sheep. The Shepherdess and the Sailor. *Unknown.* OBET

It's of a merchant's daughter. The Constant Farmer's Son. *Unknown.* OBET

It's of a pretty female as you shall understand. The Female Cabin Boy. *Unknown.* OxBSS

It's of a rich squire in Bristol doth dwell. Squire and Milkmaid; or, Blackberry Fold. *Unknown.* CoMu; OxBB (Blackberry Fold.) OBET

It's of a tradesman and his wife. How Five and Twenty Shillings Were Expended in a Week. *Unknown.* OBET

It's of a young lord o' the Hielands. Lizie Lindsay. *Unknown.* ESPB (Donald of the Isles.) OxBB

It's of flash packet, a packet of fame. The *Dom Pedro.* *Unknown.* AmFP

It's of three rioters I have to tell. Chaucer. *See* Canterbury Tales, The: Pardoner's Tale, The.

It's off in the distance. A Song of My Song, in Three Parts. *Unknown,* *tr.* by Jerome Rothenberg *and* Richard Johnny John. STP

It's on this railroad bank I stand. Careless Love. *Unknown.* UnPo

It's once I courted as pretty a lass. *Unknown.* OxNR

It's only the dawn of love, the way winds up the hill. Mohammad Taqi Mir, *tr.* by Ahmed Ali. GoT

It's only we, Grimalkin, both fond and fancy free. The Ride to Cherokee. Amelia Walstien Carpenter. AA

It's only whiskey that makes you pity me. Kagank, *tr.* by James Koller. STP

It's Over a (See Just). E. E. Cummings. OxBA; VGW

It's over now; I've known it all. Emily Brontë. NOBVV

Its owner moved out. House in the Fields. Shotetsu, *tr.* by Steven D. Carter. WFTW

Its petals do not open of their own accord. That is our part. An Artichoke for Montesquieu. Jorie Graham. NPGG

It's pleasant to remember that the world doesn't. To Mind. Clark Coolidge. UL

Its presence is not impeded by visible form. The Human Mind. Ai Shih-te, *tr.* by William C. White. TrJP

It's probably the year her marriage. Satin Doll. David Wojahn. NAmP

Its quick soft silver bell beating, beating. Auto Wreck. Karl Shapiro. CMoP; FF; LiTM; NIP; RB; VGW

It's quiet in Hell just now, it's very tame. Lament of an Idle Demon. Richard Percival Lister. FiBHP; NOBL

It's quite a walk to where a bridge and stile. Out Together. Anthony Howell. NPo

It's Raining. Guillaume Apollinaire, *tr. fr. French.* POS, *tr.* by Roger Shattuck; POS, *tr.* by Michael Benedikt; SOTW, *tr.* by Kenneth Koch; TTTS, *tr.* by Kenneth Koch

It's raining,/ it rains in Lima with a frivolous drizzle. Composition 1. Francisco Carrillo, *tr.* by Maureen Ahern *and* David Tipton. Per

It's raining again in the Southwest. Rain in the Southwest. Reeve Spencer Kelley. AmFN

It's raining, but you say, "Go away!" Emperor Go-Shirakawa, *tr. fr. Japanese by* Hiroaki Sato. *Fr.* Ryojin Hisho. FCEI

It's raining, it's pouring. *Unknown.* OxNR

It's raining like the day you walked out. The Traveler. Cleopatra Mathis. PPR

It's raining outside, the child is talking. The Child Plays. Katri Vala, tr. by Aili Jarvenpa. SOP

It's raining today, a dark rain. Birthday. P. J. Kavanagh. NAs

It's really nothing. On the Beach. Claribel Alegría, tr. by Darwin J. Flakoll. DMH

Its retributions work like clockwork. Under the Eyes. Tom Paulin. CIP

It's right to call you son. That cursing alcoholic. Letter to an Absent Son. Madeline DeFrees. NMM

Its roof among the stars projected. Phantasus. Arno Holz, tr. by Ludwig Lewisohn. AWP

Its rope broken. Teika, tr. by Steven D. Carter. WFTW

It's said that children should not use. School Policy on Stickmen. Sam Hunt. ATNZ

It's Saturday afternoon at the edge of the world. Laguna Blues. Charles Wright. GeTw

It's Saturday night, and I'm feeling reckless. Saturday Night. Sir Alan Patrick Herbert. NBLV

It's seldom wise to generalize. Homage to Texas. Robert Graves. LiTB

Its sloughed-off shell. Joso, tr. by Geoffrey Bownas and Anthony Thwaite. PeBJV

"It's snowed!" I think. Village Snowfall. Tamemasa, tr. by Steven D. Carter. WFTW

It's so dark now. The Tip. Albert Goldbarth. HCAP

"It's so good to talk with somebody." He Runs into an Old Acquaintance. Alden Nowlan. GOYP

It's so hard to say in a son's words. Prayer to My Mother. Pier Paolo Pasolini, tr. by Norman MacAfee and Luciano Martinengo. PFI

It's so hot it makes him squat. Unknown, tr. fr. Japanese by Hiroaki Sato. Fr. Inutsukuba Shu. FCEI

Its sound today. Early Autumn. Shotetsu, tr. by Steven D. Carter. WFTW

It's spring!/ when threads of the green willow. Tsurayuki, tr. fr. Japanese by Burton Watson. Fr. Kokin Shu. FCEI

It's spring! nameless mountains. Basho, tr. fr. Japanese by Burton Watson. Fr. Seventy-six Hokku. FCEI

It's Spring Returning, It's Spring and Love. Unknown. HAP

It's spring; the City, wrapped. To His Chi Mistress. George Starbuck. NYBP

It's startling when a dog enters. The Stagger of the Wind That I Think Is Your Turning. Jane Miller. KS

It's step her to your weev'ly wheat. Weevily Wheat. Unknown. AS

It's still a good time. To Friends Who Have Also Considered Suicide. Phyllis Webb. NOBC

It's strange what the past brings back. Driving through Tennessee. Charles Wright. CAPP

It's strangely like a man. A Film. Albert Goldbarth. MAYP

It's such a/ Bore. Ennui. Langston Hughes. OBAL; OBCA

It's such a little thing to weep. Emily Dickinson. RB (Life's Trades.) AnAmPo

It's such a shock, I almost screech. Two Sad. William Cole. RAR

It's such a static reference; looking. Epistrophe. Imamu Amiri Baraka. PoNe

It's summer and the dogs decline in heat. Blues for Old Dogs. Paul Zimmer. BLA

It's summer; then. Onitsura, tr. by Geoffrey Bownas and Anthony Thwaite. PeBJV

It's ten. Evening. The room is in half light. My Sister. Alfonsina Storni, tr. by Aliki and Willis Barnstone. BoWoP

It's that they want to know whose they are. On Difficulty. Jorie Graham. BAP

It's that vague feeling of panic. Commuters. Edward Hirsch. NAmP

It's the anarchy of poverty. The Poor. William Carlos Williams. MoAB; MoAmPo; NoP; PPP

It's the boat plowing in its own furrow. Reflections. Zsuzsa Beney, tr. fr. Hungarian by Jascha Kessler. Fr. A Broken Glass. FOC

"It's the east wind blowing." Taigi, tr. by Geoffrey Bownas and Anthony Thwaite. PeBJV

It's the first night, I suppose. A First Night. Peter Kane Dufault. DiPo

It's the first of May. The Anniversary. Roberta Spear. MAYP

It's the lie I've grown used to. The Custody of the Eyes. Carolyne Wright. NAmP

It's the Little Towns I Like. Thomas Lux. NAmP

It's the long road to Guinea. Guinea. Jacques Roumain, tr. by Langston Hughes. TTY

It's the might, it's the fight. A Football Game. Alice Van Eck. RHPC

It's the muse that encourages the poets. Bitter Sonnet to a Cup of Coffee. Ricardo Castorrivas, tr. by Cecilia Guidos. Vol

It's the one thing you've asked for—your medicine now, not. Hunter Radiation Center: Halloween. Alice Mattison. PPR

It's the poor first light of morning. The Obscure. Norman Dubie. NoAM

It's the Spring. Pastoral: "It's the Spring." W. E. Henley. Fr. In Hospital, XXII. BrPo

It's the start of spring, they say. Teika, tr. fr. Japanese by Hiroaki Sato. Fr. A Compendium of Good Tanka. FCEI

It's the Syme the Whole World Over. Unknown. AS, with music (It's the Syme the Wide World Over.) BeLS

It's the way you perceive the world I love. The First Love Poem. Myra Glazer Schotz. VWA

It's the world's longest car, I swear. Longmobile. Shel Silverstein. AiP

It's the yellow time when tamarack sheds. Hunting for Grouse. Roseann Lloyd. TSL

It's there/ in the hole of the sea. The Hole in the Sea. Marvin Bell. NYBP

It's there you'll see confectioners with sugar sticks and dainties. Galway Races. Unknown. OxBoLi; SD

It's this crazy weather we've been having. Crazy Weather. John Ashbery. AnAn; PoE

It's Three No Trumps. Guy Innes. FiBHP

It's Time. Ian Wedde. Fr. Earthly: Sonnets for Carlos, 2. ATNZ

It's time for bloody Watusis to romp through the streets. Time Poem. Quentin Hill. NBP

It's time I told you why. The Hindoo: He Doesn't Hurt a Fly or a Spider Either. A. K. Ramanujan. OxBC

It's time, my dear, it's time! The heart demands its quittance. Pushkin, tr. by Alan Myers. AAA

It's time to make love. Douse the glim. Conrad Aiken. NBLV (Limberick: "It's time to make love. Douse the glim.") FiBHP (Limerick: "It's time to make love. Douse the glim.") FaBoNo

It's to you that I speak, men of the Southern hemisphere. By the Waters of Babylon. Benjamin Fondane, tr. by Edouard Roditi. VWA

It's too cold to swim, so you're taking the children. Cool Day in July. Alice Mattison. PPR

It's too dark to see black. A Mother Speaks: The Algiers Motel Incident, Detroit. Michael S. S. Harper. AmPA; BPo

It's Tough Being American. Mark Irwin. SoTCo

It's true. I met the Centaur. It was on a Breton road. Centaur. Max Jacob, tr. by Armand Schwerner. RHTwFP

Its trunk as of dead silver cast. The Felled Plane Tree. Anna Hajnal, tr. by William Jay Smith. BoWoP; MHuP

It's 12:21 in New York a Thursday. In Blue. D. C. Berry. BXAP

It's up Glenbarchan's braes I gaed. Sir Walter Scott. PBBP

It's Useless. Gloria Fuertes, tr. fr. Spanish by Philip Levine. AnAn

It's Venice, late August, outside after lunch, and Hart. Portrait of the Artist with Hart Crane. Charles Wright. GeTw

It's very hard to be polite. Under the Table Manners. Unknown. CRH

Its wednesday night baby. Master Charge Blues. Nikki Giovanni. OBAL

It's wet around the well. Ozaki Hosai, tr. fr. Japanese by Hiroaki Sato. Fr. One Hundred Haiku in Free Form. FCEI

Its wingéd lion stands up straight to hide. Venice. Howard Moss. MoAB

It's wonderful how I jog. Animals Are Passing from Our Lives. Philip Levine. CAPP; CoAP; NOBA; SM; TAP; TW

Its wrinkled foreskin, twisting open, opens. Morning Glory. Howard Moss. DiPo

ITT Alcan Kaiser. I Fight Back. Lillian Allen. PBCV

Itt [or It] rely is ridikkelus. Bobby's First Poem. Norman Gale. FiBHP; MoShBr

'Ittle Touzle Head. Ray Garfield Dandridge. BANP

Itum Paradism all clothed in green. Unknown. GBP

Itylus. Swinburne. ChTr

Ivanhoe, sel. Sir Walter Scott. Rebecca's Hymn. Fr. ch. 39. EnRP

I've always been going somewhere—Vancouver. The Madwoman on the Train. Alfred Wellington Purdy. NoAM

I've always liked this lonely hill. The Infinite. Giacomo Leopardi, tr. by William Jay Smith. CT; PFI

I've always thought Polonius a dry. Lines to His Son on Reaching Adolescence. John Logan. NePoEA-2

I've always wanted brook trout. Looking for Work. Raymond Carver. GeTw

I've always wanted one. Wanting a Mummy. Sandra McPherson. AmPA; LCAP

I've always wanted to say something of you. To Teresa. Iván Silén, tr. by Julio Marzán. InW

I've an ingle, shady ingle, near a dusky bosky dingle. Midsummer Jingle. Newman Levy. BoNaP

I've aye been keen on the heich hills. Ane to Anither. Duncan Glen. PoSH

"I've become so lonely, I could die"—he writes. Ireland 1977. Paul Durcan. FaBCIP

I've been a moonshiner for seventeen long years. Kentucky Moonshiner. *Unknown.* AS; OBAL

I've been after the exotic. The Ethnic Life. Daniel Halpern. AmPA

I've been called sway. It's in the Name. Kitty Tsui. BrSi

I've been chanting poems for forty years. Chanting Poems. Wang Chiu-ssu, *tr. by* Jonathan Chaves. CoBLCP

I've been driving for hours. Looking for a Rest Area. Stephen Dunn. AmPA

I've been given this triangular face to wear. Self-Portrait. Nina Cassian, *tr. by* Herbert Kuhner. VWA

I've been giving a lot of thought. Sea Things. Gwendolyn MacEwen. FaBoWP

I've been going around everywhere without any skin. Josephine Miles. IHMS

I've been in jail from slander. The Rocky Mountains. *Unknown.* AmFP

I've been in love for long. In Love for Long. Edwin Muir. BoLoP; LiTM; MoBrPo

I've been list'nin' to them lawyers. The Lawyers' Ways. Paul Laurence Dunbar. AnAmPo

I've been plannning to tell you. Hesitating Ode. Miklós Radnóti, *tr. by* Steven Polgar, Stephen Berg *and* S. J. Marks. LLLT

I've been restless today. Haircut. Sue May. DT

I've Been to a Marvelous Party. Noel Coward. NBLV

I've been to Palestine. John Brown. Vachel Lindsay. *Fr.* The Booker Washington Trilogy, II. MoAmPo

I've been trying for hours to figure out who I was reminded of. Combat. C. K. Williams. AnAn

I've been trying to fashion a wifely ideal. A Plea for Trigamy. Sir Owen Seaman. NOBL

I've Been Waiting These Thirty Years. Anna Swirszczynska, *tr. fr. Polish by* Magnus Jan Krynski *and* Robert A. Maguire. PwPP; SaC

I've Been Workin' on the Railroad. *Unknown.* FaFP; SaC

I've borne full many a sorrow, I've suffered many a loss. The Heaviest Cross of All. Katherine Eleanor Conway. AA

I've brewed myself a whole bunch of trouble. To the Tune "Moon Over West River." Yang Shen, *tr. by* Jonathan Chaves. CoBLCP

I've brought you nuts and hops. October. Christina Rossetti. BoTP

I've built a castle in the sand. Castles in the Sand. Dorothy Baker. BoTP

I've called in guests from the seaside village for a cup of New Years wine. New Years Day at the Official Lodge. Michizane, *tr. by* Burton Watson. JLIC-1

I've climbed in trees. The Plum's Heart. Gary Soto. NAmP

I've colored a picture with crayons. Crayons. Marchette Chute. RAR

I've come again to Yen Bend and built a hut of thatch. Huang Tsung-hsi, *tr. fr. Chinese by* Lynn Struve. *Fr.* Songs from Living in the Mountains, V. WFTU

I've come back. Past Love. Anne Keiter. GOYP

I've come back many times today. Gift from Kenya. May Miller. BlSi

I've come back to my city. These are my own old tears. Leningrad. Osip Mandelstam, *tr. by* W. S. Merwin *and* Clarence Brown. FaBoPV

I've come by the May-tree all times o' the year. The May Tree. William Barnes. LiTB

I've come down here to live on a bed of weeds. The Old Lady under the Freeway. Diana O Hehir. NPGG

I've come this far to freedom and I won't turn back. Midway. Naomi Long Madgett. BlSi; BPo; PoNe

I've come to close your door, my handsome, my darling. Bereaved Child's First Night. Frances Bellerby. FaBoWP

I've come to give you fruit from out my orchard. The Crossed Apple. Louise Bogan. HeIP

I've come to see Miss Jennian Jones. Miss Jennian Jones. *Unknown.* AmFP

I've Come to the Simplest Words. Amir Gilboa, *tr. fr. Hebrew by* Warren Bargad *and* Stanley F. Chyet. IP

I've crossed the sea after truth. Kakua, *tr. by* Lucien Stryk *and* Takashi Ikemoto. ZPCJ

I've decided to return to the emperor's court. The Return of the Proconsul. Zbigniew Herbert, *tr. by* Czeslaw Milosz. FaBoPV; PwPP

I've decided to study agriculture. Li K'ai-hsien, *tr. fr. Chinese by* Jonathan Chaves. *Fr.* Pleasures among the Fields during the Four Seasons. CoBLCP

I've discovered a way to stay friends forever. Friendship. Shel Silverstein. ILY; NTCP

I've dispatch'd, my dear madam, this scrap of a letter. Sent to a Patient, with the Present of a Couple of Ducks. Edward Jenner. FaBoUs

I've drawn a salary in the capital for forty years now. Yang Shih-ch'i, *tr. fr. Chinese by* Jonathan Chaves. *Fr.* Sent to All My Nephews and Nieces at Tung-ch'eng. CoBLCP

I've Dreamed of You So Much. Robert Desnos, *tr. fr. French by* Michael Benedikt. POS

I've dug up all my garden. Sowing Seeds. Ursula Cornwall. BoTP

I've ever lost were. For Both of Us at Fisk. Sharon Scott. JB

I've finished with the listlessness. The Man Who Knew Too Much. David Wojahn. MAYP

I've followed the billowing dust as a traveler too long. Li K'ai-hsien, *tr. fr. Chinese by* Jonathan Chaves. *Fr.* Pleasures among the Fields during the Four Seasons. CoBLCP

I've forgotten what day, but late in December. The Basilisk. Philip Child. CaP

I've found a small dragon in the woodshed. A Small Dragon. Brian Patten. AmMo

I've found out why, that day, that suicide. John Berryman. PoE

I've found three people now who claim they've seen. Ghost Story. Robert Pack. MOWH

I've gathered more data on a towered city. Northern Romance. Haim Guri, *tr. by* Warren Bargad *and* Stanley F. Chyet. IP

I've given up poetry—I have no new manuscripts. Yang Chi, *tr. fr. Chinese by* Jonathan Chaves. *Fr.* Living in a Riverside Village—Miscellaneous Impressions. CoBLCP

I've Gone and Stained with the Color of Love. Milton Acorn. NeAC

I've gone to him. Komachi, *tr. fr. Japanese by* Burton Watson. *Fr.* Kokin Shu. FCEI

I've got a bow and arrow. Robin Hood. Rachel MacAndrew. BoTP

I've Got a Dog. *Unknown.* RHPC

I've got a feeling. Blue Spruce. Mark Halliday. PPR

I've Got a Home in That Rock. Raymond R. Patterson. FF; PoBA; PoNe

I've got a lovely home. Best of All. J. M. Westrup. BoTP

I've got a mule and her name is Sal. The Erie Canal. William S. Allen. AmFN; AS, *with music;* ILY

I've Got a New Book from My Grandfather Hyde. Leroy F. Jackson. FaPON

I've got a pony. The Pony. Rachel MacAndrew. BoTP

I've got a rocket. A Rocket in My Pocket. *Unknown.* RHPC

I've got a silk-worm. Theobald James. J. B. Morton. *Fr.* When We Were Very Silly. FaBoPa

I've Got No Use for the Women. *Unknown.* AmFP

I've got the best seat in the boat. Fishing. Solveig Nilsen. TSL

I've got the children to tend. Woman Work. Maya Angelou. SaC

I've Got the Giggles Today. Sir Alan Patrick Herbert. FiBHP

I've got the wiggly-wiggles today. Wiggly Giggles. Stacy Jo Crossen *and* Natalie Anne Covell. RHPC

I've got this flat, see. E Flat. Peter Olds. ATNZ

I've grown a goitre by dwelling in this den. To Giovanni da Pistoia on the Painting of the Sistine Chapel, 1509. Michelangelo, *tr. by* John Addington Symons. PFI

I've grown distant from my grandfather. War Confession. Natan Zach, *tr. by* Warren Bargad *and* Stanley F. Chyet. IP

I've grown so wretched. Komachi, *tr. fr. Japanese by* Burton Watson. *Fr.* Kokin Shu. FCEI

I've grown used to the pine door unclosed. Princess Shikishi, *tr. fr. Japanese by* Hiroaki Sato. *Fr.* Seventy-eight Tanka. FCEI

I've had enough. The Bridge Poem. Kate Rushin. GLP

I've Had Many an Aching Pain. John Clare. NOBVV

I've had my share of mountain days in snow and rain and sun. Mountain Days. Barclay Fraser. PoSH

I've had tangled feelings lately. Breakthrough. Carolyn M. Rodgers. BPo

I've heard all about musicians. Saxophonetyx. Cyn Zarco. BrSi; UL

I've heard it said that Sir Barnabas Beer. Endurance Test. Dacre Balsdon. FiBHP

I've heard strange tales of haunted trails. Voices in the Night. Melvin L. Whipple. CowP

I've heard that holy madness is a state. Buzzard. George Garrett. MT

I've heard the case for clarity. I know. Giant Killer. George Garrett. CRP

I've heard the lilting at our yowe-milking. *See* I've heard them lilting at our yowe-milking.

I've heard the sea upon the troubled rocks. The Man Whom the Sea Kept Awake. Robert Bly. NePoEA

I've heard the talk. Guillaume de Poitiers, *tr. by* Paul Blackburn. Pro

I've heard them lilting at loom and belting. C. Day Lewis. *Fr.* Two Songs. HAP; NoAM; OBMV

I've heard them [*or the*] lilting at our yowe-milking [*or the ewe-milking*]. The Flowers of the Forest. Jane Elliot. CH; FaBoCh; FaBoRV; GoTS; OxBS; WPE

(Lament for Flodden, The.) GTBS; GTBS-P; OBEV

I've juist been thinkin', neebour Johnie. Rhymes for the Times. Janet Hamilton. PF

I've jumped from myself to dawn. The Tree of Diana. Alejandra Pizarnik, *tr. by* Yishai Tobin. VWA

I've just come up. Joso, *tr. by* Kenneth Koch and Harold Henderson. TTTS

I've just had an astounding dream as I lay in the straw. Minstrel's Song. Ted Hughes. OxBA

I've kept a haughty heart thro' grief and mirth. To My Mother. Heine, *tr. by* Matilda Dickson. AWP

(Sonnet to My Mother, A.) TrJP, *tr. by* Emma Lazarus

I've kissed thee, sweetheart, in a dream at least. Sleep. Theophile de Viau, *tr. by* Sir Edmund Gosse. AWP

I've known ere now an interfering branch. The Axe-Helve. Robert Frost. OxBA

I've known rivers. The Negro Speaks of Rivers. Langston Hughes. AiP; AmFN; AmNP; BANP; BPo; CDC; HAP; HCAP; HeIP; IDB; NAAL-2; NIP; NoAM; NOBA; NoP; OBCA; PoBA; PoNe; TAP; TTY; WeW

I've known the indifference. Mohammad Taqi Mir, *tr. by* Ahmed Ali. GoT

I've known you since the time/ you were amphibian. Songs to a Lady Moonwalker. Abraham Sutskever, *tr. by* Ruth Whitman. VWA

I've lately been in great distress. Beatrice, Countess de Die, *tr. by* Meg Bogin. WT

I've learnt to laugh now at adversity. Ilyas Farhat, *tr. by* Salma Khadra Jayyusi and John Heath-Stubbs. MAP

I've left mine own old home of homes. The Flitting. John Clare. FaBoPV

I've listened, when to school I've gone. The Landrail. John Clare. PBBP

I've looked behind the shed. Gone. David McCord. TDD

I've Lost My———. Henry Cholmondeley-Pennell. CenHV

I've mastered form, can feel and think. Still Life. Roy Blount, Jr. SoTCo

I've moved here to the Immortal's place. Staying in the Mountains in Summer. Yü Hsüan-chi, *tr. by* Geoffrey Waters. BoWoP

I've multiplied, I'm 2. Number Song. Anne Waldman. UL

I've Never Been Lost. Itsik Fefer, *tr. fr. Yiddish by* John Hollander. PeBMYV

I've Never Come Away, You Know. Anna Hajnal, *tr. fr. Hungarian by* Jascha Kessler. FOC

I've Never Got Anything. Gloria Fuertes, *tr. fr. Spanish by* Philip Levine. OV

I've never known a dog to wag. The Dog. *Unknown.* WBLP

I've never known how to tan or sew. Ravidas, *tr. by* John Stratton Hawley and Mark Juergensmeyer. SSI

I've never known them served in restaurants. A Private Feast. Judson Jerome. SoTCo

I've never really understood Samson's hair. Samson's Hair. Natan Zach, *tr. by* Warren Bargad and Stanley F. Chyet. IP

I've Never Written a Baseball Poem. Elisavietta Ritchie. ASP

I've no tooth to sing you the song. Pat Cloherty's Version of *The Maisie*. Richard Murphy. IPY; RB

I've not forgotten you chose me. Letter to Madame la Marquise de S[imiane], on Sending Her Tobacco. Mme De C———, *tr. by* Dorothy Backer. DMF

I've oft been told by learned friars. An Argument. Thomas Moore. BoLoP; EnLoPo; OxBS

I've often heard my mother say. The Unknown Color. Countee Cullen. FaPON; OBCA

I've paid for your sickest fancies; I've humoured your crackedest whim. The *Mary Gloster*. Kipling. BeLS

I've picked a grave site. Written when He Was Well Over Eighty. Shunzei, *tr. fr. Japanese by* Burton Watson. *Fr.* Thirty Tanka. FCEI

I've planned my life in an eternity. 1st April 1984. Peter Russell. NPo

I've plowed and sown my field. Keizan, *tr. by* Lucien Stryk and Takashi Ikemoto. ZPCJ

I've plucked the berry from the bush, the brown nut from the tree. Sing On, Blithe Bird. William Motherwell. GN

I've poached a pickle paitricks. Poaching *in Excelsis*. G. K. Menzies. FaBoCo

I've rambled and gambled all my money away. Rabble Soldier. *Unknown.* AS

I've reached my seventy-seventh year. Gyozan, *tr. by* Lucien Stryk and Takashi Ikemoto. ZPCJ

I've Reached the Land of Corn and Wine. Edgar P. Stites. AH

I've read that Luther said (it's come to me). The Author to the Reader. Randall Jarrell. OxBC

I've read the propaganda. Amazing Gracious Living on I-93. George Starbuck. PPR

I've remained in Mokuchin thirty years. Mokuchin Juro, *tr. by* Lucien Stryk and Takashi Ikemoto. ZPCJ

I've rode the Southern, I've rode the L. & N. I Rode Southern, I Rode L & N. *Unknown.* AmFP

I've saved the milk crystal stone. Palinode. Maura Stanton. MAYP

I've seen a dying eye. Emily Dickinson. AmPP; BoWoP; FPL; NOBA; PoEL-5; PoLF

Ive seen all the sunrises since u left me. Sex Play in Four Acts. Doug Fetherling. NeAC

I've seen caravans. Caravans. Irene Thompson. BoTP

"I've seen it all." Joso, *tr. by* Geoffrey Bownas and Anthony Thwaite. PeBJV

I've seen one flying saucer. Only when. David McCord. *Fr.* Go Fly a Saucer. FaPON; ImOP

I've seen the grey-haired lyrists come down from the hills. Grand Finale. Irving Layton. NOBC

I've seen the Thousand Islands. Tadoussac. Charles Bancroft. BLPA

I've served my country nine and twenty years. Edward Thompson. *Fr.* An Humble Wish; off Porto-Sancto, March 29, 1779. NOEC

I've shore at Burrabogie, and I've shore at Toganmain. Flash Jack from Gundagai. *Unknown.* PoAu-1

I've shorn over two hunn'ert in a day. Big Sheep Knocks You About. Sharon Bryan. MAYP; PPR

I've sixpence in my pocket and I've worked hard for it. The Beggar. *Unknown.* OBET

I've Slept. Gloria Fuertes, *tr. fr. Spanish by* Philip Levine. AnAn

I've soaked weeks-old bread in water. Love and Misery. Jotie T'Hooft, *tr. by* James S. Holmes. DuIn

I've spent the night at the table. Appealing to the Imagination. Ad Zuiderent, *tr. by* Scott Rollins. DuIn

I've spent the whole year. Quijote. Marco Martos, *tr. by* David Tipton. Per

I've spoken of home before and spotted crows. Autobiographical Flashback: Puma and Pokeweed. Jim Barnes. NOVW

I've stalked the world. Issan, *tr. by* Lucien Stryk and Takashi Ikemoto. ZPCJ

I've stayed in the front yard all my life. A Song in the Front Yard. Gwendolyn Brooks. *Fr.* A Street in Bronzeville. CAPP; IDB; NAAL-2; NoAM; NOBA; PoBA

I've stitched my dress with continents. Knowledge. Nina Cassian, *tr. by* Michael Impey and Brian Swann. BoWoP

I've suffered bitterness from tyrant fate. The Moth. Ahmad al-Safi al-Najafi, *tr. by* Salma Khadra Jayyusi and John Heath-Stubbs. MAP

I've survived, I've survived. Issa, *tr. fr. Japanese by* Hiroaki Sato. *Fr.* Forty-four Hokku. FCEI

I've swallowed the Eastern Ocean's iron ball. Giten, *tr. by* Lucien Stryk and Takashi Ikemoto. ZPCJ

I've taken my fun where I've found it. The Ladies. Kipling. MoBrPo; NAEL-2

I've taken the police squad outline from where you fell. The Immigration Act of 1924. Laureen Mar. BrSi

I've Tasted My Blood. Milton Acorn. MoCV; NOBC

I've Thirty Months. J. M. Synge. OBMV

I've thought of names. Labour of the Brain, Ballad of the Body. Nicole Forman. NMM

I've told you many a tale, my child, of the old heroic days. Madeleine Verchères. William Henry Drummond. CaP

I've tossed an apple at you; if you can love me. The Apple. *At. to* Plato. WeW

I've tried to seal it in. The Knot. Stanley Kunitz. CAPP; HAP

I've tried to trace the reverie. Mood Indigo. Ira Sadoff. BLA

I've walked the world over. Issan, *tr. by* Lucien Stryk and Takashi Ikemoto. ZPCJ

I've wandered to the village, Tom, I've sat beneath the tree. Twenty Years Ago. *At. to* A. J. Gault *and also to* Dill Armor Smith. BLPA

I've watched you now a full half-hour. To a Butterfly. Wordsworth. FM

I've waxed you. A Cabinet. Eugène Guillevic, *tr. by* Teo Savory. RHTwFP

I've wined and dined on Mulligan stew. The Lady Is a Tramp. Lorenz Hart. OBAL

I've won Yasumiko! Kamatari. *Fr.* Manyo Shu. FCEI

I've worked on the Nine-Mile, likewise on the River. The Broken-down Digger. *Unknown.* PoAu-1
I've Worn My Bits o' Shoon Away. Edwin Waugh. PF
I've written you a song. Blah, Blah, Blah. Ira Gershwin. OBAL
Ivied Tree-Top, An. *Unknown.*
Ivory. Mario Luzi, *tr. fr. Italian by* I. L. Salomon. PFI
Ivory, bamboo, and kingfisher bed, An. An Earthen *K'ang.* Sung Wan, *tr. fr. Chinese by* William Schultz. *Fr.* Songs Composed in Prison, II. WFTU
Ivory Bed, The. Winfield Townley Scott. ErPo
Ivory, Coral, Gold, The. William Drummond of Hawthornden. ELP
　(Madrigal: "Ivory, coral, gold, The.") EIL
Ivory Gate, The, *sel.* Thomas Lovell Beddoes.
　Mighty Thoughts of an Old World, The. GoJo
　(Stanzas from "The Ivory Gate.") EnRP
　(Stanzas: "Mighty thought of an old world, The.") TrGrPo
Ivory in her black, and all intent. Jesu, Joy of Man's Desiring. Robert Fitzgerald. NYBP
Ivory Masks in Orbit. Keorapetse Kgositsile. PoBA
Ivory Tower, The. Robert Hillyer. NYBP
Ivry. Macaulay. FaBV; GN
Ivy, chefe of trees it is. In Praise of Ivy. *Unknown.* MeEL
Ivy Crest, The. *Unknown, tr. fr. Old Irish by* Robin Flower. AnIL
Ivy Crown, The. William Carlos Williams. NAAL-2; NoAM; NoP; PrIm
Ivy Green, The. Charles Dickens. *Fr.* The Pickwick Papers, *ch.* 6. BoNaP
Ivy o'er the mouldering wall, The. The Sun-Dial. Thomas Love Peacock. *Fr.* Melincourt. OBNC
Iwa flies heavy to nest in the brush, The. Love by the Water-Reeds. *Unknown, tr. by* M. W. Beckwith. WTO
Iwamaro, I tell you. Yakamochi. *Fr.* Manyo Shu. Ma
Iwamaro, look! Yakamochi. *Fr.* Manyo Shu. PeBJV
Iwamaro, these words. Yakamochi. *Fr.* Manyo Shu. FCEI
Iwori wotura. Oracle. *Yoruba Oral Tradition, tr. by* Ulli Beier. WTO
I'yehe! my children. *Unknown, tr. fr. Sioux Indian by* James Mooney. *Fr.* Ghost Dance Songs. STP
Izaac Walton, Cotton, and William Oldways. Walter Savage Landor. PoEL-4
Izumi River: like the bubbles on a pole. Teika, *tr. fr. Japanese by* Hiroaki Sato. *Fr.* Eighty-four Tanka. FCEI

J

J. A. G. Julia Ward Howe. PAH
J. Alfred Prufrock to. Said. George Starbuck. OBAL
J. B. H. C. Bunner. AA
J. B., *sel.* Archibald MacLeish.
　Curse God and Die, You Said to Me. EaLo
J. J. Walter de la Mare. FaBoNo
J. M. W. Turner on Switzerland. Consolations of Art. Roy Fuller. OxBC
J. S. Mill. E. C. Bentley. *See* John Stuart Mill.
J. V. Cunningham Gets Hung Up on a Dirty, of All Things, Joke. Henry Taylor. BXAP
Ja-Nez—burro with the long ears. Burro with the Long Ears. *Unknown, tr. by* Hilda Faunce Wetherill. FaPON
Jabberwocky. "Lewis Carroll." *Fr.* Through the Looking-Glass, *ch.* 1. AmMo; EBEV; EBVV; FaBoBe; FaBoCo; FaBoNo; FaBV; FaFP; FaPON; FF; FiBHP; FPL; GoJo; HeIP; HoPM; InPK; InPS; LiTB; NA; NAEL-2; NBLV; NIP; NoAM; NOBE; NOBL; NOBVV; NoP; NTCP; OAEL-2;OPOP; OxBChV; PoRA; PPP; RB; RHPC; TEP; TTTS
Jacaranda. Roo Borson. NOBC
Jacaranda. Myra Cohn Livingston. TSS
Jack. Louis Golding. TrJP
Jack. Charles Henry Ross. OxBChV; RHPC
Jack, Afterwards. Philip Dacey. SM
Jack and Dinah Want Freedom. *Unknown.* BPo
Jack and Gye. *Unknown.* OxNR
Jack and Jill. Charles Battell Loomis. BXAP
Jack and Jill. Harriet S. Morgridge. *Fr.* Mother Goose Sonnets. AA
Jack and Jill. Charles Powell. BXAP
Jack and Jill—as Kipling Might Have Written It. Anthony C. Deane. *See* Here Is the Tale.
Jack and Jill went up the hill. Mother Goose. FaBoBe; FaFP; OxBoLi; OxNR

Jack and Jill went up the hill/ To fetch some heavy water. Paul Dehn. *Fr.* Rhymes for a Modern Nursery. FiBHP
Jack and Joan they think no ill. Thomas Campion. AAS; OBSC
　(Jack and Joan.) FaBoCh; FaPoR
Jack and Roger. *At. to* Benjamin Franklin. ChTr; FaBoEE; NOBL
Jack and the Beanstalk. Kenneth Rosen. NAmP
Jack Barrett went to Quetta. The Story of Uriah. Kipling. BrPo; NOBVV; SCV
Jack be nimble. Mother Goose. OxNR
Jack Creamer. James Jeffrey Roche. PAH
Jack Denver died on Talbragar when Christmas Eve began. Talbragar. Henry Lawson. PoAu-1
Jack, eating rotten cheese, did say. Jack and Roger. *At. to* Benjamin Franklin. ChTr; FaBoEE; NOBL
　(Impromptu.) NOBL
　(Sampson Imitated.) FaBoEE
Jack Ellyat Heard the Guns. Stephen Vincent Benét. *Fr.* John Brown's Body. PoLF
"Jack fell as he'd have wished," the Mother said. The Hero. Siegfried Sassoon. OBWP
Jack Frenchman's Defeat. Congreve. APAS
Jack Frost. Helen Bayley Davis. RAR
Jack Frost. Cecily E. Pike. BoTP
Jack Frost. "Gabriel Setoun." BoTP
Jack Frost. Celia Thaxter. OBCA
Jack Frost in the Garden ("Jack Frost was in the garden"). John P. Smeeton. BoTP
Jack Giantkiller took and struck. Driving Cross-Country. X. J. Kennedy. TwCP
Jack Haggerty. *Unknown.* AmFP
Jack Hall. *Unknown.* OBET
Jack-in-the-Boat. Allen Curnow. ATNZ
Jack in the Pulpit. *Unknown.* OxNR
Jack Monroe. *Unknown.* AmFP
Jack o' Diamonds. *Unknown.* AmFP
Jack o' the Inkpot. Algernon Blackwood. BoTP
Jack Potter's Courtin'. S. Omar Barker. CowP
Jack Rabbit. Adrien Stoutenburg
Jack Robinson. *Unknown.* OBET
Jack scrubs the smell of hemp and tar from his hands. Traveling through Ports That Begin with "M." Christy Sheffield Sanford. UL
Jack Sprat could eat no fat. Mother Goose. FaBoBe; FaFP; OxNR
Jack Sprat's Cat ("Jack Sprat/ Had a cat"). *Unknown.* OxNR
Jack Tar. Emile Jacot. BoTP
Jack Tar. *Unknown.* OxBSS
Jack the Giant Queller; an Antique History, *sels.* Henry Brooke. NOEC
　"Arise, arise, arise!"
　"For often my mammy has told."
Jack the Jolly Tar. *Unknown.* AmFP
Jack the Piper. *Unknown.* See As I was going up the hill.
Jack the Ripper. Allan M. Laing. FiBHP
Jack Yazzie's Girl. Pamela Stewart. NAmP
Jackdaw, The. Vincent Bourne, *tr. fr. Latin by* William Cowper. PBBP
Jackdaw of Rheims, The ("Jackdaw sat on the Cardinal's chair").
　"Thomas Ingoldsby." *Fr.* The Ingoldsby Legends. FaBoCo; OBNV; OnMSP
Jackey Jackey gallops on a horse like a swallow. A Bushranger. Kenneth Slessor. CBAP
Jackfish in dry death, The. Returning. Kate Shanley. GOS
Jackfruit, The. Ho Xuan Huong, *tr. fr. Vietnamese by* Nguyen Ngoc Bich. PBWP
Jackie. King D. Kuka. VoR
Jackie Faa. *Unknown. See* Gypsies they came to my Lord Cassilis yett, The.
Jackie Kennedy Onassis, working at Woolworth's. Dream. Harold Witt. SM
Jackie Robinson. Lucille Clifton. ASP
Jackie Tar. *Unknown.* OxBSS
Jackie's gone a-sailing with trouble on his mind. Jack Monroe. *Unknown.* AmFP
Jackknife swandive gainer twist. Elegy for a Diver. Peter Meinke. Psk
Jacklight. Louise Erdrich. HATNAP; NOVW; TSL
Jackpot. Jorie Graham. KS
Jackson. *Unknown.* AS, *with music*
Jackson at New Orleans. Wallace Rice. PAH
Jackson is on sea, Jackson is on shore. Jackson. *Unknown.* AS, *with music*
Jackson, Mississippi. Margaret Walker. FB

Jackson Pollock had a quaint. Squeeze Play. Phyllis McGinley. *Fr.* Spectator's Guide to Contemporary Art. FaBoEE; OBSV
Jacky, come give me thy fiddle. Mother Goose. OxNR
Jacob. Phoebe Cary. OBAL
Jacob. George Garrett. CRP
Jacob. Ruth Gilbert. *Fr.* Leah, II. PeNZ
Jacob. Else Lasker-Schüler, *tr. fr. German.* BoWoP, *tr. by* Rosemarie Waldrop; VWA, *tr. by* Joachim Neugroschel.
Jacob. Bin Ramke. NAmP
Jacob. Charles Reznikoff. VWA
Jacob. Delmore Schwartz. VWA
Jacob: a bull among his herd. Else Lasker-Schüler, *tr. by* Rosemarie Waldrop. BoWoP
Jacob and Esau. Else Lasker-Schüler, *tr. fr. German by* Rosemarie Waldrop. BoWoP
Jacob and the Angel. Stephen Mitchell. VWA
Jacob Epstein. *Unknown.* FaBoCo
Jacob Godbey. Edgar Lee Masters. *Fr.* Spoon River Anthology. LiTA
Jacob, hear! Jacob's Destiny. Richard Beer-Hofmann, *tr. fr. German by* Ida Bension Wynn. *Fr.* Jacob's Dream. TrJP
Jacob Studies "The Selling of Joseph" with His Sons. Itzig Manger, *after* Genesis 37-50, *tr. fr. Yiddish by* Leonard Wolf. PeBMYV
Jacob was the buffalo of his herd. Jacob. Else Lasker-Schüler, *tr. by* Joachim Neugroschel. VWA
Jacobean. Clifton Fadiman. FiBHP
Jacobite Scot in Satire on England's Unparalleled Loss, A. *Unknown.* APAS
Jacobite Toast. John Byrom. FaBoCo; FaBoEE
Jacobite's Epitaph, A. Macaulay. FaPoR; NOBE; OBEV; OBNC
Jacob's Destiny. Richard Beer-Hofmann, *tr. fr. German by* Ida Bension Wynn. *Fr.* Jacob's Dream. TrJP
Jacob's Dream, *sel.* Richard Beer-Hofmann, *tr. fr. German by* Ida Bension Wynn.
   Jacob's Destiny. TrJP
Jacob's Ladder, The. Denise Levertov. AmPP; CAPP; PoM; PPP
Jacob's Well. *Unknown.* OBET
Jacob's Winning. Richard Sherwin. VWA
Jacques Cartier. Thomas D'Arcy McGee. CaP
Jade Butterflies. Sun Kuang-hsien, *tr. fr. Chinese by* Lois Fusek. ATF
Jade Butterflies. Wen T'ing-yün, *tr. fr. Chinese by* Lois Fusek. ATF
Jade cave, ten thousand flowering peach trees of immortality, A. Painting. Chang Yü, *tr. by* Jonathan Chaves. CoBLCP
Jade Flower Palace. Tu Fu, *tr. fr. Chinese by* Kenneth Rexroth. NaP
Jade trees from the rear courtyard of the empire of Ch'en. Li K'ai-hsien, *tr. fr. Chinese by* Jonathan Chaves. *Fr.* On Snow. CoBLCP
Jaffar. Leigh Hunt. BeLS
Jagg'd mountain peaks and skies ice-green. Breughel's Winter. Walter de la Mare. SeCePo
Jagged are the rocks. *Unknown, tr. by* Arthur Waley. BoS
Jagged cliffs overhang the soaring peaks of Mount Wu. Immortal at the River. Niu Hsi-chi, *tr. by* Lois Fusek. ATF
Jaguar, The. Ted Hughes. LiTM
Jah Son/ Another Way. Kendel Hippolyte. PVCV
Jahr der Seele, Das, *sel.* Stefan George, *tr. fr. German by* Daisy Broicher.
   "No way too long—no path too steep." AWP
Jaikur and the City. Badr Shakir al-Sayyah, *tr. fr. Arabic by* Lena Jayyusi *and* Christopher Middleton. MAP
Jaikur, your shadows of palm trees. Shadows of Jaikur. Badr Shakir al-Sayyab, *tr. by* Abdullah al-Udhari. MPAW
Jailbird. Vernon Scannell. OxBC
Jake Balokowsky, my biographer. Posterity. Philip Larkin. OxBC
Jake's store past Pindaric mountain. Purchase of a Blue, Green, or Orange Ode. Josephine Miles. NoP
Jake's Wharf. Philip Booth. NYBP
Jalan Thamrin in Denpasar. Walking down Jalan Thamrin. R. F. Brissenden. CBAP
Jam Fish, The. Edward Abbott Parry. AmMo; OxBChV
Jam on Gerry's Rock, The. *Unknown.* AmFP; AS, *with music*; FaBoBa
Jam Trap, The. Charles Tomlinson. MoBrPo
Jamaica. Louis Simpson. PBCV
Jamaica, a Poem in Three Parts, Written in That Island in the Year 1776, *sel. Unknown.*
   "And can the muse reflect her tear-stain'd eye." PBCV
Jamaica Market. Agnes Maxwell-Hall. TTY
Jamaican Bus Ride. A. S. J. Tessimond. OBTV; OxBTC
Jamaican Fisherman. Philip Sherlock. PBCV

James Alan Park/ Came naked stark. Thomas Erskine, 1st Baron Erskine. FaBoEE
James Bird. *Unknown.* AmFP
James Bond Movie, The. May Swenson. FaBoWP
James Grant. *Unknown.* ESPB
James Harris. *Unknown. See* "O where have you been, my long, long love."
James Hatley. *Unknown.* ESPB
James Honeyman. W. H. Auden. MoBS
James Hugo Johnston. Maggie Pogue Johnson. CBWP-4
James James. Disobedience. A. A. Milne. NTCP
James Lee's Wife, *sel.* Robert Browning.
   Among the Rocks. OxBSP
James McCosh. Robert Bridges. AA
James Powell on Imagination. Larry Neal. BPo
James Rigg. James Hogg. BXAP; Par
James Wetherell. E. A. Robinson. MoAmPo
James Whaland. *Unknown.* AS
Jamestown. Randall Jarrell. GOA
Jamie Douglas. *Unknown. See* Waly, Waly ("O waly, waly, up the bank").
Jamie Telfer of [*or* in] the Fair Dodhead. *Unknown.* ESPB; OxBB
Jamila. Nazik al-Mala'ika, *tr. fr. Arabic by* Kamal Boullata. WPOW
Jan van Hogspeuw staggers to the door. The Card-Players. Philip Larkin. OxBC
Jan Vermeer/ liked to paint a tankard of beer. Vonna Adrian. SoTCo
Jane Austen at the Window. Patricia Beer. FaBoWP
Jane awoke Ralph so gently on one morning. Morning. John Crowe Ransom. AmPP
Jane, Jane,/ Tall as a crane. Edith Sitwell. CMoP; MoAB; MoBrPo; MoP; NoAM; PoRA
Jane looks down at her organdy skirt. In Bertram's Garden. Donald Justice. BoLoP; ErPo; MT; NePoEA; VGW
Jane Seagrim's Party. Leonard Nathan. GOYP
Jane Williams had a lover true. Shocking Rape and Murder of Two Lovers. *Unknown.* CoMu
Jane won't touch a caterpillar. Why Run? Norah Smaridge. RHPC
Jane's Village. Koh Chang-soo, *tr. fr. Korean by the author.* ACKP
Janet Waking. John Crowe Ransom. CMoP; InPK; MoAB; MoAmPo; MoP; NAAL-2; NoAM; NoP; OBD; PoE; RB; TAP
Janie Swecker and Me and Gone with the Wind. David Huddle. GrPl
Janitor's Boy, The. Nathalia Crane. PoLF
Jankin [the Clerical Seducer]. *Unknown. See* Kyne, so kyne.
Janna. King D. Kuka. VoR
Jansenist Journey. Denis Devlin. IPY
Januar: by this fire [*or* thys fyre] I warme my handes. *Unknown.* EBEV (Labours of the Months.) GBP; OxBLMV; SaC
Januaries, Nature greets our eyes. Brazil, January 1, 1502. Elizabeth Bishop. FaBoWP; NoAM
January. Geoffrey Dutton. PoAu-2
January. Douglas Gibson. OBCP
January. H. R. Hays. EAS
January. Robert Hass. NPGG
January. John Heath-Stubbs. OBCP
January. Weldon Kees. CoAP
January. Nishiwaki Junzaburo, *tr. fr. Japanese by* Hiroaki Sato. FCEI
January. Daniel James O'Sullivan. NeIP
January. Henrietta Cordelia Ray. CBWP-3
January. James Reaney. *Fr.* A Suit of Nettles. OBCV
January. Folgore Da San Gimignano, *tr. fr. Italian by* Dante Gabriel Rossetti. *Fr.* Sonnets of the Months. PFI
January. John Updike. PDV; RHPC
January. Ellen Bryant Voigt. NoP
January. William Carlos Williams. MoAB; MoAmPo
January brings the snow. The Garden Year. Sara Coleridge. FaBoBe (Months, The.) OxBChV; RHPC
January cold and desolate. The Months. Christina Rossetti. FaPON
January Eclogue. Spenser. *Fr.* The Shepheardes [*or* Shepeards *or* Shepherd's] Calender. FiP
January 18, 1979. John Yau. UL
January falls the snow. Calendar Rhyme. Flora Willis Watson. BoTP
January 15 as a National Holiday. Carter Revard. VoR
January 1st. Anne Sexton. HCAP
January first isn't New Year's. Happy New Year, Anyway. Joanna Cole. NTCP
January Man. Dave Goulder. OBET
January Morning, A. Archibald Lampman. OBCV
January Morning. William Carlos Williams. InPS; SOTW
January night, A. Moonlight. Significant Fevers. Alison Fell. BrRo

January 1940. Roy Fuller. LiTM; SeCePo; WaP
(War Poet.) HoPM
January 1939. Dylan Thomas. EAS
January 30. A. Leyeles, *tr. fr. Yiddish by* Benjamin *and* Barbara Harshav. *Fr.* Fabius Lind's Diary. AYP
January 3, 1970. Mae Jackson. PoBA
January 28. A. Leyeles, *tr. fr. Yiddish by* Benjamin *and* Barbara Harshav. *Fr.* Fabius Lind's Diary. AYP
January 25th. Maxine W. Kumin. SM
January wraps up the wound of his arm. Charles Henri Ford. EAS
January's grey and slushy. English Weather. Wendy Cope. SoTCo
Janus. Madeline Mason. GoYe
Janus. Laurence Perrine. InPK
Janus Season. Derek Stanford. NPo
Japan. Anthony Hecht. LiTM
Japanese. Stephen Stepanchev. SoTCo
Japanese Archery. Aleksander Wat, *tr. fr. Polish by* Richard Lourie TOF
Japanese Beetles. X. J. Kennedy. OBAL
Japanese Birthday Wish, A. Thomas Burnett Swann. GoYe
Japanese Consulate, The. Frank Polite. UL
Japanese Fan. James Kirkup. GrPl
Japanese Girl with Red Table. Stephen Dobyns. MAYP
Japanese have funny things, The. A Rhyme Sheet of Other Lands. Hugh Chesterman. BoTP
Japanese Hokku. Lewis Alexander. CDC
Japanese house has a low roof, The. Roof. Ishigaki Rin, *tr. by* Hiroaki Sato. FCEI
Japanese Lovers, The. *Unknown.* BeLS; BLPA
Japanese Lullaby. Eugene Field. AnAmPo
Japanese next to me at the bar, The. In a Bar near Shibuya Station, Tokyo. Paul Engle. AmFN
Japanese Print. Austin Clarke. IPY; NOIV
Japanesque. Oliver Herford. FiBHP
Jaquerie, The, *sels.* Sidney Lanier.
Betrayal. AA
Hound, The. AA
Jar, The. Richard Henry Stoddard. AA
Jar of cider and my pipe, A. The Sluggard. W. H. Davies. OBMV
Jar of Nations, The. A. E. Housman. LiTB
Jarring the air with rumour cool. Small Fountains. Lascelles Abercrombie. *Fr.* Emblems of Love: What shall we do for Love these days? CH
Jars. Paul Raboff. VWA
Jason. Anthony Hecht. DiL
Jason and Medea. John Gower. *Fr.* Confessio Amantis, V. ACP
Jasper Cloud Monastery, The. Wu Wen, *tr. fr. Chinese by* Chang Yin-nan. WFTU
Jaunty crop-haired graying, The. Poem about People. Robert Pinsky. NPGG
Jaunty traveller that comes to peer, The. Llyn y Gadair. T. H. Parry-Williams, *tr. by* Anthony Conran. OBWVE
Jawbone is a platter for the face, The. Dog. D. C. Berry. BXAP
Jay a-Pass'd. William Barnes. NOBVV
Jay Gould's Daughter. *Unknown.* AS, *with music*
Jazz. Frank London Brown. PoNe
Jazz. Carolyn M. Rodgers. JB
Jazz Band in a Parisian Cabaret. Langston Hughes. BANP; MoAmPo
Jazz Fantasia. Carl Sandburg. AiP; MoAB; MoAmPo; PoNe
Jazz Station. Michael S. S. Harper. NoAM
Jazz Vamp. Maurice B. Cloud. VVA
Jazzonia. Langston Hughes. AmNP; BANP
"Je Ne Sais Quoi," The. William Whitehead. SoSe
Je ne veux de personne aupres de ma tristesse. Henri de Regnier, *tr. fr. French by* "Seumas O'Sullivan." AWP
Je Suis une Table. Donald Hall. EAS; NePoEA
Je T'Adore. Thomas Kinsella. MoP; NoAM
Jealous Adam. Itzig Manger, *tr. fr. Yiddish by* Jacob Sonntag. TrJP
Jealous Brothers, The. *Unknown.* AmFP
Jealous girls these sometimes were. How Marigolds Came Yellow. Robert Herrick. ChTr; TTTS
Jealous Lovers, The. Donald Hall. NYBP
Jealous Man, A. Robert Graves. CMoP
Jealous Wife, The. Vernon Scannell. ErPo
Jealousie Is the Rage of a Man. Anne Finch, Countess of Winchilsea. FM
Jealousy. Mary Elizabeth Coleridge. CH; EnLoPo; OBNC; WPE
Jealousy. John Donne. *Fr.* Elegies, I. FF
Jealousy. Esther Johnson. OxBSP
Jealousy. *Malay Oral Tradition, tr. by* R. J. Wilkinson *and* R. O. Winstedt. WTO
Jealousy. Valerie Sinason. DT
Jealousy. Stephen Vincent. NeAC
Jealousy's an awful thing and foreign to my nature. I Can't Think What He Sees in Her. A. P. Herbert. FiBHP
Jean. Burns. *See* Of A' the Airts [the Wind Can Blaw].
Jean, death comes close to us all. The Child Bearers. Anne Sexton. BoWoP
Jean, Jean, Jean. Cat at the Cream. *Unknown.* GBP
Jean Maillard lies buried here. Epitaph for Jean Maillard. *Unknown.* PeHV
Jean Richepin's Song. Herbert Trench. OBMV
Jeanie, come tie my. *Unknown.* BoTP
Jeanie with the Light Brown Hair. Stephen Collins Foster. AnAmPo; FaFP
Jeanne d'Arc. Louise Glück. GeTw
Jeanne d'Arc. Susan Ludvigson. MT
Jeanne Dixon's America. Gerald Costanzo. MAYP
Jeanne Manon Philipon-Roland. Kathinka Zitz-Halein, *tr. fr. German by* Susan L. Cocalis *and* Gerlinde Geiger. DMG
Jeannette. Otto Julius Bierbaum, *tr. fr. German by* Jethro Bithell. AWP
Jeannette and Jeannot. Charles Jefferys. BLPA
Jeannie Marsh. George Pope Morris. AA
Jeannot's Answer. Charles Jefferys. BLPA
Jeat Ring Sent, A. *See* Thou art not so black as my heart.
Jeff Buckner. Frank Beddo. WTO
Jefferson D. Henry Sylvester Cornwell. PAH
Jefferson Davis. Walker Meriwether Bell. PAH
Jefferson Valley. John Hollander. PPP
Jehovah. Israel Zangwill. WGRP
Jehovah, God, Who Dwelt of Old. Lewis R. Amis. AH
Jehovah, Lord and Majesty. Conrad Weiser, *tr. fr. German by* Sheema Z. Buehne. AH
Jehovah Our Righteousness. William Cowper. NOCV
Jehu. Louis MacNeice. LiTM; MoAB; WaP
Jelka Revisited ("Jelka's profile decorates the doorway"). James Tate. PPR
Jellicle Cats are black and white. The Song of the Jellicles. T. S. Eliot. FaBoCh; FaBoNo; OxBChV
Jellon Grame. *Unknown.* EBEV; ESPB; OxBB
Jelly Belly bit. The Dreadful Doings of Jelly Belly. Dennis Lee. RAR
Jellyfish, A. Marianne Moore. OxBSP; PCP
Jellyfish, The. Ogden Nash. FaPON
Jemima. Mother Goose. *See* There Was a Little Girl.
Jemima is my name. Mima. Walter de la Mare. BrPo
Jennie Jenkins. *Unknown.* AmFP
Jennifer Gentle and Rosemary. *Unknown. See* There was a knicht riding frae the east.
Jenny. John Mann Astrachan. TSM
Jenny. Dante Gabriel Rossetti. PoEL-5
Jenny and Johnny. Dorothy King. BoTP
Jenny and Me were engaged, you see. Pink Dominoes. Kipling. CenHV
Jenny come tie my. The Bonny Cravet. Mother Goose. OxNR
Jenny gay and Johnny grim. Jenny and Johnny. Dorothy King. BoTP
Jenny had hoops she could sling in the air. Jenny the Juvenile Juggler. Dennis Lee. RR
Jenny Kiss'd [*or* Kissed] Me. Leigh Hunt. BLPA; FaBoBe; FaFP; FPL; NBLV; NTCP; OBEV; PoRA
(Rondeau, A: "Jenny kissed me when we met.") EnRP; FaBV; FF; HoPM; InPK; NOBE; NOBVV; TEP
Jenny kiss'd me in a dream. "Such Stuff as Dreams." Franklin P. Adams. FiBHP
Jenny kiss'd me when we met. Paul Dehn. *Fr.* A Leaden Treasury of English Verse. FiBHP
Jenny Kissed Me. Leigh Hunt. *See* Jenny Kiss'd Me.
Jenny the Juvenile Juggler. Dennis Lee. RR
Jenny White and Johnny Black. Eleanor Farjeon. FaPON
Jenny Wren. W. H. Davies. MoBrPo
Jenny Wren fell sick. Ungrateful Jenny. Mother Goose. OxNR
Jenny Wren's got a house. The Secret. Elizabeth Fleming. BoTP
Jenny, your mind commands. Reading the Brothers Grimm to Jenny. Lisel Mueller. NYBP
Jephthah's Daughter, *sel.* Charles Heavysege.
"Oh! think how hard it is to die when young!" CaP
Jephthah's Daughter. "Yehoash," *tr. fr. Yiddish by* Alter Brody. TrJP
Jerboa, The, *sel.* Marianne Moore. FYAP
"Roman had an, A/ artist, a freedman." CMoP
Jeremiad. Oscar Williams. LiTA
Jeremiah, *sels.* Bible, *O.T.*
As Fowlers Lie in Wait. *Fr.* V: 26-31. TrJP
But Fear Thou Not, O Jacob. *Fr.* XLVI: 27-28. TrJP

Cry of the Daughter of My People, The. *Fr.* VIII: 18-23. TrJP

Cursed Be the Day. *Fr.* XX: 14-18. TrJP

"For Thus saith The Lord to the men of Judah and Jerusalem." *Fr.* IV: 3-31. OBVE

O Lord, Thou Hast Enticed Me. *Fr.* XX: 7-10. TrJP

Oh That I Were in the Wilderness. *Fr.* IX: 1-10. TrJP

Jeremiah, *sels.* Stefan Zweig, *tr. fr. German by* Eden *and* Cedar Paul. TrJP

Chosen of God.

Flowering Without End.

Jeremiah, blow the fire. *Unknown.* OxNR

Jeremy. Jeffrey Miller. UL

Jeremy Hobbler. *Unknown.* BoTP

Jericho. Haim Gouri, *tr. fr. Hebrew by* Warren Bargad *and* Stanley F. Chyet. IP

Jericho is on the inside. The Walls of Jericho. Blanche Taylor Dickinson. CDC

Jericho's Blind Beggar. Longfellow. WBLP

Jerome. Randall Jarrell. PPP

Jerome in Solitude. James Wright. AnAn

Jeronimo's House. Elizabeth Bishop. NoP

Jerry, Go an' Ile That Car. *Unknown.* AS

Jerry Hall,/ He is so small. Mother Goose. OxNR

Jerry Perm Poem. Carole Stewart. WS

Jersey Bait Shack. Peter Balakian. MAYP

Jersey Cattle. Ralph Nixon Currey. OxBTC

Jersey Marsh, The. David Galler. NYBP

Jerusalem. Rose Ausländer, *tr. fr. German by* Ewald Osers. VWA

Jerusalem, *sels.* Blake.

"But still the thunder of Los peals loud and thus the thunder's cry." OAEL-2

"England! awake! awake! awake!" *Fr.* IV, Prologue. EnRP; NoP (Prelude: "England! awake! awake! awake!".) OBNC

"Fearing that Albion should turn his back against the Divine Vision." OAEL-2

Fields from Islington to Marybone, The. *Fr.* II, Prologue. ChTr, *4 sts.;* FaBoPV; OBNV (Prelude: "Fields from Islington to Marybone, The.") OBNC

"I saw a Monk of Charlemaine." *Fr.* III, Prologue. EnRP

In Deadly Fear. SeCePo

"It is easier to forgive an enemy than to forgive a friend." OAEL-2

Male & Female Loves in Beulah. *Fr.* III. OBNC

Monk, The. EnRP

"Shuddring the Spectre howls, his howlings terrify the night." OAEL-2

To the Christians. *Fr.* IV, Prologue. EnRP; WGRP (Epigraph.) OBNC

Jerusalem. Blake. *See* Milton: And Did Those Feet in Ancient Time.

Jerusalem, *sel.* Uri Zvi Greenberg, *tr. fr. Hebrew by* Charles A. Cowen. Jerusalem the Dismembered. TrJP

Jerusalem. Judah Halevi, *tr. fr. Hebrew by* David Goldstein. TOF

Jerusalem. Ruben Kanalenstein, *tr. fr. Spanish by* Yishai Tobin. VWA

Jerusalem. Jon Silkin. VWA

Jerusalem. Antoni Slonimski, *tr. fr. Polish by* Isaac Komen. VWA

Jerusalem. Shlomo Vinner, *tr. fr. Hebrew by* Laya Firestone *and* Howard Schwartz. VWA

Jerusalem and the Hour. Rashid Husain, *tr. fr. Arabic by* Lena Jayyusi *and* Peter Porter. MAP

Jerusalem in the Snow. Anath Bental, *tr. fr. Hebrew by* Howard Schwartz. VWA

Jerusalem is a limestone cracked. Guide to Jerusalem. Dennis Silk. VWA

Jerusalem is Sodom's sister city. Sodom's Sister City. Yehuda Amichai, *tr. by* Shirley Kaufman. VWA

Jerusalem, My Happy Home. *Unknown.* PoE

Jerusalem 1967, *sels.* Yehuda Amichai, *tr. fr. Hebrew by* Warren Bargad *and* Stanley F. Chyet. IP

"Light on the Tower of David, light on the Church of St. Mary." *Fr.* 3.

"This year I traveled far." *Fr.* 1.

Jerusalem, Port City. Yehuda Amichai, *tr. fr. Hebrew by* Shirley Kaufman. VWA

Jerusalem Sonnets, *sels.* James Keir Baxter.

"Bees that have been hiving above the church pond, The." *Fr.* II. ATNZ; PeNZ

"Colin, you can tell my words are crippled now." *Fr.* XXXVII. PeNZ

"Small grey cloudy louse that nests in my beard, The." *Fr.* I. ATNZ; NoP; PeNZ

"Three dark buds for the Trinity." *Fr.* XXVII. ATNZ

"Yesterday I planted garlic." *Fr.* XVIII. ATNZ; PeNZ

Jerusalem Street and Paradise Square. Closing Time. James Michie. NePoEA-2

Jerusalem the Dismembered. Uri Zvi Greenberg, *tr. fr. Hebrew by* Charles A. Cowen. *Fr.* Jerusalem. TrJP

Jerusalem the Golden. Bernard of Cluny, *tr. fr. Latin by* John Mason Neale. *Fr.* De Contemptu Mundi. WGRP, *shorter sel.*

Jerusalem's autumn has prepared a text. Autumn Music. Gabriel Preil, *tr. by* Howard Schwartz. VWA

Jervis Bay, The. *Unknown.* OxBSS

Jes' beyan a clump o' pines. The Corn Song. John Wesley Holloway. BANP

Jesous Ahatonhia. Jesse Edgar Middleton. CaP; OBCP

Jesse James. William Rose Benét. FYAP; MoAmPo; TrGrPo

Jesse James ("It was on a Wednesday night, the moon was shining bright"). *Unknown.* AS; BeLS; FaBoBe; UnPo; WiR

Jesse James ("Jesse James was a lad who killed many a man"). *Unknown.* AmFP

Jesse James ("Jesse James was a man, and he had a robber band"). *Unknown.* AmFN

Jesse James was a two-gun man. Jesse James. William Rose Benét. FYAP; MoAmPo; TrGrPo

Jessica Jane ("Jessica Jane is the kind of cook"). May Justus. RHPC

Jessie ("Jessie is both young and fair"). Bret Harte. GN

Jessie Mitchell's Mother. Gwendolyn Brooks. BoWoP; NAs; NMM

Jessie, my cousin, remembers there were gypsies. Gypsies. Alden Nowlan. NeAC

Jest, The. Austin Clarke. BIrV

Jest a-wearyin' for you. Wearyin' for You. Frank Lebby Stanton. AnAmPo

Jest 'fore Christmas. Eugene Field. FaBV; FaFP; FaPON; FPL; OHFP; PoLF

Jester in the Trench, The. Leon Gellert. PoAu-1

Jester shook his hood and bells, and leap'd upon a chair, The. The Jester's Sermon. George Walter Thornbury. BeLS

Jester walked in the garden, The. The Cap and Bells. W. B. Yeats. BrPo; ChTr; NoAM; NoP; OnMSP; RB; WSC

Jester's Plea, The. Frederick Locker-Lampson. CenHV

Jester's Sermon, The. George Walter Thornbury. BeLS

Jesu. George Herbert. MeLP

Jesu,/ if Thou wilt make. A Page's Road Song. William Alexander Percy. TrPWD

Jesu Christ, My Leman Swete. Jesus, My Sweet Lover. *Unknown.* MeEL

Jesu, Come on Board. Johann C. Pyrlaeus, *tr. fr. German by* Sheema Z. Buehne. AH

Jesu! for thy mercy endelesse. Jesu! Send Us Peace. *Unknown.* MeEL

Jesu is in my heart, his sacred name. Jesu. George Herbert. MeLP (Iesu.) OBS

Jesu, Joy of Man's Desiring. Robert Fitzgerald. NYBP

Jesu, Lord, welcom thou be. A Prayer to the Sacrament of the Altar. *Unknown.* MeEL

Jesu, Lorde, that madest me. A Hymn to Jesus. Richard of Caistre. MeEL

Jesu, Maria—I am near to death. Cardinal Newman. *Fr.* The Dream of Gerontius. ACP

Jesu, no more! It is full tide. Richard Crashaw. *Fr.* On the Bleeding Wounds of Our Crucified Lord. TrGrPo

Jesu! Send Us Peace. *Unknown.* MeEL

Jesu, sweete sone dear. The Virgin's Song. *Unknown.* NOBE

Jesu, that hast me dere iboght. A Devout Prayer of the Passion. *Unknown.* MeEL

Jesu, to Thee My Heart I Bow. Nicolaus L. Zinzendorf, *tr. fr. German by* John Wesley. AH

Jesukin ("Jesukin, nursed by me. . .") *At. to* Saint Ita, *tr. fr. Irish.* TIRV, *tr. by* George Sigerson. (Vision of Ita, The.) AnIL, *tr. by* Whitley Stokes.

Jesus. Francis Lauderdale Adams. OxBS

Jesus. James McAuley. CBAP

Jesus. Theodore Parker. AA

Jesus a Child His Course Begun. Margaret Fuller. AH

Jesus, almighty King of Blis. The Nativity. *Unknown.* MeEL

Jesus and His Mother. Thom Gunn. EaLo; OxBC

Jesus and I. Dan Crawford. BLRP

Jesus Bids Man Remember. *Unknown.* MeEL

Jesus Borned in Bethlea. *Unknown.* AmFP

Jesus Christ ("Jesus Christ was a man that travelled through the land"). Woody Guthrie. WTO

Jesus Christ our Lord. Christmas. Koh Chang-soo, tr. by the author. ACKP

Jesus Comforts His Mother. Unknown. See Baby is born, us bliss to bring, A.

Jesus Contrasts Man and Himself ("Jesus doth him bimene"). Unknown. MeEL

Jesus Drum. Pearl Cleage Lomax. CNA

Jesus, Enthroned and Glorified. Zachary Eddy. AH

Jesús, Estrella, Esperanza, Mercy. Middle Passage. ·Robert Hayden. AmNP; BPo; IDB; InPS; NoAM; PoBA

Jesus, grant us all a blessing. Shouting Song. Unknown. AmFP

Jesus Himself. Henry Burton. BLRP

Jesus, I Come to Thee. Nathan S. S. Beman. AH

Jesus, I Live to Thee. Henry Harbaugh. AH

Jesus, in Sickness and in Pain. Thomas H. Gallaudet. AH

Jesus, Keep Me Near the Cross. Fanny Crosby. AH

Jesus, Lover of My Soul. Charles Wesley. WGRP
(In Temptation.) NOEC; PoEL-3

Jesus Loves Me, This I Know. Anna Bartlett Warner. AH

Jesus, Master, O Discover. Unknown. AH

Jesus, Merciful and Mild! Thomas Hastings. AH

Jesus' mother never had no man. Conception. Waring Cuney. BANP

Jesus! my Shepherd, Husband, Friend. John Newton. Fr. The Name of Jesus. TrPWD

Jesus, My Sweet Lover. Unknown. MeEL

Jesus on the Sabbath. Unknown, tr. fr. Irish by Brendan Kennelly. TIRV

Jesus, our brother, kind [or strong] and good. The Friendly Beasts. Unknown. FaPON; ILY; OnMSP; PChr

Jesus Reassures His Mother. Unknown. MeEL

Jesus Reproaches His People. Unknown. MeEL

Jesus said/ we are all brothers. ZINZ. Alma Villanueva. CCP

Jesus Saviour, Pilot Me. Edward Hopper. AH; BLRP

Jesus Shall Reign Where'er the Sun. Isaac Watts. WGRP
(King Triumphant.) BLRP

Jesus, Shepherd of Thy Sheep. George Washington Bethune. AH

Jesus, son of the living God. Jesus on the Sabbath. Unknown, tr. by Brendan Kennelly. TIRV

Jesus Spreads His Banner o'er Us. Roswell Park. AH

Jesus, teach me how to be. The Housewife. Catherine Cate Coblentz. BLRP; TrPWD

Jesus Tender Shepherd. Mary Lundie Duncan. BLRP

Jesus, there is no dearer name than thine. Jesus. Theodore Parker. AA

Jesus, These Eyes Have Never Seen. Ray Palmer. AH

Jesus, thou art the sinner's friend. 'Tis Sweet to Rest in Lively Hope. Unknown. AmFP

Jesus, Thou Divine Companion. Henry van Dyke. AH

Jesus, Thou Joy of Loving Hearts. Saint Bernard of Clairvaux, tr. fr. Latin. WGRP

Jesus to Those Who Pass By. Unknown. MeEL

Jesus Understands. Unknown. BLRP

Jesus Was Crucified or: It Must Be Deep. Carolyn M. Rodgers. BlSi; PoBA

Jesus, Won't You Come B'm-By? Unknown. AS

Jesus woundes so wide. The Wells of Jesus Wounds. Unknown. MeEL

Jet. John Travers Moore. RR

Jet Ring Sent, A. John Donne. OxBSP

Jew. Pierre Morhange, tr. fr. French by Edouard Roditi. VWA

Jew. James A. Randall, Jr. BPo

Jew, The. Isaac Rosenberg. MoBrPo; VWA

Jew. Karl Shapiro. VWA

Jew at Christmas Eve, The. Karl Shapiro. VGW

Jew in the painting by Chagall, The. Painting. A. C. Jacobs. VWA

Jew of Malta, The, sel. Christopher Marlowe.
Mine Argosy from Alexandria. Fr. I, i. ChTr

Jew to Jesus, The. Florence Kiper Frank. WGRP

Jew Walks in Westminster Abbey, A. Aubrey Hodes. TrJP

Jew was always treated, The. Dubrovnik Poem (Emilio Tolentino). Anthony Rudolf. VWA

Jew Wrecked in the German Cell, The. W. H. Auden. WaP

Jewel, The. James Wright. CAPP; CoAP; NAAL-2

Jewel of the secret treasury, The. Hafiz, tr. fr. Persian by Gertrude Lowthian Bell. Fr. Odes, VI. AWP

Jewel Stairs' Grievance, The ("The jewelled steps are already quite white with dew"). Li Po, tr. fr. Chinese by Ezra Pound. NOBA; OBVE

Jewel towers relay to jewel towers. Amy Károlyi, tr. fr. Hungarian by Laura Schiff. Fr. The Third House, VI. OV

Jewelled mine of the pomegranate, whose hexagons of honey, The. The Pomegranate. Louis Dudek. OBCV

Jewels, The. Baudelaire, tr. fr. French. BoLoP, tr. by Roy Campbell; ErPo, tr. by Paul Blackburn; NAWM-2, tr. by David Paul

Jewels, The. Austin Clarke. MoAB

Jewish Arabic Liturgies. Unknown, tr. fr. Arabic by Hartwig Hirschfeld. TrJP

Jewish Cemetery, The. César Tiempo, tr. fr. Spanish by Angela McEvan-Alvarado. VWA

Jewish Cemetery at Newport, The. Longfellow. AmPP; HAP; HeIP; HoPM; NOBA; NoP; OxBA; TAP

Jewish Cemetery near Leningrad, A. Joseph Brodsky, tr. fr. Russian by Dimitry Pospielovsky and Keith Bosley. VWA

Jewish Child Prays to Jesus, A. Ilse Blumenthal-Weiss, tr. fr. German by Erna Baber Rosenfeld. VWA

Jewish Conscript, The. Florence Kiper Frank. TrJP

Jewish Girls, The. Berta Lask, tr. fr. German by Susan L. Cocalis. DMG

Jewish Graveyards, Italy. Philip Levine. BLA

Jewish king now walks at large and sound, The. Zaph Describes the Haunts of Malzah. Charles Heavysege. Fr. Saul. OBCV

Jewish Kingdoms. Jacob Glatstein, tr. fr. Yiddish by Benjamin and Barbara Harshav. AYP

Jewish Main Street. Irving Layton. CaP; VWA

Jewish May, The. Morris Jacob Rosenfeld, tr. fr. Yiddish by Rose Pastor Stokes and Helena Frank. TrJP

Jewish Poet Counsels a King, A. Santob de Carrion, tr. fr. Spanish. Fr. Consejos y Documentos al Rey Dom Pedro. TrJP

Jewish Woman, The. Gertrud Kolmar, tr. fr. German by Henry A. Smith. VWA

Jews, The. George Herbert. JCP

Jews, The. Mieczyslaw Jastrun, tr. fr. Polish by Isaac Komem. VWA

Jews, The. Henry Vaughan. OBS

Jews at Haifa. Randall Jarrell. MoAMPo

Jew's Calendar, A. Karen Gershon. CN

Jews in Hell, The. Isaac Goldemberg, tr. fr. Spanish by David Unger. VWA

Jews in the Land of Israel. Yehuda Amichai, tr. fr. Hebrew by Warren Bargad and Stanley F. Chyet. IP

Jews of Brisk, The. Judd Teller, tr. fr. Yiddish by Grace Schulman. PeBMYV

Jezebel: Her Progress, sels. Gillian Eve Hanscombe.
"Men made myths." AIW
"Mrs. Snatcher Thatcher." BrRo

Jezreel. Thomas Hardy. NoP

Jig, A. Robert Greene. See Menaphon: Doron's Jigge.

Jig for Sackbuts. D. B. Wyndham Lewis. ErPo

Jig Tune: Not for Love. Thomas McGrath. VGW

Jigger Bush hollered horses, The. Buckin' Horse Ballet. Lucky Whipple. CowP

Jigsaw Puzzle. Russell Hoban. NTCP

Jigsaw Puzzles. K. Schippers, tr. fr. Dutch by Peter Nijmeijer. DuIn

Jill. Ronald David Laing. WeW

Jill, Afterwards. Philip Dacey. MOWH; SM

Jillian of Berry. Beaumont and Fletcher. Fr. The Knight of the Burning Pestle, IV, v. EIL
(Another Song.) OBS

Jilted Nymph, The. Thomas Campbell. EnLoPo

Jim. Hilaire Belloc. See Jim, Who Ran Away from His Nurse, and Was Eaten by a Lion.

"Jim." Bret Harte. AA; AnAmPo

Jim and I as children played together. Oh Lucky Jim! Unknown. ChTr; GBP

Jim Bludso of the Prairie Belle. John Milton Hay. AA; AnAmPo; BeLS; FaBoBe; FaFP

Jim Crow Cars. Lizelia Augusta Jenkins Moorer. CBWP-3

Jim Desterland. Hyam Plutzik. RB; VGW

Jim Dumps was a most unfriendly man. Force. Unknown. FaBoUs

Jim Fisk. Unknown. AS

Jim I Would Like to Know. Hans Lodeizen, tr. fr. Dutch by Peter Nijmeijer. DuIn

Jim Jay. Walter de la Mare. BrPo; CenHV; SD; SO

Jim Jones. Unknown. CBAP; PoAu-1

Jim says a sailor man. When We Are Men. Stella Mead. BoTP

Jim the Splitter. Henry Clarence Kendall. PoAu-1

Jim, Who Ran Away from His Nurse, and Was Eaten by a Lion. Hilaire Belloc. CenHV; ChTr; OxBChV
(Jim.) CenHV; ChTr; NoAM

Jiminy Whillikers/ Admiral Samuel. Monarch of the Sea. George Starbuck. OBAL

Jimmie's got a goil. E. E. Cummings. RR

Jimmy Drummond used bad language at school.   Clear the Way.   John Montague.   FaBCIP
Jimmy Jet and His TV Set.   Shel Silverstein.   OBCA; RHPC
Jimmy Judge.   *Unknown*.   AmFP
Jimmy the Mowdy.   Greedy Tom.   *Unknown*.   OxNR
Jimmy's Enlisted; or, The Recruited Collier.   *Unknown*.   CoMu; EBEV; OBET
Jimson weed.   Magnetized.   Arthur Sze.   BrSi
Jinan means eternal waiting.   Descent of Abu Nuwas.   Hasab al-Shaikh Jafar, *tr. by* Diana Der Hovanessian *and* Salma Khadra Jayyusi. MAP
Jingle Bells.   James S. Pierpont.   FaFP
Jingle bells! jingle, bells!   *Unknown*.   OxNR
Jinny the Just.   Matthew Prior.   NOBE; NOEC; OBEV; PoEL-3
Jitterbugging in the Streets.   Calvin C. Hernton.   PoBA
Jittery Jim.   William Jay Smith.   RHPC
Jittoku, Buddhist Mystic—15th Century.   Jane Cooper.   ER
Jo Jo, My Child.   *Unknown, tr. fr. Hebrew by* Immanuel Olsvanger. TrJP
Joachim of Flora.   Charles Spear.   ATNZ
Joan/ did you never hear.   To Joan.   Lucille Clifton.   GeTw
Joan Benoit.   Rina Ferrarelli.   ASP
Joan Brown, about Her Painting.   Kathleen Fraser.   NPGG
Joan Miró.   Ruthven Todd.   EAS
Joan of Arc.   Hugh McCrae.   PoAu-1
Joan of Arc to the Tribunal.   Anthony Frisch.   CaP
João was young like us.   The Poem of João.   Noémia da Sousa, *tr. by* Margaret Dickinson.   WMBCH
Job ("There was a man in The Land of Uz whose name was Job").   Bible, *O.T.*   NAWM-1, *abr.*
Sels.
   "Behold, God is great, and we know him not," XXXVI: 26–30, 32. ImOP
   "Canst thou draw out Leviathan with an hook[e]?"   MOS, XLI: 1–10; OBVE, XLI.
      (Leviathan, XLI: 1–21)   TrGrPo
   Job's Comforters, XI: 7–8 *Moulton, Modern Reader's Bible*. WGRP
   Let the Day Perish [Wherein I Was Born].   NAs, III; OBVE, III: 3-26; TrJP, III.
      (Job Complains, III: 3–26.)   TrGrPo
      (Job's Curse, III: 3–26.)   AWP
   "Man, that is borne of a woman is of a few dayes, and full of trouble," XIV.   ChTr, XIV: 1-2; OBVE
      (Immortality, XIV: 1–12.)   WGRP
      (Job Cries Out.)   TrGrPo
      (Job's Entreaty.)   AWP
         "For there is hope for a tree," XIV: 7–17.   DL
   "Moreover the Lord answered Job, and said," XL.   OBVE
      Out of the Whirlwind, XL: 7–XLI.   AWP, XXXVIII: 2–XXXIX.
   My Soul Is Weary of My Life, X: 1–22.   EaLo
   Not Flesh of Brass, VI: 1-13.   TrJP
   " 'Surely there is a mine for silver,' "   XXVIII: 1–11.   SaC
      (Price of Wisdom.)   TrGrPo
   Then the Lord Answered ("Who is this that darkeneth counsel by words without knowledge?")   XXXVIII: 2–XXXIX.   AWP
      "Wilt thou hunt the prey for the lion?"   XXXVIII: 38–XXXIX. FM
      "Where wast thou when I laid the foundations of the earth?" XXXVIII: 4–38.   ImOP, *abr.*
      "Knowest thou the time when the wild goates of the rocke bring forth?" XXXIX.   OBVE
      Hast Thou Given the Horse Strength, XXXIX: 19–25.   ChTr
         (Horse, The.)   FaPON, *abr.*; TrGrPo
      God Replies, XXXVIII: 2–41
      "Then the Lord answered Job out of the whirlewind, and sayd," XXXVIII.   AWP; OBVE
      "Knowest thou the time when the wild goates of the rocke bring forth," XXXIX.   OBVE
Job.   Elizabeth Sewell.   EaLo
Job Davies, eighty-five.   Lore.   R. S. Thomas.   OxBC; RB
Job's Ancient Lament.   Owen Dodson.   FB
Job's Comforters.   Bible, *O.T.*   *Fr.* Job, XI: 7–8 *Moulton, Modern Reader's Bible*.   WGRP
Job's Curse.   Bible, *O.T.*   *See* Job: Let the Day Perish [Wherein I Was Born].
Job's Entreaty.   Bible, *O.T.*   *See* Job: Man, that is borne of a woman is of a few dayes, and full of trouble.
Jobson's Amen.   Kipling.   OBTV
Jock o' Dreams.   Rose Fyleman.   BoTP
Jock o' the Side.   *Unknown*.   ESPB; OxBB

Jock of [*or* o'] Hazeldean.   Sir Walter Scott.   BeLS; EnRP; GN; GTBS; GTBS-P; NAEL-2; OxBS; TEP
Jock the Leg and the Merry Merchant.   *Unknown*.   ESPB
Jockey, A.   Ron Koertge.   TSL
Joe Bowers.   *Unknown*.   AmFP;
Joe Gillon Hypnotizes His Son.   Albert Goldbarth.   SM
Joe Green Joe Green O how are you doing today?   An Old Inmate. Kenneth Mackenzie.   PoAu-2
Joe Hill.   Alfred Hayes.   UnPo
Joe Turner Blues.   *Unknown*.   AS
Joe's No Saint.   John D. Sheridan.   TIRV
Jog On, Jog On.   *Unknown*.   ChTr; GBP
Jog On, jog on, the footpath way.   Shakespeare.   *Fr.* The Winter's Tale, IV, ii.   FaBoCh; GN
   (Autolycus's Song ("Jog on, jog on, the footpath way").)   OBSC
   (Merry Heart, A.)   EiL; TrGrPo
   (Merry Heart, The.)   BoTP
   (Song: "Jog on, jog on, the footpath way.")   OxBSP
Jogger from Schönbrunn, The.   Hermann Jandl, *tr. fr. German by* Beth Bjorklund.   CoAuP
Jogging Injury, A.   Fleda Brown Jackson.   TSL
Jogging out of a stand of pin oak and.   Still Life.   Mike Angelotti. MOWH
Johann Joachim Quantz's Five Lessons.   William Sydney Graham. FaBoMo
Johannes Agricola in Meditation.   Robert Browning.   TOF
Johannes Milton, Senex.   Robert Bridges.   CMoP; LiTB; PoEL-5
John.   Bible, *N.T.*   *See* St. John.
John.   N. M. Bodecker.   RHPC
John.   Ebenezer Elliott.   Son
John Adams lies here, of the parish of Southwell.   On a Carrier Who Died of Drunkenness.   Abel Byron.   NBLV
John Adkins' Farewell.   *Unknown*.   AmFP
John and Peter and Robert and Paul.   The Chemistry of Character. Elizabeth Dorney.   BLPA
John Anderson.   Burns.   *See* John Anderson, My Jo ("John Anderson my jo, John,/ When we were first acquent").
John Anderson My Jo ("John Anderson my jo, John,/ I wonder what you mean").   *At.* to Burns.   CoMu; ErPo; OxBS
John Anderson, My Jo ("John Anderson my jo, John,/ When we were first acquent").   Burns.   AWP; BoLoP; EnRP; FaBV; FF; HeIP; InPK; NOBE; NOEC; NoP; OBEV; PoE; PrIm; TrGrPo
   (John Anderson.)   GTBS; GTBS-P; LiTB; WBLP
John B. Sails, The.   *Unknown*.   AS
John Barleycorn.   Burns.   FaBoCh
   ("There was three kings into the east.")   RB
John Barleycorn.   *Unknown*.   OBET
John Barley-Corn, My Foe.   Charles Follen Adams.   OBAL
John Barleycorn's Diary: An Uncoloured Picture ("John Barleycorn walked eawt one morn").   Cornelius McManus.   PF
John Berryman asked me to write a poem about roosters.   A Poem with Capital Letters.   Jane Cooper.   FaBoWP
John Betjeman's Brighton.   Gavin Ewart.   FaBoPa
John Bird, a laborer, lies here.   Sylvia Townsend Warner.   MoBrPo
John Bright.   Francis Barton Gummere.   AA
John Brown.   Harry Lyman Koopman.   AA
John Brown.   Vachel Lindsay.   *Fr.* The Booker Washington Trilogy, II. MoAmPo
John Brown.   Edna Dean Proctor.   PAH
John Brown; a Paradox.   Louise Imogen Guiney.   PAH
John Brown died on the scaffold for the slave.   John Brown.   Edna Dean Proctor.   PAH
John Brown in Kansas settled, like a steadfast Yankee farmer.   How Old Brown Took Harper's Ferry.   Edmund Clarence Stedman.   OnMSP; PAH; PoNe
John Brown of Ossawatomie spake on his dying day.   Brown of Ossawatomie.   Whittier.   PAH
John Brown's Body, *sels.*   Stephen Vincent Benét.
   Battle of Gettysburg, The.   BeLS
   "He was a farmer, he didn't think much of towns."   AiP
   Jack Ellyat Heard the Guns.   PoLF
   John Brown's Prayer.   PoNe
   Love Came By from the Riversmoke.   MoAmPo
   Robert E. Lee.   AmFN
   Song of the Riders.   MoAmPo
   Three Elements.   EaLo
John Brown's Prayer.   Stephen Vincent Benét.   *Fr.* John Brown's Body. PoNe
John Brown's Prayer.   *At. to* Charles Sprague Hall *and to* Thomas Brigham Bishop.   FaFP
   (Glory Hallelujah! or, John Brown's Body.)   PAH

John Bull, Esquire, my jo John. A New Song to an Old Tune. *Unknown.* PAH
John Bun. *Unknown.* FaBoCo; NBLV
John Burns of Gettysburg. Bret Harte. AnAmPo; OHIP; PAH
John Butler Yeats. Jeanne Robert Foster. GoYe
John Button Birthday. Frank O'Hara. NAs
John Cabot, out of Wilma, once a Wycliffe. Riot. Gwendolyn Brooks. BPo; PoBA; TAP
John Chapman. Richard Wilbur. OxBC
John Charles Frémont. Charles Fletcher Lummis. PAH
John Cherokee. *Unknown.* GBP
John Clare. Jon Anderson. AmPA
John Clare. Mark Halperin. SM
John Clare and the Acts of Enclosure. Neil Curry. NPo
John Coltrane—an Impartial Review. Alfred B. Spellman. CNA; PoBA
John Cook had a little grey mare. Mother Goose. OxNR
John could take his clothes off. John. N. M. Bodecker. RHPC
John Donne. James Simmons. CIP
John Donne's Statue. John Peale Bishop. EyDe
John Dory. *Unknown.* ESPB; OxBSS, *with music*
John Douglas White. Mabel Ferrett. CN
John Endicott, *sels.* Longfellow. PAH
  Proclamation, The.
  "To-night we strive to read, as we may best."
John Evereldown. E. A. Robinson. AnAmPo; CMoP; OxBA
John Fane Dingle. Glaucopis. Richard Hughes. OBMV
John Filson. William Henry Venable. PAH
John Garfield. Nicholas Christopher. MAYP
John Gibson's Bat. Michael S. Harper. AnAn
John Gilpin. William Cowper. InVP
  (Diverting History of John Gilpin, The.) BeLS; FaBoBe; FiP; GN; OBNV
John Gorham. E. A. Robinson. MoAB; MoAmPo
John Graydon. Wilson Pugsley MacDonald. CaP
John Grumlie. Allan Cunningham. GBP; PoLF; SaC
John Hardy. *Unknown.* AmFP; FaBoBa
John Harralson, John Harralson, you are a wretched creature. Two Appeals to John Harralson, Agent. *Unknown.* OBAL
John Henry. *Unknown.* FaBoBa; FaFP; NOBA; OxBoLi; TrGrPo
  ("John Henry tol' his cap'n.") AS; BeLS
  ("When John Henry was a little babe [*or* fellow].") AmFP; BPo
  ("When John Henry was nothin' but a baby.")
John Henry, Cardinal Newman. Maurice Sagoff. SoTCo
John Henry was a lil [*or* little] baby. John Henry. *Unknown.* FaBoBa; FaFP; NOBA; OxBoLi; TrGrPo
  ("John Henry tol' his cap'n.") AS; BeLS
  ("When John Henry was a little babe [*or* fellow].") AmFP; BPo
  ("When John Henry was about three days old"). AmFN
  ("When John Henry was nothin' but a baby.") FaBoBe
John Hielandman. *Unknown.* GBP
John. In the sound of that rebellious word. John. Ebenezer Elliott. Son
John J. Curtis. Joseph Gallagher. AmFP
John-John. Thomas MacDonagh. AWP
John Jones. Swinburne. *Fr.* The Heptalogia. NA
  (At the Piano.) FaBoNo
John Keats. Byron. *See* Who Kill'd John Keats?
John Kinsella's Lament for Mrs. Mary Moore. W. B. Yeats. CMoP; LiTM; MoAB; NoP; OAEL-2; RB
John Knox. Iain Crichton Smith. OxBS
John L. Sullivan Enters Heaven. Robert Frost. BXAP
John Landless Leads the Caravan. Iwan Goll, *tr. fr.* French by William Carlos Williams. TrJP
John, look what Mis' Nelson give me. The Easter Bonnet. Clara Ann Thompson. CBWP-2
John Masefield Relates the Story of Tom, Tom, the Piper's Son. Louis Untermeyer. *Fr.* Mother Goose Up-to-Date. MoAmPo
John Maynard. Horatio Alger, Jr. BeLS; BLPA; FaBoBe
John Mouldy. Walter de la Mare. OxBChV; RB
John of Gaunt's Dying Speech. Shakespeare. *Fr.* King Richard II. FiP
  John of Gaunt Speaks. FaBoPP; FaPoR
  (This Blessed Plot. This England.) FaBV
John of Hazelgreen. *Unknown.* ESPB
John of Tours. *Unknown, tr. fr.* French by Dante Gabriel Rossetti. AWP
John Peel. John Woodcock Graves. CH; OxBoLi; SD
John Pelham. James Ryder Randall. AA; PAH

John Quincy Adams. Rosemary *and* Stephen Vincent Benét. OBCA
John Rabbit, by Dame Eagle chased. The Eagle and the Beetle. La Fontaine, *tr. by* Elizur Wright. OBVE
John Rogers' Exhortation to His Children. *Unknown. Fr.* The New England Primer. OBCA
John Skelton. Robert Graves. BrPo
John Smith, fellow fine. *Unknown.* OxNR
John Smith is my name. *Unknown.* FaBoUs
John Smith of His Friend Master John Taylor. John Smith. SCAP
John Smith's Approach to Jamestown. James Barron Hope. PAH
John Stuart Mill. E. C. Bentley. *Fr.* Clerihews. FaBoCo; FiBHP
  (J. S. Mill.) OxBoLi
John Sutter. Yvor Winters. MoAmPo; MoP; NoAM; NOBA; QFR
John the Baptist. Louis Simpson. NePoEA
John Thomson and the Turk. *Unknown.* ESPB, (A *and* B *vers.*)
John, Tom, and James. Charles Henry Ross. NBLV; OxBChV; RHPC
John Underhill. Whittier. PAH
John warns me of nostalgia. Not Wholly Lost. Raymond Souster. OBCV
John was a bad boy, and beat a poor cat. John, Tom, and James. Charles Henry Ross. NBLV; OxBChV; RHPC
John Webster. Swinburne. *Fr.* Sonnets of English Dramatic Poets. InVP; Son
John Wesley Gaines. *Unknown.* FiBHP
John while swimming in the ocean. Brats. X. J. Kennedy. NBLV
John Winter. Laurence Binyon. MOS
John, you were figuring in the gay career. To John Lamb, Esq.: Of the South-Sea House. Charles Lamb. Son
Johnie Armstrang. *Unknown.* ESPB; OxBB
Johnie Armstrong. *Unknown.* ESPB, A *vers.*; FaBoBa; HoPM, *cond.*; NoP, A *vers.*; TrGrPo
Johnie Blunt. *Unknown.* OxBB, *with music*
Johnie Cam to Our Toun. *Unknown.* GBP
Johnie Cock. *Unknown.* ESPB, (B *vers.*)
Johnie Cock. *Unknown.* ESPB, (C *vers.*)
Johnie Cock. *Unknown.* ESPB, (A *vers.*); FaBoBa
Johnie Cock. *Unknown.* ESPB
  (Johnie o' Cocklesmuir.) OxBB
Johnie Scot. *Unknown.* ESPB
Johnna at the Windmill. Diane Glancy. CRP
Johnnie Cope. Adam Skirving. OxBS
Johnnie Courteau. William Henry Drummond. CaP
Johnnie Crack and Flossie Snail. Dylan Thomas. *Fr.* Under Milk Wood. FaPON; FiBHP; GoJo; PDV; RHPC
Johnnie Norrie. *Unknown.* OxNR
Johnny. Marci Ridlon. RAR
Johnny Appleseed. Arthur Stanley Bourinot. CaP
Johnny Appleseed. Vachel Lindsay. FaPON
Johnny Appleseed. William Henry Venable. PAH
Johnny Armstrong killed a calf. *Unknown.* OxNR
Johnny Carroll's Camp. *Unknown.* AmFP
Johnny Cock, in a May morning. Johnie Cock. *Unknown.* ESPB, (C *vers.*)
Johnny Dow [*or* Doo]. *Unknown.* FaBoCo; FaBoEE; FiBHP
Johnny Dyers. *Unknown.* AmFP
Johnny Faa, the Lord of Little Egypt. *Unknown. See* Gypsy Laddie, The.
Johnny Gallagher. *Unknown.* AmFP
Johnny German. *Unknown.* AmFP
Johnny had a little dove. Johnny's Farm. H. M. Adams. BoTP
Johnny he's risen up in the morn. Johnny of Cockley's Well. *Unknown.* EnSB
Johnny, I Hardly Knew Ye. *Unknown.* BIrV; ELP; FaBoBa; GBP; OxBoLi; WaaP
Johnny made a custard. Some Cook. John Ciardi. PDV
Johnny of Cockley's Well. *Unknown.* EnSB
Johnny Raw and Polly Clark. *Unknown.* CoMu
Johnny Sands ("A man whose name was Johnny Sands"). *Unknown.* CoMu; OBET
Johnny Sands ("There was a man named Johnny Sands, who married Betty Hague"). *Unknown.* AmFP
Johnny shall have a new bonnet. Mother Goose. OxNR
Johnny, since today is. Many Happy Returns. W. H. Auden. NAs

Johnny Spain's White Heifer. Hayden Carruth. MOWH

Johnny, take a gun—take a gun—take a gun. Take a Gun. Nancy Price. CN

Johnny Tek Away Mi Wife. Slim Beckford *and* Sam Blackwood. PBCV

Johnny Thomson, so they say. Mrs. Vickers' Daughter. *Unknown.* AmFP

Johnny's Farm. H. M. Adams. BoTP

Johnny's Hist'ry Lesson. Nixon Waterman. FPL; PoLF

Johnny's into England gane. McNaughtan. *Unknown.* OxBB

Johnny's Pet Superstition. Clara Ann Thompson. CBWP-2

Johnny's Team. Eugene Field. PWR

Johnny's the Lad I Love. *Unknown.* OxBoLi

John's manners at the table. The Visitor. Katharine Pyle. OnUR

John's words were the words. After the Rain. Stanley Crouch. CNA

Johnshaven. *Unknown.* GBP

Johnson Brothers Ltd. Rutger Kopland, *tr. fr. Dutch by* Ria Leigh-Loohuizen. DuIn

Johnson, he was riding along, as fast as he could ride. Johnson-Jinkson. *Unknown.* AmFP

Johnson-Jinkson. *Unknown.* AmFP

Johnson's Cabinet Watched by Ants. Robert Bly. MoP; NOBA

"Johnsons have her and so must we, The." Piano Lessons. Baron Wormser. MAYP

Johny Faa. *Unknown.* OxBB

Johny he has risen up i' the morn. Johnie Cock. *Unknown.* ESPB, (A vers.); FaBoBa

Joie de Vivre. Joel Dailey. UL

Join with the noble-hearted. Distich. Shuraikh. TrJP

Joined the Blues. John Jerome Rooney. AA

Joining, The. Gerda Norvig. VWA

Joining Sir Ulick's at the river's bend. Lord Crashton: The Absentee Landlord. William Allingham. *Fr.* Laurence Bloomfield in Ireland. NOIV

Jojina, My Love. *Zulu Oral Tradition, tr. by* H. Tracey. WTO

Joke, The. *Unknown.* RHPC

Joke Versified, A. Thomas Moore. FaBoCo

Joke you just told isn't funny one bit, The. The Joke. *Unknown.* RHPC

Jokesmith's Vacation, The. Don Marquis. FiBHP

Joking and somber. Crossing Ontario. Robert Grenier. IAT

Jolly Beggar, The. *At. to* James V, King of Scotland. CoMu; OxBB

Jolly Beggars, The. Burns. EnRP, *sl. diff. vers.*; NBLV; PoEL-4 *Sels.*
　Drinking Song. TrGrPo
　"I am a bard of no regard." PoE
　I Once Was a Maid. *Fr.* OxBoLi.
　"See the smoking bowl before us." GoTS
　　(Drinking Song.) TrGrPo
　"When jurt leaves bestrow the yird." NOEC

Jolly blond musician played, A. At My Wedding. Yankev-Yitskhok Segal, *tr. by* Grace Schulman. PeBMYV

Jolly boating weather. Eton Boating Song. William Johnson Cory. ELP

Jolly Driver, The. *Unknown.* CoMu

Jolly Good Ale and Old. *At. to* William Stevenson *and also to* John Still. *Fr.* Gammer Gurton's Needle: Back and Side Go Bare, Go Bare. NoP; OBEV; TrGrPo

Jolly Jankin. *Unknown.* GBP; NoP; OxBLMV; OxBoLi; PoE
　(Jankin.) NOBE
　(Jankin, the Clerical Seducer.) MeEL

Jolly Jugger, The. *Unknown. See* Draw me nere [*or* near], draw me nere [*or* near].

Jolly old sow once lived in a sty, A. The Three Little Pigs. Sir Alfred Scott Gatty. BoTP; OxBChV

Jolly Pinder of Wakefield, The. *Unknown.* ESPB, A *and* B *vers.*

Jolly Plowboy, The. *Unknown.* AmFP

Jolly Sailor's True Description of a Man-of-War, The. *Unknown.* OxBSS

Jolly Shepherd, The. *Unknown.* NOBE

Jolly shepherd, shepherd on a hill. In Praise of His Love. Sir John Wotton. EIL

Jolly Shilling, The. *Unknown.* OBET

Jolly Soldier ("I once was a seaman stout and bold"). *Unknown.* AmFP; OFD

Jolly Soldier, The. (" 'Tis of a jolly soldier that lately came from war"). *Unknown.* AmFP

Jolly Thresherman, The. *Unknown.* AmFP

Jolly Trades-Men, The. *Unknown.* CoMu

Jolly Waggoner, The. *Unknown.* OBET

Jolly Woodchuck, The. Marion Edey *and* Dorothy Grider. FaPON; PDV

Jolly Young Waterman, The. Charles Dibdin. NOEC

Jollymerry/ hollyberry. The Computer's First Christmas Card. Edwin Morgan. FaBoCo; NIP; PChr

Jonah. Zbigniew Herbert, *tr. fr. Polish by* Czeslaw Milosz. PwPP

Jonah. Aldous Huxley. ChTr

Jonah, *sel.* Bible, *O.T.*
　Jonah's Prayer. *Fr.* II: 3–11. TrJP

Jonah. *Unknown. Fr.* Patience. ACP

Jonah and the Whale. *Unknown.* BLPA

Jonah son of Amittai. Jonah. Zbigniew Herbert, *tr. by* Czeslaw Milosz. PwPP

Jonah was an immigrant, so runs the Bible tale. Darky Sunday School. *Unknown.* OxBoLi

Jonah's Canticle. Jean-Paul de Dadelsen, *tr. fr. French by* Anselm Hollo. RHTwFP

Jonah's Prayer. Bible, *O.T. Fr.* Jonah, II: 3–11. TrJP

Jonas Kindred's Household. George Crabbe. *Fr.* Tales: The Frank Courtship. OBNC

Jonathan. Rachel, *tr. fr. Hebrew by* L. V. Snowman. TrJP

Jonathan. Yona Wallach, *tr. fr. Hebrew by* Warren Bargad *and* Stanley F. Chyet. IP

Jonathan,/ Winesap,/ Sheep-nose. Cider Song. Mildred Weston. BoNaP

Jonathan Bing. Beatrice Curtis Brown. FaPON; OnMSP; PDV; RHPC

Jonathan Blake. After the Party. William Wise. FaPON

Jonathan Houghton. Edgar Lee Masters. *Fr.* Spoon River Anthology. OxBA

Jonathan Swift/ Had the gift. Lines on Swift's Ancestors. Pope. FaBoCo

Jonathan Swift Somers. Edgar Lee Masters. *Fr.* Spoon River Anthology. OBAL

Jonathan to John. James Russell Lowell. *Fr.* The Biglow Papers: 2d Series, No. II. PAH

Jones! as from Calais southward you and I. Composed near Calais, on the Road Leading to Ardres, August 7, 1802. Wordsworth. FaBoPV

Jonquils and violets smelling sweet. Before Spring. P. A. Ropes. BoTP

Jordan ("When first my lines of heav'nly joyes made mention"). George Herbert. MePo; NAEL-1; OAEL-1; OBS; OBWVE; PPP; SeCP

Jordan ("Who say[e]s that fictions on[e]ly and false hair"). George Herbert. HAP; InPS; JCP; LiTB; MeLP; MePo; NAEL-1; NOCV; NoP; OAEL-1; OBS; PoE; PoEL-2; PPP; SeCP; TEP; TrCP

Jorkyns was great; he labored in the City. The Tale of Jorkyns and Gertie; or, Vice Rewarded. R. P. Lister. NYBP

Josefa, when you sing. Spain. Arthur Symons. OBTV

Joseph and Mary walked one day. The Cherry-Tree Carol. *Unknown.* AmFP

Joseph, being seventeen years old, was feeding the flock with his brethren. Bible, *O.T. Fr.* Genesis, XXXVII: 2-35, *abr.* NAWM-1

Joseph Ben Tachfin came from the Sahara. Marrakech. Ralph Nixon Currey. PeSA

Joseph, honoured from sea to sea. The Man of the House. Katharine Tynan. TIRV

Joseph, I afraid of stars. Holy Night. Lucille Clifton. GeTw

Joseph, Jesus and Mary. *Unknown.* OHIP

Joseph Mallord Turner/ no slow learner. Vonna Adrian. SoTCo

Joseph was an old man. The Cherry-Tree Carol. *Unknown.* AmFP; ChTr; EBEV; ELP; EnSB; ESPB; FaBoBa; GBP; HeIP; OAEL-1; OBCP; OBET; OFD; OnMSP; OxBB; OxBoLi; TrGrPo

Joseph were a young man, a young man were he. The Cherry-Tree Carol. *Unknown.* AmFP

Joseph, you are crying, but you have cried enough! Song for Joseph. *Unknown, tr. by* Margaret Orbell. PeNZ

Joseph, you move beneath the blankets. I uncover you. Buchenwald, 1945. Ai. *Fr.* He Kept On Burning, II. AnAn

Josephine. Alexander Resnikoff. RHPC

Joseph's Suspicion. Rainer Maria Rilke, *tr. fr. German by* J. B. Leishman. TrCP

Joshua Fit De [*or* Fought the] Battle of [*or* ob] Jericho. *Unknown.* BPo; NOBA; TAP; TrGrPo

Joshua the son of Nun. *Unknown.* FaBoUs

Joshua's Face. Amir Gilboa, *tr. fr. Hebrew* by Shirley Kaufman. VWA

Josie. *Unknown. See* Frankie and Johnny [*or* Johnnie *or* Albert].

Josie Bliss, October 1971. Carolyne Wright. NAmP

Josina, You Are Not Dead. Samora M. Machel. WMBCH

Jottings of New York. William McGonagall. OBTV

Journal. John Ciardi. PoA

Journal, *sel.* Gayl Jones.
　3-31-70. BISi

Journal, *sels.* Edna St. Vincent Millay.

"I read with varying degrees." ImOP
"In the evening I would sit." SaC
Journal from France, A, *sel.* Gillian Clarke.
    Seamstress at St. Léon. OBTV
Journal of Albion Moonlight, The, *sels.* Kenneth Patchen. NaP
    "But there is no black jaw which cannot be broken by our word."
    "I/ want you/ to listen."
Journal of Society, The. Godfrey Turner. NOBL
Journal of the Storm. Greg Kuzma. AmPA
Journal to Stella. Morton Dauwen Zabel. PoA
Journey, The. Aidan Clarke. BoTP
Journey, *sels.* Elizabeth Cook-Lynn. HATNAP
    Dream. *Fr.* I.
    Memory. *Fr.* II.
    Sacristans. *Fr.* III.
Journey. Roy Daniells. MoCV
Journey, The. Vivienne Finch. TSM
Journey. Sam Harrison. NeIP
Journey, The. David Ignatow. Psk
Journey, The. Dan Pagis, *tr. fr. Hebrew* by Bernhard Frank. MHeP
Journey, The. Margaret Reckord. AIW
Journey. Diane Wakoski. IHMS
Journey, The. James Wright. CAPP; NoAM; PoE
Journey and Observations of a Countryman, The, *sel.* John Hawthorn.
    Deathbed, A. NOEC
Journey Back to Christmas. Gwen Dunn. OBCP
Journey in the Orient. Maria Luisa Spaziani, *tr. fr. Italian by* Ruth
    Feldman. BoWoP
Journey into France, The. *Unknown.* CoMu; FaBoBa; OBTV
Journey is a short one, The. Shunzei, *tr. fr. Japanese* by Burton Watson.
    Fr. Thirty Tanka. FCEI
Journey Nears the Road-End, The. Rabindranath Tagore, *tr. fr. Bengali*
    by Amiya Chakravarty. DL
Journey of the Magi. T. S. Eliot. EaLo; FaBoCh; FaBoMo; FaFP; HAP;
    HeIP; InPK; LiTA; LiTM; MoAB; MoAmPo; NAEL-2; NIP; NOCV;
    NoP; OBCP; OBMV; OxBTC; PChr; PoE; SoSe; TAP; TrGrPo; TwCP
Journey Onwards, The. Thomas Moore. GTBS; GTBS-P; SeCePo
Journey round the World. Ingrid Jonker, *tr. fr. Afrikaans* by Jack Cope
    and William Plomer. PBWP
Journey through the Moonlight, A. Russell Edson. LCAP
Journey through the Night. John Holloway. NePoEA
Journey to a Parallel. Bruce McM. Wright. PoNe
Journey to a Village. Wang Yü-ch'eng, *tr. fr. Chinese* by Burton Watson.
    CoBCP
Journey to Hell, A; or, A Visit Paid to the Devil, *sel.* Edward Ward.
    Parish Poor-Officers, The. NOEC
Journey to Iceland. W. H. Auden. OBTV; PoA
Journey to the Insane Asylum, The. Alfred Lichtenstein, *tr. fr. German*
    by Mary Zilzer. VWA
Journey to the Interior. Theodore Roethke. LCAP; NYBP; VGW
Journey to the Interior. William Jay Smith. DiPo
Journey toward Evening. Phyllis McGinley. GoYe; NYBP
Journey with Hands and Arms, The. Benjamin Saltman. VWA
Journeys. Meg Campbell. PeNZ
Journeys. Gary Snyder. NU
Journey's End. Humbert Wolfe. TrJP
Jove descends in sleet and snow. The Storm. Alcaeus, *tr. by* John
    Hermann Merivale. AWP
Jove for Europa[e]s love took[e] shape of bull. Barnabe Barnes. *Fr.*
    Parthenophil and Parthenophe, LXIII. AAS
Jovial Beggar, The. *Unknown.* BoTP
Jovial Marriner; or, The Sea-Man's Renown, The. John Playford. CoMu
Jovial Shepheard's Song, The. Michael Drayton. *See* Shepherd's Sirena,
    The: Trent, The.
Jovial Tinker; or, The Willing Couple, The. *Unknown.* CoMu
Jowl, Jowl and Listen. *Unknown.* OBET
Joy. Gavin Bantock. OxBTC
Joy. Robert Creeley. PPP
Joy. Clarissa Scott Delany. CDC; PoNe
Joy. Robinson Jeffers. CMoP
Joy—a beginning. Anguish, ardor. Relearning the Alphabet. Denise
    Levertov. NOBA
Joy and anger are not caused by outside things. Miscellaneous Feelings in
    the Sui Garden. Yüan Mei, *tr. by* Jonathan Chaves. CoBLCP
Joy and Peace in Believing. William Cowper. NOCV
Joy and Pleasure. W. H. Davies. OBMV
Joy and rage are not caused by things. Yüan Mei, *tr. fr. Chinese by*
    Anthony C. Yu. *Fr.* Life at the Sui Garden, II. WFTU
Joy and the soul are mates, as heart and sorrow. The Cruse. Louise
    Townsend Nicholl. NYBP
Joy at Renewal. Mao Wen-hsi, *tr. fr. Chinese* by Lois Fusek. ATF
Joy at Renewal. Niu Hsi-chi, *tr. fr. Chinese* by Lois Fusek. ATF
Joy, did I [*or* I did] lock thee up; but some bad man. The Bunch of
    Grapes. George Herbert. NAEL-1; TOF
Joy Enough. Barrett Eastman. AA
Joy for the sturdy trees. Tree-planting. Samuel Francis Smith. OHIP
Joy, I did lock thee up; but some bad man. *See* Joy, did I lock thee up;
    but some bad man.
Joy in rebel Plymouth town, in the spring of sixty-four. "Albemarle"
    Cushing. James Jeffrey Roche. PAH
Joy is a trick in the air. Birth-Dues. Robinson Jeffers. MoAB;
    MoAmPo
Joy May Kill. Michelangelo, *tr. fr. Italian* by John Addington Symonds.
    AWP
Joy of a Singer, The. Piuvkaq, *tr. fr. Eskimo.* WTO
Joy of Church Fellowship Rightly Attended, The. Edward Taylor. *Fr.*
    God's Determinations. AmPP; NAAL-1; OxBA; SCAP
    (In Heaven Soaring Up.) AH, *with music.*
Joy of Cooking, The. Elaine Magarrell. SoTCo
Joy of Cooking, The, *sel.* David Mus.
    Conserves. PoA
Joy of every drop, The. Asadullah Khan Ghalib, *tr. fr. Urdu* by Ahmed
    Ali. GoT
Joy of Fishes, The. Chuang Tzu, *tr. fr. Chinese* by Thomas Merton.
    Mes
Joy of Knowledge. Isidor Schneider. TrJP
Joy of Life. Moses ibn Ezra, *tr. fr. Hebrew* by Solomon Solis-Cohen.
    Fr. The Book of Tarshish. TrJP
Joy of Love, The. Allan Dowling. ErPo
Joy of Meeting, The. Hsüeh Chao-yün, *tr. fr. Chinese* by Lois Fusek.
    ATF
Joy of my life, full oft for loving you. Spenser. *Fr.* Amoretti, LXXXII.
    HeIP
Joy of My Life! While Left Me Here. Henry Vaughan. SeCV-1
    (Joy of My Life.) OBS
Joy of the Morning. Edwin Markham. AA; FaPON
Joy of the Yiddish Word, The, *sel.* Jacob Glatstein, *tr. fr. Yiddish* by
    Benjamin *and* Barbara Harshav.
    "Oh, let me through to the joy of the Yiddish word." AYP
Joy of Union, The. Yang Fang, *tr. fr. Chinese* by Burton Watson.
    CoBCP
Joy of Writing, The. Wisława Szymborska, *tr. fr. Polish* by Czeslaw
    Milosz. PwPP
Joy Road and Livernois. Marge Piercy. ER
Joy shakes me like the wind that lifts a sail. Joy. Clarissa Scott Delany.
    CDC; PoNe
Joy, Shipmate, Joy! Walt Whitman. MoAmPo; MOS; OHIP; TAP
Joy so short alas, the pain so near, The. Sir Thomas Wyatt. SiPS
Joy to Philip, he this day. Going into Breeches. Charles Lamb *and* Mary
    Lamb. OxBChV
Joy to the bridegroom and the bride. The Milkmaid's Epithalamium.
    Thomas Randolph. BoLoP
Joyce: By Herself and Her Friends. Joyce Grenfell. OBD
Joyce was afraid of thunder. Volcano. Derek Walcott. OxBC
Joyce's Repentance, The. *Unknown, tr. fr. Irish* by Douglas Hyde.
    TIRV
Joyful. Rose Burgunder. RAR; RHPC
Joyful [*or* Joyfull] New Ballad, A. Thomas Deloney. CoMu; OxBSS,
    with music
Joyful Noise, A. Donald Finkel. CoAP
Joyful Sound It Is, A. George Strebeck. AH
Joyfully, Joyfully Onward I Move. William Hunter. AH
Joyless/ what I have done. Liadan Laments Cuirithir. *Unknown, tr. by*
    John Montague. BIrV; PBWP
Joyous birds, hid under greenewood shade, The. Tasso, *tr. fr. Italian by*
    Edward Fairfax. *Fr.* Godfrey of Bulloigne; or, The Recoverie of
    Jerusalem, XVI. OBVE; PFI
Joys. James Russell Lowell. BoTP
Joys of Mary, The. *Unknown.* AmFP
Joys of the Country: Seven Poems, *sel.* Wang Wei, *tr. fr. Chinese* by
    Burton Watson.
    "Lush, lush, fragrant grasses in autumn green." *Fr.* 4. CoBCP
Joys of the Road, The. Bliss Carman. AnAmPo
J's the jumping Jay-walker. Phyllis McGinley. *Fr.* All around the Town.
    FaPON; RHPC
Juan Belmonte, Torero. Donald Finkel. NePoEA
Juan de Juni the priest said. Aodh Ruadh O'Domhnaill. Thomas
    MacGreevy. CIP; OBMV
Juan de Pareja: Painted by Velazquez. Richard A. Long. AmNP
Juan embark'd—the ship got under way. Byron. *Fr.* Don Juan, II.
    MOS
Juan in England. Byron. *Fr.* Don Juan, XI. FiP

Juan knew several languages—as well. Byron. *Fr.* Don Juan, XI.
OAEL-2
Juan Rulfo Moved Away. Alberto Rios. UL
Juan, the moron next door. Report from the Correspondent They Fired.
David McElroy. AmPA
Juan who has eaten circles all his life. The Man of O. Marina Rivera.
FIA
Juana. Alfred de Musset, *tr. fr. French by* Andrew Lang. AWP
Juanita. Joaquin Miller. AA
Juanita, Wife of Manuelito. Simon J. Ortiz. MAYP
Juan's Song. Louise Bogan. NYBP
Jubilant Poem. Roque Dalton, *tr. fr. Spanish by* Barbara Paschke *and*
David Volpendesta. Vol
Jubilant the music through the fields a-ringing. World Music. Frances
Louisa Bushnell. AA
Jubilate Agno, *sels.* Christopher Smart.
   "For I bless the Prince of Peace and pray that all the guns may be nail'd
   up." InPS
   For I Will Consider My Cat Jeoffry [*or* Jeoffrey]. CTC; FM; HAP;
   HeIP; NAEL-1; NOEC; NoP; OAEL-1; OBWVE; PoEL-3; PPP; Prf;
   SCV; TTTS; WeW
   (My Cat Jeoffry.) ChTr; FaBoCh; LiTB; PoE; RB; SeCePo; WiR
   (Of Jeoffry, His Cat.) NU; PrIm
   "For the air is purified by prayer which is made aloud." Prf
   "For the doubling of flowers is the improvement of the gardners talent."
   NOEC
   "For the spiritual musick is as follows." NOEC
   "Let Elizur[e] rejoice with the Partridge." OAEL-1; PoEL-3
   "Let Ephah rejoice with Buprestis, the Lord endue us with temperance
   and humanity." NOEC
   "Let Shobi rejoice with the Kastrel—blessed be the name Jesus."
   NOEC
   Rejoice in God. PoE
Jubilate Canis. Erica Jong. MAYP
Jubilate Herbis. Norma Farber. PChr
Jubilation T. Cornpone. Johnny Mercer. OBAL
Jubilee before Revolution. Andrew Lang. BXAP
Jubilo. Allen Tate. WaP
Jud' Süss Oppenheimer on His First Visit with Professor Sigmund Freud.
Judah Leib Teller, *tr. fr. Yiddish by* Benjamin *and* Barbara Harshav.
Fr. Psychoanalysis. AYP
Jud' Süss Tells about Them and about Himself. Judah Leib Teller, *tr. fr.*
Yiddish by Benjamin *and* Barbara Harshav. *Fr.* Psychoanalysis.
AYP
Judaeus Errans. Louis Golding. TrJP
Judah in Exile Wanders. George Sandys. AH
Judaism. Cardinal Newman. ACP
Judas. Gerhard Fritsch, *tr. fr. German by* Beth Bjorklund. CoAuP
Judas. Vassar Miller. MoAmPo
Judas. *Unknown.* ESPB
Judas, 2 *vers. Unknown.* ESPB; PoE
Judas Goat, The. Susan Musgrave. NIP; NOBC
Judas Iscariot. Countee Cullen. PoLF
Judas Iscariot. R. A. K. Mason. ATNZ; PeNZ
Judas Iscariot. Stephen Spender. MoAB; MoBrPo; NIP
Judas Iscariot/ sat in the upper. Judas Iscariot. R. A. K. Mason.
ATNZ; PeNZ
Judas Iscariot dour and dark. Descent for the Lost. Philip Child. CaP
Judas Maccabeus. Bible, Apocrypha. *Fr.* First Maccabees, III: 1-9.
TrJP
Judas Sells His Lord. *Unknown.* MeEL
Judean Summer. Fay Lipshitz. VWA
Judeebug's Country. Joe Johnson. PoBA
Judezmo Writer in Turkey Angry, A. Stephen Levy. VWA
Judge, judge, tell the judge. *Unknown.* OxBoLi
Judge Me, O God. Joel Barlow. AH
Judge me, O God. Psalm XLIII ("Judge me, O God. "). Bible, *O.T.*
Fr. Psalms.
   (Search, The, XLII *and* XLIII *Moulton, Modern Reader's Bible.*)
   WGRP
Judge Not. Josephine D. Henderson Heard. CBWP-4
Judge Not According to the Appearance. Christina Rossetti. TrPWD
Judge said "Stand up, boy, and dry up your tears," The. Twenty-one
Years. *Unknown.* AmFP
Judge Somers. Edgar Lee Masters. *Fr.* Spoon River Anthology.
FaBoEE; OBSV
Judge, who lives impeccably upstairs, The. Upstairs Downstairs. Hervey
Allen. PoA; PoNe
Judge with the Sore Rump, The. St. George Tucker. OBAL
Judged by my goddess' doom to endless pain. William Percy. *Fr.*
   Coelia, I. Son

Judged by the Company One Keeps. *Unknown.* BLPA; FPL; NBLV
Judgement. George Herbert. SeCP
Judgement Day. *Unknown.* WTO
Judgement of Paris. Robert Graves. KS
Judgement of Tiresias, The. Hildebrand Jacob. NOEC
Judges, *sel.* Bible, *O.T.*
   Song of Deborah, The. *Fr.* V: 1-31. AWP; BoWoP; PBWP
   (Then Sang Deborah and Barak.) TrJP
   "Blessed above women/ shall Jael the wife of Heber the Kenite be."
   Fr. V:24-31.WPOW
Judges, Judges. Gene Baro. NePoEA-2
Judging Distances. Henry Reed. *Fr.* Lessons of the War, II. BoLoP;
   GTBS-P; MoAB; NIP; NOBE; NoP; SoSe
Judging from the pictures. *Unknown, tr. fr. Japanese by* Geoffrey Bownas
   and Anthony Thwaite. PeBJV
Judgment. William Rose Benét. AnAmPo
Judgment, The. Dora Read Goodale. AA
Judgment, The. Kathleen Spivack. BoWoP
Judgment Day. Robert Garioch, *after the Italian of* Giuseppe Belli.
   OBVE
Judgment Day. William Dean Howells. AA
Judgment Day. R. S. Thomas. CRP
Judgment in Heaven, A, *sel.* Francis Thompson.
   "Heaven, which man's generations draws." MoAB; MoBrPo
Judgment of Paris, The. W. S. Merwin. NAAL-2; NNaP
Judgment of Paris, The, *sels.* Ralph Schomberg. TrJP
   Ay or Nay?.
   Courtier's a Riddle, A.
   Like Birds of a Feather.
Judgment of the Light. Aimé Césaire, *tr. fr. French by* Michael Benedikt.
   POS
Judgment of the May, The. Richard Watson Dixon. OBNC
Judicious Observation of That Dreadful Comet, A. Ichabod Wiswall.
   SCAP
Judith, *sel.* Lascelles Abercrombie.
   "Balkis was in her marble town." MoBrPo
Judith. Eloise Bibb. CBWP-4
Judith. Adah Isaacs Menken. CBWP-1
Judith, *sel.* Bible, Apocrypha.
   With Timbrels. TrJP
Judith. William Young. AA
Judith of Bethulia. John Crowe Ransom. FaBoMo; FYAP; LiTA; LiTM;
   NoAM; NOBA
Judith Recalls Holofernes. Maura Stanton. AmPA
Judy-One. Don L. Lee. TAP
Judy Sugden! Judy, I made you caper. Barnsley and District. Donald
   Davie. NoAM; OxBC
Jug Brook. Ellen Bryant Voigt. MAYP; MT
Jug, jug! Fair fall the nightingal. The Nightingale. Richard Brathwaite.
   Fr. Nature's Embassy. EiL; PBBP
Jug of water in the hand, and on, A. Dawn. Rachel, *tr. by* A. M. Klein.
   TrJP
Juggle of Myrtle Twigs, A. Edward Codish. VWA
Juggler, The. Austin Straus. TSL
Juggler. Lucien Stryk. CAPP
Juggler. Richard Wilbur. CMoP; LiTM; MoAB; NePoEA; NYBP; TAP
Jugglers keep six bottles in the air. Hazardous Occupations. Carl
   Sandburg. SaC
Juggles old bones. Morning Star Man. George Keithley. NPGG
Juggling Jerry. George Meredith. BeLS; SeCePo
Juggy's Christening. *Unknown.* NOEC
Jugs, The. Paul Celan, *tr. fr. German by* Christopher Middleton. OBVE
Jugurtha. Longfellow. AA
Juice of apples climbs in me, The. The Forbidden. Phyllis Haring.
   PeSA
JuJu. Askia Muhammad Touré. PoBA
Juju of My Own, A. Lebert Bethune. PoBA; PoNe
Juke Box Love Song. Langston Hughes. GrPl; IDB; PoBA; TTTS
Julia. Wendy Rose. STE
Julia, how Irishly you sacrifice. Reproach to Julia. Robert Graves.
   FaBoEE
Julia, if I chance to die. His Request to Julia. Robert Herrick. CaPo;
   OBS
Julia, my wife, has grown quite rude. From a Connecticut Newspaper.
   Levi Rockwell. FaBoUs
Julia, when thy Herrick dies. To Julia. Robert Herrick. CaPo
Julian and Maddalo. Shelley. OAEL-2, *abr.*
   "I rode one evening with Count Maddalo," *sel.* OBTV
Julian Barely Misses Zimmer's Brains. Paul Zimmer. GOYP
Juliana, *sel.* Cynewulf, *tr. fr. Anglo-Saxon by* Charles W. Kennedy.
   "I have great need that the Saint grant help." AnOE

Julia's Petticoat. Robert Herrick. CaPo
Juliet. Hilaire Belloc. BoLoP; EnLoPo
Juliet, farewell. I would not be forgiven. Wilfrid Scawen Blunt. *Fr.* The
    Love Sonnets of Proteus: Farewell to Juliet, XXXIX. TrGrPo
Julius Caesar, *sels.* Shakespeare.
    Antony's Oration [over Caesar's Body]. *Fr.* III, iii. LiTB; TrGrPo
    (Mark Antony Addresses the Mob.) FaPoR
    "Cowards die many times before their deaths." *Fr.* II, ii. FF
    (That Men Should Fear.) TrGrPo
    Portrait of Brutus. *Fr.* V, v. TrGrPo
    (Noblest Roman, The.) FaFP
    Portrait of Caesar. *Fr.* I, ii. TrGrPo
Julius Caesar. *Unknown.* InPK
Julius Caesar and the Honey-Bee. Charles Tennyson Turner. FM
July. Henrietta Cordelia Ray. CBWP-3
July. Folgore Da San Gimignano, *tr. fr. Italian by* Dante Gabriel
    Rossetti. *Fr.* Sonnets of the Months. AWP
July. Susan Hartley Swett. GN
July 4, 1984: For Buck. June Jordan. NoAM
July 4th. May Swenson. PoA
July 4th. Anne Waldman. UL
July 4th, 1981 and all is Hell. Elegy for the Forgotten Oldsmobile.
    Adrian C. Louis. STE
July in Indiana. Robert Fitzgerald. AiP; NYBP
July in Washington. Robert Lowell. LCAP; NAAL-2; NaP; Prf
July Morning. Andreas Okopenko, *tr. fr. German by* Beth Bjorklund.
    Fr. Summer Fragments, II. CoAuP
July 1914. "Anna Akhmatova," *tr. fr. Russian by* Stanley Kunitz.
    WPOW
July sun burns down on the sandy beaches. To the Atoyac. Ignacio
    Manuel Altamirano, *tr. by* Samuel Beckett. MexPo
July the First. Robert Currie. Psk
July the first, of a morning clear, one thousand six hundred and ninety.
    The Boyne Water. *Unknown.* FaPoR; NOIV
July: The Succession of the Four Sweet Months. Robert Herrick. *See*
    First, April, she with mellow showers.
July the twenty-second day. The Descent on Middlesex. Peter St. John.
    PAH
July 31. Norman Jordan. PoBA
7,22,66. Sandra McPherson. AnAn
July Wakes. Richard Pomfret. OBET
Jumbled in the Common Box. W. H. Auden. PoRA
Jumbled rocks push up through flowers' roots. Brown Oxen Knoll. Chu
    Yi-tsun, *tr. fr. Chinese by* Irving Lo. *Fr.* Quatrains on Peking's
    Western Suburb, VI. WFTU
Jumbled sight, A. Paperclips. X. J. Kennedy. TSS
Jumblies, The. Edward Lear. BLPL; ChTr; EBEV; FaBoBe; FaBoNo;
    FaFP; GoJo; LiTB; MOS; NA; NAEL-2; OnMSP; OxBChV; OxBoLi;
    PoRA; TEP; WiR
Jump bigness upward. Mwilu/ or Poem for the Living. Don L. Lee. JB
Jump Cabling. Linda Pastan. InPK
Jump—jump—jump—Jump away. The Little Jumping Girls. Kate
    Greenaway. FaPON
Jump or Jiggle. Evelyn Beyer. RAR
Jump over the wall and come to me. Come to Me. *Gond Oral
    Tradition,* tr. by V. Elwin *and* S. Hivale. WTO
Jump-Rope Rhyme. *Unknown.* NTCP
Jump Shooter, The. Dennis Trudell. TSL
Jump shot? It's all in the wrist, The. Nothing but Net. Roy Scheele.
    ASP; TDD
Jump stone hand leaf shadow sun. The Fire. Robert Duncan. *Fr.*
    Passages. VGW
Jumper. Tony Harrison. NPo
Jumping Bean. Mary Ann Hoberman. TSS
Jumping into Joy. Marg Yeo. DT
Jumping-Jack Flash. Leslie Scalapino. BAP
Juncture. Rea Lubar Duncan. PoNe
June. Bryant. AA
June. Elaine Feinstein. BrRo
June. Aileen Fisher. PDV
June. Mary Weston Fordham. CBWP-2
June. Francis Ledwidge. BIrV; NOIV
June ("Over his keys the musing organist"). James Russell Lowell. *See*
    Vision of Sir Launfal, The: Over his keys the musing organist.
June ("What is so rare as a day in June?"). James Russell Lowell. *See*
    Vision of Sir Launfal, The: What [*or* And what] Is So Rare as a Day
    in June?
June. Wilson Pugsley MacDonald. CaP
June. Medbh McGuckian. FaBCIP
June. Irene F. Pawsey. BoTP
June. Theodore Harding Rand. CaP

June. Henrietta Cordelia Ray. CBWP-3
June. Folgore Da San Gimignano, *tr. fr. Italian by* Dante Gabriel
    Rossetti. *Fr.* Sonnets of the Months. AWP
June. Jane G. Stewart. BoTP
June Bracken and Heather. Tennyson. EnLoPo
June in Wiltshire. Geoffrey Grigson. WaP
June Morning. Hugh McCrae. PoAu-1
June Song of a Man Who Looks Two Ways. Leslie Daiken.
    NeIP
June sun in an orchard, A. My Mother's Burying. Sean O Riordain, *tr.
    by* Valentine Iremonger. TIRV
June 10. Magdalena de Rodriguez, *tr. fr. Spanish by* Nina Serrano.
    WPOW
June Thunder. Louis MacNeice. CMoP
June Twilight. John Masefield. GoYe
June war is over, The. Nizar Qabbani, *tr. fr. Arabic by* Diana Der
    Hovanessian *and* Lena Jayyusi. *Fr.* The Actors, IX. MAP
June Weather. James Russell Lowell. *See* Vision of Sir Launfal, The:
    For a cap and bells our lives we pay.
Junes were free and full, driving through tiny, The. June Thunder. Louis
    MacNeice. CMoP
Jung-sup Lee I Saw. Ruth Kim Chun-soo, *tr. fr. Korean by* Koh Chang-
    soo. ACKP
Jungle, The. Diane DiPrima. PoM
Jungle. Phyllis Haring. PeSA
Jungle, The. Alun Lewis. OBWVE
Jungle. Mary Carter Smith. PoNe
Jungle, The. Randolph Stow. *Fr.* Thailand Railway. CBAP
Jungle/ takes over the garden. The Indolent Gardener. Mary Kennedy.
    BoNaP
Jungle Book, The, *sel.* Kipling.
    Seal Lullaby. FaPON; SoSe
Jungle Café, The. Gary Soto. NoAM
Jungle Husband, The. Stevie Smith. FaBoWP; NBLV; RB
Jungle is the frame for the machine, The. The Bulldozer. Donald A.
    Stauffer. WaP
Jungle Mammy Song. *Unknown.* AS
Jungle spreads, The. In Praise of a Cremation Ground. Kataiyan
    Kannanar, *tr. by* A. K. Ramanujan. PLW
Jungle Taste. Edward S. Silvera. CDC
Jungle Trees, The. Marjorie Wilson. BoTP
Junglegrave. S. E. Anderson. PoBA
Jungles, *sel.* Kamal Sabti, *tr. fr. Arabic by* Lena Jayyusi *and* Naomi
    Shihab Nye.
    "What remains in the hands." MAP
Junior Addict. Langston Hughes. BPo; CNA
Juniper. Eileen Duggan. PChr
Juniper. Robert Francis. VGW
Juniper, aspen, blue spruce, just thawing snow. The Call of Nature.
    Tony Harrison. NoAM
Juniper, juniper. *Unknown.* BoTP
Juniper Moon Pulls at My Bones, The. Earle Thompson.
    HATNAP
Junk. Berysh Vaynshteyn, *tr. fr. Yiddish by* Benjamin *and* Barbara
    Harshav. *Fr.* New York Everywhere. AYP
Junk. Richard Wilbur. HAP; NoP; SaC; SM; WeW
Junk Shop, The. Henri Coulette. NYBP
Junkie with a Flute in the Rain, A. David Fisher. NPGG
Junkies loved Charles Parker and the sports, The. Historiography.
    Lorenzo Thomas. UL
Jupiter and Ganimede. Thomas Heywood. PeHV
Jupiter and Ten. James Thomas Fields. AnAmPo; OBAL
Jupiter uninhabited. Ernst Jandl, *tr. by* Beth Bjorklund. CoAuP
Jurgis Petrakas, the Workers' Angel, Organizes the First Miners' Strike in
    Exeter, Pennsylvania. Anthony Petrosky. FYAP
Just. Judith Johnson Sherwin. TAP
Just a few feet away, a temple from the Six Dynasties. Yang Chi, *tr. fr.
    Chinese by* Jonathan Chaves. *Fr.* Living in a Riverside Village—
    Miscellaneous Impressions. CoBLCP
Just a few of the roses we gathered from the Isar. Roses on the Breakfast
    Table. D. H. Lawrence. BrPo
Just a few steps. Why? A. Leyeles, *tr. by* Benjamin *and* Barbara
    Harshav. AYP
Just a herd of Negroes. Share-Croppers. Langston Hughes. SaC
Just a line to remind my friends that after much trouble. Dear Folks.
    Patrick Kavanagh. FaBoTw
Just a Little Wind. Ruth Kim Chun-soo, *tr. fr. Korean by* Koh Chang-
    soo. ACKP
Just a minute. Memory. Pierre Reverdy, *tr. by* Kenneth Rexroth.
    RHTwFP
Just a Smack at Auden. William Empson. FaBoCo; LiTM; MoBrPo;
    UnPo

Just a While. Frantisek Gottlieb, *tr. fr. Czech by* Ewald Osers. VWA
Just about Asleep Together. Molly Peacock. SM
Just about at the triple-barreled pistol. Armor. Sharon Olds. InPS
Just after Noon with Fierce Shears. Tram Combs. TwCP
Just an Old Man. Mary Goose. STE
Just an Old Sweet Song. Donagh MacDonagh. CIP
Just and fit actions Ptolemy (he saith). Lucan, *tr. fr. Latin by* Ben Jonson. *Fr.* Pharsalia, VII. OBVE
Just are the ways of God. The Transcendence of God. Milton. *Fr.* Samson Agonistes. OBS
Just as a year might end. Nightsong. Louis O. Coxe. FYAP
Just as eventide draws near. Song of Longing. *Unknown, tr. by* John White. WTO
Just as he is growing a beard. Flaccus. PeHV
Just as I joy at noble autumn. To the Tune "Partridge Sky." Yang Shen, *tr. by* Jonathan Chaves. CoBLCP
Just as I stood up. Exercise ("Just as I stood up"). Pat Nolan. UL
Just as I was about to call your name. Fiesta. Paul Hannigan. PPR
Just as my fingers on these keys. Peter Quince at the Clavier. Wallace Stevens. AmPP; CMoP; HeIP; InPK; InPS; LiTM; MoAB; MoAmPo; NAWM-2; NoAM; NOBA; OxBA; PoE; PPP; TAP; TrGrPo; TwCP
Just as the earth puckered its mouth. The Abortion. Anne Sexton. CAPP
Just as the hour was darkest. The Ballad of New Orleans. George Henry Boker. PAH
Just as the signal tower lights flash. Night at an Airport. David Ignatow. NNaP
Just as the Small Waves Came Where No Waves Were. Pamela Millward. NU
Just as the spring came laughing through the strife. John Pelham. James Ryder Randall. AA; PAH
Just as the Tide Was a-Flowing. *Unknown.* OBET
Just as the twilight's holy hour. To an Infant. Mary Weston Fordham. CBWP-2
Just as those swans are, poets must be rare. On Poets. Ariosto, *tr. fr. Italian by* Edwin Morgan. *Fr.* Orlando Furioso, XXXV. PFI
Just as Thou Art. Russell Sturgis Cook. AH
Just as we were amazed to learn. The Psychopathology of Everyday Life. William Matthews. AnAn
Just as You See Me, That's How I Am. Yocheved Bat-Miriam, *tr. fr. Hebrew by* Bernhard Frank. MHeP
Just at the self-same beat of Time's wide wings. The Bruised Titans. Keats. *Fr.* Hyperion; a Fragment. OBNC
Just Be Glad. James Whitcomb Riley. WBLP
Just Because. Moyshe-Leyb Halpern, *tr. fr. Yiddish by* Ruth Whitman. VWA
Just because I forget. Letter for Duncan. Larry Eigner. PoM
Just because I smile and smile. Because. B. W. Vilakazi. PeSA
Just because some teachers go away. Brain Drain. "The Mighty Chalkdust." PBCV
Just because you said, "I'll come right away." Teika, *tr. fr. Japanese by* Hiroaki Sato. *Fr.* A Compendium of Good Tanka. FCEI
Just before midnight down by the waterfront. In the Eyes of the Gods. André Breton, *tr. by* Michael Benedikt. POS
Just behind the Battle, Mother. *Unknown.* FiBHP
Just biding my time. The Moon. Tamesada, *tr. fr. Japanese by* Steven D. Carter. *Fr.* The Moon. WFTW
Just broke from school, pert, impudent, and raw. Soame Jenyns. *Fr.* The Modern Fine Gentleman. OBSV
Just Dessert. Colette Inez. SoTCo
Just Dropped In. William Cole. FiBHP; GoJo
Just ere the darkness is withdrawn. Sleep and His Brother Death. William Hamilton Hayne. AA
Just falling asleep is accidental. An Old Man's Thought. Natsume Seibi, *tr. fr. Japanese by* Hiroaki Sato. *Fr.* Twenty-seven Hokku. FCEI
Just Folks. Edgar Albert Guest. FaFP
Just for a cup of coffee? How exactly should one put it? The Mad Town. István Vas, *tr. fr.* William Jay Smith. MHuP
Just for a handful of silver he left us. The Lost Leader. Robert Browning. FaBoPV; NAEL-2; PWR; TrGrPo
Just for a handful of summits he left us. The Lost Leader. Douglas Fraser. PoSH
Just for a moment on the first day. Persephone. Keith Abbott. UL
Just for a space that I met her. Incognita. Austin Dobson. CenHV; EBVV
Just for One Day. Lillian Morrison. RHPC
Just for the Ride. *Unknown.* FaFP
Just for To-Day. Ernest R. Wilberforce. PWR
Just Forget. Myrtle May Dryden. WBLP
Just Friends. Robert Creeley. NeAP
Just God! and these are they. Clerical Oppressors. Whittier. NAAL-1; PAH
Just got used to. Sneakers. Judith Herzberg, *tr. by* Scott Rollins. DuIn

Just How Crazy Brenda Is. Melinda Goodman. GLP
Just How It Happened. Priscilla Jane Thompson. CBWP-2
Just imagine yourself seated on a shadowy terrace. That Reminds Me. Ogden Nash. FiBHP
Just in the gray of the dawn, as the mists uprose from the meadows. The Expedition to Wessagusset. Longfellow. *Fr.* The Courtship of Miles Standish. PAH
Just Instinct and Brute Reason. *Unknown.* PF
Just Jumbo. Eileen Mathias. BoTP
Just Keep On. Clifton Abbott. WBLP
Just life and death make up our worldly state. Ilyas Farhat, *tr. by* Salma Khadra Jayyusi *and* John Heath-Stubbs. MAP
Just like a Man. *Unknown.* BoTP
Just like an hour with neighbors, I would think. How Did It Seem to Sylvia? Gjertrud Schnackenberg. SM
Just like Me. P. W. Sinks. BLRP
Just Like Me. *Unknown.* BoTP
Just like That. Sam Hunt. ATNZ
Just like that. When he brings the new bike home. The Bicycle Rider. Thomas William Shapcott. CBAP
Just likc the heart that breaks at the onset of absence. Too Bad for Me. Louis Aragon, *tr. by* Joachim Neugroschel. POS
Just Like This. D. A. Olney. BoTP
Just listen to the grumbles of. Counting-Song. *Unknown, tr. by* Geoffrey Bownas *and* Anthony Thwaite. PeBJV
Just look at those hands! Soap. Martin Gardner. RHPC
Just look, Manetto, at that wry-mouth'd minx. Sonnet: Of an Ill-Favored Lady. Guido Cavalcanti, *tr. by* Dante Gabriel Rossetti. AWP
Just look, 'tis a quarter past six, love. The Coming Woman. Mary Weston Fordham. CBWP-2
Just Looking, Thank You. Leonard Nathan. BLA
Just lost, when I was saved! Emily Dickinson. AmPP; NOBA; NOCV; Prf
(Called Back.) AA; MoAmPo
Just Making It. Richard W. Thomas. PoNe
Just man followed then his angel guide, The. Lot's Wife. "Anna Akhmatova," *tr. by* Richard Wilbur. BoWoP; PBWP
Just Me. Margaret Hillert. RHPC
Just north of the Yaak River, one man sits bolt up-right. Mount Caribou at Night. Charles Wright. LCAP
Just Now. Ted Kooser. KS
Just Now. Benjamin Péret, *tr. fr. French by* Michael Benedikt. POS
Just now/ Out of the strange. The Warning. Adelaide Crapsey. WPE; WSC
(Cinquain: A Warning.) WeW
Just now, if I look back down. Just Now. Ted Kooser. KS
Just now the lilac is in bloom. The Old Vicarage, Grantchester. Rupert Brooke. BrPo; FaBoPP; FaBV; GoTL; MoBrPo; OBTV; OxBTC; PoRA
Just now, when frost flies and the moon wears a halo. View from the Pavilion on a Moonlit Night. Ch'en San-li, *tr. by* Irving Lo. WFTU
Just off the highway to Rochester, Minnesota. A Blessing. James Wright. CAPP; GrPl; InPK; InPS; LLLT; NAAL-2; NaP; NoAM; NOBA; NoP; PoE; PPP; TwCP
Just once. That Day. David Kherdian. SaC
Just One Book. *Unknown.* BLRP
Just One Day. Susan E. Gammons. PWR
Just one evening snipe. Kaya Shirao, *tr. fr. Japanese by* Hiroaki Sato. *Fr.* Twenty-four Hokku. FCEI
Just one hundred poems in this little book. Reading the Poetry Collection of Lü Fang-ch'ing. Chang Yü, *tr. by* Jonathan Chaves. CoBLCP
Just one mosquito raises a fuss. Issa, *tr. fr. Japanese by* Hiroaki Sato. *Fr.* Forty-four Hokku. FCEI
Just one room away, from time to time you sighed. Yosano Akiko, *tr. fr. Japanese by* Hiroaki Sato. *Fr.* Thirty-nine Tanka. FCEI
Just One Signal. *Unknown.* PAH
Just out of San Francisco one cold December day. The Dying Hobo. *Unknown.* AmFP
Just over the edge. Bus Depot Reunion. David Allan Evans. TSL
Just Passing. *Unknown.* BLRP
Just past those distressing days of languor. Summer Solstice. P'eng Sun-yü, *tr. by* William H. Nienhauser, Jr. WFTU
Just seen the bottom of the water. Joso, *tr. fr. Japanese by* Hiroaki Sato. *Fr.* Fifteen Hokku. FCEI
Just sitting around smoking, drinking and telling stories. And with March a Decade in Bolinas. Joanne Kyger. UL
Just smiling and flattering the whole day through. Mannequins. Mascha Kaléko, *tr. by* Susan L. Cocalis. DMG
Just so a person has heart. *Unknown, tr. fr. Japanese by* Burton Watson. *Fr.* Kangin Shu. FCEI
Just so it goes—the day, the night. An Ordinary Evening in Cleveland. Lewis Turco. NYBP

Just-So Stories, *sel.* Kipling.
  Hump, The. OxBChV
Just so that each stark. Crows. Charles Simic. GeTw
Just so you shouldn't have to ask again. What Kind of a Guy Was He?
  Howard Nemerov. PCP
Just stand aside and watch yourself go by. Watch Yourself Go By.
  Strickland W. Gillilan. BLPA
  (Cure for Fault Finding, A.) PWR; WBLP
Just Taking Note. Sharon Scott. JB
Just the ants at the bottom of the burning sky. Ozaki Hosai, *tr. fr.
  Japanese by* Hiroaki Sato. *Fr.* One Hundred Haiku in Free Form.
  FCEI
Just the lessons given you now. Maxims in Rhyme for the Young. J.
  Clark. PWR
"Just the place for a Snark!" the Bellman cried. The Hunting of the
  Snark. "Lewis Carroll." FaBoNo; FiBHP; NOBVV; OBNC;
  OBNV; OnMSP; PoEL-5
Just the Same To-Day. *Unknown.* BLRP; WBLP
Just the Two of Us. Tomioka Taeko, *tr. fr. Japanese.* FCEI, *tr. by*
  Hiroaki Sato; WPOW, *tr. by* Harry *and* Lynn Guest *and* Kajima
  Shozo
Just then, forgetful of the strict command. Homer, *tr. fr. Greek by*
  William Cowper. *Fr.* Odyssey, XII. OBVE
Just Think. Paul Celan, *tr. fr. German by* Joachim Neugroschel. VWA
Just This. István Vas, *tr. fr. Hungarian by* Jascha Kessler. FOC; VWA
Just this morning I signed the contract. Pearl Harbor Day 1970. Dick
  Lourie. NeAC
Just Three. William Wise. RAR
Just to be tender, just to be true. God's Will for Us. *Unknown.* BLRP;
  WBLP
  (God's Will for You and Me.) SoSe
Just Try This. *Unknown.* WBLP
Just Try to Be the Fellow That Your Mother Thinks You Are. Will S.
  Adkin. WBLP
Just Walking Around. John Ashbery. NAAL-2
Just Watch. Myra Cohn Livingston. RAR
Just what is there to do? Eat. Between Words. Gary Soto. NAmP
Just when each bud was big with bloom. Birth. Grace Raymond. AA
Just when he said the tornado. The Tornado. Norman H. Russell. STE
Just when I'm ready to. Naughty Soap Song. Dorothy Aldis. RAR
Just when our drawing-rooms begin to blaze. Winter Evening ("Just when
  our drawing-rooms begin to blaze"). William Cowper. *Fr.* The
  Task. NOEC
Just when you're able to admit. Corps d'Esprit. Heather McHugh.
  AmPA
Just where do you find. Kenko, *tr. fr. Japanese by* Steven D. Carter.
  WFTW
Just where the Treasury's marble front. Pan in Wall Street. Edmund
  Clarence Stedman. AA; AnAmPo
Justice. Langston Hughes. BPo
Justice. Petra von Morstein, *tr. fr. German by* Rosemarie Waldrop.
  BoWoP
Justice Denied in Massachusetts. Edna St. Vincent Millay. AiP; GOA;
  MoAmPo
Justice Is Reason Enough. Diane Wakoski. AmPA
Justice of Men! I Look for You. Rosalía de Castro, *tr. fr. Spanish by*
  Kate Flores. DMH
Justice of the Peace, The. Hilaire Belloc. NOBVV; OBSV
Justice to Scotland. *At. to* Burns. NBLV
Justification of the Horned Lizard. Pattiann Rogers. NAmP
Justified Mother of Men, The. Walt Whitman. OHIP
Justify all those renowned generations. The Renowned Generations. W.
  B. Yeats. OxBoLi
Justiniano Lamé Has Been Killed. Jimmie Durham. HATNAP
Justus Quidem Tu Es, Domine. Gerard Manley Hopkins. *See* Thou Art
  Indeed Just, Lord, If I Contend.
Jute Mill Song, The. *Unknown.* OBET
Juventius, could you not find in this great crowd of men. Catullus, *tr.
  fr. Latin.* PeHV
Juventius, my honey, while you played. Catullus, *tr. fr. Latin by* James
  Michie. PeHV
Juxta. Grover Jacoby. GoYe
Juxtaposition. Arthur Hugh Clough. *Fr.* Amours de Voyage, Canto III,
  vi. OBNC

K

K***. Pushkin, *tr. fr. Russian by* Alan Myers. AAA
K for the Klondyke, a country of gold. Hilaire Belloc. *Fr.* A Moral
  Alphabet. NoAM

Ka 'Ba. Amiri Baraka. BPo; CNA; TAP
Ka-la-kaua, a great name. Praise Song for King Kalakaua. *Unknown, tr.
  by* N. B. Emerson. WTO
Kabbalist, The. Deborah Eibel. VWA
Kabbalists in Safed. H. Leivick, *tr. fr. Yiddish by* Benjamin *and* Barbara
  Harshav. AYP
Kabir:/ Even worthless bushes. Kabir, *tr. fr. Hindi by* John Stratton
  Hawley *and* Mark Juergensmeyer. SSI
Kabir:/ My mind was soothed. Kabir, *tr. fr. Hindi by* John Stratton
  Hawley *and* Mark Juergensmeyer. SSI
Kabir:/ The hut was made of sticks. Kabir, *tr. fr. Hindi by* John Stratton
  Hawley *and* Mark Juergensmeyer. SSI
Kabir:/ The instrument is still. Kabir, *tr. fr. Hindi by* John Stratton
  Hawley *and* Mark Juergensmeyer. SSI
Kabir is done with stretching thread and weaving. Kabir, *tr. fr. Hindi by*
  John Stratton Hawley *and* Mark Juergensmeyer. SSI
Kabul town's by Kabul river. Ford o' Kabul River. Kipling. FaBoTw
Kaddish. Allen Ginsberg. HCAP; NAAL-2; NeAP; NOBA; PoM;
  VWA
Kaddish. David Ignatow. NU; VWA
Kaddish. Levi Yitzhok, *tr. fr. Yiddish by* Joseph Leftwich. TrJP
Kadia the Young Mother Speaks. Jessie E. Sampter. TrJP
Kafka's Other Metamorphosis. Len Gasparini. NeAC
Kafoozalum. *Unknown.* BeLS; BLPA
Kagu-yama/ The Heavenly Hill afar. Hitomaro. *Fr.* Manyo Shu. Ma
Kaisarion. Constantine P. Cavafy, *tr. fr. Greek by* Edmund Keeley *and*
  Philip Sherrard. MNV
Kaiser Dead. Matthew Arnold. FM
Kalahari. Luis Palés Matos, *tr. fr. Spanish by* Rachel Benson. InW
Kalahari Bushman fires flowing. Firebowl. Sydney Clouts. VWA
Kalaloch. Carolyn Forché. AmPA; AnAn; NOAM
Kalapuya Prophecy, A. *Unknown, tr. fr. Kalapuya Indian by* Jarold
  Ramsey. STP
Kaleidoscope, The. David Gill. OBTV
Kaleidoscope. G. K. Page. NoAM
Kaleidoscope, A. Sunfish Races. James Preston. InPK
Kalenda Maya. Raimbaut de Vaqueiras, *tr. fr. Provençal by* Paul
  Blackburn. Pro
Kallundborg Church. Whittier. BeLS
Kamal is out with twenty men to raise the Border side. The Ballad of
  East and West. Kipling. FaBoBe
Kanawâki—"By the Rapid." The Caughnawaga Beadwork Seller.
  William Douw Lighthall. CaP
Kane. Fitz-James O'Brien. PAH
Kangaroo. D. H. Lawrence. EBEV; InPS; OBTV; OxBTC
Kangaroo by Nightfall ("Kangaroo by the roadside, The"). Noel
  Macainsh. PoAu-2
Kangin Shu, *sels. Unknown, tr. fr. Japanese by* Burton Watson.
  FCEI
  "Because for one night you don't come."
  "Behind your fan."
  "Even the little minnows under the bridge."
  "Hey, crazy!/ when you know I have a husband."
  "I just had to start a conversation."
  "I wanted so to see you."
  "I'm on his mind."
  "It was just one night."
  "Just so a person has heart."
  "Wait for me."
Kansas Boy. Ruth Lechlitner. AmFN
Kansas Boys. *Unknown.* AS
Kansas City. Oscar Hammerstein II. OBAL
Kansas City West Bottoms. Edward Dahlberg. PoA
Kansas Emigrants, The. Whittier. OPP; PAH
Kanyariri, Village of Toil. The Village. Marina Gashe. PBA
Karamazov. Ben Belitt. DiL
Karate. Stanley Plumly. ASP
Karazah to Karl. Adah Isaacs Menken. CBWP-1
Kari Sober. Kapilar, *tr. fr. Tamil by* A. K. Ramanujan. PLW
Karl ("All day he stood at Weeping Cross"). Charles Spear. ATNZ
Karl ("Outside among the talking criss-cross reeds"). Charles Spear.
  ATNZ
Karl, from your beachhead on that hollow island. V-Letter to Karl
  Shapiro in Australia. Selden Rodman. WaP
Karl Heinrich Marx. Hans Magnus Enzensberger, *tr. fr. German by*
  Michael Hamburger. FaBoPV
Karl Marx. Al Lee. AmPA
Karl Marx Died 1883 Aged 65. Antonio Cisneros, *tr. fr. Spanish by*
  Maureen Ahern *and* David Tipton. Per
Karma. Pierre Kemp, *tr. fr. Dutch by* Fred van Leeuwen. DuIn
Karma. E. A. Robinson. AmPP; CMoP; HeIP; MoAB; MoAmPo; OFD;
  TrCP

Karolin's Song. Ben Jonson. *See* Sad Shepherd, The: Though I Am Young and Cannot Tell.

Karoo Town. Robert Dederick. PeSA

Karshish, the picker-up of learning's crumbs. An Epistle Containing the Strange Medical Experience of Karshish, the Arab Physician. Robert Browning. NAEL-2

(Karshish, the Arab Physician.) WGRP

Kashmiri Song. Laurence Hope. BLPA; BLPL; FaBoBe; FaFP

Kashrut. Edouard Roditi. VWA

"Kat" can play ball, Man, The. Funky Football. Ruby C. Saunders. BlSi

Kate and I. Susan Navarre Tarrant. TDD

Kate and the Cowhide. *Unknown.* AmFP

Kate Dalrymple. *Unknown.* GBP

Kate Kearney. Sady Morgan. BLPA; FaBoBe

Kate meets me at the top of the stairs. At Veronica's. Robert Peterson. NeAC

Kate rose up early as fresh as a lark. Wind's Work. T. Sturge Moore. BrPo

Kathaleen Ny-Houlahan. William Heffernan, *tr. fr. Irish by* James Clarence Mangan. NOIV

Katharine Jaffray. *Unknown.* ESPB, (A, B *and* C *vers.*)

Käthe Kollwitz. Muriel Rukeyser. NMM

Katherine is warm. Why? Melba Joyce Boyd. BlSi

Katherine Jaffray. *Unknown.* OxBB

Kathleen Mavourneen. *At. to* Louisa Macartney Crawford. FaBoBe

Kathleen ni Houlihan. The Celtic Fringe. Stevie Smith. FaBoNo

Katie Lee and Willy [*or* Willie] Grey. *At. to* Josie R. Hunt *and to* J. H. Pixley. BeLS; BLPA

Katskills Kiss Romance Goodbye, The. Ishmael Reed. UL

Katydid stops chirping, A. Kaya Shirao, *tr. fr. Japanese by* Hiroaki Sato. *Fr.* Twenty-one Hokku. FCEI

Katydids. Amy Lowell. PBWP

Katzenjammer Kids, The. James Reaney. MoCV; OBCV

Kavin Again. Richard Hovey. AnAmPo

Kay-You-Enn-Aye Radio, Iowa. Michael Augustin, *tr. fr. German by* Margitt Lehbert. WCI

Kayak, The. *Unknown.* FaPON

Kayak Song, A. Lucy Diamond. BoTP

Kayenta Times Yet Dreaming On. Nia Francisco. HATNAP

Kearney at Seven Pines. Edmund Clarence Stedman. AA; AnAmPo; PAH

Kearsarge. Silas Weir Mitchell. PAH

Kearsarge, The. James Jeffrey Roche. AA; PAH

Kearsarge and *Alabama. Unknown.* PAH

Keats. Longfellow. Son; TAP

Keats. William Wilberforce Lord. *Fr.* Ode to England. AA

Keats. Lizette Woodworth Reese. AA

Keats to Fanny Brawne. Edgar Lee Masters. PoA

Keelhauled across the star-wrecked death of God. George Barker. *Fr.* Sonnets of the Triple-headed Manichee, II. PoA

Keel's echo small stagger. Ripe Tack. Ray DiPalma. LP

Keen hawk, on that elm-bough gravely sitting. Just Instinct and Brute Reason. *Unknown.* PF

Keen stars were twinkling, The. To Jane. Shelley. Mes; NoP

Keen Thyself, Poor Wight. Geoffrey Keating, *tr. fr. Irish by* Padraic Pearse. TIRV

Keen to the danger. A Perilous Love Affair. Saigyo, *tr. fr. Japanese by* Burton Watson. *Fr.* Sixty-four Tanka. FCEI

Keenan's Charge. George Parsons Lathrop. AA; PAH

Keener tempests come, The: and fuming dun. James Thomson. *Fr.* The Seasons: Winter. EBEV; EnRP; NoP

Keening of Mary, The. *Unknown, tr. fr. Irish by* Padraic Pearse. TIRV

Keep a brave spirit, and never despair. Press Onward. *Unknown.* FaFP

Keep a Dime. Debra Swallow. GOS

Keep a-Goin'. Frank Lebby Stanton. FaFP; OHFP; PWR; WBLP

Keep a Good Thought in Your Head. Martin Parker. CoMu

Keep a Hand on Your Dream. X. J. Kennedy. Psk

Keep a Poem in Your Pocket. Beatrice Schenk de Regniers. PDV; RHPC

Keep a Stiff Upper Lip. Phoebe Cary. FaFP

Keep away from roads' webs, they always lead. Directions to a Rebel. W. R. Rodgers. LiTM

Keep back the one word more. Reserve. Lizette Woodworth Reese. AA

Keep bees and. Advice to the Young. Miriam Waddington. NOBC

Keep Cool. Marcus Garvey. PBCV

Keep fresh the grass upon his grave. Wordsworth's Grave. Matthew Arnold. *Fr.* Memorial Verses. FaBoPP

Keep Hidden from Me ("Keep from me all that I might comprehend!"). Rachel Korn, *tr. fr. Yiddish by* Carolyn Kizer. PBWP

Keep in a Cool Place. Allen Curnow. ATNZ

Keep in God's way; keep pace with evry hour. To Be Engraven on a Dial. Samuel Sewall. SCAP

Keep in the heart the journal nature keeps. Conrad Aiken. *Fr.* Preludes for Memnon; or, Preludes to Attitude. CMoP; OxBA

Keep It Dark. *Unknown, tr. fr. Zezuru by* Hugh Tracey. PBA

"Keep left! To the left!" *Unknown, tr. by* Geoffrey Bownas *and* Anthony Thwaite. PeBJV

Keep Love in Your Life. Thomas Curtis Clark. WBLP

Keep Me. Malka Heifetz-Tussman, *tr. fr. Yiddish by* Kathryn Hellerstein. AYP

Keep me as your servant, O Girdhar. Mirabai, *tr. fr. Medieval Hindi by* Usha Nilsson. PBWP

Keep me clean. Chamber-Pot Rhyme. *Unknown.* GBP

Keep me from bitterness. It is so easy. Prayer in Affliction. Violet Alleyn Storey. TrPWD

Keep me, I pray, in wisdom's way. The Bibliomaniac's Prayer. Eugene Field. AA

Keep Me, Jesus, Keep Me ("Keep me 'neath Thy mighty wing"). Waverly Turner Carmichael. BANP

Keep Me Still, for I Do Not Want to Dream. Larry Eigner. NeAP

Keep Not Thou Silence. Bible, *O.T. See* Psalms: Psalm LXXXIII ("O God, keep not Thou silence").

Keep On Praying. Roger H. Lyon. BLRP

Keep on Pushing. David Henderson. PoBA

Keep pushing—'tis wiser than sitting aside. Never Say Fail. *Unknown.* PWR

Keep Smiling. *Unknown.* WBLP

Keep smoking swamp. Have No Mercy. Aimé Césaire, *tr. by* Clayton Eshleman *and* Annette Smith. RHTwFP

Keep Talking. Philip Levine. WeW

Keep the commandments, Trapp, and go no further. Abel Evans. FaBoEE

Keep the dream alive and growing always. Edwin Rolfe. TrJP

Keep the Glad Flag Flying. *Unknown.* FaFP

Keep this little light, O Father. A Birthday Prayer. John Finley. TrPWD

Keep Thou My Way, O Lord. Fanny Crosby. TrPWD

Keep to yourself your kisses. Taisigh Agat Fein Do Phog. *Unknown, tr. by* Maire Cruise O'Brien. BIrV

Keep Ye Holy Sabbath Rest. *Unknown, tr. fr. Hebrew by* Herbert Loewe. TrJP

Keep you these calm and lovely things. To the Liffey with the Swans. Oliver St. John Gogarty. AnIL

Keep your copper coin, save your cup of wheat. Never Ask Me Why. Silvia Margolis. GoYe

Keep your eyes open when you kiss: do: when. John Berryman. BoLoP

Keep your kiss to yourself. *Unknown, tr. fr. Irish by* Thomas Kinsella. NOIV

Keep your whiskers crisp and clean. The King of Cats Sends a Postcard to His Wife. Nancy Willard. OBCA

Keeper, The. William Carpenter. Psk

Keeper of the Midnight Gate, The. George Mackay Brown. OxBC

Keeping Christmas. Eleanor Farjeon. OBCP

Keeping Hair. Ramona Wilson. VoR

Keeping On. Arthur Hugh Clough. *See* Say Not the Struggle Nought Availeth.

Keeping the Horses. Roy Scheele. MOWH

Keeping Their World Large. Marianne Moore. WaP

Keeping Things Whole. Mark Strand. CoAP; HCAP; HeIP; LCAP; PPP; TAP

Keepsake. Lawrence Durrell. PoPo

Keepsake Corporation, The. David Fisher. NPGG

Keepsake from Quinault. Dorothy Alyea. GoYe

Kehama's Curse. Robert Southey. *Fr.* The Curse of Kehama. OBNC

Kehi Shrine. *Unknown, tr. fr. Japanese by* Hiroaki Sato. FCEI

Keith of Ravelston. Sydney Thompson Dobell. *See* Nuptial Eve, A: Ballad of Keith of Ravelston, The.

Kekchi Warrior. Marco Antonio Flores, *tr. fr. Spanish by* David Volpendesta. VoI

Kelly. Robert Hershon. NeAC

Kelly Square Smoke Shop closes its doors, The. Outside Baby Moon's. Paul Violi. UL

Kellyburnbraes. *Unknown.* OxBB

Kelly's kept an unlicensed bull, well away. The Outlaw. Seamus Heaney. MoP; NIP; OxBC

Kelp. Nora Dauenhauer. HATNAP

Kelpius's Hymn. Arthur Peterson. AA

Kemp Owyne. *Unknown.* EnSB; ESPB, (A *and* B *vers.*)

(Kempion.) OxBB, *with music*

Ken when to spend and when to spare. *Unknown.* FaBoUs

Keng-tzu (1180), First Month, Fifth Day, Dawn. Yang Wan-li, *tr. fr. Chinese by* Burton Watson. CoBCP
Kenny and I down a few beers. Detroit Hymns, Christmas Eve. Jim Daniels. SoTCo
Keno. Dara Wier. MAYP
Kenst doo hoo. The Miller's Wife's Lullaby. *Unknown.* GBP
Kent State, May 4, 1970. Paul Goodman. MAT
Kentucky, *sel.* Yisroel-Yankev Schwartz, *tr. fr. Yiddish by* Seymour Levitan.
Climb Up, The. PeBMYV
Kentucky Babe. Richard Henry Buck. AA
Kentucky Belle. Constance Fenimore Woolson. BeLS; BLPA; FaBoBe; PAH
Kentucky Moonshiner. *Unknown.* AS; OBAL
Kentucky Mountain Farm, *sel.* Robert Penn Warren.
History among the Rocks. GOA; MoAmPo
Kentucky water, clear springs: a boy fleeing. The Swimmers. Allen Tate. InPS; MoAmPo; NoAM; NOBA
Kepe well x, and flee fro vii. Ten Commandments, Seven Deadly Sins, and Five Wits. *Unknown.* ChTr; FaBoEE
Kept Indoors on a Winter Evening. Tameko, *tr. fr. Japanese by* Steven D. Carter. WFTW
Kéramos, *sel.* Longfellow.
Potter's Song, The. PoEL-5
Kerria roses on the banks. Tsurayuki, *tr. fr. Japanese by* Burton Watson. *Fr.* Kokin Shu. FCEI
Kerr's Ass. Patrick Kavanagh. FaBCIP; NOIV; RB
Kerve thy brede note to thynne. Table Manners. *Unknown.* OxBLMV
Kettle descants in a cosy drone, The. At Tea. Thomas Hardy. *Fr.* Satires of Circumstance, I. BrPo
Kettle sang the boy to a half-sleep, The. Halibut Cove Harvest. Kenneth Leslie. CaP; NOBC
Kevin Barry. *Unknown.* AS
Kevin Barry: Died for Ireland, 1st November, 1920. *Unknown.* FaBoBa
Key, The. Max Jacob, *tr. fr. French by* Ron Padgett. RHTwFP
Key. The door. Open, A. Tom. James Schuyler. GLP
Key to Everything, The. May Swenson. IHMS; NePoEA
Key to the City, The. Anne Winters. PPR
Key West. Hart Crane. CMoP
Keyhole in the Door, The. *Unknown.* CoMu
Keys of Canterbury, The. *Unknown.* AmFP
Keys of Morning, The. Walter de la Mare. NoP
Keys turning. The Liberator. Emily Holmes Coleman. EAS
Keziah. Gwendolyn Brooks. RAR; RHPC
Khalida/ Sadness around which. A Mirror to Khalida. "Adunis," *tr. by* Lena Jayyusi *and* John Heath-Stubbs. MAP
Khamsin. Clinton Scollard. AA
Khamsin of Nisan. Leah Goldberg, *tr. fr. Hebrew by* Bernhard Frank. MHeP
Khrushchev is coming on the right day! Frank O'Hara. NeAP; PoM
Kiang and the Han sweep by, The. *Unknown, tr. fr. Chinese by* Arthur Waley. BoS
Kiang parts and joins, The. *Unknown, tr. fr. Chinese by* Arthur Waley. BoS
Kibbutz Sabbath. Levi ben Amittai, *tr. fr. Hebrew by* Simon Halkin. EaLo
Kibune River—/ the rocky waves of its rapids. Shunzei, *tr. fr. Japanese by* Burton Watson. *Fr.* Thirty Tanka. FCEI
Kick at the rock, Sam Johnson, break your bones. Epistemology. Richard Wilbur. CRP; NePoEA; NoAM; NOBA; OxBSP
Kicker's Last Steps, The. William Meissner. TSL
Kicking from Centre Field. David McFadden. NeAC
Kicking his mother until she let go of his soul. Mundus et Infans. W. H. Auden. LiTB; LiTM; MoAB; MoBrPo; NAs; NoAM
Kicking Mule, The. *Unknown.* AmFP
Kicking the Habit. Jotie T'Hooft, *tr. fr. Dutch by* James S. Holmes. DuIn
Kicking the Leaves. Donald Hall. CAPP
Kickoff. In the Beginning Was the. Lee Murchison. SD
Kid, The. Ai. GeTw; NoAM
Kid, The, *sel.* Conrad Aiken.
Proem to "The Kid." MoAB
Kid, The. Kevin Bezner. ASP
Kid Has Gone to the Colors, The. William M. Herschell. PoLF
Kid is so dumb, The. How Dumb Is He? Claudia Nabors. SoTCo
Kid Solos, The. Bob Schild. CowP
Kid Stuff. Frank Horne. AmNP; PChr; PoBA; PoNe
Kidded in April above Glencolumbkille. Care. Richard Murphy. IPY
Kidnap Poem. Nikki Giovanni. AmNP; BPo; GOYP; TAP
Kidnaper. Tess Gallagher. AmPA
(Kidnapper.) AnAn

Kidnapping of Sims, The. John Pierpont. PAH
Kids are asleep, The. It's a Different Story When You're Going into the Wind. David McFadden. NeAC
Kilbarchan now may say alas! The Life and Death of [Habbie Simson] the Piper of Kilbarchan. Robert Sempill. OBS; OxBS
Kilcash. *Unknown, tr. fr. Irish by* Frank O'Connor. BIrV; OBMV
Kilfenora Teaboy, The. Paul Durcan. FaBCIP
Kilkenny Boy, The. Eileen Shanahan. NeIP
Kilkenny Cats, The. *Unknown.* CRH; FaFP
(Limerick: "There once were two cats of Kilkenny.") CenHV
Kill a robin or a wren. *Unknown.* PBBP
Kill Me. Anna Swirszczynska, *tr. fr. Polish by* Czeslaw Milosz. PwPP
Kill me not every day. Affliction. George Herbert. TEP
Kill or be killed, the sergeant cried. The Killer Too. Walker Gibson. FF
Kill yourselves with knives and poisoned gas. Strangers Are We All upon the Earth. Franz Werfel, *tr. by* Edith Abercrombie Snow. TrJP
Killed at the Ford. Longfellow. OHIP
Killed by an omnibus—why not? On a Man Run Over by an Omnibus. Henry Luttrell. FaBoEE
Killed in Action. Juliette de Bairacli-Levy. CN
Killer, The. A'yunini, *tr. fr. Cherokee Indian by* Jerome Rothenberg. STP
Killer Too, The. Walker Gibson. FF
Killers That Run, The. Leonard Cohen. NOBC
Killigrew Wood, The. Norman Dubie. AmPA
Killing. Samuel Greenberg. LiTA
Killing, The. George MacBeth. FaBoMo
Killing anything was pure accident. The Hunting. Thomas Lux. PPR
Killing No Murder. Sylvia Townsend Warner. MoBrPo
Killing of the Birds, The. Shirley Williams. BoWoP
Kilmeny. James Hogg. *Fr.* The Queen's Wake. OBEV
(Bonny Kilmeny Gaed Up the Glen.) GoTS
Kilpeck. Fleur Adcock. ATNZ
Kilroy. Eugene McCarthy. AiP
Kilroy. Peter Viereck. FF; MoAmPo
(Kilroy Was Here.) PoRA
Kilroy is gone. Kilroy. Eugene McCarthy. AiP
Kilroy Was Here. Peter Viereck. *See* Kilroy.
Kilruddery Hunt, The. Thomas Mozeen. BIrV
Kiltartan Legend. Padraic Fallon. NOIV
Kim, *sel.* Kipling.
Prodigal Son, The. NoAM
Kimono. Jorie Graham. MAYP; PPR
Kin. Michael S. Harper. LCAP
Kin: quiet grasses. Deborah as Scion. James Dickey. SV
Kinaxixi. Agostinho Neto, *tr. fr. Portuguese by* Marga Holness. WMBCH
Kincora [or Lamentation of Mac Liag for Kincora]. *Unknown, tr. fr. Middle Irish by* James Clarence Mangan. AnIL
Kind. A. R. Ammons. NoP; PrIm
Kind Are Her Answers. Thomas Campion. BoLoP; ELP; OBSC; TrGrPo
(Kinde Are Her Answeres.) PoEL-2
Kind country-men listen I pray. All Things Be Dear but Poor Mens Labour; or, The Sad Complaint of Poor People. *Unknown.* CoMu
Kind Deeds. Isaac Watts. BoTP
Kind friends, you must pity my horrible tale. The Dreary Black Hills. *Unknown.* AmFP
Kind gentlemen, will you be patient awhile? Robin Hood's Birth, Breeding, Valor, and Marriage. *Unknown.* ESPB
Kind Heaven, assist the trembling muse. The Wyoming Massacre. Uriah Terry. PAH
Kind Inn, A. George Dillon. GoYe
Kind Keeper, The, *sel.* Dryden.
Song from the Italian, A. SeCV-2
Kind lovers, love on. John Crowne. *Fr.* Calisto. InvP; OxBSP
Kind Miss. *Unknown.* AS
Kind Mousie, The. Natalie Joan. BoTP
Kind o'er the kinderbank leans Myfanwy. Myfanwy. Sir John Betjeman. BoLoP
Kind of Act Of, The. Robert Creeley. NeAP
Kind of an Ode to Duty. Ogden Nash. TrGrPo
Kind of change came in my fate, A. Byron. *Fr.* The Prisoner of Chillon. NOBE
Kind of empty in the way it sees everything, the earth gets to its feet. For John Clare. John Ashbery. FYAP
Kind of Loss, A. Ingeborg Bachmann, *tr. fr. German by* Beth Bjorklund. CoAuP
Kind of rose she wants called John F. Kennedy, The. Fourth Ode to Persephone. Robert Kelly. *Fr.* The Book of Persephone, 16. PoM

Kind of slant—the way a ball will glance, A. Gary Miranda. SM
Kind of Thanks, A. Joseph C. Fischer. *Fr.* From the XXIII Summer Olympics, the Poet as Report, XVI. TSL
Kind pity [*or* Kinde pitty] chokes my spleen[e]; brave scorn forbids. John Donne. *Fr.* Satires, III. EBEV; JCP; OAEL-1; OBS; PoEL-2; SeCV-1
  (Religion.) NoP
  (Satyre III.) MeLP
  (Satyre III: On Religion.) NAEL-1; SeCP
  (Satyre: Of Religion.) MePo; PoE
Kind Saint! who loved the garden flowers. Saint Fiacre. John Irvine. TIRV
Kind Sir: These Woods ("Kind Sir: This is an old game"). Anne Sexton. GoYe
Kind voice, A, calls, "Come, little ones." Crocuses. Anna M. Platt. BoTP
Kind Words Can Never Die. Abby Hutchinson. AH
Kinde Are Her Answeres. Thomas Campion. *See* Kind Are Her Answers.
Kinder- und Hausmärchen. Brian Alderson. Mes
Kindergarten. Ron Rogers. NOVW
Kindergarten. Dennis Schmitz. NPGG
Kindergarten children first come forth, The. The May Day Dancing. Howard Nemerov. NYBP
Kindertotenlieder. Michael Longley. CIP
Kindle the Taper. Emma Lazarus. AH
Kindler of glory's embers. In Praise of Aed. *Unknown, tr. by* Robin Flower. AnIL
Kindliest thing God ever made, The. Shade. Theodosia Pickering Garrison. OHIP
Kindly Deed, A. Priscilla Jane Thompson. CBWP-2
Kindly Unhitch That Star, Buddy. Ogden Nash. LiTA
Kindly Vision. Otto Julius Bierbaum, *tr. fr. German by* Jethro Bithell. AWP
Kindly watcher by my bed, lift no voice in prayer. Music. George Du Maurier, *after the French of* Sully-Prudhomme. OBEV
Kindness. Catherine Davis. NYBP
Kindness. Thomas Sturge Moore. OBMV
Kindness. Sylvia Plath. FaBoWP
Kindness. Mary E. Tucker. CBWP-1
Kindness glides about my house. Kindness. Sylvia Plath. FaBoWP
Kindness to Animals. Joseph Ashby-Sterry. NA
Kindness to Animals. Laura E. Richards. NTCP
Kindness to Animals. *Unknown.* BoTP; FaBoUs
Kinds of Luck. Abraham Reisen, *tr. fr. Yiddish by* Leonard Wolf. PeBMYV
Kinds of Shel-fish. William Wood. SCAP
Kinds of Trees to Plant. Spenser. *Fr.* The Faerie Queene, I, 1. OHIP
Kineo Mountain. Celeste Turner Wright. Psk
Kinfauns Castle, *sel.* William Montgomerie.
  "Is there no vision in a lovely place?." OxBS
King, a pope, and a kaiser, A. The Ship. Charles MacKay. BLPA
King and Queen of Cantelon. Babylon. *Unknown.* ChTr
King and Queen of the Pelicans we. The Pelican Chorus. Edward Lear. FaBoNo
King Arthur, *sels.* Dryden.
  Harvest Home. PrIm
    (Song: "Your hay it is mow'd, and your corn is reap'd.") SeCV-2
  Song of Venus. OxBoLi; PoEL-3
King Arthur and King Cornwall. *Unknown.* ESPB
King Arthur Growing Very Tired Indeed. Mortimer Collins. *See* Salad: After Tennyson.
King Arthur made new knights to fill the gap. Pelleas and Ettarre. Tennyson. *Fr.* Idylls of the King. NAEL-2
  "Rose, but one, none other rose had I, A." PoEL-5
King Arthur's Death. *Unknown.* ACP
King Arthur's Dream. *Unknown.* ACP
King Arthur's Waes-hael. Robert Stephen Hawker. OBEV
King asked, The. The King's Breakfast. A. A. Milne. CenHV; OxBChV
King Berdok. *Unknown.* OxBS
King Bruce of Scotland flung himself down. Try Again. Eliza Cook. BoTP
King but an' his nobles a', The. Brown Robin. *Unknown.* ESPB; OxBB
King Canute. Stanley J. Sharpless. BXAP
King Charles on [*or* upon] the Scaffold. Andrew Marvell. *Fr.* An Horatian Ode upon Cromwell's Return from Ireland. ChTr; FaBoRV
King Charles the First. *Unknown.* *See* As I was going by Charing Cross.
King Charles the First walked and talked. *Unknown.* OxNR

King Christian. Johannes Evald, *tr. fr. Danish by* Longfellow. AWP
King Cobra as Political Assassin, The. Ray A. Young Bear. HATNAP
King David and King Solomon. James Ball Naylor. CenHV (Authorship.) NBLV
King David Dances. John Berryman. OxBC; OxBSP
King Don Luis. O. V. de L. Milosz, *tr. fr. French by* John Peck. RHTwFP
King Duffus. Sylvia Townsend Warner. FaBoWP
King Easter has courted her for her gowd. Fause Foodrage. *Unknown.* ESPB
  (Fa'se Footrage.) OxBB
King Edward the Fourth and a Tanner of Tamworth. *Unknown.* ESPB
King Edward the Third, *sel.* Blake.
  War Song to Englishmen, A. CH; OHIP; WaaP
  (War Song, A.) OHIP
King Enjoys His Own Again, The. Martin Parker. FaBoCh; OBS; OxBoLi
King Estmere. *Unknown.* ESPB; OBNV; OxBB
King Ethelred the Unready. Bill Greenwell. BXAP
King Fisher courted Lady Bird. The King-Fisher Song. "Lewis Carroll." *Fr.* Sylvie and Bruno Concluded. FaBoNo
King Francis was a hearty king, and loved a royal sport. The Glove and the Lions. Leigh Hunt. BeLS; FaPON; GN; WBLP
King George, observing with judicious eyes. Joseph Trapp. FaBoCo ("King, observing with judicious eyes, The.") FaBoEE
King had dropped his crown, A. Out of Whack. Russell Edson. LCAP
King Hancock sat in regal state. A Song about Charleston. *Unknown.* PAH
King Hart, ("King Hart, into his cumlye castell strong"), *sel.* Gawin Douglas.
  Hart's Castle. PoEL-1
King has written a braid letter, The. Lord Derwentwater. *Unknown.* ESPB
King he hath been a prisoner, The. Willie o Winsbury. *Unknown.* ESPB
King [he] sits in Dunfermline [*or* Dumferling] town [*or* toune], The. Sir Patrick Spens [*or* Spence]. *Unknown.* AmFP; AWP; CH; EBEV; ELP; EnRP; EnSB; ESPB, (A, B *and* G *vers.*); ESPB; FaBoBa; FaBoCh; FaPoR; FF; GN; GoJo; HAP; HoPM; HoPM; InPS; InvP; InVP; LiTB; MOS; NIP; NOBE; NoP, (A *vers.*); NoP; OAEL-1, *with music*; OAEL-1; OBEV; OxBB, (B *vers., with music)*; OxBB; OxBS; PoEL-1; PPP; PrIm; TrGrPo; UnPo; WeW
  ("King sits in Dunferline town, The.") NAEL-1; RB
  ("King sits in Dunferling toune, The.") InPK; NIP; PoE
King he wrote a love-letter, The. Lord Derwentwater. *Unknown.* AmFP
King Henry. *Unknown.* ESPB; OxBB, *with music*
King Henry IV, Pt. I. Shakespeare. NAEL-1
  At My Nativity. *Fr.* III, i. NAs
King Henry IV, Pt. II, *sels.* Shakespeare.
  Cares of Majesty, The. *Fr.* III, i. LiTB
  (O Gentle Sleep.) FaBoRV
  (Soliloquy on Sleep.) FiP
  "My liege, I did deny no prisoners." *Fr.* I, iii. WaaP
  "Wilt thou upon the high and giddy mast." *Fr.* III, i. MOS
King Henry V, *sels.* Shakespeare.
  Commonwealth of the Bees, The. GN
  Henry V before Agincourt. *Fr.* IV, iii. FaPoR
  (St. Crispin's Day.) FF
  Now Entertain Conjecture of a Time. *Fr. Prologue to* IV. RB; WaaP
  (Before Agincourt.) ChTr; EBEV
    "From camp to camp, through the fool womb of time." FaBoRV
  "O for a Muse of fire, that would ascend." *Fr. Prologue to* I. SCV
  (Muse of Fire, A, 2 *ll.*) ChTr
  "Once more unto the breach, dear friends, once more." *Fr.* III, i. FaBV; WaaP
  (Blast of War, The.) TrGrPo
  "Suppose that you have seen." *Fr.* III. MOS
  "Thus with imagin'd wing our swift scene flies." *Fr. Prologue to* III. EBEV
  "We few, we happy few, we band of brothers." *Fr.* IV, iii. UnPo
  Yon Island Carrions Desperate of Their Bones. *Fr.* IV, ii. RB
King Henry VI, Pt. I, *sel.* Shakespeare.
  King Is Dead, A. *Fr.* I, i. ChTr
King Henry VI, Pt. III, *sel.* Shakespeare.
  "Now sways it this way, like a mighty sea." *Fr.* II, v. MOS
King Henry VIII, *sels.* Shakespeare *and probably* John Fletcher.
  Ambition. *Fr.* III, ii. TrGrPo
  Cranmer's Prophecy of Queen Elizabeth. *Fr.* V, v. WGRP

Orpheus with His Lute [Made Trees]. *Fr.* III, i. ChTr; GN; OBS; TrGrPo
(Music.) FaBoCh
(Orpheus.) EIL; OBEV; UnS
(Song: "Orpheus with his Lute made Trees.") PoEL-2
(Sweet Music's Power.) NOBE
This Royal Infant. *Fr.* V, iv. NAs
Wolsey. FaBoRV
Wolsey's Farewell to His Greatness. *Fr.* III, ii. OHFP
(Cardinal Wolsey's Farewell.) LiTB
(Farewell to Greatness.) TrGrPo
King Henry Fifth's Conquest of France. *Unknown.* ESPB
(Henry V's Conquest of France.) OBET
King Henry to Rosamond. Michael Drayton. *Fr.* England's Heroical Epistles. OBSC
King I saw who walked a cloth of gold, The. Cloth of Gold. Francis Reginald. MoCV
King in May, The. Michael Dennis Browne. NYBP
King Is Dead, A. Shakespeare. *Fr.* King Henry VI, Pt. I, I, i. ChTr
King is man and beggar too. Man. Vali Mohammad Nazir, *tr. by* Ahmed Ali. GoT
King is out a-hunting, The. The King's Wood. C. S. Holder. BoTP
King is someone who came from the dark water, The. We Do Not Know the Name of the King. Takahashi Mutsuo, *tr. by* Hiroaki Sato. FCEI
King James and Brown. *Unknown.* ESPB
King James II. Dryden. *Fr.* The Hind and the Panther, III. ACP
King Jamie hath made a vow. Flodden Field. *Unknown.* ESPB
King John, *sels.* Shakespeare.
"Grief fills the room up of my absent child." *Fr.* III, iv. OBD
To Gild Refinèd Gold. *Fr.* IV, ii. LiTB
King John and the Abbot of Canterbury. *Unknown.* BoTP; EnSB; GN; TrGrPo
King John and the Bishop. *Unknown.* ESPB, (A *and* B *vers.*)
King Killi in Combat. Cattantaiyar, *tr. fr. Tamil by* A. K. Ramanujan. PLW
King Kong Meets Wallace Stevens. Michael Ondaatje. HeIP
King Lear, *sels.* Shakespeare.
Blow, Winds. *Fr.* III, ii. TrGrPo
(Lear's Speech to the Storm.) TW
Death of Lear. *Fr.* V, iii. FiP
Dover, the Samphire Cliff. *Fr.* IV, vi. FaBoPP
"He wakes; speak to him." SCV, IV, vii.
"How does my royal lord? How fares your Majesty?." Prf
"Howl, howl, howl! O! you are men of stones." *Fr.* V, iii. OBD
Lear and Cordelia. *Fr.* V, iii. FiP
Lear's Curse on Goneril. *Fr.* I, iv. TW
"Please you, draw near.—Louder the music there!" *Fr.* IV, vii. EBEV
Take Physic, Pomp. *Fr.* III, iv. TrGrPo
"This is the foul fiend Flibbertigibbet: he begins at." *Fr.* III, iii. WSC
King Lives. Jill Witherspoon Boyer. CNA
King Lot's Envoys. Drummond Allison. OxBSP
King Louis on his bridge is he. Le Père Sévère. *Unknown, tr. by* Andrew Lang. AWP
King luikit owre his castle wa', The. Sir Colin. *Unknown.* OxBB
King, majestic and glorious, The. *Unknown, tr. by* Arthur Waley. BoS
King Midas. Howard Moss. CoAP; TAP
(King's Speech, The.) PoA
King Midas. Ovid, *tr. fr. Latin by* Arthur Golding. *Fr.* Metamorphoses, XI. CTC
King Midas Has Asses' Ears. Donald Finkel. NePoEA-2
King must rule kingdom. Cities are seen from afar. Maxims (Cotton MS.). *Unknown, tr. by* Charles W. Kennedy. AnOE
King, observing with judicious eyes, The. Joseph Trapp. *See* Epigram: "King George, observing with judicious eyes."
King of Ai, The. Hyam Plutzik. LiTM; VWA
King of Asini, The. George Seferis, *tr. fr. Greek by* Edmund Keeley *and* Philip Sherrard. VMG
King of Brentford's Testament *abr, The.* Thackeray. OBNV
King of Canoodle-Dum, The. W. S. Gilbert. CenHV
King of Cats Sends a Postcard to His Wife, The. Nancy Willard. OBCA
King of China's Daughter, The. Dame Edith Sitwell. BoTP; FaBoMo; MoBrPo
King of Cuckooz, The. Kenneth Slessor. *Fr.* The Atlas. PoAu-2
King of Denmark's Ride, The. Caroline E. Norton. BeLS; GN
King of France, the king of France, The/ with forty thousand men. Mother Goose. OxNR
King of Glory sends his Son, The. Miracles at the Birth of Christ. Isaac Watts. NOCV

King of Huai-nan, The. In Imitation of "The King of Huai-nan." Pao Chao, *tr. by* Burton Watson. CoBCP
King of Ireland's Cairn, The. "Ethna Carbery." WPE
King of Ireland's Son, The. Nora Hopper. AnIL
King of Kings. Hubert Witheford. ATNZ
King of Owls, The. Louise Erdrich. NoAM
King of stars. The Open Door. *Unknown, tr. by* Frank O'Connor. KiLC
King of Sweden, The. Stefan Themerson. NPo
King of the Belgians. Marion Couthouy Smith. PAH
King of the Castle. *Unknown.* OxNR
King of the Cats is Dead, The. Peter Porter. NoAM
King of the Hobbledygoblins, The. Laura E. Richards. OBCA
King of the perennial holly-groves, the riven sandstone. Geoffrey Hill. *Fr.* Mercian Hymns, I. FaBoMo; HAP; NoAM
King of Thule, The. Goethe, *tr. fr. German by* James Clarence Mangan. AWP
King of waters, the sea shouldering whale, The. William Wood. SCAP
King of Yellow Butterflies, The. Vachel Lindsay. OBCA
King of Yvetot, The. Pierre Jean de Béranger, *tr. fr. French by* William Toynbee. AWP
King Oliver of New Orleans. Satchmo. Melvin Beaunearus Tolson. BPo
(Lamda.) PoNe
King once own a flea, A. Mephisto's Flea Song. Richard Frost. SoTCo
King, once summoned his favorites, A. The King's Favorites. Priscilla Jane Thompson. CBWP-2
King Orfeo. *Unknown.* ESPB; OxBB, *with music;* OxBoLi
King over Israel. Dahlia Ravikovich, *tr. fr. Hebrew by* Warren Bargad *and* Stanley F. Chyet. IP
King Paladin plunged on his moon-coloured mare. Mad Marjory. Hugh McCrae. PoAu-1
King Pellam's Launde. David Jones. *Fr.* In Parenthesis, IV. OAEL-2
"So thus he sorrowed till it was day." NoAM
King Philip had vaunted his claims. A Ballad to Queen Elizabeth. Austin Dobson.
(Ballade of the Armada, A.) FaPoR
King Philip's Last Stand. Clinton Scollard. PAH
King Richard II, *sels.* Shakespeare.
John of Gaunt's Dying Speech. FiP
John of Gaunt Speaks. FaBoPP; FaPoR
(This Blessed Plot. This England.) FaBV
Let's Talk of Graves. *Fr.* III, ii. FaBoBe
Death of Kings, The. TrGrPo
"For God's sake, let us sit upon the ground." HoPM
"O, but they say the tongues of dying men." *Fr.* II, i. OBD
(Tongues of Dying Men, The.) FaBoRV
This England. *Fr.* II, i. BoTP; TrGrPo
King Richard III, *sels.* Shakespeare.
"As we paced along/ Upon the giddy footing of the hatches." *Fr.* I, iv. MOS
Dream of Wrecks, A. *Fr.* I, iv. ChTr
Methought That I Had Broken from the Tower. *Fr.* I, iv. RB
"Now is the winter of our discontent." *Fr.* I, i. PoE
(Hate the Idle Pleasures.) TrGrPo
King Richard hearing of the pranks. The King's Disguise, and Friendship with Robin Hood. *Unknown.* ESPB
King Robert of Sicily (The Sicilian's Tale). Longfellow. *Fr.* Tales of a Wayside Inn, *pt.* I. BeLS; OHIP
King Saul. Allan Kolski Horvitz. VWA
King Saul was disconcerted. David and Goliath. Priscilla Jane Thompson. CBWP-2
King scrapes the sweat, The. When a King Asks for a Chieftain's Daughter. Maturai Marutan Ilanakanar, *tr. by* A. K. Ramanujan. PLW
King sent for his wise men all, The. W. W. James Reeves. ChTr; NTCP
King sent his lady on the first Yule day, The. The Yule Days. *Unknown.* ChTr; GBP
King Shabtai Tsvi. Uri Zvi Greenberg, *tr. fr. Yiddish by* Robert Friend. PeBMYV
King Shall Reign in Righteousness, A. Sebastian Streeter. AH
King sits in Dumferline toun, The. The New Ballad of Sir Patrick Spens. Sir Arthur Quiller-Couch. BXAP
King sits in Dumferline town [*or* Dumferling toune], The. *Unknown.* *See* Sir Patrick Spens [*or* Spence].
King Solomon stood in the house of the Lord. The Dead Solomon. John Aylmer Dorgan. AA

King Solomon Vistas. Ian Wedde. ATNZ; PeNZ

King still lives. King Lives. Jill Witherspoon Boyer. CNA

King, this is Mihyar, A. Mihyar, A King! "Adunis," tr. by Lena Jayyusi and John Heath-Stubbs. MAP

King to Oxford sent a troop of horse, The. Sir William Browne. FaBoCo; FaBoEE

King Triumphant. Isaac Watts. See Jesus Shall Reign Where'er the Sun.

King walked in his garden green, The. The Three Singing Birds. James Reeves. PDV

King was on his throne, The. The Vision of Belshazzar. Byron. GN; OnMSP

King was sick, The. His cheek was red. The Enchanted Shirt. John Hay. BLPA; GN

King Wên is on high. Unknown, tr. by Arthur Waley. BoS

King William Was King George's Son. Unknown. AmFP

King William's Dispatch to Queen Augusta. Coventry Patmore. FaBoEE

King Winter sat in his Hall one day. Outside. Hugh Chesterman. BoTP

King with all his kingly train, The. Louis XV. John Sterling. BeLS

Kingcups. Sacheverell Sitwell. MoBrPo

Kingdom. Sir Edward Dyer. See My Mind [or Minde or Mynde] to Me a Kingdom [or Kyngdome] Is.

Kingdom, The, sels. Louis MacNeice. LiTM
   "Take this old man with the soldierly straight back."
   "Under the surface of flux and of fear there is an underground movement."

Kingdom, The. Jon Swan. NYBP

Kingdom of God, The. Rab, tr. fr. Hebrew. TrJP

Kingdom of God, The. Francis Thompson. BrPo; EaLo; FaPoR; GTBS-P; NOCV;
   (In No Strange Land.) HAP; LiTB; MoAB; MoBrPo; NOBE; OBEV; TrCP; TrGrPo; WGRP

Kingdom of God, The. Richard Chenevix Trench. WBLP

Kingdom of Heaven. Léonie Adams. MoAB; MoAmPo

Kingdom of heaven is likened unto a man which sowed good seed in his field, The. The Parable of the Good Seed. Bible, N.T. Fr. St. Matthew, XIII: 24-30. InPK

Kingdom of Number is all boundaries, The. W. H. Auden. Fr. Numbers and Faces. ImOP

Kingdom of Silence. Amir Gilboa, tr. fr. Hebrew by Warren Bargad and Stanley F. Chyet. IP

Kingdom of the heart, The. Mohammad Taqi Mir, tr. by Ahmed Ali. GoT

Kingdoms fall in sequence, like the waves on the shore, The. The Sparrow's Skull. Ruth Pitter. EaLo; FaBoWP

Kinge Arthur lives in merry Carleile. The Marriage of Sir Gawain. Unknown. ESPB

Kingfisher, The. Amy Clampitt. HCAP; SM

Kingfisher, The. W. H. Davies. NOBE; OBEV; OBWVE

Kingfisher. Eleanor Farjeon. RR

Kingfisher, The. Andrew Marvell. Fr. Upon Appleton House, to My Lord Fairfax. ChTr

Kingfisher blue along a tangled bank. Poem to the Tune "Riverbank Willows." Yü Hsüan-chi, tr. by Geoffrey Waters. BoWoP

Kingfisher Flat. William Everson. PoM

Kingfisher green lines the deserted shore. Composed on the Theme "Willows by the Riverside." Yü Hsüan-chi. WPOW, tr. by Jan W. Walls

Kingfishers, The. Charles Olson. CMoP; InPS; NAAL-2; NeAP; NOBA; PoM

Kingfisher's Boxing Gloves, The. James Fenton. NoAM

Kingfishers frolic among the orchid blossoms. Poem on the Wandering Immortal. Kuo P'o, tr. by Burton Watson. CoBCP

Kingfisher's naked arc alight, A. Allen Curnow. Fr. A Small Room with Large Windows, IV. PeNZ

Kingis Quair, The, abr. James I, King of Scotland. OxBS
Sels.
   He Sees His Beloved. GoTS; PoEL-1
   "Now was there maid fast by the towris wall." EBEV

Kingly lyon, and the strong arm'd beare, The. William Wood. SCAP

Kings. Unknown, tr. fr. Sanskrit by Arthur Ryder. Fr. The Panchatantra. AWP

Kings/ like golden gleams. A History Lesson. Miroslav Holub, tr. by George Theiner. RB

Kings and Emperors. Cheng Hsieh, tr. fr. Chinese by Jan and Yvonne Walls. WFTU

Kings and Queens of England, The. Unknown. FaBoUs

Kings and Stars. John Erskine. TrCP

King's Breakfast, The. A. A. Milne. CenHV; OxBChV

Kings Came Riding. Charles Williams. OBCP

King's College Chapel. Charles Causley. TOF

King's Daughter!/ Wouldst thou be all fair. Everymaid. John Oxenham. TrCP

King's Disguise, The, sel. John Cleveland.
   "And why so coffined in this vile disguise." JCP

King's Disguise, and Friendship with Robin Hood, The. Unknown. ESPB

Kings do not touch doors. The Pleasures of the Door. Francis Ponge, tr. by Raymond Federman. RHTwFP

King's Dochter Lady Jean, The. Unknown. AmFP; ESPB

Kings don't touch doors. The Delights of the Door. Francis Ponge, tr. by Robert Bly. NU

King's Double Nature, A. Kakkai Patiniyar Naccellaiyar, tr. fr. Tamil by A. K. Ramanujan. PLW

King's Entertainment, The. Thomas Dekker. See Entertainment to James.

King's Epitaph, The. Earl of Rochester. SeCePo

King's Favorites, The. Priscilla Jane Thompson. CBWP-2

Kings from the East, The. Heine. See Wise Men Ask the Children the Way, The.

Kings go by with jeweled crowns, The. The Choice. John Masefield. Fr. Lollingdon Downs, VIII. MoAB; MoBrPo

King's Highway, The. John Masefield. BLRP

King's Highway to the Dare-Not-Know, The. "Dreams Are the Royal Road to the Unconscious." Paul Goodman. PoA

King's Last Words, A. Ceraman Kanaikkal Irumporai, tr. fr. Tamil by A. K. Ramanujan. PLW

King's Men, The. William Heyen. PoA

King's Missive, The. Whittier. PAH

King's most faithful Subjects we, The. England's Triumph. Unknown. CoMu

Kings of France. Mary W. Lincoln. BLPA

Kings of the East, The. Katharine Lee Bates. WGRP

Kings of the world are growing old, The. Rainer Maria Rilke, tr. by Robert Bly. NU

King's Own Regulars, The. Unknown. PAH

King's poet was his captain of horse in the wars, The. Mount Badon. Charles Williams. FaBoTw

Kings River Canyon. Kenneth Rexroth. NaP

King's Son, The. Thomas Boyd. OBMV

King's Speech, The. Howard Moss. See King Midas.

Kings who have died. Guillaume Apollinaire, tr. fr. French by Roger Shattuck. Fr. Heart, Crown, and Mirror. TTTS

Kings who slept in the caves are awake and out, The. The National Gallery. Louis MacNeice. EyDe

Kings, who would have good subjects, must. Loyalty. W. H. Davies. BrPo

King's Wood, The. C. S. Holder. BoTP

King's young dochter was sitting in her window, The. The King's Dochter Lady Jean. Unknown. AmFP; ESPB

Kingship of the Hills, The. Will H. Ogilvie. PoSH

Kinkaiders, The. Unknown. AS

Kinky Hair Blues. Una Marson. PBCV

Kinloch, sel. Dorothy Nash.
   Road Moves On, The. PoSH

Kinloch Ainort. Sorley MacLean. PoSH

Kinmont Willie. Unknown. ESPB; OxBB

Kinned by hieroglyphic. Kinship. Seamus Heaney. IPY

Kinneret. Judith Herzberg, tr. fr. Dutch by Shirley Kaufman. VWA

Kinnereth. Rachel, tr. fr. Hebrew by A. M. Klein. TrJP

Kinsey Report. Jutta Schutting, tr. fr. German by Beth Bjorklund. CoAuP

Kinship. Seamus Heaney. IPY

Kinship. Sir Charles G. D. Roberts. CaP

Kinsman, A. Jim Wayne Miller. MOWH

"Kio" sings the oriole. Unknown, tr. by Arthur Waley. BoS

Kirilov on a Skyscraper. Randall Jarrell. CAPP

Kirk Lonegren's Home Movie Taking Place Just North of Prince George, with Sound. Sharon Thesen. NOBC

Kirk of the Birds, Beasts and Fishes, The. Unknown. GBP

Kirk's Alarm, The. Burns. OxBoLi

Kirkyaird by the Sea, The, sel. Douglas Young, after the French of Paul Valéry.
   "Steekit, consecrat, fou o fire but fuel." OBVE

Kirov was shot, Solon will rot in jail. Once More. George Jonas. NeAC

Kirsten. Ted Berrigan. TTTS

Kirsten. Hugo Williams. Fr. Calling Your Name in the Zoo. NPo

Kiss, The. George Bogin. MOWH

Kiss, A. William Drummond of Hawthornden. EIL
Kiss, A. Robert Herrick. CaPo
Kiss, The. Bill Manhire. ATNZ
Kiss, The. Thomas Moore. EnLoPo
Kiss, The. Ned O'Gorman. FYAP
Kiss, The. Charles, d' Orléans. *See* My Ghostly Father, I me confess.
Kiss, The. Coventry Patmore. *Fr.* The Angel in the House. BoLoP; EnLoPo; FiBHP; NOBVV, *fr.* II, viii.
Kiss, The. Dante Gabriel Rossetti. *Fr.* The House of Life, VI. Son
Kiss, The. Siegfried Sassoon. MMA
Kiss, A. Mary E. Tucker. CBWP-1
Kiss, The. John Yau. UL
Kiss. Al Young. PoBA
Kiss, A ("He's my doll!"). *Unknown, tr. fr. Irish by* Frank O'Connor. KiLC
Kiss ("I close my eyes, the world recedes"). Tanikawa Shuntaro, *tr. fr. Japanese by* Hiroaki Sato. FCEI
Kiss ("She came home, smelling of another man"). Tanikawa Shuntaro, *tr. fr. Japanese by* Hiroaki Sato. FCEI
Kiss? A. Pray tell me, what is in a kiss. A Kiss. Mary E. Tucker. CBWP-1
Kiss, if you can: Resistance if she make. Ovid, *tr. fr. Latin by* Dryden. *Fr.* The Art of Love. ErPo
Kiss in the Morning Early, A. *Unknown.* GBP
Kiss in the Rain, A. Samuel Minturn Peck. OBAL
Kiss in the Ring. *Unknown.* OxBoLi
Kiss me again, re-kiss and kiss me whole. Louise Labé. WPOW, *tr. by* Raymond Oliver
    (Sonnet XVIII: "Kiss me again, rekiss, kiss me more.") BoWoP, *tr. by* Willis Barnstone
Kiss me and hug me. *Unknown, tr. by* Willis Barnstone. BoWoP
Kiss[e] me, sweet: the wary [*or* warie] Lover. To Celia. Ben Jonson. AWP; EIL; JCP; OAEL-1; OBVE; SeCP; SeCV-1
Kiss me then, my merry May. *Unknown, tr. by* John Addington Symonds. AWP
"Kiss me there where pride is glistening." Aria. Delmore Schwartz. ErPo
Kiss my grey hair, oh, my love. Healing. Abraham Reisen, *tr. by* Joseph Leftwich. TrJP
Kiss of God, The. G. A. Studdert-Kennedy. BLRP
Kiss once breathed life into me, A. The Dream Kiss. Karoline von Günderode, *tr. by* Susan L. Cocalis. DMG
Kiss'd Yestreen. *Unknown.* ErPo; GBP
Kisses. *At. to* Thomas Campion. EIL; OBSC
Kisses. *Malay Oral Tradition, tr. by* R. J. Wilkinson *and* R. O. Winstedt. WTO
Kisses Desired. William Drummond of Hawthornden. EnLoPo
Kisses in the Train. D. H. Lawrence. MoAB; MoBrPo
Kisses Loathesome. Robert Herrick. CaPo; OxBSP
Kissie Lee. Margaret Abigail Walker. BlSi; NMM
Kissin.' *Unknown.* FiBHP
Kissing. Herbert of Cherbury. EnLoPo; ViBoPo
Kissing Game. Bob Rosenthal. UL
Kissing Helena. Plato, *tr. fr. Greek by* Shelley. OBVE
Kissing her hair, I sat against her feet. Swinburne. BLPL; FaBoBe
Kissing Hippomenes, I crave. Paulos, *tr. by* Andrew Miller. PeHV
Kissing Natalia. Eldon Grier. NOBC
Kissing of My Dame. *Unknown.* GBP
    ("Sing jigmijole, the pudding bowl.") OxNR
Kit, the recording angel wrote. Kitty's "No." Arlo Bates. *Fr.* Conceits. AA
Kitchen Chimney, The. Robert Frost. EyDe
Kitchen Door Blues. Tennessee Williams. GrPl; OBAL
Kitchen fire that wakes so soon, The. Fires. Elizabeth Fleming. BoTP
Kitchen Poem. Francis Scarfe. EAS
Kitchen Range. Umberto Saba, *tr. fr. Italian by* William Jay Smith. CT; PFI
Kitchen Window. James Edward Hervey MacDonald. CaP
Kitchenette Building. Gwendolyn Brooks. *Fr.* A Street in Bronzeville. BPo; FaBoWP; FF; NAAL-2; NoP; PoE; PoNe; UnPo
Kitchie-Boy, The. *Unknown.* ESPB
Kite, The. Harry Behn. FaPON
Kite, A, *sels.* Hsü Wei, *tr. fr. Chinese by* Jonathan Chaves. CoBLCP
    Rock among Bamboo.
    "When the wind is gentle."
Kite. Laura Jensen. LCAP
Kite. John Robert Lee. PVCV
Kite. David McCord. PDV
Kite, The. Pearl Forbes MacEwen. BoTP

Kite, The. Adelaide O'Keeffe. OxBChV
Kite, The. Mark Strand. NYBP
Kite, A. *Unknown.* RAR
Kite, completed thus, is borne along, The. Samuel Bowden. *Fr.* The Paper Kite. NOEC
Kite-Flying. Kath McKay. DT
Kite for Michael and Christopher, A. Seamus Heaney. PPR
Kite Is a Victim, A. Leonard Cohen. NOBC; SD
Kite Poem. James Merrill. TwCP
Kites and vultures cannot smell out carrion. Peire Cardenal, *tr. by* Paul Blackburn. Pro
Kite's Feathers, The. Basho *and others, tr. fr. Japanese by* Geoffrey Bownas *and* Anthony Thwaite. PeBJV
Kithairon sang of cunning Kronos. Korinna, *tr. by* Willis Barnstone. BoWoP
Kitten, A. Eleanor Farjeon. CRH
Kitten. Judith Herzberg, *tr. fr. Dutch by the author*. DuIn
Kitten, The. Ogden Nash. CRH; FaPON; MoShBr
Kitten, The. Mary Oliver. CAPP
Kitten and the Falling Leaves, The, *sels.* Wordsworth.
    Kitten at Play, The. FaPON
    "Where is he, that giddy sprite." PBBP
Kitten at Play, The. Wordsworth. *Fr.* The Kitten and the Falling Leaves. FaPON
Kitten can, A. Where Knock Is Open Wide. Theodore Roethke. HAP; VGW
Kitten twirls around, A. Issa, *tr. fr. Japanese by* Hiroaki Sato. *Fr.* Forty-four Hokku. FCEI
Kittiwakes and cormorants go to sleep, The. Nightfall in Inishtrahull. Daniel James O'Sullivan. NeIP
Kitty. Doug McLeod. CRH
Kitty. Elizabeth Prentiss. BoTP; MoShBr
Kitty Bhan. Edward Walsh. ACP
Kitty-Cat Bird, The. Theodore Roethke. OBAL
Kitty Cornered. Eve Merriam. CRH
Kitty Hawk, *sel.* Robert Frost.
    But God's Own Descent. EaLo
Kitty Kline. *Unknown.* AmFP
Kitty Morey. *Unknown.* AmFP
Kitty: What She Thinks of Herself. William Brighty Rands. *See* I am the cat of cats. I am.
Kitty's Laugh. Arlo Bates. *Fr.* Conceits. AA
Kitty's "No." Arlo Bates. *Fr.* Conceits. AA
Kivers. Ann Cobb. AmFN
Kiwi Bird, The. Nina Cassian, *tr. fr. Rumanian by* Laura Schiff. OV
Kiwi Bird in the Kiwi Tree, The. Charles Bernstein. UL
Klabauterwife's Letter. Christian Morgenstern, *tr. fr. German by* W. D. Snodgrass *and* Lore Segal. WSC
Kleine Nachtmusik, *sel.* Jacob Glatstein, *tr. fr. Yiddish by* Chana Bloch.
    "Trust me from here to there." PeBMYV
Kleomedes. David Wright. MoP
Klondike, The. E. A. Robinson. PAH
Klupzy Girl, The. Charles Bernstein. IAT
Knave of darkness, limber in the leaves, The. Death for the Dark Stranger. Thomas McGrath. VGW
Knedneuch land. In the Pantry. "Hugh MacDiarmid." NoAM
Knee. Christian Morgenstern, *tr. fr. German by* W. D. Snodgrass *and* Lore Segal. RB
Knee-deep in June. James Whitcomb Riley. OHFP
Knee on Its Own, The. Christian Morgenstern, *tr. fr. German by* R. F. L. Hull. FaBoNo
Kneegrows niggas. Be Cool, Baby. Rob Penny. PoBA
Kneel then with me, fall worm-like on the ground. Night. George Chapman. *Fr.* The Shadow of Night. OBSC
Kneeling Camel, The. Anna Temple Whitney. BLPA
    (Submission and Rest.) BLRP
Kneeling Down to Look into a Culvert. Robert Bly. NoAM
Kneeling Here, I Feel Good. Marge Piercy. NeAC
Kneeling in the sheepshit. Mountain Oysters. Patrick Lane. NeAC
Knell, The. Muhammad Al-Fituri, *tr. fr. Arabic by* Samir M. Zoghby. TTY
Knell that dooms the voiceless and obscure, The. Survival. Florence Earle Coates. AA
Knicht had two sons o sma fame, A. Sir Lionel. *Unknown.* ESPB
Knife, The. Keith Douglas. NoAM
Knife, The. Juan Gelman, *tr. fr. Spanish by* Yishai Tobin. VWA
Knife, The. Milton Kaplan. TrJP
Knife, The. Richard Tillinghast. MAYP; MT
Knife, The. Jean Valentine. LCAP

Knife All Blade, A. João Cabral de Melo Neto, *tr. fr. Portuguese by* Galway Kinnell. ATCBP

Knife Whetter. Takamura Kotaro, *tr. fr. Japanese by* Hiroaki Sato. FCEI

Knife's edge, moon's edge, water's edge. Edge. Robert D. Fitzgerald. CBAP

Knight and a lady, A. *Unknown.* BoTP

Knight and a lady once met in a grove, A. Sympathy. Reginald Heber. BeLS

Knight and Shepherd's Daughter, The. *Unknown.* ESPB
    (Shepherd's Dochter, The.) OxBB

Knight and the Lady, The. William Cornish. *See* Desire.

Knight and the Shepherd's Daughter, The. *Unknown.* AmFP; ESPB, (A *and* B *vers.*)
    (Shepherd's Dochter, The.) OxBB

Knight, Death, and the Devil, The. Randall Jarrell. WeW

Knight Fallen on Evil Days, The. Elinor Wylie. MoAmPo

Knight from the world's end, The. A Dream of Governors. Louis Simpson. NYBP

Knight had ridden down from Wensley Moor, The. Hart-Leap Well. Wordsworth. BeLS

Knight in the Bower, The. *Unknown. See* Heron flew east, the heron flew west, The.

Knight in the Wood, The. Lord De Tabley. NOBVV

Knight knocked at the castle gate, The. Desire. William Cornish. Mes; OBSC
    (Knight and the Lady, The.) NOBE

Knight Knocked at the Castle Gate, The. *Unknown.* OxBLMV

Knight of Curtesy, The. ("In Faguell, a fayre countré"). *Unknown.* OxBLMV

Knight of Curtesy, The, *sel. Unknown, tr. fr. Middle English by* Pearl London.
    Eaten Heart, The. TrGrPo

Knight of Liddesdale, The. *Unknown.* ESPB

Knight of My Maiden Love. Priscilla Jane Thompson. CBWP-2

Knight of "silver tongue" and stately grace, A. Wendell Phillips. Henrietta Cordelia Ray. CBWP-3

Knight of the Burning Pestle, The, *sels.* Beaumont *and* Fletcher.
    Come, You Whose Loves Are Dead. *Fr.* IV, iv. EIL
    Jillian of Berry. *Fr.* IV, v. EIL
        (Another Song.) OBS
    Merrythought's Song. *Fr.* IV, i. OBS
    Mirth. *Fr.* II, viii. EIL
        (Laugh and Sing.) TrGrPo
    Month of May, The. *Fr.* IV, v. ChTr
    "Nose, nose, jolly red nose." *Fr.* I, iii. FaBoCh

Knight of the Grail, The. *Unknown. See* Lully, lullay [*or* lulley], lully, lullay [*or* lully].

Knight once lay beside and with, A. Gaucelm Faidit, *tr. by* Paul Blackburn. Pro

Knight Sings, The. Judah Leib Teller, *tr. fr. Yiddish by* Benjamin *and* Barbara Harshav. AYP

Knight Stained from Battle, The. William Herebert. MeEL

Knight stands in the stable-door, The. Young Johnstone. *Unknown.* ESPB

Knight there was, and that a worthy man, A. Chaucer. *See* Canterbury Tales, The: Prologue.

Knight with starry shield, The. Sir Roland; a Fragment. Robert Merry. NOEC

Knight, with Umbrella. Elder Olson. FiBHP

Knight without a Name, The. *Unknown.* WiR

Knightliest of the knightly race, The. The Virginians of the Valley. Francis Orrery Ticknor. AA; PAH

Knight's Ghost, The. *Unknown.* ESPB

Knight's Prayer, The. *Unknown.* BoTP

Knight's Tale, The. Chaucer. *Fr.* The Canterbury Tales.
    "But in the dome of mighty Mars the red." OBWP, *mod. version by* Dryden.

Knight's Tomb, The. Samuel Taylor Coleridge. EnRP; FaBoCh; GN; RB

Knitters, The. Padraic Colum. SaC

Knitting. Mary E. Tucker. CBWP-1

Knives are on their feet, The. Highway Single Sun. Tristan Tzara, *tr. by* Charles Simic *and* Michael Benedikt. POS

Knob and hump upon this tree. A Gnarled Riverina Gum-Tree. Ernest G. Moll. PoAu-2

Knock at the doorie. *Unknown.* OxNR

Knock here's where I live. Message. Gyorgy Raba, *tr. by* Jascha Kessler. VWA

"Knock-me-down sermon, and worthy of Birch, A." An Old Buffer. Frederick Locker-Lampson. CenHV

Knock on Wood. Henry Dumas. CNA; PoBA

Knocking Around. John Ashbery. NoAM

Knockout, The. Lillian Morrison. RHPC

Knockout. John Skoyles. NAmP

Knole. Charles Hubert Sisson. NOCV

Knolege, aquayntance, resort, favour with grace. Knowledge, Acquaintance. John Skelton. AAS

Knot, The. Stanley Kunitz. CAPP; HAP

Knot which first my heart did strain, The. Sir Thomas Wyatt. SiPS

Know, The. Kathleen Fraser. NPGG

Know Celia, (since thou art so proud). Ingrateful [I] Beauty Threatened. Thomas Carew. CaPo; InvP; MeLP; OBEV; OBS; SeCP; SeCV-1

Know him for a white man. Passing into Storm. Patrick Lane. NOBC

Know I not who thou mayst be. At the Hacienda. Bret Harte. AA

Know, that I would accounted be. To Ireland in the Coming Times. W. B. Yeats. NoAM; NOIV
    (Apologia Addressed to Ireland in the Coming Days.) BrPo

Know then:/ Toward summer when the sun is in Hyades. Ezra Pound, *after the Chinese Book of Rites.* OBVE

Know then, I was born in a strange country. To My People. Edwin Seaver. TrJP

Know then, my brethren, heaven is clear. *Unknown. Fr.* The Song of Anarchus. FaBoCo

Know then thyself, presume not God to scan. Pope. *Fr.* An Essay on Man, Epistle II. BLPL, *ll.* 1–18; LiTB, *fr.* II *and* IV; NAEL-1; NOEC, *ll.* 1–18; NoP; OAEL-1, *ll.* 1–18; PoEL-3; SeCePo, *ll.* 1–18; TrGrPo, *ll.* 1–18.
    (Know Thyself.) NOBE, *fr. ll.* 1-18.
    (Man.) PrIm, *fr. ll.* 1-18.
    (Paragon of Animals, The.) ACP, *ll.* 1–30.
    (Proper Study of Mankind, The.) FiP, *ll.* 1–30.
    (Riddle of the World.) FaFP, *ll.* 1–18.

Know this. Manifesto of the Soldier Who Went Back to War. Angel Miguel Queremel, *tr. by* Donald Devenish Walsh. WaaP

Know Thyself. Kenneth Burke. OBAL

Know Thyself. Pope. *See* Essay on Man, An: Know then thyself, presume not God to scan.

Know what I'll promise you? *Unknown, tr. by* Jerome Rothenberg. STP

Know ye the man whom God has blessed. Lines to the Hon. George L. Knox. Eloise Bibb. CBWP-4

Know ye the willow-tree. The Willow-Tree. Thackeray. CenHV

Know ye the witch's dell? Lincolnshire; from the Wolds to the Fens. Ben Jonson. *Fr.* The Sad Shepherd, II, vii. FaBoPP

Know you faire, on what you looke. On Mr. G. Herberts Booke Intituled the Temple of Sacred Poems, Sent to a Gentlewoman. Richard Crashaw. SeCV-1

Know your number. From an Inmate Rule Book. Joseph Bruchac. NOVW

Knowest thou the land where bloom the lemon trees. Goethe. *See* Wilhelm Meister's Apprenticeship: Mignon.

Knowest thou the time when the wild goates of the rocke bring forth. Bible, *O.T. Fr.* Job: Then the Lord Answered ("Who is this that darkeneth counsel by words without knowledge?"), XXXIX. OBVE

Knowing. Mary Coghill. BrRo

Knowing her is not knowing her. An Afterword: For Gwen Brooks. Don L. Lee. JB

Knowing I Live in a Dark Age. Milton Acorn. NOBC

Knowing that the music knows. *Unknown, tr. fr. Tepehua Indian by* Charles Boilès. *Fr.* Tepehua Thought-Songs, I. STP

Knowledge. Louise Bogan. PoA

Knowledge. Nina Cassian, *tr. fr. Rumanian by* Michael Impey *and* Brian Swann. BoWoP

Knowledge, Acquaintance. John Skelton. AAS

Knowledge and Reason. Sir John Davies. *See* Nosce Teipsum: What Is This Knowledge?

Knowledge, I know, is sure, of gradual thought. Young Knowledge. Robin Hyde. PeNZ

Knowledge of Light, The. Henry Rago. VGW

Knowledge of What Is. Jan G. Elburg, *tr. fr. Dutch by* Koos Schuur. DuIn

Knowledge That Comes through Experience, The. Jane Cooper. NMM

Knowledgeable Child, The. L. A. G. Strong. OBMV

Knowlt Hoheimer. Edgar Lee Masters. *Fr.* Spoon River Anthology. OxBA

Known. Joel Dailey. UL

Known Soldier, The. Kenneth Patchen. WaaP

Knows he that never took a pinch. To My Nose. Alfred A. Forrester. BLPA

Knoxville, Tennessee. Nikki Giovanni. AmNP; BlSi; BPo; CNA; PoBA; SO

Knuckles over the flame. Paradigms of Fire. Brian Swann. AmPA
Knyght knokett at the castell gate, The. The Knight Knocked at the Castle Gate. *Unknown.* OxBLMV
Knyght ther[e] was, and that a worthy man, A. Chaucer. *Fr.* The Canterbury Tales: Prologue. InPS
("Knight there was, and that a worthy man, A.") TrGrPo, *orig. and mod. version by* Louis Untermeyer.
Ko-Ishin-Mit Goes Fishing. George Clutesi. HATNAP
Ko-jin goes west from Ko-kaku-ro [*or* Ko-keku-to]. Separation on the River Kiang. Li Po, *tr. by* Ezra Pound. InPS; SOTW; UnPo
Ko-Ko's Song ("As some day it may happen that a victim should be found"). W. S. Gilbert. *Fr.* The Mikado.
Ko-Ko's Song ("On a tree by a river a little tom-tit"). W. S. Gilbert. *See* Mikado, The: Ko-Ko's Winning Song.
Ko-Ko's Winning Song. W. S. Gilbert. *Fr.* The Mikado, II. LiTB
(Ko-Ko's Song ("On a tree by a river a little tom-tit").) FaFP (Titwillow.) NoP
Koala. Alan Ross. OBTV
Kob Antelope. *Unknown, tr. fr. Yoruba by* Ulli Beier. *Fr.* Hunter Poems of the Yoruba. RB; WTO
Kodak; Tregantle, A. Horatio Brown. PeHV
Koheleth. Louis Untermeyer. TrJP
Kojiki, The, *sels. Unknown, tr. fr. Japanese by* Hiroaki Sato. FCEI
Emperor Ojin's Song.
Song of a Lady from Mie.
Songs Exchanged between Prince Okuninushi and Princess Nunakawa ("Divine prince of eight thousand spears").
Songs Exchanged between Prince Okuninushi and Princess Nunakawa ("The divine prince of eight thousand spears/ great ruler of our land").
Songs Exchanged between Prince Okuninushi and Princess Nunakawa ("When, having carefully put on").
Susano-o's Song.
Koka Shu, *sel. Unknown, tr. fr. Japanese by* Geoffrey Bownas *and* Anthony Thwaite.
"Through the chinks." PeBJV
Kokin Shu, *sels. Unknown, tr. fr. Japanese.*
"Along the Yodo." Tsurayuki, *tr. by* Burton Watson. FCEI
"Although it is not plainly visible to the eye." Fujiwara no Toshiyuki, *tr. by* Arthur Waley. AWP
"As autumn mists." Tsurayuki, *tr. by* Burton Watson. FCEI
"As for people—well." Tsurayuki, *tr. by* Burton Watson. FCEI
"Autumn chrysanthemums." Tsurayuki, *tr. by* Burton Watson. FCEI
"Autumn mists/ don't rise up this morning!" *Unknown, tr. by* Burton Watson. FCEI
"Beating their wings." *Unknown, tr. by* Geoffrey Bownas *and* Anthony Thwaite. PeBJV
"Beauty of the flowers faded, The." Komachi, *tr. by* Burton Watson. FCEI
"Because I fell asleep." Komachi, *tr. by* Burton Watson. FCEI
"Because I loved someone." *Unknown, tr. by* Burton Watson. FCEI
"Before we've had our fill." Narihira, *tr. by* Burton Watson. FCEI
"Beloved person must I think, The." Ki no Akimine, *tr. by* Arthur Waley. AWP
"Blossoms, at least wait." Tsurayuki, *tr. by* Burton Watson. FCEI
"Born here, you never lived." Tsurayuki, *tr. by* Burton Watson. FCEI
"Cherry blossoms." Narihira, *tr. by* Burton Watson. FCEI
"Cherry flowers." *Unknown, tr. by* Burton Watson. FCEI
"Did I ever think." Ono no Takamura, *tr. by* Arthur Waley. AWP
"Did you come here?." *Tr. by* Burton Watson. FCEI
"Dimly in the dawn mist." *Unknown, tr. by* Geoffrey Bownas *and* Anthony Thwaite. PeBJV
"Even before they fall." *Unknown, tr. by* Burton Watson. FCEI
"Even in the roaring torrent." *Unknown, tr. by* Burton Watson. FCEI
"Even the old Nagara Bridge in Naniwa." Lady Ise, *tr. by* Burton Watson. FCEI
"Ever since I dozed off." Komachi, *tr. by* Burton Watson. FCEI
"Fifth-month hills." Tsurayuki, *tr. by* Burton Watson. FCEI
"Foot-wearying mountain." Tsurayuki, *tr. by* Burton Watson. FCEI
"For all I know, I myself." Tsurayuki, *tr. by* Burton Watson. FCEI
"Forgotten by the one." Komachi, *tr. by* Burton Watson. FCEI
"Grass of Kasuga Moor." *Unknown, tr. by* Geoffrey Bownas *and* Anthony Thwaite. PeBJV
"Have the spring mists." Tsurayuki, *tr. by* Burton Watson. FCEI
"Hoping all the time." *Unknown, tr. by* Arthur Waley. AWP
"Hours of the spring night are not many, The." Michizane, *tr. by* Burton Watson. FCEI
"How I think of it!" *Unknown, tr. by* Burton Watson. FCEI
"I dip with my hands." Tsurayuki, *tr. by* Burton Watson. FCEI

"I found lodging." Tsurayuki, *tr. by* Burton Watson. FCEI
"I lost my way." Narihira, *tr. by* Burton Watson. FCEI
"I pity those rice stalks." Komachi, *tr. by* Burton Watson. FCEI
"I put in for a five-day leave." Michizane, *tr. by* Burton Watson. FCEI
"I smell the smell." *Unknown, tr. by* Geoffrey Bownas *and* Anthony Thwaite. PeBJV
"I want to see him." Lady Ise, *tr. by* Burton Watson. FCEI
"I was certain that lute and calligraphy would help my studies." Michizane, *tr. by* Burton Watson. FCEI
"If a seed is there." *Unknown, tr. by* Burton Watson. FCEI
"If I had known." *Unknown, tr. by* Geoffrey Bownas *and* Anthony Thwaite. PeBJV
"If I'd known/ it was old age calling." *Unknown, tr. by* Burton Watson. FCEI
"If love could be bought." *Unknown, tr. by* Burton Watson. FCEI
"If only my body." Lady Ise, *tr. by* Burton Watson. FCEI
"If only, when one heard." *Unknown, tr. by* Arthur Waley. AWP
"If there were no such thing." Narihira, *tr. by* Burton Watson. FCEI
"I'm getting older." Narihira, *tr. by* Burton Watson. FCEI
"In springtime/ when the plum trees bloom." Tsurayuki, *tr. by* Burton Watson. FCEI
"In the end." Narihira, *tr. by* Burton Watson. FCEI
"In the end I find." Narihira, *tr. by* Burton Watson. FCEI
"In the spring haze." *Unknown, tr. by* Geoffrey Bownas *and* Anthony Thwaite. PeBJV
"In this world." *Unknown, tr. by* Burton Watson. FCEI
"In this world." Tsurayuki, *tr. by* Burton Watson. FCEI
"In this world." Narihira, *tr. by* Burton Watson. FCEI
"In this world is there." *Unknown, tr. by* Geoffrey Bownas *and* Anthony Thwaite. PeBJV
"In waking hours." Komachi, *tr. by* Burton Watson. FCEI
"It grows dark, it seems." *Unknown, tr. by* Geoffrey Bownas *and* Anthony Thwaite. PeBJV
"It was not the wind—the oil is gone." Michizane, *tr. by* Burton Watson. FCEI
"It's spring!/ when threads of the green willow." Tsurayuki, *tr. by* Burton Watson. FCEI
"I've gone to him." Komachi, *tr. by* Burton Watson. FCEI
"I've grown so wretched." Komachi, *tr. by* Burton Watson. FCEI
"Kerria roses on the banks." Tsurayuki, *tr. by* Burton Watson. FCEI
"Kudzu vines clinging to." Tsurayuki, *tr. by* Burton Watson. FCEI
"Like a wild cherry." Tsurayuki, *tr. by* Burton Watson. FCEI
"Like the light snow." *Unknown, tr. by* Burton Watson. FCEI
"May our friend endure." *Unknown, tr. by* Geoffrey Bownas *and* Anthony Thwaite. PeBJV
"Mists rise, tree buds swell." Tsurayuki, *tr. by* Burton Watson. FCEI
"My heart, so entranced." Tsurayuki, *tr. by* Burton Watson. FCEI
"My hut is at the foot." *Unknown, tr. by* Burton Watson. FCEI
"My longings unbearable." Tsurayuki, *tr. by* Burton Watson. FCEI
"My love/ Is like the grasses." Ono no Yoshiki, *tr. by* Arthur Waley. AWP
"My love is as endless." Lady Ise, *tr. by* Burton Watson. FCEI
"My thoughts of you are endless." Komachi, *tr. by* Burton Watson. FCEI
"Neither waking or sleeping." Narihira, *tr. by* Burton Watson. FCEI
"No seaweed in this bay." Komachi, *tr. by* Burton Watson. FCEI
"No way to meet him." Komachi, *tr. by* Burton Watson. FCEI
"Now summer's come." *Unknown, tr. by* Burton Watson. FCEI
"Now that I've built my house." *Unknown, tr. by* Burton Watson. FCEI
"Now when spring mists rise." Lady Ise, *tr. by* Burton Watson. FCEI
"O Cuckoo." *Unknown, tr. by* Arthur Waley. AWP
"On autumn nights." *Unknown, tr. by* Burton Watson. FCEI
"On summer nights." Tsurayuki, *tr. by* Burton Watson. FCEI
"Orange blossoms that came." *Unknown, tr. by* Burton Watson. FCEI
"Pushing home at dawn." Narihira, *tr. by* Burton Watson. FCEI
"Rays of the autumn moon, The." Tsurayuki, *tr. by* Burton Watson. FCEI
"Sad—the end that waits me." Komachi, *tr. by* Burton Watson. FCEI

"Seen, and yet not seen." Narihira, *tr. by* Burton Watson. FCEI

"Shallow river of tears, A." Narihira, *tr. by* Burton Watson. FCEI

"Sheer fiction/ that autumn nights are longer." Komachi, *tr. by* Burton Watson. FCEI

"She's dead—but in my grief." Tsurayuki, *tr. by* Burton Watson. FCEI

"Since Amaro died I cannot sleep at night." Michizane, *tr. by* Burton Watson. FCEI

"Since I heard." Mitsune, *tr. by* Arthur Waley. AWP

"Since I was suddenly sent away." Michizane, *tr. by* Burton Watson. FCEI

"So fleeting/ that dream of a night." Narihira, *tr. by* Burton Watson. FCEI

"So much to ask." Narihira, *tr. by* Burton Watson. FCEI

"Some, childless when they left." Tsurayuki, *tr. by* Burton Watson. FCEI

"Someone must be." Narihira, *tr. by* Burton Watson. FCEI

"Speak of this to no one." Lady Ise, *tr. by* Burton Watson. FCEI (Sleeping with Someone Who Came in Secret.) LLLT

"Spring rains weaving." Lady Ise, *tr. by* Burton Watson. FCEI

"Stalks of rice." Tsurayuki, *tr. by* Burton Watson. FCEI

"Submit to you." Komachi, *tr. by* Burton Watson. FCEI

"Surely this is the moon." Narihira, *tr. by* Burton Watson. FCEI

"That cuckoo who sang." *Unknown, tr. by* Burton Watson. FCEI

"That hill where." Tsurayuki, *tr. by* Burton Watson. FCEI

"That's how life is." Tsurayuki, *tr. by* Burton Watson. FCEI

"They change/ though you can't see it." Komachi, *tr. by* Burton Watson. FCEI

"Thing which fades, A." Komachi, *tr. by* Arthur Waley. AWP; BoWoP; PBWP

"This stream that." Lady Ise, *tr. by* Burton Watson. FCEI

"This thing called parting." Tsurayuki, *tr. by* Burton Watson. FCEI

"Those who were here are gone." Komachi, *tr. by* Burton Watson. FCEI

"Though I know in time." Tsurayuki, *tr. by* Burton Watson. FCEI

"Though the Asuka River." Lady Ise, *tr. by* Burton Watson. FCEI

"Though winds blow." Narihira, *tr. by* Burton Watson. FCEI

"Three lonely months and more without news." Michizane, *tr. by* Burton Watson. FCEI

"Through autumn fields of bush clover." *Unknown, tr. by* Burton Watson. FCEI

"Time comes when, A." Komachi, *tr. by* Burton Watson. FCEI

"To plant plum-flowers." *Unknown, tr. by* Geoffrey Bownas *and* Anthony Thwaite. PeBJV

"Waters we dipped from." Tsurayuki, *tr. by* Burton Watson. FCEI

"We part/ I go beyond the." *Unknown, tr. by* Burton Watson. FCEI

"Well matched, well matched to mine." Lady Ise, *tr. by* Burton Watson. FCEI

"We've hardly parted." Tsurayuki, *tr. by* Burton Watson. FCEI

"What do you tell me now." Komachi, *tr. by* Burton Watson. FCEI

"What is constant." *Unknown, tr. by* Burton Watson. FCEI

"When a thousand birds." *Unknown, tr. by* Geoffrey Bownas *and* Anthony Thwaite. PeBJV

"When I see the moonlight pouring." *Unknown, tr. by* Burton Watson. FCEI

"When longings/ press too fiercely." Komachi, *tr. by* Burton Watson. FCEI

"When night fell, when day broke." Tsurayuki, *tr. by* Burton Watson. FCEI

"When the dawn comes." *Unknown, tr. by* Arthur Waley. AWP

"When the moonlight." *Unknown, tr. by* Geoffrey Bownas *and* Anthony Thwaite. PeBJV

"When torches cast their light." Tsurayuki, *tr. by* Burton Watson. FCEI

"Whether winds from the mountain." Lady Ise, *tr. by* Burton Watson. FCEI

"Whether you might come." *Unknown, tr. by* Geoffrey Bownas *and* Anthony Thwaite. PeBJV

"You bloom/ with a color and fragrance." Tsurayuki, *tr. by* Burton Watson. FCEI

"Your sisters all must stay at home." Michizane, *tr. by* Burton Watson. FCEI

Kol Nidra. Joseph Leiser. TrJP

Kol-Nidre. Moyshe-Leyb Halpern, *tr. fr. Yiddish by* Benjamin *and* Barbara Harshav *and* Kathryn Helle. AYP

Kol Nidre. Sharon A. Stern. TSM

Kola Run, The. D. S. Goodbrand. OxBSS

Kona Sea, The. *Unknown, tr. fr. Hawaiian by* N. B. Emerson. WTO

Kong Hits the Road with Dan-Dee Carnivals, Inc. William Trowbridge. SoTCo

Konskiwolie, Mazelbozec, Korznice. Jewish Kingdoms. Jacob Glatstein, *tr. by* Benjamin *and* Barbara Harshav. AYP

Koocoo, The. *Unknown.* GBP; TTTS

Kopis'taya. Paula Gunn Allen. HATNAP; STE

Kore. Robert Creeley. InPS; PoE

Korea Bound, 1952. William Childress. AmFN

Korean Woman Seated by a Wall, A. William Meredith. NePoEA

Korets Landscape. Yankev-Yitskhok Segal, *tr. fr. Yiddish by* Grace Schulman. PeBMYV

Korf has a distant aunt, you know. Korf's Enchantment. Christian Morgenstern, *tr. by* W. D. Snodgrass *and* Lore Segal. WSC

Korf invents some jokes of a new sort. Delayed Action. Christian Morgenstern, *tr. by* W. D. Snodgrass *and* Lore Segal. RB

Korf's Clock. Christian Morgenstern, *tr. fr. German by* Geoffrey Grigson. FaBoNo

Korf's Enchantment. Christian Morgenstern, *tr. fr. German by* W. D. Snodgrass *and* Lore Segal. WSC

Koskiusko. Samuel Taylor Coleridge. EnRP

Kou-chien, king of Yüeh, came back from the broken land of Wu. In Yüeh Viewing the Past. Li Po, *tr. by* Burton Watson. CoBCP

Kowloon-Canton Railway, The. Yu Kuang-chung, *tr. fr. Chinese by* Dominic Cheung. IFON

Koyorogi. *Unknown, tr. fr. Japanese by* Hiroaki Sato. FCEI

Kraa. William Pitt Root. SM

Kraken, The. Tennyson. AmMo; NAEL-2; NoP; OAEL-2; OBNC; PoEL-5; TOF; WiR; WSC

Kral Majales. Allen Ginsberg. PoM

Krankenhaus of Leutkirch, The. Richmond Lattimore. NYBP

Kree. A. C. Gordon. AA

Kreutzer Sonata. Ted Hughes. FaBoMo

Krinio. Rita Boumi-Pappas, *tr. fr. Greek by* Eleni Fourtouni. AIW

Krishna, Krishna,/ Now as I look on. Debate between Arjuna and Sri Krishna. *Unknown, tr. by* Swami Prabhavananda *and* Christopher Isherwood. WaaP

Krismas Dinnah. Maggie Pogue Johnson. CBWP-4

Kropotkin Poems, The, *sel.* Phyllis Webb. "Syllables disintegrate ingrate alphabets." NOBC

Ku Klux. Madison Cawein. AA; PAH

Ku Klux. Langston Hughes. BPo

Ku Li. Robin Hyde. PeNZ

Kû! Listen! In Alahíyi you repose, O Terrible Woman. Sacred Formula to Attract Affection. *Unknown, tr. by* James Mooney. LiTA

Kubla Khan; or, A Vision in a Dream. Samuel Taylor Coleridge. AWP; CH; ChER; ChTr; ELP; EnRP; EyDe; FaBoBe; FaBoCh; FaBV; FaFP; FF; FiP; FPL; GN; GoJo; HAP; HeIP; HoPM; InPK; InPS; InvP; LiTB; MAT; NAEL-2; NAWM-2; NIP; NOBE; NoP; OAEL-2; OBEV; OBNC; OPOP; PoE; PoEL-4; PoRA; PrIm; SCV; SoSe; TEP; TOF

Kudzu Spreads Till It Darkens the Brier, The. *Unknown, tr. fr. Chinese by* Burton Watson. CoBCP

Kudzu vines clinging to. Tsurayuki, *tr. fr. Japanese by* Burton Watson. Fr. Kokin Shu. FCEI

Kula. a Homecoming. Diane Mei Lin Mark. BrSi

Kumara God. Peter Bland. ATNZ

Kumulipo, The; a Creation Chant, *sels.* Keaulumoku, *tr. fr. Hawaiian by* M. W. Beckwith. WTO
  Birth of Sea and Land Life.
  Crawlers, The.
  Dawn of Day, The.
  Dog Child, The.

Kunai-mai-pa Mo. Ethel Anderson. PoAu-2

Kung walked/ by the dynastic temple. Ezra Pound. *Fr.* Cantos, XIII. CMoP; FaBoMo; PoE

Kupris bears trophies away. Sophocles, *tr. fr. Greek by* Ezra Pound. *Fr.* Women of Trachis. CTC

Kutune Shirka (The Ainu Epic), *sel.* Wakarpa, *tr. by* Arthur Waley. Golden Sea-Otter, The. WTO

Kwa Mama Zetu Waliotuzaa. Sonia Sanchez. ER

Kwatz too weak, stick too short. Seisen, *tr. by* Lucien Stryk *and* Takashi Ikemoto. ZPCJ

Kyng Jamy/ Jamy your Joye is all go. A Ballade of the Scottyshe Kynge. John Skelton. CoMu; FaBoBa

Kyoto: March. Gary Snyder. PPP

Kypros! Andromache's Wedding. Sappho, *tr. by* Willis Barnstone. BoWoP

Kyran's Christening. Alden Nowlan. NeAC

Kyrie Eleison! The Funeral of Philip Sparrow. John Skelton. *Fr.* Phyllyp Sparowe [*or* Philip Sparrow]. ACP, *abr.*

"Kyrie, so kyrie." Jolly Jankin. *Unknown.* GBP; NoP; OxBoLi; PoE
　(Jankin.) NOBE
　(Jankin, the Clerical Seducer.) MeEL
Kythans. Stewart McGavin. PoSH
Kyuko and I Stayed at Rittei's. Taigi, *tr. fr. Japanese by* Hiroaki Sato.
　Fr. Twenty-nine Hokku. FCEI

L

L(a. E. E. Cummings. NIP; NoP; RR
La Bagarède. Galway Kinnell. NYBP
La Banditaccia, 1979. Rika Lesser. MAYP
La Bella Bona Roba. Richard Lovelace. CaPo; EBEV; OAEL-1;
　PoEL-3; SeCP
La Belle Confidente. Thomas Stanley. JCP; MeLP; MePo; OBS
La Belle Dame sans Merci. T. Griffiths. BXAP
La Belle Dame sans Merci. Keats. AWP; BeLS; BLPA; CH; ChTr;
　ELP; EnRP; FaBoBe; FaBoCh; FaFP; FiP; FPL; GoJo; GTBS;
　GTBS-P; HAP; HeIP; InPS; InvP; LiTB; NAEL-2; NAWM-2; NOBE;
　NoP; OAEL-2; OBEV; OBNC; PoE; PoEL-4; PoRA; Prf; PrIm; RB;
　SCV; SoSe; TEP; TrGrPo; UnPo; VVA; WeW
La Belle Dame Sans Merci. Eugenio Montale, *tr. fr. Italian by* G. Singh.
　PFI
La Belle Dame sans Mercy. *At. to* Alain Chartier, *tr. fr. French by* Sir
　Richard Ros. *See* Belle Dame sans Mercy, La.
La Belle Morte. Conrad Aiken. VVA
La Belle Sauvage. John Hunter-Duvar. *Fr.* De Roberval. OBCV
La Brea. Richard Kenney. DiPo
La Carte. Justin Richardson. FiBHP
La Chute. Charles Olson. InPK
La Condition Botanique. Anthony Hecht. NePoEA
La Corona ("Deigne at my hands this crown of power and praise."), *sels.*
　John Donne. OBS; Son
　Annunciation. TrCP
　Ascension [*or* Ascention].
　Crucifying.
　Nativitie. OBS
　Nativity [*or* Nativitie]. OBS; Son
　Resurrection.
　Temple.
La Crosse at Ninety Miles an Hour. Richard Eberhart. AmFN
La Cucaracha. *Unknown.* AS
La Donna È Mobile. "A. K." FiBHP
La Donna E Perpetuum Mobile. Irwin Edman. FiBHP; NYBP
La Fayette. Dolly Madison. AiP; PAH
La Figlia Che Piange. T. S. Eliot. FaBoTw; GBL; HeIP; LiTA; MAT;
　OPOP; OxBTC; PoA; VGW
La Fontaine de Vaucluse. Marilyn Hacker. FYAP
　Sels.
　Azure Striation Swirls beyond the Stones. *Fr.* I. Son
　We May Be Learning How to Tell the Truth. *Fr.* VII. Son
La Grande Jeanne. Luciano Erba, *tr. fr. Italian by* Lawrence R. Smith.
　NItP
La Grisette. Oliver Wendell Holmes. AA
La Guerre. E. E. Cummings. MoAB; MoAmPo
La, La, La! Thomas M. Disch. NBLV
La-la-llamas rate as mammals. In Praise of Llamas. Arthur Guiterman.
　FiBHP
La Llorona. Greg Pape. AmPA
La Madonna dell' Acqua. John Ruskin. NOBVV
La Máquina a Houston. Edward Dorn. PoM
La Misère. Philip Appleman. BXAP
La Mort d'Arthur. William Edmonstoune Aytoun. FaBoPa
La Noche Triste. Robert Frost. FL
La Nuit Blanche. Kipling. MoBrPo
La Plata, Missouri: Clear November Night. Jim Barnes. HATNAP
La Préface. Charles Olson. PoM
La Promessa Sposa. Walter Savage Landor. NOBVV
La Reproduction Interdite/ Not to Be Reproduced. Kathleen Fraser. NPGG
La Selva. Cid Corman. VGW
La Tricoteuse. George Walter Thornbury. BeLS
La Vie C'est la Vie. Jessie Redmond Fauset. BANP; CDC; PoNe
La Vita Nuova. Weldon Kees. VGW
La Voix du Peuple. Hans Lodeizen, *tr. fr. Dutch by* James S. Holmes.
　DuIn
Laban, I curse you for this trick you played! Jacob. Ruth Gilbert. *Fr.*
　Leah, II. PeNZ
Labasheedy (the Silken Bed). Nuala Ni Dhomhnaill, *tr. fr. Irish by* The
　Author. CIP

Labienus, each hair on your bosom that grows. To Labienus. Martial.
　PeHV
Labor. Lucille Day. VWA
Labor Day. Louise Glück. NoAM
Labor raises honest sweat. The Dignity of Labor. Robert Bersohn.
　NBLV
Laboratories explain it away in retrospect as chemistry, The. Sea-Grape
　Tree and the Miraculous. William Pitt Root. GeTw
Laboratory; Ancien Régime, The. Robert Browning. NAEL-2; OBEV
Laboratory Midnight, The. Reuel Denney. ImOP
Laboratory Poem. James Merrill. CAPP; InPK; MAT; NePoEA-2; TwCP
Laborer, The. Samuel Chimsoro. WMBCH
Laborer, The. Richard Dehmel, *tr. fr. German by* Jethro Bithell. AWP
Laborer, The. José-Maria de Heredia, *tr. fr. French by* Wilfrid Thorley.
　AWP
Laborers of Christ! Arise. Lydia Huntley Sigourney. AH
"Laborers Together with God." Lucy Alice Perkins. BLRP
Laboring and Heavy Laden. Jeremiah Eames Rankin. AH
Laboring men, please all attend. Free Silver. *Unknown.* AmFP
Laborintus, *sel.* Edoardo Sanguineti, *tr. fr. Italian by* Lawrence R.
　Smith.
　"Compound earths in structural compositions are Palus Putredinis."
　NItP
Labors of Hercules, The. Marianne Moore. OxBA
Labour. "Marie." PF
Labour. M. Saint-Marthe, *tr. fr. French.* *Fr.* Paedotrophiae; or, The Art
　of Bringing Up Children. FaBoUs
Labour of the Brain, Ballad of the Body. Nicole Forman. NMM
Labour Pains. Yosano Akiko, *tr. fr. Japanese by* Kenneth Rexroth *and*
　Ikuko Atsumi. AIW
Labour Song. James Syme. PF
Labourer, The. Iolo Goch, *tr. fr. Welsh by* Gwyn Williams. OBWVE
Labourer's Song, A. James Dawson. PF
Labourer's Wife, A. John Davidson. *Fr.* To the Street Piano. EBVV
Labouring Man, The. *Unknown.* OBET
Labouring man, that tills the fertile soil, The. Pains and Gains. Edward,
　17th Earl of Oxford De Vere. ElL
Labouring poor, in spite of double pay, The. Daniel Defoe. *Fr.* The
　True-born Englishman, II. NOBL; SaC
Labours of the Months. *Unknown.* *See* Januar: by this fire I warme my
　handes.
Labyrinth, The. W. H. Auden. LiTA
Labyrinth, The. Edwin Muir. CMoP; MoBrPo
Lac Courte Orielles; 1936. Phyllis Wolf. STE
Lace grows in her eyes like. Waiting, the Hallways under Her Skin Thick
　with Dreamchildren. Lyn Lifshin. NeAC
Lace Pedlar, The. Catherine A. Morin. BoTP
Lace Tell. *Unknown.* OBET
Lacemaker (Vermeer, The). Anne Marx. GoYe
Lachesis. Victor James Daley. CBAP
Lachesis. Hilaire Kirkland. *Fr.* Clotho, Lachesis, Atropos, II. PeNZ
Lachesis. Kathleen Jessie Raine. NYBP
Lachesis Net. P. Mustapää, *tr. fr. Finnish by* Aili Jarvenpa. SOP
Lachin y Gair. Byron. OxBS
Lachrimae, *sels.* Geoffrey Hill.
　Lachrimae Verae. *Fr.* I. NAEL-2; NoAM; NoP
　Masque of Blackness, The. *Fr.* II. NoAM
Lachrimae Amantis. Geoffrey Hill. NOCV
Lachrimae Verae. Geoffrey Hill. *Fr.* Lachrimae, I. NAEL-2; NoAM;
　NoP
Lacking samite and sable. May Probyn. ACP
Lacking Sense, The. Thomas Hardy. CMoP; PoEL-5
Laconic. Odysseus Elytis, *tr. fr. Greek by* Edmund Keeley *and* Philip
　Sherrard. VMG
Laconic as anglers and, like them, submissive. At the Ferry. U. A.
　Fanthorpe. FaBoWP
Laconic crow flies by, A. Issa, *tr. fr. Japanese by* Hiroaki Sato. *Fr.*
　Forty-four Hokku. FCEI
Lacquer Liquor Locker, The. David McCord. FiBHP
Lacrimas or There Is a Need to Scream. K. Curtis Lyle. PoBA
Lacy mobile changing lazily, A. Watching a Cloud. Dannie Abse.
　OxBC; TEP
Lad of Athens, faithful be. Emily Dickinson. FaBoEE
Lad Philisides, The. A Country Song. Sir Philip Sidney. *Fr.* Arcadia.
　OBSC; SiPS
Lad when at school, one day stole a pin, A. The Results of Stealing a
　Pin. *Unknown.* FaBoUs
Ladd I the dance a Midsomer Day. A Night with a Holy-Water Clerk.
　Unknown. MeEL
Ladder, The. Gene Baro. NePoEA-2
Ladder, The. István Vas, *tr. fr. Hungarian by* Jascha Kessler. FOC

Ladder ascends and descends, A. The Drunkenness of Pain. Aliza Shenhar, *tr.* by Linda Zisquit. VWA

Ladder-Climbing and Grocery. Cheng Ch'ou-yu, *tr. fr. Chinese by* Dominic Cheung. IFON

Ladder Has No Steps, The. Jorge Plescoff, *tr. fr. Spanish by* Yishai Tobin. VWA

Ladder-seller/ Hears the cry "Swords drawn!," The. *Unknown, tr. by* Geoffrey Bownas *and* Anthony Thwaite. PeBJV

Laddie, little laddie, come with me over the hills. A Cry from the Canadian Hills. Lilian Leveridge. BLPA

Ladie stude in her bour-door, The. Young Hunting. *Unknown.* ESPB

Ladies, The. Kipling. MoBrPo; NAEL-2

Ladies' Aid, The. *Unknown.* PoLF

Ladies and gentlemen. An Apology for a Short Speech. Abdul Wahab al-Bayati, *tr.* by Abdullah al-Udhari. MPAW

Ladies and gentlemen. Complaint of the Oblivion of the Dead. Jules Laforgue, *tr.* by William Jay Smith. CT

Ladies and gentlemen:/ This broadcast comes to you from the city. Voice of the Studio Announcer. Archibald MacLeish. *Fr.* The Fall of the City. HoPM

Ladies and gentlemen:/ I have only one question. I Move the Meeting Be Adjourned. Nicanor Parra, *tr. fr. Spanish by* Miller Williams. *Fr.* Manifesto. HoPM

Ladies and Gentlemen,/ List to my song. Temperance Song. *Unknown.* FaBoUS

Ladies and gentlemen and children, too. Boogie Chant and Dance. *Unknown, tr.* by Ewald Osers. RR

Ladies and Gentlemen, my mother is. Honor Moore. *Fr.* Mourning Pictures. TV

Ladies and gentlemen, that is the end of the programme. Epilogue to a Poetry Reading. M. K. Joseph. ATNZ; PeNZ

Ladies and Gentlemen This Little Girl. E. E. Cummings. CMoP; PoE

Ladies and gents, you are here assembled. Gas from a Burner. James Joyce. TW

Ladies bow, and partners set, The. Soliloquy of a Maiden Aunt. Dollie Radford. NOBVV

Ladies' Eyes Serve Cupid Both for Darts and Fire. "A. W." OBSC

Ladies, I do here present you. A Present to a Lady. *Unknown.* ErPo

Ladies in town can't begin, The. Calling. H. Edgar Hix. SoTCo

Ladies of Bygone Days, The. Otto Orban, *tr. fr. Hungarian by* Edwin Morgan. MHuP

Ladies of London, both wealthy and fair. Advice to the Ladies of London in the Choice of Their Husbands. *Unknown.* CoMu

Ladies of St. James's, The. Austin Dobson. PoRA

Ladies of the morning gauze their mouths, The. Canonical Hours. William Dickey. CoAP

Ladies Prayer to Cupid, A. Thomas Carew. *See* Lady's Prayer to Cupid, A.

Ladies reading. Rites of the Eastern Star. Janine Pommy-Vega. UL

Ladies that have intelligence in love. Dante, *tr. fr. Italian by* Dante Gabriel Rossetti. *Fr.* La Vita Nuova, X. AWP

Ladies, though to your conquering eyes. Sir George Etherege. *Fr.* The Comical Revenge, V, iii. OBS; OxBSP

Ladies to Mademoiselle de Scudéry: Ode, The. Anne de La Vigne, *tr. fr. French by* Dorothy Backer. DMF

Ladies, to this advice give heed. A Maxim Revised. *Unknown.* BLPA; FPL; NBLV; WBLP

Ladies' Voices. Gertrude Stein. SOTW

Lads and lasses gathering. The Willow-Boughs. Alexander Block. BoTP

Lads in Their Hundreds, The. A. E. Housman. *Fr.* A Shropshire Lad, XXIII. MoBrPo; OxBTC

Lads of the Village, The. Stevie Smith. OxBSP

Lads of Wamphray, The. *Unknown.* ESPB

Lady. Ted Berrigan. UL

Lady. Jules Laforgue, *tr. fr. French by* William Jay Smith. CT

Lady, A. Amy Lowell. AnAmPo; MoAmPo

Lady, The, *sel.* Christine de Pisan, *tr. fr. French by* Naomi Lewis. From Darts of Love That Do Such Dole. *Fr.* VIII. DMF

Lady, A. W. D. Snodgrass. TW

Lady,/ baby. *Unknown.* OxNR

Lady/ I clear myself toward you. Bertrans de Born, *tr.* by Paul Blackburn. Pro

Lady,/ You, who are pattering to your carriage door. Genius. Louis Saunders Perkins. PeHV

Lady A. L., My Asylum in a Great Extremity, The. Richard Lovelace. CaPo

Lady Adeline Amundeville. Byron. *Fr.* Don Juan, XIII. PoEL-4

Lady Again Complains, The. Earl of Surrey. SiPS

Lady Alice ("George Collins come home last Friday night"). *Unknown.* AmFP

Lady Alice ("George Collins came home last Saturday night"). *Unknown.* AmFP

Lady Alice ("George Collins drove home one cold winter night"). *Unknown.* AmFP

Lady Alice ("Giles Collin he said to his mother one day"). *Unknown.* ESPB, (C *vers.*)

Lady Alice ("Giles Collins he said to his old mother"). *Unknown.* ESPB, (B *vers.*)

Lady Alice ("Lady Alice was sitting in her bower-window"). *Unknown.* ESPB, (A *vers.*)

Lady Alice ("She says the coffin to be opened"). *Unknown.* AmFP

Lady Alice was sitting in her bower-window. Lady Alice. *Unknown.* ESPB

Lady Almucs, with your permission. Almucs de Castelnau *and* Iseut de Capio, *tr.* by Meg Bogin. WT

Lady and gentlemen fays, come buy! The Elfin Pedlar. George Darley. BoTP

Lady and Queen and Mystery manifold. Ballade to Our Lady of Czestochowa. Hilaire Belloc. ACP

Lady and the Bear, The. Theodore Roethke. GoJo; NBLV; SO

Lady and the Gypsy, The. Vernon Scannell. Mes

Lady and the Unicorn, The. May Sarton. ER

Lady Anne Bathing. Anthony Delius. PeSA

Lady asks me, A. Canzone: Donna Mi Priegha. Guido Cavalcanti, *tr.* by Ezra Pound. CTC

(Donna Mi Priegha.) OBVE

Lady at the Castle, The. John Hollander. NoAM

Lady Byron's Reply to Lord Byron's "Fare Thee Well." *Unknown.* BLPA

Lady came to a bear by a stream, A. The Lady and the Bear. Theodore Roethke. GoJo; NBLV; SO

Lady Carenza of the lovely, gracious body. Alais, Iselda *and* Carenza. WT, *tr.* by Meg Bogin

(Lady Carenza, with the Lovely, Charming Body.) DMF, *tr.* by Joan H. Ferrante

Lady Clare. Tennyson. BeLS; FaPON; OnMSP

Lady Clothed in Flame, The. Dante, *tr. fr. Italian by* C. H. Sisson. *Fr.* Divina Commedia: Purgatorio, III. PFI

Lady Comes to an Inn, A. Elizabeth J. Coatsworth. MoAmPo; SO

Lady Complains of Her Lover's Absence, A. Earl of Surrey. *See* Complaint of the Absence of Her Lover Being upon the Sea.

Lady Day. Padraic Fallon. NeIP

Lady Diamond. *Unknown.* ESPB

Lady director is a gentle guide, The. Changsha Shoe Factory. Willis Barnstone. SaC

Lady Elspat. *Unknown.* ESPB

Lady Erskine sits in her chamber. Child Owlet. *Unknown.* ESPB

Lady, farewell, whom I in silence serve. A Poem Put into My Lady Laiton's Pocket. Sir Walter Ralegh. SiPS

Lady Fortune is both friend and foe, The. Fortune. *Unknown.* ACP; HeIP

Lady Franklin's Lament for Her Husband. *Unknown.* OxBSS

Lady Greensleeves. *Unknown. See* Greensleeves.

Lady, helpe! Jesu mercy! In His Utter Wretchedness. John Audelay. MeEL

Lady I Know, A. Countee Cullen. *See* Four Epitaphs

Lady, I loved you all last year. A Song of Impossibilities. Winthrop Mackworth Praed. NA

Lady, I trust it is not to do harm. A Volume of Chopin. James Picot. PoAu-2

Lady in a Distant Face. James Welch. AmPA

Lady in Kicking Horse Reservoir, The. Richard Hugo. CoAP; LCAP; NAAL-2; NoAM; NoP

Lady in the Barbershop, The. Raphael Rudnik. NYBP

Lady in the Pink Mustang, The. Louise Erdrich. HATNAP; NOVW

Lady Is a Tramp, The. Lorenz Hart. OBAL

Lady Isabel. *Unknown.* ESPB

Lady Isabel and the Elf-Knight [*or* The Elfin Knight]. *Unknown.* CH; ESPB; FaBoBa; GBP

Lady Isabel and the Elf Knight (Pretty Polly). *Unknown.* AmFP

Lady Isabella's Tragedy, The. *Unknown.* GBP

Lady Jane. Sir Arthur Quiller-Couch. FiBHP

Lady Jane, The; a Humorous Novel in Rhyme, *sels.* Nathaniel Parker Willis. OBAL

"If, in well-bred society, ('hear! hear!')."

"Some men, 'tis said, prefer a woman fat."

Lady, Lady. Anne Spencer. BlSi; PoBA

Lady, lady, I saw your face. Lady, Lady. Anne Spencer. BlSi; PoBA

Lady, lady, lady fair. The Suffolk Miracle. *Unknown.* AmFP

Lady, lady should you meet. Social Note. Dorothy Parker. *Fr.* Some Beautiful Letters. FaBoUs
Lady, lady, should you meet. Social Note. Dorothy Parker. AnAmPo
Lady Lazarus. Sylvia Plath. CAPP; FaBoWP; HCAP; MAT; MoP; NAAL-2; NaP; NIP; NoAM; NOBA; NoP; PrIm; TAP; VGW
Lady lived in Lancaster, A. Kate and the Cowhide. *Unknown.* AmFP
Lady Lost. John Crowe Ransom. MoAB; MoAmPo; TrGrPo; UnPo
Lady Love. Paul Eluard, *tr. fr. French.* OBVE, *tr. by* Samuel Beckett; RHTwFP
(Beloved, The.) POS
Lady Luck. Ann Gottlieb. NMM
Lady Maisdry was a lady fair. Lord Ingram and Chiel Wyet. *Unknown.* ESPB
Lady Maisry ("Oh she called to her little page boy"). *Unknown.* OBET
Lady Maisry ("The young lords o' the north country"). *Unknown.* ESPB, A *and* B *vers.*; OBET; OxBB, *with music.*
Lady Maisry lives intill a bower. Thomas o Yonderdale. *Unknown.* ESPB
Lady Margaret sat in her bower-door. Prince Heathen. *Unknown.* ESPB, (A *and* B *vers.*)
Lady Margaret sat in her bowry all alone. Sweet William's Ghost. *Unknown.* AWP, (A, B, F *and* G *vers.*); ESPB, (A, B, F *and* G *vers.*)
Lady Margaret sits in her bower door. Hind Etin. *Unknown.* ESPB
Lady Margery May sits in her bower. Prince Heathen. *Unknown.* ESPB
Lady Maria, in you merit and distinction. Bieiris de Romans. PeHV; WT, *tr. by* Meg Bogin
Lady Mary Villiers lies, The. Epitaph on the Lady Mary Villiers. Thomas Carew. CaPo; FaBoEE; NOBE; OBEV; SeCV-1
Lady Moon, The. Kate Louise Brown. BoTP
Lady Moon. Richard Monckton Milnes. BoTP; MoShBr; OxBChV
Lady Moon is sailing, The. The Lady Moon. Kate Louise Brown. BoTP
Lady Moon, Lady Moon, where are you roving. Lady Moon. Richard Monckton Milnes. BoTP; MoShBr; OxBChV
Lady Murasaki says. Murasaki Shikibu, *tr. fr. Japanese by* Kenneth Rexroth *and* Ikuko Atsumi. *Fr.* The Tale of Genji. BoWoP
Lady, my lady, come from out the garden. To a Certain Lady, in Her Garden. Sterling A. Brown. CDC
Lady My Treasure. Sir Philip Sidney. GBL
Lady of all the essences, full light. Inanna and the Divine Essences. Enheduanna, *tr. by* W. W. Hallo *and* J. J. A. van Dijk. BoWoP
Lady, of anonymous flesh and face. J. V. Cunningham. HoPM
Lady of Arngosk, The. *Unknown.* ESPB
Lady of Carlisle, The. *Unknown.* AmFP
Lady of Castlenoire. Thomas Bailey Aldrich. BeLS
Lady of Chaos. Ali Ja far al-Allaq, *tr. fr. Arabic by* Sharif Elmusa *and* Thomas G. Ezzy. MAP
Lady of dusk-wood fastnesses. First Praise. William Carlos Williams. VGW
Lady of Heaven and earth, and therewithal. His Mother's Service to Our Lady. Villon, *tr. by* Dante Gabriel Rossetti. AWP; CTC
Lady of Heaven, Queen of the world. Villon's Prayer for His Mother to Say to the Virgin. Villon, *tr. by* Robert Lowell. OBD
Lady of Heaven, queen terrestrial. Ballade which Villon Made. Donagh MacDonagh. TIRV
Lady of High Degree, A. *Unknown, tr. fr. French by* Andrew Lang. AWP
Lady of Life, The. Thomas Michael Kettle. ACP
Lady of Miracles. Nina Cassian, *tr. fr. Rumanian by* Laura Schiff. AIW; WPOW
Lady of Shalott, The. Tennyson. BeLS; BLPL; FaFP; FiP; GN; InPS; NAEL-2; NOBE; OAEL-2; OBEV; OBNV; PoE; TEP; TOF; WiR
Lady of shrouding hair. *Unknown.* NOIV
Lady of the bright coils and curlings. Eire. David O'Bruadair, *tr. by* Austin Clarke. BIrV
Lady of the crescent moon. Indian Love Letter. Soge Track. NOVW
Lady of the Ferry Inn. Gwerfyl Mechain, *tr. fr. Welsh.* BoWoP, *tr. by* Willis Barnstone
Lady of the house is on her benders, The. Five Domestic Interiors. Vernon Scannell. OxBC
Lady of the Lake, The, *sels.* Sir Walter Scott.
Alice Brand. *Fr.* IV. BeLS; OnMSP
Chase, The. *Fr.* I. EnRP
Coronach. *Fr.* III. CH; EnRP; GTBS; GTBS-P; OHIP; TrGrPo; WiR
Farewell, Thou Minstrel Harp. *Fr.* VI. OBNC
Gathering, The. OBNC
Hail to the Chief Who in Triumph Advances. *Fr.* II. EnRP; PoEL-4

Hymn to the Virgin. *Fr.* III. EnRP
"Now, yield thee, or by Him who made." *Fr.* V. OxBS
Soldier Rest! [Thy Warfare O'er]. *Fr.* I. AWP; GN; MoShBr; NOBE; PoRA; TrGrPo
(Song: "Soldier rest! thy warfare o'er.") OBNC
Toils Are Pitched, The. *Fr.* IV. EnRP
Western Waves of Ebbing Day, The. *Fr.* I. PoEL-4
Lady of the Lambs, The. Alice Meynell. *See* Shepherdess, The.
Lady of the legless world I have. Notes after Blacking Out. Gregory Corso. NeAP
Lady of the Manor, The. George Crabbe. *Fr.* The Parish Register: Burials. NOBE; OBNC
Lady of the Manor was dressing for the ball, The. The Highland Tinker. *Unknown.* CoMu
Lady of the Pearls, The, *sel.* Alexandre Dumas, *tr. fr. French by* Gerard Manley Hopkins.
"We set out yesterday upon a winter drive." TTY
Lady Picking Flowers, A. Shen Chou, *tr. fr. Chinese by* Jonathan Chaves. CoBLCP
Lady Pitcher, The. Cynthia MacDonald. Psk
Lady Poverty, The. Alice Meynell. NOBVV; OBMV
Lady Prayeth the Return of Her Lover Abiding on the SeasThe. *Unknown.* EIL; GBL
(Seafarer, The.) OBSC
(To Her Sea-faring Lover.) OBEV
Lady-Probationer. William Ernest Henley. *Fr.* In Hospital, IX. BrPo
Lady Queen Anne she sits in the sun. *Unknown.* OxNR
Lady Ralegh's Lament. Robert Lowell. OxBSP
Lady red upon the hill, A. Emily Dickinson. AA; BoNaP; OHIP
Lady Resists the Lover's Pleas, The. At. to Alain Chartier, *tr. fr. French by* Sir Richard Ros. *Fr.* La Belle Dame sans Mercy. OxBLMV
Lady "Rogue" Singleton. Stevie Smith. FaBoWP; OxBSP
Lady Sara Bunbury Sacrificing to the Graces, by Reynolds. Daryl Hine. EyDe
Lady Sayo of Matsura, as her name tells. *Unknown. Fr.* Manyo Shu. Ma
Lady says: "The cock has crowed," The. *Unknown, tr. by* Arthur Waley. BoS
Lady Sings, The. Milton. *See* Comus; a Masque Presented at Ludlow Castle: Echo.
Lady stands in her bower door, The. The Twa Magicians. *Unknown.* ESPB; GBP; OAEL-1; OxBB
(Two Magicians, The.) ChTr; OAEL-1; OxBoLi
Lady Stood, A. Dietmar von Aist, *tr. fr. German by* Jethro Bithell. AWP
Lady Suro. Park Je-chun, *tr. fr. Korean by* Koh Chang-soo. ACKP
Lady Tactics. Anne Waldman. PoM
Lady, tell me, will you, pray. Found—Who Lost? Mary E. Tucker. CBWP-1
Lady that hast my heart within thy hand. Hafiz, *tr. fr. Persian by* Gertrude Lowthian Bell. *Fr.* Odes, VIII. AWP
Lady That in the Prime. Milton. Son
Lady, the birds right fairly. *Unknown.* PBBP
Lady, the meshes of your coiling hair. He Praises Her Hair. *Unknown, tr. by* Earl of Longford. AnIL
Lady, the shepherds have all gone. Ya Se Van Los Pastores. Dudley Fitts. FYAP
Lady! the songs of Spring were in the grove. To the Lady Beaumont. Wordsworth. ChER
Lady, there is a hope that all men have. William Ellery Channing. *Fr.* A Poet's Hope. AA
Lady walked by the ocean strand, The. Strand-Thistle. Gustav Falke, *tr. by* Jethro Bithell. AWP
Lady walked down a roadbed, A. Gentle Heart, A: Two. Judith Johnson Sherwin. BoWoP
Lady, when you were alive. The Mortician's Twelve-year-old Son. Ai. GeTw
Lady Who Offers Her Looking-Glass to Venus, The. Matthew Prior, *after the Greek of* Plato. AWP; FaBoEE; NOEC; OBEV; OxBSP
(Farewell, A: "Venus, take my votive glass.") AWP
Lady who signs herself "Vexed," The. Edward Gorey. OBAL
Lady, whose ancestor/ Fought for Prince Charlie. The Stirrup Cup. Douglas Ainslie. GoTS
Lady with a Falcon on Her Fist, A. Richard Lovelace. CaPo
Lady with Technique, The. Hughes Mearns. *Fr.* Later Antigonishes. FiBHP
Lady with the Unicorn, The. Vernon Watkins. LiTB; TwCP
Lady with thine eyes of beauty. The Valentine. Mary Weston Fordham. CBWP-2

Lady without Paragon, A. Chaucer. *See* Legend of Good Women, The: Prologue:
Hyd, Absalon, thy gilte tresses clear.
Lady, you are with beauties so enriched. Francis Davison. ElL
Lady, you think too much of speeds. Statistics. Stephen Spender. MoBrPo
Ladybird. Ingrid Jonker, *tr. fr. Afrikaans by* Jack Cope *and* William Plomer. OV
Ladybird. Clive Sansom. GrPl
Ladybird, The. *Unknown.* GBP
Ladybird! Ladybird! Emily Brontë. OnUR
Ladybird, Ladybird fly away home. Mother Goose. FaPON; OxNR
Ladybird sat in the linden tree, The. Sirvente of the Linden Tree. Wesli Court. SoTCo
Ladybug. Joan Walsh Anglund. RHPC
Ladybug. François Dodat, *tr. fr. French by* Bert *and* Odette Meyers. TSS
Ladybug. Raymond Souster. MoCV
Ladybugs. Peggy Shumaker. TDD
Ladybug's Christmas. Norma Farber. PChr
Lady's Complaint, The. John Heath-Stubbs. TwCP
Lady's Diary, The. Charles Dibdin. NOEC
Lady's Dressing Room, The. Swift. ErPo; NoP; TEP
Lady's love is gained, A. The Price of Disrespect. Lizelia Augusta Jenkins Moorer. CBWP-3
Lady's-Maid 's Song, The. John Hollander. ErPo; LiTM; NePoEA; TW; TwCP
Lady's Prayer to Cupid, A. Thomas Carew, *after* Giovanni Battista Guarini. CaPo
(Ladies Prayer to Cupid, A.) OBVE
Lady's Receipt for a Beau's Dress, The. *Unknown.* CoMu
Lady's Resolve, The. Lady Mary Wortley Montagu. BoWoP; OxBSP
Lady's Song. Milton. *See* Comus; a Masque Presented at Ludlow Castle: Echo.
Lady's Song in Leap Year, The. *Unknown.* GBP
Lady's Third Song, The. W. B. Yeats. *Fr.* The Three Bushes. FaBoTw
LaFayette. Samuel Taylor Coleridge. EnRP
Lafayette to Washington. Maxwell Anderson. *Fr.* Valley Forge. OPP
Lagoon, The. Ashton Greene. NePoAm
Lagoons, Hanlan's Point. Raymond Souster. NOBC
Laguna Blues. Charles Wright. GeTw
Laguna man said. Wind and Glacier Voices. Simon J. Ortiz. HATNAP
Laid in My Quiet Bed [in Study as I Were]. Henry Howard, Earl of Surrey. CH; InvP
(How No Age Is Content.) LiTB
(How No Age Is Content with His Own Estate.) EIL
(Youth and Age.) SiPS
Laid on Thine Altar. *Unknown.* TrPWD
Laid-out Body, The. Alistair Campbell. *Fr.* Elegy, 8. ATNZ
Laid out for dead, let thy last kindness be. To Robin Redbreast. Robert Herrick. OBS; PBBP; PoE; TrGrPo
Laid with papyrus to catch fire. Martial, *tr. by* James Michie. FaBoEE
Laieikawai's Lament after Her Husband's Death. *Unknown, tr. fr. Hawaiian by* M. W. Beckwith. WTO
Laila Boasting. Laila Akhyaliyya, *tr. fr. Arabic by* Willis Barnstone. BoWoP
Laily Worm and the Machrel of the Sea, The. *Unknown.* ChTr; ESPB; InvP; OxBB; PoEL-1
Laird, a lord, A. *Unknown.* OxNR; SaC
Laird o' Cockpen, The. Lady Nairne, 2 added sts. by Susan Ferrier. BeLS; WPE
Laird o Drum, The. *Unknown.* ESPB
Laird o' Logie, The. *Unknown.* CH; ESPB, A *and* B *vers.*
Laird o' Ochiltree Wa's, The. *Unknown.* OxBB
Laird of Bristoll's daughter was in the woods walking, The. Captain Wedderburn's Courtship. *Unknown.* ESPB
Laird of Leys is on to Edinbrugh [*or* Edinburgh], The. The Baron o [*or* of] Leys. *Unknown.* ESPB; OxBB
Laird of Wariston, The ("Down by yon garden green"). *Unknown.* ESPB
Laird of Wariston, The ("It was at dinner as they sat"). *Unknown.* ESPB
Lairdless Place, The. Kate Rennie Archer. GoYe
Lairig, The. J. C. Milne. PoSH
Lais. Hilda Doolittle. MoAmPo
Lais. Elaine Feinstein. FaBoWP
Lais, courtesan of Corinth, why has. Lais. Elaine Feinstein. FaBoWP
Lais now old, that erst attempting lass. *Unknown, after the Greek of* Plato. FaBoEE
Lais to Aphrodite. E. A. Robinson, *after* Plato. FaBoEE

Lak of Stedfastnesse. Chaucer. AWP
Lake, A/ Is a river curled and asleep like a snake. A Lake. Thomas Lovell Beddoes. NOBVV
Lake, The. Louis O. Coxe. NYBP
Lake, The. Ted Hughes. FaBoTw; NYBP
Lake. Miyoshi Tatsuji, *tr. fr. Japanese by* Geoffrey Bownas *and* Anthony Thwaite. PeBJV
Lake, The. Poe. NAAL-1
Lake. R. A. Simpson. CBAP
Lake, The. James Stephens. MoBrPo
Lake allows an average father, walking slowly, A. Lakes. W. H. Auden. NePoAm
Lake blue below the hill, The. L'Oiseau Bleu. Mary Elizabeth Coleridge. BoTP
("Lake lay blue below the hill, The.") CH
Lake Chelan. William Stafford. NaP
Lake Chemo. James Wilton Rowe. AmFP
Lake in the Sky, The. John Haines. LCAP
Lake is blue with morning, The; and the sky. Morning on the Shore. Wilfred Campbell. NOBC
Lake is deserted now, The. The Dispossessed. Thomas Kinsella. NOCV
Lake is known as West Branch Pond, The. The Ballad of Blossom. Mona Van Duyn. EOEF; SM
Lake is sharp along the shore, The. Lakeshore. F. R. Scott. MoCV; NOBC; OBCV
Lake Isle, The. Ezra Pound. FaBoCo; FaBoPa; OxBSP; PoA
Lake Isle of Innisfree, The. W. B. Yeats. BrPo; CMoP; FaBoPP; FaBV; FaFP; FaPON; FaPoR; FPL; HeIP; InPK; InPS; LiTM; MoAB; MoBrPo; MoP; NAEL-2; NoAM; NoBE; NOBE; NoP; OBEV; OxBTC; PoE; PoRA; PrIm; TEP; TrGrPo; WeW
Lake lay blue below the hill, The. Mary Elizabeth Coleridge. *See* Lake blue below the hill, The.
Lake Leman. Byron. *See* Childe Harold's Pilgrimage:
Lake Leman woos me with its crystal face.
Lake Leman ("Clear, placid Leman! thy contrasted lake"). Byron. *Fr.* Childe Harold's Pilgrimage: It Is the Hush of Night. OBNC, *sl. diff. sel.*
Lake Leman woos me with its crystal face. Byron. *Fr.* Childe Harold's Pilgrimage, III. InPS
(Lake Leman.) PoEL-4
Lake lies blind and glinting in the sun, The. Virginia Lake. James Keir Baxter. PeNZ
Lake loon paddles, A. Rokwaho. STE
Lake of Gaube, The. Swinburne. NAEL-2; OAEL-2
Lake of Katsumata, The. *Unknown. Fr.* Manyo Shu. Ma
Lake of night is still in the valley, The. The Pine. Saunders Lewis, *tr. by* Gwyn Morgan. OBWVE
Lake of pain, an absence, A. But What Is the Reader to Make of This? John Ashbery. InPS
Lake of the Caogama, The. *Unknown.* WTO
Lake of the Dismal Swamp, The. Thomas Moore. BLPA
Lake Song. Jean Starr Untermeyer. TrJP
Lake Success. Robert Conquest. OxBC
Lake sunken among, A. Woman Skating. Margaret Atwood. FaBoWP; IHMS
Lake Superior. Samuel Griswold Goodrich. AA
Lake Superior. Lorine Niedecker. FaBoWP
Lake that held a mirror to the sun, The. Northamptonshire Fens. John Clare. *Fr.* Child Harold. FaBoPP
Lake water lifted a little and fell, The. Crab Orchard Sanctuary, Late October. Thomas Kinsella. IPY
Lakes. W. H. Auden. NePoAm
Lakes. David Donnell. NoAM
Lakes. Gabriel Preil, *tr. fr. Hebrew by* Bernhard Frank. MHeP
Lakes of the Atchafalaya, The. Longfellow. *Fr.* Evangeline. PoEL-5
Lakeshore. F. R. Scott. MoCV; NOBC; OBCV
Lakeside Hotel. Tanaka Fuyuji, *tr. fr. Japanese by* Geoffrey Bownas *and* Anthony Thwaite. PeBJV
Lakeside Incident. Robin Skelton. NOBC
Lakshmi. Padraic Fallon. NOIV
Laleham: Matthew Arnold's Grave. Lionel Johnson. FaBoPP
Lalela Zulu. *Unknown, tr. fr. Zulu.* PeSA
Lalique. Hal Porter. PoAu-2
Lalla Halima! Protect abandoned girls! Like Smoke. Mririda n'Ait Attika, *tr. by* Daniel Halpern *and* Paula Paley. PBWP
Lalla Rookh, *sels.* Thomas Moore.
"Fly to the desert, fly with me." *Fr.* The Story of the Sultana Nourmahal. BIrV
Golden Hour, The. OBNC

Light of the Harem [*or* Haram], The. *Fr.* The Story of the Sultana Nourmahal. EnRP; TEP

Peri's Lament for Hinda, The. OBNC

Lalla Rookh/ Is a naughty book. On Thomas Moore's Poems. *Unknown.* FaBoCo; FiBHP

L'Allegro. Milton. AWP; FaFP; FiP; GTBS; GTBS-P; HAP; HoPM; InPS; JCP; LiTB; NAEL-1; NoP; OAEL-1; OBEV; OBS; PoE; PPP; SeCePo; TEP; TrGrPo

"Haste thee, nymph, and bring with thee," *sel.* GN (Mirth, with Thee I Mean to Live.) FaBV

Laly, Laly. Mark Van Doren. SO

Lama, The. Ogden Nash. *See* One-l lama, the.

Lamarck Elaborated. Richard Wilbur. NePoEA

Lamb, The. Blake. *Fr.* Songs of Innocence. BLPL; BoTP; CH; EaLo; EnRP; FaBoBe; FaBoCh; FaPON; GoJo; HeIP; InPS; LiTB; NAEL-2; NAWM-2; NIP; NOEC; NoP; OAEL-2; OxBChV; PoE; SoSe; TEP; TrCP; TrGrPo; UnPo; WGRP

Lamb. Michael Dennis Browne. NU

Lamb, The. Keith Wilson. Psk

Lamb and Bear; Jet Landing. Laurence Lieberman. DiL

Lamb Was Bleating Softly, The. Juan Ramón Jiménez, *tr. fr. Spanish by* Robert Bly. NU; PChr

Lamb was so skinny I thought it was a baby goat, The. Children among the Hills. Linda Gregg. NPGG

Lambeth Lyric. Lionel Johnson. NOBVV

Lambs at Play. Christina Rossetti. BoTP

Lambs of Grasmere, 1860, The. Christina Rossetti. FM

Lambs that learn to walk in snow. First Sight. Philip Larkin. BoNaP; NTCP

Lamda. Melvin Beaunearus Tolson. *See* Satchmo.

Lame Angel. Donald Finkel. VWA

Lame Beggar, A. John Donne. FF

Lamed-Vov, The. Rose Ausländer, *tr. fr. German by* Ewald Osers. VWA

Lament: "And what shall I be today, what." Faye Kicknosway. ER

Lament: "Because the moon became my mother." Joseph Stroud. NPGG

Lament: "Diameter of the bomb was thirty centimeters, The." Yehuda Amichai. *See* Diameter of the Bomb Was Thirty Centimeters, The.

Lament: "Even beauty must die! That which subdues both gods and mortals." Schiller. OBD

Lament: "Farewell Mercy, farewell thy piteous grace." John Lydgate. *Fr.* Court of Sapience. PoEL-1

Lament, A: "Gizzard and some ruby inner parts, A." Margaret Avison. HAP

Lament, A: "I have grown old." Shotetsu, *tr. by* Steven D. Carter. WFTW

Lament: "I lie in darkness, as the dead shades gather." Matangi Hauroa, *tr. by* Barry Mitcalfe. WTO

Lament: "In that strident summer of battle." Hone Tuwhare. ATNZ

Lament: "Listen, children:/ Your father is dead." Edna St. Vincent Millay. DL

Lament: "My man is a bone ringèd with weed." Brenda Chamberlain. WPE; WPOW

(First Woman's Lament.) NeIP

Lament: "My old red Schwinn had a carrier over the back fender." George Roberts. GOYP

Lament, A: "O world! O life! O time!" Shelley. ChER; ChTr; EnRP; GTBS; GTBS-P; NAEL-2; NOBE; PoRA; TEP; TrGrPo

Lament: "Oh, everything is far." Rainer Maria Rilke, *tr. by* C. F. MacIntyre. TrJP

Lament: "One sore thing is the way." Gibbons Ruark. MT

Lament: "Someone is dead." Anne Sexton. WPE

Lament: "Spell, treasure-bearing spell, prop up the sky standing above." *Unknown, tr. by* Margaret Orbell. PeNZ

Lament: "Those we love die like birds." Mai Sayigh, *tr. by* Charles Doria *with* Salma Khadra Jayyusi. MAP

Lament: "We knelt on the rocks by the dark green pools." Frances Mayo. CN

Lament: "We who are left, how shall we look again." W. W. Gibson. MMA; OxBTC

Lament: "What face, in the water." William Carlos Williams. VGW

Lament: "What moved me, was the way your hand." Dorothy Livesay. CaP

Lament: "When I was a windy boy and a bit." Dylan Thomas. ErPo; OPOP; PPP

Lament: "You did not suck at my mother's breast." Yonathan Ratosh, *tr. by* Howard Schwartz. VWA

Lament: "Your dying was a difficult enterprise." Thom Gunn. GLP

Lament after Her Husband Bishr's Murder. Al-Khirniq, *tr. fr. Arabic by* Willis Barnstone. BoWoP

Lament City. Thomas Lux. AmPA

Lament, 1547, A. Alexander Scott. *See* Lament of the Master of Erskine.

Lament for a Cornish Soldier. Agnes Grozier Herbertson. CN

Lament for a Cricket Eleven. Kenneth Allott. OxBTC

Lament for a Dead Lover. Siraad Haad, *tr. fr. Somali by* B. W. Andrzejewski *and* I. M. Lewis. WTO

Lament for a Husband. *Unknown, tr. fr. Papuan by* Don Laycock. BoWoP

Lament for a Leg. John Ormond. OBWVE

Lament for a Sailor. Paul Dehn. WaP

Lament for a Warrior. *Unknown, tr. fr. Sotho by* Dan Kunene *and* Jack Cope. PeSA

Lament for Adonis. Bion, *tr. fr. Greek by* John Addington Symonds. AWP

Lament for Apirana Ngata. Arnold Reedy, *tr. fr. Maori by* Barry Mitcalfe. WTO

Lament for Art O Laoghaire, The, *sel.* Eibhlin Dhubh Ni Chonaill, *tr. fr. Irish by* Thomas Kinsella.

"My steadfast love!" NOIV

Lament for Art [*or* Arthur] O'Leary, The. Eibhlin Dubh O'Connell, *tr. fr. Irish by* Eilis Dillon *and* John Montague. BIrV; PBWP

Lament for Art O'Leary, The. Eileen O'Leary, *tr. fr. Irish by* Frank O'Connor. AnIL

Lament for Azazel. Francis Landy. VWA

Lament for Banba. At. *to* Egan O'Rahilly, *tr. by* James Clarence Mangan. AWP

Lament for Barney Flanagan. James Keir Baxter. ATNZ; NoP

Lament for Better or Worse. Gene Baro. NePoEA-2

Lament for Bion. Moschus, *tr. fr. Greek by* George Chapman. AWP

Lament for Chaucer. Thomas Hoccleve. *Fr.* De Regimine Principum. OBEV; OxBLMV

Lament for Culloden. Burns. *See* Lovely Lass o' Inverness, The.

Lament for Daphnaida. Spenser. FiP

Lament for Fearghal Ruadh. Tadhg Og O'Huiginn. NOIV

Lament for Flodden, The. Jane Elliot. *See* Flowers of the Forest, The.

Lament for Glasgerion. Elinor Wylie. PoA

Lament for Ignacio Sánchez Mejías. Federico García Lorca, *tr. fr. Spanish.* NAWM-2, *tr. by* Stephen Spender *and* J. L. Gili; OBVE, *tr. by* A. L. Lloyd

Lament for Kepa Anaha Ehau. Arapeta Awatere, *tr. fr. Maori by the author.* PeNZ

Lament for Lleucu Llwyd. Llywelyn Goch ap Meurig Hen, *tr. fr. Welsh by* Joseph P. Clancy. OBWVE

Lament for Llywelyn ap Gruffudd. Gruffudd ab yr Ynad Coch, *tr. fr. Welsh by* Joseph P. Clancy. OBWVE

Lament for Lost Lodgings. Phyllis McGinley. NYBP

Lament for Mafukuzela. *Zulu Oral Tradition, tr. by* H. Tracey. WTO

Lament for Maurice Bishop. Howard Fergus. PBCV

Lament for Myself, A, *sel.* Yün Shou-p'ing, *tr. fr. Chinese by* Jonathan Chaves.

"As old age approaches." CoBLCP

Lament for Our Lady's Shrine at Walsingham, A. *Unknown. See* In the wracks of Walsingham.

Lament for Pasiphae. Robert Graves. FaBoTw

Lament for Seán. Daniel James O'Sullivan. NeIP

Lament for Siôn y Glyn. Lewis Glyn Cothi, *tr. fr. Welsh by* Joseph P. Clancy. OBWVE

Lament for Tadhg Cronin's Children. Michael Hartnett. RB

Lament for Taramoana. Makere, *tr. fr. Maori by* Barry Mitcalfe. WTO

Lament for Tawhiao. *Unknown, tr. fr. Maori by* Margaret Orbell. PeNZ

Lament for Te Heuheu Herea. Te Heuheu Tukino, *tr. fr. Maori by* Margaret Orbell. PeNZ

Lament for Te Iwi—ika. *Unknown, tr. fr. Maori by* Margaret Orbell. PeNZ

Lament for the Alamo. Arthur Guiterman. AmFN

Lament for the Cuckoo. Alcuin, *tr. fr. Latin by* Helen Waddell. PeHV

Lament for the Death of Eoghan Ruadh O'Neill. Thomas Osborne Davis. NOIV

Lament for the Death of Thomas Davis. Sir Samuel Ferguson. BIrV; NOIV; OnYI

Lament for the Dorsets. Alfred W. Purdy. NoAM; NoP

Lament for the European Exile. A. L. Strauss, *tr. fr. Hebrew by* A. C. Jacobs. VWA

Lament for the Graham. Henry the Minstrel. *See* Wallace, The: Wallace's Lament for the Graham.

Lament for the Great Music, *sel.* "Hugh MacDiarmid."

"Yet there is no great problem in the world today." OxBTC

Lament for the Makaris. William Dunbar. ACP; ChTr; EBEV; GoTS; HAP; NoP; OxBS

(Fear of Death Confounds Me, The.) MeEL

(Lament for the Makers.) OAEL-1; OBEV; PoEL-1
(Timor Mortis Conturbat Me.) FaBoRV; NOBE, *abr.*
Lament for the Makers. William Dunbar. *See* Lament for the Makaris.
Lament for the O'Neills. John Montague. CIP
Lament for the Poets: 1916. Francis Ledwidge. AWP
Lament for the Priory of Walsingham, A. *Unknown.* FaBoPP; GBP
(Lament for Our Lady's Shrine at Walsingham, A.) PoEL-2
(Wreck of Walsingham, The.) ACP
"Bitter was it, Oh to view," *sel.* ChTr
Lament for the Sailing of the Crusade. Rinaldo D'Aquino, *tr. fr. Italian by* T. G. Bergin. PFI
Lament for the Two Brothers Slain by Each Other's Hand. Aeschylus, *tr. fr. Greek by* A. E. Housman. *Fr.* The Seven against Thebes. AWP
Lament for the Willows outside the City Walls, A. Yün Shou-p'ing, *tr. fr. Chinese by* Jonathan Chaves. CoBLCP
Lament for Thomas MacDonagh. Francis Ledwidge. BIrV
(Thomas MacDonagh.) NOIV
Lament for Those Who Hanged Themselves, A. Cheng Chen, *tr. fr. Chinese by* William Schultz. WFTU
Lament for Timoleague. Sean O'Coileain, *tr. fr. Irish by* Sir Samuel Ferguson. TIRV
Lament for Turlough O'Carolan. David Brendon Hopes. SM
Lament for Una, A, *sel.* Tomas Costello, *tr. fr. Gaelic by* Frank O'Connor.
"Young Una, you were a rose in a garden." WTO
Lament for Urien, The. *Unknown, tr. fr. Middle Welsh by* Ernest Rhys. *Fr.* The Red Book of Hergest. OBMV
Lament him, Mauchline husbands a.' On a Wag in Mauchline. Burns. FiBHP
(Epitaph for James Smith.) EBEV
Lament in Autumn. Harold Stewart. PoAu-2
Lament in rhyme, lament in prose. Poor Mailie's Elegy. Burns. FM
Lament, lament, Sir Isaac Heard. Epitaph on Tuft-Hunter. Thomas Moore. FaBoCo; FaBoEE
Lament my losse, my labor, and my payne. Sir Thomas Wyatt. AAS
Lament for a Man for His Son. *Unknown, tr. fr. Paiute Indian by* Mary Austin. AWP; DL
(Lament of a Young Man for His Son.) DL
Lament of a Mocking-Bird. Frances Anne Kemble. AA
Lament of a Slug-a-Bed's Wife. Stevie Smith. Mes
Lament of a Young Man for His Son. *Unknown.* *See* Lament of a Man for His Son.
Lament of an Idle Demon. Richard Percival Lister. FiBHP; NOBL
Lament of Anastasius. William Bourne Oliver Peabody. AA
Lament of Edward Blastock, The. Dame Edith Sitwell. OBMV
Lament of Eve, The. *Unknown.* ACP
Lament of Hsi-chün. Hsi-chün, *tr. fr. Chinese.* BoWoP, *tr. by* Arthur Waly
Lament of Maev Leith-Dherg, The. *Unknown, tr. fr. Middle Irish by* Thomas W. H. Rolleston. OBWP
Lament of my Father, Lakota. Paula Gunn Allen. NOVW
Lament of Orpheus, The. István Kormos, *tr. fr. Hungarian by* Edwin Morgan. MHuP
Lament of Professor Turbojet, The. James Laughlin. SoTCo
Lament of the Banana Man, The. Evan Jones. PBCV
Lament of the Border Widow, The. *Unknown.* GBP; Mes; OxBB, *with music*
(Bonnie Bower, The.) CH
Lament of the Farm Wife of Wu. Su Tung-p'o, *tr. fr. Chinese by* Burton Watson. CoBCP
Lament of the Flowers, The. Jones Very. AnAmPo; NOBA; OxBA
Lament of the Flutes. Christopher Okigbo. PBA
Lament of the Frontier Guard. Li Po, *tr. fr. Chinese by* Ezra Pound. OBVE; OBWP; VGW; WaaP
Lament of the Jewish Women for Tammuz. Charles Reznikoff. VWA
Lament of the Lovely Helmet-Dealer. Villon, *tr. fr. French by* Hubert Creekmore. ErPo
Lament of the Master of Erskine. Alexander Scott. GBL
(Lament, 1547, A.) CH
Lament of the Sodomites. George Lestey. *Fr.* Fire and Brimstone; or, The Destruction of Sodom. PeHV
Lament of the Unmarried Girl, The. Brian Merriman, *tr. fr. Modern Irish by* Frank O'Connor. *Fr.* The Midnight Court. OBVE
Lament of the Virtues and Verses on Account of the Death of Don Guido. Antonio Machado, *tr. fr. Spanish by* Charles Tomlinson *and* Henry Gifford. OBVE
Lament over the Ruins of the Abbey of Teach Molaga. *Unknown, tr. fr. Irish by* James Clarence Mangan. NOIV
Lament the falling leaves:/ The falling leaves, let them fall in spring. Ch'ü Ta-chün, *tr. fr. Chinese by* Irving Lo. *Fr.* Tune: Dreaming of the South. WFTU

Lament the falling leaves:/ The falling leaves sever the date of return. Ch'ü Ta-chün, *tr. fr. Chinese by* Irving Lo. *Fr.* Tune: Dreaming of the South. WFTU
Lament to My Mother, A. Guy C. Z. Mhone. WMBCH
Lament while Descending a Shaft. *Unknown.* AmFP
Lament, with Flesh and Blood. Sandra McPherson. SM
Lamentable Ballad of the Bloody Brook, The. Edward Everett Hale. PAH
Lamentable Case, A. Charles Hanbury-Williams. ErPo
Lamentation, A. Thomas Campion. CH; OHIP
Lamentation. Nissim Ezekiel. VWA
Lamentation, A. Carl Rakosi. VWA
Lamentation. Bible, *O.T.* *Fr.* Ezekiel, XIX: 2-9. TrJP
Lamentation for Celin, The. *Unknown, tr. fr. Spanish by* John Gibson Lockhart. AWP
Lamentation of Chloris, The. *Unknown.* CoMu
Lamentation of Enion, The. Blake. *Fr.* Vala; or The Four Zoas, The Four Zoas. OBNC
Lamentation of the Old Pensioner, The. W. B. Yeats. HAP; lnPK; NoAM; TW; WeW
Lamentation on My Dear Son Simon, A. John Saffin. SCAP
Lamentation on Ninety-Mile Beach. Barry Mitcalfe. PeNZ
Lamentation on the Death of the Duke of Wellington. *Unknown.* OBET
Lamentations. Alter Brody. TrJP; VWA
Lamentations. Norman Dubie. NoAM
Lamentations. Louise Glück. BoWoP; HCAP; MAYP
Lamentations. Siegfried Sassoon. OBSV
Lamentations, *sels.* Bible, *O.T.*
Affliction. *Fr.* III: 1–15. TrJP
Desolation in Zion. *Fr.* I: 12–17. TrJP
How Is the Gold Become Dim. ChTr
Misery of Jerusalem, The. *Fr.* I. AWP
Lamentations of an Au Pair Girl. Susan Feldman. AmPA
Lamentations of the Fallen Angels. *Unknown, tr. fr. Anglo-Saxon by* Charles W. Kennedy. *Fr.* Christ and Satan. AnOE
Lamenting for Kao Ch'ing-ch'iu, Chi-ti. Chang Yü, *tr. fr. Chinese by* Jonathan Chaves. CoBLCP
Lamenting for My Late Daughter. Wu Wei-yeh, *tr. fr. Chinese by* Jonathan Chaves. CoBLCP
Lamenting for My Wife. Wang Shih-chen, *tr. fr. Chinese by* Jonathan Chaves. CoBLCP
Lamenting Life. Ma Chih-yüan, *tr. fr. Chinese by* Jonathan Chaves. *Fr.* Three Poems to the Tune "Ssu-k'uai yü", 3. CoBLCP
Lamenting Maid, The. *Unknown.* OBET
Lamenting Noble Scholar Chu. Ni Tsan, *tr. fr. Chinese by* Jonathan Chaves. CoBLCP
Lamenting Tauba. Laila Akhyaliyya, *tr. fr. Arabic by* Willis Barnstone. BoWoP
Lamenting the Dead. P'an Yüeh, *tr. fr. Chinese by* Burton Watson. CoBCP
Lamenting the Taoist Wei Kung-yüan. Chao Meng-fu, *tr. fr. Chinese by* Jonathan Chaves. CoBLCP
Laments. Dolores Veintimilla de Galindo, *tr. fr. Spanish by* Robert L. Smith *and* Judith Candullo. DMH
Laments on the War Dead, *sel.* Yehuda Amichai, *tr. fr. Hebrew by* Warren Bargad *and* Stanley F. Chyet.
"Is all this sorrow? I don't know." *Fr.* 6. IP
Lamia. Keats. EnRP; NAEL-2; VVA
Banquet, The, *sel.* SeCePo
Lamilia's Song. Robert Greene. *See* Greene's Groatsworth of Wit: Fie, Fie on Blind Fancy!
L'Amitié et l'Amour. John Swanwick Drennan. BIrV
Lamkin ("Balankin was as gude a mason"). *Unknown.* ESPB
Lamkin ("Bolakins was a very fine mason"). *Unknown.* AmFP
Lamkin ("It's Lamkin was a mason good"). *Unknown.* ESPB; FaBoBa; OxBB
Lamkin ("My lord said to my lady"). *Unknown.* ESPB
Lamorna Cove. William Henry Davies. BrPo
Lamp, The. Sarah Pratt McLean Greene. AA
Lamp, The. Charles Whitehead. OBEV
Lamp are you, above all stars of night, A. The Pole Star. Coslett Coslett, *tr. by* Kenneth Hurlstone Jackson. OBWVE
Lamp burns blue, everyone asleep, The. Sharing Lodging with Hsieh Shih-hou. Mei Yao-ch'en, *tr. by* Burton Watson. CoBCP
Lamp burns long in the cottage, The. There's Money in Mother and Father. Morris Bishop. FiBHP
Lamp burns sure, within, The. Emily Dickinson. LiTA
Lamp by the yellow chrysanthemums, A. A Parting Talk with Seigan. Rai San'yo, *tr. by* Burton Watson. FCEI; JLIC-2
Lamp, don't moan. The Air Vision. Jakov van Hoddis, *tr. by* Charles Guenther. VWA

Lamp Flower, The. Margaret Cecilia Furse. BoTP

Lamp Goes Out, The. Michizane, *tr. fr. Chinese by* Burton Watson. JLIC-1

Lamp in the West, The. Ella Higginson. AA

Lamp must be replenish'd, but even then, The. Manfred. Byron. EnRP; NAEL-2

Lamp Now Flickers, The. Alfred Grünewald, *tr. fr. German by* Edouard Roditi. VWA

Lamp of a lily will give birth to so great a prince, The. Drugstore Conscience. Tristan Tzara, *tr. by* Michael Benedikt. POS

Lamp of heaven's crystal hall that brings the hours. William Drummond. JCP

Lamp[e], The. Henry Vaughan. QFR

Lamplight from our kitchen window-pane. Again. Glyn Jones. OBWVE

Lamplight in the window at slow dawn, A. Teika, *tr. fr. Japanese by* Hiroaki Sato. *Fr. Eighty-four Tanka.* FCEI

Lamplighter, The. "Seumas O'Sullivan." BIrV

Lamplighter, The. Robert Louis Stevenson. *Fr.* A Child's Garden of Verses. EBVV; FaFP; OxBChV; SaC

Lamplighter: 1914. Stanley Kunitz. BLA

Lamprey, glowing with uncommon fires, The. William Diaper, *after the Greek of* Oppian. *Fr.* Halieutica. OBVE

Lamps all lit up and in the shouting. General Strike 1969. Amelia Rosselli, *tr. by* Lawrence R. Smith. NItP

Lamps Are Burning, The. Charles Reznikoff. TrJP

Lamps burn all the night. The Fifth Sense. Patricia Beer. MoBS

Lamps now glitter down the street, The. Armies in the Fire. Robert Louis Stevenson. *Fr.* A Child's Garden of Verses. EBVV

Lan Nguyen; the Uniform of Death, 1971. David Mura. BrSi

L'An Trentiesme de Mon Eage. Archibald MacLeish. LiTM; MoP; NOBA

(In My Thirtieth Year.) MoAmPo

Lana Turner has collapsed! Frank O'Hara. CAPP; VGW

Lancashire Born. *Unknown.* GBP

Lancashire Lads. *Unknown.* CoMu

Lancashire Puritane, The. *Unknown.* CoMu

Lancashire Winter. Tony Connor. OxBTC

Lancelot. Arna Bontemps. CDC

Lancelot and Elaine. Tennyson. *Fr.* Idylls of the King. Song of Love and Death, The. OBNC

Lancer. A. E. Housman. MoBrPo; OBWP

Lancet, The. Denis Devlin. NOIV

Land. Carroll Arnett. VoR

Land, The. Kipling. MoBrPo; OnMSP

Land, The, *sel.* V. Sackville-West. Spring. PeHV

Land and Sea. Luciano Erba, *tr. fr. Italian by* Lawrence R. Smith. NItP

Land and Sea Tales, *sel.* Kipling. Nurses, The. NoAM

Land baron. For the Land Barons. Gasper García Laviana, *tr. by* Alejandro Murguía. Vol

Land Called Scotia, The. St. Donatus, *tr. fr. Latin.* NOIV

Land Dirge, A. John Webster. *See* White Devil, The: Call for the Robin Redbreast and the Wren.

Land earth-root. Nakasuk. WTO

Land-Fall. George M. Brady. NeIP

Land floats by under us, The. Love Making. James Tate. EAS

Land I Came Thro' Last, The. Christopher John Brennan. *Fr.* The Wanderer. PoAu-1

Land is cold and its men gather earth for no reason, The. A Woman's Song. Colleen J. McElroy. BlSi

Land Is Gone, The. *Unknown, tr. fr. Maori by* Margaret Orbell. PeNZ

Land is lonely now, The: Anathema. Robert Stephen Hawker. *Fr.* The Quest of the Sangraal. EBVV

Land Laws, The. Merimeri Penfold, *tr. fr. Maori by* Margaret Orbell. PeNZ

Land lies in water; it is shadowed green. The Map. Elizabeth Bishop. NOBA

Land-Mine, The. George MacBeth. OBWP

Land-Mine Casualty Amman 1970. Ian Wedde. *Fr.* Earthly: Sonnets for Carlos, 37. ATNZ

Land not mine, still, A. "Anna Akhmatova," *tr. by* Jane Kenyon. NU

Land o' the Leal, The. Carolina Oliphant, Baroness Nairne. GTBS; GTBS-P; OBEV; OxBS; WBLP; WGRP

Land of Beginning Again, The. Louisa Fletcher. BLPA

Land of Cokaygne, The. *Unknown.* NOIV

Land of Counterpane, The. Robert Louis Stevenson. BrPo; EBEV; FaBoBe; FaFP; NBLV; NTCP; OxBChV; PWR

Land of Dreams, The. Blake. BeLS; CH

Land of gold!—thy sisters greet thee. California. Lydia Huntley Sigourney. PAH

Land of Heart's Desire, The, *sel.* W. B. Yeats. Wind Blows out of the Gates of the Day, The. RB (Fairy Song.) MoBrPo

Land of Hope and Glory. A. C. Benson. FaPoR

Land of Indolence, The. James Thomson. *See* Castle of Indolence, The: In lowly dale, fast by a river's side.

Land of leaning ice, A. North Labrador. Hart Crane. CMoP; FaBoMo

Land of Little Sticks, 1945. James Tate. MAYP

Land of Look Beyond, The. Michelle Cliff. ER

Land of Metamorphoses, The. René Daumal, *tr. fr. French by* Michael Benedikt. POS

Land of my birth! though now, alas! no more. William Charles Wentworth. *Fr.* Australasia. PoAu-1

Land of my heart,/ What future is before thee? William Dudley Foulke. *Fr.* Ad Patriam. PGD

Land of Nod, The. Robert Louis Stevenson. PWR

Land of Our Birth. Kipling. BoTP

Land of Potpourri, The. Jack Prelutsky. RHPC

Land of Story-Books, The. Robert Louis Stevenson. FaBoBe; FaPON; PWR

Land of the Evening Mirage, The. *Unknown, tr. fr. Sioux Indian by* A. M. Bede. WGRP

Land of the Free. Arthur Nicholas Hosking. BLPA; OPP

Land of the Free. Archibald MacLeish. AmFN "We wonder whether the dream of American liberty," *sel.* MoAB

Land of the White Lily. Jukka Vieno, *tr. fr. Finnish by* Aili Jarvenpa. SOP

Land of the Wilful Gospel. Sidney Lanier. *Fr.* Psalm of the West. PAH

Land of unconquered Pelayo! land of the Cid Campeador! The Surrender of Spain. John Milton Hay. AA

Land of Yamato is a land, The. *Unknown, tr. fr. Japanese.* *Fr.* Manyo Shu. Ma

Land of Yamato over which reigns, The. Tanabe Sakimaro, *tr. fr. Japanese.* *Fr.* Manyo Shu. Ma

Land, that, from the rule of kings, The. The Bartholdi Statue. Whittier. PAH

Land that is lonelier than ruin, A. Swinburne. *Fr.* By the North Sea, I. PoEL-5

Land That We Love. Richard Watson Gilder. OPP

Land wants me to come back, The. Dust Bowl. Langston Hughes. PoA

Land was ours before we were the land's, The. The Gift Outright. Robert Frost. AiP; AmFN; AmPP; CMoP; GOA; LiTM; MoAB; MoAmPo; MoP; NAAL-2; NoAM; NOBA; NoP; OPP; OxBA; PPP; WaP

Land was white, The. *Unknown.* ChTr; OxNR

Land Where Hate Should Die, The. Denis A. McCarthy. OPP

Land where I was born sits by the seas, The. Francesca of Rimini. Dante, *tr. fr. Italian by* Byron. *Fr.* Divina Commedia: Inferno, V. PFI

Land where we were born, The. Here We Were Born. Marcelino dos Santos, *tr. by* Margaret Dickinson. WMBCH

Land Which No Mortal May Know, The. Bernard Barton. PWR

Land without presence. We stand. In Our Manner of Speaking. Kendrick Smithyman. ATNZ

Landcrab. Margaret Atwood. SoSe

Landed: A Valentine. Richard Howard. PoA

Landfall, The. James Dickey. PoA

Landfall. *Maori Oral Tradition, tr. by* A. S. Thomson. WTO

Landfall in Unknown Seas. Allen Curnow. ATNZ

Landfill. Michael S. Harper. LCAP

Landing. Michael Guttenbrunner. CoAuP

Landing, The. Daniel Halpern. AmPA

Landing. Antonia Pozzi, *tr. fr. Italian by* Brenda Webster. OV

Landing of the Pilgrim Fathers [in New England], The. Felicia Dorothea Hemans. BeLS; BLPA; FaBoBe; FaBV; FaFP; FaPON; GN; OHIP; OPP; PAH; WBLP; WPE

(Pilgrim Fathers, The.) BoTP

Landing on the Moon. May Swenson. TAP

Landlady, The. P. K. Page. CaP; SoSe

Landlord, landlord. Ballad of the Landlord. Langston Hughes. HCAP; NOBA

Landlord's Wife, The. Marilyn Chin. BrSi

Landmark by camel and shipsail we take. Cargoes of the Radanites. Harry Alan Potamkin. TrJP

Landor. John Albee. AA

Landowner, The. Samuel Bamford. PF

Landrail, The. John Clare. PBBP

Lands around my dwelling, The. *Unknown, tr. fr. Eskimo by* Knud Rasmussen. ILY

Landscape. Federico García Lorca, *tr. fr. Spanish by* William Jay Smith. *Fr.* Songs of Childhood. CT

Landscape. David Gascoyne. FaBoMo

Landscape. Anne Hébert, *tr. fr. French by* Kathleen Weaver. OV

Landscape. Horiguchi Daigaku, *tr. fr. Japanese by* Geoffrey Bownas *and* Anthony Thwaite. PeBJV

Landscape. Ishigaki Rin, *tr. fr. Japanese by* Hiroaki Sato. FCEI

Landscape. Koh Chang-soo, *tr. fr. Korean by the author.* ACKP

Landscape, A/ full of holes. Loose Woman Poem. Sharon Thesen. NOBC

Landscape. Octavio Paz, *tr. fr. Spanish.* OBVE, *tr. by* Charles Tomlinson

Landscape. Lucio Piccolo, *tr. fr. Italian by* Charles Tomlinson. *Fr.* Anna Perenna. PFI

Landscape. Alfred W. Purdy. CaP

Landscape. Abraham Sutskever, *tr. fr. Yiddish.* VWA, *tr. by* Ruth Whitman

Landscape. Judah Leib Teller, *tr. fr. Yiddish by* Benjamin *and* Barbara Harshav. AYP

Landscape, sel. Yün Shou-p'ing, *tr. fr. Chinese by* Jonathan Chaves. "Brush in rocks, draw a stream." CoBLCP

Landscape and Figure. Thomas Kinsella. IPY

Landscape as a Nude. Archibald MacLeish. *Fr.* Frescoes for Mr. Rockefeller's City, I. AmPP; CMoP

Landscape as Metal and Flowers. Winfield Townley Scott. AmFN; GoJo

Landscape at times lets a bird fly away, The. Landscape. Koh Chang-soo, *tr. by the author.* ACKP

Landscape, Deer Season. Barbara Howes. GoJo

Landscape, Dense with Trees. Ellen Bryant Voigt. BLA; MT

Landscape he saw in a German etching, A. Etching. Tamura Ryuichi, *tr. by* Sato. FCEI

Landscape in a Pot. Lo Ch'ing, *tr. fr. Chinese by* Dominic Cheung. IFON

Landscape Inspector, The. Miyazawa Kenji, *tr. fr. Japanese by* Hiroaki Sato. FCEI

Landscape Left Behind. Gerrit Kouwenaar, *tr. fr. Dutch by* Adrian Henri. DuIn

Landscape Lies within My Head, The. Gervase Stewart. WaaP

Landscape near an Aerodrome, The. Stephen Spender. LiTM; MoAB; MoBrPo; NoAM; OxBTC

Landscape of a Child on His Way to the Place of the Regents. Jean Follain, *tr. fr. French by* W. S. Merwin. RHTwFP

Landscape of a Face. Alfred Gesswein, *tr. fr. German by* Beth Bjorklund. CoAuP

Landscape of Domestic Life. David Graham. KS

Landscape of loneliness. Knowledge of What Is. Jan G. Elburg, *tr. by* Koos Schuur. DuIn

Landscape of Love, The. Thomas Cole. NePoAm

Landscape of Screams. Nelly Sachs, *tr. fr. German by* Michael Roloff. NYBP

Landscape of the Heart, The. Geoffrey Grigson. LiTB; WaP

Landscape of Violence. Ralph Nixon Currey. PeSA

Landscape Painted on a Fan, A. Chu Yün-ming, *tr. fr. Chinese by* Jonathan Chaves. CoBLCP

Landscape Philosophy. Wang Jun-hua, *tr. fr. Chinese by* Dominic Cheung. IFON

Landscape: 7. Ono Tozaburo, *tr. fr. Japanese by* Hiroaki Sato. FCEI

Landscape: 6. Ono Tozaburo, *tr. fr. Japanese by* Hiroaki Sato. FCEI

Landscape (the landscape!) again, The: Gloucester. The Librarian. Charles Olson. CAPP

Landscape Vignettes, sels. Rai San'yo, *tr. fr. Chinese by* Burton Watson. JLIC-2

"I put away my book, chin in hand, alone." *Fr.* II.

"Out the gate I meet a friend." *Fr.* III.

Landscape was, The. Coon Fire. Tom Weatherly. *Fr.* Cantos, 5. PoBA

Landscape where I lie, The. Song for a Lyre. Louise Bogan. LiTA

Landscape white-washed by water the wind. Sunday on Riverside Drive. Rose Ausländer, *tr. by* Beth Bjorklund. CoAuP

Landscape with Figures. Keith Douglas. NePoEA

Landscape with Leaves and Figure. Olga Broumas. BoWoP

Landscape with Little Figures. Donald Justice. CAPP; LCAP

Landscape with Mountain. Sándor Weöres, *tr. fr. Hungarian by* Peter Redgrove. MHuP

Landscape with Next of Kin. Olga Broumas. BoWoP

Landscape with the Fall of Icarus. William Carlos Williams. *Fr.* Pictures from Brueghel, II. LCAP; NAAL-2; NOAM; PPP

Landscape with Tractor. Henry Taylor. MAYP; PPR

Landscapeople. John Ashbery. HCAP

Landscapes, *sels.* T. S. Eliot.

Cape Ann. *Fr.* V. GoJo; NAEL-2; NoAM; RB

New Hampshire. *Fr.* I. FaBoCh; GTBS-P; NoAM; RB; WeW

Rannoch, by Glencoe. *Fr.* IV. FaBoPP; NAEL-2; PoSH; RB

Usk. *Fr.* III. FaBoCh; NOCV; RB

Virginia. *Fr.* II. InPK; RB

Landscape's private and all that it contains, The. Artillery Shoot. James Forsyth. WaP

Landslides like fingers. Because in Destroying He Creates. Alain Delahaye, *tr. by* Paul Auster. RHTwFP

Lane County Bachelor, The. *Unknown. See* Starving to Death on a Government Claim.

Lanes in Summer. Malcolm Hemphrey. BoTP

Lang Johnny More. *Unknown.* ESPB

Langston. Mari E. Evans. CNA

Langston Blues. Dudley Randall. CNA; FB

Langston Hughes. Lew Blockcolski. VoR

Language, The. Robert Creeley. CAPP; TAP

Language, The. Anselm Hollo. UL

Language. Nizar Qabbani, *tr. fr. Arabic by* Diana Der Hovanessian *and* Lena Jayyusi. MAP

Language, The/ comes loose in the head. The Language. Anselm Hollo. UL

Language Ah Now You Have Me. William Sydney Graham. AnAn

Language As Inevitable Metaphor. Idea As Inevitable Figment. Hayden Carruth. BLA

Language has not the power to speak what love indites. John Clare. FaBoEE; OAEL-2; OBNC; OxBSP; PoEL-4

Language is the first perversion of the senses. Genesis. Brian Higgins. FaBoTw

Language Lesson, 1976. Heather McHugh. MAYP

Language of Ancients. Hayim Lenski, *tr. fr. Hebrew by* Pearl Grodensky. VWA

Language of Fossils, The. Anita Endrezze-Danielson. HATNAP

Language of walls, The. Hieroglyph. Paul Auster. VWA

Language of Weather, The. Ray A. Young Bear. HATNAP

Language on which the sun flows, A. Epos. Harold Rosenberg. PoA

Language was used sparingly. My Parent's House. Adriaan Morriën, *tr. by* Ria Leigh-Loohuizen. DuIn

Languages We Are, The. Frederick Bryant, Jr.. NBP

Langue d'Oc, sel. Ezra Pound, *after the Provençal of* Arnaut Daniel. Alba ("When the nightingale to his mate"). OBVE; VGW; WeW

Languid walls. Woman in Rain. Judah Leib Teller, *tr. by* Benjamin *and* Barbara Harshav. AYP

Languishing Moon, The. Sir Philip Sidney. *See* Astrophel and Stella: XXXI. "With how sad steps, O [*or* Oh] Moon, thou climb'st the skies!"

Langwell. Kingsley Amis. *Fr.* The Evans Country. NOBL; OxBC

Lanigan's Ball. *Unknown.* OxBoLi

Lanky Hank Farrow. Harold Witt. ASP

Lanky hank of a she in the inn over there, The. A Glass of Beer. James Stephens. CMoP; FaBoCo; FiBHP; InPK; MoP; NBLV; OBMV; OxBS; OxBTC; RB; SeCePo; TW

(Righteous Anger.) MoAB; MoBrPo

Lantern light from deeper in the barn, A. The Fear. Robert Frost. BeLS

Lantern out of Doors, The. Gerard Manley Hopkins. CMoP; LiTB; TrCP

Lanternslides grinding out B-flat minor, The. Lunch. Kenneth Koch. SOTW

Lanty Leary. *Unknown.* ChTr

Laocoon. Don Gordon. WaaP

Laocoön. Wilson Harris. PBCV

Laodamia. Wordsworth. EnRP

Lapis. Shawn Wong. BrSi

Lapis Lazuli. W. B. Yeats. CMoP; FaBoMo; FaBoTw; FF; HeIP; InPS; LiTB; LiTM; MAT; MoP; NAEL-2; NAWM-2; NoAM; NOBE; NoP; OAEL-2; TEP

"L'Apparition" of Gustave Moreau. Gordon Bottomley. BrPo

Lapping of lake water, The. Lake Song. Jean Starr Untermeyer. TrJP

Laprairie Hunger Strike. Ronald G. Everson. MoCV

L'Après-Midi d'un Faune. Stéphane Mallarmé, *tr. fr. French by* Aldous Huxley. AWP

L'Après Midi d'une Fille aux Cheveux de Lin. Ronald McCuaig. PoAu-2

Lapse of time and rivers is the same, The. A Comparison. William Cowper. OxBSP

Lapsed Meadow. Stanley Plumly. AnAn

Lapstrake. Ted Greenwald. LP

Lapsus Linguae. Keith Preston. NBLV; OBAL

Lara, *sel.* Byron.
    "In him inexplicably mixed appeared." OAEL-2
Larch Trees. Kitahara Hakushu, *tr. fr. Japanese by* Hiroaki Sato. FCEI
Larch Wood Secrets. Ivy O. Eastwick. BoTP
Larches. Ivor Gurney. FaBoPP
Larches. Kitahara Hakushu, *tr. fr. Japanese by* Geoffrey Bownas *and* Anthony Thwaite. PeBJV
Large Bad Picture. Elizabeth Bishop. EyDe; NoP; NYBP; OxBC
Large, colored dyke from Atlanta, A. *Unknown.* PeHV
Large glooms were gathered in the mighty fane. James Thomson ("B. V."). *Fr.* The City of Dreadful Night, XIV. EBEV; OAEL-2
Large porcupine breathes smaller ones, The. There Won't Be Another. Diane Glancy. STE
Large Red Man Reading. Wallace Stevens. HAP; LCAP
Large, slow snowflakes fall from an ashen heaven: the noisy. A Snow-Storm. Giosuè Carducci, *tr. by* G. L. Bickersteth. PFI
Large transparent baby like a skeleton in a red tree, A. The Visible Baby. Peter Redgrove. NAs
Large tree shakes and the, A. Matinal. Marguerite Clerbout, *tr. by* Kathleen Weaver. OV
Large yellow wings, black-fringed, The. Butterfly on Rock. Irving Layton. NoAM; NOBC
Larger Hope, The. Tennyson. *See* In Memoriam A. H. H.: Oh yet We Trust.
Larger Prayer, The. Edna D. Cheney. BLRP; WGRP
Largess, The. Richard Eberhart. LiTA
Largest Life, The. Archibald Lampman. CaP
Largest stock of armaments allows me, The. Civilian. Josephine Miles. WPE
Largo. Dunstan Thompson. LiTA; WaP
Largo e mesto. William Ernest Henley. *Fr.* London Voluntaries, IV. BrPo
Lariat snaps; the cowboy rolls, The. The Closing of the Rodeo. William Jay Smith. AiP; ASP; GOA; NePoEA; SaC; SD; TwCP
Larikie, larikie, lee! *Unknown.* PBBP
Lark, The. Bernart de Ventadorn, *tr. fr. Provençal.* CTC, *tr. by* Ezra Pound; Pro, *tr. by* Paul Blackburn
Lark, A. Tonna, *tr. fr. Japanese by* Steven D. Carter. WFTW
Lark, The ("The giddy lark reacheth the steepy air"). *Unknown.* PBBP
Lark, The ("Learned in music sings the lark"). *Unknown, tr. fr. Irish by* Robin Flower. TIRV
Lark, The ("Liverockie, liverockie, lee"). *Unknown.* GBP
Lark, The ("Malisons, malisons, more than ten"). *Unknown.* GBP; PBBP
Lark, The ("Swift through the yielding air I glide"). *Unknown.* OBS
Lark along the Road, A. Tamemasa, *tr. fr. Japanese by* Steven D. Carter. WFTW
Lark as small as a flint arrow, A. The Round Barrow. Andrew Young. SeCePo
Lark Ascending, The. George Meredith. PBBP; WiR
Lark begins to go up, The. Skylarks. Ted Hughes. HAP
Lark drinks, The. Water. Sa'di Yusuf, *tr. by* Abdullah al-Udhari. MPAW
Lark drives invisible pitons in the air. Movements. Norman MacCaig. OxBC
Lark in the Morning, The. *Unknown. See* Pretty Ploughboy, The.
Lark Now Leaves His Water [*or* Wat'ry] Nest. Sir William Davenant. CH; ChTr; InvP; OxBSP; PoRA
    (Aubade: "Lark now leaves his watery [*or* wat'ry] nest, The.") NOBE; OBEV
    (Morning.) ACP
    (Morning Song.) TrGrPo
    (Song: "Lark now leaves his wat'ry [watery] nest, The.") AWP; GBL; MeLP; MePo; PBBP; SeCV-1
Larkin. Gibbons Ruark. DiPo
Larkin Automatic Car Wash, The. Gavin Ewart. NoAM
Larkinesque. Michael Ryan. NAmP
Lark's Nest, The. John Clare. PBBP
Lark's Nest, A. Christopher Smart. *See* Hymns for the Amusement of Children: For Saturday.
Lark's Song, The. Blake. *See* Milton: Thou hearest the nightingale begin the song of spring.
Larks trill in the quiet glen. The Quiet Glen. Douglas Fraser. PoSH
Lars Porsena of Clusium. Horatius at the Bridge. Macaulay. *Fr.* Lays of Ancient Rome. BeLS; FaBoCh; FaFP; FaPoR; OBNV, *abr.*; OBWP; OHFP, *abr.*; PoLF
L'Art. Frederick Feirstein. SM
L'Art, 1910. Ezra Pound. HeIP; OxBA
Las casitas near the gray cannery. Freeway 280. Lorna Dee Cervantes. NoAM
Las' Rights. Brian Meeks. PBCV

Las Trampas U.S.A. Charles Tomlinson. TwCP
Lasca. Frank Desprez. BeLS; BLPA; FaBoBe
Laser. A. R. Ammons. CAPP; NAAL-2; NoAM; NOBA
Lashes of my eye are clipped away, The. Cataract. Margoret Smith. NYBP
Lass from Bally-na-Lee, The. Anthony Raftery, *tr. fr. Irish by* Desmond O'Grady. BIrV
Lass in Wonderland, A. Francis Reginald. MoCV
Lass of Aughrim, The. Paul Muldoon. NoAM
Lass of Islington, The. *Unknown.* CoMu
    (Fair Lass of Islington, The.) OxBB, *with music*
Lass of Lynn's New Joy, for Finding a Father for Her Child, The. *Unknown.* CoMu
Lass of Roch Royal, The. *Unknown.* AmFP; ESPB
Lass That Made the Bed for Me, The. Burns. InvP
Lass, when they talk of love, laugh in their face. Love. Francis Jammes, *tr. by* Jethro Bithell. AWP
Lass with a Lump of Land. Allan Ramsay. NOEC
Lasses dance and tread the ground, The. Hitomaro, *tr. fr. Japanese. Fr.* Manyo Shu. Ma
Lasses, like nuts at bottom brown. Allan Ramsay. FaBoEE
Lassie, can ye say. For a Wife in Jizzen. Douglas Young. OxBS
Lassie, What Mair Wad You Hae? Heine, *tr. fr. German into Scottish by* Alexander Gray. GoTS; OxBS
Lassie, with the lips sae rosy. Mädchen mit den rothen Mündchen. Heine, *tr. by* Sir Theodore Martin. AWP
Lassitude. Paul Verlaine, *tr. fr. French by* Lawrence M. Bensky. ErPo
Last, The. Ezra Zussman, *tr. fr. Hebrew by* D. Shnayorson. VWA
Last Address to My Ghosts, A. Gregory Orr. GeTw
Last Affair: Bessie's Blues Song. Michael S. S. Harper. GeTw; HCAP; LCAP
Last All Saints' holy-day, even now gone by. Sonnet: Of Beatrice de' Portinari, on All Saints' Day. Dante, *tr. by* Dante Gabriel Rossetti. AWP
Last and greatest herald of Heaven's King, The. Saint John Baptist. William, of Hawthornden Drummond. EaLo; GTBS; GTBS-P; NOBE; OBEV; TrCP
    (For the Baptist.) GoTS; OBS
    (The Baptist.) TrGrPo
Last Appendix to "Yankee Doodle," The. *Unknown.* PAH
Last Apple. Malka Heifetz-Tussman, *tr. fr. Yiddish by* Marcia Falk. PeBMYV
Last autumn, as we sat, ere fall of night. Cader Idris at Sunset. Charles Tennyson Turner. FaBoPP
Last Baseball Samurai, The. Tom Clark. ASP
Last Betrayal, The. Guido Gozzano, *tr. fr. Italian by* Michael Palma. PFI
Last Bison, The, *sel.* Charles Mair.
    "Hear me, ye smokeless skies and grass-green earth." NOBC
Last Bowstrings, The. Edward Lucas White. AA
Last Breath. Laura Chester. NPGG
Last bridge I won't. Marina Tsvetayeva, *tr. fr. Russian by* Elaine Feinstein *and* Angela Livingstone. *Fr.* Poem of the End, VIII. OV
Last Brightness. Leah Goldberg, *tr. fr. Hebrew by* Robert Alter. OV
Last Buccaneer, The. Charles Kingsley. BeLS; EBVV; FaBoBe. (Old Buccaneer, The.) MoShBr
Last Buckaroo, The. Dick Gibford. CowP
Last Bus, The. E. V. Knox. BXAP
Last Bus, The. Mark Strand. TwCP
Last Came, and Last Did Go. Milton. *Fr.* Lycidas. TW
Last Campaign, The. Geoffrey Lehmann. PoAu-2
Last chair finally was carried out, The. The House. Paula Nelson. GoYe
Last Chance, The. Andrew Lang. NOBVV; SD
Last Chantey, The. Kipling. FaBoCh; MoBrPo; MOS
Last Chapter, The. Walter de la Mare. CMoP; MoBrPo
Last Child. X. J. Kennedy. OxBSP
Last Chrysanthemum, The. Thomas Hardy. CMoP; LiTB
Last Class, The. Ellen Bryant Voigt. MT
Last Coachload, The. Walter de la Mare. SeCePo
Last Confession, A. W. B. Yeats. BoLoP; CMoP; ELP; ErPo; HAP; NIP; OAEL-2; WeW
Last Conqueror, The. James Shirley. *See* Cupid and Death: Victorious Men of Earth.
Last Corn Shock, The. Glenn Ward Dresbach. FaPON
Last Cry of the Damp Fly, The. Dennis Lee. NTCP
Last Cup of Canary, The. Helen Gray Cone. AA
Last dark violet, The. Poetry. Abraham Sutskever, *tr. by* Ruth Whitman. VWA
Last Day, The. George Seferis, *tr. fr. Greek by* Edmund Keeley *and* Philip Sherrard. VMG

Last Day and the First, The. Theodore Weiss. TwCP; VGW

Last day of May, of the last May, The. May 1964. Tuomas Anhava, tr. by Aili Jarvenpa. SOP

Last Day of the Year (New Year's Eve), The. Annette von Droste-Hülshoff, tr. fr. German by Willis Barnstone. BoWoP

Last Day of the Year; or, New Year's Eve, The. Mrs. Henry Linden. CBWP-4

Last Days. Richard Hugo. PoA

Last Days. Elizabeth Stoddard. AA

Last Days of Alice. Allen Tate. NAAL-2; NOBA; OxBA; UnPo

Last days of November, and everything so green, The! The Volunteer's Thanksgiving. Lucy Larcom. OBCA

Last decent man alive, The. Across to the Peloponnese. James Welch. CDW

Last Defile, The. Amy Carmichael. TrCP

Last Dream, The. Ray A. Young Bear. STE

Last Easter I was married, that night I went to bed. The Lowlands of Holland. *Unknown.* AmFP

Last Enemy, The. Ishihara Yoshiro, tr. fr. Japanese by Hiroaki Sato. FCEI

Last eve I passed beside of a blacksmith's door. The Anvil—God's Word. John Clifford. BLPA

(Hammers and Anvil, The.) BLRP

("I paused last eve beside of a blacksmith's door.") WBLP

Last Evening. Rainer Maria Rilke, tr. fr. German. OBWP, tr. by J. B. Leishman; WaaP, tr. by C. F. MacIntyre.

Last evening you were drinking deep. Hangover Cure. Alexis. FaBoUs

Last Farewell, The. Miyazawa Kenji, tr. fr. Japanese by Hiroaki Sato. FCEI

Last Farewell to the Hills, sel. Duncan Ban MacIntyre, tr. fr. Gaelic by Robert Buchanan.

On Ben Dorain. PoSH

Last Fierce Charge, The. *Unknown.* AmFP

Last Fight, The. Lewis Frank Tooker. AA; FaBoBe

Last Fire, The. Moishe Steingart, tr. fr. Yiddish by Gabriel Preil. VWA

Last, for December, houses on the plain. December. Folgore Da San Gimignano, tr. fr. Italian by Dante Gabriel Rossetti. Fr. Sonnets of the Months. PFI

Last Friday, in the big light of last Friday night. Reality Is an Activity of the Most August Imagination. Wallace Stevens. NoAM

Last Fruit Off an Old Tree, The, sels. Walter Savage Landor.

I Strove with None. ChTr; EnRP; FaPoR; NOBE; OBNC

(Dying Speech of an Old Philosopher.) FaBoEE; GTBS-P; HeIP; NOBVV; NoP

(End, The.) SeCePo

(Finis.) OBEV

(On His Seventy-fifth Birthday.) AWP; BLPL; EBEV; LiTB; OAEL-2; TrGrPo

"There falls with every wedding chime." SeCePo

Last Furrow, The. Edwin Markham. AA

Last Galway Hooker, The. Richard Murphy. IPY

Last Game. Cary Waterman. TSL

Last Gate, The. Stella Mead. BoTP

Last Gift, The. Peter Cooley. NAmP

Last Good-by, The. Louise Chandler Moulton. AA

Last Hill in a Vista. Louise Bogan. FaBoWP

Last hour nears, The. Pshytik. Nahum Bomze, tr. by Gabriel Preil. VWA

Last Hunt, The. William Roscoe Thayer. AA; FaBoBe

Last Hymn, The. "Marianne Farningham." BLPA

Last Impression of New York. Mason Jordan Mason. PoNe

Last Instructions to a Painter, The. Andrew Marvell. APAS; OBSV Sels.

"After two sittings, now our Lady State." OBSV

Dutch in the Medway, The. OBS

"Paint Castlemaine in colours that will hold." OBSV

"Paint last the King, and a dead shade of night." OBSV

(Charles II.) OBS

Last Invocation, The. Walt Whitman. MoAmPo; OBD; OxBA; OxBSP; PoEL-5; TrGrPo; TrPWD

(Imprisoned Soul, The.) OBEV; WGRP

Last Journey, The. John Davidson. Fr. The Testament of John Davidson. GoTS

"Oh, long before the bere was steeped for malt." PoSH

Last Journey. Enrique Gonzáles Martínez, tr. fr. Spanish by Samuel Beckett. MexPo

Last Journey, The. Leonidas of Tarentum, tr. fr. Greek by Charles Merivale. AWP; OBD

Last Journey. John Montague. CIP; FaBCIP

Last Judgment, The. Giuseppe Gioacchino Belli, tr. fr. Italian by Anthony Burgess. OBD; PFI

Last Judgment. John Gould Fletcher. AWP

Last Judgment, The. *Unknown, tr. fr. Anglo-Saxon by Charles W. Kennedy. Fr.* Christ 3. AnOE

Last July 4th, like every July 4th for four years. Triple Trouble. Assotto Saint. GLP

Last Landlord, The. Elizabeth Akers Allen. AA

Last Lap, The. Kipling. OxBTC

Last Lauch. Douglas Young. FaBoCo; NBLV; OxBS; SeCePo

Last Laugh, The. Sir John Betjeman. PoPo

Last Laugh. Robert Penn Warren. MT

Last Leaf, The. Oliver Wendell Holmes. AA; AmPP; AnAmPo; FaBoBe; FaPON; NAAL-1; PoLF; PWR; WBLP

Last Leave of the Hills. Duncan Ban MacIntyre, tr. fr. Gaelic. GoTS

Last leaves fell like notes from a piano, The. Forest of Europe. Derek Walcott. PBCV

Last Lesson of the Afternoon. D. H. Lawrence. NoAM

Last Letter to Pablo. Pat Lowther. NOBC

Last Letter to the Western Civilization. D. T. Ogilvie. NBP

Last Light. Robert Kelly. VGW

Last light has gone out of the world, except, The. Liberty. Edward Thomas. MoAB; OAEL-2

Last light lingers, The. Premonition. Antonia Pozzi, tr. by Muriel Kittel. DMI

Last light muffles itself in cloud and goes, The. Mise en Scène. Robert Fitzgerald. NYBP; VGW

Last Lines. X. J. Kennedy. OBAL

Last Lines, sel. "Owen Meredith."

"Lord! if in love, though fainting oft, I have tended thy gracious Vine." TrPWD

Last Lines on a Wrestler. X. J. Kennedy. CRP

Last Look at La Plata, Missouri. Jim Barnes. CDW

Last Love. Fyodor Tyutchev, tr. fr. Russian by Alan Myers. AAA

Last Love. Fyodor Tyutchev, tr. fr. Russian by Vladimir Nabokov. BoLoP

Last Man, The, sel. Thomas Lovell Beddoes.

Crocodile, A. FM; NOBVV; OBTV; RB

Last Man, The. Thomas Campbell. EnRP

Last Man Killed by Indians in Kimble County, Texas, The. Mike Angelotti. MOWH

Last Man's Club, The. James Galvin. AnAn

Last Mathematician. Hyman Edelstein. CaP

Last May. Carroll Arnett. STE

Last May-day fair I search'd to find a snail. John Gay. Fr. The Shepherd's Week: Thursday; or, The Spell. FaBoUs

Last meal together, Leeds, the Queen's Hotel. The Queen's English. Tony Harrison. DiPo

Last Meeting. Gwen Harwood. PoAu-2

Last Meeting. Robert Penn Warren. DiPo

Last Meeting of Pocahontas and the Great Captain, The. Margaret Junkin Preston. PAH

Last Memo. Philip Hobsbaum. NPo

Last Month. John Ashbery. CoAP

Last month in your little Roman house, The. On the Death of Keats. John Logan. Prf

Last Moriori, The. Kendrick Smithyman. ATNZ

Last Mountain Lion on Maple Crest Mountain, The. Peter Meinke. MOWH

Last Night. Ilse Aichinger, tr. fr. German by Beth Bjorklund. CoAuP

Last night/ the moon let her uncarded wool. Fogbound. Roberta Hill Whiteman. ER

Last Night. David Ignatow. VGW

Last Night. Oku Onuora. PBCV

Last night a baby gargled in the throes. A Widow in Wintertime. Carolyn Kizer. CAPP; ER

Last night a sword-light in the sky. Stone Trees. John Freeman. BoNaP

Last night, above the whistling wind. A Sanitary Message. Bret Harte. AnAmPo

Last night, ah, yesternight, betwixt her lips and mine. Non Sum Qualis Eram Bonae sub Regno Cynarae [or Cynara]. Ernest Dowson. AWP; BeLS; BLPA; BoLoP; BrPo; EBVV; EnLoPo; FaBoBe; FaFP; FPL; GBL; GTBS-P; HAP; HeIP; LiTB; MoBrPo; NOBE; NoP; OAEL-2; OBEV; OBMV; OBNC; PoRA; PrIm; TEP; TrGrPo; UnPo (Cynara.) NAEL-2

Last night Alicia wore a Tuscan bonnet. Alicia's Bonnet. Elisabeth Cavazza Pullen. AA

Last night along the river banks. The Boats Are Afloat. Chu Hsi, tr. by Kenneth Rexroth. NaP

Last night, among his fellow roughs. Private of the Buffs; or, The British Soldier in China. Sir Francis Hastings Doyle. OBEV; OBTV

Last night as I lay beside you all the desire had gone out of me. House. Murray Edmond. *Fr.* Poems of the End Wall. ATNZ; PeNZ

Last night at black midnight I woke with a cry. The Ghosts of the Buffaloes. Vachel Lindsay. MoAmPo

Last night at Bon Odori the drums of Kinnara Taiko. Letter to Tina Koyama from Elliot Bay Park. Jim Mitsui. BrSi

Last night at midnight. Tune: The Taoist Priestess. Wei Chuang, *tr. by* Burton Watson. CoBCP

Last night at the movie theater. The Prejohn. Hunt Hawkins. KS

Last night, by the Klondike River. By the Klondike River. Alan Coren. OnUR

Last night came calling out of the dark. Mother. Peter Bland. ATNZ

Last night, December 24th, 1966. Report for Isolda. Julio Ortega, *tr. by* David Tipton. Per

Last night did Christ the Sun rise from the dark. Easter Sunday. Sedulius Scottus. OFD, *tr. by* Helen Waddell

Last night for the first time since you were dead. To L. H. B. Katherine Mansfield. ATNZ

Last night—I couldn't sleep. The Aging Poet. Hans Warren, *tr. by* James S. Holmes. DuIn

Last night I did not fight for sleep. In Hospital: Poona, I. Alun Lewis. OBWVE; SeCePo

"Last night I dreamed a ghastly dream." Ballad of the Flood. Edwin Muir. MoBS

Last night I dreamed I was the first man to love a woman. Like Wings. Philip Schultz. MAYP

Last night I dreamed of an old lover. Grandmother, Rocking. Eve Merriam. GrPl; PCP

Last night I dreamed of storms. Through all my skin. The Peacock Woman. László Nagy, *tr. by* George MacBeth. MHuP

Last night I dreamed you drank coffee. One More Sign. Roberta Hill Whiteman. HATNAP

Last night I dreamt in Chinese. Modern Secrets. Shirley Lim. UAS

Last Night I Felt a Poem on My Lips. Rokhl Korn, *tr. fr. Yiddish by* Seymour Levitan. PeBMYV

Last night I had a dream. A Dream about an Aged Humorist. Aaron Zeitlin, *tr. by* Ruth Whitman

Last night I had a dream bad 'cess to my dreaming. Dream, The. *Unknown.* WTO

Last night I heard a strange. Mohammad Taqi Mir, *tr. by* Ahmed Ali. GoT

Last night I heard him in the woods. The Woodpecker. Joyce Sambrook. BoTP

Last night I heard wolves howling. Wolves. John Haines. LCAP

Last night I lay a-sleeping. The Holy City. Frederic Edward Weatherly. BLRP; WBLP

Last night I licked. In Celebration. Ellen Bass. NMM

Last night, I saw a documentary. Losing Track. Cathy Song. BrSi

Last night I saw a silver road. The Silver Road. Hamish Hendry. BoTP

Last night I saw Merce Cunningham. Merce Cunningham and the Birds. Lisel Mueller. GrPl

Last night I saw the monster near; the big. The White Monster. W. H. Davies. AmMo; LiTB

Last night I saw the savage world. Song for a Birth or a Death. Elizabeth Jennings. EBEV

Last night I saw you in my sleep. Bad Dreams. Robert Browning. OxBSP

Last night I saw you in the sky. Starfish. Winifred Welles. FaPON

Last night I saw your corpse. Joyce Mansour, *tr. by* Willis Barnstone. BoWoP

Last night I spoke to a dead woman with green face. Last Night. David Ignatow. VGW

Last night I supped on lobster; it nearly drove me mad. Dream, The. *Unknown.* OxBoLi

Last night I tossed and could not sleep. God Prays. Angela Morgan. WGRP

Last night I walked with you again. Sleepwalking. Gerrit Achterberg, *tr. by* James Brockway. DuIn

Last night I was grieved for love's lovelorn face and hair. Asadullah Khan Ghalib, *tr. by* Ahmed Ali. GoT

Last night I watched my brothers play. The Brothers. Edwin Muir. GTBS-P; HeIP; Mes; NoP; PrIm

Last Night in Calcutta. Allen Ginsberg. NoAM

Last night in dream so clear I saw her. To the Tune "Child at Play." Yang Shen, *tr. by* Jonathan Chaves. CoBLCP

Last night in La Plata an avalanche of stars. La Plata, Missouri: Clear November Night. Jim Barnes. HATNAP

Last Night in London Airport. Christopher Logue. PoPo

Last Night in Sisseton, S. D. Mary Goose. STE

Last night in stomped. Dardanelles 1916. Padraic Fallon. CIP

Last night in the open shippen. Christmas Day. Andrew Young. OBCP

Last night knives flashed. LeChien cried. The Wolves. Galway Kinnell. NePoEA-2

Last night my boy [*or* little boy] confessed to me. The Two Prayers. Andrew Gillies. BLRP

Last night my friend—he says he is my friend. I Hear It Said. Barbara Young. BLPA

Last night my little boy confessed to me. *See* Last night my boy confessed to me.

Last night my soul departed. Muireadhach Albanach O Dalaigh. NOIV

Last Night of the Third Moon, The. Chia Tao, *tr. fr. Chinese by* Burton Watson. CoBCP

Last night returning from my twilight walk. A Ballad of Past Meridian. George Meredith. OAEL-2

Last night that she lived, The. Emily Dickinson. BoWoP; CMoP; LiTA; NAAL-1; OxBA; PoEL-5; QFR; SOTW

Last night the carol-singers came. The Carol Singers. Margaret G. Rhodes. BoTP

Last night the cold wind and the rain blew. Sunday at the End of Summer. Howard Nemerov. BoNaP

Last night the first light frost, and now sycamore. Long Walks in the Afternoon. Margaret Gibson. MAYP

Last night the gypsies came. Gypsies. Rachel Field. BoTP

Last night the rainbow. Moon Shadow. George Bowering. MoCV

Last night the tales died. Entrance. Mihály Ladányi, *tr. fr. Hungarian by* Jascha Kessler. *Fr.* Sketchbook. FOC

Last night thin rain, gusty wind. Li Ch'ing-chao, *tr. fr. Chinese by* Willis Barnstone *and* Sun Chu-chin. BoWoP

Last night thou didst invite me home to eat. Upon Showbread: Epigram. Robert Herrick. CaPo

Last night under the stars. Stags. William Montgomerie. PoSH

Last night watching the Pleiades. An Autumn Morning in Shokoku-ji. Gary Snyder. *Fr.* Four Poems for Robin. HAP; NNaP; NoAM; NOBA; NoP; SOTW; VGW

Last night we anchored in. Arrival, New York Harbor. Robert Peters. GOA

Last night we had a thunderstorm in style. Robert Louis Stevenson. NOBVV

Last night we slept in Miami in the house of. September 30. Dick Lourie. NeAC

Last night we started with some dry vermouth. Ballade of Liquid Refreshment. E. C. Bentley. FaBoCo

Last night, when my tired eyes were shut with sleep. A Gazelle. Richard Henry Stoddard. AA

Last night when the yellow moon. Wadasa Nakamoon, Vietnam Memorial. Ray A. Young Bear. HATNAP

Last night, while/ cabbage stuffed with/ brown-sugar. The Other Night (Comet Kohoutek). Diane Ackerman. BWV

Last night within my dream. Mohammad Taqi Mir, *tr. by* Ahmed Ali. GoT

Last night, within my dreaming. Pine Music. Kate Louise Brown. BoTP

Last night you would not come. John Logan. CAPP

Last Night Your Lost Memory. Faiz Ahmad Faiz, *tr. fr. Urdu by* Mahmood Jamal. PBMUP

Last Night's Dream. Denise Levertov. NoAM

Last night's planets and stars, last night's wind. Li Shang-yin, *tr. fr. Chinese by* Burton Watson. CoBCP

Last o' the Tinkler, The. Violet Jacob. OxBS

Last of His Tribe, The. Henry Clarence Kendall. CBAP; PoAu-1

Last of last words spoken is, Good-bye, The. Good-bye. Walter de la Mare. NoP

Last of the Fire Kings, The. Derek Mahon. FaBCIP; FaBoPV

Last of the Grand Old Masters, The. Tom Patey. PoSH

Last of the Poet's Car. Tony Connor. OxBTC

Last of the poets, first of the undead. The Mole. Dennis Schmitz. AmPA

Last of the Princes, The. A. K. Ramanujan. OxBC

Last on legs, last on sax. "Bird Lives": Charles Parker in St. Louis. Michael S. Harper. AmPA

Last One, The. W. S. Merwin. LCAP; NoAM; VGW

Last one, The/ to die here. Nelly Sachs, *tr. fr. German by* Arthur Wensinger. BoWoP

Last Ones, The. Robin Hyde. ATNZ; PeNZ

Last Ones, The. Dan Pagis, *tr. fr. Hebrew by* Stephen Mitchell. VWA

Last pale rank of poplar-trees, The. Aubade Triste. Agnes Mary Frances Robinson. NOBVV

Last Plea. Jean Starr Untermeyer. TrPWD

Last Poem. Ted Berrigan. UL
Last Poem. Charles Donnelly. BIrV
  (Poem: "Between rebellion as a private study and the public.") CIP
Last Poem. Po Chü-i, tr. fr. Chinese by Arthur Waley. OBD
Last pose flickered, failed, The. Rain after a Vaudeville Show. Stephen
  Vincent Benét. MoAmPo
Last Post, The. Robert Graves. MMA
Last Prayer, A. Helen Hunt Jackson. AA; TrPWD
Last Quarter Moon of the Dying Year, The. Jonathan Henderson Brooks.
  CDC
Last Quatrain of the Ballad of Emmett Till, The. Gwendolyn Brooks.
  CNA; PoBA; WPE
Last Rebirth, The. Coleman Barks. KS
Last Refuge, The. Augustus Young. BIrV
Last Republicans, The. Austin Clarke. CIP
Last Reservation, The. Walter Learned. AA; PAH
Last Ride Together, The. Robert Browning. BoLoP; FiP; LiTB;
  NAEL-2; OBEV; PoEL-5; UnPo
Last Ride Together (from Her Point of View), The. James Kenneth
  Stephen. BXAP; CenHV; FaBoCo; Par; UnPo
Last Rites. Christina Rossetti. OxBChV; RHPC
Last Rose of Summer, The. Thomas Moore. See 'Tis the Last Rose of
  Summer.
Last Round, The. Anna Wickham. MoBrPo
Last Scene in the First Act. Marge Piercy. NoAM
Last sea-thing dredged by sailor Time from Space. Australia. Bernard
  O'Dowd. PoAu-1
Last settlement scraggled out with a barbed wire fence, The. The Flight in
  the Desert. William Everson. VGW
Last Sheet. Roy Fuller. TEP
Last Sight, The. Robert Louis Stevenson. BrPo
Last, since a pinch of dust may quench the eyes. Lilith on the Fate of
  Man. Christopher John Brennan. Fr. Lilith. PoAu-1
Last Snow. Andrew Young. OxBTC
Last Song. James Guthrie. PDV
Last Song of Sappho, The. Giacomo Leopardi, tr. fr. Italian by Patrick
  Creagh. PFI
Last Song of the Angel of Bad Luck. Philip Levine. KS
Last Songs. Galway Kinnell. CAPP
Last Sonnet. Bill Manhire. ATNZ
Last spring carried love's garlands—this season a wreath. Spring 1940.
  Prudence Macdonald. CN
Last Statement. Vladimir Mayakovsky, tr. fr. Russian by Tom Paulin.
  FaBoPV
Last Statement for a Last Oracle. Alan Dugan. CAPP; NoAM
Last Stop. George Seferis, tr. fr. Greek by Edmund Keeley and Philip
  Sherrard. VMG
Last Straw. George Starbuck. SoTCo
Last Street, The. Abraham Reisen, tr. fr. Yiddish by Leonard Wolf.
  PeBMYV
Last Summer, The. Vivian Smith. PoAu-2
Last Summer, and at Midnight. The Guttural Muse. Seamus Heaney.
  NOIV; NoP
Last summer, in the blue heat. La Vita Nuova. Weldon Kees. VGW
Last sunbeam, The. Dirge for Two Veterans. Walt Whitman.
  AnAmPo; MoAmPo; PoEL-5
  (Two Veterans.) GN
Last Sunday petrified. Wingwalking in Oregon. Robert Peterson.
  NeAC
Last Supper, The. Jacques Prévert, tr. fr. French. POS; tr. by Michael
  Benedikt; RHTwFP, tr. by Lawrence Ferlinghetti.
Last Supper, The. Stan Rice. NPGG
Last Supper, The. Rainer Maria Rilke, tr. fr. German by M. D. Herter
  Norton. OFD
Last Supper, The. Oscar Williams. FaFP; LiTA; LiTM
Last Supper, The. Yusuf al-khal, tr. fr. Arabic by Abdullah al-Udhari.
  MPAW
Last Survivor's Speech, The. Unknown, tr. fr. Anglo-Saxon by Alfred
  David. Fr. Beowulf. NAEL-1
Last thin acre of stalks that stood, The. Immortal. Mark Van Doren.
  MoAmPo
Last thing I put on, The. Vital Message. Robert Phillips. GeTw
Last Thing I Say, The. Marvin Bell. CAPP
Last thing, the very, The. Mountain Creed. Hugh C. Rae. PoSH
Last Things. William Meredith. NoAM
Last things/ the turning leaves slip in the wind. Vincent O'Sullivan. Fr.
  Brother Jonathan, Brother Kafka, 40. PeNZ
Last Things. Kathleen Jessie Raine. NYBP
Last Things, Black Pines at 4 a.m. Robert Lowell. NOBA
Last time around the forest floor. Rainier. Jim Tollerud. VoR
Last time I kissed her, The. Almost Ninety. Ruth Whitman. PCP

Last time I saw Donald Armstrong, The. The Performance. James
  Dickey. CAPP; CoAP; LiTM; MoP; NePoEA-2; NOBA; PoE
Last time I saw my high school football coach, The. Execution. Edward
  Hirsch. TSL
Last time i was home, The. Mothers. Nikki Giovanni. CNA; TV;
  UnPo
Last Tournament, The, sels. Tennyson. Fr. Idylls of the King.
  "As the crest of some slow-arching wave." FaBoPP
  Tristram's Song. FaBoRV
  Lincolnshire Shores. FaBoPP
Last train to Barcelona, The. Sa'di Yusuf, tr. fr. Arabic by Sargon
  Boulus and Naomi Shihab Nye. Fr. Three Dispositions Regarding
  One Woman, II. MAP
Last Trial, The. Petrarch. Fr. Sonnets to Laura: To Laura in Life,
  CXIII, tr. unknown. OBSC
Last Trial, The. Unknown. OBSC
Last truly foolish thing I did was some years ago, The. The Void.
  Gwendolyn MacEwen. Fr. The T. E. Lawrence Poems. NOBC
Last two Februarys have passed, The. St. Bridget's Cross. Anne
  Hartigan. CIP
Last Utterance of the Delphic Oracle, The. Unknown, tr. fr. Greek by
  Kenneth Rexroth. OBVE
Last Verses. Thomas Chatterton. TrGrPo
Last Violet, The. Oliver Herford. OHIP
Last Visit. Robert Finch. NOBC
Last wall between us fell down, The. From Our Yoke. Jacob Glatstein,
  tr. by Benjamin and Barbara Harshav. AYP
Last War, The. Kingsley Amis. OBSV; OxBC; SoSe
Last weak rays, The. Emperor Kogon, tr. fr. Japanese by Steven D.
  Carter. WFTW
Last week I stopped by the grocer's. Shopping. Cees Buddingh', tr. by
  James S. Holmes. DuIn
Last week; the lawns, the sycamores. Janus Season. Derek Stanford.
  NPo
Last Will and Testament, A. Unknown. MeEL
Last Will and Testament, A. John Winstanley. OBSV
Last Will of the Drunk. Myra von Riedemann. OBCV
Last winter I tore up poems full of animals. A Summer Storm. Anne
  French. ATNZ
Last winter we were/ short of firewood. A Letter to Hitler. James
  Laughlin. LiTA; WaP
Last Wish, The. Sir Edward Bulwer-Lytton. OxBSP
Last Word, The. Matthew Arnold. FiP; NOBE; OAEL-2; OBNC;
  PoEL-5; TrGrPo
Last Word, The. Peter Davison. InPK
Last Word, A. Ernest Dowson. MoBrPo
Last Word: For My Son Yung. Chin Jen-Jui, tr. fr. Chinese by Irving Lo.
  WFTU
Last Word of a Bluebird, The. Robert Frost. FaPON; GoJo; GrPl; SO
Last Words. Emily Brontë. WPE
Last Words. John Hollander. OBAL
Last Words. Richard Howard. Fr. Ithaca: The Palace at Four A.M..
  DiPo
Last Words, The. Maurice Maeterlinck, tr. fr. French by Frederick York
  Powell. AWP
Last Words. James Merrill. TAP
Last Words. Linda Pastan. BLA
Last Words. Sylvia Plath. FYAP
Last Words, The. Alma Villanueva. CCP
Last Words before Winter. Louis Untermeyer. MoAmPo
Last Words, 1968. Lance Henson. CDW
Last Words of Don Henriquez, The. Zalman Schneour, tr. fr. Yiddish by
  Joseph Leftwich. TrJP
Last Words of My English Grandmother, The. William Carlos Williams.
  RB; SOTW
Last Words to a Dumb Friend. Thomas Hardy. FM
Last Words to James Wright. Richard Hugo. KS
Last World, A. John Ashbery. PoM
Last year among the flowers I saw you off. To Send to Li Tan and Yüan
  Hsi. Wei Ying-wu, tr. by Burton Watson. CoBCP
Last year at the Feast of Lanterns. Lost. Chu Shu-chen, tr. by Kenneth
  Rexroth. BoWoP
Last year changed its seasons. In Retrospect. Maya Angelou. UnAS
Last Year in Capricorn. Eeva-Liisa Manner, tr. fr. Finnish by Aili
  Jarvenpa. SOP
Last year in spring. Masaoka Shiki, tr. fr. Japanese by Burton Watson.
  Fr. Fifteen Haiku. FCEI
Last year my old friend, His Excellency Wang. When I Reached the Post
  Station at Kaya. Michizane, tr. by Burton Watson. JLIC-1
Last year, Orlando. The Political Orlando. George MacBeth. NOBL

Last year service in the eastern hills. Written When Appointed Commander of the Western Sea Marches. Umakai, *tr.* by Burton Watson. JLIC-1

Last year the child died. Olive Senior. PBCV

Last year the war was in the northeast. War. Li Po, *tr.* by Rewi Alley. ChTr

Last year we parted as the flowers began to bloom. A Lady Picking Flowers. Shen Chou, *tr.* by Jonathan Chaves. CoBLCP

Last year when I accompanied you. To a Traveler. Su Tung-p'o, *tr.* by Kenneth Rexroth. HoPM

Last year, with jade hands, you offered cups of tea. Liu E, *tr. fr. Chinese* by Jonathan Chaves. *Fr.* Poems for Yukiko of Tamba. CoBLCP

Last Years, The. W. H. Davies. FM

Last year's decencies. Odysseus. Padraic Fallon. CIP

Last Year's Discussion: The Nobel Russian. Phyllis McGinley. FaBoEE

Lasting as tell the *tsuga*-trees. Yakamochi, *tr. fr. Japanese*. *Fr.* Manyo Shu. Ma

Lastly came Winter cloathèd all in frize. Winter. Spenser. *Fr.* The Faerie Queene, VII, 7. GN

Lastly, stood war, in glittering arms yclad. The Shield of War. Thomas Sackville. *Fr.* Induction to "A Mirror for Magistrates." AAS; OBSC

Lastness. Galway Kinnell. NNaP

"Black bear sits alone, A," *sel.* DiL

Lat never a man a wooing wend. King Henry. *Unknown.* ESPB; OxBB, *with music*

Lat no man booste of conning not vertu. Transient as a Rose. John Lydgate. MeEL

Lat Take a Cat. Chaucer. *Fr.* The Canterbury Tales: The Manciple's Tale. ChTr

Late. Louise Bogan. PBWP; VGW

Late. Helen Salz. GoYe

Late afternoon light slices through the dormer window. The Gun. Stephen Dobyns. AnAn

Late Afternoon on a Good Lake. Dara Wier. MAYP

Late April and you are three; today. W. D. Snodgrass. *Fr.* Heart's Needle, II. NePoEA

Late April. Taking stock. Generalities. Robert Conquest. OxBC

Late as last summer. Thou Didst Say Me. Miriam Waddington. OBCV

Late at een, drinkin' the wine. The Dowie Houms o' Yarrow. *Unknown.* GoTS; OBEV; OBS; OxBS (Braes o' Yarrow, The.) ESPB

Late at Night. Rudolf Bayer, *tr. fr. German* by Beth Bjorklund. CoAuP

Late at Night. William Stafford. NNaP; RFM

Late at night. Kyogoku Tamekane, *tr. fr. Japanese* by Burton Watson. *Fr.* Twenty-three Tanka. FCEI

Late at night. The Beads. Jaime Jacinto. BrSi

Late at Night During a Visit of Friends. Robert Bly. InPS

Late at night our hands stop working. Return to a Place Lit by a Glass of Milk. Charles Simic. GeTw

Late at night we wrench open a crab. Crab. Fleur Adcock. ATNZ

Late Aubade, A. Richard Wilbur. SM; SoSe

Late August, given heavy rain and sun. Blackberry-picking. Seamus Heaney. BoNaP

Late Blossoms in the Cold Mountains. Gyoko, *tr. fr. Japanese* by Steven D. Carter. WFTW

Late Child. Robert Pinsky. *Fr.* Three on Luck. AnAn

Late Comer. Fanny de Groot Hastings. GoYe

Late Conversation. Mark Doty. NAmP

Late Dandelions. Ben Belitt. NYBP

Late Dispatch. Judah Leib Teller, *tr. fr. Yiddish* by Benjamin *and* Barbara Harshav. AYP

Late Fall. René Altmann, *tr. fr. German* by Beth Bjorklund. CoAuP

Late-flowering Lust. Sir John Betjeman. CMoP; ErPo; TW

Late Gothic. Phyllis Gotlieb. NOBC

Late Hour. A. Leyeles, *tr. fr. Yiddish* by Benjamin *and* Barbara Harshav. AYP

Late Hour, The. Mark Strand. HCAP

Late, I was in the back circle. Auction. William Heyen. MAYP

Late in an evening forth as I went. Archie o Cawfield. *Unknown.* ESPB

Late in Fall. Ramona Wilson. VoR

Late in my life I come to you. Yehuda Amichai, *tr. fr. Hebrew* by Warren Bargad *and* Stanley F. Chyet. IP

Late in the afternoon. Spring Burning. Patrick Roland. PeSA

Late in the afternoon the light. Crepuscular. Richard Howard. TwCP

Late in the evening the ale graines and blood. Baits for Various Fish. Thomas Barker. *Fr.* The Art of Angling. FaBoUs

Late in the season the world digs in, the fat blossoms. Over and Over Stitch. Jorie Graham. HCAP

Late in the spring night. Song of the Water Clock at Night. Mao Wen-hsi, *tr.* by Lois Fusek. ATF

Late in the Year K'uei-yu. Yü Chi, *tr. fr. Chinese* by Jonathan Chaves. CoBLCP

Late into the lulling night the pickers toiled. Uneasy Peace. Edmund Blunden. BrPo

Late into the night. Emperor Fushimi, *tr. fr. Japanese* by Steven D. Carter. WFTW

Late it was in the night, with the wind. Lament for Turlough O'Carolan. David Brendon Hopes. SM

Late, just past midnight. Off from Swing Shift. Garrett Kaoru Hongo. MAYP

Late Last Night. Arthur Gregor. VGW

Late last night I was a-making my rounds. Bad Man Ballad. *Unknown.* AmFP

Late, Last Rook, The. Ralph Hodgson. MoBrPo

Late lies the wintry sun a-bed. Winter Time. Robert Louis Stevenson. *Fr.* A Child's Garden of Verses. EBVV; MoBrPo; OxBChV

Late Light. Edmund Blunden. EnLoPo

Late Light. Barbara Bellow Watson. NYBP

Late Manuscript at the Schocken Institute, A. Gabriel Preil, *tr. fr. Hebrew* by Gabriel Levin. VWA

Late Miss H. came to us Wednesday at four, The. Swansong. Carol Muske. AmPA

Late Moon. Philip Levine. LCAP

Late moon, shut out of the town, A. Ozaki Hosai, *tr. fr. Japanese* by Hiroaki Sato. *Fr.* One Hundred Haiku in Free Form. FCEI

Late Mother, The. Cynthia MacDonald. Psk

Late Naps. Marvin Bell. AnAn

Late night wheat flour spilled. Ozaki Hosai, *tr. fr. Japanese* by Hiroaki Sato. *Fr.* One Hundred Haiku in Free Form. FCEI

Late night, with my bundle of new straws. The Burden of Decision. Peter Everwine. NNaP

Late November. Sherod Santos. Son

Late November, driving to Wichita. For a Friend. Ted Kooser. GOYP

Late November evening in Vienna. Deportation. Judah Leib Teller, *tr.* by Benjamin *and* Barbara Harshav. AYP

Late November in a Field. James Wright. CAPP; NAAL-2; NNaP

Late October. Sara King Carleton. GoYe

Late October sun. White Earth. Gerald Vizenor. HATNAP (White Earth Reservation 1980). STE

Late, of a late summer night, almost white. Night-Piece. Kendrick Smithyman. ATNZ

Late one afternoon we walk along the flank of a hill. South Seas. Cesare Pavese, *tr.* by William Arrowsmith. AnAn

Late or soon, which is it, lonely flower? The November Primrose. John Dacres Devlin. PF

Late Passenger, The. C. S. Lewis. TrCP

Late, Passing Prairie Farm. William Stafford. GOYP

Late Reflections. Babette Deutsch. NYBP

Late, retarding, and unsettled season, The. Autumn; an Ode. Charles Gullans. NePoEA

Late Return. E. A. Markham. PVCV

Late Rising on Spring Days. Wei Chuang, *tr. fr. Chinese* by Burton Watson. CoBCP

Late Saturday afternoons in Emeryville. Butcherboy. Tom Schmidt. NeAC

Late Show, The. Janet Sylvester. MAYP

Late singer of a sunless day. The Linnet in November. Francis Turner Palgrave. EBVV

Late Snow and Lumber Strike of the Summer of Fifty-four, The. Gary Snyder. NaP

Late Sonnet. Hayden Carruth. SM; Son

Late Spring. Robert Hass. GeTw; MAYP

Late Spring. W. S. Merwin. AnAn

Late spring. Onitsura, *tr. fr. Japanese* by Hiroaki Sato. *Fr.* Twenty-three Hokku. FCEI

Late Spring, A. James Scully. NYBP

Late Spring. Ts'ao Chen-chi, *tr. fr. Chinese* by William H. Nienhauser, Jr. WFTU

Late Spring: A Heaving, a Turning. John Gill. NeAC

Late Spring: Eastport, A. Philip Booth. Psk

Late spring has snatched away the blossoms. Impromptu; Late Spring at Pan-shan. Wang An-shih, *tr.* by Burton Watson. CoBCP

Late spring in the Shang-yang Palace! Pure Serene Music. Wen T'ing-yün, *tr.* by Lois Fusek. ATF

Late Spring—Traveling through the Mountains. Chu Yün-ming, *tr. fr. Chinese* by Jonathan Chaves. CoBLCP

Late Starting Dawn. Richard Brautigan. PCP

Late Stravinsky Listening to Late Beethoven. Stephen Spender. AnAn

Late Summer. Kinoshita Yuji, *tr. fr. Japanese by* Geoffrey Bownas *and* Anthony Thwaite. PeBJV
Late summer, and at midnight. The Guttural Muse. Seamus Heaney. NOIV; NoP
Late that summer. Surrendered Names. Gerald Vizenor. HATNAP
Late Tutorial. Vincent Buckley. PoAu-2
Late 'twas in June, the fleece when fully grown. Michael Drayton. *Fr.* The Shepherd's Garland, Eclogue IX (1606 ed.). OBSC
Late Victorian Girl, The. Bill Manhire. PeNZ
Late Winter. James McAuley. PoAu-2
Late Winter Snow. Brian Turner. ATNZ
Late Wisdom. George Crabbe. *Fr.* Reflections. OBEV; TrGrPo
Lately, Alas, I Knew a Gentle Boy. Henry David Thoreau. PeHV
Lately his haunch has grown stiff. Father. Jean Lipkin. AIW; PeSA
Lately I saw a sight most quaint. "Gross, Coarse, Hideous" (Police Description of My Pictures). D. H. Lawrence. FaBoEE
Lately, I think of my love for you and the rose. The Rose Growing into the House. Gibbons Ruark. InPK
Lately, I've become accustomed to the way. Preface to a Twenty Volume Suicide Note. Amiri Baraka. AmNP; PoBA; PoM; PoNe; PPP; TTY
Lately I've become religious about atoms. Metamorpho I. Joe Rosenblatt. MoCV
Lately I've felt a grave concern. Countess Beatritz de Die, *tr. fr. Provençal by* Willis Barnstone. BoWoP
Lately my neighbor wheezes. Running. Leslie Ullman. NAmP
Lately Our Poets. Walter Savage Landor. LiTB; OAEL-2; PoEL-4 ("Lately our poets loitered in green lanes.") FaBoEE; GTBS-P
Lately, there's no trace left. 1919. Jacob Glatstein, *tr. by* Benjamin *and* Barbara Harshav *and* Kathryn Helle. AYP
Later afternoons, The. End of a Summer Sunday. Andreas Okopenko, *tr. fr. German by* Beth Bjorklund. *Fr.* Summer Fragments, I. CoAuP
Later Antigonishes, *sel.* Hughes Mearns.
  Lady with Technique, The. FiBHP
Later I would say, I have cut myself free from order. Sun Moon Kelp Flower or Goat. Linda Gregg. NPGG
Later Life, *sels.* Christina Rossetti.
  Before the Mountains Were Brought Forth. *Fr.* I. Son
  "Something this foggy day, a something which." *Fr.* XVII. NAEL-2
  This Life Is Full of Numbness. *Fr.* XXVI. Son
  To Love and to Remember. *Fr.* VII. Son
Later Note on Letter 15, A. Charles Olson. *Fr.* The Maximus Poems. CAPP
Later, Spending Some Time at Bokusetsu's Hut in Otsu. Basho, *tr. fr. Japanese by* Burton Watson. *Fr.* Seventy-six Hokku. FCEI
Later that week, when the reddish. Spring Floods. Gregory Orr. GeTw
Latest Decalogue, The. Arthur Hugh Clough. ChTr; EBEV; EBVV; FaBoCo; FaBoEE; FF; GTBS-P; HAP; HoPM; NAEL-2; NIP; NOBE; NOBVV; OAEL-2; OBNC; OBSV; OPOP; PPP; WeW; WGRP
Latest Diet, The. Jim Young. SoTCo
Latest Hotel Guest Walks over Particles That Revolve in Seven Other Dimensions Controlling Latti, The. Ruth Stone. BAP
Latest in Guillotines, The. Giuseppe Giusti, *tr. fr. Italian by* Nigel Dennis. PFI
Latest poems, like the most recent, The. Dispatch Number Sixteen. Doug Fetherling. NeAC
Latet Languis. William Cornish. *See* You and I and Amyas.
Latin. Latin is a dead tongue. *Unknown.* ChTr
Latin Dances. Mark Doty. NAmP
Latin is a dead tongue. Latin. *Unknown.* ChTr
Latter Day. Rae Armantrout. LP
Latter Day, The. Thomas Hastings. *See* Hail to the Brightness of Zion's Glad Morning.
Latter-day Geography Lesson. R. A. K. Mason. ATNZ; PeNZ
Latter Day Lysistrata. Lauris Edmond. PeNZ
Latter Day Psalms. Cliff Ashby. NOCV
Latter Purification, A. Haim Guri, *tr. fr. Hebrew by* Mark Elliott Shapiro. VWA
Laudanum. *Unknown.* NOEC
Laudate Dominum. Bible, *O.T. See* Psalms: Psalm CL ("O praise God in his holiness").
Laude, honor, praisingis, thankis infinite. The Difficulties of Translation. Gawin Douglas. *Fr.* Prologues to the Aeneid, *bk.* I, Prologue. GoTS
Lauds. John Berryman. HAP
Lauds. W. H. Auden. *Fr.* Horae Canonicae. TrCP
Laugh and Be Merry. John Masefield. FaFP; MoBrPo
Laugh and Sing. Francis Beaumont *and* Fletcher. *See* Knight of the Burning Pestle, The: Mirth.

Laugh, and the world laughs with you. Solitude. Ella Wheeler Wilcox. AnAmPo; FaFP; FPL; OHFP; PoLF; PWR
  (Way of the World, The.) WBLP
Laugh It Off. Henry Rutherford Elliot. WBLP
Laugh now but by tomorrow you may weep. After Laughter. Grace Buchanan Sherwood. GoYe
Laugh on, laugh on at all the dreams. i Believe. Saul Tchernichowsky, *tr. by* Reginald V. Feldman. TrJP
Laughed at the old deliberate ways. Repression. Timothy Corsellis. WaP
Laughed every goblin. Christina Rossetti. *Fr.* Goblin Market. BrRo
Laughing Angel: Reims, The. Liz Socolow. PPR
Laughing Backwards. Jim Hall. GOYP
Laughing, before the lamps, we pour each other. The Year *I-mao* (1555), New Year's Eve. Wen Cheng-ming, *tr. by* Jonathan Chaves. CoBLCP
Laughing Child. Carl Sandburg. PCP
Laughing eyes followed. Asante Sana, Te Te. Thadious M. Davis. BISi
Laughing Hyena, by Hokusai, The. Dennis Joseph Enright. TwCP
Laughing, merry, childish voices, woke us in their eager glee. Christmas, South, 1866. Mary E. Tucker. CBWP-1
Laughing Song. Blake. *Fr.* Songs of Innocence. BoTP; NAEL-2 (When the Green Woods Laugh.) CH; EnRP; GoJo; NBLV; OxBChV
Laughing Time. William Jay Smith. FaPON
Laughs the happy April morn. Anterotics. William Ernest Henley. *Fr.* In Hospital, XXVI. BrPo
Laughter. Isabella Valancy Crawford. CaP
Laughter. Olive Enoch. BoTP
Laughter. Wislawa Szymborska, *tr. fr. Polish by* Czeslaw Milosz. PwPP
Laughter of children brings. Early Supper. Barbara Howes. GoJo; GrPl; SM
Laughter of the lesser lynx, The. The Lesser Lynx. Emile Victor Rieu. CenHV; FiBHP; RHPC
Laughter wears a lilied gown. Laughter. Isabella Valancy Crawford. CaP
Launch, The. Alice Meynell. WPE
Launched upon ether float the worlds secure. Authority. William Reed Huntington. AA
Laundress, The. Thomas Kinsella. IPY
Laundry. Bruce Smith. Son
Laundry. Berysh Vaynshteyn, *tr. fr. Yiddish by* Benjamin *and* Barbara Harshav *and* Kathryn Hellerstein. *Fr.* Negroes. AYP
Laundry and School Epigrams. Bernadette Mayer. UL
Laundryman—/ By his neighbours', The. *Unknown, tr. by* Geoffrey Bownas *and* Anthony Thwaite. PeBJV
Laura. Thomas Campion. *See* Rose-cheeked [*or* cheekt] Laura, Come.
Laura, *sels.* Robert Tofte.
  "Rich damask roses in fair cheeks do bide." EIL
  Unto Thy Favor. *Fr.* I, xxx. Son
  When She Was Born. *Fr.* III, vii. Son
Laura and Lizzie Asleep. Christina Rossetti. *Fr.* Goblin Market. PeHV
Laura is my friend, and as I shade my eyes. Red Seeds Opening in the Shade. Sandra McPherson. NAmP
Laura Sleeping. Charles Cotton. ELP; OBS; ViBoPo
Laura Sleeping. Louise Chandler Moulton. AA
Laurana's Song. Richard Hovey. AA; AnAmPo
Laureate, The. William Edmonstoune Aytoun. BXAP; Par
Laureate, The. Robert Graves. BIrV; FaBoTw; OBSV
Laureate's Complaint, The. Gavin Ewart. SoTCo
Laurel Axe, The. Geoffrey Hill. *Fr.* An Apology for the Revival of Christian Architecture in England, 9. NAEL-2; NoAM; NoP; PoE
Laurel ratio sharp or hard. Codex. Clark Coolidge. IAT
Laurel Tree, The. Louis Simpson. NNaP
Laurels and Immortelles. *Unknown.* BLPA
Laurence Bloomfield in Ireland, *sels.* William Allingham.
  Eviction, The. BIrV; NOIV
  Lord Crashton: The Absentee Landlord. NOIV
Laurentian Shield. F. R. Scott. NOBC; OBCV
L'Aurore Grelottante. Peter Levi. NePoEA-2
Laus Deo! Whittier. AmPP; PAH
Laus Mariae. Sidney Lanier. Son
Laus Veneris. Louise Chandler Moulton. AA
Laus Virginitatis. Arthur Symons. EnLoPo
Lausanne. Thomas Hardy. FaBoRV; FaBoTw; OBTV
Lauzengiers and the deceitful spies, The. Clara d'Anduza, *tr. by* Meg Bogin. WT
Lavender Bush, The. Elizabeth Fleming. BoTP
Lavender Kitten, The. Alonzo Lopez. NOVW

Lavender's Blue. *Unknown.* CH; PYC
   ("Lavender's blue, diddle diddle.") OxNR
Law, The. Samuel Butler. NBLV
Law, The. Albert E. Haynes, Jr. NBP
Law, The. Abraham Ibn Ezra, *tr. fr. Hebrew by* Alice Lucas. TrJP
Law, The. Ella Wheeler Wilcox. PWR
Law against Lovers, The, *sel.* Sir William Davenant.
   Wake All the Dead. ELP; FaBoCh; HAP; SeCePo
Law allows our feasting, The. *Unknown. Fr.* Manyo Shu. Ma
Law can take a purse in open court, The. The Law. Samuel Butler.
   NBLV
Law firm commanding, A. Help Wanted. Franklin Waldheim. BLPA
Law in the Country of the Cats. Ted Hughes. TW
Law makes long spokes of the short stakes of men. Legal Fiction.
   William Empson. CMoP; FaBoMo; LiTB; LiTM; MoP; NoAM; NoP
Law of Averages, The. "Troubadour." FiBHP
Law of Jehovah is perfect, restoring the soul, The. God's Precepts
   Perfect. Bible, *O.T. Fr.* Psalms: Psalm XIX ("The heavens declare
   the glory of God"), 7-9. BLRP
   (Glory of God, The.) TrJP
   (God's Glory.) TrGrPo
   (Heavens, The, 1-6.) ChTr
   (Heavens Above and the Law Within, The, *Moulton, Modern Reader's
   Bible.*) WGRP
   ("Heavens doe declare, The," *Bay Psalm Book.*) SCAP
   (Psalm XIX: "Heavenly frame sets forth the fame, The," *paraphrased
   by* Sir Philip Sidney.) OBVE
   (Psalm XIX: "Spacious firmament on high, The.") WGRP
Law of the Jungle, The. Kipling. LiTB; PoEL-5
Law of the Yukon, The. Robert W. Service. CaP
Law there is of ancient fame, A. Tit for Tat; a Tale. John Aikin.
   OxBChV
Law, the: unchain/ The mind from all. To One Who Reveres Buddhism.
   Bunan, *tr. by* Lucien Stryk *and* Takashi Ikemoto. ZPCJ
Lawd, Dese Colored Chillum. Ruby C. Saunders. BlSi
Lawd, I'm broke and hungry, ragged and dirty, too. Ragged and Dirty.
   Unknown. AmFP
Lawlands o' Holland, The. *Unknown.* CH
Lawlands o' Holland, The. *Unknown. See* Lowlands o' [*or* of] Holland,
   The.
Lawn as white as driven snow. Autolycus as Peddler. Shakespeare. *Fr.*
   The Winter's Tale, IV, iii. OAEL-1
   (Autolycus's Song ("Lawn as white as driven snow").) OBSC
   (Come Buy! Come Buy!) ElL
   (Pedlar, The.) WiR
   (Pedlar's Song, The.) CH
Lawn Roller, The. Robert Layzer. NePoEA
Lawn-Tennisonian Idyll, A. *Unknown.* FaBoPa
Lawns darken, evening broods in the black, The. Tennyson. Alan
   Ansen. CoAP
Lawrence here for ever blames. D. H. Lawrence and James Joyce.
   Humbert Wolfe. FaBoEE
Lawrence—not the bearded one—the one. Any Complaints? Vernon
   Scannell. OxBTC
Lawrence, of virtuous father virtuous son. To Mr. Lawrence. Milton.
   AWP; GTBS; GTBS-P; OBEV; PoE
   (Sonnet.) OBS
Laws-a-massey, what have you done? Negro Reel. *Unknown.* AS
Laws are the secret avengers, The. The Avengers. Edwin Markham.
   MoAmPo
Laws of God, The. A. E. Housman. *See* Laws of God, the Laws of
   Man, The.
Laws of God, the Laws of Man, The. A. E. Housman. MoAB;
   MoBrPo; NOBVV; OBSV; PeHV
   (Laws of God, The.) OxBoLi; PPP
Lawyer had a legal mouse, A. A Legal Mouse. Lizelia Augusta Jenkins
   Moorer. CBWP-3
Lawyers, Bob, know too much, The. The Lawyers Know Too Much.
   Carl Sandburg. CMOP; PoE
Lawyer's Invocation to Spring, The. Henry Howard Brownell. PoLF
Lawyers Know Too Much, The. Carl Sandburg. CMOP; PoE
Lawyers may revere that tree, The. Epigram on a Lawyer's Desiring One
   of the Tribe to Look with Respect to a Gibbet. Robert Fergusson.
   OxBS
Lawyers' Ways, The. Paul Laurence Dunbar. AnAmPo
Lay a garland on my hearse. Francis Beaumont *and* Fletcher. *Fr.* The
   Maid's Tragedy, II, i. ElL; GBL
Lay aside phrases; speak as in the night. This Is Not Death. Humbert
   Wolfe. MoBrPo
Lay down the axe; fling by the spade. Our Country's Call. Bryant.
   PAH

Lay down these words. Riprap. Gary Snyder. CAPP; HCAP; NAAL-2;
   NeAP; NoAM; NOBA; PoM
Lay his dear ashes where ye will. President Lincoln's Grave. Caroline
   Atherton Briggs Mason. OHIP
Lay in the house mostly living. Madness. James Dickey. NYBP
Lay me down beneaf de willers in de grass. A Death Song. Paul
   Laurence Dunbar. BANP; CDC; PoLF; PoNe
Lay me in the woodbox. Last Will of the Drunk. Myra von Riedemann.
   OBCV
Lay me in yon place, lad. The Last o' the Tinkler. Violet Jacob.
   OxBS
Lay me on an anvil, O God. Prayers of Steel. Carl Sandburg. CMoP;
   FaPON; MoAmPo; PDV; TrCP; TrPWD
Lay me to sleep in [the] sheltering flame. The Mystic's Prayer. "Fiona
   Macleod." TrPWD; WGRP
Lay not up for yourselves treasures upon the earth. Treasures. Bible,
   N.T. Fr. St. Matthew, VI: 19-21. TrGrPo
Lay of Finn, The. *Unknown, tr. fr. Anglo-Saxon by* Charles W. Kennedy.
   Fr. Beowulf. AnOE
Lay of Ike, The. John Berryman. *Fr.* Dream Songs. LCAP
Lay [*or* Short Lay] of Sigurd, The. *Unknown, tr. fr. Old Norse by*
   William Morris *and* Eirikur Magnusson. *Fr.* The Elder Edda. AWP
   "And now one prayer," *sel.* OBVE
Lay of the Battle of Tombland, The. Dunstan Thompson. LiTA
Lay of the Captive Count, The. Goethe, *tr. fr. German by* James
   Clarence Mangan. AWP
Lay of the Ettercap, The. John Leyden. BXAP
Lay of the Honeysuckle, The. Marie de France, *tr. fr. French by* Robin
   Johnson. WPE
Lay of the Labourer, The. Thomas Hood. SaC
Lay of the Last Minstrel, The, *sels.* Sir Walter Scott.
   Breathes There the [*or* a] Man [with Soul So Dead]. *Fr.* VI. BLPA;
   EnRP; FaFP; FPL; OPP; OxBS
   Father's Notes of Woe, A. *Fr.* IV. OBNC
   Hunting Song. EnRP; GN; GTBS; GTBS-P; TrGrPo; WiR
   Melrose Abbey. *Fr.* II. FaBoPP; SeCePo
   (Sir William of Deloraine at the Wizard's Tomb.) OBNC
   Minstrel Responds to Flattery, The. *Fr.* V. OBNC
   Rosabelle. *Fr.* VI. BeLS; GTBS; GTBS-P
   (Harold's Song: Rosabelle.) EnRP
   Song of Albert Graeme. *Fr.* VI. EnRP
Lay of the Lovelorn, The. William Edmonstoune Aytoun *and* Sir
   Theodore Martin. FaBoCo
   (Cry of the Lovelorn, The.) CenHV
Lay of the Trilobite, The. May Kendall. CenHV
Lay out the minutes, row on ordered row. Time Out. Frances Westgate
   Butterfield. GoYe
Lay Preacher Ponders, The. Idris Davies. OxBTC
Lay to Eliza, The. Spenser. *See* Shepheardes [*or* Shepeards *or*
   Shepherd's] Calender, The: Aprill.
Lay Your Arms Aside. Pierce Ferriter, *tr. fr. Irish by* Eilean Ni
   Chuilleanain. BIrV
Lay Your Head on My Shoulder. Yehuda Amichai, *tr. fr. Hebrew by*
   Robert Friend. VWA
Lay your sleeping head, my love. W. H. Auden. CMoP; GLP; HAP;
   LLLT; MoP; NAEL-2; NoAM; NOBE; OAEL-2; OxBTC; PoE; PPP;
   UnPo; WeW
   (Lay Your Sleeping Head, My Love.) BoLoP
   (Song XI: "Lay your sleeping head, my love.") EnLoPo
Lay your weapons down, young lady. Piaras Feiritear, *tr. fr. Irish by*
   Thomas Kinsella. NOIV
Layer on layer of hemp leaves, jute leaves shining. Tune: Sand of Silk-
   washing Stream. Su Tung-p'o, *tr. by* Burton Watson. CoBCP
Layer upon layer, with clay and bricks and hard work. A Witch Going
   Down to Egypt. Raquel Chalfi. VWA, *tr. by* Alexandra Meiri *and*
   Myra Glazer Schotz
Layers of eightfold kerria roses in such a glow. Princess Shikishi, *tr. fr.
   Japanese by* Hiroaki Sato. *Fr.* Seventy-eight Tanka. FCEI
Laying a fart. *Unknown, tr. by* Burton Watson. FCEI
Lays of Ancient Rome, *sels.* Macaulay.
   Horatius. OBWP
   Horatius at the Bridge. BeLS; FaBoCh; FaFP; FaPoR; OBNV, *abr.*;
   OBWP; OHFP, *abr.*; PoLF
Lazarus, kindling at the breath of pain. The Second Life of Lazarus.
   Gwen Harwood. CBAP
Lazarus-like, I am restored. Covering All Bases. Evelyn Thomas.
   TSM
Lazily through the clear. The Goldfish. Audrey Alexandra Brown.
   CaP
Laziness and Silence. Robert Bly. PPP

Lazy and slow, through the snags and trees. In the Bayou. Don Marquis. AmFN

Lazy-bones, lazy-bones, wake up and peep! Nonsense Verses. Charles Lamb. NA

Lazy deuks that sit i' the coal-neuks. *Unknown*. OxNR

Lazy laughing languid Jenny. Jenny. Dante Gabriel Rossetti. PoEL-5

Lazy Man's Song. Po Chü-i, *tr. fr. Chinese by* Arthur Waley. OBVE

Lazy Mary. *Unknown*. AmFP

Lazy People, The. Shel Silverstein. NTCP

Lazy petals of magnolia-bloom float down the sluggish river. Elegy on a Nordic White Protestant. John Gould Fletcher. PoNe

Lazy Pussy, The. Palmer Cox. OBCA

Lazy Roof, The. Gelett Burgess. NA

Lazy sheep, pray tell me why. The Sheep. Ann Taylor. BoTP; OxBChV

Lazy Witch. Myra Cohn Livingston. RHPC

Le Balcon. Baudelaire, *tr. fr. French by* Lord Alfred Douglas. AWP

Le Chariot. John Wieners. VGW

Le Christianisme. Wilfred Owen. BrPo

Le Hibou et la Poussiquette. Francis Steegmuller. NYBP

Le Jardin. Oscar Wilde. *Fr.* Impressions. SeCePo (Garden, The.) PoRA

Le Jazz Hot. Anselm Hollo. PoM

Le Journal. Sándor Weöres, *tr. fr. Hungarian by* Edwin Morgan. MHuP

Le Livre Est sur la Table. John Ashbery. EAS

Le Marais du Cygne. Whittier. PAH

Le Médecin Malgré Lui. William Carlos Williams. PoA; SaC

Le Monocle de Mon Oncle. Wallace Stevens. LiTM; MoAB

Le Musée Imaginaire. Charles Tomlinson. NePoEA-2

Le Père Sévère. *Unknown, tr. fr. French by* Andrew Lang. AWP

Le Sacré-Coeur. Charlotte Mew. OBTV

Le Tombeau de Frank O'Hara. Art Lange. UL

Le Tombeau de Pierre Falcon. James Reaney. MoCV

Le Touquet. Mark Jarman. BLA

Leac A'Chlarsair. Lucy Taylor. PoSH

Lead. Jayne Cortez. PoBA

Lead gently, Lord, and slow. After Reading "Lead, Kindly Light." Paul Laurence Dunbar. TrPWD

Lead me, O God, and thou my Destiny. God Leads the Way. Cleanthes, *tr. by* C. C. Martindale. EaLo

Lead On, O King Eternal. Ernest W. Shurtleff. AH

Lead Plates at the Rom Press, The. Abraham Sutskever, *tr. fr. Yiddish by* Neal Kozodoy. PeBMYV

Lead the black bull to slaughter, with the boar. Upon Master Walter Montagu's Return from Travel. Thomas Carew. CaPo

Lead us, Evolution, lead us. Evolutionary Hymn. C. S. Lewis. NOBL

Lead Us, O Father, in the Paths of Peace. William Henry Burleigh. AH

Leadbelly Gives an Autograph. Imamu Amiri Baraka. CNA

Leaden Echo and the Golden Echo, The. Gerard Manley Hopkins. BrPo; CMoP; FaFP; GTBS-P; LiTB; LiTM; MoAB; MoBrPo; NOBVV; OBMV; OBNC; SOTW

Leaden-eyed, The. Vachel Lindsay. CMoP; FaBoEE; LiTA; OxBSP; PoE; RB

Leaden summer fog, The. The Excommunication. Melech Ravitch, *tr. by* Miriam Waddington. PeBMYV

Leaden Treasury of English Verse, A, *sels.* Paul Dehn.
   "Jenny kiss'd me when we met." FiBHP
   "Nuclear wind, when wilt thou blow." FiBHP

Leader, The. Hilaire Belloc. ACP

Leader. Bruce Bennett. InPK

Leader, The. Dorothy Livesay. MoCV

Leaders. *Unknown*. WBLP

Leaders of the Crowd, The. W. B. Yeats. EBEV; MoAB; MoBrPo

Leading a goat to pasture like playing with a toy. Maybe You Cannot Comprehend. Salvador Villanueva, *tr. by* Julio Marzán. InW

Leading liot act to foriage is activity. On Autumn Lake. John Ashbery. LCAP

Leading to your Hands. Patricia Hampl. NAmP

Leaf. John Hewitt. NeIP

Leaf, A. Ludwig Uhland, *tr. fr. German by* John S. Dwight. AWP

Leaf bug comes from an egg in June, A. Cockroaches. Kaye Starbird. RHPC

Leaf-eater. Thomas Kinsella. FaBCIP

Leaf falls softly at my feet, A. A Leaf. Ludwig Uhland, *tr. by* John S. Dwight. AWP

Leaf floats in endless space, A. Seeking a Mooring. Wang Wei, *tr. by* Kenneth Rexroth *and* Ling Chung. BoWoP; WPOW

Leaf from freedom's golden chaplet fair, A. To My Father. Henrietta Cordelia Ray. BlSi; CBWP-3; Son

Leaf gold, Lord of thy golden wedge o'erlaid. Edward Taylor. *Fr.* Preparatory Meditations before My Approach to the Lord's Supper, XVI. NAAL-1

Leaf in Love and War, A. Veripatiya Kamakkanniyar, *tr. fr. Tamil by* A. K. Ramanujan. PLW

Leaf is not too little, A. A world may rest. At My Father's Grave. John Ciardi. SM

Leaf knows sorrow in this time of thorns, The. Anglo-American Chainpoem. *Unknown*. EAS

Leaf-Makers, The. Harold Stewart. PoAu-2

Leaf of lehua and noni-tint, the Kona Sea. The Kona Sea. *Unknown, tr. by* N. B. Emerson. WTO

Leaf-picking, The. Frédéric Mistral, *tr. fr. French by* Harriet Waters Preston. AWP

Leaf-Treader, A. Robert Frost. MoAmPo

Leaf upon leaf dancing in the western window. Bananas. Yu T'ung, *tr. by* Paul W. Kroll. WFTU

Leaf will wrinkle to decay, The. The Crest Jewel. James Stephens. AnIL; MoAB; MoBrPo

Leafbud straggles forth, The. Upper Broadway. Adrienne Rich. HCAP; LiPS

Leafless are the trees; their purple branches. The Golden Mile-Stone. Longfellow. PoEL-5

Leafless Trees, Chickahominy Swamp. Dave Smith. MAYP

Leafy-with-love banks and the green waters of the canal. Canal Bank Walk. Patrick Kavanagh. CIP; CMoP; FaBoTw; IPY; MoBrPo; NoAM

League of Nations, The. Mary Siegrist. PAH

Leagues north, as fly the gull and auk. The *Palatine*. Whittier. MOS

Leah, *sel.* Ruth Gilbert.
   Jacob. *Fr.* II. PeNZ

Leah. Shirley Kaufman. VWA

Leak in the Dike, The. Phoebe Cary. FaFP; FaPON

Lean and tall and stringy are the Navajo. The Navajo. Elizabeth Jane Coatsworth. AmFN

Lean back, and get some minutes' peace. Faustine. Swinburne. BeLS; PeHV

Lean close and set thine ear against the bark. Heart of Oak. Charles Henry Lüders. AA

Lean Day in a Convict's Suit, A. Jean Wahl, *tr. fr. French by* Charles Guenther. VWA

Lean doe, The. Kabir, *tr. fr. Hindi by* John Stratton Hawley *and* Mark Juergensmeyer. SSI

Lean forward Spring and touch these iron trees. Post-War Christmas. Phoebe Hesketh. CN

Lean Gaius, who was thinner than a straw. Lucilius, *tr. by* Peter Porter. OBVE

Lean in the greenhood of my fearful years. Fool Song. Cornel Lengyel. GoYe

Lean out of the Window. Goldenhair. James Joyce. *Fr.* Chamber Music, V. BoTP; ChTr

Lean out the window: down the street. A Man with a Little Pleated Piano. Winifred Welles. FaPON

Lean Street. G. S. Fraser. OxBS

Lean strips hang like, The. Biltong. James Twala. WMBCH

Leander. Hugh Henry Brackenridge *and* Philip Freneau. *Fr.* The Rising Glory of America. AiP

Leander Stormbound. Sydney Goodsir Smith. OxBS

Leander to the envious light. Chapman. *Fr.* Hero and Leander, Third Sestiad *argument*. OAEL-1

Leane, The. William Barnes. EBVV

Leaning against the golden undertow. Kenneth Slessor. *Fr.* Out of Time. CBAP

Leaning back on this sofa. Man Seated. Ferreira Gullar, *tr. by* William Jay Smith. CT

Leaning back, smoking, without a word. We Think Farewell. Kurt Klinger, *tr. by* Beth Bjorklund. CoAuP

Leaning on clouds, hugging rocks, slanting every way. Wu Chen, *tr. fr. Chinese by* Jonathan Chaves. *Fr.* Poems Inscribed on Paintings of Bamboo, 3. CoBLCP

Leaning on the chest of your seasick young mother. Wakayama Bokusui, *tr. fr. Japanese by* Hiroaki Sato. *Fr.* Forty-four Tanka. FCEI

Leaning on the oars, I watch the fire of the fireflies. The Fire of the Fireflies. Hung Sheng, *tr. by* Paul W. Kroll. WFTU

Leaning out of my Boston window. Spring at Arm's Length. Charles Vandersee. KS

Leaning Over. Janet Sutherland. DT

Leaning towers the slanted skies, The. Volt. Tristan Tzara, *tr. by* Lee Harwood. RHTwFP

Leap, The. James Dickey. NIP

Leap before You Look. W. H. Auden. NoAM

Leap-Centuries. Paul Celan, *tr. fr. German by* Michael Hamburger. OBVE
Leap in the Dark. Roberta Hill. WPOW
Leap in the Smoke. John Buchan. *Fr.* From the Pentlands. PoSH
Leap of the salmon, The. The Shannon Estuary Welcoming the Fish. Nuala Ni Dhomhnaill, *tr. by the author.* CIP
Leap out, chill water, over reeds and brakes. The River God. Sacheverell Sitwell. MoBrPo
Leap to the highest height of spring. An Early Bluebird. Maurice Thompson. AA
Leap Yeah Party, De. Maggie Pogue Johnson. CBWP-4
Leap year is given, when four will divide. Memorial Verses, Adapted to the Gregorian Account, or New Style. *Unknown.* FaBoUs
Leaping Fire, The. John Montague. IPY
"Old lady, I now celebrate." CIP
(Little Flower's Disciple, The.) TIRV
Leaping from oak to oak, tangled-up in the woods. Sacrifice of a Red Squirrel. Joseph Langland. NYBP
Leaping into the Gulf. Patricia Beer. OxBC
Leaping Laughers, The. George Barker. OBMV
Leaps over the Aisle of Syllogism. D. C. Berry. BXAP
Lear. William Carlos Williams. NAAL-2; NOBA; PoA
Lear and Cordelia. Shakespeare. *Fr.* King Lear, V, iii. FiP
Lear and Cordelia. 'twas an ancient tale. To England. George Henry Boker. AA
Learn from me, Son of Kunti! also this. *Unknown, tr. fr. Sanskrit by* Sir Edwin Arnold. *Fr.* The Bhagavad-Gita. TOF
Learn, lads and lasses, of my garden. Francis Daniel Pastorius. SCAP
"Learn to live, and live and learn." The Saturday Review. Dora Greenwell. EBVV
Learn to mak your bed, Annie. Fair Annie. *Unknown.* OxBB
Learn women all from this housewifery. Sir Richard Fanshawe, *after the Italian of* Giovanni Battista Guarini. *Fr.* Il Pastor Fido. OBVE
Learned and a happy ignorance, A. Eden. Thomas Traherne. PoEL-2; SeCV-2; TrGrPo
Learned in music sings the lark. The Lark. *Unknown, tr. by* Robin Flower. TIRV
Learned Man, A. Stephen Crane. *Fr.* The Black Riders, XX. LiTA; MoAmPo
Learned Men, The. Archibald MacLeish. MoAB
Learned Mistress, A. *Unknown, tr. fr. Irish by* Frank O'Connor. OBMV
Learned Song, A. *Unknown.* *Fr.* Mother Goose's Melody. FaBoUs
Learning. George Chapman. *Fr.* Euthymiae Raptus; or, The Teares of Peace. SeCePo
Learning. Earl Simpson. GrPl
Learning by Doing. Howard Nemerov. HAP; TwCP; WeW
Learning Destiny. Herman Charles Bosman. PeSA
Learning Experience. Marge Piercy. FF; NoAM
Learning the Spells; a Diptych. Anita Endrezze-Danielson. CDW
Learning to Count. Alberta Turner. LCAP
Learning to love differently is hard. To Have without Holding. Marge Piercy. NIP
Learning to Read. Frances Ellen Watkins Harper. BlSi
Learning to Speak. Peter Everwine. NNaP
Learning to Type. Diana O Hehir. NPGG
Lear's Curse on Goneril. Shakespeare. *Fr.* King Lear, I, iv. TW
Lear's Speech to the Storm. Shakespeare. *See* King Lear: Blow, Winds.
Lease Hound, The. Wallace McRae. CowP
Least it could do, The. Ryoshun, *tr. fr. Japanese by* Steven D. Carter. WFTW
Least of Carols, The. Sophie Jewett. OHIP
Leather Bar, The. Ralph Pomeroy. PeHV
Leather belt white shirt black pants. Telegram. Dick Lourie. NeAC
Leather-skinned wrinkled old man, A. Rock Painting. Jack Cope. PeSA
Leave Caelia, leave the woods to chase. On His Mistris That Lov'd Hunting. *Unknown.* OBS
Leave, Cytherea, Your Enchanted Isle. Lorenzo de' Medici, *tr. fr. Italian by* Marya Zaturenska. PFI
Leave Everything the Way It Is. Liesl Ujvary, *tr. fr. German by* Beth Bjorklund. CoAuP
Leave go my hands, let me catch breath and see. In the Orchard. Swinburne. BoLoP
Leave Helen to her lover. Draw away. The White Isle of Leuce. Sir Herbert Read. FaBoTw
Leave Her, Johnny, Leave Her. *Unknown.* *See* Across the Western Ocean *or* Leave Her, Bullies, Leave Her.
Leave him alone, sweet enemy. The Lonely Traveller. Kwesi Brew. PBA; TTY
Leave him: he's quiet enough: and what matter. Here Lies a Prisoner. Charlotte Mew. MoBrPo

Leave Him Now Quiet. Trumbull Stickney. LiTA
Leave It to Me Blues. Joel Oppenheimer. VGW
Leave It with Him. *Unknown.* BLRP
Leave Krete and come to this holy temple. Sappho, *tr. fr. Greek by* Willis Barnstone. BoWoP
Leave, leave, converted publican! lay down. Christus Mattaeum et Discipulos Alloquitur. Sir Edward Sherburne. ACP
Leave, me all sweet refrains my lip hath made. Luis de Camões, *tr. by* Richard Garnett. AWP
Leave Me Alone. Felice Holman. RHPC
Leave me, dawn! I'm in wretched fettle. Richard Moore. SoTCo
Leave me, my love, it's time to part. Ibrahim Naji, *tr. by* Issa Boullata *and* John Heath-Stubbs. MAP
Leave Me, O Love. Sir Philip Sidney. EIL; FaBoRV; LiTB; NAEL-1; PoE; PoRA; PPP; SeCePo; TrCP
("Leave me, O Love, which reachest but to dust.") GBL; HeIP; NIP; Son; TEP; TrPWD
(Splendidis Longum Valedico Nugis.) NOBE; NOCV; OBEV; OBSC; SiPS
Leave me, O propitious spirits. *Unknown, tr. fr. Japanese.* *Fr.* Manyo Shu. Ma
Leave me: oh! leave me. Dying. Adah Isaacs Menken. CBWP-1
Leave off, good Beroe, now. To an Old Gentlewoman That Painted Her Face. George Turberville. OxBSP
Leave Poem. Anne Bulley. CN
Leave-Taking. Giosuè Carducci, *tr. fr. Italian by* William Jay Smith. CT; PFI
Leave-Taking, A. Arno Holz, *tr. fr. German by* Jethro Bithell. AWP
Leave-taking, A. Swinburne. CH; NOBE; NOBVV; OBNC; OPOP; PoEL-5; PoLF
Leave the bars lying in the grass. Fall. Robert Francis. VGW
Leave the Miracle to Him. Thomas H. Allan. BLRP
Leave the Thread with God. *Unknown.* BLRP
Leave the window open. Death Song ("Leave the window open"). *Unknown, tr. by* Reza Baraheni *and* Zahra-Soltan Shokoohtaezeh. BoWoP
Leave the Word Alone. Edward Marshall. NeAP
Leave Them Alone. Patrick Kavanagh. OxBSP
Leave thine own home, O youth, seek distant shores! Encouragement to Exile. Petronius Arbiter, *tr. by* Howard Mumford Jones. AWP
Leave this chanting and singing and telling of beads. Rabindranath Tagore. *Fr.* Gitanjali, XI. WGRP
Leave this gaudy gilded stage. John Wilmot, 2nd Earl of Rochester. OxBSP
Leave Us Alone. Tadeusz Rozewicz, *tr. fr. Polish by* Czeslaw Milosz. PwPP
Leave Us Religion. Blanaid Salkeld. NeIP
Leave your home behind, lad. The Recruit. A. E. Housman. FaPoR
Leaves. Frank Asch. NTCP
Leaves. W. H. Davies. MoBrPo
Leaves. Malka Heifetz-Tussman, *tr. fr. Yiddish by* Marcia Falk. OV
Leaves. Ted Hughes. OxBC
Leaves. Katharine Tynan. BoTP
Leaves, The. *Unknown.* *See* Leaves had a wonderful frolic, The.
Leaves. Paul Walker. PDV
Leaves/ Murmuring by myriads in the shimmering trees. From My Diary, July 1914. Wilfred Owen. FaBoMo; LiTM; MoAB; MoBrPo
Leaves a-Vallen. William Barnes. NOBVV
Leaves are fading and falling, The. November. Alice Cary. OBCA
Leaves are sere, The. November. Henrietta Cordelia Ray. CBWP-3
Leaves are still; not a breath is heard, The. William James Linton. PF
Leaves at My Window. John James Piatt. AA
Leaves Come Again, The. Henry Vaughan *and* Thomas Stanley. *See* In March birds couple, a new birth.
Leaves Compared with Flowers. Robert Frost. NOBA
Leaves fall, The. Leaves. Paul Walker. PDV
Leaves fall, and, The. After the Leaves Fall. Ruth Kim Chun-soo, *tr. by* Koh Chang-soo. ACKP
Leaves fall, fall as if from far away, The. Autumn. Rainer Maria Rilke, *tr. by* C. F. MacIntyre. TrJP
Leaves fall from my fingers, The. October. Charles Wright. MT
Leaves fall, slanting sun lights the river. Tune: Palace of Night Revels. Chou Pang-yen, *tr. by* Burton Watson. CoBCP
Leaves fall turning turning to the ground. Han Yü, *tr. fr. Chinese by* Burton Watson. *Fr.* Autumn Thoughts, 8. CoBCP
Leaves falling/ on top of the smoke. Kyotai, *tr. fr. Japanese by* Burton Watson. *Fr.* Sixteen Hokku. FCEI
Leaves Falling at Dusk. Tameshige, *tr. fr. Japanese by* Steven D. Carter. WFTW

Leaves Falling on a Bridge. Tamemasa, *tr. fr. Japanese by* Steven D. Carter. WFTW

Leaves fritter. Single Most. Rae Armantrout. IAT

Leaves from eternity are simple things. The Eternity of Nature. John Clare. EBEV

Leaves had a wonderful frolic, The. The Leaves in a Frolic. *Unknown.* OnUR

(Leaves, The.) BoTP

Leaves have fallen, The. Saigyo, *tr. fr. Japanese by* Burton Watson. *Fr.* Sixty-four Tanka. FCEI

Leaves have their time to fall. The Hour of Death. Felicia Dorothea Hemans. OBNC

Leaves in a Frolic, The. *Unknown.* OnUR

Leaves like Fish. Gladys Cardiff. CDW

Leaves looked in at the window, The. The House across the Way. Ralph Hodgson. FaBoTw

Leaves Making a Sound as They Fall. Shotetsu, *tr. fr. Japanese by* Steven D. Carter. WFTW

Leaves of bamboo near my window stirring with the wind. Princess Shikishi, *tr. fr. Japanese by* Hiroaki Sato. *Fr.* Seventy-eight Tanka. FCEI

Leaves of Grass. Walt Whitman. *See* Song of Myself: Child said, A *What is the grass?*

Leaves of Life, The. *Unknown.* OBET

Leaves of the Fig-Tree. Nakahara Chuya, *tr. fr. Japanese by* Geoffrey Bownas *and* Anthony Thwaite. PeBJV

Leaves of the small oaks, The. Sanetomo, *tr. fr. Japanese by* Burton Watson. *Fr.* Twenty-four Tanka. FCEI

Leaves of the summer, lovely summer's pride. Sonnet: Leaves. William Barnes. BoNaP; ChTr; FaBoRV; OBNC

Leaves of trees rend, The. Shiba Sonome, *tr. fr. Japanese by* Hiroaki Sato. *Fr.* Fifteen Hokku. FCEI

Leaves sleeping under the winds, The. The Wound. "Adunis," *tr. by* Abdullah al-Udhari. MPAW

Leaves that rustled on this oak-crowned hill, The. Wordsworth. FM

Leavetaking. Eve Merriam. PDV

Leaving. Cathy Song. NoAM

Leaving. Jenny Vuglar. DT

Leaving Barra. Louis MacNeice. EBEV

Leaving beer and apples. For a Friend. Lyn Lifshin. NeAC

Leaving behind us the alien, foreign city of Dublin. Going Home to Mayo, Winter, 1949. Paul Durcan. CIP

Leaving Buffalo. Charles Martin. PoA

Leaving Crete, come visit again our temple. Sappho, *tr. by* John Frederick Nims. WeW

Leaving Forever. Denise Levertov. InPK

Leaving Inishmore. Michael Longley. FaBCIP

Leaving Itami in Early February. Onitsura, *tr. fr. Japanese by* Hiroaki Sato. *Fr.* Twenty-three Hokku. FCEI

Leaving kids alone is no problem. Fire the Babysitter. David Avidan, *tr. by* Warren Bargad *and* Stanley F. Chyet. IP

Leaving Knee-prints in the Warm Earth. Cheng Wen-tao. WCI

Leaving Mendota, 1956. Lawrence Locke. GrPl

Leaving my gate, I too am someone. Buson, *tr. fr. Japanese by* Hiroaki Sato. *Fr.* Eighty-seven Hokku. FCEI

Leaving My Post to Retire at the Sui Garden. Yüan Mei, *tr. fr. Chinese by* Anthony C. Yu. WFTU

Leaving of Liverpool, The. *Unknown.* OxBSS

Leaving Oklahoma Again. Barney Bush. NOVW

Leaving only the noise of dead leaves. Ozaki Hosai, *tr. fr. Japanese by* Hiroaki Sato. *Fr.* One Hundred Haiku in Free Form. FCEI

Leaving Port Authority for the St. Regis Rezz. Wendy Rose. HATNAP

Leaving Seoul; 1953. Walter Lew. BrSi

Leaving Smoke's. Gordon Henry. STE

Leaving Something Behind. David Wagoner. CoAP

Leaving Southern Screen Hill at Dawn and Crossing the Lake. Li E, *tr. fr. Chinese by* Irving Lo. WFTU

Leaving the Atocha Station. John Ashbery. CAPP

Leaving the bar slack-watered, I have left. Two Voyages. Maurice James Craig. NeIP

Leaving the capital/to return to my fief in the East. Rhyme-Prose on the Goddess of the Lo. Ts'ao Chih, *tr. by* Burton Watson. CoBCP

Leaving the City. Liu K'o-chuang, *tr. fr. Chinese by* Burton Watson. CoBCP

Leaving the Dance. Alexander Whitaker. NIP

Leaving the Door Open, *sels.* David Ignatow. CAPP

"He got his friends to agree to shoot him standing against a stone wall."

"In the spaces between the stars still water dances."

"Lying quietly on the bed."

(Leaving the island, she believes, to go to the child.). Monique Laederach, *tr. fr. French by* Charles Guenther. *Fr.* Penelope. BoWoP

Leaving the Motel. W. D. Snodgrass. FF; NIP

Leaving the Mountains in the Rain from Yellow Dragon Temple. Yi Shun-ting, *tr. fr. Chinese by* Timothy C. Wong. WFTU

Leaving the snows. At the Shelter-Stone. Brenda G. Macrow. PoSH

Leaving the Tate. Fleur Adcock. ATNZ

Leaving the viaduct on the left, and coming over the hill. St. Ursanne. Michael Roberts. LiTM

Leaving the white glow of filling stations. The Strand at Lough Beg. Seamus Heaney. AnAn; CIP; NoAM; NoP; OBWP

Leaving them, children of the Sun, to their perpetual. Perseus. James Keir Baxter. ATNZ

Leaving them, running. 28 VIII 69. Laura Chester. IHMS

Leaving tropic parallels. Northbound. Larry Rubin. OPP

Leaving T'u-sung at Dawn. Wu Wei-yeh, *tr. fr. Chinese by* Marie Chan. WFTU

Leaving us behind. After the Death of Her Daughter in Child-birth. Izumi Shikibu, *tr. by* Edwin A. Cranston. PBWP

Leaving, where to go? Staying, where? Shoten, *tr. by* Lucien Stryk *and* Takashi Ikemoto. ZPCJ

Leavings. Gerard Benson. BXAP

Leawood Hall. Ernest Charles Jones. PF

Lebanon. Khalil Hawi, *tr. fr. Arabic by* Abdullah al-Udhari. MPAW

Lecompton's Black Brigade. Charles Graham Halpine. PAH

Lector Aere Perennior. J. V. Cunningham. QFR

Lecture. Anselm Hollo. UL

Lecture, A. Gabriel Preil, *tr. fr. Yiddish by* Grace Schulman. PeBMYV

Lecture Hall. Patrick Kavanagh. FaBoTw

Lecture upon the Shadow, A. John Donne. AWP; NAEL-1; OBS; SeCP; TEP; UnPo

Lectured by Pa and Ma o'er night. The Lady's Diary. Charles Dibdin. NOEC

Lecturing on the Theme of Motherhood. Michael S. S. Harper. AnAn

Led by the Hebrew School Rabbi. Judith Baumel. ASP

Led by the light of an unusual star. W. H. Auden. *Fr.* For the Time Being; a Christmas Oratorio. PChr

Leda. Hilda Doolittle ("H. D."). NAAL-2

Leda. Rainer Maria Rilke, *tr. fr. German by* Robert Bly. NU

Leda. Mona Van Duyn. NMM

Leda and Her Swan. Olga Broumas. PeHV

Leda and the Swan. Oliver St. John Gogarty. AnIL; HAP

Leda and the Swan. Jerzy Harasymowicz, *tr. fr. Polish by* Czeslaw Milosz. PwPP

Leda and the Swan. W. B. Yeats. AnIL; CMoP; EBEV; ErPo; FF; FPL; GTBS-P; HAP; HeIP; InPK; LiTM; MoAB; MoBrPo; MoP; NAEL-2; NAWM-2; NIP; NoAM; NOBE; NoP; OAEL-2; PBBP; PoE; PPP; PrIm; SCV; Son; SoSe; SoSe; TEP; TEP; TrGrPo; WeW

Leda in Stratford, Ont. Anne Wilkinson. MoCV

Leda Reconsidered. Mona Van Duyn. NMM

Leda's Sister and the Geese. Katharyn Machan Aal. SoTCo

Leda's Version. James Harrison. NIP

Lede guiterriste was a craftie ladde, The. The Probatioun Officeres Tale. Gerard Benson. BXAP; NBLV

Lee-ers of Hew. James Cunningham. JB

Lee to the Rear. John Randolph Thompson. PAH

Leering across Pearl Street. Trouble. James Wright. FF

Lee's Parole. Marion Manville. PAH

Leesome Brand ("My boy was scarcely ten years auld"). *Unknown.* ESPB

Leesome Brand ("There is a feast in your father's house"). *Unknown.* ESPB

Leetla Giorgio Washeenton. T. A. Daly. FaPON

Leetle Bateese. William Henry Drummond. CaP

Leezie Lindsay. *Unknown.* FaBoCh

Left at home. Prince Hozumi. *Fr.* Manyo Shu. PeBJV

Left-Behind, The. Louis MacNeice. *Fr.* A Hand of Snapshots. FaBCIP

Left by his friend to breakfast alone on the white. Edward Lear. W. H. Auden. InvP

Left leg flung out, head cocked to the right. Poet. Karl Shapiro. CMoP; LiTM; MoAB; MoAmPo; NoAM

Left like an unknown's breath on mirrors. Visitations. Lawrence Durrell. *Fr.* Eight Aspects of Melissa. MoBrPo

Left like water in glasses overnight. Love from My Father. Carole Gregory Clemmons. CNA; PoBA

Left right. left right. . after a Thirties Poet. Peter Titheradge. *Fr.* Teatime Variations. FaBoPa

Left side of her world is gone, The. Strokes. William Stafford. PCP

Left to itself the heart continues, as the tamarind. How Morning Glories Could Bloom at Dusk. Jorie Graham. NPGG

Leg, The. Karl Shapiro. HAP; MoAB; MoAmPo; TrGrPo; UnPo; WeW

Leg in a Plaster Cast, A. Muriel Rukeyser. MoAmPo
Leg in the Subway, The. Oscar Williams. LiTM
Leg over leg. Mother Goose. OxNR
Legacy. Amiri Baraka. MoP; NoAM; NOBA; PoBA
Leg-acy of a Blue Capricorn. James Cunningham. JB
Legacy [or Legacie], The. John Donne. SeCP; TrGrPo
Legacy. Gena Ford. IHMS
Legacy. Márton Kalász, tr. fr. Hungarian by Jascha Kessler. FOC;
   MHuP
Legacy. Maurice Kenny. HATNAP
Legacy, The. Judith Minty. GeTw
Legacy, The. Bible, O.T. Fr. Proverbs, IV: 13. TrJP
Legacy: My South. Dudley Randall. PoBA; PoNe
Legal Fiction. William Empson. CMoP; FaBoMo; LiTB; LiTM; MoP;
   NoAM; NoP
Legal Mouse, A. Lizelia Augusta Jenkins Moorer. CBWP-3
Legem Tuam Dilexi. Coventry Patmore. Fr. The Unknown Eros, X.
   PoEL-5
Legend. Charles Causley. TOF
Legend. Hart Crane. InPS; OxBA
Legend. Ralph Gustafson. CaP
Legend. Jules Laforgue, tr. fr. French by Louis Simpson. Prf
Legend, A. At. to Peter Ilich Tchaikovsky, tr. fr. Russian by Nathan
   Haskell Dole. OHIP
Legend. John Van Alstyn Weaver. AmFN
Legend. Judith Wright. RB; SO
Legend of Alhambra, A. Richard Chenevix Trench. OBTV
Legend of Britomartis, or of Chastitie, The. Spenser. Fr. The Faerie
   Queene, III. NAEL-1, much abr.
   Britomart in the House of Busirane. Fr. III, 11–12.FiP
Legend of Camelot, A. George Du Maurier. CenHV
Legend of Felix is ended, the toiling of Felix is done, The. Henry Van
   Dyke. Fr. The Toiling of Felix. BLPA
Legend of Ghost Lagoon, The, sel. Joseph Schull.
   Pirates' Fight, The. CaP
Legend of Good Women, The: Prologue, sels. Chaucer.
   "And as for me, though that I konne [or can] but [or my wit be] lyte."
   CH; HeIP; ViBoPo
   "Hyd, Absalon, thy gilte tresses clear." HAP
   (Balade: "Hide [or Hyd], Absalon, thy gilte tresses clere.") AWP;
   ChTr; EBEV; FiP; GBL; NOBE; OAEL-1; OBEV
   (Lady without Paragon, A.) MeEL
   This Fresshe Flour. SeCePo
Legend of His Lyre. Aaron Schmuller. GoYe
Legend of Montrose, The, sel. Sir Walter Scott.
   Annot Lyle's Song. Fr. ch. 6. EnRP
Legend of Paul Bunyan, A. Arthur Stanley Bourinot. AmFN
   Paul Bunyan, sel. FaPON
Legend of Robert, Duke of Normandy, The, sel. Michael Drayton.
   Fame and Fortune. OBSC
Legend of Success, The Salesman's Story, The. Louis Simpson. NYBP
Legend of Tea, The. Chang Ts'o, tr. fr. Chinese by Dominic Cheung.
   IFON
Legend of the Admen, The. Everett W. Lord. BLPA
Legend of the Easter Eggs, The. Fitz-James O'Brien. BeLS
Legend of the First Cam-u-el, The. Arthur Guiterman. CenHV
Legend of the Hive, A. Robert Stephen Hawker. EBVV
Legend of the Knight of the Red Cross, or of Holiness, The. Spenser.
   Fr. The Faerie Queene, I, 1-12. NAEL-1
   (Invocation to the Faerie Queene.) FiP
   ("Lo! I the man, whose muse whilome did maske.") OAEL-1
Legend of the Northland, A. Phoebe Cary. OBCA; OnMSP
Legend of the Organ-Builder, The. Julia Caroline Ripley Dorr. BeLS;
   BLPA; FaBoBe
Legend of Versailles, A. Melvin Beaunearus Tolson. BPo
Legend of Walbach Tower, The. George Houghton. PAH
Legend of Waukulla, The. Hezekiah Butterworth. PAH
Legend: The god in the sun made two men. J. Michael Yates. Fr. The
   Great Bear Lake Meditations. HoPM
Legendary muscle that wants and grieves, The. The Hearts. Robert
   Pinsky. BAP
Legends of Evil I, The. Kipling. MoShBr
Legerdemain. Kenneth Mackenzie. PoAu-2
Legion, The. Robert Graves. BrPo
Legion Club, The, sel. Swift.
   "As I strole the city, oft I." BIrV
Legion hall in Atherton contains, The. By-Products. Baron Wormser.
   MAYP
Legree's big house was white and green. Simon Legree—a Negro
   Sermon. Vachel Lindsay. Fr. The Booker Washington Trilogy, I.
   LiTA; TAP
   (Negro Sermon, A—Simon Legree.) MoAmPo

Legs, The. Robert Graves. LiTB; LiTM; RB
Legs!/ How we have suffered each other. Poem in Which My Legs Are
   Accepted. Kathleen Fraser. AmPA; LLLT; NMM
Legs of the elk punctured the snow's crust, The. To Christ Our Lord.
   Galway Kinnell. NIP; PrIm; RFM; SM; TwCP
Legs v-ed out from the groin's nugget. The Gymnasts. Irving Feldman.
   ASP
Legsby, Lincolnshire. Unknown. GBP
Lehayyim, my brethren, Lehayyim, I say. Simhat Torah. Judah Leib
   Gordon, tr. by Alice Lucas and Helena Frank. TrJP
Lehmann does well with Largactil. Laprairie Hunger Strike. Ronald G.
   Everson. MoCV
Leicester Chambermaid, The. Unknown. CoMu; OBET
Leichhardt in Theatre, sel. Francis Webb.
   Room, The. PoAu-2
Leisure. W. H. Davies. AWP; BoNaP; BoTP; CH; FaBoBe; FaFP;
   FaPON; FaPON; LiTB; LiTM; MoBrPo; MoShBr; NOBE; OBEV;
   OBMV; PoRA; SeCePo; TrGrPo
Leisure hills, motorway connected. Hills. Robin Munro. PoSH
Leisurely she binds her shining black hair. The Drunken Gentleman.
   Hsüeh Chao-yün, tr. by Lois Fusek. ATF
Leisurely Stroll, A, sel. Hsü Pen, tr. fr. Chinese by Jonathan Chaves.
   "Mountain of green trees and orioles everywhere!" CoBLCP
Leit. Marcos Rodríguez Frese, tr. fr. Spanish by Julio Marzán.
   InW
Leit-Motif: Oh Great City of Lima. Mirko Lauer, tr. fr. Spanish by David
   Tipton. Per
Leith police dismisseth us, The. Unknown. OxNR
Leith Races, sel. Robert Fergusson.
   My Winsome Dear. SeCePo; VGW
Lela's Charms. L. A. J. Moorer. CBWP-3
L'Elisir d'Amore. Dallas E. Wiebe. MAT
L'Embarquement pour Cythère. John Manifold. CBAP
Lementable New Ballad upon the Earle of Essex Death, A. Unknown.
   CoMu
Lemme be wid Casey Jones. Odyssey of Big Boy. Sterling A. Brown.
   BANP; CDC
Lemmings, The. John Masefield. CMoP
Lemmings, The. Donald A. Stauffer. WaP
Lemon. Mario Satz, tr. fr. Spanish by Willis Barnstone. VWA
Lemon Elegy. Takamura Kotaro, tr. fr. Japanese by Sato. FCEI
Lemon Pie. Edgar A. Guest. OBAL
Lemonade. Unknown. GBP
   (Picnic Rhyme.) FaBoNo
Lemons. Ted Walker. NYBP
Lemons, Lemons. Al Young. HeIP
Lemoshl: for example. A Few Words in the Mother Tongue. Irena
   Klepfisz. ER
Lemuel's Blessing. W. S. Merwin. NYBP
Lend me cruel light. To an Angry God. X. J. Kennedy. CRP
Lend me thy fillet, Love! The Lover's Song. Edward Rowland Sill.
   AA
Lend me thy great noise, thy powerful, gentle gait. Valery Larbaud, tr.
   by William Jay Smith. CT; RHTwFP
Lend me your arm. Little Song of the Maimed. Benjamin Péret, tr. by
   David Gascoyne. OBWP
Lend me your song, ye nightingales! oh, pour. James Thomson. Fr. The
   Seasons: Spring. PBBP
Lending a branch of his antlers. Issa, tr. fr. Japanese by Hiroaki Sato.
   Fr. Forty-four Hokku. FCEI
L'Enfant Glacé. Harry Graham. FaBoCo; NBLV
Length o' days ageän do shrink, The. The Fall. William Barnes.
   PoEL-4
Length of Days. Horatius Bonar. PWR
Length of Life, The. Amos Russel Wells. PWR
Length of Moon. Arna Bontemps. CDC; LiTM; PoNe
Lenin. Mihály Ladányi, tr. fr. Hungarian by Edwin Morgan. MHuP
Lenin, sel. Dorothy Wellesley.
   "So I came down the steps to Lenin." OBMV
Leningrad. Osip Mandelstam, tr. fr. Russian by W. S. Merwin and
   Clarence Brown. FaBoPV
Leningrad brimming with rivers and canals. Leningrad: Picture Postcard.
   Meir Wieseltier, tr. by Warren Bargad and Stanley F. Chyet. IP
Leningrad Cemetery, Winter of 1941. Sharon Olds. NIP
Leningrad: 1943. Vera Inber, tr. fr. Russian by Dorothea Prall Radin and
   Alexander Kaun. Fr. The Pulkovo Meridian. WaaP
Leningrad: Picture Postcard. Meir Wieseltier, tr. fr. Hebrew by Warren
   Bargad and Stanley F. Chyet. IP
Lennox Island. David McFadden. NOBC
Lenny Bruce Fixes. Jotie T'Hooft, tr. fr. Dutch by Scott Rollins. DuIn
Lenore. Poe. AA; AmPP; AnAmPo; LiTA
Lenox Avenue. Sidney Alexander. PoNe

Lenox Avenue is a big street. Keep on Pushing. David Henderson. PoBA

Lenox Avenue Mural, *sels.* Langston Hughes. AmNP; HoPM
Harlem ("What happens to a dream deferred"). AmNP; AmPP; HeIP; HoPM; InPS; NoP; PoNe
(Dream Deferred.) FF; LiTM; PoBA; PPP; SoSe
Same in Blues. InPS

Lenox Christmas Eve 68. Sam Cornish. CNA

Lens. Michael Palmer. LP

Lens. Anne Wilkinson. MoCV; NOBC; OBCV

Lent. W. R. Rodgers. AnIL

Lent in a Year of War. Thomas Merton. EAS

Lent Lily, The. A. E. Housman. *Fr.* A Shropshire Lad, XXIX. OHIP

Lente, Lente. Ovid, *tr. fr. Latin by* Kirby Flower Smith. *Fr.* Elegies, I, 14. AWP

Lenten has brought us, as I understand. *Unknown. Fr.* Two Old Lenten Rhymes, II. ACP

Lenten Is [*or* Ys] Come [with Love to Toune]. *Unknown.* HAP; MeEL
("Lenten is come with love to towne.") EBEV; PBBP
(Spring-Tide.) OBEV

Lenten stuff is come to the town. Two Old Lenten Rhymes, I.
Unknown. ACP

Lentil, a lentil, a lentil, a stone, A. The Woman Cleaning Lentils.
Zehrd, *tr. by* Diana der Hovanessian *and* Marzbed Margossian. TSS

Lentinus! thou dost nought but fume, and fret. Martial, *tr. by* Sir Edward Sherburne. OBVE

Lenton has brought us, as I understand. Two Old Lenten Rhymes, II.
Unknown. ACP

L'Envoi: "Now in a thought, now in a shadowed word." E. A. Robinson.
TrCP

L'Envoi: "O love triumphant over guilt and sin." Frederic Lawrence Knowles. TrPWD

L'Envoi: "There's a whisper down the field where the year has shot her yield." Kipling. OBEV
(Long Trail, The.) FaBV; MOS

L'Envoi: "What is the moral? Who rides may read." Kipling. *See* Story of the Gadsbys, The: Winners, The

L'Envoi: "When Earth's last picture is painted, and the tubes are twisted and dried." Kipling. FaFP; OHFP; PWR; WGRP
(When Earth's Last Picture Is Painted.) LiTB

Leo to His Mistress. Henry Dwight Sedgwick. BLPA

Leolin and Edith. Tennyson. *Fr.* Aylmer's Field. GN

Leon, A? No. Chippewa Love Song. *Unknown, tr. by* Frances Densmore. BoWoP

Leona, dear, twelve months ago. Eloise Bibb. CBWP-4

Leonardo Da Vinci's. Marianne Moore. NYBP

Leonardo, Leonardo, you old rascal! Mona Leo. Bob McKenty.
SoTCo

Leonardo's Secret. Robert Bly. NNaP

Leopard. Gretchen Kreps. RHPC

Leopard, The. Lorenzo Thomas. UL

Leopard. *Yoruba Oral Tradition, tr. by* Ulli Beier. WTO

Leopard. *Unknown, tr. fr. Yoruba by* Ulli Beier. *Fr.* Hunter Poems of the Yoruba. RB

Leopard came to drink, A. Snow Fell. Timothy Ho!mes. UAS

Leopard, nocturnal, with eyes infernal, The. Tuvia Rübner, *tr. by* Bernhard Frank. MHeP

Lepanto. G. K. Chesterton. FaBV; FaPoR; GoTL; MoBrPo; MOS;
OBMV; OBNV; RB

Leper, The. Ka-'ehu, *tr. fr. Hawaiian by* M. K. Pukui *and* A. L. Korn.
WTO

Leper, The. Swinburne. GBL; NOBVV

Leper, The. Nathaniel Parker Willis. WGRP

Leper Cleansed, The. John Collop. TrGrPo

Lepers Cry. Peter Orlovsky. GLP

Leprechaun, The—the omadhaun!—that lives in County Clare. Of Certain Irish Fairies. Arthur Guiterman. PoLF

Leroy. Amiri Baraka. BPo; PoBA

Les Ballons. Oscar Wilde. NOBVV

Les Chasse-Neige. Ralph A. Lewin. FiBHP

Les Demoiselles de Sauve. John Gray. NOBVV

Les Enfants du Paradis. Doris Mühringer, *tr. fr. German by* Beth Bjorklund. CoAuP

Les Estreines. Matthew Prior. OxBSP

Les Halles d'Ypres. Edmund Blunden. MMA

Les Hiboux. Baudelaire, *tr. by* Arthur Symons. AWP

Les Jours Gigantesques/The Titanic Days. Kathleen Fraser. NPGG

Les Luths. Frank O'Hara. NoAM; NOBA

Les Morts Vont Vite. H. C. Bunner. AA

Les Planches-en-Montagnes. Michael Roberts. OBMV

Les Silhouettes. Oscar Wilde. *See* Impressions:
Sea is flecked with bars of grey, The.

Les Sylphides. Louis MacNeice. BoLoP

Lesbia. Richard Aldington. PoLF

Lesbia. Catullus, *tr. fr. Latin by* Sheridan Baker. PrIm

Lesbia. Congreve. OxBSP

Lesbia Forever on Me Rails. Catullus, *tr. by* Swift. OBVE
(Lesbia Railing.) AWP

Lesbia loads me night and day with her curses. Catullus, *tr. by* Peter Whigham. BoLoP

Lesbia Railing. Catullus. *See* Lesbia Forever on Me Rails.

Lesbian. Paula Jennings. PeHV

Lesbian born under Pisces, A. *Unknown.* PeHV

Lesbian girl of Khartoum, A. *Unknown.* NOBL

Lesbian Hell, The. Aleister Crowley. PeHV

Lesbian Play on T.V. Caroline Gilfillan. PeHV

Lesbian Poem. Robin Morgan. IHMS

Lesbos. Lawrence Durrell. EBEV

Leslie. Marvin Wyche, Jr.. AmNP

Lesotho. B. Makalo Khaketla, *tr. fr. Sotho by* Dan Kunene *and* Jack Cope. PeSA

Less and Less Human, O Savage Spirit. Wallace Stevens. VGW

Less Nonsense. A. P. Herbert. OxBTC

Less said about Edward's slut the better, The. Bliss. George Johnston.
NOBC

Less said the better. Missing. John Pudney. OxBTC

Less than two hours it took the Iroquois. E. J. Pratt. *See* Brébeuf and His Brethren: Martyrdom of Brébeuf and Lalemant, 16 March 1649, The.

Less troublesome than unforgettable. Lady Izumi, *tr. fr. Japanese by* Hiroaki Sato. *Fr.* Fifty-one Tanka. FCEI

Lesser Evil, The. George Orwell. OBTV

Lesser Lynx, The. Emile Victor Rieu. CenHV; FiBHP; RHPC

Lesser proof than old Voltaire's, yet greater, A. Orange Buds by Mail from Florida. Walt Whitman. NAAL-1

Lesson, The. Robert Lowell. CMoP; LCAP

Lesson, The. Edward Lucie-Smith. OxBTC; TwCP

Lesson. Susan Ludvigson. KS

Lesson, The. Paul Mariani. MAYP

Lesson, The. Larry Rubin. GoYe

Lesson, The. Charles Simic. HCAP

Lesson, A. Wordsworth. GTBS; GTBS-P

Lesson for Dreamers. Paul B. Janeczko. PCP

Lesson for Mamma, A. Sydney Dayre. OBCA; OxBChV

Lesson for Today, The. Robert Frost. LiTA; LiTM; WaP

Lesson from Golf, A. Edgar Albert Guest. ASP

Lesson from Van Gogh, A. Howard Moss. MoAB

Lesson in Detachment, A. Vassar Miller. NePoEA-2

Lesson in Handwriting, A. Alastair Reid. NYBP

Lesson in Love, A. Philip Hobsbaum. OxBTC

Lesson in Translation, A. Gabriel Preil, *tr. fr. Hebrew by* Howard Schwartz. VWA

Lesson of Silence, A. Tymoteusz Karpowicz, *tr. fr. Polish by* Czeslaw Milosz. PwPP

Lesson on the Facts of Life. Karin Kiwus, *tr. fr. German by* Susan L. Cocalis. DMG

Lessons. Mekeel McBride. NAmP

Lessons in Parsing. Rashid Husain, *tr. fr. Arabic.* MAP, *tr. by* Lena Jayyusi *and* Peter Porter; MPAW, *tr. by* Abdullah al-Udhari

Lessons of Nature, The. William Drummond of Hawthornden. *See* Book, The.

Lessons of the War, *sels.* Henry Reed. HeIP; LiTB; OBWP
Judging Distances. *Fr.* II. BoLoP; GTBS-P; MoAB; NIP; NOBE;
NoP; SoSe
Naming of Parts. *Fr.* I. FF; GoJo; HoPM; InPS; MoAB; MoBrPo;
NOBE; NoP; OxBTC; PoRA; PrIm; SeCePo; SoSe; TrGrPo; UnPo;
WaP

Unarmed Combat. HeIP; LiTB

Lessons of the Year. *Unknown.* BLRP

Lest any doubt that we are glad that they were born today. Emily Dickinson. NAs

Lest it may more quarrels breed. Twelve Articles. Swift. NBLV

Lest men suspect your tale to be untrue. The Devil's Advice to Story-Tellers. Robert Graves. LiTM; MoP; NAEL-2; NoAM

Lest men suspect your tale untrue. The Painter Who Pleased Nobody and Everybody. John Gay. BeLS

Lest the ripple deceive us. Winter Pond. Ben Belitt. NYBP

Lest you should think that verse shall die. The Immortality of Verse.
Horace, *tr. fr. Latin.* Fr. Odes, IV, 9. AWP, *tr. by* Pope.

Lestenyt, lordynges, both elde and yinge. Of a Rose, a Lovely Rose.
Unknown. OBEV

Lester Leaps In. Al Young. NPGG; SM

Lester Tells of Wanda and the Big Snow. Paul Zimmer.
MOWH

Lester Young. Ted Joans. AmNP

Let Age no longer toil with feeble strife. The Poor. John Langhorne.
   Fr. The Country Justice. NOEC

Let all chaste matrons, when they chance to see. Upon a Young Mother
   of Many Children. Robert Herrick. CaPo

Let All Created Things. Artis Seagrave. AH

Let all the family gather. Light Another Candle. Miriam Chaikin.
   NTCP

Let all the little poets be gathered together in classes. To School! Stevie
   Smith. FaBoEE

Let All Things Pass Away. W. B. Yeats. ChTr

Let all who will. Militant. Langston Hughes. PoBA

Let Allen's eyes be a jukebox of light plugged into the navel of Whitman's
   verb. Leaps over the Aisle of Syllogism. David Chapman Berry.
   BXAP

Let America Be America Again. Langston Hughes. AiP; PoNe

Let azure eyes with coral lips unite. The Value of Dentistry. Solyman
   Brown. *Fr.* Dentologia; a Poem on the Diseases of the Teeth and
   Their Proper Remedies. FaBoUs

Let baths and wine-butts be November's due. November. Folgore Da
   San Gimignano, *tr. fr. Italian by* Dante Gabriel Rossetti. *Fr.* Sonnets
   of the Months. AWP

Let Be. *Unknown.* WBLP

Let Beryl Cook paint this triptych. First. Holiday Girls. Vicki Raymond.
   UAS

Let Bourbons fight for status quo. Status Quo. Binga Dismond. PoNe

Let but a thrush begin. John Hewitt. NeIP

Let but the son of earth. The Ages of Man. *At. to* Abraham Ibn Ezra,
   tr. by Nina Davis Salaman. TrJP

Let but thy voice engender with the string. Upon Her Voice. Robert
   Herrick. CaPo

Let by Rain. Edward Taylor. *See* Address to the Soul Occasioned by a
   Rain, An.

Let certain holdings of stocks and bonds. Codicil. Mabel MacDonald
   Carver. GoYe

Let Christian Hearts Rejoice Today. *Unknown, tr. fr. French by* Francis
   X. Curley. AH

Let Christmas celebrate greenly. For the fir is king. Jubilate Herbis.
   Norma Farber. PChr

Let clownish Cymon, in fond rustic strains. St. Anthony and His Pig; a
   Cantata. Frederick Forrest. NOEC

Let Cynics bark, and the stern Stagirite. The Paradox. *Unknown.*
   APAS

Let dainty wits cry on the Sisters nine. Astrophel and Stella, III. Sir
   Philip Sidney. OAEL-1; OBSC; SiPS

"Let dainty wits cry on the Sisters nine." Sir Philip Sidney. *Fr.*
   Astrophel and Stella, III. OAEL-1; OBSC; Son

Let day, let night, come no more. Auvaiyar, *tr. by* A. K. Ramanujan.
   PLW

Let de peoples know (unnh). Blues for Bessie. Myron O'Higgins.
   PoNe

Let dirty streets be paved with flow'ry green. *Unknown.* *Fr.* The
   Comparison. NOEC

Let down, I stood in the hall. Ishikawa Takuboku, *tr. fr. Japanese by*
   Hiroaki Sato. *Fr.* Forty-seven Tanka in Three Lines. FCEI

Let due civilities be strictly paid. John Gay. *Fr.* Trivia; or, The Art of
   Walking the Streets of London, II. OAEL-1

Let each man first seek out his proper totem. A Joyful Noise. Donald
   Finkel. CoAP

Let Elizur[e] rejoice with the Partridge. Christopher Smart. *Fr.* Jubilate
   Agno. OAEL-1; PoEL-3

Let 'em censure: what care I? In Imitation of Anacreon. Matthew Prior.
   FaBoEE

Let Ephah rejoice with Buprestis, the Lord endue us with temperance and
   humanity. Christopher Smart. *Fr.* Jubilate Agno. NOEC

Let Erin Remember the Days of Old. Thomas Moore. EnRP

Let fools great Cupid's yoke disdain. Song: The Willing Prisoner to His
   Mistress. Thomas Carew. CaPo

Let foreign nations of their language boast. The Son. George Herbert.
   Fr. The Temple. Son

Let forrain nations of their language boast. The Sonne. George Herbert.
   SeCP

Let go of the present and death. Once Again. Liz Sohappy Bahe.
   CDW; NOVW

Let go of the unicorn's reins. The Beast That Rode the Unicorn. Conny
   Hannes Meyer. VWA, *tr. by* Herbert Kuhner

Let hammer on anvil ring. The Armorer's Song. Harry Bache Smith.
   AA; OHIP

Let happy throats be mute. Donald Jeffrey Hayes. AmNP

Let her be the mother of this sea. Brief Reflections on an Ancient and
   Beautiful City on the Coast of the Mediterranean Sea. Mahmoud
   Darwish, *tr. by* Abdullah al-Udhari. MPAW

Let Her Give Her Hand. *Unknown.* ELP

Let her lie naked here, my hand resting. News of the World III. George
   Barker. FaBoTw; LiTB; LiTM

Let her who walks in Paphos. Lais. Hilda Doolittle ("H.D.").
   MoAmPo

Let Heroes Account to Love. Alan Dugan. NoAM

Let him answer as he will. The Companion. E. A. Robinson. NoAM

Let him that will, ascend the tottering seat. Seneca. *See* Thyestes: Stond
   [*or* Stand] who so list upon the slipper toppe.

Let him who may. To Be Recited to Flossie on Her Birthday. William
   Carlos Williams. VGW

Let Him with Kisses of His Mouth. *Unknown.* AH

Let it be alleys. Let it be a hall. A Lovely Love. Gwendolyn Brooks.
   BPo

Let it be anywhere. For Her. Mark Strand. GOYP

Let it be forgotten, as a flower is forgotten. Sara Teasdale. AnAmPo;
   MoAmPo; PoA; TrGrPo

Let it be Sabbath, Sabbath! Eternal Sabbath. Isaac Leibush Peretz, *tr. by*
   Joseph Leftwich. TrJP

Let it disturb no more at first. Fountain. Elizabeth Jennings. WPE

Let it end here where the blueprint. Making Chicago. Dennis Schmitz.
   LCAP; NPGG

Let It Go. William Empson. FaBoMo; OPOP; OxBSP; OxBTC

Let it no longer be a forlorn hope. On the Baptized Ethiopian (*or*
   Aethiopian). Richard Crashaw. FaBoEE; NoP; SeCV-1

Let it not come near me, let it not. Fragment for the Dark. Elizabeth
   Jennings. FaBoWP

Let it not come unto you, all ye that pass by. Desolation in Zion. Bible,
   O.T. *Fr.* Lamentations, I: 12–17. TrJP

Let it not your wonder move. His Excuse for Loving. Ben Jonson. *Fr.*
   A Celebration of Charis in Ten Lyrick Peeces. JCP; PoEL-2; QFR;
   SeCP; SeCV-1

Let it start to rain. There. Franz Wright. PPR

Let kings command, and do the best they may. The Power in the People.
   Robert Herrick. CaPo

Let lordlings sign, and ladies cling, to wealth, and fame, and place. A
   Workman's Home. Thomas Ince. PF

Let love come under your roof. Carol for Advent. John Heath-Stubbs.
   OxBC

Let man's soul be a sphere, and then, in this. Good Friday [*or*
   Goodfriday], 1613. Riding Westward. John Donne. InPS; JCP;
   MeLP; MePo; NAEL-1; NOCV; NoP; OAEL-1; OBS; PoE; PoEL-2;
   PPP; SeCP; SeCV-1; TEP

Let me be. Hilda Doolittle ("H. D."). *Fr.* Sigil, X. AnAn

Let me be a little kinder, let me be a little blinder. My Daily Creed.
   Unknown. PWR

Let me be a mummy. Wake me up. Some Futureplans. David Avidan,
   tr. by Warren Bargad *and* Stanley F. Chyet. IP

Let me be at the place of the castle. Psalm Concerning the Castle.
   Denise Levertov. TwCP; WPE

Let me be buried as flesh, not burned, I say. Earth Buried. Kenneth
   Mackenzie. CBAP

Let me be buried in the rain. Helene Johnson. AmNP; BANP; PoNe

Let Me Be Held When the Longing Comes. Stephany Fuller. BPo

Let me be my own fool. A Counterpoint. Robert Creeley. NeAP

Let me be prodigal as sun in praising you. Geography of Music.
   Kenneth Patchen. UnAS

Let me be that huge red peony. Peony. Jackie Kay. DT

Let me be the mane that swings. Poem for a Singer. Milton Acorn.
   NeAC

Let me be what I am, as Virgil cold. Ben Jonson. PoEL-2; SeCP

Let Me Begin Again. Philip Levine. CAPP

Let me but live from year to year. The Zest of Life. Henry van Dyke.
   Fr. The Three Best Things. WBLP

Let me call a ghost. Song of Three Smiles. W. S. Merwin. CoAP;
   NOBA; VGW

Let me celebrate you. I. A Dialogue of Watching. Kenneth Rexroth.
   UnAS

Let me come in where you sit weeping, ay. Bereaved. James Whitcomb
   Riley. AA

"Let me confess that we two must be twain." Shakespeare. *Fr.* Sonnets,
   XXXVI. PeHV

Let me die in spring. Saigyo, *tr. fr. Japanese by* Burton Watson. *Fr.*
   Sixty-four Tanka. FCEI

Let me die in the Spring, said a sweet young girl. The Time to Die.
   Matilda Caroline Edwards. PWR

Let me die now. *Unknown.* *Fr.* Manyo Shu. FCEI

Let me do my work each day. Max Ehrmann. BLPA; BLPL; FaBoBe

Let Me Enjoy [(Minor Key)]. Thomas Hardy. AWP; FaBV

Let me fall down about your feet oh Christ. Oils and Ointments. R. A.
   K. Mason. ATNZ

Let me fetch sticks. Bliss. Eleanor Farjeon. RHPC

Let me find time. Two African Breasts. Nizar Qabbani, *tr. by* Diana Der Hovanessian *and* Lena Jayyusi. MAP

Let Me Flower as I Will. Lew Sarett. TrPWD

Let Me Get Up Early. Eugène Guillevic, *tr. fr. French by* Teo Savory. RHTwFP

Let Me Go. *Gond Oral Tradition, tr. by* V. Elwin *and* S. Hivale. WTO

Let Me Go Back. Mary E. Albright. BLRP

Let Me Go Down to Dust. Lew Sarett. TrPWD

Let me go forth, and share. Ode in May. Sir William Watson. OBEV; WGRP

Let Me Go Warm. Luis de Góngoray, *tr. fr. Spanish by* Longfellow. AWP

Let Me Go Where Saints Are Going. Lewis Hartsough. AH

Let me go where'er I will. Music. Emerson. FaBV; WGRP

Let Me Grow Lovely. Karle Wilson Baker. BLPA; FaBoBe; TrPWD

Let me grow older! I would become. Details. Dezsö Tandori, *tr. by* Daniel Hoffman. MHuP

Let me have a scarlet maple. The Grave-Tree. Bliss Carman. CaP

Let me just finish off my slender fiddle. My Fiddle. Leib Kwitko. VWA, *tr. by* Keith Bosley.

Let me know right away if I'm disturbing you. He Stepped inside my Door. Eeva Kilpi, *tr. by* Aili Jarvenpa. SOP

Let me lay it to you gently, Mr. Gone! Ray Bremser. *Fr.* Poem of Holy Madness. NeAP

Let me learn now where Beauty is. Questing. Anne Spencer. CDC

Let me live harmlessly; and near the brink. The Angler's Song. John Dennys. *Fr.* The Secrets of Angling. EIL

Let me look at what I was, before I die. Jamestown. Randall Jarrell. GOA

Let me look back upon thee, O thou wall. Timon Curses Athens and Mankind. Shakespeare. *Fr.* Timon of Athens, IV, i. TW

Let me make the songs for the people. Songs for the People. Frances Ellen Watkins Harper. PWR

Let Me Not Die. Edith Lovejoy Pierce. TrPWD

Let me not die for ever, when I'm gone. A Wish. Fanny Kemble. WPE

Let me not die till death is due to come. Let Me Not Die. Edith Lovejoy Pierce. TrPWD

Let me not know how sins and sorrows glide. James Elroy Flecker. TrPWD

Let me not live, if I not love. On Himself. Robert Herrick. CaPo

"Let me not to the marriage of true minds." Shakespeare. *Fr.* Sonnets, CXVI. AWP; EIL; EnLoPo; FaBV; FaFP; FPL; GBL; HAP; HeIP; InPS; InvP; LiTB; NAEL-1; NIP; NiP; NOBE; NoP; OAEL-1; OBEV; OBSC; PeHV; PoE; PoEL-2; PoRA; PPP; PrIm; SCV; SeCePo; Son; SoSe; TEP; TrGrPo; UnPo; WeW (True Love.) GTBS; GTBS-P

Let me now set down a picture of New England that will show it to you and explain it. Praise of New England. Thomas Caldecot Chubb. GoYe

Let me obtain forgiveness of thee, Samson. Milton. *Fr.* Samson Agonistes. EBEV

Let me play Love's last card. Poem to a Young Man. Lindolf Bell, *tr. by* William Jay Smith. CT

Let Me Play the Fool. Shakespeare. *Fr.* The Merchant of Venice, I, i. TrGrPo

Let me play to you tunes without measure or end. Bagpipe Music. "Hugh MacDiarmid." OAEL-2

Let me pour [*or* powre] forth. A Valediction: Of Weeping. John Donne. HAP; HeIP; InPS; MeLP; MePo; NAEL-1; NoP; OAEL-1; OBS; PoE; SeCP; WeW

Let me put it this way. George Jonas. NeAC

Let me say (in anger) that since the day we were married. The Crisis. Robert Creeley. FF; PPP

Let me see if Philip can. The Story of Fidgety Philip. Heinrich Hoffmann. OxBChV

Let me see you. Mirabai, *tr. fr. Hindi by* Willis Barnstone *and* Usha Nilsson. BoWoP

Let me show you my love. Webern. Thomas W. Shapcott. *Fr.* Piano Pieces. CBAP

Let Me Sing of My Well-beloved. Bible, *O.T. Fr.* Isaiah, V. TrJP

Let me speak, sir,/ For Heaven now bids me. Cranmer's Prophecy of Queen Elizabeth. Shakespeare *and probably* John Fletcher. *Fr.* King Henry VIII, V, v. WGRP

Let me strap/ the baby in the seat. If He Let Us Go Now. Shirley Williams. BoWoP

Let me take a good look. Saigyo, *tr. fr. Japanese by* Burton Watson. *Fr.* Sixty-four Tanka. FCEI

Let me take this other glove off. In Westminster Abbey. Sir John Betjeman. CMoP; FaBoCo; InPK; NBLV; NIP; NoAM; NOBL; OAEL-2; OBSV; TOF

Let me tell to you the story. Edith Agnew. PChr

Let me tell you a little story. Miss Gee. W. H. Auden. OxBTC

Let Me Tell You about Myself. Tomioka Taeko, *tr. fr. Japanese by* Hiroaki Sato. FCEI

Let me tell you my love the hardest things to learn. What Sheila Tells Him, Softly. Vincent O'Sullivan. ATNZ

Let me weep. He has left. The Abandoned. Mririda n'Ait Attik, *tr. by* René Euloge, *English vers. by* Daniel Halpern *and* Paula Paley. OV

Let me work and be glad. Theodosia Pickering Garrison. TrPWD

Let me wrap a poem around you. Gift. Judith Hemschemeyer. PCP

Let men take note of her, touching her shyness. The Gift of Song. Anthony Hecht. NYBP

Let Mine Eyes See Thee. St. Theresa of Avila, *tr. fr. Spanish by* Arthur Symons. AWP

Let mine not be the saddest fate of all. Uselessness. Ella Wheeler Wilcox. TrPWD

Let mother Earth now deck herself in flowers. Sir Philip Sidney. *Fr.* Arcadia. SiPS

Let my sweet song be pleasing unto Thee. Judah Halevi, *tr. by* Nina Davis Salaman. TrJP

Let no blasphemer till the sacred earth. Benediction. Mark Turbyfill. PoA

Let No Charitable Hope. Elinor Wylie. LiTA; LiTM; MoAB; MoAmPo; NAAL-2; OxBA; OxBSP; TrGrPo; VGW

Let no girl wait on you on that day when you bind your wild. The Alchemy of Day. Anne Hébert, *tr. by* A. Poulin, Jr. BoWoP

Let no man cum into this hall. Now Is the Time of Christmas. *Unknown.* MeEL

Let no one consider the original noise. Relays. Barrett Watten. LP

Let no one mourn his mount, upholstered bone. Epitaph for a Horseman. Michael Hamburger. NePoEA-2

Let no one speak to me of love and matrimony, please. A Maid's Fortune. Sidonie Hedwig Zäunemann, *tr. by* Susan L. Cocalis *and* Gerlinde Geiger. DMG

Let no rain fall to drench me through. *Unknown. Fr.* Manyo Shu. Ma

Let none, born after me. Hitomaro. *Fr.* Manyo Shu. Ma

Let none but guests or clubbers hither come. Ben. Johnsons Sociable Rules for the Apollo. Ben Jonson, *tr. by* Alexander Brome. SeCV-1

Let not Chloris think, because. *Unknown.* OBSC

Let not Death boast his conquering power. On Eleanor Freeman, Who Died 1650, Aged 21. *Unknown.* OBEV

Let not his humble vesture make thee blind. The Poor Scholar. Abraham Ibn Chasdai, *tr. by* J. Chotzner. TrJP

Let not old age disgrace my high desire. Old Age. Sir Philip Sidney. *Fr.* Arcadia. SiPS

Let not our town be large, remembering. On the Building of Springfield. Vachel Lindsay. OHFP

Let not the sluggish sleep. *Unknown.* ACP; OxBSP

Let not thy beauty make thee proud. Aurelian Townshend. JCP

Let not us that youngmen be. Youth. *Unknown.* OBSC

Let not young souls be smothered out before. The Leaden-eyed. Vachel Lindsay. CMoP; FaBoEE; LiTA; OxBSP; PoE; RB

Let nothing disturb thee. Lines Written in Her Breviary. St. Theresa of Avila, *tr. by* Longfellow. AWP; EaLo (Bookmark.) CTC; WPOW (St. Theresa's Book-Mark.) PoEL-5

Let oken club now strike, and poast of might. Seneca, *tr. fr. Latin by* Jasper Heywood. *Fr.* Hercules Furens, IV. OBVE

Let only your soul dwell. *Unknown. Fr.* Manyo Shu. Ma

Let other mount aloft, let other sore. Seneca, *tr. fr. Latin by* John Studley. *Fr.* Hercules Oetaeus, II. OBVE

Let other people come as streams. Charles Reznikoff. VGW (Dew.) VWA

Let others better mold the running Mass. The Sixth Book of the Aeneis. Virgil, *tr. fr. Latin, tr. by* Dryden. *Fr.* The Aeneid [*or* Eneados]. SeCV-2

Let others chaunt a country praise. London Town. Lionel Johnson. FaBoPP

Let others cheer the winning man. A Smile. *Unknown.* BLPA; WBLP

Let others from the town retire. Nonpareil. Matthew Prior. EnLoPo

Let others lie about the universe. The Physicist's Purpose. Adrianne Marcus. BWV

Let others of the world's decaying tell. William Alexander, Earl of Stirling. *Fr.* Aurora. EIL

Let others pile their yellow ingots high. A Pastoral Elegy. Albius Tibullus, *tr. by* Sir Charles Abraham Elton. AWP

Let others pray for the passenger pigeon. Elegy for the Giant Tortoises. Margaret Atwood. BoWoP

Let Others Share. Edward Anthony. RHPC

Let others sing of knights and paladins [*or* palladines]. Samuel Daniel. *Fr.* To Delia. AAS; NOBE; NoP; OBEV; OBSC (Sonnet: "Let others sing of knights and paladin[e]s.") EIL

Let others speak. Canticle. Joseph Bruchac. NOVW

Let our love be made as plain. *Unknown. Fr.* Manyo Shu. Ma

Let passion's swelling tide my senses drown! Ibnu 'I-Farid, *tr. by* R. A. Nicholson. TOF

Let poetry be/ like an air conditioner. Ars Poetica. Arturo Trías. InW, *tr. by* Julio Marzán

Let poets praise the softer winds of spring. J. B. Morton. FaBoEE

Let readers say (description or abuse). The Lemmings. Donald A. Stauffer. WaP

Let sailors watch the waning Pleiades. Cleonicos. Edward Cracroft Lefroy, *after the Greek of* Theocritus. *Fr.* Echoes from Theocritus, XXVII. AWP

Let school-masters puzzle their brain. Goldsmith. *Fr.* She Stoops to Conquer, I, ii. BIrV; NOIV
(Three Jolly Pigeons, The.) PoRA
(Three Pigeons, The.) ELP

Let Shobi rejoice with the Kastrel—blessed be the name Jesus. Christopher Smart. *Fr.* Jubilate Agno. NOEC

Let shrieking steel and gray stone be set. Psalmodist. Mani Leib. VWA, *tr. by* David G. Roskies *and* Hillel Schwartz

Let sleep take her, let sleep take her, let sleep. Fourth Song the Night Nurse Sang. Robert Duncan. VGW

Let Sol his annual journeys run. Hint from Voiture. William Shenstone. EnLoPo

Let some sad trumpeter stand. Back on Times Square, Dreaming of Times Square. Allen Ginsberg. PoE

Let some things remain unsaid. Let Us Leave Something Unsaid. Munir Niazi, *tr. by* Mahmood Jamal. PBMUP

Let Sporus tremble—"What? That thing of silk." Pope. *Fr.* Epistle to Dr. Arbuthnot. SCV
(Sporus.) AWP; ChTr; NOBE; OBSV

Let the arched knife. Pruning. John Philips. *Fr.* Cyder. FaBoUs

Let the bells ring, and let the boys sing. John Fletcher. *Fr.* The Spanish Curate, III, ii. OBS

Let the bird of loudest [*or* lowdest] lay. The Phoenix and the Turtle. Shakespeare. LiTB; NOBE; NoP; OAEL-1; OBEV; OBSC; PoEL-2; SeCePo; TEP

Let the boy try along this bayonet-blade. Arms and the Boy. Wilfred Owen. BrPo; CMoP; FaFP; HAP; LiTB; LiTM; MoAB; MoBrPo; OAEL-1; OAEL-2; OxBSP; PoE; WaP; WeW

Let the crows go by hawking their caw and caw. River Roads. Carl Sandburg. VGW

Let the damned ride their earwigs to Hell, but let me not join them. Rock Pilgrim. Herbert Edward Palmer. OxBTC

Let the Day Perish [Wherein I Was Born]. Bible, *O.T. Fr.* Job. NAs, III; OBVE, III: 3-26; TrJP, III.
(Job Complains, III: 3-26) TrGrPo
(Job's Curse, III: 3-26) AWP

Let the Dead Depart in Peace. *Yoruba Oral Tradition, tr. by* Ulli Beier. WTO

Let the Deep Organ Swell. Constantine Pise. AH

Let the exiles in-gather. Evening of the Rose. Anthony Rudolf. VWA

Let the eye remember the loved face. The Soul Remembers. Richard Burdick Eldridge. GoYe

Let the flowers make a journey. The Fury of Flowers and Worms. Anne Sexton. BoWoP

Let the foul Scene proceed. The Marionettes. Walter de la Mare. MMA

Let the knowing speak. Adjuration. Charles Enoch Wheeler. AmNP; PoNe

Let the Light Enter. Frances E. W. Harper. PoNe

Let the mountains stand forth! Hamilton Warren. GoYe

Let the Nations Be Glad. Bible, *O.T. See* Psalms: Psalm LXVII ("God be merciful unto us. . .").

Let the night keep. Night. William Rose Benét. MoAmPo

Let the Nile cloak his head in the clouds, and defy. On the Discoveries of Captain Lewis. Joel Barlow. AmPP; PAH

Let the only consistency. In the Fall. "Hugh MacDiarmid." *Fr.* In Memoriam James Joyce. FaBoMo, *st.* 1; InPS

Let the pines rock in torment of the storm. Horatian Ode. Joseph Warren Beach. PoA

Let the pure sky ahead, this sky of long. Illumination. Simone Weil, *tr. by* Carol Cosman. OV

Let the rain kiss you. April Rain Song. Langston Hughes. FaPON; NTCP; OBCA; PDV; RHPC

Let the rain plunge radiant. The Way Through. Denise Levertov. NeAP; PoM

Let the Rest of the World Go By. J. Keirn Brennan. UnPo

Let the rich man fill his belly. Antonio Machado, *tr. fr. Spanish by* Havelock Ellis. *Fr.* Spanish Folk Songs. AWP

Let the Roots Speak. Yusuf al-Khal, *tr. fr. Arabic by* Abdullah al-Udhari. MPAW

Let the shark keep to the shelves and closets of coral. From a Litany. Mark Strand. PPP

Let the snake wait under. A Sort of a Song. William Carlos Williams. HoPM; NAAL-2; NoP; OxBSP; TAP

Let the tale's sailor from a Christian voyage. Dylan Thomas. *Fr.* Altarwise by Owl-Light, X. CMoP; FaBoMo; OAEL-2

Let the wick burn low: and suddenly I remember. The Sleepers. Randolph Stow. *Fr.* Thailand Railway. CBAP

Let the Wind Blow High or Low. *Unknown.* OBET

Let the Wind Recite. Yang Mu, *tr. fr. Chinese by* Dominic Cheung. IFON

Let the wood be pulled. Surprised by Me. Walter Darring. NYBP

Let the world's sharpness, like a clasping knife. Elizabeth Barrett Browning. *Fr.* Sonnets from the Portuguese, XXIV. NOBVV

Let the youth hardened by a sharp soldier's life. III, 2. "Let the youth hardened by a sharp soldier's life" ("Angustam amice"). Horace, *tr. fr. Latin. Fr.* Odes. WaaP, *tr. by* Gardner Taplin *and* Richard Eberhart.
("Disciplined in the school of hard campaigning.") OBWP, *tr. by* James Michie.

Let them bestow on every airth a limb. On Himself, upon Hearing What Was His Sentence. James, Marquess of Montrose Graham. OBS; SeCePo
(His Metrical Prayer.) OxBS; PrIm
(Verses Composed on the Eve of His Execution.) ChTr; FaBoEE

Let them bury your big eyes. Edna St. Vincent Millay. *Fr.* Memorial to D. C., V. CMoP; MoAB; MoAmPo; PoRA
("O, loveliest throat of all sweet throats.") OxBA

Let them count scalps under the barroom wall. Lying in a Yuma Saloon. Jim Barnes. CDW

Let them keep it. And Was Not Improved. Lerone Bennett, Jr.. CNA; PoBA

Let them say to my lover. Amor Mysticus. Sister Marcela de Carpio de San Felix, *tr. by* John Hay. AWP

Let there be laid, when I am dead. Posthumous Coquetry. Théophile Gautier, *tr. by* Arthur Symons. AWP; OBD

Let there be life, said God. And what He wrought. The Power and the Glory. Siegfried Sassoon. OBMV

Let There be Light. William M. Vories. AH

"Let there be light!" said God, and there was light! Byron. *Fr.* Don Juan, VII. OBWP

Let there be many windows to your soul. Progress. Ella Wheeler Wilcox. BLPA; FPL

Let there be no flowery banks. A Garden of Situations. Jack Anderson. PoA

Let this day's air praise the Lord. Rinsed with Gold, Endless, Walking the Fields. Robert Siegel. GeTw

"Let those who are in favour with their stars." Shakespeare. *Fr.* Sonnets, XXV. OBSC

Let those who from the frozen Arctos reach. The Advantages of Washing. John Armstrong. *Fr.* The Art of Preserving Health. FaBoUs

Let those with cost deck their ill-fashioned clay. Thomas Rymer. OxBSP

Let thy gold be cast in the furnace. Cleansing Fires. Adelaide Anne Procter. WGRP

Let Thy Kingdom. *Unknown.* AH

Let thy tears, Le Vayer, let them flow. To Monsieur de la Mothe le Vayer. Molière, *tr. by* Austin Dobson. AWP

Let Tyrants Shake Their Iron Rod. William Billings. AH

Let uh revolution come. uh. U Name This One. Carolyn M. Rodgers. BlSi; NMM; PoBA

Let Us. Jacob Glatstein, *tr. fr. Yiddish by* Benjamin *and* Barbara Harshav. AYP

Let us abandon then our gardens and go home. Justice Denied in Massachusetts. Edna St. Vincent Millay. AiP; GOA; MoAmPo

Let Us All Be Unhappy on Sunday. Lord Neaves. FaBoCo

Let us ask ourselves some questions; for that man is truly wise. The Higher Catechism. Sam Walter Foss. WGRP

Let us ask you a few questions, without rancor. For Any Member of the Security Police. Josephine Jacobsen. NePoAm

Let us await the great American novel! Critical Observations. Archibald MacLeish. OBAL

Let Us Be Frank. Alfred Cruickshank. PBCV

Let us be friends, said Walt. Communion. David Ignatow. CAPP

Let us be guests in one another's house. Any Wife or Husband. Carol Haynes. BLPA

Let us be still. To Usward. Gwendolyn B. Bennett. BlSi

Let us become the overhanging day. Shelley. *Fr.* Epipsychidion. OAEL-2

Let us begin and carry up this corpse. A Grammarian's Funeral. Robert Browning. NAEL-2; NOBVV; WGRP

Let us begin and portion out these sweets. A Girtonian Funeral. *Unknown.* FaBoCo; Par

Let Us Believe. Hildegarde Flanner. WPE

Let us believe—the fangs do not quite close. And let our confidence. Leviathan. Ernest Bryll, *tr.* by Czeslaw Milosz. PwPP

Let Us Break Bread Together. *Unknown.* AH, *with music*

Let us bring out those heavy dice. Birth. Gabriela Melinescu. BoWoP, *tr. by* Willis Barnstone *and* Matei Calinescu

"Let us build bridges," said he. Building Bridges. Solomon Mahaka. WMBCH

Let us celebrate the single-cloaked beings. Psalm to the Creatures. Gwilym R. Jones, *tr.* by Joseph P. Clancy. OBWVE

Let Us Cheer the Weary Traveler. *Unknown.* AH

Let us come in to worship Jehovah. Come In. Isaiah Shembe, *tr. by* H. Tracey. WTO

Let us consider. Last Words. Linda Pastan. BLA

Let Us Consider Where the Great Men Are. Delmore Schwartz. *Fr.* Shenandoah. MoAB; MoAmPo

Let us dance and let us sing. The Fairy Ring. *Unknown.* BoTP

Let us deal kindly with a heart of old by sorrow torn. Saadabad. James Elroy Flecker. SeCePo

Let us do something grand. To the Poem. Frank O'Hara. SM

Let Us Drink. Alcaeus, *tr. fr. Greek* by John Hermann Merivale. AWP

Let us drink and be merry, dance, joke, and rejoice [*or* rejoyce]. The Careless Gallant. Thomas Jordan. CoMu; HAP; OxBoLi (Coronemus Nos Rosis Antequam Marcescant.) OBEV (Epicure, The, Sung by One in the Habit of a Town Gallant.) NOBE

Let us exchange tonight. Oath. Gabriella Sica, *tr.* by Muriel Kittel. DMI

Let us forgive Ty Kendricks. Southern Cop. Sterling Allen Brown. NIP; SoSe

Let Us Gather at the River. Marge Piercy. GeTw

Let us gather hand in hand. A Medieval Poem of the Nativity. *Unknown.* TrCP

Let us gather up the sunbeams. Scatter Seeds of Kindness. May Riley Smith. WBLP

Let us give thanks for the things of the north. The Things of the North. Rennie McOwan. PoSH

Let us give thanks to God above. Thanksgiving. Lizelia Augusta Jenkins Moorer. CBWP-3

Let us give up our trips. Direction. Barbara Guest. WPE

Let Us Go Down, the Long Dead Night Is Done. Christopher Brennan. *Fr.* Towards the Source. PoAu-1

Let us go hence, my songs; she will not hear. A Leave-taking. Swinburne. CH; NOBE; NOBVV; OBNC; OPOP; PoEL-5; PoLF

Let us go hence: the night is now at hand. A Last Word. Ernest Dowson. MoBrPo

Let Us Go, Then, Exploring. Virginia Woolf. BoNaP

Let us go then, you and I. The Love Song of J. Alfred Prufrock. T. S. Eliot. AmPP; AWP; CMoP; EBEV; FF; HAP; HeIP; HoPM; InPK; InPS; LiTB; LiTM; MoAB; MoAmPo; MoP; NAAL-2; NAEL-2; NAWM-2; NIP; NoAM; NOBA; NOBE; NoP; OAEL-2; OxBTC; PoA; PoE; PoRA; PPP; PrIm; SoSe; SOTW; TAP; TrGrPo; TwCP; WeW

Let us go to a realm beyond going. Mirabai, *tr.* by John Stratton Hawley *and* Mark Juergensmeyer. SSI

Let us have a rest about the sunset. To the Poets. *Unknown.* PeNZ

Let us have winter loving that the heart. Winter Love. Elizabeth Jennings. BoLoP; NePoEA

"Let us hold our hands tight." The Song of Greece. Chiang Hsun, *tr.* by Dominic Cheung. IFON

Let Us Laugh. Zvi Shargel, *tr. fr. Yiddish* by Gabriel Preil. VWA

Let us lay, and dance, and sing. The Vision of Delight Presented at Court in Christmas, 1617. Ben Jonson. SeCV-1

Let Us Learn. Melech Ravitch, *tr. fr. Yiddish* by Seymour Mayne *and* Rivka Augenfeld. VWA

Let us leave behind this city. City of Light. Nahum Bomze, *tr.* by Gabriel Preil *and* Howard Schwartz. VWA

Let us leave our island woods grown dim and blue. "Æ." TIRV

Let Us Leave Something Unsaid. Munir Niazi, *tr. fr. Urdu* by Mahmood Jamal. PBMUP

Let us leave talking of angelic hosts. Elinor Wylie. *Fr.* One Person. OxBA

Let us make the test. Say God wants you. Gnostics on Trial. Linda Gregg. NPGG

Let us move the stone gentleman to the toadstool wood. The Stone Gentleman. James Reeves. OxBSP

Let us not look upon. Witter Bynner. EaLo

Let us not make apologies. Instructions. Anita Skeen. IHMS

"Let us not speak, for the love we bear one another." In a Bath Teashop. Sir John Betjeman. EnLoPo

"Let Us Now Praise Famous Men." C. Day Lewis. CMoP

Let us now praise famous men. Bible, Apocrypha. *Fr.* Ecclesiasticus, XLIV: 1–15. ChTr; OBVE (Our Fathers.) TrJP

Let us now praise famous men; and the children. Dostoievsky's Daughters. Michael Hamburger. NAs

Let us play, and dance, and sing. The Vision of Delight. Ben Jonson. PoEL-2

Let us praise our Maker, with true passion extol Him. W. H. Auden. NOCV

Let us record/ The evenings when we were innocents of twenty. Winfield Townley Scott. *Fr.* Biography for Traman. ErPo

Let us rejoice on our cots, for His nocturnal miracles. Lauds. John Berryman. HAP

Let us remember the yellow. In the Month of Green Fire. Sophie Himmell. GoYe

Let us remember Treverton in all his youth and glory. Lament for a Cornish Soldier. Agnes Grozier Herbertson. CN

Let us return from Ilium, and no more. Independence. Guy Mason. CaP

Let Us Rise Up and Live. Francis Sherman. CaP

Let us save the babies. The Babies. Mark Strand. GeTw; NYBP

Let us say good-bye. Bags Packed and We Expected This. Ramona Wilson. VoR

Let us seek the past. Saigyo, *tr. fr. Japanese* by Burton Watson. *Fr.* Sixty-four Tanka. FCEI

Let us sing of it ever and long. Song of Sukkaartik, the Assistant Spirit. Ajukutooq. WTO

Let us sit by the hissing steam radiator a winter's day, grey wind. Horses and Men in the Rain. Carl Sandburg. PoLF

Let Us Smile. Wilbur Dick Nesbit. WBLP

Let us stiffen. The Covenant. James Cunningham. JB

Let Us Strive to Do Something. Mrs. Henry Linden. CBWP-4

Let us suppose the mind. Barbara Moraff. IHMS

Let us suppose, valleys and such ago. John Berryman. *Fr.* Dream Songs. NaP; PPP

Let us synge unto the Lorde, for he is become glorious. Bible, *O.T. Fr.* Exodus, XV: 1-8. OBVE

Let us take the road. The Highwaymen. John Gay. *Fr.* The Beggar's Opera, II, i. WiR

Let us take to our hearts a lesson. The Tapestry Weavers. Anson G. Chester. BLPA; BLRP; WBLP

Let us thank Almighty God. Creatrix. Anna Wickham. MoBrPo

Let us to-day. Song for Memorial Day. Clinton Scollard. OHIP

Let us tunnel. Ronald Johnson. *Fr.* Letters to Walt Whitman, I. VGW

Let us use it while [*or* whilst] we may. Of Beauty. Sir Richard Fanshawe, *after the Italian of* Giovanni Battista Guarini. *Fr.* Il Pastor Fido. BoLoP (Beauty.) GBL (Nymph's Song.) OxBSP

Let us walk in the white snow. Velvet Shoes. Elinor Wylie. CH; FaPON; FPL; GoJo; MoAB; MoAmPo; TrGrPo

Let Us with a Gladsome Mind. Milton. FL; WGRP (Praise the Lord.) FaBoCh

Let us with a gladsome mind. Bible, *O.T. See* Psalms: Psalm CXXXVI ("O give thanks unto the Lord; for he is good").

Let us worry around us. Let Us. Jacob Glatstein, *tr.* by Benjamin *and* Barbara Harshav. AYP

Let War's Tempests Cease. Longfellow. OHIP

Let who so lyst with might mace to raygne. Seneca. *See* Thyestes: Stond [*or* Stand] who so list upon the slipper toppe.

Let Y stand for you who says. You. Kenneth Rexroth. *Fr.* A Bestiary. HoPM

Let your beard grow. The Reading. Hermann Jandl, *tr.* by Beth Bjorklund. CoAuP

Let your eyes look at old people. In Respect of the Elderly. Thomas Peacock. VoR

Let your longing for me, my love. Sulpicia, *tr.* by John Dillon. PBWP

Let your song be delicate. Song Be Delicate. John Shaw Neilson. PoAu-1

Let Zeus Record, *sel.* Hilda Doolittle ("H. D."). "Stars wheel in purple, yours is not so rare." MoAmPo; NOBA; TAP

Let Zulu Be Heard. Isaiah Shembe, *tr. fr. Zulu* by G. C. Oosthuizen. WTO

Lethal Relief. André Breton, *tr. fr. French* by Samuel Beckett. RHTwFP

Lethal Thought, The. Mary Boyd Wagner. GoYe

Lethargy. Donald Justice. CRP

Lethargy of evil in her eyes, The. A Dying Viper. "Michael Field." FM

Lethe. Hilda Doolittle ("H. D."). AnAmPo; CMoP; FaBoWP; LiTM; MoAmPo; PoRA; TrGrPo; VGW; ViBoPo

Lethe. Georgia Douglas Johnson. CDC

L'étrangère. O. V. de L. Milosz, *tr. fr. French by* John Peck. RHTwFP

Let's agree to meet in our dreams. You're So Far Away. Iyamide Hazeley. DT

Let's All Hear It for Mildred Bailey! James Schuyler. BAP

Let's Be Merry. Christina Rossetti. *Fr.* Sing-Song. FaPON

Let's build bridges here and there. Interracial. Georgia Douglas Johnson. PoNe; TTY

Let's celebrate the feast of the red horse. Dalmatian Ballad. Doris Mühringer, *tr. by* Beth Bjorklund. CoAuP

Let's contend no more, Love. A Woman's Last Word. Robert Browning. BLPA; BLPL; FaBoBe; FaFP; NAEL-2; TrGrPo

Let's count the bodies over again. Counting Small-boned Bodies. Robert Bly. CAPP; EAS; NaP

Let's Do It. Cole Porter. OBAL

Let's enjoy, while the season invites us. "Giovinette, Che Fate All'Amore." Lorenzo Da Ponte, *tr. fr. Italian by* Natalie MacFarren. *Fr.* Don Giovanni. TrJP

Let's face it. Thought While Dressing to Meet the "Girls." Alma Denny. SoTCo

Let's fold perhaps. Origami for Two. Peter Dominick. RR

Let's get going. Leylâ Hanim, *tr. fr. Turkish by* Tâlat S. Halman. PBWP

"Let's get hold of one of those deer." Prospero Dreams of Arnaud Daniel Inventing Love in the Twelfth Century. Jack Gilbert. NPGG

Let's give sake to the planters today. Unknown, *tr. by* Hiroaki Sato. FCEI

Let's Go, Mets. Lillian Morrison. ASP

Let's go—much as that dog goes. Overland to the Islands. Denise Levertov. UnPo

Let's go see Old Abe. Lincoln Monument: Washington. Langston Hughes. OFD

Let's Go to Bed. Unknown. ChTr

Let's go to the wood, says this pig. Unknown. OxNR

Let's go up to the hillside today. Play Song. Peter Clarke. PBA

Let's go, you and I. Adultery at a Las Vegas Bookstore. Stephen Shu Ning Liu. BrSi

Let's have a hole in my poor. Definitive Declaration. Louis Aragon, *tr. by* Michael Benedikt. POS

Let's have less nonsense from the friends of Joe. Less Nonsense. A. P. Herbert. OxBTC

Let's hear it for the toads. Toad Song. D. Brennan. NPo

Let's let the good man sign the bill. The Man of Property. Charles G. Ballard. NOVW

Let's live, my Lesbia, and love. Lesbia. Catullus, *tr. by* Sheridan Baker. PrIm

Let's look. Confirmation. Art Lange. UL

Let's look around ourselves. Three Moral Tales. Emmanuel Hocquard, *tr. by* Michael Palmer. RHTwFP

Let's make love. The night has turned. Emperor Go-Shirakawa, *tr. fr. Japanese by* Hiroaki Sato. *Fr.* Ryojin Hisho. FCEI

Let's make sake, strong and clear, from early rice. Unknown, *tr. by* Hiroaki Sato. FCEI

Let's not be ruthless to ourselves: we must. Cognition, Language, Poetry. László Nagy, *tr. by* Jascha Kessler. FOC

Let's not be slow in knowing. On Calvary's Lonely Hill. Herbert Clark Johnson. PoNe

Let's Not Think about That. Fran Landesman. DT

Let's not think of tomorrow. The Trimdon Grange Explosion. Thomas Armstrong. OBET

Let's not use eyes anymore. Dialogue—2 Dollmakers. Gregory Corso. NeAP

Let's paddle, dear, by yonder fort. Invitation. *Malay Oral Tradition, tr. by* R. J. Wilkinson *and* R. O. Winstedt. WTO

Let's scatter petals on the coffin. Funeral Song. Maruyama Kaoru, *tr. by* Hiroaki Sato. FCEI

Let's sing a song together once. Louis Simpson. NePoAm

Let's sing the new ministry's praise. The Procession: a New Protestant Ballad. Unknown. APAS

Let's skip a few short years of hollow peace. George the Third. Byron. *Fr.* The Vision of Judgment. FiP
(George III.) TW, *abr.*

Let's spit the two of us let's spit. Poem to Shout in the Ruins. Louis Aragon, *tr. by* Geoffrey Young. RHTwFP

Let's step on daddy's head shout. Step on His Head. James Laughlin. VGW

Let's straighten this out, my little man. To a Small Boy Standing on My Shoes While I Am Wearing Them. Ogden Nash. FiBHP

Let's take a carriage—if indeed a shade. Einem alten Architekten in Rom. Joseph Brodsky, *tr. by* George L. Kline. AnAn

Let's Talk, Mother. Edith Bruck, *tr. fr. Italian by* Anita Barrows. VWA

Let's talk of graves, of worms, and epitaphs. The Death of Kings. Shakespeare. *Fr.* King Richard II: Let's Talk of Graves. TrGrPo
"For God's sake, let us sit upon the ground." HoPM
(Let's Talk of Graves.) FaBoBe

Let's think of eggs. The Poultries. Ogden Nash. CenHV

Let's write a poem about lazy people. The Lazy People. Shel Silverstein. NTCP

Letter, The. W. H. Auden. FaBoTw; MoP; NoAM

Letter, The. Patricia Beer. OxBC

Letter. Alexander Bergman. TrJP

Letter, The. John Blight. CBAP

Letter. Philip Dow. NPGG

Letter, A. Emerson. OxBA

Letter. Franco Fortini, *tr. fr. Italian by* Lawrence R. Smith. NItP

Letter. Janet Frame. PeNZ

Letter, A. Anthony Hecht. NYBP; OxBC

Letter. Langston Hughes. PoE

Letter, A. Jenny Joseph. NPo

Letter, A. Rachel Korn, *tr. fr. Yiddish by* Ruth Whitman. VWA

Letter. W. S. Merwin. HAP

Letter, The. Beatrice M. Murphy. PoNe

Letter, The. Wilfred Owen. OBD

Letter, A. Dan Pagis, *tr. fr. Hebrew by* Warren Bargad *and* Stanley F. Chyet. IP

Letter, A. Sir Arthur Quiller-Couch. CenHV

Letter, The. Charles Reznikoff. VWA

Letter. Mark Strand. NoAM

Letter, The. Tennyson. TTTS

Letter, A ("This kind o' sogerin' ain't a mite like our October trainin' "). James Russell Lowell. *Fr.* The Biglow Papers: 1st Series, No. II. OxBA

Letter, A ("Thrash away, you'll hev to rattle"). James Russell Lowell. *Fr.* The Biglow Papers: 1st Series, No. I. AmPP; OxBA
(Mr. Hosea Biglow Speaks.) PAH

Letter across Doubt and Distance. M. Carl Holman. AmNP; PoNe

Letter arrived from the town of my birth, A. 1981. Abraham Sutskever, *tr. fr. Yiddish by* Cynthia Ozick. *Fr.* Poems from a Diary. PeBMYV

Letter Catches Up with Me, A. Eric Chaet. VWA

Letter VIII. Randall Swingler. WaP

Letter V. W. S. Graham. OxBTC

Letter for a Daughter. Lorrie Goldensohn. PPR

Letter for Allhallows, A. Peter Kane Dufault. NYBP

Letter for Duncan. Larry Eigner. PoM

Letter for Marian, A. Thomas McGrath. VGW

Letter IV. William Empson. LiTB

Letter IV. Angelos Sikelianos, *tr. fr. Greek by* Edmund Keeley *and* Philip Sherrard. VMG

Letter from a Black Soldier. Bill Anderson. VGW

Letter from a Contract Worker. Antonio Jacinto, *tr. fr. Portuguese by* Margaret Dickinson. WMBCH

Letter from a Coward to a Hero. Robert Penn Warren. MoAmPo

Letter from a Friend, A. IHMS

Letter from a Girl to Her Own Old Age, A. Alice Meynell. FaBoRV; GoTL; LiTB; MoBrPo

Letter from a man, A. Unknown, *tr. by* Geoffrey Bownas *and* Anthony Thwaite. PeBJV

Letter from a State Hospital. Frank Mundorf. GoYe

Letter from a Wife. S. Carolyn Reese. PoNe

Letter from an Institution: III. Michael Ryan. AmPA

Letter from an Island. John Malcolm Brinnin. TAP

Letter from Aragon, A. John Cornford. OBWP

Letter from Artemisia in the Town, to Chloe [*or* Cloe], in the Country, A. Earl of Rochester. PoE; SeCV-2

Letter from Berlin, A. Jon Stallworthy. MoP; OBWP; OxBC

Letter from Brooklyn, A. Derek Walcott. OxBTC

Letter from Home, A. Li Nan, *tr. fr. Chinese by* Dominic Cheung. IFON

Letter from Italy [to the Right Honourable Charles Lord Halifax], A ("While you, my lord, the rural shades admire."), *sel.* Joseph Addison. NOEC
"Immortal glories in my mind revive." OBTV

Letter from Li Po, A, *sel.* Conrad Aiken.
"Winds of doctrine blow both ways at once, The." VGW

Letter from Mama Dot. Frederick D'Aguiar. PVCV

"Letter from my love today, A!" A Ballad of Hell. John Davidson. HoPM; MoBrPo
(Christmas Eve.) EBVV; OHIP

Letter from Oregon. William Stafford. NaP

Letter from Phillis Wheatley, A. Robert Hayden. NoAM

Letter from Pretoria Central Prison. Arthur Nortje. WMBCH
Letter from School, A. Thomas Love Peacock. FaBoUs
Letter from Sicily. Emanuel di Pasquale. ILY
Letter from Slough Pond. Isabella Gardner. CAPP
Letter from Smyrna to His Sisters at Crux-Easton, 1733. Thomas Lisle.
    OBTV
Letter from the Alpes-Maritimes. Marilyn Hacker. EOEF
Letter from the Caribbean, A. Barbara Howes. CoAP; UnPo
Letter from the Mountain Sanitarium. Alfredo Giuliani, tr. fr. Italian by
    Lawrence R. Smith. NItP
Letter from the Pygmies, A. Theodore Weiss. VGW
Letter from the Vieux Carre. Ethel Green Russell. GoYe
Letter from Thurlby Domain. Charles Brasch. ATNZ
Letter from Underground. Ronald G. Everson. MoCV
Letter from Vermont. Ellen Bryant Voigt. AnAn
Letter in the Present and Present Perfect. Daria Menicanti, tr. fr. Italian
    by Muriel Kittel. DMI
Letter in Winter. Raymond R. Patterson. PoBA
Letter lies unanswered, thus free of lies, The. Correspondence. Henri
    Coulette. DiPo
Letter No. 18. Dennis Brutus. WMBCH
Letter of a Mother. Robert Penn Warren. MoAmPo
Letter of Advice, A. Winthrop Mackworth Praed. NOBL; OxBoLi
Letter of Compleynt of Canace, The. John Lydgate. Fr. The Fall of
    Princes, I. OxBLMV
Letter of Cupid, The, sel. Thomas Hoccleve.
    Cupid Defends Women. OxBLMV
Letter of Dydo to Eneas, The. Chaucer. OxBLMV
Letter on the Lake, A. Carl Dennis. BLA
Letter I. William Empson. LiTB
Letter I. Randall Swingler. WaP
Letter Out of the Gray. Gabriel Preil, tr. fr. Hebrew by Shirley Kaufman
    and Howard Schwartz. VWA
Letter Sent by the Mayor and Inhabitants of the, A, sel. Unknown.
    "O thow archbishop and metropolitan." NOIV
Letter VI. William Sydney Graham. FaBoMo
Letter to a Bedouin Informer. Khalifa al-Wugayyan, tr. fr. Arabic by
    Lena Jayyusi and John Heath-Stubbs. MAP
Letter to a Censor. Kelly Cherry. KS
Letter to a Chinese Poet, sels. Ruth Dallas.
    Autumn Wind. Fr. VIII. PeNZ
    Beating the Drum. ATNZ
    Clouds on the Sea. Fr. IV. PeNZ
Letter to a Friend. Lilian Moore. ILY
Letter to a Friend. Jon Stallworthy. NoAM
Letter to a Friend. John Thompson. PoAu-2
Letter to a Friend. Robert Penn Warren. MoAmPo
Letter to a Friend in an Unknown Place. Anita Barrows. NMM
Letter to a Librarian. Irving Layton. MAT; TW
Letter to a Live Poet, A. Rupert Brooke. BrPo
Letter to a Mute. Thomas James. AmPA
Letter to a Sister Who Lives in a Distant Country. Daisy Zamora, tr. fr.
    Spanish by Barbara Paschke. Vol
Letter to a Substitute Teacher. Gary Gildner. Psk
Letter to a Young Friend. Burns. See I lang hae thought, my youthfu'
    friend.
Letter to Alex Comfort. Dannie Abse. FaBoTw; TwCP
Letter to an Absent Son. Madeline DeFrees. NMM
Letter to an American Visitor. Alex Comfort. OxBTC
Letter to an Imaginary Friend, Part One, sels. Thomas McGrath. NNaP
    "And I hear the pad of feet to the union hall." Fr. II, 2.
    "We go out in the stony midnight." Fr. VIII, 4.
Letter to an Imaginary Friend, Part Two, sels. Thomas McGrath. NNaP
    "And I hear the pad of feet to the union hall." Fr. II, 2.
    "Begun before Easter. / Sign of the Fish." Fr. VI, 4.
    "Evening—another evening—and the lights flare." Fr. V, 2.
    "We go out in the stony midnight." Fr. VIII, 4.
    "Windless city built on decaying granite, loose ends." Fr. II, 2–5.
Letter to Anne Ridler. George Sutherland Fraser. OxBS
Letter to Be Disguised as a Gas Bill. Marge Piercy. WPE
Letter to Bell from Missoula. Richard Hugo. NNaP
Letter to Ben, 1972. Paul Durcan. FaBCIP
Letter to Daphnis. Anne Finch, Countess of Winchilsea. EnLoPo
Letter to David Campbell on the Birthday of W. B. Yeats, 1965, A. Alec
    Derwent Hope. NAs
Letter to Derek Mahon. Michael Longley. CIP; FaBCIP
Letter to E. Franklin Frazier. Amiri Baraka. BPo; PoBA
Letter to Evelyn Baring, A. Edward Lear. FaBoNo
Letter to Graham and Anna. Louis MacNeice. OBTV
Letter to Her Father, A. Inib-sarri, tr. fr. Akkadian by Willis Barnstone.
    BoWoP
Letter to Her Husband, A. Anne Bradstreet. AnAmPo; LiTA

Letter to Her Husband, Absent upon Public Employment, A ("As loving
    hind"). Anne Bradstreet. OxBA; WPE
    (Another ("As loving hind").) SCAP
Letter to Her Husband, Absent upon Public[k] Employment, A. Anne
    Bradstreet. HAP; HeIP; NAAL-1; NoP; SCAP
Letter to Her Mother, A. Eristi-Aya, tr. fr. Akkadian by Willis Barnstone.
    BoWoP
Letter to His Friend Isaac, A. Judah Halevi, tr. fr. Hebrew by Emma
    Lazarus. TrJP
Letter to Hitler, A. James Laughlin. LiTA; WaP
Letter to Jean-Paul Baudot, at Christmas. Lucien Stryk. CAPP
Letter to John Donne, A. C. H. Sisson. NOCV
Letter to John Dryden, A, sel. James McAuley.
    "Dear John, whoever now takes pen to write." CBAP
Letter to Kafka. Maura Stanton. AmPA
Letter to Lady Margaret Cavendish Holles-Harley, When a Child, A.
    Matthew Prior. See Letter to the Honourable Lady Miss Margaret
    Cavendish Holles-Harley, A.
Letter to Levertov from Butte. Richard Hugo. NNaP
Letter to Logan from Milltown. Richard Hugo. NNaP
Letter to Lord Byron, sels. W. H. Auden.
    "England, my England—you have been my tutrix." OBSV
    "I like your muse because she's gay and witty." NOBL
    "Now for the spirit of the people. Here." FaBoPV
    "Ottava Rima would, I know, be proper." NOBL
    "Thought of writing came to me today, The." NOBL
    "You lived and moved among the best society." OBSV
Letter to Madame la Marquise de C——— Louise Geneviève de
    Sainctonge, tr. fr. French by Dorothy Backer. DMI
Letter to Madame la Marquise de S[imiane], on Sending Her Tobacco.
    Mme De C———, tr. fr. French by Dorothy Backer. DMF
Letter to Mantsch from Havre. Richard Hugo. TSL
Letter to Maria Gisborne, sels. Shelley.
    To Maria Gisborne in England, from Italy. NOBE
    "You are now/ In London, that great sea." ChER; EBEV
Letter to Mariana Ziegler. Anna Helena Volckmann, tr. fr. German by
    Susan L. Cocalis. DMG
Letter to Medea. Helga Novak, tr. fr. German by Susan L. Cocalis.
    DMG
Letter to My Daughter at the End of Her Second Year. Donald Finkel.
    CoAP
Letter to My Mother. Salvatore Quasimodo, tr. fr. Italian by Jack Bevan.
    PFI
Letter to My Mother. Anita Skeen. IHMS
Letter to My Sister. Anne Spencer. AmNP; BlSi; PoBA; PoNe
Letter to My Wife. Miklós Radnóti, tr. fr. Hungarian by Emery George.
    VWA
Letter to My Wife. Keidrych Rhys. WaP
Letter to Myself. Christopher Reid. FaBoPa
Letter to N. Y. Elizabeth Bishop. CAPP; NoP; TwCP
Letter to P. Robert Friend. NYBP
Letter to Paul Celan in Memory, A. Jerome Rothenberg. VWA
Letter to Pearse Hutchinson. Eiléan Ni Chuilleanáin. FaBoWP
Letter to Peter, A. Fay Chiang. BrSi
Letter to R. Willard Maas. WaP
Letter to Reed from Lolo. Richard Hugo. NNaP
Letter to Robert. Mary Fabilli. IHMS
Letter to Robert Fergusson. Alexander Scott. OxBS
Letter to Robert Frost, A. Robert Hillyer. MoAmPo
Letter to Ron Silliman on the Back of a Map of the Solar System, A.
    Dennis Schmitz. LCAP
Letter to Scanlon from Whitehall. Richard Hugo. NNaP
Letter to Seamus Heaney. Michael Longley. FaBCIP
Letter to Sigmund Freud. Judah Leib Teller, tr. fr. Yiddish by Benjamin
    and Barbara Harshav. Fr. Psychoanalysis. AYP
Letter to Sir H. Wotton at His Going Ambassador to Venice. John
    Donne. See To Sir H. W. at His Going Ambassador to Venice.
Letter to Statues. John Malcolm Brinnin. EyDe
Letter to the Actor Charles Laughton concerning the Work on the Play
    "The Life of Galileo." Bertolt Brecht, tr. fr. German by Michael
    Hamburger. AnAn
Letter to the Child Lady Margaret Cavendish Holles-Harley, A. Matthew
    Prior. See Letter to the Honourable Lady Miss Margaret Cavendish
    Holles-Harley, A.
Letter to the City Clerk. Frederick Adams Wright. FaFP
Letter to the Countess of Denbigh. Richard Crashaw. See To the Noblest
    and Best of Ladies, the Countess of Denbigh.
Letter to the Earl of Middleton, A. Sir George Etherege. OBTV
Letter to the Front. Muriel Rukeyser. WaP
    Even During War. Fr. II. TrJP
    To Be a Jew in the Twentieth Century.
    Fr. VII. TrJP

Letter to the Honourable Lady Miss Margaret Cavendish Holles-Harley, A. Matthew Prior. NoAM; NOEC; NoP; OxBC; OxBSP; SeCePo
(Letter to Lady Margaret Cavendish Holles-Harley, When a Child, A.) NOBE; OBEV
(Letter to the Child Lady Margaret Cavendish Holles-Harley, A.) OxBChV
Letter to the Immigration Officer. Jan Kemp. PeNZ
Letter to the Little Shell. Gretchen Cotrell. GOS
Letter to the Revolution. Susan Griffin. NPGG
Letter to Three Irish Poets, A. Michael Longley. BIrV
Letter to Tina Koyama from Elliot Bay Park. Jim Mitsui. BrSi
Letter to Wagoner from Port Townsend. Richard Hugo. NNaP
Letter to Welch from Browning. Richard Hugo. NNaP
Letter to William Carlos Williams, A. Kenneth Rexroth. NNaP
Letter to Women. Constance-Marie de Salm-Dyck, *tr. fr. French by* Dorothy Backer. DMF
Letter II. William Sydney Graham. NePoEA
Letter with a Black Border. Sandra McPherson. GeTw
Letter Written on a Ferry while Crossing Long Island Sound. Anne Sexton. CoAP; NAAL-2; NYBP; TwCP
Letter you sent me touched my heart, The. Thank You for Your Letter. Ch'ao Li-houa, *tr. by* Kenneth Rexroth. ILY
Letters. Bruce Andrews. IAT
Letters. Remco Campert, *tr. fr. Dutch by* James S. Holmes. DuIn
Letters. Emerson. · OxBSP
Letters. Bernard Spencer. WaP
Letters & Other Worlds. Michael Ondaatje. NoAM; NOBC; NoP
Letters at School, The. Mary Mapes Dodge. OBCA
Letters Come to Prison. Shahid. GLP
Letters [*or* Notes] Found near a Suicide ("My little stone"), *sels.* Frank Horne. AmNP; CDC; PoBA; PoNe
To "Chick." BPo
To James. BPo
To Mother. BPo
To You. BPo
Letters from a Father. Mona Van Duyn. ER; FYAP; PPR
Letters from a Married Man, *sel.* Don Mager.
"Beloved,/ What does it take to put a house in order?" GLP
Letters from Kazuko (Kyoto, Japan—Summer 1980). Alan Chong Lau. BrSi
Letters from Teignmouth, *sel.* Winthrop Mackworth Praed.
Our Ball. EnRP
Letters from Vicksburg, *sel.* Gary Gildner.
"Dear wife and bosom friend I hat seen hart." SM
Letters I, your lone friend, write in sorrow, The. From William Tyndale to John Frith. Edgar Bowers. NePoEA; QFR
Letters, like blood along a weakening body. Letters. Bernard Spencer. WaP
Letters of the Book, The. Rose Drachler. VWA
Letters of the Dead. Wislawa Szymborska, *tr. fr. Polish by* Czeslaw Milosz. PwPP
Letters of the Jews as strict as flames, The. The Alphabet. Karl Shapiro. NoAM; PoA; VWA
Letters she left to clutter up the desk. A Gesture by a Lady with an Assumed Name. James Wright. LiTM
Letters to a Stranger. Thomas James. AmPA
Letters to Live Poets, *sels.* Bruce Beaver. CBAP
"I shop in the streets of my hometown with/ my family." *Fr.* II.
"I welcome the anonymity of the middle years." *Fr.* XIX.
"Mid-day and a heat haze over all." *Fr.* XXXIV.
"Sou'wester whips the day awake, The." *Fr.* X.
"Three anti-depressants and one diuretic a day." *Fr.* XII.
"Three images of dying stick in my mind like morbid transfers." *Fr.* V.
"Today the self-destroying anger." *Fr.* XXX.
Letters to My Daughters, No. 3. Judith Minty. TV
Letters to Walt Whitman, *sels.* Ronald Johnson. VGW
"But are these landscapes to be imagined." *Fr.* IX.
"I, too, have plucked a stalk of grass." *Fr.* V.
"Let us tunnel." *Fr.* I.
"Slant sheen/ wrinkled silver." *Fr.* II.
Letters to Walt Whitman, II. Ronald Johnson. VGW
Lettie Walker was 71. The Older American. Cheryl Clarke. GLP
Letting in Cold. Marvin Bell. DiL
Letting My Feelings Out. Yü Hsüan-chi, *tr. fr. Chinese by* Geoffrey Waters. BoWoP
Letting rip a fart. *Unknown, tr. by* Geoffrey Bownas *and* Anthony Thwaite. PeBJV
Letting us know for certain you didn't want that kind of Jew. Fairy Straighttalk. Carl Morse. GLP
Lettuce Pause. Alma Denny. SoTCo
Letty's Globe. Charles Tennyson Turner. NOBVV; OBEV; OnUR

Levant. Lawrence Durrell. OBTV
Levantine, A. William Plomer. OBMV
Levavi Oculos. Marion Campbell. PoSH
Levedy, ic thonke thee. Thanks and a Plea to Mary. *Unknown.* MeEL
Levee Moan ("Ah'm goin' whah nobody knows mah name, Lawd, Lawd"). *Unknown.* AS
Levee Moan ("O baby, where you been so long? Lord, Lord, Lord, Lord"). *Unknown.* AS
Level and the Square, The. Robert Morris. BLPA
Level fields expand into lakes. Inscribed on the Painting "Meaning of a Poem by Wang Wei." Li Tung-yang, *tr. by* Jonathan Chaves. CoBLCP
Level forest stretching far and wide, A. Wu Chen, *tr. by* Jonathan Chaves. CoBLCP
Level ground breathing clouds of vapor. Isuzu River. Rai San'yo, *tr. by* Burton Watson. JLIC-2
Level lake brings news of wild geese returning, The. An Autumn Song. Wang Fu-chih, *tr. by* Irving Lo. WFTU
Level lake, mist on the waters, obscure and indistinct, A. White Lotus Flowers. Ts'ao Chen-chi, *tr. by* William H. Nienhauser, *tr. by* WFTU
Level ocean lies immeasurably blind, The. The Flying Fish. Jack Cope. PeSA
Level slope of colored sea, The. Metaphysical. Robert Fitzgerald. PoA
Level with duty, days ride a city-express across the calendar page. Coin in the Fist. Florence Kerr Brownell. GoYe
Leveling his pole like some quixotic lance. Challenge. Samuel Hazo. SD
Levelled Churchyard, The. Thomas Hardy. NOBL
Lever de Rideau. Mary Ursula Bethell. ATNZ
Levi Yitzhok:/ binding tefillin on. The Morning Prayers of the Hasid, Rabbi Levi Yitzhok. Phyllis Gotlieb. VWA
Leviathan. Ernest Bryll, *tr. fr. Polish by* Czeslaw Milosz. PwPP
Leviathan. Jay Macpherson. MoCV
Leviathan. W. S. Merwin. MoP; NePoEA; NoAM; NOBA
Leviathan. Milton. *See* Paradise Lost:
There Leviathan/ Hugest of living creatures, on the deep.
Leviathan, *sel.* Peter Quennell.
"Music met Leviathan returning, A." MoBrPo
Leviathan. Bible, *O.T. See* Job: Canst thou draw out Leviathan with an hook[e]?
Leviathan; or, A Hymn to Poor Brother Ben. *Unknown.* APAS
Leviathan the ocean, spiked and mailed. Off Cape Leeuwen. M. K. Joseph. ATNZ
Levin, on his way to Kitty's love. Secular Games. Richard Howard. PoA
Lewd Love Is Loss. Robert Southwell. ACP
Lewesdon Hill, *sel.* William Crowe.
"Up to thy summit, Lewesdon, to the brow." NOEC
Lewis Carroll. Eleanor Farjeon. OxBChV
Lewis Has a Trumpet. Karla Kuskin. PDV
Lewis, the Lost Lover. Sir Thomas More. OBSC
Lewti. Samuel Taylor Coleridge. EnRP
Lexington. Oliver Wendell Holmes. PAH
Lexington. Sidney Lanier. *Fr.* Psalm of the West. PAH
Lexington. Whittier. PAH
L'Homme Moyen Sensuel, *sels.* Ezra Pound. OBSV
"Alas, eheu, one question that sorely vexes."
"'Tis of my country that I would endite."
Li Hsü of Ch'ien-chou is an old friend of mine. Yang Shih-ch'i, *tr. fr. Chinese by* Jonathan Chaves. *Fr.* Rhymed Words Sent to My Eldest Son. CoBLCP
Li Po on board, ready to push off. Presented to Wang Lun. Li Po, *tr. by* Burton Watson. CoBCP
Li-T'ai-Po, three Jewish boys. Three Jewish Boys Write to an Ancient Chinese Poet. Judd Teller, *tr. by* Grace Schulman. PeBMYV
Liadain. *Unknown, tr. by* Frank O'Connor. WPOW
Líadan and Cuirithir. *Unknown.* NOIV
Liadan Laments Cuirithir. *Unknown, tr. fr. Irish by* John Montague. BIrV; PBWP
Liang Family Pool. Yang Shih-ch'i, *tr. fr. Chinese by* Jonathan Chaves. *Fr.* Ten Scenes at the Hsiao Family Stone Ridge. CoBLCP
Liao-ling. Po Chü-i, *tr. fr. Chinese by* Burton Watson. CoBCP
Liar, The. Amiri Baraka. AmPP; NOBA
Liar, The. *Unknown, tr. fr. Irish by* Frank O'Connor. KiLC
Liar and bragger. Peregrine. Elinor Wylie. BLPL
'Lias! 'Lias! Bless de Lawd! In the Morning. Paul Laurence Dunbar. BPo
Libation./ Hey sisters, we the color of our men. Ceremony. Jewel C. Latimore. BlSi
Libation Bearers, The. Aeschylus, *tr. fr. Greek by* Robert Fagles. NAWM-1

Libationer Hu Became Ill from Eating Sunflowers, *sel.* Yang Shih-ch'i, *tr. fr. Chinese by* Jonathan Chaves.
  "After the rain, the vegetables from your garden." CoBLCP
Liber doth vaunt how chastely he hath liv'd. In Librum. Sir John Davies. FaBoEE
Libera nos, Domine—Deliver us, O Lord. Emancipation from British Dependence. Philip Freneau. PAH
Liberace. Jonathan Holden. MAYP
Liberal. Vincent O'Sullivan. *Fr.* The Pilate Tapes. ATNZ
Liberal arts lie eastward of this shore, The. The Seven Sleepers. Mark Van Doren. FYAP
Liberal, blue-eyed, shivering, trying not. The Blue-eyed Precinct Worker. Henri Coulette. MAT
Liberals raised this in their finest hour. Norris Dam. Selden Rodman. PoNe
Liberation. Diane Mei Lin Mark. BrSi
Liberation. Ruth Stone. BoWoP
Liberator, The. Emily Holmes Coleman. EAS
Liberator of the laboring, The. Talking Union: 1964. L. E. Sissman. TW
Liberia?/ No micro-footnote in a bunioned book. On the Founding of Liberia. Melvin B. Tolson. *Fr.* Libretto for the Republic of Liberia. UnPo
  (Do.) PoNe
Libertine, The. Louis MacNeice. MoP; NoAM
Liberty. Paul Éluard, *tr. fr. French by* W. S. Merwin. POS; RHTwFP
  "On my school notebooks," *sel.* TTTS
Liberty. John Hay. AA
Liberty. Archibald MacLeish. GOA
Liberty. Chiara Matraini, *tr. fr. Italian by* Muriel Kittel. DMI
Liberty. Edward Thomas. MoAB; OAEL-2
Liberty, *sel.* Wordsworth.
  "Beetle loves his unpretending track, The." FaBoCo; FiBHP; Par
Liberty. Sir Thomas Wyatt. *See* Lover Rejoiceth, The.
Liberty and Peace. Phillis Wheatley. AiP
  "Lo! Freedom comes. Th' prescient Muse foretold," *sel.* BlSi
Liberty Enlightening the World. Edmund Clarence Stedman. PAH
Liberty for All. William Lloyd Garrison. AA
Liberty Pole, The. *Unknown.* PAH
Liberty Tree. Thomas Paine. OPP; PAH
Librarian, The. Charles Olson. CAPP
Library, The. Barbara A. Huff. FaPON; RHPC
Library. Louis Jenkins. NU
Library, The. Aidan Carl Mathews. CIP
Library, The. Frank Dempster Sherman. AA
Library Is Burning, The. Michael Palmer. LP
Libretto for the Republic of Liberia, *sel.* Melvin B. Tolson.
  On the Founding of Liberia. UnPo
  (Do.) PoNe
Lice Seekers, The. Rimbaud, *tr. fr. French by* Kenneth Koch *and* George Guy. *Fr.* Illuminations. SOTW
Lichen. Mary Elizabeth Fullerton. PoAu-1
Lichen-crusted frogs croak. Frogs Croaking. Masso, *tr. by* Lucien Stryk *and* Takashi Ikemoto. ZPCJ
Licia, *sels.* Giles Fletcher the Elder.
  Are Those Two Stars. *Fr.* XLIII. Son
  "I wish sometimes, although a worthlesse thing." *Fr.* XII. AAS
  "In time [*or* tyme] the strong and stately [*or* statelie] turrets fall." *Fr.* XXVIII. AAS; EBEV; NIP
  (Time.) OBSC
  "Like [*or* Lyke] Memnons rock, touched [*or* rocke toucht] with the rising sun[ne]." *Fr.* XLVII. AAS; FF
  (Sonnet: "Like Memnon's rock, touched with the rising sun.") ElL
  Sad, All Alone, Not Long I Musing Sat. *Fr.* I. Son
Lick your lips, X. darling, it may be the last. The Summer Ending. Glenway Wescott. PoA
Licorice Fields at Pontefract, The. Sir John Betjeman. CMoP
Lid broke, and suddenly the child, The. Skater in Blue. Jay Parini. ASP
Liddell and Scott; on the Completion of Their Lexicon. Thomas Hardy. OxBoLi
Liddesdale Crosiers hae ridden a race, The. The Death of Parcy Reed. *Unknown.* ESPB
Lidia Rosa: today is Tuesday and it is cold. In your house. Forgetting. Alfonsina Storni, *tr. by* Kate Flores. DMH
Lido, The. Edmund Wilson. ErPo
Lie, The. Kipling. NOBL
Lie, The. Al Lee. AmPA
Lie, The. Howard Moss. LiTM; MoAB; NePoAm

Lie, The. Sir Walter Ralegh. AAS; ChTr; CTC; EBEV; FaBoPV; HAP; InvP; LiTB; NAEL-1; NOBE; NoP; OBSC; OPOP; PoEL-2; QFR; RB; SCV; SiPS; TEP; TrGrPo; WGRP
Lie back, daughter, let your head. First Lesson. Philip Booth. SD; SM; TwCP
Lie down at the foot of the elm. Country Night. Rocco Scotellaro, *tr. by* Lawrence R. Smith. NItP
Lie down on the bright hill. The Dress. Mark Strand. GeTw
Lie Easy in Your Secret Cradle. John Wain. *Fr.* Wildtrack. NAs
Lie here, without a record of thy worth. Tribute to the Memory of the Same Dog. Wordsworth. FM
Lie on the mats and sweat in summer. Things to Do around Kyoto. Gary Snyder. NaP
"Lie still, my newly married wife." The Griesly Wife. John Manifold. MoBrPo; MoBS
Lie, that we come from water, A. Landcrab. Margaret Atwood. SoSe
Lie up nearer, brother, nearer, for my limbs are growing cold. The Dying Californian. *Unknown.* AmFP
Lie where you fell and longed. Letter V. W. S. Graham. OxBTC
Lieder. Rosalía de Castro, *tr. fr. Spanish by* Angel Flores *and* Kate Flores. DMH
Liefer would I turn and love. Deranged. Padraic Fiacc. NeIP
Lies. Ted Greenwald. LP
Lies on one hip by the fire. The Girl Writing Her English Paper. Robert Wallace. Psk
Lieutenant Dawson said he'd known the girl. He Remembers How He Didn't Understand What Lieutenant Dawson Meant. James Whitehead. MT
Lif of this world, the. This Life. *Unknown.* FaBoRV
Life. Francis Bacon. *See* Life of Man, The.
Life. Anna Laetitia Barbauld. BLPA; FaFP; GTBS; GTBS-P; OBEV; PWR
Life, A. Chana Bloch. MAYP
Life. Alice Brown. AA
Life. Samuel Taylor Coleridge. EnRP
Life, The. Philip Dow. AmPA
Life. Paul Laurence Dunbar. AmNP; AnAmPo; CDC
Life. Jean Follain, *tr. fr. French by* Keith Waldrop. RHTwFP
Life. Artie Gold. NOBC
Life. George Herbert. FaBoRV; JCP; LiTB; MeLP; MePo; NoP; OBS; SeCP; SeCV-1
Life. Longfellow. *Fr.* A Psalm of Life. GN
Life, A. Sylvia Plath. NOBA
Life. Henrietta Cordelia Ray. CBWP-3
Life. Nan Terrell Reed. BLPA
Life. Shin Dong-jip, *tr. fr. Korean by* Koh Chang-soo. ACKP
Life. Edward Rowland Sill. BLRP
Life, A, *sel.* Iain Crichton Smith.
  Aberdeen University 1945-49: I. UAS
Life. Clark Stillman. SoTCo
Life. Grace Treasone. InPK
Life. Mary E. Tucker. CBWP-1
Life, The. James Wright. LCAP; NaP
Life/ anthology of bewilderments. Violins in Repose. Jorge Plescoff, *tr. by* Yishai Tobin. VWA
Life!/ I came to your door like a beggar. Mustafa Zaidi, *tr. fr. Urdu by* Mahmood Jamal. *Fr.* Renewal, I. PBMUP
Life/ is at 2 playing. Childhood. Jewel C. Latimore. JB
Life/ Is not worth the trouble and grief of being lived. Anthology. Manuel Bandeira, *tr. by* Jean R. Longland. ATCBP
Life,/ preserved in amber. Christine Busta, *tr. by* Beth Bjorklund. CoAuP
Life Above, the Life on High, The. St. Theresa of Avila, *tr. fr. Spanish by* Edward Caswall. WGRP
Life after Death. Pindar, *tr. fr. Greek by* Walter Headlam. EaLo
Life after Death. Richard W. Thomas. PoBA
Life Again. Keats. *Fr.* Endymion [a Poetic Romance]. SeCePo
Life Ahead, The. Philip Levine. NoAM
Life and Adventure of Bob Thin, The. William James Linton. *Fr.* Bob Thin; or, the Poorhouse Fugitive. PF
Life and Character of Dean Swift, The, *sel.* Swift.
  "Day will come, when't shall be said, The." NOIV
Life and Death. Sir William Davenant. *Fr.* The Christian's Reply to the Philosopher. OBS
Life and Death. Lilla Cabot Perry. AA
Life and Death. Walter James Turner. FaBoTw
Life and Death of [Habbie Simson] the Piper of Kilbarchan, The. Robert Sempill. OBS; OxBS
Life and Death of Jason, The, *sel.* William Morris.
  Garden by the Sea, A. *Fr.* IV. CH; NOBE; OAEL-2; OBNC; PoEL-5
  (Nymph's Song to Hylas, The.) OBEV

Life and Death of William Longbeard, The, *sels.* Thomas Lodge.
Her Rambling. OBSC
My Mistress. TrGrPo
Rose, The. OBSC
(Fancy, A.) EIL
Life and death? Shoving a cart. Jittei, *tr. by* Lucien Stryk *and* Takashi Ikemoto. ZPCJ
Life and Genuine Character of Dean Swift, The, *sel.* Swift.
"Wise Rochefoucault a maxim writ." NOBL
Life and Impellance. William Frederick Stevenson. NOBVV
Life and Love. Whittier. BLRP
Life and Lucubrations of Crispinus Scriblerus, The, *sels.* James Woodhouse. NOEC
Birmingham and Wolverhampton.
Tribulations of an Uneducated Poet in the 1760's, The.
Life and the Universe show spontaneity. The Positivists. Mortimer Collins. EBVV
Life and the Weaver. A. W. Dewar. BLRP; WBLP
Life and Thought. Matthew Arnold. *Fr.* Empedocles on Etna. FiP, *fr.* II.
Life at last I know is terrible. What Is Terrible. Roy Fuller. WaP
Life at the Sui Garden, *sels.* Yüan Mei, *tr. fr. Chinese by* Anthony C. Yu. WFTU
"Eyes, nose, ears, mouth and mind." *Fr.* VI.
"Flowers will arrive with spring." *Fr.* V.
"In building houses, I'm content with few." *Fr.* IV.
"Joy and rage are not caused by things." *Fr.* II.
"You mustn't laugh at my tall tower." *Fr.* X.
Life at War. Denise Levertov. NMM; VGW
Life contracts and death is expected. The Death of a Soldier. Wallace Stevens. OBWP; OFD; OxBSP; QFR
Life Cycle of Common Man. Howard Nemerov. NBLV; NIP
Life Death Does End. Gerard Manley Hopkins. *See* No Worst, There Is None.
Life did not bring me silken gowns. Red Geraniums. Martha Haskell Clark. BLPA
Life drains out. In drops and spurts it flows, The. The Arena. Hubert Witheford. ATNZ
Life Drawing. Steve Orlen. BLA
Life Encompassed. Donald Davie. PoPo
Life eternal—useless to talk of that. Shadow Replies to Substance. T'ao Ch'ien, *tr. fr. Chinese by* Burton Watson. *Fr.* Substance, Shadow, and Spirit. CoBCP
Life Explains and Death Spies Out. Washington Delgado, *tr. fr. Spanish by* Maureen Ahern *and* David Tipton. Per
Life flows to death as rivers to the sea. J. V. Cunningham. VGW
Life, friends, is boring. We must not say so. John Berryman. *Fr.* Dream Songs. CAPP; HAP; HCAP; HeIP; LiTM; MoP; NAAL-2; NaP; NoAM; NOBA; PrIm; TAP; TwCP
Life from the Lifeless. Robinson Jeffers. CMoP
Life-Giving, The. Brad Leithauser. PPR
Life has conquered, the wind has blown away. Hope. Frank O'Connor, *tr. by* the author. CIP; KiLC
Life has its nauseating ironies. Sonnet Ending with a Film Subtitle. Marilyn Hacker. MAYP; SM
Life has loveliness to sell. Barter. Sara Teasdale. FaBV; FaPON; SoSe
Life has stumbled, stumbled, unraveled. Surdas, *tr. by* John Stratton Hawley *and* Mark Juergensmeyer. SSI
Life-Hook. Juana de Ibarbourou, *tr. fr. Spanish by* Marti Moody. AIW; WPOW
Life, hope, they conquer death, generally, always. After the Convention. Robert Lowell. NoAM
Life! I know not what thou art. Life. Anna Laetitia Barbauld. BLPA; FaFP; GTBS; GTBS-P; OBEV; PWR
Life impaled him high on a cliff. Biography of an Agnostic. Louis Ginsberg. TrJP
Life in a day: he took his girl to the ballet. Les Sylphides. Louis MacNeice. BoLoP
Life in a Love. Robert Browning. OBNC; TrGrPo
Life-in-Love. Dante Gabriel Rossetti. *Fr.* The House of Life, XXXVI. HAP
Life in the Boondocks. A. R. Ammons. HAP
Life in the Castle. Anne Hébert, *tr. fr. French by* Aliki *and* Willis Barnstone. BoWoP
Life in the cellars. In the Cellars. Jiri Gold, *tr. by* Jaroslav Kotan *and* Daniel Weissbort. VWA
Life in the City: In Memoriam Edward Gibbon. Philip Whalen. PoM
Life in Uncle Sam's Backyard. Valerie Bloom. WS

Life is a bitter aspic. We are not. Wallace Stevens. *Fr.* Esthétique du Mal. CMoP
Life Is a Dream, *sel.* Pedro Calderón de la Barca, *tr. fr. Spanish by* Arthur Symons.
"We live, while we see the sun." AWP
Life is a game with a glorious prize. Playing the Game. *Unknown.* PWR
Life is a glass wherein we dimly see. Life's Boundary. Henrietta Cordelia Ray. CBWP-3
Life is a jest; and all things show it. My Own Epitaph. John Gay. FaBoEE; FF; NIP; NOEC; OBD; SeCePo
Life is a long discovery, isn't it? Discovery. Hilaire Belloc. OxBSP
Life is a pilgrimage, they say. Cockle-Shell and Sandal-Shoon. Herbert T. J. Coleman. CaP
Life Is a Platform, *sel.* Peter Levi.
"Smoke when the sun fell and when it rose." FaBoTw
Life is a poet's fable. *Unknown.* OBSC
Life is a Shylock; always it demands. The Law. Ella Wheeler Wilcox. PWR
Life is a stage, and we are the actors. A Variant. A. Leyeles, *tr. by* Benjamin *and* Barbara Harshav. AYP
Life is a woven fabric. Life and the Weaver. A. W. Dewar. BLRP; WBLP
Life is butter, life is butter. *Unknown.* FaBoNo
Life Is Fine. Langston Hughes. NBLV
Life is full of mirth and pleasure. Adieu. Mary E. Tucker. CBWP-1
Life is inadequate, but there are many real. Independence Day. William Jay Smith. TwCP
Life is like a jagged tooth. Life. Grace Treasone. InPK
Life is like a river. Monish. Isaac Leibush Peretz, *tr. by* Seymour Levitan. PeBMYV
Life is long that loathsomely doth last, The. Elegy Wrote in the Tower, 1554. John Harington. EIL
Life Is More True. E. E. Cummings. WaP
Life Is Motion. Wallace Stevens. SD
Life is *not* a horse win a winner's garland. Look Sheila Seeing You've Asked Me. Vincent O'Sullivan. PeNZ
Life is not made for meetings. Presented to Wei Pa, Gentleman in Retirement. Tu Fu, *tr. by* Burton Watson. CoBCP
Life is ours like the real. Theme One: The Variations. August Wilson. PoBA
Life is real, life is earnest. A Parody on "A Psalm of Life." *At. to* Oliver Wendell Holmes. BLPA
Life is simple and gay. For the Moment. Pierre Reverdy, *tr. by* Ron Padgett. RHTwFP; TTTS
Life is the desert, life the solitude. Edward Young. *Fr.* The Revenge. OBD
Life leavened him. Baker. Gloria A. Maxson. *Fr.* Epitaphs. SoTCo
"Life! length of life!" for this, with earnest cries. Juvenal, *tr. fr. Latin by* William Gifford. *Fr.* Satires, X. OBVE
Life-Lesson, A. James Whitcomb Riley. AA; FPL; PoLF
Life like the periodical not yet. James Merrill. *Fr.* The Book of Ephraim. HCAP
Life-long, Poor Browning. Anne Spencer. CDC; PoNe
Life Mask. Charles Brasch. PeNZ
Life may change, but it may fly not. Shelley. *Fr.* Hellas: Choruses from "Hellas," 1. EnRP
Life-Mosaic. Frances Ridley Havergal. TrPWD
Life—not coming. Gyokuchu, *tr. by* Lucien Stryk *and* Takashi Ikemoto. ZPCJ
Life of. . . , The. Theodore Weiss. NYBP
Life of Ages, Richly Poured, *with music.* Samuel Johnson. AH
(Inspiration.) AA; TrPWD; WGRP
Life of Hard Times, The. Joshua Tan Pai, *tr. fr. Hebrew by* Yishai Tobin. VWA
Life of Hubert, The, *sels.* Thomas Cole. NOEC
Memories of a Dorset Childhood in the 1730's.
"Time allowed for sleep at length elapsed, The."
Life of Life. Shelley. *Fr.* Prometheus Unbound, II, v. CH; FiP; NOBE; PoE; PoEL-4
(Hymn to the Spirit of Nature.) GTBS; GTBS-P
Life of Lincoln West, The. Gwendolyn Brooks. FB; NoAM
Life of Man, The. Francis Bacon. EIL; GTBS; OBSC
(Life.) GTBS-P
Life of Man, The. Barnabe Barnes. *See* Divine Century of Spiritual Sonnets, A:
Blast of wind, a momentary breath, A.
Life of man, The. The Flight of the Arrow. Richard Henry Stoddard. AA
Life of my learning, fire of all my Art. Mary Elizabeth Coleridge. TrPWD

Life of my life, take not so soon thy flight. To His Dying Brother, Master William Herrick. Robert Herrick. CaPo; SeCV-1

Life of Service, The. Donald Davie. NYBP

Life of spring is no more than, The. Mirza Mohammad Rafi Sauda, *tr. by* Ahmed Ali. GoT

Life of T. S. Eliot. Michael Frayn. FaBoPa

Life of the Blessed, The. Luís de León, *tr. fr. Spanish by* Bryant. AWP

Life of the Letters. Emily Borenstein. VWA

Life of the Mannings. *Unknown.* FaBoBa

Life of the Wolf, The. Gary Gildner. AmPA

Life on Earth, *sel.* Frank O'Hara.
   "Shine, "O world!" don't weary the gulping Pole." UnPo

Life on the Ocean Wave, A. Epes Sargent. AA; AnAmPo; FaBoBe; GN

Life on This Star. Christine Busta, *tr. fr. German by* Beth Bjorklund. CoAuP

Life pours out images, the accidental. The Rokeby Venus. Robert Conquest. MoP

Life (priest and poet say) is but a dream. The Dragon-Fly. Walter Savage Landor. OBEV
   (Lines to a Dragon-Fly.) FM; OBNC

Life-Saving Medal. Philippe Soupault, *tr. fr. French.* POS, *tr. by* Michael Benedikt; RHTwFP, *tr. by* Rosmarie Waldrop.

Life Sculpture. George Washington Doane. BLPA; OHFP; WBLP

Life Sentence. Pierre Kemp, *tr. fr. Dutch by* Fred van Leeuwen. DuIn

Life Story. Tomioka Taeko, *tr. fr. Japanese by* Harry *and* Lynn Guest *and* Kajima Shozo. WPOW

Life Story. Tennessee Williams. GLP; PeHV

Life Study. Steve Orlen. MAYP

Life That Counts, The. "A. W. S." FaFP; WBLP

Life that is free as the bandits' of old, A. Brave Donahue. *At. to* Jack Donahue. PoAu-1

Life the hound. The Hound. Robert Francis. SoSe

Life to the bigot is a whip. Epitaph for a Bigot. Dorothy Vena Johnson. PoNe

Life today is hectic. What's Going to Happen to the Tots? Noel Coward. NBLV

Life was a narrow lobby, dark. For the Bicentenary of Isaac Watts. Norman Nicholson. EaLo

Life we find is nevermore. Deception. Josephine D. Henderson Heard. CBWP-4

Life will keep hammering the grass blades into the ground. Force. Derek Walcott. OxBC

Life without Hari is no life, friend. Mirabai, *tr. by* John Stratton Hawley *and* Mark Juergensmeyer. SSI

Life without Passion. Shakespeare. *See* Sonnets: XCIV. "They that have power to hurt, and will do none."

Life would be an easy matter. Nixon Waterman. *Fr.* If We Didn't Have to Eat. FiBHP; OBAL

Lifeboat/ drown. Ernst Jandl. CoAuP

Lifeguard, The. James Dickey. ASP; NoP; NYBP

Lifeguard's whistle organized our swimming, The. The River. Dabney Stuart. NYBP

Lifeless solitude—an angry waste, A. On the Telescopic Moon. John Swanwick Drennan. BIrV

Lifelines. Gavin Ewart. EAS

Lifelong. Rachel Boimwall, *tr. fr. Yiddish by* Gabriel Preil *and* Howard Schwartz

Lifers file into the hall, The. In the Cage. Robert Lowell. FF; NOBA; SM; Son

Life's a Funny Proposition after All. George M. Cohan. PoLF

Life's a Game. *Unknown.* BLPA

Life's Boundary. Henrietta Cordelia Ray. CBWP-3

Life's Circumnavigators. W. R. Rodgers. GTBS-P

Life's Common Duties. Minot Judson Savage. WBLP

Life's Common Things. Alice E. Allen. WBLP

Life's Evening. Dudley Foulke. WGRP

Life's Golden Sunset. Mrs. Henry Linden. CBWP-4

Life's Journey. Ella Wheeler Wilcox. PWR

Life's Last Scene. Samuel Johnson. *Fr.* Vanity of Human Wishes, The: The Tenth Satire of Juvenal Imitated. SeCePo

Life's leisure is a mirror of the hundred hues. Asadullah Khan Ghalib, *tr. by* Ahmed Ali. GoT

Life's Lessons. *Unknown.* BLRP; FPL; PoLF

Life's Mirror. "Madeline Bridges." BLPA; FaBoBe; PWR; WBLP

Life's Morning. Howell Elvet Lewis, *tr. fr. Welsh by* H. Idris Bell. OBWVE

Life's Parallels, A. Christina Rossetti. NAEL-2; PoEL-5

Life's pathway to me is dreary. The Opium-Eater. Mary E. Tucker. CBWP-1

Life's Poor Play. Pope. *Fr.* An Essay on Man, Epistle II. SeCePo

Life's Scars. Ella Wheeler Wilcox. BLPA

Life's sorrows and regrets—who can escape them? Tune: Song of Tzu-yeh. Li Yü, *tr. by* Burton Watson. CoBCP

Life's stormy surge had scarcely touched. The Grafted Bud. Mary Weston Fordham. CBWP-2

Life's Testament, *sels.* William Baylebridge. PoAu-1
   "All that I am to Earth Belongs." *Fr.* XI.
   "Brain, the blood, the busy thews, The." *Fr.* II.
   "Choir of spirits on a cloud, A." *Fr.* XVII.
   "God, to get the clay that stayed me." *Fr.* XIII.
   "I worshipped, when my veins were fresh." *Fr.* VI.
   "This miracle in me I scan." *Fr.* VIII.

Life's Trades. Emily Dickinson. *See* It's such a little thing to weep.

Life's Will. Abu al-Qasim al-Shabbi, *tr. fr. Arabic by* Sargon Boulus *and* Christopher Middleton. MAP

Life's wisdom is best found in living drunk. The Wisdom of Life. "Al-Akhtal al-Saghir," *tr. by* Issa Boullata *and* Thomas G. Ezzy. MAP

Lifesaving. Sandra McPherson. MAYP

Lift Every Voice and Sing. James Weldon Johnson. FaBV; OPP; PoNe

Lift her up tenderly. Song of the Ballet. J. B. Morton. FiBHP

Lift latch, step in, be welcome, Sir. A Luncheon. Max Beerbohm. FaBoCo; NOBL; OBSV; OxBTC

Lift Me Higher. Mary E. Tucker. CBWP-1

Lift me, O God, above myself. Per Ardua ad Astra. John Oxenham. TrPWD

Lift not the painted veil which those who live. Shelley. EnRP; OBNC; Son

Lift, O dark and glorious Wonder. A Hymn to God in Time of Stress. Max Eastman. TrPWD

Lift up thy lips, turn round, look back for love. Hermaphroditus. Swinburne. TEP

Lift up, ye poor! your everlasting prayer! The Poor of London. William Forster. CBAP

Lift up your eyes on high. Erige Cor Tuum ad Me in Caelum. Hilda Doolittle ("H. D."). CMoP

"Lift up your hartes and be glad." A Cheerful Welcome. *Unknown.* MeEL

Lift Up Your Heads. Bible, *O.T. See* Psalms: Psalm XXIV ("The Earth is the Lord's").

Lift Up Your Heads, Rejoice! Thomas T. Lynch. TrCP; WGRP

Lift your arms to the stars. Love and Liberation. John Hall Wheelock. MoAmPo

Lift your feet and you sink deeper in the mud! Ruinous Rains. Fu Hsien, *tr. by* Burton Watson. CoBCP

Lift Your Glad Voices in Triumph on High. Henry Ware, Jr. AH

Lifting and Leaning. Ella Wheeler Wilcox. BLPA; WBLP

Lifting, both hands pulling whitely. Grandpa's .45. W. M. Ransom. CDW

Lifting hands, I climb the south star. Godai Chitsu, *tr. by* Lucien Stryk *and* Takashi Ikemoto. ZPCJ

Lifting his slowly trickling years. Tête-à-Tête. Edwin Honig. NoAM

Lifting Illegal Nets by Flashlight. William Stafford. NNaP

Lifting my fingers. Frozen Hands. Joseph Bruchac. CDW

Lifting of the Cloud, The. Thomas McDonagh. TIRV

Lifting the thunder of their acclamation. Shelley. *Fr.* The Revolt of Islam, V. ChER

Ligeia, *prose tale, sel.* Poe.
   Conqueror Worm, The. AA; AWP; BLPL; LiTA; NOBA
   (Emperor Worm, The.) DL

Light. Frank Bidart. *Fr.* Elegy, IV. HCAP

Light. Francis William Bourdillon. *See* Night Has a Thousand Eyes, The.

Light. Carol Coates. CaP

Light, The. John Holloway. NePoEA

Light. Richard Kenney. Son

Light. Milton. *See* Paradise Lost: Hail holy light, ofspring [*or* offspring] of Heav'n first born.

Light, The. Gregory O'Brien. *Fr.* Bride of the Disappearing Man. ATNZ

Light a Candle. Zelda, *tr. fr. Hebrew by* Marcia Falk. VWA

Light across the courtyard. Saint's Bridge. Lola Ridge. WPE

Light after darkness, gain after loss. Afterwards. Frances Ridley Havergal. BLRP

Light along the hills in the morning, The. Notice What This Poem Is Not Doing. William Stafford. LCAP

Light and Rejoicing to Israel. *Unknown, tr. fr. Hebrew by* Israel Abrahams. TrJP

Light and warmth, The. From the Depth of the Abyss. Paul Éluard, *tr. by* Stephen Spender *and* Frances Cornford. RHTwFP

Light Another Candle. Miriam Chaikin. NTCP

Light as a leaping faun! Doris Ferne. CaP

Light became her grace and dwelt among, The. Ballatetta. Ezra Pound. NIP; VGW

Light Breaks Where No Sun Shines. Dylan Thomas. CMoP; ErPo; FaBoMo; LiTB; MoAB; MoBrPo; OxBTC; SeCePo

Light Breather, A. Theodore Roethke. NoP

Light breeze rustles the reeds, A. Night Thoughts while Travelling. Tu Fu, *tr. by* Kenneth Rexroth. NaP

Light Bulbs and Bananas. Hal J. Daniel III. SoTCo

Light clouds at the first clearing after rain. Southern Pavilion. Chu Yi-tsun, *tr. fr. Chinese by* Irving Lo. *Fr.* Quatrains on Yung-chia, VII. WFTU

Light come from my head, A. The Island. James Dickey. SM

Light dies in the eyes, hearing. Etsuzan, *tr. by* Lucien Stryk *and* Takashi Ikemoto. ZPCJ

Light diffusing my likeness. Legend of His Lyre. Aaron Schmuller. GoYe

Light do I see within my Lady's eyes. Guido Cavalcanti, *tr. by* Ezra Pound. CTC; PFI

Light drizzle falling off, A. Taking a Captive/ 1984. Barney Bush. HATNAP

Light everywhere, I live in all. Chosetsu, *tr. by* Lucien Stryk *and* Takashi Ikemoto. ZPCJ

Light exists in spring, A. Emily Dickinson. BoWoP; LiTA; NOBA; OxBA

Light fell from the window and the day was done, The. "The Truth Is Blind." David Gascoyne. EAS

Light flooding both banks. A Death in Spring. Amir Gilboa, *tr. by* Warren Bargad *and* Stanley F. Chyet. IP

Light flows our war of mocking words, and yet. The Buried Life. Matthew Arnold. NAEL-2; OAEL-2

Light foot hears you and the brightness begins, The. A Poem Beginning with a Line by Pindar. Robert Duncan. NeAP; NNaP; PoM

Light forgetting itself light falling loosely. Locations. Kathleen Fraser. NPGG

Light founders. Rain puckers the ocean, The. On the Coast. Wayne Brown. UAS

Light from Within, The. Jones Very. WGRP

Light Furs, Fat Horses. Po Chü-i, *tr. fr. Chinese by* Burton Watson. CoBCP

Light glows bright, The. The Parade. Liz Sohappy Bahe. NOVW

Light going out in the forehead, A. Swimming by Night. James Merrill. NYBP; SM; VGW

Light has come again and found. Ark of the Covenant. Louise Townsend Nicholl. ImOP

Light-hearted Fairy, The. *Unknown.* BoTP; FaPON

Light-hearted I walked into the valley wood. Conversion. T. E. Hulme. FaBoMo; OxBSP

Light Hotel. Peter Redgrove. PoE

Light-House Keeper's White-Mouse, The. John Ciardi. PDV

Light in Darkness. Mary E. Tucker. CBWP-1

Light, in light breezes and a favoring sun. Watching Tennis. John Heath-Stubbs. Son

Light in my heart, O Saviour, is Thy heart, The. A Poem to the Heart of Jesus. Teig Gaelach O'Sullivan, *tr. by* Thomas Kinsella. TIRV

Light in the Window, The. C. L. Erickson. PWR

Light in the window seemed perpetual, The. The Room above the Square. Stephen Spender. NOBE

Light into the olive entered. After Greece. James Merrill. CAPP; NOBA; NYBP

Light is a distant world. Touching. Christopher Gilbert. MAYP

Light is around the petals, and behind them. Looking at Some Flowers. Robert Bly. NaP; NOBA

Light is burning late, A. Herbert Street Revisited. John Montague. CIP; FaBCIP; IPY

Light is excessive, The. Revolution in Summertime. René Daumal, *tr. by* Michael Benedikt. POS

Light is like a spider, The. Tattoo. Wallace Stevens. LiTA

Light is on in my father's study, A. Working late. Louis Stimson. DiL; PBCV

Light is on my body also, The. Lilith. Linda Gregg. WPOW

Light Is Sweet, The. Bible, *O.T. Fr.* Ecclesiastes, XI: 7. FaPON

Light is the inside, The. Girl Powdering Her Neck. Cathy Song. MAYP

Light-Keeper, The, *sel.* Robert Louis Stevenson.

"Brilliant kernel of the night, The." EBVV

Light keeps on breaking. Breaklight. Lucille Clifton. CAPP

Light lifts from the water. Basil Bunting. *Fr.* Briggflatts [An Autobiography], V. OAEL-2; PoPo

"Light, light, light, my little Scotch-ee." Little Scotch-ee. *Unknown.* AS

Light Listened. Theodore Roethke. MoAmPo

Light little zephyr came flitting, A. Morning Compliments. Sydney Dayre. OxBChV

Light looks from a dazzled leaf. Dazzle. Dorothy Roberts. NOBC

Light may be had for nothing. Little Candle. Carl Sandburg. GoYe

Light mist, then dense fog. Li Ch'ing-chao, *tr. by* Kenneth Rexroth. BoWoP

"Light! more light! the shadows deepen." Let the Light Enter. Frances E. W. Harper. PoNe

Light—My Word. Moyshe-Leyb Halpern, *tr. fr. Yiddish by* John Hollander. PeBMYV

Light now meets, The. Outside. Robert Creeley. CAPP

Light of Asia, The, *sel.* Sir Edwin Arnold.

"Painted streets alive with hum of noon, The." OBTV

Light of dim mornings; shield from heat and cold. To Duty. Thomas Wentworth Higginson. AA

Light of dimmed stars goes on, The. The Life of Hard Times. Joshua Tan Pai, *tr. by* Yishai Tobin. VWA

Light of evening, Lissadell, The. In Memory of Eva Gore-Booth and Con Markiewicz. W. B. Yeats. FaBoPV; MoAB; NoAM; OAEL-2; OBMV; OxBTC

Light of Faith, The. Edgar Dupree. BLRP

Light of four suns, five moons, The. May I Be Beautiful. *Malay Oral Tradition, tr. by* W. W. Skeat. WTO

Light of Judea. Claude Vigée, *tr. fr. French.* VWA

Light of Life, The. "Hugh MacDiarmid." CMoP

Light of Love, The. John Hay. AnAmPo

Light of Other Days, The. Thomas Moore. *See* Oft, in the Stilly Night.

Light of our cigarettes, The. Pastel: Masks and Faces. Arthur Symons. NOBVV

Light of spring, The. Alice Duer Miller. AA

Light of Stars, The. William Henry Furness. *See* Slowly, by God's hand unfurled.

Light of the Blade, The. André du Bouchet, *tr. fr. French by* Paul Auster. RHTwFP

Light of the Harem [*or* Haram], The. Thomas Moore. *Fr.* Lalla Rookh, The Story of the Sultana Nourmahal. EnRP; TEP

Light of the moon that crosses the Plain of Heaven, The. Teika, *tr. fr. Japanese by* Hiroaki Sato. *Fr.* Eighty-four Tanka. FCEI

Light of the World, The. B. Alquit, *tr. fr. Yiddish by* Howard Schwartz. VWA

Light of the World. John Samuel Bewley Monsell. TrPWD

Light on his pins. Roethke Plain. John Malcolm Brinnin. TAP

Light on his thigh was like, The. The King of the Cats is Dead. Peter Porter. NoAM

Light on the Tower of David, light on the Church of St. Mary. Yehuda Amichai, *tr. fr. Hebrew by* Warren Bargad *and* Stanley F. Chyet. *Fr.* Jerusalem 1967, 3. IP

Light opens its eyes, The. Futile Rhetoric No. 1. Park Je-chun, *tr. by* Koh Chang-soo. ACKP

Light or Sheade. William Barnes. NOBVV

Light Passages, The. Debora Greger. MAYP

Light passes, The. Evening. Hilda Doolittle ("H. D."). CMoP; FaBoMo; VGW; WPE

Light pink, The. Saito Mokichi, *tr. by* Geoffrey Bownas *and* Anthony Thwaite. PeBJV

Light projected lifetimes ago. Telescope. Sydney Lea. BLA

Light pulling away from trees, The. Distance. Peter Everwine. NNaP

Light rustle of rain laid down now, A. Afterglow. Jack Butler. MT

Light sails set and swelling breach the clearing evening sky. Crossing the River at Kuan-yin Gate after Rain. Wang Shih-chen, *tr. by* Daniel Bryant. WFTU

Light seen suddenly in the storm, snow, A. Melancholia. Robert Bly. NoP

Light Shining Out of Darkness. Jane Borthwick. BLRP

Light Shining out of Darkness. William Cowper. EaLo; EBEV; EnRP; FaBoCh; FaFP; FPL; HeIP; LiTB; NOBE; NOCV; NOEC; NoP; PoEL-3; PWR; SeCePo; TOF; TrGrPo; WGRP

(God Moves in a Mysterious Way.) ELP; FiP

Light, so low upon earth. Marriage Morning. Tennyson. GBL

Light stands over me, The. Descartes at Daybreak. Aidan Carl Mathews. CIP

Light, sun, open air. The Engineer. João Cabral de Melo Neto, *tr. by* William Jay Smith. CT

Light That Came, The. Lucille Clifton. GeTw

Light That Failed, The, *sel.* Kipling.

Mother o' Mine. FaFP; WBLP

Light that fills thy house at morn, The. The Gifts of God. Jones Very. AA

Light that labored to an early fall, The. The Lake. Louis O. Coxe. NYBP

Light, that out of the west looked back once more. Night Thoughts in Age. John Hall Wheelock. NYBP

Light the candle I will return. Near. Abba Kovner, tr. by Shirley Kaufman. VWA

Light the Festive Candles. Aileen Fisher. RHPC

Light the fire so I can see in the mirror of the flames. The Will of a Man Dying in Exile. Samih al-Qasim, tr. by Abdullah al-Udhari. MPAW

Light the first light of evening, as in a room. Final Soliloquy of the Interior Paramour. Wallace Stevens. HAP; HCAP; LCAP

Light the first of eight tonight. Light the Festive Candles. Aileen Fisher. RHPC

Light the Lamps Up, Lamplighter! Eleanor Farjeon. CH

Light under the Door. Marilyn Nelson Waniek. MAYP

Light up My world for Me. God to Man. Unknown, tr. fr. Hebrew. Fr. The Talmud. TrJP

Light up thy homes, Columbia. Illumination for Victories in Mexico. "Grace Greenwood." PAH

Light wake early in this house. Various Wakings. Vincent Buckley. PoAu-2

Light was burning very dim, The. In the Night. Elizabeth Madox Roberts. WSC

Light white, a disgrace, an ink spot, a rosy charm, A. A Petticoat. Gertrude Stein. Fr. Tender Buttons. TTTS

Light-winged Smoke, Icarian Bird. Henry David Thoreau. Fr. Walden, ch. 13. NOBA; TAP

(Smoke.) AA; AWP; HeIP; NoP; OxBA

Light Woman's Song, The. Judith Johnson Sherwin. TAP

Light Year, The. John Ridland. OFD

Light you down, light you down, love Henry, she said. Young Hunting. Unknown. FaBoBa

Light young man lay with a lighter woman, A. On Tom Holland and Nell Cotton. Unknown. FaBoEE

Lightening/ is the future brightening. Mabrak. "Bongo Jerry." PBCV

Lighter. Sargon Boulus, tr. fr. Arabic by Sargon Boulus and Alistair Elliot. MAP

Lighter than dandelion down. Silkweed. Philip Henry Savage. AA

Lighthearted William. William Carlos Williams. SO

Lighthouse, The. Marjorie Wilson. BoTP

Lighthouse in Maine, A. Derek Mahon. FaBCIP; OBTV

Lighthouse in the Night. Alfonsina Storni, tr. fr. Spanish by Aliki and Willis Barnstone. BoWoP

Lighthouse Invites the Storm, The. Malcolm Lowry. NOBC

Lighthouses. Dorothy Wellesley. WPE

Lighting a Fire. X. J. Kennedy. TSS

Lighting a spill late in the afternoon. A Winter Talent. Donald Davie. NePoEA-2; OAEL-2

Lighting the Colony. Steve Rasnic Tem. BWV

Lighting the Night Sky. Kenneth O. Hanson. FYAP

Lightless, unholy, eldritch thing. The Bat. Ruth Pitter. FM

Lightly clad, on tiptoe, the little rain has just run into the garden. The Approaching Silence. Gyula Illyés, tr. by William Jay Smith. MHuP

Lightly forsaking/ the spring mist as it rises. Seeing the Returning Geese. Lady Ise, tr. by Etsuko Terasaki and Irma Brandeis. BoWoP

Lightly stepped a yellow star. Emily Dickinson. MoAmPo; MoShBr; OxBA

Lightness Remembered. Nancy Willard. LCAP

Lightning. D. H. Lawrence. CMoP; MoAB; MoBrPo

Lightning. Tamehide, tr. fr. Japanese by Steven D. Carter. WFTW

Lightning: a man walking. Natsume Seibi, tr. fr. Japanese by Hiroaki Sato. Fr. Twenty-seven Hokku. FCEI

Lightning: again the sky's morning glow. Kikaku, tr. fr. Japanese by Hiroaki Sato. Fr. Thirty-three Hokku. FCEI

Lightning and thunder, The. A Baby-Sermon. George Macdonald. OxBChV

Lightning Bug. Robert Morgan. GeTw

Lightning Bugs. Ernest Slyman. SoTCo

Lightning Flash, The. Unknown. AmFP

Lightning flashes, The! Basho, tr. by Earl Miner. SoSe

Lightning flashes soar like rain before your eyes. When You're Not a Poet. Yona Wallach, tr. by Warren Bargad and Stanley F. Chyet. IP

Lightning gets to be terrifying. Kaya Shirao, tr. fr. Japanese by Hiroaki Sato. Fr. Twenty-one Hokku. FCEI

Lightning gleam, A. Basho, tr. by Harold G. Henderson. SoSe

Lightning: going in the dark side. Basho, tr. fr. Japanese by Burton Watson. Fr. Seventy-six Hokku. FCEI

Lightning heat of heart's anguish filled the cloud, The. Asadullah Khan Ghalib, tr. by Ahmed Ali. GoT

Lightning hits the roof. Woman to Man. Ai. NoAM

Lightning in my hand. Basho, tr. fr. Japanese by Burton Watson. Fr. Seventy-six Hokku. FCEI

Lightning in the clouds! Basho. WeW

Lightning: in the east yesterday. Kikaku, tr. fr. Japanese by Hiroaki Sato. Fr. Thirty-three Hokku. FCEI

Lightning is a yellow fork, The. Emily Dickinson. InPK

Lightning Rod Salesman, The. M. L. Hester. CRP

Lightning scratched our sugar maple, blood. Injured Maple. Ronald G. Everson. NOBC

Lightning spills a noise. Buson, tr. fr. Japanese by Hiroaki Sato. Fr. Eighty-seven Hokku. FCEI

Lightning-stricken giant gum, The. The Wood-Swallows. "Fiona Macleod." Fr. Australian Transcripts. FM

Lightning struck, The. Lightning. Tamehide, tr. by Steven D. Carter. WFTW

Lightning Victory. René Char, tr. fr. French by W. S. Merwin. RHTwFP

Light'ood Fire, The. John Henry Boner. AA

Lights, The. J. J. Bell. BoTP

Lights among Redwood. Thom Gunn. OBTV

Lights are burning. Bus Stop. Donald Justice. CAPP; FYAP; LCAP

Lights from the parlor and kitchen shone out, The. Escape at Bedtime. Robert Louis Stevenson. TrGrPo

Light's glittering morn bedecks the sky. Hymn for Easter Morn. John Mason Neale. TrCP

Lights in the farmhouses, The. A Valley Called Moonshine. Sam Hunt. ATNZ

Lights in the Sky are Stars, The, sel. Kenneth Rexroth. Heart of Herakles, The. NU

Lights in the theater fail, The. The long racks. A Dancer's Life. Donald Justice. LCAP

Lights, lights/ and the lament of tired ships. A Night at a Port. Munir Niazi, tr. by Mahmood Jamal. PBMUP

Lights of a hundred cities are fed by its midnight power, The. The River of Stars. Alfred Noyes. OnMSP

Lights of Dublin, The. Patrick O'Connor. TIRV

Lights out. Child's Blackness. Jean Follain, tr. by Keith Waldrop. RHTwFP

Lights out. How to Meditate. Jack Kerouac. PoM

Lights Out. Edward Thomas. BrPo; Mes; MMA; NOBE; OBD

Lights out! And a prow turned towards the South. The Race of the Oregon. John James Meehan. PAH

Lights out. Shades up. Girl in a Nightgown. Wallace Stevens. OxBA

Lights were drowned in fog, The. Mustafa Zaidi, tr. fr. Urdu by Mahmood Jamal. Fr. Renewal, II. PBMUP

Lights were red, refused to change, The. Hold-up. Louis MacNeice. FaBCIP

Like/ treasure hidden in the ground. Mahadevi, tr. by A. K. Ramanujan. WPOW

Like a Beach. Harvey Shapiro. VWA

Like a Bird Dead in the Stream. Esther Raab, tr. fr. Hebrew by Bernhard Frank. MHeP

Like a bird in the butcher's palm you flutter in my hand. Revolt. Rachel, tr. by Robert Friend. VWA

Like a boatman. Yoshitada, tr. by Geoffrey Bownas and Anthony Thwaite. PeBJV

Like a bolt of silk, the rippled course of this southern river. Evening Scene at Twin Forests. Chin Nung, tr. by Jonathan Chaves. CoBLCP

Like a bread without the spreadin'. Smile. Unknown. BLPA; WBLP

Like a bubbling stream. Wakayama Bokusui, tr. by Geoffrey Bownas and Anthony Thwaite. PeBJV

Like a bullet. A Knife All Blade. João Cabral de Melo Neto, tr. by Galway Kinnell. ATCBP

Like a bulwark against fate. At Rest in the Blast. Marianne Moore. MoAB; MoAmPo

Like a child, down onto her heart he fell there. Strangers. Mani Leib, tr. by John Hollander. PeBMYV

Like a child the wise porpoise. The Zoo. John Logan. LCAP

Like a cloud haunted by the moon. Amy Károlyi, tr. fr. Hungarian. Fr. The Third House, I. OV, tr. by Laura Schiff. ("Like moon-hunted clouds, the two.") MHuP, tr. by Edwin Morgan.

Like a cloud the feathered albatross. Haka: The Feathered Albatross. Muru Walters, tr. by the author. PeNZ

Like a convalescent, I took the hand. Seamus Heaney. Fr. Station Island, XII. FaBoPV; NoAM; TOF

Like a coy maiden, ease, when courted most. Ease. William Cowper. Fr. The Task, I. TEP

Like a crumpled paper cutout. Days Ago. Dianne Hai-Jew. BrSi

Like a cuckoo. Cuckoo. Roland Jooris, tr. by Theo Hermans. DuIn

Like a deserted beach. The Man Closing Up. Donald Justice. CoAP

Like a dog before the dog-catcher's sling. Conscience. Melech Ravitch, *tr.* by Keith Bosley. VWA

Like a dragon you have filled the land. Inanna and An. Enheduanna, *tr.* by Aliki *and* Willis Barnstone. BoWoP

Like a drifter returning after thirty-one years. From Old Mrs. Mo of Heng Yang: A Letter to My Son, Lo Fu. Yip Wai-lim, *tr.* by Dominic Cheung. IFON

Like a drummer's brush. Rain. Emanuel diPasquale. InPK

Like a dry fish flung inland far from shore. Lost Anchors. E. A. Robinson. CMoP

Like a Field Waiting. Raquel Chalfi, *tr. fr. Hebrew* by Myra Glazer Schotz. VWA

Like a flat sea. Population. George Oppen. PoA

Like a flight of arrows the wind. Stormy Night in Autumn. Chu Shu-chen, *tr.* by Kenneth Rexroth. BoWoP

Like a forsaken theatre art thou. By Cobequid Bay. Alexander Louis Fraser. CaP

Like a fruit wine with earth. Cider and Vesalius. John Peck. AmPA

Like a gaunt, scraggly pine. Lincoln. John Gould Fletcher. MoAmPo

Like a gondola of green scented fruits. Images. Richard Aldington. MoBrPo; PoA

Like a great rock, far out at sea. Lady Sanuki, *tr. fr. Japanese* by Curtis Hidden Page. *Fr.* Hyaku-Nin-Isshu. AWP

Like a hidden spring. My Love-Song. Else Lasker-Schüler, *tr.* by Jethro Bithell. TrJP

Like a hot stone your cock weighs on mine, young man. Long Lines: Youth and Age. Paul Goodman. GLP; PeHV

Like a hound with nose to the trail. Michaelmas. Norman Nicholson. MoBrPo

Like a hungry fledgeling that watches and hears. Vittoria da Colonna, *tr.* by Lynne Lawner. PBWP

Like a hunted deer. Relations. Orerulavanar, *tr.* by A. K. Ramanujan. PLW

Like [*or* Lyke] a huntsman after weary chase [*or* chace]. Spenser. *Fr.* Amoretti, LXVII. GBL; HeIP; NAEL-1; NoP; PoE; PoEL-1; SeCePo; Son; TrGrPo

Like a king on a surly island. A Thousand Nights and Days. Cees Nooteboom, *tr.* by Peter Nijmeijer. DuIn

Like a kinsman. The Tollund Man. Hugo Claus, *tr.* by Theo Hermans. DuIn

Like a ladder I lean over and put. The Winter's Glance. Tomas Tranströmer, *tr.* by Samuel Charters. AnAn

Like a lit-up Christmas Tree. The Lover and the Syringa-Bush. Herman Melville. AnAmPo; OBAL

Like a little boat pushing through reeds. *Unknown. Fr.* Manyo Shu. FCEI

Like a lizard in the sun, though not scuttling. The Laureate. Robert Graves. BIrV; FaBoTw; OBSV

Like a lone Arab, old and blind. Love's Apparition and Evanishment. Samuel Taylor Coleridge. EnRP

Like a long line of high-flying herons. A Parade. Perunkunrur Kilar, *tr.* by A. K. Ramanujan. PLW

Like a long step. Dance. Haim Guri, *tr.* by Warren Bargad *and* Stanley F. Chyet. IP

Like a loose island on the wide expanse. To a Deaf and Dumb Little Girl. Hartley Coleridge. PoEL-4

Like a mad lion, like a wild bull. The Race. Nuala Ni Dhomhnaill, *tr.* by Michael Hartnett. CIP

Like a madwoman and almost alone. Interior Landscape. Gloria Fuertes. BoWoP, *tr.* by Willis Barnstone

Like a man pleading for his life. The Means of Production. Michael Hofmann. NPo

Like a map blanketing a bed. Patches of Sky. Debora Greger. MAYP

Like a mountain stream whose rapids are blocked. Teika, *tr. fr. Japanese* by Hiroaki Sato. *Fr.* A Compendium of Good Tanka. FCEI

Like a mountain whirlwind. Sappho, *tr.* by Willis Barnstone. BoWoP

Like a Mourningless Child. Kenneth Patchen. MoAmPo

Like a pair of companionable porcupines. Baucis and Philemon. Katherine Hoskins. PoA

Like a passion-plant pattern. Narihira, *tr.* by Geoffrey Bownas *and* Anthony Thwaite. PeBJV

Like a Pearl. Hayim Naggid, *tr. fr. Hebrew* by Shlomo Vinner *and* Howard Schwartz. VWA

Like a private eye she searches. The Jealous Wife. Vernon Scannell. ErPo

Like a quetzal plume, a fragrant flower. Friendship. *Unknown, tr.* by John Bierhorst. ILY

Like a rainstorm, he said, the braided colors. Worsening Situation. John Ashbery. NOBA

Like a ravaged sea/ this bed. Lady Ise, *tr.* by Etsuko Terasaki *and* Irma Brandeis. BoWoP

Like a rich has-been. The Second Winery. Hsin Mu, *tr.* by Dominic Cheung. IFON

Like a river she was. The Memory. Robert Creeley. CAPP; VGW

Like a rose, a scar. The Last Enemy. Ishihara Yoshiro, *tr.* by Hiroaki Sato. FCEI

Like a round loaf, that's how small you were. To the Newborn. Judit Tóth, *tr.* by Laura Schiff. MHuP; WPOW

Like a sailor in the shrouds he slipped over the tropic of Cancer. Anges Sont Blancs, Les. George Seferis, *tr.* by Edmund Keeley *and* Philip Sherrard. VMG

Like a scared rabbit running over and. Jack Spicer. *Fr.* Graphemics, 1. VGW

Like a serpent that ascends the rivers. Hatefully Poetry My Love. André Frénaud, *tr.* by Serge Gavronsky. RHTwFP

Like a Shabbos Goy. Elsewhere. Linda Pastan. VWA

Like a she-camel with a large bell. Fortitude. *Somali Oral Tradition, tr.* by B. W. Andrzejewski *and* I. M. Lewis. WTO

Like a Shower of Rain. Quintus Ennius, *tr. fr. Latin* by John Wight. *Fr.* Annales. WaaP

Like a silkworm weaving. Mahadevi, *tr.* by A. K. Ramanujan. PBWP

Like a single wall stretching on athwart the sky. Written at the Year's End, While Visiting Chien-ling. Ch'ü Ta-chün, *tr.* by Paul W. Kroll. WFTU

Like a skein of loose silk blown against a wall. The Garden. Ezra Pound. AWP; HeIP; LiTA; MoAB; MoAmPo; NIP; NoP; OxBSP; PPP; SOTW; TwCP

Like a sledge through snow. Erik Satie. J. Bernlef, *tr.* by Theo Hermans. DuIn

Like a small gray/ coffee-pot. The Gray Squirrel. Humbert Wolfe. GoJo; MoBrPo

Like a spider through ink, someone says, mocking: see it. Arabic Script. Anthony Thwaite. OBTV

Like a sweet apple reddening on the high. Sappho, *tr.* by Willis Barnstone. BoWoP

Like a throng of warriors. Yakamochi. *Fr.* Manyo Shu. FCEI

Like a tower above the tortuous. The Pilgrimage to Testour. Ryvel, *tr.* by Edouard Roditi. VWA

Like a trapped bird. First Day at Boarding School. Prunella Power. Mes

Like a veiled dream thy memory comes. To a Loved One of Other Days. Matilda Caroline Edwards. PWR

Like a voyeur. The Maker. Gyula Illyés, *tr.* by Daniel Hoffman. MHuP

Like a weak-minded scout. Ishikawa Takuboku, *tr. fr. Japanese* by Hiroaki Sato. *Fr.* Forty-seven Tanka in Three Lines. FCEI

Like a Whisper. Ethan Ayer. GoYe

Like a wild cherry. Tsurayuki, *tr. fr. Japanese* by Burton Watson. *Fr.* Kokin Shu. FCEI

Like a Woman. Uri Zvi Greenberg, *tr. fr. Hebrew* by Robert Mezey *and* Ben Zion Gold. VWA

Like a woman you've longed to make love to, and finally did. Pennsylvania Winter Indian 1974. Harold Littlebird. VoR

Like a Young Levite. Osip Mandelstam, *tr. fr. Russian* by Daniel Weissbort. VWA

Like Abraham and Sarah by the trees of Mamre. Song at the Skirts of Heaven. Uri Zvi Greenberg, *tr.* by Zvi Jagendorf. VWA

Like Achilles you had a goddess for mother. On Looking into E. V. Rieu's Homer. Patrick Kavanagh. NOIV

Like air on skin, coolness of yachts at mooring. Yachts on the Nile. Bernard Spencer. NoAM

Like all visitors my son disturbed me. Speaking of Gabriel. Rosario Castellanos, *tr.* by Kate Flores. DMH

Like an Adventurous Seafarer Am I. Michael Drayton. *Fr.* Idea, I. Son

Like an animal on all fours. Occupation. Michael Guttenbrunner, *tr.* by Beth Bjorklund. CoAuP

Like an army of locusts. Reflections. Constance E. Studer. TSM

Like an arrow shot/ To Death from Birth. Wine. Micah Joseph Lebensohn, *tr.* by A. M. Klein. TrJP

Like an elephant. Mahadevi, *tr.* by A. K. Ramanujan. PBWP

Like an home-reared animal in a quiet nook. King Pellam's Launde. David Jones. *Fr.* In Parenthesis, IV. OAEL-2

"So thus he sorrowed till it was day." NoAM

Like an invader, not a guest. Winter's Troops. Charles Cotton. *Fr.* Winter. ChTr

Like an Object. Gerrit Kouwenaar, *tr. fr. Dutch* by Koos Schuur. DuIn

Like an Old Proud King in a Parable. A. J. M. Smith. OBCV

Like an Orchid in Deep Muddy Water. Nilene O. A. Foxworth. AIW

Like any grey old-timer droving dreams. The Town. David Rowbotham. PoAu-2

Like any of us—you or me. Old Man Pot. Lyon Sharman. CaP

Like Any Other Man. Gregory Orr. FF

Like as a flamelet blanketed in smoke. After. W. E. Henley. *Fr.* In Hospital, VI. BrPo

Like as a ship, that through the ocean wyde. Spenser. *Fr.* The Faerie Queene, VI, 12. MOS

Like as the armed knight. The Ballad Which Anne Askew Made and Sang When She Was in Newgate. Anne Askew. WPE

Like as the Bay, that bears on branches sweet. In Praise of His Lady. Matthew Grove. *Fr.* Pelops and Hippodamia. EIL

Like as the bird in the cage enclosed. Sir Thomas Wyatt. SiPS

Like as the damask rose you see. Man's Mortality. *At. to* Simon Wastell. *Fr.* Microbiblion. FaBoCh (Verses of Man's Mortalitie.) OBS

Like as the divers-fretchled Butterfly. The Muse Reviving. Sir John Davies. SiPS

Like as the doleful dove delights alone to be. No Pains Comparable to His Attempt. *Unknown.* PBBP

Like as the Dove. Sir Philip Sidney. SiPS

Like as the dumb solsequium, with care ourcome. The Solsequium. Alexander Montgomerie. GoTS; NoP

Like as the fountaine of all light created. Incarnatio Est Maximum Donum Dei. William Alabaster. MePo

Like as the Lark. Thomas William Parsons. AA

Like as the rage of rain. The Uncertain State of a Lover. *Unknown.* EIL

Like as the swan towards her death. Sir Thomas Wyatt. SiPS

Like as the tide that comes from th' Ocean main. Spenser. *Fr.* The Faerie Queene, IV, 3. HoPM

"Like as the waves make towards the pebbled shore." Shakespeare. *Fr.* Sonnets, LX. ChTr; EBEV; EIL; FPL; LiTB; NIP; NOBE; OBSC; PeHV; PoRA; Son; TEP; UnPo (Like as the Waves.) FaFP (Revolutions.) GTBS; GTBS-P

Like Attracts Like. Emmett Williams. WeW

Like Barbarossa's beard bright with oil. Boys in October. Irving Layton. OBCV

Like battered old millhands, they stand in the orchard. Old Apple Trees. W. D. Snodgrass. CAPP; FYAP; SV

Like Birds of a Feather. Ralph Schomberg. *Fr.* The Judgment of Paris. TrJP

Like birds when first light breaks. Children Waking: Indian Hill Station. Ralph Nixon Currey. PeSA

Like blood, like good, and like age. *Unknown.* FaBoUs

Like broken-down actors who never made it. In the Tavern. Zishe Landau, *tr. by* Irving Feldman. PeBMYV

Like burnt-out torches by a sick man's bed. The Grave of Shelley. Oscar Wilde. OBTV

Like butterflies but lately come. Beautiful Creatures Brief as These. Douglas G. Jones. MoCV

Like Chaff. Jacob Glatstein, *tr. fr. Yiddish by* Benjamin *and* Barbara Harshav *and* Kathryn Helle. AYP

Like chapters of prophecy my days burn, in all the revelations. With My God, the Smith. Uri Zvi Greenberg, *tr. by* Robert Mezey *and* Ben Zion Gold. VWA

Like Chopin, not even showing my puss. Impromptu. Márton Kalász, *tr. by* Jascha Kessler. FOC

Like crystal through the mountains. Kanamura. *Fr.* Manyo Shu. PeBJV

Like cutting the dry rot out of a potato. Dark Conclusions. Ruth Stone. BoWoP

Like David. Gabriel Preil, *tr. fr. Hebrew by* Laya Firestone. VWA

Like divers, we ourselves must make the jump. The Springboard. Adrienne Rich. ASP

Like dives in the deeps of hell. Save the Boys. Frances E. W. Harper. PWR

Like Dogs. Amryl Johnson. WS

Like Dolmens Round My Childhood, the Old People. John Montague. EBEV; FaBCIP; IPY

Like dreamy youngsters. We, of the Singing Swords. Jacob Glatstein, *tr. by* Benjamin *and* Barbara Harshav. AYP

Like dust swirling. Takahama Kyoshi, *tr. by* Geoffrey Bownas *and* Anthony Thwaite. PeBJV

Like Etna's dread volcano see the ample forge. The Anchorsmiths. Charles Dibdin. NOEC

Like Feathers. Gabriel Preil, *tr. fr. Yiddish by* Grace Schulman. PeBMYV

Like fire-flies that the peasant on the hill. Dante, *tr. fr. Italian by* Laurence Binyon. *Fr.* Divina Commedia: Inferno, XXVI. Prf

Like Flowers We Spring. *Unknown.* EIL

Like foxgloves in the school of the grass moon. The Flower Master. Medbh McGuckian. FaBCIP

Like Galen even him. Elegy for Aisha. Abd al-Wahhab al-Bayyati, *tr. by* Sargon Boulus *and* Christopher Middleton. MAP

Like Ghosts of Eagles. Robert Francis. GOA; LCAP

Like Goethe at Weimar you ignore everything. Roman Epigram. Giovanni Giudici, *tr. by* Lawrence R. Smith. NItP

Like gossamer/ On the swift breath of morn, the vessel flew. Ever as We Sailed. Shelley. *Fr.* The Revolt of Islam, XII. SeCePo

Like green fruit, many dawns. Hitomaro. Anzai Hitoshi, *tr. by* Hiroaki Sato. FCEI

Like gript stick. The Sermon. Richard Hughes. OBMV

Like Groping Fingers. Abraham Sutskever, *tr. fr. Yiddish by* Joseph Leftwich. TrJP

Like Gulliver. Nina Cassian, *tr. fr. Rumanian by* Willis Barnstone *and* Matei Calinescu. BoWoP; VWA

Like Hamlet you began at thirty handing out. The Comedy of Art: Henri de Toulouse Lautrec. Richard Howard. AnAn

Like icing on a cake. Sunset. Mafika Pascal Gwala. WMBCH

Like It or Not. Bill Simpson. CowP

Like Jonah in the green belly of the whale. Emily Carr. Wilfred Watson. MoCV; NOBC; OBCV

Like lamp of intricate stained glass which hangs. From Ancient Fangs. Peter Viereck. LiTA

Like leaves on trees the race of man is found. Homer, *tr. fr. Greek by* Pope. *Fr.* The Iliad, VI. OBVE

Like liquid gold the wheat-field lies. A Dakota Wheat-Field. Hamlin Garland. OBCA

Like Lise, moreover, my mother was white. The Black Man's Son. Oswald Durand, *tr. by* Edna Worthley Underwood. TTY

Like lotus eaters none refused the fare. Toast for the Original Survivors. Kathryn Rantala. BWV

Like Loving Chekhov. Denise Levertov. InPS

Like many a one, when you had gold. The Old Story. Marcus Argentarius, *tr. by* E. A. Robinson. AWP

Like marble, nude, against the purple sky. The Diver. John Frederic Herbin. CaP

Like [*or* Lyke] Memnons rock, touched [*or* rocke toucht] with the rising sun[ne]. Giles Fletcher the Elder. *Fr.* Licia, XLVII. AAS; FF (Sonnet: "Like Memnon's rock, touched with the rising sun.") EIL

"Like men riding." Nelly Trim. Sylvia Townsend Warner. ErPo; MoAB; MoBrPo

Like milk. What She Said. Kollan Alici, *tr. by* A. K. Ramanujan. PLW

Like moon-hunted clouds, the two. Amy Károlyi. *See* Third House, The: Like a cloud haunted by the moon.

Like moss on water. What She Said. Paranar, *tr. by* A. K. Ramanujan. PLW

Like most, one way or another, ours. Marriage on a Mountain Ridge. Stewart Conn. PoSH

Like Mother, like Son. Margaret Johnston Grafflin. *See* To My Son.

Like mourners filing into church at a funeral. Trees on the Calais Road. Edmund Blunden. BrPo

Like musical instruments. Dispersion and Convergence. Tom Clark. UL

Like new waters that form nightly. Blessing of the Firstborn. Howard Schwartz. VWA

Like Noah's Weary Dove. William Augustus Mühlenberg. AH

Like Odysseus under the ram. Archilochus, *tr. by* Guy Davenport. OBVE

Like one who'in her third widdowhood doth professe. To Mr. Rowland Woodward. John Donne. MePo

Like our father Abraham. With My Grandfather. Zelda, *tr. by* Marcia Falk. VWA

Like pianos advancing on ice, each moment's. Trumpet Voluntary. Paul Hoover. UL

Like Plump Birds along the Shore. Lyn Hejinian. LP

Like plump green floor plans. Rotation. Julian Bond. FF

Like prize wine. After Sin, Penitence. F. Richard Thomas. SoTCo

Like Rachel. Dahlia Ravikovich, *tr. fr. Hebrew by* Warren Bargad *and* Stanley F. Chyet. IP

Like rain falling. The Camel. Al-Munsif al-Wahaybi, *tr. by* Salma Khadra Jayyusi *and* Naomi Shihab Nye. MAP

Like rain it sounded till it curved. Emily Dickinson. RB

Like right now it's the summertime. The Old O. O. Blues. Al Young. NPGG

Like Ripples on the Water. *Gond Oral Tradition, tr. by* V. Elwin *and* S. Hivale. WTO

Like Rousseau. Amiri Baraka. PoA

Like ruminating cattle on the sands. Women Damned. Baudelaire, *tr. by* Joanna Richardson. PeHV

Like Sand. Natan Zach, *tr. fr. Hebrew by* Warren Bargad *and* Stanley F. Chyet. IP

Like shuttles fleet the clouds, and after. Oxford Bells. Gerard Manley Hopkins. FaBoPP

Like Sieur Montaigne's distinction. Golfers. Irving Layton. SD

Like silver dew are the tears of love. A. E. Coppard. OBMV

Like small curled feathers, white and soft. While Shepherds Watched Their Flocks by Night. Margaret Deland. GN

Like Smoke. Mririda n'Ait Attika, *tr. fr. French vers. by* Daniel Halpern *and* Paula Paley. PBWP

Like snakes of golden autumn fire. Nevada. Lawrence Gurney. GoYe

Like snooker balls thrown on the table's faded green. A Poet's Progress. Michael Hamburger. NePoEA

Like Snow on the Alps. Celia Dropkin, *tr. fr. Yiddish by* Grace Schulman. PeBMYV

Like some ailing leaf. Teika, *tr. fr. Japanese by* Hiroaki Sato. *Fr.* Eighty-four Tanka. FCEI

Like some kind of ruin, but domed. In a Museum Cabinet. May Swenson. WSC

Like some school master, kind in being stern. Unanswered Prayers. Ella Wheeler Wilcox. WGRP

Like something very precious, he holds it in his hands. A Question of Art. Deborah Kendrick. TSM

Like South Sea stock, expressions rise and fall. Time's Changes. James Bramston. *Fr.* The Art of Politics. NOEC

Like Stephen Vincent Benét, I have fallen in love with American names. Ill Met by Zenith. Ogden Nash. NYBP

Like summer's first rain drops are the candle's waxen tears. Mirza Mohammad Rafi Sauda, *tr. by* Ahmed Ali. GoT

Like tall men with a battering-plank—the colt. Letter from Underground. Ronald G. Everson. MoCV

Like that again. Satie. Jan G. Elburg, *tr. by* André Lefevere. DuIn

Like that dying woman in Mexico. If. Patrick Lane. NOBC

Like the beautiful bodies of those who died before growing old. Longings. C. P. Cavafy, *tr. by* Edmund Keeley *and* Philip Sherrard. VMG

Like the bole of a fallen mountain tree. The Corpse. Salvador Díaz Mirón, *tr. by* Samuel Beckett. MexPo

Like the bubbles on the water. Hitomaro, *tr. fr. Japanese. Fr.* Manyo Shu. Ma

Like the cadence of an old love song. Child Life. Mary E. Tucker. CBWP-1

Like the crane whose cry. Lady Kasa, *tr. fr. Japanese. Fr.* Manyo Shu. FCEI

Like the crash of the thunder. Zionist Marching Song. Naphtali Herz Imber, *tr. by* Israel Zangwill. TrJP

Like the dark germs across the filter clean. Loss. Charles Madge. FaBoMo

Like the Eyes of Wolves. Nachum Yud, *tr. fr. Yiddish by* Joseph Leftwich. TrJP

Like the few ears salvaged. *Unknown. Fr.* Manyo Shu. PeBJV

Like the fey goose-girl in the enchanted wood. Horror. Henry Treece. EAS

Like the flash and roar near the clouds of heaven. *Unknown. Fr.* Manyo Shu. Ma

Like the foam on the ever-flowing Thinking River. Teika, *tr. fr. Japanese by* Hiroaki Sato. *Fr.* A Compendium of Good Tanka. FCEI

Like the Greeks, we believe that every well educated person should know. Me Too Boogie. Blaise Cendrars, *tr. by* Anselm Hollo. RHTwFP

Like the high fanning tufts on swift horses. What She Said ("Like the high fanning tufts on swift horses"). Orampokiyar, *tr. fr. Tamil by* A. K. Ramanujan. *Fr.* Five on the Riverside Cane, 4. PLW

Like the honeycomb dropping honey. Hildegard von Bingen, *tr. by* Patrick Diehl. WPOW

Like the huts. *Unknown. Fr.* Manyo Shu. FCEI

Like the Idalian Queen[e]. William Drummond of Hawthornden. ElL; ELP; GBL; InvP; NOBE; OAEL-1; OBEV; OBS; PoEL-2

Like the idle fingers of wind caressing the forehead of God. The Falling of the Snow. Raymond Souster. CaP

Like the leaves of kudzu vines. Kehi Shrine. Kagura, *tr. by* Hiroaki Sato. FCEI

Like the light snow. *Unknown, tr. fr. Japanese by* Burton Watson. *Fr.* Kokin Shu. FCEI

Like the orange-flowers that blow. Yakamochi. *Fr.* Manyo Shu. Ma

Like the pearl of dew. Lady Kasa. *Fr.* Manyo Shu. PeBJV

Like the red flame. Peyanar, *tr. fr. Tamil by* A. K. Ramanujan. *Fr.* Seven Said by the Foster-Mother, 4. PLW

Like the sails spread on the fishing-boats. *Unknown. Fr.* Manyo Shu. Ma

Like the Sea, Kisses. Vicente Aleixandre, *tr. fr. Spanish by* Perry Higman. LPSS

Like the sedge of Naniwa. Lady Otomo no Sakanoe. *Fr.* Manyo Shu. PeBJV

Like the silkworm in the cocoon. Hitomaro. *Fr.* Manyo Shu. Ma

Like the stalks of wheat in the fields. Heine, *tr. fr. German. Fr.* The North Sea. TrJP, *tr. by* Emma Lazarus.
(Epilog: "Like the ears of wheat in a wheat-field growing.") AWP, *tr. by* Louis Untermeyer.

Like the stench and smudge of the old dump-heap. Dream, Dump-Heap, and Civilization. Robert Penn Warren. NoP

Like the steps of footsore armies. Waiting for Death. Mordecai Gebirtig, *tr. by* Joseph Leftwich. TrJP

Like the sun frozen. Walls of Ice. Janet Campbell Hale. STE

Like the sweet apple which reddens upon the topmost bough. One Girl. Sappho, *tr. by* Dante Gabriel Rossetti. AWP

Like the tides' flood. *Unknown, tr. by* Kenneth Rexroth. UnAS

Like the Touch of Rain. Edward Thomas. BoLoP; EnLoPo; GBL

Like the tribes of Israel. Sherman's in Savannah. Oliver Wendell Holmes. PAH

Like the universe. Science as Art. Hugh Seidman. AmPA

Like the very gods in my sight is he. Sappho, *tr. by* Richmond Lattimore. WPOW

Like the White. Qasim Haddad, *tr. fr. Arabic by* Sharif Elmusa *and* Charles Doria. MAP

Like the white cloud on the green hill. Prince Yuhara. *Fr.* Manyo Shu. Ma

Like the white dewdrop that forms at the leaf-tip. Teika, *tr. fr. Japanese by* Hiroaki Sato. *Fr.* A Compendium of Good Tanka. FCEI

Like the white whale, born black, myself grows brighter. Pervigilium Veneris. Suzanne Noguere. PoA

Like the wife of the full moon, she rolls. Fat Mama at Swenson's. E. Castendyk Briefs. SoTCo

Like the yu'ub wood bell tied to gelded camels that are running away. Raage Ugaas, *tr. by* B. W. Andrzejewski *and* I. M. Lewis. OBD
(Poet's Lament on the Death of His Wife.) WTO

Like thee I once have stemm'd the sea of life. James Beattie. OBEV

Like This. Lajos Kassák, *tr. fr. Hungarian by* Edwin Morgan. MHuP

Like this I'll wait for you, my love. *Unknown. Fr.* Manyo Shu. FCEI

Like This Together. Adrienne Rich. VGW

Like those boats which are returning. Saigyo Hoshi, *tr. by* Arthur Waley. AWP

Like Those Sick Folks. Sir Philip Sidney. OxBSP

Like thousands, I took just pride and more than just. Reading Myself. Robert Lowell. HCAP; NAAL-2; TAP

Like tinkling gems, neither dewdrops nor tears stay. Teika, *tr. fr. Japanese by* Hiroaki Sato. *Fr.* Eighty-four Tanka. FCEI

Like to a baker's oven is the grave. Francis Jeffrey. FaBoEE
(Epitaph in Christ Church, Bristol, on Thomas Turner, Twice Master of the Company of Bakers.) OxBoLi
(In Christ Church, Bristol, on Thomas Turner, Twice Master of the Company of Bakers.) NBLV

Like to a Coin. Arlo Bates. AA

Like to a god he seems to me. Sappho. Catullus, *tr. by* William Ellery Leonard. AWP

Like to an hermit poor, in place obscure. *At. to* Sir Walter Ralegh. ElL
(Like to a Hermit Poor.) GBL

Like to Diana in her summer weed[e]. Doron's Description of Samela. Robert Greene. *Fr.* Menaphon. PoEL-2
(Samela.) ElL; GBL; NOBE; OBEV; OBSC

Like to the Arctic Needle. Francis Quarles. *Fr.* Emblems, V, 4. EBEV; NOCV; OAEL-1
(I Am My Beloved's, and His Desire Is towards Me.) OBS

Like to the clear in highest sphere. Rosaline. Thomas Lodge. *Fr.* Rosalynde; or Euphues' Golden Legacy. GTBS; GTBS-P; LiTB; OBEV
(Rosalind [*or* Rosalynde].) ElL; TrGrPo
(Rosalind's Description.) OBSC

Like to the damaske rose you see. Hos Ego Versiculos. Francis Quarles. *Fr.* Argalus and Parthenia. OBS, *See also* Man's Mortality, *sl. diff. vers. at. to* Simon Wastell, *fr.* Microbiblion.

Like to the falling of a star. Sic Vita. *At. to* Henry King. ELP; FF; FF; MePo; NOBE; OBS; OxBSP; SeCePo; SeCP
(Of Human Life.) TrGrPo

Like to the Grass That's Green Today. Peter Bulkeley the Younger. AH

Like to the leaf that falls. Epicedium. Horace L. Traubel. AA

Like to the marigold, I blushing close. Edward Taylor. *Fr.* Preparatory Meditations before My Approach to the Lord's Supper, III. SCAP

Like to the Thundering Tone. Richard Corbet. NA
(Nonsense.) FaBoNo

Like to these unmesurable montayns. Jacopo Sannazaro, tr. by Sir Thomas Wyatt. AAS
(Like to These Unmeasurable Mountains.) PoE

Like torn-up newsprint the nonchalant snow. 1894 in London. Charles Spear. ATNZ

Like trains of cars on tracks of plush. The Bee. Emily Dickinson. GN; MoAB; MoAmPo

Like trees buried in the shallows of Natori River. Teika, tr. fr. Japanese by Hiroaki Sato. Fr. A Compendium of Good Tanka. FCEI

Like truthless dreams, so are my joys expired. Farewell to the Court. Sir Walter Ralegh. OBSC; SiPS
(Like Truthless Dreams.) Son

Like two proud armies marching in the field. Unknown. OBSC
(Your Beauty and My Reason.) TrGrPo

Like two somnambulists we entered the dawn sun. Hunting for Blueberries. Thomas James. AmPA

Like Two Stones at the Bottom of a Slope. Yehuda Amichai, tr. fr. Hebrew by Bernhard Frank. MHeP

Like unto Them That Dream. Bible, O.T. See Psalms: Psalm CXXVI ("When the Lord brought back...").

Like Water down a Slope. Zalman Schneour, tr. fr. Hebrew by Harry H. Fein. TrJP

Like water pouring from a pitcher, my mouth on your nipples! Sparrow Hills. Robert Lowell. NaP

Like Weary Trees. Jacob Glatstein, tr. fr. Yiddish by Ruth Whitman. VWA

Like when the burning sun doth rise. Strato, tr. by Sydney Oswald. PeHV

Like wild oxen in dusty panic. Wilhelm Stekel Gives Up Life. Judah Leib Teller, tr. fr. Yiddish by Benjamin and Barbara Harshav. Fr. Psychoanalysis. AYP

Like Wings. Philip Schultz. MAYP

Like wolves in periods of drought. Winter. Muhammad al-Maghut, tr. by Abdullah al-Udhari. MPAW

Like women who are loved very much and are still not sated. Years. Anna Margolin, tr. by Ruth Whitman. VWA

Likelihood is, The. Children. Bill Manhire. ATNZ; PeNZ

Likeness, A. Robert Browning. CTC

Likeness, The. Arthur Gregor. VGW

Likeness has made them animal and shy. The Twins. Karl Shapiro. MoAmPo; TrJP

Likkle seed/ of her love fe a man, A. Belly Woman's Lament. Lillian Allen. PBCV

Lil' Bro.' Karama Fufuka. RHPC

Lilac, The. Humbert Wolfe. FaPON

Lilac Blossoms. Ruth Kim Chun-soo, tr. fr. Korean by Koh Chang-soo. ACKP

Lilac Garden. Yoshioka Minoru, tr. fr. Japanese by Sato. FCEI

Lilac in my garden comes to bloom, The. My Garden. W. H. Davies. BoNaP

Lilac ribbon is unbound, A. Country of No Lack. Jean Starr Untermeyer. MoAmPo

Lilacs. Amy Lowell. BLPL; MoAmPo; OxBA; PoRA

Lilacs and the Roses, The. Louis Aragon, tr. fr. French by Louis MacNeice. OBWP; RHTwFP

Lilacs wither in the Carolinas, The. In the Carolinas. Wallace Stevens. VGW

Lilian's Song. George Darley. OBNC

Lilies, The. Wendell Berry. GeTw

Lilies, The. Richard Emil Braun. NoAM

Lilies are white. Unknown. BoTP; OxNR

Lilies for the Prophet. Nazik al-Mala'ika, tr. fr. Arabic by Matthew Sorenson, modified and abr. by Christopher Middleton. MAP

Lilies lie in my lady's bower, The. Oh! Weary Mother. Barry Pain. Fr. The Poets at Tea, VIII. NA; Par

Lilies of the Valley. Jon Silkin. NoAM

Lilies say on Easter day, The. The Song of the Lilies. Lucy Wheelock. OHIP

Lilies swinging censers fair. Easter Carol. Henrietta Cordelia Ray. CBWP-3

Lilith, sels. Christopher John Brennan. PoAu-1
Adam to Lilith.
Anguish'd Doubt Broods over Eden, The.
Lilith on the Fate of Man.

Lilith. Ruth Fainlight. VWA

Lilith. Ruth Feldman. VWA

Lilith. Donald Finkel. VWA

Lilith. Iwan Goll. VWA

Lilith. Linda Gregg. WPOW

Lilith. Allen Grossman. VWA

Lilith. Primo Levi, tr. fr. Italian by Ruth Feldman and Brian Swann. VWA

Lilith. Dante Gabriel Rossetti. See House of Life, The: Body's Beauty.

Lilith, Adam's first companion. Lilith. Ruth Fainlight. VWA

Lilith on the Fate of Man. Christopher John Brennan. Fr. Lilith. PoAu-1

Lilith our second kinswoman. Lilith. Primo Levi, tr. by Ruth Feldman and Brian Swann. VWA

Lilith Re-Tells Esther's Story. Michelene Wandor. AIW

Lilith's Child. Edward Francisco. DL

Lilli Burlero [or Lillibulero]. Thomas, Lord Wharton. APAS; OxBoLi (New Song, A.) CoMu

Lilli Burlero. Unknown. NOIV

Lilliput Levee. William Brighty Rands. CenHV

Lilliputian Ode on Their Majesties' Accession, A. Henry Carey. NOEC

Lilliputian's Beer Song. Septimus Winner. OBAL

Lillium Regis. Francis Thompson. WGRP

Lilly in a Christal, The. Robert Herrick. PoEL-3; SeCP (Lily in a Crystal, The.) NAEL-1; NoP; SeCePo

Lilt Your Johnnie. Unknown. BXAP

Lily. Rosanna Warren. MAYP

Lily Adair. Thomas Holley Chivers. OBAL

Lily in a Crystal, The. Robert Herrick. See Lilly in a Christal, The.

Lily in a twilight place?, A. The Vampire. Madison Cawein. VVA

Lily, Lois & Flaubert; the Site of Loss. Kathleen Fraser. NPGG

Lily of the West, The. Unknown. AmFP

Lily of Yorrow, The. Henry van Dyke. AA

Lily on liquid roses floating. Champagne Rosée. John Kenyon. OBEV

Lily-white Rose, The. Unknown. MeEL

Lily's marking stock in the back. My Father's Store. Caroline Finkelstein. PPR

Lily's withered chalice falls, The. Le Jardin. Oscar Wilde. Fr. Impressions. SeCePo
(Garden, The.) PoRA

Limb of forests rises up, The. Yvonne Caroutch, tr. by David Cloutier. BoWoP

Limerick: "It's time to make love. Douse the glim." Conrad Aiken. See It's time to make love. Douse the glim.

Limbo. Samuel Taylor Coleridge. OAEL-2

Limbo. Alfred Gong, tr. fr. German by Beth Bjorklund. CoAuP

Limbo. Seamus Heaney. CIP; NoAM; OxBC

Limbo. Unknown. OBET

Limbs are caught in each other, The. Complicity. Tess Gallagher. GeTw

Lime condensed on the ceiling, or maybe. Living in the Boneyard. John Oliver Simon. NeAC

Limeraiku. Ted Pauker. NOBL

Limeratomy, The, sel. Anthony Euwer.
As a Beauty I Am Not a Star. InvP
(Face, The.) OBAL
(My Face.) FaFP; PoLF

Limerick [or An Eggstravagance or Henry Ward Beecher]. At. to Oliver Wendell Holmes. CenHV; ChTr; FaBoNo

Limerick: "Aging old queers are no treat." Unknown. PeHV

Limerick: "Anal erotic named Herman, An." Unknown. PeHV

Limerick: "Angry young husband called Bicket, An." John Galsworthy. CenHV

Limerick: "Animula vagula blandula." Conrad Aiken. FaBoNo; OBAL

Limerick: "Argentine gaucho named Bruno, An." Unknown. NOBL

Limerick: "Big bull-dyke, surly and sallow, A." Unknown. PeHV

Limerick: "Breasts of a barmaid of Crale, The." Unknown. NOBL

Limerick: "Certain young gourmet of Crediton, A." Charles Cuthbert Inge. CenHV

Limerick: "Charlotte Brontë said, "Wow, sister! What a man!"" Victor Gray. NOBL

Limerick: "Cleopatra, who thought they maligned her." Newton Mackintosh. NA

Limerick: "Clergyman in want, A." Ronald Arbuthnott Knox. OxBoLi

Limerick: "Consider the lowering Lynx." Langford Reed. CenHV

Limerick: "Decrepit old gas man named Peter, A." Unknown. See Decrepit Old Gasman, A.

Limerick: "Eccentric old person of Slough, An." George Robey. CenHV

Limerick: "Epicure, dining at Crewe, An." Unknown. See Epicure, Dining at Crewe, An.

Limerick: "Evangelical vicar in want." Ronald Arbuthnott Knox. CenHV

Limerick: "Fire Island pixie called "Mary," A." Unknown. PeHV

Limerick: "H was an indigent Hen." Bruce Porter. NA

Limerick: "Hermaphrodite fairy of Kew, A." Unknown. PeHV

Limerick: "I sat next to the Duchess at tea." *Unknown.* SoSe
Limerick: "I wish that my room had a floor." Gelett Burgess. FiBHP;
  InvP; OBCA
Limerick: "I'd rather have habits than clothes." Gelett Burgess. NA
Limerick: "In a high-fashion journal for queers." *Unknown.* PeHV
Limerick Is Furtive and Mean, The. Morris Bishop. NBLV
Limerick: "It's time to make love. Douse the glim." Conrad Aiken. *See*
  It's time to make love. Douse the glim.
Limerick: "Large, colored dyke from Atlanta, A." *Unknown.* PeHV
Limerick: "Lesbian born under Pisces, A." *Unknown.* PeHV
Limerick: "Lesbian girl of Khartoum, A." *Unknown.* NOBL
Limerick: "Man hired by John Smith and Co., A." "Mark Twain."
  FaBoNo; InPK
Limerick: "My name's Mister Benjamin Bunny." Frederic Edward
  Weatherly. CenHV
Limerick: "Old East End worker called Jock, An." Victor Gray. NOBL
Limerick: "On the deck of a ship called the Masm." Conrad Aiken.
  FaBoNo
Limerick: "One morning old Wilfrid Scawen Blunt." Victor Gray.
  NOBL
Limerick: "Our ambassador to Venus, Mz Abner." *Unknown.* PeHV
Limerick: "Pretty young actress, a stammerer, A." Eille Norwood.
  CenHV
Limerick: "Professional dancer, Miss Fairleigh, A." Laurence Perrine.
  SoTCo
Limerick: "Roared her father, severest of men." Laurence Perrine.
  SoTCo
Limerick: "Smooth-bottomed fellow named Fritz, A." *Unknown.* PeHV
Limerick: "Staid schizophrenic named Struther, A." *Unknown.* NIP
Limerick: "Taxi-cab whore out at Iver, A." Victor Gray. NOBL
Limerick: "That famous old pederast, Wilde." *Unknown.* PeHV
Limerick: "There is an old he-wolf named Gambart." Dante Gabriel
  Rossetti. CenHV; FaBoEE
Limerick: "There once was a girl of New York." Cosmo Monkhouse.
  NA
Limerick: "There once was a girl of Pitlochry." *Unknown.* CenHV
Limerick: "There once was a man of Bengal." *Unknown.* CenHV
  (Bengal.) OnUR
Limerick: "There once was a man who said "God." Ronald Arbuthnott
  Knox. *See* There once was a man who said "God."
Limerick: "There once was a man who said, "How." *Unknown.* NA
Limerick: "There once was a painter named Scott." Dante Gabriel
  Rossetti. CenHV
Limerick: "There once was a person of Benin." Cosmo Monkhouse. NA
Limerick: "There once was a Renaissance man." *Unknown.* PeHV
Limerick: "There once was a warden of Wadham." *Unknown.* PeHV
Limerick: "There once was a wonderful wizard." Conrad Aiken.
  FaBoNo
Limerick: "There once was an old man of Blackheath." *Unknown.*
  CenHV
Limerick: "There once was an old man of Lyme." *At. to* Edward Lear
  and Cosmo Monkhouse. NA
Limerick: "There once was an old man of Lyme." Edward Lear. *See*
  There was an old party of lyme.
Limerick: "There once were two cats of Kilkenny." *Unknown. See*
  Kilkenny Cats, The.
Limerick: "There was a dear lady of Eden." *Unknown.* NA
Limerick: "There was a faith-healer of Deal." *Unknown.* CenHV
  (Faith-Healer.) FaFP
  (Mind and Matter.) FaBoCo
Limerick: "There was a gay damsel of Lynn." *Unknown.* NA
Limerick: "There was a good Canon of Durham." William Ralph Inge.
  CenHV
Limerick: "There was a kind curate of kew." *Unknown.* CenHV
Limerick: "There was a poor chap called Rossetti." Dante Gabriel
  Rossetti. CenHV
Limerick: "There was a princess of Bengal." *At. to* Walter Parke. NA
Limerick: "There was a queer fellow named Woodin." "Cuthbert Bede."
  CenHV
Limerick: "There was a young bard of Japan." *Unknown.* CenHV
Limerick: "There was a young critic of King's." Arthur Clement Hilton.
  CenHV
Limerick: "There was a young curate of Hants." E. V. Knox. CenHV
Limerick: "There was a young fellow called Crouch." Victor Gray.
  NOBL
Limerick: "There was a young fellow called Green." *Unknown.* CenHV
Limerick: "There was a young fellow named Nutz." *Unknown.* PeHV
Limerick: "There was a young Fellow of Caius." *Unknown.* NOBL
Limerick: "There was a young Fellow of Ceuta." *Unknown.* CenHV
Limerick: "There was a young Fellow of King's." *Unknown.* NOBL
Limerick: "There was a young Fellow of Wadham." *Unknown.* NOBL

Limerick: "There was a young genius of Queens."' Arthur Clement
  Hilton. CenHV
Limerick: "There was a young gourmand of John's." Arthur Clement
  Hilton. CenHV
Limerick: "There was a young lady called Starky." *Unknown.* CenHV
Limerick: "There was a young lady named [*or* called] Bright." *At. to*
  Arthur Buller. CenHV; NOBL; OxBoLi
  (Relativity.) FaBoCo; FaFP; ImOP
  (Young Lady Named Bright, A.) FaPON
Limerick: "There was a young lady of Corsica." Edward Lear. CenHV;
  ChTr; FaBoNo
Limerick: "There was a young lady of Ealing." *Unknown.* CenHV
Limerick: "There was a young lady of Flint." *Unknown.* CenHV
Limerick: "There was a young lady of Hull." Edward Lear. MoShBr
Limerick: "There was a young lady of Kent." *Unknown.* CenHV; ILY
Limerick: "There was a young lady of Limerick." Andrew Lang.
  CenHV
Limerick: "There was a young lady of Lynn." *Unknown. See* Young
  Lady of Lynn, A.
Limerick: "There was a young lady of Milton." *Unknown.* NA
Limerick: "There was a young lady of Niger." Cosmo Monkhouse. *See*
  There Was a Young Lady of Niger.
Limerick: "There was a young lady of Riga." *Unknown.* CenHV;
  FaBoCo
Limerick: "There was a young lady of Russia." Edward Lear. MoShBr
Limerick: "There was a young lady of Spain." Monica Raymond.
  SoTCo
Limerick: "There was a young lady of station." "Lewis Carroll." *See*
  There Was a Young Lady of Station.
Limerick: "There was a young lady of Wales." *Unknown.* NA
Limerick: "There was a young lady whose eyes." Edward Lear. *See*
  There was a young lady whose eyes.
Limerick: "There was a young maid who said, "Why." *Unknown.* NA;
  SoSe
Limerick: "There was a young man of Cohoes." Robert J. Burdette.
  NA
Limerick: "There was a young man of Devizes." *At. to* Archibald
  Marshall. CenHV
Limerick: "There was a young man of Montrose." Arnold Bennett.
  CenHV; FaBoNo; OxBoLi
  (It Pays.) FaFP
Limerick: "There was a young man who was bitten." *At. to* Walter Parke.
  NA
Limerick: "There was a young person of Crete." Edward Lear.
  FaBoNo
Limerick: "There was a young person of Smyrna." Edward Lear.
  OxBoLi; TEP
Limerick: "There was a young poet of Thusis." *Unknown.* OxBoLi
Limerick: "There was a young woman called Starky." *Unknown. See*
  Mendelian Theory.
Limerick: "There was a young woman named Plunnery." Edward Gorey.
  OBAL
Limerick: "There was an auld birkie ca'ed Milton." Andrew Lang.
  CenHV
Limerick: "There was an old fellow of Trinity." *At. to* Arthur Clement
  Hilton. CenHV
Limerick: "There was an old man in a boat." Edward Lear. EBEV;
  FaBoNo
  (Floating Old Man, The.) WiR
Limerick: "There was an old man in a pew." Edward Lear. MoShBr
Limerick: "There was an old man in a tree." Edward Lear. *See* There
  Was an Old Man in a Tree.
Limerick: "There was an old man in a trunk." Ogden Nash. CenHV
  (Ultimate Reality.) FaBoCo
Limerick: "There was an old man of Bengal." "F. Anstey." CenHV
Limerick: "There was an old man of Blackheath." *Unknown.* PDV
Limerick: "There was an old man of Boulogne." *Unknown. See* There
  Was an Old Man of Boulogne.
Limerick: "There was an old man of Cape Horn." Edward Lear. EBEV
Limerick: "There was an old man of Dunblane." Edward Lear. EBEV
Limerick: "There was an old man of Dundee." Edward Lear. FaBoNo
Limerick: "There was an old man of El Hums." Edward Lear. FaBoNo
Limerick: "There was an old man of Girgenti." Edward Lear. FaBoNo
Limerick: "There was an old man of Hong Kong." Edward Lear.
  FaBoCo
Limerick: "There was an old man of Ibreem." Edward Lear. EBEV
Limerick: "There was an old man of Kamschatka." Edward Lear. NA;
  NOBL
Limerick: "There was an old man of Khartoum." *At. to* William Ralph
  Inge. *See* There Was an Old Man of Khartoum.
Limerick: "There was an old man of Leghorn." Edward Lear. NA

Limerick: "There was an old man of Madras." Edward Lear. FaBoNo
Limerick: "There was an old man of [or from] Peru/ Who dreamt he was eating his shoe." *Unknown.* CenHV; PDV; SoSe
Limerick: "There was an old man of Spithead." Edward Lear. FaBoNo
Limerick: "There was an old man of the coast." Edward Lear. CenHV; MoShBr
Limerick: "There was an old man of the Dargle." Edward Lear. ChTr
Limerick: "There was an old man of the Dee." Edward Lear. FaBoNo
Limerick: "There was an old man of Thermopylae." Edward Lear. EBEV; FaBoNo; NA; NOBL
Limerick: "There was an old man of Three Bridges." Edward Lear. FaBoNo
Limerick: "There was an old man of Vesuvius." Edward Lear. FaBoNo
Limerick: "There was an old man of Whitehaven." Edward Lear. EBEV
Limerick: "There was an old man on the Border." Edward Lear. CenHV; EBEV
Limerick: "There was an old man who said 'Do.' " *Unknown. See* There Was an Old Man Who Said, "Do."
Limerick: "There was an old man who said: "How." Edward Lear. OxBChV
Limerick: "There was an old man who said, "Hush!" Edward Lear. FaBoCo; GoJo; NA; NOBL; OxBChV; OxBoLi; TEP
Limerick: "There was an old man who supposed." Edward Lear. NA; NAEL-2; NOBVV
(There Was an Old Man Who Supposed.) NoP
Limerick: "There was an old man whose despair." Edward Lear. FaBoNo
Limerick: "There was an old man with a gong." Edward Lear. GoJo
Limerick: "There was an old man with a ribbon." Edward Lear. FaBoNo
Limerick: "There was an old person of Anerley." Edward Lear. FaBoCo
Limerick: "There was an old person of Bar." Edward Lear. FaBoNo
Limerick: "There was an old person of Brussels." Edward Lear. FaBoNo
Limerick: "There was an old person of Crowle." Edward Lear. FaBoNo
Limerick: "There was an old person of Dean." Edward Lear. MoShBr; TSS
Limerick: "There was an old person of Diss." Edward Lear. GoJo
Limerick: "There was an old person of Dover." Edward Lear. FaBoNo
Limerick: "There was an old person of Grange." Edward Lear. FaBoNo
Limerick: "There was an old person of Gretna." Edward Lear. ChTr; OxBChV
Limerick: "There was an old person of Harrow." Edward Lear. FaBoNo
Limerick: "There was an old person of Hove." Edward Lear. FaBoNo
Limerick: "There was an old person of Lear." Edward Lear. CenHV
Limerick: "There was an old person of Philae." Edward Lear. FaBoNo
Limerick: "There was an old person of Skye." Edward Lear. ChTr
Limerick: "There was an old person of Twickenham." Edward Lear. FaBoNo
Limerick: "There was an old person of Ware." Edward Lear. NA
(Old Person of Ware, An.) RAR
Limerick: "There was an old person of Wick." Edward Lear. FaBoNo; NA
Limerick: "There was an old person of Woking." Edward Lear. NA
Limerick: "There was an old person whose habits." Edward Lear. FaBoNo
Limerick: "There was an old stupid who wrote." At. to Walter Parke. NA
Limerick: "There was an old tailor of Bicester." *Unknown.* CenHV
Limerick: "There was once a man with a beard." Edward Lear. NA
Limerick: "There was once a young lady of Ryde." *Unknown.* CenHV; PDV
Limerick: "There's a combative artist named Whistler." Dante Gabriel Rossetti. CenHV; FaBoEE
Limerick: "There's a notable family named Stein." *Unknown.* NOBL
Limerick: "There's a Portuguese person named Howell." At. to Dante Gabriel Rossetti. CenHV
Limerick: "There's an Irishman, Arthur O'Shaughnessy." Dante Gabriel Rossetti. CenHV
Limerick: "They say that I was in my youth." *Unknown.* CenHV
Limerick: "Though the music of love is Schubérty." *Unknown.* PeHV
Limerick: "Treatment by old Mr. Mears, The." *Unknown.* PeHV
Limerick: "Tutor who tooted a flute, A." Carolyn Wells. SoSe
Limerick: "Two brothers devised what at sight." Laurence Perrine. SoTCo
Limerick: "Two dykes went their separate routes." *Unknown.* PeHV
Limerick: "Vice most obscene and unsavoury, A." *Unknown.* NOBL
Limerick: "Well-bred young girl of Gomorrah, A." *Unknown.* PeHV
Limerick: "Well-buggered boy named Delpasse, A." *Unknown.* PeHV
Limerick: "Well, it's partly the shape of the thing." *Unknown.* SoSe
Limerick: "When Arthur was homeless and broke." *Unknown.* PeHV

Limerick: "When Gauguin was visiting Fiji." Victor Gray. NOBL
Limerick: "When our dean took a pious young spinster." Victor Gray. NOBL
Limerick: "When that Seint George hadde sleyne ye draggon." *Unknown.* NA
Limerick: "While Titian was grinding rose madder." *Unknown.* NOBL
Limerick: "While visiting Arundel Castle." Victor Gray. NOBL
Limerick: "Wonderful bird is the pelican, A." Dixon Lanier Merritt. CenHV
Limerick: "Young engine-driver called Hunt, A." Victor Gray. NOBL
Limerick: "Young fairy with habits perverse, A." *Unknown.* PeHV
Limerick: "Young Frederick the Great was a beaut." *Unknown.* PeHV
Limerick: "Young Harvard man, sweet and tender, A." *Unknown.* PeHV
Limerick: "Young lady of fair Mytilene, A." *Unknown.* CenHV
Limestone Cowboy's Luck Runs Out, The. Greg German. SoTCo
Limitations. Henrietta Cordelia Ray. CBWP-3
Limitations. Siegfried Sassoon. MoBrPo
Limited. Carl Sandburg. HAP; MoAB; MoAmPo; OxBA
Limited, The. Robert Penn Warren. PoA
Limited Access. Mary Pierce Brosmer. ER
Limits. Emerson. FM; OxBSP; PoEL-4
Limits of Physics, The. Dan Pagis, *tr. fr. Hebrew by* Warren Bargad *and* Stanley F. Chyet. IP
Limits of Submission, The. Faarah Nuur, *tr. fr. Somali.* TTY, *tr. by* B. W. Andrzejewski *and* I. M. Lewis; WTO, *tr. by* B. W. Andrzejewski *and* I. M. Lewis
Limits of the sphere of dream, The. Goethe, *tr. fr. German by* Shelley. *Fr.* Faust. WSC
Limp as unwatered flowers, the grey limbs. Homage to the Carracci. Tom Disch. PoA
Limpid river/ rippling in dawn light. Inscribed on a Landscape by Mi Yüan-hui. Chao Meng-fu, *tr. by* Jonathan Chaves. CoBLCP
Limpid shimmering sea is like a turquoise, The. The Silent Day. Luis G. Urbina, *tr. by* Samuel Beckett. MexPo
Limping past the Guthrie theater. Indians at the Guthrie. Gerald Vizenor. STE; VoR
Limpopo and Tugela churned. The Scorpion. William Plomer. OBMV
L'Imprévisibilité. Zinaida Hippius, *tr. fr. Russian by* Temira Pachmuss. PBWP
Limrick's writtn to plas, A. Laurence Perrine. SoTCo
Lincoln. George Henry Boker. OHIP
Lincoln. John Vance Cheney. OHIP
Lincoln. John Gould Fletcher. MoAmPo
Lincoln, *sel.* John Gould Fletcher. MoAmPo
"There was a darkness in this man." *Fr.* II. OFD
Lincoln. Jane L. Hardy. OHIP
Lincoln. Vachel Lindsay. *Fr.* Litany of the Heroes. OHIP
Lincoln. S. Weir Mitchell. PAH
Lincoln. Harriet Monroe. *Fr.* Commemoration Ode. AA
Lincoln. Henrietta Cordelia Ray. CBWP-3
Lincoln. James Whitcomb Riley. OHIP
Lincoln. Corinne Roosevelt Robinson. OHIP
Lincoln. Nancy Byrd Turner. FaPON; RHPC
Lincoln. *Unknown.* OHIP
Lincoln and Liberty. *Unknown.* AS
Lincoln at Gettysburg. Bayard Taylor. *Fr.* The Gettysburg Ode. OHIP; PAH
Lincoln Leads. Minna Irving. OHIP
Lincoln Monument: Washington. Langston Hughes. OFD
Lincoln Statue, The. W. F. Collins. OHIP
Lincoln the Great Commoner. Edwin Markham. *See* Lincoln, the Man of the People.
Lincoln, the Man of the People. Edwin Markham. MoAmPo; OHFP; OHIP; PAH; TrGrPo
(Lincoln the Great Commoner.) GN
"Up from the log cabin to the capitol," *sel.* OFD
Lincoln! When men would name a man. Lincoln. *Unknown.* OHIP
Lincoln's Grave, *sel.* Maurice Thompson.
Prophecy, A. AA
Lincolnshire; from the Wolds to the Fens. Ben Jonson. *Fr.* The Sad Shepherd, II, vii. FaBoPP
Lincolnshire Poacher, The. *Unknown.* CH; GBP; OnMSP; OxBoLi; SD
(Poacher, The.) WiR
Lincolnshire Shepherd, A. *Unknown.* OBET
Lincolnshire Shores. Tennyson. *Fr.* Idylls of the King: The Last Tournament. FaBoPP
Lincolnshire Shores ("A still salt pool locked in with bars of sand"). Tennyson. *Fr.* The Palace of Art. FaBoPP

Lincolnshire Wolds and Lincolnshire Sea. Tennyson. *See* In Memoriam A. H. H.: Calm Is the Morn.

Lincolnshire's Holland Speaks of Her Waterfowl. Michael Drayton. *Fr.* Polyolbion, Five and Twentieth Song. FaBoPP

Lindamira's Complaint. Mary Sidney Wroth, Countess of Montgomery. *Fr.* Urania. WPE

Lindbergh. *Unknown.* AmFP

Lindedi Singing. Innocent Banda. WMBCH

Linden blossomed, the nightingale sang, The. Heine, *tr. by* John Todhunter. AWP

Lindie, chile, fo' Lawd sake, tell me. After the Quarrel. Priscilla Jane Thompson. CBWP-2

Line between the city and the, The. Topography. Mark A.R. Facknitz. KS

Line-Gang, The. Robert Frost. OxBSP

Line has been cast and all's preordained, The. The Anglers. Yekhi'el Mar, *tr. by* Bernhard Frank. MHeP

Line in long array where they wind betwixt green islands, A. Cavalry Crossing a Ford. Walt Whitman. AA; AiP; AmPP; ChTr; HeIP; InPK; InPS; MoP; NAAL-1; NoAM; NoP; OxBA; PPP; TAP; UnPo

Line is a crack, A. Wall Rev. Jackson Mac Low. LP

Line Like. Nelly Sachs, *tr. fr. German by* Michael Hamburger. BoWoP

Line of Beauty, The. Arthur William Edgar O'Shaughnessy. TIRV

Line to Heaven by Christ Was Made, The. *Unknown.* BXAP

Line-up, The. Joan Swift. SM

Line-up for Yesterday. Ogden Nash. SD

Lineage. Frank Bidart. *Fr.* Elegy, V. HCAP

Lineage. Robert Farren. TIRV

Lineage. Margaret Abigail Walker. BlSi; CNA; NMM; PBWP; PoBA

Linear, encircled youth, The. On Alexander and Aristotle, on a Black-on-Red Greek Plate. Alan Dugan. PPP

Linen Bands. Vance Thompson. AA

Linen Industry, The. Michael Longley. CIP; UAS

Linen Weaver, The. *Unknown.* NOEC

Linen Workers, The. Michael Longley. CIP; FaBCIP

Liner She's a Lady, The. Kipling. FaBV

Lines: "Anchoring, I watched him climb." Barbara Smith. TSL

Lines: "Cold earth slept below, The." Shelley. ChER; EnRP

Lines: "From fair Jamaica's fertile plains." "Ada." BlSi

Lines: "Here often, when a child, I lay reclined." Tennyson. FaBoPP

Lines: "His cock is big and red when I am there." Paul Goodman. PeHV

Lines———: "I have been cherish'd and forgiven." Hartley Coleridge. PoEL-4

Lines: I Praise God's Mankind in an Old Woman. Wilfred Watson. NOBC

Lines: Inspired by the Controversy on the Value or Otherwise of Old English Studies. Anthony Burgess. FaBoCo

Lines: "Other day I was loving a sweet little fruitpie-and-cream, The." Gavin Ewart. EAS

Lines: "Singularly and in pairs the decade has been ripped by bullets." Herbert Martin. PoBA

Lines: "Some are waiting, some can't wait." Heather McHugh. MAYP

Lines: To a Movement in Mozart's E-Flat Symphony. Thomas Hardy. ELP; NoAM

Lines: "When the lamp is shattered." Shelley. *See* When the Lamp Is Shattered.

Lines: "When youthful faith hath fled." John Gibson Lockhart. OBEV

Lines are keen against today's bad sky, The. The Church on Comiaken Hill. Richard Hugo. LCAP; Prf; SM

Lines by a Fond Lover. *Unknown.* NA

Lines by a Medium. *Unknown.* NA

Lines by a Person of Quality. *At. to* Pope, *and to* Swift. NA

Lines Composed a Few Miles above Tintern Abbey on Revisiting the Banks of the Wye during a Tour, July 13, 1798. Wordsworth. BLPL; ChER; EnRP; FaBoPP; FF; FiP; GoTL; HAP; HeIP; InPS; LiTB; NAEL-2; NAWM-2; NIP; NoP; OAEL-2; OBNC; PoE; PoEL-4; PPP; PrIm; SeCePo; TEP; TrGrPo

Sels.
 "For I have learned." NU
 "For thou art with me here upon the banks." Prf
 "Sounding cataract, The/ Haunted me like a passion." WGRP

Lines Composed at Hope Ranch. Tom Clark. PPR

Lines Composed in a Wood on a Windy Day. Anne Brontë. EBVV

Lines Concerning the Unknown Soldier, *sel.* Osip Mandelstam, *tr. fr. Russian by* James Greene.
 Arteries Juicy with Blood. NAs

Lines Declining a Transatlantic Dinner Invitation. Marilyn Hacker. MAYP

Lines Descriptive of Thomson's Island. Benjamin Lynde. SCAP

Lines for a Bed at Kelmscott Manor. William Morris. *See* Wind's on the wold, The.

Lines for a Christmas Card. Hilaire Belloc. TW

Lines for a Hard Time. Gena Ford. IHMS

Lines for a Wedding Gift. W. Wesley Trimpi. NePoEA

Lines for a Worthy Person Who Has Drifted by Accident into a Chelsea Revel. Sir Alan Patrick Herbert. NOBL

Lines for a Young Wanderer in Mexico. John Logan. PoA

Lines for an Interment. Archibald MacLeish. CMoP; NOBA

Lines for an Old Man. T. S. Eliot. FaBoTw; RB; TW

Lines for Cuscuscaraway and Mirza Murad Ali Beg. T. S. Eliot. FiBHP; NBLV; OBAL

Lines for Marking Time. Roberta Hill Whiteman. BoWoP; CDW

Lines for Roethke Twenty Years after His Death. Duane Niatum. HATNAP

Lines for the Ancient Scribes. Harvey Shapiro. VWA

Lines for Those to Whom Tragedy Is Denied. Joyce Carol Oates. IHMS

Lines from Catullus. Sir Walter Ralegh. *See* Sun [*or* Sunne] may set and rise, The.

Lines from Love Letters, *sels. Unknown.* OBEV
 "A celuy que plus eyme en mounde." *Fr.* I.
 "A soun tres chere et special." *Fr.* II.

Lines grow slack in our hands at full high-water, The. Rock Carving. Douglas Stewart. SeCePo

Lines I Told Myself I Wouldn't Write. Paul Mariani. MAYP

Lines in Praise of a Self-Chiming Clock. Hsüan-yeh, *tr. fr. Chinese by* Jonathan D. Spence. WFTU

Lines in Ridicule of Certain Poems Published in 1777. Samuel Johnson. *See* Lines on Thomas Warton's Poems *or* Lines in Ridicule of Certain Poems Published in 1777.

Lines Left at Mr. Theodore Hook's House in June, 1834. "Thomas Ingoldsby." FaBoUs

Lines Occasioned by the Burning of Some Letters. Sarah Dixon. NOEC

Lines of a poem, long, short: each joined to the end decreed for it. Outside the Line. Dan Pagis, *tr. by* Warren Bargad *and* Stanley F. Chyet. IP

Lines of this new song are nothing, The. Louis Zukofsky. VGW

Lines of your arteries, The. Robert. Wendy Rose. HATNAP

Lines on a Dead Girl. Priscilla Jane Thompson. CBWP-2

Lines on a Mysterious Occurrence. Alfred Denis Godley. CenHV

Lines on a Purple Cap Received as a Present from My Brother. George Alsop. SCAP

Lines on a Young Lady's Photograph Album. Philip Larkin. EnLoPo; HAP; OAEL-2; WeW

Lines on Being Refused a Guggenheim Fellowship. Reed Whittemore. TW

Lines on Bounce. Pope. FM

Lines on Carmen Sylva. Emma Lazarus. TrJP

Lines on Hearing That Lady Byron Was Ill. Byron. EBEV

Lines on Hearing the Organ. Charles Stuart Calverley. CenHV; FaBoCo; FiBHP; NOBL

Lines on Leaving a Scene in Bavaria. Thomas Campbell. OBNC

Lines on Milton. Dryden. *See* Three poets, in three distant ages born.

Lines on Receiving My Mother's Picture Out of Norfolk. William Cowper. *See* Oh that those lips had language! Life has passed.

Lines on Succession of the Kings of England. *Unknown.* FaBoUs

Lines on Swift's Ancestors. Pope. FaBoCo

Lines on the Back of a Confederate Note. Samuel Alroy Jonas. BLPA; OPP

Lines on the Death of Bismarck. John Jay Chapman. PoEL-5

Lines on the Death of the Rev. S. K. Talmage. Mary E. Tucker. CBWP-1

Lines on the Execution of King Charles I. James, Marquess of Montrose Graham. *See* Great, good and just, could I but rate.

Lines on the Mermaid Tavern. *Unknown.* EnRP; PoRA
 (Mermaid Tavern, The.) BLPL; FaBoBe; GTBS; GTBS-P

Lines on the Sea. Dilys Bennett Laing. NYBP

Lines on the Succession of the Kings of England (Reversed). *Unknown.* FaBoUs

Lines on the Tombs in Westminster. *At. to* Francis Beaumont *and to* William Basse. ACP; CH; FaPoR; GTBS; GTBS-P; NOBE; OBEV; TrGrPo
 (A Memento for Mortality.) EIL; FaBoCh; HAP; OBS
 ("Martalitie, behold and fear.") OBS

Lines on Thomas Warton's Poems *or* Lines in Ridicule of Certain Poems Published in 1777. Samuel Johnson. FaBoCo; FaBoEE
 (Lines in Ridicule of Certain Poems Published in 1777.) FaBoCo

Lines parallel. The Room. De Leon Harrison. PoBA

Lines Printed under the Engraved Portrait of Milton [in Tonson's Folio of the "Paradise Lost"]. Dryden. HeIP; InPK; SeCV-2
  (Epigram on Milton.) TrGrPo
  (Lines on Milton.) OAEL-1
  (Portrait of Milton, The.) ACP
Lines Spoken by the Ghost of John Dennis at the Devil Tavern. Thomas Gray. FL
Lines, Suggested on Reading "An Appeal to Christian Women of the South" by A. E. Grimké. "Ada." BlSi
Lines To———: "O come to me in my dreams love!" Mary Weston Fordham. CBWP-2
Lines to a Blind Girl. Thomas Buchanan Read. AA
Lines to a Don. Hilaire Belloc. FaBoCo; MoBrPo; OBSV; TW
Lines to a Dragon-Fly. Walter Savage Landor. *See* Life (priest and poet say) is but a dream.
Lines to a Friend in Trouble. W. S. Di Piero. MAYP
Lines to a Graduate. Lizelia Augusta Jenkins Moorer. CBWP-3
Lines to a Lady-Bird. Lord De Tabley. FM
Lines to a Nasturtium. Anne Spencer. AmNP; CDC; PoNe
Lines to a Reviewer. Shelley. OxBSP
Lines to a Seagreen Lover. Isabella Gardner. CAPP
Lines to a Tree. Judah Leib Teller, *tr. fr. Yiddish.* VWA, *tr. by* Gabriel Preil *and* Howard Schwartz
Lines to a World-famous Poet Who Failed to Complete a World-famous Poem; or, Come Clean, Mr. Guest! Ogden Nash. OBAL
Lines to Accompany Flowers for Eve. Carolyn Kizer. BoWoP
Lines to an Indian Air. Shelley. *See* I arise from dreams of thee.
Lines to an Old Dress. Mary E. Tucker. CBWP-1
Lines to an Old School-House. Priscilla Jane Thompson. CBWP-2
Lines to Be Embroidered on a Bib; or, The Child Is Father of the Man, but Not for Quite a While. Ogden Nash. FaBoUs
Lines to Do with Youth. Witter Bynner. PoA
Lines to Dr. Ditmars. Kenneth Allan Robinson. ImOP
Lines to Emma. Priscilla Jane Thompson. CBWP-2
Lines to Fanny, *sel.* Keats.
  "Where shall I learn to get my peace again?." ChER
Lines to Florence. Mary Weston Fordham. CBWP-2
Lines to His Son on Reaching Adolescence. John Logan. NePoEA-2
Lines to Miss Florence Huntingdon. *At. to* James De Mille. NA
Lines to Mother. Rose M. Stein. PWR
Lines to Mrs. Isabel Peace. Mary Weston Fordham. CBWP-2
Lines to Mrs. M. C. Turner. Eloise Bibb. CBWP-4
Lines to My Father. Leslie Daiken. NeIP
Lines to My Grandfathers. Tony Harrison. *Fr.* The School of Eloquence. NoAM
Lines to Our Elders. Countee Cullen. CDC
Lines to Ralph Hodgson, Esqre. T. S. Eliot. NBLV; OBAL
Lines to Ratclif. Earl of Surrey. *See* My Ratcliffe, when thy retchlesse youth offendes.
Lines to the Blessed Sacrament. *Unknown, tr. fr. Irish by* Jeremiah J. Callanan. TIRV
Lines to the Hon. George L. Knox. Eloise Bibb. CBWP-4
Lines Where Beauty Lingers. Franklin Pierce Adams. OBAL
Lines with a Gift of Herbs. Janet Lewis. QFR
Lines Written after the Discovery by the Author of the Germ of Yellow Fever. Sir Ronald Ross. ImOP
Lines Written among the Euganean Hills. ("Many a green isle needs must be"). Shelley. EnRP; GTBS; GTBS-P; PoEL-3
  (Written in the Euganean Hills, North Italy.) GTBS; GTBS-P
  "'Mid the mountains Euganean," *sel.* PBBP
Lines Written at Bridgewater, 27 July 1797, *sel.* John Thelwall.
  "Day of my double birth, if such the year." NOEC
Lines Written at Cambridge, to W. R., Esquire. Phineas Fletcher. *Fr.* To My Ever-honoured Cousin W. R. Esquire. EiL
Lines Written at the Grave of Alexander [*or* Alexandre] Dumas. Gwendolyn B. Bennett. CDC; PoNe
Lines Written beneath a Picture. Byron. OxBSP
Lines Written by a Bear of Very Little Brain. A. A. Milne. FaBoNo
Lines Written during a Period of Insanity. William Cowper. EBEV; FaBoRV; FiP; HAP; NOEC; NoP; OAEL-1; OPOP; PPP; Prf; TW
  (Lines Written under the Influence of Delirium.) PoEL-3
Lines Written for Gene Kelly to Dance To. Carl Sandburg. AiP
Lines Written Immediately after Parting from a Lady. Sir Samuel Egerton Brydges. NOEC
Lines Written in a Blank Leaf of the Prometheus Unbound. Thomas Lovell Beddoes. OAEL-2
Lines Written in a Mausoleum. Lillian Grant. GoYe
Lines Written in Dejection. W. B. Yeats. NAs
Lines Written in Early Spring. Wordsworth. EnRP; FPL; GTBS; GTBS-P; NAEL-2; OAEL-2; PoLF
  (Written in Early Spring.) GTBS; GTBS-P

Lines Written in Her Breviary. St. Theresa of Avila, *tr. fr. Spanish by* Longfellow. AWP; EaLo
  (Bookmark.) CTC; WPOW
  (St. Theresa's Book-Mark.) PoEL-5
Lines Written in Kensington Gardens, *sel.* Matthew Arnold. FaBoPP; NAEL-2; NIP
  Calm Soul of All Things! [Make It Mine]. TrPWD; WGRP
Lines Written in Oregon. Vladimir Nabokov. NYBP
Lines Written in the Album at Elbingerode, in the Hartz Forest. Samuel Taylor Coleridge. OBTV
Lines Written in the Bay of Lerici. Shelley. NAEL-2; OAEL-2
Lines Written in the Dog-Days. William Woty. NOEC
Lines Written in the Front of a Well-read Copy of Burns's *Songs:* To the Reader. *Unknown.* FaBoUs
Lines Written in Windsor Forest. Pope. EBEV
  (Hymn Written in Windsor Forest, A.) NOEC; OxBSP
Lines Written near Linton, on Exmoor. Daniel Hoffman. BXAP
Lines Written on a Farewell View of the Franconia Mountains at Twilight. Henrietta Cordelia Ray. CBWP-3
Lines Written on a Seat on the Grand Canal, Dublin. Patrick Kavanagh. BIrV; CMoP; InPS; IPY; NOIV
Lines Written on a Very Boisterous Day in May, 1844. John Clare. OxBSP
Lines Written on a Window at The Leasowes. William Shenstone. OxBSP
Lines Written on Hearing the News of the Death of Napoleon. Shelley. ChER
Lines Written on New Year's Day, *sel.* Wen Cheng-ming, *tr. fr. Chinese by* Jonathan Chaves.
  "There was no reason to expect sadness." CoBLCP
Lines Written under the Influence of Delirium. William Cowper. *See* Hatred and vengeance, my eternal portion.
Lines Written upon a Window-Shutter at Weston. William Cowper. NOEC
Lingam and the Yoni, The. Alec Derwent Hope. MAT; NoAM
Lingering scripture of bleach, The. Transmigration. Mekeel McBride. NAmP
Lingua, *sel.* Thomas Tomkis.
  Gordion Knot, The. EiL
Lining Track. *Unknown.* AmFP
Linked to a clod, harassed, and sad. Circumstance. Thomas Bailey Aldrich. AA
Links. Guillaume Apollinaire, *tr. fr. French by* Michael Benedikt. POS
Links. Turner Cassity. SM
Links are chance, the chain is fate, The. Mathematics of Love. Michael Hamburger. NePoEA-2; UnAS
Links interwoven. Indian Education. Adrian C. Louis. STE
Links of fear. The Sacrifice. Moshe Yungman, *tr. by* Marcia Falk. VWA
Linnet, The. Robert Bridges. *See* I Heard a Linnet Courting.
Linnet, The. Walter de la Mare. LiTB
Linnet in November, The. Francis Turner Palgrave. EBVV
Linnet in the rocky dells, The. Emily Brontë. HAP; OBNC
Linnet who had lost her way, A. Tenebris Interlucentem. James Elroy Flecker. MoBrPo
Linnets. Larry Levis. LCAP
Linoleum: Breaking Down. Stanley Plumly. AnAn
Linstead Market. *Unknown.* PBCV
Lintie in a Cage. Alice V. Stuart. OxBS
Lion, The. Hilaire Belloc. MoBrPo; NBLV
Lion. Mary Elizabeth Fullerton. PoAu-1
Lion, The. Mary Howitt. FaPON
Lion, The. Ogden Nash. CenHV
Lion, The. Jack Prelutsky. RHPC
Lion. Kenneth Rexroth. *Fr.* A Bestiary. HoPM
Lion. William Jay Smith. RHPC
Lion, The. May Swenson. LiTM; SoSe
Lion, The. W. J. Turner. MoBrPo
Lion. *Unknown, tr. fr. Hottentot.* PeSA
Lion, The. István Vas, *tr. fr. Hungarian by* Jascha Kessler. FOC
Lion and Álbert, The. Marriott Edgar. OBNV
Lion and his shadow the lioness, The. Girl with Pitcher. Ruth Dallas. PeNZ
Lion and the Cub, The. John Gay. *Fr.* Fables. GN
Lion and the Mouse, The. Eliezer Shteynbarg, *tr. fr. Yiddish by* Leonard Wolf. PeBMYV
Lion and the Mouse, The. Jeffreys Taylor. OnMSP
Lion and the unicorn, The. Mother Goose. BoTP; OxBoLi; OxNR
Lion and the Wave, The. William Allingham. FM

Lion cub, of sordid mind, A. The Lion and the Cub. John Gay. GN

Lion dishonoured bids death come, The. Reversionary. Stevie Smith. FaBoEE

Lion, even when full of mud, with burrs, The. Birds. Ruth Miller. PeSA

Lion for Real, The. Allen Ginsberg. GLP; HCAP; RB

Lion Gate. Vera Rich. PoSH

Lion has a golden mane, The. The Lion. Jack Prelutsky. RHPC

Lion-Hunt, The. Thomas Pringle. OBTV

Lion Hunts. Patricia Beer. OxBTC

Lion is called the king, The. Lion. Kenneth Rexroth. *Fr.* A Bestiary. HoPM

Lion is never a lion in a royal hunt, A. Lion Hunts. Patricia Beer. OxBTC

Lion is the [*or* a] beast to fight, The. Sir Arthur Quiller-Couch. CenHV (Sage Counsel.) NA; NBLV

Lion, Leopard, Lady. Douglas Le Pan. OBCV

Lion Named Passion, A. John Hollander. NePoEA-2; NoAM

Lion of my sun, my fiery joy. Psalm of St. The Priapus. James Richard Broughton. ErPo

Lion of St. Mark's upon the glass, The. Her Dead Brother. Robert Lowell. NePoEA

Lion of Winter, The. Shakespeare. *See* Midsummer Night's Dream, A: Now the Hungry Lion Roars.

Lion over the Tomb of Leonidas, The. *Unknown, tr. fr. Greek by* Walter Leaf. AWP

Lion, ruler over all the beasts, The. Lion. William Jay Smith. RHPC

Lion Skin, The. James Keir Baxter. ATNZ

Lion sleeps with open eyes, The. Faces from a Bestiary. X. J. Kennedy. NePoEA-2

Lion tamers wrestle with the lions in a cage, The. Apex. Nate Salsbury. NBLV

Lion, the Lion, he dwells in the waste, The. The Lion. Hilaire Belloc. MoBrPo; NBLV

Lion with the heat oppressed, A. The Lion and the Mouse. Jeffreys Taylor. OnMSP

Lioness whelped, and the sturdy cub, The. The Eagle's Song. Richard Mansfield. PAH

Lions and tigers dominate. Jungle. Mary Carter Smith. PoNe

Lion's Bride, The. Gwen Harwood. BoWoP

Lion's Cub, The. Maurice Thompson. AA

Lions of fire, The. Kenneth Patchen. VGW

Lions of the hill are gone, The. Deirdre's [*or* Deidre's] Lament for the Sons of Usnach. *Unknown, tr. by* Sir Samuel Ferguson. NOIV; SeCePo

Lion's Skeleton, The. Charles Tennyson Turner. FM; NOBVV

Lions who ate the Christians on the sands of the arena, The. Sunt Leones. Stevie Smith. NoAM

Lip. J. V. Cunningham. *See* Five Epigrams:
Lip was a man who used his head.

Lip and the Heart, The. John Quincy Adams. AA

Lip was a man who used his head. J. V. Cunningham. *Fr.* Five Epigrams. OBAL
(Lip.) ErPo

Lip which had once been stolid, now moving, A. Divine Love. Michael Benedikt. AmPA; CoAP

Lipman and Cohen, butchers, Hercules Lane. At the Jaffé Memorial Fountain, Botanic Gardens. Frank Ormsby. CIP

Lipogram. Sacha Rabinovitch. NPo

Lips and Eyes. Giovanni Battista Marino, *tr. fr. Italian by* Thomas Carew. OBVE; OxBSP; PFI

Lips and Nose. Rodney Hall. *Fr.* The Owner of My Face. CBAP

Lips and tongue. A Hand of Solo. Thomas Kinsella. CIP; NOIV

Lips caked with lipstick. Fille de Joie: Congo. Michael Jackson. ATNZ

Lips of the one I love are my perpetual pleasure, The. Hafiz, *tr. by* Peter Avery *and* John Heath-Stubbs. NBLV

Lips of the Wise, The. Bible, *O.T. Fr.* Proverbs, XV: 1-5, 7-8, 15-17. TrGrPo

Lips That Touch Liquor. George W. Young. NBLV

Liquor and Longevity. *Unknown.* FPL

Liquor, you turn us into kings. What Matter? *Gond Oral Tradition, tr. by* V. Elwin *and* S. Hivale. WTO

Lis/ -ten/ you know what I mean. Listen. E. E. Cummings. WaaP

Lisa. Constance Carrier. SoSe

Lisbon. *Unknown.* AmFP

Lisbon Earthquake, The, *sel.* Voltaire, *tr. fr. French by* Tobias Smollet. "Moralist still obstinate replies, The." OBD

Lisbon Packet, The. Byron. NBLV

Lise. Rose Terry Cooke. AA

Lisnagade. *Unknown.* WTO

Lissome and green, I bow in the mist as if in parting. The Willow Branches. Ho Ning, *tr. by* Lois Fusek. ATF

List, The. Carl Dennis. KS

List, The. Michael McClure. NU

List, I hear the church bells ring. The Church Bells. Mrs. Henry Linden. CBWP-4

List! list! the sleigh bells peal across the snow. December. Henrietta Cordelia Ray. CBWP-3

List the harp in window wailing. The Aeolian Harp. Herman Melville. AmPP

List to that bird! His song—what poet pens it? The Mocking-Bird. Ednah Proctor Clarke. AA

List to the sad wind, drearily moaning. Autumn ("List to the sad wind, drearily moaning"). Priscilla Jane Thompson. CBWP-2

List while the poet trolls. The Rival Curates. W. S. Gilbert. CenHV

Listen. Sophia de Mello Breyner Andresen, *tr. fr. Portuguese by* Ruth Fainlight. OV

Listen. E. E. Cummings. WaaP

Listen. Jessica Hagedorn. WPOW

Listen! Lilian Moore. NTCP

Listen. Charles Patterson. NBP

Listen!/ Listen to the witch! Listen! Lilian Moore. NTCP

Listen/ My friend. What the Girl Friend Said to the Foster-Mother. Kapilar, *tr. by* A. K. Ramanujan. PLW

Listen:/ There roams, far away, by the waters of Clead. Nikolai Gumilev, *tr. fr. Russian by* C. M. Bowra. *Fr.* The Giraffe. FaPON

Listen. / With faint dry sound. November Night. Adelaide Crapsey. FaPON

Listen all ye, 'tis the Feast o' St. Stephen. Feast o' St. Stephen. Ruth Sawyer. OHIP

Listen, and when thy hand this paper presses. A Letter from a Girl to Her Own Old Age. Alice Meynell. FaBoRV; GoTL; LiTB; MoBrPo

Listen awhile and I here will unfold. The Golden Voyage; or, The Prosperous Arrival of the *James and Mary. Unknown.* OxBSS

Listen, children:/ Your father is dead. Edna St. Vincent Millay. DL

Listen Children. Lucille Clifton. CNA; PoBA

Listen, for example, to the thudding of the winter stream. An Inconclusive Evening. Frances Bellerby. FaBoTw

Listen, for the Lord. Acknowledgement. Roberta Hill Whiteman. ER

Listen, good people, and you shall hear. The Ballad of Barnaby. W. H. Auden. OBNV

Listen—help me! Ears. Sonja Akesson, *tr. by* Joanna Bankier. WPOW

Listen here, Joe. Without Benefit of Declaration. Langston Hughes. AmNP; TTY

Listen! In the April rain. In the April Rain. Mary Anderson. BoTP

Listen! It is the summer's self that ambles. The Good Humor Man. Phyllis McGinley. MoShBr

Listen, listen! The small song bird. Song to Imogen [in Basic English]. Richard L. Greene. BXAP

Listen, lively lordings all. The Rising in the North. *Unknown.* ACP; ESPB

Listen, Lord—[a Prayer]. James Weldon Johnson. BANP; BPo

Listen lordings both great and small. The Murder of Saint Thomas of Kent. *Unknown.* ACP

Listen more often. Breaths. Birago Diop, *tr. by* Anne Atik. TTY

Listen, my children, and you shall hear. Paul Revere's Ride (The Landlord's Tale). Longfellow. *Fr.* Tales of a Wayside Inn, Pt. I. AiP; AnAmPo; BeLS; BLPA; FaBoBe; FaBoTw; FaBV; FaFP; FaPON; FaPoR; FPL; OBAL; OBCA; OBNV; OHFP; OPP; PAH; PWR; TrGrPo; WBLP

Listen, my dearest, once this flesh of mine. Two Hearts Divided. R. Williams Parry, *tr. by* Joseph P. Clancy. OBWVE

Listen natives of a dry place. The Old Boast. W. S. Merwin. NOBA

Listen, nephew/ When I opened the cantina. The Tale of Sunlight. Gary Soto. NoAM

Listen now and ye may lere. The Burgesses of Calais. Laurence Minot. ACP

Listen! Now I have come to step over your soul. Sacred Formula to Destroy Life. *Unknown, tr. by* James Mooney. LiTA

"Listen, now, verse should be as natural." Poetry for Supper. R. S. Thomas. OxBC

Listen old man listen. Sweat-House Ritual No. 1. *Unknown, tr. by* Jerome Rothenberg *from* Alia Fletcher *and* Francis La Flesche. STP

Listen. Put on Morning. William Sydney Graham. FaBoTw; LiTM

Listen! The garbage pouring down the chutes. For David Shapiro. David Lehman. PoA

Listen, the hay-bells tinkle as the cart. The Holy Innocents. Robert Lowell. InvP; MoAB; MoAmPo; NePoEA; OBCP; OxBC

Listen. These voices are under attack. Under Attack. Margaret Randall. AIW; ER

Listen to Me. Kishwar Naheed, *tr. fr. Urdu by* Mahmood Jamal. PBMUP

Listen to me, as when ye heard our father. Canadian Boat Song. *At. to* John Galt *and also to* "Christopher North." BLPA; CaP; FaBoCh; FaPoR; OBEV; OBNC

Listen to the Bird. Laya Firestone. VWA

Listen to the call of the muezzin. A Denunciation. Mahammed Abdille Hassan, *tr. by* B. W. Andrzejewski. WTO

Listen to the cicada's burning drone. The Cicada. H. M. Green. PoAu-1

Listen to the coal. In Memoriam John Coltrane. Michael Stillman. InPK; RR

Listen to the exhortation of the dawn! The Salutation of the Dawn. *Unknown.* PoLF

Listen to the Kitchen Clock. The Old Kitchen Clock. Ann Hawkshawe. BoTP

Listen to the phone calls they do not. Metaphor as Illness. Chuck Ortleb. GLP

Listen to the song. Wandering Jack. Emile Jacot. BoTP

Listen to the sounds of the warriors' elbow-guards. Empress Gemmyo. *Fr. Manyo Shu.* Ma

Listen to the story of Willie the Weeper. Willie the Weeper. *Unknown.* BeLS; BLPA; OBAL

Listen to the tale. Slim Greer. Sterling Allen Brown. BANP

Listen to the voice at its root. Ernst David, *tr. fr. German by* Beth Bjorklund. CoAuP

Listen to the water-mill. The Water Mill. Sarah Doudney. BLPA; WGRP

Listen to this story. This Island Mopsy. Victor Questel. PBCV

Listen, waves, tell of this, beach. Emperor Go-Shirakawa, *tr. fr. Japanese by* Hiroaki Sato. *Fr. Ryojin Hisho.* FCEI

Listen, what a legend. Khwaja Haider Ali Atish, *tr. by* Ahmed Ali. GoT

Listen, you drawing men. Snapshots of the Cotton South. Frank Marshall Davis. PoBA

Listen, you know the pains of love. Meleager, *tr. by* Peter Whigham. PeHV

Listen, you who have just arrived. Asadullah Khan Ghalib, *tr. by* Ahmed Ali. GoT

Listen Zulus. Lalela Zulu. *Unknown.* PeSA

Listenen to Big Black at S. F. State. Sonia Sanchez. BPo

Listeners, The. Walter de la Mare. AWP; BLPL; BrPo; CMoP; FaFP; FaPON; HAP; HeIP; HoPM; InPK; InvP; LiTB; LiTM; MoAB; MoBrPo; MoP; NoAM; NOBE; NoP; OBEV; OBMV; OnMSP; PoRA; SoSe; TrGrPo; WeW; WSC

Listener's Guide to the Birds, A. Elwyn Brooks White. NYBP

Listening. Alice Corbin, *after Chippewa Indian.* BPAW

Listening. Aileen Fisher. NTCP

Listening. Hanny Michaelis, *tr. fr. Dutch by* Marjolijn de Jager. VWA

Listening. William Stafford. RFM

Listening for the sound. Pinkie Gordon Lane. BlSi

Listening, listening; it is never still. The Märchen. Randall Jarrell. CMoP

Listening Nydia. Henrietta Cordelia Ray. CBWP-3

Listening Rock, The. Ray A. Young Bear. NOVW

Listening to/ the earth's code. September Heath. Otto Laaber, *tr. by* Beth Bjorklund. CoAuP

Listening to a Broadcast. John Manifold. WaP

Listening to Baseball in the Car. Gail Mazur. ASP

Listening to Beethoven on the Oregon Coast. Henry Carlile. Psk

Listening to Confucius. Henryk Grynberg, *tr. fr. Polish by* Issac Komem. VWA

Listening to Grownups Quarreling. Ruth Whitman. NTCP

Listening to Her. Natan Zach, *tr. fr. Hebrew by* Laya Firestone. VWA

Listening to Red Maples on an Empty Mountain. Lan Ling, *tr. fr. Chinese by* Dominic Cheung. IFON

Listening to the Lute. Jakuan, *tr. fr. Chinese by* Lucien Stryk *and* Takashi Ikemoto. ZPCJ

Listening to the man. Poem for Otis Redding. Joyce Carol Thomas. CNA

Listening to the Mountain. Brian Turner. ATNZ

Listening to the music. Listening. Hanny Michaelis, *tr. by* Marjolijn de Jager. VWA

Listening to the Music of Arsenio Rodríguez Is Moving Closer to Knowledge. Victor Hernandez Cruz. UL

Listening to the Rain. K'ang Hai, *tr. fr. Chinese by* Jonathan Chaves. CoBLCP

Listens/ to the falling snow. Robinson. Alfred Gong, *tr. by* Beth Bjorklund. CoAuP

Listeth, lordes, in good entent [*or* intent]. Sir Thopas. Chaucer. *Fr. The Canterbury Tales.* Par

(Sir Thopas's Tale.) NAEL-1

(Tale of Sir Thopas.) BXAP

Listless beauty of the hour, The. History. D. H. Lawrence. BrPo

Listless he eyes the palisades. In the Prison Pen. Herman Melville. PoEL-5; TAP

Listless morning, A. Bleak. Sándor Weöres, *tr. by* Jascha Kessler. FOC

Listless the silent ladies sit. Music. William Bell Scott. NOBVV

Listlessness. Ch'en Wei-sung, *tr. fr. Chinese by* Madeline Chu. WFTU

Lists became shorter, The. Making Lists. Gladys Cardiff. HATNAP

Liszt. E. C. Bentley. *Fr.* Clerihews. UnS

Lit. Crit. Christopher Logue. NPo

Litanie, The ("Father of heaven, and him, by whom."), *sels.* John Donne. PoEL-2

   Father, The. NOCV

   Holy Ghost, The. NOCV

   Son, The. NOCV

Litanies, *sels.* Hertha Kräftner, *tr. fr. German by* Beth Bjorklund. CoAuP

   "I idolize you with litanies."

   "You, pushed-in window in terribly beautiful countries!"

   "You stony angel over the pain."

Litanies of Julia Pastrana (1832-1860, The. Thomas William Shapcott. CBAP

Litany, The: "From a ruler that's a curse." Charles Cotton. OBSV

Litany, A: "Ring out your bells." Sir Philip Sidney. *See* Ring Out Your Bells.

Litany: "When the sun rises on another day." Charles Angoff. TrPWD

Litany for Dictatorships. Stephen Vincent Benét. OxBA

Litany for Latter-Day Mystics, A. Cale Young Rice. WGRP

Litany for Old Age, A. Una W. Harsen. TrPWD

Litany in Time of Plague, A. Thomas Nashe. *See* Summer's Last Will and Testament: Adieu, Farewell, Earth's Bliss[e].

Litany of [*or* at] Atlanta, A. William Edward Burghardt Du Bois. BANP; CDC; PoNe

Litany of Hate, A. Renée Vivien, *tr. fr. French by* Beth Archer. DMF

Litany of Sleep, *sel.* Tristan Corbière, *tr. fr. French by* Christopher Pilling.

   "You who snore with your sleeping wife so near." OBVE

Litany of the Dark People, The. Countee Cullen. EaLo; TrPWD

Litany of the Heroes, *sel.* Vachel Lindsay.

   Lincoln. OHIP

Litany of the Rooms of the Dead. Franz Werfel, *tr. fr. German by* Edith Abercrombie Snow. TrJP

Litany to Our Lady. *Unknown, tr. fr. Irish by* Eugene O'Curry. TIRV

Litany to Satan. Baudelaire, *tr. fr. French by* James Elroy Flecker. AWP

Litany to the Holy Spirit. Robert Herrick. *See* In the hour of my distress.

Literally thin-skinned, I suppose, my face. Weathering. Fleur Adcock. DiPo

Literary Dinner, A. Vladimir Nabokov. FiBHP; OBAL

Literary Exile, The. Kevin Ireland. ATNZ

Literary Importation. Philip Freneau. TAP

Literary Life in the Golden West. Philip Whalen. NAs

Literary Man Observes a Window to the Sky, The. Kevin Ireland. ATNZ

Literary Manners I. Max Jacob, *tr. fr. French by* Jerome Rothenberg. RHTwFP

Literary Manners II. Max Jacob, *tr. fr. French by* Jerome Rothenberg. RHTwFP

Literary Squabble, A. James Robinson Planché. CenHV

Literary Tag, A. Kevin Ireland. ATNZ

Literature and Poetry. Max Jacob, *tr. fr. French by* John Ashbery. RHTwFP

Litrajure of Everyday Life, The. Michael C. Blumenthal. NoAM

Little. Dorothy Aldis. FaPON; NTCP

Little Ah Sid. *Unknown.* AS

Little Alabama Coon. Hattie Starr. AA

Little and Great. Charles MacKay. PoLF

Little anna brown anna. Anna. Joe Johnson. CNA

Little bat, little bat. To the Bat. Edith King. BoTP

Little Beach-Bird, The. Richard Henry Dana. AA; AnAmPo

Little Beauty That I Was Allowed, The. Elinor Wylie. *Fr.* One Person, V. Son

Little bee returns with evening's gloom, The. A Summer Night in the Beehive. Charles Tennyson Turner. FM

Little Bell. Mary E. Tucker. CBWP-1

Little Bell. Thomas Westwood. GN

Little Benny sat one evening. Misplaced Sympathy. Charles Follen Adams. OBAL

Little Bessie. *Unknown.* AmFP

Little Betty Blue. Betty Blue. Mother Goose. OxNR

Little Betty Blue. Agnes Grozier Herbertson. BoTP

Little Betty Pringle she had a pig. Betty Pringle's Pig. Mother Goose. OxNR

Little Big Horn. Ernest McGaffey. PAH

Little Billee. Thackeray. CenHV; FaBoCh; FaBoCo; MOS; NA; NOBL (Three Sailors, The.) OxBB

Little Billy. *Unknown.* GBP

Little Billy Breek. *Unknown.* OxNR

Little Birches. Mary Effie Lee Newsome. PoNe

Little Bird. Julia Cunningham. TSS

Little Bird, The. Walter De la Mare. NAs

Little Bird, The. *Unknown, tr. by* Rolf Italiaander. PBA

Little bird, The. *Unknown. Fr.* Four Glosses. NOIV

Little bird, a tender bird, A. The Siren Bird. Henrietta Cordelia Ray. CBWP-3

Little bird flew through the dell, A. Autumn Song. Johann Ludwig Tieck, *tr. by* James Clarence Mangan. AWP

Little Bird I Am, A. Mme. Guyon, *tr. fr. French by* T. C. Upham. WGRP

Little bird of paradise. *Unknown.* OxNR

Little bird with tuneful throat. My Canary. Josephine D. Henderson Heard. CBWP-4

Little Birds. Jacob Sternberg, *tr. fr. Yiddish by* Joseph Leftwich. TrJP

Little Birds, The. *Unknown.* NTCP

Little birds in a row. Little Birds. Jacob Sternberg, *tr. by* Joseph Leftwich. TrJP

Little birds ("Little birds are playing"). "Lewis Carroll." *Fr.* Sylvie and Bruno Concluded. FaBoNo; OxBoLi

Little birds sit in their nest and beg, The. The Little Birds. *Unknown.* NTCP

Little birds sleep sweetly. Evening Song. Cecil Frances Alexander. OHIP

Little Bird's Song, A. Margaret Rose. BoTP

Little birds warble their song in the tree, The. The Bird Song. Mrs. Henry Linden. CBWP-4

Little bit of blowing, A. Thoughts for a Cold Day. *Unknown.* BoTP

Little Bits of Soft-boiled Egg. Fay Maschler. RHPC

Little Black Boy, The. Blake. *Fr.* Songs of Innocence. AWP; CH; EnRP; HeIP; NAEL-2; NAWM-2; NOEC; NoP; OAEL-2; OBEV; OBNC; OxBChV; PoE; PoEL-4; PoNe; TrGrPo

Little Black boy. Nigger. Frank Horne. BANP; CDC

Little Black Bug. Margaret Wise Brown. FaPON; NTCP

Little black bull kem down de medder, De. Hoosen Johnny. *Unknown.* AS; FaPON

Little Black Dog, The. Elizabeth Gardner Reynolds. PoLF

Little black dog ran round the house, The. *Unknown.* OxNR

Little Black-eyed Rebel, The. Will M. Carleton. FaPON; PAH

Little Black Rose, The. Aubrey Thomas De Vere. ACP; BIrV

Little Black Rose. *Unknown, tr. fr. Irish by* Thomas Kinsella. NOIV

Little Black Sheep, The. Paul Laurence Dunbar. WBLP

Little black thing among the snow, A. The Chimney Sweeper ("A little black thing among the snow"). Blake. *Fr.* Songs of Experience. NAEL-2; NAWM-2; NOEC; OAEL-2; PPP; RB; SaC; TEP

Little Black Train, The. *Unknown.* AmFP

Little blessed Earth that turns, The. O Earth, Turn! George Johnston. MoCV

Little blind girl wandering, A. The Brook. William Wilberforce Lord. AA

Little blood, more or less, he said, A. Great and Strong. Miroslav Holub, *tr. by* George Theiner. RB

"Little Blue Apron." *Unknown.* BoTP

Little Blue Ben, who lives in the glen. *Unknown.* OxNR

Little Blue Betty lived in a den. *Unknown.* OxNR

Little Bo-Peep,/ Had lost her sheep. The Fairy Sleep and Little Bo-Peep. *Unknown.* BoTP

Little Bo-Peep has lost her sheep. Mother Goose. FaBoBe; OxNR

Little boat at anchor, The. Fourth of July Night. Carl Sandburg. OFD

Little boat floats by the dock, The. Inscribed on a Painting. Tao-chi, *tr. by* Jonathan Chaves. CoBLCP

Little boat, tied up at the dock, The. Painting a Picture "The Tranquil Boat." Wen Cheng-ming, *tr. by* Jonathan Chaves. CoBLCP

Little boat—untie the line. To the Tune, "Ch'ing-p'ing Yüeh." Yang Shen, *tr. by* Jonathan Chaves. CoBLCP

Little boat with no treadboard. Saigyo, *tr. fr. Japanese by* Burton Watson. *Fr.* Sixty-four Tanka. FCEI

Little Boats of Britain, The. Sara E. Carsley. CaP

Little Bob Robin. Bob Robin. Mother Goose. OxNR

Little Book 107. Hannah Weiner. IAT

Little Book 124. Hannah Weiner. IAT

Little boy, The. Junior Addict. Langston Hughes. BPo; CNA

Little Boy, A. Ruth Kim Chun-soo, *tr. fr. Korean by* Koh Chang-soo. ACKP

Little Boy and the Old Man, The. Shel Silverstein. RHPC

Little Boy Blue. Eugene Field. AA; AnAmPo; BeLS; FaFP; FaPON; FPL; OBAL; OBCA; OHFP; PoLF; SoSe

Little Boy Blue. John Crowe Ransom. LiTM

Little Boy Blue, come blow up your horn. Mother Goose. BoTP; FaBoBe; FaFP; OxNR

Little Boy Found, The. Blake. *Fr.* Songs of Innocence. EnRP; NoP

Little boy is fishing, The. The Fisherman. David McCord. PDV

Little boy kneels at the foot of the bed. Vespers. Alan Alexander Milne. OxBChV

Little boy, laid sick and low, A. The Dying Child's Request. Hannah Flagg Gould. OBCA

Little boy, little boy, where wast thou born? Lancashire Born. *Unknown.* GBP

Little Boy Lost, A. Robert Blake. TOF

Little Boy Lost, The. Stevie Smith. FaBoTw

Little Boy Lost, A ("Nought loves another as itself"). Blake. *Fr.* Songs of Experience. EnRP

Little boy lost in the lonely fen, The. The Little Boy Found. Blake. *Fr.* Songs of Innocence. EnRP; NoP

Little Boy Lost, The ("Father, father, where are you going?"). Blake. *Fr.* Songs of Innocence. EnRP; NoP

Little boy on August first night, A. Warren Phinney. Bernadette Mayer. UL

Little boy once played so loud, A. Extremes. James Whitcomb Riley. FaPON

Little Boy, to show his might and power, The. The Metamorphosis. Sir John Suckling. CaPo; FaBoEE

Little boy was looking for his voice, The. The Little Mute Boy. Federico García Lorca, *tr. by* W. S. Merwin. RB

Little boy who would not say "Thank you" and "If you please," The. *Unknown.* FaBoUs

Little boys and little maidens. Little Catkins. Aleksandr Aleksandrovich Blok, *tr. by* Babette Deutsch. EaLo; OFD

Little Boy's Vain Regret, A. Edith M. Thomas. AA

Little breast/ O/ clouds. Flower Market. Pierre Reverdy, *tr. by* Kenneth Rexroth. RHTwFP

Little Breeches. John Milton Hay. AA; AnAmPo; BeLS; FaBoBe

Little Britain. *Unknown.* NOEC

Little brooklet trilled a song, A. The Brooklet. Joseph Skipsey. PF

Little Brother, The. James Reeves. OxBTC

Little Brother of the Rich, A. Edward Sandford Martin. AA

Little Brother's Secret. Katherine Mansfield. FaPON; NAs

Little Brown Baby. Paul Laurence Dunbar. BANP; NoP; PoNe

Little brown boy. Helene Johnson. AmNP; BANP; CDC; PoBA

Little brown brother, oh! little brown brother. Baby Seed Song. Edith Nesbit. FaPON

Little Brown Bulls, The. *Unknown.* AmFP

Little Brown Celery, The. George MacBeth. TSS

Little brown house mouse, laugh and leap. The House Mouse. Jack Prelutsky. RAR

Little Brown Jug. At. to Joseph E. Winner. FaFP; OBAL

Little Brown Seed. Rodney Bennett. BoTP

Little Brown Seed, The. Harriett Mulford Lothrop. PWR

Little brown squirrel hops in the corn, The. The Rejected "National Hymns." "Orpheus C. Kerr." OBAL

Little bunches of/ grass pretend they are bushes. Stories from Kansas. William Stafford. RFM

Little buoy said, A, "Mother, deer." A Misspelled Tail. Elizabeth T. Corbett. OBCA

Little by Little. *Unknown.* PWR

Little by little my gender drifts away. Apostrophe to a Dead Friend. Maxine W. Kumin. CAPP

Little Cabin, A. Charles Bertram Johnson. BANP

Little Candle. Carl Sandburg. GoYe

Little Car, The. Guillaume Apollinaire, *tr. fr. French.* POS, *tr. by* Michael Benedikt; RHTwFP, *tr. by* Ron Padgett *and others*; SOTW, *tr. by* Ron Padgett *and others.*

Little cares that fretted me, The. Out in the Fields with God. *At. to* Elizabeth Barrett Browning *and to* Louis Imogen Guiney. BLRP; WBLP; WGRP

(Song from Sylvan, A.) BLPA

Little Carol of the Virgin, A. Lope de Vega. PChr

Little Cat, The. *Unknown, tr. fr. Medieval Latin by* Helen Waddell. CRH

Little Cat Angel, The. Leontine Stanfield. BLPA

Little caterpillar creeps, The. Cocoon. David McCord. OBCA

Little Catkins. Aleksandr Aleksandrovich Blok, *tr. fr. Russian by* Babette Deutsch. EaLo; OFD

Little Charlie Chipmunk. Helen Cowles LeCron. FaPON

Little Cheat. *Malay Oral Tradition, tr. by* R. J. Wilkinson *and* R. O. Winstedt. WTO

Little Child, The. Albert Bigelow Paine. AA

Little child, A. Puer Aeternus. Kathleen Jessie Raine. NYBP

Little child, I counsel you that ye. Customs Change. *Unknown.* OxBChV

Little child sat on the floor, A. Where Do School Days End? Josephine D. Henderson Heard. CBWP-4

Little children here ye may lere. Manners at Table When Away from Home. *Unknown.* OxBChV

Little children, never give. Kindness to Animals. *Unknown.* BoTP; FaBoUs

Little children you will all go. Song of Man Chipping an Arrowhead. W. S. Merwin. InPK

Little Chisel, The. N. P. van Wyck Louw, *tr. fr. Afrikaans by* Jack Cope *and* Uys Krige. PeSA

Little Clan, The. F. R. Higgins. OBMV

Little Clotilda. *Unknown.* BoTP; RHPC

Little Cock Robin. *Unknown.* PBBP

Little cock sparrow sat on a green tree, A. Mother Goose. OxNR

Little cock sparrow sat on a tree, A. *Unknown.* BoTP

Little cousin is dead, by foul subtraction, The. Dead Boy. John Crowe Ransom. CMoP; FaBoMo; LiTA; Mes; NoAM; NoP; OBD; OxBA; PoE; TwCP

Little Cradle Rocks Tonight in Glory, The. *Unknown.* AmFP

Little Dame Crump. *Unknown.* BoTP

Little Dancers, The. Laurence Binyon. BoTP; CH; MoBrPo; OxBTC

Little Dandelion, The. Lula Lowe Weeden. CDC

Little dark Cape girl why is it you roam. Wordspinning. Olga Kirsch, *tr. by* Jack Cope. PeSA

Little Death. Gwyn Thomas, *tr. fr. Welsh by* Joseph P. Clancy. OBWVE

Little Diary on Growing Old, *sel.* Carlo Betocchi, *tr. fr. Italian by* i. L. Salomon.
"At noon I watch the sun shine." PFI

Little Dicky Dilver. *Unknown.* OxNR

Little Dog-Angel, A. Norah M. Holland. PoLF

Little Dog under the Wagon, The. *Unknown.* PoLF

Little Doll, The. Charles Kingsley. *See* Water Babies, The: Lost Doll, The.

Little Donkey, The. Francis Jammes, *tr. fr. French by* Lloyd Alexander. PChr

Little Donkey Close Your Eyes ("Little donkey on the hill."). Margaret Wise Brown. PDV

Little Dove, The. *Unknown.* AmFP

Little drops of water. Kind Deeds. Isaac Watts. BoTP

Little drops of water. Little Things. *At. to* Julia A. Fletcher Carney. BLPA; BLPL; FaBoBe; FaFP; FaPON; OxBChV

Little Drummer, The. Richard Henry Stoddard. AmFP; PAH

Little Drummer, The. *Unknown.* AmFP

Little drunk he walked back slowly, A. Providence. David St. John. NAmP

Little Dunkeld. *Unknown.* GBP

Little Dutch Garden, A. Harriet Whitney Durbin. AA

Little East of Jordan, A. Emily Dickinson. Mes

Little Elegy. Denis Devlin. NOIV

Little Elegy. X. J. Kennedy. CoAP; GoJo; HoPM

Little Elegy. Elinor Wylie. ILY

Little elephant was crying, The. Cradle Song of the Elephants. Adriano Del Valle, *tr. by* Alida Malkus. FaPON

Little Elf, The. John Kendrick Bangs. AA; FaBoBe; NTCP; OBCA; RAR
(Little Elfman, The.) OnUR; PDV

Little Ellie sits alone. Romance of the Swan's Nest. Elizabeth Barrett Browning. GN

Little Exercise at 4. A.M. Elizabeth Bishop. CoAP; MoAB; MoAmPo; NYBP; UnPo

Little face there was, A. In Rama. George Alfred Townsend. AA

Little Factory Girl to a More Fortunate Playmate, The. *Unknown.* SaC

Little fairy comes at night, A. The Dream Fairy. Thomas Hood. BoTP

Little Falls. Robert Hogg. MoCV

Little Farm. James Reeves. Mes; SO

Little Farm; or, The Weary Ploughman, The. *Unknown.* CoMu

Little Father Poem. Marvin Bell. LCAP

Little Fay's Thanksgiving. Henrietta Cordelia Ray. CBWP-3

Little fellow, you're amusing. Song of the Ogres. W. H. Auden. RHPC

Little Finger Game, A. E. J. Falconer. BoTP

Little Fir Tree, The. Margaret Rose. BoTP

Little Fire in the Woods, The. Hayden Carruth. DiL

Little Fish. D. H. Lawrence. OxBTC; RB; SOTW; TTTS

Little fish are silent, The. Fish. Arthur Stanley Bourinot. RAR

Little fish swim in the river, big fish swim in the sea. I Don't Let the Girls Worry My Mind. *Unknown.* AmFP

Little fish that in the stream doth fleet, The. To Alexander Neville. Barnabe Googe. NoP

Little Fish That Would Not Do as It Was Bid, The. Ann Taylor *and* Jane Taylor. OHIP

Little fishes in a brook. *Unknown.* OxNR

Little flocks of peaceful clouds. The Black Cloud. W. H. Davies. RB

Little flowers came through the ground, The. At Easter Time. Laura Elizabeth Richards. OHIP

Little Flower's Disciple, The. John Montague. *See* Leaping Fire, The: Old lady, I now celebrate.

Little Fly,/ Thy summers play. Blake. *Fr.* Songs of Experience. NAEL-2; NBLV
(Fly, The.) FM; TrGrPo

Little fogs were gathered in every hollow. The Country Wedding (A Fiddler's Story). Thomas Hardy. UnPo

Little French Lawyer, The, *sel.* John Fletcher.
Song in the Wood. EIL

Little Garaine. Sir Gilbert Parker. FaPON

Little General Monk. *Unknown.* OxNR

Little Gidding. T. S. Eliot. *Fr.* Four Quartets. FaBoMo; FaBoPV; FaBoTw; GTBS-P; MoP; NAEL-2; NAWM-2; NoAM; NOBA; NOBE; OAEL-2; OxBTC; PrIm; TAP
"We shall not cease from exploration." *Fr.* V.ImOP
"Ash on an old man's sleeve." *Fr.* II.FaBoTw

Little Giffen. Francis Orrery Ticknor. AA; GOA; PAH
(Little Giffen of Tennessee.) AnAmPo

Little Girl, A. Charles Angoff. GoYe

Little Girl, The. Nicholas Moore. ErPo

Little Girl. Mother Goose. OxNR

Little Girl, Be Careful What You Say. Carl Sandburg. GoYe

Little Girl Blue. "Yvonne." TSL

Little girl called Silé Javotte. Christmas 1970. Spike Milligan. OBCP

Little girl crouches with her little brother, A. The Journey to the Insane Asylum. Alfred Lichtenstein, *tr. by* Mary Zilzer. VWA

Little girl dressed, The. Celebration. Ray A. Young Bear. CDW

Little girl I'd known, The. Flora. Ray Fraser. NeAC

Little girl knew, The. Girl, Prince, Lizard. Heather Ross Miller. MT

"Little girl, little girl." *Unknown.* BoTP

Little girl, little girl,/ Where have you been? Little Girl. Mother Goose. OxNR

Little girl marched around her Christmas tree, A. Ogden Nash. *Fr.* The New Nutcracker Suite. PChr

Little Girl, My Stringbean, My Lovely Woman. Anne Sexton. NYBP

Little girl riding the fallen tree like a spindly horse, The. Light Hotel. Peter Redgrove. PoE

Little girl that I was, A. Laughter. Wislawa Szymborska, *tr. by* Czeslaw Milosz. PwPP

Little Girl That Lost a Finger, The. Gabriela Mistral, *tr. fr. Spanish by* Muna Lee. FaPON

Little Girl Wakes Early. Robert Penn Warren. PoE

Little Girl with Bands on Her Teeth, The. Genevieve Taggard. VGW

Little girl with scarlet enameled fingernails, A. Melodic Trains. John Ashbery. NoP

Little girl won't eat her sandwich, The. Blasting from Heaven. Philip Levine. CoAP

Little girls/ on the sidewalk. Chinatown Games. Wing Tek Lum. BrSi

Little girls—/ You are gay. Day's End. Lesbia Harford. PoAu-1

Little Girl's Dream World, A. Della Burt. BISi

Little girls' frocks are frilly, The. Ballroom Dancing Class. Phyllis McGinley. MoShBr

Little Girl's Show, A. Su Shao-lien, *tr. fr. Chinese by* Dominic Cheung. IFON

Little girls smearing. Schoolyard in April. Kenneth Koch. PoA

Little goat, The. April. Yvor Winters. RFM

Little gold in law will make, A. Isabella Whitney. *Fr.* Sweet Nosegay, A, or Pleasant Posy. WPE

Little green frog lived under a log, A. Strange Talk. L. E. Yates. BoTP

Little green frog once lived in a pool, A. The Frog. Rose Fyleman. BoTP

Little Guinever. Annie Fields. AA .

Little Gustava. Celia Thaxter. FaPON
Little Half-Brother, Little Black Star. George Barlow. NAmP
"Little Haly! Little Haly!" cheeps the robin in the tree. On the Death of
    Little Mahala Ashcraft. James Whitcomb Riley. AA
Little hand is knocking at my heart, A. The Return. Arthur Symons.
    Fr. Amor Triumphans. BrPo
Little hedgerow birds, The. An Old Man [or Old Man Travelling].
    Wordsworth. FaBoCh; OBWP
Little Herd-Boy's Song, The. Robert Buchanan. BoTP
Little Hiawatha, The. Longfellow. Fr. The Song of Hiawatha, III.
    OnUR
Little hiders hide in the hills and groves. Refuting the "Invitation to
    Hiding." Wang K'ang-chü, tr. by Burton Watson. CoBCP
Little hill climbs up to the village and puts its green hands, The. Kenneth
    Patchen. Fr. The Hunted City. NaP
Little Horned Toad. Unknown, tr. fr. Navajo Indian by Hilda Faunce
    Wetherill. FaPON
Little horses trotting, The. Rondeau of the Little Horses. Manuel
    Bandeira, tr. by Richard Wilbur. ATCBP
Little hours: two lovers herd upstairs, The. Almost Aubade. Marilyn
    Hacker. NoAM
Little House in Lithuania, The. Samuel Marshak, tr. fr. Russian by
    Daniel Weissbort. VWA
Little house there stood within a glen, A. A Deathbed. John Hawthorn.
    Fr. The Journey and Observations of a Countryman. NOEC
Little Hundred. Unknown. OxNR
Little Hunger. Richard Murphy. BIrV
Little Hymn to Mary, A. Unknown. MeEL
Little I ask; my wants are few. Contentment. Oliver Wendell Holmes.
    Fr. The Autocrat of the Breakfast Table, 11. AmPP; AnAmPo; OxBA;
    PWR.
Little, I ween, did Mary guess. His Mother's Joy. John White
    Chadwick. AA
Little Indian, Sioux, or Crow. Foreign Children. Robert Louis
    Stevenson. BoTP; GoJo
Little inmate, full of mirth. The Cricket. Vincent Bourne, tr. by William
    Cowper. PoLF
Little Jack Dandy-prat. Unknown. OxNR
Little Jack Horner. Mother Goose. FaBoBe; FaFP; OxNR, (orig. and
    parody); SoSe
Little Jack Sprat/ Once had a pig. Unknown. OxNR
Little Jenny Wren. Unknown. BoTP
Little Jesus came to town, The. A Christmas Folk-Song. Lizette
    Woodworth Reese. FaPON; OBCA; OHIP; OnMSP; TrCP
Little Jesus of the Barren, The. László Nagy, tr. fr. Hungarian by Jascha
    Kessler. FOC
Little Jesus wast Thou shy. Ex Ore Infantium. Francis Thompson.
    BoTP; FaBV; OHIP; OxBChV
    (Child's Prayer, A.) OHIP
Little Jew lived in a little straw hut, A. Biography. A. M. Klein. TrJP
Little joe gould has lost his teeth and doesn't know where. E. E.
    Cummings. NoAM
Little John a Begging ("All you that delight to spend some time").
    Unknown. ESPB
Little John a Begging. ("'Beggar,' he sayes"). Unknown. ESPB
Little John Bottlejohn. Laura E. Richards. PDV
Little John Jiggy Jag. Unknown. OxNR
Little John Nobody. Unknown. OxBoLi
Little Jumping Girls, The. Kate Greenaway. FaPON
Little King Pippin. Mother Goose. BoTP
Little Kingdom I Possess, A. Louisa May Alcott. AH
Little Kings and Queens of May. For Good Luck. Juliana Horatia
    Ewing. FaPON
    (Little Kings and Queens of the May.) BoTP
Little Knight in Green, The. Katharine Lee Bates. AA
Little Knight, you are amusing. Song of the Enchanters. W. H. Auden.
    AnAn
Little lad, little lad. Unknown. OxNR
Little ladies, white and green. Snowdrops. L. Alma Tadema. BoTP
Little lady lairdie, The. Unknown. OxNR
Little Lady Wren. Tom Robinson. FaPON
Little lamb, who made thee? The Lamb. Blake. Fr. Songs of
    Innocence. BLPL; BoTP; CH; EaLo; EnRP; FaBoBe; FaBoCh;
    FaPON; GoJo; HeIP; InPS; LiTB; NAEL-2; NAWM-2; NIP; NOEC;
    NoP; OAEL-2; OxBChV; PoE; SoSe; TEP; TrCP; TrGrPo; UnPo;
    WGRP
Little lambs, little lambs. Baby Beds. Unknown. BoTP
Little lame tailor, The. The Starling. Robert Buchanan. FM
Little lamps of the dusk. Fireflies. Carolyn Hall. FaPON
Little Landscape, A. Chu Yün-ming, tr. fr. Chinese by Jonathan Chaves.
    CoBLCP

Little Landscape by Chao Ch'ien-li, A. Yü Chi, tr. fr. Chinese by
    Jonathan Chaves. CoBLCP
Little Landscape by Yen Wen-kuei, A. Yü Chi, tr. fr. Chinese by
    Jonathan Chaves. CoBLCP
Little Language, A. Robert Duncan. NoAM
Little learning is a dangerous thing, A. Pope. Fr. Essay on Criticism,
    pt. II. FPL; HAP; HoPM; PoLF; TrGrPo
    (Alps on Alps.) FaFP
    (Little Learning, A.) ChTr; LiTB; NOBE; SeCePo
Little leaves green-skinned, white-toothed roots. Planting
    Chrysanthemums. Michizane, tr. by Burton Watson. JLIC-1
Little Libbie. Julia A. Moore. OBAL
Little Light. Jim Brodey. UL
Little light is going by, A. Firefly. Elizabeth Madox Roberts. GoJo;
    NTCP; PDV; RAR; TSS
Little Litany to St. Francis, A. Philip Murray. NePoAm
Little lonely child am I, A. The Moon-Child. "Fiona Macleod." CH
Little Lough, The. John Hewitt. NeIP
Little Love-God, The. Meleager, tr. fr. Greek by Walter Headlam.
    AWP
Little Lucy Lavender. Lucy Lavender. Ivy O. Eastwick. BoTP
Little Lucy Lester. M. Steel. BoTP
Little Lullaby. Irving Feldman. NYBP
Little lute, when I am gone. Richard Corbet. FaBoEE
Little Lyric (of Great Importance). Langston Hughes. NBLV; OBAL
Little Madness in the spring, A. Emily Dickinson. TAP
Little Maid, The. Anna Maria Wells. OBCA
Little Maid and the Cowslips, The. John Clare. BoTP
Little maid of Astrakan, A. The Divan. Richard Henry Stoddard.
    AA
Little maid, pretty maid,/ Whither goest thou? Mother Goose. OxNR
Little Man, The. Hughes Mearns. See Little Man Who Wasn't There,
    The.
Little Man. Alfonsina Storni, tr. fr. Spanish by Perry Higman. LPSS
Little man I always see on the streetcar, The. Ishikawa Takuboku, tr. fr.
    Japanese by Hiroaki Sato. Fr. Forty-seven Tanka in Three Lines.
    FCEI
Little man in coal pit. Putting On Nightgown. Unknown. OxNR
Little Man That Had a Little Gun, The. "Lewis Carroll." See In stature,
    the Manlet was dwarfish.
Little Man Who Wasn't There, The. Hughes Mearns. FaFP; FaPON
    (Antigonish.) BLPL; NBLV; PoLF
    (Case, A.) FaBoCo
    (I Met a Man.) OnUR
    (Little Man, The.) RHPC
    (Man Who Wasn't There, The.) PYC
Little Marble Boy. James Wright. EyDe
Little Marg'et sitting in her high hall door. Fair Margaret and Sweet
    William. Unknown. AMFP
Little marsh-plant, yellow green, A. The Sundew. Swinburne. ELP;
    NoP; OBNC
Little Mary Bell had a fairy in a nut. Long John Brown and Little Mary
    Bell. Blake. RB
Little masters, hat in hand. Clover. John Banister Tabb. AA
Little Men, The. Flora Fearne. BoTP
Little Milliner, The. Robert Buchanan. BeLS
Little Miss and Her Parrot. John Marchant. OxBChV
Little Miss Muffet. Unknown. BXAP; FaBoPa
Little Miss Muffet/ Crouched on a tuffet. Paul Dehn. Fr. Rhymes for a
    Modern Nursery. FiBHP
Little Miss Muffet/ Sat on a tuffet. Mother Goose. FaBoBe; FaFP;
    OxNR
Little Miss Muffet discovered a tuffet. The Embarrassing Episode of Little
    Miss Muffet. Guy Wetmore Carryl. FaPON; OBCA; OnMSP
Little Mistress Comfort got up early one fine day. Mistress Comfort.
    Elizabeth Gould. BoTP
Little Mohea, The. Unknown. AmFP
Little monkey goes like a donkey that means to say, A. A Dog.
    Gertrude Stein. Fr. Tender Buttons. TTTS
Little months little smokes. Comrade. Philippe Soupault, tr. by Pat
    Nolan. RHTwFP
Little Moon, The. Longfellow. BoTP
Little More about the Brothers and Sisters, A. Sharon Scott. JB
Little more tired at the close of the Day, A. Growing Old [or Growing
    Older]. Rollin J. Wells. BLPA; WBLP
Little Morning Music, A. Delmore Schwartz. BoNaP; NYBP
Little moths are creeping, The. Interior. Padraic Colum. MoBrPo
Little mountain spring I found, A. The Spring. Rose Fyleman. FaPON
Little Mr. Browny Bee. Browny Bee. Irene F. Pawsey. BoTP
Little Musgrave and Lady Barnard. Unknown. AmFP; ErPo; ESPB;
    FaBoBa; InvP; OBET; OxBB

Little Mute Boy, The. Federico García Lorca, *tr. fr. Spanish by* W. S. Merwin. RB

Little Nancy [*or* Nanny] Etticoat. Mother Goose. ChTr; OxNR

Little nearer, this time, A. After the Second Operation. Patricia Goedicke. TAP

Little noises of the house, The. During a Bombardment by V-Weapons. Roy Fuller. OxBSP

Little Ode. Paul Goodman. PoA

Little Ode for X. Maura Stanton. MAYP

Little of brilliance did they write or say. The Stricken Average. William Rose Benét. AnAmPo

Little old-fashioned girl, The. At Grandfather's. Clara Doty Bates. OBCA

Little Old Lady, The. Rodney Bennett. BoTP

Little Old Lady in Lavender Silk, The. Dorothy Parker. NBLV; NIP

Little old man of Derby, A. *Unknown.* OxNR

Little old man of the sea, A. The Ingenious Little Old Man. John Bennett. FaPON

Little Old Sod Shanty. *Unknown.* AmFP; AS, *with music*

Little old woman, A. Bramble Jam. Irene F. Pawsey. BoTP

Little old woman, A. Good Neighbors. May Justus. RAR

Little one, come to my knee! A Night with a Wolf. Bayard Taylor. GN

Little one sleeps in its cradle, The. Walt Whitman. *Fr.* Song of Myself, VIII. TrGrPo

Little Ones' A. B. C., The, *sel.* Noel Coward.
"A. Stands for Absolutely Anything." NBLV

Little onion lay by the fireplace, A. Nicholas Moore. EAS

Little onward lend thy guiding hand, A. Samson before the Prison in Gaza. Milton. *Fr.* Samson Agonistes. FaBoPV

Little Orphant Annie. James Whitcomb Riley. AA; AnAmPo; FaFP; FaPON; MoShBr; NBLV; OBAL; OBCA; OxBChV

Little Papoose. Hilda Conkling. FaPON

Little Parable, A. Anne Reeve Aldrich. AA

"Little, passionately, not at all, A?" Villanelle of Marguerites. Ernest Dowson. MoBrPo

Little Peach, The. Eugene Field. AnAmPo; OBAL

Little Peach, The. *Unknown.* NA

Little People. Isaac Leibush Peretz, *tr. fr. Yiddish by* Joseph Leftwich. TrJP

Little Pets of Saint Mochua, The. John Irvine. TIRV

Little Pig, Zishe Landau, *tr. fr. Yiddish.* PeBMYV, *tr. by* Irving Feldman; VWA, *tr. by* Ruth Whitman

Little Pig. *Unknown.* OxNR

Little pig lived in a sty, A. The Greedy Little Pig. Irene F. Pawsey. BoTP

Little Piggies, The. Thomas Hood. BoTP

Little plum/ said the mother to her son. Hansel and Gretel. Anne Sexton. InPS

Little Poem. Max Jacob, *tr. fr. French by* William Jay Smith. CT

Little poem for the individual, A. Fatal Longing. A. Leyeles, *tr. by* Benjamin *and* Barbara Harshav. AYP

Little Poll Parrot. *Unknown.* OxNR

Little Polly Flinders. Mother Goose. OxNR

Little poppies, little hell flames. Poppies in July. Sylvia Plath. FaBoWP; LCAP; NaP; RB

Little Prayer, A. Paul Goodman. LiTA

Little Pretty Bonny Lass, A. *Unknown.* EIL

Little pretty Nancy girl. *Unknown.* OxNR

The little pretty nightingale. The Nightingale. *Unknown.* TrGrPo

Little priest of Felton, The. Priest of Felton. *Unknown.* OxNR

Little prince of long ago, A. Sons of the King. Joan Agnew. BoTP

Little Pudding. Mary M. Roberts. BXAP

Little Puppy. *Unknown, tr. fr. Navajo Indian by* Hilda Faunce Wetherill. FaPON

Little ragged girl, our ball-boy, A. A Game at Salzburg. Randall Jarrell. NoAM

Little Rain, The. Tu Fu, *tr. fr. Chinese by* L. Cranmer-Byng. FaPON

Little rain clouds from Yunnan-Tee. My Chinese Summer. Barbara Frischmuth, *tr. by* Beth Bjorklund. CoAuP

Little Raindrops. *At. to* Ann Hawkshawe, *also to* Jane Euphemia Browne. BoTP; OxBChV

Little Random Creatures, The. *Unknown, tr. fr. Fox Indian by* Armand Schwerner. STP

Little red lark, The. Morning. Ivy O. Eastwick. BoTP

Little Red Riding Hood. Guy Wetmore Carryl. FiBHP

Little Rhyme and a Little Reason, A. Henry Anstadt. BLRP

Little river twittering in the twilight, The. Bei Hennef. D. H. Lawrence. BrPo

Little robber girl, you sleep. The Story of Good. Phyllis Janik. IHMS

Little Robin Redbreast. *Unknown.* BoTP

Little Robin Redbreast/ Came to visit me. Visitor. *Unknown.* OxNR

Little Robin red breast/ I hear you sing your song. Robin Red Breast. Lula Lowe Weeden. CDC

Little Robin Redbreast/ Sat upon a rail. Niddle Noddle. Mother Goose. OxNR; PBBP

Little Robin Redbreast sat upon a tree. Catch. Mother Goose. OxNR

Little Robin Redbreast sat upon a tree. Little Robin Redbreast. *Unknown.* BoTP

Little room, depressing, old, A. The Tailor. "S. Ansky," *tr. by* Joseph Leftwich. TrJP

Little Rose Tree, The. Rachel Field. FaPON

Little saint best fits a little shrine, A. A Ternarie of Littles, upon a Pipkin of Jellie [*or* Jelly] Sent to a Lady. Robert Herrick. FaBoCh; FaBoUs; GoJo; PoEL-3
(Littles.) BoTP

Little Sally Waters. *Unknown.* AmFP, (2 *vers.*)

Little Sam Clemens, one night back in Hannibal, The. Last Laugh. Robert Penn Warren. MT

Little scavenger away. Flute Song. Hilda Doolittle ("H. D."). AnAmPo

Little Scotch-ee. *Unknown.* AS

Little sculptured animals, young deer. Greek Antiquities: First Floor. Lauris Edmond. UAS

Little seed, A. Maytime Magic. Mabel Watts. RHPC

Little Seeds. Else Holmelund Minarik. RAR

Little sharp vexations, The. The Unfailing One. Phillips Brooks. BLRP

Little Shon a [*or* Johnny] Morgan, shentleman [*or* gentleman] of Wales. Shon a Morgan. *Unknown.* GBP; OxNR

Little shrivelled and humpbacked creature, The! Tim, the Fairy. Florence Randal Livesay. CaP

Little sibilance, as of dry leaves, A. Murmur. Anthony Hecht. BLA

Little Sir Hugh. *Unknown.* OBET

Little Sleep's-Head Sprouting Hair in the Moonlight. Galway Kinnell. InPS; LCAP

Little slender lad, toad-headed. The Ambrosia of Dionysus and Semele. Robert Graves. NYBP

Little Snail. Hilda Conkling. FaPON

Little snail,/ Dreaming you go. Snail. Langston Hughes. FaPON

Little snatch of an ancient song. Of an Old Song. William E. H. Lecky. WGRP

Little Son. Georgia Douglas Johnson. CDC

Little Song, A. Charles O. Hartman. SM

Little Song of Life, A. Lizette Woodworth Reese. FaPON; OBCA

Little Song of Seville. Federico García Lorca, *tr. fr. Spanish by* William Jay Smith. *Fr.* Songs of Childhood. CT

Little Song of the Maimed. Benjamin Péret, *tr. fr. French by* David Gascoyne. OBWP

Little Song of Work, A. Sarah Elizabeth Sprouse. BLRP

Little Songs. Marjorie Pickthall. CaP

Little songs of summer are all gone today, The. End-of-Summer Poem. Rowena Bastin Bennett. FaPON

Little soul so sleek and smiling. The Emperor Hadrian to His Soul. Hadrian, *tr. by* Stevie Smith. OBVE

Little sound, A. Many a Mickle. Walter De la Mare. FaBV

Little Sparrow. *Unknown.* AmFP

Little sparrows, The. William Carlos Williams. TwCP

Little square of earth. Undefeated. Robert Froman. ILY

Little Sticks. Eric Rolls. PoAu-2

Little stones chuckle among the fields, The. At Toledo. Arthur Symons. BrPo

Little Stream, A. Philippe Thoby-Marcelin, *tr. fr. French by* William Jay Smith. CT

Little stream used to cross my land, A. Su Tung-p'o, *tr. fr. Chinese by* Burton Watson. *Fr.* Eastern Slope. CoBCP

Little sycamore, The. *Unknown, tr. by* J. E. Manchip White. TTY

Little Talk. Aileen Fisher. FaPON

Little Talk, A. *Unknown.* RAR

Little Te Deum of the Commonplace, A, *sels.* John Oxenham.
We Thank Thee, Lord. WBLP
"With hearts responsive." TrPWD

Little Tee-wee. *Unknown.* OxNR

Little Testament. Eugenio Montale, *tr. fr. Italian.* AnAn, *tr. by* William Arrowsmith; PFI, *tr. by.* Robert Lowell.

Little Things. *At. to* Julia A. Fletcher Carney. BLPA; BLPL; FaBoBe; FaFP; FaPON; OxBChV

Little Things. Eileen Mathias. BoTP

Little Things. James Stephens. EaLo; FaPON; GoJo; MoBrPo; PDV; PoRA; RHPC; TSS

Little things that crawl and creep. Green Stems. Margaret Wise Brown. RHPC

Little Things That Happen, The. Marjorie Wilson. BoTP
Little things, that run, and quail. Little Things. James Stephens. EaLo; FaPON; GoJo; MoBrPo; PDV; PoRA; RHPC; TSS
Little thinks, in the field, yon red-cloaked clown. Each and All. Emerson. AA; AmPP; AnAmPo; AWP; BLPL; NAAL-1; NOBA; OHFP; OxBA; TAP; WGRP
Little think'st thou, poor [or poore] flower. The Blossom [or Blossome]. John Donne. AWP; LiTB; MeLP; NAEL-1; OBS; SeCP; UnPo
Little tigers are at rest, The. Tom Hood. CenHV
Little time for laughter, A. After. Philip Bourke Marston. NOBVV
Little toe, big toe, three toes between. Close Quarters. John Banister Tabb. OBAL
Little toe is attractive, The. "The Time of Man." Phyllis Webb. MoCV
Little Tom Tittlemouse/ Lived in a bell-house. Unknown. OxNR
Little Tom Tittlemouse/ Lived in a bell-house. Unknown. OxNR
Little Tommy Tacket. Unknown. OxNR
Little Tommy Tiddler. Paul Edmonds. BoTP
Little Tommy Tittlemouse/ Lived in a little house. Mother Goose. OxNR
Little Tommy Tucker. Tommy Tucker. Mother Goose. OxNR
Little Tommy Yesterday. Alex Glasgow. OBET
Little too abstract, a little too wise, A. Return. Robinson Jeffers. GoYe
Little toy dog is covered with dust, The. Little Boy Blue. Eugene Field. AA; AnAmPo; BeLS; FaFP; FaPON; FPL; OBAL; OBCA; OHFP; PoLF; SoSe
Little tree. E. E. Cummings. Fr. Chansons Innocentes, II. NTCP; OBCP; PChr; PDV
Little Trotty Wagtail. John Clare. BoTP; FaPON; OnUR; RB; UnPo
Little Trumpet, The. Corrado Govoni, tr. fr. Italian by Carlo L. Golino. PFI
Little Tumescence, A. Jonathan Williams. ErPo; NeAP; PoM
Little Turtle, The. Vachel Lindsay. FaPON; GoJo; NTCP; OBAL; OBCA; PDV; RAR
Little Vagabond, The. Blake. Fr. Songs of Experience. NBLV; OBSV
Little Viennese Waltz. Federico García Lorca, tr. fr. Spanish by William B. Logan. SOTW
Little Way, A. Frank Lebby Stanton. AA
Little way below her chin, A. On Some Buttercups. Frank Dempster Sherman. AA
Little way to walk with you, my own, A. A Little Way. Frank Lebby Stanton. AA
Little While, a Little While, A. Emily Brontë. OBNC
Little while (my life is almost set!), A. Paul Hamilton Hayne. AA; AnAmPo
Little Whistler, The. Frances Mary Frost. PDV
Little white clouds are racing over the sky, The. Magdalen Walks. Oscar Wilde. EBVV; MoBrPo
Little white lilies, The. Widows' Rice. Okkur Macattanar, tr. by A. K. Ramanujan. PLW
Little white mermaidens live in the sea, The. The Mermaidens. Laura Elizabeth Richards. OBCA
Little White Schoolhouse Blues. Florence Becker Lennon. PoNe
Little Wild Baby. "Margaret Vandegrift." AA
Little wild bird sometimes at my ear, A. Ballata: Of True and False Singing. Unknown, tr. by Dante Gabriel Rossetti. AWP
Little wild birds have come flying, The. Unknown, tr. by W. R. S. Ralston. AWP
Little Willie ("Little Willie from his mirror"). Unknown. MoShBr
Little Willie ("Little Willie hung his sister"). Unknown. NA
Little Willie ("Willie saw some dynamite"). Unknown. FaPON
Little Wind. Kate Greenaway. GoJo; RAR
Little woman looks out the window, A. Cosmic Tapestry. Anna Kiss, tr. by Jascha Kessler. FOC
Little Word, The. Unknown. PWR
Little Work, A. George Du Maurier. Fr. Trilby, pt. VIII. FaBoBe; PoLF
Little Wren, A. Priscilla Jane Thompson. CBWP-2
Little Wren of tender mind, The. The Wren. Unknown. OxBChV
Little yellow buttercup, A. A Buttercup. Unknown. BoTP
Little young lambs, oh! why do you stay. The Wolf and the Lambs. Ivy O. Eastwick. BoTP
Littleblood. Ted Hughes. Fr. Crow. PoE
Littles. Robert Herrick. Fr. A Ternarie of Littles. See Little saint best fits a little shrine, A.
Littoral. Hjalmar Flax, tr. fr. Spanish by Julio Marzán. InW
Liu Ch'e. Ezra Pound. OBVE; VGW
Live Acts. Charles Bernstein. UL
Live all thy sweet life thro'. A Summer Wish. Christina Rossetti. OBNC
Live Blindly ("Live blindly and upon the hour"). Trumbull Stickney. LiTA; TrGrPo

Live Christ. John Oxenham. BLRP
Live ever here, Lorenzo?—shocking thought! Edward Young. Fr. Night Thoughts, Night III. EnRP
Live fish—someone's New Year's gift to me. On New Year's Day of the Year Kuei-ssu. Wang T'ing-hsiang, tr. by Jonathan Chaves. CoBLCP
Live Flesh. Pierre Reverdy, tr. fr. French by Kenneth Rexroth. RHTwFP
Live for It. Ellen Bass. ER
Live fowl squatting on the grapefruit and bananas, The. Jamaican Bus Ride. A. S. J. Tessimond. OBTV; OxBTC
Live here for awhile. Kenko, tr. fr. Japanese by Steven D. Carter. WFTW
Live here, great heart; and love and dy and kill. Richard Crashaw. Fr. The Flaming Heart. OBS
Live, live with me, and thou shalt see. To Phyllisto Love and Live with Him. Robert Herrick. CaPo
Live lizard; dead lizard. Witches' Menu. Sonja Nikolay. RHPC
Live so that you. Certain Maxims of Archy. Don Marquis. OBAL
Live storm went through last night, The. Glad at the Cold (1955). Alan Dugan. NoAM
Live thy Life,/ Young and old. The Oak. Tennyson. FaPON
Lived on one's back. Vigil. W. E. Henley. Fr. In Hospital, VII. BrPo
Liveliest effigy of the human race. Ralph Chubb. Fr. The Book of God's Madness. PeHV
Lively young turtle lived down by the banks, A. The Song of the Turtle and the Flamingo. James Thomas Fields. GN
(Turtle and Flamingo, The.) AnAmPo
Liverockie, liverockie lee. The Lark. Unknown. GBP
Liverpool. Unknown. AmFP
Liverpool Girls. Unknown. OxBSS
Liverpool John. Phil and June Colclough. OxBSS
Lives. Cyril Dabydeen. BrSi
Lives. Derek Mahon. FaBCIP
Lives. Henry Reed. BoNaP; LiTB
Lives and times of Oedipus and Elektra, The. This One's on Me. Phyllis Gotlieb. MoCV; NOBC
Lives in winter. Unknown. NTCP
Lives of Famous Men, The. Jack Gilbert. NPGG
Lives of football men remind us. Dedicated to F. W. Ernest Hemingway. ASP
Lives of Great Men ("Lives of great men all remind us/ As their pages o'er we turn"). Unknown. FaFP
(After Emerson.) NOBL
Lives of great men all remind us. Life. Longfellow. Fr. A Psalm of Life. GN
Lives of Gulls and Children, The. Howard Nemerov. NePoEA
Lives of the Great Composers. Dana Gioia. EOEF
Lives of the Poets, sels. Richard O'Connell. SoTCo
	Arthur Hugh Clough.
	Sir John Suckling.
Livid sky on London, A. The Old Song. G. K. Chesterton. FaBoTw
Livin in Uncle Sam's backyard ain't easy. Life in Uncle Sam's Backyard. Valerie Bloom. WS
Living, A. D. H. Lawrence. RFM
Living. Denise Levertov. VGW; WPE
Living, The. Gloria A. Maxson. Fr. Two Guitars. TSM
Living. Harold Monro. LiTB; SeCePo
Living, The. Robert Pinsky. NoAM
Living. Unknown. BLPA; FaBoBe
Living alone is like floating on blue. So, When I Swim to the Shore. Molly Peacock. MAYP
Living among the Dead. William Matthews. GeTw
Living and Dying Prayer for the Holiest Believer in the World, A. Augustus Montague Toplady. See Rock of Ages.
Living being, the Temple was killed, A. The Temple. Gustave Kahn, tr. by Edouard Roditi. VWA
Living Book, The. Charlotte Fiske Bates. AA
Living by the Red River. James Wright. NNaP
Living God, The. Daniel ben Judah, tr. fr. Hebrew by Israel Zangwill. TrJP
Living God, The. Charlotte Perkins Gilman. WGRP
Living God, The. Abraham Ibn Ezra, tr. fr. Hebrew by Alice Lucas. TrJP
Living God O magnify and bless, The. The Living God. Daniel ben Judah, tr. by Israel Zangwill. TrJP
Living here. Unknown, tr. fr. Sanskrit by W. S. Merwin and Moussaieff Masson. UnAS
Living Here. Cilla McQueen. ATNZ

Living in a Riverside Village—Miscellaneous Impressions, *sels.* Yang Chi, *tr. fr. Chinese by* Jonathan Chaves. CoBLCP
  "I planned to get drunk to ease my sadness."
  "I've given up poetry—I have no new manuscripts."
  "Just a few feet away, a temple from the Six Dynasties."
  "Reflections in the river: trembling spring trees."
  "Suddenly, warm weather, I change to lighter clothes."
  "Three feet of mud in this narrow alley."
Living in a wide landscape are the flowers. Desert Flowers. Keith Douglas. FaBoTw
Living in its shell. Conch. Raymond Queneau. OBD
Living in Master Fang's Garden, *sels.* Yang Chi, *tr. fr. Chinese by* Jonathan Chaves. CoBLCP
  "Autumn season comes to the country, The."
  "You remove a jade pendant—to exchange for a lute."
  "Your garden hut stands by the green waters."
Living in Retirement at Te-ch'ing. Chao Meng-fu, *tr. fr. Chinese by* Jonathan Chaves. CoBLCP
Living in Sin. Adrienne Rich. FF; IHMS; NePoEA; NoP; NYBP; SoSe; TAP; UnPo
Living in the air. A Native Woman—1982. Karen Cooper. GOS
Living in the Boneyard. John Oliver Simon. NeAC
Living in the Cave. Adrienne Rich. AnAn
Living in the Country at Kou-ch'ü in Autumn—Miscellaneous Impressions, *sels.* Yang Chi, *tr. fr. Chinese by* Jonathan Chaves. CoBLCP
  "Shut in behind the window, a glittering candle."
  "This place is near Hua-yang Mountain."
  "This thatched hut, its master returned."
Living in the earth-deposits of our history. Power. Adrienne Rich. TAP
Living in the Mountains ("It's not easy to live in the mountains"). Sen of Kyuho, *tr. fr. Chinese by* Lucien Stryk *and* Takashi Ikemoto. ZPCJ
Living in the Mountains ("What good's world—profit, fame?"). Sen of Kyuho, *tr. fr. Chinese by* Lucien Stryk *and* Takashi Ikemoto. ZPCJ
Living in the Woods, *sel.* Wang Chiu-ssu, *tr. fr. Chinese by* Jonathan Chaves.
  "I love the serenity of living in the woods." CoBLCP
Living in the World. Alan Chong Lau. BrSi
Living Juliet, The. Shakespeare. *See* Romeo and Juliet: He Jests at Scars [That Never Felt a Wound].
Living Memory, A. William Augustus Croffut. AA
Living mother-of-pearl of a salmon, The. A Hazel Stick for Catherine Ann. Seamus Heaney. FaBCIP; NoAM
Living or dead, the one I love. Philippe Thoby-Marcelin, *tr. by* William Jay Smith. CT
Living? Our Supervisors Will Do That for Us! David Holbrook. NePoEA-2
Living paradise of flowers, land of honey. Merioneth. John Machreth Rees, *tr. by* Kenneth Hurlstone Jackson. OBWVE
Living Pearl, A. Kenneth Rexroth. LiTM
Living Poetry. Hugo Margenat, *tr. fr. Spanish by* Julio Marzán. InW
Living quality of, The. Haymaking. William Carlos Williams. *Fr.* Pictures from Brueghel, VI. NoAM
Living Room, The. Gjertrud Schnackenberg. FYAP
Living someplace else is wrong. The Spring Offensive of the Snail. Marge Piercy. TAP
Living Temple, The. Oliver Wendell Holmes. *Fr.* The Autocrat of the Breakfast Table. AA, *fr.* 7.
Living Tenderly. May Swenson. OBCA
Living Truth, The. Sterling Plumpp. PoBA
Living useless to the world is more abhorrent than death. Upon Returning to the Capital in 1923. Cheng Hsiao-hsü, *tr. by* Irving Lo. WFTU
Living with Children. Jim Wayne Miller. GOYP
Living with You. Angela Langfield. FF
Livings, *sel.* Philip Larkin.
  Seventy Feet Down. RB
Living's getting harder day by day. My Village Home. Lu Yu, *tr. by* Burton Watson. CoBCP
Liza! call dat chile. Meal Time. Maggie Pogue Johnson. CBWP-4
Liza in the Summer Time (She Died on the Train). *Unknown.* AS
Liza Jane. *Unknown.* AS
Lizard. D. H. Lawrence, *tr. by* W. S. Merwin. RB
Lizard, The. John Gardner. RHPC
Lizard, The. Rona Murray. NOBC
Lizard, The. Theodore Roethke. GrPl; RHPC
Lizard fidgets in the sun, A. Under Creag Mhor. Stewart Conn. PoSH
Lizard is a timid thing, The. The Lizard. John Gardner. RHPC
Lizard ran out on a rock and looked up, listening, A. Lizard. D. H. Lawrence, *tr. by* W. S. Merwin. RB
Lizards and Snakes. Anthony Hecht. FaBoMo; TwCP

Lizie Lindsay. *Unknown.* ESPB, (A *and* B *vers.*) (Donald of the Isles.) OxBB
Lizie Wan. *Unknown.* AmFP
Lizzie and Joe Catch a Thief. Edward Cordle. PBCV
Lizzie and Joe in Court. Edward Cordle. PVCV
Lizzie Borden took an axe. *Unknown.* CenHV (Crimes of Lizzie Borden, The.) FaBoCo; FaFP
Lizzie Discourses on the Small-Pox. Edward Cordle. PBCV
Lizzie, Six. Carol Ann Duffy. NPo
Llama, The. Hilaire Belloc. FaBoCh; FaBoNo; FiBHP
Llangollen Vale, *sel.* Anna Seward.
  "Now with a vestal lustre glows the Vale." PeHV
Llewellyn and the Tree. E. A. Robinson. BeLS
Lloyd George. *Unknown.* FaBoCo
Lloyd George and Woodrow Wilson and Clemenceau. A Legend of Versailles. Melvin B. Tolson. BPo
Llyn y Gadair. T. H. Parry-Williams, *tr. fr. Welsh by* Anthony Conran. OBWVE
LMFBR. Gary Snyder. PoM
Lo! above the mournful chanting. Kol Nidra. Joseph Leiser. TrJP
Lo, alas, I look and seek. The Ageing Hunter. Avane. WTO
Lo and behold, on a cloudless day. The Cutting Off. Uri Zvi Greenberg, *tr. by* Bernhard Frank. MHeP
Lo as I pause in the alien vale of the airport. Twenty-third Flight. Earle Birney. HeIP; OxBC; SoSe
Lo! As the Potter Mouldeth. *Unknown, tr. fr. Hebrew by* Elsie Davis. TrJP
Lo! Beauty flashed forth sweetly; from his eyes. Meleager, *tr. by* Sydney Oswald. PeHV
Lo, between the Myrtles Standing. Ann Griffiths, *tr. fr. Welsh by* H. Idris Bell. OBWVE
Lo! Death has reared himself a throne. The City in the Sea *or* The Doomed City. Poe. AA; AmPP; AnAmPo; LiTA; MAT; MOS; NAAL-1; NOBA; NoP; OxBA; PoE; PoEL-4; SCV; TAP; TrGrPo
Lo, fainter now lie spread the shades of night. Morning Hymn. Saint Gregory the Great, *tr. by* Edward Caswell. WGRP
Lo, for I to myself am unknown, now in God's name what must I do? Jalal ed-Din Rumi, *tr. by* R. A. Nicholson. TOF
Lo! Freedom comes. Th' prescient Muse foretold. Phillis Wheatley. *Fr.* Liberty and Peace. AiP; BlSi
Lo from our loitering ship. Iceland First Seen. William Morris. OBTV
Lo, he comes! Capability Brown. William Cowper. SaC
Lo here hath been dawning. Morning. Thomas Carlyle. PWR
Lo here I sit at holy head. Holyhead, Sept. 25th, 1727. Swift. BIrV ("Lo here I sit at Holyhead.") NOIV
Lo! Here the Gentle Lark. Shakespeare. *Fr.* Venus and Adonis. ChTr
Lo, here the state of every mortal wight. Respice Finem. Edna Dean Proctor. OBSC
Lo! here we come a-reaping, a-reaping. Song. George Peele. *Fr.* The Old Wife's Tale. OBSC
Lo, how I seek and sue to have. Sir Thomas Wyatt. SiPS
Lo! how the lark soars upward and is gone. The Death of Leander. Thomas Hood. *Fr.* Hero and Leander. EnRP
"Lo, I am black but I am comely too." The Dark Brother. Lewis Alexander. CDC
Lo! I am come to autumn. Gold Leaves. G. K. Chesterton. OxBTC
Lo, I Am Stricken Dumb. *Unknown, tr. fr. Hebrew by* Theodor H. Gaster. *Fr.* The Dead Sea Scrolls. TrJP
Lo, I have given thee wings wherewith to fly. To Kuvos. Theognis, *tr. by* G. Lowes Dickinson. PeHV
Lo! I have learned of the loveliest of lands. *Unknown, tr. fr. Anglo-Saxon by* Charles W. Kennedy. *Fr.* The Phoenix. AnOE; OAEL-1
Lo, I have opened unto you the wide gates of my being. Psalm to My Beloved. Eunice Tietjens. ErPo
Lo, I the Man. William Browne. *Fr.* Caelia, I. Son
Lo I the man, whose Muse whilome [*or* whylome] did maske. The Legend of the Knight of the Red Crosse, or of Holinesse. Spenser. *Fr.* The Faerie Queene, I, 1-12. NAEL-1; OAEL-1, *abr.* (Invocation to the Faerie Queene.) FiP, *induction only.*
Lo! I will tell the dearest of dreams. A Dream of the Rood. *At. to* Cynewulf, *tr. fr. Anglo-Saxon by* Charles W. Kennedy. AnOE; OAEL-1
Lo, if some pen should write upon your rafter. The Inner Light. F. W. H. Myers. *Fr.* Saint Paul. WGRP
Lo! in the mute, mid wilderness. The Unicorn. George Darley. *Fr.* Nepenthe. ChTr; OBNC; PoEL-4
Lo! in the West, fast fades the ling'ring light. Henry Kirke White. *Fr.* Clifton Grove. OBNC
Lo it is dawn, so rise and let us part. Veiled Land. Kahlil Gibran, *tr. by* Adnan Haydar *and* Michael Beard. MAP

Lo, Joseph dreams his dream again. The League of Nations. Mary Siegrist. PAH

Lo, Lord, Thou ridest! The Hurricane. Hart Crane. CMoP; MoAB; MoAmPo; OxBA; TrCP

Lo now he shineth yonder. Epitaph on Prince Henry. Hugh Holland. FaBoEE

Lo! now with red rent cloak and bonnet black. George Crabbe. *Fr.* Phoebe Dawson. EBEV

Lo, our great sovereign, a goddess. Hitomaro, *tr. fr. Japanese. Fr.* Manyo Shu. Ma

Lo Que Digo. *Unknown, tr. fr. Spanish.* AS

Lo! sun and moon, these minister for aye. Israel's Duration. Judah Halevi, *tr. by* Nina Davis Salaman. TrJP

Lo, the afternoon of Grand Old Men! Afternoon of Grand Old Men. Sandor Csoori, *tr. by* Jascha Kessler. FOC

Lo! the foolish fell. Killing. Samuel Greenberg. LiTA

Lo! the glorious dawn is breaking. Easter Morn. Josephine D. Henderson Heard. CBWP-4

Lo, the lilies of the field. Providence. Reginald Heber. GN; OHIP

Lo, the moon's self! Phases of the Moon. Robert Browning. *Fr.* One Word More. ChTr

Lo, the poor Indian! whose untutor'd mind. Pope. *Fr.* An Essay on Man, Epistle I. NU

Lo! the Sun, among the daughters. Sunset in the Sea. Tom Hood. FaBoNo

Lo! the unsullied stream of the Yoshinu. Kanamura. *Fr.* Manyo Shu. Ma

Lo, the Winter Is Past. Bible, *O.T. See* Song of Solomon, The: For, lo, the winter is past.

Lo! There towers the lofty peak of Fuji. Mushimaro. *Fr.* Manyo Shu. Ma

Lo, thou, my Love, art fair. Christ to His Spouse [*or* The Beloved to the Spouse]. William Baldwin. ElL; NOCV; OBSC

Lo! through a shadowy valley. The Funeral of Time. Henry Beck Hirst. AA

Lo, thus, as prostrate, "In the dust I write. James Thomson ("B. V."). *Fr.* The City of Dreadful Night. GoTS; OxBS; ViBoPo (City, The.) NOBE

Lo, 'Tis a gala night. The Conqueror Worm. Poe. *Fr.* Ligeia *prose tale.* AA; AnAmPo; AWP; BLPL; LiTA; NOBA; OBD (Emperor Worm, The.) DL

Lo, upon the carpet, where. Tamerlane. Victor James Daley. PoAu-1

Lo! we have listened to many a lay. Beowulf. *Unknown, tr. by* Charles W. Kennedy. OAEL-1

Lo, we were plucking the white millet. *Unknown, tr. by* Arthur Waley. BoS

Lo, What Enraptured Songs of Praise. Sebastian Streeter. AH

Lo! what [*or* quhat] it is to love [*or* lufe]. A Rondel of Luve [*or* Love]. Alexander Scott. BoLoP; OBEV; OxBS

Lo, where envy and where lies. Written on the Walls of His Dungeon. Luís De León, *tr. by* Thomas Walsh. TrJP

Lo, where left 'mid the sheaves, cut down by the iron-/ fanged reaper. On a Forsaken Lark's Nest. Mathilde Blind. FM

Lo! where the four mimosas blend their shade. For an Epitaph at Fiesole. Walter Savage Landor. FaBoEE; OBNC

Lo! where the rosy-bosomed Hours. Ode on the Spring. Thomas Gray. GTBS; GTBS-P; NOEC

Lo, Who Could Stand. *Unknown, tr. fr. Hebrew by* Israel Zangwill. TrJP

Lo worms enjoy the seat of bliss. Burns. FaBoEE

Lo-yang. Emperor Ch'ien Wen-ti, *tr. fr. Chinese by* Arthur Waley. AWP

Lo! yon phantom army marching across Heaven. Indian Night Tableau. Hyman Edelstein. CaP

Lo! you appear, illustrious and learned shade. Reply to the Shade of Descartes. Anne de La Vigne, *tr. by* Dorothy Backer. DMF

Load of brushes and baskets and cradles and chairs, A. No Buyers; a Street Scene. Thomas Hardy. LiTB; NoP

Loaded with gallant soldiers. Ready. Phoebe Cary. PAH

Loads of trash and we light the match. Landfill. Michael S. Harper. LCAP

Loadstone beckons to the long needle, The. The Joy of Union. Yang Fang, *tr. by* Burton Watson. CoBCP

Loath to pass by her gate. *Unknown. Fr.* Manyo Shu. Ma

Loathing both seas of life and death. *Unknown. Fr.* Manyo Shu. Ma

Loaves, The. Ronald G. Everson. TDD

Loba, *sels.* Diane di Prima. ER
"Day lay like a pearl on her lap, The."
Loba Recovers the Memory of a Mare, The.
"O lost moon sisters."
Ruses: A Coyote Tale, The.

Loba Recovers the Memory of a Mare, The. Diane di Prima. *Fr.* Loba. ER

Lobbed ball plops, then dribbles to the cup, The. Ford Madox Ford. Robert Lowell. OxBC; TwCP

Lobo. Charles Lillard. NOBC

Lobotomy. Kenneth Pitchford. PoA

Lobster, The. "Lewis Carroll." *See* Alice's Adventures in Wonderland: Alice's Recitation.

Lobster. Anne Sexton. AnAn

Lobster Cove Shindig. Lillian Morrison. BoNaP

Lobster Quadrille, The. "Lewis Carroll." *See* Alice's Adventures in Wonderland:
"Will you walk a little faster?" said a [*or* the] whiting to a [*or* the] snail.

Lobsters and the Fiddler Crab, The ("The lobsters came ashore one night"). Frederick J. Forster. RHPC

Lobsters in the Window. W. D. Snodgrass. HeIP; NYBP; TAP

Local Allosaurus, The. Steven Utley. BWV

Local Contractor Flees His Winter Trouble and Saves Some Lives in a Knoxville Motel Room, A. James Whitehead. MT

Local groceries are all out of broccoli, The. Against Broccoli. Roy Blount, Jr.. NBLV; OBAL

Local I'll bright my tale on, how. The Children of Greenock. William Sydney Graham. FaBoTw

Local Man Goes to the Killing Ground, A. James Whitehead. MT

Local Man Remembers Betty Fuller, A. James Whitehead. MT

Local Motions. Laurence Price. IAT

Local News. Loretta Merenda, *tr. fr. Italian by* Muriel Kittel. DMI

Local Note. Arthur Guiterman. NBLV

Local Places. Howard Moss. NePoEA-2

Local Politics. Robert Pinsky. MAYP

Locale. Penelope Shuttle. BrRo

Localities. Carl Sandburg. AmFN

Locate I/ love you. The Language. Robert Creeley. CAPP; TAP

Locating the anger. Full Circle. Maud Sulter. DT

Location. Knute Skinner. MAT

Locations. Kathleen Fraser. NPGG

Locations. Jim Harrison. AmPA

Loch Luichart. Andrew Young. PoSH

Loch Ossian. Syd Scroggie. PoSH

Lochan. Roger Smith. PoSH

Lochiel's Warning ("Lochiel, Lochiel! beware of the day"). Thomas Campbell. EnRP

Lochinvar. Sir Walter Scott. *Fr.* Marmion, V. BeLS; BOTP; EnRP; FaBoBe; FaBV; FaFP; FaPON; FPL; GN; GoTS; NOBE; OBNV; OxBS; PoRA
(Young Lochinvar.) OBNV

Lochmaben Harper, The. *Unknown.* ESPB; OxBB, *with music*

Lock the dairy door. *Unknown.* OxNR; PBBP

Lock the Door, Lariston. James Hogg. GoTS; OxBS

Lock the Place in Your Heart. Zindzi Mandela. LLLT

Lock up, fair lids, the treasure of my heart. Sleep. Sir Philip Sidney. *Fr.* Arcadia. OBSC; SiPS
(Sonnet: "Lock up, fair lids, the treasure of my heart.") ElL

Locke sank into a swoon. W. B. Yeats. NoAM; PrIm

Locked arm in arm they cross the way. Tableau. Countee Cullen. AmFN; BANP; PoBA

Locked Doors. Anne Sexton. KS

Locked lagoon is ice, the lake beyond, The. Double Mock Sonnet. Charles O. Hartman. SM

Locked up, inside. Feline. Ronald Wallace. TDD

Locked up within the prison I. Mohammad Taqi Mir, *tr. by* Ahmed Ali. GoT

Lockless Door, The. Robert Frost. NOBA; WSC

Locks. Kenneth Koch. CoAP

Locks and Bolts. *Unknown.* OBET

Locks between her chamber and his will, The. Midnight. Shakespeare. *Fr.* The Rape of Lucrece. OBSC

Locksley Hall ("Comrades, leave me here a little, while as yet 'tis early morn."), *sels.* Tennyson. BLPL; EBEV; FaBoBe; FaFP; NAEL-2; OAEL-2
For I Dipped [*or* Dipt] into the Future. PoLF
(Prophecy.) WBLP
"In the Spring." BoNaP
"Make me feel the wild pulsation that I felt before the strife." SaC

Locrine, *sel.* *At.* to Charles Tilney.
Cobbler's Song, The. OBSC
Locus, The. Cid Corman. VGW
Locus. Robert Hayden. FYAP
Locust, The. *Unknown, tr. fr. Malagasy.* FaPON, *tr.* by Frank Cushing;
RB, *tr.* by A. Marre *and* Willard R. Trask
(Coyote and the Locust, The.) AWP
Locust, locust, playing a flute. The Coyote and the Locust. *Unknown.*
AWP
Locust Tree in Flower, The. William Carlos Williams. SOTW; TTTS
Locusts of Silence. Seymour Mayne. VWA
Locusts, or Appolyonists, The, *sels.* Phineas Fletcher.
"Of Men, nay Beasts: worse, Monsters: worst of all." *Fr.* I.
SeCV-1
Sin, Despair, and Lucifer. *Fr.* I. OBS
Locusts' wings say "throng, throng", The. *Unknown, tr.* by Arthur
Waley. BoS
Lodestoned salmon, hurtling, The. Weir Bridge. Padraic Fallon.
CIP
Lodgepole/ cone/seed waits for fire. Gary Snyder. *Fr.* Myths and Texts:
Logging, XV. NaP
Lodger, The. Michael Longley. FaBCIP
Lodgers. Julian Tuwim, *tr. fr. Polish* by Isaac Komem. VWA
Lodging for the Night, A. Elinor Wylie. ErPo
Lodging-House Fuchsias, The. Thomas Hardy. OxBSP
Lodging in a hut where the Naniwa men burn reeds. Teika, *tr. fr.*
Japanese by Hiroaki Sato. *Fr.* A Compendium of Good Tanka.
FCEI
Lodging in the puddle from the straw coat. Kitsujo, *tr. fr. Japanese* by
Hiroaki Sato. FCEI
Lodging the fireflight from a fire. Wakayama Bokusui, *tr. fr. Japanese* by
Hiroaki Sato. *Fr.* Forty-four Tanka. FCEI
Lodging with the Old Man of the Stream. Po Chü-i, *tr. fr. Chinese* by
Arthur Waley. AWP
Loe! formest of a rout that follow'd him. Virgil, *tr. fr. Latin* by the Earl
of Surrey. *Fr.* The Aeneid [*or* Eneados], II. OBVE
Loe here the precious dust is laid. Epitaph on Maria Wentworth.
Thomas Carew. PoEL-3
Loew's Bridge, a Broadway Idyl. Mary E. Tucker. CBWP-1
Loft. Michael Dransfield. CBAP
Lofty against our Western dawn uprises Achilles. Song, Youth, and
Sorrow. William Cranston Lawton. AA
Lofty beyond the mountains. Ikenushi. *Fr.* Manyo Shu. Ma
Lofty-brow-flourishers. On Philosophers. *Unknown.* TW
Lofty elm-trees darkly dream, The. The Rookery at Sunrise. "Fiona
Macleod." *Fr.* Transcripts from Nature. FM
Lofty Lane. Edwin Gerard. PoAu-1
Lofty mountains and the seas, The. *Unknown. Fr.* Manyo Shu. Ma
Lofty poetry, the sun sets, sun rises. The Sun Sets, Sun Rises. Pentti
Saarikoski, *tr.* by Aili Jarvenpa. SOP
Lofty ship from Salcombe came, A. The Salcombe Seaman's Flaunt to
the Proud Pirate. *Unknown.* ChTr
Lofty young squire from Portsmouth he came, A. The Golden Glove.
Unknown. AmFP
Log Jam, The. William Henry Drummond. NOBC
Logan at Peach Tree Creek. Hamlin Garland. PAH
Logan Braes. John Mayne. OxBS
Logarithm, The. The fraction. The bead of dew. America the Beautiful.
Stan Rice. NPGG
Logbook. Dan Pagis, *tr. fr. Hebrew* by Warren Bargad *and* Stanley F.
Chyet. IP
Logbook of a Lost Caravan. Gyula Illyés, *tr. fr. Hungarian* by William
Jay Smith. MHuP
Logging. Gary Snyder. *Fr.* Myths and Texts.
"Each dawn is clear." *Fr.* VIII.NaP
"Groves are down, The." *Fr.* XIV.NaP
"Again the ancient, meaningless." *Fr.* V.NaP
"Stood straight/ holding the choker high." *Fr.* III.NaP; NOBA
"Lodgepole/ cone/seed waits for fire." *Fr.* XV.NaP
Logic. Alain Delahaye, *tr. fr. French* by Anthony Barnett.
RHTwFP
Logic. *Unknown.* FaBoUs
Logic does well at school. Scholars. Walter de la Mare.
NoAM
Logic is my eye. Seeing. John Lyle Donaghy. NeIP
Logical Song, A. *Unknown.* ErPo
Logical Vegetarian, The. G. K. Chesterton. CenHV
Logs, at the door, by the fence; broadcast over the paddock. B. E.
Baughan. *Fr.* A Bush Section. ATNZ; PeNZ
Lohengrin. William Morton Payne. AA
L'Oiseau Bleu. Gordon Bottomley. BrPo

L'Oiseau Bleu. Mary Elizabeth Coleridge. BoTP
("Lake lay blue below the hill, The.") CH
Lola. Yona Wallach, *tr. fr. Hebrew* by Warren Bargad *and* Stanley F.
Chyet. IP
Lolek. John Jordan. TIRV
Lollay, Lollay, Little Child! An Adult Lullaby. *Unknown.* MeEL
Lollingdon Downs. John Masefield. LiTB, I-XV.
Sels.
Choice, The. *Fr.* VIII. MoAB; MoBrPo
"I could not sleep for thinking of the sky." *Fr.* V. LiTM
"Night is on the downland, on the lonely moorland." *Fr.* XVIII.
GoYe; LiTM
(Night on the Downland.) MoBrPo
"Here in the self is all that men can know." AWP
Lollocks. Robert Graves. ChTr; RB
Lolo died yesterday. Cyn Zarco. BrSi
Lolotte, who attires my hair. Noblesse Oblige. Jessie Redmond Fauset.
CDC
Lombard-Venetian. Luciano Erba, *tr. fr. Italian* by Lawrence R. Smith.
NItP
London. John Davidson. NOBE; OBNC
London. Daniel Defoe. *Fr.* Reformation of Manners. NOEC
London. Dryden. *See* Annus Mirabilis: New London, The.
London. Samuel Johnson. PoEL-3; TEP
London. J. R. Rowland. CBAP
London: A Poem in Imitation of the Third Satire of Juvenal, *sels.* Samuel
Johnson. GoTL; PoEL-3; TEP
"By numbers here from shame or censure free." NOEC; OBSV
(Poverty in London.) ChTr
"Prepare for death, if here at night you roam." OAEL-1
London Adulterations. *Unknown.* OBET
London after the Great Fire, 1666. Dryden. *See* Annus Mirabilis: New
London, The.
London at Night. John Gay. *Fr.* Trivia; or, The Art of Walking the
Streets of London. FaBoPP
London Bells. *Unknown. See* Bells of London, The.
London Bridge. *Unknown.* CH; ChTr; GBP; OxBoLi; OxNR
("London Bridge is falling down, falling down, falling down.")
EyDe
London Bridge Is a-Burning Down. *Unknown.* AmFP
London Bridge is broken down. London Bridge. *Unknown.* CH; ChTr;
GBP; OxBoLi; OxNR
("London Bridge is falling down, falling down, falling down.")
EyDe
London Bridge is falling down, falling down, falling down. *Unknown.*
See London Bridge.
London Bridge was built. Stranger than the Worst. Babette Deutsch.
WPE
London City. *Unknown.* AS
London Despair. Frances Cornford. OBMV
London, 1802 ("Milton! thou should'st be living at this hour").
Wordsworth. AWP; EnRP; FaBoPV; FaBV; FF; HAP; HeIP; InvP;
LiTB; NAEL-2; NIP; NoP; OBNC; PoEL-4; PoRA; Son; TEP
(England, 1802, II.) OBEV
(Milton.) FaPoR
(Same, The.) GTBS; GTBS-P
(To Milton.) TrGrPo
London, MDCCCII ("O friend! I know not which way I must look").
Wordsworth. GTBS; GTBS-P
London Evening Post, *sel. Unknown.*
"Ye Beauties, Beaux, ye Pleaders at the Bar." FaBoUs
London Fete, A. Coventry Patmore. EBVV; HAP
London, from Hampstead Heath. Wordsworth. *Fr.* Extempore Effusion
upon the Death of James Hogg. FaBoPP
London, hast thou [*or* thow] accused me. A Satire on London. Henry
Howard, Earl of Surrey. AAS; SiPS
London ("I wander through each chartered street"). Blake. *Fr.* Songs of
Experience. AWP; ChER; ChTr; EnRP; FaBoPP; FaBoPV; FF; HAP;
HeIP; InPK; InPS; LiTB; MAT; Mes; NAEL-2; NAWM-2; NIP;
NOBE; NOEC; NoP; OAEL-2; OBNC; PoE; PoEL-4; PrIm; RB; SCV;
SeCePo; TEP; UnPo; WeW
London in 1646. Henry Vaughan. FaBoPP
London Interior. Harold Monro. BrPo
London Is a Fine Town. *Unknown.* CoMu
London is full of chickens, on electric spits. Peter Porter. *Fr.*
Annotations of Auschwitz. OxBTC
London is painted round them: burly railings. Street Performers, 1851.
Terence Tiller. GTBS-P
"London: John Lane, The Bodley Head." On the Imprint of the First
English Edition of "The Works of Max Beerbohm." Max Beerbohm.
InPK

London Lackpenny. *Unknown. See* London Lickpenny.
London Lickpenny. *Unknown, tr. fr. Middle English.* CoMu; FaBoPP; OBSV
   (London Lackpenny.) ChTr
   (London Lyckpeny.) OxBLMV
London Lyckpeny. *Unknown. See* London Lickpenny.
London Nightfall. John Gould Fletcher. MoAmPo
London Pavement Artist. James Schevill. TAP
London Prentice, The. *Unknown.* CoMu
London Rain. Louis MacNeice. HeIP; NoP
London Sad London. *Unknown.* OBS
London Snow. Robert Bridges. BoNaP; BrPo; CH; ChTr; CMoP; EBEV; EBVV; FaBoPP; GTBS-P; LiTB; LiTM; MoAB; MoBrPo; MoP; NoAM; NoBE; NOBVV; OAEL-2; OBNC; OxBTC; PoEL-5; SeCePo; TrGrPo; WiR
London Spring. Antoni Slonimski, *tr. fr. Polish by* Frances Notley. TrJP
London Suburbs. William Cowper. *Fr.* Retirement. FaBoPP
London ("There souls of men are bought and sold"). Blake. *Fr.* The Human Image. ChTr
London, thou art of townes. To the City of London [*or* In Honour of the City of London]. William Dunbar. ChTr; EBEV; FaBoPP; OBEV
London, to thee I do present the merry month of May. The Month of May. Beaumont *and* Fletcher. *Fr.* The Knight of the Burning Pestle, IV, v. ChTr
London Town. Lionel Johnson. FaBoPP
London Trees. Beryl Netherclift. BoTP
London versus Epping Forest. John Clare. *Fr.* Child Harold. FaBoPP
London Voluntaries, *sels.* William Ernest Henley. BrPo
  Largo e mesto. *Fr.* IV.
  Scherzando. *Fr.* III.
Londoners Gent to the King do present, The. On the Lord Mayor and Court of Aldermen, Presenting the Late King and Duke of York Each with a Copy of Their Freedoms. Andrew Marvell. CoMu; FaBoBa (Upon His Majesty's Being Made Free of the City.) APAS
Lone am I, and would be. Christine de Pisan, *tr. by* Tom Vaughan. AIW
Lone and forgotten/ Through a long sleeping. The Lonely. "Æ." AWP
Lone and weary as I wander'd by the bleak shore of the sea. Lament for Timoleague. Sean O'Coileain, *tr. by* Sir Samuel Ferguson. TIRV
Lone Bather. A. M. Klein. HeIP
Lone crow caws from the tall dead gum, The. Sheaf-Tosser. Eric Rolls. PoAu-2
Lone cuckoo, A. Mushimaro. *Fr.* Manyo Shu. FCEI
Lone Dog. Irene Rutherford McLeod. FaPON; PDV; RHPC
Lone egret flies in a clear sky across the open fields, A. Heaven's Immortal. Huang-fu Sung, *tr. by* Lois Fusek. ATF
Lone figure is waving, A. A Postcard from North Antrim. Seamus Heaney. FaBCIP; IPY
Lone Founts. Herman Melville. LiTA
Lone Gentleman. Pablo Neruda, *tr. fr. Spanish by* Clayton Eshleman. ErPo
Lone heart, learning. Vigils. Siegfried Sassoon. CMoP
Lone Huntsman. Christie Jeffries. GoYe
Lone Kauri Road ("First time I looked seaward, westward"). Allen Curnow. *Fr.* Trees, Effigies, Moving Objects, I. ATNZ; PeNZ
Lone Kauri Road ("Too many splashes, too many gashes"). Allen Curnow. *Fr.* Trees, Effigies, Moving Objects, XVII. ATNZ; PeNZ
Lone knee wanders through the world, A. The Knee on Its Own. Christian Morgenstern, *tr. by* R. F. L. Hull. FaBoNo
Lone, one, and lone I stand. The Myall in Prison. Mary Gilmore. CBAP; PoAu-1
Lone, phallic, Alet's get. Tour de Force. Peter Kane Dufault. ErPo
Lone seas are ominous. Lone Huntsman. Christie Jeffries. GoYe
Lone Star Trail, The. *Unknown.* AS
Lone Striker, A. Robert Frost. SaC
Lone Swordsman, The. Lo Ch'ing, *tr. fr. Chinese by* Dominic Cheung. IFON
Lone watch of the moon over mountains old, The. Mortality. James Devaney. PoAu-1
Lone Wild Fowl, The. H. R. MacFayden. AH
Lone Woman Asleep, A. Pierre Jean Jouve, *tr. fr. French by* David Gascoyne. RHTwFP
Lonelier still than last year. Old Man's Thoughts, An ("Lonelier still than last year"). Buson, *tr. fr. Japanese by* Hiroaki Sato. *Fr.* Eighty-seven Hokku. FCEI
Loneliness. Hayden Carruth. SM
Loneliness. Edwin Essex. TrPWD

Loneliness. Faiz Ahmad Faiz, *tr. fr. Urdu by* Mahmood Jamal. PBMUP
Loneliness. Robert Frost. *Fr.* The Hill Wife. VGW
Loneliness. Felice Holman. ILY
Loneliness. Amjad Nasir, *tr. fr. Arabic by* May Jayyusi *and* Charles Doria. MAP
Loneliness. Loyal Shegonee. NOVW
Loneliness. Franz Werfel, *tr. fr. German by* Edith Abercrombie Snow. TrJP
Loneliness. Yang Mu, *tr. fr. Chinese by* Dominic Cheung. IFON
Loneliness. Al Young. PoBA
Loneliness and July Ninth. Claribel Alegría, *tr. fr. Spanish by* Aliki *and* Willis Barnstone. BoWoP
Loneliness has no special color. Teika, *tr. fr. Japanese by* Hiroaki Sato. *Fr.* A Compendium of Good Tanka. FCEI
Loneliness is more intense with frost than with snow. Teika, *tr. fr. Japanese by* Hiroaki Sato. *Fr.* Eighty-four Tanka. FCEI
Loneliness leapt in the mirrors, but all week. Departure's Girl-Friend. W. S. Merwin. LCAP
Loneliness of the Long Distance Runner, The. Alden Nowlan. TW
Loneliness 2. Antonio Cisneros, *tr. fr. Spanish by* Maureen Ahern *and* David Tipton. Per
Lonely, The. "Æ." AWP
Lonely. Bloke Modisane. PBA
Lonely. André Spire, *tr. fr. French by* Jethro Bithell. AWP; TrJP
Lonely and big. First Pregnancy. Alta. NMM
Lonely and cold and fierce I keep my way. Gulf Stream. "Susan Coolidge." AA
Lonely and dreary was the day. Heart's Ease. Mary E. Tucker. CBWP-1
Lonely and not quite lonely. *Unknown, tr. by* Sato. FCEI
Lonely Are the Fields of Sleep. Mary Newton Baldwin. GoYe
Lonely Beauty. Samuel Daniel. *Fr.* The Complaint of Rosamond. CTC; OBSC
Lonely-Bird, The. Harrison Smith Morris. AA
Lonely Bugle Grieves, The. Grenville Mellen. *Fr.* Ode on the Celebration of the Battle of Bunker Hill, June 17, 1825. AA
Lonely Cloud of Care, The. Coventry Patmore. *Fr.* The Victories of Love, II, vii. FaBoRV
Lonely Isle, The. Claudian, *tr. fr. Latin by* Howard Mumford Jones. AWP
Lonely Land, The. A. J. M. Smith. CaP; NOBC
Lonely Love. Edmund Blunden. OxBTC
Lonely Man, The. Randall Jarrell. OxBC
Lonely Monday. J. Patrick Lewis. ILY
Lonely moon beside the village, A. Leaving T'u-sung at Dawn. Wu Wei-yeh, *tr. by* Marie Chan. WFTU
Lonely Mother, The. Fenton Johnson. PoNe
Lonely pond in age-old stillness sleeps, A. Basho, *tr. by* Curtis Hidden Page. AWP
Lonely Road. Peter Abrahams. PBA
Lonely rock above a midnight plain, A. Te Whetu Plains. Edward Tregear, *tr. by* Alan Myers. ATNZ; PeNZ
Lonely room, fiddling with a brush as the years go by. To Inscribe on My Portrait. Ema Saiko, *tr. by* Burton Watson. JLIC-2
Lonely, save for a few faint stars, the sky. The Little Dancers. Laurence Binyon. BoTP; CH; MoBrPo; OxBTC
Lonely Scarecrow, The. James Kirkup. GrPl; PDV
Lonely season in lonely lands, when fled, The. November. Robert Bridges. OBNC; PBBP; PoEL-5
Lonely Settler, The. Oliver Goldsmith, the Younger. *See* Rising Village, The:
  What noble courage must their hearts have fired.
Lonely Shell, The. Martha Eugenie Perry. CaP
Lonely sound—/ simmering in the firepit. Masaoka Shiki, *tr. fr. Japanese by* Burton Watson. *Fr.* Thirty-nine Haiku. FCEI
Lonely—still, I've forgotten. Buson, *tr. fr. Japanese by* Hiroaki Sato. *Fr.* Eighty-seven Hokku. FCEI
Lonely Street, The. William Carlos Williams. PoA; TwCP
Lonely student in a silent room, A. International Brigade Dead. Thomas O'Brien. NeIP
Lonely the Sea-Bird Lies at Her Rest. W. B. Yeats. RB
Lonely Traveller, The. Kwesi Brew. PBA; TTY
Lonely wanderer, wounded with iron, A. A Shield: "Lonely wanderer, wounded with iron. *Unknown, formerly at. to* Cynewulf, *tr. fr. Anglo-Saxon by* Charles W. Kennedy. *Fr.* Riddles (Exeter Book). AnOE
Lonely Woman's Room, The. Ahmad Abd al-Muti Hijazi, *tr. fr. Arabic by* Sargon Boulus *and* Peter Porter. MAP
Lonely World. Mrs. Henry Linden. CBWP-4
Lonesome. Myra Cohn Livingston. ILY
Lonesome Dove. *Unknown.* AmFP

Lonesome Dream, The. Lisel Mueller. CoAP
Lonesome in the Country. Al Young. MAT; NPGG
Lonesome scenes of winter incline to frost and snow, The. The Rejected
    Lover. *Unknown.* AmFP
Lonesome Water. Roy Helton. AmFN; MoAmPo
Long after, Carl. Exercise in Preparation for a Pindaric Ode to Carl
    Hubbell. Delmore Schwartz. ASP
Long after dark. Scroll. Stanley Moss. VWA
Long after he'd wearied of the work. The Swimming Pool. Jonathan
    Holden. MAYP
Long after you have swung back. Losing Track. Denise Levertov.
    HeIP; MoP; NaP; NOBA; PoE; PoM
Long afterward, Oedipus, old and blinded. Myth. Muriel Rukeyser.
    FaBoWP; IHMS; NNaP
Long afterwards. The Judgment of Paris. W. S. Merwin. NAAL-2;
    NNaP
Long Ago. Murakami Bussan, *tr. fr. Chinese by* Burton Watson. JLIC-2
Long Ago. Syd Scroggie. PoSH
Long Ago, The. Benjamin Franklin Taylor. *See* Isle of the Long Ago,
    The.
Long ago a young girl. The Sun Witness. Nurunnessa Choudhury, *tr. by*
    Nurunnessa Choudhury *and* Paul Joseph Thompson. AIW
Long ago, at fourteen or fifteen. Juan Chi, *tr. fr. Chinese by* Burton
    Watson. *Fr.* Singing of Thoughts. CoBCP
Long ago her mother. What the Informant Said to Franz Boas in 1920.
    Unknown, tr. by Armand Schwerner. STP
Long ago how fine was everything! Disillusion. *Unknown, tr. by* H. J.
    Spinden. WTO
Long ago I learned how to sleep. Wind Song. Carl Sandburg. MoAB;
    MoAmPo; MoShBr
Long Ago I Lived in the Country. Su Tung-p'o, *tr. fr. Chinese by* Burton
    Watson. CoBCP
Long ago I made that journey, fall rain coming down lightly. I Had
    Occasion to Tell a Visitor about an Old Trip I Took. Lu Yu, *tr. by*
    Burton Watson. CoBCP
Long ago, in Kentucky, I, a boy stood. Tell Me a Story. Robert Penn
    Warren. *Fr.* Audubon, VII. MT
Long ago in the north. Songs in the Turtle Dance at Santa Clara.
    Unknown, tr. by H. J. Spinden. WTO
Long ago powerful snake when men also. The Deluge. *Unknown, tr. fr.
    Delaware (Lenape) Indian by* C. S. Rafinesque. *Fr.* Walam [*or*
    Wallum*] Olum; or, Red Score. LiTA
Long ago, when Emperor Shun of Kuei was still minister to Yao of T'ang.
    Rhyme-Prose on the Sea. Mu Hua, *tr. by* Burton Watson. CoBCP
Long and gray and gaunt he lies. At the Dog Show. Christopher
    Morley. MoShBr
Long and Happy Life, A. Simon Schuchat. UL
Long and Lazy. Robert Herrick. FaBoEE
Long and Lonely Winter, The. Dave Goulder. OBET
Long anxiety and time of school, The. Childhood. Rainer Maria Rilke,
    tr. by M. D. Herter Norton. SOTW
Long arm embossed with gold slides from the tree tops, A. Léon-Paul
    Fargue, *tr. by* Kenneth Rexroth. RHTwFP
Long as I can call to mind. A Childish Game. Reinmar von Hagenau,
    tr. by Jethro Bithell. AWP
Long as the Darkening Cloud Abode. George Richards. AH
Long as the foot-wearying mountain. Teika, *tr. fr. Japanese by* Hiroaki
    Sato. *Fr.* A Compendium of Good Tanka. FCEI
Long as thine art shall love true love. Dear Land of All My Love.
    Sidney Lanier. *Fr.* The Centennial Meditation of Columbia. GN
Long Barren. Christina Rossetti. PBWP; TrCP
Long beardes heartles. The English. *Unknown.* GBP
Long before a woman knows she's pregnant. Progression of the Species.
    Brian W. Aldiss. FF
Long before I first left home, my father. Breakings. Henry Taylor.
    GrPl
Long before I hear it, Naples bright. Napoli Again. Richard Hugo.
    LCAP
Long before long ago. Impressions of My Village. Wu Sheng, *tr. by*
    Dominic Cheung. IFON
Long before the adult flora of. The Grace of Animals. Richard Harteis.
    GLP
Long before the sun cast a shadow. Gathering the Sparks. Howard
    Schwartz. VWA
Long-billed Gannets. Frances D. Emery. GoYe
Long Boat, The. Stanley Kunitz. BLA
Long by the willow-trees. The Willow-Tree. Thackeray. CenHV
Long canoe, The. Robert Hillyer. DuDa; FaPON
Long closed door, oh open it again, The. Judah al-Harizi, *tr. by* Emma
    Lazarus. TrJP

Long colonnades of slender, stone gladiolas. Tao. A. Leyeles, *tr. by*
    Benjamin *and* Barbara Harshav. AYP
long, dark night is fire, The. In Fire. H. Leivick, *tr. by* Benjamin *and*
    Barbara Harshav. AYP
Long day on the road, R. H., and three trips now. Note to R. H. from
    Strongsville. Richard Hugo. AnAn
Long desired, the dead return. They Return. Jay Macpherson. *Fr.* The
    Way Down. NOBC; PoA
Long desired, the journey is begun. The suppliants. Landscapeople.
    John Ashbery. HCAP
Long did I look into the dark eyes of my brother. Hamletism. Antoni
    Slonimski, *tr. by* Peter Dale Scott *and* Czeslaw Milosz. PwPP
Long Distance. Tony Harrison. NAEL-2
Long Distance. Dana Naone. CDW
Long Distance. William Stafford. SO; WSC
Long distance is expensive. For Avi Killed in Lebanon. Mark Osaki.
    BrSi
Long division and underprivilege. A Scottish Bride. Bill Manhire.
    ATNZ
Long-drawn-out autumn, The. Sanetomo, *tr. fr. Japanese by* Burton
    Watson. *Fr.* Twenty-four Tanka. FCEI
Long-expected one and twenty. A Short Song of Congratulation
    [*or* To a Young Heir]. Samuel Johnson. EBEV; ELP; HAP; InPK;
    InPS; InVP; NOBE; NOEC; NoP; OBSV; PoE; PoEL-3; TEP; UnPo
Long Feud. Louis Untermeyer. MoAmPo
Long Garden, The. Patrick Kavanagh. FaBCIP; IPY
Long glances heavy as lead. End Song. Shlomoh Tan'ee, *tr. by*
    Bernhard Frank. MHeP
Long Gone. Jack Prelutsky. RHPC
Long Gone. Sterling A. Brown. BANP; BPo; CDC
Long grass searches the wind, The. Shearing Grass. Peter Redgrove.
    NePoEA-2
Long, gray moss that softly swings, The. In Louisiana. Albert Bigelow
    Paine. AA; AmFN
Long green shutters are drawn, The. Elsewheres. Donald Justice.
    LCAP
Long had passed the hour of midnight. Dawn. *Malay Oral Tradition, tr.
    by* R. J. Wilkinson. WTO
Long had the proud Spaniard advanced to conquer us. The Winning of
    Cales. Thomas Deloney. CoMu; OBTV
Long had this nation been amused in vain. The Spanish Descent. Daniel
    Defoe. APAS
Long Hair. Gary Snyder. NOBA
Long hair, endless curls trained by the devoted. Strato, *tr. by* Teddy
    Hogge. PeHV
Long-haired preachers come out every night. The Preacher and the Slave .
    At. to Joe Hill. AS, *with music;* GBP; WTO
    (Pie in the Sky.) GBP
Long Handscroll of Bamboo by Wang Meng-tuan, The. Li Tung-yang, *tr.
    fr. Chinese by* Jonathan Chaves. CoBLCP
Long Harbour, The. Mary Ursula Bethell. ATNZ; PeNZ
Long has the summer sunlight shone. Incognita of Raphael. William
    Allen Butler. AA
Long hast thou, friend! been absent from thy soil. Mr. Pope's Welcome
    from Greece. John Gay. EBEV, *abr.;* OxBoLi, *abr.;* PoEL-3
Long have I beat with timid hands upon life's leaden door. The Suppliant.
    Georgia Douglas Johnson. CDC; PoBA; PoNe
Long have I framed weak phantasies of Thee. Agnosto Theo (To an
    Unknown God). Thomas Hardy. WGRP
Long have I looked for my lost child. The Lost Child. James Reaney.
    NOBC
Long have I loved the terrible clouds that loom. Prayer for Dreadful
    Morning. E. Merrill Root. TrPWD
Long have I yearned and sought for beauty. I Sit and Wait for Beauty.
    Mae V. Cowdery. BlSi
Long-Head Poem, The. John Woods. SoTCo
Long-headed, from northern Europe. The Long-Head Poem. John
    Woods. SoTCo
Long hears have left their writing on my brow. "George Eliot." *Fr.*
    Brother and Sister, II. GN
Long Hill, The. Sara Teasdale. LiTA; MoAmPo
Long History of the Short Poem. Paul Hoover. UL
Long hoe, long hoe, handle of white wood. Tu Fu, *tr. fr. Chinese by*
    Burton Watson. *Fr.* Seven Songs Written During the Ch'ien-yüan
    Era, 2. CoBCP
Long I followed [*or* follow'd] happy guides. Forerunners. Emerson.
    AA; OBEV; OxBA
Long I Have Loved to Stroll. T'ao Ch'ien, *tr. fr. Chinese by* William
    Acker. ChTr
Long I looked for what I did not need, then. Peire Vidal, *tr. by* Paul
    Blackburn. Pro

Long I Thought That Knowledge Alone Would Suffice. Walt Whitman.
NOBA
Long in thy shackles, liberty. To Lucasta, from Prison. Richard
Lovelace. CaPo
Long is the night. Curriculum Vitae. Ingeborg Bachmann. BoWoP, *tr.*
by Jerome Rothenberg
Long Island. Marvin Bell. BLA; CAPP
Long Island. Marcy S. Powell. SoTCo
Long Island Springs. Howard Moss. UnPo
Long John. Padraic Fallon. NeIP
Long John Brown and Little Mary Bell. Blake. RB
Long Joke, The. R. T. Smith. STE
Long Journey, A. Pentti Saarikoski, *tr. fr. Finnish by* Aili Jarvenpa.
SOP
Long lay the ocean-paths from man conceal'd. The Inspiration. James
Montgomery. *Fr.* The West Indies. PAH
Long-legged Fly. W. B. Yeats. CMoP; FaBoMo; FaBoTw; InPS; LiTM;
MoP; NAEL-2; NoAM; NOBE; NOP; NoP; OPOP; PoE; TEP
Long legs, crooked thighs. Mother Goose. GBP; OxNR
Long life to old Whalan of Waitin' a While. Whalan of Waitin' a While.
James William Gordon. PoAu-1
Long Lines. Paul Goodman. VGW
(Long Lines: Youth and Age.) GLP; PeHV
Long lines of cliff breaking have left a chasm. Enoch Arden. Tennyson.
BeLS
Long lines of coral light. Autumn. Wallace Stevens. FL
Long Lines: Youth and Age. Paul Goodman. *See* Long Lines.
Long live our dear and noble Queen. Edward Edwin Foot. *Fr.* On the
Inauguration of the Memorial Statue. FaBoCo
Long Live the Weeds. Theodore Roethke. NoAM; NOBA; PoA
Long, Long Ago. *Unknown.* FaPON; OHIP; PChr; PDV
Long, long ago, beyond the misty space. The Celts. Thomas D'Arcy
Magee. TIRV
Long, long ago now. Kyoroku, *tr. by* Geoffrey Bownas *and* Anthony
Thwaite. PeBJV
Long long ago on Calvary. Victory. *Unknown.* CoMu; WGRP
Long long ago, they say. The Hare in the Moon. Ryokan, *tr. by*
Geoffrey Bownas *and* Anthony Thwaite. PeBJV
Long long ago when the world was a wild place. Bedtime Story. George
MacBeth. MoP; NePoEA-2; SoSe
Long, Long Be My Heart with Such Memories Filled. Thomas Moore.
BLPL; FaBoBe
Long, long before the Babe could speak. At Bethlehem. John Banister
Tabb. *Fr.* The Child. AA
Long, long days. Blood, the Note "B." Yves Bonnefoy, *tr. by* Anthony
Rudolf. RHTwFP
Long long journey down the open road, The. Return to an Evil Domain.
René Daumal, *tr. by* Michael Benedikt. POS
Long March, The. Joyce Peseroff. PPR
Long May. Rosalía de Castro, *tr. fr. Galician by* Benjamin M.
Woodbridge, Jr. PBWP
"Long may the lonely one wait for comfort." The Wanderer. *Unknown.*
AnOE, *tr. by* Charles W. Kennedy; OAEL-1, *tr. by* Charles W.
Kennedy; TEP, *tr. by* Mark Caldwell
Long Mountain, rise. Pocomania. Philip Sherlock. PBCV
Long Nature travailed, till at last she bore. Nature's Travail. *Unknown,*
tr. by Goldwin Smith. AWP
Long neglect has worn away. Emily Brontë. NOBVV
(Long Neglect Has Worn Away.) NoP; PoE
Long night/ when the waterfall. Masaoka Shiki, *tr. fr. Japanese by*
Burton Watson. *Fr.* Thirty-nine Haiku. FCEI
Long night drags on and on, The. In the Ancient Manner. Chao Meng-
fu, *tr. by* Jonathan Chaves. CoBLCP
Long Night Home, The. Charles F. Gordon. NBP
Long night: I wake up, A. Taigi, *tr. fr. Japanese by* Hiroaki Sato. *Fr.*
Twenty-nine Hokku. FCEI
Long night succeeds thy little day. Margaret Love Peacock [for Her
Tombstone, 1826]. Thomas Love Peacock. OBNC
Long nights when he neglects me—where's he gone? Tune: Telling of
Innermost Feelings ("Long nights when he neglects me—where's he
gone?"). Ku Hsiung, *tr. by* Burton Watson. CoBCP
Long Overdue Thankyou Note to the Girl Who Taught Me Loving, A.
Tom Schmidt. NeAC
Long past midnight I sit here. Forsaken. Zalman Schneour, *tr. by* Joseph
Leftwich. TrJP
Long Person. Gladys Cardiff. CDW; STE
Long Picnic, The. Russell Edson. LCAP
Long placid evening. Tune: The Butterfly Woos the Blossoms.
Li Ching-chao, *tr. by* C. H. Kwock *and* Vincent McHugh. PBWP
Long Plighted. Thomas Hardy. NOBVV

Long Poem, The. Yusuf al-Khal, *tr. fr. Arabic by* Abdullah al-Udhari.
MPAW
Long poles support the branches of the orchards in New Hampshire.
Apples in New Hampshire. Marie Emilie Gilchrist. BoNaP
Long Prologue to a Short Play, A. Sir Henry Sheers. APAS
Long reach the garland has, A. Magnetic. Sándor Weöres, *tr. by* Jascha
Kessler. FOC
Long reaches of the street, The. The Anecdote That Went with It. Ray
DiPalma. LP
Long, rich breadth of Holland lace, A. Old Flemish Lace. Amelia
Walstien Carpenter. AA
Long River, The. Donald Hall. LCAP; NePoEA-2; SM
Long Road, The, *sel.* John Gray.
Gazelles and Unicorn. ChTr
Long road and a village, A. Holy Family. Muriel Rukeyser. MoAmPo
Long robes, or short. Yüan Mei, *tr. fr. Chinese by* Jonathan Chaves.
Fr. Miscellaneous Poems on Growing Old. CoBLCP
Long rolling, The. The Main-Deep. James Stephens. MoBrPo; MOS;
OBMV; RR; UnPo
Long shines the line of wet lamps dark in gleaming. Rainy Midnight.
Ivor Gurney. FaBoPP
Long Sigh. Lu Yu, *tr. fr. Chinese by* Burton Watson. CoBCP
Long since I'd ceased to care. The Parrot. W. W.Gibson. OBMV
Long Since Last. Ruth Miller. PeSA
Long Small Room, The. Edward Thomas. BrPo; Mes
Long spiraling. Stairs. W. S. Merwin. KS
Long spring day, The. Prince Ikusa. *Fr.* Manyo Shu. FCEI
Long steel grass. Trio for Two Cats and a Trombone. Dame Edith
Sitwell. *Fr.* Façade. NAEL-2; PBWP
Long-Suffering of God. Christopher Smart. *Fr.* Hymns for the
Amusement of Children, XXIX. NOCV
Long Summer. Laurie Lee. BoNaP
Long summer, perpetual days. Pine Waves. Yu Kuang-chung, *tr. by*
Dominic Cheung. IFON
Long-tailed pig, A. Mother Goose. OxNR
Long-tailed ponies go nosing the pine-lands. Parochial Theme. Wallace
Stevens. LiTA
Long the proud Spaniard. The Winning of Cales. Thomas Deloney.
CoMu; OxBSS
Long the tyrant of our coast. On the Capture of the *Guerrière*. Philip
Freneau. PAH
Long they pine in weary woe, the nobles of our land. Kathaleen Ny-
Houlahan. William Heffernan, *tr. by* James Clarence Mangan. NOIV
Long Time a Child. Hartley Coleridge. EnRP; PoEL-4; Son
(Sonnet.) OBNC
Long time ago, A. T'ao Ch'ien, *tr. by* Arthur Waley. FaBoCh
Long Time Ago. Leslie Silko. NoAM
Long Time Ago, A. *Unknown.* AmFP
Long time ago/ in the beginning. The Invention of White People. Leslie
Silko. STP
Long time has passed since the last rain was heard, A. Body of Summer.
Odysseus Elytis, *tr. by* Edmund Keeley *and* Philip Sherrard. VMG
Long time he lay upon the sunny hill. Childhood. Edwin Muir. CMoP;
HeIP; NoP; SeCePo
Long time in one place and I always think of moving, A. Cold Night.
Ch'en Shih-tao, *tr. by* Burton Watson. CoBCP
Long time in some forgotten churchyard earth of Warwickshire. Who
Were before Me. John Drinkwater. OBMV
Long time I've wanted to live in the southern village, A. Moving House
("A long time I've wanted to live in the southern village"). T'ao
Ch'ien. CoBCP
Long time, many years, we've had these wars, A. On a Certain
Engagement South of Seoul. Hayden Carruth. AmFN
Long time now I've lain in wait for you, A. Sparta. Angelos Sikelianos,
tr. by Edmund Keeley *and* Philip Sherrard. VMG
Long time Plain Dealing in the haughty town. Plain Dealing's Downfall.
Unknown. OBSV
Long time since it seems to-day, A. W. H. Auden. *Fr.* New Year
Letter. GOA
John Peale Bishop. LiTA
Long Tom. W. W. Gibson. OxBTC
Long, Too Long America. Walt Whitman. GOA
Long Tour: The Country Music Star Explains Why He Put off the Bus and
Fired a Good Lead Guitar in West Texas. James Whitehead. MT
Long Trail, The. Kipling. *See* L'Envoi: "There's a whisper down the
field where the year has shot her yield."
Long Trip. Langston Hughes. MOS
Long tyme hathe Christ (long tyme I must confese). On the Reed of Our
Lord's Passion. William Alabaster. PoEL-2
Long walk, A. Robert Grenier. IAT

Long Walk before the Snows Began, A. Robert Bly. LCAP
Long Walks in the Afternoon. Margaret Gibson. MAYP
Long War, The. Li Po, *tr. fr. Chinese* by Cheng Yu Sun. WaaP
Long war had ended, The. The Next War. Sir Osbert Sitwell. MMA
Long Waters, The. Theodore Roethke. NYBP
Long waves of form, and what if under a sandhill. A Path among the
   Dunes. Marvin Bell. BLA
Long Way outside Yellowstone, A. Thomas McGrath. VGW
Long ways, A. A Remembrance of a Color inside a Forest. Ray A.
   Young Bear. CDW
Long white barn, A. *Unknown.* ChTr; GBP
Long White Seam, The. Jean Ingelow. GN; NOBVV
Long Winter Night. Ryokan, *tr. fr. Japanese* by Burton Watson. FCEI;
   JLIC-2
Long winter nights. In Snow. H. Leivick, *tr.* by Benjamin *and* Barbara
   Harshav. AYP
Long-wished-for rain has fallen, The. Yakamochi. *Fr.* Manyo Shu. Ma
Long years ago I wandered here. On Recrossing the Rocky Mountains
   after Many Years. John Charles Frémont. AiP
Long years ago there came to me in sleep. The Beautiful. F. S.
   Woodley. PeHV
Long years beheld me Patton's mansion grace. A Favourite Cat's Dying
   Soliloquy. Anna Seward. FM
Long years have passed since first a merry child. To One Who Sleepeth.
   Mary E. Tucker. CBWP-1
Long[e] love that in my thought doth harbour, The. Alas! So All Things
   Now Do Hold Their Peace. Petrarch, *tr. fr. Italian.* *Fr.* Sonnets to
   Laura: To Laura in Life, CIX, *tr.* by Sir Thomas Wyatt. NAEL-1;
   NoP; OAEL-1; OBVE
   (Lover for Shamefastnesse Hideth His Desire within His Faithfull
   Hart, The.) AAS, 2 *versions.*
Longer to muse. Sir Thomas Wyatt. SiPS
Longest and much the dearest. Book Review. Russell Davies. FaBoEE
Longest day will drive a crack, The—til Jubilate windows in. Go Round.
   Laura Chester. NPGG
Longest Tyranny that ever sway'd, The. To My Friend, Dr. Charleton, on
   His Learned and Useful Works; and More Particularly This of Stone-
   Heng, by Him Restored to the True Founders. Dryden. SeCV-2
Longface Mahoney Discusses Heaven. Horace Gregory. VGW
Longfellow. Henrietta Cordelia Ray. CBWP-3
Longfellow. James Whitcomb Riley. AA
Longfellow's Visit to Venice. Sir John Betjeman. NOBL
Longing. Matthew Arnold. FPL; PoLF
Longing. Judah Halevi, *tr. fr. Hebrew* by Nina Davis Salaman. TrJP
Longing. George Herbert. SeCV-1
Longing. Rachel Korn, *tr. fr. Yiddish* by Ruth Whitman. VWA
Longing. James Russell Lowell. AnAmPo
Longing. *Gond Oral Tradition, tr.* by V. Elwin *and* S. Hivale. WTO
Longing at twilight the lovesick Adam saw. The Begetting of Cain.
   Hyam Plutzik. VWA
Longing for Death because of Feebleness. Stevie Smith. OBD
Longing for death so scorched me that my brightness returned. Laconic.
   Odysseus Elytis, *tr.* by Edmund Keeley *and* Philip Sherrard. VMG
Longing for Heaven. Anne Bradstreet. *See* As Weary Pilgrim, Now at
   Rest.
Longing for Home. Jean Ingelow. *Fr.* Songs of Seven. WGRP
Longing for Jerusalem. Judah Halevi, *tr. fr. Hebrew* by Emma Lazarus.
   TrJP
Longing for that true comrade of my need. To Liebig. August, Graf von
   Platen, *tr.* by Reginald Bancroft Cooke. PeHV
Longing for the Birds of Solomon. Joseph L. Baird. TSM
Longing for the Emperor. Empress Iwa no Hime, *tr. fr. Japanese.*
   BoWoP, *tr.* by Geoffrey Bownas *and* Anthony Thwaite
Longing for you, my love. *Unknown.* *Fr.* Manyo Shu. FCEI
Longing, I have seen you in the water. Talking Myself to Sleep in the
   Mountain. Gibbons Ruark. MAYP
Longing nostrils move. Evening Motif. Judah Leib Teller, *tr.* by
   Benjamin *and* Barbara Harshav. AYP
Longing to Be Saved, The. Maxine W. Kumin. CAPP
Longings. C. P. Cavafy, *tr. fr. Greek* by Edmund Keeley *and* Philip
   Sherrard. VMG
Longitudinal corridor between vast subterranean foundations. River.
   Philippe Soupault, *tr.* by Rosmarie Waldrop. POS
Longmobile. Shel Silverstein. AiP
Longshore Intellectual. Sean Lucy. CIP
Longterm Hatred. David Avidan, *tr. fr. Hebrew* by Warren Bargad *and*
   Stanley F. Chyet. IP
Lonnie Kramer. Geary Hobson. STE
Lonnie said before this, "I'm." Commanding Elephants. Philip Levine.
   NaP

Lon's away,/ Cill Garad is sad today. Saint Columcille, *tr. fr. Old Irish*
   by Robin Flower. *Fr.* On a Dead Scholar. AnIL
Loo-wit. Wendy Rose. HATNAP; STE
Look, The. Elizabeth Barrett Browning. TrCP
Look, The. Elizabeth Daryush. PoA
Look. Philip Levine. BLA
Look. Charlotte Zolotow. RAR
Look/ There/ The smiling infant. Cold. Brian Coffey. CIP
Look a Man Goes to Kansas. Bert Schierbeek, *tr. fr. Dutch* by Charles
   McGeehan. DuIn
Look, alas, the weather's turning. Five-Minute Water Color. Jules
   Laforgue, *tr.* by William Jay Smith. CT
Look and remember. Look upon this sky. Travelogue for Exiles. Karl
   Shapiro. MoAmPo; TrJP
Look Askance, A. James Merrill. AnAn
Look at All Those Monkeys. Spike Milligan. OnUR
Look at her, calm and benign. A Bronze Statuette of Kwan-yin. Charles
   Wharton Stork. GoYe
Look at him, over there. Disillusion. Maureen Burge. AIW; BrRo
Look at him there in his stovepipe hat. American Primitive. William Jay
   Smith. DiL; FF; InPK; MoAmPo; NePoEA; OxBSP; TwCP
Look at it well. This was the good town once. The Good Town. Edwin
   Muir. CMoP
Look at itsy-bitsy Mitzi! The Pizza. Ogden Nash. RHPC
Look at Jonah embarking from Joppa, deterred by. Tom Fool at Jamaica.
   Marianne Moore. NYBP
Look at me 8th. Sonia Sanchez. PoBA
Look at me move. The Amputee Soldier. Philip Dacey. GOYP
Look at me: my mouth unlearned complaining early. Mother of
   Fishermen. Henriëtte Roland-Holst, *tr.* by Ria Leigh-Loohuizen.
   PBWP
Look at me now I stand before you here. The Gorgeous Redhead.
   Guillaume Apollinaire, *tr.* by Michael Benedikt. POS
Look at me sleeping I am somewhat disfigured. Lachesis. Hilaire
   Kirkland. *Fr.* Clotho, Lachesis, Atropos, II. PeNZ
Look at my continent containing. Human Geography. Gloria Fuertes, *tr.*
   by Willis Barnstone. BoWoP
Look at My Face, a Collage. Carolyn M. Rodgers. JB
Look at my knees. I Wonder What It Feels Like to Be Drowned? Robert
   Graves. BrPo; MoBrPo
Look at pretty little kitty. Kitty. Doug McLeod. CRH
Look at Six Eggs. Carl Sandburg. *Fr.* Prairie. FaPON
Look at That Gal. Julian Bond. PoNe; TTY
Look at that little bay of the Ch'i. *Unknown, tr.* by Arthur Waley. BoS
Look at the aeroplane. The Aeroplane. Jeannie Kirby. BoTP
Look at the bulbul and the rose. Mohammad Taqi Mir, *tr.* by Ahmed Ali.
   GoT
Look at the eyes look from my tail! Peacock and Nightingale. Robert
   Finch. OBCV
Look at the foothills of Mount Han. *Unknown, tr.* by Arthur Waley.
   BoS
Look at the little sandpiper. The Sandpiper. Charlotte Zolotow. TSS
Look at the Lo river. *Unknown, tr.* by Arthur Waley. BoS
Look at the mountain. Wakayama Bokusui, *tr. fr. Japanese* by Hiroaki
   Sato. *Fr.* Forty-four Tanka. FCEI
Look at the path, look at her waving her sleeve! *Unknown, tr.* by Sato.
   FCEI
Look at the rat; he has a skin. *Unknown, tr.* by Arthur Waley. BoS
Look at the soul floating in the empty space. Festival in Fishing Village
   No. 3. Park Je-chun, *tr.* by Koh Chang-soo. ACKP
Look at the stars! look, look up at the skies! The Starlight Night. Gerard
   Manley Hopkins. ACP; BrPo; GTBS-P; InPS; LiTM; MoAB;
   MoBrPo; NAEL-2; PoE; PPP; SeCePo; WSC
Look at the way it's truly lovely, and ample. The Hand Is a Cake.
   Hagiwara Sakutaro, *tr.* by Sato. FCEI
Look at them flit. Fish. Mary Ann Hoberman. RAR
Look at this red pear. The Indigestion of the Vampire. W. S. Merwin.
   NaP
Look at this skin—at fourscore years. Robert Barnabas Brough. *Fr.* The
   Marquis of Carabas. FiBHP
Look at this village boy, his head is stuffed. Farm Child. R. S. Thomas.
   BoNaP
"Look at us now, then." The Dead Cities Speak to the Living Cities.
   Edmond Fleg, *tr.* by Anthony Rudolf. VWA
Look at your corn in May. *Unknown.* FaBoUs
Look Away child. Susan Cavin. GLP
Look away now from the high lonesome hills. Admonition for Spring.
   L. A. MacKay. CaP; OBCV
Look Back. Carroll Arnett. STE
Look between the bow and the bowstring, beneath. Backgrounds to Italian
   Paintings: Fifteenth Century. Anne Ridler. WPE

Look Closely. Morton Marcus. FF

Look, Delia, how we esteem the half-blown rose. Samuel Daniel. *Fr.* To Delia. HeIP; NoP; OBSC

(Half-blown Rose, The.) SeCePo

(Sonnet: "Look, Delia, how we esteem the half-blown rose.") EIL

Look down; be still. Wonga Vine. Judith Wright. PoAu-2

Look down on me, a little one. A Child's Morning Prayer. J. Kirby. BoTP

Look down. The dead have life. Gravestones. Vernon Watkins. TEP

Look down the slope of the pavement. A Touch of the Hand. Allen Curnow. ATNZ

Look, Edwin! Edna St. Vincent Millay. GoJo

Look for Me on England. Herbert B. Mallalieu. WaP

Look forth and tell me what they do. Hammer and Anvil. Samuel Valentine Cole. PoLF

Look forward, truant, to your second childhood. The Death Room. Robert Graves. NYBP

Look from the sphere of endless day. Other Sheep I Have, Which Are Not of This Fold. Bryant. TrPWD

Look, God, I have never spoken to You. Conversion. Frances Angermayer. PoLF

Look, he is superfluous—for of what use was it to be born? Ovid, *tr. fr. Latin by* L. R. Lind. *Fr.* Tristium, XIII. NAs

Look: Here our bodies lie in a long, long line. But We Shall Bloom. Haim Guri, *tr. by* David Kuselewitz. TrJP

Look here, Petah! whut's dis here. The Examination. Priscilla Jane Thompson. CBWP-2

Look him. As quiet as a July river-/ bed. Grampa. Dennis Scott. PBCV

Look Home. Robert Southwell. NOCV

Look how evening comes and around us the barbed-wire-hemmed, wild. Seventh Eclogue. Miklós Radnóti, *tr. by* Emery George. VWA

Look how her close defences laddered now. Apollo and Daphne. W. R. Rodgers. ErPo; LiTB

Look how peaceful these wooden figures are, going to their death. The War against the Jews. Gerald Stern. CAPP

Look! how the clouds are flying south! The Snow-Man. "Marian Douglas." OBCA

Look how the flower which lingeringly *or* ling'ringly doth fade. Thy Sun Posts Westward. William Drummond of Hawthornden. SeCePo

Look how the industrious bee in fragrant May. The Bee. Charles Fitz-Geffry. *Fr.* Sir Francis Drake. EIL

Look how these young, bare, bullock faces know. Soldiers on the Platform. Frances Cornford. CN

Look in my face; my name is Might-have-been. A Superscription. Dante Gabriel Rossetti. *Fr.* The House of Life, XCVII. EBVV; GTBS-P; NAEL-2; NoP; OAEL-2; OBNC; PoEL-5; SeCePo

Look, in the attic, the unentered room. Before the Carnival. Thom Gunn. NePoEA

Look, in the Labyrinth of Memory. Delmore Schwartz. TrJP

Look in the Landscape. Gerhard Fritsch, *tr. fr. German by* Beth Bjorklund. CoAuP

Look in this crystal pool, and you will see. To———, with an Ivory Hand-Glass. Lord Alfred Douglas. FaBoUs

Look in this mirror, tell me what you see. Glass Dialectic. Howard Nemerov. WaP

"Look in thy glass, and tell the face thou viewest." Shakespeare. *Fr.* Sonnets, III. LiTB; NAEL-1; OBSC

Look into the Gulf, A. Edwin Markham. AA

Look, Loig, behind. The Only Jealousy of Emer. *Unknown, tr. by* John Montague. BIrV

Look! Look at me! Tree Birthdays. Mary Carolyn Davies. OHIP

Look, look! rejoice and wonder! The Return of Astraea. Ben Jonson. NOBE

Look! look! the spring is come. First Spring Morning. Robert Bridges. BoNaP; BoTP

Look, Medusa! Suniti Namjoshi. AIW

Look, my friend, look at Hari's nimble eyes. Surdas, *tr. by* John Stratton Hawley *and* Mark Juergensmeyer. SSI

Look, my King, they're everywhere. Faith, Hope and Charity. Juan Gonzalo Rose, *tr. by* Ena Hollis. Per

Look, my Samsons are coming back, the gates of Gaza on their shoulders. My Samsons. Haim Guri. IP, *tr. by* Warren Bargad *and* Stanley F. Chyet; VWA, *tr. by* Mark Elliott Shapiro

Look: no one ever promised for sure. An Introduction to Some Poems. William Stafford. CAPP

Look Not in My Eyes, for Fear. A. E. Housman. *Fr.* A Shropshire Lad, XV. PeHV; PoEL-5

Look Not Thou. Sir Walter Scott. *See* Bride of Lammermoor, The: Lucy Ashton's Song.

Look not thou on beauty's charming. Lucy Ashton's Song. Sir Walter Scott. *Fr.* The Bride of Lammermoor, *ch.* 3. EnRP; GoTS; NOBE; OBEV; OxBS

(Look Not Thou.) OxBSP

Look now, at this February street in April. A Street in April. Louis Dudek. OBCV

Look now, bride of God. In Praise of Virginity. Hroswitha, *tr. by* John Dillon. PBWP

Look now, directed by yon candle's blaze. Fiction. Charles Sprague. *Fr.* Curiosity. AA

Look off, dear Love, across the sallow sand. Evening Song. Sidney Lanier. AnAmPo; UnPo

Look on Him Whom They Pierced, and Mourn. Isaac Watts. NOCV

Look on that form, once fit for the sculptor! Working and Waiting. Adah Isaacs Menken. CBWP-1

Look—on the topmost branches of the world. Sunday Evening in the Common. John Hall Wheelock. MoAmPo

Look on this cast, and know the hand. The Hand of Lincoln. Edmund Clarence Stedman. AA; AnAmPo; OHIP

Look on this maid of honour, now. Philip Massinger. *Fr.* The Maid of Honour, V, ii. ACP

Look once more ere we leave this specular Mount. Milton. *Fr.* Paradise Regained, *bk.* IV, *ll.* 236-284. OBTV

(Athens.) OBS, *fr. ll.* 236-364.

Look one way and the sun is going down. The Mockingbird. Randall Jarrell. DuDa; NYBP; RFM

Look or You Leap. Jasper Heywood. EIL

(Lookers-On, The.) ACP

Look our ransomed shores around. Additional Verses to Hail Columbia. Oliver Wendell Holmes. PAH

Look Out Below! Charles Robert Thatcher. PoAu-1

Look out how you use proud words. Primer Lesson. Carl Sandburg. FaPON; MoAmPo; MoShBr

Look out, inhabitants of earth. Europa Rides a Black Bull. Antonio Porta, *tr. by* Lawrence R. Smith. NItP

Look out! look out! Jack Frost. Cecily E. Pike. BoTP

Look out! Look out, boys! Clear the track! Oliver Wendell Holmes. *Fr.* The Broomstick Train. FaPON

Look out there. *Unknown.* NOIV

Look out upon the stars, my love. Edward Coote Pinkney. AA; AnAmPo

Look round our world; behold the chain of love. Pope. *Fr.* An Essay on Man, Epistle III. OBD

Look round: You see a little supper room. De Coenatione Micae. Martial, *tr. by* Robert Louis Stevenson. FaBoCh

Look Sheila Seeing You've Asked Me. Vincent O'Sullivan. PeNZ

Look, so many pockets. Pockets. Ernst Jandl, *tr. by* Beth Bjorklund. CoAuP

Look, son, what a skyscraper. My Son Doesn't See a Thing. Tomás Rivera, *tr. by* Toni Empringham. FIA

Look soul. Animula. W. S. Merwin. CAPP

Look, stranger, on this island now. On This Island. W. H. Auden. CMoP; NAEL-2; PoE

(Look, Stranger.) MoAB; MoBrPo; TrGrPo

(Look, Stranger, on This Island.) InVP

(Seascape.) GTBS-P

Look. The land ends up. Some Grand River Blues. Daniel David Moses. HATNAP

Look, the trees. In Blackwater Woods. Mary Oliver. CAPP

Look there at the star! Shepherd's Song at Christmas. Langston Hughes. PChr

Look, this must be love that fills the sky! Teika, *tr. fr. Japanese by* Hiroaki Sato. *Fr.* Eighty-four Tanka. FCEI

Look, Thoughts and Dreams. Yehuda Amichai, *tr. fr. Hebrew by* Warren Bargad *and* Stanley F. Chyet. IP

Look thy last on all things shitty. Shitty. Kingsley Amis. OxBC; TW

Look to the Back of the Hand. Judith Minty. PoA

Look! Unlearn your bookish lore. Song of the Knight of the Mirrors. W. H. Auden. *Fr.* Man of La Mancha. AnAn

Look Up *or* Lend a Hand. Edward Everett Hale. FaBoBe; FaFP

Look up and not down. Look Up *or* Lend a Hand. Edward Everett Hale. FaBoBe; FaFP

Look up, dear one, nor be cast down. Truth. Josephine D. Henderson Heard. CBWP-4

Look up into the dome. Altitudes. Richard Wilbur. CMoP

Look up into the light of the lantern. Night Song. Louise Glück. MAYP; SV

"Look up," she said; and all the heavens blazed. Starlight. John White Chadwick. AA

Look up this river in the book of rivers. Border River. Alfred Goldsworthy Bailey. CaP

Look up, you men. Men there at the fire. Rainer Maria Rilke, *tr. fr. German* by M. D. Herter Norton. *Fr.* Annunciation over the Shepherds. PChr

Look up. From bleakening hills. Snow. Adelaide Crapsey. QFR

Look, we don't give a hoot if Zippo-Fasteners have gone to war. Memorial to the Great Big Beautiful Self-sacrificing Advertisers. Frederick Ebright. WaP

Look where the mist. Mist over Pukehina. *Maori Oral Tradition, tr. by* E. Shortland. WTO

Look you child, I signify three hundred years in swarm. Policeman Cleared in Jaywalking Case. Claire Harris. PBCV

Look, You Have Cast Out Love! Kipling. *Fr.* Plain Tales from the Hills. OxBSP

"Lookatitthisway: I have seen some." Where Have All the Indians Gone? Janet Campbell Hale. STE

Look[e] how the pale Queen[e] of the silent night. A Sonnet of the Moon. Charles Best. CH
(Moon, The.) OBSC
(Of the Moon.) EIL

Looke well about, ye that lovers be. Against Women. *Unknown.* MeEL

Lookers-On, The. Jasper Heywood. *See* Look or You Leap.

Looking as I've looked before, straight down the heart. The Stranger. Adrienne Rich. NNaP

Looking at a Chagall Painting. Eli Netser, *tr. fr. Hebrew by* Bernhard Frank. MHeP

Looking at a Dead Wren in My Hand. Robert Bly. NNaP

Looking at a Dry Canadian Thistle Brought In from the Snow. Robert Bly. NNaP

Looking at a passing cloud. Buson, *tr. fr. Japanese by* Hiroaki Sato. *Fr.* Eighty-seven Hokku. FCEI

Looking at a Photograph on My Forty-Fourth Birthday. Carl Dennis. BLA

Looking at a Picture on an Anniversary. Thomas Hardy. EyDe

Looking at Chrysanthemums. Chang Yü, *tr. fr. Chinese by* Jonathan Chaves. *Fr.* Seven Poems on Living in the Mountains: Seeing Off. CoBLCP

Looking at Each Other. Muriel Rukeyser. GLP; NNaP

Looking at Henry Moore's Elephant Skull Etchings in Jerusalem during the War. Shirley Kaufman. LCAP

Looking at it, just thinking about it. Teika, *tr. fr. Japanese by* Hiroaki Sato. *Fr.* A Compendium of Good Tanka. FCEI

Looking at Kapiti. Alistair Campbell. ATNZ

Looking at My Grandchildren. Lady Izumi, *tr. fr. Japanese by* Hiroaki Sato. *Fr.* Fifty-one Tanka. FCEI

Looking at New-fallen Snow from a Train. Robert Bly. NaP

Looking at Old Note-Books. C. H. Sisson. NPo

Looking at Pictures to Be Put Away. Gary Snyder. FF; NNaP

Looking at Quilts. Marge Piercy. SaC

Looking at Some Flowers. Robert Bly. NaP; NOBA

Looking at the moon, I feel sad. Teika, *tr. fr. Japanese by* Hiroaki Sato. *Fr.* A Compendium of Good Tanka. FCEI

Looking at the open page of the psalm book. Prayer Service in an English Church. Robert Bly. KS

Looking at the standards. High Jumper. Don Welch. TSL

Looking at the willows. At the Ferry in Kuwana. Chiyojo, *tr. fr. Japanese by* Hiroaki Sato. *Fr.* Seventeen Hokku. FCEI

Looking at you, my beauty. Emperor Go-Shirakawa, *tr. fr. Japanese by* Hiroaki Sato. *Fr.* Ryojin Hisho. FCEI

Looking Back, *sel.* John Dyer.
Grongar Hill. ChTr; EnRP; FaBoPP; GoTL; NOEC; NoP; PoEL-3

Looking back in my mind I can see. The Elementary Scene. Randall Jarrell. CMoP; LCAP; PoE

Looking back, the language scribbles. Rereading Old Writing. David Ferry. DiPo; PPR

Looking Before and After. Carter Revard. HATNAP

Looking Both Ways. Jane O. Wayne. GOYP

Looking by chance in at the open window. The Foreboding. Robert Graves. ELP; GBL; PoA

Looking Down a Hill. A. R. Thompson. PoSH

Looking down into my father's/ dead face. "Good Night, Willie Lee, I'll See You in the Morning." Alice Walker. WeW

Looking Down on Nether Stowey. Samuel Taylor Coleridge. *Fr.* Fears in Solitude. FaBoPP

Looking for a Country under Its Original Name. Colleen J. McElroy. BlSi

Looking for a Recluse but Failing to Find Him. Chia Tao, *tr. fr. Chinese by* Burton Watson. CoBCP

Looking for a Rest Area. Stephen Dunn. AmPA; AnAn

Looking for a Ship. Harry Aisthorpe. OxBSS

Looking for Buddha. Jaime Jacinto. BrSi

Looking for love, she read cookbooks. The Woman Who Loved to Cook. Erica Jong. TAP

Looking for Lu Hung-chien but Failing to Find Him. Chiao-jan, *tr. fr. Chinese by* Burton Watson. CoBCP

Looking for Maimonides: Tiberias. Shirley Kaufman. VWA

Looking for Mountain Beavers. David Wagoner. VGW

Looking for Mushrooms at Sunrise. W. S. Merwin. NaP; NOBA

Looking for My Old Indian Grandmother in the Summer Heat of 1980. Diane Glancy. STE

Looking for Poetry. Carlos Drummond de Andrade, *tr. fr. Portuguese by* Mark Strand. AnAn

Looking for something in the Sunday paper. The Sunday News. Dana Gioia. GOYP

Looking for the Melungeon. Dave Smith. HCAP

Looking for Work. Raymond Carver. GeTw

Looking for you everywhere, but unable to find you. The Story of Bitter Tea. Lo Ch'ing, *tr. fr. Chinese by* Dominic Cheung. IFON

Looking Forward. Robert Louis Stevenson. *See* When I am grown to man's estate.

Looking-Glass, A. Thomas Carew. CaPo

Looking Glass, The. Kipling. FaBoTw; OBMV

Looking-Glass for Smokers, A, *sel.* Lawrence Spooner.
On Giving Up Smoking. NOEC

Looking in a thicket. Sweetheart. Phil Hey. GOYP

Looking into a Face. Robert Bly. CAPP; NOBA

Looking into a Tide Pool. Robert Bly. CAPP; MAT

Looking into History. Richard Wilbur. VGW

Looking into my daughter's eyes I read. For My Daughter. Weldon Kees. CoAP; SM

Looking like a guide to the Joined Bridge. Fuboku, *tr. by* Sato. FCEI

Looking like a wild deer sleeping against the cliffs. Presented to a Mountain Dweller. Chao Chih-hsin, *tr. by* Michael S. Duke. WFTU

Looking like all outdoors. For Richard Chase. Jim Wayne Miller. GOYP

Looking north you try to break through the sky. The Chicago Odyssey. Jim Barnes. NOVW

Looking On. Anthony Thwaite. NePoEA-2

Looking Out. Helen Chasin. NMM

Looking out toward the stars. A. L. Hendricks. *Fr.* D'Où Venons Nous? Que Sommes Nous? Où Allons Nous. PBCV

Looking over Poems by Persons of Long Ago. Shunzei, *tr. fr. Japanese by* Burton Watson. *Fr.* Thirty Tanka. FCEI

Looking through. Masaoka Shiki, *tr. by* Geoffrey Bownas *and* Anthony Thwaite. PeBJV

Looking through boxes. The Toy Bone. Donald Hall. CAPP

Looking to the sea, it is a line. The Innocence. Robert Creeley. NeAP

Looking up/ I find myself written. The Paisley Ceiling. Lila Arnold. IHMS

Looking Up at Leaves. Barbara Howes. BoNaP

Looking up at the stars, I know quite well. The More Loving One. W. H. Auden. HoPM; TOF

Looking West. William Stafford. NYBP

Lookout on a Rock on the Heights of Mount Hermon. Abba Kovner, *tr. fr. Hebrew by* Warren Bargad *and* Stanley F. Chyet. IP

Lookout watch must climb and climb, The. Crow's Nest. Richard F. Armknecht. GoYe

Looks as if about to snatch the blossoms. *Unknown, tr. fr. Japanese by* Hiroaki Sato. *Fr.* Inutsukuba Shu. FCEI

Looks of a Lover Enamoured, The. George Gascoigne. EIL; SeCePo

Loom of Time, The. *Unknown.* BLPA

Looms are sept an' brass is drawn. July Wakes. Richard Pomfret. OBET

Loon/ I thought it was, A. My Love Has Departed. *Unknown, tr. by* Frances Densmore. OV

Loon, The. Theodore Harding Rand. CaP

Loon, The. Alfred Billings Street. AA

Loon?, A, No. Chippewa Love Song. *Unknown.* BoWoP, *tr. by* Frances Densmore

Loon I Thought It Was, A. *Unknown, tr. fr. Chippewa Indian by* Frances Densmore. OBVE, *See also* Chippewa Love Song

Loon's Egg, The. Peter Dale Scott. MoCV

Loons going now, whose range we lay awake. October Cycle. John Peck. AnAn

Loon's long night call, A. Three Seasons. Francis Sparshott. NOBC

Loop of rusty cable incises, The. "Luckies." Reginald Gibbons. MAYP

Loose earth falls in the grave like a peaceful regular breathing, The. A Dog's Death. J. C. Squire. FM

Loose eyes of an old man, The. Negroes. Maxwell Bodenheim. PoNe

Loose Saraband, A. Richard Lovelace. CaPo; PoEL-3

Loose Woman. X. J. Kennedy. WeW

Loose Woman Poem. Sharon Thesen. NOBC

Loosed from its bonds my spirit fled away. A Dream, or the Type of the Rising Sun. Jean Adams. NOEC

Loosely from the Latin. David Galef. SoTCo

Loot. Thom Gunn. ErPo; NePoEA-2

Loping along on the day's patrol. The Sheepherder. Lew Sarett. AmFN; FaPON

Loppèd tree in time may grow [or goe] again by twins [or turnes]. Robert Southwell. ACP; ElL; LiTB; OBSC; PoEL-2

Lopsided with God. On the Road to Vicenza. Ralph Gustafson. CaP

Loquat. Nishiwaki Junzaburo, tr. fr. Japanese by Hiroaki Sato. FCEI

Lord, The. Erika Mitterer, tr. fr. German by Beth Bjorklund. CoAuP

Lord/ forgive me/ if I twist the sunset. The Hungry Black Child. Adam David Miller. PoBA

Lord,/ I am the cat. The Prayer of the Cat. Carmen Bernos de Gasztold, tr. by Rumer Godden. CRH; PDV

Lord,/ we have been watching over him. Act of Faith. Arturo Trías. InW, tr. by Julio Marzán

Lord,/ What a menagerie! Noah's Prayer. Carmen Bernos de Gasztold, tr. by Rumer Godden. TrCP

Lord Abbott. Hilaire Belloc. FaBoNo

Lord above gave man an arm of iron, The. With a Little Bit of Luck. Alan Jay Lerner. FaFP

Lord above, in tender love, The. Thanksgiving Hymn. Unknown. PAH

Lord, aid my work this day. Morning Prayer. Geoffrey Mac Briain Mac An Bhaird, tr. by Earl of Longford. TIRV

Lord Alcohol. Thomas Lovell Beddoes. WiR

Lord, all I am and hope to be. An Offering. Eloise Bibb. CBWP-4

Lord among the Clouds, The. Unknown, tr. fr. Chinese by Burton Watson. Fr. Nine Songs. CoBCP

Lord Apollo, who has never died, The. Many Are Called. E. A. Robinson. OxBA

Lord, art thou at the table head above. Edward Taylor. Fr. Preparatory Meditations before My Approach to the Lord's Supper, IV. AmPP; OxBA

(Reflexion, The.) AmPP; OxBA

Lord, as the grain which once on upland acres. Communion Hymn. George Seaver. TIRV

Lord, as thou wilt, bestow. Eduard Friedrich Mörike, tr. by John Drinkwater. TrPWD

Lord, at this Closing Hour. Eleazar Thompson Fitch. AH

Lord Barrenstock. Stevie Smith. FaBoNo; NBLV; OBSV

Lord Bateman. Unknown. See Young Beichan.

Lord bless thee and keep thee, The. Benediction. Bible, O.T. Fr. Numbers, VI: 24–26. TrGrPo

(Blessing of the Priests.) TrJP

("Lorde blesse the and kepe the, The," tr. by William Tyndale) OBVE, VI: 24–27.

Lord Buddha is present everywhere. Emperor Go-Shirakawa, tr. fr. Japanese by Hiroaki Sato. Fr. Ryojin Hisho. FCEI

Lord Buddha's yellow flowers, The. Ozaki Hosai, tr. fr. Japanese by Hiroaki Sato. Fr. One Hundred Haiku in Free Form. FCEI

Lord, by whose breath all souls and seeds are living. Andrew Young. EaLo

"Lord Byron" was an Englishman. Sketch of Lord Byron's Life. Julia A. Moore. FiBHP; OBAL

Lord, can a crumb of dust the earth outweigh. Edward Taylor. Fr. Preparatory Meditations before My Approach to the Lord's Supper. NAAL-1

Lord Chancellours Villanies Discovered; or, His Rise and Fall in the Four Last Years, The. Unknown. CoMu

Lord Clive. Edmund Clerihew Bentley. See Clerihews: What I like about Clive.

Lord Cockroach, Old Sir Empty Belly. A Curse against the Owner. Barton Sutter. TW

Lord, confound this surly sister. The Curse. John Millington Synge. ChTr; FaBoCo; FaBoEE; NOIV; TW

Lord Coningsby's Epitaph. Pope. FaBoEE

Lord Cozens Hardy. Sir John Betjeman. OxBTC

Lord Crashton: The Absentee Landlord. William Allingham. Fr. Laurence Bloomfield in Ireland. NOIV

Lord Cray. Edward Gorey. RHPC

Lord, Dear God! to Thy Attending. Heinrich Otto, tr. fr. German by Sheema Z. Buehne. AH

Lord Delamere. Unknown. ESPB

Lord, Deliver, Thou Canst Save. Eliza Lee Follen. AH

Lord Derwentwater ("The king has written a braid letter"). Unknown. ESPB

Lord Derwentwater ("The king he wrote a love-letter"). Unknown. AmFP

Lord Derwentwater ("Our king has wrote a long letter"). Unknown. ESPB

Lord Descended from Above, The. Thomas Sternhold. AH

(Majesty of God, The.) WGRP

Lord Douglas. Unknown. See Jamie Douglas.

Lord Douglas. Unknown. See Waly, Waly ("O waly, waly, up the bank").

Lord Erlinton had ae daughter. Erlinton. Unknown. ESPB, A and B vers.

Lord Expositor, if I had a horse. Peire Vidal, tr. by Paul Blackburn. Pro

Lord Finchley. Hilaire Belloc. FaBoCo; FaBoEE; FiBHP; NBLV; NoAM; NOBL; OxBoLi

Lord Fluting Dreams of America on the Eve of His Departure from Liverpool. Paul Zimmer. VGW

Lord, for the erring thought. A Thanksgiving. William Dean Howells. TrPWD

(Prayer, A: "Lord, for the erring thought.") WGRP

Lord, for to-morrow and its needs. Just for To-Day. Ernest R. Wilberforce. PWR

Lord, Forgive a Spirit. Gerald Stern. CAPP

Lord frowned down from every wall, The. Childhood. Donagh MacDonagh. NeIP

Lord Galloway. Burns. OxBoLi

Lord gie you chile de spirit. Gettin de Spirit. Una Marson. PBCV

Lord, Glory of the Universe. To Christ. Fadwa Tuqan, tr. by Abdullah al-Udhari. MPAW

Lord, God, forgive white Europe. Prayer for Peace: II. Léopold Sédar Senghor, tr. by John Reed and Clive Wake. TTY

Lord God, how full our cup of happiness! The Cup of Happiness. Gilbert Thomas. TrPWD

Lord God, I saw the son-of-a-bitch uncoil. The Rural Carrier Stops to Kill a Nine-Foot Cottonmouth. T. R. Hummer. SM

Lord God in Paradise. Grace for Gardens. Louise Driscoll. TrPWD

Lord God of Hosts. Shepherd Knapp. AH

Lord, God of love, the wedded hearts. The Sanctum. T. A. Daly. TrPWD

Lord God of the oak and the elm. George Villiers. TrPWD

Lord God of trajectory and blast. Man unto His Fellow Man. Norman Corwin. Fr. On a Note of Triumph. TrJP

Lord God Planted a Garden, The. Dorothy Frances Gurney. BLPA; FaBoBe; FPL; WGRP

Lord God! this was a stone. The Stone. Thomas Vaughan. OBS; OBWVE

Lord Gorbals. Harry Graham. FaBoCo

Lord had a job for me, The. Get Somebody Else. Paul Laurence Dunbar. BLRP

(Too Busy.) WBLP

Lord Has a Child, The. Langston Hughes. AH

Lord, hast Thou set me here. The Priest's Lament. Robert Hugh Benson. ACP

Lord, Have Mercy. Nahum Tate. TIRV

Lord, Have Mercy on Us. Thomas Nashe. See Summer's Last Will and Testament: Adieu, Farewell, Earth's Bliss[e].

Lord Hay's Mask, sel. Thomas Campion. Roses. OBSC

Lord, he thought he'd make a man. Dese Bones Gwine to Rise Again. Unknown. AS, with music; OxBoLi

Lord, Hear My Prayer. John Clare. NOCV; NoP; TrCP

Lord, help me live from day to day. Others. Charles D. Meigs. WBLP

Lord here my prayre and let my crye passe. Psalm CII ("Lord here my prayre and let my crye passe"). Bible, O.T. Fr. Psalms. OBVE

Lord Heygate. Hilaire Belloc. OxBoLi

Lord High-Bo. Hilaire Belloc. FiBHP

Lord Hippo. Hilaire Belloc. NoAM

Lord, how are they increased that trouble me! Psalm III ("Lord, how are they increased that trouble me!"). Bible, O.T. Fr. Psalms.

(Psalm III: "Lord how many are my foes," paraphrased by Milton) OBVE

Lord, how can man preach thy eternall word? The Windows. George Herbert. MeLP; NOCV; NoP; SeCP; SeCV-1; TrCP

(Church Windows, The.) OBS

Lord, how delightful 'tis to see. For the Lord's Day Evening. Isaac Watts. OxBChV

Lord Hsieh's youngest, his favorite child. Airing Painful Memories. Yüan Chen, tr. by Burton Watson. CoBCP

Lord, hush this ego as one stops a bell. Vassar Miller. Fr. Love's Bitten Tongue. MT

Lord, I am like to mistletoe. To God. Robert Herrick. TrPWD; WGRP

Lord, I am lonely. A Stranger in This Land. Cliff Ashby. NOCV

Lord I am not entirely selfish. Gavin Ewart. OxBC

Lord, I am not one of the just. Seder, 1944. Friedrich Torberg. VWA, *tr. by* Erna Baber Rosenfeld

Lord, I am poor; but it becomes. I Have a Roof. Ada Jackson. TrPWD

Lord, I Am Thine. Samuel Davies. AH

Lord, I give thanks! Thanksgiving. Susie Montgomery Best. TrPWD

Lord, I have knelt and tried to pray to-night. Communion. Edward Dowden. TrPWD

Lord, I have not time to pray. Helene Magaret. *Fr.* Impiety. TrPWD

Lord, I have sinn'd, and the black number swells. The Penitent. Jeremy Taylor. OBS

Lord, I Know Thy Grace Is nigh Me. Hervey Doddridge Ganse. AH

Lord, I remember, and am sore amazed. Hymn of Weeping. Amittai ben Shefatiah, *tr. by* Nina Davis Salaman. TrJP

Lord, I say nothing: I profess. Christ, the Man. W. H. Davies. WGRP

Lord, I Want to Be a Christian. *Unknown.* AH

Lord! if in love, though fainting oft, I have tended thy gracious Vine. "Owen Meredith." *Fr.* Last Lines. TrPWD

Lord, If Thou Art Not Present. John Gray. TrPWD

Lord, I'm done for: now Margot. Vincent Voiture, *tr. by* William Jay Smith. CT; FiBHP

Lord in His wisdom made the fly, The. The Fly. Ogden Nash. FaPON

Lord, in my silence how do I despise. Frailty. George Herbert. NOCV

Lord in the Wind, The. James Picot. PoAu-2

Lord, in this day of battle. Prayer during Battle. Hermann Hagedorn. TrPWD

Lord, in this dust Thy sovereign voice. A Thanksgiving. John Henry, Cardinal Newman. TrPWD

Lord, in Thy Presence Here. Jesse L. Holman. AH

Lord Ingram and Chiel Wyet. *Unknown.* ESPB, (A, B *and* C *vers.*) (Lady Maisry.) OBET; OxBB, *with music*

Lord into His Garden Comes, The. *Unknown.* AH

Lord Is a Man of War, The. Bible, *O.T. Fr.* Exodus, XV: 3-10. WaaP

Lord Is King, The. *Unknown, tr. fr. Hebrew by* Solomon Solis-Cohen. TrJP

Lord is my light and my salvation, The; whom shall I fear? Psalm XXVII ("The Lord is my light"). Bible, *O.T. Fr.* Psalms.
(Deliverance of Jehovah, The, *Moulton, Modern Reader's Bible*) WGRP
Serenity of Faith, The. *Fr.* 7-14. BLRP

Lord is my shepherd, I shall not, The. Neo-Thomist Poem. Ernest Hemingway. OBAL

Lord is my shepherd, I shall not want, The. Psalm XXIII ("The Lord is my shepherd "). Bible, *O.T. Fr.* Psalms. AWP; BLPL; FaBoBe; FaPON; FPL; NAWM-1; NIP; OHIP; PoLF; TrGrPo; TrJP
("Lord to me a shepherd is, The," *Bay Psalm Book*) OBCA
(Lord's My Shepherd, The, *Scottish Psalter*) AH, *with music; WBLP, ad. by* Francis Rous.
(Protection of Jehovah, The, *Moulton, Modern Reader's Bible*) WGRP
(Psalm XXIII: "Lord my shepherd, me His shepe, The," *paraphrased by* George Sandys) JCP
(Psalm XXIII: "Lorde is my shepherde, The; therfore can I lack nothing.") OBVE, *tr. by* Miles Coverdale.

Lord it is my chief complaint. William Cowper. *Fr.* Lovest Thou Me?. TrPWD

Lord, it is not Life to live. Augustus Montague Toplady. *Fr.* Happiness Found. TrPWD

Lord, it is time. The summer was too long. Autumn Day. Rainer Maria Rilke, *tr. by* C. F. MacIntyre. TrJP

Lord, it's very hard to get. Silent Prayer of Peasants. Imre Csanádi, *tr. by* Edwin Morgan. MHuP

Lord Jesus Christ, We Humbly Pray. Henry Eyster Jacobs. AH

Lord Jesus, make Thyself to me. My Prayer. *Unknown.* BLRP

Lord Jesus, Thou hast known. A Mother's Birthday. Henry van Dyke. OHIP

Lord Jesus, who would think that I am Thine? Christina Rossetti. NOBVV

Lord, knights, and squires, the num'rous band. To a Child of Quality of Five Years Old, the Author Supposed Forty. Matthew Prior. NOEC

Lord Lavel he stands at his stable-door. *See* Lord Lovel he stands at his stable-door.

Lord, lay the taste of prayer upon my tongue. The Taste of Prayer. Ralph W. Seager. TrPWD

Lord, lay your fingers on. Closing Prayer. Johnstone G. Patrick. TrPWD

Lord! Lead the Way the Saviour Went. William Croswell. AH

Lord, let me be the torch that springs to light. The Torch. Theodosia Pickering Garrison. BLPA

Lord, let me live like a Regular Man. Berton Braley. BLPA

Lord, let me make this rule. School Days. Maltbie Davenport Babcock. PWR

Lord, let the angels praise thy name. Miserie. George Herbert. PoEL-2

Lord, let war's tempests cease. Let War's Tempests Cease. Longfellow. OHIP

Lord, Listen. Else Lasker-Schüler, *tr. fr. German.* VWA, *tr. by* Edouard Roditi

Lord Livingston. *Unknown.* ESPB; OxBB

Lord, Lord—these miracles, the streets, all say. Stone Too Can Pray. Conrad Aiken. EaLo

Lord, Lord to Thee. A Sailor's Prayer. George Hornell Morris. TrPWD

Lord Lovel ("Lord Lovel [*or* Lavel] he stands at his stable-door"). Lord Lovel. *Unknown.* AmFP; AS, *with music;* BLPA; ESPB, (B *and* D *vers.*); ESPB; FaPON

Lord Lovel ("Lord Lovel he stood at his castle gate"). *Unknown.* AmFP; AS, *with music;* BLPA; ESPB, (A, B, *and* D *vers.*); FaPON

Lord Lovell he stood at his own front door. The Tale of Lord Lovell. *Unknown.* NOBL

Lord Lundy. Hilaire Belloc. FaBoCo; NBLV; OBSV; OxBoLi

Lord, Make a Regular Man out of Me. Edgar Albert Guest. BLPA; BLPL

Lord, make me an instrument of Your peace. Prayer of St. Francis of Assisi for Peace. St. Francis of Assisi. FPL; PoLF

Lord, make me sensitive to the sight. Barbara Marr. TrPWD

Lord, Make Me to Know Mine End. Bible, *O.T. See* Psalms: Psalm XXXIX ("I said: 'I will take heed to my ways' ").

Lord, make my soul. The Mirror. Blanche Mary Kelly. TrPWD

Lord, Many Times Thou Pleased Art. George Wither. AH

Lord Maxwell's Last Goodnight ("Good Lord of the Land."). *Unknown.* ESPB, (A *vers.*); OxBB, *with music*

Lord, mind your trees today! The Bushfeller. Eileen Duggan. ATNZ

Lord, mine eye offended. Matthew V. 29-30. Derek Mahon. CIP

Lord, my God. Malka Heifetz Tussman, *tr. by* Kathryn Hellerstein. AYP

Lord my shepherd, me His sheep, The. George Sandys. *Fr.* Paraphrase on the Psalms of David. JCP

Lord, My Weak Thought in Vain Would Climb. Ray Palmer. AH

Lord Myth. Norman Dubie. NAmP

Lord North's Recantation. *Unknown.* PAH

Lord, not for light in darkness do we pray. John Drinkwater. TrPWD; WGRP

Lord, now lettest thou thy servant depart in peace. Nunc Dimittis. Bible, *N.T. Fr.* St. Luke, II: 29-32. WGRP

Lord of a castle. *Unknown, tr. by* Burton Watson. FCEI

Lord of All Being, Throned Afar. Oliver Wendell Holmes. *Fr.* The Professor at the Breakfast Table. AH
(Sun-Day Hymn.) TrPWD; WGRP

Lord of all, himself through all diffused, The. William Cowper. *Fr.* The Task, VI. OAEL-1

Lord of all, who reigned supreme, The. Adon 'Olam. *Unknown, tr. by* F. De Sola Mendes. EaLo

Lord of Braj, the memory of my passion remains. Surdas, *tr. by* John Stratton Hawley *and* Mark Juergensmeyer. SSI

Lord of Dreams. Abba Kovner, *tr. fr. Hebrew by* Warren Bargad *and* Stanley F. Chyet. IP

Lord of Each Soul. Paul Engle. AH

Lord of Elbë, on Elbë hill. A.G.A. to A.E. Emily Brontë. FL

Lord of Life, All Praise Excelling. Clement Clarke Moore. AH

Lord of Lorn and the False [*or* Fals] Steward, The. *Unknown.* ESPB, *with music;* OxBB, *with music*

Lord of My Heart's Elation. Bliss Carman. AH, *with music;* NOBC; OBCV; TrPWD

Lord of my years, can life be bare. Common Blessings. Thomas Curtis Clark. TrPWD

Lord of Rosslyn's daughter gaed through the wud her lane, The. Captain Wedderburn's Courtship. *Unknown.* ESPB

Lord of Sea and Earth and Air. Prayer for a Pilot. Cecil Roberts. FaPON
(Prayer for the Pilot.) TrPWD

Lord of the Dance. Sydney Carter. OBET

Lord of the Far Horizons. Bliss Carman. TrPWD

Lord of the grass and hill. Overlord. Bliss Carman. CaP
(Veni Creator.) WGRP

Lord of the Isle, The. Stefan George, *tr. fr. German by* Ludwig Lewisohn. AWP

Lord of the lands, beneath Thy bending skies. A Hymn for Canada. Albert Durrant Watson. CaP

Lord of the Mountain. Prayer to the Mountain Spirit. *Unknown, tr. by* G. W. Cronyn. WGRP

Lord of the pots and pipkins, since I have not time to be. The Divine Office of the Kitchen. Cecily Hallack. BLRP; PoLF

Lord of the River. *Unknown, tr. fr. Chinese by* Burton Watson. *Fr.* Nine Songs. CoBCP

Lord of the Winds. Mary Elizabeth Coleridge. TrPWD

Lord of the World. *Unknown, tr. fr. Hebrew by* D. A. de Sola. TrJP

Lord of the Worlds Below! James Freeman. AH

Lord Our God Alone Is Strong, The. Caleb T. Winchester. AH

Lord over all! whose power the sceptre swayed. Lord of the World. *Unknown, tr. by* D. A. de Sola. TrJP

Lord over life and all the ways of breath. Ernest Dowson. *Fr.* De Amore. TrPWD

Lord, pity such sinners. Monday afternoon. A Devotional Sonnet. Timothy Steele. CRP

Lord, purge our eyes to see. Judge Not According to the Appearance. Christina Rossetti. TrPWD

Lord Rameses of Egypt sighed. Birthright. John Drinkwater. CH; OxBTC

Lord Randal. *Unknown.* ESPB

Lord Randal [*or* Rendal]. *Unknown.* EnSB; ESPB, J *vers.*

Lord Randal. *Unknown.* AmFP; AWP; EBEV; EnRP; ESPB, A, B *and* J *vers.*; FaBoBa; FF; FPL; HAP; HeIP; HoPM; LiTB; NoP, A *vers.*; OAEL-1, *with music;* OxBS, *with music;* OxBS; TrGrPo; WeW

Lord Randall. *Unknown.* NAEL-1

Lord reigneth; he is apparelled with majesty, The. Psalm XCII: "Jehovah's Immovable Throne." Bible, *O.T. Fr.* Psalms. WGRP

Lord returning home, A. Sanu Chigami, *tr. fr. Japanese. Fr.* Manyo Shu. Ma

Lord, rust my forks. Prayers of a Repentant Gentleman. Antonio Cisneros, *tr. by* Maureen Ahern *and* David Tipton. Per

Lord Saltoun and Auchanachie. *Unknown.* ESPB

Lord, Save Us, We Perish. Christina Rossetti. TrPWD

Lord, shall I find it in Thy Holy Church. Truth. Claude McKay. BPo

Lord she's gone done left me done packed/ up and split. Feeling Fucked Up. Etheridge Knight. NNaP

Lord, since the strongest human hands I know. In the Dark. Sophie Jewett. TrPWD

Lord Sits with Me Out in Front, The. Jack Gilbert. NPGG

Lord, speak to me, that I may speak. For Every Day. Frances Ridley Havergal. *Fr.* A Teacher's Prayer. BLRP, 3 *st.*

Lord Tennyson and Lord Melchett. D. H. Lawrence. FaBoEE

Lord, the Roman hyacinths are blooming in bowls. A Song for Simeon. T. S. Eliot. EaLo; LiTB; NAs; NOCV

Lord, the snowful sky. Sailor's Carol. Charles Causley. OBCP

Lord, Thine humble servants hear. Hymn for Atonement Day. Judah Halevi, *tr. by* Solomon Solis-Cohen. TrJP

Lord—Thine the Day. Dag Hammarskjöld, *tr. by* Leif Sjöberg *and* W. H. Auden. EaLo

Lord, this woman who fell into many sins. Mary Magdalene Kassia, *tr. by* Aliki *and* Willis Barnstone *and* Elene Kolb. BoWoP

Lord Thomas and Fair Annet. *Unknown.* AmFP; ESPB, A *and* D *vers.*; FaBoBa; OxBB, *with music.*

(Lord Thomas and Fair Ellinor.) OBET

Lord Thomas and Fair Ellinor. *Unknown. See* Lord Thomas and Fair Annet.

Lord Thomas and Lady Margaret. *Unknown.* ESPB

Lord Thomas is to the hunting gone. Lord Thomas and Lady Margaret. *Unknown.* ESPB

Lord Thomas Stuart. *Unknown.* ESPB

Lord, Thou art mine, and I am Thine. Clasping of Hands. George Herbert. PoEL-2

Lord, Thou Clepedest Me. *Unknown.* OxBSP

Lord, Thou Hast Been Our Dwelling Place. Bible, *O.T. See* Psalms: Psalm XC ("Lord, thou hast been our dwelling place in all generations").

Lord, Thou hast given me a cell. A Thanksgiving to God for His House. Robert Herrick. BLPL; ChTr; FaBoBe; HAP; OBS; OFD; OHIP; PoRA; SeCP; SeCV-1; TrCP; TrPWD; WGRP

Lord, Thou hast made this world below the shadow of a dream. McAndrew's Hymn. Kipling. OxBTC

(M'Andrew's Hymn.) PoEL-5

Lord, Thou Hast Promised. Samuel K. Cox. AH

Lord, Thou who art like the sea. The Night Prayer of Glückel of Hameln. Edouard Roditi. CRP

Lord, thus I sin, repent, and sin again. A Sinner's Lament. Lord Herbert of Cherbury. SeCP

Lord 'tis midnight. Three Phases of Africa. Francis Ernest Kobina Parkes. PBA

Lord to me a shepherd is, The. Bible, *O.T. See* Psalms: Psalm XXIII ("The Lord is my shepherd").

Lord to me a shepherd is, The. *Unknown. Fr.* The Bay Psalm Book. OBCA

Lord Ullin's Daughter. Thomas Campbell. BeLS; BoTP; EnRP; FaPON; FaPoR; GN; GTBS; GTBS-P; WBLP

Lord, very fair my lot and beautiful my story. Very Fair My Lot. Jacob David Kamzon, *tr. by* Sholom J. Kahn. TrJP

Lord Walter's Wife. Elizabeth Barrett Browning. BeLS; HAP

Lord Waterford. *Unknown.* ChTr; GBP

Lord, we look to once for all, The. The Heretic's Tragedy. Robert Browning. OAEL-2

Lord! what a busy [*or* busie], restles[s] thing. The Pursuit[e]. Henry Vaughan. SeCP; TrCP; TrPWD

Lord, what a change within us one short hour. Richard Chenevix Trench. WBLP; WGRP

(Prevailing Prayer.) BLRP

(Sonnet.) TrPWD

Lord! what a goodly thing is want of shirts. John Cleveland. *Fr.* The Rebel [*or* Rebell] Scot. OBSV

Lord, what a thoughtless wretch was I. *Unknown.* AmFP

Lord, what am I, that, with unceasing care. To-Morrow. Félix Lope de Vega Carpio, *tr. by* Longfellow. AWP; TrPWD

Lord, what are the sins. In a U-Haul North of Damascus. David Bottoms. FYAP; MAYP; MT

Lord what is man, that he should find. Bible, *O.T. Fr.* Psalms: Psalm VIII ("O Lord our Lord, how excellent is thy name."), 4-6 *paraphrased by* Christopher Smart.

Lord, what is man? why should he cost thee. Charitas Nimia; or, The Dear[e] Bargain. Richard Crashaw. JCP; MePo; NOCV

Lord, what these weathers [*or* weders] are [*or* ar] cold, and I am ill happend [*or* happid]. The Second Shepherds' Play. *Unknown.* NAEL-1; PoEL-1

(Wakefield Second Shepherds Play, The.) OAEL-1, *mod. vers.*

Lord, when arming me for living, The. A. K. Tolstoy, *tr. by* Alan Myers. AAA

Lord, when I look at lovely things which pass. In the Fields. Charlotte Mew. BoNaP; MoAB; MoBrPo

Lord, when the clock strikes. The Reader. Thomas Merton. CRP

Lord, when the sense of Thy sweet grace. Richard Crashaw. TrPWD

Lord, when the wise men came from far[r]. Sidney Godolphin. HAP; JCP; MeLP; MePo; NOCV; OBS

(Wise Men and Shepherds.) BLPL; NOBE

Lord! when Thou didst thy self undress. The Incarnation and Passion. Henry Vaughan. TrCP

Lord! when Thou wentest from this place. The Lament of Eve. *Unknown.* ACP

Lord, when will it be? Myself with a Glory Hole. Takahashi Mutsuo, *tr. by* Sato. FCEI

Lord, Where Shall I Find Thee? Judah Halevi, *tr. fr. Hebrew by* Nina Davis Salaman. TrJP

Lord, While for All Mankind. John R. Wreford. TrPWD

Lord, who am I to teach the way. The Teacher. Leslie Pinckney Hill. BANP; PoNe; TrPWD

Lord! Who Art Merciful as Well as Just. Robert Southey. TrPWD

(Imitated from the Persian.) EnRP

Lord, who createdst man in wealth and store. Easter Wings. George Herbert. HAP; HeIP; InPK; InPS; LiTB; MeLP; MePo; NAEL-1; NIP; NoP; OAEL-1; OBS; PoE; PoEL-2; PPP; SeCP; TEP; TOF; TrCP; WeW

Lord, who hast formed me out of mud. Trinity Sunday. George Herbert. OxBSP

Lord who ordainst for mankind. The Mother's Hymn. Bryant. OHIP

Lord, Who's the Happy Man. Nahum Tate *and* Nicholas Brady. AH

Lord Will Happiness Divine, The. William Cowper. NOCV

Lord William; or, Lord Lundy. *Unknown.* ESPB

Lord Willoughby. *Unknown.* CoMu

Lord, with glowing heart I'd praise thee. Francis Scott Key. TrPWD

Lord, with what care hast thou begirt us round! Sin. George Herbert. NoP

Lord, within thy fold I be. Priscilla Jane Thompson. CBWP-2

Lord, You may not recognize me. The Gift. Louise Glück. FaBoWP

Lord, you visited Paris on the day of your birth. Paris in the Snow. Léopold Sédar Senghor, *tr. by* Ulli Beier. PBA

Lorde blesse and kepe the, The. Bible, *O.T. See* Numbers: Benediction.

Lordinges, listen, and hold you still. Durham Field. *Unknown.* ESPB

"Lordings [or Lordinges or Lordynges]," quod he, "in chirches whan I preche." The Pardoner's Prologue. Chaucer. *Fr.* The Canterbury Tales. NAEL-1; NoP; OAEL-1; PoE

("In churches," said the Pardoner, "when I preach.","," *mod. vers.* by Theodore Morrison) NAWM-1

Lordings, Listen to Our Lay. *Unknown.* OHIP

Lordly and Isolate Satyrs, The. Charles Olson. CoAP; NeAP; PoM

Lordly Hudson, The. Paul Goodman. CoAP; VGW

Lords and ladies, The. *Unknown. Fr.* Manyo Shu. Ma

Lord's Chameleons, The. Peter Klappert. AmPA

Lords do crave all, The. A Postscript to Verses on the History of France. *Unknown.* NOIV

Lords have been made whose hired robes have hidden. On the Relinquishment of a Title. Geoffrey Grigson. FaBoEE

Lords, knights, and squires, the numerous band. To a Child of Quality [Five Years Old, the Author Supposed Forty]. Matthew Prior. GN; LiTB; NIP; NOBE; OBEV; PoEL-3

Lord's lost Him His mockingbird. Mourning Poem for the Queen of Sunday. Robert Hayden. HCAP; NoAM; NoP; PoBA

Lord's Mask[e], The, *sel.* Thomas Campion.
Stars Dance, The. OBSC

Lord's My Shepherd, The. Bible, *O.T. See* Psalms: Psalm XXIII ("The Lord is my shepherd").

Lord's name be praised, The. The Litanies of Julia Pastrana (1832-1860). Thomas William Shapcott. CBAP

Lords of Creation, The. *Unknown.* PoLF

Lords of life, the lords of life, The. Experience. Emerson. FPL; LiTA; PoEL-4; TAP

Lords of Maussane, The. René Char, *tr. fr. French* by James Wright. RHTwFP

Lords of the Main, The. Joseph Stansbury. PAH

Lord's Prayer in Verse, The. Aaron Hill. FaBoUs

Lore. R. S. Thomas. OxBC; RB

Lorelei. Heine, *tr. fr. German.* TrJP, *tr.* by Emma Lazarus (Loreley, The.) WSC, *tr.* by Aaron Kramer

Loren Eiseley's Time Passages. Robert Frazier. BWV

Lorena. H. D. L. Webster. BLPA

Lorenzo dwelt at Heighington. Fragment of a Song. "Lewis Carroll." FaBoNo

Lorenzo! Such the glories of the world! The Consolation. Edward Young. *Fr.* Night Thoughts, Night IX. NOEC

Lorna Slope. Andrea Zanzotto, *tr. fr. Italian* by Lawrence R. Smith. NItP

Los Angeles Nocturne. Xavier Villaurrutia, *tr. fr. Spanish* by Perry Higman. LPSS

Los Mineros. Edward Dorn. PoM

Lose This Day Loitering. Goethe, *tr. fr. German. Fr.* Faust. PoLF, *tr.* by John Anster.

Loser, The. Charles Bukowski. ASP

Losers. Jonathan Holden. MAYP

Losers. Carl Sandburg. CMoP; MoAB; MoAmPo; NoAM; TrGrPo

Losing a Slave-Girl. Po Chü-i, *tr. fr. Chinese* by Arthur Waley. AWP

Losing in Love. *Unknown, tr.* by Geoffrey Bownas *and* Anthony Thwaite. PeBJV

Losing It. Alice Fulton. BAP

Losing the Marbles. James Merrill. DiPo

Losing the Straight Way, *sels.* Ian Wedde. ATNZ
"I imagine the womb as a honeycomb." *Fr.* III.
"That autumn day suddenly broken into." *Fr.* II.

Losing Track. Denise Levertov. HeIP; MoP; NaP; NOBA; PoE; PoM

Losing Track. Cathy Song. BrSi

Loss. Richard Aldington. BrPo

Loss. Alex Kuo. BrSi

Loss. Charles Madge. FaBoMo

Loss falls from the air as the tables turn. Complaint. Joseph Deericks Bennett. LiTA

Loss in Delay. Robert Southwell. OBSC

Loss, my molester, at last patient be. Pamphilia's Sonnet. Mary Sidney Wroth, Countess of Montgomery. *Fr.* Urania. WPE

Loss of an Oil Tanker. Charles Causley. OxBC

Loss of our learning brought darkness, weakness and woe. *Unknown, tr.* by Thomas Kinsella. NOIV

Loss of Strength, The. Austin Clarke. IPY

Loss of the *Amphitrite. Unknown.* OxBSS

Loss of the *Due Dispatch,* The. *Unknown.* AmFP

Loss of the *Evelyn Marie,* The. *Unknown.* OxBSS

Loss of the *New Columbia,* The. *Unknown.* AmFP

Loss of the *Royal George.* William Cowper. *See* Toll for the brave.

Losses. Randall Jarrell. HCAP; LCAP; LiTM; OxBA; PoA; TAP; UnPo; WaP

Lost, The. *Malay Oral Tradition, tr.* by R. J. Wilkinson *and* R. O. Winstedt. WTO

Lost. Millen Brand. NYBP

Lost. David Fisher. NPGG

Lost. Bruce Ignacio. NOVW

Lost. Orkhan Muyassar, *tr. fr. Arabic* by Lena Jayyusi *and* Samuel Hazo. MAP

Lost. Carl Sandburg. AmPP; CMoP; PDV

Lost. Chu Shu-chen, *tr. fr. Chinese* by Kenneth Rexroth. BoWoP

Lost. Stephen Spender. PoPo

Lost, The. *Malay Oral Tradition, tr.* by R. J. Wilkinson *and* R. O. Winstedt. WTO

Lost, The. Jones Very. NOBA; QFR

Lost. David Wagoner. PoA

Lost Acres. Robert Graves. NoAM

Lost among secrets in a tangle. First Days. Tuvia Ruebner, *tr.* by A. C. Jacobs. VWA

Lost Anchors. E. A. Robinson. CMoP

Lost and bewildered in the thickening mist. On the Great Fog in London, December 1762. James Eyre Weeks. NOEC

Lost and Found. George Macdonald. WGRP

Lost and Given Over. E. J. Brady. PoAu-1

Lost Angel, The. Philip Levine. NOBA

Lost Baby, The. *Unknown.* AmFP

Lost Baby Poem, The. Lucille Clifton. BlSi; CAPP; WPE

Lost Beauty. Roger Giroux, *tr. fr. French* by Anthony Barnett. RHTwFP

Lost Carnival, The. Fred Chappell. GOYP

Lost Cat, The. Emile Victor Rieu. CRH

Lost Child, The. James Reaney. NOBC

Lost Children, The. Randall Jarrell. CoAP; PrIm; TAP

Lost Children, The. Gregory Orr. GeTw

Lost Chord, A. Adelaide Anne Procter. FaFP; WBLP; WGRP

Lost City. Ingrid Jonker, *tr. fr. Afrikaans* by Jack Cope *and* Ruth Miller. PeSA

Lost Colors, The. Elizabeth Stuart Phelps Ward. AA

Lost Continent, The. Jenny Joseph. BrRo

Lost Dancer, The. Jean Toomer. PoBA

Lost Desire. Meleager, *tr. fr. Greek* by William M. Hardinge. AWP

Lost Doll, The. Charles Kingsley. *Fr.* The Water Babies. FaPON; MoShBr
(Little Doll, The.) OxBChV

Lost Eurydice who in the odours. Sonnet to Eurydice. Sophia de Mello Breyner Andresen, *tr.* by Ruth Fainlight. OV

Lost Explorer. Edmund Pennant. GoYe

Lost Fan, Hotel Californian, Fresno, 1923. Larry Levis. AnAn

Lost for a Rose's Sake. *Unknown, tr.* by Andrew Lang. AWP

Lost Garden. "Katherine Hale." CaP

Lost Genius, The. John James Piatt. AA

Lost God, A, *sel.* Francis William Bourdillon.
"Ah, happy who have seen Him, whom the world." WGRP

Lost Goldfish in a Dream. Doris Mühringer, *tr. fr. German* by Beth Bjorklund. CoAuP

Lost Heifer, The. Austin Clarke. BIrV

Lost Illusion, A. George Du Maurier. CenHV

Lost in dream I slept. Mohammad Taqi Mir, *tr.* by Ahmed Ali. GoT

Lost in Heaven. Robert Frost. MoAmPo

Lost in the white world. Winter Climb. Beinn Eunaich. PoSH

Lost in the words. Davening. Rochelle Ratner. VWA

Lost in thought—even the firefly from the marsh. Lady Izumi, *tr. fr. Japanese* by Hiroaki Sato. *Fr.* Fifty-one Tanka. FCEI

Lost in Translation. James Merrill. *Fr.* The Book of Ephraim. FYAP; HCAP; NAAL-2; NoAM

Lost Jewel, The. Robert Graves. EnLoPo; NYBP

Lost Jimmie Whalen. *Unknown.* AmFP

Lost Johnny. *Unknown.* AmFP

Lost Lady, The, *sel.* Sir William Berkeley.
"Where did you borrow that last sigh." OxBSP

Lost Lane. Dorothy Wellesley. WPE

Lost Leader, The. Robert Browning. FaBoPV; NAEL-2; PWR; TrGrPo

Lost Leader, The. Douglas Fraser. PoSH

Lost Letter to James Wright, with Thanks for a Map of Fano. Gibbons Ruark. MAYP; MT

Lost Lines from Chaucer's Prologue to "The Canterbury Tales." *Unknown.* PeHV

Lost Little Sister, The. William Barnes. PoEL-4

Lost! lost! lost! Advertisement of a Lost Day. Lydia Huntley Sigourney. WBLP

Lost! lost! lost! Anne Boleyn. Eloise Bibb. CBWP-4

Lost—lost—lost! Into the Depths. Adah Isaacs Menken. CBWP-1

Lost Love. Robert Graves. AWP; CH; FaBoCh; Mes; MoAB; MoBrPo; NoP

Lost Love. Edward Rowland Sill. AnAmPo

Lost Love. *Unknown, tr. fr. Tewa Indian by* H. J. Spinden. WTO

Lost Love, The. Wordsworth. *See* Lucy: She Dwelt among the Untrodden Ways.

Lost manor where I walk continually. The Pier-Glass. Robert Graves. CMoP; MoAB; NoAM

Lost Mistress, The. Robert Browning. BoLoP; FiP; NOBE; OBEV; OBNC

Lost Mohican Visits Hell's Kitchen, A. A. K. Redwing. VoR

Lost Moment. Hoyt W. Fuller. PoBA

Lost Moments. Glover Davis. SM

Lost objects, The. The Found. H. H. ter Balkt, *tr. by* Scott Rollins. DuIn

Lost Occasion, The. Whittier. BLPL; NOBA

Lost on a fogbound spit of sand. W. H. Auden. FaBoEE

Lost on Both Sides. Dante Gabriel Rossetti. *Fr.* The House of Life, XCI. NoP; SeCePo

Lost on September Trail, 1967. Alberto Ríos. FYAP

Lost, One Soul. Sandy McIntosh. AIW

Lost Opportunities. Henrietta Cordelia Ray. CBWP-3

Lost Orchard, The. Edgar Lee Masters. CMoP

Lost Parasol, The. *sel.* Sándor Weöres, *tr. fr. Hungarian by* Edwin Morgan. MHuP

"Where metalled road invades light thinning air." OBVE

Lost Parents. Lawrence Ferlinghetti. PoM

Lost Picture. Ray Fraser. NeAC

Lost Pictures, The. Hollis Spurgeon Summers. HoPM

Lost Pilot, The. James Tate. CoAP; DiL; NoAM; NoP; OBWP; TwCP; UnPo

Lost Pleiad, The. William Gilmore Simms. AA

Lost Shipmate, The. Theodore Goodridge Roberts. CaP

Lost Silvertip. J. D. Reed. NYBP

Lost Sister. Cathy Song. NoAM

Lost Son, The, *sels.* Theodore Roethke. DiL; HAP; HCAP; LiTM; VGW
    Flight, The. NAAL-2; RB; TrGrPo
    Gibber, The. NAAL-2
    It Was Beginning Winter. NAAL-2
    Pit, The. NAAL-2
    Return, The. NAAL-2

Lost Soul, A. Jay Macpherson. NOBC

Lost Teddy Bear, The. Maggie Pogue Johnson. CBWP-4

Lost: The Original, Its Reason and Its Rhyme. Translation. Rika Lesser. PoA

Lost Tradition, A. John Montague. CIP

Lost Tribe, The. Robert Finch. CaP

Lost Tribe, The. Ruth Pitter. WPOW

Lost Valley, The. Gordon J. Gadsby. PoSH

Lost War-Sloop, The. Edna Dean Proctor. PAH

Lost Word of Jesus, A. Henry Van Dyke. TrCP; WGRP

Lost World, A. Robert Graves. NYBP

Lost Youth. Sir Roger Casement. TIRV

Lot has changed here since the day, A. Zig-Zag up a Thistle. Rachel McAlpine. ATNZ

Lot Later. Howard Nemerov. HoPM

Lot of folks/ don't know it. Stacademia. George Barlow. NAmP

Lot of girls lived in the castle, A. Swedish Organs. Paul Snoek, *tr. by* James S. Holmes. DuIn

Lot of love is chosen, The. I learnt that much. Chosen. W. B. Yeats. BoLoP; CMoP

Lot of Night Music, A. Anthony Hecht. NIP; OxBC; PPR

Lot of sky litters my view of home, A—oh. Alsace-Lorraine. Fanny Howe. IAT

Lot of the old folks here, A—all that's left. Reflections in a Slum. "Hugh MacDiarmid." FaBoTw

Lot of times I've thought about suicide, A. Testament. Bill Zavatsky. UL

Loth to depart, but yet at last, each one. The Parting Verse, the Feast There Ended. Robert Herrick. SeCV-1

Lotos-Eaters, The. Tennyson. ChTr; FiP; LiTB; NAEL-2; NoP; OAEL-2; OnMSP; PoEL-5; TEP

Lotos-Eaters, The ("Courage!' he said, and pointed toward the land."), *sel.* Tennyson. ChTr, 5 *sts.;* FiP; GoTL; LiTB; NAEL-2; NoP; OAEL-2; OnMSP; PoEL-5; TEP
    There Is Sweet Music Here. FaBV
    (Choric Song of the Lotus-Eaters.) FaFP
    (Choric Song: "There is sweet music here that softer falls.") HeIP; OBNC
    (Song of the Lotus-Eaters.) NOBE; OBEV

Lotos Eating. Mortimer Collins. NOBVV

Lots of empty. History. Art Lange. UL

Lots of truisms don't have to be repeated. The Anatomy of Happiness. Ogden Nash. LiTA; TAP

Lot's Wife. "Anna Akhmatova," *tr. fr. Russian by* Richard Wilbur. BoWoP; PBWP

Lot's Wife. Celia Gilbert. ER

Lotus, *sel.* Hsü Wei, *tr. fr. Chinese by* Jonathan Chaves. "Fifth day of the fifth month." CoBLCP

Lotus. Huan Fu, *tr. fr. Chinese by* Dominic Cheung. IFON

Lotus buds softly perfume the mist-covered island, The. The Beautiful Lady Yü. Lu Ch'ien-i, *tr.* by Lois Fusek. ATF

Lotus-flower doth languish, The. Die Lotusblume ängstigt. Heine, *tr. by* James Thomson. AWP

Lotus Flowers, The. Ellen Bryant Voigt. BLA; MAYP; MT

Lotus flowers will one day burst out in golden whiskers. Bamboo Branch Song. Wang Fu-chih, *tr. by* Irving Lo. WFTU

Lotus Lake. Ts'ao P'i, *tr. fr. Chinese by* Burton Watson. CoBCP

Lotus Leaf Cup. Ku Hsiung, *tr. fr. Chinese by* Lois Fusek. ATF

Lotus Leaf Cup. Wei Chuang, *tr. fr. Chinese by* Lois Fusek. ATF

Lotus Leaf Cup. Wen T'ing-yün, *tr. fr. Chinese by* Lois Fusek. ATF

Lotus leaves, how plump and full. Lotus Pond. Ch'ien Ch'ien-yi, *tr. fr. Chinese by* Ronald Miao. *Fr.* Two Quatrains on the "Awash-in-Springtime Garden." WFTU

Lotus Pond. Ch'ien Ch'ien-yi, *tr. fr. Chinese by* Ronald Miao. *Fr.* Two Quatrains on the "Awash-in-Springtime Garden." WFTU

Lotus Sutra/ the lips are busy with it. *Unknown, tr. by* Burton Watson. FCEI

Lotus Viewing. Su Tung-p'o, *tr. fr. Chinese by* Burton Watson. CoBCP

Lotuses have withered, they put up no umbrellas to the rain. Presented to Liu Ching-wen. Su Tung-p'o, *tr. by* Burton Watson. CoBCP

Loud deep calls me home even now to feed it, The. Shelley. *Fr.* Prometheus Unbound, III, i. ChER

Loud drums are rolling, the mad trumpets blow, The! Battle Cry. William Henry Venable. PAH

Loud he sang the psalm of David! The Slave Singing at Midnight. Longfellow. GOA

Loud mockers in the roaring street. The Second Crucifixion. Richard Le Gallienne. WGRP

Loud report through Lybian cities goes, The. Virgil, *tr. fr. Latin by* Dryden. *Fr.* The Aeneid [*or* Eneados], IV. OBVE

Loud through the still November air. The Church of the Revolution. Hezekiah Butterworth. PAH

Loud tumultuous and troubled world, The. Holy Night. Nathaniel Anketell Benson. CaP

Loud voices are needed. Nelo Risi, *tr. fr. Italian by* Gavin Ewart. *Fr.* Elementary Thoughts, XXI. PFI

Loud were they, loud, as they rode o'er the hill. Charms for a Sudden Stitch. *Unknown, tr. by* Charles W. Kennedy. AnOE

Loudens the sea-wind, downward plunge the bows. To D'Annunzio: Lines from the Sea. Robert Nichols. OBMV

Louder than gulls the little children scream. The Beach. Robert Graves. OxBSP

Loudon Hill; or, Drumclog. *Unknown.* ESPB

Loudspeaker screamed, The. The Akedah. Aliza Shenhar. VWA, *tr. by* Linda Zisquit

Lough Derg. Denis Devlin. BIrV; CIP; IPY

Louie. José Montoya, *tr. fr. Spanish by* Toni Empringham. FIA

Louie was buried today. Louie. José Montoya, *tr. by* Toni Empringham. FIA

Louis B. Russell. Bruce Guernsey. InPK

Louis XV. John Sterling. BeLS

Louis XIV also called the Sun King. The Eclipse. Jacques Prévert, *tr. by* Michael Benedikt. POS

Louis XVI. Blake. *Fr.* The French Revolution. ChER

Louis XVI Goes to the Guillotine. Benjamin Péret, *tr. fr. French by* Charles Simic. POS; RHTwFP

Louisa. Wordsworth. EnRP; GBL

Louisa May Alcott. Louise Chandler Moulton. AA

Louisburg. *Unknown.* PAH

Louise, have you forgotten yet. Old Loves. Henry Murger, *tr. by* Andrew Lang. AWP

Louise on the Door-Step. Charles MacKay. EBVV

Louisiana. Steve Crow. HATNAP

Louisiana Perch. Ron Padgett. UL

Louisiana Weekly #4, The. David Henderson. PoBA

Louisville Feared in Mideast. Steven Bryan Bieler. TSL

Lounge in the shade of the luxuriant laurel's. Anyte, *tr. by* Willis Barnstone. BoWoP
Lourenço Marques. Charles Eglington. PeSA
Louse Crept Out of My Lady's Shift, A. Gordon Bottomley. ChTr
Louse Hunting. Isaac Rosenberg. EBEV; NAEL-2; NoAM; NoP; OxBTC
Lousy Miner. *Unknown.* AmFP
Love. Henry Baker. NOEC
Love. Joseph Beaumont. OBS
Love. Ted Berrigan. UL
Love. Robert Browning. EnLoPo
Love, *sel.* Samuel Butler.
  "Lovers, like wrestlers, when they do not lay." ErPo
Love. Charles Stuart Calverley. FiBHP
Love. Kelly Cherry. CRP
Love. Samuel Taylor Coleridge. BeLS; ChER; EnRP; GTBS; GTBS-P; OBEV
Love. Abraham Cowley, *after the Greek of* Anacreon. AWP; OBVE
Love. *At. to.* Roy Croft. BLPA; FaBoBe
Love. Samuel Daniel. *See* Hymen's Triumph: Love Is a Sickness.
Love. Dryden. *Fr.* The Conquest of Granada, *pt.* II, Act III, sc. iii. FiP
Love/ is the hurt at being separated from you. Four Attempts at Definition. Ernst Jandl, *tr. by* Beth Bjorklund. CoAuP
Love. Nilene O. A. Foxworth, *tr. by the author.* AIW
Love. Jorie Graham. NPGG
Love. George Granville. BoLoP
Love ("Immortal Love, author of this great frame"). George Herbert. HoPM; SeCV-1
Love ("Love bade me welcome; yet my soul drew back"). George Herbert. AWP; CH; ChTr; EBEV; FaBV; HeIP; InPK; JCP; LiTB; MAT; MeLP; MePo; NAEL-1; NOBE; NOCV; NoP; OAEL-1; OBEV; OBS; OBWVE; PoEL-2; PoLF; PPP; Prf; SCV; SeCePo; SeCP; SeCV-1; TEP; TOF; TrCP; TrGrPo; WeW
Love. Immanuel di Roma, *tr. fr. Italian by* J. Chotzner. TrJP
Love. Francis Jammes, *tr. fr. French by* Jethro Bithell. AWP
Love. Tymoteusz Karpowicz, *tr. fr. Polish by* Czeslaw Milosz. PwPP
Love. Thomas Kinsella. FaBCIP
Love. Kito, *tr. fr. Japanese by* Hiroaki Sato. *Fr.* Twenty-four Hokku. FCEI
Love. Patrick Lane. NeAC
Love. Gordon LeClaire. CaP
Love. Pierre Louÿs, *tr. fr. French.* *Fr.* Chansons de Bilitis. PeHV
Love. "Hugh MacDiarmid." CMoP; PoE
Love. Nicholas Moore. ErPo
Love. Anthony Munday. *Fr.* Zelanto, the Fountain of Fame. OBSC
Love. Carol Sue Muth. RR
Love. John Oxenham. BLRP
Love. George Peele. *See* Hunting of Cupid, The: What Thing Is Love.
Love. Samuele Romanelli, *tr. fr. Hebrew by* A. B. Rhine. TrJP
Love. Sappho, *tr. fr. Greek by* William Ellery Leonard. AWP
Love. Shakespeare. *See* Merchant of Venice, The: Tell Me Where Is Fancy [*or* Fancie] Bred.
Love. Shelley. *See* To———: "One word is too often profaned."
Love. William Jay Smith. RHPC
Love. Edith Södergran, *tr. fr. Swedish by* Joanna Bankier. OV
Love. Spenser. *See* Faerie Queene, The:
  Rugged forhead that with grave foresight, The.
Love. Tasso, *tr. fr. Italian by* John Hermann Merivale. AWP
Love. Thomas Traherne. SeCV-2
Love. Katrina Trask. AA
Love. *Unknown.* TTY
Love. *Unknown, tr. fr. Irish by* John Montague. BIrV
Love. *Unknown.* SoSe
Love, *sel.* Alice Walker.
  "Old man in white, An." NMM
Love. Sir William Watson. *Fr.* Two Epigrams. TrGrPo
Love a woman! y'are an ass. Earl of Rochester. TEP
  (Song: "Love a Woman! y'are an ass.") GBL; NBLV; NOBL; PeHV; TW
Love Affair, A. Arnold Bennett. OxBTC
Love Affair, The. Russell Edson. NAmP
Love Again. Pierre Reverdy, *tr. fr. French by* John Ashbery. POS; RHTwFP
Love all the senses doth beguile. Of Love. James Sandford. EIL
Love among the Ruins. Robert Browning. FaBV; HAP; NAEL-2; NOBE; OAEL-2; OBEV; PoEL-5; PrIm
Love among the Ruins of London. Muriel Grainger. CN
Love and a Question. Robert Frost. MoBS
Love and Age. Walter Savage Landor. GBL

Love and Age. Thomas Love Peacock. *Fr.* Gryll Grange. NOBVV; OBEV; OBNC
Love and Death. Byron. EBEV; NOBE
Love and Death. Catullus, *tr. fr. Latin by* H. W. Garrod. AWP
Love and Death. Margaret Deland. AA
Love and Death. John Frederick Nims. HoPM; SM; WeW (Finisterre.) KS
Love and Death. Tennyson. OBD
Love and Discipline. Henry Vaughan. TrPWD
Love and Folly. La Fontaine, *tr. fr. French by* Bryant. AWP
Love and forgetting might have carried them. Two Look at Two. Robert Frost. MoAB; MoAmPo; NU
Love and Fortune. Fulke Greville. *See* Caelica:
  Faction, that ever dwells.
Love and Friendship. Emily Brontë. EBVV; ELP; InPK
Love and Hate. *Unknown, tr. fr. Irish by* Frank O'Connor. TW
Love and Honour. Fulke Greville. *See* Caelica:
  In the window of a grange.
Love and How It Becomes Important in Our Day to Day Lives. Miller Williams. MT
Love and Jealousy. Robert Greene. EIL
Love and Jealousy. Sir Philip Sidney. *Fr.* Arcadia. SiPS
Love and Jealousy. William Walsh. BoLoP
Love and Knowledge. Robert Penn Warren. *Fr.* Audubon, VI.
Love and Language. Louisa S. Guggenberger. NOBVV
Love and Liberation. John Hall Wheelock. MoAmPo
Love and Life. Julie Mathilde Lippmann. AA
Love and Life. Earl of Rochester. BoLoP; ELP; EnLoPo; FF; GBL; HAP; MePo; NOBE; OBEV; OBS; PoEL-3; SeCV-2; TrGrPo
Love and Lust. Isaac Rosenberg. TrJP
Love and Marriage. Ray Mathew. PoAu-2
Love and Misery. Jotie T'Hooft, *tr. fr. Dutch by* James S. Holmes. DuIn
Love and Music. *Gond Oral Tradition, tr. by* V. Elwin *and* S. Hivale. WTO
Love and Philosophy. George Chapman. *See* Coronet for His Mistress Philosophy, A: Muses That Sing Love's Sensual Empery.
Love and Poverty. Elisabeth Jones Cavazza Pullen. AA
Love and Reason. Sir Philip Sidney. *Fr.* Arcadia. SiPS
Love and Sleep. Swinburne. BoLoP
Love and the gentle heart are one same thing. Dante, *tr. fr. Italian by* Dante Gabriel Rossetti. *Fr.* La Vita Nuova, XI. AWP
Love and the Lady Lagia, Guido and I. Sonnet: On the Detection of a False Friend. Guido Cavalcanti, *tr. by* Dante Gabriel Rossetti. AWP
Love and the Mountains. Antonio Machado, *tr. fr. Spanish by* Perry Higman. LPSS
Love and Time. Sir Walter Ralegh. *See* Nature, That Washed *or* Washt Her Hands in Milk[e].
Love And Work: Apple Picking. Barry Goldensohn. NAmP
Love at First Sight. Christopher Marlowe. *Fr.* Hero and Leander, First Sestiad. NOBE
"Love at first sight," some say, misnaming. At First Sight. Robert Graves. FaBoEE; OxBSP
Love at Large. Coventry Patmore. *Fr.* The Angel in the House. EBVV, *fr.* I, ii; NOBVV, *fr.* I, ii.
Love at Roblin Lake. Alfred W. Purdy. NoP
Love at Sea. Swinburne. AWP
Love at the closing of our days. Last Love. Fyodor Ivanovich Tyutchev, *tr. by* Vladimir Nabokov. BoLoP
Love at the Door. Meleager, *tr. fr. Greek by* John Addington Symonds. AWP
Love at the lips was touch. To Earthward. Robert Frost. BLPL; LiTA; MoAB; MoAmPo; MoP; NoAM; NOBA; NoP; OxBA; TAP
Love bade me welcome; yet my soul drew back. Love. George Herbert. AWP; CH; ChTr; EBEV; FaBV; HeIP; InPK; JCP; LiTB; MAT; MeLP; MePo; NAEL-1; NOBE; NOCV; NoP; OAEL-1; OBEV; OBS; OBWVE; PoEL-2; PoLF; PPP; Prf; SCV; SeCePo; SeCP; SeCV-1; TEP; TOF; TrCP; TrGrPo; ViBoPo; WeW
Love between Brothers and Sisters. Isaac Watts. FaBoUs
Love Bit, The. Joel Oppenheimer. PoM
Love—bittersweet, irrepressible. Sappho, *tr. by* Willis Barnstone. BoWoP
Love, brave vertue's younger brother. Love's Horoscope. Richard Crashaw. MeLP; OBS
Love brought by night a vision to my bed. Lost Desire. Meleager, *tr. by* William M. Hardinge. AWP
Love brought me quietly in the dreaming night. Meleager, *tr. by* Sydney Oswald. PeHV
Love brought me to a silent grove. Upon Love. Robert Herrick. TrGrPo

Love built a stately house; where Fortune came. The World. George Herbert. OBS; SeCV-1

"Love, by sure proof I may call thee unkind." Sir Philip Sidney. *Fr.* Astrophel and Stella, LXV. Son

Love by the Water-Reeds. *Unknown, tr. fr. Hawaiian by* M. W. Beckwith. WTO

Love Calls Us to the Things of This World. Richard Wilbur. AmPP; CAPP; CMoP; HAP; HeIP; InPS; MoAmPo; NePoEA; NIP; NoAM; PoE; PoRA; PPP; TAP; TrGrPo; UnPo; VGW

Love Came By from the Riversmoke. Stephen Vincent Benét. *Fr.* John Brown's Body. MoAmPo

Love can do all but raise the dead. Emily Dickinson. LiTA

Love Cannot Live. *Unknown.* EiL

Love Charm. *Malay Oral Tradition, tr. by* R. O. Winstedt. WTO

Love Charm Songs, *sels. Unknown, tr. fr. Chippewa Indian by* Frances Densmore. OV
   "I can charm the man."
   "In the center of the earth."

Love-Charms. Thomas Campion. *See* Thrice Toss [*or* Tosse] These Oaken Ashes in the Air [*or* Ayre].

Love Child—a Black Aesthetic. Everett Hoagland. BPo

Love Comes Quietly. Robert Creeley. LLLT

Love Constraining to Obedience. William Cowper. NOCV

Love Dies. George Meredith. *See* Modern Love:
   In our old shipwrecked days there was an hour.

Love Dirge. *Unknown, tr. fr. Maori by* John White. WTO

Love Dirge to the Whitehouse, A. Bob Fletcher. NBP

Love Divine, All Loves Excelling. Charles Wesley. NOCV (Divine Love.) WGRP

Love doth again. Sir Thomas Wyatt. SiPS

Love, drunk the other day, knocked at my breast. The Dual. Richard Lovelace. CaPo

Love Enthroned. Richard Lovelace. CaPo

Love Enthroned. Dante Gabriel Rossetti. *Fr.* The House of Life, I. OBNC

Love Equals Swift and Slow. Henry David Thoreau. NoP

Love essential unto youth. Ninety. "E." CBAP

Love ever gives. Love's Prerogative. John Oxenham. BLRP

Love Ever Green. Henry VIII, King of England. MeEL

Love Expresses with Candle as a Metaphor. Tamemasa, *tr. fr. Japanese by* Steven D. Carter. WFTW

Love Feast, The. W. H. Auden. ErPo

Love feeds, like Intellect, his lamp with truth. William Baylebridge. *Fr.* Love Redeemed, XXXII. PoAu-1

Love flies with bow unstrung when Time appears. Love and Age. Walter Savage Landor. GBL

Love Flows from God. Mechthild von Magdeburg, *tr. fr. German by* Lucy Menzies. WPOW

Love Flows Not from My Liver. George Chapman. *Fr.* A Coronet for His Mistress Philosophy, III. Son

Love for a Beautiful Lady. *Unknown. See* Blow, Northern Wind.

Love for a Hand. Karl Shapiro. CoAP; NYBP

Love for a Hare. Melvin Walker La Follette. NePoEA-2

Love for an Island. Phyllis Allfrey. PBCV

Love for Love, *sel.* Congreve.
   Soldier and a Sailor, A. CoMu

Love for love, the willow grows distant. Parting. Kito, *tr. fr. Japanese by* Hiroaki Sato. *Fr.* Twenty-four Hokku. FCEI

Love for Patsy, A. John Thompson, Jr.. LiTA; WaP

Love for such a cherry lip. Thomas Middleton. *Fr.* Blurt, Master Constable. EIL

Love from My Father. Carole Gregory Clemmons. CNA; PoBA

Love, give me leave to serve thee, and be wise. Thomas Randolph. MePo

Love gives its best. Love. John Oxenham. BLRP

Love God—/ my mother said. The Will's Love. Besmilr Brigham. IHMS

Love Gone Cold. Lindsay MacRae. DT

Love-grip, first excited by the eye, The. In Panelled Rooms. Ruth Herschberger. LiTA

Love Guards [*or* Guides] the Roses of Thy Lips. Thomas Lodge. *Fr.* Phyllis, XIII. EiL; Son
   (Phillis 2.) OBEV

Love has changed the face of distances. Nineteenth Telegram ("Love has changed the face of distances"). Abd al-Aziz al-Maqalih, *tr. fr. Arabic by* Lena Jayyusi *and* Christopher Middleton. *Fr.* Telegrams of Tenderness for Sanaa. MAP

Love Has Eyes. William Forster. CBAP

Love has gone and left me, and the days are all alike. Ashes of Life. Edna St. Vincent Millay. BLPL; FaBoBe

Love has its morn, its noon, its eve, and night. Too Late. Philip Bourke Marston. OBNC

Love has its secrets, joy has its revealings. The Love Secret. *Unknown, tr. by* Wilfrid Scawen Blunt. AWP

Love has never read the Ave Maria. Love. Immanuel di Roma, *tr. by* J. Chotzner. TrJP

Love has seven names. Hadewijch, *tr. by* Willis Barnstone *and* Elene Kolb. BoWoP

Love hath me brought in evil thought. A Rhyme-Beginning Fragment. *Unknown.* AnIL

Love hath so long possessed me for his own. Dante, *tr. fr. Italian by* Dante Gabriel Rossetti. *Fr.* La Vita Nuova, XVIII. AWP

Love he to morrow, who lov'd never. *Unknown, tr. fr. Latin by* Thomas Stanley. *Fr.* The Vigil of Venus. OBVE

Love heeds no more the sighing of the wind. The Garden of Shadow. Ernest Dowson. OBNC

Love her he doesn't but the thought he puts. John Berryman. *Fr.* Dream Songs. FaBoMo

Love, hide me in your breast. The Ship of Love. Salma Khadra Jayyusi, *tr. by the author and* Charles Doria. MAP

Love, how thou'rt tired out with rhyme! Margaret Cavendish, Duchess of Newcastle. EnLoPo

Love, I adore the contours of thy shape. To a Sicilian Boy. Theodore Wratislaw. PeHV

Love, I am sick for thee, sick with an absolute grief. The Grief of Love. *Unknown, tr. by* Wilfrid Scawen Blunt. AWP

Love, I have lain awake by night. J. V. Cunningham Gets Hung Up on a Dirty, of All Things, Joke. Henry Taylor. BXAP

Love, I have warmed the car. News from the House. Michael Dennis Browne. NYBP

Love I love whose lips I love, A. The Accomplices. Conrad Aiken. NOBA

Love, I should be content. Duality. Katherine Thayer Hobson. GoYe

Love, I think, is a disease. Maghnas O Domhnaill. NOIV

Love, if a God thou art. To Cupid. Francis Davison. OBSC

Love ("Immortal heat, O let thy greater flame"). George Herbert. *Fr.* The Temple. Son

Love ("Immortal love, author of this great flame"). George Herbert. *Fr.* The Temple. HoPM; SeCV-1; Son

Love in a Cottage. J. A. R. McKellar. *Fr.* Fourth Napoleon. PoAu-2

Love in a Life. Robert Browning. InVP; NOBE; NOBVV; OBNC

Love in a Valley, *sel.* George Meredith.
   White Owl, The. ChTr

Love in a Village, *sel.* Isaac Bickerstaffe.
   "There was a jolly miller once." *Fr. st.* 1. OxNR

Love in a Warm Room in Winter. James Wright. OBAL

Love in America. Marianne Moore. AiP; GOA

Love in Brooklyn. John Wakeman. SoSe

Love in Exile, *sels.* Mathilde Blind.
   "Dost thou remember ever, for my sake." OBNC
   "I charge you, O winds of the West, O." TrJP

Love in fantastic [*or* fantastique] triumph sate [*or* satt]. Aphra Behn. *Fr.* Abdelazer. NOBE; WPE
   (Song: "Love in fantastic triumph sate.") OBEV; TrGrPo

Love in Her Eyes. John Gay. *Fr.* Acis and Galatea. ELP

Love in her sunny eyes does basking play. The Change. Abraham Cowley. *Fr.* The Mistress. MeLP; MePo; OBS; SeCP; SeCV-1

Love-in-Idleness. Shakespeare. *Fr.* A Midsummer Night's Dream, II, i. TrGrPo

Love in Labrador. Carl Sandburg. VGW

Love in many forms. Buson, *tr. fr. Japanese by* Hiroaki Sato. *Fr.* Eighty-seven Hokku. FCEI

Love in May. Jean Passerat, *tr. fr. French by* Andrew Lang. AWP

Love in my bosom like a bee. Rosalind's [*or* Rosalynd's] Madrigal[l]. Thomas Lodge. *Fr.* Rosalynde; or Euphues' Golden Legacy. EiL; InvP; NOBE; NoP; OBEV; OBSC; PoEL-2; SeCePo; TrGrPo

Love in Spring. Shotetsu, *tr. fr. Japanese by* Steven D. Carter. WFTW

Love in the City. Mascha Kaléko, *tr. fr. German by* Susan L. Cocalis. DMG

Love in the Museum. Adrienne Rich. NePoEA; NYBP

Love in the Night. Emperor Hanazono, *tr. fr. Japanese by* Steven D. Carter. WFTW

Love in the Nuclear Age. Linda Pastan. SoTCo

Love in the peaceful u.s.a. Love u.s.a. Kathleen Spivack. BoWoP

Love in the Valley. George Meredith. AWP; EBVV; ErPo; LiTB; NOBE; OAEL-2; OBEV, *abr.;* TrGrPo
   "Under yonder beech-tree single on the greensward," *sel.* ErPo; TrGrPo

Love in the Winds. Richard Hovey. AA

Love in Vain. Robert Johnson. UnPo

Love Indestructible. Robert Southey. *Fr.* The Curse of Kehama. OBNC

Love Is. Ann Darr. GrPl

Love is a circle that doth restless[e] move. Love What It Is. Robert Herrick. FaBoEE; GBL

Love is a funny thing. Love. *Unknown*. TTY

Love Is a Keeper of Swans. Humbert Wolfe. MoBrPo

Love Is a Law. *Unknown, at. to* John Webster *and* William Rowley. *Fr.* The Thracian Wonder, I, i. EIL; GBL

Love is a place. E. E. Cummings. FaBoEE

Love Is a Secret Feeding Fire. *Unknown*. OxBSP

Love Is a Shark. *Unknown, tr. fr. Hawaiian by* N. B. Emerson. WTO

Love Is a Sickness. Samuel Daniel. *Fr.* Hymen's Triumph. ELP; NOBE; OBEV; PoEL-2

(Love.) EIL; OBSC

Love is a torment. *Unknown*. *Fr.* Manyo Shu. Ma

Love is a universal migraine. Symptoms of Love. Robert Graves. BoLoP

"Love is all/ Unsatisfied." Crazy Jane on the Day of Judgment. W. B. Yeats. CMoP; SOTW

Love is and was my lord and king. Tennyson. *Fr.* In Memoriam A. H. H., CXXVI. NOBE; NOCV; OBEV; OBNC

(My Lord and King.) ChTr

Love is begot by fancy, bred. Love. George Granville. BoLoP

Love Is Bitter. *Unknown*. PeSA

Love is cruel, Love is sweet. Thomas MacDonagh. ACP

Love Is Enough, *sel.* William Morris.

"Love is enough: though the World be a-waning." FaBV; OBEV; PoEL-5

Love Is Life. Richard Rolle of Hampole. PoEL-1

Love Is Life. Richard Rolle of Hampole. *Fr.* A Song of the Love of Jesus. ACP; PoEL-1

Love is like butter, Evans mused, and stuck. Pendydd. Kingsley Amis. *Fr.* The Evans Country. NOBL

Love is like the wild rose-briar. Love and Friendship. Emily Brontë. EBVV; ELP; InPK

Love is not all; it is not meat nor drink. Edna St. Vincent Millay. *Fr.* Fatal Interview. CMoP; FPL; HAP; HeIP; NoAM; OxBA; TAP

(Love Is Not All.) InPS; PrIM; Son

Love Is Not Cleansed by Fire. Viljo Kajava, *tr. fr. Finnish by* Aili Jarvenpa. SOP

Love is not mocked whatever use. Jack Spicer. *Fr.* Graphemics, 10. VGW

Love is not worth so much. Coda. James Tate. AmPA; NYBP

Love is pain and cure. Mohammad Taqi Mir, *tr. by* Ahmed Ali. GoT

Love Is Strong. Richard Burton. AA

Love Is Teasing. *Unknown*. OBET

Love is that later thing than death. Emily Dickinson. LiTA

Love is that madness which all lovers have. Love. Dryden. *Fr.* The Conquest of Granada, pt. II, Act III, sc. iii. FiP

Love Is That Orbit. George Henry Boker. Son

Love is the blossom where there blows. Wooing Song. Giles Fletcher the Younger. *Fr.* Christ's Victory and Triumph: Christ's Victory on Earth, II. EIL; OBEV

Love is the center and circumference. What Love Is. Ella Wheeler Wilcox. PWR

Love is the peace, whereto all thoughts do[e] strive. Fulke Greville. *Fr.* Caelica, LXXXV. AAS

(Sonnet: "Love is the peace, whereto all thoughts do strive.") JCP

Love is the plant of peace and most precious of virtues. Et Incarnatus Est. William Langland. *Fr.* The Vision of Piers Plowman. NOBE, *fr.* Passus II (C *text*).

"Love is too young to know what conscience is." Shakespeare. *Fr.* Sonnets, CLI. EBEV; HeIP; PoE; PoEL-2

Love is what lacks then: but what does it mean to you? A Remonstrance. James Kenneth Stephen. NOBVV

Love, it is night. The orb of day. The Passionate Professor. Bert Leston Taylor. NBLV

Love It Is Pleasing. *Unknown*. OBET

Love, it was good to talk to you tonight. Rondeau after a Transatlantic Telephone Call. Marilyn Hacker. NoAM; SM

Love—its long spoon, its promise, and its threat. Nourishment. Rachel Hadas. BAP

Love-Joy. George Herbert. OAEL-1

Love-Knot, The. Nora Perry. AA

Love laid his sleepless head. Swinburne. TrGrPo

Love Leave to Urge. Mary Sidney Wroth, Countess of Montgomery. *Fr.* Urania. Son

Love-Lesson, A. Clément Marot, *tr. fr. French by* Leigh Hunt. AWP

Love Letter. Carole C. Gregory. AIW; BlSi

Love Letter. Sylvia Plath. NOBA

Love Letter. David Ray. TW

Love Letter. Karl Shapiro. *See* V-Letter.

Love-letter, A. Mary E. Tucker. CBWP-1

Love Letter, A. *Unknown*. MeEL

Love Letter from an Impossible Land. William Meredith. WaP

Love Letter from Mars. John Ciardi. BWV

Love-Letter One ("To C———her lover."). *Unknown*. PeHV

Love Letter to Elizabeth Thatcher, A. Thomas Thatcher. SCAP

Love-Letter Two. *Unknown*. PeHV

Love Letters. Josephine D. Henderson Heard. CBWP-4

Love, like a bird, hath perched upon a spray. Love. Sir William Watson. *Fr.* Two Epigrams. TrGrPo

Love, like a mountain-wind upon an oak. Love. Sappho, *tr. by* William Ellery Leonard. AWP

Love Likened to Clouds. Tamesada, *tr. fr. Japanese by* Steven D. Carter. WFTW

Love long dormant showing itself. Palais des Arts. Louise Glück. AnAn; MAYP

Love-lorn microbe met by chance, A. The Microbe's Serenade. George Ade. OBAL

Love, love. What His Friend Said, Teasing the Man in Love. Milaipperun Kantan, *tr. by* A. K. Ramanujan. PLW

Love, love, a lily's my care. Words for the Wind. Theodore Roethke. CoAP; NOBA

Love, love today, my dear. Charlotte Mew. MoBrPo

Love ("Love was before the light began"). *Unknown, tr. fr. Arabic by* E. Powys Mathers. *Fr.* The Thousand and One Nights. AWP

Love, love! What nonsense it is. Natalya Yevgenevna Gorbanyevskaya, *tr. by* Daniel Weissbort. WPOW

Love, love, what wilt thou with this heart of mine? Jean Froissart, *tr. by* Longfellow. AWP

Love Made in the First Age: To Chloris. Richard Lovelace. CaPo; JCP; NAEL-1; OAEL-1; SeCP

Love Making. James Tate. EAS

Love Me! Stevie Smith. OxBSP

Love Me. Maria Wine, *tr. fr. Swedish by* Nadia Christensen. PBWP

Love Me Again. *Unknown*. EIL

Love me and leave me; what love bids retrieve me? John Jones. Swinburne. *Fr.* The Heptalogia. NA

(At the Piano.) FaBoNo

Love Me, for I Love You. Christina Rossetti. *Fr.* Monna Innominata, VII. Son

Love Me - I Love You. Christina Rossetti. BoTP

Love Me Little, Love Me Long. Robert Herrick. BLPA; CaPo; EIL; FaBoBe; FaFP; NoP

Love me, Love me, I cried to the rocks and the trees. Love Me! Stevie Smith. OxBSP

Love Me Not for Comely Grace. *Unknown*. *See* Love Not Me for Comely Grace.

Love Me, O Love. Sir Philip Sidney. HeIP

Love Me or Not. Thomas Campion. EIL

Love me with the left hand. The Light Woman's Song. Judith Johnson Sherwin. TAP

Love Medicine, A. Louise Erdrich. HATNAP

Love Medley: Patrice Cuchulain. Michael S. S. Harper. GeTw

Love, Meet Me in the Green Glen. John Clare. ELP

Love mocks us all. Then cast aside. I, 33. Albi, Ne Doreas. Horace, *tr. fr. Latin.* *Fr.* Odes. AWP, *tr. by* Austin Dobson.

"Love my heart for an hour, but my bone for a day." Street Song. Edith Sitwell. CMoP

Love Necessitates. Eugene B. Redmond. CNA

Love not a loveliness too much. Ownership. Lizette Woodworth Reese. MoAmPo

Love Not Me for Comely Grace. *Unknown*. BLPL; CH; EIL; ELP; FaFP; LiTB; PoLF

(Love Me Not for Comely Grace.) GTBS; GTBS-P; OBEV; OxBSP

Love not too much. But how. The Affliction of Richard. Robert Bridges. QFR

Love now no fire hath left him. Giovanni Battista Marino, *tr. by* Richard Crashaw. OBVE

Love of a woman, The. Robert Creeley. VGW

Love of Country. Sir Walter Scott. *See* Lay of the Last Minstrel, The

Love of Fame, the Universal Passion, *sels.* Edward Young. OBSV

"Britannia's daughters, much more fair than nice." *Fr.* Satire V.

"Love of praise, howe'er concealed by art, The." *Fr.* Satire I.

"See commons, peers, and ministers of state." *Fr.* Satire III.

"These all their care expend on outward show." *Fr*. Satire II.

"With what, O Codrus! is thy fancy smit?." *Fr*. Satire II.

Love of field and coppice, The. My Country. Dorothea MacKellar. PoAu-1

Love of God, The. Bernard Rascas, *tr. fr. Provençal by* Bryant. WGRP

Love of Hell, The. Abraham Burstein. TrJP

Love of Lettuce, The. Marge Piercy. CAPP

Love of man and woman is as fire, The. My Comrade. James Jeffrey Roche. AA

Love of men for each other, The—so tender, heroic, constant. Edward Carpenter. *Fr*. A Mightier than Mammon. PeHV

Love of Nature. Mark Akenside. *Fr*. The Pleasure of Imagination, III. NOEC

Love of Older Men, The. James Kirkup. PeHV

Love of praise, howe'er concealed by art, The. Edward Young. *Fr*. Love of Fame, the Universal Passion, Satire I. OBSV

Love of the Father, The. *Unknown*. BLRP

Love of the Scorching Wind. László Nagy, *tr. fr. Hungarian by* Kenneth McRobbie. MHuP

Love, of this clearest, frailest Glass. In a Glass-Window for Inconstancy. Lord Herbert Cherbury. OxBSP; SeCP

Love, oh love, oh careless love. Careless Love. *Unknown*. AS

Love on a day (wise poets tell). How Violets Came Blue. Robert Herrick. CaPo; TTTS

Love on the Farm. D. H. Lawrence. CMoP; ErPo; FaBV; FF; MoAB; MoBrPo; NAEL-2; NoAM; TrGrPo

Love opened a vista rare with stars. Love's Vista. Henrietta Cordelia Ray. CBWP-3

Love Overgrows a Rock. Eric Roach. PVCV

Love Pictures You as Black and Long-faced. Lance Jeffers. FB

Love Play. William Cavendish, Duke of Newcastle. ErPo

Love plays a lute, and Thought an organ grand. The Two Musicians. Henrietta Cordelia Ray. CBWP-3

Love Poem. Maurice James Craig. NeIP

Love Poem. Lindsay MacRae. DT

Love Poem. Ron Padgett. UL

Love Poem, A: "And they have to get it right. We just need." John Ashbery. HCAP

Love Poem: "Black biplane crashes into [*or* through] the window, The." Gregory Orr. GeTw; MAT

Love Poem: Dispossessed, The. T. R. Hummer. MAYP

Love Poem: Extended Sonnet on the Death of Isaac Danziger. Meir Wieseltier, *tr. fr. Hebrew by* Warren Bargad *and* Stanley F. Chyet. IP

Love Poem, A: "Greyish yellow is the color of the dust." Meir Wieseltier, *tr. by* Warren Bargad *and* Stanley F. Chyet. IP

Love Poem, A: "He made no promise." Empress Eifuku, *tr. by* Steven D. Carter. WFTW

Love Poem: "I like/ the feel of your pulsating fibers." Yuri Kageyama. BrSi

Love Poem, A: "In sad revery." Tameko, *tr. by* Steven D. Carter. WFTW

Love Poem, A: "In your quest or request God is remote." Huda Na mani, *tr. by* Lena Jayyusi *and* Samuel Hazo. MAP

Love Poem: "Instinctively, unwittingly." Janet Lewis. QFR

Love Poem: "Kind of slant—the way a ball will glance, A." Gary Miranda. SM

Love Poem: "Last night you would not come." John Logan. CAPP

Love Poem: "My clumsiest dear, whose hands shipwreck vases." John Frederick Nims. FF; HoPM; InPK; SoSe

Love Poem: "My love the sun sets." Valerie Sinason. DT

Love Poem, A: "Night has fallen, The." Empress Eifuku, *tr. by* Steven D. Carter. WFTW

Love Poem: "Rain smell comes with the wind." Leslie Marmon Silko. UnPo; VoR

Love Poem: "Six o'clock and/ the sun rises. ." Miller Williams. MAT

Love Poem: "Speak earth and bless me with what is richest." Audre Lorde. GLP; NoAM

Love Poem, A: "That widowed crow." Emperor Kogon, *tr. by* Steven D. Carter. WFTW

Love Poem: "There is a white mare that my love keeps." Alex Comfort. *Fr*. The Postures of Love. ErPo

Love Poem: "When you are in love, we love the grass." Robert Bly. PCP

Love Poem: "Written under Capricorn, a land." Chris Wallace-Crabbe. PoAu-2

Love Poem, A: "Year is ending, The." Teika, *tr. by* Steven D. Carter. WFTW

Love Poem: "Yours is the face that the earth turns to me." Kathleen Jessie Raine. LiTB; MoAB; MoBrPo

Love Poem for My Country, A. Frank Mkalawile Chipasula. WMBCH

Love Poem—1940. Miriam Hershenson. GoYe

Love Poem No. 2. Yona Wallach, *tr. fr. Hebrew by* Warren Bargad *and* Stanley F. Chyet. IP

Love Poem on Theme by Whitman. Allen Ginsberg. CAPP; NaP

Love poems they read. Uses of Poetry. Winfield Townley Scott. PoA

Love Pursued. *Unknown, at. to* John Webster *and* William Rowley. *See* Thracian Wonder, The: Art Thou Gone in Haste?

Love, Reason, Hate, did once bespeak. A Barley-Break. Sir John Suckling. CaPo; SeCV-1

Love Redeemed, *sels*. William Baylebridge.

     "As fire, unfound ere pole approaches pole." *Fr*. LXXXVIII. PoAu-1

     "Love feeds, like Intellect, his lamp with truth." *Fr*. XXXII. PoAu-1

     "Quiet moon, immaculate of face, The." *Fr*. CVII. CBAP

     "Who questions if the punctual sun unbars." *Fr*. LXXXII. PoAu-1

Love Rejected. Lucille Clifton. BPo

Love scorch'd my finger, but did spare. Upon Love. Robert Herrick. SeCV-1

Love Scorns Degrees. Paul Hamilton Hayne. *Fr*. The Mountain of the lovers. AnAmPo

Love Secret, The. *Unknown, tr. fr. Arabic by* Wilfrid Scawen Blunt. AWP

Love seeketh not itself to please. The Clod and the Pebble. Blake. *Fr*. Songs of Experience. EnLoPo; EnRP; FaBV; InPS; NAEL-2; NOBE; NoP; OBNC; OxBSP; PoE; PrIm; RB; SCV; TEP; TrGrPo

Love Serviceable. Coventry Patmore. *Fr*. The Angel in the House, I, vi. EnLoPo

Love set you going like a fat gold watch. Morning Song. Sylvia Plath. BoWoP; HCAP; HeIP; IHMS; InPK; InPS; LCAP; NAAL-2; NAs; NOBA; PrIm

Love Sets Order in the Elements. Thomas Nabbes. *Fr*. Microcosmus. UnS

Love Should Grow Up like a Wild Iris in the Fields. Susan Griffin. NPGG

Love should intend realities: good-bye! Exit Line. John Ciardi. WeW

Love signed the contract blithe and leal. John Swanwick Drennan. BIrV

Love Sleeping. Plato, *tr. fr. Greek by* Thomas Stanley. AWP; FaBoEE

Love Somebody, Yes I Do. *Unknown*. AS

Love-Song. Else Lasker-Schüler, *tr. fr. German by* Jethro Bithell. TrJP

Love Song. Elio Pagliarani, *tr. fr. Italian by* Lawrence R. Smith. NItP

Love Song. Pattiann Rogers. NAmP

Love Song. Constance Lindsay Skinner. *Fr*. Three Songs from the Haida. AWP

Love-Song, A, *sel*. Thomas of Hales.

     Where is Paris and Heleyne?. ChTr

Love Song. *Unknown, tr. fr. Bagirmi by* H. Gaden. BoWoP

Love Song: "Arrow rides upon the sky, An." Samuel Allen

Love-song, A: "Beautiful, delicate bright gazelle, The." Walter James Turner. OBMV

Love Song: "Beautiful is she, this woman." *Unknown, tr. by* Constance Lindsay Skinner. AWP

Love Song, A: "By the fierce flames of love I'm in a sad taking." Royall Tyler. TAP

Love Song, A: "Come to me in the night—we shall sleep closely together [*or* Let us sleep entwined]." Else Lasker-Schüler. BoWoP, *tr. by* Michael Gillespie; OV, *tr. by* Robert Alter; TrJP, *tr. by* Michael Gillespie

Love Song: "Do not love me, my friend." Flavien Ranaivo, *tr. by* Miriam Koshland. PBA

Love Song: "Early I rose." *Unknown, tr. by* Mary Austin. AWP; LiTA

Love Song, A: "Had I concealed my love." Elinor Wylie. BLPL

Love Song, A: "He is a heart." *Unknown, tr. by* Myles Dillon. AnIL

Love Song: I and Thou. Alan Dugan. CAPP; FF; HoPM; InPK; MoP; NoAM; SoSe

Love Song: "I know not how to speak to thee, girl (damselle?)." Reed Whittemore. AmFN

Love Song: "I painted my eyes with black antimony." *Unknown, tr. by* H. Gaden. BoWoP

Love Song: "I passed by the house of the young man who loves me." *Unknown, tr. by* J. E. Manchip White. TTY

Love Song: "In the light of the moon." Hayim Be'er, *tr. by* Stephen Mitchell. VWA

Love Song, A: "Let my sweet song be pleasing unto Thee." Judah Halevi, *tr. by* Nina Davis Salaman. TrJP

Love Song: "Little sycamore, The." *Unknown, tr. by* J. E. Manchip White. TTY

Love-Song: "Little wild birds have come flying, The." *Unknown, tr. by* W. R. S. Ralston. AWP

Love Song: "Long closed door, oh open it again, The." Judah al-Harizi, *tr. by* Emma Lazarus. TrJP

Love Song: "My boat sails downstream." *Unknown, tr. by* J. E. Manchip White. TTY

Love Song: "My love is a lotus blossom." *Unknown, tr. by* J. E. Manchip White. TTY

Love Song: "My loved one is unique, without a peer." *Unknown, tr. by* J. E. Manchip White. TTY

Love Song: "On the hill tops I visit the snares." *Unknown, tr. by* Margaret Orbell. PeNZ

Love Song: "One with eyes the fairest." Euripides, *tr. fr. Greek by* Shelley. *Fr.* Cyclops. AWP

Love-Song: "Out of one golden breath." Else Lasker-Schüler, *tr. by* Jethro Bithell. TrJP

Love Song, The: "Out of the blackthorn hedges." Ivor Gurney. EnLoPo

Love Song: "See'st thou o'er my shoulders falling." Judah Halevi, *tr. by* Emma Lazarus. TrJP

Love Song: "She is a reed swaying in blue." Earle Thompson. HATNAP

Love Song: "Sweep the house clean." William Carlos Williams. MoAB; MoAmPo

Love Song: "That haughty tyranny of thine." Luís de León, *tr. by* Thomas Walsh. TrJP

Love Song: "Though to think/ Rejoiceth me." Margot Ruddock. OBMV

Love Song: "Tiny children." Yityangu Ejong, *tr. by* Frank Wordick. CBAP

Love Song, A: "Yes, I will love thee when the sun." W. F. Hawley. OBCV

Love Song: "You've got nice knees." Gavin Ewart. OxBTC

Love-Song by a Lunatic, A. *Unknown.* NA

Love-Song for Words. Nazik al-Mala'ika, *tr. fr. Arabic by* Matthew Sorenson *and* Christopher Middleton. MAP

Love Song ("I am a bunch of red roses"). *Unknown, tr. fr. Turkish by* Reza Baraheni *and* Zahra-Soltan Shokoohtaezeh. BoWoP

Love Song of J. Alfred Prufrock, The. T. S. Eliot. AiP, *abr.;* AmPP; AWP; CMoP; EBEV; FF; HAP; HeIP; HoPM; InPK; InPS; LiTB; LiTM; MoAB; MoAmPo; MoP; NAAL-2; NAEL-2; NAWM-2; NIP; NoAM; NOBA; NOBE; NoP; OAEL-2; OxBTC; PoA; PoE; PoRA; PPP; PrIm; SoSe; SOTW; TAP; TrGrPo; TwCP; WeW

Love Song of J. Alfred Prufrock, The. J. Walker. BXAP

Love-Song of the Water Carriers. *Unknown, tr. fr. Zulu.* PeSA

Love Song ("Our roofs are adjacent"). *Unknown, tr. fr. Turkish by* Reza Baraheni *and* Zahra-Soltan Shokoohtaezeh. BoWoP

Love Song out of Nothing. Vassar Miller. NePoEA

Love Song to a Stranger. Joan Baez. UnAS

Love Song to Eohippus. Peter Viereck. MoAmPo

Love Song to King Shu-Suen. Kubatum, *tr. fr. Sumerian by* Thorkild Jacobsen. WPOW

Love Song ("Your handkerchief should be blue"). *Unknown, tr. fr. Turkish by* Reza Baraheni *and* Zahra-Soltan Shokoohtaezeh. BoWoP

Love Songs. Mina Loy. VGW; WPE, *abr*

Love-Songs, at Once Tender and Informative. Samuel Hoffenstein. OBAL

Love-songs, at Once Tender and Informative, *sel.* Samuel Hoffenstein. "Your little hands." NBLV

Love Songs (Dadaria). *Gond Oral Tradition, tr. by* V. Elwin *and* S. Hivale. WTO

Love Songs in Age. Philip Larkin. PPP

Love Sonnet. John Updike. Son

Love Sonnet, A. George Wither. *See* I Loved a Lass.

Love Sonnets, *sels.* Zora Cross. CBAP
"In me there is a vast and lonely place." *Fr.* XLIX.
"What have you more than I, who crave you so?." *Fr.* LIV.

Love Sonnets of Proteus, The, *sels.* Wilfrid Scawen Blunt.
As to His Choice of Her. *Fr.* VIII. Son
Depreciating Her Beauty. *Fr.* VI. OBMV
Falcon, The. *Fr.* II. ACP
Farewell to Juliet.
"Juliet, farewell. I would not be forgiven." *Fr.* XXXIX.TrGrPo
Farewell to Juliet ("I see you, Juliet, still, with your straw hat").
Fr. XLVII.BoLoP; EnLoPo; OxBTC
St. Valentine's Day. *Fr.* LV. EnLoPo
Woman with a Past, A. *Fr.* XLIX. Son

Love Sonnets, VIII. Charles Harpur. PoAu-1

Love steered my course, while yet the sun rode high. Of Fiammetta Singing. Boccaccio, *tr. fr. Italian by* Dante Gabriel Rossetti. *Fr.* Sonnets. AWP

"Love still a boy and oft a wanton is." Sir Philip Sidney. *Fr.* Astrophel and Stella, LXXIII. AWP

Love still has something of the sea. Sir Charles Sedley. GBL; NOBE; OBS; SeCV-2

Love Story, A. Robert Graves. CMoP; FaBoTw; LiTB; NAEL-2

Love Story. Adrian Henri. UnAS

Love, strong as Death, is dead. An End. Christina Rossetti. FaBoRV; GBL

Love Suicides at Sonezaki, The, *sel.* Chikamatsu Monzaemon, *tr. fr. Japanese.*
"To this world, farewell." *Tr. by* Geoffrey Bownas *and* Anthony Thwaite. PeBJV
("Farewell to the world, and to the night farewell.") DL

Love-Talker, The. "Ethna Carbery." CH; WPE

Love, That Doth Reign [*or* Raine] and Live WithinMy Though. Petrarch, *tr. by* the Earl of Surrey. AAS; HeIP; NAEL-1; OAEL-1; OBVE; NoP
(Complaint of a Lover Rebuked.) AWP; Son; TrGrPo
("Love that liveth and reigneth in my thought.") SiPS

Love, that drained her, drained him she'd loved, though each. The Turtle Dove. Geoffrey Hill. FaBoTw; NePoEA

"Love that I hae chosen, The." The Lawlands o' Holland. *Unknown.* CH

Love that is alone with love. Love and Language. Louisa S. Guggenberger. NOBVV

Love that liveth and reigneth in my thought. Petrarch. *See* Sonnets to Laura: To Laura in Life.

Love That's Pure, Itself Disdaining. Johann A. Gruber, *tr. fr. German by* Sheema Z. Buehne. AH

Love, the delight of all well-thinking minds. Fulke Greville. *Fr.* Caelica, I. GBL; OBSC

Love, the great master of true eloquence. Love. Tasso, *tr. by* John Hermann Merivale. AWP

Love, the Light-Giver [*or* To Tommaso de' Cavalieri]. Michelangelo, *tr. fr. Italian by* John Addington Symonds. AWP; PeHV

Love the Ruins. Malka Heifetz-Tussman, *tr. fr. Yiddish by* Marcia Falk. VWA

Love the unholy, that frost which quickens summer. Didactic Sonnet. Melvin Walker La Follette. NePoEA; PoA

Love the Wild Swan. Robinson Jeffers. MoAB; MoAmPo; NoAM; Son; TW

Love thee? Yes, I'm sure I love thee. The City by the Sea. Josephine D. Henderson Heard. CBWP-4

Love, thou art absolute, sole Lord. Richard Crashaw. *Fr.* A Hymn to the Name and Honour of the Admirable Saint[e] Teresa. HAP; JCP; NOBE; NoP; OBEV; OBS; PoEL-2; SeCV-1, *abr.*
(Hymn to Saint Teresa.) ACP; EBEV; MeLP; MePo; WGRP

Love thou saist. Milton. *Fr.* Paradise Lost, *Bk.* VII, *ll.* 612–629. TOF

Love thou thy dream. Ezra Pound. FL

Love thy God and love Him only. Reality. Sir Aubrey De Vere. WGRP

Love Tight. Ted Joans. CNA

Love to the Church. Timothy Dwight. *See* I Love Thy Kingdom, Lord.

Love Triumphant, *sel.* Dryden.
Prologue to "Love Triumphant." OxBoLi

Love, 20 Cents the First Quarter Mile. Kenneth Fearing. HAP; WeW

Love twists. The Pressures. Imamu Amiri Baraka. BPo

Love Unchangeable. Rufus Dawes. AA

Love Unfeigned, The. Chaucer. OBEV

Love Unfeigned. Chaucer. *Fr.* Troilus and Criseyde [*or* Criseide], V. NOBE; OBEV

Love Unknown. George Herbert. JCP; Prf

Love Unlike Love. *Unknown. See* Christ made [*or* maketh] to man a fair present.

Love unreturn'd, how ere the flame. Constancye. Sidney Godolphin. MePo

Love Unsought. Emma Catherine Embury. AA

Love u.s.a. Kathleen Spivack. BoWoP

Love was before the light began. Love ("Love was before the light began"). *Unknown, tr. fr. Arabic by* E. Powys Mathers. *Fr.* The Thousand and One Nights. AWP

Love was true to me. John Boyle O'Reilly. ACP

Love, we curve downwards, we are set to night. After Midsummer. E. J. Scovell. OxBTC

Love we define for ourselves, The. Prothalamion. Michael Ryan. AmPA

Love we thought would never stop, The. Ending. Gavin Ewart. NBLV; OxBSP

Love wears roses' elegance. Sister Bertke. LLLT

Love What It Is. Robert Herrick. FaBoEE; GBL

Love Which Frees. Gloria Fuertes, *tr. fr. Spanish by* Philip Levine. WPOW

Love, which is least sure and most dared, the pure, keen. Peyton Houston. *Fr.* Sonnet Variations, CVI, ii. Son

Love which is the most difficult mystery. Psyche with the Candle. Archibald MacLeish. PCP

Love, Whose Month Was Ever May. Ulrich von Liechtenstein, tr. fr. German by Jethro Bithell. AWP

Love, why have you led me here. The Young Cordwainer. Robert Graves. MoBS

Love Will Find Out the Way. *Unknown.* FaBoCh; FaFP; GBL; GN; GTBS; GTBS-P; OBEV; WiR
(Great Adventure, The.) FaFP; GTBS-P

Love will not have me cry. Canzonetta: He Will Neither Boast nor Lament to His Lady. Jacopo da Lentino, tr. by Dante Gabriel Rossetti. AWP

Love winged my hopes and taught me how to fly. *Unknown.* OBSC
(Icarus.) OBEV
(Love Winged My Hopes.) EiL; TrGrPo

Love without a Truce. Antonin Artaud, tr. fr. French by Michael Benedikt. POS

Love without Hope. Robert Graves. BoLoP; ChTr; FaBoEE; GBL; GTBS-P; NAEL-2; OAEL-2

Love without Love. Luis Lloréns Torres, tr. fr. Spanish. InW, tr. by Julio Marzán

Love you alone have been with us. Jalal ed-Din Rumi, tr. by W. S. Merwin and Talat Sait Halman. LLLT

Love, You have struck me straight, my Lord! Resolution. Charles L. O'Donnell. TrPWD

"Love you?" said I, then I sighed, and then I gazed upon her sweetly. Ferdinando and Elvira, or the Gentle Pieman. W. S. Gilbert. FaBoCo; FaBoNo; FiBHP; NA

Love Your Enemy. Yusef Iman. BPo; TTY

"Love your neighbor as yourself." Thoughts on the Commandments. George Augustus Baker. AA

Love your toys, my darling. Toys. Abraham Sutskever, tr. by Seymour Levitan. VWA

Love, you're always. Because I Did Not Want to Ask. Jolanda Insana, tr. by Keala Jane Jewell. DMI

Love, You've Been a Villain. James Robinson Planché. NOBL

Lovebirds. William Jay Smith. ErPo

Loved I am, and yet complain[e] of Love. Complaint of Love. Sir Philip Sidney. *Fr.* Arcadia. PoEL-1; SiPS

Loved of My Soul. Israel Najara, tr. fr. Hebrew by Nina Davis Salaman. TrJP

Loved One, The. Joseph Hansen. NYBP

Loved ones' irresistible ways, The. Khwaja Mir Dard, tr. by Ahmed Ali. GoT

Loved stream, that meanders along. Memories of Childhood. John Carr. *Fr.* Derwent; an Ode. NOEC

Loveliest dawn of gold and rose. The Least of Carols. Sophie Jewett. OHIP

Loveliest girl in Vienna, The. Alma. Tom Lehrer. NBLV

Loveliest of Counties, Shropshire Now. Ian Sainsbury. BXAP

Loveliest of Pies. Peter De Vries. OBAL

Loveliest of streets, the High Street now. An Urban Lad. David Cram. SoTCo

Loveliest of streets will come to an end by and by, The. The Streets at Their Leisure Rise. David Avidan, tr. by Bernhard Frank. MHeP

Loveliest of Trees [the Cherry Now]. A. E. Housman. *Fr.* A Shropshire Lad, II. AWP; BLPL; BoNaP; ChTr; CMoP; ELP; FaBoBe; FaBV; FaFP; FF; HAP; HeIP; InPK; LiTB; LiTM; MoAB; MoBrPo; MoP; NAs; NoAM; NoP; OAEL-2; OHIP; OxBTC; PoE; PoLF; PrIm; RB; SoSe; TEP; TrGrPo

Loveliest of trees, the cherry now. In a Town Garden. Donald Mattam. FiBHP

Loveliest of what I leave. Adonis, Dying. Praxilla, tr. by Richard Lattimore. PBWP; WPOW

Loveliest Poem. Arvo Turtiainen, tr. fr. Finnish by Aili Jarvenpa. SOP

Lovelight. Georgia Douglas Johnson. AmNP

Loveliness. Christopher Smart. *Fr.* Hymns for the Amusement of Children, XIV. NOCV

Loveliness of Love, The. George Darley. *See* It Is Not Beauty I Demand.

Lovel's Song. Ben Jonson. *See* New Inn, The: It Was a Beauty That I Saw.

Lovely! all the essential parts. These Purists. William Carlos Williams. OBAL

Lovely are curves of the white owl sweeping. The White Owl. George Meredith. *Fr.* Love in a Valley. ChTr

Lovely body of the dead, The. Lament for Glasgerion. Elinor Wylie. PoA

Lovely boy, thou art not dead. Francis Davison. OBSC

Lovely cherries on the tree. Adjectives. Moishe Nadir, tr. by Joseph Leftwich. TrJP

Lovely companionship of school, lovely those days. Thoughts on Schoolchildren. Ahmad Shauqi, tr. by M. Mustafa Badawi and John Heath-Stubbs. MAP

"Lovely courier of the sky." Anacreon's Dove. Samuel Johnson. AWP

Lovely Étan, The. *Unknown.* NOIV

Lovely Fia was the summer queen. A Mare. Kate Barnes. NYBP

Lovely form there sate beside my bed, A. Phantom or Fact. Samuel Taylor Coleridge. EnRP

Lovely girl, you look at me through the window. Praxilla, tr. by John Dillon. PBWP

Lovely grapes and apples. A Tabernacle Thought. Israel Zangwill. TrJP

Lovely Green Lady, A. The Green Lady. Charlotte Druitt Cole. BoTP

Lovely hill-torrents are. W. J. Turner. GoJo; MoBrPo

Lovely in the winter sunshine lies the Haslemere Hotel. John Betjeman's Brighton. Gavin Ewart. FaBoPa

Lovely kind, and kindly loving. An Odd Conceit. Nicholas Breton. EiL; OBSC

Lovely Lady. Tu Fu, tr. fr. Chinese by Burton Watson. CoBCP

Lovely lady, fairest of the time. Lovely Lady. Tu Fu, tr. by Burton Watson. CoBCP

Lovely lady, rein thy will. Death's Warning to Beauty. *Unknown,* tr. by Robin Flower. AnIL

Lovely Lass o' Inverness, The. Burns. GoTS
(Lament for Culloden.) GTBS; GTBS-P; OBEV

Lovely Lass to a Friar Came, A. At. to. Earl of Rochester. CoMu

Lovely, lasting peace of mind! A Hymn to Contentment. Thomas Parnell. NOEC

Lovely Love, A. Gwendolyn Brooks. BPo

Lovely maid, with rapture swelling. Lines by a Fond Lover. *Unknown.* NA

Lovely of hair and breast and face. The Question. Norman Gale. FiBHP

Lovely Pamela, who found. Epitaph on a Party Girl. Richard Usborne. FaBoEE

Lovely Rivers and Lakes of Maine, The. George B. Wallis. BLPA

Lovely rock buried under the seaweed, A. Teika, tr. fr. Japanese by Hiroaki Sato. *Fr.* A Compendium of Good Tanka. FCEI

Lovely Rose Is Sprung, A. *Unknown,* tr. fr. German by Margarete Münsterberg. AWP

Lovely Shall Be Choosers, The. Robert Frost. MoAB; MoAmPo; NOBA; OxBA; PoE

Lovely Things. H. M. Sarson. BoTP

Lovely to look at. Arnaut de Mareuil, tr. by Paul Blackburn. Pro

Lovely Village Fair; or, I Dont Mean to Tell You Her Name, The. *Unknown.* CoMu

Lovely viper, haste not on. A Song of the Cannibals. Countess of Winchilsea. PoE

Lovely was the death. Samuel Taylor Coleridge. *Fr.* Religious Musings. EnRP

Lovely White Flowers. Constantine P. Cavafy, tr. fr. Greek by Edmund Keeley and Philip Sherrard. OBD

Lovely whore though. Cathleen. *Unknown,* tr. by Thomas MacIntyre. BIrV

Lovely young lady I mourn in my rhymes, A. George John Cayley. FiBHP

Lovely Young Moor, A. *Unknown,* tr. by Willis Barnstone. BoWoP

Lovelye William. *Unknown.* AmFP

Lovemaker, The. Robert Mezey. NePoEA-2

Lovemusic. Carolyn Kizer. ErPo

Lover, The. Robert Duncan. PeHV

Lover, The. Richard Henry Stoddard. AA

Lover. Isobel Thrilling. DT

Lover; a Ballad, The. Lady Mary Wortley Montagu. NAEL-1; NoP

Lover Abused Renounceth Love, The, *sel.* George Turberville.
"Was never day came on my head." EiL

Lover and Philosopher. Sir William Davenant. ACP; MePo; NOBE; OBEV; Prf

Lover and the Syringa-Bush, The. Herman Melville. AnAmPo; OBAL

Lover Compareth His State to a Ship in Perilous Storm Tossed on the Sea, The. Petrarch. *See* Sonnets to Laura: To Laura in Life.

Lover Compareth Himself to the Painful Falconer, The. *Unknown.* PBBP

Lover Complaineth the Unkindness of His Love, The. Sir Thomas Wyatt. AAS; EBEV; EiL; ELP; GBL; HAP; InPS; NAEL-1; NoP; OAEL-1; PoEL-1; SiPS

(Lover Complaineth, The.) TrGrPo
(To His Lute.) BoLoP; NOBE; OBEV; OBSC; QFR
Lover Consults with Reason, The. Thomas Carew. *See* Lover, upon an
Accident Necessitating His Departure, Consults with Reason, A.
Lover Deceived Writes to His Lady, The, *sel.* Thomas Howell.
Who Would Have Thought. EiL
Lover Exhorteth His Lady to Be Constant, The. *Unknown.* OBSC
Lover for Shamefastnesse Hideth His Desire within His Faithfull Hart, The.
Petrarch. *See* Sonnets to Laura: To Laura in Life.
Lover Having Dreamed Enjoying of His Love, Complaineth That the
Dreame Is Not either Longer or Truer, The. Sir Thomas Wyatt.
AAS
Lover in Liberty Smileth at Them in Thraldom, That Sometime Scorned
His Bondage, The. *Unknown.* EiL
Lover in Winter Plaineth for the Spring, The. *Unknown. See* Western
Wind.
Lover is a slender, glowing urn, A. A Fantastic Simile. Thomas Lovell
Beddoes. Son
Lover Left Alone, A. *Unknown.* MeEL
Lover Mourns for the Loss of Love, The. W. B. Yeats. WeW
Lover of Love. Hagiwara Sakutaro, *tr. fr. Japanese by* Hiroaki Sato.
FCEI
Lover of mine, if upland you journey. Ave Atque Vale. *Malay Oral
Tradition, tr. by* R. J. Wilkinson *and* R. O. Winstedt. WTO
Lover of swamps. To the Snipe. John Clare. FaBoPV; OBNC
Lover of the Lord. *Unknown.* AmFP
Lover of the moorland bare, A. To K[atharine de M]attos. Robert Louis
Stevenson. OBNC
Lover Proved False, The. *Unknown.* AmFP
Lover Rejoiceth, The. Sir Thomas Wyatt. SiPS; TrGrPo
(Liberty.) OBSC
("Tanglid I was yn love's snare.") AAS
Lover Rejoiceth the Enjoying of His Love, The. Sir Thomas Wyatt.
AAS; BoLoP; SiPS
(Promise, A.) OBSC
Lover Remembereth Such as He Sometimes Enjoyed and Showeth How He
Would Like to Enjoy Her Again, The. Leon Stokesbury. SM
Lover Renounceth Love, The. Sir Thomas Wyatt. *See* Sonnet:
"Farewell, love, and all thy laws [*or* lawes] for ever."
Lover Showeth How He Is Forsaken of Such as He Sometime Enjoyed,
The. Sir Thomas Wyatt. *See* They Flee [*or* Fle] from Me That
Sometime Did Me Seek [*or* Seke].
Lover Tells of the Rose in His Heart, The. W. B. Yeats. CMoP
(Aedh Tells of the Rose in His Heart.) BrPo; MoBrPo
Lover That I Hope You Are. Milton Acorn. NeAC
Lover to Himself, The. David Phillips. NeAC
Lover to His Lady, The. *At.* to Plato, *tr. fr. Greek by* George Turberville.
CTC; FaBoEE; FF; OBSC
Lover to the Thames of London, to Favour [*or* Favor] His Lady Passing
Thereon, The. George Turberville. ChTr; EiL; NoP; OBSC
Lover, under burthen of his mistress' love, the. Sir John Davies. *Fr.*
The Gulling Sonnets. EiL
Lover, upon an Accident Necessitating His Departure, Consults with
Reason, A. Thomas Carew. CaPo
(Lover Consults with Reason, The.) TrGrPo
Loverd, thou clepedest me. Wait a Little! *Unknown.* NOCV
Lovers, The. Conrad Aiken. NYBP
Lovers, The. Alex Comfort. PoA
Lovers. Mary Elizabeth Fullerton. PoAu-1
Lovers, The. William Robert Rodgers. BIrV; OxBSP
Lovers, The. William Jay Smith. MoAmPo
Lovers, The. Marya Zaturenska. MoAmPo
Lovers already at eight in the morning? Mattina. Kurt Klinger, *tr. by*
Beth Bjorklund. CoAuP
Lovers, and a Reflection. Charles Stuart Calverley. FaBoCo; FaBoPa;
NA
Lovers and madmen have such seething brains. The Lunatic, the Lover,
and the Poet. Shakespeare. *Fr.* A Midsummer Night's Dream, V, i.
FiP
(Imagination.) LiTB
Lover's Anger, A. Matthew Prior. ErPo
Lover's Appeal, The. Sir Thomas Wyatt. *See* And Wilt Thou Leave Me
Thus?
Lover's Arithmetic, The. *Unknown.* OxBoLi
Lovers conceits are like a flattring glasse. *Unknown.* OBS
Lover's Confession, A. Charles, Duc d' Orléans. *See* My Ghostly
Father, I me confess.
Lovers' Debouchment. William Zaranka. BXAP
Lovers everywhere are bringing babies into the world. Make Love Not
War. Howard Nemerov. NAs

Lover's eyes will gaze an eagle blind, A. Shakespeare. *Fr.* Love's
Labour's Lost, IV, iii. GBL
Lovers, fast in their longing, The. March. William Everson. ErPo
Lovers, forget your love. Wind and Window Flower. Robert Frost.
AnAmPo
Lovers Go Fly a Kite, The. W. D. Snodgrass. NYBP
Lovers How They Come and Part. Robert Herrick. GBL; OxBoLi;
OxBSP; PoEL-3
Lovers in Fall. Yehuda Amichai, *tr. fr. Hebrew by* Warren Bargad *and*
Stanley F. Chyet. IP
Lovers in ladies' magazines. Thomas McGrath. VGW
Lovers in the act dispense. The Thieves. Robert Graves. BoLoP;
CMoP; GTBS-P; LiTM; OAEL-2
Lovers in Winter. Robert Graves. FaBoEE; NYBP
Lovers' Infiniteness [e]. John Donne. EiL; LiTB; MeLP; OAEL-1; OBS;
PoEL-2; SeCP; SeCV-1
Lover's Lament, A. ("I once did court a damsel"). *Unknown.* AmFP
Lover's Lament, The. ("My dearest dear, the time draws near").
Unknown. AS
Lover's Lament *or* The Willows by the Water Side, A. *Unknown, tr. fr.
Tewa Indian by* H. J. Spinden. AWP
(Willows by the Water Side, The.) WTO
Lover's Lament for Her Sailor, The. *Unknown.* AmFP
Lover's Lane. Paul Laurence Dunbar. BANP
Lover's Leap; a Tale, The. Andrew Macdonald. NOEC
Lovers, like wrestlers, when they do not lay. Samuel Butler. *Fr.* Love.
ErPo
Lovers loitered on the deck talking, The. The Feast. Robert Hass.
GeTw
Lover's Lullaby, A. George Gascoigne. *See* Lullaby [*or* Lullabie] of a
Lover, The.
Lovers' Mass, The. *Unknown.* OxBLMV
Lovers may find similitudes. The Cascade. Edgell Rickword. FaBoTw
Lover's Meeting. Ray Mathew. CBAP
Lover's Melancholy, The, *sels.* John Ford.
Dawn. OBEV, V, i.
"If thou canst wake with me, forget to eate." *Fr.* IV, ii. PoEL-2
"Minutes are numbered by the fall of sands." *Fr.* IV, iii. PoEL-2
Lover's New Year's Gift, A. John Lydgate. PoEL-1
"Lovers of Israel" at the Belzhets Death Camp, The. Itzig Manger, *tr. fr.
Yiddish by* Leonard Wolf. PeBMYV
Lovers of pleasure more than God. Lover of the Lord. *Unknown.*
AmFP
Lovers of the Poor, The. Gwendolyn Brooks. CAPP; MoP; NAAL-2;
NoAM; NOBA
Lover's Plea, A. Thomas Campion. *See* Shall I Come, Sweet Love, to
Thee?
Lover's Posy, The. Rufinus Domesticus, *tr. fr. Greek by* W. H. D.
Rouse. AWP
Lover's Prayer, The. *Malay Oral Tradition, tr. by* R. J. Wilkinson *and*
R. O. Winstedt. WTO
Lover's Progress, The, *sel.* John Fletcher.
Dead Host's Welcome, The. *Fr.* III, i. TrGrPo
Lover's Question, A. James Baldwin. GLP
Lovers Rejoice! Francis Beaumont *and* Fletcher. *Fr.* Cupid's Revenge.
EiL
Lover's Reply to Good Advice. Richard Hughes. MoBrPo
Lover's Resolution, A. George Wither. *See* Fair Virtue, the Mistress of
Philarete: Shall I Wasting in Despair.
Lover's Song, The. Edward Rowland Sill. AA
Lovers who/ came to me. Ghost Poem Five. Sister Mary Norbert Körte.
IHMS
Lovers who are young indeed, and wish to know the sort of life. Love,
You've Been a Villain. James Robinson Planché. NOBL
Lovers whose lifted hands are candles in winter. For a Child Expected.
Anne Ridler. LiTM; SeCePo
Love's Alchemy [*or* Alchemie]. John Donne. MePo; NAEL-1; NoP;
OAEL-1; PoE; SeCP
Love's an headstrong wild desire. Love. Henry Baker. NOEC
Loves and sorrows of those who lose an orchard. The Lost Orchard.
Edgar Lee Masters. CMoP
Love's Apparition and Evanishment. Samuel Taylor Coleridge. EnRP
Love's as Warm as Tears. C. S. Lewis. TIRV
Love's Bitten Tongue, *sel.* Vassar Miller.
"Lord, hush this ego as one stops a bell." MT
Love's Change. Anne Reeve Aldrich. AA
Love's Clock. Sir John Suckling. *See* That None Beguiled Be.
Love's Coming. John Shaw Neilson. PoAu-1
Love's Coming. Ella Wheeler Wilcox. AnAmPo
Love's Consolation, *sel.* Richard Watson Dixon.
"All who have loved, be sure of this from me." OBNC

Love's Cure, *sel.* Francis Beaumont *and* Fletcher.
"Turn, turn thy beauteous face away." PoEL-2
Love's Deity [*or* Deitie]. John Donne. AWP; EIL; GBL; LiTB; MePo; SeCePo; SeCP; SeCV-1
Love's Despair. Dryden. *See* Spanish Friar [*or* Fryar], The: Farewell, Ungrateful Traitor.
Love's Despair. Richard Lynche. *Fr.* Diella, XIII. EIL
Love's Despair. Shakespeare. *See* Twelfth Night: Come Away, Come Away, Death.
Love's domain, supernal Zion. Brynbwrla. Kingsley Amis. *Fr.* The Evans Country. NOBL
Love's Emblem. John Clare. NIP
Love's Emblems. John Fletcher. *See* Tragedy of Valentinian, The: Now the Lusty Spring [Is Here].
Loves End. Lord Herbert of Cherbury. SeCP
Love's Ending. *Unknown.* OBSC
Love's Entreaty. Michelangelo. *See* Thou knowest, love, I know that thou dost know.
Love's Epitaph. William Cavendish, Duke of Newcastle. OxBSP
Love's Fancy. Dryden. *See* Evening's Love, An: After the Pangs of a Desperate Lover.
Love's Farewell. Michael Drayton. *See* Idea:
Since there's [*or* ther's] no help[e], come let us kiss[e] and part.
Love's Fidelity. Petrarch. *See* Sonnets to Laura: To Laura in Life.
Loves flies with bow unstrung when Time appears. Love and Age. Walter Savage Landor. GBL
Love's Flight. Else Lasker-Schüler, *tr. fr. German by* Jethro Bithell. TrJP
Love's Fool. Margit Szécsi, *tr. fr. Hungarian by* Kenneth McRobbie. MHuP
Love's Force. Thomas Carew. CaPo
Love's Franciscan. Henry Constable. ACP
Love's Glory. Fulke Greville. *See* Caelica:
Fie [*or* Fye], foolish Earth, think[e] you the heaven wants glory.
Love's god is a boy. Cupid. *Unknown.* EIL
Love's Grave. George Meredith. *See* Modern Love:
Mark where the pressing wind shoots javelin-like:
Love's Grave. Thomas Watson. *See* Hecatompathia; or, Passionate Century of Love: Here Lieth Love.
Love's Growth. John Donne. JCP; MePo; NoP; SeCV-1
Love's Guerdons. Edith Nesbit. NOBVV
Love's hidden pearl is shining yet. Hafiz, *tr. by* R. A. Nicholson. TOF
Love's Horoscope. Richard Crashaw. MeLP; OBS
Love's Immaturity. Edith Jay Scovell. GBL; LiTB
Love's Justification. Michelangelo. *See* Yes! hope may with my strong desire keep pace.
Love's Labour Lost. Robert Tofte. *Fr.* Alba. EIL
Love's Labour's Lost, *sels.* Shakespeare.
Did Not the Heavenly Rhetoric of Thine Eye. *Fr.* IV, iii. LiTB; Son
"If she be made of white and red." *Fr.* I, ii. CTC
"Lover's eyes will gaze an eagle blind, A." *Fr.* IV, iii. GBL
On a Day—Alack the Day. *Fr.* IV, iii. EIL
(Blossom, The.) OBEV
(Dumain's Rhymes.) OBSC
(Love's Perjuries.) GTBS; GTBS-P
So Sweet a Kiss. *Fr.* IV, iii. EIL; InvP
When Daisies Pied [and Violets Blue]. *Fr.* V, ii. FF; InPK; NAEL-1; NOBE; NoP; PoRA; PrIm
("Now daisies pied, and violets blue.") BoTP
(Song: "When daisies pied and violets blue.") FiP; PBBP; PoEL-2
(Spring.) EIL; HAP; HeIP; NBLV; NIP; OAEL-1; OBEV; PoEL-2; SeCePo; TEP; TrGrPo; UnPo
(Ver.) OBSC
When Icicles Hang by the Wall. *Fr.* V, ii. AWP; FaPON; FF; GN; GoJo; InPK; InPS; LiTB; NAEL-1; NOBE; PoRA; PrIm
(Hiems.) FaBoCh; OBSC
(Merry Note, A.) WiR
(Song: "When icicles hang by the wall.") FiP; PBBP; PoEL-2
(Tu-Whit To-Who.) CH
(Winter.) BoNaP; ChTr; EIL; GTBS; GTBS-P; HAP; HeIP; NIP; OAEL-1; OBEV; SeCePo; TEP; TrGrPo; UnPo; WeW
Love's Land. Isabella Valancy Crawford. CaP
Love's Language. Donagh MacDonagh. NeIP
Love's Last Resource. Sadi, *tr. fr. Persian by* L. Cranmer-Byng. *Fr.* The Gulistan. AWP
Love's Limit. *Unknown.* TrGrPo
Love's Martyr, *sels.* Sir Robert Chester. EIL
Her Hair.
Love's Martyrs. John Ford. *See* Broken Heart, The:
Oh [*or* O], no more, no more, too late.
Love's Matrimony. William Cavendish. SeCePo

Love's memories haunt my footsteps still. John Clare. NOBVV
Love's multitudinous boneyard. Jack Kerouac. *Fr.* Mexico City Blues, 230. NeAP
Love's night and a lamp. Meleager, *tr. by* Peter Whigham. BoLoP
Loves of the Birds. *Malay Oral Tradition, tr. by* R. J. Wilkinson *and* R. O. Winstedt. WTO
Loves of the Plants, The. Erasmus Darwin. *Fr.* The Botanic Garden, *pt.* II.
Vegetable Loves. SeCePo
Nightmare. NOEC
Loves of the Puppets. Richard Wilbur. OxBC
Loves of the Triangles, The, *sel.* John Hookham Frere.
"Stay your rude steps, or e'er your feet invade." FaBoNo
Love's Offence. Sir John Suckling. CaPo
Love's Old Sweet Song. G. Clifton Bingham. FaBoBe
Love's Omnipresence. Joshua Sylvester. *See* Were I as Base as Is the Lowly Plain.
Love's Pains. John Clare. NOBVV
Love's pallor and the semblance of deep ruth. Dante, *tr. fr. Italian by* Dante Gabriel Rossetti. *Fr.* La Vita Nuova, XXIV. AWP
Love's Perjuries. Shakespeare. *See* Love's Labour's Lost: On a Day—Alack the Day.
Love's Philosophy. Shelley. BLPA; BLPL; BoLoP; EnRP; FaBoBe; FaBV; GTBS; GTBS-P; HoPM; TrGrPo
Love's Pilgrims. Thomas Campion. *See* What Faire Pompe.
Love's Prayer. James Whitcomb Riley. AA
Love's Prerogative. John Oxenham. BLRP
Love's Primal Want. William Ellery Leonard. *Fr.* Two Lives. Son
Love's Progress. John Donne. *Fr.* Elegies, XVIII. LiTB; OAEL-1
Love's Promises. Alastair Fowler. NPo
Love's Protestation. Thomas Lodge. *See* Rosalynde; or Euphues' Golden Legacy: Fancy, A.
Love's Rebel. Earl of Surrey. OBSC; SiPS
("When sommer toke in hand the winter to assail.") AAS
Love's Remorse. Edwin Muir. OxBTC
Love's Résumé. Heine, *tr. by* J. F. C.. TrJP
Love's Resume. Heine. *See* Die Rose, die Lilie, die Taube, die Sonne.
Love's Resurrection Day. Louise Chandler Moulton. AA
Love's Rocky Forest. Arto Melleri, *tr. fr. Finnish by* Aili Jarvenpa. SOP
Love's Rosary. George Edward Woodberry. AA
Love's secret had remained concealed. Mohammad Taqi Mir, *tr. by* Ahmed Ali. GoT
Love's Servile Lot. Robert Southwell. ACP
Loves She Like Me? Samuel Woodworth. AA
Love's Siege. Sir John Suckling. *See* 'Tis Now, Since I Sat[e] Down Before.
Love's Stratagems. Donald Justice. NYBP
Love's the boy stood on the burning deck. Casabianca. Elizabeth Bishop. FaBoWP; OxBSP
Loves Victory. Aurelian Townshend. *See* To the Countesse of Salisbury.
Love's Vision. Edward Carpenter. WGRP
Love's Vista. Henrietta Cordelia Ray. CBWP-3
Love's Votary. George Augustus Simcox. NOBVV
Loves who many years held all my mind, The. Walter Savage Landor. GBL
Love's Will. Lewis Warsh. UL
Love's Wisdom. Margaret Deland. AA
Love's Witchery. Thomas Moore. EIL
Love's without Reason. Alexander Brome. OBS
Loves Witness. Aphra Behn. BoWoP
Loves World. Sir John Suckling. SeCV-1
Love's worshipers alone can know. Love and Folly. La Fontaine, *tr. by* Bryant. AWP
Love's Young Dream. Thomas Moore. WBLP
Lovesight. Dante Gabriel Rossetti. *Fr.* The House of Life, IV. EBVV; GTBS-P; NAEL-2; OBNC; TrGrPo
Lovesleep, The. Gavin Ewart. OxBC
Lovest Thou Me?, *sel.* William Cowper.
"Lord it is my chief complaint." TrPWD
Lovewell's Fight. *Unknown.* PAH
Loving. Shirley Kaufman. VWA
Loving. Jane Stembridge. NMM
Loving and Beloved. Sir John Suckling. CaPo; NAEL-1; OBS
Loving and Liking. Dorothy Wordsworth. OxBChV
Loving care! Leave Me Alone. Felice Holman. RHPC
Loving Henry. *Unknown.* AmFP
"Loving in truth, and fain in verse my love to show." Sir Philip Sidney. *Fr.* Astrophel and Stella, I. AWP; BLPL; EBVV; GBL; HAP; InPS; LiTB; NAEL-1; NoP; OAEL-1; OBSC; PoE; SeCePo; Son; TEP; TrGrPo

Loving looks the large-eyed cow. A Christmas Prayer. George Macdonald. PChr

Loving Mad Tom. *Unknown. See* Tom o' Bedlam's Song.

Loving My Grandchild. Kaai Chigetsu, *tr. fr. Japanese* by Hiroaki Sato. *Fr.* Thirteen Hokku. FCEI

Loving She Stood Apart. Patrick Lane. NeAC

Loving someone/ who doesn't love you. Lady Kasa. *Fr.* Manyo Shu. FCEI

Loving the rituals that keep men close. Palladas, *tr.* by Tony Harrison. OBVE

Loving the watery stairs. Some Love. Peter Redgrove. NPo

Loving this man who is far away. Like Loving Chekhov. Denise Levertov. InPS

Loving You Less than Life, a Little Less. Edna St. Vincent Millay. NAAL-2

Loving you, my heart may shatter. Lady Izumi, *tr. fr. Japanese* by Hiroaki Sato. *Fr.* Fifty-one Tanka. FCEI

Loving you was difficult. Dear John. Lindsay MacRae. DT

Lovingly I turn me down. After Mass. "Michael Field." WPE

Low-anchored Cloud. Henry David Thoreau. *Fr.* A Week on the Concord and Merrimack Rivers. ImOP; NoP
   (Mist.) AA; AmPP; AnAmPo; AWP; OxBA

Low Barometer. Robert Bridges. CMoP; LiTB; MoP; NoAM; NOCV; OBNC; QFR

Low beating of the tom-toms, The. African Dance. Langston Hughes. FaPON

Low-built houses of the poor, The. Look. Philip Levine. BLA

Low Church. Stanley J. Sharpless. NBLV

Low Doun in the Broom. *Unknown.* GoTS

Low Fields and Light. W. S. Merwin. LCAP

Low hedges bent by the wind. Impressions of the Countryside. Ito Togai, *tr.* by Burton Watson. JLIC-2

Low in the eastern sky. To the Maiden in the East. Henry David Thoreau. AnAmPo; OxBA

Low in thy grave with thee. David's Lament for Jonathan. Peter Abelard, *tr.* by Helen Waddell. PeHV

Low prayer, a high prayer, I send through space, A. *Unknown, tr.* by Douglas Hyde. WTO

Low sandy beach and the thin scrub pine, The. Cape Cod. George Santayana. AnAmPo

Low-set island this September, A. Tresco. Geoffrey Grigson. FaBoPP

Low spake the knight to the peasant maid. The Rose and the Gauntlet. John Wilson. BeLS

Low sun whitens on the flying squalls, The. Rounding the Cape. Roy Campbell. PeSA

Low Tide on Grand Pré. Bliss Carman. CaP; NOBC; OBCV

Low Trick, A. Gelett Burgess. OBCA

Low was our pretty cot: our tallest rose. Reflections on Having Left a Place of Retirement. Samuel Taylor Coleridge. EnRP

Low ye hills in ocean lie. My Heart Is in Merioneth. *Unknown, tr. by* Richard Llwyd. OBWVE

Lowdown Dirty Blues. *Unknown.* AmFP

Lowell. James Russell Lowell. *Fr.* A Fable for Critics. AmPP; NOBA; OxBA; TAP
   (On Himself.) AA

Lower Forms of Life. Mary Winter. GoYe

Lower the flags. Special Bulletin. Langston Hughes. PoBA

Lower the Standard: That's My Motto. Karl Shapiro. MoP; NoAM

Lowermost leaves, The. Ietaka, *tr.* by Steven D. Carter. WFTW

Lowery Cot. L. A. G. Strong. MoBrPo

Lowest Place, The. Christina Rossetti. NOBVV; TrPWD

Lowest Trees Have Tops, The. Sir Edward Dyer. OPOP; OxBSP; RB

Lowlands. *Unknown.* ChTr; OxBoLi

Lowlands Away ("Lowlands, Lowlands away, my John"). *Unknown.* GBP

Lowlands o' [or of] Holland, The. *Unknown.* AmFP, *diff. version;* OxBB, *with music*
   (Lawlands o' Holland, The.) CH

Lowlands of Holland, The. *Unknown.* AmFP

Lowlands of Holland, The. *Unknown.* OxBB

Lowly Bard, The. "Fanny Forester." PF

Lowly Peasant, The. *Unknown, tr.* by Rina Benmayor. PBWP

Lowpin owre a burn. O Aa the Manly Sports. J. K. Annand. PoSH

Lowriders #2 ("Lowriders/ cruising the barrio"). Reyes Cárdenas, *tr. fr. Spanish* by Toni Empringham. FIA

Lowveld, The. Charles Eglington. PeSA

Loyal. William Matthews. MAYP

Loyal General, The, *sel.* Nahum Tate.
   "If yet there be a few that take delight," (*by* Dryden) SeCV-2

"Loyal Hearts of London City, come I pray, and sing my ditty." The Dutchess of Monmouth's Lamentation for the Loss of Her Duke. *Unknown.* CoMu; FaBoBa

Loyal Sins. Jacob Glatstein, *tr. fr. Yiddish* by Ruth Whitman. VWA

Loyal subject, thou, to that bright Queen, A. To W. L. G. on Reading His "Chosen Queen. Charlotte Forten. BlSi

Loyalty. Berton Braley. BLPA

Loyalty. Allan Cunningham. *See* Hame, Hame, Hame.

Loyalty. William Henry Davies. BrPo

Loyalty. Leslie Ullman. NAmP

Loyalty Confin'd. Sir Roger L'Estrange. OBS

Loyalty to the Flag. Lizelia Augusta Jenkins Moorer. CBWP-3

L's live in caves under the earth, The. Summer Letters. Michael Davidson. IAT

Lu wine like amber. In Reply When Lesser Officials of Chung-tu Brought a Pot of Wine and Two Fish to My Inn as Gifts. Li Po, *tr.* by Burton Watson. CoBCP

Lubber Breeze. T. Sturge Moore. CH

Lucasia, Rosania and Orinda Parting at a Fountain, July 1663. Katherine Philips. PeHV

Lucasta, frown and let me die. To Lucasta: Her Reserved Looks. Richard Lovelace. CaPo; SeCV-1

Lucasta Laughing. Richard Lovelace. PoEL-3

Lucasta's Fan, with a Looking-Glass in It. Richard Lovelace. CaPo

Lucasta's World. Richard Lovelace. CaPo; SeCP

Lucent lake was lit with sheen, The. A Thought of Lake Ontario. Henrietta Cordelia Ray. CBWP-3

Lucia, *sel.* Giles Fletcher the Elder.
   First Did I Fear. *Fr.* XX. Son

Lucifer, The. Guy Glover. CaP

Lucifer/ you called yourself. Names. Maria Neef-Uthoff, *tr.* by Susan L. Cocalis. DMG

Lucifer in Starlight. George Meredith. AWP; CH; EBVV; FF; HAP; InPK; LiTB; Mes; NAEL-2; NOBE; NOBVV; NoP; OAEL-2; OBEV; OBNC; PoE; PoEL-5; Son; TrGrPo; UnPo; WeW

Lucifer in the Train. Adrienne Rich. EaLo; NePoEA; NePoEA-2

Lucilia, wedded to Lucretius, found. Lucretius. Tennyson. OAEL-2

Lucinda Matlock. Edgar Lee Masters. *Fr.* Spoon River Anthology. CMoP; FaBV; FF; HAP; LiTA; LiTM; MoAmPo; MoP; NoAM; NOBA; OxBA

Lucindy, who you 'spose I seed. A Common Occurrence. Priscilla Jane Thompson. CBWP-2

Luck. W. W. Gibson. MoShBr; OBMV

Luck. Evan V. Shute. CaP

Luck has no songs, luck has no thoughts, luck has nothing. Pain. Edith Södergran, *tr. by* Jaakko A. Ahokas. PBWP; WPOW

Luck? I am upset. My dog is ill. A Rune for C. Barbara Howes. NYBP; SM

Luck is not smiling upon us. Smile at Me. Musa Moris Farhi. VWA

Luck is something I do not understand. The Lover Remembereth Such as He Sometimes Enjoyed and Showeth How He Would Like to Enjoy Her Again. Leon Stokesbury. SM

Luck of Edenhall, The. Ludwig Uhland, *tr. fr. German* by Longfellow. AWP

Luck, we've had it; our character the public's. It Did. Robert Lowell. NoAM

Luckes, my faire falcon, and your fellowes all. Sir Thomas Wyatt. *See* Epigram: "Lux my fair falcon, and your fellows all."

"Luckies." Reginald Gibbons. MAYP

Luckily, I take great joy of love. Guillaume de Poitiers, *tr.* by Paul Blackburn. Pro

Luckless man/ Avoids the miserable bodkin's point. Man's Anxious, but Ineffectual Guard against Death. Thomas Lovell Beddoes. ChER

Luck's Shining Child. George Garrett. MT

Lucky. Cathy Song. BrSi

Lucky and Unlucky. William Matthews. BLA

Lucky bridegroom. Sappho, *tr. by* Josephine Balmer. AIW

Lucky Chance, The, *sel.* Aphra Behn.
   "Oh! Love, that stronger art than wine." WPE; WPOW

Lucky Coin, The. Austin Clarke. NeIP

Lucky day, fifth of the week, A. *Unknown, tr.* by Arthur Waley. BoS

Lucky like Cook to travel and return. "Heureux Qui comme Ulysse." John Manifold. WaaP; WaP

Lucky Lion! *Zulu Oral Tradition, tr.* by H. Tracey. WTO

Lucky Marriage, The. Thomas Blackburn. GTBS-P

Lucky Sailor; or, The Sailor's Invitation to Go with Admiral Anson, The. *Unknown.* OxBSS

Lucky the husband. Mabel Kelly. Turlough Carolan, *tr. by* Austin Clarke. BIrV; CIP
Lucky the living child, born in a land. American Child. Paul Engle. AmFN
Lucretius. Tennyson. OAEL-2
Lucretius could not credit centaurs. Invitation to Juno. William Empson. CMoP; FaBoMo
Lucretius felt the change of the world in his time. Prescription of Painful Ends. Robinson Jeffers. LiTA; MoAB; MoAmPo; OxBA
Lucy. Walter de la Mare. CMoP
Lucy, *complete, in 5 parts* ("Strange fits of passion have I known."). Wordsworth. EBEV, *pt. 1;* EnRP; FiP; GBL, *pt. 1;* NOBE; OAEL-2; OBEV; OBNC; TrGrPo
Sels.
　I Traveled [*or* travell'd] among Unknown Men. AWP; EnRP; FaBV; GTBS; GTBS-P; OBNC
　She Dwelt among the Untrodden Ways. AWP; BLPA; BoLoP; ELP; EnLoPo; EnRP; FaBV; FF; FPL; HAP; HeIP; LiTB; NIP; NoP; OxBSP; PPP; PrIm; PWR; TEP; UnPo; WeW
　(Lost Love, The.) GTBS; GTBS-P
　Slumber Did My Spirit Seal, A. AWP; BLPL; ELP; EnLoPo; EnRP; FaBoCh; GTBS; GTBS-P; HAP; HeIP; InPK; InPS; InvP; NoP; PoEL-4; PoRA; PPP; PrIM; SCV; TEP; UnPo; WeW
　Three Years She Grew in Sun and Shower. EnRP; FiP; GN; HAP; NoP; PoEL-4
　(Education of Nature, The.) GTBS; GTBS-P
Lucy Ashton's Song. Sir Walter Scott. *Fr.* The Bride of Lammermoor, *ch. 3.* EnRP; GoTS; NOBE; OBEV; OxBS
　(Look Not Thou.) OxBSP
Lucy goes down the celestial escalator in light. Lucy Taking Birth. Diana Scott. BrRo
Lucy Gray; or, Solitude. Wordsworth. BeLS; CH; EnRP; FiP; NAEL-2; OAEL-2; OxBChV; TEP
Lucy Lake. Newton Mackintosh. BXAP
Lucy Lavender. Ivy O. Eastwick. BoTP
Lucy Locket lost her pocket. Mother Goose. OxBoLi; OxNR
Lucy Taking Birth. Diana Scott. BrRo
Lucy, you brightnesse of our spheare, who are. To Lucy, Countesse of Bedford, with Mr. Donnes Satyres. Ben Jonson. OBS; SeCV-1
Lud! what a group the motley scene discloses! Goldsmith. *Fr.* Epilogue to "The Sister." OBSV
Ludicrous Stick. Tina Darragh. LP
Luf es lif that lastes ay, thar it in Christe es feste. Love Is Life. Richard Rolle of Hampole. PoEL-1
Lugete O Veneres. R. A. K. Mason. ATNZ
Lugubrious Whing-Whang, The. James Whitcomb Riley. NA
Lui et Elle. D. H. Lawrence. NoAM
Luis de Camões. Roy Campbell. FaBoTw; PeSA
Luke XI: Blessed Be the Paps Which Thou Hast Sucked. Richard Crashaw. BXAP; JCP
Luke and John. Handwriting on the Wall. *Unknown.* AmFP
Luke Havergal. E. A. Robinson. AA; AmPP; AWP; GBL; LiTA; LiTM; MoAB; MoAmPo; NAAL-2; NoAM; NOBA; PoEL-5; QFR; UnPo
Luke Preach-Ill admires what we laymen can mean. The Insatiable Priest. Matthew Prior. OxBSP
Luke. Bible, *N.T. See* St. Luke.
Lula Vires. *Unknown.* AmFP
Lulee, lullay. Janet Lewis. NOCV
Lull, The. Molly Peacock. MAYP
Lullabie. *See* Lullaby.
Lullaby: "Beloved, may your sleep be sound." W. B. Yeats. BoLoP; FaBoTw; OBMV
Lullaby: "Din of work is subdued, The." W. H. Auden. FaBoMo; GLP; NoAM
Lullaby, A: "For wars his life and half a world away." Randall Jarrell. HCAP; OxBC
Lullaby: "Go to sleep, my baby." *Unknown, tr. by* Geoffrey Bownas *and* Anthony Thwaite. PeBJV
Lullaby: "Golden slumbers kiss your eyes." Thomas Dekker *and others. See* Pleasant Comedy of Patient Grissell [*or* Grissel *or* Grissill], The: Golden Slumbers.
Lullaby: "Hare, Mr. Hare." *Unknown, tr. by* Geoffrey Bownas *and* Anthony Thwaite. PeBJV
Lullaby: "Huge snowflakes dancing down." *Unknown, tr. by* Geoffrey Bownas *and* Anthony Thwaite. PeBJV
Lullaby: "Hush dove the summer." Miriam Waddington. CaP
Lullaby: "Hush, lullay." Léonie Adams. MoAB; MoAmPo
Lullaby, A: "Hush ye, hush ye! honey, darlin.'" Clara Ann Thompson. CBWP-2
Lullaby: "I wish to God my child was born." *Unknown.* AmFP
Lullaby: "In my memory you flare." Gerrit Achterberg, *tr. by* James Brockway. DuIn

Lullaby: "Is she sound asleep?" *Unknown, tr. by* Geoffrey Bownas *and* Anthony Thwaite. Mes; PeBJV
Lullaby: "Lay your sleeping head, my love." W. H. Auden. CMoP; GLP; HAP; LLLT; MoP; NAEL-2; NoAM; NOBE; OAEL-2; OxBTC; PoE; PPP; UnPo; WeW
　(Lay Your Sleeping Head, My Love.) BoLoP
　(Song XI: "Lay your sleeping head, my love.") EnLoPo
Lullaby: "Leopard, nocturnal, with eyes infernal, The." Tuvia Rübner, *tr. by* Bernhard Frank. MHeP
Lullaby: "Long canoe, The." Robert Hillyer. DuDa; FaPON
Lullaby: "Lullaby baby, lullaby baby." John Phillip. ELI
Lullaby: "Lullaby, lullaby." Phyllis L. Garlick. BoTP
Lullaby: "Lullee, lullay." Janet Lewis. CRP; NOCV
Lullaby: "More than all the stars in the sky." *Unknown, tr. by* Geoffrey Bownas *and* Anthony Thwaite. PeBJV
Lullaby: "O! hush thee, my darling, sleep soundly my son." *Unknown, tr. by* Alice Lucas. TrJP
Lullaby: "O men from the fields." Padraic Colum. *See* O men from the fields.
Lullaby: "O my son, born on a winter's morn." Noho-mai-te-Rangi, *tr. by* Barry Mitcalfe. WTO
Lullaby: Puva, puva, puva. *Unknown, tr. fr. Hopi Indian by* Natalie Curtis. TTTS
Lullaby: "Rockaby, lullaby, bees in the clover!" Josiah Gilbert Holland. *Fr.* The Mistress of the Manse. AA
Lullaby: "Sleep, baby, sleep." *Unknown, tr. by* Geoffrey Bownas *and* Anthony Thwaite. NOBE; PeBJV
Lullaby: "Sleep, little one, sleep." *Unknown, tr. by* Geoffrey Bownas *and* Anthony Thwaite. PeBJV
Lullaby: "Sleep, my little baby, sleep." Samuel Hoffenstein. TrJP
Lullaby: "Sleep now." Shlomo Vinner, *tr. by* Laya Firestone. VWA
Lullaby: "Someone would like to have you for her child." *Unknown.* TTTS
Lullaby, A: "Speak roughly to your little boy." "Lewis Carroll." *See* Alice's Adventures in Wonderland: Speak roughly to your little boy.
Lullaby: "Sweet and low, sweet and low." Tennyson. *See* Princess, The: Sweet and Low [Sweet and Low].
Lullaby: "Sweet love, everything/ closes its eyes now to sleep." Steve Kowit. TDD
Lullaby: "Than mind a child/ That yelps like this/ I'd all day work." *Unknown, tr. by* Geoffrey Bownas *and* Anthony Thwaite. Mes; PeBJV
Lullaby: "Though the world has slipped and gone." Dame Edith Sitwell. CMoP; LiTM; WaP
Lullaby: "Upon my lap my sovereign sits." Richard Verstegan. CH; EIL; OBEV
Lullaby: "Where has the guardian of sleep gone?" *Unknown, tr. by* Geoffrey Bownas *and* Anthony Thwaite. PeBJV
Lullaby: "Wide as this night, old as this night is old and young as it is young." Kenneth Fearing. CMoP
Lullaby: "Wind whistled loud at the window-pane, The." William Brighty Rands. BoTP
Lullaby: "With lights for eyes, our city turns." Dom Moraes. NePoEA-2
Lullaby: "You, orphan child." *Unknown, tr. by* Geoffrey Bownas *and* Anthony Thwaite. PeBJV
Lullaby, a Farewell, A. Sonya Dorman. BWV
Lullaby baby, lullaby baby. John Phillip. ELI
Lullaby for an Emigrant. Benjamin Fondane, *tr. fr. French by* Keith Bosley. VWA
Lullaby for Ann-Lucian. Calvin Forbes. PoBA
Lullaby for Familiars. Nancy Willard. BLA
Lullaby for Miriam. Richard Beer-Hofmann, *tr. fr. German by* Jonathan Griffin. VWA
Lullaby for My Dead Child. Denise Jallais, *tr. fr. French by* Maxine *and* Judith Kumin. BoWoP
Lullaby for the Hungry. Muhammad Mahdi al-Jawahiri, *tr. fr. Arabic by* Issa Boullata *and* John Heath-Stubbs. MAP
Lullaby for Titania. Shakespeare. *See* Midsummer Night's Dream, A: You Spotted Snakes [with Double Tongue].
Lullaby in Auschwitz. Pierre Morhange, *tr. fr. French by* Edouard Roditi. VWA
Lullaby, lullaby. Phyllis L. Garlick. BoTP
Lullaby, my little cat. Lullaby for Familiars. Nancy Willard. BLA
Lullaby, my little one. Carl Michael Bellman. FaPON
"Lullaby, O, lullaby!" A Serenade. Thomas Hood. *Fr.* Domestic Poems. NBLV
Lullaby [*or* Lullabie] of a Lover, The. George Gascoigne. AAS; EBEV; EIL; HAP; NAEL-1; QFR
　(A Lover's Lullaby.) OBEV

(Gascoigne's Lullaby [*or* Lullabie].) NoP; PoEL-1; TrGrPo
(Sing Lullaby, as Women Do.) InvP
Lullaby of an Infant Chief. Sir Walter Scott. EnRP; FaPON; OxBChV
Lullaby of the Nativity, A. *Unknown.* MeEL
Lullaby, sweet baby mine! A Danish Cradle Song. *Unknown.* BoTP
Lullaby Town. John Irving Diller. BLPA
Lullay, lullay, la, lullay. Jesus Reassures His Mother. *Unknown.* MeEL
Lullay My Liking. *Unknown. See* Lullaby of the Nativity, A.
Lulled, at silence, the spent attack. Baggot Street Deserta. Thomas Kinsella. CIP; CMoP; FaBCIP; IPY; NoAM
Lullee, lullay. Janet Lewis. CRP
Lulls swears he is all heart, but you'll suppose. Upon Lulls. Robert Herrick. CaPo
Lully, Lulla. *Unknown. See* Coventry Carol.
Lully, lulla, thou little tiny child. Coventry Carol. *Unknown.* ELP; MeEL; OFD; PChr; TTTS
Lully, lullay, lully, lullay. Corpus Christi Carol. *Unknown.* ChTr; GBP; MeEL; NAEL-1; NOBE; NoP; OAEL-1; OBD; SCV
(Bereaved Maid, The.) TrGrPo
(Corpus Christi.) FaBoBa
(Falcon, The.) ACP; LiTB; NU
(Knight of the Grail, The.) OBEV
(Lully, Lulley, Lully, Lulley.) CH; EBEV; HAP; WeW
Lumber of a London-going dray, The. An Incident in the Early Life of Ebenezer Jones, Poet, 1828. Sir John Betjeman. CMoP; MoP; NoAM
Lumber of Spring. Anne Ridler. NYBP
Lumbering tractor rolls its panting round, The. The Agricultural Show, Flemington, Victoria. "Furnley Maurice." CBAP
Lumberman's Alphabet, The. *Unknown.* AmFP
Lumberyard, The. Ruth Herschberger. LiTA; WPE
Luminare. Scott Minar. KS
Luminary of the Birds expires, The. To the Admirable Transubstantiation of the Roses into the Marvellous Image of Our Lady of Guadalupe. Luis de Sandoval y Zapata, *tr. by* Samuel Beckett. MexPo
Luminous, The. Barbara Guest. PoM
Luminous blaze! An Ode on Gas. *Unknown.* OBAL
Luminous cows, mysterious cows. The Cows of Heaven. Saleem Barakat, *tr. by* Lena Jayyusi *and* Naomi Shihab Nye. MAP
Luminous Night. Louis Simpson. CAPP
Lumps. Judith Thurman. RHPC
Lumumba's Grave ("Lumumba was black"). Langston Hughes. CNA
Luna puella pallidula. September 13, 1959 (Variation). Andrea Zanzotto, *tr. by* Lawrence R. Smith. NItP
Lunar Baedeker. Mina Loy. VGW
Lunar Eclipse. Diane Glancy. STE
Lunar Eclipse. Mei Yao-ch'en, *tr. fr. Chinese by* Burton Watson. CoBCP
Lunar Games, The. Eeva-Liisa Manner, *tr. fr. Finnish by* Jaakko A. Ahokas. WPOW
Lunar Stanzas. Henry Coggswell Knight. FaBoNo; NA
Lunatic, the Lover, and the Poet, The. Shakespeare. *Fr.* A Midsummer Night's Dream, V, i. FiP
(Imagination.) LiTB
Lunch. Kenneth Koch. SOTW
Lunch at the Coq d'Or. Peter Davison. TwCP
Lunch with Girl Scouts. Sharon Bryan. MAYP
Luncheon, A. Max Beerbohm. FaBoCo; NOBL; OBSV; OxBTC
Luncheon of the Boating Party, The. Leon Stokesbury. MT
Lunchroom bus boy who looked like Orson Welles, The. They Were All like Geniuses. Horace Gregory. *Fr.* The Passion of M'Phail. NYBP
Lungs draw in the air and rattle it out again, The. Remorse. Sir John Betjeman. MoBrPo; OxBSP
Lupercalia. Ted Hughes. CMoP
Lupus in Fabula. Malcolm Lowry. OBCV
(Xochitepec.) NOBC
Lurching from gloomy limousines we slip. My Father's Funeral. Karl Shapiro. DiL
Lure, The. John Boyle O'Reilly. TIRV
Lure, The. Steve Sneyd. BWV
Lure, falconers, lure! give warning to the field! For the Hern and Duck. *Unknown.* PBBP
Luriana, Lurilee. Charles Elton. Mes
Luscious and Sorrowful. Christina Rossetti. PoEL-5; SeCePo
Luscious lobster, with the crabfish raw, The. Kinds of Shel-fish. William Wood. SCAP
Lush emerald the summer color becomes. Teika, *tr. fr. Japanese by* Hiroaki Sato. *Fr.* Eighty-four Tanka. FCEI

Lush, lush, fragrant grasses in autumn green. Wang Wei, *tr. fr. Chinese by* Burton Watson. *Fr.* Joys of the Country: Seven Poems, 4. CoBCP
Lusiads, The, *sels.* Luis de Camões, *tr. fr. Portuguese by* Sir Richard Fanshawe. OBVE
"Now through the ocean in great haste they flunder."
"Shores are crown'd with people, The."
Luss! be for ever sunk beneath. Mercury; on Losing My Pocket Milton at Luss near Ben Lomond, and Other Mountains. Robert Andrews. NOEC
Lust. William Matthews. PCP
Lust of Gold, The. James Montgomery. *Fr.* The West Indies. PAH
Lustily, Lustily. *Unknown. Fr.* Common Conditions. OxBSS
Lustra, *sels.* Ezra Pound.
"Come, my songs, let me express our baser passions." PoA
(Further Instructions.) TwCP
"O helpless few in my country." PoA
(Rest, The.) AmPP; MoAB; MoAmPo; NoAM; NOBA; OxBA
Lustre of the flowers, The. Komachi, *tr. by* Geoffrey Bownas *and* Anthony Thwaite. PeBJV
Lusty Fryer of Flanders, The. *Unknown.* CoMu
Lusty is the young millet. *Unknown, tr. by* Arthur Waley. BoS
Lusty Juventus. Charles Madge. FaBoMo
Lusty Juventus, *sel.* Robert Wever.
"In a herber [*or* a harbour *or* an arbour] green [*or* grene], asleep [*or* aslepe] whereas [*or* where as *or* where] I lay."
(In an Arbour Green.) ELP
(In Youth Is Pleasure.) ChTr; NOBE; OBEV
(Of Youth He Singeth.) EIL
(Youth.) OBSC
Lusty May. *Unknown.* OBEV
(Four May Poems.) OxBS
Lute and the pear are your half sisters, The. A Flock of Guinea Hens Seen from a Car. Eudora Welty. GrPl; NYBP; PrIm
Lute, companion of my calamity. Louise Labé, *tr. by* Aliki *and* Willis Barnstone. BoWoP
Lute Music. Kenneth Rexroth. TAP
Lute Obeys, The. Sir Thomas Wyatt. *See* Blame Not My Lute for He Must Sound *or* Sownde.
Lutea Allison. Sir John Suckling. ErPo
Luther B——stepped from his air-conditioned house. I Hear America Griping. Morris Bishop. AmFN
Luther to a Bluebottle Fly. Eugene Lee-Hamilton. *Fr.* Imaginary Sonnets. Son
Lutra, the Fisher. James McMichael. AmPA
Luvin' wumman is a licht, A. Love. "Hugh MacDiarmid." CMoP; PoE
Lux in Tenebris. Katharine Tynan. TrPWD
Lux my fair falcon, and your fellows all. Sir Thomas Wyatt. NoP; OxBSP
(Epigram: "Lux, my fair falcon, and your fellows all.") SiPS
("Luckes, my faire falcon, and your fellowes all.") AAS
Luxurious house had a huge mirror, The. The Mirror in the Front Hall. Constantine P. Cavafy, *tr. by* Edmund Keeley *and* Philip Sherrard. PeHV
Luxurious man, to bring his vice in use. The Mower against Gardens. Andrew Marvell. EBEV; FaBoPV; LiTB; NAEL-1; NoP; OAEL-1; PoE; PoEL-2; PPP; SeCV-1
Luxury. Donald Justice. HeIP
Luxury of Sin. Joyce Carol Oates. KS
Luxury, then, is a way of. Political Poem. Amiri Baraka. CoAP; MoP; NAAL-2; NoAM
Luzumiyya. Abd al-Wahhab al-Bayyati, *tr. fr. Arabic by* Salma Khadra Jayyusi *and* Christopher Middleton. MAP
Luzzato. Charles Reznikoff. VWA
Lwonesomeness. William Barnes. NOBVV
Lyce. William Walsh. BoLoP
Lychee, The. Wang I, *tr. fr. Chinese by* Arthur Waley. FaBoCh
Lycias. Earl of Rochester. ErPo
Lycidas ("Yet once more, O ye laurels, and once more"). Milton. AWP; ChTr; EBEV; FiP; GTBS; GTBS-P; HAP; InPS; JCP; LiTB; NOBE; NoP; OAEL-1; OBEV; OBS; PoEL-3; PPP; PrIm; TrGrPo; UnPo; WeW; WGRP
Sels.
"Ay me! whilst thee the shores and sounding seas." Prf
Last Came, and Last Did Go. TW
"Weep no more, woful shepherds weep no more." FaBoRV
Lycidas and Moeris. Virgil, *tr. fr. Latin by* Dryden. *Fr.* Eclogues, IX. AWP
Lycon begin—begin the mournful tale. William Diaper. *Fr.* Nereides; or, Sea-Eclogues. SeCePo

Lycoris darling, once I burned for you. Martial, *tr. by* Peter Porter. BoLoP

Lydia. Lizette Woodworth Reese. AA

Lydia and Shirley have. Two Friends. Nikki Giovanni. ILY

Lydia, in Heavens Name. Horace, *tr. fr. Latin by* Sir Richard Fanshawe. *Fr.* Odes, I, 8. "Lydia, in Heaven's Name" ("Lydia, dic, per omnes"). OBVE

Lydia Is Gone This Many a Year. Lizette Woodworth Reese. CH; GoJo

Lydia Pinkham. *Unknown.* AS

Lying. Thomas Moore. FiBHP

Lying. Richard Wilbur. BLA; DiPo; HCAP; SV

Lying/ Lying as if dead. With Closed Eyes. Alois Vogel, *tr. by* Beth Bjorklund. CoAuP

Lying abed I heard the din of magpies in the grove. On Rising at Dawn and Seeing the Mountains. Hung Sheng, *tr. by* Paul W. Kroll. WFTU

Lying along the wide branch. Tiger People. Geary Hobson. STE

Lying apart now, each in a separate bed. One Flesh. Elizabeth Jennings. AIW; FaBoWP; OxBTC; PBWP

Lying asleep between the strokes of night. Love and Sleep. Swinburne. BoLoP

Lying at Leisure during Rain. Kao Ch'i, *tr. fr. Chinese by* Jonathan Chaves. CoBLCP

Lying at night poised between sleep and waking. East Coast—Canada. Elizabeth Brewster. CaP

Lying Awake. Thomas Hardy. FaBoRV

Lying Awake. W. D. Snodgrass. HoPM; MoAmPo; NYBP

Lying Awake Endlessly in Old Age. Kaai Chigetsu, *tr. fr. Japanese by* Hiroaki Sato. *Fr.* Thirteen Hokku. FCEI

Lying awake quietly at daybreak. Emperor Go-Shirakawa, *tr. fr. Japanese by* Hiroaki Sato. *Fr.* Ryojin Hisho. FCEI

Lying close to your heart-beat, my lips. Before Sleep. Fleur Adcock. *Fr.* Night-Piece, II. PeNZ

Lying disconsolate in new spring white wadded robes. Spring Rain. Li Shang-yin, *tr. by* Burton Watson. CoBCP

Lying Down. Robert Desnos, *tr. fr. French by* Bill Zavatsky. RHTwFP

Lying Down. *Unknown, tr. fr. Bella Bella Indian by* Franz Boas. STP

Lying here, everything in me. Margaret Atwood. NeAC

Lying here quietly beside you. Quietly. Kenneth Rexroth. ErPo

Lying in a Hammock at William Duffy's Farm in Pine Island, Minnesota. James Wright. CAPP; HAP; HCAP; HoPM; NaP; NOBA; OPOP

Lying in a Yuma Saloon. Jim Barnes. CDW

Lying in bed I hear two come nose to nose. Drag Race. Dave Smith. AnAn

Lying in bed in the dark, I hear the bray. Weather Ear. Norman Nicholson. OxBSP

Lying in the dark music. The Enigma Variations. Paul Petrie. NYBP

Lying in the dark together. One, Two. Mervyn Morris. PBCV

Lying in the Grass. Sir Edmund Gosse. EBVV

Lying in the sunshine among the buttercups and dandelions. Tribute to Grass. John James Ingalls. WBLP

Lying is an occupation. Laetitia Pilkington. WPE

Lying Muslims. *Yoruba Oral Tradition, tr. by* Ulli Beier. WTO

Lying on a Bridge. Van K. Brock. MT; SM

Lying on my pillow, I am startled to see. New Year's Day—Following the Rhymes of Inspector Luan-chiang. Pien Kung, *tr. by* Jonathan Chaves. CoBLCP

Lying on the ground, I pick young herbs. Issa, *tr. fr. Japanese by* Hiroaki Sato. *Fr.* Forty-four Hokku. FCEI

Lying quietly on the bed. David Ignatow. *Fr.* Leaving the Door Open. CAPP

Lying south of sweet Northumber. Rhymed Mnemonic of the Forty Counties of England. Donald Monat. FaBoUs

Lying under the stars. The Heart of Herakles. Kenneth Rexroth. *Fr.* The Lights in the Sky are Stars. NU

Lying with no love on the paper. Untidy Dreadful Table. William Sydney Graham. PoPo

Lying with unstable pego 'twixt a brace of vigorous boys. To Phoebus. Martial. PeHV

Lying, with You. Ernst Jandl, *tr. fr. German by* Beth Bjorklund. CoAuP

Lyk as the dum. The Solsequium. Alexander Montgomerie. GoTS; NoP; OxBS

Lyke as a huntsman after weary chace. *See* Like as a huntsman after weary chace.

Lyke-Wake Dirge, The [*or* A]. *Unknown.* CH; ChTr; EaLo; FaBoCh; FaBoRV; GBP; HAP; HoPM; NOBE; NoP; OBEV; PoEL-1; WeW

Lynched Negro. Maxwell Bodenheim. PoNe

Lynching, The. Claude McKay. BANP; IDB; PoBA

Lynching. Lizelia Augusta Jenkins Moorer. CBWP-3

Lynching. Berysh Vaynshteyn, *tr. fr. Yiddish by* Benjamin *and* Barbara Harshav. *Fr.* Negroes. AYP

Lynching and Burning. Primus St. John. PoBA

Lynx, The. Charles Edward Eaton. DiPo

Lynx. Ben Howard. GrPl

Lynx. Mirko Lauer, *tr. fr. Spanish by* David Tipton. Per

Lynx. R. A. D. Ford. CaP

Lyons Pawes. Shakespeare. *See* Sonnets, XIX.

Lyre-Bird, The. Roland Robinson. PoAu-2

Lyre of the sonnet, that fully many a time. Written December 1790. Anna Seward. Son

Lyre Player, The. Stefan George, *tr. by* Carol North Valhope *and* Ernst Morowitz. PeHV

Lyrebirds. Judith Wright. GoJo

Lyric: "Embodiment of what, The." Arthur Gregor. TAP

Lyric: "From now on kill America out of your mind." James Agee. GOA

Lyric: "I touched a shining mote of sand." Philip Child. CaP

Lyric, A: "If time and space, as sages say." T. S. Eliot. FL

Lyric: "Let but a thrush begin." John Hewitt. NeIP

Lyric: You Would Have Understood Me. Paul Verlaine, *tr. fr. French by* Ernest Dowson. BoLoP; MoBrPo; NOBVV

Lyric Barber. Liboria E. Romano. GoYe

Lyric by Nine. *Unknown.* EAS

Lyric from a Play, A. *Unknown.* MeEL

Lyric[k] for Legacies. Robert Herrick. FaBoRV; JCP; OBS

Lyric night of the lingering Indian Summer. September Midnight. Sara Teasdale. PoA

Lyric to Mirth, A. Robert Herrick. CaPo

Lyric to Spring. Joseph W. Stilwell. OBAL

Lyrics, *sels.* James Agee. MoAmPo
   "I loitered weeping with my bride for gladness."
   "No doubt left. Enough deceiving."
   "Not met and marred with the year's whole turn of grief."

Lyrics of the Bon Dance. *Unknown, tr. fr. Japanese by* Geoffrey Bownas *and* Anthony Thwaite. PeBJV

Lysidike dedicates. Kenneth Rexroth, *after the Greek of* Asklepiades. NNaP

Lysistrata, *sel.* Aristophanes, *tr. fr. Greek by* B. B. Rogers. How the Women Will Stop War. WaaP

Lytell Treatyse for to Lerne Englysshe and Frens, A, *sels. Unknown.* OxBLMV
   For to Aske the Waye.
   Pour demander le chemin.

Lyth and listen, gentlemen. Robin Hood and the Beggar, II. *Unknown.* ESPB

Lythe and listin, gentilmen. A Gest of Robyn Hode. *Unknown.* ESPB; OxBB

Lyttel Boy, The. Eugene Field. AA

Lyve thowe gladly, yff so thowe may. Sir Thomas Wyatt. AAS

M

M. A. P. Calvin Forbes. MAYP

M. Crashaw's Answer for Hope. Richard Crashaw. *See* For Hope.

M. le professeur in prominent senility. My Neighbor in the Mirror. Louise Glück. Son

M. l'Epicier in his white hat. Soissons. Keith Douglas. NoAM

M Sgt. Robert G. Levi 1915-1943. Uncle Robert. Robert Morgan. GeTw

M., Singing. Louise Bogan. GoJo; LiTA; NoAM

M 13. Harry Bose. *Fr.* Seven One-Line Poems. BWV

Ma & I were at Louise's house. The Contest of Nerves. Patricia Traxler. TV

Ma Canny Hinny. *Unknown.* FaBoPP; GBP

Ma Jesus. Troubled Jesus. Waring Cuney. BANP

Ma lass by munelicht fesht me frae the fail. The Deean Tractorman, Deleerit. Edith Anne Robertson. OxBS

Ma-wei. Yüan Mei, *tr. fr. Chinese by* Jonathan Chaves. CoBLCP

Mab. Ben Jonson. *See* Satyr, The: Mab the Mistress-Fairy.

Mab the Mistress-Fairy. Ben Jonson. *Fr.* The Satyr. ElL

Mabel Kelly. Turlough Carolan, *tr. fr. Irish by* Austin Clarke. BIrV; CIP

Mabel Woo. Belle Randall. *Fr.* A Hundred Ways of Playing Solitaire. CRP

Mabrak. "Bongo Jerry." PBCV

Macadam, gun-grey as the tunny's belt. Van Winkle. Hart Crane. *Fr.* The Bridge: Powhatan's Daughter. AmPP; FaBV; MoAB; MoAmPo

Macadam Road Remembers, The. István Csukás, *tr. fr. Hungarian by* Barbara Howes. MHuP

McAfee's Confession ("Draw near, young men, and learn of me"). *Unknown.* AmFP

Macaffie's Confession ("Now come young men and list to me"). *Unknown.* BeLS

McAndrew's Hymn. Kipling. OxBTC
   (M'Andrew's Hymn.) PoEL-5

Macaulay at Tea. Barry Pain. *Fr.* The Poets at Tea, I. CenHV; Par

Macavity: The Mystery Cat. ("Macavity's a mystery cat"). T. S. Eliot. CenHV; CRH; FaBoCo; InPS; NBLV; NOBL; OBCA; OnUR; OxBChV; PoRA; RB

Macaw preens upon a branch outspread, A. Decoration. Louise Bogan. MoAB; MoAmPo

Macbeth. Andrew of Wyntoun. OxBS

Macbeth, *sels.* Shakespeare.
   "Hang out our banners on the outward walls." *Fr.* V, v. EBEV
   "I have done the deed—Didst thou not hear a noise?." *Fr.* II, ii. EBEV
   (Macbeth Does Murder Sleep.) FiP
   I Have Lived Long Enough. *Fr.* V, iii. TrGrPo
   "If it were done when 'tis done, then 'twere well." *Fr.* I, vii. UnPo
   (Vaulting Ambition.) FiP
   O! Full of Scorpions. *Fr.* III, ii. FiP
   "She should have died hereafter." *Fr.* V, v. DL; SoSe
   "Wherefore was that cry?" FiP, *sl. longer sel.*
   Song of the Witches. RHPC
   (Charm, The.) EiL
   Tomorrow, and Tomorrow, and Tomorrow. FaBoRV; FaFP; FF; LiTB; TrGrPo, *sl. shorter sel.*
   (Out, Out, Brief Candle!) ChTr
   Thrice the Brinded Cat Hath Mewed. *Fr.* IV, i. InVP; OFD; RB; WSC

Macbeth. Horace *and* James Smith Smith. BXAP

Macbeth Does Murder Sleep. Shakespeare. *See* Macbeth:
   I have done the deed—Didst thou not hear a noise?

McCaffery. *Unknown.* OBET

McDonald's, New Hartford, NY. Valerie Worth. AiP

Macdonald's Raid. Paul Hamilton Hayne. PAH

McDonogh Day in New Orleans. Marcus B. Christian. AmNP; PoNe

MacDuff. Charles Tomlinson. NAs; OxBC

Maceo. Luis Lloréns Torres, *tr. fr. Spanish.* InW, *tr. by* Julio Marzán

MacFlecknoe; or, A Satire [*or* Satyr] upon the True-Blue [*or*-Blew] Protestant Poet T. S. ("All human[e] things are subject to decay."), *sel.* Dryden. HAP, *abr.*; NoP; OAEL-1; OBSV; OxBoLi; QFR; TEP
   "All human[e] things are subject to decay." SCV; TrGrPo
   (Crown Prince of Dullness, The.) NOBE
   (Poet Shadwell, The.) FiP
   (Primacy of Dullness, The.) OBS

MacGregor's Gathering. Sir Walter Scott. OxBS

Machberoth, *sels.* Immanuel di Roma, *tr. fr. Hebrew by* J. Chotzner. TrJP
   Oh, Let Thy Teachings.
   Virtue.

Macheath and Polly. John Gay. *See* Beggar's Opera, The: Were I laid on Greenland's coast.

Machine-gun bullets, The. Mexico, August 20, 1940. Ai. NoAM

Machine gunner aims, A. El Alamein. Steve Crow. HATNAP

Machine to make noise, A. Useless Machine. André Frénaud, *tr. by* Serge Gavronsky. RHTwFP

Machu Picchu, Peru. Fred Red Cloud. NOVW

Machupuchare. What the Mountain Said. Shaking the Dead Bones, Christmas Eve, 1974. Joseph Stroud. NPGG

McIlrath of Malate. John Jerome Rooney. PAH

Macinnes's Mountain Patrol. Tom Patey. PoSH

McIntosh Apple. Steven Kroll. RHPC

McIntyre and Ross. Sorley MacLean. PoPo

Mackerel. Wayne Brown. UAS

Mackerel-man drives down the street, The. A Pretty Ambition. Mary E. Wilkins Freeman. OBCA

Mackerel sky. *Unknown.* *Fr.* Weather Wisdom. FaBoUs; OxNR

McKinley. *Unknown.* PAH

Mackinnon's Boat. Charles Tomlinson. AnAn

McLean's Welcome. James Hogg. OxBS

McLuhan Transposed. Suzette Haden Elgin. BWV

McNaughtan. *Unknown.* OxBB

Macquarie Place. Robert David Fitzgerald. PoAu-2

Macrinus against Trees. "Michael Field." WPE

Macrocarpas. Michael Jackson. PeNZ

Macrocosm. Philip Child. CaP

Mad, The. Robert Pinsky. *Fr.* Essay on Psychiatrists, XVIII. NoAM

Mad Answer of a Madman, A. Robert Hayman. FF

Mad are predators, The. Too often lately they harbor. Geoffrey Hill. *Fr.* Mercian Hymns, VIII. NoP

Mad as the Mist and Snow. W. B. Yeats. ChTr

Mad Berkeley believed, with his gay cavaliers. The Burning of Jamestown. Thomas Dunn English. PAH

Mad Day in March. Philip Levine. NYBP

Mad Dogs and Englishmen. Noel Coward. CenHV; FiBHP; NBLV; NOBL; OBTV

Mad Fight Song for William S. Carpenter, 1966, A. James Wright. NoAM

Mad Gardener's Song, The. "Lewis Carroll." *Fr.* Sylvie and Bruno. BLPL; FaBoCo; FaBoNo; FiBHP, 6 *sts.*; NA; OnUR, 4 *sts.*; OxBChV; WiR

Mad girl with the staring eyes and long white fingers, The. Cassandra. Robinson Jeffers. HeIP; LiTA; LiTM; WaP

Mad Hatter's Song, The. "Lewis Carroll." *Fr.* Alice's Adventures in Wonderland, *ch.* 7. FaBoNo; NOBL; Par

Mad Lover, The, *sels.* John Fletcher.
   Arm, Arm, Arm, Arm! *Fr.* V, iv. EiL
   "O divine star of heaven." *Fr.* IV, i. GBL
   "Orpheus I am, come from the deeps below." *Fr.* IV, i. GBL

Mad Maid's Song, The. Robert Herrick. AWP; CaPo; CH; EnLoPo; OAEL-1; OBEV; SeCV-1; TrGrPo; WiR

Mad Marjory. Hugh McCrae. PoAu-1

Mad Negro Soldier Confined at Munich, A. Robert Lowell. FaBoMo; OxBC

Mad of mind, The. Asadullah Khan Ghalib, *tr. by* Ahmed Ali. GoT

Mad Patsy said, he said to me. In the Poppy Field. James Stephens. PoRA

Mad Pomegranate Tree, The. Odysseus Elytis, *tr. fr. Greek by* Edmund Keeley *and* Philip Sherrard. VMG

Mad Queen Aeronautical Corporation. . Cyclone. 3030. Telephone Directory. Harry Crosby. EAS

Mad Scene, The. James Merrill. CoAP; NOBA; PoA; PoE; TAP

Mad Song. Blake. *Fr.* Poetical sketches. EnRP; NAEL-2; NOEC; OAEL-2; PoE; PoEL-4; PrIm; TEP; TrGrPo

Mad Song. Denise Levertov. TAP

Mad Sonnet 1. Michael McClure. PoM

Mad Sweeney. *Unknown.* *See* Sweeney the Mad.

Mad Sweeny. John Montague. FaBCIP

Mad Town, The. István Vas, *tr. fr. Hungarian by* William Jay Smith. MHuP

Mad Woman. Suad al-Mubarak al-Sabah, *tr. fr. Arabic by* May Jayyusi *and* John Heath-Stubbs. MAP

Mad Woman of Punnet's Town, The. L. A. G. Strong. MoBrPo

Mad Words. Yüan Mei, *tr. fr. Chinese by* J. P. Seaton. WFTU

Madaket Beach. Isabel Harriss Barr. GoYe

Madam,/ If you're deceived, it is not by my cheat. A Very Heroical Epistle in Answer to Ephelia. John Wilmont, 2nd Earl of Rochester. APAS

Madam and the Minister. Langston Hughes. NOBA

Madam Eglantine. Chaucer. *See* Canterbury Tales, The: Prologue.

Madam Hickory. Wilbur Larremore. AA

Madam if you please. Christopher Smart. FL

Madam Life's a Piece in Bloom. W. E. Henley. EBVV; NAEL-2; OPOP
   (Madam Life.) MoBrPo; TrGrPo
   (To W. R.) NOBVV; OBD

Madam Mouse Trots. Edith Sitwell. FaBoCh

Madam, no more! The time has come to eat. A. D. Hope. ErPo; NoP

Madam, 'tis true, your beauties move. Sidney Godolphin. JCP

Madam, twice through the Muses Grove I walkt. Upon Mrs. Anne Bradstreet Her Poems. John Rogers. SCAP

Madam, wearing a wig, has the calm jaws of a cow. Roxy's. Patrick Conrad, *tr. by* Peter Nijmeijer. DuIn

Madam, withouten Many Words. *See* Madame, withouten Many Wordes.

Madam would speak with me. So, now it comes. George Meredith. *Fr.* Modern Love, XXXIV. NOBVV

Madam, you are right, the fight was a great pity. To the Woman in Bond Street Station. Edward Weismiller. LiTA; WaP

Madam, your face half-hidden by your hair. Stephen Spender. FL

Madame. George McWhirter. UAS

Madame d'Albert's Laugh. Clément Marot, *tr. fr. French by* Leigh Hunt. AWP

Madame Dill. *Unknown.* FiBHP

Madame, had all antiquitie been lost. To Mary Lady Wroth. Ben Jonson. OBS

Madame hates men who with a look will gnash. The Woman in the Arts. Gerrit Komrij, tr. by Jacob Lowland. DuIn

Madame, his grace will not be absent long. Cyril Tourneur. Fr. The Revenger's Tragedy, III, v. PoEL-2

Madame, I Have Come a-Courting. Unknown. AmFP

Madame Maynard of the hard pebble. Stranded in My Ontario. Ronald G. Everson. NOBC

Madame Orchidée. Sherod Santos. AnAn

Madame [or Madam], withouten Many Wordes [or Words]. Sir Thomas Wyatt. AAS; EnLoPo; NAEL-1; NoP; OBVE; OxBSP; SiPS
(To a Lady to Answer Directly with Yea or Nay.) EiL
(To His Lady.) OBSC; SeCePo

Madame, ye been [or ben] of alle [or all or al] beautee [or beaute] shrine [or shryne]. To Rosamond. Chaucer. NoP
(Ballade to Rosamund.) MeEL
(To Rosamound.) OAEL-1; PoE

Madam's Past History. Langston Hughes. MoP; NoAM

Madboy's Song. Muriel Rukeyser. MoAmPo; TrJP

Mädchen mit dem rothen Mündchen. Heine, tr. fr. German by Sir Theodore Martin. AWP

Made in his maker's image? Tree of Knowledge. Edward Lowbury. VWA

Made in the Hot Weather. W. E. Henley. See Fountains that frisk and sprinkle.

Made Shine. Josephine Miles. NoAM

Made up in death as never in life. Hands. Anne Stevenson. BLA

Madeleine Verchères. William Drummond of Hawthronden. CaP

Madge Wildfire Sings. Sir Walter Scott. See Heart of Midlothian, The: Proud Maisie ("Proud Maisie is in the wood").

Madge Wildfire's [Death] Song. Sir Walter Scott. See Heart of Midlothian, The: Proud Maisie ("Proud Maisie is in the wood").

Madhav, even those who haven't a shred of worth. Surdas, tr. by John Stratton Hawley and Mark Juergensmeyer. SSI

Madhav, please, control that cow. Surdas, tr. by John Stratton Hawley and Mark Juergensmeyer. SSI

Madhav, you'll find none duller than I. Tulsidas, tr. by John Stratton Hawley and Mark Juergensmeyer. SSI

Madhouse, The. Jared Carter. MOWH

Madhouse. Calvin C. Hernton. IDB; PoNe
(Patient: Rockland County Sanitarium, The.) PoBA

Madhouse. Mustafa Zaidi, tr. fr. Urdu by Mahmood Jamal. PBMUP

Madison Square. A. Leyeles, tr. fr. Yiddish. Fr. New York. AYP, tr. by Benjamin and Barbara Harshav; VWA, tr. by Keith Bosley.

Madly Singing in the Mountains. Po Chü-i, tr. fr. Chinese by Arthur Waley. Mes

Madman, The. S. J. Pretorius, tr. fr. Afrikaans by Uys Krige and Jack Cope. PeSA

Madman's Song, The. John Webster. Fr. The Duchess of Malfi, IV, ii. EiL
(Song: "O, let us howl some heavy note.") InvP

Madman's Song. Elinor Wylie. MoAB; MoAmPo; PoRA

Madman's Wife, The. Steve Orlen. MAYP

Madness. John Armstrong. Fr. The Art of Preserving Health. NOEC

Madness. Robert Browning. Fr. The Dance of Death. FL

Madness. James Dickey. NYBP

Madness. Yoshihara Sachiko, tr. fr. Japanese by James Kirkup and Shozo Tokunaga. BoWoP

Madness, I shall betray you. In all my poems. The Break-up. László Nagy, tr. by George MacBeth. MHuP

Madness of King Goll, The. W. B. Yeats. NAEL-2

Madonna. Ian Wedde. Fr. Earthly: Sonnets for Carlos, 1. ATNZ

Madonna in the Subway, The. A. Leyeles, tr. fr. Yiddish by Benjamin and Barbara Harshav. AYP

Madonna Natura. "Fiona Macleod." WGRP

Madonna of the Evening Flowers. Amy Lowell. PeHV; UnAS

Madras,/ 1965, and rain. Some Indian Uses of History on a Rainy Day. A. K. Ramanujan. OxBC

Madre Sofía. Alberto Ríos. NoAM

Madrid. "Pai Wei", tr. fr. Chinese by Kenneth Rexroth and Ling Chung. PBWP

Madrigal. Francis Davison. See Some there are as fair to see too.

Madrigal, A: "Crabbed age and youth." Shakespeare. See Passionate Pilgrim, The: Crabbed Age and Youth.

Madrigal: "Ay me, alas, heigh ho, heigh ho!" Thomas Weelkes. FaBoCh; OxBLi

Madrigal: "Beauty [or Beautie], and the life, The." William Drummond of Hawthornden. EiL; PoEL-2
(Her Passing.) OBEV

Madrigal: "Come let's begin to revel't out." Unknown. BoTP

Madrigal: "Dear, when I did from you remove." Lord Herbert of Cherbury. EiL

Madrigal: "Diana, naked in the shadowy pool." Petrarch, tr. by Morris Bishop. PFI

Madrigal: "Ha ha! ha ha! This world doth pass." Unknown. See Fara Diddle Dyno.

Madrigal: "How should I love my best?" Herbert of Cherbury. PoEL-2; SeCP

Madrigal: "I always loved to call my lady Rose." Unknown. EiL

Madrigal: "Ivory, coral, gold, The." William Drummond of Hawthornden. See Ivory, Coral, Gold, The.

Madrigal: "Like the Idalian Queen [e]." William Drummond of Hawthornden. EiL; ELP; GBL; InvP; NOBE; OAEL-1; OBEV; OBS; PoEL-2
(Inexorable.) NOBE; OBEV
(Like the Idalian Queen.) GoTS; SeCePo

Madrigal: "Love now no fire hath left him." Giovanni Battista Marino, tr. by Richard Crashaw. OBVE

Madrigal: Madrigal. William Drummond of Hawthornden. CH; EiL; GTBS; GTBS-P; OAEL-1; OBS; SeCePo; TrGrPo
(This Life.) CH; TrGrPo

Madrigal: "My love in her attire doth show her wit." Unknown. See My Love in Her Attire.

Madrigal: "My mistress frowns when she should play,." John Hilton. OxBoLi
(Fa La La.) CH

Madrigal: "My mistress is as fair as fine." Thomas Ravenscroft. CH; OxBoLi

Madrigal 121: "Now Love, see how this lady, young and fair." Petrarch, tr. by Marion Shore. PFI

Madrigal: "Poor turtle, thou bemoans." William Drummond of Hawthornden. PBBP

Madrigal: "Ravished by all that to the eyes is fair." Michelangelo. See Three Poems: Ravished by all that to the eyes is fair.

Madrigal: "Since Bonny-boots was dead, that so divinely." Unknown. See Since Bonny-Boots Was Dead.

Madrigal: "Sister, awake! close not your eyes." Unknown. See Sister, Awake!

Madrigal: "Some there are as fair to see to." Francis Davison. EiL

Madrigal: "Sound of thy sweet name, my dearest treasure, The." Francis Davison. EiL

Madrigal: "Tell me where is fancy bred." Shakespeare. See Merchant of Venice, The: Tell Me Where Is Fancy [or Fancie] Bred.

Madrigal: "This world a hunting is." William Drummond of Hawthornden. OxBSP

Madrigal: "To be a whore. . ." Charles Cotton. FaBoEE

Madrigal: To His Lady Selvaggia Vergiolesi; Likening His Love to a Search for Gold. Cino da Pistoia, tr. fr. Italian by Dante Gabriel Rossetti. AWP; PFI

Madrigal: "Unhappie Light." William Drummond of Hawthornden. OBS

Madrigal: "When in her face mine eyes I fix." William Alexander, Earl of Stirling. Fr. Aurora. EiL

Madrigal: "Why dost thou haste away?" Sir Philip Sidney. Fr. Arcadia. OBSC; SiPS

Madrigal: "You kiss me like a sister." Pauline de Simiane, tr. by Dorothy Backer. DMF

Madrigal: "Your love is dead, lady, your love is dead." Ronald Stuart Thomas. BoLoP; EnLoPo

Madrigal de Verano. Federico García Lorca, tr. fr. Spanish by Paul Blackburn. ErPo

Madroño. Bret Harte. AA

Madwoman at Rodmell. Michele Roberts. BrRo

Madwoman of Papine, The. Abdur-Rahman Slade Hopkinson. PBCV

Madwoman on the Train, The. Alfred Wellington Purdy. NoAM

Madwomen of the Plaza del Mayo, The. Eli W. Mandel. NOBC

Mae West. Edward Field. FYAP

Mae's Rent Party. Ernest J. Wilson, Jr.. PoNe

Maesia's Song. Robert Greene. Fr. Farewell to Folly. CTC; OBSC; UnPo
(Mind Content, A.) EiL; ViBoPo
(Poor Estate, The.) TrGrPo
(Song: "Sweet are the thoughts that savour of content.") PoEL-2

Maestro's Barber Shop, The. Ricardo Vásquez, tr. fr. Spanish by Toni Empringham. FIA

Mafukuzela, rain-giving clouds. Lament for Mafukuzela. Zulu Oral Tradition, tr. by H. Tracey. WTO

Mag Uidhir's Winter Campaign. Eochadh O'Hussey. NOIV

Magaiça. Noémia da Sousa, tr. fr. Portuguese by Margaret Dickinson. WMBCH

Magalu. Helene Johnson. BlSi; CDC; PoBA; PoNe

Magazine Fort, Phoenix Park, Dublin, The. William Wilkins. SeCePo

Magdalen, The. Sir Edward Sherburne. *See* And She Washed His Feet with Her Tear[e]s, and Wiped Them with the Hairs of Her Head.
Magdalen at Michael's gate. At Glastonbury. Henry Kingsley. PoRA
Magdalen Walks. Oscar Wilde. EBVV; MoBrPo
Maggie. Duane Niatum. HATNAP
Maggie. *Unknown.* OnUR
Maggie and Milly and Molly and May. E. E. Cummings. NoAM; NOBA; RB; RHPC
Maggie Lauder. *At.* to Francis Sempill. OBS; OxBS
Maggie Mac. *Unknown.* AmFP
Maggie's Star. Charles Tennyson Turner. FM
Magi, The. George Garrett. MT
Magi, The. Louise Glück. PoA
Magi, The. Ramon Guthrie. PoE
Magi, The. Milton. *Fr.* On the Morning of Christ's Nativity, 2 *ll.* ChTr
Magi, The. W. B. Yeats. BrPo; CMoP; FaBoRV; HAP; InPK; NoAM; OAEL-2; OFD; PChr; PoA; PoE; TrCP
Magi in Europe, The. Khalil Hawi, *tr. fr. Arabic by* Diana Der Hovanessian *and* Lena Jayyusi. MAP
Magic. Judith Herzberg, *tr. fr. Dutch by the author.* DuIn
Magic. Ovid, *tr. fr. Latin. Fr.* Metamorphoses, VII. AWP, *tr. by* Shakespeare.
   Medea's Incantation. OBVE, *tr. by* Arthur Golding.
Magic. Shakespeare. *See* Tempest, The: Ye elves of hill, brooks, standing lakes, and groves.
Magic/ my man. Black Magic. Sonia Sanchez. BPo
Magic Apple Tree, The. Elaine Feinstein. BrRo
Magic Car Moved On, The. Shelley. *Fr.* Queen Mab, I. GN
Magic Casements. Keats. *Fr.* Ode to a Nightingale. FaBV
Magic dance, The. After the Ball. Imamu Amiri Baraka. NAAL-2
Magic dragon may hibernate in here, A. Cutstone Pond. Chao Meng-fu, *tr. fr. Chinese by* Jonathan Chaves. *Fr.* Twenty-Eight Poems Inscribed on T'ien-kuan Mountai. CoBLCP
Magic Flute, The. W. D. Snodgrass. NYBP
Magic Fox. James Welch. CDW; HATNAP; NoAM
Magic Mist, A. Owen Roe O'Sullivan, *tr. fr. Irish by* Thomas Kinsella. NOIV
Magic mists twirl around the sky. Inscribed on a Painting ("Magic mists twirl around the sky"). Yün Shou-p'ing, *tr. by* Jonathan Chaves. CoBLCP
Magic Mountain, A. Czeslaw Milosz, *tr. fr. Polish by* Lillian Vallee. AnAn
Magic of the day is the morning, The. Ballad of the Morning Streets. Imamu Amiri Baraka. CNA; SOTW; TTTS
Magic Piper, The. E. L. Marsh. BoTP
Magic step of unfinished nights. Approach. Tristan Tzara, *tr. by* Lee Harwood. RHTwFP
Magic Whistle, The. Margaret Rose. BoTP
Magic Wood, The. Henry Treece. EAS
Magic Words [for Hunting Caribou]. *Unknown, tr. fr. Eskimo by* Jerome Rothenberg *and* Johnny John. NU; STP
Magic Words for Hunting Seal. *Unknown, tr. fr. Eskimo by* Edward Field. STP
Magic Words to Feel Better. Nakasuk, *tr. fr. Eskimo by* Jerome Rothenberg. STP
Magical course of unending nights. Approach. Tristan Tzara, *tr. by* Michael Benedikt. POS
Magical Eraser. Shel Silverstein. WSC
Magical Mouse, The. Kenneth Patchen. SO
Magical prognosticator. Halloween Witches. Felice Holman. WSC
Magician, The. Gary Miranda. SM
Magician, The. Bin Ramke. MAYP; NAmP
Magician and the Baron's Daughter, The. *Unknown. See* Draw me nere [or near], draw me nere [or near].
Magician Suspends the Children, The. Carole Oles. SoSe
Magma. G. J. F. Dutton. PoSH
Magna Est Veritas. Coventry Patmore. *See* Unknown Eros, The: Here, in This Little Bay.
Magna Est Veritas. Stevie Smith. OxBC
Magnanimous, The. Ellen de Young Kay. NePoEA
Magnet, The. Thomas Stanley. MePo; NOBE
Magnet, The. Ruth Stone. MoAmPo
Magnet hung in a hardware shop, A. The Fable of the Magnet and the Churn. W. S. Gilbert. *Fr.* Patience. FaPON; OnMSP
Magnetic. Sándor Weöres, *tr. fr. Hungarian by* Jascha Kessler. FOC
Magnetic Mountain, The, *sels.* C. Day Lewis.
   Nearing Again the Legendary Isle. *Fr.* VI. FaBoTw; LiTB; MoAB; MoBrPo

Tempt Me No More. *Fr.* XXIV. MoAB; MoBrPo; OBMV; PoA
Third Enemy Speaks. *Fr.* XXI. EaLo
Magnetized. Arthur Sze. BrSi
Magnificat. Michele Roberts. BrRo
Magnificat, The. Bible, *N.T. Fr.* St. Luke, I: 46-56. BoWoP; WGRP ("And Marie said, My soule doth magnifie the Lord.") OBVE
Magnificent Bull, The. *Dinka Oral Tradition.* TTTS
Magnificent snow/ Has fallen here at my place. Emperor Temmu. *Fr.* Manyo Shu. Ma
Magnolia. Mary Weston Fordham. CBWP-2
Magnolia Flower, The. Mao Hsi-chen, *tr. fr. Chinese by* Lois Fusek. ATF
Magnolia Flower, The. Wei Ch'eng-pan, *tr. fr. Chinese by* Lois Fusek. ATF
Magnolia Flower, The. Wei Chuang, *tr. fr. Chinese by* Lois Fusek. ATF
Magnolia trees, The. Genealogy. Frank Lamont Phillips. AmNP
Magnolia's Shadow, The. Robert Lowell. NaP, *ad. fr. the Italian of* Eugenio Montale.
Magpie. Peter Davison. GrPl
Magpie and Pines. Louis Johnson. ATNZ; PeNZ
Magpie, magpie, flutter and flee. *Unknown.* OxNR
Magpie Rhyme, Northumberland, A. *Unknown.* GBP
Magpie Song. *Unknown, tr. fr. Navajo Indian by* Washington Matthews. AnAmPo
Magpie! The Magpie! Here underneath, The. Magpie Song. *Unknown, tr. by* Washington Matthews. AnAmPo
Magpie vicious or mute on his frozen tree, The. Vincent O'Sullivan. *Fr.* Brother Jonathan, Brother Kafka, 42. ATNZ
Magpies, The. Denis Glover. ATNZ; PeNZ
Magpies in Picardy. T. P. Cameron Wilson. MMA
Mag's Song. *Unknown.* AS
Maguire is not afraid of death, the Church will light him a candle. Patrick Kavanagh. *Fr.* The Great Hunger. CIP
Magus, A. John Ciardi. MAT
Magus, The. James Dickey. NAs
Mahabalipuram. Louis MacNeice. OBTV
Mahabharata, The, *sel. Unknown, tr. fr. Sanskrit by* Franklin Edgerton. "So, pure and dutiful, she sought that place." DL
Maharani of midnight tresses, The. In the Seraglio. David R. Slavitt. ErPo; PeHV
Mahler, *sel.* Jonathan Williams.
   Symphony No. 3, in D Minor. VGW
Mahoney. Sean Jennett. NeIP
Mahony's Mountain. Douglas Stewart. PoAu-2; SeCePo
Mahratta Ghats, The. Alun Lewis. OBTV; OBWVE
Mahuta. Alistair Campbell. ATNZ
Maid, The. Theodore Goodridge Roberts. MoShBr
Maid and the Palmer, The. *Unknown.* ACP; ESPB
Maid comes into the hall, The. Lunar Eclipse. Mei Yao-ch'en, *tr. by* Burton Watson. CoBCP
Maid Freed from the Gallows, The. *Unknown.* AMFP; AS, *with music*; AWP; ESPB
Maid, I dare not tell her name, A. The Nameless Maiden. *Unknown.* ErPo
Maid in the Mill, The, *sel.* John Fletcher *and* William Rowley. "Now having leisure, and a happy wind." *Fr.* V, i. GBL
Maid Marian, *sels.* Thomas Love Peacock.
   For the Slender Beech and the Sapling Oak. EnRP
   (Song: "For the tender beech and the sapling oak.") OHIP Friar, The. SD
Maid Marjory sits at the castle gate. Medieval Norman Song. *Unknown, tr. by* John Addington Symonds. AWP
Maid o' the West, The. John Clare. OAEL-2
Maid of Arc, The. Gordon Bottomley. GoTL
Maid of Athens [Ere We Part]. Byron. EBEV; EnRP; FaBV; FaFP; PrIm
Maid of Brenten Arse, A. *Unknown.* GBP
Maid of Ehrenthal, The. Henrietta Cordelia Ray. CBWP-3
Maid of Honour, The, *sel.* Philip Massinger. "Look on this maid of honour, now." *Fr.* V, ii. ACP
Maid of Kent, A. *Unknown.* OxBoLi
Maid of Monterey, The. *Unknown.* AmFP
Maid of Neidpath, The. Thomas Campbell. GoTS; GTBS; GTBS-P
Maid of Neidpath, The. Sir Walter Scott. BeLS; EnRP; GTBS; GTBS-P
Maid of Orleans, The. Schiller, *tr. fr. German by* James Clarence Mangan. AWP
Maid of the Moor, The; or, The Water-Fiends, *sel.* George Colman the Younger. "Cold blows the blast—the night's obscure." NOEC
Maid of Tottenham, The. *Unknown.* CoMu

Maid she[e] went to the well to wash[e], The.   The Maid and the Palmer.
  Unknown.   ACP; ESPB
Maid to help me, I pick my way home, The.   Coming Home at Night in
  the Snow.   Yanagawa Koran, *tr. by* Burton Watson.   JLIC-2
Maid was thoroughly drilled.   Work and slave, The.   The Homecoming.
  Gerrit Komrij, *tr. by* Jacob Lowland.   DuIn
Maid, where's my lawrel? Oh my rageing soul!   The Enchantment.
  Theocritus, *tr. fr. Greek by* Thomas Creech.   *Fr.* Idylls, II.   CTC;
  OBVE
Maid who binds her warrior's sash, The.   The Brave at Home.   Thomas
  Buchanan Read.   AnAmPo
Maiden, The.   Peter Hille, *tr. fr. German by* Jethro Bithell.   AWP
Maiden.   Márton Kalász, *tr. fr. Hungarian by* Jascna Kessler.   FOC
Maiden, The.   Rochelle Ratner.   PCP
Maiden and Her Hair, A.   W. H. Davies.   BrPo
Maiden, and mistress of the months and stars.   Swinburne.   *Fr.* Atalanta
  in Calydon.   PoEL-5
Maiden and River.   Mary Weston Fordham.   CBWP-2
Maiden caught me in the wild, The.   The Crystal Cabinet.   Blake.   CH;
  FaBoCh; OAEL-2; OBNC; PoEL-4
Maiden in the Moor [*or* Mor], A.   *Unknown.*   PoEL-1
  (Maiden Lay in the Wilds, The.)   MeEL
Maiden Lies in Her Chamber, A.   Heine, *tr. fr. German by* Louis
  Untermeyer.   AWP
Maiden Name.   Philip Larkin.   GTBS-P
Maiden of the Smile, The.   Alfred Austin.   TEP
Maiden ran away to fetch the clothes, The.   Deluge.   John Clare.
  BoNaP
Maiden sat in an apple-tree, A.   The Apple-Tree.   Brian Vrepont.
  PoAu-2
Maiden There Lived, A.   *Unknown.*   NOBL
Maiden Unai of Ashinoya, The.   Mushimaro.   *Fr.* Manyo Shu.   Ma
Maiden walks alone, A.   Mushimaro.   *Fr.* Manyo Shu.   Ma
Maidenhair Tree, The.   Neil Curry.   NPo
Maidenhead.   "Ephelia."   WPE
Maiden's Best Adorning, The.   *Unknown.*   OxBChV
Maidens Came, The.   *Unknown.*   GBL; PoEL-1
  (Bailey Beareth the Bell Away, The.)   LiTB; SeCePo
Maiden's Denial, A.   *Unknown.*   ErPo
Maidens, kilt your skirts and go.   Celia's Home-coming.   Agnes Mary
  Frances Robinson.   OBEV
Maiden's Lament, A.   Pernette Du Guillet, *tr. fr. French by* Dorothy
  Backer.   *Fr.* The Triumph of the Muses over Love.   DMF
Maiden's Plight, The.   Brian Merriman, *tr. fr. Modern Irish by* Frank
  O'Connor.   *Fr.* The Midnight Court.   BIrV
Maidens shall weep at merry morn.   The Summer Malison.   Gerard
  Manley Hopkins.   CMoP; PoEL-5
Maidens who this bursting [*or* burning] May.   A Young Man's Song.
  William Bell.   FaBoTw; NePoEA
Maidens, why spare ye?   To Cupid.   Michael Drayton.   EIL
Maidens young and virgins tender.   Horace.   *See* Odes: I, 21. To Apollo
  and Diana ("Dianam tenerae dicite virgines").
Maid's Complaint for Want of a Dil Doul, The.   *Unknown.*   CoMu
Maids Conjuring Book, The.   *Unknown.*   CoMu
Maid's Fortune, A.   Sidonie Hedwig Zäunemann, *tr. fr. German by* Susan
  L. Cocalis *and* Gerlinde Geiger.   DMG
Maid's Lament, The.   Walter Savage Landor.   *Fr.* The Citation and
  Examination of William Shakespeare.   OBEV; OBNC
Maid's letter, The.   *Unknown, tr. by* Geoffrey Bownas *and* Anthony
  Thwaite.   PeBJV
Maids, not to you my mind doth change.   "Michael Field."   *Fr.*
  Variations on Sappho.   PeHV
Maids of Honour, The.   *Unknown.*   CoMu
Maid's Thought, The.   Robinson Jeffers.   ErPo
Maids to bed and cover coal.   The Bellman's Song.   *Unknown.*   EBEV;
  EIL; SeCePo
Maid's Tragedy, The, *sels.*   Beaumont *and* Fletcher.
  Bridal Song ("Cynthia, to thy power").   *Fr.* I, ii.   OBEV
  Bridal Song ("Hold back thy hours").   *Fr.* I, ii.   EIL; ErPo; TrGrPo
  "Lay a garland on her hearse."   *Fr.* II, i.   EIL; GBL
Maidservant, the man yawns.   I call!   Poem for Valery Larbaud.   "St.-
  John Perse", *tr. by* Richard Howard.   RHTwFP
Mail Boat, *Leinster*, The.   *Unknown.*   OxBSS
Mail Call.   John Bensko.   MAYP
Mail Has Come, The.   Mary E. Tucker.   CBWP-1
Mailman, The.   Mark Strand.   CAPP
Mailman brings, The.   A Letter from Home.   Li Nan, *tr. by* Dominic
  Cheung.   IFON
Maim'd Debauchee, The.   Earl of Rochester.   *See* As some brave
  Admiral, in former war.

Maimed and enormous in the air.   The Feast.   David Wagoner.
  NePoEA-2
Main artery of fighting.   War.   Guillaume Apollinaire, *tr. by* Jessie Degen
  and Richard Eberhart.   WaaP
Main-Deep, The.   James Stephens.   MoBrPo; MOS; OBMV; RR; UnPo
Main-Truck; or, A Leap for Life, The.   *At. to.* George Pope Morris.
  AnAmPo; BLPL; PoLF
Maine.   Philip Booth.   AmFN
Maine.   Elinor Nauen.   UL
Maine Lake at Night.   Harry Morris.   CRP
Maine Vastly Covered with Much Snow.   John Tagliabue.   InPK
Mainly I was led to them, the casinos of aluminium.   Painting Mount
  Taranaki.   David Eggleton.   PeNZ
Mainspring, The.   Martha Eugenie Perry.   CaP
Maintrunk Country Roadsong.   Sam Hunt.   PeNZ
Maitreya! Maitreya!   Hotei, *tr. by* Lucien Stryk *and* Takashi Ikemoto.
  ZPCJ
Majestuous and sapphirine, it rears.   The Chest of Perote.   Joaquín
  Arcadio Pagaza, *tr. by* Samuel Beckett.   MexPo
Majesty and Mercy of God, The.   Sir Robert Grant.   OHIP; WGRP
Majesty of God, The.   Thomas Sternhold.   *See* Lord Descended from
  Above, The.
Major abstraction is the idea of man, The.   Wallace Stevens.   *Fr.* Notes
  toward a Supreme Fiction.   NOBA
Major André.   *Unknown.*   AmFP
Major Bowes' Diary.   Imamu Amiri Baraka.   NAAL-2
Major-General Scott.   On to Richmond.   John Reuben Thompson.   PAH
Major Macroo.   Stevie Smith.   NBLV
Major, with wonderful force, A.   An Atrocious Pun.   *Unknown.*   RHPC
Majuba Hill.   Roy Macnab.   PeSA
Makar, The.   William Soutar.   OxBS
Make a jigsaw puzzle from an amateur photo.   Jigsaw Puzzles.   K.
  Schippers, *tr. by* Peter Nijmeijer.   DuIn
Make a joyful noise unto the Lord, all ye lands.   Psalm C ("Make a joyful
  noise. ").   Bible, *O.T.*   *Fr.* Psalms.   BLRP; OFD; OHIP
  (Be Thankful unto Him.)   FaPON
  ("Enter into His gates with thanksgiving.")
  (Giving Thanks, 4.)   BLRP
  (Old Hundredth, *metrical vers. by* William Kethe)   FaPoR; NOCV
  (Scotch Te Deum.)   WGRP
Make all your sorrow neat.   The Young Wife.   Derek Walcott.   DiPo
Make every bargain clear and plain.   *Unknown.*   FaBoUs
Make for Him a Revolution, If You Can!   Moyshe-Leyb Halpern, *tr. fr.
  Yiddish by* Benjamin *and* Barbara Harshav.   AYP
Make it sweet and delicate to eat.   The Eaten Heart.   *Unknown, tr. fr.
  Middle English by* Pearl London.   *Fr.* The Knight of Curtesy.
  TrGrPo
Make Love Not War.   Howard Nemerov.   NAs
Make me a bowl, a mighty bowl.   The Cup.   John Oldham.   AWP
Make me a captive, Lord.   Christian Freedom.   George Matheson.
  TrPWD
Make me a grave where'er you will.   Bury Me in a Free Land.   Frances
  Ellen Watkins Harper.   BPo
Make me a heaven, and make me there.   The Eye.   Robert Herrick.
  CaPo
Make me content, O Lord, with daily bread.   Prayer for Contentment.
  Edwin McNeill Poteat.   TrPWD
Make me, dear Lord, polite and kind.   A Child's Prayer.   John Banister
  Tabb.   FaPON
Make me feel the wild pulsation that I felt before the strife.   Tennyson.
  Fr. Locksley Hall.   SaC
Make Me Hear You.   Reginald Gibbons.   MAYP
Make me, O Lord, thy spinning [*or* spining] wheel[e] complete [*or
  compleat or* compleate] [*or* of use for thee].   Huswifery.   Edward
  Taylor.   EaLo; FaBV; LiTA; NAAL-1; NIP; NOBA; NOBE; NoP;
  OxBA; SaC; SCAP; TAP
  (Housewifery.)   LiTA; NoP
Make me over, mother April.   Spring Song.   Bliss Carman.   AnAmPo
Make me too brave to lie or be unkind.   A Prayer for Every Day.   Mary
  Carolyn Davies.   BLPA; FaBoBe
Make miniatures of the once-monstrous theme.   A Short History of British
  India.   Geoffrey Hill.   OxBC
Make Music with Your Life.   Bob O'Meally.   CNA
Make my mortal dreams come true.   Whittier.   *Fr.* Andrew Rykman's
  Prayer.   TrPWD
Make new friends, but keep the old.   New Friends and Old Friends.
  Joseph Parry.   BLPA; BLPL
Make no mistake: if He rose at all.   Seven Stanzas at Easter.   John
  Updike.   EaLo; TrCP
Make-off.   Karin Kiwus, *tr. fr. German by* Susan L. Cocalis.   DMG

Make room, all ye kingdoms, in history renown'd. American Independence. Francis Hopkinson. PAH
Make room on our banner bright. Song of Texas. William Henry Cuyler Hosmer. PAH
Make sure the engraving is done skillfully. Philhellene. Constantine P. Cavafy, *tr. by* Edmund Keeley *and* Philip Sherrard. VMG
Make this night loveable. W. H. Auden. TW
Make this thing plain to us, O Lord! Clean Hands. Austin Dobson. TrPWD
Make three fourths of a cross, and a circle complete. *Unknown*. OxNR
Make us Thy mountaineers. The Last Defile. Amy Carmichael. TrCP
Make Way. Steven Lavoie. UL
Make Way! Ada Negri, *tr. fr. Italian by* Lynne Lawner. PBWP
Make way, make way. The Stream's Song. Lascelles Abercrombie. OBMV
Make we mirth. Sing We Yule. *Unknown*. MeEL
Make Ye a Joyful Sounding Noise. *Unknown*. AH
Maker, The. Gyula Illyés, *tr. fr. Hungarian by* Daniel Hoffman. MHuP
Maker-of-Sevens in the scheme of things. The Wife-Woman. Anne Spencer. BANP
Makers, The. David Galler. NYBP
Makers, The. Howard Nemerov. DiPo; FYAP
Makers. Nancy Dingman Watson. RAR
Makes no difference to the flowers. Naming the Flowers. Anne Stevenson. ER
Makes the Little Ones Dizzy. Samuel Hoffenstein. BXAP
Makes up the game. The Announcer. Austin Straus. TSL
Makhno's Philosophers. John Manifold. CBAP
Makin' Jump Shots. Michael S. Harper. ASP; PoE
Making a Door. Dennis Schmitz. LCAP
Making a Fist. Naomi Shihab Nye. MAYP
Making a Man. Nixon Waterman. BLPA
Making a Season. Nicki Jackowska. DT
Making Chicago. Dennis Schmitz. LCAP; NPGG
Making Contact. John Manifold. CBAP
Making Feet and Hands. Benjamin Péret, *tr. fr. French by* David Gascoyne. EAS; RHTwFP
Making Fun of the Well at the Inn below the Mountain. Chu Yün-ming, *tr. fr. Chinese by* Jonathan Chaves. CoBLCP
Making her doll. *Unknown, tr. by* Geoffrey Bownas *and* Anthony Thwaite. PeBJV
Making his advances. Tortoise Gallantry. D. H. Lawrence. CMoP; MoP
Making It Simple December 8, 1969. David McElroy. AmPA
Making it up. *Unknown, tr. by* Geoffrey Bownas *and* Anthony Thwaite. PeBJV
Making Lists. Gladys Cardiff. HATNAP
Making Love outside Aras an Uachtaráin. Paul Durcan. FaBCIP
Making Love to Myself. James L. White. GLP
Making Money: Drought Year in Minkler, California. Gary Soto. NoAM
Making Music. Judith Minty. GeTw
Making no sound. Shigeyuki, *tr. by* Geoffrey Bownas *and* Anthony Thwaite. PeBJV
Making of Birds, The. Katharine Tynan. TIRV
Making of Color, The. Hugh Seidman. AmPA
Making of Man, The. John White Chadwick. AA
Making of the Cross, The. William Everson. VGW
Making out she doesn't know. *Unknown, tr. by* Geoffrey Bownas *and* Anthony Thwaite. PeBJV
Making Peace. Denise Levertov. ER
Making Poetry. Anne Stevenson. DiPo
Making Tens. M. M. Hutchinson. BoTP
Making the Jam without You. Maxine W. Kumin. ER; TV
Making the Move. Paul Muldoon. NoAM
Making these word things to. Report from a Far Place. William Stafford. CAPP
Making toast at the fireside. Misfortunes Never Come Singly. Harry Graham. FaFP
Making Up for a Soul. David Wagoner. VGW
Malacoda. Samuel Beckett. CIP
Malady of Love Is Nerves, The. Petronius Arbiter, *tr. fr. Latin by* Howard Mumford Jones. AWP
Malady smote the earth one year, A. The Animals Sick of the Plague. Marianne Moore, *ad. fr.* La Fontaine. InPS
Malaga. Pearse Hutchinson. BIrV
Malawi. Innocent Banda. WMBCH
Malcolm. Lucille Clifton. CNA
Malcolm. Welton Smith. BPo
Malcolm, a Thousandth Poem. Conrad Kent Rivers. CNA
Malcolm Lowry. Malcolm Lowry. OBD

Malcolm X. Gwendolyn Brooks. CNA; OFD; PoBA; TTY
Malcolm X—an Autobiography. Larry Neal. AmNP; BPo
Malcolm's Katie, *sels*. Isabella Valancy Crawford. OBCV
"Bite deep and wide, O Axe, the tree."
"South Wind laid his moccasins aside, The."
Malcontent, The, *sel*. John Marston.
"I cannot sleepe, my eyes ill neighbouring lids." PoEL-2
Malcontents, The. Dryden. *Fr.* Absalom and Achitophel, Pt. I. OBS
Maldive Shark, The. Herman Melville. AmPP; AnAmPo; MOS; NAAL-1; NOBA; NoP; OxBA; PoE; PoEL-5; RB; TAP; TW
Male & Female Loves in Beulah. Blake. *Fr.* Jerusalem, III. OBNC
Male Rage Poem. Pier Giorgio Di Cicco. NOBC
Male Rain. Laura Tohe. STE
Male Torso. Christopher Middleton. NePoEA-2
Malediction. Barry Spacks. TW
Malefic Return, The. Ramón López Velarde, *tr. fr. Spanish by* Samuel Beckett. MexPo; OBVE
Malemute Dog, A. Pat O'Cotter. BLPA
Malest Cornifici Tuo Catullo. Allen Ginsberg. NeAP
Malfeasance, The. Alan Bold. AmMo
Malice of Innocence, The. Denise Levertov. NNaP
Malicious Envy rode. Envy. Spenser. *Fr.* The Faerie Queene, I, 4. TW
Malign my character, but do it under a willow. Direct Address. Amy Gerstler. UL
Malignant planets! do ye still combine. The Sow of Feeling. Robert Fergusson. UL
Malison of the Stone-chat. *Unknown*. GBP
Malisons, malisons more than ten. The Lark. *Unknown*. GBP; PBBP
Mallard Lake Boating Songs, *sels*. Chu Yi-tsun, *tr. fr. Chinese by* Irving Lo. WFTU
"Sandbar egrets, sleeping, nestle close to my boat." *Fr.* II.
"Wind above Long River spreads the scent of lotus, leaf after leaf, The." *Fr.* XXXI.
Mallards call with evening from the reeds, The. "Tajihi." *Fr.* Manyo Shu. Ma
Mallee in October. Flexmore Hudson. PoAu-2
Maltese Dog, A. Tymnes, *tr. fr. Greek by* Edmund Blunden. FaBoCh; FaBoEE; OBD
Malum Opus. James Appleton Morgan. FaBoCo; NA
Malvern Hill. Herman Melville. AmPP; FPL; PAH; TAP
Malvern Hills, *sel*. Joseph Cottle.
Industrial Evils. NOEC
Malvern Waters ("Malvern Water, says Dr. John Wall"). *Unknown*. FaBoEE
Malvolio. Walter Savage Landor. Par
Malzah's Song. Charles Heavysege. *Fr.* Saul. OBCV
Mam-maw's losing touch at last: her face. Beside My Grandmother. Al Lee. SM
Mama. Rita Anyiam-St. John. WS
Mama/ eats death/ tastes like fish. Monogram 4. Martina Werner, *tr. by* Rosemarie Waldrop. BoWoP
Mama/ I wish I were silver. Silly Song. Federico García Lorca, *tr. by* M. D. Herter Norton. TTTS
Mama,/ papa,/ and us. An Inconvenience. John Raven. BPo; CRP
Mama/ today it's my turn. Mama. Rita Anyiam-St. John. WS
Mama and Daughter. Langston Hughes. UnPo
Mama Have You Heard the News. *Unknown*. AS
Mama is a tree. Papa and Mama. Li Nan, *tr. by* Dominic Cheung. IFON
Mama Julinda is let down into a hole. Island Funeral. Frank Stanford. MT
Mama Knows. Sharon Scott. JB
Mama never rocked me. For Mama. Deborah Kendrick. TSM
Mama, please brush off my coat. Mama and Daughter. Langston Hughes. UnPo
Mama writes. Under Your Voice, among Legends. Phyllis Beauvais. NMM
Mamana Saquina. José Craveirinha, *tr. fr. Portuguese by* Margaret Dickinson. WMBCH
Mamano. José Craveirinha, *tr. fr. Portuguese by* Chris Searle. WMBCH
Mama's Promise. Marilyn Nelson Waniek. ER
Mamba the Bright-eyed, *sel*. George Gordon McCrae.
"Day had fled, the moon arose, The." PoAu-1
Mamie and I, we haven't known. A President in His Country Residence. Remco Campert, *tr. by* James Brockway. DuIn
Mamma! Frank Horne. BPo
Mamma sent me to the spring, she told me not to stay. Chewing Chawing Gum. *Unknown*. AmFP

Mammals are a varied lot. Dogs and Cats and Bears and Bats. Jack
    Prelutsky. RHPC
Mammon Marriage. George Macdonald. BoLoP; EBVV
Mammoth morning moved grey flanks and groaned, A. Walking
    Wounded. Vernon Scannell. OBWP
Mammy Hums. Carl Sandburg. PoNe
Mamparra M'gaiza. José Craveirinha, tr. fr. Portuguese by Margaret
    Dickinson. WMBCH
Mamua, when our laughter ends. Tiare Tahiti. Rupert Brooke. BrPo
Mamzelle. Mary Wilson. AIW
Man, A. Nina Cassian, tr. fr. Rumanian by Roy MacGregor-Hastie. OV
Man, The. Robert Creeley. OBAL
Man. Sir John Davies. Fr. Nosce Teipsum. EIL
    (I Know Myself a Man.) ChTr
    "I know my soul hath power to know all things." OBEV
Man. Armanda Guiducci, tr. fr. Italian by Muriel Kittel. DMI
Man. George Herbert. MePo; NAEL-1; NoP; PoEL-2; SeCP; SeCV-1;
    TrGrPo; TrPWD, abr
Man. Mieczyslaw Jastrun, tr. fr. Polish by Czeslaw Milosz. PwPP
Man. Vali Mohammad Nazir, tr. fr. Urdu by Ahmed Ali. GoT
Man. Pope. See Essay on Man, An: Know then thyself, presume not
    God to scan.
Man! A. Clinton Scollard. OHIP
Man. Swinburne. See Atalanta in Calydon: Before the Beginning of
    Years.
Man. Margit Szécsi, tr. fr. Hungarian by Laura Schiff. MHuP
Man. Henry Vaughan. MeLP; MePo; NOBE; NOCV; OBEV; OBS;
    PoEL-2; SeCV-1
Man. Humbert Wolfe. MoBrPo
Man, A (a Tom, a Dick, or some such epithet). The Bayonet and the
    Needle. Eliezer Steinbarg, tr. by Curt Leviant. VWA
Man Adrift on a Slim Spar, A. Stephen Crane. MOS; NAAL-2
Man against the Sky, The. Edwin Arlington Robinson. AmPP; CMoP;
    LiTA; OxBA
Man All Grown Up Is Supposed To, A. Terry Stokes. AmPA
Man Alone. Louise Bogan. NYBP
Man Alone. Denise Levertov. CAPP
Man alone gets up while the sea's still dark, The. Morning Star. Cesare
    Pavese, tr. by William Arrowsmith. PFI
Man and a woman, A. To Stay Alive. Elizabeth McKim. ER
Man and a woman walk out into the summer night, A. Such Comfort as
    the Night Can Bring to Us. Peter Cooley. MAYP; NAmP
Man and Bat. D. H. Lawrence. RB
Man and Cows. Andrew Young. EBEV
Man and Dog. Edward Thomas. FM
Man and His Image, The. La Fontaine, tr. fr. French by Elizur Wright.
    OBVE
Man and His Wife, A. Peter Redgrove and Penelope Shuttle. PoPo
Man and Nature. Robert Kelley Weeks. AA
Man and the maid go side by side, The. Sunday Afternoon in Italy. D.
    H. Lawrence. BrPo
Man and the Weasel, The. Phaedrus, tr. fr. Latin by Christopher Smart.
    AWP
Man and Wife. Mitchell Goodman. VGW
Man and Wife. Robert Lowell. AmPP; BoLoP; CAPP; NAAL-2
Man and Wife. Anne Sexton. CAPP
Man and Wife Is One Flesh. Ann Deagon
Man and Woman. Robert Conquest. OxBTC
Man and Woman. Don L. Lee. NeAC
Man and woman, A. The Woman's Dream. Frances Horovitz. BrRo
Man and Woman Absolutely White, A. André Breton, tr. fr. French by
    David Antin. POS
Man and woman lie on a white bed, A. Happiness. Louise Glück.
    MAYP
Man and woman, they enter the sea. The Bathers. Karl Shapiro. ASP
Man Arrested in Hacking Death Tells Police He Mistook Mother-in-Law
    for Raccoon. Susan Ludvigson. MAYP; MT
Man Asleep in a Child's Bed. Thomas Lux. AnAn
Man Asleep in the Desert. Thomas Lux. LCAP
Man at the moment of departure, turning, A. Ritual of Departure.
    Thomas Kinsella. CIP; CMoP
Man Awakened by a Song above His Roof, The. Tomas Tranströmer, tr.
    fr. Swedish by Robert Bly. EAS
Man, be merry, I thee rede. Unknown. Fr. Three Christmas Carols, II.
    ACP
Man behind the book may not be man, The. The Intellectual. Karl
    Shapiro. CMoP
Man bent over his guitar, The. Wallace Stevens. See Man with the Blue
    Guitar, The: I cannot bring a world quite round.
Man bent over his guitar, The. The Man with the Blue Guitar. Wallace
    Stevens. CMoP; LiTA; NoAM

Man-brained and man-handed ground-ape, physically, The. Original Sin.
    Robinson Jeffers. MoAB; MoAmPo
Man by the Name of Bolus, A. James Whitcomb Riley. AA
Man by the wall snores, The. Unknown, tr. fr. Middle Irish by J. G.
    O'Keefe. Fr. Sweeney the Mad. AnIL
Man came into the store, A. Inventory. Frank Stanford. MT
Man came slowly from the setting sun, A. The Death of Cuchulain. W.
    B. Yeats. ChTr
    (Cuchulain's Fight with the Sea.) AnIL
Man Can Complain, Can't He?, A. Ogden Nash. NBLV
Man Cannot Name Himself. Luci Shaw. TrCP
Man Carrying Bale. Harold Monro. BrPo; MoBrPo
Man Closing Up, The. Donald Justice. CoAP
Man comes home in the morning and finds himself waiting, A. Three
    Self-Plagiarisms. David Avidan, tr. fr. Hebrew by Warren Bargad
    and Stanley F. Chyet. Fr. Traveling in the City, 4. IP
Man comes home to find his wife in bed, A. The Face in the Ceiling.
    Stephen Dobyns. BLA
Man Coming toward You, The. Oscar Williams. LiTA
Man Dancing with a Baby. Susan Stewart. NAmP
Man dat wahs de slickest tile, De. Appearances. Ben King. AnAmPo
Man, dream[e] no more of curious mysteries. Fulke Greville. Fr.
    Caelica, LXXXVIII [LXXXIX]. MePo; QFR
    (Sonnet: "Man, dream[e] no more of curious mysteries.") JCP; OBS
Man Exalted. Unknown. MeEL; NoP
Man Falling. Zoltán Zelk, tr. fr. Hungarian by Daniel Hoffman. MHuP
Man-Fate, The. William Everson. NoAM
Man feared that he might find an assassin, A. Stephen Crane. Fr. The
    Black Riders, LVI. NAAL-2
Man fell out of grace, A. A Funny Joke. Leon Stokesbury. MAYP
Man first hangs an apron from his thin neck, The. The Past. Yoshioka
    Minoru, tr. by Hiroaki Sato. FCEI
Man Flammonde, from God knows where, The. Flammonde. Edwin
    Arlington Robinson. AmPP; CMoP; LiTA; LiTM; NoAM
Man! Foolish Man! On Exodus 3: 14: "I am that I am." Matthew Prior.
    NOCV
Man fools about with self-analysis. The Collective Portrait. Robert
    Finch. MoCV
Man Frail, and God Eternal. Isaac Watts. See O God, Our Help in Ages
    Past.
Man free as the sky, no ties, no entanglements, A. Sudden Inspiration on
    a Summer Day. Michizane, tr. by Burton Watson. JLIC-1
Man from Inversnaid, The. Robert Fuller Murray. SD
Man from Ironbark, The. A. B. Paterson. PoAu-1
Man from Snowy River, The. A. B. Paterson. CBAP; PoAu-1
Man from the Crowd, The. Sam Walter Foss. PoLF
Man from the Top of the Mind, The. David Wagoner. NePoEA-2
Man from the Woods, The. John Ciardi. SO
Man from Up-Country Talking, The. João Cabral de Melo Neto, tr. fr.
    Portuguese by W. S. Merwin. ATCBP
Man from Washington, The. James Welch. CDW; HATNAP; NoAM;
    NOVW
Man had just married an automobile, A. The Automobile. Russell
    Edson. LCAP
Man had wronged a woman. It was, A. A Modern Woman. Marie
    Janitschek, tr. by Susan L. Cocalis and Gerlinde Geiger. DMG
Man has been drowned in this lake, they think, A. Lake. Miyoshi
    Tatsuji, tr. by Geoffrey Bownas and Anthony Thwaite. PeBJV
Man has been standing, A. The Tunnel. Mark Strand. HeIP; TwCP;
    WeW
Man has separated lust and sorrow. All Is God's. Jakov de Haan, tr. by
    David Soetendorp. VWA
Man He Killed, The. Thomas Hardy. BrPo; CMoP; DL; FaFP; FF;
    HAP; HeIP; LiTB; LiTM; MoAB; MoBrPo; NIP; OBWP; RB; WaaP;
    WeW
Man, hef in mind and mend thy mis. Remember the Last Things.
    Unknown. MeEL
Man Hidden behind the Drapes, The. Pattiann Rogers. MAYP
Man hired by John Smith and Co., A. "Mark Twain." FaBoNo; InPK
Man, husband existence: ne'er launch on the sea. Epitaph of Cleonicus.
    Theocritus, tr. by Charles Stuart Calverley. FaBoEE
Man, I Felt Like Running All Night. Salomón R. Baldenegro, Jr., tr. fr.
    Spanish by Toni Empringham. FIA
Man I had a love for, The. An Old Woman's Lamentations. Villon, tr.
    by J. M. Synge. MoBrPo; OBMV
Man I left behind, The. Song of the Ringing in the Ear. Ishihara
    Yoshiro, tr. by Hiroaki Sato. FCEI
Man I love. Even Tho. Grace Nichols. WS
Man I saw in the forest, The. Dream 2: Brian the Still-Hunter. Margaret
    Atwood. BoWoP
Man, if I said once, "I know." The Islands. Randall Jarrell. EAS

Man in Black, The. Mark Strand. EAS

Man in Hangchou Spread Word That I Had Died, A. Ni Tsan, *tr. fr. Chinese by* Jonathan Chaves. CoBLCP

Man in his secret shrine. Hymn in Columbus Circle. Stephen Vincent Benét. OBAL

Man in Nature. William Roscoe Thayer. AA

Man in righteousness arrayed, The. Horace. *See* Odes: I, 22. "Virtue, dear friend, needs no 'defence'" ("Integer vitae").

Man in righteousness arrayed, The. To Sally. John Quincy Adams, *after* Horace. AA; AWP; OBAL

Man in terror of impotence, A. The Ninth Symphony of Beethoven Understood at Last as a Sexual Message. Adrienne Rich. NoP; TAP

Man in That Airplane, The. Oscar Williams. WaP

Man in the Dead Machine, The. Donald Hall. CAPP

Man in the Dream Is Death, The. Lynne Butler. IHMS

Man in the feed store called them mountain beavers, The. Looking for Mountain Beavers. David Wagoner. VGW

Man in the Mirror, The. Mark Strand. NYBP

Man in the moon, The/ Came down too soon [*or* Came tumbling down]. *Unknown.* OxBoLi; OxNR

Man in the Moon. Linda Hogan. HATNAP

Man in the Moon, The. James Whitcomb Riley. NA

Man in the Moon, The. *Unknown.* MeEL; PYC

Man in the Moon Drinks Claret [*or* Clarret], The. *Unknown.* OxNR; CoMu

Man in the Moon, The ("Mon in the mone stond and strit"). *Unknown.* MeEL

Man in the moon was caught in a trap, The. *Unknown.* OxNR

Man in the mune, The/ is making shune. *Unknown.* OxNR

Man in the Onion Bed, The. John Ciardi. SO

Man in the Rain, The. Van K. Brock. MT

Man in the red scarf comes—from five split places, The. The Raspberry in the Pudding. Philip O'Connor. EAS

Man in the Street. Robert Penn Warren. OBAL

Man in the street is fed, The. Carl Sandburg. OxBA

Man in the Tree, The. Mark Strand. EAS

Man in the wilderness asked [of] me [*or* said to me], The [*or* A]. Mother Goose. BoTP; FaBoCh; FaBoCo; FaBoNo; GBP; NA; OxNR

Man in the yellow hard hat, The. Consecration. Susan Stewart. NAmP

Man into a Churchyard. Bernard Gutteridge. EAS

Man, introverted man, having crossed. Science. Robinson Jeffers. NU; OxBA

Man Is a Fool. *Unknown.* FaFP

Man is a lumpe, where all beasts kneaded bee. To Sir Edward Herbert at Julyers. John Donne. SeCV-1

Man is a sacred city built of marvelous earth. John Masefield. *Fr.* The Tragedy of Pompey the Great. WGRP

Man Is a Spirit. Stevie Smith. OxBC

Man Is a Weaver. Moses ibn Ezra, *tr. fr. Hebrew by* Emma Lazarus. TrJP

Man Is an Animal That Laughs. Raquel Jodorowsky, *tr. fr. Spanish by* Kate Flores. DMH

Man Is Beaten Up, A. Gábor Garai, *tr. fr. Hungarian by* Edwin Morgan. MHuP

Man Is but a Castaway. Clarence Day. ImOP

Man Is God's Nature. Richard Eberhart. EaLo

Man Is in Pain. Philip Lamantia. NeAP

Man is leaning on a cold iron rail, A. The Man Who Loved Islands. Derek Walcott. NoAM

Man Is Nothing But. Saul Tchernichovsky, *tr. fr. Hebrew by* Robert Friend. VWA

Man Is What He Wills to Be. Mrs. Henry Linden. CBWP-4

Man knows not love—such love as woman feels. Woman's Love. *Unknown.* WBLP

Man knows where first he ships himself, but he. Man's Dying-Place Uncertain. Robert Herrick. CaPo

Man, like others, formed by God, A. The Saxons of Flint. *Unknown, tr. by* Mary C. Llewelyn. OBWVE

Man looking into the sea. A Grave. Marianne Moore. CMoP; FaBoWP; HAP; HeIP; LiTA; MoP; MOS; NAAL-2; NoAM; NOBA; PoE; TAP; UnPo; WeW; WPE

Man loosened his shoe, A. The Hourglass. Russell Edson. AnAn

Man Lying on a Wall. Michael Longley. FaBCIP

Man-made bay, its fat weeds, The. Mission Bay. John Koethe. PoA

Man, Man, Man. *Unknown.* ErPo; FaFP
    (Man, Man, Man Is for the Woman Made.) Prf

Man, matron, maiden. Sir Robert Baden-Powell. CenHV

Man may be martyred in bondage. The Mainspring. Martha Eugenie Perry. CaP

Man may work from sun to sun. *Unknown.* SaC

Man Meeting Himself. Howard Sergeant. EAS

Man Missing. Charles Brasch. ATNZ

Man more kindly, in his careless way, A. A Portrait. Caroline Duer. AA

Man-Moth, The. Elizabeth Bishop. CAPP; LiTA; LiTM; MAT; MoAB; MoAmPo; MoP; NoAM; NOBA; PPP

Man-muckle was I or I saw. What Finer Hills? J. K. Annand. PoSH

Man must tempt his heart with fancy, A. World of Fancy. Sami Mahdi, *tr. by* May Jayyusi. MAP

Man never is; yet here are men. Building Programme. Kendrick Smithyman. ATNZ

Man, Not His Arms. Selden Rodman. WaP

Man o' War Bird. Derek Walcott. TTY

Man, obsessed by people, A. A Man Rises from the Cave of Hira.' Al-Munsif al-Wahaybi, *tr. by* Salma Khadra Jayyusi *and* Naomi Shihab Nye. MAP

Man of Action, A. Charles B. Stetler. GOYP

Man of bone confirms his throne, The. The New Ancient of Days. Herman Melville. OBAL

Man of Calvary, The, *sel.* "Sin-Killer" Griffin.
    "Roman soldiers come riding in full speed." AmFP

Man of Glass, The. Gordon Challis. ATNZ

Man of Green Hill. The Song of the Man of Green Hill. Kao Ch'i, *tr. by* Jonathan Chaves. CoBLCP

Man of independent means, A. No Occupation. George Rostrevor Hamilton. FaBoEE

Man of Kerioth, The, *sel.* Robert Norwood.
    "But, this I found." *Fr.* V. CaP

Man of La Mancha, *sels.* W. H. Auden. AnAn
    Don Quixote's Credo.
    Don Quixote's Farewell.
    Finale.
    Golden Age, The.
    Highway to Glory Song.
    Sancho Panza's Dream.
    Song of Dejection.
    Song of the Barber.
    Song of the Knight of the Mirrors.
    Song of the Quest.

Man of Life Upright, The. Thomas Campion. AAS; EiL; OBSC; PoRA

Man of marble holds the throne, A. The Roman Stage. Lionel Johnson. BrPo; NOBVV

Man of Mystery. Dahlia Ravikovich, *tr. fr. Hebrew by* Warren Bargad *and* Stanley F. Chyet. IP

Man of O, The. Marina Rivera. FIA

Man of Peace, The. Bliss Carman. OHIP

Man of Prayer, The. Christopher Smart. *Fr.* A Song to David. LiTB

Man of Property, The. Charles G. Ballard. NOVW

Man of Rain, A. Arlindo Barbeitos, *tr. fr. Portuguese by* Donald Burness. WMBCH

Man of Tao—his iron flute plays music, The. Yang Wei-chen, *tr. fr. Chinese by* Jonathan Chaves. *Fr.* Songs of Lake Tung-t'ing, II. CoBLCP

Man of Taste, The, *sels.* James Bramston.
    "Huge commentators grace my learned shelves." FaBoCo
    "Whoe'er he be that to a taste aspires." NOEC

Man of Taste, The. William Parsons. OBTV

Man of the House, The. Katharine Tynan. TIRV

Man of the House, The. David Wagoner. NoAM

Man of the Stone City. Mahmoud al-Buraikan, *tr. fr. Arabic by* Lena Jayyusi *and* Naomi Shihab Nye. MAP

Man of the Time, The. Edwin Waugh. PF

Man of the World. Michael Hamburger. NePoEA-2

Man of Thessaly, The. *Unknown.* FaBoCo
    ("There was a man of Thessaly.") FaBoNo; OxNR

Man of Tyre, The. D. H. Lawrence. TOF

Man of Valour to His Fair Lady, The. William Dunbar. MeEL

Man-of-War's Garland, The. *Unknown.* OxBSS

Man of Words, A. John Ashbery. PoA

Man of Words, A. *Unknown.* FaFP; FF

Man on a Raft. John Russell Hervey. ATNZ

Man on his own in a car, A. Meditation on the A30. Sir John Betjeman. RB

Man on the Bed, The. Debora Greger. MAYP

Man on the dubious waves of error toss'd. William Cowper. *Fr.* Truth. NOCV

Man on the Dump, The. Wallace Stevens. HAP; NAWM-2; NoAM

Man on the Flying Trapeze, The. *Unknown, also at. to* George Leybourne. BeLS; BLPA; FaBoBe; FaFP; OxBoLi

Man on Wheels. Karl Shapiro. PCP

Man or woman walking today, A. To Xanadu, Which Is Beth Shaul. Arye Sivan, *tr. by* Anthony Rudolf *and* Natan Zach. VWA

Man—pitiful insect. Ch'i-yü-ko. *Unknown, tr. by* Burton Watson. CoBCP

Man proposes, God in His time disposes. On a Dead Child. Richard Middleton. SoSe

Man Ray is blowing out fuses in a French room. Time; or, How the Line about Chagall's Lovers Disappears. Jane Miller. SM

Man rejects imprisonment. Fall To. Howard Jones. NBP

Man Rises from the Cave of Hira', A. Al-Munsif al-Wahaybi, *tr. fr. Arabic by* Salma Khadra Jayyusi *and* Naomi Shihab Nye. MAP

Man Said to the Universe, A. Stephen Crane. *Fr.* War Is Kind, XXI. AmPP; FaBoEE; FF; ImOP; LiTM; NAAL-2, *sect.* 96; OBAL; OBSV; PrIm; TAP; WeW

Man Sails the Deep a While. Robert Louis Stevenson. MOS

Man sat in the felon's tank, alone, A. In the Tank. Thom Gunn. NoAM

Man Saw a Ball of Gold in the Sky, A. Stephen Crane. *Fr.* The Black Riders, XXXV. LiTA

Man says lilacs against white houses, two sparrows, one streaked, A. Spring Drawing II. Robert Hass. MAYP

Man Seated. Ferreira Gullar, *tr. fr. Portuguese by* William Jay Smith. CT

Man Sentenced to Death, The, *sel.* Jean Genet, *tr. fr. French by* Steven Finch.
"Murderers of the wall wrap themselves in sunrise, The." PeHV

Man shall come into this land, A. Bard's Chant. James Shirley. *Fr.* Saint Patrick for Ireland. ACP

Man She Called Honey, and Married, The. Alberto Ríos. MAYP

Man she had was kind and clean, The. Tombstones in the Starlight: The Fisherwoman. Dorothy Parker. NIP

Man shot himself, A. Leader. Bruce Bennett. InPK

Man should never earn his living, A. A Living. D. H. Lawrence. RFM

Man sits at the table, The. Peter Rosei, *tr. by* Beth Bjorklund. CoAuP

Man sits in a timelessness, The. The Rescue. Robert Creeley. CAPP; CRP

Man Splitting Wood in the Daybreak, The. Galway Kinnell. AnAn

Man, standing in the shadows of a, A. For H. W. Fuller. Carolyn M. Rodgers. BPo

Man still light of foot, but ageing, took, A. Thinking of Mr. D. Thomas Kinsella. NoAM

Man stood in the laurel tree, A. Things. Louis Simpson. OxBC

Man stoops low on the overcast plain, A. He is earthing. Landscape and Figure. Thomas Kinsella. IPY

Man stumbled on some rat droppings, A. The Rat's Tight Schedule. Russell Edson. AnAn

Man talks/ the woman listens, The. The Meaningful Exchange. Marge Piercy. AIW

Man that had six mortal wounds, a man, A. Cuchulain Comforted. W. B. Yeats. CMoP; LiTM; OAEL-2; TOF

Man, that is borne of a woman of a few dayes, and full of trouble .
Bible, *O.T. Fr.* Job, XIV. ChTr, XIV: 1-2; OBVE
(Immortality, XIV: 1–12.) WGRP
(Job Cries Out.) TrGrPo
(Job's Entreaty.) AWP
"For there is hope for a tree" XIV: 7–17. DL

Man that joins in life's career, The. The Parting Glass. Philip Freneau. AA

Man That Lives, The. *Unknown.* OBET

Man that mates wi' Poverty, The. Comfort in Puirtith. Helen B. Cruickshank. OxBS

Man that never will declare his thought, The. On the Deception of Appearances. Sadi, *tr. fr. Persian by* L. Cranmer-Byng. *Fr.* The Gulistan. AWP

Man that sees by chance his picture made, A. Robert Bridges. *Fr.* The Growth of Love, XXXIX. NoAM

Man, the egregious egoist. Cold-blooded Creatures. Elinor Wylie. ImOP; OxBSP

Man the Enemy of Man. Sir Walter Scott. *Fr.* Rokeby, III. WBLP

Man the hare has met, The. The Names of the Hare. *Unknown, tr. by* Seamus Heaney. RB

Man, them revolutionary niggers is all. Just Taking Note. Sharon Scott. JB

Man Then Suddenly Stops Moving, A. Alberto Ríos. NoAM

Man Thinking about Woman. Don L. Lee. CNA; MoP

Man travels (eyes head and face of the servingmen), A. Trip with Knives. Armando, *tr. by* James S. Holmes. DuIn

Man under the Bed, The. Erica Jong. AmPA

Man unto His Fellow Man. Norman Corwin. *Fr.* On a Note of Triumph. TrJP

Man upon mold, whatsoever thou be. Money Is What Matters. *Unknown.* MeEL

Man Upright, The. Thomas MacDonagh. BIrV

Man Walking through Clachtoll, A. Norman MacCaig. NPo

Man Walking through the Snow, A. Shotetsu, *tr. fr. Japanese by* Steven D. Carter. WFTW

Man walks beside them, A. White Oxen. Louis Simpson. NoAM

Man walks into a room, A. There is a corpse on the floor. Gorg, a Detective Story. B. P. Nichol. NOBC

Man walks towards town, A. The Late Hour. Mark Strand. HCAP

"Man wants but little here below." The Wants of Man. John Quincy Adams. OBAL, *abr.;* PoLF

Man was called Methuselah I remember, The. Methuselah. Rosemary Dobson. *Fr.* The Devil and the Angel. PoAu-2

Man was sitting underneath a tree, A. Seumas Beg. James Stephens. FaPON; GrPl; OxBTC

Man Watching, The. Rainer Maria Rilke, *tr. fr. German by* Robert Bly. NU

Man Watching His Wife in a Play. Elizabeth Smither. ATNZ

Man waxy, The—he jogs along the fields. Napoleon after Sedan. Arthur Rimbaud, *tr. fr. French by* Robert Lowell. *Fr.* Eighteen-Seventy. FaBoPV; OBWP

Man went a-hunting at Reigate, A. *Unknown.* BoTP

Man went forth one day at eve, A. Tragedy. "Æ" MoBrPo

Man went forth with gifts, A. Martin Luther King, Jr. Gwendolyn Brooks. CNA; PoBA

Man White, Brown Girl and All That Jazz. Gloria C. Oden. PoBA

Man Who Became Old, The. Alberto Ríos. NoAM

Man Who Buys Hides, The. Dennis Schmitz. LCAP

Man Who Dreamed of Faeryland, The. W. B. Yeats. CMoP; NAEL-2; NoAM; NoP

Man who drew his strength from all, A. The Lincoln Statue. W. F. Collins. OHIP

Man who feels not, more or less, somewhat, The. Sonnet: Of Love in Men and Devils. Cecco Angiolieri da Siena, *tr. by* Dante Gabriel Rossetti. AWP

Man Who Finds That His Son Has Become a Thief, The. Raymond Souster. NOBC; OBCV

Man who follow English ways. Civil Irish and Wild Irish. Laoiseach Mac an Bhaird, *tr. by* Kenneth Jackson. AnIL

Man who found the aardvark, The. A Bestiary. Kenneth Rexroth. OBAL

Man Who Frets at Worldly Strife, The. Fitz-Greene Halleck *and* Joseph Rodman Drake. *Fr.* The Croaker Papers. AA

Man Who Had Fallen among Thieves, A. E. E. Cummings. HAP; LiTM; MoP; NoAM; NOBA; OxBA; TAP

Man, who had no rivals in the love, A. The Man and His Image. La Fontaine, *tr. by* Elizur Wright. OBVE

Man who has grown distant, A. Saigyo, *tr. by* Geoffrey Bownas *and* Anthony Thwaite. PeBJV

Man who, having collapsed, rises, takes steps, is insane, The. Forced March. Miklós Radnóti, *tr. by* Emery George. VWA

Man Who Hid His Own Front Door, The. Elizabeth MacKinstry. FaPON

Man who in his life trusts in this world, A. *Unknown.* TrJP

Man who is tied to a tree, The. The Hanged Man. John Oliver Simon. BWV

Man who just made this fiery speech, The. My Friend Abul Haul. Akhtar-ul-Iman, *tr. by* Mahmood Jamal. PBMUP

Man who keeps a diary, pays, A. Writing. William Allingham. NOBVV

Man Who Knew Too Much, The. David Wojahn. MAYP

Man who lies on his back under huge trees, The. Breathing Space July. Tomas Tranströmer, *tr. by* Robert Bly. RB

Man Who Loved Islands, The. Derek Walcott. NoAM

Man who loves hiking, A. Hiking. Joseph Bruchac. CDW

Man Who Made Me Love Him, The. Bruce Weigl. NAmP

Man Who Married Magdalene, The. Louis Simpson. MoP; NePoEA; NoAM; SM; TAP

Man Who Owned Cars, The. Elliot Fried. GOYP

Man Who Rode to Conemaugh, The. John Eliot Bowen. PAH

Man Who Sang the Sillies, The. John Ciardi. OBCA

Man who saw the light hanging on the tall end, The. The Borrower of Salt. Oscar Williams. *Fr.* Variations on a Theme, III. LiTA

Man who seeks one thing in life, and but one, The. One Thing. "Owen Meredith." WBLP

Man who sits on the bottom step, The. Rude Awakenings. Bob Rosenthal. UL

Man who sold his lawn to standard oil, The. The War against the Trees. Stanley Kunitz. CAPP; HAP

Man who stood beside me, The. Sweet Will. Philip Levine. BLA

Man who tells you which is the whiter wash, The. Love and How It Becomes Important in Our Day to Day Lives. Miller Williams. MT

Man Who Thinks He Can, The. Walter D. Wintle. *See* Thinking.

Man who touches a cabbage is seldom sorry, A. Proverbs. Donald Hall. SoTCo

Man Who Wasn't There, The. Hughes Mearns. *See* Little Man Who Wasn't There, The.

Man Who Went Absent from the Native Literature, The. Anthony Cronin. CIP

Man Who Would Be a Mother, The. Herbert Scott. NAmP

Man who would woo a fair maid, A. W. S. Gilbert. *Fr.* Yeoman of the Guard. FaBoUs

Man whom many held for wise, A. Memo. Hans Sahl, *tr. by* Edouard Roditi. VWA

Man Whom the Sea Kept Awake, The. Robert Bly. NePoEA

Man whose height his fear improved he, The. Medgar Evers. Gwendolyn Brooks. NoP; PoBA

Man whose name was Johnny Sands, A. Johnny Sands *Unknown.* CoMu; OBET

Man will keep a horse for prestige, A. Gateposts. Medbh McGuckian. FaBCIP

Man with a Little Pleated Piano, A. Winifred Welles. FaPON

Man with a marvelous mug, A. A Ballad in "G." Eugene Fitch Ware. PoLF

Man with a scythe: the torrent of his swing. Gardens No Emblems. Donald Davie. LiTM; NePoEA-2; OAEL-2

Man with a thousand hearts, The. Image-Nation 13 (the Telephone). Robin Blaser. PoM

Man with his burning soul. Truth. John Masefield. WGRP

Man with his lion under the shed of wars, The. The Song of the Borderguard. Robert Duncan. NeAP; PoM

Man with No Family to Take Leave of, The. Tu Fu, *tr. fr. Chinese by* Burton Watson. CoBCP

Man with One Small Hand. Patricia K. Page. MoCV; OBCV

Man with the blood in his sight, The. To Strike for Night. Lebert Bethune. NBP

Man with the Blue Guitar, The, *sels.* Wallace Stevens. LiTA
    "I cannot bring a world quite round." *Fr.* II. CMoP
        ("Man bent over his guitar, The.") CMoP; MoP; NoAM
    "Tom-tom, c'est moi. The blue guitar." *Fr.* XII. CMoP
    "Tune beyond us as we are, A." *Fr.* VI. CMoP

Man with the camera comes, The. Reservation Special. Lew Blockcolski. VoR

Man with the Hoe, The. Edwin Markham. AA; AnAmPo; BLPA; BLPL; EaLo; FaFP; LiTA; MoAmPo; OHFP; PrIm; SaC; TrGrPo; WBLP; WGRP

Man with the Hoe; a Reply, The. John Vance Cheney. AA

Man with the Hollow Breast, The. Tania Van Zyl. PeSA

Man with the red hat, The. Glazunoviana. John Ashbery. LCAP

Man with the Wooden Leg, The. Katherine Mansfield. ATNZ

Man without feelings, A. Saigyo, *tr. by* Geoffrey Bownas *and* Anthony Thwaite. PeBJV

Man without Sense of Direction. John Crowe Ransom. LiTM; OxBA

Man would like to fly off. Feathers. Paul Eluard, *tr. by* Michael Benedikt. POS

Man you/ are/ a liar. Insult before Gift-Giving. Frank Bolton, *tr. by* Armand Schwerner. STP

Man, you are at the first door. The Seven Houses. George Mackay Brown. NAs

Man you know, assured and kind, The. Almost Human. C. Day Lewis. NoAM

"Man, you too, aren't you, one of these rough followers of the criminal?" In the Servants' Quarters. Thomas Hardy. MoAB; MoBrPo

Manahatta. / A lovely name, he thought, and a lovely island. Early Dutch. Jennie M. Palen. GoYe

Manassas. Catherine Anne Warfield. PAH

Manatee, The. Carey Blyton. AmMo

Manchán's Prayer. Saint Manchán. NOIV

Manchester. John Bolton Rogerson. PF

Manchester Ship Canal, The. Oh the SS Irwell left this port the stormy sea to cross. *Unknown.* OBET

Manchester Ship Canal, The. I sing a theme deserving praise. *Unknown.* OBET

Manciple's Tale, The. Chaucer. *Fr.* The Canterbury Tales.
    Lat Take a Cat. ChTr
    Controlling the Tongue. OxBChV

Mandalay. Kipling. BrPo; FaBV; FPL; LiTB; MoBrPo; NOBE; OBTV; TrGrPo

Mandarin/ in a silent film. The Yellow Bird. James W. Thompson. PoBA

Mandarin Duck Lake is at Chia-ho. Ni Tsan Poem Following Rhyme-Words of Wu Chen. Wu Chen, *tr. by* Jonathan Chaves. CoBLCP

Mandarin ducks coze in the warmth of the quiet river. Echoing Heaven's Everlastingness. Mao Wen-hsi, *tr. by* Lois Fusek. ATF

Mandarin ducks swim in the warmth of the clear pond. The Beautiful Lady Yü. Mao Wen-hsi, *tr. by* Lois Fusek. ATF

Mandarin ducks were in flight. *Unknown, tr. by* Arthur Waley. BoS

Mandelstam. Richard Burns. VWA

Mandelstam. David Young. AmPA

Mandoline. Paul Verlaine, *tr. fr. French by* Arthur Symons. AWP; OBMV

Mandrake Hert, The. Sydney Goodsir Smith. OxBS

Mandrakes for Supper. James K. Baxter. OxBC

Mandrill, The. Conrad Aiken. RHPC

Maneuvers. Nelo Risi, *tr. fr. Italian by* Lawrence R. Smith. NItP

Manfred: A Dramatic Poem, *sel.* Byron. EnRP; NAEL-2
    "Stars are forth, the moon above the tops, The." *Fr.* III, iv. OAEL-2

Mangin Street. Berysh Vaynshteyn, *tr. fr. Yiddish by* Benjamin *and* Barbara Harshav. *Fr.* New York Everywhere. AYP

Mango on the Mango Tree, The. Robert Penn Warren. *Fr.* Mexico Is a Foreign Country: Four Studies in Naturalism, IV. MoP; NoAM

Mango Tree, The. Eric Chock. BrSi

Mangoes grow in clusters, The. So Close Should Be Our Love. *Gond Oral Tradition, tr. by* V. Elwin *and* S. Hivale. WTO

Mangy god is stoking this fire, A. Goldrush. H. C. ten Berge, *tr. by* Wanda Boeke. DuIn

Manhattan. Morris Abel Beer. AmFN

Manhattan. Lorenz Hart. OBAL

Manhattan. H. R. Hays. EAS

Manhattan. Osbert Lancaster. *Fr.* Afternoons with Baedeker. NOBL

Manhattan Bridge. A. Leyeles, *tr. fr. Yiddish by* Benjamin *and* Barbara Harshav. *Fr.* New York. AYP

Manhattan is no island, it. Under. George Bowering. NeAC

Manhattan Lullaby. Rachel Lyman Field. AmFN

Manhattan Menagerie. Joseph Cherwinski. GoYe

Manhole Covers. Karl Shapiro. AmFN; GoJo; NoAM

Manhood. Adela Zamudio, *tr. fr. Spanish by* Kate Flores. DMH

Manichaeans, The. Gary Snyder. VGW

Manichean Geography I. Tom Paulin. FaBCIP

Manicheans did no idols make, The. Fulke Greville. *Fr.* Caelica, LXXXIX. NOCV

Manifest Destiny. Anita Endrezze-Danielson. CDW

Manifest Destiny. Anselm Hollo. UL

Manifest Destiny. Pearse Hutchinson. CIP

Manifesto, *sel.* Nicanor Parra, *tr. fr. Spanish by* Miller Williams. I Move the Meeting Be Adjourned. HoPM

Manifesto for the Faint-Hearted, A. Carole Oles. SM

Manifesto of the Soldier Who Went Back to War. Angel Miguel Queremel, *tr. fr. Spanish by* Donald Devenish Walsh. WaaP

Manifold Little Hills. Ho Ning, *tr. fr. Chinese by* Lois Fusek. ATF

Manifold Little Hills. Hsüeh Chao-yün, *tr. fr. Chinese by* Lois Fusek. ATF

Manifold Little Hills. Mao Hsi-chen, *tr. fr. Chinese by* Lois Fusek. ATF

Manifold Little Hills. Wei Chuang, *tr. fr. Chinese by* Lois Fusek. ATF

Manila. Eugene Fitch Ware. FiBHP

Manila Bay. Arthur Hale. PAH

Mankend I cale. Christ Calls Man Home. *Unknown.* MeEL

Mankind, *sel. Unknown.*
    "Very fownder and begynner of owr fyrst creacyon, The." OxBLMV

Mankind and man's world. Tameko, *tr. by* Steven D. Carter. WFTW

Manless Society, The. Pierre Unik, *tr. fr. French.* EAS, *tr. by* David Gascoyne

Manlet, The. "Lewis Carroll." BXAP; Par
    (Little Man That Had a Little Gun, The.) FaBoNo

Manlius to Coeymans. Clark Coolidge. LP

Manly Heart, The. George Wither. *See* Fair Virtue, the Mistress of Philarete: Shall I Wasting in Despair.

Manly Man, The. *Unknown.* BLPA; WBLP

Mannahatta. Walt Whitman. AA; EyDe; GOA; MoAmPo

Mannequins. Daniel Mark Epstein. MAYP

Mannequins. Mascha Kaléko, *tr. fr. German by* Susan L. Cocalis. DMG

Manner of Speaking, A. Jack Myers. NAmP

Mannerly Margery Mylk and Ale. John Skelton. AAS; FaBoNo; NAEL-1; NoP

Manners. Howard Nemerov. NBLV

Manners. Edith Marcombe Shiffert. WPE

Manners. Mariana Griswold Van Rensselaer. FaPON; RHPC

Manners at Table When Away from Home. *Unknown.* OxBChV

Manners [for a Child of 1918]. Elizabeth Bishop. GOYP; OxBC; RB
Manners in the dining-room. *Unknown.* OxNR
Manoeuvre, The. William Carlos Williams. PCP
Manomin. Phyllis Wolf. STE
Manong Benny. Virginia Cerenio. BrSi
Manong Federico Delos Reyes and His Golden Banjo. Al Robles. BrSi
Manong Jacinto Santo Tomas. Al Robles. BrSi
Manor Garden, The. Sylvia Plath. FaBoWP; LCAP
Manor Lord, The. George Houghton. AA
Manor Water. *Unknown.* GBP
Manos Karastefanís. James Merrill. TAP
"Man's a man, A," says Robert Burns. For A' That and A' That. *Unknown.* BXAP
Man's a Man for A' That, A. Burns. *See* For A' That and A' That ("Is there, for honest poverty").
Man's a poor deluded bubble. Robert Dodsley. OxBSP
Man's Amazement. *Unknown.* CoMu
Man's and woman's bodies lay without souls. A Childish Prank. Ted Hughes. OAEL-2; OxBC
Man's Anxious, but Ineffectual Guard against Death. Thomas Lovell Beddoes. ChER
Man's Days. Eden Phillpotts. OBEV; OxBTC
Man's Dying-Place Uncertain. Robert Herrick. CaPo
Man's Going Hence. Samuel Rogers. *Fr.* Human Life. OBNC
Man's Inhumanity to Man. Burns. BLPA; FaFP
Man's Life. William Hammond. OBS
Man's life is death. Yet Christ endured to live. Wednesday in Holy Week. Christina Rossetti. TrCP
Man's life is laid in the loom of time. The Loom of Time. *Unknown.* BLPA
Man's life is like a rose that in spring. Meditation. Philip Pain. *Fr.* Meditations for July 26, 1666. NOBA; SCAP
Man's life is well compared to a feast. A Comparison of the Life of Man. Richard Barnfield. OBSC; OxBSP
Man's life was once a span; now one of those. Man's Life. William Hammond. OBS
Man's life's a tragedy: his mother's womb. De Morte. Sir Henry Wotton. OBS; OxBSP
Man's Littleness in Presence of the Stars. Henry Kirke White. WBLP
Man's Mortality. *At. to* Simon Wastell. *Fr.* Microbiblion. FaBoCh (Verses of Man's Mortalitie.) OBS
Man's Need. *Gond Oral Tradition,* tr. by V. Elwin *and* S. Hivale. WTO
Man's parts tell us such a lot, A! Parts. Zishe Landau, *tr. by* Ruth Whitman. VWA
Man's Pillow. Irving Browne. AA
Man's Prayer, The. T. A. Daly. TrPWD
Mans restlesse soule hath restlesse eyes and ears. Roger Williams. SCAP
Man's Sliding Mood, A. Mary Elizabeth Fullerton. CBAP
Man's Song, about His Daughter, A. *Unknown, tr. fr. Eskimo by* Armand Schwerner. STP
Man's Vocation Is Nobody's Business, A. James Galvin. KS
Man's woe and misery. Reminder. John D. Engle, Jr.. SoTCo
Man's Woman, A. Mary Carolyn Davies. PoLF
Man's years fall short of a hundred. *Unknown, tr. fr. Chinese by* Burton Watson. *Fr.* Nineteen Old Poems of the Han, XV. CoBCP
Manservants on the last trains. North to Milwaukee. Gerald Vizenor. VoR
Mantelpiece of Shells, A. Ruthven Todd. NYBP
Mantis. David McCord. OBAL
Mantle. William Heyen. MAYP; TSL
Mantle ran so hard, they said. Mantle. William Heyen. MAYP; TSL
Mantle So Green, The. *Unknown.* AmFP
Mantova. James Wright. LCAP; NNaP
Manual, The. Larry Rubin. MT
Manuelzinho. Elizabeth Bishop. FaBoWP; NYBP
Manufactured Gods. Carl Sandburg. WGRP
Manumission. Barbara Burford. DT
Manure Book, The. Russell Edson. AnAn
Many a fairer face than yours. To a Lady. Franklin P. Adams. FiBHP
Many a green isle needs must be. Lines Written among the Euganean Hills. Shelley. EnRP; GTBS; GTBS-P; PoEL-4
Many a hearth upon our dark globe sighs after many a vanish'd face. Vastness. Tennyson. OPOP
Many a lip is gaping for drink. Eliza Cook. *Fr.* Song of the Seaweed. FiBHP
Many a long, long year ago. The Alarmed Skipper. James Thomas Fields. AnAmPo; NBLV
Many a Mickle. Walter De la Mare. FaBV

Many a summer is dead and buried, A. Spirits Everywhere. Ludwig Uhland, *tr. by* James Clarence Mangan. AWP
Many American flags, The. The Grand Entry. Gary Snyder. NoAM
Many and sharp the numerous ills. Man's Inhumanity to Man. Burns. BLPA; FaFP
Many animals that our fathers killed in America. Fear Is What Quickens Me. James Wright. CAPP
Many Are Called. Edwin Arlington Robinson. OxBA
Many are the joys. Intimations of Sublimity. Wordsworth. *Fr.* The Prelude [or, Growth of a Poet's Mind]: School-Time. OBNC
Many are the sayings of the wise. The Ways of God to Men. Milton. *Fr.* Samson Agonistes. OBS
Many are the ways and many the recipes. Recipe: Hare. Archestratus. FaBoUs
Many are thy tones, O Ocean. Sea Cadences. Henrietta Cordelia Ray. CBWP-3
Many as noticed by the one, The. De Imagine Mundi. John Ashbery. FaBoMo
Many Birds. Anne Welsh. PeSA
Many colors will take you to themselves. Never Seek to Tell Thy Love. John Ashbery. HCAP; InPS
Many days of sorrow, many nights of woe. Chain Gang Blues. *Unknown.* WTO
Many desire, but few or none deserve. The Advice. Sir Walter Ralegh. AAS; SiPS
Many Die Here. Gayl Jones. BlSi
Many fingers point. She Is Not Mute. Chan Ch'e, *tr. by* Dominic Cheung. IFON
Many Happy Returns. W. H. Auden. NAs
Many husbands are missing tonight. The Beautiful Urinals of Paris. C. D. Wright. MT
Many in aftertimes will say of you. Christina Rossetti. *Fr.* Monna Innominata. OBNC
Many Indeed Must Perish in the Keel. Hugo von Hofmannsthal, *tr. fr. German by* Jethro Bithell. AWP; TrJP
Many ingenious lovely things are gone. W. B. Yeats. *Fr.* Nineteen Hundred and Nineteen, I. BiRV; LiTB; MoAB; PoE
Many liberals don't just. Respectabilities. Jon Silkin. NePoEA-2
Many little cuss words, bother, dash and blow. *Unknown.* FaBoUs
Many long years ago, I loved a youth. The Blight of Love. Mary E. Tucker. CBWP-1
Many love music but for music's sake. On Music. Walter Savage Landor. GoJo
Many-maned scud-thumper, tub. Winter Ocean. John Updike. InPK; MOS; SoSe
Many mosquitoes bloated with blood. Taigi, *tr. fr. Japanese by* Hiroaki Sato. *Fr.* Twenty-nine Hokku. FCEI
Many of us are still sitting. Report on the Situation. Helga Novak, *tr. by* Susan L. Cocalis. DMI
Many paths lead. Paths to God. Musa Moris Farhi, *tr. by the author.* VWA
Many people have been frighted & died in cemeteries. My Gang. Jack Kerouac. PoM
Many people have gathered together. Foot Race Song. *Unknown, tr. by* Frank Russell. NU; OBVE
Many people seem to think. Nonsense Quatrains. Gelett Burgess. CenHV; FaBoNo (Parisian Nectar.) FaBoNo
Many prophets have failed, their voices silent. Ode to Failure. Allen Ginsberg. CAPP
Many red devils ran from my heart. Stephen Crane. *Fr.* The Black Riders, XLVI. TAP
Many shapes of wings. Environs. Larry Eigner. NeAP
Many ships have asked for sanctuary. Free Harbor. Suad al-Mubarak al-Sabah, *tr. by* May Jayyusi *and* John Heath-Stubbs. MAP
Many strange mountains in Shu and Han. Imitating the Old Poems. Pao Chao, *tr. by* Burton Watson. CoBCP
Many things I might have said today. Aprons of Silence. Carl Sandburg. NOBA
Many Things Thou Hast Given Me, Dear Heart. Alice Wellington Rollins. AA
Many Times November Has Come Back. Margherita Guidacci, *tr. fr. Italian by* Muriel Kittel. DMI
Many times the size of man. The Horse. Francis Ponge, *tr. by* Beth Archer. NU
Many trees can stand unshaded. Trees and Cattle. James Dickey. NePoEA-2
Many-volumned authoresses. Agatha Christie and Beatrix Potter. John Updike. AnAmPo
Many Wagons Ago. John Ashbery. HCAP

Many weary weeks divide me. The Ship's Cook, a Captive Sings. Hugo von Hofmannsthal, *tr. by* Charles Wharton Stork. TrJP
Many were happy. Fresh News from the Past. Marvin Bell. LCAP
Many without Elegy. William Sydney Graham. OxBS
Many women call on me to sleep with them. A Mourning-Song for Rangiaho. Te Heuheu Herea, *tr. by* Barry Mitcalfe. WTO
Many Workmen. Stephen Crane. *Fr.* The Black Riders, XXXI. LiTA; TAP
Many worship you, Sunday, throw into you feverishly. The Bliss of Sunday. László Nagy, *tr. by* Edwin Morgan. MHuP
Many years ago. Arlindo Barbeitos, *tr. fr. Portuguese by* Ronald Rassner. WMBCH
Many years back was an evening. Then and Now. Anne B. Murray. PoSH
Manyo Shu, *sels. Various Authors, tr. fr. Japanese.*
"Above the cascade running down the rocks." Prince Shiki, *tr. by* Hiroaki Sato. FCEI
"Above the cascade tumbling down the rocks." Prince Shiki. Ma
"Above the height of Mikasa in Kasuga." *Unknown.* Ma
"Above the north mountain-range." Empress Jito. Ma
"Absurd!/ at my age." *Unknown, tr. by* Burton Watson. FCEI
"Across the river of Asuka where the birds fly." Hitomaro, *tr. by* Hiroaki Sato. FCEI
"Across the river of the bird-flying Asuka." Hitomaro. Ma
"After five years passed in the country." Okura. Ma
"After his weary travels." "Tsuki." Ma
"After travelling from the Imperial City." *Unknown.* Ma
"After we, dear friends, have drunk together." Lady Otomo no Sakanoe. Ma
"Ah, must I leave you dear." Hasetsukabe Tori. Ma
"Ah, that rascal love." Prince Hozumi. Ma
"Alas, the Garden Palace of my prince." *Unknown.* Ma
"All creatures that live." Tabito, *tr. by* Geoffrey Bownas *and* Anthony Thwaite. PeBJV
"All over the meadow." Princess Takata. Ma
"All unaware, it may be." Hitomaro. Ma
"Along the coast of Tsunu." Hitomaro. Ma
"Along the path of Iware." Prince Yamakuma. Ma
"Although across the plains of the sea I came." *Unknown.* Ma
"Although I am on a journey." Mibu Utamaro. Ma
"Am I a man of the days gone by." Furuhito. Ma
"Am I the son my father and mother cherish." Yakamochi. Ma
"And this/ is all there is." Yakamochi, *tr. by* Burton Watson. FCEI
"Are there no gods of heaven and earth?." *Unknown.* Ma
"Are these truly the fisher-maids." Tanabe Akiniwa. Ma
"As evening falls the autumn wind is cold." *Unknown.* Ma
"As far as sleeping goes." *Unknown, tr. by* Burton Watson. FCEI
"As for me, I can take." Tamatsukuribe Hirome. Ma
"As I pass over Mount Shiotsu." Kanamura. Ma
"As I sit worn and weary." *Unknown.* Ma
"As if a cloud were sailing." Lady Otomo no Sakanoe. Ma
"As if to foreshadow." *Unknown.* Ma
"As if to say that I may die." Hitomaro. Ma
"As if to say the land will prosper." *Unknown.* Ma
"As if with wardens posted." *Unknown.* Ma
"As in the autumn paddies rice stalks lean only one way." Princess Tajima, *tr. by* Hiroaki Sato. FCEI
"As long as I live." Lady Kasa, *tr. by* Burton Watson. FCEI
"As one hears the rumbling thunder." Kuramochi Chitose. Ma
"As people have told from mouth to mouth." *Unknown.* Ma
"As spring has come when the mist trails." Kamo Taruhito. Ma
"As the moon sinks on the mountain-edge." *Unknown.* Ma
"As the mountain torrents roar and roar again." Hitomaro. Ma
"As the seasons change." Yakamochi. Ma
"As the *yu*-cloth is dyed fast and deep." Hitomaro. Ma
"As we go fast, rowing the huge ship." Hanishi Mitoshi. Ma
"As we row round the jutting beaches." Kurohito. Ma
"As you, honoured Lord, travelled all the way." Mushimaro. Ma
"At every trotting sound of a horse's hoofs." *Unknown.* Ma
"At home the *hagi* flowers of autumn." Lady Otomo no Tamura. Ma
"At Iwashiro I bind." Prince Arima. Ma
"At Iwashiro I tie together branches of a beach pine." Prince Arima, *tr. by* Hiroaki Sato. FCEI
"At Misaka, the Pass of the Gods." Kamutobe Kooshio. Ma
"At my home." Lady Kasa, *tr. by* Burton Watson. FCEI
"At our awful Sovereign's word." *Unknown.* Ma
"At our dread Sovereign's word." Yuki Yakamaro. Ma
"At the beginning of heaven and earth." Hitomaro. Ma
"At the bidding of my great Sovereign." Yakamochi. Ma
"At the coming of the New Year." Prince Funado. Ma

"At the corner of the reed fence." *Unknown, tr. by* Hiroaki Sato. FCEI
"At the headland of Kashima." Mushimaro. Ma
"At the house where the Saburu girl." Yakamochi. Ma
"At the palace of Kukuri." *Unknown.* Ma
"At the post station." *Unknown, tr. by* Hiroaki Sato. FCEI
"At the Table Island." *Unknown.* Ma
"At the upper course of the river." *Unknown.* Ma
"At this time of the year when the white-clouded Tatsuta Hill." Mushimaro. Ma
"At wave-bright Naniwa." Lady Otomo no Sakanoe. Ma
"Away from the sight of my dear wife." Akahito. Ma
"Away, you who rattle at my door." *Unknown.* Ma
"Awesome beyond speech." Hitomaro. Ma
"Be not concerned, O my Sovereign." Princess Minabe. Ma
"Be not hasty." Kojima. Ma
"Be strong like a mansion built." Sakatabe Obitomaro. Ma
"Beach is beautiful; and there grow, The." Kuramochi Chitose. Ma
"Beacons of the fishing-boats, The." *Unknown, tr. by* Geoffrey Bownas *and* Anthony Thwaite. PeBJV
"Beautiful is the moon-lit night." Yotsuna. Ma
"Beauty was hers that glowed like autumn mountains." Hitomaro. Ma
"Because he is young." Okura, *tr. by* Arthur Waley. AWP
"Because I am human and unable to be near a god." *Unknown, tr. by* Hiroaki Sato. FCEI
"Because of the slanderous tongues." Princess Tajima. Ma
"Because of your errant love for a maid." *the wife of* Isonokami Otomaro. Ma
"Because people's words are rampant and the rumor pains me." Princess Tajima, *tr. by* Hiroaki Sato. FCEI
"Because spring's here." Yakamochi, *tr. by* Burton Watson. FCEI
"Before me on my track." Kisakibe Isoshima. Ma
"Behind my parents' house." Ikutamabe Tarukuni, *tr. by* Geoffrey Bownas *and* Anthony Thwaite. PeBJV
"Behind the mountain ledge." *Unknown, tr. by* Geoffrey Bownas *and* Anthony Thwaite. PeBJV
"Bell has rung, the sign, The." Lady Kasa, *tr. by* Geoffrey Bownas *and* Anthony Thwaite. PeBJV
"Bell lily blooming under a shrub in the summer field, A." Lady Otomo no Sakanoe, *tr. by* Hiroaki Sato. FCEI
"Bells are tolling, The." Lady Kasa. Ma
"Beloved one, my lord." *Unknown, tr. by* Burton Watson. FCEI
"Better than to say things like a wise fellow." Tabito, *tr. by* Hiroaki Sato. FCEI
"Beyond the waves rearing a thousandfold." Hitomaro. Ma
"Birds of the Island Palace, The." Hitomaro. Ma
"Boil water, my lads." Naga Okimaro. Ma
"Brave liegeman like you, A." Kanamura. Ma
"Breakers of the Ise Sea, The." Lady Kasa, *tr. by* Geoffrey Bownas *and* Anthony Thwaite. PeBJV
"Breaking and spreading for a bed." *the wife of* Go Dan-ochi. Ma
"Breezes blowing/ through the little clumps." Yakamochi, *tr. by* Burton Watson. FCEI
"Brief is this mortal life." Yakamochi. Ma
"Burgeoning anew in spring." *Unknown.* Ma
"But a fisherman's daughters." Tabito. Ma
"By all the routes under heaven." Yakamochi. Ma
"By the light of the flares." *Unknown, tr. by* Burton Watson. FCEI
"By the light of the Moon God." Prince Yuhara. Ma
"By the sea-shore of Mitsu, that reminds one." Tajihi Kasamaro. Ma
"By way of pretext." Yakamochi, *tr. by* Arthur Waley. AWP
"Calm and knowing ways." Tabito, *tr. by* Geoffrey Bownas *and* Anthony Thwaite. PeBJV
"Can only a spring rain so drench." *Unknown.* Ma
"Can the prime of youth come back to me?." Tabito. Ma
"Children, The/ who cried." *Unknown, tr. by* Hiroaki Sato. FCEI
"Choosing "sage" as a name for sake." Tabito, *tr. by* Hiroaki Sato. FCEI
"City of Nara of good blue clay, The." Ono no Oyu, *tr. by* Hiroaki Sato. FCEI
"Clear and loud." Hitomaro, *tr. by* Geoffrey Bownas *and* Anthony Thwaite. PeBJV
"Clear is the bottom of the lake." Yakamochi. Ma
"Clearly I see the pebbles in the water." *Unknown.* Ma
"Climbing the peaks of Tsukuba." Mushimaro. Ma
"Clinging to this transient life." Prince Omi. Ma
"Cloud clings, The." *Unknown.* Ma
"Cloud drifting over the brows, The." Hitomaro. Ma
"Cold dew of heaven has fallen, The." Lady Otomo no Sakanoe. Ma
"Come, my men, let us hasten to Yamato!" Okura. Ma

"Come, then, my men." Emperor Ojin, *tr. by* Geoffrey Bownas *and* Anthony Thwaite. PeBJV

"Come to me, my dearest." *Unknown.* Ma

"Come to see me through the spaces." *Unknown, tr. by* Hiroaki Sato. FCEI

"Continuously, as their name tells." Akahito. Ma

"Could a little spring rain." *Unknown, tr. by* Burton Watson. FCEI

"Could my great ship take you in." *Unknown.* Ma

"Countless are the mountains in Yamato." Emperor Jomei. Ma

"Court ladies may board a boat, The." Hitomaro. Ma

"Cowherd, since parting with the Princess Weaver, The." Okura, *tr. by* Hiroaki Sato. FCEI

"Cranes fly calling towards Sakurada Fields." Kurohito. Ma

"Crickets chirp at my bedside, The." *Unknown.* Ma

"Crow that feeds on the rice, A." Prince Takamiya. Ma

"Dainty water-weeds, growing up-stream." Hitomaro. Ma

"Darting over the cedar brakes." Yakamochi, *tr. by* Burton Watson. FCEI

"Day I go, The/ to pick arrowhead." *Unknown, tr. by* Burton Watson. FCEI

"Day in, day out." Yosami. Ma

"Dear child, my daughter, who stood." Lady Otomo no Sakanoe. Ma

"Dear old man's verse, The." *Unknown.* Ma

"Debate not who I am." Hitomaro. Ma

"Deer that seeks the *hagi* flowers for mate, A." *Unknown.* Ma

"Deer that weds, The." *Unknown, tr. by* Burton Watson. FCEI

"Did men living long ago." Hitomaro. Ma

"Divine prince, born and descended." Lady Otomo no Sakanoe, *tr. by* Hiroaki Sato. FCEI

"Do it up!'" *the wife of* Mikata Shami. Ma

"Do not burn the brake." *Unknown.* Ma

"Do not tether a horse." *Unknown.* Ma

"Do the courtiers even now." Nakatomi Yakamori. Ma

"Do the vast oceans die?." *Unknown.* Ma

"Do you desire our love to endure?." Lady Otomo no Sakanoe. Ma

"Don't cut the bamboo grass under the elm." *Unknown, tr. by* Hiroaki Sato. FCEI

"Don't cut the shrub on Idemi Beach." *Unknown, tr. by* Hiroaki Sato. FCEI

"Don't go!/ now with the night so far gone." *Unknown, tr. by* Burton Watson. FCEI

"Don't think about useless things." *Unknown.*

"Don't wilt and brood on things." *Unknown, tr. by* Hiroaki Sato. FCEI

"Dread imperial command, The." Mononobe Akimochi. Ma

"Dreadful order, The." Mononobe Akimochi, *tr. by* Geoffrey Bownas *and* Anthony Thwaite. PeBJV

"Dress that my brother has put on is thin, The." Lady Otomo no Sakanoe, *tr. by* Arthur Waley. AWP

"Dripping dew of the foot-wearying mountain, The." Lady Ishikawa, *tr. by* Hiroaki Sato. FCEI

"Drum that the watchman beats, The." *Unknown.* Ma

"Ducks along the reedy shore, The." Prince Shiki, *tr. by* Hiroaki Sato. FCEI

"Echoing with the cries." Yakamochi, *tr. by* Burton Watson. FCEI

"Eight hundred days." Lady Kasa, *tr. by* Burton Watson. FCEI

"Eighty are the harbours." *Unknown.* Ma

"Empty house, The." Tabito, *tr. by* Geoffrey Bownas *and* Anthony Thwaite. PeBJV

"'Enough!' I say." Lady Shii, *tr. by* Burton Watson. FCEI

"Even a breeze may fail me." Princess Kagami. Ma

"Even a flaming fire can be snatched." Empress Jito. Ma

"Even a priceless jewel." Tabito, *tr. by* Geoffrey Bownas *and* Anthony Thwaite. PeBJV

"Even after my locks." Manzei. Ma

"Even as the snow falls to-day." Yakamochi. Ma

"Even if you bore them to the deepest sea." Tsukan. Ma

"Even if you say, 'I come.'" Lady Otomo no Sakanoe. Ma

"Even in a strange land I see." Hasetsukabe Mamaro. Ma

"Even in the heat." *Unknown.* Ma

"Even jewels that flash." Tabito, *tr. by* Geoffrey Bownas *and* Anthony Thwaite. PeBJV

"Even on spring days you work the fields." *Unknown, tr. by* Hiroaki Sato. FCEI

"Even the grains of sand." Lady Kasa, *tr. by* Geoffrey Bownas *and* Anthony Thwaite. PeBJV

"Even the sands uncounted of a long." Lady Kasa. Ma

"Even the wild-ducks skimming." Princess Ki. Ma

"Even to-day, were I in the city." Nakatomi Yakamori. Ma

"Even when no thunder sounds." Hitomaro. Ma

"Evening moon shines, The." Prince Yuhara. Ma

"Ever since heaven and earth were parted." Akahito. Ma

"Ever since the day he started." Minaka. Ma

"Everyone says 'It's so long—put it up!'" Mikata no Sami, *tr. by* Hiroaki Sato. FCEI

"Far off as the reed-plain of Manu." Lady Kasa. Ma

"Father and mother/ patting my head." *Unknown, tr. by* Hiroaki Sato. FCEI

"Fearsome even to allow in mind." Hitomaro, *tr. by* Hiroaki Sato. FCEI

"Field of Omi in Inami Plain, The." Akahito. Ma

"Fisher-maids at Shika, The." Kimiko. Ma

"Fishing fires far away, The." *Unknown.* Ma

"Five hundred rocks by the river." Lady Fuki. Ma

"Flocks of birds are singing." *Unknown, tr. by* Burton Watson. FCEI

"Flowering herbs of spring, The." Prince Ichihara. Ma

"Flowers have blossomed in my garden, The." Yakamochi. Ma

"Flowers of spring must now." Yakamochi. Ma

"Flowers that blow, The." Okura. Ma

"For my sister's sake." Hitomaro, *tr. by* Arthur Waley. AWP

"For the time that you return." Sanu Chigami. Ma

"For you, who journey to Shiragi." *Unknown.* Ma

"For your sake, O slave." Lady Ki. Ma

"Forget not, I pray, your Eastland girl." *Unknown.* Ma

"Forth to the field of spring." Akahito. Ma

"Fringed pink in my garden, The." *Unknown.*

"From bamboo groves." Yakamochi, *tr. by* Burton Watson. FCEI

"From Mitsu Beach." *Unknown, tr. by* Geoffrey Bownas *and* Anthony Thwaite. PeBJV

"From Mitsu, dearest shore to me." *Unknown.* Ma

"From Mount Kamunabi of Mimoro." *Unknown.* Ma

"From Saiga's plain, where we serve." Akahito. Ma

"From the age of the gods." Empress Kogyoku, *tr. by* Geoffrey Bownas *and* Anthony Thwaite. Ma; PeBJV

"From the mulberry-rope country of Silla." Lady Otomo no Sakanoe, *tr. by* Hiroaki Sato. FCEI

"From this time on." Yakamochi. Ma

"From to-morrow ever." Princess Oku. Ma

"Frontier-guard, A/ I set out in the morning." *Unknown.* Ma

"Frontier-guard when I set out, A." Wakatoneribe Hirotari. Ma

"Gallant courtier, A." Tanushi. Ma

"Garment is thin, The." Lady Otomo no Sakanoe. Ma

"Gazing at the hand you squeezed." Lady Heguri. Ma

"Gem that gleams at night it may be, A." Tabito, *tr. by* Hiroaki Sato. FCEI

"Gentle winds at Asuka, The." Prince Shiki. Ma

"Go not away, dear heart." *Unknown.* Ma

"Going alone to the western market." *Unknown.* Ma

"Grass of love would load, The." Princess Hirokawa, *tr. by* Geoffrey Bownas *and* Anthony Thwaite. PeBJV

"Great earth itself, The." Hitomaro. Ma

"Had he been at home, he would have slept." Prince Shotoku. Ma

"Had I foreknown my sweet lord's coming." *Unknown.* Ma

"Had not there been the man." Wakamiya Ayumaro. Ma

"Had we foreknown." Princess Nukada. Ma

"Hark! even here, into the chambers of the Palace." Naga Okimaro. Ma

"Hark, the bells are ringing." *Unknown.* Ma

"Having met you as in a dream." *Unknown.* Ma

"Having seen your smile." Yakamochi. Ma

"He lies unloosened of his white clothes." Tanabe Sakimaro. Ma

"He who burns the sere weeds." *Unknown.* Ma

"Heaven and earth." Hitomaro, *tr. by* Geoffrey Bownas *and* Anthony Thwaite. PeBJV

"Her husband is gone towards Naniwa." Tajihi Yanushi. Ma

"Here at the river neck." *Unknown.* Ma

"Here I thought I was." *Unknown, tr. by* Burton Watson. FCEI

"Here in a beautiful dell where the river runs." Akahito. Ma

"Here in the capital I wonder." Tabito. Ma

"Here is the water by which." Azumabito. Ma

"Here where stands the Palace of Yoshinu." Akahito. Ma

"Here where the wild ducks." Taniha Ome. Ma

"High in the sanctuary." Ishikawa Toshitari. Ma

"High on the peak of Mikasa." Akahito, *tr. by* Geoffrey Bownas *and* Anthony Thwaite. PeBJV

"Highway of Shinanu, The." *Unknown.* Ma

"Highway to Shinano, The." *Unknown, tr. by* Geoffrey Bownas *and* Anthony Thwaite. PeBJV

"Hill of secluded Hatsuse, The." *Unknown.* Ma

"Horse is loose, The." Ojibe Kurome, *tr. by* Geoffrey Bownas *and* Anthony Thwaite. PeBJV

"How awesome/ the imperial command." *Unknown, tr. by Hiroaki Sato.* FCEI

"How distinct is Matokata, the Target Bay." "Toneri." Ma

"How fortunate he is!" *Unknown.* Ma

"How gladdening would be this falling snow." Empress Komyo. Ma

"How I regret it now." Udobe Ushimaro. Ma

"How I waste and waste away." Yakamochi. Ma

"How marvelous a fellow." *Unknown, tr. by Burton Watson.* FCEI

"How named is the god." Hitomaro. Ma

"How plainly one may see." Hitomaro. Ma

"How sorely the rain besets me!" Naga Okimaro. Ma

"How to speak of it." Tabito, *tr. by Geoffrey Bownas and Anthony Thwaite.* PeBJV

"How truly now I understand." *Unknown.* Ma

"How ugly—take a good look at a man who acts wise." Tabito, *tr. by Hiroaki Sato.* FCEI

"How will you manage." Princess Daihaku, *tr. by Arthur Waley.* AWP

"How winsome are the lilies of my garland." Yakamochi. Ma

"However long I wait for him." *Unknown.* Ma

"However loud I call to the man." *Unknown.* Ma

"However much I beat him." *Unknown.* Ma

"I, a dear child to my father." Isonokami Otomaro. Ma

"I am at my post." *Unknown.* Ma

"I am of this world." *Unknown, tr. by Geoffrey Bownas and Anthony Thwaite.* PeBJV

"I am on a journey." *Unknown, tr. by Geoffrey Bownas and Anthony Thwaite.* PeBJV

"I am sick body and soul." *The Wife of* Kuramochi. Ma

"I came to this spring field to pick violets." Akahito, *tr. by Hiroaki Sato.* FCEI

"I can bear/ not seeing you." Lady Kasa, *tr. by Burton Watson.* FCEI

"I cherished you, my darling." Lady Otomo no Sakanoe. Ma

"I deliver the jewel." Lady Otomo no Sakanoe. Ma

"I didn't take/ a good look at him." *Unknown, tr. by Burton Watson.* FCEI

"I don't know how to say it, what to do about it." Tabito, *tr. by Hiroaki Sato.* FCEI

"I dreamed I was holding." Lady Kasa. Ma

"I dreamt/ I clasped a sword." Lady Kasa, *tr. by Burton Watson.* FCEI

"I dreamt of a great sword." Lady Kasa, *tr. by Geoffrey Bownas and Anthony Thwaite.* PeBJV

"I dusted the bed." *Unknown, tr. by Burton Watson.* FCEI

"I eat my food." *Tr. by Burton Watson.* FCEI

"I gather shells and pebbles." Kamatari. Ma

"I go on loving him." Lady Kasa, *tr. by Burton Watson.* FCEI

"I have determined that my dear lord's name." *Unknown.* Ma

"I have lived my life." Momoyo. Ma

"I have lost a true man's mettle." Hitomaro. Ma

"I have not met her for so long." Prince Kadobe. Ma

"I have waited on my lord." *Unknown.* Ma

"I hear the bell striking." Lady Kasa, *tr. by Burton Watson.* FCEI

"I hear the twang of the mid-string." Empress Kogyoku. Ma

"I heard that you were." Lady Ishikawa. Ma

"I know well this body of mine." Yakamochi. Ma

"I leave my father and mother behind." Hasetsukabe Hitomaro. Ma

"I love you/ do not forget me." Lady Kasa, *tr. by Burton Watson.* FCEI

"I love you,/ it's utterly hopeless." Lady Kasa, *tr. by Burton Watson.* FCEI

"I loved her like the leaves." Hitomaro, *tr. by Geoffrey Bownas and Anthony Thwaite.* PeBJV

"I make a pillow of a rock-root on Mount Kamo." Hitomaro, *tr. by Hiroaki Sato.* FCEI

"I, Okura, must excuse myself now." Okura, *tr. by Hiroaki Sato.* FCEI

"I, Okura, will leave now." Okura. Ma

"I pound the rice." *Unknown, tr. by Geoffrey Bownas and Anthony Thwaite.* PeBJV

"I put good rice in water." *Unknown, tr. by Burton Watson.* FCEI

"I remember ever so long." *Unknown.* Ma

"I saw the sun set in clouds." Emperor Tenji, *tr. by Hiroaki Sato.* FCEI

"I saw this house." Prince Odai. Ma

" 'I shall forget,' I said." Akinoosa Obitomaro, *tr. by Geoffrey Bownas and Anthony Thwaite.* PeBJV

"I shall think of nothing more now." Lady Abe. Ma

"I stand and gaze at the tomb." Tanabe Sakimaro. Ma

"I thought I would wear it." *Unknown.* Ma

"I thought there could be." Princess Hirokawa. Ma

"I, thy humble subject." Ama-no-Inukai Okamaro. Ma

"I told the water god on my hill to let the snow fall." Emperor Temmu, *tr. by Hiroaki Sato.* FCEI

"I turn and gaze far." Empress Yamato-hime. Ma

"I waited and I." Princess Nukada, *tr. by Geoffrey Bownas and Anthony Thwaite.* PeBJV

"I was not to know." *Unknown, tr. by Geoffrey Bownas and Anthony Thwaite.* PeBJV

"I who have counted me for a strong man." *Unknown.* Ma

"I will not comb my morning hair." *Unknown.* Ma

"I will not from to-day." Imamatsuribe Yosofu. Ma

"I will think of you, love." *Unknown.* Ma

"I will tread the sharpness of the." Hitomaro. Ma

"I wish I could lend a coat." Akahito, *tr. by Arthur Waley.* AWP

"I wish I had a pony." *Unknown, tr. by Hiroaki Sato.* FCEI

"I wish I had the leisure." Mononobe Komaro. Ma

"I wish there were a man going to my home." Otomobe Fushimaro. Ma

"I would make my way without a thought of you." *Unknown.* Ma

"I would quickly reach my loved one's dwelling." Hitomaro. Ma

"I'd like to see you as in a clear mirror." *Unknown, tr. by Hiroaki Sato.* FCEI

"If I am left behind and long for you." *Unknown, tr. by Hiroaki Sato.* FCEI

"If I buy a horse." *Unknown, tr. by Burton Watson.* FCEI

"If I come, surprising her." *Unknown.* Ma

"If I come to her." *Unknown.* Ma

"If I could see the capital." Tabito. Ma

"If I enjoy myself in this world." Tabito, *tr. by Hiroaki Sato.* FCEI

"If I get a horse, my beloved." *Unknown.* Ma

"if I go/ when she's not expecting me." *Unknown, tr. by Burton Watson.* FCEI

"If I leave her and go away." *Unknown, tr. by Hiroaki Sato.* FCEI

"If I leave you behind." *Unknown.* Ma

"If I revel." Tabito, *tr. by Geoffrey Bownas and Anthony Thwaite.* PeBJV

"If I sent my forlorn love." Lady Otomo no Sakanoe. Ma

"If I'd known you were coming, love." *Unknown, tr. by Hiroaki Sato.* FCEI

"If it were death to love." Lady Kasa. Ma

"If my recent love-labours." *Unknown, tr. by Geoffrey Bownas and Anthony Thwaite.* PeBJV

"If need be, I'd follow you." *Unknown.* Ma

"If one can die of love." Lady Kasa, *tr. by Burton Watson.* FCEI

"If only I had time." *Unknown, tr. by Hiroaki Sato.* FCEI

"If the gods of heaven and earth." Lady Kasa. Ma

("If the gods/ of heaven and earth.") FCEI, *tr. by Burton Watson.*

"If the thunder rolls for a while." Hitomaro. Ma

"If there be a law that allows." *Unknown.* Ma

"If tied, it would slip off." Mikata Shami. Ma

"If you lack, makers of Buddhas." Omiwa Okimori. Ma

"If you so heed your mother." *Unknown.* Ma

"I'll not die of love." *Unknown, tr. by Burton Watson.* FCEI

"Imperial City of fairest Nara, The." Ono Oyu. Ma

"In a creek in Muko Bay." *Unknown, tr. by Geoffrey Bownas and Anthony Thwaite.* PeBJV

"In all-under-heaven where our sovereign." Hitomaro, *tr. by Hiroaki Sato.* FCEI

"In building the great sanctuary." Kose Natemaro. Ma

"In calling it 'sage.' " Tabito, *tr. by Geoffrey Bownas and Anthony Thwaite.* PeBJV

"In Katsushika of the grebes." *Unknown, tr. by Hiroaki Sato.* FCEI

"In my dream said a plum-blossom." Tabito. Ma

"In my garden." Yakamochi, *tr. by Burton Watson.* FCEI

"In my garden fall the plum-blossoms." Tabito. Ma

"In my morning bed." Yakamochi, *tr. by Burton Watson.* FCEI

"In my morning bed I listen." Yakamochi. Ma

"In O-Yashima, the dominion under heaven." Tanabe Sakimaro. Ma

"In obedience to the imperial command." Yakamochi. Ma

In 728, Longing for His Deceased Wife. Tabito, *tr. by Hiroaki Sato.* FCEI

"In that little ugly hut." *Unknown, tr. by Burton Watson.* FCEI

"In that most wretched hovel." *Unknown.* Ma

"In the Akitsu Dale of Yoshinu." Akahito. Ma

"In the bay of Matsuho of Awaji Island." Kasa no Kanamura, *tr. by Hiroaki Sato.* FCEI

"In the Bay of Naniwa." *Unknown, tr. by Geoffrey Bownas and Anthony Thwaite.* PeBJV

"In the cock-crowing land of Azuma." Mushimaro. Ma

"In the days when my wife lived." Hitomaro. Ma

"In the dew dripping." Prince Otsu, *tr. by* Geoffrey Bownas *and* Anthony Thwaite. PeBJV

"In the dripping dew of the foot-wearying mountain." Prince Otsu, *tr. by* Hiroaki Sato. FCEI

"In the evening." Tajihi, *tr. by* Geoffrey Bownas *and* Anthony Thwaite. PeBJV

"In the far realm of our Lord." Yakamochi, *tr. by* Geoffrey Bownas *and* Anthony Thwaite. PeBJV

"In the field I've roped off, thinking to pick spring herbs." Akahito, *tr. by* Hiroaki Sato. FCEI

"In the garden of spring." Yakamochi. Ma

"In the Garden Palace." *Unknown.* Ma

"In the glorious age of the Emperor, a god." Yakamochi. Ma

"In the great ship, full-oared." Empress Otomaro. Ma

"In the hills of Nara." Sena Gyomon. Ma

"In the Kamunabi Mountains." *Unknown.* Ma

"In the Lake of Omi." *Unknown, tr. by* Geoffrey Bownas *and* Anthony Thwaite. PeBJV

"In the land of Azuma." Mushimaro. FCEI, *tr. by* Hiroaki Sato; PeBJV, *tr. by* Geoffrey Bownas *and* Anthony Thwaite.

"In the land of Koshi." Yakamochi. Ma

"In the land of Yamato." Emperor Jomei, *tr. by* Geoffrey Bownas *and* Anthony Thwaite. PeBJV

"In the land where our Sovereign rules." Yotsuna. Ma

"In the land where white clouds hover." *Unknown.* Ma

"In the leafy tree-tops." Yakamochi. Ma

"In the loneliness of my heart." Lady Kasa. Ma

"In the palace and beyond." Yakamochi, *tr. by* Burton Watson. FCEI

"In the reign of/ that far-off ancestor too." Yakamochi, *tr. by* Burton Watson. FCEI

"In the remote age of the gods." Yakamochi. Ma

"In the river of Matsura." Tabito. Ma

"In the scramble to get away." Udobe Ushimaro, *tr. by* Geoffrey Bownas *and* Anthony Thwaite. PeBJV

"In the sea of Iwami." Hitomaro. Ma

"In the service of/ My mighty Lord." Yakamochi, *tr. by* Geoffrey Bownas *and* Anthony Thwaite. PeBJV

"In the spring meadow." *Unknown, tr. by* Geoffrey Bownas *and* Anthony Thwaite. PeBJV

"In the tranquil sun of spring." Yakamochi. Ma

"In the twilight." *Unknown, tr. by* Hiroaki Sato. FCEI

"In the twilight darkness." "Oyakeme." Ma

"In the Uji, the river of eighty clans of officials." Hitomaro, *tr. by* Hiroaki Sato. FCEI

"In the wave-bright Naniwa Bay." *Unknown.* Ma

"In this distant outpost." Yakamochi, *tr. by* Burton Watson. FCEI

"In vine-trailing Iwami's sea." Hitomaro, *tr. by* Hiroaki Sato. FCEI

"Inlet of Okura is echoing, The." Hitomaro. Ma

"Instead of wasting thoughts on unavailing things." Tabito. Ma

"Is he here? Is he here?." *Unknown, tr. by* Burton Watson. FCEI

"Is it because our mighty Sovereign stays." Yakamochi. Ma

"Is it that summer and winter." Yakamochi. Ma

"Is the Prince of Omi a fisherman?." Prince Omi. Ma

"It snowed yesterday." Akahito. Ma

"It was for you, my slave." Lady Ki, *tr. by* Geoffrey Bownas *and* Anthony Thwaite. PeBJV

"It was I who did command." Lady Fujiwara. Ma

"I've won Yasumiko!" Kamatari, *tr. by* Hiroaki Sato. FCEI

"Iwamaro, I tell you." Yakamochi. Ma

"Iwamaro, look!" Yakamochi, *tr. by* Geoffrey Bownas *and* Anthony Thwaite. PeBJV

"Iwamaro, these words." Yakamochi, *tr. by* Burton Watson. FCEI

"Kagu-yama/ The Heavenly Hill afar." Hitomaro. Ma

"Lady Sayo of Matsura, as her name tells." *Unknown.* Ma

"Lake of Katsumata, The." *Unknown.* Ma

"Land of Yamato is a land, The." *Unknown.* Ma

"Land of Yamato over which reigns, The." Tanabe Sakimaro. Ma

"Lasses dance and tread the ground, The." Hitomaro. Ma

"Lasting as tell the *tsuga*-trees." Yakamochi. Ma

"Law allows our feasting, The." *Unknown.* Ma

"Leave me, O propitious spirits." *Unknown.* Ma

"Left at home." Prince Hozumi, *tr. by* Geoffrey Bownas *and* Anthony Thwaite. PeBJV

"Let me die now." *Unknown, tr. by* Burton Watson. FCEI

"Let no rain fall to drench me through." *Unknown.* Ma

"Let none, born after me." Hitomaro. Ma

"Let only your soul dwell." *Unknown.* Ma

"Let our love be made as plain." *Unknown.* Ma

"Like a little boat pushing through reeds." *Unknown, tr. by* Burton Watson. FCEI

"Like a throng of warriors." Yakamochi, *tr. by* Burton Watson. FCEI

"Like crystal through the mountains." Kanamura, *tr. by* Geoffrey Bownas *and* Anthony Thwaite. PeBJV

"Like the bubbles on the water." Hitomaro. Ma

"Like the crane whose cry." Lady Kasa, *tr. by* Burton Watson. FCEI

"Like the few ears salvaged." *Unknown, tr. by* Geoffrey Bownas *and* Anthony Thwaite. PeBJV

"Like the flash and roar near the clouds of heaven." *Unknown.* Ma

"Like the huts." *Unknown, tr. by* Burton Watson. FCEI

"Like the orange-flowers that blow." Yakamochi. Ma

"I ike the pearl of dew." Lady Kasa, *tr. by* Geoffrey Bownas *and* Anthony Thwaite. PeBJV

"Like the sails spread on the fishing-boats." *Unknown.* Ma

"Like the sedge of Naniwa." Lady Otomo no Sakanoe, *tr. by* Geoffrey Bownas *and* Anthony Thwaite. PeBJV

"Like the silkworm in the cocoon." Hitomaro. Ma

"Like the white cloud on the green hill." Prince Yuhara. Ma

"Like this I'll wait for you, my love." *Unknown, tr. by* Hiroaki Sato. FCEI

"Listen to the sounds of the warriors' elbow-guards." Empress Gemmyo. Ma

"Lo, our great sovereign, a goddess." Hitomaro. Ma

"Lo! the unsullied stream of the Yoshinu." Kanamura. Ma

"Lo! There towers the lofty peak of Fuji." Mushimaro. Ma

"Loath to pass by her gate." *Unknown.* Ma

"Loathing both seas of life and death." *Unknown.* Ma

"Lofty beyond the mountains." Ikenushi. Ma

"Lofty mountains and the seas, The." *Unknown.* Ma

"Lone cuckoo, A." *Unknown, tr. by* Hiroaki Sato. FCEI

"Long spring day, The." Prince Ikusa, *tr. by* Burton Watson. FCEI

"Long-wished-for rain has fallen, The." Yakamochi. Ma

"Longing for you, my love." *Unknown, tr. by* Hiroaki Sato. FCEI

"Lord returning home, A." Sanu Chigami. Ma

"Lords and ladies, The." *Unknown.* Ma

"Love is a torment." *Unknown.* Ma

"Loving someone/ who doesn't love you." Lady Kasa, *tr. by* Burton Watson. FCEI

"Magnificent snow/ Has fallen here at my place." Emperor Temmu. Ma

"Maiden Unai of Ashinoya, The." Mushimaro. Ma

"Maiden walks alone, A." Mushimaro. Ma

"Mallards call with evening from the reeds, The." "Tajihi." Ma

"Maples, The/ of Mount Komochi." *Unknown, tr. by* Hiroaki Sato. FCEI

"May no one take the path." *Unknown, tr. by* Hiroaki Sato. FCEI

"May the men who are born." Hitomaro, *tr. by* Arthur Waley. AWP

"Men of the court go forth, The." Akahito. Ma

"Men of valor, The." Akahito, *tr. by* Arthur Waley. AWP

"Mere echo, The/ of a horse's hoof." *Unknown, tr. by* Burton Watson. FCEI

"Mirrored in the waters of the Kamunabi River." Prince Atsumi. Ma

"Mists of spring, The." Taruhito, *tr. by* Geoffrey Bownas *and* Anthony Thwaite. PeBJV

"Mists trailing over them." Yakamochi, *tr. by* Burton Watson. FCEI

"More sad thoughts crowd into my mind." Lady Kasa. Ma

"More than the gems." Lady Otomo no Sakanoe, *tr. by* Geoffrey Bownas *and* Anthony Thwaite. PeBJV

"Morning air is cold on Mount Ujima, The." Prince Nagaya. Ma

"Morning sky was overcast, The." *Unknown.* Ma

"Mortal creature as I am." *Unknown.* Ma

"Mount Futagami, round which flow." Yakamochi. Ma

"Mount Kagu strove with Mount Miminashi." Emperor Tenji. Ma

"Mouth of the mare, The." *Unknown.* Ma

"My beloved brother, born of my own parents." Tanabe Sakimaro. Ma

"My darling gazed at the juniper." Tabito. Ma

"My dear wife loved my arm." Tabito. Ma

"My friend, you are setting out." *Unknown.* Ma

"My good sirs." *Unknown, tr. by* Geoffrey Bownas *and* Anthony Thwaite. PeBJV

"My hands so chapped from rice-pounding." *Unknown.* Ma

"My heart, thinking." Lady Otomo no Sakanoe, *tr. by* Arthur Waley. AWP

"My house forsaken by my love." Tabito. Ma

"My keepsake/ look at it and think of me." Lady Kasa, *tr. by* Burton Watson. FCEI

"My life vanishing." Hitomaro. Ma

"My lord came to survey." Mushimaro, *tr. by* Geoffrey Bownas *and* Anthony Thwaite. PeBJV

"My Lord has departed." Empress Iwa no Hima, *tr. by* Geoffrey Bownas *and* Anthony Thwaite. PeBJV

"My love for you, O mother." Abe Okina. Ma

" 'My love?' I said." *Unknown, tr. by* Burton Watson. FCEI
"My love must sigh after me." *Unknown.* Ma
"My love stands in my sight." *Unknown.* Ma
"My love-thoughts these days." *Unknown.* Ma
"My love's labours of these days." *Unknown.* Ma
"My prince, graceful as the pliant bamboo." Prince Niu. Ma
"My prince, who bent to me." Princess Niu, *tr. by* Geoffrey Bownas *and* Anthony Thwaite. PeBJV
"My shame I will bear." *Unknown.* Ma
"My tangled hair." *Unknown, tr. by* Geoffrey Bownas *and* Anthony Thwaite. PeBJV
"My thought and my tongue." Yakamochi. Ma
"My thought is held with awe." Yakamochi. Ma
"My tongue is awed." Okura. Ma
"My very soul, it seems." Lady Abe. Ma
"My wife and I are one in heart." Yakamochi. Ma
"My wife is far away." Prince Aki, *tr. by* Burton Watson. FCEI
"My wife thinks of me much, I know." Wakayamatobe Mumaro. Ma
"My wife whom I hid under the holy elm in Hatsuse." *Unknown, tr. by* Hiraoki Sato. FCEI
"Never can I forget the words." Hasetsukabe Inamaro. Ma
"Never do I doubt your heart." *Unknown.* Ma
"Night crow calls as if to tell of dawn, The." *Unknown.* Ma
"Night far gone." Yakamochi, *tr. by* Burton Watson. FCEI
"Night hours have advanced, The." Hitomaro. Ma
"No more," I say to her." Empress Jito. Ma
"No more," I say to you." Lady Shihi. Ma
"No, no! I say,/ But still you command." Lady Shihi, *tr. by* Geoffrey Bownas *and* Anthony Thwaite. PeBJV
"No, no! I say/ To Shii's far-fetched tales." Empress Jito, *tr. by* Geoffrey Bownas *and* Anthony Thwaite. PeBJV
"No way of consoling myself for this love." *Unknown, tr. by* Hiraoki Sato. FCEI
"No ways are left me now to meet my love." *Unknown.* Ma
"Not knowing that the long spring day." Prince Ikusa. Ma
"Now I know." *Unknown.* Ma
"Now that I am brought to know." Tabito. Ma
"Now that I am here." Isonokami Otomaro. Ma
"Now that I have uttered my name." Hitomaro. Ma
"Now the *uguisu* must be warbling." Yakamochi. Ma
"O boy cutting grass." Hitomaro, *tr. by* Arthur Waley. AWP
"O cuckoo, you were born." Mushimaro. Ma
"O for a fire from heaven." Sanu Chigami. Ma
"O for a sight once more." Hasetsukabe Taruhito. Ma
"O for my couriers." *Unknown.* Ma
"O for the body of my darling wife." *Unknown.* Ma
"O Futagi Palace where is enthroned high." Tanabe Sakimaro. Ma
"O good friend, dear master." *Unknown.* Ma
"O Juniper, that grasps the rocks of the beach." Tabito. Ma
"O Minume Bay, chosen by all Yashima's shipmen." Tanabe Sakimaro. Ma
"O moon god seated high in heaven." Prince Yuhara. Ma
"O pine-tree standing." Hakutsu, *tr. by* Arthur Waley. AWP
"O plovers flying over the evening waves." Hitomaro. Ma
"O Sanuki of beautiful seaweed." Hitomaro. Ma
"O solitary pine, how many." Prince Ichihara. Ma
"O that I were the cloud." *Unknown.* Ma
"O that I'd had." Mononobe Furumaro, *tr. by* Geoffrey Bownas *and* Anthony Thwaite. PeBJV
"O that my father and my mother were flowers." Hasetsukabe Kuromasa. Ma
"O that she might rather die." Hitomaro. Ma
"O that sweet mountain of Miwa." Princess Nukada. Ma
"O that the bridge to heaven were longer." *Unknown.* Ma
"O that the hill, the stony road." Hitomaro. Ma
"O the Palace of Yoshinu." Tabito. Ma
"O what an ugly sight." Tabito, *tr. by* Geoffrey Bownas *and* Anthony Thwaite. PeBJV
"O you, who were voyaging to the Land of Kara." *Unknown.* Ma
"Obedient to our mighty Sovereign's word." *Unknown.* Ma
"Obedient to our Sovereign's command." Yakamochi. Ma
"Obedient to our Sovereign's orders." Yakamochi. Ma
"Of the ways to play." Tabito, *tr. by* Geoffrey Bownas *and* Anthony Thwaite. PeBJV
"Of those abalone pearls." Yakamochi. Ma
"Oh how steadily I love you." Lady Kasa. Ma
"Oh, my dear love far away!" Prince Aki. Ma
"Oh, our heaven-born god." Lady Otomo no Sakanoe. Ma
"Oh, plovers on the river-shore." Prince Kadobe. Ma
"Oh, that my dear mother." Tsumori Okurusu. Ma
"Oh, the autumn foliage." Empress Jito. Ma

"Oh, the pain of my love that you know not." Lady Otomo no Sakanoe. Ma
"Oh, when will this night end." *Unknown.* Ma
"Oh, Yasumiko I have won!" Kamatari. Ma
"Old, old woman that I am." Lady Ishikawa. Ma
"On a journey and lonesome, I see below a hill." Kurohito, *tr. by* Hiraoki Sato. FCEI
"On a misty day in spring." Mushimaro, *tr. by* Geoffrey Bownas *and* Anthony Thwaite. PeBJV
"On a spring day/ the trailing windows." Yakamochi, *tr. by* Burton Watson. FCEI
"On cold nights." Okura, *tr. by* Geoffrey Bownas *and* Anthony Thwaite. PeBJV
"On frost-filled nights." *Unknown, tr. by* Hiraoki Sato. FCEI
"On looming Mount Hatsuse." Hitomaro, *tr. by* Hiraoki Sato. FCEI
"On Matsuho's shore of Awaji Island." Kanamura. Ma
"On Mikasa, a peak of Mount Kasuga." Akahito. Ma
"On Mount Kasuga of the spring days." Akahito, *tr. by* Hiraoki Sato. FCEI
"On Mount Tsukuba where eagles dwell." Mushimaro. Ma
"On my lofty ship." *Unknown, tr. by* Geoffrey Bownas *and* Anthony Thwaite. PeBJV
"On nights when, wind mixing in, the rain falls." Okura, *tr. by* Hiraoki Sato. FCEI
"On river flats, too." Yakamochi, *tr. by* Burton Watson. FCEI
"On Tatsuta Hill." Mushimaro, *tr. by* Geoffrey Bownas *and* Anthony Thwaite. PeBJV
"On the beach of Iwashiro." Prince Arima, *tr. by* Geoffrey Bownas *and* Anthony Thwaite. PeBJV
"On the beach where you sleep." *Unknown, tr. by* Geoffrey Bownas *and* Anthony Thwaite. PeBJV
"On the desolate stony shore." *Unknown.* Ma
"On the hill slope of Sada." *Unknown.* Ma
"On the miscanthus of my garden." Yakamochi. Ma
"On the moor of Kasuga." Hitomaro, *tr. by* Arthur Waley. AWP
"On the mountain of Mifune." Kanamura. Ma
"On the night when the rain beats." Okura. Ma
"On the ocean where no islands are in sight." *Unknown.* Ma
"On the peak of Mimiga of fair Yoshinu." Emperor Temmu. Ma
"On the peak of Ogura above the rapids." Mushimaro. Ma
"On the pool of the River of Natsumi." Prince Yuhara. Ma
"On the road to the palace." Hitomaro, *tr. by* Geoffrey Bownas *and* Anthony Thwaite. PeBJV
"On the road to Yamashiro." *Unknown, tr. by* Geoffrey Bownas *and* Anthony Thwaite. PeBJV
"On the roads of Yamashiro." *Unknown, tr. by* Burton Watson. FCEI
"On the sea of heaven the waves of cloud arise." Hitomaro. Ma
"On the shore of Nawa." *Unknown.*
"On the Tamashima River." *Unknown.* Ma
"On the vast lake of Omi." Empress Yamato-hime. Ma
"On the way to the lustrous shrine." *Unknown, tr. by* Hiraoki Sato. FCEI
"On this New Year's Day." Fujii Moroai. Ma
"On Tsukuba mountain." Mushimaro, *tr. by* Hiraoki Sato. FCEI
"On Tsukuba peak." *Unknown, tr. by* Hiraoki Sato. FCEI
"Once I saw it with uncaring eyes." Yakamochi. Ma
"Once in the long-gone age." Yakamochi. Ma
"Once—only once." Ato Tobira. Ma
"One of your cords of Koguryo brocade." *Unknown, tr. by* Hiraoki Sato. FCEI
"Others may cease to remember." Empress Yamato-hime. Ma
"Our boat shall harbour at the port of Hira." Kurohito. Ma
"Our comrade, crossing." *Unknown, tr. by* Geoffrey Bownas *and* Anthony Thwaite. PeBJV
"Our great Empress." Hitomaro, *tr. by* Geoffrey Bownas *and* Anthony Thwaite. PeBJV
"Our great prince who orders." Hitomaro, *tr. by* Geoffrey Bownas *and* Anthony Thwaite. PeBJV
"Our great sovereign, a goddess." Hitomaro. Ma
"Our great Sovereign who rules in peace,/ Offspring of the Bright One on high,/ Has begun to build." *Unknown.* Ma
"Our great Sovereign who rules in peace,/ Offspring of the Bright One on high,/ Wills, as a goddess." *Unknown.* Ma
"Our lord and prince, ruling in peace." Okisome no Azumabito. Ma
"Our noble prince, child of the Bright One on high." Hitomaro. Ma
"Our prince, offspring of the Bright One on high." Hitomaro. Ma
"Our prince, pliant as the soft bamboo." Prince Niu, *tr. by* Hiraoki Sato. FCEI
"Our sovereign, a god." Miyuki. Ma
"Our sovereign familiar with the eight corners." Hitomaro, *tr. by* Hiraoki Sato. FCEI

"Our sovereign familiar with the eight corners/ being a god, rules on high." Akahito, *tr.* by Hiroaki Sato. FCEI
"Our sovereign familiar with the eight corners/ his eternal palace where we serve." Akahito, *tr.* by Hiroaki Sato. FCEI
"Our Sovereign has come to dwell." Akahito. Ma
"Our Sovereign who rules in peace." *Unknown*. Ma
"Our Sovereign's far-off court." Yakamochi. Ma
"Over Kohata, the hill in Yamashina." Hitomaro. Ma
"Over Shimotsuke fields." *Unknown, tr.* by Hiroaki Sato. FCEI
"Over the big." Mushimaro, *tr.* by Hiroaki Sato. FCEI
"Over the branches of the cryptomerias." Hitomaro. Ma
"Over the far ocean plains." Kose Sukunamaro. Ma
"Over the hills and mountains I came." Yakamochi. Ma
"Over the river ferry of Saho." Yakamochi. Ma
"Over the River of Heaven." *Unknown*. Ma
"Over the spring field trails the mist." Yakamochi. Ma
"Oxherd and the Weaver Maid standing, The." Okura. Ma
"Palace of Hishiro at Makimuku, The." Prince Kinashi no Karu, *tr.* by Geoffrey Bownas *and* Anthony Thwaite. PeBJV
"Palace of Naniwa, whither often comes, The." Tanabe Sakimaro. Ma
"Palace of Yoshino where our Sovereign, The." Akahito, *tr.* by Hiroaki Sato. FCEI
"Passing shower, A." *Unknown*. Ma
"Passing the shore of Minume." Hitomaro. Ma
"Pay no mind to my mother." *Unknown, tr.* by Burton Watson. FCEI
"Peerless are the gems." Prince Ichihara. Ma
"People throng the sun-lit Palace-road." Hitomaro. Ma
"Perhaps, Cape Karasaki of Shiga." Toneri Kine. Ma
"Person can die of love, A." Lady Kasa, *tr.* by Burton Watson. FCEI
"Pine bloom, though you, The." Lady Heguri. Ma
"Plovers over the evening waves of Lake Omi." Hitomaro, *tr.* by Hiroaki Sato. FCEI
"Plum-blossom, The." Akahito, *tr.* by Arthur Waley. AWP
"Plums already blooming." Yakamochi, *tr.* by Burton Watson. FCEI
"Post-horse bells are tinkling, The." *Unknown*. Ma
"Praying to the gods of heaven and earth." Otabe Aramimi. Ma
"Priceless treasure it may be, A." Tabito, *tr.* by Hiroaki Sato. FCEI
"Prime of my life has far declined, The." Tabito. Ma
"Province of Sanuki, renowned for lovely seaweed, The." Hitomaro, *tr.* by Hiroaki Sato. FCEI
"Pushing freely through the bush-clovers." Naga Okimaro. Ma
"Putting a boat in the River of Eternal Heaven." Okura, *tr.* by Hiroaki Sato. FCEI
"Quilted silk from Tsukushi, The." Manzei. Ma
"Rain beats on me, I make a shelter, The." *Unknown*. Ma
"Rain-drops, The/ That fall this evening." *Unknown*. Ma
"Rather than be a so-so human being." Tabito, *tr.* by Hiroaki Sato. FCEI
"Rather than be wise." Tabito, *tr.* by Geoffrey Bownas *and* Anthony Thwaite. PeBJV
"Rather than stay behind to languish." Princess Tajima. Ma
"Rather than that I should remain at home." *The father of* Kusakabe Minaka. Ma
"Rather than that I should thus pine." Yakamochi. Ma
"Rather than worry." Tabito, *tr.* by Geoffrey Bownas *and* Anthony Thwaite. PeBJV
"Reaper on the Suminoe fields." Hitomaro. Ma
"Red pony cannot be fetched, The." Ujibe Kurome. Ma
"Resting my eyes on the bay of Miho." Masuhito. Ma
"Rice-abounding Land of Reed Plains, The." Hitomaro. Ma
River of Heaven, The. *Unknown, tr.* by Lafcadio Hearn. AWP
"River plovers crying." Yakamochi, *tr.* by Burton Watson. FCEI
"Road to Shinano, The." *Unknown, tr.* by Hiroaki Sato. FCEI
"Scratching your eyebrows, sneezing." *Unknown, tr.* by Hiroaki Sato. FCEI
"Season has come, The." Yakamochi, *tr.* by Burton Watson. FCEI
"Seasons when the spring sun." Mushimaro, *tr.* by Burton Watson. FCEI
"Sedge of the marsh where irises bloom, The." *Unknown, tr.* by Hiroaki Sato. FCEI
"See, neighbour,/ Washing morning greens in the river." *Unknown*. Ma
"Sending my dear brother." Princess Oku, *tr.* by Geoffrey Bownas *and* Anthony Thwaite. PeBJV
"Seven treasures, The." Okura, *tr.* by Geoffrey Bownas *and* Anthony Thwaite. PeBJV
"Seven types of treasures, The." Okura, *tr.* by Hiroaki Sato. FCEI
"Shall I be false to friends." *Unknown*. Ma
"Shall we make love." *Unknown, tr.* by Arthur Waley. AWP
"Shallow is the mountain well-pool." *Unknown*. Ma
" 'Shame it is,' I say and sigh." Prince Toneri. Ma

"She came from distant Shiragi." Lady Otomo no Sakanoe. Ma
"She goes to the sun-bright palace." Sukunamaro. Ma
"Sheaves of my love-thoughts, The." Princess Hirokawa. Ma
"Should a horse-load of love." Yakamochi. Ma
"Should I, a man, die in vain." Okura. Ma
"Should I be favoured with a happy lease of life." Hozumi Oyu. Ma
"Should the time come." Hitomaro. Ma
"Should you hide in the rock tomb." *Unknown, tr.* by Burton Watson. FCEI
"Sight of our parents, The." Okura. Ma
"Silkworms my mother rears, The." Hitomaro, *tr.* by Geoffrey Bownas *and* Anthony Thwaite. PeBJV
"Since all living things die in the end." Tabito, *tr.* by Hiroaki Sato. FCEI
"Since by the imperial order to serve." Yakamochi. Ma
"Since heaven and earth parted." Akahito, *tr.* by Hiroaki Sato. FCEI
"Since I came by chance into this life." Kanamura. Ma
"Since I had shut the gate." *Unknown*. Ma
"Since I left the loving hands of my mother." Hitomaro. Ma
"Since in Karu lived my wife." Hitomaro. Ma
"Since our ancestral gods." Yakamochi. Ma
"Since that time far off." Yakamochi, *tr.* by Burton Watson. FCEI
"Since the age of the gods it has always been said." Okura. Ma
"Since the era of that sage sovereign." Hitomaro. Ma
"Since the far beginning of heaven and earth." Yakamochi. Ma
"Since the reign of Kashihara's sun-ruler." Hitomaro, *tr.* by Hiroaki Sato. FCEI
"Since the time of the gods." Yakamochi. Ma
"Since thy reign is to endure." Emperor Junnin. Ma
"Since you, my Lord, were gone." Empress Iwa no Hime. Ma
"Slave, it seems, The." Yakamochi, *tr.* by Geoffrey Bownas *and* Anthony Thwaite. PeBJV
"Sleepless with longing for my love." Hitomaro. Ma
"Slight not these flowers!" Hirotsugu. Ma
"So I refused to see them." Kurohito. Ma
"So it is, my dearest lover." *Unknown*. Ma
"So long as lasts the span of life." Okura. Ma
"So loud the deer cries, calling to his mate." Yakamochi. Ma
"So that no one will see." *Unknown, tr.* by Burton Watson. FCEI
"So to the mud-bed." *Unknown*. Ma
"Sojourner in Mika's plains, A." Kanamura. Ma
"Sooner than be a man." Tabito, *tr.* by Geoffrey Bownas *and* Anthony Thwaite. PeBJV
"Soot-black as she is, like the shed." *Unknown*. Ma
"Spacious Land of Yamato, The." Empress Koken. Ma
"Spring comes/ and the night sadly wanes away." Yakamochi, *tr.* by Burton Watson. FCEI
"Spring garden, The." Yakamochi, *tr.* by Burton Watson. FCEI
"Spring has passed." Empress Jito, *tr.* by Burton Watson. FCEI
"Spring has passed away." Empress Jito. Ma
"Stag of the Ogura mountain, The." Emperor Jomei. Ma
"Stag that calls on Mount Ogura when the evening comes, The." Emperor Jomei, *tr.* by Hiroaki Sato. FCEI
"Stairway up to heaven, The." *Unknown, tr.* by Geoffrey Bownas *and* Anthony Thwaite. PeBJV
"Standing or sitting/ I know not what to do." *Unknown*. Ma
"Starting in the morning from the sea of Suzu." Yakamochi. Ma
"Starting out on my travels." *Unknown*. Ma
"Staying here at home." *The father of* Kusakabe Omininaka, *tr.* by Geoffrey Bownas *and* Anthony Thwaite. PeBJV
"Steeds the prince of Minu keeps, The." *Unknown*. Ma
"Steep mountain-road of Ashigara, The." Shidoribe Karamaro. Ma
"Strange land is hard to live in, A." Sanu Chigami. Ma
"Straw matting/ to sleep on." *Unknown, tr.* by Burton Watson. FCEI
"Strong man as I am." Hitomaro. Ma
"Succeeding to the Celestial Throne." Yakamochi. Ma
"Such a fleeting life though we shared together." Yakamochi. Ma
"*Susuki*, growing along the way to my beloved." *Unknown*. Ma
"Swift over the plains of Shimotsuke." Ma
"Tending the hallowed tomb." Princess Nukada. Ma
"Terrible are the ocean billows." *Unknown*. Ma
"That fording place in the Saho." Yakamochi, *tr.* by Burton Watson. FCEI
"That girl/ lovely as the little oaks." *Unknown, tr.* by Hiroaki Sato. FCEI
"That I who thought myself a strong man." Tabito. Ma
"That meadow which my heart loved." *Unknown*. Ma
"That morning I set off." *Unknown, tr.* by Hiroaki Sato. FCEI
"That path through the azaleas." *Unknown*. Ma
"That wife of mine." Wakayama Mimaro, *tr.* by Geoffrey Bownas *and* Anthony Thwaite. PeBJV

"That you like me not." *Unknown*. Ma
"There lived a maiden Tamana." Mushimaro. Ma
"These are the clothes your dainty girl." Sanu Chigami. Ma
"These dream meetings." Yakamochi, *tr. by* Burton Watson. FCEI
"These hands all chapped." *Unknown, tr. by* Hiroaki Sato. FCEI
"These hemp-clothes which you take." *Unknown*. Ma
"Thick sea-pine, The." Hitomaro, *tr. by* Geoffrey Bownas *and* Anthony Thwaite. PeBJV
"Thine is a happy name." Emperor Shomu. Ma
"Thinking sad thoughts over and over." Yakamochi. Ma
"Thinking "Today! Today!" I wait for you." Yosami, *tr. by* Hiroaki Sato. FCEI
"This being a place over which." Tabito. Ma
"This crab—where does it come from?." Emperor Ojin, *tr. by* Geoffrey Bownas *and* Anthony Thwaite. PeBJV
"This evening on my journey far from home." *Unknown*. Ma
"This evening so cold and chill." Prince Shiki. Ma
"This is our Sovereign's distant court." Yakamochi. Ma
"This is the arrow which I, a warrior, shot." Kanamura. Ma
"This is the cloth I wove for my lord." Hitomaro. Ma
"This is the cloth I've woven for you." *Unknown, tr. by* Hiroaki Sato. FCEI
"This is the mountain souvenir." Empress Gensho. Ma
"This is what/ the villagers told me." *Unknown, tr. by* Burton Watson. FCEI
"This wine I have brewed for you." Tabito. Ma
"This world is so full." Princess Takata. Ma
"Those pines standing in rows." Mononobe Mashima. Ma
"Those sedges in light-flooded Naniwa." Lady Otomo no Sakanoe, *tr. by* Hiroaki Sato. FCEI
"Those seven wise men of the past." Tabito, *tr. by* Hiroaki Sato. FCEI
"Though clear and bright." *Unknown*. Ma
"Though I am chidden like a horse." *Unknown*. Ma
"Though I have silks." *Unknown*. Ma
"Though I only/ saw you dimly." Lady Kasa, *tr. by* Burton Watson. FCEI
"Though I see the white azaleas on the shore." *Unknown*. Ma
"Though I tried to forget, as I came." Akino Osamaro. Ma
"Though I try to calm down my soul." Sanu Chigami. Ma
"Though I'm old now." *Unknown, tr. by* Burton Watson. FCEI
"Though, in the land where rules our sovereign." Hitomaro. Ma
"Though it be the night when I make." *Unknown*. Ma
"Though many are the lofty mountains." Tajihi Kunihito. Ma
"Though many were the hot springs." Akahito. Ma
"Though men say/ An autumn night is long." *Unknown*. Ma
"Though my eyes could see your spirit soar." Empress Yamato-hime. Ma
"Though my love, long standing at the gate." *Unknown*. Ma
"Though my thoughts of her." Hitomaro. Ma
"Though not commanded." Okura, *tr. by* Geoffrey Bownas *and* Anthony Thwaite. PeBJV
"Though not sure of the tale of old." *Unknown*. Ma
"Though the hemp you've spun." *Unknown, tr. by* Hiroaki Sato. FCEI
"Though the land of wave-bright Naniwa." Kanamura. Ma
"Though there are men without number." *Unknown*. Ma
"Though they say her tomb is here." Akahito. Ma
"Though, waiting for you to come." Okura. Ma
"Though you say, "Do not grieve!"" Yosami. Ma
"Though your season is not over." Yamochi. Ma
"Thousand times a day, A." *Unknown*. Ma
"Thousand years, you said, A." Lady Heguri, *tr. by* Geoffrey Bownas *and* Anthony Thwaite. PeBJV
"Through the bright gleaming." Yakamochi, *tr. by* Burton Watson. FCEI
"Through the plain of Miyake." *Unknown*. Ma
"Thus let us drink and be merry!" Lady Otomo no Sakanoe. Ma
"Thus say the famished she-devils." "Ikeda." Ma
"Till my black hair be white." "Takahashi." Ma
"Till my hair is white like the falling snow." Tachihana Moroe. Ma
"Till they see it." *Unknown, tr. by* Hiroaki Sato. FCEI
"Tired of sitting indoors all day long." Yakamochi. Ma
"To-day, taking my last sight of the mallards." Prince Otsu. Ma
"To-day, when people in China, it is said." Yakamochi. Ma
"To gather the wave-borne pearls." *Unknown*. Ma
"To go up to the sun-lit Imperial City." Okura. Ma
"To keep silent and act wise." Tabito, *tr. by* Hiroaki Sato. FCEI
"To love a man without return." Lady Kasa, *tr. by* Geoffrey Bownas *and* Anthony Thwaite. PeBJV
"To love you who love me not." Lady Kasa. Ma

"To meet my love." *Unknown, tr. by* Geoffrey Bownas *and* Anthony Thwaite. PeBJV
"To-night he makes his one journey of the year." *Unknown*. Ma
"To-night I am coming." *Unknown*. Ma
"To speed my brother." Princess Oku. Ma
"To the hill of Kasuga where *kuzu* vines creep." *Unknown*. Ma
"To the pit of my heart I pine." Yakamochi, *tr. by* Geoffrey Bownas *and* Anthony Thwaite. PeBJV
"To this land of Tsukushi." Okura. Ma
"To what shall I compare this world?." Manzei, *tr. by* Hiroaki Sato. FCEI
"To you, brave warrior, starting for the Land of Kara." Tajihi Takanushi. Ma
"Today, today,/ I wait for him." Yosami, *tr. by* Geoffrey Bownas *and* Anthony Thwaite. PeBJV
"Together with my wife I passed." Tabito. Ma
"Told from age to age." Yakamochi. Ma
"Tons of snow have fallen in my village." Emperor Temmu, *tr. by* Hiroaki Sato. FCEI
"Tread not the snow." Mikata Shami. Ma
"Troubles are many in the path of a little boat." *Unknown*. Ma
"Tumbling water breaks upon the rocks, The." *Unknown*. Ma
"Unaware that the ships must wait." *Unknown*. Ma
"Unchanging as the *tsuga*-trees." Yakamochi. Ma
"Unknown love/ Is as bitter a thing." Lady Otomo no Sakanoe. AWP, *tr. by* Arthur Waley; PBWP, *tr. by* Arthur Waley.
  ("Unknown love/ is bitter.") BoWoP, *tr. by* Willis Barnstone; LLLT, *tr. by* Willis Barnstone.
"Unlike the cloud that dwells on Mount Mifune." Prince Yuge. Ma
"Unresting, like the people." *Unknown*. Ma
"Village-folk told me, saying, The." *Unknown*. Ma
"Vivid smile of my sweetheart, The." *Unknown*. Ma
"Waiting for me." Lady Ishikawa, *tr. by* Geoffrey Bownas *and* Anthony Thwaite. PeBJV
"Waiting for you." Prince Otsu. Ma
"Waiting for you, I am filled with longing." Princess Nukada, *tr. by* Hiroaki Sato. FCEI
"Warriors go forth, The." Kanamura. Ma
"Was it only last night." *Unknown, tr. by* Hiroaki Sato. FCEI
"Was it pleasing to my prince's soul?." Princess Tamochi. Ma
"Water at Ayuchi in Oharida, The." *Unknown*. Ma
"Waves lingering about the fish-weir stakes, The." Hitomaro. Ma
"Waves toss high, The." *Unknown*. Ma
"We are helpless before time." Okura. Ma
"We are helpless in this world." Okura, *tr. by* Geoffrey Bownas *and* Anthony Thwaite. PeBJV
"We built mountain paddies." Prince Kinashi no Karu, *tr. by* Geoffrey Bownas *and* Anthony Thwaite. PeBJV
"We think our boat is alone." *Unknown, tr. by* Geoffrey Bownas *and* Anthony Thwaite. PeBJV
"We wait for the moon." Princess Nukada, *tr. by* Geoffrey Bownas *and* Anthony Thwaite. PeBJV
"Wear yourself not out." *Unknown*. Ma
"Well do I know that human life is passing." Yakamochi. Ma
"Well do I remember how she wept." Osakabe Chikuni. Ma
"Well is the hill of Mimoro guarded." *Unknown*. Ma
"Were it not for the dresses." Nakatomi Yakamori. Ma
"Were the Itada bridge to crumble." *Unknown*. Ma
"Were these flowers broken off." *Unknown*. Ma
"We've traveled a road." *Unknown, tr. by* Hiroaki Sato. FCEI
"What am I to do with my sister?." Prince Yuhara, *tr. by* Arthur Waley. AWP
"What can I do with you." Prince Yuhara. Ma
"What do I care for life or death." Otoneribe Chifumi. Ma
"What do I care if my name." The elder daughter of Lady Otomo no Sakanoe. Ma
"What pain and distress." Yakamochi. Ma
"What the seven sages, too." Tabito, *tr. by* Geoffrey Bownas *and* Anthony Thwaite. PeBJV
"What worth to me the seven treasures." Okura. Ma
"When, after holing up for winter, the spring comes." Princess Nukada, *tr. by* Hiroaki Sato. FCEI
"When, at our Sovereign's command." Yakamochi. Ma
"When autumn comes we shall meet." *Unknown*. Ma
"When autumn is here." *Unknown, tr. by* Geoffrey Bownas *and* Anthony Thwaite. PeBJV
"When evening comes." Yakamochi. AWP, *tr. by* Arthur Waley; FCEI, *tr. by* Burton Watson; PeBJV, *tr. by* Geoffrey Bownas *and* Anthony Thwaite.
"When evening mist." *Unknown, tr. by* Hiroaki Sato. FCEI
"When I am parted from you, my dearest." *Unknown*. Ma

"When I eat melon." Okura. Ma
"When I lie sleepless, longing for Yamato." Empress Otomaro. Ma
"When I look up and gaze." Yakamochi. Ma
"When I love her/ so much." *Unknown, tr. by* Burton Watson. FCEI
"When I meet you." *Unknown.* Ma
"When I see a woman." *Unknown.* Ma
"When I sleep alone, in the Imperial City." Tabito. Ma
"When I started out from home." Mononobe Tatsu. Ma
"When I take the *koto*, sobs break forth." *Unknown.* Ma
"When I trusted as one trusts in a great ship." *Unknown.* Ma
"When I was a new-born babe." *Unknown.* Ma
"When, in spring, the sun is misted." Mushimaro. Ma
"When last I journeyed down." *Unknown.* Ma
"When, loosened from the winter's bonds." Princess Nukada. Ma
"When mist rises on the seashore." *Unknown.* Ma
"When on my travels I pine for home." Kurohito. Ma
"When she was alive, now a memory." Hitomaro, *tr. by* Hiroaki Sato. FCEI
"When so little of his life remained." Kon Myogun. Ma
"When spring comes round." *Unknown.* Ma
"When the cherry-flower blooms." *Unknown.* Ma
"When the hills of spring." "Owari." Ma
"When the moon that shines." *Unknown.* Ma
"When the plum-blossoms are gone." Sakiko. Ma
"When the spring comes." Princess Nukada, *tr. by* Geoffrey Bownas *and* Anthony Thwaite. PeBJV
"When winter is gone and spring comes." *Unknown.* Ma
"When with the first month comes the spring." Ki. Ma
"When you are away, wherefore should I adorn myself?." *Unknown.* Ma
"When you are thus gone." Emperor Shomu. Ma
"When you well might have wished to live." Fujii Kooyu. Ma
"When you're unfilled in ways of worldly entertainment." Tabito, *tr. by* Hiroaki Sato. FCEI
"Where is my husband trudging on his journey?." *The wife of* Tagima Maro. Ma
"Where others' husbands ride on horseback." *Unknown.* Ma
"Where shall I seek shelter." Kurohito. Ma
"Where the spring mist slowly drifts." *Unknown.* Ma
"Where will it find harbor." Kurohito, *tr. by* Hiroaki Sato. FCEI
"Where will that boat find harbour." Kurohito. Ma
"While at Nigitazu we await the moon." Princess Nukada. Ma
"While I behold the brightness of the fallen snow." Ki Kiyohito. Ma
"While I wait and long for you." Hitomaro. Ma
"While I waited and wondered." Yakamochi. Ma
"While, sleeping in your clothes." Kurahashibe Otome. Ma
"While the leaves of the bamboo rustle." *Unknown, tr. by* Geoffrey Bownas *and* Anthony Thwaite. PeBJV
"While, waiting for you." Princess Nukada. Ma
"While with my sleeves I sweep the bed." *Unknown.* Ma
"White gem unknown of men, A." *Unknown.* Ma
"White pearl, sunk under the deep sea, The." *Unknown.* Ma
"White snow which lies so deep, The." Yakamochi. Ma
"Who has broken the tops of the reeds in the port?." *Unknown, tr. by* Hiroaki Sato. FCEI
"Whole day's light is not enough, The." Masuhito. Ma
"Whose husband this time." *Unknown, tr. by* Hiroaki Sato. FCEI
"Whose man goes." *Unknown, tr. by* Geoffrey Bownas *and* Anthony Thwaite. PeBJV
"Wind and waves sinking low, The." Yakamochi. Ma
"Wind blew: for you, The." Princess Kagami, *tr. by* Geoffrey Bownas *and* Anthony Thwaite. PeBJV
"Wind that sweeps down Ikaho, The." *Unknown, tr. by* Geoffrey Bownas *and* Anthony Thwaite. PeBJV
"With a basket, a lovely basket." Emperor Yuryaku, *tr. by* Hiroaki Sato. FCEI
"With grass for a pillow, on a journey." Hitomaro, *tr. by* Hiroaki Sato. FCEI
"With her basket, her basket." Emperor Yuryaku, *tr. by* Geoffrey Bownas *and* Anthony Thwaite. PeBJV
"With his lady your slave must be in love." Yakamochi. Ma
"With morning you leave." *Unknown, tr. by* Hiroaki Sato. FCEI
"With my axe I felled the trees." *Unknown.* Ma
"With reverence I compose these words." *Unknown.* Ma
"With the bounteous wine the doughty warrior blesses." Prince Yuhara. Ma
"With the jewels of my anklets." *Unknown.* Ma
"With the ninth month when the thunder." *Unknown.* Ma
"With the ships all in trim." Mariko Omaro. Ma
"Within the bounds of heaven and earth." Sanu Chigami. Ma
"Wonderful is the sea." *Unknown.* Ma

"World has so many eyes, The." Lady Kasa, *tr. by* Burton Watson. FCEI
"Would I had been, beloved." Lady Ishikawa. Ma
"Would my love were a bracelet." Furu Tamuke. Ma
"Would that I had stayed." Princess Oku. Ma
"Would that they were flowers." Prince Aki. Ma
"Would there were a land." *Unknown.* Ma
"Yamato has clusters of mountains." Emperor Jomei, *tr. by* Hiroaki Sato. FCEI
"Yon white cloud blown." *Unknown.* Ma
"Yonder in the plum-tree." *Unknown.* Ma
"Yonder on the plain of Kasuga." *Unknown.* Ma
"You are like those scarves, those white beach waves." *Unknown, tr. by* Hiroaki Sato. FCEI
"You are to me my breath, my life." *Unknown, tr. by* Hiroaki Sato. FCEI
"You care naught for the living." Okura. Ma
"You, dear husband, who have gone forth." Kanamura. Ma
"You, for whom I have longed standing across the River of Heaven." Okura, *tr. by* Hiroaki Sato. FCEI
"You had better tell." *Unknown.* Ma
"You seem to have lived, my lady." Miyori. Ma
"You start so early this morning." Hitomaro. Ma
"You stood at a bend." Osakabe Ataechikuni, *tr. by* Geoffrey Bownas *and* Anthony Thwaite. PeBJV
"You went to fields madder-red." Princess Nukada, *tr. by* Geoffrey Bownas *and* Anthony Thwaite. PeBJV
"You who are constantly on my mind." Kanamura. Ma
"You who journey to Shiragi." *Unknown, tr. by* Geoffrey Bownas *and* Anthony Thwaite. PeBJV
"Your basket, with your pretty basket." Emperor Yuryaku. Ma
"Your hair comes undone when you put it up." Mikata no Sami, *tr. by* Hiroaki Sato. FCEI
Manzanita, The. Yvor Winters. VGW
Manzini; Escape Artist. Gwendolyn MacEwen. NOBC
Map, The. Elizabeth Bishop. NOBA
Map, The. G. C. Oden. AmNP; PoNe
Map. Murilo Mendes, *tr. fr. Portuguese by* W. S. Merwin. ATCBP
Map, The/ takes me back. Passover. Rose Ausländer, *tr. by* Ewald Osers. VWA
Map. Marcos Konder Reis, *tr. fr. Portuguese by* Mark Strand. ATCBP
Map, The. Gary Soto. MAYP; NoAM
Map, The. Mark Strand. NYBP
Map of Mock-Begger Hall, The. *Unknown.* CoMu
Map of Montana in Italy, A. Richard Hugo. LCAP
Map of My Country, A. John Holmes. AiP; AmFN
Map of Places, The. Laura Riding. LiTA
Map of the City, A. Thom Gunn. NAEL-2; PoE
Map of the Western Part of the County of Essex in England, A. Denise Levertov. CoAP; NAAL-2
Map Reference T994724. John Pudney. WaP
Map shows me where it is you are, The. A Private Letter to Brazil. Gloria C. Oden. AmNP; PoNe
Maple and Sumach. Cecil Day Lewis. FaBoMo; Son
Maple buds are red, are red, The. A Song of Waking. Katharine Lee Bates. OHIP
Maple buds were blossoming reddish tufts, The. The Grotto. Ray Fraser. NeAC
Maple Feast. Frances Mary Frost. RHPC
Maple is a dainty maid, The. Autumn Fancies. *Unknown.* FaPON
Maple Leaves. Thomas Bailey Aldrich. GN
Maple leaves fill the emerald mountain. Boiling Falls. Liu E, *tr. by* Jonathan Chaves. CoBLCP
Maple, oak, poplar, gingko. Walking the New York Bedrock Alive in the Sea of Information. Gary Snyder. BAP
Maple Syrup. Donald Hall. CAPP
Maples. Philip Appleman. BXAP
Maples, The/ of Mount Komochi. *Unknown. Fr.* Manyo Shu. FCEI
Maples flare among the spruces, The. Harvest Home. Arthur Guiterman. RHPC
Maples have turned, The. Fire snaps on my tongue. On a Recent Protest against Social Conditions. David Posner. NYBP
Mapmaker on His Art, The. Howard Nemerov. NYBP
Mappemounde. Earle Birney. OBCV
Maps. Robert Hass. NPGG
Maps. Dorothy Brown Thompson. RHPC
Maps to Nowhere. David Rosenberg. VWA
Maquillage. Arthur Symons. OxBSP
Maratea Porto: Saying Goodbye to the Vitolos. Richard Hugo. MAT
Marathon Runner, The. Fenton Johnson. CDC

Marban, a Hermit Speaks. *Unknown, tr. fr. Irish by* Michael Hartnett. BIrV; CIP

Marble Floor. Karol Wojtyla. CRP

Marble mausoleum solemnly holds the rich, A. Quatrains. Salah Jahin, *tr. by* Samir M. Zoghby. TTY

Marble Nor Monuments whereof Then We Spoke. John Berryman. *Fr.* Sonnets, XL. Son

Marble Statuette Harpist. Sara Van Alstyne Allen. GoYe

Marble-streeted Town, The. Thomas Hardy. FaBoPP

Marble the stone-cool the, The. Friederike Mayröcker, *tr. by* Beth Bjorklund. CoAuP

Marble-Top. E. B. White. FiBHP; OBAL

Marble, weepe, for thou dost cover. On Margaret Ratcliffe. Ben Jonson. SeCP

Marbles. Joan LaBombard. TDD

Marbles. Valerie Worth. TSS

Marceline, to Her Husband. Elizabeth Libbey. AmPA

Marcellus. Virgil, *tr. fr. Latin by* Dryden. *Fr.* The Aeneid [*or* Eneados], VI. OBS

March. Ilse Aichinger, *tr. fr. German by* Beth Bjorklund. CoAuP

March. Bryant. GN

March. Elizabeth Jane Coatsworth. PDV; RHPC

March. Hart Crane. BoNaP

March. William Everson. ErPo

March, *sel.* Daryl Hine.
    "Once when I was coming from art class they surprised me." GLP

March. A. E. Housman. FaBoCh

March. Roy McFadden. TIRV

March. Henrietta Cordelia Ray. CBWP-3

March. Folgore Da San Gimignano, *tr. fr. Italian by* Dante Gabriel Rossetti. *Fr.* Sonnets of the Months. AWP

March, The. Sir John Collings Squire. OHIP

March. *Unknown.* GBP

March. Charles Henry Webb. AA

March Calf, A. Ted Hughes. NoP

March Day, 1941. Joyce Grenfell. CN

March Evening. L. A. G. Strong. MoBrPo

March 1st. Kathleen Spivack. NYBP

March, flickering dirge. March, Vigilant Fire. Delia Quiñónez, *tr. by* David Volpendesta. Vol

March 4th Anno 1698/9; a Charracteristicall Satyre. John Saffin. *See* Satyretericall Charracter of a Proud Upstart, A.

March Hares. Walter de la Mare. FaBoNo

March has come to the bridge head. Poem by the Bridge at Ten-shin. Li Po, *tr. by* Ezra Pound. OBVE

March in the Ranks Hard-Prest, and the Road Unknown, A. Walt Whitman. AmPP; NAAL-1; OxBA

March into Virginia, The. Herman Melville. BLPL; HAP; LiTA; NAAL-1; NoP; PoE; TAP; TrGrPo; WaaP

March Journal. Charles Wright. BLA

March, march, Ettrick and Teviotdale. Border Ballad. Sir Walter Scott. *Fr.* The Monastery, *ch.* 25. GN
    (Blue Bonnets over the Border.) OxBS
    (Border March.) EnRP

March, march, head erect. Mother Goose. OxNR

March! March! March! from sunrise till it's dark. The Marching Song of Stark's Men. Edward Everett Hale. PAH

March, May, July, October; these are they. The Roman Calendar. Benjamin Hall Kennedy. AAA

March 19, 1823. V. A. Zhukovsky, *tr. fr. Russian by* Alan Myers. AAA

March, 1941. Paul Goodman. LiTA

March of the Three Kings. *Unknown.* OHIP

March of the Women, The. Cicely Hamilton. BrRo

March 1, The. Robert Lowell. HCAP; NoP

March said to Averil. The Borrowing Days. *Unknown.* GBP

March 2, The. Robert Lowell. NoP

March Snow. Don McKay. NOBC

March. . .someone has walked across the snow. Vacancy in the Park. Wallace Stevens. LCAP

March the 3rd. Edward Thomas. NAs

3-31-70. Gayl Jones. *Fr.* Journal. BlSi

March to Moscow, The. Robert Southey. FaBoCo

March, Upstate. William Bronk. NYBP

March, Vigilant Fire. Delia Quiñónez, *tr. fr. Spanish by* David Volpendesta. Vol

March Weather. Jon Swan. NYBP

March Wind, The. E. H. Henderson. BoTP

March Wind, The. *Unknown.* RHPC

March Wind. Lewis Warsh. UL

March Winds. Cecil Francis Lloyd. CaP

March winds and April showers. *Unknown. Fr.* Weather Wisdom [*or* Weather Wise]. FaBoBe; OxNR

March with his wind hath struck a cedar tall. On Queen Anne's Death. *Unknown.* EIL

March yeans the lammie. March. *Unknown.* GBP

Marchant was ther with a forked berd, A. Chaucer. *Fr.* The Canterbury Tales: Prologue. CTC, *abr.*

Märchen, The. Randall Jarrell. CMoP

Märchenbilder. John Ashbery. KS; LCAP; NOBA

Marching. Isaac Rosenberg. BrPo

Marching Litany to Our Martyrs, A. Jack A. Mapanje. WMBCH

Marching 'round the Levee. *Unknown.* AmFP

Marching Song. Dana Burnet. PAH

Marching Song. Robert Louis Stevenson. BoTP; FaPON

Marching Song of Stark's Men, The. Edward Everett Hale. PAH

Marching through Georgia. Henry Clay Work. FaPoR; PAH

Marching to Quebec. *Unknown.* AmFP

Marching to Utah. *Unknown.* AmFP

Marcia and I went over the curve. Millions of Strawberries. Genevieve Taggard. FaPON; ILY; MoShBr

Marcia Thompane was light and compact. Dancing School. Jonathan Holden. Psk

Marco Bozzaris, *sel.* Fitz-Greene Halleck. AA; AnAmPo; BeLS; GN; WBLP
    "At midnight, in his guarded tent." HoPM

Marcus Antoninus Cui Cognomen Erat Aurelius. Burns Singer. OxBS

Marcus Aurelius. C. H. Sisson. OxBC

Marcus Curtius. Oliver St. John Gogarty. OBMV

Marcus, the sluggard, dreamed he ran a race. The Sluggard. Lucilius, *tr. by* Humbert Wolfe. SD

Mare, A. Kate Barnes. NYBP

Mare, The. Vernon Watkins. OBWVE

Mare Liberum. Henry Van Dyke. PAH

Mare lies down in the grass where the nest of the skylark is hidden, The. The Mare. Vernon Watkins. OBWVE

Mare Nostrum. Joel Oppenheimer. NeAP

Mare ran into the yard, A. Le Journal. Sándor Weöres, *tr. by* Edwin Morgan. MHuP

Mares of the Camargue, The. Frédéric Mistral, *tr. fr. Provençal by* George Meredith. *Fr.* Mirèio. AWP

Mare's skeleton in the clearing: another sign of life, The. Adrienne Rich. *Fr.* Shooting Script, 11. FaBoWP

Marezle toats. *Unknown.* FaBoNo

Margaret. Charles Cotton. *See* Marg'ret of Humbler Stature by the Head.

Margaret Are You Drug. George Starbuck. InPK; MAT

Margaret, are you grieving. Spring and Fall. Gerard Manley Hopkins. BrPo; CMoP; EBEV; ELP; FaBoUs; FF; GTBS-P; HAP; HeIP; HoPM; InPK; InPS; LiTM; MAT; NAEL-2; NIP; NoAM; NOBE; NoP; OBD; PoE; PoEL-5; PPP; RB; SCV; SOTW; TEP; TOF; WeW
    (Spring and Fall: To a Young Child.) ChTr; GoJo; LiTB; MoAB

Margaret Fuller. Amos Bronson Alcott. AA

Margaret Grady—I fear she will burn. The Witch. Katharine Tynan. NOBVV

Margaret Love Peacock [for Her Tombstone, 1826]. Thomas Love Peacock. OBNC

Margaret mentioned Indians. Indians. John Fandel. AmFN; NYBP

Margaret my sweetest, Margaret I must go. The Souldiers Farewel to His Love. *Unknown.* CoMu

Margarita first possest. The Chronicle; a Ballad. Abraham Cowley. SeCV-1

Margarite of America, A, *sel.* Thomas Lodge.
    "O shady vales, O fair enriched meads." EIL; OBSC

Margery Mutton-pie. Mother Goose. OxNR

Marginal Field, The. Stephen Spender. PoA

Marginalia, *sel.* W. H. Auden.
    "Dead man, A/ who never caused others to die." OAEL-2

Marginalia. György Somlyó, *tr. fr. Hungarian by* Jascha Kessler. FOC

Marginalia. Richard Wilbur. CMoP; PoA

Margined by dirty snow-heaps, pavements puffed and clean. Snowy Morning, 1940. N. K. Cruikshank. CN

Marg'ret of Humbler Stature by the Head. Charles Cotton. *Fr.* Resolution in Four Sonnets, of a Poetical Question Put to Me by a Friend, Concerning Four Rural Sisters, II. PoEL-3; Prf; Son
    (Margaret.) TrGrPo
    (Two Rural Sisters.) BoLoP; EnLoPo

Mari Magno, *sel.* Arthur Hugh Clough.
    "Have you the Giesbach seen? a fall." OBTV

María Belén, María Belén, María Belén. Elegy for María Belén Chacón. Emilio Ballagas, *tr. by* Perry Higman. LPSS

Maria Enchained. Juana Castro, *tr. fr. Spanish by* Kate Flores. DMH

Maria intended a letter to write. How to Write a Letter. Elizabeth Turner. MoShBr; OxBChV

Maria Wentworth. Thomas Carew. CaPo; JCP; MeLP; MePo; OBD; OBS; SeCV-1

Mariam, *sels*. Lady Elizabeth Carey. WPE
   "Fairest action of our human life, The." *Fr.* IV.
   "'Tis not enough for one that is a wife." *Fr.* III.

Mariana. Tennyson. AWP; CH; ChER; InPS; NAEL-2; NOBE; NoP; OAEL-2; OBEV; OBNC; PoE; PoEL-5; TEP; TrGrPo; UnPo; WiR

Marianne, Madeline, Alys. Three Little Girls. Richard Aldington. BrPo

Marichi. Kenneth Rexroth. PPR

Marie Hamilton. *Unknown. See* Mary Hamilton.

Marie Hamilton's to the kirk gane. The Queen's Marie. *Unknown.* OBEV

Marie Magdalens Complaint at Christs Death. Robert Southwell. MePo

Marigold, The. William Forrest. ACP

Marigold, The. George Wither. OBS

Marigolds. Louise Driscoll. BoTP

Marigolds. Robert Graves. BrPo

Marin. Philip Booth. AiP; NYBP

Marina. T. S. Eliot. CMoP; FaBoMo; GTBS-P; HeIP; LiTA; MOS; NAEL-2; NOBE; NOCV; PoE; TOF

Marina. O. B. Hardison, Jr. AiP; CRP

Marina Mother. Lucha Corpi, *tr. fr. Spanish by the author and* Catherine Rodríguez-Nieto. *Fr.* I. CCP; OV

Marina of the Rocks. Odysseus Elytis, *tr. fr. Greek by* Edmund Keeley *and* Philip Sherrard. VMG

Marina Poems, The, *sels*. Lucha Corpi, *tr. fr. Spanish by the author and* Catherine Rodríguez-Nieto. CCP; OV
   Devil's Daughter, The. *Fr.* III.
   Marina Mother. *Fr.* I.
   Marina Virgin. *Fr.* II.
   She (Marina Distant). *Fr.* IV.

Marina Tsvetayeva. Derek Walcott. AnAn

Marina Virgin. Lucha Corpi, *tr. fr. Spanish by the author and* Catherine Rodríguez-Nieto. *Fr.* The Marina Poems, II. CCP; OV

Marina's gone, and now sit I. Celadyne's Song. William Browne. *Fr.* Britannia's Pastorals, III, Song 1. OBS

Marine Aquarium, The. Louis Dudek. *Fr.* Atlantis. MoCV

Marine Biology. Israel Efrat, *tr. fr. Hebrew by* Bernhard Frank. MHeP

Mariner, in the green spire. Land-Fall. George M. Brady. NeIP

Mariner sat on the shrouds one night, A. The Drowned Mariner. Longfellow. SHA

Mariner that on smooth waves doth glide, The. Anne Bradstreet. *Fr.* Contemplations. WPOW

Mariner, what of the deep? Deep Sea Soundings. Sarah Williams. WGRP

Mariners' Carol. W. S. Merwin. EaLo

Mariner's Dream, The. William Dimond. BeLS

Mariner's Song, The. Sir John Davies. OBSC

Marionette. Dahlia Ravikovich, *tr. fr. Hebrew by* Warren Bargad *and* Stanley F. Chyet. IP

Marionettes, The. Walter de la Mare. MMA

Mariposa Lily, The. Ina Coolbrith. AA

Maritae Suae. William Philpot. OBEV

Marital Problem, The. Sonja Åkesson, *tr. fr. Swedish by* Joanna Bankier. OV

Maritimes. Penelope Shuttle. BrRo

Marjorie's Almanac. Thomas Bailey Aldrich. FaPON

Mark. Bible, N.T. *See* St. Mark.

Mark. Ernest McGaffey. AA

Mark. John Tranter. NoAM

Mark Anderson. W. W. Gibson. MMA

Mark Antony Addresses the Mob. Shakespeare. *See* Julius Caesar: Antony's Oration [over Caesar's Body].

Mark but this flea, and mark in this. The Flea. John Donne. BLPL; BoLoP; EBEV; FF; FM; HoPM; InPK; InPS; JCP; LiTB; MAT; MePo; NAEL-1; NBLV; NIP; OAEL-1; PoE; SCV; SeCP; SeCV-1; SoSe; TEP; TrGrPo

Mark finished it himself, choosing midnight. Mark. John Tranter. NoAM

Mark how the bashful morn in vain. Boldness[e] in Love. Thomas Carew. CaPo; ErPo; MePo; SeCV-1

Mark how the feathered tenants of the flood. Water Fowl. Wordsworth. FM

Mark how the lanterns cloud mine eyes! A Non Sequitor. Richard Corbet. FaBoNo

Mark how the lark and linnet sing. Dryden. *Fr.* An Ode on the Death of Mr. Henry Purcell. PBBP

Mark how yon eddy steals away. To My Mistress Sitting by a River's Side; an Eddy. Thomas Carew. CaPo

Mark me how still I am!—The sound of feet. The Statue of Lorenzo de' Medici. James Ernest Nesmith. AA

Mark the dark rook, on pendent branches hung. George Canning. *Fr.* The Progress of Man. FaBoNo

Mark Tobey's Legacy. Wieland Schmied, *tr. fr. German by* Beth Bjorklund. CoAuP

Mark well my heavy doleful tale . A Carol for Twelfth Day. *Unknown.* OHIP

Mark when she smiles with amiable cheer. Spenser. *Fr.* Amoretti, XLL. AWP

Mark where the pressing wind shoots javelin-like. George Meredith. *Fr.* Modern Love, XLIII. EnLoPo; GBL; NOBE; OBNC; PoEL-5; TEP (Love's Grave.) OBEV

Mark yon round parson, fat and sleek. Robert Lloyd. *Fr.* A Familiar Epistle to J. B. Esq. OBSV

Mark you how the peacock's eye. Gerard Manley Hopkins. FM

Mark you the floor [*or* floore]? that square and speckled stone. The Church-Floor [*or* Floore]. George Herbert. EBEV; MeLP; OAEL-1; OBS; SeCePo

Marke but this flea, and marke in this. *See* Mark but this flea, and mark in this.

Marke how the bashfull morne in vaine. *See* Mark how the bashful morn in vain.

Marke, when the Evenings cooler wings. To Amoret. Henry Vaughan. SeCP

Marked with D. Tony Harrison. *Fr.* The School of Eloquence. NAEL-2; NoAM

Marker slants, flowerless, day's almost done, The. John Berryman. *Fr.* Dream Songs. CAPP; DiL; HCAP

Markers. Frank Steele. GOYP

Market Basket in the Car, A. Thomas MacDermot. PVCV

Market Day. Roberto Roversi, *tr. fr. Italian by* Lawrence R. Smith. NItP

Market Day. Mary Webb. CH

Market Economy, The. Marge Piercy. GeTw

Market Place. "Sahir Ludhianvi," *tr. fr. Urdu by* Mahmood Jamal. PBMUP

Market square's admiring throngs, The. Goethe, *tr. fr. German by* John Weiss. *Fr.* West-Easterly Divan, *bk.* 9. PeHV

Market torches, boat lanterns: a jumble of fireflies. An Evening Prospect: City Lights. Chiang Shih-ch'üan, *tr. by* Irving Lo. WFTU

Market Women. Angela Figueroa-Aymerich, *tr. fr. Spanish by* Kate Flores. DMH

Marketing. E. J. Falconer. BoTP

Marketplace sleeps, its booths like skulls, The. Perets Markish, *tr. by* Leonard Wolf. PeBMYV

Marketwoman, The. Agostinho Neto, *tr. fr. Portuguese by* Marga Holness. WMBCH

Markings. Frank Steele. Psk

Marks. Linda Pastan. NIP

Mark's Fingers. Mary O'Neill. RHPC

Marl white road, the Dorée rushing cool, The. Tales of the Islands. Derek Walcott. OxBTC

Marlborough, *sel*. Charles Hamilton Sorley.
   "So, there, when sunset made the downs look new." WGRP

Marlburyes Fate. Benjamin Tompson. SCAP

Marlow and Nancy. Sandra McPherson. AmPA

Marlowe. Arthur Bayldon. PoAu-1

Marm Grayson's Guests. Mary Eleanor Wilkins Freeman. OBCA

Marmalade Man Makes a Dance to Mend Us, The. Nancy Willard. ILY

Marmion, *sels*. Sir Walter Scott.
   Battle, The ("But as they left the dark'ning heath"). *Fr.* VI. ELP
   Battle, The ("By this, though deep the evening fell"). *Fr.* VI. PoEL-4
   Battle, The ("Not for advanc'd was morning day"). *Fr.* VI. EnRP
   Edinburgh from the Pentland Hills. *Fr.* IV. FaBoPP
   Ettrick Forest in November. *Fr. Introd. to* I. FaBoPP
   "Heap on more wood!—the wind is chill." *Fr. introd. to* VI. OBCP (Christmas in England, *abr.*) GN
   Lochinvar. *Fr.* V. BeLS; BOTP; EnRP; FaBoBe; FaBV; FaFP; FaPON; FPL; GN; GoTS; NOBE; OBNV; OxBS; PoRA (Young Lochinvar.) OBNV
   Marmion and Douglas. *Fr.* VI. OHFP
   Nelson, Pitt, Fox. *Fr. Introd. to* I. OBEV
   "Where shall the lover rest." *Fr.* III. CH, *abr.*; EnRP; GTBS; GTBS-P

Maroon Girl, The. Walter Adolphe Roberts. PVCV

Marpessa's Choice. Yannis Ritsos, *tr. fr. Greek by* Edmund Keeley. AnAn

Marquis de Sade, The. André Breton, *tr. fr. French by* Keith Waldrop. POS; RHTwFP

Marquis of Carabas, The, *sel.* Robert Barnabas Brough.
  "Look at this skin—at fourscore years." FiBHP
Marrakech. Ralph Nixon Currey. PeSA
Marrakech. Richard Eberhart. LiTM
Marriage, A. Anthony Barnett. VWA
Marriage. Blake. *See* When a Man Has Married a Wife.
Marriage. Raymond Carver. GeTw
Marriage. Austin Clarke. BIrV; GTBS-P
Marriage. Mary Elizabeth Coleridge. PeHV
Marriage. Gregory Corso. CoAP; LiTM; MoP; NeAP; NoP; OBAL;
  PPP; PrIm; TAP
Marriage. Nathaniel Cotton. *See* Those awful words "Till death do
  part."
Marriage, A. Robert Creeley. LiTM; NeAP
Marriage. Elaine Feinstein. AIW
Marriage. Mary Weston Fordham. CBWP-2
Marriage, The, *sels.* Witold Gombrowicz, *tr. fr. Polish by* Louis Iribarne.
  PwPP
  "Game/ Suppose it's just a game, A." *Fr.* Act III.
  "Oh, the insanities I took part in!" *Fr.* Act II.
Marriage. Donald Hall. NePoEA
Marriage, A. Michael Jackson. ATNZ
Marriage, *sels.* Robert Lowell. NAS
  Ninth Month. *Fr. st.* 11.
  Overhanging Cloud. *Fr. st.* 14.
  Robert Sheridan Lowell. *Fr. st.* 13.
Marriage. Marianne Moore. NOBA
Marriage. Mary Ellen Solt. BoWoP
Marriage, The. Mark Strand. EAS; NoAM
Marriage ("Here we go around this ring"). *Unknown.* AmFP
Marriage ("Put your hand in the creel"). *Unknown.* GBP
Marriage, The. Anna Wickham, *tr. fr. Hungarian.* AIW
Marriage. William Carlos Williams. PoA
Marriage, The. Yvor Winters. QFR
Marriage à la Mode, *sels.* Dryden.
  Whil'st Alexis Lay Prest [*or* Press'd]. *Fr.* IV, ii. ErPo; FF; PrIm
    (Song: "Whilst Alexis lay pressed.") BoLoP
  Why Should a Foolish Marriage Vow. *Fr.* I, i. HeIP; NAEL-1; NIP
    (Song: "Why should a foolish marriage vow.") AWP; SeCV-2
Marriage and Midsummer's Night. Linda Gregg. NAmP; NPGG
Marriage and Money. Sir Charles Sedley. *Fr.* The Happy Pair. OBSV
Marriage betwixt Scrape, Monarch of the Maunders, and Blobberlips,
  Queen of the Gypsies, A, *sel.* Alexander Pennecuik.
  "Below fair Peebles, on the river's side." NOEC
Marriage Couplet. William Cole. OBAL
Marriage in Eden, The. William Williams, *tr. fr. Welsh by* Lewis
  Saunders *and* Gwyn Jones. *Fr.* A View of Christ's Kingdom.
  OBWVE
Marriage is a lovely thing. Christine de Pisan, *tr. fr. French by* Joanna
  Bankier. WPOW
Marriage is not/ a house or even a tent. Habitation. Margaret Atwood.
  BoWoP; FaBoWP
Marriage Morning. Tennyson. GBL
Marriage of a Virgin, The. Dylan Thomas. ErPo
Marriage of Earth and Heaven, The. Jay Macpherson. OBCV
Marriage of Heaven and Earth, The. Howard Nemerov. NYBP
Marriage of Heaven and Hell, The, *sels.* Blake. EnRP; OAEL-2
  "In seed time learn, in harvest teach, in winter enjoy." FF
    (Proverbs of Hell.) NAEL-2
  Memorable Fancy, A ("Angel came to me and said"). NU
  Memorable Fancy, A ("As I was walking among the fires of hell"). NU
  "Pride of the peacock is the glory of God, The." FF
  "Rintrah roars & shakes his fires in the burdend air." *Fr.* Argument.
    NAEL-2
  Voice of the Devil, The. NU
Marriage of Hector and Andromache, The. Sappho, *tr. fr. Greek by* Guy
  Davenport. OBVE
Marriage of Pocahontas, The. Mary Morison Webster. PAH
Marriage of Sir Gawain, The. *Unknown.* ESPB
Marriage of the Frog and the Mouse, The. *Unknown.* EBEV
Marriage on a Mountain Ridge. Stewart Conn. PoSH
Marriage Poem, A. Ellen Bryant Voigt. PPR
Marriage Portrait. James Applewhite. MT
Marriage Prospect, A. William Hurrell Mallock. NOBVV
Marriage Ring, A. George Crabbe. BoLoP; EnLoPo; OBEV
Marriage Song. Judah Halevi, *tr. fr. Hebrew by* Alice Lucas. TrJP
Marriage Toast. William Rossa Cole. SoTCo
Marriage Vow. Mrs. Henry Linden. CBWP-4
Marriage, which might have been a mateship sweet. Elizabeth
  Wolstenholme-Elmy. *Fr.* Woman Free. BrRo
Marriage Wig, The. Ruth Whitman. IHMS

Marriages. George Crabbe. *Fr.* The Parish Register, *pt.* II.
  "Disposed to wed, e'en while you hasten, stay." FaBoUs
Marrie dear. When in Rome. Mari E. Evans. AmNP; SoSe
Married. Moyshe-Leyb Halpern, *tr. fr. Yiddish by* Benjamin *and* Barbara
  Harshav. AYP
Married academic woman ten. My Mother's Novel. Marge Piercy. TV
Married and Single Life. *Unknown.* AmFP
Married, but they seem to wait for the night. *Unknown, tr. fr. Japanese
  by* Hiroaki Sato. FCEI
Married for one year. Making It Simple December 8, 1969. David
  McElroy. AmPA
Married Love. Kuan Tao Sheng, *tr. fr. Chinese by* Kenneth Rexroth *and*
  Ling Chung. UnAS
Married Love. Liz Rosenberg. NIP
Married Love. Sherod Santos. Son
Married Lover, The. Coventry Patmore. *Fr.* The Angel in the House, II,
  xii. OBEV; TrGrPo
Married Man, The. Robert Phillips. GeTw
Married man comes nearest to the dead, A. Samuel Butler. FaBoEE
Married to rural goldmines. The Dark Way Home: Survivors. Michael
  S. S. Harper. CNA
Marrog, The. R. C. Scriven. AmMo; RHPC
Marrow, The. Theodore Roethke. NYBP
Marrow of My Bone. Mari E. Evans. BPo
Marrows. Louis Johnson. PeNZ
Marry in Lent. *Unknown.* FaBoUs
Marry in May. *Unknown.* FaBoUs
Marry the Lass? Andrew Greig. PoSH
Marrying Again. Mei Yao-ch'en, *tr. fr. Chinese by* Burton Watson.
  CoBCP
Marrying left your maiden name disused. Maiden Name. Philip Larkin.
  GTBS-P
Marrying the Hangman. Margaret Atwood. NOBC
Mars and Venus. Robert Greene. *Fr.* Tullie's Love. OBSC
Mars in a fury 'gainst love's brightest queen. Mars and Venus. Robert
  Greene. *Fr.* Tullie's Love. OBSC
Mars is braw in crammasy. The Bonnie Broukit Bairn. "Hugh
  MacDiarmid." FaBoCh; HAP; InPS
Marseillaise, The. Claude Joseph Rouget de Lisle, *tr. fr. French by*
  Charles H. Kerr. WBLP
Marsh, The. Beatrice Hawley. PPR
Marsh, The. W. D. Snodgrass. BoNaP; NePoEA
Marsh, The. Marcia Southwick. MAYP
Marsh bank, lotus rank. Confucius, *tr. fr. Chinese by* Ezra Pound. *Fr.*
  Songs of Ch'en. CTC
Marsh Leaf. David Wagoner. PoA
Marsh, New Year's Day, The. Peter Everwine. NNaP
Marsh Song—at Sunset. Sidney Lanier. NOBA
Marshall, the thinges for to attayne. *See* Martial, the things that do attain.
Marshes, The. Jane Mayhall. TAP
Marshes of Glynn, The. Sidney Lanier. AA; AmPP; AnAmPo; LiTA;
  NOBA; OxBA; PrIm; WGRP
Marshlands. Pauline E. Johnson. NOBC
Marston. Stephen Spender. FaBoTw
Marsyas. Hugo Claus, *tr. fr. Dutch by* James S. Holmes. DuIn
Martha. Walter de la Mare. MoBrPo
Martha/ Mary passed this morning. Mary Passed This Morning. Owen
  Dodson. PoBA
Martha Blake. Austin Clarke. TIRV
Martha Blake at Fifty-one. Austin Clarke. CIP; IPY; NOIV
Martha Graham. James Laughlin. RR
Martha Is Not So Tall. Charles Cotton. *Fr.* Resolution in Four Sonnets,
  of a Poetical Question Put to Me by a Friend, Concerning Four Rural
  Sisters, IV. PoEL-3; Prf; Son
Martha Nelson Speaks. George Bogin. MOWH
Marthe Away (She Is Away). Kenneth Rexroth. UnAS
Marthy Virginia's Hand. George Parsons Lathrop. PAH
Martial Cadenza. Wallace Stevens. OxBA; VGW
Martial [*or* Marshall *or* My Friend], the thing[e]s that do [*or* for to] attain
  [*or* attayne]. The Happy Life. Martial, *tr. by* Earl of Surrey.
  NOBE; OBVE; SiPS
  (Martial's Quiet Life.) OBSC
  (Means to Attain Happy Life, The.) ElL; FaBoEE; OBEV
  (My Friend, the Things That Do Attain.) NAEL-1; NoP
  (Things That Cause a Quiet Life, The.) TrGrPo
Martial Variations, *sel.* Amelia Rosselli, *tr. fr. Italian.*
  "In the lethargy which follows the machinations." *Tr. by* Lawrence R.
  Smith. NItP
Martial's Quiet Life. Martial. *See* Martial, the things that do attain.
Martian Sends a Postcard Home, A. Craig Raine. NAEL-2; NoAM; NoP
Martin Buber in the Pub. Max Harris. PoAu-2

Martin cat long shaged of courage good, The. John Clare. FM
Martin, I wonder who makes all the songs. Child and Boatman. Jean Ingelow. *Fr.* Songs on the Voices of Birds. FM
Martin Luther at Potsdam. Barry Pain. NA
Martin Luther King. Myra Cohn Livingston. RHPC
Martin Luther King, Jr. Gwendolyn Brooks. CNA; PoBA
Martin said to his man. *Unknown.* FaBoNo
    (Martin to His Man.) NA
Martin sat young upon his bed. St. Martin and the Beggar. Thom Gunn. Mes; MoBS
Martin to His Man. *Unknown.* NA
Martin's Blues. Michael S. Harper. CNA; HCAP; PoBA
Martyr. "E." CBAP
Martyr. Mary Elizabeth Fullerton. CBAP
Martyr, The. Herman Melville. PoEL-5; TAP; TrGrPo
Martyr, The. Ibrahim Tuqan, *tr. fr. Arabic by* Lena Jayyusi *and* John Heath-Stubbs. MAP
Martyr poets —did not tell, The. Emily Dickinson. EyDe
Martyrdom. "Rufus Learsi." TrJP
Martyrdom. Richard W. Thomas. PoBA
Martyrdom: A Love Poem. Bin Ramke. KS
Martyrdom of Brébeuf and Lalemant, 16 March 1649, The. E. J. Pratt. *Fr.* Brébeuf and His Brethren. NOBC; OBCV
Martyrdom of Father Campion. Henry Walpole. ACP
Martyrdom of Mary, Queen of Scots, The. Robert Southwell. ACP
Martyrdom of St. Theresa, The. A. D. Hope. CBAP
Martyrdom of Two Pagans. Philip Whalen. NeAP
Martyred Democrat, The. C. J. Dennis. CBAP
Martyred Earth, The. Ewart Milne. BIrV
Martyred Saint, he lies upon his bier, A. Lincoln. Corinne Roosevelt Robinson. OHIP
Martyred Widow Liu of Hai-ling: A Ballad. Cheng Hsieh, *tr. fr. Chinese by* Jan *and* Yvonne Walls. WFTU
Martyrs, The. Jay Macpherson. MoCV
Martyr's Death, A. Menahem ben Jacob, *tr. fr. Hebrew.* TrJP
Martyr's Memorial. Louise Imogen Guiney. AA
Martyrs of the *Maine*, The. Rupert Hughes. PAH
Marunouchi Building, The. Nakahara Chuya, *tr. fr. Japanese by* Geoffrey Bownas *and* Anthony Thwaite. PeBJV
Marvaill no more all tho. Sir Thomas Wyatt. *See* Fortune.
Marvel, The. Keith Douglas. RB
Marvel, A. Carolyn Wells. OBCA
Marvel Down. Shin Shalom, *tr. fr. Hebrew by* Bernhard Frank. MHeP
Marvel [*or* Marvaill] no more although [*or* all tho]. Fortune. Sir Thomas Wyatt. AAS; OBSC; SiPS
Marvel of Marvels. Christina Rossetti. NOBE; WGRP
Marvell! I think you'd neither seen nor smelt. Hibernia. Stuart Howard-Jones. NOBL
Marvellous Martin. Charles Harpur. CBAP
Marvell's Garden. Phyllis Webb. OBCV
Marvell's Ghost. John Ayloffe. APAS
Marvelous. Allan Kaplan. MHeP
Marvin Pickett. Mel Glenn. ASP
Marx the Sign Painter. Edgar Lee Masters. *Fr.* The New Spoon River. NoAM; TAP
Mary. John Clare. *See* It is the evening hour.
Mary Ackerman, 1938. Diane Glancy. STE
Mary Ames. *Unknown.* NA
Mary and the Baby, Sweet Lamb. *Unknown.* AmFP
Mary and the Bramble. Lascelles Abercrombie. OBMV
Mary Ann ("Mary Ann has gone to rest"). *Unknown.* FaBoCo
Mary Arnold the Female Monster. *Unknown.* GBP; OBET
Mary Booth. Thomas William Parsons. AA
Mary Complains to Other Mothers. *Unknown.* MeEL
Mary, for the love of thee. Carol: The Five Joys of the Virgin. *Unknown.* ACP
Mary Gloster, The. Kipling. BeLS
Mary Gravely Jones. Adrienne Rich. *Fr.* Grandmothers. NAAL-2
Mary Gulliver to Captain Lemuel Gulliver. John Gay *and* Alexander Pope. OAEL-1
Mary had a little bird. The Canary. Elizabeth Turner. OxBChV
Mary had a little lamb. Mary's Lamb [*or* Mary and Her Lamb]. Sarah Josepha Hale. FaBoBe; FaFP; FaPON; OBCA; OxBChV; OxNR
Mary Had a William Goat. *Unknown.* AS
Mary Hamilton. *Unknown.* ESPB, A *and* B *vers.*; FaBoBa; NOBE; NoP; OxBB
    ("Word has come from the kitchen.") AmFP
Mary! I want a lyre with other strings. To Mary Unwin [*or* Sonnet to Mrs. Unwin]. William Cowper. GTBS; GTBS-P; OBEV; TrGrPo
Mary in the Silvery Tide. *Unknown.* OBET

Mary is a gentle name. Gentle Name. Selma Robinson. MoShBr
Mary Is Black. Charles Cotton. *Fr.* Resolution in Four Sonnets, of a Poetical Question Put to Me by a Friend, Concerning Four Rural Sisters, III. PoEL-3; Prf; Son
Mary Is with Child. *Unknown.* MeEL
Mary Jane. *Unknown.* NA
Mary laid her Child among. Norman Nicholson. OBCP
Mary Lifted from the Dead. William Alfred. AH
Mary, long by Boss's kisses bored. Don't Look Now but Mary Is Everybody. Peter Viereck. LiTA
Mary McGuire's our cook, you know. This and That. Florence Boyce Davis. FaPON
Mary Magdalene. Saunders Lewis, *tr. fr. Welsh by* Gwyn Morgan. OBWVE
Mary Magdalene, that easy woman. Lent. W. R. Rodgers. AnIL
Mary, Mary. Anthony C. Deane. FaBoPa
Mary, Mary [*or* Mistress Mary], quite contrary. Mother Goose. FaBoBe; FaFP; OxNR
Mary Middling. Rose Fyleman. RAR
Mary mild, good maiden. Saint Columcille. NOIV
Mary Morison. Burns. EnRP; GTBS; GTBS-P; OBEV; OxBS; TrGrPo
"Mary mother, dost thou sleep?" Mary's Dream. *Unknown, tr. by* C. C. Bell. OBWVE
Mary, Mother of Christ. Countee Cullen. PChr
Mary Passed This Morning. Owen Dodson. PoBA
Mary, pray for Paris. Dumb Oxen. Sister Mary Madeleva. *Fr.* Of Mary. CRP
Mary, Queen of Heaven. *Unknown.* MeEL
Mary, Queen of Scots. Henry Glassford Bell. BeLS; BLPA; FaBoBe
Mary sat musing on the lamp-flame at the table. The Death of the Hired Man. Robert Frost. AmPP; CMoP; HeIP; HoPM; MoAB; MoAmPo; NAAL-2; NoP; OxBA; SoSe; TrGrPo
Mary stood in the kitchen. Ballad of the Bread Man. Charles Causley. RB
Mary Stuart. Edwin Muir. RB
Mary Suffers with Her Son. *Unknown.* MeEL
Mary, the Blessed Virgins name. Profit and Loss: An Elegy upon the Decease of Mrs. Mary Gerrish. John Danforth. SCAP
Mary, the Christ long slain, passed silently. Motherhood. Agnes Lee. BLPA
Mary the Cook-Maid's Letter to Dr. Sheridan. Swift. OxBoLi
Mary, The Mother of Jesus. Ada Belle Gardner. PWR
Mary, the mother, sits on the hill. Langdon E. Mitchell. OHIP
Mary Weeps for Her Child. *Unknown.* OxBoLi
Mary, will you ever grow? Water, blessed by bishops. Song for Healing. Roberta Hill. CDW
Mary Winslow. Robert Lowell. PPP
Mary Wyatt and Henry Green. *Unknown.* AmFP
Marye, maide, milde and fre. A Song to Mary. *At. to* William of Shoreham. MeEL
Maryland Battalion, The. John Williamson Palmer. AA; PAH
Maryland Resolves. *Unknown*
Maryland Virginia Caroline. Emblems. Allen Tate. AWP; VGW
Mary's Dream. *Unknown, tr. fr. Welsh by* C. C. Bell. OBWVE
Mary's Ghost. Thomas Hood. FiBHP
Mary's Girlhood. Dante Gabriel Rossetti. WGRP
Mary's gone a-milking. Milking Pails. *Unknown.* CH
Mary's Lamb [*or* Mary and Her Lamb]. Sarah Josepha Hale. FaBoBe; FaFP; FaPON; OBCA; OxBChV; OxNR
Mary's Song. Charles Causley. OBCP
Mary's Song. Sylvia Plath. CAPP; FaBoMo; FaBoWP
Maryuma. Frank Lamont Phillips. AmNP
Mas' Charley. *Unknown.* PBCV
Masaccio's Expulsion. Jorie Graham. AnAn
Masai warrior is not, The. Outbreak. Bill Anderson. VGW
Mashed potatoes cannot hurt you, darling. Giving Potatoes. Adrian Mitchell. NBLV; RB
Mashkin Hill. Louis Simpson. SaC
Mask, The. Elizabeth Barrett Browning. OBNC
Mask. Elizabeth Cox. GoYe
Mask, The. Clarissa Scott Delany. CDC; PoNe
Mask, The. Patty L. Harjo. VoR
Mask, The. Valery Larbaud, *tr. fr. French.* CT, *tr. by* William Jay Smith. RHTwFP, *tr. by* Ron Padgett *and* Bill Zavatsky.
Mask, The. Irma McClaurin. BlSi
Mask, A. Milton. *See* Comus; a Masque Presented at Ludlow Castle: Star that bids the shepherd fold, The.
Mask. Stephen Spender. MoAB; MoBrPo
Mask and the Poem, The. Alejandra Pizarnik, *tr. fr. Spanish by* Alina Rivero. VWA
Mask-Maker. Michael Jackson. PeNZ

Mask [*or* Masque] of Anarchy, The, *sel.* Shelley. EnRP
  "As I lay asleep in Italy." Mes; OBSV; RB; SCV
Mask of Cupid, The. Spenser. *Fr.* The Faerie Queene, III, 12.
  OBSC
  (Masque of Cupid, The.)
  "Noble Mayde, still standing, all this vewd, The." PoEL-1
  "First was Fancy, like a lovely boy, The." NOBE
Mask of Evil, The. Bertolt Brecht, *tr. fr. German by* Michael Hamburger.
  AnAn
Mask of Love. Thomas Kinsella. CMoP
Mask of Mutability, The. Spenser. *Fr.* The Faerie Queene, VII, 7.
  OBSC
  (Seasons, The.) GN
Masked by the pines. *Unknown, tr. by* Geoffrey Bownas *and* Anthony
  Thwaite. PeBJV
Masked by the snowflakes. Ono Takamura, *tr. by* Geoffrey Bownas *and*
  Anthony Thwaite. PeBJV
Masked Shrew, The. Isabella Gardner. ImOP
Masks. Thomas Bailey Aldrich. AA
Masks. Elizabeth Fenton. NMM
Masochist, The. Maxine W. Kumin. IHMS; PoA
Mason lives, The. Symbolum. Goethe, *tr. by* Tom Paulin.
  FaBoPV
Mason's Trick. James Hayford. InPK
Masons, when they start upon a building. Scaffolding. Seamus Heaney.
  GOYP
Masque of Balliol, The. *Var. authors. See* Balliol Rhymes.
Masque of Blackness, The. Geoffrey Hill. *Fr.* Lachrimae, II. NoAM
Masque of Christmas, The. Ben Jonson. OxBoLi
Masque of Cupid, The. Spenser. *See* Faerie Queene, The: Mask of
  Cupid, The.
Masque of Queens, The, *sels.* Ben Jonson.
  "What our Dame bids us do." OFD; WSC
  Witches' Charms, The. EiL
  (Witches' Sabbath, The.) WSC
  (Witches' Charm, The.) FaBoCh
  (Charme.) FM
Masque of the Inner Temple and Gray's Inne, The, *sels.* Francis
  Beaumont.
  "More pleasing were these sweet delights." *Fr.* III. OBS
  "On blessed youths, for Jove doth pause." *Fr.* II. OBS
  "Peace and silence be the guide." *Fr.* V. OBS
  "Shake off your heavy trance!" *Fr.* I. OBS; TrGrPo
  (Fit Only for Apollo.) ChTr
  (Song for a Dance.) EiL; FaBoCh
  "Ye [*or* You] should stay longer if we durst." *Fr.* IV. OBS;
  TrGrPo
Masque of the Middle Temple and Lincoln's Inn, The, *sels.* George
  Chapman.
  Bridal Song. EiL; OxBSP
  Descend, Fair Sun! EiL
Masque of the Twelve Months, The, *sel. At. to* George Chapman.
  Shine Out, Fair Sun, with All Your Heat. ChTr; ELP
  (Song: "Shine out, fair sun, with all your heat.") EiL
Masque of the Virtues against Love. Mary Monck. NOEC
Masquerade. Carolyn M. Rodgers. BlSi
Mass at Dawn. Roy Campbell. PeSA
Mass for the Day of St. Thomas Didymus, *sel.* Denise Levertov.
  Credo. AIW
Mass hysteria, wave after breaking wave. Willowware Cup. James
  Merrill. NoP
Mass of leaves shot through with green and red, A. A Lecture. Gabriel
  Preil, *tr. by* Grace Schulman. PeBMYV
Mass of van contemplation to intercede crush of. For Love Has Such a
  Spirit That If It Is Portrayed It Dies. Charles Bernstein. IAT
Massa ob de sheepfol', De. De Dheepfol'. Sarah Pratt McLean Greene.
  AA
Massachusetts Song of Liberty. *At. to* Mrs. Mercy Warren.
  PAH
Massacre of the Innocents, The, *sel.* Giovanni Battista Marino, *tr. fr.
  Italian by* Richard Crashaw.
  "Yet on the other side, faine would he start." OBVE
Massacre of the Innocents. Tadeusz Rózewicz, *tr. fr. Polish by* Jan
  Darowski. OBD
Massacre of the Innocents, The. William Jay Smith. EaLo
Massacre of the Macpherson, The. William Edmonstoune Aytoun.
  BXAP; CenHV; ChTr; FaBoCo
Massada, *sel.* Yitzhak Lamdan, *tr. fr. Hebrew by* A. C. Jacobs.
  "On an autumn night, lying restless, far from her broken homeland."
  VWA
Massa's in de Cold Cold Ground. Stephen Collins Foster. AA
Massasauga. Hamlin Garland. AA

Massenet/ Never wrote a Mass in A. Antony Butts. FiBHP
Masses. César Vallejo, *tr. fr. Spanish. Fr.* España, Aparta de me Este
  Caliz. LPSS, *tr. by* Lynn C. Jacox *and* Perry Higman; RB, *tr. by*
  Robert Bly.
Masses of sweet snowy apricot blooms cover the branches. The Foreign
  Woman's Complaint. Wen T'ing-yün, *tr. by* Lois Fusek.
  ATF
Massive engines lift beautifully from the deck. The Teeth Mother Naked
  at Last. Robert Bly. NNaP
Massive rains darken the marshes and slopes. Dreaming of Master Chung-
  lu. K'ang Hai, *tr. by* Jonathan Chaves. CoBLCP
Mast Year, The. Medbh McGuckian. CIP
Master, The. "C. G. L." ImOP
Master, The. W. S. Merwin. NePoEA
Master, The. E. A. Robinson. LiTA; LiTM; MoAB; MoAmPo;
  OHIP
Master and Boatswain. W. H. Auden. *See* Sea and the Mirror, The:
  Song of the Master and Boatswain.
Master and Man. Mother Goose. NA; OxNR
Master and Man. Sir Henry Newbolt. OxBTC
Master Brunetto, this my little maid. Sonnet: To Brunetto Latini. Dante,
  tr. by Dante Gabriel Rossetti. AWP
Master Charge Blues. Nikki Giovanni. OBAL
Master Cheng is thirty—and doesn't have a job! Cheng Hsieh, *tr. fr.
  Chinese by* Jonathan Chaves. *Fr.* Seven Songs. CoBLCP
Master City, The. Rose J. Orente. GoYe
Master Francesco, I have come to thee. Petrarch. Giosuè Carducci, *tr.
  by* William Dudley Foulke. AWP
"Master has come over Jordan, The." Christ and the Little Ones. Julia
  Gill. BLPA
Master Hugues of Saxe-Gotha. Robert Browning. OAEL-2
Master I have, and I am his man. Master and Man. Mother Goose.
  NA; OxNR
Master Jen has long been famous. Thanking Doctor Jen. Li K'ai-hsien,
  tr. by Jonathan Chaves. CoBLCP
Master McGrath. *Unknown. See* Eighteen sixty nine being the date of
  the year.
Master Mo Tzu and Master Lao Tzu. Inspector Hsü Claims He Has
  Found the Secret of Youth. T'ang Hsien-Tsu, *tr. by* Jonathan
  Chaves. CoBLCP
Master, No Offering. Edwin Pond Parker. AH
Master of beauty, craftsman of the snowflake. John Berryman. *Fr.*
  Eleven Addresses to the Lord, I. UnPo
Master of blood I am yours. Nocturnal Heart. Anne-Marie Kegels, *tr. by*
  W. S. Merwin. BoWoP
Master of discords John. The Harper. *Unknown, tr. by* Frank O'Connor.
  AnIL
Master of human destinies am I! Opportunity. John James Ingalls. AA;
  AnAmPo; FaFP; OHFP; PoLF; WBLP
Master of spirits! hear me: King of souls! The Darkness. Lionel
  Johnson. BrPo
Master of the world! Forgotten. Malka Heifetz Tussman, *tr. by* Kathryn
  Hellerstein. AYP
Master-Player, The. Paul Laurence Dunbar. AnAmPo
Master said, The: "The Fang bird does not come." A Chinese Mural.
  Carlos Baker. *Fr.* A Visit to the Art Gallery. EyDe
Master Shih's medical fame, because of Master Ch'en. Sent to the Master
  Physician, "Almond Orchard" Shih. Li K'ai-hsien. CoBLCP
Master Singers, The. Rhys Carpenter. WGRP
Master Sky-Lark, *sels.* John Bennett. AA
  Sky-Lark's Song, The.
  Song of the Hunt, The.
Master-songs are ended, and the man, The. Walt Whitman. E. A.
  Robinson. OxBA
Master stood in His garden, The. For the Master's Use [*or* The Watered
  Lilies]. *Unknown.* BLPA; BLRP
Master Suian's Birthplace. Sekirin, *tr. fr. Chinese by* Lucien Stryk *and*
  Takashi Ikemoto. ZPCJ
Master, the swabber, the boatswain and I, The. Shakespeare. *Fr.* The
  Tempest, II, ii. MOS
  (Sea Song, A: "Master, the swabber, the boatswain and I, The.")
  NBLV
  (Song: "Master, the swabber, the boatswain and I, The.") FF;
  NOBL; OxBSP
Master, they say that when I seem. C. S. Lewis. TIRV; TrCP
Master, to do great work for Thee my hand. Life-Mosaic. Frances
  Ridley Havergal. TrPWD
Master, whose fire kindled our glad surprise. The Master. "C. G. L."
  ImOP
Masterpiece of the taxidermist's art, A. Phar Lap in the Melbourne
  Museum. Peter Porter. PoAu-2
Masters. Kingsley Amis. NePoEA

Masters, be kind to the old house that must fall. Rockland. Julia Randall. WPE

Master's hut is as tiny as that of Wan-ch'iu, The. Dawn Snow. Huang Ching-jen, *tr.* by Daniel Bryant. WFTU

Masters, in This Hall. William Morris. ChTr

Master's Invitation, The. Anson Davies Fitz Randolph. AA

Master's Touch, The. Horatius Bonar. TrPWD

Mastery. Sara Teasdale. WGRP

Masts at Dawn. Robert Penn Warren. NAAL-2

Mata Hari/ Was later sorry. Paul Curry Steele. SoTCo

Matadero, Riley and Company. Paul Mariani. BLA

Matadors, The. Josephine Jacobsen. TAP

Matauwhi Bay V. Amanda Eason. DT

Match, The. Andrew Marvell. EBEV

Match, A. Swinburne. ELP; NOBVV

Match at Football, A, *sel.* Matthew Concanen. Heaps on Heaps. SD

Match-bark of the younger dog sets fire to, The. Table-Birds. Kenneth Mackenzie. PoAu-2

Match with the Moon, A. Dante Gabriel Rossetti. NOBVV

Matches among other things that were not allowed. The Burnt Child. W. S. Merwin. NoAM

Matching a Poem by Secretary Kuo. T'ao Ch'ien, *tr. fr. Chinese by* Burton Watson. CoBCP

Matching Green Ribbon. Jim Hofer. CowP

"Mater á Dios, preserve us." With Cortez in Mexico. Wilfred Campbell. PAH

Mater Amabilis. Emma Lazarus. OHIP

Mater Dei. Padraic Fallon. NOCV

Mater Dei. Katharine Tynan. TIRV

Mater Dolorosa. William Barnes. CH; NOBE; OBEV

"Mater dulcissima, now the mists are descending." Letter to My Mother. Salvatore Quasimodo, *tr.* by Jack Bevan. PFI

Materia Nupcial. Pablo Neruda, *tr. fr. Spanish by* Clayton Eshleman. ErPo

Material of our lives increases, and, The. March Wind. Lewis Warsh. UL

Materialism. C. E. M. Joad. FaBoCo

Materialized into an Owl. Louis Oliver. STE

Maternal Despotism; or, The Rights of Infants. Richard Graves. NOEC

Maternal Earth stirs redly from beneath. Roy Campbell. *Fr.* The Flaming Terrapin, I. MoBrPo

Maternity. Jean Ingelow. *Fr.* Songs of Seven. OHIP

Maternity. Alice Meynell. OxBSP

Maternity Gown. David Holbrook. OxBTC

Math Class. Myra Cohn Livingston. TSS

Mathematical Problem, A. Samuel Taylor Coleridge. FaBoUs

Mathematician. Bruce Boston. BWV

Mathematics for the Women's Movement. Sigrid Weigel, *tr. fr. German by* Susan L. Cocalis. DMG

Mathematics of Encounter. Isabella Gardner. ErPo

Mathematics of Love. Michael Hamburger. NePoEA-2; UAS

Mathematics or the Gift of Tongues. Anna Hempstead Branch. ImOP

Mathmid, The. Hayyim Nahman Bialik, *tr. fr. Hebrew by* Maurice Samuel. AWP

Matilda. Hilaire Belloc. CenHV; FaBoCh; NOBE; OnMSP; OxBChV

Matilda Maud Mackenzie frankly hadn't any chin. How a Girl Was Too Reckless of Grammar [by Far]. Guy Wetmore Carryl. AnAmPo; FiBHP; OBAL

Matilda told such dreadful lies. Matilda. Hilaire Belloc. CenHV; FaBoCh; NOBE; OnMSP; OxBChV

Matin Hymn. Josephine D. Henderson Heard. CBWP-4

Matin Pandemoniums, The. Richard Eberhart. NYBP

Matin Song. Thomas Heywood. *See* Rape of Lucrece, The: Pack, Clouds, Away.

Matinal. Marguerite Clerbout, *tr. fr. French by* Kathleen Weaver. OV

Matinal. Cilla McQueen. ATNZ

Matinees. James Merrill. HCAP; NOBA; Prf

Mating Answer. Ronald Bottrall. PoA

Mating the Goats. Aliki Barnstone. BoWoP

Matins. Denise Levertov. AmPP; FaBoWP; IHMS; MoP; NoAM; NOBA

Matins, or Morning Prayer. Robert Herrick. CaPo

Matlock Bath. Sir John Betjeman. NYBP

Matmiya. Mary TallMountain. HATNAP

Matrimony. John Williams. NOEC

Matrix, *sel.* Dorothy Wellesley. "Spiritual, the carnal, are one, The." OBMV

Matronita. Dennis Silk. VWA

Matt Casey formed a social club that beat the town for style. The Band Played On. John F. Palmer. OBAL

Mattens. George Herbert. TrPWD

Matter is palsy: the land heaving, water. From Heraclitus. Alan Dugan. PoA

Matter of Fact. Bruce Andrews. LP

Matter of Urgency. Louis Johnson. ATNZ

Matter whose movement moves us all. Entropy. Theodore Spencer. ImOP

Matters have become very simple. Stone. Aharon Amir, *tr. by* Bernhard Frank. MHeP

Matthew. Bible, *N.T. See* St. Matthew.

Matthew and Mark and Luke and holy John. Epi-strauss-ium. Arthur Hugh Clough. NAEL-2

Matthew V. 29-30. Derek Mahon. CIP

Matthew, Mark, Luke, and John/ Bless the bed that I lie on. *Unknown.* FaBoCh; OxNR
(Before Sleeping.) CH
(Prayer: "Matthew, Mark, Luke, and John.") OxBoLi
(White Paternoster, The.) GBP

Matthew, Mark, Luke and John./ Hold my horse till I leap on. *Unknown.* OxNR; PYC

Matthew, Mark, Luke, and John./ The Book of Acts then think upon. The New Testament. *Unknown.* FaBoUs

Matthew X. 28. Roger Wolcott. SCAP

Mattina. Kurt Klinger, *tr. fr. German by* Beth Bjorklund. CoAuP

Maturity. J. Elgar Owen. WaP

Maturity. Tristan Tzara, *tr. fr. French by* Michael Benedikt. POS

Maturity. Isabelle Vuckovic, *tr. fr. French by* Kathleen Weaver. OV

Mauberley. Ezra Pound. *See* Hugh Selwyn Mauberley: Turned from the eau forte.

Maud. Mary Swander. MOWH

Maud, *sels.* Tennyson.
"Ah, what shall I be at fifty." *Fr. Pt.* I, i. NAEL-2
"Birds in the high Hall-garden." *Fr. Pt.* I, xii. NAEL-2
"Catch not my breath, O clamorous heart." *Fr. Pt.* I, xvi. NAEL-2
"Come into the garden, Maud." *Fr. Pt.* I, xxii. EBVV; FaBV; FiP; NOBE; NOBVV; OAEL-2; PoE
(Maud.) OBEV
(Song: "Come into the garden, Maud.") AWP
"Dead, long dead." *Fr. Pt.* II, v. OAEL-2
"Go not, happy day." *Fr. Pt.* I, xvii. EBVV
"I hate the dreadful hollow behind the little wood." *Fr. Pt.* I, i. FaBoPV
"I have led her home, my love, my only friend." *Fr. Pt.* I, xviii. ChER; EBVV; ELP; FiP; NAEL-2; NOBVV; PoEL-5
"I was walking a mile." *Fr. Pt.* I, ix. EBVV
"My life has crept so long on a broken wing." *Fr. Pt.* III. OAEL-2; OBWP
"O let the solid ground." *Fr. Pt.* I, xi. NAEL-2; NOBVV
"O [*or* Oh] that 'twere possible." *Fr. Pt.* II, iv. BoLoP; NAEL-2; NOBE; NOBVV; OAEL-2; OBEV; PoE
"See what a lovely shell." *Fr. Pt.* II, ii. BoNaP; GoJo; PoEL-5
(Shell, The.) GN
"She came to the village church." *Fr. Pt.* I, viii. EBVV; NAEL-2
Sleeping House, The. *Fr. Pt.* I, xiv. OBNC
There Is None like Her. *Fr. Pt.* I, xviii. OBNC

Maud Muller. Whittier. AA; AnAmPo; BeLS; BLPL; FaBoBe; OHFP; PoLF; TAP; WBLP

Maud Muller all that summer day. Mrs. Judge Jenkins (Being the Only Genuine Sequel to "Maud Muller"). Bret Harte. BxAP; FiBHP

Maud went to college. Sadie and Maud. Gwendolyn Brooks. InPK; MoP; NoAM; NOBA; TAP

Maude Clare. Christina Rossetti. BeLS; EBVV

Maudle-in Ballad, A. *Unknown.* BXAP; FaBoPa

Maui. Meg Campbell. PeNZ

Maui's Fish, *sel.* Blanche Baughan. "Toward the dawn." PeNZ

Maumee Ruth. Sterling A. Brown. CDC

Maunder's Praise of His Strowling Mort, The. *Unknown.* OxBoLi

Maunding Soldier; or, The Fruits of Warre Is Beggery, The. Martin Parker. CoMu; WaaP

Maureen Dean, wearing persimmon summer silk. On the Watergate Women. Robin Morgan. GLP

Maureen in England, Joseph in Guelph. The Wishbone. Paul Muldoon. CIP

Maurice de Guérin. Maurice Francis Egan. AA

Maurice was in an Exhibition Hall. Austin Clarke. *Fr.* Mnemosyne Lay in Dust, V. IPY; PoE

Mavrone. Arthur Guiterman. BXAP; FiBHP

Maw Bonnie Lad. *Unknown.* GBP

Max Ernst. Paul Eluard, *tr. fr. French by* Robery Bly. POS

Max Ernst's Walk. Wieland Schmied, *tr. fr. German by* Beth Bjorklund. CoAuP

Max Is Dead. Natan Zach, *tr. fr. Hebrew by* Warren Bargad *and* Stanley F. Chyet. IP

Max Schmitt in a Single Scull. Richmond Lattimore. AiP; EyDe

Maxie Allen. Gwendolyn Brooks. NAAL-2

Maxim Revised, A. *Unknown.* BLPA; FPL; NBLV; WBLP

Maxims (Cotton MS.). *Unknown, tr. fr. Anglo-Saxon by* Charles W. Kennedy. AnOE

Maxims (Exeter Book). *Unknown, tr. fr. Anglo-Saxon by* Charles W. Kennedy. AnOE

Maxims in Rhyme for the Young. J. Clark. PWR

Maximus. D. H. Lawrence. TOF

Maximus Poems, The, *sels.* Charles Olson.
    Celestial Evening, October 1967. PoM
    Cole's Island. PoM
    "Colored pictures." *Fr.* I. NoAM
    I, Maximus of Gloucester, to You ("By ear, she sd"). *Fr.* NeAP.
    I, Maximus of Gloucester, to You ("Off-shore, by islands hidden in the blood"). LiTM; NoAM; PoM
    Later Note on Letter 15, A. CAPP
    Maximus, to Gloucester, Letter 19. CMoP
    Maximus, to Gloucester, Letter 27. NOBA; PoE
    Maximus, to Gloucester, Letter 2. NoAM
    Maximus, to Gloucester, Sunday, July 19. NAAL-2
    Maximus, to Himself. CAPP; CMoP; CMOP; NeAP; NOBA; PoE; PoM; VGW
    Songs of Maximus. NeAP
        "This morning of the small snow." *Fr.* III. PPP
        (All/ wrong.) NoAM
        "Colored pictures/ of all things to eat: dirty." *Fr.* I. NeAP; NoAM

Maxixe. Sir Osbert Sitwell. PoA

Maxwell[1] ton['s] braes are bonnie. Annie Laurie. William Douglas, *revised by* Lady Jane Scott. FaBoBe; FaBV; FaFP; GN; WBLP

May. William Barnes. *Fr.* May. ChTr

May. Thomas Dekker. *See* Shoemaker's Holiday, The: O, the Month of May.

May. Richard Edwards. OBSC

May. Edward Hovell-Thurlow. OBEV

May. Mrs. Henry Linden. CBWP-4

May. John Shaw Neilson. PoAu-1

May. James Gates Percival. BoTP

May. Henrietta Cordelia Ray. CBWP-3

May. Christina Rossetti. GBL; NOBVV

May. Folgore Da San Gimignano, *tr. fr. Italian by* Dante Gabriel Rossetti. *Fr.* Sonnets of the Months. PFI

May. Spenser. *Fr.* The Faerie Queene, VII, 7. GN

May. *Unknown, tr. fr. Old Irish by* Frank O'Connor. AnIL

May. John Updike. *Fr.* A Child's Calendar. OBCA

May afternoon with birds in every bush. Poem in May. John Hewitt. NeIP

May All Earth Be Clothed in Light. George Hitchcock. VGW

May all my enemies go to hell. Lines for a Christmas Card. Hilaire Belloc. TW

May all that dread the cruel feind of night. Warning to Travailers Seeking Accomodations at Mr. Devills Inn. Sarah Kemble Knight. SCAP

May all your tears, wanderer. Song of the Wanderer. Wang T'ing-hsiang, *tr. by* Jonathan Chaves. CoBLCP

"May an unforeseen disaster." The Horse and the Whip. Eliezer Steinbarg, *tr. by* Curt Leviant. VWA

May and Death. Robert Browning. FaBoRV; NOBE

May, and the air is light. The Road's End. John Montague. *Fr.* A Severed Head, I. IPY

May, and the wall was warm again. For miles. Winter's Cold. William Robert Rodgers. EnLoPo

May! be thou never graced with birds that sing. [Epitaph] In Obitum M.S., X[D]G/ Maij [*or* Maii], 1614. William Browne. EIL; FaBoEE; JCP; NOBE; OBEV; OBS

May Bright Mushrooms Grow. Innocent Banda. WMBCH

May Carol. *Unknown.* OBET

May Collin. Lady Isabel and the Elf-Knight. *Unknown.* ESPB

May Colven. *Unknown.* OxBB; TrGrPo

May come up with bird-din. Nuts in May. Louis MacNeice. MoAB; MoBrPo

May-Day, *sel.* Emerson.
    April and May. GN; OHIP

May-Day. Aaron Hill. NOEC

May Day. Sara Teasdale. BoNaP

May Day, A. Sir Henry Wotton. *See* And now all nature seem'd in love.

May Day Dancing, The. Howard Nemerov. NYBP

May Day, hurrah! Kalenda Maya. Raimbaut de Vaqueiras, *tr. by* Paul Blackburn. Pro

May Day Rounds: Renfrew County, *sel.* Joan Finnigan.
    "Stoop on the log-house is brown with sweet rain-rot, The." WPE

May de Lord—He will be glad of me. Bright Sparkles in de Churchyard. *Unknown.* AA

May Evening. Eileen Brennan. NeIP

May 1506 (Christopher Columbus Speaking). Winfield Townley Scott. GOA

May 15th. Raymond Souster. MoCV

May God above. A Curse on Mine-Owners. *Unknown.* TW

May God be praised for woman. On Woman. W. B. Yeats. CMoP

May God bless your home. Marriage Vow. Mrs. Henry Linden. CBWP-4

May God Give Strength. Peter Van Wynen. BLRP

May has come out from the showers. The Jewish May. Morris Jacob Rosenfeld, *tr. by* Rose Pastor Stokes *and* Helena Frank. TrJP

May has her beauties like another month. Waking. C. H. Sisson. NPo

May have killed the cat; more likely. Curiosity. Alastair Reid. SoSe

May he fall in with beasts that scatter fire. Ballad against the Enemies of France. Villon, *tr. by* Swinburne. AWP

May he have new life like the fall. John Coltrane: An Impartial Review. Alfred B. Spellman. CNA; PoBA

May he lose his way on the cold sea. Archilochus, *tr. by* Guy Davenport. OBVE

May Heaven guard and keep you. *Unknown, tr. by* Arthur Waley. BoS

May His Body make me safer. Thanksgiving after Communion. *Unknown, tr. by* Douglas Hyde. WTO

May I Be Beautiful. *Malay Oral Tradition, tr. by* W. W. Skeat. WTO

May I Feel Said He. E. E. Cummings. BoLoP; ErPo; FF; HeIP; LiTA; NBLV; NOBE

May I find a woman fair. True Beauty. Francis Beaumont. EIL

May I for my own self song's truth reckon. The Seafarer. *Unknown, tr. by* Ezra Pound. CTC; FaBoTw; HeIP; LiTA; NoP; OxBA; RB

May I forever a Muse-/ um. Vow. John Updike. NYBP

May I learn the shape of that hurt. Don. Anthony McNeill. PBCV

May I put my head on your shoulder, Mr. Mac Adams, Sr.? Nuts and Bolts Poem for Mr. Mac Adams, Sr. Kathleen Fraser. NPGG

May in the Green-Wood. *Unknown.* OBEV

May Is Building Her House. Richard Le Gallienne. OHIP

May is the moneth maist amene. Of May. Alexander Scott. OxBS

May It Be. Boris Pasternak, *tr. fr. Russian by* C. M. Bowra. TrJP

May it be you or I. Mohammad Taqi Mir, *tr. by* Ahmed Ali. GoT

May It Not Run Down. Anna Hajnal, *tr. fr. Hungarian by* Jascha Kessler. FOC

May-June, 1940. Robinson Jeffers. LiTA; MoAB; MoAmPo; WaP
    (Battle.) LiTM

May Margret stood in her bouer door. Hind Etin. *Unknown.* ESPB, (A *and* B *vers.*); OxBB

May Morn. Michael McClure. EAS

May Morning. Celia Thaxter. AA

May My Heart Always. E. E. Cummings. OxBSP

May my Irish grandfather from Tyrells Pass. The Buzz Plane. Robert Francis. TW

May 1964. Tuomas Anhava, *tr. fr. Finnish by* Aili Jarvenpa. SOP

May no one take the path. *Unknown. Fr.* Manyo Shu. FCEI

May nothing evil cross this door. Prayer for This House. Louis Untermeyer. BLPL; FaPON; PoLF
    (Prayer for a New House.) TrPWD

May our friend endure. *Unknown, tr. fr. Japanese by* Geoffrey Bownas *and* Anthony Thwaite. *Fr.* Kokin Shu. PeBJV

May peace be established throughout the land. Te Atairangikaahu. Kingi M. Ihaka, *tr. by* Kingi M. Ihaka. PeNZ

May poverty, without offence, approach. Nicholas James. *Fr.* The Complaints of Poverty. NOEC

May! queen of blossoms. May. Edward Hovell-Thurlow. OBEV

May rain: in front of a wide river. Buson, *tr. fr. Japanese by* Hiroaki Sato. *Fr.* Eighty-seven Hokku. FCEI

May rain: marks on each wall. Rakushisha. Basho, *tr. fr. Japanese by* Burton Watson. *Fr.* Seventy-six Hokku. FCEI

May rain: paddy by paddy. Buson, *tr. fr. Japanese by* Hiroaki Sato. *Fr.* Eighty-seven Hokku. FCEI

May rain: the muddy water thrusts. Buson, *tr. fr. Japanese by* Hiroaki Sato. *Fr.* Eighty-seven Hokku. FCEI

May rains! Sanpu, *tr. by* Kenneth Koch *and* Harold Henderson. TTTS

May seven tears in every week. A Wish. J. M. Synge. FaBoEE

May Song. *Unknown.* OBET

May Sun Sheds an Amber Light, The. Bryant. AA

May 10th. Maxine W. Kumin. BoNaP; NYBP; RFM

May that lovely young body of yours. Maiden. Márton Kalász, *tr. by* Jascha Kessler. FOC

May the Babylonish curse. A Farewell to Tobacco. Charles Lamb. OxBoLi

May the ethereal elements not rise up as enemies. Prayer for Guidance. *Unknown, tr. fr. Tibetan by* W. Y. Evans-Wentz. *Fr.* The Tibetan Book of the Dead. OBD

May the grace of the Holy Ghost be gained by us. The Graces of the Holy Ghost. *Unknown, tr. by* Douglas Hyde. TIRV

May the harpoon rust, may the cold steel be gone. Blood on the Sails. Phil *and* June Colclough. OBET

May the man who gained my trust yet did not come. Ryojin Hisho. BoWoP

May the man who has cruelly murdered his sire. A Counterblast against Garlic. Horace, *tr. fr. Latin by* Roswell Martin Field. *Fr.* Epodes, III. NBLV

May the men who are born. Hitomaro. *Fr.* Manyo Shu. AWP

May the Saddest Memory. Birthday Wishes to a Husband. Lizelia Augusta Jenkins Moorer. CBWP-3

May the very ugly ones forgive me, but. Woman Recipe. Vinícius de Moraes, *tr. by* Paul Blackburn. ATCBP

May the will come from Thee. Annul Wars. Rabbi Nahman of Bratzlav, *tr. by* Jacob Sloan. TrJP

May the wrath of the heart of my god be pacified! *Unknown.* WGRP

May they come, may they come. Song of the Highest Tower. Rimbaud, *tr. by* Edgell Rickword. AWP

May they stumble [*or* wander], stage by stage. The Travel[l]er's Curse after Misdirection. Robert Graves. BrPo; CMoP; FiBHP; HoPM; LiTM; MoAB; MoBrPo; NBLV; TW

May 30, 1893. John Kendrick Bangs. AA

May this carnation announce to you [*or* tell you]. Carnation, The ("May this carnation announce to you"). Guillaume Apollinaire, *trs. by* Michael Benedikt *and by* Roger Shattuck. POS

May-Time. *Unknown.* BoTP

May Time. Sir Thomas Wyatt. *See* Sonnet: "You that in love find[e] luck[e] and abundaunce [*or* habundance]."

May Tree, The. William Barnes. LiTB

May Trees in a Storm. Geoffrey Grigson. GBL

May with its light behaving. W. H. Auden. EBEV

Maya in the city has a dream. The Book of Ephraim. James Merrill. *Fr.* The Changing Light at Sandover. NAAL-2

Mayakovsky was right. Kiss. Al Young. PoBA

Mayan Ruins. Ory Bernstein, *tr. fr. Hebrew by* Warren Bargad *and* Stanley F. Chyet. *Fr.* Poems from Mexico. IP

Maybe all I saw was the mirror. Vision. Delmira Augustini, *tr. by* Marti Moody. WPOW

Maybe all that my verses have expressed. It May Be. Alfonsina Storni, *tr. by* Mark I. Smith. OV

Maybe Alone on My Bike. William Stafford. NYBP

Maybe Dats Your Pwoblem Too. Jim Hall. MT

Maybe Elegies. Sandor Csoori, *tr. fr. Hungarian by* Jascha Kessler. FOC

Maybe he dreamed of/ new snow. Retired Farmer. David Allan Evans. Psk

Maybe I am what she always wanted. Why My Mother Made Me. Sharon Olds. ER

Maybe I should go back to the white leather. Desnos Reading the Palms of Men on Their Way to the Gas Chambers. Stephen Berg. VWA

Maybe it is true we have to return. Obsessions. Denise Levertov. LiTM; NePoEA-2; SM

Maybe it was the way. Finding You. Virginia Gilbert. IHMS

Maybe it's so. Snail's Pace. Aileen Fisher. RAR

Maybe Love. Allen Ginsberg. PeHV

Maybe morning lightens over. For My Grandmother, Bridget Halpin. Michael Hartnett. BIrV

Maybe no one can distinguish which voice. The Creation of the Inaudible. Pattiann Rogers. KS

Maybe the street is tired of being a street. New Year. Naomi Shihab Nye. MT

Maybe this is the final battle. No One's Land. Janet Dubé. DT

Maybe this is what ghost is. Recovery. Patricia Y. Ikeda. BrSi

Maybe we knew each other better. Coda. Louis MacNeice. FaBCIP

Maybe we should start small, in a cradle. Beginning. Jacob Glatstein, *tr. by* Benjamin *and* Barbara Harshav. AYP

Maybe You Cannot Comprehend. Salvador Villanueva, *tr. fr. Spanish.* InW, *tr. by* Julio Marzán

Maybe you ranted in the grove. Ezry. Archibald MacLeish. NOBA

Maybrick trial is over now, there's been a lot of jaw, The. Penal Servitude for Mrs. Maybrick. *Unknown.* OxBoLi

Mayday. Ed Roberson. PoBA

Mayde ther was, y-clept Joan Hunter Dunn, A. The Summonee's Tale. Stanley J. Sharpless. BXAP; FaBoPa

Mayde's Metamorphosis, The, *sels. At. to* John Lyly *and to* Thomas Ravenscroft.

  By the Moon ("By the moon we sport and play"). CH

  (Fairy Dances.) ElL

  (Urchin's Dance, The.) BoTP

  Elves' Dance, The. CH; FaPON

Mayflower, The. Erastus Wolcott Ellsworth. AA; FaBoBe; PAH

Mayflower. John Boyle O'Reilly. AA; PAH

Mayor has angrily banished the seven deadly, The. The Exiles. Paul Ramsey. *Fr.* Three Epigrams. CRP

Mayor of Fukui, The. Gust Gils. *Fr.* Two Japanese Poems, II. DuIn

Mayor of Lagos. *Yoruba Oral Tradition, tr. by* Ulli Beier. WTO

Mayor of Scuttleton, The. Mary Mapes Dodge. NA

Mayors, The. Blake. *See* Island in the Moon, An: Good English Hospitality.

May's Invocation after a Tardy Spring. Henrietta Cordelia Ray. CBWP-3

May's the merriest time of all. May. *Unknown, tr. by* Frank O'Connor. AnIL

Mayst thou die desp'rate in some dirty pool. An Adieu to My Landlady. George Farewell. NOEC

Maytide's evenen wer a-dyen, A. Light or Sheade. William Barnes. NOBVV

Maytime. Thomas Dekker. *See* Shoemaker's Holiday, The: O, the Month of May.

Maytime. *Unknown, tr. fr. Chinese by* L. Cranmer-Byng. *Fr.* Shi King. AWP

Maytime, loveliest season. Sadness in Spring. *Unknown, tr. by* Gwyn Jones. OBWVE

Maytime Magic. Mabel Watts. RHPC

Mazeppa. Byron. EnRP

Mazilla and Mazura. *Unknown.* ChTr

Mbuyazi of the Bay! Praises of Henry Francis Fynn. *Zulu Oral Tradition, tr. by* T. Cope. WTO

$MC^2=E$. Lois Wickstrom. BWV

Me. Karla Kuskin. RHPC

Me. Walter de la Mare. FaPON; RHPC

Me a poet! My daughter with maimed limb. Self Justification. Tony Harrison. *Fr.* The School of Eloquence. NoAM

Me Alone. Lula Lowe Weeden. CDC

Me and Hercule Poirot. Deborah Kendrick. TSM

Me and my brother. My Brother, Beautiful Shinault, That Goat. David Huddle. GrPl

Me and My Dog. *Unknown.* PoAu-1

Me and the boys. Like It or Not. Bill Simpson. CowP

Me and the Mule. Langston Hughes. IDB

Me clairvoyant. Old King Cole ("Me clairvoyant"). G. K. Chesterton. *Fr.* Variations on an Air Composed on Having to Appear in a Pageant as Old King Cole. BXAP; FaBoPa; NOBL; Par

Me, Colored. Peter Abrahams. *Fr.* Tell Freedom. PBA

Me! dutiful son going back to South Wales, this time afraid. Down the M4. Dannie Abse. OxBC

Me happy, night, night full of brightness. Elegy VII. Ezra Pound. *Fr.* Homage to Sextus Propertius. ErPo; InvP; VGW

Me I Am! Jack Prelutsky. RHPC

Me—I Am but One. Amir Gilboa, *tr. fr. Hebrew by* Bernhard Frank. MHeP

Me I will throw away. The Self-slaved. Patrick Kavanagh. MoBrPo

Me, I'm the man that dug the Murray for Sturt to sail down. They'll Tell You about Me. Ian Mudie. PoAu-2

Me Imperturbe. Walt Whitman. NOBA

Me, in Kulu Se and Karma. Carolyn M. Rodgers. PoBA

Me list no more to sing. Sir Thomas Wyatt. AAS; SiPS

Me Lord? can'st Thou mispend. Phineas Fletcher. *Fr.* The Divine Wooer. Tof; TrPWD

"Me miserable! which way shall I fly." Milton. *Fr.* Paradise Lost, *Bk.* IV, *ll.* 73–535. PoE

Me nappy hair dream child. Image in the Mirror. Peggy Susberry Kenner. JB

Me one, way out in the crowd. Valley Prince. Mervyn Morris. PBCV

Me Polytimus vexes and provokes. Martial. PeHV

Me Rueth, Mary. *Unknown.* *See* Now Goeth [*or* goth *or* goothe] Sun [*or* Sunne] under Wood.

Me so oft my fancy drew. The Choice. George Wither. OBEV

Me take my cutacoo. A Negro Song. *Unknown.* PBCV

Me Tarzan. Tony Harrison. *Fr.* The School of Eloquence. NoAM

Me that 'ave been what I've been. Chant-Pagan. Kipling. FaBoPV

Me, the kid, and some other boys was playin' a hand of cards. The Kid Solos. Bob Schild. CowP

Me thinkes this draught such vertue does infuse. The Office of Poetry. Nathaniel Whiting. *Fr.* Il Insonio Insonado. OBS

Me thinks I see our mighty monarch stand. *Unknown.* *Fr.* The Royal Angler. OBSV

Me thinks [*or* Methinks], I see, with what a busie [*or* busy] hast[e]. On Zacheus [*or* Zacchaeus]. Francis Quarles. HAP; MePo; OBS

Me thoughte thus: that [h]it was May. The Dream. Chaucer. *Fr.* The Book of the Duchesse. FiP; PBBP

Me to You. Alastair Reid. NYBP

Me Too Boogie. Blaise Cendrars, *tr. fr. French by* Anselm Hollo. RHTwFP

Me Up at Does. E. E. Cummings. NYBP; OxBSP; WeW

Mea Culpa. "Ethna Carbery." TrPWD

Meadow-Field, The. Charles Sangster. *Fr.* Pleasant Memories. OBCV

Meadow is poisonous but pretty in the fall, The. Saffron. Guillaume Apollinaire, *tr. by* Roger Shattuck. POS

Meadow Lark, The. Hamlin Garland. AA

Meadow Mouse, The. Theodore Roethke. HeIP; NaP; NIP; RB

Meadow upon the Mercy of Heaven, The. Hsin Mu, *tr. fr. Chinese by* Dominic Cheung. IFON

Meadows, The. Jane *and* Ann Taylor. BoTP

Meadows are empty, The. There are two villages. The Hours. Norman Dubie. GeTw

Meadows of cella-anemonies. Photomicrograph: Last Centimeter of the Human Airway. S. R. Compton. BWV

Meadowsweet. William Allingham. OBNC

Meal, The. Karla Kuskin. RAR

Meal Time. Maggie Pogue Johnson. CBWP-4

Mean Drunk Poem. Sharon Thesen. NOBC

Mean Rufus Throw-Down. David Smith. TDD

Mean the same thing, like flammable and inflammable. Lucky and Unlucky. William Matthews. BLA

Meandering abroad in the Lincolnshire meadows day. George Barker. *Fr.* Calamiterror, VI. EAS

Meandering Wye. Robert Bloomfield. *Fr.* The Banks of Wye. OBNC

Meanest trick I ever knew, The. A Low Trick. Gelett Burgess. OBCA

Meaning, The. Ralph Gustafson. OBCV

Meaning a context or vision to confer with this which could be a book. Approximately. Diane Ward. LP

Meaning and Truth. Stefan Themerson. NPo

Meaning of Africa, The. Abioseh Nicol. PBA

Meaning of Love, The. *Malay Oral Tradition, tr. by* R. O. Winstedt. WTO

Meaning of the Look, The. Elizabeth Barrett Browning. TrCP

Meaning of the word: independent country, The. I Talked to a Frenchman. Adam Zagajewski, *tr. by* Antony Graham. PwPP

Meaningful Exchange, The. Marge Piercy. AIW

Meanings in the Pattern, The. Judy Grahn. UL

Means of Production, The. Michael Hofmann. NPo

Means of Propulsion for Steam-Ships. Thomas Baker. *Fr.* The Steam Engine; or, The Power of the Flame. FaBoUs

Means to Attain Happy Life, The. Martial. *See* My friend, the things that do attain.

Meantime. Heather McHugh. GeTw

Meanwhile. Joel Dailey. UL

Meanwhile surely there must be something to say. The Constructed Space. W. S. Graham. PoA

Meanwhile the adversary of God and man. Milton. *Fr.* Paradise Lost, *Bk.* II. DL, *ll.* 629–841; EBEV, *ll.* 629–734.
(Sin and Death.) OBNV, *ll.* 629–889.

Meanwhile the choleric Captain strode wrathful away to the council. The War-Token. Longfellow. *Fr.* The Courtship of Miles Standish. PAH

Meanwhile the tepid caves and fens and shores. Milton. *Fr.* Paradise Lost, Bk. VII, *ll.* 417–448. PBBP

Meanwhile the troops beneath Patroclus' care. Homer, *tr. fr. Greek by* Pope. *Fr.* The Iliad, XVI. OBVE

Meanwhile the woman, from her strawberry lips. Metamorphoses of the Vampire. Baudelaire, *tr. by* Jackson Mathews. ErPo

Meare's milk and deer's milk. A Witch's Spell [*or* Witch's Milking Charm]. *Unknown.* ChTr; GBP
(Witch's Milking Charm.) GBP

Measles. Kaye Starbird. RHPC

Measles in the Ark. "Susan Coolidge." OxBChV

Measure. Gillian Eve Hanscombe *and* Suniti Namjoshi. DT

Measure. Robert Hass. GeTw

Measure, The. Patrick Lane. NOBC

Measure for Measure, *sels.* Shakespeare.
"Any [*or* Aye], but to die, and go we know not where." *Fr.* III, i. OBD; RB
Be Absolute for Death. *Fr.* III, i. FaBoRV
On Death. *Fr.* III, i. FiP
"Sense of death is most in apprehension, The." *Fr.* III, i. OBD
Take, O Take Those Lips Away (*also given, with add. st., in* The Bloody Brother *by* John Fletcher *and others*). *Fr.* IV, i. AWP; EBEV; EIL; ELP; EnLoPo; FaBV; GBL; HeIP; InPS; LiTB; NoP; OAEL-1; OBEV
(At the Moated Grange.) NOBE
(Seals of Love.) TrGrPo
(Song at the Moated Grange, A.) OBSC
(Song: "Take, O take those lips away.") FiP; PoEL-2

Measure is a guess the mind makes about itself. Telemann to A.C. Helen Chasin. TV

Measure Me, Sky. Leonora Speyer. FaPON

Measure of a Man, The. *Unknown.* BLPL; PoLF

Measure of freedom, A. Mike, floating. Handicapped Children Swimming. Michael Dennis Browne. TSL

Measure time. Metronome. János Pilinszky, *tr. by* William Jay Smith. MHuP

Measured blood beats out the year's delay, The. Simple Autumnal. Louise Bogan. MoAB; MoAmPo; QFR; Son

Measurement. A. M. Sullivan. RHPC

Measures. Jackson MacLow. LP

Measuring worm with a hump on his back, A. Pedagogical Principles. Harry Amoss. CaP

Mechanic, The. Robert Creeley. NaP

Mechanic, The. Diane Wakoski. AmPA

Mechanical/ Oracles dot the sky. Gods in Vietnam. Eugene B. Redmond. NBP; PoBA

Mechanical digger wrecks the drill, A. At a Potato Digging. Seamus Heaney. CIP; IPY

Mechanical Doll. Forugh Farrokhzad, *tr. fr. Persian by* Deirdre Lashgari. OV

Mechanism. Archie Randolph Ammons. HAP

Mechanophilus, *sel.* Tennyson.
"Dash back that ocean with a pier." FaBoCo

Mecklenburg Declaration, The. William C. Elam. PAH

Mecox Road. Marc Cohen. BAP

Medal [*or* Medall], The, *sel.* Dryden.
Vox Populi. NOBE
"Almighty crowd, thou shorten'st all dispute." OBS

Medal of John Bays; a Satire against Folly and Knavery, The. Thomas Shadwell. APAS

Medal Reversed, The. Elkanah Settle. APAS

Medall, The. Dryden. *See* He preaches to the crowd that power is lent.

Medallion. Sylvia Plath. HeIP; NoP; SM

Medals and Money: A Re-evaluation. Barbara Lamblin. ASP

Meddlesome Matty. Ann Taylor. OnMSP; OxBChV

Meddow Verse; or, Aniversary to Mistris Bridget Lowman, The. Robert Herrick. SeCV-1

Medea. Euripides, *tr. by* Rex Warner. NAWM-1

Medea, *sel.* Lord De Tabley.
"Sweet are the ways of death to weary feet." OBEV

Medea, *sels.* Seneca, *tr. fr. Latin by* John Studley. OBVE
"Her chaunging lookes no colour longe can holde." *Fr.* IV.
"That Orpheus Calliops sonne who stayde the running brooke." *Fr.* III.

Medea in Athens, *sel.* Augusta Davies Webster.
"Oh smooth adder/ who with fanged kisses changedst my natural blood." BrRo

Medea, you beautiful woman, don't turn around. Letter to Medea. Helga Novak, *tr. by* Susan L. Cocalis. DMG

Medea's Incantation. Ovid, *tr. fr. Latin.* *Fr.* Metamorphoses: Magic. OBVE, *tr. by* Arthur Golding.

Medgar Evers. Gwendolyn Brooks. NoP; PoBA

Mediator, The. Elizabeth Barrett Browning. TrPWD

Medical Aid. Walter Hard. BXAP

Medicine. Alice Walker. NMM

Medicine Bearer. Gail Tremblay. HATNAP

Medicine-fetcher, The. *Unknown, tr. by* Geoffrey Bownas *and* Anthony Thwaite. PeBJV

Medicine plants blooming beneath. Another Old Song. Barney Bush. STE

Medieval Mirth. *Unknown.* *Fr.* The Squire of Low Degree. ACP

Medieval Norman Song ("Alas, poor heart, I pity thee"). *Unknown, tr. fr. French by* John Addington Symonds. AWP
Medieval Norman Song ("Before my lady's window gay"). *Unknown, tr. fr. French by* John Addington Symonds. AWP
Medieval Norman Song ("Beneath the branch of the green may"). *Unknown, tr. fr. French by* John Addington Symonds. AWP
Medieval Norman Song ("Drink, gossips mine!"). *Unknown, tr. fr. French by* John Addington Symonds. AWP
Medieval Norman Song ("Fair is her body, bright her eye"). *Unknown, tr. fr. French by* John Addington Symonds. AWP
Medieval Norman Song ("In this merry morn of May"). *Unknown, tr. fr. French by* John Addington Symonds. AWP
Medieval Norman Song ("My love for him shall be."). *Unknown, tr. fr. French by* John Addington Symonds. AWP
Medieval Norman Song ("They lied, those lying traitors all"). *Unknown, tr. by* John Addington Symonds. AWP
Medieval Poem of the Nativity, A. *Unknown.* TrCP
Medieval town, with frieze, The. What Is Poetry. John Ashbery. LCAP
Meditating on Star Light While Traveling Highway. Anita Endrezze-Danielson. HATNAP
Meditatio. Ezra Pound. FaBoCh; OBAL
Meditation. Baudelaire, *tr. fr. French by* Robert Lowell. InPK; NAWM-2
Meditation, A. Richard Eberhart. LiTA
Meditation. Anthony Hecht. BLA; EOEF
Meditation. Mikhail Yurevich Lermontov, *tr. fr. Russian by* Alan Myers. AAA
Meditation, A. Herman Melville. GOA
Meditation, A. János Pilinszky, *tr. fr. Hungarian by* Jascha Kessler. FOC
Meditation. Carl Rakosi. VWA
Meditation. Beyle Schaechter-Gottesman, *tr. fr. Yiddish by* Gabriel Preil. VWA
Meditation. Shin Dong-jip, *tr. fr. Korean by* Koh Chang-soo. ACKP
Meditation at Kew. Anna Wickham. FaBoTw; MoBrPo
Meditation at Lagunitas. Robert Hass. AnAn; MAYP; NoP; NPGG
Meditation at Oyster River. Theodore Roethke. CAPP; CMoP; MoAmPo; NYBP
Meditation at Seventy. Rudolf Henz, *tr. fr. German by* Beth Bjorklund. CoAuP
Meditation at Stuyvesant Church. Judah Leib Teller, *tr. fr. Yiddish by* Benjamin *and* Barbara Harshav. AYP
Meditation at the Threshold. Rosario Castellanos, *tr. fr. Spanish by* Kate Flores. DMH
Meditation 8 ("Scarce do I pass a day but that I hear"). Philip Pain. NOBA; OxBSP; QFR
Meditation for a Pickle Suite. Richard H. W. Dillard. HoPM; MT
Meditation for Christmas, A. Selwyn Image. OBEV
Meditation for His Mistress[e], A. Robert Herrick. CaPo; JCP; NOBE; OBEV; OBS; SeCP
Meditation 9 ("Man's life is like a rose that in Spring"). Philip Pain. *Fr.* Meditations for July 26, 1666. NOBA; SCAP
Meditation of a Mariner. Dorothy Auchterlonie. CBAP
Meditation on a Bone. A. D. Hope. NoAM; TW
Meditation on a Memoir. J. V. Cunningham. QFR
Meditation on Communion with God. Judah Halevi, *tr. fr. Hebrew by* Solomon Solis-Cohen. TrJP
Meditation on John Constable, A. Charles Tomlinson. NePoEA-2
Meditation on Rhode Island Coal, A. Bryant. TAP
Meditation on Statistical Method. J. V. Cunningham. CoAP; QFR; VGW
Meditation on the A30. Sir John Betjeman. RB
Meditation on the Lake. Gasper García Laviana, *tr. fr. Spanish by* Alejandro Murguía. Vol
Meditation on the Nativity. Elizabeth Jennings. NAs
Meditation Rock, The. Mo Shih-lung, *tr. fr. Chinese by* Jonathan Chaves. CoBLCP
Meditation 62 ("How is it that I am so careless here"). Philip Pain. NOBA
Meditation 10 ("Alas, what is the world?"). Philip Pain. NOBA
Meditation 29 ("How mutable is every thing that here"). Philip Pain. *Fr.* Meditations for July 26, 1666. NOBA
Meditation upon the Toothache, A. Laurence Lerner. NePoEA-2
Meditations. Solomon ibn Gabirol, *tr. fr. Hebrew by* Emma Lazarus. TrJP
Meditations for a Savage Child. Adrienne Rich. LCAP
Meditations for August 1, 1666. Philip Pain. SCAP
Meditations for July 26, 1666, *sels.* Philip Pain.
    Meditation 9 ("Man's life is like a rose that in Spring"). SCAP
    Meditation 29 ("How mutable is every thing that here"). NOBA; SCAP

Meditations for July 19, 1666. Philip Pain. SCAP
Meditations for July 25, 1666. Philip Pain. SCAP
Meditations in an Emergency. Frank O'Hara. CAPP; TAP
Meditations in Time of Civil War, *sels.* W. B. Yeats.
    Ancestral Houses. *Fr.* I. LiTB; OAEL-2
    I See Phantoms of Hatred and of the Heart's Fullness and of the Coming Emptiness. *Fr.* VII. LiTB
    My Descendants. *Fr.* IV. LiTB
    My House. *Fr.* II. LiTB
    My Table. *Fr.* III. LiTB
    Road at My Door, The. *Fr.* V. BIrV; LiTB; NOBE; PoE
    Stare's Nest by My Window, The. *Fr.* VI. BIrV; GTBS-P; InPS; LiTB; NOBE
    ("Bees in the crevices, The.") FaBoPV
Meditations of a Hindu Prince. Sir Alfred Comyn Lyall. WGRP
Meditations of a Parrot. John Ashbery. TTTS
Meditations of a Tortoise Dozing under a Rosetree Near a Beehive at Noon While a Dog Scampers About and a Cuckoo Calls from a Distant Wood. Emile Victor Rieu. FiBHP
Meditations of an Old Woman, *sels.* Theodore Roethke. NaP
    First Meditation. LCAP; NOBA
    I'm Here. CoAP; NYBP
Meditations on the Moon. Paula Gunn Allen. HATNAP
Meditations on the Sepulchre in the Garden. Philip Doddridge. NOCV; NOEC
Meditatioun in Wyntir. William Dunbar. OxBS; SeCePo
Mediterranean. Israel Pincas, *tr. fr. Hebrew by* A. C. Jacobs. VWA
Mediterranean, The. Allen Tate. FaBoMo; GOA; HAP; LiTA; LiTM; MoAB; MoAmPo; MOS; VGW; WeW
Mediterranean. Ruth Whitman. VWA
Mediterranean Woman. Kondo Azuma, *tr. fr. Japanese by* Geoffrey Bownas *and* Anthony Thwaite. PeBJV
Medium, The. Elaine Feinstein. BrRo
Medium IV: Sights, The. Carl Rakosi. InPS
Medium Poem. Eileen Myles. UL
Medlars and Sorb-Apples. D. H. Lawrence. NoAM; OAEL-2
Medusa. Louise Bogan. AWP; BoWoP; HoPM; MoAB; MoAmPo; NoAM; NoP; WPE
Medusa. Vincent O'Sullivan. ATNZ
Medusa. Robert Kelley Weeks. AA
Medusa living on a remote shore. Look, Medusa! Suniti Namjoshi. AIW
Medusa. Sit down. Take. Eve Meets Medusa. Michelene Wandor. AIW
Medusas. Paul Eluard, *tr. fr. French by* Michael Benedikt. POS
Medusa's Hair Was Snakes. Was Thought, Split Inward. Kathleen Fraser. NPGG
Mee-ow, mee-ow. Pussy-Cat and Puppy-Dog. Lilian McCrea. BoTP
Meek and the Proud, The. Abraham ibn Chasdai, *tr. fr. Hebrew by* J. Chotzner. TrJP
Meek dew shone, the grass lay prostrate, The. The Tree. Ilya Grigoryevich Ehrenburg, *tr. by* Babette Deutsch. TrJP
Meek Francis lies here, friend, without stop or stay. Matthew Prior. FaBoEE
Meet Me in St. Louis, Louis. Andrew B. Sterling. OBAL
Meet me to-night, lover, meet me. Moonlight. *Unknown.* AS
Meet me tonight. Jackie. King D. Kuka. VoR
Meet me tonight as usual at nine. Love Poem—1940. Miriam Hershenson. GoYe
Meet-on-the-Road. *Unknown.* TTTS
Meet Rabbi Shatz in his correct black homburg. Tales of Shatz. Dannie Abse. OxBC; VWA
Meet the Supremes. David Trinidad. UL
Meet was at "The Cock and Pye," The. John Masefield. *Fr.* Reynard the Fox. OxBTC
Meet women with tender bearing. The Voice of Experience. Goethe, *tr. by* Walter Kaufman. ErPo
Meeting. Matthew Arnold. *Fr.* Switzerland, I. ELP
Meeting, The. Louise Bogan. NoAM; NYBP
Meeting, A. C. Day Lewis. NYBP
Meeting, The. Gerald Costanzo. MAYP
Meeting, The. George Crabbe. OBEV
Meeting, The. Tess Gallagher. GeTw
Meeting. Sam Harrison. NeIP
Meeting, The. Nicki Jackowska. BrRo
Meeting, The. Pierre Louÿs, *tr. fr. French. Fr.* Chansons de Bilitis. PeHV
Meeting, The. Howard Moss. GOYP; NYBP
Meeting. Christina Rossetti. GBL; Mes
Meeting, The. Muriel Rukeyser. MoAmPo; TrJP
Meeting, The. Kathleen Spivack. NMM
Meeting, The. Ramona Wilson. VoR

Meeting a Bear. David Wagoner. HAP

Meeting after Long Absence, sels. Lilla Cabot Perry. AA
As It Was. *Fr.* II.
As She Feared It Would Be. *Fr.* I.

Meeting after Separation. Marula, tr. fr. *Sanskrit by* Tambimuttu *and* G. V. Vaiyda. BoWoP

Meeting and Passing. Robert Frost. OxBA

Meeting at a Salesyard. John Ennis. CIP

Meeting at Night. Robert Browning. AWP; BoLoP; ELP; FaBV; FF; FiP; GBL; HeIP; InPS; InvP; MOS; NAEL-2; NOBE; NOBVV; OBEV; OBNC; OPOP; OXBSP; PoRA; SCV; SeCePo; SoSe; TrGrPo; UnPo; WeW

Meeting by the Gjulika Meadow. Geoffrey Grigson. WaP

Meeting Etsujin. Boncho, tr. fr. *Japanese by* Hiroaki Sato. *Fr.* Twenty-one Hokku. FCEI

Meeting his mother makes him lose ten years. Between the Porch and the Altar. Robert Lowell. NePoEA

Meeting-House Hill. Amy Lowell. MoAmPo; OxBA; PoRA

Meeting-house is not what it used to be, The. Elegy in a Presbyterian Burying-Ground. Robert Noble Denison Wilson. BIrV

Meeting in the Forest, A. Yrjö Jylhä, tr. fr. *Finnish by* Aili Jarvenpa. SOP

Meeting Master Oryu taught me this. Rodohin, tr. by Lucien Stryk *and* Takashi Ikemoto. ZPCJ

Meeting Mick Jagger. Robert Peters. BXAP

Meeting My Best Friend from the Eighth Grade. Gary Gildner. ASP; SM

Meeting My Fellow Countryman, Yü Wu-chung. Yang Chi, tr. fr. *Chinese by* Jonathan Chaves. CoBLCP

Meeting Myself. Edward Lucie-Smith. NePoEA-2

Meeting of Cultures, A. Donald Davie. OBTV; OxBC

Meeting of the Waters, The. Thomas Moore. AnIL; NOIV; OxBoLi; PoEL-4

Meeting Point. Louis MacNeice. FaBCIP

Meeting the British. Paul Muldoon. CIP; FaBoPV; NoAM

Meeting the Dead. Alicia Ostriker. ER

Meeting the first time for many years. A Meeting. C. Lewis. NYBP

Meeting the Mountains. Gary Snyder. NoAM; TAP

Meeting the Reincarnation Analyst. Gary Gildner. AmPA

Meeting Together of Poles & Latitudes: In Prospect. Margaret Avison. NOBC; OBCV

Meeting Trappers on the Road in Heavy Snow. Li K'ai-hsien, tr. fr. *Chinese by* Jonathan Chaves. CoBLCP

Meeting Up. Vincent O'Sullivan. ATNZ

Meeting when all the world was in the bud. Loves of the Puppets. Richard Wilbur. OxBC

Meeting with Giorgio de Chirico. Wieland Schmied, tr. fr. *German by* Beth Bjorklund. CoAuP

Meeting with Time, "Slack thing," said I. Time. George Herbert. NAEL-1; TEP

Meetings. János Pilinszky, tr. fr. *Hungarian by* William Jay Smith. MHuP

Meetings and Absences. Roy Fuller. OnUR

Meetings meetings meetings. Yuh Lookin Good. Carolyn M. Rodgers. BPo

Meg/ Likes/ A regular egg. Meg's Egg. Mary Ann Hoberman. RHPC

Meg Merrilies [or Merrilees]. Keats. BoTP; ELP; FaBoCh; FaPON; FiP; OxBChV; TEP

Megaceph, chosen to serve the State. Ambrose Bierce. *Fr.* The Devil's Dictionary. OBAL

Megga/ your child dying in the street! Dying in the Street. Amryl Johnson. WS

Meg's Egg. Mary Ann Hoberman. RHPC

Mein Herz, Mein Herz Ist Traurig. Heine, tr. fr. *German by* James Thomson. AWP

Mein Kind, wir waren Kinder. Heine. *See* My child, we were two children.

Mein Liebchen, wir sassen zusammen. Heine, tr. fr. *German by* James Thomson. AWP

Melampus. George Meredith. PoEL-5

Melampus, when will love be void of fears? Song of Coridon and Melampus. George Peele. *Fr.* The Hunting of Cupid. OBSC

Melancholetta, sel. "Lewis Carroll."
"My dismal sister! Couldst thou know." FiBHP

Melancholia. Robert Bly. NoP

Melancholia. Robert Bridges. CMoP

Melancholia. Stephen Plaice. NPo

Melancholia. *Unknown.* NA

Melancholy. John Fletcher. *Fr.* The Nice Valor. GTBS; GTBS-P; OBEV
(O Sweetest Melancholy.) TrGrPo

(Passionate Man's Song, The.) OBS
(Song: "Hence all you vaine delights.") PoEL-2

Melancholy. Thomas Lodge. *See* Scilla's Metamorphosis: Earth, Late Choked with Showers, The.

Melancholy. Edward Thomas. NoP

Melancholy Conceit. Samuel Rowlands. OxBSP

Melancholy days are come, the saddest of the year, The. The Death of the Flowers. Bryant. AA; AnAmPo; BLPL; BoNaP; GN; OBCA; PoLF; WBLP

Melancholy days come once a year, The. A View on Death. Roy W. Watson. PWR

Melancholy days have come, The. Autumn Leaves. Charles H. Webb. OBAL

Melancholy desire of ancient things, A. On an Air of Rameau. Arthur Symons. OBNC

Melancholy face Charles Carville had, A. Charles Carville's Eyes. E. A. Robinson. AnAmPo; CMoP; OxBA; TAP

Melancholy green of November. November. A. Leyeles, tr. by Benjamin *and* Barbara Harshav. AYP

Melancholy Knight, The, sels. Samuel Rowlands.
Poetaster, The. EIL
Sir Eglamour. EIL; FaBoCh; FaBoNo; InvP

Melancholy Lay, A. Marjory Fleming. FaBoCh; FiBHP; NBLV

Melancholy Pig, The. "Lewis Carroll." *See* Sylvie and Bruno
Concluded: Pig-Tale, A.

Melancholy slackening that ensued, The. Cambridge and the Alps. Wordsworth. *Fr.* The Prelude [or, Growth of a Poet's Mind], VI. FiP; ImOP; PoEL-4
"But 'twas a time when Europe was rejoiced." FaBoPV
Crossing the Alps. OBTV; RB
Imagination ("Imagination—here the power so called"). FiP
"'Tis told by one whom stormy waters threw." ImOP
"When from the Vallais we had turned." TOF

Meleager. Ovid, tr. fr. *Latin by* Arthur Golding. *Fr.* Metamorphoses, VIII. CTC

Melhill Feast. William Barnes. OBNC

Melincourt, sel. Thomas Love Peacock.
Sun-Dial, The. OBNC

Melinda, who had never been. The Coquette. Aphra Behn. TrGrPo

Melissa Finnan Haddie. Miss M. F. H. E. I. I. Jones. Karla Kuskin. ILY

Melissima's Waltz. Christopher Logue. NPo

Mellifluous as bees, these brittle men. On First Looking in on Blodgett's Keats's "Chapman's Homer." George Starbuck. OBAL

Mellisandra. Harriet Rose. BrRo

Mellow moon hangs golden in the sky, The. October. Henrietta Cordelia Ray. CBWP-3

Mellow the moonlight to shine is beginning. The Spinning-Wheel. John Francis Waller. ChTr

Mellow year is hasting to its close, The. November. Hartley Coleridge. *Fr.* Sonnets to the Seasons.

Mellowness and Flight. George Barlow. CNA

Melmac Year, The. David Hilton. UL

Melodic Trains. John Ashbery. NoP

Melodies of Time, The. Thomas Hood. *Fr.* The Plea of the Midsummer Fairies. OBNC

Melodious Birds. Timothy Holmes. UAS

Melody. Shmuel Moreh, tr. fr. *Arabic by* Yoffee Berkovitz. VWA

Melody in C. Wei Ch'eng-pan, tr. fr. *Chinese by* Lois Fusek. ATF

Melon-Slaughterer; or, A Sick Man's Praise for a Well Woman. Robert Peters. BXAP

Melons. Moshe Yungman, tr. fr. *Yiddish by* Gabriel Preil *and* Howard Schwartz. VWA

Melpomene (at whose mischeifous tove). Carmen Elegiacum. Thomas Morton. SCAP

Melpomene, the Muse of tragic songs. Oenone's Complaint. George Peele. *Fr.* The Arraignment of Paris. EIL; OBSC

Melrose Abbey. Sir Walter Scott. *Fr.* The Lay of the Last Minstrel, II. FaBoPP; SeCePo
(Sir William of Deloraine at the Wizard's Tomb.) OBNC

Melt all the butter. What Her Girl Friend Said to Her Lover on His Return. Kakkai Patiniyar Naccellaiyar, tr. by A. K. Ramanujan. PLW

Melt the money down and take. Memento Vitae. Heather McHugh. NAmP

Melting, The. Russell Edson. PPR

Melting in thin mist and heavy clouds. Li Ch'ing-chao, tr. by J. P. Seaton. BoWoP

Melting Pot. Michael Echeruo. TTY

Melting Pot, The. Dudley Randall. BPo

Melting snow. Issa, *tr. by* Geoffrey Bownas *and* Anthony Thwaite. PeBJV

Melting snow/ among deep mountains clouded over. Kyotai, *tr. fr. Japanese by* Burton Watson. *Fr.* Sixteen Hokku. FCEI

Melton Mowbray Pork Pie, A. Richard Le Gallienne. BXAP; Par

Member of the modern great, A. John Cunningham. FaBoEE

Memento for Mortality, A. *At. to* Francis Beaumont *and to* William Basse. *See* Mortality, behold and fear.

Memento Mori. Moyshe-Leyb Halpern, *tr. fr. Yiddish by* Benjamin *and* Barbara Harshav *and* Kathryn Helle. AYP

Memento Vitae. Heather McHugh. NAmP

Memento Vivendi. Eva Brudne. VWA

Mementos, I: "Sorting out letters and piles of my old." W. D. Snodgrass. FF; HeIP; MoAmPo; NePoEA-2; UnPo

Mementos, II: "I found them there today." W. D. Snodgrass. NePoEA-2

Mementos of the dead. *Unknown, tr. by* Burton Watson. FCEI

Memnon. Clinton Scollard. AA

Memo. Charles G. Ballard. VoR

Memo. Kenneth Fearing. CMoP; PoE

Memo. Hildegarde Flanner. NYBP

Memo. Charles Lynch. PoBA

Memo. Hans Sahl, *tr. fr. German by* Edouard Roditi. VWA

Memo from the Desk of X. Donald Justice. TwCP

Memo to Mr. Auden, 29/8/66. Alistair Campbell. ATNZ

Memoir. Honor Moore. GLP

Memoirs, The. Carl Rakosi. PoA

Memoirs of a Spinach-Picker. Sylvia Plath. GrPl

Memoirs of a Turcoman Diplomat, *sel.* Denis Devlin.
  "Evenings ever more willing lapse into my world's evening." IPY; NOIV

Memorabilia. Robert Browning. FiP; NAEL-2; NOBVV; NoP; OAEL-2; OBNC; PoE; RB; SeCePo

Memorable Fancy, A ("Angel came to me and said"). Blake. *Fr.* The Marriage of Heaven and Hell. NU

Memorable Fancy, A ("As I was walking among the fires of hell."). Blake. *Fr.* The Marriage of Heaven and Hell. NU

Memorandum. Rudy Bee Graham. PoNe

Memorandum. William Stafford. NYBP

Memorandum/ The Accountant's Notebook. Kathleen Norris. OBAL

Memoria Technica for the Books of the Bible. *Unknown.* FaBoUs

Memoria Technica for the Plays of Shakespeare. *Unknown.* FaBoUs

Memorial. Rigoberto Paredes, *tr. fr. Spanish by* Walter Martínez. VoI

Memorial. Robert Pinsky. HCAP; SM

Memorial. Sonia Sanchez. BlSi

Memorial Couplets for the Dying Ego. George Barker. EBEV

Memorial Day. Michael Anania. NoAM

Memorial Day. Theodosia Garrison. OHIP

Memorial Day. Richard Watson Gilder. OHIP

Memorial Day. Emma A. Lent. WBLP

Memorial Day. Josephine Miles. NoP

Memorial Day. Clara Ann Thompson. CBWP-2

Memorial Day. Annette Wynne. OHIP

Memorial Day; a Collaboration, *sel.* Anne Waldman *and* Ted Berrigan.
  "And now the book is closed." EAS

Memorial Days. Ira Sadoff. BLA

Memorial for a Fisherman. Johannes Bobrowski, *tr. fr. German by* Don Bogen. AnAn

Memorial in Aachen. Franz Richter, *tr. fr. German by* Beth Bjorklund. CoAuP

Memorial Lines on the Gender of Latin Substantives. Benjamin Hall Kennedy. FaBoUs

Memorial Ode. Chief John Buck. GOA

Memorial: On the Slain at Chickamauga. Herman Melville. AA

Memorial I. Audre Lorde. AIW

Memorial Poem. Roy Fuller. OxBSP

Memorial Poem. Jacob Glatstein, *tr. fr. Yiddish by* Ruth Whitman. VWA

Memorial Rain. Archibald MacLeish. AmPP; CMoP; LiTA; MoAB; MoAmPo; OBWP

Memorial Service for the Invasion Beach Where the Vacation in the Flesh Is Over. Alan Dugan. TwCP

Memorial to a Missionary. Keith Sinclair. ATNZ; PeNZ

Memorial to D. C., *sel.* Edna St. Vincent Millay.
  "Let them bury your big eyes." *Fr.* V. CMoP; MoAB; MoAmPo; PoRA
  ("O, loveliest throat of all sweet throats.") OxBA

Memorial to the Great Big Beautiful Self-sacrificing Advertisers. Frederick Ebright. WaP

Memorial to the Vicars of Urswick. Neil Curry. NPo

Memorial Verses, *sel.* Matthew Arnold. FiP; NAEL-2; OAEL-2; Wordsworth's Grave. FaBoPP

Memorial Verses, Adapted to the Gregorian Account, or New Style. *Unknown.* FaBoUs

Memorial Verses for Travellers. Sir Anthony Fitzherbert. *Fr.* Husbandry. FaBoUs

Memorial Wreath. Dudley Randall. CNA; IDB; PoBA; PoNe

Memories. Thomas Bailey Aldrich. AA

Memories. Horiguchi Daigaku, *tr. fr. Japanese by* Geoffrey Bownas *and* Anthony Thwaite. PeBJV

Memories. George Denison Prentice. AA

Memories. Walt Whitman. PCP

Memories glide. Into Snowy Night. Hannu Mäkelä, *tr. by* Aili Jarvenpa. SOP

Memories of a Dorset Childhood in the 1730's. Thomas Cole. *Fr.* The Life of Hubert. NOEC

Memories of a Lost War. Louis Simpson. OBWP; VGW

Memories of Aunt Maria-Martha. William Zaranka. BXAP

Memories of Childhood. John Carr. *Fr.* Derwent; an Ode. NOEC

Memories of Her Friend Who Died. Ory Bernstein, *tr. fr. Hebrew by* Warren Bargad *and* Stanley F. Chyet. IP

Memories of Italy (Broken Sestina). John Ash. BAP; NPo

Memories of President Lincoln, *sels.* Walt Whitman.
  O Captain! My Captain! AA; FaBoBe; FaBoCh; FaBv; FAFP; FaPon; FaPoR; FPL; GN; GOA; ImPk; LitA; MoAmPo; MOS; OBCA; OHFP; OHIP; PAH; PoLF; TAP; TrGrPo
  When Lilacs Last in the Dooryard Bloom'd. AmPP; AWP; FPL; HAP; LiTA; MoAmPo; NAAL-1; NOBA; NoP; OFD, , 24 *ll.*; OxBA; PoEL-5; PoRA; PPP; TAP; TrGrPo
    "Come lovely and soothing death." SCV
    (Carol of Death, The.) DL
    "In the swamp in secluded recesses." RFM

Memories of the Village School. Al-Tijani Yusuf Bashir, *tr. fr. Arabic by* Issa Boullata *and* John Heath-Stubbs. MAP

Memories of Verdun. Alan Dugan. OxBSP; RB

Memories of West Street and Lepke. Robert Lowell. AmPP; CAPP; CMoP; InPS; NAAL-2; NaP; NoAM; NOBA; PoE

Memoriter. Charles Spear. ATNZ; PeNZ

Memory. Thomas Bailey Aldrich. AA; AnAmPo; BoNaP; PoLF

Memory. Anne Brontë. EBVV

Memory, A. Rupert Brooke. BrPo

Memory. William Browne. *See* Britannia's Pastorals:
  So shuts the marigold her leaves.

Memory. Elizabeth Cook-Lynn. *Fr.* Journey, II. HATNAP

Memory, The. Robert Creeley. CAPP; VGW

Memory. Babette Deutsch. PoA

Memory. Goldsmith. *See* Captivity, The: O Memory, Thou Fond Deceiver.'

Memory. Michael Hamburger. OxBTC

Memory. Helen Hoyt. PoLF

Memory. Kitahara Hakushu, *tr. fr. Japanese by* Hiroaki Sato. FCEI

Memory. Walter Savage Landor. EBEV; NOBVV; OAEL-2

Memory. Abraham Lincoln. BLPA; FaBoBe; FPL; WBLP

Memory. Norman MacCaig. NPo

Memory, A. Adah Isaacs Menken. CBWP-1

Memory, A. P. Mustapää, *tr. fr. Finnish by* Aili Jarvenpa. SOP

Memory. Edward Coate Pinkney. AnAmPo

Memory. Pierre Reverdy, *tr. fr. French by* Kenneth Rexroth. RHTwFP

Memory. Christina Rossetti. OBNC

Memory. Dante Gabriel Rossetti. OxBSP

Memory. Erik Johann Stagnelius, *tr. fr. Swedish by* Sir Edmund Gosse. AWP

Memory, A. L. A. G. Strong. FaBoCo; NOBL

Memory. Joseph Stroud. NPGG

Memory. Tennyson. FL

Memory. Unsi al-Haj, *tr. fr. Arabic by* Abdullah al-Udhari. MPAW

Memory. W. B. Yeats. BIrV; PoE

Memory I. George Seferis, *tr. fr. Greek by* Edmund Keeley *and* Philip Sherrard. VMG

Memory Air. Charles Dobzynski, *tr. fr. French by* Anita Barrows. VWA

Memory cannot linger long. So Wags the World. Ellen Mackay Hutchinson Cortissoz. AA

Memory! dear enchanter! Memory. Tennyson. FL

Memory: farfields of morning. Persephone. Robert Duncan. NOBA

Memory feeds us on a prison diet. Mandrakes for Supper. James K. Baxter. OxBC

Memory Gardens. Allen Ginsberg. NNaP

Memory has no end here and no beginning. Rehearsing for Death. Angelos Sikelianos, *tr. by* Edmund Keeley *and* Philip Sherrard. VMG

Memory, hither come. Blake. NAEL-2; PoEL-4
Memory: I can take my head and strike it on a wall on Cumberland Island. The Shark's Parlor. James Dickey. MT; NYBP
Memory, magnesium flare, you single. Circus at the Barber's Shop. Kendrick Smithyman. PeNZ
Memory of a Rose. Koh Chang-soo, *tr. fr. Korean by the author.* ACKP
Memory of Another Climate. Gabriel Preil, *tr. fr. Hebrew by* Jeremy Garber. VWA
Memory of Boxer Benny (Kid) Paret, The. Frank Lima. PoNe
Memory of Brother Michael. Patrick Kavanagh. FaBCIP; MoAB; OnYI
Memory of Dust and Light. Julio Ortega, *tr. fr. Spanish by* David Tipton. Per
Memory of Elena, The. Carolyn Forché. ER; MAYP; NoAM
Memory of France. Paul Celan, *tr. fr. German by* Joachim Neugroschel. AnAn
Memory of Hills, *sel.* Rex Ingamells.
  "There are rock-rooted ranges to dominate." CBAP
Memory of my Father. Patrick Kavanagh. FaBCIP; InPS; RB
Memory of my father is wrapped in white paper, The. My Father. Yehuda Amichai, *tr. by* Warren Bargad *and* Stanley F. Chyet. IP
Memory of Pinks. Kitahara Hakushu, *tr. fr. Japanese by* Hiroaki Sato. FCEI
Memory of summer is winter's consciousness. Early Winter. Weldon Kees. NaP
Memory of the face, A. After the War. Hayim Naggid. VWA, *tr. by* Shlomo Vinner *and* Howard Schwartz
Memory of the Hill, A. Kapilar, *tr. fr. Tamil by* A. K. Ramanujan. PLW
Memory of the Players in a Mirror at Midnight, A. James Joyce. InvP
Memory of the Present. David Shapiro. UL
Memory pales in the face of the moon. On Leaving Baltimore. Duane Niatum. CDW
Memory Sire, The. Barney Bush. HATNAP
Memory System, A. *Unknown.* PWR
Memory II. George Seferis, *tr. fr. Greek by* Edmund Keeley *and* Philip Sherrard. VMG
Memphis Blues. Sterling Allen Brown. BANP
Men. Archibald MacLeish. AmFN; MoAB
Men against the Sky. John Haines. LCAP
Men and Women. David Dabydeen. PBCV
Men and women sang and played, The. World's Bliss. Alice Notley. UL
Men Are Children of This World. Moses Ibn Ezra, *tr. fr. Hebrew by* Solomon Solis-Cohen. TrJP
Men are children of this world. Meditation. Carl Rakosi. VWA
Men Are Coming Back! The. Barry Cole. OxBTC
Men are drawn to my ass by. Being Aware. Dennis Cooper. GLP; UL
Men are running across a field. Letter. Mark Strand. NoAM
Men are what they are, and what they do. Intimate Parnassus. Patrick Kavanagh. MoBrPo
Men are what they do, women are what they are. In Nature There Is neither Right nor Left nor Wrong. Randall Jarrell. OxBC
Men at Forty. Donald Justice. CAPP; DiL; LCAP; MT; NoAM; PPP; Prf
Men behind the Guns, The. John Jerome Rooney. AA; BLPA; FaBoBe; PAH
Men beren eek the wommen upon honde. Cupid Defends Women. Thomas Hoccleve. *Fr.* The Letter of Cupid. OxBLMV
Men, brother men, that after us yet live. The Epitaph in Form of a Ballad. Villon, *tr. by* Swinburne. CTC
Men call you fair [*or* fayre]. Spenser. *Fr.* Amorette, LXXIX. AWP; FaBoBe; NAEL-1; NoP; Son
  (Sonnet: "Men call you fair.") BLPL
Men chase the boy into the hog shed, The. Rape. Thomas Rabbitt. MAYP
Men choose a crystal goblet filled with wine. God's Ways, Not Our Ways. Henrietta Cordelia Ray. CBWP-3
Men cut windows into ice, The. Ice-Fishing. Denise Pendleton. ASP
Men, do not dishonor. Stanzas Written in Great Haste in Reply to Some Proposing That Women Are Fickle. Marcia Belisarda, *tr. by* Kate Flores. DMH
Men do not long endure the light. Fleur de Lys. Rayner Heppenstall. WaP
Men dying make their wills—but wives. Woman's Will. John Godfrey Saxe. FaFP
Men Fade Like Rocks. Walter James Turner. OBMV
Men Fishing in the Arno. Elizabeth Jennings. OBTV
Men Folks ob Today, De. Maggie Pogue Johnson. CBWP-4
Men grew sae cauld, maids sae unkind. The Blind Boy's Pranks. William Thom. OBEV

Men halt in the littered spot before the bank. Saturday in the County Seat. Elijah L. Jacobs. AmFN
Men have come again to move partitions, The. I Am Getting a Mountain View. Floyd Skloot. SoTCo
Men have made them gods of love. Pain. "Æ" MoBrPo
Men heard this roar of parleying starlings, saw. February Afternoon. Edward Thomas. NoAM
Men if you love us, play no more. In the Person of Woman Kind. Ben Jonson. NIP; SeCP; SeCV-1
Men in Aïda, they appeal, eh? A day, O Achilles! David Melnick. IAT
Men! In exchange for a good piece. With Lamp in Hand. Agnes Gergely, *tr. by* Daniel Hoffman. MHuP
Men in Green. David Campbell. PoAu-2
Men in her department envied her, The. Sayre. Lynn Strongin. IHMS
Men in the City. Alfonsina Storni, *tr. fr. Spanish.* PBWP, *tr. by* Rachel Benson
Men laughed and baaed like sheep, The. Memories of Verdun. Alan Dugan. OxBSP; RB
Men lean toward the wood. Lynching and Burning. Primus St. John. PoBA
Men like not prosy tales: we'll try. The Life and Adventure of Bob Thin. William James Linton. *Fr.* Bob Thin; or, the Poorhouse Fugitive. PF
Men love papers, The. They love to sign them, file them and. Larry Mitchell. GLP
Men Loved Wholly beyond Wisdom. Louise Bogan. LiTA; LiTM; VGW
Men made myths. Gillian Eve Hanscombe. *Fr.* Jezebel: Her Progress. AIW
Men Made out of Words. Wallace Stevens. MoAB; NOBA; OxBSP; TAP; VGW
Men may leue alle gamys. The Pilgrims' Sea Voyage and Seasickness. *Unknown.* OBTV
  (By Sea to Santiago.) OxBLMV
Men May Talk of Country-Christmasses. Philip Massinger. OBCP
Men meet and part. Words Made of Water. Burns Singer. NePoEA-2
Men moving in a trench, in the clear noon. These Men. Leon Gellert. PoAu-1
Men never know. The Radical. Waring Cuney. CDC
Men of Ch'ing are in P'eng, The. *Unknown, tr. by* Arthur Waley. BoS
Men of England, wherefore plough. Song to the Men of England. Shelley. EnRP; FiP; InPS; SaC; TrGrPo
  (Song: "Men of England", A.) NAEL-2
Men of Gotham, The. Thomas Love Peacock. *See* Nightmare Abbey: Wise Men of Gotham, The.
Men of Old, The. Richard Monckton Milnes. OBEV
Men of steel and sons of Mars. Ski Song of the U.S. Army's Tenth Mountain Division. W. T. Levitt. ASP
Men of Sudbury, The. Carlos Baker. GOA
Men of the Alamo, The. James Jeffrey Roche. PAH
Men of the court go forth, The. Akahito. *Fr.* Manyo Shu. Ma
Men of the East, The. Feathers of Snow. *Unknown.* GBP
Men of the *Maine*, The. Clinton Scollard. PAH
Men of the *Merrimac*, The. Clinton Scollard. PAH
Men of the North. John Neal. AA
Men of the North and West. Richard Henry Stoddard. PAH
Men of the Rocks, *sels.* Joseph Gordon MacLead. OxBS
  "Below the dancing larches freckled."
  "Fire the heather."
  "Our pastures are bitten and bare."
Men of valor, The. Akahito. *Fr.* Manyo Shu. AWP
Men on Ice, *sel.* Andrew Greig.
  On Falling. PoSH
Men Only Pretend. *Unknown.* MeEL
Men openly call you the enemy, call you the swine. Take Down the Fiddle, Karl! Shaw Neilson. CBAP
Men plow, and know everything about "late" and "early", The. Li K'ai-hsien, *tr. fr. Chinese by* Jonathan Chaves. *Fr.* Pleasures among the Fields during the Four Seasons. CoBLCP
Men Po Men with Glasses. Thérèse Plantier, *tr. fr. French by* Mary Ann Caws. DMF
Men proffer presents here to my people. Wulf and Eadwacer. *Unknown.* TrGrPo
Men rent me on rode. Jesus Bids Man Remember. *Unknown.* MeEL
Men said at vespers: "All is well!" Chicago. Whittier. PAH
Men saw no portents on that night. Young Lincoln. Edwin Markham. OHIP
Men say the sullen instrument. In the Twilight. James Russell Lowell. AA
Men Say They Know Many Things. Henry David Thoreau. ImOP

Men seem as alike as the leaves on the trees. The Man from the Crowd. Sam Walter Foss. PoLF

Men seldom make passes. News Item. Dorothy Parker. *Fr.* Some Beautiful Letters. FaBoUs; OBAL

Men share perceptions. The Switch Blade; or, John's Other Wife. Jonathan Williams. NeAP

Men, some to bus'ness, some to pleasure take. Pope. *Fr.* Moral Essays: Epistle to a Lady: Of the Characters of Women. OBSV

Men spread disease among the faggots, one of the things they, The. Larry Mitchell. GLP

Men Tell and Talk. Nia Francisco. STE

Men that are safe, and sure, in all they doe. An Epistle Answering to One That Asked to be Sealed of the Tribe of Ben. Ben Jonson. SeCV-1

Men, that delight to multiply desire. Fulke Greville. *Fr.* Caelica, XCIV.
   (Sonnet: "Men, that delight to multiply desire.") OBS

Men That Don't Fit In, The. Robert W. Service. BLPA; BLPL

Men That Once Were, The, *sel.* Owen Gruffydd, *tr. fr. Welsh by* Anthony Conran.
   "Old, old/ To live on, wretched to behold." OBWVE

Men that worked for England, The. Elegy in a Country Churchyard. G. K. Chesterton. FaPoR; MMA; MoBrPo; OBWP; OxBSP; TrGrPo

Men Told Me, Lord! David Starr Jordan. WGRP

Men tortured children. Children of Auschwitz. Naum Korzhavin, *tr. by* Daniel Weissbort. VWA

Men Walked To and Fro. Blanaid Salkeld. NeIP

Men went to Catraeth, keen their war-band. Aneirin, *tr. fr. Welsh by* Joseph P. Clancy. *Fr.* The Gododdin. OBWVE

Men went to Gododdin, laughter-loving. Aneirin, *tr. fr. Welsh by* Joseph P. Clancy. *Fr.* The Gododdin. OBWP

Men went up on these sands along the sea. Children's Song. Arye Sivan, *tr. by* David Shevin. VWA

Men were looking up. Austin Clarke. *Fr.* Mnemosyne Lay in Dust, III. IPY

Men Who Hunger. Yisroel Shtern, *tr. fr. Yiddish by* Robert Friend. PeBMYV

Men who killed poetry, The. García Lorca: A Photograph of the Granada Cemetery, 1966. Larry Levis. AnAn

Men Who March Away. Thomas Hardy. *Fr.* The Dynasts, *Pt.* I, Act I, sc. i. CH; MMA; OBWP

Men Who Wear My Clothes, The. Vernon Scannell. PoPo

Men! whose boast it is that ye. Stanzas on Freedom. James Russell Lowell. OHIP; PoNe

Men with crew-cuts. Crew-cuts. Donald Hall. MAT

Men with the fire of deep desire. Asadullah Khan Ghalib, *tr. by* Ahmed Ali. GoT

Men with the heads of eagles. Margaret Atwood. *Fr.* Circe/ Mud Poems. NoAM

Men with ventilators of black straw, The. Confab. Kenneth Rosen. AmPA

Men Working. Edna St. Vincent Millay. SaC

Men would never have come to need an attic. Up There. W. H. Auden. OxBTC

Menace of the Flower, The. Alfonso Reyes, *tr. fr. Spanish by* Samuel Beckett. MexPo

Menacing machine turns on and off, The. Terror Conduction. Philip Lamantia. NeAP

Menagerie, The. William Vaughn Moody. AnAmPo

Menaphon, *sels.* Robert Greene.
   Doron's Description of Samela. PoEL-2
      (Samela.) EiL; GBL; NOBE; OBEV; OBSC
   Doron's Jigge. PoEL-2
      (Jig, A.) EiL
   Menaphon's Ditty. OBSC
   Menaphon's Song. OBSC
   Of His Mistress. EiL
   Sephestia's Song to Her Child[e]. ELP; PoEL-2; TrGrPo
      (Sephestia's Lullaby.) NOBE; OBEV
      (Sephestia's Song.) OBSC
      (Weep Not My Wanton.) EiL; SeCePo

Mend my broken mood. Prayer for Song. Fay Lewis Noble. TrPWD

Mendacious Song. Yisroel Rabon, *tr. fr. Yiddish by* Robert Friend. PeBMYV

Mendacity. A. E. Coppard. OBMV

Mendelian Theory. *Unknown.* FaBoCo
   (Limerick: "There was a young woman called Starky.") NOBL

Mending Crab Pots. Dave Smith. GeTw; MT

Mending Sump. Kenneth Koch. BXAP; HeIP; InPK; MoP; NeAP; NoAM; NoAM

Mending the Adobe. Hayden Carruth. EyDe; Psk

Mending Wall. Robert Frost. AmFN; AmPP; AnAmPo; CMoP; FaBoPV; FaBV; FaFP; FPL; HeIP; HoPM; InPS; LiTA; LiTM; MoAB; MoAmPo; MoP; NAAL-2; NoAM; NOBA; NoP; OHFP; OxBA; PoE; PrIm; SCV; SoSe; TAP; VGW; ViBoPo; WeW

Mendings. Muriel Rukeyser. SaC

Mene Mene. Ory Bernstein, *tr. fr. Hebrew by* Warren Bargad *and* Stanley F. Chyet. IP

"Mene, Mene, Tekel, Upharsin." Madison Cawein. PAH

Menelaus and Helen. Rupert Brooke. SeCePo

Meng-ch'eng Hollow. Wang Wei, *tr. fr. Chinese by* Burton Watson. *Fr.* Twenty Views of Wang-ch'uan, 1. CoBCP

Menodotis. Leonidas of Alexandria, *tr. fr. Greek by* Richard Garnett. AWP

Menopause—word used as an insult. Something to Look Forward To. Marge Piercy. ER

Men's can at Café Society Uptown, The. Let's All Hear It for Mildred Bailey! James Schuyler. BAP

Men's hearts, like the nets. *Unknown, tr. fr. Japanese by* Geoffrey Bownas *and* Anthony Thwaite. PeBJV

Men's hearts love gold and jade. Lodging with the Old Man of the Stream. Po Chü-i, *tr. by* Arthur Waley. AWP

Men's Impotence. *Unknown, tr. fr. Eskimo.* WTO

Men's loving is a false affection. *Unknown.* NOIV

Men's Room in the College Chapel, The. W. D. Snodgrass. MoAmPo; PPP

Men's Voices. Inger Christensen, *tr. fr. Danish by* Nadia Christensen. BoWoP

Menstruation at Forty. Anne Sexton. CAPP

Mental Cases. Wilfred Owen. BrPo; CMoP; FaBoMo; MMA; NoAM; WaP

Mental Hospital Garden, The. William Carlos Williams. FYAP

Mental Traveller, The. Blake. EnRP; NAEL-2; OAEL-2; OPOP; PoE; PoEL-4

Mention trusty as a talk of marching, orders. Prosperity. Diane Ward. LP

Menu. Edward Lear. FaBoNo

Menzi son of Ndaba! Senzangakhona. *Zulu Oral Tradition, tr. by* T. Cope. WTO

Mephisto, *sel.* Uri Zvi Greenberg, *tr. fr. Yiddish by* Robert Friend.
   "Why is it then that early-spring blue is so deeply distressed?." PeBMYV

Mephistopheles enters. Choosing the Devil. Linda Gregg. NPGG

Mephisto's Flea Song. Richard Frost. SoTCo

Mer-Man, and Marstig's Daughter, The. *Unknown, tr. fr. Danish by* Robert Jamieson. AWP

Mercado. Greg Pape. AmPA

Merce Cunningham and the Birds. Lisel Mueller. GrPl

Merce of Egypt. Charles Olson. NoP

Merced. Adrienne Rich. NOBA

Mercedes. Elizabeth Stoddard. AA

Mercedes, Her Aloneness. Colette Inez. IHMS

Mercenaries. Ahmad Faraz, *tr. fr. Urdu by* Mahmood Jamal. PBMUP

Merchandise. Sean Jennett. NeIP

Merchant and the Fidler's Wife, The. *Unknown.* CoMu; OxBB

Merchant, as crafty a man is he, The. Do You Plan to Speak Bantu? Ogden Nash. FiBHP

Merchant at Yokohama, The. Osman Edwards. *Fr.* Residential Rhymes, I. OBTV

Merchant Marine. Josephine Miles. TAP; VGW

Merchant of Venice, The, *sels.* Shakespeare.
   All That Glisters Is Not Gold. *Fr.* II, vii. CTC
   Fire Seven Times Tried This, The. *Fr.* II, ix. CTC
   How Sweet the Moonlight Sleeps. *Fr.* V, i. FaBoRV; TrGrPo
      (Moonlight.) OHFP
   Let Me Play the Fool. *Fr.* I, i. TrGrPo
   "Moon shines bright, The. In such a night as this." *Fr.* V, i. GBL
   Power of Music, The. *Fr.* V, i. GN
   Quality of Mercy [Is Not Strain'd], The. *Fr.* IV, i. FaFP; LiTB
      (Mercy.) OHFP; TrGrPo; WBLP
   Tell Me Where Is Fancy [*or* Fancie] Bred. *Fr.* III, ii. CH; EiL; ELP; LiTB; NAEL-1; OAEL-1
      (Casket Song, A.) OBSC
      (Fancy.) FaPON; TrGrPo
      (Love.) OBEV
      (Madrigal: "Tell me where is fancy bred.") GTBS; GTBS-P
      (Song: "Tell me where is fancy bred.") CTC; PoEL-2

Merchant Shipping Act, The. *Unknown.* OxBSS

Merchant, to secure his treasure, The. Matthew Prior. AWP; EnLoPo; GTBS; GTBS-P; NOEC; NoP; PoRA
   (Song: "Merchant, to secure his treasure, The.") OBEV; TrGrPo

Merchant's boat is piled high with goods, The. Ballad of the Merchant. Hsü Pen, *tr. by* Jonathan Chaves. CoBLCP

Merchants from Cathay. William Rose Benét. MoAmPo

Merchants have multiplied more than the stars of heaven. The Executive's Death. Robert Bly. CoAP; NaP

Merchant's Joy, The. Chang Yü, *tr. fr. Chinese by* Jonathan Chaves. CoBLCP

Merchant's Joy, The. Lu Yu, *tr. fr. Chinese by* Burton Watson. CoBCP

Merchants of London, The. Mother Goose. *See* Hey diddle dinkety, poppety, pet.

Mercian Hymns, *sels.* Geoffrey Hill.
  "And it seemed, while we waited, he began to walk." *Fr.* XXX. NoAM; NoP
  "At Pavia, a visitation of some sorrow. Boethius' dungeon." *Fr.* XVIII. FaBoMo
  "Brooding on the eightieth letter of Fors Clavigera." *Fr.* XXV. HAP; PoE
  "Clash of salutation. As keels thrust into shingle." *Fr.* XVI. NoAM; NoP
  "Coins handsome as Nero's; of good substance and weight." *Fr.* XI. FaBoMo; HAP; NoAM
  "Dismissing reports and men, he put pressure on the wax." *Fr.* XIV. HAP
  "Gasholders, russet among fields." *Fr.* VII. HAP; NoAM; NoP
  "He adored the desk, its brown-oak inlaid with ebony." *Fr.* X. HAP; NoAM; NoP
  "I was invested in mother-earth, the crypt of roots." *Fr.* IV. NoAM
  "King of the perennial holly-groves, the riven sandstone." *Fr.* I. FaBoMo; HAP; NoAM
  "Mad are predators, The. Too often lately they harbor." *Fr.* VIII. NoP
  "Not strangeness, but strange likeness." *Fr.* XXIX. FaBoMo; HAP; NoAM
  "On the morning of the crowning we chorused our remission from school." *Fr.* III. HAP
  "Pet-name, a common name. Best-selling brand, curt, A." *Fr.* II. NoAM
  "Princes of Mercia were badger and raven, The." *Fr.* VI. HAP; NAEL-2; NoAM; NoP; PoE
  "Processes of generation; deeds of settlement." *Fr.* XXVIII. NoP
  "So much for the elves' wergild, the true governance." *Fr.* V. NoAM
  "Strange church smelled a bit 'high,' of censers, The." *Fr.* IX. PoE
  "Their spades grafted through the variably-resistant." *Fr.* XII. PoE
  "Trim the lamp; polish the lens; draw, one by one, rare coins." *Fr.* XIII. FaBoMo
  "We ran across the meadow scabbed with the cow-dung." *Fr.* XXII. HAP

Mercies of the Year, The. John Danforth. SCAP

Merciles[s] Beaute [*or* Beautée *or* Beauty], *sel.* Chaucer. CTC; EBEV; EnLoPo; HAP; NoP
  (Three Roundels of Love Unreturned.) MeEL

Merciless Beauty, *mod. vers. Fr.* I. ACP, *mod. vers.*; BoLoP; NAEL-1
  (Rondel of Merciles Beaute, A.) TrGrPo
  (Rondel of Merciless Beauty, A, *mod. vers.* by Louis Untermeyer.) TrGrPo
  (Three Roundels of Love Unreturned.) NoP

Merciless love, whom nature hath denied. John Fletcher. *Fr.* The Chances, III, ii. GBL

Mercury Bay Eclogue. M. K. Joseph. ATNZ; PeNZ

Mercury; on Losing My Pocket Milton at Luss near Ben Lomond, and Other Mountains. Robert Andrews. NOEC

Mercury shew'd Apollo, Bartas Book. Nathaniel Ward. SCAP

Mercury's Song [to Phaedra]. Dryden. *See* Amphitryon: Fair Iris I love, and hourly I die.

Mercutio Describes Queen Mab. Shakespeare. *See* Romeo and Juliet: O [*or* Oh], then, I see Queen Mab hath been with you.

Mercutio's Queen Mab Speech. Shakespeare. *See* Romeo and Juliet: O [*or* Oh], then, I see Queen Mab hath been with you.

Mercy. Joy Harjo. ER

Mercy. Shakespeare. *See* Merchant of Venice, The: Quality of Mercy [Is Not Strain'd], The.

Mercy and Love. Robert Herrick. SeCV-1

Mercy is whiter than laundry. Angels in Winter. Nancy Willard. LCAP

Mercy Pleads for Mankind. Giles Fletcher the Younger. *Fr.* Christ's Victory and Triumph: Christ's Victory in Heaven, I. JCP

Mere echo, The/ of a horse's hoof. *Unknown, tr. fr. Japanese. Fr.* Manyo Shu. FCEI

Meredith Phyfe. Edgar Lee Masters. *Fr.* The New Spoon River. GOA

Merely the landscape of a vanished whim. Versailles. Adrienne Rich. NePoEA

Merida, 1969. William Matthews. EOEF

Meridians are a net. Objects. Richard Wilbur. FF; NoP

Merie sungen the muneches binnen Ely. Cnut's Song. *Unknown. Fr.* Canute at Ely. PoE

Merioneth. John Machreth Rees, *tr. fr. Welsh by* Kenneth Hurlstone Jackson. OBWVE

Merit of True Passion, The. *At. to* Sir Robert Ayton. *See* Silent Lover, The: Wrong Not, Sweete Empress of My Heart.

Merle Bascom's .22. Donald Hall. TSL

Merlin. Emerson. AmPP; NOBA
  Sels.
  Merlin ("Rhyme of the poet, The"). *Fr.* II. PoEL-4
  Merlin ("Thy trivial harp will never please"). *Fr.* I. AA; NAAL-2; OxBA

Merlin. Geoffrey Hill. InPK

Merlin. Edwin Muir. FaBoTw; OxBS; RB

Merlin and the Gleam. Tennyson. OAEL-2

Merlin and the Snake's Egg. Leslie Norris. WSC

Merlin and Vivien. Tennyson. *Fr.* Idylls of the King.
  In Love, If Love Be Love. PoEL-5; TrGrPo
  (All in All.) LiTB
  (Vivien's Song.) OBNC

Merlin Enthralled. Richard Wilbur. CMoP; NePoEA; NYBP

Merlin in the Cave: He Speculates without a Book. Thom Gunn. NePoEA

Merlin's Riddling. Tennyson. *Fr.* Idylls of the King: The Coming of Arthur. FaBoRV

Mermaid, The. Ben King. AnAmPo; OBAL

Mermaid, The. Tennyson. BOTP, *abr.*; FaPON; GN; WSC

Mermaid, The ("One [*or* 'Twas a] Friday morn"). *Unknown.* AmFP
  (One Friday Morn.) CH; ESPB; OnMSP

Mermaid, The ("To you fausse stream"). *Unknown.* CH

Mermaid, The. *Unknown. See* Seamen's Distress, The.

Mermaid Tavern, The. *Unknown. See* Lines on the Mermaid Tavern.

Mermaiden, A. Thomas Hennell. FaBoTw

Mermaidens, The. Laura Elizabeth Richards. OBCA

Mermaidens' Vesper-Hymn, The. George Darley. *Fr.* Syren Songs, VI. GBL; NAEL-2; OBNC; PoEL-4
  (Siren Chorus.) BIrV; FaBoRV; WSC

Mermaids. Kenneth Slessor. The Atlas. PoAu-2

Mermaids, The. Spenser. *Fr.* The Faerie Queene, II, 12. ChTr

Mermaids, The. Walter de la Mare. BrPo

Mermaid's not a human thing, A. Lost and Given Over. E. J. Brady. PoAu-1

Mermaid's tears, A. Burning Bright. Lillian Morrison. TSS

Merman, The. Tennyson. BoTP, *abr.*; FaPON; GN; WSC

Merops. Emerson. OxBA

Merrie World did on a day, The. *See* Merry World did on a day, The.

Merrily, merrily,/ All the spring. Merry Birds. Rodney Bennett. BoTP

Merrily swinging on brier and weed. Robert of Lincoln. Bryant. FaBoBe; FaPON; OBCA; WBLP, *abr.*

Merritt Parkway. Denise Levertov. AmPP; NeAP; PoM

Merry Are the Bells. *Unknown.* MoShBr

Merry Bagpipes, The. *Unknown.* CoMu

Merry Birds. Rodney Bennett. BoTP

Merry Christmas. Aileen Fisher. RHPC

Merry Country Lad, The. Nicholas Breton. *Fr.* The Passionate Shepherd. EiL
  (Happy Countryman, The, *shorter sel.*) CH
  (Pastoral: "Who can live in heart so glad.") ELP
  (Shepherd and Shepherdess.) OBSC

Merry Cuckold, The. *Unknown.* CoMu

Merry cuckoo, messenger of spring, The. Spenser. *Fr.* Amoretti, XIX. OBSC

Merry-go-round. Langston Hughes. PoNe

Merry-go-round. Oliver Jenkins. GoYe

Merry-go-round. James McAuley. CBAP

Merry-go-round. Gloria Rawlinson. ATNZ

Merry-go-round, The. Rainer Maria Rilke, *tr. fr. German by* C. F. MacIntyre. WeW

Merry-go-round. Mark Van Doren. SO

Merry-go-rounds go round, The. Artifice Afire. René Daumal, *tr. by* Michael Benedikt. POS

Merry have we met. A Party Song. *Unknown.* BoTP

Merry Hay-Makers; [or, Pleasant Pastime between the Young-Men and Maids, in the Pleasant Meadows], The. *Unknown.* CoMu; ErPo

Merry Heart, A [*or* The]. Shakespeare. *See* Winter's Tale, The: Jog On, jog on, the footpath way.
Merry Hoastess, The. *Unknown.* CoMu
Merry Imagination, The. Zelda, *tr. fr. Hebrew by* Bernhard Frank. MHeP
Merry It Is. *Unknown.* HAP
    (How Long This Night Is.) MeEL
    ("Mirie it is, while sumer ilast.") HAP; MeEL
Merry it is in May morning. By a Chapel as I Came. *Unknown.* ChTr; GBP
Merry it is in the good greenwood. Alice Brand. Sir Walter Scott. *Fr.* The Lady of the Lake, IV. BeLS; OnMSP
Merry Jovial Beggar, The. Peter Casey, *tr. fr. Irish by* Douglas Hyde. TIRV; WTO
Merry Little Maid and Wicked Little Monk, The. *Unknown.* ErPo
Merry Little Men. Kathleen M. Chaplin. BoTP
Merry-ma-Tanzie, The. *Unknown.* GBP
    ("Here we go dancing jingo-ring.") OxNR
Merry March wind is a boisterous fellow, The. The March Wind. E. H. Henderson. BoTP
Merry [*or* Mirry] Margaret,/ As midsummer flower. To Mistress [*or* Maystres] Margaret Hussey. John Skelton. *Fr.* The Garlande [*or* Garlands] of Laurell. AAS; ACP; EBEV; EnLoPo; GN; GoJo; HeIP; HoPM; InPS; NAEL-1; NBLV; NOBE; NoP; OAEL-1; OBEV; OBSC; OPOP; PoE; PoEL-1; PoRA; PPP; SCV; TrGrPo
    (Mistress Margaret Hussey.) FaBoCh
Merry May the Keel Row. *Unknown.* GBP
Merry may the maid be. The Miller. Sir John Clerk. ChTr
Merry, Merry Is My Lord. *Unknown, tr. fr. Chinese by* Burton Watson. CoBCP
Merry, merry, merry, cheery, cheery, cheery! Harvest. Thomas Nashe. *Fr.* Summer's Last Will and Testament. OBSC
Merry, merry sparrow! The Blossom. Blake. *Fr.* Songs of Innocence. GoJo; PBBP
Merry Month of March, The. Wordsworth. *See* Cock is crowing, The.
Merry Note, A. Shakespeare. *See* Love's Labour's Lost: When Icicles Hang by the Wall.
Merry Pieman's Song, The. John Bennett. ILY
Merry sang the monks who in Ely fare. The Monks of Ely. *Unknown.* ACP
Merry the green, the green hill shall be merry. Another Song. Donald Justice. NePoEA-2; VGW
    (Tune for a Lonesome Fife.) NYBP
Merry tongues in the lit fireplace. The Heart Will Have Its Way. Israel Efrat, *tr. by* Bernhard Frank. MHeP
Merry voices chatterin.' Two-an'-Six. Claude McKay. BANP
Merry wind danced over the hill, A. Such a Blustery Day! Elizabeth Gould. BoTP
Merry Window, The. Francis Scarfe. EAS
Merry [*or* Merrie] World did on a day, The. The Quip. George Herbert. JCP; LiTB; OBS; SeCP; SeCV-1
Merrythought's Song. Francis Beaumont *and* Fletcher. *Fr.* The Knight of the Burning Pestle, IV, i. OBS
Meru. W. B. Yeats. NoAM; OAEL-2; PoA
Mery Gest How a Sergeaunt Wolde Lerne to Be A Frere, A. Sir Thomas More. AAS
Mery it was in grene forest. Adam Bel [*or* Bell], Clym [*or* Clim] of the Clough[e], and Wyllyam [*or* William] of Cloudesle [*or* Cloudesly]. *Unknown.* ESPB; OxBB
Meseem'd that Love, with swifter feet than fire. An Utter Passion Uttered Utterly. John Todhunter. BXAP
Meseemeth I heard cry and groan. The Complaint of the Fair Armoress [*or* Armouress]. Villon, *tr. by* Swinburne. AWP; CTC; OBVE
Mesh cast for mackerel. Fishermen. Basil Bunting. PoA
Meshed in a glow of nickel, glass. Ballad of the Drinker in His Pub. N. P. van Wyck Louw, *tr. by* Uys Krige, Jack Cope *and* Ruth Miller. PeSA
Mesnevi. Sadi, *tr. fr. Persian by* L. Cranmer-Byng. *Fr.* The Gulistan. AWP
Mesón Brujo. E. A. Lacey. PeHV
Mesopotamia. Kipling. MMA
Mesopotamian wind. 7 Days in Another Town. Kit Robinson. IAT
Mess Deck Casualty. Alan Ross. *Fr.* Five Songs. WaP
    (Epilogue: " 'O where are you going?' said reader to rider.") FaBoCh; LiTM
Mess is all asleep, my candle burns, The. A Wry Smile. Roy Fuller. WaaP; WaP
Mess of Love, The. D. H. Lawrence. OAEL-2
Mess Sergeant. Garry Geddes. UAS
Message, A. Fleur Adcock. DiPo

Message. Hayyim Nahman Bialik, *tr. fr. Hebrew by* Bernhard Frank. MHeP
Message. Fred Chappell. BLA
Message, The. John Donne. EIL; MeLP; OBS
Message. Allen Ginsberg. NeAP; VGW
Message, The. Heine, *tr. fr. German by* Kate Freiligrath Kroeker. AWP
Message, A. George Ives. PeHV
Message. Renata Pallottini, *tr. fr. Portuguese by* Monique *and* Carlos Altschul. WPOW
Message, The. Jacques Prévert, *tr. fr. French by* John Frederick Nims. WeW
Message. Gyorgy Raba, *tr. fr. Hungarian by* Jascha Kessler. VWA
Message. Dorothy M. Richardson. PoA
Message, A. Elizabeth Stuart Phelps Ward. PAH
Message at Sunset for Bishop Berkeley. Heather McHugh. GeTw
Message from a Mouse, Ascending in a Rocket. Patricia Hubbell. RHPC
Message from a secretary tells me first, A. Elegy for Frank Stanford. Thomas Lux. AnAn
Message from her set his brain aflame, A. George Meredith. *Fr.* Modern Love, V. NOBVV
Message from Home. Kathleen Jessie Raine. ImOP; WPE
Message from Ohanapecosh Glacier. W. M. Ransom. CDW
Message of Peace, A. Longfellow. *Fr.* The Arsenal at Springfield. WBLP
Message of the March Wind, The. William Morris. OBNC; WiR
Message of the Rain, The. Norman H. Russell. STE
Message to a Loved One Dead, A. Josephine D. Henderson Heard. CBWP-4
Message to Siberia. Pushkin, *tr. fr. Russian.* AAA, *tr. by* Alan Myers; AWP, *tr. by* Max Eastman; TTY, *tr. by* Max Eastman
Message to the Bard. William Livingston, *tr. fr. Gaelic.* GoTS
Messages. Francis Thompson. CH
Messages, The. W. W. Gibson. OHIP
Messe of Nonsense, A. *Unknown.* OBS
Messenger, The. Frances Horovitz. BrRo
Messenger, The, *sel.* Thomas Kinsella.
    "Inside, it is bare but dimly alive." CIP
Messenger, The. Grace Schulman. AnAn
Messenger, The. Jean Valentine. LCAP
Messenger dispatch'd, again she view'd, The. Ave atque Vale. Dryden. *Fr.* Sigismonda and Guiscardo. OBS
Messenger from Rome. A Defence of Poetry. Giolla Brighde Mac Con Midhe. NOIV
Messengers. Louise Glück. AnAn; HCAP
Messengers, The. Thom Gunn. PoA
Messengers, The. Henrietta Cordelia Ray. CBWP-3
Messiah, *sel.* Pope.
    Rise, Crowned with Light Imperial Salem Rise. WGRP
Messiah, The. Bible, *O.T. Fr.* Isaiah, VII: 14–25. AWP
Messiah, The. Virgil, *tr. fr. Latin. Fr.* Eclogues, IV. AWP, *tr. by* Dryden.
Messiah, The. Moshe Yungman, *tr. fr. Yiddish by* David G. Roskies *and* Hillel Schwartz. VWA
Messiah, The ("So they in Heav'n their odes and vigils tun'd.") Milton. *Fr.* Paradise Regained, *bk.* I, *ll.* 182–293. OBS
Messiah will not come. The Field of Night. Miriam Waddington. VWA
Messmates. Sir Henry Newbolt. CH; EBVV
Messy is the stew in the pot. *Unknown, tr. fr. Chinese by* Arthur Waley. BoS
Meta-social, The. Lecture. Anselm Hollo. UL
Metagnomy. N. H. Pritchard II. NBP
Metal. Granite. Uproar. Racket. Clatter. New York. A. Leyeles, *tr. by* Benjamin *and* Barbara Harshav. AYP
Metallic apparition whirring. Hummingbird. Marge Piercy. GeTw
Metallic weight of iron, The. De Profundis. Walter de la Mare. OBD
Metamorpho I. Joe Rosenblatt. MoCV
Metamorphoses. Roy Fuller. OxBTC
Metamorphoses. Howard Nemerov. EyDe; HCAP
Metamorphoses, *sels.* Ovid, *tr. fr. Latin.*
    Acteon. *Fr.* III, *tr. by* Arthur Golding. CTC
    "And from the Citie Tegea there came the Paragone." *Fr.* X, *tr. by* Arthur Golding. OBVE
    Daedalus. *Fr.* VIII. CTC, *tr. by* Arthur Golding; OBVE, *tr. by* Arthur Golding.
    ("Now in this while gan Daedalus a weariness to take.") OBVE
    Daphne and Apollo. *Fr.* I, *tr. by* Matthew Prior. NOEC

Death of Eurydice and Orpheus' Journey to Hell, The. *Tr.* by George Sandys. JCP

"Floods, by nature enemies to land, The." *Fr.* I. OBVE, *tr.* by Dryden.

   Flood, The. ChTr

"I pray thee Nymph Penaeis stay, I chase not as a fo." *Fr.* I, *tr.* by Arthur Golding. OBVE

"In the Shire of Phestos hard by Cnossus dwelt of yore." *Fr.* IX, *tr.* by Arthur Golding. PeHV

King Midas. *Fr.* XI, *tr.* by Arthur Golding. CTC

Magic. *Fr.* VII. AWP, *tr.* by Shakespeare.

   Medea's Incantation. OBVE, *tr.* by Arthur Golding.

Meleager. *Fr.* VIII, *tr.* by Arthur Golding. CTC

"More whyght thou art than primrose leaf my Lady Galatee." *Fr.* VIII. OBVE, *tr.* by Arthur Golding.

   (Cyclops.) CTC, *tr.* by Arthur Golding.

"My intention is to tell of bodies changed." *Fr.* I, *tr.* by Rolfe Humphries. NAWM-1

"Near the Cymmerians, in his dark abode." *Fr.* XI, *tr.* by Dryden. OBVE

"Neare Enna walles there standes a Lake Pergusa is the name." *Fr.* V, *tr.* by Arthur Golding. OBVE

"Northern breath, that freezes floods, he binds, The." *Fr.* I, *tr.* by Dryden. OBVE

"Not Pallas, not ev'n Spleen it self could blame." *Fr.* VI, *tr.* by John Gay. OBVE

"Now have I brought a woork to end which neither Joves fierce [*or* feerce] wrath." *Fr.* XV, *tr.* by Arthur Golding. OBVE

   (Conclusion.) CTC

"Now in this while gan Daedalus a wearinesse to take." *Fr.* VIII, *tr.* by Arthur Golding. OBVE

   (Daedalus.) CTC

"Now whyle Hippomenes/ Debates theis things." *Fr.* X. OBVE, *tr.* by Arthur Golding.

Of the Pythagorean Philosophy. *Fr.* XV, *tr.* by Dryden.

   "But this by sure experiment we know." FM

   "This let me further add, that nature knows." OBVE

Philemon and Baucis. *Fr.* VIII, *tr.* by Arthur Golding. CTC

   "Upon the hills of Phrygie near a teyle there stands a tree." OBSC, *tr.* by Arthur Golding.

   (Baucis and Philemon.)

   "Then Lelex rose, an old experienced man." AWP *and* OBVE, *tr.* by Dryden.

   "Heaven's power is infinite; earth, air, and sea." OAEL-1, *tr.* by Dryden.

Phoenix Self-born, The. *Fr.* XV, *tr.* by Dryden. ChTr

"Pygmalion seeing these to spend their times." *Fr.* X.

Pygmalion's Statue Comes to Life. *Fr.* X, *tr.* by Arthur Golding. OAEL-1

"Seeing as the father saw the rosy morn." *Fr.* II, *tr.* by Joseph Addison. OBVE

"Stones (a miracle to mortal view), The." *Fr.* I, *tr.* by Dryden. OBVE

"Then sprang up first the golden age, which of itself maintained." *Fr.* I, *tr.* by Arthur Golding. NAEL-1

   (Golden Age, The.) OAEL-1

"Then thus the sire of gods, with look serene." *Fr.* VIII, *tr.* by Dryden. OBD

"There was a man here, Samian born, but he." *Fr.* XV, *tr.* by Rolfe Humphries. NAWM-1

"To thee obeyeth all the East as far as Ganges goes." *Fr.* IV, *tr.* by Arthur Golding. OBVE

Metamorphoses of M. John Peale Bishop. ErPo

Metamorphoses of the Vampire. Baudelaire, *tr. fr. French.* ErPo, *tr.* by Jackson Mathews; VVA, *tr.* by Arthur Symons.

Metamorphosis. Michael Guttenbrunner, *tr. fr. German* by Beth Bjorklund. CoAuP

Metamorphosis. Sylvia Plath. PoA

Metamorphosis. Peter Porter. OxBTC

Metamorphosis. Wallace Stevens. InPK; VGW

Metamorphosis, The. Sir John Suckling. CaPo; FaBoEE

Metamorphosis. Jane Yolen. BWV

Metamorphosis of Aunt Jemima, The. William Childress. MAT

Metamorphosis of Lovers, The. Robert Marteau, *tr. fr. French* by John Montague. RHTwFP

Metamorphosis of Pygmalion's Image, The, *sel.* John Marston.

   "O gracious gods, take compassion." OAEL-1

Metamorphosis of the Carnation, *sel.* Rafael Alberti, *tr. fr. Spanish* by Mark Strand.

   "I went away." AnAn

Metaphor as Degeneration. Wallace Stevens. LCAP

Metaphor as Illness. Chuck Ortleb. GLP

Metaphors. Sylvia Plath. HeIP; InPK; SoSe

Metaphors. Miklós Radnóti, *tr. fr. Hungarian* by Steven Polgar *and* Stephen Berg *and* S. J. Marks. VWA

Metaphors of a Magnifico. Wallace Stevens. SOTW

Metaphysic of Snow. Donald Finkel. PoA

Metaphysical. Robert Fitzgerald. PoA

Metaphysical Amorist, The. J. V. Cunningham. VGW

Metaphysical Paintings, The. John Perreault. EAS

Metaphysical Sectarian, The ("He was in logick a great critic"). Samuel Butler. *Fr.* Hudibras. MeLP, *fr.* I, 1.

   (Hudibras, the Presbyterian Knight, *abr.*) OxBoLi

   (Portrait of Hudibras.) PoEL-3

   (Presbyterian Knight and Independent Squire, *abr.*) OBS

   (Sir Hudibras, His Passing Worth.) FaBoCo

Metaphysical Shock while Watching a TV Cartoon. Stan Rice. NPGG

Metaphysician. Robert Fitzgerald. PoA

Metaphysics. Oliver Herford. NA

Meteor/ Meteor. Winslow Crater. Edward Bryant. BWV

Meteor's arc of quiet, The; a voiceless rain. Faint Music. Walter de la Mare. FaBoCh

Methinks all things have travelled since you shined. On the Sun Coming Out in the Afternoon. Henry David Thoreau. OxBSP; PoEL-4

Methinks already, from this chymick flame. The New London. Dryden. *Fr.* Annus Mirabilis. FaBoCh; OBS

   (London.) SeCePo

   (London after the Great Fire, 1666.) NOBE

Methinks, dear Tom, I see thee stand demure. To the Revd. Mr. — — — on His Drinking Sea-Water. John Winstanley. NOEC

Methinks Death like one laughing lyes. Epitaph. Caecil. Boulstr. Lord Herbert of Cherbury. SeCP

Methinks heroick poesie till now. To Sir William Davenant, Upon His Two First Books of Gondibert. Abraham Cowley. SeCV-1

Methinks How Dainty Sweet It Were. Charles Lamb. Son

Methinks I am a prophet new inspir'd. John of Gaunt's Dying Speech. Shakespeare. *Fr.* King Richard II. FiP

   John of Gaunt Speaks. FaBoPP; FaPoR

   (This Blessed Plot. This England.) FaBV

Methinks I see great Diocletian walk. Great Diocletian. Abraham Cowley. *Fr.* The Garden. ChTr

Methinks I See Some Crooked Mimic Jeer. Michael Drayton. *Fr.* Idea, XXXI. Son

Methinks I see with what a busy haste. On Zacchaeus. Francis Quarles. OxBSP

Methinks I spy Almighty holding in. Edward Taylor. *Fr.* Preparatory Meditations before My Approach to the Lord's Supper, LXVIII. HAP

Methinks the poor town has been troubled too long. Charles Sackville. SeCV-2

Methinks thou writhest as in rage. To a Worm Which the Author Accidentally Trode Upon. William Hawkins. FM

Methinks 'Tis Pretty Sport [to Hear a Child]. Thomas Bastard. ElL; InvP

   (De Puero Balbutiente.) OxBSP

Method, The. J. D. McClatchy. EOEF

Method must be purest meat, The. On Burroughs' Work. Allen Ginsberg. NAAL-2; NOBA

Method of Preserving Hay from Being Mow-Burnt, or Taking Fire, A. Robert Dodsley. *Fr.* Agriculture. FaBoUs

Methodist, The, *sels.* Evan Lloyd.

   Religion and the Lower Classes. NOEC

   "Sons of War sometimes are known, The." OBSV

Methods of Cooking Trout. Thomas Barker. *Fr.* The Art of Angling. FaBoUs

Methought I lived in the icy times forlorn. Great Britain Through the Ice: Or, Premature Patriotism. Charles Tennyson Turner. Son

Methought I Saw. Milton. *See* On His Deceased Wife.

Methought I saw/ Life swiftly treading over endless space. The Sea of Death. Thomas Hood. LiTB; OBNC; PoEL-4

Methought I saw (as I did dream in bed). The Vision. Robert Herrick. CaPo

Methought I saw my late espoused saint. On His Deceased Wife. Milton. BLPL; FaFP; LiTB; OBEV; PoE; SCV; TEP

   (Methought I Saw.) NoP; Son

   ("Methought I saw my late espoused saint.") BoLoP; EnLoPo; NAEL-1

   (On His Dead Wife.) GBL; HAP; NOBE; WeW

   (On His Late Wife.) PoEL-3

   (Sonnet: "Methought I saw my late espoused saint.") EBEV; OAEL-1; OBS

Methought I saw the grave where Laura lay.   A Vision upon This Conceit of the Fairy Queen.   Sir Walter Ralegh.   *Fr.* Commendatory Verses to Edmund Spenser's Fairy Queen.   OBSC; Son
("Methought I saw the grave where Laura lay.")   NAEL-1
(Of Spenser's Faery Queen.)   SiPS

Methought I stood where trees of every clime.   A Dream.   Keats.   *Fr.* The Fall of Hyperion, I.   OAEL-2; OBNC

Methought, on this aspiring form I gazed.   Thomas Cooper.   *Fr.* The Purgatory of Suicides.   PF

Methought That I Had Broken from the Tower.   Shakespeare.   *Fr.* King Richard III, I, iv.   RB

Methuselah.   Rosemary Dobson.   *Fr.* The Devil and the Angel.   PoAu-2

Methuselah ("Methuselah ate what he found on his plate").   *Unknown.*   BLPA; BLPL; FaBoBe

Meticulous, past midnight in clear rime.   Hart Crane.   *Fr.* Voyages (I–VI), V.   NAAL-2; PoE

Metonymy as an Approach to a Real World.   William Bronk.   VGW

Metre Colombian, The.   *Unknown.*   BXAP; Par

Metric Figure.   William Carlos Williams.   MoAB; MoAmPo

Metrical Index to the Bible, A, *sel.*   Josiah Chorley.
"All things created, Moses writes."   FaBoUs

Metrical Version of the Bible, Said to Have Been Composed by a Negro Christian in the State of Massachusetts, and Published in Louisville, Kentucky, in 1858, A, *sel.   Unknown.*
"Adam was de first man and Eve was de udder."   FaBoUs

Métro Balard-Charenton.   Peter Handke, *tr. fr. German by* Beth Bjorklund.   CoAuP

Metronome.   János Pilinszky, *tr. fr. Hungarian by* William Jay Smith.   MHuP

Metropolitan Nightmare.   Stephen Vincent Benét.   ImOP; NYBP

Metropolitan Railway, The.   Sir John Betjeman.   EBEV; OxBTC

Metrum Parhemiacum Tragicum.   Eugenius Vulgarius, *tr. fr. Latin by* Helen Waddell.   WaaP

Mewlips, The.   John R. R. Tolkien.   AmMo; SO; WSC

Mews Flat Mona.   William Plomer.   FaBoTw

Mexican dwarfs can dance for miles, The.   Maxixe.   Sir Osbert Sitwell.   PoA

Mexican Market Woman.   Langston Hughes.   SaC

Mexican Serenade.   Arthur Guiterman.   FiBHP

México.   Lorna Dee Cervantes.   *Fr.* Visions of Mexico While at a Writing Symposium in Port Townsend, Washington.   FIA; NoAM

Mexico, *sels.*   Robert Lowell.
"Difficulties, the impossibilities, The."   *Fr.* 1.   HCAP
"South of Boston, south of Washington."   *Fr.* 4.   HCAP

Mexico, 1940.   Ai.   NoAM

Mexico, August 20, 1940.   Ai.   NoAM

Mexico City Blues, *sels.*   Jack Kerouac.
"Big Engines, The."   *Fr.* 146.   NeAP
"Essence of Existence, The."   *Fr.* 182.   NeAP
"Glenn Miller and I were heroes."   *Fr.* 179.   NeAP
"Got up and dressed up."   *Fr.* 113.   NeAP
"In the ocean there's a very sad turtle."   *Fr.* 229.   PoM
"Love's multitudinous boneyard."   *Fr.* 230.   NeAP
"Nobody knows the other side."   *Fr.* 127.   NeAP
"Old Man Mose."   *Fr.* 221.   NeAP
"Only awake to Universal Mind."   *Fr.* 183.   NeAP
"Praised be man, he is existing in milk."   *Fr.* 228.   NeAP
"Saints, I give myself up to thee."   *Fr.* 219.   NeAP
"Void that's highly embraceable, The."   *Fr.* 225.   NeAP
"Wheel of the quivering Meat, The."   *Fr.* 211.   NeAP; PoM

Mexico City, 150 Pesos to the Dollar.   Jim Mitsui.   BrSi

Mexico Is a Foreign Country: Four Studies in Naturalism, *sel.*   Robert Penn Warren.

Mango on the Mango Tree, The.   *Fr.* IV.   MoP; NoAM

Mezzo Cammin.   Longfellow.   FPL; NAAL-1; NoP; PoE; TAP

Mezzo Cammin.   Judith Moffett.   SM

M'Fingal, *sels.*   John Trumbull.
"At once with resolution held."   AmPP
"Rise then, ere ruin swift surprize."   GOA

Mi Abuelo.   Alberto Ríos.   MAYP

Mi cyaan believe it.   For Michael.   Valerie Bloom.   WS

Mia Carlotta.   T. A. Daly.   NBLV

Miami.   Daniel Mark Epstein.   MAYP

Mica shines on the beach.   Extract.   Paul Bowles.   PoA

Micah, *sel.*   Bible, *O.T.*
Woe Is Me! VII: 1-6.   *Fr.* VII: 1-6.   TrJP

Mice.   Rose Fyleman.   BoTP; FaPON; NTCP; PDV; RAR; RHPC

Mice in the garbage.   For Rosa Yen, Who Lived Here.   Greg Pape.   AmPA

Mice in the Hay.   Leslie Norris.   OBCP; PChr

Mice masticate from crumb to tooth.   Repast.   Gertrude Tiemer-Wille.   GoYe

Michael.   Sandra McPherson.   LCAP

Michael.   Michael Sheridan.   NAmP

Michael.   Wordsworth.   EnRP; GoTL; NAEL-2; OAEL-2

Michael, Archangel of the King of Kings.   A Sequence for Saint Michael.   Alcuin, *tr. by* Helen Waddell.   TIRV

Michael Met a Duck.   J. Dupuy.   BoTP

Michael Robartes and the Dancer.   W. B. Yeats.   OAEL-2

Michael Robartes Bids His Beloved Be at Peace.   W. B. Yeats.   BrPo; MoP; NoAM

Michael Robartes Remembers Forgotten Beauty.   W. B. Yeats.   *See* He Remembers Forgotten Beauty.

Michael Walked in the Wood.   Robert Greacen.   NeIP

Michaelmas.   Norman Nicholson.   MoBrPo

Michael's Song.   W. W. Gibson.   BoTP

Micheál Mac Liammóir.   Paul Durcan.   FaBCIP

Michigan-I-O.   *Unknown.*   AmFP

Micmac woman's body has been disinterred and her, The.   Report on Her Remains.   Daniel David Moses.   HATNAP

Microbe's Serenade, The.   George Ade.   OBAL

Microbiblion, *See also* Hos Ego Versiculos, *sl. diff. vers. by* Francis Quarles, *Fr.* Argalus and Parthenia, *sel. At. to* Simon Wastell.
Man's Mortality.   FaBoCh
(Verses of Man's Mortalitie.)   OBS

Microcosmos.   Peter Payack.   BWV

Microcosmus, *sel.*   Thomas Nabbes.
Love Sets Order in the Elements.   UnS

Micromutations.   James Wright.   NYBP

Microscope.   Gwyn Thomas, *tr. fr. Welsh by* Joseph P. Clancy.   OBWVE

Microscosmos.   Susan Miles.   OxBTC

'Mid all the ceaseless rush of life.   Refuge.   Mabel E. McCartney.   BLRP

Mid-August at Sourdough Mountain Lookout.   Gary Snyder.   HAP; InPK; MAT; NaP; NoP; TAP

Mid-autumn late autumn.   His Running My Running.   Robert Francis.   ASP

Mid-Autumn Moon.   Su Tung-p'o, *tr. fr. Chinese by* Burton Watson.   CoBCP

Mid-Autumn Night, A.   Chao Chih-hsin, *tr. fr. Chinese by* Michael S. Duke.   WFTU

Mid-Country Blow.   Theodore Roethke.   BoNaP

Mid-day and a heat haze over all.   Bruce Beaver.   *Fr.* Letters to Live Poets, XXXIV.   CBAP

Mid-Noon in January.   "Fiona Macleod."   *Fr.* Australian Transcripts.   FM

Mid-Ocean in War-Time.   Joyce Kilmer.   MOS

'Mid pleasures and palaces though we may roam.   "Home, Sweet Home," with Variations ("Mid pleasures and palaces though we may roam").   H. C. Bunner.   *Fr.* Home.   OBAL

Mid pleasures and palaces though we may roam.   Home, Sweet Home.   John Howard Payne.   *Fr.* Clari, the Maid of Milan.   AA; AnAmPo; BLPA; FaBoBe; FaFP; WBLP

Mid-Rapture.   Dante Gabriel Rossetti.   *Fr.* The House of Life, XXVI.   BLPL; FaBoBe

Mid-Term Break.   Seamus Heaney.   InPS; NIP; NoP

'Mid the flower-wreathed tombs I stand.   Decoration.   Thomas Wentworth Higginson.   AA; OHIP

'Mid the half-lit air, and the lonely place.   In the Graveyard.   Macdonald Clarke.   PWR

'Mid the mountains Euganean.   Shelley.   *Fr.* Lines Written among the Euganean Hills.   PBBP

Mid the squander'd colour.   Cheddar Pinks.   Robert Bridges.   SeCePo

Mid the white spouses of the Sacred Heart.   To St. Mary Magdalen.   Benjamin Dionysius Hill.   AA

Mid-Winter.   Sue Roe.   NPo

Mid Winter.   Hubert Witheford, *tr. fr. Maori by* Sam Karetu.   PeNZ

Mid-Winter Waking.   Robert Graves.   MoAB

Midafternoon in Norfolk.   At the Swings.   Henry Taylor.   MT

Midas, *sels.*   John Lyly.
Daphne.   EIL
(Song of Daphne to the Lute, A.)   OBSC
Pan's Syrinx.   *Fr.* IV, i.   ELP
(Pan's Song.)   OBSC
(Syrinx.)   EIL; SeCePo
Song of Apollo.   OBSC

Midas, they say, possessed the art of old.   "Peter Pindar."   NIP

Midas watched the golden crust.   The Ungrateful Garden.   Carolyn Kizer.   CAPP; NePoEA-2

Midas, we are in story told.   The Fable of Midas.   Swift.   APAS

Midden of rotting bodies of men, A. Corpses in the Wood. Ernst Toller, *tr. by* E. Ellis Roberts. TrJP

Middle. Jimmie Durham. HATNAP

Middle Age. Patricia Beer. FaBoWP

Middle Age. Paula Rankin. MAYP; MT

Middle age—I grow somewhat fond of the way. At My Country Home in Chung-nan. Wang Wei, *tr. by* Burton Watson. CoBCP

Middle-aged, The. Adrienne Rich. HCAP; NePoEA-2

Middle-aged farm-labourer lived here, A. A Son. Lilian Bowes-Lyon. CN

Middle-aged king, The. King Saul. Allan Kolski Horvitz. VWA

Middle-aged life is merry, and I love to lead it. Peekaboo, I Almost See You. Ogden Nash. PoLF

Middle Ages, The. John Haines. LCAP

Middle Ages. Siegfried Sassoon. SO

Middle-elderly have wrinkled necks, The. Sonnet from Below the Age Gap. Keith Sinclair. PeNZ

Middle of a War, The. Roy Fuller. OBWP

Middle of the Night, The. Karla Kuskin. RHPC

Middle of the Way. Galway Kinnell. NU

Middle of the World. D. H. Lawrence. HAP; NoAM

Middle Passage. Robert Hayden. AmNP; BPo; IDB; InPS; NoAM; PoBA

Middle Years, The. Anthony Cronin. CIP

Middleaged Man, The. Louis Simpson. NNaP

Middleness of the Road, The. Robert Frost. LiTA; NOBA

Middlesex. Sir John Betjeman. OxBTC

Midewiwan. Phyllis Wolf. STE

Midges Dance aboon the Burn, The. Robert Tannahill. BoNaP

Midget, The. Philip Levine. NaP

Midlandfall. Alfred A. Yuson, *tr. by* Satoru Sato. WCI

Midnight. Mary Ursula Bethell. ATNZ; PeNZ

Midnight. Dryden. ACP

Midnight. Baljit Kang. Mes

Midnight. Archibald Lampman. OBCV

Midnight. John Masefield. BrPo

Midnight. Thomas Middleton. *Fr.* Blurt, Master Constable. EIL; SeCePo

Midnight. Gabriela Mistral, *tr. fr. Spanish by* David Garrison. BoWoP

Midnight. Arthur Nortje. WMBCH

Midnight. Henrietta Cordelia Ray. *Fr.* Idyl. CBWP-3

Midnight. Michael Roberts. OBMV

Midnight. Shakespeare. *Fr.* The Rape of Lucrece. OBSC

Midnight. Judah Leib Teller, *tr. fr. Yiddish by* Benjamin *and* Barbara Harshav. *Fr.* Three Poems of Nightmare. AYP

Midnight/ The Graveyard Is Silent. Midnight. Baljit Kang. Mes

Midnight and Ten Minutes. Shlomo Vinner, *tr. fr. Hebrew by* Laya Firestone *and* Howard Schwartz. VWA

Midnight at Baiae; a Dream Fragment of Imperial Rome. John Addington Symonds. PeHV

Midnight at sea like so many other midnights at sea. Valery Larbaud, *tr. fr. French by* William Joy Smith. *Fr.* Europe, I. CT

Midnight Court, The (" 'Twas my pleasure to walk in the river meadows"). Brian Merriman, *tr. fr. Modern Irish.* AnIL, *tr. by* Frank O'Connor; NOIV, *tr. by* Thomas Kinsella

Sels.

  Country's Crisis, The. *Tr. by* David Marcus. BIrV

  Husband's Lament, The. *Tr. by* Frank O'Connor. OBVE

  Irish Marriage Night, An. *Tr. by* Frank O'Connor. BIrV

  Lament of the Unmarried Girl, The. *Tr. by* Frank O'Connor. OBVE

  Maiden's Plight, The. *Tr. by* Frank O'Connor. BIrV

  Now God Stand Up for Bastards. *Tr. by* Arland Ussher. BIrV

  Old Man's Tale, The. *Tr. by* David Marcus. BIrV

  Solution, The. *Tr. by* Arland Ussher. BIrV

  Walk. *Tr. by* Brendan Behan. BIrV

Midnight cry appalls the gloom, A. Johnny Appleseed. William Henry Venable. PAH

Midnight Dancer. Langston Hughes. FF

Midnight dreams broken by the hissing roar. Atami. Chugan Engetsu, *tr. by* Burton Watson. FCEI; JLIC-2

Midnight: I still haven't gotten to sleep. At Night, Hearing Someone Singing in the House Next Door. Mei Yao-ch'en, *tr. by* Burton Watson. CoBCP

Midnight in Bonnie's Stall. Siddie Joe Johnson. PChr

Midnight is no time for. No Time for Poetry. Julia Fields. AmNP

Midnight Lamentation, *sel.* Harold Monro. BrPo; OxBTC

  "When you and I go down." OBMV

Midnight ("Midnight was come, when every vital thing"). Thomas Sackville, *fr.* A Mirror [*or* Mirour] for Magistrates. *Fr.* Induction to "A Mirror for Magistrates." CH

Midnight moonlight mobbed Dante's bridge. Bill Berkson. UL

Midnight on Front Street. Roberta Hill. CDW

Midnight on the Great Western. Thomas Hardy. CH; NOBE

Midnight plane with its riding lights, The. Night Plane. Frances Mary Frost. FaPON; PDV

Midnight Prayer. Hayyim Nahman Bialik, *tr. fr. Hebrew by* Helena Frank. TrJP

Midnight Ramble, The. Charles Woodward. NOEC

Midnight—September 19, 1881. John Boyle O'Reilly. PAH

Midnight Show. Karl Shapiro. OxBA

Midnight shower—that crying. Issa, *tr. by* Hiroaki Sato. FCEI

Midnight Skaters, The. Edmund Blunden. FaBoTw; GoJo; GTBS-P; MoBrPo; NOBE; OBD

Midnight Special. Kenneth Patchen. VGW

Midnight Special. *Unknown.* AS

Midnight streets as I walk back, The. Letter I. Randall Swingler. WaP

Midnight Tennis Match, The. Thomas Lux. AmPA; ASP; TSL

Midnight Train, The. *Unknown.* AS

Midnight was come, when every vital thing. Midnight ("Midnight was come, when every vital thing.") Thomas Sackville, *fr.* A Mirror [*or* Mirour] for Magistrates. *Fr.* Induction to "A Mirror for Magistrates." CH

Midnightmouse, The. Christian Morgenstern, *tr. fr. German by* W. D. Snodgrass *and* Lore Segal. RB

Midnight's bell goes ting, ting, ting, ting, ting. Midnight. Thomas Middleton. *Fr.* Blurt, Master Constable. EIL; SeCePo (Noises in the Night.) Mes

Midocean like a pale blue morning-glory. Calm Morning at Sea. Sara Teasdale. MOS

Midpoint. Charles Simic. GeTw

Midrash on Hamlet. Francis Landy. VWA

Midshipman, The. William Falconer. MOS

Midst the fair range of buildings which, new-reared. George Keate. *Fr.* A Burlesque Ode, on the Author's Clearing a New House of Some Workmen. NOEC

Midst the opacous gloom. Feast by the Manzanares. Juan Ruiz de Alarcón, *tr. fr. Spanish by* Samuel Beckett. *Fr.* The Suspicious Truth, I. MexPo

Midstream. D. J. Enright. OxBC

Midstream. Mao Tse-tung, *tr. fr. Chinese by* Earle Birney. MoCV

Midsummer. Robert Fitzgerald. PoA

Midsummer. Thomas Kinsella. IPY

Midsummer. Sydney King Russell. BLPA; FaBoBe

Midsummer. James Scully. NYBP; TwCP

Midsummer. John Townsend Trowbridge. AA

Midsummer. Derek Walcott. NAEL-2

Midsummer, *sel.* Derek Walcott.

  "Rest, Christ! from tireless war. See, it's midsummer." TOF

Midsummer Day in France. Alexander Hume. *Fr.* Of the Day Estivall. FaBoPP

Midsummer Jingle. Newman Levy. BoNaP

Midsummer Moon. "E. M. G. R." BoTP

Midsummer Night. Elizabeth Gould. BoTP

Midsummer Night's Dream, A, *sels.* Shakespeare.

  Asleep, My Love?. *Fr.* V, i. CTC

  Bottom's Song. *Fr.* III, i. CTC; PBBP

  Flower of This Purple Dye. *Fr.* III, ii. CTC

  Helena and Hermia. *Fr.* III, ii. GN

  "How now, spirit! whither wander you?." GN

  Love-in-Idleness. *Fr.* II, i. CTC

  Lunatic, the Lover, and the Poet, The. *Fr.* V, i. FiP (Imagination.) LiTB

  Now the Hungry Lion Roars. *Fr.* V, ii. CH; ChTr; CTC; EIL; LiTB; OBSC; WSC

    (Epilogue: "Now the hungry lion roars.") OBSC

    (Fairy Blessing, The.) OxBoLi

    (Fairy Songs ("Now the hungry lion roars.").) TrGrPo

    (Lion of Winter, The.) WiR

    (Puck's Song.) MoShBr

  Now, Until the Break of Day. *Fr.* V, ii. NAs

    (Fairy Songs ("Now, until the break of day.").) TrGrPo

  Over Hill, over Dale. *Fr.* II, i. EIL

    (Fairy Land, 1.) OBEV

    (Fairy Song ("Over hill, over dale").) NOBE; OBSC; TrGrPo

    (Fairy's Wander-Song.) FaPON

    (Puck and the Fairy.) GN

    (Song: "Over hill, over dale.") InvP

  Sunrise on the Sea. *Fr.* III, ii. ChTr

  Through the Forest Have I Gone. *Fr.* II, ii. CTC

  Through the House. *Fr.* V, ii. CTC

    (Oberon and Titania to the Fairy Train.) GN

  Up and Down. *Fr.* III, ii. CTC

Violet Bank, A. *Fr.* II, i. FaPON
("I know a place whereon the wild thyme blows.") BoNaP
(Where the Wild Thyme Blows.) TrGrPo
Yet but Three?. *Fr.* III, ii. CTC
You Spotted Snakes [with Double Tongue.] *Fr.* II, ii. BoTP; InvP;
   LiTB; NOBE; PoRA; WSC
(Fairies' Lullaby, The.) EIL
(Fairy Land, 2.) OBEV
(Fairy Lullaby.) FaPON
(Fairy Songs: "You spotted snakes with double tongue.") OBSC;
   TrGrPo
(Lullaby for Titania.) GN
(Song: "You spotted snakes with double tongue.") FiP
"Midsummer Night's Dream" in Regent's Park, A. Derwent May. Mes
Midsummer Noon in the Australian Forest, A. Charles Harpur. PoAu-1
Midsummer Song, A. Richard Watson Gilder. BoNaP
Midsummer stretches before me with a cat's yawn. Port of Spain. Derek
   Walcott. NoAM
Midsummer's Rose, A. Eeva Kilpi, *tr. fr. Finnish* by Aili Jarvenpa.
   SOP
Midway. Robert Desnos, *tr. fr. French* by George Quasha. RHTwFP
Midway. Naomi Long Madgett. BlSi; BPo; PoNe
Midway between Mecca and Medina. To a Hero Dead at al-Safra. Hind
   bint Uthatha, *tr.* by Bridget Connelly *and* Deirdre Lashgari. WPOW
Midway in our life's journey, I went astray. Inferno. Dante, *tr. fr.*
   Italian. *Fr.* Divina Commedia. NAWM-1, *tr.* by John Ciardi.
   "And now we walked along the solid mire." *Fr.* XV. OBVE
   Francesca of Rimini. *Fr.* V. PFI
   Gates of Hell, The. *Fr.* III. PFI
   "Like fire-flies that the peasant on the hill." *Fr.* XXVI. Prf
   "Now the hard margin bears us on, while steam." PeHV
   Pier delle Vigne. *Fr.* XII. HoPM
   "Through me you enter the city of lament." *Fr.* III. OBD
   Ugolino. *Fr.* XXXII-XXXIII. AnAn; FaBoPV; FPI, *fr.* XXXIII.
Midway the hill of science, after steep. To Mr. S. T. Coleridge. Anna
   Laetitia Barbauld. NOEC
Midways of a walled garden. William Morris. *Fr.* Golden Wings.
   ChTr
(Ancient Castle, The.) SeCePo
Midweek. Josephine Miles. NoP
Midwest Town. Ruth Delong Peterson. AmFN
Midwife Cat. Mark Van Doren. CRH
Midwife laid her hand on his thick skull, The. Thomas Shadwell the Poet.
   Dryden *and* Nahum Tate. *Fr.* Absalom and Achitophel: Part II.
   ChTr
Midwife puts a rag in the dead woman's hand, The. Obedience of the
   Corpse. C. D. Wright. MT
Midwife's Story; Two, A. Anne Szumigalski. NOBC
Midwinter. John Townsend Trowbridge. AA; AnAmPo; GN
Midwinter spring is its own season. Little Gidding. T. S. Eliot. *Fr.*
   Four Quartets. FaBoMo; FaBoPV; FaBoTw; GTBS-P; MoP;
   NAEL-2; NAWM-2; NoAM; NOBA; NOBE; OAEL-2; OxBTC; PrIm;
   TAP
   "Ash on an old man's sleeve." *Fr.* II. FaBoTw
   "We shall not cease from exploration." *Fr.* V. ImOP
Midwinter Stars. Roberta Hill Whiteman. STE
Midwinter Thaw. Lenore Pratt. CaP
Midwinter Warm. Gillian Stone. NPo
Might and Right. Clarence Day. NBLV
Might as well bury her. Maumee Ruth. Sterling A. Brown. CDC
Might have been. This Place Rumord to Have Been Sodom. Robert
   Duncan. NeAP; NOBA; PoM; PPP
Might have been a merchant's home. A Fighting Position. Sa'di Yusuf,
   tr. by Abdullah al-Udhari. MPAW
Might have known it. Unknown, *tr.* by Jerome Rothenberg. STP
Might I, if you can find it, be given. Saint Nicholas. Marianne Moore.
   NYBP; WPE
"Might Is Right." Israel Zangwill. TrJP
Mightier Storms than This. George Santayana. AnAmPo
Mightier storms than this are brewed on earth. George Santayana. *Fr.*
   Sonnets. AnAmPo
Mightier than Mammon, A, *sel.* Edward Carpenter.
   "Love of men for each other, The—so tender, heroic, constant." PeHV
Mightier than the sword thou art. The Pen. Mary Weston Fordham.
   CBWP-2
Mightiest of all heights is the Peak. Unknown, *tr.* by Arthur Waley. BoS
Mighty are you, Hou Chi. Unknown, *tr.* by Arthur Waley. BoS
Mighty bell is six o'clock, A. Six to Six. Unknown, *tr.* by A. C.
   Jordan. PBA
Mighty change it is, and ominous, A. The Winter Shore. Thomas Wade.
   OAEL-2

Mighty creature is the germ, A. The Germ. Ogden Nash. CenHV;
   MoShBr; RB
Mighty Fortress, A. Bible, *O.T.* *See* Psalms: Psalm XCI ("He that
   dwelleth.")
Mighty Fortress Is Our God, A. Martin Luther, *tr. fr. German.* AWP;
   EaLo; PWR, *tr. by* Frederick Henry Hedge
   (Feste Burg Ist Unser Gott, Ein.) CTC, *tr. by* M. Woolsey Stryker
   (Hymn: "Mighty fortress is our God, A.") WGRP
   (Paraphrase of Luther's Hymn.) AA
Mighty hand, from an exhaustless urn, A. The Flood of Years. Bryant.
   AA
Mighty Heart, The. Emerson. *Fr.* Woodnotes II ("As sunbeams stream
   through liberal space.") AA
Mighty Hunter, The. J. B. Worley. PoLF
Mighty is God on high. Unknown, *tr.* by Arthur Waley. BoS
Mighty is Mount Liang. Unknown, *tr.* by Arthur Waley. BoS
Mighty Love. John Fletcher. *See* Tragedy of Valentinian, The: Hear, Ye
   Ladies [That Despise].
Mighty Mary, hear me. Muireadhach Albanach O Dalaigh. NOIV
Mighty mother, and her son who brings, The. Pope. *Fr.* The Dunciad,
   I. OBSV; PoE
Mighty One, before Whose Face. Bryant. AH
Mighty, praised beyond compare. Rock of My Salvation. Mordecai, *tr.*
   by Solomon Solis-Cohen. TrJP
Mighty river flowing dark and deep, The. James Thomson ("B. V.").
   Fr. The City of Dreadful Night, XIX. EBVV
Mighty Runner, A. E. A. Robinson. OBAL; SD
Mighty soul that is ambition's mate, The. Disenchantment. Charles
   Leonard Moore. AA
Mighty spirit, and its power, which stains, The. Inebriety. George
   Crabbe. BXAP
Mighty this people of Chou! Unknown, *tr.* by Arthur Waley. BoS
Mighty Thoughts of an Old World, The. Thomas Lovell Beddoes. *Fr.*
   The Ivory Gate. GoJo
   (Stanzas from "The Ivory Gate.") EnRP
   (Stanzas: "Mighty thought of an old world, The.") TrGrPo
Mighty waste of moaning waters lay, The. The Deep Dark Night.
   Tennyson. *Fr.* The Devil and the Lady. SeCePo
Mighty wave rush'd o'er him as he spoke, A. Homer, *tr. fr. Greek by*
   Pope. *Fr.* Odyssey, V. OBVE
Mignon. Goethe, *tr. fr. German by* Robert Bly. *Fr.* Wilhelm Meister's
   Apprenticeship, *bk.* I *ch.* 1. NU
   ("Knowest thou the land where bloom the lemon trees.") AWP, *tr.*
   by James Elroy Flecker.
Mignon. Henrietta Cordelia Ray. CBWP-3
Migod, a picture window. The One-Night Stand: An Approach to the
   Bridge. Paul Blackburn. ErPo
Migrant, The. A. L. Hendricks. PBCV
Migrants. Sylvia Lynd. CN
Migration. Carole Gregory Clemmons. *See* Ghetto Lovesong—
   Migration.
Migration. Pinkie Gordon Lane. BlSi
Migration of Darkness, The. Peter Payack. BWV
Migration of the Grey Squirrels, The. William Howitt. OxBChV
Mihailovich. Roy McFadden. NeIP
Mihyar, A King! "Adunis", *tr. fr. Arabic by* Lena Jayyusi *and* John
   Heath-Stubbs. MAP
Mikado, The, *sels.* W. S. Gilbert.
   Ko-Ko's Song ("As some day it may happen that a victim must be
      found"). LiTB
   Ko-Ko's Winning Song. *Fr.* II. LiTB
   (Ko-Ko's Song ["On a tree by a river a little tom-tit"].) FaFP
   (Titwillow.) NoP
   Mikado's Song, The. LiTB
   To Sit in Solemn Silence. FiBHP
Mike 65. Lennox Raphael. PoBA
Miklos Radnoti. Willis Barnstone. VWA
Milan August 1943. Salvatore Quasimodo, *tr. fr. Italian by* Jack Bevan.
   PFI
Mild and slow and young. Girl Help. Janet Lewis. HeIP; InPK; QFR
Mild is the parting year, and sweet. Walter Savage Landor. *Fr.* Ianthe.
   EnLoPo; TEP
   (Autumn.) TrGrPo
Mild, melancholy, and sedate, he stands. The Hottentot. Thomas
   Pringle. OBTV
Mild offspring of a dark and sullen sire! To an Early Primrose. Henry
   Kirke White. OBNC
Mild the mist upon the hill. Emily Brontë. NOBVV
Mild yoke of Christ, most harsh to me not bearing. Paradox. Vassar
   Miller. NePoEA

Mildest of all the powers of earth: no lightnings. Gravity. John Frederick Nims. BLA

Mildred's Doves. Henrietta Cordelia Ray. CBWP-3

Mile an' a Bittock, A. Robert Louis Stevenson. NOBVV; OxBS; SeCePo

Mile and mile and mile; but no one would gather. The Sea. Francis Webb. CBAP; PoAu-2

Mile behind is Gloucester town, A. Gloucester Moors. William Vaughn Moody. AnAmPo; NOBA; OxBA

Mile Hill. Dennis Schmitz. LCAP

Mile more down the flat fast road, the homestead, A. Serpent Knowledge. Robert Pinsky. Fr. An Explanation of America. NAAL-2

Mile out in the marshes, under a sky, A. The Town Dump. Howard Nemerov. CMoP; MAT

Mile with Me, A. Henry van Dyke. BLPA; FPL

Miles, and miles, and miles of desolation! Suffolk. Swinburne. Fr. By the North Sea, III. FaBoPP

Miles and miles of pasture. The Lavender Kitten. Alonzo Lopez. NOVW

Miles' Delight ("Miles Davis"). Ted Joans. PoNe

Miles Keogh's Horse. John Milton Hay. PAH

Miles of glittering/ Whales. Corruption of Metals. Sonya Dorman. BWV

Miles of pram in the wind and Pam in the gorse track. Potpourri from a Surrey Garden. Sir John Betjeman. CenHV; FiBHP; NOBL

Militant. Langston Hughes. PoBA

Military Harpist, The. Ruth Pitter. FaBoTw

Military Occupations, sel. Dionne Brand.
    "In the 5 a.m. dusk." PBCV

Militerotics. Chuck Ortleb. GLP

Militia, The. Dryden. Fr. Cymon and Iphigenia. OBSV

Milk at the Bottom of the Sea. Oscar Williams. LiTA

Milk Boy. Dorothy Wellesley. CN

Milk for the Cat. Harold Monro. BoTP; FaBoBe; FaFP; MoBrPo; OBMV

Milk White Doe, The. Unknown, tr. fr. French by Andrew Lang. AWP

Milk-white Dove. Unknown. See Song of the Murdered Child.

Milk white Hind, immortal and unchang'd, A. Dryden. Fr. The Hind and the Panther, I. SeCV-2
    (Churches of Rome and of England, The, much abr.) ACP

Milk-white Moon, Put the Cows to Sleep. Carl Sandburg. FaPON

Milk-white mouse immortal and unchang'd, A. The Town Mouse and the Country Mouse. Matthew Prior. BXAP

Milke before wine, I would 'twere mine. Unknown. FaBoUs

Milking before Dawn. Ruth Dallas. PeNZ

Milking-Maid, The. Christina Rossetti. BeLS

Milking Pails. Unknown. CH

Milking Shed, The. John Clare. CH

Milking Time. Elizabeth Madox Roberts. FaPON; GoJo; OBCA

Milkmaid. Laurie Lee. BoLoP; FaBoTw

Milkmaid, The. Unknown. AmFP

Milkmaid's Epithalamium, The. Thomas Randolph. BoLoP

Milkman, The. Isabella Gardner. CAPP

Milkman, The. Clive Sansom. BoTP

Milkman and His Son, The. Thomas Lux. PPR

Milkweed. Philip Levine. LCAP

Milkweed, A. Richard Wilbur. Fr. Two Voices in a Meadow. CRP

Milkweed. James Wright. LCAP; NaP; NU

"Milkweed, and a buttercup, and cowslip, A," said sweet Mary. Her Dairy. Peter Newell. NA

Milkweed Pods in Winter. Lisel Mueller. KS

Milky Way, The. Jon Anderson. MAYP

Milky Way/ Milky Way. Tune: Flirtatious Laughter. Wei Ying-wu, tr. by Burton Watson. CoBCP

Milky Way above, The. Fire Island. May Swenson. PoA; TAP

Milky Way still warns of the fate of the Clear One, The. Upon Reading the Boudoir Poem of Mei-ts'un. Ch'ien Ch'ien-yi, tr. by Irving Lo. WFTU

Milky Way's silver river, The. Song of the Waterfall at Mount Lu. Yang Wei-chen, tr. by Jonathan Chaves. CoBLCP

Mill, A. William Allingham. FaBoEE; OxBSP; SeCePo

Mill, The. H. H. ter Balkt, tr. fr. Dutch by Scott Rollins. DuIn

Mill, The. William Heyen. EyDe

Mill, The. E. A. Robinson. CMoP; DL; HAP; NAAL-2; NoAM; NoP; PrIm; SoSe; WeW
    (Miller's Wife, The.) TAP

Mill, The. Richard Wilbur. Psk; SoSe

Mill goes toiling slowly around, The. Nightfall in Dordrecht. Eugene Field. AA

Mill-Pond, The. Edward Thomas, tr. fr. German. RB

Mill-stream, now that noises cease, The. A. E. Housman. GBL

The mill that hangs open like a mouth. The Mill. H. H. ter Balkt, tr. by Scott Rollins. DuIn

Mill Valley. Myra Cohn Livingston. RFM

"Millennium," yes; "pandemonium!" Hometown Piece for Messrs. Alston and Reese. Marianne Moore. OBAL

Miller, The. Sir John Clerk. ChTr

Miller and His Sons, The. Unknown. OBET

Miller, Miller. Ivy O. Eastwick. BoTP

Miller of Dee, The. Unknown. GBP

Miller was a stout carl, for the nones, The. Chaucer. Fr. The Canterbury Tales: Prologue. TrGrPo
    ("Miller, stout and sturdy as the stones, The," mod. vers. by Louis Untermeyer) TrGrPo

Miller's daughter, The. Spinning Song. Edith Sitwell. MoAB; MoBrPo

Miller's Daughter, The. Tennyson. OBEV; TrGrPo

Miller's mill-dog lay at the mill-door, The. Bingo. Unknown. CH; TTTS

Miller's Prologue, The. Chaucer. Fr. The Canterbury Tales.
    ("Whan that the knight had [or hadde] thus his tale ytold.") NAEL-1; OAEL-1

Miller's [or Milleres] Tale, The. Chaucer. Fr. The Canterbury Tales. NAEL-1; OAEL-1; OxBoLi
    ("Sometime ago there was a rich old codger," mod. vers. by Nevill Coghill) TEP
    ("There used to be a rich old oaf who made," mod. vers. by Theodore Morrison) NAWM-1
    "Fair was this yonge wyf, and therwithal." EBEV

Miller's wife had waited long, The. The Mill. E. A. Robinson. CMoP; DL; HAP; NAAL-2; NoAM; NoP; PrIm; SoSe; WeW
    (Miller's Wife, The.) TAP

Miller's Wife's Lullaby, The. Unknown. GBP

Millery, millery, dustipole. Unknown. OxNR

Millibars of Storm. Aimé Césaire, tr. fr. French by Michael Benedikt. POS

Millicent can play the flute. Broom Balancing. Kathleen Fraser. RHPC

Millie's Date. Dannie Abse. NPo

Million, A. Yonathan Ratosh, tr. fr. Hebrew by Bernhard Frank. MHeP

Million, The. Peter Redgrove. OxBC

Million butterflies rose up from South America, A. Annual Legend. Winfield Townley Scott. CoAP; LiTA; LiTM; WaP

Million Little Diamonds, A. Mary Frances Butts. AA

Million stars are dreaming out, A. Frank O'Hara. SM

Million years of death some star, A. Micromutations. James Wright. NYBP

Millionaires, presidents—even kings. Everyday Things. Jean Ayer. BoTP

Millions and millions of years. The Garden. Jacques Prévert, tr. by Michael Benedikt. POS

Millions of Strawberries. Genevieve Taggard. FaPON; ILY; MoShBr

Millions who pass you see. To a Blue Hippopotamus. Ellen de Young Kay. NePoEA

Mills of the Gods, The. Unknown. BLPA; FPL

Milltown Union Bar, The. Richard Hugo. NoAM

Milne's Bar. Norman MacCaig. FaBoTw

Milo's from home; and, Milo being gone. Martial, tr. by Elijah Fenton. OBVE

Milton, sels. Blake.
    And Did Those Feet in Ancient Time. Fr. Preface. AWP; EnRP; FaBoCh; FaBoPV; FaBV; HAP; HeIP; InPS; MAT; NAEL-2; NAWM-2; NoP; OAEL-2; PoE; PoEL-4; PoRA; PrIm; WGRP
    (Jerusalem.) BoTP; EaLo; FaPoR; NOBE; NOCV; OBEV; RB; WaaP
    (New Jerusalem, A.) LiTB; TrGrPo
    (Prelude: "And did those feet in ancient time.") OBNC
    Reason and Imagination. Fr. II. EnRP
    "Then Milton rose up from the heaven of Albion ardorous!" Fr. I. OAEL-2
    "This wine-press is call'd war on earth." Fr. I. EBEV
    (Wine-Press of Los, The.) EnRP
    "Thou hearest the nightingale begin the song of spring." Fr. II. PBBP
    (Choir of Day, The.) EnRP
    (Lark's Song, The.) WiR
    (Vision of Beulah, The: "Thou hearest the nightingale begin the song of spring.") NOBE
    (Vision of the Lamentation of Beulah, A.) OBNC
    Vision of Beulah, The ("There is a place where contrarieties are equally true"). Fr. II. OAEL-2
    Wild Thyme, The. Fr. II. WiR

Milton. Longfellow. AA; AmPP; AWP; NoP; TAP; TrGrPo

Milton. Lloyd Mifflin. AA
Milton. H. Cordelia Ray. BlSi; CBWP-3
Milton. Wordsworth. *See* London, 1802 ("Milton! thou should'st be living at this hour.")
Milton by Firelight. Gary Snyder. CAPP; CoAP; InPS; NAAL-2; PPP
Milton! I think thy spirit hath passed away. To Milton. Oscar Wilde. BrPo
Milton: On the Busts of Milton, in Youth and Age, sels. William Lisle Bowles. Son
  In Age.
  In Youth.
Milton! thou should'st be living at this hour. London, 1802. Wordsworth. AWP; EnRP; FaBoPV; FaBV; FF; HAP; HeIP; InvP; LiTB; NAEL-2; NIP; NoP; OBNC; PoEL-4; PoRA; Son; TEP
  (England, 1802, II.) OBEV
  (Milton.) FaPoR
  (Same, The.) GTBS; GTBS-P
  (To Milton.) TrGrPo
Milton, who made his illiterate daughters. Eve of Easter. Bernadette Mayer. UL
Miltonic Sonnet for Mr. Johnson on His Refusal of Peter Hurd's Official Portrait, A. Richard Wilbur. TW
Milton's Prayer for [*or* of] Patience. Elizabeth Lloyd Howell. AA; WGRP
Milton's the prince of poets—so we say. Byron. *Fr.* Don Juan, III. NOBL; OAEL-2
Milwaukee Fire, The. *Unknown.* AmFP
Mima. Walter de la Mare. *Unknown.* BrPo
Mima'amakim. H. Leivick, *tr. fr. Yiddish by* Benjamin *and* Barbara Harshav. AYP
Mime. John Updike. RR
Mimesis. György Somlyó, *tr. fr. Hungarian by* Jascha Kessler. FOC
Mimesis. Barrett Watten. LP
Mimi, do you remember. Biftek aux Champignons. Henry Augustin Beers. AA
Mimic Muse, The, *sel.* Samuel Hoffenstein.
  "With rue my heart is laden." NBLV
Mimnermus in Church. William Johnson Cory. NOBE; OBEV
Mimnermus Incert. Walter Savage Landor. PoEL-4
Mimosa. Cleopatra Mathis. MAYP
Minaret, The. "Adunis," *tr. fr. Arabic by* Abdullah al-Udhari. MPAW
Mince-Python, The. Carolyn Wells. *Fr.* A Baker's Dozen of Wild Beasts. OBCA
Mincemeat. Elizabeth Gould. BoTP
Mind. Jorie Graham. HCAP
Mind, The, *sel.* Charles Swain.
  "Thin are, oh Mind!—the colours which delight." PF
Mind. Richard Wilbur. CMoP; HCAP; HoPM; NePoEA; OxBSP; PPP
Mind a clutter: sick with love for another. Night Trip across the Chesapeake and After. Sydney Lea. MAYP
Mind and environment—you have quieted both. Wu Shan-yang. Yang Chi, *tr. fr. Chinese by* Jonathan Chaves. *Fr.* Thinking of My Friends at Kou-jung Subprefecture. CoBLCP
Mind and Matter. *Unknown. See* Limerick: "There was a faith-healer of Deal."
Mind and object scrapped. Daio, *tr. by* Lucien Stryk *and* Takashi Ikemoto. ZPCJ
Mind Content, A. Robert Greene. *See* Farewell to Folly: Maesia's Song.
Mind drowned in the sun may dream of birds, The. A Balcony with Birds. Howard Moss. NePoEA
Mind Emerges, The. Pierre Reverdy, *tr. fr. French by* William Jay Smith. CT
Mind Flying Afar. Edgar Lee Masters. PoA
Mind has shown itself at times, The. For the Marriage of Faustus and Helen. Hart Crane. InPS; NoAM; NOBA
Mind in its [*or* the] purest play is like some bat. Mind. Richard Wilbur. CMoP; HCAP; HoPM; NePoEA; OxBSP; PPP
Mind, Intractable Thing, The. Marianne Moore. LiTM; NYBP
Mind Is an Ancient and Famous Capital, The ("The mind is a city like London.") Delmore Schwartz. NoAM; TAP
Mind Is an Enchanting Thing, The. Marianne Moore. CMoP; HeIP; InPK; InvP; MoAB; MoAmPo; NAAL-2; OxBA; PoE; PPP; WPOW
Mind is not, The. The Perishing Bird. Douglas G. Jones. MoCV
Mind, mind, mind—above the Path. Zengetsu, *tr. fr. Chinese by* Lucien Stryk *and* Takashi Ikemoto. *Fr.* Twenty-four Poems of Living in the Mountains. ZPCJ
Mind of Man is fram'd even like the breath, The. In Patterdale. Wordsworth. *Fr.* The Prelude [or, Growth of a Poet's Mind]: Childhood and School-Time. FaBoRV
Mind of the people is like mud, The. Talking with Soldiers. W. J. Turner. MoBrPo

Mind-Reader, The, *sel.* Richard Wilbur. NAAL-2; NoAM
  "What should I tell them?" CRP
Mind remembers, The. Images. Merle Collins. WS
Mind went away, The. Time When the Day Ended. Michael Burkard. NAmP
Mind, with its own eyes and ears, The. The Mind's Liberty. W. H. Davies. MoBrPo
Mindful of the/ shambles of the day. Nightwalker. Thomas Kinsella. IPY
Minding Ruth. Aidan Carl Mathews. CIP
Minds awake in bodies that were asleep. Pandora and the Moon. Merrill Moore. MoAmPo
Mind's eye aches from Henry James, The. Satie, at the End of Term. Simon Curtis. NOBL
Mind's Liberty, The. W. H. Davies. MoBrPo
Mind's no solid. Waka. Dogen, *tr. by* Lucien Stryk *and* Takashi Ikemoto. ZPCJ
Mine. Frank Polite. NYBP
Mine. Mary E. Tucker. CBWP-1
Mine Argosy from Alexandria. Christopher Marlowe. *Fr.* The Jew of Malta, II, i. ChTr
Mine be a cot beside the [*or* a] hill. A Wish. Samuel Rogers. FaPoR; GTBS; GTBS-P; NOBE; OBEV
Mine—by the right of the white election! Emily Dickinson. NAAL-1; NoP
Mine enemy is growing old. Emily Dickinson. TW
"Mine eye and heart are at a mortal war." Shakespeare. *Fr.* Sonnets, XLVI. EyDe
Mine eye bewrays. Love Cannot Live. *Unknown.* EIL
"Mine eye hath play'd the painter, and hath steel'd." Shakespeare. *Fr.* Sonnets, XXIV. EyDe
Mine eye, mine ear, my will, my wit, my heart. Sir John Davies. *Fr.* The Gulling Sonnets. Son
Mine eyes beheld the blessed pity spring. Dante, *tr. fr. Italian by* Dante Gabriel Rossetti. *Fr.* Vita Nuova, La, XXIII. AWP
Mine eyes have seen the glory of the coming of the Lord. The Battle Hymn of the [American] Republic. Julia Ward Howe. AA; AH, *with music;* AnAmPo; BLPA; CH; EaLo; FaBoBe; FaFP; FaPON; FaPoR; GN; NOBA; NOCV; OBWP; OHIP; OPP; PAH; PWR; SCV; TAP; WBLP; WGRP; WPE
Mine Host of "The Golden Apple." Thomas Westwood. GN; OHIP
Mine is the freedom of the tranquil hills. Freedom of the Hills. Douglas Fraser. PoSH
"Mine, O Thou Lord of Life, Send My Roots Rain." Lorna Goodison. UAS
Mine old dear enemy, my froward master. Translation from Petrarch. Petrarch, *tr. by* Sir Thomas Wyatt. SiPS
Mine Own John Poins [*or* Poyntz]. Sir Thomas Wyatt. *Fr.* Satires. AAS; NoP; OBSV; OBVE; PoEL-1; SiPS
  (Of the Courtier's Life.) OBSC
Mine owne good Bat, before thou hoyse up saile. Councell Given to Master Bartholmew Withipoll. George Gascoigne. AAS
Mine was a Midwest home—you can keep your world. One Home. William Stafford. AmFN; CoAP; VGW
Minemyme but where. Innery. Reinhard Priessnitz, *tr. by* Beth Bjorklund. CoAuP
Miner Boy, The. *Unknown.* AmFP
Miner Coming Home One Night, A. *Unknown.* GBP
Mineral Kingdom. Jacques Dupin, *tr. fr. French by* Paul Auster. RHTwFP
Minerals of Cornwall, Stones of Cornwall. Peter Redgrove. FaBoMo
Miners. Wilfred Owen. BrPo; MoAB; MoBrPo; NAEL-2; NOBE; OBWVE
Miner's Doom, The. *Unknown.* AmFP
Miner's Helmet, The. George MacBeth. OxBTC
Miner's Lament, The. *Unknown.* AmFP
Miner's Life, A. *Unknown.* OBET
Miners' Wives. Joe Corrie. OxBS
Ming the Merciless. Jessica Hagedorn. BrSi
Mingled/ breath and smell. Subway Rush Hour. Langston Hughes. InPK
Mingled aye with fragrant yearnings. Blue Moonshine. Francis G. Stokes. NA
Mingled the moonlight with daylight. Thomas Hardy. Walter de la Mare. NoAM
Mingled Yarns. X. J. Kennedy. OBCA
Mingiing my prayer. Saigyo Hoshi, *tr. fr. Japanese by* Arthur Waley. AWP
Mingling with the Wind. Ryokan, *tr. fr. Japanese by* Burton Watson. FCEI
Mingus. Bob Kaufman. PoBA

Mini-Samizdat of New River Rhymes, A, *sels.* William Rossa Cole.
    SoTCo
    "Anna Livia Plurabelle."
    "On Ireland's Roaringwater Bay."
    "On the beach near Port St. Joe."
    "Sailing on Lac d'Annecy."
    "When she lived near St. Lawrence."
    "With Robert Hughes on Botany Bay."
Miniature. Eden Phillpotts. OxBSP
Miniatures. Anna Kiss, *tr. fr. Hungarian by* Jascha Kessler. FOC
Miniatures IV. Lynn Strongin. IHMS
Minimal. Roland Jooris, *tr. fr. Dutch by* Peter Nijmeijer. DuIn
Minimal, The. Theodore Roethke. HCAP; MoP; NoAM; NOBA; RB;
    TSS
Mining in Killdeer Alley. Dabney Stuart. MT
Minion Wife, A. Nicholas Udall. *Fr.* Ralph Roister Doister. ElL
Minister at Chiuzenji, The. Osman Edwards. *Fr.* Residential Rhymes,
    III. OBTV
Minister of birds, islands, and pools. Cortege for Colette. Jean Garrigue.
    NYBP
Minister of War. *Unknown, tr. by* Arthur Waley. BoS
Minister said it wad [*or* wald] dee, The. Last Lauch. Douglas Young.
    FaBoCo; NBLV; OxBS; SeCePo
Minister, why do you direct your artillery against. A Fisher's Apology.
    Unknown, tr. by Arthur Johnstone. GoTS
Ministers who've sold the King. Are You Glad? *Mongol Oral Tradition,
    tr. by* C. R. Bawden. WTO
Miniver Cheevy. E. A. Robinson. AmPP; AWP; ChTr; CMoP; FaBoCh;
    FaBV; FaFP; FF; FPL; HeIP; LiTA; LiTM; MoAB; MoAmPo; MoP;
    NAAL-2; NBLV; NIP; NoAM; NOBA; NoP; OBSV; OxBA; PoEL-5;
    PoLF; PoRA; SCV; TAP; TrGrPo
Miniver Cheevy, Jr. David Fisher Parry. BXAP; NBLV
Minneapolis Poem, The. James Wright. FYAP; NoAM; UnPo
Minnesota Camp Grounds. Gerald Vizenor. STE
Minnesota Thanksgiving. John Berryman. GOA
Minnie and Her Dove. Charles Tennyson Turner. FM
Minnie and Mattie. Christina Rossetti. *Fr.* Sing-Song. GoJo; InvP
Minnie and Mrs. Hoyne. Kenneth Fearing. PoRA
Minnie and Winnie. Tennyson. NA; OxBChV; TTTS
Minnie, I canna caa my wheel. Douglas Young, *after the Greek of*
    Sappho. OBVE
Minnows. Keats. *Fr.* I Stood Tiptoe [upon a Little Hill]. FaPON; GN
Minor. Judd Teller, *tr. fr. Yiddish by* Grace Schulman. PeBMYV
Minor Bird, A. Robert Frost. CMoP
Minor Elegy. Henriqueta Lisboa, *tr. fr. Portuguese by* Willis Barnstone
    and Nelson Cerqueira. BoWoP
Minor Key. Judah Leib Teller, *tr. fr. Yiddish.* VWA, *tr. by* Gabriel
    Preil *and* Howard Schwartz
Minor Mythology. David Avidan, *tr. fr. Hebrew by* Warren Bargad *and*
    Stanley F. Chyet. IP
Minor Prophet, A, *sel.* "George Eliot."
    Tide of Faith, The. WGRP
Minor Things. Heather Ross Miller. MT
Minority Report. John Updike. GOA
Minotaur. Robert Fisher. AmMo
Minotaur Poems, *sels.* E. W. Mandel.
    "It has been hours in these rooms." OBCV, I.
    "My father was always out in the garage." *Fr.* II. MoCV; OBCV
    Orpheus. *Fr.* VI. OBCV
Minstrel, The, *sels.* James Beattie.
    Nature and the Poets. SeCePo
    Youth of a Poet, The. *Fr.* I. NOEC
Minstrel, The. Goethe, *tr. fr. German by* James Clarence Mangan.
    AWP
Minstrel, The. Joseph Skipsey. PF
Minstrel and Genius, to whose songs or sighs. Autumnal Ode. Aubrey
    Thomas De Vere. OBNC
Minstrel Boy, The. Thomas Moore. ACP; AnIL; FaBoBe; FaFP; GN;
    OnYI; PrIm
Minstrel Responds to Flattery, The. Sir Walter Scott. *Fr.* The Lay of the
    Last Minstrel, V. OBNC
Minstrels and Maids. William Morris. *See* Earthly Paradise, The:
    Outlanders, The.
Minstrel's Last Lay, The. John Barth. OBAL
Minstrel's Lot, The. John Bolton Rogerson. PF
Minstrels sing the jasmine songs. Peyanar, *tr. fr. Tamil by* A. K.
    Ramanujan. *Fr.* Seven Said by the Foster-Mother, 6. PLW
Minstrel's Song. Thomas Chatterton. *See* Aella; a Tragycal Enterlude:
    Oh! sing unto my roundelay [*or* O! Synge untoe mie roundelaie].
Minstrel's Song. Ted Hughes. OBCP
Mint bed is in, The. Sunday. James Schuyler. TTTS

Mint Julep, The. Charles Fenno Hoffman. AA
Minuet, The. Mary Mapes Dodge. OHFP
Minuet on Reaching the Age of Fifty, A. George Santayana. BLPL;
    FaFP
Minute I heard my first love story, The. Jalal ed-Din Rumi, *tr. by* John
    Moyne *and* Coleman Barks. UnAS
Minute-Men of Northboro', The. Wallace Rice. PAH
Minutes. Denis Johnson. MAYP
Minutes are numbered by the fall of sands. John Ford. *Fr.* The Lover's
    Melancholy, IV, iii. PoEL-2
Minyan, The. Jack Myers. VWA
Mips and Ma the Mooly Moo. Theodore Roethke. *Fr.* Praise to the End!
    NBLV; RB
Mir träumte von einem Königskind. Heine, *tr. fr. German by* Richard
    Garnett. AWP
Mir träumte wieder der alte Traum. Heine, *tr. fr. German by* James
    Thomson. AWP
Mira is dancing with bells tied on her ankles. Mirabai, *tr. by* Willis
    Barnstone *and* Usha Nilsson. BoWoP
Mirabeau Bridge, The. Guillaume Apollinaire, *tr. fr. French.* BoLoP,
    tr. by Quentin Stevenson; OBVE, *tr. by* W. S. Merwin; RHTwFP, *tr.*
    by Richard Wilbur.
Mirabell: Books of Number, *sels.* James Merrill.
    "And Maddening—it's all by someone else!" *Fr. Bk.* 9. NAAL-2
    "It starts in the small hours. An interlude." *Fr. Bk.* 8. NoAM
    "World was everything that was the case? The." *Fr. Bk.* 9. HCAP
Miracle. Liberty Hyde Bailey. OHIP
Miracle, The. Walter de la Mare. LiTB; UnPo
Miracle, The. Allan Dowling. ErPo
Miracle, The. Emerson. FM
Miracle, The. Chaim Grade, *tr. fr. Yiddish.* VWA, *tr. by* Ruth Whitman
Miracle, The. Maureen Hawkins. AIW; WS
Miracle, The. Sir John Suckling. CaPo
Miracle for Breakfast, A. Elizabeth Bishop. LiTA
Miracle Hill. Emerson Blackhorse Mitchell. NOVW
Miracle in Milan. Kurt Klinger, *tr. fr. German by* Beth Bjorklund.
    CoAuP
Miracle Indeed, A. Swami Purohit. OBMV
Miracle of the world, I never will deny. Henry Constable. *Fr.* Diana.
    OBSC
Miracles. Conrad Aiken. MoAmPo
Miracles. Arna Bontemps. PoNe
Miracles. Julia Randall. CRP
Miracles. Walt Whitman. AnAmPo
Miracles at the Birth of Christ. Isaac Watts. NOCV
Miracles Real Miracles. Max Jacob, *tr. fr. French by* Armand Schwerner.
    RHTwFP
Miraculous Dawn. R. Williams Parry, *tr. fr. Welsh by* Joseph P. Clancy.
    OBWVE
Miraculous part of our relationship is being apart, The. Last Word: For
    My Son Yung. Chin Jen-Jui, *tr. by* Irving Lo. WFTU
Miraculously in the autumn twilight, out of. The Boy. Ruth Dallas.
    ATNZ
Miraculously, through prayer to Saint Anthony. Robert Fitzgerald. *Fr.*
    Adulescentia. SD
Mirage. Christina Rossetti. BoLoP; LLLT; PoRA
Mirage. Amber Coverdale Sumrall. TSM
Mirage, The. Oscar Williams. LiTM
Mirage has offered its solace to my heart, A. Dark Mirage. "Badawi
    al-Jabal," *tr. by* Christopher Tingley *and* Richard Wilbur. MAP
Miramar Beach. J. V. Cunningham. *Fr.* To What Strangers, What
    Welcome. PoA
Miramichi Fire, The. *Unknown.* AmFP
Miramichi Lightning. Alfred Goldsworthy Bailey. OBCV
Miranda. W. H. Auden. *Fr.* The Sea and the Mirror. NoAM
Miranda, as usual, indefatigable. Elephant. Louis Johnson. ATNZ
Miranda in Reno. Nicholas Christopher. BAP
Mira's Will. Mary Leapor. NOEC
Mirèio, *sels.* Frédéric Mistral, *tr. fr. Provençal.* AWP
    Cocooning, The. *Tr. by* Harriet Waters Preston.
    Mares of the Camargue, The. *Tr. by* George Meredith.
Miriam, *sel.* Whittier.
    Book Our Mothers Read, The. BLRP
Miriam and Horlick spend a great deal of time putting off going to bed.
    Goodnight. Stevie Smith. FaBoWP
Miriam Tazewell. John Crowe Ransom. TW
Mirie it is, while sumer ilast. *Unknown. See* Merry It Is.
Mirkayan, don't show your love, simply relish. Do Not Show Your Love.
    Said Aql, *tr. by* Matthew Sorenson *and* Naomi Shihab Nye. MAP
Mirror, The. Edgar Bowers. QFR
Mirror, The. Chan Ch'e, *tr. fr. Chinese by* Dominic Cheung. IFON

Mirror. Tada Chimako, *tr. fr. Japanese by* Kenneth Rexroth *and* Ikuko Atsumi. BoWoP

Mirror. Peter De Vries. PoA

Mirror, The. Louise Glück. GeTw; MAYP

Mirror, The. Judah Halevi, *tr. fr. Hebrew by* Emma Lazarus. TrJP

Mirror, The. Blanche Mary Kelly. TrPWD

Mirror. James Merrill. CoAP; NePoEA-2; SM

Mirror, The. John N. Morris. PoA

Mirror, The. Paul Muldoon, *tr. fr. Irish by* Michael Davitt. CIP

Mirror. Sylvia Plath. FaBoWP; HAP; NYBP

Mirror, The. Isaac Rosenberg. NoAM

Mirror above my fireplace reflects the reflected, The. Reflections. Louis MacNeice. FaBCIP

Mirror copies everything it sees, A. Reflections on Mirrors. Elder Olson. CRP

Mirror Fantasy. Koh Chang-soo, *tr. fr. Korean by the author.* ACKP

Mirror for Autumn, A. "Adunis", *tr. fr. Arabic by* Abdullah al-Udhari. MPAW

Mirror for Poets, A. Thom Gunn. LiTM; NePoEA

Mirror for the Barnyard. Jack Myers. AmPA

Mirror for the Twentieth Century, A. "Adunis", *tr. fr. Arabic by* Abdullah al-Udhari. MPAW

Mirror in February. Thomas Kinsella. CIP; FaBCIP; GTBS-P; NoAM

Mirror in the Front Hall, The. Constantine P. Cavafy, *tr. fr. Greek by* Edmund Keeley *and* Philip Sherrard. PeHV

Mirror in Which Two Are Seen as One, The. Adrienne Rich. NAAL-2; NNaP

Mirror of Knighthood, The, *sels.* Robert Parry. EIL
   Except I Love.
   "Fond affection, hence, and leave me!"

Mirror of men's eyes delights me less, The. Laus Virginitatis. Arthur Symons. EnLoPo

Mirror of poets, mirror of our age. Upon Ben Johnson. Edmund Waller. SeCV-1

Mirror Perilous, The. Alan Dugan. LiTM; TwCP

Mirror Poems, The. Toi Derricotte. ER

Mirror to Khalida, A. "Adunis," *tr. fr. Arabic by* Lena Jayyusi *and* John Heath-Stubbs. MAP

Mirrored in the waters of the Kamunabi River. Prince Atsumi. *Fr.* Manyo Shu. Ma

Mirrorment. A. R. Ammons. PCP

Mirrors, The. Sophia de Mello Breyner Andresen, *tr. fr. Portuguese by* Allan Francovich. PBWP

Mirrors. Elizabeth Jennings. NePoEA

Mirrors. Fu'ad Rifqa, *tr. fr. Arabic by* Sargon Boulus *and* Samuel Hazo. MAP

Mirrors, let us pass through the glass. The Flight into Egypt. W. H. Auden. *Fr.* For the Time Being; a Christmas Oratorio. OxBA

Mirrors, no one yet has really described. Rainer Maria Rilke, *tr. fr. German by* Christopher Hawthorne. *Fr.* Sonnets to Orpheus. SOTW

Mirrors of Jerusalem, The. Barbara F. Lefcowitz. VWA

Mirth. Beaumont *and* Fletcher. *Fr.* The Knight of the Burning Pestle, II, viii. EIL
   (Laugh and Sing.) TrGrPo

Mirth. Robert Herrick. LiTB

Mirth. Christopher Smart. *Fr.* Hymns for the Amusement of Children, XXV. OxBChV

Mirth and Melancholy. Margaret Cavendish, Duchess of Newcastle. WPE

Mirth, with Thee I Mean to Live. Milton. *See* L'Allegro: Haste thee, nymph, and bring with thee.

Mirthful Lunacy. Thomas Tod Stoddart. *Fr.* The Death-Wake or Lunacy, Lunacy. ONBC

Mis-shapen Time, copesmate of ugly Night. Shakespeare. *Fr.* The Rape of Lucrece. OAEL-1

Mis' Smith. Albert Bigelow Paine. PoLF

Misael, civil servant in the Ministry of Labor, 63 years old. Brazilian Tragedy. Manuel Bandeira, *tr. by* Elizabeth Bishop. ATCBP

Misanthropos, *sel.* Thom Gunn.
   "Serving man, A. Curled my hair." OxBC

Misapprehension. Paul Laurence Dunbar. BPo

Miscellaneous Feelings, *sel.* T'ang Yin, *tr. fr. Chinese by* Jonathan Chaves.
   "Galloping around, north and south." CoBLCP

Miscellaneous Feelings at West Lake, *sels.* Ch'ien Ch'ien-i, *tr. fr. Chinese by* Jonathan Chaves. CoBLCP
   "Desolate poems of chaotic times—could I bear."
   "In hermit's robe, clean and simple."

Miscellaneous Feelings in the Sui Garden. Yüan Mei, *tr. fr. Chinese by* Jonathan Chaves. CoBLCP

Miscellaneous Impressions of T'an-chou, *sel.* Yang Chi, *tr. fr. Chinese by* Jonathan Chaves.
   "Up at the prow, I wash my mouth, dripping water on my robe." CoBLCP

Miscellaneous Poems, *sels.* Wu Chia-chi, *tr. fr. Chinese by* John E. Willis, Jr.. WFTU
   "Beside the road the *wu t'ung* tree." *Fr.* I.
   "I have beaten my sword into an axe." *Fr.* II.

Miscellaneous Poems Composed While Drinking Wine, *sels.* Cheng Chen, *tr. fr. Chinese by* Irving Lo. WFTU
   "Butterflies and dragonflies come in succession." *Fr.* X.
   "Tall willows canopy the thrashing ground with their shade." *Fr.* IV.

Miscellaneous Poems of the Year *Chi-hai, sels.* Kung Tzu-chen, *tr. fr. Chinese by* Shirleen S. Wong. WFTU
   "By chance I composed "Ascending the Clouds," by chance I grew tired of flying." *Fr.* CXXXV.
   I Saw a Professional Juggler by the Roadside and Presented Him with This Poem. *Fr.* XIX.
   "Tending a bare hill takes no small talent." *Fr.* CCII.
   "This trip shall take me through hills to the north and east." *Fr.* IV.
   "View phenomena as void, view phenomena as appearance, such is the ultimate view." *Fr.* CCXXVI.

Miscellaneous Poems on Growing Old, *sels.* Yüan Mei, *tr. fr. Chinese by* Jonathan Chaves. CoBLCP
   "After half a minute of conversation."
   "I write characters in lamplight."
   "Long robes, or short."
   "Old habits it seems cannot be swept away."

Miscellaneous Poems on Living in the Woods, *sel.* Wang Chiu-ssu, *tr. fr. Chinese by* Jonathan Chaves.
   "Total failure—Master Han Shan, A." CoBLCP

Miscellaneous Poems on Mountain Travel, *sels.* Chao Chih-hsin, *tr. fr. Chinese by* James M. Hargett. WFTU
   "Evening clouds suddenly scatter and peaks come into view." *Fr.* II.
   "Where the summit road twists and turns, I'm soon to lose my way." *Fr.* I.

Miscellaneous Poems on Spirit-Valley Temple, *sels.* Wang T'ing-hsiang, *tr. fr. Chinese by* Jonathan Chaves. CoBLCP
   Pagoda of Master Chih, The.
   Wall Painting by Wu Wei, A.

Miscellaneous Poems Written in My Studio on an Autumn Day, *sels.* Chu Yün-ming, *tr. fr. Chinese by* Jonathan Chaves. CoBLCP
   "Bamboo bed, rattan pillow, A."
   "Rumble of thunder brings evening rain, The."

Miscellaneous Poems Written while in Jail. Ch'ien Ch'ien-i, *tr. fr. Chinese by* Jonathan Chaves. CoBLCP

Miscellaneous Songs of the Four Seasons East of the Kamo, *sels.* Nakajima Soin, *tr. fr. Chinese by* Burton Watson. JLIC-2
   "Before Gion Shrine, determined to drive away poverty."
   "No more light from second-story lamps."

Miscellaneous Verses on Living in the Mountains, *sels.* Wen T'ing-shih, *tr. fr. Chinese by* Timothy C. Wong. WFTU
   "I diligently concoct my elixir in a crucible of Himalayan bamboo." *Fr.* I.
   "Out of the floodgate of stone, just closed, a three-foot cataract." *Fr.* II.

Miscellaneous Words on the Lake, *sels.* Tsung Ch'en, *tr. fr. Chinese by* Jonathan Chaves. CoBLCP
   "Glittering, glittering, fireflies in the grass."
   "Night of rain on the autumn river, A."
   "Scorching sun, enough to parch the Yangtze!, A."
   "White-haired man, holding a fishing pole, The."
   "White snow fills the lakeside village."

Miscellany, A. Wang Fu-chih, *tr. fr. Chinese by* Irving Lo. WFTU

Miscellany on the Garden of Autumn Clouds: Peach-Blossom Pond, A. Sung Wan, *tr. fr. Chinese by* Yin-nan Chang. WFTU

Misconception, A. James Russell Lowell. OBAL

Misconceptions. Robert Browning. OBEV

Misdeeming eye! that stoopest to the lure. Lewd Love Is Loss. Robert Southwell. ACP

Mise en Scène. Robert Fitzgerald. NYBP; VGW

Miser. Gordon LeClaire. CaP

Miser. Gloria A. Maxson. *Fr.* Epitaphs. SoTCo

Miserable change now at my end, The. Shakespeare. *Fr.* Antony and Cleopatra, IV, xiii. EBEV

Miserable day, his dog had leapt, A. Riven Doggeries. James Tate. MAYP

Miserere, *sels.* David Gascoyne.
   Ecce Homo. LiTM; OBWP
   Ex Nihilo. GTBS-P

Miserere, My Maker. *Unknown.* NOCV

Misericordia! James Lipton. NBLV
Misericordia. Margaret Mead. PoA
Miserie. George Herbert. PoEL-2
Miserimus. Adah Isaacs Menken. CBWP-1
Miserly Patron, A. *Unknown, tr. fr. Old Irish by* Myles Dillon. AnIL
Misery. John Holmes. NYBP
Misery etcetera. The Day of the Sentry. David St. John. AnAn
Misery is a good thing if misery is spread. Misery. John Holmes. NYBP
Misery is when your. Langston Hughes. ILY
Misery of Jerusalem, The. Bible, *O.T. Fr.* Lamentations, I. AWP
Misery of Mechanics, The. Philip Booth. MAT
Misfortune is as huge/ and heavy as this cold. Snow-Girl. Yunna Moritz, *tr. by* Elaine Feinstein. VWA
Misfortune to have lived not knowing thee. Emerson. Amos Bronson Alcott. AA
Misfortunes Never Come Singly. Harry Graham. FaFP
Misfortunes of Elphin, The, *sels.* Thomas Love Peacock.
  Song of the Four Winds, The. WiR
  War Song of Dinas Vawr, The. AWP; EnRP; FaBoCh; FaPoR; HAP; InvP; NOBE; OAEL-2; OnMSP; PrIm; WaaP; WeW; WiR
Misgivings. Herman Melville. NAAL-1; NOBA; OxBA
Mishka. John Gray. NOBVV
Mishnah says I blind you with my hair, The. The Marriage Wig. Ruth Whitman. IHMS
Misnomer. Eve Merriam. RHPC
Misnomer really, A. With a few exceptions. Squares. Michael Hamburger. FF
Misogynist, The. Jean Morgan. FF
Misplaced Sympathy. Charles Follen Adams. OBAL
Misplacing—Mistaking. On Sir Nathaniel Wraxall the Historian. George Colman, the Younger. FaBoEE
Miss Babian Tending a Bar on the Atlantic Coast ("Miss Babian, in this coast bar"). Fanor Tellez, *tr. fr. Spanish by* Alejandro Marguía. Vol
Miss Bailey's Ghost. George Colman, the Younger. *See* Unfortunate Miss Bailey.
Miss Betty's Singing-Bird. John Winstanley. NOEC
Miss Bitter. N. M. Bodecker. NTCP
Miss Blues'es Child. Langston Hughes. TTTS
Miss Brown, before these walls unquote. Notation in Haste. Elias Lieberman. GoYe
Miss Buss and Miss Beale. *Unknown.* CenHV; FaBoEE
Miss Carney handed us out blank paper and marla. Model School, Inchicore. Thomas Kinsella. CIP
Miss Cho Composes in the Cafeteria. James Tate. SM; WeW
Miss Creighton. Henry Taylor. GrPl
Miss Crustacean. Robert Phillips. GeTw
Miss Dickinson is gone. A New England Sampler. John Malcolm Brinnin. GOA
Miss Ellen Gee of Kew. *Unknown.* FaBoNo
Miss Emily Brittle Sails for India. Sir George Dallas. *Fr.* India Guide, The; or, Journal of a Voyage to the East Indies in 1780. NOEC
Miss Euphalime. John Crowe Ransom. CMoP
Miss Flora McFlimsey, of Madison Square. Nothing to Wear. William Allen Butler. OBAL; PoLF
Miss Foggerty's Cake. *Unknown.* BLPA; NBLV
Miss Gee. W. H. Auden. OxBTC
Miss Geeta. Margaret Reckord. AIW
Miss Grant. Freda Downie. FaBoWP
Miss Helen Slingsby was my maiden aunt. Aunt Helen. T. S. Eliot. AnAmPo; OBAL; PoA
Miss her, Catullus? don't be so inept to rail. Catullus, *tr. by* Celia and Louis Zukofsky. OBVE
Miss Ivy, tell me supmn. Wha Fe Call I.' Valerie Bloom. AIW
Miss J. Hunter Dunn, Miss J. Hunter Dunn. A Subaltern's Love-Song. Sir John Betjeman. BoLoP; HAP; NoAM; NOBL; OxBTC; TwCP
Miss James. A. A. Milne. MoShBr
Miss Jennian Jones. *Unknown.* AmFP
Miss Kilmansegg and Her Precious Leg, *sels.* Thomas Hood.
  "Born in wealth and wealthily nursed." EBVV
  Her Accident. EBVV
  Her Christening. NOBVV
  Her Death. NOBVV
  Her Education. EBVV
  Her Precious Leg. NOBVV
  What Different Dooms Our Birthdays Bring! NAs (Miss Kilmansegg's Birth.) OxBoLi
Miss Lavender. Jon Stallworthy. OxBC
Miss Lemonada. Shauqi Abi Shaqra, *tr. fr. Arabic by* Abdullah al-Udhari. MPAW

Miss Loo. Walter de la Mare. CMoP; OxBTC
Miss M. F. H. E. I. I. Jones. Karla Kuskin. ILY
Miss Marnell. Austin Clarke. IPY
Miss Melerlee. John Wesley Holloway. BANP; PoNe
Miss Millay Says Something Too. Samuel Hoffenstein. BXAP; NBLV
Miss Nancy Ellicott. Cousin Nancy. T. S. Eliot. AnAmPo; OBAL; OxBSP
Miss Norma Jean Pugh. Mary O'Neill. RHPC
Miss One, Two, and Three. *Unknown.* OxNR
Miss Pheasant. Walter de la Mare. FaBoNo
Miss Rafferty wore taffeta. The Private Dining Room. Ogden Nash. NYBP
Miss Ravenel's Conversion, *sel.* John William De Forest.
  National Hymn, A. OPP
Miss Rosie. Lucille Clifton. AmPA; BlSi; CAPP; CNA; NMM; PoBA; TwCP
Miss Summerfest. Susan Firer. TSL
Miss T. Walter de la Mare. CenHV; FaBoBe; GoJo; GrPl; MoShBr; NTCP; OnUR; PDV
Miss Tourist. "Lord Kitchener." PBCV
Miss Twye. Gavin Ewart. ErPo; FiBHP; NOBL
"Miss Ulalume, there are questions that linger here." Abbreviated Interviews with a Few Disgruntled Literary Celebrities. Reed Whittemore. FiBHP
Miss Wagnalls, when I brought you here. The Girl I Took to the Cocktail Party. Trevor Williams. FiBHP
Miss You. David Cory. BLPA; FaBoBe
Missed a last shot. Gary Snyder. *Fr.* Myths and Texts: Hunting. NoBA; NU
Misshapen, black, unlovely to the sight. A Bulb. Richard Kendall Munkittrick. AA
Missing. W. H. Auden. *See* From Scars Where Kestrels Hover.
Missing. A. A. Milne. MoShBr; PDV
Missing. John Pudney. OxBTC
Missing. John Banister Tabb. TrPWD
Missing. *Unknown.* WGRP
Missing Beat. Carolyn M. Rodgers. JB
Missing Dates. William Empson. CMoP; HAP; LiTB; LiTM; MoAB; MoBrPo; MoP; NoAM; NOBE; NoP; OAEL-2; PoE; UnPo
Missing from the map, the abandoned roads. Old Roads. Eiléan Ní Chuilleanáin. CIP
Missing Link, The. Oliver Herford. CenHV
Missing My Daughter. Stephen Spender. GTBS-P
Missing Person, The. Donald Justice. CAPP; NYBP
Missing, Presumed Killed. Pamela Holmes. CN
Missing you. Love. Ted Berrigan. UL
Missing You. Charlotte Zolotow. ILY
Mission. *Unknown.* AmFP
Mission Bay. John Koethe. PoA
Mission of the Flowers, The. Frances E. W. Harper. BlSi
Mission Tire Factory, 1969. Gary Soto. NPGG
Missionaries in the Jungle. Linda Piper. BlSi
Missionary, The. Mrs. Henry Linden. CBWP-4
Missionary at Karnizawa, The. Osman Edwards. *Fr.* Residential Rhymes, II. OBTV
Missionary from the Mau Mau told me, A. A Magus. John Ciardi. MAT
Missionary Hymm. James Burke. TIRV
Missionary Visits Our Church in Scranton, The. Jay Parini. MAYP
Mississippi Blues. *Unknown.* AmFP
Mississippi Born. Pearl Cleage Lomax. CNA
Mississippi Mornings. Tom Dent. UL
Mississippi Sawyer. *Unknown.* AmFP
Missives, fleeting, my lover's only trace. Teika, *tr. fr. Japanese by* Hiroaki Sato. *Fr.* Eighty-four Tanka. FCEI
Missoula Softball Tournament. Richard Hugo. TSL
Missouri Sequence, *sel.* Brian Coffey.
  Nightfall, Midwinter, Missouri. CIP
Missouri Traveller Writes Home: 1830, A. Robert Bly. NePoEA
Misspelled Tail, A. Elizabeth T. Corbett. OBCA
Misspelt scrawl, upon the wall, The. In an Album. James Russell Lowell. AnAmPo; OBAL
"Missy Sick." *Unknown.* CoMu
Mist. Gyoko, *tr. fr. Japanese by* Steven D. Carter. WFTW
Mist. Gill Man. PoSH
Mist. Henry David Thoreau. AnAmPo
Mist. Henry David Thoreau. *See* Week on the Concord and Merrimack Rivers, A: Low-anchored Cloud.
Mist. Andrew Young. PoSH
Mist and All, The. Dixie Willson. FaPON

Mist and cold descend from the hills of Wales.   Evening in Camp.
  Patricia Ledward.   CN; WaP
Mist and fog shroud out the dust of the world.   Sitting Alone in the
  Mountains.   Tami No Kurohito, tr. by Burton Watson.   JLIC-1
Mist and water of Five Lakes, this body not gone home.   Ni Tsan, tr. fr.
  Chinese by Jonathan Chaves.   Fr. Two Poems to the Tune "Hsiao-
  t'iao hung", II.   CoBLCP
Mist clears and the cavities, The.   Derry Morning.   Derek Mahon.
  NOIV
Mist clears away, The.   Emperor Hanazono, tr. by Steven D. Carter.
  WFTW
Mist clings to bank upon bank of willows.   Willow Creek.   Ch'ien
  Ch'ien-yi, tr. fr. Chinese by Irving Lo.   Fr. Two Quatrains on the
  "Awash-in-Springtime Garden."   WFTU
Mist condenses, The.   A Warm Winter Day.   Julian Cooper.   BoNaP
Mist dissolves above the mountains in spring.   Mountain Hawthorns.   Niu
  Hsi-chi, tr. by Lois Fusek.   ATF
Mist Forms.   Carl Sandburg.   CMoP
Mist in the palace willows, The.   Echoing Old Man Mu's Poem.   Wang
  Shih-chen, tr. by Jonathan Chaves.   CoBLCP
Mist in the valley.   Plymouth Women.   Lyn Lifshin.   ER
Mist Maiden, The.   Henrietta Cordelia Ray.   CBWP-3
Mist—no sky.   Mist.   Gill Man.   PoSH
Mist of pain has covered my dour old heart, A.   Valentine Browne.   Egan
  O'Rahilly, tr. by Thomas Kinsella.   NOIV
Mist of snowflakes swirling in the street, A.   Quilt Song.   Mark Vinz.
  GOYP
Mist on the Willows.   Mao Wen-hsi, tr. fr. Chinese by Lois Fusek.   ATF
Mist over Pukehina, The.   Maori Oral Tradition, tr. by E. Shortland.
  WTO
Mist rauk is hanging, The.   John Clare.   NOBVV
Mist. Say/ nothing now.   Density.   Roland Jooris, tr. by Peter Nijmeijer.
  DuIn
Mist stretches without end, The.   Song of the Southern Country.   Li
  Hsün, tr. by Lois Fusek.   ATF
Mist that from the moor arose, A.   Tregardock.   Sir John Betjeman.
  FaBoPP
Mist was driving down the British Channel, A.   The Warden of the
  Cinque Ports.   Longfellow.   AA
Mistah Berrybones, you daid?   William Zaranka.   BXAP
Mistake.   Haim Guri, tr. fr. Hebrew by Warren Bargad and Stanley F.
  Chyet.   IP
Mistake, The.   Sami Mahdi, tr. fr. Arabic by May Jayyusi.   MAP
Mistake, The.   Theodore Roethke.   Fr. Three Epigrams, 2.   NBLV
Mistaken fair, lay Sherlock by.   Verses Written in a Lady's Sherlock
  "Upon Death."   Earl of Chesterfield.   EBEV
  (To a Lady on Reading Sherlock "Upon Death.")   NOEC
Mistaken for a blind man.   Basho, tr. fr. Japanese by Burton Watson.
  Fr. Seventy-six Hokku.   FCEI
Mistakes are dredged up again.   Unalterables.   Arthur Gregor.   NYBP
Mistaking birds for leaves.   Chiyojo, tr. fr. Japanese by Hiroaki Sato.
  Fr. Seventeen Hokku.   FCEI
Mister.   See also Mr.
Mister Alley Cat.   John McGowan.   CRH
Mister Backlash, Mister Backlash.   The Backlash Blues.   Langston
  Hughes.   BPo
Mister Beers.   Hugh Lofting.   FaPON
Mister Francis Beaumont's Letter to Ben Johnson.   Francis Beaumont.
  OBS
Mister Johnson.   Ben Harney.   OBAL
Mister Socrates Snooks, a lord of creation.   Socrates Snooks.   Fitz Hugh
  Ludlow.   BLPA
Mister Williams/ lets youn me move.   Uncle Iv Surveys His Domain from
  His Rocker.   Jonathan Williams.   NBLV; OBAL
Mistletoe.   Walter de la Mare.   SO
Mistletoe, The.   Jack Prelutsky.   RAR
Mistletoe.   Mary E. Tucker.   CBWP-1
Mistletoe Bough, The.   Thomas Haynes Bayly.   BLPA
Mistral.   Barbara Howes.   NYBP
Mistral.   John Koethe.   BAP
Mistral blows, the plane leaves, The.   On the Eve of the Plebiscite.
  Kenneth Rexroth.   NNaP
Mistress.   See also Mrs.
Mistress, The.   Joan Barton.   OxBTC
Mistress, The, sels.   Abraham Cowley.
  Against Hope.   LiTB; MeLP; OBS; SeCV-1
  (On Hope.)   MePo; NOBE
  Change, The.   MeLP; MePo; OBS; SeCP; SeCV-1
  Clad All in White.   SeCV-1
  Platonic[k] Love.   NoP; SeCV-1
  Spring, The.   HAP; JCP; MeLP; OBS

Thief, The.   JCP
Thraldome, The.   SeCV-1
Welcome, The.   BoLoP; SeCV-1
Wish, The.   LiTB; NOBE; NoP; OBEV; OBS; SeCV-1; TrGrPo
Written in Juice of Lem[m]on.   SeCP; SeCV-1
Mistress, The.   Sir William Davenant.   JCP
Mistress; a Song, The.   Earl of Rochester.   EBEV; MePo; NOBE; OBS
Mistress allows an average lover, A.   To His Coy Mistress.   John Flood.
  BXAP; FaBoPa
Mistress, Behold, in This True-Speaking Glass.   Barnabe Barnes.   Fr.
  Parthenophil and Parthenophe, I.   Son
Mistress Comfort.   Elizabeth Gould.   BoTP
Mistress Hale of Beverly.   Lucy Larcom.   PAH
Mistress Margaret Hussey.   John Skelton.   See Garlande [or Garlands] of
  Laurell, The: To Mistress [or Maystres] Margaret Hussey.
Mistress of the Manse, The, sel.   Josiah Gilbert Holland.
  "Rockaby, lullaby, bees in the clover!"   AA
Mistress of the Matchless Mine.   Clyde Robertson
Mistress of Vision, The.   Francis Thompson.   BrPo; CH, abr.
Mistress Penelope Penwick, she.   The Ballad of Sweet P.   Virginia
  Woodward Cloud.   PAH
Mistress, Since You So Much Desire.   Thomas Campion.   OAEL-1
Mistress, The; a Song.   Earl of Rochester.   EBEV; MePo; NOBE; OBS
Mistress Towl.   Unknown.   FaBoNo
Mistress without Compare, A.   At. to Charles d'Orléans.   MeEL
Mistrustful minds be moved.   Sir Thomas Wyatt.   SiPS
Mists above the crimson leaves.   Teika, tr. fr. Japanese by Hiroaki Sato.
  Fr. Eighty-four Tanka.   FCEI
Mists Are Rising Now, The.   Hasye Cooperman.   GoYe
Mists of spring, The.   Taruhito.   Fr. Manyo Shu.   PeBJV
Mists rise over, The.   Yamabe no Akahito, tr. by Kenneth Rexroth.
  HoPM
Mists rise, tree buds swell.   Tsurayuki, tr. fr. Japanese by Burton Watson.
  Fr. Kokin Shu.   FCEI
Mists trailing over them.   Yakamochi.   Fr. Manyo Shu.   FCEI
Misty and dim, a bush in the wilds of Kapa'a.   Kaiama, tr. by N. B.
  Emerson.   WTO
Misty Island, The.   Unknown.   PoSH
Misty-Moisty Was the Morn.   Unknown.   GBP
  (How Do You Do?)   ChTr
Misunderstood.   Lizelia Augusta Jenkins Moorer.   CBWP-3
Mitching.   Michael Smith.   CIP
Mite, The.   Boynton Merrill, Jr.   CRP
Mites go up, The.   Stalagmites and Stalactites.   Unknown.   FaBoUs
Mither's Lament, The.   Sydney Goodsir Smith.   OxBS
Mithraic Emblems, sel.   Roy Campbell.
  To the Sun.   EaLo
Mithras, God of the morning, our trumpets waken the wall!   A Song to
  Mithras.   Kipling.   Fr. Puck of Pook's Hill.   NoAM
Mithridates.   Emerson.   AnAmPo; NOBA
Mitten Song, The.   Marie Louise Allen.   NTCP; RAR
Mittens tucked fat in my armpit.   The Iceball.   William Hathaway.
  NAmP
Mix a Pancake.   Christina Rossetti.   Fr. Sing-Song.   NTCP; RAR
  (Pancake, The.)   BoTP
Mix honey and semen.   Second Position.   Mary Mackey.   Fr.
  Arabesque: Five Poems for Women without Children.   ER
Mixed Feelings.   John Ashbery.   HAP
Mixed Sketches.   Don L. Lee.   BPo; TAP
Mixed-Up School.   X. J. Kennedy.   TDD
Mixer, The.   Louis MacNeice.   FaBoTw
Mizpah.   Julia Aldrich Baker.   BLPA; FaBoBe
MJQ, The.   Joyce Carol Thomas.   CNA
Mme. Argel, awful is your name.   Verses against Argula.   Argula von
  Grumbach, tr. fr. German by Susan L. Cocalis.   Fr. An Answer in
  Verse for Someone Studying in Ingolst.   DMG
Mnemosyne.   Trumbull Stickney.   LiTA; NOBA; OxBA
Mnemosyne Lay in Dust, sels.   Austin Clarke.
  "Maurice was in an Exhibition Hall."   Fr. V.   IPY; PoE
  "Men were looking up."   Fr. III.   IPY
  "One night he heard heart-breaking sound."   Fr. VI.   CIP; CMoP; IPY
  "Past the house where he was got."   Fr. I.   CMoP; IPY; PoE
  "Rememorised, Maurice Devane."   Fr. XVIII.   CMoP, (1970 ed.);
    IPY
  "Straight-jacketing sprang to every lock."   Fr. II.   CMoP; IPY
  "Summer was sauntering by."   Fr. XVII.   IPY
  "Tall, handsome, tweeded Dr. Leeper."   Fr. IV.   IPY
Moanish Lady.   Unknown.   AS, with music
Mobile, immaculate and austere.   Geoffrey Hill.   NePoEA-2
Moby Dick, sel.   Herman Melville.

Ribs and Terrors in the Whale, The. *Fr. ch.* 9. EaLo
  (Whale, The.) TrGrPo
Moccasins of an Old Man, The. Ramona Carden. NOVW
Mock Charon, A. Richard Lovelace. CaPo
Mock Invocation to Genius, A, *sel.* William Woty.
  "I now solicit not the Muses nine." NOEC
Mock-Medicine. *Unknown.* MeEL
Mock On, Mock On, Voltaire, Rousseau. Blake. EnRP; HAP; NAEL-2;
  NAWM-2; NoP; OAEL-2; OBNC; OxBSP; PoE; PoEL-4; PPP; PrIm
  (Scoffers, The.) LiTB; UnPo
Mock Orange. Louise Glück. MAYP; NoAM
Mock Song, A. Richard Lovelace. CaPo
Mock Translation from the Greek. Alan Dugan. PPR
Mock Turtle's Song, The. "Lewis Carroll." *See* Alice's Adventures in
  Wonderland: "Will you walk a little faster?" said a [*or* the] whiting
  to a [*or* the] snail.
Mock up again, summer, the sooty altars. Spectacular Blossom. Allen
  Curnow. ATNZ; PeNZ
Mockado, Fustian, and Motley. John Taylor. *See* Odcomb's Complaint:
  Sweet semi-circled Cynthia played at maw.
Mocking-Bird, The. Ednah Proctor Clarke. AA
Mocking Bird, The. Paul Hamilton Hayne. AnAmPo
Mocking Bird, The. Sidney Lanier. AA
Mocking-Bird, The. Frank Lebby Stanton. AA
Mocking-Bird, The. Henry Jerome Stockard. AA
Mocking Bird, The. *Unknown.* AmFP
Mocking-bird on a branch, A. Wyncote, Pennsylvania: A Gloss.
  Thomas Kinsella. NOIV
Mocking Fairy, The. Walter de la Mare. MoBrPo; MoShBr
Mocking Myself. Chao Yi, *tr. fr. Chinese by* Shirleen S. Wong. WFTU
Mocking Myself. Ku Yen-wu, *tr. fr. Chinese by* J. P. Seaton. WFTU
Mocking Song against Qaqortingneq. Piuvkaq, *tr. fr. Eskimo.* WTO
Mocking Spectacles. Yüan Mei, *tr. fr. Chinese by* Anthony C. Yu.
  WFTU
Mockingbird, The. Randall Jarrell. DuDa; NYBP; RFM
Mockingbird of Mockingbirds, The. Denise Levertov. ER
Mode Z. Barrett Watten. LP
Model Church, The. John H. Yates. PWR
Model for the Laureate, A. W. B. Yeats. CMoP
Model School, Inchicore. Thomas Kinsella. CIP
Model Sermon, A. *Unknown.* FaBoEE
Model 3/ Melpomene. Friederike Mayröcker, *tr. fr. German by* Beth
  Bjorklund. CoAuP
Model yourself upon the hill. To a Nude Walking. Raymond Radiguet,
  tr. by William Jay Smith. CT
Moderation. Robert Herrick. FaBoEE
Moderation. Christopher Smart. *Fr.* Hymns for the Amusement of
  Children, IX. NOCV
Modern Baby, The. William Croswell Doane. BLPA
Modern Critics. Samuel Taylor Coleridge. FaBoEE
Modern Dragon, A. Rowena Bastin Bennett. PDV; RAR
Modern Fable, The. Nishiwaki Junzaburo, *tr. fr. Japanese by* Hiroaki
  Sato. FCEI
Modern Fine Gentleman, The, *sel.* Soame Jenyns.
  "Just broke from school, pert, impudent, and raw." OBSV
Modern Fine Lady, The, *sel.* Soame Jenyns. NOEC
  "For love no time has she, or inclination." OBSV
Modern Hiawatha, The. George A. Strong. *Fr.* The Song of
  Milkanwatha. FaBoPa; FaFP; FaPON; FiBHP; MoShBr; NA; Par;
  RHPC
Modern Jonas, The. *Unknown.* PAH
Modern Kabbalist. Marcia Falk. VWA
Modern Love. Keats. OBNC
Modern Love, *sels.* George Meredith.
  "Along the garden terrace, under which." *Fr.* XXXVII. NOBVV
  "Am I failing? For no longer can I cast." *Fr.* XXIX. GBL
  "At dinner, she is hostess, I am host." *Fr.* XVII. HeIP; NOBVV;
  NoP; PoE
  (At Dinner, She Is Hostess.) Son
  "But where began the change; and what's my crime?" *Fr.* X. PoEL-5
  "By this he knew she wept with waking eyes." *Fr.* I. EnLoPo; HeIP;
  NAEL-2; NOBVV; NoP; OAEL-2; PoE; PoEL-5; Son
  (End of Love, The.) HoPM
  "He felt the wild beast in him betweenwhiles." *Fr.* IX. NOBVV
  "He found her by the ocean's moaning verge." *Fr.* XLIX. NoP;
  OAEL-2
  "Here Jack and Tom are paired with Moll and Meg." *Fr.* XVIII.
  InvP; PoEL-5
  "I am to follow her. There is much grace." *Fr.* XLII. NAEL-2;
  NOBVV
  "I play for seasons, not eternities!" *Fr.* XIII. OBNC

"I think she sleeps: it must be sleep, when low." *Fr.* XV.
  NAEL-2
"In our old shipwrecked days there was an hour." *Fr.* XVI. BoLoP;
  NOBVV
  (Love Dies.) SeCePo
"It chanced his lips did meet her forehead cool." *Fr.* VI. NOBVV
"It is no vulgar nature I have wived." *Fr.* XXXV. NAEL-2
"It is the season of the sweet wild rose." *Fr.* XLV. GBL; PoEL-5
"Madam would speak with me. So, now it comes." *Fr.* XXXIV.
  NOBVV
"Mark where the pressing wind shoots javelin-like." *Fr.* XLIII.
  EnLoPo; GBL; NOBE; OBNC; PoEL-5; TEP
  (Love's Grave.) OBEV
"Message from her set his brain aflame, A." *Fr.* V. NOBVV
"My lady unto Madam makes her bow." *Fr.* XXXVI. NOBVV
"Not solely that the future she destroys." *Fr.* XII. GBL; TEP
"Out in the yellow meadows, where the bee." *Fr.* XI. GBL
"She issues radiant from her dressing-room." *Fr.* VII. NOBVV
"Their sense is with their senses all mixed in." *Fr.* XLVIII. NAEL-2;
  NoP; OAEL-2
"This golden head has wit in it. I live." *Fr.* XXXI. NOBVV
This Was the Woman. *Fr.* III. Son
"Thus piteously Love closed what he begat." *Fr.* L. EBEV; EnLoPo;
  GTBS-P; HAP; NOBE; NOBVV; NoP; OAEL-2; OBNC; PoE;
  PoEL-5; SeCePo; Son; TrGrPo
  (Dusty Answer, A.) SeCePo
"'Tis Christmas weather, and a country house." *Fr.* XXIII. NAEL-2;
  NOBVV
"We saw the swallows gathering in the sky." *Fr.* XLVII. EnLoPo;
  GTBS-P; Mes; NOBE; NOBVV; OAEL-2; OBNC
  (We Saw the Swallows.) ELP
"We three are on the cedar-shadowed lawn." *Fr.* XXI. NOBVV
"What are we first? First, animals; and next." *Fr.* XXX. GBL; HAP;
  NoP; PoEL-5
"You like not that French novel? Tell me why." *Fr.* XXV.
  NOBVV
Modern Love Songs. *Unknown, tr. fr. Somali.* TTY, *tr. by* B. W.
  Andrzjewski *and* I. M. Lewis; WTO, *tr. by* B. W. Andrzejewski *and*
  M. Laurence.
Modern Major-General, The. W. S. Gilbert. *See* Pirates of Penzance,
  The: I Am the Very Model [*or* Pattern] of a Modern Major-General.
Modern malady of love is nerves, The. Nerves. Arthur Symons. BrPo;
  FaBoTw
Modern on the Surface. Nia Francisco. HATNAP
Modern Poem in Response to "Wild Geese on the Lake" by Shen Yüeh, A.
  Li Chien, *tr. fr. Chinese by* Irving Lo. WFTU
Modern Poetry. Anita Skeen. IHMS
Modern Romans, The. Charles Frederick Johnson. AA
Modern Secrets. Shirley Lim. UAS
Modern Theologian, A. Paul Ramsey. *Fr.* Three Epigrams. CRP
Modern Woman, A. Marie Janitschek, *tr. fr. German by* Susan L.
  Cocalis *and* Gerlinde Geiger. DMG
Modern World, The. Colin Ellis. FaBoEE
Modernists, The. Tom MacInnes. CaP
Modes of Pleasure. Thom Gunn. PeHV; PPP
Modes of the Court, The. John Gay. *Fr.* The Beggar's Opera, III, iv.
  HeIP
Modes of Vallejo Street, San Diego, Los Angeles, The, *sels.* Hugh
  Seidman. UnPo
  "He imagines her." *Fr.* 3.
  "He knows he must explain this." *Fr.* 9.
Modest and needy is my destiny in thy world, O God! Kibbutz Sabbath.
  Levi ben Amittai, *tr. by* Simon Halkin. EaLo
Modest front of this small floore, The. An Epitaph upon Mr. Ashton, a
  Conformable Citizen. Richard Crashaw. OBS
Modest Wit, A. Selleck Osborn. BLPA
Modestly we violets cower. Violets. P. A. Ropes. BoTP
Modesty. Aaron Hill. OxBSP
Modo and Alciphron. Sylvia Townsend Warner. MoBrPo
Moenkopi. Arthur Sze. BrSi
Mog the Brunette. *Unknown.* CoMu
Mogami River has poured the hot sun into the sea, The. Basho, *tr. fr.*
  Japanese by Burton Watson. *Fr.* Seventy-six Hokku. FCEI
Mogami's tea-house. *Unknown, tr. by* Geoffrey Bownas *and* Anthony
  Thwaite. PeBJV
Moguls and Monks. Lewis MacAdams. UL
Mohajir. Fahmida Riaz, *tr. fr. Urdu by* Mahmood Jamal. PBMUP
Mohammed and Seid. Harrison Smith Morris. AA
Mohammed Ibrahim Speaks. Martha Beidler. FF
Mohini Chatterjee. W. B. Yeats. NoAM

Móir Hatching. Nuala Ni Dhomhnaill, *tr. fr. Gaelic* by Joan Keefe. OV

Moiré. Michael McClure. EAS

Moishe Leib stood up. Just Because. Moyshe-Leyb Halpern, *tr.* by Ruth Whitman. VWA

Moist Moon People. Carl Sandburg. MoAmPo

Moist [*or* Moyst] with one drop of thy blood, my dry soul[e]. Resurrection. John Donne. *Fr.* La Corona. OBS; Son

Moistened osier of the hoary willow, The. The Coracle. Lucan, *tr.* by Sir Walter Ralegh. ChTr

Mokau roars, Tamaki roars. Lament for Tawhiao. *Unknown, tr.* by Margaret Orbell. PeNZ

Molasses River. Richard Kendall Munkittrick. OBCA

Mold-brown, moss-green, broad trunk of my wake, The. Rowing Early. John Peck. SM

Mole, The. Dennis Schmitz. AmPA

Mole and the Eagle, The. Sarah Josepha Hale. OBCA

Mole Catcher. Edmund Blunden. OBMV

Mole is blind, and under ground, The. The Mole and the Eagle. Sarah Josepha Hale. OBCA

Mole makes his pole redhot. Alonzo Gonzales , *tr.* by Jerome Rothenberg. STP

Mole who knows. Back to Base. Jenny Joseph. BrRo

Molecatcher. Albert D. Mackie. GoTS

Moles. William Stafford. NYBP; RFM

Moll-in-the-wad and I fell out. *Unknown.* OxNR

Mollis Abuti. Swift. ChTr

Molly Means. Margaret Abigail Walker. AmNP; BlSi; NMM; PoNe

Molly Mog; or, The Fair Maid of the Inn. John Gay. CoMu

Molly Moor. George Farewell. NOEC

Molly of the North Country. *Unknown.* OBET

Molly Pitcher. Laura E. Richards. PAH

Molly Pitcher. Kate Brownlee Sherwood. PAH

Molokai. Tomas Tranströmer, *tr. fr. Swedish* by Samuel Charters. AnAn

Moly. Thom Gunn. HAP; MoP; NoAM; PrIm

Mom says she won't; we'll have to clean them, though. Cleaning the Fish. Robert Pack. SM

Moment. Robert Creeley. CAPP

Moment, The. Theodore Roethke. NYBP

Moment, The. William Stafford. NNaP

Moment. Zoltán Zelk, *tr. fr. Hungarian* by Daniel Hoffman. MHuP

Moment after the Rain. Jeannie Ebner, *tr. fr. German* by Beth Bjorklund. CoAuP

Moment Ago, A. David Avidan, *tr. fr. Hebrew* by Warren Bargad *and* Stanley F. Chyet. IP

Moment at the Louvre, A. Dan Pagis, *tr. fr. Hebrew* by Bernhard Frank. MHeP

Moment by Moment. Daniel W. Whittle. BLRP

Moment I saw the strangers at the door, The. Lot's Wife. Celia Gilbert. ER

Moment in Summer, A. Charlotte Zolotow. RHPC

Moment in the morning, ere the cares of day begin, A. To Begin the Day. *Unknown.* BLRP

Moment is what moves us, after all, The. A Discussion of the Vicissitudes of History under a Pine Tree. Katha Pollitt. MAYP

Moment Musical in Assynt. Norman MacCaig. PoSH

Moment of Calm. Aimé Césaire, *tr. fr. French* by Michael Benedikt. POS

Moment of desire, The! the moment of desire! the virgin. Blake. *Fr.* Visions. ErPo

Moment of My Father's Death, The. Sharon Olds. ER

Moment of silence first, then there it is, A. The Dial Tone. Howard Nemerov. NYBP

Moment of the Rose, The. Dunstan Thompson. LiTA

Moment of Truth. Rowley Habib. PeNZ

Moment of War, A. Laurie Lee. OBWP

Moment Please, A. Samuel Allen. AmNP; IDB; PoBA

Moment the wild swallows like a flight, A. A Thunderstorm. Archibald Lampman. CaP; NOBC

Moment to/ moment the/ body seems. Time. Robert Creeley. LCAP

Momentariness. Stefan Brecht. BAP

Moments. Ivor Gurney. OxBSP

Moments. Marcel Schwob, *tr. fr. French* by William Brown Meloney. TrJP

Moments He Remembers, The. Mark Van Doren. NYBP

Moments of Fullfillment—Writing Down Miscellaneous, *sels.* Yüan Mei, *tr. fr. Chinese* by Jonathan Chaves. CoBLCP
  "As I grow old, and weaker grow my eyes."
  "Do not say that time once gone can never be returned!"
  "My whole family floats out on the lake."
  "Three magnolias, identical."

Moments of happiness, The. Mohammad Taqi Mir, *tr.* by Ahmed Ali. GoT

Moments-of-Past-Happiness Quilt, The. Kathleen Spivack. ER

Moments of Vision. Thomas Hardy. OAEL-2

Momist. Amy Groesbeck. GoYe

Momma Momma Momma. Getting Down to Get Over. June Jordan. ER; TAP

Momma said I had eyes like a hawk. Trading Post—Winslow, Arizona. Terri Meyette. GOS

Mommy/ Daddy/ quick! The Mistletoe. Jack Prelutsky. RAR

"Mommy, take me home. I'm a changed boy!" Ontogeny. Jarold Ramsey. NIP

Mom's Homecooked Trees. Michael Stephens. UL

Momus' Song to Mars. Dryden. *Fr.* The Secular Masque. OxBSP

Mon cher maitre, could even you have mastered. Howard's Way. Richard Howard. PPR

Mon dieu mon dieu. H. C. Artmann, *tr.* by Beth Bjorklund. CoAuP

Mon-Goos, The. Oliver Herford. *Fr.* Child's Natural History. AA

Mon in the mone stond and strit. The Man in the Moon. *Unknown.* MeEL; PYC

Mon that wist for raine, The. Amedie Eva List. BXAP

Mona Leo. Bob McKenty. SoTCo

Mona Lisa, A. Angelina Weld Grimké. BlSi; CDC

Mona Lisa. Walter Pater. OBMV

Monadnock, The. John Gould Fletcher. PoA

Monangamba. Antonio Jacinto, *tr. fr. Portuguese.* TTY, *tr.* by Alan Ryder; WMBCH, *tr.* by Margaret Dickinson

Monarch oak, the patriarch of the trees, The. The Oak. Dryden. OHIP

Monarch of Gods and Dæmons, and all Spirits. Shelley. *Fr.* Prometheus Unbound, I. EnRP; FiP, *abr.*; NAEL-2; OAEL-2

Monarch of the Sea. George Starbuck. OBAL

Monarch sat on his judgment-seat, The. The Fay's Sentence. Joseph Rodman Drake. *Fr.* The Culprit Fay. AA

Monarche, The, *sel.* Sir David Lindsay.
  After the Flood. OxBS

Monarchs, the butterflies, are commanded, The. Alan Dugan. AnAn

Monasteries Lift Gold Domes, The. Yocheved Bat-Miriam, *tr. fr. Hebrew* by Robert Friend. VWA

Monastery, The, *sels.* Sir Walter Scott.
  Border Ballad. *Fr. ch.* 25. GN
  (Blue Bonnets over the Border.) OxBS
  (Border March.) EnRP
  Sir Walter Scott's Tribute. *Fr. ch.* 12. WBLP
  (Bible, The.) BLRP

Monastery on Athos. Richmond Lattimore. EyDe

Monday. William Stafford. NYBP

Monday Christine Street. Guillaume Apollinaire, *tr. fr. French* by Michael Benedikt. POS

Monday I found a boot. Beachcomber. George Mackay Brown. OxBC

Monday, Monday. David Trinidad. UL

Monday's child is fair of face. Mother Goose. BLPA; BLPL; BoTP; FaBoBe; FaBoCh; MoShBr; NBLV; OxNR; PYC

Mondays sweating the flat smell. Days through Starch and Bluing. Alice Fulton. GOYP

Monet: "Les Nymphéas." W. D. Snodgrass. CoAP

Monet never knew. Monet's Lilies Shuddering. Lawrence Ferlinghetti. CAPP

Monet Refuses the Operation. Lisel Mueller. FYAP

Monet's Lilies Shuddering. Lawrence Ferlinghetti. CAPP

Monet's "Waterlilies." Robert Hayden. CAPP

Money. Richard Armour. FaFP; NBLV

Money. W. H. Davies. OBEV; OBMV

Money. Howard Nemerov. OxBC; WeW

Money. C. H. Sisson. OxBSP

Money. *Unknown.* AS

Money. Yüan Mei, *tr. fr. Chinese* by J. P. Seaton. WFTU

Money and a Friend. *Unknown.* BLPA

Money burns the pocket, pocket hurts. Seventh Street. Jean Toomer. NAAL-2

Money Cry, The. Peter Davison. FYAP

Money Gets the Mastery. Robert Herrick. CaPo

Money is the rich. In the Blood. Gerald Costanzo. SoTCo

Money Is What Matters. *Unknown.* MeEL

Money Isn't Everything! Oscar Hammerstein II. OBAL

Money Makes the Mirth. Robert Herrick. CaPo

Money men collect in high rise, The. Thumbing Old Magazines. Gerald Vizenor. VoR

Money! Money! *Yoruba Oral Tradition, tr.* by O. Ogunba. WTO

Money, thou bane of bliss and source of woe. Avarice. George. FaBoRV; LiTB

Money thou ow'st me; prithee fix a day. Upon Bunce: Epigram. Robert Herrick. CaPo

Money was once well known, like a townhall or the sky. Behaviour of Money. Bernard Spencer. LiTB

Moneyless Men, The. Henry T. Stanton. BLPA

Mongol Libation. Victor Segalen, *tr. fr. French by* Nathaniel Tarn. RHTwFP

Mongoloid boy is astounded, The. In the Dome Car of the "Canadian." Sid Marty. NOBC

Mongoloid Child Handling Shells on the Beach, A. Richard Snyder. InPK

Mongols Are Coming, The. Rai San'yo, *tr. fr. Chinese by* Burton Watson. JLIC-2

'Mongst all the hard names that denote reproach. Burnet's Character. *Unknown.* APAS

Mongst all the Palaces in Hells command. Sospetto d'Herode. Giovanni Battista Marino, *tr. fr. Italian by* Richard Crashaw. *Fr.* La Strage degli Innocenti, II. SeCV-1

Monish. Isaac Leibush Peretz, *tr. fr. Yiddish by* Seymour Levitan. PeBMYV

Monk, The. Blake. *Fr.* Jerusalem. EnRP

Monk, The. Cheng Hsieh, *tr. fr. Chinese by* Jan W. Walls. WFTU

Monk and His Pet Cat, The. *Unknown, tr. fr. Old Irish.* CH

Monk carries a pine, The. Outdoor Collections. Wang Jun-hua, *tr. by* Dominic Cheung. IFON

Monk from Etsu Returning to a Hermitage. Enkei, *tr. fr. Chinese by* Lucien Stryk *and* Takashi Ikemoto. ZPCJ

Monk in the Kitchen, The. Anna Hempstead Branch. MoAmPo

Monk Kudo Asked Me, 'What's Your Haikai Eye Like?' Onitsura, *tr. fr. Japanese by* Hiroaki Sato. *Fr.* Twenty-three Hokku. FCEI

Monk of Casal-Maggiore, The (The Sicilian's Tale). Longfellow. *Fr.* Tales of a Wayside Inn, *pt.* III. AmPP; OxBA

Monk of Great Renown, The. *Unknown.* CoMu

Monk sat in his den, The. The Weak Monk. Stevie Smith. BoWoP; FaBoTw

Monk, step further off. *Unknown.* NOIV

Monk there was, a monk of mastery, A. Chaucer. *See* Canterbury Tales, The: Prologue.

Monkey, The. Cees Buddingh', *tr. fr. Dutch by* James S. Holmes. DuIn

Monkey, The. Mary Howitt. GN

Monkey. Josephine Miles. LiTM

Monkey. Shotetsu, *tr. fr. Japanese by* Steven D. Carter. WFTW

Monkey—a hairless body, A. Night in Manhattan. Moyshe-Leyb Halpern, *tr. by* Benjamin *and* Barbara Harshav. AYP

Monkey cries out, A. Monkey. Shotetsu, *tr by* Steven D Carter. WFTW

Monkey curled his tail about, The. Before the Monkey's Cage. Edna Becker. RAR

Monkey Difference. Barbara Howes. AnAn

Monkey, lap-dog, parrot, and her Grace, The. Sir Charles Hanbury Williams. *Fr.* Isabella; or, The Morning. NOEC

Monkey, little merry fellow. The Monkey. Mary Howitt. GN

Monkey married the Baboon's sister, The. The Monkey's Wedding. *Unknown.* AS, *with music;* BLPA, *with music;* NA, *with music*

Monkeyland. Sándor Weöres, *tr. fr. Hungarian by* Edwin Morgan. MHuP; RB

Monkeys. Frank A. Collymore. PBCV

Monkeys. Padraic Colum. Mes; OxBTC

Monkeys, The. Marianne Moore. CMoP; LiTA; NOBA; OxBA

Monkeys and the Crocodile, The. Laura E. Richards. FaPON

Monkey's Glue, The. Goldwin Goldsmith. NA

Monkeys in a forest. Where. Walter de la Mare. NYBP

Monkeys on Mt. Hiei. Edith Marcombe Shiffert. WPE

Monkey's Wedding, The. *Unknown.* AS, *with music;* BLPA, *with music;* NA, *with music*

Monkeys winked too much and were afraid of snakes, The. The Monkeys. Marianne Moore. LiTA; OxBA

Monks at Ards, The. Patrick Maybin. NeIP

Monks of Ely, The. *Unknown.* ACP

Monk's season has come, The. January. Nishiwaki Junzaburo, *tr. by* Hiroaki Sato. FCEI

Monna Innominata, *sels.* Christina Rossetti.
I Wish I Could Remember. Son
(First Day, The.) BLPL; BoLoP; FaBoBe; GBL
Love Me, for I Love You. *Fr.* VII. Son
"Many in aftertimes will say of you." OBNC
"Youth gone, and beauty gone if ever there." GBL; OBNC; Son

Monody. Herman Melville. LiTA; NAAL-1; OxBSP; PoE; PoEL-5

Monody on a Century. Earle Birney. CaP

Monogamy, *sel.* Gerald Gould.

Monody to the Sound of Zithers. Kay Boyle. PoA
"You were young—but that was scarcely to your credit." OxBTC

Monogram 4. Martina Werner, *tr. fr. German by* Rosemarie Waldrop. BoWoP

Monogram 29. Martina Werner, *tr. fr. German by* Rosemarie Waldrop. BoWoP

Monogram 23. Martina Werner, *tr. fr. German by* Rosemarie Waldrop. BoWoP

Monologue, A. Clark Coolidge. BAP

Monologue. Hone Tuwhare. PeNZ

Monologue of a Dying Beast. Mark Ameen. GLP

Monologue of the Inhabitant. Washington Delgado, *tr. fr. Spanish by* David Tipton. Per

Monostichs de la Guerre de Petite-Sparte, *sel.* Ian Hamilton Finlay. "Classical warfare." PoPo

Monserrat. William Edwin Collin. CaP

Monsieur AA, Antiphilosopher. Tristan Tzara, *tr. fr. French by* Richard Howard. RHTwFP

Monsieur Etienne de Silhouette. Some Frenchmen. John Updike. FaBoCo; NBLV

Monsieur Ezra Pound croit que. Another Canto. John Bingham Morton. FaBoPa

Monsieur Gaston. A. M. Klein. MoCV

Monsoon. Kenneth Slade Alling. NePoAm

Monsoon. David Wevill. NYBP

Monsoon History. Shirley Lim. UAS

Monster/ sleeps, A. Cloud Shadow. Lilian Moore. TDD

Monster, The. Greg Kuzma. AmPA

Monster, The. Edward Lowbury. AmMo

Monster, The. David Lunde. BWV

Monster, The. Henry Rago. PoA

Monster Alphabet. Robert Fisher. AmMo

Monster has escaped from the dungeon, The. Frankenstein. Edward Field. FF

Monster, in a course of vice grown old, A. The Monument. Samuel Wesley. OxBSP

Monster-Mender, The. René Daumal, *tr. fr. French by* Michael Benedikt. POS

Monster rests upon my roof, A. The Chimera. Alfred Mombert, *tr. by* Erna Baber Rosenfeld. VWA

Monster taught, A/ To come to hand. Song of a Train. John Davidson. BrPo

Monster who lives in Loch Ness, A. The Monster. Edward Lowbury. AmMo

Monstering horror swallows, A. Thanksgiving (1956). E. E. Cummings. FaBoPV

Monstrous Regiment, The. Alice Coats. CN

Monstrous, uncouth, their vast leaves amply spread. Palm House, Botanic Gardens. George Hetherington. NeIP

Mont Blanc. Shelley. EnRP; ErNP; InPS; NAEL-2; NIP; NoP; OAEL-2; OBTV; TEP

Montague Michael. *Unknown.* CRH

Montalbert, *sel.* Charlotte Smith.
"Swift fleet the billowy clouds along the sky." BoWoP; WPE

Montana Eclogue. William Stafford. NYBP

Montana Fifty Years Ago. J. V. Cunningham. Prf

Montana Pastoral. J. V. Cunningham. MAT; MoAmPo; PrIm; VGW

Montana Ranch Abandoned. Richard Hugo. CAPP

Montana Remembered from Albuquerque; 1982. Ron Rogers. STE

Montana Wives. Gwendolen Haste. AmFN

Montanus' Sonnet. Thomas Lodge. *Fr.* Rosalynde; or Euphues' Golden Legacy. PoEL-2

Montcalm and Wolfe. *Unknown.* AmFP

Monte Albán. Joseph Stroud. NPGG

Monte Cassino 1945. Marion Coleman. CN

Montefiore. Ambrose Bierce. AA

Montefiore in Vilna. Leyzer Volf, *tr. fr. Yiddish by* Robert Friend. PeBMYV

Monterey. Charles Fenno Hoffman. AA; AnAmPo; FaBoBe; PAH

Monterrey Sun. Alfonso Reyes, *tr. fr. Spanish by* Samuel Beckett. MexPo

Montgomery. Sam Cornish. CNA; PoBA; Psk

Montgomery at Quebec. Clinton Scollard. PAH

Month is amber, The. October. John Updike. PDV

Month of few days. Lorna Slope. Andrea Zanzotto, *tr. by* Lawrence R. Smith. NItP

Month of January. Frankie Armstrong. BrRo

Month of June: 13½, The. Sharon Olds. BLA
Month of leaves. June. Irene F. Pawsey. BoTP
Month of May, The. Beaumont *and* Fletcher. *Fr.* The Knight of the
　　Burning Pestle, IV, v. ChTr
Month of the drowned dog, The. After long rain the land. November.
　　Ted Hughes. CMoP; GTBS-P; NePoEA-2; NoP
Month or twain to live on honeycomb, A. Before Parting. Swinburne.
　　NOBVV
Month when my cord to the womb was cut, yet almost hot. Sereno.
　　Sydney Lea. BLA
Months, The. Chaucer. OxBLMV
Months, The. Sara Coleridge. *See* January brings the snow.
Months, The. Christina Rossetti. FaPON
Months, The. *Unknown.* ChTr
Months after the Muse. The Illustration—a Footnote. Denise Levertov.
　　PoA
Months in the house have steamed them open. Milkweed Pods in Winter.
　　Lisel Mueller. KS
Month's last day, no moon, The. Basho, *tr. fr. Japanese by* Burton
　　Watson. *Fr.* Seventy-six Hokku. FCEI
Months of the Year, The. Richard Grafton. FaBoUs
Months of the Year, The. *Unknown.* FaBoUs
Monticello. Robert Hass. AnAn
Monticello. May Sarton. GOA
Montjuich. Philip Levine. AnAn
Montreal. A. M. Klein. CaP; MoCV; OBCV
Montrose to His Mistress, *sel.* James Graham, Marquess of Montrose.
　　"My dear and only Love, I pray." OxBS
Monument. Milton Acorn. NeAC
Monument, The. Elizabeth Bishop. HCAP; LiTA; NoAM; NOBA
Monument, A. Charles Madge. FaBoMo
Monument. A. M. Sullivan. GoYe
Monument, The. Samuel Wesley. OxBSP
Monument and the Shrine, The. John Logan. LCAP
Monument Mountain. Bryant. BeLS
Monument of Cleita, The. Edward Cracroft Lefroy, *after the Greek of*
　　Theocritus. *Fr.* Echoes from Theocritus, XXIX. AWP
Monument speaks correctly, The. Position. Barrett Watten. IAT
Monument to Pushkin. Joseph Brodsky, *tr. fr. Russian by* Dimitry
　　Pospielovsky *and* Keith Bosley. VWA
Monumental Memorial of Marine Mercy, A. Richard Steere. SCAP
Monuments. John Hollander. KS
Monuments for a Friendly Girl at a Tenth Grade Party. William Stafford.
　　NoAM
Monuments of Hiroshima, The. D. J. Enright. OxBSP
Monumentum Aere, Etc. Ezra Pound. NOBA
Many one talks [*or* speaks] o the grass, the grass. C *vers., st.* Willie
　　and Earl Richard's Daughter. *Unknown.* ESPB
Moo! Robert Hillyer. OBAL
Moo-Cow-Moo, The. Edmund Vance Cooke. FaFP; MoShBr
Moochie ("Moochie likes to keep on playing"). Eloise Greenfield. NTCP
Mood. David Gascoyne. FL
Mood, A. Winifred Howells. AA
Mood, The. Quandra Prettyman. PoBA
Mood, A. Amélie Rives. AA
Mood Apart, A. Robert Frost. OxBSP
Mood comes on—I want to cross Hsi-ling, The. Tao-chi, *tr. by* Jonathan
　　Chaves. CoBLCP
Mood Indigo. Ira Sadoff. BLA
Moods. Leib Kwitko, *tr. fr. Yiddish by* Joseph Leftwich. TrJP
Moods, The. W. B. Yeats. CTC
Moods of Rain. Vernon Scannell. BoNaP
Mookie and Hubie and Strawberry. Let's Go, Mets. Lillian Morrison.
　　ASP
"Mooly cow, mooly cow, home from the wood." The Cow-Boy's Song.
　　Anna Maria Wells. OBCA
Moom moom. Troll Chanting. Anselm Hollo. *Fr.* Out of the
　　"Kalevala." WSC
Moon, The. Emily Dickinson. BoTP
Moon/ Have you met my mother? Karla Kuskin. ILY
Moon. Antonin Artaud, *tr. fr. French by* Michael Benedikt. POS
Moon, The. Charles Best. *See* Sonnet of the Moon, A.
Moon, The. Robert Creeley. VGW
Moon, The. W. H. Davies. BrPo; MoBrPo
Moon, The. Gyoko, *tr. fr. Japanese by* Steven D. Carter. WFTW
Moon. Frances Horovitz. BrRo
Moon, The. Howard Moss. EOEF
Moon, The. Henry Rowe. OBEV
Moon, The. Shelley. *See* Waning Moon, The.

Moon. William Jay Smith. CRH; PDV
Moon, The. Robert Louis Stevenson. PWR
Moon, The. Tamesada, *tr. fr. Japanese by* Steven D. Carter. WFTW
Moon. Derek Walcott. MoP
Moon, a sweeping scimitar, dipped in the stormy straits, The. Winged
　　Man. Stephen Vincent Benét. MoAmPo
Moon about to set, The. Buson, *tr. fr. Japanese by* Hiroaki Sato. *Fr.*
　　Eighty-seven Hokku. FCEI
Moon above the clouds doesn't look like the moon, The. Lady Izumi, *tr.
　　fr. Japanese by* Hiroaki Sato. *Fr.* Fifty-one Tanka. FCEI
Moon above the milky field, The. Night-Piece. Léonie Adams. MoAB;
　　MoAmPo
Moon after rain—who's that! Buson, *tr. by* Hiroaki Sato. FCEI
Moon and a Cloud, The. W. H. Davies. RB
Moon and Candle-light. William Renton. NOBVV
Moon and seven Pleiades have set, The. Alone. Sappho, *tr. by* William
　　Ellery Leonard. AWP
Moon and the Night and the Men, The. John Berryman. CoAP; VGW;
　　WaP
Moon and the Nightingale, The. Milton. *See* Paradise Lost:
　　Now came still evening on, and twilight gray.
Moon and the Salt Flats, The. Mary Di Michele. NOBC
Moon and the Yew Tree, The. Sylvia Plath. CoAP; FaBoMo; FaBoWP;
　　NaP; NYBP; PPP; VGW; WPE; WPOW
Moon appears from the mouth of the sheer bluff, The. Aboard a Boat at
　　Night, Drinking with My Wife. Mei Yao-ch'en, *tr. by* Burton
　　Watson. CoBCP
Moon as Medusa. Vinnie-Marie D'Ambrosio. IHMS
Moon as your guide, The. Basho, *tr. fr. Japanese by* Burton Watson.
　　Fr. Seventy-six Hokku. FCEI
Moon at evening, The. Emperor Kogon, *tr. by* Steven D. Carter.
　　WFTW
Moon at heaven's center. Buson, *tr. fr. Japanese by* Hiroaki Sato. *Fr.*
　　Eighty-seven Hokku. FCEI
Moon at the Fortified Pass, The. Li Po, *tr. fr. Chinese by* Witter Bynner
　　and Kiang Kang-hu. WaaP
Moon at the full. Europe has burst its banks. The Inundation. Howard
　　Sergeant. EAS
Moon at Three A.M. Lance Henson. CDW
Moon beams and yams. Rapping Along with Ronda Davis. James
　　Cunningham. JB
Moon behind High Tranquil Leaves, The. Robert Nichols. OBMV
Moon behind the Hill, The. *Unknown.* WTO
Moon Bird, The. V. C. Vickers. AmMo
Moon Boat. Charlotte Pomerantz. RAR
Moon boat floats by misty shores. Singing of the Moon. Emperor
　　Mommu, *tr. by* Burton Watson. JLIC-1
Moon-Bone Song [*or* Cycle], *sels.* Aborigine Oral Tradition, *tr. by* R. M.
　　Berndt. CBAP
　Birds, The. WTO
　Evening Star, The. WTO
　New Moon. WTO
Moon Bright. Park Je-chun, *tr. fr. Korean by* Koh Chang-soo. ACKP
Moon came to the forge, The. Ballad of Luna, Luna. Federico García
　　Lorca, *tr. by* William B. Logan. SOTW
Moon-Child, The. "Fiona Macleod." CH
Moon-Come-Out. Eleanor Farjeon. RAR
Moon comes from the blue sky, The. The Moon in a Winecup. Shen
　　Chou, *tr. by* Jonathan Chaves. CoBLCP
Moon cuts through, The. Somewhere near Phu Bai. Yusef Komunyakaa.
　　MAYP
Moon Dips in the Puddle's Flow, The. Dov Khomsky, *tr. fr. Hebrew by*
　　Bernhard Frank. MHeP
Moon dips low and the stars grow dim, The. Song of the Wine Spring.
　　Wei Chuang, *tr. by* Lois Fusek. ATF
Moon Eclipse Exorcism. *Unknown, tr. fr. Alsea Indian by* Armand
　　Schwerner. STP
Moon-faced baby with cocaine arms. Blues for Sister Sally. Lenore
　　Kandel. NMM
Moon Festival. Tu Fu, *tr. fr. Chinese by* Kenneth Rexroth.
　　NaP
Moon Fishing. Lisel Mueller. CoAP
Moon, Flowers, Man. Su Tung-p'o, *tr. fr. Chinese by* Kenneth Rexroth.
　　NaP
Moon from a Boat, The. Gyoko, *tr. fr. Japanese by* Steven D. Carter.
　　WFTW
Moon goes over the water, The. Half Moon. Federico García Lorca, *tr.
　　by* W. S. Merwin. RFM
Moon going orange, The. The Point. Gary Soto. MAYP

Moon had climbed the highest hill, The. The Banks of Dee. *Unknown.* AmFP

Moon had risen an hour or more, The. Crescent Moon. William Renton. NOBVV

Moon had risen on the eastern hill, The. The Sailor and His Bride. *Unknown.* AmFP

The moon has a face like the clock in the hall. The Moon. Robert Louis Stevenson. PWR

Moon has gone to her rest, The. Wilfrid Scawen Blunt. OBMV

Moon has left the sky, The. A Night in Lesbos. George Horton. AA

Moon Has Set, The. Sappho, *tr. fr. Greek.* ChTr

Moon has mare, all silver-bright, The. The Chase. W. H. Davies. BrPo

Moon hung low 'mid clouds enshrined, The. The Fading Skiff. Henrietta Cordelia Ray. CBWP-3

Moon in a Winecup, The. Shen Chou, *tr. fr. Chinese by* Jonathan Chaves. CoBLCP

Moon, in her pride, once glanced aside, The. The Moon Sings. *Unknown.* OxBoLi

Moon in the bureau mirror, The. Insomnia. Elizabeth Bishop. LLLT

Moon in the cold, The. Miura Chora, *tr. fr. Japanese by* Hiroaki Sato. *Fr.* Sixteen Hokku. FCEI

Moon in the garden. Tamekane, *tr. by* Steven D. Carter. WFTW

Moon in your eyes is best, The. Tracking Rabbits: Night. Jim Barnes. CDW

Moon in Your Hands, The. Hilda Doolittle ("H. D."). BoWoP; NYBP

Moon is a dusty place, The. Moon-Witches. Ted Hughes. WSC

Moon is a poor woman, The. Sidney Keyes. *Fr.* The Foreign Gate. OBWP

Moon is a sow, The. Song for Ishtar. Denise Levertov. MoP; NaP; NMM; NoAM; PoM

Moon is a still presence, The. Flowers Fill the Palace. Yin O, *tr. by* Lois Fusek. ATF

Moon is able to command the valley tonight, The. Moist Moon People. Carl Sandburg. MoAmPo

Moon Is Always Female, The. Marge Piercy. NoAM

Moon is an ivory tusk in the Utah sky, The. The Moon and the Salt Flats. Mary Di Michele. NOBC

Moon is at her full, and, riding high, The. The Tides. Bryant. TAP

Moon is down, The. Night up There. G. D. Valentine. PoSH

Moon is eaten and renewed, The. The Lunar Games. Eeva-Liisa Manner, *tr. by* Jaakko A. Ahokas. WPOW

Moon is fully risen, The. Der Mond ist aufgegangen. Heine, *tr. by* James Thomson. AWP

Moon is like a lamp, The. The Weathercock. Rose Fyleman. BoTP

Moon is lovely when it's full, The. Asadullah Khan Ghalib, *tr. by* Ahmed Ali. GoT

Moon is not green cheese, The. Night Light. Nancy Willard. LCAP

Moon is salmon as a postage-stamp, The. Power-Cut. Medbh McGuckian. FaBCIP

Moon is slowly sinking, The. Delight in the High-Flying Orioles. Hsüeh Chao-yün, *tr. by* Lois Fusek. ATF

Moon Is Teaching Bible, The. Zelda, *tr. fr. Hebrew by* Marcia Falk. VWA

Moon is the companion, The. To the Tune "The Southerner." Yang Shen, *tr. by* Jonathan Chaves. CoBLCP

Moon Is the Number 18, The. Charles Olson. CMoP; PoE

Moon Is to Blood. Richard Duerden. NeAP

Moon is up, The. Old Mole. James Reeves. WSC

Moon Is Up, The. *Unknown.* NA

Moon-like Is All Other Love. *Unknown, tr. fr. Middle English by* Donald Davie. NOCV

Moon lives by damaging the ocean, The. A Song about the Moon. Bill Manhire. ATNZ

Moon lives in all the alone places, The. Meditations on the Moon. Paula Gunn Allen. HATNAP

Moon-Man. Dorothy Hewett. CBAP

Moon Mattress. Diane DiPrima. NMM

Moon mentions, The. Grunion. Myra Cohn Livingston. RFM

Moon, moon/ Mak' me a pair o'shoon. *Unknown.* OxNR

Moon moon moon moon moon this. This May Be Your Captain Speaking. Christian Karlson Stead. ATNZ

Moon Now Rises to Her Absolute Rule, The. Henry David Thoreau. PoEL-4

Moon of Huckleberries. Phillip William George. VoR

Moon of Id came, The. Nur, Empress Jahan, *tr. fr. Persian by* Willis Barnstone. BoWoP

Moon of Mobile, The. Thomas Holley Chivers. OBAL

Moon of the Earth. *Gond Oral Tradition, tr. by* V. Elwin *and* S. Hivale. WTO

Moon on a Spring Dawn. Sanetaka, *tr. fr. Japanese by* Steven D. Carter. WFTW

Moon on the Night of the Third of the Month, The. Chiang Ch'un-lin, *tr. fr. Chinese by* Irving Lo. WFTU

Moon on the one hand, the dawn on the other, The. The Early Morning. Hilaire Belloc. BoNaP; BoTP; OxBSP

Moon over the Mountain Pass. Hsü Ts'an, *tr. fr. Chinese by* Pao Chia-lin. WFTU

Moon over the Ruined Castle. Tsuchii Bansui, *tr. fr. Japanese by* Geoffrey Bownas *and* Anthony Thwaite. PeBJV

Moon Poems. John Wieners. VGW

Moon Pond, The. Medbh McGuckian. FaBCIP

Moon/ real/ estate and scree cascading 9. Three. Marilyn Kitchell. UL

Moon Rises, The. Federico García Lorca, *tr. fr. Spanish by* William Bryant Logan. SOTW; TTTS

Moon rises, The, a vengeance on anguish. Sleepwalkers. Bella Akhmadulina, *tr. by* Barbara Einzig. BoWoP

Moon rising white, A. *Unknown, tr. by* Arthur Waley. BoS

Moon setting, crows cawing, frost filling the sky. Tying Up for the Night at Maple River Bridge. Chang Chi, *tr. by* Burton Watson. CoBCP

Moon Shadow. George Bowering. MoCV

Moon shines across miles of purple frontier, The. Pacifying the Western Barbarians. Niu Chiao, *tr. by* Lois Fusek. ATF

Moon Shines Bright, The ("Moon shines bright, and the stars give a light, The"). *Unknown.* GBP; OBET; OxNR

Moon shines bright, The; and the stars give a light. The Moon Shines Bright. *Unknown.* GBP; OBET

Moon shines bright, The. In such a night as this. Shakespeare. *Fr.* The Merchant of Venice, V, i. GBL

Moon shines clear as silver, The. Sun and Moon. Charlotte Druitt Cole. BoTP

Moon shines in front of the red tower, The. Song of Ho Man-tzu. Mao Wen-hsi, *tr. by* Lois Fusek. ATF

Moon shines over the hill field, The. *Unknown, tr. by* Geoffrey Bownas *and* Anthony Thwaite. PeBJV

Moon silvers the bay, she waxes, she wanes, The. The Eternal Kinship. Maurice E. Peloubet. GoYe

Moon Sings, The. *Unknown.* OxBoLi

Moon, sinking, drops beside my pillow, A. A Random Poem. Cheng Hsiao-hsü, *tr. by* Irving Lo. WFTU

Moon-soaked/ she emitted. The Journey. Margaret Reckord. AIW

Moon Solo. Jules Laforgue, *tr. fr. French by* William Jay Smith. CT

Moon Song. Chuba Nweke. PBA

Moon Song, Woman Song. Anne Sexton. PPP

Moon splashes, The. Venetian Fragment. Alois Hergouth, *tr. by* Beth Bjorklund. CoAuP

Moon, Sun, Sleep, Birds, Live. Kenneth Patchen. WeW

Moon that now and then last night, The. Snow Harvest. Andrew Young. BoNaP

Moon, The? It is a griffin's egg. Yet Gentle Will the Griffin Be. Vachel Lindsay. *Fr.* Poems about the Moon, II. PDV

Moon, they say, called Mantis, The. How Death Came. *Unknown, tr. by* W. H. I. Bleek. PeSA; TTY

Moon upon her fluent route, The. Emily Dickinson. QFR

Moon-viewings in the capital. Saigyo, *tr. fr. Japanese by* Burton Watson. *Fr.* Sixty-four Tanka. FCEI

Moon was like a full cup tonight, The. The Cows at Night. Hayden Carruth. SV

Moon was round, The. The Whisperer. James Stephens. WGRP

Moon was shining brightly upon the battle plain, The. The Maid of Monterey. *Unknown.* AmFP

Moon Watching by Lake Chapala. Al Young. NPGG

Moon white? No, it was not. Water Hyacinth. Kitahara Hakushu, *tr. by* Hiroaki Sato. FCEI

Moon Window, the. Chang Yü, *tr. fr. Chinese by* Jonathan Chaves. *Fr.* Twelve Miscellaneous Poems on the Fang Garden. CoBLCP

Moon-Witches. Ted Hughes. WSC

Moon, with the pace of a wolf, The. Harvest Poem. David Fisher. NPGG

Moonbeams over Arno's vale in silver flood were pouring, The. The Veery. Henry van Dyke. AA

Moone-Calfe, The, *sel.* Michael Drayton. "It was not long e're he perceiv'd the skies." PoEL-2

Mooni. Henry Clarence Kendall. OBEV

Moonless night—a friendly one, A. Running the Batteries. Herman Melville. PAH

Moonlight. Walter de la Mare. EnLoPo

Moonlight, The. Ann Hawkshawe. BoTP

Moonlight. Berta Hart Nance. AmFN

Moonlight. Vali Mohammad Nazir, *tr. fr. Urdu by* Ahmed Ali. GoT

Moonlight. Shakespeare. *See* Merchant of Venice, The: How Sweet the Moonlight Sleeps.

Moonlight. Jacques Tahureau, *tr. fr. French by* Andrew Lang. AWP

Moonlight. Sara Teasdale. GOYP; VGW

Moonlight among the Pines. "Hugh MacDiarmid." OAEL-2

Moonlight Bay. Wu Chen, *tr. fr. Chinese by* Jonathan Chaves. CoBLCP

Moonlight breaks upon the city's domes, The. A Song of the Moon. Claude McKay. PoNe

Moonlight—fluorescently shining. Materialized into an Owl. Louis Oliver. STE

Moonlight has touched them all, The. Ryder. John Haines. LCAP

Moonlight in front of my bed. Still Night Thoughts. Li Po, *tr. by* Burton Watson. CoBCP; TTTS

Moonlight in the Forest. Aaro Hellaakoski, *tr. fr. Finnish by* Aili Jarvenpa. SOP

Moonlight is and is not as of old, The. Princess Shikishi, *tr. fr. Japanese by* Hiroaki Sato. *Fr.* Seventy-eight Tanka. FCEI

Moonlight is good, good for solitary sitting, The. Pine Sounds. Po Chü-i, *tr. by* Burton Watson. CoBCP

Moonlight Night. Tu Fu, *tr. fr. Chinese by* Burton Watson. CoBCP

Moonlight Night: Carmel. Langston Hughes. MOS

Moonlight on Lake Sydenham. Wilson Pugsley MacDonald. CaP

Moonlight remains, The. Gyoko, *tr. by* Steven D. Carter. WFTW

Moonlight ripples, ripples, The. Moonlight Bay. Wu Chen, *tr. by* Jonathan Chaves. CoBLCP

Moonlight shines on the jade tower as spring rushes by. Song of the Jade Tower in Spring. Ku Hsiung, *tr. by* Lois Fusek. ATF

Moonlight Song of the Mocking-Bird. William Hamilton Hayne. AA

Moonlight streams down unbroken until it ruffles my cloak. Strolling under the Moon. Li Chien, *tr. by* Irving Lo. WFTU

Moonlight, The: Juice flowing from an overripe pomegranate. Enchantment. Lewis Alexander. PoBA

Moonlight through my gauze curtains. The Skein. Carolyn Kizer. PrIm; VGW

Moonlight washes the west side of the house. Winter Verse for His Sister. William Meredith. NYBP; TAP

Moonlight. Scattered Clouds. Robert Bloomfield. *Fr.* The Farmer's Boy. OBNC

Moonlit Apples. John Drinkwater. BoNaP; BoTP; OBMV; OxBTC; PoRA

Moonlit night, A. Mist. Gyoko, *tr. by* Steven D. Carter. WFTW

Moonlit night I return. Ozaki Hosai, *tr. fr. Japanese by* Hiroaki Sato. *Fr.* One Hundred Haiku in Free Form. FCEI

Moonmoth and grasshopper that flee our page. A Name for All. Hart Crane. VGW

Moonrise. D. H. Lawrence. LiTM; PoA

Moonrise. Hilda Doolittle ("H. D."). PoA

Moonrise. Gerard Manley Hopkins. FaBoPP; MoAB; MoBrPo; NOBVV; RB; SeCePo

Moonrise. Frank Dempster Sherman. AA

Moonrise in the Rockies. Ella Higginson. AA

Moon's a devil jester, The. The Traveler. Vachel Lindsay. MoAmPo

Moon's a little arch, The. A Classic Case. Gilbert Sorrentino. NeAP

Moon's a path, The. Hansel, Gretel and Ruby Redlips. Anita Endrezze-Danielson. HATNAP

Moon's glow by seven fold multiplied, turned red. After Reading St. John the Divine. Gene Derwood. LiTM; WPE

Moon's greygolden meshes make, The. Alone. James Joyce. InvP

Moon's little skullcap, The. Front Street. Howard Moss. NYBP

Moon's my constant mistress, The. Tom o' Bedlam. *Unknown.* CH; FaBoCh; PoRA

Moon's on the lake, and the mist's on the brae, The. MacGregor's Gathering. Sir Walter Scott. OxBS

Moon's small aura pins, The. A Natural Shame. Sydney Lea. NAmP

Moon's the North Wind's Cooky, The. Vachel Lindsay. FaFP; FaPON; OBCA; PDV; RAR; RHPC

Moon's up-riding makes a line, The. Night Scenes. Robert Duncan. VGW

Moonset. Sir Henry Newbolt. EBVV

Moonset, Gloucester, December 1, 1957, 1:58 A.M. Charles Olson. CAPP

Moonsheep, The. Christian Morgenstern, *tr. fr. German by* Geoffrey Grigson. FaBoNo

Moonshine. Walter de la Mare. FiBHP

Moonshine. Richard Murphy. PoPo

Moonshot Sonnet. Mary Ellen Solt. BoWoP

Moonstruck. "Hugh MacDiarmid." NAEL-2

Moonstruck/ I/ bereft of everything. Yearning for the Shore. Saqi Farooqi, *tr. by* Mahmood Jamal. PBMUP

Moonsweet the summer evening locks. Sheepbells. Edmund Blunden. BrPo

Moontan. Mark Strand. NYBP

Moonwalk. John Engels. MAT

Moor, The. Ralph Hodgson. MoBrPo

Moor, The. R. S. Thomas. OBWVE

Moorburn in Spring. *Unknown.* PoSH

Moored. Philippe Denis, *tr. fr. French by* Paul Auster. RHTwFP

Moored to your blood. Moored. Philippe Denis, *tr. by* Paul Auster. RHTwFP

Moorhen. William Logan. DiPo

Mooring at Hsai-k'ou at Night. Li Meng-yang, *tr. fr. Chinese by* Jonathan Chaves. CoBLCP

Mooring at K'ou-ch'üeh, *sels.* Pien Kung, *tr. fr. Chinese by* Jonathan Chaves. CoBLCP

    "Apricot trees form a grove." *Fr.* I.

    This year of famine, old and young suffer many strange diseases. *Fr.* II.

Mooring at Night. T'an Ssu-t'ung, *tr. fr. Chinese by* Timothy C. Wong. WFTU

Mooring at Night at Kao-yu. Wang Shih-chen, *tr. fr. Chinese by* Jonathan Chaves. CoBLCP

Mooring at Night at the River Mouth, I Heard a Flute. Wang Shih-chen, *tr. fr. Chinese by* Jonathan Chaves. CoBLCP

Mooring in the Evening at Plum Village, *sel.* P'eng Sun-yü, *tr. fr. Chinese by* Daniel Bryant.

    "As the tenth month comes to a river district." *Fr.* II. WFTU

Mooring in the Rain at Kao-yu. Wang Shih-chen, *tr. fr. Chinese by* Daniel Bryant. WFTU

Mooring in the Rain at Sung-ling. Chin Nung, *tr. fr. Chinese by* Jonathan Chaves. CoBLCP

Mooring My Boat at Pan-ch'a. Shen Te-ch'ien, *tr. fr. Chinese by* Marie Chan. WFTU

Mooring My Boat on the Ssu River and Watching the Moon. Wen Cheng-ming, *tr. fr. Chinese by* Jonathan Chaves. CoBLCP

Mooring Our Boat at Tan-yang Harbor. Kao Ch'i, *tr. fr. Chinese by* Jonathan Chaves. CoBLCP

Moorings. Norman MacCaig. OxBTC

Moorish Frigate: 2, A. Hans Warren, *tr. fr. Dutch by* James S. Holmes. DuIn

Moorland sheep is frightened and amazed, The. Philosophy Is Born. Christian Morgenstern, *tr. by* Geoffrey Grigson. FaBoNo

Moorlands of the Not. *Unknown.* NA

Moose, The. Elizabeth Bishop. DiPo; FaBoWP; NAAL-2

Mop-eyed I am, as some have said. Upon Himself. Robert Herrick. OxBSP

Mopoke. Louis Lavater. PoAu-1

Moral, The. David Avidan, *tr. fr. Hebrew by* Warren Bargad *and* Stanley F. Chyet. *Fr.* Samson, Our Hero, 9. IP

Moral, The. Theodore Weiss. Prf

Moral Alphabet, A, *sels.* Hilaire Belloc.

    "A stands for Archibald who told no lies." NoAM

    "B stands for Bear. When bears are seen." NoAM

    "Dreadful Dinotherium he, The." NOBL

    "E stands for egg." NoAM

    "K for the Klondyke, a country of gold." NoAM

    "R the reviewer, reviewing my book." NoAM

Moral Essays, *sels.* Pope.

    Duke of Buckingham, The. *Fr.* Epistle III. NOBE

    (Death of Buckingham, The.) FiP

    Epistle to a Lady: Of the Characters of Women. *Fr.* Epistle II. NAEL-1; NOEC; OAEL-1; OxBoLi, *shorter sel..*

        "Yet Chloe [*or* Cloe] sure was formed without a spot." ErPo; OBSV.

        (Timon's Villa.) PoE

        (Chloe.) AWP; NOBE

        "Men, some to bus'ness, some to pleasure take." OBSV

    To Richard Boyle, Earl of Burlington: Of the Uses of Riches. *Fr.* Epistle IV. NOEC; OAEL-1; OBSV; PoEL-3; PPP

        "At Timon's villa let us pass a day." NOEC; OAEL-1; OBSV; PoEL-5; PPD

        (Timon's Villa.) PoE

Moral Ode. David Rosenmann-Taub, *tr. fr. Spanish by* Charles Guenther. VWA

Moral Poem, A. J. V. Cunningham. VGW

Moral Poem Freely Accepted from Sappho, A. James Wright. CAPP

Moral Story II. David Wright. PeSA

Moral Taxi Ride, The. Erich Kästner, *tr. fr. German by* Jerome Rothenberg. ErPo

Moral Tetrastich, A. Sir William Jones. *See* Epigram: "On parent knees, a naked new-born child."

Moralist still obstinate replies, The. Voltaire, *tr. fr. French by* Tobias Smollet. *Fr.* The Lisbon Earthquake. OBD

Morality, thou deadly bane. Burns. *Fr.* A Dedication to G**** H******* Esq. OBSV

Morals. James Thurber. *Fr.* Further Fables for Our Time. FaBV

Morden Lecture, 1978. Ursula K. Le Guin. BWV

More. Philip Appleman. BXAP

More. Yrjö Jylhä, *tr. fr. Finnish by* Aili Jarvenpa. SOP

More, The. Eli Netser, *tr. fr. Hebrew by* Bernhard Frank. MHeP

More. Gertrude Stein. *Fr.* Tender Buttons. PBWP

More amazed than anything. The Kitten. Mary Oliver. CAPP

More Ancient Mariner, A. Bliss Carman. AnAmPo; OBAL

More and more. *Unknown, tr. by* Geoffrey Bownas *and* Anthony Thwaite. PeBJV

More Animals, *sel.* Oliver Herford.
  Cow, The. NA

More Ballads! here's a spick and span new Supplication. A Free Parliament Litany. *Unknown.* OxBoLi

More beautiful and soft than any moth. The Landscape near an Aerodrome. Stephen Spender. LiTM; MoAB; MoBrPo; NoAM; OxBTC

More beautiful than any gift you gave. The Token. F. T. Prince. FaBoTw; OxBTC

More beautiful than the notable moon and its ennobled light. To the Sun. Ingeborg Bachmann. BoNaP, *tr. by* Michael Hamburger; CoAuP, *tr. by* Beth Bjorklund

More Beautiful Than Your Eyes. Said Aql, *tr. fr. Arabic by* Matthew Sorenson *and* Naomi Shihab Nye. MAP

More Clues. Muriel Rukeyser. IHMS

More discontents I never had. Discontents in Devon. Robert Herrick. CaPo; OxBSP; SeCV-1

More distant than the dead sea. Nadia Tuéni, *tr. by* Carol Cosman. PBWP

More Foreign Cities. Charles Tomlinson. NePoEA-2

More gaily, dance. Quick-Step. Robert Creeley. VGW

More Girl Than Boy. Yusef Komunyakaa. PPR

More grotesque than a row of laundromats. The Novelty Shop. Duane Niatum. CDW

More haughty than the rest, the wolfish race. The Presbyterians. Dryden. *Fr.* The Hind and the Panther, I. OBS

More humane Mikado never, A. The Mikado's Song. W. S. Gilbert. *Fr.* The Mikado. LiTB

More ill at ease was never man than Walbach, that Lord's day. The Legend of Walbach Tower. George Houghton. PAH

More It Snows, The. A. A. Milne. NTCP; PYC; RAR; RHPC

More Joy in Heaven. Howard Nemerov. NoAM

More kicks than pence. To Hell with Commonsense. Patrick Kavanagh. FaBoTw

More Letters Found near a Suicide. Frank Horne. BANP

"More Light! More Light!" Anthony Hecht. CoAP; HAP; NePoEA-2; NoAM; NOBA; NoP; OBWP; RB; SM; SoSe; TwCP; UnPo; VGW; VWA

More like the candle going out. Nancy Sullivan. *Fr.* Two Orgasms, I. NIP

More Love. *Unknown.* AH

More love or more disdain I crave. Against Indifference. Charles Webbe. OBEV

More Love to Thee, O Christ. Elizabeth Payson Prentiss. AH

More Lovely Grows the Earth. Helena Coleman. CaP

More Loving One, The. W. H. Auden, *tr. by the author.* HoPM; TOF

More Luck to Honest Poverty. Shirley Brooks. BXAP
  (For A' That and A' That.) FaBoCo; NOBL; Par

More melancholy than the bright moon. Teika, *tr. fr. Japanese by* Hiroaki Sato. *Fr.* Eighty-four Tanka. FCEI

More Nudes for Florence. Harold Witt. ErPo

More of a Corpse than a Woman. Muriel Rukeyser. NMM

More of Thee. Horatius Bonar. BLRP

More oft than once Death whispered in mine ear. Sonnet: Death's Last Will. William Drummond, of Hawthornden. JCP

More pleasing were these sweet delights. Francis Beaumont. *Fr.* The Masque of the Inner Temple and Gray's Inne, III. OBS

More Power. Egan O'Rahilly, *tr. fr. Modern Irish by* John Montague. BIrV

More Powerful than the Sea. Zoltán Zelk, *tr. fr. Hungarian by* Barbara Howes. MHuP

More Questions. Ory Bernstein, *tr. fr. Hebrew by* Warren Bargad *and* Stanley F. Chyet. IP

More Reformation, *sel.* Daniel Defoe.
  "To sin's a vice in nature, and we find." OBSV

More reminiscent than distressed, you say. To a Blind Student Who Taught Me to See. Samuel Hazo. GOYP

More sad thoughts crowd into my mind. Lady Kasa. *Fr.* Manyo Shu. Ma

More shower than shine. Valentines to My Mother, 1880. Christina Rossetti. OFD

More shy than the shy violet. Quaker Ladies. Ellen Mackay Hutchinson Cortissoz. AA

More Songs from Vagabondia, *sel.* Richard Hovey.
  "Whose furthest footstep never strayed." AA

More Sonnets at Christmas, *sels.* Allen Tate. LiTA; LiTM; WaP
  "Citizen myself, or personal friend." WaP
  "Gay citizen, myself, and thoughtful friend." *Fr.* IV. LiTA; LiTM

More Stanzas Applied to Spiritual Things. Saint John of the Cross, *tr. fr. Spanish by* K. Kavanaugh *and* O. Rodrigues. TOF

More Strong Than Time. Victor Hugo, *tr. fr. French by* Andrew Lang. AWP

More than a beggar I dare not. Peire Vidal, *tr. by* Paul Blackburn. Pro

More than a year has reeled and clamoured by. For Freda. Margery Smith. CN

More than all the stars in the sky. *Unknown, tr. by* Geoffrey Bownas *and* Anthony Thwaite. PeBJV

More than Fifty. Jack Gilbert. NPGG

More than honey the words you speak are sweet. *Unknown, tr. by* L. R. Lind. PFI

More than leaves, more than flakes. More. Philip Appleman. BXAP

More than Morgan, I desire to eat people. Morgan. John Blight. CBAP

More than most fair, full of that heavenly fire. Fulke Greville. *Fr.* Caelica, III. EIL
  (To His Lady.) OBSC

More Than Most People. Eldon Grier. MoCV

More than novelty crooked its finger—silent, austere. Melissa Green. DiPo

More than once I have heard. Lindedi Singing. Innocent Banda. WMBCH

More than People. Robin Fulton. *Fr.* A Cleared Land. PoSH

More than the ash stays you from nothingness! The Phoenix. J. V. Cunningham. QFR

More than the gems/ locked away and treasured. Sent from the Capital to Her Elder Daughter. Lady Otomo no Sakanoe, *tr. by* Geoffrey Bownas *and* Anthony Thwaite. AIW; BoWoP; PeBJV; WPOW

More than the shortest distance. A Barbed Wire Fence Meditates upon the Goldfinch. Don McKay. NOBC

More than We Ask. Faith Wells. BLRP

More things are wrought by prayer. Tennyson, *incorporated in* Idylls of the King *with changes, as* The Passing of Arthur. *Fr.* Morte d'Arthur. BLRP

More we live, more brief appear, The. The River of Life. Thomas Campbell. FaFP; GTBS; GTBS-P; LiTB
  (Thought Suggested by the New Year, A.) OBNC

More whyght thou art than primrose leaf my Lady Galatee. Ovid, *tr. fr. Latin by* Arthur Golding. *Fr.* Metamorphoses, VIII. OBVE
  (Cyclops.) CTC,

More wild, more rash, Eve, admit it. The Voices of Eden. Else Lasker-Schüler, *tr. by* Robert Alter. OV

More years ago than I can state. My Last Illusion. John Kaye Kendall. FiBHP

Morea's Sonnet. Mary Sidney Wroth, Countess of Montgomery. *Fr.* Urania. WPE

Morels. William Jay Smith. BoNaP; MAT; NYBP; RFM

Moreover the Lord answered Job, and said. Bible, *O.T.* *Fr.* Job, XL. OBVE
  Out of the Whirlwind. *Fr.* XL: 7–XLI. AWP

Moreton Bay. *Unknown.* CBAP

Morgan. John Blight. CBAP

Morgan. Edward Harrington. PoAu-1

Morgan. Edmund Clarence Stedman. AA

Morgan Stanwood. Hiram Rich. PAH

Morgante and the Boars. Luigi Pulci, *tr. fr. Italian by* Byron. PFI

Morgante Maggiore, Il, *sel.* Luigi Pulci, *tr. fr. Italian.*
  Prophecy. PAH

Morgue, The. James Keir Baxter. ATNZ

Morituri Salutamas, *sel.* Longfellow.
  It Is Too Late. BLPL; PoLF
  (Too Late?) WBLP

Moriturus. "Marie Madelaine," *tr. fr. French by* Ferdinand E. Kappey. PeHV

Moriturus. Edna St. Vincent Millay. LiTA

Morley's light went out. Power Failure. Michael Dennis Browne. AmPA

Mormons, led by Colonel Cooke, The. On the Road to California; or, The Buffalo Bullfight. *Unknown.* AmFP

Morn. Josephine D. Henderson Heard. CBWP-4

Morn. Helen Hunt Jackson. AA

Morn hath risen clear and bright, The. The Expulsion of Hagar. Eloise Bibb. CBWP-4

Morn was cloudy and dark and gray, The. The Battle of Morris' Island. *Unknown.* PAH

Morning. Mir Babbar Ali Anis, *tr. fr. Urdu by* Ahmed Ali. GoT

Morning. Blake. FaBoCh; OAEL-2

Morning. Charles Stuart Calverley. FiBHP

Morning. Thomas Carlyle. PWR

Morning. Chu Shu-chen, *tr. fr. Chinese by* Kenneth Rexroth. BoWoP

Morning. John Cunningham. NOEC

Morning. Sir William Davenant. *See* Lark Now Leaves His Water [*or* Wat'ry] Nest.

Morning. Emily Dickinson. *See* Will there really be a morning?

Morning. Tove Ditlevsen, *tr. fr. Danish by* Nadia Christensen. PBWP

Morning. Ivy O. Eastwick. BoTP

Morning. Keats. *See* now Morning from her orient chamber came.

Morning. Sami Mahdi, *tr. fr. Arabic by* May Jayyusi. MAP

Morning. José Manuel Martínez de Navarrete, *tr. fr. Spanish by* Samuel Beckett. MexPo

Morning. John Crowe Ransom. AnAmPo

Morning. Alberto Ríos. MAYP

Morning. Philip Henry Savage. AA

Morning, A. Mark Strand. GeTw; HCAP

Morning. Giuseppe Ungaretti, *tr. fr. Italian by* William Jay Smith. CT; PFI

Morning. *Unknown.* NOEC

Morning/ and she awoke to. Five Sense. Marvin Wyche, Jr. AmNP

Morning/ broods. Strawberrying. Maurice Kenny. HATNAP

Morning, about six, as I look at the rim of the hill. *Unknown, tr. by* Hiroaki Sato. FCEI

Morning After, The. Heine, *tr. fr. German by* Louis Untermeyer. ErPo

Morning After. Langston Hughes. MoP; NAAL-2; NBLV; NoAM

Morning After. The. Dorothy Wellesley. OBMV

Morning after death on the bar was calm. Paul Henderson. ATNZ

Morning after she's gone, The. *Unknown, tr. by* Geoffrey Bownas *and* Anthony Thwaite. PeBJV

Morning after. Love, The. Kattie M. Cumbo. BlSi

Morning again, nothing has to be done. Second Poem. Peter Orlovsky. NeAP

Morning air is cold on Mount Ujima, The. Prince Nagaya. *Fr.* Manyo Shu. Ma

Morning and evening. Goblin Market. Christina Rossetti. BoTP; EBEV; GoTL; NAEL-2; NOBVV; OBNV

Morning and Evening. Antoni Slonimski, *tr. fr. Polish by* Watson Kirkconnell. TrJP

Morning and evening, drunk and singing. For Kuo Hsiang. Yü Hsüah-chi, *tr. by* Geoffrey Waters. BoWoP

Morning and evening, sleep she drove away. The Spinning Woman. Leonidas of Tarentum, *tr. by* Andrew Lang. AWP

Morning and Evening Star. Plato. *See* Astrophel and Stella: First Song.

Morning and Myself. Nia Francisco. STE

Morning and reverent. Funnels In. Bruce Andrews. IAT

Morning, and streaks of heavenly blue. London Spring. Antoni Slonimski, *tr. by* Frances Notley. TrJP

Morning, and the poet up again and out and about. The Poet's Day. Richard Weber. CIP

Morning and the snow might fall forever. Going to Remake This World. James Welch. CDW

Morning at Arnheim. William Jay Smith. NePoEA

Morning at nine, seven ultra-masculine men. In Your Bad Dream. Richard Hugo. LCAP

Morning at Point Dume. May Swenson. DiPo

Morning at the Window. T. S. Eliot. AWP; PoA

Morning Athletes. Marge Piercy. AIW; ASP; NIP

Morning Bird Songs. Tomas Tranströmer, *tr. fr. Swedish by* Robert Bly. InPS

Morning: blue, cold, and still. January. Weldon Kees. CoAP

Morning breaks like a pomegranate, The. Wedding Morn. D. H. Lawrence. MoAB; MoBrPo

Morning Bright, with Rosy Light, The. Thomas O. Summers. AH

Morning Bus. John Coulter. CaP

Morning by morning the breath of the wind grows stronger. Wind and Rain. Michizane, *tr. by* Burton Watson. JLIC-1

Morning comes, and thickening clouds prevail, The. The Clouded Morning. Jones Very. NOBA

Morning comes, the night decays, the watchmen leave their stations, The. Empire Is No More. Blake. *Fr.* America; a Prophecy. EnRP

Morning comes. The old woman, a spot, The. Grief. Wendell Berry. GeTw; MT

Morning comes to consciousness, The. T. S. Eliot. *Fr.* Preludes, II. HeIP; LiTA; NoP; OBMV; PPP; SeCePo; SOTW; TwCP; UnPo; VGW; WeW

Morning Compliments. Sydney Dayre. OxBChV

Morning drum-call on my eager ear, The. Robert Louis Stevenson. NOBVV

Morning Duke Ellington Praised the Lord and Six Little Black Davids Tapped Danced Unto, The. Owen Dodson. FB

Morning finds the self-sequester'd man, The. The Garden. William Cowper. *Fr.* The Task, III. PoE

Morning fodder: a frog. Ranchiku, *tr. by* Hiroaki Sato. FCEI

Morning fog/ one man's got a fire going. Masaoka Shiki, *tr. fr. Japanese by* Burton Watson. *Fr.* Thirty-nine Haiku. FCEI

Morning-Glories. Rokunyo, *tr. fr. Chinese by* Burton Watson. JLIC-2

Morning glories: a single flower. Buson, *tr. fr. Japanese by* Hiroaki Sato. *Fr.* Eighty-seven Hokku. FCEI

Morning-glories' white continues to bloom. Ozaki Hosai, *tr. fr. Japanese by* Hiroaki Sato. *Fr.* One Hundred Haiku in Free Form. FCEI

Morning-Glory, The. Maria White Lowell. AA

Morning Glory. Howard Moss. DiPo

Morning Glory. Ruth Pitter. FaBoWP

Morning Glory. Siegfried Sassoon. TrCP

Morning Glory, The. *Unknown, tr. fr. Chinese by* Helen Waddell. *Fr.* Shi King. AWP

Morning Glory Pool. Sandra McPherson. LCAP

Morning Has No House. Rosemarie Waldrop. MAT

Morning he had gone. My Face Is My Own, I Thought. Tom Raworth. EAS

Morning Hymn. Joseph Beaumont. TrPWD

Morning Hymn. Saint Gregory the Great, *tr. fr. Latin by* Edward Caswell. WGRP

Morning Hymn. John Keble. *See* New every morning.

Morning Hymn. Thomas Ken. FaFP; OBS

Morning Hymn, A. Christopher Smart. OxBChV

Morning Hymn. Charles Wesley. TOF

Morning Hymn of Adam. Milton. *See* Paradise Lost: These are thy glorious works, Parent of good.

Morning, if this late withered light can claim. The Zonnebeke Road. Edmund Blunden. MMA; OBWP

Morning in Christchurch. Lauris Edmond. UAS

Morning in Spring. Louis Ginsberg. GoYe

Morning in the Hills. Bliss Carman. NOBC

Morning in the North-west. Arthur Stringer. CaP

Morning is bright and sunlit, and the west wind running smoothly, The. Message to the Bard. William Livingston. GoTS

Morning is cheery, my boys, arouse, The! Reveille. Michael O'Connor. AA

Morning is clean and blue and the wind blows up the clouds, The. John Gould Fletcher. *Fr.* Irradiations, V [XXII]. MoAmPo

Morning is hot and windy, The. Lonnie Kramer. Geary Hobson. STE

Morning is lost in a maze. We're OK. Gloria Fuertes, *tr. by* Philip Levine. WPOW

Morning is the gate of day, The. The Sentinel. *Unknown.* BLRP

Morning Letter, A. Robert Duncan. PoA

Morning Light. Mary Effie Lee Newsome. AmNP; CDC; PoBA; PoNe

Morning Light, The. Louis Simpson. NNaP

Morning light floods my room overlooking the lake. Chiang Shih, *tr. fr. Chinese by* Irving Lo. *Fr.* Getting Up Early at Lakeside Pavilion. WFTU

Morning Light Is Breaking, The. Samuel Francis Smith. AH, *with music;* WGRP (Daybreak.) BLRP

Morning Light Song. Philip Lamantia. NeAP

Morning like an upturned jewel. Weather. Nishiwaki Junzaburo, *tr. by* Geoffrey Bownas *and* Anthony Thwaite. PeBJV

Morning like others, and a father, A. Why I Am Afraid to Have Children. Bin Ramke. MAYP

Morning, May rain. The Man Awakened by a Song above His Roof. Tomas Tranströmer, *tr. by* Robert Bly. EAS

Morning mists still haunt the stony street, The. Enter Patient. W. E. Henley. *Fr.* In Hospital, I. BrPo

'Morning, Morning. Ray Mathew. PoAu-2

Morning, Noon, and. Hawley Truax. NYBP

Morning of a cold month, The. The International Brigade Arrives at Madrid. Pablo Neruda, *tr. by* Angel Flores. WaaP

Morning of evanescent shadow, of laughter, A. What She Wanted to Be. Ory Bernstein, *tr. by* Warren Bargad *and* Stanley F. Chyet. IP

Morning of our rest has come, The. The Poor Man's Sunday Walk. Charles MacKay. EBVV

Morning, on a beach. A man & woman sitting by fire. Moon Is to Blood. Richard Duerden. NeAP

Morning on the Lièvre. Archibald Lampman. SD

Morning on the misty highlands. Sandpipers. Helen Merrill Egerton. CaP

Morning on the St. John's. Jane Cooper. NYBP

Morning on the Shore. Wilfred Campbell. NOBC

Morning ought not. Pas de Deux for Lovers. Michael Dransfield. CBAP

Morning-Piece; or, An Hymn for the Hay-Makers, A. Christopher Smart. NOEC

Morning Prayer. Aua, tr. fr. Eskimo. WTO

Morning Prayer. Geoffrey Mac Briain Mac An Bhaird, tr. fr. Irish by Earl of Longford. TIRV

Morning Prayer. Ogden Nash. GrPl; OxBChV

Morning Prayers of the Hasid, Rabbi Levi Yitzhok, The. Phyllis Gotlieb. VWA

Morning rain, evening rain, little plums turned yellow. Feeling Sorry for Myself. Lu Yu, tr. by Burton Watson. CoBCP

Morning road's fogged in. My circle speeds, The. Bridegroom. Gerrit Achterberg, tr. by James S. Holmes. DuIn

Morning Scene, A. Wu Sheng, tr. fr. Chinese by Dominic Cheung. IFON

Morning-Selah. Amir Gilboa, tr. fr. Hebrew by Warren Bargad and Stanley F. Chyet. IP

Morning service! parson preaches. The House of God. A. D. Hope. OxBC

Morning sky glitters, The. De Civitate Hominum. Thomas MacGreevy. CIP

Morning sky was overcast, The. Unknown. Fr. Manyo Shu. Ma

Morning Song. A. A. Fet, tr. fr. Russian by Max Eastman. AWP

Morning Song. Conrad Aiken. See Senlin; a Biography: It is morning, Senlin says, and in the morning.

Morning Song. Henry Blakely. CNA

Morning Song. Sir William Davenant. See Lark Now Leaves His Water [or Wat'ry] Nest.

Morning Song. Charlotte DeClue. STE

Morning Song. Gregory Orr. MAYP

Morning Song. Sylvia Plath. BoWoP; HCAP; HeIP; IHMS; InPK; InPS; LCAP; NAAL-2; NAs; NOBA; PrIm

Morning Song, A. Shakespeare. See Cymbeline: Hark! Hark! the Lark.

Morning Song. Solomon ibn Gabirol, tr. fr. Hebrew by Nina Davis Salaman. TrJP

Morning Song. Kurt M. Stein. FiBHP

Morning Song. Sara Teasdale. AnAmPo

Morning Song in the Jungle. Kipling. NoAM

Morning Song of Senlin. Conrad Aiken. See Senlin; a Biography: It is morning, Senlin says, and in the morning.

Morning Sounds. Saqi Farooqi, tr. fr. Urdu by Mahmood Jamal. PBMUP

Morning spent looking for my calendar. Losing the Marbles. James Merrill. DiPo

Morning spreads over. May All Earth Be Clothed in Light. George Hitchcock. VGW

Morning Star, The. Emily Brontë. ChTr

Morning Star. Thomas Hornsby Ferril. VGW

Morning Star. Cesare Pavese, tr. fr. Italian by William Arrowsmith. PFI

Morning Star, The. Primus St. John. PoBA

Morning Star Man. George Keithley. NPGG

Morning Star, O Cheering Sight! Unknown. AH

Morning Stillness. Klaus Demus, tr. fr. German by Beth Bjorklund. CoAuP

Morning Sun. Louis MacNeice. MoAB; MoBrPo; TwCP

Morning sun, The. Poem for Myself and Mei: Abortion. Leslie Marmon Silko. VoR

Morning sun climbs the eastern peak, The. Pien Kung, tr. fr. Chinese by Jonathan Chaves. Fr. Paintings, I. CoBLCP

Morning Swim. Maxine W. Kumin. CAPP; SM; WPE

Morning Thanksgiving. John Drinkwater. BoTP

Morning: the caged baby. A Marriage Poem. Ellen Bryant Voigt. PPR

Morning: the soft release. Meditation for a Pickle Suite. Richard H. W. Dillard. HoPM; MT

Morning They Shot Tony Lopez, Barber and Pusher Who Went Too Far, 1958, The. Gary Soto. MAYP

Morning Track, The. Edward Parone. NYBP

Morning trickles over the bruised vegetables. The Manless Society. Pierre Unik, tr. by David Gascoyne. EAS

Morning trumpets hail us the elders and children of the/ morning. No. 65. Lajos Kassák, tr. by Jascha Kessler. FOC

Morning uptown, quiet on the street. Song Form. Imamu Amiri Baraka. SOTW; TTTS

Morning Vigil. Phillip William George. VoR

Morning Watch, The. Henry Vaughan. LiTB; MePo; OBS; SeCePo

Morning Work. D. H. Lawrence. MoAB; MoBrPo

Morning Workout. Babette Deutsch. SD

Mornings/ before the sun's liquid. Lagoons, Hanlan's Point. Raymond Souster. NOBC

Mornings/ I got up early. The Way It Was. Lucille Clifton. WPE

Mornings After. Fleur Adcock. ATNZ

Mornings are his, The. Waterwings. Cathy Song. NoAM

Morning's at seven. Pippa Passes, But I Can't Get Around This Truck. Margaret Blaker. NBLV

Mornings everything is grey. Morning Has No House. Rosemarie Waldrop. MAT

Mornings, from my upstairs window, I can see a gray. Permission to Speak. Steve Orlen. MAYP

Morning's roof. Yonder. Itamar Ya'oz-kest, tr. by Bernhard Frank. MHeP

Morning's sudden and extravagant. Familiar Landscapes. Lawrence Raab. BLA

Morning's underplayed resistance, The. White Zombie. Harrison Fisher. UL

Mornings up before the rooster calls. Autumn Thoughts. Lu Yu, tr. by Burton Watson. CoBCP

Mornings when sky is white as dried gristle. The Onion. Margaret Gibson. MT

Mornin's Mornin, The. Gerald Brennan. BLPA

Morns are meeker than they were, The. Emily Dickinson. AA; BoNaP; FaPON; OBCA

Moro Assassinato, sel. Allen Curnow.
  An Urban Guerrilla. Fr. II. PeNZ

Morphine. Nizar Qabbani, tr. fr. Arabic by Abdullah al-Udhari. MPAW

Morrigan, The. Unknown, tr. fr. Irish by Thomas Kinsella. BIrV

Morrissey and the Russian Sailor,. Unknown. AS

Morrow every listen. Colloam. P. Inman. LP

Mors Benefica. Edmund Clarence Stedman. AA

Mors et Vita. Richard Henry Stoddard. AA

Mors Iabrochii. Unknown. NA

Mort aux Chats. Peter Porter. OxBC

Mortal Combat. Countess Alice Fay di Castagnola. GoYe

Mortal creature as I am. Unknown. Fr. Manyo Shu. Ma

Mortal flesh is full of grief. The Vanity of the World. Siôn Cent, tr. by Joseph P. Clancy. OBWVE

Mortal mixed of middle clay. Guy. Emerson. NOBA

Mortal my mate, bearing my rock-a-heart. To His Watch. Gerard Manley Hopkins. MoAB; MoBrPo

Mortal never won to view thee. Hafiz, tr. by R. A. Nicholson. TOF

Mortal Prudence, handmaid of divine Providence. The Testament of Perpetual Change. William Carlos Williams. GOA

Mortal, Sneer Not at the Devil. Heine, tr. fr. German by Emma Lazarus. Fr. Homeward Bound. TrJP

Mortality. James Devaney. PoAu-1

Mortality. Naomi Long Madgett. PoBA; PoNe

Mortality [or Mortalitie], behold and feare! Lines on the Tombs in Westminster. At. to Francis Beaumont and to William Basse. ACP; CH; FaPoR; GTBS; GTBS-P; NOBE; OBEV; TrGrPo
  (A Memento for Mortality.) EiL; FaBoCh; HAP; OBS

Mortally smitten by a feather'd dart. The Wounded Bird. La Fontaine, tr. by Edward Marsh. OBD

Mortar Salvos. Jaroslav Seifert, tr. fr. Czech by Jeffrey Fiskin and Erik Vestville. AnAn

Morte d'Arthur, sels. Tennyson, Incorporated in Idylls of the King with changes, as The Passing of Arthur. DL; FaBoBe; FaBoRV; FiP; NIP; NOBVV; OAEL-2; OBNV; PoEL-5
  "And answer made King Arthur, breathing hard." EBEV
  "But now farewell. I am going a long way."" FaBoRV
  Sir Gawain Encounters Sir Priamus. PoEL-1
  "So all day long the noise of battle rolled." FaBoRV
  "Then loudly cried the bold Sir Bedivere." TOF

Mortician's Twelve-year-old Son, The. Ai. GeTw

Mortification. George Herbert. MePo; SeCP

Mortified Genius, The. James Graeme. NOEC

Mortifying Mistake, A. Anna Maria Pratt. AA

Mortmain, sel. Robert Penn Warren.
  "In Time's concatenation and/ Carnal conventicle." Fr. I. NOBA; Prf
  (After Night Flight.) DiL

Morvin. John Fuller. NePoEA-2

Mosaic Worker, The. Arthur Wallace Peach. BLRP

Mosby at Hamilton. Madison Cawein. PAH

Moschatel. Daniel James O'Sullivan. NeIP

Moschus Moschiferus. A. D. Hope. CBAP; GrPl

Moscow Night, End of December 1934. A. Leyeles, *tr. fr. Yiddish by* Benjamin *and* Barbara Harshav. AYP

Moses. Amir Gilboa, *tr. fr. Hebrew by* Stephen Mitchell. VWA

Moses. Sydney Tremayne. OxBS

Moses. *Unknown.* OxNR; RHPC

Moses' Account. Milan Fuest, *tr. fr. Hungarian by* André Ungar. VWA

Moses and Jesus. Israel Zangwill. TrJP

Moses and Joshua. Else Lasker-Schüler, *tr. fr. German by* Joachim Neugroschel. VWA

Moses, from whose loins I sprung. The Jew. Isaac Rosenberg. MoBrPo; VWA

Moses on Mount Nebo. Abraham Regelson, *tr. fr. Hebrew by* Richard Flantz. VWA

Moses supposes his toeses are roses. Moses. *Unknown.* OxNR; RHPC

Mosquito, The. D. H. Lawrence. RB
  (Mosquito Knows, The.) FaBoEE; OxBTC

Mosquito, The. Rodney Jones. MAYP; MT

Mosquito. John Updike. AnAmPo

Mosquito-buzz. Buson, *tr. by* Geoffrey Bownas *and* Anthony Thwaite. PeBJV

Mosquito Knows, The. D. H. Lawrence. *See* Mosquito, The.

Mosquito larva plays alone, A. Issa, *tr. fr. Japanese by* Hiroaki Sato. *Fr.* Forty-four Hokku. FCEI

Mosquito whirs each time, A. Buson, *tr. fr. Japanese by* Hiroaki Sato. *Fr.* Eighty-seven Hokku. FCEI

Mosquitoes. José Emilio Pacheco, *tr. fr. Spanish by* Alastair Reid. TSS

Mosquitoes came in, and while the two. Raizan, *tr. fr. Japanese by* Hiroaki Sato. *Fr.* Thirteen Hokku. FCEI

Mosquitoes come in stately rank. I Hate Mosquitoes. Shu Wei, *tr. by* Barry L. Gartell. WFTU

Moss below the Stairs. Kao Ch'i, *tr. fr. Chinese by* Jonathan Chaves. CoBLCP

Moss-gathering. Theodore Roethke. RFM; VGW

Moss of His Skin, The. Anne Sexton. CoAP; IHMS; SM

Moss Supplicateth for the Poet, The. Richard Henry Dana. AA

Mossbawn: Two Poems in Dedication, *sels.* Seamus Heaney.
  Mossbawn Sunlight. *Fr.* I. BIrV
  (Sunlight.) FaBCIP; NoP
  Seed Cutters, The. FaBCIP

Mossy Stane, The. Robert Nicoll. PF

Most Acceptable Gift, The. Matthias Claudius, *tr. fr. German by* J. M. Campbell. BLRP

Most-Age, The. Mihály Váci, *tr. fr. Hungarian by* Edwin Morgan. MHuP

Most all of you boys have rode hosses like that. That Little Blue Roan. Bruce Kiskaddon. CowP

Most alluring clouds that mount the sky, The. Wordsworth. NOBVV

Most animals have no houses, only holes. Housing Starts. Peter Davison. EyDe

Most are innocent, shy, will not undress. Angels. Dannie Abse. PoA

Most Beautiful, The. Guido Gozzano, *tr. fr. Italian by* Victoria Pesce. TTTS

Most Beautiful Girl in the World, The. Lorenz Hart. OBAL

Most beautiful is the object, The. Study of the Object. Zbigniew Herbert, *tr. by* Czeslaw Milosz. PwPP

Most beautiful of things I leave is sunlight. Praxilla, *tr. by* Willis Barnstone. BoWoP

Most beautiful! the red-flowering eucalyptus. The Torso: Passages 18. Robert Duncan. CAPP

Most Beautiful Woman at My Highschool Reunion, The. Ellen Marie Bissert. GLP; PeHV

Most beds are beds. Sylvia Plath. *Fr.* The Bed Book. PYC

Most Expensive Picture in the World, The. Howard Nemerov. EyDe

Most folks believe in doctors, but there's my old girl she don't. Household Remedies. *Unknown.* OBET

Most glorious Lord of Life [*or* Lyfe]! that on this day. *Fr.* Amoretti, LXVIII Spenser. EIL; HAP; InPS; LiTB; NAEL-1; NOCV; NoP; PoE; Son; TrPwP
  (Easter.) NOBE; OBEV
  (Easter Morning.) OHIP

Most glorious of all the Undying, many-named, girt round with awe! Hymn to Zeus. Cleanthes, *tr. by* Edward Hayes Plumptre. WGRP

Most Gracious Queen, we thee implore. On Queen Caroline. *Unknown.* FaBoEE

Most happy letters framed by skillfull trade. Spenser. *Fr.* Amoretti, LXXIV. NAEL-1

Most high Lord. Cantico del Sole. Saint Francis of Assisi, *tr. by* Ezra Pound. CTC

Most Holy Night, that still dost keep. The Night. Hilaire Belloc. OBEV

Most holy Satyr. Holy Satyr. Hilda Doolittle ("H. D."). MoAmPo

Most inexplicable the wiles of boys I deem. Rhianus, *tr. by* Sydney Oswald. PeHV

Most Ingenious Paradox, A. W. S. Gilbert. *Fr.* The Pirates of Penzance. NAs

Most is your name the name of this dark stone. Rainy Mountain Cemetery. N. Scott Momaday. CDW; HATNAP

Most Like an Arch This Marriage. John Ciardi. WeW

Most Lovely Shade ("Most lovely dark, my Æthiopia born"). Edith Sitwell. FaBoTw; GTBS-P

Most men know love but as a part of life. Quatorzain. Henry Timrod. AnAmPo
  (Most Men Know Love.) Son
  (Sonnet.) AA

Most men use/ their eyes. The Mechanic. Diane Wakoski. AmPA

Most modern nature lovers have a personal scale of values that tells them. William Wordsworth (1770-1850). Gavin Ewart. NoAM

Most mornings we go running side by side. Morning Athletes. Marge Piercy. AIW; ASP; NIP

Most near, most dear, most loved and most far. Sonnet to My Mother. George Barker. FaFP; LiTB; MoAB; SeCePo; WaP
  (To My Mother.) FaBoMo; FF; LiTM; OxBTC; Son; TwCP

Most needy aren oure neighebores, The. The Poor. William Langland. *Fr.* The Vision of Piers Plowman. PoEL-1

Most of his friends, as expected. As Expected. Thom Gunn. GLP

Most of It, The. Robert Frost. HAP; NAAL-2; NoP; NU; TOF; WeW

Most of my days are passed away, yet my heart is still impure. The Worthless Heart. Immanuel di Roma. TrJP

Most of the houses along the river are those of fisherfolk. Wang Shih-chen, *tr. fr. Chinese by* Daniel Bryant. *Fr.* Chen-chou Quatrains, IV. WFTU

Most of the mornings here, when we awaken. For a Suicide, a Little Early Morning Music. Gibbons Ruark. MT

Most of the walls. Taranto. James Wright. AnAn

Most of your life we have kept our separate places. Discovering My Daughter. Dabney Stuart. SM

Most poets to a muse that is stone-deaf cry. On the Oxford Book of Victorian Verse. "Hugh MacDiarmid." MoBrPo

Most prefer not to know, proceed by faith and chance. Matter of Urgency. Louis Johnson. ATNZ

Most present of all the watchers where we camped, The. When We Looked Back. William Stafford. NYBP

Most Quietly at Times. Cäsar Flaischlen, *tr. fr. German by* Jethro Bithell. AWP

Most reverend Father, I have borne all wrong. Two Souls. Marjorie Pickthall. NOBC

Most reverend lords, the church's joy and wonder. On Calamy's Imprisonment and Wild's Poetry. *Unknown.* APAS

Most Saturday afternoons. The Weepies. Paul Muldoon. NoAM

Most souls, 'tis true, but peep out once an age. Pope. *Fr.* Elegy to the Memory of an Unfortunate Lady. CH
  (Dull, Sullen Prisoners.) FaBoRV

Most Sovereign Lady. *Unknown.* MeEL

Most stupendous show they ever gave, The. In Memory of the Circus Ship *Euzkera*. Walker Gibson. FiBHP

Most Sweet It Is with Unuplifted Eyes. Wordsworth. EnRP
  (Inner Vision, The.) GTBS; GTBS-P

Most that can be said, The. Parade's End. Barbara Guest. PoM

Most that I know but one. Care. Josephine Miles. NYBP

Most Unloving One, The. Samuel Daniel. *See* To Delia:
  My spotless love hovers, with purest wings.

Most virile of beings—man. Rhyme-Prose on the Marriage of Man and Woman. Asatsuna, *tr. by* Burton Watson. FCEI; JLIC-1

Most Vital Thing in Life, The. Grenville Kleiser. SoSe

Most weeds, whilst young. Francis Daniel Pastorius. SCAP

Most worthy of praise were the virtuous ways. Little Red Riding Hood. Guy Wetmore Carryl. FiBHP

Most worthye she is in towne, The. In Praise of Ivy. *Unknown.* MeEL

Most wounds can Time repair. At Ease. Walter de la Mare. GTBS-P

Most wretched heart, most miserable. Sir Thomas Wyatt. SiPS

Mostly it was starlings. Shooting Crows. David Huddle. GOYP

Mot eran dous miei cossir. Arnaut Daniel, *tr. by* Harriet Waters Preston. AWP

Motel. William Mills. MT

Motel: "I am a young girl." *Unknown, tr. by* Carol Cosman. PBWP

Motet: "I am merry,/ Pretty, pleasing." *Unknown, tr. by* Muriel Kittel. DMF

Motet ("My love, how could your heart consider"). *Unknown, tr. fr. Old French by* Carol Cosman. PBWP

Motet: "O God! I have no husband." *Unknown, tr. by* Patricia Terry. DMF

Motet, A: "Stranger here, as all my fathers were, A." John Amner. OxBSP

Motets, The, *sels.* Eugenio Montale, *tr. fr. Italian by* Dana Gioia. PFI
  "Gondola that glides, The." *Fr.* XIII.
  "I run my hand across your forehead." *Fr.* XII.
  "Reed that sheds its, The." *Fr.* XIX.
  "Why are you waiting? The squirrel in the pine tree." *Fr.* X.
  "You know this: I must lose you again and cannot." *Fr.* I.

Moth, The. Ahmad al-Safi al-Najafi, *tr. fr. Arabic by* Salma Khadra Jayyusi *and* John Heath-Stubbs. MAP

Moth, A. Henry Bellyse Baildon. NOBVV

Moth, A. Confusion. Victor Hernandez Cruz. UL

Moth. Lance Henson. VoR

Moth, The. Walter de la Mare. BrPo

Moth, The. Vernon Scannell. OxBC

Moth ate a word. To me it seemed, A. Book Moth. *Unknown, formerly at. to* Cynewulf, *tr. fr. Anglo-Saxon by* Charles W. Kennedy. *Fr.* Riddles (Exeter Book). AnOE

Moth flew a bee-line, The. Mothy Monologue. Ralph Gustafson. NOBC

"Moth has got into it, The." The Moth. Vernon Scannell. OxBC

Moth-Song. Ellen Mackay Hutchinson Cortissoz. AA

Moth-Terror. Benjamin De Casseres. TrJP

Mother. Peter Bland. ATNZ

Mother, The. Gwendolyn Brooks. *Fr.* A Street in Bronzeville. BlSi; BPo; CAPP; FaBoWP; NMM

Mother. Aldo Camerino, *tr. fr. Italian by* Anita Barrows. VWA

Mother, The. Hugo Claus, *tr. fr. Dutch by* James S. Holmes. DuIn

Mother. Herman de Coninck, *tr. fr. Dutch by* James S. Holmes. DuIn

Mother. Philip Dow. NPGG

Mother, The. S. S. Gardons. NePoEA-2

Mother. Seamus Heaney. NAs

Mother. Josephine D. Henderson Heard. CBWP-4

Mother. Theresa Helburn. FaPON; OHIP

Mother. Erica Jong. TV

Mother. Daniel Lawrence Kelleher. NeIP

Mother. Sharon Mayer Libera. IHMS

Mother, The. Catulle Mendès, *tr. fr. French by* W. J. Robertson. TrJP

Mother. José Montoya, *tr. fr. Spanish by* Toni Empringham. FIA

Mother. Nancy Morejón, *tr. fr. Spanish by* Kathleen Weaver. AIW

Mother. Nagase Kiyoko, *tr. fr. Japanese by* Kenneth Rexroth *and* Ikuko Atsumi. AIW; BoWoP

Mother, The. Nettie Palmer. PoAu-1

Mother, The. Padraic Pearse. TIRV

Mother. Julian Przybos, *tr. fr. Polish by* Czeslaw Milosz. PwPP

Mother. Hettye Rayburn Ramsey. PWR

Mother. Anwar Shaul, *tr. fr. Arabic by* Yoffee Berkovitz. VWA

Mother, The. W. D. Snodgrass. CAPP

Mother. Kate Starbird. TDD

Mother. Julian Tuwim, *tr. fr. Polish by* Isaac Komem. VWA

Mother, The. *Unknown, tr. fr. Chinese by* George Barrow. OHIP

Mother. Stephen Vincent. NeAC

Mother. Rosanna Warren. *Fr.* Funerary Portraits, I. NOAM

Mother. Whittier. *Fr.* Snow-bound; a Winter Idyl. AA; OHIP

Mother,/ If I am where I am. From an Asylum; Kathy Chattle to Her Mother, Ruth Arbeiter. Anne Stevenson. BrRo

Mother,/ You did not leave me an inheritance of necklaces for a wedding. Mother's Inheritance. Fawziyya Abu Khalid, *tr. by* Kamal Boullata. WPOW

Mother, among the Dustbins. Stevie Smith. PBWP

Mother and Child. Penelope Shuttle. AIW

Mother and Her Son on the Cross, The. *Unknown.* MeEL

Mother and listener she is, but she does not listen. The Question. Muriel Rukeyser. IHMS; WPOW

Mother and Poet. Elizabeth Barrett Browning. NAEL-2

Mother and Son. William Heyen. GeTw

Mother and Son. Allen Tate. LiTA; MoAB; MoAmPo

Mother Asks What I'm Put To. Julia Alvarez. *Fr.* 33. Son

Mother, because you never spoke to me. More Clues. Muriel Rukeyser. IHMS

Mother Bombie, *sel.* John Lyly.
  O Cupid! Monarch over Kings. EIL
  (Fools in Love's College.) TrGrPo
  (Song of Accius and Silena.) OBSC

Mother Cat. John Montague. AnAn; NOIV

Mother Cat's Purr. Jane Yolen. RAR

Mother Country, The. Benjamin Franklin. AiP; PAH

Mother Crab and Her Family, The. L. T. Manyase, *tr. fr. Xhosa by* Jack Cope *and* C. M. Mcanyangwa. PeSA

Mother Dark. Francesca Yetunde Pereira. PBA

Mother darling, I cannot work the loom. Sappho, *tr. by* Willis Barnstone. BoWoP

"Mother dear, may I go downtown." Ballad of Birmingham. Dudley Randall. BPo; HeIP; InPK; MoP; NIP; NoAM

Mother Dear, O! Pray for Me. *Unknown.* AH

Mother/ Deer/ Lady. Harold Littlebird. VoR

Mother, did we laugh or did we cry? Did We Laugh or Did We Cry? Patu Simoko. WMBCH

Mother Dies. Saito Mokichi, *tr. fr. Japanese by* Hiroaki Sato. FCEI

Mother does knitting, The. Familial. Jacques Prévert, *tr. by* D. J. Enright. OBD

Mother Doesn't Want a Dog. Judith Viorst. NBLV; RHPC

Mother Duck. *Unknown.* BoTP

Mother Earth. Anna Margolin, *tr. fr. Yiddish by* Keith Bosley. VWA

Mother Earth; Her Whales. Gary Snyder. LCAP; WeW

Mother England. Edith M. Thomas. AA

Mother, for months a mist has been before me. Light in Darkness. Mary E. Tucker. CBWP-1

Mother Goose Rhyme. Kenneth Rexroth. ErPo

Mother Goose Sonnets, *sel.* Harriet S. Morgridge.
  Jack and Jill. AA

Mother Goose Up-to-Date, *parodies, sels.* Louis Untermeyer.
  Archibald MacLeish Suspends the Five Little Pigs. MoAmPo
  Edgar A. Guest Considers "The Good Old Woman Who Lived in a Shoe" and the Good Old Truths Simultaneously. NIP
    (Edgar A. Guest Considers "The Old Woman Who Lived in a Shoe" and the Good Old Verities at the Same Time.) FiBHP; OBAL
    (Edgar A. Guest Syndicates the Old Woman Who Lived in a Shoe.) MoAmPo
  Edna St. Vincent Millay Exhorts Little Boy Blue. MoAmPo
  John Masefield Relates the Story of Tom, Tom, the Piper's Son. MoAmPo
  Walter de la Mare Tells the Listener about Jack and Jill. MoAmPo

Mother Goose's Garland. Archibald MacLeish. AnAmPo; OBAL

Mother Goose's Melody, *sel. Unknown.*
  Learned Song, A. FaBoUs

Mother has lupus. Dear World. Paula Gunn Allen. HATNAP

Mother-heart doth yearn at eventide, The. When Even Cometh On. Lucy Evangeline Tilley. AA

Mother, here there are shadowy salmon. Letter from Oregon. William Stafford. NaP

Mother, Home, Heaven. William Goldsmith Brown. FaBoBe

Mother, I Am. Lucille Clifton. GeTw

Mother!, I am sick. For an Obligate Parasite. Alan Dugan. TW

Mother, I am something more. Looking Out. Helen Chasin. NMM

Mother, I Cannot Mind My Wheel. Walter Savage Landor, *first st. par. fr. the Greek of* Sappho. AWP, *st.* 1; BoLoP; EnRP; GBL; NAEL-2; NOBE; OBEV; OBVE; TEP; TrGrPo

Mother, I haven't forgotten you who told. Mother, I Won't Forget. Cesare Vivaldi, *tr. by* Lawrence R. Smith. NItP

Mother, I long to get married. Whistle, Daughter, Whistle. *Unknown.* AIW; AmFP; ErPo; OBET; OxNR, *shorter vers*
  ("Mother, I longs to get married.") ErPo
  ("O mother, I longs to get married.") OBET

Mother, I may do violence to you. Mother. Sharon Mayer Libera. IHMS

Mother, I want to go. *Unknown, tr. by* Willis Barnstone. BoWoP

Mother, I went to China this morning. Who Can Say. Alastair Reid. NePoEA

Mother, I Won't Forget. Cesare Vivaldi, *tr. fr. Italian by* Lawrence R. Smith. NItP

Mother in Egypt, A. Marjorie Pickthall. CaP

"Mother-in-Law Is Cruel." Cheng Hsieh, *tr. fr. Chinese by* Jonathan Chaves. CoBLCP

Mother in the House, The. Hermann Hagedorn. OHIP

Mother in the Snow-Storm, The. Sebald Smithon. MoCV

Mother is drinking to forget a man. Frying Trout While Drunk. Lynn Emanuel. MAYP

Mother is gone. Bird songs wouldn't let her breathe. William Stafford. NaP

Mother, is this the darkness of the end. For "Our Lady of the Rocks." Dante Gabriel Rossetti. EBEV

Mother knits/ the son makes war, The. Familial. Jacques Prévert, *tr. by* Mark Strand *and* Jean Ballard. POS

Mother Land/ Long lain asleep. Mother Dark. Francesca Yetunde Pereira. PBA

Mother-land'scape (Letters). William Harmon. PPR

Mother, let me congratulate you on/ the birthday of your son. Birthday. Yevgeny Yevtushenko, *tr. by* Peter Levi *and* Robin Milner-Gulland. NAs

Mother Maudlin the Witch. Ben Jonson. *Fr.* The Sad Shepherd. ChTr

Mother, May I? Alma Villanueva. CCP; WPOW

Mother, May I Go Out to Swim? *Unknown.* FaPON; OxNR

"Mother, may I stay up tonight?" Conversation. David McCord. GrPl; SO

Mother, mother,/ Why is it not you? The One Who Struggles. Ernst Toller, *tr. by* E. Ellis Roberts. TrJP

Mother, Mother, Are You All There? Felicia Lamport. NBLV

Mother, mother, I feel sick. *Unknown.* OBD

Mother, Mother, Make My Bed. *Unknown.* ELP

Mother Mother shave me. *Unknown, tr. by* Ulli Beier. BoWoP

Mother, mother, what illbred aunt. The Disquieting Muses. Sylvia Plath. NMM; TV

Mother, my eyes wait on you, unfulfilled. Mother. Anwar Shaul, *tr. by* Yoffee Berkovitz. VWA

Mother, my Mary Gray. The Division of Parts. Anne Sexton. NePoEA-2

Mother Night. James Weldon Johnson. Son

Mother o' blossoms, and ov all. William Barnes. *Fr.* May. ChTr

Mother o' Mine. Kipling. *Fr.* The Light That Failed. FaFP; WBLP

Mother of composition, arrangement, The. Three Songs. William Dickey. BLA

Mother of Dante, The. Angelos Sikelianos, *tr. fr. Greek by* Edmund Keeley *and* Philip Sherrard. VMG

Mother of Fishermen. Henriëtte Roland-Holst, *tr. by* Ria Leigh-Loohuizen. PBWP

Mother of God, in this brazen sun. Denis Glover. *Fr.* Arawata Bill. ATNZ

Mother of God! no lady thou. Our Lady. Mary Elizabeth Coleridge. OBEV; OBMV; WPE

Mother of God! Our Lady! For Eleanor and Bill Monahan. William Carlos Williams. CRP, *abr.;* VGW

Mother of God that's Lady of the Heavens. Prayer of the Old Woman. Villon, *tr. by* J. M. Synge. MoBrPo

Mother of God, whose burly love. On the Eve of the Feast of the Immaculate Conception: 1942. Robert Lowell. WaaP

"Mother of heaven, regina of the clouds." Le Monocle de Mon Oncle. Wallace Stevens. LiTM; MoAB

Mother of Hermes! and still youthful Maia! Fragment of an Ode to Maia Written on May Day, 1818. Keats. EnRP; OAEL-2; OBEV; PoEL-4

Mother of Man. Vesna Parun, *tr. fr. Croatian by* Mary Coote. PBWP

Mother of memories! O mistress-queen! Le Balcon. Baudelaire, *tr. by* Lord Alfred Douglas. AWP

Mother of musings, contemplation sage. The Pleasures of Melancholy. Thomas Warton the Younger. EnRP

Mother of my birth, for how long were we together. Kaddish. David Ignatow. NU; VWA

Mother of nations, of them eldest we. America to England. George Edward Woodberry. AA

Mother of Nothing. Naomi Shihab Nye. NAmP

Mother of roots, you have not seeded. Goodbye to the Poetry of Calcium. James Wright. CAPP

Mother of the Groom. Seamus Heaney. OxBSP

Mother of the muses, we are taught, The. Memory. Walter Savage Landor. EBEV; NOBVV; OAEL-2

Mother Poem. Joel Oppenheimer. PoM

Mother presses her head to her hand, already, The. Mother. Rosanna Warren. *Fr.* Funerary Portraits, I. NOAM

Mother said if I wore this hat. My Hat. Stevie Smith. BrRo

Mother said to call her if the H bomb exploded. Belief. Josephine Miles. FaBoWP; MoP; NoAM; TAP

Mother Sarah's Lullaby ("Mother Sarah rocks the cradle.") Itzik Manger, *tr. fr. Yiddish by* Jacob Sonntag. TrJP

Mother shake the cherry-tree. Let's Be Merry. Christina Rossetti. *Fr.* Sing-Song. FaPON

Mother, she asks, with what can I worship? Ravidas, *tr. by* John Stratton Hawley *and* Mark Juergensmeyer. SSI

Mother Shipton's Prophecies. *At. to* Charles Hindley. BLPA

Mother Speaks: The Algiers Motel Incident, Detroit, A. Michael S. S. Harper. AmPA; BPo

Mother Tabbyskins. Elizabeth Anna Hart. CenHV; OxBChV

Mother, The ("From out the south the genial breezes sigh.") *Unknown, tr. fr. Chinese by* George Barrow. OHIP

Mother the Wardrobe Is Full of Infantrymen. Roger McGough. MAT

Mother to Her Waking Infant, A. Joanna Baillie. NOEC

Mother to Son. Langston Hughes. AmNP; CDC; NAAL-2; NTCP; OBCA; PoNe; SO; TTY

Mother Tongue. Jon Stallworthy. NoAM

Mother was a crack of light. Three Floors. Stanley Kunitz. SM

Mother was a wolf; snarled her long. Recollection. Donald D. Govan. NBP

Mother watched her daughter kneeling, The. Fish Story. Sharon Olds. TV

Mother Wept. Joseph Skipsey. EBVV; PF

Mother wept, A: where were You, God. Calvary. Libby Stopple. GoYe

Mother what happened in the beginning. Sister Mother. Franca Maria Catri, *tr. by* Muriel Kittel. DMI

Mother Who Died Too, The. Edith M. Thomas. AA

Mother with Child. Lenore Keeshig-Tobias. GOS

Motherhood. Charles Stuart Calverley. FM

Motherhood. Agnes Lee. BLPA

Motherhood. May Swenson. CoAP

Motherless I have become. When Mother Died. Natsume Seibi, *tr. fr. Japanese by* Hiroaki Sato. *Fr.* Twenty-seven Hokku. FCEI

Mothers. Auvaiyar, *tr. fr. Tamil by* A. K. Ramanujan. PLW

Mothers. Angela Figueroa-Aymerich, *tr. fr. Spanish by* Kate Flores. DMH

Mothers. Nikki Giovanni. CNA; TV; UnPo

Mothers. Kakkai Patiniyar Naccellaiyar, *tr. fr. Tamil by* A. K. Ramanujan. PLW

Mothers. Kavarpentu, *tr. fr. Tamil by* A. K. Ramanujan. PLW

Mothers. Maturaipputan Ilankanar, *tr. fr. Tamil by* A. K. Ramanujan. PLW

Mothers. Punkanuttiraiyar, *tr. fr. Tamil by* A. K. Ramanujan. PLW

Mothers. Tristan Tzara, *tr. fr. French by* Willis Barnstone *and* Matei Calinescu. VWA

Mothers/ cranking the machine. The Greater Friendship Baptist Church. Carole C. Gregory. BlSi

Mothers,/ That hope of yours, your joyful burden. To the Mothers. Ernst Toller, *tr. by* E. Ellis Roberts. TrJP

Mothers: A Meditation. Mary Pierce Brosmer. ER

Mother's Advice. *Unknown.* AmFP

Mothers—and Others. Amos R. Wells. WBLP

Mothers are hardest to forgive. The Adversary. Phyllis McGinley. OBCA

Mother's Birthday, A. Henry Van Dyke. OHIP

Mother's Birthday. Lydia Wagenlander. PWR

Mother's Choice, The. *Unknown.* OxBoLi

Mothers, Daughters. Shirley Kaufman. BoWoP; NMM; TV

Mother's Day. Edwin Becker. PWR

Mother's Day. Sandie Castle. UL

Mother's Day. Jerome Sala. UL

Mother's face looked tired and worn, The. The Skeptic. Clara Ann Thompson. CBWP-2

Mother's got salve. Color of Honey. Anne Waldman. TV

Mother's Habits. Nikki Giovanni. BlSi

Mother's hardest to forgive, A. The Adversary. Phyllis McGinley. FaBoEE; OBCA; OxBSP

Mother's Hymn, The. Bryant. OHIP

Mother's Inheritance. Fawziyya Abu Khalid, *tr. fr. Arabic by* Kamal Boullata. WPOW

Mother's Joy, A. Ruth Fortney Maxwell. PWR

Mother's Lament, The. Mary E. Tucker. CBWP-1

Mother's Lament for the Death of Her Son, A. Burns. HoPM

Mother's List of Duties, A. Ponmutiyar, *tr. fr. Tamil by* A. K. Ramanujan. PLW

Mother's Love. Ross B. Clapp. WBLP

Mother's Love, A. Josephine D. Henderson Heard. CBWP-4

Mother's Lullaby, The. John Clare. NAs

Mother's Malison; or, Clyde's Water, The. *Unknown.* ESPB

Mother's Nerves. X. J. Kennedy. GrPl; RHPC

Mothers of America. Ave Maria. Frank O'Hara. HCAP; NAAL-2; NNaP; NoP; PoM

Mothers of Men, The. Joaquin Miller

Mothers of our forest-time, The! The Mothers of the West. William Davis Gallagher. PAH

Mothers of sailors, I hope you will draw nigh. Johnny Gallagher. *Unknown.* AmFP

Mothers of Sons. Lesley Saunders. BrRo

Mothers of the West, The. William Davis Gallagher. PAH

Mother's Picture, A. Edmund Clarence Stedman. OHIP

Mother's Prayer, A. Margaret Elizabeth Sangster. TrPWD

Mother's Recall. Mary Weston Fordham. CBWP-2

Mother's Song, The. Virginia Woodward Cloud. AA

Mother's Song. *Unknown, tr. by* Willis Barnstone. BoWoP

Mother's Song, The. *Unknown, tr. fr. Eskimo by* Peter Freuchen. OBCP; WTO

Mother's Song. *Unknown.* GN

Mother's Voice. Robert Creeley. CAPP; NIP

Mothers who clutch the hands of your children. Dancing on Water. Harold Bond. TSM

Moths. Julia Fields. *Fr.* Poems: Birmingham 1962–1964. PoBA; PoNe
Moths, The. Michael Jackson. ATNZ; PeNZ
Moths, The. W. S. Merwin. HeIP
Moths, The. Sean O Riordain, *tr. fr. Irish* by Thomas Kinsella. NOIV
Moth's kiss, first, The! Robert Browning. *Fr.* In a Gondola. BoLoP; GBL; OBEV
   (Song: "Moth's kiss, first, The!") TrGrPo
Mothy Monologue. Ralph Gustafson. NOBC
Motion of gathering loops of water, The. The Glass Bubbles. Samuel Greenberg. LiTA
Motion of the Earth, The. Norman Nicholson. ImOP
Motion Which Disestablishes Organizes Everything. A. R. Ammons. BAP
Motionless Clouds. T'ao Ch'ien, *tr. fr. Chinese* by Burton Watson. CoBCP
Motionless—His sons. Death Bed. Thomas Kinsella. CIP
Motions and means, on land and sea at war. Steamboats, Viaducts, and Railways. Wordsworth. NAEL-2
Motion's Holdings. A. R. Ammons. NoAM
Motion's the dead giveaway. Viable. A. R. Ammons. TAP
Motive. Muriel Rukeyser. PoA
Motive for Mercy. Ken Milburn. PoSH
Motive for Metaphor, The. Wallace Stevens. MoAB; MoAmPo
Motley. Peter Davison. NBLV
Motley. Walter de la Mare. HoPM; MMA
Motley's the Only Wear. Shakespeare. *Fr.* As You Like It, II, vii. TrGrPo
Motor Bus. Alfred Denis Godley. FaBoCo; NOBL
   (On the Motor Bus.) FaBoNo
Motor Cars. Rowena Bastin Bennett. FaPON
Motorbike, A. Ted Hughes. InPS
Motorboat stalling, The. Port Morazán. Carlos Martínez Rivas, *tr.* by Alejandro Murguía *and* Walter Martínez. Vol
Motorcycle. Benjamin Sturgis Pray. GoYe
Motorcycle Evolution. Peter Payack. BWV
Motorcycle Irene. Skip Spence. MAT
Motorcycle Racer Thinks of Quitting. Grace Butcher. ASP
Motorcyclists, The. James Tate. MAYP; NoAM
Motown/ Smokey Robinson. Jessica Hagedorn. BrSi; UL
Motto, The. Abraham Cowley. SeCP
Motto. Langston Hughes. PoBA; PoNe
Motto for a Sundial. *Unknown.* FaBoEE
Motto Vision 1971. Delano Abdul Malik de Coteau. PBCV
Mottoes. Basho, *tr. fr. Japanese* by Burton Watson. *Fr.* Seventy-six Hokku. FCEI
Mould of Castile. Jack R. Clemo. NOCV
Mouldering Vine, The. *Unknown.* AmFP
Mound, The. Thomas Hardy. OxBTC
Mound, The, *sels.* Perets Markish, *tr. fr. Yiddish* by Leonard Wolf. PeBMYV
   "After you, the killed of the Ukraine."
   "No! Heavenly tallow, don't lick my gummy beards."
Mounds of Human Heads Are Wandering into the Distance. Osip Mandelstam, *tr. fr. Russian* by W. S. Merwin *and* Clarence Brown. FaBoPV
Mounds of humped rust-colored hills. Safed. Dovid Knut, *tr.* by Daniel Weissbort. VWA
Mount, The. Léonie Adams. MoAB; MoAmPo
Mount Arachi so steep. Saigyo, *tr. fr. Japanese* by Burton Watson. *Fr.* Sixty-four Tanka. FCEI
Mount Badon. Charles Williams. FaBoTw
Mount Caribou at Night. Charles Wright. LCAP
Mount Fuji, Opus 5. Kusano Shimpei, *tr. fr. Japanese* by Geoffrey Bownas *and* Anthony Thwaite. PeBJV
Mount Futagami, round which flow. Yakamochi. *Fr.* Manyo Shu. Ma
Mount Gilboa. Malka Heifetz-Tussman, *tr. fr. Yiddish* by Marcia Falk. PBWP
Mount Kagu strove with Mount Miminashi. Emperor Tenji. *Fr.* Manyo Shu. Ma
Mount Lykaion. Trumbull Stickney. *Fr.* Sonnets from Greece. OxBA; Son; TrGrPo
Mount—mount for the hunting—with musket and spear! The Lion-Hunt. Thomas Pringle. OBTV
Mount of the Muses, The. Robert Herrick. CaPo
Mount Sumeru mallet firmly gripped, The. Shonen, *tr.* by Lucien Stryk *and* Takashi Ikemoto. ZPCJ
Mount Vernon. *Unknown.* AmFP; OFD
Mount Vernon, the Home of Washington. William Day. OHIP
Mount Yoshino/ looking at pines awhile. *Unknown, tr.* by Burton Watson. FCEI

Mount Yoshino, *sels.* Rai San'yo, *tr. fr. Chinese* by Burton Watson. JLIC-2
   "I attend her palanquin a hundred miles." *Fr.* I.
   "On flowered paths, squeaks of flying squirrels." *Fr.* III.
   "Ten thousand heaps of fragrant snow fallen in the dust." *Fr.* II.
Mount Zion. *Unknown.* AmFP
Mountain, The. Robert Finch. CaP
Mountain, The. Robert Frost. FaBV
Mountain, The. Louise Glück. NoAM
Mountain, The. Shirley Kaufman. TV
Mountain, The. Mikhail Yurevich Lermontov, *tr. fr. Russian* by Max Eastman. AWP
Mountain, The. W. S. Merwin. VGW
Mountain, The. Musaemura Bonus Zimunya. WMBCH
Mountain Afterglow, The. James Laughlin. VGW
Mountain Altar, The. Brian O'Higgins. TIRV
Mountain Barrier. Su Shao-lien, *tr. fr. Chinese* by Dominic Cheung. IFON
Mountain Bride. Robert Morgan. GeTw; MAYP; MOWH; MT
Mountain Brook. Elizabeth Jane Coatsworth. RHPC
Mountain Cemetery, The. Edgar Bowers. NePoEA
Mountain clouds half colored. On the Road to Takaya. Kan Sazan, *tr. by* Burton Watson. JLIC-2
Mountain colors, whether near or far. Distant Mountains. Ou-yang Hsiu, *tr. by* Burton Watson. CoBCP
Mountain Convent. Laura Benét. GoYe
Mountain Corral. Helen Sorrells. WPE
Mountain Creed. Medora Addison Nutter. GoYe
Mountain Creed. Hugh C. Rae. PoSH
Mountain Days. Barclay Fraser. PoSH
Mountain Drive. Cothrai Gogan. TIRV
Mountain Dwelling. Ching An, *tr. fr. Chinese* by Irving Lo. WFTU
Mountain, Fire, Thornbush. Harvey Shapiro. VGW
Mountain Flowers. Ho Ning, *tr. fr. Chinese* by Lois Fusek. ATF
Mountain Girl. Rafaela Chacón Nardi, *tr. fr. Spanish* by Margaret Randall. AIW
Mountain Greenery. Lorenz Hart. OBAL
Mountain Hawthorns. Chang Pi, *tr. fr. Chinese* by Lois Fusek. ATF
Mountain Hawthorns. Niu Hsi-chi, *tr. fr. Chinese* by Lois Fusek. ATF
Mountain Hawthorns. Sun Kuang-hsien, *tr. fr. Chinese* by Lois Fusek. ATF
Mountain Hawthorns. Wei Ch'eng-pan, *tr. fr. Chinese* by Lois Fusek. ATF
Mountain Haze. Keiun, *tr. fr. Japanese* by Steven D. Carter. WFTW
Mountain held the town as in a shadow, The. The Mountain. Robert Frost. FaBV
Mountain Hut in a Storm. Tamekane, *tr. fr. Japanese* by Steven D. Carter. WFTW
Mountain in Labor, The. Aesop, *tr. fr. Greek* by William Ellery Leonard. AWP
Mountain is a sort of music, A: theme. Moment Musical in Assynt. Norman MacCaig. PoSH
Mountain is the father of the clouds, The. A Painting in the Style of Secretary Kao. Yün Shou-p'ing, *tr. by* Jonathan Chaves. CoBLCP
Mountain is wild with men, The. Matronita. Dennis Silk. VWA
Mountain Lion. D. H. Lawrence. Mes; OBTV; OxBTC; RB; RFM
Mountain Meadows. Martha Keller. BoNaP
Mountain Medicine. Elizabeth-Ellen Long. AmFN
Mountain mist: a horse-dung cleaner. Issa, *tr. fr. Japanese* by Hiroaki Sato. *Fr.* Forty-four Hokku. FCEI
Mountain of green trees and orioles everywhere! Hsü Pen, *tr. fr. Chinese* by Jonathan Chaves. *Fr.* A Leisurely Stroll. CoBLCP
Mountain of the lovers, The, *sel.* Paul Hamilton Hayne.
   Love Scorns Degrees. AnAmPo
Mountain our life is, overlooking, A. The Abyss of Death. Ma ruf al-Rasafi, *tr. by* Issa Boullata *and* Christopher Middleton. MAP
Mountain Oysters. Patrick Lane. NeAC
Mountain pass is magnificent, yet the road is arduous, The. Blocked by Snow. Wu Wei-yeh, *tr. by* Marie Chan. WFTU
Mountain path is steep, The. An Sending Spring Love to Tzu-. Yü Hsüan-Chi, *tr. by* Kenneth Rexroth *and* Ling Chung. UnAS
Mountain pavilion is silent—few people visit me here, The. T'ang Yin, *tr. fr. Chinese* by Jonathan Chaves. *Fr.* Poems Inscribed on Paintings. CoBLCP
Mountain people/ making their way toward home, The. Leaves Falling at Dusk. Tameshige, *tr. by* Steven D. Carter. WFTW
Mountain Rain. Ho Shao-chi, *tr. fr. Chinese* by J. D. Schmidt. WFTU
Mountain Residence of Secretary Cheng Ching-ssu, The. Hsü Pen, *tr. fr. Chinese* by Jonathan Chaves. CoBLCP
Mountain Retreat of a Recluse, The. Chang Yü, *tr. fr. Chinese* by Jonathan Chaves. CoBLCP

Mountain road is steep, the stone steps are dangerous, The. Spring Thoughts Sent to Tzu-an. Yü Hsüan-chi, *tr. by* Geoffrey Waters. BoWoP

Mountain sat upon the plain, The. Emily Dickinson. FaBV

Mountain Sculpture. James Will. PoSH

Mountain sheep are sweeter, The. The War Song of Dinas Vawr. Thomas Love Peacock. *Fr.* The Misfortunes of Elphin. AWP; EnRP; FaBoCh; FaPoR; HAP; InvP; NAEL-2; NOBE; OAEL-2; OnMSP; PrIm; WaaP; WeW; WiR

Mountain slopes crawl with lumberjacks, The. Chin-doba, *tr. by* Lucien Stryk *and* Takashi Ikemoto. ZPCJ

Mountain snow. Seasons in Santa Fe. Gerald Vizenor. HATNAP

Mountain soars and the sea sings on its side, The. Wakayama Bokusui, *tr. fr. Japanese by* Hiroaki Sato. *Fr.* Forty-four Tanka. FCEI

Mountain Soprano. Martha McFerren. KS

Mountain Spirit, The. *Unknown, tr. fr. Chinese by* Burton Watson. *Fr.* Nine Songs. CoBCP

Mountain spring: near the black sleeve, A. Sampu, *tr. by* Sato. FCEI

Mountain stood here once, The. Excerpts from the Modern Tragedy. Sándor Weöres, *tr. by* Jascha Kessler. FOC

Mountain Stream, The. John Ceiriog Hughes, *tr. fr. Welsh by* Kenneth Hurlstone Jackson. OBWVE

Mountain stream, The. Shunzei, *tr. fr. Japanese by* Burton Watson. *Fr.* Thirty Tanka. FCEI

Mountain Study. Peter Van Toorn. NOBC

Mountain summits sleep, The: glens, cliffs, and caves. Sleep Upon the World. Alcman, *tr. by* Thomas Campbell. ChTr (Fragment: "Mountain summits sleep, glens, cliffs, and caues, The.") AWP

Mountain Talk. A. R. Ammons. HCAP

Mountain teeth, tips of anemious rippled stone. On the Subject of Waves. Eldon Grier. MoCV

Mountain temple dim and far away, its back against the setting sun, A. Wang Kuo-wei, *tr. by* Ching-i Tu. WFTU

Mountain temple: no one comes, A. Miura Chora, *tr. fr. Japanese by* Hiroaki Sato. *Fr.* Sixteen Hokku. FCEI

Mountain tips are white and dead, The. The River. Leo Vroman. VWA

Mountain-Toilet Thief, A. Al Robles. BrSi

Mountain Tops. Lizelia Augusta Jenkins Moorer. CBWP-3

Mountain Town—Mexico. Eldon Grier. NOBC

Mountain Tree, The. Hugh Connell. NeIP

Mountain Vigil. Douglas Fraser. PoSH

Mountain was in great distress and loud, A. The Mountain in Labor. Aesop, *tr. by* William Ellery Leonard. AWP

Mountain water, trickly. Ozaki Hosai, *tr. fr. Japanese by* Hiroaki Sato. *Fr.* One Hundred Haiku in Free Form. FCEI

Mountain where I danced on moonlit stones, The. Cairngorm, November 1971. Martyn Berry. PoSH

Mountain Whippoorwill, The. Stephen Vincent Benét. TrGrPo

Mountain Wind, A. "Æ." AWP

Mountain Wind. Barbara Kunz Loots. RHPC

Mountain wind, The. Kyogoku Tamekane, *tr. fr. Japanese by* Burton Watson. *Fr.* Twenty-three Tanka. FCEI

Mountain wind blows, The. Tonna, *tr. by* Steven D. Carter. WFTW

Mountain windows scan the deep valley. Autumn Day at the Home of Prince Nagaya. Hironiwa, *tr. by* Burton Watson. JLIC-1

Mountain winds, The. Tamesuke, *tr. by* Steven D. Carter. WFTW

Mountaineer, The. Robert Nathan. TrJP

Mountaineer is working with his Bible, The. Quatrina. Joseph Deericks Bennett. LiTA

Mountaineering Bus. Rennie McOwan. PoSH

Mountains. W. H. Auden. FaBoPV

Mountains, The. Louis Dudek. CaP

Mountains, The. Walker Gibson. SD

Mountains. Lucy Larcom. WBLP

Mountains, The. Walter de la Mare. BrPo

Mountains after mountains, road upon road scramble. Galilee. Perets Markish, *tr. by* Leonard Wolf. PeBMYV

Mountains and cold places on the earth. The Cloud Factory. John Haines. EAS

Mountains and rivers are like discarded shoes. Kings and Emperors. Cheng Hsieh, *tr. by* Jan *and* Yvonne Walls. WFTU

Mountains and Rivers without End: The Market, *sel.* Gary Snyder. "Seventy-five feet hoed rows equals." NaP

Mountains, and the lonely death at last, The. To a Traveler. Lionel Johnson. MoBrPo

Mountains are dragons, The. Nightmare on Rhum. James Macmillan. PoSH

Mountains are low, The. Buson, *tr. fr. Japanese by* Hiroaki Sato. *Fr.* Eighty-seven Hokku. FCEI

Mountains are moving, rivers. The Redwoods. Louis Simpson. AmFN; CoAP

Mountains are steadfast but the mountain streams. Hwang Chin-i, *tr. by* Peter H. Lee. PBWP

Mountains beyond the city fade to nothingness, The. Bamboo Branch Song of Han-chia. Wang Shih-chen, *tr. by* Jonathan Chaves. CoBLCP

Mountains by the seaside—sharp pointed swords. A Poem to Send to Friends in the Capital. Liu Tsung-yüan, *tr. by* Burton Watson. CoBCP

Mountains cannot block this dreamlike song, The. Hearing a Flute on the River Chi. Wen Cheng-ming, *tr. by* Jonathan Chaves. CoBLCP

Mountains carry snow, the season fails, The. The Homer Mitchell Place. John Engels. SM

Mountains darkened, The. Buson, *tr. fr. Japanese by* Hiroaki Sato. *Fr.* Eighty-seven Hokku. FCEI

Mountains, darkening, have robbed. Buson, *tr. fr. Japanese by* Hiroaki Sato. *Fr.* Eighty-seven Hokku. FCEI

Mountains far away. Landscape Philosophy. Wang Jun-hua, *tr. by* Dominic Cheung. IFON

Mountain's giddy height I sought, A. The Lay of the Trilobite. May Kendall. CenHV

Mountains grow unnoticed, The. Emily Dickinson. MoAB; MoAmPo; TrGrPo

Mountains have gathered in the distance. Sleep on the Fraser. Patrick Lane. NeAC

Mountains loom upon the path we take. Song to the Mountains. *Unknown, tr. by* Alice C. Fletcher. AWP

Mountains nuzzle mountains. The Scene. Denis Glover. *Fr.* Arawata Bill. ATNZ

Mountains of Ch'u are dark green, The. Song of the Fisherman. Li Hsün, *tr. by* Lois Fusek. ATF

Mountains on the screen shimmer in the golden dawn, The. Deva-like Barbarian. Wen T'ing-yün, *tr. by* Lois Fusek. ATF

Mountains ring, the wild wind comes, The. Wild Wind. Li Meng-yang, *tr. by* Jonathan Chaves. CoBLCP

Mountains shine through forest breaks, bamboo hides the wall. Tune: Partridge Sky. Su Tung-p'o, *tr. by* Burton Watson. CoBCP

Mountain's Side, The. Shmu'el Shatal, *tr. fr. Hebrew by* Bernhard Frank. MHeP

Mountains taught us speechlessness, The. Alps. Rosanna Warren. MAYP

Mountains that I like, The. Homeward Bound. Ezekiel Mphahlele. WMBCH

Mountaintop: as far as I can see. Wakayama Bokusui, *tr. fr. Japanese by* Hiroaki Sato. *Fr.* Forty-four Tanka. FCEI

Mountebanks, The. Charles Henry Lüders. AA

Mountebank's Mask, The, *sel.* Thomas Campion. Hours of Sleepy Night, The. EIL (Dismissal.) OBSC

Mounted on a mule, to ford the shallow stream. P'eng Sun-yü, *tr. fr. Chinese by* Daniel Bryant. *Fr.* North-of-the-River Rhymes, III. WFTU

Mounting lark, day's herald, got on wing, The. William Browne. *Fr.* Britannia's Pastorals, I, Song 3. PBBP

Mountown! thou sweet retreat from Dublin cares. William King. *Fr.* Mully of Mountown. FaBoPP; OBTV

Mourn for Yourself. Geoffrey Keating, *tr. fr. Irish by* Sean Lucy. BIrV

Mourn, hapless Caledonia, mourn. The Tears of Scotland. Tobias Smollett. NOEC

Mourn No More. At. to John Fletcher. See Queen of Corinth, The: Weep No More.

Mourn Not for Adonais. Shelley. See Adonais; an Elegy on the Death of John Keats: Peace, peace! he is not dead, he doth not sleep.

Mourn not, friends, mourn not, bereaved. Lines on the Death of the Rev. S. K. Talmage. Mary E. Tucker. CBWP-1

Mourn, ye wee songsters o' the wood. Burns. *Fr.* Elegy on Captain Matthew Henderson. PBBP

Mourners, The. Bevil Higgons. APAS

Mourners drive away, The. The Mowing Crew. Baron Wormser. MAYP

Mournful Dove, The. *Unknown.* AmFP

Mournful is the remembrance which awakes. William Haygarth. *Fr.* Greece. OBTV

Mournful wind. Gyodai, *tr. by* Geoffrey Bownas *and* Anthony Thwaite. PeBJV

Mourning. Andrew Marvell. SeCP

Mourning a Lost Poem. Ed Coletti. SoTCo

Mourning and Melancholia. Alfred Alvarez. VWA

Mourning Conquest; or, The Woman's Sad Complaint, and Doleful Cry to See Her Love in Fainting Fits to Lye, The. *Unknown.* CoMu

Mourning for Lü Hui-chiu, *sel.* Yün Shou-p'ing, *tr. fr. Chinese by* Jonathan Chaves.
  "Facing you, on the wall, across from your bed." CoBLCP

Mourning for My Son Jun-erh, *sels.* Cheng Hsieh, *tr. fr. Chinese by* Jonathan Chaves. CoBLCP
  "At the dawn of your life, you ate gruel."
  "When a wax candle burns down, ashes are left behind."

Mourning for My Teacher Hokuju. Buson, *tr. fr. Japanese by* Hiroaki Sato. FCEI

Mourning for My Younger Sister. Rai San'yo, *tr. fr. Chinese by* Burton Watson. JLIC-2

Mourning Letter from Paris, A. Conrad Kent Rivers. BPo

Mourning Pablo Neruda. Robert Bly. LCAP

Mourning Picture. Adrienne Rich. CoAP

Mourning Pictures, *sel.* Honor Moore.
  "Ladies and Gentlemen, my mother is." TV

Mourning Poem for the Queen of Sunday. Robert Hayden. HCAP; NoAM; NoP; PoBA

Mourning Song. Robert Pearl, *tr. fr. Tsimshian Indian by* Armand Schwerner. STP

Mourning-Song for Rangiaho, A. Te Heuheu Herea, *tr. fr. Maori by* Barry Mitcalfe. WTO

Mouse, The. Elizabeth Jane Coatsworth. BoTP; FaPON; MoShBr; OBCA

Mouse, The. Jean Garrigue. TwCP

Mouse, The. Louis Johnson. ATNZ

Mouse, The. Hugh McCrae. PoAu-1

Mouse, The. Laura Elizabeth Richards. OBCA

Mouse, The. Thirza Wakley. BoTP

Mouse and the Cake, The. Eliza Cook. OxBChV

Mouse-brown foal that fain had fed, The. The Foal. William Renton. NOBVV

Mouse Dinner. Aileen Fisher, *tr. fr. Armenian.* TSS

Mouse Dinners, The. Russell Edson. SoSe

Mouse doesn't dine, A. Mouse Dinner. Aileen Fisher. TSS

Mouse found a beautiful piece of plum cake, A. The Mouse and the Cake. Eliza Cook. OxBChV

Mouse in the Wainscot, The. Ian Serraillier. PDV

Mouse, The Frog and The Little Red Hen, The. *Unknown.* BoTP

Mouse the trap had slapped on, but not caught, A. Ballad of the Mouse. Robert Wallace. NYBP

Mousemeal. Howard Nemerov. TwCP

Mouse's Lullaby, The. Palmer Cox. OBCA

Mouse's Nest. John Clare. ChTr; InPK; LiTB; NAEL-2; RB

Mouse's Petition, The. Anna Laetitia Barbauld. FM; OxBChV

Mouse's Tale, The. "Lewis Carroll." *See* Alice's Adventures in Wonderland: Fury Said to a Mouse.

Mousie, mousie. Conversation. Rose Fyleman. BoTP

Mouth. Clarisse Nicoïdski, *tr. fr. Judezmo by* Stephen Levy. VWA

Mouth. Dennis Scott. PBCV

Mouth and the Ears, The. Shem-Tob ben Joseph Palquera, *tr. fr. Hebrew by* J. Chotzner. TrJP

Mouth. Can blow or breathe, A. Cardinal Ideograms. May Swenson. OBCA

Mouth like old silk soft with use, A. A Levantine. William Plomer. OBMV

Mouth of the Hudson, The. Robert Lowell. AiP; AmFN; NaP

Mouth of the mare, The. *Unknown. Fr.* Manyo Shu. Ma

Mouth of the sealed well. Dream. Malka Heifetz Tussman, *tr. by* Kathryn Hellerstein. AYP

Mouth of the Wen River—240 feet wide, The. On Board a Boat at Chi-ning. Yüan Hung-tao, *tr. by* Jonathan Chaves. CoBLCP

Mouth should launch words gracefully, A. James Weigel, Jr. *Fr.* Testament, XXX. TSM

Mouth to mouth joined we lie, her naked breasts. Tantalos. Paulus Silentiarius, *tr. by* Dudley Fitts. ErPo

Move Continuing, The. Al Young. PoBA

Move him into the sun. Futility. Wilfred Owen. CMoP; FaBoMo; GTBS-P; MMA; MoAB; MoBrPo; NAEL-2; NoAM; NoP; OBWP; RB; SeCePo; TrGrPo

Move into/ the past tense. Grammar Lesson. Linda Pastan. Psk

Move On, Yiddish Poet. Jacob Glatstein, *tr. fr. Yiddish by* Ruth Whitman. VWA

Move over, Ali Baba! Now there comes. Autosonic Door. Dorothy Brown Thompson. GoYe

Move over, ham. Hiding Place. Richard Armour. NIP

Move to the front. The Death of a Parent. Linda Pastan. BLA

Moved by the miracles of saints. The Raising of the Dead. Rosemary Dobson. PoAu-2

Moved towards a Future. Laura Chester. NPGG

Movement. Denise Levertov. LLLT

Movement along the Frieze. Caroline Knox. BAP

Movement of Fish, The. James Dickey. NYBP; VGW

Movement, she explained, would bring poetry to the rich, The. Ralph Hodgson. *Fr.* Flying Scrolls. FaBoTw

Movement Song. Audre Lorde. CNA

Movements. Norman MacCaig. OxBC

Movie Actors Scribbling Letters Very Fast in Crucial Scenes. Jean Garrigue. TAP

Movie-Going. John Hollander. CoAP

Movie Run Backward, The. Robert Creeley. CAPP

Movie within a Movie. Denis Johnson. NAmP

Movies, The. Jack Gilbert. NPGG

Movies are badder. Saturday Afternoon at the Movies. John Logan. NNaP

Movies for the Home. Howard Moss. NePoEA-2; NYBP

Movies, Left to Right. Robert Sward. NYBP

Moviestar. Thulani Davis. ER

Moving/ resting is meaningless. Unoku, *tr. by* Lucien Stryk *and* Takashi Ikemoto. ZPCJ

Moving. Darrell Gray. UL

Moving. P. J. Kavanagh. PoPo

Moving. Janet Reed McFatter. GrPl

Moving. Frank Steele. GOYP; MOWH

Moving Ahead. Rainer Maria Rilke, *tr. fr. German by* Robert Bly. NU

Moving between Beloit and Monroe. Bink Noll. GrPl

Moving form or rigid mass, A. Song of the Screw. *Unknown.* NA

Moving from Cheer to Joy, from Joy to All. Next Day. Randall Jarrell. HAP; HCAP; MoP; NAAL-2; NoAM; NoP; NYBP; WeW

Moving from left to left, the light. View of the Capitol from the Library of Congress. Elizabeth Bishop. AmFN

Moving House ("A long time I've wanted to live in the southern village"). T'ao Ch'ien, *tr. fr. Chinese.* CoBCP

Moving House ("In spring and fall there are many days"). T'ao Ch'ien, *tr. fr. Chinese by* Burton Watson. CoBCP

Moving In. Paul Engle. PoA

Moving In. Josephine Miles. NoP

Moving In. Karl Shapiro. NAs

Moving: New York—New Haven Line. Alfred Corn. MAYP

Moving of stones, that sly jockeying thrust, The. Stones. Maxine W. Kumin. CAPP

Moving on or going back to where you came from. A Procession at Candlemas. Amy Clampitt. FaBoWP; HCAP

Moving Out. Robley Wilson, Jr. KS

Moving out. Thing Poem. Petra von Morstein, *tr. by* Rosemarie Waldrop. BoWoP

Moving over the hills, crossing the irrigation. Some San Francisco Poems. George Oppen. NNaP

Moving shadows, The. Virgil Hutton. InPK

Moving sun-shapes on the spray, The. Going and Staying. Thomas Hardy. CMoP; NoAM

Moving through the silent crowd. Stephen Spender. NOBE

Moving to the Cottage of Pine and Bamboo, *sels.* Chang Wen-t'ao, *tr. fr. Chinese by* William Schultz.
  "Pure is the sandalwood incense—a good place to live." *Fr.* I. WFTU
  "This floating life—a grain of millet on a boundless sea!" *Fr.* II. WFTU

Mower, The. *Unknown.* CoMu; OBET

Mower against Gardens, The. Andrew Marvell. EBEV; FaBoPV; LiTB; NAEL-1; NoP; OAEL-1; PoE; PoEL-2; PPP; SeCV-1

Mower in Ohio, The. John James Piatt. AA

Mower to the Glow-Worms [or Glowworms], The. Andrew Marvell. AWP; ELP; InvP; NAEL-1; NOBE; NoP; OAEL-1; OxBoLi; PPP; TrGrPo
  (Mower to the Glo-Worms, The.) EnLoPo; MePo; OBS; PoEL-2; SeCP

Mowers: An Anticipation of the Cholera, 1848, The. Charles MacKay. EBVV

Mowers begin, The. Watchers. W. S. Merwin. NaP

Mower's Song, The. Andrew Marvell. NAEL-1; PoEL-2; PPP; SeCP; SeCV-1

Mowers, weary and brown, and blithe. Scythe Song. Andrew Lang. GN

Mowing. Robert Frost. AnAmPo; BLPL; CMoP; HoPM; LiTA; NAAL-2; NOBA; OxBA; PPP; VGW

Mowing, The. Sir Charles G. D. Roberts. NOBC; OBCV

Mowing Crew, The. Baron Wormser. MAYP

Mowing the Lawn. John Bensko. MAYP
Moxford Book of English Verse, The, *sels.* Archibald Stodart-Walker. CenHV
  Counsel to Girls.
  Early Bacon.
  Inflictis.
Moyshe-Leib stops in the middle of the night. Why Not. Moyshe-Leyb Halpern, *tr. by* Benjamin *and* Barbara Harshav *and* Kathryn Helle. AYP
Moyst with one drop of thy blood, my dry soule. Resurrection. John Donne. OBS
Mozart. Jacob Glatstein, *tr. fr. Yiddish.* PeBMYV, *tr. by* Cynthia Ozick; VWA, *tr. by* Ruth Whitman
Mozart. John Heath-Stubbs. EBEV
Mozart, Goethe, and the Duke of Wellington. The Augsburg Adoration. Randall Jarrell. NYBP
Mozart's Grave. Paul Scott Mowrer. GoYe
Mr. *See also* Mister.
Mr. and Mrs. Discobbolos. Edward Lear. BLPL
Mr. and Mrs. Spikky Sparrow. Edward Lear. OxBChV
Mr. and Mrs. Vite's Journey. *Unknown.* NOBL
Mr. Aplinio Morales has reported this. Incident at Imuris. Alberto Rios. UL
Mr. Apollinax. T. S. Eliot. PoA
Mr. Artesian's Conscientiousness. Ogden Nash. NBLV
Mr. Attila. Carl Sandburg. ImOP
Mr. Beetle. Emily Hover. BoTP
Mr. Bernard Shaw. E. C. Bentley. *Fr.* Clerihews. CenHV
Mr. Bidery's Spidery Garden. David McCord. RHPC
Mr. Billings of Louisville. Eugene Field. NBLV
Mr. Bleaney. Philip Larkin. HoPM; InPS; NePoEA-2; OxBC; PoE
Mr. Brodsky. Charles Tomlinson. MoP; NoAM; OxBC
Mr. Brokaw's enunciation. Anchors Weighed. Peter McMillan. SoTCo
Mr. Brown. Rodney Bennett. BoTP
Mr. Brunt. Robert Siegel. GeTw
Mr. Coggs. E. V. Lucas. BoTP
  (Mr. Coggs, Watchmaker.) FaPON
Mr. Cogito—The Return. Zbigniew Herbert, *tr. fr. Polish by* John Carpenter *and* Bogdana Carpenter. AnAn
"Mr. Colwell"/ says Sharon the nurse. The Cry of an Aged One. Ray Fraser. NeAC
Mr. Cooper. Anthony Thwaite. OxBTC
Mr. Cromek [to Mr. Stothard]. Blake. ChTr; FaBoEE
Mr. Davis's Experience. *Unknown.* AmFP
Mr. Edward Fordham. Mary Weston Fordham. CBWP-2
Mr. Edwards and the Spider. Robert Lowell. CAPP; CMoP; CoAP; FaBoMo; HeIP; InPS; LiTM; MoAB; NAAL-2; NePoEA; NOBA; NoP; SM; SoSe; TwCP
Mr. Eliot Pastor of the Church of Christ at Roxbury. Edward Johnson. SCAP
Mr. Eliot's Day. Robert Francis. NYBP
Mr. Finney's Turnip. *Unknown.* NA
Mr. Flood's Party. E. A. Robinson. AmPP; AWP; BLPL; CMoP; FaFP; FF; HAP; HeIP; HoPM; LiTA; LiTM; MAT; MoAB; MoAmPo; MoP; NAAL-2; NIP; NoAM; NOBA; NoP; OxBA; PoE; PoRA; PPP; PrIm; SoSe; TAP; TrGrPo; UnPo; WeW
Mr. Francis Beaumont's Letter from the Country [to Jonson]. Francis Beaumont. OBS; SeCP
Mr. Frog Went a-Courting. *Unknown. See* Frog He Would A-Wooing Go, A.
Mr. Frost Goes South to Boston. Firman Houghton. Par
Mr. G., my instructor, with wild eyes. Ophelia. Brenda Hillman. MOWH
Mr. 'Gator. N. M. Bodecker. NTCP; OnUR
Mr. Giraffe. Geoffrey LaPage. OnUR
Mr. Gunman. Vin Garbutt. OBET
Mr. Hansen, the cop at the campus gate. Officers. Josephine Miles. FaBoWP
Mr. Heath-Stubbs as you must understand. John Heath-Stubbs. NePoEA; OxBTC
Mr. Hilaire Belloc. E. C. Bentley. *Fr.* Clerihews. CenHV
Mr. Hosea Biglow to the Editor of the Atlantic Monthly. James Russell Lowell. *Fr.* The Biglow Papers: 2d Series, No. X. AA, *abr.*
  ("Beaver roars hoarse with meltin' snows.") PoEL-5
Mr. Housman's Message. Ezra Pound. FaBoEE; FaBoPa
Mr. Hughes. David Campbell. CBAP
Mr. Ibister, and Betsy his sister. Mr. Ibister. *Unknown.* OxNR
Mr. Johnson's Policy of Reconstruction. Charles Graham Halpine. PAH

Mr. Jones. Harry Graham. CenHV; FaBoCo; FaFP
  (Common Sense.) FiBHP
Mr. Kartoffel. James Reeves. RHPC
Mr. Klein says, "Milagres, hold Angelo's hand." The Retarded Class at F. A. O. Schwarz's Celebrates Christmas. David Fisher. NPGG
Mr. Leach made a speech. Forensic Jocularities. Sir George Rose. OxBoLi
  (Chancery Suit, A.) FaBoCo
Mr. Lear, I'm the Akond of Swat. A Reply from the Akond of Swat. Ethel Talbot Scheffauer. FiBHP
Mr. Lizard is Crying. Federico García Lorca, *tr. fr. Spanish by* William Bryant Logan. TTTS
Mr. MacCall at Cleveland Hall. James Thomson. NOBVV
Mr. McGregor's Garden. Medbh McGuckian. CIP; FaBCIP
Mr. Macklin's Jack O'Lantern ("Mr. Macklin takes his knife"). David McCord. FaPON
Mr. Meant-to. *Unknown.* WBLP
Mr. Merry's Lament for "Long Tom." John Gardiner Calkins Brainard. AA
Mr. Moon. Bliss Carman. FaPON
Mr. Murple's got a dog that's long. Noctambule. George Johnston. MoCV
Mr. Muscle-On. Faye Kicknosway. GeTw
Mr. Nixon. Ezra Pound. *Fr.* Hugh Selwyn Mauberley. (Life and Contacts). MoAmPo
Mr. Nobody. *Unknown.* BOTP; FaPON
"Mr. Nowlan, are you asleep?" Semi-Private Room. Alden Nowlan. NeAC
Mr. Ody met a body. Edith Nesbit. CenHV; FaBoNo
Mr. Over. Stevie Smith. NoP
Mr. P.—I have heard it rumored. Letter to a Librarian. Irving Layton. MAT; TW
Mr. Pennycomequick. P. M. Stone. BoTP
Mr. Pope. Allen Tate. MoAB; NoAM; NOBA; TwCP; VGW
Mr. Pope's Welcome from Greece. John Gay. EBEV, *abr.;* OxBoLi, *abr.;* PoEL-3
Mr. Pratt ("Mr. Pratt has never left"). Myra Cohn Livingston. RHPC
Mr. Pratt, your sheep are very fat. The Norfolk Rebellion. *Unknown.* GBP
Mr. Pyme. Harry Behn. PDV
Mr. Rhind is very kind. The Schoolmaster. *Unknown.* GBP
Mr. Rockefeller's Hat. Helen Smith Bevington. OBAL
Mr. Roosevelt Regrets. Pauli Murray. PoBA
Mr. Scarecrow. Sheila Braine. BoTP
Mr. Shareholder, Mr. Civil-Servant. Pure Thoughts. Washington Delgado, *tr. by* David Tipton. Per
Mr. Slimmer's Funeral Verses for the *Morning Argus.* "Max Adeler." CenHV
  (Out of the Hurly-Burly.) OBAL
Mr. Smith. William Jay Smith. FiBHP
Mr. Speeds will clean his auto. Some Who Do Not Go to Church. *Unknown.* WBLP
Mr. Squirrel. V. M. Julian. BoTP
Mr. Strugnell. Wendy Cope. FaBoPa
Mr. Symons at Richmond, Mr. Pope at Twickenham. Julian Symons. WaP
Mr T./ bareheaded. The Artist. William Carlos Williams. InPS; LCAP; NYBP; RB
Mr. T. S. Eliot Cooking Pasta. József Tornai, *tr. fr. Hungarian by* Richard Wilbur. GrPl; MHuP
Mr. Thomas Shepeard. Edward Johnson. SCAP
Mr. Tom Narrow. James Reeves. SO
Mr. U Will Not Be Missed. E. E. Cummings. FaBoEE; VGW
Mr. Vachel Lindsay Discovers Radio. Samuel Hoffenstein. BXAP
Mr. Vanessa took the phone. Parallax. Maxwell Anderson. NYBP
Mr. Wakeville on Interstate 90. Donald Hall. BLA
Mr. Walter de la Mare Makes the Little Ones Dizzy. Samuel Hoffenstein. Par
Mr. Ward of Anagrams Thus. Nathaniel Ward. SCAP
Mr. Wells. Elizabeth Madox Roberts. FaPON
Mr. Whittier. Winfield Townley Scott. VGW
Mr. Z. M. Carl Holman. SoSe
Mririda. Mririda n'Ait Attik, *tr. fr. Berber into French by* René Euloge; *English vers. by* Daniel Halpern *and* Paula Paley. AIW; WPOW
Mrs. *See also* Mistress.
Mrs. Albion You've Got a Lovely Daughter. Adrian Henri. OxBTC
Mrs. Alfred Uruguay. Wallace Stevens. TwCP
Mrs. Applebaum's Sunday Dance Class. Philip Schultz. MAYP
Mrs. Brown. Rose Fyleman. BoTP; OxBChV
Mrs. Bubb was gay and free, fair, fat and forty-three. The One Horse Chay. *Unknown.* OxBoLi

Mrs. Busk. Sir Osbert Sitwell. OxBTC
Mrs. Chub was rich and portly. Jupiter and Ten. James Thomas Fields.
  AnAmPo; OBAL
Mrs. Coley's three-flat brick. The Vacant Lot. Gwendolyn Brooks.
  NoAM; NOBA
Mrs. E. Cohrs Brown. Mary Weston Fordham. CBWP-2
Mrs. Evans Fach, You Want Butter Again. Idris Davies. OBWVE
Mrs. Golightly. Gertrude Hall. AA
Mrs. Hamer. Jane Stembridge. NMM
Mrs. Hopley, on Seeing Her Children Say Goodnight to Their Father.
  Gerard Manley Hopkins. FaBoEE
Mrs. Indiarubber Duck. D. Carter. BoTP
Mrs. Jaypher. Edward Lear. FaBoNo
Mrs. Jaypher on Lemons. Edward Lear. FaBoNo
Mrs. Jenny Wren. Rodney Bennett. BoTP
Mrs. Johnson Objects. Clara Ann Thompson. AIW; BISi; CBWP-2
Mrs. Judge Jenkins (Being the Only Genuine Sequel to "Maud Muller").
  Bret Harte. BXAP; FiBHP
Mrs. Kriss Kringle. Edith M. Thomas. OBCA
Mrs. Loewinsohn &c. Ron Loewinsohn. NeAP
Mrs. Louise B. Weston. Mary Weston Fordham. CBWP-2
Mrs. McGrath. *Unknown.* FaBoBa
Mrs. Macintosh. Rodney Hall. CBAP
Mrs. MacQueen (or The Lollie-Shop). Walter de la Mare. BoTP
Mrs. Malone. Eleanor Farjeon. OxBChV
Mrs. Marmaduke Moore, at the age of ten. The Seven Spiritual Ages of
  Mrs. Marmaduke Moore. Ogden Nash. MoAmPo
Mrs. Mary Blaize. Goldsmith. *See* Elegy on That Glory of Her Sex,
  Mrs. Mary Blaize, An.
Mrs. Mary Furman Weston Byrd. Mary Weston Fordham. CBWP-2
Mrs. Mason's Basin ("Mrs. Mason bought a basin"). *Unknown.*
  OxNR
Mrs. Masters's fuchsias hung. The Lodging-House Fuchsias. Thomas
  Hardy. OxBSP
Mrs. Myrick's Lecture. Mary E. Tucker. CBWP-1
Mrs. Noah in the Ark. The Ballad of Mrs. Noah. Robert Duncan.
  MoP; NoAM; NOBA
Mrs. Peck-Pigeon. Eleanor Farjeon. NTCP; OnUR; PDV
Mrs. Rebecca Weston. Mary Weston Fordham. CBWP-2
Mrs. Sadie Grindstaff, Weaver and Factotum. Jonathan Williams.
  OBAL
Mrs. Saunder's Experience. *Unknown.* AmFP
Mrs. Severin. Winfield Townley Scott. InPK
Mrs. Snatcher Thatcher. Gillian Eve Hanscombe. *Fr.* Jezebel: Her
  Progress. BrRo
Mrs. Snipkin and Mrs. Wobblechin. Laura E. Richards. OxBChV
Mrs. Someone's been to Asia. An Importer. Robert Frost. FaBoCo
Mrs. Spider. Myra Cohn Livingston. PDV
Mrs. Throckmorton's bull-finch sang a song. Homage to William Cowper.
  Donald Davie. NePoEA
Mrs. Trollope in America ("Mrs. Trollope took a doleful view").
Mrs. Vickers' Daughter. *Unknown.* AmFP
Mrs. Walpurga. Muriel Rukeyser. NMM
Mrs. West of West Village ("Mrs. West's hands are younger than her
  age"). Ruth Kim Chun-soo, *tr. fr. Korean by* Koh Chang-soo.
  ACKP
Mrs.Coley's three-flat brick. The Vacant Lot. Gwendolyn Brooks.
  NAAL-2; NoAM; NOBA
MS Found in a Bottle. Yang Mu, *tr. fr. Chinese by* Dominic Cheung.
  IFON
Ms Understood. Sherma Springer. WS
Ms. Whatchamacallit Thingamajig. Miriam Chaikin. RHPC
Ms World. Caeia March. DT
Mu'allaqa. Antar, *tr. by* A. J. Arberry. TTY
Mu'allaqat, The, *sels. Unknown.*
  Abla. Antar, *tr. by* E. Powys Mathers. AWP
  "Have the poets left a single spot for a patch to be sewn?" Antar, *tr. by*
    A. J. Arberry. TTY
  "Weep, ah weep love's losing." Imr el Kais, *tr. by* Lady Anne Blunt
    and Wilfrid Scawen Blunt. AWP
  Pour Us Wine. Ibn Kolthum, *tr. by* E. Powys Mathers. AWP
Much Ado about Nothing, *sels.* Shakespeare.
  Beauty Is a Witch. *Fr.* II, i. TrGrPo
  Claudio's Lament: "Pardon, goddess of the night." *Fr.* V, iii. OBSC
    (Song: "Pardon, goddess of the night.") CTC
  "Done to death by slanderous tongues." *Fr.* V, iii. CTC
    (Claudio's Lament: "Done to death by slanderous tongues.") OBSC
  Sigh No More, Ladies [Sigh No More]. *Fr.* II, iii. AWP; CTC; EIL;
    ELP; FF; LiTB; TrGrPo
Much Ado about Nothing in the City. *Unknown.* FaBoPa

Much as he left it when he went from us. Why He Was There. E. A.
  Robinson. CMoP; NOBA
Much cry and little wool. Back. Weldon Kees. NaP; PrIm
Much did I rage when young. Youth and Age. W. B. Yeats.
  FaBoEE
Much-discerning public hold, A. La Nuit Blanche. Kipling. MoBrPo
Much Distressed. *Unknown.* CBAP
Much earlier than most he found. Childhood of a Spy. Dick Davis.
  DiPo
Much had passed/ Since last we parted. Byron Recollected at Bologna.
  Samuel Rogers. *Fr.* Italy. OBNC
Much happens in silence. Return. Michael Guttenbrunner, *tr. by* Beth
  Bjorklund. CoAuP
Much Has Been Said. *Unknown.* CoMu
Much have I labored, much read o'er. Alas for Youth. Firdausi, *tr. by*
  R. A. Nicholson. AWP
Much have I roved by Sandy River. By Sandy Waters. Jesse Stuart.
  AmFN
Much have I spoken of the faded leaf. November. Elizabeth Stoddard.
  AA
Much have I travail'd in the realms of gold. On First Looking into the
  Dark Future. Roger Lancelyn Green. CenHV
Much have I travell'd [*or* travelled *or* traveled] in the realms of gold. On
  First Looking into Chapman's Homer. Keats. BLPA; CH; ChER;
  ChTr; EnRP; FaBoBe; FaBoCh; FaBV; FaFP; FF; FiP; FPL; GN;
  GTBS; GTBS-P; HAP; HeIP; HoPM; InPK; LiTB; NAWM-2; NIP;
  NOBE; NoP; OAEL-2; OBAL; OBEV; OBNC; PoE; PoEL-4; PPP;
  PrIm; Son; SoSe; TEP; TrGrPo
    (Ode: On First Looking into Champan's Homer.) NAEL-2
    (Sonnet: On First Looking into Chapman's Homer.) ChER
Much have I travelled in East Lothian and Dundee. On First Looking into
  Chapman's Homer. W. S. Brownlie. BXAP
Much-hugged rag-doll is oozing cotton from her ruined figure, The.
  September. Robert Lowell. NaP
Much Knowledge, Little Reason. Sir John Davies. *See* Nosce Teipsum:
  What Is This Knowledge?
Much madness is divinest sense. Emily Dickinson. AmPP; BoWoP;
  CMoP; HeIP; LiTM; MAT; NAAL-1; NAWM-2; NoAM; NOBA;
  NoP; OxBA; WPE
    (Much Madness.) LiTA
Much, much in love, you see her by chance. Emperor Go-Shirakawa, *tr.*
  fr. Japanese by Hiroaki Sato. Ryojin Hisho. FCEI
Much remains hidden, but much much. Step by Step. Cees Buddingh',
  tr. by James S. Holmes. DuIn
Much suspected by me. Written with a Diamond on Her Window at
  Woodstock. Elizabeth I, Queen of England. PBWP; WPE
Much tobacco is burnt. Rolling Thunder. Phyllis Wolf. STE
Muckers. Carl Sandburg. SaC
Mucus that runs from you nose your eyes. Kicking the Habit. Jotie
  T'Hooft, *tr. by* James S. Holmes. DuIn
Mud. Polly Chase Boyden. RAR
Mud dark above the stream the factory's finger. The Refugee. Marjorie
  Battcock. CN
Mud ("Mud is very nice to feel"). Polly Chase Boyden. FaBV; NTCP;
  RHPC
Mud of the bulk of the back yard, The. Clark Coolidge. IAT
Mud packing her gullet the robin pecks. A Pinto Mare. Dave Smith.
  BLA
Mud turkle settin' on de end of a log. The Turtle's Song. *Unknown.*
  BPo
Mud Turtle, The. Howard Nemerov. NYBP
Muddled Metaphors. Tom Hood. NA
Muddling up the wooden stairs one night, in my socks. Spiders. David
  Wevill. MoCV
Muddy Madrigal. Léon-Paul Fargue, *tr. fr. French by* William Jay Smith.
  CT
Muddy meek river, oh, it was splendid sport. Big Dam. William Robert
  Moses. AmFN
Muddy Puddle, The. Dennis Lee. RHPC
Muddy-wheeled cart goes lurching, A. The Plain. Sándor Weöres, *tr. by*
  Jascha Kessler. FOC
Mufaddaliyat, The, *sels. Unknown, tr. fr. Arabic by* Sir Charles Lyall.
  AWP
  Gone Is Youth. Salamah, son of Jandal.
  His Camel. Alqamah.
  Old Age. Al-Aswad, Son of Ya'fur.
Muffin Man, The. Ann Croasdell. BoTP
Muffin-Man's Bell, The. Ann Hawkshawe. BoTP
Muffled drum's sad roll has beat, The. The Bivouac of the Dead.
  Theodore O'Hara. AA; AnAmPo; BLPA; PAH

Mug for the camera with your hand on the door. The Dream as Calculation. Barry Goldensohn. NAmP

Mugford's Victory. John White Chadwick. PAH

Mugging. Allen Ginsberg. NoAM

Mugging, *sel.* Allen Ginsberg.
"Tonite I walked out of my red apartment door on East tenth street's dusk." HCAP

Mugo's life cry: "Don't be." Jakushitsu, *tr. by* Lucien Stryk *and* Takashi Ikemoto. ZPCJ

Muhammedan Call to Prayer. Bilal, *tr. fr. Arabic by* Raoul Abdul. TTY

Muirland Meg. Burns. ErPo

Mukhammas. Khwaja Mir Dard; *tr. fr. Urdu by* Ahmed Ali. GoT

Mulatta as Penelope, The. Lorna Goodison. PBCV

Mulatto. Langston Hughes. NAAL-2

Mulberry Garden, The, *sels.* Sir Charles Sedley.
Ah Cloris! That I Now Could Sit. *Fr.* III. OBS
Child and Maiden. GTBS; GTBS-P
("Ah, Chloris! Could I now but sit.") OBS
(Song: "Ah Cloris! That I could now sit.") SeCV-2
(To Chloris.) OBEV

Mulberry Mountain. *Unknown.* AmFP

Mulberry on the lowland, how graceful!, The. *Unknown, tr. by* Arthur Waley. BoS

Mule, The. Boynton Merrill, Jr. CRP

Mule Skinner's Song. *Unknown.* AS

Mule Team and Poster. Donald Justice. AnAn

Mules. Ted Walker. NYBP

Mulford. Whittier. AA

Mulish. Hans Andreus, *tr. fr. Dutch by* James Brockway. DuIn

Mullabinda. David Rowbotham. CBAP; PoAu-2

Mullins Farm, The. Richard H. W. Dillard. MT

Mullion. A. P. Herbert. SD

Mully of Mountown, *sels.* William King.
"How fleet is air! how many things have breath." FM
Mountown! Thou Sweet Retreat. FaBoPP
"Mountown! thou sweet retreat from Dublin cares." OBTV

Multicoloured mushroom seems, The. Haiku of the Flowerpot. José Juan Tablada, *tr. by* Samuel Beckett. MexPo

Multitudes Turn in Darkness. Conrad Aiken. PoA

Multitudinous Stars, *sel.* "Ping Hsin," *tr. fr. Chinese by* Kenneth Rexroth *and* Ling Chung.
"Void only." PBWP

"Multum Dilexit." Hartley Coleridge. EnRP

Mumford. Ina M. Porter. PAH

Mummia. Rupert Brooke. BrPo

Mummies, The. Maxine W. Kumin. Psk

Mummy of a Lady Named Jemutesonekh XXI Dynasty. Thomas James. AmPA; SM

Mummy Slept Late and Daddy Fixed Breakfast. John Ciardi. PDV; RHPC

Mumps. Elizabeth Madox Roberts. FaPON

Munching a plum on/ the street. To a Poor Old Woman. William Carlos Williams. AnAmPo; OBAL; SOTW; TAP; TTTS

Munch's Scream. Donald Hall. NePoEA

Mundus et Infans. W. H. Auden. LiTB; LiTM; MoAB; MoBrPo; NAs; NoAM

Mundus Morosus. Frederick William Faber. ACP

Mundus Qualis. Joshua Sylvester. FaBoEE

Munich Elegy No. 1. George Barker. SeCePo; WaP

Munich Mannequins, The. Sylvia Plath. CAPP; NaP

Municipal. Kipling. BrPo; BXAP

Municipal Gallery Revisited, The. W. B. Yeats. GTBS-P; LiTB; OxBTC

Munition Workers, The. Diana James. CN

Muppim and Huppim! Strike blows on your drums! The Dance of Despair. Hayyim Nahman Bialik, *tr. by* A. M. Klein. TrJP

Mural, *sel.* Vincente Rodríguez Nietzche, *tr. fr. Spanish by* Julio Marzán.
"We must burn up." InW

Murali sounds on the banks of the Jumna. Mirabai, *tr. by* John Stratton Hawley *and* Mark Juergensmeyer. SSI

Murder in the Cathedral, *sels.* T. S. Eliot.
"We do not wish anything to happen." OxBTC
Forgive Us, O Lord. EaLo

Murder of a Community. Daniel Weissbort. VWA

Murder of a Spanish Lady by a Pirate. Richard Henry Dana. AnAmPo

Murder of Goins, The. *Unknown.* AmFP

Murder of Maria Marten, The. W. Corder. CoMu; OBET

Murder of Moses, The. Karl Shapiro. EaLo

Murder of Saint Thomas of Kent, The. *Unknown.* ACP

Murder of the customs inspector was magnificent what with, The. For a Daylight Dream. Robert Desnos, *tr. by* Michael Benedikt. POS

Murder of William Remington, The. Howard Nemerov. CMoP; CoAP

Murder self slowly. And die like ants shuffling up under. Reckoning A.M. Thursday. Doris Turner. JB

Murder Trial, The. Perseus Adams. PeSA

Murdered Girl Is Found on a Bridge, The. Jane Hayman. NYBP

Murdered, I went, risen. The Life. James Wright. LCAP; NaP

Murdered Little Bird. *Unknown.* FiBHP

Murderer, The. Paul Petrie. NYBP

Murderer, The. Stevie Smith. FaBoWP; OxBSP; TEP

Murderer came down the chimney, The. On History. Paul Hoover. UL

Murderers/ of Emmett Till. Salute. Oliver Pitcher. PoBA

Murderers of Kings, The. Zbigniew Herbert, *tr. fr. Polish by* John Carpenter *and* Bogdana Carpenter. AnAn

Murderers of the wall wrap themselves in sunrise, The. Jean Genet, *tr. fr. French by* Steven Finch. *Fr.* The Man Sentenced to Death. PeHV

Murie Sing. Archibald Y. Campbell. FaBoPa

Murmur. Anthony Hecht. BLA

Murmur of a bee, The. Emily Dickinson. MoAmPo

Murmur of the mourning ghost, The. The Ballad of Keith of Ravelston. Sydney Dobell. *Fr.* A Nuptial Eve. CH; OBEV
(Keith of Ravelston.) CH

Murmurers, The. Josephine Jacobsen. GrPl

Murmuring in empty shells, A. The Relic. Robert Hillyer. GoYe; UnS

Murph and McClop. *Unknown.* CowP

Murukan: His Places. Nakkiranar, *tr. fr. Tamil by* A. K. Ramanujan. PLW

Murukan, the Red One. Nakkiranar, *tr. fr. Tamil by* A. K. Ramanujan. PLW

Musa, Musae,/ The Gods were at tea. The Muses. *Unknown.* FaBoNo

Muscle and Bone of Song. Hone Tuwhare. ATNZ

Muscovy Drake, The. E. A. S. Lesoro, *tr. fr. Sotho by* Dan Kunene *and* Jack Cope. PeSA

Muse, The. E. A. Baratynsky, *tr. fr. Russian by* Alan Myers. AAA

Muse, The. Barry Spacks. MAT

Muse, The. W. H. Davies. BrPo

Muse. David Wagoner. PoA

Muse and Poet. Robert Bridges. OBMV

Muse as Medusa, The. May Sarton. ER

Muse, bid the morne awake. To His Valentine. Michael Drayton. PoEL-2

Muse, disgusted at an age and clime, The. On the Prospect of Planting Arts and Learning in America. George Berkeley. AiP; FaFP; NOEC; OBTV; TrGrPo
(Verses on the Prospect of Planting Arts and Learning in America.) SeCePo

Muse, first of Arden tell, whose footsteps yet are found. The Dwindling Forest of Arden. Michael Drayton. *Fr.* Polyolbion, Thirteenth Song. FaBoPP

Muse-haunted. Hugh McCrae. PoAu-1

Muse in Late November. Jonathan Henderson Brooks. PoNe

Muse in the New World, The. Walt Whitman. *Fr.* Song of the Exposition. MoAmPo

Muse, June, Related, *sel.* Brian Coffey.
"Blooms such as wither at finger-touch." BIrV

Muse of Amergin, The. *Unknown, tr. fr. Irish by* John Montague. BIrV

Muse of Fire, A. Shakespeare. *See* King Henry V: O for a Muse of fire, that would ascend.

Muse of native land! loftiest Muse! Keats. *Fr.* Endymion [a Poetic Romance], IV. EnRP

Muse of Poetry came down one day, The. In Memoriam Paul Laurence Dunbar. Henrietta Cordelia Ray. CBWP-3

Muse of the many-twinkling feet! whose charms. Byron. *Fr.* The Waltz. OBSV

Muse of Water, A. Carolyn Kizer. NMM

Muse Poem. Kathryn Van Spanckeren. FF

Muse Reviving, The. Sir John Davies. SiPS

Muse should be sprightly, The. A Skeltoniad. Michael Drayton. PoEL-2

Muse, sing the stir that happy Whitbread made. George III Visits Whitbread's Brewery. "Peter Pindar." *Fr.* Instructions to a Celebrated Laureat. NOEC

Muse that stirs my blood, The. Bird and the Muse. Marya Zaturenska. PoA

Muse to an Unknown Poet, The. Paul Potts. FaBoTw

Muse with the hero's brave deeds being fired, The. Captain Death. *Unknown.* CoMu

Muse, you have left me at last. How did I come. Cooking Eggs. Dave Smith. AnAn; BLA

Musée des Beaux Arts. W. H. Auden. CMoP; FaFP; FF; GTBS-P; HAP; HeIP; InPK; InPS; LiTB; LiTM; MoAB; MoP; NAEL-2; NIP; NoAM; NOBE; NoP; PoE; PoRA; PPP; PrIm; SCV; SeCePo; SoSe; TEP; TrCP; TrGrPo; TwCP; WeW
Muses, The. *Unknown.* FaBoNo
Muse's Answer, The. Gibbons Ruark. MT
Muses' Elysium [*or* Elizium], *sels.* Michael Drayton.
  "Clear [*or* Cleere] had the day been [*or* bin] from the dawn [*or* dawne]." BoTP
  (Fine Day, A.) GN
  (Sixt Nimphall, The.) OBS
  Description of Elizium, The. OAEL-1
  (Poet's Paradise, The.) WiR, *much abr.*
  Second Nimphall, The. PBBP
    "I have two sparrows white as snow," *sel.* PBBP
  Tenth Nimphall, The. JCP
Muse's Favor, The. Priscilla Jane Thompson. CBWP-2
Muses' friend, The (grey-eyed Aurora), yet. William Browne. *Fr.* Britannia's Pastorals, II, Song 2. JCP
Muses That Sing Love's Sensual Empery. George Chapman. *Fr.* A Coronet for His Mistress Philosophy, I. EiL; Son
  (Love and Philosophy.) OBSC; SeCePo
Muses wrapped in mysteries of light, The. The Whirlwind Road. Edwin Markham. AA
Museum, The. William Abrahams. WaP
Museum. Robert Hass. NPGG
Museum is gone from my bones, The. Calling the Scientists Home. Wendy Rose. BWV
Museum of Man. Earle Birney. OxBC
Museum of Modern Art on West Fifty-third Street, The. Tulips and Addresses. Edward Field. NYBP; Psk
Museum of the Second Creation, The. Sandra McPherson. LCAP
Museum-Piece. Audrey Alexandra Brown. CaP
Museum Piece. Lawrence P. Spingarn. GoYe
Museum Piece. Richard Wilbur. CMoP; FaBoMo; InPK; NIP; NoP; TAP
Museums. Louis MacNeice. MoBrPo
Museums and stockmarkets protect me, The. Four Stanzas Written in Anxiety. George Jonas. MoCV
Museums offer us, running from among the buses. Museums. Louis MacNeice. MoBrPo
Musgrove. *Unknown.* AmFP
Mushroom Gatherer Deep in the Mountains, A. Hsü Wei, *tr. fr. Chinese by* Jonathan Chaves. CoBLCP
Mushroom Gatherers, The. Donald Davie. NePoEA-2
Mushroom Hunting in Late August, Peterborough, N.H. Michael C. Blumenthal. MAYP
Mushroom, Soft Ear, Old Memory. Bring the North. William Stafford. LCAP
Mushrooms. Basil Dowling. ATNZ
Mushrooms. Sylvia Plath. BoNaP; FaBoWP; NePoEA-2; RB; WeW; WPOW
Mushrooms grew near the tree. Peter Rabbit. Sandra McPherson. LCAP
Music. Conrad Aiken. *See* Calyx of the Oboe Breaks, The.
Music, A. Wendell Berry. VGW
Music. Bible, *Apocrypha. Fr.* Ecclesiasticus, XXXII: 5–6. TrJP
Music. George Du Maurier, *after the French of* Sully-Prudhomme. OBEV
Music. Alice Dunbar-Nelson. BlSi
Music. Emerson. FaBV; WGRP
Music. Josephine D. Henderson Heard. CBWP-4
Music. Robert Herrick. CaPo
Music, The. Everett Hoagland. CNA
Music. Frank O'Hara. NoP
Music. William Bell Scott. NOBVV
Music. Shakespeare *and probably* John Fletcher. *See* King Henry VIII: Orpheus with His Lute [Made Trees].
Music. Shelley. *See* Music, When Soft Voices Die.
Music. *Malay Oral Tradition, tr. by* R. O. Winstedt. WTO
Music after Reading. Valery Larbaud, *tr. fr. French by* Ron Padgett *and* Bill Zavatsky. RHTwFP
Music and feasting are done, the moon is just full, The. Speaking of Love. Wei Ch'eng-pan, *tr. by* Lois Fusek. ATF
Music and its harmony, The. The Design. Clarence Major. PoBA
Music and Memory. John Albee. AA
Music and song wandering beyond the clouds. Powerful Officials. Cheng Hsieh, *tr. by* Jan W. Walls. WFTU
Music Crept by Us, The. Leonard Cohen. FF
Music ("Down the quiet eve"). W. E. Henley. *Fr.* In Hospital, XXIII. BrPo

Music emerges from the windows. Romance. Antonin Artaud, *tr. by* Michael Benedikt. POS
Music first and foremost of all! Art Poétique. Paul Verlaine, *tr. by* Arthur Symons. AWP
"Music for a while." Song at Night. Norman Nicholson. FaBoTw
Music God. Mark Van Doren. UnS
Music had the heat of blood, The. During Music. Arthur Symons. NOBVV
Music I heard with you was more than music. Conrad Aiken. *Fr.* Discordants, I. AWP; BLPL; CMoP; FaFP; LiTA; LiTM; NOBA; OxBA; PoRA
  (Bread and Music.) MoAB; MoAmPo
Music in an Empty House. Hugh Sykes Davies. EAS
Music in Camp. John R. Thompson. AA; BLPA
Music in my head again, The. Coda: Greed Part 12—Looking for Beethoven in Las Vegas. Diane Wakoski. ER
Music in the Air. Ronald McCuaig. ErPo
Music in the Night. Harriet Prescott Spofford. AA
Music in the Rec Hut. Hubert Creekmore. WaP
Music in Venice. Louis Simpson. NYBP
Music Is Unevennesses. Geoffrey Lehmann. *Fr.* Ross's Poems. CBAP
Music leads you out, The. Driving into the Storm: The Art of Poetry. Ian Wedde. ATNZ
Music Lessons. Mary Oliver. CAPP
Music lifting and falling. Aria. Rolfe Humphries. NYBP
Music! Lilting, soft and languorous. Music. Alice Dunbar-Nelson. BlSi
Music Makers, The. Cees Buddingh', *tr. fr. Dutch by* James S. Holmes. DuIn
Music Makers, The. Arthur William Edgar O'Shaughnessy. *See* We Are the Music Makers.
Music met Leviathan returning, A. Peter Quennell. *Fr.* Leviathan. MoBrPo
Music of a Tree, The. Walter James Turner. MoBrPo
Music of Colours: The Blossom Scattered. Vernon Watkins. LiTB
Music of Colours—White Blossom. Vernon Watkins. LiTM; WaP
Music of Forefended Spheres, The. Coventry Patmore. *Fr.* The Victories of Love, I, ii. FaBoRV
Music of His Steps, The. Samuel Wakefield. AH
Music of Hungary. Anne Reeve Aldrich. AA
Music of the Future, The. Oliver Herford. CenHV
Music of the Night. John Neal. AA
Music of the Spheres, The. Marvin Bell. PoA
Music on the Water. George Johnston. MoCV
Music rises in a wall of light, The. On a Bomb Heard through a Violin Concerto. Christina Chapin. CN
Music stirs me, for you. Ricarda Huch, *tr. by* Susan C. Strong. PBWP
Music [*or* Musick], thou queen of heaven, care-charming spell. To Music: A Song. Robert Herrick. CaPo; UnS
Music, thou queen of souls, get up and string. Thomas Randolph. OxBSP
Music, thou queen of heaven, care-charming spell. Music. Robert Herrick. CaPo
"Music[k] to hear[e], why hear'st thou music[k] sadly?" Shakespeare. *Fr.* Sonnets, VIII. PoEL-2
Music touches me with your hands, The. Leit. Marcos Rodríguez Frese, *tr. by* Julio Marzán. InW
Music was going on, The. At the Fillmore. Philip Levine. NNaP
Music, When Soft Voices Die. Shelley. FaBV; GTBS; GTBS-P; LiTB; NOBE; OBEV; OxBSP; PCP; TrGrPo
  (Music.) CH
  (To———.) AWP; EnRP; FiP; HeIP; NoP; OBNC; PoEL-4; SeCePo
Musica No. 3. Richard Duerden. NeAP
Musical Critic Anticipates Eternity, A. Siegfried Sassoon. UnS
Musical Instrument, A. Elizabeth Barrett Browning. EBVV; FaBoBe; FaPON; NAEL-2; NoP; OAEL-2; OBEV; OnMSP; PoE; WPE
Musical instruments in Sicily, The. Sicilian Airs. Leonard Wallace Robinson. SoTCo
Musical Lion, The. Oliver Herford. OBCA
Musical man is walking along the shore, A. Telemachus with a Transistor. Ruth Dallas. PeNZ
Musical Orchard, The. Douglas Dunn. FaBoMo
Musical Shuttle. Harvey Shapiro. VWA
Musician. Louise Bogan. GoJo; NYBP
Musician of Saint-Merry, The. Guillaume Apollinaire, *trs. fr. French by* Michael Benedikt *and by* Roger Shattuck. POS
Musicians Wrestle Everywhere. Emily Dickinson. UnS
Music[k]'s Duel[l]. Richard Crashaw. OAEL-1; OBS; SeCP; SeCV-1
Music's Silver Sound. Shakespeare. *Fr.* Romeo and Juliet, IV, v. GN

Musidora's Vision. Henrietta Cordelia Ray. CBWP-3

Musing beneath a Pine. P'eng Sun-yü, *tr. fr. Chinese by* Daniel Bryant. WFTU

Musing on roses and revolutions. Roses and Revolutions. Dudley Randall. BPo; CNA; PoBA; TAP

Musing upon the restless bisinesse. Thomas Hoccleve. *Fr.* De Regimine Principium. PoEL-1

Musings. William Barnes. HAP; NOBE; OBNC

Musings. Patty L. Harjo. NOVW

Musk-ox smells, The. The Long River. Donald Hall. LCAP; NePoEA-2; SM

Musk Oxen. Igjugarjuk, *tr. fr. Eskimo.* WTO

Muskogee's hokpi, The. The Sharpbreasted Snake. Louis Oliver. STE

Muskrat. John Engels. AnAn

Muslims are still lying, The. Lying Muslims. *Yoruba Oral Tradition, tr. by* Ulli Beier. WTO

Musmee, The. Sir Edwin Arnold. OBTV

Musophilus; or, Defence of All Learning, *sels.* Samuel Daniel.
   English Poetry. OBSC
   (Heavenly Eloquence.) NOBE
   O Blessed Letters. FaBoRV
   Poet and Critic. OBSC

Mussel Hunter at Rock Harbor. Sylvia Plath. NYBP

Musselburgh Field. *Unknown.* ESPB

Mussels. Mary Oliver. NU

Must all successful rebels grow. 1912–1952, Full Cycle. Peter Viereck. OBAL

Must be a good day. Issa, *tr. fr. Japanese by* Hiroaki Sato. *Fr.* Forty-four Hokku. FCEI

Must Be Freed. Lizelia Augusta Jenkins Moorer. CBWP-3

Must Be the Season of the Witch. Alurista, *tr. fr. Spanish by* Toni Empringham. FIA

Must delicate women die in vain. The Pill. Austin Clarke. TW

Must hapless man, in ignorance sedate. Celestial Wisdom. Juvenal, *tr. fr. Latin by* Samuel Johnson. *Fr.* Satires, X. AWP

Must I go bound and you go free. *Unknown.* WTO

Must I shoot the. Watts. Conrad Kent Rivers. PoBA

Must I tell again. The Daemon. Louise Bogan. NYBP

Must I then see, alas! eternal night. Elegy over a Tomb. Lord Herbert of Cherbury. EIL; MeLP; MePo; NOBE; OBEV; OBS; OBWVE; PoEL-2; QFR

Must noble Hastings immaturely die. Upon the Death of the Lord Hastings. Dryden. SeCV-2

"Must represent the governess." Xenophobia. Rae Armantrout. IAT

Must we part, Von Hügel, though much alike. W. B. Yeats. *Fr.* Vacillation. OBMV

Mustacheless Bard, A. J. Gordon Coogler. OBAL

Mustapha, *sels.* Fulke Greville.
   Chorus Primus: Wise Counsellors. OBS
   Chorus Quintus: Tartarorum. OBS
   Chorus Sacerdotum. HAP; InvP; JCP; LiTB; MePo; NAEL-1; NOBE; OAEL-1; OBS; PoEL-1; PPP; SeCePo
   Chorus Tertius: Of Time; Eternitie. OBS
      Eternity's Speech against Time. JCP

Multipara: Gravida 5. Marie Ponsot. VGW

Mutability. Rupert Brooke. BrPo

Mutability. Shelley. EnRP; NAEL-1; NoP; OBNC; TEP

Mutability. W. D. Snodgrass. DiPo

Mutability. Spenser. *Fr.* The Faerie Queene, VII, 7 *and* 8. PoEL-1

Mutability. Wordsworth. *Fr.* Ecclesiastical Sonnets, III, XXXIV. EBEV; EnRP; HeIP; InPK; LiTB; NOBE; NoP; OAEL-2; OBEV; PoEL-4; PrIm

Mutability ("When these were past, thus gan the Titanesse"). Spenser. PoEL-1

Mutations of the Phoenix, *sel.* Sir Herbert Read.
   "Phoenix, bird of terrible pride." FaBoTw

Mute/ the hand moves from the heart. Miniatures IV. Lynn Strongin. IHMS

Mute bird sidles through soft valleys of air, A. Afternoon in Anglo-Ireland. Bruce Williamson. NeIP

Mute City, The. Lazer Eichenrand, *tr. fr. Yiddish by* Gabriel Preil *and* Howard Schwartz. VWA

Mute figures with bowed heads. The Refugees. Sir Herbert Read. BrPo

Mute he sat in the saddle—mute 'midst our full acclaim. A Christopher of the Shenandoah. Edith M. Thomas. PAH

Mute Opinion. Thomas Hardy. CMoP

Mute Phenomena, The. Derek Mahon. FaBCIP

Mute, sightless visitant. Helen Keller. Edmund Clarence Stedman. AA

Muted. Paul Verlaine, *tr. fr. French by* C. F. MacIntyre. UnAS

Muted Music. Robert Penn Warren. KS

Muted Screen of Graham Greene, The. Phyllis McGinley. FaBoEE

Muted wood-wind is one noise of the traffic, and there is a second. The Empire Clock. Bernard Spencer. OBTV

Mutes, The. Denise Levertov. IHMS; NaP; NOBA

Mutilated choir boys, The. Heine, *tr. fr. German by* Ezra Pound. *Fr.* Heimkehr, Die. AWP

Mutilated Soldier, The. David Fisher. NPGG

Muttering. Sándor Weöres, *tr. fr. Hungarian by* Jascha Kessler. FOC

Muttering at the crowd, indifferent. The Death of an Old Man. Michael Hamburger. NePoEA

Mutterings over the Crib of a Deaf Child. James Wright. LCAP

Mutton. *Unknown.* BXAP

Mutton and Leather. *Unknown.* CoMu

Mutual Congratulations of the Poets Anna Seward and Hayley, The. Richard Porson. FaBoEE; OBSV

Mutual Forgiveness of each Vice. For the Sexes; the Gates of Paradise. Blake. LiTB; PoEL-4

Mutual Love. William Hammond. JCP

Mutual magnetism of love, The. Physics of Love. Charles Brasch. ATNZ

Mutual Problem. William Cole. OBAL

Mutual Subjection. Christopher Smart. *Fr.* Hymns for the Amusement of Children, XXVI. NOCV

Muu's Way; or Pictures from the Uterine World. *Unknown, tr. fr. Cuna Indian by* Jerome Rothenberg. STP

Muvver was barfin' 'er biby one night, A. Dahn the Plug'ole. *Unknown, tr. by* Robert Bly. RB
   ("Biby's" Epitaph.) FiBHP

Muzik of blood. Bass Culture. Linton Kwesi Johnson. PBCV

Muzzle and jowl and beastly brow. Fearfull Symmetry. Basil Bunting. PoA

Muzzy with drink, I let my humor recline. The Ghost of an Education. James Michie. NYBP

Mwilu/ or Poem for the Living. Don L. Lee. JB

My/ father/ dreams. The Eyes of Flesh. Sandra Hochman. NMM

My absent daughter—gentle, gentle maid. A Living Memory. William Augustus Croffut. AA

My adored statue. The Arid Husband. E. L. T. Mesens. EAS

My Africa. Michael Dei-Anang. PBA

My age? Around middle. Perspective. John H. Dromey. SoTCo

My age fallen away like white swaddling. Age. Philip Larkin. CMoP

My age is three hundred and seventy-two. The Sleepy Giant. Charles Edward Carryl. OnUR

My aged friend, Miss Wilkinson. The Bards. Walter de la Mare. FaBoNo; NOBL

My Aim. George Linnaeus Banks. *See* I live for those that love me.

My Ain Countree. Mary Lee Demarest. WGRP

My Ain Fireside. Elizabeth Hamilton. FaBoBe

My Ain Kind Dearie, O. Burns. GoTS

My airplane in flames my Rhinewine-flooded castle. Hello. Benjamin Péret, *tr. by* Michael Benedikt. POS

My Alba. Allen Ginsberg. NOBA

My ambition as I remember and. Love at Roblin Lake. Alfred W. Purdy. NoP

My American host in Madras in his moist air-conditioned apartment. Americans Are Afraid of Lizards. Karl Shapiro. AmFN

My ancestor was called on to go out. The Wind at Your Door. Robert David Fitzgerald. PoAu-2

My ancestors are nearer. Ancestral Poem. Olive Senior. PBCV

My ancestors were fine, long men. Square-toed Princes. Robert Peter Tristram Coffin. AmFN

My Angel. Jonathan Henderson Brooks. PoNe

My Angel, I Never Knew What Angel. Amelia Rosselli, *tr. fr. Italian by* Muriel Kittel. DMI

My Angeline. Harry B. Smith. NBLV

My annals have it so. Emus. Mary Elizabeth Fullerton. PoAu-1

My Answer. Ralph Adamo. MT

My answer would have to be music. The Medium. Elaine Feinstein. BrRo

My apartment building has 5 stories. A Citizen's Dissertation on His Neighborhood. Avraham Shlonsky, *tr. by* Bernhard Frank. MHeP

My Apologies. Buland al-Haidari, *tr. fr. Arabic by* Abdullah al-Udhari. MPAW

My ardours for emprize nigh lost. On an Invitation to the United States. Thomas Hardy. AiP; AWP

My Arkansas. Maya Angelou. BlSi

My arm sweeps down. Gesture. Donald Finkel. InPK

My arm, the pillow of hemp cloth my dear one used to sleep on. In 728, Longing for His Deceased Wife. Tabito. *Fr.* Manyo Shu. FCEI

My Arms Are Raised towards You.   Esther Raab, *tr. fr. Hebrew by*
Bernhard Frank.   MHeP
My arms are round you, and I lean.   To the Oaks of Glencree.   J. M.
Synge.   MoBrPo; NOIV
My Arms Became the Month of October.   Shauqi Abi Shaqra, *tr. fr.
Arabic by* Abdullah al-Udhari.   MPAW
My arms didn't clasp.   *Unknown, tr. by* Geoffrey Bownas *and* Anthony
Thwaite.   PeBJV
My arms smell good. Think.   Please Forward.   James Welch.   CDW
My aspens dear, whose airy cages quelled.   Binsey Poplars (Felled 1879).
Gerard Manley Hopkins.   BoNaP; BrPo; EBVV; ELP; FaBoPP; InPS;
Mes; NAEL-2; NoAM; NoP; RB
My Atlas Poet.   George Bowering.   NeAC
My attention is a wild/ animal.   Pet Panther.   A. R. Ammons.   NoP
My Atthis, although our dear Anaktoria.   Sappho, *tr. by* Willis Barnstone.
BoWoP
My attire is noiseless when I tread the earth.   Wild Swan: "My attire is
noiseless when I tread the earth."   *Unknown, formerly at. to*
Cynewulf, *tr. fr. Anglo-Saxon.   Fr.* Riddles (Exeter Book).   AnOE,
tr. by Charles W. Kennedy.
   (Riddle: Mute Swan.)   PBBP
My Auld Wife.   *Unknown.*   GBP
My Aunt.   Oliver Wendell Holmes.   AmPP; TAP
My Aunt.   Ted Hughes.   WSC
My Aunt Bebe.   The Aga Khan.   Steve Orlen.   Psk
My aunt! my dear unmarried aunt!   My Aunt.   Oliver Wendell Holmes.
AmPP; TAP
My aunt she died a month ago.   Death of My Aunt.   *Unknown.*
OxBoLi
My aunt was an herb doctor, one-eyed with crooked yellow teeth.   To-ta
Ti-om.   Peter Blue Cloud.   HATNAP; STE
My aunts washed dishes while the uncles.   Paper Matches.   Paulette Jiles.
Mes; NIP; NOBC
My Aunty Jean.   Tide and Time.   Roger McGouch.   TDD
My author and disposer, what thou biddest.   Milton.   *Fr.* Paradise Lost,
bk. IV, *ll.* 635–658.
   (Thus Eve to Adam.)   FaBV
My Autobiography.   Ted Berrigan.   BAP
My Autumn Walk.   Bryant.   AA
My Babes in the Wood.   Sarah Morgan Bryan Piatt.   AA
My Baby Has No Name Yet.   Kim Nam Jo, *tr. fr. Korean by* Ko Won.
AIW; PBWP
My ball is in a bunch of fern.   Mullion.   A. P. Herbert.   SD
My bands of silk and miniver.   Full Moon.   Elinor Wylie.   MoAB;
MoAmPo; OPOP; VGW
My banks they are furnished with bees.   William Shenstone.   *Fr.* Pastoral
Ballad.   BoNaP
   (Shepherd's Home, The.)   GN
My banks they are furnished with bees.   The Shepherd's Home.   William
Shenstone.   GN
My Baptismal Birthday.   Samuel Taylor Coleridge.   NOCV
My Barcelona—the stone pavement shaded deep with weariness.   Dream
of Barcelona: My Ancient World.   Takahashi Mutsuo, *tr. by* Hiroaki
Sato.   FCEI
My barefoot steps lie broad and big.   Spring.   Moishe Kulbak, *tr. by*
Ruth Whitman.   VWA
My beak is bent downward, I burrow below.   Plow: "My beak is bent
downward, I burrow below."   *Unknown, formerly at. to* Cynewulf, *tr.
fr. Anglo-Saxon.   Fr.* Riddles (Exeter Book).   AnOE
My beautiful! my beautiful! that standest meekly by.   The Arab to His
Favorite Steed.   Caroline Norton.   BeLS
   (Arab's Farewell to His Horse, The.)   BLPA
My beautiful one gave it to me when we parted.   Feelings Wakened by a
Mirror.   Po Chü-i, *tr. by* Burton Watson.   CoBCP
My beautiful picture of pirates and treasure.   Jigsaw Puzzle.   Russell
Hoban.   NTCP
My beauty is not wine to me.   The Song of the Narcissus.   *Unknown, tr.
fr. Arabic by* E. Powys Mathers.   *Fr.* The Thousand and One Nights.
AWP
My bed concealed by a folding screen.   Lying at Leisure during Rain.
Kao Ch'i, *tr. by* Jonathan Chaves.   CoBLCP
My Bed Is a Boat ("My bed is like a little boat").   Robert Louis
Stevenson.   PWR
My being not yet done.   Ancient Song.   Amir Gilboa, *tr. by* Warren
Bargad *and* Stanley F. Chyet.   IP
My beloved brother, born of my own parents.   Tanabe Sakimaro.   *Fr.*
Manyo Shu.   Ma
My beloved has already been.   The Snake Star.   Michael Guttenbrunner,
tr. by Beth Bjorklund.   CoAuP
My beloved hath a vineyard.   The Vineyard of My Beloved.   Priscilla
Jane Thompson.   CBWP-2

My Beloved Is Mine, and I Am His; He Feedeth among the Lillies.
Francis Quarles.   *Fr.* Emblems, V, 3.   MeLP; MePo; NOBE; OBEV;
OBS; TrGrPo, *abr.*
   (Divine Rapture.)   OBEV
My beloved land.   Minority Report.   John Updike.   GOA
My beloved little billiard balls.   Poem to Some of my Recent Poems.
James Tate.   NAmP; NoAM
My best belovit brother of the band.   To R. Hudson.   Alexander
Montgomerie.   OxBS
My Best Clothes.   Eli Netser, *tr. fr. Hebrew.*   MHeP, *tr. by* Bernhard
Frank
My best friend's name is Billy.   Puzzle.   Arnold Spilka.   ILY; RHPC
My better half, why turn a peevish scold.   Epigram.   Martial.   PeHV
My bibliography has grown.   Dallas E. Wiebe.   TW
My biggest worry is this.   In a Time of Sickness.   Orpingalik, *tr. by*
Edward Field.   STP
My Bird.   Ingeborg Bachmann, *tr. fr. German by* Beth Bjorklund.
CoAuP
My Bird.   "Fanny Forester."   AA
My Birth.   Minot Judson Savage.   AA; WGRP
My Birthday.   George Crabbe.   OxBSP
My birthdays take so long to start.   Between Birthdays.   Ogden Nash.
OnUR
My black-eyed lover broke my back.   The Masochist.   Maxine W.
Kumin.   IHMS; PoA
My black face fades.   Facing It.   Yusef Komunyakaa.   MT
My black hills have never seen the sun rising.   Shancoduff.   Patrick
Kavanagh.   BIrV; CIP; FaBCIP; FaBoTw; IPY; NoP
My black mothers I hear them singing.   Black Star Line.   Henry Dumas.
CNA; PoBA
My Black Triangle.   Grace Nichols.   WS
My Blackness Is the Beauty of This Land.   Lance Jeffers.   NBP; PoBA
My Blessed Lord, how doth thy Beautious Spouse.   Edward Taylor.   *Fr.*
Preparatory Meditations before My Approach to the Lord's Supper,
CL.   SCAP
My blessed mother dozing in her chair.   A Valentine to My Mother.
Christina Rossetti.   OHIP
My blood so red.   The Call.   *Unknown.*   OBEV
My bloodstream chokes on gall and spleen.   Quatrain.   Barend Toerien,
tr. by author.   PeSA
My Boat.   Raymond Carver.   TSL
My boat goes west, yours east.   Chao Li-hua, *tr. by* J. P. Seaton.
BoWoP
My boat is on the shore.   To Thomas Moore.   Byron.   EnRP
My boat sails downstream.   *Unknown, tr. by* J. E. Manchip White.   TTY
My body/ she says.   Cleopatra.   Mary Mackey.   AIW
My Body.   Jacques Dupin, *tr. fr. French by* Paul Auster.   RHTwFP
My Body.   Rachel Korn, *tr. fr. Yiddish by* Ruth Whitman.   VWA
My body.   What She Said ("My body").   Ammunavar, *tr. by* A. K.
Ramanujan.   PLW
My body a rounded stone.   Living Tenderly.   May Swenson.   OBCA
My body answers you, my blood.   Music of Hungary.   Anne Reeve
Aldrich.   AA
My body as an act of derision.   Bill Manhire.   ATNZ
My body being dead, my limbs unknown.   The Preparative.   Thomas
Traherne.   PoEL-2
My body, eh? Friend Death, how now?   Habeas Corpus.   Helen Hunt
Jackson.   AA; WGRP
My body fell asleep years ago. Cut off.   The Tingle.   Norman Andrew
Kirk.   TSM
My body heavy with poverty (starch).   Today's News.   Ted Berrigan.
UL
My body holds its shape. The genius is intact.   Mummy of a Lady Named
Jemutesonekh XXI Dynasty.   Thomas James.   AmPA; SM
My Body in the Walls Captived.   Sir Walter Ralegh.   SeCePo; SiPS
My body is like/ a field wasted by winter.   On Seeing the Field Being
Singed.   Lady Ise.   BoWoP, *tr. by* Etsuko Terasaki *and* Irma
Brandeis
My body is made of waves and foam.   Sea-Games.   Aliza Shenhar, *tr. by*
Linda Zisquit.   VWA
My body is weary to death of my mischievous brain.   Nebuchadnezzar.
Elinor Wylie.   MoAmPo
My body knows it will never bear children.   Waiting.   Jane Cooper.
TAP
My body opens over San Francisco like the daylight.   Splittings.
Adrienne Rich.   CAPP
My body's like a tree trunk in the wood.   My Body.   Rachel Korn, *tr. by*
Ruth Whitman.   VWA
My body's passion-hide.   Two Times Two Is Four.   H. Leivick, *tr. by*
Ruth Whitman.   VWA

My Bonny Black Bess. *Unknown. See* Dick Turpin's Ride ("Dick Turpin bold! Dick, hie away").

My bonny keel laddie, my canny keel laddie. The Bonny Keel Laddie. *Unknown.* GBP

My bonny lass, thine eye. Love's Witchery. Thomas Lodge. ElL

My bonny moorhen, my bonny moorhen. The Bonny Moorhen. *Unknown.* GBP

My Book. Louise Ackermann, *tr. fr. French* by Beth Archer. DMF

My Books. Longfellow. AA

My books, my sword, the wind-swept curtain. Remembering My Late Wife. Chu Yün-ming, *tr.* by Jonathan Chaves. CoBLCP

My bootheels and my cane. Death Stairs/Life House. Jack Hand. TSM

My Boy Kree? Kree. A. C. Gordon. AA

My Boy Tammy. Hector MacNeill. CH

My boy was scarcely ten years auld. Leesome Brand. *Unknown.* ESPB

My boys walk down the range intent to find. Archery Instructor. Richard Aldridge. TSL

"My brain dried like spread turf, my stomach." Seamus Heaney. *Fr.* Station Island, IX. CIP

My brain is like the ravaged shores—the sand. At Night. Frances Cornford. MoBrPo

My brain's gutterings unwind. Internus. Sándor Weöres, *tr.* by Edwin Morgan. MHuP

My breadwinner. The Breadwinner. Amrita Pritam, *tr.* by Charles Brasch *and* Amrita Pritam. OV

My breast is rent asunder. Asadullah Khan Ghalib, *tr.* by Ahmed Ali. GoT

My Breath. Orpingalik, *tr. fr. Eskimo* by K. Rasmussen. WTO

My brethren all attend. The Zealous Puritan. *Unknown.* OBS

"My brethren. . . ." And a bland, elastic smile. The Evangelist. Donald Davie. NePoEA

"My bride is not coming, alas!" says the groom. At the Altar-Rail. Thomas Hardy. *Fr.* Satires of Circumstance, IX. BrPo; MoAB; MoBrPo

My Brigantine. James Fenimore Cooper. *Fr.* The Water Witch, *ch.* 15. AA; MOS

My Brother. Patricia Parker. GLP

My Brother. Marci Ridlon. RHPC

My Brother, Beautiful Shinault, That Goat. David Huddle. GrPl

My Brother Bert. Ted Hughes. RHPC

My brother Cain, the wounded, liked to sit. Abel. Demetrios Capetanakis. GTBS-P; WaaP

My brother came back from the field. My Brother Was Silent. Amir Gilboa, *tr.* by A. C. Jacobs. VWA

My brother comes home from work. You Can Have It. Philip Levine. AnAn; CAPP

My Brother Flies Over Low. David Huddle. TDD

My brother has a little flute. The Fairy Flute. Rose Fyleman. BoTP

My brother has on/ a thin robe. Lady Otomo of Sakanoe, *tr.* by Willis Barnstone. BoWoP

My brother is skull and skeleton now. William Montgomerie. OxBS

My brother Jack was nine in May. The Baby's Debut. Horace Smith *and* James Smith. Par

My brother Jamie lost me all. Mary Stuart. Edwin Muir. RB

My Brother: ("My brother is not he who was born"). *Unknown.* WMBCH

My brother was not a camel driver. On Her Brother. Al-Khansa, *tr.* by Willis Barnstone. BoWoP

My Brother Was Silent. Amir Gilboa, *tr. fr. Hebrew* by A. C. Jacobs. VWA

My brother wrote to tell me. Revolution. Musaemura Bonus Zimunya. WMBCH

My Brothers. Anna Walters. VoR

My brother's worth about two cents. My Brother. Marci Ridlon. RHPC

My brudder sittin' on de tree of life. Roll, Jordan, Roll. *Unknown.* AA

My bull is white like silver fish in the river. The Magnificent Bull. *Dinka Oral Tradition.* TTTS

My bully boys of Liverpool. The Banks of Newfoundland. *Unknown.* GBP

My Buried Friends. *Unknown.* AmFP

My burned stabbed single seeing eye's a cave agape. In My Eye. Martin Seymour-Smith. NPo

My Burned Suit. Ilyas Farhat, *tr. fr. Arabic* by Salma Khadra Jayyusi *and* John Heath-Stubbs. MAP

My Cabinets Are Oyster-Shells. Margaret Cavendish, Duchess of Newcastle. *Fr.* The Convent of Pleasure. ELP
(Song: "My cabinets are oyster-shells.") WPE

My camel kneels at Ibn Marwan's door. Camel. Laila Akhyaliyya, *tr.* by Willis Barnstone. BoWoP

My Camping Ground. Morris Jacob Rosenfeld, *tr. fr. Yiddish* by Aaron Kramer. TrJP

My Canary. Josephine D. Henderson Heard. CBWP-4

My candle burns at both ends. First Fig. Edna St. Vincent Millay. AiP; FaBoWP; NoAM

My candle burns up lank and fair. Resurrection. Margiad Evans. OBWVE

My Captain. Dorothea Day. BLPA

My Care. Peter Fallon. CIP

My cares draw on mine everlasting night. Samuel Daniel. *Fr.* To Delia. OBSC

My case is this. Sir John Davies. *Fr.* The Gulling Sonnets. Son

My cat/ Is quiet. Cat. Dorothy W. Baruch. CRH

My cat. Territory. Jean Chapman. CRH

My Cat and I. Roger McGough. OxBTC

My cat can look at a king. No-Kings and the Calling of Spirits. Nancy Willard. LCAP

My cat has got no name. Cat. Vernon Scannell. CRH

My Cat Jeoffry. Christopher Smart. *See* Jubilate Agno: For I Will Consider My Cat Jeoffry [*or* Jeoffrey].

My Cat Mrs. Lick-a-Chin. John Ciardi. CRH

My Catbird. William Henry Venable. AA

My Cats. Stevie Smith. FaBoNo

My ceramic lake in dawn, water settled clear. Han Yü, *tr. fr. Chinese* by Burton Watson. *Fr.* A Pond in a Jardiniere, 3. CoBCP

My Chakabuku Mama. Jewelle Gomez. GLP

My Cheap Lifestyle. Eileen Myles. UL

My cheap toy lamp. Child's Song. Robert Lowell. RB

My cheek on the earth. With Teeth in the Earth. Malka Heifetz-Tussman, *tr.* by Kathryn Hellerstein. AYP

My Child. Susan Griffin. NPGG

My Child. John Pierpont. AA

My child and I hold hands on the way to school. September, the First Day of School. Howard Nemerov. OxBC

My child deep in the/ snow of illusion. My Child. Susan Griffin. NPGG

My child is still not twenty. Emperor Go-Shirakawa. *See* Ryojin Hisho: My son must be twenty by now.

My child, the Duck-billed Plat-y-pus. The Platypus. Oliver Herford. FiBHP; NA

My child, we were two children. Heine, *tr.* by Elizabeth Barrett Browning. OBVE
(Mein Kind, wir waren Kinder.) AWP; TrJP

My child (whichever) my love for you's more dear. To My Daughters. Martin Seymour-Smith. NPo

My childhood all a myth. The Myth. Edwin Muir. CMoP

My childhood is a long way off. Tourist. Muhammad al-Maghut, *tr.* by May Jayyusi *and* John Heath-Stubbs. MAP

My childhood is a sphere. Childhood. Thomas Traherne. TrGrPo

My childhood was like a dark passage. Intimations. Alma Johanna Koenig, *tr.* by Edouard Roditi. VWA

My childhood's home I see again. Memory. Abraham Lincoln. BLPA; FaBoBe; FPL; WBLP

My children/ when at first I liked the whites. *Unknown, tr. fr. Sioux Indian* by James Mooney. *Fr.* Ghost Dance Songs. STP

My children learn. If Our Dogs Outlived Us. Debra Hines. MOWH

My children, my little dears. The Mother Crab and Her Family. L. T. Manyase, *tr.* by Jack Cope *and* C. M. Mcanyangwa. PeSA

My children! speak not ill of one another. To Poets. Walter Savage Landor. FaBoEE

My Children's-Children's Past. Jacob Glatstein, *tr. fr. Yiddish* by Benjamin *and* Barbara Harshav. AYP

My Chinese Summer. Barbara Frischmuth, *tr. fr. German* by Beth Bjorklund. CoAuP

My Chinese uncle, gouty, deaf, half-blinded. Grotesques. Robert Graves. CMoP

My Christmas gifts were few: to one. To a Lady. Thomas William Parsons. AA

My Christmas; Mum's Christmas. Sarah Forsyth. OBCP

My Church ("My church has but one temple"). "E. O. G." BLPA; SoSe

My City. Faiz Ahmad Faiz, *tr. fr. Urdu* by Mahmood Jamal. PBMUP

My City. James Weldon Johnson. BANP; CDC; PoNe

My city collapsed. The Clock on the War. Samih al-Qasim, *tr.* by Abdullah al-Udhari. MPAW

My city mine. No more can I. Amir Gilboa, *tr.* by Warren Bargad *and* Stanley F. Chyet. IP

My city slept. The Beginning of a Long Poem on Why I Burned the City. Lawrence Benford. NBP; TTY

My claw is tired of scribing! Saint Columcille. NOIV

My Cleo's blush is tender, slow. Tender, Slow. *Unknown, tr.* by Wallace Rice. ErPo

My clothes are perfectly contoured. Success Story. Terence Winch.
   UL
My clothes are silent when I walk on the earth. Riddle: Mute Swan.
   Unknown. PBBP
My clothing was once of the linsey woolsey fine. Poor Old Horse.
   Unknown. CH; OBET
My clumsiest dear, whose hands shipwreck vases. John Frederick Nims.
   FF; HoPM; InPK; SoSe
My coachman, in the moonlight there. Without and Within. James
   Russell Lowell. AnAmPo
My Cobra Girl. *Gond Oral Tradition, tr. by* V. Elwin *and* S. Hivale.
   WTO
My cock? Chicken. Dennis Kelly. PeHV
My cocoon tightens—Colors tease. Emily Dickinson. NAAL-1
My Coffin Is a Deckchair. Rodney Hall. *Fr. Black Bagatelles.*
   CBAP
My comforts drop and melt away like snow. The Answer. George
   Herbert. FaBoRV; TEP
My Company. Sir Herbert Read. BrPo; MMA
My Comrade. Edwin Markham. AA
My Comrade. James Jeffrey Roche. AA
My conscience has given me several twitches. To My Cousin Mary, for
   Mending My Tobacco Pouch. Francis Scott Key. OBAL
My counterpane is soft as silk. A Child's Song of Christmas. Marjorie
   Pickthall. BoTP
My Country. Dorothea MacKellar. PoAu-1
My Country. Zindzi Mandela. AIW
My Country. Julio Ortega, *tr. fr. Spanish by* Ena Hollis. Per
My Country, *sels.* George Edward Woodberry.
   "O destined Land, unto thy citadel." AA
   O Land Beloved. PAH
My country,/t'is of thee/ I sing. A Lover's Question. James Baldwin.
   GLP
My country is handed over from one tyrant. From Exile to Exile. Abd-
   Allah al-Baraduni, *tr. by* Diana Der Hovanessian *and* Sharif Elmusa.
   MAP
My country is not a country. Eli W. Mandel. NOBC
My country need not change her gown. Emily Dickinson. AmFN; GOA
"My country, 'tis of thee." Assembly: Harlem School. Eugene T.
   Maleska. GoYe
My country, 'tis of thee. America. Samuel Francis Smith. AA; AiP;
   AnAmPo; FaBoBe; FaFP; FaPON; OPP; PoLF; WBLP
My Country, to Thy Shore. Theodore Chickering Williams. AH
My countryman, the poet, wears a Stetson. David Wright. *Fr.* Seven
   South African Poems. PeSA
My countrymen have now become too base. April 1962. Paul Goodman.
   VGW
My Cousin Agueda [*or Agatha*]. Ramón López Velarde, *tr. fr. Spanish.*
   LPSS, *tr. by* Perry Higman; MexPo, *tr. by* Samuel Beckett; OBVE
My Cousin German came from France. *Unknown.* FaBoCh
My Creed. Alice Cary. WGRP
My Creed. Jeanette Leonard Gilder. WGRP
My Creed. Howard Arnold Walter. FaFP; PoLF; WBLP
My crown desired, my true love and joy. A Love Letter to Elizabeth
   Thatcher. Thomas Thatcher. SCAP
My Crying-Out-Loud. Moyshe-Leyb Halpern, *tr. fr. Yiddish by* Benjamin
   and Barbara Harshav. AYP
My curse be on the day when first I saw. Sonnet: To the Lady Pietra
   degli Scrovigni. Dante, *tr. by* Dante Gabriel Rossetti. AWP
My cuticles are a mess. Oh honey, by the way. The Motorcyclists.
   James Tate. MAYP; NoAM
My dad gave me one dollar bill. Smart. Shel Silverstein. RHPC
My dad was a fisherman bold and he lived till he grew old. The
   Candlelight Fisherman. *Unknown.* OxBSS
My daddie is a cankert carle. Low Doun in the Broom. *Unknown.*
   GoTS
My Daddy baptized me. A Testimony. George Ella Lyon. GOYP
My daddy don't know. For Sapphires. Carolyn M. Rodgers. CNA
My Daddy has paid the rent. Good Times. Lucille Clifton. AmNP;
   AmPA; BPo; CNA; FF; GrPl; InPS; PoBA; TAP; TwCP
My daddy is an engineer. Wanderin'. *Unknown.* AS
My daddy played the market. January 1st. Anne Sexton. HCAP
My Dad's Dinner Pail. Edward Harrigan. BLPA
My Daily Creed. *Unknown.* PWR
My Daily Prayer. Grenville Kleiser. BLRP
My dame hath a lame tame crane. *Unknown.* OxNR
My Damon was the first to wake. Meeting. George Crabbe. OBEV
My Dancing Day. *Unknown.* OxBoLi
My dancing is, in my opinion, good. Of Dancing. Alan Brownjohn.
   FaBoMo

My Daphne's hair is twisted gold. Daphne. John Lyly. *Fr.* Midas.
   EIL
   (Song of Daphne to the Lute, A.) OBSC
My Dark Fathers. Brendan Kennelly. BIrV; CIP
My darkling child the stars have obeyed. George Barker. *Fr.* To My
   Son, I. TwCP
My darling gazed at the juniper. Tabito. *Fr.* Manyo Shu. Ma
My darling, my love. Desmond O'Grady, *tr. fr. Irish by the author.* *Fr.*
   In the Greenwood, I. CIP
My darling, we sat together. Mein Liebchen, wir sassen zusammen.
   Heine, *tr. by* James Thomson. AWP
My Darling's on the Deep Blue Sea. *Unknown.* AmFP
My Daughter. Habib Jalib, *tr. fr. Urdu by* Mahmood Jamal. PBMUP
My daughter, at eleven. Little Girl, My Stringbean, My Lovely Woman.
   Anne Sexton. NYBP
My Daughter Considers Her Body. Floyd Skloot. SM
My daughter cries, and I. Child Crying. Anthony Thwaite. NePoEA-2
My daughter cries when we have to talk about money. The Money Cry.
   Peter Davison. FYAP
My daughter denies she is like me. Breaking Tradition. Janice
   Mirikitani. BrSi
My daughter is a mystic about cats. Waiting for the Transformation.
   Judith Minty. TV
My daughter must be past ten by now. Emperor Go-Shirakawa, *tr. fr.*
   Japanese by Hiroaki Sato. *Fr.* Ryojin Hisho. FCEI
My daughter plays on the floor. Spelling. Margaret Atwood. NoAM;
   NoP
My daughter pleads with me. Chile. Susan Griffin. NPGG
My daughter spreads her legs. After Reading *Mickey in the Night Kitchen*
   for the Third Time before Bed. Rita Dove. ER
My daughter who's not yet born and who's name is Hagar. The Boring
   Orbit. Samih al-Qasim, *tr. by* Abdullah al-Udhari. MPAW
My daughter, you must care for your toys. Toys. Abraham Sutskever,
   tr. by Chana Bloch. PeBMYV
My Daughter's Ring. Barbara Eve Reiss. TV
My Days Among the Dead are Past. Robert Southey. EnRP; TEP
   (His Books.) OBEV
My Days are Gliding Swiftly By. David Nelson. AH
My days' delights, my springtime joys fordone. A Poem Entreating of
   Sorrow. Sir Walter Ralegh. SiPS
My Days of Love Are Over. Byron. *Fr.* Don Juan, I. OBNC
My Dead. Frederick Lucian Hosmer. WGRP
My Dead. Rachel, *tr. fr. Hebrew by* Robert Mezey. VWA
My dead Love came to me, and said. The Apparition. Stephen Phillips.
   OBEV
My dear/ for seven years. A Dog Poem. Saqi Farooqi, *tr. by* Mahmood
   Jamal. PBMUP
My dear,/ Today a letter from Berlin. A Letter from Berlin. Jon
   Stallworthy. MoP; OBWP; OxBC
My dear and only love, I pray. James Graham, Marquess of Montrose.
   Fr. Montrose to His Mistress. JCP; OxBS
   (I'll Never Love Thee More.) GBL; NOBE; OBEV
   (My Dear and Only Love.) OBS
My dear brother Burritt, you asked me to-day. My Latest Publication.
   Edward Capern. PF
My dear brother Ned. The *South Carolina. Unknown.* PAH
My dear child, first thyself enable. The Boy Serving at Table. John
   Lydgate. OxBChV
My dear Daddie bought a mansion. The Little Bird. Walter De la Mare.
   NAs
My dear, darkened in sleep turned from the moon. To Judith Asleep.
   John Ciardi. LiTM
My dear deaf father, how I loved him then. Sir John Betjeman. *Fr.*
   Summoned by Bells. OxBTC
My dear, do you know. The Babes in the Wood. *Unknown.* OxBChV;
   PBBP
My dear, do you remember that country. Remember That Country. Jean
   Garrigue. VGW
My dear, dumb friend, low lying there. To My Dog "Blanco." Josiah
   Gilbert Holland. PoLF
"My dear fellow!" said the great poet. Fiction: A Message. Gavin
   Ewart. OxBC
My dear, I wonder if before the end. To D——, Dead by Her Own
   Hand. Howard Nemerov. PoA
"My dear, indulgent, older (by five minutes) brother." Clayfeld's Twin.
   Robert Pack. BLA
My Dear Lady. *Unknown.* EIL
My dear little crane. A Pet Crane. *Unknown, tr. by* Myles Dillon.
   AnIL
My dear Magritte, I have been ill. Again. Personal Values. Richard
   Howard. SM

My dear, mere words have no power. Afanasi Afanasievich Fet, *tr. by* Alan Myers. AAA

My dear mistress has a heart. Earl of Rochester. SeCV-2

My dear Mr. Murray. Epistle to Mr. Murray. Byron. FaBoUs

My dear, my dear, I know. To a Young Girl. W. B. Yeats. EBEV

My dear, naïve, ingenuous child. Don't Say You Like Tchaikowsky. Paul Rosner. FiBHP

My dear, observe the rose! though she desire it. William Bell. NePoEA

My dear one is mine as mirrors are lonely. Miranda. W. H. Auden. *Fr.* The Sea and the Mirror. NoAM

My dear Orange brothers, have you heard of the news. The Orange Lily. *Unknown.* NOIV

My Dear Son John's deceas'd ah! gone from hence. A Brief Elegie on My Dear Son John. John Saffin. SCAP

My Dear, we have been invited to a ball our first night. Donna Anna Writes to Her Sister. Tom Disch. SoTCo

My dear, when I was very young. To a Lady on Her Marriage. William Bell. NePoEA

My dear wife loved my arm. Tabito. *Fr.* Manyo Shu. Ma

My dear young friend, whose shining wit. Comic Miseries. John Godfrey Saxe. AnAmPo

My dear young maiden clingeth. The Vampire. Heinrich August Ossenfelder, *tr. by* Aloysius Gibson. VVA

My dearest dear, the time draws near. The Lover's Lament. *Unknown.* AS

My dearest dust, could not thy hasty day. Epitaph on the Monument of Sir William Dyer at Colmworth, 1641. Lady Catherine Dyer. *Fr.* Sir William Dyer, Knight. BoLoP; EnLoPo

My dearest Rival, least our Love. Sir John Suckling. MeLP

My Dearling. Elizabeth Akers Allen. AA

My dearly loved friend how oft have we. To My Most Dearly-loved Friend, Henry Reynolds, Esquire, of Poets and Poesy. Michael Drayton. OBS
(First Steps Up Parnassus.) NOBE, *abr.*

My dears, 'tis said in days of old. The Bee, the Ant, and the Sparrow. Nathaniel Cotton. OxBChV

My Death. A. J. M. Smith. OBCV

My Death. Carl Zuckmayer, *tr. fr. German by* E. B. Ashton. TrJP

My death was arranged by special plans in Heaven. A New England Bachelor. Richard Eberhart. MoAmPo; NoAM

My Deery Honey. *Unknown.* PBCV

My Delight and Thy Delight. Robert Bridges. CMoP; NOBE; OBEV; PoEL-5

My Descendants. W. B. Yeats. *Fr.* Meditations in Time of Civil War, IV. LiTB

My desire for revenge, the bitterness. Till Death Do Us Part. Leila Miccolis, *tr. by* Willis Barnstone *and* Nelson Cerqueira. BoWoP

My desk's at the back of the class. The Marrog. R. C. Scriven. AmMo; RHPC

My desolation does begin to make. Shakespeare. *Fr.* Antony and Cleopatra, V, ii. OBD

My destiny has been to prune one tree. They. Marvin Bell. CAPP

"My deth I love, my lif ich hate." A Cleric Courts His Lady. *Unknown.* MeEL

My dismal sister! Couldst thou know. "Lewis Carroll." *Fr.* Melancholetta. FiBHP

My Dog. John Kendrick Bangs. BLPA; BLPL; FaBoBe

My Dog. Marchette Chute. FaPON; PDV

My Dog Dash. John Ruskin. FM

My Dog I was ever well pleased to see. My Dog Tray. John Byrom. SeCePo

My dog lay dead five days without a grave. The Pardon. Richard Wilbur. MoP; NePoEA; NIP; NoAM; NOBA; NoP; OBD

My Dog Ponto. Edgar Lee Masters. FM

My Dog, Spot. Rodney Bennett. BoTP

My Dog Tray. John Byrom. SeCePo

My dog went mad and bit my hand. D is for Dog. W. H. Davies. OxBSP

My Doggie. C. Nurton. BoTP

My dog's assumed my alter ego. The Strange Case. Michael Ondaatje. NIP

My dog's so furry I've not seen. The Hairy Dog. Herbert Asquith. FaPON; PDV; RHPC

My dolour is ane cup. Ressaif My Saul. R. Crombie Saunders. OxBS

My Dolphin, you only guide me by surprise. Dolphin. Robert Lowell. NoAM; NOBA

My donkey has a bridle. The Donkey. Rose Fyleman. BoTP

My Dragon. X. J. Kennedy. RAR

My Dream. Lew Blockcolski. VoR

My Dream. Christina Rossetti. BrRo

My Dream. *Unknown.* NA

My dreams/ Watching me said. Note. Paul Potts. PoPo

My dreams always returned. Afterthoughts. Tachihara Michizo, *tr. by* Geoffrey Bownas *and* Anthony Thwaite. PeBJV

My dreams are above all a liquor. The Bad Dreamer. Antonin Artaud, *tr. by* Michael Benedikt. POS

My Dreams are lucid. Dreams. Anne Bloch. Mes

My dreams are so full of longing. Longing. Rachel Korn, *tr. by* Ruth Whitman. VWA

My Dreams by Henry James. Michael Ryan. SV

My dreams foam cherry blossom. Fair in Frosty May. László Nagy, *tr. by* Tony Connor. MHuP

My Dreams, My Works, Must Wait Till after Hell. Gwendolyn Brooks. NoP

My Drinking Song. Richard Dehmel, *tr. fr. German by* Ludwig Lewisohn. AWP

My drum, hollowed out thru the thin slit. La Chute. Charles Olson. InPK

My duchess was the werst she laffed she bitte. Sonnet. Ernest Walsh. ErPo

My ducks are so funny, I think. Peter and Wendy. Wymond Garthwaite. RAR

My dugout canoe goes. Paddling Song. *Unknown, tr. by* Max Exner. PBA

My dumb ox loyalty is. Remember Medusa? Eunice De Souza. AIW

My eager waiting heart can bear no more. He Comes Not To-night. Josephine D. Henderson Heard. CBWP-4

My Early Home. John Clare. BoTP; PoLF

My early Mistress, now my ancient Muse. Preface to The Progress of Learning. Sir John Denham. OxBSP

My Early Religious Education. Sally Fisher. SoTCo

My Easter Dove. Henrietta Cordelia Ray. CBWP-3

My ecstasy is that I have met you. Said Aql, *tr. fr. Arabic by* Matthew Sorenson *and* Naomi Shihab Nye. *Fr.* The Book of Roses. MAP

My Elbow Ancestry. Larry Mollin. NeAC

My elder,/ Born into death like a message into a bottle. To My Brother Hanson. W. S. Merwin. NAAL-2

My elder sister stays by my side. Happy about Being Old. Yüan Mei, *tr. by* Jonathan Chaves. CoBLCP

My eldest sister arrived home that morning. Cuba. Paul Muldoon. CIP; PPR

My embarrassment at his nakedness. The Pool. Robert Creeley. CoAP

My Enemy. Alice Williams Brotherton. AA

My enemy came nigh. Hate. James Stephens. MoAB; MoBrPo

My enemy had bidden me as guest. The Compassionate Fool. Norman Cameron. GTBS-P; OxBSP; OxBTC; RB

My energy is going, been spent. Old Man. Faye Kicknosway. UL

My Epitaph. H. J. Daniel. FaBoEE

My Epitaph. David Gray. EBVV

My Epitaph. Alexis Piron, *tr. fr. French.* OBD

My epitaph write on your heart. Love's Epitaph. William Cavendish, Duke of Newcastle. OxBSP

My Erotic Double. John Ashbery. LCAP; PoE

My erstwhile glance, once cast at a river. Beyond the Imaginary Garden. Gabriel Preil, *tr. by* Bernhard Frank. MHeP

My ethics were. Basketball: A Retrospective. Stephen Dunn. ASP

My Evening Prayer. Charles H. Gabriel. BLPA; FaBoBe

My eye cried and woke me. The Night. Al-Khansa, *tr. by* Willis Barnstone. BoWoP

My eye descending from the Hill, surveys. Sir John Denham. *Fr.* Cooper's Hill. OAEL-1
(Thames from Cooper's Hill, The.) OBS; SeCePo

My eyelids red and heavy are. A Poor Scholar of the 'Forties. Padraic Colum. AnIL; NOIV

My eyes are dim, my hands are clumsy. Getting on Horseback. Yü Chi, *tr. by* Jonathan Chaves. CoBLCP

My eyes are dry of tears. Mohammad Taqi Mir, *tr. by* Ahmed Ali. GoT

My eyes are filmed, my beard is grey. The Time of the Barmecides. James Clarence Mangan. EnRP

My eyes are on a butterfly. Who Are You? "Adunis," *tr. by* Lena Jayyusi *and* John Heath-Stubbs. MAP

My eyes are the enemy's eyes. The Enemy's Eyes. Emma Lee Warrior. HATNAP

My eyes are thirsty. Mirabai, *tr. by* Willis Barnstone *and* Usha Nilsson. BoWoP

My eyes are white stones. River God's Song. Anne Ridler. NYBP

My eyes catch ruddy necks. Marching. Isaac Rosenberg. BrPo

My eyes have telescopes. João Cabral de Melo Neto, *tr. by* W. S. Merwin. ATCBP

My eyes may close in the last remaining. Constant Love Even beyond Death. Francisco de Quevedo, *tr. by* Perry Higman. LPSS

My eyes went away from me. The Fickle One. Pablo Neruda, *tr. by* Donald D. Walsh. FF

My Face. Anthony Euwer. *See* Limeratomy, The: As a Beauty I Am Not a Star.

My face is black. See the moon? My eyes. Crystal. Faye Kicknosway. IHMS

My face is grass. Legacy. Maurice Kenny. HATNAP

My Face Is My Own, I Thought. Tom Raworth. EAS

My face is wet with rain. Walking at Night. Amory Hare. PoLF

My face will be dark. Myself of the Onan Legend. Takahashi Mutsuo, *tr. by* Hiroaki Sato. FCEI

My Faces. Gyorgy Raba, *tr. fr. Hungarian by* Jascha Kessler. FOC

My faint spirit was sitting in the light. From the Arabic; an Imitation. Shelley. OBEV

My Fair Lady. *Unknown.* EnLoPo; PoEL-1

My fair, look from those turrets of thine eyes. Michael Drayton. *Fr.* Idea's Mirrour, XXXIV. OBSC

My fairest child, I have no song to give you. Charles Kingsley. BLPA; EBVV; GN; OxBChV

My fairest child, I have no song to sing thee. A Farewell, To C. E. G. Charles Kingsley. BoTP

My Fairy. "Lewis Carroll." FaBoNo

My Faith. Ananda Acharya. WGRP

My Faith Looks Up to Thee. Ray Palmer. AH, *with music;* WGRP (Faith.) AA

My faithful friend, if you can see. Impossibilities to His Friend. Robert Herrick. OxBSP

My Familiar. John Godfrey Saxe. AnAmPo

My family has married me. Song of Sorrow. *Unknown, tr. by* Burton Watson. CoBCP

My family slept those level miles. Across Kansas. William Stafford. CAPP

My Fancy. "Lewis Carroll." *See* I painted her a gushing thing.

My Father. Vicente Aleixandre, *tr. fr. Spanish by* Perry Higman. LPSS

My Father. Yehuda Amichai, *tr. fr. Hebrew.* IP, *tr. by* Warren Bargad *and* Stanley F. Chyet; MHeP, *tr. by* Bernhard Frank.

My Father. James Berry. PBCV

My Father. Hayyim Nahman Bialik, *tr. fr. Hebrew by* Bernhard Frank. MHeP

My Father. Abraham Chalfi, *tr. fr. Hebrew by* Shlomo Vinner *and* Howard Schwartz. VWA

My Father. Rae Dalven. GoYe

My Father. Pablo Guevara, *tr. fr. Spanish by* David Tipton. Per

My Father, *sel.* H. Leivick, *tr. fr. Yiddish by* Benjamin *and* Barbara Harshav.

Sturdy in Me, The. AYP

My Father. Tuvia Rübner, *tr. fr. Hebrew by* Bernhard Frank. MHeP

My father/ lets his hair down now. Father Takes to the Road and Lets His Hair Down. Alan Chong Lau. BrSi

My Father after Work. Gary Gildner. Psk

My father and his muscles. My Father Toured the South. Jeannette Nichols. ASP

My father and mother held me in their arms. I Accompanied My Mother on a Visit to the Itsukushima Shrine. Rai San'yo, *tr. by* Burton Watson. JLIC-2

My father and mother left me a good living. Han-shan, *tr. by* Burton Watson. CoBCP

My father and mother, my brother and sister. The Sightseers. Paul Muldoon. CIP

My father and mother (what ails 'em?). The Rural Lass. Catherine Jemmat. NOEC

My father and my mother never quarrelled. Because. James McAuley. CBAP

My father and my uncle. I Accompanied My Uncle Shumpo on an Outing to Lake Biwa. Rai San'yo, *tr. by* Burton Watson. FCEI; JLIC-2

My father asks me how I stand it all. Parents. Vincent Buckley. CBAP

My father at the dictionary-stand. Supernatural Love. Gjertrud Schnackenberg. DiPo; NoAM

My father bequeathed me no wide estates. Heirloom. A. M. Klein. NIP; NOBC; OBCV; TrJP

My father brought that dog home. Bony. Simon J. Ortiz. CDW

My father brought the emigrant bundle. Europe and America. David Ignatow. AmFN; NNaP; UnPo

My father by some strange conjunction had mice for sons. In All the Days of My Childhood. Russell Edson. AmPA

My father came in the darkness. Hyena. *Unknown, tr. by* George Economou. TTY

My father casts a stone whose ripples ride. L. E. Sissman. *Fr.* Going Home, 1945. DiL

My father comes to see me on Friday night. Bar Mitzvah. Isaac Goldemberg, *tr. by* David Unger. VWA

My father coming home. One Summer. Robert Mezey. DiL

My father could go down a mountain faster than I. That Dark Other Mountain. Robert Francis. CRP; SD

My father could hear a little animal step. Listening. William Stafford. RFM

My father died a month ago. *Unknown.* OxNR

My father died at the age of eighty. Honey. James Wright. KS

My father died nine months before. Birth of a Son. Sam Hunt. PeNZ

My Father Died This Spring. Joanne Kyger. PoM

My father engraved his life in stone. Copy. Ben-Zion Tomer, *tr. fr. Hebrew by* Bernhard Frank. *Fr.* Song Sequence. MHeP

My father entered the kingdom of roots. 1933. Philip Levine. VWA

My father, folding toward the earth again, plays. Waving Good-bye to My Father. Michael C. Blumenthal. DiL

My father found it after the war. The House on Buder Street. Gary Gildner. TAP

My father, fresh out of dental school. Old Photo, 1942. George Uba. BrSi

My father, gasping, in his white calked shoes. The Course. Robert Huff. CoAP

My father got on his horse and went to the field. Infancy. Carlos Drummond de Andrade, *tr. by* Elizabeth Bishop. ATCBP

My father had a glass eye. My Father's Eye. Eléni Vakaló, *tr. by* Kimon Friar. BoWoP

My father had terrible words for you. For My Brother Jesus. Irving Layton. NoP

My father has big skin like a soldier's cape. Venus Khoury-Gata, *tr. by* Carol Cosman. OV

My father hated moonlight. Moonlight. Berta Hart Nance. AmFN

My father haunts me in the old men that I find. Pain-Killers. Tony Harrison. NPo

My father he died, but I can't tell you how. Mother Goose. OxNR

My father, he was a mountaineer. The Ballad of William Sycamore. Stephen Vincent Benét. MoAmPo; PoRA

My father, his mouth full of nails. Nails. Gary Gildner. TAP

My father in his. Beryl. Lyn Lifshin. NeAC

My Father in the Night Commanding No. Louis Simpson. CoAP; DiL; HeIP; LCAP; NePoEA-2; NoAM; NOBA; NYBP; SM; TAP; TwCP; VGW

My father is a fugitive/ from the villages of Chagall. Two Refugees. Mordecai Marcus. VWA

My father is a hard man. The Armorer's Daughter. Debora Greger. MAYP

"My father is a knight and a man of high renown." The Bold Dragoon. *Unknown.* OBET

My father is a quiet man. Fruit of the Flower. Countee Cullen. PoLF

My father is dead. Song of the Bush-Shrike. *Unknown.* PeSA

My father is dead and there is nothing left. Not Saying Much. Linda Gregg. AiP; NPGG

My Father—Is the Root, *sel.* Itamar Ya'oz-kest, *tr. fr. Hebrew by* Bernhard Frank.

"Flag on the house you dwelled in the wind blows now and then, The." MHeP

My Father Kept a Horse. *Unknown.* GBP

My Father Kept His Cats Well Fed. Kenneth Sherman. HeIP

My Father Knows. Wilbur Fisk Tillett. BLRP

My father leads me by the hand to synagogue. Holiday. H. Leivick, *tr. fr. Yiddish by* Benjamin *and* Barbara Harshav. *Fr.* Remembrances. AYP

My father left me a book of Hemingway's stories. The Hemingway House in Key West. Philip Schultz. MAYP

My father left me three acres of land. Three Acres of Land. *Unknown.* NA; OxNR

(Sing Ivy.) BoTP

My father, let no similes eclipse. In Memoriam. Michael Longley. FaBCIP

My father lies black and hushed. The Worker. Richard W. Thomas. PoBA; PoNe

My father limps on the leg that healed short. Hook. Floyd Skloot. ASP

My father listening to opera, that's me. David Ignatow. DiL

My father, looking for trouble, would find it. The Man of the House. David Wagoner. NoAM

My father made a synagogue of a boat. Two Fishermen. Stanley Moss. CoAP; VWA

(Fisherman.) DiL

My Father Moved through Dooms of Love. E. E. Cummings. CMoP; DiL; FYAP; HAP; LiTA; MoAB; MoP; NAAL-2; NoAM; NOBA; NoP; OxBA; TAP; UnPo

My father moves through the South hunting duck. Treetops. Marvin Bell. AmPA; DiL

My Father, My Son. John Malcolm Brinnin. DiL; NYBP

My Father; October 1942. William Stafford. CAPP; DiL; NaP
My father once broke a man's hand. Winter Stars. Larry Levis. DiL; MAYP; NAmP
My Father Owns the Butcher Shop. *Unknown.* FaFP; RAR; RHPC
My father paces the upstairs hall. Spree. Maxine W. Kumin. NoAM
My Father Paints the Summer. Richard Wilbur. DiL; NOBA
My father played the melodion. Patrick Kavanagh. *Fr.* A Christmas Childhood. PChr; RB
My father promised. Private Acts. Leslie Ullman. NAmP
My father recommended safety. Belonging to a New Family. Mohammad Bennis, *tr. by* Sharif Elmusa *and* Charles Doria. MAP
My father remembered what it was to be small. In the Giant's Castle. Ruth Dallas. PeNZ
My father returned. The Return. Shmuel Moreh. VWA, *tr. by* Yoffee Berkovitz
My father said quicksand. Lesson. Susan Ludvigson. KS
My father sang the songs. Yiddish. Judith Herzberg. DuIn, *tr. by* Manfred Wolf; VWA, *tr. by* Shirley Kaufman
My Father Scything. Sam Hunt. ATNZ; PeNZ
My father, severe because he was shy. Foreword. Jules Laforgue, *tr. by* William Jay Smith. CT
My father smiled this morning when. Keep Smiling. *Unknown.* WBLP
My father stands in the warm evening. Starlight. Philip Levine. CAPP
My father talked too much. How My Father Died. Nissim Ezekiel. VWA
My father taught. Whose Voice. Barney Bush. STE
My father, the least happy. The Cage. John Montague. CIP; FaBCIP
My father thought that fact was dull. Garland for a Storyteller. Jessie Farnham. GoYe
My Father Today. Sam Hunt. PeNZ
My father tore out his native roots. My Father. Rae Dalven. GoYe
My Father Toured the South. Jeannette Nichols. ASP
My father used to say. Silence. Marianne Moore. AnAmPo; CMoP; FaBoMo; FaBoWP; InPS; LiTA; NOBA; QFR
My Father Used to Tell of An. A. R. Ammons. DiL
My father was a farmer gay. One-and-Twenty. *Unknown.* AmFP
My father was a Frenchman. *Unknown.* OxNR
My father was a sailor. Antonio Machado, *tr. Spanish by* Havelock Ellis. *Fr.* Spanish Folk Songs. AWP
My father was a tough cookie. My Mother Really Knew. Wing Tek Lum. MOWH
My father was always out in the garage. E. W. Mandel. *Fr.* Minotaur Poems, II. MoCV; OBCV
My father was born with a spade in his hand and traded it. John Ciardi. DiL
My father was hung from a star. Song of the Last Jewish Child. Edmond Jabès, *tr. by* Anthony Rudolf. VWA
My father was sixty when I was born. My Father Scything. Sam Hunt. ATNZ; PeNZ
My Father Washes His Hands. Fred Chappell. MT
My father! when I saw thee last. To Father. Mary E. Tucker. CBWP-1
My father who forgets that yesterday. Bagatelles. Steve Orlen. NAmP
My father who found the English landscape tame. Woods. Louis MacNeice. FaBCIP
My father, who works with stone. A Story of How a Wall Stands. Simon J. Ortiz. HATNAP; MAYP
My Father, Who's Still Alive. José Kozer, *tr. fr. Spanish by* Jorge Guitart. VWA
My father woke at dawn. Winter. Yankev-Yitskhok Segal, *tr. by* Grace Schulman. PeBMYV
My father wore it working coal at Shotts. The Miner's Helmet. George MacBeth. OxBTC
My father worked with a horse-plough. Follower. Seamus Heaney. FaBCIP; IPY
My father would have saved us, had the occasion of fire arisen. Netting. Jorie Graham. NPGG
My father would walk about for hours with a lit cigarette. The Stranger. Juan Gelman, *tr. by* Yishai Tobin. VWA
My father writes from Arizona. Latin Dances. Mark Doty. NAmP
My Fatherland. William Cranston Lawton. AA
My Father's a Still Day. Geoffrey Lehmann. *Fr.* Ross's Poems. CBAP
My father's body was a globe of fear. Letters & Other Worlds. Michael Ondaatje. NoAM; NOBC; NoP
My Fathers Came from Kentucky. Vachel Lindsay. AmFN
My Father's Child. "Stuart Sterne." AA
My Father's Close. *Unknown, tr. fr. French by* Dante Gabriel Rossetti. AWP
My fathers come to me in an old film. The Worm. Willis Barnstone. VWA
My Father's Cot, *sel.* J. C. Squire.
  "I left thee with a courage high." BXAP

My Father's Death. Ugo Foscolo, *tr. fr. Italian by* Lorna de' Lucchi. PFI
My Father's Dream. Sargon Boulus, *tr. fr. Arabic by* Sargon Boulus *and* Alistair Elliot. MAP
My Father's Eye. Eléni Vakaló, *tr. fr. Modern Greek by* Kimon Friar. BoWoP
My Father's Face. Hayden Carruth. DiL
My father's face is brown with sun. Father. Frances M. Frost. FaPON
My father's friend came once to tea. A Recollection. Frances Cornford. FaBoWP
My Father's Funeral. Karl Shapiro. DiL
My Father's Garden. David Wagoner. DiPo
My father's in business, takes it a day at a time. Ballade of the Back Road. Ron Block. SM
My Father's Leaving. Ira Sadoff. AmPA; DiL
My father's life is alchemy. Words and Legacy. Cyril Dabydeen. PBCV
My father's lips that might be blessing someone. Of Things Past. Shmuel Halkin, *tr. by* Hillel Halkin. PeBMYV
My father's loud call like a crest of feathers. To a Dead Childhood. Rodolfo Hinostroza, *tr. by* Maureen Ahern *and* David Tipton. Per
My Father's Martial Art. Stephen Shu Ning Liu. BrSi; InPK
My Father's Memorial Day. Yehuda Amichai, *tr. fr. Hebrew by the author and* Ted Hughes. OBD
My father's memory book. Coat of Arms. Alan Dugan. DiL
My father's mother had the second sight. Second Sight. Michael Longley. FaBCIP
My father's name is Frankenstein. Father and Mother. X. J. Kennedy. GrPl; RHPC
My Fathers sit on benches. Song for the Old Ones. Maya Angelou. SaC
My Father's Song. Simon J. Ortiz. HATNAP; MAYP; STE
My Father's Store. Caroline Finkelstein. PPR
My Father's Story. Priscilla Jane Thompson. CBWP-2
My Father's Voice in Prayer. May Hastings Nottage. BLRP
My Father's Watch. John Ciardi. ImOP
My Father's Wedding. Robert Bly. CAPP; DiL; InPS; NoAM
My fathers wrote their names in sweat. Signatures. Candace Thurber Stevenson. AmFN
My fault, my greatest fault. The Child Scribbles. Nizar Qabbani, *tr. by* Diana Der Hovanessian *and* Lena Jayyusi. MAP
My favorite student lately is the one who wrote about feeling clumbsy. The Spell against Spelling. George Starbuck. FYAP
My Feet. Gelett Burgess. NA
My feet are elms, roots in the earth. They Tell Me I Am Lost. Maurice Kenny. HATNAP; STE
My feet have felt the sands. Determination. John Henrik Clarke. CNA; PoBA
My feet strike an apex of the apices of the stairs. Infinity. Walt Whitman. *Fr.* Song of Myself, XLIV–XLV. AA
My feet taste funny. Why I Didn't Go to Delphi. James Welch. CDW
My feet, they haul me round the house. My Feet. Gelett Burgess. NA
My, Fellowship, with, God. José Garcia Villa. EaLo
My female friends, whose tender hearts. Swift. *Fr.* Verses on the Death of Doctor Swift [D.S.P.D., Occasioned by Reading a Maxim in Rochefoucauld]. NOBL; SeCePo
My Fiddle. Leib Kwitko, *tr. fr. Yiddish by* Keith Bosley. VWA
My Fiddle. James Whitcomb Riley. AnAmPo
My fifthe housbonde, god his soule blesse! Chaucer. *Fr.* The Canterbury Tales: The Wife of Bath's Prologue. FiP
My 50th year having arrived. On the Birth of Dan Goldman. Daniel Berrigan. NAs
My Final Agonies. Benjamin Péret, *tr. fr. French by* James Laughlin. POS
My fingers are but stragglers at the rear. Stragglers. Pietro Aretino, *tr. by* Samuel Putnam. ErPo
My first big love was cosmically correct. My Chakabuku Mama. Jewelle Gomez. GLP
My First Forty Years. Kevin Ireland. PeNZ
My First Love. Harry Graham. FiBHP
My first love sighed for brooches. Prices. Louis Ginsberg. TrJP
My first Sabbath cigarette between my lips. The First Cigarette. Joseph Rolnik, *tr. by* Irving Feldman. PeBMYV
My first thought was, he lied in every word. "Childe Roland to the Dark Tower Came." Robert Browning. NAEL-2; NOBVV; NoP; OAEL-2; OBNV; PoE; PPP
My first vivid memory of you. To Jesus Villanueva, with Love. Alma Villanueva. CCP
My fixed abode is Glen Bolcain. Suibne Geilt. NOIV
My flattering fortune, look thou never so fair. To Fortune. Sir Thomas More. ACP

My flesh is racked by plague. The New Ahasuerus. Jozsef Kiss, *tr. by* André Ungar. VWA

My flock feeds not, my ewes breeds not. The Unknown Shepherd's Complaint. Richard Barnfield. EIL
(Shepherd's Complaint, A.) OBSC

My flower beds were trampled down. The Gardener. Herbert Zand, *tr. by* Beth Bjorklund. CoAuP

My flowery and green age was passing away. Petrarch, *tr. fr. Italian. Fr.* Sonnets to Laura: To Laura in Death, XLVII, *prose tr. by* J. M. Synge. OBMV
(He Understands the Great Cruelty of Death.) BIrV

My foe was dark, and stern, and grim. My Enemy. Alice Williams Brotherton. AA

My folk, now answere me. Jesus Reproaches His People. *Unknown.* MeEL

My food was pallid till I heard it ring. King Midas. Howard Moss. CoAP; TAP
(King's Speech, The.) PoA

My foolish heart keeps beckoning to me. Ilyas Farhat, *tr. by* Salma Khadra Jayyusi *and* John Heath-Stubbs. MAP

My foolish heart what is ailing thee? Asadullah Khan Ghalib, *tr. by* Ahmed Ali. GoT

My foot-steps grew where, centuries ago. The Red Men. Charles Sangster. CaP

My forehead's lined, my eyes intense, deep-set. Self-Portrait. Ugo Foscolo, *tr. by* William Jay Smith. CT; PFI

My fortitude is all awry. She Sees Another Door Opening. Firman Houghton. Par

My forty-year-old father learned to fly. The Hang-Glider's Daughter. Marilyn Hacker. MAYP

My foster-brother and foster-sister. The Golden Sea-Otter. Wakarpa. *Fr.* Kutune Shirka (The Ainu Epic). WTO

My four steeds are weary. *Unknown, tr. by* Arthur Waley. BoS

My frame of nature is a ruffled sea. The Hurry of the Spirits, in a Fever and Nervous Disorders. Isaac Watts. NOEC

My freshmen/ settle in. Achilles. Freshmen. Barry Spacks. NYBP

My Friend. Samuel Allen. FB

My Friend. Philip Appleman. BXAP

My friend. We Laughed. Rochelle Kraut. UL

My Friend Abul Haul. Akhtar-ul-Iman, *tr. fr. Urdu by* Mahmood Jamal. PBMUP

My friend and I. Same But Different. Merle Collins. WS

My friend cannot speak any more. Waiting for a Second Time. Tauhindauli. STE

My friend from Asia has powers and magic. Credo. Robinson Jeffers. MoAB; MoAmPo

My friend, have you heard of the town of Nogood. The Town of Nogood. W. E. Penny. BLPA

My friend is always doing good. Faith and Works. Muriel Spark. OxBSP

My friend is lodging high in the Eastern Range. To Tan Ch'iu. Li Po, *tr. by* Arthur Waley. AWP

My friend! Miserable grass. Letter to a Bedouin Informer. Khalifa al-Wugayyan, *tr. by* Lena Jayyusi *and* John Heath-Stubbs. MAP

My friend must be a bird. Emily Dickinson. TAP

"My friend, my friend." Ballad of My Beautiful Lady. *Unknown, tr. by* Perry Higman. LPSS

My friend says I was not a good son. Yesterday. W. S. Merwin. DiL; FYAP

My friend, speak always once, but listen twice. The Mouth and the Ears. Shem-Tob ben Joseph Palquera, *tr. by* J. Chotzner. TrJP

My friend, the poet Ted. Cellars and Attics. Malka Heifetz Tussman, *tr. by* Kathryn Hellerstein. AYP

My Friend, the Things That Do Attain. Martial, *tr. fr. Latin by* the Earl of Surrey. NAEL-1; NoP

My Friend the Wind. King D. Kuka. VoR

My friend, this body is made of bone. The Origin of the Praise of God. Robert Bly. NU

My friend thy beauty seemeth good. The Penurious Quaker; or, The High Priz'd Harlot. *Unknown.* CoMu

My friend who married the girl I. Watts. Shirley Kaufman. NMM

My friend, who was a heroin addict. Certain Choices. Richard Shelton. Psk

My friend, you are setting out. *Unknown. Fr.* Manyo Shu. Ma

My friend, you don't understand. My Friend. Philip Appleman. BXAP

My friend, your face. Who Is My Brother? Pinkie Gordon Lane. BISi

My friends,/ I am amazed. Acceptance Speech. Marvin Bell. AmPA

My friends all know that I am shy. The Chipmunk. Ogden Nash. NIP

My friends are borne to one another. Martin Buber in the Pub. Max Harris. PoAu-2

My friends are on vacation. Mothers. Tristan Tzara, *tr. by* Willis Barnstone *and* Matei Calinescu. VWA

My friend's father, I love this story. Enos Slaughter. Jim Lavella Havelin. ASP

My friends hunted in packs, had themselves photographed. Ancient Evenings. Michael Hofmann. NPo

My friend's knife by my side. On the Gift of a Knife. Muireadhach Albanach O Dalaigh. NOIV

My friends, my sweet barbarians. A Breakfast for Barbarians. Gwendolyn MacEwen. NOBC

My Friends, This Storm. Kizito Z. Muchemwa. WMBCH

My funeral-shaft, and marble shapes that dwell. Baucis. Erinna, *tr. by* Richard Garnett. AWP

My galleon of adventure. San Francisco. Walter Adolphe Roberts. PoNe

My Galley. Petrarch, *tr. fr. Italian by* Sir Thomas Wyatt. InPS; NAEL-1

My galley [*or* galy] charged with forgetfulness. My Galley. Petrarch, *tr. fr. Italian by* Sir Thomas Wyatt. *Fr.* Sonnets to Laura: To Laura in Life, CLVI. AAS; HAP; InPS; MOS; NAEL-1; NoP; OAEL-1; OBVE; PPP; SiPS; Son
(Galley, The.) OBSC
(Lover Comparath His State to a Ship in Perilous Storm Tossed on the Sea, The.) EIL; GBL; HeIP; PoEL-1

My Gang. Jack Kerouac. PoM

My garage is a structure of excessive plainness. Detail. Mary Ursula Bethell. ATNZ; PeNZ

My Garden. Thomas Edward Brown. BLPL; FaBV; InPK; OBEV; PoLF; WBLP; WGRP

My Garden. W. H. Davies. BoNaP

My Garden. Norah Hussey. BoTP

My Garden. J. A. Lindon. InPK

My Garden. Janice Appleby Succorsa. HoPM

My garden blazes brightly with the rose-bush and the peach. In Springtime. Kipling. BrPo

My garden is a pleasant place. Louise Driscoll. BLPA; FaBoBe

My Garden, My Daylight. Jorie Graham. HCAP; MAYP

My gaze comes to rest. Emperor Fushimi, *tr. by* Steven D. Carter. WFTW

My gentle child, behold this horse. The Racing-Man. A. P. Herbert. FiBHP

My gentle father. Feliks Skrzynecki. Peter Skrzynecki. CBAP

My ghost pets are like shadows on the wall. Ghost Pet. Horatio Colony. GoYe

My Ghostly Father, I me confess. Charles, Duc d' Orléans. BoLoP
(Confession.) ChTr
(Confession of a Stolen Kiss.) MeEL
(Lover's Confession, A.) NOBE
("My ghostly fadir I me confess.") GBL
(My Gostly Fader, I Me Confesse.) EnLoPo
(The Kiss.) ACP

My Gift. Christina Rossetti. *Fr.* A Christmas Carol, *st.* 5. FaPON; PChr

My gift is scant, my voice lacks force behind it. E. A. Baratynsky, *tr. by* Alan Myers. AAA

My girl hath violet eyes and yellow hair. The Little Milliner. Robert Buchanan. BeLS

My girl, thou gazest much. The Lover to His Lady. *At. to* Plato, *tr. by* George Turberville. CTC; FaBoEE; FF; OBSC

My glad feet shod with the glittering steel. The Skater. Sir Charles G. D. Roberts. NoBC

"My glass shall not persuade me I am old." Shakespeare. *Fr.* Sonnets, XXII. OBSC; Son

My glittering sky, high, clear, profound. The Lovers. Marya Zaturenska. MoAmPo

My glory, honor, all depend. The Gentleman. Menahem ben Judah Lonzano, *tr. by* A. B. Rhine. TrJP

My Glumdalclitch, come here and sit with me. A Tryst in Brobdingnag. Adrienne Rich. NYBP

My God. Solomon Ibn Gabirol, *tr. fr. Hebrew by* Alice Lucas. *Fr.* The Royal Crown. TrJP

My God, a verse is not a crown. The Quidditie. George Herbert. PoEL-2

My God, how gracious art thou! I had slipt. The Relapse. Henry Vaughan. TrCP

My God, how perfect are thy ways! Jehovah Our Righteousness. William Cowper. NOCV

My God, How Wonderful Thou Art. Frederick William Faber. *Fr.* Our Heavenly Father. TrPWD

My God, I heard this day. Man. George Herbert. MePo; NAEL-1; NoP; PoEL-2; SeCP; SeCV-1; TrGrPo; TrPWD, *abr.*

My God, I know that those who plead. My God. Solomon Ibn Gabirol, *tr. fr. Hebrew by* Alice Lucas *sel. Fr.* The Royal Crown. TrJP

My God, I love thee, not because. Saint Francis Xavier. WGRP

My God, I Thank Thee. Andrews Norton. AH

My God, I thank Thee who hast made. Thankfulness. Adelaide Anne Procter. TrPWD

My God is just, yes he is. *Unknown, tr. by* Saduddin Shpoon. PBWP

My God is not a chiselled stone. True Knowledge. Panatattu. WGRP

My God, like a beloved great-uncle. Invitation. Kadya Molodovsky, *tr. by* Irving Feldman. PeBMYV

My God! looke on me with thine eye. His Ejaculation to God. Robert Herrick. SeCV-1

My God, my God, have mercy on my sin. Ash Wednesday. Christina Rossetti. TrCP

My God, my God, let me for once look on thee. Robert Browning. *Fr.* Pauline. TrPWD

My God, My God, Look upon Me. Chad Walsh. *Fr.* The Psalm of Christ. TrCP

My God, my god, what queer corner am I in? In the Deep Museum. Anne Sexton. MoAmPo; Prf

My God, my God, why hast thou forsaken me? Psalm XXII ("My God, my God.") Bible, *O.T. Fr.* Psalms. (Cry in Distress, A, 1-15) TrGrPo

My God (oh, let me call Thee mine). Anne Brontë. TrPWD

My God, sometimes I cannot pray. Unuttered Prayer. Josephine D. Henderson Heard. CBWP-4

My God, the bitter-tasting mouth was me. Homage. R. J. Schoeck. GoYe

My God, when I walk in those groves. Religion. Henry Vaughan. NOCV; OAEL-1; OBS; TOF

My God, where is that ancient heat towards thee. George Herbert. FL; OAEL-1

My god you shall not thus forsake me, you. Prayer of a Little Hope. Jean Wahl, *tr. by* Charles Guenther. VWA

My godmother invited my cousin. My Cousin Agueda [*or* Agatha]. Ramón López Velarde. LPSS, *tr. by* Perry Higman; MexPo, *tr. by* Samuel Beckett; OBVE

My good sirs. *Unknown. Fr.* Manyo Shu. PeBJV

My good wife was born in the Capital. Fan Tseng-hsiang, *tr. fr. Chinese by* J. P. Seaton. *Fr.* Random Verses from a Boat, III. WFTU

My Gostly Fader, I Me Confesse. Charles, Duc d' Orléans. *See* My Ghostly Father, I me confess.

My Grace Is Sufficient. Josephine D. Henderson Heard. CBWP-4

"My Grace Is Sufficient for Thee." *Unknown.* BLRP

My gracious Lord, I would thee glory doe. Edward Taylor. *Fr.* Preparatory Meditations before My Approach to the Lord's Supper, IV. SCAP

My Grandaddy Mostly with His Knife. David Huddle. GrPl

My Grandchild-Generation. Jacob Glatstein, *tr. fr. Yiddish by* Benjamin *and* Barbara Harshav. AYP

My Grandfather in Search of Moonshine. George Ella Lyon. GOYP

My grandfather killed a mule with a hammer. Short Story. Ellen Bryant Voigt. BLA; PPR

My grandfather leads me through snow. Blessing. Melvin Wilk. VWA

My grandfather lived five thousand years or so. Mendacious Song. Yisroel Rabon, *tr. by* Robert Friend. PeBMYV

My grandfather placed wood. Mythology. Earle Thompson. HATNAP; STE

My grandfather said to me. Manners [for a Child of 1918]. Elizabeth Bishop. GOYP; OxBC; RB

My grandfather used to pray. The Wicked Neighbor. Zelda, *tr. by* Hannah Hoffman. WPOW

My Grandfather Was a Quantum Physicist. Duane Big Eagle. STE

My grandfather was always sad. The Last Man's Club. James Galvin. AnAn

My grandfather was an elegant gentleman. David Wright. *Fr.* Seven South African Poems. PeSA

My grandfather worked when he was very young. An Old Man's Advice. *Unknown.* OBET

My grandfather's beard/ Was blacker than God's. On the Photograph of a Man I Never Saw. Hyam Plutzik. VWA

My Grandfather's Church Goes Up. Fred Chappell. SM

My grandfather's clock was too large for the shelf. Grandfather's Clock. Henry Clay Work. BLPA; FaFP

My Grandfather's Days. *Unknown.* OBET

My Grandfather's Funeral. James Applewhite. MT

My grandfather's kinsman, a Jew who tamed bears. Ten Commandments. Moishe Kulbak, *tr. by* Leonard Wolf. PeBMYV

My Grandmama/ dont believe they walked in space. It's All the Same. Thadious M. Davis. BiSi

My Grandmother. Perseus Adams. PeSA

My Grandmother. Maureen Ismay. WS

My Grandmother. Karl Shapiro. VGW

My grandmother. The Dust Will Settle. Luci Tapahonso. STE

My Grandmother Green. *Unknown.* AmFP

My grandmother grew tiny grapes and tiger-lilies. Her Garden. Freda Downie. FaBoWP

My grandmother had braids. Keeping Hair. Ramona Wilson. VoR

My grandmother is old, not old. Grandmother Poems. Marilyn Chin. BrSi

My grandmother lived in yonder little lane. Grandma's Advice. *Unknown.* OBET

My grandmother lived on yonder green. My Grandmother Green. *Unknown.* AmFP (Grandma's Advice.) OBET

My grandmother moves to my mind in context of sorrow. My Grandmother. Karl Shapiro. VGW

My grandmother sent me a new-fashioned three-cornered cambric country-cut handkerchief. *Unknown.* OxNR

My grandmother, she, at the age of eighty-three. Grandmother's Old Armchair. *Unknown.* BLPA

My grandmother was a wrinkled little girl. Genealogy. Eléni Vakaló, *tr. by* Paul Merchant. PBWP

My Grandmother was buried here. Epitaph in a Churchyard at Thetford, in Norfolk. *Unknown.* FaBoUs

My Grandmother Washes Her Feet. Fred Chappell. MT

My Grandmother Washes Her Vessels. Fred Chappell. MT

My grandmother's/brother here. At a Chinaman's Grave. Wing Tek Lum. BrSi

My Grandmother's Burial Ground. Elizabeth Cook-Lynn. HATNAP

My Grandmother's Funeral. Thomas Lux. WeW

My Grandmother's Ghost. James Wright. Son

My Grandmother's Love Letters. Hart Crane. BLPL; CMoP; FaBoBe; HeIP; InPK; MoAB; NoAM; NOBA; NoP

My grandmothers were strong. Lineage. Margaret Abigail Walker. BiSi; CNA; NMM; PBWP; PoBA

My Grandpa lives in a wonderful house. The Painted Ceiling. Amy Lowell. OBAL

My grandparents lived to a great age in the cold. Cold. Dorothy Roberts. NOBC

My great-aunt Elizabeth Fortune. Strawberry Moon. Mary Oliver. InPS

My great brother. A Psalm Praising the Hair of Man's Body. Denise Levertov. CAPP

My great-grandfather spoke to Edmund Burke. The Seven Sages. W. B. Yeats. NOIV

My Great-Grandfather's Slaves. Wendell Berry. GeTw

My Great Great etc. Uncle Patrick Henry. James Tate. OBAL

My great wars close. Treaties. A. R. Ammons. HCAP

"My green leaves are more beautiful." Leaves. Frank Asch. NTCP

My grey-barked trees wave me in. I Stroll. Peter Redgrove. NePoEA-2

My grey-eyed father kept pigs on his farm. The Pigs. Geoffrey Lehmann. CBAP

My grief on the ocean. *Unknown, tr. by* Thomas Kinsella. NOIV

My Grief on the Sea. *Unknown, at. to* Biddy Cussrooee, *tr. fr. Modern Irish by* Douglas Hyde. AnIL; OBEV; WTO

My grief, quoth I, is called Ignorance. Rachel Speght. *Fr.* A Dream. WPE

My Guardian Angel Stein. Philip Schultz. InPS; KS; MAYP

My gudame wes a gay wif, bot scho wes ryght gend. The Ballad of Kynd Kittok. William Dunbar. GoTS; OxBoLi

My guest! I have not led you thro.' Interlude. Walter Savage Landor. GTBS-P

My Guests. Faiz Ahmad Faiz, *tr. fr. Urdu by* Mahmood Jamal. PBMUP

My guts worn out by debts. No. 12. Lajos Kassák, *tr. by* Jascha Kessler. FOC

My hair/ my head/ my eyes. Property Is Theft. Gerhard Rühm, *tr. by* Beth Bjorklund. CoAuP

My hair has dried. Self Dirge. Wendy Rose. CDW

My hair is gray, but not with years. The Prisoner of Chillon. Byron. EnRP; PoLF

My hair is springy like the forest grasses. Black Woman. Naomi Long Madgett. BiSi; FB; PoBA

My Hairt Is Heich Aboif. *Unknown.* OxBS

My hand. Comparison of Hands One Day Late Summer El Sobrante. Wendy Rose. HATNAP

My hand is lonely for your clasping, dear. You and I. Henry Alford. BLPA; FaBoBe

My hand is weary with [or has a pain from] writing. St. Columcille the Scribe. *At.* to Saint Columcille, *tr. by* Kuno Meyer. AnIL, *tr. by* Kuno Meyer; BIrV, *tr. by* Flann O'Brien

My hand on your breasts the kitchen. The Knife. Juan Gelman, *tr. by* Yishai Tobin. VWA

My hand plunged into the waters of night. Memory of Another Climate. Gabriel Preil, *tr. by* Jeremy Garber. VWA

My hand waving from the window. Platform Goodbye. Herbert B. Mallalieu. WaP

My hands/ Open the curtains of your being. Touch. Octavio Paz. BoLoP, *tr. by* Charles Tomlinson

My hands are tender feathers. Calypso's Song to Ulyssess. Adrian Mitchell. GBL

My hands are withered. *Unknown.* NOIV

My hands did numb to beauty. I Held a Shelley Manuscript. Gregory Corso. VGW

My hands have developed eyes! Conversion. Geof Hewitt. NeAC

My hands have not touched water since your hands. Carrier Letter. Hart Crane. BoLoP

My hands have tried. Teaching My Students Prosody. Jay Rogoff. KS

My hands here, gentle, where her breasts begin. No Continuing City. Michael Longley. FaBCIP

My hands in pockets worn out at the seams. The Strolling Player. Rimbaud, *tr. by* William Jay Smith. CT; GrPl

My hands, my fists, my small bells. Oh Yes. William Matthews. AmPA

My hands of silk and miniver. Full Moon. Elinor Wylie. MoAB

My hands so chapped from rice-pounding. *Unknown. Fr.* Manyo Shu. Ma

My Handsome Gilderoy. *Unknown. See* Gilderoy.

My Happiness. Greg Pape. MAYP; MOWH

My Harry was a gallant gay. Highland Harry Back Again. *At.* to Burns. EBEV

My harte of golde as true as stele. *See* My heart of gold as true as steel.

My Hat. Stevie Smith. BrRo

My hated birthday is here, and I must go. Sulpicia, *tr. by* Aliki *and* Willis Barnstone. BoWoP

My hazard wouldn't be yours, not ever. Advice. Ruth Stone. NMM

My head aches. Going through Changes. Jean Tepperman. NMM

My head and shoulders, and my book. The Signature of All Things. Kenneth Rexroth. NNaP; NU

My head is bald, my breath is bad. Late-flowering Lust. Sir John Betjeman. CMoP; ErPo; TW

My head is drawing closer to the bar again. Indian Guys at the Bar. Simon J. Ortiz. STE

My head, my heart, mine eyes, my life, nay more. A Letter to Her Husband, Absent upon Public[k] Employment. Anne Bradstreet. HAP; HeIP; NAAL-1; NoP; SCAP

My head on moss reclining. *Unknown.* NOEC

My Head on My Shoulders. Jeremy Ingalls. GoYe

My Heart. H. C. Artmann, *tr. fr. German by* Beth Bjorklund. CoAuP

My heart aches and a drowsy numbness pains. Ode to a Nightingale. Keats. AWP; BLRP; ChER; EBEV; EnRP; FaBoBe; FaFP; FiP; GTBS; GTBS-P; HAP; HeIP; InPS; LiTB; NAEL-2; NAWM-2; NOBE; NoP; OAEL-2; OBEV; OBNC; OPOP; PBBP; PoE; PoEL-4; PoRA; PPP; PrIm; RB; SoSe; TEP; TOF; TrGrPo; UnPo; WeW (To a Nightingale.) ChTr

My Heart Atones. Ramón López Velarde, *tr. fr. Spanish by* Samuel Beckett. MexPo

My heart beating, my blood running. Time's Dedication. Delmore Schwartz. VGW

My heart beats to the feet of the first faithful. An Interlude. Robert Duncan. CMoP

My Heart Belongs to Daddy. Cole Porter. OBAL

My Heart Burns for Him. *Gond Oral Tradition, tr. by* V. Elwin *and* S. Hivale. WTO

My heart could never win your heart. Mohammad Taqi Mir, *tr. by* Ahmed Ali. GoT

My heart cried like a beaten child. Song Making. Sara Teasdale. WGRP

My heart doth in the Lord rejoice [or rejoiceth in the Lord], that living Lord of might. Hannah's Song of Thanksgiving. Bible, *O.T. Fr.* First Samuel, II: 1–10. AWP (Song of Hannah, The.) TrCP, *ad. by* Michael Drayton.

My heart grows sick before the wide-spread death. The Grave-Yard. Jones Very. NOBA

My heart has an opening that discharges blood. The Heart. David Ignatow. VWA

My heart has grown rich with the passing of years. The Solitary. Sara Teasdale. MoAmPo

My heart has thank'd thee, Bowles! for those soft strains. To the Reverend W. L. Bowles. Samuel Taylor Coleridge. EnRP; Son

My Heart, How Very Hard It's Grown. Cotton Mather. AH

My heart, I cannot still it. Auspex. James Russell Lowell. PoEL-5; TAP

My heart, imprisoned in a hopeless isle. Michael Drayton. *Fr.* Idea's Mirrour, XXII. OBSC

My heart in pieces like the bits. Climbing. Tom Clark. UL

My heart is a-breaking, dear tittie. Tam Glen. Burns. AWP; OxBS

My heart is a temple of fire. Asadullah Khan Ghalib, *tr. by* Ahmed Ali. GoT

My heart is an oil lamp. A Rapier of Treason. *Unknown, tr. by* Willis Barnstone. BoWoP

My heart is capable of every form. Ibnu 'L-arabi, *tr. by* R. A. Nicholson. TOF

My heart is clear now. A Storm at a House in the Hills. Yoshimoto, *tr. by* Steven D. Carter. WFTW

My heart is constant and of him. Insha Allah Khan Insha, *tr. by* Ahmed Ali. GoT

My heart is empty. All the fountains that should run. The Naked Seed. C. S. Lewis. TrCP

My heart is filled to overflowing. Mohammad Taqi Mir, *tr. by* Ahmed Ali. GoT

My Heart Is High Above. *At.* to Alexander Scott. OBEV (My Heart is Heich Above [or Abufe].) ErPo; GoTS

My Heart Is in Merioneth. *Unknown, tr. fr. Welsh by* Richard Llwyd. OBWVE

My Heart Is in the East. Judah Halevi, *tr. fr. Hebrew.* TrJP

My heart is in woe. The Downfall of the Gael. Fearflatha O'Gnive, *tr. by* Sir Samuel Ferguson. AWP

My heart is just as heavy. Grief. *Unknown, tr. by* Aneirin Talfan Davies. OBWVE

My heart is lighter than the poll. The New-slain Knight. *Unknown.* ESPB

My heart is like a fountain true. Mother's Song. *Unknown.* GN

My Heart Is like a Ship. "E. C." *Fr.* Emaricdulfe, XXIX. Son

My heart is like a singing bird. A Birthday. Christina Rossetti. AWP; BLPL; CH; FaFP; InvP; LiTB; NA; NAEL-2; NOBE; NOBVV; OAEL-2; OBEV; PoE; TrGrPo; TTTS; WiR; WPE

My heart is like one asked to dine. An Unexpected Pleasure. *Unknown.* FaBoCo

My heart is moved. Empress Eifuku, *tr. by* Steven D. Carter. WFTW

My heart is on my fist. The Tomb of the Kings. Anne Hébert, *tr. by* Aliki *and* Willis Barnstone. BoWoP

My heart is set upon a lusty pin. Queen Elizabeth of York. WPE

My heart leaps up when I behold. Song to be Sung by the Father of Infant Female Children. Ogden Nash. MoAmPo

My Heart Leaps Up [When I Behold]. Wordsworth. EnRP; FaBV; FaFP; GTBS; GTBS-P; InPK; InPS; NAEL-2; NOBE; NoP; OAEL-2; OBNC; OxBSP; TEP; TrGrPo (Rainbow, The.) BLPA; FPL; LiTB; OBEV

My heart like an upside down flame. Guillaume Apollinaire, *tr. fr. French by* Roger Shattuck. *Fr.* Heart, Crown, and Mirror. TTTS

My heart, loyal, atones in the darkness. My Heart Atones. Ramón López Velarde, *tr. by* Samuel Beckett. MexPo

My heart, my heart is mournful. Mein Herz, Mein Herz Ist Traurig. Heine, *tr. by* James Thomson. AWP

My heart, my tired heart, sings elegies. In the End-of-Summer Light. Yisroel-Yankev Schwartz, *tr. by* Seymour Levitan. PeBMYV

My heart no longer is. Momin Khan Momin, *tr. by* Ahmed Ali. GoT

My heart [or heart] of gold[e] as true as steel [or stele]. A Nonsense Carol. *Unknown.* OxBoLi (Carol: "My heart of gold as true as steel.") FaBoCo; FaBoNo (Nonsense Song, A.) OxBLMV

My heart sharpened to a point. Mother and Child. Penelope Shuttle. AIW

My heart, so entranced. Tsurayuki, *tr. fr. Japanese by* Burton Watson. *Fr.* Kokin Shu. FCEI

My heart still hovering round about you. Robert, Earl Nugent. NOEC

My heart stirs quietly now to think. A Hermit's Song. *Unknown, tr. by* James Simmons. BIrV

My heart that was so passionless. Rencontre. Jessie Redmond Fauset. CDC

My heart, thinking/ "How beautiful he is." The Lady of Sakanoye, *tr. by* Arthur Waley. AWP; PBWP

My heart, thinking. Lady Otomo no Sakanoe. *Fr.* Manyo Shu. AWP

My heart throbbed like a boat on the water. Hamlet in Russia, A Soliloquy. Boris Pasternak, *tr. by* Robert Lowell. FaBoPV

My heart was fired, as from his sight it turned. The Dream of Dakiki. Firdausi, *tr.* by A. V. Williams Jackson. WGRP

My heart was heavy, for its trust had been. Forgiveness. Whittier. TrCP

My Heart Was Wandering in the Sands. Christopher Brennan. *Fr.* The Twilight of Disquietude. PoAu-1

My heart's afflictions and its pain. Mohammad Taqi Mir, *tr.* by Ahmed Ali. GoT

My heart's friend, will you tell me who this mischievous youngster is? Dancing-Girl's Song. Kshetrayya, *tr.* by Tambimuttu *and* R. Appalaswamy. BoWoP

My Heart's in the Highlands. Burns. AWP; EnRP; FaFP

My heart's so heavy with a hundred things. Sonnet: In Absence from Becchina. Cecco Angiolieri da Siena, *tr.* by Dante Gabriel Rossetti. AWP

My help, my hope, my strength shall be. The Law. Abraham Ibn Ezra, *tr.* by Alice Lucas. TrJP

My Hereafter. Juanita de Long. WGRP

My Heritage. Adah Isaacs Menken. CBWP-1

My Hero. Benjamin Brawley. BANP; PoNe

My highway is unfeatured air. Hymn of the Earth. William Ellery Channing. AA

My history crucified, buried under the muddy flood of time. The Rusted Chain. Yosef Damana ben Yeshaq, *tr.* by Ephraim Isaac. VWA

My history extends/ Where moved my tourist hands. Abroad Thoughts from Home. Donald Hall. NePoEA

My hoary locks I dye with care. Self-Defense. Santob de Carrion, *tr.* by George Ticknor. TrJP

My home? I'm stopping near the town. Stopping Wine. T'ao Ch'ien, *tr.* by Burton Watson. CoBCP

My home is a house. The Country Child. Irene Thompson. BoTP

My home is the mountain. Akhtar Amiri, *tr.* *Farsi* by Fereshte Mahamadi. *Fr.* I Am a Woman. WPOW

My Home ("My home is on the rolling deep.") *Unknown.* NA

My home, where all I touch. Issa, *tr.* by Geoffrey Bownas *and* Anthony Thwaite. PeBJV

My homeless one, will you ever fly again? Perets Markish, *tr.* *fr.* *Yiddish* by Leonard Wolf. *Fr.* To a Jewish Dancer. PeBMYV

My home's in Montana, I wear a bandanna. Cowboy's Lament, The Smoky Mountains. *Unknown.* AmFP

My homestead's with lightning aflame. The Meaning of Love. *Malay Oral Tradition,* *tr.* by R. O. Winstedt. WTO

My Honey, My Love. Joel Chandler Harris. *Fr.* Uncle Remus and His Friends. AA; FaBoBe

My hope, alas, hath me abused. Sir Thomas Wyatt. SiPS

My Hope, My Love. *Unknown, tr. fr. Irish* by Edward Walsh. BIrV

My hopes retire; my wishes as before. Walter Savage Landor. *Fr.* Ianthe. GBL; OBNC

My horny feet are cutting through the fog. Satyr. Charles Gullans. PoA

My horse threads a mountain trail through bamboos just yellowing. Journey to a Village. Wang Yü-ch'eng, *tr.* by Burton Watson. CoBCP

My hour switched on the cameras take. The Voice of America, 1961. James Liddy. CIP

My House. Robert Adamson. CBAP

My House. George Bruce. OxBS

My House. Claude McKay. CDC

My House. W. B. Yeats. *Fr.* Meditations in Time of Civil War, II. LiTB

My house forsaken by my love. Tabito. *Fr.* Manyo Shu. Ma

My house, I say. But hark to the sunny doves. Robert Louis Stevenson. FM; NOBVV

My house is granite. My House. George Bruce. OxBS

My house is not quiet, I am not loud. Fish in River. *Unknown, formerly at. to* Cynewulf, *tr. fr. Anglo-Saxon* by Charles W. Kennedy. *Fr.* Riddles (Exeter Book). AnOE

My house is red—a little house. A Happy Child. Kate Greenaway. BoTP

My house, my fairy/ palace. Jeronimo's House. Elizabeth Bishop. NoP

My house was built in just one night. The House. Uuno Kailas, *tr.* by Aili Jarvenpa. SOP

My humble Muse sad, and in lonely state. To His Excellency Joseph Dudley. John Saffin. SCAP

My humid hand against your/ breast. An Island. Shawn Wong. BrSi

My Husband. *Unknown.* CoMu

My husband gives me an A. Marks. Linda Pastan. NIP

My husband is the same who took my maidenhead. Silabhattarika, *tr. fr. Sanskrit* by Daniel H. H. Ingalls. *Fr.* Wanton. PBWP
   ("My husband is the same man who first pierced me.") BoWoP, *tr. by* Willis Barnstone.

My Husband Says. Alice Walker. MT

My husband smiles in sleep beside me. Charlotte Nicholls. Jack R. Clemo. NAs

My husband's a jockey, a jockey, a jockey. My Husband. *Unknown.* CoMu

My Husband's Birthday. Josephine D. Henderson Heard. CBWP-4

My Hut. Eileen Mathias. BoTP

My Hut. Wu Chia-chi, *tr. fr. Chinese* by Jonathan Chaves. CoBLCP

My hut is at the foot. *Unknown, tr. fr. Japanese* by Burton Watson. *Fr.* Kokin Shu. FCEI

My Iambic Pentameter Lines. Robert Crawford. InPK

My infinite child, hold me to sleep. David Ignatow. *Fr.* Sunlight: A Sequence for My Daughter. CAPP

My Infundibuliform Hat. Charles Follen Adams. OBAL

My Inmost Hope. Sarah Copia Sullam, *tr. fr. Italian.* TrJP

My inquisitive little brown children. Song for My Little Friends. Leonard Adame, *tr.* by Toni Empringham. FIA

My Insect Soul. N. M. Rashed, *tr. fr. Urdu* by Mahmood Jamal. PBMUP

My Inside-Self. Rachel Lyman Field. FaPON

My intention is to tell of bodies changed. Ovid, *tr. fr. Latin* by Rolfe Humphries. *Fr.* Metamorphoses, I. NAWM-1

My Jacket Old. Herman Melville. SaC

My Jacobean Fatigues. Miron Bialoszewski, *tr. fr. Polish* by Czeslaw Milosz. PwPP

My Jesus, as Thou wilt! Consecration. Benjamin Schmolck. BLRP

My Johnny. *Unknown.* OBET

My Joy, My Jockey, My Gabriel. George Barker. *Fr.* First Cycle of Love Poems, V. ErPo; MoBrPo

My Joy, my Life, my Crown! A True Hymn. George Herbert. InvP; NOCV

My jumping jack. Children's Carnival. Juliane Windhager, *tr.* by Beth Bjorklund. CoAuP

My Kate. Elizabeth Barrett Browning. OHFP; WBLP

My keepsake/ look at it and think of me. Lady Kasa. *Fr.* Manyo Shu. FCEI

My ketch must lead into the fray. Parting at Dawn. *Malay Oral Tradition,* *tr.* by R. J. Wilkinson *and* R. O. Winstedt. WTO

My Kin Talk. Anna Margolin, *tr. fr. Yiddish* by Keith Bosley. VWA

My kite is three feet broad, and six feet long. The Kite. Adelaide O'Keeffe. OxBChV

My kitty cat has nine lives. Nine Lives. *Unknown.* CRH

My knee against the ground. The Ladder Has No Steps. Jorge Plescoff, *tr.* by Yishai Tobin. VWA

My Laddie's Hounds. Marguerite Elizabeth Easter. AA

My ladies haire is threeds of beaten gold. Fidessa, More Chaste than Kind, XXXIX. Bartholomew Griffin. *Fr.* AAS

My lady/ fair with. A Token. Robert Creeley. VGW

My Lady Carenza of the lovely body. *Unknown, tr.* by Willis Barnstone. BoWoP

My lady carries love within her eyes. Dante, *tr. fr. Italian* by Dante Gabriel Rossetti. *Fr.* Vita Nuova, La, XII. AWP

My Lady Is a Pretty One. *Unknown.* OxBoLi

My lady looks so gentle and so pure. Dante, *tr. fr. Italian* by Dante Gabriel Rossetti. *Fr.* Vita Nuova, La, XVI. AWP

My Lady mine, I send. Canzonetta: Of His Lady, and of His Making Her Likeness. Jacopo da Lentino, *tr.* by Dante Gabriel Rossetti. AWP

My Lady Pleases Me. Robert Bridges. *Fr.* The Growth of Love, XXX. Son

My Lady Spring. *Unknown.* BoTP

My Lady the Lake. Peter Davidson. WeW

My lady unto Madam makes her bow. George Meredith. *Fr.* Modern Love, XXXVI. NOBVV

My lady walks her morning round. The Henchman. Whittier. OBEV

My lady was found mutilated. Leonard Cohen. OBCV

My lady went to Canterbury [or Caunterbury]. *Unknown.* FaBoCo; FaBoNo
   (Nonsense Song, A.) OxBLMV

My lady woke upon a morning fair. On His Lady's Waking. Pierre de Ronsard, *tr.* by Andrew Lang. AWP

My Lady's face it is they worship there. Sonetto XXXV: To Guido Orlando. Guido Cavalcanti, *tr.* by Ezra Pound. CTC

My lady's presence makes the roses red. Henry Constable. *Fr.* Diana. EiL; NIP; OBSC

My Lady's Tears. *Unknown.* *See* I Saw My Lady Weep.

My Lai/ Remuera/ Ponsonby. David Mitchell. PeNZ

My lamp, full charged with its sweet oil, still burns. Hero Entombed I. Peter Quennell. LiTB

My land is bare of chattering folk. Sanctuary. Dorothy Parker. NBLV

My land is fair for any eyes to see. Jesse Stuart. FaPON

My Language. Ida Hahn-Hahn, *tr. fr. German by* Susan L. Cocalis. DMG

My lank limp lily, my long lithe lily. A Maudle-in Ballad. *Unknown.* BXAP; FaBoPa

My Last Afternoon with Uncle Devereux Winslow. Robert Lowell. NAAL-2; NoP; VGW

My Last Duchess. Robert Browning. AWP; BeLS; EBVV; FaBoPV; FaFP; FF; FiP; FPL; GTBS-P; HAP; HeIP; HoPM; InPK; InPS; LiTB; MAT; NAEL-2; NIP; NOBE; NOBVV; NoP; OAEL-2; OBNC; PoE; PoEL-5; PoLF; PPP; PrIm; SCV; SoSe; TEP; TrGrPo; WeW

My Last Illusion. John Kaye Kendall. FiBHP

My Last Poem. Manuel Bandeira, *tr. by Portuguese by* Elizabeth Bishop. ATCBP

My Latest Publication. Edward Capern. PF

My Latest Sun Is Sinking Fast. Jefferson Haskell. AH

My least height flowers late with buds. Where Unimaginably Bright. Oliver Hale. GoYe

My lefe is faren in a lond. The One I Love Is Gone Away. *Unknown.* MeEL

(Separated Lovers.) OAEL-1

My left eye is blind and jogs like. Sketch for a Job Application Blank. Jim Harrison. AmPA; MoP

My left hand's like after a vow. It hurts. I'm trying to dream again. Amir Gilboa, *tr. by* Warren Bargad *and* Stanley F. Chyet. IP

My legs break. Haiti: Skin Diving. Jane Shore. ASP

My Lesbia let us love and live. Catullus, *tr. by* Wordsworth. OBVE

My Lessons in the Jail. Miriam Waddington. MoCV

My Letter. Grace Denio Litchfield. AA

My letters! all dead paper, mute and white. Elizabeth Barrett Browning. *Fr.* Sonnets from the Portuguese, XXVIII. HAP

My Lief Is Faren in Londe. *Unknown.* NAEL-1

My liege, I did deny no prisoners. Shakespeare. *Fr.* King Henry IV, Pt. II, I, iii. WaaP

My Life. Max Jacob, *tr. fr. French by* Ron Padgett. RHTwFP

My Life. Mark Strand. NoAM

My life/ is/ a/ bald headed match. Black Taffy. Peggy Susberry Kenner. JB

My life closed twice before its close. Emily Dickinson. AmPP; BoLoP; BoWoP; GBL; HeIP; MoAmPo; MoP; NAAL-1; NIP; NoAM; NOBA; OxBA; OxBSP; PPP; SCV; SoSe; TrGrPo

(My Life Closed Twice.) MoAB

My life gives out no ray of light. Bahadur Shah Zafar, *tr. by* Ahmed Ali. GoT

My life had stood—a loaded gun. Emily Dickinson. AmPP; HAP; InPK; NAAL-1; NAWM-2; NIP; NoP; WeW; WPOW

My life had taken the shape of the small square. The Small Square. Sophia de Mello Breyner Andresen, *tr. by* Alexis Levitin. WPOW

My life has crept so long on a broken wing. Tennyson. *Fr.* Maud, *pt.* III. OAEL-2; OBWP

My Life Is a Bowl. May Riley Smith. BLPA

My life is a story for the world to hear. Nawab Mirza Khan Dagh, *tr. by* Ahmed Ali. GoT

My life is a wearisome journey. The End of the Way. Harriet Cole. BLRP

My life is cast. Sifting. Victor Emanuel Beck. GoYe

"My life is done, yet all remains." Robert the Bruce. Edwin Muir. OxBS

My life is engraved on my poems. Of Myself. Leah Goldberg, *tr. by* Ramah Commanday. BoWoP

My life is like a music-hall. Prologue to "London Nights." Arthur Symons. BrPo

My life is like a stroll upon the beach. The Fisher's Boy. Henry David Thoreau. AA; ChTr; MOS

My Life Is like the Summer Rose. Richard Henry Wilde. AnAmPo

(Stanzas: "My life is like the summer rose.") AA

My life is measur'd by this glass[e], this glass[e]. On an Hour[e]-Glass[e]. John Hall. MeLP; MePo; OPOP

My life is the great expanse. Asadullah Khan Ghalib, *tr. by* Ahmed Ali. GoT

My life must touch a million lives in some way ere I go. My Prayer. *Unknown.* BLRP

My Life, the Quality of Which. Etheridge Knight. NNaP

My life—to Discontent a prey. Rhymes (?) Henry S. Leigh. NOBL

My life vanishing. Hitomaro. *Fr.* Manyo Shu. Ma

My life was never so precious. Inscription for the Tank. James Wright. TwCP

My Life, your light green eyes. Last Words. James Merrill. TAP

My Life's Delight. Thomas Campion. ElL; InvP; OBSC; TrGrPo

My light will tip tankards of fire in the sky. A Constant Labor. James W. Thompson. BPo

My lines falter. Arriving. Gabriel Preil, *tr. by* Robert Friend. VWA

My lips from this day forgot how to smile. Auguste Lacaussade, *tr. fr. French.* Fr. Les Salaziennes. TTY

My lips lack prophecy. Lamentation. Nissim Ezekiel. VWA

My lips murmur. The Vigil. Shlomo Reich, *tr. by* Mira Reich. VWA

My little Ben, whilst thou art young. To His Son Bennet. John Hoskyns. FaBoEE

My Little Bird. Bunyan. OBS

(Of the Child with the Bird on the Bush.) OxBChV

My Little Birds. *Unknown, tr. fr. Arabic by* Henrietta Siksek-Su'ad. FaPON

My little boat emerges at Heng-t'ang. Late Spring—Traveling through the Mountains. Chu Yün-ming, *tr. by* Jonathan Chaves. CoBLCP

My little boy Kun-shih. Poem for My Little Boy. Li Shang-yin, *tr. by* Burton Watson. CoBCP

My little breath, under the willows by the water-side we used to sit. A Lover's Lament *or* The Willows by the Water Side. *Unknown, tr. by* H. J. Spinden. AWP

(Willows by the Water Side, The.) WTO

My little cousin, if you'll be. To My Youngest Kinsman, R. L. Abraham Chear. OxBChV

My little dears, who learn to read, pray early learn to shun. Cautionary Verses to Youth of Both Sexes. Theodore Hook. OxBChV

(Address to Children.) FaBoUs

My Little Dog. Pearl Forbes MacEwen. BoTP

My little Dreams. Georgia Douglas Johnson. BANP; BlSi; CDC; PoNe

My little finger's stuck in a/ Coca-Cola bottle. Constant Defender. James Tate. MAYP

My Little Garden. Li Chien, *tr. fr. Chinese by* Irving Lo. WFTU

My Little Girl. Samuel Minturn Peck. AA

My Little House. J. M. Westrup. BoTP

My Little Lize. James Martinez. PBCV

My little lord, methinks 'tis strange. A Prognostication on Will Laud, Late Archbishop of Canterbury. *Unknown.* OxBoLi

My Little Love Lies on the Ground. Larin Paraske, *tr. fr. Finnish by* Jaakko A. Ahokas. PBWP

My little Mädchen found one day. A Chrysalis. Mary Emily Bradley. AA

My Little Neighbor. Mary Augusta Mason. AA

My little old man and I fell out. Mother Goose. OxNR

My little one begins his feet to try. The First Step. Andrew Bice Saxton. AA

My little ones pull. Bloomfield, Inc. Richard Katrovas. NAmP

My little pretty patch of wilderness. Touching Heartsease. Janet Sutherland. DT

My little scholar, to thy book inclined. A Schoolmaster's Precepts. John Penkethman. OxBChV

My Little Sister. William Wise. RHPC

My little snowman has a mouth. Snowman. David McCord. RAR

My little son enters. Transformations. Tadeusz Rozewicz, *tr. by* Czeslaw Milosz. PwPP

My little son, I have cast you out. Choosing a Name. Anne Ridler. NOBE

My little son, when you could command marvels. Geoffrey Hill. *Fr.* Funeral Music, VI. NoAM

My little son, who looked from thoughtful eyes. The Toys. Coventry Patmore. *Fr.* The Unknown Eros, I, x. ACP; BeLS; EBEV; EBVV; FaFP; NOBVV; OBEV; SoSe; TrGrPo; TrPWD

My little soul, my vagrant charmer. Emperor Hadrian, *tr. fr. Latin by* J.V. Cunningham. OBVE

My Little Stone. Frank Horne. *Fr.* Letters Found Near a Suicide. AmNP; CDC; PoBa; PoNe

My lizard just beyond the lamp's shine. The Small Lizard. Linda Gregg. MAYP

My lizard, my lively writher. Wish for a Young Wife. Theodore Roethke. MoP; NAAL-2; NoAM; NoP; OxBSP; TAP

My loathsome uncle chews his rasher. Ballywaire. Tom Paulin. FaBCIP

My locker, green steel. Game Resumed. Richmond Lattimore. NYBP

My lodging it is on the cold ground. Sir William Davenant. *Fr.* The Rivals. JCP

My loneliness/ I snuggle it up. *Unknown, tr. by* Burton Watson. FCEI

My long nose sticks out like a knife. Life-Saving Medal. Philippe Soupault, *tr. by* Michael Benedikt. POS

My long two-pointed ladder's sticking through a tree. After Apple-picking. Robert Frost. AmPP; AnAmPo; CMoP; FPL; InPS; LiTA; MoAB; MoAmPo; MoP; NAAL-2; NoAM; NOBA; NU; OxBA; PoE; PPP; PrIM; TAP; UnPo

My longings unbearable. Tsurayuki, *tr. fr. Japanese by* Burton Watson. *Fr.* Kokin Shu. FCEI

My Lord/ if I worship Thee from fear of Hell. Rabi'a al-Adawiyya, *tr.* by Margaret Smith. WPOW

My Lord and King. Tennyson. *See* In Memoriam A. H. H.: Love is and was my lord and king.

My lord came to survey. Mushimaro. *Fr.* Manyo Shu. PeBJV

My Lord, fallen, sin-stained. Sticheron for Matins, Wednesday of Holy Week. Mary Magdalene Kassia, *tr.* by Patrick Diehl. WPOW

My Lord has departed. Longing for the Emperor. Empress Iwa no Hime. *Fr.* Manyo Shu. BoWoP, *tr.* by Geoffrey Bownas *and* Anthony Thwaite; PeBJV, *tr.* by Geoffrey Bownas *and* Anthony Thwaite.

My lord has great shoulders. A Woman in Love with a Captive King. Nakkannaiyar, *tr.* by A. K. Ramanujan. PLW

My lord, I was accustomed to swill about the sky. The Dove Apologizes to His God for Being Caught by a Cat. Anthony Eaton. PeSA

My lord is all a-glow. *Unknown*, *tr.* by Arthur Waley. BoS

My lord is on service. *Unknown*, *tr.* by Arthur Waley. BoS

My lord must be secretly coming in. *Unknown*, *tr.* by Hiroaki Sato. FCEI

My Lord, my life, can envy ever bee. Edward Taylor. *Fr.* Preparatory Meditations before My Approach to the Lord's Supper, XXIII. PoEL-3

My lord said to my lady. Lamkin. *Unknown*. ESPB

My Lord Tomnoddy. Robert Barnabas Brough. FiBHP

My Lord, What a Morning. Waring Cuney. TTY

My Lord, what a morning when de stars begin to fall. Judgement Day. *Unknown*. WTO

My Lord's Gone to Service. *Unknown*, *tr. fr. Chinese by* Burton Watson. CoBCP

My Lords, my Lord of Warwick. Joan of Arc to the Tribunal. Anthony Frisch. CaP

My lords, with your leave. A New War Song by Sir Peter Parker. *Unknown*. PAH

My Lost Youth. Longfellow. AA; AmPP; AnAmPo; AWP; FaBoBe; FaBV; FaFP; FaPoR; FPL; GoJo; LiTA; NAAL-1; NOBA; OBEV; OxBA; PoEL-5; PoLF; PoRA; TAP

My loud machine for making hay. An Old Field Mowed. William Meredith. NYBP

My lov'd, my honour'd, much respected friend! The Cotter's Saturday Night. Burns. EnRP

My Love. E. E. Cummings. ErPo; LiTM; VGW

My Love. Bartholomew Griffin. *See* Fidessa, More Chaste than Kind: Faire Is My Love.

My Love. James Russell Lowell. BLPL; FaBoBe

My Love. Richard Shelton. GOYP

My love/ Is like the grasses. Ono no Yoshiki, *tr. fr. Japanese by* Arthur Waley. *Fr.* Kokin Shu. AWP

My love affair is like the clumps of bush clover. Teika, *tr. fr. Japanese by* Hiroaki Sato. *Fr.* A Compendium of Good Tanka. FCEI

My love and I for kisses play'd. William Strode. FaBoEE

My love and my delight. The Lament for Art O'Leary. Eileen O'Leary, *tr.* by Frank O'Connor. AnIL

My Love behind Walls. Heather Spears. OBCV

My Love bound me with a kiss. Kisses. *At.* to Thomas Campion. ElL; OBSC

My love came back to me. All Souls' Night. Frances Cornford. EnLoPo; OBD; OxBSP; OxBTC

My Love Eats an Apple. Ralph Gustafson. MoCV

My love for him shall be. Medieval Norman Song. *Unknown*, *tr.* by John Addington Symonds. AWP

"My love for you has faded"—thus the Bad. Versions of Love. Roy Fuller. LiTM

My love for you, O mother. Abe Okina. *Fr.* Manyo Shu. Ma

My love forever! The Lament for Art [*or* Arthur] O'Leary. Eibhlin Dubh O'Connell, *tr.* by Eilis Dillon *and* John Montague. BIrV; PBWP

"My love has built a bonny ship, and set her on the sea." The Lowlands o' [*or* of] Holland. *Unknown*. AmFP, *diff. version*; OxBB, *with music*
(Lawlands o' Holland, The.) CH

My Love Has Departed. *Unknown*, *tr. fr. Chippewa Indian by* Frances Densmore. OV

My love has gone down to his garden. Bible, *O.T. Fr.* The Song of Solomon. BoWoP, *ad.* by Willis Barnstone.

My love has left me has gone from me. Souvenirs. Dudley Randall. BPo

My love he built me a bonnie bower. The Lament of the Border Widow. *Unknown*. GBP; Mes; OxBB, *with music*
(Bonnie Bower, The.) CH

My love he is fairer than a summer day. The Drynaun Dhun. *Unknown*. GBP

My love he was a fisher lad and when he came on shore. The Fisher Lad of Whitby. *Unknown*. OxBSS

My love, how could your heart consider. Motet. *Unknown*, *tr.* by Carol Cosman. PBWP

My Love, I cannot thy rare beauties place. William Smith. *Fr.* Chloris. ElL; InvP

My Love I Gave for Hate. *Unknown*, *tr. fr. Irish by* George Hay. BIrV

My love I give to you a threefold thing. Branwell's Sestina. James Reaney. *Fr.* A Suit of Nettles. MoCV

My love I learned. Poem for a Marriage. Christine Craig. AIW

"My love?" I said. *Unknown*. *Fr.* Manyo Shu. FCEI

My Love in Her Attire. *Unknown*. BLPL; FF; GTBS; GTBS-P; HeIP; LiTB; NIP; NiP; OxBSP
(Madrigal: "My love in her attire doth show her wit.") BoLoP; EiL; NAEL-1; NOBE; OBEV; OBSC

My love is a lotus blossom. *Unknown*, *tr.* by J. E. Manchip White. TTY

"My love is as a fever [*or* feaver], longing still." Shakespeare. *Fr.* Sonnets, CXLVII. EBEV; HoPM; NAEL-1; PoEL-2; TEP

My love is as endless. Lady Ise, *tr. fr. Japanese by* Burton Watson. *Fr.* Kokin Shu. FCEI

My love is but a shepherd lad. The Shepherd and the Shepherdess. *Unknown*. OBET

My Love Is Dead. Thomas Chatterton. *See* Aella; a Tragycal Enterlude: Oh! sing unto my roundelay [*or* O! Synge untoe mie roundelaie].

My love is in my house. Mirabai, *tr. fr. Hindi by* Willis Barnstone *and* Usha Nilsson. BoWoP

My Love is Like a Myrtle. Moses ibn Ezra, *tr. fr. Hebrew by* Solomon Solis-Cohen. TrJP

My love is like the silk on the loom. Ancient Sentiments. Wu Wei-yeh, *tr.* by Irving Lo. WFTU

My love is like to ice, and I to fire. Spenser. *Fr.* Amoretti, XXX. ErPo; FF; FPL; LiTB; TrGrPo

My love is neither young nor old. *Unknown*. OBSC

My love is no short year's sentence. Love. *Unknown*, *tr.* by John Montague. BIrV

My love is o' comely height, an' straight. White an' Blue. William Barnes. GBL; GTBS-P

My love is of a birth as rare. The Definition of Love. Andrew Marvell. BLPL; BoLoP; EBEV; GBL; HoPM; InPS; JCP; LiTB; MeLP; MePo; NAEL-1; NOBE; NoP; OAEL-1; OBEV; OBS; PoEL-2; SeCePo; SeCP; SeCV-1; TEP; TrGrPo; UnPo

My Love Is Past. Thomas Watson. PBBP

My love is playing on a fiddle. *Gond Oral Tradition*, *tr.* by V. Elwin *and* S. Hivale. WTO

My Love Is Sleeping. Kenneth Leslie. OBCV

"My love is strengthen'd, though more weak in seeming." Shakespeare. *Fr.* Sonnets, CII. AWP; EiL; OBEV; OBSC

My love is tasting the fragrance. *Unknown*, *tr.* by Saduddin Shpoon. PBWP

My love is the maid o' all maidens. In the Spring. William Barnes. GBL

My Love is the voice of a song. David McKee Wright. *Fr.* Dark Rosaleen, IX. PoAu-1

My love is white and ruddy. Bible, *O.T. Fr.* The Song of Solomon. BoWoP, *ad.* by Willis Barnstone.

My Love Is Young. Earle Birney. NOBC

My Love Late Walking. James Keir Baxter. ATNZ

My love leads the white bulls to sacrifice. Processionals. Alice Archer James. AA

My love lies in the gates of foam. The Churchyard on the Sands. Lord De Tabley. CH, *abr.*; FaBoPP; GBL; OBNC

My love lies underground. Hymn to Priapus. D. H. Lawrence. CMoP; MoAB; OBMV; PoE

My love, like the vast majority. José Luis Vega, *tr. fr. Spanish*. *Fr.* Erotic Suite. InW

My love looks like a girl to-night. The Bride. D. H. Lawrence. NoAM; OxBTC

My love must sigh after me. *Unknown*. *Fr.* Manyo Shu. Ma

My love, my lord. Verses Expressing the Feelings of a Lover. Sister Juana Inés de la Cruz, *tr.* by Samuel Beckett. MexPo

My love on Wednesday letting fall her body. In Crisis. Lawrence Durrell. LiTM

My love sent me a chicken without e'er a bone. *Unknown*. OxNR

My love she is a gentlewoman. Auld Matrons. *Unknown*. ESPB

My Love She Passed Me By. *Unknown*. AmFP

My love she was born in the north country wide. Molly of the North Country. *Unknown*. OBET

My Love-Song. Else Lasker-Schüler, *tr. fr. German by* Jethro Bithell. TrJP

My love stands in my sight. *Unknown*. *Fr.* Manyo Shu. Ma

My love takes an apple to bed. Evesong. Maureen Duffy. PeHV
My love the sun sets. Valerie Sinason. DT
My love, this is the bitterest, that thou. Any Wife to Any Husband. Robert Browning. OBNC
My love-thoughts these days. *Unknown. Fr.* Manyo Shu. Ma
My love too stately is to be but fair. Electra. Francis Howard Williams. AA
My love took scorn my service to retain. Sir Thomas Wyatt. SiPS
My Love Was Light. Tennessee Williams. PoA
My love was so overwhelming it would not bear the telling. Personal Problems. David Avidan, *tr. by* Bernhard Frank. MHeP
My Love When This Is Past. Stephany Fuller. BPo
My love whose bangles. What He Said. Ammuvanar, *tr. by* A. K. Ramanujan. PLW
My love will come. Waiting. Yevgeny Yevtushenko, *tr. by* Robin Milner-Gulland *and* Peter Levi. LLLT; UnAS
My loved, my honored, much-respected friend! The Cotter's Saturday Night. Burns. BeLS; FaBoBe; PoLF
My loved one is unique, without a peer. *Unknown, tr. by* J. E. Manchip White. TTY
My lovely child all clothed in blue. Lullaby in Auschwitz. Pierre Morhange, *tr. by* Edouard Roditi. VWA
My lover capable of terrible lies. Kaccipettu Nannakaiyar, *tr. by* A. K. Ramanujan. BoWoP; PBWP; WPOW
My lover never danced with me. Lines to a Seagreen Lover. Isabella Gardner. CAPP
My lovers/ (Simple chaps). Ode: To My Lovers. Paul Verlaine, *tr. by* J. Murat *and* W. Gunn. PeHV
My lover's a cowboy, wild broncos he breaks. Bucking Bronco. *Unknown.* AmFP
My lovers do not belong to the two rich classes. Thousands and Three. Paul Verlaine, *tr. by* François Pirou. PeHV
My love's eyes are red as the sargasso. The Talking Fish. Ruth Stone. BoWoP
My Love's Guardian Angel. William Barnes. GBL; PoEL-4
My love's labours of these days. *Unknown. Fr.* Manyo Shu. Ma
My love's manners in bed. The Way. Robert Creeley. BoLoP; LiTM; NeAP; PPP
My loyal sins. Loyal Sins. Jacob Glatstein, *tr. by* Ruth Whitman. VWA
My Lulu. *Unknown.* AS
My Lute and I. Sir Thomas Wyatt. MeEL; SiPS
My lute, awake! perform at last. The Lover Complaineth the Unkindness of His Love. Sir Thomas Wyatt. AAS; EBEV; EIL; ELP; GBL; HAP; InPS; NAEL-1; NoP; OAEL-1; PoEL-1; SiPS
(Lover Complaineth, The.) TrGrPo
(To His Lute.) BoLoP; NOBE; OBEV; OBSC; QFR
My lute, be as thou wast [*or* wert] when thou didst grow. William Drummond of Hawthornden. EIL; OBS; Son
(To His Lute.) GTBS; GTBS-P
My Luve. Burns. *See* O my love is like a red, red rose.
"My luve she lives in Lincolnshire." Alison and Willie. *Unknown.* ESPB
My Luve's in Germany. *Unknown.* CH
My Luve's like a Red, Red Rose. Burns. EnRP; FaBoBe; HoPM
My mad despair is the enemy. Asadullah Khan Ghalib, *tr. by* Ahmed Ali. GoT
My madman bathes in the golden tank. The Right True End. *Gond Oral Tradition, tr. by* V. Elwin *and* S. Hivale. WTO
My madness is dear to me. Mad Song. Denise Levertov. TAP
My Madonna. Robert W. Service. BLPA
"My magic is dead," said the witch. "I'm astounded." The Witch's Cat. Ian Serraillier. SO; WSC
My maid Mary,/ She minds the dairy. Mother Goose. OxNR
My Maisters all attend you. Turners Dish of Lentten Stuffe or A Galymaufery. William Turner. CoMu
My Maker shunneth me. Spiritual Isolation. Isaac Rosenberg. TrJP
My Makeup. Rochelle Kraut. UL
My Mall, I mark that when you mean to prove me. The Author to His Wife, of a Woman's Eloquence. Sir John Harington. BoLoP; ErPo
My Mama Moved among the Days. Lucille Clifton. BlSi; PoBA; TV
My Mamma is a mean old sing. Insulted. Priscilla Jane Thompson. CBWP-2
My mamma is dead and she's buried. My Darling's on the Deep Blue Sea. *Unknown.* AmFP
My mammy she told me to open the door. Old Gray Beard a-Shaking. *Unknown.* AmFP
My Mammy Was a Wall-eyed Goat. *Unknown.* ChTr; FaBoNo
My mammy's in the cold, cold ground. Po' Boy. *Unknown.* AS

My man is a bone ringèd with weed. Brenda Chamberlain. WPE; WPOW
(First Woman's Lament.) NeIP
My Man John. *Unknown.* OBET
My man loved me so much. So Long. Jayne Cortez. BoWoP
My Man Pa Replies. Li Ho, *tr. fr. Chinese by* Burton Watson. CoBCP
My Many-Coated Man. Laurie Lee. NYBP
My Marriage with Mrs. Johnson. Jack Gilbert. NPGG
My Mary. William Cowper. *See* To Mary.
My Maryland. James Ryder Randall. AA; AnAmPo; FaBoBe; FaFP; PAH
My Master and I. *Unknown.* CoMu; OBET
My master gave me a black cow to tend. A Cowherd's Song: In Imitation of Chang Chi. Li E, *tr. by* Irving Lo. WFTU
My Master Hath a Garden. *Unknown.* CH
My master who lived on honey. At Gesthemane. Ruth Kim Chun-soo, *tr. by* Koh Chang-soo. ACKP
My masters twain made me a bed. Said the Canoe. Isabella Valancy Crawford. NOBC
(Canoe, The.) OBCV
My Mate Bill. George Herbert Gibson. PoAu-1
My meal finished, one short nap. After Eating. Po Chü-i, *tr. by* Burton Watson. CoBCP
My meaning, my experiences have nothing to do with Li Po or Tu Fu. Discussing Poetry with Shu-yüan. K'ang Yu-wei, *tr. by* Irving Lo. WFTU
My meaning passes like wild nightbirds. Credo. Brewster Ghiselin. PoA
My Midnight Meditation. Henry King. MePo; OBS
"My milk-white doo," said the young man. The Young Man and the Young Nun. A. D. Mackie. OxBS
My mill grinds pepper and spice. *Unknown.* OxNR
My mind i th' mines of rich Philosophy. On My Lord Bacon. John Danforth. SCAP
My Mind is Dry Boughs. Kim Hyun-sung, *tr. fr. Korean by* Koh Chang-soo. ACKP
My mind is intact, but the shapes. Riddle in the Garden. Robert Penn Warren. NoAM
My mind is made up. Tamekane, *tr. fr. Japanese by* Steven D. Carter. WFTW
My mind is sad and weary thinking how. Odell. James Stephens. MoAB; MoBrPo
My mind is so evil and unjust. Human Relations. C. H. Sisson. TW
My mind is stuffed with tablecloths. Poland/ 1931 "The Wedding." Jerome Rothenberg. PoM; Prf
My mind lets go a thousand things. Memory. Thomas Bailey Aldrich. AA; AnAmPo; BoNaP; PoLF
My mind on the form. Nagachika, *tr. by* Steven D. Carter. WFTW
My mind shrugs off his threadbare winter poems. Time Out. Donald Finkel. HoPM
My Mind [*or* Minde *or* Mynde] to Me a Kingdom [*or* Kyngdome] Is. *Wr. at. to* Edward Dyer. BLPL; EIL; FaBoBe; LiTB; NIP; NOBE; PoEL-1; TrGrPo; WGRP
(In Praise of a Contented Mind.) NAEL-1
(Kingdom.) OBSC
My mind was once the true survey. The Mower's Song. Andrew Marvell. NAEL-1; PoEL-2; PPP; SeCP; SeCV-1
My mirror is always a little taller than I am. Mirror. Tada Chimako, *tr. by* Kenneth Rexroth *and* Ikuko Atsumi. BoWoP
My Mistress. Thomas Lodge. *Fr.* The Life and Death of William Longbeard. TrGrPo
My Mistress. William Warner. EIL
"My mistress' eyes are nothing like the sun." Shakespeare. *Fr.* Sonnets, CXXX. AWP; BoLoP; EBEV; FF; HAP; HoPM; InPK; InPS; InvP; LiTB; NAEL-1; NIP; NoP; OAEL-1; PoE; PPP; PrIm; Son; SoSe; TEP; WeW
My mistress frowns when she should play. John Hilton. OxBoLi
(Fa La La.) CH
My Mistress is a paragon. My Mistress. William Warner. EIL
My mistress is as fair as fine. Thomas Ravenscroft. CH; OxBoLi
My mistress sayes she'll marry none but me. Catullus, *tr. by* Richard Lovelace. OBVE
My mistress when she goes. Her Rambling. Thomas Lodge. *Fr.* The Life and Death of William Longbeard. OBSC
My mither sent me to the well. Whistle o'er the Lave o't. *Unknown.* GBP
My Mocking Bird. Josephine D. Henderson Heard. CBWP-4
My mom says I'm her sugarplum. Some Things Don't Make Any Sense at All. Judith Viorst. RHPC
My money! O, my money! Mavimbela, *tr. by* H. Tracey. WTO
My mortal love's a rabbit skin. Apology. Vassar Miller. NePoEA

My most distinguished guest and learnèd friend. Edna St. Vincent Millay. VGW

My most pious songs I have written. God's Gifts. Jakov de Haan, *tr. by* David Soetendorp. VWA

My Mother. Alistair Campbell. ATNZ

My Mother. Josephine Rice Creelman. OHIP

My Mother. Francis Ledwidge. OHIP; TIRV

My Mother. Robert Mezey. NaP; SM

My Mother. Hayim Naggid, *tr. fr. Hebrew by* Rose Drachler. VWA

My Mother. Ann Taylor. BLPA; BLPL; OHIP; OxBChV

My Mother. John Wieners. GLP

My mother. Farewell at the Hour of Parting. Agostinho Neto, *tr. by* Marga Holness. WMBCH

My mother/sits. My Mother Takes a Bath. Yuri Kageyama. BrSi

My mother/ the magician. Tricks. Sharon Olds. TV

My mother/ used to speak about Coyote. What Frank, Martha and I Know about the Desert. Alice Sadongei. GOS

My mother always said. Sappho, *tr. by* Willis Barnstone. BoWoP

My mother and I debate. The Black Walnut Tree. Mary Oliver. CAPP

My Mother and the Bed. Lyn Lifshin. ER; TV

My Mother and the Touched Old Woman. Gary Gildner. MOWH; SoTCo

My mother and your mother. *Unknown.* OxNR

My mother babbles. A salad of noises. Nursing Home. Barry Spacks. PPR

My mother bore me. Foolish Child. *Unknown, tr. by* J. B. Danquah. PBA

My mother bore me in the heat of summer. On Approaching My Birthday. Vassar Miller. IHMS; NMM

My mother bore me in the southern wild. The Little Black Boy. Blake. *Fr.* Songs of Innocence. AWP; CH; EnRP; HeIP; NAEL-2; NAWM-2; NOEC; NoP; OAEL-2; OBEV; OBNC; OxBChV; PoE; PoEL-4; PoNe; TrGrPo

My mother called me on her deathbed side, these words she said to me. Coon Can (Poor Boy). *Unknown.* AS

My mother called my father "Mr. Hunt." Stabat Mater. Sam Hunt. ATNZ

My mother came/ From a village of grasses. Beginnings. Erez Biton, *tr. by* Judith Katz. VWA

My mother could lie down. Harvest. Philip Levine. AnAn

My mother gave me a bitter tongue. Rhyme of My Inheritance. Joan Larkin. GLP

My mother groan'd! my father wept. Infant Sorrow. Blake. *Fr.* Songs of Experience. InPS; NAEL-2; NAs; OBNC; OxBSP; PoEL-4; RB

My mother grumbles. A Bard's Family. Peruncittiranar, *tr. by* A. K. Ramanujan. PLW

My mother had no patio garden. Mother. Nancy Morejón, *tr. by* Kathleen Weaver. AIW

My mother had two faces and a frying pot. From the House of Yemanjá. Audre Lorde. NoAM; NoP

My mother has the prettiest tricks. Song for My Mother, A: Her Words. Anna Hempstead Branch. *Fr.* Songs for My Mother. FaPON

My mother laid me by the fence. The Foundling. Nathan Alterman, *tr. by* Bernhard Frank. MHeP

My mother lives in a house. My House. Robert Adamson. CBAP

My mother, my two brothers, myself. Segregation. Carlos German Belli, *tr. by* Maureen Ahern. Per

My mother never forgave my father. The Portrait. Stanley Kunitz. CAPP; DiL; Psk

My mother of the blue/ Anglo-Saxon eyes. The Eyes, the Blood. David Meltzer. PoM; VWA

My Mother on an Evening in Late Summer. Mark Strand. FYAP; GeTw

My Mother Once Told Me. Yehuda Amichai, *tr. fr. Hebrew by* Assia Gutmann. NYBP

My mother once was a doe. My Nightingale. Rose Ausländer, *tr. by* Ewald Osers. VWA

My Mother Pieced Quilts. Teresa Palma Acosta. FIA; WPOW

My mother—preferring the strange to the tame. The Intruder. Carolyn Kizer. BoWoP; ER; InPK; NePoEA-2

My mother punches my father today. Mother's Day. Jerome Sala. UL

My Mother Really Knew. Wing Tek Lum. MOWH

My mother said I must not have a collier. I'll Have a Collier for My Sweetheart. William Oliver. WTO

My mother said, "If just once more." Mother's Nerves. X. J. Kennedy. GrPl; RHPC

My mother said that I never should. Gypsies in the Wood. *Unknown.* BoTP; OxBoLi; OxBSP; OxNR

My mother sate me at her glass. The Comb. Walter de la Mare. FaBoRV

My mother saw the green tree toad. Lorine Niedecker. VGW

My mother says/ If the neighbor boys. Mother. Kate Starbird. TDD

My mother says I must not pass. The Witch in the Glass. Sarah Morgan Bryan Piatt. AA

My mother sent us to the school. The Shoemakker. *Unknown.* OBET

My mother she's so good to me. A Boy's Mother. James Whitcomb Riley. OHIP

My Mother Shoots the Breeze. Fred Chappell. MT

"First time I met your Pa he took my slip off," *sel.* NBLV

My mother sliced the south for us. Lullaby for Ann-Lucian. Calvin Forbes. PoBA

My Mother Spinning. Peter Olds. ATNZ; PeNZ

My Mother Takes a Bath. Yuri Kageyama. BrSi

My mother thinks. Living in the World. Alan Chong Lau. BrSi

My mother took me because she couldn't. Madre Sofía. Alberto Ríos. NoAM

My mother took us, when we went walking. The Dell. Gavin Ewart. OxBC

My Mother Tries to Visit Me in the Dead of Night. Diane Wakoski. TV

My mother twice in her life on worn feet. Frederick Douglass. Sam Cornish. PoBA

My mother used to work for me. Patches. Thomas Russell Shelton. PWR

My mother wanted to name me after an Irish thinker. Boxing towards My Birth. Jack Driscoll. TSL

My Mother Was Always Dressed. Abigail Luttinger. TV

My mother was an ill woman. The Death of Lord Warriston. *Unknown.* OxBB

My mother wept loudly. Austin Clarke. *Fr.* Tiresias. CIP

My mother, when young, scrubbed laundry in a tub. In an Iridescent Time. Ruth Stone. MoAmPo

My mother whispers to my father. At Wonder Donut. Laureen Mar. BrSi

My mother whistled softly. The Little Whistler. Frances Mary Frost. PDV

My Mother, Who Came from China, Where She Never Saw Snow. Laureen Mar. WPOW

My mother, who has a hide. The Hide of My Mother. Edward Dorn. NeAP

My mother who loses a piece. Now It Is Broccoli. Jeff Tagami. BrSi

My Mother! With the angels now. Mrs. Louise B. Weston. Mary Weston Fordham. CBWP-2

My Mother Would Be a Falconress. Robert Duncan. CAPP; GLP; PoM

My mother writes from Trenton. My Mother. Robert Mezey. NaP; SM

My Mother's Bible. George Pope Morris. AA; AnAmPo; BLRP; WBLP

My Mother's Birthday, *sel.* Kathleen Jessie Raine.

I Used to Watch You, Sleeping. NAs

My Mother's Body. Marge Piercy. ER

My Mother's Breakfront. Janet Sternburg. TV

My mother's brother hauled me to the big-boys' club. Fall In. Lincoln Kirstein. MoP

My Mother's Burying. Sean O Riordain, *tr. fr. Irish by* Valentine Iremonger. TIRV

My Mother's College. Sharon Olds. ER

My mother's Council house is occupied. Ornaments. Frank Ormsby. CIP

My Mother's Feet. Stanley Plumly. GeTw

My mother's form was spare and keen. Generations. Robert Clark. PoAu-2

My Mother's Garden. Alice E. Allen. BLPA; BLPL; FaBoBe

My mother's hands are cool and fair. A Song for My Mother: Her Hands. Anna Hempstead Branch. OHIP

My Mother's House, *sel.* Leah Goldberg, *tr. fr. Hebrew.*

"My mother's mother died." MHeP, *tr. by* Bernard Frank; PBWP, *tr. by* Robert Alter.

(From My Mother's Home.) VWA, *tr. by* Robert Friend.

My mother's lamp once out. Scenes of Childhood. James Merrill. CoAP; DiL

My mother's maids [*or* maydes], when they did sew and spin [*or* sowe and spynne]. Sir Thomas Wyatt. *Fr.* Satires, II. AAS; SiPS

My Mother's Mother, Dearly Beloved. Elizabeth Nannestad. ATNZ

My mother's mother died. Leah Goldberg, *tr. fr. Hebrew. Fr.* My Mother's House. MHeP, *tr. by* Bernhard Frank; PBWP, *tr. by* Robert Alter.

(From My Mother's Home.) VWA, *tr. by* Robert Friend.

My Mother's Novel. Marge Piercy. TV

My mother's phantom hovers here. Fadwa Tuqan, *tr. fr. Arabic by* Hatem Hussaini. *Fr.* Behind Bars, I. OV

My Mother's Prayer. T. C. O'Kane. BLPA; FaBoBe

My Mother's Shoes. Rayzel Zychlinska, *tr. fr. Yiddish by* Marc Kaminsky. VWA

My Mother's Sister. Cecil Day Lewis. OxBTC

My mother's uncle was physician to the Persian Shah. Eternal Now. Gabriel Preil, *tr. by* Grace Schulman. PeBMYV

My Mother's Voice. Mary E. Tucker. CBWP-1
My mountains, God has company in heaven. In High Places. Harriet Monroe. PoA
My Mouth. Arnold Adoff. RHPC
"My mouth doth water, and my breast doth swell." Sir Philip Sidney. Fr. Astrophel and Stella, XXXVII. NAEL-1; Son
My mouth is often joined against his mouth. Rimbaud, tr. by François Pirou. PeHV
My mouth's full of snow. The Print of Your Hand. Sandor Csoori, tr. by Jascha Kessler. FOC
My Muse. Valery Larbaud, tr. fr. French. CT, tr. by William Jay Smith; RHTwFP, tr. by Ron Padgett and Bill Zavatsky.
My muse in meads has spent her many hours. To Mistress Katherine Bradshaw, the Lovely, That Crowned Him with Laurel. Robert Herrick. CaPo
My muse is in the sulks to-day. Knitting. Mary E. Tucker. CBWP-1
My Muse, though airy, glides softly along. The Song of the Pen. Judah al-Harizi, tr. by J. Chotzner. TrJP
My muse, what ails this ardour? Sappho, tr. by Sir Philip Sidney. OBVE
My Muse will now by chymistry draw forth. To the Learned and Reverend Mr. Cotton Mather, on His Excellent Magnalia. Grindall Rawson. SCAP
My, my! My, oh my! Shu Wei, tr. fr. Chinese by Barry L. Gartell. Fr. Impressions of Things Encountered. WFTU
My Naked Aunt. Archibald MacLeish
My naked simple life was I. My Spirit. Thomas Traherne. SeCV-2
My Name. John Wain. PoPo
My Name and I. Robert Graves. Mes; NoAM; NYBP
My name engraved herein. A Valediction: Of My Name in the Window. John Donne. QFR
My Name in the Star Registry. Michael Bachstein. TSM
My Name Is. Pauline Clarke. RHPC
My Name Is Afrika. Keorapetse Kgositsile. PoBA
My name is Captain Hall. Captain Hall. Unknown. GBP
My name is Captain Kid, who has sailed. Captain Kid's Farewell to the Seas; or, The Famous Pirate's Lament. Unknown. OxBSS
My name is Colin Clout. The Prelates. John Skelton. Fr. Colin Clout. TrGrPo
My name is David Lowston, I did seal, I did seal. David Lowston. Unknown. PeNZ
My name is Ebenezer Brown. Epigram. J. V. Cunningham. RB
My name is Edgar Poe and I was born. On the Edge. Philip Levine. CoAP; TAP
My name is Edward Hollander, as you may understand. The Flying Cloud. Unknown. AmFP; OBET; OxBSS
My name is Frank Taylor [or Frank Bolar] a [or 'nole] bachelor I am. Starving to Death on a Government Claim. Unknown. AmFP; OBAL
(Lane County Bachelor, The.) AS
My name is George Nathaniel Curzon. John William Mackail and Cecil Arthur Spring-Rice. Fr. Balliol Rhymes. FaBoCo; FaBoEE; NOBL
My name is "I am living." I Have Bowed before the Sun. Anna Walters. WPOW
My name is Icarus. Wings. Elissa Hamilton Malcohn. BWV
My name is James A. Wright, and I was born. At the Executed Murderer's Grave. James Wright. HCAP
My name is John J. Curtis. John J. Curtis. Joseph Gallagher. AmFP; NoAM
My name is Johnson. Madam's Past History. Langston Hughes. MoP; NoAM
My name is Judith meaning. Judy Grahn. Fr. Confrontations with the Devil in the Form of Love. ER
My name is not my own. The Meeting. Tess Gallagher. GeTw
My name is O'Kelly, I've heard the Revelly. Shillin' a Day. Kipling. NoAM
My name is old Jack Palmer. The Old Keg of Rum. Unknown. PoAu-1
My name is Parrot, a byrd of paradise. John Skelton. Fr. Speak [or Speke], Parrot. OxBoLi
(Parrot, The.) ACP
(Parrot's Soliloquy.) PoEL-1
My name is Peter Emily. Peter Amberley. John Calhoun. AmFP
My name is Phyllis Janik. In the Field. Phyllis Janik. IHMS
My name is Samuel Hall, Samuel Hall. Sam Hall. Unknown. AmFP
(Samuel Hall.) ChTr. See also Oh My Name it is Sam Hall, it is Sam Hall.
My name is Sanford Barney, and I came from Little Rock town. Sanford Barney. Unknown. AmFP
My name is Severino. João Cabral de Melo Neto, tr. fr. Portuguese by Elizabeth Bishop. Fr. The Death and Life of a Severino, I. ATCBP
My name is Sluggery-wuggery. My Name Is. Pauline Clarke. RHPC

My name is Solomon Levi. An Old Cracked Tune. Stanley Kunitz. SM
My name it is Jack Hall, chimney sweep, chimney sweep. Jack Hall. Unknown. OBET
My name it is [or is] Joe Bowers, I have [or I've got] a brother Ike. Joe Bowers. Unknown. AmFP; FSW
My name it is Nell, quite [or right] candid I tell. Nell Flaherty's Drake. Unknown. TW
My name—my country—what are they to thee? No Matter. Paulus Silentarius, tr. by William Cowper. AWP
(Epitaph: "My name—my country—what are they to thee.") FaBoEE; OBVE
My Name Was Legion. Hildegarde Hoyt Swift. AmFN
My name was Pat. We used to read Poe in bed. Joy Road and Livernois. Marge Piercy. ER
My name's Mister Benjamin Bunny. Frederic Edward Weatherly. CenHV
My name's Polly Parker I come o'er. The Collier Lass. Frankie Armstrong. BrRo
My Nannie's Awa.' Burns. GN
My native clay. Growing in Grace. Jack R. Clemo. NOCV
My Native Land. Sir Walter Scott. See Lay of the Last Minstrel, The: Breathes there the man.
My Native Land, thy Puritanic stock. The Rejected "National Hymns." "Orpheus C. Kerr." OBAL
My native town. Mukai Kyorai, tr. by Geoffrey Bownas and Anthony Thwaite. PeBJV
My nature singing in me is your nature singing. Singing & Doubling Together. A. R. Ammons. NAAL-2; NoAM
My neck, where love ran. Good Old Days. Elma Mitchell. PoPo
My necktie, my gloves. Charlie's Sad Date. Rafael Alberti, tr. by Mark Strand. AnAn
My neighbor, a scientist and art-collector, telephones me. The Burning of Paper instead of Children. Adrienne Rich. LCAP
My neighbor brings me bottom fish. My Garden, My Daylight. Jorie Graham. HCAP; MAYP
My neighbor frets about his lawn. Summer. Lucien Stryk. CAPP
My neighbor Hunks's house and mine. Near Neighbors. Martial, tr. by Swift. AWP
My Neighbor in the Mirror. Louise Glück. Son
My neighbor shares his stereo. Interference. Scott Keyes. SoTCo
My Neighbor to the South, the Office Clerk Hsiao, Came in the Evening to Say Good-bye. Mei Yao-ch'en, tr. fr. Chinese by Burton Watson. CoBCP
My neighbor's boy has lifted his father's shotgun and stolen. Snowy Egret. Bruce Weigl. MAYP
My Neighbor's Roses. Abraham L. Gruber. BLPA
My neighbor's willow sways its frail. The Willow. Tu Fu, tr. by Kenneth Rexroth. NaP
My nephew sleeping in a basement room. Rain on the Roof. Janet Frame. ATNZ
My net/ Is heavy with weed. The Disappointed Shrimper. P. A. Ropes. BoTP
My new-cut ashlar takes the light. Kipling. PoEL-5
My New Garden Field. Unknown. AmFP
My new province is a land of bamboo-groves. Eating Bamboo-Shoots. Po Chü-i, tr. by Arthur Waley. OBVE
My New Rabbit. Elizabeth Gould. BoTP
My New Umbrella. M. M. Hutchinson. BoTP
My New World. Irving Browne. AA
My Nightingale. Rose Ausländer, tr. fr. German by Ewald Osers. VWA
My Nkosi you loved me. I Am the Beginning. Isaiah Shembe, tr. by G. C. Oosthuizen. WTO
My noble, lovely, little Peggy. A Letter to the Honourable Lady Miss Margaret Cavendish Holles-Harley. Matthew Prior. NoAM; NOEC; NoP; OxBC; OxBSP; SeCePo
(Letter to Lady Margaret Cavendish Holles-Harley, When a Child, A.) NOBE; OBEV
(Letter to the Child Lady Margaret Cavendish Holles-Harley, A.) OxBChV
My normal dwelling is the lungs of swine. Autobiography of a Lungworm. Roy Fuller. MoP; NoAM; NoP; OxBC
My northern pines are good enough for me. Boston. E. A. Robinson. AnAmPo
My Nose. Dorothy Aldis. RHPC
"My nose is blue." Me. Karla Kuskin. RHPC
My nose long like a knife. Life-Saving Medal. Philippe Soupault, tr. by Rosmarie Waldrop. RHTwFP
My November Guest. Robert Frost. BLPL; OxBA; PoLF
My Occupations. Henri Michaux, tr. fr. French by Richard Ellman. RHTwFP
My Ol' Stetson. Owen Barton. CowP

My Old Bible. *Unknown*. BLRP

My Old Black Billy. Edward Harrington. PoAu-1

My Old Cat. Hal Summers. CRH; OBD; OxBTC

My old companion! and my friend! To My Worthy Friend, Mr. James Bayley. Nicholas Noyes. SCAP

My Old Counselor. Gertrude Hall. AA

My old flame, my wife! The Old Flame. Robert Lowell. BoLoP; NoAM; NOBA

My old friend, Lord O., owned a parcel of land. False Dawn. Walter de la Mare. FaBoNo

My old friend takes leave of the west at Yellow Crane Tower. At Yellow Crane Tower Taking Leave of Meng Hao-jan. Li Po, *tr. by* Burton Watson. CoBCP

My Old Hammah. *Unknown*. AS

My Old Kentucky Home, [Good Night]. Stephen Collins Foster. AA; AnAmPo; FaBoBe; FaBV; FaFP; PoLF; TrGrPo

My old lady died. Kitchen Door Blues. Tennessee Williams. GrPl; OBAL

My old man's a white old man. Cross. Langston Hughes. AmNP; BANP; IDB; LiTM; PoBA; PoLF; SoSe; TAP

My Old Man's Dawdling. Gyula Illyés, *tr. fr. Hungarian by* Jascha Kessler. FOC

My old Mistiss promise me. Promises of Freedom. *Unknown*. BPo

My old mule. Me and the Mule. Langston Hughes. IDB

My old red Schwinn had a carrier over the back fender. George Roberts. GOYP

My Old Straw Hat. Eliza Cook. BrRo

My Old Wife's a Good Old Cratur. *Unknown*. OBET

My Olson Elegy. Irving Feldman. Prf

My once dear love; hapless that I no more. The Surrender. Henry King. BoLoP; EBEV; JCP; MePo; TrGrPo

My one aim, to be a wandering monk. Ryokan, *tr. by* Burton Watson. JLIC-2

My one and only. The 49. Nila NorthSun. GOS

My One Voice. Bob Perelman. IAT

My only desire was to make myself over. The Outwit Song. Daniel Hoffman. SaC

My Only Son. Moyshe-Leyb Halpern, *tr. fr. Yiddish by* Benjamin *and* Barbara Harshav *and* Kathryn Helle. AYP

My only son, more God's than mine. Jesus and His Mother. Thom Gunn. EaLo; OxBC

My Only Star. Francis Davison. EIL

My only wealth is my pain. Stray Prostrations. Kaifi A'Zmi, *tr. by* Mahmood Jamal. PBMUP

My Orcha'd in Linden Lea. William Barnes. EBVV; NOBVV

My ornaments are arms. The Wandering Knight's Song. John Gibson Lockhart. ChTr

My Other Chinee Cook. Brunton Stephens. PoAu-1

My Other Me. Grace Denio Litchfield. AA

My Own Cáilin Donn. George Sigerson. FaBoBe

My own dark head (my own, my own). *Unknown, tr. by* Thomas Kinsella. NOIV

My own dim life should teach me this. Tennyson. *Fr.* In Memoriam A. H. H., XXXIV. SeCePo

My Own Epitaph. John Gay. FaBoEE; FF; NIP; NOEC; OBD; SeCePo

My own flesh and blood—dear sister, dear Ismene. Antigone. Sophocles, *tr. by* Robert Fagles. NAWM-1

My Own Hallelujahs. Zack Gilbert. PoBA

My own head. Seen in mirrors. Cleanly axed. Edward Lucie-Smith. *Fr.* Caravaggio Dying, Porto Ercole, July 1610, Aged 36, II. PeHV

My own heart let me more have pity on. Gerard Manley Hopkins. BrPo; FaBoMo; InPS; LiTM; MoAB; MoBrPo; NOBVV; NoP; TOF

My Own Hereafter. Eugene Lee-Hamilton. WGRP

My Own Hills. Robert Story. PF

My own in a foreign land. The Jewish Conscript. Florence Kiper Frank. TrJP

My Ox Duke. John Dyer. NOEC

My pa held me up to the moo-cow-moo. The Moo-Cow-Moo. Edmund Vance Cooke. FaFP; MoShBr

My Packard Bell was set up in the vacant lot near the stump. The Campaign. Josephine Miles. WPE

My Papa's Waltz. Theodore Roethke. AnAmPo; CAPP; CMoP; DiL; FF; HAP; HCAP; HeIP; HoPM; InPK; InPS; LCAP; LiTM; MoAB; MoP; NAAL-2; NBLV; NIP; NoAM; NOBA; NoP; PoE; PPP; PrIm; SM; TAP; VGW; WeW

My parents are making the journey. Spirit-like before Light. Arthur Gregor. VWA

My Parents, as If Enemies. *Unknown, tr. fr. Spanish by* Kate Flores. DMH

My parents couldn't know, in 1950. Corner Lot. Sharon Bryan. MAYP

My parents felt those rumblings. The Hongo Store 29 Miles Volcano Hilo, Hawaii. Garrett Kaoru Hongo. MAYP; MOWH

My parents have come to town for my wedding. The Form and Function of the Novel. Albert Goldbarth. GeTw

My Parent's House. Adriaan Morriën, *tr. fr. Dutch by* Ria Leigh-Loohuizen. DuIn

My parents raised me tenderly. The Girl I Left behind Me. *Unknown*. AmFP

My parents stand by my bed. Scenario. Barbara Eve Reiss. TV

My Paris is a land where twilight days. Paris. Arthur Symons. NOBVV

My Parker, paper, pen, and ink were made to write. To Parker. George Turberville. OBTV

My Party. Queenie Scott-Hopper. BoTP

My passion is as mustard strong. A New Song of New Similies. John Gay. FaBoCo; NOBL

My passion is like turbulence at the head of waters. *Unknown, tr. by* Willis Barnstone. BoWoP

My Past. Dennis Cooper. GLP; UL

My "Patch of Blue." Mary Newland Carson. BLPA

My patent pardouns ye may see. Sir David Lindsay. *Fr.* Ane Satire [*or* Satyre] of the Three [*or* Thrie] Estaitis. OBSV

My pathway breaks off. Fallen Leaves in a Valley. Sogi, *tr. by* Steven D. Carter. WFTW

My pathway lies through worse than death. Conquest. Georgia Douglas Johnson. AmNP

My paycheck/ blew down the street. Paycheck. Michael Dennis Browne. SoTCo

My Peggy [Is a Young Thing]. Allan Ramsay. *Fr.* The Gentle Shepherd. GN; OxBS
(Peggy.) OBEV

My Pen. Take Pain a Little Space. Sir Thomas Wyatt. SiPS
(To His Pen.) OBSC

My pensioners who daily. Pensioners. W. M. Letts. BoTP

My pensive Sara! thy soft cheek reclined. The Eolian [*or* Aeolian] Harp. Samuel Taylor Coleridge. EnRP; NAEL-2; NoP; OAEL-2

My Penultimate Speech at a Meeting of Some People of Good Will. J. Monika Walther, *tr. fr. German by* Susan L. Cocalis. DMG

My People. Margery Himel. IHMS

My People. Else Lasker-Schüler, *tr. fr. German by* Michael Hamburger. WPOW

My People Came to This Country. Struthers Burt. OPP

My people have married me. Lament of Hsi-chün. Hsi-chün, *tr. by* Arthur Waly. BoWoP

My people? Who are they? Who Are My People? Rosa Zagnoni Marinoni. BLPA

My period had come for prayer. Emily Dickinson. EaLo

My Persecutor. Malka Heifetz-Tussman, *tr. fr. Yiddish by* Kathryn Hellerstein. AYP

My Phillis hath the morning sun. Phillis. Thomas Lodge. *Fr.* Phyllis. OBSC
(Phillis 1.) OBEV
(Phyllis.) ACP; EIL

My Philosofy. James Whitcomb Riley. AnAmPo

My photograph already looks historic. The Middle of a War. Roy Fuller. OBWP

My Picture-Gallery. Walt Whitman. NAAL-1

My Picture Left in Scotland. Ben Jonson. MePo; NAEL-1; PoEL-2; QFR; SeCP; SeCV-1

My pictures blacken in their frames. Death of the Day. Walter Savage Landor. NoP

My Pilgrimage. Sir Walter Ralegh. *See* Give me my scallop shell of quiet.

My Place. David Ignatow. CAPP

My plaid awa, my plaid awa. Lady Isabel and the Elf-Knight [*or* The Elfin Knight]. *Unknown*. CH; FaBoBa; GBP

My Plan. Marchette Chute. FaPON

My plan was to generate light. The Project. Gregory Orr. GeTw

My Playmate. Mary I. Osborn. BoTP

My Playmate. Whittier. AnAmPo; NOBA

My Poem. Nikki Giovanni. AmNP; BPo; PoBA

My poem would eat nothing. The Poem You Asked For. Larry Levis. AmPA; GOYP

My Poems. A. Leyeles, *tr. fr. Yiddish by* Benjamin *and* Barbara Harshav. AYP

My poems. Poems. Bruce Severy. NOVW

My poet, thou canst touch on all the notes. Elizabeth Barrett Browning. *Fr.* Sonnets from the Portuguese, XVII. BrRo

My Poker Girl. Tom Masson. OBAL

My Polish Grandma. Edward Field. Prf

My poor body is alas unworthy. Ch'in Chia's Wife's Reply. *Unknown*, *tr. by* Arthur Waley. BoWoP

My Poor Exploited Language. Herbert Zand, *tr. fr. German by* Beth Bjorklund. CoAuP

My poor old bones—I've only two. The Lonely Scarecrow. James Kirkup. GrPl; PDV

My poor Pegasus must go on foot. In Life's Stable. Kadya Molodovsky, *tr. by* Ruth Whitman. VWA

My poplars are like ladies trim. The Poplars. Theodosia Garrison. OHIP

My portion is defeat—today. Emily Dickinson. OBWP

My Portrait. Moyshe-Leyb Halpern, *tr. fr. Yiddish by* Joseph Leftwich. TrJP

My Prairies. Hamlin Garland. FaPON

My Prayer. Horatius Bonar. BLRP

My Prayer. Patrick O'Connor. TIRV

My Prayer. *Unknown.* BLRP

My prayer is that I have friends. My Prayer. Patrick O'Connor. TIRV

My precious life I spent considering. Take the Crust. Sadi, *tr. fr. Persian by* L. Cranmer-Byng. *Fr.* The Gulistan. AWP

My precious life was spent. Mohammad Taqi Mir, *tr. by* Ahmed Ali. GoT

"My present mother." *Unknown*, *tr. by* Geoffrey Bownas *and* Anthony Thwaite. PeBJV

My Pretty [Little] Pink, *with music. Unknown.* AmFP; AS

My pretty Marten, my winter friend. The Dead Marten. Walter Savage Landor. FM

My Pretty Rose Tree. Blake. *Fr.* Songs of Experience. BoLoP; NAEL-2

My prime of youth is but a frost of cares. Tichborne's Elegy. Chidiock Tichborne. EIL; FaBoRV; FF; HAP; HeIP; InPS; NoP; OAEL-1; OBD

    (Elegy for Himself.) RB

    (Elegy: "My prime of youth is but a frost of cares.") ChTr; EBEV; NOBE; OBSC; WeW

    (Elegy, Written with His Own Hand in the Tower before His Execution.) DL; InPK

    (On the Eve of His Execution.) TrGrPo

    (Retrospect.) ACP

    (Written on the Eve of Execution.) LiTB

    (Written the Night before His Execution.) SCV

My prince, graceful as the pliant bamboo. Prince Niu. *Fr.* Manyo Shu. Ma

My prince, who bent to me. Princess Niu. *Fr.* Manyo Shu. PeBJV

My prow is tending toward the west. My New World. Irving Browne. AA

My puberty tree swayed big, saw-edged leaves. The Puberty Tree. D. M. Thomas. TOF

My Puritan Grandmother!—I see her now. Sea Lavender. Louise Morey Bowman. CaP

My purpose is to tell my own true tale. The Seafarer. *Unknown*, *tr. by* John Wain. EBEV

My Purse. *Unknown.* EBEV

    ("Singe we alle and say we thus.") EBEV

My Queen. William Winter. AA

My quiet kin, must I affront you. Preliminary to Classroom Lecture. Josephine Miles. MoP; NoAM

My quietness has a man in it, he is transparent. In Memory of My Feelings. Frank O'Hara. NAAL-2; NeAP; PoM

My quill is charged with fire. Song of Hate. Jacob ben David Frances, *tr. by* A. B. Rhine. TrJP

My race began as the sea began. Names. Derek Walcott. AnAn

My raiment is my weapons. Ballad of Constancy. *Unknown*, *tr. by* Perry Higman. LPSS

My Ratclif [*or* Ratcliffe], when the retchlesse [*or* rechless] youth offendes. Exhortation to Learn of Others' Trouble. Earl of Surrey. FaBoEE

    (Lines to Ratclif.) SiPS

    ("My Ratclif, when thy retchlesse youth offendes.") AAS

My ravist spreit in that desart terribill. Nightmare. Gawin Douglas. *Fr.* The Palace [*or* Palice] of Honor [*or* Honour]. PoEL-1

My reason which was once severed. Hidden Reason. Margot Jordan. WS

My Recollectest Thoughts. Charles Edward Carryl. *Fr.* Davy and the Goblin, *ch.* 7. NA

My red engine goes chuff-chuff-choo! chuff-chuff-choo! My Toys. Lilian McCrea. BoTP

My reflection. Ray A. Young Bear. STP

My Regrets. Michael Andre. UL

My report is not of schools. Return from Luluabourg. Michael Jackson. ATNZ; PeNZ; UAS

My Restlessness Is of a Wolf. Moyshe-Leyb Halpern, *tr. fr. Yiddish by* Benjamin *and* Barbara Harshav *and* Kathryn Helle. AYP

My Return to Czechoslovakia. Murray Edmond. ATNZ

My Right Hand Don't Leave Me No More. Carter Revard. HATNAP

My Rival. Kipling. OxBTC

My room in Florence was the color of air. Above the Arno. May Swenson. NYBP

My room is shaped like a cage. Hotel. Guillaume Apollinaire, *tr. by* Michael Benedikt. POS

My room is so small. Leah Goldberg, *tr. fr. Hebrew by* Ramah Commanday. *Fr.* Nameless Journey. BoWoP

My room opens like a flower. Monologue of the Inhabitant. Washington Delgado, *tr. by* David Tipton. Per

My room's a square and candle-lighted boat. The Country Bedroom. Frances Cornford. MoBrPo

My room's bigger than a coffin. On Saint-Urbain Street. Milton Acorn. NeAC; NOBC

My rug is red. My couch, whereon I deal. The Map. G. C. Oden. AmNP; PoNe

My ruminations/ are still far from exhausted. Ietaka, *tr. by* Steven D. Carter. WFTW

My sacred sword's invisible. Ingen, *tr. by* Lucien Stryk *and* Takashi Ikemoto. ZPCJ

My Sad Captains. Thom Gunn. CMoP; FaBoMo; LiTM; NAEL-2; NePoEA-2; NoAM; PoCH

My Sad Self. Allen Ginsberg. UnPo

My Sadness Sits around Me. June Jordan. BPo

My Samsons. Haim Guri, *tr. fr. Hebrew.* IP, *tr. by* Warren Bargad *and* Stanley F. Chyet; VWA, *tr. by* Mark Elliott Shapiro

My sange es in sihting. A Song of Love for Jesus. Richard Rolle. MeEL

My saull and lyfe, stand up and see. Ane Sang of the Birth of Christ, with the Tune of Baw Lula Low. Martin Luther, *tr. by* John Wedderburn. ChTr

My Savior, let me hear Thy voice tonight. I'll Follow Thee. Clara Ann Thompson. CBWP-2

My script soars up, flies away, but I'm too drunk to know. Chang Wen-t'ao, *tr. by* William Schultz. WFTU

My second daughter, I loved her so much! Seeing Flowers I Remember My Late Daughter, Shu. Kao Ch'i, *tr. by* Jonathan Chaves. CoBLCP

My Second Marriage to My First Husband. Alice Fulton. NAmP

My secret way of waking. Waking. Lilian Moore. RHPC

My secrets cry aloud. Open House. Theodore Roethke. NoAM; NOBA; NoP

My serious son! I see thee look. Before a Saint's Picture. Walter Savage Landor. OxBChV

My servant wakes at break of dawn. Rough Ridge. Yüan Mei, *tr. by* Jonathan Chaves. CoBLCP

My seven sons came back from Indonesia. Homecoming. Peter Viereck. CoAP

My seven year old friend. The World Is with Me Just Enough. Sam Abrams. UL

My 71st Year. Walt Whitman. NAs

My sexual feats. Fred Apollus at Fava's. Nicholas Moore. ErPo

My Shadow. Robert Louis Stevenson. FaBoBe; FaBV; FaPON; OnUR; OxBChV; PDV; PWR; TEP

My shadow swims before me. The Harbor. John Engels. KS

My shag-hair Cyclops, come, lets ply. Vulcan's Song. John Lyly. *Fr.* Sapho and Phao. EBEV; EIL

    (Song in Making of the Arrows.) OBSC

My shame I will bear. *Unknown. Fr.* Manyo Shu. Ma

My shattred phancy stole away from mee. Edward Taylor. *Fr.* Preparatory Meditations before My Approach to the Lord's Supper, XXIX. SCAP

My Sheep Are Thoughts. Sir Philip Sidney. *Fr.* Arcadia. SiPS

My Shepherd Is the Living Lord. Thomas Sternhold. AH

My Shepherd's unkind; alas, what shall I do? The Lamentation of Chloris. *Unknown.* CoMu

My Shifting ground from season. Blue Crest of Fondness. Unsi al-Haj, *tr. by* Sargon Boulus *and* Alistair Elliot. MAP

My ship passes over-slowly through the foreign lands. First Prelude. Dream in Ohio; the Father. John Logan. *Fr.* Poem in Progress. LCAP

My ship stopped, I've come upon this country. Wakayama Bokusui, *tr. fr. Japanese by* Hiroaki Sato. *Fr.* Forty-four Tanka. FCEI

My Ships. Ella Wheeler Wilcox. PoLF

My Shoes. Charles Simic. CoAP; HCAP

My shoes./ I have just taken them off. 17. IV. 71. Paul Blackburn. PoM

My shoes are almost dead. Caesar. W. S. Merwin. LCAP; NaP

My shoes are in their firing squad position. First Day of Spring. Robert Long. NAmP

My short and happy day is done. The Stirrup-Cup. John Hay. AA

My shrink told me it was unnatural to be. Invisible History. Walta Borawski. GLP

My signs are a rain-proof coat, good shoes, a staff cut from the woods. Walt Whitman. *Fr.* Song of Myself, XLVI. Prf

My silent jailers, well experienced. Who love me. Pictures of Jews. Haim Guri, *tr.* by Warren Bargad *and* Stanley F. Chyet. IP

My silks and fine array. Blake. EnRP; OBNC; TrGrPo (My Silks and Fine Array.) ChTr; ELP; GBL; TEP; UnPo

My sin! my sin, my God, these cursed dregs. Edward Taylor. *Fr.* Preparatory Meditations before My Approach to the Lord's Supper, XXXIX. SCAP

My sinnes are like the haires upon my head. The Authour's Dreame. Francis Quarles. *Fr.* Argalus and Parthenia. OBS

My sins in their completeness. Mael Isu O Brolchain. NOIV

My Sister. Muhammad al-Ghuzzi, *tr. fr. Arabic by* May Jayyusi *and* John Heath-Stubbs. MAP

My Sister. Abba Kovner, *tr. fr. Hebrew by* T. Carmi. TOF

My Sister. Pertti Nieminen, *tr. fr. Finnish by* Aili Jarvenpa. SOP

My Sister. Alfonsina Storni, *tr. fr. Spanish by* Aliki *and* Willis Barnstone. BoWoP

My sister and I. Plans. Helen Morgan Brooks. PoNe

My sister and I when we were close together. Sisters. Dorothy Roberts. CaP

My sister comes from. The Student. Shauqi Abi Shaqra, *tr. by* Sargon Boulus *and* Peter Porter. MAP

My sister in her well-tailored silk blouse hands me. The Photos. Diane Wakoski. NIP

My Sister Jane. Ted Hughes. OnUR; SO

My sister Laura's bigger than me. My Sister Laura. Spike Milligan. NTCP; RAR

My sister! my sweet sister! if a name. Epistle to Augusta. Byron. EnRP

My sister rubs the doll's face in mud. The Kid. Ai. GeTw; NoAM

My sister says. Rhinos Purple, Hippos Green. Michael Patrick Hearn. RHPC

My Sister She Works in a Laundry, *with music. Unknown.* AS

My sister, you are a stranger to this place. God Hasn't Made Room. Mririda n'Ait Attika, *tr. by* Daniel Halpern *and* Paula Paley. PBWP

My Sisters. Bill Kushner. UL

My Sisters, O My Sisters. May Sarton. ER

My sisters played beyond the doorway. Detail from an Annunciation by Crivelli. Rosemary Dobson. PoAu-2

My Sister's Sleep. Dante Gabriel Rossetti. NAEL-2

My Six Toothbrushes. Phyllis McGinley. GoYe

My skin is black, my arms are long. Four Women. Nina Simone. MAT

My skin is so thin. And Yet. Kadya Molodovsky, *tr. by* Seymour Levitan. VWA

My skinny horse. The Shrine of General Pien. Chu Yün-ming, *tr. by* Jonathan Chaves. CoBLCP

My slain! Oh silver-hoof! Oh clover breath! Unbridled Now. Laura Lourene LeGear. GoYe

My Small Daughter. Huang Tsun-hsien, *tr. fr. Chinese by* J. D. Schmidt. WFTU

My snow-flakes jump. Absolute Faith. Kim Hyun-sung, *tr. by* Koh Chang-soo. ACKP

My soft woman, what do you smell of. Ode to Her Aroma. Pablo Neruda, *tr. by* Perry Higman. LPSS

My softness heaves its spiral canopy. Snail. Elisabeth Eybers, *tr. by* Elisabeth Eybers. PeSA

My Son. James D. Hughes. BLPA

My Son. Uuno Kailas, *tr. fr. Finnish by* Aili Jarvenpa. SOP

My Son. Ruth Stone. WPE

My Son and I. Philip Levine. DiL

My Son and I. Rosemary Norman. BrRo

My son & I, between *Fu-Sang* and/ Cathay. Philip Dow. *Fr.* Sussyissfriin. NPGG

My Son Doesn't See a Thing. Tomás Rivera, *tr. fr. Spanish by* Toni Empringham. FIA

My Son, Forsake Your Art. Mahon O'Heffernan, *tr. fr. Irish by* Maire Cruise O'Brien. BIrV

My son has birds in his head. Daedalus. Alastair Reid. NYBP

My son invites me to witness with him. Mousemeal. Howard Nemerov. TwCP

My son, keep well thy tongue, and keep thy friend. Controlling the Tongue. Chaucer. *Fr.* The Canterbury Tales: The Manciple's Tale. OxBChV

My son must be twenty by now. Emperor Go-Shirakawa, *tr. fr. Japanese by* Hiroaki Sato. *Fr.* Ryojin Hisho. FCEI ("My child is still not twenty.") PeBJV, *tr. by* Geoffrey Bownas *and* Anthony Thwaite.

My Son, My Executioner. Donald Hall. CAPP; DiL; NePoEA; SM

My son tells his aunt. A San Diego Poem. Simon J. Ortiz. CDW

My son, thou wast my heart's delight. On the Death of My Son Charles. Daniel Webster. AA

My son was killed while laughing at some jest. A Son. Kipling. *Fr.* Epitaphs of the War, 1914–1918. FaBoEE

My son wears a nappy. My Son and I. Rosemary Norman. BrRo

"My son!" What simple, beautiful words! To My Unborn Son. Cyril Morton Thorne. BLPA

My son who is stranger. A Variation. Robert Creeley. DiL

My son, you loved telling the story of Prince Nata. T'ang Hsien-Tsu, *tr. fr. Chinese by* Jonathan Chaves. *Fr.* Twenty-two Quatrains on Receiving the Obituary Notice for my Son Shih-Chü. CoBLCP

My Song. Hayyim Nahman Bialik, *tr. fr. Hebrew by* Ruth Nevo. VWA

My Song. King D. Kuka. VoR

My Song. Rabindranath Tagore. OHIP

My song, I fear that thou wilt find but few. Epipsychidion. Shelley. EnRP

My Song Is Love Unknown. Samuel Crossman. OxBChV

My Song to the Jewish People. Leib Olitski, *tr. fr. Yiddish by* Jacob Sonntag. TrJP

My song today is the storm-cock's song. The Storm-Cock's Song. "Hugh MacDiarmid." OxBTC

My Songs Are Poisoned ("My songs, they say, are poisoned.") Heine, *tr. fr. German by* Louis Untermeyer. AWP

My Sons. Ron Loewinsohn. NeAP

My sons/ sometimes I can. Efficiency Apartment. Gerald William Barrax. PoBA

My sons' dreams smell of clay and grass. I Drink the Wine of Your Dreams. Pertti Nieminen, *tr. by* Aili Jarvenpa. SOP

My Sons Have Grown to Manhood. Helena Anhava, *tr. fr. Finnish by* Aili Jarvenpa. SOP

My Son's One-Year Test: Improvised, *sel.* Wen Cheng-ming, *tr. fr. Chinese by* Jonathan Chaves.

"Smiling, we set the testing tray before the hall." CoBLCP

My sorrow, Donncha, my thousand-cherished. Padraig O Heigeartaigh, *tr. by* Thomas Kinsella. NOIV

My sorrow is so wide. Kings River Canyon. Kenneth Rexroth. NaP

My sorrow makes you sad, alas. Asadullah Khan Ghalib, *tr. by* Ahmed Ali. GoT

My sorrow that I am not by the little dún. The Starling Lake. "Seumas O'Sullivan." AWP

My sorrow, when she's here with me. My November Guest. Robert Frost. BLPL; OxBA; PoLF

My Sort o' Man. Paul Laurence Dunbar. AmNP

My soul, be not disturbed. Address to My Soul. Elinor Wylie. AWP; LiTM; OxBA

My Soul before Thee Prostrate Lies. C. F. Richter, *tr. fr. German by* John Wesley. AH

My soul, calm sister, towards thy brow, whereon scarce grieves. Sigh. Stéphane Mallarmé, *tr. by* Arthur Symons. AWP

My Soul Doth Pant towards Thee. Jeremy Taylor. TrPWD

My soul, guard against pomp and glory. The Ides of March. C. P. Cavafy, *tr. by* Edmund Keeley *and* Philip Sherrard. VMG

My soul has solitudes. Loneliness. Edwin Essex. TrPWD

My Soul Hovers over Me. Joshua Tan Pai, *tr. fr. Hebrew by* Yishai Tobin. VWA

My Soul in the Bundle of Life. *Unknown, tr. fr. French by* E. Margaret Rowley. *Fr.* The Dead Sea Scrolls. TrJP

My Soul in the Palm of Your Hand. Levi Ben-Amittai, *tr. fr. Hebrew by* Bernhard Frank. MHeP

My soul is an Elysium of shades. Fyodor Ivanovich Tyutchev, *tr. by* Alan Myers. AAA

My soul is awakened, my spirit is soaring. Lines Composed in a Wood on a Windy Day. Anne Brontë. EBVV

My soul is like a well of dead, deep water. The Well. Luis Palés Matos, *tr. by* Donald Walsh. InW

My soul is like the oar that momently. Struggle. Sidney Lanier. LiTA; OxBA

My soul is the veil of his love. Solomon Hafiz, *tr. by* R. A. Nicholson. TOF

My Soul Is Weary of My Life. Bible, *O.T. Fr.* Job, X: 1–22. EaLo

My soul looked down from a vague height, with Death. The Show. Wilfred Owen. LiTB; LiTM; MoAB; MoBrPo; OBWVE; OxBTC; WaaP; WaP

My soul magnifies the Lord. The Magnificat. Bible, *N.T. Fr.* St. Luke, I: 46-56. BoWoP; WGRP ("And Marie said, My soule doth magnifie the Lord.") OBVE

My soul, my pleasant soul and witty. Animula Vagula, Blandula. Emperor Hadrian, *tr. by* Henry Vaughan. FaBoRV

My soul of heaven's light blue. Love. Edith Södergran, *tr. by* Joanna Bankier. OV

My soul, sit thou a patient looker-on. Francis Quarles. NOBE

(Epigram: Respice Finem.) OBEV
(My Soul, Sit Thou a Patient Looker-on.) NIP
My soul stands at the window of my room. Nostalgia. Karl Shapiro.
   CMoP; CoAP; TrJP; TwCP; WaaP
My soul surcharged with grief now loud complains. Rachel Morpurgo, tr.
   by Nina Davis Salaman. TrJP
My Soul, there is a country [or countrie]. Peace. Henry Vaughan.
   AWP; ChTr; EaLo; EBEV; ELP; FaBoCh; GN; HAP; MePo; NOBE;
   NOCV; OBD; OBEV; OBS; PoE; SeCV-1; TEP; TOF; TrCP; WeW;
   WGRP
My Soul Thirsteth for God. Bible, O.T. See Psalms: Psalm XLII ("As
   the hart panteth after the water brooks").
My Soul Thirsts for God. William Cowper. TrCP
My soul, thy love is dear: 'twas thought a good. Francis Quarles. Fr.
   Emblems, V, 4. OAEL-1
My soul thy sacrifice! I choose thee out. Poems of the Arabic.
   Unknown, tr. fr. Arabic by Sir Richard Burton. Fr. The Thousand
   and One Nights. ErPo
My soul to-day. Drifting. Thomas Buchanan Read. AA; AnAmPo;
   GN
My Soul Wanders About. Amir Gilboa, tr. fr. Hebrew by Warren Bargad
   and Stanley F. Chyet. IP
My soul was an old horse. Pegasus. Patrick Kavanagh. MoAB
My Soul, Weigh Not Thy Life. Leonard Swain. AH
My soul, what's lighter than a feather? Wind. Francis Quarles.
   FaBoEE
My Soul Would Fain Indulge a Hope. Joseph Steward. AH
My South. Don West. PoNe
My specialty is living said. E. E. Cummings. NOBA
My Spectre around Me Night and Day. Blake. OAEL-2
My Spirit. Thomas Traherne. SeCV-2
My spirit is a pestilential city. Desolate. Claude McKay. CDC
My spirit is too weak—mortality. On Seeing the Elgin Marbles. Keats.
   BLPL; EnRP; EyDe; LiTB; NAEL-2; NIP; PrIm; TrGrPo
My spirit leans in joyousness tow'rd thine. Lines Suggested in Reading
   "An Appeal to Christian Women of the South," by A. E. Grimke.
   "Ada." BlSi
My Spirit Longeth for Thee. John Byrom. BLPL; NOBE
(Desponding Soul's Wish, The.) TrPWD
My Spirit Will Not Haunt the Mound. Thomas Hardy. MoBrPo; OBNC;
   QFR
My Spirit's Complement. Henrietta Cordelia Ray. CBWP-3
My spotless love hovers, with purest wings. Samuel Daniel. Fr. To
   Delia. OBEV; OBSC
(Most Unloving One, The.) SeCePo
My spouse, Chunaychunay. Unknown, tr. by W. S. Merwin. BoWoP
My Spring Thing. Everett Hoagland. BPo
My Springs. Sidney Lanier. UnPo
My Star. Robert Browning. FaPON; SoSe; TrGrPo
My star, star-gazing?—if only I could be. Aster. Plato, tr. by Peter Jay.
   PeHV
My stare like God's in space. The Well-aimed Stare. Hugo Margenat,
   tr. by Julio Marzán. InW
My Stars. Abraham Ibn Ezra, tr. fr. Spanish by Robert Mezey.
   OFD
My steadfast love! Eibhlin Dhubh Ni Chonaill, tr. fr. Irish by Thomas
   Kinsella. Fr. The Lament for Art O Laoghaire. NOIV
My Stearine Candles. James Henry. NOBVV
My steps are wet from the cold death. Old Jewish Cemetery in Worms.
   Alfred Kittner, tr. by Herbert Kuhner. VWA
My stick fingers click with a snicker. Player Piano. John Updike. RR;
   WeW
"My stick!" he says, and turns in the lane. Outside the Window.
   Thomas Hardy. Fr. Satires of Circumstance.
My stock lies dead, and no increase. Grace. George Herbert. JCP;
   SeCV-1
My stocking's where. David McCord. Fr. A Christmas Package. PChr;
   RHPC
My stomach is of many minds. Stomach. Kathleen Norris. OBAL
My Strawlike Hair. Asya, tr. fr. Yiddish by Gabriel Preil and Howard
   Schwartz. VWA
My straying thoughts, reduced stay. Anne Collins. WPE
My Street—Sheepshead Bay. Berysh Vaynshteyn, tr. fr. Yiddish by
   Benjamin and Barbara Harshav. AYP
My street thunders like. Zimmer's Street. Paul Zimmer. TDD
My students look at me expectantly. The Mountain. Louise Glück.
   NoAM
My Students Who Stand in Snow. Michael S. S. Harper. AnAn
My stupefied uncles lay in the old hut. Winter at Night in the Old Hut.
   Moishe Kulbak, tr. fr. Yiddish by Leonard Wolf. Fr. Byelorussia.
   PeBMYV
My Subtle and Proclamant Song. Sean Jennett. NeIP

My summer jacket. In a Strong Wind at the Suma Seashore. Masaoka
   Shiki, tr. fr. Japanese by Burton Watson. Fr. Thirty-nine Haiku.
   FCEI
My Sun,/ You smile at the granite of Milton. The Street of Named
   Houses. Robert David Cohen. NYBP
My Sun-killed Tree. Marguerite Harris. GoYe
My sunlight came pre-packaged. Nomen. Naomi Long Madgett.
   BlSi
My Swallows. Gerald Stern. KS
My sweet did sweetly sleep. Stolen Pleasure. William Drummond of
   Hawthornden. EnLoPo
My Sweet Gazelle! Immanuel di Roma, tr. fr. Italian. TrJP
My Sweet Old Etcetera. E. E. Cummings. AmPP; AnAmPo; CMoP; FF;
   HeIP; InPS; OBAL; OBWP; OxBA; PPP; SOTW; WaaP; WaP
My Sweet Sweeting. Unknown. CH
My Sweetest Lesbia [Let Us Live and Love]. Thomas Campion, after the
   Latin of Catullus. AAS; AWP; EIL; FF; GBL; HAP; HeIP; InPS;
   NAEL-1; NIP; NoP; OAEL-1; OBSC; OBVE; PoE; PoRA; PrIm; TEP;
   TrGrPo; WeW
(To Lesbia.)
(Vivamus, Mea Lesbia, atque Amemus.) EBEV
My sweetheart in the rippling hills of sand. Unknown, tr. by S. H. Elbert
   and N. Mahoe. WTO
My Sweetheart's Dainty Lips. Judah Halevi, tr. fr. Hebrew by Emma
   Lazarus. TrJP
My Sweetie's a Mule in the Mine. Unknown. AmFP
My swirling wants. Your frozen lips. A Valediction Forbidding
   Mourning. Adrienne Rich. NAAL-2; NoAM; NoP
My sword I shook. The Sword. Abu Bakr, tr. by A. J. Arberry.
   TTY
My Table. W. B. Yeats. Fr. Meditations in Time of Civil War, III.
   LiTB
My tail is not impresssive. Ode to the Pig: His Tail. Walter Rollin
   Brooks. RHPC
My tailor is against parting. Against Parting. Natan Zach, tr. by Jon
   Silkin. VWA
My tale remained, alas, untold within my heart. Mohammad Taqi Mir, tr.
   by Ahmed Ali. GoT
My tangled hair. Unknown. Fr. Manyo Shu. PeBJV
My Task. Maude Louise Ray. PWR
My Tea. Kenneth Rosen. NAmP
My tea is nearly ready and the sun has left the sky. The Lamplighter.
   Robert Louis Stevenson. Fr. A Child's Garden of Verses. EBVV;
   FaFP; OxBChV; SaC
My teacher and I sit down. Playing Solitaire. Steven Fortney. TSL
My tears are blue. Siege. Muhammad al-Maghut, tr. by Abdullah al-
   Udhari. MPAW
My tears are true, though others be divine. Henry Constable. Fr. Diana.
   OBSC
My tears were Orion's splendor with sextuple suns. Tears. Edith Sitwell.
   CMoP
My Teddy Bear. Marchette Chute. RAR
My Teddy Bear. Margaret Hillert. RAR
My teeth dare not trust you. Bridgework. Annette Lynch. FF
My temples throb, my pulses boil. To Minerva. Thomas Hood. ChTr;
   FaBoCo; FaBoNo; FiBHP; NBLV; NOBL; OxBoLi
My tender parents brought me here. Wexford Girl, The. Unknown.
   AmFP
My theory withstood the light of the Hyades. Einstein's Exile in an Old
   Dutch Winter. Norman Dubie. NAmP
My Thing Is My Own. Unknown. CoMu
My thirsty soul desires her drought. A Prisoner's Song of Jerusalem.
   Unknown. ACP
My Thirty Years. Juan Fransico Manzano, tr. fr. Spanish by Oliver
   Cobarn and Ursula Lehrburger. TTY
My thought and my tongue. Yakamochi. Fr. Manyo Shu. Ma
My thought awaked me with Thy Name. Meditation on Communion with
   God. Judah Halevi, tr. by Solomon Solis-Cohen. TrJP
My thought grows like rock azaleas. Teika, tr. fr. Japanese by Hiroaki
   Sato. Fr. A Compendium of Good Tanka. FCEI
My thought is caught in the eyes of love. Entanglement. Francis
   Sparshott. MoCV
My thought is held with awe. Yakamochi. Fr. Manyo Shu. Ma
My thoughts are as a garden-plot, that knows. Thy Garden. "Mustafa",
   tr. by Dulcie L. Smith. AWP
My Thoughts Are Not Your Thoughts. Bible, O.T. Fr. Isaiah, LV: 8–
   13. TrJP
My thoughts are winged with hopes. At. to Sir Walter Ralegh and to
   George Clifford. EIL; GBL
(To Cynthia.) OBSC
My Thoughts Do Harbour. Shakespeare. Fr. The Two Gentlemen of
   Verona, III, i. CTC

My thoughts flow in streams around this tower. Liu E, *tr. fr. Chinese by* Jonathan Chaves. *Fr.* On the Fifteenth Day of the Eighth Month. CoBLCP

My thoughts hold mortal[l] strife. Madrigal. William Drummond of Hawthornden. EiL; GTBS; GTBS-P; OBS; OxBSP (Inexorable.) NOBE; OBEV

My thoughts impelled me to the resting-place. Moses Ibn Ezra, *tr. by* Emma Lazarus. TrJP

My thoughts, like sailors becalmed in Cape Town harbor. Sailor's Harbor. Henry Reed. MoAB; MoBrPo; MOS

My thoughts, my grief! are without strength. A Poem Written in Time of Trouble by an Irish Priest Who Had Taken Orders in France. *Unknown, tr. by* Lady Gregory. OBMV

My thoughts of you are endless. Komachi, *tr. fr. Japanese by* Burton Watson. *Fr.* Kokin Shu. FCEI

My thoughts on the past. Sanetaka, *tr. by* Steven D. Carter. WFTW

My thoughts, useless dreams in midair. Teika, *tr. fr. Japanese by* Hiroaki Sato. *Fr.* Eighty-four Tanka. FCEI

My Thread. Dovid Hofstein, *tr. fr. Yiddish by* Joseph Leftwich. TrJP

My three sisters are sitting. Women. Adrienne Rich. NMM

My Three Wives. *Unknown, after* Etienne Pasquier. FaBoEE

My tidings for you: the stag bells. Summer Is Gone. *Unknown, tr. by* Kuno Meyer. FaBoCh

My time is carved in my poems. On Myself. Leah Goldberg, *tr. by* Robert Alter. OV

My time, my monster, who will be able. The Age. Osip Mandelstam, *tr. by* Peter Russell. AnAn

My Times Are in Thy Hand. Anna L. Waring. PWR

My times that passed away. In Mourning for the Summer. Tachihara Michizo, *tr. by* Sato. FCEI

My Toe. Felice Holman. TSS

My tongue is awed. Okura. *Fr.* Manyo Shu. Ma

"My tongue—tied muse in manners holds her still." Shakespeare. *Fr.* Sonnets, LXXXV. Son

"My towers at last!" Herman Melville. Conrad Aiken. AnAmPo; NoAM; NOBA; TAP

My townspeople, beyond in the great world. Gulls. William Carlos Williams. NoP; OxBA

My Toys. Lilian McCrea. BoTP

My trade takes me frequently into decaying houses. From a Museum Man's Album. John Hewitt. OxBTC

My train passes Ono Station. Wakayama Bokusui, *tr. fr. Japanese by* Hiroaki Sato. *Fr.* Forty-four Tanka. FCEI

My traveling provisions are short, and won't see me through. Sufi Quatrain. Rabi'a bint Isma'il of Syria, *tr. by* Deirdre Lashgari. WPOW

My Triumph. Whittier. NOBA

My triumph lasted till the drums. Emily Dickinson. OBWP; WaaP

My true love breathed her latest breath. The Murderer. Stevie Smith. FaBoWP; OxBSP; TEP

"My True Love Hath My Heart and I Have His." Mary Elizabeth Coleridge. BoLoP

My True Love Hath My Heart [and I Have His]. Sir Philip Sidney. *Fr.* Arcadia. BoLoP; CH; FaBoBe; GBL; PoE; PoEL-1; TrGrPo (Arcadian Duologue.) SiPS (Bargain, The.) NOBE; OBEV (Ditty, A: "My true love hath my heart, and I have his.") AWP; GTBS; GTBS-P (Heart Exchange.) LiTB (Sonnet: "My true love hath my heart.") EiL (True Love.) ChTr; OBSC

My true love makes me happy. Beatrice, Countess de Die, *tr. by* Doris Earnshaw. WPOW

My True Memory. Asya, *tr. fr. Yiddish by* Gabriel Preil *and* Howard Schwartz. VWA

My Trundle Bed. J. G. Baker. BLPA; FaBoBe

My Trust, *sel.* Whittier.
"Picture memory brings to me, A." OHIP, *first 3 sts.*

My trusty warhorse, spirited yet mild. To Fido, His Horse. Vittorio Alfieri, *tr. by* Barbara Howes. PFI

My tune is of troubadours who sing variously. Peire d'Alvernhe, *tr. by* Paul Blackburn. Pro

My twenty-six-year-old ensign. To a Portrait of Lermontov. Margarita Aliger, *tr. by* Elaine Feinstein. VWA

My Uncle. William Corbett. PPR

My uncle, a craftsman of hammers and wood. Willy Lyons. James Wright. HCAP; NNaP; PoE

My Uncle Daniel. E. E. Cummings. AnAmPo

My uncle had a birthmark. My Uncle. William Corbett. PPR

My uncle is a small man. Hills Brothers Coffee. Luci Tapahonso. STE

My Uncle Jehoshaphat. Laura E. Richards. OxBChV

My Uncle Paul of Pimlico. Mervyn Laurence Peake. OnUR

My uncle played the fiddle—more elegantly the violin. The Country Fiddler. John Montague. FaBCIP

My uncle sleeps in the image of death. Lawrence Durrell. *Fr.* Death of General Uncebunke, The; a Biography in Little. FaBoMo

My Uncle Tum. Elijah Ridings. PF

My uncle was Sabbath crazed. Ichthycide. Joe Rosenblatt. NOBC

My Uninvited Guest. May Riley Smith. AA; WGRP

My urine smells of smoke. Desert in the Sea. Brian Swann. AmPA

My Valentine. Robert Louis Stevenson. *See* I will make you brooches and toys for your delight.

My various fleets for fowl, O who is he can tell. Michael Drayton. *Fr.* Polyolbion, Fifth and Twentieth Song. PBBP

My very soul, it seems. Lady Abe. *Fr.* Manyo Shu. Ma

My Village Home. Lu Yu, *tr. fr. Chinese by* Burton Watson. CoBCP

My Voice. Amalia Guglielminetti, *tr. fr. Italian by* Muriel Kittel. DMI

My Voice. Oscar Wilde. BrPo; EBVV

My voice is thin I stand in the shower what's that I ask. The Shower. Linda Smukler. GLP

My voice, plucked from the air. Fingers, Fists, Gabriel's Wings. Michael Cleary. TSM

My voice rings down through thousands of years. Sappho's Reply. Rita Mae Brown. PeHV

My Wage. Jessie Belle Rittenhouse. BLPA

My walls outside must have some flowers. Truly Great. W. H. Davies. OBMV

My walls tonight are lined with ancestors. Ancestors. Harold Schimmel. VWA

My Wander-Brother. Jacob Glatstein, *tr. fr. Yiddish by* Benjamin *and* Barbara Harshav. AYP

My way is in the sand flowing. Samuel Beckett. NOIV

My Way Is Not Thy Way. D. H. Lawrence. CMoP

My wearied bark, O let it now be crowned! To Crown It. Robert Herrick. CaPo

My wedding-ring lies in a basket. Wedding-Ring. Denise Levertov. CAPP

My well-beloved was stripped. Knowing my whim. The Jewels. Baudelaire, *tr. by* Roy Campbell. BoLoP

My well-dressed friend. What She Said to Her Girl Friend, after a Tryst at Night (Which Turned Out to Be a Fiasco). Kapilar, *tr. by* A. K. Ramanujan. PLW

My Wellington boots go. Boots and Shoes. Lilian McCrea. BoTP

My whining lover, what needs all. Against Absence. Sir John Suckling. CaPo

My whiskey is/ a tough way of life. Drink. William Carlos Williams. OxBA

My White Book of Poems. "Rachel", *tr. fr. Hebrew by* "N. N." VWA

My white canoe, like the silvery air. The Camp of Souls. Isabella Valancy Crawford. NOBC

My whole eye was sunset red. Eye and Tooth. Robert Lowell. CAPP; NAAL-2

My whole family floats out on the lake. Yüan Mei, *tr. fr. Chinese by* Jonathan Chaves. *Fr.* Moments of Fullfillment—Writing Down Miscellaneous. CoBLCP

My whole life. At the Well. Malka Heifetz-Tussman, *tr. by* Marcia Falk. VWA

My whole life coming to this place. Port Jefferson. Louis Simpson. CAPP

My whole life has been a chronology of—changes. For Malcolm: After Mecca. Gerald William Barrax. CNA; OFD; PoBA

My Wicked Uncle. Derek Mahon. FaBCIP; OxBC

My wife already there to comfort. The Berries. William Heyen. GeTw; MAYP

My Wife and I. Saibara, *tr. fr. Japanese by* Hiroaki Sato. FCEI

My wife and I are one in heart. Yakamochi. *Fr.* Manyo Shu. Ma

My wife and I lived all alone. Ballad of the Despairing Husband. Robert Creeley. NeAP; NoP; OBAL; SM

My wife and I lived [or live] all alone. Little Brown Jug. *At. to* Joseph E. Winner. FaFP; OBAL

My wife broke a dollar tube of perfume. The Problem. Paul Blackburn. NeAP

My wife bursts into the room. The Loneliness of the Long Distance Runner. Alden Nowlan. TW

My wife exclaims, "Qué Macho!" A Manner of Speaking. Jack Myers. NAmP

My wife had an ulcer. Pain Paint. Peter Minck. FaBoUs

My wife is far away. Prince Aki. *Fr.* Manyo Shu. FCEI

My wife is left-handed. For Hettie. Imamu Amiri Baraka. NeAP; NOBA

My Wife Is My Shirt. Stephen Tropp. InPK

My wife looks bright—her heart is light. The Toiler's Wife. George Hull. PF

My wife rushing around, hair like a tangle of hemp.   Written on New
   Year's Eve.   Rai San'yo, *tr. by* Burton Watson.   JLIC-2
My wife sits reading in a garden chair.   October.   Barry Spacks.   PoA;
   SM
My wife sleeps soundly beside me.   Shooting the Loop.   Michael
   Sheridan.   NAmP
My wife thinks of me much, I know.   Wakayamatobe Mumaro.   *Fr.*
   Manyo Shu.   Ma
My wife went away, left me.   Katda, *tr. by* James Koller.   STP
My wife whom I hid under the holy elm in Hatsuse.   *Unknown.   Fr.*
   Manyo Shu.   FCEI
My wife whose hair is a brush fire.   Free Union.   André Breton, *tr. by*
   David Antin.   POS; RHTwFP; TTTS
My wife with the hair of a wood fire.   Freedom of Love.   André Breton,
   tr. by Edouard Roditi.   EAS
My Wife's a Wanton Wee Thing.   *Unknown.*   CoMu
My window, framed in pear-tree bloom.   Villeggiature.   Edith Nesbit.
   NOBVV
My window is the open sky.   Immortality.   Arthur Sherburne Hardy.
   AA
My window opens out into the trees.   Solace.   Clarissa Scott Delany.
   AmNP; CDC; PoBA; PoNe
My window shows the travelling clouds.   The Alchemist in the City.
   Gerard Manley Hopkins.   NoP
My windows now are giant drops of dew.   A Bright Day.   W. H. Davies.
   OBWVE
My Winsome Dear.   Robert Fergusson.   *Fr.* Leith Races.   SeCePo;
   VGW
My Winter Past.   Eldon Grier.   NOBC
My wish for you/ that God should make your love.   Rabi'a of Balkh, *tr.*
   fr. Farsi by Deirdre Lashgari.   WPOW
My wives do not write.   Memory.   Michael Hamburger.   OxBTC
My Woe Must Ever Last.   Sir Walter Ralegh.   EIL
My woman has picked.   New Season.   Michael S. S. Harper.   CAPP
My woman weeping under a bush of stars.   Simple Ode.   Kendrick
   Smithyman.   ATNZ
My Woodcock.   Patrick Reginald Chalmers.   CenHV
My word/ Hand caught in the door.   Safety Lock.   Louis Aragon, *tr. by*
   Michael Benedikt.   POS
My Words.   William Hathaway.   EOEF
My words and thoughts do both express this notion.   Our Life Is Hid with
   Christ in God.   George Herbert.   OAEL-1
My words for you.   The Words of Finn.   *Unknown.*   ChTr
My world is a painted fresco, where coloured shapes.   Dreams Old and
   Nascent.   D. H. Lawrence.   WGRP
My worthy [*or* woorthy] Lord, I pray you wonder not.   Gascoigne's
   Woodmanship.   George Gascoigne.   AAS; PoEL-1; QFR
My Young Days Were Oppressed with Cares.   Anna Louisa Karsch, *tr. fr.*
   German by Susan L. Cocalis.   DMG
My young grandfather, for the me of four.   Links.   Turner Cassity.   SM
My young love said to me, "My brothers won't mind."   She Moved
   through the Fair.   Padraic Colum.   BIrV; InvP; NOIV
My young Mary do's mind the Dairy.   The Happy Husbandman; or,
   Country Innocence.   *Unknown.*   CoMu
My Young Mother.   Jane Cooper.   FaBoWP; NMM
My younger brother and sister ran up to me.   The Writing of the Character
   "Tree."   Lo Ch'ing, *tr. by* Dominic Cheung.   IFON
My Youngest Daughter Getting Up in the Morning.   Adèle Davide.   Mes
My youth? I hear it mostly in the long, volleying.   The Poet at Seventeen.
   Larry Levis.   NAmP
My youth is.   Yacht for Sale.   Archibald MacLeish.   ASP
My zazen platform, my cushion—they made off with both!   Visited by
   Thieves.   Ryokan, *tr. by* Burton Watson.   JLIC-2
Myall in Prison, The.   Mary Gilmore.   CBAP; PoAu-1
Mycenae.   David Fisher.   NPGG
Mycilla dyes her locks, 'tis said.   On an Old Woman.   Lucilius, *tr. by*
   William Cowper.   AWP
Mye love toke skorne my servise to retaine.   Sir Thomas Wyatt.   AAS
Myfanwy.   Sir John Betjeman.   BoLoP
Myne [*or* Mine] owne John Poyntz, sins [*or* since] ye delight to know, I.
   Mine Own John Poins [*or* Poyntz].   Sir Thomas Wyatt.   *Fr.* Satires.
   AAS; NoP; OBSV; OBVE; PoEL-1; SiPS
   (Of the Courtier's Life.)   OBSC
Mynstrelles Songe: "Angelles bee wrogte to bee of neidher kynde."
   Thomas Chatterton.   *Fr.* Aella; a Tragycal Enterlude.   EnLoPo
Mynstrelles Songe ("Boddynge flourettes bloshes atte the lyghte.").
   Thomas Chatterton.   *See* Aella; a Tragycal Enterlude: Budding
   floweret blushes at the light, The.
Mynstrelle's Songe ("O! synge untoe mie roundelaie").   Thomas
   Chatterton.   *See* Oh! sing unto my roundelay [*or* O! Synge untoe mie
   roundelaie].

Myopia.   Giancarlo Majorino, *tr. fr. Italian by* Lawrence R. Smith.   NItP
Myra.   Fulke Greville.   *See* Caelica: I, with whose colors [*or* colours]
   Myra dressed [*or* dress'd] her head.
Myra Song, The ("Myra, Myra, sing-song").   John Ciardi.   RHPC
Myriad affairs all end in silence and extinction.   Elegy for Myself.   Ching
   An, *tr. by* Irving Lo.   WFTU
Myriad leaves hanging on a thousand twigs, The.   Moon Bright.   Park
   Je-chun, *tr. by* Koh Chang-soo.   ACKP
Myriads and myriads plumed their glittering wings.   Leaves.   Katharine
   Tynan.   BoTP
Myriads of motley molecules through space.   Soul and Sense.   Hannah
   Parker Kimball.   AA
Myriads of wasps now also clustering hang.   How to Catch Wasps.   John
   Philips.   *Fr.* Cyder.   FaBoUs
Myris: Alexandria, A.D. 340.   C. P. Cavafy, *tr. fr. Greek by* Edmund
   Keeley *and* Philip Sherrard.   AnAn; VMG
Myrtilla, early on the lawn.   Sweet Slug-a-Bed.   *Unknown.*   FaBoCo
Myrtle.   Ted Kooser.   GOYP
Myrtle, and eglantine.   The Flower-Seller.   William Young.   *Fr.*
   Wishmakers' Town.   AA
Myrtle bush grew shady, The.   Jealousy.   Mary Elizabeth Coleridge.
   CH; EnLoPo; OBNC; WPE
Myrtle for Two.   Horace.   *See* Odes: I, 38. Simplicity.
Myrtle Tree, The.   Nikos Gatsos, *tr. fr. Greek by* Edmund Keeley *and*
   Philip Sherrard.   *Fr.* Four Songs.   VMG
Myself.   Edgar Albert Guest.   BLPA; BLPL
Myself.   Adah Isaacs Menken.   CBWP-1
Myself.   Waring.   PWR
Myself.   Walt Whitman.   *See* Song of Myself: I celebrate myself, and
   sing myself.
Myself am Hang the buccaneer.   The Flying Fish.   John Gray.   NOBVV
Myself Departing.   Takahashi Mutsuo, *tr. fr. Japanese by* Hiroaki Sato.
   FCEI
Myself in an Anatomical Chart of Sexual Intercourse.   Takahashi Mutsuo,
   tr. fr. Japanese by Hiroaki Sato.   FCEI
Myself in the Disguise of an Ancient Goddess.   Takahashi Mutsuo, *tr. fr.*
   Japanese by Hiroaki Sato.   FCEI
Myself of the Onan Legend.   Takahashi Mutsuo, *tr. fr. Japanese by*
   Hiroaki Sato.   FCEI
Myself unto myself will give.   The Holy Office.   James Joyce.   FaBoTw;
   NoAM; OxBTC
Myself When I Am Real.   Al Young.   CNA; PoBA
Myself When Young.   Tom Donnelly.   BXAP
Myself when young did eagerly frequent.   Omar Khayyám, *tr. fr. Persian*
   by Edward Fitzgerald.   *Fr.* The Rubáiyát of Omar Khayyám of
   Naishápúr.   EaLo; WGRP
Myself with a Glory Hole.   Takahashi Mutsuo, *tr. fr. Japanese by* Sato.
   FCEI
Myselves/ the grievers.   Ceremony after a Fire Raid.   Dylan Thomas.
   CMoP; WaP
Mysteries.   Dannie Abse.   PoPo
Mysteries.   Terence Winch.   UL
Mysteries of Life.   Mary E. Tucker.   CBWP-1
Mysteries Remain, The.   Hilda Doolittle ("H. D.").   NOBA; TAP; VGW;
   WPOW
Mysteries Revealed after Death.   John Reynolds.   *Fr.* Death's Vision.
   NOEC
Mysterious Biography.   Carl Sandburg.   OFD
Mysterious Cat, The.   Vachel Lindsay.   ChTr; FaPON; GoJo; OBCA
Mysterious East.   William Cole.   OBAL
Mysterious Geometry.   Max Hölzer, *tr. fr. German by* Beth Bjorklund.
   CoAuP
Mysterious Night! when our first parent knew.   To Night.   Joseph Blanco
   White.   EBEV; OBEV; Son; WGRP
Mysterious Presence! Source of All.   Seth Curtis Beach.   AH
Mysterious things within you, The.   Ahmad al-Mushari al-Udwani, *tr. fr.*
   Arabic by Hilary Kilpatrick *and* Charles Doria.   *Fr.* Signs, VI.
   MAP
Mystery, The.   *At. to* Amergin, *tr. fr. Irish by* Douglas Hyde.   TIRV
Mystery, The.   Ralph Hodgson.   CH; MoAB; MoBrPo; WGRP
Mystery, The.   Lilian Whiting.   AA
Mystery.   "Yehoash", *tr. fr. Yiddish by* Marie Syrkin.   TrJP
Mystery Baseball.   Philip Dacey.   TSL
"Mystery Boy' Looks for Kin in Nashville."   Robert Hayden.   LCAP;
   NoAM; PoE
Mystery of Cro-a-tàn, The.   Margaret Junkin Preston.   PAH
Mystery of Emily Dickinson, The.   Marvin Bell.   CAPP; LCAP; NIP
Mystery of Life, The.   John Gambold.   NOEC
Mystery of the Caves, The.   Michael Waters.   GeTw; MAYP
Mystery of the Charity of Charles Péguy, The, *sel.*   Geoffrey Hill.
   "Dear lords of life, stump-toothed, with ragged breath."   DiPo

Mystery of the Three Horns, The.   Jules Laforgue, *tr. fr. French by*
    William Jay Smith.   CT
Mystery Story.   Howard Nemerov.   NBLV
Mystic.   Sylvia Plath.   NYBP
Mystic, The.   Cale Young Rice.   WGRP
Mystic and Cavalier.   Lionel Johnson.   MoBrPo; SeCePo
Mystic as Soldier, A.   Siegfried Sassoon.   WGRP
Mystic Borderland, The.   Helen Field Fischer.   WBLP
Mystic Drum, The.   Gabriel Okara.   TTY
Mystic finishes in Time, The.   The Insomniacs.   Adrienne Rich.
    NYBP
Mystic in the morning, half asleep, A.   Bachelor.   William Meredith.
    NoAM
Mystic Magi, The.   Robert Stephen Hawker.   ChTr; OBCP
Mystic Moment.   James Tate.   NAmP
Mystic Pig, The.   Richard Katrovas.   NAmP
Mystic River.   John Ciardi.   NYBP
Mystic Song, A.   *Unknown, tr. fr. French by* Percy Allen.   WGRP
Mystical Beast in the Shadows, The.   Richard Eberhart.   BLA
Mystical cycle of seven times five.   Villanelle of the Mystical Cycle.   A.
    Leyeles, *tr. by* Benjamin *and* Barbara Harshav.   AYP
Mystical strains unheard.   A Clymène.   Paul Verlaine, *tr. by* Arthur
    Symons.   AWP
Mysticism, but let us have no words.   Conrad Aiken.   *Fr.* Time in the
    Rock [or, Preludes to Definition], XI.   VGW
Mystic's Prayer, The.   "Fiona Macleod."   TrPWD; WGRP
Myth, A.   Charles Kingsley.   GN
Myth, The.   Edwin Muir.   CMoP
Myth.   Muriel Rukeyser.   FaBoWP; IHMS; NNaP
Myth lilies. A smog-edge sky blurs his eyes.   Crow's Way.   Duane
    Niatum.   CDW
Myth-maker drags his myth, The.   Alone by the Road's Edge.   Diana O
    Hehir.   NPGG
Myth on Mediterranean Beach: Aphrodite as Logos.   Robert Penn Warren.
    HAP; WeW
Mythic Fragment.   Louise Glück.   NoAM
Mythical Journey, The.   Edwin Muir.   NoAM; OxBS
Mythics.   Helen Chasin.   IHMS
Mythistorima, *sels.*   George Seferis, *tr. fr. Greek by* Edmund Keeley *and*
    Philip Sherrard.
    "And if the soul."   *Fr.* IV.   VMG
    "Angel/ three years we waited intently for him, The."   *Fr.* I.   VMG
    "Harbor is old, I can't wait any longer, The."   *Fr.* IX.   VMG
    "I woke with this marble head in my hands."   *Fr.* III.   VMG
    "On the track, on the track again, on the track."   *Fr.* VI.   VMG
    "Our country is closed in, all mountains."   *Fr.* X.   VMG
    "Sleep wrapped you in green leaves like a tree."   *Fr.* XV.   VMG
    "So very much having passed before our eyes."   *Fr.* XXII.   VMG
    "We didn't know them."   *Fr.* V.   VMG
Mythmaking.   Kathleen Spivack.   NMM
Mythological Sonnets, *sels.*   Roy Fuller.
    "How startling to find the portraits of the gods."   *Fr.* XVI.   ErPo; Son
    "Suns in a skein, the uncut stones of night."   *Fr.* VIII.   GTBS-P
    There Actually Stood.   *Fr.* II.   Son
    Well Now, the Virgin.   *Fr.* VII.   Son
Mythology.   Lawrence Durrell.   OxBTC
Mythology.   Marilyn Hacker.   NoAM
Mythology.   Earle Thompson.   HATNAP; STE
Mythology.   Michael Waters.   MAYP
Mythos of Samuel Huntsman, The.   Hyam Plutzik.   LiTM
Myths.   Guy Butler.   PeSA
Myths and Texts, *sels.*   Gary Snyder.
    Burning, *abr.*   NeAP; PoM
    "After scanning its face again and again. John Muir on Mt. Ritter."
        Fr. VIII.   NOBA
    "He's out stuck in a bird's craw."   *Fr.* IV.   NaP
    "If, after attaining Buddhahood, anyone in my land."   *Fr.* X.   NaP
    "Night here, a covert."   *Fr.* IX.   NaP
    Second Shaman Song.   *Fr.* I.   NeAP; NOBA; PoM
    "Sourdough mountain called a fire in."   *Fr.* XVII.   NAAL-2; NaP;
        NoP
    "Spikes of new smell driven up nostrils."   *Fr.* XIII.   NaP
    "Stone-flake and salmon."   *Fr.* XV.   NaP
    Hunting.
    "All beaded with dew."   *Fr.* VII.   NaP
    "Birds in a whirl, drift to the rooftops."   *Fr.* III.   NaP
    First Shaman Song.   *Fr.* I.   NOBA
    "How rare to be born a human being!"   *Fr.* XVI.   NaP
    "Out the Greywolf valley."   *Fr.* XII.   NaP
    "Swallow-shell that eases birth, The."   *Fr.* IV.   NaP
    This Poem Is for Bear.   *Fr.* VI.   NoBA; NU
        ("Bear down under the cliff, A.")   HCAP; NaP

This Poem is for Deer.   *Fr.* VIII.   NaP; NOBA
    ("Missed a last shot.")   NoBA; NU
Logging.
    "Again the ancient, meaningless."   *Fr.* V.   NaP
    "Each dawn is clear."   *Fr.* VIII.   NaP
    "Groves are down, The."   *Fr.* XIV.   NaP
    "Lodgepole/ cone/seed waits for fire."   *Fr.* XV.   NaP
    "Stood straight/ holding the choker high."   *Fr.* III.   NaP; NOBA
Myxomatosis.   Philip Larkin.   CMoP; MoP; NoAM; NoP

N

N.   Hugh Seidman.   PoA
N. B., Symmetrians.   Gene Derwood.   LiTA
N blo Win.   Writing through a Text by Chris Mann.   John Cage.   EOEF
N. N./ seated on a stool, in a bar, without companions.   Cruel Photograph
    without Light at Daybreak.   Mirko Lauer, *tr. by* David Tipton.   Per
Nabara, The.   C. Day Lewis.   OBNV
Nabokov's Death.   William Matthews.   AnAn
Naboth's Vineyard.   John Caryll.   APAS
Nadar.   Richard Howard.   AnAn
Nae man wha loves the lawland tongue.   The Makar.   William Soutar.
    OxBS
Nagyszombat, 1704.   István Vas, *tr. fr. Hungarian by* William Jay Smith.
    MHuP
Nahant.   Emerson.   AA
    (Waves.)   AmPP
Naiad, hid beneath the bank.   William Johnson Cory.   OBNC
Nail, The.   Vasco Popa, *tr. fr. Serbo-Croatian by* Anne Pennington.   *Fr.*
    Games.   RB
Nail that sticks up will be hammered down, The.   Japanese.   Stephen
    Stepanchev.   SoTCo
Nailed to a cross, your beauty still aglow.   Crucifixion.   "Marie
    Madelaine", *tr. by* Ferdinand E. Kappey.   PeHV
Nails.   Gary Gildner.   TAP
Nails and a Cross.   R. A. K. Mason.   ATNZ
Naked/ Come shivering.   Roger Giroux, *tr. by* Anthony Barnett.
    RHTwFP
Naked/ have lain in beastly days.   Dawn.   Alejandra Pizarnik, *tr. by*
    Alina Rivero.   VWA
Naked and Alone and Unwary You Caught Me.   Veronica Franco, *tr. fr.*
    Italian by Muriel Kittel.   DMI
Naked and knowing my heart my love had left on.   The Jewels.
    Baudelaire.   BoLoP, *tr. by* Roy Campbell; ErPo, *tr. by* Paul
    Blackburn; NAWM-2, *tr. by* David Paul
Naked and the Nude, The.   Robert Graves.   NYBP; SoSe
Naked Ape, The.   John Updike.   EOEF
Naked as from the earth we came.   Submission to Afflictive Providences.
    Isaac Watts.   NOCV
Naked before the glass she said.   Young Woman.   Howard Nemerov.
    ErPo
Naked earth is warm with Spring, The.   Into Battle.   Julian Grenfell.
    FaPoR; MMA; OBEV; OBMV; OBWP; OxBTC; WaaP
Naked Eve shared the last bite.   Like Weary Trees.   Jacob Glatstein,
    tr. by Ruth Whitman.   VWA
Naked Girl Swimming, A.   Arthur Rex Dugard Fairburn.   PeNZ
Naked, he lies in the blinded room.   Soledad.   Robert Hayden.   CAPP
Naked house, a naked moor, A.   The House Beautiful.   Robert Louis
    Stevenson.   NOBE
Naked I Came.   Palladas, *tr. fr. Greek by* A. J. Butler.   NIP
Naked I came, naked I leave the scene.   Epitaph for Someone or Other.
    J. V. Cunningham.   *Fr.* Five Epigrams.   OBAL; SM
    (Epigram: "Naked I came, naked I leave the scene.")   VGW
Naked I came when I began to be.   Nudus Redibo.   Thomas Flatman.
    OxBSP
Naked I reached the world at birth.   Naked I Came.   Palladas, *tr. by* A.
    J. Butler.   NIP
Naked I saw thee.   Ideal.   Padraic Pearse, *tr. by* Thomas MacDonagh.
    AWP
Naked I saw thee.   Renunciation.   Padraic Pearse, *tr. by the author.*
    NOIV
Naked in Borneo.   May Swenson.   NYBP
Naked is the earth.   Antonio Machado, *tr. fr. Spanish by* John Dos Passos.
    Fr. Poems.   AWP
Naked Land, The.   Kenneth Patchen.   EAS
Naked little bird just out of the egg, A.   Slavery.   Malka Heifetz-
    Tussman, *tr. by* Kathryn Hellerstein.   AYP
Naked out of the dark we came.   Kenneth Rexroth.   FaBoEE
Naked Poetry.   Peter Cooley.   SM

Naked Seed, The. C. S. Lewis. TrCP

Naked she lay, clasped in my longing arms. The Imperfect Enjoyment. Earl of Rochester. BoLoP; ErPo

Naked Town, A. Zbigniew Herbert, *tr. fr. Polish* by Czeslaw Milosz. PwPP

Naked vastness forms your eyes, A. The Tree and the Bird: A Duet. Lo Men, *tr.* by Dominic Cheung. IFON

Naked War. Michael Heffernan. BXAP

Naked woman, black woman. Black Woman. Léopold Sédar Senghor, *tr.* by Anne Atik. TTY

Naked woman chained against a cliff, A. Starchart. Jan Kuijper, *tr.* by Jacob Lowland. DuIn

Naked World, The. Sully-Prudhomme, *tr. fr. French* by William Dock. ImOP

Nakhman of Bratslav to His Scribe. Jacob Glatstein, *tr. fr. Yiddish* by Benjamin *and* Barbara Harshav. AYP

Nam. Mike Lowery. Psk

Namby-Pamby; or, A Panegyric on the New Versification. Henry Carey. FaBoNo; FaBoPa; NOEC, *abr.;* OBSV; Par

Name, A. Maxine Chernoff. UL

Name, *sel.* Alan Davies.
   "If the devices fail pens." LP

Name, The. Jalal ed-Din Rumi. NU, *ad. from* Persian by Robert Bly

Name, The/ never left his lips. Scribe. Paul Auster. VWA

Name for All, A. Hart Crane. VGW

Name Giveaway. Phillip William George. VoR

Name, if you can, your shadow, your fear. One Word Will Do. René Daumal, *tr.* by Michael Benedikt. POS

Name in a footnote. Faceless name. Crispus Attucks. Robert Hayden. CNA

Name in block letters. *None that signified.* A Form of Epitaph. Laurence Whistler. GTBS-P; Mes

Name in the Sand, A. Hannah Flagg Gould. AA

Name is hard, The. On the 25th Anniversary of the Liberation of Auschwitz. Eli W. Mandel. NOBC

Name is immortal but only the name, for the rest, The. Jew. Karl Shapiro. VWA

Name known, but no relations or kin in this place. Ishikawa Takuboku, *tr. fr. Japanese* by Hiroaki Sato. *Fr.* Forty-seven Tanka in Three Lines. FCEI

Name of God Is, The. Jeanine Hathaway. KS

Name of it is "Autumn," The. Emily Dickinson. ImOP
   (Name—of it—is "Autumn," The.) InPS

Name of Jesus, The, *sel.* John Newton. NOEC
   (How Sweet the Name of Jesus Sounds.) NOCV
   "Jesus! my Shepherd, Husband, Friend." TrPWD

Name of King Ram: think of it with love, The. Tulsidas, *tr.* by John Stratton Hawley *and* Mark Juergensmeyer. SSI

Name of my heroine, simply "Rose." The Tale of a Pony. Bret Harte. OBNV

Name of Old Glory, The. James Whitcomb Riley. GN

Name of Our Country, The. Dennis Schmitz. AmPA

Name of the beast is, The. Small Comment. Sonia Sanchez. NBP

Name of the game is beat the lame, The. The Hustler. *Unknown.* TW

Name of the product I tested is "Life," The. A Consumer's Report. Peter Porter. FaBoCo; NOBL

Name of this poem is, The. Cameo No. II. June Jordan. BPo

Name they gave me is lost, The. The Privilege. Alejandra Pizarnik, *tr.* by Yishai Tobin. VWA

Name thou wearest does thee grievous wrong, The. The Mocking-Bird. Henry Jerome Stockard. AA

Named Kovacs went down. A Jockey. Ron Koertge. TSL

Named them. Orpheus. Donald Davie. TEP

Nameless. Natan Zach, *tr. fr. Hebrew* by Warren Bargad [*and*] Stanley F. Chyet. IP

Nameless Doon [*or* Dun]. William Larminie. AnIL; BIrV

Nameless Epitaph, A. Matthew Arnold. FaBoEE

Nameless, he crept from the hutch of creation. Love for a Hare. Melvin Walker La Follette. NePoEA-2

Nameless Journey, *sel.* Leah Goldberg, *tr. fr. Hebrew* by Ramah Commanday.
   "My room is so small." BoWoP

Nameless Maiden, The. *Unknown.* ErPo

Nameless One, A. Margaret Avison. HeIP; NOBC

Nameless One, The. James Clarence Mangan. ACP; BIrV; EnRP; NOIV; OBEV

Nameless one. Ina, 1979. Bea Medicine. GOS

Nameless Ones, The. Conrad Aiken. AnAmPo; OxBA

Nameless Saints, The. Edward Everett Hale. WGRP

Names, The. Lauris Edmond. ATNZ

Names. Dennis Joseph Enright. FaBoCo

Names. Maria Neef-Uthoff, *tr. fr. German* by Susan L. Cocalis. DMG

Names. Derek Walcott. AnAn

Names and Order of the Books of the Old Testament, The. Thomas Russell. BLPA

Names for everything I touch. The Hollow Thesaurus. Roger McDonald. CBAP

Names from the War. Bruce Catton. AmFN

Names in Monterchi: To Rachel. James Wright. AnAn; NNaP

Names of Georgian Women, The. Bella Akhmadulina, *tr. fr. Russian.* BoWoP, *tr.* by Stanley Noyes *and* Olga Carlisle

Names of Horses. Donald Hall. CAPP; HAP; InPK; LCAP; LLLT

Names of the Hare, The. *Unknown, tr. fr. Middle English* by Seamus Heaney. RB

Names of the Humble, The. Les A. Murray. CBAP

Names of the Idols, The. József Tornai, *tr. fr. Hungarian* by Jascha Kessler. FOC

Names of things, The—sparks! Resigning from a Job in a Defense Industry. Sandra McPherson. LCAP

Naming. Joseph Stroud. NPGG

Naming of Cats, The. T. S. Eliot. NBLV

Naming of Parts. Henry Reed. *Fr.* Lessons of the War, I. FF; GoJo; HoPM; InPS; MoAB; MoBrPo; NOBE; NoP; OxBTC; PoRA; PrIm; SeCePo; SoSe; TrGrPo; UnPo; WaP

Naming of Private Parts. John Lloyd Williams. BXAP; FaBoPa

Naming of the Beasts, The. Francis Sparshott. NIP; NOBC

Naming the Flowers. Anne Stevenson. ER

Namkwin Pul. Bernard Gutteridge. WaP

Nanak and the Sikhs, *sel. Unknown, tr. fr. Hindustani.*
   "How shall I address Thee, O God? how shall I praise Thee?." WGRP

Nancibel. Bliss Carman. AnAmPo

Nancy Hanks. Rosemary *and* Stephen Vincent Benét. FaBV; FaPON; NTCP

Nancy Hanks. Harriet Monroe. OHIP

Nancy Hanks dreams by the fire. Fire-Logs. Carl Sandburg. AnAmPo

Nancy Hanks, Mother of Abraham Lincoln. Vachel Lindsay. CMoP

Nancy, Jimmy, Larry, Frank, and Berdie. Lady. Ted Berrigan. UL

Nancy, the hogs don't know us. Mirror for the Barnyard. Jack Myers. AmPA

Nani. A. A. Ríos. SM

Nano's Song. Ben Jonson. *See* Volpone: Fools, they are the only nation.

Nansen said: It's everywhere. Chosha, *tr.* by Lucien Stryk *and* Takashi Ikemoto. ZPCJ

Nanta was nominated for a W(hore). Aenigma on the Six Cases. *Unknown.* FaBoUs

Nantucket. William Carlos Williams. AnAmPo; HAP; InPS; OxBA; SOTW; TAP; WeW

Naomi. Gwendolyn Brooks. NAAL-2

Naomi and Ruth. Bible, *O.T. Fr.* Ruth, I: 8-17. TrJP

Naomi (Omie) Wise. *Unknown.* AmFP

Napa, California. Ana Castillo. WPOW

Napkin and Stone. Vernon Watkins. NYBP

Naples. Samuel Rogers. OBTV

Naples Again. Arthur Freeman. NYBP

Napoleon. Walter de la Mare. FaBoCh; FaBoTw; NOBE; RB

Napoleon after Sedan. Arthur Rimbaud, *tr. fr. French* by Robert Lowell. *Fr.* Eighteen-Seventy. FaBoPV; OBWP

Napoleon and the British Sailor. Thomas Campbell. BeLS

Napoleon hoped that all the world would fall beneath his sway. *Unknown.* FaBoCo

Napoleon is charging our squares. Keith Douglas. *Fr.* Waterloo. FL

Napoleon is standing with his pants upon the floor. The Poor Old Prurient Interest; Blues. John Hartford. MAT

Napoli Again. Richard Hugo. LCAP

Nappy Edges (A Cross Country Sojourn). Ntozake Shange. BlSi

Narcissa. Gwendolyn Brooks. GrPl; NTCP

Narcissus./ Your fragrance. Federico García Lorca, *tr.* by William Jay Smith. CT

Narcissus. Israel Efrat, *tr. fr. Hebrew* by Bernhard Frank. MHeP

Narcissus. Charles Gullans. NePoEA

Narcissus. Donald Petersen. NePoEA-2

Narcissus. Paul Valéry, *tr. fr. French* by Joseph T. Shipley. AWP

Narcissus and chrysanthemum. Ch'ien Ch'ien-i, *tr. fr. Chinese* by Jonathan Chaves. *Fr.* In Lamplight, Watching My Wife Preparing a Flower. CoBLCP

Narcissus and Echo. Fred Chappell. MT

Narcissus and Some Tadpoles. Victor James Daley. PoAu-1

Narcissus, Come Kiss Us! *Unknown.* ErPo

Narcissus in a Cocktail Glass. Frances Minturn Howard. GoYe

Narcissus in Camden. Helen Gray Cone. BXAP

Narcissus Pseudonarcissus. Elio Pagliarani, *tr. fr. Italian* by Lawrence R. Smith. NItP

Narcissus: To Himself. David Galler. PoA
Narcolepsy. Maureen Owen. TTTS
Narcotic plash of water from the kitchen sink. The Girl Who Learned to
    Sing in Crow. Paul Mariani. GeTw
Narnian Suite. C. S. Lewis. RR
Narration. George Seferis, *tr. fr. Greek by* Edmund Keeley *and* Philip
    Sherrard. VMG
Narrative. Russell Atkins. PoBA
Narrative. Louis Dudek. CaP
Narrative. Elisabeth Eybers, *tr. fr. Afrikaans by the author.* PeSA
Narrative Hooper and L.D.O. Sestina with a Long Last Line, The. James
    Whitehead. HoPM
Narrator's Trance, The, *sels.* James Cunningham. JB
  "And birds came crying."
  "Song thumbed down a cruiser for a ride, A."
  "There were blood spots on the skirt."
  "Woods are overhead over everywhere, The."
Narrow fellow in the grass, A. Emily Dickinson. AmPP; BoWoP;
    CMoP; FaFP; FM; FPL; GoJo; HAP; HoPM; LiTM; NAAL-1; NIP;
    NoAM; NOBA; NoP; OBCA; OxBA; PoE; PoEL-5; PoLF; PPP; RB;
    SoSe; TAP; WeW
  (Snake, The.) LiTA; MoAB
Narrow glade unfolded, such as Spring, A. An Interview near Florence.
    Samuel Rogers. *Fr.* Italy. OBNC
Narrow path: frog, A. Korin, *tr. by* Hiroaki Sato. FCEI
Narrow Sea, The. Robert Graves. FaBoEE; FaBoMo; MOS
Narrow, thorny path he trod, The. The Ascetic. Victor James Daley.
    PoAu-1
Narrowing of knowledge to one window to a door, A. Elegy for William
    Soutar. William Montgomerie. OxBS
Narrowing sea embraces it forever, The. The Urumbula Song.
    Unknown, tr. by T. G. H. Strehlow. CBAP
Narrows of Birth, The. William Everson. PoM
Nasal whine of power whips a new universe. Hart Crane. *Fr.* The
    Bridge: Cape Hatteras. MoAB
  (Power.) MoAmPo
Nashoba. Jim Barnes. *Fr.* Four Things Choctaw. HATNAP
Naskeag. Alfred Corn. BLA
Naso, you are many men's man; and yet. To Naso. Catullus, *tr. by* Jack
    Lindsay. ErPo
Nastasya. Moishe Kulbak, *tr. fr. Yiddish by* Leonard Wolf. *Fr.*
    Byelorussia. PeBMYV
Nasturtiums with. Rainbow Writing. Eve Merriam. GrPl
Nasty surprise in a sandwich, A. God, A Poem. James Fenton. DiPo;
    NoAM
Nat Turner. Samuel Allen. CNA; FB
Nata Natal. Juan Gonzalo Rose, *tr. fr. Spanish by* Ena Hollis. Per
Natalya Nikolayevna Goncharov. Don Coles. NOBC
Nathan Hale. Francis Miles Finch. PAH
Nathan Hale. William Ordway Partridge. OPP
Nathan Hale. *Unknown.* PAH
Nathan, lay off thinking today. The Bratslaver to His Scribe. Jacob
    Glatstein. PeBMYV, *tr. by* Leonard Wolf.
    (Nathan, no thought today. The Bratzlav Rabbi to His Scribe.).
    TrJP, *tr. by* Jacob Sloan.
Nathaniel Lee to Sir Roger L'Estrange. Nathaniel Lee. FaBoEE
Nation. Charlie Cobb. PoBA
Nation. Mendel Naigreshel, *tr. fr. Yiddish by* Joachim Neugroschel.
    VWA
Nation of trees, drab green and desolate gray, A. Australia. A. D.
    Hope. NoAM; NoP
Nation Once Again, A. Thomas Davis. NOIV
Nation shattered, hills and streams remain, The. Spring Prospect. Tu Fu,
    tr. by Burton Watson. CoBCP
Nation Wrapped in Stone, A. Roberta Hill. BoWoP; CDW
National Anthem. Egbert Martin. PVCV
National Cemetery, Beaufort, South Carolina, The. Josephine D.
    Henderson Heard. CBWP-4
National Cold Storage Company. Harvey Shapiro. MAT; VGW
National Federation is a grand and glorious band, The. All We Ask Is
    Justice. Mrs. Henry Linden. CBWP-4
National Gallery, The. Louis MacNeice. EyDe
National Hymn, A. John William De Forest. *Fr.* Miss Ravenel's
    Conversion. OPP
National Library. Oswald de Andrade, *tr. fr. Portuguese by* Jean R.
    Longland. ATCBP
National Miner, The. *Unknown.* AmFP
National Ode, July 4, 1876, The, *sel.* Bayard Taylor. PAH
  America. AA
National Paintings, The. Fitz-Greene Halleck *and* Joseph Rodman Drake.
    Fr. The Croaker Papers. AA

National Security. Archibald MacLeish. GOA
National Song. William Henry Venable. PAH
National Trust. Tony Harrison. NAEL-2
National Winter Garden. Hart Crane. *Fr.* The Bridge: Three Songs.
    ErPo; InPS; LiTM; NAAL-2; OxBA
Nationality. Mary Gilmore, *tr. fr. Eskimo.* CBAP; PoAu-1; WTO
Nation's Strength, A, *sel. Wr. at. to* Emerson. OPP
  "Not gold, but only man can make." AmFN; FaPON
Nations That Long in Darkness Walked. John Barnard. AH
Native, The. W. S. Merwin. NePoEA-2; PoRA
Native Born. Eve Langley. PoAu-2; WPE
Native Land. M. Y. Lermontov, *tr. fr. Russian by* Alan Myers. AAA
Native Land. Sir Walter Scott. *See* Lay of the Last Minstrel, The
Native Moments. Walt Whitman. OPOP; OxBA
Native Origin. Beth Brant. STE
Native Woman—1982, A. Karen Cooper. GOS
Natives, The. David Mura. BrSi
Natives here have given up their backyards, The. Champagne. Rita
    Dove. MAYP
Natives of America, The. Ann Plato. BlSi
Natives were all in their houses, The. Ceylon. Nishiwaki Junzaburo, *tr.*
    by Hiroaki Sato. FCEI
Nativitie, The. William Drummond of Hawthornden. *See* Flowers of
    Sion: Angels, The.
Nativity [*or* Nativitie]. John Donne. *Fr.* La Corona. OBS; Son
Nativity, The. Mary Weston Fordham. CBWP-2
Nativity, A. Kipling. NAs
Nativity. Aquah Laluah. CDC; PBA; TTY
Nativity, The. C. S. Lewis. TrCP
Nativity. James Montgomery. NOCV
Nativity, The. *Unknown.* MeEL
Nativity Chant, The. Sir Walter Scott. *Fr.* Guy Mannering. ChTr;
    FaBoCh; NAs
Nativity of Our Lord and Saviour Jesus Christ, The. Christopher Smart.
    Fr. Hymns and Spiritual Songs, XXXII. EBEV; HAP; NOBE;
    NOCV; PoEL-3
  (Christmas Day, *sts.* 6–9) ChTr; OBCP
  (Hymn.) NAs; NOEC
Nativity Song. Jacopone da Todi, *tr. fr. Latin.* OHIP, *ad. from Latin by*
    Sophia Jewett
Natura Naturans. Arthur Hugh Clough. HAP; NOBVV
Natura Naturans. Kathleen Jessie Raine. NYBP
Natural Grace, A. C. K. Stead. ATNZ
Natural History. Richard Howard. TAP
Natural History, *sel.* Harold Monro.
  "Vixen woman, The." OBMV
Natural History. Robert Penn Warren. FF; NAAL-2
Natural History of Unicorns and Dragons My Daughter and I Have Known,
    A. William Pitt Root. SM
Natural Ice Cream. Jack Myers. NAmP
Natural Order of Things, The. Harley Elliott. NeAC
Natural pussy. Bitter Herbs. Alta. NMM
Natural Shame, A. Sydney Lea. NAmP
Natural silence of a tree, The. Fortune. Charles Madge. FaBoMo
Natural Stockade at Bamboo Lake, The. Yang Shih-ch'i, *tr. fr. Chinese*
    by Jonathan Chaves. *Fr.* Ten Scenes at the Hsiao Family Stone
    Ridge. CoBLCP
Natural Tears. Thomas Hood. *See* After such years of dissention and
    strife.
Natural Theology, A. James Whitehead. BLA; MT
Natural world is a spiritual house, The. Intimate Associations.
    Baudelaire, *tr. by* Robert Bly. NU
Naturalist's Summer-Evening Walk, The. Gilbert White. NOEC;
    PBBP
Naturally. Audre Lorde. BlSi; CNA
Naturally it is night. Air. W. S. Merwin. CAPP; NaP
Naturally the Foundation Will Bear Your Expenses. Philip Larkin.
    FaBoPV
Nature. Emerson. AWP
Nature. Longfellow. AA; BoNaP; FaBoBe; FPL; PoLF; TAP; TrGrPo
Nature. Walter Stone. NYBP
Nature. Andrew Taylor. UAS
Nature. Henry David Thoreau. AiP; BLPL; FaBoBe
Nature. Alfred de Vigny, *tr. fr. French by* Margaret Jourdain. AWP
Nature and Nature's laws lay hid in Night. Pope. FaBoCo; FaBoEE
  (Epitaph Intented for Sir Isaac Newton.) ImOP
  (Epitaph on Sir Isaac Newton.) FiP
  (Intended for Sir Isaac Newton.) InPK; WeW
Nature and the Child. John Lancaster Spalding. *Fr.* God and the Soul.
    AA

Nature and the Poets. James Beattie. *Fr.* The Minstrel. SeCePo
Nature Be Damned. Anne Wilkinson. NOBC; OBCV
Nature, creations law, is judg'd by sense. Upon Love Fondly Refus'd for
    Conscience's Sake. Thomas Randolph. OAEL-1
Nature especially abhors the smell of vacuums. Specimen of an Induction
    to a Poem. Alan Bernheimer. UL
Nature Green Shit. Gary Snyder. LCAP
Nature had long a treasure made. The Match. Andrew Marvell. EBEV
Nature had made them hide in crevices. New Hampshire, February.
    Richard Eberhart. LiTM; TwCP
Nature has endowed her with complete charm. T'ang Yin, *tr. fr. Chinese
    by* Jonathan Chaves. *Fr.* On a Painting of a Woman Shown Half-
    Length, I. CoBLCP
Nature herself doth Scotchmen beasts confess. John Cleveland. *Fr.* The
    Rebel [*or* Rebell] Scot. OBSV
Nature in Couplets. Charlton Ogburn. GrPl
Nature in her wisdom has formed the human head. Four Heads & How to
    Do Them. John Forbes. CBAP
Nature Is. Jack Prelutsky. RHPC
Nature is rising from the dead. Epigram on the First of April. John
    Winstanley. NOEC
Nature is the endless sky. Nature Is. Jack Prelutsky. RHPC
Nature isn't enough. Those. Nature. Andrew Taylor. UAS
Nature Morte. Alastair Fowler. NPo
Nature Morte. Louis MacNeice. NoAM
Nature Morte. Heidi Pataki, *tr. fr. German by* Beth Bjorklund. CoAuP
Nature most calm is often a crisis. Chesapeake. Gerta Kennedy. NYBP
Nature Notes, *sels.* Louis MacNeice. FaBCIP
    Cats.
    Corncrakes.
    Dandelions.
    Sea, The.
Nature nothing shows more rare. Shells. T. Sturge Moore. SeCePo
Nature of an Action, The. Thom Gunn. NePoEA
Nature of creation itself, The. Asadullah Khan Ghalib, *tr. by* Ahmed Ali.
    GoT
Nature of Love, The. James Kirkup. EaLo
Nature of Man, The. C. H. Sisson. FaBoTw
Nature of the Eagle, The. *Unknown, tr. fr. Middle English. Fr.* The
    Bestiary. PBBP
Nature of the Turtle Dove, The. *Unknown, tr. fr. Middle English. Fr.*
    The Bestiary. PBBP
Nature of these birds, The. On Some Partridges Sent to Her Alive.
    Florencia del Pinar, *tr. by* Kate Flores. DMH
Nature one hour appears a thing unsexed. Francis Thompson. *Fr.*
    Contemplation. OBNC
Nature reads not our labels, "great" and "small." The Man with the Hoe;
    a Reply. John Vance Cheney. AA
Nature requires five; custom gives seven. Hours of Sleep. *Unknown.*
    NBLV
Nature selects the longest way. A Northern Suburb. John Davidson.
    NOBVV; OBNC
Nature—sometimes sears a sapling. Emily Dickinson. NAAL-1
Nature Study. Craig Raine. NoAM
Nature Study, after Dufy. Helen Smith Bevington. NYBP
Nature that day a woman was in weakness. A Storm in Summer. Wilfrid
    Scawen Blunt. FaBoTw
Nature That Framed Us of Four Elements. Christopher Marlowe. *Fr.*
    Tamburlaine the Great, *pt.* I, Act II, sc. vii. PoEL-2; TrGrPo
    (Perfect Bliss and Sole Felicity.) SeCePo
Nature, That Washed [*or* Washt] Her Hands in Milk[e]. Sir Walter
    Ralegh. NoP
    (Love and Time.) SiPS
Nature: The Artist. Frederic Lawrence Knowles. AA
Nature, which is the vast creation's soul. To Mr. Henry Lawes.
    Katherine Philips. WPE
Nature withheld Cassandra in the skies. Fragment of a Sonnet. Pierre de
    Ronsard, *tr. by* Keats. AWP; OBVE
Nature's Cook, *sel.* Margaret Cavendish, Duchess of Newcastle.
    "Death is the cook of nature, and we find." PBWP
Nature's Creed. *Unknown.* OHIP
Nature's Easter Music. Lucy Larcom. OHIP
Nature's Embassy, *sel.* Richard Brathwaite.
    Nightingale, The. ElL; PBBP
Nature's first green is gold. Nothing Gold Can Stay. Robert Frost.
    AmPP; GrPl; MoAB; MoAmPo; NAAL-2; NOBA; PPP; SoSe; TAP;
    VGW
Nature's Influence on Man. Mark Akenside. *Fr.* The Pleasures of
    Imagination, III. NOEC .
    (Love of Nature.) NOEC

Nature's lay idiot, I taught thee to love. John Donne. *Fr.* Elegies, VII.
    NoP
    (Elegie: "Nature's lay ideot, I taught thee to love.") SeCP
Nature's Lineaments. Robert Graves. FaBoTw; RB
Nature's Minor Chords. Henrietta Cordelia Ray. CBWP-3
Nature's Questioning. Thomas Hardy. TEP
Nature's Reply to Mutability. Spenser. *Fr.* The Faerie Queene, VII, 7
    and VIII, 1. NOBE
Nature's Travail. *Unknown, tr. fr. Greek by* Goldwin Smith. AWP
Nature's Uplifting. Henrietta Cordelia Ray. CBWP-3
Nature's workings made this gentle place. Yün Shou-p'ing, *tr. fr. Chinese
    by* Jonathan Chaves. *Fr.* On the Painting "Mist over Ten Thousand
    Mountains." CoBLCP
Naught but liberty was ever. Liberty. Chiara Matraini, *tr. by* Muriel
    Kittel. DMI
Naught remains of the dying glow, past and present, on the waters of
    Ch'in-huai. Remembering the Past at Chin-ling. Wei Yüan, *tr. by*
    Irving Lo. WFTU
Naughty Boy. Robert Creeley. HeIP; NoAM; NOBA
Naughty Lord and the Gay Young Lady Damages, $10,000, The.
    Unknown. CoMu
Naughty Paughty Jack-a-Dandy. Namby-Pamby; or, A Panegyric on the
    New Versification. Henry Carey. FaBoNo; FaBoPa; NOEC, *abr.;*
    NOEC; OBSV; Par
Naughty Preposition, The. Morris Bishop. FiBHP; NBLV; NYBP
Naughty Soap Song. Dorothy Aldis. RAR
Nausea. Catherine Davis. NePoEA
Nausicaa. Homer, *tr. fr. Greek by* George Chapman. *Fr.* Odyssey, VI.
    OBS
Nausicäa. Irving Layton. ErPo
Nausicaa with Some Attendants. Tom Lowenstein. VWA
Nautical Ballad, A. Charles Edward Carryl. *See* Davy and the Goblin:
    Walloping Window-Blind, The.
Nautilus Island's hermit. Skunk Hour. Robert Lowell. AmPP; CAPP;
    CMoP; CoAP; FaBoMo; HAP; HCAP; HeIP; InPK; InPS; LCAP;
    MoAmPo; MoP; NAAL-2; NIP; NoAM; NOBA; NoP; OPOP; OxBC;
    PoE; PPP; PrIm; PrIm; SCV; TAP; WeW
Nauty Pauty Jack-a-Dandy. *Unknown.* OxNR
Nauvoo. Bayard Taylor. OBAL
Navaho Sings. Nan Benally. GOS
Navajo, The. Elizabeth Jane Coatsworth. AmFN
Navajo Girl of Many Farms. Charles G. Ballard. NOVW
Navajo Signs. Winifred Fields Walters. NOVW
Naval Photograph: 25 October 1942: What the Hand May Be Saying.
    David Bottoms. BLA
Nave of the church, The. St. Nicholas. Juliane Windhager, *tr. by* Beth
    Bjorklund. CoAuP
Navel. Dennis Schmitz. AnAn
Navigators, The. W. J. Turner. OBMV
Nay, but of such an one. *Unknown, tr. fr. Sanskrit by* Sir Edwin Arnold.
    Fr. The Bhagavad-Gita. TOF
Nay but you, who do not love her. Robert Browning. TrGrPo
Nay do not smile: my lips shall rather dwell. One Desiring Me to Read,
    But Slept It Out, Wakening. George Daniel. OxBSP
Nay, gather not that filbert, Nicholas. The Filbert. Robert Southey.
    FM
Nay, I have loved thee. Theseus and Ariadne. Lloyd Mifflin. AA
Nay, Ivy, Nay, *sel. Unknown. Fr.* Holly and Ivy. MeEL
    "Holly stand in the hall." CH
Nay, lady, one frown is enough. To Helen in a Huff. Nathaniel Parker
    Willis. AnAmPo; OBAL
Nay, Lord, not thus! white lilies in the spring. Sonnet on Hearing the
    Dies Irae Sung in the Sistine Chapel. Oscar Wilde. TrPWD
Nay! Nay! Ivy! Holly against Ivy. *Unknown.* MeEL
    (Holly Beareth Berries.) PBBP, *abr.*
Nay, nay, my boy—'tis not for me. Horace. *See* Odes: I, 38.
    Simplicity.
May, 1945. Peter Porter. OxBC
Nay, painter, if thou dar'st design that fight. The Second Advice to a
    Painter. Andrew Marvell. APAS
Nay, pish; nay, phew! nay, faith and will you? fie! A Maiden's Denial.
    Unknown. ErPo
Nay, prethee *or* prithee dear, draw nigher. A Loose Saraband. Richard
    Lovelace. CaPo; PoEL-3
Nay, prithee tell me, Love, when I behold. The Transfiguration of
    Beauty. Buonarroti Michelangelo, *tr. by* John Addington Symonds.
    AWP
Nay, tempt me not, my Corydon; I tell you once again. Football and
    Rowing—an Eclogue. Alfred Denis Godley. CenHV
Nay, tempt me not to love again. Thomas Moore. *Fr.* Odes to Nea.
    OBNC

Nay then, farewell, if this be so. To Avisa. Henry Willoby. *Fr.* Willobie His Avisa. EIL

"Nay then," quoth Adon, "you will fall again." Venus Abandoned. Shakespeare. *Fr.* Venus and Adonis. OBSC

Nay, thou art my eternal attribute. Whym Chow. "Michael Field." FM

Nay, Xanthias, feel unashamed. II, 4. Ad Xanthiam Phoceum ("Ne sit ancillae"). Horace, *tr. fr. Latin.* AWP, *tr. by* Franklin P. Adams.

Nazca Pottery. Javier Sologuren, *tr. fr. Spanish by* Maureen Ahern *and* David Tipton. Per

Nazis. Ira Sadoff. BLA

Ndaaya's Kàsàlà, *sel.* Citèkù Ndaaya, *tr. after French-Luba texts by* Judith Gleason.
"Ndaaya, I, am so poor." PBWP

Ne Plus Ultra. Samuel Taylor Coleridge. OAEL-2

Ne trellisses, no vines. Iron Landscapes (and the Statue of Liberty). Thom Gunn. OBTV

Neaera when I'm there is adamant. J. V. Cunningham, *after the Latin of* George Buchanan. OBVE

Neap-tide and the ebbing days slide. A Song of Sickness. Hine Tangikuku, *tr. by* Barry Mitcalfe. WTO

Near. Abba Kovner, *tr. fr. Hebrew by* Shirley Kaufman. VWA

Near a fence, young, small grasses. Taigi, *tr. fr. Japanese by* Hiroaki Sato. Fr. Twenty-nine Hokku. FCEI

Near a lifeless stump in a fertile lea. The Ailing Eagle. Annette von Droste-Hülshoff, *tr. by* Susan L. Cocalis *and* Gerlinde Geiger. DMG

Near a shady wall a rose once grew. The Rose Still Grows beyond the Wall. A. L. Frink. BLPA

Near a Waterfall at Ryumon. Lady Ise, *tr. fr. Japanese by* Etsuko Terasaki *and* Irma Brandeis. BoWoP

Near an Old Prison. Frances Cornford. OBMV

Near Anahorish. Seamus Heaney. PPR

Near autumn our hearts are close. On the Twenty-first of the Seventh Month of the Seventh Year of Genroku, at Bokusetsu's Hut. Basho, *tr. fr. Japanese by* Burton Watson. *Fr.* Seventy-six Hokku. FCEI

Near Avalon. William Morris. OAEL-2

Near Death. Stef Pixner. AIW

Near Dover, September 1802. Wordsworth. EnRP
(Sonnet september, 1802.) ChER

Near Dusk. Joseph Auslander. FaPON

Near Helikon. Trumbull Stickney. LiTA

Near Lake Suwa in Shinshu. Tsuetsuki Pass. Ishigaki Rin, *tr. by* Hiroaki Sato. FCEI

Near Lanivet, 1872. Thomas Hardy. AWP; CMoP; NoAM

Near Myth. Marian Gleason. SoTCo

Near Neighbors. Martial, *tr. fr. Latin by* Swift. AWP

Near Perigord. Ezra Pound. FaBoMo; LiTA; LiTM

Near Rhydcymerau. Rhydcymerau. David Gwenallt Jones, *tr. by* Anthony Conran. OBWVE

Near strange, weird temples, where the Ganges' tide. The Bayadere. Francis Saltus Saltus. AA

Near the beginning of his first journey. Ibn Battuta. Dick Davis. NPo

Near the Border of Insanities. Dannie Abse. PoA

Near the celebrated Lido where the breeze is fresh and free. Longfellow's Visit to Venice. Sir John Betjeman. NOBL

Near the City of Petersburg. The V. N. and C. I. Maggie Pogue Johnson. CBWP-4

Near the cliff's sharp edge, on high. The Vampyre. Vasile Alecsandri, *tr. by* William Beatty-Kingston. VVA

Near the Cymmerians, in his dark abode. Ovid, *tr. fr. Latin by* Dryden. *Fr.* Metamorphoses, XI. OBVE

Near the dry river's water-mark we found. A Note Left in Jimmy Leonard's Shack. James Wright. HCAP; NoP

Near the edge, as on a shelf. Cat on the Porch at Dusk. Dorothy Harriman. GoYe

Near the end we will travel as two old men. Whatever It Is. Jim Simmerman. BLA

Near the goal, head sunk into his shoulders. Soccer at the Meadowlands. Diane Ackerman. ASP

Near the headwaters of the longest river. The Banished Gods. Derek Mahon. OxBC

Near the Lake. George Pope Morris. AA

Near the mountain's summit, when the bells. The Fox. R. Williams Parry, *tr. by* Gwyn Williams. OBWVE

Near the Ocean. Robert Lowell. NOBA

Near the river with white waves, we probed. Apology of the Young Scientists. Celia Dimmette. GoYe

Near the salt pans. What Her Girl Friend Said to Him. Centan Kannanar, *tr. by* A. K. Ramanujan. PLW

Near the School for Handicapped Children. Thomas W. Shapcott. CBAP

Near the sea. Today's Ferns. Ono Tozaburo, *tr. by* Hiroaki Sato. FCEI

Near the top a bad turn some dare. Whether There Is Sorrow in the Demons. John Berryman. LiTM

Near the village where quails call. Travelogue. Nishiwaki Junzaburo, *tr. by* Hiroaki Sato. FCEI

Near the Vipsanian columns where the aqueduct. Martial, *tr. by* Peter Porter. OBVE

Near this spot. Epitaph to a Dog. Byron. BLPA

Near to disgust, close to calling quits with song. Peire Vidal, *tr. by* Paul Blackburn. Pro

Near to me as my flesh, my flesh and blood. Allen Tate. *Fr.* Sonnets of the Blood, II. PoA

Near[e] to the silver Trent. The Trent. Michael Drayton. *Fr.* The Shepherd's Sirena. FaBoPP; OBEV; PoEL-2
(Jovial Shepheard's Song, The.) PoEL-2
(Sirena.) OBEV

Near Twelve Mile Point. Lance Henson. HATNAP

Near where I live there is a lake. Fringed Gentians. Amy Lowell. FaPON

Near Wilton sweet huge heaps of stone are found. Stonehenge. Sir Philip Sidney. *Fr.* The Seven Wonders of England. FaBoPP

Near yonder copse, where once the garden smiled. The Village Parson. Goldsmith. *Fr.* The Deserted Village. BeLS; EnRP; FaFP; GoTL; LaA; NOEC; NoP; OAEL-1; PoEL-3; TEP
(Village Preacher, The.) TIRV

Neare Enna walles there standes a Lake Pergusa is the name. Ovid, *tr. fr. Latin by* Arthur Golding. *Fr.* Metamorphoses, V. OBVE

Nearer. Judith Herzberg, *tr. fr. Dutch by* Shirley Kaufman. BoWoP; VWA

Nearer Home. Phoebe Cary. AA; BLRP; FaFP; PWR; WBLP; WGRP
(One Sweetly Solemn Thought.) AH

Nearer, My God, to Thee. Sarah Flower Adams. BLRP; FaBoBe; FaFP; WBLP; WGRP

Nearing Again the Legendary Isle. C. Day Lewis. *Fr.* The Magnetic Mountain, VI. FaBoTw; LiTB; MoAB; MoBrPo

Nearing La Guaira. Derek Walcott. TTY

Nearing Winter. Ernest Sandeen. NYBP

Nearly dark; warm stones of the wall in the woods. The Owl. Thorkild Bjornvig, *tr. by* Robert Bly. NU

Nearly Nameless. Márton Kalász, *tr. fr. Hungarian by* Jascha Kessler. FOC

Nearly right, The. To the Tune of the Coventry Carol. Stevie Smith. FaBoTw; OPOP

Nearly winter. All day the sky gray. Earth heavy. A Long Walk before the Snows Began. Robert Bly. LCAP

Nearsighted child has taken off her glasses, The. Country Stars. William Meredith. GrPl

Neat little packet from Hobart set sail, A. The Waterwitch. *Unknown.* PoAu-1

'Neath blue-bell or streamer. Song from "Al Aaraaf." Poe. *Fr.* Al Aaraaf. AmPP; AnAmPo; OxBA

'Neath northern skies thou hid'st thy punctual nest. The Loon. Theodore Harding Rand. CaP

Neatly/ and well/ ordered. Peter Zumpf, *tr. by* Beth Bjorklund. CoAuP

Nebraska. Jon Swan. RFM

Nebuchadnezzar. Elinor Wylie. MoAmPo

Nebuchadnezzar, von Hoffman the Great, then. Lines I Told Myself I Wouldn't Write. Paul Mariani. MAYP

Nebulous. Benjamin Péret, *tr. fr. French by* Michael Benedikt. POS

Necessary Miracle, A. Eda Lou Walton. NYBP

Necessitarian's Epitaph, A. Thomas Hardy. FaBoEE

Necessities of Life. Adrienne Rich. HCAP; NIP; NOBA

Necessity. Langston Hughes. NOBA

Necessity Is the Mother of the "Bullet." Patrick Worth Gray. TSL

Necessity of Falling, The. William Mills. MT

Nechama. Shirley Kaufman. LCAP

Necklace of beads loops round her white throat, A. Gathering the Mulberry. Ho Ning, *tr. by* Lois Fusek. ATF

Necklace of flame, little dropped hearts. Tattoos. Charles Wright. HCAP

Necromance. Rae Armantrout. LP

Necropolis. Karl Shapiro. MoAB; PoA

Nectar, puff of sails, lily. To a Young Girl. David Rosenmann-Taub, *tr. by* Charles Guenther. VWA

Ned Braddock. John Williamson Palmer. PAH

Ned Christie. Robert J. Conley. STE

Ned knew I was short of tobacco one day. Ned's Delicate Way. Henry Lawson. CBAP

Ned Vaughan. Walter de la Mare. FaBoEE

Neddy Nibble'm and Biddy Finn. *Unknown.* GBP

Ned's Delicate Way. Henry Lawson. CBAP

Need. Babette Deutsch. PCP

Need, The. Siegfried Sassoon. TrPWD

Need from excess—excess from folly growing. Samuel Bishop. NOEC

Need Is Our Name. Luci Shaw. TrCP

Need of an Angel. Raymond Souster. CaP

Need of Being Versed in Country Things, The. Robert Frost. NoAM; NoBA; OxBA; UnPo

Need of Loving. Strickland W. Gillilan. BLPA; WBLP

Need to explore, The. Explorers as Seen by the Natives. Doug Fetherling. NOBC

Need to Love, The. Shlomo Vinner, tr. fr. Hebrew by Laya Firestone and Howard Schwartz. VWA

Need to Win, The. Thomas Merton. ASP

Needing/ to go separate. Ama Credo. Margaret Reckord. AIW

Needing one, I invented her. Aunt Leaf. Mary Oliver. TDD

Needle, The. Grace Cornell Tall. GoYe

Needle, The. Samuel Woodworth. GN

Needle and Thread. Pan Chao, tr. fr. Chinese by Richard Mather and Rob Swigart. WPOWA

Needle quivering from its pole, The. To a Lady, with a Compass. George Napier. FaBoUs

Needles and Pins. Mark Van Doren. SO

Needles and pins, needles and pins. Proverb. Unknown. FaBoBe

Needles are starved, brown, The. Acceleration near the Point of Impact. Joyce Carol Oates. GeTw

Needle's Eye, The. Unknown. AmFP

Needles' Lighthouse from Keyhaven, Hampshire, The. Charles Tennyson Turner. FaBoPP

Needless Alarm, The. John Ruskin. FM

Needless Return. Dan Pagis, tr. fr. Hebrew by Warren Bargad and Stanley F. Chyet. IP

Needless to catalogue heroes. No Man Knows War. Edwin Rolfe. TrJP; WaP

Needs. A. R. Ammons. NIP; OBAL

Needs must I leave and yet needs must I love. Henry Constable. Fr. Diana. InvP; OBSC

"Needy knife-grinder! whither are you going?" The Friend of Humanity and the Knife Grinder. George Canning and John Hookham Frere. BXAP; FaBoCo; Par

(Sapphics.) NOEC

Needy were lined up by order of famine, The. The Offended. Anne Hébert, tr. by Willis Barnstone. BoWoP

Negation is the spectre, the reasoning power in man, The. Reason and Imagination. Blake. Fr. Milton, II. EnRP

Negative. Yoshioka Minoru, tr. fr. Japanese by Hiroaki Sato. FCEI

Negative in an enlarger, A. A Slice of Life. Lois Wickstrom. BWV

Negative Passage. Michael Newman. PoA

Negative Space. Michael Waters. NAmP

Negative tree, you are belief. Bound. Theodore Roethke. PoA

Negatives, The. Philip Levine. NePoEA-2

Negatives. Charles Wright. PoA

Neglected long had been my useless lyre. On the Defeat at Ticonderoga or Carilong. Unknown. PAH

Neglectful Edward. Robert Graves. BrPo; MoBrPo

Neglectful, I have not died of love. Teika, tr. fr. Japanese by Hiroaki Sato. Fr. Eighty-four Tanka. FCEI

Neglectful, we've yet. Saigyo, tr. fr. Japanese by Burton Watson. Fr. Sixty-four Tanka. FCEI

Negligently the day opens before I have time to sleep. Teika, tr. fr. Japanese by Hiroaki Sato. Fr. Eighty-four Tanka. FCEI

Negritude. James A. Emanuel. BPo; CNA

Negro, The. James A. Emanuel. HoPM; InPK

Negro/ With the trumpet at his lips, The. Trumpet Player. Langston Hughes. NAAL-2; TTY

Negro Ballot, The. Lizelia Augusta Jenkins Moorer. CBWP-3

Negro Cemetery Next to a White One, A. Howard Nemerov. OxBSP

Negro Dreams. Doughtry Long, Jr.. PoBA

Negro Geo'ge. Berysh Vaynshteyn, tr. fr. Yiddish by Benjamin and Barbara Harshav. Fr. Negroes. AYP

Negro Has a Chance, The. Maggie Pogue Johnson. CBWP-4

Negro Hero. Gwendolyn Brooks. CAPP

Negro Heroines. Lizelia Augusta Jenkins Moorer. CBWP-3

Negro holds firmly the reins of his four horses, The. The Drayman. Walt Whitman. Fr. Song of Myself, XIII. PoNe

"Oxen that rattle the yoke and chain or halt in the leafy shade." FM

Negro Love Song, A. Paul Laurence Dunbar. BANP; PoNe

Negro Peddler's Song, A. Fenton Johnson. AmNP

Negro Poets. Charles Bertram Johnson. BANP

Negro Reel. Unknown. AS

Negro Schools, The. Lizelia Augusta Jenkins Moorer. CBWP-3

Negro Serenade. James Edwin Campbell. BANP

Negro Sermon, A—Simon Legree. Vachel Lindsay. See Booker Washington Trilogy, The: Simon Legree—a Negro Sermon.

Negro Servant. Langston Hughes. VGW

Negro Singer, The. James David Corrothers. BANP

Negro Soldiers, The. Roscoe Conkling Jamison. BANP

Negro Soldier's Civil War Chant. Unknown. BPo

Negro Soldier's Viet Nam Diary, A. Herbert Martin. PoBA

Negro Song, A. Unknown. PBCV

Negro Song at Cornwall. Unknown. PBCV

Negro Speaks of Rivers, The. Langston Hughes. AiP; AmFN; AmNP; BANP; BPo; CDC; HAP; HCAP; HeIP; IDB; NAAL-2; NIP; NoAM; NOBA; NoP; OBCA; PoBA; PoNe; TAP; TTY; WeW

Negro Spiritual. Perient Trott. PoNe

Negro Spirituals. Rosemary Benét and Stephen Vincent Benét. AmFN; FaPON

Negro sprouts from the pavement like an asparagus, A. Stumpfoot on 42nd Street. Louis Simpson. NNaP; UnPo; VGW

Negro Village. Berysh Vaynshteyn, tr. fr. Yiddish by Benjamin and Barbara Harshav. Fr. Negroes. AYP

Negro Woman. Lewis Alexander. CDC; PoBA

Negroes. Maxwell Bodenheim. PoNe

Negroes, sels. Berysh Vaynshteyn, tr. fr. Yiddish. AYP
   Harlem Negroes. Tr. by Benjamin and Barbara Harshav.
   Laundry. Tr. by Benjamin and Barbara Harshav and Kathryn Hellerstein.
   Lynching. Tr. by Benjamin and Barbara Harshav.
   Negro Geo'ge. Tr. by Benjamin and Barbara Harshav.
   Negro Village. Tr. by Benjamin and Barbara Harshav.

Negroes/ Sweet and docile. Warning. Langston Hughes. BPo

Negroes, labouring, The. Guadalupe, W.I. Nicolás Guillén, tr. by Anselm Hollo. TTY

Negro's Tragedy, The. Claude McKay. BPo

Neighbor, A/ rejects chemotherapy and the hospital. The Cloud Chamber. Arthur Sze. BrSi

Neighbor thought that they, A. The Planetary Arc-Light. August Derleth. GoYe

Neighbors. A. R. Ammons. CAPP

Neighbors. David Allan Evans. Psk

Neighbors. Marilyn Francis. GoYe

Neighbors. Mary Ann Hoberman. ILY

Neighbors. Joseph Rolnik, tr. fr. Yiddish by Irving Feldman. Fr. Poets. PeBMYV

Neighbors. Anne Spencer. CDC

Neighbors. James Tate. BAP

Neighbors of Bethlehem, The. Unknown, tr. fr. French. OHIP

Neighbour mine not long ago there was, A. A Tale for Husbands. Sir Philip Sidney. Fr. Arcadia. SiPS

Neighing North, The. Annie Charlotte Dalton. CaP

Neïla. Iwan Goll, tr. fr. French by Anthony Rudolf. VWA

Neither blemish this book, nor the leaves double down. Unknown. FaBoUs

Neither does the heart remain. Mohammad Taqi Mir, tr. by Ahmed Ali. GoT

Neither Here nor There. W. R. Rodgers. LiTB; LiTM; MoAB; MoBrPo

Neither Hook nor Line. Bunyan. SD

Neither in idleness consume thy days. Walter Savage Landor. FaBoEE

Neither love, the subtlety of refinement. The Presence. William Everson. ErPo

Neither of them was better than the other. From Plane to Plane. Robert Frost. MoAmPo

Neither on horseback nor seated. Walt Whitman at Bear Mountain. Louis Simpson. CAPP; LiTM; NePoEA-2; PoCH

Neither our vices nor our virtues. Poetry, a Natural Thing. Robert Duncan. CAPP; NoAM; NOBA

Neither Out Far nor In Deep. Robert Frost. AmPP; ChTr; HAP; LiTA; MoAB; MoP; MOS; NAAL-2; NoAM; NOBA; NoP; TAP; WeW

Neither Poverty nor Riches. Bible, O.T. Fr. Proverbs, XXX: 7-9. TrJP

Neither Shadow of Turning. Jack R. Clemo. NOCV

Neither snow, nor rain. On Their Appointed Rounds. Unknown. FaPON

Neither the actors nor the audience knew what was coming next. Amnesia. David Lehman. EOEF

Neither the harps nor the crowns amused, nor the. The Return of the Children. Kipling. OBD

Neither the interminable patches of land. Like This. Lajos Kassák, tr. by Edwin Morgan. MHuP

Neither the little Jewshops nor the complex wooden churches. Ghost Psalms. Márton Kalász, tr. by Jascha Kessler. FOC

Neither This nor That. Luis Palés Matos, tr. fr. Spanish by Julio Marzán. InW

Neither tribal nor trivial he shouts. Newsboy. Irving Layton. CaP

Neither waking or sleeping. Narihira, *tr. fr. Japanese by* Burton Watson. *Fr.* Kokin Shu. FCEI
Neither will I put myself forward as others may do. Eternal Masculine. William Rose Benét. AWP; MoAmPo
Neither yielding to rain. November 3rd. Miyazawa Kenji, *tr. by* Hiroaki Sato. FCEI
Nell. Raymond Knister. *Fr.* A Row of Stalls. Mes; NOBC; OBCV
Nell Flaherty's Drake. *Unknown.* TW
Nellie Rakerfield. Nell. Raymond Knister. *Fr.* A Row of Stalls. Mes; NOBC; OBCV
Nelly Kelly loved baseball games. Take Me Out to the Ball Game. Jack Norworth. ASP; OBAL
Nelly, methinks, 'twixt thee and me. To a Cat. Hartley Coleridge. FM
Nelly Trim. Sylvia Townsend Warner. ErPo; MoAB; MoBrPo
Nelson, Pitt, Fox. Sir Walter Scott. *Fr.* Marmion, I, *introd.* OBEV
Nelson's Death. *Unknown.* OBET
Nelson's Death and Victory. *Unknown.* OxBSS
Nemea. Emerson. NOBA
Neo-Classical Poem. William Jay Smith. WaP
Neo-Classical Urn, The. Robert Lowell. NAAL-2
Neo-Thomist Poem. Ernest Hemingway. OBAL
Neoplatonic Soliloquy. Donald Campbell Babcock. NePoAm
Nepenthe, *sels.* George Darley.
  Hundred-gated Thebes. NOBE
  In Dreamy Swoon. OBNC
  O Blest Unfabled Incense Tree. BIrV; ChER; FaBoCh; FaBoRV; PBBP
  (Hundred-sunned Phenix.) OBNC
  ("O fast her amber blood doth flow.") OBEV
  (Phoenix, The.) ChTr; NOBE; OAEL-2; WiR
  Onward to Far Ida. OBNC
  "Solitary wayfarer!" PBBP
  (Hoopoe.) OBNC
  Unicorn, The. ChTr; OBNC; PoEL-4
Nephelidia. Swinburne. *Fr.* The Heptalogia. BXAP; FaBoCo; FaBoNo; FaBoPa; HoPM, *first sixteen lines*; NA; Par
Neptune and Mars in council sate. Louisburg. *Unknown.* PAH
Neptune—Polka. Dame Edith Sitwell. NOBE
Neptune Rising. Jane Yolen. BWV
Neptune's Triumph, *sel.* Ben Jonson.
  "Spring all the Graces of the age." OBS
Nereides; or, Sea-Eclogues, *sel.* William Diaper.
  "Lycon begin—begin the mournful tale." SeCePo
Nero ("Nero/ you died"). Tanikawa Shuntaro, *tr. fr. Japanese by* Hiroaki Sato. FCEI
Nerves. David Huddle. *Fr.* Tour of Duty. Son
Nerves. "Sagittarius." OxBTC
Nerves. Arthur Symons. BrPo; FaBoTw
Nervous hose is dribbling on the tar, A. The Roof Garden. Howard Moss. MAT
Nervous Miracles. Jim Gustafson. UL
Nervous Prostration. Anna Wickham. AIW; FaBoWP; TW
Nervy with neons, the main drag. At Barstow. Charles Tomlinson. MoP; NoAM; TwCP
Nessa. Paul Durcan. FaBCIP
Nessie. Ted Hughes. AmMo
Nest, The. Marvin Bell. CAPP
Nest Eggs. Robert Louis Stevenson. FM
Nest in a Wall, A. Richard Murphy. CIP
Nesting. Dennis Saleh. NeAC
Nesting among Clouds. Yang Chi, *tr. fr. Chinese by* Jonathan Chaves. CoBLCP
Nesting Time. Douglas Stewart. PoAu-2
Nestle-down Cottage. Mary Weston Fordham. CBWP-2
Nests well hidden. Secret Places. Irene Thompson. BoTP
Nestus Gurley. Randall Jarrell. HeIP; TwCP
Net, The. Fleur Adcock. ATNZ; PeNZ
Net, The. W. R. Rodgers. AnIL; BoLoP; CIP; ErPo
Net, The. Joseph Rolnik, *tr. fr. Yiddish by* Irving Feldman. PeBMYV
Net and the Sword, The. Douglas Le Pan. NOBC
Net for a Night Raven, A. *Unknown.* OxBSS
Net Menders, The. Brian Vrepont. PoAu-2
Net of Moon, The. Mitchell, *tr. fr. Pawnee Indian by* Jerome Rothenberg. STP
Net rests on the water's surface, The. Elena Clementelli, *tr. fr. Italian by* Ruth Feldman and Brian Swann. *Fr.* Etruscan Notebook. PBWP
Net to Snare the Moonlight, A. Vachel Lindsay. PoLF
Netherlands, The. Samuel Taylor Coleridge. OBTV
Netley Abbey. William Lisle Bowles. Son

Netley Abbey; Midnight. William Sotheby. NOEC
Nets are real, The—heroin (sniffed) clears them. For Artaud. Michael McClure. NeAP
Nets to Catch the Wind. John Webster. *See* Devil's Law Case, The: All the Flowers of the Spring.
Netting. Jorie Graham. NPGG
Nettles, The. Thomas Hardy. OxBSP
Nettles. Neil Munro. PoSH
Nettles in May. Euros Bowen, *tr. fr. Welsh by the author.* OBWVE
Network, The. Robert Finch. CaP
Network, The. Arthur Sze. AiP
Neural Folds. Lucille Day. BWV
Neurasthenia. Agnes Mary Frances Robinson. NOBVV
Neurophysiologist, The. Jonathan V. Post. BWV
Neutral, The. Wrenne Jarman. CN
Neutral British Gentleman, The. "Orpheus C. Kerr." OBAL
Neutral Tones. Thomas Hardy. BrPo; CMoP; EBVV; HAP; HeIP; InPK; InPS; MoBrPo; MoP; NAEL-2; NoAM; NOBVV; OAEL-2; PPP; TEP; UnPo
Neutrality. Sidney Keyes. MoAB; MoBrPo
Neutrality Loathsome. Robert Herrick. LiTB; NoP
Neutrinos. Georgette Perry. BWV
Nevada. Lawrence Gurney. GoYe
Never. Afanasi Afanasievich Fet, *tr. fr. Russian by* Alan Myers. AAA
Never. Kurt Klinger, *tr. fr. German by* Beth Bjorklund. CoAuP
Never. George Reavey. BIrV
Never a beak has my white bird. Thistle-Down. Clara Doty Bates. AA
Never a careworn wife but shows. Wives in the Sere. Thomas Hardy. BrPo; NOBE; NOBVV
Never a trial that He is not there. Moment by Moment. Daniel W Whittle. BLRP
Never Admit the Pain. Mary Gilmore. PoAu-1
Never afflict yourself to know the cause. Refrain. Mary Jo Salter. EOEF
Never afraid of those huge creatures. Horseback. Carolyn Kizer. ASP
Never Again, The. Charles Dobzynski, *tr. fr. French by* Anita Barrows. VWA
Never Again. Richard Henry Stoddard. *See* There Are Gains for All Our Losses.
Never again, Orpheus. Antipater of Sidon, *tr. fr. Greek by* Kenneth Rexroth. OBVE
Never again shall we beat out to sea. Fiddler's Green. Theodore Goodridge Roberts. CaP
Never Again Would Birds' Song Be the Same. Robert Frost. FYAP; HAP; InPK; NIP; NoAM; NoP; Son; VGW
Never and never, my girl riding far and near. In Country Sleep. Dylan Thomas. LiTB
Never another garden where the clock. The Seventh Garden. Sándor Weöres, *tr. by* Daniel Hoffman. MHuP
Never Ask Me Why. Silvia Margolis. GoYe
Never ask of money spent. The Hardship of Accounting. Robert Frost. FaBoCh; FaBoCo; FaFP; OBAL
Never Be As Fast As I Have Been. Robert Hahn. ASP
Never believe all you hear. Wolf. Kenneth Rexroth. *Fr.* A Bestiary. NNaP
Never believe I leave you. Hiding Our Love. Carolyn Kizer. UnAS
Never, believe me/ Appear the Immortals. The Visit of the Gods. Schiller, *tr. by* Samuel Taylor Coleridge. OBVE
Never can I forget the words. Hasetsukabe Inamaro. *Fr.* Manyo Shu. Ma
Never consider yourself. Obligations of the Poet. Giaconda Belli, *tr. by* Barbara Paschke. Vol
Never could I think/ Our love a worldly commonplace. Izumi Shikibu, *tr. fr. Japanese by* Edwin A. Cranston. PBWP
Never do I doubt your heart. *Unknown. Fr.* Manyo Shu. Ma
Never forget this when the talk is clever. The Sacred Order. May Sarton. ImOP
Never forget who brings the rain. Turn of the Moon. Robert Graves. TEP
Never Give a Bum an Even Break. James Welch. NoAM
Never Give All the Heart. W. B. Yeats. BoLoP; CMoP
Never have I seen the sky more clear. Depressed by the Death of the Horse That He Bought from Robert Bly. Henry Taylor. BXAP
Never, in all your career of worrying, did you imagine. The Flying Cat. Naomi Shihab Nye. TDD
Never in My Life. Walter McDonald. MT
Never May the Fruit Be Plucked. Edna St. Vincent Millay. NAAL-2; OxBSP
Never mind avarice; the hills. Thinking of Hölderlin. Christopher Middleton. NePoEA-2

Never mind the clouds which gather. I Have Always Found It So. Birdie Bell. BLRP

Never mind the day we left, or the way the women clung to us. The Klondike. E. A. Robinson. PAH

Never More, Sailor. Walter de la Mare. MOS

Never more will the wind. Hilda Doolittle ("H. D."). *Fr.* Hymen. CTC; TrGrPo

Never, Never Can Nothingness Come. Norma Keating. GoYe

Never, never let your gun. A Rule for Shooting. *Unknown.* FaBoUs

Never, never may the fruit be plucked from the bough. Never May the Fruit Be Plucked. Edna St. Vincent Millay. NAAL-2; OxBSP

Never on this side of the grave again. A Life's Parallels. Christina Rossetti. NAEL-2; PoEL-5

Never once—since the world began. God's Sunshine. John Oxenham. WBLP

Never Pain to Tell Thy Love. Blake. *See* Never Seek to Tell Thy Love.

Never pass a nun. How to Walk in a Crowd. Robert Hershon. FF

Never presume that in this marble stable. The Brass Horse. Drummond Allison. FaBoTw

Never reaching the promised land in Canada. A Tribute to Chief Joseph. Duane Niatum. NOVW

Never Really. Stanislaw Baranczak, *tr. fr. Polish by* Magnus Jan Krynski *and* Robert A. Maguire. PwPP

Never Said a Mumbalin' Word. *Unknown.* GBP

Never saw him. The Negro. James A. Emanuel. HoPM; InPK

Never Say Fail. *Unknown.* PWR

Never Seek to Tell Thy Love. John Ashbery. HCAP; InPS

Never Seek to Tell Thy Love. Blake. ChER; ELP; EnLoPo; EnRP; FaBV; InPS; NOBE; OBNC; PoEL-4

(Never Pain to Tell Thy Love.) NAEL-2; OAEL-2

"Never shall a young man." For Anne Gregory. W. B. Yeats. CMoP; CMoP; FaFP; LiTM; NAEL–2; SOTW

Never so much befuddled. Thirteen White Chrysanthemums. Chou Meng-tieh, *tr. by* Dominic Cheung. IFON

Never Such Love. Robert Graves. BoLoP

Never take her away. Vinícius de Moraes, *tr. by* Richard Wilbur. ATCBP

Never talk down to a glowworm. Glowworm. David McCord. NTCP

Never Tell. *Unknown, tr. fr. Welsh by* Anthony Conran. OBWVE

Never the Time and the Place. Robert Browning. EnLoPo

Never the tramp of foot or horse. Farewell to Anactoria. Sappho, *tr. by* Allen Tate. AWP

Never think she loves him wholly. Appraisal. Sara Teasdale. MoAmPo

Never think you fortune can bear the sway. On Fortune. Elizabeth I, Queen of England. PBWP; WPE

Never to be lonely like that. Face to Face. Adrienne Rich. LiTM; NAAL-2; NoAM; NoP

Never to see a nation born. James Russell Lowell. *Fr.* Under the Old Elm, VII. GOA

Never to see ghosts? Then to be. Ghosts. Alastair Reid. NYBP

Never Too Late, *sels.* Robert Greene.

Infida's Song. OBSC

Palmer's Ode, The. CTC; OBSC

Never turn your back on the sea. A Dead Lamb. Allen Curnow. ATNZ

Never twice that river. By the River Eden. Kathleen Jessie Raine. NYBP

Never until the mankind making. A Refusal to Mourn the Death, by Fire, of a Child in London. Dylan Thomas. BLPL; CMoP; EBEV; FaBoMo; FaFP; FF; GTBS-P; HeIP; HoPM; LiTB; LiTM; MoAB; MoBrPo; MoP; NoAM; NOBE; NoP; OAEL-2; OBWVE; OxBTC; PoE; SeCePo; TEP; TwCP; UnPo; WaaP

Never we needed Thee so sore. In Time of Need. Katharine Tynan. TrPWD

Never Weather-beaten Sail[e]. Thomas Campion. ChTr; ElL; OAEL-1; OBSC; OxBSP; PoEL-2

(O Come Quickly!) NOBE; OBEV

Never will I forget the days when father waited for me on the horizon. A Stray Bird's Homeland. Liu K'o-hsiang, *tr. by* Dominic Cheung. IFON

Never Will I Hear the Sweet Voice of God. Yona Wallach, *tr. fr. Hebrew by* Warren Bargad *and* Stanley F. Chyet. IP

Never will I leave you. Never. Kurt Klinger, *tr. by* Beth Bjorklund. CoAuP

Never yet was a springtime. Awakening. Margaret E. Sangster. AA

Nevermore/ Shall the shepherds of Arcady follow. The God-Maker, Man. Don Marquis. WGRP

Nevertheless. Gustav Davidson. GoYe

Nevertheless. Marianne Moore. CMoP; MoAB; NAAL-2; OxBA; SoSe

Nevertheless I prefer. . .1968. . . Petra von Morstein, *tr. by* Rosemarie Waldrop. BoWoP

Nevertheless you've seen a strawberry. Nevertheless. Marianne Moore. CMoP; MoAB; NAAL-2; OxBA; SoSe

New Age. Keorapetse Kgositsile. WMBCH

New Age, The. Stevie Smith. NAEL-2

New Ahasuerus, The. Jozsef Kiss, *tr. fr. Hungarian by* André Ungar. VWA

New air has come around us. Dakota: October, 1822, Hunkpapa Warrior. Rod Taylor. WeW

New Ancient of Days, The. Herman Melville. OBAL

New and Old Gospel. Nate Mackey. CNA

New Apartment, Minneapolis, The. Linda Hogan. ER; HATNAP

New Approach Needed. Kingsley Amis. NoAM; OxBTC

New Arrival, The. George Washington Cable. AA

New Ballad, A. Arthur Mainwaring. APAS

New Ballad, A ("I am a senseless thing"). *Unknown.* APAS

New Ballad, A ("Rouse, Britons! at length"). *Unknown.* PAH

New Ballad of Sir Patrick Spens, The. Sir Arthur Quiller-Couch. BXAP

New Ballad, to an Old Tune, Called, I Am the Duke of Norfolk, etc, A. *Unknown.* APAS

New Ballade of the Marigolde, A. William Forrest. CoMu

New Balow, The. *Unknown.* CoMu

New Bath Guide, The, *sel.* Christopher Anstey.

"Hearken, Lady Betty, hearken." NOEC

New Birth, The. Jones Very. NOBA

New-born moon gives little light, The. To the Tune "New Moon." Yang Shen, *tr. by* Jonathan Chaves. CoBLCP

New Brooms. Robert Wilson. *Fr.* The Three Ladies of London. ElL (Conscience's Song.) OBSC

New Bundling Song, A. *Unknown.* ErPo

New Bury Loom, The. *Unknown.* OBET

New Canaans Genius; Epilogus. Thomas Morton. SCAP

New Castalia, The. William Hayes Ward. AA

New Catch in Praise of the Reverend Bishops, A. *Unknown.* APAS

New Cecilia, The. Thomas Lovell Beddoes. OAEL-2

New Chitons for Old Gods, *sel.* David McCord.

Euterpe; a Symmetric. UnS

New-Chum's First Trip, The. *Unknown.* FaBoBa

New Church Organ, The. Will M. Carleton. PoLF

New Coasts and Poseidon's Son. Homer, *tr. fr. Greek by* Robert Fitzgerald. *Fr.* Odyssey, IX. WTO

New Colossus, The. Emma Lazarus. AiP; AmFN; FaBV; FaFP; FaPON; FPL; OPP; PoLF; PrIm; Son; WPE

New Colour in the Colour of Sunlight, A. Munir Niazi, *tr. fr. Urdu by* Mahmood Jamal. PBMUP

New-come buckra/ He get sick. *Unknown.* *Fr.* Songs, I. PBCV

New-come Chief, The. James Russell Lowell. *Fr.* Under the Old Elm, III. PAH

New Courtly Sonnet of the Lady Greensleeves, A. *Unknown.* *See* Greensleeves.

New Cup and Saucer, A. Gertrude Stein. *Fr.* Tender Buttons. TTTS

New Dance, A. S. E. Anderson. NBP

New-dated from the terms that reappear. To Oxford. Gerard Manley Hopkins. BrPo; FaBoPP

New Day, The, *sels.* Richard Watson Gilder.

"Night was dark, though sometimes a faint star, The." PoLF

"Not from the whole wide world I chose thee." AA

"Years have flown since I knew thee first." AA

New Day, The. Fenton Johnson. BANP

New Day. Naomi Long Madgett. BlSi

New Dial, The. *Unknown.* OBET

New Diary, A. Dannie Abse. NoAM

New Direction, The. Emerson Blackhorse Mitchell. NOVW

New doth the sun appear. Change Should Breed Change. William Drummond of Hawthornden. OBEV

New Dress, A. Rachel Korn, *tr. fr. Yiddish by* Ruth Whitman. VWA

New Duckling, The. Alfred Noyes. BoTP; FaPON

New Dust. Eleanor Ross Taylor. PFR

New Emigration, The. Kay Boyle. WPE

New England. James Gates Percival. AA

New England. George Denison Prentice. AA

New England. E. A. Robinson. GOA; HeIP; MoAB; MoAmPo; NAAL-2; NOBA; NoP; OxBA; TAP

New England Bachelor, A. Richard Eberhart. MoAmPo; NoAM

New-England Boy's Song about Thanksgiving Day, The. Lydia Maria Child. *See* Thanksgiving Day.

New England Church, A. Wilson Agnew Barrett. WGRP

New England Interlude. Madeline DeFrees. PPR

New England Is New England Is New England. Brenda Heloise Green. GoYe

New England Primer, The, *sels.* *Unknown.*

"In Adam's fall/ We sinned all." OBCA

(ABC, An.) GBP
John Rogers' Exhortation to His Children. OBCA
New England Sampler, A. John Malcolm Brinnin. GOA
New England, Springtime. Norman Dubie. NAmP
New England Verses, sel. Wallace Stevens.
   Statue against a Clear Sky. EyDe
New England's Annoyances. Unknown. PAH
   (Old Song, Wrote by One of Our First New-England Planters, An.)
   SCAP
New England's Chevy Chase. Edward Everett Hale. PAH
New-Englands Crisis. Benjamin Tompson. SCAP
New England's Dead! Isaac McLellan, Jr.. AA
New England's Growth. William Bradford. PAH
New English Canaan; Prologue. Thomas Morton. SCAP
New every morning. John Keble. FaPoR
   (Hymn: "New every morning is thy love.")
   (Morning Hymn.) NOCV
New every morning is the love. Prime. Donald Davie. Fr. Horae
   Canonicae. CRP
New every morning now the clerk docks off. Summer Holidays.
   William Robert Rodgers. LiTB
New Ezekiel, The. Emma Lazarus. AA
New Face. Alice Walker. AIW
New Faces, The. W. B. Yeats. GTBS-P
New Farm Tractor. Carl Sandburg. FaPON
New-fashioned Farmer, The. Unknown. OBET
New Fashions. George Moses Horton. OBAL
New follies spring; and now we must be taught. Picturesque; a Fragment.
   John Aikin. NOEC
New Friends and Old Friends. Joseph Parry. BLPA; BLPL
New Garden Fields. Unknown. OBET
New Genesis, A. Avraham Shlonsky, tr. fr. Hebrew by Francis Landy.
   VWA
New God, The. Witter Bynner. Fr. The New World. WGRP
New God, The. James Oppenheim. WGRP
New Graveyard: Jerusalem. Shirley Kaufman. VWA
New Guinea. James McAuley. NOCV; PoAu-2
New Guinea Time. Louis Johnson. ATNZ; PeNZ
New Hampshire. T. S. Eliot. Fr. Landscapes, I. FaBoCh; GTBS-P;
   NoAM; RB; WeW
New Hampshire. Donald Hall. LCAP; NePoEA-2
New Hampshire Farm Woman. Rachel Graham. GoYe
New Hampshire, February. Richard Eberhart. LiTM; TwCP
New Heart, The. Unknown, tr. fr. Chinese. WGRP
New Heaven and Earth. D. H. Lawrence. CMoP
New Heaven, New War [re]. Robert Southwell. MePo; NOBE; NoP;
   OBSC
New Holland is a barren place, in it there grows no grain. The Lowlands
   of Holland. Unknown. OxBB
New home at the mouth of Meng-ch'eng, A. Meng-ch'eng Hollow.
   Wang Wei, tr. fr. Chinese by Burton Watson. Fr. Twenty Views of
   Wang-ch'uan, 1. CoBCP
New House, A. Bertolt Brecht, tr. fr. German by Michael Hamburger.
   AnAn
New House, The. Joseph Easton McDougall. CaP
New House. Rai San'yo, tr. fr. Chinese by Burton Watson. FCEI;
   JLIC-2
New House, The. Vern Rutsala. GOYP
New House, The. Edward Thomas. EBEV; MoAB; MoBrPo; NOBE;
   OBEV; OBWVE
New Household, A. Longfellow. Fr. The Hanging of the Crane. GN
New Hunting Song, A. Unknown. CoMu; OBET
New Hymns for Solitude, sel. Edward Dowden.
   "I found Thee in my heart, O Lord." TrPWD
New Improved Sonnet XVIII. Peter Titheradge. FaBoPa
New Indian Medicine. Emma Lee Warrior. HATNAP
New Inn, The, sel. Ben Jonson.
   It Was a Beauty That I Saw. OBS
   (Lovel's Song.) TrGrPo
New Jail. Unknown. AmFP
New Jersey. Will Bennett. UL
New Jersey Turnpike. Richard Cumbie. NBLV
New Jersey White-tailed Deer. Joyce Carol Oates. GeTw
New Jerusalem, A. Blake. See Milton: And Did Those Feet in Ancient
   Time.
New Jerusalem, The. Bible, N.T. Fr. Revelation, XXI: 1-6, 10-12, 21,
   23-25. TrGrPo
New Jerusalem, The. Unknown. See Hierusalem, my happy [or happie]
   home.
New Jewish Hospital at Hamburg, The. Heine, tr. fr. German by Charles
   Godfrey Leland. TrJP

New Journey, A. Javier Heraud, tr. fr. Spanish by Maureen Ahern. Per
"New King Arrives in His Capital by Air. "—Daily Newspaper. Sir John
   Betjeman. NOBE; OxBoLi
   (Death of King George V.) NOBE; OxBS
New Lady Barber at Ralph's Barber Shop, The. Leo Dangel. MOWH
New Leaf, A. Kathleen Wheeler. BLRP; WBLP
New Life. Joseph E. Kariuki. TTY
New Light, A. William Hawkins. MoCV
New light gives new directions, fortunes new. Chapman. Fr. Hero and
   Leander, Third Sestiad. OAEL-1
New Lines for Cuscuscaraway and Mirza Murad Ali Beg. Louis Simpson.
   OBAL
New Litany, The. Rita Mae Brown. PeHV
New Litany in the Year 1684, A. Unknown. APAS
New London, The. Dryden. Fr. Annus Mirabilis. FaBoCh; OBS
   (London.) SeCePo
   (London after the Great Fire, 1666.) NOBE
New Man, The. Jones Very. NOBA
New man flies in from Manchester, A. A New Poet Arrives. Gavin
   Ewart. OxBTC
New Manong, The. Luis Syquia. BrSi
New Married Couple; or, A Friendly Debate between the Country Farmer
   and His Buxome Wife, The. Unknown. CoMu
New Maths. Tom Lehrer. FaBoUs
New mercies, new blessings, new light on the way. A New Year Wish.
   Frances Ridley Havergal. BLRP
New Mexican Mountain. Robinson Jeffers. GOA; InPS; MoP; NoAM
New Mistress, The. A. E. Housman. Fr. A Shropshire Lad, XXXIV.
   MoBrPo
New Moon, The. Edmund Blunden. BrPo
New Moon. D. H. Lawrence. BoNaP
New Moon. Aborigine Oral Tradition. Fr. Moon-Bone Song [or Cycle].
   WTO
New moon hangs like an ivory bugle, The. The Penny Whistle. Edward
   Thomas. MoAB; MoBrPo
New moon hung in the sky, The. Prescience. Thomas Bailey Aldrich.
   AA
New moon, new moon, I hail thee! Unknown. FaBoUs
New moon, of no importance, The. New Moon. D. H. Lawrence.
   BoNaP
New Morality, sel. George Canning and John Hookham Frere.
   "From mental mists to purge a nation's eyes." NOEC
New-mown hay smell and wind of the plain. Population Drifts. Carl
   Sandburg. OxBA
New Music. Gwen Harwood. CBAP
New National Hymn. Francis Marion Crawford. PAH
New Navigation, The. John Freeth. OBET
New Negro, The. James Edward McCall. CDC
New Night Thoughts on Death; a Parody. William Whitehead. NOEC
New Noah, The. "Adunis", tr. fr. Arabic by Abdullah al-Udhari.
   MPAO
New Notebook, The. Maria Banus, tr. fr. Rumanian by Laura Schiff and
   Dana Beldiman. AIW; PBWP
New Nutcracker Suite, The, sel. Ogden Nash.
   "Little girl marched around her Christmas tree, A." PChr
New Order, The. Phyllis McGinley. AmFN
New Order of Chivalry, A. Thomas Love Peacock. CenHV
New Organ, The. Josephine D. Henderson Heard. CBWP-4
New Orleans. Hayden Carruth. AmFN
New Orleans. Joy Harjo. HATNAP; STE
New Pastoral, The, sel. Thomas Buchanan Read.
   Blennerhassett's Island. PAH
New Physics, The. Al Zolynas. BWV
New Pietà: For the Mothers and Children of Detroit, The. June Jordan.
   PoBA
New Platform Dances, The. Jack A. Mapanje. WMBCH
New Poem, A. Robert Duncan. NNaP; PoM
New Poem, The. Charles Wright. CAPP; GeTw; HCAP
New Poet Arrives, A. Gavin Ewart. OxBTC
New Potatoes. Ken Belford. NeAC
New Prince, New Pomp. Robert Southwell. ELP; GN; NOBE; NOCV;
   OBSC; OHIP; TrCP
New Proverb. Shirley Brooks. FaBoNo
New Reality Is Better Than a New Movie!, A. Imamu Amiri Baraka.
   NoAM
New Republic, The. Marcelin Pleynet, tr. fr. French by John Ashbery.
   RHTwFP
New Republic Is Infuriated at the News Coverage, The. George Starbuck.
   BLA
New River Head, a Fragment, The. E. Dower. NOEC
New road runs into, The. Directions. William Matthews. AmPA

New Romance. Nellie Wong. BrSi
New Roof, The. Francis Hopkinson. PAH
New Saddhus, The. Robert Pinsky. MAYP
New Sea Song. *Unknown.* OxBSS
New Season. Michael S. S. Harper. CAPP
New season brought sure the visible good. Restoration. Woodridge
  Spears. GoYe
New Shakespeare, A. Andrew Lang. CenHV
"New Shirt, A!" Why? Paul Grano. PoAu-2
New shoes, new shoes. Choosing Shoes. ffrida Wolfe. PYC
New Sights. *Unknown.* BoTP
New-silver-crescented the moon forth came. The New Moon. Edmund
  Blunden. BrPo
New-slain Knight, The. *Unknown.* ESPB
New Song, A. Seamus Heaney. CIP; FaBoTw
New Song, A. Joseph Stansbury. PAH
New Song, A. Thomas, Lord Wharton. *See* Lilli Burleo [*or*
  Lilliburlero].
New Song, A. *Unknown.* PAH
New Song called The Curling of the Hair, A. *Unknown.* CoMu
New Song, Called the Frolicsome Sea Captain; or, Tit for Tat, A.
  Unknown. OxBSS
New Song Called the Gaspee, A. *Unknown.* PAH
New Song Called the *Victory*, A. *Unknown.* OxBSS
New Song Composed on the Death of Lord Nelson, A. *Unknown.* *See*
  Death of Nelson, The.
New Song Entitled the Warming Pan, A. *Unknown.* CoMu
New Song of an Orange, A. *Unknown.* CoMu
New Song of Mary, A. *Unknown.* MeEL
New Song of New Similies, A. John Gay. FaBoCo; NOBL
New Song of Wood's Halfpence, A. *At. to* Swift. OxBoLi
New Song on the Birth of the Prince of Wales, A. *Unknown.* CoMu;
  FaBoBa; NOBVV
New Song on the *Blandford* Privateer, A. *Unknown.* OxBSS
New Song on the Taxes, A. *Unknown.* WTO
New Song on the Total Defeat of the French Fleet, A,. *Unknown.*
  OxBSS
New Song to an Old Tune, A. *Unknown.* PAH
New Spoon River, The, *sels.* Edgar Lee Masters.
  Benjamin Franklin Hazard. GOA
  Marx the Sign Painter. NoAM; TAP
  Meredith Phyfe. GOA
  Unknown Soldiers. NoAM; TAP
  Willis Beggs. SaC
New Spring, A. Albert D. Mackie. OxBS
New Storefront. Russell Atkins. FB
New Story, A. Simon J. Ortiz. STE
New Strain. George Starbuck. TwCP
New Style, The. David O'Bruadair, *tr. fr. Irish by* John Montague.
  BIrV
New Tenants, The. E. A. Robinson. NoAM
New Testament, The. *Unknown.* FaBoUs
New Thatched Hall, A. Po Chü-i, *tr. fr. Chinese by* Burton Watson.
  CoBCP
New ties, fifteen each, ten. Ties. Raymond Souster. MoCV; OBCV
New Time. *Unknown.* BLRP
New Vestments, The. Edward Lear. NOBVV; RHPC
New Vicar of Bray, The. Colin Ellis. NOBL
New Victory, The. Margaret Widdemer. WGRP
New Vintage, The. Douglas Le Pan. OBCV
New volcano has erupted, A. Crusoe in England. Elizabeth Bishop.
  HCAP
New War Song by Sir Peter Parker, A. *Unknown.* PAH
New Way, Old Way. David W. Martinez. NOVW
New Wife. *Gond Oral Tradition, tr. by* V. Elwin *and* S. Hivale. WTO
New Wings for Icarus, *sel.* Henry Beissel.
  "In the one-two domestic goose one-two one-two step." MoCV
New Words, *sel.* Coleman Barks.
  "So it is." CRP
New World, The. Imamu Amiri Baraka. NoAM; NoP
New World, The, *sel.* Louis James Block.
  Final Struggle, The. PAH
New World, The, *sel.* Witter Bynner.
  New God, The. WGRP
New World, The. Paul Engle. AmFN
New World, The, *sel.* Edgar Lee Masters.
  "This America is an ancient land." AmFN
New World, A. Shelley. *See* Hellas: Choruses from "Hellas."
New World, The. Jones Very. AA
New World. Derek Walcott. OxBC
New world/ artful as monkeys, A. Ray DiPalma. *Fr.* Planh, V. IAT

New World in the Morning. Norman German. TSL
New World Symphony, A. Kit Wright. NBLV
New Worlds. Milton. *See* Paradise Lost:
  As when a Scout/ through dark and desart wayes with peril gone.
New Worlds for Old. Louis Johnson. ATNZ
New Year. Nazik Al-Mala'ika, *tr. fr. Arabic by* Abdullah al-Udhari.
  MPAW
New Year. Alfred Corn. BAP
New Year, The. Charles Cotton. GoTL; OBS
New Year. Gail N. Harada. BrSi
New Year, The. Homera Homer-Dixon. BLRP
New Year. Naomi Shihab Nye. MT
New Year. Stephen Spender. AWP
New Year, The. Mark Strand. *Fr.* Elegy for My Father. UnPo
New Year, The ("I am the little New Year"). *Unknown.* BoTP
New Year, The ("Oh! I'm the New Year"). *Unknown.* BoTP
New Year Carol, A. *Unknown.* BoTP; CH; OxBoLi
  (New Year, The.) OBCP
  (New Year's Water.) GBP; OFD
New Year for Trees, The. Howard Schwartz. VWA
New year has dawned and we meet it with gladness, The. New Year's
  Morning; or, the First Day of the Year. Mrs. Henry Linden.
  CBWP-4
New Year Letter, *sels.* W. H. Auden.
  "Long time since it seems to-day, A." GOA
  "Our news is seldom good: the heart." FaBoRV
New Year on Dartmoor. Sylvia Plath. FaBoWP
New Year Wish, A. Frances Ridley Havergal. BLRP
New Year Wish, A. *Unknown.* BLRP
New yeares, expect new gifts: Sister, your Harpe. Ben Jonson. SeCP
New-Yeares-Gift Sung to King Charles, 1635, A. Ben Jonson. SeCP
New Year's ("Solid houses in the mist, The."), *sel.* Charles Reznikoff.
  VGW
"This is the autumn and our harvest." OFD
New Year's Blizzard, The. Su Tung-p'o, *tr. fr. Chinese by* Burton
  Watson. CoBCP
New Year's Carol. *Unknown.* OBET
New Year's Day/ Dawns clear, and sparrows. Ransetsu, *tr. by* Geoffrey
  Bownas *and* Anthony Thwaite. PeBJV
New Year's Day. Richard Crashaw. JCP
New Year's Day. Robert Lowell. AmPP; LiTM; NePoEA
New Year's Day. Rai San'yo, *tr. fr. Chinese by* Burton Watson. JLIC-2
New Years Day at the Official Lodge. Michizane, *tr. fr. Chinese by*
  Burton Watson. JLIC-1
New Year's Day—Following the Rhymes of Inspector Luan-chiang. Pien
  Kung, *tr. fr. Chinese by* Jonathan Chaves. CoBLCP
New Year's Days. Celia Standish. BoTP
New Year's Eve. John Berryman. LiTM
New Year's Eve, *sel.* John Davidson.
  Imagination. MoBrPo
New Year's Eve. Thomas Hardy. MoBrPo; NoAM
New Year's Eve. D. H. Lawrence. BoLoP; ErPo
New Year's Eve. Liu E, *tr. fr. Chinese by* Jonathan Chaves. CoBLCP
New Year's Eve. Herbert B. Mallalieu. WaP
New Year's Eve. Su Tung-p'o, *tr. fr. Chinese by* Burton Watson.
  CoBCP
New Year's Eve. Wen Cheng-ming, *tr. fr. Chinese by* Jonathan Chaves.
  CoBLCP
New Year's Eve in Solitude. Robert Mezey. NaP; VWA
New Year's Eve in the Year *Keng-tzu*. Chu Hsiao-tsang, *tr. fr. Chinese
  by* Li Chi *and* Michael Patrick O'Connor. WFTU
New Year's Eve in Troy. Adrienne Rich. NePoEA-2
New-Year's Gift Sent to Sir Simeon Steward, A. Robert Herrick. CaPo
New-Years-Gift to Brian Lord Bishop of Sarum, A. William Cartwright.
  MePo
New Year's morning. After the Gentle Poet Kobayashi Issa. Robert
  Hass. GeTw
New Year's Morning; or, the First Day of the Year. Mrs. Henry Linden.
  CBWP-4
New Year's Poem. Margaret Avison. LiTM; NOBC; OBCV
New Year's Promise, A. *Unknown.* BLRP
New Year's Sacrifice: To Lucinda, A. Thomas Carew. CaPo
New Year's [*or* Year] Song. Ted Hughes. OBCP; OFD
New Year's Water. *Unknown.* *See* New Year Carol, A.
New Year's Wish, A. "J. H. S." BLRP
New Year's Wishes. Frances Ridley Havergal. BLRP
New-Yeeres Gift, or Circumcisions Song, Sung to the King in the Presence
  at White Hall, The. Robert Herrick. SeCV-1
New York. "Æ." OBMV
New York. Federico García Lorca, *tr. fr. Spanish by* Robert Bly. NU

New York, *sels*. A. Leyeles, *tr. fr. Yiddish* by Benjamin *and* Barbara Harshav. AYP
  Evening.
  In the Subway ("Rush hour").
  In the Subway ("Wall, A").
  In the Subway ("Walled-in").
  Madison Square.
  Manhattan Bridge.
  Night.
  On Broadway.
  Wall Street.
New York. William Logan. EOEF
New York. Marianne Moore. NAAL-2
New York! At first I was confused by your beauty, by those great golden long-legged girls. To New York. Léopold Sédar-Senghor, *tr.* by Ulli Beier. PBA
New York City. George Abbe. GoYe
New York City—1935. Gregory Corso. Psk
New York—December, 1931. Babette Deutsch. ImOP
New York Everywhere, *sels.* Berysh Vaynshteyn, *tr. fr. Yiddish* by Benjamin *and* Barbara Harshav. AYP
  Division Street.
  Junk.
  Mangin Street.
  New York Everywhere.
  People Who Talk to Themselves.
  Sheep in New York.
New York in a Jewish Mood. Judah Leib Teller, *tr. fr. Yiddish* by Benjamin *and* Barbara Harshav. AYP
New York Landscapes. Judah Leib Teller, *tr. fr. Yiddish* by Benjamin *and* Barbara Harshav. AYP
New York, Summer. Jack Gilbert. NPGG
New York Woman, The. L. E. Sissman. MAT
New York's lovely weather. Bean Spasms. Ted Berrigan. EAS
New Zealand. James Keir Baxter. NoP
Newark Abbey. Thomas Love Peacock. NOBE; OBNC
Newark, for Now (68). Carolyn M. Rodgers. PoBA
Newberry. *Unknown*. AmFP
Newborn greylag geese follow anyone who moves. The Romance of Imprinting. Christy Sheffield Sanford. UL
Newborn Neurological Exam. Mary Baron. MOWH
Newborn, on the naked sand. Song for the Newborn. *Unknown, tr.* by Mary Austin. OFD; WPE
Newcomers. Abraham Reisen, *tr. fr. Yiddish* by Keith Bosley. VWA
Newcomer's Wife, The. Thomas Hardy. BoLoP; OxBTC
Newes from Virginia. Richard Rich. PAH
Newest Banana Plant Leaf, The. Ingrid Wendt. NMM
Newgate's Garland. John Gay. FaBoBa
Newsletter from My Mother. Michael S. Harper. PoBA
Newly Discovered "Homeric" Hymn, A. Charles Olson. MoP; NeAP; NoAM; PoM
Newly Pressed Suit, The. Roger McGough. MoP
Newly shaven, your eyes only slightly bloodshot. Desires. Connie Bensley. FaBoWP
Newlyweds, The. Cloyd Mann Criswell. PoLF
Newmarket Song, The. *Unknown*. APAS
Newness. Tom Paulin. FaBCIP
News. Louis Dudek. *Fr.* Provincetown. MoCV
News, The. Tuini Ngawai, *tr. fr. Maori* by Kumeroa Ngoingoi Pewhairangi. PeNZ
News, The. John Godfrey Saxe. NBLV
News. Dennis Schmitz. NPGG
News, The. Charles Sprague. *Fr.* Curiosity. AA
News. Thomas Traherne. *Fr.* The Third Century. MePo; NOBE; OBEV; SeCV-2
  (On News.) QFR
News & the Weather, The. Rika Lesser. MAYP
News for the Delphic Oracle. W. B. Yeats. CMoP; FaBoMo; LiTB; LiTM; NoAM
News from a foreign [*or* forein *or* forrein] country came. News. Thomas Traherne. *Fr.* The Third Century. MePo; NOBE; OBEV; SeCV-2
  (On News.) QFR
News from a Pacified Area. James Keir Baxter. OxBC
News from abroad does a secret reveal, The. An Excellent New Song Called "Mat's Peace." Arthur Mainwaring. APAS
News from Actium, about the outcome of the sea-battle, was of course unexpected, The. In a Township of Asia Minor. C. P. Cavafy, *tr.* by Edmund Keeley *and* Philip Sherrard. VMG
News from Mount Amiata. Robert Lowell. NaP, *ad. from the Italian of* Eugenio Montale

News from Norwood. Christopher Middleton. FaBoMo; NePoEA-2
News from Paris. Charles Spear. ATNZ
News from the Basement Laundromat. G. N. Gabbard. SoTCo
News from the Cabin. May Swenson. NYBP
News from the Court. David Wagoner. NePoEA-2
News from the heavens! All wars are at an end. Rare News. Nicholas Breton. NIP
News from the House. Michael Dennis Browne. NYBP
News from Yorktown. Lewis Worthington Smith. PAH
News, Indeed!—pray do you call it news, The. The News. John Godfrey Saxe. NBLV
News is of camps, outpost, little progress, The. Lecturing on the Theme of Motherhood. Michael S. Harper. AnAn
News Item. Dorothy Parker. *Fr.* Some Beautiful Letters. FaBoUs; OBAL
News lapped at us out of all, The. The Sirens. Donald Finkel. NePoEA
News of Old Girls. Elizabeth Baines. NPo
News of the Occluded Cyclone. Alice Fulton. NAmP
News of the palace. Lady Ise, *tr.* by Etsuko Terasaki *and* Irma Brandeis. BoWoP
News of the Phoenix. A. J. M. Smith. MoCV
News of the World I ("Cold shuttered loveless star, skulker in clouds"). George Barker. LiTB
News of the World III. George Barker. FaBoTw; LiTB; LiTM
News of the World II. George Barker. FaBoTw; LiTB
News Reel. David Ross. GoYe
News Report. David Ignatow. ErPo; TwCP
News That Stays News. Paul Mariani. BLA; GeTw
News, The! our morning, noon, and evening cry. The News. Charles Sprague. *Fr.* Curiosity. AA
Newsboy. Irving Layton. CaP
Newspaper appears in the morning, The. Khalifa al-Wugayyan, *tr.* by Lena Jayyusi *and* John Heath-Stubbs. MAP
Newspaper Is a Collection of Half-Injustices, A. Stephen Crane. *Fr.* War Is Kind, XII. AmPP; NAAL-2, *sect.* 87.
Newspapers aged the couch. Marina Tsvetayeva. Derek Walcott. AnAn
Newspapers rise high in the air over Maryland. At a March against the Vietnam War. Robert Bly. EAS
Newsreel. C. Day Lewis. MoAB; MoBrPo
Newsreel. Adrienne Rich. *Fr.* Shooting Script, 9. FaBoWP; HCAP
Newstead Abbey. Byron. ChER
Newsvendor with his hut and crutch, The. The Imprisoned. Robert Fitzgerald. TwCP
Newton. Wordsworth. *Fr.* The Prelude [or, Growth of a Poet's Mind]: Residence at Cambridge. ImOP
Newton to Einstein. Jeannette Chappell. GoYe
Newton's Statue. Wordsworth. *See* Prelude [or, Growth of a Poet's Mind], The: Residence at Cambridge.
Next. Tina Koyama. BrSi
Next after comes coyote, Stretched-out-in-Dew. Scalp Dance Song. *Unknown, tr.* by H. J. Spinden. WTO
Next bidding all draw near on bended knees. Pope. *Fr.* The Dunciad, IV. OBSV
Next came one/ Who mourn'd in earnest. Milton. *Fr.* Paradise Lost, *bk.* I, *ll.* 457–489. EBEV
Next Day. Randall Jarrell. HAr; HCAP; MoP; NAAL-2; NoAM; NoP; NYBP; WeW
Next Day the Fog Was Even Worse, The. Yüan Mei, *tr. fr. Chinese* by Jonathan Chaves. CoBLCP
Next day they rambled round the town, and swore. James Bisset. *Fr.* Ramble of the Gods through Birmingham. NOEC
Next died the Lady, who yon Hall possess'd. The Lady of the Manor. George Crabbe. *Fr.* The Parish Register: Burials. NOBE; OBNC
Next, for October, to some sheltered coign. Sonnets of the Months: October. Folgore da San Geminiano, *tr.* by Dante Gabriel Rossetti. AWP
  (October). PFI
Next grand adjunct to our Hero's cause, The. The Electric Telegraph. Thomas Baker. *Fr.* The Steam Engine; or, The Power of the Flame. FaBoUs
Next Heaven, my vows to thee, O sacred Muse! Upon the Saying That My Verses Were Made by Another. Anne Killigrew. WPE
Next him Jac! Squire through his own tear-drops sploshes. Roy Campbell. *Fr.* The Georgiad. OxBTC
Next his chamber, beside his study. The Bishop's Harp. Robert Mannyng. ACP

Next is your lot, fair, to be numbered one. To His Kinswoman, Mistress Penelope Wheeler. Robert Herrick. CaPo
Next of Kin. Herbert B. Mallalieu. WaP
Next, Please. Philip Larkin. MoBrPo; NePoEA
Next Poem, The. Dana Gioia. DiPo
Next Table, The. C. P. Cavafy, tr. fr. Greek by John Mavrogordato. PeHV
Next These, a troop of busy [or buisy] spirits press. John Dryden and Nahum Tate. Fr. Absalom and Achitophel: Part II. PPP; SeCV-2
Next to my counsels an attention pay. Hesiod, tr. fr. Greek by Thomas Cooke. Fr. Works and Days. FaBoUs
Next of Course God America I. E. E. Cummings. AmFN; AmPP; FaBoPV; InPK; LiTM; NAAL-2; NBLV; NoP; OBWP; OFD; OPOP; OxBA; TAP; VGW; WaaP
Next to the Apostolic Church of God. The Maestro's Barber Shop. Ricardo Vásquez, tr. by Toni Empringham. FIA
Next to the fresh grave of my beloved grandmother. Ireland 1972. Paul Durcan. FaBCIP
Next to will/ I value reason. Swimming Pool. Maria Teresa Horta, tr. by Suzette Macedo. PBWP
Next War, The. Robert Graves. BrPo
Next War, The. Wilfred Owen, tr. fr. Turkish. OBD; Son; WaP
Next War, The. Sir Osbert Sitwell. MMA
Next whose fortune 't was a tale to tell, The. Fitz Adam's Story. James Russell Lowell. AmPP
Next Year, in Jerusalem. Shirley Kaufman. VWA
Next year the grave grass will cover us. Street Corner College. Kenneth Patchen. MoAmPo
Next year we are to bring the soldiers home. Homage to a Government. Philip Larkin. EBEV; FaBoPV; NoAM
"Next year you must come again." Liu E, tr. fr. Chinese by Jonathan Chaves. Fr. Poems for Yukiko of Tamba. CoBLCP
Ngaa. now then. Paddy Biran's Song. Paddy Biran, tr. by R. M. W. Dixon. CBAP
Ngoni Burial Song. Unknown, tr. fr. Zulu. PeSA
NHR. Jack Hirschman. VWA
Ni Tsan Poem Following Rhyme-Words of Wu Chen. Wu Chen, tr. fr. Chinese by Jonathan Chaves. CoBLCP
Niagara Falls. Alan Dugan. PoA
Niagara Falls. Narushima Ryuhoku, tr. fr. Chinese by Burton Watson. JLIC-2
Niagara Falls Nocturne. Len Gasparini. NeAC
Nibble, nibble, little sheep. Sheep. Samuel Hoffenstein. TrJP
Nicander, ooh, your leg's got hairs! Alkaios, tr. by Tony Harrison. PeHV
Nice Day for a Lynching. Kenneth Patchen. PoNe
Nice Mrs. Eberle early had been told. La Donna E Perpetuum Mobile. Irwin Edman. FiBHP; NYBP
Nice Part of Town, A. Alfred Hayes. NYBP
Nice priest! After he'd left us we saw him fly over the lake. Miracles Real Miracles. Max Jacob, tr. by Armand Schwerner. RHTwFP
Nice Valor, The, sel. John Fletcher.
   Melancholy. GTBS; GTBS-P; OBEV
   (O Sweetest Melancholy.) TrGrPo
   (Passionate Man's Song, The.) OBS
   (Song: "Hence all you vaine delights.") PoEL-2
Nice young man about the town, A. I've Got the Giggles Today. A. P. Herbert. FiBHP
Nicest child I ever knew, The. Charles Augustus Fortescue. Hilaire Belloc. NoAM
Nichita Stanescu. Brian Turner. PeNZ
Nicholas Ned. Unknown. NTCP
Nicholas Nye. Walter de la Mare. BoTP
Nick and the Candlestick. Sylvia Plath. CAPP; CoAP; LCAP; PBWP
Nickleplate moon, The. Kansas City West Bottoms. Edward Dahlberg. PoA
Nicky, the word has come to the West Coast. Smoke. Charles Wright. NYBP
Nicolas Gatineau. Arthur Stanley Bourinot. CaP
Nid-nod through shuttered streets at dead of night. The Last Bus. E. V. Knox. BXAP
Niddle Noddle. Mother Goose. OxNR; PBBP
Nietzsche is pietsche. Graffiti. James. NBLV
Nievie nievie nick nack. Unknown. OxNR
Nigerian Unity/ or Little Niggers Killing Little Niggers. Don L. Lee. NeAC
Nigga Section, The. Welton Smith. BPo
Nigger. Frank Horne. BANP; CDC
Nigger. Sonia Sanchez. BPo
Nigger. Karl Shapiro. OxBA

Nigger/ Can you kill. True Import of Present Dialogue, Black vs, The Negro. Nikki Giovanni. BPo; PoBA
Nigger mighty happy w'en he layin' by co'n. The Plough-Hands' Song. Joel Chandler Harris. Fr. Uncle Remus and His Friends. AA
Nigger Song: An Odyssey. Rita Dove. AmPA
Nigh to a grave that was newly made. The Old Sexton. Park Benjamin. AA
Night, The. Al-Khansa, tr. fr. Arabic by Willis Barnstone. BoWoP
Night, The. Hilaire Belloc. OBEV
Night. William Rose Benét. MoAmPo
Night. Hayyim Nahman Bialik, tr. fr. Hebrew by Maurice Samuel. AWP
Night. Blake. Fr. Songs of Innocence. BLPL; BoNaP; BoTP; CH; EnRP; FaBoBe; FaPON; OBEV; OxBChV; PoLF; WiR
Night. Robert Bly. NaP
Night. Louise Bogan. UnPo
Night. Aldo Camerino, tr. fr. Italian by Anita Barrows. VWA
Night. George Chapman. Fr. The Shadow of Night. OBSC
Night, sel. Thomas Cleaver.
   "Day is o'er! yet pleasure, commerce, gain, The." PF
Night, sel. Victor James Daley.
   "Suns, planets, stars, in glorious array." PoAu-1
Night. Peter Everwine. NNaP
Night. Donald Jeffrey Hayes. CDC
Night. Josephine D. Henderson Heard. CBWP-4
Night. Charles Heavysege. OBCV
Night. Anne Hébert, tr. fr. French by Kathleen Weaver. OV
Night. Hermann Hesse, tr. fr. German by Ludwig Lewisohn. AWP
Night, The. Rodolfo Hinostroza, tr. fr. Spanish by Maureen Ahern and David Tipton. Per
Night. Mary Ann Hoberman. RHPC
Night. Patricia Hubbell. PDV
Night. Solomon ibn Gabirol, tr. fr. Hebrew by Emma Lazarus. TrJP
Night. Robinson Jeffers. AWP; LiTA; MoAmPo; NOBA; OxBA
Night. Miyazawa Kenji, tr. fr. Japanese by Hiroaki Sato. FCEI
Night, The. Helen Leuty. BoTP
Night. A. Leyeles, tr. fr. Yiddish by Benjamin and Barbara Harshav. Fr. New York. AYP
Night, The. Myra Cohn Livingston. PDV
Night. Richard Lovelace. CaPo
Night. Joyce Carol Oates. GeTw
Night. Anne Radcliffe. WPE
Night. Henri de Regnier, tr. fr. French by "Seumas O'Sullivan." AWP
Night. Shelley. See Swiftly walk o'er the western wave.
Night. Tanikawa Shuntaro, tr. fr. Japanese by Hiroaki Sato. FCEI
Night. Sir Philip Sidney. Fr. Arcadia. SiPS
Night. Robert Southey. GN
Night, The. James Stephens. BoTP
Night. Earl of Surrey. See Alas, so all things now.
Night. S. D. R Sutu, tr. fr. Sotho by Dan Kunene and Jack Cope. PeSA; TTY
Night. Sara Teasdale. FaPON
Night. Unknown. BoTP
Night, The, sel. Henry Vaughan. EBEV; LiTB; MeLP; MePo; NAEL-1; NOBE; NOCV; NoP; OAEL-1; OBEV; OBS; OBWVE; PoEL-2; SeCV-1; TOF
   "Dear Night! this world's defeat." TrGrPo
Night. Edward Young. See Night Thoughts: Tired nature's sweet restorer, balmy Sleep!
Night. V. A. Zhukovsky, tr. fr. Russian by Alan Myers. AAA
Night/ And death rides fast on foul breath. Night Slivers. Darwin T. Turner. NBP
Night/ and in the warm blackness. Upon Your Leaving. Etheridge Knight. NeAC; NNaP
Night,/ And the yellow pleasure of candlelight. Song of the Rain. Hugh McCrae. CBAP; PoAu-1
Night, The/ creeps in. The Night. Myra Cohn Livingston. PDV
Night, A: mysterious, tender, quiet, deep. A Common Inference. Charlotte Perkins Gilman. AA; WGRP
Night a Sailor Came to Me in a Dream, The. Diane Wakoski. TAP; VGW
Night above the Town. Thomas Lux. NAmP
Night after night. Desire. Dinah Livingstone. AIW
Night after Night. "Stuart Sterne." AA
Night after night. The Survivors. Judith Hemschemeyer. TV
Night after Night I Come to Worship. Manfred Winkler, tr. fr. Hebrew by Bernhard Frank. MHeP
Night after night, I crack. A Basket of Walnuts. George MacBeth. NPo
Night along the Mackinac Bridge. Roberta Hill. CDW; STE
Night; an Epistle to Robert Lloyd, sels. Charles Churchill.

Nut, a World, a Squirrel, and a King, A.   FaBoRV
"Spectators only on this bustling stage."   OBSV
What Is't to Us?.   SeCePo
Night and a Distant Church.   Russell Atkins.   PoBA
Night and a starless sky.   Shipwreck.   Mary Weston Fordham, *tr. by* Mary Ann Caws.   CBWP-2
Night and Day.   Michael Drayton.   *See* Idea:
   Deare [*or* Dear], why should you command [*or* commaund] me to my rest.
Night and Day.   Sidney Lanier.   AA
Night and day arrive, and day after day goes by.   For My Son, Noah, Ten Years Old.   Robert Bly.   CAPP; DiL; InPS
Night and day under the rind of me.   Parodies of Cole Porter's "Night and Day."   Ring Lardner.   OBAL
Night, and its muffled creakings, as the wheels.   The Shako.   Robert Lowell.   Son
Night and Morning.   Austin Clarke.   AnIL; CIP; IPY; MoAB; NeIP
Night and Morning.   *Unknown, tr. fr. Welsh by* R. S. Thomas.   OBWVE
Night, and on all sides only the folding quiet.   Night.   S. D. R Sutu, *tr. by* Dan Kunene *and* Jack Cope.   PeSA; TTY
Night and Sleep.   Coventry Patmore.   EBVV
   (Shadow of Night, The.)   CH
Night and the Child.   Judith Wright.   SeCePo
Night and the distant rumbling; for the train.   The Last Evening.   Rainer Maria Rilke, *tr. by* C. F. MacIntyre.   WaaP
Night, and the down by the sea.   Rain on the Down.   Arthur Symons.   *Fr.* At Dieppe.   BrPo; OBNC
Night, and the heavens beam serene with peace.   Night.   Solomon ibn Gabirol, *tr. by* Emma Lazarus.   TrJP
Night and the hood.   Conrad Kent Rivers.   PoBA
Night and the Pines.   Duncan Campbell Scott.   OBCV
Night and we heard heavy and cadenced hoofbeats.   The Return.   John Peale Bishop.   LiTA; OxBA; WaP
Night and Wind.   Arthur Symons.   BrPo
Night arches England, and the winds are still.   Peace.   Walter de la Mare.   MoAB; MoBrPo
Night at a Port, A.   Munir Niazi, *tr. fr. Urdu by* Mahmood Jamal.   PBMUP
Night at an Airport.   David Ignatow.   NNaP
Night at an Inn: Written in the Style of Meng Chiao.   Chiang Shih, *tr. fr. Chinese by* Irving Lo.   WFTU
Night at Gettysburg.   Don C. Seitz.   OHIP
Night at My Lodge, A.   Ch'en San-li, *tr. fr. Chinese by* Irving Lo.   WFTU
Night at the End of the Year.   Tamemasa, *tr. fr. Japanese by* Steven D. Carter.   WFTW
Night attendant, a B.U. sophomore, The.   Waking in the Blue.   Robert Lowell.   CoAP; HCAP; MoAMP; UnPo
Night bangs around its stars, The.   Gold Medal.   Philippe Soupault, *tr. by* Michael Benedikt.   POS
Night, Be Mood to Me.   Jacob Glatstein, *tr. fr. Yiddish by* Benjamin *and* Barbara Harshav.   *Fr.* From the Nursery.   AYP
Night before a Journey.   Charles Causley.   PoPo
Night before Christmas, The.   Clement Clarke Moore.   *See* Visit from St. Nicholas, A.
Night before Larry Was Stretched, The.   *Unknown.*   BIrV; FaBoBa; GBP; NOBL; NOIV; OxBoLi
Night before my uncle Carter got shot, The.   Support Your Local Police Dog.   Carter Revard.   VoR
Night before the Battle of Waterloo, The.   Byron.   *See* Childe Harold's Pilgrimage: There was a sound of revelry by night.
Night before they meant to pluck his eyes, The.   Among Philistines.   R. S. Gwynn.   MT; SoTCo
Night before Waterloo, The.   Byron.   *See* Childe Harold's Pilgrimage: There was a sound of revelry by night.
Night Bell on the Mountain.   Shotetsu, *tr. fr. Japanese by* Steven D. Carter.   WFTW
Night Blessing.   Phil George.   NOVW
Night-blooming Cactus, The.   John Bensko.   MAYP
Night-blooming Cereus, The.   Robert Hayden.   CAPP; FB; NoP; NU
Night-blooming Cereus, The.   Roger Weingarten.   NAmP
Night Blooming Flowers.   Katha Pollitt.   MAYP
Night Boat.   Audrey Alexandra Brown.   CaP
Night Braid, *sel.*   Faye Kicknosway.
   "I am the woman of sweaty language, the belly."   ER
Night breaths, short ones.   In the Hospital.   Laura Jensen.   AmPA
Night by nightfall more benighted.   Garcia Lorca Murdered in Granada.   John Manifold.   CBAP
Night by the Sea, A.   Heine, *tr. fr. German by* Howard Mumford Jones.   *Fr.* The North Sea.   AWP
Night Catch.   Heather McHugh.   AmPA

Night Clouds.   Amy Lowell.   AnAmPo; MoAmPo
Night Club.   Louis MacNeice.   OxBSP
Night Club.   F. R. Scott.   NOBC
Night Comes.   Beatrice Schenk de Regniers.   RAR; RHPC
Night comes and, drowsy with drink, I'm slow to shed my ornaments.   Tune: Telling of Innermost Feelings.   Li Ch'ing-chao, *tr. by* Burton Watson.   CoBCP
Night comes.   Day runs for its life into my eyes.   Gil Orlovitz.   *Fr.* Art of the Sonnet.   PoA
Night comes now.   Black-Out.   Valentine Ackland.   CN
Night comes to the man who can pray.   New Year's Eve in Solitude.   Robert Mezey.   NaP; VWA
Night Crackles.   Elizabeth Woody.   STE
Night Crawler.   N. M. Bodecker.   TDD
Night Cries, Wakari Hospital, *sels.*   Charles Brasch.
   Tempora Mutantur.   ATNZ
   Winter Anemones.   ATNZ; PeNZ
Night Crow.   Theodore Roethke.   HoPM; InPK; OxBSP; VGW
Night crow calls as if to tell of dawn, The.   *Unknown.* *Fr.* Manyo Shu.   Ma
Night Dances, The.   Sylvia Plath.   LCAP
Night, Death, Mississippi.   Robert Hayden.   CAPP; FF; LCAP; VGW
Night deepening.   Myoe, *tr. fr. Japanese by* Burton Watson.   *Fr.* Ten Tanka.   FCEI
Night deepens, the sound of water trickling, The.   Princess Shikishi, *tr. fr. Japanese by* Hiroaki Sato.   *Fr.* Seventy-eight Tanka.   FCEI
Night Dive.   Don Johnson.   MAYP
Night Don Juan came to pay his fees, The.   Don Juan in Hell.   Baudelaire, *tr. by* James Elroy Flecker.   AWP
Night draws itself as tight.   Lord, Listen.   Else Lasker-Schüler.   VWA, *tr. by* Edouard Roditi.
Night Drive.   Seamus Heaney.   FaBCIP
Night envelops us: clouds rest, darkness drizzles.   At the Turning Point of Life.   Gyula Illyés, *tr. by* William Jay Smith.   MHuP
Night Expedition from Ben Alder Cottage.   Roger A. Redfern.   PoSH
Night, expositor of love.   Musical Shuttle.   Harvey Shapiro.   VWA
Night falls between the hills as if they were real, The.   End of Autumn.   Julio Ortega, *tr. by* Ena Hollis *and* David Tipton.   Per
Night far gone.   Yakamochi.   *Fr.* Manyo Shu.   FCEI
Night Feeding.   Muriel Rukeyser.   NMM; WPE
Night Fishing for Blues.   Dave Smith.   GeTw
Night Flight.   Franz Richter, *tr. fr. German by* Beth Bjorklund.   CoAuP
Night Flight.   George Whalley.   CaP
Night Flute.   Fei Ma, *tr. fr. Chinese by* Dominic Cheung.   IFON
Night flutters.   Hasidim Dance.   Nelly Sachs, *tr. fr. German by* Keith Bosley.   VWA
Night Fog, The.   Kim Hyun-sung, *tr. fr. Korean by* Koh Chang-soo.   ACKP
Night Fun.   Judith Viorst.   RAR
Night Funeral in Harlem.   Langston Hughes.   InPS
Night Game in Menomonie Park, A.   Susan Firer.   TSL
Night gathers.   Outside.   Kinder- und Hausmärchen.   Brian Alderson.   Mes
Night Gives Old Woman the Word.   Gail Tremblay.   HATNAP
Night Grew Late in Kuzuha Village in Hirakata, The.   Onitsura, *tr. fr. Japanese by* Hiroaki Sato.   *Fr.* Twenty-three Hokku.   FCEI
Night growing late.   Ryota, *tr. by* Geoffrey Bownas *and* Anthony Thwaite.   PeBJV
Night grows no flower children.   Ascendancy.   Herbert A. Simmons.   NBP
Night Guards.   Wu T'e-Liang, *tr. fr. Chinese by* Dominic Cheung.   IFON
Night hailstones fall so hard.   Kaya Shirao, *tr. fr. Japanese by* Hiroaki Sato.   *Fr.* Twenty-one Hokku.   FCEI
Night Has a Thousand Eyes, The.   Francis William Bourdillon.   BoLoP; FaFP; OBEV; OHFP; OxBSP; WBLP
   (Light.)   BLPA; BLPL; FaBoBe
Night has come.   Let us go then, Goddess of my dreams.   Egyptian Serenade.   Ali Mahmud Taha, *tr. by* Issa Boullata *and* Thomas G. Ezzy.   MAP
Night has come on like a woman sleeping, The.   Moon Poems.   John Wieners.   VGW
Night has fallen, The.   Empress Eifuku, *tr. by* Steven D. Carter.   WFTW
Night has secreted us.   Amen.   Richard W. Thomas.   PoBA
Night Has Twenty-four Hours, The.   Pedro Juan Pietri.   InW
Night he died, earth's images all came, The.   Poet.   Peter Viereck.   HoPM; MoAmPo
Night held me as I crawled and scrambled near.   The Turkish Trench Dog.   Geoffrey Dearmer.   Mes

Night here, a covert. Gary Snyder. *Fr.* Myths and Texts: Burning, IX. NaP

Night Heron. Frances Frost. RHPC

Night hides our thefts; all faults then pardoned be. In the Dark None Dainty. Robert Herrick. CaPo

Night hours have advanced, The. Hitomaro. *Fr.* Manyo Shu. Ma

Night huddled our town. In Dear Detail, by Ideal Light. William Stafford. NaP

Night hung o'er Virginia's forest wild, The. Capt. Smith and Pocahontas. Eloise Bibb. CBWP-4

Night Hymns on Lake Nipigon. Duncan Campbell Scott. OBCV

Night, I know you are powerful and artistic. For Bill Hawkins, a Black Militant. William J. Harris. PoBA

Night I seldom remember, A. Obeah Night. Jean Rhys. PVCV

Night in a Village, A. Ivan Savvich Nikitin, *tr. fr. Russian by* P. E. Matheson. AWP

Night in June, A. Duncan Campbell Scott. OBCV

Night in June, A. Wordsworth. BoTP

Night in Lesbos, A. George Horton. AA

Night in Manhattan. Moyshe-Leyb Halpern, *tr. fr. Yiddish by* Benjamin *and* Barbara Harshav. AYP

Night in Odessa, A. Louis Simpson. NNaP

Night in Prison, A. Sibilla Aleramo, *tr. fr. Italian by* Muriel Kittel. DMI

Night in the bloodstained snow: the wind is chill. Hjalmar Speaks to the Raven. Leconte de Lisle, *tr. by* James Elroy Flecker. AWP

Night. In the darkest places sparkle traces. We the Wordproletariat. Jacob Glatstein, *tr. by* Benjamin *and* Barbara Harshav. AYP

Night in the Forest. Galway Kinnell. TAP

Night in the House by the River. Tu Fu, *tr. fr. Chinese by* Kenneth Rexroth. NaP

"Night" in the Medici Chapel. Michelangelo, *tr. by* William Jay Smith. PFI

Night in the Red Sea, A. Sir Alfred Comyn Lyall. OBTV

Night in the Royal Ontario Museum, A. Margaret Atwood. PBWP

Night, in the sweetness of his murky dominion. Nocturnal Thoughts. Avraham Huss, *tr. by* Mark Elliott Shapiro. VWA

Night in which one re-reads the sentences, The. Alfred Kolleritsch, *tr. by* Beth Bjorklund. CoAuP

Night Interpreted. Everett Hoagland. NBP

Night Is a Big Black Cat, The. G. Orr Clark. RHPC

Night is a furrow, a queasy, insistent wound, The. Nightletter. Charles Wright. PoA

Night is a purple pumpkin. Night. Patricia Hubbell. PDV

Night is beautiful, The. Langston Hughes. CDC

Night is black swan wholly adrift. Hotel in Paris. Dennis Trudell. PoA

Night is blue, stains, The. In a Minor Key. Judah Leib Teller, *tr. by* Benjamin *and* Barbara Harshav. AYP

Night is blue, the blanket, The. Minor. Judd Teller, *tr. by* Grace Schulman. PeBMYV

Night is calm, the cygnet's down, The. On a Calm Summer's Night. John Nicholson. EnLoPo

Night is cold and frosty, The. A Winter Night. Priscilla Jane Thompson. CBWP-2

Night is cold on the Great Bog, The. *Unknown. Fr.* Toward Winter. NOIV

Night is come, but not too soon, The. The Little Moon. Longfellow. BoTP

Night is come, like to the day, The. A Colloquy with God. Sir Thomas Browne. *Fr.* Religio Medici. OBS

Night is coming softly, slowly, The. Night. Mary Ann Hoberman. RHPC

Night is coming to the islands. The Vision of Marsden Hartley. John Haines. BLA

Night is covered with signs, The. Akiba. Muriel Rukeyser. VWA

Night is dark, The. And Yet. Errol B. Sloan. BLRP

Night Is Dark, The. H. Leivick, *tr. fr. Yiddish by* Meyer Schapiro. PeBMYV

Night is dark, the wind has dashed, The. Midnight Prayer. Hayyim Nahman Bialik, *tr. by* Helena Frank. TrJP

Night Is Darkening round Me. Emily Brontë. NOBVV; OBNC; PoEL-5 (Spellbound.) NOBE

Night Is Freezing Fast, The. A. E. Housman. CMoP; LiTM; OxBSP; PrIm

Night is light and chill, The. Night and Wind. Arthur Symons. BrPo

Night is long, The. Grandpa Bear's Lullaby. Jane Yolen. RHPC

Night is my sister, and how deep in love. Edna St. Vincent Millay. HAP

Night Is Near [*or* Neir] Gone, The. Alexander Montgomerie. GoTS; OBEV; OxBS
(Hey! Now the Day Dawns.) CH

Night is o'er England, and the winds are still. Peace. Walter de la Mare. MMA; MoAB; MoBrPo

Night is on the downland, on the lonely moorland. John Masefield. *Fr.* Lollingdon Downs, XVIII. GoYe; LiTM
(Night on the Downland.) MoBrPo

Night is soft with summer, The; yon faint arch. John Plummer Derwent Llwyd. *Fr.* The Vestal Virgin. CaP

Night is still silky, The. Curtains are drawn. Observation at Dawn. Abba Kovner, *tr. by* Shirley Kaufman. VWA

Night is still. The unfailing surf, The. Miramar Beach. J. V. Cunningham. *Fr.* To What Strangers, What Welcome. PoA

Night is tranquil, the w ᴅ-blown curtain, The. Spring Night. Chang Yü, *tr. fr. Chinese by* Jonathan Chaves. *Fr.* Twelve Miscellaneous Poems on the Fang Garden. CoBLCP

Night is very dark, The. Assassination Poems. John Ridland. MAT; OFD

Night is warm and clear and without wind, The. Poem after Leopardi. Mark Strand. AnAn

Night is warm and hot, my arms, The. Death Is a Second Cousin Dining with Us Tonight. Geraldine Kudaka. BrSi

Night is white, The. Birch Trees. John Richard Moreland. OHIP; RHPC

Night it was a holy night, The. Godly Girzie. Burns. CoMu; ErPo

Night it was horribly dark, The. Measles in the Ark. "Susan Coolidge." OxBChV

Night John Henry is born an ax, The. The Birth of John Henry. Melvin Beaunearus Tolson. *Fr.* Harlem Gallery. BPo; TTY

Night Journal. Charles Wright. BLA

Night Journey, The. Rupert Brooke. BrPo

Night Journey. Theodore Roethke. AmFN; GOA; NYBP; RR

Night Landscape. Joan Aiken. DuDa

Night Las Vegas caught fire, The. The Case. H. R. Hays. EAS

Night Letter. Marge Piercy. NMM

Night lies blue and white, The. Minor Key. Judah Leib Teller. VWA, *tr. by* Gabriel Preil *and* Howard Schwartz

Night-life. Letters, journals, bourbon. Origins and History of Consciousness. Adrienne Rich. NIP

Night Light. Nancy Willard. LCAP

Night like a silver peacock in the sky. Poetry and Science. W. J. Turner. SeCePo

Night like purple flakes of snow. Night. Donald Jeffrey Hayes. CDC

Night! loathèd jailor of the locked-up sun. Night. Richard Lovelace. CaPo

Night Mail, The. W. H. Auden. ChTr; GrPl; OxBTC

Night Mail North, The. Henry Cholmondeley-Pennell. EBVV

Night makes no difference 'twixt the priest and clerk. No Difference in the Dark. Robert Herrick. CaPo

Night-March, The. Herman Melville. LiTA

Night Mare. Anita Endrezze-Danielson. STE

Night Meeting. Gyorgy Raba, *tr. fr. Hungarian by* Jascha Kessler. FOC

Night, metamorphoser of forms. Shlomo Molkho Sings on the Eve of His Burning. A. Leyeles, *tr. by* Benjamin *and* Barbara Harshav. AYP

Night Mirror, The. John Hollander. NYBP; Prf

Night mist leaves us yearnng for a new location, The. Floating Houses. David Wojahn. SM

Night Mists. William Hamilton Hayne. AA

Night, more night: love now a fact. The Faithful Lovers. Jorge Guillén, *tr. by* Perry Higman. LPSS

Night-Music. Philip Larkin. InPS

Night music slanted. Cell Song. Etheridge Knight. NNaP; PoBA

Night Nurse Goes Her Round, The. John Gray. OBNC

Night of Battle. Yvor Winters. PoA

Night of darkness and of storms!, A. Robert Southey. *Fr.* Thalaba the Destroyer. VVA

Night of Death, The. Frances Ellen Watkins Harper. PWR

Night of iron wheels and rain, A. The Red Flag. Michael Jackson. PeNZ

Night of love, A. The Second Madrigal. Anna Swirszczynska, *tr. by* Czeslaw Milosz. PwPP

Night of My Return, The. Philippe Thoby-Marcelin, *tr. fr. French by* William Jay Smith. CT

Night of rain on the autumn river, A. Tsung Ch'en, *tr. fr. Chinese by* Jonathan Chaves. *Fr.* Miscellaneous Words on the Lake. CoBLCP

Night of Sine. Léopold Sédar-Senghor, *tr. fr. French by* Ulli Beier. PBA

Night of Souls. Ann Stanford. WPE

Night of Spring. Thomas Westwood. BoTP; SoSe

Night of the Dance, The. Thomas Hardy. BrPo

Night of the eclipse we're parallel, The. Total Eclipse. Michael J. Rosen. DiPo

Night of the Fifteenth, Second Month. Yüan Mei, *tr. fr. Chinese by* Jonathan Chaves. CoBLCP

Night of the First Full Moon, The. Li K'ai-hsien, *tr. fr. Chinese*. CoBLCP, *tr. by* Jonathan Chaves; WFTU, *tr. by* Cecile Chu-chin Sun.

Night of the Fourteenth. Ho Ching-ming, *tr. fr. Chinese by* Jonathan Chaves. CoBLCP

Night of the Full Moon. Cheng Hsiao-hsü, *tr. fr. Chinese by* Irving Lo. WFTU

Night of the Seventeenth, The. Li K'ai-hsien, *tr. fr. Chinese by* Jonathan Chaves. CoBLCP

Night of Trafalgar, The. Thomas Hardy. *Fr.* The Dynasts, *pt.* I, Act V, sc. vii. ChTr; FaBoCh; MoBrPo; MOS; OBMV (Trafalgar.) CH

Night of utter silences, A. Shadows. "Yehoash", *tr. by* Elias Lieberman. TrJP

Night of Wind. Frances Frost. FaPON

Night on Clinton. Robert Mezey. AmPA; NaP

Night on earth and sky. A Terrible Thought. Eliezer Steinbarg, *tr. by* Joseph Leftwich. TrJP

Night on the Downland. John Masefield. *See* Lollingdon Downs: Night is on the downland, on the lonely moorland.

Night on the Prairies. Walt Whitman. RFM, (*ll.* 1–5)

Night on the shores, your voice is no stranger. A Song of Job. Khalil Touma, *tr. by* Lena Jayyusi *and* Samuel Hazo. MAP

Night opens like an almond. Yvonne Caroutch, *tr. by* Elene Kolb. BoWoP

Night, our black summer, simplifies her smells. Nights in the Gardens of Port of Spain. Derek Walcott. OxBC

Night Out. R. A. Simpson. PoAu-2

Night-owl shrieked, The: a gibbous moon peered pallid o'er the yew. The Conscience-Curst! "F. Anstey." CenHV

Night passd and Enitharmon eer the dawn returnd in bliss. Song of Enitharmon. Blake. *Fr.* Vala; or The Four Zoas. OAEL-2

Night passed and the fog froze. Anne Ridler. *Fr.* Still Life. PoPo

Night-Piece. Léonie Adams. MoAB; MoAmPo

Night-Piece, *sel.* Fleur Adcock.
   Before Sleep. *Fr.* II. PeNZ

Night Piece. John Manifold. LiTM; MoBrPo; WaP

Night-Piece. Raymond R. Patterson. PoBA; WSC; WSC

Night-Piece. Kendrick Smithyman. ATNZ

Night Piece. *Unknown*. OBSC

Night-Piece, A. Wordsworth. EnRP

Night-Piece on Death, A. Thomas Parnell. NOEC; SeCePo

Night Piece on Death ("By the blue taper's trembling light."), *sel.* Thomas Parnell. NOEC; SeCePo
   "Up yonder hill, behold how sadly slow." OBD

Night-Piece; or, Modern Philosophy, A. Christopher Smart. NOEC

Night-Piece, to Julia, The. Robert Herrick. CaPo; CH; ELP; InvP; JCP; LiTB; NAEL-1; NoP; OAEL-1; OBEV; OBS; PoE; PoEL-3; PoRA; SeCP; SeCV-1; TEP
   (On a Dark Road.) BoTP

Night Plane. Frances Frost. FaPON; PDV

Night Poem in an Abandoned Music Room. William Pillen. VWA

Night Practice. May Swenson. RR

Night Prayer. *Unknown, tr. fr. Irish by* Douglas Hyde. TIRV

Night Prayer of Glückel of Hameln, The. Edouard Roditi. CRP

Night Prayers. Dinah Livingstone. DT

Night Quarters. Henry Howard Brownell. GN

Night Rain: A Wall Collapses. Yang Shih-ch'i, *tr. fr. Chinese by* Jonathan Chaves. CoBLCP

Night Rain beneath the City Walls of P'i-chou. Yang Shih-ch'i, *tr. fr. Chinese by* Jonathan Chaves. CoBLCP

Night rendezvous/ mosquitoes squashed to death. *Unknown, tr. by* Burton Watson. FCEI

Night Robbers. Ishihara Yoshiro, *tr. fr. Japanese by* Sato. FCEI

Night Runner's Prayer. Mykie Silz Reidy. TSL

Night sank upon the dusky beach, and on the purple sea. Macaulay. *Fr.* Armada, The [a Fragment]. OBNC

Night saw the crew like pedlars with their packs. Lunar Stanzas. Henry Coggswell Knight. FaBoNo; NA

Night, say all, was made for rest, The. Upon Visiting His Lady by Moonlight. "A. W." CTC; OBSC

Night Scenes. Robert Duncan. VGW

Night sea quickens, The. On the shoal or rock. Lighthouses. Dorothy Wellesley. WPE

Night seems endless, The. Tune: Fragrant Wandering: A Song. Wu Tsao, *tr. by* Julie Landau. WFTU

Night Serene, The. Luís de León, *tr. fr. Spanish by* Thomas Walsh. TrJP

Night Shore. Barry O. Higgs. PeSA

Night Sits in This Chair, The. Alice Notley. UL

Night Sky. Louise Erdrich. HATNAP

Night Sky, The. *Unknown*. BoTP

Night sleeps, but the chill, The. The Harp of David. Jacob Cohen, *tr. by* Sholom J. Kahn. TrJP

Night Slivers. Darwin T. Turner. NBP

Night Snow. Emperor Kogon, *tr. fr. Japanese by* Steven D. Carter. WFTW

Night Snow. Po Chü-i, *tr. fr. Chinese by* Burton Watson. CoBCP

Night Song. Frances Cornford. FM

Night Song. Louise Glück. MAYP; SV

Night Song at Amalfi. Sara Teasdale. MoAmPo

Night Song for a Child. Charles Williams. OBEV

Night Song for a Woman. Alfred W. Purdy. NOBC

Night Song for Two Mystics. Paul Blackburn. NeAP

Night Song: How to Defend against Tree Shadows, A. Yang Mu, *tr. fr. Chinese by* Dominic Cheung. IFON

Night Song of a Traveller. Tachihara Michizo, *tr. fr. Japanese by* Geoffrey Bownas *and* Anthony Thwaite. PeBJV

Night Sowing. David Campbell. CBAP; PoAu-2

Night stilled the field, and every golden stook. Cornfield. Leo Cox. CaP

Night stirs the trees. By Achmelvich Bridge. Norman MacCaig. OxBS

Night Storm. William Gilmore Simms. MOS

Night, street, a lamp, a chemist's window. Aleksandr Aleksandrovich Blok, *tr. fr. Russian by* Jon Stallworthy *and* Peter France. *Fr.* Dances of Death. OBVE

Night Sweat. Robert Lowell. NAAL-2; TAP; VGW

Night sweat: my temperature spikes to 102. December 27, 1966. L. E. Sissman. DiPo; SM

Night that devil danced on me, The. Dear Mom. Paul Zarzyski. TSL

Night that has no star lit up by God, The. The New World. Jones Very. AA

Night, that old woman, jabs the sun. 29 (A Dream in Two Parts). Ai. MAYP

Night, the black summer, simplifies her smells. Nights in the Gardens of Port of Spain. Derek Walcott. NAAL-2; OxBC

Night the cold the solitude, The. From Outside. Paul Eluard, *tr. by* Michael Benedikt. POS

Night the Eighth (The Eternal Man). Blake. *Fr.* Vala; or The Four Zoas. PoE

Night, the rain, who could forget, The? In the Street. John Shaw Neilson. CBAP

Night the Second (Enion's Lament). Blake. *See* Vala; or The Four Zoas: Price of Experience, The.

Night, the Starless Night of Passion, The. William Alabaster. *Fr.* Divine Meditations, I. Son

Night Thought. Gerald Jonas. NYBP

Night Thought of a Tortoise Suffering from Insomnia on a Lawn. E. V. Rieu. FiBHP

Night Thoughts. Henri Coulette. FYAP

Night Thoughts. Elaine Feinstein. PoPo

Night-Thoughts. Solomon Ibn Gabirol, *tr. fr. Hebrew by* Emma Lazarus. TrJP

Night Thoughts. Ozaki Bunki, *tr. fr. Chinese by* Burton Watson. JLIC-2

Night Thoughts, *sels.* Edward Young.
   Consolation, The. *Fr.* Night IX. NOEC
   "How poor, how rich, how abject, how august." *Fr.* Night I. OAEL-1
   Infidel Reclaimed, The. *Fr.* Night VII. NOEC
   "Live ever here, Lorenzo?—shocking thought!" *Fr.* Night III. EnRP
   "Thy nature, immortality! who knows?" *Fr.* Night VI. OBD
   "Tired nature's sweet restorer, balmy Sleep!" *Fr.* Night I. EnRP; NOEC
   (Night.) SeCePo, *much abr.*.
   "Where dwells that which most ardent of the wise?" OBD
   "Where, thy true treasure? Gold says, 'Not in me.'" *Fr.* Night VI. OAEL-1

Night Thoughts: Baby & Demon. Gwen Harwood. CBAP

Night Thoughts in Age. John Hall Wheelock. NYBP

Night Thoughts over a Sick Child. Philip Levine. NePoEA-2; SM

Night Thoughts while Travelling. Tu Fu, *tr. fr. Chinese by* Kenneth Rexroth. NaP

Night, too long illumined, comes a stranger, The. In the Proscenium. Gene Derwood. LiTA

Night too struggled to escape this pitted field, The. The Spoilers and the Spoils. Judith Johnson Sherwin. SM

Night Train. Hagiwara Sakutaro, *tr. fr. Japanese by* Hiroaki Sato. FCEI

Night Train. Adrien Stoutenburg. PDV

Night trembles in the black storm, The. The Rain. Muhammad al-Mahdi al-Majdhoub, *tr. by* Matthew Sorenson. MAP

Night Trip across the Chesapeake and After. Sydney Lea. MAYP

Night up There. G. D. Valentine. PoSH

Night usually computes itself in stars. News of the Occluded Cyclone. Alice Fulton. NAmP

Night Visitors. Kadya Molodovsky, *tr. fr. Yiddish by* Ruth Whitman. VWA

Night Walk. Eli Netser, *tr. fr. Hebrew by* Bernhard Frank. MHeP

Night Walk. Sylvia Plath. *See* Hardcastle Crags.

Night was again descending, when my mule. The Great St. Bernard. Samuel Rogers. OBTV

Night was clear, sea calm; I came on deck, The. Crossing Cook Straight. James Keir Baxter. ATNZ

Night was coming very fast, The. The Hens. Elizabeth Madox Roberts. GoJo; OBCA; PDV

Night was creeping on the ground, The! Check. James Stephens. AnIL; OnUR; RHPC

Night was dark and fearful, The. The Watcher. Sarah Josepha Hale. AA

Night was dark, the rain came down, The. Over the Top with Pershing. Zelda Sayre Fitzgerald. AiP

Night was dark, though sometimes a faint star, The. Richard Watson Gilder. *Fr.* The New Day. PoLF

Night was faint and sheer, The. A Nocturne for October 31st. Yvor Winters. PoA

Night was growing old, The. In the Night. *Unknown.* FaBoNo; NA; NBLV

Night was growing old, The. *Unknown. See* In the Night.

Night was made for rest and sleep, The. Interim. Clarissa Scott Delany. CDC; PoNe

Night was stormy and dark, The. The Speculators. Thackeray. OBSV

Night was thick and hazy, The. Robinson Crusoe. Charles Edward Carryl. *Fr.* Davy and the Goblin, *ch.* 11. AA
(Robinson Crusoe's Story.) BeLS; FiBHP; PoRA

Night was winter in his roughest mood, The. William Cowper. *Fr.* The Task, VI. EnRP; TEP

Night was winter in his roughest mood, The. A Winter Walk at Noon. William Cowper. *Fr.* The Task, VI. EnRP; TEP
"No noise is here, or none that hinders thought." PBBP

Night Washes over the Mind. Mario Luzi, *tr. fr. Italian by* Dana Gioia. PFI

Night Watch. Margo Magid. NMM

Night Watch, The. William Winter. AA

Night-watchmen think of dawn and things auroral. Blindman's Buff. Peter Viereck. LiTM; MoAmPo

Night we parted in the red tower was hard to endure, The. Deva-like Barbarian. Wei Chuang, *tr. by* Lois Fusek. ATF

Night we went to see the Brisbane River, The. Profiles of My Father. Rhyll McMaster. CBAP

Night Will Never Stay, The. Eleanor Farjeon. BoTP; CH; NTCP; OxBChV

Night Wind, The. Emily Brontë. ChER; ChTr; EBVV; NAEL-2; TEP

Night Wind, The. Eugene Field. FaPON

Night wind/ rips a cloud sheet, The. Rags. Judith Thurman. TDD

Night-wind veering, the smell of the spilt wine, The. California. Bernice Zamora. CCP

Night Winds. Adelaide Crapsey. QFR

Night with a Friend, A. Li Po, *tr. fr. Chinese by* Burton Watson. CoBCP

Night with a Holy-Water Clerk, A. *Unknown.* MeEL

Night with a Wolf, A. Bayard Taylor. GN

Night with Cindy at Heitman's, A. Richard Hugo. AnAn

Night without Light, A. István Vas, *tr. fr. Hungarian by* Jascha Kessler. FOC

Night Works, The. Antonin Artaud, *tr. fr. French by* Michael Benedikt. POS

Nightbreak. Adrienne Rich. IHMS

Nightdream. Charles Wright. CAPP; LCAP

Nightfall, *sel.* Herbert Asquith.
"Hooded in angry mist, the sun goes down." OBD

Nightfall. Walter Davies, *tr. fr. Welsh by* Anthony Conran. OBWVE

Nightfall. Robert Desnos, *tr. fr. French by* Michael Benedikt. POS

Nightfall. Cassiano Ricardo, *tr. fr. Portuguese by* Barbara Howes. ATCBP

Nightfall comes like. Nightfall in Soweto. Mbuyiseni Oswald Mtshali. WMBCH

Nightfall in Dordrecht. Eugene Field. AA

Nightfall in Inishtrahull. Daniel James O'Sullivan. NeIP

Nightfall in Soweto. Mbuyiseni Oswald Mtshali. WMBCH

Nightfall, Midwinter, Missouri. Brian Coffey. *Fr.* Missouri Sequence. CIP

Nightfall on Sedgemoor. Andrew Young. FaBoPP

Nightfall, that saw the morning-glories float. On the Skeleton of a Hound. James Wright. LiTM; NePoEA

Nighthawks circle/ through the midwestern elms. For a Winnebago Brave. Joseph Bruchac. CDW

Nightingale/ From singing, The. *Unknown, tr. by* Geoffrey Bownas *and* Anthony Thwaite. PeBJV

Nightingale, The. Mark Akenside. *See* Ode to the Evening Star *or* The Nightingale.

Nightingale, The. Richard Barnefield. *See* Passionate Pilgrim, The:
As it fell upon a day.

Nightingale, The. Richard Barnfield. *See* Affectionate Shepherd, The:
As it fell upon a day.

Nightingale, The. Richard Brathwaite. *Fr.* Nature's Embassy. EIL; PBBP

Nightingale, The. John Clare. EBVV

Nightingale, The. Samuel Taylor Coleridge. EnRP; FM; PBBP

Nightingale, The, *sels.* Samuel Taylor Coleridge. EnRP; FM
Nightingales. ChTr
"No cloud, no relique of the sunken day." PBBP

Nightingale, The. Marie de France, *tr. fr. French by* Patricia Terry. BoWoP

Nightingale, The. William Strode, *after the Latin of* Famianus Strada. OBVE

Nightingale, The. Katharine Tynan. BoTP

Nightingale, The ("Little pretty nightingale, The"). *Unknown.* TrGrPo

Nightingale, The ("One morning, one morning, one morning in May"). *Unknown. See* One morning, one morning . . .

Nightingale and the Glowworm, The. William Cowper. OnMSP; PBBP

Nightingale, in dead of night, The. The Happy Nightingale. *Unknown.* OxBChV

Nightingale near the House, The. Harold Monro. MoBrPo

Nightingale, that all day long, A. The Nightingale and the Glowworm. William Cowper. OnMSP; PBBP

Nightingale, the organ of delight, The. *Unknown.* PBBP

Nightingale, whose happy noble hart, The. The Steele Glas. George Gascoigne. AAS

Nightingales. Robert Bridges. BrPo; CMoP; LiTB; LiTM; MoAB; MoBrPo; NOBE; OAEL-2; OBEV; OBMV; OBNC; PBBP; TrGrPo; UnPo

Nightingales. Samuel Taylor Coleridge. *Fr.* The Nightingale. ChTr

Nightingales Are Not Singing. Moshe Dor, *tr. fr. Hebrew by* Dennis Johnson. VWA

Nightingales grow out of my warm thighs, The. Fertile. Gerrit Komrij, *tr. by* Jacob Lowland. DuIn

Nightingales of Spring, The. *Unknown.* AmFP

Nightingales warble about it. The Secret. George Edward Woodberry. *Fr.* Wild Eden, VI. AA

Nightingales warbled without. In the Garden at Swainston. Tennyson. OBEV; OBNC

Nightingales won't let you sleep in Plates. Helen. George Seferis. VMG

Nightjar, The. Sir Henry Newbolt. Mes

Nightletter. Charles Wright. PoA

Nightly tormented by returning doubt. The Struggle. Sully-Prudhomme, *tr. by* Arthur O'Shaughnessy. AWP

Nightmare. Erasmus Darwin. *Fr.* The Botanic Garden: The Loves of the Plants. NOEC

Nightmare. Gawin Douglas. *Fr.* The Palace [*or* Palice] of Honor [*or* Honour]. PoEL-1

Nightmare. James A. Emanuel. BPo

Nightmare. Isabella Gardner. CoAP

Nightmare. W. S. Gilbert. *Fr.* Iolanthe. NOBL; NoP; OxBoli; PoRA
(Chancellor's Nightmare, The.) FaBoNo

Nightmare. Lyall Wilkes. OBD

Nightmare Abbey, *sels.* Thomas Love Peacock.
Song by Mr. Cypress. *Fr. ch.* 11. OAEL-2; OBNC; Par
Wise Men of Gotham, The. *Fr. ch.* 11. BXAP; FaBoNo
(Men of Gotham, The.) CH
(Seamen Three.) WiR
(Three Men of Gotham.) FaBoCh; OBEV

Nightmare at Noon. Stephen Vincent Benét. OxBA

Nightmare Begins Responsibility. Michael S. S. Harper. CAPP; DiL; GeTw; HCAP; LCAP; TAP

Nightmare Inspection Tour for American Generals. Gibbons Ruark. TW

Nightmare leaves fatigue. Louis MacNeice. *Fr.* Autumn Journal. AnIL; BIrV; CIP; FaBCIP

Nightmare Number Three. Stephen Vincent Benét. MoAmPo; SaC

Nightmare of beasthood, snorting, how to wake. Moly. Thom Gunn. HAP; MoP; NoAM; PrIm

Nightmare of Mouse. Robert Penn Warren. SO

Nightmare on Rhum. James Macmillan. PoSH

Nightmare shower room, The. My tormentor leers. Days of 1941 and '44. James Merrill. GLP

Nightmare, with Angels. Stephen Vincent Benét. MAT

Nightmares. Siv Cedering Fox. WSC

Nightpiece. James Joyce. PoA

Nights. Cyn Zarco. UL

Nights along the River. Charles Sullivan. AiP

Nights and days we stumble over each other. Stumbling. Dick Lourie. NeAC

Nights are long and I cannot sleep. *Unknown. See* Tzu Yeh Songs: All night I could not sleep.

Nights bring you the fever. Prometheus. Jenny Mastoraki. BoWoP, *tr. by* Nikos Germanakos

Night's diadem around thy head. Fairest of Freedom's Daughters. Jeremiah Eames Rankin. PAH

Night's drifts, The. A Winter Daybreak above Vence. James Wright. InPS; LCAP

Night's first sweet silence fell, and on my bed. The Malady of Love Is Nerves. Petronius Arbiter, *tr. by* Howard Mumford Jones. AWP

Nights here are usually clear and the shadows, The. Addio a la Mamma. Noe Jitrik, *tr. by* Yishai Tobin. VWA

Nights in Hackett's Cove. Mark Strand. GeTw

Nights in the Gardens of Port of Spain. Derek Walcott. NAEL-2; OxBC

Night's Invitation. Ishihara Yoshiro, *tr. fr. Japanese by* Hiroaki Sato. FCEI

Nights Passed on Ward's Island, Toronto Harbour. Doug Fetherling. NeAC

Night's ride's over. Anselm Hollo. UL

Nights, seasons, dates, times. Nanak, *tr. by* John Stratton Hawley *and* Mark Juergensmeyer. SSI

Night's still silken. Curtains spread red silk, The. Dimmed Observation. Abba Kovner, *tr. by* Warren Bargad *and* Stanley F. Chyet. IP

Nights when the muddy river. Kyotai, *tr. fr. Japanese by* Burton Watson. *Fr.* Sixteen Hokku. FCEI

Nights you wake to sudden stars. Wolf Hunting near Nashoba. Jim Barnes. STE

Nightsea and violet wave. A Storm of Love. Hilary Corke. NYBP

Nightsong. Louis O. Coxe. FYAP

Nightswim. William Pitt Root. MAYP

Nighttime. The faithful prison guard. Bedtime Story. Lou Lipsitz. VGW

Nightwalker. Thomas Kinsella. IPY

Nightwalker ("Mindful of the/ shambles of the day."), *sel. Thomas* Kinsella. IPY

  "I must lie down with them all soon and sleep." BIrV

Nightwatch, *sel.* Khairi Mansour, *tr. fr. Arabic by* Lena Jayyusi.

  "I see trees breaking off their branches." MAP

Nightwind sings and rustles through the reeds, The. Nocturne in G Minor. Karl Gustav Vollmoeller, *tr. by* Ludwig Lewisohn. AWP

Nightwood. William Jay Smith. PoA

Nihil Humani Alienum. Titus Munson Coan. AA

Nijiko. Basho, *tr. fr. Japanese by* Burton Watson. *Fr.* Seventy-six Hokku. FCEI

Nijinsky. Parker Tyler. PoA

Nike. Ernest Bryll, *tr. fr. Polish by* Czeslaw Milosz. PwPP

Nike. Adam Wazyk, *tr. fr. Polish by* Isaac Komem. VWA

Nikki-Rosa [*or* Nikki-Roasa]. Nikki Giovanni. AIW; AmNP; BlSi; HeIP; IHMS; MoP; NBP; PoBA; TAP

Niko pirosmanashvili is my name. Song Encountered in the Landscape. H. C. ten Berge, *tr. by* Theo Hermans. DuIn

Nikolina. Celia Thaxter. GN

Nile, The. Leigh Hunt. EBEV; EnRP; NOBE; OBNC

Nilotic Elegy. George Sutherland Fraser. WaP

Nima, The. Jorge Isaacs, *tr. fr. Spanish by* Alice Jane McVan. TrJP

Nimble as dolphins to. Gimboling. Isabella Gardner. ErPo

Nimble cat and lazy maid, A. On Maids and Cats. Henricus Selyns. SCAP

Nimble sigh, on thy warm wings. To Amoret. Henry Vaughan. EnLoPo

Nimbus. Douglas Le Pan. MoCV; OBCV

Nimium Fortunatus. Robert Bridges. *See* Fortunatus Nimium.

Nimphs Reply to the Sheepheard, The. Sir Walter Ralegh. *See* Nymph's Reply to the Shepherd, The.

Nina loved compromising. Three Women. Alan Dienstag. ErPo

Nina Simone. Lance Jeffers. CNA

Nina's cross: her alphabet. Cubes. Mary Elizabeth Fullerton. PoAu-1

Nine, The. John Sheffield. APAS

Nine adulteries, 12 liaisons, 64 fornications and something approaching a rape. The Temperaments. Ezra Pound. BoLoP; ErPo; NoAM; NOBA

9:00 A.M. Imre Oravecz, *tr. fr. Hungarian by* Jascha Kessler. FOC

Nine Below. Joy Harjo. ER

Nine Birds. E. E. Cummings. UnPo

Nine Charms against the Hunter. David Wagoner. ASP; TW

Nine drops of water bead the jessamine. A Wet August. Thomas Hardy. PPP

Nine grenadiers, with bayonets in their guns. The Dream of a Boy Who Lived at Nine Elms. William Brighty Rands. OxBChV

Nine Inch Will Please a Lady. Burns. ErPo

Nine Little Goblins, The. James Whitcomb Riley. OBCA

Nine Lives. *Unknown.* CRH

Nine Men out of a Minyan. Haim Guri, *tr. fr. Hebrew by* Mark Elliott Shapiro. VWA

Nine months I waited in the dark beneath. Pro Sua Vita. Robert Penn Warren. MoAmPo

Nine Nectarines and Other Porcelain. Marianne Moore. OxBA

Nine o'Clock. Katharine Pyle. *Fr.* The Wonder Clock. OBCA

Nine-o'clock Bell! School-Bell. Eleanor Farjeon. FaPON

Nine o'clock, the radios in the building have shut. 9:00 A.M. Imre Oravecz, *tr. by* Jascha Kessler. FOC

Nine on Happy Reunion, sels. Peyanar, *tr. fr. Tamil by* A. K. Ramanujan. PLW

  What He Said ("As the deer begin to hide"). *Fr.* 5.

  What He Said ("As wild oxen bellowed"). *Fr.* 3.

  What He Said ("Because peacocks moved like you"). *Fr.* 2.

  What He Said ("In this time of rain and thunder"). *Fr.* 1.

  What He Said ("The red earth"). *Fr.* 4.

  What Her Girl Friend Said ("As the cassias blossom"). *Fr.* 6.

  What Her Girl Friend Said ("Her eyes lined with kohl"). *Fr.* 9.

  What Her Girl Friend Said ("Saying to himself"). *Fr.* 8.

  What Her Girl Friend Said ("Your arms are beautiful again"). *Fr.* 7.

999 Call. Elizabeth Bartlett. FaBoWP

Nine Poems for the Unborn Child, *sel.* Muriel Rukeyser.

  They Came to me and Said, "There Is a Child." *Fr.* II. Son

Nine Reasons Why. Deborah Levy. DT

Nine Songs, *sels. Unknown, tr. fr. Chinese by* Burton Watson. CoBCP

  Lord among the Clouds, The.

  Lord of the River.

  Mountain Spirit, The.

  Those Who Died for Their Country.

9000 Jackals Swimming to Boston. Lucebert, *tr. fr. Dutch by* Peter Nijmeijer. DuIn

Nine Times. James Michie. DiPo

Nine Times a Night. *Unknown.* OBET

Nine Triads. Lillian Morrison. ASP

9 Verses of the Same Song, *sel.* Wendell Berry.

  "And my love has come to me." LLLT

Nine white chickens come. A Black November Turkey. Richard Wilbur. LCAP; MoAB; NAAL-2

1918-1941. Robert David Fitzgerald. CBAP

1980. Abraham Sutskever, *tr. fr. Yiddish by* Cynthia Ozick. *Fr.* Poems from a Diary. PeBMYV

1981. Abraham Sutskever, *tr. fr. Yiddish by* Cynthia Ozick. *Fr.* Poems from a Diary. PeBMYV

1955. Bruce Weigl. MAYP; NAmP

1905. David Ignatow. VWA

1945. Sheila Cussons, *tr. fr. Afrikaans by* Jack Cope *and* Uys Krige. PeSA

1945. Sir Herbert Read. OxBTC

1944—On the Invasion Coast. Jack Beeching. WaP

1941. Everette Maddox. MT

1943. Naomi Mitchison. CN

1943. Sandra McPherson. FaBoWP

1904. Frederick Morgan. BLA

1914, *sels.* Rupert Brooke.

  Dead, The ("Blow out, you bugles, over the rich dead!"). *Fr.* III. WGRP

  Dead, The ("These hearts were woven"). *Fr.* IV. BrPo; CH; LiTB; MMA; PoA

  Peace. *Fr.* I. MMA; OBWP; PoA; WGRP

  Safety. *Fr.* II. BrPo; EnLoPo

  Soldier, The. *Fr.* V. BrPo; FaBV; FaFP; FaPoR; FF; FPL; HeIP; LiTB; LiTM; MoBrPo; NAEL-2; NIP; NOBE; OBEV; OBWP; OxBTC; PoA; PoLF; PoRA; Son; TEP; TrGrPo; WaP

MCMXIV. Philip Larkin. EBEV; NAEL-2; NoAM; OBWP

Nineteen Hundred and Nineteen. W. B. Yeats. BIrV; LiTB; MoAB

Nineteen Hundred and Nineteen, *sels.* W. B. Yeats. PoE

  "Many ingenious lovely things are gone." *Fr.* I.

  "Some moralist or mythological poet." *Fr.* III.

Nineteen long lines hanging over my door. Lace Tell. *Unknown.* OBET

1909. Guillaume Apollinaire, *tr. fr. French by* Robert Bly. POS; RHTwFP
1919. Jacob Glatstein, *tr. fr. Yiddish.* AYP, *tr. by* Benjamin *and* Barbara Harshav *and* Kathryn Helle; PeBMYV, *tr. by* Cynthia Ozick.
Nineteen Old Poems of the Han, *sels. Unknown, tr. fr. Chinese by* Burton Watson. CoBCP
"Clear moon brightly shining in the night." *Fr.* VII.
"Far far away, the Herdboy Star." *Fr.* X.
"First month of winter: cold air comes." *Fr.* XVII.
"Frail frail, lone-growing bamboo." *Fr.* VIII.
"Green green, river bank grasses." *Fr.* II.
"Green green the cypress on the ridge." *Fr.* III.
"I drive my carriage from the Upper East Gate." *Fr.* XIII.
"I turn the carriage, yoke and set off." *Fr.* XI.
"Man's years fall short of a hundred." *Fr.* XV.
"Northwest the tall tower stands." *Fr.* V.
"On and on, going on and on." *Fr.* I.
"We hold a splendid feast today." *Fr.* IV.
Nineteen Pieces for Love, *sel.* Susan Griffin.
Trying to Say, #15. LLLT
1970s. Liu K'o-hsiang, *tr. fr. Chinese by* Dominic Cheung. IFON
1975. Remco Campert, *tr. fr. Dutch by* James S. Holmes. DuIn
1975. Abraham Sutskever, *tr. fr. Yiddish by* Cynthia Ozick. *Fr.* Poems from a Diary. PeBMYV
1974. Marilyn Hacker. GLP
1974. Abraham Sutskever, *tr. fr. Yiddish by* Cynthia Ozick. *Fr.* Poems from a Diary. PeBMYV
1974—The Sounds. Christina Beer. PeNZ
1976. Abraham Sutskever, *tr. fr. Yiddish by* Cynthia Ozick. *Fr.* Poems from a Diary. PeBMYV
1976 Ford, A. A shiny lacquered. Front Page. Abba Kovner, *tr. by* Warren Bargad *and* Stanley F. Chyet. IP
1916. R. S. Gwynn. MT
1916. Mirko Lauer, *tr. fr. Spanish by* David Tipton. Per
1916 Seen from 1921. Edmund Blunden. MMA
1968. Petra von Morstein, *tr. fr. German by* Rosemarie Waldrop. BoWoP
1964 and I'm parked. White. Christopher Buckley. MOWH
1930. Kathleen Fraser. NPGG
1935. Stephen Vincent Benét. MoAmPo
Nineteen Thirty-Nine, *sel.* Charles Brasch.
City, The. ATNZ
1939 Somewhere in England. Virginia Graham. CN
1933. Philip Levine. VWA
1930's. Robert Lowell. NoP
1912–1952, Full Cycle. Peter Viereck. OBAL
1925. Edwin Honig. *Fr.* To Restore a Dead Child, I. NoAM
1929. W. H. Auden. SOTW
1926. Weldon Kees. CoAP; NaP
19 years old and going nowhere. At Bessemer. Philip Levine. BLA
Nineteenth Century and After, The. W. B. Yeats. FaBoEE
Nineteenth of April, The. Lucy Larcom. PAH
Nineteenth Telegram ("Love has changed the face of distances"). Abd al-Aziz al-Maqalih, *tr. fr. Arabic by* Lena Jayyusi *and* Christopher Middleton. *Fr.* Telegrams of Tenderness for Sanaa. MAP
Ninetieth Psalm, The. Isaac Watts. *See* O God, Our Help in Ages Past.
Ninety. "E." CBAP
98 Fahrenheit. Judah Leib Teller, *tr. fr. Yiddish by* Benjamin *and* Barbara Harshav. AYP
Ninety-fifth. Isaac Watts. AmFP
90 North. Randall Jarrell. CAPP; CoAP; FYAP; MoAB; MT; NAAL-2; NoAM; NOBA; TAP
Ninety percent of the mass of the Universe. Certainty before Lunch. John Berryman. LCAP; OxBC
Nineveh, Tyre. Memphis Blues. Sterling Allen Brown. BANP
Nino, the Wonder Dog. Roy Fuller. FF
9th July, 1932. Mary Ursula Bethell. PeNZ
Ninth Month. Robert Lowell. *Fr.* Marriage, *st.* 11. NAS
Ninth Month, Tenth Day. Michizane, *tr. fr. Chinese by* Burton Watson. JLIC-1
Ninth of Av. Myra Sklarew. CRP
Ninth of July, The. John Hollander. CoAP
Ninth Symphony of Beethoven Understood at Last as a Sexual Message, The. Adrienne Rich. NoP; TAP
Ninth Telegram ("Trains roll over my heart, The"). Abd al-Aziz al-Maqalih, *tr. fr. Arabic by* Lena Jayyusi *and* Christopher Middleton. *Fr.* Telegrams of Tenderness for Sanaa. MAP
Niobe, *sel.* Aeschylus, *tr. fr. Greek by* C. M. Bowra.
"Alone of gods death has no love for gifts." OBD
Niobe. Henrietta Cordelia Ray. CBWP-3

Niobe on Phrygian sands. The Wish. Thomas Stanley. AWP
Niplets. *Unknown, tr. fr. Greek by* Wallace Rice. ErPo
Nirvana. John Hall Wheelock. MoAmPo
Nisei Picnic, A. David Mura. BrSi
NN 616410. Bill Tulloch. PoSH
No/ that I always wanted to say, The. Peter Turrini, *tr. by* Beth Bjorklund. CoAuP
No, The. Philip Dacey. NAmP
No,/ people are feared to fall off. On Falling. Andrew Greig. *Fr.* Men on Ice. PoSH
No! Thomas Hood. ChTr; FiBHP; GN
(November.) ChTr
No/ No/ No/ I am not doing. Our Lives. Sharon Scott. JB
No,/ I cannot/ turn from love. To Turn from Love. Sarah Webster Fabio. BlSi
No/ Don't look for me. Where I Am. Marcelino dos Santos, *tr. by* Chris Searle. WMBCH
No. Natan Zach, *tr. fr. Hebrew by* Laya Firestone. VWA
No Accident. Norman MacCaig. PoSH
No argument, no anger, no remorse. Hedges Freaked with Snow. Robert Graves. OxBTC
No Bargains Today. Peggy Susberry Kenner. JB
No bars are set too close, no mesh too fine. The Sparrow in the Zoo. Howard Nemerov. MoP
(Epigram: Political Reflection.) NIP
No beggar she in the mighty hall where her bay-crowned sisters wait. Arizona. Sharlot M. Hall. PAH
No bells rang in her house. The silver plate. Miss Marnell. Austin Clarke. IPY
No berserk thirst of blood had they. Lexington. Whittier. PAH
No better lost than any other woman. Marilyn Hacker. NoAM
No better than the ordinary in talent. Ishikawa Takuboku, *tr. fr. Japanese by* Hiroaki Sato. *Fr.* Forty-seven Tanka in Three Lines. FCEI
No bird, no fabled fowl it is. Little Cheat. *Malay Oral Tradition, tr. by* R. J. Wilkinson *and* R. O. Winstedt. WTO
No bitterness: our ancestors did it. Ave Caesar. Robinson Jeffers. FaBoPV; MoP; NoAM; NOBA; OxBA; OxBSP
No black and swirling cloak, no faceless grin. Waiting for the Post. Dorothy Auchterlonie. CBAP
No blacker than others in winter, but. Burning Mountain. W. S. Merwin. NYBP
No bottom,/ Mark four. *Unknown.* AmFP
No boy chooses war. Sailors on Leave. Owen Dodson. AmNP
No branch nor the last grass. Fossil. E. D. Blodgett. NOBC
No breath of wind. Snow. Walter de la Mare. OnUR
No breeze stirs. *Unknown, tr. by* Arthur Waley. BoS
No butler, no second maid, no blood upon the stair. Crime Club. Weldon Kees. NaP
No Buyers; a Street Scene. Thomas Hardy. LiTB; NoP
No by torchlight, The. Kawahigashi Hekigoto, *tr. by* Geoffrey Bownas *and* Anthony Thwaite. PeBJV
No camellia. Yosano Akiko, *tr. fr. Japanese.* PBWP, *tr. by* Geoffrey Bownas *and* Anthony Thwaite; PeBJV, *tr. by* Geoffrey Bownas *and* Anthony Thwaite
No Categories! Stevie Smith. NoP
No ceaseless vigil with hard toil we keep. Compensation. Thomas Stephens Collier. AA
No Chance Operations. James Sherry. LP
No Change in Me. *Unknown.* AmFP
No Change of Place. W. H. Auden. *See* Who Will Endure.
No changes of support—only. Last Month. John Ashbery. CoAP
No charm can stay, no medicine can assuage. Walter Savage Landor. FaBoEE
No Child. Padraic Colum. OBMV
No, children, my trips are over. The Engineer's Story. *Unknown.* BeLS
No citizen is melancholy. Joie de Vivre. Joel Dailey. UL
No city in the spacious universe. London. Daniel Defoe. *Fr.* Reformation of Manners. NOEC
No city primness train'd my feet. Rustic Childhood. William Barnes. OBNC
No cloud can hide the glow of living faith. The Light of Faith. Edgar Dupree. BLRP
No cloud, no relique of the sunken day. Samuel Taylor Coleridge. *Fr.* The Nightingale. EnRP; FM; PBBP
No clouds are in the morning sky. Going a-Nutting. Edmund Clarence Stedman. GN
No coins to buy my firewood. Sweeping Leaves. Ryushu Shutaku, *tr. by* Burton Watson. FCEI
No Cold Approach. *At. to* Burns. EBEV

No Coming to God without Christ. Robert Herrick. OxBSP
No Complaints. Anselm Hollo. UL
No Continuing City. Michael Longley. FaBCIP
No Country You Remember. Robert Mezey. FF
No Coward Soul [Is Mine]. Emily Brontë. BrRo; EaLo; EBVV; FaFP; HeIP; LiTB; NAEL-2; NoP; OBNC; PoEL-5; TIRV; TOF; TrCP; TrPWD
No Coward's Song. James Elroy Flecker. OxBSP
No Credit. Kenneth Fearing. CMoP
No crooked leg, no bleared eye. Written in Her French Psalter. Elizabeth I, Queen of England. PBWP; WPE
No crunch of boots. Winter Pause: Mt. Liberty, N.H. Martin Robbins. RR
No, Daisy! lift not up thy ear. To a Spaniel. Walter Savage Landor. FM
No date of birth, nor place, background unknown. Wild Grass. Akhtar-ul-Iman, tr. by Mahmood Jamal. PBMUP
No David could send a stone as high. Central Park West. Stanley Moss. PCP
No Dawns. Julianne Perry. PoBA
No day was sad as the day Sakhr. On Her Brother Sakhr. Al-Khansa. BoWoP, tr. by Willis Barnstone
No Dead Ends. Cathleen Quirk. PPR
No Denying. Mihály Ladányi, tr. fr. Hungarian by Jascha Kessler. FOC
No Deposit. Earle Thompson. HATNAP
No Dialects Please. Merle Collins. WS
No Difference in the Dark. Robert Herrick. CaPo
No different, I said, from rat's or chicken's. Not to Be Born. David Sutton. OBD
No dignity without a chromium. Ballad of Faith. William Carlos Williams. OBAL
No Discharge. Arthur Waley. OBD
No doubt at all. Marcabrun, tr. by Paul Blackburn. Pro
No doubt in the mind of Brébeuf that this was the last. The Martyrdom of Brébeuf and Lalemant, 16 March 1649. E. J. Pratt. Fr. Brébeuf and His Brethren. NOBC; OBCV
("Less than two hours it took the Iroquois.") OBCV
No doubt left. Enough deceiving. James Agee. Fr. Lyrics. MoAmPo
No doubt: the sun. Monterrey Sun. Alfonso Reyes, tr. by Samuel Beckett. MexPo
No doubt this way is best. No Use. W. D. Snodgrass. BoLoP
No doubt to-morrow I will hide. At Mass. Vachel Lindsay. VGW
No dream of mortal joy. Love and Lust. Isaac Rosenberg. TrJP
No dreams through the night. Elegies for Prince Atsumichi. Lady Izumi, tr. fr. Japanese by Hiroaki Sato. Fr. Fifty-one Tanka. FCEI
No dust have I to cover me. An Inscription by the Sea. E. A. Robinson, after Glaucus. AWP; ChTr; FaBoEE
No ears could hear then the mutter of the Milky Way. Prophecy. Eileen Duggan. PeNZ
No earthquake. Chapped, a lifting in this field. Dead Center. Chester Kallman. PoA
No Easy Harbour. Anne Hartigan. CIP
No End of No-Story. George MacDonald. NOBVV
No end to roofs' cry. Madison Square. A. Leyeles, tr. fr. Yiddish by Benjamin and Barbara Harshav. Fr. New York. AYP
No Escape. Harriet L. Delafield. GoYe
No "fan is in his hand" for these. The Threshing Machine. Alice Meynell. SeCePo; WPE
No farther/ than to the Milky Way. From the Milky Way. Otto Laaber, tr. by Beth Bjorklund. CoAuP
No fence will keep a growing boy outside. Father of the Man. Elizabeth Mabel Bryan. GoYe
No fields, no house, one poor scholar. Rai San'yo, tr. fr. Chinese by Burton Watson. Fr. Shortly after I Married, I Had to Go into Mourning, I. FCEI; JLIC-2
No first-class war can now be fought. Civil Defense. Kenneth Burke. OBAL
No fledgling feeds the fatherbird. Child Labor. Charlotte Perkins Gilman. AnAmPo
No Flowers. Ch'ien Ch'ien-i, tr. fr. Chinese by Jonathan Chaves. CoBLCP
No flowers!/ Let's blame the god in charge of flowers. Poem on Drinking Wine with the Degree-Holder Ku. Ch'ien Ch'ien-i, tr. by Jonathan Chaves. CoBLCP
No flute, The. Unknown, tr. by Geoffrey Bownas and Anthony Thwaite. PeBJV
No, for I'll save it! Seven years since. Apparent Failure. Robert Browning. NAEL-2; NOBE
No for you, my queyn, will I prepare. The Real Muse. Tom Scott. PoA
No Foundation. John Hollander. OBAL

No freeman, saith the wise, thinks much on death. The End. Wallace Rice. AA
No Funeral Gloom. Ellen Terry. BLPA
No funeral gloom, my dears, when I am gone. William Allingham. NOBVV
No Furlough. Stephen Stepanchev. WaP
No Generation. Rutger Kopland, tr. fr. Dutch by Ria Leigh-Loohuizen. DuIn
No Chost Is True. Leslie A. Fiedler. PoA
No Girls Allowed. Jack Prelutsky. RHPC
No gorgeous coat has he. My Mocking Bird. Josephine D. Henderson Heard. CBWP-4
No great house is finer. An Ivied Tree-Top. Unknown. NOIV
No Great Matter. David Lawson. VGW
No Grounds for Prosecution. André Breton, tr. fr. French by Paul Auster. RHTwFP
No hand has been allowed to touch. Inscription on a Chemise. Unknown, tr. fr. Arabic by E. Powys Mathers. Fr. The Thousand and One Nights. ErPo
No Haste but Good. George Gascoigne. Fr. Gascoigne's Memories. AAS; Son
No hawk hangs over in this air. The Snow Storm. Edna St. Vincent Millay. NAAL-2; PoA
No, He is too quick. We never. Getting Inside the Miracle. Luci Shaw. TrCP
No! Heavenly tallow, don't lick my gummy beards. Perets Markish, tr. fr. Yiddish by Leonard Wolf. Fr. The Mound. PeBMYV
No heavier lies the everlasting snow. Truth. Cecil Francis Lloyd. CaP
No help I'll call till I'm put in the narrow coffin. Egan O'Rahilly, tr. by Thomas Kinsella. NOIV
No Hiding Place Down There. Unknown. GBP
No high mountains. Ito Sachio, tr. by Geoffrey Bownas and Anthony Thwaite. PeBJV
No Hint of Stain. William Vaughn Moody. Fr. An Ode in Time of Hesitation. AA
No hint upon the hill top shows. Inspiration. John Banister Tabb. WGRP
No Holes Marred. Suzanne Douglass. RHPC
"No home, no home," cried an orphan girl. The Orphan Girl. Unknown. AmFP; AS, with music.
No, Honoria, I am greatly flattered. Time's Revenges. Sir Owen Seaman. FaBoUs
No hoofprints planned. Buckskin Flats. Gordon Eastman. CowP
No hope have I to live a deathless name. Poietes Apoietes. Hartley Coleridge. OBNC
No house of stone. The Elements. William Henry Davies. MoBrPo
No hungr[y] hawke poore patridge to devoure. Mr. Thomas Shepeard. Edward Johnson. SCAP
No, I Am Not as Others Are. Villon, tr. fr. French by Arthur Symons. AWP
No, I am not death wishes of sacred rapists. I, Too, Know What I Am Not. Bob Kaufman. NBP
No, I am through and you can call in vain. Admonition. Philip Stack. BLPA
No, I don't believe, as they say, that I. Moment after the Rain. Jeannie Ebner, tr. by Beth Bjorklund. CoAuP
No, I don't love you. Anti-Love Poems. Elizabeth Brewster. NOBC
No, I had set no prohibiting sign. Trespass. Robert Frost. FaBV
No, I have never found. Places, Loved Ones. Philip Larkin. CMoP; NePoEA
"No, I have tempered haste." The Mount. Léonie Adams. MoAB; MoAmPo
No—I'll endure ten thousand deaths. Chaste Florimel. Matthew Prior. BoLoP; ErPo
No, I'm not afraid of death. Soliloquy I. Richard Aldington. BrPo
No. I'm not an Englishman with a partisan religion. Tragic Guilt. Keidrych Rhys. WaP
No, I'm not Byron, it's my role. Mikhail Yurevich Lermontov, tr. by Alan Myers. AAA
No Images. Waring Cuney. AmNP; BANP; CDC; MAT; NIP; TTY
No Imposter. Duane Reece. CowP
No! Indeed. Sir Thomas Wyatt. See Rondeau: "What no, perdy! ye may be sure!"
No Irish Need Apply. Unknown. WTO
No, it is not an elephant or any such grasshopper. Nessie. Ted Hughes. AmMo
No, it is not in heaven that we find the dry. Not in Heaven. Iain Crichton Smith. NPo

No, it's a tenement. "It's a Whole World, the Body. A Whole World!" Swami Satchidananda. David Young. FF
No. It's an impudent falsehood. Men did not. On a Vulgar Error. C. S. Lewis. OxBTC
No-Kings and the Calling of Spirits. Nancy Willard. LCAP
No Labor-saving Machine. Walt Whitman. PCP
No, Lady, the shepherds have not gone. No Se Van Los Pastores. Charles Squier. SoTCo
No Land like Ours. J. R. Barrick. OPP
No Laws. Brian Allwood. WaP
No leaf is left unmoistened by the dew. Prayer by Moonlight. Roberta Teale Swartz. TrPWD
No Less than Prisoners. Frederick Thomas Bennett Macartney. CBAP
No, let it stay. It speaks but truth. The First Grey Hair. Mary E. Tucker. CBWP-1
No Letter. Mary E. Tucker. CBWP-1
No life in earth, or air, or sky. Crotalus. (Bret Harte). AA
No lifeless thing of iron and stone. Brooklyn Bridge. Sir Charles G. D. Roberts. PAH
No light except the stars, but from the cliff. The Sea Birds. Van K. Brock. NYBP; SM
No light within the court, and moss climbs the stairs. Written in a Cool Breeze. Fan Tseng-hsiang, tr. by J. P. Seaton. WFTU
No Loathsomnesse in Love. Robert Herrick. GBL
No Lock against Lechery. Robert Herrick. CaPo
No longer aware of mind and object. Daio, tr. by Lucien Stryk and Takashi Ikemoto. ZPCJ
No longer can the ear. Limbo. Alfred Gong, tr. by Beth Bjorklund. CoAuP
No longer casual hand to lip. Blind, I Speak to the Cigarette. Joanne de Longchamps. GoYe
"No longer mourn for me when I am dead." Shakespeare. Fr. Sonnets, LXXI. AWP; EBEV; EIL; FaBoRV; GBL; HAP; LiTB; NAEL-1; NoP; OBSC; PoRA; Son; TEP; TrGrPo
(Triumph of Death, The.) GTBS; GTBS-P
No longer the feather. Guilt. Lorenzo Thomas. UL
No longer throne of a goddess to whom we pray. Full Moon. Robert Hayden. BPo
No longer to lie reading Strauss's Life. Memories of Aunt Maria-Martha. William Zaranka. BXAP
No longer to lie reading Tess of the d'Urbervilles. The Lesson. Robert Lowell. CMoP; LCAP
No, Love Is Not Dead. Robert Desnos, tr. fr. French by Bill Zavatsky. RHTwFP; UnAS
No Love, to Love of Man and Wife. Richard Eedes. InvP
(Of Man and Wife.) EIL
No McTavish. Genealogical Reflection. Ogden Nash. OBAL
No man can bid a fool or sage. The Power of Thought. Süsskind von Trimberg. TrJP
No man can serve two masters. Bible, N.T. Fr. St. Matthew, VI: 24-29. OBVE
No man can utterly fulfill what he has in his heart. Aimeric de Belenoi, tr. by Paul Blackburn. Pro
No man could have been more unfaithful. The Turkish Carpet. Paul Durcan. CIP
No man could have that woman, Mouth-of-the-River. The Boy Who Became Sky. David Wagoner. AnAn
No Man, if Men Are Gods. E. E. Cummings. InvP; VGW
No Man Knoweth His Sepulchre. Bryant. AnAmPo
No Man Knows War. Edwin Rolfe. TrJP; WaP
No man lives now. Yoshitsune, tr. by Geoffrey Bownas and Anthony Thwaite. PeBJV
No man outlives the grief of war. The Permanence of the Young Men. William Soutar. OxBS
No Man's Land. Eric Bogle. OBET
No Man's Land. Gloria Escoffery. PVCV
No man's trust let woman claim. The Roman Earl. Unknown, tr. by Douglas Hyde. OBVE
No Marvel Is It. Bernard de Ventadour, tr. fr. Provençal by Harriet Waters Preston. AWP
No Matter. Paulus Silentarius, tr. fr. Greek by William Cowper. AWP
(Epitaph: "My name—my country—what are they to thee.") FaBoEE; OBVE
No matter how fast I run. Night. Tanikawa Shuntaro, tr. by Hiroaki Sato. FCEI
No matter how hard I listen, the wind speaks. For Zbigniew Herbert, Summer, 1971, Los Angeles. Larry Levis. FYAP; LCAP
No matter how hard I try to forget you. I Cannot Forget You. Unknown, tr. by Frances Densmore. ILY
No Matter What, after All, and That Beautiful Word So. Hayden Carruth. BLA

No matter what life you lead. Snow White and the Seven Dwarfs. Anne Sexton. HCAP
No matter what we are and who. Routine. Arthur Guiterman. RHPC
No matter why, nor whence, nor when she came. The Story of the Ashes and the Flame. E. A. Robinson. AnAmPo
No Mean City. Patrick MacDonogh. BIrV; OxBSP
No. Merely to have writ. Peruke of Poets. William Zaranka. BXAP
No mo meetings. Listenen to Big Black at S. F. State. Sonia Sanchez. BPo
No Money in Art. Jim Gustafson. UL
No monuments or landmarks guide the stranger. A Country without a Mythology. Douglas Le Pan. MoCV; NOBC
No moon. Night water shapes all light. Night Dive. Don Johnson. MAYP
No moon, no chance to meet. Ono no Komachi, tr. by Rob Swigart. WPOW
No moon No road No thunder. Poem on the Suicide of My Teacher. Joseph Stroud. NPGG
No Moon, No Star. Babette Deutsch. NYBP
No More. Carl Clark. JB
No more alone sleeping, no more alone waking. Marriage. Mary Elizabeth Coleridge. PeHV
No more, America, in mournful strain. Phillis Wheatley. Fr. To the Right Honourable William, Earl of Dartmouth. WPOW
No More Apologizing the No More Little Laughing Blues, The. Lyn Lifshin. ER
No More Auction Block. Unknown. BPo
"No more be grieved at that which thou hast done." Shakespeare. Fr. Sonnets, XXXV. NAEL-1; PeHV; PoE; TEP; UnPo
No More Beneath the Oppressive Hand. Unknown. AH
No More Booze. Unknown. OBAL
(Fireman Save My Child.) AS, with music
No more chant your old rhymes about bold Robin Hood. General Ludd's Triumph. Unknown. OBET
No more exercises of style for him. A Younger Poet. Peter Schjeldahl. PoA
No More Fighting. Meiling Jin. WS
No more for them shall evening's rose unclose. Epicedium. J. Corson Miller. PAH
"No more," I say to her. Empress Jito. Fr. Manyo Shu. Ma
"No more," I say to you. Lady Shihi. Fr. Manyo Shu. Ma
No more in any house can I be at peace. A Dream. Charles Williams. OBEV
No More Lewd Lays. Barnabe Barnes. Fr. A Divine Century of Spiritual Sonnets. Son
No more light from second-story lamps. Nakajima Soin, tr. fr. Chinese by Burton Watson. Fr. Miscellaneous Songs of the Four Seasons East of the Kamo. JLIC-2
No More Love Poems #1. Ntozake Shange. Fr. For Colored Girls Who Have Considered Suicide When the Rainbow Is Enuf. BlSi
"No more, my dear, no more these counsels try." Sir Philip Sidney. Fr. Astrophel and Stella, LXIV. OBSC
No more my visionary soul shall dwell. Pantisocracy. Samuel Taylor Coleridge. EnRP
No more, no more,/ We are already pin'd. Alexander Brome. OBS
No more, no more Jewish townships in Poland. Antoni Slonimski, tr. by Isaac Komem. VWA
No more—no more—Oh! never more on me. My Days of Love Are Over. Byron. Fr. Don Juan, I. OBNC
No More, O My Spirit. Euripides, tr. fr. Greek by Hilda Doolittle ("H. D."). Fr. Hippolytus. AWP
No more of talk where God or Angel Guest. Milton. Fr. Paradise Lost, Bk. IV complete. NAEL-1, fr. ll. 1–1189; NAWM-1; NoP; TOF, fr. ll. 1–47.
(Subject of Heroic Song, The.) OBS, fr. ll. 1–47.
No more of your titled acquaintances boast. Burns. FaBoEE
No more post-stops on the road. Following the Rhymes of Yang T'ing-ho's Poem "On the Road Back." Li Tung-yang, tr. by Jonathan Chaves. CoBLCP
No more sand art, no sand book, no masters. Paul Celan, tr. by Beth Bjorklund. CoAuP
No more shall I see. Frithiof's Farewell. Esaias Tegnér, tr. fr. Swedish by Longfellow. Fr. Frithiof's Saga. AWP
No more shall I, since I am driven hence. To Larr. Robert Herrick. CaPo; SeCV-1
No more shall I work in the factory. The Factory Girl. Unknown. SaC
No more shall walls, no more shall walls confine. Hosanna. Thomas Traherne. PoEL-2; SeCV-2
No More Soft Talk. Diane Wakoski. FF; IHMS
No More than Five. Fred Levinson. AmPA

No more the battle or the chase. Indian Summer. John Banister Tabb. AA

No more the English girls may go. High Germany. Edward Shanks. OBMV

No More the Slow Stream. Floris Clark McLaren. OBCV

No more the swanboat on the artificial lake. Blind Date. Conrad Aiken. DL

No More the Thunder of Cannon. Julia Caroline Ripley Dorr. OHIP

No more wine? Then we'll push back chairs and talk. Bishop Blougram's Apology. Robert Browning. OBNC; PoEL-5

No more with candied words infect mine ears. Tell Me No More. William Drummond of Hawthornden. TrGrPo

No more with overflowing light. For a Dead Lady. E. A. Robinson. CMoP; DL; FYAP; HeIP; HoPM; InvP; LiTA; LiTM; MoAB; MoAmPo; MoP; NoAM; NOBA; OxBA; PoEL-5; PoRA

No More Words. Franklin Lushington. PAH

No more words! To the field, to arms. Veronica Franco, tr. by Lynne Lawner. PBWP

No more work and no more play. Good Night. Ruth Ainsworth. BoTP

No more your name, not your face. I Have Never Forgotten You. André Frénaud, tr. by Kenneth Rexroth. RHTwFP

"No mortal man beneath the sky." Epitaph for George Moore. Thomas Hardy. FaBoEE

No mortal thing enthralled these longing eyes. Celestial Love. Michelangelo, tr. by John Addington Symonds. AWP

No motion and/ no sound. Newborn Neurological Exam. Mary Baron. MOWH

No mountains moved in the heart of the seas. Barges, Rivers. Hans Tentije, tr. by Scott Rollins. DuIn

No need for confusion if we but recall. Rhyme for Remembering the Date of Easter. Justin Richardson. FaBoUs

No Need for Nuremberg. Erica Marx. CN

No need to dial the doctor. I have. The Legacy. Judith Minty. GeTw

"No need to get home early." Father's voice. William Stafford. RFM

No need to look up. Rain Games. Tony Beyer. ATNZ

No need to squeeze out half a tube. Toothsome. Norah Smaridge. RAR

No! never such a draught was poured. A Ballad of the Boston Tea-Party. Oliver Wendell Holmes. PAH

No, Never Think. Pushkin, tr. fr. Russian by Babette Deutsch. ErPo

No new delights to our desire. Singers to Come. Alice Meynell. WPE

No New Music. Stanley Crouch. PoBA

No New Thing. Vincent Buckley. CBAP

No News at All. Jack Butler. TSL

No news of navies burnt at seas. A New-Year's Gift Sent to Sir Simeon Steward. Robert Herrick. CaPo

No news whatever came of those. Insha Allah Khan Insha, tr. by Ahmed Ali. GoT

No! No!/ Bird in the darkness singing. The Tsigane's Canzonet. Edward King. AA

No, no, don't, please. Crimes of Passion: The Phone Caller. Terry Stokes. AmPA

No, no, fair heretic[k], it needs must be. Sir John Suckling. Fr. Aglaura, IV, i. CaPo; OBS; PrIm

"No, no; for my virginity." A True Maid. Matthew Prior. ErPo; FaBoEE; FaBoEE; NAEL-1; NIP; NOEC

No, no! Go from me. I have left her lately. A Virginal. Ezra Pound. CMoP; MoAB; MoAmPo; NAAL-2; NIP; NOBA; OxBA; Son; TAP

No, no! go not to Lethe, neither twist. Ode on Melancholy. Keats. EnRP; FiP; HAP; HeIP; InPK; InPS; LiTB; MAT; NAEL-2; NAWM-2; NOBE; NoP; OAEL-2; OBEV; OBNC; PoE; PoEL-4; PoRA; PPP; PrIm; TEP; TrGrPo

No, no I did not bargain for so much. Too Much. Edwin Muir. LiTB

No, no, I don't like it. To Someone. Takamura Kotaro, tr. by Hiroaki Sato. FCEI

No, no! I say/ To Shii's far-fetched tales. Empress Jito. Fr. Manyo Shu. PeBJV

No, no! I say,/ But still you command. Lady Shihi. Fr. Manyo Shu. PeBJV

No, no, I well remember—proofs, you said. The Demon-Lover. James Abraham Hillhouse. Fr. Hadad. AA

No, no, no, I know I was not important as I moved. Come Dance with Kitty Stobling. Patrick Kavanagh. FaBCIP; MoP; NoAM

No, no, no, no, I cannot have my foe. Sir Philip Sidney. SiPS

No no: of course they. Testimony. Dan Pagis, tr. by Warren Bargad and Stanley F. Chyet. IP

No, No, Poor Suffering Heart. Dryden. Fr. Cleomenes, II, ii. LiTB; QFR; ViBoPo

(One Happy Moment.) OBEV

(Song: "No, no, poor suff'ring Heart no Change endeavour.") SeCV-2

No, no, this bitterness is no new thing. Northwind. Gene Baro. NePoEA-2

No noise is here, or none that hinders thought. William Cowper. Fr. The Task: A Winter Walk at Noon. PBBP

No, not in the halls of the noble and proud. The Quakeress Bride. Elizabeth Clementine Kinney. AA

No not that way she'd. My Mother and the Bed. Lyn Lifshin. ER; TV

No not this old whalehall can whelm us. Mappemounde. Earle Birney. OBCV

No, not tonight. In Teesdale. Andrew Young. FaBoPP; OxBSP

No, not under an alien sky. "Anna Akhmatova", tr. fr. Russian by Doris Earnshaw. Fr. Requiem 1935-1940. OV

No, not under the vault of another sky. Requiem 1935—1940. "Anna Akhmatova", tr. by Richard McKane. BoWoP

No, nothing is asleep in this demesne. The Sleeping Beauty. Robert Layzer. NePoEA

No Occupation. George Rostrevor Hamilton. FaBoEE

No Offence. D. J. Enright. OxBTC

No One. Amelia Rosselli, tr. fr. Italian by Lawrence R. Smith. NItP

No one alive has seen such ice but the five-mile floor. Photographic Plate, Partly Spidered, Hampton Roads, Virginia, with Model T Ford Mid-Channel. Dave Smith. MAYP

No one alone could detail that falling—the immediate. The Pieces of Heaven. Pattiann Rogers. NAmP

No one can communicate to you. Face of Poverty. Lucy Smith. PoNe

No one can hurt me. They've tried to kill me. Alone. "Anna Akhmatova", tr. by Stephen Berg. BoWoP

No one can order his face in advance. He Who Calls Himself Leader. Moyshe-Leyb Halpern, tr. by Benjamin and Barbara Harshav and Kathryn Helle. AYP

No one can tell you why. W. D. Snodgrass. Fr. Heart's Needle, IV. NePoEA

No one cares about the flowers. I Feel Sorry for the Garden. Forugh Farrokhzad, tr. by Deirdre Lashgari. OV

No one comes. The Old Place. Hone Tuwhare. ATNZ

No one comes to this deserted mountain. The Cliff of the Ancient Tomb. Chang Yü, tr. fr. Chinese by Jonathan Chaves. Fr. Seven Poems on Living in the Mountains: Seeing Off. CoBLCP

No one could have a blacker tail. Othello Jones Dresses for Dinner. Ed Roberson. PoBA; PoNe

No one could perceive the perfume. Ghazel of Unforseen Love. Federico García Lorca, tr. by Perry Higman. LPSS

No one could tell me where my Soul might be. The Search. Ernest Crosby. AA

No one disputes that sex. Toward a Better Love. Roque Dalton, tr. by Jack Hirschman. VoI

No one ever comes to this region of stillness. Mountain Dwelling. Ching An, tr. by Irving Lo. WFTU

No one ever walking this our only earth. Muriel Rukeyser. NNaP

No one for spelling at a loss is. What's the Plural? Unknown. FaBoUs

No one has sung "Let the world know!" Antiphonal Hymn in Praise of Inanna. Enheduanna. BoWoP

No one in the garden. Laughter. Olive Enoch. BoTP

No one introduces the show. A Little Girl's Show. Su Shao-lien, tr. by Dominic Cheung. IFON

No one kneads us again out of earth and clay. Paul Celan, tr. by Joachim Neugroschel. VWA

("No one moulds us again out of earth and clay.") CoAuP, tr. by Beth Bjorklund; OBVE, tr. by Michael Hamburger

No one knew the secret of my flutes. Something Whispered in the Shakuhachi. Garrett Kaoru Hongo. InPS

No one knows how old this tree is, standing before the mountain. Song of the Old Oak. Chang Yü, tr. by Jonathan Chaves. CoBLCP

No one knows the man who throws out the season's first ball. Mystery Baseball. Philip Dacey. TSL

No one knows the way out of his mother. String. Dennis Schmitz. LCAP

No one moulds us again out of earth and clay. Paul Celan. See Psalm: "No one kneads us again out of earth and clay."

No one need feel alone looking up at leaves. Looking Up at Leaves. Barbara Howes. BoNaP

No one noticed it at the housewarming of our new home. Between You and Me. Shmu'el Shatal, tr. by Bernhard Frank. MHeP

No One Remembers Abandoning the Village of White Fir. Duane Niatum. CDW

No One So Much as You. Edward Thomas. GBL

No one spoke. Ryota, tr. by Kenneth Rexroth. TTTS

No one standing. How the Joy of It Was Used Up Long Ago. Linda Gregg. NPGG

No one this far south chances ice. Ice. David Bottoms. BLA

No one to lose his way among the heaped up leaves. Princess Shikishi, *tr. fr. Japanese* by Hiroaki Sato. *Fr.* Seventy-eight Tanka. FCEI

No one understands the Windigo, his voice like. Windigo. Paulette Jiles. NOBC

No one wants to hear about the war. Nam. Mike Lowery. Psk

No one was in the fields. Tom's Angel. Walter de la Mare. Mes

No one would mistake a watermelon for a meteorite. Six Ways of Eating Watermelons. Lo Ch'ing, *tr.* by Dominic Cheung. IFON

No one writes to me. Letter Out of the Gray. Gabriel Preil, *tr.* by Shirley Kaufman *and* Howard Schwartz. VWA

No one's been told. Black Study. Michael S. S. Harper. CAPP

No one's dancing here tonight. The Dance. Daniel Halpern. MAYP

No one's fated or doomed to love anyone. Adrienne Rich. *Fr.* Twenty-one Love Poems, XVII. GLP

No one's going to read. A Dance for Militant Dilettantes. Al Young. PoBA

No One's Land. Janet Dubé. DT

No Ordinary Sun. Hone Tuwhare. ATNZ; PeNZ

No Other Choice. Tobias Hume. *See* Fain Would I Change That Note.

No other road, no other way. Love's Rocky Forest. Arto Melleri, *tr.* by Aili Jarvenpa. SOP

No, our kind cannot live with these. Oreads. Kathleen Jessie Raine. PoSH

No Pains Comparable to His Attempt. *Unknown.* PBBP

No pavement chalks the plain with memories. Beginning the Year at Rosebud, S. D. Roberta Hill. CDW

No people are uninteresting. People. Yevgeny Yevtushenko, *tr.* by Robin Milner-Gulland *and* Peter Levi. DL

No photographs exist. This man. Crazy Horse Returns to South Dakota. Harley Elliott. NeAC

No Place Like Home. Llawdden, *tr. fr. Welsh* by Gwyn Jones. OBWVE

No place seemed farther than your death. And I Am Old to Know. Pauline Hanson. TAP

No Place So Grand. *Unknown.* WTO

No Platonic [*or* Platonique] Love. William Cartwright. ErPo; GBL; InvP; JCP; LiTB; OAEL-1; PoEL-2

No Pleasure without Some Pain. Lord Thomas Vaux. ElL

No poet should set store by public acclamation. To a Poet. Pushkin, *tr.* by Alan Myers. AAA

No point now my friend in telling. Heemi. Hone Tuwhare. PeNZ

No pornographic film. On Obscenity. Tanikawa Shuntaro, *tr.* by Hiroaki Sato. FCEI

No porter guards the passage of your door. Dryden. *Fr.* To My Honour'd Kinsman, John Driden, of Chesterton. EBEV

No Possum, No Sop, No Taters. Wallace Stevens. HCAP; OxBA; TAP; VGW

No prayer marks my forehead. Apology. Amiq Hanafi, *tr.* by Mahmood Jamal. PBMUP

No private grudge they need, no personal spite. Modern Critics. Samuel Taylor Coleridge. FaBoEE

No quirt—right?—nor spur. To My Mouse-colored Mare. Tristan Corbière, *tr.* by C. F. MacIntyre. ErPo

No rack can torture me. Emily Dickinson. MoAB

No rain, and yet my saddle is damp. Fog at Liang-hsiang. Yüan Mei, *tr.* by Jonathan Chaves. CoBLCP

No Regret. Rochelle Kraut. UL

No Regrets. Ned Pastor. SoTCo

No Remedy. Drummond Allison. OxBTC

No Reparation. Charles Brasch. ATNZ

No rest! No rest on this bleak earth for me. Crazed. Mary E. Tucker. CBWP-1

No Road. Philip Larkin. EBEV; MoBrPo

No robe, no sleeves, my hair uncombed. Chu Yün-ming, *tr. fr. Chinese* by Jonathan Chaves. *Fr.* Improvisations, II. CoBLCP

No rock along the road but knows. Poet. Donald Jeffrey Hayes. AmNP; PoNe

No rooftops to rest on. Madison Square. A. Leyeles, *tr.* by Keith Bosley. VWA

No room for mourning: he's gone out. William Wordsworth. Sidney Keyes. OxBTC; SeCePo

No room in the inn, of course. What the Donkey Saw. U. A. Fanthorpe. OBCP

No rooster wakes them. A donkey brays. In the Madison Zoo. Roberta Hill. CDW

No round-shouldered pitchers here, no stewards. Cana Revisited. Seamus Heaney. FaBoMo

No runner clears the final fence. The Unfinished Race. Norman Cameron. OxBS

"No," said Charles Peace. E. C. Bentley. *Fr.* Clerihews. NOBL

No saint on a disc of snow. Emily Dickinson Postage Stamp. Lynn Strongin. NMM

No Say. Millie Murray. WS

No Se Van Los Pastores. Charles Squier. SoTCo

No season/ brings conclusion. Outlook Uncertain. Alastair Reid. NePoEA-2

No seaweed in this bay. Komachi, *tr. fr. Japanese* by Burton Watson. *Fr.* Kokin Shu. FCEI

No Second Troy. W. B. Yeats. BrPo; CMoP; EnLoPo; GTBS-P; MoP; NAEL-2; NoAM; NOBE; OAEL-2; OxBTC; PoEL-5; PPP; SeCePo; WeW

No Sects in Heaven. Elizabeth H. Jocelyn Cleaveland. BLPA

No Sense Grieving. Ilya Rubin, *tr. fr. Russian* by Linda Zisquit. VWA

No sense like the strong magnetic feel. Noh Play. Jim Brodey. UL

No shade for halting the horse to shake my sleeves. Teika, *tr. fr. Japanese* by Hiroaki Sato. *Fr.* Eighty-four Tanka. FCEI

No shelter in sight. Teika, *tr.* by Steven D. Carter. WFTW

No ship of all that under sail or steam. Immigrants. Robert Frost. GOA

No Shop Does the Bird Use. Elizabeth J. Coatsworth. OBCA

No sickness worse than secret love. *Unknown.* NOIV

No sign is made while empires pass. Continuity. "Æ" MoBrPo

No single hour can stand for naught. John Clare. OBNC

No Single Thing Abides. Lucretius, *tr. fr. Latin* by W. H. Mallock. *Fr.* De Rerum Natura (On the Nature of Things). AWP; ImOP, *abr.*.

No, Sir, No. *Unknown.* AmFP

"No, sir," said General Sherman. E. C. Bentley. *Fr.* Clerihews. NOBL

No sleep for twelve days. What Happened to a Young man in a Place Where He Turned to Water. *Unknown, tr.* by Anselm Hollo. STP

No sleep! I rise and burn the night away. The Protagonist. Peter Hopegood. PoAu-2

No sleep. The sultriness pervades the air. The House-Top. Herman Melville. LiTA; NAAL-1; NOBA; Prf

No sleep tonight. Summary. Sonia Sanchez. BPo

No sly usurping dream defeats the will. The Settled Men. George M. Brady. NeIP

No Smiles. Frank Lamont Phillips. AmNP

No snow falls from blue sky. Spinal Guard. Alan Bernheimer. IAT

No song of a soldier riding down. The Ride of Collins Graves. John Boyle O'Reilly. PAH

No sooner came, [*or* come] but gone, and fall'n asleep. On My Dear Grandchild Simon Bradstreet. Anne Bradstreet. NAAL-1; SCAP

No sooner had I drunk. Oliver Johnson Comes Back to Bed the Morning after the Ice Storm and Tells His Wife Why. David Jauss. MOWH

No sooner had I learned to get along without. And Dreams Paled. Eeva Kilpi, *tr.* by Aili Jarvenpa. SOP

No sooner had I left A. Midpoint. Charles Simic. GeTw

No sooner had th' Almighty ceas't, but all. Milton. *Fr.* Paradise Lost, Bk. III, *ll.* 344–371. (Heaven.) OBS

No soothing time for someone who thinks of blossoms. Lady Izumi, *tr. fr. Japanese* by Hiroaki Sato. *Fr.* Fifty-one Tanka. FCEI

No sound of any storm that shakes. Hillcrest. E. A. Robinson. MoAB; OxBA

No sound—yet my room fills up with thunder. The Peeper. Peter Davidson. ErPo

No specious splendour of this stone. The Cornelian. Byron. PeHV

No Speech from the Scaffold. Thom Gunn. OxBTC

No spot of earth where men have so fiercely for ages of time. Antrim. Robinson Jeffers. BIrV; NOBA; VGW

No Spring, nor Summer Beauty hath such grace. The Autumnal[l]. John Donne. *Fr.* Elegies, IX. InPS; JCP; PoEL-2; SeCV-1; TEP

No Stars Her Eyes. Thomas Lodge. *Fr.* Phyllis, VIII. Son

No stately column marks the hallowed place. Alamance. Seymour W. Whiting. PAH

No Stewart art thou, Galloway. On Lord Galloway. Burns. FaBoEE

No stir in the air, no stir in the sea. The Inchcape Rock. Robert Southey. BeLS; ChTr; FaBoBe; GN; OBNV

No storm, but the forest is drumming. Frost, the Red-nosed. AAA Nikolai Alekseyevich Nekrasov, *tr. fr. Russian* by Alan Myers. *Fr.*

No strength of Nature can suffice. Love Constraining to Obedience. William Cowper. NOCV

No such luck under the lush, bumpy orange and leaf sky, the owner. Americans in an Orange Grove. Arthur Vogelsang. MAYP

No Sufferer for Her Love. *Unknown, tr. fr. Late Middle Irish* by Robin Flower. AnIL

No sun—no moon! No! Thomas Hood. ChTr; FiBHP; GN (November.) ChTr

No sunny ray, no silver night. Threnody. Thomas Lovell Beddoes. EnRP

No Swan So Fine. Marianne Moore. AnAmPo; EyDe; NoP; OxBA; PoA; PrIm; UnPo

No syrup or perfume. Nox. Salvador Díaz Mirón, *tr. by* Samuel Beckett. MexPo

No table there is spread. John Derricke. *Fr.* The Image of Irelande. OBTV

No Taker for the Small Shoes. Sue Roe. NPo

No teacher I of boys or smaller fry. Allen Beville Ramsay. CenHV

No tears. The Face of Christ. Ch'iao Lin, *tr. by* Dominic Cheung. IFON

No Thank You. John Skoyles. NAmP

"No, Thank You, John." Christina Rossetti. NAEL-2; TEP

No, the Queen must not look upon. The Rain (Rapa Nui). Pablo Neruda, *tr. by* Lynn C. Jarox. LPSS

No, the serpent did not. Theology. Ted Hughes. FaBoMo; NAEL-2; NoAM

No, the serpent was not. Reveille. Ted Hughes. PPP

No, the solution is not. Meditation at the Threshold. Rosario Castellanos, *tr. by* Kate Flores. DMH

No Theory. David Ignatow. NNaP

No, they are come; their horn is lifted up. Gerard Manley Hopkins. *Fr.* Six Epigrams. SeCePo

No thing/ no-thing. Cathexis. F. J. Bryant, Jr.. PoBA

No this isn't a road intersected by enemy lines or foreign tongues or silence. Piyyut for the New Year. Haim Guri, *tr. by* Warren Bargad *and* Stanley F. Chyet. IP

No Thoroughfare. Ruth Holmes. BoTP

No! those days are gone away. Robin Hood. Keats. AWP; EnRP

No, thou hast never griev'd but I griev'd too. Walter Savage Landor. GBL

No thunder blasts Jove's plant, nor can. Occasioned by Seeing a Walk of Bay Trees. Mildmay Fane, Earl of Westmorland. OxBSP

No thyng is to man so dere. Praise of Women. Robert Mannyng. OBEV

No Time Ago. E. E. Cummings. OxBSP

No Time for God. Norman L. Trott. BLRP

No Time for Lamentation Now. Milton. *See* Samson Agonistes: Come, come, no time for lamentation now.

No Time for Poetry. Julia Fields. AmNP

No time, no time. The Suburb. Anne Stevenson. NMM

"No, Time, thou shalt not boast that I do change!" Shakespeare. *Fr.* Sonnets, CXXIII. OBSC; Son; TrGrPo

No title. Henry Howard, Earl of Surrey. *See* Complaint of the Absence of Her Lover Being upon the Sea.

No title, no lands—no worries either. Pronouncement on Returning Home. Narushima Ryuhoku, *tr. by* Burton Watson. JLIC-2

No towers tremble now at the blast of my sighs. De Profundis. László Kálnoky, *tr. by* Edwin Morgan. MHuP

No trace left these last days. 1919. Jacob Glatstein, *tr. by* Cynthia Ozick. PeBMYV

No trace of verdant hillside, nor of meadow. A Steppe in the Nazas Country. Manuel José Othón, *tr. by* Samuel Beckett. MexPo

No trellisses, no vines. Iron Landscapes (and the Statue of Liberty). Thom Gunn. FaBoPV

No trust to metals nor to marbles, when. Epitaph on the Tomb of Sir Edward Giles and His Wife. Robert Herrick. QFR

No two eyes gaze alike. Janus. Madeline Mason. GoYe

No Use. W. D. Snodgrass. BoLoP

No use, no use, now, begging Recognize! Amnesiac. Sylvia Plath. NYBP

No use to speak, no good to tell you that. Communication. Elizabeth Jennings. NePoEA

No use waiting for it to stop. Apples. Shirley Kaufman. NMM

No Voice of Man. Raymond Falconer. PoSH

No War. Judith Kazantzis. AIW

No warm, downy pillow His sweet head pressed. The Heavenly Stranger. Ada Blenkhorn. BLRP

No water is still, on top. The Movement of Fish. James Dickey. NYBP; VGW

"No water so still as the/ dead fountains of Versailles." No Swan So Fine. Marianne Moore. AnAmPo; EyDe; NoP; OxBA; PoA; PrIm; UnPo

No way of consoling myself for this love. *Unknown.* *Fr.* Manyo Shu. FCEI

No Way of Knowing. John Ashbery. AnAn

No way to meet him. Komachi, *tr. fr. Japanese by* Burton Watson. *Fr.* Kokin Shu. FCEI

No way too long—no path too steep. Stefan George, *tr. fr. German by* Daisy Broicher. *Fr.* Jahr der Seele, Das. AWP

No ways are left me now to meet my love. *Unknown.* *Fr.* Manyo Shu. Ma

No, we will not make vows to the ever-winning goddess. What She Said to Her Girl Friend. Korran, *tr. by* A. K. Ramanujan. PLW

No wind of Life may strike within. Dutch Seacoast. Kenneth Slessor. *Fr.* The Atlas. PoAu-2

No wind, still the dry side-oat's stems are swaying. Gathering Cattle in the Deertracks Pasture. Drummond Hadley. CowP

No woman's pleasure did I feel. Evidence at the Witch Trials. James Keir Baxter. OxBC

No wonder the birds make whittlings of sound, that the hemlock. Sun-up in March. Abbie Huston Evans. NePoAm

No wonder Wendy's coat blew off. Wendy in Winter. Kaye Starbird. RHPC

No wonder you're grieved this morning. Lady Izumi, *tr. fr. Japanese by* Hiroaki Sato. *Fr.* Fifty-one Tanka. FCEI

No Word. Barry Goldensohn. NAmP

No word, keep secret and withhold. Silentium. Fyodor Ivanovich Tyutchev, *tr. by* Alan Myers. AAA

No word, no lie, can cross a carven lip. Silence. Thomas Sturge Moore. QFR

No, worldling, no, 'tis not thy gold. The Second Rapture. Thomas Carew. CaPo; OPOP

No Worst, There Is None. Gerard Manley Hopkins. BrPo; CMoP; EBVV; FaBoMo; GTBS-P; HeIP; InPS; LiTB; LiTM; MoAB; MoBrPo; MoP; NAEL–2; NoAM; NoAM; NOBE; NOBVV; NoP; OAEL–2; OPOP; PoE; PoEL-5; PPP
(Life Death Does End.) SeCePo
(Sonnet: "No worst, there is none.") OBNC

Noah. Chana Bloch. VWA

Noah. Wayne Brown. PBCV

Noah. Roy Daniells. Mes

Noah, *sel. Unknown.*
"I thank the, Lord so dere, that wold vowchsayf." PoE

Noah an' Jonah an' Cap'n John Smith. Don Marquis. PoLF

Noah at Sea. Kathryn Rantala. BWV

Noah in New England. Tom Lowenstein. VWA

Noah sailed his ark and skimmed his inner world. Proust on Noah. Eisig Silberschlag. VWA

Noah, 30 days out and hard alee. Noah at Sea. Kathryn Rantala. BWV

Noah's Ark. Marguerite Young. WPE

Noah's daughter. Sibyl of the Waters. Ruth Fainlight. VWA

Noah's Flood. Caedmon, *tr. fr. Anglo-Saxon by* C. W. Kennedy. *Fr.* Genesis. AnOE

Noah's Flood, *sels.* Michael Drayton.
"And as our God the beasts had given in charge." PBBP
"Eternall and all-working God, which wast." PoEL-2

Noah's Prayer. Carmen Bernos de Gasztold, *tr. fr. French by* Rumer Godden. TrCP

Noah's Raven. W. S. Merwin. HCAP

Noah's Song. Evan Jones. PoAu-2

Nobility. Alice Cary. OHFP; WBLP

Noble, The. Wordsworth. *Fr.* The Prelude [or, Growth of a Poet's Mind]: Residence in France, 3 *ll.*. ChTr

Noble Balm, The. Ben Jonson. OBEV

Noble [*or* Brave Old] Duke of York, The. *Unknown.* GBP
(Brave Old Duke of York, The.) OxNR
("O, the grand old Duke of York.") GBP

Noble executors of the munificent testament. Application for a Grant. Anthony Hecht. SaC

Noble Fisherman; or, Robin Hood's Preferment, The. *Unknown.* ESPB

Noble hart, that harbours vertuous [*or* virtuous] thought, The. The Fight of the Red Cross Knight and the Heathen Sansjoy. Spenser. *Fr.* The Faerie Queene, I, 5. FiP

Noble horse with courage in his eye, The. Aristocrats. Keith Douglas. FaBoMo; NAEL-2; NePoEA; NoAM; OBWP

Noble is he who falls in front of battle. How Can Man Die Better. Tyrtaeus, *tr. by* T. F. Higham. WaaP

Noble King of Brentford, The. The King of Brentford's Testament *abr.* Thackeray. OBNV

Noble Love. Richard Flecknoe. ACP

Noble Mayde, still standing, all this vewd, The. Spenser. *Fr.* The Faerie Queene: The Mask of Cupid. PoEL-1

Noble, nasty course he ran, A. Epitaph on the Late King of the Sandwich Isles. Winthrop Mackworth Praed. FiBHP

Noble Nature, The. Ben Jonson. *See* To the Immortal[l] Memory [*or* Memorie] and Friendship of That Noble Pair[e], Sir Lucius Cary and Sir Henry Morrison: It Is Not Growing Like a Tree.

Noble range it was, of many a rood, A. Leigh Hunt. *Fr.* The Story of Rimini, III. EnRP

Noble Ritter Hugo, Der. Ballad by Hans Breitmann. Charles Godfrey Leland. BXAP; CenHV; NOBL
(Ballad of the Mermaid.) FiBHP

Noble Scholar Playing the Lute, A. Yang Chi, *tr. fr. Chinese by* Jonathan Chaves. CoBLCP

Noble Servant, The. Philippe Thoby-Marcelin, *tr. fr. French by* William Jay Smith. CT

Noble Tuck-Man, The. Jean Ingelow. NA

Nobleman and Thresherman, The ("Nobleman lived in a valley of late."). *Unknown.* OBET

Nobleman's House, A, *sel.* May Sarton. "After the palaces." EyDe

Nobles and heralds, by your leave. On Himself. Matthew Prior. FaBoEE

(Prior's Epitaph.) TrGrPo

Noblesse Oblige. Jessie Redmond Fauset. CDC

Noblesse Oblige. Celeste Turner Wright. Psk

Noblest Charis, you that are. His Discourse with Cupid. Ben Jonson. *Fr.* A Celebration of Charis in Ten Lyrick Peeces. SeCP

Noblest Roman, The. Shakespeare. *See* Julius Caesar: Portrait of Brutus.

Nobly Born, The. Frances Ellen Watkins Harper. PWR

Nobly, nobly Cape Saint Vincent to the northwest died away. Home Thoughts, from the Sea. Robert Browning. NAEL-2

Nobody. Brenda Agard. WS

Nobody but Lester let Lester leap. Lester Leaps In. Al Young. NPGG; SM

Nobody but me can know the sorrow that wrings me. Complaint of a Young Girl. Wang Chung-ju, *tr. by* Kenneth Rexroth. PCP

Nobody comes to the graveyard on the hill. The Hill above the Mine. Malcolm Cowley. SaC

Nobody comes up from the sea as late as this. You Will Know When You Get There. Allen Curnow. ATNZ; PeNZ

Nobody could believe/ my brother ever got through. My Brother Flies Over Low. David Huddle. TDD

Nobody could touch me. Nobody. Brenda Agard. WS

Nobody heard him, the dead man. Not Waving but Drowning. Stevie Smith. FaBoWP; FF; GTBS-P; HAP; HeIP; MoP; NAEL-2; NoAM; NOBE; NoP; OAEL-2; OxBTC; PoE; PPP; PrIm; TEP; WeW

Nobody I know would like to be buried. Thanksgiving for a Habitat. W. H. Auden. NYBP

Nobody in the lane, and nothing, nothing but blackberries. Blackberrying. Sylvia Plath. HAP; HCAP; NAAL-2; NoAM; NOBA; NYBP

Nobody is dead yet and won't be. Right. A Local Contractor Flees His Winter Trouble and Saves Some Lives in a Knoxville Motel Room. James Whitehead. MT

Nobody knew when it would start again. Schizophrenic. Patricia K. Page. HeIP

Nobody knows/ Whither our delirium. The Need. Siegfried Sassoon. TrPWD

Nobody Knows but Mother. Mary Morrison. BLPA

Nobody Knows de Trouble I've Seen,. *Unknown.* AH, *with music*

Nobody knows the other side. Jack Kerouac. *Fr.* Mexico City Blues, 127. NeAP

Nobody knows the world but me. Professor Noctutus. George MacDonald. NOBVV

Nobody knows what I say. Alone. Itzig Manger. VWA, *tr. by* Ruth Whitman

Nobody knows what love is anymore. For a Masseuse and Prostitute. Kenneth Rexroth. NNaP

Nobody knows what's growing in Bridget. The Bulge. George Johnston. MoCV

Nobody lies in this earth. Cemetery in Pernambuco. João Cabral de Melo Neto, *tr. by* Jane Cooper. ATCBP

Nobody lives in the cottage now. Fairy Feet. Phyllis L. Garlick. BoTP

Nobody Lives on Arthur Godfrey Boulevard. Gerald Costanzo. MAYP

Nobody Loses All the Time. E. E. Cummings. CMoP; DL; FaBoCo; FF; LiTM; NAAL-2; NBLV; NOBA; RB; TwCP

Nobody loves you Chloe, you sly minx. To His Coy Mistress. Edward Bird. BXAP; FaBoPa

Nobody mentioned war. Malcolm. Lucille Clifton. CNA

Nobody noogers the shaff of a sloo. On a Flimmering Floom You Shall Ride. Carl Sandburg. GoYe; OBAL

Nobody on earth has a book of matches. Race of the Kingfishers. Ray A. Young Bear. HATNAP

Nobody painted Mrs. Aherne's store. Dakota: Five Times Six. Joseph Hansen. NYBP

Nobody planted roses, he recalls. "Summertime and the Living." Robert Hayden. PoBA; PPP; TwCP

Nobody Riding the Roads Today. June Jordan. BPo; NoAM

Nobody said Apples for nearly a minute. Political Intelligence. Arthur James Marshall Smith. EAS

Nobody sees what I can see. Just Me. Margaret Hillert. RHPC

Nobody stays here long. Not in the Guide-Books. Elizabeth Jennings. LiTM; NePoEA

Nobody stuffs the world in at your eyes. Snow. Margaret Avison. NOBC

Nobody wanted this infant born. Burial. Mark Van Doren. MoBS

Nobody will open the door for you. Blanca Varela, *tr. by* Willis Barnstone. BoWoP

Nobody will quarrel with the woodcock. Quarrel. *Yoruba Oral Tradition, tr. by* Ulli Beier. WTO

Nobody will sing a mass. Anniversary. Heine, *tr. by* Alistair Elliot. OBD

Noch Einmal, an Orpheus. George Bradley. BAP

Nocht o' Mortal Sicht. Bessie J. B. Macarthur. OxBS

Noctambule. George Johnston. MoCV

Nocturn: "At the barren heart of midnight." W. E. Henley. *Fr.* In Hospital, XXVII. BrPo

Nocturn at the Institute. David McElroy. Psk

Nocturnal Festival. Antonin Artaud, *tr. fr. French by* Michael Benedikt. POS

Nocturnal Heart. Anne-Marie Kegels, *tr. fr. French by* W. S. Merwin. BoWoP

Nocturnal Journey. Ory Bernstein, *tr. fr. Hebrew by* Warren Bargad *and* Stanley F. Chyet. IP

Nocturnal Landscape. Malcolm Cowley. PoA

Nocturnal Reverie, A. Countess of Winchilsea. EBEV; GoTL; NAEL-1; NOEC; NoP; PBWP; PoE; PoEL-3; SeCePo; WPE

Nocturnal Sketch, A. Thomas Hood. FaBoCo; FiBHP

Nocturnal Sounds. Kattie M. Cumbo. BlSi

Nocturnal Sunscape. Lucha Corpi. CCP

Nocturnal Thoughts. Avraham Huss, *tr. fr. Hebrew by* Mark Elliott Shapiro. VWA

Nocturnal water, primaeval silences. Useless Day. Rosario Castellanos, *tr. by* Maureen Ahern. WPOW

Nocturnal[l] upon Saint Lucy's [or S. Lucies] Day, Being the Shortest Day, A. John Donne. EBEV; GBL; JCP; LiTB; MeLP; MePo; NAEL-1; NOBE; NoP; OAEL-1; OBS; PoE; PoEL-2; PPP; SeCP; SeCV-1; TEP

Nocturne: "Be thou at peace this night." Edward Davison. CH

Nocturne: "Blade of a knife, The." Richard Murphy. IPY

Nocturne: Georgia Coast. Daniel Whitehead Hicky. AmFN

Nocturne: "I love the languor of your sensual lips." Renée Vivien, *tr. by* Beth Archer. DMF

Nocturne: "If the deep wood is haunted." Robert Hillyer, *tr. by* John Moyne *and* Coleman Barks. FYAP; UnAS

Nocturne: "Listening for the sound." Pinkie Gordon Lane. BlSi

Nocturne: "long arm embossed with gold slides from the tree tops, A." Léon-Paul Fargue, *tr. by* Kenneth Rexroth. RHTwFP

Nocturne, A: "Moon has gone to her rest, The." Wilfrid Scawen Blunt. OBMV

Nocturne: "Over New England now, the snow." Frances Mary Frost. BoNaP

Nocturne: "Red flame flowers bloom and die, The." Crosbie Garstin. CH

Nocturne: "Softly blow lightly." Donald Jeffrey Hayes. CDC

Nocturne: "Song of a blackbird in my ears." Eino Leino, *tr. by* Aili Jarvenpa. SOP

Nocturne: "This cool night is strange." Gwendolyn B. Bennett. BANP

Nocturne: "Today now at this moment the world flies against me." Rossana Ombres, *tr. by* Muriel Kittel. DMI

Nocturne: "Toughs walk by in groups explosive." David Kirby. SoTCo

Nocturne: "Wildness of haggard flights." Roussan Camille, *tr. by* Seth L. Wolitz. TTY

Nocturne at Bethesda. Arna Bontemps. AmNP; BANP; CDC; PoNe

Nocturne for Freedom. Tirso Canales, *tr. fr. Spanish by* Juan Felipe Herrera. VoI

Nocturne for October 31st, A. Yvor Winters. PoA

Nocturne in a Deserted Brickyard. Carl Sandburg. MoAmPo

Nocturne in G Minor. Karl Gustav Vollmoeller, *tr. fr. German by* Ludwig Lewisohn. AWP

Nocturne in the Women's Prison. Maria Beneyto, *tr. fr. Spanish by* Catherine Rodriguez-Nieto. WPOW

Nocturne of the Self-evident Presence. Thomas MacGreevy. BIrV; CIP

Nocturne of the Wharves. Arna Bontemps. BANP; BPo; PoNe

Nocturne Varial. Lewis Alexander. PoBA; PoNe

Nod. Will Bennett. UL

Nod. Walter de la Mare. BoTP; MoAB; MoBrPo; OxBTC

Nodding and beckoning across, observed of Attaché and Guardsman. Arthur Hugh Clough. *Fr.* The Bothie of Tober-na-Vuolich, *Bk.* I. FaBoPV

Nodding, its great head rattling like a gourd. Original Sin; a Short Story. Robert Penn Warren. HoPM; LiTA; LiTM; NOCV; PPP; SM; TAP

Nodding Off. Kao Ch'i, *tr. fr. Chinese by* Jonathan Chaves. CoBLCP

Noe more unto my thoughts appeare. Sidney Godolphin. MeLP; MePo (Quatrains.) OBS

Noel. Richard Watson Gilder. AA

Noel; Christmas Eve, 1913. Robert Bridges. LiTB; NOCV; OBCP; PoEL-5

Noel, noel, noel. Out of Your Sleep Arise and Wake. *Unknown.* NoP

Noel of the marvelous night. To Noel. Gabriela Mistral, *tr. by* Doris Dana. PChr

Noël Tragique. Ramon Guthrie. ErPo

Noelle. Hugo Williams. *Fr.* Calling Your Name in the Zoo. NPo

Noh Play. Jim Brodey. UL

Noh Plays, The. Lauris Edmond. ATNZ

Noise: a scarecrow fell by itself, A. "Not a Bird Singing, the Mountain Is All the More Quiet." Boncho, *tr. fr. Japanese by* Hiroaki Sato. *Fr.* Twenty-one Hokku. FCEI

Noise began in my belly, The. For Carlos Charles Bucillio. Alice Sadongei. HATNAP

Noise Grimaced. Larry Eigner. NeAP

Noise in Darkness. Sándor Weöres, *tr. fr. Hungarian by* Jascha Kessler. FOC

Noise of hammers once I heard. The Hammers. Ralph Hodgson. GoJo; MoBrPo; NOBE; OxBTC

Noise of passing feet, The. Listening. Alice Corbin, *after Chippewa Indian*

Noise of the Village, The. *Unknown, tr. fr. Chippewa Indian by* Frances Densmore. OBVE

Noise of trampling, the wind of trumpets, The. Louis XVI. Blake. *Fr.* The French Revolution. ChER

Noise of water teased his literal ears, The. Persistent Explorer. John Crowe Ransom. OxBA

Noise That Time Makes, The. Merrill Moore. MoAmPo; TrGrPo

Noiseless Patient Spider, A. Walt Whitman. AmPP; AnAmPo; AWP; BLPL; FF; HAP; HeIP; InPK; InPS; LiTA; MoAmPo; NAAL-1; NIP; NOBA; NoP; OxBA; OxBSP; PoE; SCV; SoSe; TAP; TrGrPo; WiR

Noiselessly/ in the blue of night this heart of mine. The Beggar. Muhammad al-Ghuzzi, *tr. by* May Jayyusi *and* John Heath-Stubbs. MAP

Noises. Fred Johnson. CNA

Noises in the Night. Lilian McCrea. BoTP

Noises in the Night. Thomas Middleton. Mes

Noises of the harbour die, the smoke is petrified, The. The Statue. John Fuller. NePoEA-2; NOBE

Noises of the street come up subdued, The. An Upper Room. Daniel Lawrence Kelleher. NeIP

Noises round my house, The. On cobbles bounding. Regent's Park Terrace. Bernard Spencer. FaBoPP

Noisette on my garden path, A. The Shadow Rose. Robert Cameron Rogers. AA

Noisy cricket, The. Watanabe Suiha, *tr. by* Geoffrey Bownas *and* Anthony Thwaite. PeBJV

Noisy politicians confuse the world. Rhyming with a Friend. Yü Hsüan-chi, *tr. by* Geoffrey Waters. BoWoP

Noisy urchins scampered round, The. Much Distressed. *Unknown.* CBAP

Nokes went, he thought, to Styles's wife to bed. A Case to the Civilians. *Unknown.* FaBoEE

Noli Me Tangere, The. Robert Lowell. *See* Death of the Sheriff, The.

Nomad's Utopia. Antonio Porta, *tr. fr. Italian by* Lawrence R. Smith. NItP

Noman, the King of Hira, sat one day. The Abdication of Noman. Richard Henry Stoddard. AnAmPo

Nomen. Naomi Long Madgett. BlSi

Nomenclature. Stephen Vincent Benét. AnAmPo

Nominativo hic gallant asse. The Declining of a Gallant. *Unknown.* FaBoUs

Nomine Domini/ Theotocopoulos. High Renaissance. George Starbuck. NBLV; OBAL

Non Amo Te. Thomas Brown. *See* I do not love thee, Doctor Fell.

Non-Commitment. Chinua Achebe. UAS

Non Dolet. Oliver St. John Gogarty. OBMV

Non ego hoc ferrem calida juventâ. At Thirty Years. Byron. *Fr.* Don Juan, I. FiP

Non Nobis. Henry Cust. OBEV

Non Omnis Moriar. Manuel Gutiérrez Nájera, *tr. fr. Spanish by* Samuel Beckett. MexPo

Non Piangere, Liù. Peter Porter. OxBC

Non Que Je Veuille Ôter la Liberté. Pernette de Guillet, *tr. fr. French by* Raymond Oliver. WPOW

Non Sequitor, A. Richard Corbet. FaBoNo

Non Sum Qualis Eram Bonae sub Regno Cynarae [*or* Cynara]. Ernest Dowson. AWP; BeLS; BLPA; BoLoP; BrPo; EBVV; EnLoPo; FaBoBe; FaFP; FPL; GBL; GTBS-P; HAP; HeIP; LiTB; MoBrPo; NOBE; NoP; OAEL-2; OBEV; OBMV; OBNC; PoRA; PrIm; TEP; TrGrPo; UnPo

Non Sum Qualis Eram in Bona Urbe Nordica Illa. John Hollander. ErPo

Non Ti Fidar. Louis Zukofsky. VGW

Nona poured oil on the water and saw the eye. The Evil Eye. John Ciardi. MoBS; NAs

Nondescript express in from the South, A. Gare du Midi. W. H. Auden. OxBSP

None. Josephine Miles. VGW

None but a Muse in love, can tell. On Fruition. Sir Charles Sedley. ErPo

None but the mouse-brown wren. The Young Martins. Andrew Young. FM

None call thee flower! I will not so malign. To the Milkweed. Lloyd Mifflin. AA

None could ever say that she. True or False. Catullus, *tr. by* Walter Savage Landor. AWP; OBVE

None ever was in love with me but grief. "My True Love Hath My Heart and I Have His." Mary Elizabeth Coleridge. BoLoP

None Is Happy. Hartmann von Aue, *tr. fr. German by* Jethro Bithell. AWP

None knows since when the sea. Mohammad Taqi Mir, *tr. by* Ahmed Ali. GoT

None of it true; for Christ's sake, spill the ink. Robin Hyde. *Fr.* The Houses, V. ATNZ; PeNZ

None of our warnings sank in. Contentment. Mark Osaki. BrSi

None of Self and All of Thee. Theodore Monod. BLRP

None of the easy remedies have proved effective. Christine Lavant, *tr. by* Beth Bjorklund. CoAuP

None of the sweetest things in this world. Eterna Voluttà, L.' Valery Larbaud, *tr. by* William Jay Smith. CT

None of this seems real, seen from the east. New England Interlude. Madeline DeFrees. PPR

None of us ever doubted. 20th Century Requiem. Patricia M. Saunders. CN

None other fame mine unambitious muse. Samuel Daniel. *Fr.* To Delia. AAS

None Other Lamb None Other Name. Christina Rossetti. TrPWD

None saw their spirits' shadow shake the grass. Isaac Rosenberg. *Fr.* Dead Man's Dump. OBD

None shall gainsay me. I will lie on the floor. Gloriana Dying. Sylvia Townsend Warner. FaBoWP

None walked behind that shoddy rain-swept hearse. Mozart's Grave. Paul Scott Mowrer. GoYe

Nonetheless Ali Baba had no richer cave. Quebec Liquor Commission Store. A. M. Klein. OBCV

Nonexistent are men. Mohammad Taqi Mir, *tr. by* Ahmed Ali. GoT

Nonny, The ("Nonny-bird, I love particularly, The"). James Reeves. AmMo

Nonpareil. Matthew Prior. EnLoPo

Nonpareil's Grave, The. M. J. McMahon. SD

Nonsense. Richard Corbet. *See* Like to the Thundering Tone.

Nonsense. Thomas Moore. FaBoEE; NA

Nonsense! Jack Prelutsky. RHPC

Nonsense. *Unknown. See* Oh that my lungs could bleat like butter'd pease.

Nonsense Carol, A. *Unknown.* OxBoLi

Nonsense Quatrains. Gelett Burgess. *See* Ah, Yes, I Wrote the "Purple Cow."

Nonsense Quatrains: "I sent my Collie to the wash." Gelett Burgess. CenHV

Nonsense Song, A. *Unknown. See* My lady went to Canterbury.

Nonsense Song ("My heart of gold."). *Unknown.* OxBLMV

Nonsense? That's what makes no sense. Nonsense! Jack Prelutsky. RHPC

Nonsense Verses. Charles Lamb. NA

Noodle-Vendor's Flute, The. D. J. Enright. NoP

Nooksack Valley. Gary Snyder. NaP

Noon. John Clare. SeCePo

Noon. "Michael Field." NOBVV

Noon. Robinson Jeffers. MoAmPo

Noon heat in the yard, The. Hen Woman. Thomas Kinsella. CIP; IPY

Noon is beautiful, The: the perfect wheel. Yvor Winters. VGW

Noon of the Sunbather. Marge Piercy. NMM

Noon on the mountain! Walt Whitman. Emanuel Carnevali. PoA

Noon sun beats down the leaf; The noon. Grapes Making. Léonie Adams. FYAP; UnPo

Noon. The luminous tide. Ballydavid Pier. Thomas Kinsella. BIrV; FaBCIP

Noonday April Sun, The. George Love. IDB

Noonday Sun. Kathryn Byron Jackson. FaPON

Noonday Sun and the Shade, The. Muhammad al-Maghut, *tr. fr. Arabic*. MPAW, *tr. by* Abdullah al-Udhari.

Noonday Thought. Henrietta Cordelia Ray. *Fr.* A Group of Musings. CBWP-3

Noonlight is sudden full of the spirits. The Storm. Robert Wallace. NYBP

Noon's Dream-Song. Eugene Lee-Hamilton. NOBVV

Noontide. Henrietta Cordelia Ray. *Fr.* Idyl. CBWP-3

Nooses of double meanings swing. Conversation Piece. Arthur Freeman. ErPo

Nor do these heads sing. Lightness Remembered. Nancy Willard. LCAP

Nor dread nor hope attend. Death. W. B. Yeats. OxBSP

Nor exults he nor complains he; silent bears whate'er befalls him. Ever Watchful. Ta' Abbata Sharra, *tr. by* W. G. Palgrave. AWP

Nor Hammond's love nor Shenstone's was sincere. John Maclaurin. NOEC

Nor happiness, nor majesty, nor fame. Political Greatness. Shelley. EnRP

Nor Is It Written. Laura Riding. *Fr.* Three Sermons to the Dead, III. LiTA

Nor less the spaniel, skillful to betray. John Gay. *Fr.* Rural Sports. PBBP

Nor lingered Paris in the lofty house. Homer, *tr. fr. Greek by* Tennyson. *Fr.* The Iliad, VI. OBVE

Nor long the trench or lofty walls oppose. Homer, *tr. fr. Greek by* Pope. *Fr.* The Iliad, XII. OBVE

Nor practising virtue nor committing crime. Geoffrey Taylor. FaBoEE

Nor shall you for your fields neglect your stock. Young Stock. Victoria Mary Sackville-West. OxBTC

Nor skin nor hide nor fleece. Lethe. Hilda Doolittle ("H. D."). AnAmPo; CMoP; FaBoWP; LiTM; MoAmPo; PoRA; TrGrPo; VGW; ViBoPo

Nor think, in nature's state they blindly trod. Pope. *Fr.* An Essay on Man, Epistle III. OAEL-1

Nor truth nor good did they know. Gloss. Padraic Fiacc. CIP

Nor was this fellowship vouchsaf'd to me. Wordsworth Skates on Esthwaite Water. Wordsworth. *Fr.* The Prelude [or, Growth of a Poet's Mind]: Childhood and School-Time. FaBoPP

Nor when the youthful pair more closely join. Concerning the Nature of Love. Lucretius, *tr. fr. Latin by* Dryden. *Fr.* De Rerum Natura (On the Nature of Things), IV. ErPo

Nor, will anyone dare say to. Sharon Will Be No/Where on Nobody's Best-selling List. Sharon Scott. JB

Nor will the search be hard or long. Epistle to the President of the Scottish Society of Antiquaries: On Being Chosen a Correspondent Member. Alexander Geddes. OxBS

Nor with less waste the whisker'd vermin race. How to Exterminate Rats. James Grainger. *Fr.* The Sugar Cane. FaBoUs

Nor writ in water nor in mist. For John Keats, Apostle of Beauty. Countee Cullen. *Fr.* Four Epitaphs. AmNP; CDC; PoBA

Nor yet do I, your knowing lover. Portrait. John Lyle Donaghy. BIrV

Norembega. Whittier. PAH

Norfolk Memorials, *sels.* Coman Leavenworth.
  North Pickenham. *Fr.* I. LiTA
  "We learned to laugh. Although the flying bombs." *Fr.* II. LiTA
  Wendling. *Fr.* III. LiTA

Norfolk Rebellion, The. *Unknown.* GBP

Norfolk sprang [*or* sprung] thee, Lambeth holds thee dead. Epitaph on Thomas Clere. Earl of Surrey. AAS; OBWP; SiPS

Normally, who can explain the hurtful spring. Tune: Willow Branch. Cheng Wen-cho, *tr. by* William Schultz. WFTU

Norman conquest all historians fix, The. The English Succession. *Unknown.* OxBChV

Norman Morrison. Adrian Mitchell. FF

Norman; or, The Fungus among Us. Bruce Bennett. SoTCo

Norris Dam. Selden Rodman. PoNe

Norse am I when the first snow falls. The Song of the Ski. Wilson MacDonald. CaP

Norse Lullaby. Eugene Field. BoTP

Norsemen, The. Whittier. PAH

North. Philip Booth. NePoEA

North. Seamus Heaney. InPS

North. Lance Henson. HATNAP; STE

North, The. Barry McKinnon. NOBC

North, The. Stephen Spender. *See* our single purpose was to walk through snow.

North American Sequence. Theodore Roethke. NaP

North and South. Claude McKay. AmPP

North Atlantic. Carl Sandburg. MOS

North Country. Kenneth Slessor. CBAP

North Country Collier, The. *Unknown.* OxBSS

North Country Maid, The. *Unknown.* OBET

North-country maid up to London had stray'd, A. The Oak and the Ash. *Unknown.* FaBoCh

(North County Maid, The.) OBET

North Dakota, North Light. N. Scott Momaday. HATNAP

North Express. Joyce Mansour, *tr. fr. French by* author. WPOW

North Haven. Elizabeth Bishop. CAPP; HCAP

North Haven. Philip Booth. BLA

North is weather, Winter, and change. North. Philip Booth. NePoEA

North Labrador. Hart Crane. CMoP; FaBoMo

North of my grandfathers house. North. Lance Henson. HATNAP; STE

North of my lodge, south of my lodge, spring rivers all. A Guest Arrives. Tu Fu, *tr. by* Burton Watson. CoBCP

North of Santa Monica. Carter Revard. VoR

North-of-the-River Rhymes, *sels.* P'eng Sun-yü, *tr. fr. Chinese by* Daniel Bryant. WFTU
  "From withered trees we gather the silkworm floss." *Fr.* II.
  "Mounted on a mule, to ford the shallow stream." *Fr.* III.

North Percy, *sel.* Paul Goodman.
  Pagan Rites. DiL

North Philadelphia, Trenton, and New York. Richmond Lattimore. NYBP

North Pickenham. Coman Leavenworth. *Fr.* Norfolk Memorials, I. LiTA

North Pole Story, A. Menella Bute Smedley. OxBChV

North Sea, The, *sels.* Heine, *tr. fr. German.*
  "Like the stalks of wheat in the fields." TrJP, *tr. by* Emma Lazarus. (Epilog: "Like the ears of wheat in a wheat-field growing.") AWP, *tr. by* Louis Untermeyer.
  Evening Twilight. *Tr. by* John Todhunter. AWP
  Night by the Sea, A. *Tr. by* Howard Mumford Jones. AWP

North Sea Undertaker's Complaint, The. Robert Lowell. NePoEA

North Ship, The. Philip Larkin. RB

North Star, The. John Morris-Jones, *tr. fr. Welsh by* Anthony Conran. OBWVE

North to Milwaukee. Gerald Vizenor. VoR

North Wales girl was once my passion, A. Two-Faced Too. *Unknown, tr. by* Glyn Jones. OBWVE

North we climb the T'ai-hang Mountains. Song on Enduring the Cold. Susan Ts'ao Ts'ao, *tr. by* Burton Watson. CoBCP

North Wind, The. Dorothy Graddon. BoTP

North Wind. Benjamin Péret, *tr. fr. French by* Michael Benedikt. POS

North wind blowing through the barren willows, The. Singde, *tr. fr. Chinese by* William Schultz. *Fr.* In Imitation of Ancient-Style Poetry, XL. WFTU

North wind blows, cracking the earth, The. New Year's Eve. Liu E, *tr. by* Jonathan Chaves. CoBLCP

North wind blows, scattering the third-watch snow, The. Singde, *tr. by* William Schultz. WFTU

North wind doth blow, The. Mother Goose. OnUR; OxNR; PBBP

North wind heard is heard always, A. Reverberation. Maurice Kenny. HATNAP

North wind shakes my studio window, The. Returning to Nanking. Cheng Hsiao-hsü, *tr. by* Irving Lo. WFTU

North winds send hail, south winds bring rain. The Winds. Thomas Tusser. WiR

Northamptonshire Fens. John Clare. *Fr.* Child Harold. FaBoPP

Northboun.' Lucy Ariel Williams Holloway. BANP; BlSi; CDC; PoNe

Northbound. Larry Rubin. OPP

Northeast wind was the wind off the lake, The. Weather. Archibald MacLeish. MoAmPo

Northern breath, that freezes floods, he binds, The. Ovid, *tr. fr. Latin by* Dryden. *Fr.* Metamorphoses, I. OBVE

Northern Building Society Office Showing Police Headquarters, Auckland. Riemke Ensing. ATNZ

Northern Cobbler, The. Tennyson. EBEV

Northern Farmer. Tennyson. NAEL-2

Northern Ireland: Two Comments. Seamus Deane. CIP

Northern Legion, A. Sir Herbert Read. SeCePo

Northern light should have been veiled like Venus, with, A. This Poem Should Have Etc. Yona Wallach, *tr. by* Warren Bargad *and* Stanley F. Chyet. IP

Northern pair, we waive the name, A. The Power of Innocence. "C. G. H." NOEC

Northern Pike. James Wright. NAAL-2

Northern Romance. Haim Guri, *tr. fr. Hebrew by* Warren Bargad *and* Stanley F. Chyet. IP

Northern Seas, The. William Howitt. GN

Northern showers come out of the mountains, The. Teika, a No Play. *at.* to Komparu Zenchiku, *tr.* by Hiroaki Sato. FCEI
Northern Spring, A. Gene Baro. NePoEA-2
Northern Spring, A, *sel.* Frank Ormsby.
 "Some of us stayed forever, under the lough." CIP
Northern Suburb, A. John Davidson. NOBVV; OBNC
Northern Vigil, A. Bliss Carman. OBEV
Northern Wind/ sweeping down from the Sahara. Exile in Nigeria. Ezekiel Mphahlele. PBA
Northhanger Ridge. Charles Wright. HCAP
Northland in Cold, The. Li Ho, *tr. fr. Chinese* by Burton Watson. CoBCP
North/South. Paul Mariani. BLA
Northumberland Betray[e]d by Douglas [*or* Dowglas]. *Unknown.* ESPB; OxBB
Northward bound/ the ice mumbled. Drumlin Prayer. Tom MacIntyre. CIP
Northwest Airlines. Fred Chappell. HoPM
Northwest the tall tower stands. *Unknown, tr. fr. Chinese* by Burton Watson. *Fr.* Nineteen Old Poems of the Han, V. CoBCP
Northwind. Gene Baro. NePoEA-2
Northwind dies half way to the Gobi Desert, A. I Lie on the Chilled Stones of the Great Wall. Stephen Shu Ning Liu. BrSi
Northwind fallen, in the newstarrèd night, The. The Hesperides. Tennyson. OAEL-2
Norway. Norman Dubie. GeTw
Nosce Teipsum. Sir John Davies. SiPS
 Sels.
 Affliction. NOBE; OBSC
 In What Manner the Soule Is United to the Body. CTC; LiTB; NOBE; OBSC; PoEL-2
 (Soul and the Body, The.) CTC; NOBE; OBSC
 Man. EIL
 (I Know Myself a Man.) ChTr
 "I know my soul hath power to know all things." OBEV
 To Queen Elizabeth. OBSC
 (Dedication I: "To that clear majesty which in the north.")
 What Is This Knowledge?. FaBoRV
 (Knowledge and Reason.) OBSC
 (Much Knowledge, Little Reason.) ChTr
Nose, The. Iain Crichton Smith. RB
Nose becomes a triangular history, The. Terra Cotta. K. Curtis Lyle. CNA
Nose, nose, jolly red nose. Mother Goose, *also appears in* Beaumont *and* Fletcher. FaBoCh; OxNR
Nose, nose, jolly red nose. Beaumont *and* Fletcher. *Fr.* The Knight of the Burning Pestle, I, iii. FaBoCh
Nose only above water. Sandra: At the Beaver Trap. Michael S. Harper. NoAM
Nose went away, by itself, The. The Nose. Iain Crichton Smith. RB
Nosegay. Elizabeth Jane Coatsworth. OBCA
Nosegay, A. John Reynolds. OBEV
Nosegay Always Sweet, for Lovers to Send for Tokens of Love at New Year's Tide, or for Fairings, A ("Nosegay, lacking flowers fresh,"). William Hunnis. EIL
Nostalgia. Walter de la Mare. LiTM
Nostalgia. D. H. Lawrence. PoA
Nostalgia. Amy Lowell. AnAmPo
Nostalgia. Bin Ramke. MT
Nostalgia. Karl Shapiro. CMoP; CoAP; TrJP; TwCP; WaaP
Nostalgia. Wu T'e-Liang, *tr. fr. Chinese* by Dominic Cheung. IFON
Nostalgia. Yu Kuang-chung, *tr. fr. Chinese* by Dominic Cheung. IFON
Nostalgia and Complaint of the Grandparents. Donald Justice. NoAM
Nostalgia is the elixir drained. Lyn Hejinian. UL
Nostalgia of the Lakefronts. Donald Justice. BAP
Nostalgias. Derek Mahon. FaBCIP
Nostalgie d'Automne. Leslie Daiken. NeIP
"Not a Bird Singing, the Mountain Is All the More Quiet." Boncho, *tr. fr. Japanese* by Hiroaki Sato. *Fr.* Twenty-one Hokku. FCEI
Not a Christian, not a Buddhist, not a Confucian either. Natsume Soseki, *tr.* by Burton Watson. JLIC-2
Not a day goes by without someone borrowing books from me. Li K'ai-hsien, *tr. fr. Chinese* by Jonathan Chaves. *Fr.* Early Summer: At the Riverside. CoBLCP
Not a drum was heard, not a funeral note. The Burial of Sir John Moore after [*or* at] Corunna. Charles Wolfe. ChTr; EnRP; FaBoPa; FaBoRV; FaFP; FaPoR; GN; GTBS; GTBS-P; NOBE; OBEV; OBWP; OnYI; PoRA; PWR; WaaP; WBLP
Not a laugh was heard, not a frivolous note. The Burial of the Bachelor. *Unknown.* FaBoPa
"Not a leaf shall stay." Tameuji, *tr.* by Steven D. Carter. WFTW

Not a line of her writing have I. Thoughts of Phena [at News of Her Death]. Thomas Hardy. EBVV; NOBVV; NoP; OxBTC
Not a rabbit. In the Picture. Thomas M. Disch. BWV
Not a sign of life we rouse. Battery Moving Up to a New Position from Rest Camp: Dawn. Robert Nichols. MMA
Not a single word. *Unknown, tr.* by Geoffrey Bownas *and* Anthony Thwaite. PeBJV
Not a soul is left. Teika, *tr.* by Steven D. Carter. WFTW
Not a sound disturbs the air. A Midsummer Noon in the Australian Forest. Charles Harpur. PoAu-1
Not a sound to pull. There Is Something I Want to Say. Alex Kuo. BrSi
Not a Sous Had He Got. "Thomas Ingoldsby." *Fr.* The Ingoldsby Legends: The Cynotaph. FaBoCo
Not a squeak. Not a rustle. Don't dare make a sound. The Pig and the Nightingale. Eliezer Shteynbarg, *tr.* by Leonard Wolf. PeBMYV
Not a Thing of Paint or Feathers. Joseph Bruchac. NOVW
Not a thing on the river McCluskey did fear. The Little Brown Bulls. *Unknown.* AmFP
Not a thousand gold will make me part with the moon tonight. Night of the Full Moon. Cheng Hsiao-hsü, *tr.* by Irving Lo. WFTU
Not a trace is left. Teika, *tr.* by Steven D. Carter. WFTW
Not a tree but the tree. There Is Only One of Everything. Margaret Atwood. NOBC
Not a viper with milk beneath its tongue. Who Will Give Cover? Anadad Eldan. VWA, *tr.* by Ruth Nevo
Not Adlestrop. Dannie Abse. NoAM
Not All Immaculate. Laura Riding. *Fr.* Three Sermons to the Dead, II. LiTA
Not all of them must suffer. Some. Saints. George Garrett. EaLo
Not all of them were human. The Village of Tudda. Kenneth Patchen. VGW
Not all of us were warm, not all of us. Spring. James Still. GrPl; MT
Not all pale Hecate's direful charms. Lines Occasioned by the Burning of Some Letters. Sarah Dixon. NOEC
Not all the swallows have left with the spring. Swallows. Wu Tsao, *tr.* by Irving Lo. WFTU
Not all the time. People. Orban Veli Kanik, *tr.* by Talat Sait Halman. LLLT
Not All There. Robert Frost. FaBoCo
Not all thy flushing suns are set. An Ode to Master Endymion Porter, upon His Brother's Death. Robert Herrick. CaPo
Not Allowed to Make a Movie in This Country. David Avidan, *tr. fr. Hebrew* by Warren Bargad *and* Stanley F. Chyet. *Fr.* Traveling in the City, 18. IP
Not Allowed to Write. Gloria Fuertes, *tr. fr. Spanish* by Robert L. Smith *and* Judith Candullo. DMH
Not Alone for Mighty Empire. William Pierson Merrill. AH, *with music;* OPP; TrPWD
Not alwayes give a melting kiss. Johannes Secundus, *tr. fr. Latin by* Thomas Stanley. *Fr.* Basia, VIII. OBVE
Not always as the whirlwind's rush. The Call of the Christian. Whittier. NOCV
Not always to the swift race. The Law of Averages. "Troubadour." FiBHP
Not an editorial-writer, bereaved with bartlett. Portrait of the Poet as Landscape. A. M. Klein. NoAM; NOBC
Not another bite, not another cigarette. Search. Raymond Souster. OBCV
Not Any Higher Stands the Grave. Emily Dickinson. AnAmPo
Not any more distant, somewhere on a mountain. February 23. A. Leyeles, *tr. fr. Yiddish by* Benjamin *and* Barbara Harshav. *Fr.* Fabius Lind's Diary. AYP
Not as all other women are. My Love. James Russell Lowell. BLPL; FaBoBe
"Not as Black Douglas, bannered, trumpeted." Two Wise Generals. Ted Hughes. MoBS
Not as height rises into lightness. Breadth. Circle. Desert. Monarch. Month. Wisdom. John Hollander. PoA
Not as the white nations. The Black Madonna. Albert Rice. CDC
Not as we are but as we must appear. Geoffrey Hill. *Fr.* Funeral Music, VIII. NoAM
Not as when some great Captain falls. Abraham Lincoln. Richard Henry Stoddard. AA; AnAmPo; FaBoBe; GN; OHIP; PAH
Not as Wont. Joseph Skipsey. NOBVV
Not as you had dreamed was the battle's issue. To a Young Leader of the First World War. Stefan George, *tr.* by E. B. Ashton. WaaP
Not Ashurbanipal. Wall Street. A. Leyeles, *tr. fr. Yiddish by* Benjamin *and* Barbara Harshav. *Fr.* New York. AYP
Not at midnight, not at morning, O sweet city. Caryatid. Léonie Adams. LiTM

Not at night, no, altogether, tomorrow. No. Natan Zach, *tr. by* Laya Firestone. VWA

Not at the first sight, nor with a dribbed shot. Sir Philip Sidney. *Fr.* Astrophel and Stella, II. NAEL-1; OAEL-1

Not because of their beauty—though they are slender. The Twins. Judith Wright. PoAu-2

Not because of victories. Te Deum. Charles Reznikoff. TrJP; VWA

Not because of you, not because of me, just that. Natalya Gorbanyevskaya, *tr. by* Daniel Weissbort. BoWoP

Not because you didn't call. The Heart Has Its Reasons. Felice Picano. PeHV

Not being Breedlove, whose immortal skid. To Dorothy on Her Exclusion from the *Guinness Book of World Records*. X. J. Kennedy. Psk

Not Being Oedipus. John Heath-Stubbs. OxBC; TEP

Not-Being was not, Being was not then. Brahma, the World Idea. *Unknown, tr. fr. Sanskrit by* Romesh Dutt. *Fr.* Vedic Hymns. WGRP

Not born to the forest are we. Song of the Camels. Elizabeth Jane Coatsworth. FaPON

Not but they die, the teasers and the dreams. The Teasers. William Empson. OxBTC

Not by Bread Alone. *Unknown, tr. fr. Greek by* James Terry White. PoLF

Not by hammering the furious word. Harlem Riot, 1943. Pauli Murray. PoBA

Not by lost killers stranded. The Biggest Killing. Edward Dorn. VGW

Not by the ball or brand. Vanquished. Francis Fisher Browne. AA

Not by the city bells that chime the hours. A Summer Day. Florence Harrison. BoTP

Not by the poets. Discovery of This Time. Archibald MacLeish. LiTA; WaP

Not by wayout hairdos, bulbous Afro blowouts and certainly. Only in This Way. Margaret Goss Burroughs. BlSi

Not by Wind Ravaged. Hone Tuwhare. ATNZ

Not Canaan and its cities, the splendor of towers. Moses on Mount Nebo. Abraham Regelson, *tr. by* Richard Flantz. VWA

Not caring to observe the Wind. Of Loving at First Sight. Edmund Waller. SeCP

Not, Celia, that I juster am. Sir Charles Sedley. GTBS; GTBS-P (Song to Celia.) OBS; SeCePo (To Celia.) AWP; NOBE; OBEV

Not content, the violets have dyed. Shiba Sonome, *tr. fr. Japanese by* Hiroaki Sato. *Fr.* Fifteen Hokku. FCEI

Not Dead, but Sleeping. Clara Ann Thompson. CBWP-2

Not different the fate of bards. McIntyre and Ross. Sorley MacLean. PoPo

Not drowsihood and dreams and mere idleness. In Sleep. Richard Burton. AA

Not drunk but with a buzz on maybe, he. In Memory of W. H. Auden. David R. Slavitt. SM

Not easy to state the change you made. Love Letter. Sylvia Plath. NOBA

Not entirely enviable, however envied. The Master. W. S. Merwin. NePoEA

Not even. Albert Speer. W. D. Snodgrass. NoAM

Not even dried-up leaves. Thesis, Antithesis and Nostalgia. Alan Dugan. PCP

Not even for a moment have we joined. Princess Shikishi, *tr. fr. Japanese by* Hiroaki Sato. *Fr.* Seventy-eight Tanka. FCEI

Not even for a moment. He knew, for one thing, what he was. Leda. Mona Van Duyn. NMM

Not even in dreams/ Can I meet him anymore. Lady Ise, *tr. fr. Japanese by* Donald Keene. WPOW

Not even the cops who can do anything could do this. Laundry. Bruce Smith. Son

Not even the moon. Chikako, *tr. by* Steven D. Carter. WFTW

Not even trying to touch the hot blood-tide. Yosano Akiko, *tr. fr. Japanese by* Hiroaki Sato. *Fr.* Thirty-nine Tanka. FCEI

Not even waiting. Tameyo, *tr. by* Steven D. Carter. WFTW

Not ever knowing what she does in the shower. A Fixture. Bill Berkson. UL

Not Every Day Fit for Verse. Robert Herrick. PoRA

Not every man can own as Tomas does. A Private Life. Celia Gilbert. ER

Not every man has gentians in his house. Bavarian Gentians. D. H. Lawrence. CMoP; CMoP; FaBoCh; FaBoMo; GoJo; GTBS-P; GTBS-P; HAP; InPK; InPK; InPS; LiTB; MoP; NAEL-2; NoAM; NOBE; NoP; OAEL-2, 2 *versions;* PoE; SOTW; TTTS; ViBoPo

Not every skin-teeth. Skin-Teeth. Grace Nichols. AIW

Not far advanc'd was morning day. Battle, The ("Not for advanc'd was morning day"). Sir Walter Scott. *Fr.* Marmion, VI. EnRP

Not far beyond the town wild flowers grow. Sanctuary. Clifford Dyment. PoA

Not far from the palace. Ruins. Mark Strand. BLA

Not far from these Phoenician Dido stood. Dido among the Shades. Virgil, *tr. fr. Latin by* Dryden. *Fr.* The Aeneid [*or* Eneados], VI. OBS

Not fifty summers yet have passed thy clime. Oliver Goldsmith, the Younger. *Fr.* The Rising Village. OBCV

Not Flesh of Brass. Bible, *O.T.* *Fr.* Job, X: 1–22. TrJP

Not for all of beauty. Commentary Applied to Spiritual Things. Saint John of the Cross, *tr. by* K. Kavanaugh *and* O. Rodrigues. TOF

Not for Its Own Sake. Hazel Littlefield. GoYe

Not for me a giantess. Requirements. Niarchus, *tr. by* Wallace Rice. ErPo

Not for nothing did we let them know. Our Jewish Quarter. Jacob Glatstein, *tr. by* Cynthia Ozick. PeBMYV

Not for Sale. Hans Vlek, *tr. fr. Dutch by* James S. Holmes. DuIn

Not for That City. Charlotte Mew. MoBrPo

Not for the promise of the laboured field. Ode to the Poppy. Henrietta Oneil. WPE

Not for us this shell grew like a lily. A Striped Shell. Ruth Dallas. ATNZ

Not for You. Ory Bernstein, *tr. fr. Hebrew by* Bernhard Frank. MHeP

Not forgetting Ko-jen, that. More Foreign Cities. Charles Tomlinson. NePoEA-2

Not Fortune's worshipper, nor Fashion's fool. Apologia pro Vita Sua. Pope. *Fr.* Epistle to Dr. Arbuthnot. NOBE

Not from my reverent sires hath come. Poet's Prayer. Adelaide Love. TrPWD

Not from successful love alone. Halcyon Days. Walt Whitman. OxBA

Not from that/ could you get it. The City. Robert Creeley. LCAP

Not from the earth, or skies. Health of Body Dependent on Soul. Jones Very. WGRP

Not from the glory of the cloud's pile and rift. Elegy on the Eve. George Barker. WaaP

Not from the stars do I my judgement pluck. Shakespeare. *Fr.* Sonnets, XIV. Son

Not from the unmapped valleys of darkness, nor. Hall of Ocean Life. John Hollander. PoA

Not from the whole wide world I chose thee. Richard Watson Gilder. *Fr.* The New Day. AA

Not from This Anger. Dylan Thomas. LiTB

Not from Titania's Court do I. Hob Gobbling's Song. James Russell Lowell. OBCA

Not furred nor wet, the pointing words yet make. Beaver Pond. Anne Marriott. NOBC

Not going in. *Unknown, tr. by* Geoffrey Bownas *and* Anthony Thwaite. PeBJV

Not Going with It. Zali Gurevitch, *tr. fr. Hebrew by* Gabriel Levin. VWA

Not gold, but only man can make. *Unknown.* *Fr.* A Nation's Strength. AmFN; FaPON

Not greatly moved with awe am I. The Two Deserts. Coventry Patmore. BoNaP

Not guns, not thunder, but a flutter of clouded drums. Fireworks. Babette Deutsch. NYBP; OFD

Not happy with what he has. What Her Girl Friend Said to Her. Palaipatiya Perunkatunko, *tr. by* A. K. Ramanujan. PLW

Not he who holds the sceptre high atop the eagle's throne. Why the Resurrection Was Revealed to Women. Catharina Regina von Greiffenberg, *tr. by* Michael Hamburger. PBWP

Not hell but a street, not. 209 Canal. Richard Howard. TAP

Not Here. Edmund Wilson. PoA

Not Here, O Apollo. Matthew Arnold. *See* Empedocles on Etna: Song of Callicles, The.

"Not home! Not home!" Natsume Seibi, *tr. fr. Japanese by* Hiroaki Sato. *Fr.* Twenty-seven Hokku. FCEI

Not honey/ not the plunder of the bee. Hilda Doolittle ("H. D."). NAAL-2

Not—"How did he die?" But—"How did he live?" The Measure of a Man. *Unknown.* BLPL; PoLF

Not I. Robert Louis Stevenson. NA; NOBL

Not I ("Not I, but Christ"). *Unknown.* BLRP

Not I, not I, but the wind that blows through me! Song of a Man Who Has Come Through. D. H. Lawrence. CMoP; FaBoMo; GTBS-P; InPS; LiTM; OxBTC; PoE

Not Ideas about the Thing but the Thing Itself. Wallace Stevens. HAP; HCAP; LCAP; TAP

Not if men's tongues and angels' all in one. Shakespeare. Swinburne. TrGrPo

Not, I'll not, carrion comfort, Despair, not feast on thee. Carrion Comfort. Gerard Manley Hopkins. CMoP; HeIP; LiTB; NAEL-2; NoAM; NoP; OAEL-2; PoE; PoEL-5; PPP; Son; TEP; TOF ("Sonnet: "Not, I'll not, carrion comfort, Despair, not feast on thee.") OBNC

Not in a silver casket cool with pearls. Edna St. Vincent Millay. CMoP; VGW

Not in Dumb Resignation. John Milton Hay. WGRP

Not in Heaven. Iain Crichton Smith. NPo

Not in my saddle, but above it. Indian Summer: Montana, 1956. W. M. Ransom. CDW

Not in our time, O Lord. Hilda Doolittle ("H. D."). *Fr.* Tribute to the Angels. NOBA

Not in sleep I saw it, but in daylight. Kindly Vision. Otto Julius Bierbaum, *tr. by* Jethro Bithell. AWP

Not in the ancient abbey. Threnody for a Poet. Bliss Carman. CaP

Not in the cities, nor among fabricated towers. Boulder Dam. May Sarton. SaC

Not in the crises of events. The Spirit's Epochs. Coventry Patmore. *Fr.* The Angel in the House, I, viii. EBEV; GBL; OxBSP

Not in the dire, ensanguined front of war. The Men of the *Maine*. Clinton Scollard. PAH

Not in the Guide-Books. Elizabeth Jennings. LiTM; NePoEA

Not in the Poet. George Barker. OxBSP

Not in the sepulchre Thou art. Passiontide Communion. Katharine Tynan. TrPWD

Not in the silence only. My Prayer. Horatius Bonar. BLRP

Not in the sky. The Lost Pleiad. William Gilmore Simms. AA

Not in the world of light alone. The Living Temple. Oliver Wendell Holmes. *Fr.* The Autocrat of the Breakfast Table. AA

Not in those climes where I have late been straying. Dedication: To Ianthe. Byron. *Fr.* Childe Harold's Pilgrimage. OBNC

Not in thy body is thy life at all. Life-in-Love. Dante Gabriel Rossetti. *Fr.* The House of Life, XXXVI. HAP

Not in Vain. *Unknown.* BLRP

Not just folklore, or. Fast Ball. Jonathan Williams. NeAP

Not Just for the Ride. Cosmo Monkhouse. *See* There Was a Young Lady of Niger.

Not just the sizes named (like miniatures). Taxonomical Note. David Sutton. Mes

Not Just Yet. Carter Revard. VoR

Not Knowing, *sel.* Mary Gardiner Brainard. PWR

"I know not what will befall me: God hangs a mist o'er my eyes." AA

Not knowing in what season this again. Parting: 1940. John Frederick Nims. PoA

Not knowing that the long spring day. Prince Ikusa. *Fr.* Manyo Shu. Ma

Not knowing the dream without beginning has been a dream. Princess Shikishi, *tr. fr. Japanese by* Hiroaki Sato. *Fr.* Seventy-eight Tanka. FCEI

Not knowing where he was or how he got there. A Bewilderment at the Entrance of the Fat Boy into Eden. Daryl Hine. NOBC; OBCV

Not least, 'tis ever my delight. Morning. Philip Henry Savage. AA

Not less because in purple I descended. Tea at the Palaz of Hoon. Wallace Stevens. FaBoMo; PoA

Not less delighted do I call to mind. Recollections of a Day's Journey in Spain. Robert Southey. OBTV

Not light of love, lady! The Lover Exhorteth His Lady to Be Constant. *Unknown.* OBSC

Not like a Cypress. Yehuda Amichai, *tr. fr. Hebrew by* Stephen Mitchell. VWA

Not like a suddenly-extinguished light. Triumphs. Petrarch, *tr. by* Morris Bishop. OBD

Not like an ordinary cloud. Teika, *tr. fr. Japanese by* Hiroaki Sato. *Fr.* Eighty-four Tanka. FCEI

Not like the brazen giant of Greek fame. The New Colossus. Emma Lazarus. AiP; AmFN; FaBV; FaFP; FaPON; FPL; OPP; PoLF; PrIm; Son; WPE

Not like we used to with pipes. Bubbles. George Garrett. MT

Not liking what life has in it. Wet Are the Boards. John Ashbery. BLA; NPo

Not lips of mine have ever said. In Youth. Evaleen Stein. AA

Not long ago a man was smoking on a balcony. Birth of the Cool. C. D. Wright. MT

Not long ago from hence I went. The Lusty Fryer of Flanders. *Unknown.* CoMu

Not Lost, but Gone Before. Caroline Norton. BLRP; WBLP

Not lost or won but above all endeavor. Fidelity. Trumbull Stickney. LiTA

Not Lotte. Katherine Hoskins. ErPo

Not Machines. Peter Redgrove. NPo

Not magnitude, not lavishness. Greek Architecture. Herman Melville. NoP

Not many days have passed. Teika, *tr. fr. Japanese by* Hiroaki Sato. *Fr.* A Compendium of Good Tanka. FCEI

"Not Marble nor the Gilded Monuments." Archibald MacLeish. BoLoP; CMoP; HoPM; MoAB; PoRA; TwCP

Not marble, nor the gilded monuments. Shakespeare. *Fr.* Sonnets, LV. AWP; BLPL; CTC; FaFP; FF; HeIP; LiTB; NAEL-1; NIP; NOBE; NoP; OAEL-1; OBSC; PeHV; PoE; PoEL-2; PoRA; Son; TEP; TrGrPo

Not Marching Away to Be Killed. Jean Overton Fuller. FF

Not Me. Shel Silverstein. *See* Slithergadee has crawled out of the sea, The.

Not merely for our pleasure, but to purge. "Ej Blot til Lyst." William Morton Payne. AA

Not met and marred with the year's whole turn of grief. James Agee. *Fr.* Lyrics. MoAmPo

Not midst the lightning of the stormy fight. Stonewall Jackson. Henry Lynden Flash. AA; PAH

Not Mine. Julia Caroline Ripley Dorr. PWR

Not mine own fears nor the prophetic soul. Shakespeare. *Fr.* Sonnets, CVII. AWP; CTC; EBEV; FiP; HAP; LiTB; NAEL-1; NoP; OAEL-1; OBSC

Not mine to draw the cloth-yard shaft. The Satirist. Harry Lyman Koopman. AA

Not much more than being. Louis Zukofsky. *Fr.* 29 Poems, 2. PoE

Not Much Talking. *Unknown.* PWR

Not My Best Side. U. A. Fanthorpe. FaBoWP

Not my hands but green across you now. The Lady in Kicking Horse Reservoir. Richard Hugo. CoAP; LCAP; NAAL-2; NoAM; NoP

Not now, but in the coming years. Some Time We'll Understand. Maxwell N. Cornelius. BLRP; WBLP

Not now expecting to live forever. Dublin Bay. Ewart Milne. NeIP

Not o'er thy dust let there be spent. Whittier. Paul Laurence Dunbar. AnAmPo

Not of All My Eyes See. Gerard Manley Hopkins. OxBSP

Not, of course, the monster hunched downtown. Dome Poem. Dave Smith. PoA

Not of Itself but Thee. *Unknown, tr. fr. Greek by* Richard Garnett. AWP

Not of ourselves are we free. Heritage. Mary Gilmore. CBAP

Not of the princes and prelates with periwigged charioteers. A Consecration. John Masefield. MoAB; MoBrPo

Not Often. Ray Fraser. NeAC

Not often *con brio*, but *andante, andante.* Stanley Matthews. Alan Ross. OxBTC

Not on a prayerless bed, not on a prayerless bed. Exhortation to Prayer. Margaret Mercer. AA

Not on an altar shall mine eyes behold thee. Real Presence. Ivan Adair. WGRP

Not on our golden fortunes builded high. The Forgotten Man. Edwin Markham. BLPL; PoLF

Not one not dandled a man high up in the air. White Pines, Felled 1984. Richard Eberhart. BLA

Not one poem about an animal, she said. Florida. Dannie Abse. OxBC

Not Only around Our Infancy. James Russell Lowell. *Fr.* The Vision of Sir Launfal, Prelude to *Pt.* I. FaFP

Not only how far away, but the way that you say it. Judging Distances. Henry Reed. *Fr.* Lessons of the War, II. BoLoP; GTBS-P; MoAB; NIP; NOBE; NoP; SoSe

Not only the soot from the city air. The Floor Is Dirty. Edward Field. NeAP

Not only we, the latest seed of Time. Godiva. Tennyson. BeLS

Not Only Where God's Free Winds Blow. Shepherd Knapp. AH

Not only with no sense of shame. Tennyson. FaBoEE

Not out of the war, not out of the agitated. Man on a Raft. John Russell Hervey. ATNZ

Not overwhelming, this morning's little dream. The Know. Kathleen Fraser. NPGG

Not Palaces [an Era's Crown]. Stephen Spender. CMoP; FaBoMo; LiTB; LiTM; MoAB; MoBrPo; NoAM; NoP; WaP

Not pall, but shadows. My Words. William Hathaway. EOEF

Not Pallas, not ev'n Spleen it self could blame. Ovid, *tr. fr. Latin by* John Gay. *Fr.* Metamorphoses, VI. OBVE

Not perched on the top of the hill. At Mrs. Alefounder's. Barbara Howes. AnAn

Not picnics or pageants or the improbable. Terror. Robert Penn Warren. PoA; WaP

Not power nor the storied hand of God. Allen Tate. *Fr.* Sonnets of the Blood, IX. PoA

Not Provable. Ilse Tielsch, *tr. fr. German by* Beth Bjorklund. CoAuP
Not Quite Spring. Lyn Lifshin. NeAC
Not Ragged-and-Tough. *Unknown.* ChTr; FaBoNo
Not realizing. Six Feet Under. Janet Campbell Hale. VoR
Not Rice, Not Water. Mocikiranar, *tr. fr. Tamil by* A. K. Ramanujan. PLW
Not rose of death. Rose in the Afternoon. Jenny Joseph. BrRo
Not satisfied/ with the expanse of the waves. The Moon from a Boat. Gyoko, *tr. by* Steven D. Carter. WFTW
Not Saying Much. Linda Gregg. AiP; NPGG
Not Seeing Is Believing. Paul Petrie. TAP
Not seeing that a "Zen man" is no Zen man. Guchu, *tr. by* Lucien Stryk *and* Takashi Ikemoto. ZPCJ
Not serried ranks with flags unfurled. What Makes a Nation Great? Alexander Blackburn. WBLP
Not she with traitorous kiss her Saviour stung. Woman. Eaton Stannard Barrett. TIRV
Not single filmy threads. A Shower of Cobwebs. Gilbert White. TSS
Not slowly wrought, nor treasured for their form. Snowflakes. Howard Nemerov. HCAP; PCP
Not so awful long ago. The Book. Waddie Mitchell. CowP
Not so, for living yet are those. A Dead Past. At. *to* C. C. Munson. BLRP; WBLP
Not-so-good Earth, The. Bruce Dawe. CBAP
Not so much you yourself. Fabius Lind to Comrade Death. A. Leyeles, *tr. by* Benjamin *and* Barbara Harshav. AYP
Not sobered up from my muddy Kao-yang drunk. Yang Shih-ch'i, *tr. fr. Chinese by* Jonathan Chaves. *Fr.* Hsi-li Echoed My Poems, and I Respond to Him. CoBLCP
Not solely that the future she destroys. George Meredith. *Fr.* Modern Love, XII. GBL; TEP
Not soon shall I forget—a sheet. Katharine Tynan. CH
Not speaking many words. Wakayama Bokusui, *tr. fr. Japanese by* Hiroaki Sato. *Fr.* Forty-four Tanka. FCEI
Not speaking of the way. Yosano Akiko, *tr. by* Kenneth Rexroth. UnAS
Not speaking of the Way. Yosano Akiko, *tr. fr. Japanese by* Hiroaki Sato. *Fr.* Thirty-nine Tanka. FCEI
Not strangeness, but strange likeness. Geoffrey Hill. *Fr.* Mercian Hymns, XXIX. FaBoMo; HAP; NoAM
Not Such Your Burden. Agathias, *tr. fr. Greek by* William M. Hardinge. AWP
Not that by this disdain. The Repulse. Thomas Stanley. MeLP; MePo; OBS
Not That Far. May Miller. BISi
Not that God's dead. Jacob's Winning. Richard Sherwin. VWA
Not that he promised not to windowshop. One Man's Wife. Philip Booth. NIP; VGW
Not that her blooms are marked with beauty's hue. To Mr. Gray. Thomas Warton, the Younger. Son
Not that I have cause for celebration. New Year's Eve. Herbert B. Mallalieu. WaP
Not that I wish to take the liberty. Non Que Je Veuille Ôter la Liberté. Pernette de Guillet, *tr. by* Raymond Oliver. WPOW
Not that my hand could make of stubborn stone. Death-Bed Reflections of Michel-Angelo. Hartley Coleridge. EyDe
Not that the earth is changing, O my God! On Refusal of Aid between Nations. Dante Gabriel Rossetti. EBEV
Not that the tree in my garden does not bloom. Harp Song. Lu Yu, *tr. by* Burton Watson. CoBCP
Not that thy hand is soft, is sweet, is white. Henry Constable. *Fr.* Diana. OBSC
Not that we are weary. In the Trenches. Richard Aldington. MMA
Not the Arms Race. Sam Abrams. UL
Not the attendance of stones. Black Maps. Mark Strand. PoA
Not the beautiful youth with features of bloom & brightness. Beauty. Walt Whitman. WeW
Not the city lights. We want. View. Rae Armantrout. IAT
Not the dark café, not today; I want color. The Summer's Cold. Max Hölzer, *tr. by* Beth Bjorklund. CoAuP
Not the dead shall praise you, Lord, today. Of the Travelers That Won't Come Again. Benyamin Galai, *tr. by* Bernhard Frank. MHeP
Not the delicate mare who came nosing. White Horse of the Father, White Horse of the Son. William Pitt Root. MAYP
Not the intimacy of your forehead clear as a celebration. Amorous Anticipation. Jorge Luis Borges, *tr. by* Perry Higman. LPSS
Not the milk, but the color of milk. Taking the Milk to Grandmother. William Kloefkorn. KS
Not the night of shepherds. Noise in Darkness. Sándor Weöres, *tr. by* Jascha Kessler. FOC
Not the respiration. The gasping. Exhortation. János Pilinszky, *tr. by* Ted Hughes. MHuP

Not the round natural world, not the deep mind. Frederick Goddard Tuckerman. *Fr.* Sonnets, I, xxviii. NoP
Not these appal/ The soul. Faith's Difficulty. Theodore Maynard. TrPWD
Not Thinking of America. Judith Kroll. AmPA
Not those patient men who knocked and were unheeded. 1918-1941. Robert David Fitzgerald. CBAP
Not those slim-flanked fillies. Tim. John Montague. FaBCIP
Not Thou but I. Philip Bourke Marston. BLPA; BLPL
Not to Be Born. David Sutton. OBD
Not to Be Ministered To. Maltbie Davenport Babcock. TrPWD
Not to dance with her. A Triviality. Waring Cuney. CDC
Not to do but work. The Sum of Life. Ben King. CTC
Not to Forget Miss Dickinson. Marshall Schacht. LiTM
Not to Keep. Robert Frost. CMoP; OxBA
Not to know vice at all, and keepe true state. Epode. Ben Jonson. SeCP; SeCV-1
Not to lose the feel of the mountains. The Double-headed Snake. John Newlove. MoCV
Not to Love. Robert Herrick. CaPo
Not to say what everyone else was saying. Different. Clere Parsons. FaBoTw
Not to sigh and to be tender. Aphra Behn. BoWoP
Not to the butcher did he pass. The Old Ox. George Rostrevor Hamilton, *after the Greek of* Addaios of Makedon. FaBoEE
Not to the swift, the race. Reliance. Henry van Dyke. FaFP
Not to the weak alone. The Call to the Strong. William Pierson Merrill. BLRP
Not to Us, Not unto Us, Lord. *Unknown.* AH
Not tomorrow night. Not Yet. Joanne Kyger. UL
Not Tonight, Josephine. Colin Curzon. ErPo
Not too chary, not too fast. Requirements ("Not too chary, not too fast."). Rufinus Domesticus, *tr. by* Wallace Rice. ErPo
Not too far north from where I write set dawn. Hint for the Incomplete Angler. Kendrick Smithyman. ATNZ; PeNZ
Not too lean, and not too fat. Requirements ("Not too lean, and not too fat"). Rufinus Domesticus, *tr. by* Wallace Rice. ErPo
Not too old, and not too young. Requirements ("Not too old, and not too young"). Honestus, *tr. by* Wallace Rice. ErPo
Not too pallid, as if bleacht. Requirements ("Not too pallid, as if bleacht"). Xenos Palaestes, *tr. by* Wallace Rice. ErPo
Not Ulysses, no, nor any other man. Louise Labé, *tr. by* Willis Barnstone. BoWoP
Not Understood. Thomas Bracken. BLPA
Not unto us, O Lord. Non Nobis. Henry Cust. OBEV
Not upon earth, as you suppose. "Tu Non Se' in Terra, Si Come Tu Credi." Kathleen Jessie Raine. WPE
Not us, I say, not us. Psalm CXV ("Not unto us, O Lord. . ."). Bible, *O.T. Fr.* Psalms.
   (Psalm CXV: "Not unto us, O Lord, not unto us," *paraphrased by the* Countess of Pembroke) NOCV
Not waking, in my dreams, my dreams. Infidelity. Olga Berggolts, *tr. by* Daniel Weissbort. BoWoP
Not Wanting Myself. Linda Gregg. NPGG
Not Waving but Drowning. Stevie Smith. FaBoWP; FF; GTBS-P; HAP; HeIP; MoP; NAEL-2; NoAM; NOBE; NoP; OAEL-2; OxBTC; PoE; PPP; PrIm; TEP; WeW
Not weaned yet, without comprehension loving. Love's Immaturity. Edith Jay Scovell. GBL; LiTB
Not what, but Whom, I do believe. Credo. John Oxenham. BLRP
Not what I am, O Lord, but what Thou art. More of Thee. Horatius Bonar. BLRP
Not what we expected. And dark in there. Remodeling the Hermit's Cabin. Fred Chappell. MOWH
Not when leaves are brown and sere. When I Would Die. Josephine D. Henderson Heard. CBWP-4
Not when, with self dissatisfied. With Self Dissatisfied. Frederick L. Hosmer. TrPWD
Not where the battle red. On the Death of "Jackson." *Unknown.* PAH
Not while, but long after he had told me. Each Bird Walking. Tess Gallagher. FaBoWP; MAYP; SV
Not Wholly Lost. Raymond Souster. OBCV
Not wide but a wing. The Table. Ray DiPalma. LP
Not wishing to pronounce the taboo word. Tuberculosis. Dannie Abse. NPo
Not with a club the heart is broken. Emily Dickinson. LiTA
Not with more glories, in th' ethereal plain. Pope. *Fr.* The Rape of the Lock, II. EBEV; NOEC
   (Voyage on the Thames, The.) NOBE
Not with my hands. Benediction. Donald Jeffrey Hayes. AmNP; PoNe

Not with slow, funereal sound. An Ode, on the Unveiling of the Shaw Memorial on Boston Common, May 31st, 1897. Thomas Bailey Aldrich. AA; PAH

Not with vain tears, when we're beyond the sun. Rupert Brooke. BrPo

Not without Beauty. John A. B. McLeish. CaP

Not working, not breathing. Autumn. Bella Akhmadulina, *tr.* by Barbara Einzig. BoWoP; OV

Not wrongly moved by this dismaying scene. William Empson. LiTM; WaP

"Not ye who have stoned, not ye who have smitten us," cry. Arraignment. Helen Gray Cone. AA

Not Yet. Joanne Kyger. UL

Not yet dark, but stars glitter. Buson, *tr. fr. Japanese* by Hiroaki Sato. *Fr.* Eighty-seven Hokku. FCEI

Not yet dead, not yet alone. Osip Mandelstam, *tr.* by James Greene. OBVE

Not yet enslaved, not wholly vile. O My Mother Isle! ("Not yet enslaved, not wholly vile"). Samuel Taylor Coleridge. *Fr.* Ode on the Departing Year. FaBoPP

Not yet five, and the light. After Hours. Robert Mezey. NaP

Not yet in sight. 'Twere well to step aside. At the Polo-Ground. Samuel Ferguson. NOIV

Not yet, not yet. The Tree. Joel Sloman. VGW

"Not yet, not yet; steady, steady!" Bunker Hill. George Henry Calvert. BeLS; FaBoBe; PAH

Not yet will those measureless fields be green again. The Cenotaph. Charlotte Mew. MMA; WPE

Not you, lean quarterlies and swarthy periodicals. To the Film Industry in Crisis. Frank O'Hara. NOBA; OBAL; SOTW

Nota: man is the intelligence of his soil. The Comedian as the Letter C. Wallace Stevens. OxBA

Notable Dinner, A. Lizelia Augusta Jenkins Moorer. CBWP-3

Notably fond of music, I dote on a sweeter tone. The Clink of the Ice. Eugene Field. AnAmPo

Notation in Haste. Elias Lieberman. GoYe

Note. Paul Potts. PoPo

Note. Meir Wieseltier, *tr. fr. Hebrew* by Warren Bargad *and* Stanley F. Chyet. IP

Note apropos a Light Breeze and an Elderly Couple on a Bench, Together, in the National Park at Ram. Abba Kovner, *tr. fr. Hebrew* by Bernhard Frank. MHeP

Note apropos the Neighbor's Garden. Abba Kovner, *tr. fr. Hebrew* by Bernhard Frank. MHeP

Note-Book of a European Tramp, The, *sel.* Michael Hamburger. "Townsman on his yielding bed, The." NePoEA

Note Delivered by a Female Impersonator. Heather McHugh. AmPA

Note how the desert takes form, easily as wax. It moves. In Scorching Time. Alex Stevens. KS

Note Left in Jimmy Leonard's Shack, A. James Wright. HCAP; NoP

Note/ O. O. Gabugah writes that he "was born in a taxicab right smack on 125th." "Boogie with O. O. Gabugah." Al Young. NPGG

Note of Humility, A. Arna Bontemps. PoNe

Note on Feeding. *Unknown.* FaBoUs

Note on Intellectuals. W. H. Auden. FiBHP

Note on Local Flora. William Empson. EBEV; FaBoMo

Note on Propertius I.5. Fleur Adcock. ATNZ; BoLoP; PeNZ

Note on the Latin Gerunds, A. Richard Porson. FaBoCo; FaBoEE

Note on the Social Arts, A. Kendrick Smithyman. ATNZ

Note on Wyatt, A. Kingsley Amis. WeW

Note that the fire. The Fire Poem. Theodore Enslin. CRP

Note the stump, a peach tree. We had to cut it down. Places and Ways to Live. Richard Hugo. NIP

Note this survivor, bearing the mark of the violator. Swedenborg's Skull. Vernon Watkins. FaBoTw

Note to Isolationists 1940. F. Tennyson Jesse. CN

Note to My Friends, While Slightly Ill, A. Huang Ching-jen, *tr. fr. Chinese* by Daniel Bryant. WFTU

Note to R. H. from Strongsville. Richard Hugo. AnAn

Note to the Difficult One, A. William Sydney Graham. AnAn

Note to the Previous Tenants. John Updike. GOYP

Note to Wang Wei. John Berryman. NYBP

Noted outside the window: a fly, the sun on his back. Cold Fly. Yang Wan-li, *tr.* by Burton Watson. CoBCP

Notepad-pain. Paul Celan, *tr.* by Beth Bjorklund. CoAuP

Notes. Cecilia Bustamante, *tr. fr. Spanish* by David Tipton. Per

Notes after Blacking Out. Gregory Corso. NeAP

Notes for a History of Poetry. David Daiches. PoA

Notes for a Lecture. David Ignatow. NNaP

Notes for a Movie Script. M. Carl Holman. AmNP; PoBA; PoNe

Notes for a Revised Sonnet. Edward Pygge. BXAP

Notes for a Sonnet. Edward Pygge. BXAP

Notes for a Southern Road Map. Phyllis McGinley. NBLV

Notes for Albuquerque. Roberta Hill Whiteman. STE

Notes for an Elegy: for John Gardner. Linda Pastan. AnAn

Notes for Echo Lake 5. Michael Palmer. NPGG

Notes for My Son. Alex Comfort. *Fr.* The Song of Lazarus, VI. LiTM; MoBrPo; SeCePo

Notes for the Chart in 306. Ogden Nash. NYBP

Notes for the Legend of Salad Woman. Michael Ondaatje. NoAM

Notes Found near a Suicide. Frank Horne. *See* Letters Found near a Suicide.

Notes from a Chicana "COED." Bernice Zamora. CCP

Notes from an Analyst's Couch. Anita Endrezze Probst. CDW

Notes Made in the Piazza San Marco. May Swenson. CoAP

Notes on a Girl. Peter Kane Dufault. ErPo

Notes on a Life to Be Lived. Robert Penn Warren. NYBP

Notes on a Long Evening. David Phillips. NeAC

Notes on a Track Meet. David McCord. SD

Notes on Life at Home, February, 1942. Valentine Ackland. CN

Notes on My Father, *sel.* Katerina Anghelaki-Rooke. "Old man moved into his night, The." PBWP

Notes on Saint Maurice. Judit Tóth, *tr. fr. Hungarian* by Laura Schiff. MHuP

Notes on the Book of Defeat, *sel.* Nizar Qabbani, *tr. fr. Arabic* by Diana Der Hovanessian *and* Lena Jayyusi. "If an audience could be arranged." MAP

Notes on the Book of Defeat. Nizar Qabbani. *See* Friends.

Notes on the Moving of a Corpse. Mirko Lauer, *tr. fr. Spanish* by David Tipton. Per

Notes on the Peanut. June Jordan. NoAM

Notes to the Books of the Old Testament. Aleksander Wat, *tr. fr. Polish* by Czeslaw Milosz. PwPP

Notes to the Reader. Robert Bringhurst. NOBC

Notes toward a Supreme Fiction, *sels.* Wallace Stevens. "And for what, except for you, do I feel love?." NOBA "Begin, ephebe, by perceiving the idea." NOBA "Bethou me, said sparrow, to the crackled blade." LiTM "First idea was not our own, The. Adam." NOBA Great Statue of the General Du Puy, The. LiTA "It feels good as it is without the giant." NOBA "Major abstraction is the idea of man, The." NOBA President Ordains the Bee to Be, The. LiTA Soldier, There Is a War between the Mind. LiTM; NoAM Whistle Aloud, Too Weedy Wren. LiTA

Notes towards a Poem That Can Never Be Written. Margaret Atwood. NOBC

Notes Written in Obory, *sel.* Aleksander Wat, *tr. fr. Polish* by Czeslaw Milosz. "X was asked." PwPP

Nothin very bad happen to me lately. John Berryman. *See* Nothing very bad . . .

Nothing. Julia de Burgos, *tr.* by Aliki *and* Willis Barnstone. BoWoP

Nothing. Walter de la Mare. WSC

Nothing. James Sherry. LP

Nothing. Charles Simic. NNaP

Nothing. Burns Singer. OxBS

Nothing/ substance utters or time. The Word. Basil Bunting. PoA

Nothing and Something. Frances Ellen Watkins Harper. PWR

Nothing at All. I. A. Richards. CRP

Nothing bestial or human remains. From the Workshop of Brancusi and Giancometti. John Haines. BLA

Nothing but a hovel now. The Rain. Dafydd ap Gwilym, *tr.* by Rolfe Humphries. OBVWE

Nothing but a man. Nadia Tuéni, *tr.* by Willis Barnstone. BoWoP

Nothing but Death. Pablo Neruda, *tr. fr. Spanish* by Robert Bly. EAS

Nothing but innocent, stubborn stone, originally. Double Jade Ring Grievance. Chang Ts'o, *tr.* by Dominic Cheung. IFON

Nothing but Net. Roy Scheele. ASP; TDD

Nothing but no and I, and I and no. Michael Drayton. *Fr.* Idea, V. GBL; PoEL-2

Nothing could be secondhand that's so full of love. In the Luxembourg Gardens. Thomas McCarthy. WCI

Nothing could make me sooner to confess. Of the Progres of the Soule; the Second Anniversary. John Donne. SeCP

Nothing Could Take Away the Bear-King's Image. Ray A. Young Bear. HATNAP

Nothing derivative here. The Litrajure of Everyday Life. Michael C. Blumenthal. NoAM

Nothing Elegant. Gertrude Stein. *Fr.* Tender Buttons. PBWP

Nothing for a dirty man. All That Is Lovely in Men. Robert Creeley. NaP

Nothing from a straight line swerves. Samuel Hoffenstein. *Fr.* Songs about Life and Brighter Things Yet. NBLV

Nothing Gold Can Stay. Robert Frost. AmPP; GrPl; MoAB; MoAmPo; NAAL-2; NOBA; PPP; SoSe; TAP; VGW

Nothing grows in vain. Use plants to heal. Creed of Mr. Nicholas Culpeper. Patricia Beer. OxBC

Nothing grows on the laborer's skin. The Laborer. Samuel Chimsoro. WMBCH

Nothing Happened. Betty Adcock. KS

Nothing has happened yet. Linda Pastan. KS

Nothing here is bitter. Wisdom. Phyllis Hanson. GoYe

Nothing human is alien to me. Human Qualities. Dahlia Ravikovich, tr. by Warren Bargad and Stanley F. Chyet. IP

Nothing if not utterly in death. So? James P. Vaughn. AmNP

Nothing in Heaven Functions as It Ought. X. J. Kennedy. SM; Son

Nothing in our lives to stop us. Following the Rhymes of Kao Chi-ti's Poem "We Had Planned to Travel to Cloud Cliff." Hsü Pen, tr. by Jonathan Chaves. CoBLCP

Nothing in this bright region melts or shifts. From the Highest Camp. Thom Gunn. Son; TwCP

Nothing Is. Sun-Ra. PoBA

Nothing is better, I well think. The Leper. Swinburne. GBL; NOBVV

Nothing Is Enough. Laurence Binyon. MoBrPo

Nothing is left now. Emperor Hanazono, tr. by Steven D. Carter. WFTW

Nothing Is Lost. Anne Ridler. WPE

Nothing is more cruel than to see. Salah Fa'iq, tr. by Patricia Alanah Byrne and Salma Khadra Jayyusi. MAP

Nothing is new: we walk where others went. Nothing New. Robert Herrick. CaPo

Nothing is plumb, level or square. Love Song: I and Thou. Alan Dugan. CAPP; FF; HoPM; InPK; MoP; NoAM; SoSe

Nothing is quite so quiet and clean. Snow in Town. Rickman Mark. BoTP

Nothing is so beautiful as spring. Spring. Gerard Manley Hopkins. BoNaP; BrPo; EBVV; FaBV; HAP; InvP; LiTM; MoAB; MoBrPo; NAEL-2; NoAM; NOBE; NOBVV; OAEL-2; OBMV; OBNC; RB; SoSe; TrCP

Nothing like that road runs from me. A Cabin in Minnesota. Marvin Bell. HoPM

Nothing More Will Happen. Marge Piercy. NeAC

Nothing move thee. St. Theresa of Avila, tr. by Yvor Winters. CRP

Nothing much to say about the jonquil smiling at me like a garlic clove. To Be Continued. Benjamin Péret, tr. by Michael Benedikt. POS

Nothing nastier than a white person! The Great Palaces of Versailles. Rita Dove. NAmP; NoAM

Nothing New. Robert Herrick. CaPo

Nothing, no one, gives me rest. In Memoriam. Tom Disch. BAP

Nothing now to mark the spot. Rachel Field. Fr. A Circus Garland. OBCA

Nothing on her has any effect. Momin Khan Momin, tr. by Ahmed Ali. GoT

Nothing out of which to create a new, A. None. Josephine Miles. VGW

Nothing remained: Nothing, the wanton name. The Annihilation of Nothing. Thom Gunn. NePoEA-2

Nothing Sacred. Roger Woddis. NOBL

Nothing Said. Brenda Agard. WS

Nothing sings from these orange trees. On Watching the Construction of a Skyscraper. Burton Raffel. PCP

Nothing so difficult as a beginning. Romantic to Burlesque. Byron. Fr. Don Juan, IV. EnRP; FiP; OAEL-2

Nothing so sharply reminds a man he is mortal. Departure in the Dark. C. Day Lewis. TwCP

Nothing so startles us as tumbleweeds in December. Weeds. Ann Stanford. GrPl

Nothing so true as what you once let fall. Epistle to a Lady: Of the Characters of Women. Pope. Fr. Moral Essays, Epistle II. NAEL-1; NOEC; OAEL-1; OxBoLi, shorter sel.

"Yet Chloe [or Cloe] sure was formed without a spot." ErPo; OBSV (Chloe.) AWP; NOBE

"Men, some to bus'ness, some to pleasure take." OBSV

Nothing Strange. Tom Kryss. NeAC

Nothing that is said or done. At First. C. H. Sisson. OxBC

Nothing there but. Kawabata Bosha, tr. by Geoffrey Bownas and Anthony Thwaite. PeBJV

Nothing! thou elder brother ev'n to shade. Upon Nothing. Earl of Rochester. MePo; OBS; OBSV; PoEL-3; TrGrPo

Nothing to Be Said. Philip Larkin. OxBTC

Nothing to be said about it, and everything. Dying. Robert Pinsky. HCAP; MAYP

Nothing to do but work. The Pessimist. Ben King. AnAmPo; BLPA; FaBoCo; FaBoNo; FaFP; NA; NBLV; OBAL (Sum of Life, The.) CTC

Nothing to Fear. Kingsley Amis. ErPo; OxBC

Nothing to Save. D. H. Lawrence. SOTW

Nothing to Say. Monique Griffiths. WS

Nothing to say? Then we'll say nothing. Conrad Aiken. Fr. Preludes for Memnon; or, Preludes to Attitude. LiTA

Nothing to Steal. John Ashbery. BLA

Nothing to Wear. William Allen Butler. OBAL; PoLF

Nothing to Write Home About. Joe Brainard. PPR

Nothing under the bowl—it's shifted again! Playing Bowl-and-Bead. Tate Ryuwan, tr. by Burton Watson. JLIC-2

Nothing [or Nothin] very bad happen to me lately. Henry's Confession. John Berryman. Fr. Dream Songs. LCAP; MoP; NAAL-2; NoAM; PoE; TwCP

Nothing was left of me. A Dream of Burial. James Wright. NaP

Nothing west beyond. Geo. Ray DiPalma. IAT

Nothing will ever change beside this river. Changeless Shore. Sarah Leeds Ash. GoYe

Nothing will fill the salt caves our youth wore. Alone. Edith Jay Scovell. GBL

Nothing will give delight. Nausea. Catherine Davis. NePoEA

Nothing would sleep in that cellar, dank as a ditch. Root Cellar. Theodore Roethke. AmPP; AnAmPo; BoNaP; HeIP; InPK; NoP; PPP

Nothing you could know, or name, or say. Peppergrass. Stanley Plumly. LCAP

Nothingness. Aharon Amir, tr. fr. Hebrew. VWA

Nothingness, for the, The. Paul Celan, tr. by Beth Bjorklund. CoAuP

Nothing's going to become of anyone. Play. A. R. Ammons. PoA

Notice. Robert Lowell. NoAM

Notice at the factory gate, The. Hands. Alex Glasgow. OBET

Notice the Convulsed Orange Inch of Moon. E. E. Cummings. VGW

Notice the oak, the high. Baii. Jim Barnes. Fr. Four Things Choctaw. HATNAP

Notice What This Poem Is Not Doing. William Stafford. LCAP

Noticing from what they talk about, and how they stand, or walk. Remembering Lunch. Douglas Dunn. OxBC

Notify someone of authority. If You See This Man. Thomas Lux. AmPA

Notions of freedom are tied up with drink. The Drunkards. Malcolm Lowry. NYBP

Notorious Glutton, The. Ann Taylor. OxBChV

Notre Dame. Osip Mandelstam, tr. fr. Russian by James Greene. OBVE

Notre Dame Victory March, The. John Shea. ASP

Nottamun Town. Unknown. FaBoNo; OxBoLi

Nottingham Fair. Unknown. AmFP

Nottinghamshire Poacher, The. Unknown. OBET

Nought is on earth more sacred or divine. Spenser. Fr. The Faerie Queene, V, 7. OAEL-1

Nought loves another as itself. Little Boy Lost, A ("Nought loves another as itself"). Blake. Fr. Songs of Experience. EnRP

Nouner, A. The Death of Floyd Collins. Clark Coolidge. LP

Nourishment. Rachel Hadas. BAP

Nova. Robinson Jeffers. CMoP; HAP

Novas. Van K. Brock. MT

Novelettes, sel. Louis MacNeice. Gardener, The. Fr. III. FaBCIP

Novella. Robert Hass. NAmP

Novella. Adrienne Rich. PPP

Novelty Shop, The. Duane Niatum. CDW

November. Margaret Atwood. NOBC

November. Robert Bridges. OBNC; PBBP; PoEL-5

November. Bryant. AnAmPo; Son

November. Alice Cary. OBCA

November. Hartley Coleridge. Fr. Sonnets to the Seasons, XII. OBNC

November. Elizabeth Daryush. QFR

November. F. W. Harvey. OxBTC

November. Thomas Hood. See No!

November. Ted Hughes. CMoP; GTBS-P; NePoEA-2; NoP

November. John Keble. Fr. Forest Leaves in Autumn. OBEV ("Red o'er the forest glows the setting sun.") OBNC

November. A. Leyeles, tr. fr. Yiddish by Benjamin and Barbara Harshav. AYP

November. Itzig Manger, tr. fr. Yiddish by Leonard Wolf. PeBMYV

November. Giovanni Pascoli, tr. fr. Italian by William Jay Smith. CT; PFI

November. Henrietta Cordelia Ray. CBWP-3

November. James Reaney. Fr. A Suit of Nettles. OBCV

November. Margaret Rose. BoTP

November. Folgore Da San Gimignano, *tr. fr. Italian by* Dante Gabriel Rossetti. *Fr.* Sonnets of the Months. AWP
November. Spenser. *Fr.* The Shepheardes [*or* Shepeards *or* Shepherd's] Calender. PoEL-1
  Dido My Dear, Alas, Is Dead. ChTr
November. Elizabeth Stoddard. AA
November. Frederick Goddard Tuckerman. NOBA
November air, The. Hotel Sierra. David St. John. MAYP
November Blue. Alice Meynell. MoBrPo
November Calf. Jane Kenyon. InPS
November Cotton Flower. Jean Toomer. CDC; MoP; NoAM; UnPo
November dawns and dewy-glooming downs. November in the Isle of Wight. Tennyson. *Fr.* Enoch Arden. FaBoPP
November Day at McClure's. Robert Bly. NU
November, 1806. Wordsworth. OBWP
November Fugitive. Henry Morton Robinson. GoYe
November Harvest. Anita Endrezze-Danielson. HATNAP
November is in the Isle of Wight. Tennyson. *Fr.* Enoch Arden. FaBoPP
November is a spinner. November. Margaret Rose. BoTP
November is come and I wait for you still. Pursuit of an Ideal. Patrick Kavanagh. FaBCIP
November Morning Near Abingdon. Valery Larbaud, *tr. fr. French by* Ron Padgett *and* Bill Zavatsky. RHTwFP
November Night. Adelaide Crapsey. FaPON
November 1918. Joseph Mills Hanson. OPP
November 1956. Evan Jones. PBCV
November 1968. Adrienne Rich. CAPP; NMM
November 1967. Paul Durcan. FaBCIP
November Poppies. Hilary Corke. NYBP
November Primrose, The. John Dacres Devlin. PF
November '73. Dan Pagis, *tr. fr. Hebrew by* Warren Bargad *and* Stanley F. Chyet. IP
November Song. Mark Vinz. Psk
November Sunday Morning. Alvin Feinman. CoAP
November Surf. Robinson Jeffers. NAAL-2; OxBA
November the Fifth. Leonard Clark. OnUR
November 3rd [*or* Third]. Miyazawa Kenji, *tr. fr. Japanese.* FCEI, *tr. by* Hiroaki Sato; PeBJV, *tr. by* Geoffrey Bownas *and* Anthony Thwaite.
November through a Giant Copper Beech. Edwin Honig. NoAM; NYBP
November Twenty-sixth Nineteen Hundred and Sixty-three. Wendell Berry. LiTM
November woods are bare and still. Down to Sleep. Helen Hunt Jackson. GN
November's misty sunshine on the streets of Paris lay. November 1918. Joseph Mills Hanson. OPP
Novembers or Straight Life. Maureen Owen. UL
November's sky is chill and drear. Ettrick Forest in November. Sir Walter Scott. *Fr.* Marmion, *Introd. to* I. FaBoPP
Novena. Mary Swander. KS
Novice, The. Edward Davison. ErPo
Novice was sitting on a cornice, A. Illustration. John Ashbery. NAAL-2
Novice when I came beneath thy gaze, A. Stanzas Concerning Love. Stefan George, *tr. by* Ludwig Lewisohn. AWP
Novices, The. Denise Levertov. NaP
Now. Sarah Knowles Bolton. PWR
Now. Mary Barker Dodge. AA
Now. Gloria Fuertes, *tr. fr. Spanish by* Philip Levine. OV
Now. Christopher Gilbert. MAYP
Now. Sarah Knowles. PWR
Now. William Stafford. NNaP
Now/ As the sad rain. From the Threshold to the Sky. Muhammad al-Maghut, *tr. by* May Jayyusi *and* John Heath-Stubbs. MAP
Now,/ At the third hour of the twentieth century. The Tattoo. Muhammad al-Maghut, *tr. by* May Jayyusi *and* John Heath-Stubbs. MAP
Now/ the polar nights. White Bears. Veronica Porumbacu, *tr. by the author and* Kathleen Weaver. OV
Now/ with the lead melted for divination. George Seferis, *tr. fr. Greek by* Edmund Keeley *and* Philip Sherrard. *Fr.* Three Secret Poems, III: 14. VMG
Now/ with your head thrown back. I Tell of Another Young Death. César Tiempo, *tr. by* Donald Devenish Walsh. TrJP
Now, after a party with the consul and our best friend. Summer, 1970. Daniel Halpern. AmPA
Now after David had lived seventy years. The Death of David. Hayyim Nahman Bialik, *tr. by* Herbert Danby. TrJP
Now Ain't That Love? Carolyn M. Rodgers. BPo
Now al is done; bring home the bride againe. Spenser. *Fr.* Epithalamion. FiP

Now all aloud the wind and rain. The Watercress Seller. Thomas Miller. OxBChV
Now all day long the man who is not dead. Mother and Son. Allen Tate. LiTA; MoAB; MoAmPo
Now all is calm. The window-lights spent. Night. A. Leyeles, *tr. fr. Yiddish by* Benjamin *and* Barbara Harshav. *Fr.* New York. AYP
Now all of change. Sir Thomas Wyatt. SiPS
Now all our hurries that hung up on hooks. War-Time. W. R. Rodgers. OxBSP
Now all the cloudy shapes that float and lie. Such Stuff as Dreams Are Made Of. Thomas Wentworth Higginson. AA
Now all the dogs with folded paws. Suburban Song. Elizabeth Riddell. CBAP
Now all the flowers that ornament the grass. Unreturning. Elizabeth Stoddard. AA
Now all the lights of Dublin. The Lights of Dublin. Patrick O'Connor. TIRV
Now all the peacefull regents of the night. George Chapman. *Fr.* Bussy d'Ambois, II, ii. PoEL-2
Now all the truth is out. To a Friend Whose Work Has Come to Nothing. W. B. Yeats. AWP; InPK; LiTM; MoAB; MoBrPo; OAEL-2; OBMV; PoA
Now and Afterwards. Dinah Maria Mulock Craik. PoLF; WGRP
Now and, I fear, again. Table Talk. Donald Mattam. FiBHP
Now and Then. Eileen Blacker Peterson. SoTCo
Now and then there will arise. *Unknown, tr. by* Frances Densmore. OBVE
Now another day is breaking. Morning Prayer. Ogden Nash. GrPl; OxBChV
Now are our labours crowned with their reward. Hops along the Medway. Christopher Smart. *Fr.* The Hop-Garden. FaBoPP
Now are our prayers divided, now. At the "Ye That Do Truly." Charles Williams. NOCV
Now are the bells unlimbered from their spires. Pilgrimage. Eileen Duggan. ATNZ
Now are the forests dark and the ways full. Southern Summer. Francis Stuart. NeIP
Now are the winds about us in their glee. Song in March. William Gilmore Simms. AA
Now Arethusa from her snow couches arises. Shelley's "Arethusa" Set to New Measures. Robert Duncan. CMoP
Now art thou fair, Diodorus. Strato, *tr. by* Sydney Oswald. PeHV
Now as at all times I can see in the mind's eye. The Magi. W. B. Yeats. BrPo; CMoP; FaBoRV; HAP; InPK; NoAM; OAEL-2; OFD; PChr; PoA; PoE; TrCP
Now as even's warning bell. Solitude. John Clare. EnRP
Now as I took a walk down Grand Street I stepped into Paddy West's house. Paddy West. *Unknown.* OxBSS
Now as I was young and easy under the apple boughs. Fern Hill. Dylan Thomas. CMoP; FaBoPP; FaBV; FPL; GoJo; GTBS-P; HAP; HeIP; InPK; InPS; LiTB; LiTM; MoAB; MoBrPo; MoP; NAEL-2; NIP; NoAM; NOBE; NoP; OAEL-2; OBWVE; OxBTC; PoE; PoLF; PoRA; PPP; SoSe; TrGrPo; TwCP; WeW
Now, as Never. Ramón López Velarde, *tr. fr. Spanish by* Samuel Beckett. MexPo
Now as the river fills the ice. Crew Cut. David McCord. SD
Now as the train bears west. Night Journey. Theodore Roethke. AmFN; GOA; NYBP; RR
Now as Then. Anne Ridler. CN; WaP
Now as these slaughtered seven hundreds hear. On the *Struma* Massacre. Ralph Gustafson. OBCV
Now as we cross this white page together. The Escape. William Stafford. NNaP
Now at long last. Yoshimoto, *tr. by* Steven D. Carter. WFTW
Now at the dark's perpetual descent. By the Beautiful Ohio. Joan LaBombard. SM
Now, at the time that was before agreed. Spenser. *Fr.* The Faerie Queene, VII, 7. OAEL-1
Now austere lips are laid. The Hard Lovers. George Dillon. PoA
Now Autumn comes, the wise fool of the year. Autumn. Frances Winwar. GoYe
Now be for ever still. To Himself. Giacomo Leopardi, *tr. by* John Heath-Stubbs. PFI
Now Be the Gospel Banner. Thomas Hastings. AH
Now be ye lords or commoners. The Tod's Hole. *Unknown.* GBP
Now beginneth Glutton [*or* biginneth Glotoun] for to go to shrift[e]. The Glutton [*or* Glutton in the Tavern]. William Langland. *Fr.* The Vision of Piers Plowman. ACP; PoE
Now Behold the Saviour Pleading. John Leland. AH

Now, being invisible, I walk without mantilla. The Souls of Women at Night. Wallace Stevens. CMoP

Now Bekotsidi, that am I. For them I make. The Song of Bekotsidi. *Unknown, tr. by* Washington Matthews. OBVE

Now Blue October. Robert Nathan. FYAP; UAS

Now bold Robin Hood to the north would go. Robin Hood and the Scotchman. *Unknown.* ESPB

Now burley's curing in the high-tiered barn. Squirrel Stand. Jim Wayne Miller. MT

Now burst above the city's cold twilight. Six o'Clock. Trumbull Stickney. AnAmPo; OxBA

Now call to mind Edom, remember well. The Church of England's Glory. *Unknown.* APAS

Now came still evening on, and twilight gray. Milton. *Fr.* Paradise Lost, *Bk.* IV.
    (Evening in Paradise.) GN, *fr. ll.* 598–609; NOBE, *fr. ll.* 598–656.
    (Moon and the Nightingale, The.) ChTr

Now can you see the monument? It is of wood. The Monument. Elizabeth Bishop. HCAP; LiTA; NoAM; NOBA

Now Cape Clear it is in sight. Whip Jamboree. *Unknown.* OxBSS

Now chaos has pitched a tent. Revival. George Garrett. MT

Now children may. May. John Updike. *Fr.* A Child's Calendar. OBCA

Now Christendom bids her cathedrals call. Elegy X. William Bell. NePoEA

Now Christmas Day is drawing near at hand. Christmas Now Is Drawing Near. *Unknown.* OBET

Now Christmas is come. *Unknown.* PChr

Now Clear the Triple Region of the Air. Christopher Marlowe. *Fr.* Tamburlaine the Great, *Pt.* I, Act IV, sc. ii. TrGrPo

Now close your eyes. Wedding Reception. Melinda Goodman. GLP

Now coldness comes sifting down, layer after layer. Flute Notes from a Reedy Pond. Sylvia Plath. FaBoMo

Now come young men and list to me. Macaffie's Confession. *Unknown.* BeLS
    (McAfee's Confession.) AmFP

Now comes, indeed, the end of all delight. To Billy, My Son. Vera Bax. CN

Now Comes the Good Rain Farmers Pray for (and). E. E. Cummings. NoAM

Now comes the graybeard of the north. Winter Days. Henry Abbey. AA

Now cometh alle ye that ben ibroght. Huc omnes pariter. Boethius, *tr. fr. Latin by* John Walton. *Fr.* The Consolation of Philosophy, III, 2 OBLMV

Now corn pushes past the foam. Ode to a Dead Dodge. David McElroy. AmPA

Now crouch, ye kings of greatest Asia. The Bloody Conquests of Mighty Tamburlaine. Christopher Marlowe. *Fr.* Tamburlaine the Great, *Pt.* II, Act IV, sc. iii. ChTr
    (Emperor of the Threefold World.) TrGrPo

Now Cunningham, who rhymed by fits and starts. Terse Elegy for J.V. Cunningham. X. J. Kennedy. DiPo

Now Cynthia shone serene, and ev'ry star. The Daventry Wonder. "Agricola." NOEC

Now daisies pied, and violets blue. Shakespeare. *See* Love's Labour's Lost: When Daisies Pied [and Violets Blue].

Now dandelions in the short, new grass. Dandelions. John Albee. AA

Now day and night sit balanced. Spring Equinox. Peter Blue Cloud. *Fr.* Within the Seasons. HATNAP

Now do our eyes behold. Lament for the Two Brothers Slain by Each Other's Hand. Aeschylus, *tr. fr. Greek by* A. E. Housman. *Fr.* The Seven against Thebes. AWP

Now Does Our World Descend. E. E. Cummings. NYBP

Now dreams. Oppression. Langston Hughes. CNA

Now Dreary Dawns the Eastern Light. A. E. Housman. CMoP

Now each creature joys the other. Samuel Daniel. EIL; OBSC

Now England lessens on my sight. To England. Charles Leonard Moore. AA

Now Entertain Conjecture of a Time. Shakespeare. *Fr.* King Henry V, *Prologue to* IV. RB; WaaP
    (Before Agincourt.) ChTr; EBEV
    "From camp to camp, through the fool womb of time." FaBoRV

Now especially, each flower moves. Variation on the Gothic Spiral. W. S. Merwin. PoA

Now even the sound. Tameyo, *tr. by* Steven D. Carter. WFTW

Now Evening Puts Amen to Day. Paul Horgan. AH

Now evermore, lest some one hope might ease. The Portents. Lucan, *tr. fr. Latin by* Christopher Marlowe. *Fr.* Pharsalia, I. OBSC

Now every man at my request. *Unknown.* OBCP

Now every thing that shadowy thought. In Festubert. Edmund Blunden. OBMV

Now ev'ning fades! her pensive step retires. Night. Anne Radcliffe. WPE

Now Fade the Rose and Lily-Flower. *Unknown, tr. fr. Middle English by* Brian Stone. NOCV

Now fades the last long streak of snow. Tennyson. *Fr.* In Memoriam A. H. H., CXV. FaBoRV; GTBS-P; NOBE; OBNC

Now ferkes to the firthe thees fresche men of armes. Sir Gawain Encounters Sir Priamus. Tennyson, *Incorporated in* Idylls of the King *with changes, as* The Passing of Arthur. *Fr.* Morte d'Arthur. PoEL-1

Now, fie on foolish love! It not befits. Fie on Love. James Shirley. OxBSP

Now fie upon that everlasting life, I dye! Valiant Love. Richard Lovelace. SeCP

Now first, as I shut the door. The New House. Edward Thomas. EBEV; MoAB; MoBrPo; NOBE; OBEV; OBWVE

Now first of all he means the night. A Song for the Middle of the Night. James Wright. SM; WeW

"Now for a brisk and cheerful fight!" The Fight at [the] San Jacinto. John Williamson Palmer. AA; PAH

Now for a little I have fed on loneliness. Fruit of Loneliness. May Sarton. PoA

Now, for the last time, total solitude. Cunard Liner 1940. Phyllis Shand Allfrey. CN

Now for the spirit of the people. Here. W. H. Auden. *Fr.* Letter to Lord Byron. FaBoPV

Now for your sixtieth birthday am I to send you. To Wystan Auden. Geoffrey Grigson. NAs

Now from each van. War Poetry. John Philips. *Fr.* Blenheim. NOEC

Now from Labor and from Care. Thomas Hastings. AH

Now from Leander's place she rose, and found. Chapman. *Fr.* Hero and Leander, Fourth Sestiad. EBEV

Now from the darkness of myself. Escape and Return. Elizabeth Jennings. NePoEA

Now from the east. Masahongva, *tr. fr. Hopi Indian by* Natalie Curtis. WTO

Now from their slumber waking. Comrades. Henry R. Dorr. PAH

Now front to front the hostile armies stand. Homer, *tr. fr. Greek by* Pope. *Fr.* The Iliad, III. OBVE

Now frost has broken summer like a glass. Der Abschied. May Sarton. ER

Now gather round, you stroppy Jacks who serve the peacetime Andrew. The Kola Run. D. S. Goodbrand. OxBSS

Now Gen'ral. I am the nightwatch frontier guard, come. Floral Invasions. Hsiang Yang, *tr. by* Dominic Cheung. IFON

Now gently winding up the fair ascent. Homer, *tr. fr. Greek by* Pope. *Fr.* Odyssey, XXI. OBVE

Now get thee back, retreat, depart, O Serpent. He Overcometh the Serpent of Evil in the Name of Ra. *Unknown, tr. fr. Egyptian by* Robert Hillyer. *Fr.* Book of the Dead. AWP

Now, Gibbon has told the story of old. Fighting McGuire. William Percy French. CenHV

Now Gilderoy was a bonny boy, and he would not the ribbons wear. Gilderoy. *Unknown.* OBET
    (My Handsome Gilderoy.) CH

Now ginnes this goodly frame of temperaunce. The Bower of Bliss. Spenser. *Fr.* The Faerie Queene, II, 12. PoEL-1
    "Thence passing forth, they shortly do arruve." FiP
    "Eftsoones they heard a most melodious sound." NOBE; OBSC; SCV
    "And in the midst of all, a fountaine stood."

Now glory to the Lord of Hosts, from whom all glories are! Ivry. Macaulay. FaBV; GN
    (The Battle of Ivry.) WBLP

Now, God be thanked Who has matched us with His hour. Peace. Rupert Brooke. *Fr.* 1914, I. MMA; OBWP; PoA; WGRP

Now God preserve, as you well do deserve. The Masque of Christmas. Ben Jonson. OxBoLi

Now God Stand Up for Bastards. Brian Merriman, *tr. fr. Modern Irish by* Arland Ussher. *Fr.* The Midnight Court. BIrV

Now Goeth [*or* goth *or* goothe] Sun [*or* Sunne] under Wood. *Unknown.* NoP
    (Me Rueth, Mary.) GBP
    (Pity for Mary.) MeEL
    (Sunset on Calvary.) NAEL-1

Now gowans sprout, an' lavrocks sing. Ode to Mr. F—[*or* Mr. Forbes]. Allan Ramsay, *after* Horace. NOEC; OBVE

Now grace, strength and pride. The Laid-out Body. Alistair Campbell. *Fr.* Elegy, 8. ATNZ

Now gracious plenty rules the board. Thanksgiving. Florence Earle Coates. TrPWD

Now grapes are plush upon the vines. Contrary Theses (I). Wallace Stevens. OxBA

Now grimy April comes again. For City Spring. Stephen Vincent Benét. BXAP; NBLV

Now had th' Almighty Father from above. Milton. *Fr.* Paradise Lost, *bk.* III, *ll.* 54–76. NIP

"Now half a hundred years had I been born." His Statement of the Case. James Herbert Morse. AA

Now hand in hand, you little maidens, walk. Spring. André Spire, *tr. by* Jethro Bithell. AWP

Now hardly here and there a hackney-coach. A Description of the Morning. Swift. EBEV; FF; HAP; HelP; InPS; NOBE; NOEC; NoP; OAEL-1; PPP; Prf; SoSe; TEP; WeW

Now has ended the battle of Saul. Saul. Nathan Alterman, *tr. by* Dov Vardi. TrJP

Now haste, my Muse, pursue thy destin'd way. Soame Jenyns. *Fr.* The Art of Dancing. FaBoUs

Now hath Flora robbed her bowers. Roses. Thomas Campion. *Fr.* Lord Hay's Mask. OBSC

Now hath my life across a stormy sea. On the Brink of Death. Buonarroti Michelangelo, *tr. by* John Addington Symonds. AWP

Now haud your tongue, baith wife and carle. Red Harlaw. Sir Walter Scott. *Fr.* The Antiquary, *ch.* 40. OxBB

Now have I brought a woork to end which neither Joves fierce [*or* feerce] wrath. Ovid, *tr. fr. Latin by* Arthur Golding. *Fr.* Metamorphoses, XV. OBVE (Conclusion.) CTC

Now have I see, in Graisivaudan's vale. From Grenoble. James Elroy Flecker. OBTV

Now having leisure, and a happy wind. John Fletcher *and* William Rowley. *Fr.* The Maid in the Mill, V, i. GBL

Now hawk, wind's jockey, sitting tight. Kite. John Robert Lee. PVCV

Now he has seen the girl Hsiang-Hsiang. Chinese Ballad. Mao Tse-tung, *tr. by* William Empson. Mes

Now He Is Dead. Alistair Campbell. *Fr.* Elegy, 2. ATNZ

Now he is gone and we had not understood one another. The Year's Ending. St. J. Page Yako, *tr. by* C. M. Mcanyangwa *and* Jack Cope. PeSA

Now he who knows old Christmas. Old Christmas. Mary Howitt. GN

Now hear this! Marcabrun, *tr. by* Paul Blackburn. Pro

Now Help Us, Lord. *Unknown.* AH, *ad. by* Charles E. Ives

Now here, now there, lightheaded, crazed with grief. A Psalm of the Early Buddhist Sisters. *Unknown.* WGRP

Now high and low, where leaves renew. Autet e bas. Arnaut Daniel, *tr. by* Ezra Pound. CTC

Now his nose's bridge is broken, one eye. On Hurricane Jackson. Alan Dugan. CoAP; SD

Now hollow fires burn out to black. A. E. Housman. *Fr.* A Shropshire Lad, LX. NOBVV

Now homing tradesmen scatter through the streets. Place Pigalle. Richard Wilbur. HelP

Now I am blind; I've shunned Hari's name. Surdas, *tr. by* John Stratton Hawley *and* Mark Juergensmeyer. SSI

Now I am dead you sing to me. An Upbraiding. Thomas Hardy. OPOP

Now I am getting light as cotton candy. Snakebite. Thomas James. SM

Now I am slow and placid, fond of sun. With Child. Genevieve Taggard. AIW; MoAmPo

Now I am still and spent. Words Asleep. Laurie Lee. PoPo

Now I am thankful this unbroken flesh. Fisherman's Son. Charles Bruce. CaP

Now I am tired of being Japanese. Picture of a Castle. William Meredith. NePoEA

Now I believe tradition, which doth call. Upon the Author; by a Known Friend. Benjamin Woodbridge. SCAP

Now I can be sure of my sleep. On the Hill below the Lighthouse. James Dickey. NePoEA-2; SM

Now I can catch and throw a ball. Big. Dorothy Aldis. RAR

Now, I cannot tell. Tsurayuki, *tr. by* Geoffrey Bownas *and* Anthony Thwaite. PeBJV

Now I feel good when Dave Winfield. Empathy for David Winfield. David Shapiro. BAP

Now I find thy looks were feigned. Thomas Lodge. *Fr.* Phyllis. EIL; OBSC

Now I go down here and bring up a moon. Auctioneer. Carl Sandburg. PDV

Now I have come to reason. Cecil Day Lewis. CMoP

Now I Have Forgotten All. David Vogel, *tr. fr. Hebrew by* A. C. Jacobs. VWA

Now I have found thee I will evermore. Upon the Crucifix. William Alabaster. PoEL-2

Now I have known, O Lord. Al-Junaid, *tr. by* A. J. Arberry. TOF

Now I have lost you, I must scatter. Farewell, Sweet Dust. Elinor Wylie. LiTA

Now I Have Nothing. Stella Benson. OxBTC

Now I have touched you near the grated bone. Postscript. Mary Mills. NePoAm

Now I knew I lost her. Emily Dickinson. PeHV

Now I know. *Unknown. Fr.* Manyo Shu. Ma

Now I know I never shall. Ted Hughes. *Fr.* Prometheus on His Crag, IX. AnAn

Now I lay me down to sleep. Compline. Donald Davie. *Fr.* Horae Canonicae. CRP

"Now I Lay Me Down to Sleep." Eugene Henry Pullen. AA; FaBoBe

Now I Lay me Down to Sleep. *Unknown.* OBD

Now I Lay Me Down to Take My Sleep. *Unknown.* BLRP; FaFP; GBP; OxNR

Now I love you/ as the sea loves its water. Pedro Salinas, *tr. fr. Spanish by* Linda Gutierrez *and* Lawrence Pitkethly. *Fr.* Razón de Amor. LLLT

Now I must betray myself. Prothalamion. Delmore Schwartz. OxBA

Now I out walking. Away! Robert Frost. NOBA

Now I pray the man who may love this lay. Cynewulf, *tr. fr. Anglo-Saxon by* Charles W. Kennedy. *Fr.* Fates of the Apostles. AnOE

Now I realize/ it is my sovereign's light. Masayori, *tr. by* Steven D. Carter. WFTW

Now I see its whiteness. The Dead Butterfly. Denise Levertov. NoP

Now I see the leaves tilting. Variations on a Still Morning. Thomas Cole. NePoAm

Now I see their faces stamped forever. Why I Can't Write a Poem about Lares. Iván Silén, *tr. by* Julio Marzán. InW

Now I see you. Grandfather. Joseph Stroud. NPGG

Now I shall reach over. With Lilacs in My Eye. Lucile Coleman. GoYe

Now, I think, finally. After Reading the Poetry of Yannis Ritsos. Friederike Mayröcker, *tr. by* Beth Bjorklund. CoAuP

Now I understand. Saigyo, *tr. fr. Japanese by* Burton Watson. *Fr.* Sixty-four Tanka. FCEI

Now I wake and see the light. Eugene Henry Pullen. BLRP

Now I walk with you through the ruins of the city. Some Walks with You. John Hollander. NoAM

Now I wear my named pants. Glose. Michael Malinowitz. EOEF

"Now I will abandon the route of my life." Mr. Wakeville on Interstate 90. Donald Hall. BLA

Now I will do nothing but listen. Walt Whitman. *Fr.* Song of Myself, XXVI. HoPM

Now I will fashion the tale of a fish. The Whale. *Unknown, tr. fr. Anglo-Saxon by* Charles Kennedy. *Fr.* Physiologus. AnOE; MOS ("To explain the nature of fishes in craft of verse."). EBEV

Now I will make fat puddings. Advent. Anne Hartigan. CIP

Now I would remind you, brethren. Bible, *N.T. Fr.* First Corinthians, XV: 1-8. DL

Now ich see blostme springe. Of Jesu Christ I Sing. *Unknown.* PoE

Now if ever it is time to cleanse Helicon. Ezra Pound. *Fr.* Homage to Sextus Propertius. VGW

"Now, if the fish will only bite, we'll have some royal fun." Timid Hortense. Peter Newell. NA

Now if thou hast one dram of grace. Nahum Tate, *after the Latin of* Catullus. OBVE

Now if you want an onion, just consider. Recipe: Onions. Philemon. FaBoUs

Now if you will listen I'll tell you a story. The New-Chum's First Trip. *Unknown.* FaBoBa

Now I'm Easy. Eric Bogle. OBET

Now I'm going to tell you. Now. Gloria Fuertes, *tr. by* Philip Levine. OV

Now I'm leaving old England, the land that I love. The First of the Emigrants. *Unknown.* OxBSS

Now in a thought, now in a shadowed word. E. A. Robinson. TrCP

Now in her green mantle blythe nature arrays. My Nannie's Awa.' Burns. GN

Now in middle age, my blood like a thief who. Irish Music. Larry Levis. MAYP

Now in my/ heart I/ see clearly. Sappho, *tr. fr. Greek by* Willis Barnstone. BoWoP

Now in my Samarkand of blue enamels. Journey in the Orient. Maria Luisa Spaziani, *tr. by* Ruth Feldman. BoWoP

Now in old age, quiet in his tent. Isaac. Barry Holtz. VWA

Now in the Bloom. Florence Kiper Frank. GoYe
Now in the dawn before it dies, the eagle swings. The Story of a Well-made Shield. N. Scott Momaday. CDW; GrPl; HATNAP
Now, in the evenings, when the light. The Generations. George M. Brady. OnYI
Now in the garden Spring's the saki. Mir Sirajuddin Siraj, tr. by Ahmed Ali. GoT
Now in the Palace Gardens. Trumbull Stickney. Fr. Eride, V. LiTA
Now in the patron's mansion see the wight. Richard Savage. Fr. The Progress of a Divine. OBSV
Now in the Storm. Yehuda Amichai, tr. fr. Hebrew by Warren Bargad and Stanley F. Chyet. IP
Now in the suburbs and the falling light. Father and Son. Stanley Kunitz. CAPP; DiL; MoP; TwCP
Now in the third voice. William Sydney Graham. Fr. The Dark Dialogues, III. OxBS
Now in this mirthfull tyme of May. Four May Poems, II. Unknown. OxBS
Now in this while gan Daedalus a wearinesse to take. Daedalus. Ovid, tr. fr. Latin. Fr. Metamorphoses, VIII. CTC, tr. by Arthur Golding; OBVE, tr. by Arthur Golding.
("Now in this while gan Daedalus a weariness to take.") OBVE
Now in thy dazzling half-oped eye. A Mother to Her Waking Infant. Joanna Baillie. NOEC
Now, innocent, within the deep. M., Singing. Louise Bogan. GoJo; LiTA; NoAM
Now into the saddle, and over the grass. The Pony Express. Dorothy Brown Thompson. AmFN
Now is a bursting in me. Argent Solipsism. Howard Blake. PoA
Now Is Farewell. Blanaid Salkeld. NeIP
Now is it most like as if on ocean. The Voyage of Life. Cynewulf, tr. fr. Anglo-Saxon by Charles W. Kennedy. Fr. Christ 2. AnOE; MOS
Now is it pleasant in the summer-eve. George Crabbe. Fr. The Borough, Letter IX. FM
Now is mon hol and soint. When Death Comes. Unknown. MeEL
Now is my Chloris fresh as May. Unknown. OBSC
Now is my father. Poem for My Father's Ghost. Mary Oliver. InPS
Now is my misery full, and namelessly. Pieta. Rainer Maria Rilke, tr. by M. D. Hester Norton. OFD
Now is Past. John Clare. Mes
Now is the fox drevin to hole! hoo to hym, hoo, hoo! Unknown. OxBLMV
Now is the globe shrunk tight. Snowdrop. Ted Hughes. FaBoMo
Now is the hour when, swinging in the breeze. Harmonie du Soir. Baudelaire, tr. by Lord Alfred Douglas. AWP
Now is the month of maying. Unknown. EBEV; OBSC
Now is the time for mirth. To Live Merrily, and to Trust to Good Verses. Robert Herrick. AWP; CaPo; InvP; OBS; SeCP; SeCV-1
Now is the time for the burning of the leaves. The Burning of the Leaves. Laurence Binyon. GTBS-P; NOBE; OxBTC
Now Is the Time of Christmas. Unknown. MeEL
Now is the time, when all the lights wax dim. To Anthea ("Now is the time, when all the lights wax dim"). Robert Herrick. OBS; PoEL-3
Now is the winter of our discontent. Shakespeare. Fr. King Richard III, I, i. PoE
(Hate the Idle Pleasures.) TrGrPo
Now is the world withdrawn all. Carol. Howard Nemerov. TrCP
Now Israel May Say, and That Truly. William Whittingham. AH
Now it appears very clear. Hilda Doolittle ("H. D."). Fr. The Walls Do Not Fall. NAAL-2
Now It Can Be Told. Philip Levine. VWA
Now it grows dark. Hymn to Night. Melville Cane. MoAmPo
Now it is autumn and the falling fruit. The Ship of Death. D. H. Lawrence. CMoP; FaBoRV; FaBoTw; GTBS-P; LiTB; MoAB; MoBrPo; MoP; MOS; NAEL-2; NoAM; NoP; OAEL-2; PrIm
Now It Is Broccoli. Jeff Tagami. BrSi
Now it is fashionable among painters. Painting. Stanislaw Grochowiak, tr. by Czeslaw Milosz. PwPP
Now it is fifteen years you have lain in the meadow. Lines for an Interment. Archibald MacLeish. CMoP; NOBA
Now it is only hours before you wake. Letter to My Daughter at the End of Her Second Year. Donald Finkel. CoAP
Now it is winter and the fallen snow. Los Mineros. Edward Dorn. PoM
Now it seems an old forgotten fable. H.M.S. Glory at Sydney. Charles Causley. OBTV
Now it was Spring. Grant at Appomattox. Gertrude Claytor. GoYe
Now it was that the Morrigan settled in bird shape. The Morrigan. Unknown, tr. by Thomas Kinsella. BIrV

Now it's July, hot and sleepy and still. Summer Journey. W. R. Rodgers. OBTV
Now it's styrofoam pellets. White Trash. Jim Hall. MT
Now, it's three long years since we made her pay. The Final Trawl. Archie Fisher. OxBSS
Now it's Uncle Sam sitting on top of the world. Carl Sandburg. Fr. Good Morning America, XIV. OFD
Now Jentil Belly Down. Unknown. GBP
Now Johnson would go up to join the great simulacra of men. Up Rising. Robert Duncan. Fr. Passages. NNaP
Now, jolly Swains! the harvest of your cares. How to Shear Sheep. John Dyer. Fr. The Fleece, II. FaBoUs
Now Jones had left his new-wed bride. A Code of Morals. Kipling. FaBoCo
Now, Joy is born of parents poor. Joy and Pleasure. W. H. Davies. OBMV
Now keep that long revolver at your side. George Hetherington. NeIP
Now Kindness. Peter Viereck. LiTA
Now kisse me, lovely Ganimed, for see. Jupiter and Ganimede. Thomas Heywood. PeHV
Now, ladies, if you'll listen, a story I'll relate. Pearl Bryan. Unknown. AmFP
Now landed Trader, that, with haughty stare. Ebenezer Elliott. Fr. The Village Patriarch, V. PF
Now leave the check-reins slack. To the Man after the Harrow. Patrick Kavanagh. CIP; FaBCIP; GTBS-P
Now let my thoughts be like the Arrow, wherein was gold. Holiday Piece. Denis Glover. ATNZ
Now let no charitable hope. Let No Charitable Hope. Elinor Wylie. LiTA; LiTM; MoAB; MoAmPo; NAAL-2; OxBA; OxBSP; TrGrPo; VGW
Now Let Our Hearts Their Glory Wake. Elizabeth Scott. AH
Now let the cycle sweep us here and there. Hilda Doolittle ("H. D."). Fr. Sigil, XIV. AnAn; VGW
Now let the legless boy show the great lady. In the Children's Hospital. "Hugh MacDiarmid." NAEL-2; NoP
Now let us praise heaven's Emperor. Caedmon's Hymn. Unknown, tr. by Walter Kendrick. TEP
Now Liddesdale [or Liddisdale] has ridden a raid. Jock o' the Side. Unknown. ESPB; OxBB
Now Liddisdale has lain long in. Dick o' the Cow. Unknown. ESPB; OxBB
Now light the candles; one; two; there's a moth. Repression of War Experience. Siegfried Sassoon. BrPo; CMoP; MMA; NIP; NoAM; PoE
Now lighted windows climb the dark. Manhattan Lullaby. Rachel Lyman Field. AmFN
Now, like a magpie, he collects the bright. "Trade" Rat. Eleanor Glenn Wallis. NePoAm
Now like my tears these April blossoms fall. Parting in April. Pamela Holmes. CN
Now, like the gods, he is invulnerable. On the Death of Francisco López Merino. Jorge Luis Borges, tr. by Norman Thomas di Giovanni. OBD
Now list and lithe, you gentlemen. Northumberland Betray[e]d by Douglas [or Dowglas]. Unknown. ESPB; OxBB
Now list you, lithe you, gentlemen. Robin Hood and Queen Katherine. Unknown. ESPB
Now listen I am speaking to you through the miracle of rice through steelwool through Japanese micro. Election Speech for the Presidency of the United States of Chinamerica. David Avidan, tr. by Warren Bargad and Stanley F. Chyet. IP
Now listen to boasting which leaves the heart dazed. Al-Samau'al Ibn Adiya, tr. fr. Arabic by Hartwig Hirschfeld. Fr. Are We Not the People. TrJP
Now, listen, Ye who established the Great League. Memorial Ode. Chief John Buck. GOA
Now Little Billy is gone to the kirk. Little Billy. Unknown. GBP
Now look here. ! H. C. Artmann, tr. by Beth Bjorklund. CoAuP
Now Look What Happened. Molly Peacock. MAYP
Now look, you see, it's this way like. The Road to Hogan's Gap. Andrew Barton Paterson. CBAP
Now, Lord, or never, they'll believe on thee. On the Miracle of Loaves. Richard Crashaw. ACP; OxBSP
Now Love, see how this lady, young and fair. Petrarch, tr. by Marion Shore. PFI
Now lufferis cummis with larges lowd. The Petition of the Gray Horse, Auld Dunbar. William Dunbar. OxBS
Now manhood and garbroyls I chaunt. Virgil, tr. fr. Latin by Richard Stanyhurst. Fr. The Aeneid [or Eneados], I. BIrV; OBVE

Now may we turn aside and dry our tears. Inis Fal. Egan O'Rahilly, *tr. by* James Stephens. BIrV; OBMV

Now milkmaids' pails are deckt with flowers. Stool Ball. *Unknown.* CH

Now, miners, if you'll listen, I'll tell you quite a tale. Coming around the Horn. John A. Stone. AmFP

Now mirk December's dowie face. The Daft Days. Robert Fergusson. NOEC

Now Mister Johnson had troubles of his own. The Cat Came Back. *Unknown.* CRH

Now more and more on my concern with the lifted waves of genius gaining. On the Ocean Floor. "Hugh MacDiarmid." FaBoMo; HAP

Now Morn her rosy steps in the eastern clime. Milton. *Fr.* Paradise Lost, *Bk.* V, *ll.* 1–128. NAEL-1; OAEL-1

Now Morning from her orient chamber came. Imitation of Spenser. Keats. EnRP; FL
(Morning.) GN

Now Mr. Boomer Johnson was a gettin' old in spots. Boomer Johnson. Henry Herbert Knibbs. CowP

Now Mrs. Eberle early had been told. La Donna È Perpetuum Mobile. Irwin Edman. FiBHP

Now Muse assist me, aptly to describe. A. D. Hope. *Fr.* Dunciad Minor, *bk.* V. BXAP

Now must all satisfaction. Certain Mercies. Robert Graves. GTBS-P

Now must I learn to live [*or* lerne to lyve] at rest. Sir Thomas Wyatt. AAS; SiPS

Now must I these three praise. Friends. W. B. Yeats. MoP; NoAM

Now must I wait. The Blank Book Letter. Samuel Greenberg. LiTA

Now must we praise of heaven's kingdom the keeper. Caedmon's Hymn. Caedmon. OAEL-1

Now my charms are all o'erthrown. Shakespeare. *Fr.* The Tempest, V, i. CTC

Now, my co-mates and brothers in exile. The Uses of Adversity. Shakespeare. *Fr.* As You Like It, II, i. LiTB; TrGrPo

Now my days are all undone. Complaint after Psycho-Analysis. Edgell Rickword. PoPo

Now my fair'st friend. Some Flowers o' the Spring. Shakespeare. *Fr.* The Winter's Tale: Here's flowers for you. ChTr

Now, my friends, please hear. The Song of a Dream. *Unknown, tr. by* John Bierhorst. ILY

Now my heart turns to and fro. Hatshepsut, *tr. fr. Egyptian by* Mariam Lichtheim. *Fr.* Obelisk Inscriptions. WPOW

Now my legs begin to wale. Thaw in the City. Lou Lipsitz. MAT

Now, my son, is life for you. Wishes for My Son. Thomas MacDonagh. TIRV

Now, My Usefullness Over. Edwin Honig. NoAM

Now new-vamped silks the mercer's window shows. A Description of Spring in London. *Unknown.* NOEC

Now, night; and once again. Avalon. Audrey McGaffin. NePoAm

Now no. But when I am child my parents. Ideas. James Merrill. PPR

Now, not a tear begun. A Woman Mourned by Daughters. Adrienne Rich. IHMS; TV

Now, now's the time so oft by Truth. An Epithalamy to Sir Thomas Southwell and His Lady. Robert Herrick. CaPo

Now o'er the rugged peasants' cot. Ye Simple Men. John Stuart Blackie. PoSH

Now of all the trees by the king's highway. Aunt Mary. Robert Stephen Hawker. OHIP

Now of that vision I, bereaven. Francis Thompson. *Fr.* Grace of the Way. MoAB; MoBrPo

Now, on a sudden, I know it, the secret, the secret of life. Revealed. Harry Lyman Koopman. AA

Now on the verge of spring the icy silver leaf. Return to Spring. Florence Ripley Mastin. GoYe

Now once again the gloomy scene explore. The Pauper's Funeral. George Crabbe. *Fr.* The Village. OBNC

Now once upon a time the King of Astrakhan, at that. The Lacquer Liquor Locker. David McCord. FiBHP

Now one and all, you roses. A Wood Song. Ralph Hodgson. GoJo

Now only rarely. The Cherry Blossoms at Shiga. Kaneyoshi, *tr. by* Steven D. Carter. WFTW

Now only the moon. Shinkei, *tr. by* Steven D. Carter. WFTW

Now or Never. Astra. AIW; BrRo

Now or Never. Judith Moffett. SM; Son

Now orange blossoms filigree. Ain't Nature Commonplace! Arthur Guiterman. FiBHP

Now o'er the sea from her old love comes she. Ovid, *tr. fr. Latin by* Christopher Marlowe. *Fr.* Amores, 1, 13. OBVE

Now Phillipa Is Gone. Anne Ridler. FaBoTw

Now Phoebus did the world with frowns survey. Abigail's Lamentation for the Loss of Mr. Harley. William Walsh. APAS

Now Poem. For Us. Sonia Sanchez. CNA; PoBA

Now ponder well, you parents dear. The Babes in the Wood. *Unknown.* OBNV
(Children in the Wood, The.) EnSB

"Now, pray, where are you going, child?" said Meet-on-the-Road. Meet-on-the-Road. *Unknown.* TTTS

Now, put me near your chess. Argument One: The Lady Shews How She Is Foresaken for a Piece of Wood. Judith Emlyn Johnson. TSL

"Now rede me, dear mither, a sonsy rede." The Mer-Man, and Marstig's Daughter. *Unknown, tr. by* Robert Jamieson. AWP

Now rest for evermore, my weary heart! A Sè Stesso. Giacomo Leopardi, *tr. by* Lorna De' Lucchi. AWP

Now Robin Hood, Will Scadlock and Little John. Robin Hood and the Prince of Aragon. *Unknown.* ESPB

Now rock the boat to a fare-thee-well. Rite of Passage. Audre Lorde. CNA; PoBA

Now, rocking horse! rocking horse! where shall we go? Through Nurseryland. *Unknown.* BoTP

Now ropin' bears (says Uncle Sid) is sure a heap of fun. Bear Ropin' Buckaroo. S. Omar Barker. CowP

Now secretness dies of the open. For the Nightly Ascent of the Hunter Orion over a Forest Clearing. James Dickey. TwCP

Now seven days from land the gulls still wheel. Transport. William Meredith. WaP

Now shal y tellen to ye, y wis. The Lay of the Ettercap. John Leyden. BXAP

Now shall I make my soul. W. B. Yeats. *Fr.* The Tower. OBD

Now shall I walk. The Best Friend. W. H. Davies. OBMV

Now shall we see, that nature hath no end. George Chapman. *Fr.* Bussy d'Ambois, V, ii. PoEL-2

Now she burnes as well as I. Song: To Her Againe, She Burning in a Feaver. Thomas Carew. SeCP

Now She Is like the White Tree-Rose. C. Day Lewis. *Fr.* From Feathers to Iron. CMoP; FaBoTw; MoBrPo

Now she will lean away to fold. A Girl in a Window. James Wright. ErPo

Now she's borne her brat. *Unknown, tr. by* Geoffrey Bownas *and* Anthony Thwaite. PeBJV

Now she's got a baby. *Unknown, tr. by* Geoffrey Bownas *and* Anthony Thwaite. PeBJV

Now she's ninety I walk through the local park. A Winter Visit. Dannie Abse. KS; NoAM

Now shout into my dream. These trumpets snored. Farewell in a Dream. Stephen Spender. MoAB; MoBrPo

Now show thy joy, frolic in Angels' sight. Leviathan. Jay Macpherson. MoCV

Now side by side, with like unweary'd care. Homer, *tr. fr. Greek by* Pope. *Fr.* The Iliad, XIII. OBVE

"Now since mine even is come at last." The Ride to the Lady. Helen Gray Cone. AA

Now since the members of the world we view. Lucretius, *tr. fr. Latin by* Thomas Creech. *Fr.* De Rerum Natura (On the Nature of Things), I. OBVE

Now sinks another day to rest. The Bull. V. Sackville-West. WPE

Now sleep, bind fast the flood of air. Bridal Song. George Chapman. *Fr.* The Masque of the Middle Temple and Lincoln's Inn. ElL; OxBSP

Now Sleep My Little Child So Dear. Casper Kriebel, *tr. fr. German by* Sheema Z. Buehne. AH

Now Sleeps the Crimson Petal. Tennyson. *Fr.* The Princess, *pt.* VII. BoLoP; ChER; EBEV; EBVV; ELP; FiP; GBL; GTBS-P; LLLT; NAEL-2; NIP; NOBE; NoP; OBNC; PoEL-5; PPP; SCV; TrGrPo
(Song: "Now sleeps the crimson petal, now the white.") BLPL; FaBoBe
(Summer Night.) OBEV; SeCePo

Now Snow Descends. Jean Garrigue. WPE

Now so high. The Swing. Mary I. Osborn. BoTP

Now so many people that are in this place. Thank You: A Poem in Seventeen Parts. *Unknown, tr. by* Richard Johnny John *and* Jerome Rothenberg. STP

Now some may drink old vintage wine. Early Morning Meadow Song. Charles Dalmon. CH

Now some people thinks it's jolly for to lead a single life. Wedding Song. *Unknown.* OBET

Now south and south and south the mallard heads. The North Sea Undertaker's Complaint. Robert Lowell. NePoEA

Now spears lift them by their ribs. Dog Sacrifice at Lake Ronkonkoma. William Heyen. AmPA

Now springes the spray. Now Springs the Spray. *Unknown.* OAEL-1; PoE
   (Singing Maid, The.) MeEL

Now spring's over, I know not. Jakuren, *tr. by* Geoffrey Bownas *and* Anthony Thwaite. PeBJV

Now Springs the Spray. *Unknown.* OAEL-1; PoE
   (Singing Maid, The.) MeEL

Now stamp the Lord's Prayer on a grain of rice. Dylan Thomas. *Fr.* Altarwise by Owl-Light, VII. FaBoMo

Now stands our love on that still verge of day. James Agee. *Fr.* Sonnets, XX. MoAmPo

Now stoops the sun, and dies day's cheerful light. The Gauls Sacrifice. C. M. Doughty. *Fr.* The Dawn in Britain. FaBoTw

Now stop you noses, Readers, all and come. Og [and Doeg]. Dryden *and* Nahum Tate. *Fr.* Absalom and Achitophel: Part II. AWP; FiP; TW

Now strike your sailes, ye jolly mariners. Spenser. *Fr.* The Faerie Queene, I, 12 *and* II, 6. MOS

Now, suddenly, the table rocks, a bell. Séance. William Abrahams. NYBP

Now Summer finds her perfect prime. Heaven, O Lord, I Cannot Lose. Edna Dean Proctor. AA

Now summer's come. *Unknown, tr. fr. Japanese by* Burton Watson. *Fr.* Kokin Shu. FCEI

Now sunk the sun, now twilight sunk, and night. A Rhapsody, Written at the Lakes in Westmorland. John Brown. NOEC

Now swarthy Summer, by rude health embrowned. Summer Images. John Clare. OBNC

Now sways it this way, like a mighty sea. Shakespeare. *Fr.* King Henry VI, Pt. III, II, v. MOS

Now take your fill of love and glee. A Double Ballad of Good Counsel. Villon, *tr. by* Swinburne. AWP

Now that black ground and bushes. Winter Sketches. Charles Reznikoff. PoA

Now that Fate is dead and gone. Edith Sitwell. MoAB; MoBrPo

Now that he's left the room. Univac to Univac. Louis B. Salomon. FF

Now that high, oft-affronted bosom heaves. To the Lady Portrayed by Margaret Dumont. John Hollander. OBAL; PoA
   (For the Passing of Groucho's Pursuer.) PoA

Now that his fatherland has darkened on earth. Odysseus Elytis, *tr. fr. Greek by* Edmund Keeley *and* Philip Sherrard. *Fr.* Heroic and Elegiac Song for the Lost Second Lieute, VIII. VMG

Now that I am brought to know. Tabito. *Fr.* Manyo Shu. Ma

Now that I am fifty-six. Muriel Rukeyser. FF

Now That I Am Forever with Child. Audre Lorde. PoBA

Now that I am here. Isonokami Otomaro. *Fr.* Manyo Shu. Ma

Now That I Am Oxford Professor of Poetry. Unsolicited Letters to Five Artists. Clive James. FaBoPa

Now that I have lighted my smoke. Smoking My Prayers. Simon J. Ortiz. NOVW

Now that I have uttered my name. Hitomaro. *Fr.* Manyo Shu. Ma

Now that I have your face by heart, I look. Song for the Last Act. Louise Bogan. NePoAm; NoP; NYBP; UnPo; WPE

Now that I have your hand, let me persuade you. One Last Word. John Glassco. NOBC

Now that I know. Knowledge. Louise Bogan. PoA

Now that I, tying thy glass mask tightly. The Laboratory; Ancien Régime. Robert Browning. NAEL-2; OBEV

Now That I'm Young. *Unknown, tr. fr. Spanish by* William M. Davis. DMH

Now that I've built my house. *Unknown, tr. fr. Japanese by* Burton Watson. *Fr.* Kokin Shu. FCEI

Now that I've nearly done my days. The Things That Matter. Edith Nesbit. OxBTC

Now that I've taken a wife. The Groom's Lament. Robert Peterson. NeAC

Now that I've wasted. My Alba. Allen Ginsberg. NOBA

Now That My Father Lies Down beside Me. Stanley Plumly. DiL; GeTw

Now that my seagoing self-possession wavers. Autobiography. Charles Causley. LiTM; Son

Now that night is creeping. Evensong. C. S. Lewis. TIRV; TrCP

"Now that of absence the most irksome night." Sir Philip Sidney. *Fr.* Astrophel and Stella, LXXXIX. NAEL-1

Now that our love has drifted. Finis. Waring Cuney. AmNP; BANP

"Now that poor, wayward Jane is big with child." Repentance. Louis Untermeyer. NBLV

Now that the April of your youth adorns. A Ditty in Imitation of the Spanish ["Entre Tanto Que L'Avril"]. Herbert of Cherbury. ElL; OBS

Now that the barbarians have got as far as Picra. Translation. Roy Fuller. NOBE; OxBTC

Now that the day is done. Centaur Song. Hilda Doolittle ("H. D."). VGW

Now That the Flowers. Cullen Jones. GoYe

Now that the harth [*or* hearth] is crown'd with smiling fire. Ode to Sir William Sydney, on His Birth-Day. Ben Jonson. NAs; WiR
   (Another Birthday.) WiR

Now that the others are gone, all of them, forever. Tomorrow. Kenneth Fearing. CMoP

Now that the red glare of thy fall is blown. Francis Thompson. *Fr.* Ode to the Setting Sun. OBNC

Now that the time has come wherein. Advice from Poor Robin's Almanack. *Unknown.* OBCP

Now That the Truth Is Tried. Thomas Whythorne. EIL

Now that the Village-Reverence doth lye hid. A New-Years-Gift to Brian Lord Bishop of Sarum. William Cartwright. MePo

Now that the winter's gone, the earth hath lost. The Spring. Thomas Carew. CaPo; GN; NoP; PoE; PoEL-3; SeCV-1; TEP; TrGrPo; WiR

Now that the world is all in a maze. The Unconcerned. Thomas Flatman. FaBoCh

Now that the young buds are tipped with a falling sun. Early Spring. Sidney Keyes. MoBrPo

Now that these wings to speed my wish ascend. The Philosophic Flight. Giordano Bruno, *tr. by* John Addington Symonds. AWP

Now that they have grown to the age of killers. My Sons Have Grown to Manhood. Helena Anhava, *tr. by* Aili Jarvenpa. SOP

Now that we're almost settled in our house. In Memory of Major Robert Gregory. W. B. Yeats. AnIL; EBEV; OAEL-2

Now that we're alone we can talk prince man to man. Elegy of Fortinbras. Zbigniew Herbert, *tr. by* Czeslaw Milosz. FaBoPV; PwPP

Now that we've done our best and worst, and parted. The Busy Heart. Rupert Brooke. MoBrPo

Now that you lie. Before Sleep. Anne Ridler. CN

Now the bat circles on the breeze of eve. Anne Radcliffe. WPE

Now the bird of my being sings. The Bird of My Being. Israel Efrat, *tr. by* Bernhard Frank. MHeP

Now the bitter pangs of hope deferred. The Mail Has Come. Mary E. Tucker. CBWP-1

Now the bright crocus flames, and now. In the Spring. Meleager, *tr. by* Andrew Lang. AWP

Now the bright morning star, day's [*or* dayes] harbinger. Song on [*or* of] May Morning. Milton. BoNaP; CH; GN; TrGrPo

Now the crops grow green and the fields flourish with life. Request for Meat and Drink. Sedulius Scottus. NOIV

Now the day is over. Sabine Baring-Gould. OxBChV

Now the declining fulgent orb of day. J. C. Squire. *Fr.* Doris and Philemon. BXAP

Now the declining sun 'gan downwards bend. The Nightingale. William Strode, *after the Latin of* Famianus Strada. OBVE

Now the dreary winter's over. Spring Song. Nahum. *tr. by* Emma Lazarus. TrJP

Now the Earth, the Skies, the Air. *Unknown.* EIL

Now the first silly bastard he got in an aeroplane. Ops in a Wimpey. *Unknown.* CoMu

Now the frog, all lean and weak. The Sweet o' the Year. George Meredith. BoNaP

Now the frosty stars are gone. Ariel in the Cloven Pine. Bayard Taylor. AA

Now the golden morn aloft. Thomas Gray. *Fr.* Ode on the Pleasure Arising from Vicissitude. GTBS; GTBS-P; NOEC

Now the good man's away from home. Sally Sweetbread. Henry Carey. CoMu

Now the hard margin bears us on, while steam. Dante, *tr. fr. Italian by* Dorothy L. Sayers. *Fr.* Divina Commedia: Inferno. PeHV

Now the heart sings with all its thousand voices. The Gateway. A. D. Hope. BoLoP; ErPo

Now the Holy Lamp of Love. Patrick MacDonogh. BIrV

Now the Hungry Lion Roars. Shakespeare. *Fr.* A Midsummer Night's Dream, V, ii. CH; ChTr; CTC; EIL; LiTB; OBSC; WSC
   (Epilogue: "Now the hungry lion roars.") OBSC
   (Fairy Blessing, The.) OxBoLi
   (Fairy Songs ["Now the hungry lion roars."].) TrGrPo
   (Lion of Winter, The.) WiR
   (Puck's Song.) MoShBr

Now the ice lays its smooth claws on the sill. Scotland's Winter. Edwin Muir. OxBS; OxBTC

Now the joys of the road are chiefly these. The Joys of the Road. Bliss Carman. AnAmPo

Now the Laborer's Task Is O'er. John Lodge Ellerton. BLPA; WGRP

Now the last day of many days. To Jane: The Recollection. Shelley. ChER; GTBS; OBNC
(The Recollection.) GTBS-P
Now the late fruits are in. For a Wine Festival. Vernon Watkins. OxBTC
Now the Leaves Are Falling Fast. W. H. Auden. CMoP
Now the light o' the west is a-turn'd to gloom. Evenen in the Village. William Barnes. EBVV
Now the long blade of the sun, lying. Thebes of the Seven Gates. Sophocles, *tr. fr. Greek by* Dudley Fitts *and* Robert Fitzgerald. *Fr.* Antigone. WaaP
Now the lotuses in the imperial lake. Wang Ch'ing-hui, *tr. fr. Chinese by* Kenneth Rexroth *and* Ling Chung. BoWoP
Now the Lusty Spring [Is Here]. John Fletcher. *Fr.* The Tragedy of Valentinian, II, iv. ELP; ErPo; FF
(Love's Emblems.) BoLoP; EIL; NIP; NOBE
Now the magpie had a nest. *Unknown, tr. by* Arthur Waley. BoS
Now the man has a child. *Unknown, tr. by* Geoffrey Bownas *and* Anthony Thwaite. PeBJV
Now the moisty wood discloses. Spring Morning. Frances Cornford. BoTP
Now the moon is. Sinking Rising. Dahlia Ravikovich, *tr. by* Warren Bargad *and* Stanley F. Chyet. IP
Now the Most High Is Born. James Ryman. MeEL
Now the narrowing track. The Look. Elizabeth Daryush. PoA
Now the New Moon is hanging, having cast away his bone. New Moon. *Aborigine Oral Tradition. Fr.* Moon-Bone Song [*or* Cycle]. WTO
Now the People Have the Light. Charles G. Ballard. NOVW; VoR
Now the pines lift. Burning the Tomato Worms. Carolyn Forché. AmPA
Now! The Red Tobacco has come to strike your soul. *Unknown, tr. fr. Cherokee Indian. Fr.* Run toward the Nightland. STP
Now the rich cherry, whose sleek wood. Country Summer. Léonie Adams. GoJo; LiTM; MoAB; MoAmPo; TrGrPo
Now the river is rich, but her voice is low. The River in March. Ted Hughes. OxBC
Now the shiades o' the elems da stratch muore an muore. Evening, and Maidens. William Barnes. OBEV
Now the snow hides the ground, little birds leave the wood. The Robin. John Clare. FL
Now the stone house on the lake front is finished and the workmen are beginning the fence. A Fence. Carl Sandburg. WeW
Now the storm begins to lower. The Fatal Sisters. Thomas Gray, *after the Icelandic.* EnRP
Now the sun's gane out o' sight. Up in the Air. Allan Ramsay. NOEC
Now the thinkers our old ones remember. Dance of the Rain Gods. *Unknown, tr. by* Anselm Hollo. STP
Now the trouble with SETting down a: written calypso. Calypsomania. Anthony Brode. FiBHP
Now the *uguisu* must be warbling. Yakamochi. *Fr.* Manyo Shu. Ma
Now the universe wants to be known for. Dog Star Sale. Douglas Crase. BAP
Now the vapour hot and damp. Song of the Evil Spirit of the Woods. Thomas Moore. OBTV
Now the white-buskined lamb. At Bungendore. James McAuley. PoAu-2
Now the white roses, wilted and yellowing fast. Lament of the Jewish Women for Tammuz. Charles Reznikoff. VWA
Now the wild bees that hive in the rocks. The Brown Bear. Mary Austin. FaPON
Now the winter is gone and the summer is come. As I Walked through the Meadows. *Unknown.* OBET
Now Thebes stood in good estate, now Cadmus might thou say. Acteon. Ovid, *tr. fr. Latin by* Arthur Golding. *Fr.* Metamorphoses, III. CTC
Now then, take your seats! for Glasgow and the North. The Night Mail North. Henry Cholmondeley-Pennell. EBVV
Now then, what are you up to, Dai? Langwell. Kingsley Amis. *Fr.* The Evans Country. NOBL; OxBC
Now there are gold reflections on the water. In Time of Gold. Hilda Doolittle ("H. D."). PoA
Now there are no bonds except the flesh; listen. Manzini; Escape Artist. Gwendolyn MacEwen. NOBC
Now there comes/ The Christmas rose. New Year's [*or* Year] Song. Ted Hughes. OBCP; OFD
Now there's many fool things a woman will do. Gold Tooth Blues. Tennessee Williams. OBAL
Now they are resting. Fine Work with Pitch and Copper. William Carlos Williams. OxBA

Now they have two cars to clean. Do It Yrself. Larry Eigner. NeAP; PoM
Now they're pillaging the last coast. The Vandals. Jenny Mastoraki, *tr. by* Nikos Germanakos. BoWoP
Now they're ready, now they're waiting. Football. F. Scott Fitzgerald. ASP
Now this is my first counsel. Counsels of Sigrdrifa. *Unknown, tr. fr. Old Norse by* William Morris *and* Eirikr Magnusson. *Fr.* The Elder Edda. AWP
(Part of the Lay of Sigrdrifa.) OBVE
Now this is new: that I (habitué). First Day of Teaching. Bonaro W. Overstreet. TrPWD
Now this is the Law of the Jungle—as old and as true as the sky. The Law of the Jungle. Kipling. LiTB; PoEL-5
Now this particular girl. Spinster. Sylvia Plath. FaBoWP
Now those that are low spirited I hope won't think it wrong. A New Hunting Song. *Unknown.* CoMu; OBET
Now thou art dead, no eye shall ever see. Upon His Spaniell Tracie. Robert Herrick. FM
Now thou hast lov'd me one whole day. Woman's Constancy. John Donne. NBLV; NoP; SeCV-1
Now thought seeks shelter, lest the heart melt. Recovery. F. R. Scott. CaP
Now Thrice Welcome Christmas. *Unknown.* OHIP
Now through Night's Caressing Grip. W. H. Auden. PoRA
Now through the ocean in great haste they flunder. Luis de Camões, *tr. fr. Portuguese by* Sir Richard Fanshawe. *Fr.* The Lusiads. OBVE
Now Time's Andromeda on this rock rude. Andromeda. Gerard Manley Hopkins. EBEV; FaBoMo; LiTB
Now to attune my dull soul, if I can. Bleue Maison. Edmund Blunden. BrPo
Now to be clean he must abandon himself. The Swan Bathing. Ruth Pitter. MoBrPo
Now to Blackwall Docks we bid adieu. Homeward Bound. *Unknown.* OxBSS
Now to dispose the dead, the care remains. Homer, *tr. fr. Greek by* Pope. *Fr.* Odyssey, XXII. OBVE
Now to Great Britain we must make our way. Of England, and of Its Marvels. Fazio degli Uberti, *tr. by* Dante Gabriel Rossetti. AWP
Now, today, I'll lose myself. Teika, *tr. fr. Japanese by* Hiroaki Sato. *Fr.* A Compendium of Good Tanka. FCEI
Now toils the Heroe; trees on trees o'erthrown. Homer, *tr. fr. Greek by* Pope. *Fr.* Odyssey, V. OBVE
Now Tomlinson gave up the ghost in his house in Berkeley Square. Tomlinson. Kipling. BeLS
Now touch the air softly. A Pavane for the Nursery. William Jay Smith. DuDa; GoJo; MoAmPo
Now tow'rd the Hunter's gloomy sides we came. The Hospital Prison Ship. Philip Freneau. *Fr.* The British Prison Ship, III. AmPP
Now, Until the Break of Day. Shakespeare. *Fr.* A Midsummer Night's Dream, V, ii. NAs
(Fairy Songs ("Now, until the break of day.").) TrGrPo
Now upon sale, a bankrupt island. Four Epigrams on the Naturalization Bill. John Byrom. NOBL
Now upon this piteous year. The Stranger. Jean Garrigue. LiTA; LiTM; NOBA; TwCP
Now van to van the foremost squadrons meet. Dryden. *Fr.* Annus Mirabilis. OBWP
Now Venus is an evening star. Waiting. Hilary Corke. ErPo
Now vows connubial chain the plighted pair. Reproduction of Life. Erasmus Darwin. *Fr.* The Temple of Nature; or, The Origin of Society, II. PBBP
Now—wagon full of thunder. Wagon Full of Thunder. Louis Oliver. HATNAP; STE
Now war is all the world about. Ode on His Majesty's Proclamation. Sir Richard Fanshawe, *after the Italian of* Giovanni Battista Guarini. *Fr.* Il Pastor Fido. NOBE
(Ode, upon Occasion of His Majesties Proclamation in the Year 1630, An.) MePo; OBS
Now was there maid fast by the towris wall. James I, King of Scotland. *Fr.* The Kingis Quair. EBEV
Now watch this autumn that arrives. Song at the Beginning of Autumn. Elizabeth Jennings. OxBTC
Now we are civilized, the old men die. Old Men's Ward. Elma Dean. GoYe
Now we are come to the cold time. Azalais de Porcairages, *tr. by* Meg Bogin. WT
Now we are fleshing islands. The Aging of Clones. Andrew Joron *and* Robert Frazier. BWV
Now we are forced to contemplate the sky. Sky-Conscious. Alice Coats. CN

Now we are left out. Funeral Song. *Unknown, tr. by* Dan Kunene *and* Jack Cope. PeSA

Now we are like a snail. June. Medbh McGuckian. FaBCIP

Now We Are Sick. J. B. Morton. *Fr.* When We Were Very Silly. FaBoPa

Now we are thirty-five we no longer enjoy red neon. Literary Life in the Golden West. Philip Whalen. NAs

Now we begin another day together. Prayer at Dawn. Edwin McNeill Poteat. TrPWD

Now we enter a strange world, where the Hessian Christmas. After the Industrial Revolution, All Things Happen at Once. Robert Bly. CoAP

Now we gathered for the match. The Volleyball Match. Bill Pearlman. ASP

Now we have always with us these men—these men! Memo. Hildegarde Flanner. NYBP

Now we must get up quickly. Two Lines from the Brothers Grimm. Gregory Orr. AmPA

Now we must praise heaven-kingdom's Guardian. Caedmon, tr. by D. K. Fry. TrCP

Now weave the winds to music of June's lyre. June. Theodore Harding Rand. CaP

Now Welcom[e], Somer [*or* Summer]. Chaucer. *Fr.* The Parlement of Foules. HAP; SeCePo
(Birds' Rondel, The, *mod. vers. by* Louis Untermeyer) TrGrPo
(Foules Rondel.) TrGrPo
(Qui Bien Aime a Tard Oublie.) EnLoPo
(Roundel: "Now welcom[e], somer, with thy sunne [*or* sonne] softe.") CTC; OAEL-1; OxBSP
(Welcome, Summer.) MeEL

Now wend we to the Palmalle. Domine, Quo Vadis? *Unknown.* ACP

Now we're met, my brethren Benchers. The Humours of the King's Bench Prison, a Ballad. Leonard Howard. NOEC

Now we're stuck there. Heaving the Lead Line. *Unknown.* AmFP

Now westward Sol had spent the richest beam[e]s. Music[k]'s Duel[l]. Richard Crashaw. GoTL; OAEL-1; OBS; SeCP; SeCV-1

Now we've made a child. And What About the Children. Audre Lorde. PoBA

Now what do you think. *Unknown.* OxNR

Now what in the world shall we dioux. The Sioux. Eugene Field. FiBHP; GoJo

Now what will we do for timber. Cill Chais. *Unknown, tr. by* Thomas Kinsella. NOIV

Now when I have thrust my body. To Forget Me. Theodore Weiss. CoAP

Now, when my vision turns in on itself. Shards. Perets Markish, *tr. by* Leonard Wolf. PeBMYV

Now when spring mists rise. Lady Ise, *tr. fr. Japanese by* Burton Watson. *Fr.* Kokin Shu. FCEI

Now, when the cheerless empire of the sky. Winter. James Thomson. *Fr.* The Seasons: Winter. OxBA

Now, when the rozier blows. Bernart Arnaut de Moncuc, *tr. by* Paul Blackburn. Pro

Now when the solemn rites of pray'r were past. Homer, *tr. fr. Greek by* Dryden. *Fr.* The Iliad, I. OBVE

Now, when thou hast decreed to seize their stores. The Care of Bees. Virgil, *tr. fr. Latin by* Dryden. *Fr.* Georgics, IV. FaBoUs

Now, when twelve days complete had run their race. Homer, *tr. fr. Greek by* Dryden. *Fr.* The Iliad, I. OBVE

Now where's a song for our small dear. The Unwritten Song. Ford Madox Ford. BoTP

Now whether folks are Methodists. The Radio Religion. William Ludlum. WBLP

Now, whether it were by peculiar grace. Wordsworth. *Fr.* Resolution and Independence. Par

Now which is wrong or right? Too glib we talk. Falkland at Newbury, 1643. Hugh Conway. EBVV

Now, while amid those dainty downs and dales. To His Pandora, from England. Alexander Craig. Son

Now while Rogero learns the arms and name. Angelica and the Ork. Ariosto, *tr. fr. Italian by* Sir John Harington. *Fr.* Orlando Furioso, X. OBSC

Now, while the birds thus sing a joyous song. Wordsworth. *Fr.* Ode: Intimations of Immortality from Recollections of Early Childhood. Prf

Now, while thou hast the wondrous power of word. The Gift of Speech. Sadi, *tr. fr. Persian by* L. Cranmer-Byng. *Fr.* The Gulistan. AWP

Now Whitehall's in the grave. A Mock Song. Richard Lovelace. CaPo

Now who is he on earth that lives. Medieval Norman Song. *Unknown, tr. by* John Addington Symonds. AWP

Now whyle Hippomenes/ Debates theis things. Ovid, *tr. fr. Latin.* Fr. Metamorphoses, X. OBVE, *tr. by* Arthur Golding.

Now will I a lover be. The Combat. Thomas Stanley. AWP

Now will you stand for me, in this cool light. Love in the Museum. Adrienne Rich. NePoEA; NYBP

Now winter downs the dying of the year. Year's End. Richard Wilbur. CAPP; CoAP; HeIP; LiTM; NAAL-2; NePoEA; SM (At Year's End.) NYBP

Now Winter Nights Enlarge. Thomas Campion. AAS; EBEV; EIL; ELP; HeIP; NoP; OBSC; QFR; SeCePo; TEP

Now Winter's winds are banished from the sky. Spring. Meleager, *tr. by* William M. Hardinge. AWP

Now with a general peace the world was blest. Dryden. *Fr.* Astraea Redux. OBS

Now with a still wind in his quiet hair. Odysseus Elytis, *tr. fr. Greek by* Edmund Keeley *and* Philip Sherrard. *Fr.* Heroic and Elegiac Song for the Lost Second Lieute, IV. VMG

Now with a vestal lustre glows the Vale. Anna Seward. *Fr.* Llangollen Vale. PeHV

Now with earth riven and a bloodied sun. We Shall Say. Miriam Allen DeFord. GoYe

Now with the coming in of the spring the days will stretch a bit. The County Mayo. Anthony Raftery, *tr. by* James Stephens. AnIL

Now with the springtime the days will grow longer. County Mayo. Anthony Raftery, *tr. by* Frank O'Connor. KiLC

Now, with your palms on the blades of my shoulders. Dead Still. Andrei Voznesensky, *tr. by* Richard Wilbur. BoLoP

Now wolde I sing [*or* faine some merthes] mak[e]. Song for My Lady. A. Godwin. OxBoLi
(Now Wolde.) CH
(Song in His Lady's Absence, A.) MeEL

Now would to God swift ships had ne'er been made! Sopolis. Callimachus, *tr. by* William M. Hardinge. AWP

Now write down. Seven Mysteries. Michael Jackson. ATNZ

Now, yield thee, or by Him who made. Sir Walter Scott. *Fr.* The Lady of the Lake, V. OxBS

Now you are going, what can I do but wish you. The Poet's Farewell to His Teeth. William Dickey. PoA

Now you are holding my skull in your hand. A Meditation. Richard Eberhart. LiTA

Now you are one with us, you know our tears. To America, on Her First Sons Fallen in the Great War. E. M. Walker. PAH

Now you are standing face to face with the clear light. Prayer for the Little Daughter between Death and Burial. Diana Scott. BrRo

Now you can't expect a cowboy to agitate his shanks. The Cowboy's Dance Song. James Barton Adams. CowP

Now you come again. Happiness of 6 A.M. Harvey Shapiro. NYBP

Now you depart, and though your way may lead. To a Friend Going on a Journey. Mahammed Abdille Hassan, *tr. by* M. Laurence. WTO

Now, you great stanza, you heroic mold. Single Sonnet. Louise Bogan. Son

Now You Have Burned. John Thompson. NOBC

Now you have freely given me leave to love. To a Lady That Desired I Would Love Her. Thomas Carew. CaPo; MeLP; MePo; OBS; SeCV-1

Now you have stabbed her good. Kreutzer Sonata. Ted Hughes. FaBoMo

Now "you," if you are still yourself. Witness. Jon Anderson. MAYP

Now you love me. Divorce Song. *Unknown, tr. by* Carl Cary. STP

"Now you must die," the young one said. The Rite. Dudley Randall. HoPM

Now you take ol Rufus. He beat drums. For Freckle-faced Gerald. Etheridge Knight. BPo; NeAC

Now you think that is right, sah? Talk the truth. The Carpenter's Complaint. Edward Baugh. PVCV

Now young Jack Potter was a man who knowed the ways of steers. Jack Potter's Courtin.' S. Omar Barker. CowP

Now You're Content. André Spire, *tr. fr. French by* Stanley Burnshaw. TrJP

Nowadays the mess is everywhere. The Survivors. Daryl Hine. TwCP

Nowel! nowel! nowel! Man Exalted. *Unknown.* MeEL

Nowel! nowel! nowel! Mary Is with Child. *Unknown.* MeEL

Nowhere. John Berryman. AnAn

Nowhere are we safe. Hymn Written after Jeremiah Preached to Me in a Dream. Owen Dodson. AmNP

Nowhere did I ever meet. Mohammad Taqi Mir, *tr. by* Ahmed Ali. GoT

Nowhere else does screened porch wire. Marriage Portrait. James Applewhite. MT

Nowhere, No Trace Can I Discover. Faiz Ahmad Faiz, *tr. fr. Urdu by* Mahmood Jamal. PBMUP

Nowhere, not among the warriors at their festival. Atimantiyar, *tr. fr. Tamil by* A. K. Ramanujan. WPOW
Now's the time for mirth and play. For Saturday. Christopher Smart. *Fr.* Hymns for the Amusement of Children, XXXIII. FaBoCh; NOEC; OxBChV
(Hymn for Saturday.) OxBChV
(Lark's Nest, A.) FaBoCh
Nox. Salvador Díaz Mirón, *tr. fr. Spanish by* Samuel Beckett. MexPo
"Nox Nocti Indicat Scientiam." William Habington. *Fr.* Castara, III. ACP; JCP; MeLP; MePo; NOBE; OBEV; OBS
Nox was lit by lux of Luna, The. Carmen Possum. *Unknown.* BLPA; NBLV
Ntabuu/ Ntabuu Selina and. The Sisters. Alexis De Veaux. GLP
Nu-numma-kwiten formerly sang. The Song of Nu-Numma-Kwiten. *Unknown.* PeSA
Nuala's Fiddle. Tomas O Canainn. NPo
Nuances of a Theme by Williams. Wallace Stevens. CMoP; LiTA
Nuclear Unit. Valerie Sinason. DT
Nuclear wind, when wilt thou blow. Paul Dehn. *Fr.* A Leaden Treasury of English Verse. FiBHP
Nude. Daniel Halpern. MAYP
Nude. Harold Witt. ErPo
Nude Descending a Staircase. X. J. Kennedy. CoAP; HoPM; NePoEA; NePoEA-2; NIP; OxBSP; PoA; SM
Nude in a Fountain. Norman MacCaig. OxBS
Nude Kneeling in Sand. John Logan. ErPo
Nude on the Bathroom Wall, The. Gena Ford. IHMS
Nude Reclining at Word Processor, in Pastel. Carl Conover. GOYP
Nude Swim, The. Anne Sexton. ASP; WPE
Nudes. Anthony Howell. NPo
Nudes—stark and glistening. Louse Hunting. Isaac Rosenberg. EBEV; NAEL-2; NoAM; NoP; OxBTC
Nudging and thrusting to the light. Gideon at the Well. Geoffrey Hill. NePoEA
Nudities. André Spire, *tr. fr. French.* AWP, *tr. by* Jethro Bithell; ErPo, *tr. by* Jethro Bithell; TrJP, *tr. by* Stanley Burnshaw; VWA, *tr. by* Stanley Burnshaw.
Nudus Redibo. Thomas Flatman. OxBSP
Nuit Blanche: North End. Conrad Aiken. OxBA
Numb, stiff, broken by no sleep. Night Thoughts over a Sick Child. Philip Levine. NePoEA-2; SM
No. 42. Lajos Kassák, *tr. fr. Hungarian by* Jascha Kessler. FOC
Number Four. Doughtry Long, Jr... CNA; PoBA; SO
No. 96. Lajos Kassák, *tr. fr. Hungarian by* Jascha Kessler. FOC
Number One/ I slouch in bed. Two Hangovers. James Wright. LCAP
Number one is a good clean number, The. The Million. Peter Redgrove. OxBC
No. 65. Lajos Kassák, *tr. fr. Hungarian by* Jascha Kessler. FOC
Number Song. Anne Waldman. UL
No. 12. Lajos Kassák, *tr. fr. Hungarian by* Jascha Kessler. FOC
Number two priest, The. *Unknown, tr. by* Geoffrey Bownas *and* Anthony Thwaite. PeBJV
Numbering at Bethlehem, The. Albert Goldbarth. NAmP
Numberless days of the past fill our bodies and minds. Meditation. Shin Dong-jip, *tr. by* Koh Chang-soo. ACKP
Numbers, *sels.* Bible, *O.T.*
Balaam's Blessing. *Fr.* XXIV: 5–9. TrGrPo
("How goodly are the tentes of Jacob and thine habitacions Israel," *tr. by* William Tyndale) OBVE
Benediction. *Fr.* VI: 24–26. TrGrPo
(Blessing of the Priests.) TrJP
("Lorde blesse and kepe the, The," *tr. by* William Tyndale) OBVE, VI: 24–27.
Song of the Well. *Fr.* XXI: 17–18. TrJP
Numbers and Faces, *sel.* W. H. Auden.
"Kingdom of Number is all boundaries, The." ImOP
Numbers, Letters. Imamu Amiri Baraka. BPo; NOBA
Numbness. Friederike Mayröcker, *tr. fr. German by* Beth Bjorklund. CoAuP
Numerella Shore, The. "Cockatoo Jack." PoAu-1
Numerous Celts. Sir John Collings Squire. BXAP
Numerous host of dreaming saints succeed, A. Zimri: The Duke of Buckingham. Dryden. *Fr.* Absalom and Achitophel, Pt. I. NOBE; OBSV
(Zimri ("Numerous host of dreaming saints succeed.").) AWP; SeCePo
Nummum et secalis sacculum cantate! Four and Twenty Merulae. J. Moyr Smith. FaBoNo
Numskull for eighty-five years!, A. Kogetsu, *tr. by* Lucien Stryk *and* Takashi Ikemoto. ZPCJ
Nun, The. Arthur Symons. BrPo

Nun walked on her prayer, The. The Friar and the Nun. *Unknown.* GBP
Nunaptigne. In our land—*ahe, ahe, ee, ee, iee.* The Wind Has Wings. *Unknown, tr. by* Raymond de Coccola *and* Paul King. GrPl
Nunc Dimittis. Bible, *N.T. Fr.* St. Luke, II: 29-32. WGRP
Nunc Scio, Quid Sit Amor. L. A. MacKay. OBCV
Nunc Viridant Segetes. Sedulius Scottus, *tr. fr. Medieval Latin by* Helen Waddell. BIrV
Nuns at Eve. John Malcolm Brinnin. MoAB; TwCP
Nuns Fret Not at Their Convent's Narrow Room. Wordsworth. EBEV; EnRP; NIP; NoP; Son
(Sonnet: "Nuns fret not at their convent's narrow room.") OBEV
Nuns, his nieces, bring the priest in the next. A Far Cry after a Close Call. Richard Howard. NYBP; UnPo
Nuns in the Wind. Muriel Rukeyser. NNaP
Nun's Priest's Prologue, The. Chaucer. *Fr.* The Canterbury Tales. OAEL-1
("Stop!" cried the kinght. "No more of this good sir!"") NAWM-1
Nun's Priest's Tale, The. Chaucer. *Fr.* The Canterbury Tales. FiP; NAEL-1; NoP; OAEL-1; PoEL-1; TrGrPo, , *orig. and mod. vers. by* Frank Ernest Hill.
(Cock and the Hen, The.) OBNV
("Once a poor widow, aging year by year.") NAWM-1, *tr. by mod. version by* Theodore Morrison.
("Once, long ago, set close beside a wood.") TrGrPo
("There liv'd, as authors tell, in days of yore.") OBVE
"This Chauntecleer stood hye up-on his toos."
Chauntecleer. FiP
"There liv'd, as authors tell, in days of yore," *mod. version by* Dryden OBVE
"His comb was redder than the fine coral." PBBP
Nuptial. Joan Drew Ritchings. SoTCo
Nuptial Dialogues, *sel.* Edward Ward.
Dialogue between a Squeamish Cotting Mechanic and His Sluttish Wife, in the Kitchen. NOEC
Nuptial Eve, A, *sel.* Sydney Thompson Dobell. OBNC
Ballad of Keith of Ravelston, The. CH; OBEV
(Keith of Ravelston.) CH
Nuptial Hymn. Henry Peacham. *Fr.* The Period of Mourning. EIL
Nuptial Sleep. Dante Gabriel Rossetti. *Fr.* The House of Life, VI. EBVV; NAEL-2
Nuptial Song. Lord De Tabley. GTBS-P
Nuptial Song. Henricus Selyns. *See* O! days light transcending.
Nuptial[l] Song, or Epithalamie [or Epithalamy], on Sir Clipseby Crew and His Lady, A. Robert Herrick. CaPo; JCP; PoEL-3; SeCP; SeCV-1
Nuremberg. Longfellow. AmPP
Nurse believed the sick man slept, The. Charlotte Brontë. NOBVV
Nurse-life wheat, within his greene huske growing, The. Fulke Greville. *Fr.* Caelica, XL. AAS
(Sonnet: "Nurse-life wheat within his green husk growing, The.") JCP
(Youth and Maturity.) OBSC
Nurse No Long Grief. Mary Gilmore. PoAu-1
Nursery, The. Fanny Howe. UL
Nursery boast, The. On Seeing My Birthplace from a Jet Aircraft. John Pudney. NYBP
Nursery Rhyme. Kenneth Burke. OBAL
Nursery Rhyme of Innocence and Experience. Charles Causley. GoJo
Nursery Rhymes for the Tender-hearted, *sel.* Christopher Morley.
"Scuttle, scuttle little roach." *Fr.* I. FaFP
Nurses, The. Kipling. *Fr.* Land and Sea Tales. NoAM
Nurse's Dole in the Medea, The. Byron. OBVE
Nurse's hand taking my pulse, The. Ishikawa Takuboku, *tr. fr. Japanese by* Hiroaki Sato. *Fr.* Forty-seven Tanka in Three Lines. FCEI
Nurse's Lament, The. Mary Elizabeth Coleridge. NOBVV; OxBSP
Nurse's Song. Blake. *Fr.* Songs of Experience. EnRP; FF; NAEL-2
Nurse's Song. Blake. *Fr.* Songs of Innocence. AWP; BLPL; CH; EnRP; FaBoBe; NAEL-2; OxBChV
(Play Time.) FaPON
Nurse's Song. M. K. Joseph. ATNZ
Nursing Home. Barry Spacks. PPR
Nursing your nerves. The Afterwake. Adrienne Rich. NOBA; Prf
Nut, a World, a Squirrel, and a King, A. Charles Churchill. *Fr.* Night; an Epistle to Robert Lloyd. FaBoRV
Nut-brown Maid, The. *Unknown.* OBEV; OBSC
Nut Tree, A. *Unknown.* TTTS
Nutcrackers and the Sugar-Tongs, The. ("Nutcrackers sate by a plate on the table, The"). Edward Lear. BLPL; Mes; PoLF
Nutgrass still grows on the hill, The. *Unknown, tr. by* Arthur Waley. BoS
Nuts and Bolts Poem for Mr. Mac Adams, Sr. Kathleen Fraser. NPGG

Nuts in May. Louis MacNeice. MoAB; MoBrPo
Nutting. Wordsworth. EnRP; NAEL-2; NU; OAEL-2; RB
NW5 and N6. Sir John Betjeman. SCV
N.Y. to L.A. by Jet Plane. Sonya Dorman. GOA
Nyanu was appointed. Early Losses; a Requiem. Alice Walker. BlSi
Nymph and Her Fawn, The. Andrew Marvell. Fr. The Nymph
  Complaining for the Death of Her Faun. FaBoCh
Nymph and shepherd raise electric tridents. Chances "R." Allen
  Ginsberg. HCAP
Nymph Complaining for the Death of Her Fawn, The. Andrew Marvell.
  CH; FM; GoTL; HeIP; MePo; NAEL-1; OAEL-1; OBS, abr.; PoEL-2;
  SeCP; SeCV-1
Nymph I come once more awooing. Ay or Nay? Ralph Schomberg.
  Fr. The Judgment of Paris. TrJP
Nymph in vain bestows her pains, The. Anne Finch, Countess of
  Winchilsea. OxBSP
Nymph, nymph, what are your beads? Overheard on a Saltmarsh.
  Harold Monro. BoTP; CH; FaPON; GoJo; Mes; MoShBr; SO; WSC
"Nymph of the garden where all beauties be." Sir Philip Sidney. Fr.
  Astrophel and Stella, LXXXII. InvP; PoE
Nymph turnd home, The. He fell to felling downe. Homer, tr. fr. Greek
  by George Chapman. Fr. Odyssey, V. OBVE
Nymphidia, sels. Michael Drayton.
  Pigwiggin Arms Himself. MoShBr
  (Arming of Pigwiggen, The.) GN
  Queen's Chariot, The. OBS
Nymphs, The, sel. Leigh Hunt.
  "There are the fair-limbed nymphs o' the woods." OBNC
Nymphs and Shepherds. Milton. Fr. Arcades. ELP
  (Song: "Nymphs and shepherds dance no more.") FiP
Nymph's Disdain of Love, A. Unknown. EiL
Nymphs of Fiesole, sel. Boccaccio, tr. fr. Italian by Joseph Tusiani.
  Rape of Mensola, The. PFI
Nymphs of sea and land, away. Nuptial Hymn. Henry Peacham. Fr.
  The Period of Mourning. EiL
Nymph's Reply to the Passionate Shepherd. Sir Walter Ralegh. See If
  all the world and love were young.
Nymph's Reply to the Shepherd, The. Sir Walter Ralegh. CTC; EiL;
  FF; HAP; HeIP; HoPM; InPK; InPS; LiTB; NAEL-1; NBLV; NIP;
  NOBE; NoP; PoE; PPP; RB; SeCePo; SiPS; TrGrPo; WeW
  (Answer to Marlowe.) OAEL-1; OBSC
  (Her Reply.) BoLoP; OBEV
  (Nimphs Reply to the Sheepheard, The.) AAS
  (Nymph's Reply to the Passionate Shepherd.) FaBoPa
Nymph's Secret, A. Ben Jonson. OBEV
Nymph's Song. Sir Richard Fanshawe, after the Italian of Giovanni
  Battista Guarini. See Let us use it while we may.
Nymph's Song to Hylas, The. William Morris. See Life and Death of
  Jason, The: Garden by the Sea, A.
Nymphs! your fine hands ethereal floods amass. The Action of Electricity.
  Erasmus Darwin. Fr. The Economy of Vegetation. FaBoUs

O

Ö. Rita Dove. HCAP; MAYP
O. Richard Wilbur. LiTA
O/ Holy/ Wood. Sister Mary Madeleva. CRP
O/ out of a bed of love. Holy Spring. Dylan Thomas. WaP
O/ spare/ us/ from/ the/ need. Clobber the Lobber. Felicia Lamport.
  RR
O, a dainty plant is the Ivy green. The Ivy Green. Charles Dickens.
  Fr. The Pickwick Papers, ch. 6. BoNaP
O a little lonely in Cambridge all that first Fall. Transit. John Berryman.
  AnAn
O a' the isles of this braid sea. Skye. John Gawsworth. PoSH
O a year from tomorrow I left my own people. Clonmel Jail. Unknown,
  tr. by Valentin Iremonger. BIrV
O Aa the Manly Sports. J. K. Annand. PoSH
O Abishag, my little serving-maid. Abishag. André Spire, tr. by
  Emanuel Eisenberg. TrJP
O ah drove three mules foh Gawge McVane. Mule Skinner's Song.
  Unknown. AS
O Alison Gross, that lives in yon tower [or tow'r]. Alison [or Allison]
  Gross. Unknown. CH; ESPB; FaBoCh; OxBB; WSC
O All Down within the Pretty Meadow. Kenneth Patchen. HAP; WeW
O all the problems other people face. Alcoholic. John Berryman.
  NOCV
O all ye fair ladies with your colours and your graces. The Revenant.
  Walter de la Mare. GBL

O all you little blackey tops. Scaring Crows. Unknown. BoTP; OxNR;
  PBBP
O all your ages at the mercy of my loves. John Berryman. Fr. Homage
  to Mistress Bradstreet. NOBA
O Amber Day, amid the Autumn Gloom. William Talbot Allison. CaP
O amiable prospect! New Lines for Cuscuscaraway and Mirza Murad Ali
  Beg. Louis Simpson. OBAL
O an old King in a story. After W. B. Yeats. G. K. Chesterton.
  NOBL
O another deluge of wind and rain. Cathedral in the Thrashing Rain.
  Takamura Kotaro, tr. by Hiroaki Sato. FCEI
O antique city on St. Lawrence shore. Quebec. Henrietta Cordelia Ray.
  CBWP-3
O apple blossoms. Japanese Hokku. Lewis Alexander. CDC
O! Are Ye Sleepin [or Sleeping], Maggie? Robert Tannahill. OxBS
O Artemis and your virgin girls. Telesilla, tr. by Willis Barnstone.
  BoWoP
O Atthis. Ezra Pound. PoA
O Autumn, laden with fruit, and stained. To Autumn. Blake. BoNaP;
  NAEL-2; WiR
O baby, where you been so long? Lord, Lord, Lord, Lord. Levee Moan.
  Unknown. AS
O bards! weak heritors of passion and of pain! Miserimus. Adah Isaacs
  Menken. CBWP-1
O barn reality! I saw you swimming. Iowa Land. Marvin Bell. SaC
O batsman, rise and go and stop the rot. The Extra Inch. Siegfried
  Sassoon. FL
O, Be Not Too Hasty, My Dearest. "Orpheus C. Kerr." OBAL
O be swift. The Helmsman. Hilda Doolittle ("H. D."). CMoP; OxBA
O beams of steel are slim and black. Song of the Builders. Jessie
  Wilmore Murton. AmFN
O beautiful calm. Tu-kehu and Wetea, tr. by J. C. Andersen. WTO
O beautiful for spacious skies. America the Beautiful. Katharine Lee
  Bates. BLPA; EaLo; FaBoBe; FaBV; FaFP; FaPON; GOA; OPP;
  TAP; WBLP; WGRP
O Beautiful Forever! I Saw Eternity. Louise Bogan. LiTA
O Beautiful, My Country. Frederick L. Hosmer. AH, with music; OPP
O, Beautiful They Move. William Pillen. VWA
O beauty (beams, nay, flame). A Description of Beauty. Samuel Daniel.
  OBSC
O beech, unbind your yellow leaf, for deep. Ghostly Tree. Léonie
  Adams. MoAB; MoAmPo
O Bessie Bell and Mary Gray. Bessy [or Bessie] Bell and Mary Gray.
  Unknown. ESPB; OxBB
O Billie, billie, bonny billie. The Battle of Bothwell Bridge. Unknown.
  OxBB, with music
  (Bothwell Bridge.) ESPB
O Billows Bounding Far. A. E. Housman. BoNaP
  (Profoundly True Reflections on the Sea.) FaBoNo
O Bird at night, who, hearing, could forget. Bird at Night. Marion Ethel
  Hamilton. GoYe
O bird crying in the acacia tree, alike are our sorrows. An Andalusian
  Exile. Ahmad Shauqi, tr. by M. Mustafa Badawi and John Heath-
  Stubbs. MAP
O Bird, So Lovely. Louis Golding. TrJP
O Bird, thou dartest to the sun. Maria White Lowell. AA
O Black and Unknown Bards. James Weldon Johnson. AmNP; BANP;
  BPo; HeIP; PoBA; PoNe; TTY; UnPo
O blackbird! sing me something well. The Blackbird. Tennyson. FM;
  PBBP
O Blackbird, what a boy you are! Vespers. T. E. Brown. BoTP
O blazing Sun, how happy you are there. Louise Labé, tr. by Willis
  Barnstone. BoWoP
O Blessèd House, That Cheerfully Receiveth. Karl Johann Philipp Spitta,
  tr. fr. German by Charles William Schaeffer. TrPWD
O Blessed Letters. Samuel Daniel. Fr. Musophilus; or, Defence of All
  Learning. FaBoRV
O blessed man, that in th' advice. Bible, O.T. See Psalms: Psalm I
  ("Blessed is the man. . .").
O Blessed man, that in th'advice. Unknown. Fr. The Bay Psalm Book.
  SCAP
O Blest Estate, Blest from Above. George Sandys. AH
O Blest Unfabled Incense Tree. George Darley. Fr. Nepenthe. BIrV;
  ChER; FaBoCh; FaBoRV; PBBP
  (Hundred-sunned Phenix.) OBNC
  ("O fast her amber blood doth flow.") OBEV
  (Phoenix, The.) ChTr; NOBE; OAEL-2; WiR
O blisful light, of which the beames clere. Wooing of Criseide, The, III.
  Chaucer. Fr. Troilus and Criseyde [or Criseide]. PoEL-1
O blithe new-comer! I have heard. To the Cuckoo. Wordsworth.
  BoTP; ELP; EnRP; FaFP; FiP; GTBS; GTBS-P; PoLF; TrGrPo

O blue is such a fatal colour. September Blue. Barbara Burford. DT
O blush not so! O blush not so! Sharing Eve's Apple. Keats. ChER; ErPo; NBLV
O Bois de Boulogne, don't you remember. Bois de Boulogne. Ahmad Shauqi, tr. by M. Mustafa Badawi and John Heath-Stubbs. MAP
O Bonny Baby Livingston. Bonny Baby Livingston. Unknown. ESPB
O bonny, bonny sang the bird. The Unquiet Grave. Unknown. EnSB
O, born in luckless hour, with every muse. To the Editor of Mr. Pope's Works. Thomas Edwards. Son
O Boston, though thou now art grown. Of Boston in New England. William Bradford. SCAP
O Boston wives and maids, draw near and see. To the Boston Women. Unknown. PAH
O boy cutting grass. Hitomaro. Fr. Manyo Shu. AWP
O Brazil, the Isle of the Blest. Gerald Griffin. ACP (Hy-Brasail—the Isle of the Blest.) BLPA
O bretheren, my way. My Way's Cloudy. Unknown. BoAN-1
O [or Oh], Brignal[l] banks are wild and fair. Brignall Banks. Sir Walter Scott. Fr. Rokeby, III. EnRP; OBEV (Edmund's Song.) PoRA (Outlaw, The.) GTBS; GTBS-P
O broad-breasted queen among nations! Boston. John Boyle O'Reilly. PAH
O brother, as you've given me so much. Bride's Farewell: Two Songs. Gond Oral Tradition, tr. by V. Elwin and S. Hivale. WTO
O brother in the restless rest of God! Zora Cross. Fr. Elegy on an Australian Schoolboy. PoAu-1
O brother, lift a cry, a long world cry. Peace. Edwin Markham. WBLP
O brothers mine, take care! Take care! The White Witch. James Weldon Johnson. BANP; CDC
O brothers mine, today we stand. Fifty Years. James Weldon Johnson. BANP
O brothers, why do you talk. Mahadevi, tr. fr. Kannada by A. K. Ramanujan. WPOW
O Bury Me Beneath the Willow,. Unknown. AS
"O [or Oh] bury me not on the lone prairie." Bury Me Not on the Lone Prairie. Unknown. AS; FaBV; FaFP (Dying Cowboy, The.) FaBoBe
O, but how white is white, white from shadows come. Music of Colours: The Blossom Scattered. Vernon Watkins. LiTB
O, but I saw a solemn sight. The Wicked Hawthorn Tree. W. B. Yeats. WSC
O but there is wisdom. Consolation. W. B. Yeats. OxBSP
O, but they say the tongues of dying men. The Tongues of Dying Men. Shakespeare. Fr. King Richard II, II, i. FaBoRV
O but we talked at large before. Sixteen Dead Men. W. B. Yeats. FaBoPV; OBWP
O By the By. E. E. Cummings. OxBA
O Caledonia! Sir Walter Scott. Fr. The Lay of the Last Minstrel. FaBoPP
O California. Alejandro Murguía, tr. fr. Spanish by Toni Empringham. FIA
O' cam' ye here to hear a lilt. The Battle of Glentilt (1847). Sir Douglas Maclagan. PoSH
O cam ye in by the House o Rodes. John Thomson and the Turk. Unknown. ESPB, (A and B vers.)
O Cambridge, attend. Satire upon the Heads. Thomas Gray. FaBoCo
O camp of flowers, with poplars girdled round. Memory. Erik Johann Stagnelius, tr. by Sir Edmund Gosse. AWP
O Captain! My Captain! Walt Whitman. See When lilacs last in the dooryard blomm'd.
O Carib Isle! Hart Crane. NoAM; PoA; VGW
O Cat of Carlishkind. John Skelton. Fr. Phyllyp Sparowe [or Philip Sparrow]. ChTr
O catch Miss Daisy Pinks. Daisy Pinks. Alistair Campbell. ATNZ
O chansons foregoing. Ezra Pound. OxBA
O Charnwood, be thou called the choicest of thy kind. Charnwood Forest. Michael Drayton. Fr. Polyolbion, Sixth and Twentieth Song. FaBoPP
O Cheese. Donald Hall. DiPo
O child, had I thy lease of time! such unimagined things. A Child of To-Day. James Buckham. AA
O Child of Lowly Manger Birth,. Ferdinand Q. Blanchard. AH
O Children, Would You Cherish? Christopher Dock, tr. fr. German by Samuel W. Pennypacker. AH
O child's tremble. Forming Child Poems. Simon J. Ortiz. CDW
O chillen, run, Cunjah man. De Cunjah Man. James Edwin Campbell. BANP
O Christ of Bethlehem. H. Glenn Lanier. AH

O Christ of God! whose life and death. Vesta. Whittier. TrPWD
O Christ of Olivet, you hushed the wars. Edwin Markham. Fr. The Christ of the Andes. TrPWD
O Christ, the glorious Crown. Philip Howard. ACP
O Christ, Thou Art within Me Like a Sea. Edith Lovejoy Pierce. TrPWD
O Christ, Who Died. John Calvin Slemp. TrPWD
O Christ, who in Gethsemane. Henrietta Cordelia Ray. CBWP-3
O Christmas Night. Henricus Selyns, tr. fr. Dutch by Howard Murphy. AH, sts. 1, 2, 4, 6 with music (Nuptial Song) SCAP
O city metropole, isle riverain! Montreal. A. M. Klein. CaP; MoCV; OBCV
O city of the world, with sacred splendor blest. Longing for Jerusalem. Judah Halevi, tr. by Emma Lazarus. TrJP
O close of night, I would have you linger. "Adunis", tr. by Lena Jayyusi and John Heath-Stubbs. MAP
O cloud that wants to be the sky's arrow. Rosario Castellanos, tr. fr. Spanish by Willis Barnstone. BoWoP
O Columbia, the gem of the ocean. Columbia, the Gem of the Ocean. David T. Shaw. FaBoBe (Red, White and Blue.) WBLP
O Come, All Ye Faithful. Unknown, tr. fr. Latin by Frederick Oakeley. FaFP (Adeste Fideles.) WGRP
O come and take thy mother/ Beneath thy wing. Beneath Thy Wing. Hayyim Nahman Bialik, tr. by Helena Frank. TrJP
O come let us sing unto the Lord [or Jehovah]. Bible, O.T. Fr. Psalms, XCV. AWP; BLRP, abr.; OHIP, abr.
O come, my body is alone. Come Laugh with Me. Gond Oral Tradition, tr. by V. Elwin and S. Hivale. WTO
O come, our Lord and Saviour. Unknown. BLRP
O Come Quickly! Thomas Campion. See Never Weather-beaten Sail[e].
O come, soft rest of cares, come Night. Bridal Song. Chapman. Fr. Hero and Leander, Fifth Sestiad. NOBE; OBEV
O come to me in my dreams love! Mary Weston Fordham. CBWP-2
O come to me, my brother Green, for I am shot and bleeding. Brother Green. Unknown. AmFP
O come with me, thus ran the song. Emily Brontë. NOBVV
O come you pious youth! adore. Jupiter Hammon. Fr. An Address to Miss Phillis Wheatley. AmPP
O commemorate me where there is water. Lines Written on a Seat on the Grand Canal, Dublin. Patrick Kavanagh. BIrV; CMoP; InPS; IPY; NOIV
O comrades, come gather and join in my ditty. The Cumberland's Crew. Unknown. AmFP
O cool in the summer is salad. Salad: After Swinburne. Mortimer Collins. Fr. Salad. Par
"O Cormac, grandson of Conn," said Carbery. Unknown, tr. fr. Irish by Kuno Meyer. Fr. The Instructions of King Cormac. BIrV
O Could I Find from Day to Day. Benjamin Cleavland. AH
O courteous Christkind guest, most gracious host. To a Crucifix. Anna Wickham. MoBrPo
O crescent of the waning moon. Crescent Moon. Gabriele D'Annunzio, tr. by George Campster. PFI
O cricket, from your cheery cry. Basho, tr. fr. Japanese by Curtis Hidden Page. AWP
"O crikey, Bill!" she ses to me, she ses. Culture in the Slums. W. E. Henley. CenHV
O crimson blood. Hildegard von Bingen, tr. fr. Latin by Patrick Diehl. WPOW
O crownless soul of Ishmael! Hemlock in the Furrows. Adah Isaacs Menken. CBWP-1
O cruel!—could thy cruel bosom find. To a Little Boy, Who Had Destroyed a Nest of Young Birds. Unknown. FaBoUs
"O cruel Death, give three things back." Three Things. W. B. Yeats. OBMV
O cruel Death! thou hast cut down. Epitaph—on the Wife of Dr. Greenwood. Dr. ——— Greenwood. FaBoUs
O cruel Love! on thee I lay. Sapho's Song. John Lyly. Fr. Sapho and Phao. OBSC
O Cuckoo. Unknown, tr. fr. Japanese by Arthur Waley. Fr. Kokin Shu. AWP
O Cuckoo! shall I call thee Bird. To the Cuckoo. F. H. Townsend. ChTr; FaBoNo
O cuckoo that sang to us and art fled. Lament for the Cuckoo. Alcuin, tr. by Helen Waddell. PeHV
O cuckoo, you were born. Mushimaro. Fr. Manyo Shu. Ma
O Cupid! Monarch over Kings. John Lyly. Fr. Mother Bombie. ElL (Fools in Love's College.) TrGrPo (Song of Accius and Silena.) OBSC

O curfew of the setting sun! O Bells of Lynn! The Bells of Lynn. Longfellow. AA

"O. D." Zack Gilbert. CNA

O Daedalus, Fly Away Home. Robert Hayden. HAP; IDB; PoBA; PoNe; WeW

O Dandelion. *Unknown.* BoTP

O dappled throat of white! Shy, hidden bird! The Lonely-Bird. Harrison Smith Morris. AA

O dark-haired girl, let us now. From an Irish-Latin Macaronic. Geoffrey Taylor. NeIP

O David, highest in the list. Christopher Smart. *Fr.* A Song to David. NOEC

O David, if I had. That Harp You Play So Well. Marianne Moore. MoAB; MoAmPo; PoA

O dawn upon me slowly, Paradise. Come Slowly, Paradise. James Benjamin Kenyon. AA

O Day most calm, most bright. Sunday. George Herbert. OBS; SeCV-1; TrCP

O Day of God, Draw Nigh. Robert Balgarnie Young Scott. AH

O Day of Light and Gladness. Frederick Lucian Hosmer. AH

O Day of Rest and Gladness. Christopher Wordsworth. WGRP

O, de birds ar' sweetly singin'. 'Weh Down Souf'. Daniel Webster Davis. BANP

O, de light-bugs glimmer down de lane. Negro Serenade. James Edwin Campbell. BANP

O' de wurl' ain't flat! Northboun'. Lucy Ariel Williams Holloway. BANP; BlSi; CDC; PoNe

O dear and loving God. Prayer for Living and Dying. Christopher La Farge. TrPWD

O dear! I cannot choose but write. Eve. Oliver Herford. OBAL

O Dear O. *Unknown.* ErPo

O dearest, canst thou tell me why. Warum sind denn die Rosen so blass. Heine, *tr. by* Richard Garnett. AWP

O Dearest Dread, most glorious King. A Prayer unto Christ the Judge of the World. Michael Wigglesworth. SCAP

O dearly-bought revenge, yet glorious! Heroic Vengeance. Milton. *Fr.* Samson Agonistes. OBS

O Death. *Unknown.*

O Death. Bible, Apocrypha. *Fr.* Ecclesiasticus, XLI: 1-4. TrJP

O Death, Rock Me Asleep. *At. to* George Boleyn, *also at. to* Anne Boleyn. EiL; FaBoRV; FF; TrGrPo; WPE (Death.) OBSC (O Death, Rock Me on Sleep.) ChTr

O death, thy certainty is such. Henry Luttrell. FaBoEE

O Death! Why dost thou steal the great. In Memoriam Frederick Douglass. Eloise Bibb. CBWP-4

O death you dark master. H. C. Artmann, *tr. by* Beth Bjorklund. CoAuP

O deep and clear as is the sky. To Silence. T. S. Moore. BrPo

O deep-blue sea, O god Uli! Prayer of the Fishing Net. *Unknown, tr. by* N. B. Emerson. WTO

O deep, creating Light. Eagle Song. Gordon Bottomley. *Fr.* Suilven and the Eagle. MoBrPo

O depth sufficient to desire. Adam's Song to Heaven. Edgar Bowers. QFR

O Desolate Eves. Christopher John Brennan. *Fr.* The Wanderer. PoAu-1

O destined Land, unto thy citadel. George Edward Woodberry. *Fr.* My Country. AA

O Deus, Ego Amo Te. Gerard Manley Hopkins. TrPWD

O Did you ever hear of the brave Earl Brand. Earl Brand. *Unknown.* OxBB

O did you see a troop go by. The Camp within the West. Roderic Quinn. PoAu-1

O Diodorus, in a storm of spring. *Unknown, tr. by* Sydney Oswald. PeHV

O Dirty Bird Yr Gizzard's Too Big & Full of Sand. James Koller. PoM

O distant Christ, the crowded, darkening years. Doubt. Margaret Deland. TrPWD

O distant cuckoo. Nagachika, *tr. by* Steven D. Carter. WFTW

O divine star of heaven. John Fletcher. *Fr.* The Mad Lover, IV, i. GBL

O do not grieve, Dear Heart, nor shed a tear. Margaret Cavendish, Duchess of Newcastle. EnLoPo

O do not use me/ After my sinnes! Sighs and Grones. George Herbert. PoEL-2

O Doctor Dear My Love. Anne Halley. NMM

O Domine Deus! Speravi in te. Prayer before Execution. Mary Queen of Scots, *tr. by* John Fawcett. WGRP

O Donal[l] Oge, if you go across the sea. Donal[l] Oge: Grief of a Girl's Heart. *Unknown.* GBL, *tr. by* Lady Gregory; PBWP, *tr. by* Lady Gregory

O don't, don't ever ask me for alms. Death and the Plowman. Sidney Keyes. OxBTC

O Doomsday come, shake up the world. Momin Khan Momin, *tr. by* Ahmed Ali. GoT

O down in the orchard. Apple Harvest. Helen Leuty. BoTP

O dream from the blackness. Sappho, *tr. by* Willis Barnstone. BoWoP

O dream, where art thou now? Emily Brontë. NOBVV

O Dreams, O Destinations, *sel.* C. Day Lewis. "To travel like a bird, lightly to view." GTBS-P

O dull, cold northern sky. Robert Louis Stevenson. EBVV

O Duty,/ Why hast thou not the visage of a sweetie or a cutie? Kind of an Ode to Duty. Ogden Nash. TrGrPo

"O Earl Rothes, an thou wert mine." Earl Rothes. *Unknown.* ESPB

O early one morning I walked out like Agag. The Streets of Laredo. Louis MacNeice. ChTr; MoBS; OBWP

O Earnest Be. *Unknown.* AH

O Earth, adore creative power. Creation. Mary Weston Fordham. CBWP-2

O Earth! Art Thou Not Weary? Julia Caroline Ripley Dorr. AA

O earth, lie heavily upon her eyes. Rest. Christina Rossetti. NOBE; OAEL-2; OBEV; OBNC; TrGrPo

O Earth, O dewy mother, breathe on us. Archibald Lampman. TrPWD

O Earth, Sufficing All Our Needs. Sir Charles G. D. Roberts. CaP

O Earth, thou hast not any wind that blows. The Word. Richard Realf. AA; WGRP

O Earth, throughout thy borders. Easter Carol. George Newell Lovejoy. OHIP

O Earth, Turn! George Johnston. MoCV

O elephant, possessor of a savings-basket full of money. Salute to the Elephant. Odeniyi Apolebieji, *tr. by* S. A. Babalola. WTO

O England, Country of My Heart's Desire. E. V. Lucas. BoTP

O Englishwoman on the Pincian. Thomas Edward Brown. *Fr.* Roman Women. NOBVV; OBNC

O eternal grass. On the Meadow. "Katri Vala," *tr. by* Jaakko A. Ahokas. PBWP

O Eternal, in thy majesty ride. Jewish Arabic Liturgies. *Unknown, tr. by* Hartwig Hirschfeld. TrJP

O ever beauteous, ever friendly, tell. Elegy to the Memory of an Unfortunate Lady. Pope. ACP

O everie living warldly wight. Of Gods Omnipotencie. Alexander Hume. NOCV

O everlasting Kingdom of the Scepter. He Maketh Himself One with the Only God, Whose Limbs Are the Many Gods. *Unknown, tr. fr. Egyptian by* Robert Hillyer. *Fr.* Book of the Dead. AWP

O eye, weep for a rider. Rain to the Tribe. Al-Khansa, *tr. by* Willis Barnstone *and* Tony Nawfal. BoWoP

O eyes clear with beauty, O tender gaze. Louise Labé, *tr. by* Willis Barnstone. BoWoP

O fair is our Lord's own city. Fair is Our Lord's Own City. *Unknown, tr. by* Coslett Quin. TIRV

O fair! O sweet! when I do look on thee. Sir Philip Sidney. SiPS

O faire sweet face, O eyes celestiall bright. John Fletcher. *See* Oh fair sweet face, Oh eyes.

O faithless thorn. *Gond Oral Tradition, tr. by* V. Elwin *and* S. Hivale. WTO

O Fall of the leaf, I am tired. Leaf. John Hewitt. NeIP

O, Falmouth is a fine town with ships in the bay. Home *or* Falmouth. W. E. Henley. GN; MoBrPo; MOS; PoLF

O false and treacherous Probability. Fulke Greville. *Fr.* Caelica, CIII [CIV]. AAS (Sonnet: "O false and treacherous Probability.") OBS

O fan of white silk. Fan-Piece, for Her Imperial Lord. Ezra Pound. MoAB

O far, fantastic line of notch and spire. A'Chuilionn. A. G. Hutchison. PoSH

O far withdrawn into the lonely West. To K. H. Thomas Edward Brown. OBNC

O far-off darling in the South. Coeur de Lion to Berengaria. Theodore Tilton. AA

O fare ye weel, my auld wife! My Auld Wife. *Unknown.* GBP

"O fare you well, my darling." Ten Thousand Miles. *Unknown.* AmFP

O fast her amber blood doth flow. George Darley. *See* Nepenthe: O Blest Unfabled Incense Tree.

O, fastidious mind, gorging on absolutes, remember. Promises. Ruth Forbes Sherry. GoYe

O Father, we approach Thy throne. Adam's Hymn in Paradise. Joost van den Vondel, *tr. by* Sir John Bowring. WGRP

O, father's gone to market town, he was up before the day. A Midsummer Song. Richard Watson Gilder. BoNaP

O favorable spirit, propitious guest. Milton. *Fr.* Paradise Lost, *bk.* V, *ll.* 507–543. (Adam Unfallen.) NOCV

O fearfull, frowning nemesis. Samuel Daniel. *Fr.* Cleopatra. PoEL-2

O Felix Culpa! *Unknown. See* Adam Lay Ibounden [*or* Ibowndyn *or* Ybounden].

O first created and creating source. Ode to the Sea. Howard Baker. OxBA

O Flame of Living Love. Saint John of the Cross, *tr. fr. Spanish.* AWP, *tr. by* Arthur Symons

O flower fawn. Five Flower World Variations. *Unknown, tr. by* Jerome Rothenberg. STP

O flower of all that springs from gentle blood. Gabriello Chiabrera, *tr. by* Wordsworth. *Fr.* Epitaphs, VII. AWP

O flower of all wind-flowers and sea-flowers. Sark. Swinburne. *Fr.* The Garden of Cymodoce. FaBoPP

O flowers of Mekhmekh, give us peace! *Unknown, tr. by* Ezra Pound *and* Noel Stock. BoWoP

O Fly My Soul. James Shirley. *Fr.* The Imposture, II, ii. OBS (Song of Nuns, A.) ACP

O fond, but fickle and untrue. Walter Savage Landor. GBL

O fons Bandusiae. The First Forgotten. James Keir Baxter. FL

O foolish tears, go back! In Vain. Adah Isaacs Menken. CBWP-1

O foolishnes of men! that lend their ears. Comus's Praise of Nature. Milton. *Fr.* Comus; a Masque Presented at Ludlow Castle. PoEL-3

O for a babe still at the breast. *Unknown, tr. by* Geoffrey Bownas *and* Anthony Thwaite. PeBJV

O for a Booke. *Unknown.* CH

O! [*or* Oh] for a bowl of fat canary. John Lyly. *Fr.* Alexander and Campaspe, I, iii *Also in* A Mad World, My Masters (*by* Thomas Middleton).
(Oh, for a Bowl of Fat Canary.) NoP
(Serving Men's Song, A.) NOBE; OBSC

O [*or* Oh] for a Closer Walk with God. William Cowper. FiP; OxBoCh (Walking with God.) EnRP; NOCV; NOEC; OBEC; PoEL-3; TEP; TOF

O for a faith that will BLRP

O for a ferryman to steer my yearning. Home-Sickness. Hedwig Lachmann, *tr. by* Jethro Bithell. TrJP

O for a fire from heaven. Sanu Chigami. *Fr.* Manyo Shu. Ma

O for a muse of fire, a sack of dough. Sonnet with a Different Letter at the End of Every Line. George Starbuck. OBAL

O for a Muse of fire, that would ascend. Shakespeare. *Fr.* King Henry V, *Prologue to* I. SCV
(Muse of Fire, A, , 2 *ll.*) ChTr

O for a sculptor's hand. Balaam. John Keble. OBNC

O for a sight once more. Hasetsukabe Taruhito. *Fr.* Manyo Shu. Ma

O for a toe, such as the funeral pyre. Sir Thomas Browne. FaBoEE

O for my couriers. *Unknown. Fr.* Manyo Shu. Ma

O for one hour of youthful joy! The Old Man Dreams. Oliver Wendell Holmes. AnAmPo; BLPL; PoLF

O for one minute hark what we are saying! Frederic William Henry Myers. TrPWD

O for our upland meads. Shepherd and Shepherdess. Thomas Hennell. FaBoTw

O! for some honest lover's ghost. *See* Oh! for some honest lover's ghost.

O for ten years, that I may overwhelm. Keats. *Fr.* Sleep and Poetry. NAEL-2; OAEL-2

O for that warning voice, which he who saw. Milton. *Fr.* Paradise Lost, *Bk.* IV. OAEL-1, *complete; TEP, ll.* 1–324.
(Prospect of Eden, The.) PoEL-3, *ll.* 1–775.

O for the body of my darling wife. *Unknown. Fr.* Manyo Shu. Ma

O for the Happy Hour. George Washington Bethune. AH

O for the perfumes that arise. Non Sum Qualis Eram in Bona Urbe Nordica Illa. John Hollander. ErPo

O for the time when I shall sleep. Emily Brontë. *Fr.* Enough of Thought, Philosopher. OBD

O for the Wings of a Dove. Euripides, *tr. fr. Greek by* Gilbert Murray. *Fr.* Hippolytus. AWP

O fortunate, O happy day. A New Household. Longfellow. *Fr.* The Hanging of the Crane. GN

O fountain of Bandusia. Horace, *tr. fr. Latin by* Eugene Field. *Fr.* Odes, III, 13. To the Fountain[s] of Bandusia ("O fons Bandusiae"). AA; AWP

O Frail Adam. Epitaph for Mr. Moses Levy. *Unknown.* TrJP

O Friend! I know not which way I must look. Written in London, September, 1802. Wordsworth. FaBoPV; TrGrPo
(England, 1802, I.) OBEV
(In London, September, 1802.) EnRP
(London, MDCCCII.) GTBS; GTBS-P
(Sonnet: Written in London, September, 1802.) ChER

O friends! who have accompanied thus far. Walter Savage Landor. GBL

O friends! with whom my feet have trod. The Eternal Goodness. Whittier. AA; OHFP; WGRP

O Friendship! Friendship! the shell of Aphrodite. Walter Savage Landor. GBL

O, from your sweet mouth I have come. The Shulamite. Else Lasker-Schüler, *tr. by* Robert Alter. OV

O! Full of Scorpions. Shakespeare. *Fr.* Macbeth, III, ii. FiP

O furrowed plaintive face. The Hurrier. Harold Monro. MoBrPo

O Futagi Palace where is enthroned high. Tanabe Sakimaro. *Fr.* Manyo Shu. Ma

O Future bards. A Prophecy. Allen Ginsberg. TAP

O gallant brothers of the generous South. Henry Peterson. *Fr.* Ode for Decoration Day. AA; FaBoBe

O, Gambler, Git Up Off o' Yo' Knees. *Unknown.* BoAN-1

O generation of the thoroughly smug and thoroughly uncomfortable. Salutation. Ezra Pound. HeIP; MoAB; MoAmPo; NOBA; OxBA; TAP; VGW

O gentle, gentle land. Night Sowing. David Campbell. CBAP; PoAu-2

O gentle, gentle summer rain. Invocation to Rain in Summer. William Cox Bennett. GN

O Gentle Love. George Peele. *Fr.* The Arraignment of Paris. EIL (Colin's Passion of Love.) OBSC

O gentle Love, do not forsake the guide. Upon Some Alterations in My Mistress, after My Departure into France. Thomas Carew. CaPo

O Gentle Ships. Meleager, *tr. fr. Greek by* Andrew Lang. AWP

O Gentle Sleep. Shakespeare. *See* King Henry IV, Pt. II: Cares of Majesty, The.

O gentle Sleep, come, wave thine opiate wing. On Dreams, October 15, 1782. Sir Samuel Egerton Brydges. Son

O gentle sleep! do they belong to thee. To Sleep. Wordsworth. Son

O gie the lass her fairin' lad. Gie the Lass her Fairin.' Burns. CoMu; ErPo

O gifted men, vainglorious for first place. Oderisi D'Agobbio on Pride. Dante, *tr. fr. Italian by* John Ciardi. *Fr.* Divina Commedia: Purgatorio, IX. PFI

O Gin My Love Were Yon Red Rose. *Unknown.* GBP

O girl, you torment me, you are so deceiving. *Gond Oral Tradition, tr. by* V. Elwin *and* S. Hivale. WTO

O give thanks unto the Lord, for He is good. Bible, *O.T.* Psalms, CVII, *sel.*
(O give yee thanks unto the Lord, *Bay Psalm Book*) SCAP
They That Go Down to the Sea. ChTr, 23-31; FaPON, 23-24; MOS, 23-30.
(Ocean, The, *Moulton, Modern Reader's Bible*) WGRP, (23-33).

O give thanks unto the Lord, for He is good/ because his mercy endureth forever. Bible, *O.T.* Psalms, CXVIII. TrJP

O give thanks unto the Lord; for he is good;/ for his mercy endureth forever. Bible, *O.T.* Psalms, CXXXVI. AWP; OHIP, *abr.*
("Let us with a gladsome mind," *paraphrased by* Milton) FL

O give us skulls of hot coals. Antonin Artaud, *tr. by* Michael Benedikt. POS

O give yee thanks unto the Lord. Bible, *O.T. See* Psalms: Psalm CVII.

O Glorious Childbearer. Joseph Campbell. TIRV

O Glorious Christ of God; I live. Cotton Mather. SCAP

O glowing walls of this city. Calcutta. Gábor Garai, *tr. by* Daniel Hoffman. MHuP

"O go again," said the King. King Arthur's Death. *Unknown.* ACP

O God,/ forever I turn in this hard crystal. The Prayer of the Goldfish. Carmen Bernos de Gasztold. PDV

O god above, relent. Here Followeth the Songe of the Death of Mr. Thewlis. *Unknown.* CoMu

O God, above the Drifting Years. John Wright Buckham. AH

O God, Accept the Sacred Hour *with music.* Samuel Gilman. AH

O God, Great Father, Lord, and King. E. Embree Hoss. AH

O God! Have Mercy, in This Dreadful Hour. Robert Southey. MOS; TrPWD

O God, I Cried, No Dark Disguise. Edna St. Vincent Millay. AH

O God! I have no husband. *Unknown, tr. by* Patricia Terry. DMF

O God, I love thee, I love thee. O Deus, Ego Amo Te. Gerard Manley Hopkins. TrPWD

O God! if this indeed be all. If This Be All. Anne Brontë. TrPWD

O God, in Restless Living. Harry Emerson Fosdick. TrPWD

O God, in the dream the terrible horse began. The Dream. Louise Bogan. InPK; LiTA; LiTM; MAT; MoAB; MoAmPo; NoAM

O God, in whom my deepest being dwells. Edmund Blunden. TrPWD

O God, in Whom the Flow of Days. Donald Campbell Babcock. AH

O God, in whom we half believe. Offertorium. Cecil Day Lewis. *Fr.* Requiem for the Living. TIRV

O God, in Whose Great Purpose. James G. Gilkey. AH

O God, keep not thou silence.　Bible, *O.T.*　Psalms, LXXXIII.
(Keep Not Thou Silence.)　TrJP
O God, my dream! I dreamed that you were dead.　On the Threshold.
Amy Levy.　NOBVV
O God, my master God, look down and see.　The Artisan.　Alice Brown.
TrPWD
O God! O Montreal!　Samuel Butler.　FaBoCo; OBSV; OxBoLi
(Psalm of Montreal, A.)　OBTV
O God, O Venus, O Mercury, patron of thieves.　The Lake Isle.　Ezra
Pound.　FaBoCo; FaBoPa; OxBSP; PoA
O God of battles, who art still.　On the Eve of War.　Danske Bedinger
Dandridge.　PAH
O God of Bethel.　Philip Doddridge.　WTO
O God of Calvary and Bethlehem.　The Hem of His Garment.　Anna
Elizabeth Hamilton.　TrPWD
O God of earth and altar.　A Hymn [*or* Prayer].　G. K. Chesterton.
TrPWD; WGRP
O God of goodness, forwardness, and fulness.　Doris Hedges.　GoYe
O God of love unbounded! Lord supreme!　Prayer to God.　"Placido", *tr.*
by Raoul Abdul.　TTY
O God of Mercy.　God of Mercy.　Kadya Molodovsky, *tr. by* Irving
Howe.　PeBMYV; WPOW
O God of My Salvation, Hear.　Joel Barlow.　AH
O God of Stars and Distant Space.　John Franzen.　AH
O God of Youth.　Bates G. Burt.　AH
O God, our Father, if we had but truth!　Edward Rowland Sill.　AA
O God, Our Help in Ages Past.　Isaac Watts.　EaLo; FaPoR; WGRP
See also Our God Our Help in Ages Past.
(Man Frail, and God Eternal.)　NOCV
(Ninetieth Psalm, The.)　BLRP
(Recessional.)　WBLP
O God, our loving Father, help us.　A Christmas Prayer.　Robert Louis
Stevenson.　TrCP
O God, Send Men.　Elizabeth Burrowes.　AH
O God, the cleanest offering.　Father Damien.　John Banister Tabb.
ACP
O God, the heathen are come into Thine inheritance.　Bible, *O.T.*
Psalms, LXXIX.
(Heathen Are Come into Thine Inheritance, The.)　TrJP
O God, the Rock of Ages.　Edward Henry, Bishop of Exeter Bickersteth.
BLPA; FPL
O God, though Countless Worlds of Light.　James D. Knowles.　AH
O God, thy moon is on the hills.　Kelpius's Hymn.　Arthur Peterson.
AA
O God, unknown, invisible, secure.　John Addington Symonds.　*Fr.* An
Invocation.　TrPWD
O God, when You send for me, let it be.　Prayer to Go to Paradise with
the Asses.　Francis Jammes, *tr. by* Jethro Bithell.　AWP
O God, where do they tend—these struggling aims?　Robert Browning.
Fr. Pauline.　WGRP
O God, who made me.　The Prayer of the Donkey.　Carmen Bernos de
Gasztold.　PChr
O God, whose daylight leadeth down.　George Macdonald.　*Fr.* Evening
Hymn.　TrPWD
O God Whose Presence Glows in All.　Nathaniel Langdon Frothingham.
AH
O God! whose thunder shakes the sky.　Resignation.　Thomas Chatterton.
TrCP
O God, why hast thou cast us off for ever?　Bible, *O.T., paraphrased by*
the Countess of Pembroke.　Psalms, LXXIV.　NOCV
O Goddess! hear these tuneless numbers, wrung.　Ode to Psyche.　Keats.
ChER; EnRP; InPS; LiTB; NAEL-2; NOBE; NoP; OAEL-2; OBEV;
OBNC; PoE; PoEL-4; PPP; TOF
O goddess Laka!　Altar Prayers.　*Unknown, tr. by* N. B. Emerson.
WTO
O gold, a deep contempt for you I own.　Ilyas Farhat, *tr. fr. Arabic by*
Salma Khadra Jayyusi *and* John Heath-Stubbs.　MAP
O gold Hyperion, love-lorn Porphyro.　Keats.　William Wilberforce Lord.
Fr. Ode to England.　AA
O Golden Fleece ("O golden fleece she is where she lies tonight.")
George Barker.　*Fr.* Secular Elegies, V.　ErPo; LiTM; MoAB;
MoBrPo
O golden-tongued romance, with serene lute!　On Sitting Down to Read
"King Lear" Once Again.　Keats.　EBEV; EnRP; NAEL-2; NoP
O Gongyla, my darling rose.　Sappho, *tr. fr. Greek by* Willis Barnstone.
BoWoP
O good friend, dear master.　*Unknown, tr. fr. Japanese.*　*Fr.* Manyo Shu.
Ma
"O good Lord Judge, and sweet Lord Judge."　The Maid Freed from the
Gallows.　*Unknown.*　AWP; ESPB
O good painter, tell me true.　An Order for a Picture.　Alice Cary.
BLPA

O good Sun,/ Look thou down upon us.　Song for Fine Weather.
Unknown, tr. by Constance Lindsay Skinner.　AWP
O Goodly Hand.　Sir Thomas Wyatt.　InvP; SiPS
(His Lady's Hand.)　OBSC
O Gracious Father of Mankind.　Henry Hallam Tweedy.　AH
O gracious gods, take compassion.　John Marston.　*Fr.* The
Metamorphosis of Pygmalion's Image.　OAEL-1
O Gracious Jesus, Blessed Lord!　Andrew Fowler.　AH
O gracious moon, I call to mind again.　To the Moon.　Giacomo
Leopardi, *tr. by* John Heath-Stubbs.　PFI
"O grammar-rules, O now your virtues show."　Sir Philip Sidney.　*Fr.*
Astrophel and Stella, LXIII.　AAS; SiPS
(Grammar-Rules.)　FaBoUs
O grandest of the Angels, and most wise.　Litany to Satan.　Baudelaire,
tr. by James Elroy Flecker.　AWP
O grasses wet with dew, yellow fallen leaves.　A Glimpse.　Frances
Cornford.　OBMV
O Great Apposition.　Michel Deguy, *tr. fr. French by* Clayton Eshleman.
RHTwFP
O Great Mary.　Litany to Our Lady.　*Unknown, tr. by* Eugene O'Curry.
TIRV
O Great Spirit!　A Voyager's Prayer.　*Unknown, tr. by* Tanner.　WGRP
O great tone-master! low thy massive head.　Beethoven.　Henrietta
Cordelia Ray.　CBWP-3
O great white-winged blackbird slowly, slowly word veering.　Flight.
Paul-Jean Toulet, *tr. by* William Jay Smith.　CT
O Grief!　*Unknown.*　EiL
O guide my judgment and my taste.　Taste.　Christopher Smart.　*Fr.*
Hymns for the Amusement of Children, XV.　NOCV
O guns, fall silent till the dead men hear.　The Anxious Dead.　John
McCrae.　OHIP
O had truth power, the guiltless could not fall.　His Petition to Queen
Anne of Denmark (1618).　Sir Walter Ralegh.　SiPS
O Hada Cibernetica.　Carlos German Belli, *tr. fr. Spanish by* Maureen
Ahern *and* David Tipton.　Per
O handsome chestnut eyes, evasive gaze.　Louise Labé, *tr. by* Willis
Barnstone.　BoWoP
O happy [*or* happie] dames, that may embrace.　Complaint of the Absence
of Her Lover Being upon the Sea.　Henry Howard, Earl of Surrey.
AAS; EBEV; EiL; ELP; GBL; NOBE; OBEV
(The Seafarer.)　SiPS
O happy golden age.　*See* O lovely age of gold!
O happy Tithon! if thou know'st thy hap.　Aurora.　William Alexander,
Earl of Stirling.　OBEV
O hard endeavor, to blend in with these.　Frederick Goddard Tuckerman.
Fr. Sonnets, II, xx.　QFR
"O hark, the drums do beat, my love, I can no longer stay."　The Banks
of the Nile.　*Unknown.*　OBET
O hark! 'tis the note of the Schmaltztenor!　Schmaltztenor!　M. W
Branch.　FiBHP
O Hark to the Herald.　Eleazar Ben Kalir, *tr. fr. Hebrew by* Israel
Zangwill.　TrJP
O harmless feast.　Barten Holyday.　*Fr.* Technogamia.　EiL
O Harry Heine, curses be.　Translator to Translated.　Ezra Pound.
FaBoEE
O hate me not for my grey hair.　A Song: In the Name of a Lover, to His
Mistress; Who Said, She Hated Him for His Grey Hairs, Which He
Had at Thirty.　William Wycherley.　SeCV-2
O hateful harm! condicion of poverte!　Prologue to the Man of Law's
Tale.　Chaucer.　*Fr.* The Canterbury Tales.　FiP
O, have ye been in love, me boys.　I Met Her in the Garden Where the
Praties Grow.　*Unknown.*　AS
O have ye na heard o' the fause Sakelde?　Kinmont Willie.　*Unknown.*
ESPB; OxBB
O, have you been in Gudbrand's dale, where Laagen's mighty flood.
Thoralf and Synnöv.　Hjalmar Hjorth Boyesen.　AA
O Have You Caught the Tiger?　A. E. Housman.　BXAP; FaBoNo
O, have you seen the leper healed.　The Healing of the Leper.　Vernon
Watkins.　FaBoTw
O have you seen the Stratton flood.　Stratton Water.　Dante Gabriel
Rossetti.　OxBB
O hear a pensive prisoner's prayer.　The Mouse's Petition.　Anna Laetitia
Barbauld.　FM; OxBChV
O Hear My Prayer, Lord.　John Craig.　AH
O hear ye that foul and fiendish laughter.　War!　James Gilchrist Lawson.
WBLP
O heard ye never of Wat o' the Cleuch?　Walsinghame's Song.　James
Hogg.　BXAP
O heard ye of a silly Harper.　The Lochmaben Harper.　*Unknown.*
OxBB
O heard ye of Sir James the Rose.　Sir James the Rose.　*Unknown.*
ESPB

O hearken, all ye little weeds. Candlemas. Alice Brown. AA

O hearken and hear, and I will you tell. Friar in the Well. *Unknown.* ESPB

O heart/ sorrowing. A Young Warrior. Ponmutiyar, *tr. by* A. K. Ramanujan. PLW

O heart of mine, we shouldn't worry so! Just Be Glad. James Whitcomb Riley. WBLP

O heart, small urn. Hilda Doolittle ("H. D."). *Fr.* The Walls Do Not Fall. LLLT

O Heart! the equal poise of love's both parts. Richard Crashaw. *Fr.* The Flaming Heart. TrGrPo

O heart, why dost thou sigh, and wilt not break? When He Thought Himself Contemned. Thomas Howell. EIL

O Heaven Indulge. Stephen Tilden. AH

O heavenly color, London town. November Blue. Alice Meynell. MoBrPo

O Heavy Step of Slow Monotony. Ernst Toller, *tr. fr. German by* Ashley Dukes. TrJP

O Hector, thou wert rooted in my heart. Helen's Lamentation. Homer, *tr. fr. Greek by* Congreve. *Fr.* The Iliad, XXIV. OBVE

O Heitsi-Eibib. Hunter's Prayer. *Unknown.* PeSA

O hell, what do mine eyes. Milton by Firelight. Gary Snyder. CAPP; CoAP; InPS; NAAL-2; PPP

O hell! what do mine eyes with grief behold! Milton. *Fr.* Paradise Lost, *Bk.* IV, *ll.* 358–392.
(Satan Beholds Adam and Eve.) TW

O helpless few in my country. Ezra Pound. *Fr.* Lustra. PoA
(Rest, The.) AmPP; MoAB; MoAmPo; NoAM; NOBA; OxBA

O hermitage well found. The Young Pilgrim Finds Refuge with the Goatherds. Luis de Góngora y Argote, *tr. fr. Spanish by* Edward Meryon Wilson. *Fr.* The First Solitude. OBVE

O Hesperus! thou bringest all good things. Evening. Byron. *Fr.* Don Juan, III. TrGrPo
(Hesperus the Bringer.) AWP

O hideous little bat, the size of snot. The Fly. Karl Shapiro. LiTM; MoP; NIP; NoAM; TW

O Holy Aether, and swift-wingèd Wings. The Wail of Prometheus Bound. Aeschylus, *tr. fr. Greek by* Elizabeth Barrett Browning. *Fr.* Prometheus Bound. WGRP

O Holy City Seen of John. Walter Russell Bowie. AH

O Holy Ghost, whose temple I. The Holy Ghost. John Donne. *Fr.* The Litanie. NOCV

O Holy, Holy, Holy, Lord. James Wallis Eastburn. AH

O holy Jerusalem, Vision of peace. *Unknown, tr. fr. Anglo-Saxon. Fr.* Christ 1: Advent Lyrics, III. AnOE, *tr. by* Charles W. Kennedy. EIL

O holy Love, religious saint! Sir Robert Chester. *Fr.* Love's Martyr. EIL

O Holy Mother, thou who still dost send. At the Tomb of Rachel. "Yehoash", *tr. by* Isidore Goldstick. TrJP

O holy night as it was in the beginning. Canticle for Xmas Eve. David Wagoner. SM

O holy virgin! clad in purest white. To Morning. Blake. EnRP

O Holy Water. Margot Ruddock. OBMV

O! Honour! Honour! Honour! Oh! the Gain! God's Selecting Love in the Decree. Edward Taylor. *Fr.* God's Determinations. PoEL-3

O how canst thou renounce the boundless store. The Youth of a Poet. James Beattie. *Fr.* The Minstrel, I. NOEC

O, how comely it is, and how reviving. *See* Oh, how comely it is, and how reviving.

O, how I remember the pain of it. Blood. Nina Cassian, *tr. by* Herbert Kuhner. VWA

O how lightly in youth we achieved our disinterested. Friends. Richard Moore. SM

"O [*or* Oh], how much more doth beauty beauteous seem." Shakespeare. *Fr.* Sonnets, LIV. AWP; EIL; OBEV; OBSC; PoE

O how my mind. Confusion. Christopher Hervey. BXAP; Par

O! how my poet's-spirit doth it vex. Henry F. Lott. PF

O! How my thoughts do beat me. *Unknown.* OBSC

O how often I have thought of those tears. The Death of Atahuallpa. Valery Larbaud, *tr. by* William Jay Smith. CT

O how righteous, X, are all your days! The Separateness of the Fingers in Trance. Kit Robinson. IAT

O! How shall I picture, in delicate strain. Miss Emily Brittle Sails for India. Sir George Dallas. *Fr.* India Guide, The; or, Journal of a Voyage to the East Indies in 1780. NOEC

O How Sweet Are Thy Words! Anne Steele. BLRP

O, how this spring of love resembleth. This Spring of Love. Shakespeare. *Fr.* The Two Gentlemen of Verona, I, iii. ChTr

O how this sullen, careless world. The Idiot. John Ashbery. *Fr.* Two Sonnets. VGW

O, hungry heart. Heart-Hungry. Josephine D. Henderson Heard. CBWP-4

O hurry where by water among the trees. The Ragged Wood. W. B. Yeats. GBL

O, hush thee, my babie [*or* baby], thy sire was a knight. Lullaby of an Infant Chief. Sir Walter Scott. EnRP; FaPON; OxBChV

O! hush thee, my darling, sleep soundly my son. *Unknown, tr. by* Alice Lucas. TrJP

O hushed October morning mild. October. Robert Frost. GoJo

O Hymen! O Hymenee! Walt Whitman. ErPo

O hymned in many a poet's strain. A Legend of Alhambra. Richard Chenevix Trench. OBTV

O! I do love thee, meek simplicity. To Simplicity. Samuel Taylor Coleridge. *Fr.* Sonnets Attempted in the Manner of Contemporary Writers. Son

O, I don't give a shit. On the Death of Robert Lowell. Eileen Myles. UL

O I feel like the kinks in the paws of the Sphinx! Hotel Continental. William Jay Smith. WaP

"O I forbid you, maidens a' [*or* all]." Tam Lin. *Unknown.* ESPB; FaBoBa; NOBE; OBEV; OBNV; OxBB; OxBS
(Tamlane.) WSC

O I gaed furth and far awa to see what he cou'd see. Dolomites. J. C. Milne. PoSH

O I had a future. I Had a Future. Patrick Kavanagh. BIrV; NoAM

O I had been to sunny Spain. On First Looking into Chapman's Homer. I. T. Griffiths. BXAP

O, I hae come from far away. The Witch's Ballad. William Bell Scott. NOBVV; OBEV
(Witches' Ballad, The.) CH

O I Have Dined on This Delicious Day. Richard Snyder. TDD

O, I wad like to ken—to the beggar-wife says I. The Spaewife. Robert Louis Stevenson. BrPo; OxBS

O I went into the stable. Our Goodman. *Unknown.* AmFP; ESPB, (A *and* B *vers.*)

O I will sing to you a sang. The Clerk's Twa Sons O Owsenford. *Unknown.* ESPB

O if all the young maidens was blackbirds and thrushes. Blackbirds and Thrushes. *Unknown.* GBP

O, if Thou knew'st how Thou Thyself doest harm. *See* Oh, if Thou knew'st how Thou Thyself doest harm.

O, Inexpressible as Sweet. George Edward Woodberry. *Fr.* Wild Eden, VII. AA

O, insatiable monster! Could'st thou not. A Requiem. Mary Weston Fordham. CBWP-2

O interminable desires, O futile hope. Louise Labé, *tr. fr. French by* Willis Barnstone. BoWoP

"O, is that what they think!" Physics. Cees Buddingh', *tr. by* James S. Holmes. DuIn

O Isis, Mother of God, to thee I pray! Prayer to Isis. Christina Walsh. BrRo

O "Isles" (as Byron said) "of Greece!" The Schoolmaster Abroad. Sir Owen Seaman. OBTV

O islets green, Nature's immortal gems. Hymn to the Thousand Islands. Henrietta Cordelia Ray. CBWP-3

O it fell out upon a day. The Laird o Drum. *Unknown.* ESPB

O, it is great for our country to die, where ranks are contending! Elegiac. James Gates Percival. AA

O, it is hard to work for God. The Right Must Win. Frederick William Faber. PWR

O Italy, I see the lonely towers. To Italy. Giacomo Leopardi, *tr. by* Romilda Rendel. AWP

O it's best to be a total boor. David O'Bruadair, *tr. by* Thomas Kinsella. NOIV

O it's up in the Highlands, and along the sweet Tay. Bonnie James Campbell. *Unknown.* ESPB

O Jean Baptiste, pourquoi. Pourquoi You Greased. *Unknown.* ChTr

O Jean, my Jean, when the bell ca's the congregation. Tam i' the Kirk. Violet Jacob. GBL; GoTS

O Jellon Grame sat in Silver Wood. Jellon Grame. *Unknown.* EBEV; ESPB; OxBB

O Jenny, don't sobby! vor I shall be true. William Barnes. BoLoP

O Jesus Christ, True Light of God, *with music.* John F. Ernst. AH

O Jesus, I have promised. To the End. John E. Bode. BLRP

O Jesus, My Savior, I Know Thou Art Mine. Caleb J. Taylor. AH

O John "Doctor" Donne, O John "Doctor" Donne. Death Again. T. Hope. BXAP

O Johney was as brave a knight. Johnie Scot. *Unknown.* ESPB

O Jojina my love, I always miss you. Jojina, My Love. *Zulu Oral Tradition, tr. by* H. Tracy. WTO

O joy of creation. What the Bullet Sang. Bret Harte. AA; OBEV

O joy! that in our embers. Wordsworth. *Fr.* Ode: Intimations of Immortality from Recollections of Early Childhood. Prf

"O joy too high for my low style to show!" Sir Philip Sidney. *Fr.* Astrophel and Stella, LXIX. NAEL-1; TrGrPo

O joys [*or* joyes]! Infinite sweetness! with what flowers [*or* flowres]. The Morning Watch. Henry Vaughan. LiTB; MePo; OBS; SeCePo

O Juniper, that grasps the rocks of the beach. Tabito. *Fr.* Manyo Shu. Ma

O Kane, O Ku-ka-Pao. Old Creation Chant. *Unknown.* WTO

O Kane, O Lono of the blue sea. *Unknown, tr. fr. Hawaiian by* N. B. Emerson. WTO

O keen pellucid air! nothing can lurk. A Brilliant Day. Charles Tennyson Turner. NOBVV

O Keeper of the Sacred Key. Forceythe Willson. *Fr.* In State. AA

O keeper of the tavern. Mohammad Taqi Mir, *tr. by* Ahmed Ali. GoT

O Kentucky! my parents were driving. A Poem of the Forty-eight States. Kenneth Koch. NNaP; OBAL

O King, I know you gave me poison. Mirabai, *tr. fr. Medieval Hindi by* Usha Nilsson. PBWP; WPOW

O King of Saints, We Give Thee Praise and Glory. Mary A. Thomson. AH

O King of the Friday. *Unknown, tr. by* Douglas Hyde. BIrV

O King of the starry sky. Starry Sky. *Unknown, tr. by* Sean O'Faolain. AnIL

O King of the World. *Unknown, tr. by* Douglas Hyde. WTO

"O kiss, which dost those ruddy gems impart." Sir Philip Sidney. *Fr.* Astrophel and Stella, LXXXI. NAEL-1; Son

O knit me, that am crumbled dust! the heape. Distraction. Henry Vaughan. SeCP

O Lady amorous,/ Merciless lady. Canzonetta: A Bitter Song to His Lady. Pier Moronelli da Fiorenza, *tr. by* Dante Gabriel Rossetti. AWP; OBVE

O lady full of guile. Geoffrey Keating, *tr. by* Thomas Kinsella. NOIV

O lady leal and lovesomest. To Our Lady. Robert Henryson. ACP

O Lady Moon. Christina Rossetti. OxBChV

O lady of all truths bright light going forth. Enheduanna, *tr. fr. Sumerian by* Anne Draffkorn Kilmer *based on a text by* W. W. Hallo *and* J. J. A. van Dijk. *Fr.* Inanna Exalted. WPOW

O Lady, rock never your young son young. Young Hunting. *Unknown.* ESPB; OxBB

O lady, when the tipped cup of the moon blessed you. Ted Hughes. LLLT

O Lamb Give Me My Salt. *Unknown, tr. fr. Ibo by* Dennis C. Osadebay. PBA

O Land Beloved. George Edward Woodberry. *Fr.* My Country. PAH

O Land, of every land the best. Peace. Phoebe Cary. PAH

O land of mine where I was bred. A. K. Tolstoy, *tr. by* Alan Myers. AAA

O lapwing, thou fliest around the heath. O Lapwing! Blake. FaBoEE; PBBP

(O Lapwing.) ChTr

O, Lay Thy Hand in Mine, Dear! Gerald Massey. EBVV

O leafy yellowness you create for me. October. Patrick Kavanagh. CIP; GTBS-P

O lend to me, sweet nightingale. The Daughter of Mendoza. Mirabeau Buonaparte Lamar. AA

O let me be in loving nice. Punctilio. Mary Elizabeth Coleridge. OBEV

O let the days spin out. Leave Poem. Anne Bulley. CN

O let the solid ground. Tennyson. *Fr.* Maud, *pt.* I, xi. NAEL-2; NOBVV

O let your strong imagination turn. Sir John Collings Squire. *Fr.* The Birds. PBBP

O Life That Maketh All Things New. Samuel Longfellow. AH

O, Lift One Thought. Samuel Taylor Coleridge. *See* Epitaph: "Stop, Christian passer-by!—Stop, child of God."

O Light Invisible, we praise Thee! T. S. Eliot. *Fr.* The Rock, Chorus X. TrPWD

O Light, 'tis I, who from death's other shores. Helen. Paul Valéry, *tr. by* William Jay Smith. CT

O lily of the King! low lies the silver wing. Lillium Regis. Francis Thompson. WGRP

O, listen for a moment, lads, and hear me tell my tale. Jim Jones. *Unknown.* CBAP; PoAu-1

(Jim Jones at Botany Bay.) GBP

O listen, gude peopell, to my tale. The Laird o' Logie. *Unknown.* CH; ESPB, (A *and* B *vers.*)

O [*or* Oh] listen, listen, ladies gay! Rosabelle. Sir Walter Scott. *Fr.* The Lay of the Last Minstrel, VI. BeLS; GTBS; GTBS-P

(Harold's Song: Rosabelle.) EnRP

O little buds, break not so fast! Budding-Time Too Brief. Evaleen Stein. AA

"O little cloud," the virgin said, "I charge thee tell to me." Blake. *Fr.* The Book of Thel. OBD

O little fleet! that on thy quest divine. Columbus and the Mayflower. Richard Monckton Milnes. PAH

O little friend, your nose is ready; you sniff. Dog. Harold Monro. MoBrPo

O little hearts, beat home, beat home. Swallow Song. Marjorie Pickthall. CaP

O little Land of lapping seas. The Promised Land. Jessie E. Sampter. TrJP

O little mouse, so frightened of each sound. O Pity Our Small Size. Benjamin Rosenbaum. TrJP

O little self, within whose smallness lies. John Masefield. *Fr.* Sonnets. WGRP

O little soldier with the golden helmet. Dandelion. Hilda Conkling. FaPON; PDV; RHPC

O Little Town of Bethlehem. Phillips Brooks. AA; AH, *with music;* AnAmPo; BLRP; FaFP; FaPON; GN; OHIP; WBLP; WGRP

O little well, you give no water. *Gond Oral Tradition, tr. by* V. Elwin *and* S. Hivale. WTO

O littleblood, hiding from the mountains in the mountains. Littleblood. Ted Hughes. *Fr.* Crow. PoE

O Living Always, Always Dying. Walt Whitman. NOBA

O living image of eternal youth! Trilby. Alice Brown. AA

"O living will that shalt endure." Tennyson. *Fr.* In Memoriam A. H. H., CXXXI. FaBoBe

(Prayer, The: "O living will that shalt endure.") WGRP

O London is a dainty place. London Is a Fine Town. *Unknown.* CoMu

O lonely bay of Trinity. The Cable Hymn. Whittier. PAH

"O lonely workman, standing there." In the Moonlight. Thomas Hardy. *Fr.* Satires of Circumstance, XV. BrPo; NoAM

O lonesome sea-gull, floating far. Sea-Birds. Elizabeth Akers Allen. AA; FaBoBe

O look how the loops and balloons of bloom. Stormy Day. W. R. Rodgers. LiTB

O, Lord/ If in life eternal. "Ping Hsin," *tr. fr. Chinese by* Kai-yu Hsu. *Fr.* Spring Waters. WPOW

O Lord,/ Thou hast given me a body. Thanksgiving for the Body. Thomas Traherne. ImOP

O Lord, Almighty God. *Unknown.* AH

O Lord, at Joseph's humble bench. The Carpenter. George Macdonald. TrPWD

O Lord, Bow Down Thine Ear. Thomas Prince. AH

O Lord, grant each his own, his own death indeed. Rainer Maria Rilke, *tr. fr. German by* J. B. Leishman. *Fr.* The Book of Hours. OBD

O Lord, How Lovely Is the Place. *Unknown.* AH

O Lord, I been a-working. Trifling Women. *Unknown.* AmFP

O Lord, I Come Pleading. James Gilchrist Lawson. BLRP

O Lord, I pray/ That for this day. Not to Be Ministered To. Maltbie Davenport Babcock. TrPWD

O Lord, I pray: that for each happiness. Petition. John Drinkwater. TrPWD

O Lord, I wonder at thy lov. Thomas Traherne. *Fr.* The Approach. TrPWD

O Lord, in me there lieth nought. Psalm CXXXIX. Bible, *O.T.*, *paraphrased by* Countess of Pembroke. NOCV; OBSC; WPE

O Lord, in your courtesy. Praise of Diseases. Jacopone da Todi, *tr. by* L. R. Lind. PFI

O Lord! methought, what pain it was to drown! A Dream of Wrecks. Shakespeare. *Fr.* King Richard III, I, iv. ChTr

O Lord of Life. Washington Gladden. AH

O Lord, our God, Thy mighty hand. Peace Hymn of the Republic. Henry Van Dyke. AH

(America Befriend.) OPP

O Lord our Lord, how excellent is thy name. Bible, *O.T.* *Fr.* Psalms, VIII. AWP; NAWM-1

(How Glorious Is Thy Name.) TrJP

(Psalm VIII: "O Lord, that rul'st the human heart," *paraphrased by* Christopher Smart) OBVE

(Psalm VIII: "O Lorde oure governoure, howe excellent is thy name.") OBVE, *tr. by* Miles Coverdale.

(What Is Man?) TrGrPo

"Lord what is man, that he should find." *Fr.* 4-6 *paraphrased by* Christopher Smart.

When I Consider Thy Heavens. FaPON, 3-5; ImOP, 3-8.

O Lord, rebuke me not in thine anger. Bible, *O.T.* *Fr.* Psalms, VI.

(Psalm VI: "O lord, I dred, and that I did not dred.") OBVE, *ad. by* Sir Thomas Wyatt.

O Lord, Save We Beseech Thee. *Unknown.* TrJP

O Lord, seek us, O Lord, find us. Lord, Save Us, We Perish. Christina Rossetti. TrPWD

O Lord, since we have feasted thus. Grace after Dinner. Burns. FaBoEE

O Lord, That Art My God and King. John Craig. AH

O Lord, the hard-won miles. Paul Laurence Dunbar. TrPWD

O Lord, Thou Hast Been to the Land. *Unknown.* AH

O Lord, Thou Hast Enticed Me. Bible, *O.T. Fr.* Jeremiah, XX: 7-10. TrJP

O Lord, thou hast searched me. Bible, *O.T. Fr.* Psalms, CXXXIX.
   (Psalm CXXXIX: Domine, Probasti.) WPE
   (Psalm CXXXIX: "O Lord, in me there lieth nought", *paraphrased by* the Countess of Pembroke) NOCV; OBSC, (1-6); OBVE, (7-10).

O Lord, Turn Not Away Thy Face. *At. to* John Marckant. AH

O Lord, we come this morning. Listen, Lord—[a Prayer]. James Weldon Johnson. BANP; BPo

O Lord! who seest from yon starry height. The Image of God. Francesco de Aldana, *tr. by* Longfellow. WGRP

O Lord whose mercy never fails. Pro Libra Mea. Joseph I. C. Clarke. TrPWD

O Lord, why must thy poets peak and pine. Priest or Poet. Sir Shane Leslie. WGRP

O Lord, you know my inmost hope and thought. My Inmost Hope. Sarah Copia Sullam. TrJP

O Loss of sight, of thee I most complain. The Blindness of Samson. Milton. *Fr.* Samson Agonistes. LiTB
   "I, dark in light, exposed." TrGrPo, 5 *ll.*

O lost moon sisters. Diane di Prima. *Fr.* Loba. ER

O love, Answer. Anne Ridler. SeCePo

O love, be fed with apples while you may. Sick Love. Robert Graves. BoLoP; CMoP; EBEV; GTBS-P; HAP; NOBE; OAEL-2
   (O Love in Me.) FaBoMo

O Love Divine, That Stooped to Share. Oliver Wendell Holmes. *Fr.* The Professor at the Breakfast Table, *ch.* 11. AH
   (Hymn of Trust.) AA; TrPWD

O Love, give me a passionate heart. Irene Rutherford McLeod. TrPWD

O Love, how strangely sweet. John Marston. ElL

O love, how thou art tired out with rhyme! Of the Theme of Love. Margaret Cavendish Newcastle. OxBSP

O love, I never, never thought. Juan II of Castile, *tr. by* George Ticknor. AWP

O Love in Me. Robert Graves. *See* O love, be fed with apples while you may.

O, love, in your sweet name enough. Anne Finch. *Fr.* Essay on Marriage. FaBoTw

O Love, Love, Love! O withering might! Fatima. Tennyson. GBL; SeCePo; UnPo

O Love, my love, and perfect bliss! Medieval Norman Song. *Unknown, tr. by* John Addington Symonds. AWP

O love! O glory! what are you who fly. Byron. *Fr.* Don Juan, VII. OAEL-2

O Love, O thou that, for my fealty. Sonnet: To Love, In Great Bitterness. Cino da Pistoia, *tr. by* Dante Gabriel Rossetti. AWP

O love of God, God's love, love that alone. For All Sorts and Conditions. Norman Nicholson. EaLo

O Love of God incarnate. Incarnate Love. Wilbur Fisk Tillett. BLRP

O love, so sweet at first. Disarmed. Laura Redden Searing. AA

O Love, That Dost with Goodness Crown. John White Chadwick. TrPWD

O Love That Lights the Eastern Sky. Louis FitzGerald Benson. AH

O Love That Wilt Not Let Me Go. George Matheson. TrPWD; WGRP

O love, the interest itself in thoughtless heaven. W. H. Auden. EBEV; FaBoMo

O love triumphant over guilt and sin. Frederic Lawrence Knowles. TrPWD

O love, turn from the unchanging sea, and gaze. October. William Morris. *Fr.* The Earthly Paradise. OBNC

O love, what hours were thine and mine. The Daisy. Tennyson. EnLoPo; NOBVV; OBNC; PoEL-5

O Love, when in my day of doom. The Gardener. Laurence Housman. TrPWD

O Love, who all this while hast urged me on. Canzone: To Love and to His Lady. Guido delle Colonne, *tr. by* Dante Gabriel Rossetti. AWP

O Love, whose patient pilgrim feet. The Golden Wedding. David Gray. FaBoBe

O, loveliest throat of all sweet throats. Edna St. Vincent Millay. *See* Memorial to D. C.: Let them bury your big eyes.

O lovely age of gold! Tasso, *tr. fr. Italian. Fr.* Aminta. OBVE, *tr. by* Leigh Hunt.

   (Golden Age, The.) AWP, *tr. by* Leigh Hunt; PFI, *tr. by* Leigh Hunt.
   (Pastoral[1], A: "Oh [*or* O] happy golden age.") OAEL-1, *tr. by* Samuel Daniel; OBSC, *tr. by* Samuel Daniel; PoEL-2, *tr. by* Samuel Daniel.

O lovely April, rich and bright. Gustave Kahn, *tr. by* Ludwig Lewisohn. TrJP

O lovely maiden, thou hast drawn my heart. The Unhappy Lover. Judah Al-Harizi, *tr. by* J. Chotzner. TrJP

O lovely O most charming pug. A Sonnet on a Monkey. Marjory Fleming. FaBoCo; FaFP; FiBHP
   (Sonnet, A: "O lovely O most charming pug.") FaBoCo; NBLV

O [*or* Oh], lovers' eyes are sharp to see. The Maid of Neidpath. Sir Walter Scott. BeLS; EnRP; GTBS; GTBS-P

O ludicrous and pensive trinity. Romeo and Juliet. H. Phelps Putnam. ErPo

O luely, luely, cam she in. The Tryst [*or* Trysting Place]. William Soutar. EBEV; ErPo; GoTS; OxBS
   (Trysting Place, The.) BoLoP

O Lusty May, with Flora queen! Lusty May. *Unknown.* OBEV
   (Four May Poems.) OxBS

O luxury! Thou curst by Heaven's decree. Goldsmith. *Fr.* The Deserted Village. BIrV

O Lyric Love. Robert Browning. *Fr.* The Ring and the Book, I. FiP

O Lyric Love. Winfield Townley Scott. VGW

"O madam, I will give to thee a new silk gown." My Man John. *Unknown.* OBET

O madam, I will give to you the keys of Canterbury. The Keys of Canterbury. *Unknown.* AmFP

O Magi of the East, did you continue? The Magi in Europe. Khalil Hawi, *tr. by* Diana Der Hovanessian *and* Lena Jayyusi. MAP

O magic sleep! O comfortable bird. Life Again. Keats. *Fr.* Endymion [a Poetic Romance]. SeCePo

O maister deere and fader reverent! Thomas Hoccleve. *Fr.* De Regimine Principum. EBEV

O Maistres Myn. *Unknown. See* O Mistress Mine ("O mistress mine, till you I me commend").

O make me a mask and a well to shut from your spies. Dylan Thomas. PoA

O Mally's Meek, Mally's Sweet. Burns. GN

O Man of mine own people, I alone. The Jew to Jesus. Florence Kiper Frank. WGRP

O man of the seashore. What Her Girl Friend Said to Him When He Wanted to Come by Day. Ammuvanar, *tr. by* A. K. Ramanujan. PLW

O! Mankinde. See! Here, My Heart. *Unknown.* MeEL

O, many a day have I made good ale in the glen. *See* Oh, many a day have I made good ale in the glen.

O many-petaled light where. Lament of my Father, Lakota. Paula Gunn Allen. NOVW

O Marduk, lord of countries, terrible one. *Unknown, tr. fr. Assyrian. Fr.* Hymn to Marduk. WGRP

O Martyred Spirit. George Santayana. TrPWD

O [*or* Oh] Mary, at the window be. Mary Morison. Burns. EnRP; GTBS; GTBS-P; OBEV; OxBS; TrGrPo
   (Song: Mary Morison.) AWP

O [*or* Oh] Mary, go and call the cattle home. The Sands of Dee. Charles Kingsley. *Fr.* Alton Locke, *ch.* 26. BeLS; CH; EBVV; FaBoPP; FaPON; FaPoR; GN; WBLP

O Mary Hamilton to the kirk is gane. Mary Hamilton. *Unknown.* NOBE; OxBB

O Mary Mary lying on the wheel. Visitor's Parking. Anne Szumigalski. NOBC

O Master, Let Me Walk with Thee. Washington Gladden. AH, *with music;* PWR; WGRP
   (Service.) BLRP

O Master Masons. Ernst Toller, *tr. fr. German by* Ashley Dukes. TrJP

O Master of the heart, whose magic skill. To the Author of Clarissa. Thomas Edwards. Son

O Master-Workman of the Race. Jay Thomas Stocking. AH, *with music*

O Matre Pulchra. Charles Spear. ATNZ

O [*or* Oh] may I join the choir invisible. The Choir Invisible. "George Eliot." EBVV; OBD; OBNC; OHFP; WBLP; WGRP

O may I with myself agree. John Dyer. *Fr.* Grongar Hill. TrGrPo

O May she comes, and May she goes. The Bonny Hind. *Unknown.* ESPB
   (Bonny Heyn, The.) OxBB

O me, oh my, oh you. Does the Spearmint Lose Its Flavor on the Bedpost Overnight? Billy Rose. OBAL

"O me! what eyes hath love put in my head." Shakespeare. *Fr.* Sonnets, CXLVIII.
   (Blind Love.) GTBS; GTBS-P

"O 'Melia, my dear, this does everything crown!" The Ruined Maid. Thomas Hardy. BoLoP; BrPo; CMoP; ErPo; FiBHP; HeIP; LiTB; NAEL-2; NBLV; NOBL; NoP; NOP; OxBTC; SCV; TEP; WeW

O memory, could I but loose thee now. Lindamira's Complaint. Mary Sidney Wroth, Countess of Montgomery. *Fr.* Urania. WPE

O Memory, Thou Fond Deceiver.' Goldsmith. *Fr.* The Captivity, I. OxBSP
   (Memory.) OBEV

O men from the fields! A Cradle Song. Padraic Colum. TIRV
   (Lullaby.) WTO

O men, the beautiful world is going to be spoiled. Suez Crisis. *Somali Oral Tradition, tr.* by B. W. Andrezjewski. WTO

O men, walk on the hills. Maxwell Bodenheim. TrJP

O merciful Father, my hope is in thee! Prayer Before Execution. Mary Queen of Scots, *tr.* by John Fawcett. WGRP

O merciful God, hear this our request. A Prayer to Be Said When Thou Goest to Bed. Francis Seager. OxBChV

O Merlin in your crystal cave. Merlin. Edwin Muir. FaBoTw; OxBS; RB

O! mestress, why. Distant as the Duchess of Savoy. *Unknown.* MeEL

O Michael, you are at once the enemy. Garden-Lion. "Evelyn Hayes." ChTr

O mickle yeuks the keckle doup. Justice to Scotland. *At.* to Burns. NBLV

O might those sighes and teares returne againe. John Donne. *Fr.* Holy Sonnets, III. OBS

O Mighty Nothing! unto thee. And He Answered Them Nothing. Richard Crashaw. MePo

O Mighty, powerful, strong one of Ashur. *Unknown, tr. fr.* Assyrian. *Fr.* Hymn to Marduk. WGRP

O mighty river! strong, eternal Will. The Great River. Henry Van Dyke. TrPWD

O Mind of God, Broad as the Sky. Oliver Huckel. TrPWD

O mine own sweet heart. Simon and Susan. *Unknown.* OxBoLi

O Minume Bay, chosen by all Yashima's shipmen. Tanabe Sakimaro. *Fr.* Manyo Shu. Ma

O miserable sorrow, withouten cure. Sir Thomas Wyatt. SiPS

O Mister Giraffe, you make me laugh. Mr. Giraffe. Geoffrey LaPage. OnUR

O [or Oh] Mistress Mine [Where Are You Roaming?]. Shakespeare. *Fr.* Twelfth Night, II, iii. AWP; CTC; EIL; ELP; FaBV; FaFP; GBL; HAP; HeIP; InPS; LiTB; NAEL-1; NBLV; NOBE; NoP; OAEL-1; OxBoLi; OxBSP; PoRA; TrGrPo
   (Carpe Diem.) GTBS; GTBS-P
   (Feste's Song ("O mistress mine! where are you roaming?").) BoLoP; OBSC
   (Song: "O mistress mine! where are you roaming?.") FiP; GoJo
   (Sweet-and-Twenty.) OBEV; PoE

O Mistress Mine ("O mistress mine, till you I me commend"). *Unknown.* GoTS; MeEL
   (O Maistres Myn.) OxBS

O money is the meat in the cocoanut. Money. *Unknown.* AS

O money, money, tell me why. N. M. Yazykov, *tr.* by Alan Myers. AAA

O months of blossoming, months of transfigurations. The Lilacs and the Roses. Louis Aragon, *tr.* by Louis MacNeice. OBWP; RHTwFP

O moon at dawn. Tameyo, *tr.* by Steven D. Carter. WFTW

O moon god seated high in heaven. Prince Yuhara. *Fr.* Manyo Shu. Ma

O Moon, Mr. Moon. Mr. Moon. Bliss Carman. FaPON

O Moon! the oldest shades 'mong oldest trees. Keats. *Fr.* Endymion [a Poetic Romance], III. EnRP

O more, and more! this was so well. Ben Jonson. *Fr.* Pleasure Reconciled to Virtue. NAEL-1

O Morning-Maker, deign that ray. Plea for Hope. Francis Carlin. TrPWD

O Mors! Quam Amara Est Memoria Tua Homini Pacem Habenti in Substantiis Suis. Ernest Dowson. BrPo; OBMV

O mortal folk you may behold and see. The Epitaph of Graunde [or La Graunde] Amoure. Stephen Hawes. *Fr.* The Pastime of Pleasure, 42. ChTr; EBEV; FaBoRV; OBSC
   (Epitaph, An: "O mortal folk you may behold and see.") ACP; OBEV; TrGrPo
   (Epitaphy of la Graunde Amoure.) FaBoEE

O mortal man, that lives by bread. *At.* to Julius Caeser Ibbetson. ChTr; FaBoEE
   (Sally Birkett's Ale.)

O most unconscious daisy! To a School-Girl. Neilson. PoAu-1

O Mother Dear, Jerusalem. "F. B. P." WGRP

O Mother-heart! when fast the arrows flew. Niobe. Henrietta Cordelia Ray. CBWP-3

O mother, I longs to get married. *Unknown.* Whistle, Daughter, Whistle. AmFP; *sl. diff.*; ErPo; OBET; OxNR, *shorter vers.*

O mother, lay your hand on my brow! The Sick Child. Stevenson. CH

O mother-maid! O maiden-mother free! Chaucer. *Fr.* The Canterbury Tales: The Prologue of the Prioress's Tale.

O mountain O dolomites like a bird's heart beneath my childlike hands. Inclination. Aimé Césaire, *tr.* by Michael Benedikt. POS

O mud, mud, how fluid! Words Heard, by Accident, over the Phone. Sylvia Plath. AnAn

O [or Oh] my aged uncle Arly! Incidents in the Life of My Uncle Arly. Edward Lear. FaBoNo; FPL; MoShBr; NA; OAEL-2; OxBoLi; TrGrPo

O My Belly. *Unknown.* GBP

O my black[e] soul[e]! now thou art summoned. *See* Oh my black[e] soul[e]! now thou art summoned.

O my body! I dare not desert the likes of you in other men and women, nor the likes of the parts of you. Walt Whitman. *Fr.* I Sing the Body Electric. ErPo

O My Bonny, Bonny May. *Unknown.* GBP

O my brother I heard u. Before/ and After. Jewel C. Latimore. JB

O my comrade, it is cold. Cold and Heat. *Unknown, tr.* by M. W. Beckwith. WTO

O my cousin, my beloved. Girl's Song. *Unknown, tr.* by Willard Trask. LLLT

O my coy darling, still. Ode to a Dressmaker's Dummy. Donald Justice. NoAM

O [or Oh] my dark Rosaleen. Dark Rosaleen. *At.* to Owen Roe MacWard *and to* Hugh O'Donnell, *tr.* by James Clarence Mangan. ACP; AnIL; AWP; BIrV; CH; EnRP; NOIV; OBEV

O my deir hert, young Jesus sweit. Balulalow. John James *and* Robert Wedderburn. EaLo; OBEV

O my earliest love, who, ere I number'd. First Love. Charles Stuart Calverley. FiBHP

O my eyes where are you, you that found a face so wonderful? Old Age. Milán Füst, *tr.* by Edwin Morgan. MHuP

O my God, thou hast wounded me with love. A Confession. Paul Verlaine, *tr.* by Arthur Symons. WGRP

O my Heart, my Mother, my Heart, my Mother. He Approacheth the Hall of Judgment. *Unknown, tr. fr. Egyptian* by Robert Hillyer. *Fr.* Book of the Dead. AWP

O My Honey, Take Me Back. *Unknown.* AS

O my hornbill husband, you have a bad smell. Lament for a Husband. *Unknown, tr.* by Don Laycock. BoWoP

O My Invisible Estate. Bruce Smith. Son

O my lady, the Anunna, the great gods. Inanna and the Anunna. Enheduanna, *tr.* by Aliki *and* Willis Barnstone. BoWoP

O my land! O my love! Lament for Banba. *At.* to Egan O'Rahilly, *tr.* by James Clarence Mangan. AWP

O my life is so simple and the world. The Fiddlehead. David McFadden. NeAC

O my Lord, if I worship you from fear of Hell. Rabi'a al-Adawiyya, *tr. fr. Arabic* by Willis Barnstone. BoWoP

O my Lord, the stars glitter and eyes of men are closed. Rabi'a al-Adawiyya. BoWoP

O my lost husband! let me ever mourn. Andromache's Lamentation. Homer, *tr. fr. Greek* by Congreve. *Fr.* The Iliad, XXIV. OBVE

O my love/ The pretty towns. Kenneth Patchen. VGW

O my love, my wife! Shakespeare. *Fr.* Romeo and Juliet, V, iii. OBD

O my lover, blind me. The Tired Woman. Anna Wickham. MoBrPo

O my Lucasia, let us speak our love. To My Lucasia, in Defence of Declared Friendship. Katherine Phillips. MeLP

O my luve's like a red, red rose. A Red, Red Rose. Burns. AWP; BoLoP; ChTr; FaBV; FaFP; FF; GBL; HAP; HeIP; InvP; NAEL-2; NIP; NOBE; NOEC; NoP; OAEL-1; OBEV; OxBS; PoEL-4; PoLF; PrIm; SoSe; TEP
   (My Luve.) FPL; TrGrPo

O My Mother Isle! ("Not yet enslaved, not wholly vile."). Samuel Taylor Coleridge. *Fr.* Ode on the Departing Year. FaBoPP

O My Mother Isle! ("O native Britain! O my Mother Isle!"). Samuel Taylor Coleridge. *Fr.* Fears in Solitude. FaBoPP

O My Poor Darling. Wilfred Watson. EnLoPo

O my pretty pink frock. The Pink Frock. Thomas Hardy. OxBSP

O my sinner, let us spend this night together. Tonight, at Least, My Sinner. *Gond Oral Tradition, tr.* by V. Elwin *and* S. Hivale. WTO

O my son,/ Only your name remains. Lament for Taramoana. Makere, *tr.* by Barry Mitcalfe. WTO

O my son, born on a winter's morn. Noho-mai-te-Rangi, *tr.* by Barry Mitcalfe. WTO

O my songs. Coda. Ezra Pound. NOBA

O my soul be patient, she is very beautiful. She Is Not for Me. *Gond Oral Tradition, tr. by* V. Elwin *and* S. Hivale. WTO
O my soul, keep the rest unknown! He Resolves to Say No More. Thomas Hardy. TEP
O my soul, my string of gems. Princess Shikishi, *tr. by* Geoffrey Bownas *and* Anthony Thwaite. PeBJV
O My Swallows! Ernst Toller, *tr. fr. German by* Ashley Dukes. TrJP
O my thoughts' sweet food, my only owner. Lady My Treasure. Sir Philip Sidney. GBL
O my trade it is the rarest one. The Stranger's Song. Thomas Hardy. BrPo
O my winged ancestors! Queen Tatavane. Sándor Weöres, *tr. by* Edwin Morgan. MHuP
O native Britain! O my Mother Isle! O My Mother Isle! Samuel Taylor Coleridge. *Fr.* Fears in Solitude. FaBoPP
O Nature! I do not aspire. Nature. Henry David Thoreau. AiP; BLPL; FaBoBe
O Nectar! O Delicious Stream! Love. Thomas Traherne. SeCV-2
O Ness, let all men stand. The Song of Childbirth. *Unknown, tr. by* Eleanor Hull. TIRV
"O [*or* Oh]! Never say that I was false of heart." Shakespeare. *Fr.* Sonnets, CIX. EIL; NOBE; OBEV; OBSC
(Unchangeable, The.) GTBS; GTBS-P
O New England, thou canst not boast. A Word to New England. William Bradford. SCAP
O Night! dark Night! wrapped round with Stygian gloom! New Night Thoughts on Death; a Parody. William Whitehead. NOEC
O Night Flower. Arlindo Barbeitos, *tr. fr. Portuguese by* Donald Burness. WMBCH
O Night, O jealous Night, repugnant to my pleasures [*or* measures]. A Night Piece. *Unknown.* OBSC
(To Night.) EIL
O Night O Trembling Night. Stephen Spender. ErPo
O Night of the Crying Children. Nelly Sachs, *tr. fr. German by* Keith Bosley. VWA
O night, the ease of care, the pledge of pleasure. Night. Sir Philip Sidney. *Fr.* Arcadia. SiPS
O nightingale of woodland gay. Medieval Norman Song. *Unknown, tr. by* John Addington Symonds. AWP
O nightingale, the poet's bird. A Song about Singing. Anne Reeve Aldrich. AA
O Nightingale! Thou Surely Art. Wordsworth. PBBP
O, no iron, no Rio, no. Six of Ox Is. Lydia Tomkiw. BAP
O, No, John [*or* No John] [*or* The One Answer]. *Unknown.* ErPo; OBET; PDV
O, no more, no more, too late. *See* Oh, no more, no more.
O noble brow, so wise in thought! Washington. Mary Wingate. OHIP
O noble England, fall down upon thy knee. A Joyful [*or* Joyfull] New Ballad. Thomas Deloney. CoMu; OxBSS, *with music*
O noble Oisin, son of the king. Oisin in the Land of Youth. Michael Comyn, *tr. by* Tomás O'Flannghaile. AnIL
O nothing in this corporal earth of man. Francis Thompson. *Fr.* The Heart. OBMV
(All's Vast.) MoAB; MoBrPo; Son
(Correlated Greatness.) GTBS-P
O, now for ever/ Farewell the tranquil mind! Farewell content. Shakespeare. *Fr.* Othello, III, iii. TrGrPo
O now I know: a smile. Rest O Sun I Cannot. Joseph Tusiani. GoYe
O Now the Drenched Land Wakes. Kenneth Patchen. PoA
O now you come in rut. To Frighten a Storm. Gladys Cardiff. CDW; STE
O nymph, compar'd with whose young bloom. To Lady Anne Fitzpatrick, When about Five Years Old, with a Present of Shells, 1772. Horace Walpole. NOEC
O-o-o-oh, lil' man. Chahcoal Man. *Unknown.* AS
O once I loved a bonnie lass. Burns. FL
O only Source of all our light and life. Qui Laborat, Orat. Arthur Hugh Clough. TrPWD
O, Open the Door to Me, O! Burns. *See* Open the Door to Me, Oh!
O, Opportunity, thy guilt is great. Opportunity. Shakespeare. *Fr.* The Rape of Lucrece. LiTB; OBSC; PoEL-2
(Outcry upon Opportunity, An.) NOBE
O oriole, yellow bird. *Unknown, tr. by* Arthur Waley. BoS
O [*or* Oh] Paddy, dear, and [*or* an'] did you hear the news that's going [*or* goin'] 'round? The Wearing of [*or* Wearin' o'] the Green. *Unknown.* AnIL; AWP; FaFP; FaPoR; GBP; OxBoLi; WTO
O Paleys [*or* palace], whylom [*or* whilom] croune [*or* crown] of houses all[e]. The Complaint of Troilus. Chaucer. *Fr.* Troilus and Criseyde [*or* Criseide], V. NOBE; OBEV
O Paradise! O Paradise! Frederick William Faber. WGRP
O Parcy Reed has Crozer ta'en. Parcy Reed. *Unknown.* OxBB

"O Passenger, pray list and catch." The Levelled Churchyard. Thomas Hardy. NOBL
O Patrick, hail, who once the wand'ring race. Saint Patrick. Sir Shane Leslie. TIRV
O peerless marble marvel! what of grace. The Venus of Milo. Henrietta Cordelia Ray. CBWP-3
O peony, O pink inverted bell. A Peony for Apollo. Charles Edward Eaton. GoYe
O people-chosen! are ye not. To the Thirty-ninth Congress. Whittier. PAH
O people who live in the world. Andal, *tr. by* Willis Barnstone. BoWoP
O perfite light, quhilk schaid away. Of the Day Estivall. Alexander Hume. NOCV; OxBS
O Peter, O Apostle, hast thou seen my bright love. The Keening of Mary. *Unknown, tr. by* Padraic Pearse. TIRV
O Phoebus embattling the high wall of Ilium. Chorus: The Kings of Troy. Euripides, *tr. fr. Greek by* George Allen. *Fr.* Andromache. WaaP
O piano I heard at evening. Piano at Evening. Palea, *tr. by* M. K. Pukui *and* A. L. Korn. WTO
O pine-tree standing. Hakutsu. *Fr.* Manyo Shu. AWP
O Pioneers! John Peale Bishop. VGW
O piteous race! Judaism. Cardinal Newman. ACP
O Pity Our Small Size. Benjamin Rosenbaum. TrJP
O pitying angel, pause, and say. In Paradise. Arlo Bates. AA
O pleasant exercise of hope and joy! Wordsworth. *Fr.* The Prelude (or, Growth of a Poet's Mind): France. HAP; OBNC
("France leered me forth; the realm that I had crossed.") FaBoPV
(French Revolution, The.) FiP
(Residence in France [Continued].) PoEL-4
O Pleasing Thoughts. Thomas Lodge. *Fr.* Phyllis, I. Son
O plovers flying over the evening waves. Hitomaro. *Fr.* Manyo Shu. Ma
O, po' sinner, O, now is yo' time. What Yo' Gwine to Do When Yo' Lamp Burn Down? *Unknown.* BPo
O poet gifted with the sight divine! Milton. H. Cordelia Ray. BlSi; CBWP-3
O poet of the future! I. The Future. George Frederick Cameron. OBCV
O poet rare and old! Astræa. Whittier. AA
O poet strutting from the sandbagged portal. As One Non-Combatant to Another. George Orwell. OxBTC
O poet, what do you do? I praise. Praise. Rainer Maria Rilke. ChTr
O Polly, you might have toy'd and kist. John Gay. *Fr.* The Beggar's Opera, I, i. EnLoPo
O poppy Death!—sweet poisoner of sleep! Scylla's Lament. Thomas Hood. *Fr.* Hero and Leander. EnRP
O potent Earth, and Heaven god-built. Earth and Sky. Euripides, *tr. by* C. M. Bowra. EaLo
O pour upon my soul again. Rosalie. Washington Allston. AA
O power of Love, O wondrous mystery! Love. Katrina Trask. AA
O Powers Celestial, with what sophistry. Barnabe Barnes. *Fr.* Parthenophil and Parthenophe. EnLoPo
O, praise an' tanks! De Lord he come. Song of the Negro Boatman. Whittier. *Fr.* At Port Royal. GN
O praise God in his holiness: praise him in the firmament of his power. Psalm CL. Bible, *O.T. Fr.* Psalms.
(Laudate Dominum.) ChTr
O praying one, who long has prayed. Ask, and Ye Shall Receive. Mrs. Havens. BLRP
O precious codex [*or* code], volume, tome. To a Thesaurus. Franklin P. Adams. BLPL; NBLV
O Prince of Life, Thy Life hath tuned. The Prince of Life. John Oxenham. TrPWD
O pumpkins! O periwinkles! Wet Weather at Cannes. Edward Lear. FaBoNo
O quick quick quick, quick hear the song sparrow. Cape Ann. T. S. Eliot. *Fr.* Landscapes, V. GoJo; NAEL-2; NoAM; RB
O quondam pre-and-post-bellum. The Bitch-Kitty. Jonathan Williams. PoM
O, Rachel, your very gait. A Vilna Puzzle. Sasha Chorny, *tr. by* Daniel Weissbort. VWA
O radiant luminary of light interminable. A Prayer to the Father of [*or* in] Heaven. John Skelton. HoPM; TrPWD
O raging seas, and mighty Neptune's reign! Coming Homeward out of Spain. Barnabe Googe. EIL
O rain at seven. Virginia. Hart Crane. *Fr.* The Bridge. NAAL-2
O rain, depart with blessings. Song of the Dew. *Unknown, tr. by* Solomon Solis-Cohen. TrJP
O! raise the woefull Pillalu. An Irish Lamentation. Goethe, *tr. by* James Clarence Mangan. AWP
O [*or* Oh] rare Harry Parry. Harry Parry. *Unknown.* GBP; OxNR

O rare Narcissus! sunny-haired! Echo's Complaint. Henrietta Cordelia Ray. CBWP-3

O Reader! hast thou ever stood to see. The Holly Tree. Robert Southey. EnRP

O Realm Bejewelled. Forugh Farrokhzad, *tr. fr. Farsi by* Jascha Kessler *and* Amin Banani. WPOW

O reapers and gleaners. Harvest Song. Joseph Campbell. OFD

O Restless Heart, Be Still! Henrietta Cordelia Ray. CBWP-3

O, rich young lord, thou ridest by. Compensation. James Edwin Campbell. BANP

O Ride On, Jesus. *Unknown.* AH

O Risen Lord upon the Throne. Louis F. Benson. AH

O river, green and still. Boy in Ice. Laurie Lee. NYBP

O rocking boat, rocking boat poised on the wave. Boat Song. Henrietta Cordelia Ray. CBWP-3

O rose and hyacinth, honeysuckle and peony. Power of the Flowers. Ferenc Juhász, *tr. by* Kenneth McRobbie. MHuP

O Rose the Red and White Lil[l]y. Rose the Red and White Lil[l]y. *Unknown.* ESPB; OxBB

O Rose, thou art sick! The Sick Rose. Blake. *Fr.* Songs of Experience. AWP; BoLoP; ChER; ChTr; ELP; EnLoPo; HAP; HeIP; InPK; InPS; NAEL-2; NAWM-2; NIP; NOBE; NOEC; NoP; OAEL-2; OBNC; OxBSP; PoE; PoEL-4; PPP; RB; SoSe; TrGrPo; WeW

O Ross, thou wale of hearty cocks. To Mr. Alexander Ross. James Beattie. OxBS

O Rourk's noble fare. The Description of an Irish Feast. Aodh MacGabhrain, *tr. by* Swift. NOIV

O roving muse, recall that wondrous year. The Great Frost. John Gay. *Fr.* Trivia; or, The Art of Walking the Streets of London. SeCePo

O ruddier than the cherry! John Gay. *Fr.* Acis and Galatea. ELP; NAEL-1; NOEC

    (Song: "O ruddier than the cherry.") NOBE

O ruddy Lover. The Clover. Margaret Deland. AA

O ruined father dead, long sweetly rotten. For the Word Is Flesh. Stanley Kunitz. DiL; VGW

O sacred poesie, thou spirit of artes. Ben Jonson. *Fr.* The Poetaster, I, ii. PoEL-2

O sad for me Glen Aora. Nettles. Neil Munro. PoSH

O sailing stars! Star Song. Henrietta Cordelia Ray. CBWP-3

O sailor, come ashore. Christina Rossetti. *Fr.* Sing-Song. FM; BOTP

O Saki, hold my hand awhile. Insha Allah Khan Insha, *tr. by* Ahmed Ali. GoT

"O Sally my dear, shall I come up to see you?" Hares on the Mountain. *Unknown.* ErPo; OBET

O Sanuki of beautiful seaweed. Hitomaro. *Fr.* Manyo Shu. Ma

O Saviour of a World Undone. Leonard Withington. AH

O, saw ye bonny Lesley. Bonnie Lesley. Burns. CTC; GTBS; GTBS-P; NOBE; OBEV

    (Saw Ye Bonny Lesley.) OxBS

"O saw ye my father? or saw ye my mother?" The Grey Cock, or, Saw You My Father? *Unknown.* ESPB

O saw ye not fair Ines? Fair Ines. Thomas Hood. EnRP; OBEV

O, Saw Ye the Lass. Richard Ryan. FaBoBe

O [*or* Oh] say, can you see, by the dawn's early light. The Star-spangled Banner. Francis Scott Key. AA; AiP; AnAmPo; BLPA; FaBoBe; FAFP; FaPON; OPP; PAH; TAP; WBLP

O say, have you seen at the Willows so green. The Ballad of the Emeu. Bret Harte. NBLV

O say, my flattering heart. Loves She Like Me? Samuel Woodworth. AA

O say what is that thing call'd Light. The Blind Boy. Colley Cibber. GTBS; GTBS-P; NOEC; OxBChV

O sea goddess Nuliajuk. Magic Words for Hunting Seal. *Unknown, tr. by* Edward Field. STP

O see how narrow are our days. Prayer of the Maidens to Mary. Rainer Maria Rilke, *tr. by* Jethro Bithell. AWP

O seeded grass, thou army of little men. John Gould Fletcher. *Fr.* Irradiations, IV *or* IX [XV]. MoAmPo

O, Seeger, the night you tied the cabbie. Quarry/Rock. Paul Mariah. GLP; PeHV

O seeker of Greater Light. The Circle. Carol Coates. CaP

O! sely anker, that in thy celle. Go, Sad Complaint. Charles d'Orléans. MeEL

O shady vales, O fair enriched meads. Thomas Lodge. *Fr.* A Margarite of America. EiL; OBSC

O Shannadore, I love your daughter. The Wide Mizzoura. *Unknown.* AS

O she looked out of the window. The Two Magicians. *Unknown.* ChTr; OxBoLi

O, she walked unaware of her own increasing beauty. She Walked Unaware. Patrick MacDonogh. NeIP

O she was full of loving fuss. One of the Principal Causes of War. "Hugh MacDiarmid." OxBSP

O ship incoming from the sea. Off Rivière du Loup. Duncan Campbell Scott. OBCV

O Ship of State. Longfellow. *See* Building of the Ship, The: Thou, too, sail on, O Ship of State!

O, Shmuel My Brother! Moyshe-Leyb Halpern, *tr. fr. Yiddish by* John Hollander. PeBMYV

O Sicily, O Tuscany, where I. Easter Sunday, 1945. G. A. Borgese. NePoAM

O sight of pity, shame and dole! The Singer in the Prison. Walt Whitman. BeLS

O Silent God, Thou whose voice afar in mist and mystery. A Litany of [*or* at] Atlanta. William Edward Burghardt Du Bois. BANP; CDC; PoNe

O silent wood, I enter thee. A Silent Wood. Elizabeth Siddal. NOBVV

O silver splendor, marvelous! A Vision of Moonlight. Henrietta Cordelia Ray. CBWP-3

O [*or* Oh] silver-throated swan. The Dying Swan. T. Sturge Moore. OBMV; SeCePo

O Simplicitas. Madeleine L'Engle. *Fr.* Three Songs of Mary. OBCP; PChr

O Sing to Me of Heaven. Mary Stanley Bunce Dana. AH

Oh! sing unto my roundelay [*or* O! Synge untoe mie roundelaie]. Thomas Chatterton. *Fr.* Aella; a Tragycal Enterlude. CH; LiTB; Mes; NOBE

    (Minstrel's Song.) HAP; TrGrPo, *sl. abr.*

    (My Love Is Dead.) WiR

    (Mynstrelle's Songe ("O! synge untoe mie roundelaie").) EnLoPo; EnRP; NOEC

    (Song: "O sing into my roundelay.") OBEV

O [*or* Oh] sing unto the Lord [*or* Jehovah] a new song. Psalm XCVIII ("O sing unto the Lord."). Bible, *O.T. Fr.* Psalms. TrJP

    (Floods Clap Their Hands, The.) TrGrPo

    (O Sing unto the Lord a New Song.) EaLo

    (Sing unto Jehovah.) BLRP

O Sing unto the Lord a New Song. Bible, *O.T. See* Psalms: Psalm XCVIII ("O sing unto the Lord.").

O! sing ye a dirge for the loved and the lost. Tribute to a Lost Steamer. Mary Weston Fordham. CBWP-2

O singer of Persephone! Theocritus. Oscar Wilde. NOBE

O singing wind. The Fir-Tree. Edith Matilda Thomas. OHIP

O Sion, Haste, Thy Mission High Fulfilling. Mary A. Thomson. AH

O! sisters too. The Coventry Carol. *Unknown.* MeEL

O sixteen hundred and ninety one. The Two Witches. Robert Graves. SO

O sleep, my babe, hear not the rippling wave. Sara Coleridge. *Fr.* Phantasmion. OBNC

O Sleep, O tranquil son of noiseless Night. To Sleep. Giovanni della Casa, *tr. by* John Addington Symonds. AWP

O sleeper rise, if thou would'st see. Sleeper Rise. *Gond Oral Tradition, tr. by* V. Elwin *and* S. Hivale. WTO

O sleepy city of reeling wheelchairs. The Wheelchair Butterfly. James Tate. NoAM

O smooth flatterers, go over sea. Reflection and Advice. Ezra Pound. OBSV

O [*or* Oh] snatch'd away in beauty's bloom! Byron. EnRP; FiP; GTBS; GTBS-P

O snowflake clouds, O feath'ry clouds. Cloud Song. Henrietta Cordelia Ray. CBWP-3

O so gay, The. Children among the Tombstones. John Russell Hervey. ATNZ

O soft embalmer of the still midnight. To Sleep. Keats. ChTr; EnRP; FaBoRV; NIP; OBEV; PoEL-4; PrIm; Son; TEP

    (Sonnet to Sleep.) NAEL-2

"O soldier, O soldier, won't you marry me now." Soldier, Won't You Marry Me? *Unknown.* AmFP; OxBoLi

O soldiers, soldiers, get ye back, I pray! Saved. Adah Isaacs Menken. CBWP-1

O solo mio, hot diggety, nix. "I wather think I can." Frank O'Hara. TTTS

O solemn procession of magnificent suns. Funeral March for the Death of the Earth. Jules Laforgue, *tr. by* William Jay Smith. CT

O Solitary of the Austere Sky. Sir Charles G. D. Roberts. CaP

O solitary pine, how many. Prince Ichihara. *Fr.* Manyo Shu. Ma

O Solitude! if I must with thee dwell. Solitude. Keats. EnRP

O sometimes in the street, or in the Paris Metro. Remembrance. Antoni Slonimski, *tr. by* Frances Notley. TrJP

O Son of God, it would be sweet. Saint Columcille. NOIV

O Son of God, who seeing two things. The Son. John Donne. *Fr.* The Litanie. NOCV

O son of man, by lying tongues adored. On the Russian Persecution of the Jews. Swinburne. Son

O Son of Man, Thou Madest Known. Milton S. Littlefield. AH, *with music;* TrPWD

O son of man, when thou findest wine. Five Arabic Verses in Praise of Wine. *Unknown, tr. by* Hartwig Hirschfeld. TrJP

O son of mine, when dusk shall find thee bending. From Generation to Generation. Sir Henry Newbolt. FaBoTw

O Son of the living God. Manchán's Prayer. Saint Manchán. NOIV

O song as yet unsung! A Song as Yet Unsung. "Yehoash", *tr. by* Isidore Goldstick. TrJP

O sons of men. *Unknown, tr. fr. Arabic by* E. Powys Mathers. *Fr.* The Thousand and One Nights. OBD

O sons of men, that toil, and love with tears! The Fair Maid and the Sun. Arthur O'Shaughnessy. BeLS

O! sop of sorrow, sonkin into cair. Cresseid's Complaint against Fortune. Robert Henryson. *Fr.* The Testament of Cresseid. MeEL

O Sorrow,/ Why dost borrow. Song of the Indian Maid. Keats. *Fr.* Endymion [a Poetic Romance], IV. NOBE; OBEV (O Sorrow!, *abr.*) CH

O sorrow, cruel fellowship. Tennyson. *Fr.* In Memoriam A. H. H., III. HAP

O sorrow! He is one who jumps. Springbok. *Unknown.* PeSA

O sorrowful and ancient days. Metrum Parhemiacum Tragicum. Eugenius Vulgarius, *tr. by* Helen Waddell. WaaP

O soul, canst thou not understand. Aridity. "Michael Field." OBMV

O soul, 'tis thine in season meet. Ode on Theoxenos. Pindar. PeHV, *tr. by* John Addington Symonds

O soul, why shouldst thou downcast be? Hope Thou in God. Josephine D. Henderson Heard. CBWP-4

O Soul, with Storms Beset. Solomon Ibn Gabirol, *tr. fr. Hebrew by* Alice Lucas. TrJP

O sovereign power of love! O grief! O balm! Keats. *Fr.* Endymion [a Poetic Romance], II. EnRP; OBNC

O spare a tear for poor Tom Hood. Elegy on Thomas Hood. Martin Fagg. FaBoPa; NOBL

(Elegy: "O spare a tear for poor Tom Hood.") BXAP

O sperm, testes, paradidymus! o scrotum, septum, and rectum! Gay Epiphany. James Mitchell. PeHV

O spirit of Venus whom I adore. *Unknown.* PeHV

O spread agen your leaves an' flow'rs. The Woodlands. William Barnes. BoNaP

O spring, O spring. Ode to Spring. Walter Rollin Brooks. RAR; RHPC

O Spring, thou youthful beauty of the year. Spring. Giovanni Battista Guarini, *tr. by* Leigh Hunt. AWP

O spring's a pleasant time. Aye Waukin' O! *Unknown.* GoTS

O stagnant east-wind, palsied mare. A Room on a Garden. Wallace Stevens. NoP

O Star (the fairest one in sight). Choose Something like a Star. Robert Frost. MoAB; MoAmPo

O! Start a Revolution. D. H. Lawrence. FaBoEE

O Stay, Sweet Love. *Unknown.* TrGrPo

O stay that covetous hand! First turn all eye. Upon the Curtain of Lucasta's Picture It Was Thus Wrought. Richard Lovelace. CaPo

O steadfast trees that know. Man and Nature. Robert Kelley Weeks. AA

O stealthily-creeping *Merrimac.* The Victory-Wreck. Will M. Carleton. PAH

O stiffly shapen houses that change not. Suburbs on a Hazy Day. D. H. Lawrence. OBMV

O stony grey soil of Monaghan. Stony Grey Soil. Patrick Kavanagh. CIP

O stoodent A has gone and spent. Ballad with an Ancient Refrain. *Unknown.* NA

O strange devices that alone divide. Eyes. Walter de la Mare. BrPo

O Strassburg. *Unknown, tr. fr. German by* C. F. MacIntyre. WaaP

O strategic map of disasters, hungry America. On Walt Whitman's Birthday. Anne Waldman. UL

O Strong to Bless. Elizabeth Daryush. QFR

O strong was the wood in the ashen oar. Lament for Seán. Daniel James O'Sullivan. NeIP

O, Struck beneath the Laurel. George Edward Woodberry. *Fr.* Wild Eden, XXXIII. AA

O such a commotion under the ground. Flower Chorus. Emerson. BoTP

O Suen, the usurper Lugalanne means nothing to me! Appeal to the Moongod Nanna-Suen to Throw Out Lugalanne. Enheduanna, *tr. by* Aliki *and* Willis Barnstone. BoWoP

O suitably-attired-in-leather-boots. Fragment of a Greek Tragedy. A. E. Housman. CenHV; FaBoNo; NOBL; Par

O sun, ah, moon. *Unknown, tr. by* Arthur Waley. BoS

O sun, and moonlight shining in the woods. Carmen Saeculare. Charles Hubert Sisson, *after the Latin of* Horace. OBVE

O sun, be his protection. Branwen's Starling. R. Williams Parry, *tr. by* Gwyn Jones. OBWVE

O Sun, when I stand in my green leaves. To the Sun from a Flower. Guido Gezelle, *tr. by* Jethro Bithell. FaPON

O suns [or sun] and skies and clouds of June. October's Bright Blue Weather. Helen Hunt Jackson. BLPA; BLPL; FaBoBe; GN

O Susanna. Margaret Wainwright. CN

O swan, come slowly from the sky. Song of Poverty. *Gond Oral Tradition, tr. by* V. Elwin and S. Hivale. WTO

O, sweep of stars over Harlem streets. Stars. Langston Hughes. GLP

O Sweet Anne Page. William Shenstone. SeCePo

O sweet are tropic lands for waking dreams. North and South. Claude McKay. AmPP

O sweet everlasting voices be still. The Everlasting Voices. W. B. Yeats. AWP

O sweet is the fair face of nature, when Spring. The Awakening of the People. Gerald Massey. PF

O sweet, sad, singing river. Henrietta Cordelia Ray. CBWP-3

O sweet September! thy first breezes bring. Sweet September. George Arnold. GN

O Sweet Spontaneous. E. E. Cummings. MoP; NAAL-2; NoAM; NoP; PrIm

O sweet the time, when neither folly might. Truth's Complaint over England. Thomas Lodge. ACP

O sweet woods, the delight of solitariness. Solitariness. Sir Philip Sidney. *Fr.* Arcadia. OBSC; SiPS

O sweete and bitter monuments of paine. Upon the Ensignes of Christes Crucifyinge. William Alabaster. MePo

O Sweetest Melancholy. John Fletcher. *See* Nice Valor, The: Melancholy.

O sylvan priest of nature! rightly thou. A Thought at Walden. Henrietta Cordelia Ray. CBWP-3

O Sylvan prophet, whose eternal fame. Hymn for St. John's Eve. *Unknown, tr. by* Dryden. AWP

O Sylvia, Sylvia. Sylvia's Death. Anne Sexton. NAAL-2

O take me to the sullen flats. From the Righteous Man Even the Wild Beasts Run Away. David Bromwich. PoA

O Taste and See. Denise Levertov. NoP; PBWP; PPP; TAP

"O tears, no tears, but rain from beauty's skies." Sir Philip Sidney. *Fr.* Astrophel and Stella, C. Son

O tell me, little children, have you seen her. Nikolina. Celia Thaxter. GN

O tell me, pretty river! The River. *Unknown.* PWR

O tell me whence that joy doth spring. The Queer. Henry Vaughan. PoEL-2

O tender-heartedness right bitter grown. Fragmenti. Ezra Pound. PoA

O Tender under Her Right Breast. George Barker. *Fr.* Second Cycle of Love Poems, II. MoAB; MoBrPo

O tenderly the haughty day. Emerson. AA; GN

O terrible is the highest thing. Kenneth Patchen. VGW

O Thalassa! Thalassa! Where, where. The Singers. George Bruce. OxBS

O that I could a sin once see! Sin. George Herbert. NoP; OxBSP

O, That I Had Some Secret Place. *Unknown.* AmFP

O that I were the cloud. *Unknown. Fr.* Manyo Shu. Ma

O that I'd had. Mononobe Furumaro. *Fr.* Manyo Shu. PeBJV

"O that mastering tune!" And up in the bed. In the Nuptial Chamber. Thomas Hardy. *Fr.* Satires of Circumstance, X. BrPo; InPK

O that mine eyes might closed be. Thomas Elwood. PWR

O that my father and my mother were flowers. Hasetsukabe Kuromasa. *Fr.* Manyo Shu. Ma

"O That My Love Were in My Arms." *Malay Oral Tradition, tr. by* R. J. Wilkinson *and* R. O. Winstedt. WTO

O that our dreamings all, of sleep or wake. Keats. *Fr.* Epistle to John Hamilton Reynolds. OAEL-2

O that she might rather die. Hitomaro *Fr.* Manyo Shu. Ma

O that sweet mountain of Miwa. Princess Nukada. *Fr.* Manyo Shu. Ma

O that the bridge to heaven were longer. *Unknown. Fr.* Manyo Shu. Ma

O that the hill, the stony road. Hitomaro. *Fr.* Manyo Shu. Ma

O, that the Holy Angels would indite. The Quarto Centennial. Josephine D. Henderson Heard. CBWP-4

O that the rain would come—the rain in big battalions. Precursors. Louis MacNeice. OxBSP

O, that the years had language! time would/ tell. Judith. Eloise Bibb. CBWP-4

O, that this too too solid flesh would melt. Shakespeare. *Fr.* Hamlet, I, i. SCV
  (Frailty, Thy Name is Woman.) TrGrPo
O [*or* Oh] that 'twere possible. Tennyson. *Fr.* Maud, II, iv. BoLoP; NAEL-2; NOBE; NOBVV; OAEL-2; OBEV; PoE
O the aching of that long, long night. Sundered. John Barford. PeHV
O the Chimneys. Nelly Sachs, *tr. fr. German by* Keith Bosley. VWA
O the cuckoo she's a pretty bird. The Cuckoo. *Unknown.* GBP; RB
  See also Cuckoo is a bonny [*or* fine *or* merry] bird, The.
O, the days gone by! O, the days gone by! The Days Gone By. James Whitcomb Riley. OBCA
O the days of the Messiah are at hand, are at hand! Ballad of the Days of the Messiah. A. M. Klein. TrJP
O the evening's for the fair, bonny lassie O! Bonny Lassie O! John Clare. CH
O [*or* Oh] the French are on the sea [*or* say]. The Shan Van Vocht. *Unknown.* AnIL; FaBoPV; GBP; OxBoLi
O, the fun, the fun and frolic. Interlude: "O, the fun, the fun and frolic." W. E. Henley. *Fr.* In Hospital, XVII. BrPo
O the goose and the gander walk'd over the green. The Goose and the Gander. *Unknown.* GBP; RB
O, the grand old Duke of York. *Unknown. See* Noble [*or* Brave Old] Duke of York, The.
O the green glimmer of apples in the orchard. Ballad of Another Ophelia. D. H. Lawrence. ChTr
O the green things growing, the green things growing. Green Things Growing. Dinah Maria Mulock Craik. FaFP; GN; OHIP
O the hog-eye men are all the go. The Hog-Eye Man. *Unknown.* AS
O the hurt, the hurt, and the hurt of love! The Hurt of Love. George Macdonald. TrCP
O the instrument draws close. The Wasp. Joyce Carol Oates. GeTw
O the little rusty dusty miller. *Unknown.* OxNR
O, the lovely rivers and lakes of Maine! The Lovely Rivers and Lakes of Maine. George B. Wallis. BLPA
O, the Month of May. Thomas Dekker. *Fr.* The Shoemaker's Holiday, III, v. EIl
  (May.) OBSC
  (Maytime.) TrGrPo
  (Song: "O the month of May, the merry month of May.") PBBP
O the opal and the sapphire of that wandering western sea. Beeny Cliff. Thomas Hardy. OBNC; RB
O the Palace of Yoshinu. Tabito. *Fr.* Manyo Shu. Ma
O the Ploughboy was a-ploughing. The Simple Ploughboy. *Unknown.* FaBoCh
O the pride of Portsmouth water. The Lost War-Sloop. Edna Dean Proctor. PAH
O the Raggedy Man! He works fer Pa. The Raggedy Man. James Whitcomb Riley. FaPON; OBCA; OxBChV
O, the rain, the weary, dreary rain. Twenty Golden Years Ago. James Clarence Mangan. NOBVV
O the sad day! The Sad Day. Thomas Flatman. OBEV
O the Spring will come. The Spring Will Come. H. D. Lowry. BoNaP
O the vines were golden, the birds were loud. Frederic Prokosch. WaP
O the warm, sweet, mellow summer noon. The Favorite Flower. Celia Thaxter. AiP
O the wonder man rides his space ship. African Things. Victor Hernandez Cruz. InW
O [*or* Oh], then, I see Queen Mab hath been with you. Shakespeare. *Fr.* Romeo and Juliet, I, iv. WSC
  (Mercutio's Queen Mab Speech.) LiTB
  (Queen Mab.) FaPON; FiP
  ("She is the fairies' midwife, and she comes.") RB
  (Mercutio Describes Queen Mab.) TrGrPo
O, there are times/ When all this fret. Daily Trials. Oliver Wendell Holmes. PoEL-5
O there is blessing in this gentle breeze. Wordsworth. *Fr.* The Prelude; or, Growth of a Poet's Mind. NAEL-2, *Complete.*
O [*or* Oh] there was a woman, and she was a widow. Flowers in the Valley. *Unknown.* OnMSP; OxBoLi
O [*or* Oh] there was an old soldier and he had a wooden leg. There Was an Old Soldier. *Unknown.* AS
O these wakeful wounds of thine! On the Wounds of Our Crucified Lord. Richard Crashaw. NAEL-1
O Thirsty Wind. *Unknown, tr. fr. Hawaiian by* N. B. Emerson. WTO
O this fair volume which we World do name. On the Margin Wrought. William Drummond of Hawthornden. SeCePo
O thorn-crowned Sorrow, pitiless and stern. Sorrow. Katrina Trask. AA
O Thou/ God of all long desirous roaming. Rupert Brooke. *Fr.* The Song of the Pilgrims. TrPWD
O thou afflicted, drunken not with wine! Dirge for the Ninth of Ab. *Unknown, tr. by* Nina Davis Salaman. TrJP

O thou all-eloquent, whose mighty mind. Man's Going Hence. Samuel Rogers. *Fr.* Human Life. OBNC
O Thou almighty will. Strength, Love, Light. Robert II, King of France. WGRP
O thou bright jewel in my aim I strive. On Virtue. Phillis Wheatley. TAP
O thou by Nature taught. Ode to Simplicity. William Collins. EnRP; NOBE; OBEV; TEP
O, Thou Eternal One! Gavril Romanovich Derzhavin, *tr. fr. Russian by* Sir John Bowring. WGRP
O Thou Eternal Source of Life. Rolland W. Schloerb. TrPWD
O Thou Eternal Victim Slain. Charles Wesley. NOCV
O thou fair silver Thames. Michael Drayton. *Fr.* The Shepherd's Garland, Eclogue III (1593 ed.). OBSC
O Thou Great Being! what Thou art. Prayer under the Pressure of Violent Anguish. Burns. TrPWD
O Thou great Friend to all the sons of men. The Way, the Truth, and the Life. Theodore Parker. TrPWD; WGRP
O thou great Movement of the Universe. Bryant. *Fr.* An Evening Revery. AA
O thou great wrong, that, through the slow-paced years. The Death of Slavery. Bryant. AA
O Thou Immortal Deity. Shelley. TrPWD
O thou in heaven and earth the only place. Milton. *Fr.* Paradise Lost, *Bk.* III, *ll.* 274–343.
  (Plan of Salvation, The.) WGRP
O thou Moor of Morería. Abenamar, Abenamar. *Unknown, tr. by* Robert Southey. AWP
O Thou Most High Who Rulest All. Anne Bradstreet. AH
O thou, my lovely boy, who in thy power. Shakespeare. *Fr.* Sonnets, CXXVI. NAEL-1
O Thou my monster, Thou my guide. Prayer in Mid-Passage. Louis MacNeice. EaLo
O Thou my soule, Jehovah blesse. Bible, *O.T. See* Psalms: Psalm CIII ("Bless the Lord, O my soul.").
O Thou my soule, Jehovah blesse. *Unknown. Fr.* The Bay Psalm Book. SCAP
O thou newcomer who seek'st Rome in Rome. Rome. Joachim du Bellay, *tr. by* Ezra Pound. AWP
O Thou not made with hands. The City of God. Francis Turner Palgrave. WGRP
O thou of little faith. Hitherto Hath the Lord Helped. *Unknown.* BLRP
O thou that achest, pulse o' the unwed vast. Adam to Lilith. Christopher John Brennan. *Fr.* Lilith. PoAu-1
O Thou, that dost cover the heavens. Song of the Wind and the Rain. Solomon Ibn Gabirol, *tr. by* Solomon Solis-Cohen. TrJP
O thou that from thy mansion. For My Funeral. A. E. Housman. CMoP; TrPWD
O thou that held'st the blessed Veda dry. Hymn to Vishnu. Jayadeva, *tr. fr. Sanskrit by* Sir Edwin Arnold. *Fr.* The Gita Govinda. AWP
O Thou, that in the heavens does dwell. Holy Willie's Prayer. Burns. EBEV; GoTS; NOEC; OBSV; OxBS; PoE; PoEL-4; PPP; TW
  (O Thou, wha in the heavens dost dwell.) EnRP; InPS; NoP; OAEL-1; OxBoLi
O thou that often hast within thine eyes. Sonnet: He Speaks of a Third Love of His. Guido Cavalcanti, *tr. by* Dante Gabriel Rossetti. AWP
O thou, that sendest out the man. England and America in 1782. Tennyson. PAH
O thou, that sit'st (*or* sitst) upon a throne. A Song to David. Christopher Smart. ChTr; EBEV; LaA; NAEL-1; NOBE; OAEL-1; OBWVE; PoE; PoEL-3; TrGrPo
O Thou That Sleep'st like Pig in Straw. Sir William Davenant. InvP
O [*or* Oh] thou that swing'st upon the waving hair [*or* haire *or* ear *or* eare]. The Grasshopper. Richard Lovelace. CaPo; EBEV; FaBoPV; JCP; NOBE; NoP; OAEL-1; OBEV; OBS; PPP; SeCePo; SeCV-1
  (Grasse-Hopper, The.) MeLP; MePo
O thou that to the moonlight vale. Ode: To the Nightingale. Joseph Warton. PBBP
O thou that with surpassing glory crown'd. Milton. *Fr.* Paradise Lost, *Bk.* IV, *ll.* 32–113.
  (Satan's Soliloquy.) LiTB; OBS
O Thou! the first fruits of the dead. Buriall. Henry Vaughan. SeCV-1
O thou undaunted daughter of desires! Richard Crashaw. *Fr.* The Flaming Heart. HAP
  (Upon the Book and Picture of the Seraphical Saint Teresa.) NOBE; OBEV
O Thou unknown, Almighty Cause. A Prayer in the Prospect of Death. Burns. TrPWD; WGRP
O Thou, wha in the heavens dost dwell. Burns. *See* O Thou that in the heavens dost dwell.

O thou! whatever title suit thee. Address to the Deil. Burns. EnRP; GoTS; NOEC; OAEL-1; OxBS; PoEL-4

O Thou who all-things has of nothing made. Deo Opt. Max. George Sandys. *Fr.* Paraphrase on the Psalms of David. OBS

O thou who art of all that is. Through Unknown Paths. Frederick L. Hosmer. TrPWD

O Thou Who Art Our Author and Our End. Sir John Beaumont

O Thou who bidst the torrent flow. Whittier. *Fr.* Hymn from the French of Lamartine. TrPWD

O thou who camest from above. Charles Wesley. SeCePo; TrPWD (Inextinguishable Blaze.) NOEC

O thou who didst furnish. Hymn to Moloch. Ralph Hodgson. OxBTC

O Thou, Who Didst Ordain the Word. Edwin Hubbell Chapin. AH

O thou, who lately closed my eyes. A Morning Hymn. Christopher Smart. OxBChV

O Thou, who man of baser earth didst make. Omar Khayyám, *tr. fr. Persian* by Edward Fitzgerald. *Fr.* The Rubáiyát of Omar Khayyám of Naishápúr. EaLo

O thou who movest onward. Gabriello Chiabrera, *tr. by* Wordsworth. *Fr.* Epitaphs. AWP

O thou who never harbored fear. Eloise Bibb. CBWP-4

O thou, who passest through our valleys in. To Summer. Blake. WiR

O thou, who plumed with strong desire. The Two Spirits [an Allegory]. Shelley. CH; OAEL-2; Prf; WiR

O Thou who speedest Time's advancing wing. He Asketh Absolution of God. *Unknown, tr. fr. Egyptian by* Robert Hillyer. *Fr.* Book of the Dead. AWP

O thou whom Poetry (*or* Poesy) abhors. On Elphinston's Translation of Martial. Burns. FaBoCo; FaBoEE (Epigram on Elphinstone's Translation of Martials' Epigrams.) TW

O Thou whose equal purpose runs. Wendell Phillips Stafford. TrPWD

O thou, whose eyes were closed in death's pale night. Epitaph on a Child Killed by Procured Abortion. *Unknown.* NOEC

O thou whose face hath felt the Winter's wind. What the Thrush Said. Keats. EBEV

O thou! whose fancies from afar are brought. To H. C. Wordsworth. ChER; EnRP; PoEL-4

O Thou Whose Feet Have Climbed Life's Hill. Louis FitzGerald Benson. AH

O Thou, whose glorious orbs on high. Hymn of [*or* to] the West. Edmund Clarence Stedman. PAH (Hymn to the West.) TrPWD

O Thou Whose Gracious Presence Blest. Louis FitzGerald Benson. TrPWD

O Thou Whose Gracious Presence Shone. Marion Franklin Ham. AH

O Thou Whose Image. Arthur Hugh Clough. TrPWD

O thou, whose mighty palace roof doth hang. Hymn to Pan. Keats. *Fr.* Endymion [a Poetic Romance], I. ChER; PoEL-4

O thou whose name shatters the universe. Eli the Thatcher. Max Beerbohm *and* William Rothenstein. FaBoNo

O Thou Whose Own Vast Temple Stands. Bryant. AH

O thou whose pow'r o'er moving worlds presides. Boethius, *tr. fr. Latin by* Samuel Johnson. *Fr.* The Consolation of Philosophy, III, 9. OBVE; TrPWD

O Thou! Whose Presence Went Before. Whittier. AH

O thou, with dewy locks who lookest down. To Spring. Blake. BLPL; BoNaP; BoTP; EnRP; NAEL-2; NOEC; OAEL-2; OBEV; PoEL-4; PoLF; PPP; WiR

O thow archbishop and metropolitan. *Unknown. Fr.* A Letter Sent by the Mayor and Inhabitants of the. NOIV

O thow Lucyna, qwene and empyresse. On the Departing of Thomas Chaucer. John Lydgate. OxBLMV

O [*or* Oh] thy bright eyes must answer now. Plead for Me. Emily Brontë. PoEL-5 (God of Visions.) TrGrPo (O Thy Bright Eyes Must Answer Now.) BrRo

O tide-enwreathed and time-tormented Man. The Gatineaus. James Wreford Watson. CaP

O Time the fatal wrack of mortal things. Anne Bradstreet. *Fr.* Contemplations. PBWP; WPOW

O Time, whence comes the Mother's moody look amid her labours. The Lacking Sense. Thomas Hardy. CMoP; PoEL-5

O Time! who know'st a lenient hand to lay. Time and Grief. William Lisle Bowles. OBEV (Influence of Time on Grief.) EnRP

O times most bad. Upon the Troublesome Time. Robert Herrick. CaPo

O to Be a Dragon. Marianne Moore. CTC; GoYe

O to be blind! The Blind Man at the Fair. Joseph Campbell. AWP

O to break loose, like the chinook. Waking Early Sunday Morning. Robert Lowell. FaBoMo; HCAP; NOBA; OxBC

O [*or* Oh], to have a little house! An Old Woman of the Roads. Padraic Colum. BoTP; CH; FaBoBe; FaPON; FYAP; MoBrPo; NOIV; OBEV; PoRA

O to lie in long grasses! In the Grass. Hamlin Garland. AA

O to scuttle from the battle and to settle on an atoll far from brutal mortal neath a wattle portal! What'll Be the Title? Justin Richardson. FiBHP

O touch me not, unless thy soul. Unless. Ella Dietz Glynes. AA

O Trade! O Trade! would thou wert dead! The Symphony. Sidney Lanier. AmPP; LiTA

O tragic hours when lovers leave each other! Partings. Charles Guérin, *tr. by* Jethro Bithell. AWP

O transitory season, lightningless. Rhapsody on Time. István·Simon, *tr. by* Edwin Morgan. MHuP

O traveler, cosmopolite! At present. The Old Station of Cahors. Valery Larbaud, *tr. by* William Jay Smith. CT

O treacherous scent, O thorny sight. Another for the Briar Rose. William Morris. NOBVV

O trees, to whom the darkness is a child. Advice to a Forest. Maxwell Bodenheim. TrJP

O tremble, all ye earthly princes. The Revolutionaries. Richard Percival Lister. NOBL

O tremble! O tremble, O tremble. Six Sunday. Hart Leroi Bibbs. NBP

"O Troy Muir, my lily-flower." The Queen of Scotland. *Unknown.* ESPB

O. T.'s Blues. Waring Cuney. MAT

O [*or* Oh] turn away those cruel eyes. The Relapse. Thomas Stanley. OBEV

O Turn Ye, O Turn Ye. Josiah Hopkins. AH

O 'twas on a bright mornin' in summer. Who's the Pretty Girl Milkin' the Cow? *Unknown.* AS

O Tweed! a stranger, that with wandering feet. The Tweed Visited. William Lisle Bowles. Son

O-U-G-H. Charles Battell Loomis. NBLV

O universal Mother, who dost keep. Hymn to Earth the Mother of All. *Unknown, tr. fr. Greek by* Shelley. *Fr.* Homeric Hymns. AWP

O Urizen! Creator of men! mistaken Demon of heaven! Take Thy Bliss, O Man. Blake. *Fr.* Visions of the Daughters of Albion. EnRP

O valiant Hearts, who to your glory came. The Supreme Sacrifice. John S. Arkwright. WGRP

O, very gloomy is the House of Woe. Thomas Hood. *Fr.* The Haunted House. SeCePo

O vile ingratefull me. Biothanatos. Joseph Beaumont. OBS

O Virgin. *Unknown, tr. fr. Gaelic by* Douglas Hyde. WTO

O Virtuous Light. Elinor Wylie. MoAB; MoAmPo

O Visionary who adjust your lens. The Higher Empiricism. Francis C. Golffing. PoA

O wad this braw hie-heapit toun. The Prows o' Reekie. Lewis Spence. OxBS

O Wahkonda (Master of Life) pity me! A Dance Chant. *Unknown, tr. by* D. G. Brinton. WGRP

O wall-flower! or ever thy bright leaves fade. The Wall-Flower. Henrik Arnold Thaulov Wergeland, *tr. by* Sir Edmund Gosse. AWP

O Waly, Waly. *Unknown. See* O waly, waly, up the bank.

"O waly, waly, my gay goss-hawk." The Gay Goshawk [*or* Goss-Hawk] . *At. to* Anna Gordon Brown. ESPB, (A *and* E *vers.*); GN; OxBB, *with music;* WPE

O waly, waly, up the [*or* yon] bank. Waly, Waly. *Unknown.* EnLoPo; EnSB; FaBoBa; GBP; HAP; OBEV; OxBS (Forsaken Bride, The.) GTBS; GTBS-P (Jamie Douglas.) ESPB (Lord Douglas.) OxBB (O Waly, Waly.) ELP; GoTS; OBS (Waly, Waly, Love Be Bonny.) PrIm

O waly waly waly waly. The Holloe Menn. Harrison Everard. BXAP

O warm, enthusiastic maid. Joseph Warton. *Fr.* Ode to Fancy. NOEC

O wastfull riot, never well content. Lucan, *tr. fr. Latin by* Sir Walter Raleigh. *Fr.* Pharsalia, IV. OBVE

O water-girl! with tinkling anklets. Water-Girl. *Gond Oral Tradition, tr. by* V. Elwin *and* S. Hivale. WTO

O! we know not we know not, what future joys. There's a Silvery Lining to Every Cloud. Matilda Caroline Edwards. PWR

O, we loved long and happily, God knows! The Custom of the World. Louis Simpson. BoLoP

O we sailed to Virginia and thence to New York. The Death of Admiral Benbow. *Unknown.* OxBSS

"O we were sisters seven, Maisry." Fair Mary of Wallington. *Unknown.* ESPB (The Bonny Earl of Livingston.) OxBB

O we were sisters, sisters seven. Earl Crawford. *Unknown.* ESPB

O wearisome condition of humanity. *See* Oh wearisome condition of humanity.

O weary Champion of the Cross, lie still. Cardinal Newman. Christina Rossetti. NAEL-2

O Weary Pilgrims. Robert Bridges. *Fr.* The Growth of Love, XXIII. MoAB; MoBrPo

O weel may the boatie row and better may she speed. The Boatie Rows. *Unknown.* OxBSS

"O well is [*or* well's] me, [o] my gay goshawk." The Gay Goshawk. *Unknown.* ESPB; GN; OxBB; WPE

O wen, wen, O little wennikins. A Charm. *Unknown, tr. by* Richard Hammer. RB

O Wendy, Arthur. Maurice Kenny. HATNAP

O Were My Love Yon Lilac Fair. Burns. ChTr; GBL; OBEV

O [*or* Oh], Wert Thou in the Cauld Blast. Burns. EBEV; ELP; EnRP; HAP; HeIP; NOBE; NoP; OxBS; TrGrPo

O wha my babie-clouts will buy? The Rantin' Dog, the Daddie o't. Burns. OxBoLi; PPP

"O wha will bake my bridal bread." Fair Annie. *Unknown.* ESPB

"O wha will shoe my bonny foot?" Fair Isabell of Rochroyall. *Unknown.* OxBB

"O wha will shoe my fair foot?" The Lass of Roch Royal. *Unknown.* ESPB

O wha would [*or* wou'd] wish the win to blaw. Brown Adam. *Unknown.* ESPB; OxBB

"O whare are ye gaun?" [*or* "O where are you going?"]. The False Knight upon [*or* on] the Road. *Unknown.* AmFP; CH; EnSB; ESPB; GBP (The False Knight and the Wee Boy.) FaBoCh; OxBoli; OxBS

"O whare hae ye been a' day, Lord Donald, my son?" Lord Randal. *Unknown.* ESPB

"O [*or* Oh] whare hae ye been a' day, my bonnie wee croodlin dow?" Lord Randal. *Unknown.* EnSB; ESPB, (J *vers.*)

O Whare hae ye been, my dearest dear. *See* O where have you been my dear, dear love.

O whare hae ye been, my dearest dear. The Carpenter's Wife. *Unknown.* OAEL-1; OxBB

"O whare hae ye been, Peggy?" Young Peggy. *Unknown.* ESPB

O [*or* Oh] what a cunning guest. Confession. George Herbert. JCP

O what a loud and fearful shriek was there. Koskiusko. Samuel Taylor Coleridge. EnRP

O what a tangled web we weave. A Word of Encouragement. J. R. Pope. FiBHP; FPL; NBLV; NOBL

O what an endelesse worke have I in hand. Spenser. *Fr.* The Faerie Queene, IV, 12. MOS

O what an ugly sight. Tabito. *Fr.* Manyo Shu. PeBJV

O [*or* Oh *or* Ah] what can ail thee, knight-at-arms [*or* wretched wight]. La Belle Dame sans Merci. Keats. AWP; BeLS; BLPA; CH; ChTr; ELP; EnRP; FaBoBe; FaBoCh; FaFP; FiP; FPL; GoJo; GTBS; GTBS-P; HAP; HeIP; InPS; InvP; LiTB; NAEL-2; NAWM-2; NOBE; NoP; OAEL-2; OBEV; OBNC; PoE; PoEL-4; PoRA; Prf; PrIm; RB; SCV; SoSe; TEP; TrGrPo; UnPo; VVA; WeW

O, what can be the matter with thee, Knight-at-arms. La Belle Dame sans Merci. T. Griffiths. BXAP

O what could be more nice. Light Listened. Theodore Roethke. MoAmPo

O what harper could worthily harp it. The Schoolmaster Abroad with His Son. Charles Stuart Calverley. NOBL

O What Is That Sound [Which So Thrills the Ear]. W. H. Auden. FaBoPV; LiTB; PoE; SoSe (Ballad: "O what is that sound. . . .") MoAB; MoBrPo; WaP (Quarry, The.) CMoP

O what their joy and their glory must be. Hymn for the Close of the Week. Peter Abelard. TrCP

O what transparent waves, what a tranquil sea. Vittoria da Colonna, *tr. by* Lynne Lawner. PBWP

O what's the blood that's [*or* 'at's] on your sword. Son David. *Unknown.* OxBB; OxBS

O what's the weather in a beard? Dinky. Theodore Roethke. OBAL; OBCA; RHPC; SM

O, when I hear at sea. Wind and Wave. Charles Warren Stoddard. AA; AnAmPo

O, when our clergie [*or* clergy], at the dreadful[l] day. On Those That Deserve It. Francis Quarles. MePo; NOCV; OBS

O [*or* Oh] when the saints go marchin' [*or* marching] in. When the Saints Go Marchin' [*or* Marching] In. *Unknown.* EaLo

O when, through ev'ry province, shall be raised. The Happy Workhouse and the Good Effects of Industry. John Dyer. *Fr.* The Fleece, III. NOEC

O Where Are You Going? W. H. Auden. *Fr.* The Orators. CMoP; LiTB; NOAM; NOBE; SoSe (Epilogue: " 'O where are you going?' said reader to rider.") FaBoCh (Five Songs.) LiTM (Song: " 'O Where Are You Going?' said reader to rider.") OAEL-2

O, where are you going, "Goodspeed" and "Discovery"? Southern Ships and Settlers. Rosemary *and* Stephen Vincent Benét. AmFN

O [*or* Oh] where are you going? says [*or* said] Milder to Malder. The Cutty Wren. *Unknown.* GBP; OxBoLi; WiR

O where hae ye been, my long, long, love. *See* O where have you been my dear, dear, love.

O where have you been all day. In the Woods. Dorothy Baker. BoTP

"O [*or* Oh] where have [*or* ha *or* hae] you [*or* ye] been, Lord Randal [*or* Rendal] my son?" Lord Randal. *Unknown.* AmFP; AWP; EBEV; EnRP; ESPB, (A, B *and* J *vers.*); FaBoBa; FF; FPL; HAP; HeIP; HoPM; LiTB; NoP, (A *vers.*); OAEL-1, *with music*; OxBB, *with music*; OxBS; TrGrPo; WeW

"O where [*or* whare] have you [*or* hae ye] been, my dear, dear [*or* dearest dear *or* long, long] love." The Demon Lover. *Unknown.* EnSB; HAP; LiTB; MAT; UnPo; WeW (Carpenter's Wife, The.) OAEL-1, *with music*; OBET, *diff. vers.*; OxBB, *with music* (Daemon Lover, The.) MOS, *diff. vers.*; NU (House Carpenter, The.) AMFP; AS, *with music* (James Harris.) ESPB, (A, D, *and* F *vers.*); FaBoBa

O where is tiny Hewe? The Goblin's Song. James Telfer. ChTr

O where were ye, my milk-white steed. The Broomfield Hill. *Unknown.* CH

O, where, where are the winter grounds of angels. The Angels. Marguerite Young. WPE

O while within a Jewish breast. Hatikvah—a Song of Hope. Naphtali Herz Imber, *tr. by* Henry Snowman. TrJP

O whisper, O my soul! The afternoon. The Tired Worker. Claude McKay. BANP; BPo

O whistle, and I'll come to you, my lad. Whistle, and I'll Come to You, My Lad. Burns. OxBoLi

O white and midnight sky! O starry bath! The Celestial Passion. Richard Watson Gilder. AA

O white clay, O fine clay of the earth cold. Fine Clay. Winifred Shaw. PoAu-1

O white, white, light moon, that sailest in the sky. Donald. Henry Abbey. AA

O whither goest thou, pale student. Ye Laye of Ye Woodpeckore. Henry Augustin Beers. NA

O, whither sail you, Sir John Franklin? A Ballad of Sir John Franklin. George Henry Boker. AA; AnAmPo; OnMSP

O who can ever praise enough. Poem. W. H. Auden. PoA

O who rides by night thro' the woodland so wild? The Erl-King. Goethe. AWP; OBVE; WSC; *all tr. by* Sir Walter Scott (Invisible King, The.) NU, *tr. by* Robert Bly

O [*or* Oh] who shall, from this dungeon, raise. A Dialogue between the Soul and [the] Body. Andrew Marvell. HAP; INPS; JCP; MeLP; MePo; NAEL-1; NoP; OAEL-1; OBS; PoEL-2; PPP; SeCP; SeCV-1; TEP; WeW

O, who will drive the chariot when she comes? She'll Be Comin' Round the Mountain. *Unknown.* AS, (A *and* B *vers.*, *with music*)

"O who will shoe my fair foot." Fair Annie of Lochryan. *Unknown.* AS

"O who will shoe my little feet." The Lass of Roch Royal. *Unknown.* AmFP

O who will shoe your pretty little foot. Who Will Shoe Your Pretty Little Foot? *Unknown.* AS

O who will show me those delights on high? Heaven. George Herbert. SeCP; TrCP; TrGrPo; TTTS

O who will walk a mile with me. A Mile with Me. Henry van Dyke. BLPA; FPL

"O who'll get me a healthy child." A Practical Woman. Thomas Hardy. NAs

O why do you walk through the fields in gloves. To a Fat Lady Seen from the Train. Frances Cornford. BLPA; FaBoWP; GoJo; MoBrPo; OBMV; WeW

O Why Should the Spirit of Mortal Be Proud? *See* Oh! Why Should the Spirit. . .

O, why should we the dead deplore. African Dirge. M. J. Chapman. PVCV

O wide blossom-splashed private drives. Lines Composed at Hope Ranch. Tom Clark. PPR

O wild West Wind, thou breath of Autumn's being. Ode to the West Wind. Shelley. AWP; BoNaP; CH; EBEV; EnRP; FaBoBe; FaBV; FaFP; FiP; FPL; GTBS; GTBS-P; HAP; HeIP; InPS; LiTB; MOS; NAEL-2; NIP; NOBE; NoP; OAEL-2; OBEV; OBNC; OHFP; PoE; PoEL-4; PoLF; PoRA; PPP; PrIm; TEP; TrGrPo; WeW

O Willie brew'd a peck o' maut. Willie Brew'd [*or* Brewed] a Peck o' Maut. Burns. AWP; EnRP; OxBS

O Willie's large o' limb and lith. The Birth of Robin Hood. *Unknown.* OAEL-1; OxBB (Willie and Earl Richard's Daughter.) ESPB

O Willy was as brave a lord. Willie o Douglas Dale. *Unknown.* ESPB

O wind, rend open the heat. Heat. Hilda Doolittle ("H. D."). *Fr.* The Garden. CMoP; HeIP; InPK; MoAmPo; OxBA; PrIM; TAP; UnPo

O Winter! bar thine adamantine doors. To Winter. Blake. WiR

O winter wind, lat grievin be. Margaret Winefride Simpson. OxBS

O, winter, your gesture. Winter. Bella Akhmadulina, *tr. by* Barbara Einzig. BoWoP

O Winter's a beautiful time of the year. Winter. Enid Blyton. BoTP

O with what key. Skeleton Key. John Hollander. NoP

O woe, woe,/ People are born and die. Mr. Housman's Message. Ezra Pound. FaBoEE; FaBoPa

O woman, let thy heart not cleave. Forepledged. John Lancaster Spalding. AA

O Woman of Three Cows, agra [*or* agragh]! The Woman of Three Cows. *Unknown*, *tr. by* James Clarence Mangan. AnIL; EnRP; NOIV

O Woman, Shapely as the Swan. *Unknown. See* I Shall Not Die for Thee.

O woman! Why, being so pure, are the clear rays emanating. Lieder. Rosalía de Castro, *tr. by* Angel Flores *and* Kate Flores. DMH

O women/ when in the early dawn, near men, our lovers. V. Charlotte Calmis, *tr. by* Mary Ann Caws. DMF

O women, for you I tune my lyre! Letter to Women. Constance-Marie de Salm-Dyck, *tr. by* Dorothy Backer. DMF

O wonder!/ How many goodly creatures are there here! Brave New World. Shakespeare. *Fr.* The Tempest, V, i. TrGrPo

O wonderful nonsense of lotions of Lucky Tiger. Haircut. Karl Shapiro. TwCP

O, wondrous depth to which my soul is stirr'd. Music. Josephine D. Henderson Heard. CBWP-4

"O words are lightly spoken." The Rose Tree. W. B. Yeats. CMoP; ELP; FaBoPV; OBMV

O words, which fall like summer dew on me! Rural Poesy. Sir Philip Sidney. *Fr.* Arcadia. ElL

O World. George Santayana. *See* Sonnets:
  O world, thou choosest not the better part!

O world, I cannot hold thee close enough! God's World. Edna St. Vincent Millay. BLPL; CMoP; FaBoBe; FaBV; MoAmPo; TrCP

O world invisible, we view thee. The Kingdom of God. Francis Thompson. BrPo; EaLo; FaPoR; GTBS-P; NOCV
  (In No Strange Land.) HAP; LiTB; MoAB; MoBrPo; NOBE; OBEV; TrCP; TrGrPo; WGRP

O world! O life! O time! A Lament. Shelley. ChER; ChTr; EnRP; GTBS; GTBS-P; NAEL-2; NOBE; PoRA; TEP; TrGrPo

O world that turneth as a vane that veers! Heliodore. John Daniel Logan. CaP

O world, thou choosest not the better part! George Santayana. *Fr.* Sonnets, III. AnAmPo; TrGrPo
  (Faith.) WGRP
  (O World.) FPL

O world, you old customs officer. Ego. Annie Vivanti, *tr. by* Muriel Kittel. DMI

O would I were where I would be! Suspiria. *Unknown*. OBEV

O wretch! hath madness cured thy dire despair? On Seeing an Officer's Widow Distracted. Mary Barber. NOEC

O wretched offspring! O unhappy state. Death the Consequence of the Fall. Dryden. *Fr.* The State of Innocence. NOCV

O ye, all ye that walk in Willowwood. Willowwood. Dante Gabriel Rossetti. *Fr.* The House of Life, LI. NAEL-2; OAEL-2

O ye that look on Ecstasy. Ecstasy. Rachel Annand Taylor. GoTS

O ye that put your trust and confidence. A Rueful Lamentation on the Death of Queen Elizabeth. Sir Thomas More. AAS; FaBoRV; LiTB; OBSC

O Ye That Would Swallow the Needy. Bible, *O.T. Fr.* Amos, VIII: 4–10. TrJP

O [*or* A *or* Oh] ye wha are sae guid yoursel. Address to the Unco Guid, or the Rigidly Righteous. Burns. EnRP; NOBE; NOCV; NoP; OxBS; TrGrPo

O ye who see with other eyes than ours. Life and Death. Lilla Cabot Perry. AA

O ye who tread the Narrow Way. Buddha at Kamakura. Rudyard Kipling. OBTV

O ye wretched Scots. John Skelton. *Fr.* How the Doughty Duke of Albany like a Coward Knight Ran Away Shamefully. OBSV

O Year, grow slowly. Exquisite, holy. Slow Spring. Katharine Tynan. BoTP

O years! and age! farewell. Eternity. Robert Herrick, *tr. by* Clarence Brown *and* W. S. Merwin. OBD

O yee, whome lorde of lande and waters wyde. Seneca, *tr. fr. Latin by* Jasper Heywood. *Fr.* Thyestes, III. OBVE

O yes, I love you, book of my confessions. Water under the Earth. Robert Bly. NNaP

O yes, O yes! if any maid. Cupid's Indictment. John Lyly. *Fr.* Galathea. EIL
  (Song of Diana's Nymphs, A.) OBSC

O yes, we've seen your girl friend, haven't we? Six Said by the Concubines to Him. Ammuvanar, *tr. by* A. K. Ramanujan. PLW

O you,/ Who came upon me once. Carrefour. Amy Lowell. BoWoP

O You among Women. F. R. Higgins. BIrV

O you are a rajah in your rage. Courage for the Pusillanimous. Paul Roche. GoYe

O you chorus of indolent reviewers. Hendecasyllabics. Tennyson. EBEV; FaBoCo; NOBL

O you dear trees, you have learned so much of beauty. This Way Only. Lesbia Harford. PoAu-1

O you hollow-cheeked offspring. Baboon. *Zulu Oral Tradition*, *tr. by* C. and W. Leslav. WTO

O you liar tell me this. The Liar. *Unknown*, *tr. by* Frank O'Connor. KiLC

O you not only worshipful but dear. Credo. Zona Gale. TrPWD

O you so long dead. To My Brother. Louise Bogan. AiP; NYBP

O you that hear this voice. Sir Philip Sidney. *Fr.* Astrophel and Stella. OBSC

O you unfortunate swans, who sentinel. The Death of Virgil. Angelo di Costanzo, *tr. by* David Wright. PFI

O you who come to me—alas! Laieikawai's Lament after Her Husband's Death. *Unknown*, *tr. by* M. W. Beckwith. WTO

O you, who were voyaging to the Land of Kara. *Unknown. Fr.* Manyo Shu. Ma

O you would clothe me in silken frocks. The Wild Goat. Claude McKay. CDC

O you, you wear flowers of gold. What She Said to Her Girl Friend ("O you, you wear flowers of gold"). Kapilar, *tr. by* A. K. Ramanujan. PLW

O, young Lochinvar is come out of the west. *See* Oh, young Lochinvar is come out of the west.

O young Mariner. Merlin and the Gleam. Tennyson. OAEL-2

O younge [*or* yonge] fres[s]he folkes, he or she. Love Unfeigned. Chaucer. *Fr.* Troilus and Criseyde [*or* Criseide], V. NOBE; OBEV

"O your hair," he said. What She Said (" 'O your hair,' he said"). Kapilar, *tr. by* A. K. Ramanujan. PLW

O, you're braw wi' your pearls and your diamonds. Lassie, What Mair Wad You Hae? Heine, *tr. by* Alexander Gray. GoTS; OxBS

O zummer clote! when the brook's a-glidèn [*or* a-sliden]. The Clote (Water-Lily). William Barnes. ELP; PoEL-4

O' zummer night, as day did gleam. The Lost Little Sister. William Barnes. PoEL-4

Oa! hoy! awe! ba! mey! Canedolia. Edwin Morgan. FaBoCo; PoSH

Oak. Philip Child. CaP

Oak, The. Dryden. OHIP

Oak, The. Tennyson. FaPON

Oak and Lily. Ben Jonson. *See* To the Immortal[l] Memory [*or* Memorie] and Friendship of That Noble Pair[e], Sir Lucius Cary and Sir Henry Morrison: It Is Not Growing Like a Tree.

Oak and the Ash, The. *Unknown*. FaBoCh
  (North County Maid, The.) OBET

Oak and the Brere, The. Spenser. *Fr.* The Shepheardes [*or* Shepeards *or* Shepherd's] Calender: February. OBSC

Oak and the Olive, The. George Barker. FaBoMo; OBTV

Oak Inns Creak in Their Joints as Light Declines, The. Derek Walcott. NoAM

Oak is called the king of trees, The. Trees. Sara Coleridge. BOTP; OHIP; OxBChV; RHPC

Oak Leaf Plate. Mary Ann Hoberman. TSS

Oak leaves are big as the mouse's ear. Every One to His Own Way. John Vance Cheney. AA

Oaken, broken elbow-chair, An. True and Faithful Inventory of the Goods Belonging to Dr. Swift, Vicar of Laracor, & upon Lending His House to the Bishop of Meath, till His Palace Was Rebuilt. Swift. FaBoUs

Oakey Street Evictions, The. Thomas Armstrong. OBET

Oakland Rose Garden. Jacques Roubaud, *tr. fr. French by* Neil Baldwin. RHTwFP

Oaks are old at birth and ornery. At the Woodpile. Raymond Henri. SaC

Oaks, how subtle and marine, The. Bearded Oaks. Robert Penn Warren. LiTM; MoAmPo; MoP; NAAL-2; NoAM; NOBA; PoA; PoE; TAP; TwCP

Oars fell from our hands, The. The Island. George Woodcock. MoCV

Oars stop. I go to buy dark brew, The. Drinking Wine: Second Series. Ch'ien Ch'ien-yi, *tr. by* Ronald Miao. WFTU

Oasis of Sidi Khaled, The. Wilfred Scawen Blunt. OBTV

Oath. Gabriella Sica, *tr. fr. Italian by* Muriel Kittel. DMI

Oath, The. Allen Tate. FaBoMo; LiTM; OxBA; VGW

Oath of Friendship. Li Po, *tr. fr. Chinese* by Arthur Waley. TTTS
Oatmeal was in their blood and in their names. The Gathering. E. J. Pratt. *Fr.* Towards the Last Spike. MoCV; OBCV
Ob all de subjicts I kin read. Men Folks ob Today, De. Maggie Pogue Johnson. CBWP-4
Obatala, the Creator. *Yoruba Oral Tradition, tr. by* Ulli Beier. WTO
Obeah Night. Jean Rhys. PVCV
Obedience. George Macdonald. BLRP; WGRP
Obedience of the Corpse. C. D. Wright. MT
Obedient to our mighty Sovereign's word. *Unknown. Fr.* Manyo Shu. Ma
Obedient to our Sovereign's command. Yakamochi. *Fr.* Manyo Shu. Ma
Obedient to our Sovereign's orders. Yakamochi. *Fr.* Manyo Shu. Ma
Obediently we walked. The Crystal Bridge. Lucha Corpi. CCP
Obelisk Inscriptions, *sel.* Hatshepsut, *tr. fr. Egyptian by* Mariam Lichtheim.
  "Now my heart turns to and fro." WPOW
Obermann Once More. Matthew Arnold. PoEL-5
Oberon and Titania to the Fairy Train. Shakespeare. *See* Midsummer Night's Dream, A: Through the House.
Oberon, the Fairy Prince, *sel.* Ben Jonson.
  Buz, Quoth the Blue Fly. NA; TEP
  ("Buzz, quoth the blue fly," *sl. diff.*) OxNR
  (Catch, A.) EIL
  (Satyrs' Catch, The.) FaBoNo; FM
Oberon's Feast. Robert Herrick. CaPo; SeCV-1; TrGrPo
Oberon's Palace. Robert Herrick. CaPo
Obit. Robert Lowell. HCAP
Obit on Parnassus. F. Scott Fitzgerald. NBLV; NYBP; PrIm
Obituary. Conrad Aiken. OBAL
Obituary. Anthony Brode. FiBHP
Obituary. Kenneth Fearing. VGW
Obituary. Thomas William Parsons. AA
Object among dreams, you sit here with your shoes off, An. A Girl in a Library. Randall Jarrell. NAAL-2; NoAM; NOBA; NoP
Object Lesson. Paul Henderson. ATNZ
Object of creation, The. Mohammad Taqi Mir, *tr. by* Ahmed Ali. GoT
Object of our search, The. Mohammad Taqi Mir, *tr. by* Ahmed Ali. GoT
Objection to Being Stepped On, The. Robert Frost. NBLV
Objects. Richard Wilbur. FF; NoP
Objets d'Art. Cynthia MacDonald. ER; NMM
Obligations. Jane Cooper. NePoEA-2
Obligations of the Poet. Giaconda Belli, *tr. fr. Spanish by* Barbara Paschke. Vol
Oblique light on the trite, on brick and tile. Courtyards in Delft. Derek Mahon. CIP; FaBCIP
Obliterate/ mythology as you unwind. The Cavern. Charles Tomlinson. CMoP
Oblivion. Jessie Redmond Fauset, *fr. the French of* Massillon Coicou. BANP; PoNe
Oblivion. Ellis Ayitey Komey. PBA
Oblivion. Ibrahim Naji, *tr. fr. Arabic by* Issa Boullata *and* John Heath-Stubbs. MAP
Oblivion! Skin. Nelly Sachs, *tr. by* Michael Roloff. PBWP
Oboe. Laurence McKinney. NBLV
Oboe. Eugenio Montale, *tr. fr. Italian by* Jonathan Galassi. *Fr.* Chords, V. PFI
Obon by the Hudson. Richard Oyama. BrSi
O'Bruadair. David O'Bruadair, *tr. fr. Irish by* James Stephens. BIrV
Obscene Caller, The. Philip Dacey. AmPA
Obscene Caller, The. Cheri Fein. TW
Obscure, The. Norman Dubie. NoAM
"Obscure craftsman" but my own man, An! Small Craftsman. Imre Csanádi, *tr. by* Edwin Morgan. MHuP
Obscure Martyrs. Sir Edwin Arnold. PWR
Obscure Night of the Soul, The. St. John of the Cross, *tr. by* Arthur Symons. AWP; OBMV
Obscure Pleasure of the Indistinct, The. Bin Ramke. MAYP
Obscured Prince; or, The Black Box Boxed, The. *Unknown.* APAS
Obscurely yet most surely called to praise. Praise in Summer. Richard Wilbur. CAPP; NoP
Obscurest night involved [*or* involv'd] the sky. The Castaway. William Cowper. ELP; EnRP; FiP; HeIP; MOS; NAEL-1; NOBE; NOEC; NoP; OAEL-1; PoE; PoEL-3; PPP
Obscurity has its tale to tell. Focus. Adrienne Rich. FaBoWP
Obsequies of Stuart. John Randolph Thompson. PAH
Observant of the way she told. Tact. E. A. Robinson. NoAM
Observation. Robert Herrick. FaBoUs

Observation. Dorothy Parker. *Fr.* Some Beautiful Letters. FiBHP
Observation at Dawn. Abba Kovner, *tr. fr. Hebrew by* Shirley Kaufman. VWA
Observation by a Formerly Rose-Lipt Maiden. Joyce LaMers. SoTCo
Observation Car. Alec Derwent Hope. MoP; NoAM
Observation Car and Cigar. William Stafford. LCAP
Observation of a Bee. Leah Goldberg, *tr. fr. Hebrew by* Stephen Mitchell. WPOW
Observation of Facts. Charles Tomlinson. NePoEA-2
Observation on a Small Harbor outside the Military Zone. Abba Kovner, *tr. fr. Hebrew by* Bernhard Frank. MHeP
Observation on a Solitary Tree. Abba Kovner, *tr. fr. Hebrew by* Bernhard Frank. MHeP
Observations, *sels.* Hilaire Kirkland. PeNZ
  "Arranged on the opposite porch is a male." *Fr.* I.
  "Daily the neighbour's dog is withdrawn to the park." *Fr.* II.
  "Turn again, maiden, twice slain and rotten." *Fr.* III.
Observations in a Cornish Teashop. Kenneth Rexroth. OBAL
Observe how he negotiates his way. Swimmer. Robert Francis. NePoAm; TSL; WeW
Observe! I turn the key in this new door. After the Blitz, 1941. J. R. Ackerley. PeHV
Observe. Ridged, raised, tactile, the horror. Munch's Scream. Donald Hall. NePoEA
Observe the Cat upon this page. The Cat. Oliver Herford. FaBV
Observe the daily circle of the sun. Virgil, *tr. fr. Latin by* Dryden. *Fr.* Georgics, I. FaBoUs
Observe the weary birds ere night be done. Orinda to Lucasia. Katherine Philips. PeHV
Observe the young and tender frond. Conversation in the Bush. Arthur Rex Dugard Fairburn. *Fr.* Album Leaves. ATNZ; PeNZ
Observe these pirates bold and gay. On the Dangers Attending Altruism on the High Seas. G. K. Chesterton. FaBoNo
Observe this man, he is an engineer. Revelation. Nancy Keesing. PoAu-2
Observing a Vulgar Name on the Plinth of an Ancient Statue. Walter Savage Landor. EyDe
Observing as I go along. Kyotai, *tr. fr. Japanese by* Burton Watson. *Fr.* Sixteen Hokku. FCEI
Observing Children. Saigyo, *tr. fr. Japanese by* Burton Watson. *Fr.* Sixty-four Tanka. FCEI
Observing point by point mere instances. On a Baltimore Bus. Charles G. Bell. NePoAm
Obsessed by betrayal. Palm Leaf of Mary Magdalene. Cheryl Clarke. GLP
Obsession of the snow, pearl. Snow. Antonin Artaud, *tr. by* Michael Benedikt. POS
Obsessions. Denise Levertov. LiTM; NePoEA-2; SM
Obsessive. Marvin Bell. *Fr.* The Escape into You. LCAP; SM
Obsessive memory of first. Evenings of Ink. Jean Follain, *tr. by* W. S. Merwin. RHTwFP
Obtuse Angle, Scopprell, Aradobo, and Tilly Lally. In Obtuse Angle's Study. Blake. *Fr.* An Island in the Moon. FaBoNo
Occam's Razor Starts in Massachusetts. Edward Pygge. BXAP
Occasional mornings when an early fog. Housewife. Josephine Miles. PCP
Occasional Poem. Peter Handke, *tr. fr. German by* Beth Bjorklund. CoAuP
Occasional Poem. A. E. Housman. *See* When Adam Day by Day.
Occasional Verses. Marilyn Hacker. Son
Occasional Yarrow, The. Stevie Smith. FaBoNo
Occasioned by General Washington's Arrival in Philadelphia, on His Way to His Residence in Virginia. Philip Freneau. PAH
Occasioned by Seeing a Walk of Bay Trees. Mildmay Fane, Earl of Westmorland. OxBSP
Occasions of Grace at a Poetry Performance. John Frederick Nims. SoTCo
Occupation. Michael Guttenbrunner, *tr. fr. German by* Beth Bjorklund. CoAuP
Occupation: Housewife. Phyllis McGinley. *Fr.* I Know a Village. WPE
Ocean, The. Byron. *Fr.* Childe Harold's Pilgrimage, IV. PoEL-4
  (By the Deep Sea.) OBNC, *shorter sel.*
  "Roll on, thou deep and dark blue ocean—roll!"
    (Apostrophe to the Ocean.) OHFP; WBLP
    (Deep and Dark Blue Ocean.) ChTr
    (Ocean, The.) FaBV; TrGrPo
    (Roll On, Thou Deep and Dark Blue Ocean.) FaPON; FiP
    (Sea, The.) BLPL; FaBoBe; LiTB
    (To the Ocean.) GN; WGRP
  "There is a pleasure in the pathless woods." MOS

Ocean, The. Byron. *See* Childe Harold's Pilgrimage: Ocean, The.

Ocean, The. Louis Dudek. *Fr.* Provincetown. MoCV

Ocean, The. Moschus, *tr. fr. Greek* by Shelley. AWP; MOS; OBVE

Ocean, The. Bible, *O.T. See* Psalms: Psalm CVII ("O give thanks.").

Ocean air is heavy in autumn, The. Climbing to the Top of the City Walls at Kan-yü. Wang T'ing-hsiang, *tr.* by Jonathan Chaves. CoBLCP

Ocean-Fight, The. *Unknown.* PAH

Ocean has not been so quiet for a long while, The. Evening Ebb. Robinson Jeffers. NoAM

Ocean how far ocean. Sea how lost. Midlandfall. Alfred A. Yuson, *tr.* by Satoru Sato. WCI

Ocean is a strange, The. Laura St. Martin. FF

Ocean Is like a Wreath, The. Kuapakaa, *tr. fr. Hawaiian.* WTO

Ocean Liner. Koh Chang-soo, *tr. fr. Korean* by the author. ACKP

Ocean Musing, An. Henrietta Cordelia Ray. CBWP-3

Ocean of bears, An. Browsing in *Roget's Thesaurus.* R. P. Dickey. SoTCo

Ocean of Earth. Guillaume Apollinaire. *See* Earth-Ocean.

Ocean said to me once, The. Stephen Crane. *Fr.* The Black Riders, XXXVIII. MOS

Ocean Springs Mississippy. Al Young. *Fr.* The Song Turning Back into Itself, 3. CNA; NPGG

Ocean tides curl in anger, swift winds rage. Inscribed on a Painting of Dragons by Ch'en So-weng. Hsieh Chin, *tr.* by Jonathan Chaves. CoBLCP

Ocean to Cynthia, The. Sir Walter Ralegh. *See* Ocean's Love to Cynthia, The.

Ocean too has winter-views serene, The. Winter Views Serene. George Crabbe. *Fr.* The Borough, Letter IX. OBNC

Ocean Wanderer, The. *Unknown.* NA

Oceana and Britannia. John Ayloffe. APAS

Oceanic World. Friederike Mayröcker, *tr. fr. German* by Beth Bjorklund. CoAuP

Oceanography. Bob Perelman. IAT

Oceans. Juan Ramón Jiménez, *tr.* by Robert Bly. NU

Ocean's Love to Cynthia, The. Sir Walter Ralegh. SiPS, *sl. abr*

(Ocean to Cynthia, The.) OBSC, *sl. abr*

Och hey! for the splendour of tartans! The Return. Pittendrigh Macgillivray. GoTS; OxBS

Och hon for somebody! somebody. *Unknown.* OxBS

Och! what will [*or* shall] we do for linen? What Will We Do for Linen? *Unknown.* GBP; WTO

Oche Iron. Peter Blue Cloud. HATNAP

Ochil Hills, The. *Unknown.* PoSH

Ock Gurney and old Pete were there. John Masefield. *Fr.* Reynard the Fox. CMoP

Octo-/ ber/ means/ the sun. Impression. René Altmann, *tr.* by Beth Bjorklund. CoAuP

October. Thomas Bailey Aldrich. *See* Maple Leaves.

October. Otto René Castillo, *tr. fr. Spanish* by Wilfredo Castaña. Vol

October. Mary Weston Fordham. CBWP-2

October. Robert Frost. GoJo

October. Rodney Hall. *Fr.* Black Bagatelles. CBAP

October. Donald Justice. BLA

October. Patrick Kavanagh. CIP; GTBS-P

October. William Morris. *Fr.* The Earthly Paradise. OBNC

October. Julio Ortega, *tr. fr. Spanish* by David Tipton. Per

October. Greg Pape. AmPA

October. Henrietta Cordelia Ray. CBWP-3

October. Christina Rossetti. BoTP

October. Folgore Da San Gimignano, *tr. fr. Italian* by Dante Gabriel Rossetti. *Fr.* Sonnets of the Months. PFI

October. Maurice Sendak. RHPC

October. Barry Spacks. PoA; GM

October. Spenser. *Fr.* The Shepheardes [*or* Shepeards *or* Shepherd's] Calender. NAEL-1; OAEL-1

(Contempt of Poetry.) OBSC

October. Judah Leib Teller, *tr. fr. Yiddish* by Benjamin *and* Barbara Harshav. AYP

October. Edward Thomas. NoAM

October. John Updike. PDV

October. S. W. Whitman. BoTP

October. Charles Wright. MT

October. Zoltán Zelk, *tr. fr. Hungarian* by Daniel Hoffman. MHuP

October again. My roots feel. Autumn, Iowa City. Edwin Thumboo. WCI

October, and a rain-blurred face. At a Fishing Settlement. Alistair Campbell. ATNZ

October and November. Robert Lowell. MAT

October: and the fires go out along the coast. October. Rodney Hall. *Fr.* Black Bagatelles. CBAP

October Arriving. Charles Simic. BLA

October: as a storm sweeps down Mount Mimuro. Princess Shikishi, *tr. fr. Japanese* by Hiroaki Sato. *Fr.* Seventy-eight Tanka. FCEI

October at last has come! The thicket has shaken. Autumn. Pushkin, *tr.* by Max Eastman. AWP

October Cycle. John Peck, *tr. fr. Italian.* AnAn

October 1803. Wordsworth. EnRP

October Elegy. Margaret Gibson. FYAP

October gave a party. October's Party. George Cooper. BoTP; PoLF

October. Here in this dark unfamiliar kitchen. Photograph of My Father in His Twenty-second Year. Raymond Carver. TSL

October in my country. Fugue. Shauqi Abi Shaqra, *tr.* by Sargon Boulus *and* Peter Porter. MAP

October in Tennessee. Walter Malone. AA

October in the Country: 1983. James Simmons. CIP

October is a piper. Autumn Song. Margaret Rose. BoTP

October Is Here. Mrs. Henry Linden. CBWP-4

October Journey. Margaret Abigail Walker. AmNP; IDB; PoBA; PoNe

October Magic. Myra Cohn Livingston. PDV

October Morning. Mary Ursula Bethell. ATNZ

October Morning Walk. Anita Endrezze-Danielson. GOS

October 1942. Roy Fuller. WaP

October 1. Karl Shapiro. MoAB; MoAmPo; PoA

October Poem. Tamura Ryuichi, *tr. fr. Japanese* by Geoffrey Bownas *and* Anthony Thwaite. PeBJV

October Redbreast, The. Alice Meynell. MoBrPo

October 16: The Raid. Langston Hughes. PoBA

October Thought. Seamus Heaney. FL

October Thoughts. Jean Follain, *tr. fr. French* by W. S. Merwin. RHTwFP

October turned my maple's leaves to gold. Maple Leaves. Thomas Bailey Aldrich. GN

(October.) RHPC

October XXIX, 1795. William Stanley Braithwaite. CDC

October's Bright Blue Weather. Helen Hunt Jackson. BLPA; BLPL; FaBoBe; GN

October's Party. George Cooper. BoTP; PoLF

Octopus. Ghazi al-Gosaibi, *tr. fr. Arabic* by Sharif Elmusa *and* Charles Doria. MAP

Octopus. A. C. Hilton. BXAP; CenHV; FaBoCo; FaBoPa; Par

Octopus, The. "Hugh MacDiarmid." TW

Octopus, The. James Merrill. CAPP; CoAP

Octopus, The. Ogden Nash. MOS; RB

Octopus traps: fleeting dreams. Staying Overnight at Akashi. Basho, *tr. fr. Japanese* by Burton Watson. *Fr.* Seventy-six Hokku. FCEI

Octopussycat, The. Kenyon Cox. FaPON

Octoroon eating a macaroon, An. Whalefeathers. Paul Violi. UL

Odcomb's Complaint, *sel.* John Taylor.

"Sweet semi-circled Cynthia played at maw." EIL

(Mockado, Fustian, and Motley.) FaBoNo

Odd but True. *Unknown.* FaBoCo

(Nonsense.) FaBoNo; NA

(Oh That My Lungs.) NOBL

Odd Conceit, An. Nicholas Breton. EIL; OBSC

Odd day, An. For the first time in years. The View from a Cab. Henry Taylor. NBLV

Odd rot it what a shame it is. To Miss B. John Clare. NOBVV

Odd silence, An/ Falls as we enter. Dreams of Water. Donald Justice. LCAP; NYBP

Odd to a Krokis. *Unknown.* NA

Odd way you comb your hair, The. Lady in a Distant Face. James Welch. AmPA

Oddities composed the sum of the news. For the Lost Generation. Galway Kinnell. NePoAm

Ode: "Absence, hear thou my protestation." John Hoskyns. *See* Absence.

Ode: Acme and Septimus. Catullus. *See* Whil'st on Septimius panting brest.

Ode, An: "As it fell upon a day." Richard Barnfield. *See* Affectionate Shepherd, The: As it fell upon a day.

Ode: "At her fair hands how have I grace entreated." Walter Davison. *See* At Her Fair Hands.

Ode: Autumn. Thomas Hood. *See* I saw old Autumn on the misty morn.

Ode, An: "Awake, faire Muse; for I intend." William Browne. OBS

Ode: "Bards of passion and of mirth." Keats. ChER; EnRP; OBEV

(Ode on the Poets.) GTBS; GTBS-P

Ode: First of April, The, *sel.* Thomas Warton, the Younger.

"Swallow, for a moment seen, The." PBBP

Ode: "God save the Rights of Man!" Philip Freneau. GOA

Ode: "How are thy servants blest, O Lord!" Joseph Addison. TrPWD

Ode: "How sleep the brave, who sink to rest." William Collins. *See* How Sleep the Brave.

Ode: "I am the spirit of the morning sea." Richard Watson Gilder. AA
Ode: "I hate that drum's discordant sound." John Scott of Amwell. NIP; NOEC; TW
Ode, An: "I sing a song of sixpence, and of rye." Anthony C. Deane. NOBL
Ode: "Idea of justice may be precious, An." Frank O'Hara. NeAP
Ode, An: "I'm going to write a novel, hey." John Updike. FiBHP
Ode: Intimations of Immortality from Recollections of Early Childhood, sels. Wordsworth. AWP; BLPL; ChER; EnRP; FaBoRV; FiP; HAP; HeIP; InvP; LiTB; NAs; NOBE; NoP; OAEL-2; OBEV; OBNC; PoEL-4; PPP; PrIm; TEP; TrGrPo
  (Ode on Intimations of [or on] immortality.) FaFP; GTBS; GTBS-P; OHFP
  "Now, while the birds thus sing a joyous song." Prf
  "O joy! that in our embers." Prf
  "Our birth is but a sleep and a forgetting." EaLo; WGRP
  (Intimations of Immortality.) ChTr
  (Our Birth Is But a Sleep.) FaBV
  "There was a time when meadow, grove and stream." NAEL-2; TOF
Ode: "Lend me thy great noise, thy powerful, gentle gait." Valery Larbaud, tr. by William Jay Smith. CT; RHTwFP
Ode, An: "Merchant, to secure his treasure, The." Matthew Prior. AWP; EnLoPo; GTBS; GTBS-P; NOEC; NoP; PoRA
  (Song: "Merchant, to secure his treasure, The.") OBEV; TrGrPo
Ode: "Midnight moonlight mobbed Dante's bridge." Bill Berkson. UL
Ode: "Mistah Berrybones, you daid?" William Zaranka. BXAP
Ode: "Now each creature joys the other." Samuel Daniel. ElL; OBSC
Ode, An: "Now I find thy looks were feigned." Thomas Lodge. Fr. Phyllis. ElL; OBSC
Ode: "O tenderly the haughty day." Emerson. AA; GN
Ode: Of Wit. Abraham Cowley. MeLP; MePo; NAEL-1; OAEL-1; SeCP; SeCV-1
  (Of Wit.) OBS
Ode: On First Looking into Chapman's Homer. Keats. See Much have I travell'd in the realms of gold.
Ode: On the Death of W. B. Yeats. Arthur James Marshall Smith. OBCV
Ode: "Once more the country calls." Allen Tate. WaP
Ode: "Poor bird, I do not envy thee." George Daniel. See Poor bird, I do not envy thee.
Ode: Rule, Britannia. James Thomson. NAEL-1
Ode: Salute to the French Negro Poets. Frank O'Hara. GLP; NeAP; NNaP; PoM; PoNe
Ode: "Sleep sweetly in your humble graves." Henry Timrod. GOA; NOBA; OxBA; TAP
  (At Magnolia Cemetery.) AnAmPo
  (Sleep Sweetly.) AH, with music
Ode: "Spacious firmament on high, The." Joseph Addison. BLPA; EaLo; ELP; FaBoBe; FaPoR; FPL; GN; HeIP; NOCV; NOEC; PoEL-3; TOF
Ode: Spirit Wooed, The. Richard Watson Dixon. OBNC
Ode: "That I have often been in love, deep love." "Peter Pindar." NOEC
Ode: "They journeyed,/ When the darkness of night." Ibn al-Arabi, tr. by R. A. Nicholson. AWP
Ode: To My Lovers. Paul Verlaine, tr. fr. French by J. Murat and W. Gunn. PeHV
Ode: To My Pupils. W. H. Auden. MoBrPo
Ode: "To orisons, the midnight bell." William Beckford. OBTV
Ode: To the Cuckoo. Michael Bruce. See Hail, beauteous stranger of the wood.
Ode: To the Nightingale. Joseph Warton. PBBP
Ode: To the Virginian Voyage. Michael Drayton. HAP; NAEL-1; NOBE; OBEV; OBS; PAH; PoEL-2; SeCePo; TEP
Ode: "Until thine hands clasp girdlewise the waist of the Belov'd." Sadi, tr. by R. A. Nicholson. AWP
Ode: "We are the music-makers." Arthur William Edgar O'Shaughnessy. FaPoR; OBEV; TrGrPo
  (Music Makers, The.) FaBV
Ode: "Weep, ah weep love's losing." Imr el Kais. Fr. The Mu'allaqat. AWP
Ode: "When first, descending from the moorlands." Wordsworth. See Extempore Effusion [upon the Death of James Hogg], An.
Ode: "Who can support the anguish of love?" Ibn al-Arabi, tr. by R. A. Nicholson. AWP
Ode, An: "Why doth heaven bear a sun." Barnabe Barnes. Fr. Parthenophil and Parthenophe. ElL; OBSC
Ode: "Why will they never sleep." John Peale Bishop. LiTA; LiTM

Ode against St. Cecilia's Day. George Barker. PoA
Ode for a Master Mariner Ashore. Louise Imogen Guiney. AA
Ode for a Social Meeting. Oliver Wendell Holmes. OBAL
Ode for Ben Jonson, An. Robert Herrick. AWP; InvP; SeCP; TrGrPo
  (Ode for Him, An.) CaPo; NoP; OBS; SeCV-1
Ode for Decoration Day, sel. Henry Peterson. OHIP
  "O gallant brothers of the generous South." AA; FaBoBe
Ode for Him, An. Robert Herrick. See Ah, Ben!/ Say how or when.
Ode for Soft Voice. Michael McClure. NeAP
Ode for the American Dead in Korea. Thomas McGrath. NePoEA; VGW
  (Ode for the American Dead.) AiP
Ode for the Burial of a Citizen. John Ciardi. LiTM
Ode for the New Year, An. At. to. John Gay. OxBoLi
Ode in Honour. Francis Scarfe. EAS
Ode in May. Sir William Watson. OBEV; WGRP
Ode in Memory of the American Volunteers Fallen for France. Alan Seeger. PAH
Ode in 1,000 Lines, sel. Takahashi Mutsuo, tr. fr. Japanese by Hiroaki Sato.
  Forecome and Come. FCEI
Ode in the Praise of Sack, An. Unknown. OBS
Ode in Time of Hesitation, An, sels. William Vaughn Moody. AnAmPo; OxBA; PAH
  No Hint of Stain. AA
  Robert Gould Shaw. AA
Ode Inscribed to W. H. Channing. Emerson. AmPP; HAP; NAAL-1; NOBA; NoP; OxBA; TAP
Ode Occasioned by the Death of Mr. Thomson. William Collins. NOEC; PoE
Ode of Signs, sel. Muhammad Abd al-Hayy, tr. fr. Arabic by Matthew Sorenson and Alistair Elliot.
  Adam Sign, The. Fr. I. MAP
Ode of the Birth of Our Saviour, An, sel. Robert Herrick.
  Instead of Neat Inclosures. ChTr
Ode on a Decision to Settle for Less. William Pillen. VWA
Ode on a Distant Prospect of Clapham Academy. Thomas Hood. BXAP
Ode on a Distant Prospect of Eton College. Thomas Gray. BLPL; GTBS; GTBS-P; HeIP; LiTB; NAEL-1; NOBE; NOEC; NoP; OAEL-1; PoE; PoEL-3; PrIm
Ode on a Grecian Urn. Keats. AWP; ChER; EBEV; EnRP; FaBoBe; FaFP; FF; FiP; FPL; HAP; HeIP; HoPM; InPS; LiTB; NAEL-2; NAWM-2; NIP; NOBE; NoP; OAEL-2; OBEV; OBNC; OHFP; PoE; PoEL-4; PPP; PrIm; SoSe; TEP; TOF; TrGrPo; UnPo
Ode on a Grecian Urn. E. O. Parrott. BXAP
Ode on a Grecian Urn Summarized. Desmond Skirrow. NIP; NOBL
Ode on [or to] a Jar of Pickles. Bayard Taylor. BXAP; FaBoPa
Ode on Celestial Music. Brian Patten. OxBTC
Ode on Contemplating Clapham Junction. Christopher Middleton. Fr. Herman Moon's Hourbook. NePoEA-2
Ode on Gas, An. Unknown. OBAL
Ode on His Majesty's Proclamation. Sir Richard Fanshawe, after the Italian of Giovanni Battista Guarini. Fr. Il Pastor Fido. NOBE
  (Ode, upon Occasion of His Majesties Proclamation in the Year 1630, An.) MePo; OBS
Ode on Indolence. Keats. EnRP; LiTB; NAEL-2; OBNC
Ode on Intimations of [or on] immortality. Wordsworth. See Ode: Intimations of Immortality from Recollections of Early Childhood.
Ode on Lord Macartney's Embassy to China. William Shepherd. NOEC
Ode on Melancholy. Keats. EnRP; FiP; HAP; HeIP; InPK; InPS; LiTB; MAT; NAEL-2; NAWM-2; NOBE; NoP; OAEL-2; OBEV; OBNC; PoE; PoEL-4; PoRA; PPP; PrIm; TEP; TrGrPo
Ode on St. Cecilia's Day, sel. Pope.
  Descend, Ye Nine. GN
Ode on [or to] Solitude. Pope. AWP; FiP; FL; HeIP; InvP; NAEL-1; PoRA; Prf; TEP
  (Quiet Life, The.) GTBS; GTBS-P
  (Solitude.) FaFP; TrGrPo
Ode on the Birth of Our Saviour, An. Robert Herrick. GN
Ode on the Celebration of the Battle of Bunker Hill, June 17, 1825, sel. Grenville Mellen.
  Lonely Bugle Grieves, The. AA
Ode on [or On] the Death of a Favourite [or Favorite] Cat, Drowned in a Tub [or Bowl] of Gold Fishes. Thomas Gray. EBEV; FaBoBe; FM; HoPM; NAEL-1; NBLV; NOBE; NOBL; NOEC; NoP; OAEL-1; PoE; PoEL-3; PPP; TEP
  (Cat and the Fish, The.) WiR

(On a Favorite Cat Drowned in a Tub of Gold Fishes.)
BeLS; FaBoCo; GN; GTBS; GTBS-P; InvP; LiTB;
OBEV
(On the Death of a Favorite Cat, Drowned in a Tub of Gold Fishes.)
FPL; InPS; PoLF; PoRA
Ode on the Death of Mr. Henry Purcell, An, *sel.* Dryden.
"Mark how the lark and linnet sing." PBBP
Ode on the Death of [Mr.] Thomson. William Collins. *See* In yonder
grave a Druid lies.
Ode on the Departing Year, *sel.* Samuel Taylor Coleridge.
O My Mother Isle! ("Not yet enslaved, not wholly vile").
FaBoPP
Ode on the Morning of Christ's Nativity. Milton. *See* On the Morning
of Christ's Nativity.
Ode on the Pleasure Arising from Vicissitude. Thomas Gray. GTBS;
GTBS-P
"Now the golden morn aloft," *sel.* NOEC
Ode on the Poetical Character. William Collins. EnRP; NAEL-1;
NOEC; OAEL-1; PoE; PoEL-3; TEP
Ode on the Poets. Keats. *See* Ode: "Bards of passion and of mirth."
Ode on the Popular Superstitions of the Highlands of Scotland, An.
William Collins. EnRP; NOEC; OAEL-1
Ode on the Popular Superstitions of the Highlands of Scotland [Considered
as the Subject of Poetry], An. William Collins. EnRP; NOEC;
OAEL-1
Stormy Hebrides, The, *sel.* NOBE
Ode on the Spring. Thomas Gray. GTBS; GTBS-P; NOEC
Ode on the Spring, An. Thomas Gray. GTBS
Ode on the Twentieth Century. Henrietta Cordelia Ray.
CBWP-3
Ode, on the Unveiling of the Shaw Memorial on Boston Common, May
31st, 1897, An. Thomas Bailey Aldrich. AA; PAH
Ode on Theoxenos. Pindar, *tr. fr. Greek.* PeHV, *tr.* by John Addington
Symonds
Ode on Zero. Phoebe Pettingell. PoA
Ode Recited at the Harvard Commemoration. James Russell Lowell.
AA; NOBA; OBWP, *br. sel.*; PAH
Sels.
"I praise him not." AiP
"I with uncovered head." *Fr.* VIII *and* XII. OHIP
Ode to a Beautiful Woman. Carl Clark. JB
Ode to a Butterfly. Thomas Wentworth Higginson. AA;
FaBoBe
Ode to a Country Hoyden. "Peter Pindar." NOEC
Ode to a Dead Dodge. David McElroy. AmPA
Ode to a Dental Hygienist. Earnest Albert Hooton. FiBHP
Ode to a Dressmaker's Dummy. Donald Justice. NoAM
Ode to a Lost Cargo in a Ship Called *Save.* José Craveirinha, *tr. fr.
Portuguese* by Chris Searle. WMBCH
Ode to a Model. Vladimir Nabokov. OBAL
Ode to a Nightingale. Keats. AWP; BLRP; ChER; EBEV; EnRP;
FaBoBe; FaFP; FiP; GTBS; GTBS-P; HAP; HeIP; InPS; LiTB;
NAEL-2; NAWM-2; NOBE; NoP; OAEL-2; OBEV; OBNC; OPOP;
PBBP; PoE; PoEL-4; PoRA; PPP; PrIm; RB; SoSe; TEP; TOF;
TrGrPo; UnPo; WeW
(To a Nightingale.) ChTr
Sels.
"Darkling I listen; and for many a time." OBD
Magic Casements. FaBV
Ode to a Nightingale. Roy Kelly. BXAP
Ode to a Pig while His Nose Was Being Bored. Robert Southey.
NOBL
Ode to a Skylark. Shelley. *See* Hail to thee, blithe spirit!
Ode to an Alien. Diane Ackerman. BWV
Ode to an Old Man. Yoshioka Minoru, *tr. fr. Japanese* by Hiroaki Sato.
FCEI
Ode to Anactoria. Sappho, *tr. fr. Greek* by William Ellery Leonard.
AWP
Ode to Aphrodite. Sappho, *tr. fr. Greek by* William Ellery Leonard.
AWP
Ode to Arnold Schoenberg. Charles Tomlinson.
NePoEA-2
Ode to Autumn. Keats. *See* Season of mists and mellow fruitfulness!
Ode to Beauty. Emerson. AmPP; PoEL-4
Ode to Bohemians. Ron Padgett. UL
Ode to David's Harp. Isaac Rosenberg. FL
Ode to Duty. Wordsworth. AWP; EnRP; FPL; GTBS; GTBS-P;
NAEL-2; NoP; OAEL-2; OBEV; WGRP
Ode to England, *sels.* William Wilberforce Lord. AA
Keats.
Wordsworth.

Ode to Evening. William Collins. AWP; EBEV; EnRP; FaBoBe; GTBS;
GTBS-P; HAP; LiTB; NAEL-1; NOBE; NOEC; NoP; OAEL-1;
OBEV; PoE; PoEL-3; PPP; SeCePo; TrGrPo; ViBoPo
(To Evening.) GTBS; GTBS-P
Ode to Failure. Allen Ginsberg. CAPP
Ode to Fancy, *sel.* Joseph Warton.
"O warm, enthusiastic maid." NOEC
Ode to Fanny, *sel.* Keats.
"Ah! dearest love, sweet home of all my fears." ChER
Ode to Fear. William Collins. NOEC; TrGrPo, *abr.*
Ode to Food. Darrell Gray. UL
Ode to Fortune. Fitz-Greene Halleck *and* Joseph Rodman Drake. *Fr.*
The Croaker Papers. AA
Ode to Freedom. Aaron Zeitlin, *tr. fr. Yiddish* by Keith Bosley.
VWA
Ode to Garlic. William Stafford. CAPP
Ode to Her Aroma. Pablo Neruda, *tr. fr. Spanish* by Perry Higman.
LPSS
Ode to Himself, An. Ben Jonson. HAP; JCP; LiTB; NOBE; NoP; OBS;
PoEL-2; PrIm; QFR; SeCePo; SeCP; SeCV-1
Ode to Himsel[f]e ("Come leave the loathed stage"). Ben Jonson.
NAEL-1; OAEL-1; OBS; SeCP
Ode to Jamestown. James Kirke Paulding. PAH
Ode to Joy. Frank O'Hara. GLP; NeAP; PPP
Ode to Liberty. Thomas Chatterton. *Fr.* Goddwyn.
TrGrPo
Ode to Master Endymion Porter, upon His Brother's Death, An. Robert
Herrick. CaPo
Ode to Me. Kingsley Amis. NAs
Ode to Michael Goldberg's Birth and Other Births, *sel.* Frank O'Hara.
NeAP
I Don't Remember Anything of Then. NAs
Ode to Miss Hoyland. Thomas Chatterton. BXAP
Ode to Moderation, *sel.* Annabella Plumptre.
"To thee, whose cautious step and specious air." NOEC
Ode to Mr. [*or* Master] Anthony Stafford to Hasten Him into the Country,
An. Thomas Randolph. NOBE; OBEV; OBS
Ode to Mr. F—[*or* Mr. Forbes]. Allan Ramsay, *after* Horace. NOEC;
OBVE
Ode to Naples, *sel.* Shelley.
At Pompeii. FaBoPP
Ode to Napoleon Buonaparte, *sel.* Byron.
Washington. OHIP; PAH
Ode to Peace. Mary Weston Fordham. CBWP-2
Ode to Peace. *Unknown.* PAH
Ode to Pornography. Jack Anderson. PoA
Ode to Psyche. Keats. ChER; EnRP; InPS; LiTB; NAEL-2; NOBE;
NoP; OAEL-2; OBEV; OBNC; PoE; PoEL-4; PPP; TOF
Ode to Rhys ap Maredudd of Tywyn. Dafydd Nanmor, *tr. fr. Welsh* by
H. Idris Bell. OBWVE
Ode to Salt. Pablo Neruda, *tr. fr. Spanish* by Robert Bly.
NU
Ode to Simplicity. William Collins. EnRP; NOBE; OBEV;
TEP
Ode to Sir William Sydney, on His Birth-Day. Ben Jonson. NAs
(Another Birthday.) WiR
Ode to Spring. Walter Rollin Brooks. RAR; RHPC
Ode to Spring in the Metropolis, An. Sir Owen Seaman. FiBHP
Ode to Stephen Dowling Bots, Dec'd. "Mark Twain." *See* Adventures
of Huckleberry Finn, The: Emmeline Grangerford's "Ode to Stephen
Dowling Bots, Dec'd."
Ode to Swansea. Vernon Watkins. OBWVE
Ode to Terminus. W. H. Auden. HAP
Ode to the Cameleopard. Thomas Hood. FaBoNo
Ode to the Confederate Dead. Allen Tate. AiP; FaBoMo; HeIP; LiTA;
LiTM; MoAB; MoAmPo; MoP; NAAL-2; NoAM; NOBA; NoP;
OBD, *ll.* 1-9; OBWP; OxBA; PrIm; TAP; UnPo
Ode to the Departing Year. Samuel Taylor Coleridge. EnRP
Ode to the End of Summer. Phyllis McGinley. NBLV
Ode to the Evening Star. Mark Akenside. PBBP
Ode to the Framers of the Frame Bill, An. Byron. CoMu;
SaC
Ode to the German Drama. *Unknown.* NOEC
Ode to the Hayden Planetarium. Arthur Guiterman. ImOP
Ode to the Human Heart. Laman Blanchard. NA; NOBL
Ode to the Inhabitants of Pennsylvania. Longfellow. PAH
Ode to the Lake of Geneva. William Parsons. OBTV
Ode to the Last Pot of Marmalade. "John." OBTV
Ode to the Maguire. Eochadh O'Hussey. *See* O'Hussey's Ode to the
Maguire.
Ode to the Medieval Poets. W. H. Auden. PoA

Ode to the Northeast Wind. Charles Kingsley. FaPoR; GN

Ode to the Pig: His Tail. Walter Rollin Brooks. RHPC

Ode to the Pious Memory of the Accomplished Young Lady, Mrs. Anne Killigrew. Dryden. *See* To the Pious Memory of the Accomplished [*or* Accomplisht] Young Lady, Mrs. Anne Killigrew, [Excellent in the Two Sister-Arts of Poesie and Painting].

Ode to the Poppy. Henrietta Oneil. WPE

Ode to the Protestant Poets. Paul Hoover. UL

Ode to the Sea. Howard Baker. OxBA

Ode to the Setting Sun, *sels.* Francis Thompson.
  "Now that the red glare of thy fall is blown." OBNC

Sun, The. MoAB; MoBrPo

Ode to the Spirit of Earth in Autumn. George Meredith. TEP

Ode to the Sun. Eloise Bibb. CBWP-4

Ode to the Watermelon. Pablo Neruda, *tr. fr. Spanish by* Robert Bly. EAS; NU

Ode to the West Wind. Shelley. AWP; BoNaP; CH; EBEV; EnRP; FaBoBe; FaBV; FaFP; FiP; FPL; GTBS; GTBS-P; HAP; HeIP; InPS; LiTB; MOS; NAEL-2; NIP; NOBE; NoP; OAEL-2; OBEV; OBNC; OHFP; PoE; PoEL-4; PoLF; PoRA; PPP; PrIm; TEP; TrGrPo; WeW

Ode to the Yorkshire Dales. Cees Buddingh', *tr. fr. Dutch by* Peter Nijmeijer. DuIn

Ode to Tobacco. Charles Stuart Calverley. FaBoCo; FiBHP

Ode to Walt Whitman. Federico García Lorca, *tr. fr. Spanish.* PeHV

Ode to Winter. Thomas Campbell. GTBS; GTBS-P

Ode to Zion. Judah Halevi, *tr. fr. Hebrew by* Nina Davis Salaman. TrJP

Ode, upon a Question Moved, Whether Love Should Continue Forever? An. Herbert of Cherbury. JCP; MeLP; MePo; NOBE; OBS; SeCP

Ode upon Doctor Harvey. Abraham Cowley. PoEL-2
  "Coy Nature (which remain'd, though aged grown)," *sel.* Par

Ode, upon Occasion of His Majesties Proclamation in the Year 1630, An. Sir Richard Fanshawe, *after the Italian of* Giovanni Battista Guarini. *See* Il Pastor Fido: Ode on His Majesty's Proclamation.

Ode Written during the War with America, 1814, *sel.* Robert Southey. Bower of Peace, The. *Fr.* PAH.

Ode Written in 1746. William Collins. *See* How Sleep the Brave.

Ode Written in the Beginning of the Year 1746. William Collins. *See* How Sleep the Brave.

Ode Written in the Peak[e], An. Michael Drayton. FaBoPP; OBS

Odell. James Stephens. MoAB; MoBrPo

Odeon. Aharon Amir, *tr. fr. Hebrew by* Bernhard Frank. MHeP

Oderisi D'Agobbio on Pride. Dante, *tr. fr. Italian by* John Ciardi. *Fr.* Divina Commedia: Purgatorio, IX. PFI

Odes, *sels.* Hafiz, *tr. fr. Persian.* AWP
  "Comrades, the morning breaks, the sun is up." *Fr.* II, *tr. by* Richard Le Gallienne.
  "Days of spring are here, The! the eglantine." *Fr.* X, *tr. by* Gertrude Lowthian Bell.
  "Grievous folly shames my sixtieth year, A." *Fr.* IV, *tr. by* Richard Le Gallienne.
  "I cease not from desire till my desire." *Fr.* IX, *tr. by* Gertrude Lowthian Bell.
  "I have borne the anguish of love, which ask me not to describe." *Fr.* XI, *tr. by* John Hindley.
  "I said to heaven that glowed above." *Fr.* XII, *tr. by* Emerson.
  "Jewel of the secret treasury, The." *Fr.* VI, *tr. by* Gertrude Lowthian Bell.
  "Lady that hast my heart within thy hand." *Fr.* VIII, *tr. by* Gertrude Lowthian Bell.
  "Oft have I said, I say it once more." *Fr.* XIII, *tr. by* Emerson.
  "Rose is not the rose unless thou see, The." *Fr.* III, *tr. by* Richard Le Gallienne.
  "Saki, for God's love, come and fill my glass." *Fr.* I, *tr. by* Richard Le Gallienne.
  "Where is my ruined life, and where the fame." *Fr.* V, *tr. by* Gertrude Lowthian Bell.
  "Wind from the east, oh Lapwing of the day." *Fr.* VII, *tr. by* Gertrude Lowthian Bell.

Odes, *sels.* Horace, *tr. fr. Latin.*
  I, 3. To the Ship on Which Virgil Sailed to Athens ("Sic te diva potens Cyri"). AWP, *tr. by* Dryden.
  I, 4. Ode: "Hold! pale death, at the poor man's shack and the pasha's palace." OBD, *tr. by* James Michie.
  I, 5. "What slender youth bedewed with liquid odours" ("Quis multa gracilis"). OBVE, *tr. by* Milton.
    (Another to the Same.) WiR, *tr. by* William Browne.
    (Fifth Ode of Horace, The.) EBEV, *tr. by* Milton; EnLoPo, *tr. by* Milton; PoEL-3, *tr. by* Milton.
    ("Pyrrha, what slender well-shap'd beau.") OBVE, *tr. by* Anthony Horneck.

("Say what slim youth, with moist perfumes.") OBVE, *tr. by* Christopher Smart.
    ("Tell me, Pyrrha, what fine youth.") OAEL-1, *tr. by* William Browne; WIR, *tr. by* William Browne.
    (To a Girl.) WiR, *tr. by* Milton.
    (To Pyrrha.) AWP, *tr. by* Milton.
    ("To whom now, Pyrrha, art thou kind?.") OBVE, *tr. by* Abraham Cowley.
    ("What stripling now thee discomposes.") OBVE, *tr. by* Sir Richard Fanshawe.
  I, 8. "Lydia, in Heavens Name" ("Lydia, dic, per omnes"). *Tr. by* Sir Richard Fanshawe. OBVE
  I, 9. "Behold yon mountain's hoary height." ("Vides ut alta"). OBVE, *tr. by* Dryden.
    ("Thou seest the hills candied with snow.") OBVE
    (To Thaliarchus ("Thou seest the hills").) OBVE, *tr. by* Sir Richard Fanshawe.
  I, 11. "Seek not, Leuconöe, to know how long you're going to live yet."
    (Ad Leuconöen.) AWP, *tr. by* F. P. Adams.
    ("Tu ne quaesieris".) AA, *tr. by* Eugene Field.
  I, 14. Ship of State, The ("O navis, referent"). AWP, *tr. by* William Ewart Gladstone.
  I, 21. To Apollo and Diana ("Dianam tenerae dicite virgines"). OBVE, *tr. by* Branwell Brontë.
    (Invocation: "Maidens young and virgins tender,".) AWP, *tr. by* Louis Untermeyer.
  I, 22. "Virtue, dear friend, needs no 'defence' " ("Integer vitae"). OBVE, *tr. by* Earl of Roscommon.
    ("Man in righteousness arrayed, The.") AWP
    (To Aristius Fuscus.) OBVE, *tr. by* Samuel Johnson.
    ("To man, my friend, whose conscious heart.") OBVE
    (To Sally.) AWP, *tr. by* John Quincy Adams.
  I, 23. To Chloe ("Vitas hinnuleo"). AWP, *tr. by* Austin Dobson. OBVE
  I, 25. Ribald Romeos Less and Less Berattle ("Parcius iunctas quatiunt fenestras"). MAT, *tr. by* John Frederick Nims.
    ("Bloods and bucks of this lewd town, The.") OBVE, *tr. by* the Young Gentlemen of Mr. Rule's Academy at Islington.
    (To Lydia.) OBVE, *tr. by* Philip Francis.
    ("Wanton herd of rakes profest, The.") OBVE
    ("Young bloods come round less often now, The.") BoLoP, *tr. by* James Michie.
  I, 31. By the Flat Cup ("Quid dedicatum"). CTC, *tr. by* Ezra Pound.
  I, 33. Albi, Ne Doleas. AWP, *tr. by* Austin Dobson.
  I, 38. Simplicity. InPK; NBLV
    ("Ah child, no Persian—perfect art.") OBVE, *tr. by* Gerard Manley Hopkins.
    ("Boy, I detest the Persian pomp.") InPK; NBLV
    (Chicago Analogue.) NBLV, *tr. by* Keith Preston.
    ("Davus, I detest.") NBLV
    ("Dear Lucy, you know what my wish is.") NBLV
    (Fie on Eastern Luxury.) InPK, *tr. by* Hartley Coleridge.
    ("I do not share the common craze.") NBLV
    (Myrtle for Two.) NBLV, *tr. by* George F. Whicher.
    ("Nay, nay, my boy—'tis not for me.") InPK
    ("Persian flummery.") NBLV
    (Persian Fopperies.) AWP, *tr. by* William Cowper.
    ("Persian pomps, boy, ever I renounce them.") OBVE, *tr. by* Christopher Smart.
    (Persicos Odi: Pocket Version.) NBLV
    (Preference Declared, The, *tr. by* Eugene Field) InPK; NBLV
    (Victorian Paraphrase, A.) NBLV, *tr. by* Thackeray.
  II, 4. Ad Xanthiam Phoceum ("Ne sit ancillae"). AWP, *tr. by* Franklin P. Adams.
  II, 7. "Pompeius, best of all my comrades, you and I" ("O saepe mecum"). WaaP, *tr. by* John Wight.
    ("Pompeius, chief of all my friends, with whom.") OBWP, *tr. by* James Michie.
  II, 10. "Receive, dear friend, the truths I teach" ("Rectius vives"). AWP, *tr. by* William Cowper; OBVE, *tr. by* William Cowper.
    ("Of thy lyfe, Thomas, this compass well mark.") OBVE, *tr. by* Earl of Surrey.
    (To Licinius.) AWP, *tr. by* William Cowper.
    ("You better sure shall live, not evermore.") OBVE, *tr. by* Sir Philip Sidney.
  II, 11. To an Ambitious Friend ("Quid bellicosus"). AWP, *tr. by* Matthew Arnold.
  II, 18. "Gold or iv'ry's not intended" ("Non ebur neque aureum"). OBVE, *tr. by* Christopher Smart.

III, 1. "Tread back—and back, the lewd and lay!" ("Odi profanum vulgus"). OBVE, *tr. by* Gerard Manley Hopkins.
("Hence ye prophane; I hate ye all.") OBVE, *tr. by* Abraham Cowley, 2 *sts.*.
(Profane, The.) AWP, *tr. by* Abraham Cowley.
III, 2. "Let the youth hardened by a sharp soldier's life" ("Angustam amice"). WaaP, *tr. by* Gardner Taplin *and* Richard Eberhart.
("Disciplined in the school of hard campaigning.") OBWP, *tr. by* James Michie.
III, 7. "Dear Molly, why so oft in tears?" ("Quid fles, Asterie"). OBVE, *tr. by* George Stepney.
III, 9. Dialogue between Horace and Lydia, A ("Donec gratus eram"). OBVE, *tr. by* Robert Herrick.
(Reconciliation: A Modern Version, The.) NBLV, *mod. vers. by* F. P. Adams.
("What time I was your one best bet.") NBLV
III, 10. Extremum Tanain. AWP, *tr. by* Austin Dobson.
III, 13. To the Fountain[s] of Bandusia ("O fons Bandusiae"). *Tr. by* Eugene Field. AA; AWP
III, 22. Pine Tree for Diana, The ("Montium custos nemorumque"). AWP, *tr. by* Louis Untermeyer.
III, 23. To Phidyle ("Caelo supinas si tuleris"). AWP, *tr. by* Austin Dobson.
III, 28. Holiday ("Festo quid potius die"). AWP, *tr. by* Louis Untermeyer.
III, 29. "Descended of an ancient line" ("Tyrrhena regum progenies"), *paraphrased by* Dryden. OBVE
(Happy the Man, *st. 8 only.*) FaPoR
(Horat. Ode 29. Book 3.) SeCV-2
(To Maecenas, *tr. by* Dryden) AWP, *tr. by* Dryden; OBVE, *tr. by* Dryden; SeCV-1, *tr. by* Dryden.
III, 30. This Monument Will Outlast ("Exegi momumentum aere perennius,." CTC, *tr. by* Ezra Pound.
IV, 1. To Venus ("Intermissa, Venus"). AWP, *tr. by* Ben Jonson; OBVE, *tr. by* Ben Jonson.
("Again? New tumults in my breast?.") PeHV, *tr. by* Pope.
IV, 2. Praise of Pindar, The ("Pindarum quisquis studet aemulari"). OAEL-1, *tr. by* Abraham Cowley.
IV, 7. "The snow dissolv'd no more is seen" ("Diffugere nives"). NAEL-1, *tr. by* Samuel Johnson; OBVE, *tr. by* Samuel Johnson.
(Diffugere Nives.) OBVE, *tr. by* A. E. Housman.
("Snows are fled away, leaves on the shaws, The.") OBEV
IV, 9. Immortality of Verse, The. AWP, *tr. by* Pope.
IV, 10. "O Ligurinus" ("O crudelis adhuc"). PeHV
IV, 13. Revenge ("Audivere, Lyce"). AWP, *tr. by* Louis Untermeyer.
Odes, *sels.* Albius Tibullus, *tr. fr. Latin by* John Dart. PeHV
"And you, whate'er your Fav'rite does, approve." *Fr.* I, 4. PeHV
"Far from the tender tribe of boys remove." *Fr.* I, 4.
Odes to Nea, *sels.* Thomas Moore.
"I pray you, let us roam no more." OBNC
"Nay, tempt me not to love again." OBNC
Odi et Amo. Catullus, *tr. fr. Latin.* CTC, *tr. by* Ezra Pound.
("I hate and love; wouldst thou the reason know?") OBVE, *tr. by* Richard Lovelace.
("I love and hate. Ah! never ask why so!") OBVE, *tr. by* Walter Savage Landor.)
Odiham. John Gray. FaBoCo
Odor of thyme, The. The Landing. Michael Guttenbrunner. CoAuP
Odorous shade lingers the fair day's ghost, An. Night. Henri de Regnier, *tr. by* "Seumas O'Sullivan." AWP
Odors. Mani Leib, *tr. fr. Yiddish by* John Hollander. PeBMYV
Odour, The. George Herbert. OBS
O'Driscoll drove with a song. The Host of the Air. W. B. Yeats. BrPo; CH
Odysseus. Padraic Fallon. CIP
Odysseus. Haim Guri, *tr. fr. Hebrew by* Bernhard Frank. MHeP
Odysseus. W. S. Merwin. NOBA; NoP
Odysseus has come home, to the gully farm. The Homecoming. James Keir Baxter. ATNZ
Odysseus heard the sirens; they were singing. The Sirens. John Manifold. LiTB; LiTM; MoBrPo; Son; WaP
Odysseus in Phaeacia. Gábor Devecseri, *tr. fr. Hungarian by* Robert Graves. MHuP
Odysseus' Song to Calypso. Peter Kane Dufault. ErPo
Odysseus under wet snapping sheets. C. K. Stead. *Fr.* Quesada, X. ATNZ; PeNZ
Odyssey ("Sing in me, Muse, and through me tell the story."). Homer, *tr. fr. Greek by* Robert Fitzgerald. NAWM-1
Sels.
"And now Eurynome had bath'd the king." *Fr.* XXIII, *tr. by* George Chapman. OBVE

"And now his well-known bow the master bore." *Fr.* XXI, *tr. by* Pope. OBVE
"And now man-slaughtering Pallas took in hand." *Fr.* XXII, *tr. by* George Chapman. OBVE
(End of the Suitors, The.) OBS
"And now the Queene of women had intent." *Fr.* XXI, *tr. by* George Chapman. OBVE
"Cave we found, but vacant all within, The." *Fr.* IX, *tr. by* Pope. OBVE
"Close to the gates a spacious garden lies." *Fr.* VII, *tr. by* Pope. OBVE
"For my part, I'le not meddle with the cause." *Fr.* XIV, *tr. by* George Chapman. CTC
"From her bed's high and odoriferous roome." *Fr.* IV, *tr. by* George Chapman. CTC
Gardens of Alcinous, The ("Close to the gates a spacious garden lies"). *Fr.* VII, *tr. by* Pope. OAEL-1; OBVE
Gardens of Alcinous, The ("Without the hall, and close upon the gate"). *Fr.* VII, *tr. by* George Chapman. OAEL-1; OBVE
"God who mounts the winged winds, The." *Fr.* V, *tr. by* Pope. OBVE
"He ended, nor the Argicide refus'd." *Fr.* V, *tr. by* William Cowper. OBVE
"He spake, to whom I, answ'ring, thus replied." *Fr.* XI, *tr. by* William Cowper. OBD
"Just then, forgetful of the strict command." *Fr.* XII, *tr. by* William Cowper. OBVE
"Mighty wave rush'd o'er him as he spoke, A." *Fr.* V, *tr. by* Pope. OBVE
Nausicaa. *Fr.* VI, *tr. by* George Chapman. OBS
New Coasts and Poseidon's Son. *Fr.* IX, *tr. by* Robert Fitzgerald. WTO
"Now gently winding up the fair ascent." *Fr.* XXI, *tr. by* Pope. OBVE
"Now to dispose the dead, the care remains." *Fr.* XXII, *tr. by* Pope. OBVE
"Now toils the Heroe; trees on trees o'erthrown." *Fr.* V, *tr. by* Pope. OBVE
"Nymph turnd home, The. He fell to felling downe." *Fr.* V, *tr. by* George Chapman. OBVE
Sacrifice, The. *Fr.* III, *tr. by* George Chapman. OBS
Scylla and Charybdis. *Fr.* XII, *tr. by* George Chapman. OBS
"She thus; when I had great desire to prove." *Fr.* XI, *tr. by* George Chapman. OBVE
"Then tooke they seate, and forth our passage strooke." *Fr.* XII, *tr. by* George Chapman. MOS
"There grew two olives, closest of the grove." *Fr.* V, *tr. by* Pope. OBVE
"This spoke, a huge wave tooke him by the head." *Fr.* V, *tr. by* George Chapman. MOS; OBVE
"Thus charg'd he; nor Argicides denied." *Fr.* V, *tr. by* George Chapman. OBVE
"Trembling the spectres glide, and plaintive vent." *Fr.* XXIV, *tr. by* Pope. OBVE
"Twelve herds of oxen, no less flockes of sheepe." *Fr.* XIV, *tr. by* George Chapman. CTC
Ulysses and His Dog. *Fr.* XVII, *tr. by* Pope. FiP
Ulysses in the Waves. *Fr.* V, *tr. by* George Chapman. OBS
Ulysses Leaves the Nymph Calypso. *Fr.* V, *tr. by* George Chapman. JCP
"Where neither King nor shepheard want comes neare." *Fr.* IV, *tr. by* George Chapman. CTC
"While thus he thought, a monst'rous wave up-bore." *Fr.* V, *tr. by* Pope. OBVE
"Without the hall, and close upon the gate." *Fr.* VII, *tr. by* George Chapman. OBVE
"Youth there was, Elpenor was he nam'd, A." *Fr.* X, *tr. by* Pope. OBVE
Odyssey, The. Andrew Lang. OBEV; OBNC; PoLF; PoRA
Odyssey of Big Boy. Sterling A. Brown. BANP; CDC
Oeconomy of Love; a Poetical Essay, The, *sel.* John Armstrong.
Advice to Lovers. NOEC
Oedipus. Thomas Blackburn. FaBoTw
Oedipus, *sel.* Dryden.
Incantation to Oedipus. *Fr.* III, i. OFD; WSC
(Spell, A.) WiR
Oedipus. Josephine Miles. WPE
Oedipus. Edwin Muir. CMoP
Oedipus at Colonus, *sels.* Sophocles, *tr. fr. Greek.*
"What man is he that yearneth." *Tr. by* A. E. Housman. AWP

Colonus' Praise. *Tr. by* W. B. Yeats. OBVE
"Endure what life God gives and ask no longer span." *Tr. by* W. B. Yeats. OBMV
Oedipus the King [*or* Oedipus Rex] ("Oh my children, the new blood of ancient Thebes."), *sel.* Sophocles, *tr. fr. Greek by* Robert Fagles. NAWM-1
"Oh, may my constant feet not fail." *Tr. by* Robert Whitelaw. WGRP
Oedipus to the Oracle. W. Wesley Trimpi. NePoEA
Oenone and Paris. George Peele. *See* Arraignment of Paris, The: Fair and Fair.
Oenone's Complaint. George Peele. *Fr.* The Arraignment of Paris. EIL; OBSC
O'er a low couch the setting sun had thrown its latest ray. The Baron's Last Banquet. Albert Gorton Greene, *tr. by* Alice Fletcher. AA; AnAmPo; BeLS
O'er a small suburban borough. The Domineering Eagle and the Inventive Bratling. Guy Wetmore Carryl. OBAL
O'er all my song the image of a face. The Negro Singer. James David Corrothers. BANP
O'er all the hill-tops. Goethe, *tr. fr. German. Fr.* Wanderer's Night-Songs, II. AWP
(Second Poem the Night-Walker Wrote, The.) NU, *tr. by* Robert Bly.
O'er Cambridge set the yeoman's mark. Lexington. Sidney Lanier. *Fr.* Psalm of the West. PAH
O'er Continent and Ocean. John Haynes Holmes. AH
O'er golden sands my waters flow. The Enchanted Spring. George Darley. BoNaP
O'er Huron's wave the sun was low. The Battle of Bridgewater. *Unknown.* PAH
O'er the high and o'er the lowly. Our National Banner. Dexter Smith. OPP; PAH
O'er the level plains, where mountains greet me as I go. Time's Song. Winthrop Mackworth Praed. EnRP
O'er the men of Ethiopia she would pour her cornucopia. Husband and Heathen. Sam Walter Foss. OBAL
O'er the rough main, with flowing sheet. The *Bonhomme Richard* and *Serapis.* Philip Freneau. PAH
O'er the rugged mountain's brow. Harry Graham. *Fr.* Some Ruthless Rhymes, VI. CenHV
O'er [*or* O're] the smooth enameled green. Milton. *Fr.* Arcades. OBEV; TrGrPo
(Song: "O'er The smooth enamelled green.") OxBSP
O'er the snow, through the air, to the mountain. Alpine Spirit's Song. Thomas Lovell Beddoes. OBNC; OBTV
O'er the warrior gauntlet grim. Parricide. Julia Ward Howe. PAH
O'er the waste of waters cruising. Philip Freneau. PAH
O'er the Water to Charlie. Burns. FaBoCh
O'er the wet sands an insect crept. An Autograph. James Russell Lowell. AA
O'er the Wild Gannet's Bath. George Darley. *Fr.* Ethelstan. ChTr; PoEL-4
O'er the yellow crocus on the lawn. A Russian Fantasy. Nathan Haskell Dole. AA
O'er town and cottage, vale and height. Valley Forge. Thomas Buchanan Read. *Fr.* The Wagoner of the Alleghanies. PAH
O'er Waiting Harp-Strings of the Mind. Mary Baker Eddy. AH
Of. Debora Greger. EOEF
Of a brazier's daughter who lived near. The Betrayed Maiden. *Unknown.* OBET
Of a Contented Mind. Lord Thomas Vaux. EIL
(Content.) OBSC; QFR
Of a Daw. John Heywood. PBBP
Of a Fair Lady Playing with a Snake. Edmund Waller.
Of a Fair Shrew. Sir John Harington.
Of a fallen sparrow, the prairie dog first softens. Gnawing the Breast. Sandra McPherson. LCAP
Of a lady fair to see. Lines to Mrs. M. C. Turner. Eloise Bibb. CBWP-4
Of a Lady That Refused to Dance with Him. Earl of Surrey. SiPS
Of a little take a little. *Unknown.* OxNR
Of a pendulum's mildness, with her feet up. A Timepiece. James Merrill. HoPM; NePoEA-2
Of a Rose, a Lovely Rose. *Unknown.* OBEV
Of a Sea-Born Aphrodite. Emmanuel Hocquard, *tr. fr. French by* Michael Palmer. RHTwFP
Of a Spider. Wilfred Thornley. FaPON; PDV
Of a tall stature and of sable hue. Charles II. *Unknown.* FaBoEE
(An Historical Poem.) APAS
Of A' the Airts [the Wind Can Blaw]. Burns. AWP; EnRP; GoTS; NoP; OxBS

(I Love My Jean.) GN
(Jean.) GTBS; GTBS-P; OBEV; TrGrPo
Of a' the maids o' fair Scotland. Young Benjie. *Unknown.* ESPB; OxBB, *with music*
Of a Zealous Lady. Sir John Harington, *after the Latin of* Martial. FaBoEE
Of Adam's first wife, Lilith, it is told. Body's Beauty. Dante Gabriel Rossetti. *Fr.* The House of Life, LXXVIII. OAEL-2; Son; TrGrPo
(Lilith.) PoEL-5
Of age of ours. Age of the Rubber Seals. Buland al-Haidari, *tr. by* Patricia Alanah Byrne *and* Salma Khadra Jayyusi. MAP
Of all amusements for the mind. Wishing. John Godfrey Saxe. AnAmPo
Of all creatures women be best. What Women Are Not. *Unknown.* MeEL
Of All My Loves. Abba Kovner, *tr. fr. Hebrew by* Warren Bargad *and* Stanley F. Chyet. IP
Of all our bath-house thieves the cleverest one. Catullus, *tr. by* James Michie. PeHV
Of all sins of the flesh, that reprobate. Hangover Mass. X. J. Kennedy. DiPo
Of all that Orient lands can vaunt. The Haschish. Whittier. AnAmPo; OBAL
Of all the beasts which we for our veneriall name. Michael Drayton. *Fr.* Polyolbion, Thirteenth Song. OBS
Of All the Birds I know. The Toucan. Pyke Johnson, Jr.. NTCP
Of All the Birds That I Do Know. George Gascoigne. *Fr.* The Praise of Philip Sparrow. CH; PBBP
Of all the birds that sing and fly. Samuel Hoffenstein. *Fr.* Songs about Life and Brighter Things Yet. NBLV
Of all the brave captains that ever were seen. Sir Dilberry Diddle, Captain of Militia. *Unknown.* NOEC
Of all the causes which conspire to blind. Pope. *Fr.* Essay on Criticism, *pt.* II. NOEC; NoP
Of all the creatures, in the world, that be. John Oldham, *after the French of* Boileau. *Fr.* Satires, VIII. OBVE
Of all the curst plagues that e'er fate did decree. The Sailor's Complaint *or,* The True Character of a Purser of a Ship. *Unknown.* OxBSS
Of all the famous Hangchou sights. Yüan Mei, *tr. fr. Chinese by* Jonathan Chaves. *Fr.* Five Poems on Returning to Hangchou. CoBLCP
Of all the flowers rising now. Maritae Suae. William Philpot. OBEV
Of all the gay birds that e'er I did see. *Unknown.* PBBP
Of all the girls that are so smart. Sally in Our Alley. Henry Carey. AnAmPo; AWP; BLPL; BoLoP; CoMu; FaBoBe; FaFP; GTBS; GTBS-P; NOBE; OBEV
(Ballad of Sally in Our Alley, The.) NOEC
Of all the girls that e'er were seen. John Gay. CoMu; ErPo
Of all the grain our nation yields. A Panegyric upon Oates. Richard Duke. APAS
Of all the Lombards, by their Trophies knowne. Sir William Davenant. *Fr.* Gondibert, I, i. SeCV-1
Of All the Men. Thomas Moore. FiBHP
Of all the myriad moods of mind. Longing. James Russell Lowell. AnAmPo
Of all the pleasant ways. Driving in the Park. *Unknown.* OxBoLi
Of all the rides since the birth of time. Skipper Ireson's Ride. Whittier. AA; AnAmPo; BeLS; NOBA; OBAL; OBCA; OxBA; PAH; PoLF
Of all the sayings in this world. *Unknown.* OxNR
Of all the seas that's coming. *Unknown.* EBEV
Of all the secret places. The Sound of Rain. David Allan Evans. GOYP
Of all the ships upon the blue. Captain Reece. William Schwenck Gilbert. CenHV; FiBHP; GN
Of all the souls that stand create. Emily Dickinson. AmPP; NAAL-1; TrGrPo
(Choice.) AA
Of All the Splendor. Ory Bernstein, *tr. fr. Hebrew by* Warren Bargad *and* Stanley F. Chyet. IP
Of all the stars that bathe the heavens in glory. La Donna È Mobile. "A. K." FiBHP
Of all the tales of human struggle, hear this one from Tennessee. Bryan's Last Battle. *Unknown.* AmFP
Of all the tales was ever told. Mary Arnold the Female Monster. *Unknown.* GBP; OBET
Of all the things lost there is one. Experiences. Christine Busta, *tr. by* Beth Bjorklund. CoAuP
Of all the thoughts of God that are. The Sleep. Elizabeth Barrett Browning. WGRP
Of all the torments, all the cares. Rivals. *At. to* Sir George Etherege. OBEV

Of all the trees in England. Trees. Walter de la Mare. OHIP

Of all the ways of traveling in earth and air and sea. Flight Plan. Jane Merchant. RHPC

Of all the wild deeds upon murder's black list. Verses on Daniel Good. *Unknown*. CoMu; OxBB

Of all thes kene conquerours to carpe it were kynde. The Tournament of Tottenham. *Unknown*. BoLi

Of all these, pieces from which this. Senses of Responsibility. Charles Bernstein. LP

Of All Things for You to Go Away Mad. Joanne Kyger. PoM

Of all wemen that ever were borne. Mary Complains to Other Mothers. *Unknown*. MeEL

Of Althea and Flaxie. Cheryl Clarke. GLP

Of an Heroical Answer of a Great Roman Lady to Her Husband. Sir John Harington. BoLoP; ErPo

Of an old king in a story. Old King Cole. G. K. Chesterton. *Fr.* Variations on an Air Composed on Having to Appear in a Pageant as Old King Cole. BXAP

Of an old King in a story. Variations on an Air: After W. B. Yeats. G. K. Chesterton. BXAP; FaBoPa; NOBL; Par

Of an Old Song. William E. H. Lecky. WGRP

Of an old souldier of the Queens. An Old Souldier of the Queens. *Unknown*. OBS

Of an Orchard. Katharine Tynan. WGRP

Of asphodel, that greeny flower. William Carlos Williams. *Fr.* Asphodel, That Greeny Flower. CMoP

Of Astraea. Sir John Davies. *Fr.* Hymns of Astraea. TrGrPo

Of Autumn. Veronica Porumbacu, *tr. fr. Rumanian by* Willis Barnstone *and* Matei Calinescu. BoWoP; VWA

Of Baiting the Lion. Sir Owen Seaman. NA

Of beasts am I, of men was he most brave. The Lion over the Tomb of Leonidas. *Unknown*, *tr. by* Walter Leaf. AWP

Of Beauty. Sir Richard Fanshawe, *after the Italian of* Giovanni Battista Guarini. *Fr.* Il Pastor Fido. BoLoP

(Beauty.) GBL

(Nymph's Song.) OxBSP

Of Being Numerous, *sels.* George Oppen.

It Is Difficult Now to Speak of Poetry. NNaP

Of Being Numerous #24. GOA

Of Birds and Birders. John Heywood. PBBP

Of Books. John Florio. EIL

Of Boston in New England. William Bradford. SCAP

Of Breakfast, then of walking to the pond. Good Appetite. Mark Van Doren. OxBSP

Of bricks. Who built it? Like some crazy balloon. Our Youth. John Ashbery. SOTW; VGW

Of bright cities/ and citrus. Florida. Carl Rakosi. TAP

Of Calico Cats. Kirsty Seymour-Ure. CRH

Of Certain Irish Fairies. Arthur Guiterman. PoLF

Of Change of Opinions. Victor Plarr. NOBVV

Of Coal. Marcelin Pleynet, *tr. fr. French by* John Ashbery. RHTwFP

Of comfort no man speak! Let's Talk of Graves. Shakespeare. *Fr.* King Richard II, III, ii. FaBoBe

Death of Kings, The. TrGrPo

"For God's sake, let us sit upon the ground." HoPM

Of Commerce and Society. Geoffrey Hill. NePoEA-2

Of Common Devotion. Francis Quarles. *See* Our God and soldiers we alike adore.

Of composts shall the Muse descend to sing. Compost. James Grainger. *Fr.* The Sugar Cane. NOEC

(How to Fertilize Soil.) FaBoUs

Of course/ the sun is angry. Nadia Tuéni, *tr. by* Carol Cosman. OV

Of Course I Know. Zishe Landau, *tr. fr. Yiddish by* Ruth Whitman. VWA

Of course I know, this day's without compare. Khamsin of Nisan. Leah Goldberg, *tr. by* Bernhard Frank. MHeP

Of course I prayed. Emily Dickinson. BoWoP; MoAmPo

Of course I tried to tell him. Poets Hitchhiking on the Highway. Gregory Corso. NeAP; PoM

Of course it is snowing. Dear Old Stockholm. Al Young. NPGG

Of course, the entire effort is to put myself. Thoughts during an Air Raid. Stephen Spender. MoBrPo

Of course the heart is nothing. City. Joseph Stroud. NPGG

Of course, there'll be whimpers afterward. Afterward. Gyula Illyés, *tr. by* Jascha Kessler. FOC

Of course when someone leaves you forever. Back. Angela McCabe. AmPA

"Of course you saw the Villa d'Este Gardens." Villa d'Este Gardens. Siegfried Sassoon. OBTV

Of Courtesy, it is much less. Courtesy. Hilaire Belloc. ACP

Of Cupid. Henry Chettle. *See* Piers Plainness' Seven Years' Prenticeship: Aeliana's Ditty.

Of Cynthia. *Unknown*. OBSC

Of Dancing. Alan Brownjohn. FaBoMo

Of Dandelions & Tourists. Joe Rosenblatt. NOBC

Of De Witt Williams on His Way to Lincoln Cemetery. Gwendolyn Brooks. NoAM; NOBA

Of De Witt Williams on His Way to Lincoln Cemetery. Gwendolyn Brooks. *Fr.* A Street in Bronzeville. CAPP

Of Death. Countess of Pembroke. *Fr.* Antonius. EIL

Of Difference Does It Make. Tom Paulin. FaBCIP

Of Disdainful Daphne. M. H. Nowell. EIL

Of diverse monsters I have sometimes read. Strange Monsters. Rowland Watkyns. FaBoEE

Of Drunkenness. George Turberville. NBLV; NoP

Of Dying Beauty. Louis Zukofsky. PoA

Of Edenhall the youthful lord. The Luck of Edenhall. Ludwig Uhland, *tr. by* Longfellow. AWP

Of England, and of Its Marvels. Fazio degli Uberti, *tr. fr. Italian by* Dante Gabriel Rossetti. AWP

Of English Verse. Edmund Waller. NAEL-1; OAEL-1; OBS; PoE; SeCP

Of Europe I sing, her railroads and theatres. My Muse. Valery Larbaud, *tr. by* William Jay Smith. CT

Of every kinne [*or* everykune] tree, of every kinne tree. The Hawthorn. *Unknown*. ChTr; GBP

Of every vice pursued by those. Gambling. Royall Tyler. TAP

Of fair girls the loveliest. *Unknown*, *tr. by* Arthur Waley. BoS

Of few words, Sir, you seem to be. *Unknown*. SiPS

Of Fiammetta Singing. Boccaccio, *tr. fr. Italian by* Dante Gabriel Rossetti. *Fr.* Sonnets. AWP

Of Fortune. Thomas Kyd. *Fr.* Cornelia. EIL

Of fret, of dark, of thorn, of chill. Opposition. Sidney Lanier. AnAmPo; LiTA

Of genius here at home. Once the Sole Province. Douglas Crase. EOEF

Of Glotons and Dronkardes. Alexander Barclay. *Fr.* The Ship of Fools. OxBLMV

Of God we ask one favor. Emily Dickinson. EaLo

Of Gods Omnipotencie. Alexander Hume. NOCV

Of gold or gowns my mother had not much. She Would Have Roses. Nicholas Lloyd Ingraham. PWR

Of Growing Old. D. J. Enright. AnAn

Of Heaven Considered as a Tomb. Wallace Stevens. PoA; QFR

Of Heaven or Hell I have no power to sing. An Apology. William Morris. *Fr.* The Earthly Paradise. AWP; EBVV; LiTB; NAEL-2; NoP; OAEL-2; OBNC; OPOP

Of heavenly stature, but most human smile. Written in the Visitors' Book at the Birthplace of Robert Burns. George Washington Cable. AA

Of her own accord, before the altar. Marina Virgin. Lucha Corpi, *tr. fr. Spanish by the author and* Catherine Rodríguez-Nieto. *Fr.* The Marina Poems, II. CCP; OV

Of heroes and statesmen I'll just mention. Paul Jones—a New Song. *Unknown*. PAH

Of high Honour should be her hood. The Garment of Good Ladies. Robert Henryson. ACP

(Garmont of Gude Ladies, The.) GoTS

Of Himself. Meleager, *tr. fr. Greek by* Richard Garnett. AWP

Of His Cynthia. Fulke Greville. *See* Caelica: Away with these self-loving lads.

Of His Dear Son, Gervase. Sir John Beaumont. *Fr.* Of My Dear Son, Gervase Beaumont. OBEV

Of His Death. Meleager, *tr. fr. Greek by* Andrew Lang. AWP

Of His Lady. *Unknown*. EIL

Of His Lady's Old Age. Pierre de Ronsard, *tr. fr. French by* Andrew Lang. AWP; CTC

Of His Last Sight of Fiammetta. Boccaccio, *tr. fr. Italian by* Dante Gabriel Rossetti. *Fr.* Sonnets. AWP

Of His Majesties Receiving the News of the Duke of Buckingham's Death. Edmund Waller. SeCV-1

Of His Mistress. Robert Greene. *Fr.* Menaphon. EIL

Of History More Like Myth. Jean Garrigue. NYBP

Of how your poems. A Letter to Paul Celan in Memory. Jerome Rothenberg. VWA

Of Human Learning, *sel.* Fulke Greville.

"Chiefe use then in man of that he knowes, The." OBS

Of Human Life. Henry King. *See* Sic Vita.

Of interest to John Calvin and Thomas Aquinas. Why God Permits Evil: For Answers to This Question of Interest to Many Write Bible Answers Dept. E-7. Miller Williams. MT; SM

Of Iron Am I. *Malay Oral Tradition, tr. by* W. W. Skeat. WTO

Of Jeoffry, His Cat. Christopher Smart. *See* Jubilate Agno: For I Will Consider My Cat Jeoffry [*or* Jeoffrey].

Of Jesu Christ I Sing. *Unknown.* PoE

Of Joan's Youth. Louise Imogen Guiney. AA

Of John Bunyan's Life. John James. SCAP

Of John Cabanis' wrath and of the strife. The Spooniad. Edgar Lee Masters. *Fr.* Spoon River Anthology. OBAL

Of Jolly Good Ale and Old. *At. to* William Stevenson *and also to* John Still. *See* Gammer Gurton's Needle: Back and Side Go Bare, Go Bare.

Of Kate's Baldness. John Davies of Hereford. FaBoEE

Of Kings and Dukes. Roy Fuller. AnAn

Of Late. George Starbuck. VGW

Of late from time to time there's risen. Amir Gilboa, *tr. by* Warren Bargad *and* Stanley F. Chyet. IP

Of Leeuwenhoek's. Glimmers. Jack Marshall. UL

Of Liddisdale the common thievis. Aganis the Thievis of Liddisdale. Sir Richard Maitland. GoTS

Of Life and Death, *sel.* Henry Vaughan.
Winged Heart, A. FaBoRV

Of life days like. Robert Grenier. *Fr.* A Sequence/ 28 Separate Poems. IAT

Of little use the man you may suppose. Pope. *Fr.* First Epistle of the Second Book of Horace, Imitation of. EBEV

Of living creatures most I prize. Butterfly. William Jay Smith. GoJo

Of London Bridge, and the Stupendous Sight, and Structure Thereof. James Howell. ChTr; FaBoPP

Of Love. Kahlil Gibran. *Fr.* The Prophet. PoLF

Of Love. James Sandford. EIL

Of love he sang, full hearted one. A Forced Music. Robert Graves. MoBrPo

Of loves perfection perfectly to speake. Spenser. *Fr.* Colin Clout's Come Home Again. OAEL-1

Of Loving at First Sight. Edmund Waller. SeCP

Of Maids' Inconstancy. Richard Brathwaite. *Fr.* A Strappado for the Devil. EIL

Of Man and Wife. Richard Eedes. *See* No Love, to Love of Man and Wife.

Of Manners gentle, of affections mild. On Mr. Gay; In Westminster Abbey, 1732. Pope. FiP

Of man's first disobedience, and the fruit. Milton. *Fr.* Paradise Lost, Bk. I. EBEV, *fr. ll.* 1–270; FaBoRV, *fr. ll.* 1–26; NAEL-1, *fr. complete;* NAWM-1, *fr. complete;* NIP, *fr. ll.* 1–49; NoP, *fr. ll.* 1–26; OAEL-1, *fr. ll.* 1–375; TOF, *fr. ll.* 1–26.
(Induction, The.) PoE, *fr. ll.* 1–26.
(Invocation: "Of man's first disobedience, and the fruit.") PoEL-3, *fr. ll.* 1–26.
(Of Man's First Disobedience.) FiP, *fr. ll.* 1–26.

Of many marvels in my time. A Description of a Strange (and Miraculous) Fish. Martin Parker. CoMu

Of many things adulterate. Tristan Corbière, *tr. by* Joseph T. Shipley. AWP

Of Mary. A New Song of Mary. *Unknown.* MeEL

Of Mary, *sel.* Sister Mary Madeleva.
Dumb Oxen. CRP

Of May. Alexander Scott. OxBS

Of Men, nay Beasts: worse, Monsters: worst of all. Phineas Fletcher. *Fr.* The Locusts, or Appolyonists, I. SeCV-1

Of Mere Being. Wallace Stevens. HCAP

Of Misery. Thomas Howell. EIL; FF

Of Modern Poetry. Wallace Stevens. InvP; MoP; NAAL-2; NoAM; OxBA; PrIm; TAP

Of Money. Barnabe Googe. EIL; FF; NBLV; NoP

Of mountain scenery, the Southern Screen is best. Random Poem on the Lake. Sung Wan, *tr. by* Yin-nan Chang. WFTU

Of My Dear Son [*or* Deare Sonne], Gervase Beaumont. Sir John Beaumont. *Fr.* JCP; NOBE; OBS
Of His Dear Son, Gervase, *sel.* OBEV

Of my flesh and blood, only one remains. Yüan Mei, *tr. fr. Chinese by* Jonathan Chaves. *Fr.* Five Poems on Returning to Hangchou. CoBLCP

Of My Lady Isabella Playing on the Lute. Edmund Waller. HAP; MePo
(On My Lady Isabella Playing on the Lute.) SeCP

Of my lady, wel me rejoise I may. A Description of His Ugly Lady, a. Thomas Hoccleve. MeEL

Of Myself. Abraham Cowley. *See* Vote, A:
This only grant me, that my means may lye.

Of Myself. Leah Goldberg, *tr. fr. Hebrew by* Ramah Commanday. BoWoP

Of nearness to her sundered things. Emily Dickinson. PoE

Of Nelson and the North. Battle of the Baltic. Thomas Campbell. EnRP; FaPoR; GN; GTBS; GTBS-P; OBEV

Of Neptune's empire let us sing. A Hymn[e] in Praise [*or* Prayse] of Neptune. Thomas Campion. BoNaP; MOS; NOBE; OBEV; OBSC; WiR

Of Objects Considered as Fortresses in a Baleful Place. Hyam Plutzik. VGW

Of old, a man who died. Immortal Flowers. Wallace Rice. AA

Of old when folk lay sick and sorely tried. On Hygiene. Hilaire Belloc. MoBrPo

Of old when Nature, in her verve defiant. The Giantess. Baudelaire, *tr. by* Roy Campbell. OBVE

Of old, when Scarron his companions invited. Goldsmith. *Fr.* Retaliation. LaA; NOIV; OxBoLi

Of One Dead. Tennyson. *Fr.* In Memoriam A. H. H., XIV. EBVV, *abr.*; OAEL-2, *abr.*

Of One Self-slain. Charles Hanson Towne. WGRP

Of One That Had a Great Nose. George Turberville, *after the Greek of* Trajan. FaBoEE

Of one who grew up at Gallipoli. War Story. Jon Stallworthy. OxBC

Of One Who neither Sees nor Hears. Richard Watson Gilder. AA

Of One Who Seemed to Have Failed. S. Weir Mitchell. AA

Of Only a Single Poem. G. J. F. Dutton. PoSH

Of Oystermen, Workboats. Dave Smith. MAYP

Of people running down the street. A Picture. Howard Nemerov. OxBC

Of Perfect Friendship. Henry Cheke. EIL

Of Phyllis. William Drummond of Hawthornden. EIL; GN
(Phyllis.) GN

Of Poor B.B. Bertolt Brecht, *tr. fr. German by* Michael Hamburger. RB

Of Property Naught. Margarita Hickey, *tr. fr. Spanish by* Kate Flores. DMH

Of Rama. Herman Melville. LiTA

Of Reason and Discovery. Don Mattera. WMBCH

Of Robert Frost. Gwendolyn Brooks. MoP; NoAM; NOBA

Of Rome. Herman Melville. *Fr.* Clarel. OxBA

Of Scolding Wives and the Third Day Ague. Henricus Selyns. AiP; SCAP

Of simple choice they are the villagers; their clothes come. Adrienne Rich. *Fr.* Shooting Script, 5. HCAP

Of Sitting Bear. Wayne Dodd. *Fr.* The General Mule Poems. KS

Of Snow. Norman Brick. WaP

Of Solitude, *sel.* Abraham Cowley. OBS
Solitude and Reason, in the Village. FaBoPP

Of Spenser's Faery Queen. Sir Walter Ralegh. *See* Vision upon This Conceit of the Faerie Queene, A.

Of spinach and gammon. The Right Heart in the Wrong Place. James Joyce. FaBoPV

Of Stories Fathers Tell. Roger Pfingston. SoTCo

Of Suicide. John Berryman. NoAM

Of Swimming in Lakes and Rivers. Bertolt Brecht, *tr. fr. German by* H. R. Hays. SD

Of Tact. Arthur Guiterman. MoShBr

Of Taste; an Essay, *sel.* James Cawthorn.
"Time was, an Englishman would join." NOEC

Of that Medusa strange. The Statue of Medusa. William Drummond of Hawthornden. EyDe

Of that wherein thou art a questioner. To Dante Alighieri: He Interprets Dante Alighieri's Dream. Dante da Maiano, *tr. by* Dante Gabriel Rossetti. AWP

Of the Azazmeh Too. Haim Guri, *tr. fr. Hebrew by* Warren Bargad *and* Stanley F. Chyet. IP

Of the beast. an angel. The Everlasting Contenders. Kenneth Patchen. NaP

Of the beauty of kindness I speak. Kindness. T. Sturge Moore. OBMV

Of the Beloved Caravan. Conny Hannes Meyer, *tr. fr. German by* Herbert Kuhner. VWA

Of the birds that fly in the farthest sea. John Gray. *Fr.* The Flying Fish, II. OBNC

Of the Birth and Bringing Up of Desire. Edward DeVere, 17th Earl of Oxford. FaBoEE; OBSC

Of the Blessed Sacrament of the Altar. Robert Southwell. OBEV

Of the Boy and Butterfly. Bunyan. OxBChV

Of the Child with the Bird on the Bush. Bunyan. *See* My Little Bird.

Of the Confident Stranger. Clark Coolidge. UL

Of the Courtier's Life. Sir Thomas Wyatt. *See* Satires: Mine Own John Poins [*or* Poyntz].

Of the Cuckoo. Bunyan. PBBP

Of the dark past. Ecce Puer. James Joyce. BIrV; EBEV; MoP; NAs; NoAM; OPOP; TrCP

Of the Day Estivall ("O perfite light, quhilk schaid away"). Alexander Hume. NOCV; OxBS

    Midsummer Day in France, *sel.* FaBoPP

Of the Elmira Wood. Her Apron through the Trees. Roger Weingarten. AmPA

Of the French Kings Nativity. Benjamin Harris. SCAP

Of the Going Down of the Sun. Bunyan. CH

Of the Great and Famous. Sir Francis Drake, and of My Little-Little Selfe. Robert Hayman. CH; FaBoCh; NoP

Of the Holy Eucharist. *Unknown.* ACP

Of the ills we daily see. The Social Life. Lizelia Augusta Jenkins Moorer. CBWP-3

Of the islands, Puerto Rico. *Unknown.* ILY

Of The Last Verses in the Book ("When we for age could neither read nor write."), *sels. Edmund* Waller. EBEV; FaBoRV; HAP; MePo; NoP; OBS; SeCP; SeCV-1

    "Seas are quiet when the winds give o'er, The." NOCV

    (Old Age.) BLPL; NOBE; OBEV

    Soul's Dark Cottage, The. ChTr; OBD

Of the leaning cypresses. The Cypresses. Jon Anderson. NAmP

Of the Loss of Time. John Hoskyns. FaBoEE

Of the manner in which he moves. A Walk in Early March. Paul Mariani. DiL

Of the Manner of Addressing Clouds. Wallace Stevens. PoA

    (On the Manner of Addressing Clouds.) QFR

Of the many known and proven. Curing Homosexuality. Jim Everhard. GLP

Of the Mathematician. Alice Clear Matthews. GoYe

Of the million or two, more or less. Instans Tyrannus. Robert Browning. EBEV

Of the Moon. Charles Best. *See* Sonnet of the Moon, A.

Of the myriad afflictions that beset Hellas. The Breed of Athletes. Euripides, *tr. by* Moses Hadas. SD

Of the Nativity of the Lady Rich's Daughter. Henry Constable. OBSC

Of the old house, only a few crumbled. The House That Was. Laurence Binyon. MoBrPo

Of the onset, fear-inspiring, and the firing and the pillage. The Sack of Deerfield. Thomas Dunn English. PAH

Of the Progresse of the Soule; the Second Anniversarie ("Nothing could make me sooner to confess."), *sels. John* Donne. SeCP

    Contemplation of Our State in Our Deathbed. OBS

    Our Companie in the Next World. OBS

    "Poor soul, in this thy flesh what dost thou know?." OAEL-1

    (Soules Ignorance in This Life and Knowledge in the Next, The.) OBS

Of the Pythagorean Philosophy. Ovid, *tr. fr. Latin by* Dryden. *Fr.* Metamorphoses, XV.

    "But this by sure experiment we know." FM

    "This let me further add, that nature knows." OBVE

Of the Realme of Scotland. Sir David Lindsay. *Fr.* The Dreme. OxBS

Of the Sad Lot of the Humanists in Paris. George Buchanan. *tr. fr. Latin.* GoTS

Of the Scythians. Katha Pollitt. DiPo; InPS; SM

Of the Stalking of the Stag. Sir Owen Seaman. CenHV

Of the Theme of Love. Margaret Cavendish Newcastle. OxBSP

Of the Three or Four in the Room. Yehuda Amichai, *tr. fr. Hebrew by* Bernhard Frank. MHeP

Of the three Wise Men. Carol of the Brown King. Langston Hughes. PChr

Of the Travelers That Won't Come Again. Benyamin Galai, *tr. fr. Hebrew by* Bernhard Frank. MHeP

Of the unended in the speed of. Anne-Marie Albiach, *tr. fr. French by* Paul Auster. *Fr.* État. PBWP

Of the ways to play. Tabito. *Fr. Manyo Shu.* PeBJV

Of thee (kind boy) I ask no red and white. Sir John Suckling. CaPo; MeLP; MePo; NoP; OBS; OxBoLi; SeCP; SeCV-1

Of them all—those laboring men who knew my first name. At the Sign-Painter's. Jared Carter. FYAP

Of thes four letters purpose I. A New Song of Mary. *Unknown.* MeEL

Of thes Frer Minours me thenkes moch wonder. Friars' Enormities. *Unknown.* MeEL

Of these the false Achitophel was first. Dryden. *Fr.* Absalom and Achitophel, Pt. I. HAP; InPS; PoEL-3

Of these two spitefull rocks, the one doth shove. Scylla and Charybdis. Homer, *tr. fr. Greek by* George Chapman. *Fr.* Odyssey, XII. OBS

Of things I'd rather keep in silence I must sing. Beatrice, Countess de Die, *tr. by* Meg Bogin. WT

Of Things Past. Shmuel Halkin, *tr. fr. Yiddish by* Hillel Halkin. PeBMYV

Of this bad world the loveliest and the best. On a Dead Hostess. Hilaire Belloc. MoBrPo

Of This Core I Sample the Bitter Taste. Lindolf Bell, *tr. fr. Portuguese by* William Jay Smith. CT

Of this fair[e] volume which we e World do[e] name. The Book. William Drummond of Hawthornden. CH

    (Lessons of Nature, The.) GTBS-P

    (World, The.) OBS

Of this world's theatre in which we stay. Spenser. *Fr.* Amoretti, LIV. NAEL-1; NoP; OAEL-1

Of Thomas Traherne and the Pebble Outside. Sydney Clouts. VWA

Of those abalone pearls. Yakamochi. *Fr. Manyo Shu.* Ma

Of those around thee there is none who heeds. To Bülow. August, Graf von Platen, *tr. by* Reginald Bancroft Cooke. PeHV

Of those dear friends of ours who lived in days of yore. Remembrance. V. A. Zhukovsky, *tr. by* Alan Myers. AAA

Of those few fools, who with ill stars are cursed. Congreve. *Fr.* The Way of the World. NAEL-1

Of those rebellions that we start in jest. Fear Test: Integrity of Heroes. James Simmons. CIP

Of those the gods hate more than teachers. Weather Forecasters. Eeva Kilpi, *tr. by* Aili Jarvenpa. SOP

Of those whom I have known, the few and fatal friends. Largo. Dunstan Thompson. LiTA; WaP

Of three eyes, I would still give two for one. The Third Eye. Jay Macpherson. MoCV

Of Three Friendly Warnings This Is the First. *Unknown, tr. fr. Seneca Indian by* Jerome Rothenberg *and* Richard Johnny John. STP

Of Three Friendly Warnings This Is the Second. *Unknown, tr. fr. Seneca Indian by* Jerome Rothenberg *and* Richard Johnny John. STP

Of Three Friendly Warnings This Is the Third. *Unknown, tr. fr. Seneca Indian by* Jerome Rothenberg *and* Richard Johnny John. STP

Of Three Girls and of Their Talk. Boccaccio, *tr. fr. Italian by* Dante Gabriel Rossetti. *Fr.* Sonnets. AWP; PFI

Of Three or Four in a Room. Yehuda Amichai, *tr. fr. Hebrew by* Stephen Mitchell. VWA

Of thy lyfe, Thomas, this compass well mark. Horace. *See* Odes: II, 10. "Receive, dear friend, the truths I teach" ("Rectius vives").

Of Time and River. Affonso Romano de Sant'Anna. WCI

Of Time and the Line. Charles Bernstein. UL

Of Time and Us. David R. Bunch. BWV

Of Treason. Sir John Harington. FaBoEE; FF; InPK; OxBoLi

Of True Liberty. Sir John Beaumont. OBS

Of two fair virgins, modest, though admired. On a Nun. Jacopo Vittorelli, *tr. by* Byron. AWP

    (Sonnet: "Of two fair virgins, modest, though admired.") PFI

Of Tyndarus, That Frumped a Gentlewoman. *Unknown, tr. fr. Latin.* BIrV, *tr. by* Richard Stanyhurst

Of us/ not much is known. Degli Sposi. Rika Lesser. FYAP; UnAS

Of Use. John Heywood. FaBoEE; PBBP

Of Utterances. Alma Villanueva. CCP

Of virtues I most warmly bless. Gerard Manley Hopkins. FaBoEE

Of wealthy lustre was the banquet-room. The Banquet. Keats. *Fr.* Lamia. SeCePo

Of western New York state. As You Came from the Holy Land. John Ashbery. CAPP

Of what a quality is courage made. Donagh MacDonagh. *Fr.* Charles Donnelly. CIP

"Of what are you afraid, my child?" inquired the kindly teacher. Wild Flowers. Peter Newell. NA; RHPC

Of what good can Paradise be. Paradise. Immanuel di Roma, *tr. by* J. Chotzner. TrJP

Of what mould did Nature frame me? The Tinder. Thomas Carew. CaPo

Of white and tawny, black as ink. Variation on a Sentence. Louise Bogan. FM; ImOP

Of Wit. Abraham Cowley. *See* Ode: Of Wit.
Of woman and wine, of woods and spring. Inexhaustible. Israel Zangwill. TrJP
Of Women. Richard Edwards. EIL
Of Women. *Unknown, tr. fr. Arabic by* E. Powys Mathers. *Fr.* The Thousand and One Nights. ErPo
Of Women No More Evil. *Unknown, tr. fr. Late Middle Irish by* Robin Flower. AnIL
Of woods, of plains, of hills and dales. Upon a Rich Country Gentleman. *Unknown.* FaBoEE
Of worthy Captain Lovewell I purpose now to sing. Lovewell's Fight. *Unknown.* PAH
Of writing many books there is no end. Elizabeth Barrett Browning. *Fr.* Aurora Leigh. NOBVV
Of Your Father's Indiscretions and the Train to California. Lynn Emanuel. MAYP
Of your trouble, Ben, to ease me. Her Man Described by Her Owne Dictamen. Ben Jonson. *Fr.* A Celebration of Charis in Ten Lyrick Peeces. SeCP
Of Youth He Singeth. Robert Wever. *See* Lusty Juventus:
In a herber [*or* a harbour *or* an arbour] green [*or* grene], asleep [*or* aslepe] whereas [*or* where as *or* where] I lay.
Ofay-Watcher Looks Back. Mongane Wally Serote. WMBCH
Off-/ balance, into the wide wide world. Skate. Laurel Blossom. ASP
Off a pane) the. E. E. Cummings. RR
Off a Puritane. *Unknown.* CoMu
Off all the lords in faire Scottland. The Heir of Linne. *Unknown.* ESPB
Off an ancient story Ile tell you anon. King John and the Bishop. *Unknown.* ESPB
Off at dawn to service in the walled and storied palace. Lu Chi, *tr. fr. Chinese by* Burton Watson. *Fr.* Two Poems Presented to the Gentleman in the Office of Palace Writers Ku Yen-hsien, II. CoBCP
Off at Tatsuta/ white clouds are piling up. Teika, *tr. by* Steven D. Carter. WFTW
Off Brighton Pier. Alan Ross. OBWP
Off Broadway, where they sell those photographs. Manhattan Menagerie. Joseph Cherwinski. GoYe
Off Cape Leeuwen. M. K. Joseph. ATNZ
Off Crane's Neck the sun. The Spirit of Wrath. William Heyen. AmPA
Off Februar the fyiftene nycht. The Dance of the Sevin Deidly Synnis. William Dunbar. GoTS; OxBS; PoE
Off from Boston. *Unknown.* PAH
Off from Swing Shift. Garrett Kaoru Hongo. MAYP
Off Highway 106. Cherrylog Road. James Dickey. CoAP; HAP; HCAP; InPS; MT; NAAL-2; NIP; NYBP; PrIm; TwCP; WeW
Off in the twilight hung the low full moon. Full Moon. Sappho, *tr. by* William Ellery Leonard. AWP
Off in the wilderness bare and level. The Temptations of Saint Anthony. Phyllis McGinley. OxBSP
"Off Manilly." Edmund Vance Cooke. PAH
Off Rivière du Loup. Duncan Campbell Scott. OBCV
Off-shore, by islands hidden in the blood. I, Maximus of Gloucester, to You ("Off-shore, by islands hidden in the blood"). Charles Olson. *Fr.* The Maximus Poems. LiTM; NoAM; NOBA; PoM
Off the Back of a Lorry. Tom Paulin. FaBCIP
Off the beach at dusk. Kenko, *tr. by* Steven D. Carter. WFTW
Off the beaten track. Ernst David, *tr. by* Beth Bjorklund. CoAuP
Off the coast of Hispaniola. Columbus and the Mermaids. Elizabeth J. Coatsworth. GOA
Off the track/ I blew. Phoenix. Carolyn M. Rodgers. JB
Off to hunt ducks. Song of the Duck Hunters. Kao Ch'i, *tr. by* Jonathan Chaves. CoBLCP
Off to Patagonia. Theodore Weiss. AnAn; TAP
Off to Sea Once More. *Unknown.* OxBSS
Off to the Fishing Ground. Lucy Maud Montgomery. CaP
Off to work. *Unknown, tr. by* Burton Watson. FCEI
Off We Go to Market. Gwen A. Smith. BoTP
Off with sleep, love, up from bed. Love in May. Jean Passerat, *tr. by* Andrew Lang. AWP
Off with the fetters. Vagabondia. Richard Hovey. AnAmPo
Off with your hat as the flag goes by! The Old Flag. H. C. Bunner. OPP
Off Womanheid Ane Flour Delice. *Unknown.* OxBS
Offended, The. Anne Hébert, *tr. fr. French by* Willis Barnstone. BoWoP
Offender, The. Denise Levertov. NePoEA-2
Offer, An. Arthur Guiterman. TrJP
Offer it up plank it down. Ooftish. Samuel Beckett. NoAM
An Offering. Eloise Bibb. CBWP-4

Offering. Robert Bly. NU
Offering Congratulations to the Enlightened Reign. Ou-yang Chiung, *tr. fr. Chinese by* Lois Fusek. ATF
Offering Deep Affection. Ku Hsiung, *tr. fr. Chinese by* Lois Fusek. ATF
Offering Deep Affection. Ou-yang Chiung, *tr. fr. Chinese by* Lois Fusek. ATF
An Offering for the Cat. Mei Yao-ch'en, *tr. fr. Chinese by* Burton Watson. CoBCP
Offering of the Heart Tapestry from Arras, XV Century, The. Rolfe Humphries. FYAP
Offering: Part One, The. Mary Lee, Lady Chudleigh. WPE
Offering to the Storm. Aimé Césaire, *tr. fr. French by* Michael Benedikt. POS
Offering Wine. Park Je-chun, *tr. fr. Korean by* Koh Chang-soo. ACKP
Offering Wine. Yü Wu-ling, *tr. fr. Chinese by* Burton Watson. CoBCP
Offertorium. C. Day Lewis. *Fr.* Requiem for the Living. TIRV
Offertory. John F. Deane. TIRV
Office feels like a sealed glass case today, The. What Grandma Knew. Edward Field. Psk
Office of Poetry, The. Nathaniel Whiting. *Fr.* Il Insonio Insonado. OBS
Office Party. Phyllis McGinley. OBSV
Office work: a wearisome jumble. Poem without a Category. Liu Cheng, *tr. by* Burton Watson. CoBCP
Officers. Josephine Miles. FaBoWP
Officers get all the steak, The. World War. *Unknown.* FaFP
Officers' Mess. Gavin Ewart. OxBTC
Officers' Mess (1916). Harold Monro. BrPo
Officer's Prison Camp Seen from a Troop Train, An. Randall Jarrell. WaP
Official document blows through a forest, An. The Long Picnic. Russell Edson. LCAP
Official Iconography. Roberto Roversi, *tr. fr. Italian by* Lawrence R. Smith. NItP
Off'rings of the Easterne kings of old, The. Royall Presents. Nathaniel Wanley. OBS
Offshore. Philip Booth. SD
Offshore Breeze. Milton Acorn. NeAC
Offspring. Naomi Long Madgett. FB
Offspring of modern poetry, attend. Morning. *Unknown.* NOEC
Oft am I by the women told. Age. Abraham Cowley. AWP
Oft as at pensive eve I pass the brook. Sonnet on Passing the Bridge of Alcantra, near Lisbon. William Mickle. OBS
Oft, as we run the weary way. Courage. Stopford Brooke. WGRP
Oft did I hear our eyes the passage were. Sir John Davies. *Fr.* Sonnets to Philomel. SiPS
Oft do I return/ To my little song. The Song of the Trout Fisher. Ikinilik. WTO
Oft has our Poet wisht, this happy Seat. Epilogue Spoken by Mrs. Boutell. Dryden. SeCV-2
Oft has this planet rolled around the sun. Sir Samuel Garth. *Fr.* The Dispensary. OBSV
Oft have I heard my lief[e] Corydon [*or* Coridon] report on a love-day. Hexametra Alexis in Laudem Rosamundi. Robert Greene. *Fr.* Greene's Mourning Garment. EiL; GBL; PoEL-2
Oft have I heard thee mourn the wretched lot. Charles Churchill. *Fr.* The Prophecy of Famine. OBSV
Oft have I mused, but now at length I find. Sir Philip Sidney. *Fr.* Certain Sonnets. EiL; GBL; NOBE; OBSC; SiPS
Oft have I mused the cause to find. Ladies' Eyes Serve Cupid Both for Darts and Fire. "A. W." OBSC
Oft have I played at cards and dice. The Rantin Laddie. *Unknown.* AmFP; ESPB; HAP; OxBA; TAP; ViBoPo
Oft have I said, I say it once more. Hafiz, *tr. fr. Persian by* Emerson. *Fr.* Odes, XIII. AWP
Oft have I seen, ere Time had ploughed my cheek. Decay of Piety. Wordsworth. TrCP
Oft have I wakened ere the spring of day. Will It Be So? Edith Matilda Thomas. *Fr.* The Inverted Torch. AA
Oft have I walked these woodland paths. Under the Leaves. Albert Laighton. OHIP
Oft have we heard of impious sons before. The Female Parricide. *Unknown.* APAS
Oft have you seen a swan superbly frowning. To Charles Cowden Clarke. Keats. EnRP, *abr;* PBBP, *abr*
Oft I had heard of Lucy Gray. Lucy Gray; or, Solitude. Wordsworth. BeLS; CH; EnRP; FiP; NAEL-2; OAEL-2; OxBChV; TEP
Oft I must strive with wind and wave. Anchor: "Oft I must strive with wind and wave." *Unknown, formerly at. to* Cynewulf, *tr. fr. Anglo-Saxon by* Charles W. Kennedy. *Fr.* Riddles (Exeter Book). AnOE

Oft in danger yet alive. To Mrs. Thrale [on Her Thirty-fifth Birthday]. Samuel Johnson. FaBoEE; NaS

Oft in My Thought. Charles, Duc d' Orléans. NoP

Oft in the hall I have heard my people. *Unknown, tr. fr. Anglo-Saxon by* Charles W. Kennedy. *Fr.* Beowulf. HeIP

Oft in the lone church-yard at night I've seen. Robert Blair. *Fr.* The Grave. OBD

Oft, in the silence of the night. Our Little Ghost. Louisa May Alcott. OBCA

Oft in the Silent Night. Otto Julius Bierbaum, *tr. fr. German by* Ludwig Lewisohn. AWP

Oft, in the Stilly Night. Thomas Moore. EnRP; FaBoBe; LiTB; OBNC; PoEL-4; Prf

(Light of Other Days, The.) FaFP; GTBS; GTBS-P; NOBE; OBEV

Oft it befalls by the grace of God. Fates of Men (Exeter Book). *Unknown, tr. by* Charles W. Kennedy. AnOE

Oft I've implored the Gods in vain. A Prayer for Indifference. Frances Greville. NOEC

Oft o'er my brain does that strange fancy roll. Composed on a Journey Homeward; the Author Having Received Intelligence of the Birth of a Son. Samuel Taylor Coleridge. Son

(Sonnet: Oft o'er My Brain.) ChER

Oft on a dusky night of March, I've watched. Moorburn in Spring. *Unknown.* PoSH

Oft shall the soldier think of thee. Ben Milam. William H. Wharton. PAH

Oft since thine earthly eyes have closed on mine. Sarah Helen Whitman. *Fr.* Sonnets from the Series Relating to Edgar Allan Poe, III. AA

Oft to the Wanderer, weary of exile. The Wanderer. *Unknown, tr. by* Charles W. Kennedy. AnOE; NAWM-1; OAEL-1

Oft when I'm sitting without anything to read. Lines to a World-famous Poet Who Failed to Complete a World-famous Poem; or, Come Clean, Mr. Guest! Ogden Nash. OBAL

Oft when my spirit doth spread her bolder wings. Spenser. *Fr.* Amoretti, LXXII. OBSC; Son

"Oft with true sighs, oft with uncallèd tears." Sir Philip Sidney. *Fr.* Astrophel and Stella, LXI. NAEL-1

Often, at the Dormition of Twilight, her soul took on a certain. Beauty and the Illiterate. Odysseus Elytis, *tr. by* Edmund Keeley *and* Philip Sherrard. VMG

Often, before I come home, I see. Daily Preparations. Leo Vroman. DuIn

Often beneath the wave, wide from this ledge. At Melville's Tomb. Hart Crane. HAP; MoAmPo; MoP; MOS; NAAL-2; NoAM; NoP; PoA; TAP; UnPo; VGW

Often had I found her fair. Alec Derwent Hope. ErPo

Often, half-way to sleep. In Procession. Robert Graves. TwCP

Often I Am Permitted to Return to a Meadow. Robert Duncan. CAPP; CMoP; HeIP; NOBA; NU

Often I compare my lord to heaven. Gaspara Stampa, *tr. by* Lynne Lawmer. PBWP

Often I have seen on the screen. The Vampires Won't Vampire for Me. F. Scott Fitzgerald. VVA

Often I saw, as on my balcony. Christ Church Meadows, Oxford. Donald Hall. NYBP

Often I sit in the sun and brooding over the city, always. Dennis Lee. *Fr.* Civil Elegies. NOBC

Often I talk to men, on this or that. Talk. Philip A. Stalker. FiBHP

Often I think of my Jewish friends. The Pripet Marshes. Irving Feldman. VWA

Often I think of the beautiful town. My Lost Youth. Longfellow. AA; AmPP; AnAmPo; AWP; FaBoBe; FaBV; FaFP; FaPoR; FPL; GoJo; LiTA; NAAL-1; NOBA; OBEV; OxBA; PoEL-5; PoLF; PoRA; TAP

(Sea Memories.) FaPON

Often I walked the roads round Colonos. Evening at Colonos. Nikos Gatsos, *tr. fr. Greek by* Edmund Keeley *and* Philip Sherrard. *Fr.* Four Songs. VMG

Often I would stand at the window. Grandmother. Louise Glück. *Fr.* Dedication to Hunger, II. AnAn; GeTw

Often in summer, on a tarred bridge plank standing. Wild Bees. James Keir Baxter. ATNZ; NoP

Often in the morning the fog is thick over Jersey. A View of Jersey. Edward Field. NeAP

Often, in these blue meadows. Pursuit from Under. James Dickey. HAP; PPP

Often in this life. Poem to Han-shan. Joseph Stroud. NPGG

Often I've wished that I'd been born a woman. A Wish. Laurence Lerner. FF; OxBTC

Often rebuked, yet always back returning. *At. to* Emily Brontë, *also at. to* Charlotte Brontë. ChER; LiTB; NoBVV; OAEL-2; OBNC; PBWP

(Stanza.) OBEV

Often the sudden smell of "home." Remembering England. Peter Bland. ATNZ

Often the western wind has sung to me. Alfred Bruce Douglas. TrPWD

Often this thought wakens me unawares. Night. Hermann Hesse, *tr. by* Ludwig Lewisohn. AWP

Often waking/ before the sun decreed. The Author of *Christine.* Richard Howard. CoAP

Often when alone I liken my lord/ to the cosmos. Gaspara Stampa, *tr. by* J. Vitiello. BoWoP

Often, when o'er tree and turret. Hic Vir, Hic Est. Charles Stuart Calverley. OxBoLi

Often when the night is come. To a Maid Demure. Edward Rowland Sill. AnAmPo

Often you see them sitting, solitary, on a dune. The Beach Homos. Forrest Anderson. PeHV

Often you walked at night, houselights made. In Sepia. Jon Anderson. NAmP; PoA

Oftener seen, the more I lust, The. Out of Sight, Out of Mind. Barnabe Googe. EiL; InPS

(Oftener Seen, the More I Lust, The.) InvP; OPOP

Of/To Man. Alma Villanueva. CCP

Og [and Doeg]. Dryden *and* Nahum Tate. *Fr.* Absalom and Achitophel: Part II. AWP; FiP; TW

O'Grady lived in Shantytown. O'Grady's Goat. Will S. Hays. PoLF

O'Grady's Goat. Will S. Hays. PoLF

Ogre does what ogres can, The. August 1968. W. H. Auden. OxBSP

Ogres and Pygmies. Robert Graves. CMoP; FaBoMo; LiTB; LiTM; MoP; NoAM; SeCePo

O grief! even on the bud that fairly flowered. O Grief! *Unknown.* EiL

Oh/ CRASH!/ my/ BASH! The Fourth. Shel Silverstein. RR

Oh, a capital ship for an ocean trip. Charles Edward Carryl. *See* Davy and the Goblin: *Walloping Window-Blind, The.*

Oh, a hidden power is in my breast. Song of the Moon. Priscilla Jane Thompson. CBWP-2

Oh a high holiday, on a high holiday. Little Musgrave and Lady Barnard. *Unknown.* AmFP

Oh, a lush green English meadow—it's there that I would lie. The Poplars. Bernard Freeman Trotter. CaP

Oh! a private buffoon is a light-hearted loon. The Family Fool. William Schwenck Gilbert. *Fr.* Yeoman of the Guard. NBLV

Oh, a sailor's life is the life for me. The Warrior's Lament. Sir Owen Seaman. FiBHP

Oh a shantyman's life is a wearisome [*or* drearisome] life. A Shantyman's Life. *Unknown.* AmFP; AS, *with music*

Oh, a ship she was rigged and ready for sea. The Fishes. *Unknown.* GBP

Oh [*or* O], a wonderful stream is the River Time. The Isle of the Long Ago. Benjamin Franklin Taylor. FaFP; WBLP

(Long Ago, The.) BLPA

Oh Achilles of the moleskins. To "Chick." Frank Horne. *Fr.* Letters Found near a Suicide. BPo

Oh all ye, who passe by, whose eyes and minde. The Sacrifice. George Herbert. PoEL-2

Oh angels! will ye never sweep the drifts from my door? Drifts That Bar My Door. Adah Isaacs Menken. CBWP-1

Oh, Anselm,/ take/ Schubert. H. C. Artmann, *tr. by* Beth Bjorklund. CoAuP

Oh, as I went down to Derby Town. The Derby Ram. *Unknown.* AmFP

("As I was going to Derby.") OxNR

Oh, Athelstane, the faithful! Athelstane. Priscilla Jane Thompson. CBWP-2

Oh, away down South where I was born. Roll the Cotton Down. *Unknown.* AmFP

Oh, baby, baby, baby dear. Edith Nesbit. NOBVV

Oh, band in the pine-wood, cease! The Band in the Pines. John Esten Cooke. AA

Oh, be not ether-borne, poet of earth. Poet of Earth. Stephen Henry Thayer. AA

Oh be thou blest with all that Heav'n can send. To Mrs. M. B. on Her Birthday. Pope. EnLoPo

Oh Beverly, do you remember. September 7. Ellen Bass. NMM

Oh! blame not the bard, if he fly to the bowers. Thomas Moore. NOIV

Oh blessed Lord! and wouldst thou die. On the Death of Our Lord. Richard Flecknoe. TIRV

Oh! blest [*or* bless'd] of heav'n [*or* Heaven], whom not the languid songs. Nature's Influence on Man. Mark Akenside. *Fr.* The Pleasures of Imagination, III. NOEC

(Love of Nature.) NOEC

Oh blythely [*or* blithely] shines the bonnie [*or* bonny] sun. We'll Go to Sea No More. *Unknown.* ChTr; GBP

Oh Boney's on the sea. The Shan Van Vocht. *Unknown.* OxBoLi

Oh, Bonnie is the little cow. Midnight in Bonnie's Stall. Siddie Joe Johnson. PChr

Oh, Boston, Boston, thou hast nought to boast on. Boston, Lincolnshire. *Unknown.* FaBoPP; GBP

Oh, bow your head, Tom Dooley. Tom Dooley. *Unknown.* AmFP

Oh, Breathe Not His Name! Thomas Moore. AnIL; EnRP

Oh! breathe upon this hapless world. Ode to Peace. *Unknown.* PAH

Oh, bright Heaven high above. *Unknown, tr.* by Arthur Waley. BoS

Oh Britannia's got a baby, a baby, a baby. Britannia's Baby. D. H. Lawrence. NAs

"Oh, brother, oh, brother, can you play ball." The Two Brothers. *Unknown.* AmFP

Oh brother, sister—man. Klaus Demus, *tr.* by Beth Bjorklund. CoAuP

Oh, but it is dirty! Filling Station. Elizabeth Bishop. FaBoMo; HAP; HCAP; InPK; NoP; NYBP; WeW

Oh but It Was Good. Harold Littlebird. VoR

Oh but, says one, tradition set aside. Tradition. Dryden. *Fr.* Religio Laici. OBS

Oh, call my brother back to me. The Child's First Grief. Felicia Dorothea Hemans. BLPA
(First Grief, The.) CH

Oh, cease, my wandering soul. Fulfillment. William Augustus Muhlenberg. WGRP

Oh, Charlie's sweet and Charlie's neat. Weevily Wheat. *Unknown.* AmFP; AS, *with music*

Oh child, do you know, do you know. Our Child. Pablo Neruda, *tr.* by Perry Higman. LPSS

Oh come and listen to my song. The Oxford and Hampton Railway. *Unknown.* OBET

Oh, come let us welcome sweet Sabbath the Queen! Welcome, Queen Sabbath. Zalman Schneour, *tr.* by Harry H. Fein. TrJP

Oh Come, Little Children. Phyllis McGinley. FaBV

Oh, come my joy, my soldier boy. Henry Treece. WaP

Oh, Come to Me When Daylight Sets. Thomas Moore. EnRP

Oh, come with me in my little canoe. Ossian's Serenade. Calder Campbell. BLPA

Oh, could I but sing as the minstrels of old! Lines to Emma. Priscilla Jane Thompson. CBWP-2

Oh, could we weep. Nurse No Long Grief. Mary Gilmore. PoAu-1

Oh Count, Where Has Gone. Gaspara Stampa, *tr. fr. Italian by* Muriel Kittel. DMI

Oh Cruel Was the Press-Gang. *Unknown.* GBP

Oh, Day of Days. LeRoy V. Brant. AH

Oh, de boll weevil am a little black bug. Boll Weevil Song. *Unknown.* AS

Oh, de good ole chariot swing so low. Swing Low, Sweet Chariot. *Unknown.* AA; AnAmPo

Oh, de grubbin'-hoe's a-rustin' in de co'nah. The Deserted Plantation. Paul Laurence Dunbar. AnAmPo

Oh, de ole sheep, dey know de road. De Ole Sheep Dey Know de Road. *Unknown.* BPo

Oh, de white gal ride in a automobile. De Black Girl. *Unknown.* GBP

Oh! Dear! *Unknown. See* Oh, Dear! What Can the Matter Be?

Oh dear me, the mill's ga'in' fast. The Jute Mill Song. *Unknown.* OBET

Oh, dear, what can the matter be?/ Two old women got up in an apple-tree. *Unknown.* FaBoNo

Oh, Dear! What Can the Matter Be? *Unknown.* OxNR
(Oh! Dear!) CH

Oh! dearer by far than the land of our birth. Richard Henry Wilde. GOA

"Oh, dearest grandpa, come and see." The Dead Sister. Caroline Gilman. OBCA

Oh! Death. *Unknown.* AmFP

Oh! Death will find me, long before I tire. Rupert Brooke. PoRA
(Sonnet: Death Will Find Me.) MoBrPo; Son

Oh, dere's lots o'keer an' trouble.) A Banjo Song. Paul Laurence Dunbar. AnAmPo

Oh, dewy was the morning, upon the first of May. Manila. Eugene Fitch Ware. FiBHP

Oh, dey whupped him up de hill, up de hill, up de hill. Never Said a Mumbalin' Word. *Unknown.* GBP

Oh, did you go to see the show. The Orange Lily. *Unknown.* FaBoPV; GBP

Oh! Did you ne'er hear of Kate Kearney? Kate Kearney. Lady Morgan. BLPA; FaBoBe

Oh, did you see him riding down. Riding Down. Nora Perry. AA

Oh, do buzz off, you bumptious Sun. Busy Old Fool. Ian Kelso. BXAP

Oh do not die, for I shall hate. A Fever. John Donne. OAEL-1

Oh, do not tease the Bluffalo. The Bluffalo. Jane Yolen. RHPC

Oh, do you remember sweet Betsey from Pike. Sweet Betsey from Pike. *Unknown.* AmFP; AS, *with music;* FaBoBa; OBAL; OxBoLi

Oh do[e] not wanton with those eyes. Ben Jonson. OBS; SeCP; TEP

Oh! don't you remember black Alice, Sam Holt. A Ballad of Queensland (Sam Holt). G. H. Gibson. PoAu-1

"Oh! don't you see the turtle-dove." The Turtle-Dove. *Unknown.* OxBoLi

Oh Dreams, Oh Destinations, *sel.* C. Day Lewis.
Symbols of Gross Experience. Son

Oh! Dublin sure there is no doubtin.' No Place So Grand. *Unknown.* WTO

Oh, early in the evenin', just after dark. The Blackleg Miners. *Unknown.* GBP; OBET

Oh East is East, and West is West, and never the twain shall meet. The Ballad of East and West. Kipling. BeLS; BLPL; BrPo; FaBoBe; FaBV; FaPoR; OBNV

Oh effervescent palisades of ferns in drippage. From Rome, for More Public Fountains in New York City. Alan Dugan. POS

Oh, Eleazar Wheelock was a very pious man. Eleazar Wheelock. Richard Hovey. OBAL

Oh, England./ Sick in head and sick in heart. England. *Unknown.* FaBoEE; OxBSP

Oh, England is a pleasant place for them that's rich and high. The Last Buccaneer. Charles Kingsley. BeLS; EBVV; FaBoBe
(Old Buccaneer, The.) MoShBr

Oh! Erin my country, my ancestor's home! Song to Erin. Mary Weston Fordham. CBWP-2

Oh, ever thus from childhood's hour, I've seen my fondest hopes recede. Muddled Metaphors. Tom Hood. NA
(Few Muddled Metaphors by Moore-ose Melodist.) FaBoNo

Oh everything is coming to an end. Heartbreak. Pierre Reverdy, *tr. by* Michael Benedikt. POS

Oh, everything is far. Rainer Maria Rilke, *tr. by* C. F. MacIntyre. TrJP

Oh, Fair to See. Christina Rossetti. *Fr.* Sing-Song. FaPON; OHIP

Oh [*or* O] fair[e] sweet face, oh [*or* O] eyes celestial[1] bright. John Fletcher. *Fr.* Women Pleased, III, iv. OBS; PoEL-2

Oh [*or* O] Fairest of the Rural Maids. Bryant. AA; TAP

Oh, fare you well, my darling. Fare You Well, My Darling. *Unknown.* AmFP

Oh fat world of crafty bourgeois. Challenge. Ada Negri, *tr. by* Muriel Kittel. DMI

Oh Father. Wendy Rose. CDW

Oh father, answer me. Dialogue. Howard Nemerov. NYBP

Oh Father—if Thou wouldst indeed. Father. Arthur Davison Ficke. TrPWD

"Oh father, let us hence—for hark." A Presentiment. Bryant. AnAmPo

Oh father, now that I have touched. Oh Father. Wendy Rose. CDW

Oh, fields of wonder. Birth. Langston Hughes. NAs

Oh fine, oh lovely! *Unknown, tr. by* Arthur Waley. BoS

Oh flame falling, as shaken, as the stories. The Fire. Robert Creeley. NOBA

Oh, fond attempt to give a deathless lot. On Observing Some Names of Little Note Recorded in the "Biographia Britannica." William Cowper. OBD

Oh, for a book and a shady nook. Open Sesame. *Unknown.* BoTP

Oh, for a Bowl of Fat Canary. John Lyly. *See* Alexander and Campaspe: O! [*or* Oh] for a bowl of fat canary.

Oh! for a closer walk with God. Walking with God. William Cowper. EnRP; NOCV; NOEC; PoEL-3; TEP; TOF
(O [*or* Oh] for a Closer Walk with God.) FiP

Oh, for a drink, to-night. Charmion's Lament. Eloise Bibb. CBWP-4

Oh for a lodge in some vast wilderness. The Time-Piece. William Cowper. *Fr.* The Task, II. EnRP
(Against Slavery.) NOEC

Oh for a pathway. Travel. Gyoko, *tr. by* Steven D. Carter. WFTW

Oh for a poet—for a beacon bright. Oh for a Poet—for a Beacon Bright. E. A. Robinson. OxBA

Oh for boyhood's painless play. Whittier. *Fr.* The Barefoot Boy. AiP

Oh for far-off monkeyland. Monkeyland. Sándor Weöres, *tr. by* Edwin Morgan. MHuP; RB

Oh for one hour of youthful joy! The Old Man Dreams. Oliver Wendell Holmes. BLPL; PoLF

Oh! [*or* O!] for some honest lover's ghost. Sir John Suckling. BXAP; JCP; MeLP; MePo; OBS; Par; PoEL-3; SeCP; SeCV-1
(Doubt of Martyrdom, A.) BoLoP; CaPo; NOBE; OBEV

Oh fortune, thy wresting wavering state. Written on a Wall at Woodstock. Elizabeth I, Queen of England. PBWP; WPE

Oh, foully slighted Ethiope maid! Priscilla Jane Thompson. CBWP-2

Oh, frame some little word for me. The Clue. Charlotte Fiske Bates. AA

Oh friend, we arrived too late. Friedrich Hölderlin, *tr. fr. German by* Robert Bly. *Fr.* Bread and Wine. NU

Oh, fury, equalled only by the shrieking wind. To Ariadne. Sylvia Plath. FL

Oh! fye upon care. The Ranting Wanton's Resolution; 1672. *Unknown.* CoMu

Oh gallant was our galley from her carven steering-wheel. The Galley-Slave. Kipling. BrPo

Oh, gallant was the first love, and glittering and fine. Pictures in the Smoke. Dorothy Parker. NBLV

Oh, gallantly they fared forth in khaki and in blue. America's Welcome Home. Henry van Dyke. AiP

Oh, *or* O Galuppi, Baldassaro, this is very sad to find! A Toccata of Galuppi's. Robert Browning. EBVV; GTBS-P; HAP; LiTB; Mes; NAEL-2; NOBE; NOBVV; NoP; OAEL-2; TEP

"Oh, Georgie Wedlock is my name." Georgie Wedlock. *Unknown.* AmFP

"Oh, get you forth, my son Willy." Marm Grayson's Guests. Mary Eleanor Wilkins Freeman. OBCA

Oh, Ghingeli, my bleeding heart. Oh, Ghingeli [*or* Gingilee], my bleeding heart. Moyshe-Leyb Halpern. AYP, *tr. by* Benjamin *and* Barbara Harshav *and* Kathryn Helle; TrJP, *tr. by* Joseph Leftwich

Oh gin I were a doo. Gin I Were a Doo. *Unknown.* GBP

Oh give attention, you maidens dear. Constance Kent. *Unknown.* OBET

Oh give me a home where the buffalo roam. A Home on the Range. *Unknown.* FaBoBe

Oh, Give Me the Hills. *Unknown.* AmFP

Oh! give to me of the bright green leaves. I Am Fashion's Toy. Mary E. Tucker. CBWP-1

Oh, Give Us Back the Days of Old! John Mason Neale. NOCV

Oh, give us pleasure in the flowers today. A Prayer in Spring. Robert Frost. TrCP; TrPWD

(Oh, Give Us Pleasure in the Flowers Today.) AH

Oh glorious spirits, who after all your bands. To All Angels and Saints. George Herbert. SeCV-1

Oh, gloriously did the king lead. *Unknown, tr. by* Arthur Waley. BoS

Oh, go to old Ireland and then you will know. Go to Old Ireland. *Unknown.* AmFP

Oh, God, beneath thy guiding hand. The Pilgrim Fathers. Leonard Bacon. AH, *with music;* WGRP

Oh God Forbid. Freddie Greenfield. GLP

Oh God I really went and did it this time. Went and picked up. The Blake Mistake. Sandie Castle. UL

Oh God! It's great! Chocolate Milk. Ron Padgett. TTTS

Oh, God, let me be beautiful in death. Last Plea. Jean Starr Untermeyer. TrPWD

Oh God made a trance on Sunday. God Made a Trance. *Unknown.* OBET

Oh God! my heart is thine. In the Valley. Priscilla Jane Thompson. CBWP-2

Oh, God on high, we pray to Thee. Prayer for America. Peter Marshall. OPP

Oh God, she said. Song My. Susan Griffin. NMM; WPOW

Oh, golden flower opened up. A Poem to the Mother of the Gods. *Unknown, tr. by* Edward Kissam. STP

Oh! Golden Rose! Oh. Glittering Lilly White. Edward Taylor. *Fr.* Preparatory Meditations before My Approach to the Lord's Supper, II. SCAP

Oh, good gigantic smile o' the brown old earth. Among the Rocks. Robert Browning. *Fr.* James Lee's Wife. OxBSP

Oh! Good, good, good, my Lord. What more love yet. Edward Taylor. *Fr.* Preparatory Meditations before My Approach to the Lord's Supper, CXII. NOBA

Oh! Great South China Sea with boundless magnificent outward ocean. Sea Offerings. Yu Kuang-chung, *tr. by* Dominic Cheung. IFON

Oh, great were you, King Wu! *Unknown, tr. by* Arthur Waley. BoS

Oh, greenly and fair in the lands of the sun. The Pumpkin. Whittier. OHIP

Oh, grieve not, ladies, if at night. Grieve Not, Ladies. Anna Hempstead Branch. FaFP

"Oh, hangman, hangman, slacken your rope." The Sycamore Tree. *Unknown.* AmFP

Oh, hapless sire, distraught with cares. The Yoke. Kalonymos ben Kalonymos, *tr. fr. Hebrew by* J. Chotzner. *Fr.* The Touchstone. TrJP

Oh happy golden age. *See* O lovely age of gold!

Oh, happy, happy maid. A Nuptial Eve. Sydney Thompson Dobell. OBNC

Oh happy shades! to me unblest. The Shrubbery. William Cowper. FaBoRV; NOBE

Oh happy trees that we plant today. Tree Planting. *Unknown.* OHIP

Oh, hark the dogs are barking, love. The Banks of the Condamine. *Unknown.* FaBoBa; GBP; PoAu-1

Oh, have you heard de lates.' Ballit of de Boll Weevil, De. *Unknown.* NOBA

Oh, have you seen the *Tattlesnake.* The Journal of Society. Godfrey Turner. NOBL

Oh, he is plucking cloth-creeper. *Unknown, tr. by* Arthur Waley. BoS

"Oh, hear you a horn, mother, behind the hill?" The Horn. James Reeves. SO

Oh heart rejoice! For I Have Done a Good and Kindly Deed. Franz Werfel, *tr. by* Edith Abercrombie Snow. TrJP

Oh, heavens! the weakness of my unkind father! The Obscured Prince; or, The Black Box Boxed. *Unknown.* APAS

Oh Heav'ns! I'm choack'd with smoak, I'm burn'd with fire. Lament of the Sodomites. George Lestey. *Fr.* Fire and Brimstone; or, The Destruction of Sodom. PeHV

"Oh hell, what do mine eyes." Milton by Firelight. Gary Snyder. CoAP; PPP

Oh, her beauty—the tender maid! Its brilliance gives light. Ibnu 'L-Arabi, *tr. by* R. A. Nicholson. TOF

Oh, here's a jolly lark. The Old Marquis and His Blooming Wife. *Unknown.* CoMu

Oh, Hollow! Hollow! Hollow! W. S. Gilbert. *Fr.* Patience. FaBoNo

Oh, holy cause/ That points the grass. Sung on a Sunny Morning. Jean Starr Untermeyer. TrPWD

Oh house with two doors that is mine. House with Two Doors. Enrique Gonzáles Martínez, *tr. by* Samuel Beckett. MexPo

"Oh how black the night is." The Old Man at the Window. Anthony Harvey. Mes

Oh, how can I live in a torture so wild. Disappointment. Mary E. Tucker. CBWP-1

Oh [*or* O], how comely it is, and how reviving. Milton. *Fr.* Samson Agonistes. NOBE; NOCV; OBEV

(Deliverer, The.) OBS

Oh how I hated that village, crown of thorns around my timid child's heart. Crown of Hatred and Love. Ferenc Juhász, *tr. by* Kenneth McRobbie. MHuP

Oh how I wish that an embargo. The Nurse's Dole in the Medea. Byron. OBVE

Oh, how my love/ With a whirling power. Tu-kehu, *tr. by* J. C. Andersen. WTO

Oh, how my pulse pipes to go riding, go riding. Riding. Harry Amoss. CaP

Oh how oft I wake and find. To My God. George Macdonald. TrPWD

Oh how steadily I live and find. Lady Kasa. *Fr.* Manyo Shu. Ma

Oh hush thee, little Dear-my-soul. Christmas Eve. Eugene Field. OHIP

Oh! hush thee, my baby, the night is behind us. Seal Lullaby. Kipling. *Fr.* The Jungle Book. FaPON; SoSe

Oh! hush Thee, oh! hush Thee, my Baby so small. Cradle Song at Bethlehem. E. J. Falconer. BoTP

Oh hush up. Breakfast. Everette Maddox. MT

Oh! I admit I'm dull and poor. The Claim. Edith Nesbit. NOBVV

Oh I am a cat that likes to/ Gallop. The Galloping Cat. Stevie Smith. BrRo

Oh, I am a Texas cowboy, just off the Texas plains. The Texas Cowboy. *Unknown.* AmFP

Oh, I am wild—wild! Sale of Souls. Adah Isaacs Menken. CBWP-1

Oh, I be vun of the useful troibe. A Rustic Song. Anthony C. Deane. FiBHP

Oh, I can hear you, God, above the cry. Wind in the Pine. Lew Sarett. TrPWD

Oh, I can laugh and I can sing. Whistling. Jack Prelutsky. RAR

Oh, I can smile for you, and tilt my head. A Certain Lady. Dorothy Parker. NIP

Oh I can't decide between my two loves ei! Women's Songs. *Unknown, tr. by* Margaret Orbell. PeNZ

Oh I could love him! My dreaming soul. Laments. Dolores Veintimilla de Galindo, *tr. by* Robert L. Smith *and* Judith Candullo. DMH

Oh, I don't mind the idea of heaven. Heaven. Michael Dennis Browne. SoTCo

Oh, I don't want to be a gambler. I Don't Want to Be a Gambler. *Unknown.* AS

Oh I got up and went to work. On a Seven-Day Diary. Alan Dugan. OBAL

Oh, I had a bird and the bird pleased me. The Barnyard. *Unknown.* AmFP

Oh, I had a horse and his name was Bill. The Horse Named Bill. *Unknown.* AS

Oh, I have dream'd a pleasant dream of sunny spots and dells. The Dream of the Artisan. G. R. Emerson. PF

Oh I have grown so shrivelled and sere. Body of John. R. A. K. Mason. ATNZ; PeNZ

Oh, I have no illusions as to what. Penelope. James Harrison. NIP

Oh, I have slipped the surly bonds of earth. High Flight. John Gillespie Magee, Jr. FaFP; FaPON

Oh, I laugh to hear what grown folk. Mrs. Kriss Kringle. Edith Matilda Thomas. OBCA

Oh! I love to travel far and near throughout my native land. Wizard Oil. *Unknown.* AS

Oh, I never had but one true love. The Unquiet Grave. *Unknown.* AmFP

Oh, I should love to be like one of those. The Youth Dreams. Rainer Maria Rilke, *tr.* by Ludwig Lewisohn. AWP; TrJP

Oh I suppose I should. Le Médecin Malgré Lui. William Carlos Williams. PoA; SaC

Oh, I used to sing a song. The Endless Song. Ruth McEnery Stuart. OBAL

Oh! I vu'st know'd o' my true love. Heedless o' My Love. William Barnes. GBL

Oh I want to/ tell you. Perversity. Susan Griffin. LLLT

Oh, I went to California in the spring of seventy-six. Root, Hog, or Die. *Unknown.* AmFP

Oh! I wish I were a tiny brown bird from out the south. Valentine's Day. Charles Kingsley. BoTP

Oh, I Wish I Were Single Again. *Unknown.* AmFP

Oh, I wonder where my lost Johnny's gone. Lost Johnny. *Unknown.* AmFP

Oh, I woud I wee a cose, cose fiend. Sim Ines. Jane Stubbs. FiBHP

Oh, if but a single hour. Permanence in Change. Goethe. HoPM, *tr. by* John Frederick Nims

Oh! if by any unfortunate chance I should happen to die. The Soldier. J. Y. Watson. BXAP

Oh, if I could only make you see. Her Mother. Alice Cary. OHIP

Oh, If They Only Knew! Edith L. Mapes. BLRP; WBLP

Oh, If Thou Knew'st How Thou Thyself Dost Harm. William Alexander, Earl of Stirling. *Fr.* Aurora, XXXIII. Son
(Sonnet: "Oh, if thou knew'st how thou thyself dost harm.") EiL
(To Aurora.) FaFP; GTBS; GTBS-P

Oh, ill-starred Ethiopia. Address to Ethiopia. Priscilla Jane Thompson. CBWP-2

Oh, I'm a good old Rebel. The Rebel. Innes Randolph. NBLV; OBAL; OxBoLi

Oh I'm Dirty Dan, the world's dirtiest man. The Dirtiest Man in the World. Shel Silverstein. OBCA

Oh I'm in love with the janitor's boy. The Janitor's Boy. Nathalia Crane. PoLF

Oh, I'm mad for Don Juan. How to Tell Juan Don from Another. Gardner E. Lewis. FiBHP

Oh! I'm the New Year. The New Year. *Unknown.* BoTP

Oh in eighteen hundred and forty-one. Poor Paddy Works on the Railway. *Unknown.* AS

Oh, in eighteen hundred and sixty-one. Roll, *Alabama,* Roll. *Unknown.* OxBSS

Oh, in the fourteenth the faith landed. The Land Is Gone. *Unknown, tr. by* Margaret Orbell. PeNZ

Oh, in the merry month of May. Bonny Barbara Allan. *Unknown.* AmFP

Oh in the Stonegut Sugar Works. Ballad of the Stonegut Sugar Works. James Keir Baxter. PeNZ

"Oh is it the jar of nations." The Jar of Nations. A. E. Housman. LiTB

Oh, is it, then, Utopian. De Profundis. Dorothy Parker. ErPo; NAAL-2

Oh, is not this a holy spot? On Laying the Corner-Stone of the Bunker Hill Monument. John Pierpont. PAH

"Oh! isn't it a pity, such a pretty girl as I." Harriet H. Robinson. SaC

Oh, it *is* life! to see a proud. Gallantly within the Ring. John Hamilton Reynolds. SD

Oh it was a fine and pleasant day. The Shoals of Herring. Ewan MacColl. OxBSS

Oh, it was not a pheasant cock. The Drowned Lady. *Unknown.* ChTr

Oh it's all under the leaves and the leaves of life. The Leaves of Life. *Unknown.* OBET

Oh, it's fiddle-de-dum and fiddle-de-dee. The Dancing Bear. Albert Bigelow Paine. OBCA

Oh, it's H-A-P-P-Y I am, and it's F-R-double-E. The Bells. *Unknown.* FiBHP

"Oh, it's Hynde Horn fair, and it's Hynde Horn free." Hynde Horn. *Unknown.* GN

Oh, It's Nine Years Ago I Was Digging in the Land. *Unknown.* AmFP

Oh, it's twenty gallant gentlemen. The Last Hunt. William Roscoe Thayer. AA; FaBoBe

Oh, its up on the Highlands. *See* Hie upon Hielands.

Oh, I've got no use for the women. I've Got No Use for the Women. *Unknown.* AmFP

Oh, I've ridden plenty of horses. Noonday Sun. Kathryn Byron Jackson. FaPON

Oh! kangaroos, sequins, chocolate sodas! Today. Frank O'Hara. TTTS

Oh King of Saints, how great's thy work, say we. Edward Johnson. SCAP

Oh King of stars! Hospitality in Ancient Ireland. *Unknown, tr.* by Kuno Meyer. OnYI; TIRV

Oh, kite-owl, kite-owl. *Unknown, tr.* by Arthur Waley. BoS

Oh! Ladies and gentlemen, please to draw near. Down, Down Derry Down. *Unknown.* AS

Oh, lady, wake! the azure moon. Ballad of Bedlam. *Unknown.* NA

Oh *or* O last and best of Scots! who did'st maintain. Upon the Death of the Viscount of Dundee. Dryden. OBS
(Upon the Death of the Earl of Dundee.) ACP

Oh last Thursday morning while playing at ball. Willie. *Unknown.* AmFP

Oh Lawd have mussy now upon us. Blessing without Company. *Unknown.* BPo

Oh leaden heeld. Lord, give, forgive I pray. Edward Taylor. *Fr.* Preparatory Meditations before My Approach to the Lord's Supper, I. SCAP

Oh leave his body broken on the rocks. On a Dying Boy. William Bell. NePoEA

Oh, let me run and hide. Spring Ecstasy. Lizette Woodworth Reese. MoAmPo

Oh, let me through to the joy of the Yiddish word. Jacob Glatstein, *tr. fr. Yiddish by* Benjamin *and* Barbara Harshav. *Fr.* The Joy of the Yiddish Word. AYP

Oh, Let Thy Teachings. Immanuel di Roma, *tr. fr. Hebrew by* J. Chotzner. *Fr.* Machberoth. TrJP

Oh, let us howl some heavy note. The Madman's Song. John Webster. *Fr.* The Duchess of Malfi, IV, ii. EiL
(Song: "O, let us howl some heavy note.") InvP

Oh let your shining orb grow dim. To the Sun. Roy Campbell. *Fr.* Mithraic Emblems. EaLo

Oh, let's fix us a julep and kick us a houn.' Boogie-woogie Ballads. St. Clair McKelway. PoNe

Oh, let's go up the hill and scare ourselves. The Bonfire. Robert Frost. InvP

Oh, life is a glorious cycle of song. Comment. Dorothy Parker. *Fr.* Some Beautiful Letters. AnAmPo; NBLV; NIP; OBAL

Oh, like a tree. The Tree. John Freeman. BoTP

Oh, limpid stream of Tyrus, now I hear. A Classic Ode. Charles Battell Loomis. NA

Oh List to My Song! Clara Ann Thompson. CBWP-2

Oh! Listen, man! Immortality. Richard Henry Dana. NA

Oh, little Christ, why do you sigh. Christmas Eve in France. Jessie Redmond Fauset. BANP

Oh! little loveliest lady mine. A Valentine. Laura Elizabeth Richards. AA

Oh loathsome place! where I. Earl of Surrey. SiPS

Oh! lonely is our old green fort. Old Fort Meigs. *Unknown.* PAH

Oh, long before the bere was steeped for malt. John Davidson. *Fr.* The Testament of John Davidson: The Last Journey. PoSH

Oh, long, long/ The snow has possessed the mountains. The Grass on the Mountain. *Unknown, tr.* by Mary Austin. AmFN; AWP; FaPON; GOA

Oh! Look at the Moon. Eliza Lee Follen. BoTP

Oh Lord Cozens Hardy. Lord Cozens Hardy. Sir John Betjeman. OxBTC

Oh Lord, I have been staring into a mirror. Eugene Heimler, *tr. by* Anthony Rudolf. VWA

Oh, Lord! I lift my heart. Priscilla Jane Thompson. CBWP-2

Oh Lord, I've never lived where churches grow. A Cowboy's Prayer. Badger Clark. CowP

Oh Lord! thou hast known me, and searched me out. An Hymn on the Omnipresence. John Byrom. TrPWD

Oh, Lord, we call to you from our apartment. A Gay Psalm from Fort Valley. Louie Crew. GLP

Oh Lord, when all our bones are thrust. Supplication. Edgar Lee Masters. TrCP; TrPWD

Oh lordy, lord, oh lordy, lord. Worried Life Blues. *Unknown.* AmFP

Oh, love builds on the azure sea. Love's Land. Isabella Valancy Crawford. CaP

Oh love! no habitant of earth thou art. Byron. *Fr.* Childe Harold's Pilgrimage, IV. OAEL-2

(Fatal Spell, The.) OBNC

Oh! Love, that stronger art than wine. Aphra Behn. *Fr.* The Lucky Chance. WPE; WPOW

Oh Lovely Fishermaiden. Heine, *tr. fr. German by* Louis Untermeyer. AWP

Oh, Lovely, Lovely, Lovely! *Unknown.* CRH

Oh, Lovely Rock. Robinson Jeffers. NU

Oh! lovely voices of the sky. Hymn for Christmas. Felicia Dorothea Hemans. GN

Oh Lucky Jim! *Unknown.* ChTr; GBP

Oh Madame Curie. While Dissecting Frogs in Biology Class Scrut Discovers the Intricacies of the Scooped Neckline in His Lab Partner's Dress. George Roberts. GOYP

Oh, make me, sphere-descended Queen. A Wykehamist's Address to Learning. P. N. Shuttleworth. FaBoCo

Oh, make my bed in the warm air. To Carry on Living. Yehuda Amichai, *tr. by* the author. LLLT

Oh mama dear, come and meet me. Song of the Rice Workers. *Unknown, tr. by* Muriel Kittel. DMI

"Oh, Mammy, Mammy, now I'm married." Will the Weaver. *Unknown.* AmFP

Oh [*or* O], many a day have I made good ale in the glen. The Outlaw of Loch Lene. *Unknown, tr. by* Jeremiah Joseph Callanan. BIrV; CH; GBL; OBEV

Oh, Mary and the Baby, sweet Lamb. Mary and the Baby, Sweet Lamb. *Unknown.* AmFP

Oh Mary, at the window be. *See* O Mary, at the window be.

Oh Mary, go and call the cattle home. *See* O Mary, go and call the cattle home.

Oh May, bonnie May is to the Yowe buchts gane. The Laird o' Ochiltree Wa's. *Unknown.* OxBB

Oh may I join the choir invisible. *See* O may I join the choir invisible.

Oh, may my constant feet not fail. Sophocles, *tr. fr. Greek by* Robert Whitelaw. *Fr.* Oedipus the King [*or* Oedipus Rex]. WGRP

Oh may you bless your happy lot that lies secure on shore. The Banks of Newfoundland ("Oh may you bless your happy lot that lies secure on shore"). *Unknown.* OxBSS

Oh me/ is that the ambulance chasing out of town? Alan Brunton. PeNZ

Oh me good friend, Mr. Wilberforce, make we free! Song of the King of the Eboes. *Unknown.* PBCV

Oh, meet me tonight in the moonlight. New Jail. *Unknown.* AmFP

Oh men are beaten, beaten, beaten down. The Land Laws. Merimeri Penfold, *tr. by* Margaret Orbell. PeNZ

Oh Menelaus. On Hearing the First Cuckoo. Richard Church. OBMV

Oh, merry the waves of the P'an. *Unknown, tr. by* Arthur Waley. BoS

Oh, mighty America, hast thou come to this? Fare Thee Well. Eli Siegel. GOA

Oh mighty city of New York! you are wonderful to behold. Jottings of New York. William McGonagall. OBTV

Oh Mistress Mine [Where Are You Roaming?] Shakespeare. *See* O Mistress Mine.

Oh, Molly, oh, Molly, I've told you before. Red Whiskey. *Unknown.* AmFP

Oh moon, oh moon! *Unknown, tr. by* Mari Marase. BoWoP

Oh Moon! when I look on thy beautiful face. Poetic Thought. *Unknown.* FiBHP

Oh, most high, almighty, good Lord God. Canticle of the Sun. Saint Francis of Assisi, *tr. by* Maurice Francis Egan

Oh mother, holiest mother, mother night! To Night, the Mother of Sleep and Death. John Addington Symonds. Son

Oh, mother, I shall be married to Mr. Punchinello. To Mr. Punchinello. *Unknown.* OxNR

Oh Mother of a Mighty Race. Bryant. FaBoBe; OPP; PAH (America.) AA

Oh Mother, so many times. Mother with Child. Lenore Keeshig-Tobias. GOS

Oh! mourn not for Anacreon dead. On Tom Moore's Translation of Anacreon. Thomas, 1st Baron Erskine. FaBoEE

Oh, Mr. Cross! Address to Mr. Cross, of Exeter 'Change, on the Death of the Elephant. Thomas Hood. FM

"Oh, Mrs. McGrath," the sergeant said. Mrs. McGrath. *Unknown.* FaBoBa

Oh Muse! I crave a favor. The Muse's Favor. Priscilla Jane Thompson. CBWP-2

Oh, Musgrove, he persuaded me. Musgrove. *Unknown.* AmFP

Oh my aged uncle Arly. *See* O my aged uncle Arly.

Oh my black[e] soule! now thou art summoned. John Donne. *Fr.* Holy Sonnets, IV. EBEV; JCP; OAEL-1; OBS; Son; TEP; TOF

Oh my boy: Jesus. The Confession Stone. Owen Dodson. TTY

Oh, My Darling Clementine. *At. to* Percy Montross. AmFP; AnAmPo; FaBoBe; FaFP; OBAL

Oh, my dear love far away! Prince Aki. *Fr.* Manyo Shu. Ma

Oh my fine, my honey-colored Duke of Marmalade! Elegy for the Duke of Marmalade. Luis Palés Matos, *tr. by* Julio Marzán. InW

Oh, My Geraldine. Sir Francis Cowley Burnand. NA

Oh my God, screamed Mommy, you went and ate the baby. The Snack. L. L. Zeiger. BXAP

Oh! my hips hurt so! *Unknown, tr. by* Geoffrey Bownas *and* Anthony Thwaite. PeBJV

Oh, my Lord. My Lord, What a Morning. Waring Cuney. TTY

Oh, My Love Is Like a Red, Red Rose. Burns. InPK; LiTB

Oh, my man is so unfeeling. Emperor Go-Shirakawa. *See* Ryojin Hisho: You have no heart.

Oh, my mother's moaning by the river. The Lonely Mother. Fenton Johnson. PoNe

Oh, my name is Bob the Swagman, before you all I stand. The Old Bark Hut. *Unknown.* PoAu-1

Oh! my name is John Wellington Wells. William Schwenck Gilbert. *Fr.* The Sorcerer, Mr. Wells. WSC

Oh [*or* O], my name it is Sam[uel] Hall, it is Sam[uel] Hall. Sam [*or* Samuel Hall]. *Unknown.* ChTr; TW; UnPo

Oh, my name was Robert Kidd, as I sailed, as I sailed. Captain Kidd. *Unknown.* MoShBr

Oh My People I Remember. Wendy Rose. CDW

Oh my Plutonian restaurateur! Revving Up la Rêve. Joel Dailey. UL

Oh, my wandering melody. Melody. Shmuel Moreh, *tr. by* Yoffee Berkovitz. VWA

Oh! Mystery of Man. Wordsworth. *Fr.* The Prelude [or, Growth of a Poet's Mind]: Imagination and Taste, How Impaired and Restored, XII. FiP

"Oh, Nancy, my heart." To Milk in the Valley Below. *Unknown.* OBET

Oh Neïla/ borne away by evening. Neïla. Iwan Goll, *tr. by* Anthony Rudolf. VWA

Oh never in this hard world was such an absurd. Nesting Time. Douglas Stewart. PoAu-2

Oh never marry Ishmael! Song for Unbound Hair. Genevieve Taggard. PoRA

Oh never on my youthful ear. My Mother's Voice. Mary E. Tucker. CBWP-1

Oh! Never say that I was false of heart. *See* O! Never say that I was false of heart.

Oh, never say that you have reached the very end. We Survive! Hirsch Glick, *tr. by* Ruth Rubin. TrJP

Oh never weep for love that's dead. Dead Love. Elizabeth Siddal. NOBVV

Oh nimber, nimber Will-o! Chuck Will's Widow Song. *Unknown.* BPo

Oh! ninna and anninia! Sleep, Baby Boy. *Unknown.* FaPON

Oh No. Robert Creeley. HeIP; InPK; NaP; SM

Oh No More, No More. John Ford. *See* Broken Heart, The: Oh [*or* O], no more, no more, too late.

Oh [*or* O], no more, no more, too late. John Ford. *Fr.* The Broken Heart, IV, iii. GBL; PoEL-2

(Love's Martyrs.) NOBE

(Oh No More, No More.) ELP

(Song: "Oh no more, no more, too late.") OBS; OxBSP; SeCePo

Oh, no one can deny. Self's the Man. Philip Larkin. NOBL

Oh, Noa, Noa! William Cole. NBLV

Oh, Northern men—true hearts and bold. Cast Down, but Not Destroyed. *Unknown.* PAH

Oh, not to be in England. Abroad Thoughts. Edward Blishen. NOBL

Oh, Nothing. John Ashbery. NAAL-2

"Oh, now I've come back to you, Mother." The Cripple for Life; or, The Poor Volunteer. *Unknown.* AmFP

Oh, now we're leaving home, me boys; to Ottawa we're goin.' The Lake of the Caogama. *Unknown.* WTO

Oh oh—ah ah. Ti-ch'ü Song Words. *Unknown, tr. by* Burton Watson. CoBCP

Oh! oh! is all I can say. Teishitsu, *tr. by* Geoffrey Bownas *and* Anthony Thwaite. PeBJV

Oh, oh, you will be sorry for that word! Edna St. Vincent Millay. BoWoP

Oh, on an early morning I think I shall live forever! Poem in Three Parts. Robert Bly. CAPP; NaP; NOBA

Oh, once I lived in Cottonwood and owned a little farm. Once I Lived in Cottonwood. *Unknown.* AmFP

Oh, once I was a policeman young and merry (young and merry). A Policeman's Lot. Wendy Cope. FaBoWP

Oh once I was a shepherd boy. Once I Was a Shepherd Boy. *Unknown.* OBET

Oh, open the door, my hinnie, my heart. The Padda Song. *Unknown.* GBP

Oh open the door, some pity to shew. Open the Door to Me, Oh! Burns. PoEL-4

(O, Open the Door to Me, O!) FaBoCh

Oh, our heaven-born god. Lady Otomo no Sakanoe. *Fr.* Manyo Shu. Ma

Oh our Mother the Earth oh our Father the Sky. Song of the Sky Loom. *Unknown, tr. by* Herbert J. Spinden. WTO

Oh, Paddy dear! and did ye hear the news that's goin' round? The Wearin' o' the Green. *Unknown.* NOIV

Oh, Passage town is of great renown. The Town of Passage. *Unknown.* OxBoLi

Oh, passer-by, should you inquire. Epitaph on Pegasus, a Limping Gay. "Panormitanus." PeHV

Oh, perhaps your doubt, perhaps anxiety. To My Mother. Giuseppina Turrisi Colonna, *tr. by* Muriel Kittel. DMI

Oh, Pillykin Willykin Winky Wee! Punkydoodle and Jollapin. Laura E. Richards. OBCA

Oh pleasant eventide! Twilight Calm. Christina Rossetti. BoNaP; OBNC

Oh, please don't. Lotus. Huan Fu, *tr. by* Dominic Cheung. IFON

Oh, plovers on the river-shore. Prince Kadobe. *Fr.* Manyo Shu. Ma

Oh, Poet of our Race. Poet of Our Race. Maggie Pogue Johnson. CBWP-4

"Oh [*or* O] Polly love, Oh Polly [*or* my dear] Polly, the rout [*or* war] has now begun." High Germany. *Unknown.* OBET; WaaP

Oh! poverty is a weary thing, 'tis full of grief and pain. The Sale of the Pet Lamb. Mary Howitt. CH

"Oh, pray come in." Rather Too Good, Little Peggy! Adelaide O'Keeffe. FaBoUs

Oh Promise Me. Clement Scott. FaFP

Oh, pure and sportive little child. To a Little Colored Boy. Priscilla Jane Thompson. CBWP-2

Oh quick, garner the children. Planting Children: 1939. Evan Zimroth. ER

Oh rare Harry Parry. *See* O rare Harry Parry.

Oh, rock-a-by, baby mouse, rock-a-by, so! The Mouse's Lullaby. Palmer Cox. OBCA

Oh roses for the flush of youth. Christina Rossetti. ELP; GTBS-P; NOBVV

Oh, rouse you, rouse you, men at arms. The Great Swamp Fight. Caroline Hazard. PAH

Oh, Sally Brown, of New York City. Sally Brown. *Unknown.* AmFP

Oh [*or* O], say, can you see, by the dawn's early light. The Star-spangled Banner. Francis Scott Key. AA; BLPA; FaBoBe; FaFP; FaPON; FaPoR; PAH; TAP; WBLP

Oh, say, what is this fearful, wild. The Hippopotamus. Oliver Herford. NA

Oh, say you can hear/ On the Watergate tapes. Final Curtain. Roger Woddis. FaBoPa

Oh, says the linnet, if I sing. Birds' Lament. John Clare. PoEL-4

Oh, See How Thick the Goldcup Flowers. A. E. Housman. *Fr.* A Shropshire Lad, V. FaBV; MoBrPo

Oh, see my little boat. The Boat. Caroline Gilman. OBCA

Oh, seek me not within a tomb. John G. Neihardt. WGRP

Oh send to me an apple that hasn't any kernel. *Unknown, tr. fr. Welsh by* Gwyn Williams. FaBoCh

Oh shall I never never be home again? Brumana. James Elroy Flecker. BrPo

Oh she called to her little page boy. Lady Maisry ("Oh she called to her little page boy"). *Unknown.* OBET

Oh! she is good, the little rain! and well she knows our need. The Little Rain. Tu Fu, *tr. by* L. Cranmer-Byng. FaPON

Oh, she walked unaware of her own increasing beauty. She Walked Unaware. Patrick MacDonogh. BoLoP; ErPo; FaBoTw; NeIP

Oh, Shannadore, I love your daughter. The Wide Mizzoura. *Unknown.* AS

Oh, Shenandoah, I long to hear you. Shenandoah. *Unknown.* AmFN

Oh, shield me from his rage, celestial Powers! Jealousy. Esther Johnson. OxBSP

Oh ship! new billows sweep thee out. I, 14. Ship of State, The ("O navis, referent"). Horace, *tr. fr. Latin. Fr.* Odes. AWP, *tr. by* William Ewart Gladstone.

"Oh, sick I am to see you, will you never let me be?" The New Mistress. A. E. Housman. *Fr.* A Shropshire Lad, XXXIV. MoBrPo

Oh silver-throated swan. *See* O silver-throated swan.

Oh, silver tree! Jazzonia. Langston Hughes. AmNP; BANP

Oh, sing me the song of the factory girl! Song of the Factory Girls. *Unknown.* SaC

Oh, Sing to God. Jacob Steendam, *tr. fr. Dutch.* AH

Oh sing unto the Lord [*or* Jehovah] a new song. *See* O sing unto the Lord [*or* Jehovah] a new song.

Oh, sister Phoebe, how merry were we. Tom Jones's Plum Tree. *Unknown.* AmFP

Oh Siva, great giver. Tulsidas, *tr. by* John Stratton Hawley *and* Mark Juergensmeyer. SSI

Oh, Sleep, Fond Fancy. *Unknown.* ElL

Oh, Sleep Forever in the Latmian Cave. Edna St. Vincent Millay. CMoP; LiTM; MoAmPo; NoAM; NoP

Oh! sleep in peace where poppies grow. Reply to "In Flanders Fields." John Mitchell. BLPA

Oh [*or* O], slow to smite and swift to spare. The Death of Lincoln. Bryant. NAAL-1; TAP

(Abraham Lincoln.) PAH

(To the Memory of Abraham Lincoln.) OHIP

Oh smooth adder/ who with fanged kisses changedst my natural blood. Augusta Davies Webster. *Fr.* Medea in Athens. BrRo

Oh snatch'd away in beauty's bloom! *See* O snatch'd away in beauty's bloom!

Oh soft flowing rivers. My South. Don West. PoNe

Oh some are fond of red wine, and some are fond of white. Captain Stratton's Fancy. John Masefield. MoBrPo; OBEV

Oh some have killed in angry love. A Rope for Harry Fat. James Keir Baxter. MoBS

Oh, stalwart, stalwart. *Unknown, tr. by* Arthur Waley. BoS

Oh stormy, stormy world. Happiness Makes Up in Height for What It Lacks in Length. Robert Frost. MoAB; MoAmPo

Oh, strong and faithful and enduring. The Return. Martha Ostenso. CaP

Oh strong ridged and deeply hollowed. Smell. William Carlos Williams. MoAB; MoAmPo; TAP

Oh sumptuous moment. Emily Dickinson. NAAL-1

Oh! surely for thee were the gates ajar. Rev. Samuel Weston. Mary Weston Fordham. CBWP-2

Oh! surely 'tis a theme sublime. Dedicated to the Right Rev'd D. A. Payne. Mary Weston Fordham. CBWP-2

Oh! [*or* O] Susanna. Stephen Collins Foster. AnAmPo; FaFP; OBAL

Oh, Sweet Content. W. H. Davies. CH

Oh, sweet courtly love of God, always clasp the soul in me. On the Divine Power of Courtly Love. Mechthild von Magdeburg, *tr. by* Susan L. Cocalis. DMG

Oh Sweet Souvenirs. Baldomero Garcilaso de la Vega, *tr. fr. Spanish by* Perry Higman. LPSS

Oh, take my hand and stroll with me. The Land of Potpourri. Jack Prelutsky. RHPC

Oh [*or* O], talk not to me of a name great in story. Stanzas Written on the Road between Florence and Pisa. Byron. EnRP; NAEL-2

(All for Love.) GTBS; GTBS-P

Oh, Teddy wants a nine-dollar shawl. I Wish I Was a Mole in the Ground. *Unknown.* AmFP

Oh! tell me a tale of the airly days. A Tale of the Airly Days. James Whitcomb Riley. AnAmPo

Oh! tell me have you ever seen a red, long-leg'd Flamingo? The Flamingo. Lewis Gaylord Clark. NA

"Oh, tell me, sailor, tell me true." The Gray Swan. Alice Cary. BeLS; GN

Oh thank you cowboy with four-wheel drive. For Drum Hadley. Harold Littlebird. VoR

Oh thank you for giving me the chance. Thank You. Kenneth Koch. NeAP; PoM

Oh that horse I see so high. A Gift of Great Value. Robert Creeley. LCAP; NaP

Oh, that I always breath'd in such an air. Edward Taylor. *Fr.* Preparatory Meditations before My Approach to the Lord's Supper, III.

(Experience, The.) AmPP

Oh that I had wings like a dove. Wings. Bible, *O.T. Fr.* Psalms: Psalm LV ("Give ear to my prayer. "). FaPON, 6-7.

Oh that I was the Bird of Paradise! Edward Taylor. *Fr.* Preparatory Meditations before My Approach to the Lord's Supper, 63. NOCV

Oh that I were/ Where I would be. *Unknown.* OxNR

Oh! that I were a poet now in grain! An Elegie upon that Reverend. Mr. Thomas Shepard. Urian Oakes. SCAP

Oh That I Were in the Wilderness. Bible, *O.T. Fr.* Jeremiah, IX: 1-10. TrJP

Oh! that mine eye might closed be. Thomas Ellwood. WGRP

Oh, that my dear mother. Tsumori Okurusu. *Fr.* Manyo Shu. Ma

"Oh That My Love Were in My Arms." *Malay Oral Tradition, tr. by* R. J. Wilkinson *and* R. O. Winstedt. WTO

Oh that my lungs could bleat like butter'd pease. Odd but True. *Unknown.* FaBoCo
   (Nonsense.) FaBoNo; NA
   (Oh That My Lungs.) NOBL

Oh that my soul a marrow-bone might seize! Sonnet Found in a Deserted Madhouse. *Unknown.* FaBoCo; FaBoNo; InvP; NA

Oh! That my young life were a lasting dream. Dreams. Poe. AmPP; OxBA; TAP

Oh! that the desert [*or* desart] were my dwelling-place. The Ocean. Byron. *Fr.* Childe Harold's Pilgrimage, IV. PoEL-4
   "Roll on, thou deep and dark blue ocean—roll!"
   (Apostrophe to the Ocean.) OHFP; WBLP
   (By the Deep Sea.) OBNC, *shorter sel.*
   (Deep and Dark Blue Ocean.) ChTr
   (Ocean, The.) FaBV; TrGrPo
   (Roll On, Thou Deep and Dark Blue Ocean.) FaPON; FiP
   (Sea, The.) BLPL; FaBoBe; LiTB
   (To the Ocean.) GN; WGRP
   "There is a pleasure in the pathless woods." MOS

Oh that those lips had language! Life has pass'd. William Cowper. *Fr.* On the Receipt of My Mother's Picture out of Norfolk [the Gift of My Cousin Ann Bodham]. EnRP; FiP; NOEC
   (Lines on Receiving My Mother's Picture Out of Norfolk.) CH; OHIP

Oh that thy creed were sound! The Good Samaritan. Cardinal Newman. OBTV

Oh that 'twere possible. *See* O that 'twere possible.

"Oh [*or* O]! that you were yourself! but, love, you are." Shakespeare. *Fr.* Sonnets, XIII. TEP

Oh, the autumn foliage. Empress Jito. *Fr.* Manyo Shu. Ma

Oh, the big ice axe, it hangs on the wall. The Scottish Mountaineering Club Song. John G. Stott. PoSH

Oh, the bitter shame and sorrow. None of Self and All of Thee. Theodore Monod. BLRP

Oh, the blue blue bloom. Pansy. Mary Effie Lee Newsome. CDC

Oh, the bosses' tricks of '76. Two-Cent Coal. *Unknown.* AmFP

Oh the charming month of May! Joseph Addison. NOEC

Oh, the Ch'i and the Chü. *Unknown, tr. by* Arthur Waley. BoS

Oh, the comfort—the inexpressible comfort of feeling safe with a person. Friendship. Dinah Maria Mulock Craik. BLPA

Oh, the constant leveling solitude. Torn Mountain. René Char, *tr. by* William Jay Smith. CT

Oh the corrugated-iron town. Douglas Stewart. *Fr.* The Birdsville Track. CBAP

Oh the dance of our Sister! The Dance of the Rain. Eugène Marais, *tr. by* Jack Cope *and* Uys Krige. PeSA

Oh the dances we have done! The Dance. Jim Gustafson. UL

Oh! the days are gone, when beauty bright. Love's Young Dream. Thomas Moore. WBLP

Oh, the Devil in hell they say he was chained. Hell in Texas. *Unknown.* BLPA

Oh! the dream, the dream! The Orphan. Muhammad al-Maghut. MAP, *tr. by* May Jayyusi *and* John Heath-Stubbs; MAP, *tr. by* May Jayyusi *and* John Heath-Stubbs; MPAW, *tr. by* Abdullah al-Udhari

Oh! the eastern winds are blowing. The Cornish Emigrant's Song. Robert Stephen Hawker. EBVV

Oh the falling snow! For Snow. Eleanor Farjeon. CH

Oh, the flowers of the bignonia. *Unknown, tr. by* Arthur Waley. BoS

Oh the French are on the sea. *See* O the French are on the sea.

Oh, the gen'ral raised the devil with the kernel, so 'tis said. Bugs. Will Stokes. MoShBr

Oh, the girl that I loved she was handsome. *See* Once I was happy but now I'm forlorn.

Oh, the gorgeous leaves of autumn! Autumn Leaves. Clara Ann Thompson. CBWP-2

Oh the Inconstant. N. P. van Wyck Louw, *tr. fr. Afrikaans by* Uys Krige *and* Jack Cope. PeSA

Oh, the insanities I took part in! Witold Gombrowicz, *tr. fr. Polish by* Louis Iribarne. *Fr.* The Marriage, Act II. PwPP

Oh the January man he walks abroad in woollen coat and boots of leather. January Man. Dave Goulder. OBET

Oh! the king's gane gyte. Cophetua. "Hugh MacDiarmid." OxBS

Oh the many joys of a harlot's wedding. Hail Wedded Love! Jay Macpherson. MoCV

Oh the Miller, the dusty, musty Miller. A Ballad of All the Trades. *Unknown.* CoMu; ErPo

Oh [*or* O], the noble [*or* brave *or* grand old] duke of York. The Noble [*or* Brave Old] Duke of York. *Unknown.* GBP
   (Brave Old Duke of York, The.) OxNR
   ("O, the grand old Duke of York.") GBP

Oh the noble fleet of whalers out sailing from Dundee. The *Balena.* *Unknown.* OxBSS

Oh the north countree is a hard countree. The Ballad of Yukon Jake. Edward E. Paramore, Jr. BeLS; BLPA

Oh, the old gray mare, she ain't what she used to be. Old Gray Mare. *Unknown.* AS, *with music;* AS; GBP

Oh! the old swimmin'-hole! whare the crick so still and deep. The Old Swimmin'-Hole. James Whitcomb Riley. AnAmPo; BeLS; FaFP

Oh, the pain of my love that you know not. Lady Otomo no Sakanoe. *Fr.* Manyo Shu. Ma

Oh, the Pilliwinks lived by the portals of Loo. The Cooky-Nut Trees. A. B. Paine. OBCA

Oh, the Polliwog is woggling. The Polliwog. Arthur Guiterman. RHPC

Oh, the praties they grow small. The Praties. *Unknown.* WTO
   (Famine Song.) WTO

Oh, the Rifles have stolen my dear jewel away. The Rifles. *Unknown.* OBET

Oh the rocks and the thimble. Meditations of a Parrot. John Ashbery. TTTS

Oh the sad day. Death. Thomas Flatman. OBD

Oh, the sea is deep. Song for a Suicide. Langston Hughes. PoNe

Oh, the shambling sea is a sexton old. The Gravedigger. Bliss Carman. BoNaP

Oh! the shearing is all over. The Old Bullock Dray. *Unknown.* PoAu-1

Oh, the slimy, squirmy, slithery eel! Song of Hate for Eels. Arthur Guiterman. OBAL

Oh! the snow, the beautiful snow. The Beautiful Snow. John Whittaker Watson. BLPA; WBLP

Oh the SS *Irwell* left this port the stormy sea to cross. The Manchester Ship Canal. *Unknown.* OBET

Oh the streams of lovely Nancy are divided into three parts. The Streams of Lovely Nancy. *Unknown.* FaBoBa; OBET; OxBoLi

Oh, the sun sets red, the moon shines white. The *Armstrong* at Fayal. Wallace Rice. PAH

Oh, the sweet contentment. Coridon's Song. John Chalkhill

Oh the thumb-sucker's thumb. Thumbs. Shel Silverstein. TSS

Oh, the tidal waves of our suffering. The Law. Albert E. Haynes, Jr. NBP

Oh! the time that is past. *Unknown.* BoLoP

Oh, the times are hard and the wages low. Across the Western Ocean *or* Leave Her, Bullies, Leave Her. *Unknown.* AS, *with music;* OxBSS, *with music*
   (Leave Her, Johnny, Leave Her.) OxBSS

Oh the Toe-Test! Norma Farber. RHPC

Oh, the train's off the track. The Train Is Off the Track. *Unknown.* AmFP

Oh the trawler wharf in Aberdeen. Deep Sea Tug. Harry Robertson. OxBSS

Oh, the white house, the bride's house. The Bride's Song. William Cory. OBTV

Oh, the white sea-gull, the wild sea-gull. The Sea-Gull. Mary Howitt. BoTP; OxBChV

Oh, the wild joys of living! the leaping from rock up to rock. Robert Browning. *Fr.* Saul, IX. FaBV
   (Youth.) BoTP

Oh, the wind from the desert blew in!—Khamsin. Khamsin. Clinton Scollard. AA

Oh the wine's fine. A Song for New Orleans. George Keithley. NPGG

Oh, the yogi—/ my friend, that clever one. Mirabai, *tr. by* John Stratton Hawley *and* Mark Juergensmeyer. SSI

Oh [*or* O] there is a blessing in this gentle breeze. Wordsworth. *Fr.* The Prelude [or, Growth of a Poet's Mind]: Childhood and School-Time. EnRP; OAEL-2

Oh, there once was a Puffin. There Once Was a Puffin. Florence Page Jaques. NTCP

Oh there was a jolly ship built in Nazi Germany. The Sinking of the *Graf Spee. Unknown.* OxBSS, *with music*

Oh! there was a moanish lady. Moanish Lady. *Unknown.* AS, *with music*

Oh there was a woman, and she was a widow. *See* O there was a woman, and she was a widow.

Oh, there was a youth and a noble youth. The Bailiff's Daughter of Islington. *Unknown.* AmFP; ESPB; FaBoBa; GN; OBET; OxBB, *with music;* OxBoLi

Oh there was an old soldier and he had a wooden leg. *See* O there was an old soldier and he had a wooden leg.

Oh, there were fifteen men in green. Men in Green. David Campbell. PoAu-2

Oh! these days. *Unknown, tr. by* Geoffrey Bownas *and* Anthony Thwaite. PeBJV

Oh, they love the larky lobsters. The Sadomasochistic Satisfactions of Seafood. Gavin Ewart. NPo

Oh! think how hard it is to die when young! Charles Heavysege. *Fr.* Jephthah's Daughter. CaP

Oh, this day of sacred rites. A Sacred Ceremony. Louise Aston, *tr. by* Susan L. Cocalis. DMG

Oh, this hectic world. Ryota, *tr. by* Geoffrey Bownas *and* Anthony Thwaite. PeBJV

Oh this is the animal that never was. Rainer Maria Rilke, *tr. fr. German by* Stephen Mitchell. *Fr.* The Unicorn. TTTS

Oh, this is the tale of John Cherokee. John Cherokee. *Unknown.* GBP

Oh this man. Magnificat. Michele Roberts. BrRo

Oh, this subdued, subtle beauty of middle class. Hymn to the Women of the Middle Class. Ursula Krechel, *tr. by* Susan L. Cocalis. DMG

Oh, this world of ours. Shunzei, *tr. by* Geoffrey Bownas *and* Anthony Thwaite. PeBJV

Oh those were happy days, heaped up with wineskins. Silenus in Proteus. Thomas Lovell Beddoes. EnRP

Oh thou great Power, in whom I move. A Hymn to My God in a Night of My Late Sicknesse. Sir Henry Wotton. MeLP; MePo; OBS

Oh, thou immortal bard! Byron. J. Gordon Coogler. OBAL

Oh, thou! in Hellas deemed of heavenly birth. Byron. *Fr.* Childe Harold's Pilgrimage, I. NAEL-2, *much abr.*

Oh thou, that dear and happy isle. Andrew Marvell. *Fr.* Upon Appleton House, to My Lord Fairfax. OxBoLi

Oh, thou that swing'st upon the waving hair. The Grasshopper. Richard Lovelace. NAEL-1

Oh, Thou! Who Dry'st the Mourner's Tear. Thomas Moore. TrPWD

Oh! thou—whose great imperial mind could raise. *Unknown.* OBTV

Oh thy bright eyes must answer now. *See* O thy bright eyes must answer now.

Oh! 'tis pretty to be in Ballinderry. Ballinderry. *Unknown.* WTO

Oh to be a bride. The Bride. Bella Akhmadulina. AIW; BoWoP, *tr. by* Stephan Stepanchev

Oh to be at Crowdieknowe. Crowdieknowe. "Hugh MacDiarmid." InPS; NoP; OxBS

Oh [*or* O], to be in England. Home Thoughts from Abroad. Robert Browning. AWP; BoNaP; BoTP; EBVV; FaBoBe; FaBV; FaFP; FaPON; FaPoR; FiP; FPL; GN; HeIP; LiTB; NAEL-2; NOBE; NOBVV; NoP; OBEV; OBNC; OBTV; PoLF; PoRA; PrIm; TEP; TrGrPo
(April in England.) GN

"Oh! to be in England," *par.* Home Thoughts from Abroad. *Unknown.* Par

Oh to be in England now that Winston's out. Ezra Pound. *Fr.* Cantos, LXXX. PoA

Oh, to be there to-night! Ada Cambridge. *Fr.* On Australian Hills. PoAu-1

Oh! to be wafted away. *Unknown.* NA

Oh, to feel the fresh breeze blowing. The Song of the Forest Ranger. Herbert Bashford. OHIP

Oh, to have a little house! *See* O, to have a little house!

Oh, to have a little house! An Old Woman of the Roads. Padraic Colum. TIRV

Oh! to have hidden in the undergrowth. King Lot's Envoys. Drummond Allison. OxBSP

Oh, to those who know no better. That Little Lump of Coal. *Unknown.* AmFP

Oh, to vex me, contraries [*or* contraryes] meet in one. John Donne. *Fr.* Holy Sonnets, XIX. OAEL-1; PoEL-2; Son
(Devout Fits.) SeCePo

Oh! true was his heart while he breathed. The King of Thule.¹ Goethe, *tr. by* James Clarence Mangan. AWP

Oh turn away those cruel eyes. *See* O turn away those cruel eyes.

Oh very early all in the spring. Early, Early in the Spring. *Unknown.* OBET

Oh virgin queen of mountain-side and woodland. Pine Tree for Diana, The ("Montium custos nemorumque"). Horace, *tr. fr. Latin by* Louis Untermeyer. *Fr.* Odes, III, 22. AWP

Oh! water for me! Bright water for me! The Water-Drinker. Edward Jonson. BXAP

Oh! waves in the sunlight gleaming. Sonnet to My First Born. Mary Weston Fordham. CBWP-2

Oh, way down South where I was born. Roll the Cotton Down. *Unknown.* AmFP

Oh, we come on the sloop *John B.* The *John B.* Sails. *Unknown.* AS

Oh, we started down from Roto when the sheds had all cut out. On the Road to Gundagai. *Unknown.* PoAu-1

Oh [*or* O] wearisome condition of humanity. Chorus Sacerdotum. Fulke Greville. *Fr.* Mustapha. HAP; InvP; JCP; LiTB; MePo; NAEL-1; NOBE; OAEL-1; OBS; PoEL-1; PPP; SeCePo

Oh! Weary Mother. Barry Pain. *Fr.* The Poets at Tea, VIII. NA; Par

Oh, weep for Mr. and Mrs. Bryan! The Lion. Ogden Nash. CenHV

Oh well born of Benares, I too am born well known. Ravidas, *tr. by* John Stratton Hawley *and* Mark Juergensmeyer. SSI

Oh well done Lord E——n! and better done R——r! An Ode to the Framers of the Frame Bill. Byron. CoMu; SaC

Oh, we'll rally 'round the flag, boys, we'll rally once again. The Battle Cry of Freedom. George Frederick Root. FaBoBe; PAH

Oh well tonight or some other night. Te Kaha. Rachel McAlpine. PeNZ

Oh Wellington! (Or "Villainton," for Fame). Byron. *Fr.* Don Juan, IX. OBSV; OxBoLi
(On Wellington.) FiP

Oh were I at the moss house, where the birds do increase. The Streams of Bunclody. *Unknown.* BIrV

Oh, Wert Thou in the Cauld Blast. *See* O, Wert Thou in the Cauld Blast.

"Oh whare hae ye been a' day my bonnie wee croodlin dow?" *See* "O whare hae ye been a'day my bonnie wee croodlin dow?"

Oh what a cunning guest. *See* O what a cunning guest.

Oh, what a dreary place this was when first the Mormons found it. St. George. Charlie Walker. AmFP

Oh what a host of questions in me rose. Back Again for the Holidays. Sir John Betjeman. *Fr.* Summoned by Bells. FaBoPP

Oh what a lad was Zimmer. A Zimmershire Lad. Paul Zimmer. SM

Oh, what a lark to fish for shark. The Shark. J. J. Bell. RHPC

Oh, what a night for a soul to go! Iter Supremum. Arthur Sherburne Hardy. AA

Oh [*or* O!] what a plague is Love! Phillida Flouts Me [*or* The Disdainful Shepherdess]. *Unknown.* CoMu; EIL; InVP; OBEV; OBSC; TrGrPo

Oh, what a pleasure to sing winter songs in *khamsin* days. Winter Song. Yankev Fridman, *tr. by* Ruth Whitman. PeBMYV

Oh! What a precious casket hast thou there. Sonnet: My Friend's Library. Henry F. Lott. PF

Oh, what a set of Vagabundos. Morgan. Edmund Clarence Stedman. AA

Oh! what a thing is man? Lord, who am I? Edward Taylor. *Fr.* Preparatory Meditations before My Approach to the Lord's Supper, XXXVIII. NAAL-1; NOBA; OxBA

Oh what a you say, seekers. Die in de Fiel'. *Unknown.* BoAN-1

Oh what can ail thee knight-at-arms. *See* O what can ail thee, knight-at-arms.

Oh, what can be more pleasant. Chorus of Scyrian Maidens. Philip Bainbrigge. *Fr.* Achilles in Scyros. PeHV

Oh, what can you do with a Christmas pup. Gift with the Wrappings Off. Mary Elizabeth Counselman. RHPC

Oh, what has become of us? *Unknown, tr. by* Arthur Waley. BoS

Oh! what has caused this great commotion. Tippecanoe and Tyler Too. Alexander Coffman Ross. AnAmPo

Oh, what have you got for dinner, Mrs. Bond? Dilly Dilly. *Unknown.* OxNR

Oh, what is so merry, so merry, heigh-ho! The Light-hearted Fairy. *Unknown.* BoTP; FaPON

"Oh! what is that comes gliding in." Sally Simpkin's Lament. Thomas Hood. EnRP; MOS

"Oh! what shall I do?" sobbed a tiny mole. Who'll Help a Fairy? *Unknown.* BoTP

Oh, what was your name in the States? What Was Your Name in the States? *Unknown.* AS

Oh what will I do. A Secret Affair Comes to Its End. Kenko, *tr. by* Steven D. Carter. WFTW

"Oh, what's that stain on your shirt sleeve?" Edward. *Unknown.* AmFP

Oh! what's the matter? what's the matter? Wordsworth. *Fr.* Goody Blake and Harry Gill. Par

Oh, what's the matter wi' [*or* with] you, my lass. Jimmy's Enlisted; or, The Recruited Collier. *Unknown.* CoMu; EBEV; OBET
(Recruited Collier, The.) OBET

Oh, what's the way to Arcady. The Way to Arcady. H. C. Bunner. AA; AnAmPo

Oh, when I come to die. Give Me Jesus. *Unknown.* BoAN-1, *with music;* BPo

Oh when I think of my long-suffering race. Enslaved. Claude McKay. BPo

Oh, When I Was in Love with You. A. E. Housman. *Fr.* A Shropshire Lad, XVIII. BoLoP; FaBV; LiTB; MoBrPo; TTTS

Oh, when I was single, oh then, oh then! I Wish I Were [*or* Was] Single Again. *Unknown.* AmFP, *2 versions;* AS

Oh, when I'm in trouble. Do, Lord, Remember Me. *Unknown.* AmFP

Oh, When Shall I See Jesus? *Unknown.* AH, *with music* (Ecstasy.) AmFP

Oh when the early morning at the seaside. East Anglian Bathe. Sir John Betjeman. NoP; SD

Oh when the saints go marchin' in. *See* Oh when the saints go marchin' in.

Oh, when this earthly tenement. "Ada." BlSi

"Oh, when we going to marry, to marry, to marry." Buffalo Boy. *Unknown.* AmFP

Oh, when will this night end. *Unknown. Fr.* Manyo Shu. Ma

Oh, Whence Comes the Gladness? Priscilla Jane Thompson. CBWP-2

"Oh whence do you come, my dear friend, to me." The Poor Ghost. Christina Rossetti. GBL

"Oh, where are you going, my kind old husband." The Best Old Fellow in the World. *Unknown.* AmFP

"Oh, where are you going, my little maiden fair." The Milkmaid. *Unknown.* AmFP

Oh where are you going? says Milder to Malder. *See* O where are you going? says Milder to Malder.

Oh where are you going, to all you Big Steamers. Big Steamers. Kipling. Par

Oh, where are you going to, my pretty little dear. Dabbling in the Dew. *Unknown.* CH

"Oh, where are you going with your lovelocks flowing." Amor Mundi. Christina Rossetti. NoP; PoEL-5

Oh, where do you come from. Little Raindrops. *At.* to Ann Hawkshawe *and also to* Jane Euphemia Browne. BoTP; OxBChV

"Oh where ha'e ye been, Lord Randall my son?" Lord Randall. *Unknown.* NAEL-1

"Oh, where have you been, Billy boy, Billy boy?" Billy Boy. *Unknown.* AmFP; BLPA; HoPM

("Where have ye [*or* you] been all the day,/ Billy Boy?"). OxNR

"Oh where have you been, Lord Randal, my son?" *See* O where have you been, Lord Randal, my son?

Oh, where, Kincora! is Brian the Great? Kincora [*or* Lamentation of Mac Liag for Kincora]. *Unknown, tr.* by James Clarence Mangan. AnIL

Oh where, my sweet, my dear beloved son. To Her Little Son Rinaldo When Sick. Faustina Maratti Zappi, *tr.* by Muriel Kittel. DMI

Oh where, oh where has my little dog gone? Where Is He? Mother Goose. OxNR

Oh! where shall I bury my poor dog Tray. The Cynotaph. "Thomas Ingoldsby." *Fr.* The Ingoldsby Legends. FM

Not a Sous Had He Got. FaBoCo

Oh, where the white quince blossom swings. Japanesque. Oliver Herford. FiBHP

Oh! where's the slave so lowly. Thomas Moore. NOIV

Oh, whiffaree an' a-whiffo-rye. Honey, Take a Whiff on Me. *Unknown.* OxBoLi

Oh, whisky here, and whisky there. Whisky, Johnny. *Unknown.* AmFP

Oh whither, oh why, and oh wherefore. Goosey Goosey Gander—By Various Authors (Swinburne's Version). William Percy French. CenHV

Oh, who has not heard of the Northmen of yore. America. Arthur Cleveland Coxe. PAH

Oh, who is so merry, so merry, heigh ho! The Light-hearted Fairy. *Unknown.* FaPON

Oh Who Is That Young Sinner with the Handcuffs on His Wrists? A. E. Housman. FaBoTw; NOBVV; PeHV; SoSe

Oh! who is there of us that has not felt. November. Frederick Goddard Tuckerman. NOBA

Oh! who on the mountain, the plain, or the wave. The Song of the Micmac. Joseph Howe. CaP

Oh, Who Regards ("Oh, who regards a wounded soul's lamenting"). *Unknown.* EiL

Oh who shall, from this dungeon, raise. *See* O who shall, from this dungeon, raise.

Oh who that ever lived and loved. The Egg. Clarence Day. NBLV

Oh, who will follow old Ben Milam into San Antonio? The Valor of Ben Milam. Clinton Scollard. PAH

"Oh, who will shoe your feet, my love." The Mournful Dove. *Unknown.* AmFP

Oh who'll replace this old miner. The Old Miner. *Unknown.* OBET

Oh, why did God,/ Creator wise. Milton. *Fr.* Paradise Lost, *Bk.* X, *ll.* 888–908.

(Adam Speaks.) NU

Oh, why does the white man follow my path. The Indian Hunter. Eliza Cook. BLPA

Oh, why don't you [*or* I] work like other men do? Hallelujah, I'm a Bum [*or* Hallelujah, Bum Again]. *Unknown.* AS, *with music;* GBP; SaC, *abr.*

Oh [*or* O]! Why Should the Spirit of Mortal Be Proud? William Knox. BLPA; FaFP; WBLP; WGRP

Oh! Wilberforce, our star of hope. Golden Jubilee of Wilberforce. Mrs. Henry Linden. CBWP-4

Oh, will you wear red? I'll Wear Me a Cotton Dress. *Unknown.* BPo

Oh Woman, Blessed Woman! Mrs. Henry Linden. CBWP-4

Oh, women dear, and did ye hear the news that's going round. The Purple, White and Green. L. E. Morgan-Browne. BrRo

Oh wond'rous power of words, how sweet they are. The Young Wordsworth's London. Wordsworth. *Fr.* The Prelude [or, Growth of a Poet's Mind]: Residence in London. FaBoPP

"Oh [*or* O], World-God, give me Wealth!" the Egyptian cried. Gifts. Emma Lazarus. TrJP; WGRP

Oh, worship the King all glorious above. The Majesty and Mercy of God. Sir Robert Grant. OHIP; WGRP

Oh would I could subdue the flesh. Senex. Sir John Betjeman. RB

Oh, Would That I Knew. Al-Samau'al Ibn Adiya, *tr. fr. Arabic.* TrJP

Oh would that I were a reliable spirit careering around. Longing for Death because of Feebleness. Stevie Smith. OBD

Oh would you know why Henry sleeps. Inhuman Henry. A. E. Housman. FiBHP; NBLV

Oh, Yasumiko I have won! Kamatari. *Fr.* Manyo Shu. Ma

Oh, Ye Censurers. Al-Samau'al Ibn Adiya, *tr. fr. Arabic by* Hartwig Hirschfeld. TrJP

Oh, ye lost ones, ye departed, who have passed that silent shore. Beyond. *Unknown.* PWR

Oh ye wha are sae guid yoursel. *See* O ye wha are sae guid yoursel.

Oh ye! who teach the ingenuous youth of nations. Byron. *Fr.* Don Juan, II. EnRP

Oh—Yeah! Sharon Scott. JB

Oh Yes. William Matthews. AmPA

Oh yes/ We got Mr. President Roosevelt. President Roosevelt. Big Joe Williams. FaBoPV

Oh yes, even more than this. Mechanical Doll. Forugh Farrokhzad, *tr. by* Deirdre Lashgari. OV

Oh, Yes! Oh, Yes! Wait 'til I Git on My Robe. *Unknown.* BoAN-2

Oh yes, that the hen lays, befits. Hen. Paul Eluard, *tr. by* Michael Benedikt. POS

Oh yes, we are so thankful. The Black Army. S. E. K. Mqhayi, *tr. by* C. M. Mcanyangwa *and* Jack Cope. PeSA

Oh yesterday the cutting edge drank thirstily and deep. Tomorrow. John Masefield. MoBrPo; TrGrPo

Oh! yet a few short years of useful life. Wordsworth. *Fr.* The Prelude [or, Growth of a Poet's Mind]: Conclusion ("It was a close, warm, breezeless summer night"). EBEV; OBNC; PoEL-4

Oh yet We Trust. Tennyson. *Fr.* In Memoriam A. H. H., LIV. EaLo; LiTB; NoP; OBNC; TrGrPo

(Larger Hope, The.) WGRP

Oh, you are a kilt which a young dandy set out to choose. Woman Sings of Her Love. *Somali Oral Tradition, tr. by* B. W. Andrzejwski *and* I. M. Lewis. WTO

Oh, you come along, boys, you listen to my tale. The Old Chisholm Trail. *Unknown.* AmFP

Oh, you foulbreathed destroyer of children and villages. Warming Up for the Real Thing. Lee Rudolph. TW

"Oh, you must answer my questions nine." The Devil's Nine Questions. *Unknown.* AmFP; WSC

Oh you round and liquid room: comfortable, well-situated. A Sonnet in Which I Say My Son Is a Long Way Off and Has Been for More Than a Year. Antonio Cisneros, *tr. by* Ena Hollis *and* David Tipton. Per

Oh, You Wholly Rectangular. Eugene Roger Cole. GoYe

Oh, you with the blue collar. *Unknown, tr. by* Arthur Waley. BoS

Oh [*or* O], young Lochinvar is come out of the west. Lochinvar. Sir Walter Scott. *Fr.* Marmion, V. BeLS; BOTP; EnRP; FaBoBe; FaBV; FaFP; FaPON; FPL; GN; GoTS; NOBE; OBNV; OxBS; PoRA (Young Lochinvar.) OBNV

Oh! young Lochinvar is come out of the West. Young Lochinvar. *Unknown.* FiBHP

Oh, your sweetness, softness, smoothness! Lassitude. Paul Verlaine, *tr. by* Lawrence M. Bensky. ErPo

Oh, Zarkhi, Zarkhi, you cannot cause. Zarkhi to Himself. Moyshe-Leyb Halpern, *tr. fr. Yiddish by* Benjamin *and* Barbara Harshav. *Fr.* Zarkhi on the Sea Shore. AYP

Oh, Zlochov, you my home, my town [*or* Oh Zlotchev, my home, my town]. Zlochov [*or* Zlotchev, My Home]. Moyshe-Leyb Halpern, *tr. by* Benjamin *and* Barbara Harshav. AYP; VWA, *tr. by* Richard J. Fein

Ohakune Fires. Lauris Edmond, *tr. fr. Maori by* Margaret Orbell. PeNZ

OhHeDidDidHeOK. Spin Control. George Starbuck. SoTCo

Ohio Valley Swains. James Wright. NNaP

Ohioan Pastoral. James Wright. LCAP

Ohms. Irving Layton. NeAC

Oho for the woods where I used to grow. The Song of the Christmas Tree. Blanche Elizabeth Wade. OHIP

O'Hussey's Ode to the Maguire. Eochadh O'Hussey, *tr. fr. Irish by* James Clarence Mangan. NOIV; SeCePo

(Ode to the Maguire.) BIrV

Oi! oi! firefly, here! *Unknown, tr. by* Geoffrey Bownas *and* Anthony Thwaite. PeBJV

Oil. Hansjörg Mayer. WeW

Oil. Gary Snyder. LCAP

Oil and Blood. W. B. Yeats. VVA

Oil, came, The. NHR. Jack Hirschman. VWA

Oil Painting. Walter Martínez, *tr. fr. Spanish by the author.* Vol

Oileus by his brother's side stood close. Homer, *tr. fr. Greek by* George Chapman. *Fr.* The Iliad, XIII. OBVE

"Oilfish" to "Old Chap" for "C." Tina Darragh. LP

Oils and Ointments. R. A. K. Mason. ATNZ

Oiseaurie. Margaret Widdemer. BXAP

Oisin in the Land of Youth. Michael Comyn, *tr. fr. Modern Irish by* Tomás O'Flannghaile. AnIL

Oisin, tell me the famous story. The Wanderings of Oisin. W. B. Yeats. BrPo

Ojibwa War Songs. *Unknown, tr. fr. Ojibwa Indian by* H. H. Schoolcraft. AWP

Ojisan after the Stroke; Three Notes to Himself. Tina Koyama. BrSi

Ojistoh. Pauline E. Johnson. NOBC

O.K. Ann Ziety. DT

OK, it's imperishable or a world as Will. The Same Old Jazz. Philip Whalen. NeAP

OK, love. Let's take. Tabula Rasa. Bartolo Cattafi, *tr. by* Lawrence R. Smith. NItP

OK. So she got back the baby. Onesided Dialog. June Jordan. NoAM

Okaru and Kampei. Kitahara Hakushu, *tr. fr. Japanese by* Hiroaki Sato. FCEI

Okaru is crying. Okaru and Kampei. Kitahara Hakushu, *tr. by* Hiroaki Sato. FCEI

Okay. Sharon Scott. JB

Okay, my starsick beauty. Unknown Shores. D. M. Thomas. BWV

Okay "Negroes." June Jordan. BPo

Okay, so the wheel bit was a grinding bore. Eve: Night Thoughts. Judson Jerome. SM

Okeechobee. John Allison. GrPl

O'Keeffe Retrospective. May Swenson. ER

Okefenokee Swamp. Daniel Whitehead Hicky. AmFN

Okhotsk Elegy. Miyazawa Kenji, *tr. fr. Japanese by* Hiroaki Sato. FCEI

Okinawa Kanashii Monogatari. Geraldine Kudaka. BrSi

Oklahoma, January 20, 1914. Stop Press. Blaise Cendrars, *tr. by* Anselm Hollo. RHTwFP

Oklahoma Ligno and Lithograph Co., The. Corporate Entity. Archibald MacLeish. OBAL

Oklahoma Rt. 66. Nora Naranjo-Morse. GOS

Ol' Bunk's Band. William Carlos Williams. NOBA

Ol' Doc' Hyar. James Edwin Campbell. BANP

Ol' Edgar Martin. Carlos Ashley. CowP

Ol' plantation wither. For Consciousness. Mervyn Morris. PBCV

Old. Ralph Hoyt. AA

Old/ Few years more attend me, I am redundant. Ago. Elizabeth Jennings. GOYP

Old, The/ Old winds that blew. Night Winds. Adelaide Crapsey. QFR

Old Abram Brown is dead and gone. Abram Brown. *Unknown.* OxNR

Old Adam. Thomas Lovell Beddoes. *See* Death's Jest Book: Old Adam, the Carrion Crow.

Old Adam, The. Denise Levertov. NaP; UnPo

Old Adam. *Unknown.* AS

Old Adam, the Carrion Crow. Thomas Lovell Beddoes. *Fr.* Death's Jest Book, V, iv. ChER; EBEV; EnRP; LiTB; OAEL-2; PBBP; PoEL-4

(Carrion Crow, The.) TrGrPo; WiR

(Old Adam.) ELP

(Song: "Old Adam, The carrion crow.") ChER; EBEV; LiTB; OAEL-2; PBBP; PoEL-4

Old Age. Al-Aswad, Son of Ya'fur, *tr. fr. Arabic by* Sir Charles Lyall. *Fr.* The Mufaddaliyat. AWP

Old Age. Milán Füst, *tr. fr. Hungarian by* Edwin Morgan. MHuP

Old Age. Jacob Glatstein, *tr. fr. Yiddish.* AYP, *tr. by* Benjamin *and* Barbara Harshav; PeBMYV, *tr. by* Cynthia Ozick.

Old Age. E. Keary. NOBVV

Old Age. John Morris-Jones, *tr. fr. Welsh by* Anthony Conran. OBWVE

Old Age. Sir Philip Sidney. *Fr.* Arcadia. SiPS

Old Age. Frederick Tennyson. NOBVV

Old Age. *Gond Oral Tradition, tr. by* V. Elwin *and* S. Hivale. WTO

Old Age. *Zulu Oral Tradition, tr. by* H. Tracey. WTO

Old Age. Edmund Waller. *See* Of The Last Verses in the Book: Seas are quiet when the winds give o'er, The.

Old Age Come to Us All. Hazel Williams. WS

Old Age Compensation. James Wright. NNaP

Old Age Gets Up. Ted Hughes. NoAM

Old age has come, my head is shaking. Once I Played and Danced in My Parents' Kingdom. *Gond Oral Tradition, tr. by* V. Elwin *and* S. Hivale. WTO

(Folk Song, A.) AIW

Old age has little joy. Fresh Flowers. Wang An-shih, *tr. by* Burton Watson. CoBCP

Old Age in His Ailing. Herman Melville. TAP

Old age is. To Waken an Old Lady. William Carlos Williams. HAP; InPK; NoP; QFR; WeW

"Old age never comes alone"—it brings sighs. Old Age. John Morris-Jones, *tr. by* Anthony Conran. OBWVE

Old Age of Michelangelo, The. Frank Templeton Prince. PeSA

Old Age, on tiptoe, lays her jewelled hand. A Minuet on Reaching the Age of Fifty. George Santayana. BLPL; FaFP

Old Age Pensioner, The. Joseph Campbell. AnIL

Old Age Sticks. E. E. Cummings. InPS

Old Air, An. F. R. Higgins. AnIL

Old am I in years and wisdom and. Old I Am. Herman Charles Bosman. PeSA

Old Amusement Park. Marianne Moore. NYBP

Old and abandoned by each venal friend. On Lord Holland's Seat near Margate, Kent. Thomas Gray. NOEC; OAEL-1; OPOP; TW

(Impromptu.") SeCePo

Old and alone sit we. The Old Men. Walter De la Mare. MoAB; MoBrPo

Old and New ("Farewell, Old Year!"). *Unknown.* BLRP

Old and New ("She went up the mountain to pluck wild herbs"). *Unknown, tr. fr. Chinese by* Arthur Waley. AWP

Old and New Year Ditties, *sel.* Christina Rossetti. Passing Away. *Fr.* III. NoP; OAEL-2; OBNC; WPE

Old and sick, you turn away from mirrors, whether. Late Reflections. Babette Deutsch. NYBP

Old and the New, The. Clara Ann Thompson. CBWP-2

Old and the New Courtier, The. *Unknown.* CoMu

Old and the New Masters, The. Randall Jarrell. WPE

Old Anguish, The. Chu Shu-chen, *tr. fr. Chinese by* Kenneth Rexroth. BoWoP

Old Apple-Tree, The. Paul Laurence Dunbar. AnAmPo

Old Apple Trees. W. D. Snodgrass. CAPP; FYAP; SV

Old Arm-Chair, The. Eliza Cook. AnAmPo; BrRo; InPK; WBLP

Old as I am, for ladies' love unfit. Cymon and Iphigenia. Dryden. OBNV

Old astronomer there was, An. A Marvel. Carolyn Wells. OBCA

Old Astronomer to His Pupil, The. Sarah Williams. BLPA

Old Barbarossa. Sleeping Heroes. Edward Shanks. OBMV

Old Bark Hut, The. *Unknown.* PoAu-1

Old Battalion, The. *Unknown.* OBET

Old battle field, fresh with Spring flowers again. All That Is Left. Basho, *tr. by* Curtis Hidden Page. AWP; WaaP

("Old battle field, fresh with Spring flowers again.") AWP

Old Beauty, The. Phyllis McGinley. FaBoEE

Old Ben Golliday. Mark Van Doren. SO

Old Bibles. Marilyn Nelson Waniek. MAYP

Old Bill the Whaler said to me. Bill the Whaler. Will Lawson. PoAu-1

Old bitch labrador swims, The. The End of Summer. Judith Minty. GeTw

Old black bird on a strand of silk, An. Wise Owl. Patricia Goedicke. SM

Old black dog comes in one evening, The. First Snow. Ted Kooser. GrPl

Old Black Joe. Stephen Collins Foster. FaFP

Old Black ladies. Weeksville Women. Elouise Loftin. PoBA
Old Black Men. Georgia Douglas Johnson. CDC; PoBA; PoNe
Old Black Men Say. James A. Emanuel. PoBA
Old blanket. The crumbs of rubbed wool turning up, The. Adrienne Rich. *Fr.* Shooting Script, 3. HCAP
Old Blue. *Unknown.* SD
Old Boards. Robert Bly. NaP
Old Boast, The. W. S. Merwin. NOBA
Old Boat, The. Lenore Pratt. CaP
Old Boatman of Death's River, The. R. Williams Parry, *tr. fr. Welsh by* Joseph P. Clancy. OBWVE
Old Boniface he loved good cheer. *Unknown.* OxNR
Old Books, The. Vernon Scannell. OxBC
Old Botany Bay. Mary Gilmore. PoAu-1
Old boy's seventy-three this year, The. A Eulogy on My Own Portrait. Yang Shih-ch'i, *tr. by* Jonathan Chaves. CoBLCP
Old boys, the cracked boards spread before. Bread. James Dickey. LCAP
Old Brass Wagon. *Unknown.* AS
Old Bridge at Florence, The. Longfellow. EyDe
Old brown hen and the old blue sky, The. Continual Conversation with a Silent Man. Wallace Stevens. LiTM; NoP
Old Brown Horse, The. W. F. Holmes. BoTP
Old brown thorn-trees break in two high over Cummen Strand, The. Red Hanrahan's Song about Ireland. W. B. Yeats. CMoP; FaBoCh; NOIV
Old Brown's Daughter. *Unknown.* OBET
Old Buccaneer, The. Charles Kingsley. *See* Last Buccaneer, The.
Old Buffer, An. Frederick Locker-Lampson. CenHV
Old Bullock Dray, The. *Unknown.* PoAu-1
An Old Burden. Amado Nervo, *tr. fr. Spanish by* Samuel Beckett. MexPo
Old Cabin, The. Paul Laurence Dunbar. PoLF
Old calypsonian sings, The. Politics Kaiso. Roger McTair. PBCV
Old canoe in, The. Sunrise. Jim Tollerud. VoR
Old Cat Care. Richard Hughes. OBMV
Old cat whose calm, The. Her Seventeenth Winter. John Leax. CRP
Old Cat's Confessions, An. Christopher Pearse Cranch. OBCA
Old Cat's Dying Soliloquy, An. Anna Seward. NOEC
Old Champagne Glass. Eddy van Vliet, *tr. fr. Dutch by* Theo Hermans. DuIn
Old Charcoal Seller, An. Po Chü-i, *tr. fr. Chinese by* Eugene Eoyang. SaC
Old Chaucer, like the morning Star. On Mr. Abraham Cowley, His Death and Burial amongst the Ancient Poets. Sir John Denham. OBS, *abr.*; SeCV-1
Old Chisholm Trail, The. ("Come along boys, and listen to my tale.") *Unknown.* BeLS; FaBoBe
Old Chisholm Trail, The. ("Oh, you come along, boys, you listen to my tale.") *Unknown.* AmFP
Old Christmas. Mary Howitt. GN
Old Christmas. *Unknown.* OHIP
An Old Christmas Greeting. *Unknown. See* Sing, hey! Sing, hey!/ For Christmas Day.
Old Christmas Morning. Roy Helton. MoAmPo
Old Christmas Returned. *Unknown.* GN; OHIP
Old *Chüeh-chü. Unknown, tr. fr. Chinese by* Burton Watson. CoBCP
Old Churchyard of Bonchurch, The. Philip Bourke Marston. EBVV; OBNC
Old City, The. Ruth Manning-Sanders. CH
Old Clock on the Stairs, The. Longfellow. PWR; WBLP
Old Clothes. Phil Hey. GOYP
Old cloud passes mourning her daughter. Sunset after Rain. W. S. Merwin. PoA
Old Counsel. Herman Melville. FaBoRV
Old Countryside. Louise Bogan. HAP; LiTA; WPE
Old Couple, The. F. Pratt Green. OxBTC
Old Couple. Charles Simic. HCAP
Old Cove, The. Henry Howard Brownell. PAH
Old Cowman, The. Dick Gibford. CowP
Old Coyote. "If he hadn't looked back." Telling about Coyote. Simon J. Ortiz. STP
Old Crabbed Men. James Reeves. ErPo
An Old Cracked Tune. Stanley Kunitz. SM
Old cradle of an infant world. Ode to Jamestown. James Kirke Paulding. PAH
Old Creation Chant. *Unknown, tr. fr. Hawaiian.* WTO
Old Crib, The. Mary E. Tucker. CBWP-1
Old Crow, upon the tall tree-top. The Crow. Mrs. — — — Alexander. BoTP

Old Cumberland Beggar, The. Wordsworth. EnRP; LaA
Old Damon's Pastoral. Thomas Lodge. OBSC
Old Dan'l. L. A. G. Strong. MoBrPo
Old daughter, small traveler. Making the Jam without You. Maxine W. Kumin. ER; TV
Old Davis owned a solid mica mountain. A Fountain, a Bottle, a Donkey's Ears and Some Books. Robert Frost. VGW
Old dears gardening in fur coats. The House Next Door. Douglas Dunn. OxBC
Old Deep Sing-Song. Carl Sandburg. RR
Old Doc. Mark Vinz. Psk
Old Doctor Foster. *Unknown.* OxNR
Old dog barks backward without getting up, The. The Span of Life. Robert Frost. HoPM; LiTM; SoSe
Old Dog in the Ruins of the Graves at Arles, The. James Wright. NNaP
Old Dog lay in the summer sun. Sunning. James Sterling Tippett. RHPC
Old Dog, New Dog. Sydney Lea. MAYP
Old Dominion. Robert Hass. MAYP
Old dream comes again to me, The. Mir träumte wieder der alte Traum. Heine, *tr. by* James Thomson. AWP
Old Dubuque. Dave Etter. AmFN
Old Dutch Woman, The. Gary Snyder. NAAL-2
Old earth, how she sulks. Jacaranda. Roo Borson. NOBC
Old East End worker called Jock, An. Victor Gray. NOBL
Old Eben Flood, climbing alone one night. Mr. Flood's Party. E. A. Robinson. AmPP; AWP; BLPL; CMoP; FaFP; FF; HAP; HeIP; HoPM; LiTA; LiTM; MAT; MoAB; MoAmPo; MoP; NAAL-2; NIP; NoAM; NOBA; NoP; OxBA; PoE; PoRA; PPP; PrIm; SoSe; TAP; TrGrPo; UnPo; WeW
Old Eddie's face, wrinkled with river lights. The Glory Trumpeter. Derek Walcott. NAEL-2
Old Egyptians hid their wit, The. On Mr. Nash's Picture at Full Length. Jane Brereton. WPE
Old Ellen Sullivan. Winifred Welles. FaPON
Old elm that murmured in our chimney top. The Fallen Elm. John Clare. FaBoPV
Old elm trees flock round the tiled farmstead, The. Childhood. Sir Herbert Read. BrPo
Old Emily. Hyacinthe Hill. GoYe
Old enemies. Safed and I. Molly Myerowitz Levine. VWA
Old England. Nahum Tate. APAS
Old England Forever and Do It No More. *Unknown.* GBP
Old England is eaten by Knaves. Alexander McLachlan. *Fr.* The Emigrant. NOBC; OBCV
Old England's long-expected heavy news from our fleet. Nelson's Death. *Unknown.* OBET
Old Ernie Anderson eating peanuts. Peanuts. Ken Belford. NeAC
Old Essex Door. Agnes MacCarthy Hickey. GoYe
Old Euclid drew a circle. Euclid. Vachel Lindsay. *Fr.* Poems about the Moon, I. ImOP
Old faithful horse, I find you by the creek. Old Horse. Don Ian Smith. CowP
Old Familiar Faces, The. Charles Lamb. AWP; BLPA; EnRP; FaBoBe; FaBoRV; FaFP; FaPoR; FPL; GTBS; GTBS-P; NOBE; OBEV; RB
Old Farmer Giles. *Unknown.* OxNR
Old farmer, nearing death, asked, The. Field Day. W. R. Rodgers. BIrV
Old Farmer Oats and his son Ned. John Jay Chapman. PoEL-5
Old-fashioned Garden, The. John Russell Hayes. AA
Old-fashioned Pitcher, The. George E. Phair. SoSe
Old-fashioned sketchbook, An. Good News Bad News. Keith Abbott. UL
Old Father Greybeard. *Unknown.* OxNR
Old father tongue sticking out. Rehearsal. Cyril Dabydeen. BrSi; PBCV
Old Fellow. Ernest Walsh. ErPo
Old Fence Post. Leigh Hanes. GoYe
Old Field Mowed, An. William Meredith. NYBP
Old fish fiddle with their fins and glide, The. Aquarium. George T. Wright. NYBP
Old Fisherman with Guitar. George Mackay Brown. OxBC
Old Fitz, who from your suburb grange. To E. Fitzgerald. Tennyson. NOBVV; PoEL-5
Old Flag, The. H. C. Bunner. OPP
Old Flag. W. S. Merwin. AnAn
Old Flame, The. Robert Lowell. BoLoP; NoAM; NOBA
Old Flemish Lace. Amelia Walstien Carpenter. AA
Old Flood Ireson! all too long. A Plea for Flood Ireson. Charles Timothy Brooks. PAH
Old Florist. Theodore Roethke. OxBSP; PCP; SaC

Old Folk, The. Tove Ditlevsen, *tr. fr. Danish by* Nadia Christensen. PBWP

Old Folks at Home, The. Stephen Collins Foster. AA; AnAmPo; FaBoBe; FaFP; WBLP

Old forms are like birdhouses that, The. Poetry. Greg Kuzma. PoA

Old Fort Meigs. *Unknown.* PAH

Old Fortunatus, *sels.* Thomas Dekker.
Fortune and Virtue. GoTL; OBSC
Priest's Song, A. OBSC
(Song: "Virtue's branches wither, virtue pines.") EIL

Old Forty-five Per Cent. *Unknown.* FaBoEE

Old Freedman, The. Priscilla Jane Thompson. CBWP-2

Old Friedrich Barbarossa. Barbarossa. Friedrich Rückert, *tr. by* John W. Thomas. WSC

Old friend, kind friend! lightly down. To My Old Schoolmaster. Whittier. NOBA

Old friend, you. Back from the Word-Processing Course, I Say to My Old Typewriter. Michael C. Blumenthal. GOYP; NoAM

Old friend, your place is empty now. No more. To Scott. Winifred M. Letts. PoLF

Old Fritz, on this rotating bed. A Flat One. W. D. Snodgrass. CAPP; LiTM; NePoEA-2; SM

Old Furniture. Thomas Hardy. OxBTC

Old gardens, a ruined terrace, willow trees new. At Su Terrace Viewing the Past. Li Po, *tr. by* Burton Watson. CoBCP

Old german nurse, The. Reawakening. Sharon A. Stern. TSM

Old Ghost, The. Thomas Lovell Beddoes. WiR

Old gilt vane and spire receive, The. The Late, Last Rook. Ralph Hodgson. MoBrPo

Old Girl, The. Gary Lenhart. UL

Old glass has waves and shares the bending. Luminare. Scott Minar. KS

Old Glory! say, who. The Name of Old Glory. James Whitcomb Riley. GN

Old Gods, The. Edwin Muir. EaLo

Old Grahame he is to Carlisle gone. Bewick and Graham. *Unknown.* ESPB

Old Gramophone Records. James Kirkup. NYBP

Old Grandpaw Yet. *Unknown.* AmFP

Old Graves fell asleep. George Keithley. *Fr.* The Donner Party. NPGG

Old Gray Beard a-Shaking. *Unknown.* AmFP

Old Gray Goose, The. *Unknown.* AmFP; GBP
("Go and tell Aunt Nancy.") ChTr, *sl. diff. vers.*

Old Gray Mare. *Unknown.* AS, *with music;* AS; GBP

Old Green River knife had to be scraped, An. Canst Thou Draw Out Leviathan with an Hook. Allen Curnow. ATNZ; PeNZ

Old grey hearse goes rolling by, The. The Hearse Song. *Unknown.* AS, A *and* B *vers., with music;* OxBoLi; RB

Old grey shade of the mountain, The. In the Selkirks. Duncan Campbell Scott. CaP

Old Grey Wall, The. Bliss Carman. CaP

Old Grimes. Albert Gorton Greene. BeLS

Old Guitar, The. John Hollander. DiPo

Old guy put down his beer, The. Do the Dead Know What Time It Is? Kenneth Patchen. HoPM; MoAmPo

Old Habitant, An. Frank Oliver Call. CaP

Old habits it seems cannot be swept away. Yüan Mei, *tr. fr. Chinese by* Jonathan Chaves. *Fr.* Miscellaneous Poems on Growing Old. CoBLCP

Old Haven. Jean Garrigue. WPE

Old he was but not yet wax. My Father's Face. Hayden Carruth. DiL

Old, heavy, engraved tabletop caught crumbs, The. Clues to Displaced Persons. Mark Jarman. BLA

Old Hokum Buncombe, The. Robert E. Sherwood. NBLV

Old Horse. Don Ian Smith. CowP

Old house felt unfriendly, The. The Empty House. Max Williams. CBAP

Old house from my childhood, The. Yüan Mei, *tr. fr. Chinese by* Jonathan Chaves. *Fr.* In Late Spring of the Year Keng-hsü. CoBLCP

Old house with trees and twisting river, An. A Visit to Bridge House. Richard Weber. BIrV

Old Houses of Flanders, The. Ford Madox Ford. CTC

Old houses were scaffolding once. Image. T. E. Hulme. InPK; OxBTC

Old Humpy. *Unknown.* AmFP

Old Hundredth. William Kethe. FaPoR
(Psalm C.) NOCV
(Scotch Te Deum.) WGRP

Old Hundredth. Bible, *O.T. See* Psalms: Psalm C ("Make a joyful noise. . .").

An Old Husband Suspects Adultery. Gavin Ewart. NoAM

Old Hymns, The. Frank Lebby Stanton. BLRP

Old I Am. Herman Charles Bosman. PeSA

Old I Am. Thomas Stanley, *after the Greek of* Anacreon. AWP

Old Ice Factory in Petakh Tikva, The. Yehuda Amichai, *tr. fr. Hebrew by* Bernhard Frank. MHeP

Old Inmate, An. Kenneth Mackenzie. PoAu-2

Old Inn on the Eastern Shore. William H. Matchett. NePoEA

Old Ironsides. Oliver Wendell Holmes. AA; AiP; AnAmPo; BLPA; FaBoBe; FaFP; FaPON; FPL; GN; GOA; MOS; NAAL-1; OPP; PAH; PWR; TAP

Old Ironsides at anchor lay. The Main-Truck; or, A Leap for Life . At. to George Pope Morris. AnAmPo; BLPL; PoLF

Old Jason, the Argonaut, The. Denis Glover. PeNZ

Old Jew, The. Paradise. Willis Barnstone. VWA

Old Jew asked me by the Jaffa Gate, An. Conversation with a Countryman. Antoni Slonimski, *tr. by* Isaac Komen. VWA

Old Jewish Cemetery in Worms. Alfred Kittner, *tr. fr. German by* Herbert Kuhner. VWA

Old Jockey, The. F. R. Higgins. OBMV; OxBTC

Old Joe. *Unknown.* OxBoLi

Old Joe Yazzie died after working. The Death of Old Joe Yazzie. Ron Rogers. STE

Old John Bax. Charles Henry Souter. PoAu-1

Old Joyce. Sean Jennett. NeIP

Old Keg of Rum, The. *Unknown.* PoAu-1

Old Kimball. *Unknown.* AmFP

Old King, The. John Heath-Stubbs. NePoEA

Old King Cabbage. Richard Kendall Munkittrick. OBCA

Old King Cole ("Me clairvoyant"). G. K. Chesterton. *Fr.* Variations on an Air Composed on Having to Appear in a Pageant as Old King Cole. BXAP

Old King Cole ("Of an old king in a story"). G. K. Chesterton. *Fr.* Variations on an Air Composed on Having to Appear in a Pageant as Old King Cole. BXAP

Old King Cole ("Who smoke-snorts toasts o' My Lady Nicotine"). G. K. Chesterton. *Fr.* Variations on an Air Composed on Having to Appear in a Pageant as Old King Cole. BXAP

Old King Cole was a merry old soul. Mother Goose. FaBoBe; FaFP; OxNR

Old King of Dorchester, The. The Ceremonial Band. James Reeves. OnUR

Old Kitchen Clock, The. Ann Hawkshawe. BoTP

Old Knight, The. George Peele. *See* Polyhymnia: His Golden Lock[e]s [Time Hath to Silver Turned].

Old Ladies. Will Allen Dromgoole. WeW

Old Ladies, The. Colin Ellis. OxBTC

Old lady, I now celebrate. John Montague. *Fr.* The Leaping Fire, I. CIP
(Little Flower's Disciple, The.) IPY; TIRV

Old Lady of London, The. *Unknown.* AmFP

Old lady Shih, braving acerbity, pokes in her three-foot beak. To Go with Shih K'o's Painting of an Old Man Tasting Vinegar. Huang T'ing-chien, *tr. by* Burton Watson. CoBCP

Old Lady Sitting in the Dining Room. *Unknown.* AmFP

Old Lady under the Freeway, The. Diana O Hehir. NPGG

Old lady writes me in a spidery style, An. A Letter from Brooklyn. Derek Walcott. OxBTC

Old lady's face, The. At the Bus Stop: Eurydice. David Ferry. PPR

Old Lady's Lament for Her Youth, The. Villon, *tr. fr. French by* Robert Lowell. BoLoP

Old Lambro pass'd unseen a private gate. Byron. *Fr.* Don Juan, III. EnRP

Old Leader Complains, The. Moyshe-Leyb Halpern, *tr. fr. Yiddish by* Benjamin *and* Barbara Harshav *and* Kathryn Helle. AYP

Old leaves, the perfume of moldering. Looking Both Ways. Jane O. Wayne. GOYP

Old Lem. Sterling A. Brown. BPo; FB; IDB; PoBA; PoNe; TTY

Old letters!/ I was on such familiar terms. Ishikawa Takuboku, *tr. fr. Japanese by* Hiroaki Sato. *Fr.* Forty-seven Tanka in Three Lines. FCEI

Old light & owl-light. 2nd Light Poem: For Diane Wakoski. Jackson MacLow. PoM

Old Liu's Dawn. Chan Ch'e, *tr. fr. Chinese by* Dominic Cheung. IFON

Old Log House. James S. Tippett. FaPON

Old-Long-Syne. *Unknown.* OBS

Old Loves. Henry Murger, *tr. fr. French by* Andrew Lang. AWP

Old Lutheran Bells at Home, The. Wallace Stevens. NoAM

Old, mad, blind, despised, and dying king, An. England in 1819. Shelley. EnRP; FaBoPV; FF; MAT; NAEL-2; NAWM-2; NOBE; NoP; OAEL-2; Son; TrGrPo; TW; UnPo
(Sonnet: England in 1819.) FiP; PPP; SeCePo

Old Magic. Grace Nichols. PBCV

Old maid, an old maid, An. *Unknown.* OxNR

Old Maid Early, An. Blake. OxBSP

Old Maids. *Unknown.* AmFP

Old Maid's Soliloquy. Maggie Pogue Johnson. CBWP-4

Old Maid's Song. *Unknown.* AmFP

Old Malediction, An. Anthony Hecht, *after* Horace. NoAM; TW

Old Man. Alan J. Carr

Old Man, The. David Fisher. NPGG

Old Man, The. Alfredo Giuliani, *tr. fr. Italian by* Lawrence R. Smith. NItP

Old Man. James Henry. NOBVV

Old Man. Elizabeth Jennings. NePoEA-2

Old Man. Faye Kicknosway. UL

Old Man. Edward Thomas. LiTM; SCV

Old Man [*or* Old Man Travelling], An. Wordsworth. FaBoCh; OBWP

Old man, The/ He is gone now. The Old Man Who Is Gone Now. Margarita Baldenegro Reyes. FIA

Old man/ man black man. Tony Get the Boys. D. L. Graham. PoBA

Old man, a slight smile on his lips, rides a grey deer, The. Song of the Painting of the Long-Life Star. Wang Chiu-ssu, *tr. by* Jonathan Chaves. CoBLCP

Old man accompanies, The. Ode to an Old Man. Yoshioka Minoru, *tr. by* Hiroaki Sato. FCEI

Old Man and Jim, The. James Whitcomb Riley. AA

Old Man and Young Wife, The. *Unknown.* CoMu

Old Man at the Crossing, The. Strong. OBMV

Old Man at the Window, The. Anthony Harvey. Mes

Old man bending I come among new faces, An. The Wound-Dresser. Walt Whitman. AmPP; NAAL-1; NOBA; OBWP; PrIm; TAP

Old man Brown. The Cheerful Chilterns. Frank Sidgwick. BXAP

Old man Chih-shan has a head of white hair. Chu Yün-ming, *tr. fr. Chinese by* Jonathan Chaves. *Fr.* Improvisations, I. CoBLCP

Old man dozed, The. The hospital quietened. Burns Singer. *Fr.* Sonnets for a Dying Man, XV. NePoEA-2

Old Man Dreams, The. Oliver Wendell Holmes. AnAmPo; BLPL; PoLF

Old Man from Darjeeling. *Unknown.* NTCP

Old Man from Peru, An. *Unknown. See* Limerick: "There was an old man of [*or* from] Peru/ Who dreamt he was eating his shoe."

Old man gets up turns, An. Zeimbekiko. Robin Magowan. EAS

Old man, going a lone highway, An. Building the Bridge. Will Allen Dromgoole. WeW

Old man had been listless, but he perked, The. End of Steel. Thomas Saunders. CaP

Old Man He Courted Me, An. *Unknown.* OBET

Old man howling at death, An. In Vain. Jacques Prévert, *tr. by* Teo Savory. POS

Old man in a lodge within a park, An. Chaucer. Longfellow. AA; AWP; HeIP; InvP; NOBA; NoP; OBEV; OxBA; PoE; PoRA; PrIm; Son; TAP; TrGrPo

Old Man in a Moon Loft. T. Glynne Davies, *tr. fr. Welsh by the author.* OBWVE

Old man in the crystal morning after snow. Delmore Schwartz. PoA

Old man in white, An. Alice Walker. *Fr.* Love. NMM

Old man is a greyer stone this year, The. The Birthday. Louis Johnson. ATNZ

Old man is seated, The. The Old Man. David Fisher. NPGG

Old Man Know-All. *Unknown.* BPo

Old man leaning on a gate, An. From My Window. Mary Elizabeth Coleridge. OBNC

Old Man Mose. Jack Kerouac. *Fr.* Mexico City Blues, 221. NeAP

Old man moved into his night, The. Katerina Anghelaki-Rooke. *Fr.* Notes on My Father. PBWP

Old man never had much to say. The Old Man and Jim. James Whitcomb Riley. AA

Old man now, An. Tonna, *tr. by* Steven D. Carter. WFTW

Old man of eighty. Hasidic Jew from Sadagora. Rose Ausländer. VWA, *tr. by* Ewald Osers

Old Man of Nine Dragon Mountain, The. The Long Handscroll of Bamboo by Wang Meng-tuan. Li Tung-yang, *tr. by* Jonathan Chaves. CoBLCP

Old man of the mountains loves the mountains, The. Winter. Chang Yü, *tr. fr. Chinese by* Jonathan Chaves. *Fr.* The Four Seasons in the Mountains. CoBLCP

Old man of the sea, briny bell. Now Is Farewell. Blanaid Salkeld. NeIP

Old Man of Verona, The. Claudian, *tr. fr. Latin by* Abraham Cowley. AWP; OBVE

Old Man on the River Bank, An. George Seferis, *tr. fr. Greek by* Edmund Keeley *and* Philip Sherrard. VMG

Old Man, or Lad's-Love,—in the name there's nothing. Old Man. Edward Thomas. LiTM; SCV

Old Man Pondered. John Crowe Ransom. MoAmPo

Old Man Pot. Lyon Sharman. CaP

Old Man Potchikoo, *sels.* Louise Erdrich. HATNAP
Birth of Potchikoo, The.
Death of Potchikoo, The.
How Potchikoo Got Old.
Potchikoo Marries.

Old man pushing seventy. Written in a Carefree Mood. Lu Yu, *tr. by* Burton Watson. CoBCP

Old Man Said, The. Carroll Arnett. STE

Old Man sits in wrinkled reverie, An. An Evasion. Douglas Livingstone. PeSA

Old Man Stirs the Fire to a Blaze, An. W. B. Yeats. *Fr.* The Wanderings of Oisin. RB

Old Man Sweeping. George Barlow. NAmP

Old Man, the Sweat Lodge. Phil George. GrPl; NOVW

Old Man to His Scythe, The. Denis Wrafter. NeIP

Old Man Told Me. Lance Henson. VoR

Old man was already well ahead, The. The Last Dream. Ray A. Young Bear. STE

Old man was cold, The. Translating. Ruth Whitman. VWA

Old man went to meetin', for the day was bright and fair, The. The Preacher's Vacation. *Unknown.* BLPA; BLPL

Old Man Who Is Gone Now, The. Margarita Baldenegro Reyes. FIA

Old Man Who Lived in a Wood[s], The. *Unknown. See* Father Grumble.

Old man who seined. Lorine Niedecker. VGW

Old man whose black face, An. The Rainwalkers. Denise Levertov. NePoEA-2; PPP

Old Man with a Beard. Edward Lear. *See* There was an old man with a beard.

Old man with a gold armband and a black watch, An. Pall-Bearers. Jacques Prévert, *tr. by* Teo Savory. POS

Old Man with a Mowing Machine. May Carleton Lord. GoYe

Old man with a yellow flower on his coat, The. The Lion Skin. James Keir Baxter. ATNZ

Old man, you surface seldom. Full Fathom Five. Sylvia Plath. MOS

Old Man's Advice, An. *Unknown.* OBET

Old Man's Carousal, The. James Kirke Paulding. AA

Old Man's Comforts and How He Gained Them, The. Robert Southey. HoPM; OxBChV; Par; UnPo

Old Man's Complaint, The. *Unknown.* OxBSP

Old Man's Example, The. Bill Manhire. ATNZ

Old Man's fair-haired consort, whole dewy axle-tree, The. Lente, Lente. Ovid, *tr. fr. Latin by* Kirby Flower Smith. *Fr.* Elegies, I, 14. AWP

Old Man's Idyl, An. Richard Realf. AA

Old Man's Lazy, The. Peter Blue Cloud. HATNAP

Old Man's Son, An. Russell Edson. LCAP

Old man's son was killed far away, An. The Colors of Night. N. Scott Momaday. STE

Old Man's Song, about His Wife, The. *Unknown, tr. fr. Eskimo by* Armand Schwerner. STP

Old Man's Tale, The. Brian Merriman, *tr. fr. Modern Irish by* David Marcus. *Fr.* The Midnight Court. BIrV

Old Man's Thought, An. Natsume Seibi, *tr. fr. Japanese by* Hiroaki Sato. *Fr.* Twenty-seven Hokku. FCEI

Old Man's Thoughts, An ("Lonelier still than last year"). Buson, *tr. fr. Japanese by* Hiroaki Sato. *Fr.* Eighty-seven Hokku. FCEI

Old Man's Winter Night, An. Robert Frost. AWP; HAP; MoAB; MoAmPo; NAAL-2; NoAM; OxBA; VGW

Old Man's Wish, The. Walter Pope. CoMu; OBS

Old Mansion. John Crowe Ransom. HeIP; NOBA; OxBA

Old Map of Barnstable County. Brendan Galvin. KS

Old Maps and New. Norman MacCaig. OxBC

Old Mare, The. Elizabeth J. Coatsworth. MoAmPo

Old Marlborough Road, The. Henry David Thoreau. PoEL-4

Old Marquis and His Blooming Wife, The. *Unknown.* CoMu

Old-Marrieds, The. Gwendolyn Brooks. AmNP; PoBA

Old Marse John. *Unknown.* TTY

Old master yourself now, Auden, An. As You Like It. Theodore Weiss. TAP

Old May Song. *Unknown.* BoTP; CH

Old mayor climbed the belfry tower, The. The High Tide on the Coast of Lincolnshire (1571). Jean Ingelow. BeLS; EBVV; FaBoPP; GN; Mes, *abr.*; OnMSP

Old Meg she was a gipsy [*or* gypsy]. Meg Merrilies [*or* Merrilees]. Keats. BoTP; ELP; FaBoCh; FaPON; FiP; OxBChV; TEP

Old Memories of Earth. R. A. K. Mason. ATNZ; PeNZ

Old Men, The. Cid Corman. PCP

Old Men, The. Walter De la Mare. MoAB; MoBrPo

Old Men, The. Irving Feldman. TwCP

Old Men, The. Alexander Javitz. TrJP

Old Men, The. Kipling. OBSV

Old Men. Ogden Nash. AnAmPo; InPS; RB

Old Men Admiring Themselves in the Water, The. W. B. Yeats. CMoP; FaBoCh; GoJo; PCP

Old Men and Old Women Going Home on the Street Car. Merrill Moore. MoAmPo

Old men are like little boys. Han Yü, *tr. fr. Chinese* by Burton Watson. *Fr.* A Pond in a Jardiniere, 1. CoBCP

Old men beneath the mountain. With a Sliver of Marble from Carrara. James Wright. EyDe

Old men in blue: and heavily encumbered. Pihsien Road. "Robin Hyde." ATNZ; WPE

Old Men on the Courthouse Lawn, Murray, Kentucky. James Galvin. AnAn

Old men sleeping. The List. Michael McClure. NU

Old men stand. Bulldozers. Frederick Dec. PCP

Old men, white-haired, beside the ancestral graves. Basho, *tr.* by Curtis Hidden Page. AWP

Old Menalcas on a day. The Palmer's Ode. Robert Greene. *Fr.* Never Too Late. CTC; OBSC

Old Men's Ward. Elma Dean. GoYe

Old Michael. George M. Brady. NeIP

Old Mill, The. Thomas Dunn English. AA

Old Miner, The. *Unknown.* OBET

Old Miner's Refrain, The. *Unknown.* AmFP

Old Miniatures. Leo Vroman. VWA

Old Moke. Harold Littlebird. VoR

Old Mole. James Reeves. WSC

Old Molly Means was a hag and a witch. Molly Means. Margaret Abigail Walker. AmNP; BlSi; NMM; PoNe

An old monk perches at the tip of a tree. A Wall Painting by Wu Wei. Wang T'ing-hsiang, *tr. fr. Chinese* by Jonathan Chaves. *Fr.* Miscellaneous Poems on Spirit-Valley Temple. CoBLCP

Old moon is tarnished, The. Sea Lullaby. Elinor Wylie. BoNaP; MOS

Old moon my eyes are new moon with human footprint. Poem Rocket. Allen Ginsberg. VGW

Old Morgan. G. D. Roberts. BoTP

Old Mortality, sels. Sir Walter Scott. And What though Winter Will Pinch Severe. *Fr. ch.* 19. EnRP Sound, Sound the Clarion. Thomas O. Mordaunt, *formerly at. to* Scott, *fr. ch.* 34. FaBoEE; FaPoR; NOBE (Call, The.) OBEV (One Crowded Hour.) TrGrPo

Old Mother Duck has hatched a brood. Mother Duck. *Unknown.* BoTP

Old Mother Earth woke up from her sleep. A Spring Song. *Unknown.* PoLF

Old Mother Goose. Mother Goose. BoTP; OxNR; PBBP, *st.* 1

Old Mother Hubbard. Sarah Catherine Martin. FaBoBe; OnMSP; OxNR (Comic Adventures of Old Mother Hubbard and Her Dog, The.) OxBChV

Old Mother Niddity Nod. *Unknown.* OxNR

Old Mother Shuttle. *Unknown.* OxNR

Old Mother Twitchett had [*or* has] but one eye. Mother Goose. NTCP; OxNR; TSS

Old mountain man is learning to garden, The. Vegetable Garden. Lu Yu, *tr.* by Burton Watson. CoBCP

Old Mountain Road. Charles Simic. FYAP

Old Mountaineer, The. W. K. Holmes. PoSH

Old Movies. John Cotton. FF

Old Mrs. Jarvis. Elizabeth Fleming. BoTP

Old Mrs. Tressider/ Over at Winches. The Scarf. Ivy O. Eastwick. BoTP

Old Munro Bagger, The. *Unknown.* PoSH

Old Nick in Sorel. Standish O'Grady. *Fr.* The Emigrant. OBCV

Old Nick took a fancy, as many men tell. Old Nick in Sorel. Standish O'Grady. *Fr.* The Emigrant. OBCV

Old Nick, who taught the village school. The Retort. George Pope Morris. AnAmPo

Old Night Hawk, The. Bruce Kiskaddon. CowP

Old Noah he had an ostrich farm and fowls on the largest scale. Wine and Water. G. K. Chesteron. *Fr.* The Flying Inn. ACP; CenHV; FaBoCo; FiBHP; MoBrPo

Old nursery chair; its legs, cut down, are broken. Robin Hyde. *Fr.* The Houses, I. ATNZ

Old O. O. Blues, The. Al Young. NPGG

Old oak, old timber, sunk and rooted. G. M. B. Donald Davie. OxBC

Old Oaken Bucket, The. Samuel Woodworth. AnAmPo; BLPA; FaBoBe; FaFP; FaPON; FPL; WBLP

Old oblivion-book, that I lay open. Accountability. Gerrit Achterberg, *tr.* by Adrienne Rich. DuIn

Old, old/ To live on, wretched to behold. Owen Gruffydd, *tr. fr. Welsh* by Anthony Conran. *Fr.* The Men That Once Were. OBWVE

Old, old woman that I am. Lady Ishikawa. *Fr.* Manyo Shu. Ma

Old One and the Wind, The. Clarice Short. IHMS

Old ones go to each other's funerals, The. Burials. Geoffrey Grigson. PoA

Old ones to the side. Charles Simic. AmPA; LCAP

Old ones whose ancestors hunted, The. Raven. Duane Niatum. STE

Old [*or* Ould] Orange Flute, The. *Unknown.* FaBoBa; GBP; OxBoLi; WTO

Old Ox, The. George Rostrevor Hamilton, *after the Greek of* Addaios of Makedon. FaBoEE

Old Pack, The. *Unknown.* APAS

Old Paintings on Italian Walls. Kathleen Raine. NYBP

Old Park, The. Afanasi Afanasievich Fet, *tr. fr. Russian* by Alan Myers. AAA

Old Penobscot Indian, The. Flux. Richard Eberhart. Psk; VGW

Old people are like birds. City Pigeons. Helen Chasin. WeW

Old People Dozing. Denise Levertov. AIW

Old People on the Nursing Home Porch. Mark Strand. CAPP

Old People Speak of Death, The. Quincy Troupe. CNA

Old People Working (Garden, Car). Gwendolyn Brooks. SaC

Old Person of Ware, An. Edward Lear. *See* Limerick: "There was an old person of Ware."

Old Peter Grimes made fishing his employ. Peter Grimes. George Crabbe. *Fr.* The Borough, Letter XXII. EnRP; OBNV; PoEL-4; TEP
(Poor of the Borough, The; Peter Grimes.) NoP
"Thus by himself compelled to live each day." NOBE; OBNC; SeCePo
"He built a mud-wall'd hovel, where he kept." SaC

Peter Grimes at Aldeburgh. FaBoPP

"Priest attending, found he spoke at times, The." PoE

Old Peter Prairie-Dog. Prairie-Dog Town. Mary Austin. FaPON

Old Photo, 1942. George Uba. BrSi

An Old Picture. Howard Nemerov. OxBSP

Old Pilot, The. Donald Hall. LCAP

Old pine trees, their shaggy manes. Pei-mang Cemetery. Yüan Hung-tao, *tr.* by Jonathan Chaves. CoBLCP

Old Place, The. Blanche Baughan. ATNZ; PeNZ

Old Place, The. Hone Tuwhare. ATNZ

Old Poem. *Unknown, tr. fr. Chinese.* AWP, *tr.* by Arthur Waley; BoWoP, *tr.* by Arthur Waley; CoBCP, *tr.* by Burton Watson

Old Poet, Poetry's final subject glimmers months ahead. Don't Grow Old. Allen Ginsberg. DiL

Old pond, An: a frog jumps in. Basho, *trs. fr. Japanese* by Burton Watson *and* by Hiroaki Sato. *Fr.* Seventy-six Hokku. FCEI

Old priest Peter Gilligan, The. The Ballad of Father Gilligan. W. B. Yeats. EaLo; EBVV; MoBrPo; OnYI; PoRA

Old Prison, The. Judith Wright. PoAu-2

Old professor of zoology, The. The Parrot. James Elroy Flecker. FaBoTw

Old Pro's Lament, The. Paul Petrie. TAP

Old Provincial Council Buildings, Christchurch, The. Allen Curnow. ATNZ

Old Python Nose with the wind-rolling ears. To a Dead Elephant. Douglas Livingstone. PeSA

Old Quin Queeribus. Nancy Byrd Turner. RHPC

Old Repair Man, The. Fenton Johnson. AmNP

Old Rhyme, An. *Unknown.* BoTP

Old ridiculous partner is back again, The. The She Wolf. Muriel Spark. NYBP

Old river, once blue-mercurial. We Are a Young Nation, Uncle. Marilyn Chin. BrSi

Old River Road. Blanche Whiting Keysner. GoYe

Old Road, The. Jones Very. AA

Old Roads. Eiléan Ní Chuilleanáin. CIP

Old Roadside Resorts. Molly Peacock. MAYP

Old Robin of Portingale. *Unknown.* ESPB

Old Roger. *Unknown.* OxBoLi

Old Room, The. W. S. Merwin. NYBP

Old Ross, Cockburn, and Cochrane too. The Battle of Baltimore. *Unknown.* PAH

Old rude church, with bare, bald tower, is here, The. Wordsworth's Grave. Sir William Watson. OBNC

Old Rugged Cross, The. George Bennard. AH

Old Ruralities: A Regret. Charles Tennyson Turner. EBVV; Son

Old Russian spits up a plum, The. A Man Then Suddenly Stops Moving. Alberto Ríos. NoAM

Old Rustic Mill, The. George Sands Johnson. PWR

Old Sailor, The. A. A. Milne. CenHV

Old Sailor Looking at a Container Ship. Robert Carson. AiP

Old Saint's Prayer, The. Priscilla Jane Thompson. CBWP-2

Old saltman, hair turned white, The. Wu Chia-chi, tr. by Jonathan Chaves. CoBLCP

Old Sam Smith. The Shepherd. Mary Gilmore. PoAu-1

Old Sam's Wife. Unknown. ChTr

Old sandpiper contemplates his age, The. Summer's Early End at Hudson Bay. Hayden Carruth. NYBP

Old Santa Fe Trail, The. Richard Burton. PAH

Old Scent of the Plum Tree. Ietaka, tr. fr. Japanese by E. Powys Mathers. AWP

Old School List, The. James Kenneth Stephen. CenHV

Old Scottish Cavalier, The. William Edmonstoune Aytoun. GN

Old scythe in the hedge. The Old Man to His Scythe. Denis Wrafter. NeIP

Old sea-dog on a sailor's log, An. The Powerful Eyes o' Jeremy Tait. Wallace Irwin. FiBHP

Old Seawoman. Gordon LeClaire. CaP

Old Section Boss, The. Unknown. BPo

Old Sergeant, The. Forceythe Willson. AA; BeLS

Old Sexton, The. Park Benjamin. AA

Old Shellover. Walter de la Mare. BoTP; OxBChV

Old Shepherd's Prayer. Charlotte Mew. EaLo; MoAB; MoBrPo; OBD; OxBTC; WPE

Old Ships, The. James Elroy Flecker. BrPo; CH; FaBoRV; MoBrPo; MOS; OBMV; PoRA

Old shoe, an old pot, an old skin, An. Autumn Sequence. Adrienne Rich. VGW

Old Sipsey Valley Road, The. Thomas Rabbitt. MT

Old Sir Simon the king. Unknown. OxNR

Old Skinflint. W. W. Gibson. OBMV

Old snake, old hole in the corner man. A Dead Weasel. David Helwig. NOBC

Old Snapshot. Ronald G. Everson. MoCV

Old snow gets up and moves taking its, The. December among the Vanished. W. S. Merwin. NaP

Old snow-summitted mountains, The. Monte Cassino 1945. Marion Coleman. CN

Old Soldier. Padraic Colum. OBMV

Old soldiers true, ah, them all men can trust. A Prophecy. Maurice Thompson. Fr. Lincoln's Grave. AA

Old Song. Edward Fitzgerald. GN; OBEV

Old Song, The. G. K. Chesterton. FaBoTw

Old Song, An. "Yehoash", tr. fr. Yiddish by Marie Syrkin. AWP

Old Song Ended, An. Dante Gabriel Rossetti. BoLoP; EBVV

Old song made by an old aged pate, An. The Old and the New Courtier. Unknown. CoMu

Old Song of Rejoicing, An. Unknown, tr. fr. Maori by Margaret Orbell. PeNZ

Old Song Re-sung, An. John Masefield. LiTB

Old Song Resung, An. Charles Larcom Graves. CenHV

Old Song Resung, An. W. B. Yeats. See Down by the Salley Gardens.

Old Song Written during Washington's Life. Unknown. OHIP

Old Song, Wrote by One of Our First New-England Planters, An. Unknown. See New England's Annoyances.

Old Sophora Tree, An. Hung Sheng, tr. fr. Chinese by Paul W. Kroll. WFTU

Old Souldier of the Queens, An. Unknown. OBS

Old South Boston Aquarium stands, The. For the Union Dead. Robert Lowell. AmPP; CoAP; FaBoPV; FYAP; HAP; HCAP; HeIP; InPS; LCAP; LiTM; MoP; NAAL-2; NaP; NoAM; NOBA; NoP; OBWP; PoE; SCV; TwCP; UnPo; WeW

Old spoon, An. The Spoon. Charles Simic. NNaP

Old Squire, The. Wilfrid Scawen Blunt. FaPoR; OBEV; SD

Old Station of Cahors, The. Valery Larbaud, tr. fr. French by William Jay Smith. CT

Old Stephen. Charles Tennyson-Turner. EBVV

Old Stoic, The. Emily Brontë. FaPoR; FPL; NOBE; OBEV; OBNC; PoLF; TrGrPo

Old stories of a Tyler sing. Tom Tiler; or, The Nurse. Unknown. APAS

Old Storm. David Phillips. NeAC

Old Story, The. Marcus Argentarius, tr. by E. A. Robinson. AWP

Old Story. Lance Henson. VoR

Old Story, An. Rena Lee. VWA

Old Story, The. Louis MacNeice. GBL

Old Story, An. E. A. Robinson. AnAmPo; MoAmPo; OxBSP

Old Story Is Retold, An. John Hollander. BAP

Old Street, An. Virginia Woodward Cloud. AA

Old suitcase a sock and an endive, An. It Keeps Going On. Benjamin Péret, tr. by Michael Benedikt. POS

Old Summerhouse, The. Walter de la Mare. CMoP; FaBoPP; FaBoRV; GTBS-P

Old Susan. Walter de la Mare. CMoP; MoBrPo

Old Sussex Road, The. Ian Serraillier. NTCP

Old Sweetheart of Mine, An. James Whitcomb Riley. BeLS; BLPA; FPL

Old Swimmer, The. Christopher Morley. SD

Old Swimmin'-Hole, The. James Whitcomb Riley. AnAmPo; BeLS; FaFP

Old tales were told of Sigemund's daring. The Tale of Sigemund. Unknown, tr. fr. Anglo-Saxon by Charles W. Kennedy. Fr. Beowulf. AnOE

Old tenacious boards. Interior Patio. Sebastian Salazar Bondy, tr. by David Tipton. Per

Old Tennis Player. Gwendolyn Brooks. SD

Old Testament, a bygone age, The. The Flood. Lev Mak, tr. by Neil Muhlberger and Marvin Misemer. VWA

Old Testament Contents. BLPA

Old-Testament Gospel. William Cowper. TrCP

Old, the, the mad, the blind have fairest daughters, The. The Beauty of Job's Daughters. Jay Macpherson. MoCV; NOBC

Old Theme. W. R. Moses. KS

Old thorn tree in a stony place, An. Ode: On the Death of W. B. Yeats. Arthur James Marshall Smith. OBCV

Old though I am. Shunzei, tr. fr. Japanese by Burton Watson. Fr. Thirty Tanka. FCEI

Old Thought, An. Charles Henry Lüders. AA

Old Thought for a New Couple, An. E. A. Markham. PBCV

Old Tiger. Marianne Moore. AnAn

Old-Time Childhood in Kentucky. Robert Penn Warren. AiP; BLA

Old Time is lame and halt. Wie langsam kriechet sie dahin. Heine, tr. by Richard Monckton Milnes. AWP

Old-Time Sea-Fight, An. Walt Whitman. See Song of Myself

Old-Time Service. Thomas Churchyard. Fr. A Fayned Fancy betweene the Spider and the Gowte. OBSC

Old Timers. Carl Sandburg. NoAM

Old Times. Daniel Mark Epstein. DiPo

Old Times Were the Best, The. James Whitcomb Riley. FaFP

Old Tippecanoe. Unknown. PAH

Old tips come out as good as new. John William Mackail. Fr. Balliol Rhymes. CenHV

Old town lies afar, An. There Is an Old City. Karl Bulcke, tr. by Ludwig Lewisohn. AWP

Old Tree, The. Andrew Young. GoJo

Old Triton Time. Vernon Watkins. OxBSP

Old Trouper, The. Don Marquis. Fr. Archy and Mehitabel. FaBoCo

Old Tubal Cain was a man of might. Tubal Cain. Charles MacKay. WBLP

Old Tuff. Georgie Sicking. CowP

Old Tune, An. Gérard de Nerval, tr. fr. French by Andrew Lang. AWP

Old Uncle Jim was as blind as a mole. Echoes of Childhood. Alice Corbin. PoNe

Old Vicarage, Grantchester, The. Rupert Brooke. BrPo; FaBoPP; FaBV; GoTL; MoBrPo; OBTV; OxBTC; PoRA

Old Violin, The. Maurice Francis Egan. AA

Old virgin, your airs are proper. To an Elderly Virgin. Mael Ísu O Brolcháin, tr. by Thomas Kinsella. NOIV

Old Virginny. James A. Bland. See Carry Me Back to Old Virginny.

Old Voyager. Walter Blackstock. GoYe

Old Walking Song, The. John R. R. Tolkien. RFM

Old walls creak. Restoring the Ancestral House. Katerina Te Hei Koko Mataira, tr. by Katerina Te Hei Koko Mataira. PeNZ

Old Walt. Langston Hughes. HeIP

Old War-Dreams. Walt Whitman. AnAmPo; OxBSP

Old warder of these buried bones. Tennyson. Fr. In Memoriam A. H. H., XXXIX. PoEL-5

Old watch, The: their/ thick eyes. Vapor Trail Reflected in the Frog Pond. Galway Kinnell. CAPP; NoP; OBWP; VGW

Old Waterford Woman, An. Mary Devenport O'Neill. NeIP

Old West, the old time, The. Spanish Johnny. Willa Cather. AiP; FaPON

Old Whim Horse, The. Edward Dyson. CBAP

Old Whore Speaks to a Young Poet, The. Dave Smith. SM

Old Whorehouse, An. Mary Oliver. CAPP
Old Wichet. *Unknown.* GBP
Old Wife, The. Rolly Kent. FF
Old Wife and the Ghost, The. James Reeves. PDV
Old Wife in High Spirits. "Hugh MacDiarmid." CMoP; OxBTC; PoE
Old Wife Speaks, The. Gerda Mayer. DT
Old Wife's Tale, The. *See* Old Wives' Tale.
Old wine filled him, and he saw, with eyes, The. Maurice de Guérin. Maurice Francis Egan. AA
Old wine to drink! A Winter Wish. Robert Hinckley Messinger. AA
Old Winter. Thomas Noel. GN
Old Witherington. Dudley Randall. NoAM; TW
Old Wives Prayer, The. Robert Herrick. SeCV-1
Old Wives' [*or* Wife's] Tale, The, *sels.* George Peele.
   Fair Maiden. PoEL-2
   Gently Dip. ELP; InPS
     (Fair Maiden.) PoEL-2
     (Song for the Head.) RB
     (Voice from the Well [of Life Speaks to the Maiden], The.) ChTr; NOBE
   Harvester's Song. TrGrPo
     "Lo! here we come a-reaping, a-reaping," 4 *ll.*
   Song: "Lo! here we come a-reaping, a-reaping." OBSC
   Spell, A. ChTr
   Voice [Speaks] from the Well, A. FaBoCh; NOBE; OBSC; OxBoLi
   Whenas [*or* When as] the Rye [Reach to the Chin]. ELP; EnLoPo; FaBoCh; GBL; InvP; NoP; SeCePo; TEP
     (Song: "When as [*or* whenas] the rye [*or* rie] reach to the chin.") ElL; OBSC; OxBoLi; PoEL-2
     (Summer Song, A.) NOBE; OBEV
Old Woman, The. Joseph Campbell. AWP; MoBrPo; OxBTC
Old Woman, An. David Gwenallt Jones, *tr. fr. Welsh by* H. Idris Bell. OBWVE
Old Woman, The. Beatrix Potter. GoJo; NTCP; PDV; RAR
Old Woman, An. Charles Henry Ross. OxBChV
Old Woman. Iain Crichton Smith. FaBoTw; OxBTC
Old Woman, The. Anna Swirszczynska, *tr. fr. Polish by* Czeslaw Milosz. PwPP
Old Woman. *Unknown.* AmFP
Old woman across the way, The. The Whipping. Robert Hayden. GrPl; IDB; PoBA; PoE; TW
Old Woman Awaiting the Greyhound Bus. Duane Niatum. CDW
Old woman dried an egg, The. The Egg. Jean Follain, *tr. by* W. S. Merwin. RHTwFP
Old woman has forgotten her face, The. Evasion. Blanaid Salkeld. NeIP
Old woman, her butt spread on the stoop, An. Rapunzel. Faye Kicknosway. UL
Old woman in me walks patiently to the hospital, An. Revelation. Carole C. Gregory. BlSi
Old Woman in Mongkok, An. Yu Kuang-chung, *tr. fr. Chinese by* Dominic Cheung. IFON
Old Woman Laments in Spring-Time, An. Dame Edith Sitwell. ViBoPo
Old woman likes to melt her husband, An. The Melting. Russell Edson. PPR
Old woman must stand, The. *Unknown.* OxNR
Old Woman Nature. Gary Snyder. NoAM
Old Woman of Beare Regrets Lost Youth, The. *Unknown, tr. fr. Irish by* Frank O'Connor. AnIL; OBMV
Old Woman of Harrow. *Unknown.* FaBoNo
Old Woman of the Roads, An. Padraic Colum. BoTP; CH; FaBoBe; FaPON; FYAP; MoBrPo; NOIV; OBEV; PoRA; TIRV
Old woman, old and bent and worn. Morning Bus. John Coulter. CaP
Old woman, old woman,/ Shall we go a-shearing? Mother Goose. OxNR
"Old woman, old woman, are you fond of carding?" Old Woman. *Unknown.* AmFP
Old Woman, Outside the Abbey Theater, An. L. A. G. Strong. FiBHP; MoBrPo
Old Woman Remembers, An. Sterling A. Brown. CNA; PoBA
Old woman sits on a bench before the door and quarrels, The. Fawn's Foster-Mother. Robinson Jeffers. MoP; NoAM; NOBA
Old Woman Speaks of the Moon, An. Ruth Pitter. WPE
Old woman, time and your own. To Grandmother on Her Going. Gail Tremblay. HATNAP
Old woman went to market and bought a pig, An. *Unknown.* OxNR
Old woman's hair, The. Mothers. Punkanuttiraiyar, *tr. by* A. K. Ramanujan. PLW
Old Woman's Lamentations, An. Villon, *tr. fr. French by* J. M. Synge. MoBrPo; OBMV

Old woman's shoulders, The. Mothers. Kakkai Patiniyar Naccellaiyar, *tr. by* A. K. Ramanujan. PLW
Old Woman's Song, An. Akjartoq, *tr. fr. Eskimo into Danish by* Knud Rasmussen; *English vers. by* Tom Lowenstein. WPOW
Old Women, The. George Mackay Brown. NePoEA-2; OxBS
Old women all their lives, they're a mixture of whitelime and brine. Women at the Market. Angela Figueroa-Aymerich, *tr. by* Hardie St. Martin. PBWP
Old women are gathered in the Longhouse, The. Native Origin. Beth Brant. STE
Old Women beside a Church. Keith Wilson. Psk
Old women, like the oaks and the red clay of that land, The. The Old Women Still Sing. Charles H. Rowell. CNA
Old Women of Toronto. Miriam Waddington. NIP; NOBC
Old women say that men don't know. Becoming a Dad. Edgar A. Guest. BLPL; PoLF
Old Women Still Sing, The. Charles H. Rowell. CNA
Old woodcutter of the sea, The. Song of the Woodcutter of the Sea. Pien Kung, *tr. by* Jonathan Chaves. CoBLCP
Old wooden house a soft, The. Brass Tacks. Denise Levertov. InPS
Old wooden steps to the front door, The. A Time Past. Denise Levertov. NoAM
Old, worn harp that had been played, An. The Master-Player. Paul Laurence Dunbar. AnAmPo
Old wound in my ass, The. Fabrication of Ancestors. Alan Dugan. CAPP; NoAM
Old Year, The. John Clare. NOBVV; OBCP
Old Year, The. Priscilla Jane Thompson. CBWP-2
Old Year and the New, The. Annie Johnson Flint. BLRP
Old year's gone away, The. The Old Year. John Clare. NOBVV; OBCP
Old yellow stucco, The. Winter Nightfall. J. C. Squire. OxBTC
Old yew, which graspest at the stones. Tennyson. *Fr.* In Memoriam A. H. H., II. ELP; GTBS-P; NOBE; NoP; OBNC; PoEL-5; UnPo
Olden Days, The. Joseph Hall. *See* Virgidemiarum: Time was, and that was termed the time of Gold.
Olden Love-making. Nicholas Breton. OBSC
Older American, The. Cheryl Clarke. GLP
Older and younger brother meet. Drinking Wine with Yoshiyuki and Being Very Happy. Ryokan, *tr. by* Burton Watson. FCEI; JLIC-2
Older Men. Alfred Corn. GLP
Older Now. Dave Gingell. PoSH
Older than the ancient Greeks. Pigeons. Marianne Moore. PoA
Older than the anus with which it shares. Navel. Dennis Schmitz. AnAn
Oldest of us burst into tears and cried, The. Allen Curnow. *Fr.* Tomb of an Ancestor, I. ATNZ; PeNZ
Ole Abe (God bless 'is ole soul!). Negro Soldier's Civil War Chant. *Unknown.* BPo
   (Black Soldier's Civil War Chant.) TAP
Ole Aunt Dinah, she's jes lak me. Jack and Dinah Want Freedom. *Unknown.* BPo
Ole Sheep Dey Know de Road, De. *Unknown.* BPo
Oleander on the wall, The. By the Arno. Oscar Wilde. EBVV
Oleaster, The. Robert Graves. OBTV
Olga Poems. Denise Levertov. LCAP; NNaP
   "Everything flows," *sel.* NAAL-2
Olger the Dane and Desiderio. Charlemagne. Longfellow. FaFP
Oliphaunt. John R. R. Tolkien. AmMo; RHPC
Olive, The. A. E. Housman. NoAM
Olive, The. *Unknown, tr. fr. Italian by* Grace Warwick. PFI
Olive journeys. Journey round the World. Ingrid Jonker, *tr. by* Jack Cope *and* William Plomer. PBWP
Olive Tree, The. Sabine Baring-Gould. GN
An Olive Tree in Corfu. Christine Busta, *tr. fr. German by* Beth Bjorklund. CoAuP
Olive Trees. Bernard Spencer. NoAM
Olive trees and vineyards as far as the sea. The Age of Blue Memory. Odysseus Elytis, *tr. by* Edmund Keeley *and* Philip Sherrard. VMG
Oliver Johnson Comes Back to Bed the Morning after the Ice Storm and Tells His Wife Why. David Jauss. MOWH
Oliver Twist. Marlene Philip. PBCV
Olives and Mountains. Elizabeth Barrett Browning. *Fr.* Aurora Leigh, VII. FaBoPP
Olivia. Edward Pollock. AA
Olivia. Tennyson. *Fr.* The Talking Oak. GN
Ollie, Answer Me. Stephen Berg. NaP
Ollie McGee. Edgar Lee Masters. OBD

Ol'Tunes, The. Paul Laurence Dunbar. AnAmPo
Olympian sunlight is the Poet's sphere. The Crystal. Titus Munson
Coan. AA
Olympic Event. Lois Leurgans. SoTCo
Olympic Girl, The. Sir John Betjeman. SD
Olympic projectiles we've got, The. Boomerang. David Cram.
SoTCo
Olympicus, don't look into a mirror. The Boxer's Face. Lucilius, *tr. by*
Humbert Wolfe. SD
Om. *Malay Oral Tradition, tr. by* R. O. Winstedt. WTO
Omar Rabbi Zarkhi—so said Rabbi Zarchi. From Zarkhi's Teachings.
Moyshe-Leyb Halpern, *tr. fr. Yiddish by* Benjamin *and* Barbara
Harshav. *Fr.* Zarkhi on the Sea Shore. AYP
Ombre and basset laid aside. A Song on the South Sea. Countess of
Winchilsea. NOEC
Omelet of A MacLeish, The. Edmund Wilson. NYBP; Par
Omens, The. Ann Stanford. WSC
Omens. *Unknown, tr. fr. Gaelic by* A. Carmichael. RB
Omi, emperor's city. Fujiwara no Nakamaro, Governor of Omi, Wrote
a Poem on the Two Willows. Yasu, *tr. by* Surton Watson.
JLIC-1
"Omit needless words!" Preface Shrinklit: Elements of Style. Maurice
Sagoff. NBLV
Omkar/ True name. Nanak, *tr. by* John Stratton Hawley *and* Mark
Juergensmeyer. SSI
Omnes Gentes Plaudite! *Unknown.* OxBSP
Omnia Exeunt in Mysterium. George Sterling. WGRP
Omnia Somnia. Joshua Sylvester. FaBoEE; OBS
Omnia Somnia. Joshua Sylvester. *See* Go, Silly Worm.
Omnia Vanitas. Dugald Buchanan, *tr. fr. Gaelic.* GoTS
Omnibus across the bridge, An. Symphony in Yellow. Oscar Wilde.
EBVV; FaBoPP; MoBrPo; NoAM; NoBVV; OxBSP
Omnipotent and steadfast God. John Brown's Prayer. Stephen Vincent
Benét. *Fr.* John Brown's Body. PoNe
Omnipotent confederate of all good. Amos N. Wilder. TrPWD
Omnipresence. Edward Everett Hale. WGRP
Omniscience. Blanche Mary Kelly. TrPWD
Omphalos: The Well. Sean Jennett. NeIP
On a Bad Singer. Samuel Taylor Coleridge. FaBoEE; RHPC
On a Baltimore Bus. Charles G. Bell. NePoAm
On a Bank [*or* Banck] asl I Sat [*or* Sate] a-Fishing; a Description of the
Spring. Sir Henry Wotton. OBS; SeCP
On a bare branch. Basho, *tr. by* Geoffrey Bownas *and* Anthony Thwaite.
PeBJV
On a bare tree in a garden. A Garden. John Wakeman. NPo
On a Bas-Relief. W. Wesley Trimpi. NePoEA
On a beach too small to have a name. From the Illinois Shore. Michael
Sheridan. NAmP
On a Bed of Guernsey Lilies. Christopher Smart. NOEC
On a Bicycle, *sel.* Yevgeny Yevtushenko, *tr. fr. Russian by* Robin
Milner-Gulland *and* Peter Levi.
"Under the dawn I wake my two-wheel friend." ILY
On a Birth. Geoffrey Grigson. NAs
On a Birthday. J. M. Synge. ChTr; GBL; OBMV
On a Blind Girl. Baha Ad-din Zuhayr, *tr. fr. Arabic by* E. H. Palmer.
AWP
On a board of raspberry and pure gold. Osip Mandelstam, *tr. by* W. S.
Merwin *and* Clarence Brown. AnAn
On a Bomb Heard through a Violin Concerto. Christina Chapin. CN
On a Bougainvillaea Vine at the Summer Palace [*or* in Haiti]. Barbara
Howes. MoAmPo; NYBP
On a Boy's First Reading of "King Henry V." Silas Weir Mitchell.
AA
On a Bright and Summer's Morning. *Unknown.* AmFP
On a Bust of Dante. Thomas William Parsons. AA
On a Bust of Lincoln. Clinton Scollard. OHIP
On a Calm Summer's Night. John Nicholson. EnLoPo
On a Carrier Who Died of Drunkenness. Abel Byron. NBLV
On a Cast from an Antique. George Pellew. AA
On a Catholic Childhood. Janet Campbell Hall. VoR
On a Celtic Mask by Henry Moore. Horace Gregory. PoA
On a Certain Alderman. John Cunningham, *after the Greek of* Simonides.
FaBoEE
On a Certain Effeminate Peer. John Winstanley. FaBoEE
On a Certain Engagement South of Seoul. Hayden Carruth. AmFN
On a Certain Lady at Court. Pope. NOBE; NOEC; OBEV; OxBSP;
TrGrPo
On a Certain Lord Giving Some Thousand Pounds for a House. David
Garrick. FaBoEE
On a Certain Occasion for the Year 1790. William Cowper. NOCV

On a Ch'an branch cries a valley bird. Chia Mountain Monastery. Chu
Yi-tsun, *tr. fr. Chinese by* Irving Lo. *Fr.* Quatrains on Peking's
Western Suburb, VIII. WFTU
On a Child Asleep in a Tube Shelter. Sheila Shannon. CN
On a Child Who Lived One Minute. X. J. Kennedy. HoPM; NYBP
On a Child with a Wooden Leg. Bertram J. Warr. OBCV
On a Clear Day I Can See Forever. Alex Kuo. BrSi
On a Clear Night. Ya'ir Hurvits, *tr. fr. Hebrew by* Bernhard Frank.
MHeP
On a Clergyman's Horse Biting Him. *Unknown.* FaBoCo; FaBoEE;
NBLV; OxBoLi
On a clothesline hangs the moon. Room Poems. Eli Bachar, *tr. by*
Jeremy Garber. VWA
On a Cock at Rochester. Sir Charles Sedley. FaBoEE; OPOP; TW
On a Cold Day I Climbed Tiger Hill With Professor Ho. Mo Shih-lung,
tr. fr. Chinese by Jonathan Chaves. CoBLCP
On a cold night. Solitary. Lance Henson. HATNAP
On a cold night I came through the cold rain. J. V. Cunningham. HAP;
QFR
On a cold winter day the snow came down. Proud Little Spruce Fir.
Jeannie Kirby. BoTP
On a Contentious Companion. John Hoskyns. FaBoEE
On a Country Road. Harley Elliot. NeAC
On a Curate's Complaint of Hard Day. Swift. TIRV
On a Daffodil, the First Flower the Author Had Seen That Year. Samuel
Johnson. FL
On a dark and stormy night. The Wreck of the Royal Palm. *Unknown.*
AmFP
On a dark night, as long as it's dark. Kaya Shirao, *tr. fr. Japanese by*
Hiroaki Sato. *Fr.* Twenty-one Hokku. FCEI
On a Dark Road. Robert Herrick. *See* Her eyes the glow-worme lend
thee.
On a Day—Alack the Day. Shakespeare. *Fr.* Love's Labour's Lost, IV,
iii. EIL
(Blossom, The.) OBEV
(Dumain's Rhymes.) OBSC
(Love's Perjuries.) GTBS; GTBS-P
On a day long and wet we fall upon. Arriving. Daniel Halpern. HoPM
On a Dead Babe. James Whitcomb Riley. AnAmPo
On a Dead Child. Robert Bridges. BrPo; CMoP; EBEV; LiTB; LiTM;
NoAM; NOBE; NOBVV; OBMV; OBNC
On a Dead Child. Richard Middleton. SoSe
On a Dead Hostess. Hilaire Belloc. MoBrPo
On a Dead Poet. William Rose Benét. AnAmPo
On a Dead Poet. Frances Sargent Osgood. AA
On a Dead Scholar, *sel.* Saint Columcille, *tr. fr. Old Irish by* Robin
Flower.
"Lon's away,/ Cill Garad is sad today." AnIL
On a Discovery Made Too Late. Samuel Taylor Coleridge. EnRP; Son
On a Distant Prospect of an Absconding Bookmaker. George Rostrevor
Hamilton. FaBoCo
On a Distinguished Politician. J. E. Thorold Rogers. FaBoEE
On a Doctor of Divinity. Richard Porson. *See* Here lies a Doctor of
Divinity.
On a Dog of Lord Eglinton's. Burns. OxBSP
On a Drawing by Flavio. Philip Levine. VWA
On a Dream. Keats. EnRP
On a Drop of Dew. Andrew Marvell. HAP; JCP; LiTB; MeLP; MePo;
NIP; OBS; SeCP; SeCV-1; TEP
On a Dying Boy. William Bell. NePoEA
On a Fair Beggar. Philip Ayres. EnLoPo; OBS
On a Fall Night. Levi Ben-Amittai, *tr. fr. Hebrew by* Bernhard Frank.
MHeP
On a Favorite Cat Drowned in a Tub of Gold Fishes. Thomas Gray. *See*
'Twas on a lofty vase's side.
On a Female Rope-Dancer. *Unknown.* NOEC
On a Ferry Boat. Richard Burton. AA
On a Field Trip at Fredericksburg. Dave Smith. GeTw; HCAP
On a Fifteenth-Century Flemish Angel. David Ray. CRP; NePoEA-2
On a flat road runs the well-train'd runner. The Runner. Walt Whitman.
ASP; InPK; InPS; SD
On a Flimmering Floom You Shall Ride. Carl Sandburg. GoYe; OBAL
On a Fly Drinking out of [*or* from] His Cup. William Oldys. FaFP;
OBEV; TrGrPo
On a Forsaken Lark's Nest. Mathilde Blind. FM
On a Fortification at Boston Begun by Women. Benjamin Tompson.
GOA; PAH; SCAP
On a Fowler. Isidorus, *tr. fr. Greek by* William Cowper. AWP
On a Frightful Dream. John Codrington Bampfylde. NOEC
On a General Election. Hilaire Belloc. FaBoCo; FaBoEE; NOBE;
NOBL; OBSV; OxBTC

On a Gentleman Marrying His Cook. Colin Ellis. FaBoEE
On a Gentlewoman Walking in the Snow. William Strode. *See* I saw fair[e] Chloris walk alone.
On a German Tour. Richard Porson. FiBHP
On a Girdle. Edmund Waller. AWP; BLPL; FF; GTBS; GTBS-P; HeIP; InPK; LiTB; NAEL-1; NoP; OBEV; OBS; PoE; PoRA; SeCePo; SeCV-1; TrGrPo
On a Gloomy Easter. Alice Freeman Palmer. OHIP
On a Goldfinch Starved to Death in His Cage. William Cowper. OBD
On a grassy pillow. Happy Myrtillo. Henry Carey. SeCePo
On a Grave in Christchurch, Hants. Oscar Fay Adams. AA
On a Great Election. Hilaire Belloc. *See* The accursed power which stands on privilege.
On a Great Man Whose Mind Is Clouding. Edmund Clarence Stedman. AA
On a Greek Vase. Frank Dempster Sherman. AA
On a green island in the Main Street traffic. Pro Patria. Constance Carrier. NYBP; WPE
On a Grey-haired Old Lady Knitting at an Orchestral Concert. "Furnley Maurice." CBAP
On a hill above the town. The Whistle Column. John Haines. AnAn
On a hill far away. The Old Rugged Cross. George Bennard. AH
On a hill in Frisco. Irrational. Philip Lamantia. UL
On a hill near Petersburg. James Hugo Johnston. Maggie Pogue Johnson. CBWP-4
On a hill there blooms a palm. Hayyim Nahman Bialik, *tr. fr. Hebrew by* Maurice Samuel. *Fr.* Songs of the People, II. AWP
On a hill there grows a flower. Nicholas Breton. EiL
   (Ipsa Quae.) OBSC
   (Phyllida and Corydon.) TrGrPo
On a Historical Topic. Ts'ao Chen-chi, *tr. fr. Chinese by* William H. Nienhauser, Jr.. WFTU
On a holy day when sails were blowing southward. The Straying Student. Austin Clarke. AnIL; BIrV; CIP; IPY; MoAB; NeIP; NOIV
On a Honey Bee *or* To a Honey Bee. Philip Freneau. TAP
On a Horse Carved in Wood. Donald Hall. EyDe
On a hot summer Sunday. The Cemetery at Academy, California. Philip Levine. NaP
On a Journey. Shohaku, *tr. fr. Japanese by* Steven D. Carter. WFTW
On a journey and lonesome, I see below a hill. Kurohito. *Fr.* Manyo Shu. FCEI
On a Lady Named Beloved. Anne de Rohan, *tr. fr. French by* Dorothy Backer. DMF
On a Lady Who Beat Her Husband. *Unknown.* FiBHP
On a Lady Who P-ssed at the Tragedy of Cato. Pope. OxBSP
On a Landscape by Myself. Yün Shou-p'ing, *tr. fr. Chinese by* Jonathan Chaves. CoBLCP
On a Landscape of Sestos. Carlos Baker. *Fr.* A Visit to the Art Gallery. EyDe
On a Ledge. William Bell. PoSH
On a Line in Sandburg. Ronald Stuart Thomas. NAs
On a Little Bird. Martin Armstrong. CH
On a Little Boy's Endeavouring to Catch a Snake. Thomas Foxton. OxBChV
On a little green knoll. Old Log House. James S. Tippett. FaPON
On a little piece of wood. Mr. and Mrs. Spikky Sparrow. Edward Lear. OxBChV
On a Lord. Samuel Taylor Coleridge. FaBoCo; FiBHP
On a lorry the centre of a gaping crowd. W. H. Auden. *Fr.* A Happy New Year. OBSV
On a Lover of Books. Geoffrey Grigson. FaBoEE
On a Magazine Sonnet. Russell Hillard Loines. OBAL
On a Maid [*or* Maide] of Honour Seen by a Scholar in Somerset Garden. Thomas Randolph. JCP; MePo
On a Man Run Over by an Omnibus. Henry Luttrell. FaBoEE
On a mid-December day. Since. W. H. Auden. InPS
On a midsummer night, on a night that was eerie with stars. August Night. Sara Teasdale. MoAmPo
On a Miniature. Henry Augustin Beers. AA
On a misty day in spring. Mushimaro. *Fr.* Manyo Shu. PeBJV
On a Monday mornin' it began to rain. Jay Gould's Daughter. *Unknown.* AS
On a Monday Morning. Cyril Tawney. OBET
On a Monday morning early as my wandering steps did lead me. The Boys of Mullabaun [*or* Mullaghbawn]. *Unknown.* BIrV; GBP
On a Monday morning it began to rain. On the Charlie So Long. *Unknown.* AS
On a Monument to Martí. Walter Adolphe Roberts. PBCV; TTY
On a morning such as this. Veteran. Lola Ridge. WPE
On a mountain of sugar-candy. Arno Holz, *tr. fr. German by* Babette Deutsch. *Fr.* Phantasus. PChr
On a New Duke. *Unknown.* FaBoEE

On a night of mist and rain. Phyllis. Sydney King Russell. ErPo
On a Night of Snow. Elizabeth J. Coatsworth. CRH; MoAmPo; MoShBr; OBCA
On a Night of the Full Moon. Audre Lorde. AIW; UnAS
On a Noisy Polemic. Burns. FaBoEE
On a Nomination to the Legion of Honour. *Unknown.* FaBoEE
On a Nook Called Fairyland. Henrietta Cordelia Ray. CBWP-3
On a Note of Triumph, *sel.* Norman Corwin. Man unto His Fellow Man. TrJP
On a Nun. Jacopo Vittorelli, *tr. fr. Italian by* Byron. AWP
On a Painted Woman. Shelley. FaBoCo; NBLV
On a Painting "Ancient Trees and Flowing Stream." Yün Shou-p'ing, *tr. fr. Chinese by* Jonathan Chaves. CoBLCP
On a Painting by Patient B of the Independence State Hospital for the Insane. Donald Justice. CoAP; NePoEA-2; NoAM
On a Painting of a Knight-Errant. Cheng Hsieh, *tr. fr. Chinese by* Jonathan Chaves. CoBLCP
On a Painting of a Woman Shown Half-Length, *sels.* T'ang Yin, *tr. fr. Chinese by* Jonathan Chaves. CoBLCP
   "Nature has endowed her with complete charm." *Fr.* I.
   "Who used his masterful brush to paint this romantic beauty?." *Fr.* II.
On a Painting of Mushrooms. Yün Shou-p'ing, *tr. fr. Chinese by* Jonathan Chaves. CoBLCP
On a Pair of Garters. Sir John Davies. OPOP; SiPS
On a Parisian Boulevard. James Kenneth Stephen. *Fr.* England and America. NOBL
On a patrician evening in Ireland. The Woman of the House. Richard Murphy. IPY
On a Photo of Sgt. Ciardi a Year Later. John Ciardi. AiP
On a Photograph of My Mother at Seventeen. Miller Williams. MT
On a Picture by J. M. Wright, Esq. Robert Southey. FM
On a Picture by Michele Da Verona, of Arion as a Boy Riding upon a Dolphin. Anne Ridler. PoA
On a Picture by Pippin, Called "The Den." Selden Rodman. PoNe
On a Picture by Poussin Representing Shepherds in Arcadia. John Addington Symonds. FaBoBe
On a Picture of Your House. Douglas G. Jones. NOBC
On a Piece of Unwrought Pipeclay. John Frederick Bryant. NOEC
On a Pig's Head. Charles Tomlinson. NoAM
On a Poet. Henry Parrot. FaBoEE
On a poet's lips I slept. Shelley. *Fr.* Prometheus Unbound, I. ChER; ELP; FiP; TOF; ViBoPo
   (Poet's Dream, The.) GTBS; GTBS-P
On a Political Prisoner. W. B. Yeats. FaBoPV; OAEL-2; OBMV
On a Politician. Hilaire Belloc. *See* Here, richly with ridiculous display.
On a Politician. Hilaire Belloc. TW
On a Portrait of Columbus. George Edward Woodberry. AA
On a Portrait of Mme. Rimsky-Korsakov. Kingsley Amis. NePoEA-2
On a Portrait of Wordsworth by B. R. Haydon. Elizabeth Barrett Browning. HeIP
On a potato leaf, by a dewdrop, a snail. Issa, *tr. fr. Japanese by* Hiroaki Sato. *Fr.* Forty-four Hokku. FCEI
On a Prayer Book Sent to Mrs. M.R, *sel.* Richard Crashaw. "Dear soul be strong!" ErPo
On a Puritan. Hilaire Belloc. FaBoEE
On a Puritanicall Lock-Smith. William Camden. FaBoEE
On a Quaker's Tankard. Walter Savage Landor. FaBoEE
On a Quiet Conscience. Charles I, King of England. CH
On a Rainy Evening: Written in Playful Imitation of Yi-shan's "Untitled Poems." Li Tz'u-ming, *tr. fr. Chinese by* Daniel Bryant. WFTU
On a rainy night, the house is desolate. On Seeing a Firefly in My Room. Yang Chi, *tr. by* Jonathan Chaves. CoBLCP
On a Recent Protest against Social Conditions. David Posner. NYBP
On a Return from Egypt. Keith Douglas. NePoEA
On a Rhine Steamer. James Kenneth Stephen. *Fr.* England and America. NOBL; OBTV; TW
On a rock, whose haughty brow. A Pindaric Ode. Thomas Gray. *Fr.* The Bard. SeCePo
On a Romantic Lady. Mary Monck. NOEC
On a Rose in December. Ebenezer Elliott. FaBoEE
On a Royal Demise. Thomas Hood. FiBHP
On a Ruined House in a Romantic Country. Samuel Taylor Coleridge. *Fr.* Sonnets Attempted in the Manner of Contemporary Writers. FaBoPa; Par; Son
On a Saturday afternoon in the football season. Laziness and Silence. Robert Bly. PPP
On a Schoolmaster on Cleish Parish, Fifeshire. Burns. *See* Here lie Willie Michie's bones.
On a Scooter. Desmond A. Greig. PeSA
On a Sea-Grape Leaf. Katherine Garrison Chapin. GrPl
On a Sea-Storm nigh the Coast. Richard Steere. SCAP
On a Seal. Plato, *tr. fr. Greek by* Thomas Stanley. AWP; FaBoEE
On a Seven-Day Diary. Alan Dugan. OBAL

On a shining silver morning long ago. David McKee Wright. *Fr.* Dark Rosaleen, I. PoAu-1

On a shrub in the heart of the garden. Leaf-eater. Thomas Kinsella. FaBCIP

On a Similar Occasion for the Year 1792. William Cowper. NOCV

On a Sixth Floor. A. Leyeles, *tr. fr. Yiddish by* Benjamin *and* Barbara Harshav. AYP

On a small balcony, the shadow of someone leaning against the tall sky. Written on an Autumn Day at the Garden of the Official Residence of the Governor of Kansu. T'an Ssu-t'ung, *tr. by* Timothy C. Wong. WFTU

On a small six-acre farm dwelt John Grist the miller. Under the Drooping Willow Tree. *Unknown.* OxBoLi

On a Snowy Day. Dorothy Aldis. PDV

On a Snowy Night. Koh Chang-soo, *tr. fr. Korean by the author.* ACKP

On a Snowy Night Thinking of the Bamboos at Home. Michizane, *tr. fr. Chinese by* Burton Watson. JLIC-1

On a snug evening I shall watch her fingers. Piano after War. Gwendolyn Brooks. AmNP

On a Soldier Fallen in the Philippines. William Vaughn Moody. AnAmPo; NOBA; PAH

On a Soldier Killed in the Great War. R. Williams Parry, *tr. fr. Welsh by* H. Idris Bell. OBWVE

On a Spaniel Called Beau Killing a Young Bird. William Cowper. FaBoCh

On a Splendud Match. James Whitcomb Riley. AnAmPo

On a spring day/ the trailing windows. Yakamochi. *Fr.* Manyo Shu. FCEI

On a spring day when boundless light. Teika, *tr. fr. Japanese by* Hiroaki Sato. *Fr.* A Compendium of Good Tanka. FCEI

On a spring night. Tameuji, *tr. by* Steven D. Carter. WFTW

On a squeaking cart, they push the usual stuff. A Removal from Terry Street. Douglas Dunn. FaBoMo; OxBC

On a Squinting Poetess. Thomas Moore. FaBoCo

On a Squirrel Crossing the Road in Autumn, in New England. Richard Eberhart. HeIP; LiTM; PoCH; Psk

On a starred [*or* starr'd] night Prince Lucifer uprose. Lucifer in Starlight. George Meredith. AWP; CH; EBVV; FF; HAP; InPK; LiTB; Mes; NAEL-2; NOBE; NOBVV; NoP; OAEL-2; OBEV; OBNC; PoE; PoEL-5; Son; TrGrPo; UnPo; WeW

On a starry, wintry night. The Christ Child. Mary Weston Fordham. CBWP-2

On a Statue of Sir Arthur Sullivan. G. Rostrevor Hamilton. FaBoCo

On a Steamer. Dorothy Walter Baruch. FaPON

On a Stingy Beau. John Winstanley. FaBoEE

On a Stone Thrown at a Very Great Man, But Which Missed Him. "Peter Pindar." NBLV

On a straw-colored day. Dream. Solomon Edwards. PoNe

On a street in Knoxville. Street Scene—1946. Kenneth Porter. PoNe

On a Stupendous Leg of Granite, Discovered Standing by Itself in the Deserts of Egypt, with the Inscription Inserted Below. Horace Smith. PrIm

On a summer day in the month of May. The Big Rock Candy Mountains. *Unknown.* NOBA

On a summer hill a doe appears. Gomei, *tr. by* Hiroaki Sato. FCEI

On a summer's day when the sea [*or* wave] was rippled. The Ship That Never Returned. Henry Clay Work. BLPA

On a summer's day while the waves were rippling, with a quiet and gentle breeze. The Ship That Never Returned. *Unknown.* AS

On a Sunbeam. Thomas Heyrick. MePo

On a Sunday Afternoon. Andrew B. Sterling

On a Sundial. Hilaire Belloc. FaBoEE

On a throne of new gold the Son of the Sky. The Emperor. Tu Fu, *tr. by* E. Powys Mathers. AWP

On a Time the Amorous Silvy. *Unknown.* GBL

On a train in Texas German prisoners eat. Defeat. Witter Bynner. PoNe

On a Travelling Speculator. Philip Freneau. AA

On a tree by a river, a little tom-tit. Ko-Ko's Winning Song. William Schwenck Gilbert. *Fr.* The Mikado, II. LiTB (Ko-Ko's Song ["On a tree by a river a little tom-tit"].) FaFP (Titwillow.) NoP

On a Tree Fallen across the Road. Robert Frost. RB

On a tributary of the Amazon. The Lass of Aughrim. Paul Muldoon. NoAM

On a Trip. Hagiwara Sakutaro, *tr. fr. Japanese by* Hiroaki Sato. FCEI

On a Vase of Gold-Fish. Charles Tennyson Turner. NOBVV

On a verdant summer islet. Burial of a Fairy Queen. Mary E. Tucker. CBWP-1

On a very hot Independence Day. Sonnet No. 21. Mark Ameen. GLP

On a View of Pasadena from the Hills. Yvor Winters. QFR

On a Violet in Her Breast. Thomas Stanley. OBS

On a Virtuous Young Gentlewoman That Died Suddenly. William Cartwright. HAP; OBEV

On a Visit to Ch'ung Chen Taoist Temple. Yu Hsüan-chi, *tr. by* Kenneth Rexroth *and* Ling Chung. PBWP

On a Vulgar Error. Clive Staples Lewis. OxBTC

On a Wag in Mauchline. Burns. EBEV; FiBHP

On a warm roof, working. Ozaki Hosai, *tr. fr. Japanese by* Hiroaki Sato. *Fr.* One Hundred Haiku in Free Form. FCEI

On a Watchman Asleep at Midnight. James Thomas Fields. CenHV

On a Wet Day. Franco Sacchetti. *See* As I walked thinking through a little grove.

On a wet night, laden with books for luggage. The Poet on the Island. Richard Murphy. CIP

On a Wet Summer. John Codrington Bampfylde. NOEC

On a white field. The Sower. R. Olivares Figueroa, *tr. by* Dudley Fitts. FaPON

On a Whore. John Hoskyns. FaBoEE

On A Wife. Francis Burdett Money-Coutts. OxBSP

On a windmill sail, in the golden sunset. The Tale of the Fly. Moyshe-Leyb Halpern, *tr. by* John Hollander. PeBMYV

On a Winter Day Drinking Wine at a Friend's House in the Country. I Nagashiro, *tr. fr. Chinese by* Burton Watson. JLIC-1

On a Winter Evening. Koh Chang-soo, *tr. fr. Korean by the author.* ACKP

On a winter night. Cold Night. Nakahara Chuya, *tr. by* Geoffrey Bownas *and* Anthony Thwaite. PeBJV

On a Winter Night. May Sarton. ER

On a withered branch. Basho, *tr. fr. Japanese.* WeW

On a Woman. Robert Williams, *tr. fr. Welsh by* H. Idris Bell. OBWVE

On A Woman's Inconstancy. Sir Robert Ayton. EIL

On a Young Man and an Old Man. Edward May. OxBSP

On a young rush blade a frog. Shoda, *tr. by* Hiroaki Sato. FCEI

On Acrocorinth. Angelos Sikelianos, *tr. fr. Greek by* Edmund Keeley *and* Philip Sherrard. VMG

On Addy Road. May Swenson. GOYP

On Aesthetics, More or Less. Peter Kane Dufault. NYBP

On Ageing. Maya Angelou. AIW

On Alexander and Aristotle, on a Black-on-Red Greek Plate. Alan Dugan. PPP

On Alexis. Plato, *tr. fr. Greek by* Thomas Stanley. AWP

On alien ground, breathing an alien air. Where a Roman Villa Stood, above Freiburg. Mary Elizabeth Coleridge. OBNC; OBTV

On alien ground I dwelt and also. The Dwelling. Moshe Dor, *tr. by* Dennis Johnson. VWA

On All Fours. Benjamin Perét, *tr. fr. French by* Charles Simic *and* Michael Benedikt. POS; RHTwFP

On all sides a palpitating gray. Saint Médard. István Vas, *tr. by* William Jay Smith. MHuP

On all sides I see valor pull up short. Guillem de Montanhagol, *tr. by* Paul Blackburn. Pro

On all sides the night cracks & splinters. The Metamorphosis of Lovers. Robert Marteau, *tr. by* John Montague. RHTwFP

On an Aberdeen Favourite. *Unknown.* FaBoPP ("Here lie the bones of Elizabeth Charlotte.") FaBoEE

On an Air of Rameau. Arthur Symons. OBNC

On an Anniversary. J. M. Synge. FaBoEE; NOIV; OBMV

On an apple-ripe September morning. Patrick Kavanagh. *Fr.* Tarry Flynn. FaBCIP; IPY

On an ascent of Annapurna. End of the Ice Age. Paul Snoek, *tr. by* Alasdair MacKinnon. DuIn

On an autumn night, lying restless, far from her broken homeland. Yitzhak Lamdan, *tr. fr. Hebrew by* A. C. Jacobs. *Fr.* Massada. VWA

On an early Sunday in April, a feeble day. An Extract from Addresses to the Academy of Fine Ideas. Wallace Stevens. LiTA; LiTM

On an Engraving by Casserius. A. D. Hope. CBAP

On an eve that May. Song on Beholding an Enlightenment. Matías de Bocanegra, *tr. by* Samuel Beckett. MexPo

On an evening/ aglow with the crimson. Tamekane, *tr. by* Steven D. Carter. WFTW

On an Hour[e]-Glass[e]. John Hall. MeLP; MePo; OPOP

On an Indian Tomineois, the Least of Birds. Thomas Heyrick. FM

On an Infant. Gyula Illyés, *tr. fr. Hungarian by* Jascha Kessler. FOC

On an Infant Dying as Soon as Born. Charles Lamb. GTBS; GTBS-P; OBEV

On an Infant Which Died before Baptism. Samuel Taylor Coleridge. OBD

On an Invitation to the United States. Thomas Hardy. AiP; AWP

On an Island. "Ethna Carbery." WPE

On an Island. J. M. Synge. BIrV; MoBrPo; OxBSP

On an island the soft hue of memory. Hugging the Jukebox. Naomi Shihab Nye. MAYP

On an oak in autumn. Survivor. Archibald MacLeish. PrIm

On an Old Horn. Wallace Stevens. LiTA

On an Old Muff. Frederick Locker-Lampson. CenHV

On an Old Woman. Lucilius, tr. fr. Greek by William Cowper. AWP

On an olive-crested steep. Virgil's Tomb. Robert Cameron Rogers. AA

On an onion tuft. Matsumoto Takashi, tr. by Geoffrey Bownas and Anthony Thwaite. PeBJV

On and on, going on and on. Unknown, tr. fr. Chinese by Burton Watson. Fr. Nineteen Old Poems of the Han, I. CoBCP

On Angels. W. W. Eustace Ross. MoCV

On Another's Sorrow. Blake. Fr. Songs of Innocence. AWP; EnRP; FaBV; PoEL-4

On any train. The Fat Lady Travels. Cathy Smith-Bowers. KS

On Apples. David Ross. NYBP

On Approaching Fifty. István Vas, tr. fr. Hungarian by William Jay Smith. MHuP

On Approaching My Birthday. Vassar Miller. IHMS; NMM

On Archaeanassa. Plato, tr. fr. Greek by Thomas Stanley. AWP

On Arrival. Richard Howard. TAP

On Arthur Hugh Clough. Swinburne. FaBoEE

On Australian Hills, sel. Ada Cambridge.
"Oh, to be there to-night!" PoAu-1

On Authors and Booksellers. Pope. FaBoEE

On Autumn Lake. John Ashbery. LCAP

On autumn nights. Unknown, tr. fr. Japanese by Burton Watson. Fr. Kokin Shu. FCEI

On Barclay's Apology for the Quakers. Matthew Green. NOEC

On beaches washed by seas. What She Said to Her Girl-Friend. Venmanipputi, tr. by A. K. Ramanujan. PBWP

On Behalf of Some Irishmen Not Followers of Tradition. "Æ" AnIL

On Being a Householder. Alan Dugan. NoAM

On Being a Woman. Dorothy Parker. AnAmPo; FPL; PoLF

On Being Asked for a Peace Poem. Howard Nemerov. OxBC

On Being Asked for a War Poem. W. B. Yeats. NIP; OBWP

On Being Assigned as Military Adviser to the Garrison Army. T'ao Ch'ien, tr. fr. Chinese by Burton Watson. CoBCP

On Being Brought from Africa to America. Phillis Wheatley. FF; GOA; HeIP; NAAL-1; NOBA; NOEC; TAP; TTY; WPE

On Being Head of the English Department. Pinkie Gordon Lane. BlSi

On Being Much Better Than Most and Yet Not Quite Good Enough. John Ciardi. GOYP

On Being Sixty. Po Chü-i, tr. fr. Chinese by Arthur Waley. AWP

On Being Stone. Vivienne Finch. TSM

On Being Told "You Have Stars in Your Eyes." Sandra McPherson. NAmP

On Ben Dorain. Duncan Ban MacIntyre, tr. fr. Gaelic by Robert Buchanan. Fr. Last Farewell to the Hills. PoSH

On Bertrand Russell's "Portraits from Memory." Donald Davie. FaBoTw

On black bare trees a stale cream moon. Eau-Forte. F. S. Flint. OxBTC

On blessed youths, for Jove doth pause. Francis Beaumont. Fr. The Masque of the Inner Temple and Gray's Inne, II. OBS

On blood, smoke, rain and the dead. Who Knows Where. Detlev von Liliencron, tr. by Ludwig Lewisohn. AWP

On blue summer evenings I'll go down the pathways. Sensation. Rimbaud, tr. by Kenneth Koch. SoTW; TTTS

On Board a Boat at Chi-ning. Yüan Hung-tao, tr. fr. Chinese by Jonathan Chaves. CoBLCP

On Board Ship. Constantine P. Cavafy, tr. fr. Greek by Edmund Keeley and Philip Sherrard. AnAn

On Board the Cumberland. George Henry Boker. PAH

On Board the Leicester Castle. Unknown. OxBSS

On board the noble Ann, twenty-seventh of March, from Shields to Greenland we set sail. The Greenland Men. Unknown. OxBSS

On Board the '76. James Russell Lowell. MOS

On Botching. John Heywood. FaBoCo; FaBoEE

On Broad Cairn, I remember still. Long Ago. Syd Scroggie. PoSH

On Broadway. A. Leyeles, tr. fr. Yiddish by Benjamin and Barbara Harshav. Fr. New York. AYP

On Burning a Dull Poem. Swift. TW

On Burroughs' Work. Allen Ginsberg. NAAL-2; NOBA

On Butler who can think without rage. John Oldham. Fr. A Satire. OBSV

On Button the Grave-Maker. Unknown. FaBoEE

On Buying a Dog. Edgar Klauber. NTCP

On Buying a Horse. Unknown. NBLV; RB

On Calamy's Imprisonment and Wild's Poetry. Unknown. APAS

On Calvary Street are trellises. Ballad of Calvary Street. James Keir Baxter. ATNZ

On Calvary's Lonely Hill. Herbert Clark Johnson. PoNe

On Calvert's plains new faction reigns. Maryland Resolves. Unknown

On Captiva Island I sit on a ledge beside palmettos. Dreams of Snakes, Chocolate and Men. Christy Sheffield Sanford. UL

On Cardinal Wolsey. Unknown. FaBoCo

On Catania and Syracuse Swallowed Up by an Earthquake, from the Italian of Filicaja. Anna Seward. Son

On Catching a Dog-Daisy in the Mower. Peter Redgrove. NePoEA-2

On Catullus. Walter Savage Landor. OBEV

On Cedar Lake, 1957. Ruth F. Brin. TSL

On Certain Ladies. Pope. See When other fair ones [or ladies] to the shades [or groves] go down.

On Certain Mornings Everything Is Sensual. David Jauss. GOYP

On Certain Wits. Howard Nemerov. HCAP; OxBC

On Change of Weathers. Francis Quarles. OxBSP

On charcoal dust. Kikaku, tr. fr. Japanese by Hiroaki Sato. Fr. Thirty-three Hokku. MoAmPo

On cherry petals. Blossoms at Evening. Empress Eifuku, tr. by Steven D. Carter. WFTW

On Chloris Walking in the Snow. William Strode. ELP; JCP; OAEL-1

On Christians, Mercy Will Fall. Unknown, tr. fr. Welsh by D. Myrddin Lloyd. OBWVE

On Christmas Day. Earl of Orrery. TIRV

On Christmas Day. Thomas Traherne. OBS; PoEL-2

On Christmas Day I weep. Christmas Mourning. Vassar Miller. MoAmPo

On Christmas-day in seventy-six. The Battle of Trenton. Unknown. PAH

On Christmas Day ("On Christmas Day it happened so"). Unknown. OBET

On Christmas Day to My Heart. Clement Paman. OBS

On Christmas Eve I turned the spit. Unknown. OxNR

On Christmas Eve my mother read. Christmas Eve. Edna Kingsley Walla. BoTP

On Christmas Eve the little stars. Christmas Eve. Charlotte Druitt Cole. BoTP

On Christmas Morn. Unknown. See Words from an Old Spanish Carol.

On Christmas morn awake did I. He Sports by Himself. Susan Miles. BXAP

On Clarastella Singing. Robert Heath. OBS

On Clarastella walking in Her Garden. Robert Heath. OBS

On Clark Street in Chicago. George Keithley. NPGG

On Clergymen Preaching Politics. John Byrom. SeCePo

On cold days. Becoming a Nun. Erica Jong. MAYP

On cold nights. Okura. Fr. Manyo Shu. PeBJV

On colored rubber soles of illusion. Fabius Lind to Fabius Lind. A. Leyeles, tr. by Benjamin and Barbara Harshav. AYP

On Commonwealth, on Marlborough. Technologies. George Starbuck. NYBP

On Communists. Ebenezer Elliott. See "What is a communist? One who hath yearnings."

On Court-Worme. Ben Jonson. SeCP

On crystal rims, they wheel in space. Snowflakes. Alice Behrend. GoYe

On dead branches crows remain. Basho, tr. fr. Japanese by Burton Watson. Fr. Seventy-six Hokku. FCEI

On Dean Inge. Humbert Wolfe. See Hark the herald angels sing.

On Death. Anne Killigrew. BoWoP

On Death. Walter Savage Landor. See Death Stands above Me.

On Death. Shakespeare. Fr. Measure for Measure, III, i. FiP

On Death, sel. Shelley.
"Who telleth a tale of unspeaking death?." OBD

On Death and Love. Janet Campbell Hale. VoR

On Death, thy murd'rer, this revenge I take. An Epitaph upon My Dear Brother, Francis Beaumont. Sir John Beaumont. JCP

On Death's domain intent I fix my eyes. To a Gentleman and Lady on the Death of the Lady's Brother and Sister, and a Child of the Name Avis, Aged One Year. Phillis Wheatley. BlSi

On December, the sixth. Trenton and Princeton. Unknown. PAH

On Dennis. Pope. FaBoEE

On Descending the River Po. William Parsons. OBTV
On Details. Sami Mahdi, *tr. fr. Arabic by* May Jayyusi *and* Charles Doria. MAP
On Difficulty. Jorie Graham. BAP
On Digital Extremities. Gelett Burgess. FaPON
On Disbanding the Army. David Humphreys. PAH
On Discovering a Butterfly. Vladimir Nabokov. NYBP
On Diverse Deviations. Maya Angelou. BISi
On Dives. Richard Crashaw. ACP
On Don Juan del Norte, Not Don Juan Tenorio del Sur. Alan Dugan. ErPo
On Don Surly. Ben Jonson. FaBoEE; NAEL-1
On Donne's Poem "To a Flea." Samuel Taylor Coleridge. FM
On Donne's Poetry. Samuel Taylor Coleridge. InvP; NAEL-2; NoP; OAEL-2; SeCePo
On Dorinda. Charles Sackville. *See* Dorinda's sparkling wit, and eyes.
On Double Creek. James Still. MT
On, dour! Oh, Mayflower! But enough of that. Ode to the Protestant Poets. Paul Hoover. UL
On Dr. Evans Cutting Down a Row of Trees. *Unknown.* FaBoEE
On Dr. Isaac Letsome. *Unknown.* FaBoCo
On Dr. Keene, Bishop of Chester. Thomas Gray. FaBoEE
On Dr. Lettsom. *Unknown.* FaBoEE
On Dr. Samuel Ogden. R. P. Arden. FaBoCo
On Drawing-Room Amenities. Gelett Burgess. FaBoNo
On Dreams. Swift. BIrV
On Dreams, October 15, 1782. Sir Samuel Egerton Brydges. Son
On Drinking. Wakayama Bokusui, *tr. fr. Japanese by* Hiroaki Sato. *Fr.* Forty-four Tanka. FCEI
On dry days, I remember. First Rainfall. Alan P. Lightman. BWV
On Dulcina. *At. to* Sir Walter Ralegh. CoMu
On dull mornings. Mrs. Busk. Sir Osbert Sitwell. OxBTC
On Dullness. Pope. OxBSP
On Duty. Frederick D'Aguiar. PBCV
On Dwelling. Robert Graves. CMoP; FaBoMo; OxBSP
On ear and ear two noises too old to end. The Sea and the Skylark. Gerard Manley Hopkins. FM; LiTB; OBMV
On Earth. Forugh Farrokhzad, *tr. fr. Persian by* Girdhard Tikku. BoWoP
On Earth There Is a Lamb So Small. Nicolaus L. Zinzendorf, *tr. fr. German by* Sheema Z. Buehne. AH
On Easter Day. Celia Thaxter. FaPON
On Easter Morning. Eben E. Rexford. BLRP
On Eastnor Knoll. John Masefield. CH
On Editing Scott Fitzgerald's Papers. Edmund Wilson. NYBP
On Edward Seymour, Duke of Somerset. *Unknown.* OBSC
On either side the river lie. The Lady of Shalott. Tennyson. BeLS; BLPL; FaFP; FiP; GN; InPS; NAEL-2; NOBE; OAEL-2; OBEV; OBNV; PoE; TEP; TOF; WiR
On Eleanor Freeman, Who Died 1650, Aged 21. *Unknown.* OBEV
On Elizabeth Ireland. *Unknown.* FaBoEE
On Ellson Fell. William Landles. PoSH
On Elphinston's Translation of Martial. Burns. FaBoCo
On Enclosures. *Unknown. See* 'Tis bad enough in manor woman.
On English Monsieur. Ben Jonson. NBLV; NoP
On evenings like this. Empress Eifuku, *tr. by* Steven D. Carter. WFTW
On Evergreen Hill. Yoshinobu, *tr. by* Geoffrey Bownas *and* Anthony Thwaite. PeBJV
On every branch sat birdes three. *Unknown. Fr.* The Squire of Low Degree. PBBP
On every defeat on every design they've walked with necks outstretched meticulously. On My Words. Abba Kovner, *tr. by* Warren Bargad *and* Stanley F. Chyet. IP
On every schoolhouse, ship, and staff. Half-Mast. Lloyd Mifflin. PAH
On every slave a pigeon loft to kick in the light of his decline. 9000 Jackals Swimming to Boston. Lucebert, *tr. by* Peter Nijmeijer. DuIn
On Evolution. John Ciardi. OBAL
On Exodus 3: 14: "I am that I am." Matthew Prior. NOCV
On Failing the Examination. Meng Chiao, *tr. fr. Chinese by* Burton Watson. CoBCP
On fair Augusta's towers and trees. A Tale of Drury Lane. Horace Smith. FaBoCo
On Falling. Andrew Greig. *Fr.* Men on Ice. PoSH
On Falling Asleep by Firelight. William Meredith. NoAM; NYBP
On Fanny Godwin. Shelley. ChER; OBNC
On far hills. Takahama Kyoshi, *tr. by* Geoffrey Bownas *and* Anthony Thwaite. PeBJV
On Fatherish Men. Amelia Rosselli, *tr. fr. Italian by* Muriel Kittel. DMI
On festal days; or when their work is done. James Grainger. *Fr.* The Sugar Cane. PBCV

On File. John Kendrick Bangs. WBLP
On Finding a Small Fly Crushed in a Book. Charles Tennyson Turner. FM
On Finding Out that the One You Slept with the Night Before Was Murdered the Next Day. Chuck Ortleb. GLP
On Finding the Tree of Life. Alan Dugan. CAPP
On Finding the Truth. Jones Very. TrCP
On First Entering Westminster Abbey. Louise Imogen Guiney. AA
On First Looking in on Blodgett's *Keats's "Chapman's Homer."* George Starbuck. OBAL
On First Looking into Chapman's Homer. W. S. Brownlie. BXAP
On First Looking into Chapman's Homer. I. T. Griffiths. BXAP
On First Looking into Chapman's Homer. Keats. BLPA; CH; ChER; ChTr; EnRP; FaBoBe; FaBoCh; FaBV; FaFP; FF; FiP; FPL; GN; GTBS; GTBS-P; HAP; HeIP; HoPM; InPK; LiTB; NAWM-2; NIP; NOBE; NoP; OAEL-2; OBAL; OBEV; OBNC; PoE; PoEL-4; PPP; PrIm; Son; SoSe; TEP; TrGrPo
On First Looking into Chapman's Homer II. Peter Peterson. BXAP
On First Looking into Loeb's Horace. Lawrence Durrell. FaBoMo; LiTM
On First Looking into Michael Grant's *Cities of Vesuvius.* Gavin Ewart. OBTV
On First Looking into the Dark Future. Roger Lancelyn Green. CenHV
On first-paddy maidens deep in the hills, blossoms have opened! *Unknown, tr. by* Hiroaki Sato. FCEI
On First Returning from Taking the Examinations. Wen Cheng-ming, *tr. fr. Chinese by* Jonathan Chaves. CoBLCP
On flower-lathered, green horses. A Headboard to Headboards. László Nagy, *tr. by* Jascha Kessler. FOC
On flowered paths, squeaks of flying squirrels. Rai San'yo, *tr. fr. Chinese by* Burton Watson. *Fr.* Mount Yoshino, III. JLIC-2
On Foinaven. Donald G. Saunders. PoSH
On foot I climb Pei-mang Slope. Written on Parting from Mr. Ying. Ts'ao Chih, *tr. by* Burton Watson. CoBCP
On Forgetting to Cry. Norma Thomas Colvin. TSM
On Fort Sumter. *Unknown.* PAH
On Fortune. Elizabeth I, Queen of England. PBWP; WPE
On four-horse coach, whose luggage pierced the sky. Past and Present. R. E. Egerton Warburton. NOBVV
On Freedom and Ambition. Goldsmith. *Fr.* The Travel[l]er; or, A Prospect of Society. NOIV
On Frost. Wang Fu-chih, *tr. fr. Chinese by* Irving Lo. WFTU
On frost-filled nights. *Unknown. Fr.* Manyo Shu. FCEI
On Frosty Days. David Campbell. CBAP
On Frozen Fields. Galway Kinnell. CAPP
On Fruition. Sir Charles Sedley. ErPo
On Galveston Beach. Barbara Howes. MoAmPo
On Garland Sunday, the weaver told me. Garland Sunday. Padraic Colum. GoYe
On gay Anacreon's joy-inspiring line. On the Translation of Anacreon. Horace Walpole. FaBoEE
On Gay Wallpaper. William Carlos Williams. MoAB; MoAmPo; TAP
On Genessarett. Josephine D. Henderson Heard. CBWP-4
On getting a card. William Carlos Williams. VGW
On Getting a Natural. Dudley Randall. FB; PoBA
On Giles and Joan. Ben Jonson. NAEL-1; NOBL; TEP
On Giving Up Smoking. Lawrence Spooner. *Fr.* A Looking-Glass for Smokers. NOEC
On Glaister's Hill, *sel.* William Jeffrey. Carlyle on Burns. OxBS
On Going Home. Marjorie L. Agnew. GoYe
On Going to the Wars. Earle Birney. WaP
On golden seas of drink, so the Greek poet said. Alcohol. Louis MacNeice. LiTM
On Growing Old. John Masefield. CMoP; FaFP; FPL; LiTB; LiTM; MoAB; MoBrPo; NoP; PoRA; ViBoPo
On Growing Old in San Francisco. Jack Gilbert. NPGG
On Guard. Meir Wieseltier, *tr. fr. Hebrew by* Warren Bargad *and* Stanley F. Chyet. IP
On Gustavus Adolphus, King of Sweden. Sir Thomas Roe. FaBoEE
On Gut. Ben Jonson. JCP; NoP
On gypsum slabs of preternatural whiteness. Animal, Vegetable and Mineral. Louise Bogan. FM
On Hallow-Mass Efe, ere you boune ye to rest. St. Swithin's Chair. Sir Walter Scott. WSC
On Halloween. Aileen Fisher. RAR
On Hallowe'en the old ghosts come. Hallowe'en. Eleanor Farjeon. Mes
On Hardscrabble Mountain. Galway Kinnell. RFM
On Harting Down. Thomas Sturge Moore. OxBTC
On Having Piles. Sir Walter Scott. FaBoEE

On he goes, the little one. Tortoise Family Connections. D. H. Lawrence. BrPo

On Hearing a Broadcast of Ceremonies in Connection with Conferring of Cardinals' Hats. Denis Wrafter. NeIP

On Hearing a Cricket in the Boat. Sung Wan, *tr. fr. Chinese* by William Schultz. WFTU

On Hearing a Lady Praise a Certain Rev. Doctor's Eyes. George Outram. EBVV

On Hearing a Symphony of Beethoven. Edna St. Vincent Millay. LiTA; LiTM; MoAB; MoAmPo; TrGrPo

On Hearing It Has Been Ordered in the Chapterhouse of Ireland That the Friars Make No More Songs or Verses. Padraigin Haicead, *tr. fr. Irish* by Thomas Kinsella. NOIV

On Hearing Mrs. Woodhouse Play the Harpsichord. William Henry Davies. BrPo

On Hearing Prokofieff's Grotesque for Two Bassoons, Concertina and Snare-Drums. Louis Untermeyer. BXAP

On Hearing That on the Sixteenth Day of the Tenth Month the Magistrate of Li-po, Chiang Hsiao-yün, *tzu* Chia-ku, of Shao-hsing/ Attacked the Rebels. Cheng Chen, *tr. fr. Chinese* by William Schultz. WFTU

On Hearing That San-p'ing's Newly Brewed Chrysanthemum Wine Is Ready to Drink. Pien Kung, *tr. fr. Chinese* by Jonathan Chaves. CoBLCP

On Hearing That the Market outside the East Gate of the City Has Been Burned Down. Cheng Chen, *tr. fr. Chinese* by William Schultz. WFTU

On Hearing that the Port of Shimoda Has Been Opened to the Foreigners. Gessho, *tr. fr. Chinese* by Burton Watson. JLIC-2

On Hearing That the Sea-Barbarians Are about to Attack Hu-chou. Tsung Ch'en, *tr. fr. Chinese* by Jonathan Chaves. CoBLCP

On Hearing That the Students of Our New University Have Joined the Agitation against Immoral Literature. W. B. Yeats. MoP; NoAM

On Hearing That Torture Was Suppressed throughout the Austrian Dominions. John Codrington Bampfylde. Son

On Hearing the Airlines Will Use a Psychological Profile to Catch Potential Skyjackers. Stephen Dunn. AmPA

On Hearing the Chukar. Yu T'ung, *tr. fr. Chinese* by Paul W. Kroll. WFTU

On Hearing the First Cuckoo. Richard Church. OBMV

On Hearing the Marsh Bird's Water Cry. Duane Niatum. CDW

On Heaven. Ford Madox Ford. CTC

On Hellespont, guilty [*or* guiltie] of true love's blood. Christopher Marlowe. Hero and Leander, First Sestiad. Christopher Marlowe. AAS; NAEL-1; NoP; OAEL-1; OBSC; PoEL-2; SeCePo; TEP

On her beautiful face there are smiles of grace. A Pretty Girl. J. Gordon Coogler. OBAL

On Her Brother. Al-Khansa, *tr. fr. Arabic*. BoWoP, *tr.* by Willis Barnstone

On Her Brother Sakhr. Al-Khansa, *tr. fr. Arabic*. BoWoP, *tr.* by Willis Barnstone

On Her Portrait. Sister Juana Inés de la Cruz, *tr. fr. Spanish* by Kate Flores. DMH

On her side, reclining on her elbow. So-and-So Reclining on Her Couch. Wallace Stevens. AmPP; LiTM; NOBA

On her 36th birthday, Thomas had shown her. Wingfoot Lake. Rita Dove. BLA

On her way, the little nun. Kyotai, *tr. fr. Japanese* by Burton Watson. *Fr.* Sixteen Hokku. FCEI

On her white breast a sparkling cross she wore. Pope. *Fr.* The Rape of the Lock, II. ACP

On him the unpetitioned heavens descend. A Counsel of Moderation. Francis Thompson. MoBrPo

On him was her soft dead body. The Body. Yona Wallach, *tr.* by Warren Bargad and Stanley F. Chyet. IP

On Himself. Robert Herrick. CaPo; FaBoEE; ChTr; SeCV-1; SeCP

On Himself. Walter Savage Landor. FaBoEE

On Himself. James Russell Lowell. *See* Fable for Critics, A: Lowell.

On Himself. William Oldys. FaBoEE

On Himself. Matthew Prior. FaBoEE

On Himself. Dante Gabriel Rossetti. FaBoEE

On Himself, upon Hearing What Was His Sentence. James Graham, Marquess of Montrose. OBS; SeCePo

On his airy perch among the branches. The Fox and the Crow. La Fontaine, *tr.* by Marianne Moore. OBVE; PPP

On His Blindness. Milton. *See* When I Consider How My Light Is Spent.

On His Books. Hilaire Belloc. ACP; FaBoCo; FaBoEE; MoBrPo; NBLV; OxBoLi; WeW

On His Dead Wife. Milton. *See* Me thought I saw my late espouse'd saint.

On his death-bed poor Lubin lies. A Reasonable Affliction. Matthew Prior. NOEC; NoP; TrGrPo (Cause and Effect.) NBLV

On His Deceased Wife. Milton. BLPL; FaFP; LiTB; OBEV; PoE; SCV; TEP
(Methought I Saw.) NoP; Son
("Methought I saw my late espoused saint.") BoLoP; EnLoPo; NAEL-1
(On His Dead Wife.) GBL; HAP; NOBE; WeW
(On His Late Wife.) PoEL-3
(Sonnet: "Methought I saw my late espoused saint.") EBEV; OAEL-1; OBS

On His First Sonne. Ben Jonson. *See* Farewell, thou child of my right hand, and joy!

On His Garden Book. Francis Daniel Pastorius. SCAP

On His Lady's Waking. Pierre de Ronsard, *tr. fr. French* by Andrew Lang. AWP

On his last swing around. Field Work. Doug Cockrell. Psk

On His Late Espoused Saint. Sir Kenelm Digby. ACP

On His Late Wife. Milton. *See* Me thought I saw my late espouse'd saint.

On His Life. Vittorio Alfieri, *tr. fr. Italian* by Barbara Howes. PFI

On His Mistress [*or* Mistris]. John Donne. *Fr.* Elegies, XVI. BoLoP; EBEV; LiTB; NAEL-1; PoEL-2

On His Mistress. *At.* to Henry Noel *and to* William Strode. *See* Gaze not on swans in whose soft breast.

On His Mistress Drown'd. Thomas Spratt. EnLoPo

On His Mistress Going from Home. *Unknown*. OBS

On His Mistress Looking in a Glass. Thomas Carew. CaPo

On [*or* To] His Mistress, the Queen of Bohemia. Sir Henry Wotton. EiL; ELP; EnLoPo; GBL; HAP; JCP; MeLP; MePo; NoP; OBS; SeCP; TrGrPo

On His Mistresse Going to Sea. Thomas Cary. OBS

On His Mistris That Lov'd Hunting. *Unknown*. OBS

On his morning rounds the Master. Incident Characteristic of a Favourite Dog. Wordsworth. FM

On His Ninth Decade. Walter Savage Landor. *See* To My Ninth Decade I Have Tottered On.

On His Own Deafness. Swift. BIrV; FaBoEE

On His Own Poetry. Charles Churchill. *Fr.* The Prophecy of Famine. NOEC

On His Portrait. William Cowper. EyDe

On His Queerness. Christopher Isherwood. OxBTC; PeHV

On His Royal Blindness Paramount Chief Kwangala. Jack A. Mapanje. WMBCH

On His Seventy-fifth Birthday. Walter Savage Landor. *See* I strove with none, for none was worth my strife.

On his way home, he may be watching this. Teika, *tr. fr. Japanese* by Hiroaki Sato. *Fr.* Eighty-four Tanka. FCEI

On his way to the open hearth where white-hot steel. My Father's Garden. David Wagoner. DiPo

On his wedding night. Sons of War. Samih al-Qasim, *tr.* by Abdullah al-Udhari. MPAW

On His Writing Verses. John Hawthorn. NOEC

On History. Paul Hoover. UL

On hoary Conway's battlemented height. With a Rose from Conway Castle. Julia Caroline Ripley Dorr. AA

On Honour. Bernard Mandeville. NOEC

On Hope. Lindolf Bell, *tr. fr. Portuguese* by William Jay Smith. CT

On Hope. Abraham Cowley. *See* Hope, whose weak being ruin'd is.

On Hope. Richard Crashaw. *See* For Hope.

On Hope by Way of Question and Answer between Abraham Cowley and Richard Crawshaw. Abraham Cowley *and* Richard Crashaw. *See* Hope, whose weak being ruined is.

On horseback, I am crossing the river. Crossing the River. Yang Shih-ch'i, *tr.* by Jonathan Chaves. CoBLCP

On Hot Days. James Reiss. AmPA

On hot summer mornings my aunt set glasses. Water. Leslie Norris. OBWVE

On How the Cobler. *Unknown*. SCAP

On Hubbard Street, among factory signs. On the Upside. G. E. Murray. MAYP

On humming rubber along this white concrete. Driving in Oklahoma. Carter Revard. HATNAP; VoR

On Hurricane Jackson. Alan Dugan. CoAP; SD

On Hurt. Meiling Jin. WS

On Hygiene. Hilaire Belloc. MoBrPo
On Imagination. Phillis Wheatley. AmPP; BlSi; PoNe
On Imitation. Samuel Taylor Coleridge. OxBSP
On Inclosures. *Unknown.* FaBoCo
On Independence. Jonathan Mitchell Sewall. PAH
On Inhabiting an Orange. Josephine Miles. NoAM; PoA
On Installing an American Kitchen in Lower Austria. W. H. Auden. NYBP
On Ireland's Roaringwater Bay. William Rossa Cole. *Fr.* A Mini-Samizdat of New River Rhymes. SoTCo
On Its Way. May Swenson. WPE
On itself. His red hair was standing up. "I just began to weep." The Woman Who Could Read the Minds of Dogs. Leslie Scalapino. NPGG
On J. M. S. Gent. Pope. FaBoEE
On J. W. Ward. Samuel Rogers. FaBoEE
On Jacob Tonson, His Publisher. Dryden. ChTr; FaBoEE; OBSV
On jagged steps moss grows deep. A Descriptive Piece for April, 1853. Chiang Ch'un-lin, *tr. by* Irving Lo. WFTU
On Jam. Hilaire Belloc. NBLV
On Jessy Watson's Elopement. Marjory Fleming. Mes
On Jocky Bell. *Unknown.* FaBoEE
On John Donne's Book of Poems. John Marriot. CH
On John So. *Unknown.* FaBoEE
On Jordan's Bank. Byron. ChER
On Jordan's stormy banks I stand. The Promised Land. Samuel Stennett. AmFP
On Judas Iscariot. Francis Quarles. FaBoEE
On July 5 the Associated Press gave the news to the world. Harangue on the Death of Hayyim Nahman Bialik. César Tiempo, *tr. by* Donald Devenish Walsh. TrJP
On Keats. Shelley. FaBoEE
On King Arthur's Round Table, at Winchester. Thomas Warton the Younger. Son
On King Richard the Third, Who Lies Buried under Leicester Bridge. Sir John Suckling. CaPo
On Kingston Bridge. Ellen Mackay Hutchinson Cortissoz. AA
On Knighthood. Folgore da San Geminiano, *tr. fr. Italian by* John Addington Symonds. AWP
On Ladies' Accomplishments. *Unknown.* FaBoUs
On Lady Anne Hamilton. Sheridan. FaBoEE
On Lady Poltagrue, a Public Peril. Hilaire Belloc. FaBoCo; MoBrPo
On Lake Pend Oreille. Richard Shelton. NYBP
On Late-acquired Wealth *or* Riches. *Unknown, tr. fr. Greek by* William Cowper. OBVE
On Laying the Corner-Stone of the Bunker Hill Monument. John Pierpont. PAH
On Laying Up Treasure. Lois Smith Hiers. GoYe
On Leander's Swimming over the Hellespont to Hero. Thomas Warton the Younger, *after* Martial. FaBoEE
On Leaping over the Moon. Thomas Traherne. LiTB; Mes; NAEL-1; SeCV-2
On Learning That Certain Peat Bogs Contain Perfectly Preserved Bodies. Susan Ludvigson. MAYP
On Learning to Adjust to Things. John Ciardi. OBCA
On Learning to Play the Guitar. Ray Fraser. NeAC
On Leaving. Gertrudis Gomez de Avellaneda, *tr. fr. Spanish by* Frederick Sweet. PBWP
On Leaving Baltimore. Duane Niatum. CDW
On Leaving Cuba, Her Native Land. Gertrudis Gomez de Avellaneda, *tr. fr. Spanish by* Catherine Rodriguez-Nieto. WPOW
On Leaving Holland, *sel.* Mark Akenside.
   "Farewell to Leyden's lonely bound." OBTV
On Leaving Town. Alan Dugan. CAPP
On Lebanon. David Gray. AA
On Lending a Punch-Bowl. Oliver Wendell Holmes. AA
On Liberty and Slavery. George Moses Horton. PoNe
On Lieutenant Shift. Ben Jonson. OBSV
On Linden, when the sun was low. Hohenlinden. Thomas Campbell. BeLS; CH; ChTr; EnRP; FaBoCh; FaBoRV; FaPoR; GN; GTBS; GTBS-P; NOBE; OBNC; OBWP; OnMSP; WaaP; WBLP
On Listening to a Bus Conductor. Anne Bloch. Mes
On Listening to the Spirituals. Lance Jeffers. PoBA
On Literature, *sels.* Chang Wen-t'ao, *tr. fr. Chinese by* Irving Lo. WFTU
   "Poem without a self is fit only to be excised, A." *Fr.* VII.
   "To condone rotten rubbish is to deny the miraculous." *Fr.* I.
On Lo-tien's Poem on the Three Friends of the Northern Window. Michizane, *tr. fr. Chinese by* Burton Watson. JLIC-1
On Lolham Brigs in wild and lonely mood. The Flood. John Clare. RB

On London fell a clearer light. Summer in England, 1914. Alice Meynell. BrRo; WPE
On Long Island, they moved my clapboard house. Whitman. Larry Levis. MAYP
On longer evenings. Coming. Philip Larkin. MoBrPo; OxBTC
On Looking at an Old Climbing Photograph. Douglas Fraser. PoSH
On Looking at Stubb's Anatomy of the Horse. Edward Lucie-Smith. NePoEA-2
On Looking in the Looking Glass. Isabella Gardner. CAPP
On Looking into E. V. Rieu's Homer. Patrick Kavanagh. NOIV
On Looking into Henry Moore. Dorothy Livesay. OBCV
On Looking Up by Chance at the Constellations. Robert Frost. CMoP
On Lookout Mountain. Robert Hayden. PoE
On looming Mount Hatsuse. Hitomaro. *Fr.* Manyo Shu. FCEI
On Lord Chesterfield and His Son. *Unknown.* FaBoCo
On Lord Galloway. Burns. FaBoEE
On Lord Holland's Seat near Margate, Kent. Thomas Gray. NOEC; OAEL-1; OPOP; TW
On lost Apollo's glittering. The Lure. Steve Sneyd. BWV
On Love. Tanikawa Shuntaro, *tr. fr. Japanese by* Hiroaki Sato. FCEI
On Love. Kyogoku Tamekane, *tr. fr. Japanese by* Burton Watson. *Fr.* Twenty-three Tanka. FCEI; LLLT
On love's worst ugly day. First Meditation. Theodore Roethke. *Fr.* Meditations of an Old Woman. LCAP; NOBA
On Lucretia Borgia's Hair. Walter Savage Landor. *See* Borgia, thou once were a'most too august.
On Lucy Countesse of Bedford. Ben Jonson. OBS; SeCP; SeCV-1
On Lydia Distracted. Philip Ayres. EnLoPo; Son
On Maids and Cats. Henricus Selyns. SCAP
On Malverne Hilles, the Place of Piers Plowman's Vision. William Langland. *See* Vision of Piers Plowman, The: In a summer [*or* somer] season, when soft[e] was the sun [*or* sunne *or* sonne].
On Mammon. Herman Melville. *Fr.* Clarel. OxBA
On Man. Walter Savage Landor. OBNC
On man, on nature, and on human life. Prospectus [*incl. in* The Excursion]. Wordsworth. *Fr.* The Recluse. EnRP; NoP; OAEL-2
On many a lazy river, in many a sparkling bay. The Little Boats of Britain. Sara E. Carsley. CaP
On Margaret Ratcliffe. Ben Jonson. SeCP
On Marriage. Richard Crashaw. FaBoEE
On Marriage. Thomas Flatman. FaBoUs; FiBHP; NOBL
On Mary Magdalene. William Drummond of Hawthornden. OAEL-1
On Matsuho's shore of Awaji Island. Kanamura. *Fr.* Manyo Shu. Ma
On Matsuo Beach/ I wait in the pines at dusk. Teika, *tr. by* Steven D. Carter. WFTW
On Mayday we dance. *Unknown.* BoTP
On Meall nan Con, the Peak of the Dogs. Alasdair Maclean. PoSH
On Meeting a Gentlewoman in the Dark. *Unknown.* FaBoEE
On Meeting the Clergy of the Holy Catholic Church in Osaka. Joy Kogawa. BrSi
On Mercenary and Unjust Bailiffs. Henricus Selyns. SCAP
On Middleton Edge. Andrew Young. SD
On Midsummer night the witches shriek. Owl. Sylvia Read. RHPC
On Mikasa, a peak of Mount Kasuga. Akahito. *Fr.* Manyo Shu. Ma
On Mike O'Day. *Unknown.* FaBoEE
On miserable Nearchos' bones lie lightly, earth. Last Lines. X. J. Kennedy. OBAL
On Miss Eleanor Ambrose, a Celebrated Beauty in Dublin. Philip Dormer Stanhope, 4th Earl of Chesterfield. FaBoEE
On misty waters, vast and vague. Hearing a Flute at Broken Bridge. Yün Shou-p'ing, *tr. by* Jonathan Chaves. CoBLCP
On Mites; to a Lady. Stephen Duck. FM
On Monday man gave God. Adam and God. Anne Wilkinson. MoCV
On Monday morning as we set sail. Bold General Wolfe. *Unknown.* OBET
On Monday, when the sun is hot. Lines Written by a Bear of Very Little Brain. A. A. Milne. FaBoNo
On Monsieur Coué. Charles Cuthbert Inge. FaFP
On Monsieur's Departure. Elizabeth I, Queen of England. NAEL-1; WPE
On moonlight bushes. Nightingales. Samuel Taylor Coleridge. *Fr.* The Nightingale. ChTr
On Moonlit Heath and Lonesome Bank. A. E. Housman. *Fr.* A Shropshire Lad, IX. BrPo; CMoP; SoSe
On moony nights the dogs bark shrill. Night Song. Frances Cornford. FM
On moors where people get lost and die of air. Water. Ted Hughes. OxBSP

On Motel Walls. David Wagoner. BLA; DiPo
On Mother's Day. Aileen Fisher. NTCP; RHPC
On Mount Chung-nan what is there? *Unknown, tr. by* Arthur Waley. BoS
On Mount Kasuga of the spring days. Akahito. *Fr.* Manyo Shu. FCEI
On Mount Moru where both white dew. Teika, *tr. fr. Japanese by* Hiroaki Sato. *Fr.* A Compendium of Good Tanka. FCEI
On mount Sinnin. The Bird. "Adunis", *tr. by* Abdullah al-Udhari. MPAW
On Mount Tsukuba where eagles dwell. Mushimaro. *Fr.* Manyo Shu. Ma
On Mount Yoshino. Saigyo, *tr. by* Geoffrey Bownas *and* Anthony Thwaite. PeBJV
On Mr. Abraham Cowley, His Death and Burial amongst the Ancient Poets. Sir John Denham. OBS, *abr.;* SeCV-1
On Mr. Edward Howard, upon His British Princes. Charles Sackville. OBSV
On Mr. Francis Beaumont (Then Newly Dead). Richard Corbet. OBS
On Mr. G. Herberts Booke Intituled the Temple of Sacred Poems, Sent to a Gentlewoman. Richard Crashaw. SeCV-1
On Mr. Gay; In Westminster Abbey, 1732. Pope. FiP
On Mr. Hobbs, and His Writings. John Sheffield. PoEL-3
On Mr. Milton's Paradise Lost. Andrew Marvell. JCP
On Mr. Nash's Picture at Full Length. Jane Brereton. WPE
On Mr. Nash's Present of His Own Picture at Full Length. Earl of Chesterfield. NOEC
On Mr. Paine's Rights of Man. Philip Freneau. NAAL-1
On Mr. Pitt's Hair-Powder Tax. Burns. FaBoEE
On Mr. Pricke. *Unknown.* FaBoEE
On Mrs. Reynolds's Cat. Keats. *See* To a Cat.
On Mrs. W——. Nicolas Bentley. FiBHP
On Mundane Acquaintances. Hilaire Belloc. FaBoEE; FiBHP; OxBTC
On Music. Walter Savage Landor. GoJo
On My Bed I Sought Him. Bible, *O.T. Fr.* The Song of Solomon, III: 1-5. TrJP
On My Birthday, July 21. Matthew Prior. OBEV
On My Birthday—Sick. Li K'ai-hsien, *tr. fr. Chinese by* Jonathan Chaves. CoBLCP
On my boxwood pillow. Dawn. Shunzei, *tr. fr. Japanese by* Burton Watson. *Fr.* Thirty Tanka. FCEI
On my cheeks I wear. My Makeup. Rochelle Kraut. UL
On My Dear Grandchild Simon Bradstreet. Anne Bradstreet. NAAL-1; SCAP
On my desk, a set of labels. City Gent. Craig Raine. NoAM
On my father's memorial day. My Father's Memorial Day. Yehuda Amichai, *tr. by the author and* Ted Hughes. OBD
On my 50th birthday I shall give up symbols. 50 on 50. Peter Meinke. KS
On My First Daughter. Ben Jonson. EBEV; FaBoEE; HoPM; InPS; JCP; NAEL-1; NOBE; NoP; OBS; PoE; SeCP; SeCV-1; TEP
On My First Son [*or* Sonne]. Ben Jonson. AWP; EBEV; ElL; FaBoEE; FF; HAP; HeIP; HoPM; InPK; InPS; JCP; LiTB; NAEL-1; NIP; NoP; OAEL-1; OBD; OxBSP; PoE; PoEL-2; QFR; RB; SeCP; SeCV-1; TEP; WeW
On My Fortieth Birthday. John Tripp. NAs
On My Joyful Departure from the City of Cologne. Samuel Taylor Coleridge. FaBoCo; InvP; OBTV; TW
On My Joyful Departure from the Same City. Samuel Taylor Coleridge. *See* As I am a rhymer.
On my knees. In the Garden. Tom Schmidt. NeAC
On My Lady Isabella Playing on the Lute. Edmund Waller. *See* Such moving sounds, from such a careless touch.
On my land grew a green tree. The Possessor. Arthur Rex Dugard Fairburn. *Fr.* Album Leaves. PeNZ
On My Late Dear Wife. Jonathan Richardson. NOEC
On my little guitar. On My Old Ramkiekie. C. Louis Leipoldt, *tr. by* Anthony Delius. PeSA
On my little magic whistle I will play to you all day. The Magic Whistle. Margaret Rose. BoTP
On my lofty ship. *Unknown. Fr.* Manyo Shu. PeBJV
On My Lord Bacon. John Danforth. SCAP
On My Old Ramkiekie. C. Louis Leipoldt, *tr. fr. Afrikaans by* Anthony Delius. PeSA
On My Own. Philip Levine. FYAP
On My Pretty Marten. Charles Cotton. FM
On my school notebooks. Paul Eluard, *tr. fr. French by* W. S. Merwin. *Fr.* Liberty. Pos; RHTwCP; TTTS
On My Son. Ben Jonson. *See* Farewell, thou child of my right hand, and joy.

On My Sorrowful Life. Moses ibn Ezra, *tr. fr. Hebrew by* Solomon Solis-Cohen. TrJP
On My Stand. Sharon Scott. JB
On my stupid face I see white. Kito, *tr. fr. Japanese by* Hiroaki Sato. *Fr.* Twenty-four Hokku. FCEI
On My Thirty-third Birthday. Byron. FaBoEE; NAs
On My Two-Hundredth Birthday. Jacob Glatstein, *tr. fr. Yiddish by* Benjamin *and* Barbara Harshav *and* Kathryn Helle. AYP
On my wall hangs a Japanese carving. The Mask of Evil. Bertolt Brecht, *tr. by* Michael Hamburger. AnAn
On My Wandering Flute. Abraham Sutskever, *tr. fr. Yiddish by* Ruth Whitman. VWA
On my way back from seeing you off forever. Snow. Shin Dong-jip, *tr. by* Koh Chang-soo. ACKP
On my way back home. Tameie, *tr. by* Steven D. Carter. WFTW
On My Way Home. Onitsura, *tr. fr. Japanese by* Hiroaki Sato. *Fr.* Twenty-three Hokku. FCEI
On my way home at dusk. Teika, *tr. fr. Japanese by* Hiroaki Sato. *Fr.* Eighty-four Tanka. FCEI
On my way home from school. The Testing-Tree. Stanley Kunitz. FYAP; MAT; UnPo
On my way home last night. The First Ice. Shin Dong-jip, *tr. by* Koh Chang-soo. ACKP
On my way to Mass. The Lass from Bally-na-Lee. Anthony Raftery, *tr. by* Desmond O'Grady. BIrV
On my way to Sainsbury's. Conversation with an Angel. Wanda Barford. Mes
On My Wife's Birth-Day. Christopher Smart. NAs
On my window sill. Before Their Tanks. Tawfiq Zayyad, *tr. by* Sharif Elmusa *and* Charles Doria. MAP
On My Words. Abba Kovner, *tr. fr. Hebrew by* Warren Bargad *and* Stanley F. Chyet. IP
On Myself. Edith Bone. FaBoEE
On Myself. Leah Goldberg, *tr. fr. Hebrew by* Robert Alter. OV
On Myself. Anne Finch, Countess of Winchilsea. OxBSP; TrGrPo
On Naniwa Strand. Plovers on the Coast. Kenko, *tr. by* Steven D. Carter. WFTW
On National Data Banks. Louis Phillips. SoTCo
On National Vanity. J.E. Clare McFarlane. PBCV
On Neal's Ashes. Allen Ginsberg. CAPP; PoM
On New Year's dawn. Kikaku, *tr. by* Geoffrey Bownas *and* Anthony Thwaite. PeBJV
On New Year's Day of the Year *Kuei-ssu.* Wang T'ing-hsiang, *tr. fr. Chinese by* Jonathan Chaves. CoBLCP
On New-Year's Day 1640, to the King. Sir John Suckling. SeCV-1
On New Year's Eve. Ts'uei T'u, *tr. fr. Chinese by* Witter Bynner. OFD
On New Year's Eve of the Year *Hsin-wei, sel.* Chin Nung, *tr. fr. Chinese by* Jonathan Chaves.
"Traveler, I've been through a thousand changes, A." CoBLCP
On News. Thomas Traherne. *See* News from a foreign country came.
On nights I can't sleep. The Furniture-Maker. Michael Waters. NAmP
On nights when hail/ falls noisily. Izumi Shikibu, *tr. by* Willis Barnstone. BoWoP
On nights when, wind mixing in, the rain falls. Okura. *Fr.* Manyo Shu. FCEI
On 19 December 1853, the Rebels Are Approaching the Capital. Chiang Ch'un-lin, *tr. fr. Chinese by* Irving Lo. WFTU
On No Work of Words. Dylan Thomas. LiTB; OxBSP
On Noman, a Guest. Hilaire Belloc. FaBoEE
On Not Being Milton. Tony Harrison. *Fr.* The School of Eloquence. FaBoPV; NoAM
On Not Being Your Lover. Medbh McGuckian. FaBCIP
On Not Going Out the Gate. Michizane, *tr. fr. Chinese by* Burton Watson. JLIC-1
On Not Saying Everything. Cecil Day Lewis. NoP
On November 2nd 1965. Norman Morrison. Adrian Mitchell. FF
On Obscenity. Tanikawa Shuntaro, *tr. fr. Japanese by* Hiroaki Sato. FCEI
On Observing a Large Red-Streak Apple. Philip Freneau. NAAL-1
On Observing Some Names of Little Note Recorded in the "Biographia Britannica." William Cowper. OBD
On ochre walls in ice-formed caves shaggy Neanderthals. To My Son Parker, Asleep in the Next Room. Bob Kaufman. PoBA; TwCP; VGW
On Old Olympia's Towering Top. The Cranial Nerves. *Unknown.* FaBoUs
On old slashed spruce boughs. On Hardscrabble Mountain. Galway Kinnell. RFM
On Oliver Goldsmith. David Garrick. FaBoEE
On, on, on. The Dirigible. Chris Wallace-Crabbe. CBAP

On, on the vessel flies, the land is gone. Byron. *Fr.* Childe Harold's
Pilgrimage, XIV - XIX. OBTV
On, on to the darkest continent. Dedicated to Dr. W. H. Sheppard.
Maggie Pogue Johnson. CBWP-4
On One Condition. Charles Madge. EAS
On One Dying in a Convent. Stephen Lucius Gwynn. TIRV
On one fix'd point all nature moves. On the Uniformity and Perfection of
Nature. Philip Freneau. AmPP
On one of those days with the Legion. A Day with the Foreign Legion.
Reed Whittemore. CoAP; LiTM; NePoEA
On one side of the world. At Half Past Three in the Afternoon. Jon
Stallworthy. EOEF
On one side the sun at its grandest. Summer Solstice. George Seferis,
tr. by Edmund Keeley *and* Shilip Sherrard. AnAn
On one summer's day, sun was shining fine. Bill Bailey, Won't You
Please Come Home. Hughie Cannon. OBAL
On One That Lived Ingloriously. John Hoskyns, *after the Greek of*
Simonides. FaBoEE
On One Who Died Discovering Her Kindness. John Sheffield. OBEV
On One Who Died in May. Clarence Chatham Cook. AA
On Originality. Bill Manhire. PeNZ
On other cloudy afternoons. The Double. Irving Feldman. NYBP
On Our Crucified Lord, Naked and Bloody. Richard Crashaw. *See* Upon
the Body of Our Blessed Lord Naked and Bloody.
On our lone pathway bloomed no earthly hopes. Sarah Helen Whitman.
Fr. Sonnets from the Series Relating to Edgar Allan Poe, V.
AA
On our Pharsalian Plaines, comprizing space. Seaconk Plain Engagement.
Benjamin Thompson. SCAP
On Our Thirty-ninth Wedding Day. Jonathan Odell. CaP
On Oxford. Keats. Par
On Pali Lookout. Stephen Shu Ning Liu. BrSi
On Parade. Fragano Ledgister. PBCV
On parent knees, a naked new-born child. Sir William Jones, *after the*
Sanskrit of Kalidasa. FaBoEE; OBEV
(Moral Tetrastich, A.) OxBSP
On Parting with a Friend. Mary Weston Fordham. CBWP-2
On Parting with Moses ibn Ezra. Judah Halevi, *tr. fr. Hebrew by*
Solomon Solis-Cohen. TrJP
On Passing by Those Icy Stones (and Yes, Columbia!). David R. Bunch.
BWV
On Passing the New Menin Gate. Siegfried Sassoon. NAEL-2; NoAM;
OBMV; Son
On Passing Two Negroes on a Dark Country Road Somewhere in Georgia.
Conrad Kent Rivers. IDB
On Peaks Before. Ryokan, *tr. fr. Japanese by* Burton Watson. FCEI;
JLIC-2
On, Pegasus! Why, whither turn ye? A Survey of the Amphitheatre.
Moses Browne. NOEC
On Peter Robinson. Francis Jeffrey. FaBoCo; FaBoEE; NBLV
On Philiphaugh a fray began. The Battle of Philiphaugh. *Unknown.*
ESPB
On Philosophers. *Unknown.* TW
On pillow after pillow lies. Heads in the Women's Ward. Philip Larkin.
OBD
On Playwright. Ben Jonson. NoP
On Poet-Ape. Ben Jonson. Son
On Poet Ninny. John Wilmot, 2nd Earl of Rochester. APAS
On Poetry. Chao Chih-hsin, *tr. fr. Chinese by* Irving Lo. WFTU
On Poetry, *sels.* Chao Yi, *tr. fr. Chinese by* Irving Lo. WFTU
"Best of poetry comes from the destitute, but my pocket is not yet
empty, The." *Fr.* V.
"Poems of Li Po and Tu Fu, passed along by myriad voices, The." *Fr.*
II, *tr. by* William Schultz.
"World is alive with inspiration to a potter who turns the wheel, The."
Fr. I.
On Poetry, *sels.* Sung Hsiang, *tr. fr. Chinese by* Irving Lo.
WFTU
"Did every one of the three hundred poets have a teacher?." *Fr.* I.
"Emulate Han, emulate Tu, emulate the bearded Su." *Fr.* V.
"True, one must read ten thousand volumes until threadbare." *Fr.*
VIII.
On Poetry; a Rhapsody. Swift. OBSV
Sels.
"All human race would fain be wits." HAP;
PoEL-3
"Hobbes clearly proves that every creature." HAP; SCV
(Critics.) SeCePo
On Poets. Ariosto, *tr. fr. Italian by* Edwin Morgan. *Fr.* Orlando
Furioso, XXXV. PFI
On Poets. Pope. FaBoEE

On Portents. Robert Graves. FaBoMo
On Pretext. Charles Simic. PPR
On primal rocks she wrote her name. Our Country. Julia Ward Howe.
OPP; PAH
On Primrose Hill in the early spring. Primrose Hill. Rose Fyleman.
BoTP
On Prince Frederick. *Unknown.* FaBoCo; FaBoEE; NOBL
On Professor Drennan's Verse. Roy Campbell. GTBS-P
On quarry walls the spleenwort spreads. Rockferns. Norman Nicholson.
MoBrPo
On Queen Anne's Death. *Unknown.* EiL
On Queen Caroline. *Unknown.* FaBoEE
On Queen Caroline's Deathbed. Pope. TW
On Rachmaninoff's Birthday. Frank O'Hara. PoM
On Ragged Mountain birches twists from rifts in granite. Granite and
Grass. Donald Hall. DiPo
On Rainy Shadows. Ernst Jandl, *tr. fr. German by* Beth Bjorklund.
CoAuP
On Reading. Thomas Bailey Aldrich. AA
On Reading a Poet's First Book. H. C. Bunner. AA
On Reading Aloud My Early Poems. John Williams. WeW
On Reading Poems to a Senior Class at South High. D. C. Berry. SoSe
On Receiving a Crown of Ivy from the Same. Leigh Hunt. Son
On Receiving My Letter of Termination. Yüan Hung-tao, *tr. fr. Chinese*
by Jonathan Chaves. CoBLCP
On Receiving News of the War. Isaac Rosenberg. MMA; MoBrPo;
OBWP
On Recrossing the Rocky Mountains after Many Years. John Charles
Frémont. AiP
On Refusal of Aid between Nations. Dante Gabriel Rossetti. EBEV
On Returning to Detroit. Carolyn Forché. ER
On Revisiting Cintra after the Death of Catarina. Luis de Camões, *tr. fr.*
Spanish by Richard Garnett. AWP
On Richard Hind. Francis Jeffrey. *See* Here lies the body of Richard
Hind.
On Riding to See Dean Swift in the Mist of the Morning. Pope *and*
Thomas Parnell. FaBoEE
On Riots. Cy Leslie. NBP
On Rising at Dawn and Seeing the Mountains. Hung Sheng, *tr. fr.*
Chinese by Paul W. Kroll. WFTU
On river flats, too. Yakamochi. *Fr.* Manyo Shu. FCEI
On roads, the race drew me outside. Out on the Course. William J.
Vernon. TSL
On Robert Buchanan, Who Attacked Him under the Pseudonym of
"Thomas Maitland." Dante Gabriel Rossetti. FaBoEE
On Roman Feet my stumbling Muse declines. An Elegiack Verse on
...Mr. Elijah Corlet. Nehemiah Walter. SCAP
On Roofs of Terry Street. Douglas Dunn. OxBTC
"On royal crowns and purples, I." Long John. Padraic Fallon. NeIP
On Ryñeveld, an Unpopular Dutch Judge. *Unknown.* FaBoEE
On St. Martin's evening green. Nuns at Eve. John Malcolm Brinnin.
MoAB; TwCP
On Saint-Urbain Street. Milton Acorn. NeAC; NOBC
On St. Winefred. Gerard Manley Hopkins. SaC
On Saturday night shall be my care. Mother Goose. OxNR
On Saturday sailed from Bremen. Gerard Manley Hopkins. *Fr.* The
Wreck of the *Deutschland.* SeCePo
On Saturday with joy Bill dubs his half. The Linen Weaver. *Unknown.*
NOEC
On Saying Goodbye to the Lady in Green. Ali Abdallah Khalifa, *tr. fr.*
Arabic by Lena Jayyusi *and* Alistair Elliot. MAP
On Scafell Pike. Ted Walker. NYBP
On Scaring Some Waterfowl in Loch Turit, a Wild Scene among the Hills
of Oughtertyre. Burns. PBBP
On scattered hailstones. Hara Sekitei, *tr. by* Geoffrey Bownas *and*
Anthony Thwaite. PeBJV
On scent of game from town to town he flew. On a Travelling Speculator.
Philip Freneau. AA
On Science Fiction. Thomas M. Disch. BWV
On Scotland's rolling highlands in. A History of Golf—Sort Of. Thomas
L. Hirsch. ASP
On Scott's Poem "The Field of Waterloo." Thomas Erskine, 1st Baron.
FaBoCo; FiBHP; NBLV
On Sebastian. Sebastian. Yona Wallach, *tr. by* Warren Bargad *and*
Stanley F. Chyet. IP
On Seein an Aik-Tree Sprent Wi Galls. Robert Garioch. OxBS
On Seeing a Construction of a Sheet Metal Man. S. L. Friedman. TSM
On Seeing a Fine Frigate at Anchor in a Bay off Mount Edgecumbe, *sel.*
N. T. Carrington.
"Is she not beautiful? reposing there." FaBoPP

On Seeing a Firefly in My Room. Yang Chi, *tr. fr. Chinese by* Jonathan Chaves. CoBLCP
On Seeing a Hair of Lucretia Borgia. Walter Savage Landor. HAP; WeW
On Seeing a Lady's Garter. *Unknown.* ErPo
On Seeing a Little Child Spin a Coin of Alexander the Great. Charles Tennyson Turner. NOBVV
On Seeing a Pigeon Make Love. Leigh Hunt. FM
On Seeing a Poet of the First World War on the Station at Abbeville. Charles Causley. LiTM
On Seeing a Torn Out Coin Telephone. Martin Robbins. MAT
On Seeing an Officer's Widow Distracted. Mary Barber. NOEC
On Seeing Francis Jeffrey Riding on a Donkey. *At. to* Sydney Smith. FaBoEE
On Seeing Lute Priest Off. Enkei, *tr. fr. Chinese by* Lucien Stryk *and* Takashi Ikemoto. ZPCJ
On Seeing My Birthplace from a Jet Aircraft. John Pudney. NYBP
On Seeing the Elgin Marbles. Keats. BLPL; EnRP; EyDe; LiTB; NAEL-2; NIP; PrIm; TrGrPo
On Seeing the Field Being Singed. Lady Ise, *tr. fr. Japanese by* Etsuko Terasaki *and* Irma Brandeis. BoWoP
On Seeing Two Brown Boys in a Catholic Church. Frank Horne. BANP; CDC; PoBA; PoNe; TTY
On Seeming to Presume. Lawrence Durrell. LiTM
On Shakespeare. Milton. InvP; MeLP; MePo; NAEL-1; NoP; PoE; PoRA; SeCePo; TrGrPo
On Shakespeare and Voltaire. Thomas Holcroft. NOEC
On Shakespeare Critics. A. D. Hope. *Fr.* Dunciad Minor, *Bk.* V. OxBC
On shallow straw, in shadeless glass. Take One Home for the Kiddies. Philip Larkin. OBD; OxBTC
On Shiloh's dark and bloody ground. The Drummer Boy of Shiloh. *Unknown.* AmFP
On shining heights where Thought with stately tread. Emerson. Henrietta Cordelia Ray. CBWP-3
On Shooting a Swallow in Early Youth. Charles Tennyson Turner. FM; NOBVV
On Shooting Particles beyond the World. Richard Eberhart. LiTA; LiTM; TW
On Sight of a Gentlewoman's Face in the Water. Thomas Carew. CaPo; SeCV-1
On Sir Henry Clinton's Recall. *Unknown.* PAH
On Sir John Calf. *Unknown.* PAH
On Sir John Fenwick. Henry Hall. APAS
On Sir John Hill, M. D., Playwright. David Garrick. FaBoCo; FaBoEE; NBLV
On Sir John Vanbrugh [Architect]. Abel Evans. FaBoCo; FaBoEE; FiBHP
On Sir Nathaniel Wraxall the Historian. George Colman, the Younger. FaBoEE
On Sir Philip Sidney. Matthew Royden. *Fr.* An Elegy, or Friend's Passion for His Astrophil [*or* Astrophel]. ElL
On Sitting Down to Read "King Lear" Once Again. Keats. EBEV; EnRP; NAEL-2; NoP
On Sivori's Violin. Frances Sargent Osgood. AA
On small donkeys they bring in suns. Melons. Moshe Yungman, *tr. by* Gabriel Preil *and* Howard Schwartz. VWA
On smooth sand among stones. Photographing a Rattlesnake. David Wagoner. BLA
On Snow, *sel.* Li K'ai-hsien, *tr. fr. Chinese by* Jonathan Chaves. "Jade trees from the rear courtyard of the empire of Ch'en." CoBLCP
On Snow-Flakes Melting on His Lady's Breast. William Martin Johnson. AA
On softest pillows my dim eyes unclose. Vita Benefica. Alice Wellington Rollins. AA
On Solomon Pavy, a Child of Queen Elizabeth's Chapel. Ben Jonson. *See* Weep with me, all you that read.
On Some Buttercups. Frank Dempster Sherman. AA
On Some Humming-Birds in a Glass Cage. Charles Tennyson Turner. FM
On some island I long to be. Saint Columcille, *tr. fr. Irish by* John Montague. BIrV
On Some Partridges Sent to Her Alive. Florencia del Pinar, *tr. fr. Spanish by* Kate Flores. DMH
On Some Shells Found Inland. Trumbull Stickney. LiTA; Son
On Some South African Novelists. Roy Campbell. FaBoCo; FaBoEE; GTBS-P; InPK; MoBrPo; NOBL; OxBTC
On some Vermont road. Mating the Goats. Aliki Barnstone. BoWoP
On Something Observed. Kokan Shiren, *tr. fr. Chinese by* Burton Watson. JLIC-2

On Something, That Walks [*or* Walkes] Somewhere. Ben Jonson. NAEL-1; OxBSP; PoE; SeCP; SeCV-1
On Spies. Ben Jonson. NoP; OxBSP
On spring fields there was only snow. Lady Izumi, *tr. fr. Japanese by* Hiroaki Sato. *Fr.* Fifty-one Tanka. FCEI
On Springfield Mountain there did dwell. Springfield Mountain. *Unknown.* AmFP
On starry heights. The Conflict of Convictions. Herman Melville. NOBA
On Stella's Birthday (1719). Swift. *See* Stella this day is thirty-four.
On stifling summer days/ While a listless peacock strays. Old Inn on the Eastern Shore. William H. Matchett. NePoEA
On still black waters where the stars lie sleeping. Ophelia. Rimbaud, *tr. by* Brian Hill. ChTr
On stone floors lie heavy ropes with steel anchors. On the Docks. Berysh Vaynshteyn, *tr. by* Benjamin *and* Barbara Harshav *and* Kathryn Helle. AYP
On Stopping Late in the Afternoon for Steamed Dumplings. Toi Derricotte. InPS
On Sturminster Foot-Bridge. Thomas Hardy. FaBoPP; OxBSP
On such a day as this. Soundings. Paula Gunn Allen. HATNAP
On such a day as this I think. An April Day. Joseph Seamon Cotter, Jr. CDC
On such a morning as this. In Memory of Basil, Marquess of Dufferin and Ava. Sir John Betjeman. OBWP
On summer afternoons I sit. La Vie C'est la Vie. Jessie Redmond Fauset. BANP; CDC; PoNe
On summer evenings blue, pricked by the wheat. Sensation. Rimbaud, *tr. by* Jethro Bithell. AWP
On summer nights. Tsurayuki, *tr. fr. Japanese by* Burton Watson. *Fr.* Kokin Shu. FCEI
On summer nights they swarm. Termites. Eric Chock. BrSi
On Sunday Afternoons. Sunday Afternoons. Anthony Thwaite. OxBTC
On Sunday morning, then he comes. Mr. Wells. Elizabeth Madox Roberts. FaPON
On Sunday morning well I knew. *Unknown, tr. fr. Italian by* John Addington Symonds. *Fr.* Popular Songs of Tuscany. AWP
On Sunday the hawk fell on Bigging. The Hawk. George Mackay Brown. RB
On Sunday, when she visits him, she must come prepared. Erev Shabbos. Marc Kaminsky. VWA
On Sundays friends arrive with kindly words. Air-Raid Causalties: Ashridge Hospital. Patricia Ledward. CN
On Sweet Killen Hill. Tom MacIntyre. CIP
On swift sail flaming. Stephen's Vampire Poem. James Joyce. *Fr.* Ulysses. VVA
On Sympathisers with the American Revolution. Charles Wesley. NOCV
On Tara's hill the daylight dies. The Paschal Fire. Denis Florence MacCarthy. TIRV
On Tatsuta Hill. Mushimaro. *Fr.* Manyo Shu. PeBJV
On taut air—bells; lifted, adoring eyes. Immolation. Robert Farren. TIRV
On Teaching the Young. Yvor Winters. NoAM; NOBA
On Ternissa's Death. Walter Savage Landor. *See* Hellenics, The: Ternissa! You Are Fled.
On that big estate there is no rain. Monangamba. Antonio Jacinto. TTY, *tr. by* Alan Ryder; WMBCH, *tr. by* Margaret Dickinson
On that clear, dry, cold Christmas Eve. Nagyszombat, 1704. István Vas, *tr. by* William Jay Smith. MHuP
On that last night before we went. Tennyson. *Fr.* In Memoriam A. H. H., CIII. PoEL-5
On the altar. Receiving Buddha. Ping-hsin, *tr. by* K. C. Leung. OV
On the American Rivers. James Smith. FaBoUs
On the Anniversary of Basho's Death I Visited His Grave in Kiso. Kaai Chigetsu, *tr. fr. Japanese by* Hiroaki Sato. *Fr.* Thirteen Hokku. FCEI
On the Anniversary of My Father's Death. Natsume Seibi, *tr. fr. Japanese by* Hiroaki Sato. *Fr.* Twenty-seven Hokku. FCEI
On the Antiquity of Microbes. Strickland W. Gillilan. NBLV
On the Apparition of Oneself. William Burford. PoA
On the Appeal from the Race of Sheba: II. Léopold Sédar Senghor, *tr. fr. French by* John Reed *and* Clive Wake. TTY
On the Army of Spartans, Who Died at Thermopylae. Simonides. *See* Tell them in Lacedaemon passer-by.
On the Astrologer and Almanac Maker, John Partridge. Swift. FaBoEE
On the Asylum Road. Charlotte Mew. MoBrPo
On the Atchafalaya. Longfellow. *Fr.* Evangeline. AA

On the Author of the *Treatise of Human Nature*. James Hay Beattie. FaBoCo

On the avenue the faces change each day. Hope. F. D. Reeve. PoA

On the Balcony. D. H. Lawrence. BrPo; GBL

On the balcony of La Fitte in Exile. The Mystic Pig. Richard Katrovas. NAmP

On the bamboo grass. Bamboo Grass. Kagura, *tr. by* Hiroaki Sato. FCEI

On the Banisters. Margaret E. Gibbs. BoTP

On the bank deep in smartweed, oranges perfume the winds. Sand of Silk-Washing Stream. Sun Kuang-hsien, *tr. by* Lois Fusek. ATF

On the Banks of Salee. *Unknown*. AmFP

On the Banks of the Little Eau Pleine. *Unknown*. AmFP

On the banks of the Passamaquoddy. Down East Drama. David H. Green. SoTCo

On the banks of the Potomac there's an army so grand. The Red, White and Red. *Unknown*. AmFP

On the Baptized Ethiopian (*or* Aethiopian). Richard Crashaw. FaBoEE; NoP; SeCV-1

On the bare mountain. Distant View. Uys Krige, *tr. by* Uys Krige *and* Jack Cope. PeSA

On the bare veld where nothing ever grows. A Veld Eclogue: The Pioneers. Roy Campbell. OBSV

On the Barrack Islands far out. A Rum Cove, a Stout Cove. Tom Paulin. FaBCIP

On the battlefield, the spring wind is harsh. Shih Jun-chang, *tr. fr. Chinese by* William Shultz. *Fr.* Songs on Accompanying the Governor-General, II. WFTU

On the Beach. Claribel Alegría, *tr. fr. Spanish by* Darwin J. Flakoll. DMH

On the Beach. Charles Stuart Calverley. FiBHP

On the Beach at Fontana. James Joyce. MoBrPo; OBMV; PoA; RB; SoSe

On the Beach at Night. Walt Whitman. AmPP; AWP; ChTr; MoAmPo; NOBA; NoP; OxBA

On the Beach at Night Alone. Walt Whitman. TAP

On the beach near Port St. Joe. William Rossa Cole. *Fr.* A Mini-Samizdat of New River Rhymes. SoTCo

On the beach of Iwashiro. Prince Arima. *Fr.* Manyo Shu. PeBJV

On the beach where we had been idly. Gracious Goodness. Marge Piercy. Psk

On the beach where you sleep. *Unknown*. *Fr.* Manyo Shu. PeBJV

On the Benefactions in the Late Frost. Pope. NOEC; OxBSP

On the beryl-rimmed rebecs of Ruby. Lily Adair. Thomas Holley Chivers. OBAL

On the Big Horn. Whittier. PAH

On the Birth of a Black/Baby/Boy. Etheridge Knight. DiL

On the Birth of a Posthumous Child, Born in Peculiar Circumstances of Family Distress. Burns. NAs

On the Birth of Dan Goldman. Daniel Berrigan. NAs

On the Birth of His Son. Su Tung-p'o, *tr. fr. Chinese by* Arthur Waley. AWP; OBVE; OFD

On the Birth of My Son, Malcolm Coltrane. Julius Lester. PoBA

On the black stage he. Mime. John Updike. RR

On the black tarmac playground dark. Deaf-and-Dumb School. Anthony Delius. PeSA

On the Bleeding Wounds of Our Crucified Lord, *sel.* Richard Crashaw. SeCV-1

"Jesu, no more! It is full tide." TrGrPo

On the Blessed Virgin's Bashfulness. Richard Crashaw. HAP; OxBSP

On the bluff of the Little Big Horn. Miles Keogh's Horse. John Milton Hay. PAH

On the Body. Léon-Paul Fargue, *tr. fr. French by* Lydia Davis. RHTwFP

On the bog road the blackthorn flowers, the turf-stacks. Anthony Cronin. *Fr.* R.M.S. Titanic. BIrV

On the Border, First Series, *sels.* Tu Fu, *tr. fr. Chinese by* Burton Watson. CoBCP

"If you draw a bow, draw a strong one." *Fr.* 6.

"We recruits have our commanders to send us off." *Fr.* 4.

On the boulder at the bottom. Joso, *tr. fr. Japanese by* Hiroaki Sato. *Fr.* Fifteen Hokku. FCEI

On the Breaking-up of a School. Tadhg O'g O'Huiginn, *tr. fr. Late Middle Irish by* Osborn Bergin. AnIL

On the Bridge. Kate Greenaway. RHPC

On the Bridge of Sighs. Byron. *See* Childe Harold's Pilgrimage: I stood in Venice on the Bridge of Sighs.

On the Bright Side. Carter Revard. NOVW; VoR

On the Brink of Death. Buonarroti Michelangelo, *tr. fr. Italian by* John Addington Symonds. AWP

On the British Invasion. Philip Freneau. PAH

On the British King's Speech. Philip Freneau. PAH

On the broad canvas Paros had pourtray'd. Genius and Intemperance. John Nicholson. PF

On the Building of a New Church. *Unknown*. *See* They built the front, upon my word.

On the Building of Springfield. Vachel Lindsay. OHFP

On the Burial of His Brother. Catullus, *tr. fr. Latin by* Aubrey Beardsley. AWP

On the Bus. Mitsuye Yamada. *Fr.* Camp Notes. WPOW

On the Bust of Helen by Canova. Byron. EyDe

On the Butcher Block. Jacob Glatstein, *tr. fr. Yiddish by* Benjamin *and* Barbara Harshav. AYP

On the Butterflies. T'ang Yin, *tr. fr. Chinese by* Jonathan Chaves. CoBLCP

On the Butterfly's. Philippe Denis, *tr. fr. French by* Paul Auster. RHTwFP

On the Calculus. J. V. Cunningham. QFR

On the Campagna. Elizabeth Stoddard. AA

On the Candidates for the Laurel. Pope. FaBoEE

On the Capture of the *Guerrière*. Philip Freneau. PAH

On the Cards and Dice. Sir Walter Ralegh. RB (Prognostication upon Cards and Dice, A.) SiPS

On the Castle of Chillon. Byron. *See* Prisoner of Chillon, The: Sonnet on Chillon.

On the chalk cliff edge struggles the final field. The Marginal Field. Stephen Spender. PoA

On the Charlie So Long. *Unknown*. AS

On the Chia-ling River. Wei Yüan, *tr. fr. Chinese by* Irving Lo. WFTU

On the Circuit. W. H. Auden. NOBL; OxBTC

On the Circumsision: New Year's Day. Luke Wadding. NOIV

On the Clerk of a Country Parish. William Shenstone. FaBoEE

On the Closing of Millom Ironworks. Norman Nicholson. FaBoTw

On the Coast. Wayne Brown. UAS

On the Coast of Coromandel. Sir Osbert Sitwell. MoBrPo; SeCePo

On the Coast of Coromandel. The Courtship of the Yonghy-Bonghy-Bo. Edward Lear. EnLoPo; FaBoNo; NA; OAEL-2; OnMSP; WiR

On the Cold Food Festival, Entertaining at the Southern Estate. Li K'ai-hsien, *tr. fr. Chinese by* Jonathan Chaves. CoBLCP

On the Collar of Mrs. Dingley's Lap-Dog. Swift. FaBoEE; FM

On the Columbia River near Vantage. Bobber. Raymond Carver. GeTw

On the Completion of the Pacific Telegraph. Jones Very. TAP

On the Concord River. Henrietta Cordelia Ray. CBWP-3

On the Congo. Harry Edmund Martinson, *tr. fr. Swedish by* Robert Bly. RB

On the Corner. Kit Robinson. IAT

On the corner—116th and Lenox. Harlem Freeze Frame. Lebert Bethune. PoBA

On the Couch. Oscar Williams. WaP

On the Countess Dowager of Pembroke. *At. to* William Browne. AWP; HAP; InvP; JCP; NoP; OAEL-1; PoEL-2; PoRA; WeW

On the Countess of Dorchester. Charles Sackville. *See* Dorinda's sparkling wit, and eyes.

On the craggy mountain-top the mist. Majuba Hill. Roy Macnab. PeSA

On the Creation and Ontogony. *Unknown, tr. fr. Delaware (Lenape) Indian by* C. S. Rafinesque. *Fr.* Walam [*or* Wallum] Olum; or, Red Score. LiTA

On the crest of the hill. Dawn Cherries. Hezutsu Tosaku, *tr. by* Burton Watson. FCEI

On the Crocodile. Thomas Heyrick. FM

On the crooked arm of Columbus, on his cloak. Pigeons. Alastair Reid. NePoEA; NYBP; TwCP

On the Croun o Bidean. J. K. Annand. PoSH

On the Curve-Edge. Abbie Huston Evans. NYBP

On the Dangers Attending Altruism on the High Seas. G. K. Chesterton. FaBoNo

On the Dark, Still, Dry, Warm Weather Occasionally Happening in the Winter Months. Gilbert White. NOEC

On the dark wings of the cutting blast. In the Wet Shadows. Ramón López Velarde, *tr. by* Samuel Beckett. MexPo

On the darkening road, stands the verminous man. The Crucified and the Verminous Man. Itzig Manger, *tr. by* Leonard Wolf. PeBMYV

On the day I was born. My Stars. Abraham Ibn Ezra, *tr. by* Robert Mezey. OFD

On the day I was born, many visitors come to see me. On My Birthday—Sick. Li K'ai-hsien, *tr. by* Jonathan Chaves. CoBLCP

On the day I was conceived. The Inheritance. Maureen Hawkins. WS

On the day my father died a flame-tree. Vincent O'Sullivan. *Fr.* Brother Jonathan, Brother Kafka, 8. ATNZ

On the Day of Atonement. Yehuda Amichai, *tr. fr. Hebrew*. TOF, *tr. by* T. Carmi; VWA, *tr. by* Shirley Kaufman

On the Day of Atonement we fasted. Day of Atonement. Jack Myers. VWA

On the day of death, when my bier is on the move. Jalal ed-Din Rumi, *tr. by* A. J. Arberry. OBD

On the day of the explosion. The Explosion. Philip Larkin. EBEV; FaBoMo; HAP; NAEL-2; NoAM; OxBC; RB; SCV; WeW

On the Day of the Mid-Autumn Festival of the Year, *sel.* Yün Shou-p'ing, *tr. fr. Chinese by* Jonathan Chaves.

"In a hidden spot on the northern mountain." CoBLCP

On the Day of Washing the Buddha in the Year *Ting-wei*. T'ang Hsien-Tsu, *tr. fr. Chinese by* Jonathan Chaves. CoBLCP

On the day the sienna-skinned man. Russia, 1927. Ai. NoAM

On the day the two in love set out. For Sonoda Saeko. Wakayama Bokusui, *tr. fr. Japanese by* Hiroaki Sato. *Fr.* Forty-four Tanka. FCEI

On the day the world ends. A Song on the End of the World. Czeslaw Milosz, *tr. by the author*. PwPP

On the Death-Bed. Thomas Hardy. *Fr.* Satires of Circumstance, XIII. BrPo

On the Death of a Child. Edward S. Silvera. PoNe

On the Death of a Favorite Cat, Drowned in a Tub of Gold Fishes. Thomas Gray. *See* 'Twas on a lofty vase's side.

On the Death of a Favourite Old Spaniel. Robert Southey. FM

On the Death of a Female Officer of the Salvation Army. A. E. Housman. *See* "Hallelujah!" was the only observation.

On the Death of a Lady's Owl. Moses Mendes. TrJP

On the Death of a Metaphysician. George Santayana. *Fr.* Sonnets. AnAmPo

On the Death of a Monkey. Thomas Heyrick. FM; MePo

On the Death of a New Born Child. Mei Yao-Ch'en, *tr. fr. Chinese by* Kenneth Rexroth. NaP

On the Death of a Particular Friend. James Thomson. *Fr.* On the Death of Mr. William Aikman the Painter. OBEV

On the Death of a Pious Lady. Olof Wexionius, *tr. fr. Swedish by* Sir Edmund Gosse. AWP

On the Death of a Prince; a Meditation. Thomas Philipott. JCP

On the Death of a Young and Favorite Slave. Martial, *tr. fr. Latin by* Goldwin Smith. AWP

On the Death of an Acquaintance. Oscar Williams. *Fr.* Variations on a Theme, I. LiTA

On the Death of an Emperor Penguin in Regent's Park, London. David Wright. NYBP

On the Death of Anne Brontë. Charlotte Brontë. WPE

On the Death of Benjamin Franklin. Philip Freneau. PAH

On the Death of Captain Nicholas Biddle. Philip Freneau. PAH

On the Death of Catarina de Attayda. Luis de Camões, *tr. fr. Spanish by* R. F. Burton. AWP

On the Death of Commodore Oliver H. Perry. John Gardiner Calkins Brainard. PAH

On the Death of Donne. Thomas Carew. *Fr.* An Elegy upon the Death of the Dean of [St.] Paul's, Dr. John Donne. NOBE

On the Death of Elizabeth, Queen of Henry VII, and Mother of Henry VIII. *Unknown*. FaBoRV

On the Death of Emperor Tenji. *Unknown, tr. fr. Japanese by* Geoffrey Bownas *and* Anthony Thwaite. BoWoP

On the Death of Francisco López Merino. Jorge Luis Borges, *tr. fr. Spanish by* Norman Thomas di Giovanni. OBD

On the Death of Friends in Childhood. Donald Justice. InPK; LCAP

On the Death of Her Body. James Keir Baxter. ATNZ; PeNZ

On the Death of Her Mother. Muriel Rukeyser. SM

On the Death of His Son. Charles Wesley. NOCV

On the Death of His Son Vincent. Leigh Hunt. NOBVV

On the Death of His Wife. Muireadach O'Dalaigh, *tr. fr. Irish by* Frank O'Connor. BIrV; CIP

On the Death of His Younger Sister. Kyorai, *tr. fr. Japanese by* Burton Watson. *Fr.* Twenty Hokku. FCEI

On the Death of Ho Chi Minh. Eli W. Mandel. NIP

On the Death of "Jackson." *Unknown*. PAH

On the Death of Joseph Rodman Drake. Fitz-Greene Halleck. AA; AnAmPo; BLPA; PAH; PoEL-4

On the Death of Karl Barth. Jack R. Clemo. NOCV

On the Death of Keats. John Logan. Prf

On the Death of Lisa Lyman. Della Burt. BlSi

On the Death of Little Mahala Ashcraft. James Whitcomb Riley. AA

On the Death of M. D'Ossoli and His Wife, Margaret Fuller. Walter Savage Landor. PAH

On the Death of Marie, Countesse of Pembroke. William Browne. *See* Underneath this sable hearse.

On the Death of Mistress Mary Prideaux. William Strode. JCP

On the Death of Mr. Crashaw. Abraham Cowley. MeLP; MePo; OBS; SeCP; SeCV-1

On the Death of Mr. Pope. *Unknown*. NOEC

On the Death of Mr. Richard West. Thomas Gray. *See* In vain to me the smiling mornings shine.

On the Death of Mr. [*or* Dr.] Robert Levet, a Practiser in Physic. Samuel Johnson. EBEV; HeIP; InPS; NAEL-1; NOBE; NOEC; NoP; OAEL-1; OBEV; PoE; PoEL-3; PPP; SCV; TEP

On the Death of Mr. William Aikman the Painter, *sel.* James Thomson. On the Death of a Particular Friend. OBEV

On the Death of Mr. William Hervey [*or* Harvey], *sel.* Abraham Cowley. EBEV; FaBoRV; OBEV; OBS; SeCP; SeCV-1

"It was a dismal and a fearful night." NOBE

On the Death of Mrs. Bowes. Lady Mary Wortley Montagu. BoWoP

On the Death of My Son Charles. Daniel Webster. AA

On the Death of Old Bennet the News-Crier. *Unknown*. NOEC

On the Death of Our Lord. Richard Flecknoe. TIRV

On the Death of Paul Celan (A Vindication). Doris Mühringer, *tr. fr. German by* Beth Bjorklund. CoAuP

On the Death of Phillips. *Unknown*. OBSC

On the Death of President Garfield. Oliver Wendell Holmes. PAH

On the Death of Robert Lowell. Eileen Myles. UL

On the Death of Sir Philip Sidney. Henry Constable. OBEV; OBSC

On the Death of Squire Christopher. John Wigson. OxBSP

On the Death of Sylvia Plath. Judith Herzberg, *tr. fr. Dutch*. VWA, *tr. by* Shirley Kaufman; WPOW, *tr. by* Manfred Wolf

On the Death of the Giraffe. Thomas Hood. FaBoEE; OBD

On the Death of the Great Chef Alexis Soyer. *Unknown*. FaBoEE

On the Death of the Lord Treasurer. *Unknown*. FaBoEE

On the Death of the Rev. Mr. George Whitefield. Phillis Wheatley. NAAL-1

On the Death of William Edward Burghardt Du Bois by African Moonlight and Forgotten Shores. Conrad Kent Rivers. NBP; PoBA

On the Decease of the Religious and Honourable Jno Haynes Esqr. John James. SCAP

On the Deception of Appearances. Sadi, *tr. fr. Persian by* L. Cranmer-Byng. *Fr.* The Gulistan. AWP

On the deck of a ship called the Masm. Conrad Aiken. FaBoNo

On the deck of Patrick Lynch's boat I sat in woeful plight. The County of Mayo. *At. to* Thomas Flavell, *tr. by* George Fox. BIrV; OBEV

On the Defeat at Ticonderoga or Carilong. *Unknown*. PAH

On the Defeat of Henry Clay [*or* of a Great Man]. William Wilberforce Lord. AA; PAH

On the Departing of Thomas Chaucer. John Lydgate. OxBLMV

On the Departure of Sir Walter Scott from Abbotsford, for Naples. Wordsworth. EBEV; EnRP

On the Departure of the British from Charleston. Philip Freneau. PAH

On the Departure Platform. Thomas Hardy. NOBE; OBNC; OxBTC

On the Deputy of Ireland's Child. Sir John Davies. FaBoEE

On the Desert. Stephen Crane. *Fr.* War Is Kind, XI. LiTM

On the desolate stony shore. *Unknown*. *Fr.* Manyo Shu. Ma

On the Detraction Which Followed upon My Writing Certain Treatises. Milton. PoE; Son

On the Detraction Which Followed upon My Writing Certain Treatises. Milton. FaBoPV; NoP

On the diesel train's. In the Eyes of a Screech Owl. Ono Tozaburo, *tr. by* Hiroaki Sato. FCEI

On the Discoveries of Captain Lewis. Joel Barlow. AmPP; PAH

On the Divine Power of Courtly Love. Mechthild von Magdeburg, *tr. fr. German by* Susan L. Cocalis. DMG

On the Docks. Berysh Vaynshteyn, *tr. fr. Yiddish by* Benjamin *and* Barbara Harshav *and* Kathryn Helle. AYP

On the Duke of Buckingham. James Shirley. FaBoEE

On the Duke of Buckingham, Slain by Felton, the 23rd August, 1628. Owen Felltham. JCP

On the dust-heap. Taigi, *tr. by* Geoffrey Bownas *and* Anthony Thwaite. PeBJV

On the dusty earth-drum. Rain Music. Joseph Seamon Cotter, Jr. BANP; CDC

On the dyke there is a magpie's nest. *Unknown, tr. by* Arthur Waley. BoS

On the Earl of Leicester. *Unknown*. FaBoEE

On the eastern seacoast lives a sick man. Inscribed on a Painting by Myself. Ni Tsan, *tr. by* Jonathan Chaves. CoBLCP

On the eastern sidewalk of Magdalen College a small. Notes to the Books of the Old Testament. Aleksander Wat, *tr. by* Czeslaw Milosz. PwPP

On the Eating of Mice. Russell Edson. NAmP; PPR

On the Eclipse of the Moon of October 1865. Charles Tennyson Turner. OBNC

On the Edge. Philip Levine. CoAP; TAP

On the edge of night. Morning. Giuseppe Ungaretti, *tr. by* William Jay Smith. CT; PFI

On the Edge of the Copper Pit. Pauline Henson. GoYe

On the Edition of Mr. Pope's Works with a Commentary and Notes. Thomas Edwards. TW

On the eighteenth of August, at the eighth month of the year. New Garden Fields. *Unknown*. OBET

On the eighth day, the rain stopped before dusk. The Loon's Egg. Peter Dale Scott. MoCV

On the Emigration to America [and Peopling the Western Country]. Philip Freneau. NAAL-1; PAH; TAP

On the Erection of Shakespeare's Statue in Westminster Abbey. Pope. FaBoEE

On the Erie Canal, it was. The Aged Pilot Man. "Mark Twain." OBAL

On the Esplanade des Invalides. David Fisher. NPGG

On the Eve of a Birthday. Geoffrey Grigson. NAs

On the Eve of His Execution. Chidiock Tichborne. *See* My prime of youth is but a forest of cares.

On the Eve of the Feast of the Immaculate Conception: 1942. Robert Lowell. WaaP

On the Eve of the Plebiscite. Kenneth Rexroth. NNaP

On the Eve of War. Danske Bedinger Dandridge. PAH

On the evening when, alone, I leave my village. Princess Shikishi, *tr. fr. Japanese by* Hiroaki Sato. *Fr.* Seventy-eight Tanka. FCEI

On the Extinction of the Venetian Republic. Wordsworth. EnRP; FaBoRV; GTBS; GTBS-P; NOBE; NoP; OBEV; OBNC; TrGrPo

On the Eyes of an SS Officer. Richard Wilbur. CAPP

On the fair green hills of Rio. The Burglar of Babylon. Elizabeth Bishop. InPS; NYBP; RB

On the far edge of a plain. The Watcher. John Peck. AmPA

On the far river bank. Ishikawa Takuboku, *tr. by* Geoffrey Bownas *and* Anthony Thwaite. PeBJV

On the far side. A Late Spring: Eastport. Philip Booth. Psk

On the far side of the water, high on a sand bar. Arkansas Traveller. Charles Wright. MT

On the Farm. R. S. Thomas. OxBTC

On the farm it never mattered. The Assistance. Paul Blackburn. NeAP; PoM

On the Farther Wall, Marc Chagall. Phyllis McGinley. *Fr.* Spectator's Guide to Contemporary Art. OBSV

On the Fifteenth Day of the Eighth Month, *sels.* Liu E, *tr. fr. Chinese by* Jonathan Chaves. CoBLCP

"Cotton blankets left in the cold."

"My thoughts flow in streams around this tower."

On the Fifteenth Day of the Ninth Month of the Year *Kuei-mao* of the *Chih-cheng* Period. Ni Tsan, *tr. fr. Chinese by* Jonathan Chaves. CoBLCP

On the Fifteenth Day of the Seventh Month I Came Home Late from the City. Shen Chou, *tr. fr. Chinese by* Jonathan Chaves. CoBLCP

On the Fifth Anniversary of Bluma Sach's Death. Vinnie-Marie D'Ambrosio. IHMS

On the fifth of November in 'fifty-three. Diesel and Shale. Cyril Tawney. OxBSS

On the Fine Arts Garden, Cleveland. Russell Atkins. PoBA

On the fine new robes. Tameko, *tr. by* Steven D. Carter. WFTW

On the fine wire of her whine she walked. Mosquito. John Updike. AnAmPo

On the first day/ malcolm. The Easter Bunny Blues or All I Want for Xmas Is the Loop. Ebon Dooley. PoBA

On the first day good enough father and son. Target Practice. Donald Finkel. NePoEA-2

On the first day of school the teacher asked me. How a Girl Got Her Chinese Name. Nellie Wong. WPOW

On the first day of snow, my train. Letter VIII. Randall Swingler. WaP

On the first hour of my first day. The Beginner. Kipling. *Fr.* Epitaphs of the War, 1914–1918. FaBoTw

On the first morning of the moon, in land. The Good Beasts. Willis Barnstone. VWA

On the first of March. The Rooks. *Unknown*. GBP; OxNR

On the first of May. Mountain Greenery. Lorenz Hart. OBAL

On the first of Tishre I was walking the field in the evening breeze. Tashlich. Abba Kovner, *tr. by* Warren Bargad *and* Stanley F. Chyet. IP

On the first page of my dreambook. Empire of Dreams. Charles Simic. LCAP

On the Flesh of Christ. John William Corrington. MT

On the Flightiness of Thought. *Unknown, tr. fr. Irish by* Brendan Kennelly. TIRV

On the Fly-Leaf of Manon Lescaut. Walter Learned. AA

On the Fly-Leaf of Pound's Cantos. Basil Bunting. FaBoTw; NoAM; OxBTC

On the Following Work and Its Author. Jonathan Mitchell. SCAP

On the forgotten si-/ ding. Tank Town. John Atherton. NYBP

On the Founding of Liberia. Melvin B. Tolson. *Fr.* Libretto for the Republic of Liberia. UnPo

On the Four Georges. Walter Savage Landor. *See* George the First was always reckon'd.

On the fourteenth of February we sailed from the land. Bold *Princess Royal*. *Unknown*. OxBSS

On the Frequent Review of the Troops. "M." NOEC

On the Friendship betwixt Two Ladies. Edmund Waller. PeHV

On the front steps, our mothers wait for us, flushed. Playing Time. Theresa Pappas. TSL

On the Frozen Lake. Wordsworth. *Fr.* The Prelude [or, Growth of a Poet's Mind]: Childhood and School-Time. FaBoCh; GN

On the Fushimi hills. Shunzei, *tr. fr. Japanese by* Burton Watson. *Fr.* Thirty Tanka. FCEI

On the Gift of a Knife. Muireadhach Albanach O Dalaigh. NOIV

On the Glorious Assumption of Our Blessed Lady. Richard Crashaw. OBS

On the Gold Mines. B. W. Vilakazi. *See* Rumble on, machines of the gold mines.

On the Grand Canal. David Gascoyne. SeCePo

On the Grass. Miyoshi Tatsuji, *tr. fr. Japanese by* Geoffrey Bownas *and* Anthony Thwaite. PeBJV

On the Grasshopper and [the] Cricket. Keats. BoTP; EnRP; FaBoBe; GN; LiTB; NIP; OAEL-2; Son; TrGrPo; TTTS

On the grassy banks. Lambs at Play. Christina Rossetti. BoTP

On the Great Fog in London, December 1762. James Eyre Weeks. NOEC

On the great streams the ships may go. Robert Louis Stevenson. *Fr.* The Canoe Speaks. SD

On the green banks of Shannon, when Sheelah was nigh. The Irish Harper and His Dog. Thomas Campbell. CH

On the green lawn of a city park. The Will to Live. Mekeel McBride. MAYP; NAmP

On the green sheep-track, up the healthy hill. Samuel Taylor Coleridge. *Fr.* Fears in Solitude. OBNC

On the grey sand beside the shallow stream. Ego Dominus Tuus. W. B. Yeats. CMoP

On the ground are my sketches of the contours. The Painter in the Lion Cage. Betti Alver, *tr. by* Willis Barnstone *and* Felix Oinas. BoWoP

On the ground cedar and zelkova roots. Rest. Miyazawa Kenji, *tr. by* Hiroaki Sato. FCEI

On the ground there was a tree. The Tree in the Wood. *Unknown*. AmFP

On the Hall at Stowey. Charles Tomlinson. CMoP; PoE

On the Hall of Precious Virtue. Yang Shih-ch'i, *tr. fr. Chinese by* Jonathan Chaves. CoBLCP

On the Happy Corydon and Phyllis. *At. to* Sir Charles Sedley. BoLoP; CoMu; ErPo

On the Hazards of Smoking. Leah Goldberg, *tr. fr. Hebrew by* Bernhard Frank. MHeP

On the headland's grassed and sheltered side. Storm. Judith Wright. PoAu-2; WPE

On the Heart's Beginning to Cloud the Mind. Robert Frost. CMoP

On the heavily loaded bull's head. Issa, *tr. fr. Japanese by* Hiroaki Sato. *Fr.* Forty-four Hokku. FCEI

On the Heights. Lucius Harwood Foote. AA

On the Heights. W. K. Holmes. PoSH

On the Heights. Walter Savage Landor. FaBoEE

On the heights of great endeavor. Attainment. Madison Cawein. WGRP

On the Hellenics. Walter Savage Landor. *Fr.* The Hellenics. EnRP

On the High Cost of Dairy Products. James McIntyre. FiBHP

On the high hill pastures. Wild Thyme. Joyce Sambrook. BoTP

On the high plains. No Complaints. Anselm Hollo. UL

On the highway. Está Muy Caliente. George Bowering. MoCV

On the Hill. William Soutar. PoSH

On the Hill below the Lighthouse. James Dickey. NePoEA-2; SM

On the hill slope of Sada. *Unknown. Fr.* Manyo Shu. Ma

On the hill tops I visit the snares. *Unknown, tr. by* Margaret Orbell. PeNZ

On the hill's top we stood. Distances. Jeremy Kingston. NYBP

On the Historians Freeman and Stubbs. J. E. Thorold Rogers. FaBoEE

On the holy day of your going out to war. Mohodahi, *tr. by* Willis Barnstone. BoWoP

On the hottest day of the year I rode the mail. The Insult. Robert Layzer. NePoEA

On the Hudson. A. Leyeles, tr. fr. Yiddish by Benjamin and Barbara Harshav. AYP
On the hunting field. Hawking. Keiun, tr. by Steven D. Carter. WFTW
On the Ice Islands Seen Floating in the German Ocean. William Cowper. OAEL-1; PrIm
On the idle hill of summer. A. E. Housman. Fr. A Shropshire Lad, XXXV. MoBrPo; NOBE; OAEL-2; OBNC; OBWP; SoSe
On the Ile de Gorée, M. Diop elegant. Double Take at Relais de L'Espadon. Thadious M. Davis. BlSi
On the Impermanence of Life. Saigyo, tr. fr. Japanese by Burton Watson. Fr. Sixty-four Tanka. FCEI
On the Imprint of the First English Edition of "The Works of Max Beerbohm." Max Beerbohm. InPK
On the Inauguration of the Memorial Statue, sel. Edward Edwin Foot. "Long live our dear and noble Queen." FaBoCo
On the Ineffable Inspiration of the Holy Spirit. Catharina Regina von Greiffenberg, tr. fr. German by Michael Hamburger. PBWP
On the Infancy of Our Saviour. Francis Quarles. OBS; SeCePo
On the Irish Club. Swift. OBSV
On the Island. Dennis Brutus. WMBCH
On the Island. L. E. Sissman. NYBP
On the Island, finding you naked and pearled. That Summer's Shore. John Ciardi. ErPo
On the island of Skip-scoop-anellie. Skip-Scoop-Anellie. Tom Prideaux. FiBHP
On the Isle of Man shore, I carelessly wandered. The Isle of Man Shore. Unknown. AmFP
On the isle of Penang there is 'stablished a city. Regret. Malay Oral Tradition, tr. by R. J. Wilkinson. WTO
On the Jewish Day of Judgment in the Year 1942 (5703). Jozef Wittlin, tr. fr. Polish by Isaac Komem. VWA
On the Job. Felix Munso. SoTCo
On the Journey to Your Heart. Heidi Pataki, tr. fr. German by Beth Bjorklund. CoAuP
On the Jubilee of Queen Victoria. Tennyson. UnPo
On the Lacedaemonian Dead at Plataea. Simonides, tr. fr. Greek by Richard Eberhart. WaaP
On the Lake. Victoria Mary Sackville-West. OBMV
On the Lake Poets. Charles Townsend. FaBoEE
On the lake, the autumn wind blows blue ripples. As I Looked at a Lake, My Thoughts Turned to a Certain Friend. Chu Yün-ming, tr. by Jonathan Chaves. CoBLCP
On the Lakes of Ponchartrain. Unknown. AmFP
On the Lamented Death of Mrs. Throckmorton's Bullfinch. William Cowper. NOEC; PBBP; PPP
On the last day of the year we have so much to be thankful for. The Last Day of the Year; or, New Year's Eve. Mrs. Henry Linden. CBWP-4
On the last year's trip I enjoyed this place. On the Road through Chang-te. Sun Yün-feng, tr. by Kenneth Rexroth and Ling Chung. BoWoP; WPOW
On the Late Engagement in Carles Town River. Unknown. OxBSS
On the Late Mass of Curs in Piedmont. David Shevin. SoTCo
On the Late Massacre [or Massacher] in Piedmont [or Piemont]. Milton. AWP; GTBS; GTBS-P; HAP; HeIP; LiTB; NAEL-1; NOBE; NoP; OBWP; PoEL-3; PPP; Son; UnPo; WaaP; WeW
On the Late Metamorphosis of an Old Picture of Oliver Cromwell's. Unknown. APAS
On the Late S. T. Coleridge. Washington Allston. AA
On the Late Successful Expedition against Louisbourg. Francis Hopkinson. PAH
On the Latin Gerunds. Richard Porson. See When Dido found Aeneas would not come.
On the Lawn at Ira's. Gregory Orr. GeTw
On the Lawn at the Villa. Louis Simpson. CoAP; GOA; LCAP; OBAL; OxBC; PPP
On the leanest black bough, the blackbird rests. The Blackbird. Su Shao-lien, tr. by Dominic Cheung. IFON
On the leaves of the bamboo-grass. Unknown, tr. by Geoffrey Bownas and Anthony Thwaite. PeBJV
On the Life-Mask of Abraham Lincoln. Richard Watson Gilder. AA
On the Life of Man. Sir Walter Ralegh. See What Is Our Life? A Play of Passion.
On the Life of Trees. Ernst Jandl, tr. fr. German by Beth Bjorklund. CoAuP
On the lips a taste of tolling we are blind. (Poem) (Chicago) (The Were-Age). William Knott. EAS
On the long shore, lit by the moon. The Goose Fish. Howard Nemerov. CMoP; HeIP; LiTM; NePoEA; NIP; NoAM; NoP; PoE; SM
On the Lord Gen. Fairfax at the Siege of Colchester. Milton. OBS

On the Lord Mayor and Court of Aldermen, Presenting the Late King and Duke of York Each with a Copy of Their Freedoms. Andrew Marvell. CoMu; FaBoBa
On the Loss of the Royal George. William Cowper. EBEV; FiP; GN; NOBE; TrGrPo
On the Loss of U.S. Submarine S4, sel. Harry Clifford Canfield. "Entrapped inside a submarine." FaBoCo; FiBHP
On the low table by the bed. Mark Anderson. W. W. Gibson. MMA
On the Manner of Addressing Clouds. Wallace Stevens. See Gloomy grammarians in golden gowns.
On the mantelpiece. Studio Poem. Cilla McQueen. PeNZ
On the many-leafed bedscreens, gold flickers and fades. Tune: Deva-like Barbarian ("On the many-leafed bedscreens, gold flickers and fades"). Wen T'ing-yün, tr. by Burton Watson. CoBCP
On the March. Richard Aldington. BrPo
On the Margin, sel. David Wright.
   Anniversary Approaches, An; of the Birth of God. NAs
On the Margin Wrought. William, of Hawthornden Drummond. SeCePo
On the Marginal Way. Richard Wilbur. CoAP; NOBA
On the Margins of a Poem. Jiri Mordecai Langer, tr. fr. Hebrew by Gabriel Preil and Howard Schwartz. VWA
On the Marriage of a Virgin. Dylan Thomas. EnLoPo
On the Marriage of Art and Science. Sonya Dorman. BWV
On the Marriage of T. K. and C. C., the Morning Stormy. Thomas Carew. BoLoP
On the Marshes at Dawn. David Weiss. KS
On the Masquerades. Christopher Pitt. NOEC
On the matting. The People Went to War. Antonio Jacinto, tr. by Margaret Dickinson. WMBCH
On the Meadow. "Katri Vala," tr. fr. Finnish by Jaakko A. Ahokas. PBWP
On the Meatwheel. Dick Gallup. UL
On the Meetings of the Scotch Covenanters. Unknown. FaBoEE
On the Memorial building's. Under Cancer. John Hollander. CoAP
On the Memory of Mr. Edward King, Drowned in the Irish Seas. John Cleveland. OAEL-1; OBS; SeCP
On the Miracle of Loaves. Richard Crashaw. ACP; OxBSP
On the Miracle of Multiplied Loaves. Richard Crashaw. OxBSP
On the mirror two naked boys wearing enormous fins. On the Shore. Julian Przybos, tr. by Czeslaw Milosz. PwPP
On the miscanthus of my garden. Yakamochi. Fr. Manyo Shu. Ma
On the moor of Kasuga. Hitomaro. Fr. Manyo Shu. AWP
On the morning. The Idol in the Porch. José Juan Tablada, tr. by Samuel Beckett. MexPo
On the Morning of Christ's Nativity, sels. Milton. MeLP; NAs; NOCV; NoP; OBS; PoEL-3; WGRP
   (Ode on the Morning of Christ's Nativity.) GTBS; GTBS-P; LiTB
   "But peaceful was the night." FaBoCh
   Hymn on the Morning of Christ's Nativity [or On the Morning of Christ's Nativity]. FiP; NAEL-1; NOBE; OBEV
   Magi, The. Fr. 2 ll. ChTr
On the morning of the crowning we chorused our remission from school. Geoffrey Hill. Fr. Mercian Hymns, III. HAP
On the morning of the Käthe Kollwitz exhibit, a young man and woman. Museum. Robert Hass. NPGG
On the Morning of the Third Night above Nisqually. W. M. Ransom. CDW; NU
On the morning that a typhoon was blowing. Autumn. Nishiwaki Junzaburo, tr. by Hiroaki Sato. FCEI
On the most westerly Blasket. The Given Note. Seamus Heaney. FaBCIP
On the Motor Bus. Alfred Denis Godley. See What is this that roareth thus?
On the mountain. Saito Mokichi, tr. fr. Japanese by Geoffrey Bownas and Anthony Thwaite. PeBJV
On the Mountain. Neidhart von Reuental, tr. fr. German by Jethro Bithell. AWP
On the Mountain. Ruth Stone. BoWoP
On the mountain is the thorn-elm. Unknown, tr. by Arthur Waley. BoS
On the mountain of Mifune. Kanamura. Fr. Manyo Shu. Ma
On the mountain, old trees, still green in autumn. Inscribed on a Painting ("On the mountain, old trees, still green in autumn"). T'ang Yin, tr. by Jonathan Chaves. CoBLCP
On the mountain peak, called "Going-to-the-Sun." The Apple-Barrel of Johnny Appleseed. Vachel Lindsay. AmFN; OxBA
On the mountain's blind and rugged ridge. The Crag. Joaquín Arcadio Pagaza, tr. by Samuel Beckett. MexPo
On the mountains of Judea. The Expectation. Frederick William Faber. Fr. Our Lady's Expectation. ACP
On the Move. Thom Gunn. CMoP; HAP; LiTM; NePoEA-2; NoP; OAEL-2; OxBTC; PoE; PPP; TwCP

On the Murder of Sir Edmund Berry Godfrey. *Unknown.* APAS
On the mute walls of empty shops. Perets Markish, *tr. by* Leonard Wolf. PeBMYV
On the Naming Day. Jewel C. Latimore. CNA
On the Nativity of Our Saviour. Thomas Philipott. JCP
On the navel of the Boer's domain. Lesotho. B. Makalo Khaketla, *tr. by* Dan Kunene *and* Jack Cope. PeSA
On the Needle of a Sundial. Francis Quarles. OBS; TrGrPo
On the New Forcers of Conscience Under the Long Parliment. Milton. FaBoPV; NAEL-1; Son
On the New Jersey shore he met her. Blue Springs, Georgia. Ree Young. GOYP
On the New Laureate. *Unknown.* FaBoCo
On the New Road. Lyn Lifshin. NeAC
On the new sand. What Her Girl Friend Said, the Lover within Earshot, behind a Fence. Uloccanar, *tr. by* A. K. Ramanujan. PLW
On the Night. Ivor Gurney. OxBSP
On the Night in Question. Patricia Goedicke. TAP
On the night of the Belgian surrender the moon rose. The Moon and the Night and the Men. John Berryman. CoAP; VGW; WaP
On the Night of the Fourteenth of the Eleventh Month Setting Out for Nanchang by Boat on a Moonlit Night. Ch'en San-li, *tr. fr. Chinese by* Irving Lo. WFTU
On the Night of the Sixteenth of the Eighth Month. Liu E, *tr. fr. Chinese by* Jonathan Chaves. CoBLCP
On the night road from El Rama the cows. Second Poem from Nicaragua Libre: War Zone. June Jordan. NoAM
On the night when the rain beats. Okura. *Fr.* Manyo Shu. Ma
On the Ning Nang Nong. Spike Milligan. RHPC
On the Ninth Day of the Month, Thinking of Ch'eng, *sel.* Wu Chia-chi, *tr. fr. Chinese by* John E. Wills, Jr..
  "Itinerant trade is the business of petty men." *Fr.* II. WFTU
On the Ninth, outside Feng-yi Gate, I Passed by P'ei-ts'un's Country House. Chu Hsiao-tsang, *tr. fr. Chinese by* Li Chi *and* Michael Patrick O'Connor. WFTU
On the North Shore a reptile lay asleep. The Precambrian [*or* Pre-Cambrian] Shield. E. J. Pratt. *Fr.* Towards the Last Spike. MoCV; NOBC; NoBC; OBCV
On the North Side of Suilven. Norman MacCaig. NPo
On the Occident she shed her light. Beauty on a Western Balcony. Luis de Sandoval y Zapata, *tr. by* Samuel Beckett. MexPo
On the Ocean Floor. "Hugh MacDiarmid." FaBoMo; HAP
On the ocean that hollows the rocks where ye dwell. O Brazil, the Isle of the Blest. Gerald Griffin. ACP
  (Hy-Brasail—the Isle of the Blest.) BLPA
On the ocean where no islands are in sight. *Unknown. Fr.* Manyo Shu. Ma
On the one side. Pimville Station. Sipho Sepamla. WMBCH
On the one-ton temple bell. Buson. InPK
On the Oregon Coast. Galway Kinnell. NoAM
On the Origin of Evil. John Byrom. NOEC
On the Other Side. Czeslaw Milosz, *tr. fr. Polish by* Jan Darowski. OBD
On the other side. Ohioan Pastoral. James Wright. LCAP
On the other side/ of my world. To the Man I Live With. Ann Menebroker. IHMS
On the other side of the arc-light-level window. The Second Story. T. R. Hummer. KS; NAmP
On the Other Side of the Poem. Rokhl Korn, *tr. fr. Yiddish by* Seymour Levitan. PeBMYV
On the other side of the world I heard. Elegy for a Schoolmate. Vincent O'Sullivan. ATNZ; PeNZ
On the outer Barcoo where the churches are few. A Bush Christening. A. B. Paterson. PoAu-1
On the outermost far-flung ridge of ice and snow. Inspiration. W. W. Gibson. WGRP
On the outside grows the furside. The Sleeping-bag. Herbert George Ponting. CenHV
On the Outskirts of Antioch. Constantine P. Cavafy, *tr. fr. Greek by* Edmund Keeley *and* Philip Sherrard. VMG
On the Oxford Book of Victorian Verse. "Hugh MacDiarmid." MoBrPo
On the Oxford Carrier. Milton. NA
On the Painter Val Prinsep. Dante Gabriel Rossetti. FaBoEE
On the Painting "Joys of Village Life," *sel.* Yün Shou-p'ing, *tr. fr. Chinese by* Jonathan Chaves.
  "For a hundred miles the west wind carries the fragrance of millet." CoBLCP
On the Painting "Mist over Ten Thousand Mountains," *sels.* Yün Shou-p'ing, *tr. fr. Chinese by* Jonathan Chaves. CoBLCP
  "I listen to a waterfall."
  "Nature's workings made this gentle place."

On the Path. A. L. Strauss, *tr. fr. Hebrew by* Robert Friend. VWA
On the path. Under the Maud Moon. Galway Kinnell. CAPP; NNaP
On the path winding. The Path among the Stones. Galway Kinnell. NNaP; NOBA; Prf
On the pathway mica glints. Water and Worship: An Open-Air Service on the Gatineau River. Margaret Avison. HAP
On the peak of Mimiga of fair Yoshinu. Emperor Temmu. *Fr.* Manyo Shu. Ma
On the peak of Ogura above the rapids. Mushimaro. *Fr.* Manyo Shu. Ma
On the pennants of blue are bold characters. Reviewing the Troops at Kuei-lin. Yang Chi, *tr. by* Jonathan Chaves. CoBLCP
On the phonograph, the voice. Reunion. Carolyn Forché. MAYP; NoAM
On the Photograph of a Man I Never Saw. Hyam Plutzik. VWA
On the Picture of a Child. Henrietta Cordelia Ray. CBWP-3
On the pilgrimage to Ise. *Unknown, tr. fr. Japanese by* Geoffrey Bownas *and* Anthony Thwaite. PeBJV
On the Pilgrim's Way in Kent, as It Leads to the Coldrum Stones. Asphodel. BrRo
On the plain that town flat like an iron sheet. A Naked Town. Zbigniew Herbert, *tr. by* Czeslaw Milosz. PwPP
On the Plains. Francis Brooks. *Fr.* lutaglios. AA
On the Planet of Flies. Christian Morgenstern, *tr. fr. German by* Geoffrey Grigson. FaBoNo
On the plate the pears. The Pears. Ferreira Gullar, *tr. by* William Jay Smith. CT
On the Plough-Man. Francis Quarles. OBS
On the Poet O'Shaughnessy. Dante Gabriel Rossetti. ChTr
On the Poet's Leer. David Ray. NePoEA-2
On the Pole. Uri Zvi Greenberg, *tr. fr. Hebrew by* Robert Mezey *and* Ben Zion Gold. VWA
On the pond, frost floats like rice paper. October Morning Walk. Anita Endrezze-Danielson. GOS
On the pool of the River of Natsumi. Prince Yuhara. *Fr.* Manyo Shu. Ma
On the poplars and oaks. The Bard's Song. Sir Robert Stapylton. SeCePo
On the Porch at the Frost Place, Franconia, NH. William Matthews. MAYP
On the Portrait of a Woman about to Be Hanged. Thomas Hardy. CMoP
On the Princess Mary. John Heywood. *See* Give place, you ladies, and be gone.
On the Proposal to Erect a Monument in England to Lord Byron. Emma Lazarus. AA
On the Prorogation. *Unknown.* APAS
On the Prospect of Planting Arts and Learning in America. George Berkeley. AiP; FaFP; NOEC; TrGrPo
On the prow. The Landing. Daniel Halpern. AmPA
On the quays of Papeete, the dawdling white-ducked colonists. Gauguin. Derek Walcott. NoAM
On the Queen's Return from the Low Countries. William Cartwright. MePo; OBEV
On the rapids of the St. Lawrence. Henrietta Cordelia Ray. CBWP-3
On the Receipt of My Mother's Picture out of Norfolk [the Gift of My Cousin Ann Bodham], *sel.* William Cowper. EnRP; NOEC
  (Lines on Receiving My Mother's Picture Out of Norfolk.) CH; OHIP
  "Oh that those lips had language! Life has pass'd." FiP
On the Reed of Our Lord's Passion. William Alabaster. PoEL-2
On the refrigerator a gash. The Oven Loves the TV Set. Heather McHugh. NAmP
On the Relative Merit of Friend and Foe, Being Dead. Donald Thompson. WaP
On the Religion of Nature. Philip Freneau. AmPP; NAAL-1
On the Relinquishment of a Title. Geoffrey Grigson. FaBoEE
On the Resurrection of Christ. William Dunbar. *See* Done Is a Battle.
On the Reverend Jonathan Doe. *Unknown.* ChTr; FaBoEE
On the Ridgeway. Andrew Young. FaBoPP
On the River. William Vaughn Moody. AnAmPo
On the River. Tu Fu, *tr. fr. Chinese by* Burton Watson. CoBCP
On the River, *sel.* Wang Shih-chen, *tr. fr. Chinese by* Daniel Bryant.
  "And what of the journey where the head of Wu meets the tail of Ch'u?" WFTU
On the river bank. River Messages. Wen T'ing-yün, *tr. by* Lois Fusek. ATF
On the river late in spring, the cherry-apple is fragrant. Immortal at the River. Ho Ning, *tr. by* Lois Fusek. ATF
On the River Lookout. Itamar Ya'oz-kest, *tr. fr. Hebrew by* Bernhard Frank. MHeP

On the river, the spring tides are calm. Inscribed on an Album Leaf Painted by Dr. Lin. Pien Kung, *tr. by* Jonathan Chaves. CoBLCP
On the road. Driving to the Beach. Joanna Cole. RHPC
On the Road. Tudor Jenks. NA
On the Road. Judah Leib Teller, *tr. fr. Yiddish by* Benjamin *and* Barbara Harshav. AYP
On the Road at Dusk. Emperor Hanazono, *tr. fr. Japanese by* Steven D. Carter. WFTW
On the Road at Night There Stands the Man. Dahlia Ravikovich, *tr. fr. Hebrew by* Chana Bloch. WPOW
On the road he sails like a ship. Dog On the Road. Ory Bernstein, *tr. by* Bernhard Frank. MHeP
On the Road Home. Wallace Stevens. NU
On the road I meet descendants of the Korean prisoners. Rai San'yo, *tr. fr. Chinese by* Burton Watson. *Fr.* Songs of Satsuma, II. JLIC-2
On the Road I Met a White-Haired Old Man. Michizane, *tr. fr. Chinese by* Burton Watson. JLIC-1
On the road over head. An Old Waterford Woman. Mary Devenport O'Neill. NeIP
On the road, the lonely road. The Stab. William Wallace Harney. AA
On the Road There Stands a Tree. Itzig Manger, *tr. fr. Yiddish by* Stephen Griffin. VWA
On the Road through Chang-te. Sun Yün-feng, *tr. fr. Chinese by* Kenneth Rexroth *and* Ling Chung. BoWoP; WPOW
On the road through the hills I thought I heard it. Half-heard. Christopher Koch. PoAu-2
On the Road through the Wu-i Mountains. Hsü Wei, *tr. fr. Chinese by* Jonathan Chaves. CoBLCP
On the Road to An-hsi. Hung Liang-chi, *tr. fr. Chinese by* Irving Lo. WFTU
On the Road to California; or, The Buffalo Bullfight. *Unknown.* AmFP
On the Road to Chorrera. Arlo Bates. AA
On the Road to Gundagai. *Unknown.* PoAu-1
On the Road to Hsin-ch'eng. Su Tung-p'o, *tr. fr. Chinese by* Burton Watson. CoBCP
On the Road to Pyongyang—An Improvisation. Liu E, *tr. fr. Chinese by* Jonathan Chaves. CoBLCP
On the Road to San Romano. André Breton, *tr. fr. French by* Charles Simic *and* Michael Benedikt. POS; RHTwFP
On the Road to Takaya. Kan Sazan, *tr. fr. Chinese by* Burton Watson. JLIC-2
On the Road to Tang Lake. P'eng Sun-yü, *tr. fr. Chinese by* William H. Nienhauser, Jr. WFTU
On the road to the bay was a lake of rushes. The Bay. James Keir Baxter. ATNZ; PeNZ
On the road to the palace. Hitomaro. *Fr.* Manyo Shu. PeBJV
On the Road to the Sea. Charlotte Mew. BrRo; FaBoWP; PeHV
On the Road to Vicenza. Ralph Gustafson. CaP
On the road to Yamashiro. *Unknown.* *Fr.* Manyo Shu. PeBJV
On the road with not a soul. Saigyo, *tr. fr. Japanese by* Burton Watson. *Fr.* Sixty-four Tanka. FCEI
On the roads at night I saw the glitter of eyes. Eyes of Night-Time. Muriel Rukeyser. BoWoP
On the Roads of Siberia. H. Leivick, *tr. fr. Yiddish.* AYP, *tr. by* Benjamin *and* Barbara Harshav; PeBMYV, *tr. by* Cynthia Ozick
On the roads of Yamashiro. *Unknown.* *Fr.* Manyo Shu. FCEI
On the rock overlapping the huddled rock-gorge. The Detail. Cid Corman. PCP
On the roof of a coach at night I lie. Moon Solo. Jules Laforgue, *tr. by* William Jay Smith. CT
On the Rouge. Raymond Souster. NOBC
On the rough diamond. Sign for My Father, Who Stressed the Bunt. David Bottoms. MAYP; MT
On the Ruins of a Country Inn. Philip Freneau. *See* Where now those mingled ruins lie.
On the Russian Persecution of the Jews. Swinburne. Son
On the Sabbath-day. Barbara. Alexander Smith. GoTS
On the salt water streets. Venice Recalled. Bruce Boyd. NeAP
On the Same. Roy Campbell. OxBTC
On the same. Milton. *See* Book was writ of late called Tetrachordon, A.
On the sand of a sandhill. Ishikawa Takuboku, *tr. fr. Japanese by* Hiroaki Sato. *Fr.* Forty-seven Tanka in Three Lines. FCEI
On the school platform, draping the folding seats. Political Meeting. A. M. Klein. MoCV; OBCV
On the Sea. Keats. EnRP; FF; LiTB; NoP; OAEL-2; TEP; TrGrPo
On the sea and at the Hogue, sixteen hundred ninety-two. Hervé Riel. Robert Browning. BeLS; FaBoBe; GN; MOS; OnMSP
On the sea-bed. Wakayama Bokusui, *tr. by* Geoffrey Bownas *and* Anthony Thwaite. PeBJV
On the sea god's plain the waves and the sky merge. Teika, *tr. fr. Japanese by* Hiroaki Sato. *Fr.* Eighty-four Tanka. FCEI

On the sea of heaven the waves of cloud arise. Hitomaro. *Fr.* Manyo Shu. Ma
On the Sea Wall. C. Day Lewis. SeCePo
On the sea's face, sharks. Sharks. Kaneko Mitsuharu, *tr. by* Hiroaki Sato. FCEI
On the second of August, eighteen hundred and one. Second of August. *Unknown.* OxBSS
On the second of October, a Monday at noon. Walter Lesly. *Unknown.* ESPB
On the secret map the assassins. Rivers and Mountains. John Ashbery. CoAP; NoAM; NOBA
On the Sentence Passed by the House of Lords on Dr. Sacheverell. *Unknown.* APAS
On the Setting Up of Mr. Butler's Monument in Westminster Abbey. Samuel Wesley. InvP; NBLV; NOEC; OBD; OxBSP
On the Seventh Anniversary of the Death of My Father. Robert Pack. NePoEA
On the seventh day the storm lay dead. The Dyke-Builder. Henry Treece. LiTB; WaP
On the sheep-cropped summit, under hot sun. Cat and Mouse. Ted Hughes. EaLo; OxBSP
On the sheet, on your side. Imitation of Water. João Cabral de Melo Neto, *tr. by* Ashley Brown. ATCBP
On the Shore. Aila Meriluoto, *tr. fr. Finnish by* Aili Jarvenpa. SOP
On the Shore. Julian Przybos, *tr. fr. Polish by* Czeslaw Milosz. PwPP
On the shore of Nawa. *Unknown.* *Fr.* Manyo Shu.
On the shore of the sidewalks they walk apart with downcast eyes. People Who Talk to Themselves. Berysh Vaynshteyn, *tr. fr. Yiddish by* Benjamin *and* Barbara Harshav. *Fr.* New York Everywhere. AYP
On the shores of the Nile. All the Same. Iftiqar Arif, *tr. by* Mahmood Jamal. PBMUP
On the Sicilian strand a hare well wrought. Decimus Magnus Ausonius, *tr. fr. Latin by* Richard Lovelace. OBVE
On the side of the road. Song. Edmond Jabès, *tr. by* Anthony Rudolf. VWA
On the Sidelines. Lillian Morrison. TSM
On the sidewalk/ waiting. The Way Downtown. Edward L. Hooper. TSM
On the "Sievering" Tram. Bernard Spencer. NAs
On the sightless seas of ether. Mikhail Yurevich Lermontov, *tr. fr. Russian by* Babette Deutsch *and* Avrahm Yarmolinsky. *Fr.* The Daemon. AWP
On the signboard. Climbing the Mountain. Chiang Hsun, *tr. by* Dominic Cheung. IFON
On the Site of a Mulberry-Tree Planted by William Shakespeare, Felled by the Rev. F. Gastrell. Dante Gabriel Rossetti. TW
On the Sixteenth Day I Visit the Temple Again. Pien Kung, *tr. fr. Chinese by* Jonathan Chaves. CoBLCP
On the sixteenth day of September, nineteen twenty-eight. The West Palm Beach Storm. *Unknown.* AmFP
On the Sixth Floor. Bartolo Cattafi, *tr. fr. Italian by* Lawrence R. Smith. NItP
On the Skeleton of a Hound. James Wright. LiTM; NePoEA
On the skim of the wharf where the planks split. Bucket of Sea-Serpents. Howard Ant. GoYe
On the Slaughter. Hayyim Nahman Bialik, *tr. fr. Hebrew by* Bernhard Frank. MHeP
On the Slope of the Desolate River. Rabindranath Tagore. *Fr.* Gitanjali, LXIV. OBMV
On the smooth brow and clustering hair. Walter Savage Landor. GBL
On the Snake. *Unknown.* PAH
On the snow. Kawabata Bosha, *tr. by* Geoffrey Bownas *and* Anthony Thwaite. PeBJV
On the Snuff of a Candle. Sir Walter Ralegh. FaBoEE; OBD; SiPS
On the Solitary Fells around Hawkshead. Wordsworth. *See* Prelude [or, Growth of a Poet's Mind], The: Childhood and School-Time.
On the Sonnet. Keats. NIP; NoP; OAEL-2
On the South Coast of Cornwall. John Gray. NOBVV
On the South Downs. Sara Teasdale. MoAmPo
On the southern hills grows the nutgrass. *Unknown, tr. by* Arthur Waley. BoS
On the southwest side of Capri. The Nude Swim. Anne Sexton. ASP; WPE
On the Spartan Dead at Thermopylae. Simonides. WeW
On the Speed of Sight. Raymond DiZazzo. BWV
On the spring river, you depart. Tsung Ch'en, *tr. fr. Chinese by* Jonathan Chaves. *Fr.* Song of Chiang-nan. CoBLCP
On the Spur of the Moment. Tu Fu, *tr. fr. Chinese by* Burton Watson. CoBCP
On the stage I stumbled. Indian Blood. Mary TallMountain. STE

On the stage, mirrored many times. The Stripper. Anita Endrezze Probst. CDW

On the stairway fragrance assails the bosom. A Spring Song of Tzu-yeh. Hsiao Yen, *tr. by* Jan W. Walls. LLLT

On the State of Englishness (A Fairy Tale). Deborah Levy. DT

On the steps of the bright madhouse. In the Fleeting Hand of Time. Gregory Corso. NAs

On the steps of the Pentagon I tucked my skull. Revised Notes for a Sonnet. Edward Pygge. BXAP

On the stiff twig up there. Black Rook in Rainy Weather. Sylvia Plath. LiTM; NAAL-2; NePoEA-2; NIP; SM

On the stolen. Takahama Kyoshi, *tr. by* Geoffrey Bownas *and* Anthony Thwaite. PeBJV

On the stone terrace, underneath the shade. The Summer Landscape; or, The Dragon's Teeth. Rolfe Humphries. NYBP

On the storm's freezing blast. Kyogoku Tamekane, *tr. fr. Japanese by* Burton Watson. *Fr.* Twenty-three Tanka. FCEI

On the straw roof grass grows. Ozaki Hosai, *tr. fr. Japanese by* Hiroaki Sato. *Fr.* One Hundred Haiku in Free Form. FCEI

On the Street. C. P. Cavafy, *tr. fr. Greek by* Rae Dalven. BoLoP

On the street/ Slung on his shoulder. The Shovel Man. Carl Sandburg. HAP

On the street, the sun. Bent. Martin Carter. PBCV

On the *Struma* Massacre. Ralph Gustafson. OBCV

On the Subject of Waves. Eldon Grier. MoCV

On the suburban street, guarded by patient trees. I Did Not Know the Truth of Growing Trees. Delmore Schwartz. LiTM

On the Suicide of the Refugee W. B. Bertolt Brecht, *tr. fr. German by* John Willett. OBD

On the summer road that ran by our front porch. Lizards and Snakes. Anthony Hecht. FaBoMo; TwCP

On the Sun Coming Out in the Afternoon. Henry David Thoreau. OxBSP; PoEL-4

On the Supposed Author of a Late Poem "In Defense of Satire." John Wilmont, 2nd Earl of Rochester. APAS

On the Swag. R. A. K. Mason. ATNZ; PeNZ

On the Symbolic Consideration of Hands and the Significance of Death. Miller Williams. InPK

On the table/ is a gray cloth. Some Things. Gerhard Rühm, *tr. by* Beth Bjorklund. CoAuP

On the table: fresh bread, swollen, fat. Evening Bread. Jacob Glatstein. PeBMYV, *tr. by* Cynthia Ozick; VWA, *tr. by* David G. Roskies *and* Hillel Schwartz
("On the table, a fresh bread, pregnant with promise.") AYP, *tr. by* Benjamin *and* Barbara Harshav

On the tall hill. What She Said to Her Girl Friend ("On the tall hill"). Paranar, *tr. by* A. K. Ramanujan. PLW

On the Tamashima River. *Unknown.* *Fr.* Manyo Shu. Ma

On the taut shore, the bald skull. Resurrection. Robert Pack. NePoEA-2

On the Telescopic Moon. John Swanwick Drennan. BIrV

On the temple bell. Buson, *tr. fr. Japanese by* Kenneth Koch *and* Harold Henderson. TTTS

On the Tennis Court at Night. Galway Kinnell. TSL

On the tenth day of December. Musselburgh Field. *Unknown.* ESPB

On the Tercentenary of Milton's Death. Gavin Ewart. OxBC

On the third day rose Arp. Resurrection of Arp. A. J. M. Smith. MoCV; NOBC

On the third finger of my left hand. Ceremony. William Stafford. LCAP

On the third planet too, life is found. Excerpt from a Report to the Galactic Council. Robert Conquest. OxBC

On the Thirteenth Day of Christmas. Charles Causley. OBCP

On the 31st day of the month of August 1914. The Little Car. Guillaume Apollinaire. POS, *tr. by* Michael Benedikt; SOTW, *tr. by* Ron Padgett *and others*

On the Threshold. Karl Kraus, *tr. fr. German by* Albert Bloch. TrJP

On the Threshold. Amy Levy. NOBVV

On the Threshold. *Unknown.* BLPA

On the threshold of heaven, the figures in the street. To an Old Philosopher in Rome. Wallace Stevens. MoP; NoAM; NOBA

On the tidal mud, just before sunset. Daybreak. Galway Kinnell. LCAP

On the Tomb of Kalamachius, the Jogger. Elliot Richman. TSL

On the top of the Crumpetty Tree. The Quangle Wangle's Hat. Edward Lear. AmMo; EBEV; ILY; OnUR

On the Tower. Annette von Droste-Hülshoff, *tr. fr. German.* DMG, *by* Ruth Angress; PBWP, *by* James Edward Tobin; WPON, *by* James Edward Tobin.

On the track, on the track again, on the track. George Seferis, *tr. fr. Greek by* Edmund Keeley *and* Philip Sherrard. *Fr.* Mythistorima, XVI. VMG

On the train/ old ladies playing football. Going Uptown to Visit Miriam. Victor Hernandez Cruz. FF; MAT

On the Translation of Anacreon. Horace Walpole. FaBoEE

On the tree, a peal. Jacaranda. Myra Cohn Livingston. TSS

On the Triumph of Rationalism. Alfred Ainger. FaBoCo

On the Twentieth Day. Ni Tsan, *tr. fr. Chinese by* Jonathan Chaves. CoBLCP

On the 25th Anniversary of the Liberation of Auschwitz. Eli W. Mandel. NOBC

On the Twenty-fifth of July. David Cornel DeJong. NYBP

On the Twenty-First Day of the Fifth Month, I Reached Home. Yüan Mei, *tr. fr. Chinese by* Jonathan Chaves. CoBLCP

On the Twenty-first of the Seventh Month of the Seventh Year of Genroku, at Bokusetsu's Hut. Basho, *tr. fr. Japanese by* Burton Watson. *Fr.* Seventy-six Hokku. FCEI

On the Twenty-fourth: Improvisations, *sels.* Liu E, *tr. fr. Chinese by* Jonathan Chaves. CoBLCP
"Academics? Politics? I've nothing to do with them!"
"Beautiful women—we've vowed to be lovers!"

On the Twenty-Second Night of the Seventh Month, Facing the Moon at Listening-to-the-Water Studio. Ch'en Pao-shen, *tr. fr. Chinese by* Irving Lo. WFTU

On the twenty-sixth of August, our fatal moss gave way. The Donibristle Moss Moran Disaster. *Unknown.* WTO

On the 26th of October, in the evening. Winter Journey. Stanislaw Wygodski, *tr. by* Isaac Komem. VWA

On the unbreathing sides of hills. Squatter's Children. Elizabeth Bishop. NoP

On the under-leaves. *Unknown, tr. by* Geoffrey Bownas *and* Anthony Thwaite. PeBJV

On the Uniformity and Perfection of Nature. Philip Freneau. AmPP

On the University Carrier (Who Sickn'd in the Time of His Vacancy). Milton. EBEV; FaBoCh; FaBoEE; MePo; PrIm; SaC

On the University of Cambridge's Burning the Duke of Monmouth's Picture. George Stepney. APAS

On the Unusual Cold and Rainie Weather in the Summer, 1648. Robert Heath. OBS

On the up-platform at Morpeth station. The Complaint of the Morpethshire Farmer. Basil Bunting. CTC

On the Upside. G. E. Murray. MAYP

On the Use of Jayshus. Oliver St. John Gogarty. FaBoEE

On the Use of New and Old Words in Poetry. Anna Seward. Son

On the Vanity of Earthly Greatness. Arthur Guiterman. BXAP; HeIP; HoPM; OBCA; TrJP

On the Vanity of Man's Life. *Unknown.* OBSC

On the vast lake of Omi. Empress Yamato-hime. *Fr.* Manyo Shu. Ma

On the Verge. William Winter. AA

On the violets of the field. Natsume Seibi, *tr. fr. Japanese by* Hiroaki Sato. *Fr.* Twenty-seven Hokku. FCEI

On the "Vita Nuova" of Dante. Dante Gabriel Rossetti

On the volcanic hill. Precarious Ground. Leah Bodine Drake. GoYe

On the Vowels—a Riddle. Swift. FaBoUs; OnYI

On the Wall. Immanuel di Roma, *tr. fr. Hebrew by* Solomon Solis-Cohen. TrJP

On the wall there is star-thistle. *Unknown, tr. by* Arthur Waley. BoS

On the Wallowy. Laura Chester. NPGG

On the wan sea-strand. Evening Twilight. Heine, *tr. fr. German by* John Todhunter. *Fr.* The North Sea. AWP

On the warm July river. Inner Tube. Michael Ondaatje. NoAM

On the water, cork floats. Concerning Cork. Alan Bold. NPo

On the water the first wind. Spring. W. S. Merwin. NaP

On the Watergate Women. Robin Morgan. GLP

On the Way. Jeannie Ebner, *tr. fr. German by* Beth Bjorklund. CoAuP

On the Way. Mordechai Husid, *tr. fr. Yiddish by* Seymour Mayne *and* Rivka Augenfeld. VWA

On the way, a whim, I changed my mind. Ishikawa Takuboku, *tr. fr. Japanese by* Hiroaki Sato. *Fr.* Forty-seven Tanka in Three Lines. FCEI

On the Way Back. A. Leyeles, *tr. fr. Yiddish by* Benjamin *and* Barbara Harshav. AYP

On the way down. The Way Down. Philip Levine. NOBA

On the Way to Dakar. Blaise Cendrars, *tr. fr. French by* John Dos Passos. RHTwFP

On the Way to Language. Michael Palmer. LP; NPGG

On the Way to Pa-ling. Yüan Mei, *tr. fr. Chinese by* Jonathan Chaves. CoBLCP

On the way to the lustrous shrine. *Unknown.* *Fr.* Manyo Shu. FCEI

On the Way to the Mission. Duncan Campbell Scott. CaP; NOBC

On the way up from Sheet I met some children. To Edward Thomas. Alun Lewis. WaP

On the Welsh Marches. Walter Stone. NYBP

On the wet sand the queen emerged from forest. Theseus: A Trilogy. Yvor Winters. NOBA

On the white throat of the useless passion. Ad Finem. Ella Wheeler Wilcox. BLPA; FPL

On the Wide Heath. Edna St. Vincent Millay. CMoP; WPE

On the wide level of a mountain's head. Time, Real and Imaginary. Samuel Taylor Coleridge. EnRP; NOBE; OBEV; OxBSP

On the Wide Stairs. Yehuda Amichai, tr. fr. Hebrew by Laya Firestone and Howard Schwartz. VWA

On the wind, a drifting echo. Christmas Night. Lawrence Sail. OBCP

On the wind of January. Unknown. BoTP

On the World. Francis Quarles. HAP

On the Wounds of Our Crucified Lord. Richard Crashaw. NAEL-1

On the Young Statesmen. Charles Sackville. APAS

On thee thou must take a long journey. Unknown. Fr. Everyman. OBD

On Their Appointed Rounds. Unknown. FaPON

On their hides one can still see the calm of sunny mountains. Sheep in New York. Berysh Vaynshteyn, tr. fr. Yiddish by Benjamin and Barbara Harshav. Fr. New York Everywhere. AYP

On these ancient discs, smooth-backed, severe. Old Gramophone Records. James Kirkup. NYBP

On these moth-eaten. Trinità dei Monti. Nelo Risi, tr. by Lawrence R. Smith. NItP

On these occasions, the feelings surprise. Father and Son. Delmore Schwartz. DiL; LiTA

On these white cliffs, that calm above the flood. At Dover Cliffs. William Lisle Bowles. EnRP

On things asleep, no balm. North American Sequence. Theodore Roethke. NaP

On Things Seen, sel. Tsung Ch'en, tr. fr. Chinese by Jonathan Chaves. "Rebels' cavalry are everywhere, The." CoBLCP

On Third Street there's a naked spot. The Ballad of Mary Baldwin. Stephen Sandy. MAT

On this bald hill the new year hones its edge. Parliament Hill Fields. Sylvia Plath. HCAP

On This Day. M. B. Goffstein. NTCP

On This Day I Complete My Fortieth Year. Peter Porter. NAs

On This Day I Complete My Thirty-sixth Year. Byron. EnRP; FiP; NAs; NoP; OAEL-2; OBWP; PoE

On this day man's disgust is known. On Shooting Particles beyond the World. Richard Eberhart. LiTA; LiTM; TW

On this day of my birth, I see no visitors. The Evening of My Birthday. Yang Shih-ch'i, tr. by Jonathan Chaves. CoBLCP

On this feast day, oh, cursèd day and hour! Love at First Sight. Christopher Marlowe. Fr. Hero and Leander, First Sestiad. NOBE

On this final day. The End of the Third Lunar Month. Kaneyoshi, tr. by Steven D. Carter. WFTW

On this floor. Floor: O. Stephen Vincent. Fr. Elevator Landscapes. NeAC

On this gay and slender tune. Arnaut Daniel, tr. by Paul Blackburn. Pro

On this heavenly molehill. Gaiety and Good Heart. Otto Orban, tr. by Edwin Morgan. MHuP

On this hill crossed. Galway Kinnell. NaP

On this hotel, their rumpled royalties. The West Forties: Morning, Noon, and Night. L. E. Sissman. CoAP; NYBP

On This Island. W. H. Auden. CMoP; NAEL-2; PoE

On this lone Isle, whose rugged rocks affright. Sonnet: Suppos'd to Be Written at Lemnos. Thomas Russell. NOEC

On this map white. A state thick as a fist. A Map of Montana in Italy. Richard Hugo. LCAP

On this moss-fringed isle. Providential. Sándor Weöres, tr. by Jascha Kessler. FOC

On This My Sick-Bed Beats the World. Jiri Wolker, tr. fr. Czech by Karl W. Deutsch. WaaP

On this New Year's Day. Fujii Moroai. Fr. Manyo Shu. Ma

On this piece of earth I seize a knife. Conversation. Gyorgy Raba, tr. by Jascha Kessler. VWA

On this side of the tapestry. The Tapestry. Howard Nemerov. Prf

On this spring night. Fujiwara no Teika, tr. by Steven D. Carter. WFTW

On this tree thrown up. Spindrift. Galway Kinnell. NaP; NYBP

On this trip I couldn't come with offerings. Teika, tr. fr. Japanese by Hiroaki Sato. Fr. A Compendium of Good Tanka. FCEI

On this winter night. Izumi Shikibu, tr. by Willis Barnstone. BoWoP

On this wondrous sea. Eternity. Emily Dickinson. AA

On Thomas Moore's Poems. Unknown. FaBoCo; FiBHP

On Thomas, Second Earl of Onslow. Unknown. FaBoCo

On Those That Deserve It. Francis Quarles. MePo; NOCV; OBS

On Those That Hated The Playboy of the Western World. W. B. Yeats. NOIV

On thrones from China to Peru. A Model for the Laureate. W. B. Yeats. CMoP

On thy fair bosom, silver lake. To Senaca Lake. James Gates Percival. BoTP

On Time. Lindolf Bell, tr. fr. Portuguese by William Jay Smith. CT

On Time. Richard Hughes. MoBrPo

On Time. Milton. BLPL; LiTB; MePo; OBEV; OBS

On Tintock-Tap there is a mist. Tintock. Unknown. GBP

On to Richmond. John Reuben Thompson. PAH

On to the beach the quiet waters crept. The Quiet Tide near Ardossan. Charles Tennyson Turner. FaBoPP

On to the Morgue. Unknown. AS

On to the Source. James Tate. AnAn

On Tobacco. Charles Cotton. OBSV

On Tobacco. Thomas Pestel. EIL

On Tom Holland and Nell Cotton. Unknown. FaBoEE

On Tom Moore's Translation of Anacreon. Thomas, 1st Baron Erskine. FaBoEE

On Tom-o-Combe. Unknown. FaBoEE

On Tom Onslow, Earl of Onslow. Unknown. See What can Tommy Onslow do?

On Tomato Ketchup. Unknown. FaBoUs; NBLV

On Top of Old Smoky. Unknown. FaFP

On top of that if you know me I pronounce you an ignu. Ignu. Allen Ginsberg. NaP

On top of this long hill. Among Dark Trees. Mirkka Rekola, tr. by Aili Jarvenpa. SOP

On Treason. Sir John Harington. See Treason doth never prosper: what's the reason.

On tree-topped hill, on tufted green. Tree-topped Hill. Unknown. NOEC

On Trees. Alan Dugan. NoAM

On Tsukuba mountain. Mushimaro. Fr. Manyo Shu. FCEI

On Tsukuba peak. Unknown. Fr. Manyo Shu. FCEI

On Tuesday morn at half-past six o'clock. James Rigg. James Hogg. BXAP; Par

On Twisting River Is the Old Home of My Father, sel. Chin Nung, tr. fr. Chinese by Jonathan Chaves. "I remember when he took me on a trip to this place." CoBLCP

On Two Brothers. Simonides, tr. fr. Greek by W. H. D. Rouse. AWP

On Two Monopolists. John Byrom. FaBoCo; FaBoEE

On two tables I spread out old legends. Pentti Saarikoski, tr. by Aili Jarvenpa. SOP

On Udo Beach. Suruga Dance. Unknown, tr. by Hiroaki Sato. FCEI

On Ullswater. Wordsworth. Fr. The Prelude [or, Growth of a Poet's Mind]: Childhood and School-Time. FaBoPP; RB

On Vacation. Robert Creeley. CAPP

On Vacation: a Poem to Record My Thoughts. Michizane, tr. fr. Chinese by Burton Watson. JLIC-1

On Venus, time passes slowly because. Here. Marvin Bell. AmPA

On village green, whose smooth and well-worn sod. A Disappointment. Joanna Baillie. NOEC

On Virtue. Phillis Wheatley. TAP

On Virtuous Government—For His Excellency Wang Fu-ssu, Salt Subcontroller of T'ai-chou. Wu Chia-chi, tr. fr. Chinese by John E. Wills, Jr. WFTU

On Visiting My Son, Port Angeles, Washington. Duane Niatum. CDW

On Visiting the Graves of Hawthorne and Thoreau. Jones Very. TAP

On Visiting the M. D. Anderson. Salma Khadra Jayyusi, tr. fr. Arabic by the author and Charles Doria. MAP

On Waking. Alida Carey Gulick. GoYe

On Waking from a Dreamless Sleep. Annie Fields. AA

On Walking Back to the Bus. Alan Gardner. PoSH

On Walt Whitman's Birthday. Anne Waldman. UL

On wan dark night on Lac St. Pierre. The Wreck of the Julie Plante [or The Julie Plante]. William Henry Drummond. BeLS; BLPA; CaP; FaBoBe; FaPON; NA; OBCV

On Watching Politicians Perform at Martin Luther King's Funeral. Etheridge Knight. NNaP

On Watching the Construction of a Skyscraper. Burton Raffel. PCP

On Waterloo's ensanguined plain. On Scott's Poem "The Field of Waterloo." Thomas Erskine, 1st Baron. FaBoCo; FiBHP; NBLV

On Weathering Gales. Elisavietta Ritchie. TSL

On Wednesday night. Wednesday Night Prayer Meeting. Jay Wright. PoBA

On Wellington. Byron. See Don Juan: Oh Wellington! (Or "Villainton," for Fame).

On Wenlock Edge [the Wood's in Trouble]. A. E. Housman. Fr. A Shropshire Lad, XXXI. BrPo; GTBS-P; LiTB; Mes; MoAB;

MoBrPo; NAEL-2; NOBE; NoP; OBNC; OxBTC; PoEL-5; PoRA; PrIm; RB

On western hills the sun dies, eastern hills are dusking. Song of the Sacred Strings. Li Ho, *tr. by* Burton Watson. CoBCP

On Westwall Downes [*or* On Westwell Downs]. William Strode. FaBoPP; JCP; PoEL-2

On what a brave and curious whim. Clocks. Louis Ginsberg. TrJP

On what foundation stands the warrior's pride. Samuel Johnson. *Fr.* Vanity of Human Wishes, The: The Tenth Satire of Juvenal Imitated. OBWP

(Charles XII of Sweden.) NOBE

On what long tides. Fires of Driftwood. Isabel Ecclestone MacKay. CaP

On ["Who Wrote Icon Basilike" by Dr.] Christopher Wordsworth, Master of Trinity. Benjamin Hall Kennedy. FaBoCo; FaBoEE

On whose assurance shall I pass. Mohammad Taqi Mir, *tr. by* Ahmed Ali. GoT

On wide waters, alone, my boat. Fisherman. Honei, *tr. by* Lucien Stryk *and* Takashi Ikemoto. ZPCJ

On Will Smith. *Unknown.* FaBoCo

On William Prynne. Samuel Butler. FaBoEE

On William Wilson, Tailor. *Unknown.* FaBoEE

On Windermere; Bowness Bay and Belle Isle. Wordsworth. *Fr.* The Prelude [*or,* Growth of a Poet's Mind]: Childhood and School-Time. FaBoPP

On windy days the mill. The Unfortunate Miller. A. E. Coppard. FaBoTw

On Winter Evenings; 1912, *sel.* Dovid Hofshteyn, *tr. fr. Yiddish by* Robert Friend.

    In Winter's Dusk. PeBMYV

On winter nights. The Car Cemetery. Ciaran Carson. CIP

On Wisdom. Hakuin, *tr. fr. Japanese by* Lucien Stryk *and* Takashi Ikemoto. ZPCJ

On Wodin's day, sixth of December, thirty-nine. *In re* Solomon Warshawer. A. M. Klein. MoCV

On Woman. W. B. Yeats. CMoP

On woodlands ruddy with autumn. My Autumn Walk. Bryant. AA

On wool-soft feet he peeps and creeps. Santa Claus. Walter de la Mare. PChr

On Words and Concepts and Things. Paul Ramsey. CRP

On Wordsworth. Hartley Coleridge. *See* He Lived amidst th' Untrodden Ways.

On Writing Asian-American Poetry. Geraldine Kudaka. BrSi

On Writing for the Stage. John Sheffield. *Fr.* Essay on Poetry. FaBoUs

On Yes Tor. Sir Edmund Gosse. CH

On yon hill's top which this sweet plain commands. Invites His Nymph to His Cottage. Philip Ayres. EnLoPo

On yonder hill there is a red deer. *Unknown.* ChTr; GBP

On yonder hill there stands a creature. O, No, John [*or* No John] [*or* The One Answer]. *Unknown.* ErPo; OBET; PDV

On yonder oak, upon its lordliest height. Mistletoe. Mary E. Tucker. CBWP-1

On Your Back. Gerrit Komrij, *tr. fr. Dutch by* Jacob Lowland. DuIn

On your bare rocks, O barren moors. The Barren Moors. William Ellery Channing. AA

On your dazzling throne, Aphrodite. Sappho, *tr. by* Willis Barnstone. BoWoP

On your grave. Song for the Burial of My Mother. Shimazaki Toson, *tr. by* Burton Watson. FCEI

On your slender body. For the Courtesan Ch'ing Lin. Wu Tsao, *tr. by* Kenneth Rexroth *and* Ling Chung. BoWoP; WPOW

On your soft bed my love. In the Silence of Endless Night. N. M. Rashed, *tr. by* Mahmood Jamal. PBMUP

On your soil I was destined to sing the song of your land. On Your Soil, America. Berysh Vaynshteyn, *tr. by* Benjamin *and* Barbara Harshav. AYP

On Zacheus [*or* Zacchaeus]. Francis Quarles. HAP; MePo; OBS; OxBSP

On Zion and on Lebanon. Henry Ustic Onderdonk. AH

Once. Eric N. Batterham. CH

Once. George Ives. PeHV

Once. Maud Sulter. WS

Once. *Unknown.* CH; PBBP

Once, *sels.* Alice Walker. BlSi

    "Green lawn/ a picket fence." PoBA

    "I/ never liked/ white folks." PoBA

    "It is true—/ I've always loved." NMM; PoBA

Once. Siv Widerberg, *tr. fr. Swedish by* Verne Moberg. NTCP

Once/ I went for an ocean trip. On a Steamer. Dorothy W. Baruch. FaPON

Once a Big Molicepan. *Unknown.* FaPON

Once a boy beheld a bright. The Rose. Goethe, *tr. by* James Clarence Mangan. AWP

Once a crane lived in the wilds. A Song of the Wild Crane: Presented to a Friend. Singde, *tr. by* William Schultz. WFTU

Once a day the rocks, with little warning. Naskeag. Alfred Corn. BLA

Once a dream did weave a shade. A Dream. Blake. *Fr.* Songs of Innocence. CH; EnRP

Once a gay wit, subsequently a wretched instructor. The Father. Richmond Lattimore. EyDe

Once a jolly swagman camped by a billabong. Waltzing Matilda. Andrew Barton Paterson. CBAP; ChTr; GBP; PoAu-1

Once a Kansas zephyr strayed. Zephyr. Eugene Fitch Ware. PoLF

Once, a lady of the O Moores. Parthenogenesis. Nuala Ni Dhomhnaill, *tr. by* Michael Hartnett. CIP

Once a little baby lay. The First Christmas. Emilie Poulsson. OHIP

Once a little red hen. The Mouse, The Frog and The Little Red Hen. *Unknown.* BoTP

Once a man is born he has to die. All Intents. Larry Eigner. VGW

Once a mouse, a frog, and a little red hen. The Mouse, The Frog and The Little Red Hen. *Unknown.* BoTP

Once a pallid vestal. The Vestal. Nathalia Crane. TrJP

Once a poor widow, aging year by year. Chaucer. *See* Canterbury Tales, The: Nun's Priest's Tale, The.

Once a raven from Pluto's dark shore. The True Facts of the Case. Anthony Euwer. OBAL

Once a sexton's house, constructed on. Introduction to a Pub in Limerick. Knute Skinner. SoTCo

Once a wife in Bethlehem. A Prayer for a Sleeping Child. Mary Carolyn Davies. OHIP

Once Again. Liz Sohappy Bahe. CDW; NOVW

Once again. Rudolf Henz, *tr. fr. German by* Beth Bjorklund. CoAuP

Once again. From the Liturgy. Juan Gonzalo Rose, *tr. by* David Tipton. Per

Once again a spring has come around. A Natural Theology. James Whitehead. BLA; MT

Once again, my luggage packed, I'm returning to Wu. Mooring in the Rain at Sung-ling. Chin Nung, *tr. by* Jonathan Chaves. CoBLCP

Once again seated below bright awnings, here, there. Anacreontic. István Vas, *tr. by* Jascha Kessler. FOC

Once again, tell me, what was it like? Summer. Gary Soto. WeW

Once again the great days of the crusades return! Arbitrary Destiny. Robert Desnos, *tr. by* Michael Benedikt. POS

Once again the scurry of feet—those myriads. The Face of the Waters. Robert David Fitzgerald. CBAP; PoAu-2

Once again the smell of hay. August Night. Gerhard Fritsch, *tr. by* Beth Bjorklund. CoAuP

Once again they've quarreled on a tram. Two. Margarita Aliger, *tr. by* Elaine Feinstein. VWA

Once again to see West Lake! Yüan Mei, *tr. fr. Chinese by* Jonathan Chaves. *Fr.* In Late Spring of the Year *Keng-hsü*. CoBLCP

Once Alien Here. John Hewitt. CIP; NeIP

Once an ex-con told me. The Rape Poem. Tommi Avicolli. GLP

Once, and but once found in thy company. The Perfume. John Donne. *Fr.* Elegies. IV. SeCP

Once and for All. Louis Aragon, *tr. fr. French by* Michael Benedikt. POS

Once and Future. Diana Chang. BrSi

Once and Upon. Madeline Gleason. NeAP

Once, as a child, I ate raspberries. And forgot. Raspberries. Laurence Lerner. EBEV

Once as a child I loved to hop. Adam's Footprint. Vassar Miller. MT; NePoEA

Once as Congress sat in session. The Reagan. Richard Quick. FaBoPa

Once as I travelled through a quiet evening. Egrets. Judith Wright. GoJo

Once as I went by rail to Epping Street. The Wasp. John Davidson. FM

Once [*or* Ons] as methought [*or* me thought], fortune me kissed [*or* kist *or* kyst]. The Lover Rejoiceth the Enjoying of His Love. Sir Thomas Wyatt. AAS; BoLoP; SiPS

(Promise, A.) OBSC

Once, as old Lord Gorbals motored. Lord Gorbals. Harry Graham. FaBoCo

Once as we were sitting by. Spring 1942. Roy Fuller. LiTM; OxBTC; WaaP

Once at a merry wedding feast. St. George Tucker. *Fr.* The Cynic. NBLV

Once at sunset Jesus and His disciples. Agraphon. Angelos Sikelianos, *tr. by* Edmund Keeley *and* Philip Sherrard. VMG

Once at Swanage. Thomas Hardy. FaBoPP

Once before I loved this quiet place. Returning to Lotus Village. Kao Ch'i, *tr. by* Jonathan Chaves. CoBLCP

Once before, this self-same air. Mary Mapes Dodge. AA

Once between us the Atlantic. Sundered. Israel Zangwill. TrJP

Once—but no matter when. A Chronicle. *Unknown.* BLPL; NA

Once by the Pacific. Robert Frost. CMoP; HAP; HeIP; LiTA; LiTM; MoAB; MoAmPo; MOS; NAAL-2; NOBA; PrIm; Son; VGW; WeW

Once came an exile, longing to be free. Blennerhassett's Island. Thomas Buchanan Read. *Fr.* The New Pastoral. PAH

Once did I love, and yet I live. *Unknown.* OBSC

Once did my Philomel reflect on me. Sir John Davies. *Fr.* Sonnets to Philomel. SiPS

Once Did My Thoughts. *Unknown.* EBEV; ELP

Once did she hold the gorgeous east in fee. On the Extinction of the Venetian Republic. Wordsworth. EnRP; FaBoRV; GTBS; GTBS-P; NOBE; NoP; OBEV; OBNC; TrGrPo

Once down on my knees to growing plants. A Mood Apart. Robert Frost. OxBSP

Once, Driving West of Billings, Montana. Susan Mitchell. NAmP

Once drunk, my delight knows no limits. Written When Drunk. Chang Yüeh, *tr. by* Burton Watson. CoBCP

Once each year *penitentes* in mailshirts. Penitents. Bernice Zamora. CCP

Once, ere God was crucified. The Abdication of Fergus Mac Roy. Sir Samuel Ferguson. AnIL

Once from a big, big building. A Visit to the Asylum. Edna St. Vincent Millay. SO

Once, grave Laodicean profiteer. Lourenço Marques. Charles Eglinton. PeSA

Once he asked me. Tales about My Father. Abd al-Karim Kassid, *tr. by* Lena Jayyusi *and* Anthony Thwaite. MAP

Once he puts out the light. The Hermit Has a Visitor. Maxine W. Kumin. BoWoP

Once he will miss, twice he will miss. Death ("Once he will miss, twice he will miss"). *Unknown, tr. fr. Arabic by* E. Powys Mathers. *Fr.* The Thousand and One Nights. AWP

Once hoary winter chancedalas! Why Ye Blossome Cometh Before Ye Leafe. Oliver Herford. AA

Once I am sure there's nothing going on. Church Going. Philip Larkin. CMoP; GTBS-P; HeIP; LiTM; MoBrPo; MoP; NAEL-2; NePoEA; NIP; NoAM; NoP; OAEL-2; PPP; PrIm; SCV; TwCP; UnPo

Once I courted a fair beauty bride. The Fair Beauty Bride. *Unknown.* AmFP

Once I cried for new songs to sing. I Sing No New Songs. Frank Marshall Davis. PoBA; PoNe

Once—I didn't mean to. Accidentally. Maxine W. Kumin. RHPC

Once I followed horses. Thistledown. Denis Glover. *Fr.* Sings Harry. ATNZ; PeNZ

Once I heard an old bachelor say. The Bachelor's Complaint. *Unknown.* AmFP

Once I knew a fine song. Scaped. Stephen Crane. *Fr.* The Black Riders, LXV. AA

Once I learnt in wilful hour. On A Wife. Francis Burdett Money-Coutts. OxBSP

Once I liked pablum. Once. Siv Widerberg, *tr. by* Verne Moberg. NTCP

Once I Lived in Cottonwood. *Unknown.* AmFP

Once I loved a sailor, who often enjoyed my charms. What'll the Neighbours Say? Sandra Kerr. AIW

Once I loved a spider. The Spider and the Ghost of the Fly. Vachel Lindsay. VGW

Once I Pass'd through a Populous City. Walt Whitman. AmPP; AnAmPo; NAAL-1; OxBA

Once I Played and Danced in My Parents' Kingdom. *Gond Oral Tradition, tr. by* V. Elwin *and* S. Hivale. WTO

Once I saw a little bird. Mother Goose. OxNR

Once I saw a little bird going hop, hop, hop. *Unknown.* BoTP

Once I saw it with uncaring eyes. Yakamochi. *Fr.* Manyo Shu. Ma

Once I saw mountains angry. Ancestry. Stephen Crane. *Fr.* The Black Riders, XXII. AA

Once I seen a human ruin. Ambrose Bierce. *Fr.* The Devil's Dictionary. OBAL

Once I stood in a green bough. Portrait of the Father. Lindy Hough. IHMS

Once I Thought to Die for Love. *Unknown.* ElL

Once I was a boy and I sat in a meadow with flowers in it. Time Passes. Richard Percival Lister. NYBP

Once I was a cow, a horse. Wang An-shih, *tr. fr. Chinese by* Burton Watson. *Fr.* Twenty Poems in Imitation of Han-shan and Shih-te. CoBCP

Once I was a little boy. The Foggy Dew. *Unknown.* OBET

Once I was a monarch's daughter. Once. *Unknown.* CH; PBBP

Once I was a poor man's son. Natsume Soseki, *tr. by* Burton Watson. JLIC-2

Once I was a schoolboy and stayed at home with ease. The Smacksman. Sam Larner. OxBSS

Once I Was a Shepherd Boy. *Unknown.* OBET

Once I was a young horse all in my youthful prime. Poor Old Horse. *Unknown.* OBET

Once I was good like the Virgin Mary and the Minister's wife. The Scarlet Woman. Fenton Johnson. BANP; PoBA; PoNe

Once I was happy, but now I'm forlorn. The Man on the Flying Trapeze. *Unknown.* BeLS; BLPA; FaBoBe, *at. to* George Leybourne. ("Oh, the girl that I loved she was handsome.") FaFP; OxBoLi

Once I was jealous of lovers. Now I am. The Valley. Stanley Moss. NYBP; PCP

Once I was lovely, had renown. Cadenet, *tr. by* Paul Blackburn. Pro

Once I was the master of a city. Natsume Soseki, *tr. by* Burton Watson. JLIC-2

Once I Was Young. Anna Margolin, *tr. fr. Yiddish by* Marcia Falk. PeBMYV

Once I went through the lanes, over the sharp. Spring. V. Sackville-West. *Fr.* The Land. PeHV

Once in a dream I saw the flowers. Paradise. Christina Rossetti. WGRP

Once, in a finesse of fiddles found I ecstasy. The Embankment [*or* Fantasia of a Fallen Gentleman]. T. E. Hulme. EBEV; FaBoMo; GTBS-P; OxBSP; OxBTC

(Fantasia of a Fallen Gentleman on a Cold Bitter Night on the Embankment.) SeCePo

Once, in a great while. Icon. Mark Osaki. BrSi

Once in a hundred years the lemmings come. The Lemmings. John Masefield. CMoP

Once in a Lifetime, Snow. Les A. Murray. CBAP

Once in a lifetime, we may see the veil. Midnight—September 19, 1881. John Boyle O'Reilly. PAH

Once, in a roostery. The Hen and the Carp. Ian Serraillier. OnUR

Once in a saintly passion. Once in a Saintly Passion. James Thomson. FF; NOBVV

Once in a while a curious weed unknown to me. William Jones. Edgar Lee Masters. *Fr.* Spoon River Anthology. ImOP

Once in a While a Protest Poem. David B. Axelrod. InPK

Once in a wood at winter's end. Winter's End. Howard Moss. NePoEA

Once in Aleppo. Othello's Report. Rodolfo Hinostroza, *tr. by* Maureen Ahern *and* David Tipton. Per

Once in Canandaigua, hitchhiking from Ann Arbor. Faces. John Ciardi. WeW

Once in Mexico an old man was. Visions. William Stafford. NoAM

Once in our lives,/ Let us drink to our wives. *Unknown.* FaBoEE

Once-in-Passing, The. Louis MacNeice. *Fr.* A Hand of Snapshots. FaBCIP

Once in Persia reigned a King. Even This Shall Pass Away. Theodore Tilton. BLPA; WGRP

Once in Royal David's City. Cecil Frances Alexander. OxBChV (Christmas Hymn, A: "Once in royal David's City.") OHIP

Once, in the burning age. Apprentices. Robin Munro. PoSH

Once in the dark of night. The Dark Night. Saint John of the Cross. WeW, *tr. by* John Frederick Nims (Obscure Night of the Soul, The.) AWP, *tr. by* Arthur Symons; OBMV, *tr. by* Arthur Symons

Once in the dear dead days beyond recall. Love's Old Sweet Song. G. Clifton Bingham. FaBoBe

Once in the Jurassic, about 150 million years ago. Smokey the Bear Sutra. *Unknown.* MAT

Once in the long-gone age. Yakamochi. *Fr.* Manyo Shu. Ma

Once in the past I stepped on a snail. Remembering with Feeling. Onitsura, *tr. fr. Japanese by* Hiroaki Sato. *Fr.* Twenty-three Hokku. FCEI

Once in the winter. The Forsaken. Duncan Campbell Scott. CaP; NOBC

Once, in this Tuscan garden, noon's huge ball. A Snail's Derby. Eugene Lee-Hamilton. FM

Once in your life you pass. The Place. Paul Zimmer. BLA

Once it had gorged itself. On a Pig's Head. Charles Tomlinson. NoAM

Once, it happened I'd been dining, on my couch I slept reclining. The Goblin Goose. *Unknown.* FaBoPa

Once it smiled a silent dell. The Valley of Unrest. Poe. AmPP; NAAL-1; PoEL-4

Once it was enough simply. Reaching the Horizon. Robert Mezey. NaP

Once, long ago, set close beside a wood. Chaucer. *See* Canterbury Tales, The: The Nun's Priest's Tale, The.

Once looked Gudrun. Gudrun Laments over Sigurd. *Unknown, tr. fr. Old Norse by* William Morris *and* Eirikr Magnusson. *Fr.* The Elder Edda: The First Lay of Gudrun. OBVE

Once mermaids mocked your ships. Mermaids. Kenneth Slessor. *Fr.* The Atlas. PoAu-2

Once More. Forugh Farrokhzad, *tr. by* Jascha Kessler *and* Amin Banani. BoWoP

Once More. Roger Giroux, *tr. fr. French by* Anthony Barnett. RHTwFP

Once More. George Jonas. NeAC

Once More. István Vas, *tr. fr. Hungarian by* Jascha Kessler. FOC

Once more/ to be able to say: September. Boedromion. Alfred Gong, *tr. by* Beth Bjorklund. CoAuP

Once More a-Lumbering Go. *Unknown.* AmFP

Once more around should do it, the man confided. Flight of the Roller Coaster. Raymond Souster. NOBC; SO

Once more as I gather about me the cloak of the evening. Charles Brasch. *Fr.* The Estate, XXII. ATNZ

Once more beneath my thumb the globe turns. Childhood. Donald Justice. AnAn; LCAP

Once more by the brook the alder leaves. Hayden Carruth. NNaP

Once more, Cesario. Shakespeare. *Fr.* Twelfth Night, II, iv. SCV

Once more coming through the door with rain. Fireflies. Chao Chih-hsin, *tr. by* Michael S. Duke. WFTU

Once more evening on the earth. The Lake in the Sky. John Haines. LCAP

Once More Fields and Gardens. T'ao Ch'ien, *tr. fr. Chinese by* Amy Lowell *and* Florence Ayscough. AWP

Once More Following the Rhymes of Pin-lao's Poem "Getting Up After Illness." Huang T'ing-chien, *tr. fr. Chinese by* Burton Watson. CoBCP

Once more I came to Sarum Close. The Cathedral Close. Coventry Patmore. *Fr.* The Angel in the House, I, i. EBVV (Salisbury; the Cathedral Close.) EBVV; FaBoPP

Once more I come to the white page of art. The Cost of Seriousness. Peter Porter. NoAM

Once more I move among you, dear familiar places. Amagansett Beach Revisited. John Hall Wheelock. NYBP

Once more I saw him. In the lofty room. The Last Sight. Robert Louis Stevenson. BrPo

Once more it seems. Zohara. Jack Hirschman. VWA

Once more it's spring; the meadows laugh once more. Planting a Wood. E. A. Baratynsky, *tr. by* Alan Myers. AAA

Once more, listening to the wind and rain. The Return. Arna Bontemps. CDC; PoBA; PoNe

Once more, Mother, I turn to you. From a New Height. Andrea Zanzotto, *tr. by* Lawrence R. Smith. NItP

Once more my deeper life goes on with more strength. Moving Ahead. Rainer Maria Rilke, *tr. by* Robert Bly. NU

Once More, O Lord. George Washington Doane. AH

Once More O Ye Etc. Michael Reck. PPR

Once more, once more, my Mary dear. Memories. George Denison Prentice. AA

Once more Orion and the sister Seven. A Welcome to Dr. Benjamin Apthorp Gould. Oliver Wendell Holmes. ImOP

Once More, Our God, Vouchsafe to Shine! Samuel Sewall. AH (Wednesday, January 1, 1701.) SCAP

Once, more than you wanted. To My Daughter Riding in the Circus Parade. Joan Labombard. GOYP

Once more the Ancient Wonder. Easter, 1923. John G. Neihardt. OHIP

Once more the changed year's turning wheel returns. Barren Spring. Dante Gabriel Rossetti. *Fr.* The House of Life, LXXXIII. EBVV; NoP; OAEL-2; OBNC; PoEL-5

Once more the country calls. Allen Tate. WaP

Once more the cuckoo's call I hear. Spring. Aubrey Thomas De Vere. *Fr.* A Year of Sorrow. OBNC

Once more the flower of Essex is marching to the wars. Essex Regiment March. George Edward Woodberry. PAH

Once more the liberal year laughs out. Harvest Hymn. Whittier. *Fr.* For an Autumn Festival. OHIP

Once more the miracle, still unexplained. On the Heights. W. K. Holmes. PoSH

Once more the storm is howling, and half hid. A Prayer for My Daughter. W. B. Yeats. BLPL; CMoP; HAP; LiTB; LiTM; MoAB; MoP; NAEL-2; NAs; NoAM; NoP; OxBTC; PoA; PoLF; PoRA; PrIm; TEP

Once more this autumn-earth is ripe. The Australian. Arthur H. Adams. PoAu-1

Once more time withdraws. Once More. Roger Giroux, *tr. by* Anthony Barnett. RHTwFP

Once more unto the breach, dear friends, once more. Shakespeare. *Fr.* King Henry V, III, i. FaBV; WaaP (Blast of War, The.) TrGrPo

Once Musing as I Sat. Barnabe Googe. NoP (Fly, The.) CH

Once, my braids swung heavy as ropes. The Butcher's Wife. Louise Erdrich. HATNAP

Once my parents were older. Chiyo, *tr. by* David Ray. BoWoP

Once on a morning of sweet recreation. The Blackbird. *Unknown.* NOIV

Once on a silver and green day, rich to remember. Brindabella. Douglas Stewart. PoAu-2

Once on a time, a monarch, tired with whooping. The Apple Dumplings and a King. "Peter Pindar." OBSV

Once on a time a thousand different men. James Henry. NOBVV

Once on a time did Eucritus and I. Harvest-Home. Theocritus, *tr. fr. Greek by* Charles Stuart Calverley. *Fr.* Idylls, VII. AWP

Once on a time I used to be. Harlot's Catch. Robert Nichols. ErPo; FaBoTw

Once on a time, it came to pass. The Fable of the Piece of Glass and the Piece of Ice. John Hookham Frere. OxBChV

Once on a time, some centuries ago. Monk of Casal-Maggiore, The (The Sicilian's Tale). Longfellow. *Fr.* Tales of a Wayside Inn, *pt.* III. AmPP; OxBA

Once on a time there was a pool. Rev. Homer Wilbur's "Festina Lente." James Russell Lowell. *Fr.* The Biglow Papers: 2d Series, No. IV. OBAL

Once, on that highway where a traveler works hard. Pornography, Nebraska. Sandra McPherson. MAYP

Once, once, in Washington. Patriotic Tour and Postulate of Joy. Robert Penn Warren. AiP; NYBP

"Once . . . once upon a time. . . ." Martha. Walter de la Mare. MoBrPo

Once, one of my students read a book we had. Untitled Poem. Alan Dugan. CAPP

Once—only once. Ato Tobira. *Fr.* Manyo Shu. Ma

Once or Twice. John Skoyles. NAmP

Once or twice he eyed me oddly. Once. Temptations of St. Antony by His Housekeeper. Elizabeth Smither. ATNZ; PeNZ

Once-over, The. Paul Blackburn. ErPo; NeAP; PoM

Once riding in Old Baltimore. Incident. Countee Cullen. BPo; CDC; FF; IDB; NAAL-2; NoAM; NTCP; OBCA; PoBA; PoNe; SoSe; VGW

Once she was the reason for his festivals. What Her Girl Friend Said, When the Woman Was About to Take Back Her Unfaithful Husband. Orampokiyar, *tr. by* A. K. Ramanujan. PLW

Once, so long ago. For Paddy Mac. Padraic Fallon. CIP

Once some people were visiting Chekhov. Chocolates. Louis Simpson. InPS; LCAP; Mes; OxBC

Once the Days. Denis Glover. *Fr.* Sings Harry. ATNZ; PeNZ

Once the head is gray. A Catch. Richard Henry Stoddard. AA

Once the land had no great names and no history. Names from the War. Bruce Catton. AmFN

Once, the mighty waves of ocean. The Precious Pearl. Priscilla Jane Thompson. CBWP-2

Once the nation's chief was honored by the company of one. A Notable Dinner. Lizelia Augusta Jenkins Moorer. CBWP-3

Once the Sole Province. Douglas Crase. EOEF

Once the stone god turned its. For D. S. Christine Craig. AIW

Once the voice has quietly spoken, every knight must ride alone. Song of the Quest. W. H. Auden. *Fr.* Man of La Mancha. AnAn

Once There Came a Man. Stephen Crane. AnAmPo

Once there lived a little man. *Unknown.* BoTP

Once there was a fence here. Former Barn Lot. Mark Van Doren. FaBV; MoAmPo; PDV

Once there was a King of Thule. Complaint of the King of Thule. Jules Laforgue, *tr. by* William Jay Smith. CT

Once there was a little boy whose name was Robert Reese. An Overworked Elocutionist. Carolyn Wells. BLPA; BLPL

Once there was a little Kitty. Kitty. Elizabeth Prentiss. BoTP; MoShBr

Once there was a man named Mr. Artesian and his activity was tremendous. Mr. Artesian's Conscientiousness. Ogden Nash. NBLV

Once there was a straight line which told how it got bent. Politics. Bob Perelman. BAP

Once there was a woman went out to pick beans. The Hairy Toe. *Unknown.* PYC

Once there was an elephant. Eletelephony. Laura Elizabeth Richards. FaPON; GoJo; MoShBr; NBLV; NTCP; OBCA; OnUR; OxBChV; PDV; PYC; RHPC

Once there were mallards ahead of a blizzard. Still Hunting. Don Welch. TSL

Once there were peasant pots and a dry brown hare. Joan Miró. Ruthven Todd. EAS

Once there were 3 little Indian girls. Charité Espérance et Foi. Earle Birney. OxBC

Once there were three stones sitting in a patch of soft. The Death of Potchikoo. Louise Erdrich. *Fr.* Old Man Potchikoo. HATNAP

Once this soft turf, this rivulet's sands. The Battle-Field. Bryant. AA; AnAmPo; FPL; PoLF

Once to Every Man and Nation. James Russell Lowell. *Fr.* The Present Crisis. FaPoR

Once to life I said, yes! To Life I Said Yes. Chaim Grade, *tr. by* Joseph Leftwich. TrJP

Once, twice, thrice/ I give thee warning. *Unknown.* OxNR

Once, Twice, Thrice. *Unknown.* ErPo

Once u hurl a stone. Mike 65. Lennox Raphael. PoBA

Once upon a colony. Can. Hist. Earle Birney. OxBC

Once upon a midnight dreary, eerie, scary. Ravin's of Piute Poet Poe. C. L. Edson. BXAP

Once upon a midnight dreary, while I pondered [*or* ponder'd], weak and weary. The Raven. Poe. AA; AmPP; AnAmPo; BeLS; BLPA; CH; FaBoBe; FaBoCh; FaBV; FaFP; FPL; GN; HeIP; LiTA; NAAL-1; NIP; NOBA; OBCA; OBNV; OHFP; OxBA; PoRA; PWR; TAP; WBLP

Once upon a Time. Mekeel McBride. KS

Once upon a Time. Gabriel Okara. PBA

Once upon a time/ I composed a witty rhyme. The Minstrel's Last Lay. John Barth. OBAL

Once upon a time/ Old Mr. Pyme. Mr. Pyme. Harry Behn. PDV

Once upon a time/ there was, and is, and old witch. Issa, *tr. by* Harry Behn. WSC

Once upon a time/ I caught a little rhyme. Catch a Little Rhyme. Eve Merriam. OBCA; PDV

Once upon a time/ there was a lonely wolf. János Pilinszky, *tr. fr. Hungarian.* MHuP, *tr. by* Ted Hughes; OBVE; RB, *tr. by* Ted Hughes *and* János Csokits.

Once upon a time,/ In the realm of Dewajing. Zong Belegt Baatar. *Mongol Oral Tradition, tr. by* C. R. Bawden. WTO

Once upon a time I was. To the Tune "The Fall of a Little Wild Goose." Huang O, *tr. by* Kenneth Rexroth *and* Ling Chung. AIW; WPOW

Once upon a time, in a little wee house. The Funny Old Man and His Wife. *At. to* D'Arcy Wentworth Thompson. OnUR

Once upon a time in California. A Friend of the Family. Louis Simpson. NNaP

Once upon a time there was an Italian. Columbus. Ogden Nash. NoP; OFD

Once upon a time there were three little foxes. The Three Foxes. Alan Alexander Milne. GoJo; GrPl; MoShBr; OxBChV

Once upon the earth at the midnight hour. The Wooing Lady. William Jay Smith. NePoEA

Once, walking home, I passed beneath a tree. The Music of a Tree. W. J. Turner. MoBrPo

Once, walking in the woods. Getting at the Root of the Matter. Henry Taylor. BXAP

Once was every woman the witch. Witches. Ted Hughes. GoYe

Once we dreamed of eagles. Reading Indian Poetry. Ramona Wilson. VoR

Once we laughed together. Missing You. Charlotte Zolotow. ILY

Once we lived so close to the bush. The Ghost Moth. Lauris Edmond. ATNZ

Once we were wayfarers, then seafarers, then airfarers. Post Early for Space. Peter J. Henniker-Heaton. AmFN

Once when I walked into a room. Between Ourselves. Audre Lorde. WPOW

Once when I was coming from art class they surprised me. Daryl Hine. *Fr.* March. GLP

Once when I was very scared. Charlotte Zolotow. NTCP

Once, when midnight smote the air. On Those That Hated *The Playboy of the Western World.* W. B. Yeats. NOIV

Once when my heart was passion free. Communion. John Banister Tabb. WGRP

Once, when my wife was a child. Dracula. Steve Kowit. VVA

Once when the moon was out about three quarters. White Clover. Marvin Bell. CAPP

Once when the snow of the year was beginning to fall. The Runaway. Robert Frost. AWP; CH; FaBoCh; FaPON; GoJo; MoAB; MoAmPo; PDV; TwCP; VGW

Once when the wind was on the roof. Beyond. Hannah Parker Kimball. AA

Once, when their hearts were wild with joy. On Harting Down. T. Sturge Moore. OxBTC

Once when they came to my bed in dream. The Dream of Fair Women. Carl Dennis. BLA

Once, winter stumbled into your bed. Land of the White Lily. Jukka Vieno, *tr. by* Aili Jarvenpa. SOP

Once, with a certain pride, we kept attempts. Spot the Ball. Frank Ormsby. CIP

Once with a whirl of thought oppressed. The Day of Judgment. Swift. TW

Once you said joking slyly, "If I'm killed." The Faithful. Jane Cooper. NePoEA-2; SM

Once you shone among the living as the morning star. Plato. OBD

Ondt and the Gracehoper, The. James Joyce. *Fr.* Finnegans Wake. BIrV

One, The. Patrick Kavanagh. MoBrPo; TIRV

One, The. Ida Procter. CN

One. Carolyn M. Rodgers. BPo

One after the other, they wished to predict a happy future for us. The Lords of Maussane. René Char, *tr. by* James Wright. RHTwFP

One afternoon he said to his girl. A Guerrilla's Goodbye. Javier Heraud, *tr. by* Maureen Ahern. Per

One afternoon in my room. A True Story. Marvin Bell. SV

One afternoon the last week in April. Axe Handles. Gary Snyder. CAPP; NoAM

One among friends who stood above your grave. Auden's Funeral. Stephen Spender. AnAn

One, and then another, they settled before me like flakes of air. Mining in Killdeer Alley. Dabney Stuart. MT

One-and-Twenty. *Unknown.* AmFP

One Angry Woman. Veronica Williams. WS

One arch of the sky. Love in Labrador. Carl Sandburg. VGW

One arm circles my neck. Octopus. Ghazi al-Gosaibi, *tr. by* Sharif Elmusa *and* Charles Doria. MAP

One arm hooked around the frayed strap. Yellow Light. Garrett Kaoru Hongo. InPS; MAYP

One Art. Elizabeth Bishop. CAPP; DiPo; HAP; NAAL-2; NoAM; PoE; SM; SoSe

One asked a madman if a wife he had. A Mad Answer of a Madman. Robert Hayman. FF

One asked a sign from God; and day by day. The Seekers. Victor Starbuck. WGRP

One assault of wild thunder, one assault of wind. Sudden Shower. Okubo Shibutsu, *tr. by* Burton Watson. JLIC-2

One bails out into space. Flight. Barbara Howes. NYBP

One balding forehead one pair of glasses. Inventory. Mihály Ladányi, *tr. by* Edwin Morgan. MHuP

One be the nail another the pincers. The Nail. Vasco Popa, *tr. fr. Serbo-Croatian by* Anne Pennington. *Fr.* Games. RB

One beautiful morning in the month of May all was serene and/ quiet. May. Mrs. Henry Linden. CBWP-4

One behind another the hours. Snow. Javier Sologuren, *tr. by* David Tipton. Per

One bite/ and I'm doing a dance. *Unknown, tr. by* Burton Watson. FCEI

One biting winter morning. The Spider. Hannah Flagg Gould. OBCA

One black horse standing by the gate. The Farmyard. A. A. Attwood. BoTP

One Blackbird. Harold Monro. BoTP

One bland elipse in cornflower blue. Rigor Viris. Margaret Avison. CaP

One blessing had I, than the rest. Emily Dickinson. LiTA

One bliss for which. Taboo to Boot. Ogden Nash. FiBHP; RB

One body, but heart shattered into a thousand pieces. Elegies for Prince Atsumichi ("One body, but heart shattered into a thousand pieces"). Lady Izumi, *tr. fr. Japanese by* Hiroaki Sato. *Fr.* Fifty-one Tanka. FCEI

One book has it that Eve. Eve. Jean Follain, *tr. by* W. S. Merwin. RHTwFP

One born to hardship in his place and station. Vidya, *tr. fr. Sanskrit by* Daniel H. H. Ingalls. *Fr.* Substantiations. PBWP

One boy alone in all the world for me. Epigram. Meleager, *tr. by* Sydney Oswald. PeHV

One boy, Saint Dwyn, my bauble. Lament for Siôn y Glyn. Lewis Glyn Cothi, *tr. by* Joseph P. Clancy. OBWVE

One by One. Adelaide Anne Procter. GN

One by one, as harvesters, all heavy laden. Sacheverell Sitwell. *Fr.* Agamemnon's Tomb. MoBrPo

One by one, the ancient. Next Year, in Jerusalem. Shirley Kaufman. VWA

One by one the sands are flowing. One by One. Adelaide Anne Procter. GN

One by one they appear in. My Sad Captains. Thom Gunn. CMoP; FaBoMo; LiTM; NAEL-2; NePoEA-2; NoAM

One calm and cloudless winter night. Medusa. Robert Kelley Weeks. AA

One cannot ask loneliness. Jakuren, *tr.* by Geoffrey Bownas *and* Anthony Thwaite. PeBJV

One cannot be sure. Bird. Shotetsu, *tr.* by Steven D. Carter. WFTW

One cannot possess. Heritage. Augustus Young. CIP

One canso I've made murderously. Peire Vidal, *tr.* by Paul Blackburn. Pro

One can't say it is impossible. Winter Music. Tamura Ryuichi, *tr.* by Hiroaki Sato. FCEI

One Certainty, The. Christina Rossetti. OBNC

One chain-smoked cigarettes. Grandfathers. Michael Castro. VWA

One Chip of Human Bone. Ray A. Young Bear. NOVW; STE

One Chord. Nelly Sachs, *tr. fr. German by* Keith Bosley. VWA

One Christmas-Time. Wordsworth. *Fr.* The Prelude [or, Growth of a Poet's Mind]: France. RB

One Christmastime Fats Waller in a fur coat. History of My Heart. Robert Pinsky. NAmP; NPGG

One clear glass slipper; a slender blue single-rose vase. Cranston Near the City Line. Ted Berrigan. UL

One Coat of Paint. John Ashbery. BAP

One comes to language from afar, the ear. A Vulnerary. Jonathan Williams. PoM

One Country. Frank Lebby Stanton. AA; OPP

One Crowded Hour. Thomas O. Mordaunt, *formerly at. to* Scott. *See* Old Mortality: Sound, Sound the Clarion.

One cup for my self-hood. Barry Pain. *Fr.* The Poets at Tea, X. Par

One dark world is all I am. Born Again. Forugh Farrokhzad, *tr.* by Jascha Kessler *and* Amin Banani. PBWP

One day/ You gonna walk in this house. Seduction. Nikki Giovanni. NMM

One day/ as I was lying on the lawn. The Gift. Ed Ochester. Psk

One day/ two people decide to build a bed. The Bed. Dennis Saleh. NeAC

One day/ Marilyn marched. Chic Freedom's Reflection. Alice Walker. InPS; NMM

One day, a fine day, a high-flying-sky day. The Cat Heard the Cat-Bird. John Ciardi. SO

One day a man fell in love with himself, and was unable. The Love Affair. Russell Edson. NAmP

One day across the lake where echoes come now. The Animal That Drank Up Sound. William Stafford. VGW

One day as I sat and suffered. The Heretic. Bliss Carman. WGRP

One day as I strolled down by the Royal Albion. The Young Sailor Cut Down in His Prime. *Unknown.* OxBSS

One day as I unwarily did gaze. Spenser. *Fr.* Amoretti, XVI. OAEL-1.

One day as I was a-rambling around. Wild Bill Jones. *Unknown.* AmFP

One day as I was sitting still. The Battle of Sole Bay. *Unknown.* GBP (Song on the Duke's Late Glorious Success over the Dutch, A.) OxBSS

One day between the Lip and the Heart. The Lip and the Heart. John Quincy Adams. AA

One day I complained about the periphery. Periphery. A. R. Ammons. NOBA

One day I found a lost dog in the street. Dead Dog. Vernon Scannell. OxBC

One day I met you. Song of Meeting. Tsung Ch'en, *tr.* by Jonathan Chaves. CoBLCP

One day I observed a grey hair in my head. The Grey Hair. Judah Halevi, *tr.* by J. Chotzner. TrJP

One day I saw a downy duck. Good Morning. Muriel Sipe. RAR

One day I saw a ship upon the sands. Sea Irony. John Langdon Heaton. AA

One day I shall seat you in splendour. When Nothing Remains. Stanislaw Grochowiak, *tr.* by Czeslaw Milosz. PwPP

One day I thought I'd have some fun. The Tenderfoot. D. J. O'Malley. AS
(D-2 Horse Wrangler.) CowP, *diff. vers.*

One day I walked into the shop of those who blow the glass. Mohammad Taqi Mir, *tr.* by Ahmed Ali. GoT

One day I was walking, I heard a complaining. The Housewife's Lament. *Unknown.* MAT

One day I watched Ted Williams. The Kid. Kevin Bezner. ASP

One day I went down in the golden harvest field. *Unknown.* GBP

One day I wrote her name upon the strand. Spenser. *Fr.* Amoretti, LXXV. AWP; BLPL; BoLoP; EBEV; EIL; FiP; GBL; HAP; HeIP; InPS; LiTB; NAEL-1; NoP; OAEL-1; PoE; SeCePo; Son; Wew

One day in a popular quarter of Kharkov. Images. Valery Larbaud, *tr. by* William Jay Smith. CT

One day in the Library. Further Advantages of Learning. Kenneth Rexroth. TAP

One day, not here, you will find a hand. Again. Charlotte Mew. MoAB; MoBrPo

One day on our village in the month of July. Death of an Aircraft. Charles Causley. MoBS

One day over the course of a week or so. Dream of the Artfairy. Carl Morse. GLP

One day people will touch and talk perhaps easily. Daydream. A. S. J. Tessimond. SeCePo

One day ringing men will be a race gone. The Ringers. John Peck, *tr. by* William Arrowsmith. AmPA; AnAn

One day soon he'll tell her it's time to start packing. Drifters. Bruce Dawe. CBAP; NoAM

One day Sun found a new canyon. People of the South Wind. William Stafford. NNaP

One day the cages and caverns opened. The Animal's Crusade. H. H. ter Balkt, *tr.* by Scott Rollins. DuIn

One day the Chinese Bird of Royalty, Fum. Fum and Hum, the Two Birds of Royalty. Thomas Moore. OBSV

One day the fields will be forever green. Song of Hope. Daisy Yamora, *tr.* by James Black *and* Bernardo Garcia-Pandavenes. AIW

One day the god of fond desire. James Thomson. EnLoPo

One day the letters went to school. The Letters at School. Mary Mapes Dodge. OBCA

One day the nouns were clustered in the street. Permanently. Kenneth Koch. CoAP; NoP; PoA; PoM; PPP

One day the sun was rising high. The Peddler and His Wife. *Unknown.* AmFP

One day the tired sea will open to the sun. Like a Pearl. Hayim Naggid, *tr.* by Shlomo Vinner *and* Howard Schwartz. VWA

One day, the vine. The Rebellious Vine. Harold Monro. BrPo

One day there entered an my chamber door. My Uninvited Guest. May Riley Smith. AA; WGRP

One day thou didst desert me—then I learned. To Imagination. Edith M. Thomas. AA

One day, through the primeval wood. The Calf-Path. Sam Walter Foss. PoLF

One day we took our lunches. The Circus Parade. Katharine Pyle. OBCA

One day, when childhood tumbled the spongy tufts. Crane. Joseph Langland. NYBP

One day when Coyote. One for Coyote. *Unknown, tr.* by Carl Cary. STP

One day when I was a child, long ago. Grace Paley. NMM

One Day When It Was Night Out. Robert Desnos, *tr. fr. French by* Michael Benedikt. POS

One day when the sun shone on the water. Introduction to a Prayer. Fritzi Harmsen van Beek, *tr.* by Claire Nicolas White. DuIn

One Day When We Went Walking. Valine Hobbs. RHPC

One day, while in a lonesome grove. Newberry. *Unknown.* AmFP

One day you look at the mirror and it's open. Glass. W. S. Merwin. EAS

One day you'll have to go to the City of the Dead. Elephants May Parade before Your House. *Gond Oral Tradition, tr.* by V. Elwin *and* S. Hivale. WTO

One deep in the dark. Ray DiPalma. *Fr.* Planh, X. IAT

One Desiring Me to Read, But Slept It Out, Wakening. George Daniel. OxBSP

One died, and the soul was wrenched out. Street Musicians. John Ashbery. CAPP; HCAP

One dignity delays for all. Emily Dickinson. SoSe

One document at dawn, submitted to the nine-tiered palace. Written on My Way into Exile. Han Yü, *tr.* by Burton Watson. CoBCP

"One does not bathe twice in the same stream," said the philosopher Heraclitus. The Rue Ravignan. Max Jacob, *tr.* by John Ashbery. RHTwFP

One does not have to worry if we die. 7 October, 1940. Valentine Ackland. CN

One does such work as one will not. In the Matter of Two Men. James David Corrothers. BANP

One dollar down. Abelardo. FIA

One dot/ Grainily shifting. The Bee. James Dickey. SoSe

One dove has its head turned. Girl with Doves. Stephen Gray. PeSA

One Down. Richard Armour. SD

One duck stood on my toes. Feeding Ducks. Norman MacCaig. OxBS

One—dumbbell—Two—curls. A Fitness Center Chant. James Koch. SoTCo

One eats/ the moon in a tortilla. Food. Victor M. Valle, *tr.* by Toni Empringham. FIA

One elf, I trow, is diving now. Song of the Elfin Steersman. George Hill. AA

One ends in ignominy because one begins mistakenly. Precious Mettle. Lewis Warsh. UL

One-erum, two-erum. *Unknown.* OxNR

One-ery, two-ery, [or ore-ery], ickery, Ann. *Unknown.* FaPON; OxNR

One-ery, two-ery, tickery, seven. *Unknown.* OxNR

One evening a young lady fair, her estate rode out to see. On the Banks of Salee. *Unknown.* AmFP

One evening as the sun went down [or when the sun was low]. The Big Rock Candy Mountains. *Unknown.* AmFP; ChTr; GBP; OBAL; TTTS, *shorter version*

One evening bright stars they were shining. The Brooklyn Theater Fire. *Unknown.* AmFP

One evening in November I happened for to stray. Johnny Carroll's Camp. *Unknown.* AmFP

One evening last June as I rambled. On the Banks of the Little Eau Pleine. *Unknown.* AmFP

One evening (surely I was led by her). On Ullswater. Wordsworth. *Fr.* The Prelude [or, Growth of a Poet's Mind]: Childhood and School-Time. FaBoPP; RB

One evening, when the sun was just gone down. On the Death of Old Bennet the News-Crier. *Unknown.* NOEC

One evening when we were lounging in his apartment in a relaxed mood. Rain. Anselm Hollo. PoM

One evening, while the cooler shade she sought. Dryden. *Fr.* The Hind and the Panther, I. PoEL-3

One eye without a head to wear it. On the Farther Wall, Marc Chagall. Phyllis McGinley. *Fr.* Spectator's Guide to Contemporary Art. OBSV

One Eyed Black Man in Nebraska. Sam Cornish. PoBA

One face looks out from all his canvases. In an Artist's Studio. Christina Rossetti. NAEL-2; NoP

One fall not far from Ozark, Arkansas. The Narrative Hooper and L.D.O. Sestina with a Long Last Line. James Whitehead. HoPM

One fantee wave. Edith Sitwell. *Fr.* Gold Coast Customs. OBMV

One fatal mistake that is made today is gossip. Gossip. Mrs. Henry Linden. CBWP-4

One feather is a bird. The Voice. Theodore Roethke. VGW

One fine day an old man. The Girl Warrior. *Unknown, tr. by* Angel Flores. DMH

One fine day I'll start writing. Ars Poetica. József Tornai, *tr. by* Jascha Kessler. FOC

One fine day in the middle of the night. *Unknown.* CenHV

One fine morning, in the country on a very gentle people. Royalty. Rimbaud, *tr. by* Enid Rhodes Peschal. SOTW

One fine night in a witch's cavern. Gobbolino, the Witch's Cat. G. C. Westcott. CRH

One Flesh. Elizabeth Jennings. AIW; FaBoWP; OxBTC; PBWP

One Flight Up. Bob Holman. UL

One flutter of memory, then all becomes. Burning the Letters. Gwendolyn Grew. HoPM

One Foot in Eden. Edwin Muir. CMoP; GTBS-P; NoAM; NOBE; OPOP

One foot in front of the other, heel to toe. Highway Patrol Stops Me, Going Too Slow. Robert Peterson. NeAC

One Foot in the Door. Anne Elder. CBAP

One for Coyote. *Unknown, tr. fr. Skagit Indian by* Carl Cary. STP

One for money. *Unknown.* OxNR

One for sorrow, two for joy. *Unknown.* OxNR

One for sorrow, two for mirth. *Unknown.* PBBP

One forfeit more from life the current claimed. At the Discharge of Cannon Rise the Drowned. Hubert Witheford. ATNZ; PeNZ

One Friday morn when we set sail. The Mermaid. *Unknown.* CH; ESPB; OnMSP

One from One Leaves Two, *sel.* Ogden Nash.
  "I pray the Lord my soul to take." NBLV

One Furrow, The. Ronald Stuart Thomas. HoPM; OxBC

One gets a wife, one gets a house. The Cat. Ogden Nash. CRH

One Girl. Sappho, *tr. fr. Greek by* Dante Gabriel Rossetti. AWP

One Girl at the Boys Party, The. Sharon Olds. InPK; MAYP

One girl in a red dress leaves the shopping center. Suburban Dusk. Bert Meyers. EAS

One Goes with Me along the Shore. Manfred Winkler, *tr. fr. Hebrew by* Mary Zilzer. VWA

One good crucifixion and he rose from the dead. Easter. Charles Hubert Sisson. OxBSP

One good thing about music. Trenchtown Rock. Bob Marley. PBCV

One got peace of heart at last, the dark march over. After War. Ivor Gurney. OxBSP

One granite ridge. Piute Creek. Gary Snyder. CoAP; NAAL-2; NaP; NOBA

One had a lovely face. Memory. W. B. Yeats. BIrV; PoE

One had grown almost affluent: one had. Elegy for an Estrangement. John Holloway. NePoEA

One half of me was up and dressed. The Gentle Check. Joseph Beaumont. PBBP

One hand is smaller than the other. It. Man with One Small Hand. P. K. Page. MoCV; OBCV

One hand, two hands. Nothing more. Sphinxes Inclined to Be. Olga Orozco, *tr. by* Leslie Keffer. WPOW

One Happy Moment. Dryden. *See* Cleomenes: No, No, Poor Suffering Heart.

One has a feeling it is all coming to an end. The Feeling. William Bronk. VGW

One hears Light harnessing the strong back of the sky-ox. There Are Three Bones in the Human Ear. Anita Endrezze-Danielson. STE

One heifer and one fleecy sheep. Aristeides. Antipater of Sidon, *tr. by* Charles Whibley. AWP

One hero dies,—a thousand new ones rise. Nathan Hale. William Ordway Partridge. OPP

One holy church of God appears. The Church Universal. Samuel Longfellow. WGRP

One Home. William Stafford. AmFN; CoAP; VGW

One Hope, The. Dante Gabriel Rossetti. *Fr.* The House of Life, CI. NAEL-2; OAEL-2

One-horned Ewe, The. *Unknown.* GBP

One Horse Chay, The. *Unknown.* OxBoLi

One hue of our flag is taken. The Rejected "National Hymns." "Orpheus C. Kerr." OBAL

108 Tales of a Po 'Buckra, *sel.* Will Inman.
  "Dark brother touches me, The." GLP

One hundred feet from off the ground. Long-Suffering of God. Christopher Smart. *Fr.* Hymns for the Amusement of Children, XXIX. NOCV

151st Psalm, The. Karl Shapiro. EaLo; VWA

104 Boulevard Saint-Germain. Kenneth Pitchford. NYBP

One Hundred Haiku in Free Form, *sels.* Ozaki Hosai, *tr. fr. Japanese by* Hiroaki Sato. FCEI
  "After scolding my wife."
  "Already dawn, before the Buddha's altar."
  "Althea nodding all day, it has darkened."
  "An early morning road, a dog."
  "Ants stopped coming."
  "Big pine's darkening, The."
  "Biting hard pears, arguing."
  "Blowing the evening sun."
  "Carrying fresh water with both hands."
  "Carved into Buddha's form."
  "Children are shouting."
  "Chrysanthemums have all withered."
  "Cigarette is dead, The."
  "Clipped the nails, the fingers."
  "Crow wordlessly flew away, A."
  "Daybreak, big waves, the clear sky."
  "Driving huge bulls up the hill."
  "Emptying the boat, they all climbed up."
  "Farewell said, cover lowered."
  "Festival, letting a baby sleep, A."
  "For a hollow mind."
  "For laughing, front teeth."
  "From the pipe pointing the way for me."
  "Frost-packed morning."
  "Getting time off from the Buddha."
  "Gun, glinting, deep snow, A."
  "Handkerchief still lying there, A."
  "Having washed the gravestone."
  "He moves his quiet shadow."
  "Heart that seeks something, The."
  "Here's a dying invalid."
  "Holding a child's hand intently."
  "Houses are crowding the town."
  "I cough and am still alone."
  "I go around to the back of the grave."
  "I have no vessel, I receive."
  "I hold a dog, my skin."
  "I know the footsteps of the sparrow."
  "I leave the paper doors open."
  "I look at the evening sky."
  "I look back at the shore."
  "I release a turtle."

"I rescue a needle from the ashes."
"I slip a boiled egg out of its shell."
"I walk over a moistened bridge."
"I'm looking for a single flea, midnight."
"I'm thinking of sweeping."
"In a pond of silence a turtle."
"In a sharp wind trying to part."
"In the darkness of the well."
"In the great wind, in the sky."
"In the mountain sunset the graveyard."
"In the sun, counting the money."
"It came as a stray dog and still is."
"It's been raining for days."
"It's wet around the well."
"Just the ants at the bottom of the burning sky."
"Late moon, shut out of the town, A."
"Late night wheat flour spilled."
"Leaving only the noise of dead leaves."
"Lord Buddha's yellow flowers, The."
"Moonlit night I return."
"Morning-glories' white continues to bloom."
"Mountain water, trickly."
"On a warm roof, working."
"On the straw roof grass grows."
"One or two, immersed in darkness."
"Pine cone, as it is, A."
"Pomegranate opened its mouth, A."
"Praying mantis drops with a thud, A."
"Ran and caught up, in the wind."
"Rejecting a slanderous mind."
"Right under the big sky."
"Sea becomes light, a window is open, The."
"Single set of footsteps coming, A."
"Small rural newspaper, The."
"Snake, killed, A."
"Snap, the thong broke."
"Snow fades into the river, The."
"Snow has cleared, The."
"Snowy sky turns into a single crow, The."
"Sound of the florist's scissors, The."
"Sparrows all at once are gone, The."
"Splashing hot water over my navel."
"Supper eaten, still blessed."
"Their many children each reading."
"There it was, my face."
"These are the mornings and evenings."
"Thinking about something."
"To one of the ears."
"Unable to put thread through a needle."
"Walking down to eat my meal."
"Wallet gone completely empty."
"We drained the pond."
"Wears dirty clogs."
"Where the autumn sun shines, on a stone."
"With a face saying I caught something."
"Woman in dark glasses, A."
"Woman in the newspaper, The."
"Wonderful breasts, here's a mosquito."
"101." Alan Davies. IAT
One hundred silences and not a single tear. Elul in Galilee. Leah Goldberg, tr. by Bernhard Frank. MHeP
110 Year Old House. Ed Ochester. Psk
One I love. Unknown. OxNR
One I Love Is Gone Away, The. Unknown. MeEL
One imagines the lives of the Prince. Winter in Étienburgh. Stephen Parker. NYBP
One in herself, not rent by schism, but sound. The Catholic Church. Dryden. Fr. The Hind and the Panther, II. OBS
One in ten, as the lot falls. So be it. Thorns. Haim Gouri, tr. by Warren Bargad and Stanley F. Chyet. IP
One in the boat cried out. The Door. L. A. G. Strong. MoBrPo
One Inch Tall. Shel Silverstein. OBCA
One is a bitch with stinking. The Furies. Donald Justice. AnAn
One is a sign of mischief. Unknown. PBBP
One is an ex-professor of biology. Dykes in the Garden. Sharon Barba. PeHV
One is enough, she cried. Technicalities for Jack Spicer. Philip Whalen. PoM
One is not hale until one inhales. On Apples. David Ross. NYBP
"One is reminded of a certain person." Kite Poem. James Merrill. TwCP

One is so seldom struck by lightning. For the Poet Who Said Poets Are Struck by Lightning Only Two or Three Times. Peter Klappert. NBLV
One is sorrow, two mirth. Unknown. PBBP
One Island. Naomi Shihab Nye. NAmP
One keeps a secret for me. The Secret. Mary Morison Webster. PeSA
One kind of love, a Tourist Bureau print. At the Fox Glacier Hotel. James Keir Baxter. ATNZ
One Kingfisher and One Yellow Rose. Eileen Brennan. NeIP
One king's daughter said to anither. Sheath and Knife. Unknown. CH; ESPB
One-l lama, the. Ogden Nash. FaBoCh
(The Lama.) FaPON; FiBHP
One last look at your hills, Lysander. Learning Destiny. Herman Charles Bosman. PeSA
One Last Word. John Glassco. NOBC
One late spring evening in Bohemia. The Cloud. Edwin Muir. OBTV
One-legged Man, The. Siegfried Sassoon. CMoP
One lesson, Nature, let me learn of [or from] thee. Quiet Work. Matthew Arnold. FaBoBe; TrGrPo
One Life. Dinah Butler. AIW
One little dicky-bird. Ten Little Dicky-Birds. A. W. I. Baldwin. BoTP
One little Indian boy making a canoe. Ten Little Indian Boys. M. M. Hutchinson. BoTP
One little noise of life remained—I heard. On the Eclipse of the Moon of October 1865. Charles Tennyson Turner. OBNC
One lives by commerce, said the guide. Guide to the Ruins. Howard Nemerov. EyDe
One lone pine tree. Saigyo, tr. fr. Japanese by Burton Watson. Fr. Sixty-four Tanka. FCEI
One long sigh piled on another. Long Sigh. Lu Yu, tr. by Burton Watson. CoBCP
One look at plum blossoms. Shoju-rojin, tr. by Lucien Stryk and Takashi Ikemoto. ZPCJ
One looks from the train. The Orient Express. Randall Jarrell. CMoP; CoAP; NOBA; PoE
One Lost, The. Isaac Rosenberg. MoBrPo
One lovely summer afternoon when balmy breezes blew. To Clements' Ferry. Josephine D. Henderson Heard. CBWP-4
One makes no noise. The Vigil. Philippe Jaccottet, tr. by Anthony Rudolf. RHTwFP
One Man Down. Ai. GeTw
One Man to Another. Rita Anyiam–St. John. WS
One man with a frown ruining. Country Hotel. Brian Turner. ATNZ
One Man's Wife. Philip Booth. NIP; VGW
One midnight, after a day when lilies. Digging. Donald Hall. CAPP
One midnight, deep in starlight still. Bankrupt. Cortlandt W. Sayres. PoLF
One might as well conceive this story in the cirrose. Richard Kenney. Fr. The Encantadas. EOEF
One millennium more. Asleep in the Arms of Mother Night. Andrew Joron. BWV
One misty, moisty morning. Mother Goose. BoTP; FaBoBe; OxNR; RHPC
One Modern Poet. Carl Sandburg. OBAL
One moment past our bodies cast. Morning Song in the Jungle. Kipling. NoAM
One Moment's Mirror. Paul Eluard, tr. fr. French by Michael Benedikt. POS
One monk, you have dissolved phenomena. At the Mountain of the Mysterious Tomb. Wu Wei-yeh, tr. by Jonathan Chaves. CoBLCP
One More Day's Work for Jesus. Anna B. Warner. AH
One More Explanation for the Mystery. Pierre Reverdy, tr. fr. French by Michael Benedikt. POS
One more little spirit to Heaven has flown. Little Libbie. Julia A. Moore. OBAL
One More New Botched Beginning. Stephen Spender. CMoP; NoAM; NYBP
One more night my blood. O Wendy, Arthur. Maurice Kenny. HATNAP
One more rendezvous. John G. Neihardt. Fr. The Song of Jed Smith. FYAP
One more round of trials, another ordeal endured. Sitting in Meditation: A Random Thought. Ku T'ai-ch'ing, tr. by Pao Chia-lin. WFTU
One More Sign. Roberta Hill Whiteman. HATNAP
One More Time. James Welch. NOVW
One more unfortunate. The Bridge of Sighs. Thomas Hood. BeLS; EBEV; EnRP; FaPoR; FPL; GTBS; GTBS-P; OBEV; WBLP
One morn before me were three figures seen. Ode on Indolence. Keats. EnRP; LiTB; NAEL-2; OBNC

One morn I watch'd the rain subside. Devonshire Scenes. Coventry Patmore. *Fr.* Tamerton Church-Tower or First Love. FaBoPP
One Morning. Jan Hanlo, *tr. fr. Dutch by* James S. Holmes. DuIn
One Morning. Timothy Steele. CRP
One morning a great gaggle slid. When Angels Came to Zimmer. Paul Zimmer. MOWH
One morning a weasel came swimming. The Weasel. *Unknown.* ChTr
One morning as I rambled. The Miner Boy. *Unknown.* AmFP
One morning de captain wake. Itanami. *Unknown.* PBCV
One morning ere [*or* before] Titan had thought to stir [*or* thought of stirring] his feet. The Vision. Egan O'Rahilly, *tr. by* Thomas Kinsella. NOIV
(Reverie, The.) AnIL, *tr. by* Frank O'Connor
(Reverie at Dawn.) FaBoPV, *tr. by* Frank O'Connor
One morning I call for a sedan-chair man. Yüan Mei, *tr. fr. Chinese by* Jonathan Chaves. *Fr.* Five Poems on Returning to Hangchou. CoBLCP
One Morning I got up. The Little Bird. *Unknown, tr. by* Rolf Italiaander. PBA
One Morning in May [*or* The Nightingale]. *Unknown.* AS
One Morning in May; or, The Young Girl Cut Down in Her Prime. *Unknown.* AmFP
One morning in spring. Fife Tune. John Manifold. CBAP; FaFP; GoJo; InPS; LiTB; LiTM; Mes; NBLV; WaaP; WaP
One morning in the month of June. The Royal Fisherman. *Unknown.* ChTr; GBP
One morning in the month of May. Just as the Tide Was a-Flowing. *Unknown.* OBET
One morning of ancestral ash. Without Knowing Why. Sebastian Salazar Bondy, *tr. by* Ena Hollis *and* David Tipton. Per
One Morning, Oh, So Early! Jean Ingelow. OxBChV
One morning old Wilfrid Scawen Blunt. Victor Gray. NOBL
One morning, one morning, one morning in May. One Morning in May [*or* The Nightingale]. *Unknown.* AS
(Nightingale, The.) AmFP
(Rebel Soldier, The.) OxBoLi
One morning, one morning, one morning in Spring. I'll Be Fourteen Next Sunday. *Unknown.* AmFP
One morning, reading the paper, I was flabbergasted. English—ugh! Tsuboi Shigeji, *tr. by* Geoffrey Bownas *and* Anthony Thwaite. PeBJV
One Morning the Earth Stirred. Eeva Kilpi, *tr. fr. Finnish by* Aili Jarvenpa. SOP
One Morning the World Woke Up. Oscar Williams. FaFP; WaaP; WaP
One Morning We Brought Them Order. Al Lee. FF
One morning when I went downtown. Morning in Spring. Louis Ginsberg. GoYe
One Morning When the Rain-Birds Call. Lloyd Roberts. CaP
One morning with a 12-gauge my brother shot what he said was a linnet. Linnets. Larry Levis. LCAP
One mouse adds up to many mice. Singular Indeed. David McCord. OBCA
One Mr. B,/ A joker he. Repartée. Charles Follen Adams. OBAL
One must have a mind of winter. The Snow Man. Wallace Stevens. CMoP; GoJo; HAP; HCAP; HeIP; MAT; NAAL-2; NoAM; NoP; NU; PoE; PrIm; QFR; SoSe; WeW
One needs a lyric poet in these. Julius Lester. *Fr.* In the Time of Revolution, IV. PoBA
One night/ my father saw a saint in his dream. My Father's Dream. Sargon Boulus, *tr. by* Sargon Boulus *and* Alistair Elliot. MAP
One Night. Umberto Saba, *tr. fr. Italian by* Felix Stefanile. PFI
One night a bird came to me. Night Visitors. Kadya Molodovsky, *tr. by* Ruth Whitman. VWA
"One night," a doctor said, "last fall." Ambrose Bierce. *Fr.* The Devil's Dictionary. OBAL
One night all nights and tonight like every other night. Yves Tanguy. Paul Eluard, *tr. by* Michael Benedikt. POS
One night all tired with the weary day. The Gnat. Joseph Beaumont. FM; OBS
One night as Dick lay fast asleep. Full Moon. Walter de la Mare. BoNaP
One night as I lay on my bed. Death. *Unknown, tr. by* Aneirin Talfan Davies. OBWVE; RB
One night as Polly Oliver was lying in her bed. Polly Oliver's Rambles. *Unknown.* OBET
One Night at Victoria Beach. Gabriel Okara. UAS
One Night Away from Day. John Digby. EAS
One night, being pressed by his old friend Chubb. The Undertakers' Club. *Unknown.* GBP
One night came on a hurricane. The Sailor's Consolation. *At. to* William Pitt. BeLS; FaBoCo

One-Night Expensive Hotel. Ronald G. Everson. NOBC
One-Night Fair. Nancy Price. GOYP
One night from the stern I thought, as I watched. Braemar. Galway Kinnell. PoA
One night he dreamed he was a. The Young Man Who Loved the Girl Who Took Care of Her Aged Father. Greg Kuzma. AmPA
One night he heard heart-breaking sound. Austin Clarke. *Fr.* Mnemosyne Lay in Dust, VI. CIP; CMoP; IPY
One night I dreamed I was locked in my Father's watch. My Father's Watch. John Ciardi. ImOP
One night I lay asleep in Africa. Bookra. Charles Dudley Warner. AA
One night I reached a cave: I slept, my head. Incident on a Journey. Thom Gunn. NePoEA
One night i' th' yeare [*or* in the year], my dearest Beauties, come. To His Lovely Mistresses. Robert Herrick. CaPo; CTC; SeCP
One night in late October. Judged by the Company One Keeps. *Unknown.* BLPA; FPL; NBLV
One night Jake telephoned. 26th Precinct Station. Louis Simpson. EOEF
One night of tempest I arose and went. Night and Morning. *Unknown, tr. by* R. S. Thomas. OBWVE
One night poor Jim had not a sou. Facts. W. H. Davies. BrPo
One night quite bang up to the mark, ri tol de lol. Johnny Raw and Polly Clark. *Unknown.* CoMu
One Night Stand. Amiri Baraka. NeAP
One-Night Stand: An Approach to the Bridge, The. Paul Blackburn. ErPo
One night the Brownies reached a mound. The Brownies' Celebration. Palmer Cox. OBCA
One night there was no moon, and never had been. The Thrush Relinquished. Allen Grossman. PPR
One night two hunters, drunk, came in the tent. At the Piano. Andrew Hudgins. MOWH
One night when I was in the House of Death. Birth. Harold Monro. *Fr.* Strange Meetings. PoA
One night when I was walking. Let the Wind Blow High or Low. *Unknown.* OBET
One night when I went down. The Heap of Rags. W. H. Davies. BrPo
One night, your mother is listening to the walls. How You Get Born. Erica Jong. UnPo
One noonday, at my window in the town. Ball's Bluff. Herman Melville. OBWP
One nostril means latin. Queer Things. Emanuel Carnevali. EAS
One November. Hunting Season. Mykie Silz Reidy. TSL
One No. 7. John Frederick Frank. GoYe
One ocean. Recipe for Sand. Barbara Brinson Curiel. ER
One o'Clock. Katharine Pyle. *Fr.* The Wonder Clock. OBCA
One o'clock in the letter-box. The Meeting. Muriel Rukeyser. MoAmPo; TrJP
One of Many. Stevie Smith. OxBC
One of my father; he stands. Photographs. Charles Wright. HoPM
One of Our Aircraft Failed to Return. Patricia M. Saunders. CN
One of our race's great lights has gone out to the world. Paul Laurence Dunbar. Mrs. Henry Linden. CBWP-4
One of our race's greatest needs in this country today. The Y. M. C. A. Mrs. Henry Linden. CBWP-4
One of the clock, and silence deep. One o'Clock. Katharine Pyle. *Fr.* The Wonder Clock. OBCA
One of the Dead Speaks. Cahit Sitki Taranci, *tr. fr. Turkish by* Nermin Menemencioglu. OBD
One of the difficulties is in being. Russian Asylum. Marilyn Bowering. NOBC
One of the Jews. C. P. Cavafy, *tr. fr. Greek.* TrJP
One of the Many Days. Norman MacCaig. PoSH
One of the more intelligent members. For the Fly-Leaf of a School-Book. Norman Cameron. OxBS
One of the Principal Causes of War. "Hugh MacDiarmid." OxBSP
One of the Regiment. Douglas Le Pan. CaP
One of the two according to your choice. Haidée. Byron. *Fr.* Don Juan, IV. SeCePo
"One of the wits of the school" your chum would say. Your Birthday in Wisconsin You Are 140. John Berryman. NAs
One of Their Gods. C. P. Cavafy, *tr. fr. Greek by* Edmund Keeley *and* Philip Sherrard. VMG
One of these days. A Swell Idea. Steve Kowit. UL
One of these days under the white. The Boarding. Denis Johnson. MAYP
One of these nights about twelve o'clock. The Heavenly Aeroplane. *Unknown.* NOCV
One of those days when the water. The Neurophysiologist. Jonathan V. Post. BWV

One of those golden oldies from the fifties. Golden Oldie. Paul Mariani. GeTw

One of those lubricious teenage latin beauties. Renewal. Steve Kowit. UL

One of those two-bit luncheonettes on a nothing. A Candystore in Washington Heights. James Reiss. AnAn

One of us/ will/ be. Devils. Norman Mailer. OBAL

One of Wally's Yarns. John Masefield. BrPo

One of you is a major made of cord and catskin. Lent in a Year of War. Thomas Merton. EAS

One of your cords of Koguryo brocade. *Unknown. Fr.* Manyo Shu. FCEI

"One old Chinese man told me," he said. The Mango Tree. Eric Chock. BrSi

One Old Ox. *Unknown.* ChTr; FaBoNo

One, or a thousand voices?—filling noon. The Crickets in the Fields. Edward Rowland Sill. AnAmPo

One or two, immersed in darkness. Ozaki Hosai, *tr. fr. Japanese by* Hiroaki Sato. *Fr.* One Hundred Haiku in Free Form. FCEI

One ought not to have to care. The Hill Wife. Robert Frost. CMoP; HAP; InPS; LiTM; NoP; VGW

One ounce of truth benefits. Nikki Giovanni. CNA

One paddy ceases croaking for a while. Kyorai, *tr. by* Hiroaki Sato. FCEI

One paddy planted. Stopping by Saigyo's Willow. Basho, *tr. fr. Japanese by* Burton Watson. *Fr.* Seventy-six Hokku. FCEI

One peak, stripped sheer. A Trip to Hua-yang Mountain. Tao-chi, *tr. by* Jonathan Chaves. CoBLCP

One per cent. Third World. Salah Niyazi, *tr. by* Abdullah al-Udhari. MPAW

One Perfect Rose. Dorothy Parker. FiBHP; NBLV; NIP; NoP; OBAL

One person. Issa, *tr. by* Kenneth Koch *and* Harold Henderson. TTTS

One Person, *sels.* Elinor Wylie.
"I hereby swear that to uphold your house." *Fr.* XVI. LiTA; MoAB; NAAL-2; OxBA; Son
(Sonnet from "One Person.") LiTA; MoAmPo
"In our content, before the autumn came." *Fr.* XII. NAAL-2
"Let us leave talking of angelic hosts." OxBA
Little Beauty That I Was Allowed, The. *Fr.* V. Son

One person each, out. Bob Perelman. IAT

One pillar holding up consolation. César Vallejo, *tr. by* James Wright. AnAn

One Plant for Man-made Oil. Ono Tozaburo, *tr. fr. Japanese by* Hiroaki Sato. FCEI

One Poet Visits Another. W. H. Davies. TW

One point behind, ten seconds left. The Kicker's Last Steps. William Meissner. TSL

1.1./ not the reproduction. But We'll Make Another One. Nanni Balestrini, *tr. by* Lawrence R. Smith. NItP

One potato, two potato. Counting-out Rhymes. *Unknown.* FaPON

One Presenting a Rare Book to Madame Hull. John Saffin. SCAP

One question, and master thunders. Kyochu, *tr. by* Lucien Stryk *and* Takashi Ikemoto. ZPCJ

One quick scratch. Lighting a Fire. X. J. Kennedy. TSS

One rain, and all the flowers done! Sleeplessness. Yüan Mei, *tr. by* J. P. Seaton. WFTU

One rainy night that year we saw our wives. Our Wives. Jonathan Galassi. EOEF

One Reason for Stars. Jack Butler. MT

One Red Rose. Ernie Fanning. CowP

One remains, the many change and pass, The. Shelley. *Fr.* Adonais; an Elegy on the Death of John Keats. SCV

One returns to the place where he left his life. Memorial. Rigoberto Paredes, *tr. by* Walter Martínez. Vol

One ring of clear chimes through the evening mist. Inscribed on My Little Painting of Plum Blossom and Bamboo. Tao-chi, *tr. by* Jonathan Chaves. CoBLCP

One road leads to London. Roadways. John Masefield. BoTP

One room, one bed—enough. Ryuge, *tr. by* Lucien Stryk *and* Takashi Ikemoto. ZPCJ

One rooster does not weave a morning. Weaving the Morning. João Cabral de Melo Neto, *tr. by* Galway Kinnell. ATCBP

One Rose of Stone. Keith Wilson. GOYP

One, round the candytuft. I Spy. N. E. Hussey. BoTP

One sat within a hung and lighted room. Love and Poverty. Elisabeth Jones Cavazza Pullen. AA

One Saturday. "Marian Douglas." AA

One Saturday night as we set sail. The Mermaid. *Unknown.* AmFP

One scene as I bow to pour her coffee. Vacation. William Stafford. AmFN; Psk

One seem'd all dark and red—a tract of sand. Tennyson. *Fr.* The Palace of Art. UnPo

One set on the highway to sing. Li Po, *tr. by* Ezra Pound. OxBA

One shadow glides from the dumb shore. Gloucester Harbor. Elizabeth Stuart Phelps Ward. AA

One ship drives east and another drives west. The Winds of Fate. Ella Wheeler Wilcox. AnAmPo; BLPA; FPL; WBLP

One shuts one eye. Before Play. Vasco Popa, *tr. fr. Serbo-Croatian by* Anne Pennington. *Fr.* Games. RB

One side of his world is always missing. Riding a One-eyed Horse. Henry Taylor. HeIP; InPK

One side of the potato-pits was white with frost. A Christmas Childhood. Patrick Kavanagh. AnIL; FaBCIP; IPY

One-sided Love. Kitahara Hakushu, *tr. fr. Japanese by* Hiroaki Sato. FCEI

One-Sided Love. Shunzei, *tr. fr. Japanese by* Burton Watson. *Fr.* Thirty Tanka. FCEI

One Sided Shoot-out. Don L. Lee. BPo; PoBA

One silent night of late. The Cheat of Cupid; or, The Ungentle Guest. Robert Herrick, *after* Anacreon. AWP; OBVE

One single word of heartfelt kindness. Kindness. Mary E. Tucker. CBWP-1

One slash through the dense growth—the road south of the city. Late Spring. Ts'ao Chen-chi, *tr. by* William H. Nienhauser, Jr. WFTU

One solitary bird melodiously. Evening. Charles Sangster. CaP

One Song, The. Mark Strand. CAPP

One sore thing is the way. Gibbons Ruark. MT

One sound after another. K'uang Chou-yi, *tr. by* Li Chi *and* Michael Patrick O'Connor. WFTU

One sound. Then the hiss and whir. The Garden. Louise Glück. AmPA; HCAP; NAAL-2

One spring the circus gave. A Hill of Beans. Rita Dove. BLA

One standing on the empty beach. Ballykinlar: May 1940. Patrick Maybin. NeIP

One star fell and another as we walked. Conrad Aiken. *Fr.* Preludes for Memnon; or, Preludes to Attitude. MoAmPo

One steed I have of common clay. Comrades. Henry Ames Blood. AA

One Step at a Time. *Unknown.* WBLP

One step twix't me and death, (twas Davids speech). Roger Williams. SCAP

One stone sufficeth (lo what death can do). On a Whore. John Hoskyns. FaBoEE

One stood still, looking stupid. The other. The Willets. May Swenson. WPE

One stormy day in winter. The Splinter. James Kenneth Stephen. CenHV

One stormy morn I chanced to meet. A Kiss in the Rain. Samuel Minturn Peck. OBAL

One Summer. Robert Mezey. DiL

One Summer Day, Invited by Mr. Shih Chü-an to Have a Drink. Ch'en Wei-sung, *tr. fr. Chinese by* Madeline Chu. WFTU

One Summer Evening ("One summer evening (led by her) I found"). Wordsworth. *Fr.* The Prelude [or, Growth of a Poet's Mind]: Childhood and School-Time. FiP; NU

One summer he stole the jade buttons. Of Your Father's Indiscretions and the Train to California. Lynn Emanuel. MAYP

One summer, high in Wyoming. Before the Storm. Kenneth O. Hanson. CoAP

One summer I stayed. The Two Families. Joyce L. Brisley. BoTP

One summer morning a daring band. The Ballad of Ishmael Day. *Unknown.* PAH

One summer only grant me, you powerful fates. To the Fates. Friedrich Hölderlin, *tr. by* Michael Hamburger. OBD

One Sunday morning as I went walking, by Brisbane waters I chanced to stray. Moreton Bay. *Unknown.* CBAP

One Sunday morning soft and fine. Brigadier. A. J. M. Smith. MoCV

One sweetly solemn thought. Nearer Home. Phoebe Cary. AA; BLRP; FaFP; PWR; WBLP; WGRP
(One Sweetly Solemn Thought.) AH

One Talent, The. William Cutler. PWR

One That Got Away. Jenny Joseph. NPo

One that is ever kind said yesterday. The Folly of Being Comforted. W. B. Yeats. AnIL; BrPo; GBL; HeIP; NAEL-2

One, The Other, and. Wendy Wieber. NMM

One they hunt by night, The. I Am Ham Melanite. William Millett. GoYe

One Thing. "Owen Meredith." WBLP

One thing at a time. *Unknown.* OxNR

One thing has a shelving bank. A Drumlin Woodchuck. Robert Frost. GoYe; NoAM; NOBA

One thing in all things have I seen. The Secret. "Æ." MoBrPo

One thing is sure. The Pulse. Mark Van Doren. MoAmPo
One Thing Needful, The. Max Isaac Reich. BLRP
One Thing That Can Save America, The. John Ashbery. AiP; NoAM; NOBA
One thing that literature would be greatly the better for. Very like a Whale. Ogden Nash. BLPL; HAP; InPK; InPS; PoLF; TrGrPo; WeW
One Thing to Take, Another to Keep. Crescenzo del Monte, *tr. by* Barbara Garvin. VWA
One thing work gives. Wendell Berry. *Fr.* Reverdure. SaC
One thing you left with us, Jack Johnson. Strange Legacies. Sterling A. Brown. CNA; PoBA; TTY
One thought the recurring "image" in the poet's song. Handbook of Versification. Gilbert Sorrentino. PoA
One Thousand and One Arabian Nights. Fei Ma, *tr. fr. Chinese by* Dominic Cheung. IFON
One thousand and one tumbles. Tettsu, *tr. by* Lucien Stryk *and* Takashi Ikemoto. ZPCJ
One thousand eight hundred and twenty-four. The Greenland Whale Fishery. *Unknown.* AmFP
One Thousand Fearful Words for Fidel Castro. Lawrence Ferlinghetti. VGW
One Thousand Feet of Shadow. David Craig. PoSH
1,000 Illustrations and a Complete Concordance. Michael Andre. UL
One thousand saxophones infiltrate the city. Battle Report. Bob Kaufman. AmNP; TTY
One Time. Douglas Livingstone. PeSA
One Time Henry Dreamed the Number. Doughtry Long, Jr. BPo; CNA; PoBA
One time I wanted two moons. Jacob Nibenegenesabe, *tr. fr. Cree Indian by* Howard Norman. *Fr.* The Wishing Bone Cycle. STP
One time in Alexandria, in wicked Alexandria. Thaïs. Newman Levy. FiBHP
One-time liaison officer in Babel's tower. The Oracle. Gordon Challis. ATNZ
One time my friend Tergvinder brought a large round boulder. Tergvinder's Stone. W. S. Merwin. CAPP
One Times One, *sel.* E. E. Cummings.
"Plato told/ him:he couldn't." *Fr.* XIII. CTC
One Tiny Bird. Yekhi'el Mar, *tr. fr. Hebrew by* Bernhard Frank. MHeP
One to destroy, is murder by the law. Edward Young. FF
One to Grieve, the. Rudy Thomas. GOYP
One to make ready. *Unknown.* OxNR
(The Start.) SD
One to Nothing. Carolyn Kizer. OBAL
One Token. W. H. Davies. BrPo
One, Two. Mervyn Morris. PBCV
One, two,/ Buckle my shoe. Mother Goose. BoTP; OxNR
One, two, Buckle my shoe. The Late Mother. Cynthia MacDonald. Psk
One, Two, Three. H. C. Bunner. FaPON; PoLF
One—Two—Three. Hannah Senesh, *tr. fr. Hungarian by* Peter Hay. WPOW
One, two, three,/ I love coffee. *Unknown.* OxNR
One, two, three, four,/ Mary at the cottage door. Mother Goose. OxNR
One, two, three, four, five/Once I caught a fish alive. Mother Goose. OxNR
One-two-three-four-five-six-seven. Ten-i, *tr. by* Lucien Stryk *and* Takashi Ikemoto. ZPCJ
One, Two, Three—Gough! Eve Merriam. NTCP
1-2-3 was the number he played but today the number came 3-2-1. Kenneth Fearing. FF; HeIP; HoPM; NIP; PoRA; RB; TrJP
One, two, tree/ All de same. *Unknown. Fr.* Songs, II. PBCV
One, two, whatever you do. *Unknown.* OxNR
One ugly trick has often spoiled. Meddlesome Matty. Ann Taylor. OnMSP; OxBChV
One-Upmanship. Miriam Chaikin. NTCP
One wading a fall meadow finds on all sides. The Beautiful Changes. Richard Wilbur. CMoP; CoAP; HCAP; InPS; PoE
One wants a Teller in a time like this. Gwendolyn Brooks. *Fr.* The Womanhood, XI. WPE
One was fifteen years old, the other sixteen, The. Pensionnaires. Paul Verlaine, *tr. by* François Pirou. PeHV
One was kicked in the stomach. Gangrene. Philip Levine. VGW
One Way Down. David Craig. PoSH
One Way of Looking at It. Arthur Munby. NOBVV
One-Way Song, *sel.* D. B. Wyndham Lewis.
"I would set all things whatsoever front to back." CTC
One We Knew. Thomas Hardy. NAEL-2
One wept whose only child was dead. Maternity. Alice Meynell. OxBSP

One West Coast. Al Young. NPGG
One white foot, run him for your life. How to Choose a Horse. *Unknown.* FaBoUs
One white foot, try him. On Buying a Horse. *Unknown.* NBLV; RB
One who does not love me, The. Song of Abuse. *Yoruba Oral Tradition, tr. by* Ulli Beier *and* B. Gbadamosi. WTO
One who gave the warning with his wings, The. Exile. Karl Shapiro. *Fr.* Adam and Eve. CRP
One Who Is Missing, The. Abraham Chalfi, *tr. fr. Hebrew by* Shlomo Vinner *and* Howard Schwartz. VWA
One, who is not, we see: but one, whom we see not, is. The Higher Pantheism in a Nutshell. Swinburne. *Fr.* The Heptalogia. BXAP; FaBoNo; NA; Par
One Who Is Within, The. Nia Francisco. STE
One Who Laughs and Laughs and Laughs, The. Unsi al-Haj, *tr. fr. Arabic by* Sargon Boulus *and* Alistair Elliot. MAP
One who rises, rises of himself. Ni-buttsu, *tr. by* Lucien Stryk *and* Takashi Ikemoto. ZPCJ
One who rows a storm at the inception. A Comparison. Agnes Nemes Nagy, *tr. by* Alan Dixon. MHuP
One who sees corn and is glad. Chicken. *Unknown, tr. fr. Yoruba by* Ulli Beier. *Fr.* Hunter Poems of the Yoruba. RB
One Who Skins Cats, The. Paula Gunn Allen. GOS
One Who Struggles, The. Ernst Toller, *tr. fr. German by* E. Ellis Roberts. TrJP
One Who Watches. Siegfried Sassoon. TrJP
One whom I knew, a student and a poet. Alex Comfort. MoBrPo; MOS (Poem: "One whom I knew, a student and a poet.") SeCePo
One who's asleep, The. *Unknown, tr. by* Geoffrey Bownas *and* Anthony Thwaite. PeBJV
One who's unkind is like you, The. Teika, *tr. fr. Japanese by* Hiroaki Sato. *Fr.* A Compendium of Good Tanka. FCEI
One whose love will never end. Accompanying a Gift ("One whose love will never end"). Lizelia Augusta Jenkins Moorer. CBWP-3
One whose majestic presence ever here. In Memoriam Frederick Douglass. Henrietta Cordelia Ray. CBWP-3
One Whose Reproach I Cannot Evade, The. George Hitchcock. EAS
One Wife for One Man. Frank Aig-Imoukhuede. PBA
One window for seeing. A Window. Forugh Farrokhzad, *tr. by* Deirdre Lashgari. OV
One Winter Night in August. X. J. Kennedy. OBCA
One with eyes the fairest. Euripides, *tr. fr. Greek by* Shelley. *Fr.* Cyclops. AWP
One without looks in to-night [*or* tonight]. The Fallow Deer at the Lonely House. Thomas Hardy. AWP; CH; CMoP; OxBSP; RB; TTTS
One word beyond all rules. Love. Gordon LeClaire. CaP
One word in your letter &, again, that quail trots from the vineyard, spurts. Letter. Philip Dow. NPGG
One word is too often profaned. Shelley. BLPL; BoLoP; ELP; EnRP; FaBV; GTBS; GTBS-P; LiTB; NOBE; OBEV; OBNC; OPOP; PoLF; PPP; TrGrPo
(Love.) FiP
One Word More, *sel.* Robert Browning. FiP; PoEL-5
Phases of the Moon. ChTr
One Word Will Do. René Daumal, *tr. fr. French by* Michael Benedikt. POS
One would be in less danger. Family Court. Ogden Nash. FiBHP
One would never assume, from the toy bulldogs taking the air. A Nice Part of Town. Alfred Hayes. NYBP
One writes, that "other friends remain." Tennyson. *Fr.* In Memoriam A. H. H., VI. PoEL-5
One Writing against His Prick. *Unknown.* TW
One X. E. E. Cummings. FaBoMo
One Year. Ali Sardar J'afri, *tr. fr. Urdu by* Mahmood Jamal. PBMUP
One Year Ago. Adah Isaacs Menken. CBWP-1
One year there were too many/ frogs. Calendar. Cecil Bødker, *tr. by* Nadia Christensen *and* Alexander Taylor. BoWoP
One Year to Life on the Grand Central Shuttle. Audre Lorde. CNA
Onely the Reverend Grave and Godly Mr. Buckly Remaines. Edward Johnson. SCAP
Oneness of the Philosopher with Nature, The. G. K. Chesterton. FaBoNo
One's grand flights, one's Sunday baths. The Sense of the Sleight-of-Hand Man. Wallace Stevens. HAP; LiTM; MoAB; MoAmPo; NoAM; NOBA; PoA; TwCP; WeW
Ones newly planted north of Sempu Ward, The. Plum Blossoms. Michizane, *tr. by* Burton Watson. JLIC-1
One's none. Little Hundred. *Unknown.* OxNR
One's-Self I Sing. Walt Whitman. FaBoPV; NOBA; OxBA
Ones who don't sleep in the drowsy sea, The. The Rustlers. Rocco Scotellaro, *tr. by* Lawrence R. Smith. NItP

Ones who hammer the air with fists, The. Cripples. J. D. Reed. NeAC

Ones who widened the Panama Canal, The. Poem of Love. Roque Dalton, *tr. by* Alejandro Murguía. Vol

Oneself Miss Grant. Miss Grant. Freda Downie. FaBoWP

Onesided Dialog. June Jordan. NoAM

Ongoing Story, The. John Ashbery. HCAP

Onion, The. Margaret Gibson. MT

Onion, The. John Thompson. NOBC

Onion Bucket. Lorenzo Thomas. PoBA

Onion, Memory, The. Craig Raine. NAEL-2; NoAM; NoP

Onion Skin in Barn. Kenneth Slade Alling. NePoAm

Onlie X. Fanny Howe. PPR

Onlooker, The. Wade Wellman. VVA

Only/ a little/ yellow/ school bus. Snow Country. Dave Etter. AmFN

Only/ avenue/ of/ escape. Lies. Ted Greenwald. LP

Only/ the gray wind. Something for Supper. Carroll Arnett. VoR

Only a baby, fair, and small. George Washington. *Unknown*. OHIP

Only a Blush. Mary E. Tucker. CBWP-1

Only a few will really understand. One Sided Shoot-out. Don L. Lee. BPo; PoBA

Only a fool would eat his heart out so. Ballad of the Bushman. Ellen Duggan. PeNZ

Only a fool would fail. God's Praises. *Unknown, tr. by* Brendan Kennelly. TIRV

Only a hundred yards, says Bob. Space and Time. Syd Scroggie. PoSH

Only a little drunk, I couldn't quite reach the Happy Land. A Traveler's Night. P'eng Sun-yü, *tr. by* William H. Nienhauser, Jr.. WFTU

Only [*or* Onely] a little more. His Poetry [*or* Poetrie] His Pillar. Robert Herrick. CaPo; JCP; QFR

Only a man harrowing clods. In Time of "The Breaking of Nations." Thomas Hardy. BoLoP; CMoP; EBEV; HAP; LiTB; LiTM; MMA; MoAB; MoBrPo; MoP; NAEL-2; NoAM; NOBE; NoP; OAEL-2; OBEV; OBWP; PPP; QFR; RB; WeW

Only a Miner. *Unknown*. AmFP

Only a Pin. Isaac Hinton Brown. PWR

Only a single river flowed. Gosan. Park Je-chun, *tr. by* Koh Chang-soo. ACKP

Only a small folk song. Folk Melody. P. Mustapää, *tr. by* Aili Jarvenpa. SOP

Only a tender little thing. A Snowdrop. Harriet Prescott Spofford. GN

Only a woman of this measure. Tatiana Kalatschova. William Logan. SM

Only after a couple of months of hard. Ice River. David Baker. SM

Only after, wading waist deep. The Ring. Paul Mariani. GeTw

Only awake to Universal Mind. Jack Kerouac. *Fr.* Mexico City Blues, 183. NeaP

Only Bar in Dixon, The. James Welch. AmPA; FF

Only Be Willing to Search for Poetry. Yuan Mei, *tr. fr. Chinese*. PDV

Only Beating, The. Jacques Dupin, *tr. fr. French by* Paul Auster. RHTwFP

Only brooms. Brooms. Charles Simic. AmPA; LCAP; NNaP; NNaP, *early version*

Only butterflies fly in the field. Basho, *tr. fr. Japanese by* Burton Watson. *Fr.* Seventy-six Hokku. FCEI

Only contentment for our bodies, The. Tale chante a/an. György Somlyó, *tr. by* Daniel Hoffman. MHuP

Only Daughter, The. *Unknown*. OBET

Only for these I pray. Two Prayers. Charlotte Perkins Gilman. WGRP

Only from Afar. Ory Bernstein, *tr. fr. Hebrew by* Warren Bargad *and* Stanley F. Chyet. IP

Only ghost I ever saw, The. Emily Dickinson. WSC

Only head in the sky, The. Giraffe. Stanley Plumly. AmPA

Only in sleep. The Old Wife Speaks. Gerda Mayer. DT

Only in This Way. Margaret Goss Burroughs. BISi

Only intermittent beads of water. Princess Shikishi, *tr. fr. Japanese by* Hiroaki Sato. *Fr.* Seventy-eight Tanka. FCEI

Only January 3, 1962, The. Rip. Giancarlo Majorino, *tr. by* Lawrence R. Smith. NItP

Only Jealousy of Emer, The. *Unknown, tr. fr. Irish by* John Montague. BIrV

Only Jealousy of Emer, The, *sel.* W. B. Yeats. "Woman's beauty is like a white, A." MoAB

Only joy, now here you are. Sir Philip Sidney. *Fr.* Astrophel and Stella: Fourth Song. EIL; GBL; HAP; InvP; NAEL-1; NoP; OBSC

Only kid, An! an only kid. Had Gadyaa Kid, a Kid. *Unknown*. TrJP

Only last week, walking the hushed fields. Father and Son. F. R. Higgins. BIrV; OBMV

Only leaf upon its tree of blood, The. The Red Heart. James Reaney. CaP

Only let it form within his hands once more. The Brandy Glass. Louis MacNeice. FaBCIP

Only loving, only knowing. Pier Paolo Pasolini, *tr. fr. Italian by* Lawrence R. Smith. *Fr.* The Ditchdigger's Tears. NItP

Only loving, only knowing. The Tears of the Excavator. Pier Paolo Pasolini, *tr. by* Norman Macafee *and* Luciano Martinengo. PFI

Only major city, one would hope, The. U-24 Anchors off New Orleans. Turner Cassity. MT

Only mother he could afford was a skinny old man, The. Because They Were Very Poor That Winter. Kenneth Patchen. NaP

Only My Opinion. Monica Shannon. FaPON; RAR

Only news I know, The. Emily Dickinson. NOCV

Only on the rarest occasions, when the blue air. The Mountain. W. S. Merwin. VGW

Only One. George Cooper. *See* Only One Mother.

Only one guy and. Issa, *tr. by* Cid Corman. InPK

Only One Mother. George Cooper. OHIP

Only one or two nights since winter came. Teika, *tr. fr. Japanese by* Hiroaki Sato. *Fr.* Eighty-four Tanka. FCEI

Only one thing/ can give me understanding. Autumn Evening. Tameshige, *tr. by* Steven D. Carter. WFTW

Only One Way. Ella Wheeler Wilcox. *See* However the battle is ended.

Only one who'd appreciate my daybreak's, The. My Old Man's Dawdling. Gyula Illyés, *tr. by* Jascha Kessler. FOC

Only over the river, darkness flows: fireflies. Chiyojo, *tr. fr. Japanese by* Hiroaki Sato. *Fr.* Seventeen Hokku. FCEI

Only quiet death. Waring Cuney. AmNP; BANP

Only real airship, The. The Dirigible. Ralph Wilhelm Bergengren. FaPON

Only relics left are those long, The. Monuments for a Friendly Girl at a Tenth Grade Party. William Stafford. NoAM

Only response, The. William Knott. InPK

Only Seven. Henry S. Leigh. BXAP

Only Silence. Arthur Stanley Bourinot. CaP

Only snake writes, a coil sprung in my fingers. Yetzer ha Ra. Edward Codish. VWA

Only Statues Don't Shy Away. Tsfrirah Gar, *tr. fr. Hebrew by* Bernhard Frank. MHeP

Only, sweet Love, afford me but thy heart. For Her Heart Only. *Unknown*. EIL

Only teaching on Tuesdays, book-worming. Memories of West Street and Lepke. Robert Lowell. AmPP; CAPP; CMoP; InPS; NAAL-2; NaP; NoAM; NOBA; PoE

Only the air-spirits know. Solitary Song. *Unknown*. WTO

Only the Beards Are Different. Bruce Dawe. PoAu-2

Only the compass, keeping hope alive. Logbook of a Lost Caravan. Gyula Illyés, *tr. by* William Jay Smith. MHuP

Only the Dead. Reed Whittemore. NYBP

Only the deep well. I Break the Sky. Owen Dodson. PoBA

Only the dim-witted say it's evening. What She Said ("Only the dim-witted say it's evening"). Milaipperun Kantan, *tr. by* A. K. Ramanujan. PLW

Only the Eyes. Marie Luise Kaschnitz, *tr. fr. German by* Susan L. Cocalis. DMG

Only the foreground's green. Love Overgrows a Rock. Eric Roach. PVCV

Only the Heart. Marjorie Freeman Campbell. CaP

Only the illegitimate are beautiful. Thesis. Edward Dorn. NOBA

Only the lion and the cock. After Galen. Oliver St. John Gogarty. FaBoEE; OBMV; PoRA

Only the Polished Skeleton. Countee Cullen. PrIm; VGW

Only the sand, only the sand. El Alamein Revisited. Roy Macnab. PeSA

Only the short, broad, splayed feet. Young Shepherd Bathing His Feet. Peter Clarke. PBA

Only the thief was there, no one else. What She Said ("Only the thief was there, no one else"). Kapilar, *tr. by* A. K. Ramanujan. PLW

Only the wanderer. Ivor Gurney. FaBoPP

Only the wholesomest foods you eat. Samuel Hoffenstein. *Fr.* Poems in Praise of Practically Nothing. TrJP

Only thing I have of Jane MacNaughton, The. The Leap. James Dickey. NIP

Only thing that can be relied on, The. The Snow on Saddle Mountain. Miyazawa Kenji, *tr. by* Gary Snyder. NoAM; NOBA

Only thing we know is the thing, The. Red Light. Amiri Baraka. SOTW

Only things left are my body soaked, The. Offering Wine. Park Je-chun, *tr. by* Koh Chang-soo. ACKP

Only think, dearest Louisa, what fearful scenes we have witnessed! Arthur Hugh Clough. *Fr.* Amours de Voyage, Canto II, viii. EBVV

Only this evening I saw again low in the sky. Martial Cadenza. Wallace Stevens. OxBA; VGW
Only those coral insects live. The Builders. Judith Wright. SeCePo
Only Thy Dust. Don Marquis. PoLF
Only to find Forever, blest. Heaven. Martha Gilbert Dickinson Bianchi. AA
Only to have a grief. Peeling Onions. Adrienne Rich. BoWoP; HCAP; TAP
Only today and just for this minute. The Withdrawal. Robert Lowell. NoP
Only totems protrude. An Inhabited Emptiness. Jiri Gold, *tr. by* Jaroslav Kotan *and* Daniel Weissbort. VWA
Only Tourist in Havana Turns His Thoughts Homeward, The. Leonard Cohen. MoCV; MoP
Only two beds. The Family of Eight. Abraham Reisen, *tr. by* Marcia Falk. VWA
Only two patient eyes to stare. Faded Pictures. William Vaughn Moody. AnAmPo
Only Waiting. Frances Laughton Mace. BLPA
Only way to be quiet, The. Poetry. Frank O'Hara. HCAP
Only Way to Win, The. *Unknown.* WBLP
Only we don't think that you will be able some day or. Of Coal. Marcelin Pleynet, *tr. by* John Ashbery. RHTwFP
Only what is heroic and courageous moves our blood. The Flowers of Politics, II. Michael McClure. NeAP
Only what is, is forever. Contraries. Sándor Weöres, *tr. by* Jascha Kessler. FOC
Only when she left. Pig. Vasco Popa, *tr. by* Anne Pennington. OBD
Only with Radiance. Margit Szécsi, *tr. fr. Hungarian by* Kenneth McRobbie. MHuP
Only Woman, The. Bertalicia Peralta, *tr. fr. Spanish by* Kate Flores. DMH
Only Years. Kenneth Rexroth. TAP
Only yesterday/ I had thought I must visit. Ietaka, *tr. by* Steven D. Carter. WFTW
Only yesterday I sent winter away and now it's back again. Surprised by Winter. Michizane, *tr. by* Burton Watson. JLIC-1
Onomatopoeia. Eve Merriam. RR
Ons in your grace I knowe I was. What Once I Was. Sir Thomas Wyatt. MeEL
Onset, The. Robert Frost. CMoP; MoAB; MoAmPo; OxBA; PPP
Onto the hallowit steid bryng in, thai cry. Virgil, *tr. into Middle English by* Gavin Douglas. *Fr.* The Aeneid [*or* Eneados], II. OBVE
Ontogeny. Jarold Ramsey. NIP
Onus of Mercy, The. Yehuda Amichai, *tr. fr. Hebrew by* Warren Bargad *and* Stanley F. Chyet. IP
Onward, Christian Soldiers. Sabine Baring-Gould. FaBoBe; FaPoR; WGRP
"Onward Christian Soldiers!" Frank Marshall Davis. FB
Onward, Christian soldiers! Duty's way is plain. Christians at War. John F. Kendrick. TW
Onward flies the rushing train. The Engine Driver. "G. S. O." BoTP
Onward led the road again. Hell Gate. A. E. Housman. NoAM; UnPo
Onward, Onward, Men of Heaven. Lydia Huntley Sigourney. AH
Onward to Far Ida. George Darley. *Fr.* Nepenthe. OBNC
Onwardness. Doris Hedges. CaP
Onyons. Swift. *Fr.* Verses for Fruitwomen. BIrV; FaBoUs
Oocuck, The. Justin Richardson. FiBHP
Oodles of Noodles. Lucia *and* James L. Hymes, Jr. RHPC
Ooftish. Samuel Beckett. NoAM
Oor best-lo'ed makar has but late grown cauld. Carlyle on Burns. William Jeffrey. *Fr.* On Glaister's Hill. OxBS
Opal ring and a holly tree, An. Sailor's Woman. Annette Patton Cornell. GoYe
Ope, aged Atlas, open then thy lap. Ben Jonson. *Fr.* Pleasure Reconciled to Virtue. NAEL-1
Ope your doors and take me in. The House of the Trees. Ethelwyn Wetherald. CaP
Open. Larry Eigner. NeAP
Open and Closed Space. Tomas Tranströmer, *tr. fr. Swedish by* Robert Bly. EAS
Open are the arms of the rose. Asadullah Khan Ghalib, *tr. by* Ahmed Ali. GoT
Open as experience, this day, this. Tomarata. Kendrick Smithyman. PeNZ
Open-backed dumpy junktruck. In Passing. Gerald Jonas. GrPl; TDD
Open Casket. Sandra McPherson. GeTw
Open Country. Richard Hugo. LCAP
Open country, flat sand. Hunting in the Ordos, the Pheasants and Hares Were Many. Hsüan-yeh, *tr. by* Jonathan D. Spence. WFTU
Open Door, An. Kevin Ireland. ATNZ

Open Door, The. *Unknown, tr. fr. Irish by* Frank O'Connor. KiLC
Open Earth. Clarisse Nicoïdski, *tr. fr. Judezmo by* Stephen Levy. VWA
Open House. Aileen Fisher. RAR
Open House. Theodore Roethke. NoAM; NOBA; NoP
Open Hydrant. Marci Ridlon. RHPC
Open Letter from a Constant Reader. Mona Van Duyn. PoA
Open, love. Unclench Yourself. Marge Piercy. NeAC
Open me like a meadow lily. The Seduction. Suzanne Berger Rioff. NMM
Open Range. Kathryn Jackson *and* Byron Jackson. FaPON
Open Range. Melvin L. Whipple. CowP
Open Sea, The. William Meredith. CoAP; GrPl; MOS; NePoEA; TAP; UnPo
Open Secret, An. Caroline Atherton Briggs Mason. AA
Open Sesame. *Unknown.* BoTP
Open the Door. *Unknown.* EIL; GBL
Open the Door. *Malay Oral Tradition, tr. by* R. J. Wilkinson *and* R. O. Winstedt. WTO
Open the Door to Me, Oh! Burns. PoEL-4
    (O, Open the Door to Me, O!) FaBoCh
Open the door, who's there within? Open the Door. *Unknown.* EIL; GBL
"Open the gates." The Bonny Earl of Murray. *Unknown.* ESPB
Open the Gates. *Unknown, tr. fr. Hebrew by* Israel Zangwill. TrJP
Open the Heart. Charles Brasch. ATNZ
Open the window on the high. Earth Tremor in Lugano. James Kirkup. NYBP
Open Thy Doors, O Lebanon. Bible, *O.T. Fr.* Zechariah, XI: 1-14. AWP
Open to Me! He Commandeth a Fair Wind. *Unknown, tr. fr. Egyptian by* Robert Hillyer. *Fr.* Book of the Dead. AWP
Open up, Gate. H. Leivick, *tr. fr. Yiddish by* Benjamin *and* Barbara Harshav. *Fr.* Clouds behind the Forest. AYP
Open Window in Florence. Leah Goldberg, *tr. fr. Hebrew by* Bernhard Frank. MHeP
Open wound which has been healed anew, An. Richard Chenevix Trench. TrPWD
Open your eyes and stare. Haka: Hinemotu. Te Aomuhurangi Te Maaka. PeNZ
Open Your Fist. Jukka Vieno, *tr. fr. Finnish by* Aili Jarvenpa. SOP
OPEN YR HANDS REPEAT OPEN. TELEX FOR JIX RE SUNDAY. Vincent O'Sullivan. ATNZ
Opened. Jacques Dupin, *tr. fr. French by* Paul Auster. RHTwFP
Opened, clear as a child's geography. The Summer Countries. Henry Rago. VGW
Opening a little the wheeled door at the back, I look out. *Unknown, tr. by* Sato. FCEI
Opening Day. Bruce Severy. NOVW
Opening Letter to Manufacturers of Bathroom Wallpaper. Katharine O'Brien. SoTCo
Opening on plum twigs in the unfaded snow. Princess Shikishi, *tr. fr. Japanese by* Hiroaki Sato. *Fr.* Seventy-eight Tanka. FCEI
Opening Service, An. Clara Ann Thompson. CBWP-2
Opening the door. *Unknown, tr. by* Geoffrey Bownas *and* Anthony Thwaite. PeBJV
Opening the knots of your braid. Memory of the Present. David Shapiro. UL
Opening Year, The. *Unknown, tr. fr. Latin by* F. Pott. BLRP
Openly, yes,/ with the naturalness. Black Earth. Marianne Moore. FaBoMo
Opens small notebook. The Terrorist Smiles. Anselm Hollo. UL
Opera Songstress, An. Ya Hsien, *tr. fr. Chinese by* Dominic Cheung. IFON
Operation, The. Robert Creeley. NaP
Operation. W. E. Henley. *Fr.* In Hospital, V. BrPo
Operation, The. W. D. Snodgrass. InPK; TAP
Operation Memory. David Lehman. BAP
Operative No. 174 Resigns. Kenneth Fearing. NYBP
Ophelia. Brenda Hillman. MOWH
Ophelia. Rimbaud, *tr. fr. French by* Brian Hill. ChTr
Ophelia's Death. Shakespeare. *See* Hamlet:
    There is a willow grows aslant a brook.
Ophelia's Songs, 1 ("How should I your true love know"). Shakespeare. *See* Hamlet: How Should I Your True Love Know.
Ophelia's Songs, 2 ("And will he not come again"). Shakespeare. *See* Hamlet: And Will He Not Come Again.
Ophra. Judah Halevi, *tr. fr. Hebrew by* Nina Davis Salaman. TrJP
Opinion is not worth a rush. Michael Robartes and the Dancer. W. B. Yeats. OAEL-2
Opinions about the Painter de Chirico. Wieland Schmied, *tr. fr. German by* Beth Bjorklund. CoAuP

Opinions of the New Student. Regino Pedroso, *tr. fr. Spanish by* Langston Hughes. TTY
Opium-Den. *Malay Oral Tradition, tr. by* R. J. Wilkinson *and* R. O. Winstedt. WTO
Opium-Eater, The. Mary E. Tucker. CBWP-1
Opium Fantasy, An. Maria White Lowell. AnAmPo; InPK
Opportunity. Berton Braley. WBLP
Opportunity. Madison Cawein. AA
Opportunity. Harry Graham. FaBoCo
Opportunity. John James Ingalls. AA; AnAmPo; FaFP; OHFP; PoLF; WBLP
Opportunity. Machiavelli, *tr. fr. Italian by* J. E. Flecker. AWP; PFI
Opportunity. Walter Malone. BLPA; BLPL; FaBoBe; PWR; WBLP
Opportunity. Shakespeare. *Fr.* The Rape of Lucrece. LiTB; OBSC; PoEL-2
  (Outcry upon Opportunity, An.) NOBE
Opportunity. Edward Rowland Sill. AnAmPo; BLPA; GN; OHFP; WGRP
Opposite House, The. Robert Lowell. CMoP
Opposite of Two, The. Richard Wilbur. RHPC
Opposition. Kaneko Mitsuharu, *tr. fr. Japanese by* Geoffrey Bownas *and* Anthony Thwaite. PeBJV
Opposition. Sidney Lanier. AnAmPo; LiTA
Oppressed and few, but freemen yet. The Mecklenburg Declaration. William C. Elam. PAH
Oppressing all, sunken in autumn sorrows. Princess Shikishi, *tr. fr. Japanese by* Hiroaki Sato. *Fr.* Seventy-eight Tanka. FCEI
Oppression. Langston Hughes. CNA
Ops in a Wimpey. *Unknown.* CoMu
Optimism. Blanaid Salkeld. NeIP
Optimism. Ella Wheeler Wilcox. BLPA; BLPL; FaBoBe; PWR
Optimist, The. *Unknown.* BLPA
Optimist fell ten stories, The. The Optimist. *Unknown.* BLPA
Options. "O. Henry." FiBHP
Opulent oracle—it's a terrible thing! It's a Terrible Thing! Everett Hoagland. BPo
Opusculum paedagogum. Study of Two Pears. Wallace Stevens. InPS; NAAL-2; NoAM; NU; OxBA
Or a crippled sloop falters, about to go under. The Volume. Robert Pinsky. AnAn
Or a ship's mast. Speak like Rain. Jerred Metz. VWA
Or Ever God Created Adam. *Malay Oral Tradition, tr. by* R. J. Wilkinson. WTO
Or Ever the Earth Was. Charles Leonard Moore. AA
Or from what spring doth your opinion rise. Sir John Davies. *Fr.* Orchestra; or, A Poem[e] of Da[u]ncing. UnS
"Or I shall live your epitaph to make." Shakespeare. *Fr.* Sonnets, LXXXI. OBSC
Or love me less [*or* mee lesse], or love me [*or* mee] more. Sidney Godolphin. MePo; OBS
  (Song: "Or love me less [*or* mee lesse], or love me more.") JCP
Or many things adulterate. Tristan Corbière, *tr. fr. French by* Joseph T. Shipley. AWP
Or scorne or pittie on me take. Ben Jonson. *See* Dream[e], The.
Or scorn[e] or pity [*or* pittie] on me take. The Dream[e]. Ben Jonson. NOBE
  ("Or scorne or pittie on me take.") PoEL-2
Or the black centaurs, statuesquely still. Ambuscade. Hugh McCrae. PoAu-1
Or this doll of death, hideous, we treasure. The Doll. Peyton Houston. *Fr.* Sonnet Variations, XVII. Son
Or, trying simple charms and spells. John Clare. *Fr.* The Shepherd's [*or* Shepheards] Calendar. FaBoUs
Or what is closer to the truth. When I Buy Pictures. Marianne Moore. EyDe; OxBA
Or wren or linnet. Samuel Taylor Coleridge. PBBP
Or yield or die's the word, what could he mean. Ignotum per Ignotius, or a Furious Hodge-Podge of Nonsense; a Pindaric. *Unknown.* NOEC
Oracle, The. Gordon Challis. ATNZ
Oracle. Donald Finkel. BLA
Oracle. *Yoruba Oral Tradition, tr. by* Ulli Beier. WTO
Oracles, The. A. E. Housman. HAP
Oracular Portcullis, The. James Reaney. ErPo
Oraga Haru, *sels.* Issa, *tr. fr. Japanese by* Nobuyuki Yuasa. OFD
  Buddha's Birthday: April 8, 1819.
  Buddha's Death Day: February 15, 1815.
  "For a fresh start."
Oral Messages, *sel.* Lawrence Ferlinghetti.
  "I am waiting for my case to come up." AiP; CAPP; GOA
"Oran" to "Ordain" for "J." Tina Darragh. LP
Orange. Barbara Ferland. PVCV

Orange air grows fetid with smoke, The. The uneasy dark. Mess Deck Casualty. Alan Ross. WaP
  (Epilogue: " 'O where are you going?' said reader to rider.") (Five Songs.) FaBoCh; LiTM
Orange Bears, The. Kenneth Patchen. NaP
Orange blossoms that came. *Unknown, tr. fr. Japanese by* Burton Watson. *Fr.* Kokin Shu. FCEI
Orange Buds by Mail from Florida. Walt Whitman. NAAL-1
Orange Chiffon. Jayne Cortez. BlSi
Orange fish are swimming. Watching the Sun Rise over Mount Zion. Ruth Whitman. VWA
Orange flowers scatter in a village. Teika, *tr. fr. Japanese by* Hiroaki Sato. *Fr.* Eighty-four Tanka. FCEI
Orange in the middle of a table. Against Still Life. Margaret Atwood. MoCV; NMM
Orange is a tiger lily. What Is Orange? Mary O'Neill. RHPC
Orange is the single-hearted color. I remember. Poppies. Sandra McPherson. GeTw
Orange Jews. Ted Berrigan *and* Ron Padgett. EAS
Orange Juice Song. David Phillips. NeAC
Orange leaves are gone. Izumi Shikibu, *tr. by* Willis Barnstone. BoWoP
Orange Lily, The. *Unknown.* NOIV
Orange Lily, The. *Unknown.* FaBoPV; GBP
Orange line splits the sky, An. The Flint Hills. Lew Blockcolski. VoR
Orange March. Richard Murphy. *Fr.* The Battle of Aughrim. NOIV
Orange on its way. On Its Way. May Swenson. WPE
Orange on the table, An. Alicante. Jacques Prévert, *tr. by* Lawrence Ferlinghetti. BoLoP
Orange Piano, The. David St. John. NAmP
Orange rivers and red dogs of Paul Gauguin, The. Slag. C. D. Wright. MT
Orange Tree, The. John Shaw Neilson. CBAP; PoAu-1
Orange Tree, The. Ellen Pearce. IHMS
Orange trees had put away, The. Sunscape. Lucha Corpi. CCP
Oranges, The. Abu Dharr, *tr. fr. Arabic by* A. J. Arberry. TTY
Oranges. Gary Soto. MOWH; NoAM
Oranges in a wooden bowl. Still-Life. Ronald Perry. NePoEA-2
Oranges in th bowl, Th. Windfall. David Mitchell. ATNZ
Orara. Henry Clarence Kendall. CBAP; PoAu-1
Orator. Emerson. *Fr.* Quatrains. OxBA
Orator dismal of Nottinghamshire, An. An Excellent New Song, Being the Intended Speech of a Famous Orator against Peace. Swift. APAS
Orator Prigg. Blake. OBSV
Orators, The, *sel.* W. H. Auden.
  O Where Are You Going? CMoP; LiTB; NOBE; SoSe
  (Epilogue: " 'O where are you going?' said reader to rider.") FaBoCh
  (Five Songs.) LiTM; NoAM
  (Song: " 'O Where Are You Going?' said reader to rider.") OAEL-2
Orator's Epitaph, The. Lord Brougham. NBLV
Orb. Maxine W. Kumin. KS
Orbiting, the sun itself has a sun. The Great Dark. Martin Carter. PVCV
Orchard, The. Gretel Ehrlich. MAYP
Orchard. John Engels. BLA
Orchard. Hilda Doolittle ("H. D."). CMoP; LiTA; LiTM; MoAmPo; OxBA
Orchard and the Heath, The. George Meredith. OBNC
Orchard at Avignon, An. Agnes Mary Frances Robinson. NOBVV; OBTV
Orchard beyond the wall, dripping, and a peacock, An. Cuernavaca. Ory Bernstein, *tr. fr. Hebrew by* Warren Bargad *and* Stanley F. Chyet. *Fr.* Poems from Mexico. IP
Orchard-Pit, The. Dante Gabriel Rossetti. EnLoPo; NAEL-2; OAEL-2; PoEL-5; SCV
Orchard Trees, January. Richard Wilbur. BLA
"Orchards," said Johnny Appleseed. Johnny Appleseed. Arthur Stanley Bourinot. CaP
Orchards, we linger here because. For a Second Marriage. James Merrill. NePoEA
  (Upon a Second Marriage.) NoP
Orchestra. Reg Saner. KS
Orchestra, The. William Carlos Williams. HAP
Orchestra; or, A Poem of Dancing. Sir John Davies. OBSC; SiPS
Orchestra; or, A Poem[e] of Da[u]ncing ("Where lives the man that never yet did hear."), *sels.* Sir John Davies. OBSC; SiPS
  Dance of Love, The. EIL; SeCePo
  Dancing Sea, The. ChTr
  "Dauncing (bright Lady) then began to bee." PoEL-2
  Dedications, I: To His Very Friend, Master Richard Martin. SiPS

Dedications, II: To the Prince. SiPS

"Or from what spring doth your opinion rise." UnS

"Sole heir of virtue, and of beauty both." NAEL-1

Orchestra tunes up, each instrument, The. Meditation. Anthony Hecht. BLA; EOEF

Orchid lamp burns low, The. Dreaming of the South. Huang-fu Sung, tr. by Lois Fusek. ATF

Orchid-lipped, loose-jointed, purplish, indolent flowers. Himalayan Balsam. Anne Stevenson. FaBoWP

Orchids. Judith Minty. GeTw

Orchids. Theodore Roethke. CMoP

Ordained I was a beggar. The File-Hewer's Lamentation. Joseph Mather. FaBoPV; NOEC

Ordeal. Nina Cassian, tr. fr. Rumanian by Michael Impey and Brian Swann. PBWP

Ordeal by Fire, The, sel. Edmund Clarence Stedman.

"Thou, who dost feel Life's vessel strand." WGRP

Ordeal by Fire, sels. Itamar Ya'oz-kest, tr. fr. Hebrew by Bernhard Frank. MHeP

"Children called, The."

Funeral, The.

"Railway car."

Shot.

"Suddenly a squeal."

Order for a Picture, An. Alice Cary. BLPA

Order is a lovely thing. The Monk in the Kitchen. Anna Hempstead Branch. MoAmPo

Order the ground? Versions. Robert Kelly. Fr. The Book of Persephone, 12. PoM

Ordered to strip prior to execution. Murder of a Community. Daniel Weissbort. VWA

Ordinary, The, sel. William Cartwright.

Saint Francis and Saint Benedight. Fr. III, i. EaLo

(House Blessing, A.) ChTr

Ordinary Evening in Cleveland, An. Lewis Turco. NYBP

Ordinary people are peculiar too. Conversation. Louis MacNeice. TEP

Ordinary valour only works, The. "F. Anstey." CenHV

Ordinary Women, The. Wallace Stevens. OxBA

Ore is waiting in the tubs, the snow's upon the fells, The. Fourpence a Day. Unknown. OBET

Oread. Hilda Doolittle ("H. D."). AWP; CMoP; GoJo; HeIP; InPS; MoAmPo; MoP; NAAL-2; NoAM; NOBA; OxBA; TAP

Oreads. Kathleen Jessie Raine. PoSH

Oregon Message, An. William Stafford. CoAP

Oregon Story, An. Janice Gould. GOS

Oregon Trail, The. Arthur Guiterman. FaPON

Oregon Winter. Jeanne McGahey. AmFN

Oreti Beach. Charles Brasch. ATNZ

Orf. Ted Hughes. NoAM

Organ and Sulphur. Antonin Artaud, tr. fr. French by Michael Benedikt. POS

Organist, The. George W. Stevens. BLPA

Orgasm completely, The. Tom Clark. CoAP

Orgy. Norman MacCaig. OxBC

Orgy (That Is, Vegetable Market, at Sarno). Gina Labriola, tr. fr. Italian by Edgar Pauk. WPOW

Orient Express, The. Randall Jarrell. CMoP; CoAP; NOBA; PoE

Orient Wheat. Adrienne Rich. NePoEA

Oriental Apologue, An. James Russell Lowell. PoEL-5

Oriental Ballerina, The. Rita Dove. NAmP

Oriflamme. Jessie Redmond Fauset. BANP; BlSi; PoBA

Origami for Two. Peter Dominick. RR

Origin of Baseball, The. Kenneth Patchen. ASP

Origin of Centaurs, The. Anthony Hecht. NePoEA

Origin of Cities, The. Robert Hass. NPGG

Origin of Didactic Poetry, The. James Russell Lowell. PoEL-5

Origin of Dreams. Marvin Bell. LCAP

Origin of the Praise of God, The. Robert Bly. NU

Origin of the Skagit Indians, The. Lucy Ariel Williams Holloway, tr. fr. Skagit Indian by Carl Cary. STP

Original./ Ragged-round. Malcolm X. Gwendolyn Brooks. CNA; OFD; PoBA; TTY

Original Child Bomb, sel. Thomas Merton.

In the Year 1945 an Original Child Was Born. NAs

Original Epitaph on a Drunkard. Royall Tyler. OBAL

Original face is the reality of realities. Tokugaku, tr. by Lucien Stryk and Takashi Ikemoto. ZPCJ

Original family rock is three parts restored, The. Anniversary. Daniel Weissbort. VWA

Original form, The. Remnant. Jung Han-mo, tr. by Koh Chang-soo. ACKP

Original Sin. Robinson Jeffers. MoAB; MoAmPo

Original Sin. Alexander Kinnan Laing. NYBP

Original Sin; a Short Story. Robert Penn Warren. HoPM; LiTA; LiTM; NOCV; PPP; SM; TAP

Original Strawberry. Nancy Willard. LCAP

Origins. Barbara Fiedler, tr. fr. German by Susan L. Cocalis. DMG

Origins. Keorapetse Kgositsile. PoBA

Origins and History of Consciousness. Adrienne Rich. NIP

Oriki Erinle. Unknown, tr. fr. Yoruba by Ulli Beier. PBA; TTY

Orinda to Lucasia [Parting, October, 1661, at London]. Katherine Philips. OBS; PcHV

Orinoco, 1561, The. Ai. Fr. The Gilded Man, I. AnAn

Oriole at Dawn, An. Li Meng-yang, tr. fr. Chinese by Jonathan Chaves. CoBLCP

Oriole songs hold me to look at the mountains even longer, The. Describing My Feelings While Living in Retirement by the Riverside: Seven Poems to the Tune "Ch'ing-p'ing-yüeh." Yang Chi, tr. by Jonathan Chaves. CoBLCP

Orioles chirp. Speaking of Love. Wen T'ing-yün, tr. by Lois Fusek. ATF

Orioles sing, swallows chatter, and the grass is lush, The. The Flowers in the Rear Garden. Mao Hsi-chen, tr. by Lois Fusek. ATF

Orioles trim her fragrant robe, thin as a cicada's wing. Mountain Flowers. Ho Ning, tr. by Lois Fusek. ATF

Orion. Blaise Cendrars, tr. fr. French by John Dos Passos. RHTwFP

Orion. Adrienne Rich. MoP; NAAL-2; NIP; NoAM; NoP; WPE

Orisha. Jayne Cortez. BlSi

Orishas. Larry Neal. NBP

Orlando Commercial, The. George MacBeth. NOBL

Orlando Furioso, sels. Ariosto, tr. fr. Italian.

"Alcyna met them at the outer gate." Fr. VII, tr. by Sir John Harington. OBVE

Angelica and the Ork. Fr. X, tr. by Sir John Harington. OBSC

Astolfo Visits the Moon. Fr. XXXIV, tr. by Sir John Harington. PFI

"Blessed angell not a word replies, The." Fr. XIV, tr. by Sir John Harington. OBVE

"Go soule, go sweetest soule for ever blest." Fr. XXIX, tr. by Sir John Harington. OBVE

On Poets. Fr. XXXV, tr. by Edwin Morgan. PFI

Orlando's Rhymes. Shakespeare. Fr. As You Like It, III, ii. CTC; OBSC

Orlo's Valediction. Jon Manchip White. NePoEA

Ormerod was deeply troubled. Distractions and the Human Crowd. Stevie Smith. OxBC

Ornament here, a decoration there, An. Unknown, tr. by Arthur Waley. BoS

Ornamental bung, An. Gargoyle. Robert B. Shaw. CRP

Ornaments. Frank Ormsby. CIP

Orotava Road, The. Basil Bunting. NoAM

O'Rourke's noble fare [or O'Rourke's revel rout]. The Description of an Irish Feast. Hugh MacGowran, tr. fr. Irish by Charles Wilson. NOIV; OBVE, tr. by Swift.

(O'Rourke's [or O Rourke's] Feast,) tr. by Charles Wilson. BIrV

Orphan, The. Muhammad al-Maghut, tr. fr. Arabic. MAP, tr. by May Jayyusi and John Heath-Stubbs; MPAW, tr. by Abdullah al-Udhari.

Orphan, The. Unknown, tr. fr. Chinese by Arthur Waley. PoA

Orphan beat of my heart, The. "Ping Hsin", tr. by Kenneth Rexroth and Ling Chung. BoWoP

Orphan Born. Robert Jones Burdette. OBAL

Orphan Boy, The. Unknown. OBET

Orphan Girl, An. Mrs. Henry Linden. CBWP-4

Orphan Girl, The. Unknown. AmFP; AS, with music.

"Orphan Hours, the Year is dead." Dirge for the Year. Shelley. GN

Orphan, yes, An. But not. Fragment Reflection I. Doris Turner. JB

Orphaned/ I am your child. Strings/Himo. Yuri Kageyama. BrSi

Orphan's Song, The. Sydney Thompson Dobell. CH; ELP; OBNC

Orpheus. Donald Davie. TEP

Orpheus. E. W. Mandel. Fr. Minotaur Poems, VI. OBCV

Orpheus. Robert Herrick. CaPo

Orpheus. Elizabeth Madox Roberts. MoAmPo

Orpheus. Shakespeare and probably John Fletcher. See King Henry VIII: Orpheus with His Lute [Made Trees].

Orpheus. Susan Tichy. ER

Orpheus. Yvor Winters. NOBA; VGW

Orpheus and Eurydice. Robert Browning. CTC

Orpheus and Eurydice. Geoffrey Hill. NePoEA-2

Orpheus and Eurydice. Jean Valentine. FaBoWP; LCAP

Orpheus he went (as poets tell). Orpheus. Robert Herrick. CaPo

Orpheus I am, come from the deeps below. John Fletcher. Fr. The Mad Lover, IV, i. GBL

Orpheus in Greenwich Village. Jack Gilbert. NPGG

Orpheus in the Underworld. David Gascoyne. FaBoTw

Orpheus liked the glad personal quality. Syringa. John Ashbery. HCAP; NoAM

Orpheus to Beasts. Richard Lovelace. CaPo

Orpheus to Woods. Richard Lovelace. CaPo

Orpheus with His Lute [Made Trees]. Shakespeare *and probably* John Fletcher. *Fr.* King Henry VIII, III, i. ChTr; GN; OBS; TrGrPo
  (Music.) FaBoCh
  (Orpheus.) EIL; OBEV; UnS
  (Song: "Orpheus with his Lute made Trees.") PoEL-2
  (Sweet Music's Power.) NOBE

Orson Welles/ Suffered from eating spells. Edmund Conti. SoTCo

Orthodox, Orthodox, wha believe in John Knox. The Kirk's Alarm. Burns. OxBoLi

Orthodoxy's staunch adherent. To Dr. Kipling. Richard Porson. FaBoCo

Ortho's Epitaph. Theocritus, *tr. fr. Greek by* Charles Stuart Calverley. FaBoEE

Ortiz. Hezekiah Butterworth. PAH

Orts, *sel.* Ted Hughes.
  Buzz in the Window. NoAM

Ortus. Ezra Pound. LiTA

Oscar Wilde/ Married and fathered a child. Maurice Sagoff. SoTCo

Osceola. Walt Whitman. NAAL-1

Oshun makes of her people one. I-Tie-All-My-People-Together. Michelle Cliff. ER

Oshun, the River Goddess. *Yoruba Oral Tradition, tr. by* Ulli Beier. WTO

Osip Mandelshtam. Irving Layton. NeAC

Osip Mandelshtam. Seamus Deane. FaBo

Osprey sails about the sound, The. The Fisherman's Hymn. Alexander Wilson. AA

Ossawatomie. Carl Sandburg. CMoP; OxBA

Ossian's Serenade. Calder Campbell. BLPA

Ostia Will Receive You. Friederike Mayröcker, *tr. fr. German by* Beth Bjorklund. CoAuP

'Ostler Joe. George R. Sims. BeLS; BLPA

Ostracized as we are with God. Apology of Genius. Mina Loy. QFR

Ostrich is a Silly Bird, The. Mary E. Wilkins Freeman. FaPON; OBCA

Ostriches and Grandmothers! Amiri Baraka. NeAP

Othello, *sels.* Shakespeare.
  Death of Othello. *Fr.* V, ii. FiP
  Farewell content. *Fr.* III, iii. TrGrPo
  Good Name, A. *Fr.* III, iii. FaFP
  "Her father loved me; oft invited me." *Fr.* I, iii. EBEV; SCV
  "It is the cause, it is the cause, my soul." *Fr.* V, ii. EBEV
  (Othello and Desdemona.) FiP

Othello Jones Dresses for Dinner. Ed Roberson. PoBA; PoNe

Othello's Report. Rodolfo Hinostroza, *tr. fr. Spanish by* Maureen Ahern *and* David Tipton. Per

Other, An. Thomas Carew. *See* Epitaph: Epitaph on the Lady Mary Villiers, An.

Other, The. Peter Cooley. MAYP; NAmP

Other, The. Ruth Fainlight. BrRo

Other. Lance Henson. VoR

Other bright days of action have seemed great. John Masefield. *Fr.* Biography. OxBTC

Other day a partridge, The. The Talk of the Town. Ed Fisher. FiBHP

Other day I was loving a sweet little fruitpie-and-cream, The. Gavin Ewart. EAS

Other day, when I looked at a tree, The. Roots. Louis Ginsberg. TrJP

Other days on another continent. Chamutal Reich. *Fr.* Three Poems in Black and White, 1. WCI

Other Death, The. Roberto Sosa, *tr. fr. Spanish by* Alejandro Murguía. Vol

Other end of this long bridge, The. Taigi, *tr. fr. Japanese by* Hiroaki Sato. *Fr.* Twenty-nine Hokku. FCEI

Other Fabrics, Other Mores! Anna Maria Lenngren, *tr. fr. Swedish by* Nadia Christensen *and* Marianne Tiblin. AIW; PBWP

Other Fellow's Job, The. Strickland W. Gillilan. WBLP

Other Great Composers, The. John Ash. NPo

Other Lives of the Romantics. Jane Flanders. SoTCo

Other loves I have known. Proof. Bessie Calhoun Bird. BlSi

Other men are thorn. Mahadevi, *tr. by* A. K. Ramanujan. BoWoP

Other Night (Comet Kohoutek), The. Diane Ackerman. BWV

Other One, The. Harry Thurston Peck. AA

Other patients are ill otherwise, and do. The Mad. Robert Pinsky. *Fr.* Essay on Psychiatrists, XVIII. NoAM

Other prisoners you've written to. Pen Pal. Carl Dennis. BLA

Other props are gone, The. Je T'Adore. Thomas Kinsella. MoP; NoAM

Other rules had to be learned. Notes on Saint Maurice. Judit Tóth, *tr. by* Laura Schiff. MHuP

Other Sheep I Have, Which Are Not of This Fold. Bryant. TrPWD

Other Side, The. Roy Fuller. OxBC

Other Side, The. Seamus Heaney. CIP; FaBCIP

Other Side, The. Linda Hogan. ER

Other Side, The. Nelo Risi, *tr. fr. Italian by* Lawrence R. Smith. NItP

Other Side of a Mirror, The. Mary Elizabeth Coleridge. BoWoP

Other Side of the River, The. Charles Wright. MT

Other Side of the Valley, The. *Unknown, tr. fr. Chinese by* Burton Watson. CoBCP

Other Side of This World, The. Calvin Forbes. MAYP

Other Voice, The. Tom Paulin. FaBCIP

Other Woman, The. Jane Shore. PPR

Other World, The. Harriet Beecher Stowe. AA; WGRP

Other World, The. *Unknown, tr. fr. Egyptian by* Robert Hillyer. *Fr.* Book of the Dead. AWP; OBD

Others. Charles D. Meigs. WBLP

Others abide our question. Thou art free. Shakespeare. Matthew Arnold. FiP; HeIP; InvP; NoP; OBEV; Son; TrGrPo

Others because you did not keep. A Deep-sworn Vow. W. B. Yeats. CMoP; OAEL-2; PCP; PoE; UnPo

Others have pleasantness and praise. Love's Votary. George Augustus Simcox. NOBVV

Others Hunters in the North the Cree, The. Jerome Rothenberg. PoM

Others, I am not the first. A. E. Housman. *Fr.* A Shropshire Lad, XXX. CMoP; LiTB; MoBrPo; NOBVV; OxBTC; PoE; PPP

Others, many others, must have known. Leaving Buffalo. Charles Martin. PoA

Others may cease to remember. Empress Yamato-hime. *Fr.* Manyo Shu. Ma

Others May Praise What They Like. Walt Whitman. Par

Others stand in their imported, The. Giving Up Butterflies. Geraldine Kudaka. BrSi

Others taunt me with having knelt at well-curbs. For Once, Then, Something. Robert Frost. NoAM; NOBA

Others weary of the noise. Mothers—and Others. Amos R. Wells. WBLP

Others would think I was walking somewhere. Friday Evening. Julio Marzán. InW

Otis. Lorenzo Thomas. UL

Ottava Rima would, I know, be proper. W. H. Auden. *Fr.* Letter to Lord Byron. NOBL

Otter, The. Seamus Heaney. FaBCIP; IPY; NoAM

Otter, An. Ted Hughes. CMoP; MoP; NePoEA-2; NoAM

Otter is known, The. Lutra, the Fisher. James McMichael. AmPA

Otto. Gwendolyn Brooks. PChr; PDV

Otto. Theodore Roethke. DiL

Ou Phrontis. Charles Causley. NePoEA

Oui Papa. Delano Abdul Malik de Coteau. PBCV

Ouphe and goblin! imp and sprite! Elfin Song. Joseph Rodman Drake. *Fr.* The Culprit Fay. AA

Our age bereft of nobility. A Poem for Painters. John Wieners. NeAP; PoM

Our ambassador to Venus, Mz Abner. *Unknown.* PeHV

Our Andy's gone with cattle now. Andy's Gone with Cattle. Henry Lawson. PoAu-1

Our Angels. Howard Schwartz. VWA

Our author by experience finds it true. Dryden. *Fr.* Aureng-Zebe. FiP; OBS; OxBoLi; SeCV-2

Our babysitter lives across from the Dodge Street cemetery. Adolescence. Larry Levis. NAmP

Our Backs Are to the Cypress. Leah Goldberg, *tr. fr. Hebrew by* Ramah Commanday. BoWoP

Our backyards touched somewhere upon the hill. Neighbors. Marilyn Francis. GoYe

Our Ball. Winthrop Mackworth Praed. *Fr.* Letters from Teignmouth. EnRP

Our band is few but true and tried. Song of Marion's Men. Bryant. AnAmPo; PAH

Our bark was out—far, far from land. The Sailor's Grave. *At. to* Eliza Cook. BLPA

Our Barrio. Alurista, *tr. fr. Spanish by* Toni Empringham. FIA

Our beauty is to us that which to men. Sir Richard Fanshawe, *after the Italian of* Giovanni Battista Guarini. *Fr.* Il Pastor Fido. OBVE

Our Bias. W. H. Auden. MoP; NoP

Our Biggest Fish. Eugene Field. AnAmPo

Our birth is but a sleep and a forgetting. Wordsworth. *Fr.* Ode: Intimations of Immortality from Recollections of Early Childhood. EaLo; WGRP
  (Intimations of Immortality.) ChTr
  (Our Birth Is but a Sleep.) FaBV

Our Blackness Did Not Come to Us Whole. Linda Brown Bragg. CNA

Our blue boat drifts. Birdwatching at Fan Lake. Anita Endrezze-Danielson. HATNAP

Our boat is asleep on Serchio's stream. Shelley. *Fr.* The Boat on the Serchio. Mes

Our boat shall harbour at the port of Hira. Kurohito. *Fr.* Manyo Shu. Ma

Our boats were moored where Luxor throws. Written on the Plain of Thebes. J. W. Burgon. OBTV

Our boatswain calls out for his bold British heroes. New Sea Song. *Unknown.* OxBSS

Our Bodies. Denise Levertov. NaP; PPP

Our Bog is Dood. Stevie Smith. FaBoNo; NAEL-2; NBLV; PoE; WeW

Our Bondage It Shall End. *At. to* Peter Cartwright. AH

Our bones will all be built into the runway. Gavin Ewart. NPo

Our brains ache, in the merciless iced east winds that knive us. Exposure. Wilfred Owen. FaBoMo; InPS; MMA; NoAM; OBWP; RB; WaP

Our brother Clarence goes to school. Big Brother. Elizabeth Madox Roberts. FaPON

Our brothers and mothers and cousins with strangers between their syllables. Watch Them Die. Dennis Trudell. KS

Our brown canal was endless to my thought. "George Eliot." *Fr.* Brother and Sister. NOBVV

Our bugles sang truce, for the night-cloud had lowered [*or* lower'd]. The Soldier's Dream. Thomas Campbell. BeLS; EnRP; FaPoR; GTBS; GTBS-P

Our camp-fires shone bright on the mountain. Sherman's March to the Sea. Samuel H. M. Byers. PAH

Our candles, lit, re-lit, have gone down now. Twelfth Night. Peter Scupham. OBCP

Our Canoe Idles in the Idling Current. Kenneth Rexroth. ErPo

Our Captain Cried All Hands. *Unknown.* OBET

Our captain stood upon the deck, a spyglass in his hand. Captain Bunker. *Unknown.* AmFP

Our car was fierce enough. The Trip. William Stafford. PCP

Our Caribbean/ a bandolier. Our Home. Jan Carew. PBCV

Our cat turns up her nose at mice. The Cat Who Aspired to Higher Things. X. J. Kennedy. TDD

Our caves do not go Boom! and make one nervy. Sterkfontein. Ruth Miller. PeSA

Our chariots are strong. *Unknown, tr. by* Arthur Waley. BoS

Our cherished dualism gone? Journal to Stella. Morton Dauwen Zabel. PoA

Our Child. Pablo Neruda, *tr. fr. Spanish by* Perry Higman. LPSS

Our child, our treasure. Issa, *tr. by* Hiroaki Sato. FCEI

Our Childhood Spilled into Our Hearts. David Vogel, *tr. fr. Hebrew by* A. C. Jacobs. VWA

Our children have eaten supper. Nightfall, Midwinter, Missouri. Brian Coffey. *Fr.* Missouri Sequence. CIP

Our Children's Children Will Marvel. Ilya Grigoryevich Ehrenburg, *tr. fr. Russian by* Jeannette Eyre. WaaP

Our Christmas pudding was made in November. Pudding Charms. Charlotte Druitt Cole. BoTP

Our city has sunk to the bottom of the sea. These Days. Otto Laaber, *tr. by* Beth Bjorklund. CoAuP

Our city's sons and daughters. School Days in New Amsterdam. Arthur Guiterman. FaPON

Our closest relative, but how far we have. The Monkey. Cees Buddingh', *tr. by* James S. Holmes. DuIn

Our clothes are still wet from wading. The Huts at Esquimaux. Norman Dubie. MOWH

Our Club Work. Mrs. Henry Linden. CBWP-4

Our collective wastebin. In the Outhouse. Mitsuye Yamada. *Fr.* Camp Notes. WPOW

Our Companie in the Next World. John Donne. *Fr.* Of the Progresse of the Soule; the Second Anniversarie. OBS

Our comrade, crossing. *Unknown. Fr.* Manyo Shu. PeBJV

"Our couch shall be roses all spangled with dew." A Sensible Girl's Reply to Moore's. Walter Savage Landor. FaBoEE

Our Country. Julia Ward Howe. OPP; PAH

Our Country. Henry David Thoreau. GOA

Our Country. Whittier. OPP

Our country is closed in, all mountains. George Seferis, *tr. fr. Greek by* Edmund Keeley *and* Philip Sherrard. *Fr.* Mythistorima, X. VMG

Our Country Is Divided. Faarah Nuur, *tr. fr. Somali by* B. W. Andrzejewski *and* I. M. Lewis. WTO

Our Country's Call. Bryant. PAH

Our Country's Emblem. *Unknown.* WBLP

Our cup of joy was overfilled. A Dialogue. Lizelia Augusta Jenkins Moorer. CBWP-3

Our daughter, Alicia. Hot Line. Louella Dunann. RHPC

Our day was composed of resemblances, take. Sail Away. Robert Adamson. CBAP

Our days, alas! our mortal days. The Shortness and Misery of Life. Isaac Watts. NOCV

Our Dead. Robert Nichols. WGRP

Our diaries squatted, toad-like [*or* toadlike]. Complaint of the Grandparents. Justice. BLA; CAPP (Nostalgia and Complaint of the Grandparents.) NoAM

Our dog Fred. The Diners in the Kitchen. James Whitcomb Riley. OBAL

Our doom is in our being. We began. James Agee. *Fr.* Sonnets, II. MoAmPo

Our Dreams. Amir Gilboa, *tr. fr. Hebrew by* Warren Bargad *and* Stanley F. Chyet. IP

Our dreams of love and modest glory. To Chaadaev. Pushkin, *tr. by* Alan Myers. AAA

Our earth in 1969. Doggerel by a Senior Citizen. W. H. Auden. NBLV; NOBL

Our Earth Mother. *Unknown, tr. fr. Zuni Indian by* R. Bunzel. WTO

Our efforts are those of men prone to disaster. Trojans. C. P. Cavafy, *tr. by* Edmund Keeley *and* Philip Sherrard. VMG

Our English gamesters scorne to stake. Roger Williams. SCAP

Our epoch takes a voluptuous satisfaction. Hypocrite Auteur. Archibald MacLeish. AmPP

Our Ernest. "Elmo." PWR

Our eye pupils are always honest. Green Tomatoes. Dennis Trudell. KS

Our eyeless bark sails free. The Earth. Emerson. AA

Our eyes are holden that we do not see. Faith and Sight. Anna M. King. BLRP

Our eyes have viewed the burnished vineyards where. Letter to a Friend. Robert Penn Warren. MoAmPo

Our eyes meet over other. Loyalty. Leslie Ullman. NAmP

Our eyes unlash slowly one. Bill Knott. PPR

"Our Fadder, Which are in Heaben!" He Paid Me Seven. *Unknown.* BPo

Our fairest garland, made of Beauty's flowers. Contention between Four Maids Concerning That Which Addeth Most Perfection to That Sex. Sir John Davies. SiPS

Our famous Harvey hath made good. The Circulation. Thomas Washbourne. NOCV

Our fancies are but joys all unexprest. Henrietta Cordelia Ray. CBWP-3

Our Father, by Whose Name. F. Bland Tucker. AH

Our Father, God. Adoniram Judson. AH

Our Father, grant us to lie down in peace. Evening Prayer. *Unknown, tr. by* Solomon Solis-Cohen. TrJP

Our Father in Heaven. Sarah Josepha Hale. AH

Our father our all-wielding is. The "Pater Noster. *Unknown.* ACP

Our Father, Our King. *Unknown.* TrJP

Our Father which [*or* who] art in heaven. Bible, *N.T. Fr.* St. Matthew, VI: 9-13. EaLo; PoLF; TrGrPo

Our Father! While Our Hearts Unlearn. Oliver Wendell Holmes. AH

Our Father who art in heaven/ Stay there. Pater Noster. Jacques Prévert, *tr. by* Lawrence Ferlinghetti. RHTwFP

Our Father, whose creative Will. W. H. Auden. *Fr.* For the Time Being; a Christmas Oratorio. TrPWD

Our father works in us. A Father of Women. Alice Meynell. BrRo; WPE

Our Fathers. Bible, *Apocrypha. See* Ecclesiasticus: Let us now praise famous men.

Our fathers all were poor. The Fathers. Edwin Muir. OxBS

Our fathers came to search for gold. Australia's on the Wallaby. *Unknown.* PoAu-1

Our Fathers' God. Benjamin Copeland. AH

Our fathers' God! from out whose hand. Centennial Hymn. Whittier. AA; OPP; PAH

Our Father's Hand. Annie Johnson Flint. BLRP

Our fathers in their books and speech. Orient Wheat. Adrienne Rich. NePoEA

Our father's ship. Our Island. Richard Katrovas. NAmP

Our fathers took oaths as of old they took wives. Thomas Brown. FaBoEE

Our fathers, who were wondrous wise. *Unknown.* FaBoUs

Our fathers wrung their bread from stocks and stones. Children of Light. Robert Lowell. CMoP; MoAB; NAAL-2; OxBA

Our Fear. Zbigniew Herbert, *tr. fr. Polish by* Czeslaw Milosz. PwPP

Our feet have wandered from thy path. Wanderers. Thomas Curtis Clark. TrPWD

Our feet meet the earth in this place. Marble Floor. Karol Wojtyla. CRP

Our first ancestor (Abram) alone received his religion from Heaven. Therefore We Preserve Life. Shen Ch'üan, *tr. by* William C. White. TrJP

Our First Century. George Edward Woodberry. PAH

Our Flag Was Still There. Richard Tillinghast. MAYP

Our flesh was a battle-ground. The Litany of the Dark People. Countee Cullen. EaLo; TrPWD

Our friend's feet were cold the morning we set out. Yosano Akiko, tr. fr. Japanese by Hiroaki Sato. Fr. Thirty-nine Tanka. FCEI

Our friends go with us as we go. Non Dolet. Oliver St. John Gogarty. OBMV

Our friendship, Robert, firm through twenty years. A Letter to Robert Frost. Robert Hillyer. MoAmPo

Our Garden. Moyshe-Leyb Halpern, tr. fr. Yiddish by Benjamin and Barbara Harshav and Kathryn Helle. AYP

Our garden's very near the trains. Trains. Hope Shepherd. BoTP

Our generation yearns to be free. A Song: Promoting Women's Rights. Ch'iu Chin, tr. by Pao Chia-lin. WFTU

Our geodesic dome-shaped space. The Personification of a Name. Ray A. Young Bear. HATNAP

Our glances spin silver threads. Empathy. Agnes Pratt. NOVW

Our God and Father surely knows. The Father Knows. "F. L. H." BLRP

Our God and God of our fathers. Prayer for Dew. Eleazar ben Kalir, tr. by Israel Zangwill. TrJP

Our God and soldiers we alike adore. Francis Quarles. FaBoEE (Of Common Devotion.) OxBSP

Our God, Our Help in Ages Past. Isaac Watts. OBVE; PWR; TOF. See also O God, Our Help in Ages Past. (Our God, Our Help.) NoP

Our golden age was then, when lamp and rug. Family Prime. Mark Van Doren. VGW

Our goodly ship was loaded deep. Captain Mansfield's Fight with the Turks at Sea. Unknown. OxBSS

Our Goodman. Unknown. AmFP; ESPB, A and B vers.

Our great Empress. Hitomaro. Fr. Manyo Shu. PeBJV

Our great prince who orders. Hitomaro. Fr. Manyo Shu. PeBJV

Our great sovereign, a goddess. Hitomaro. Fr. Manyo Shu. Ma

Our great Sovereign who rules in peace,/ Offspring of the Bright One on high,/ Wills, as a goddess. Unknown. Fr. Manyo Shu. Ma

Our great Sovereign who rules in peace,/ Offspring of the Bright One on high,/ Has begun to build. Unknown. Fr. Manyo Shu. Ma

Our Ground Time Here Will Be Brief. Maxine W. Kumin. ER

Our guttural muse. Traditions. Seamus Heaney. FaBoMo

Our half-thought thoughts divide in sifted wisps. Train to Dublin. Louis MacNeice. FaBCIP

Our Hands in the Garden. Anne Hébert, tr. fr. French by A. Poulin, Jr.. BoWoP

Our happiness is easily wronged by speech. Writing. Anthony Cronin. PoPo

Our haughty life is crowned with darkness. London, from Hampstead Heath. Wordsworth. Fr. Extempore Effusion upon the Death of James Hogg. FaBoPP

Our hearths are gone out, and our hearts are broken. The Raven Days. Sidney Lanier. AnAmPo; OxBA

Our hearts are filled with pride to-day. Welcome to Hon. Frederick Douglass. Josephine D. Henderson Heard. CBWP-4

Our Heavenly Father, sel. Frederick William Faber. My God, How Wonderful Thou Art. TrPWD

Our Heritage. Jesse Stuart. AmFN

Our Heroes. Phoebe Cary. BLPA

Our Hired Man (And His Daughter, Too). Monica Shannon. FaPON

Our hired man is the kindest man. The Hired Man's Way. John Kendrick Bangs. OBCA

Our History. Catherine Cate Coblentz. FaPON

Our history is grave noble and tragic. Men. Archibald MacLeish. AmFN; MoAB

Our history sings of centuries. Our History. Catherine Cate Coblentz. FaPON

Our Home. Jan Carew. PBCV

Our homes are eaten out by time. The Town Betrayed. Edwin Muir. CMoP

Our honeymoon. Bridal Piece. Louise Glück. SM

Our horse fell down the well around behind the stable. Good-By Liza Jane. Unknown. AS

Our Hoste sey wel that the brighte sonne. Introduction to the Man of Law's Prologue. Chaucer. Fr. The Canterbury Tales. FiP

Our House. Marco Martos, tr. fr. Spanish by David Tipton. Per

Our House. Dorothy Thompson. RHPC

Our house had filled with moths. The Moths. Michael Jackson. ATNZ; PeNZ

Our house had wings for children, chandeliers. The Exile. Larry Rubin. GoYe

Our house is small. Our House. Dorothy Thompson. RHPC

Our Hunting Fathers. W. H. Auden. FaBoMo; MoP; NoAM

Our images withdraw, the rose returns. Beyond Possession. Elizabeth Jennings. NePoEA

Our indolence was despair. We were still at times struck. An Interlude. John Peale Bishop. LiTA

Our Insufficiency to Praise God Suitably for His Mercy. Edward Taylor. LiTA

Our Island. Richard Katrovas. NAmP

Our Islet out of Helgoland, dismissed. Islet the Dachs. George Meredith. FM

Our Jewish Quarter. Jacob Glatstein, tr. fr. Yiddish by Cynthia Ozick. PeBMYV

Our journey had advanced. Emily Dickinson. LiTA; LiTM; MoAB; NOCV; PoEL-5; QFR

Our Joyful Feast. George Wither. See So now is come our joyful'st feast.

Our keels are furred with tropic weed that clogs the crawling tides. The Captive Ships at Manila. Dorothy Paul. PAH

Our Kind Creator. Solomon Howe. AH

Our king went forth to Normandy. The Agincourt Carol. Unknown. OAEL-1; OBET (Carol of Agincourt, A.) MeEL

Our king has wrote a lang letter. Lord Derwentwater. Unknown. ESPB

Our king he has a secret to tell. The Bonny Lass of Anglesey. Unknown. ESPB, (A and B vers.)

Our king he kept a false steward. Sir Aldingar. Unknown. ESPB; ESPB, (A, B and C vers.); OxBB

Our king lay at Westminster. Hugh Spencer's Feats in France. Unknown. ESPB

Our[e] king[e] went forth to Normandy. The Agincourt Carol. Unknown. OAEL-1; OBET (Carol of Agincourt, A.) MeEL (Deo Gracias, Anglia.) EBEV

Our King went up upon a hill high. Henry before Agincourt: October 25, 1415. John Lydgate. CH

Our Lady. Mary Elizabeth Coleridge. OBEV; OBMV; WPE

Our Lady in the Middle Ages. Frederick William Faber. ACP

Our Lady of the Waves. George Mackay Brown. NePoEA-2

Our Lady Peace. Mark Van Doren. WaP

Our Lady's Expectation, sel. Frederick William Faber. Expectation, The. ACP

Our Lady's Song. Unknown. OBEV

Our Land. Yannis Ritsos, tr. fr. Greek by Edmund Keeley. AnAn

Our last bridge. Marina Tsvetayeva, tr. fr. Russian by Paul Schmidt. Fr. The Daughter of Jairus, VIII. BoWoP

Our last free summer we mooned about at odd hours. Chrysalides. Thomas Kinsella. BIrV

Our last morning in that long room. In the Last Few Moments Came the Old German Cleaning Woman. Jane Cooper. SM

"Our Left." Francis Orrery Ticknor. PAH

Our left and right show red and green: mute phonics. Flying Friendly Skies. Turner Cassity. MT

Our Life Is Hid with Christ in God. George Herbert. OAEL-1

Our life is like a bubble. Mohammad Taqi Mir, tr. by Ahmed Ali. GoT

Our life is like a forest, where the sun. Charles Sangster. Fr. Sonnets Written in the Orillia Woods, VII. NOBC

Our life is not life, save in the fleeting. Responding Voice. Francisco A. de Icaza, tr. by Samuel Beckett. MexPo

Our life is two-fold: Sleep hath its own world. The Dream. Byron. BeLS; ChER; TEP

Our Light Afflictions. Unknown. BLRP

Our Lips and Ears. Unknown. BLPA; WBLP

Our little bird in his full day of health. The Vacant Cage. Charles Tennyson Turner. FM

Our little fleet in July first. The Armada, 1588. John Wilson. OxBChV

Our Little Ghost. Louisa May Alcott. OBCA

Our little kinsmen after rain. Emily Dickinson. FaPON; ImOP

Our little tantrum, flushed and misery-hollow. Rebeca in a Mirror. Judith Rodriguez. CBAP

Our Lives. Sharon Scott. JB

Our Lives Are Rivers. Luis G. Urbina, tr. fr. Spanish by Samuel Beckett. MexPo

Our lives are Swiss. Emily Dickinson. NOBA; TAP

Our lives float on quiet waters. Quiet Waters. Blanche Shoemaker Wagstaff. BLPA

Our lives no longer feel ground under them. The Stalin Epigram. Osip Mandelstam, tr. by W. S. Merwin and Clarence Brown. FaBoPV

Our lord and prince, ruling in peace. Okisome no Azumabito. Fr. Manyo Shu. Ma

Our lords are to the mountains gane. Hughie Graham. Unknown. OxBB

Our lord's reign. Congratulations. Shunzei, tr. fr. Japanese by Burton Watson. Fr. Thirty Tanka. FCEI

Our Love. Xavier Villaurrutia, *tr. fr. Spanish by* Perry Higman. LPSS

Our Love Is Made, Your Heavy Head. Alastair Fowler. NPo

Our Love Shall Be the Brightness. James Wreford Watson. CaP

Our Love Was a Grim Citadel. R. A. K. Mason. ATNZ

Our love was conceived in silence and must live silently. At the Dark Hour. Paul Dehn. BoLoP; WaP

Our love was pure. Song of Snow-white Heads. Cho Wen-chün, *tr. by* Arthur Waley. BoWoP

Our love will not come back on fortune's wheel. Obit. Robert Lowell. HCAP

Our man of the seashore. What Her Girl Friend Said on Her Wedding Day. Ammuvanar, *tr. by* A. K. Ramanujan. PLW

Our many years are made of clay and cloud. Destiny. Harrison Smith Morris. AA

Our March. Vladimir Mayakovsky, *tr. fr. Russian by* Babette Deutsch *and* Avrahm Yarmolinsky. AWP

Our Martyr-Chief. James Russell Lowell. OHIP

Our Master. Whittier. BLRP; WBLP

Our medieval fathers simply named. Hedge-Sparrows and House-Sparrows. Roy Fuller. AnAn

Our Modest Doughboys. Albert Charlton Andrews. PAH

Our Mother. George Cooper. *See* Hundreds of stars in the pretty sky.

Our mother bade us keep the trodden ways. "George Eliot." *Fr.* Brother and Sister, III. GN

Our Mother, loved of all thy sons. Sea and Shore. Harry Lyman Koopman. AA

Our mother makes a pot of tea. Pot of Tea. Susan Griffin. NPGG

Our mother sits by the/ pool. Sitting. Susan Griffin. NPGG

Our mother tells us it is time to clean up. Tissue. Susan Griffin. NPGG

Our mother, the pride of us all. Mugford's Victory. John White Chadwick. PAH

Our Mother Tongue. Richard Monckton Milnes. GN

Our mother was the pussy-cat, our father was the owl. The Children of the Owl and the Pussy-Cat. Edward Lear. FaBoNo

Our mother, while she turned her wheel. Mother. Whittier. *Fr.* Snowbound; a Winter Idyl. AA; OHIP

Our moulting days are in the twilight stage. Garnishing the Aviary. Margaret Danner. *Fr.* Far from Africa: Four Poems, I. BPo

Our Movements. Paul Eluard, *tr. fr. French by* Michael Benedikt. POS

Our Nation Forever. Wallace Bruce. OHIP

Our National Banner. Dexter Smith. OPP; PAH

Our Nation's birth gave history your name. Washington. John A. Prentice. OHIP

Our neighbors are so courteous, worthy and human! Peire Cardenal, *tr. by* Paul Blackburn. Pro

Our new clothes fool no one. Yom Kippur. Chana Bloch. VWA

Our new house isn't steady. Atlantis. Maura Stanton. NAmP

Our news is seldom good: the heart. W. H. Auden. *Fr.* New Year Letter. FaBoRV

Our nightshadow. Pantheism: 1968. Judah Leib Teller, *tr. by* Benjamin *and* Barbara Harshav. AYP

Our Noble Booker T. Washington. Mrs. Henry Linden. CBWP-4

Our noble prince, child of the Bright One on high. Hitomaro. *Fr.* Manyo Shu. Ma

Our Norman betters. Lines: Inspired by the Controversy on the Value or Otherwise of Old English Studies. Anthony Burgess. FaBoCo

Our Number. Martin Carter. PVCV

Our nuns come out to shop in the afternoon. Intercessors. Austin Clarke. CMoP

Our objections to the war. For the Minority. Robert Peterson. NeAC

Our Orders. Julia Ward Howe. AA

Our Own. Margaret E. M. Sangster. BLPA

Our passions are most like to floods and streams. To His Mistress. Sir Walter Ralegh. SiPS

Our pastures are bitten and bare. Joseph Gordon MacLead. *Fr.* Men of the Rocks. OxBS

Our paths began at distant points in space. Juncture. Rea Lubar Duncan. PoNe

Our People. Diane Burns. STE

Our perverse old *pisatel'* Vladimir. Something for My Russian Friends. Edmund Wilson. OBAL

Our Photograph[s]. Frederick Locker-Lampson. NBLV; NOBL

Our poets had best. Yadoyano Meshimori, *tr. by* Geoffrey Bownas *and* Anthony Thwaite. PeBJV

Our portion of fire. The Manichaeans. Gary Snyder. VGW

Our Presidents. *Unknown.* BLPA

Our prime minister made a fast move! *Unknown, tr. by* Hiroaki Sato. FCEI

Our prince, offspring of the Bright One on high. Hitomaro. *Fr.* Manyo Shu. Ma

Our prince, pliant as the soft bamboo. Prince Niu. *Fr.* Manyo Shu. FCEI

Our quarterback kept throwing higher. Necessity Is the Mother of the "Bullet." Patrick Worth Gray. TSL

Our quin's seek, an very seek. Queen Eleanor's Confession. *Unknown.* ESPB, A *and* B *vers.*; OBET; PrIm

Our Revels Now Are Ended. Shakespeare. *Fr.* The Tempest, IV, i. LiTB; RB

(Stuff of Dreams, The.) FaBV

(Such Stuff as Dreams Are Made On.) TrGrPo

Our Richard Allen in his early youth. Rt. Rev. Richard Allen. Josephine D. Henderson Heard. CBWP-4

Our roads are ridden. For Sammy Younge. Charlie Cobb. PoBA

Our Rock with loving care. Grace after Meals. *Unknown, tr. by* Alice Lucas. TrJP

Our roofs are adjacent. Love Song ("Our roofs are adjacent"). *Unknown, tr. by* Reza Baraheni *and* Zahra-Soltan Shokoohtaezeh. BoWoP

Our ruins run back to memory. Cavafy in Redondo. Mark Jarman. NAmP

Our rural ancestors, with little blest. The Ideals of Satire. Pope. *Fr.* First Epistle of the Second Book of Horace. FiP

"Our saints are poets, Milton and Blake." Encounter. Denis Devlin. BIrV

Our sardine fishermen work at night in the dark of the moon. The Purse-Seine. Robinson Jeffers. CMoP; HAP; NoAM; NOBA; NoP; OxBA; PrIm; WeW

Our Saviour/ (Paterne of true holinesse). Ensamples of Our Savior. Robert Southwell. PoEL-2

Our Saviour's Golden Rule. Isaac Watts. OxBChV

Our Saviour's Love. *Unknown.* OBET

Our scene shifts to a hunting lodge in which. The Queer Assayers of the Frontier. Peter Porter. *Fr.* Baroque Quatrains. AnAn

Our School Now Closes Out. Edmund Dumas. AH

Our share of night to bear. Emily Dickinson. AA

Our shepherds all. Boots and Saddles. Nicolas Saboly. OHIP

Our ship lay tumbling in an angry sea. On Board the '76. James Russell Lowell. MOS

Our Ship She Lies in Harbour. *Unknown.* OBET

Our ship, the Sea Smithy, swerved out of the tradewinds. On the Congo. Harry Edmund Martinson, *tr. by* Robert Bly. RB

Our short fat, lord bishop. Bad Bishop Jegon. *Unknown.* GBP

Our Silly Little Sister. Dorothy Aldis. FaPON

Our single purpose was to walk through snow. Polar Exploration. Stephen Spender. MoAB; NoAM

(North, The.) FaBoMo

Our Smoke Has Gone Four Ways. Lance Henson. CDW

Our soprano is on the wind tonight. Autumn Song on Perry Street. Lloyd Frankenberg. GrPl

Our Sorcerers. Adam Cornford. BWV

Our sorrow sends its shadow round the earth. J. A. G. Julia Ward Howe. PAH

Our sovereign, a god. Miyuki. *Fr.* Manyo Shu. Ma

Our sovereign familiar with the eight corners/ being a god, rules on high. Akahito. *Fr.* Manyo Shu. FCEI

Our sovereign familiar with the eight corners. Hitomaro. *Fr.* Manyo Shu. FCEI

Our sovereign familiar with the eight corners—/ his eternal palace where we serve. Akahito. *Fr.* Manyo Shu. FCEI

Our Sovereign has come to dwell. Akahito. *Fr.* Manyo Shu. Ma

Our Sovereign who rules in peace. *Unknown. Fr.* Manyo Shu. Ma

Our Sovereign's far-off court. Yakamochi. *Fr.* Manyo Shu. Ma

Our Stars Come from Ireland. Wallace Stevens. GOA

Our States, O Lord. John Mycall. AH

Our steel helmets. Night Guards. Wu T'e-Liang, *tr. by* Dominic Cheung. IFON

Our steps are scattered far. In the Wilderness. Edith Lovejoy Pierce. TrPWD

Our storme is past, and that storm's tyrannous rage. The Calme. John Donne. MePo; MOS

Our story is noble, tragic. Hunting Horns. Guillaume Apollinaire, *tr. by* Paul Blackburn. RHTwFP

Our Sun. George Seferis, *tr. fr. Greek by* Edmund Keeley *and* Philip Sherrard. VMG

Our Sunday morning when dawn-priests were applying. John Berryman. BoLoP

Our tarin' Dan O'Connell sure he was a mighty man. Cushendall. *Unknown.* WTO

Our Task. Henrietta Cordelia Ray. CBWP-3

Our task is done! on Gunga's breast. An Evening Walk in Bengal. Reginald Heber. OBTV

Our Teacher Moses. Jacob Glatstein, *tr. fr. Yiddish by* Benjamin *and* Barbara Harshav. AYP

Our teachers drove us nuts. The Teachers. Nicanor Parra, tr. by William Jay Smith. CT

Our tears have fallen for this world of stone. My Subtle and Proclamant Song. Sean Jennett. NeIP

Our Tense and Wintry Minds. Hayden Carruth. AH

Our tropic fruits, nurs'd 'neath a torrid sky. Unknown. Fr. A Poetical Epistle, from the Island of Jamaica. to. PBCV

Our trust is now in thee, Beauregard! Beauregard. Catherine Anne Warfield. PAH

Our Two Opinions. Eugene Field. AA

Our Two Worthies. John Crowe Ransom. OBAL

Our vernal signs the RAM begins. The Signs of the Zodiac. Ebenezer Cobham Brewer. FaBoUs

Our view of sky, jungle, and fields constricts. The Insert. R. L. Barth. InPK

Our Village—by a Villager. Thomas Hood. OBSV
(Our Village.) PoEL-4

Our vision is by nature free. Mocking Spectacles. Yüan Mei, tr. by Anthony C. Yu. WFTU

Our Voice. Noémia da Sousa, tr. fr. Portuguese into French by Jean Todrani and André Joucla-Ruau; English vers. by Kathleen Weaver. OV

Our walls were thick. Venus Khoury-Gata, tr. by Carol Cosman. OV

Our Washing Machine. Patricia Hubbell. RHPC

Our way of life. It's a Woman's World. Eavan Boland. CIP

Our window-panes enthral our summer bees. The Bee-Wisp. Charles Tennyson Turner. FM

Our Wives. Jonathan Galassi. EOEF

Our words are dead. Silence. Ghazi al-Gosaibi, tr. by Sharif Elmusa and Charles Doria. MAP

Our Youth. John Ashbery. SOTW; VGW

Our youth was happy: why repine. Walter Savage Landor. FaBoEE

Oure Hoste gan to swere as he were wood. The Introduction to the Pardoner's Prologue. Chaucer. Fr. The Canterbury Tales. NAEL-1; NoP

Oure kinge went forth to Normandy. See Our king went forth to Normandy.

Ourobouros. Jorge Plescoff, tr. fr. Spanish by Yishai Tobin. VWA

Ours are the streets where Bess first met her/ cancer. Bess. William Stafford. NNaP; NoP

Ourselves we do inter with sweet derision. Emily Dickinson. FaBoEE

Ourselves were wed one summer—dear. Emily Dickinson. PeHV

Out/ Of the self. Out of and Back in. Malka Heifetz-Tussman, tr. by Kathryn Hellerstein. AYP

Out and Back on the Fifteenth Night of the First Month. Mei Yao-ch'en, tr. fr. Chinese by Burton Watson. CoBCP

Out and Fight. Charles Godfrey Leland. PAH

Out and In Again. Malka Heifetz-Tussman, tr. fr. Yiddish by Kathryn Hellerstein. AYP

Out Early One Morning, I Met an Old Acquaintance. Shen Yüeh, tr. fr. Chinese by Burton Watson. CoBCP

Out Fishin.' Edgar A. Guest. BLPL; PoLF

Out Fishing. Barbara Howes. ASP; WPE

Out for a morning meal a little crow, drenched with dew. Unknown, tr. by Hiroaki Sato. FCEI

Out for a walk, after a week in bed. An Urban Convalescence. James Merrill. CoAP; NAAL-2; NOBA

Out for a walk the other day. A Mystic Song. Unknown, tr. by Percy Allen. WGRP

Out frae the wüd the gowk cries still. On the Hill. William Soutar. PoSH

Out from Its Fine Cage. Unknown, tr. fr. Italian by William Jay Smith. CT; PFI

Out from Lobster Cove. J. D. Reed. NeAC

Out from muted bee-sounds and musketry. Origin of Dreams. Marvin Bell. LCAP

Out from the harbor of Amsterdam. Henry Hudson's Quest. Burton Egbert Stevenson. PAH

Out from the horror of infernal deeps. Rosamond's Appeal. Samuel Daniel. Fr. The Complaint of Rosamond. OBSC

Out from the moat, a frog. Totaku, tr. by Hiroaki Sato. FCEI

Out goes the rat. Counting-out Rhymes. Unknown. FaPON
(Eena, meena, mina, mo.) OxNR

Out here in the fields, few social affairs. Returning to My Home in the Country. T'ao Ch'ien, tr. by Burton Watson. CoBCP

Out here on Cottage Grove it matters. The galloping. Pyrography. John Ashbery. PoM

Out here there are no hearthstones. Sleep in the Mojave Desert. Sylvia Plath. AiP; NoP

Out in a world of death, far to the northward lying. The Winter Lakes. Wilfred Campbell. BoNaP; NOBC; OBCV

Out in back. Train Song. Diane Siebert. RHPC

Out in the bushlands a creeper grows. Unknown, tr. by Arthur Waley. BoS

Out in the Cold. George Starbuck. NYBP

Out in the Dark. Edward Thomas. BrPo; CH; GTBS-P; LiTM; MoAB; MoBrPo; MoVE; NOBE; NoBE; OBWVE; RB

Out in the dark beyond my gates. New Year's Eve in Troy. Adrienne Rich. NePoEA-2

Out in the dark it throbs and glows. On the Verge. William Winter. AA

Out in the dark over the snow. Out in the Dark. Edward Thomas. BrPo; CH; GTBS-P; LiTM; MoAB; MoBrPo; MoVE; NOBE; NoBE; OBWVE; RB

Out in the Desert. Josephine D. Henderson Heard. CBWP-4

Out in the far distance away. Unknown Smoke. Archie Washburn. NOVW

Out in the fields which were green last May. A Child's Thought of Harvest. "Susan Coolidge." OHIP

Out in the Fields with God. At. to Elizabeth Barrett Browning and to Louis Imogen Guiney. BLRP; WBLP; WGRP
(Song from Sylvan, A.) BLPA

Out in the garden. The Pigeons. Rodney Bennett. BoTP

Out in the garden. The Blackbird. Phyllis Drayson. BoTP

Out in the garden. Bubbles. L. Nicholson. BoTP

Out in the garden. Tamekane, tr. by Steven D. Carter. WFTW

Out in the garden, sunny and still. Freedom. Joan Agnew. BoTP

Out in the late amber afternoon. In Shadow. Hart Crane. NOBA

Out in the misty moonlight. Ghosts. Richard Kendall Munkittrick. AA

Out in the night thou art the sun. Star of Ethiopia. Lucian B. Watkins. BANP

Out in the paddies. Kaneyoshi, tr. by Steven D. Carter. WFTW

Out in the rain a world is growing green. Easter Monday. Christina Rossetti. NOCV

Out in the sky the great dark clouds are massing. Ships That Pass in the Night. Paul Laurence Dunbar. AnAmPo; BANP; CDC; MOS

Out in the Woods. Carroll Arnett. NOVW

Out in the yellow meadows, where the bee. George Meredith. Fr. Modern Love, XI. GBL

Out in this desert we are testing bombs. Trying to Talk with a Man. Adrienne Rich. HCAP

Out-island once, on a south slope. Deer Isle. Philip Booth. VGW

Out it spake Lizee Linzee. Lizie Lindsay. Unknown. ESPB, A and B vers.
(Donald of the Isles.) OxBB

Out of a cavern on Parnassus' side. The New Castalia. William Hayes Ward. AA

Out of a dream of ease and indolence. Highway to Glory Song. W. H. Auden. Fr. Man of La Mancha. AnAn

Out of a fired ship, which, by no way. A Burnt Ship. John Donne. EBEV; InPK; OBWP; WaaP

Out of a gothic North, the pallid children. Good-bye to the Mezzogiorno. W. H. Auden. OxBTC

Out of a government grant to poets, I paid. Economics. Mona Van Duyn. SM

Out of a Northern city's bay. The Cruise of the Monitor,. George Henry Boker. PAH

Out of a War of Wits. Dylan Thomas. PoA

Out of adult hearing. A Picture of Okinawa. Dennis Schmitz. LCAP; NPGG

Out of and Back in. Malka Heifetz-Tussman, tr. fr. Yiddish by Kathryn Hellerstein. AYP

Out of brightness, a brightness out of brightness. The Waltz. Hilary Corke. NYBP

Out of burlap sacks, out of bearing butter. They Feed They Lion. Philip Levine. CAPP; LCAP; MAT; MoP; NNaP; NoAM; NOBA; Prf

Out of Chaos Out of Order Out. Michele Roberts. BrRo

Out of Control; the Quarry. Christopher Dewdney. NOBC

Out of Doors. E. North. BoTP

Out-of-Doors. Robert Whitaker. TrPWD

Out of every hundred of us. American Commencement. Aram Boyajian. NeAC

Out of frayed sackcloth—breasts of filthy cataracts. Perets Markish, tr. by Leonard Wolf. PeBMYV

Out of French. Sir Charles Sedley. FaBoEE

Out of friendship and a slow retreat of the blood. Ascending Red Cedar Moon. Duane Niatum. CDW

Out of gas south. Autumn. Philip Levine. NNaP

Out of her house she crept. Miss Euphemia. John Crowe Ransom. CMoP

Out of her own body she pushed. Grandmother. Paula Gunn Allen. STE

Out of him that I loved. Our Stars Come from Ireland. Wallace Stevens. GOA

Out of hir swouh whan she did abraide. The Letter of Compleynt of Canace. John Lydgate. *Fr.* The Fall of Princes, I. OxBLMV

Out of his cottage to the sun. Old Dan'l. L. A. G. Strong. MoBrPo

Out of hunger/ or out of great love. To My Child. Abraham Sutskever, *tr. by* David G. Roskies *and* Hillel Schwartz. VWA

Out of icy storms the white hare came. Ecclesiastes. Joseph Langland. NePoEA

Out of it steps the future of the poor. The Door. W. H. Auden. *Fr.* The Quest. Son

Out of Luck. Abraham ibn Ezra, *tr. fr. Hebrew by* Solomon Solis-Cohen. TrJP

Out of me unworthy and unknown. Anne Rutledge. Edgar Lee Masters. *Fr.* Spoon River Anthology. AmFN; CMoP; FaFP; HAP; LiTA; LiTM; MoAmPo; MoP; NoAM; NOBA; NoBA; OFD; OHFP; OxBA; TrGrPo

Out of Midsummer's Blazing Most Not Night. E. E. Cummings. NoAM

Out of money, so I'm sitting in the shade. More than Fifty. Jack Gilbert. NPGG

Out of my clothes, I ran past the boathouse. Under the Boathouse. David Bottoms. MAYP; MT

Out of my flesh that hungers. On a Night of the Full Moon. Audre Lorde. AIW; UnAS

Out of my heart, one day, I wrote a song. Misapprehension. Paul Laurence Dunbar. BPo

Out of my longing, dusk-aware. Candle Song. Anna Elizabeth Bennett. GoYe

Out of my own great woe. Heine, *tr. by* Elizabeth Barrett Browning. AWP

Out of my poverty. Conversation by the Body's Light. Jane Cooper. ER

Out of my sleeves ten bones protrude. James Weigel, Jr. *Fr.* Testaments, XXVIII. TSM

Out of my window I could see. Blossoms. Frank Dempster Sherman. OBCA

Out of my window late at night I gape. In the Night. Elizabeth Jennings. NePoEA; NYBP

Out of one golden breath. Else Lasker-Schüler, *tr. by* Jethro Bithell. TrJP
(Love-Song.) TrJP

Out of our daylight into death you burn. Paper Anarchist Addresses the Shade of Nancy Ling Perry. George Woodcock. NOBC

Out of Our Shame. Norman Rosten. TrJP

Out of Palestine, out of Babylon. Wandering Jews. Nancy Keesing. VWA

Out of sadness I eat fish. Kito, *tr. fr. Japanese by* Hiroaki Sato. *Fr.* Twenty-four Hokku. FCEI

Out of Sight. R. C. Shebelski. SoTCo

Out of Sight in the Direction of My Body. Paul Éluard, *tr. fr. French by* Samuel Beckett. RHTwFP

Out of Sight, Out of Mind. Barnabe Googe. ElL; InPS

Out of Sleep. Allen Curnow. ATNZ

Out of Soundings. Padraic Fallon. NeIP

Out of the bitter herb the splintered bone. Shelter Him in Milk and Meadow. Meridel LeSueur. ER

Out of the blackthorn hedges. Ivor Gurney. EnLoPo

Out-of-the-Body Travel. Stanley Plumly. AmPA; DiL; GeTw; LCAP

Out of the bosom of the air. Snow-Flakes. Longfellow. ChTr; FaBoRV; FPL; NOBA; NoP; PoEL-5; TAP; UnPo; WiR
(Snow.) BoTP

Out of the breath of Gehennah. Germination. Arlene Stone. VWA

Out of the church she followed [*or* follow'd] them. Maude Clare. Christina Rossetti. BeLS; EBVV

Out of the clover and blue-eyed grass. Driving Home the Cows. Kate Putnam Osgood. AA; BeLS; PAH

Out of the complicated house, come I. The Hills. Frances Cornford. MoBrPo

Out of the corpse-warm vestibule of heaven steps the sun. Ingeborg Bachmann, *tr. by* Janice Orion. BoWoP

Out of the Cradle Endlessly Rocking. Walt Whitman. AA; AmPP; AWP; HAP; HeIP; MoAmPo; NAAL-1; NAWM-2; NOBA; NoP; OxBA; PoE; PoEL-5; PrIm; TAP; WeW

Out of the dark raw earth. Alabama. Julia Fields. PoBA; PoNe

Out of the Dark Wood. "Peter." AmMo

Out of the Darkness. Frankie Armstrong. BrRo

Out of the Darkness. Gertrud Kolmar, *tr. fr. German by* Michael Hamburger. WPOW

Out of the deep. Clara Ann Thompson. CBWP-2

Out of the deep and the dark. The Poet. Yone Noguchi. WGRP

Out of the deeps I cry to thee, O God! Richard Le Gallienne. TrPWD

Out of the Depths. Frederic Lawrence Knowles. TrPWD

Out of the depths [*or* deep] have I cried [*or* called] (unto) Thee, O Lord. Bible, *O.T.* Psalms, CXXX. TrJP
(De Profundis.) BLRP; WGRP
(Psalm CXXX: "Ffrom depth off sinn and from a diepe dispaire," *paraphrased by* Sir Thomas Wyatt) OBVE
(Song of Supplication, A.) TrGrPo

Out of the Depths I Cry unto You, O Death! Tawfiq Sayigh, *tr. fr. Arabic by* Anne Royal *and* Samuel Hazo. MAP

Out of the depths of a heart of love. A Valentine. Priscilla Jane Thompson. CBWP-2

Out of the dusk a shadow. Evolution. John Banister Tabb. AA

Out of the earth. I Sing for the Animals. *Teton Sioux Oral Tradition.* TTTS

Out of the earth beneath the water. The Mud Turtle. Howard Nemerov. NYBP

Out of the earth, out of the air, out of the water. Rapparees. Richard Murphy. *Fr.* The Battle of Aughrim. BIrV; NOIV

Out of the earth to rest or range. The Passing Strange. John Masefield. LiTB; MoAB; MoBrPo; OBEV

Out of the factory chimney, tall. Smoke Animals. Rowena Bastin Bennett. PDV

Out of the fire they come, headlong from heart's desire. For the War-Children. Sylvia Read. CN

Out of the floodgate of stone, just closed, a three-foot cataract. Wen T'ing-shih, *tr. fr. Chinese by* Timothy C. Wong. *Fr.* Miscellaneous Verses on Living in the Mountains, II. WFTU

Out of the focal and foremost fire. Little Giffen. Francis Orrery Ticknor. AA; GOA; PAH
(Little Giffen of Tennessee.) AnAmPo

Out of the fog. The Fog Dream. Sandra M. Gilbert. PoA

Out of the Frying Pan into the Fire. James Henry. NOBVV

Out of the garden comes the tree. Because Thou Did'st Give. Harry Morris. CRP

Out of the ghetto streets where a Jewboy. Autobiographical. A. M. Klein. MoCV; NoAM

Out of the golden remote wild west where the sea without shore is. Hesperia. Swinburne. OBNC

Out of the grass in a storm. Miura Chora, *tr. fr. Japanese by* Hiroaki Sato. *Fr.* Sixteen Hokku. FCEI

Out of the gray steel of imagination. Spring & Asura. Miyazawa Kenji, *tr. by* Sato. FCEI

Out of the grey air grew snow and more snow. Snow. W. R. Rodgers. LiTM

Out of the heart there flew a little singing bird. Youth. Virginia Woodward Cloud. AA

Out of the hills of Habersham. Song of the Chattahoochee. Sidney Lanier. AA; AmFN; AnAmPo; BoNaP; FaBoBe; FaBV; LiTA; OHFP

Out of the Hitherwhere. James Whitcomb Riley. BLPA; FPL

Out of the Hurly-Burly. "Max Adeler." *See* Death-angel smote Alexander McGlue, The.

Out of the icy storms the white hare came. Ecclesiastes. Joseph Langland. NePoEA

Out of the Inner Shell of a Certain Landscape. Hagiwara Sakutaro, *tr. fr. Japanese by* Hiroaki Sato. FCEI

Out of the Italian; a Song. Richard Crashaw. SeCV-1

Out of the "Kalevala", *sel.* Anselm Hollo.
Troll Chanting. WSC

Out of the lamplight. Mice in the Hay. Leslie Norris. OBCP; PChr

Out of the Land of Heaven. Leonard Cohen. MoCV
(Poem for Marc Chagall.) OBCV

Out of the light that dazzles me. My Captain. Dorothea Day. BLPA

Out of the living word. The Book of Kells. Howard Nemerov. EaLo

Out of the midnight sky a great dawn broke. The Shepherd Speaks. John Erskine. TrCP

Out of the mighty Yule log came. The Yule Log. William Hamilton Hayne. AA

Out of the morning dark, the pale. Terra Incognita. Sherod Santos. AnAn

Out of the mud two strangers came. Two Tramps in Mud Time. Robert Frost. BLPL; CMoP; LiTA; LiTM; MoAB; MoAmPo; MoP; NAAL-2; NoAM; PrIm; TrGrPo

Out of the mud which covers me. Inflictis. Archibald Stodart-Walker. *Fr.* The Moxford Book of English Verse. CenHV

Out of the night of the sea. At Carbis Bay. Arthur Symons. FaBoPP

Out of the North the wild news came. The Rising. Thomas Buchanan Read. *Fr.* The Wagoner of the Alleghanies. PAH

Out of the Northeast. The White Horse. Tu Fu, *tr. by* Rewi Alley. ChTr

Out of the Old House, Nancy. Will M. Carleton. AA

Out of the poisonous East. Largo e mesto. W. E. Henley. *Fr.* London Voluntaries, IV. BrPo

Out of the Sea, Early. May Swenson. RFM

Out of the seething of the tool, which. Eros Possessed. Denis Roche, *tr. by Harry Mathews*. RHTwFP

Out of the shadow, I am come in to you whole a black holy man. Study Peace. Amiri Baraka. PoBA

Out of the sighs and breath of each small citizen. The City: Midnight. Bruce Dawe. PoAu-2

Out of the Strong, Sweetness. Charles Reznikoff. VWA

Out of the swirling shadow host. Chatterton. Rina Hands. Mes

Out of the table endlessly rocking. Just Friends. Robert Creeley. NeAP

Out of the tense awed darkness, my Frangepani comes. Rainy Season Love Song. Gladys May Casely Hayford. CDC

Out of the terra cotta still a voice. Etruscan Warrior's Head. Helen Rowe Henze. GoYe

Out of the tomb, we bring Badroulbadour. The Worms at Heaven's Gate. Wallace Stevens. NoAM; OBD

Out of the utmost pitch of wilderment. De Profundis. Amos Niven Wilder. TrPWD

Out of the Vastness that is God. A Litany for Latter-Day Mystics. Cale Young Rice. WGRP

Out of the Whirlwind. Bible, *O.T. Fr.* Job: Moreover the Lord answered Job, and said, XL: 7–XLI. AWP, XXXVIII: 2–XXXIX.

Out of the wild sweet grape, I have trampled a wine. On Laying Up Treasure. Lois Smith Hiers. GoYe

Out of the Wilderness. Ulrich Troubetzkoy. GoYe

Out of the winds' and the waves' riot. Ebb Tide. Marjorie Pickthall. CaP

Out of the wine-pot cry'd the fly. The Fly. Philip Ayres, *after the Spanish of* Quevedo. OBVE

Out of the wood of thoughts that grows by night. Cock-Crow. Edward Thomas. GTBS-P; MoAB; MoBrPo; OxBSP; RB

Out of these thin, thin cups I drink pale tea. Bone China. R. P. Lister. NYBP

Out of this thoughtless, formless, swarming life. Self to Self. Charles Brasch. ATNZ

Out of this ugliness may come. Glasgow Street. William Montgomerie. OxBS

Out of Time, *sel.* Kenneth Slessor.
"Leaning against the golden undertow." CBAP

Out of Tune. W. E. Henley. MoBrPo

Out of Whack. Russell Edson. LCAP

Out of what calms and pools the cool shell grows. The Atoll in the Mind. Alex Comfort. LiTB; LiTM; SeCePo

Out of Your Sleep [*or* slepe] Arise and Wake. *Unknown.* NoP; OxBLMV
(Man Exalted.) MeEL; NoP

Out on a limb and frantically sawing. Martyrdom of Two Pagans. Philip Whalen. NeAP

Out on a Nevada mountain. The Vanishing Valley. Ernie Fanning. CowP

Out on Kara Cape. Tameko, *tr. by* Steven D. Carter. WFTW

Out on the bare grey roads, I pass. Touch It. Robert Mezey. NaP

Out on the board the old shearer stands. Click Go the Shears, Boys. *Unknown.* PoAu-1

Out on the Course. William J. Vernon. TSL

Out on the high "bird islands," Ciboux and Hertford. Cape Breton. Elizabeth Bishop. InPS

Out on the lawn I lie in bed. A Summer Night. W. H. Auden. FaBoRV

Out on the margin of moonshine land. The Lugubrious Whing-Whang. James Whitcomb Riley. NA

Out on the ocean, dreary and cold. Swell My Net Full. *Unknown.* OxBSS

Out on the ocean, great wide ocean. Great *Titanic. Unknown.* AmFP

Out on the roads of sky the moon stands poised. Roy McFadden. NeIP

Out on the tormented, midnight sea. Poem and Message. Dannie Abse. TEP

Out on the wastes of the Never Never. Where the Dead Men Lie. Barcroft Henry Boake. CBAP; PoAu-1

Out on the waves. A Distant View of the Sea. Tamekane, *tr. by* Steven D. Carter. WFTW

Out on the western prairies. The Cowboy's Prayer. Curley W. Fletcher. CowP

Out on the windy hill. The Shepherd's Dog. Leslie Norris. OBCP

"Out, Out." Robert Frost. DL; FF; HAP; HeIP; NAAL-2; OxBA; RB; SoSe; UnPo; VGW; WeW

Out, Out, Brief Candle! Shakespeare. *See* Macbeth: She should have died hereafter.

Out, out, harrow! Into bale am I brought. Satan and Pilate's Wife. *Unknown.* ACP

Out shopping, little Julia spied. The Coconut. "Ande." FiBHP

Out shot Master Suian's fist. Master Suian's Birthplace. Sekirin, *tr. by* Lucien Stryk *and* Takashi Ikemoto. ZPCJ

Out that black hole of bush. Third World Snapshots. John Robert Lee. PBCV

Out the gate I meet a friend. Rai San'yo, *tr. fr. Chinese by* Burton Watson. *Fr.* Landscape Vignettes, III. JLIC-2

Out the Greywolf valley. Gary Snyder. *Fr.* Myths and Texts: Hunting, XII. NaP

Out the southern gate at sundown. *Unknown, tr. fr. Chinese by* Burton Watson. *Fr.* Tzu Yeh Songs. CoBCP

Out there, beyond the boundary fence, beyond. The Singing Bones. Randolph Stow. CBAP

Out There Somewhere. Henry Herbert Knibbs. BLPA

Out there, we've walked [*or* talked] quite friendly up to death. The Next War. Wilfred Owen. OBD; Son; WaP

Out there where Barnum Road hooks left. The Last Mountain Lion on Maple Crest Mountain. Peter Meinke. MOWH

Out there, with little else to do. Robben Island. Robert Dederick. PeSA

Out through the fields and the woods. Reluctance. Robert Frost. CMoP; MoAB; MoAmPo; OxBA

Out to Old Aunt Mary's. James Whitcomb Riley. FaFP; OHFP

Out Together. Anthony Howell. NPo

Out under the sprinkler, naked as toads. They Grow Up Too Fast, She Said. Diana O Hehir. NPGG

Out upon it! I have loved. Sir John Suckling. NBLV; PoE

Out, upon the deep old ocean. On Genessarett. Josephine D. Henderson Heard. CBWP-4

Out upon you California. Pennsylvania Places. T. A. Daly. OBAL

Out walking in the frozen swamp one gray [*or* grey] day. The Wood-Pile. Robert Frost. AnAmPo; InPK; LiTA; NAAL-2; NoAM; NoP; VGW

Out walking ties left over from a track. Cross Ties. X. J. Kennedy. HoPM

Out West. Gary Snyder. NNaP

Out West, they say, a man's a man; the legend still persists. Étude Géographique. Stoddard King. AmFN

Out Where the West Begins ("Out where the hand-clasp's a little stronger"). Arthur Chapman. AiP; BLPA; FaBoBe; FaFP

Out with the mountain moon, stinging clear. Mill Valley. Myra Cohn Livingston. RFM

Outbound, your bark awaits you. Were I one. Godspeed. Whittier. Son

Outbreak. Bill Anderson. VGW

Outcast. "Æ." OxBSP

Outcast, The. Josephine D. Henderson Heard. CBWP-4

Outcast. Claude McKay. AmNP; PoBA

Outcast, The. James Stephens. MoBrPo

Outcrop stone is miserly. Still-Life. Ted Hughes. NYBP

Outcry upon Opportunity, An. Shakespeare. *See* Rape of Lucrece, The: Opportunity.

Outdoor Anniversary with Maria. Penelope Shuttle. NPo

Outdoor Collections. Wang Jun-hua, *tr. fr. Chinese by* Dominic Cheung. IFON

Outdoor Litany, An. Louise Imogen Guiney. TrPWD

Outer Space Haiku. Thomas M. Disch. BWV

Outgoing Sabbath. *Unknown, tr. fr. Yiddish by* Joseph Leftwich. TrJP

Outhouse Blues. Sheryl L. Nelms. MOWH

Outlanders, The. Andrew Glaze. NYBP

Outlanders, The. William Morris. *Fr.* The Earthly Paradise. EBVV
(Minstrels and Maids.) GN

Outlandish Knight, The. *Unknown.* OBET

Outlandish names. *Unknown, tr. by* Geoffrey Bownas *and* Anthony Thwaite. PeBJV

Outlaw, The. Seamus Heaney. MoP; NIP; OxBC

Outlaw, The. Sir Walter Scott. *See* Rokeby: Brignall Banks.

Outlaw Murray, The. *Unknown.* ESPB; OxBB

Outlaw of Loch Lene, The. *Unknown, tr. fr. Modern Irish by* Jeremiah Joseph Callanan. BIrV; CH; GBL; OBEV

Outlaw's Song, The. Joanna Baillie. OBEV

Outlines. Audre Lorde. GLP

Outlook Uncertain. Alastair Reid. NePoEA-2

Outlook wasn't brilliant for the Mudville nine that day, The. Casey at the Bat. Ernest Lawrence Thayer. AiP; BeLS; BLPA; FaBoBe; FaFP; FaPON; FPL; OBAL; OBCA; PoRA; SD

Outlook wasn't brilliant for the Mudvillettes, it seems, The. Casey's Daughter at the Bat. Al Graham. ASP

Outside. Phyllis Beauvais. IHMS

Outside. Hugh Chesterman. BoTP

Outside. Robert Creeley. CAPP

Outside/ yellow leaves rattle. Voice in the Blood. Barney Bush. STE

Outside/ outside myself/ there is a world. William Carlos Williams. *Fr.* Paterson, II. NoAM
(Sunday in the Park.) NAAL-2

Outside, a delicate arch. The Curse. John Hollander. UnPo
Outside, affectionate eyes. Ursula. David Ray. VGW
Outside among the talking criss-cross reeds. Karl. Charles Spear. ATNZ
Outside Baby Moon's. Paul Violi. UL
Outside Bristol Rovers Football Ground. The Ballad of Billy Rose. Leslie Norris. MoBS
Outside Fargo, North Dakota. James Wright. LCAP; NNaP
Outside: forecasts of humiliating storms. A Night with Cindy at Heitman's. Richard Hugo. AnAn
Outside my cheap candle. To Myself, Late, in a Myrtle Grove. Robert Peterson. NeAC
Outside my window. Chikako, *tr. by* Steven D. Carter. WFTW
Outside New York, a high place where with one glance. Schubertiana. Tomas Tranströmer, *tr. by* Robert Bly. NU
Outside that bulbous Babylon. English Beach Memory: Mr. Thuddock. Sir Osbert Sitwell. NYBP
Outside the café of mirrors. Paschal Transfiguration. Michael Harlow. ATNZ
Outside the cats are wailing. Leah Goldberg, *tr. fr. Hebrew by* Robert Alter. *Fr.* The Symposium. PBWP
Outside the children play like flames. The Fever. Rosemary Dobson. FaBoWP
Outside the city, desolate, an ancient terrace. The Flower-Rain Terrace. Tao-chi, *tr. by* Jonathan Chaves. CoBLCP
Outside the courtroom. Sharpeville Inquiry. Anne Welsh. PeSA
Outside the Eastern Gate. *Unknown, tr. by* Arthur Waley. BoS
Outside the Holy City. James G. Gilkey. AH
Outside, the last kids holler. Leaving the Motel. W. D. Snodgrass. FF; NIP
Outside the Line. Dan Pagis, *tr. fr. Hebrew by* Warren Bargad *and* Stanley F. Chyet. IP
Outside the pavilion, the rain just cleared. In a Dream, I Visited a Place Called the Monastery of Heavenly Music. Ku T'ai-ch'ing, *tr. by* Irving Lo. WFTU
Outside, the rain, pinafore of gray water, dresses the town. Child Beater. Ai. BoWoP
Outside the second grade room. The Girl Who Loved the Sky. Anita Endrezze-Danielson. HATNAP
Outside the Supermarket. Roy Fuller. OxBC
Outside the tent on the Little Fork. Horace Kephart. Robert Morgan. MAYP
Outside the Terrace of Yellow Cranes. Mooring at Hsai-k'ou at Night. Li Meng-yang, *tr. by* Jonathan Chaves. CoBLCP
Outside the tower, the east wind's early to arrive. To the Tune "Chao-chün's Sorrow." Yang Shen, *tr. by* Jonathan Chaves. CoBLCP
Outside the town I've built this little place. Garden Living. Wu Wei-yeh, *tr. by* Jonathan Chaves. CoBLCP
Outside, the visible gale's. Storm Warning. Howard Moss, *tr. by* William Arrowsmith. AnAn
Outside the whistled gang-call, Twelfth Street Rag. Me Tarzan. Tony Harrison. *Fr.* The School of Eloquence. NoAM
Outside the window, a pistol shot. Night's Invitation. Ishihara Yoshiro, *tr. by* Hiroaki Sato. FCEI
Outside the world crackles like a daily. A lion. A Room I Once Knew. Henry Birnbaum. GoYe
Outside the world was full, plural. The Christmas Tree. Patricia Beer. OBCP
Outside White Earth. Gordon Henry. STE
Outsider, If There Were Such a Man, An. Szabolcs Várady, *tr. fr. Hungarian by* William Jay Smith. MHuP
Outspoken buttocks in pink beads. National Winter Garden. Hart Crane. *Fr.* The Bridge: Three Songs. ErPo; InPS; LiTM; NAAL-2; OxBA
Outward. Louis Simpson. NYBP
Outward Bound. Thomas Bailey Aldrich. AA
Outward Bound. James Simmons. CIP
Outward Bound. Edward Sydney Tylee. PAH
Outward Man Accused, The. Edward Taylor. LiTA
Outwardly splendid as of old. The Church Today. Sir William Watson. WGRP
Outwit me, Lord, if ever hence. Security. Charles L. O'Donnell. TrPWD
Outwit Song, The. Daniel Hoffman. SaC
Outwitted. Edwin Markham. BLPA; FPL; MoAmPo
Ovals of opal on dislustred seas. Memoriter. Charles Spear. ATNZ; PeNZ
Oven Bird, The. Robert Frost. AmPP; AWP; HeIP; MoP; NAAL-2; NoAM; NOBA; NoP; OxBA; PoE; PPP; Son; TAP
Oven Loves the TV Set, The. Heather McHugh. NAmP
Over. R. S. Thomas. FF
Over/ the angular lily. The Tear. Ramón López Velarde, *tr. by* Samuel Beckett. MexPo

Over a bloomy land, untrod. In Dreamy Swoon. George Darley. *Fr.* Nepenthe. OBNC
Over a ground of slate and light gravel. The Sanctuary. Howard Nemerov. NePoEA
Over a slow-dying fire. Lachesis. Victor James Daley. CBAP
Over a wild and stormy sea. Mother Shipton's Prophecies. *At. to.* Charles Hindley. BLPA
Over against the treasury. His Gift and Mine. *Unknown.* BLRP
Over-all picture is winter, The. The Hunters in the Snow. William Carlos Williams. *Fr.* Pictures from Brueghel, III. LCAP
Over all regions of Italy I predict. Weather Forecast. Vivian Lamarque, *tr. by* Muriel Kittel. DMI
Over all the hilltops. The Second Poem the Night-Walker Wrote. Goethe, *tr. by* Robert Bly. NU
(Wanderers Night Songs.) AWP, *tr. by* Longfellow.
Over an ash-fawn beach fronting a sea which keeps. Fiascherino. Charles Tomlinson. NoAM
Over and back. At Ithaca. Hilda Doolittle ("H. D."). VGW
Over and Over Again. Norman MacCaig. NPo
Over and over again the papers print. Once in a While a Protest Poem. David B. Axelrod. InPK
Over and over again to people. The Limits of Submission. Faarah Nuur, *tr. by* B. W. Andrzejewski *and* I. M. Lewis. TTY; WTO
Over and over I see them. Harbach 1944. János Pilinszky, *tr. by* Jascha Kessler. FOC
Over and Over Stitch. Jorie Graham. HCAP
Over and over, when the wayside dust had grayed us. To Be Said at the Seder. Karl Wolfskehl, *tr. by* Carol North Valhope *and* Ernst Morwitz. TrJP
Over back where they speak of life as staying. The Investment. Robert Frost. CMoP; OxBA
Over Bright Summer Seas. Robert Hillyer. NYBP
Over by my bedroom wall. The Ugstabuggle. Peter Wesley-Smith. AmMo
Over Case's Door. John Case. FaBoUs
Over deep cushions, drenched with drowsy scents. Damned Women. Baudelaire, *tr. by* Roy Campbell. BoLoP
Over Dragon Pool frozen clouds. To a Monk Departing for Mid Stream. Seigan, *tr. by* Lucien Stryk *and* Takashi Ikemoto. ZPCJ
Over empty limbs. Tamekane, *tr. by* Steven D. Carter. WFTW
Over England rose a star. The Vampire. Herbert Edward Palmer. VVA
Over every hill. Wanderer's Night-Song. Goethe, *tr. by* Arthur Hugh Clough. OBD
Over-Heart, The. Whittier. NOCV; WGRP
Over heavy dew. Tamenori, *tr. by* Steven D. Carter. WFTW
Over here in England I'm helpin' wi' the hay. Corrymeela. "Moira O'Neill." AWP
Over Hill, over Dale. Shakespeare. *Fr.* A Midsummer Night's Dream, II, i. EiL
(Fairy Land, 1.) OBEV
(Fairy Song ("Over hill, over dale").) NOBE; OBSC; TrGrPo
(Fairy's Wander-Song.) FaPON
(Puck and the Fairy.) GN
(Song: "Over hill, over dale.") InvP
Over hills and high mountains. The Wandering Maiden; or, True Love at Length United. *Unknown.* CoMu
Over his keys the musing organist. James Russell Lowell. *Fr.* The Vision of Sir Launfal, Prelude to *Pt.* I. LiTA
June. OHFP
Over his millions Death has lawful power. On the Death of M. D'Ossoli and His Wife, Margaret Fuller. Walter Savage Landor. PAH
Over in the corner where the bishops sit stuffing themselves. Special Preference. Louis Aragon, *tr. by* Michael Benedikt. POS
Over in the Meadow. Oliver A. Wadsworth. MoShBr
Over Japan there are stars. Stars. Takenaka Iku, *tr. by* Geoffrey Bownas *and* Anthony Thwaite. PeBJV
Over Kohata, the hill in Yamashina. Hitomaro. *Fr.* Manyo Shu. Ma
Over marsh water. Fireflies over a Marsh. Tamemasa, *tr. by* Steven D. Carter. WFTW
Over mountains, pride. The Praise of Ben Dorain. Duncan Ban MacIntyre, *tr. by* "Hugh MacDiarmid" (Christopher Murray Grieve). GoTS
Over my head, I see the bronze butterfly. Lying in a Hammock at William Duffy's Farm in Pine Island, Minnesota. James Wright. CAPP; HAP; HCAP; HoPM; NaP; NOBA; OPOP
Over my head the fan moves slowly. In the Turkish Ward. Peter Balakian. MAYP
Over my head the stars. Under the Winter Sky. János Pilinszky, *tr. by* Ted Hughes. MHuP
Over my head the woodland wall. The Scribe. *Unknown.* AnIL; TIRV, *tr. by* Robin Flower.

Over my pillow. Plum Scent through a Window closed against the Snow. Shotetsu, *tr.* by Steven D. Carter. WFTW

Over New England now, the snow. Frances Mary Frost. BoNaP

Over northeast mountains. Voyeur's Dream. Barney Bush. HATNAP

Over our heads the branches made. The Mountebanks. Charles Henry Lüders. AA

Over our heads the missiles ran. Loss of an Oil Tanker. Charles Causley. OxBC

Over rock and wrinkled ground. Beagles. W. R. Rodgers. FaBoTw; SD

Over rocks on the deserted shore, over the burning heat. Pan. Angelos Sikelianos, *tr.* by Edmund Keeley *and* Philip Sherrard. VMG

Over Salève. George Herbert Clarke. CaP

Over Shimotsuke fields. *Unknown. Fr.* Manyo Shu. FCEI

Over Sir John's Hill. Dylan Thomas. LiTB; MoAB; TOF

Over that morn hung heaviness, until. Seascape. Francis Brett Young. OxBTC

Over the Arafura sea, the China sea. For John Chappell. Gary Snyder. NNaP

Over the barbed wire is the elementary school. A Common Song. Ya Hsien, *tr.* by Dominic Cheung. IFON

Over the big. Mushimaro. *Fr.* Manyo Shu. FCEI

Over the black mountain, across the black bay, into the/ black night and beyond. Encounter. Uys Krige, *tr. by the author.* PeSA

Over the bleak and barren snow. Tony O! Colin Francis. CH; FaBoCo

Over the branches of the cryptomerias. Hitomaro. *Fr.* Manyo Shu. Ma

Over the bridge. Crossing Portsmouth Bridge. Alan Chong Lau. BrSi

Over the briny wave I go. The Kayak. *Unknown.* FaPON

Over the cities evening spreads desire. Phalanstery. Mihály Ladányi, *tr. fr. Hungarian* by Jascha Kessler. *Fr.* Sketchbook. FOC

Over the Coffin. Thomas Hardy. *Fr.* Satires of Circumstance, XIV. BrPo

Over the cradle the mother hung. Where Shall the Baby's Dimple Be. Josiah G. Holland. BLPA

Over the dark highway. Winter Twilight. Lou Lipsitz. GOYP

Over the dark water. A Kayak Song. Lucy Diamond. BoTP

Over the Dark World Flies the Wind. Tennyson. FaBoRV

Over the dim confessional cried. A Priest's Prayer. Martha Gilbert Dickinson Bianchi. AA

Over the downs there were birds flying. On the South Downs. Sara Teasdale. MoAmPo

Over the Edge. Fleur Adcock. PeNZ

Over the eroded earth. The Evening Suit. Jean Follain, *tr.* by W. S. Merwin. RHTwFP

Over the eye behind the moon's cloud. Raison d'Etre. Oliver Pitcher. AmNP

Over the far ocean plains. Kose Sukunamaro. *Fr.* Manyo Shu. Ma

Over the Field. May Swenson. RR

Over the Fields. Adeline White. BoTP

Over, the four long years! And now there rings. Oxford. Lionel Johnson. FaBoPP; OBNC

Over the granite. Sorrow. Noshiwaki Junzaburo, *tr.* by Hiroaki Sato. FCEI

Over the Great City. Edward Carpenter. WGRP

Over the gulf and soaring of the city. Diretro al Sol. Charles G. Bell. NePoAm

Over the half-finished houses. The Roofwalker. Adrienne Rich. CoAP; NAAL-2; PPP

Over the harbor at St. James. The Mill. William Heyen. EyDe

Over the hill came horsemen, horsemen whistling. A Stared Story. William Stafford. Son

Over the hill I have watched the dawning. Dawning. Richard Watson Dixon. NOBVV

Over the hill the farm-boy goes. Evening at [*or* on] the Farm. John Townsend Trowbridge. FaPON; GN
(Evening on the Farm.) MoShBr

Over the Hill to the Poor-House. Will M. Carleton. BeLS; BLPA; FaFP

Over the hills/ Where the edge of the light. The Witches' Ride. Karla Kuskin. PDV

Over the Hills and Far Away. John Gay. *See* Beggar's Opera, The: Were I laid on Greenland's coast.

Over the hills and mountains I came. Yakamochi. *Fr.* Manyo Shu. Ma

Over the hills the loose clouds rambled. The Subjection of Women. Austin Clarke. CIP

Over the ice she flies. Skating. Kipling. SD

Over the lake, the wind and snow of New Year's sky. At Shoraku-ji in Omi, First Poem of the Year. Kishun Ryuki, *tr.* by Burton Watson. FCEI

Over the land freckled with snow half-thawed. Thaw. Edward Thomas. EBEV; FaBoTw; FM; GTBS-P; MoAB; MoBrPo; OxBSP; OxBTC

Over the last century. Song of Lin Liang's Painting "Two Horned Falcons." Li Meng-yang, *tr.* by Jonathan Chaves. CoBLCP

Over the lids of thine eye. Images. Richard Schaukal, *tr.* by Ludwig Lewisohn. AWP

Over the low, barnacled, elephant-colored rocks. Meditation at Oyster River. Theodore Roethke. CAPP; CMoP; MoAmPo; NYBP

Over the monstrous shambling sea. Marsh Song—at Sunset. Sidney Lanier. NOBA

Over the mountains/ And over the waves. Love Will Find Out the Way. *Unknown.* FaBoCh; FaFP; GBL; GN; GTBS; GTBS-P; OBEV; WiR
(Great Adventure, The.) FaFP; GTBS-P

Over the mountains/ Over the plains. Trains. James S. Tippett. FaPON

Over the Phone. Mekeel McBride. MAYP

Over the plains where Persian hosts. The Cyclamen. Arlo Bates. AA

Over the plum snow, the train's blonde smoke. On Returning to Detroit. Carolyn Forché. ER

Over the quarry the children went rambling. The Fossil Raindrops. Harriet Prescott Spofford. OBCA

Over the rainy day mountain. Wishes. Patty L. Harjo. VoR

Over the right/ triangle formed. The Slogan. Paul Blackburn. PoM

Over the rim of the glass. The Ghost in the Martini. Anthony Hecht. DiPo; OxBC

Over the river and through the wood. Thanksgiving Day. Lydia Maria Child. FaPON; NTCP; OHIP; RHPC
(New-England Boy's Song about Thanksgiving Day, The.) OBCA

Over the river ferry of Saho. Yakamochi. *Fr.* Manyo Shu. Ma

Over the River of Heaven. *Unknown. Fr.* Manyo Shu. Ma

Over the roof-tops race the shadows of clouds. John Gould Fletcher. *Fr.* Irradiations, I *or* III [V]. MoAmPo

Over the sea our galleys went. The Wanderers. Robert Browning. *Fr.* Paracelsus, IV. OBEV

Over the Sea to Skye. Robert Louis Stevenson. *See* Sing me a song of a lad that is gone.

Over the sheer rocks over the gorges. Stanislav Vinaver, *tr.* by Vasa D. Mihailovich. VWA

Over the sheer stone cliff-face, over springs and star clusters. By a Waterfall. David Wagoner. BLA

Over the shingled roof the shower has passed. Princess Shikishi, *tr. fr. Japanese* by Hiroaki Sato. *Fr.* Seventy-eight Tanka. FCEI

Over the shoulders and slopes of the dune. The Daisies. Bliss Carman. AnAmPo; BoNaP

Over the Sleeping Eyes. H. Leivick, *tr. fr. Yiddish* by Benjamin *and* Barbara Harshav. AYP

Over the small Jewish graveyard. The Gray Light. A. Leyeles, *tr.* by Benjamin *and* Barbara Harshav. AYP

Over the southern hill so deep. *Unknown, tr.* by Arthur Waley. BoS

Over the spring field trails the mist. Yakamochi. *Fr.* Manyo Shu. Ma

Over the stern, my sad heart, drool. The Tortured Heart. Rimbaud. PeHV

Over the stones still rattling, up Pall Mall. Byron. *Fr.* Don Juan. NOBL, XI.

Over the street, like a towel in the swimming pool. July Morning. Andreas Okopenko, *tr. fr. German* by Beth Bjorklund. *Fr.* Summer Fragments, II. CoAuP

Over! the sweet summer closes. Tennyson. *Fr.* Becket. GBL

Over the Top with Pershing. Zelda Sayre Fitzgerald. AiP

Over the turbulence of the world. Memory. Norman MacCaig. NPo

Over the turret, shut in his ironclad tower. Craven. Sir Henry Newbolt. PAH

Over the utmost hill at length I sped. Shelley. *Fr.* The Revolt of Islam, V. OBWP

Over the Wall: Berlin, May 1975. C. H. Sisson. OBTV; OxBC

Over the warts on the bumpy. Sadie's Playhouse. Margaret Danner. PoBA

Over the water an old ghost strode. The Old Ghost. Thomas Lovell Beddoes. WiR

Over the water and over the lea. *Unknown.* OxNR

Over the west side of the mountain. Lyrebirds. Judith Wright. GoJo

Over the winter glaciers. Beyond Winter. Emerson. RHPC

Over the wintry. Soseki, *tr.* by Henry Behn. PDV

Over the wintry fields the snow drifts; falling, falling. Winter Evening. Walter de la Mare. FaBoRV

Over the years hearts have been broken on Mo-ling boats. Wang Shih-chen, *tr. fr. Chinese* by Daniel Bryant. *Fr.* Poems on the Ch'i-huai, I. WFTU

Over the years, they've darkened, like old paintings. In Memory. Katha Pollitt. MAYP

Over their edge of earth. The Little Clan. F. R. Higgins. OBMV

Over Their Graves. Henry Jerome Stockard. AA; OHIP

Over there in your fields you have. Rains for the Harvest. *Unknown, tr.* by H. J. Spinden. WTO

Over this battered track. Express Train. Karl Kraus, *tr.* by Albert Bloch. TrJP

Over Three Nipple-Stones. Paul Celan, *tr. fr. German by* Joachim Neugroschel. VWA

Over two shadowless waters, adrift as a pinnace in peril. Evening on the Broads. Swinburne. TEP

Over 2000 Illustrations and a Complete Concordance. Elizabeth Bishop. HCAP; LCAP; NAAL-2; NoAM

Over yonder's a park, which is newly begun. The Corpus Christi Carol. *Unknown.* GBP

Over you falls the sea-light, festive yet pale. Ireland. Francis Stuart. NeIP

Over your body the clouds go. Gulliver. Sylvia Plath. NOBA

Overboard. May Swenson. RR

Overcast Dawn. Roberta Hill Whiteman. NOVW

Overcome this great divide of sex. To a Man. Susana March, *tr. by* Kate Flores. DMH

Overcome with humility in the American West. A Man's Vocation Is Nobody's Business. James Galvin. KS

Overdose of beautiful words, An. 12th Raga: For John Wieners. David Meltzer. *Fr.* Ragas. NeAP

Overdue Balance Sheet. Thérèse Plantier, *tr. fr. French by* Maxine W. Kumin *and* Judith Kumin. BoWoP

Overflowing eyes. Meditation. Beyle Schaechter-Gottesman, *tr. by* Gabriel Preil. VWA

Overhanging Cloud. Robert Lowell. *Fr.* Marriage, *st.* 14. NAS

Overhead, the match burns out. Disregard. Ai. NoAM

Overheard. Denise Levertov. PoM

Overheard in an Orchard. Elizabeth Cheney. BLRP

Overheard on a Saltmarsh. Harold Monro. BoTP; CH; FaPON; GoJo; Mes; MoShBr; SO; WSC

Overheard over S. E. Asia. Denise Levertov. BoWoP

Overhung by evergreen, your house was cool. Hope. Tom Sleigh. PPR

Overland to the Islands. Denise Levertov. UnPo

Overlander, The. *Unknown.* PoAu-1

Overloaded circuit, An—lightning. Shimmering Pediment. John Yau. UL

Overlooking the River Stour. Thomas Hardy. FaBoPP

Overlooking the water, a desolate city. Sha-ch'eng, "Sand City". Yang Shih-ch'i, *tr. by* Jonathan Chaves. CoBLCP

Overlord. Bliss Carman. CaP

Overmastering of the mud, The. 4 Variations On. Gerrit Kouwenaar, *tr. by* Peter Nijmeijer. DuIn

Overnight/ My razor rusted. Boncho, *tr. by* Geoffrey Bownas *and* Anthony Thwaite. PeBJV

Overnight clouds begin to scatter. Inscribed on the Painting, "Spring Dawn at Peach Blossom Spring," by Scholar Shang Te-fu. Chao Meng-fu, *tr. by* Jonathan Chaves. CoBLCP

Overnight Guest. Ramona Wilson. VoR

Overnight in the Apartment by the River. Tu Fu, *tr. fr. Chinese by* William Hung. ChTr

Overnight the bush had been cancelled. Happy. Alastair Fowler. NPo

Overnight, very/ whitely, discreetly. Mushrooms. Sylvia Plath. BoNaP; FaBoWP; NePoEA-2; RB; WeW; WPOW

Overreacher, The. Christopher Marlowe. *Fr.* Tamburlaine the Great, *Pt.* I, Act I. NIP

Overripe Fruit. Kasmuneh, *tr. fr. Arabic.* TrJP

Overtaken by the dark. Tadanori, *tr. by* Geoffrey Bownas *and* Anthony Thwaite. PeBJV

Overthrow of Lucifer, The. Phineas Fletcher. *Fr.* The Purple Island, XII. OBS

Overtime. Moyshe-Leyb Halpern, *tr. fr. Yiddish by* Benjamin *and* Barbara Harshav *and* Kathryn Helle. AYP

Overture. Zuhur Dixon, *tr. fr. Arabic by* Patricia Alanah Byrne *and* Salma Khadra Jayyusi. MAP

Overture. Linda Pastan. BLA

Overture for Bubble-Gum and Flute. Alistair Paterson. ATNZ; PeNZ

Overture to Strangers. Phyllis Haring. PeSA

Overtures to Death, *sel.* C. Day Lewis.
     "For us, born into a still." *Fr.* VII. CMoP

Overturned Lake, The. Charles Henri Ford. EAS

Overworked Elocutionist, An. Carolyn Wells. BLPA; BLPL

Ovibos, The. Robert Beverly Hale. FiBHP

Ovid in the Third Reich. Geoffrey Hill. FaBoMo; NoAM; PoPo

Ovid is the surest guide. Written in an Ovid. Matthew Prior. FaBoEE; FaBoUs

Ovid, Meet a Metamorphodite. Jonathan Williams. PoM

Ovid on the Dacian Coast. Dunstan Thompson. NYBP

Ovid's Banquet of Sense, *sel.* George Chapman.
     Corinna Bathes. OBSC

Owed to America. Lawrence Durrell. OBTV

Owed to New York. Byron Rufus Newton. BLPA; NBLV

Owen of Carron, *sel.* John Langhorne.
     "Does nature bear a tyrant's breast?." FaBoCo

Owen's praise demands my song. The Triumphs of Owen. Thomas Gray. EnRP; PoEL-3

Ower the grey sentinel hills. No Voice of Man. Raymond Falconer. PoSH

Owl/ you/ my frightful friend. Doris Mühringer, *tr. by* Beth Bjorklund. CoAuP

Owl/ whose home was in the hemlock, The. *Unknown, tr. by* Jerome Rothenberg *and* Richard Johnny John. STP

Owl, The. Thorkild Bjornvig, *tr. fr. Danish.* NU *tr. by* Robert Bly

Owl, The. Edward Davison. PoA

Owl, The. Walter de la Mare. OxBSP

Owl. Peter Kane Dufault. NYBP

Owl, The. W. S. Merwin. PPP

Owl. Sylvia Read. RHPC

Owl. Rokwaho. STE

Owl, The. William Jay Smith. PDV

Owl, The. Tennyson. BoTP; FaBoCh; FaPON; GoJo; MoShBr

Owl, The. Edward Thomas. ChTr; EBEV; FaBoRV; FaBoTw; FF; GTBS-P; LiTB; MoP; NAEL-2; NIP; NoAM; NOBE; NoP; OAEL-2; OBWVE; PoE; RB; SoSe; UnPo

Owl, The. *Unknown.* TTTS

Owl, The. Robert Penn Warren. MoAmPo

Owl, The. Sándor Weöres, *tr. fr. Hungarian by* Jascha Kessler. FOC

Owl and Rooster. Gladys Cardiff. STE

Owl and the Crow, The. Ben King. AnAmPo

Owl and the Eel and the Warming-Pan, The. Laura E. Richards. OBCA

Owl and the Fox, The. *Unknown.* BLPA

Owl and the Nightingale, The, *sel.* At. to Nicholas de Guildford.
     "When I was in a summer valley." *Tr. fr. Middle English by* John William Hey Atkins. PBBP

Owl and the Pussy-Cat, The. Edward Lear. BeLS; BoTP; FaBoBe; FaBoCh; FaBoNo; FaFP; FaPON; FPL; GoJo; GTBS-P; MoShBr; NA; NBLV; NOBE; NoP; NTCP; OxBChV; OxBoLi; PDV; PoLF; PoRA; PYC; RHPC; TrGrPo; TTTS

Owl-Critic, The. James Thomas Fields. BLPA; CenHV; OBAL; WBLP

Owl expires, the. Eyes! Death gave the dreadful word. On the Death of a Lady's Owl. Moses Mendes. TrJP

Owl has come, The/ Right into my house. Eyes. W. H. Davies. BrPo; FM

Owl hooted and told of the morning star, The. Owl, The. *Unknown.* FaBoNo

Owl in the Oak, The. *Unknown.* FaBoNo

Owl in the Rabbi's Barn, The. Dan Jaffe. VWA

Owl in the Rearview Mirror, An. Duane Niatum. NOVW

Owl in the Sarcophagus, The. Wallace Stevens. FaBoMo

Owl is abroad, the bat and the toad, The. The Witches' Charm. Ben Jonson. *Fr.* The Masque of Queens. FaBoCh; RB (Charme.) FM

Owl Is an Only Bird of Poetry, An. Robert Duncan. NeAP; PoM

Owl that lives in the old oak tree, The. The Owl. William Jay Smith. PDV

Owl to her mate is calling, The. The Fate of the Oak. "Barry Cornwall." OHIP

Owl winks in the shadows, An. Mother Earth; Her Whales. Gary Snyder. LCAP; WeW

Owl Woman. Amber Coverdale Sumrall. GOS

Owl Woman's Death Song. *Unknown, tr. fr. Papago Indian by* Ruth Underhill. BoWoP

Owle, The, *sel.* Michael Drayton.
     "And every bird shew'd in his proper kind." FM

Owls. W. D. Snodgrass. Psk

Owl's Bedtime Story, The. Randall Jarrell. ILY

Owls have feathers lined with down, The. The Hedgehog and His Coat. Elizabeth Fleming. BoTP

Owls roost like gray lamps up there, The. Brobdingnag. Adrien Stoutenburg. NYBP

Owner of My Face, The, *sels.* Rodney Hall. CBAP
     After a Sultry Morning.
     Lips and Nose.
     Some Magnetism in the Sea.

Ownership. Lizette Woodworth Reese. MoAmPo

Ownership of the Night, The. Larry Levis. LCAP

Owning. Wilmot B. Lane. CaP

Owning a Dead Man. Marcia Southwick. MAYP

Owre the Hill. William Soutar. PoSH

Owslebury Lads, The. *Unknown.* OBET

Owt of your slepe aryse and wake. Out of Your Sleep Arise and Wake! *Unknown.* OxBLMV

Ox, The. Mary Morison Webster. PeSA

Ox-Bow. Donald Davie. DiPo

Ox Cart Man. Donald Hall. CAPP; FYAP; InPS; LCAP

Ox driver in a sudden shower. *Unknown*, tr. by Burton Watson. FCEI
Ox-Tamer, The. Walt Whitman. RB
Oxen, The. Thomas Hardy. BoTP; CMoP; EBEV; HAP; InPK; InPK; LiTM; MoAB; MoBrPo; MoP; NoAM; NoAM; NOBE; OAEL-2; OBCP; OxBTC; PChr; PPP; RB; SoSe; TOF; WeW
Oxen have voices, The. Don Giovanni on His Way to Hell. Jack Gilbert. NPGG
Oxen: Ploughing at Fiesole. Charles Tomlinson. OxBTC
Oxen that rattle the yoke and chain or halt in the leafy shade. Walt Whitman. *Fr.* Song of Myself: The Drayman. FM
Oxford, *sel.* Edward Dorn.
   Comforted by Limestone. NOBA
Oxford. Keith Douglas. NePoEA
Oxford. Lionel Johnson. FaBoPP; OBNC
Oxford and Hampton Railway, The. *Unknown.* OBET
Oxford Barber's Verses on the Queen's Death. *Unknown.* APAS
Oxford Bells. Gerard Manley Hopkins. FaBoPP
Oxford Canal. James Elroy Flecker. OxBTC
Oxford Girl; or, Expert Town, The. *Unknown.* AmFP
Oxford in Wartime. Mary Wilson. CN
Oxford Is a Stage. Edward Nolan. CenHV
Oxford Nights. Lionel Johnson. BrPo
Oxford, since late I left thy peaceful shore. To Oxford. Thomas Russell. Son
Oxford Street Museum. Margo Lockwood. PPR
Oxford to London, 1884. In a Railway Compartment. John Fuller. NePoEA-2
Oxherd and the Weaver Maid standing, The. Okura. *Fr.* Manyo Shu. Ma
Oxygen. Joan Swift. NYBP
Oxygen for a Castle in the Air. Paul Snoek, tr. fr. Dutch by Peter Nijmeijer. DuIn
Oya. Audre Lorde. CNA
Oye, oyeye. Battle Songs of the King Tshaka. *Unknown.* PeSA
Oyster-Crabs. Carolyn Wells. BXAP
Oyster in his oyster shell, The. Oyster Shell. Kambara Yumei, tr. by Geoffrey Bownas *and* Anthony Thwaite. PeBJV
Oyster of Locmariaquer, The. The Hoity-Toity Oyster. Charles W. Pratt. *Fr.* A Fable in Two Languages. SoTCo
Oyster Shell. Kambara Yumei, tr. fr. *Japanese by* Geoffrey Bownas *and* Anthony Thwaite. PeBJV
Oyster shuts his gates to form the pearl, The. The Precious Pearl. Pat Wilson. ATNZ
Oyster that went to bed x-million years ago, An. Goodnight. John Ciardi. OBAL
Oyster, The ("The oyster, about as large as a medium-sized stone"). Francis Ponge, tr. fr. *French by* Robert Bly. NU
Oystercatchers. Christopher Middleton. FaBoTw
Oystering. Richard Howard. NoAM
Oysters. Swift. ErPo
Ozymandias [*or* Ozymandias of Egypt]. Shelley. AWP; BeLS; CH; DL; EnRP; FaBoBe; FaBoCh; FaBoRV; FaFP; FaPoR; FF; FiP; FPL; GTBS; GTBS-P; HAP; HeIP; HoPM; InPK; InPS; NAEL-2; NIP; NOBE; NoP; OAEL-2; OBNC; PoE; PoLF; PoRA; PrIM; RB; SCV; Son; SoSe; TEP; TrGrPo; WeW
Ozymandias Revisited. Morris Bishop. BXAP; NBLV
Ozymandias II. Howard Nemerov. Son

P

P Is for Paleontology. Milton Bracker. FiBHP
Pa lays around 'n' loafs all day. Options. "O. Henry." FiBHP
Pa, Pa, Build Me a Boat. *Unknown.* AmFP
Pac-Man. Philip Dacey. NAmP
Pachacamac. Antonio Cisneros, tr. fr. *Spanish by* David Tipton. Per
Pachuco Remembered. Tino Villanueva. FIA
Pacific Epitaphs. Dudley Randall. MoP
Pacific Railway, The. C. R. Ballard. PAH
Pacific Sonnets, *sels.* George Barker.
   "And now there is nothing left to celebrate." *Fr.* XII. LiTM
   "At midday they looked up and saw their death." *Fr.* VII [*or* IX]. LiTM; MOS; WaP
   "From thorax of storms the voices of verbs." *Fr.* VI [*or* VIII]. LiTM; MOS; WaP
   "Seagull, spreadeagled, splayed on the wind, The." *Fr.* V [*or* VII]. LiTM; MOS; WaP
Pacifists. George Woodcock. NOBC
Pacifying the Western Barbarians. Mao Hsi-chen, tr. fr. *Chinese by* Lois Fusek. ATF

Pacifying the Western Barbarians. Niu Chiao, tr. fr. *Chinese by* Lois Fusek. ATF
Pacifying the Western Barbarians. Sun Kuang-hsien, tr. fr. *Chinese by* Lois Fusek. ATF
Pacifying the Western Barbarians. Wen T'ing-yün, tr. fr. *Chinese by* Lois Fusek. ATF
Pacing back and forth between their restless. What the Stone Dreams. James B. Hathaway. GOYP
Pacing with bag-pipe in a bosky square. Caledonia. Anthony Powell. NOBL
Pack, The. Frank Prewett. HATNAP
Pack, Clouds, Away. Thomas Heywood. *Fr.* The Rape of Lucrece. BoTP; ElL; GBL; GTBS; GTBS-P; PBBP; SoSe
   (Good Morrow.) CH
   (Matin Song.) OBEV
Pack-master strokes his whip, The. The She-Fox. Claire Goll, tr. by Mary Ann Caws. DMF
Pack Rat, The. Robert Pack. PPP
Packed in my mind lie all the clothes. The Inward Morning. Henry David Thoreau. AmPP; NoP
Packed with woodpeckers, my head knocks. Raking Leaves. Robert Pack. NYBP
Packet of Letters. Louise Bogan. GrPl; PCP
Packing a Photograph from Firenze. William H. Matchett. NePoEA
Pact. Kenneth Fearing. CMoP
Pact, A. Ezra Pound. AmPP; AnAmPo; LiTA; MoP; NAAL-2; NoAM; NOBA; OxBA; TAP
Pact that we made was the ordinary pact, The. From a Survivor. Adrienne Rich. AnAn
Padda Song, The. *Unknown.* GBP
Paddle Your Own Canoe. Sarah K. Bolton. FaFP
Paddling misty straits mid Go and Etsu. Crossing the Sento River. Masso, tr. by Lucien Stryk *and* Takashi Ikemoto. ZPCJ
Paddling Pool, The. E. M. Adams. BoTP
Paddling Song. *Unknown*, tr. fr. *Bantu by* Max Exner. PBA
Paddock's a lonely space to stay inside, The. The Gate's Open. John Blight. CBAP
Paddy Biran's Song. Paddy Biran, tr. fr. *Girramay by* R. M. W. Dixon. CBAP
Paddy, Get Back. *Unknown.* AmFP
Paddy House. Shotetsu, tr. fr. *Japanese by* Steven D. Carter. WFTW
Paddy, I have but stol'n your living. Ebenezer Elliott. FaBoEE
Paddy keeper/ has dozed off for a moment, The. The Wind at a House in the Paddies. Tameshige, tr. fr. *Japanese by* Steven D. Carter. WFTW
Paddy snail, paddy snail. *Unknown*, tr. by Geoffrey Bownas *and* Anthony Thwaite. PeBJV
Paddy West. *Unknown.* OxBSS
Padlock your garden, my dear. Miriam Yalan-Shteklis, tr. fr. *Hebrew by* Bernhard Frank. *Fr.* Prayer to Be Sung. MHeP
Padraic O'Conaire, Gaelic Storyteller. Frederick Robert Higgins. OBMV
Padstow Night Song, The. *Unknown.* ChTr; GBP
Paean. Jonathan Henderson Brooks. CDC
Paean to Eve's Apple. James Liddy. CIP
Paedotrophiae; or, The Art of Bringing Up Children, *sels.* M. Saint-Marthe, tr. fr. *French.* FaBoUs
   Choosing a Wet-Nurse.
   Cravings during Pregnancy.
   Infant Diseases and Their Treatment.
   Labour.
Pagan Fires. Tawfiq Zayyad, tr. fr. *Arabic by* Sharif Elmusa *and* Charles Doria. MAP
Pagan Isms, The. Claude McKay. BPo
Pagan Prayer. Alice Brown. WGRP
Pagan Prayer. Maria Luisa Spaziani, tr. fr. *Italian by* Muriel Kittel. DMI
Pagan Reinvokes the Twenty-third Psalm, A. Robert Wolf. TrPWD
Pagan Rites. Paul Goodman. *Fr.* North Percy. DiL
Pagan Woman. César Vallejo, tr. fr. *Spanish by* Robert Bly. AnAn
Pagan's myths through marble lips are spoken, The. Worship. Whittier. NOCV
Pagans wild confesse the bonds, The. Roger Williams. SCAP
Page. Sandra McPherson. PoA
Page from the Koran. James Merrill. KS
Pageant Verses. Sir Thomas More. *See* I am called Chyldhod, in play is all my mynde.
Pages of an Album. Dan Pagis, tr. fr. *Hebrew by* Warren Bargad *and* Stanley F. Chyet. IP
Pages of history open, The. Sandra M. Gilbert. PoA
Pages of the album, The. Sonatina in Yellow. Donald Justice. CAPP; DiL; LCAP
Page's Road Song, A. William Alexander Percy. TrPWD

Pages' Song, The. Shakespeare, *See* As You Like It: It Was a Lover and His Lass.

Pagett, M. P. Kipling. BrPo

Pagget, a schoolboy, got a sword, and then. Upon Pagget. Robert Herrick. CaPo; FaBoCh

Pagoda of Master Chih, The. Wang T'ing-hsiang, *tr. fr. Chinese by* Jonathan Chaves. *Fr.* Miscellaneous Poems on Spirit-Valley Temple. CoBLCP

"Paid by my lord, one portrait, Lady Anne." Child with a Cockatoo. Rosemary Dobson. CBAP

Paid on Both Sides, *sel.* W. H. Auden.
  Walking Tour, The. CMoP
  (Chorus: "To throw away the key and walk away.") MoBrPo

Pain. "Æ" MoBrPo

Pain. Enrique Gonzáles Martínez, *tr. fr. Spanish by* Samuel Beckett. MexPo

Pain. Jack Hand. TSM

Pain. James Henry. NOBVV

Pain. Edith Södergran, *tr. fr. Swedish by* Jaakko A. Ahokas. PBWP; WPOW

Pain. Alfonsina Storni, *tr. fr. Spanish by* Merrilee Antrim. WPOW

Pain. Herbert Zand, *tr. fr. German by* Beth Bjorklund. CoAuP

Pain and labor of oppression gave the Western world its birth. The Pharaohs of Today. Lizelia Augusta Jenkins Moorer. CBWP-3

Pain did not wish to be indebted. Asadullah Khan Ghalib, *tr. by* Ahmed Ali. GoT

Pain for a Daughter. Anne Sexton. SoSe; TV; WeW

Pain—has an element of blank. Emily Dickinson. LiTA; LiTM; MoAB; MoAmPo; NAAL-1; PPP

Pain is a blacksmith. Blacksmith Pain. Otto Julius Bierbaum, *tr. by* Jethro Bithell. AWP

Pain is a useless thing. A Personal Opinion. Dahlia Ravikovich, *tr. by* Bernhard Frank. MHeP

Pain is greater now, The. Prince Munenaga, *tr. by* Steven D. Carter. WFTW

Pain Is My Brother. Jack Hand. TSM

Pain is something useless. A Private View. Dahlia Ravikovich, *tr. by* Warren Bargad *and* Stanley F. Chyet. IP

Pain-Killers. Tony Harrison. NPo

Pain of loving you, The. A Young Wife. D. H. Lawrence. BrPo; ELP; MoBrPo

Pain of too poignant beauty fills the heart. The World's Desire. William Rose Benét. TrPWD

Pain Paint. Peter Minck. FaBoUs

Pain we have to suffer seems so broad, The. Belief. Ella Wheeler Wilcox. PWR

"Pain, who made thee?" thus I said once. Pain. James Henry. NOBVV

Painful and brief the act. Eve on the barren shore. Eve in Reflection. Jay Macpherson. OBCV

Painful Love Song, A. Yehuda Amichai, *tr. fr. Hebrew by the author.* LLLT

Painful Plough, The. *Unknown.* OBET

Painless lump, A. Cancer. Hans Verhagen, *tr. by* Peter Nijmeijer. DuIn

Pains and Gains. Edward, 17th Earl of Oxford De Vere. EIL

Pains of Education, The. Charles Churchill. *Fr.* The Author. FaBoCo (Against Education.) TW

Pains of insecurity surround me. Back Again, Home. Don L. Lee. BPo

Pains of Sleep, The. Samuel Taylor Coleridge. EnRP; NAEL-2; OBNC; SeCePo; TEP

Pains the sharp sentence the heart in whose wrath it was uttered. Pardon. Julia Ward Howe. PAH

Paint Box, The. Emile Victor Rieu. RHPC; SO

Paint Castlemaine in colours that will hold. Andrew Marvell. *Fr.* The Last Instructions to a Painter. OBSV

Paint chips slowly. Thirty Miles West of Chicago. Lyn Lifshin. ER

Paint-flaken, it is paint-flaken. March, Upstate. William Bronk. NYBP

Paint last the King, and a dead shade of night. Andrew Marvell. *Fr.* The Last Instructions to a Painter. OBSV
(Charles II.) OBS

Paint me a cavernous waste shore. Sweeney Erect. T. S. Eliot. OxBTC; VGW

Painted autumn overwhelms, The. John Meade Falkner. FaBoPP

Painted Bridge, The. Eleanor Ross Taylor. PPR

Painted Ceiling, The. Amy Lowell. OBAL

Painted Fan, A. Ellen Louise Chandler. AA

Painted Head. John Crowe Ransom. LiTA; LiTM; NoAM; NOBA; OxBA

Painted Lady, The. Margaret Danner. BPo

Painted Madonna Speaks, The. Berta Lask, *tr. fr. German by* Susan L. Cocalis. DMG

Painted Passages. Gail N. Harada. BrSi

Painted stars. Pictures on the Wall. Zvi Shargel. VWA, *tr. by* Gabriel Preil *and* Howard Schwartz

Painted streets alive with hum of noon, The. Sir Edwin Arnold. *Fr.* The Light of Asia. OBTV

Painted whore, the mask of deadly sin, A. William Lithgow. OBTV

Painted with one fish, a cucumber. Japanese Fan. James Kirkup. GrPl

Painted Words. Paul Eluard, *tr. fr. French by* Michael Benedikt. POS

Painter, The. John Ashbery. HCAP; NOBA; NoP; PoE; SOTW

Painter and poet, runner and disk-thrower. One of the Jews. Constantine P. Cavafy. TrJP

Painter, by unmatch'd desert. The Picture. Anacreon, *tr. by* Thomas Stanley. AWP

Painter in the Lion Cage, The. Betti Alver, *tr. fr. Estonian by* Willis Barnstone *and* Felix Oinas. BoWoP

Painter Jung-sup Lee. Ruth Kim Chun-soo, *tr. fr. Korean by* Koh Chang-soo. ACKP

Painter of Dante's awful ferry-ride, The. Babette Deutsch. PoA

Painter Paints, The. Natan Zach, *tr. fr. Hebrew by* Warren Bargad *and* Stanley F. Chyet. IP

Painter, thin with auburn hair, works before an easel, A. The Sketchbook Ashes of Jehoshaphat. Norman Dubie. NAmP

Painter Who Pleased Nobody and Everybody, The. John Gay. BeLS

Painters, The. Judith Hemschemeyer. Psk

Painters. Muriel Rukeyser. EyDe

Painter's Mistress, The. James Elroy Flecker. BrPo

Painting. Stanislaw Grochowiak, *tr. fr. Polish by* Czeslaw Milosz. PwPP

Painting. A. C. Jacobs. VWA

Painting: A Head. John Crowe Ransom. MoAB; MoAmPo

Painting ("A jade cave, ten thousand flowering peach trees of immortality"). Chang Yü, *tr. fr. Chinese by* Jonathan Chaves. CoBLCP

Painting a Madonna. Rosanna Warren. KS

Painting a pear today, it occurs to me that what painting. Nothing to Write Home About. Joe Brainard. PPR

Painting a picture of the same shrimp boat. Discovering Your Subject. Pattiann Rogers. MT

Painting a Picture "The Tranquil Boat." Wen Cheng-ming, *tr. fr. Chinese by* Jonathan Chaves. CoBLCP

Painting Entitled Love and the Pilgrim, A. Gregory O'Brien. ATNZ

Painting Her Nails. Yang Wei-chen, *tr. fr. Chinese by* Jonathan Chaves. CoBLCP

Painting in the Style of Secretary Kao, A. Yün Shou-p'ing, *tr. fr. Chinese by* Jonathan Chaves. CoBLCP

Painting, *"Mist and Rain on the Spring River,"* by Hsiao Chao, The. Tai Piao-yüan, *tr. fr. Chinese by* Jonathan Chaves. CoBLCP

Painting Mount Taranaki. David Eggleton. PeNZ

Painting of Bamboo by Ni Yün-lin, A. Yang Chi, *tr. fr. Chinese by* Jonathan Chaves. CoBLCP

Painting of Chrysanthemums in the Boneless Style of Hsü Ch'ung-ssu, A. Yün Shou-p'ing, *tr. fr. Chinese by* Jonathan Chaves. CoBLCP

Painting of My Father. Padraic Fallon. NOIV

Painting of One Hundred Wild Geese, A. Tai Piao-yüan, *tr. fr. Chinese by* Jonathan Chaves. CoBLCP

Painting of Peach Blossom Spring, A. Shen Chou, *tr. fr. Chinese by* Jonathan Chaves. CoBLCP

Painting of People Strolling through a Pine Forest, A. Hsü Wei, *tr. fr. Chinese by* Jonathan Chaves. CoBLCP

Painting of the Butterfly Dream by the Master Artist Li Tsai, A. Chu Yün-ming, *tr. fr. Chinese by* Jonathan Chaves. CoBLCP

Painting of Water Buffaloes, A, *sel.* Yang Shih-ch'i, *tr. fr. Chinese by* Jonathan Chaves.
  "Herdboy returns, none too early, The." CoBLCP

Painting of Yams, A. Yün Shou-p'ing, *tr. fr. Chinese by* Jonathan Chaves. CoBLCP

Painting pines. Ransetsu, *tr. by* Geoffrey Bownas *and* Anthony Thwaite. PeBJV

Painting ("Slowly I walk the gully path, alone"). Chang Yü, *tr. fr. Chinese by* Jonathan Chaves. *Fr.* Twelve Miscellaneous Poems on the Fang Garden. CoBLCP

Painting "Solitary Fisherman by a Spring River," The. Ni Tsan, *tr. fr. Chinese by* Jonathan Chaves. CoBLCP

Painting the Gate. May Swenson. WeW

Painting with Words, *sel.* Nizar Qabbani, *tr. fr. Arabic by* Diana Der Hovanessian *and* Lena Jayyusi.
  "Twenty years on the road of love." MAP

Paintings, *sels.* Chang Yü, *tr. fr. Chinese by* Jonathan Chaves. CoBLCP
  "His pole and paddle have been with him a long time."
  "I close the book in my hands."

Paintings, *sels.* Pien Kung, *tr. fr. Chinese by* Jonathan Chaves. CoBLCP

"Done playing the lute, but still full of feeling." *Fr.* II.

"Morning sun climbs the eastern peak, The." *Fr.* I.

Paintings of Fishermen, *sels.* Wu Chen, *tr. fr. Chinese by* Jonathan Chaves. CoBLCP

"Drunk, he leans back in his boat." *Fr.* II.

"West of the village, evening rays linger on red leaves." *Fr.* I.

Paintings of Ladies Engaged in Four Springtime Occ, *sel.* Yang Chi, *tr. fr. Chinese by* Jonathan Chaves.

Springtime Embroidery. CoBLCP

Paintings of Various Subjects by Fang Jih-sheng. Pien Kung, *tr. fr. Chinese by* Jonathan Chaves. CoBLCP

Paintings on My Wall Have Been Damaged by the Weather, The. T'ang Hsien-Tsu, *tr. fr. Chinese by* Jonathan Chaves. CoBLCP

Paintings with stiff. Primitives. Dudley Randall. BPo

Painture. Richard Lovelace. CaPo

Pair, A. May Swenson. RFM

Pair of angels, A. Café. Hala Baykov. Mes

Pair of blackbirds, A. In Modern Dress. Craig Raine. NoAM

Pair of dark blue panties, A. Familiar Music. Bill Berkson. UL

Pair of Fireflies, A. Stephen Shu Ning Liu. BrSi

Pair of funnels stroll by night, A. The Funnels. Christian Morgenstern, *tr. by* Geoffrey Grigson. FaBoNo

Pair of golden phoenixes wind round the lute, A. Song of the West Stream. Niu Chiao, *tr. by* Lois Fusek. ATF

Pair of Shoes, A. Theodore Weiss. NoAM

Pair of soft, black eyes, A. A Home Greeting. Priscilla Jane Thompson. CBWP-2

Pair of Wings, A. Stephen Hawes. MeEL

Paired Lives. W. R. Rodgers. CIP

Paired swallows from the eaves fly in front of her rooms. Manifold Little Hills. Mao Hsi-chen, *tr. by* Lois Fusek. ATF

Paired swallows soar above. Thoughts of the Yüeh Beauty. Chang Pi, *tr. by* Lois Fusek. ATF

Paisley Ceiling, The. Lila Arnold. IHMS

Paiute Ponies. Jim Barnes. CDW

Paki Go Home. Himani Bannerji. AIW

Pal, in the Pals of Death Club. This Is a Poem for the Fathers and for Michael Ryan. Thomas Lux. AmPA

Palabras Cariñosas. Thomas Bailey Aldrich. AA

Palabras Grandiosas. Bayard Taylor. AnAmPo; OBAL

Palace, The. Charles Stuart Calverley. EBVV

Palace, The. Rita Dove. *Fr.* Parsley, II. NoAM

Palace clocks are stiff as coats of mail, The. The King's Speech. Howard Moss. *Fr.* King Midas. PoA

Palace of Art, The, *sels.* Tennyson.

   Lincolnshire Shores ("A still salt pool locked in with bars of sand"). FaBoPP

   "One seem'd all dark and red—a tract of sand." UnPo

Palace of Hishiro at Makimuku, The. Prince Kinashi no Karu, *tr. fr. Japanese.* Manyo Shu. PeBJV

Palace [*or* Palice] of Honor [*or* Honour], The, *sels.* Gawin Douglas.

   Calliope's Nymph Brings the Poet to the Palace to Honour. OxBLMV

   Nightmare. PoEL-1

Palace of humbug, The. "Lewis Carroll." FaBoNo

Palace of Naniwa, whither often comes, The. Tanabe Sakimaro, *tr. fr. Japanese.* Manyo Shu. Ma

Palace of Pleasant Regard, The. Lady of the Assembly. *Fr.* The Assembly of Ladies. WPE

Palace of Prince Ma, The. Yang Shih-ch'i, *tr. fr. Chinese by* Jonathan Chaves. *Fr.* Three Poems on Ch'ang-sha. CoBLCP

Palace of Sun-White at Makimuku, The. Song of a Lady from Mie. *Unknown, tr. fr. Japanese by* Hiroaki Sato. *Fr.* The Kojiki. FCEI

Palace of the Gnomes. Maria Gowen Brooks. *Fr.* Zophiël. AA

Palace of Truth, The. William Langland. *Fr.* The Vision of Piers Plowman. ACP

Palace of Yoshino where our sovereign, The. Akahito, *tr. fr. Japanese. Fr.* Manyo Shu. FCEI

Palace orioles warble with the ringing Ching-yang Bell. The Flowers in the Rear Garden. Sun Kuang-hsien, *tr. by* Lois Fusek. ATF

Palace Song. Wang Chien, *tr. fr. Chinese by* Burton Watson. CoBCP

Palace with revolving doors, was mine, The. Atameros. John Beevers. EAS

Palaces are sombre cliffs by night, The. On the Grand Canal. David Gascoyne. SeCePo

Palaces of Gold. Leon Rosselson. OBET

Palaces of the House of Han lie in the setting sun, The. A Song of the Precious Knife. Ch'iu Chin, *tr. by* Pao Chia-lin. WFTU

Palais des Arts. Louise Glück. AnAn; MAYP

Palamon and Arcite, *sel.* Dryden.

   Parts of the Whole Are We; but God the Whole. NAs

Palatine, The. Whittier. MOS

Pale amber sunlight falls across. Autumnal. Ernest Dowson. EBVV; OBNC

Pale beech and pine-tree blue. In a Wood. Thomas Hardy. OBNC

Pale beryl sky, with clouds. A Winter Twilight. Arlo Bates. AA

Pale, beyond porch and portal. Proserpine. Swinburne. *Fr.* The Garden of Proserpine. ChTr

Pale Blue Casket, The. Oliver Pitcher. PoBA; TTY

Pale brown Moses went down to Egypt land. Benediction. Bob Kaufman. PoNe

Pale brows, still hands and dim hair. The Lover Mourns for the Loss of Love. W. B. Yeats. WeW

Pale, climbing disk, who dost lone vigil keep. To the Moonflower. Craven Langstroth Betts. AA

Pale darts still quivering, crocuses. Poem at Equinox. Hilary Corke. NYBP

Pale, drooping girl and the swaggering soldier, The. Just an Old Sweet Song. Donagh MacDonagh. CIP

Pale-faced rat! To Noël Coward. Noel Coward. FaBoPa

Pale Fire. Vladimir Nabokov. OBD

Pale from the watery west, with the pallor of winter a-cold. In Winter. Arthur Symons. BrPo

Pale grey, her guns hooded, decks clear of all impediment. H. M. S. *Hero.* Michael Roberts. OxBTC

Pale hands I love beside the Shalimar. Kashmiri Song. Laurence Hope. BLPA; BLPL; FaBoBe; FaFP

Pale Heinrich he came sauntering by. The Window-Glance. Heine, *tr. by* John Todhunter. AWP

Pale Italian peasant, A. At the Shrine. Richard Kendall Munkittrick. AA

Pale morning in June 4 AM, A. Country Roads. Rolf Jacobsen, *tr. by* Robert Bly. NU

Pale nuns of St. Joseph are here, The. Island of the Three Marias. Alberto Ríos. NoAM

Pale pink and green lights flush on white. Tangier: Hotel Rif. Donald Thomas. OBTV

Pale Punk drinks liquid naugahyde on porch of Cafe Flor. Round Trip. Stan Rice. NPGG

Pale-voiced, flayed. Paul Celan, *tr. by* Beth Bjorklund. CoAuP

Palely intent, he urged his keel. At the Cannon's Mouth. Herman Melville. PAH

Palestine. Whittier. WBLP

Palimpsest. Hyman Edelstein. CaP

Palindrome. Lisel Mueller. IHMS; WeW

Palinode, A. Edmund Bolton. ElL; InvP; OBSC; PoEL-2; PrIm

Palinode. Oliver St. John Gogarty. OBMV

Palinode, A. Robert Greene. *Fr.* Greene's Groatsworth of Wit. OBSC

Palinode. James Russell Lowell. AA

Palinode. Maura Stanton. MAYP

Pall-Bearers. Jacques Prévert, *tr. fr. French by* Teo Savory. POS

Palladium. Matthew Arnold. GTBS-P; OAEL-2; OBNC; PPP

Pallid and moonlike in the smog. A Man Can Complain, Can't He? Ogden Nash. NBLV

Pallid Cuckoo. David Campbell. CBAP; PoAu-2

Pallid cuckoo, The. Late Winter. James McAuley. PoAu-2

Pallid, mis-shapen he stands. The World's grimed thumb. In the Dock. Walter de la Mare. LiTM

Pallid Thunderstricken Sigh for Gain, The. Tennyson. TW

Pallid with too much longing. Laus Veneris. Louise Chandler Moulton. AA

Pallor. Agnes Mary Frances Robinson. NOBVV

Palm, The. Roy Campbell. MoBrPo

Palm at the end of the mind, The. Of Mere Being. Wallace Stevens. HCAP

Palm House, Botanic Gardens. George Hetherington. NeIP

Palm Leaf of Mary Magdalene. Cheryl Clarke. GLP

Palm of my hand touched but one spot, The. We Two. Shlomoh Tan'ee, *tr. by* Bernhard Frank. MHeP

Palm of the hand, The,/ is not aware of dying. Fumi Saito, *tr. fr. Japanese by* Edith Marcombe Shiffert *and* Yuki Sawa. BoWoP

Palm of the Hand. Rainer Maria Rilke, *tr. fr. German by* Robert Bly. NU

Palm-Sunday Hymn, A. William Herebert. MeEL

Palm Sunday: Naples. Arthur Symons. BrPo

Palm the head just so. Then. How It's Done. Alvin Aubert. MT

Palm Tree, The. Abd-ar-Rahman I, *tr. fr. Arabic by* J. B. Trend. AWP

Palm tree grows in the far bush, The. Election Songs. *Yoruba Oral Tradition, tr. by* Ulli Beier. WTO

Palm Trees. Rex Warner. OBTV

Palm trees against the sky. A Small War. Ory Bernstein, *tr. fr. Hebrew by* Warren Bargad *and* Stanley F. Chyet. *Fr.* Poems from Mexico. IP

Palmer, The. John Heywood. *Fr.* The Play of the Four P.P. ACP

Palmer, The. William Langland. *Fr.* The Vision of Piers Plowman. ACP
Palmer's Ode, The. Robert Greene. *Fr.* Never Too Late. CTC; OBSC
Palms, The. David Knight. MoCV
Palms and Myrtles. Eleazar Ben Kalir, *tr. fr. Hebrew by* Alice Lucas. TrJP
Palo Alto; the Marshes. Robert Hass. NPGG
Paltry Nude Starts on a Spring Voyage, The. Wallace Stevens. HCAP
Pamela in Town. Ellen Mackay Hutchinson Cortissoz. AA
Pampered steed, of swiftness proud. The. The Horse and the Mule. John Huddlestone Wynne. OxBChV
Pamphilia to Amphilanthus. Mary Sidney Wroth, Countess of Montgomery. *Fr.* Urania. WPE
 "Am I thus conquered? have I lost the powers." NAEL-1
 "False hope which feeds but to destroy, and spill." NAEL-1
Pamphilia's Sonnet. Mary Sidney Wroth, Countess of Montgomery. *Fr.* Urania. WPE
Pan. Angelos Sikelianos, *tr. fr. Greek by* Edmund Keeley *and* Philip Sherrard. VMG
Pan and the Cherries. Paul Fort, *tr. fr. French by* Jethro Bithell. AWP
Pan-Asian Holiday Tour. Luis Syquia. BrSi
Pan came out of the woods one day. Pan with Us. Robert Frost. OxBA
Pan Cogito's Thoughts on Hell. Zbigniew Herbert, *tr. fr. Polish by* Adam Czerniawski. FaBoPV
Pan in Battle. *Unknown.* PeNZ
Pan in Wall Street. Edmund Clarence Stedman. AA; AnAmPo
Pan leave piping, the gods have done feasting. The Green-Gown. *Unknown.* CoMu
Pan loved his neighbour Echo—but that child. Moschus, *tr. by* Shelley. OBVE
Pan Piping. Plato, *tr. fr. Greek by* Thomas Stanley. FaBoEE
Pan Recipe. John Agard. PBCV
Pan, the Pot, the Burning Fire I Have in Front of Me, The. Ishigaki Rin, *tr. fr. Japanese by* Hiroaki Sato. FCEI
Pan with Us. Robert Frost. OxBA
Panama. Amanda T. Jones. PAH
Panama. James Jeffrey Roche. PAH
Pancake, The. Christina Rossetti. *See* Mix a Pancake.
Pancake Collector, The. Jack Prelutsky. OBCA
Pancakes for the Queen of Babylon, The. Peter Levi.
 "City built in darkness and cold air, A." CRP
Panchatantra, The, *sels. Unknown, tr. fr. Sanskrit by* Arthur Ryder. AWP
 Fool and False.
 Kings.
 Penalty of Virtue, The.
 Poverty.
 True Friendship.
Panda, The. Harley Elliott. *Fr.* Animals That Stand in Dreams. NeAC
Pandemonium hews/ no clouds. Lyn Hejinian. IAT
Pandora and the Moon. Merrill Moore. MoAmPo
Pandora Speaks. William Vaughn Moody. *See* Fire-Bringer, The: I Stood within the Heart of God.
Pandosto, *sel.* Robert Greene.
 Ah Were She Pitiful. TrGrPo, *abr.*
 (Fawnia.) OBEV; OBSC
 (In Praise of His Loving and Best-beloved Fawnia.) PoEL-2
Panegyric. Harris Lenowitz. VWA
Panegyric, A. *Unknown.* APAS
Panegyric on the Author of "Absalom and Achitophel," A. *Unknown.* APAS
Panegyric[k] to My Lord Protector, A, *sel.* Edmund Waller. OBS
 "While with a strong and yet a gentle hand." JCP; OBS; SeCV-1
Panegyric to Sir Lewis Pemberton, A. Robert Herrick. CaPo
Panegyric upon Oates, A. Richard Duke. APAS
Panes of light cracking. A Wet Night. Richard Ryan. CIP
Panes of Sound, The. Antonin Artaud, *tr. fr. French by* Paul Zweig. RHTwFP
Pang of the long century of rains, The. The Lament of Edward Blastock. Edith Sitwell. OBMV
Pangloss's Song [A Comic-Opera Lyric]. Richard Wilbur. MoP; NBLV; NoAM
Pangolin, The. Marianne Moore. HAP; NoAM; NOBA; PBWP
Pangur Bán. *Unknown, tr. fr. Gaelic by* Robin Flower. AnIL; CRH; FaBoCh; RB
Pangur Bán. *Unknown.* NOIV
Panic, *sels.* Archibald MacLeish. MoAmPo
 Final Chorus.
 Panic ("Slowly the thing comes").
Panic on the Oil Rig. Paul Snoek, *tr. fr. Dutch by* Alasdair MacKinnon. DuIn

Panic ("Slowly the thing comes"). Archibald MacLeish. *Fr.* Panic. MoAmPo
Pannyra of the Golden Heel. Albert Samain, *tr. fr. French by* James Elroy Flecker. AWP
Panope. Edith Sitwell. MoAB; MoBrPo
Pan's/ spring rain. Symphony No. 3, in D Minor. Jonathan Williams. *Fr.* Mahler. VGW
Pans Anniversarie. Ben Jonson. OBS
Pans at Carnival. Henry Beissel. PVCV
Pan's Syrinx. John Lyly. *Fr.* Midas, IV, i. ELP
 (Pan's Song.) OBSC
 (Syrinx.) EIL; SeCePo
Pansies, lilies, kingcups, daisies. To the Small Celandine. Wordsworth. EnRP
Pansy. Mary Effie Lee Newsome. CDC
Pantheism: 1968. Judah Leib Teller, *tr. fr. Yiddish by* Benjamin *and* Barbara Harshav. AYP
Panther. Sam Cornish. PoBA
Panther, The. Ogden Nash. FaPON; MoShBr; OBAL; OBCA
Panther, The. Rainer Maria Rilke, *tr. fr. German by* Robert Bly. NU
Panther, The. *Unknown.* NA
Panther and Peacock. Gwen Harwood. CBAP; PoAu-2
Panther is like a leopard, The. The Panther. Ogden Nash. FaPON; MoShBr; OBAL; OBCA
Panther lies next to Wharncliffe. Appalachian Front. Robert Lewis Weeks. AmFN; NYBP
Panther Man. James A. Emanuel. BPo
Panther sure the noblest, next the Hind, The. The Church of England. Dryden. *Fr.* The Hind and the Panther, I. OBS
Pantisocracy. Samuel Taylor Coleridge. EnRP
Pantomime. Paul Verlaine, *tr. fr. French by* Arthur Symons. AWP
Pantoum. John Ashbery. SM
Pants. Lisa Vice. GLP
Papa above! Emily Dickinson. AmPP; FM
Papa and Mama. Li Nan, *tr. fr. Chinese by* Dominic Cheung. IFON
Papa called her Pearl when he came home. Taking In Wash. Rita Dove. PPR
Papa John. Jorge de Lima, *tr. fr. Portuguese by* John Nist. TTY
Papa's Letter. *Unknown.* WeW
Paper airplanes/ flooding the road. Miniatures. Anna Kiss, *tr. by* Jascha Kessler. FOC
Paper Anarchist Addresses the Shade of Nancy Ling Perry. George Woodcock. NOBC
Paper Anniverary. Muriel Rukeyser. NoAM
Paper boat sank to the bottom of the garden, The. Eden Gate. Allen Curnow. ATNZ
Paper Boats. Rabindranath Tagore. FaPON
Paper Cities. Gjertrud Schnackenberg. AnAn
Paper come out—done strewed de news. Scottsboro. *Unknown.* InPK
Paper Dragons. Susan Alton Schmeltz. RHPC
Paper Flowers. Dov Khomsky, *tr. fr. Hebrew by* Bernhard Frank. MHeP
Paper Kite, The, *sel.* Samuel Bowden.
 "Kite, completed thus, is borne along, The." NOEC
Paper Matches. Paulette Jiles. Mes; NIP; NOBC
"Paper Men to Air Hopes and Fears." Robert Francis. LCAP
Paper Nautilus, The. Marianne Moore. FaBoWP; VGW
Paper of Pins. *Unknown.* AmFP
Paper tiger thrown H-bomb in south pole. Pepsi Generation. Walasse Ting. MAT
Paper tigers roar at noon, The. Tiger. A. D. Hope. OxBC; RB
Paper universe of prime. From C. Michael Palmer. BAP
Paperclips. X. J. Kennedy. TSS
Papermill Graveyard. Ben Belitt. NYBP
Paper's whiteness, The. Sober. Gabriel Preil, *tr. by* Grace Schulman. PeBMYV
Paperweight, The. Gjertrud Schnackenberg. SM
Paphnutius, *sel.* Hroswitha von Gandersheim, *tr. fr. Latin by* Patrick Diehl.
 "I bring you a goat." WPOW
Paphos. Lawrence Durrell. NYBP
Papio. Eric Chock. BrSi
Pap's got his patent right, and rich as all creation. Back to Griggsby's Station. James Whitcomb Riley. BLPA; BLPL
Paps of Jura, The. Andrew Young. PoSH
Papuan Shepherd, A. Francis Webb. *Fr.* A Drum for Ben Boyd. PoAu-2
Parable. W. H. Auden. FaBoCo
Parable, A. Li K'ai-hsien, *tr. fr. Chinese by* Jonathan Chaves. CoBLCP
Parable. Bob Orr. PeNZ
Parable. Robert Pack. NePoEA-2
Parable. Richard Wilbur. OxBSP

Parable of the Good Seed, The. Bible, *N.T. Fr.* St. Matthew, XIII: 24-30. InPK

Parable of the Old Man and the Young, The. Wilfred Owen. FaBoRV; OPOP

Parable of Two Talents. Kendrick Smithyman. ATNZ

Parabola. A. D. Hope. PoA

Paracas. Antonio Cisneros, *tr. fr. Spanish by* Maureen Ahern *and* David Tipton. Per

Paracelsus, *sels.* Robert Browning.
   Awakening of Man, The. *Fr. V.* WGRP
   Thus the Mayne Glideth. *Fr. V.* OBEV
   Wanderers, The. *Fr.* IV. OBEV

Parachute. Dwight Okita. BrSi

Parachute Descent. David Bourne. WaP

Parachutes, My Love, Could Carry Us Higher. Barbara Guest. NeAP

Parachuting Thoor Ballylee. William Zaranka. BXAP

Parachutist, The. Jon Anderson. AmPA; NYBP

Parade, The. Liz Sohappy Bahe. NOVW

Parade. Rachel Field. *Fr.* A Circus Garland. OBCA

Parade, The. Ashton Greene. NePoAm

Parade, A. Perunkunrur Kilar, *tr. fr. Tamil by* A. K. Ramanujan. PLW

Parade: Liberation Day. Kevin Ireland. ATNZ

Parade's End. Barbara Guest. PoM

Paradigm. Babette Deutsch. TrJP

Paradigm, The. Allen Tate. NOBA

Paradigms of Fire. Brian Swann. AmPA

Parading near Saint Peter's flood. The Battle of Lake Champlain. Philip Freneau. PAH

Paradise. Willis Barnstone. VWA

Paradise. Chana Bloch. VWA

Paradise. Immanuel di Roma, *tr. fr. Hebrew by* J. Chotzner. TrJP

Paradise. George Herbert. OAEL-1; SeCP; TrGrPo

Paradise. Milton. *See* Paradise Lost: Another side, umbrageous grots and caves.

Paradise. Steve Orlen. NAmP

Paradise. Christina Rossetti. WGRP

Paradise. E. N. Sargent. NYBP

Paradise and Lunch. Jean Day. IAT

Paradise Lost, *sels.* Milton.
  "Adam the goodliest man of men since born." *Fr. Bk.* IV, *ll.* 323–355 *abr.*
   (Scene in Paradise, A.) GN
  "And God created the great whales, and each." *Fr. Bk.* VII, *ll.* 391–416. MOS
  "And God said, let the waters generate." *Fr. Bk.* VII, *ll.* 387–505.
   (Creation of the Animals.) FM
  "Another side, umbrageous grots and caves." *Fr. Bk.* IV, *ll.* 257–294.
   (Paradise.) OBS
  "As when a Scout/ through dark and desart wayes with peril gone." *Fr. Bk.* III, *ll.* 543–571.
   (New Worlds.) OBS
  "Be it so, for I submit; his doom is fair." *Fr. Bk.* X, *ll.* 770-1114. NAWM-1
  "Beneath him with new wonder now he views." *Fr. Bk.* IV, *ll.* 205–268. PPP
  "Birds their quire apply; airs, vernal airs, The." *Fr. Bk.* IV, *ll.* 264–268.
   (Eternal Spring, The.) GN
  "Brandish't sword of God before them blaz'd, The." *Fr. Bk.* XII, *ll.* 633–649.
   (Expulsion from Paradise.) ChTr
  "But he his wonted pride." *Fr. Bk.* I, *ll.* 527–699.
   (Satan and His Host.) OBS
  "Descend from Heav'n Urania, by that name." *Fr. Bk.* VII, *ll.* 1-39. EBEV; NAEL-1; OAEL-1; TOF
   (Invocation to Urania.) FiP; OBS
  "Descended, Adam to the bower where Eve." *Fr. Bk.* XII, *ll.* 607–649.
   (Adam Fallen.) NOCV
  "Dungeon horrible, on all sides round, A." *Fr. Bk.* I, *ll.* 61-74. OBD
  "Earth was form'd, but in the womb as yet, The." *Fr. Bk.* VII, *ll.* 276–309. MOS
  "Egypt, divided by the river Nile." *Fr. Bk.* XII, *ll.* 157–235. FaBoPV
  "Father, Thy word is past, man shall find grace." *Fr. Bk.* III, *ll.* 227–265.
   (Atonement, The.) OBS
  "Fiend/ Saw undelighted all delight, all kind, The." *Fr. Bk.* IV, *ll.* 285–357. FaBoPV
  "For now too nigh/ The archangel stood, and from the other hill." *Fr. Bk.* XII, *ll.* 625–649.
   (Their Banishment.) SeCePo

"Forsake me not thus, Adam, witness Heav'n." *Fr. Bk.* X, *ll.* 914–946.
   (Eve Penitent.) OBS

"Hail holy light, ofspring [*or* offspring] of Heav'n first born." *Fr. Bk.* III, *ll.* 1–55. OAEL-1; SCV; TOF
   (Hail, Holy Light.) FiP
   (Holy Light.) NOBE
   (Light.) LiTB; OBEV; OBS

"Hail wedded love, mysterious law, true source." *Fr. Bk.* IV, *ll.* 750–775.
   (Their Wedded Love.) SeCePo
   (Wedded Love.) OBS

"Half yet remains unsung, but narrower bound." *Fr. Bk.* VII, *ll.* 21–39. FaBoPV

"He ceased; and Satan stayed not to reply." *Fr. Bk.* II, *ll.* 1010–1055.
   (Satan ("He ceased; and Satan stayed not to reply").) SeCePo

"He ended, and they both descend the hill." *Fr. Bk.* XII, *ll.* 606–649. NAWM-1
   (Adam Fallen.) NOCV

"He ended; and thus Adam last replied." *Fr. Bk.* XII, *ll.* 552–649. HeIP
   (Retreat from Paradise, The.) PoEL-3

"He scarce had ceas't when the superior Fiend." *Fr. Bk.* I, *ll.* 283–313.
   (Satan and the Fallen Angels.) LiTB; OBS
   (Satan ("He scarce had ceas't when the superior Fiend").) SeCePo

"He stood and call'd/ His legions, angel forms, who lay intranced." *Fr. Bk.* I, *ll.* 300–304.
   (Satan's Legions and the Beech Leaves of the Casentino.) FaBoPP

Hell ("At once with him they rose"). *Fr. Bk.* II, *ll.* 475–628.
   (Hell.) OBS

"Her long with ardent look his eye pursu'd." *Fr. Bk.* IX, *ll.* 397–470. UnPo

"High on a throne of royal state, which far." *Fr. Bk.* II, *ll.* 1–42. NIP; OAEL-1, *fr. ll.* 1–309.

"His pride/ Had cast him out from Heaven, with all his host." *Fr. Bk.* I, *ll.* 36–75.
   (Satan ("His pride/ Had cast him out from Heaven, with all his host").) TrGrPo

"How shall I behold the face." *Fr. Bk.* IX, *ll.* 1080–1098. TOF

"How to th' ascent of that steep savage hill." *Fr. Bk.* IV, *ll.* 172–201.
   (Satan Journey's to the Garden of Eden.) ChTr

"If thou beest he; but O how fall'n! how chang'd." *Fr. Bk.* I, *ll.* 84–124. SCV

"In bower and field he sought, where any tuft." *Fr. Bk.* IX, *ll.* 417–492. TEP
   (Eve.) OBS, *fr. ll.* 417–466.

"Into thir inmost bower." *Fr. Bk.* IV, *ll.* 738–775. FF, *fr. ll.* 738–757; TOF

"Is this the region, this the soil, the clime." *Fr. Bk.* I, *ll.* 242–270. TEP
   (Fall of the Angels, The.) FiP, *fr. ll.* 242–363.
   (Satan as Rebel-Liberator.) FF, *fr. ll.* 242–255.

"Love thou saist." *Fr. Bk.* VII, *ll.* 612–629. TOF

"Me miserable! which way shall I fly."" *Fr. Bk.* IV, *ll.* 73–535. PoE

"Meanwhile the adversary of God and man." *Fr. Bk.* II. DL, *fr. ll.* 629–841; EBEV, *fr. ll.* 629–734.
   (Sin and Death.) OBNV, *fr. ll.* 629–889.

"Meanwhile the tepid caves and fens and shores." *Fr. Bk.* VII, *ll.* 417–448. PBBP

"My author and disposer, what thou biddest." *Fr. Bk.* IV, *ll.* 635–658.
   (Thus Eve to Adam.) FaBV

"Next came one/ Who mourn'd in earnest." *Fr. Bk.* I, *ll.* 457–489. EBEV

"No more of talk where God or Angel Guest." *Fr. Bk.* IV, *complete.* NAEL-1, *fr. ll.* 1–1189; NAWM-1; NoP; TOF, *fr. ll.* 1–47.
   (Subject of Heroic Song, The.) OBS, *fr. ll.* 1–47.

"No sooner had th' Almighty ceas't, but all." *Fr. Bk.* III, *ll.* 344–371.
   (Heaven.) OBS

"Now came still evening on, and twilight gray." *Fr. Bk.* IV.
   (Evening in Paradise.) GN, *fr. ll.* 598–609; NOBE, *fr. ll.* 598–656.
   (Moon and the Nightingale, The.) ChTr

"Now had th' Almighty Father from above." *Fr. Bk.* III, *ll.* 54–76. NIP

"Now Morn her rosy steps in the eastern clime." *Fr. Bk.* V, *ll.* 1–128. NAEL-1; OAEL-1

"O favorable spirit, propitious guest." *Fr. Bk.* V, *ll.* 507–543.
   (Adam Unfallen.) NOCV

"O for that warning voice, which he who saw." *Fr. Bk.* IV. OAEL-1, *complete;* TEP, *fr. ll.* 1–324.

(Prospect of Eden, The.) PoEL-3, *fr. ll.* 1–775.
"O hell! what do mine eyes with grief behold!" *Fr. Bk.* IV, *ll.* 358–392.
(Satan Beholds Adam and Eve.) TW
"O thou in heaven and earth the only place." *Fr. Bk.* III, *ll.* 274–343.
(Plan of Salvation, The.) WGRP
"O thou that with surpassing glory crown'd." *Fr. Bk.* IV, *ll.* 32–113.
(Satan's Soliloquy.) LiTB; OBS
"Of man's first disobedience, and the fruit." *Fr. Bk.* I. EBEV, *fr. ll.* 1–270; FaBoRV, *fr. ll.* 1–26; NAEL-1, *complete;* NAWM-1, *complete;* NIP, *fr. ll.* 1–49; NoP, *fr. ll.* 1–26; OAEL-1, *fr. ll.* 1–375; TOF, *fr. ll.* 1–26.
(Induction, The.) PoE, *fr. ll.* 1–26.
(Invocation: "Of man's first disobedience, and the fruit.") PoEL-3, *fr. ll.* 1–26.
(Of Man's First Disobedience.) FiP, *fr. ll.* 1–26.
"Oh, why did God,/ Creator wise." *Fr. Bk.* X, *ll.* 888–908.
(Adam Speaks.) NU
"Pensive here I sat." *Fr. Bk.* II, *ll.* 777–807. OBD
"She, as a veil down to the slender waist." *Fr. Bk.* IV, *ll.* 304–311. ErPo
(Before the Fall.) NIP, *fr. ll.* 304–355.
"So passed they naked on, nor shunned the sight." *Fr. Bk.* IV, *ll.* 319–355.
(Adam and Eve.) SeCePo
"So Satan spake, and him Beëlzebub." *Fr. Bk.* I, *ll.* 271–669.
(Council of Satan, The.) PoEL-3
"So spake our Mother Eve, and Adam heard." *Fr. Bk.* XII, *ll.* 624–649.
(Banishment, The.) NOBE; OBS
(Exit from Eden, The.) FaBoRV
"So spake th' archangel Michael; then paused." *Fr. Bk.* XII, *ll.* 466–649. FaBoPV, *fr. ll.* 466–551; NAEL-1; OAEL-1
"So spake the enemy of mankind, enclosed." *Fr. Bk.* IX, *ll.* 494–526. FM
"So spake the godlike power, and thus our sire." *Fr. Bk.* VIII, *ll.* 249–653. NAEL-1
"So stretched out huge in length the Arch-Fiend lay." *Fr. Bk.* I, *ll.* 209–238. TEP
"So to the sylvan lodge." *Fr. Bk.* V, *ll.* 377–512. NAEL-1
Standing on Earth ("Standing on Earth, not rapt above the Pole"). *Fr. Bk.* VII, *ll.* 23–39. ChTr
"Stygian council thus dissolved; and forth, The." *Fr. Bk.* II, *ll.* 506–870. OAEL-1
"Sweet is the breath of Morn, her rising sweet." *Fr. Bk.* IV.
"Then both ourselves and seed at once to free." *Fr. Bk.* X, *ll.* 999–1006. OBD
"There Leviathan/ Hugest of living creatures, on the deep." *Fr. Bk.* VII, *ll.* 412–416.
(Leviathan.) AmMo
"There stood a hill not far whose grisly top." *Fr. Bk.* I, *ll.* 670–798. OBEL-1
"There the companions of his fall, o'erwhelmed." *Fr. Bk.* I, *ll.* 76–124.
(Immortal Hate.) NOBE
"These are thy glorious works, Parent of good." *Fr. Bk.* V.
(Adam's Morning Hymn.) WGRP, *fr. ll.* 153–210.
(Morning Hymn of Adam.) TrPWD, *fr. ll.* 153–165, 195–208.
"They ended parle, and both addressed for fight." *Fr. Bk.* VI, *ll.* 296–353. OBWP
"This having learnt, thou hast attaind the summe." *Fr. Bk.* XII, *ll.* 575–649. SCV
"Th' other way Satan went down." *Fr. Bk.* X, *ll.* 414–584. NAEL-1
"Thus Adam himself lamented loud." *Fr. Bk.* X, *ll.* 845–1104. OAEL-1
"Thus began/ Outrage from lifeless things; but Discord first." *Fr. Bk.* X, *ll.* 706–1104. NAEL-1
"Thus Belial with words clothed in reason's garb." *Fr. Bk.* II, *ll.* 226–378. FaBoPV
"Thus saying, from her husband's hand her hand." *Fr. Bk.* IX, *ll.* 385–1189.
(Fall, The.) PoEL-3
"Thus saying, from her side the fatal key." *Fr. Bk.* II, *ll.* 871–1055. EBEV
"Thus talking hand in hand alone they pass'd." *Fr. Bk.* IV, *ll.* 689–775. EBEV
"Thus they in Heav'n, above the starry sphear." *Fr. Bk.* III, *ll.* 416–515. EBEV
"To whom thus also th' angel last replied." *Fr. Bk.* XII, *ll.* 574–649. FiP
"To whom thus Michael. Justly thou abhorr'st." *Fr. Bk.* XII, *ll.* 79–104. FaBoPV

"To whom thus Michael. Those whom last thou saw'st." *Fr. Bk.* XI, *ll.* 782–835. FaBoPV
"Uriel to his charge/ Returned on that bright beam." *Fr. Bk.* IV, *ll.* 589–609.
(Now Came Still Evening On.) FaBoRV
What Though the Field Be Lost?. *Fr. Bk.* I, *ll.* 105–124. EaLo
What Words Have Passed. *Fr. Bk.* IX, *ll.* 1144–1189. TrCP
"While thus he spake, th' Angelic Squadron bright." *Fr. Bk.* IV, *ll.* 977–1004. SCV
"With thee conversing, I forget all time." *Fr. Bk.* IV, *ll.* 639–656. WiR
(Eve Speaks to Adam.) ChTr; GBL
(Eve to Adam.) TrGrPo
Paradise Lost. Stanley J. Sharpless. BXAP
Paradise Lost, Book V: An Epitome. Anthony Hecht. NBLV
Paradise on earth is found, A. The Description of Elizium. Michael Drayton. *Fr.* Muses' Elysium [*or* Elizium]. OAEL-1
(Poet's Paradise, The.) WiR, *much abr.*.
Paradise on earth—that's the city of Suchou! The Scene at Heaven Gate. T'ang Yin, *tr.* by Jonathan Chaves. CoBLCP
Paradise Regained, *sels.* Milton.
"At thy nativity a glorious quire." *Fr. Bk.* I, *ll.* 242-254. PChr
"It was the hour of night, when thus the Son." *Fr. Bk.* II, *ll.* 260-389. EBEV
"Look once more ere we leave this specular Mount." *Fr. Bk.* IV, *ll.* 236-284. OBTV
(Athens.) OBS, *fr. ll.* 236-364.
Messiah, The ("So they in Heav'n their odes and vigils tun'd"). *Fr. Bk.* I, *ll.* 182–293. OBS
Parthians, The ("He look't and saw what numbers numberless"). *Fr. Bk.* III, *ll.* 310–343. OBS
Rome ("The City which thou seest no other deem"). *Fr. Bk.* IV, *ll.* 44–108. OBS
Satan's Guile ("Whom thus answer'd th' Arch Fiend now undisguis'd"). *Fr. Bk.* I, *ll.* 357-405. LiTB; OBS
Table Richly Spread, A. *Fr. Bk.* II, *ll.* 340-365. FaBoCh
"Therefore let pass, as they are transitory." *Fr. Bk.* IV, *ll.* 209-364. OAEL-1
True and False Glory ("To whom our Saviour calmly thus reply'd"). *Fr. Bk.* III, *ll.* 43–107. LiTB; OBS
Paradise Saved. Alec Derwent Hope. OxBC
Paradisi Gloria. Thomas William Parsons. AA
Paradiso. Dante, *tr. fr. Italian.* *Fr.* Divina Commedia.
"Glory of Him who moves all things rays forth, The." *Fr.* I. NAWM-1, *tr.* by John Ciardi.
"Glory of the great all-mover goes, The." *Fr.* I. OBD, *tr.* by T. W. Ramsey
"Piercing brightness of the living ray, The." *Fr.* XXXIII. TOF, *tr.* by Dorothy L. Sayers *and* Barbara Reynolds.
Saint Bernard's Hymn of Praise to the Virgin Mary. *Fr.* XXXIII. PFI, *tr.* by Dana Gioia
Saints in Glory, The. *Fr.* XXXI. WGRP, *tr.* by Henry Cary
"That sun that breathed love's fire into my youth." *Fr.* III. NAWM-1, *tr.* by John Ciardi.
"Then, in the form of a white rose, the host." *Fr.* XXXI-XXXIII. NAWM-1, *tr.* by John Ciardi.
Paradiso Terrestre. Ian Wedde. *Fr.* Earthly: Sonnets for Carlos, 3. ATNZ
Paradox, The. Paul Laurence Dunbar. PoBA
Paradox, A. Earl of Pembroke. EIL
Paradox. Angelina Weld Grimké. CDC
Paradox. Vassar Miller. NePoEA
Paradox, The. Francesca Yetunde Pereira. PBA
Paradox, A. Aurelian Townshend. SeCP
Paradox, The. *Unknown.* APAS
Paradox is eaten by the space around it, A. Plasma. Barrett Watten. IAT
Paradox of Time, The. Pierre de Ronsard, *tr. fr. French by* Austin Dobson. AWP
Paradox: That Fruition Destroys Love, *sel.* Henry King.
"Since lovers' joys then leave so sick a taste." ErPo
Paradoxes and Oxymorons. John Ashbery. CAPP; HeIP; NoAM; NoP
Paragon of Animals, The. Pope. See Essay on Man, An: Know then thyself, presume not God to scan.
Paragraph Made Up of Seven Sentences Which Have Entered My Memory, A. Chuck Wachtel. UL
Paraguay. Philip Levine. AnAn
Parakeet. Leonard Clark. Mes
Parakeet, The. Keith Sinclair. ATNZ
Parallax. Maxwell Anderson. NYBP
Parallel Bars. Jeffrey Stockwell. TSL
Paralytic. Sylvia Plath. FaBoWP

Parameter. Marcos Konder Reis, *tr. fr. Portuguese by* Mark Strand. ATCBP
Paranoia. Michael Dennis Browne. AmPA
Paranoia in Crete. Gregory Corso. NeAP
Paraphrase from the French, A. Matthew Prior. OxBoLi
Paraphrase of Luther's Hymn. Martin Luther. *See* Mighty Fortress Is Our God, A.
Paraphrase on the Psalms of David, *sels.* George Sandys. Deo Opt. Max, Psalm CIV. OBS
"As on Euphrates shady banks we lay." OBS
Paraphrase on Thomas à Kempis, A, *sel.* Pope. "Speak, Gracious Lord, oh speak; thy Servant hears." TrPWD
Parasite lichen. Lichen. Mary Elizabeth Fullerton. PoAu-1
Parasitosis. Ronda Davis. JB
Parcae, The, or Three Dainty Destinies: The Armillet. Robert Herrick. CaPo
Parched throat ashen, while sobering up. Wakayama Bokusui, *tr. fr. Japanese by* Hiroaki Sato. Fr. Forty-four Tanka. FCEI
Parchment and paper left clean. The Making of Color. Hugh Seidman. AmPA
Parcy Reed, *with music. Unknown.* OxBB
Pardon. Julia Ward Howe. PAH
Pardon, The. Richard Wilbur. MoP; NePoEA; NIP; NoAM; NoAM; NOBA; NoP; OBD
Pardon, Lord, the lips that dare. Whittier. *Fr.* Andrew Rykman's Prayer. TrPWD
Pardon, old fathers, if you still remain. W. B. Yeats. *Fr.* Responsibilities. PoEL-5
Pardon our visit to this place. The Framework-Knitters Petition. C. Briggs. CoMu
Pardoner's Prologue, The. Chaucer. *Fr.* The Canterbury Tales. NAEL-1; NoP; OAEL-1; PoE
("In churches," said the Pardoner, "when I preach," *mod. vers. by* Theodore Morrison.) NAWM-1
Pardoner's Tale, The. Chaucer. *Fr.* The Canterbury Tales. FiP; HAP; NAEL-1; NoP; OAEL-1; PoE; PoEL-1
("It's of three rioters I have to tell," *mod. vers. by* Nevill Coghill.) SCV
("There was a company of young folk living," *mod. vers. by* Theodore Morrison.) NAWM-1
Death and the Three Revellers. OBNV
"But, sires o word forgat I in my tale." EBEV
"This olde man gan looke in his visage." OBD
Parent deer hurries back at the wind, A. Issa, *tr. by* Sato. FCEI
Parent of all, omnipotent. The American Patriot's Prayer. *Unknown.* PAH
(American Patriot's Prayer 1776, The.) OPP
Parental Critic, The. Keith Preston. NBLV
Parental Ode to My Son, Aged Three Years and Five Months, A. Thomas Hood. FiBHP, *abr.*; PoLF
(To My Son, Aged Three Years and Five Months.) FaPON, *abr.*
Parental Recollections. Mary Lamb. OxBSP
Parenthood. John Chipman Farrar. OHIP
Parents. Vincent Buckley. CBAP
Parents. William Meredith. FYAP
Parents are sinful now, for they must whisper. Marriage. Austin Clarke. BIrV; GTBS-P
Parents in Winter, *sel.* L. E. Sissman. "Brick plant like a wound. The winter set, The." DiL
Parfum Exotique. Baudelaire, *tr. fr. French by* Arthur Symons. AWP
Pari! Pari! they cry. Kapilar, *tr. by* A. K. Ramanujan. PLW
Parihaka. W. H. Oliver. PeNZ
Paring the Apple. Charles Tomlinson. CMoP; NePoEA-2; OxBTC; PoE
Paris. Gregory Corso. VGW
Paris. Gertrud Kolmar, *tr. fr. German by* David Kipp. PBWP
Paris. Arthur Symons. NOBVV
Paris by Night. Gustave Kahn, *tr. fr. French by* Edouard Roditi. VWA
Pari's Green Land, Remembered. Kapilar, *tr. fr. Tamil by* A. K. Ramanujan. PLW
Pari's Hill Is Partial to Dancers. Kapilar, *tr. fr. Tamil by* A. K. Ramanujan. PLW
Paris in the Snow. Léopold Sédar Senghor, *tr. fr. French by* Ulli Beier. PBA
Pari's Parampu hill. His Hill. Kapilar, *tr. by* A. K. Ramanujan. PLW
Paris; This April Sunset Completely Utters. E. E. Cummings. SOTW
Parish. Norman Dubie. MAYP
Parish Poor-Officers, The. Edward Ward. *Fr.* Journey to Hell, A; or, A Visit Paid to the Devil. NOEC
Parish priest, The. The Preacher's Mistake. William Croswell Doane. BLPA

Parish-priest was of the pilgrim train, A. The Character of a Good Parson. Dryden. NOCV
Parish Register, The, *sels.* George Crabbe. Burials. *Fr. pt.* III. OAEL-1, *abr.*
Lady of the Manor, The. NOBE; OBNC
Ancient Virgin, An. OBNC
Marriages. *Fr. Pt.* II. "Disposed to wed, e'en while you hasten, stay." FaBoUs
Parisian Nectar. Gelett Burgess. *See* Nonsense Quatrains.
Park. David Ignatow. Psk
Park I'm describing, The. Sunday Morning in the Park. Hermann Gail, *tr. by* Beth Bjorklund. CoAuP
Park in Milan, The. William Jay Smith. CoAP
Park is filled with night and fog, The. Spring Night. Sara Teasdale. BLPL; FaBoBe; LiTA; MoAmPo
Park, the heart, you see at town's center is soft, The. Last Look at La Plata, Missouri. Jim Barnes. CDW
Parked in the fields. The Forms of Love. George Oppen. NNaP
Parklands, The. Stevie Smith. MoBS
Parks and Ponds. Emerson. PoEL-4
Park's beautiful, The. On the Fine Arts Garden, Cleveland. Russell Atkins. PoBA
Parlement of Foules, The, *sels.* Chaucer. Now Welcom[e], Somer [*or* Summer]. HAP; SeCePo
(Birds' Rondel, The, *mod. vers. by* Louis Untermeyer) TrGrPo
(Foules Rondel.) TrGrPo
(Qui Bien Aime a Tard Oublie.) EnLoPo
(Roundel: "Now welcom[e], somer, with thy sunne [*or* sonne] softe.") CTC; OAEL-1; OxBSP
(Welcome, Summer.) MeEL
"There mighte men the royal eagle find." PBBP
Parlement [*or* Parliament] of the Thre[e] Ages, The, *sel. Unknown.* "When the water fowl are found, the falconers hasten." PBBP
Parley of Beasts. "Hugh MacDiarmid." MoBrPo; MoP; NoAM; NoP; OBMV
Parley with His Empty Purse, A. Thomas Randolph. JCP; OBS
Parliament Dissolved at Oxford, The. *Unknown.* "In the reign of the second Charles." NOEC
Parliament Had Been Dissolved. Pentti Saarikoski, *tr. fr. Finnish by* Aili Jarvenpa. SOP
Parliament Hill Fields. Sir John Betjeman. FaBoTw; NOBE; OPOP
Parliament Hill Fields. Sylvia Plath. HCAP
Parliament of fowls, The. *See* Parlement of Foules.
Parliament Soldiers, The. *Unknown.* GBP; OxNR
Parnassians, The. James Merrill. BLA
Parnell. W. B. Yeats. CMoP
Parochial Theme. Wallace Stevens. LiTA
Parodie, A: "Souls joy, when thou art gone." George Herbert. OBS
Parodies of Cole Porter's "Night and Day." Ring Lardner. OBAL
Parody, A: "Come saints and sinners." Frederick Douglass. NAAL-1; NAWM-2
Parody. Martha Paley Francescato, *tr. fr. Spanish by* Willis Barnstone. BoWoP
Parody on "A Psalm of Life", A. *At. to* Oliver Wendell Holmes. BLPA
Parody on Thomas Hood's "The Bridge of Sighs." *Unknown.* FiBHP
Paros. Robin Magowan. EAS
Parrhasius. Nathaniel Parker Willis. AA
Parricide. Julia Ward Howe. PAH
Parrot, The. Thomas Campbell. FM
Parrot, The. James Elroy Flecker. FaBoTw
Parrot, The. Wilfrid Wilson Gibson. OBMV
Parrot, The. Edward Lucie-Smith. SO
Parrot. Park Je-chun, *tr. fr. Korean by* Koh Chang-soo. ACKP
Parrot, The. John Skelton. *See* Speak [*or* Speke], Parrot: My name is Parrot, a byrd of paradise.
Parrot, The. José Juan Tablada, *tr. fr. Spanish by* Samuel Beckett. MexPo
Parrot, The/ Is eating a carrot. Who Killed Lawless Lean? Stevie Smith. TEP
Parrot Cry, The. "Hugh MacDiarmid." OxBS
Parrot Fish, The. James Merrill. NOBA
Parrot, from the Spanish main, A. The Parrot. Thomas Campbell. FM
Parrot identical with that. The Parrot. José Juan Tablada, *tr. by* Samuel Beckett. MexPo
Parrot, if I had your wings. The Boy and the Parrot. John Hookham Frere. OxBChV
Parrot is a thief, The. The Parrot. Edward Lucie-Smith. SO
Parrot teased, The. Banquet. Gloria Evans Davies. NPo
Parrots, The. W. W. Gibson. CH
Parrot's Soliloquy. John Skelton. *See* Speak [*or* Speke], Parrot: My name is Parrot, a byrd of paradise.
Parrot's voice snaps out, The. "Psittachus Eois Imitatrix Ales ab Indis." Sacheverell Sitwell. MoBrPo

Parry, of all my friends the best. The Invitation. Goronwy Owen, *tr. by* George Borrow. OBWVE

Parsley. Rita Dove. ER; HCAP; NAmP

Parsley, sels. Rita Dove.
Cane Fields, The. *Fr.* I. NoAM
Palace, The. *Fr.* II. NoAM

Parsley leaf green's. Quiet House. Yoshioka Minoru, *tr. by* Hiroaki Sato. FCEI

Parsnips, those rabbis, The. In the Root Cellar. Maxine W. Kumin. FaBoWP

Parson Allen's Ride. Wallace Bruce. PAH

Parson Gray. Goldsmith. NA

Parson Grocer, The. *Unknown.* CoMu

Parson him answered, The, "Bendicite!,." The Shipman. Chaucer. *Fr.* The Canterbury Tales: The Epilogue of the Man of Law's Tale. ACP

Parson of a country town was he, The. Chaucer. *See* Canterbury Tales, The: Prologue.

Parson, these things in thy possessing. The Happy Life of a Country Parson. Pope. BXAP

Parson's Looks, The. Burns. OxBoLi

Parson's Pleasure. Barry O. Higgs. PeSA

Parson's Prologue, The. Chaucer. *Fr.* The Canterbury Tales. NAEL-1

Part for the Whole. Robert Francis. PoA

Part of a Letter. Richard Wilbur. CMoP

Part of a Novel, Part of a Poem, Part of a Play, sels. Marianne Moore.
Hero, The. CMoP; NOBA; OxBA; PoA
Steeple-Jack, The. BoWoP; CMoP; FaBoMo; FaBoWP; HAP; InPS; NoAM; NOBA; NoP; OxBA; PBWP; WeW; WPE

Part of an Ode, A. Ben Jonson. *See* To the Immortal[l] Memory [*or* Memorie*] and Friendship of That Noble Pair[e], Sir Lucius Cary and Sir Henry Morrison: It Is Not Growing Like a Tree.

Part of Plenty. Bernard Spencer. ErPo; GBL; LiTB; LiTM

Part of the Darkness. Isabella Gardner. CAPP

Part of the Lay of Sigrdrifa. *Unknown. See* Elder Edda, The: Counsels of Sigrdrifa.

Part of the Question. Ilse Aichinger, *tr. fr. German by* Beth Bjorklund. CoAuP

Part of the work remains; one part is past. The End of His Work. Robert Herrick. CaPo

Part Quake. Charles Bernstein. IAT

Part-Sequence for Change, A. Robert Duncan. VGW

Parta Quies. A. E. Housman. NOBE; TEP

Parted. Clara Ann Thompson. CBWP-2

Parted, I came away and years have passed. Ishikawa Takuboku, *tr. fr. Japanese by* Hiroaki Sato. *Fr.* Forty-seven Tanka in Three Lines. FCEI

Parted Souls. Lord Herbert of Cherbury. SeCP

Parterre, The. E. Harriet Palmer. FaBoCo; NA; NOBL

Parthenogenesis. Nuala Ni Dhomhnaill, *tr. fr. Irish by* Michael Hartnett. CIP

Parthenon, The. John Heath-Stubbs. OBTV

Parthenophil and Parthenophe, sels. Barnabe Barnes.
"Ah, sweet Content! where is thy mylde abode?." *Fr.* LXVI. AAS (Content.) OBSC
(Sonnet: "Ah, sweet Content! where is thy mild abode.") EIL
"Jove for Europa[e]s love took[e] shape of bull." *Fr.* LXIII. AAS
Mistress, Behold, in This True-Speaking Glass. *Fr.* I. Son
"O Powers Celestial, with what sophistry." EnLoPo
"Why doth heaven bear a sun." EIL; OBSC
"Soft, lovely, rose-like lips, conjoined with mine." EnLoPo
Write! Write! Help! Help! *Fr.* XVIII. Son

Parthians, The ("He look't and saw what numbers numberless"). Milton. *Fr.* Paradise Regained, *Bk.* III, *ll.* 310–343. OBS

Partholan went out one day. The First Lawcase. *Unknown, tr. by* John Montague. BIrV

Partial Accounts. William Meredith. GLP

Partial Comfort. Dorothy Parker. FaBoCo; OBAL; OBD

Partial Explanation, The. Charles Simic. NoP

Partial Luetic History of an Individual at Risk. J. M. Regan. GLP

Partial Resemblance. Denise Levertov. CoAP; NaP

Partial View of a Supernova. Terry A. Garey. BWV

Partidges. John Masefield. OxBTC

Parting. A. R. Ammons. NoAM

Parting, The. Michael Drayton. *See* Idea:
Since there's [*or* ther's] no help[e], come let us kiss[e] and part.

Parting. Judah Halevi, *tr. fr. Hebrew by* Nina Salaman. AWP; TrJP

Parting, The. Josephine D. Henderson Heard. CBWP-4

Parting, The. Elizabeth Jennings. NePoEA-2

Parting. Kito, *tr. fr. Japanese by* Hiroaki Sato. *Fr.* Twenty-four Hokku. FCEI

Parting. Thomas Middleton. *Fr.* A Chaste Maid in Cheapside. EIL

Parting. Gabriel Preil, *tr. fr. Hebrew by* Laya Firestone. VWA

Parting. Edward Thomas. Mes

Parting. *Malay Oral Tradition, tr. by* R. J. Wilkinson *and* R. O. Winstedt. WTO

Parting. Shlomo Vinner, *tr. fr. Hebrew by* Laya Firestone *and* Howard Schwartz. VWA

Parting, A. Wang Wei, *tr. fr. Chinese by* Witter Bynner *and* Kiang Kan-Hu. ILY

Parting. W. B. Yeats. FaBoTw

Parting; a Game. Lynn Sukenick. NMM

Parting, a thousand cups won't wash away the sorrow. To Tzu-an. Yü Hsüan-chi, *tr. by* Geoffrey Waters. BoWoP

Parting as Descent. John Berryman. LiTA; MoAmPo

Parting at Dawn. John Crowe Ransom. AnAmPo

Parting at Dawn. *Malay Oral Tradition, tr. by* R. J. Wilkinson *and* R. O. Winstedt. WTO

Parting at Morning. Robert Browning. AWP; FaBV; FF; FiP; HeIP; InPS; MOS; NAEL-2; NOBE; OBEV; OBNC; OxBSP; SoSe; UnPo; WiR

Parting at Morning. Dietmar von Aist, *tr. fr. German by* Frank C. Nicholson. AWP

Parting Chant. T'an Ssu-t'ung, *tr. fr. Chinese by* Timothy C. Wong. WFTU

Parting friends put me the query. Anglo-Eire Vignette. Patric Stevenson. NeIP

Parting from Liu Nan-chou, sel. Hsieh Chin, *tr. fr. Chinese by* Jonathan Chaves.
"Wait until I too "hang up my carriage."" CoBLCP

Parting from the Courtier Sung. Yin Shih, *tr. fr. Chinese by* Burton Watson. CoBCP

Parting from the dead, I've stifled my sobs. Dreaming of Li Po. Tu Fu, *tr. by* Burton Watson. CoBCP

Parting from you, I go to Inaba. Teika, *tr. fr. Japanese by* Hiroaki Sato. *Fr.* A Compendium of Good Tanka. FCEI

Parting Gift. Elinor Wylie. OxBA

Parting Glass, The. Philip Freneau. AA

Parting golden haze, A. L'Oiseau Bleu. Gordon Bottomley. BrPo

Parting Hymn, A. Charlotte Forten. BlSi

Parting Hymn We Sing, A. Aaron R. Wolfe. AH

Parting in April. Pamela Holmes. CN

Parting in Wartime. Frances Cornford. FaBoWP; NIP

Parting Is Hard. *Unknown, tr. fr. Chinese by* Geoffrey Waters. BoWoP

Parting Kiss, The. Josephine D. Henderson Heard. CBWP-4

Parting Lovers, The. Mrs. Henry Linden. CBWP-4

Parting meal, low lamp—stay and enjoy it a bit longer, A. Farewell Talk with Saiko by a Rainy Window. Rai San'yo, *tr. by* Burton Watson. FCEI; JLIC-2

Parting: 1940. John Frederick Nims. PoA

Parting of Hector and Andromache, The. Homer, *tr. fr. Greek by* William B. Smith *and* Walter Miller. *Fr.* Iliad.

Parting of the Red Sea, The. *Unknown, tr. fr. Anglo-Saxon by* Charles W. Kennedy. *Fr.* Exodus. AnOE

Parting of the Ways, The. Joseph B. Gilder. PAH

Parting of Venus and Old Age, The. John Gower. *Fr.* Confessio Amantis, VIII. PoEL-2

Parting Talk with Seigan, A. Rai San'yo, *tr. fr. Japanese by* Burton Watson. FCEI; JLIC-2

Parting. To—— Robert Frost. AnAmPo

Parting Verse, the Feast There Ended, The. Robert Herrick. SeCV-1

Parting with Lucasia; a Song. Katherine Philips. PeHV

Parting, without a Sequel. John Crowe Ransom. MoAB; MoAmPo; OxBA; SoSe

Partings. Charles Guérin, *tr. fr. French by* Jethro Bithell. AWP

Partings. Maria Jane Jewsbury. OxBChV

Partly Because. Ursula Laird. Mes

Partly to My Cat. Ellen Bass. NMM

Partly to verify the facts of a certain period. Kaisarion. Constantine P. Cavafy, *tr. by* Edmund Keeley *and* Philip Sherrard. VMG

Partner, hold me tight! Dance. N. M. Rashed, *tr. by* Mahmood Jamal. PBMUP

Partnership dissolved. Sale. Miller Williams. WeW

Parts. Zishe Landau, *tr. fr. Yiddish by* Ruth Whitman. VWA

Parts of Speech, The. *Unknown.* FaBoUs

Parts of the Whole Are We; but God the Whole. Dryden. *Fr.* Palamon and Arcite. NAs

Party, The. Margaret Avison. PoA

Party, The. Paul Laurence Dunbar. AmNP

Party, The. William Robert Rodgers. BIrV

Party, The. Jerome Sala. UL

Party, The. Reed Whittemore. CoAP

Party at Bannon Brook. Alden Nowlan. NeAC

Party at Hydra. Irving Layton. HeIP
Party balloons fondle each other. Balloons. Dan Pagis, *tr. by* Bernhard Frank. MHeP
Party Favour. Daniel David Moses. HATNAP
Party finished early, 'twas on the stroke of nine, The. The Keyhole in the Door. *Unknown.* CoMu
Party in Winter. Karl Shapiro. PCP
Party is going strong, The. Tribute to Kafka for Someone Taken. Alan Dugan. CAPP
Party Knee. John Updike. FiBHP
Party Piece. Brian Patten. BoLoP
Party Song, A. *Unknown.* BoTP
Partying by a river near Ellwood City, Pennsylvania. Coming Home in March. Harold Littlebird. STE; VoR
Pas de Deux for Lovers. Michael Dransfield. CBAP
Pasa Thalassa Thalassa. Edwin Arlington Robinson. MOS
Paschal Fire, The. Denis Florence MacCarthy. TIRV
Paschal Lamb. Robert Hass. NAmP; NPGG
Paschal Transfiguration. Michael Harlow. ATNZ
Pasolini. Kevin Killian. BAP
Pasquin to the Queen's Statue at St. Paul's. William Shippen. APAS
Pass. Edmund Vance Cooke. PWR
Pass, The. John Logan. LCAP
Pass forth, my wonted cries. Sir Thomas Wyatt. SiPS
Pass It On. Henry Burton. BLRP; PWR
Pass It On Grandson. Ted D. Palmanteer. STE
Pass Office Song. *Unknown, tr. fr. Afrikaans by* Peggy Rutherford. PBA; TTY
  ("Take off your hat.") WTO, *tr. by* H. Tracey
Pass On, You Lonely Grandfathers. Izi Kharik, *tr. fr. Yiddish by* Leonard Wolf. PeBMYV
Pass over this as well. Games. Ory Bernstein, *tr. by* Warren Bargad *and* Stanley F. Chyet. IP
Pass to thy rendezvous of light. Emily Dickinson. NAWM-2
Pass we the ills, which each man feels or dreads. Matthew Prior. *Fr.* Solomon on the Vanity of the World, *bk.* III. NOEC; PoEL-3
Pass zaps, The. Scoring. Kent Cartwright. TSL
Passage. Hart Crane. CMoP; NOBA; PoE
Passage. Denise Levertov. CAPP
Passage. John M. Roderick. GOYP
Passage of a Year, The. *Unknown, tr. fr. Middle English by* Brian Stone. *Fr.* Sir Gawain and the Green Knight. PoEL-1
Passage over Water. Robert Duncan. NoAM; NOBA
Passage Rite. John Caddy. TSL
Passage Steamer. Louis MacNeice. MOS
Passage to India, *sels.* Walt Whitman. AmPP; NAAL-1; PoEL-5
  "Ah, more than any priest, O soul, we too believe in God." WGRP
  "Bathe me O God in thee, mounting to thee." TrPWD
Passages, *sels.* Robert Duncan.
  At the Loom. VGW
  Fire, The. VGW
  Tribal Memories. NOBA
  Up Rising. NNaP
  "Willingly I'll say."
Passages. Larry Eigner. NeAP
Passed Ruin'd Ilion. Walter Savage Landor. *See* Ianthe: Past ruin'd Ilion Helen lives.
Passenger at times in your trains of vice, A. The Train to Hell. Monique Buri, *tr. by* Serge Gavronsky. DMF
Passenger Pigeons. Robert Morgan. GeTw; MAYP; MT
Passengers, The. David Antin. NYBP
Passengers. Denis Johnson. MAYP; SM
Passenjare, The. Isaac H. Bromley. FiBHP
Passer, The. George Abbe. SD
Passer Mortuus Est. Edna St. Vincent Millay. CMoP; FaBoWP; MoAmPo; OBD; OxBA
Passer-by, A. Robert Bridges. BrPo; CMoP; LiTB; LiTM; MoAB; MoBrPo; MOS; OAEL-2; OBEV; OBNC; OxBTC; WiR
Passerby being fair about sacrifice, A. Chickens the Weasel Killed. William Stafford. NaP
Passes are blocked by snow, The. Persia. Victoria Mary Sackville-West. WPE
Passetyme of Pleasure. Stephen Hawes. *See* Pastime of Pleasure.
Passin Ben Dorain. Alastair MacKie. *Fr.* At the Heich Kirk-Yaird. PoSH
Passing a dull red college-block. A Walk in Würzburg. William Plomer. NYBP
Passing across the billowy sea. *Unknown, tr. fr. Italian. Fr.* Popular Songs of Tuscany. AWP, *tr. by* John Addington Symonds
Passing an Orchard by Train. Robert Bly. CAPP
Passing and Glassing. Christina Rossetti. OBNC

Passing Away. Christina Rossetti. *Fr.* Old and New Year Ditties, III. NoP; OAEL-2; OBNC; WPE
Passing Bell, The. Thomas Heywood. *Fr.* The Rape of Lucrece. FaBoRV
Passing Bell, The. James Shirley. ACP
Passing Bell at Stratford, The. William Winter. AA
Passing between the stumbling generations. The Wandering Jew Comes to the Wall. Edmond Fleg, *tr. fr. French by* Humbert Wolfe. *Fr.* The Wall of Weeping. TrJP
Passing By. Thomas Ford. *See* There Is a Lady Sweet and Kind.
Passing by Huai-yin I Have Feelings. Wu Wei-yeh, *tr. fr. Chinese by* Jonathan Chaves. CoBLCP
Passing by the Battlefield at Feng-k'ou. Kao Ch'i, *tr. fr. Chinese by* Jonathan Chaves. CoBLCP
Passing by the Hot Springs at Hua-ch'ing Palace, *sel.* Yüan Hung-tao, *tr. fr. Chinese by* Jonathan Chaves.
  "Eastern mountains/ and western mountains." CoBLCP
Passing Chao-ling Again. Tu Fu, *tr. fr. Chinese by* Burton Watson. CoBCP
Passing into Storm. Patrick Lane. NOBC
Passing like a Strauss waltz. The Hoofer. A. K. Redwing. VoR
Passing Miscanthus on the Road. Tamesada, *tr. fr. Japanese by* Steven D. Carter. WFTW
Passing of a dream, The. John Clare. NOBVV
Passing of Arthur, The. Layamon. *Fr.* The Brut. PoE
Passing of Arthur, The. Sir John Collings Squire. BXAP
Passing of Arthur, The. Tennyson. *Fr.* Idylls of the King. NAEL-2; OBNC
  (Morte d'Arthur, *incorporated in the* Idylls *with changes, as* The Passing of Arthur) DL; FiP; OAEL-2
  "And answer made King Arthur, breathing hard." EBEV
  "But now farewell. I am going a long way.'" FaBoRV
  Prayer ("Pray for my soul. More things are wrought by prayer"). WGRP
Passing of the Forest, The. William Pember Reeves. PeNZ
Passing of the Old Year. Mary Weston Fordham. CBWP-2
Passing of the Poets, The. Fearflatha O'Gnive. NOIV
Passing of the Shee, The. John Millington Synge. BIrV; FaBoEE
Passing out of a great city. Initial. Arthur Boyars. NePoEA-2
Passing out of the shadow. Just Passing. *Unknown.* BLRP
Passing Remark. Tawfiq Zayyad, *tr. fr. Arabic by* Sharif Elmusa *and* Charles Doria. MAP
Passing Seven-Mile Rapids on a Moonlit Night. Li E, *tr. fr. Chinese by* Irving Lo. WFTU
Passing shower, A. *Unknown. Fr.* Manyo Shu. Ma
Passing Strange. Alan Bernheimer. UL
Passing Strange, The. John Masefield. LiTB; MoAB; MoBrPo; OBEV
Passing stranger! you do not know how longingly I look upon you. To a Stranger. Walt Whitman. NOBA
Passing the American graveyard, for my birthday. Poem for My Twentieth Birthday. Kenneth Koch. PoA
Passing the Bridge of Immortal Encounter Looking for the Sublime Ascent Temple. Yi Shun-ting, *tr. fr. Chinese by* Timothy C. Wong. WFTU
Passing the cedar grove at Osaka Barrier. Princess Shikishi, *tr. fr. Japanese by* Hiroaki Sato. *Fr.* Seventy-eight Tanka. FCEI
Passing the Corporate Forest. Michael McFee. SoTCo
Passing the flower-stalls there did I perceive. Strato, *tr. by* Sydney Oswald. PeHV
Passing the great plane tree in the square. The Beginning of the End. Jon Stallworthy. OxBC
Passing the Night at the Monastery of Eternal Peace. Hung Sheng, *tr. fr. Chinese by* Paul W. Kroll. WFTU
Passing the Retreat of Hsü Ching-po. Wu Chia-chi, *tr. fr. Chinese by* John E. Wills, Jr.' WFTU
Passing the shore of Minume. Hitomaro. *Fr.* Manyo Shu. Ma
Passing Through. Annie Johnson Flint. BLRP
Passing through a wood of larch trees. Larch Trees. Kitahara Hakushu, *tr. by* Hiroaki Sato. FCEI
Passing through Albuquerque where I'd read poetry. Second Prelude. Reality in Albuquerque: The Son. John Logan. *Fr.* Poem in Progress. CAPP
Passing through huddled and ugly walls. The Harbor. Carl Sandburg. TAP
Passing through South Lake Again. Li E, *tr. fr. Chinese by* Shirleen S. Wong. WFTU
Passing travelers/ making their way through this field. Passing Miscanthus on the Road. Tamesada, *tr. by* Steven D. Carter. WFTW
Passing Visit to Helen. D. H. Lawrence. CMoP
Passion, The. Ralph Knevet. JCP

Passion. Sue May. DT
Passion. Susan Prospere. AnAn
Passion According to Ravensbrück, The. János Pilinszky. *See* Passion of Ravensbrück.
Passion and Exaltation of Christ, The. Isaac Watts. NOCV
Passion Drinker, The. Anita Endrezze Probst. VoR
Passion of Christ, The. Denis Devlin. IPY
Passion of Jesus, The. *Unknown.* MeEL
Passion of M'Phail, The, *sels.* Horace Gregory.
  They Were All like Geniuses. NYBP
  This Is the Place to Wait. MoAmPo
Passion of Ravensbrück. János Pilinszky, *tr. fr. Hungarian by* Ted Hughes. MHuP
  (Passion According to Ravensbrück, The.) FOC, *tr. by* Jascha Kessler
Passion without a Name. Lucha Corpi. CCP
Passionate love is temporary. Landscape with Leaves and Figure. Olga Broumas. BoWoP
Passionate Man's Pilgrimage, The. Sir Walter Ralegh. AAS; ChTr; EiL; LiTB; MePo; NOBE; NoP; OBSC; PoE; PoEL-2; PoRA; RB; SeCePo; TrGrPo
  (His Pilgrimage.) OBEV
  (My Pilgrimage.) WGRP
  (Pilgrimage, The.) SiPS
Passionate Man's Song, The. John Fletcher. *See* Nice Valor, The: Melancholy.
Passionate Pilgrim, The, *sels.* Shakespeare *and others.*
  "As it fell upon a day." Richard Barnefield. GBL; PBBP
    (Nightingale, The.) AWP; GTBS; GTBS-P
    (Ode, An.) EiL; OBSC
    (Philomel.) CH; NOBE; OBEV
  Beauty. *Unknown, fr.* XIII. OBSC
  Crabbed Age and Youth. Shakespeare, *fr.* XII. GBL; InPS; LiTB; OBEV
    (Age and Youth.) EiL
    (Madrigal, A: "Crabbed age and youth.") GTBS; GTBS-P; InPS
    (Youth and Age.) OBSC
  Fair Is My Love. *At. to* Shakespeare, *fr.* VII. EiL
  It Was a Lording's Daughter. *At. to* Shakespeare. EiL
  Sweet Rose, Fair Flower. *At. to* Shakespeare, *fr.* X. EiL
Passionate Professor, The. Bert Leston Taylor. NBLV
Passionate Shepherd, The, *sels.* Nicholas Breton.
  Aglaia. OBSC
  Merry Country Lad, The. EiL
    (Happy Countryman, The, *shorter sel.*) CH
    (Pastoral: "Who can live in heart so glad.") ELP
    (Shepherd and Shepherdess.) OBSC
  Pretty Twinkling Starry Eyes. EiL
Passionate Shepherd to His Love, The. Christopher Marlowe. AAS; AWP; BoLoP; CTC; EiL; ELP; FaBoBe; FaFP; FF; FPL; GTBS; GTBS-P; HAP; HeIP; HoPM; InPK; InPS; LiTB; NAEL-1; NBLV; NIP; NOBE; NoP; OAEL-1; OBEV; OBSC; PoE; PoLF; PoRA; PPP; RB; SCV; SeCePo; TrGrPo; TTTS; WeW
    (Shepherd to His Love, The.) GN
    (Shepherd's Plea, The.) SiPS
Passionate Shepherd to His Love, The. Delmore Schwartz. NIP
Passionate Sword, The. Jean Starr Untermeyer. TrJP; TrPWD
Passionately joined to all things visible. Invisible Work. Margaret Gibson. MT
Passions, an Ode for [*or* to] Music, The. William Collins. GTBS; GTBS-P
Passions are liken'd best to floods and streams. The Silent Lover. Sir Walter Ralegh. *Fr.* The Silent Lover. LiTB
Passiontide Communion. Katharine Tynan. TrPWD
Passover. Rose Ausländer, *tr. fr. German by* Ewald Osers. VWA
Passover Eve. Fania Kruger. GoYe
Passport, The. Mahmoud Darwish, *tr. fr. Arabic by* Abdullah al-Udhari. MPAW
Passport. Judah Leib Teller, *tr. fr. Yiddish by* Benjamin *and* Barbara Harshav. *Fr.* Invasion. AYP
Past. Arnold Adoff. TDD
Past, The. Bryant. AA
Past, The. Emerson. FaBoCh; FPL; LiTA; PoEL-4; TAP
Past, The. Mary Weston Fordham. CBWP-2
Past. Winifred Howells. AA
Past, The. Yoshioka Minoru, *tr. fr. Japanese by* Hiroaki Sato. FCEI
Past, The. William Oandasan. STE
Past/ Is but the cinders, The. The Search. Kwesi Brew. PBA
Past, a glacier, gripped the mountain wall, The. Full Moon at Tierz; before the Storming of Huesca. John Cornford. OBWP
Past and Present. Thomas Hood. *See* I Remember, I Remember.

Past and Present. R. E. Egerton Warburton. NOBVV
Past arenas, sanctuaries. Pilgrims. Joseph Brodsky, *tr. by* Dimitry Pospielovsky *and* Keith Bosley. VWA
Past comfort, all despairing. Lament for the Sailing of the Crusade. Rinaldo D'Aquino, *tr. by* T. G. Bergin. PFI
Past exchanges have left orbits of rain around my face. An Apology. Diane Wakoski. TAP
Past factory workshops, empty. Marina Tsvetaeva, *tr. fr. Russian by* Paul Schmidt. *Fr.* The Daughter of Jairus, IX. BoWoP
Past flowershops and shoestores, bars. August 1964. Ferreira Gullar, *tr. by* William Jay Smith. CT
Past is a strange land, most strange, The. Parting. Edward Thomas. Mes
Past Is Dark with Sin and Shame, The. Thomas Wentworth Higginson. AH
Past is fresh, dust is fresh, The. Ebb. John Lyle Donaghy. NeIP
Past is past, and if one. Salute. James Schuyler. FYAP; NeAP
Past is such a curious creature, The. Emily Dickinson. Mes
Past Is the Present, The. Marianne Moore. NAAL-2
Past Love. Anne Keiter. GOYP
Past ploughed and fallow, at the top. Glenarm. John Lyle Donaghy. NeIP
Past ruin'd [*or* ruined] Ilion Helen lives. Walter Savage Landor. *Fr.* Ianthe. CTC; ELP; EnLoPo; EnRP; GBL; HAP; HeIP; NAEL; NoP; OBNC; PoRA; TrGrPo; WeW
    (Ianthe.) LiTB; PoEL-4
    (Passed Ruin'd Ilion.) AWP
    (To Ianthe.) NOBE
    (Verse: "Past ruin'd Ilion. . .") OBEV
Past scenic laybys and stag warning signs. History Classes. Tony Harrison. *Fr.* The School of Eloquence. NoAM
Past second cock-crow yacht masts in the harbor go slowly white. Masts at Dawn. Robert Penn Warren. NAAL-2
Past sends images to beach, The. Lines for the Ancient Scribes. Harvey Shapiro. VWA
Past seven o'clock: time to be gone. Moonset. Sir Henry Newbolt. EBVV
Past storefronts lit among the dusk-swept avenues. Anniversary of the Air. Michael Waters. NAmP
Past the blueing humus. Vigil of the Wounded. Phillip Yellowhawk Minthorn. STE
Past the house where he was got. Austin Clarke. *Fr.* Mnemosyne Lay in Dust, I. CMoP; IPY; PoE
Past the old barbershop on Jefferson. Gary Gotow. George Uba. BrSi
Past the school and down. Directions to the Nomad. James Welch. CDW
Past the Tin Butterflies and Plaster Gnomes. Peter Bland. ATNZ
Past them he strode. The Hinds of Kerry. William S. Wabnitz. GoYe
"Past two o'clock and Cornwallis is taken." News from Yorktown. Lewis Worthington Smith. PAH
Past walks here, noiseless, unasked, alone, The. An Old Street. Virginia Woodward Cloud. AA
Past Will Not Return, The. José Coronel Urtecho, *tr. fr. Spanish by* Tony Ryan *and* Walter Martínez. VoI
Pasta starts in teeny-weeny. A Graduation of Pasta. Willard R. Espy. SoTCo
Pastel. Francis Saltus Saltus. AA
Pastel: Masks and Faces. Arthur Symons. NOBVV
Pastel the flowers, the wreaths in the pastel gardens. Moon Mattress. Diane DiPrima. NMM
Pastime. Henry VIII, King of England. CTC; EBVV; OBSC
Pastime of Pleasure, The, *sels.* Stephen Hawes.
  Dame Music. PoEL-1
  Epitaph of Graunde [*or* La Graunde] Amoure, The. *Fr.* 42. ChTr; EBEV; FaBoRV; OBSC
    (Epitaph, An: "O mortal folk you may behold and see.") ACP; OBEV; TrGrPo
    (Epitaphy of la Graunde Amoure.) FaBoEE
  Seven Deadly Sins, The. PoEL-1
  Time and Eternity. PoEL-1
  True Knight [*or* True Knighthood], The. *Fr.* 27. ACP; OBEV; TrGrPo
Pastime with good company. Pastime. Henry VIII, King of England. CTC; EBEV; OBSC
    (Good Company.) TrGrPo
Pastor M'Gadi's startling blackness. Halo. Ralph Nixon Currey. PeSA
Pastor Speaks Out, The ("Pastor sips weak hock and seltzer, The."). David Fisher. NPGG
Pastoral, A. Nicholas Breton. *See* Honourable Entertainment Given to the Queen's Majesty in Progress at Elvetham, 1591, The: Phillida and Coridon.
Pastoral: "Afternoon wears on, The." David Wright. NYBP

Pastoral: "Annette came through the meadows." Henrietta Cordelia Ray. CBWP-3
Pastoral, A: "By the side of a green stagnate pool." George Alexander Stevens. CoMu; ErPo
Pastoral: "Crouched in the yard." Ellen Bryant Voigt. MAYP
Pastoral: "Death./ The death of a million." Ron Loewinsohn. NeAP
Pastoral: "Dominic Francis Xavier Brotherton-Chancery." Gavin Ewart. OxBC
Pastoral: "Dove walks with sticky feet, The." Kenneth Patchen. NaP
Pastoral: "Farmhouse skyline, draped with trees, The." Alan Creighton. CaP
Pastoral, A: "From thence into the open fields he fled." Spenser. *Fr.* The Faerie Queene, VI, 9. OBSC
Pastoral: "I came to a field." Charles Simic. NNaP
Pastoral: "It all happened so fast. Fenya was in the straight chair." Norman Dubie. AmPA
Pastoral: "It's the Spring." William Ernest Henley. *Fr.* In Hospital, XXII. BrPo
Pastoral: "Little sparrows, The." William Carlos Williams. TwCP
Pastoral, A: "Mobile, immaculate and austere." Geoffrey Hill. NePoEA-2
Pastoral[l], A: "Oh [*or* O] happy golden age." Tasso. *See* Aminta:
Pastoral[l], A: "On a hill there grows a flower." Nicholas Breton. ElL (Ipsa Quae.) OBSC
(Phyllida and Corydon.) TrGrPo
Pastoral: "One person each, out." Bob Perelman. IAT
Pastoral, A: "So soft in the hemlock wood." Robert Hillyer. MoAmPo
Pastoral, A: "Sweet Bird! that sit and sing amid the shady valleys." Nicholas Breton. *See* Sweet Bird! that sit . . . .
Pastoral, A: "There went out in the dawning light." *Unknown, tr. by* John Addington Symonds. AWP
Pastoral: "This is a place of ease." Marion Strobel. PoA
Pastoral: "Today in Peru, this first day of summer." Lawrence Raab. AmPA
Pastoral: "When I was younger." William Carlos Williams. AmPP; OxBA
Pastoral: "Who can live in heart so glad." Nicholas Breton. *See* Passionate Shepherd, The: Merry Country Lad, The.
Pastoral, A: "Wise old apple tree in spring, The." Robert Hillyer. BoNaP
Pastoral Ballad, *sel.* William Shenstone.
"My banks they are furnished with bees." BoNaP
(Shepherd's Home, The.) GN
Pastoral Ballad by John Bull, A. Thomas Moore. BIrV; OBSV
Pastoral Elegy, A. Albius Tibullus, *tr. fr. Latin by* Sir Charles Abraham Elton. AWP
Pastoral[l] Hymn[e], A. John Hall. MeLP; OBS; TrPWD
Pastoral; in the Modern Style, A. "Worcester." NOEC
Pastoral on the King's Death; Written in 1648, The. Alexander Brome. OBS
Pastoral Poesy. John Clare. OAEL-2
Pastorale: "Wheels fall innumerably." Yoshioka Minoru, *tr. by* Hiroaki Sato. FCEI
O lovely age of gold!
Pastorall Dialogue, A. Thomas Carew. CaPo; GBL; SeCP
Pastorals, *sel.* Pope.
Sylvan Delights. NOBE
Pastourelle. Donald Jeffrey Hayes. AmNP
Pasttime. Emilio de Grazia. TSL
Pasture, The. Robert Frost. BLPL; CMoP; FaPON; GoJo; MoAB; MoAmPo; MoShBr; NAAL-2; NOBA; OxBA; PDV; PoE; TTTS
Pasture, A. Frederic Lawrence Knowles. AA
Pasture, stone wall, and steeple. Question in a Field. Louise Bogan. NYBP
Pastures of Plenty. Woody Guthrie. WTO
Pat-a-cake, pat-a-cake, baker's man. Mother Goose. OxNR
Pat Cloherty's Version of *The Maisie.* Richard Murphy. IPY; RB
Pat Dugan. . . my grandfather. . . throat cancer. . .1947. People Who Died. Ted Berrigan. UL
Pat Young. Kenneth Mackenzie. PoAu-2
Pat your foot. Leadbelly Gives an Autograph. Imamu Amiri Baraka. CNA
Patapan. Bernard de la Monnoye, *tr. fr. French.* PChr
Patch of cloud rides the moon tonight, A. Boncho, *tr. fr. Japanese by* Hiroaki Sato. *Fr.* Twenty-one Hokku. FCEI
Patch of Old Snow, A. Robert Frost. CMoP; OxBSP; WeW
Patches. Thomas Russell Shelton. PWR
Patches of freeway still break through the meadow. 2021: Noon: Idaho. Bruce Hawkins. BWV
Patches of it. The Luminous. Barbara Guest. PoM
Patches of Sky. Debora Greger. MAYP

Patching Together, A, *sel.* Murray Edmond.
Cell Lay Inside Her Body, The. *Fr.* 3. NAs
Patching up a row. *Unknown, tr. by* Geoffrey Bownas *and* Anthony Thwaite. PeBJV
Patchwork Quilt, The. Elizabeth Fleming. BoTP
Patent No. 1. Kay Hargreaves. Mes
Pater Filio. Robert Bridges. CMoP; OBEV
Pater Noster. Jacques Prévert, *tr. fr. French by* Lawrence Ferlinghetti. RHTwFP
"Pater Noster, The." *Unknown.* ACP
Paternal, *sel.* Mariella Bettarini, *tr. fr. Italian by* Muriel Kittel.
"But then what do you know about the rights of suffocated genitals." DMI
Paternal. Ernest J. Wilson, Jr.. PoNe
Paternal house has collapsed, The. We Must Free Ourselves Today. Ida Vallerugo, *tr. by* Muriel Kittel. DMI
Pater's Bathe. Edward Abbott Parry. OxBChV
Paterson, *sels.* William Carlos Williams.
"Beautiful thing/ I saw you." CMoP
"Edward/ Paterson has grown older." *Fr. bk.* V. NoAM
Episode 17. OxBA
"Outside/ outside myself/ there is a world." *Fr.* II. NoAM
(Sunday in the Park.) NAAL-2
"Paterson lies in the valley under the Passaic Falls." *Fr. bk.* I. TAP (Delineaments of the Giants, The.) NoAM
"Rigor of beauty is the quest. But how will you find beauty when it is locked." NoAM
"To make a start." *Fr.* I. CMoP; NoAM; NOBA
"To make a start." CMoP; NoAM; NOBA
"There is a woman in our town." *Fr.* V, ii. CMoP; PoE
Paterson lies in the valley under the Passaic Falls. William Carlos Williams. *Fr.* Paterson, *bk.* I. TAP
(Delineaments of the Giants, The.) NoAM
Path, The. Edward Thomas. BrPo
Path across a meadow fair and sweet, A. Two Paths. Julia Caroline Ripley Dorr. AA
Path among the Dunes, A. Marvin Bell. BLA
Path among the Stones, The. Galway Kinnell. NNaP; NOBA; Prf
Path by which we twain did go, The. Tennyson. *Fr.* In Memoriam A. H. H., XXII. SCV
Path ending, a fragrance, The. Buson, *tr. fr. Japanese by* Hiroaki Sato. *Fr.* Eighty-seven Hokku. FCEI
Path I Must Travel, The. Emerson Blackhorse Mitchell. NOVW
Path-let. leaving home, leading out. Footpath. Stella Ngatho. WPOW
Path of the Old Spells, The. Donald Sinclair, *tr. fr. Gaelic.* GoTS
Path of the Padres, The. Edith D. Osborne. AmFN
Path of the Stars, The. Thomas S. Jones, Jr.. WGRP
Path of Wisdom, The. Bible, Apocrypha. *Fr.* Baruch, III: 9–IV: 4. TrJP
Path that Leads to Nowhere, The. Corinne Roosevelt Robinson. BLPA
Pathedy of Manners. Ellen Kay. SoSe
Pathetic Runaway, The. Philippe Thoby-Marcelin, *tr. fr. French by* William Jay Smith. CT
Pathfinder—and Path-clincher! John Charles Frémont. Charles Fletcher Lummis. PAH
Pathology of Colours. Dannie Abse. NoAM
Paths are drenched with dew, The. *Unknown, tr. by* Arthur Waley. BoS
Paths of Prayer, The. Edouard Roditi. VWA
Paths to God. Musa Moris Farhi, *tr. fr. Turkish by the author.* VWA
Patience. Elaine Feinstein. BrRo; FaBoWP
Patience, *sels.* W. S. Gilbert.
Bunthorne's Song [The Aesthete]. EBVV; FiBHP; LiTB; OAEL-2 (Aesthete, The.) EBVV
Fable of the Magnet and the Churn, The. FaPON; OnMSP
If You're Anxious for to Shine in the High Aesthetic Line. NAEL-2
"If you're anxious for to shine in the high esthetic line as a man of culture." NBLV
Oh, Hollow! Hollow! Hollow! FaBoNo
Patience. Harry Graham. FiBHP; MoShBr
Patience. Frank Horne. BPo
Patience. Bobbi Katz. RHPC
Patience. Geoffrey Anketell Studdert-Kennedy. TrPWD
Patience, *sel.* Unknown.
Jonah. ACP
Patience. Sir Thomas Wyatt. *See* Patience, Though I Have Not.
Patience! coy singers of the Delphic wood. To Poets. Walter Savage Landor. FaBoEE
Patience, for I have wrong. Sir Thomas Wyatt. SiPS
Patience for my device. Sir Thomas Wyatt. SiPS

Patience, hard thing! the hard thing but to pray. Gerard Manley Hopkins. NOBVV; OBNC
   (Patience, Hard Thing!) Prf; Son
Patience is a virtue. *Unknown.* OxNR
Patience Is When You Stop Waiting. Charles Kenneth Williams. CAPP
Patience of a People. Frederick Bryant, Jr.. CNA
Patience on all my smart. Sir Thomas Wyatt. SiPS
Patience on a Monument. Shakespeare. *Fr.* Twelfth Night, II, iv. TrGrPo
Patience, Though I Have Not. Sir Thomas Wyatt. NoP; SiPS
   (Patience.) OBSC; TrGrPo
Patience. patience. Patience. Frank Horne. BPo
Patient, The. Nicholas Moore. EAS
Patient above his tinted tiles he bent. The Mosaic Worker. Arthur Wallace Peach. BLRP
Patient bones in a sack. Beside the Bed. P. J. Kavanagh. NPo
Patient Griselda. Chaucer. *Fr.* The Canterbury Tales: The Clerk's Tale. PoRA
Patient Is Rallying, The. Weldon Kees. NaP
Patient: Rockland County Sanitarium, The. Calvin C. Hernton. *See* Madhouse.
Patiently/ the earth turns. Turns. Tymoteusz Karpowicz, tr. by Czeslaw Milosz. PwPP
Patios of Ithaca. Mirko Lauer, *tr. fr. Spanish by* David Tipton. Per
Patmos. David Gascoyne. OBVE
Patriarch, The. Burns. CoMu
Patriarch in black takes, The. The Sacrifice. Chana Bloch. VWA
Patriarch Jacob Meets Rachel, The. Itzig Manger, *tr. fr. Yiddish by* Leonard Wolf. PeBMYV
Patricians, The. Douglas Dunn. OxBC
Patrick Ewing Takes a Foul Shot. Diane Ackerman. ASP; MAYP
Patrick, you chatter too loud. The Praise of Fionn. *Unknown, tr. by* Frank O'Connor. TIRV
Patriot, The. Robert Browning. TrGrPo
Patriot, The. J. C. Milne. PoSH
Patriot, The. Sir Walter Scott. *See* Lay of the Last Minstrel, The
Patriotic Ode on the Fourteenth Anniversary of the Persecution of Charlie Chaplin. Bob Kaufman. PoBA
Patriotic Poem. Diane Wakoski. PoBA; VGW
Patriotic Reflections. Yehuda Amichai, *tr. fr. Hebrew by* Warren Bargad *and* Stanley F.Chyet. IP
Patriotic Tour and Postulate of Joy. Robert Penn Warren. AiP; NYBP
Patriotism, sel. George Richardson.
   "England! my persecuted isle." PF
Patriotism. Sir Walter Scott. *See* Lay of the Last Minstrel, The
Patriotism [I] ("Breathes there the man with soul so dead"). Sir Walter Scott. *See* Breathes There The Man.
Patriotism [II] ("To mute and to material things"). Sir Walter Scott. *See* Nelson, Pitt, Fox.
Patroclus' Body Saved. Homer, *tr. fr. Greek by* E. R. Dodds. *Fr.* The Iliad, XVII. WaaP
Patrol; Buonamary. Bernard Gutteridge. WaP
Patrolling Barnegat. Walt Whitman. MOS; NoP
Patron of all those who do good by stealth. December: Prayer to St. Nicholas. John Heath-Stubbs. OBCP
Patron of Flawless Serpent Beauty. Friederike Mayröcker, *tr. fr. German by* Michael Hamburger. WPOW
Patrum Propositum. Robert Fitzgerald. GOA
Patter of the Shingle, The. *Unknown.* BLPA
Pattern Poem with an Elusive Intruder. Reinhold Döhl. WeW
Patterns. Amy Lowell. AWP; BoWoP; DL; FaFP; FPL; LiTA; MoAmPo; OnMSP; OxBA; TrGrPo
Patterns. Roberta Hill Whiteman. HATNAP
Patterns of old green-gold trees. Autumn. D. R. Beeton. PeSA
Patty-cake, patty-cake/ Marcus Antonius. Tact. Paul Pascal. WeW
Patty, 1949–1961. Sharon Mayer Libera. IHMS
Pauca Mea, sel. Christopher Brennan.
   I Said, This Misery Must End. PoAu-1
Paudeen. W. B. Yeats. HAP; OxBSP; PoEL-5
Paul. James Wright. NePoEA
Paul and Silas, bound in jail. All Night Long. *Unknown.* AS
Paul Bunyan. Arthur Stanley Bourinot. *Fr.* A Legend of Paul Bunyan. FaPON
Paul comes from Toronto on Sunday. I Am Not a Conspiracy Everything Is Not Paranoid. Susan Musgrave. NoAM
Paul Faber, Surgeon, sel. George Macdonald.
   That Holy Thing. OBEV; TrPWD; WGRP
Paul Jones. *Unknown.* PAH
Paul Jones. *Unknown.* PAH
Paul Jones—a New Song. *Unknown.* PAH
Paul Jones's Victory. *Unknown.* AmFP
Paul Klee. John Haines. LCAP

Paul Klee. Ruthven Todd. EAS
Paul Laurence Dunbar. James David Corrothers. BANP; PoNe
Paul Laurence Dunbar. Robert Hayden. NoP
Paul Laurence Dunbar. Mrs. Henry Linden. CBWP-4
Paul Revere's Ride. Longfellow. AiP; AnAmPo; OPP
Paul Revere's Ride (The Landlord's Tale). Longfellow. *Fr.* Tales of a Wayside Inn, *Pt.* I. BeLS; BLPA; FaBoBe; FaBoTw; FaBV; FaFP; FaPON; FaPoR; FPL; OBAL; OBCA; OBNV; OHFP; PAH; PWR; TrGrPo; WBLP
Paul Robeson. Gwendolyn Brooks. CNA; PoBA
Paula Becker to Clara Westhoff. Adrienne Rich. NAAL-2
Paulina, her room behind the servants' quarters. Czeslaw Milosz, *tr. fr. Polish by the author and* Peter Dale Scott. *Fr.* Throughout Our Lands, XI. PwPP
Pauline, sels. Robert Browning.
   "My God, my God, let me for once look on thee." TrPWD
   "O God, where do they tend—these struggling aims?." WGRP
   "Thou wilt remember. Thou art no more dear." OAEL-2
Paulownia tree drops dead leaves, A. Boncho, *tr. fr. Japanese by* Hiroaki Sato. *Fr.* Twenty-one Hokku. FCEI
Paul's clock struck twelve, 'twas time to go to bed. The Midnight Ramble. Charles Woodward. NOEC
Pauper, A. Allen Tate. LiTM
Pauper Woodland. Ronald G. Everson. NOBC
Pauper's Funeral, The. George Crabbe. *Fr.* The Village. OBNC
Pause. Mary Ursula Bethell. ATNZ; PeNZ
Pause a Moment. Asya, *tr. fr. Yiddish by* Gabriel Preil *and* Howard Schwartz. VWA
Pause, courteous spirit!—Balbi supplicates. Epitaphs, IX. Gabriello Chiabrera, *tr. by* Wordsworth. AWP
Pause for Breath, A. Ted Hughes. NYBP
Pause of Thought, A. Christina Rossetti. NOBE; OBNC
Pavane for the Nursery, A. William Jay Smith. DuDa; GoJo; MoAmPo
Paved square, The. The Colors of the Windows. Pierre Reverdy, *tr. by* Michael Benedikt. POS
Pavilion. Bill Manhire. ATNZ
Pavilion for Listening to Fragrance, The. Chang Yü, *tr. fr. Chinese by* Jonathan Chaves. CoBLCP
Pavilion is empty on the pond, its screens rolled up, A. Immortal at the River. Li Hsün, *tr. by* Lois Fusek. ATF
Pavilion of the Infinite Heavens, The. Yao Nai, *tr. fr. Chinese by* Daniel Bryant. WFTU
Pavilions of dance, terraces of song. Ch'ien Ch'ien-i, *tr. fr. Chinese by* Jonathan Chaves. *Fr.* In Spring of the Year Ping-shen. CoBLCP
Pavillion-Where-the-Crane-Came, The. Chao Meng-fu, *tr. fr. Chinese by* Jonathan Chaves. CoBLCP
Pavlov. Naomi Long Madgett. BPo
Paw. Paul Eluard, *tr. fr. French by* Michael Benedikt. POS
Pawky auld carle cam[e] ower [or owre or o'er] the lea [or lee], The. The Gaberlunzie Man. *Unknown.* EnSB; GoTS; OxBB, *with music;* OxBS
Pawky Duke, The. David Rorie. GoTS
Pawn-shop man knows hunger, The. Street Window. Carl Sandburg. PCP
Pawns, The. William Young. *Fr.* Wishmakers' Town. AA
Pawnshop Window. R. H. Grenville. GoYe
Pax. D. H. Lawrence. TrCP
Pax Anima, sel. Manuel Gutiérrez Nájera, *tr. fr. Spanish by* Samuel Beckett.
   "To remember. To forgive. To have loved." *tr. by* Samuel Beckett. MexPo
Pax Paganica. Louise Imogen Guiney. AA
Pay Day [or Payday] at Coal Creek. *Unknown.* AmFP
Pay no mind to my mother. *Unknown.* *Fr.* Manyo Shu. FCEI
Pay-off. Kenneth Fearing. CMoP
Pay the Bill. Ch'iao Lin, *tr. fr. Chinese by* Dominic Cheung. IFON
Pay Your Debts. Mrs. Henry Linden. CBWP-4
Paycheck. Michael Dennis Browne. SoTCo
Paying a Sick-call to Yao Ts'un-tao in the Rain. Shen Chou, *tr. fr. Chinese by* Jonathan Chaves. CoBLCP
Paying Homage at the Golden Gate. Hsüeh Chao-yün, *tr. fr. Chinese by* Lois Fusek. ATF
Paying Homage at the Golden Gate. Niu Hsi-chi, *tr. fr. Chinese by* Lois Fusek. ATF
Paying Homage at the Golden Gate. Sun Kuang-hsien, *tr. fr. Chinese by* Lois Fusek. ATF
Paying Homage at the Golden Gate. Wei Chuang, *tr. fr. Chinese by* Lois Fusek. ATF
Payments. Diana O Hehir. NPGG
Paysage Choisi. Francis Sparshott. MoCV
Paysage Moralisé. John Hollander. ErPo; NePoEA

Paysage Moralisé. W. H. Auden. *See* Hearing of Harvests Rotting in the Valleys.

P.C. Plod versus the Dale St. Dog Strangler. Roger McGough. MoP

Pcheek pcheek pcheek pcheek pcheek. Galway Kinnell. *Fr.* The Avenue Bearing the Initial of Christ into the New World, 1. LiTM; NePoEA-2

Pea crab crawls up my leg, A. Basho, *tr. fr. Japanese by* Burton Watson. *Fr.* Seventy-six Hokku. FCEI

Pea-Fields, The. Sir Charles G. D. Roberts. *Fr.* Songs of the Common Day. NOBC; OBCV

Peace. Bhartrihari, *tr. fr. Sanskrit by* Paul Elmer More. AWP

Peace. Rupert Brooke. *Fr.* 1914, I. MMA; OBWP; PoA; WGRP

Peace. Charles Stuart Calverley. EBVV

Peace. Phoebe Cary. PAH

Peace. Walter de la Mare. MMA; MoAB; MoBrPo

Peace. Irwin Edman. TrJP

Peace. George Herbert. AWP; ChTr; ELP; NOCV; TEP

Peace. Gerard Manley Hopkins. ELP; GTBS-P; OxBSP; TrCP

Peace. Langston Hughes. BPo

Peace. George Jonas. NeAC

Peace. Patrick Kavanagh. FaBCIP

Peace. D. H. Lawrence. FaBoPP

Peace. Michael Longley. CIP

Peace. Edwin Markham. WBLP

Peace. Edwin Markham. WBLP

Peace. *Unknown.* MeEL

Peace. Henry Vaughan. AWP; ChTr; EaLo; EBEV; ELP; FaBoCh; GN; HAP; MePo; NOBE; NOCV; OBD; OBEV; OBS; PoE; SeCV-1; TEP; TOF; TrCP; WeW; WGRP

Peace. Adeline D. T. Whitney. PAH

Peace: A Study. Charles Stuart Calverley. *See* He stood, a worn-out city clerk.

Peace and Love. Ella Wheeler Wilcox. PWR

Peace and Mercy and Jonathan. First Thanksgiving of All. Nancy Byrd Turner. FaPON

Peace and silence be the guide. Francis Beaumont. *Fr.* The Masque of the Inner Temple and Gray's Inne, V. OBS

Peace at the Goal. Ella Wheeler Wilcox. PWR

Peace, Be at Peace, O Thou My Heaviness. Baudelaire, *tr. fr. French by* Lord Alfred Douglas. InPK

(Sois sage o ma douleur.) AWP

Peace be unto you,/ Ye ministering angels. Shalom Aleichem. *Unknown.* TrJP

Peace be unto you, Penglima Lenggang Laut! Invitation to a Spirit. *Malay Oral Tradition, tr. by* W. W. Skeat. WTO

Peace be with you, gentle scrivener. Sholom Aleichem. Elias Lieberman. TrJP

Peace be with you, O Tin-ore. Tin-Ore. *Malay Oral Tradition, tr. by* W. W. Skeat. WTO

Peace; come away: the song of woe. Tennyson. *Fr.* In Memoriam A. H. H., LVII. EBVV

Peace Delegate. Douglas Livingstone. PeSA

Peace Hymn of the Republic. Henry van Dyke. *See* O Lord our God, Thy mighty hand.

Peace in the sober house of Jonas dwelt. Jonas Kindred's Household. George Crabbe. *Fr.* Tales: The Frank Courtship. OBNC

Peace in the Welsh Hills. Vernon Watkins. GTBS-P; OxBTC

Peace in the World. John Galsworthy. PoLF

Peace in thy hands. The Ghost. Walter de la Mare. BrPo; CMoP; ELP; EnLoP; LiTM; MoAB; MoBrPo; NOBE; OAEL-2; OxBTC

Peace is declared, and I return. The Return. Kipling. MoBrPo

Peace is made with a warlike man. *Unknown, tr. by* John Montague. BIrV

Peace is the men not marching away to be killed. Not Marching Away to Be Killed. Jean Overton Fuller. FF

Peace Is the Mind's Old Wilderness. John Holmes. AH

Peace is written on the doorstep. Peace. D. H. Lawrence. FaBoPP

Peace Maketh Plenty. *Unknown.* OxBSP

Peace Message, The. Burton Egbert Stevenson. PAH

Peace of a Good Mind, The. Sir Thomas More. *Fr.* The Twelve Weapons of Spiritual Battle. FaBoRV

Peace of great doors be for you, The. For You. Carl Sandburg. MoAmPo

Peace of the Roses, The. Thomas Philipps. ACP

Peace of Wild Things, The. Wendell Berry. GeTw; HeIP; MT; NIP; NU; PCP; VGW

Peace-Offering, The. Thomas Hardy. OxBSP

Peace on Earth. Bacchylides, *tr. fr. Greek by* John Addington Symonds. AWP

Peace on Earth. Edmund Hamilton Sears. *See* It Came upon the Midnight Clear.

Peace on Earth. William Carlos Williams. LiTA

Peace on New England, on the shingled white houses, on golden. Jehu. Louis MacNeice. LiTM; MoAB; WaP

Peace, peace! he is not dead, he doth not sleep. Shelley. *Fr.* Adonais; an Elegy on the Death of John Keats. OBD

(Elegy on the Death of John Keats, An.) OBNC

(Mourn Not for Adonais.) NoBE

Peace, peace, my friend; these subjects fly. George Crabbe. *Fr.* Sir Eustace Grey. PoEL-4

Peace, peace, my hony [*or* honey], do not cry. Edward Taylor. *Fr.* God's Determinations. PoEL-3

(Christ's Reply.) NAAL-1

Peace, peace, peace, make no noise. A Ditty. John Day. *Fr.* Humour Out of Breath. EIL

Peace, Perfect Peace. Edward H. Bickersteth. BLRP; WGRP

Peace Poem. Maturai Velacan, *tr. fr. Tamil by* A. K. Ramanujan. PLW

Peace, Shepherd, peace! What boots it singing on? Genius Loci. Margaret L. Woods. OBEV

Peace! The perfect word is sounding, like a universal hymn. In the Dawn. Odell Shepard. WGRP

Peace, the wild valley streaked with torrents. The Straw. Robert Graves. OxBTC

Peace, there is peace in this awaking. Waking. Patrick MacDonogh. NeIP

Peace-Time. Mervyn Morris. PVCV

Peace to all such! but were there one whose fires. Atticus. Pope. *Fr.* Epistle to Dr. Arbuthnot. AWP; InPK; NoBE; SeCePo

Peace to-night, heroic spirit! Requiem for a Young Soldier. Florence Earle Coates. OHIP

Peace to these little broken leaves. Leaves. W. H. Davies. MoBrPo

"Peace upon earth!" was said. We sing it. Christmas: 1924. Thomas Hardy. FaBoEE; OBCP

Peace Walk. William Stafford. Psk

Peace, war, religion. This Tokyo. Gary Snyder. NeAP

Peace! where art thou to be found? Enquiry after Peace. A Fragment. Countess of Winchilsea. PoE

Peaceable Kingdom, The. Marge Piercy. TwCP

Peaceable Kingdom. Bible, *O.T. See* Isaiah: Wolf also shall dwell with the lamb, The.

Peaceful life, A—just toil and rest. Lincoln. James Whitcomb Riley. OHIP

Peaceful night and the unassuming gleam. The Last Song of Sappho. Giacomo Leopardi, *tr. by* Patrick Creagh. PFI

Peaceful Shepherd, The. Robert Frost. *Fr.* A Sky Pair. MoAB; MoAmPo

Peaceful Song, A. Natan Zach, *tr. fr. Hebrew by* Peter Everwine *and* Shula Starkman. VWA

Peaceful spot is Piper's Flat, A. The folk that live around. How McDougal Topped the Score. Thomas E. Spencer. PoAu-1

Peaceful times of Emperor Yang!, The. River Messages. Sun Kuang-hsien, *tr. by* Lois Fusek. ATF

Peach blossoms are adrift on rippling tides of water. Speaking of Love. Mao Wen-hsi, *tr. by* Lois Fusek. ATF

Peach Tree with Fruit. Padraic Colum. BoNaP

Peach Tree Young and Fresh. *Unknown, tr. fr. Chinese by* Burton Watson. CoBCP

Peachstone. Dannie Abse. OxBC

Peacock. D. H. Lawrence. TTTS

Peacock and Nightingale. Robert Finch. OBCV

Peacock "At Home," The. Catherine Ann Dorset. OxBChV

"Peacock colored tears and rotten oranges." Midnight on Front Street. Roberta Hill. CDW

Peacock in Leucadia loved a maid, A. From Burton the Anatomist. Maurice James Craig. NeIP

Peacock Room, The. Robert Hayden. FB

Peacock Woman, The. László Nagy, *tr. fr. Hungarian by* George MacBeth. MHuP

Peacocks. Walter Adolphe Roberts. PVCV

Peacock's Feather, A. Seamus Heaney. DiPo

Peacock's golden-threaded tail fans out behind him, The. Eight-Beat Barbarian Tune. Sun Kuang-hsien, *tr. by* Lois Fusek. ATF

Peak, The. W. W. Gibson. PoSH

Peak and Puke. Walter de la Mare. Mes

Peaks, The. Stephen Crane. *Fr.* War Is Kind, XVIII. AA; WGRP

Peanut sat on a railroad track, A. Toot! Toot! *Unknown.* RHPC

Peanuts. Ken Belford. NeAC

Peanuts. *Unknown.* FaFP

Pear, The. Vinícius de Moraes, *tr. fr. Portuguese by* Ashley Brown. ATCBP

Pear blossoms. Mizuhara Shuoshi, *tr. by* Geoffrey Bownas *and* Anthony Thwaite. PeBJV

Pear blossoms drift through the garden like fragrant snow. Deva-like Barbarian. Mao Hsi-chen, *tr. by* Lois Fusek. ATF

Pear Tree. Hilda Doolittle ("H. D."). BoWoP; CMoP; MoAmPo; NOBA; PoE; UnPo
Pear-Tree, The. Mary Gilmore. PoAu-1
Pear-Tree, The. Iwan Goll, *tr. fr. German by* Babette Deutsch *and* Avram Yarmolinsky. TrJP
Pear Tree, The. Edna St. Vincent Millay. MoAmPo
Pear-Tree, The. *Unknown, tr. fr. Chinese by* Allen Upward. *Fr.* Shi King. AWP
Pear-Tree, The. *Unknown. See* I Have a New Garden.
Pear tree, more dead than alive, The. Markers. Frank Steele. GOYP
Pearl. Barbara Brinson Curiel. ER
Pearl, The. George Herbert. EBEV; HAP; JCP; MePo; NOCV; OAEL-1; PoEL-2; SeCP
  (Pearl, The. Matth. 13.) SeCV-1
Pearl, *sels. Unknown.*
  "Perle, plesaunte to prynces paye." EBEV, *sts.* 1-5.
  Queen of Courtesy, The, *sts.* 36-8 ACP
Pearl Avenue runs past the high-school lot. Ex-Basketball Player. John Updike. ASP; InPK; NYBP; SM
Pearl Bryan. *Unknown.* AmFP
Pearl Harbor Day 1970. Dick Lourie. NeAC
Pearl of the sea! Star of the West! On Leaving Cuba, Her Native Land. Gertrudis Gomez de Avellaneda, *tr. by* Catherine Rodriguez-Nieto. WPOW
Pearl Perch. John Blight. CBAP
Pearl-teardrops roll and gather. Huang E, *tr. by* Jonathan Chaves. CoBLCP
Pearl, The. Matth. 13. George Herbert. *See* Pearl, The.
Pearls plucked,/ the oyster shells. Saigyo, *tr. fr. Japanese by* Burton Watson. *Fr.* Sixty-four Tanka. FCEI
Pearly and opaque boy, it was to you. For My Brother Who Died before I Was Born. Baron Wormser. GOYP
Pearly Beads. *Gond Oral Tradition, tr. by* V. Elwin *and* S. Hivale. WTO
Pearly Everlasting, The. Ernest Fewster. CaP
Pears, The. Ferreira Gullar, *tr. fr. Portuguese by* William Jay Smith. CT
Pears. Linda Pastan. VWA
Peas. *Unknown. See* I eat my peas with honey.
Peasant. W. S. Merwin. NYBP
Peasant, A. R. S. Thomas. OBWVE
Peasant, The. Leonard Wolf. NYBP
Peasant and Ox. Shin Dong-jip, *tr. fr. Korean by* Koh Chang-soo. ACKP
Peasant and the Sheep, The. Ivan Andreevich Kriloff, *tr. fr. Russian by* C. Fillingham Coxwell. AWP
Peasant Declares His Love, The. Emile Roumer, *tr. fr. French by* John Peale Bishop. ErPo; TTY
Peasant haled a sheep to court, A. The Peasant and the Sheep. Ivan Andreevich Kriloff, *tr. by* C. Fillingham Coxwell. AWP
Peasant Poet, The. John Clare. OAEL-2; OBNC; WGRP
Peasant stood before a king and said, A. Ahab Mohammed. James Matthew Legaré. AA
Peasant sun went crushing grapes, The. Laurence Dakin. *Fr.* Tancred, I, i. CaP
Peasants, The. Alun Lewis. LiTM
Peasants get off the mail trains, The. Market Day. Roberto Roversi, *tr. by* Lawrence R. Smith. NItP
Peasants my forebears were. Forebears. Monk Gibbon. NeIP
Peasant's Song, The. *Unknown. See* When Adam delf. . .
Pease porridge [*or* pudding] hot. Mother Goose. FaFP; OxNR, (2 *vers.*)
Pebble, The. Zbigniew Herbert, *tr. fr. Polish by* Czeslaw Milosz. PwPP
Pebble, The. Elinor Wylie. MoAmPo
Pebbles. Edith King. BoTP
Pebbles/ at ebbtide numberless. My Faces. Gyorgy Raba, *tr. by* Jascha Kessler. FOC
Peblis to the Play. *Unknown.* GoTS
Pecan, The Toucan, The. Robert Williams Wood. NBLV
Peck of Gold, A. Robert Frost. PDV; SO
Pedagogical Principles. Harry Amoss. CaP
Peddler,/ the first watch of night. Ravidas, *tr. by* John Stratton Hawley *and* Mark Juergensmeyer. SSI
Peddler,/ the fourth watch of night. Ravidas, *tr. by* John Stratton Hawley *and* Mark Juergensmeyer. SSI
Peddler,/ the second watch of night. Ravidas, *tr. by* John Stratton Hawley *and* Mark Juergensmeyer. SSI
Peddler,/ the third watch of night. Ravidas, *tr. by* John Stratton Hawley *and* Mark Juergensmeyer. SSI
Peddler and His Wife, The. *Unknown.* AmFP
Peddler's Song, A. *Unknown. See* Fine Knacks for Ladies.
Pedestrian. Thomas Lux. NAmP

Pedestrian's Plaint, The. Edward Verrall Lucas. CenHV
Pedigree. Mary Mills. NePoAm
Pedigree of honey, The. Emily Dickinson. BLPL; FaBV; MoP; NOBA
Pedlar. Confucius, *tr. fr. Chinese by* Ezra Pound. *Fr.* Wei Wind. CTC; OBVE
Pedlar. Sharon Nelson. VWA
Pedlar, The. Shakespeare. *See* Winter's Tale, The: Autolycus as Peddler.
Pedlar Jim. Florence Hoare. BoTP
Pedlar of Small-Wares, A. Sir John Suckling. CaPo
Pedlar's Caravan, The. William Brighty Rands. BoTP; OxBChV
Pedlar's Song, The. Shakespeare. *See* Winter's Tale, The: Autolycus as Peddler.
Pedlar's Song, The. Shakespeare. *See* Winter's Tale, The: When daffodils begin to peer.
Pedra. John William Burgon. BLPA
Pedro. Phoebe W. Hoffman. GoYe
Pedro. Luis Omar Salinas. FF
Peekaboo, I Almost See You. Ogden Nash. PoLF
Peel off me. Incantation to Get Rid of a Sometime Friend. Emanuel DiPasquale. TW
Peeler and the Goat, The. *Unknown.* AnIL
Peeler, hast thou found my treasure. I've Lost My———. Henry Cholmondeley-Pennell. CenHV
Peeler's Lament, The. *Unknown.* WTO
Peeling Onions. Adrienne Rich. BoWoP; HCAP; TAP
Peeling pears/ sweet juice drips. Masaoka Shiki, *tr. fr. Japanese by* Burton Watson. *Fr.* Thirty-nine Haiku. FCEI
Peeling Pears at Midnight. Lo Fu, *tr. fr. Chinese by* Dominic Cheung. IFON
Peeling Pippins. Mary TallMountain. HATNAP
Peeper, The. Peter Davidson. ErPo
Peepin' through the knothole. Go Get the Axe. *Unknown.* AS
Peeping Tom. Francis Hope. ErPo
Peer of the gods is that man, who. Sappho, *tr. fr. Greek by* William Carlos Williams. OBVE
Peer of the golden gods is he to Sappho. Ode to Anactoria. Sappho, *tr. by* William Ellery Leonard. AWP
Peering at the stars. Chora, *tr. by* Geoffrey Bownas *and* Anthony Thwaite. PeBJV
Peering into your stout you see a past of lazybeds. The Left-Behind. Louis MacNeice. *Fr.* A Hand of Snapshots. FaBCIP
Peerless are the gems. Prince Ichihara. *Fr.* Manyo Shu. Ma
Peerless yet hopeless maid of Q. Miss Ellen Gee of Kew. *Unknown.* FaBoNo
Pees maketh plente. Peace. *Unknown.* MeEL
Peeter a Whitfeild he hath slaine. Jock o' the Side. *Unknown.* ESPB
Peg of Limavaddy. Thackeray. OBTV
Pegasos are steaming, The. Winter Rains: Cataluña. Philip Levine. NaP
Pegasus. Patrick Kavanagh. MoAB
Pegasus Lost. Elinor Wylie. MoAmPo
Peggy. Allan Ramsay. *See* Gentle Shepherd, The: My Peggy [Is a Young Thing].
Peggy Browne. Turlough Carolan, *tr. fr. Irish by* Austin Clarke. BIrV
Peggy Said Good Morning. John Clare. ELP
Pei-mang Cemetery. Yüan Hung-tao, *tr. fr. Chinese by* Jonathan Chaves. CoBLCP
Peire Salvatge, it's the flowers. Pedro III, King of Aragon, *tr. by* Paul Blackburn. Pro
Pelican, The. Greg Kuzma. AmPA
Pelican Chorus, The. Edward Lear. FaBoNo
Pelicans. Robinson Jeffers. FM; MoAmPo
Pelleas and Ettarre. Tennyson. *Fr.* Idylls of the King. NAEL-2
  "Rose, but one, none other rose had I, A." PoEL-5
Pellucid moon, The. Gyoko, *tr. by* Steven D. Carter. WFTW
Pelops and Hippodamia, *sel.* Matthew Grove.
  In Praise of His Lady. EIL
Pelters of Pyramids. Richard Henry Horne. OBTV
Pen, The. Muhammad al-Ghuzzi, *tr. fr. Arabic by* May Jayyusi *and* John Heath-Stubbs. MAP
Pen, The. Mary Weston Fordham. CBWP-2
Pen-guin sits up-on the shore, The. A Penguin. Oliver Herford. FiBHP
Pen-guin. The Sword-fish, The. Robert Williams Wood. NBLV
Pen Hy Cane ("Pen Hyrogliphic Cane"). Mason Jordan Mason. PoNe
"Pen is mightier than the sword, The." A Feather's Weight. G. P. Lathrop. FaBoUs
Pen-knife, quills, ink-horn, books, paper, table-books, caps; take. Verses to Be Repeated by an Attorney Leaving His Lodging to Wait upon Judges Riding the Circuits from One County to Another, Least He Forget Some Necessary Thing. John Willis. FaBoUs

Pen Pal. Carl Dennis. BLA
Pen stops in a phrase of a letter home, The. Music in the Rec Hut. Hubert Creekmore. WaP
Penal Law. Austin Clarke. BoLoP; GTBS-P; IPY; NOIV
Penal Rock: Altamuskin. John Montague. FaBCIP
Penal Servitude for Mrs. Maybrick. *Unknown.* OxBoLi
Penalties of Baldness, The. Sir Owen Seaman. FiBHP
Penalty of Virtue, The. *Unknown, tr. fr Sanskrit by* Arthui Ryder. *Fr.* The Panchatantra. AWP
Pencil and Paint. Eleanor Farjeon. PDV
Pencilled by the Rain. Peter Hooper. PeNZ
Pencil's Dream, The. Tymoteusz Karpowicz, *tr. fr. Polish by* Czeslaw Milosz. PwPP
Pendant Watch. Madeline DeFrees. NMM
Pendydd. Kingsley Amis. *Fr.* The Evans Country. NOBL
Penelope. Janet Dubé. DT
Penelope. James Harrison. NIP
Penelope, *sels.* Monique Laederach, *tr. fr. French by* Charles Guenther. BoWoP
"And so I speak/ in place of that primordial cry."
"Leaving the island, she believes, to go to the child."
Penelope. Ursula Vaughn Williams. CN
Penelope as a *garçon manqué.* Mythology. Marilyn Hacker. NoAM
Penelope pulls home. Kiltartan Legend. Padraic Fallon. NOIV
Penelope's Despair. Yannis Ritsos, *tr. fr. Greek by* Edmund Keeley. AnAn
P'eng That Was a K'un, The. *At. to* Chuang Tzu, *tr. fr. Chinese by* Robert Graves. AmMo
Penguin, A. Oliver Herford. FiBHP
Penguin hailed me at the door, A. Penguins in the Home. Helen Smith Bevington. OBAL
Penguin on the Beach. Ruth Miller. PeSA
Penguins in the Home. Helen Smith Bevington. OBAL
Peninsula, The. Seamus Heaney. FaBCIP
Penitent, The. Edna St. Vincent Millay. AnAmPo
Penitent, The. Jeremy Taylor. OBS
Penitent Considers Another Coming of Mary, A. Gwendolyn Brooks. NoAM; PChr
Penitent Nun, The. John Lockman. ErPo
Penitent Palmer's Ode, The. Robert Greene. *Fr.* Francesco's Fortunes. OBSC
Penitential Psalm to the Goddess Anunit: "May the wrath of the heart of my god be pacified!" *Unknown, tr. fr. Babylonian.* WGRP
Penitents. Bernice Zamora. CCP
Penniless Indian fakirs and their camels, The. Avarice. Anthony Hecht. OxBSP
Pennines in April. Ted Hughes. PPP
Pennsylvania Deutsch. Christopher Morley. NBLV
Pennsylvania Places. Thomas Augustin Daly. OBAL
Pennsylvania Song. *Unknown.* PAH
Pennsylvania Station. Langston Hughes. AmNP
Pennsylvania Winter Indian 1974. Harold Littlebird. VoR
Penny and penny. *Unknown.* OxNR
Penny is heavier than the shrew, A. The Masked Shrew. Isabella Gardner. ImOP
Penny lost in the lak, The. *Unknown. Fr.* Colkelbie Sow. OxBS
Penny Trumpet. Raphael Rudnik. MAT; NYBP
Penny Whistle, The. Edward Thomas. MoAB; MoBrPo
Penny Wish, A. Irene Thompson. BoTP
Pennycandystore beyond the El, The. Lawrence Ferlinghetti. *Fr.* A Coney Island of the Mind. CAPP; HeIP; PoM; TAP
Penological Study: Southern Exposure, *sel.* Robert Penn Warren. Wet Hair: If Now His Mother Should Come. *Fr.* III. NoAM
Pensioners. W. M. Letts. BoTP
Pensionnaires. Paul Verlaine, *tr. fr. French by* François Pirou. PeHV
Pensive at Eve. Samuel Taylor Coleridge. *Fr.* Sonnets Attempted in the Manner of Contemporary Writers. Son
Pensive gnu, the staid aardvark, The. For an Amorous Lady. Theodore Roethke. NBLV
Pensive here I sat. Milton. *Fr.* Paradise Lost, *bk.* II, *ll.* 777–807. OBD
Pensive, on Her Dead Gazing, I Heard the Mother of All. Walt Whitman. RB
Pensy Ant, right trig and clean, A. The Caterpillar and the Ant. Allan Ramsay. SeCePo
Pentachromatic. Julia de Burgos, *tr. by* Julio Marzán. InW
Pentagonia. G. E. Bates. NYBP
Pentecost. Ai. GeTw
Pentecost. Adelbert Sumpter Coats. TrPWD
Pentecost Castle, The. Geoffrey Hill. HAP

Penthesileia. Robert Graves. OBD
Pentland Hills, The. *Unknown.* GBP
Pentucket. Whittier. PAH
Penumbra. Pierre Louÿs, *tr. fr. French. Fr.* Chansons de Bilitis. PeHV
Penurious Quaker; or, The High Priz'd Harlot, The. *Unknown.* CoMu
Penus envy, they call it. Alta. NMM
Peonage System, The. Lizelia Augusta Jenkins Moorer. CBWP-3
Peonies below the stairs, The. Yüan Mei, *tr. fr. Chinese by* Jonathan Chaves. *Fr.* In Late Spring of the Year *Keng-hsü.* CoBLCP
Peonies blooming on paired pillows. Written on a Boat on the Ch'ien-t'ang River. Hung Liang-chi, *tr. by* Irving Lo. WFTU
Peony. Jackie Kay. DT
Peony Fallen. Buson *and* Kito, *tr. fr. Japanese by* Sato. FCEI
Peony for Apollo, A. Charles Edward Eaton. GoYe
Peony in a wide garden. Buson, *tr. fr. Japanese by* Hiroaki Sato. *Fr.* Eighty-seven Hokku. FCEI
People, The. Tomasso Campanella, *tr. fr. Italian by* John Addington Symonds. AWP; PFI
People, The. Robert Creeley. VGW
People, The. Thomas Ince. PF
People. Orban Veli Kanik, *tr. fr. Turkish by* Talat Sait Halman. LLLT
People. X. J. Kennedy. SoTCo
People. D. H. Lawrence. BrPo
People. Lois Lenski. FaPON
People, The. Elizabeth Madox Roberts. GoJo; RHPC
People, The. W. B. Yeats. CMoP
People. Yevgeny Yevtushenko, *tr. fr. Russian by* Robin Milner-Gulland *and* Peter Levi. DL
People. Charlotte Zolotow. RHPC
People,/ male and female. Mahadevi, *tr. by* A. K. Ramanujan. BoWoP
People all over the world want proof of death. Sunken Temple. Tamura Ryuichi, *tr. by* Hiroaki Sato. FCEI
People all say the southland's better. Tune: Deva-like Barbarian. Wei Chuang, *tr. by* Burton Watson. CoBCP
People along the sand, The. Neither Out Far nor In Deep. Robert Frost. AmPP; ChTr; HAP; LiTA; MoAB; MoP; MOS; NAAL-2; NoAM; NOBA; NoP; TAP; WeW
People always say to me. The Question. Karla Kuskin. NTCP; PDV
People always tell me things. Me and Hercule Poirot. Deborah Kendrick. TSM
People are different. John Montague. *Fr.* The Well Dreams. PoPo
People are making a camp of branches in that country at Arnhem Bay, The. The Moon-Bone Song. *Unknown, tr. by* Ronald M. Berndt. CBAP
People are putting up storm windows now. Storm Windows. Howard Nemerov. InPK
People are saying that I am your enemy, The. To Julia de Burgos. Julia de Burgos, *tr. by* Grace Schulman. BoWoP; PBWP
People arrive to worship in their church. The Church. Jules Romains, *tr. by* Jethro Bithell. WGRP
People Buy a Lot of Things. Annette Wynne. PDV
People chained to aurora, A. Civilization and Its Discontents. John Ashbery. LCAP; TwCP
People comment on my cold fingers. Finger to Finger. Elizabeth Smither. ATNZ
People did die in our neighborhood. Suburban. H. R. Coursen. GOYP
People die from loneliness. One. Carolyn M. Rodgers. BPo
People do gossip. Sappho, *tr. by* Mary Barnard. PBWP
People expect old men to die. Old Men. Ogden Nash. AnAmPo; InPS; RB
People Getting Divorced. Lawrence Ferlinghetti. NoAM
People going home. Masaoka Shiki, *tr. fr. Japanese by* Burton Watson. *Fr.* Thirty-nine Haiku. FCEI
People going straight up to heaven. Amazing Grace. Anselm Hollo. PoM
People have got used to her, The. Home. Karen Gershon. CN
People I love the best, The. To Be of Use. Marge Piercy. CAPP; GeTw
People in These Houses, The. Jack Matthews. KS
People is a beast of muddy brain, The. The People. Tomasso Campanella, *tr. by* John Addington Symonds. AWP; PFI
People know, The. A Little More about the Brothers and Sisters. Sharon Scott. JB
People live forever in Jacksonville and St. Petersburg and Tampa. Come On in, the Senility Is Fine. Ogden Nash. AiP
People look at me and say. The Attaché Case. George Bogin. PPR
People made a ring, The. The Hemorrhage. Stanley Kunitz. WaP
People married by pictures then. Relocation. David Mura. BrSi
People need poetry, The. Osip Mandelstam. Seamus Heaney. FaBoPV
People of Blakeney, The. *Unknown.* GBP

People of My Country, The. Salah Abd al-Sabur, *tr. fr. Arabic by* Lena Jayyusi *and* John Heath-Stubbs. MAP
People of our race were created by heaven, The. *Unknown, tr. by* Arthur Waley. BoS
People of Spain think Cervantes, The. E. C. Bentley. *Fr.* Clerihews. CenHV; FiBHP
People of Tao-chou, The. Po Chü-i, *tr. fr. Chinese by* Arthur Waley. ChTr
People of the Future. Ted Berrigan. UL
People of the hundred-acre palace, The. Teika, *tr. fr. Japanese by* Hiroaki Sato. *Fr.* A Compendium of Good Tanka. FCEI
People of the South Wind. William Stafford. NNaP
People on This Beach Will Never, The. Yehuda Amichai, *tr. fr. Hebrew by* Bernhard Frank. MHeP
People—people of my kind, my own, The. To the Lacedemonians. Allen Tate. NAAL-2; NoAM
People say the sun is in heaven. Hsieh Chin, *tr. fr. Chinese by* Jonathan Chaves. *Fr.* What Does the Little Boy Love?, II. CoBLCP
People say they have a hard time. For de Lawd. Lucille Clifton. CNA; PoBA; TAP; TwCP
People spoiled by too many masters. Poetics. André Spire, *tr. by* Edouard Roditi. VWA
People throng the sun-lit Palace-road. Hitomaro. *Fr.* Manyo Shu. Ma
People Trying to Love. Stephen Berg. NaP
People upstairs, The. Ogden Nash. RHPC
People vs. the People, The. Kenneth Fearing. MoAmPo
People wake up in the morning. From My Royzele's Diary. Moyshe-Leyb Halpern, *tr. by* Benjamin *and* Barbara Harshav *and* Kathryn Helle. AYP
People walk upon their heads, The. Topsy-turvy Land. H. E. Wilkinson. BoTP
People Went to War, The. Antonio Jacinto, *tr. fr. Portuguese by* Margaret Dickinson. WMBCH
People were bathing and posturing themselves on the beach. The Gods! The Gods! D. H. Lawrence. CMoP
People who buy flowers in Ch'ang-an. Song of Selling Flowers. Tsung Ch'en, *tr. by* Jonathan Chaves. CoBLCP
People Who Died. Ted Berrigan. UL
People who have no children can be bard. The Children of the Poor. Gwendolyn Brooks. *Fr.* The Womanhood, I. PoA, *complete;* WPE, 1 *and* 2.
    What Shall I Give. BPo, 2 *only.*
People Who Must. Carl Sandburg. PDV
People Who Talk to Themselves. Berysh Vaynshteyn, *tr. fr. Yiddish by* Benjamin *and* Barbara Harshav. *Fr.* New York Everywhere. AYP
People who want to live beside the ocean are fundamentalists. Lakes. David Donnell. NoAM
People will live on, The. Carl Sandburg. *Fr.* The People, Yes, *Sec.* 107. MoAB; MoAmPo; NoAM; NOBA; OxBA; TrGrPo
People Will Talk. Samuel Dodge. WBLP
People, Yes, The, *sels.* Carl Sandburg.
    "Englishman in the old days, An." *Fr. Sec.* 11. FYAP
    "From the four corners of the earth." *Fr. Sec.* 1. CMoP
    "People will live on, The." *Fr. Sec.* 107. MoAB; MoAmPo; NoAM; NOBA; OxBA; TrGrPo
    "They have yarns." *Fr. Sec.* 45. AmFN; LiTA; MoAmPo
    "What the people learn out of lifting and hauling." *Fr. Sec.* 32. OBAL
    "Who shall speak for the people?" *Fr. Sec.* 24. OxBA
    "Why did the children." *Fr. Sec.* 41. OBAL
    "Why repeat? I heard you the first time." *Fr. Sec.* 42. OBAL
People's Attorney, servant of the Right! Wendell Phillips. Amos Bronson Alcott. AA
People's Literary, De. Maggie Pogue Johnson. CBWP-4
People's Prayer, The. Amos Russel Wells. OPP
People's Sabbath Prayer, The. Ebenezer Elliott. PF
People's voices: returning by this road as autumn ends. Basho, *tr. fr. Japanese by* Burton Watson. *Fr.* Seventy-six Hokku. FCEI
People's wrath finds no expression, The. N. M. Yazykov, *tr. by* Alan Myers. AAA
Pep. Grace G. Bostwick. WBLP
Pepita, my paragon, bright star of Arragon. Saragossa. Henry Sambrooke Leigh. FaBoCo
Peppergrass. Stanley Plumly. LCAP
Peppertrees, the peppertrees, The! Scenes from the Life of the Peppertrees. Denise Levertov. LiTM; NeAP; NoP; PoM
Peppery Man, The. Arthur Macy. FaPON
Pepsi Generation. Walasse Ting. MAT
Per Ardua ad Astra. John Oxenham. TrPWD

Per Iter Tenebricosum. Oliver St. John Gogarty. AnIL; OBMV
Per Pacem ad Lucem. Adelaide Anne Procter. TrPWD
Perambulator Poems, I-VII, *sel.* David McCord.
    When I Was Christened. *Fr.* V. OBCA
    (Perambulator Poem.) OFD
Perception of an object costs. Emily Dickinson. NOBA
Perchance in days to come. Strange Love. Moses Ibn Ezra, *tr. by* Solomon Solis-Cohen. TrJP
Perchance she died in age—surviving all. Rome by Metella's Tomb. Byron. *Fr.* Childe Harold's Pilgrimage, IV. FaBoPP
Perchance some coming after. Strato, *tr. by* Sydney Oswald. PeHV
Perchance that I might learn what pity is. A Prayer for Purification. Buonarroti Michelangelo, *tr. by* John Addington Symonds. AWP
Perchance, the friend who cheered thy early years. Judge Not. Josephine D. Henderson Heard. CBWP-4
Perched in a tower of this ancestral wall. At the Great Wall of China. Edmund Blunden. GTBS-P
Perched on a birch stump. The Hooded Crow. Rennie McOwan. PoSH
Perched on a great fall of air. Landscape with Figures. Keith Douglas. NePoEA
Percivale's Quest. Tennyson. *Fr.* Idylls of the King: The Holy Grail. OAEL-2
Percolating Highway. Michael Castro. VWA
Percussions. Ron Welburn. CNA
Percussive, furious, this wind. Mistral. Barbara Howes. NYBP
Percy/ 68. Glenn Myles. NBP
Percy Shelley. John Peale Bishop. ErPo
Perdita. Florence Earle Coates. AA
Perdita. Louis MacNeice. PoA
Perdition. Aimé Césaire, *tr. fr. French by* Clayton Eshleman *and* Annette Smith. RHTwFP
Perdy [*or* Perdie *or* Perdye]! I said[e] it [*or* yt] not. Constancy. Sir Thomas Wyatt. OBSC; SiPS
    (Perdye I Saide Yt Not.) PoEL-1
Père Lalement. Marjorie Pickthall. CaP; NOBC; OBCV
Peregrine. Elinor Wylie. BLPL
Peregrine Prykke's Pilgrimage, *sel.* Clive James.
    "Blood has soaked the bone which hides the stone, The." FaBoPa
Peregrine White and Virginia Dare. Rosemary *and* Stephen Vincent Benét. OBCA
Peregrine's Sunday Song. Elinor Wylie. NYBP
Perennial fluctuation. Cuvier Light. Pat Wilson. ATNZ
Perennials. Judith Kitchen. KS
Perfect. Philippe Jaccottet, *tr. fr. French by* Paul Auster. RHTwFP
Perfect. "Hugh MacDiarmid." RB
Perfect Bliss and Sole Felicity. Christopher Marlowe. *See* Tamburlaine the Great: Nature That Framed Us of Four Elements.
Perfect Child, The. Adrian Porter. NBLV
Perfect Day, A. Carrie Jacobs Bond. WBLP
Perfect dear whom no one blames, The. Lady Sara Bunbury Sacrificing to the Graces, by Reynolds. Daryl Hine. EyDe
Perfect Disc of the Moon, The. Richard Kenney. Son
Perfect Garden, The. Winifred Robertson. PoSH
Perfect Gift, The. Edmund Vance Cooke. PChr
Perfect Husband, The. Ogden Nash. FaBoUs
Perfect ice of the thin keys must break, The. Piano. Karl Shapiro. RR
Perfect is the word I can never hear. Rhymes. Charles Tomlinson. DiPo
Perfect little body, without fault or stain on thee. On a Dead Child. Robert Bridges. BrPo; CMoP; EBEV; LiTB; LiTM; NoAM; NOBE; NOBVV; OBMV; OBNC
Perfect love is nourished by despair, A. George Santayana. *Fr.* Sonnets. AnAmPo
Perfect melody—like wind. Listening to the Lute. Jakuan, *tr. by* Lucien Stryk *and* Takashi Ikemoto. ZPCJ
Perfect Mother, The. Susan Griffin. NPGG
Perfect Orchestra, The. Henrietta Cordelia Ray. CBWP-3
Perfect rainbow, A! a wide. The Storm. William Carlos Williams. PCP
Perfect Reactionary, The. Hughes Mearns. NTCP
Perfect Symbol, The. Louis Johnson. ATNZ
Perfect way out, The. Getsudo, *tr. by* Lucien Stryk *and* Takashi Ikemoto. ZPCJ
Perfect Woman. Wordsworth. *See* She Was a Phantom of Delight.
Perfection. Francis Carlin. FaFP
Perfection. Ernst Jandl, *tr. fr. German by* Beth Bjorklund. CoAuP
Perfection, if't hath ever been attayned. In the Due Honor of the Author Master Robert Norton. John Smith. SCAP

Perfection is terrible, it cannot have children. The Munich Mannequins. Sylvia Plath. CAPP; NaP
Perfection, of a kind, was what he was after. Epitaph on a Tyrant. W. H. Auden. HeIP; NoAM; OxBSP; RB
Perfection of Dentistry, The. Marvin Bell. AmPA; CoAP
Perfection of Snow, The. Andrea Zanzotto, tr. fr. Italian by Lawrence R. Smith. NItP
Perfectly happy now, he looked at his estate. Voltaire at Ferney. W. H. Auden. LiTA, LiTM; PoA
Perfectly useless concentration, A. Matadero, Riley and Company. Paul Mariani. BLA
Perfervid Roc, sitting on candle light, The. The Roc. Richard Eberhart. CMoP
Perforated Spirit, The. Morris Bishop. FiBHP
Performance, The. James Dickey. CAPP; CoAP; LiTM; MoP; NePoEA-2; NOBA; PoE
Performance at Hog Theater, A. Russell Edson. AmPA
Performances, assortments, résumés. The Tunnel. Hart Crane. Fr. The Bridge, VII. CMoP; MAT; MoAB; MoAmPo; OxBA
Performing military service for the king and bearing a child. "Oilfish" to "Old Chap" for "C." Tina Darragh. LP
Performing Seal, The. Rachel Field. Fr. A Circus Garland. OBCA; RHPC
Perfume, The. John Donne. Fr. Elegies, IV. SeCP
Perfume, The. Robert Herrick. CaPo
Perfume like an acid sword, A. Youth. Pablo Neruda, tr. by Perry Higman. LPSS
Pergamon city of the Phrygians. The Aftermath. Euripides, tr. fr. Greek by Richmond Lattimore. Fr. Iphigenia [or Iphigeneia] in Aulis. WaaP
Perhaps. Lucille Clifton. CAPP; GeTw
Perhaps. Sydney Thompson Dobell. NOBVV
Perhaps. Rachel, tr. fr. Hebrew by A. C. Jacobs. VWA
Perhaps/ You will remember/ John Brown. October 16: The Raid. Langston Hughes. PoBA
Perhaps/ This is the way. Antigone I. Herbert Martin. PoBA
Perhaps biography is the flat map. Biography. Maura Stanton. MAYP
Perhaps, Cape Karasaki of Shiga. Toneri Kine. Fr. Manyo Shu. Ma
Perhaps Eve in the garden knew the sun. The Fortunate Fall. Alfred Alvarez. VWA
Perhaps I may allow, the Dean. Swift. Fr. Verses on the Death of Doctor Swift [D.S.P.D., Occasioned by Reading a Maxim in Rochefoucauld]. NOBE
Perhaps I was meant to travel with my kind. Kong Hits the Road with Dan-Dee Carnivals, Inc. William Trowbridge. SoTCo
Perhaps if we could begin some definite way. A Bird Sings to Establish Frontiers. Jack Gilbert. NPGG
Perhaps, if you/ Are very good. Hob the Elf. Norman M. Johnson. BoTP
Perhaps it is God. J. L. Teller, tr. by Benjamin and Barbara Harshav. AYP
Perhaps it is to avoid some great sadness. Sleeping on the Wing. Frank O'Hara. InPS; NAAL-2; SOTW
Perhaps it is well now. We Who Are Left. George Whalley. CaP
Perhaps it was because. Nightswim. William Pitt Root. MAYP
Perhaps it was never so. Perhaps. Rachel, tr. by A. C. Jacobs. VWA
Perhaps it will melt into our lifeblood. Possibilities of Snow. Cheng Wen-tao. WCI
Perhaps It's as You Say. Peter Everwine. NNaP
Perhaps It's Only Music. Natan Zach, tr. fr. Hebrew by Peter Everwine and Shula Starkman. VWA
Perhaps, long hence, when I have pass'd away. She, to Him. Thomas Hardy. OBEV; OxBTC
Perhaps on a sunday. Day Song. Lance Henson. HATNAP
Perhaps she said, lively at first but once. Farmer Goes Beserk. Anne Elder. CBAP
Perhaps some needful service to the state. Gabriella Chiabrero, tr. by Wordsworth. Fr. Epitaphs. AWP
Perhaps the Best Time. William Meredith. NePoEA
Perhaps the Socrates he had never read. Why Hast Thou Forsaken Me? Chad Walsh. Fr. The Psalm of Christ. TrCP
Perhaps this valley too leads into the head of long-ago days. Grand Abacus. John Ashbery. EAS; PoA
Perhaps—well/ It may not matter! Men's Impotence. Unknown. WTO
Perhaps you expected a face that was free from tears. Narcissus. Paul Valéry, tr. by Joseph T. Shipley. AWP
Perhaps you shouldn't be sad because of what happened. The Crab-Legged Flower. Lo Fu, tr. by Dominic Cheung. IFON

Perhaps you were thinking of leaving. The Witch Sycorax Addresses Her Lover. Vicki Raymond. UAS
Pericles, sels. Shakespeare.
"Terrible childbed hast thou had, my dear, A." Fr. III, i. EBEV
Thou God of This Great Vast, Rebuke These Surges. Fr. III, i. MOS; NAs
Pericles and Aspasia, sels. Walter Savage Landor.
Behold, O Aspasia! I Send You Verses. Fr. CXC. OBNC
Corinna, from Athens, to Tanagra. Fr. XLIV. OBEV
(Corinna to Tanagra.) OBNC
(Corinna, to Tanagra, from Athens.) NOBE
Death of Artemidora, The. Fr. LXXXV. EnRP; OBNC
Dirce. Fr. CCXXX. AWP; CTC; EBEV; EnRP; FaBoEE; GBL; HAP; LiTB; NOBE; NoP; OAEL-2; OBEV; OBNC; OxBSP; PoEL-4; PoRA; TrGrPo; WeW
(Stand Close Around.) ChTr
Perilous Love Affair, A. Saigyo, tr. fr. Japanese by Burton Watson. Fr. Sixty-four Tanka. FCEI
Perils and the dangers of the voyage being past, The. Jack Robinson. Unknown. OBET
Perils of Obesity, The. Harry Graham. FiBHP
Perimedes [or Perimedes, the Blacksmith], sels. Robert Greene.
Coridon and Phillis. OBSC
Fair Is My Love. ElL
Period of Mourning, The, sel. Henry Peacham.
Nuptial Hymn. ElL
Periods of Adjustment. Shawn Wong. BrSi
Periphery. A. R. Ammons. NOBA
Periphrastic Insult, Not a Banal, A. J. V. Cunningham. TW
Peri's Lament for Hinda, The. Thomas Moore. Fr. Lalla Rookh. OBNC
Perishing Bird, The. Douglas G. Jones. MoCV
Perle, plesaunte to prynces paye. Unknown. Fr. Pearl. EBEV, sts. 1-5.
Permanence in Change. Goethe, tr. by John Frederick Nims. HoPM
Permanence in the sea of life, The. Nawab Mirza Khan Dagh, tr. by Ahmed Ali. GoT
Permanence of the Young Men, The. William Soutar. OxBS
Permanent occasion, A. Winter Garden. Donald Britton. EOEF
Permanent Tourists, The. Patricia K. Page. LiTM; NOBC
Permanently. Kenneth Koch. CoAP; NoP; PoA; PoM; PPP
Permission to Speak. Steve Orlen. MAYP
Permit me here a simple brief aside. To Calliope. Robert Graves. CMoP
Permit Me Voyage. James Agee. MoAmPo
Permit Us, Lord, to Consecrate. Joseph Green. AH
Permitted to assist you, let me see. St. Valentine. Marianne Moore. NYBP; OFD
Peroration, Concerning Genius. Robert Pinsky. Fr. Essay on Psychiatrists, XX. NoAM
Perpetuum Immobile. Bruce Dawe. CBAP
Perplex'd with trifles thro' the vale of life. A Nut, a World, a Squirrel, and a King. Charles Churchill. Fr. Night; an Epistle to Robert Lloyd. FaBoRV
Perplexity. Ibrahim Tuqan, tr. fr. Arabic by Christopher Tingley and John Heath-Stubbs. MAP
Perry's Victory—A Song. Unknown. PAH
Perse owt of[f] Northombarlande, The. Chevy Chase. Unknown. OxBB
(Ancient Ballad of Chevy-Chase, The.) EnRP
(Hunting of the Cheviot, The.) ESPB
Persephone. Keith Abbott. UL
Persephone. Robert Duncan. NOBA
Persephone. Michael Longley. FaBCIP
Persephone, 5, Outside. Keith Abbott. UL
Persephone is the woman buried. Robert Kelly. Fr. The Book of Persephone, 11. PoM
Perseus. James Keir Baxter. ATNZ
Perseus. Robert Hayden. NoAM
Perseus. Louis MacNeice. LiTM
Pershing at the Tomb of Lafayette. Amelia Josephine Burr. PAH
Persia. Victoria Mary Sackville-West. WPE
Persian, The. Stevie Smith. FaBoWP
Persian Eclogue the Second. William Collins. FL
Persian flummery. Horace. See Odes: I, 38. Simplicity.
Persian Fopperies. Horace. See Odes: I, 38. Simplicity.
Persian galleys plumed with warriors, The. Before Salamis. William Bedell Stanford. NeIP
Persian Miniature. William Jay Smith. CoAP
Persian Parables, sel. Aleksander Wat, tr. fr. Polish by Czeslaw Milosz.
"By a great, swift water." PwPP

Persian pomps, boy, ever I renounce them. Horace. *See* Odes: I, 38. Simplicity.

Persian Song of Hafiz, A. Hafiz, *tr. fr. Persian by* Sir William Jones. AWP

Persian Version, The. Robert Graves. CMoP; FaBoCo; LiTB; LiTM; MoP; NoAM; NOBL; OBWP; WeW

Persians, The, *sel.* Aeschylus, *tr. fr. Greek by* G. M. Cookson. Salamis. WaaP

Persicos Odi: Pocket Version. Horace. *See* Odes: I, 38. Simplicity.

Persimmon Tree, The. *Unknown.* GBP

Persimmons and Plums. Elizabeth Hodges. GrPl

Persistence of Memory, the Failure of Poetry, The. Robert Phillips. GeTw

Persistence of Nature in Our Lives, The. Andrew Hudgins. DiPo

Persistent Explorer. John Crowe Ransom. OxBA

Person after person. Buddha's Birthday: April 8, 1819. Issa, *tr. fr. Japanese by* Nobuyuki Yuasa. Fr. Oraga Haru. OFD

Person can die of love, A. Lady Kasa. *Fr.* Manyo Shu. FCEI

Person from Porlock, A. R. S. Thomas. TOF

Person has/ two faces, A. Festival of the Blind. Ishigaki Rin, *tr. by* Sato. FCEI

Person I meet, A. Kenko, *tr. by* Steven D. Carter. WFTW

Person is very self-conscious about his head, A. Thoughts on One's Head. William Meredith. HAP

Person who can do, The. Alan Dugan. ErPo

Personal. Langston Hughes. AmNP; NOBA; PoNe

Personal. Samuel Yellen. NYBP

Personal Column. Tom Paulin. FaBCIP

Personal Helicon. Seamus Heaney. FaBCIP; IPY

Personal Opinion, A. Dahlia Ravikovich, *tr. fr. Hebrew by* Bernhard Frank. MHeP

Personal Poem. Ingrid Wendt. NMM

Personal Problems. David Avidan, *tr. fr. Hebrew by* Bernhard Frank. MHeP

Personal Reflections, *sel.* Ahmad al-Mushari al-Udwani, *tr. fr. Arabic by* Hilary Kilpatrick *and* Charles Doria.
"I asked the grave-digger, 'Do you have.'" MAP

Personal Song. Arnatkoak, *tr. fr. Eskimo.* WTO

Personal Talk. Wordsworth. EnRP; NOBE

Personal Values. Richard Howard. SM

Personality Sketch: Bill, A. Ronda Davis. JB

Personals. Leatrice W. Emeruwa. PCP

Personification of a Name, The. Ray A. Young Bear. HATNAP

Personified Sentimental, The. Bret Harte. NA

Person's life: width of a hand, A. Proportions. Arto Melleri, *tr. by* Aili Jarvenpa. SOP

Perspective. Margaret Avison. OBCV

Perspective. John H. Dromey. SoTCo

Perspective. Coventry Patmore. *Fr.* The Angel in the House, II, i. FaBoEE; GBL

Perspective. Pierre Reverdy, *tr. fr. French by* David Gascoyne. RHTwFP

Perspective and Limits of Snapshots, The. Dave Smith. MAYP

Perspective He Would Mutter Going to Bed. Jack Gilbert. NPGG

Perspective never withers from their eyes. Quaker Hill. Hart Crane. *Fr.* The Bridge, VI. LiTM; NAAL-2

Perspective of Co-ordination. Arthur Davison Ficke. PoA

Perspectives. Dudley Randall. AmNP

Perspectives Are Precipices. John Peale Bishop. LiTA

Persuasions to Enjoy. Thomas Carew. CaPo; MePo; NOBE; OBEV; SeCP; SeCV-1
(Persuasions to Joy; a Song.) OBEV
(Song: Persuasions [*or* Persuasions] to Enjoy.) CaPo; NAEL-1; SeCP

Perturbations of Uranus, The. Roy Fuller. ErPo

Peru, 1955. Ai. *Fr.* He Kept On Burning, III. AnAn

Peru was a chimera. Imperfect Times. Washington Delgado, *tr. by* Maureen Ahern *and* David Tipton. Per

Peruke of Poets. William Zaranka. BXAP

Perverse Custom, A. *Unknown, tr. fr. Latin by* John Boswell. PeHV

Perverse habit of cat goddesses, A. Cat Goddesses. Robert Graves. NYBP; OxBSP

Perversion interests me. Note Delivered by a Female Impersonator. Heather McHugh. AmPA

Perversity. Susan Griffin. LLLT

Pervigilium Veneris. Suzanne Noguere. PoA

Pesach Has Come to the Ghetto Again. Binem Heller, *tr. fr. Yiddish by* Max Rosenfeld. TrJP

Pesci Misti. Leonard Aaronson. FaBoTw

Pessimist, The. Ben King. AnAmPo; BLPA; FaBoCo; FaBoNo; FaFP; NA; NBLV; OBAL
(Sum of Life, The.) CTC

Pet Crane, A. *Unknown, tr. fr. Old Irish by* Myles Dillon. AnIL

Pet Deer, The. James Tate. EAS

Pet Lamb, The. Wordsworth. OxBChV

Pet-name, a common name. Best-selling brand, curt, A. Geoffrey Hill. *Fr.* Mercian Hymns, II. NoAM

Pet Panther. A. R. Ammons. NoP

Pet was never mourned as you. Last Words to a Dumb Friend. Thomas Hardy. FM

Petal/ Yasmin/ Vlodostk. Frolic. Deborah Levy. DT

Petals fall in the fountain, The. Ts'ai Chi'h. Ezra Pound. NoP

Petals of the Tulips, The. Judith Hemschemeyer. TV

Pete at the Zoo. Gwendolyn Brooks. ILY; PDV

Pete Peterson, before this bit, a professional entertainer. Vaudeville. Lincoln Kirstein. MoP

Pete Rousecastle the sailor's son. Rousecastle. David Wright. MoBS

Peter. Michael Dennis Browne. NYBP

Peter. Marianne Moore. CMoP; NAAL-2; NoP; OxBA

Peter Amberley. John Calhoun. AmFP

Peter and John. Elinor Wylie. MoAB; MoAmPo; MoBS

Peter and Michael were two little menikin. *Unknown.* BoTP

Peter and Wendy. Wymond Garthwaite. RAR

Peter at some immortal cloth, it seemed. The Death of Peter Esson. George Mackay Brown. NePoEA-2

Peter Bell. John Hamilton Reynolds. OBNC; Par

Peter Bell the Third, *sels.* Shelley.
"Among the guests who often stayed." ChER
"Devil now knew his proper cue, The." OBSV
"Hell is a city much like London." OBD; OBSV

Peter Cooper. Joaquin Miller. AA

Peter Grimes. George Crabbe. *Fr.* The Borough, Letter XXII. EnRP; OBNV; PoEL-4; TEP
(Poor of the Borough, The; Peter Grimes.) NoP
"He built a mud-wall'd hovel, where he kept." SaC

Peter Grimes at Aldeburgh. FaBoPP
"Priest attending, found he spoke at times, The." PoE
"Thus by himself compelled to live each day." NOBE; OBNC; SeCePo

Peter had experienced the tight, nauseous desire. The Wickedness of Peter Shannon. Alden Nowlan. MoCV

Peter Hath Lost His Purse. *Unknown.* FF

Peter-Penny, The. Robert Herrick. CaPo

Peter, Peter, pumpkin eater. Mother Goose. FaBoBe; FaFP; OxNR

Peter Piper picked a peck of pickled peppers. Mother Goose. FaBoBe; FaFP; FaPON; OxNR

Peter Quince at the Clavier. Wallace Stevens. AmPP; CMoP; HeIP; InPK; InPS; LiTM; MoAB; MoAmPo; NAWM-2; NoAM; NOBA; OxBA; PoE; PPP; TAP; TrGrPo; TwCP

Peter Rabbit. Sandra McPherson. LCAP

Peter sleep-walks. Peter. Michael Dennis Browne. NYBP

Peter Stuyvesant's New Year's Call. Edmund Clarence Stedman. PAH

Peter White will ne'er go right. Mother Goose. OxBoLi; OxNR

Peterhead in May. Burns Singer. OxBS

Peterhof. Edmund Wilson. GoJo

Peter's not friendly. He gives me sideways looks. John Berryman. *Fr.* Dream Songs. CAPP

Petit Salon des Indépendants. Cees Buddingh', *tr. fr. Dutch by* James S. Holmes. DuIn

Petit, the Poet. Edgar Lee Masters. *Fr.* Spoon River Anthology. CMoP; MoAmPo; NoAM; NOBA; OxBA; TAP

Petite Histoire of Red Fascism, A. Andrei Codrescu. UL

Petition, A. Thomas Bailey Aldrich. AA

Petition. W. H. Auden. CMoP; LiTB; NAEL-2; Son

Petition. John Drinkwater. TrPWD

Petition. Eleanor Slater. TrPWD

Petition. R. S. Thomas. FaBoMo

Petition for an Absolute Retreat, The, *sel.* Anne Finch, Countess of Winchilsea. PoEL-3; WPE, *abr.*
"Give me, O indulgent fate!" TrGrPo

Petition for Reconciliation. Cynddelw Brydydd Mawr, *tr. fr. Welsh by* Joseph P. Clancy. OBWVE

Petition of the Gray Horse, Auld Dunbar, The. William Dunbar. OxBS

Petition of the Orangemen of Ireland, The. Thomas Moore. NOIV

Petition to Have Her Leave to Die. "A. W." *See* When will the fountain of my tears be dry?

Petrarch. Giosuè Carducci, *tr. fr. Italian by* William Dudley Foulke. AWP

Petrarch must have known why we and the goldfinch. To Michael. Norman Dubie. AnAn
Petrified Minute. Zoltán Zelk, *tr. fr. Hungarian by* Barbara Howes. MHuP
Pets. Ted Hughes. CRH
Pets are the hobby of my brother Bert. My Brother Bert. Ted Hughes. RHPC
Pettichap's Nest, The. John Clare. PBBP
Petticoat, A. Gertrude Stein. *Fr.* Tender Buttons. TTTS
Pettitoes are little feet, The. *Unknown.* OxNR
Petty sneaking knave I knew, A. Cromek [*or* On Cromek]. Blake. FaBoCo; FiBHP
Petulance is purple. Spectrum. Mari E. Evans. BPo
Peveril of the Peak, *sel.* Sir Walter Scott.
  "Speak not of niceness, when there's chance of wreck," *fr. ch.* 38. FaBoEE
Pew, pew,/ My minny me slew. Song of the Murdered Child. *Unknown.* GBP
  (Milk-white Dove.) ChTr
Pewter. Jack Gilbert. NPGG
Peyote Poem, *sel.* Michael McClure. PoM
  "Clear—the senses bright—sitting in the black chair—Rocker." NeAP
Peyote Vision. Lew Blockcolski. VoR
Phaedra. Osip Mandelstam, *tr. fr. Russian by* James Greene. OBVE
Phaedra. Jean Racine, *tr. fr. French by* Kenneth Muir. NAWM-2
Phalanstery. Mihály Ladányi, *tr. fr. Hungarian by* Jascha Kessler. *Fr.* Sketchbook. FOC
Phallic Root. Shiraishi Kazuko. WPOW
Phallus. Shiraishi Kazuko, *tr. by* Ikuko Atsumi. BoWoP
Phantasmagorillaorgasmiasmacharismamama. Poem in Nueva York. Cyn Zarco. UL
Phantasmion, *sel.* Sara Coleridge.
  "O sleep, my babe, hear not the rippling wave." OBNC
Phantasus, *sel.* Arno Holz, *tr. fr. German by* Ludwig Lewisohn. AWP
  "On a mountain of sugar-candy." *Tr. by* Babette Deutsch. PChr
Phantasy. *Unknown.* ACP
Phantom. Samuel Taylor Coleridge. NAEL-2; OAEL-2; OxBSP; PoEL-4
Phantom, The. Salvador Díaz Mirón, *tr. fr. Spanish by* Samuel Beckett. MexPo
Phantom. Tawfiq Sayigh, *tr. fr. Arabic by* Anne Royal *and* Thomas G. Ezzy. MAP
Phantom Bark, The. Hart Crane. CMoP
Phantom Horsewoman, The. Thomas Hardy. CMoP; FaBoPP; NOBE; PoEL-5; WSC
Phantom Light of the Baie des Chaleurs, The. Arthur Wentworth Hamilton Eaton. CaP
Phantom of the Clouds. Guillaume Apollinaire, *trs. fr. French by* Michael Benedikt *and by* Roger Shattuck. POS
Phantom or Fact. Samuel Taylor Coleridge. EnRP
Phantom Pain. Maxine Chernoff. EOEF
Phantom Skin, The. René Daumal, *tr. fr. French by* Michael Benedikt. POS
Phantom streams were in the distance—mocking lights of lake and pool. Christmas Creek. Henry Clarence Kendall. CBAP
Phantom-Wooer, The. Thomas Lovell Beddoes. EnRP; NAEL-2; TrGrPo; ViBoPo; WiR
Phantoms. Ben-Zion Tomer, *tr. fr. Hebrew by* Bernhard Frank. MHeP
Phantoms All. Harriet Prescott Spofford. AA
Phantoms of the Steppe. Pushkin, *tr. fr. Russian by* Edna Worthley Underwood. WSC
Phar Lap in the Melbourne Museum. Peter Porter. PoAu-2
Pharaoh and Joseph ("Pharaoh rejects his blossoming wives"). Else Lasker-Schüler, *tr. fr. German by* Joachim Neugroschel. VWA
Pharaohs of Today, The. Lizelia Augusta Jenkins Moorer. CBWP-3
Pharao's Daughter. Michael Moran. BIrV
Pharisee murmurs when the woman weeps, conscious of guilt, The. Sequaire. Godeschalk, *tr. by* Ezra Pound. CTC
Pharoah's Army Got Drownded. *Unknown.* AS
Pharsalia, *sels.* Lucan, *tr. fr. Latin.*
  "Just and fit actions Ptolemy (he saith)." *Fr.* VII, *tr. by* Ben Jonson. OBVE
  "O wastfull riot, never well content." *Fr.* IV, *tr. by* Sir Walter Ralegh. OBVE
  Portents, The. *Fr.* I, *tr. by* Christopher Marlowe. OBSC
  "Thee Pompey thy past deeds by turns infest." *Fr.* I, *tr. by* Nicholas Rowe. OBVE
Phases of Darkness, The. Paul Petrie. TAP
Phases of the Moon. Robert Browning. *Fr.* One Word More. ChTr
Pheasant. Nishiwaki Junzaburo, *tr. fr. Japanese by* Hiroaki Sato. FCEI
Pheasant. Sylvia Plath. RB
Pheasant. Sándor Rákos, *tr. fr. Hungarian by* Alan Dixon. MHuP

Phenomena. Robinson Jeffers. NOBA; OxBA
Phenomenal Survivals of Death in Nantucket. Louise Glück. AmPA; SM
Phenomenology of anger, The. Adrienne Rich. PoE
Phenomenon, The. Karl Shapiro. CMoP; NYBP
Phernazis the poet is at work. Dareios. C. P. Cavafy, *tr. by* Edmund Keeley *and* Philip Sherrard. AnAn; VMG
Philadelphia. Kipling. OBTV
Philadelphia ("Philadelphia is a handsome town"). *Unknown.* AmFP
Philander. Donald Hall. ErPo
Philanderer, The. Moses Mendes. *Fr.* The Chaplet. TrJP
Philaret on Willy cals. The Fourth Eclogue. George Wither. *Fr.* The Shephe[a]rd's Hunting. SeCV-1, *abr.*
Philarete Praises Poetry. George Wither. *Fr.* The Shephe[a]rd's Hunting: Eclogue IV. OBS
Philatelic Lessons: The German Collection. Lawrence P. Spingarn. NYBP
Philatelist Royal. Robert Graves. FaBoCo
Philemon and Baucis. Ovid, *tr. fr. Latin by* Arthur Golding. *Fr.* Metamorphoses, VIII. CTC
  "Heaven's power is infinite; earth, air, and sea." *Tr. by* Dryden. OAEL-1
  "Then Lelex rose, an old experienced man." *Tr. by* Dryden. AWP; OBVE
  "Upon the hills of Phrygie near a teyle there stands a tree." *Tr. by* Arthur Golding. OBSC
  (Baucis and Philemon.)
Philhellene. C. P. Cavafy, *tr. fr. Greek by* Edmund Keeley *and* Philip Sherrard. VMG
Philip, foozling with his cheek. Harry Graham. *Fr.* Some Ruthless Rhymes, VII. CenHV
Philip Sparrow. John Skelton. *See* Phyllyp Sparowe.
Philip van Artevelde, *sel.* Sir Henry Taylor.
  Elena's Song. *Fr.* II. OBEV
Philippines were drenched in sun, The. Portrait Philippines. Alfred A. Duckett. PoNe
Phillida and Coridon. Nicholas Breton. *Fr.* The Honourable Entertainment Given to the Queen's Majesty in Progress at Elvetham, 1591. OBEV; TTTS
  (Pastoral, A.) TrGrPo
  (Phyllida and Corydon.) EiL; SeCePo
  (Ploughman's Song, The.) NOBE; OBSC
Phillida Flouts Me [*or* The Disdainful Shepherdess]. *Unknown.* CoMu; EiL; InVP; OBEV; OBSC; TrGrPo
Phillida was a fair maid. Harpalus' Complaint of Phillida's Love. *Unknown.* OBSC
Phillips, whose touch harmonious could remove. An Epitaph upon the Celebrated Claudy Phillips, Musician, Who Died Very Poor. Samuel Johnson. NOEC
Phillis ("My Phillis hath the morning sun"). Thomas Lodge. *See* Phyllis.
Phillis for Shame Let Us Improve. Charles Sackville. OBS
  (Song: "Phillis for shame let us improve.") SeCV-2
Phillis is my only joy. Sir Charles Sedley. EnLoPo; OBS; SeCV-2
Phillis kept sheep along the western plains. Coridon and Phillis. Robert Greene. *Fr.* Perimedes [*or* Perimedes, the Blacksmith]. OBSC
Phillis, let's shun the common fate. Sir Charles Sedley. SeCV-2
Phillis on the new made hay. The Coy Shepherdess; or, Phillis and Amintas. *Unknown.* CoMu
Phillis; or, The Progress of Love. Swift. *See* Phyllis.
Phillis, shou'd we delay. To Phillis. Edmund Waller. SeCP
Phillis's [*or* Phyllis's] Age. Matthew Prior. EnLoPo;
  (Phyllis's Age.) FaBoEE
Phillis's Resolution. William Walsh. OxBSP
Philocles. Leonidas of Tarentum, *tr. fr. Greek by* F. A. Wright. AWP
Philoctetes. Lord De Tabley. NOBVV
Philodendron. Helen Armstead Johnson. AmNP
Philomel. Richard Barnfield. *See* Affectionate Shepherd, The: As it fell upon a day.
Philomel to Corydon. William Young. AA
Philomela. Matthew Arnold. OAEL-2; OBEV; PBBP; PPP; UnPo
Philomela. John Crowe Ransom. ChTr; CMoP; FaBoPP; NAAL-2; NoAM; NOBA; OBAL; OBSV; OxBA
Philomela. Yannis Ritsos, *tr. fr. Greek by* Edmund Keeley. AnAn
Philomela, the Lady Fitzwater's Nightingale, *sels.* Robert Greene.
  Philomela's Second Ode. OBSC
  "Sitting by a river['s] side." TEP
  (Philomela's Ode in Her Arbour.) OBSC
Philomela, the Nightingale, *sel.* Patrick Hannay.
  "Upon the boughs and tops of trees." PBBP
Philomela's Ode in Her Arbour. Robert Greene. *See* Philomela, the Lady Fitzwater's Nightingale: Sitting by a river['s] side.

Philomela's Second Ode. Robert Greene. *Fr.* Philomela, the Lady Fitzwater's Nightingale. OBSC

Philomena Andronico. William Carlos Williams. FaBoMo

Philon [the Shepherd]. *Unknown. See* While that the sun with his beams hot.

Philosopher, A. Sam Walter Foss. OBAL

Philosopher, The. Edna St. Vincent Millay. CMoP

Philosopher, The. Edward Rowland Sill. AnAmPo

Philosopher and Her Father, The. Shirley Brooks. CenHV

Philosopher and the Birds, The. Richard Murphy. CIP

Philosopher and the Lover: To a Mistress Dying, The. Sir William Davenant. OBD

Philosopher to His Mistress, The. Robert Bridges. LiTM; PoEL-5

Philosophers, The. Russell Edson. NAmP

Philosopher's Stone, The. *Unknown.* OxBLMV

Philosophiae Consolationis. Paul Scarron, *tr. fr. French by* G. N. Gabbard. SoTCo

Philosophic Flight, The. Giordano Bruno, *tr. fr. Italian by* John Addington Symonds. AWP

Philosophy. Paul Laurence Dunbar. BPo

Philosophy Is Born. Christian Morgenstern, *tr. fr. German by* Geoffrey Grigson. FaBoNo

Philosophy, the great and only heir. Abraham Cowley. *Fr.* To the Royal Society. JCP

Phineas dwelled midst lives of many pieces. Phineas Within and Without. Paul Zimmer. VGW

Phineas Pratt. Gloria MacArthur. GoYe

Phineas Within and Without. Paul Zimmer. VGW

Phlebas the Phoenician, a fortnight dead. Death by Water. T. S. Eliot. *Fr.* The Waste Land, IV. OBVE

Phoebe Dawson, *sel.* George Crabbe.
  "Lo! now with red rent cloak and bonnet black." EBEV

Phoebe in a Rosebush. Clyde Watson. NTCP

Phoebe on Latmus. Michael Drayton. *Fr.* Endimion and Phoebe. OBSC

Phoebe sate,/ Sweet she sate. Montanus' Sonnet. Thomas Lodge. *Fr.* Rosalynde; or Euphues' Golden Legacy. PoEL-2

Phoebus, Arise. William Drummond of Hawthornden. EiL; GoTS
  (Invocation.) OBEV
  (Song: "Phoebus, Arise.") OBS
  (Summons to Love.) GTBS; GTBS-P

Phoebus, art thou a god, and canst not give. Funeral Elegy on the Death of His Very Good Friend, Mr. Michael Drayton. Sir Aston Cokayne. OBS

Phoebus, farewell! A sweeter saint I serve. A Sweeter Saint I Serve. Sir Philip Sidney. *Fr.* Arcadia. SiPS

Phoebus, make haste: the day's too long; be gone. A Letter to Her Husband. Anne Bradstreet. AnAmPo; LiTA

Phoebus, the goddess variant and changeable. Christine de Pisan, *tr. fr. French, ad. by* Joan Keefe. *Fr.* The Epistle of Othea to Hector (A Lytil Bibell of Knyghthod). PBWP

Phoebus with Admetus. George Meredith. NOBE; OBEV

Phoenix. Ilya Abu Madi, *tr. fr. Arabic by* Issa Boullata *and* Naomi Shihab Nye. MAP

Phoenix. Rose Ausländer, *tr. fr. German by* Ewald Osers. VWA

Phoenix, The. A. C. Benson. OBEV

Phoenix, The. J. V. Cunningham. QFR

Phoenix, The. George Darley. *See* Nepenthe: O Blest Unfabled Incense Tree.

Phoenix, The. Robert Fisher. AmMo

Phoenix, The. Matti Megged, *tr. fr. Hebrew by* Howard Schwartz. VWA

Phoenix, The. Ogden Nash. CenHV

Phoenix, The. Howard Nemerov. LiTM

Phoenix. Carolyn M. Rodgers. JB

Phoenix, The. Siegfried Sassoon. ChTr

Phoenix, The, *sels. Unknown, tr. fr. Anglo-Saxon.*
  "Lo! I have learned of the loveliest of lands." *Tr. by* Charles W. Kennedy. AnOE; OAEL-1
  "When the sun comes up from the salt sea." *Tr. by* Peggy Munsterberg. PBBP

Phoenix and [the] Turtle, The ("Let the birds of loudest lay"), *sel.* Shakespeare. LiTB; MePo; NOBE; NoP; OAEL-1; OBEV; OBSC; SeCePo; TEP
  "Let the bird of lowdest lay." PoEL-2

Phoenix at Fifty, A. Lawrence Ferlinghetti. NAs

Phoenix, bird of terrible pride. Sir Herbert Read. *Fr.* Mutations of the Phoenix. FaBoTw

Phoenix comes of flame and dust, The. The Phoenix. Howard Nemerov. LiTM

Phoenix in its flight, The. The Phoenix. Robert Fisher. AmMo

Phoenix of Mozart, The. Claude Vigée, *tr. fr. French by* Anthony Rudolf. VWA

Phoenix on the hot sirocco's breath. H. B. Mallalieu. PoA

Phoenix Self-born, The. Ovid, *tr. fr. Latin by* Dryden. *Fr.* Metamorphoses, XV. ChTr

Phone Call to Rutherford. Paul Blackburn. PoM

Phone duet over the radio, A. The Louisiana Weekly #4. David Henderson. PoBA

Phone for the fish-knives, Norman. How to Get On in Society. John Betjeman. NOBL; OBSV; OxBTC

Phone Number. Jack Collom. UL

Phone vibrates all winter. The. Exterminator. Lucien Stryk. CAPP

Phono, at the Boar's Head. Henri Coulette. *Fr.* The War of the Secret Agents, IX. NePoEA-2

Photo at the Bridge. Dan Pagis, *tr. fr. Hebrew by* Warren Bargad *and* Stanley F. Chyet. IP

Photo of Emily, The. Lawrence Ferlinghetti. CAPP

Photo of someone else's childhood, A. The Old Adam. Denise Levertov. NaP; UnPo

Photo of the Author with a Favorite Pig. William Matthews. BLA

Photo shows me, The. The Others Hunters in the North the Cree. Jerome Rothenberg. PoM

Photograph, The. Barbara Drake. ASP

Photograph. Sue May. DT

Photograph. Quandra Prettyman. PoBA

Photograph at the Cloisters: April 1972. Helen Chasin. NMM

Photograph can't speak or move its face, A. Album-Leaf. Kingsley Amis. PoPo

Photograph in a Stockholm Newspaper for March 13, 1910. Don Coles. NOBC

Photograph of a Baby. Charles Brasch. ATNZ

Photograph of Haymaker, 1890. Molly Holden. OxBTC

Photograph of My Father in His Twenty-second Year. Raymond Carver. TSL

Photograph of My Room. Carolyn Forché. NAmP

Photograph of Myself, The. Jon Anderson. AmPA

Photograph the Cat Licks, The. Beatrice Walter. NMM

Photographed at midday. To Boris Pasternak. Aleksander Kushner. VWA, *tr. by* Dimitry Pospielovsky *and* Keith Bosley

Photographer. Philip Booth. EyDe

Photographer, The. Louis Simpson. LCAP

Photographic Plate, Partly Spidered, Hampton Roads, Virginia, with Model T Ford Mid-Channel. Dave Smith. MAYP

Photographing a Rattlesnake. David Wagoner. BLA

Photographs. Charles Wright. HoPM

Photographs: A Vision of Massacre. Michael S. S. Harper. PoBA

Photographs of Pioneer Women. Ruth Dallas. PeNZ

Photomicrograph: Last Centimeter of the Human Airway. S. R. Compton. BWV

Photos, The. Diane Wakoski. NIP

Photos of a Salt Mine. Patricia K. Page. NoAM; NOBC

Phrase goes on growing in my head, The. Dark Wood. Ian Wedde. ATNZ

Phrase which was to be the axis of my poem's crystallization, The. Ars Poetica. Adam Wazyk, *tr. by* Isaac Komem. VWA

Phraseology. Jayne Cortez. BISi

Phryne. John Donne. FaBoEE

Phyllida and Corydon. Nicholas Breton. *See* Honourable Entertainment Given to the Queen's Majesty in Progress at Elvetham, 1591, The: Phillida and Coridon.

Phyllidula. Ezra Pound. FaBoTw

Phyllis. Nicholas Breton. OBSC; TrGrPo
  (Pastoral, A: "Sweet Bird! that sit and sing amid the shady valleys.") EIL

Phyllis. William, of Hawthornden Drummond. *See* Of Phyllis.

Phyllis, *sels.* Thomas Lodge.
  "Devoide of reason, thrale to foolish ire." *Fr.* XXXI *after the French of* Pierre de Ronsard. AAS
  I Hope and Fear. *Fr.* XXXV. Son
  "I would in rich and golden coloured raine." *Fr.* XXXIV *after the French of* Pierre de Ronsard. AAS
  Love Guards [*or* Guides] the Roses of Thy Lips. *Fr.* XIII. EIL; Son
    (Phillis 2.) OBEV
  No Stars Her Eyes. *Fr.* VIII. Son
  O Pleasing Thoughts. *Fr.* I. Son
  Phillis ("My Phillis hath the morning sun"). OBSC
    (Phillis 1.) OBEV
    (Phyllis.) ACP; EIL

Phyllis. Thomas Randolph. BoLoP

Phyllis. Sydney King Russell. ErPo

Phyllis Corydon clutched to him. Catullus, *tr.* by Peter Whigham.
  BoLoP
Phyllis; or, The Progress of Love. Swift. OAEL-1; OBSV; PoE
  (Phillis; or, The Progress of Love.) PoEL-3
Phyllis! why should we delay. To Phyllis. Edmund Waller. TrGrPo
Phyllis's Age. Matthew Prior. EnLoPo; FaBoEE
Phyllyp Sparowe [*or* Philip Sparrow]. John Skelton. AAS; PoEL-1
  Sels.
  Commendations of Mistress Jane Scrope, The. OBSC
  Funeral of Philip Sparrow, The. ACP, *abr.*
  O Cat of Carlishkind. ChTr
  "Pla ce bo! Who is there, who?." AAS; NOBE; OAEL-1; OxBoLi,
    abr.
  "When I remember again." PBBP; SeCePo
  (Sparrow's Dirge, The.) FaBoCh; OBSC
Physical Geography. Louise Townsend Nicholl. ImOP
Physical Universe. Louis Simpson. CAPP; InPS
Physicist's Purpose, The. Adrianne Marcus. BWV
Physics. Cees Buddingh', *tr. fr. Dutch* by James S. Holmes. DuIn
Physics, A. Heather McHugh. MAYP
Physics of Love. Charles Brasch. ATNZ
Physics of Ochun, The. Victor Hernandez Cruz. UL
Physiologus, *sel. Unknown, tr. fr. Anglo-Saxon.*
  Whale, The. *Tr. by* Charles Kennedy. AnOE; MOS
    "To explain the nature of fishes in craft of verse." EBEV
Piano, The. Frank Daley. NOBC
Piano. D. H. Lawrence. BLPL; CMoP; GrPl; GTBS-P; HAP; HeIP;
  InPK; InvP; LiTB; MoAB; MoBrPo; MoP; NAEL-2; NIP; NoAM;
  NOBE; NoP; OAEL-2; OxBSP; PoE; PPP; RB; UnPo; WeW
Piano. Karl Shapiro. RR
Piano, A. Gertrude Stein. *Fr.* Tender Buttons. PBWP
Piano after War. Gwendolyn Brooks. AmNP
Piano and Drums. Gabriel Okara. NIP; PBA; TTY
Piano at Evening. Palea, *tr. fr. Hawaiian* by M. K. Pukui *and* A. L.
  Korn. WTO
Piano di Sorrento. Robert Browning. *Fr.* The Englishman in Italy.
  FaBoPP; SeCePo
  (Englishman in Italy, The ["Time for rain! for your long hot dry
    autumn"].) SeCePo
Piano hums, The. Effendi. Michael S. S. Harper. CNA; PoBA
Piano Lessons. Baron Wormser. MAYP
Piano Pieces, *sels.* Thomas W. Shapcott.
  Schoenberg Op. 11. CBAP
  Webern. CBAP
Piano Player Explains Himself, The. Allen Grossman. BAP
Piano Practice. Howard Moss. NYBP
Piano tuner spoke to me, that tenderest, The. Pyrargyrite Metal, 9.
  Cecília Meireles, *tr.* by James Merrill. ATCBP; PBWP
Piano Tuner's Wife, The. Karl Shapiro. NoAM
Piarco. Eric Roach. PVCV
Piazza di Spagna. Willard M. Grimes. GoYe
Piazza di Spagna, Early Morning. Richard Wilbur. GrPl; InPS; OxBSP;
  SM; VGW
Piazza Piece. John Crowe Ransom. AnAmPo; BoLoP; ErPo; HeIP;
  MoAB; MoAmPo; MoP; NAAL-2; NoAM; NOBA; NoP; OPOP;
  OxBA; Son; SoSe; TAP; TrGrPo
Piazza Tragedy, A. Eugene Field. FiBHP; NBLV
Piazzas. Barbara Guest. NeAP
Pibroch. Ted Hughes. FaBoMo; NePoEA-2; OAEL-2; PoCH
Pibroch of Donuil Dhu. Sir Walter Scott. EnRP; FaBoCh; OxBS;
  PoEL-4
  (Gathering Song of Donald the Black.) GTBS; GTBS-P
  (Gathering Song of Donuil Dhu.) GN
  (Pibroch.) FaPoR
Picasso didn't want to paint Guernica. Remembrances of Guernica.
  Wieland Schmied, *tr.* by Beth Bjorklund. CoAuP
Piccadilly. Ezra Pound. AnAmPo
Picciola. Robert Henry Newell. AA
Piccolomini, The, *sel.* Schiller, *tr. fr. German* by Samuel Taylor
  Coleridge.
  Thekla's Song. AWP
Pick a fern, pick a fern, ferns are high. Ezra Pound, *after the Chinese.*
  OBVE
Pick and Poke. Gerald Stern. AnAn
Pick the words. Comment on Ethnopoetics and Literacy. Wendy Rose.
  ER
Pick-up at Chef Rizal Restaurant. Virginia Cerenio. BrSi
Pickaxes, pickaxes swinging today. Bam, Bam, Bam. Eve Merriam.
  PDV
Picket Fence, The. Christian Morgenstern, *tr. fr. German* by Max Knight.
  GrPl

Picket-Guard, The. Ethel Lynn Beers. *See* All Quiet along the Potomac.
Picketing Supermarkets. Tom Wayman. NIP
Pickety fence, The. David McCord. NTCP
Pickin Em Up and Layin Em Down. Maya Angelou. NBLV
Picking Fresh Flowers. Huang-fu Sung, *tr. fr. Chinese* by Lois Fusek.
  ATF
Picking Grapes in an Abandoned Vineyard ("Picking grapes alone in the
  late autumn sun"). Larry Levis. MAYP
Picking Lilies. *Unknown.* OBET
Picking Rushes. *Unknown, tr. fr. Chinese* by Burton Watson. CoBCP
Picking through pieces. Analyst. David Fisher. NPGG
Pickpocket, The. Bill Manhire. ATNZ
Pickup in Tony's Hashhouse. Kenneth Pitchford. *Fr.* Good for Nothing
  Man. ErPo
Pickwick Papers, The, *sel.* Charles Dickens.
  Ivy Green, The. *Fr. ch.* 6. BoNaP
Picnic, The. Dorothy Aldis. RAR
Picnic. Hugh Lofting. GoJo
Picnic, The. John Logan. NePoEA-2
Picnic at the Beach. Pyke Johnson, Jr.. SoTCo
Picnic Day. Rachel Field. RAR
Picnic Remembered. Robert Penn Warren. NAAL-2
Picnic Rhyme. *Unknown. See* Lemonade.
Picnic: the Liberated. M. Carl Holman. PoBA; PoNe
Picnics. *Unknown.* BoTP
Pico della Mirandola. Mason Jordan Mason. PoNe
Pict Song, A. Kipling. *Fr.* Puck of Pook's Hill. NoAM
Pictor Ignotus. Robert Browning. CTC; TEP
Picture, The. Anacreon, *tr. fr. Greek* by Thomas Stanley. AWP
Picture, A. D. C. Cuthbertson. PoSH
Picture, A. Dora Greenwell. EBVV
Picture, A. Howard Nemerov. OxBC
Picture, A. Henrietta Cordelia Ray. CBWP-3
Picture and book remain. An Acre of Grass. W. B. Yeats. CMoP;
  NoAM
Picture book torn, The. The Fall. Alois Hergouth, *tr.* by Beth
  Bjorklund. CoAuP
Picture Bride. Cathy Song. AiP
Picture Collection. Marjorie Welish. UL
Picture from the Blitz. Lois Clark. CN
Picture memory brings to me, A. Whittier. *Fr.* My Trust. OHIP, *fr.
  first 3 sts..*
Picture my grandmother at sixty the year. Family Album. Lonny
  Kaneko. BrSi
Picture of a Castle. William Meredith. NePoEA
Picture of a Nativity. Geoffrey Hill. NoAM; OxBC
Picture of a Woman. Maureen Ismay. WS
Picture of Dorian Gray, The, *sel.* Oscar Wilde.
  "Artist is the creator of beautiful things, The." NAEL-2
Picture of J. T. in a Prospect of Stone, The. Charles Tomlinson. PPP
Picture of Little J.A. in a Prospect of Flowers, The. John Ashbery.
  CAPP; PPP
Picture of Little T. C. in a Prospect of Flowers, The. Andrew Marvell.
  JCP; LiTB; MeLP; MePo; NAEL-1; NOBE; NoP; OAEL-1; OBEV;
  OBS; PoE; PPP; PrIm; SeCP; SeCV-1
Picture of Loot. Alan Sillitoe. OxBTC
Picture of Okinawa, A. Dennis Schmitz. LCAP; NPGG
Picture of Village Happiness, A. Yün Shou-p'ing, *tr. fr. Chinese* by
  Irving Lo. WFTU
Picture Postcard of a Zoo. Oscar Williams. Son
Picture Postcards. Miklós Radnóti, *tr. fr. Hungarian* by Emery George.
  VWA
Picture-Show. Siegfried Sassoon. CMoP
Picture that, The. *Unknown, tr.* by Geoffrey Bownas *and* Anthony
  Thwaite. PeBJV
Pictures. F. Ann Elliott. BoTP
Pictures at an Exhibition. Nathan Rosenbaum. GoYe
Pictures from Brueghel, *sels.* William Carlos Williams.
  Corn Harvest, The. *Fr.* VII. PPP
  Haymaking. *Fr.* VI. NOAM
  Hunters in the Snow, The. *Fr.* III. LCAP
  Landscape with the Fall of Icarus. *Fr.* II. LCAP; NAAL-2; NOAM;
    PPP
  Self-Portrait. *Fr.* I. LCAP
Pictures in a Gallery Undersea. C.K. Stead. ATNZ
Pictures in the Smoke. Dorothy Parker. NBLV
Pictures of a Gone World, *sels.* Lawrence Ferlinghetti.
  "Away above a harborful." *Fr. Sec.* 1. BoLoP; ErPo; PoM
  "Dada would have liked a day like this." *Fr. Sec.* 23. NeAP
  "Sarolla's women in their picture hats." *Fr. Sec.* 8. NeAP; PoM

Pictures of Jews. Haim Guri, *tr. fr. Hebrew by* Warren Bargad *and* Stanley F. Chyet. IP
Pictures of the Rhine. George Meredith. OBTV
Pictures on the Wall. Zvi Shargel, *tr. fr. Yiddish by* Gabriel Preil *and* Howard Schwartz. VWA
Picturesque; a Fragment. John Aikin. NOEC
Pie Are Square. Pearl Bloch Segall. SoTCo
Pie in the Sky. Joe Hill. *See* Long-haired preachers come out ev'ry night.
Pie Problem. Shel Silverstein. RHPC
Pie sat on a pear tree, A. Hop't She. *Unknown.* GBP; PBBP
Piece by piece I seem. Necessities of Life. Adrienne Rich. HCAP; NIP; NOBA
Piece of art, a scene, a poem, A. Silence, an Eloquent Applause. Leona Gregory. TrCP
Piece of Black Bread, A. "Eduard Bagritsky," *tr. fr. Russian by* C. M. Bowra. TrJP
Piece of flesh gives off, A. The Dead Shall Be Raised Incorruptible. Galway Kinnell. NOBA; PoE
Piece of green pepper, A. Haiku Ambulance. Richard Brautigan. InPK
Piece of Rush Matting, A. Sung Wan, *tr. fr. Chinese by* William Schultz. *Fr.* Songs Composed in Prison, I. WFTU
Piece Worker, The. Emma Döltz, *tr. fr. German by* Susan L. Cocalis *and* Gerlinde Geiger. DMG
Piecemeal the summer dies. Exeunt. Richard Wilbur. BoNaP; HeIP; PoLF; Psk
Pieces. Duane Niatum. HATNAP
Pieces of Heaven, The. Pattiann Rogers. NAmP
Pieces of memory stick together. Remembering. Judit Tóth, *tr. by* Emery George. VWA
Pieces of Snot. *Unknown, tr. fr. Bella Bella Indian by* Franz Boas. STP
Pied à Terre. Anne Bloch. Mes
Pied Beauty. Gerard Manley Hopkins. AWP; BrPo; CMoP; EaLo; EBVV; FaBoMo; FaFP; GoJo; GTBS-P; HAP; HeIP; HoPM; InPK; InPS; InvP; LiTB; LiTM; MoAB; MoBrPo; MoP; NAEL-2; NoAM; NOBE; NOBVV; NoP; OAEL-2; OBEV; OBMV; OBNC; OxBSP; PoE; PoRA; PPP; PrIm; RB; SCV; SoSe; SOTW; TEP; TrGrPo; TTTS; WeW
Pied Piper of Hamelin, The ("Hamelin Town's in Brunswick"), *sel.* Robert Browning. BeLS; BLPL; FaBoBe; FaBoCh; FaFP; GN; OBNV; OxBChV
"Into the street the Piper stept." BoTP
Pier. Ivan Uriarte, *tr. fr. Spanish by* Jack Hirschman. Vol
Pier delle Vigne. Dante, *tr. fr. Italian by* John Ciardi. *Fr.* Divina Commedia: Inferno, XII. HoPM
Pier-Glass, The. Robert Graves. CMoP; MoAB; NoAM
Pier: Under Pisces, The. James Merrill. NoAM
Piercing brightness of the living ray, The. Dante, *tr. fr. Italian. Fr.* Divina Commedia: Paradiso, XXXIII. TOF, *tr. by* Dorothy L. Sayers *and* Barbara Reynolds.
Piercing Chill I Feel, The. Buson, *tr. fr. Japanese by* Harold G. Henderson. InPK
Piercing to the marrow: beyond a garden fire. Princess Shikishi, *tr. fr. Japanese by* Hiroaki Sato. *Fr.* Seventy-eight Tanka. FCEI
Piere Vidal Old. Ezra Pound. MoAB
Pierre Falcon. Le Tombeau de Pierre Falcon. James Reaney. MoCV
Pierrot, no sentimental swain. Pantomime. Paul Verlaine, *tr. by* Arthur Symons. AWP
Piers are pummelled by the waves, The. The Fall of Rome. W. H. Auden. InPS; MAT; OAEL-2; OxBTC; UnPo
Piers Gaveston, *sel.* Michael Drayton.
"This Edward in the Aprill of his age." PeHV
Piers Plainness' Seven Years' Prenticeship, *sel.* Henry Chettle.
Aeliana's Ditty. OBSC
(Of Cupid.) EIL
Piers Plowman. William Langland. *See* Vision of Piers Plowman, The.
Pietà. James McAuley. CBAP; PoAu-2
Pieta. Rainer Maria Rilke, *tr. fr. German by* M. D. Hester Norton. OFD
Pieta, The, Rhenish, 14th C., The Cloisters. Mona Van Duyn. Prf
Pig. Paul Eluard, *tr. fr. French.* POS, *tr. by* Michael Benedikt; TTTS, *tr. by* Kenneth Koch.
Pig. Anthony Hecht. OxBC
Pig, The. Ogden Nash. FPL; RB
Pig. Vasco Popa, *tr. fr. Rumanian by* Anne Pennington. OBD
Pig, The. *Unknown.* FaBoEE
Pig, The. Roland Young. RHPC
Pig and the Nightingale, The. Eliezer Shteynbarg, *tr. fr. Yiddish by* Leonard Wolf. PeBMYV
Pig, if I am not mistaken, The. The Pig. Ogden Nash. FPL; RB
Pig Is Never Blamed, A. Babette Deutsch. RHPC
Pig is not a nervous beast, The. The Pig. Roland Young. RHPC

Pig Island Letters, *sels.* James Keir Baxter.
"From an old house shaded with macrocarpas." *Fr.* II. ATNZ; PeNZ
"When I was only semen in a gland." *Fr.* VIII. PeNZ
Pig lay on a barrow dead, The. View of a Pig. Ted Hughes. LiTM; OxBTC; TwCP
Pig Song. Margaret Atwood. NoP
Pig stands squarely, The. Transubstantiation. Gary Geddes. NOBC
Pig-Tale, A. "Lewis Carroll." *Fr.* Sylvie and Bruno Concluded. WiR (Melancholy Pig, The.) FaPON
"Pig'back" she brought me where the lake surrounded. Kineo Mountain. Celeste Turner Wright. Psk
Pigeon, A. Hugo Claus, *tr. fr. Dutch by* Theo Hermans. DuIn
Pigeon. Elouise Loftin. CNA
Pigeon-Feeders in Battery Park, The. Julia Cooley Altrocchi. GoYe
Pigeon purrs in the wood; the wodd has gone, The. Idylls of the King. Geoffrey Hill. *Fr.* An Apology for the Revival of Christian Architecture in England, 11. FaBoRV; NoAM; PoE
Pigeons, The. Rodney Bennett. BoTP
Pigeons. Bert Meyers. EAS
Pigeons. Marianne Moore. PoA; RHPC
Pigeons. Alastair Reid. NePoEA; NYBP; TwCP
Pigeons are city folk. Pigeons. Marianne Moore. PoA; RHPC
Pigeons flutter'd fieldward, one and all, The. Gout and Wings. Charles Tennyson Turner. NOBVV
Pigeons on the grass alas. Gertrude Stein. *Fr.* Four Saints in Three Acts. TAP
Pigeons shake their wings on the copper church roof. Fourth Floor, Dawn, Up All Night Writing Letters. Allen Ginsberg. CAPP
Pigeon's Story, The. Jeannie Kirby. BoTP
Pigeons that peck at the grass in Trinity Churchyard, The. Trinity Place. Phyllis McGinley. MoAmPo; OxBSP; SaC
Piggie Wig and Piggie Wee. The Pigs. Emilie Poulsson. RAR
Piggy-wig found he had four little feet. What Piggy-Wig Found. Enid Blyton. BoTP
Pigmies and Cranes. Walter Savage Landor. NOBVV
Pigs. Andrea Hollander Budy. KS
Pigs, The. Geoffrey Lehmann. CBAP
Pigs, The. Emilie Poulsson. RAR
Pigs, The. Jane Taylor. FM
Pigs for Circe in May, The. Joanne Kyger. PoM
Pigs o' Pelton. *Unknown.* GBP
Pig's Tail, The. Norman Ault. BoTP
Pigtail dangled down my back, A. Ballad of the Dreamy Girl. Edith Roseveare. Mes
Pigwiggen. Michael Drayton. BoTP
Pigwiggin Arms Himself. Michael Drayton. *Fr.* Nymphidia. MoShBr (Arming of Pigwiggen, The.) GN
Pihsien Road. "Robin Hyde." ATNZ; WPE
Pike, The. Edmund Blunden. LiTM
Pike, The. John Bruce. SD
Pike. Ted Hughes. CMoP; FaBoMo; HAP; HeIP; InPS; LiTM; MAT; NAEL-2; NePoEA-2; OxBTC; PoE; SoSe; WeW
Pike, The. Theodore Roethke. ASP
Pilate Tapes, The, *sel.* Vincent O'Sullivan.
Liberal. ATNZ
Pile the bodies high at Austerlitz and Waterloo. Grass. Carl Sandburg. AWP; BLPL; FaBV; MoAB; MoAmPo; MoP; NAAL-2; NoAM; NOBA; NoP; OBWP; OHFP; OxBA; PoLF; TrGrPo; WaaP
Piled deep below the screening apple-branch. The Orchard-Pit. Dante Gabriel Rossetti. EnLoPo; NAEL-2; OAEL-2; PoEL-5; SCV
Piled on a loading dock where I walked. Desks. Dave Smith. HCAP
Piled snow hugs the bramble gates. Traveling Early through a Snowy Valley. Yü Chi, *tr. by* Jonathan Chaves. CoBLCP
Pilgrim, The. Bunyan. *See* Pilgrim's Progress, The: Who would true valour see.
Pilgrim, The. Emma C. Embury. OBCA
Pilgrim, The. "E. Foxton." AA
Pilgrim, The. Brendan Kennelly. TIRV
Pilgrim, The. Richard Wightman. WGRP
Pilgrim, The. W. B. Yeats. RB
Pilgrim am I, on my way, A. The Pilgrim. "E. Foxton." AA
Pilgrim at Rome, The. *Unknown.* AnIL
Pilgrim Cranes, The. Lord De Tabley. EBVV
Pilgrim Fathers, The. Leonard Bacon. AH, *with music;* WGRP
Pilgrim Fathers, The. Felicia Dorothea Hemans. *See* Landing of the Pilgrim Fathers [in New England], The.
Pilgrim Fathers, The. John Pierpont. AA; PAH
Pilgrim Fathers, The. Wordsworth. AiP, *abr.;* PAH
Pilgrim Fathers, The—where are they? The Pilgrim Fathers. John Pierpont. AA; PAH

"Blest leaf! whose aromatic gales dispense." BXAP; Par
"Boy! bring an ounce of Freeman's best." Par
   (Boy! Bring an Ounce.) BXAP
Piped a tiny voice hard by. The Chickadee. Emerson. FaPON
Piped the blackbird on the beechwood spray. Little Bell. Thomas
   Westwood. GN
Piper, The. Blake. *See* Songs of Innocence: Piping Down the Valleys
   Wild.
Piper, The. W. S. Merwin. NAAL-2
Piper, A [*or* The]. "Seumas O'Sullivan." BOTP; CH; FaPON; MoShBr;
   PDV
Piper o' Dundee, The. *Unknown.* OxBS
Piper's Progress, The. Francis Sylvester Mahony. FiBHP
Pipes at Lucknow, The. Whittier. GN
Pipes of the misty moorlands. The Pipes at Lucknow. Whittier. GN
Piping Down the Valleys Wild. Blake. *Fr.* Songs of Innocence.
   FaBoCh; FaBV; HeIP; InvP; NAEL-2; NAWM-2; NIP; NOBE; OnUR;
   PoE
   (Introduction to "Songs of Innocence.") EnRP; FaBoBe; GoJo; InPS;
     NOEC; NoP; OAEL-2; OBNC; PoEL-4; RHPC; SoSe; TEP; TrGrPo
   (Piper, The.) AWP; OxBChV; PDV
   (Reeds of Innocence.) LiTB; OBEV
Piping hot, smoking hot. The Hot Pease Man. Mother Goose. OxNR
Piping Peace. James Shirley. *Fr.* The Imposture. ACP; NOBE
   (Song: "You virgins that did late despair.") PoEL-2
Pipling. Theodore Roethke. *Fr.* Three Epigrams, 1. NBLV; TW
Pippa Passes, *sels.* Robert Browning.
   Service. *Fr.* Introduction. TrGrPo
   Song. ViBoPo
   Year's at the Spring, The. *Fr.* sc. 1. BLPA; FaBoBe; FaBV; WGRP
     (Pippa's Song.) BLPL; BoTP; FaFP; FaPON; GoJo; LiTB; NTCP;
     OBEV; OBNC; PDV; TEP; TrCP; UnPo
     (Song: "Year's at the Spring, The.") SoSe; TrGrPo
Pippa Passes, But I Can't Get Around This Truck. Margaret Blaker.
   NBLV
Pippa's Song. Robert Browning. *See* Pippa Passes: Year's at the Spring,
   The.
Pippity poppity. Portrait of the Consort to Louis XIV. Blossom S.
   Kirschenbaum. SoTCo
Piraeus. Haim Guri, *tr. fr. Hebrew* by Warren Bargad *and* Stanley F.
   Chyet. IP
Pirate, The, *sels.* Sir Walter Scott.
   Song of the Mermaids and Mermen. *Fr. ch.* 16. WSC
   Song of the Reim-Kennar, The. *Fr. ch.* 6. OAEL-2; OBNC
Pirate Ditty. Robert Louis Stevenson. *Fr.* Treasure Island. NOBVV
Pirate Don Durk of Dowdee, The. Mildred Plew Meigs. OnUR; PDV
Pirate Story. Robert Louis Stevenson. BeLS; FaPON
Pirates' Fight, The. Joseph Schull. *Fr.* The Legend of Ghost Lagoon.
   CaP
Pirates of Penzance, The, *sels.* William Schwenck Gilbert.
   I Am the Very Model [*or* Pattern] of a Modern Major-General. NBLV;
     NOBL; NOP
   (Modern Major-General, The.) NBLV
   Most Ingenious Paradox, A. NAs
   Policeman's Lot, A [*or* The]. NOBL; SaC; TrGrPo
Pirates' Tea-Party, The. Dorothy Una Ratcliffe. BoTP
Pirithous being over hault or mynde and such a one. Philemon and
   Baucis. Ovid, *tr. fr. Latin* by Arthur Golding. *Fr.* Metamorphoses,
   VIII. CTC
   "Upon the hills of Phrygie near a teyle there stands a tree." OBSC, *tr.*
     by Arthur Golding.
     (Baucis and Philemon.)
   "Then Lelex rose, an old experienced man." AWP, *tr.* by Dryden.
     OBVE, *tr.* by Dryden.
   "Heaven's power is infinite; earth, air, and sea." OAEL-1, *tr.* by
     Dryden.
Piscatorie Eclogues, *sel.* Phineas Fletcher.
   "Fisher-lad, A (no higher dares he look)." *Fr.* III. SeCV-1
Pisces. R. S. Thomas. OxBC
Pisces Child. Sandra McPherson. NMM
Pisgah. Willard Austin Wattles. WGRP
Piss Artist, The. W. G. Shepherd. NPo
Pissing and trembling. Issa, *tr. fr. Japanese* by Hiroaki Sato. *Fr.* Forty-
   four Hokku. FCEI
Pistyll Rhaeadr and Wrexham steeple. The Seven Wonders of North
   Wales. *Unknown.* OBWVE
Pit, The. Suad al-Mubarak al-Sabah, *tr. fr. Arabic* by May Jayyusi *and*
   John Heath-Stubbs. MAP
Pit, The. Theodore Roethke. *Fr.* The Lost Son. NAAL-2
Pit, pat, well-a-day. Mother Goose. OxNR
Pit Viper. N. Scott Momaday. CDW; HATNAP; NOVW

Pit Viper. George Starbuck. NYBP
Pitch and quantity struggle in our words. Rhythm. Veijo Meri, *tr. by*
   Aili Jarvenpa. SOP
Pitch-Ball. Yang Chi, *tr. fr. Chinese* by Jonathan Chaves. *Fr.* Ten
   Poems on the Tuan-yang Festival. CoBLCP
Pitch here the tent, while the old horse grazes. Juggling Jerry. George
   Meredith. BeLS; SeCePo
Pitch pines fade, The. The Quiet Fog. Marge Piercy. UnPo
Pitch Seven. Hamish Brown. PoSH
Pitcher. Robert Francis. NePoAm; OxBSP; SD; SoSe; WeW
Pitcher, The. Yüan Chen, *tr. fr. Chinese* by Arthur Waley. AWP
Pitcher of Mignonette, A. H. C. Bunner. AA
Pith of faith is gone, The. And as there lie. Child of Loneliness.
   Norman Gale. WGRP
Pithecanthropus erectus. On Evolution. John Ciardi. OBAL
Pitiful mouth, saith he, that living gavest. Henry's Lament. Samuel
   Daniel. *Fr.* The Complaint of Rosamond. OBSC
Pitifully baby frogs. Kifu, *tr.* by Sato. FCEI
Pitiless heat from heaven pours. The Seasons. Kalidasa, *tr.* by Arthur
   W. Ryder. AWP
Pitt-Rivers Museum, Oxford, The. James Fenton. FaBoMo
Pitter-patter, hear it raining? Rain. Lilian McCrea. BoTP
Pittsburgh. Witter Bynner. AmFN
Pitty Patty Polt! *Unknown.* BoTP
Pity. William Mills. MT
Pity beyond all telling, A. The Pity of Love. W. B. Yeats. CMoP;
   NOBVV
Pity for him who suffers from his waste. Suffer the Children. Audre
   Lorde. PoBA
Pity for Mary. *Unknown.* *See* Now Goeth [*or* goth *or* goothe] Sun [*or*
   Sunne] under Wood.
Pity, how the dew must spill from grass leaves. Teika, *tr. fr. Japanese* by
   Hiroaki Sato. *Fr.* A Compendium of Good Tanka. FCEI
Pity me on my pilgrimage to Lock Derg! At Saint Patrick's Purgatory.
   Donnchadh Mor O'Dala, *tr.* by Sean O'Faolain. AnIL; TIRV
Pity me, your child. *Unknown, tr.* by Arthur Waley. BoS
Pity! mourn in plaintive tone. The Death of Lesbia's Bird. Catullus, *tr.*
   by Samuel Taylor Coleridge. AWP
   (Death of the Starling, The.) PBBP
Pity now poor Mary Ames. Mary Ames. *Unknown.* NA
Pity of It, The. Thomas Hardy. CMoP; LiTM; WaP
Pity of Love, The. W. B. Yeats. CMoP; NOBVV
Pity of the Leaves, The. E. A. Robinson. AA; AnAmPo; MoAmPo
Pity, pity, pity. A True Love Ditty. Thomas Middleton. *Fr.* Blurt,
   Master Constable. EIL
Pity Poor Labourers. *Unknown.* OBET
Pity poor lovers who may not do what they please. The Envy of Poor
   Lovers. Austin Clarke. CIP; CMoP; IPY
Pity, Religion has so seldom found. William Cowper. WGRP
Pity the girl with crystal hair. Joan Aiken. WSC
Pity the Man Who English Lacks. Michael Hartnett, *tr. fr. Irish by* the
   author. CIP
Pity the nameless, and the unknown, where. The Nameless Ones.
   Conrad Aiken. AnAmPo; OxBA
Pity the sorrows of a poor old man! The Beggar. Thomas Moss.
   NOEC
Pity the sweetfish after spawning. Kaya Shirao, *tr. fr. Japanese* by
   Hiroaki Sato. *Fr.* Twenty-one Hokku. FCEI
Pity This Busy Monster, Manunkind. E. E. Cummings. AmPP; LiTA;
   LiTM; NAAL-2; NOBA; OxBA; PPP; TAP
Pity this girl. The Stranger. William Everson. FF
Pity those men who from the start. A Song about Great Men. Michael
   Hamburger. NePoEA
Pity; We Were Such a Good Invention, A. Yehuda Amichai, *tr. fr.*
   Hebrew by Assia Gutmann. BoLoP
Pity would be no more. The Human Abstract. Blake. *Fr.* Songs of
   Experience. EnRP; NAEL-2; NOEC; OAEL-2; PoE; PoEL-4; PPP
Pitying a Woman Who Has Many Affairs. Kito, *tr. fr. Japanese* by
   Hiroaki Sato. *Fr.* Twenty-four Hokku. FCEI
Pitying the Farmer. Li Shen, *tr. fr. Chinese* by Burton Watson.
   CoBCP
Piute Creek. Gary Snyder. CoAP; NAAL-2; NaP; NOBA
Pixies, slipping, dipping, stealing. Cornish Magic. Ann Durell.
   FaPON
Piyyut for Rosh Hashana. Haim Guri, *tr. fr. Hebrew.* OFD, *tr.* by Ruth
   Finer Mintz; IP, *tr.* by Warren Bargad *and* Stanley F. Chyet.
Pizza, The. Ogden Nash. RHPC
Pizza Joint in Cranston, A. Craig Weeden. BXAP
Pizza, pickle. Three Tickles. Dennis Lee. RAR
Pla ce bo! Who is there, who? John Skelton. *Fr.* Phyllyp Sparowe [*or*
   Philip Sparrow]. AAS; NOBE; OAEL-1; OxBoLi, *abr.*.

Pilgrim from the East, The. Gustave Kahn, *tr. fr. French by* Jethro Bithell. TrJP

Pilgrim Song, The. Bunyan. *See* Pilgrim's Progress, The: Who would true valor see.

Who would true valour see.

Pilgrim Song. Florence Earle Coates. OHIP

Pilgrimage. Austin Clarke. CIP; IPY; TIRV

Pilgrimage. Eileen Duggan. ATNZ

Pilgrimage, The. George Herbert. ChTr; FaBoRV; NAEL-1; PoE

Pilgrimage, The. Sir Walter Ralegh. *See* Passionate Man's Pilgrimage, The.

Pilgrimage Song. *Unknown, tr. fr. Pueblo Indian by* Mary Austin. WPE

Pilgrimage to Testour, The. Ryvel, *tr. fr. French by* Edouard Roditi. VWA

Pilgrims. Joseph Brodsky, *tr. fr. Russian by* Dimitry Pospielovsky *and* Keith Bosley. VWA

Pilgrims. William Stafford. BLA

Pilgrims. Jean Valentine. LCAP; TAP

Pilgrims Came, The. Annette Wynne. OHIP

Pilgrims in Mexico. *Unknown.* OBCP

Pilgrims of the trackless deep. Pilgrim Song. Florence Earle Coates. OHIP

Pilgrim's Problem. C. S. Lewis. TrCP

Pilgrim's Progress, The, *sels.* Bunyan.
"He that is down needs fear no fall." EBEV
(Enough!) BLRP
(Shepherd Boy Sings [in the Valley of Humiliation], The.) EaLo; GN; NOBE; OBEV; WGRP
(Shepherd Boy's Song, The.) BoTP
(Song of the Shepherd Boy.) OxBSP
(Song of the Shepherd in the Valley of Humiliation, The.) OBS
"What danger is the pilgrim in." EBEV
"Who would true valour see." EBEV
(Pilgrim, The.) BoTP; GN
(Pilgrim Song, The.) CoMu; ELP; NOCV; OBS
(Pilgrim's Song, The.) WiR
(To Be a Pilgrim, *sl. diff. vers.*) FaPoR

Pilgrims' Sea Voyage and Seasickness, The. *Unknown.* OBTV
(By Sea to Santiago.) OxBLMV

Pilgrim's Song. Bernard S. Ingemann, *tr. fr. Danish by* Sabine Baring-Gould. WGRP

Pilgrim's Song, The. Bunyan. *See* Pilgrim's Progress, The: Who would true valor see.

Pilgrim's Song, The. Bible, *O.T. See* Psalms: Psalm CXXI ("I will lift up mine eyes unto the hills").

Pill, The. Austin Clarke. TW

Pillar of Fame, The. Robert Herrick. CaPo; JCP; NIP; SeCP

Pillar of fire by night, A. The Song of Sherman's Army. Charles Graham Halpine. PAH

Pillar perished is whereto I leant, The. Sir Thomas Wyatt. *See* Piller pearisht is whearto I lent, The.

Pillar Towers of Ireland, The. Denis Florence MacCarthy. TIRV

Piller pearisht is whearto I lent, The. Sir Thomas Wyatt, *after the Italian of* Petrarch. AAS; OBVE
(Pillar perished is whereto I leant, The.) FaBoPV

Pillory, The. Renée Vivien, *tr. fr. French by* Sandia Belgrade. PeHV

Pillow hard as stone! Kawabata Bosha, *tr. by* Geoffrey Bownas *and* Anthony Thwaite. PeBJV

Pillows wet our faces with, The. New and Old Gospel. Nate Mackey. CNA

Pilot, The. Russell Edson. LCAP

Pilotless in youth was my life's ship. The Ship of Life. Ahmad al-Safi al-Najafi, *tr. by* Salma Khadra Jayyusi *and* John Heath-Stubbs. MAP

Pilots, The. Denise Levertov. InPS

Pilots, Man Your Planes. Randall Jarrell. MoAB; MoAmPo

Pilpul. Rodger Kamenetz. UL; VWA

Pimpernel. Charlotte Druitt Cole. BoTP

Pimville Station. Sipho Sepamla. WMBCH

Pin, The. Ann Taylor. OxBChV

Pin-swin or spine-swine, The. His Shield. Marianne Moore. LiTM

Pin-up Girl. Louis O. Coxe. WaP

Pinay. Virginia Cerenio. BrSi

Pinch him, pinch him, black and blue. A Fairy Song. John Lyly. *Fr.* Endymion. OBSC

Pinch of Salt, A. Robert Graves. MoBrPo

Pindar. Antipater of Sidon, *tr. fr. Greek by* John Addington Symonds. AWP

Pindar is imitable by none. The Praise of Pindar ("Pindarum quisquis studet aemulari"). Horace, *tr. fr. Latin by* Abraham Cowley. *Fr.* Odes, IV, 2. OAEL-1

Pindaric Ode, A. Thomas Gray. *Fr.* The Bard. SeCePo

Pindaric on the Grunting of a Hog, A. Samuel Wesley. NOBL

Pindarique Ode on the Arrival of His Excellency, A, *sel. Unknown.*
"Sing first the heroe in his goodly ship." PBCV

Pindar's Revenge. Edward Sanders. PoM

Pine, The. Saunders Lewis, *tr. fr. Welsh by* Gwyn Morgan. OBWVE

Pine, The. Augusta Webster. OHIP

Pine and cypress by the old tomb. Yoshino. Fujii Chikugai, *tr. by* Burton Watson. JLIC-2

Pine at Timber-Line, The. Harriet Monroe. PoA

Pine bloom, though you, The. Lady Heguri. *Fr.* Manyo Shu. Ma

Pine boat a-shift. Ezra Pound, *fr. the Chinese.* OBVE

Pine cone, as it is, A. Ozaki Hosai, *tr. fr. Japanese by* Hiroaki Sato. *Fr.* One Hundred Haiku in Free Form. FCEI

Pine Gum. W. W. E. Ross. OBCV

Pine Music. Kate Louise Brown. BoTP

Pine needles cover the silent ground. Woodlands. Sir Herbert Read. BrPo

Pine Pavilion Hill. Chu Yi-tsun, *tr. fr. Chinese by* Irving Lo. *Fr.* Quatrains on Yung-chia, I. WFTU

Pine Point, You Are. Gordon Henry. STE

Pine Resin. Moritake, *tr. fr. Japanese by* Sato. FCEI

Pine Sounds. Po Chü-i, *tr. fr. Chinese by* Burton Watson. CoBCP

Pine-Tree Buoy, A. Harrison Smith Morris. AA

Pine-tree grew in the wood, The. Three Trees. C. H. Crandall. OHIP

Pine-tree standeth lonely, A. Ein Fichtenbaum steht einsam. Heine, *tr. by* James Thomson. AWP

Pine Tree Tops. Gary Snyder. NOBA; Prf

Pine Waves. Yu Kuang-chung, *tr. fr. Chinese by* Dominic Cheung. IFON

Pines, The. Julie Mathilde Lippmann. AA

Pines, The. Harriet Prescott Spofford. AA

Pines along the Coast. Tameko, *tr. fr. Japanese by* Steven D. Carter. WFTW

Pines and cedars, a hundred feet of green, clinging to the earth. T'ang Yin, *tr. fr. Chinese by* Jonathan Chaves. *Fr.* Poems Inscribed on Paintings. CoBLCP

Pines and the Sea, The. Christopher Pearse Cranch. AA

Pines are capped with snow, The. Inscribed on a Painting. Yü Chi, *tr. by* Jonathan Chaves. CoBLCP

Pines of Karasaki, The. Basho, *tr. fr. Japanese by* Burton Watson. *Fr.* Seventy-six Hokku. FCEI

Pines were dark on Ramoth hill, The. My Playmate. Whittier. AnAmPo; NOBA

Piney Woods. Malcolm Cowley. NYBP

Pining for one who does not come. Teika, *tr. by* Geoffrey Bownas *and* Anthony Thwaite. PeBJV

Pinionjay shits pebbles. *Unknown, tr. by* Jerome Rothenberg. STP

Pink Almond. Katharine Tynan. BoTP

Pink confused with white. The Pot of Flowers. William Carlos Williams. QFR

Pink Dominoes. Kipling. CenHV

Pink Frock, The. Thomas Hardy. OxBSP

Pink Slip at Tool & Dye. Dave Smith. NoAM

Pink, small and punctual. Emily Dickinson. FaBV

Pink tender hand. Tune: Phoenix Hairpin. Lu Yu, *tr. by* Burton Watson. CoBCP

Pinkletinks. Grace Elisabeth Allen. GoYe

Pinks and a Blue Cat. Hagiwara Sakutaro, *tr. fr. Japanese by* Hiroaki Sato. FCEI

Pino the Lizard in his patent leather shoes. Four Brothers. W. S. Di Piero. MAYP

Pins of the slack pin seine, The. Our Number. Martin Carter. PVCV

Pint of Water, A. *Unknown.* FaBoUs

Pinta, the Nina and the Santa Maria, The. John Tagliabue. AmFN

Pinto Mare, A. Dave Smith. BLA

Pints and the pistols, the pike-staves and pottles, The. *At. to* Winthrop Mackworth Praed. SoSe

Pinwheel's Song, The. John Ciardi. PDV; SO

Pioneer Woman. Vesta Pierce Crawford. AiP

Pioneer Woman—in the North Country, The. Eunice Tietjens. AmFN

Pioneers. Charles Badger Clark, Jr. FaBoBe

Pioneers. Hamlin Garland. AA

Pioneers! O Pioneers! Walt Whitman. FaBoBe; OPP

Pious Selinda [or Celinda]. Congreve. ELP; ErPo; NOBE
(Song: "Pious Selinda goes to prayers.") BoLoP; FaBoCo; NBLV; NOEC; OxBSP

Pipe and Can, I ("The Indian weed withered quite"). Robert Wisdome. *See* Indian weed [now] withered quite, The.

Pipe and Can II. Thomas Bonham. *See* Whenas [or When as or When that] the chill sirocco [or charokko or charocco] blow[e]s.

Pipe of Tobacco, A, *sels.* Isaac Hawkins Browne.

"Blest leaf! whose aromatic gales dispense." BXAP; Par
"Boy! bring an ounce of Freeman's best." Par
  (Boy! Bring an Ounce.) BXAP
Piped a tiny voice hard by. The Chickadee. Emerson. FaPON
Piped the blackbird on the beechwood spray. Little Bell. Thomas
  Westwood. GN
Piper, The. Blake. *See* Songs of Innocence: Piping Down the Valleys
  Wild.
Piper, The. W. S. Merwin. NAAL-2
Piper, A [*or* The]. "Seumas O'Sullivan." BOTP; CH; FaPON; MoShBr;
  PDV
Piper o' Dundee, The. *Unknown.* OxBS
Piper's Progress, The. Francis Sylvester Mahony. FiBHP
Pipes at Lucknow, The. Whittier. GN
Pipes of the misty moorlands. The Pipes at Lucknow. Whittier. GN
Piping Down the Valleys Wild. Blake. *Fr.* Songs of Innocence.
  FaBoCh; FaBV; HeIP; InvP; NAEL-2; NAWM-2; NIP; NOBE; OnUR;
  PoE
  (Introduction to "Songs of Innocence.") EnRP; FaBoBe; GoJo; InPS;
    NOEC; NoP; OAEL-2; OBNC; PoEL-4; RHPC; SoSe; TEP; TrGrPo
  (Piper, The.) AWP; OxBChV; PDV
  (Reeds of Innocence.) LiTB; OBEV
Piping hot, smoking hot. The Hot Pease Man. Mother Goose. OxNR
Piping Peace. James Shirley. *Fr.* The Imposture. ACP; NOBE
  (Song: "You virgins that did late despair.") PoEL-2
Pipling. Theodore Roethke. *Fr.* Three Epigrams, 1. NBLV; TW
Pippa Passes, sels. Robert Browning.
  Service. *Fr.* Introduction. TrGrPo
  Song. ViBoPo
  Year's at the Spring, The. *Fr.* sc. 1. BLPA; FaBoBe; FaBV; WGRP
    (Pippa's Song.) BLPL; BoTP; FaFP; FaPON; GoJo; LiTB; NTCP;
    OBEV; OHIP; PDV; TEP; TrCP; UnPo
    (Song: "Year's at the Spring, The.") SoSe; TrGrPo
Pippa Passes, But I Can't Get Around This Truck. Margaret Blaker.
  NBLV
Pippa's Song. Robert Browning. *See* Pippa Passes: Year's at the Spring,
  The.
Pippity poppity. Portrait of the Consort to Louis XIV. Blossom S.
  Kirschenbaum. SoTCo
Piraeus. Haim Guri, *tr. fr. Hebrew* by Warren Bargad *and* Stanley F.
  Chyet. IP
Pirate, The, *sels.* Sir Walter Scott.
  Song of the Mermaids and Mermen. *Fr.* ch. 16. WSC
  Song of the Reim-Kennar, The. *Fr.* ch. 6. OAEL-2; OBNC
Pirate Ditty. Robert Louis Stevenson. *Fr.* Treasure Island. NOBVV
Pirate Don Durk of Dowdee, The. Mildred Plew Meigs. OnUR; PDV
Pirate Story. Robert Louis Stevenson. BeLS; FaPON
Pirates' Fight, The. Joseph Schull. *Fr.* The Legend of Ghost Lagoon.
  CaP
Pirates of Penzance, The, *sels.* William Schwenck Gilbert.
  I Am the Very Model [*or* Pattern] of a Modern Major-General. NBLV;
    NOBL; NOP
    (Modern Major-General, The.) NBLV
  Most Ingenious Paradox, A. NAs
  Policeman's Lot, A [*or* The]. NOBL; SaC; TrGrPo
Pirates' Tea-Party, The. Dorothy Una Ratcliffe. BoTP
Pirithous being over hault or mynde and such a one. Philemon and
  Baucis. Ovid, *tr. fr. Latin* by Arthur Golding. *Fr.* Metamorphoses,
  VIII. CTC
  "Upon the hills of Phrygie near a teyle there stands a tree." OBSC, *tr.*
    by Arthur Golding.
    (Baucis and Philemon.)
  "Then Lelex rose, an old experienced man." AWP, *tr.* by Dryden;
    OBVE, *tr.* by Dryden.
  "Heaven's power is infinite; earth, air, and sea." OAEL-1, *tr. by*
    Dryden.
Piscatorie Eclogues, *sel.* Phineas Fletcher.
  "Fisher-lad, A (no higher dares he look)." *Fr.* III. SeCV-1
Pisces. R. S. Thomas. OxBC
Pisces Child. Sandra McPherson. NMM
Pisgah. Willard Austin Wattles. WGRP
Piss Artist, The. W. G. Shepherd. NPo
Pissing and trembling. Issa, *tr. fr. Japanese* by Hiroaki Sato. *Fr.* Forty-
  four Hokku. FCEI
Pistyll Rhaeadr and Wrexham steeple. The Seven Wonders of North
  Wales. *Unknown.* OBWVE
Pit, The. Suad al-Mubarak al-Sabah, *tr. fr. Arabic* by May Jayyusi *and*
  John Heath-Stubbs. MAP
Pit, The. Theodore Roethke. *Fr.* The Lost Son. NAAL-2
Pit, pat, well-a-day. Mother Goose. OxNR
Pit Viper. N. Scott Momaday. CDW; HATNAP; NOVW

Pit Viper. George Starbuck. NYBP
Pitch and quantity struggle in our words. Rhythm. Veijo Meri, *tr. by*
  Aili Jarvenpa. SOP
Pitch-Ball. Yang Chi, *tr. fr. Chinese* by Jonathan Chaves. *Fr.* Ten
  Poems on the Tuan-yang Festival. CoBLCP
Pitch here the tent, while one horse grazes. Juggling Jerry. George
  Meredith. BeLS; SeCePo
Pitch pines fade, The. The Quiet Fog. Marge Piercy. UnPo
Pitch Seven. Hamish Brown. PoSH
Pitcher. Robert Francis. NePoAm; OxBSP; SD; SoSe; WeW
Pitcher, The. Yüan Chen, *tr. fr. Chinese* by Arthur Waley. AWP
Pitcher of Mignonette, A. H. C. Bunner. AA
Pith of faith is gone, The. And as there lie. Child of Loneliness.
  Norman Gale. WGRP
Pithecanthropus erectus. On Evolution. John Ciardi. OBAL
Pitiful mouth, saith he, that living gavest. Henry's Lament. Samuel
  Daniel. *Fr.* The Complaint of Rosamond. OBSC
Pitifully baby frogs. Kifu, *tr. by* Sato. FCEI
Pitiless heat from heaven pours. The Seasons. Kalidasa, *tr. by* Arthur
  W. Ryder. AWP
Pitt-Rivers Museum, Oxford, The. James Fenton. FaBoMo
Pitter-patter, hear it raining? Rain. Lilian McCrea. BoTP
Pittsburgh. Witter Bynner. AmFN
Pitty Patty Polt! *Unknown.* BoTP
Pity. William Mills. MT
Pity beyond all telling, A. The Pity of Love. W. B. Yeats. CMoP;
  NOBVV
Pity for him who suffers from his waste. Suffer the Children. Audre
  Lorde. PoBA
Pity for Mary. *Unknown. See* Now Goeth [*or* goth *or* goothe] Sun [*or*
  Sunne] under Wood.
Pity, how the dew must spill from grass leaves. Teika, *tr. fr. Japanese* by
  Hiroaki Sato. *Fr.* A Compendium of Good Tanka. FCEI
Pity me on my pilgrimage to Lock Derg! At Saint Patrick's Purgatory.
  Donnchadh Mor O'Dala, *tr.* by Sean O'Faolain. AnIL; TIRV
Pity me, your child. *Unknown, tr.* by Arthur Waley. BoS
Pity! mourn in plaintive tone. The Death of Lesbia's Bird. Catullus, *tr.*
  by Samuel Taylor Coleridge. AWP
  (Death of the Starling, The.) PBBP
Pity now poor Mary Ames. Mary Ames. *Unknown.* NA
Pity of It, The. Thomas Hardy. CMoP; LiTM; WaP
Pity of Love, The. W. B. Yeats. CMoP; NOBVV
Pity of the Leaves, The. E. A. Robinson. AA; AnAmPo; MoAmPo
Pity, pity, pity. A True Love Ditty. Thomas Middleton. *Fr.* Blurt,
  Master Constable. EiL
Pity Poor Labourers. *Unknown.* OBET
Pity poor lovers who may not do what they please. The Envy of Poor
  Lovers. Austin Clarke. CIP; CMoP; IPY
Pity, Religion has so seldom found. William Cowper. WGRP
Pity the girl with crystal hair. Joan Aiken. WSC
Pity the Man Who English Lacks. Michael Hartnett, *tr. fr. Irish* by the
  author. CIP
Pity the nameless, and the unknown, where. The Nameless Ones.
  Conrad Aiken. AnAmPo; OxBA
Pity the sorrows of a poor old man! The Beggar. Thomas Moss.
  NOEC
Pity the sweetfish after spawning. Kaya Shirao, *tr. fr. Japanese* by
  Hiroaki Sato. *Fr.* Twenty-one Hokku. FCEI
Pity This Busy Monster, Manunkind. E. E. Cummings. AmPP; LiTA;
  LiTM; NAAL-2; NOBA; OxBA; PPP; TAP
Pity this girl. The Stranger. William Everson. FF
Pity those men who from the start. A Song about Great Men. Michael
  Hamburger. NePoEA
Pity; We Were Such a Good Invention, A. Yehuda Amichai, *tr. fr.*
  Hebrew by Assia Gutmann. BoLoP
Pity would be no more. The Human Abstract. Blake. *Fr.* Songs of
  Experience. EnRP; NAEL-2; NOEC; OAEL-2; PoE; PoEL-4; PPP
Pitying a Woman Who Has Many Affairs. Kito, *tr. fr. Japanese* by
  Hiroaki Sato. *Fr.* Twenty-four Hokku. FCEI
Pitying the Farmer. Li Shen, *tr. fr. Chinese* by Burton Watson.
  CoBCP
Piute Creek. Gary Snyder. CoAP; NAAL-2; NaP; NOBA
Pixies, slipping, dipping, stealing. Cornish Magic. Ann Durell.
  FaPON
Piyyut for Rosh Hashana. Haim Guri, *tr. fr. Hebrew.* OFD, *tr. by* Ruth
  Finer Mintz; IP, *tr. by* Warren Bargad *and* Stanley F. Chyet.
Pizza, The. Ogden Nash. RHPC
Pizza Joint in Cranston, A. Craig Weeden. BXAP
Pizza, pickle. Three Tickles. Dennis Lee. RAR
Pla ce bo! Who is there, who? John Skelton. *Fr.* Phyllyp Sparowe [*or*
  Philip Sparrow]. AAS; NOBE; OAEL-1; OxBoLi, *abr.*.

Plaça Santiago, The. "George Eliot." *Fr.* The Spanish Gypsy. OBTV

Place, The. Janet Frame. PeNZ

Place, The. Paul Zimmer. BLA

Place a custard stand in a garden. The Invention of New Jersey. Jack Anderson. TW

Place at Albert Bay, The. Muriel Rukeyser. PoA

Place changes, dawn breaks. Song of a Girl Journeying to the Country of the Dead. *Unknown.* OV

Place flickers. It always does, A. Sententiae. Vincent O'Sullivan. ATNZ

Place for No Story, The. Robinson Jeffers. AiP

Place in evidence. Lamberto Pignotti, *tr. fr. Italian by* Lawrence R. Smith. *Fr.* Zero Life. NItP

Place in thy memory, dearest, A. Gerald Griffin. BLPA

Place is called the Golden Cock, The. Lunch at the Coq d'Or. Peter Davison. TwCP

Place is calm, dusty worries clear, The. On the Twentieth Day. Ni Tsan, *tr. by* Jonathan Chaves. CoBLCP

Place is growing difficult, The. Flails of bramble. The Secret Garden. Thomas Kinsella. IPY; TwCP

Place is the focus. What is the language. In Defense of Metaphysics. Charles Tomlinson. MoBrPo

Place Me in the Breach. Yehuda Karni, *tr. fr. Hebrew by* Sholom J. Kahn. TrJP

Place Me under Your Wing. Hayyim Nahman Bialik, *tr. fr. Hebrew by* Gabriel Levin. VWA

Place-Names of China. Alan Bennett. FaBoPa; NOBL

Place no longer exists, The. At Sea. Yona Wallach, *tr. by* Warren Bargad *and* Stanley F. Chyet. IP

Place of Backs, The. W. S. Merwin. HoPM

Place-of-Many-Swans. Charlotte DeClue. STE

Place of O, The. Ray A. Young Bear. VoR

Place of Rest, The. "Æ" WGRP

Place of the Damn'd, The. Swift. FaBoEE; OBSV

Place of the Fian is bare tonight, The. *Unknown.* NOIV

Place of the Salamander. Yves Bonnefoy, *tr. fr. French by* Galway Kinnell. RHTwFP

Place of V, The. Ray A. Young Bear. VoR

Place on a Grave. Frank Stanford. MT

Place Pigalle. Richard Wilbur. HeIP

Place: Somewhere. Gerrit Kouwenaar, *tr. fr. Dutch by* Peter Nijmeijer. DuIn

Place we could never enter hides away still, The. Last Visit. Robert Finch. NOBC

Place where my mother, The. Garden Moss under Snow. Kaneyoshi, *tr. by* Steven D. Carter. WFTW

Place where our two gardens meet, The. The Wall. Henry Reed. LiTB

Place Where the Rainbow Ends, The. Paul Laurence Dunbar. PWR

Place your hand. Love Tight. Ted Joans. CNA

Pla ce bo,/ Who is there, who? Phyllyp Sparowe. John Skelton. AAS; OxBoLi

(Philip Sparrow.) NOBE; OAEL-1; PoEL-1

(Sparrow's Dirge, The.) OBSC

Placed in the west, Manukau spreads out. Tamaki of a Hundred Lovers. Merimeri Penfold, *tr. by* Margaret Orbell. PeNZ

Placed on this isthmus of a middle state. Pope. *Fr.* An Essay on Man, Epistle II. WeW

Places and Ways to Live. Richard Hugo. NIP

Places I go, leaning on my bramble cane, The. Inscribed on a Painting ("The places I go, leaning on my bramble cane"). T'ang Yin, *tr. by* Jonathan Chaves. CoBLCP

Places, Loved Ones. Philip Larkin. CMoP; NePoEA

Placid Man's Epitaph, A. Thomas Hardy. NoBrPo

Placid, rotted harbour has no voice, The. Arrival and Departure. Charles Eglington. PeSA

Placing a $2 Bet for a Man Who Will Never Go to the Horse Races Any More. Diane Wakoski. UnPo

Plague is Love, a plague, A! but yet. The Little Love-God. Meleager, *tr. by* Walter Headlam. AWP

Plague of Dead Sharks. Alan Dugan. LiTM; NoAM

Plague of Starlings, A. Robert Hayden. NoAM

Plague Sermon. William Heyen. KS

Plague take all your pedants, say I! Sibrandus Schafnaburgensis. Robert Browning. *Fr.* Garden Fancies, II. CTC; EBVV; TEP

Plague take them, every female! The Girls of Llanbadarn. Dafydd ap Gwilym, *tr. by* Leslie Norris. DiPo

Plain, The. Sándor Weöres, *tr. fr. Hungarian by* Jascha Kessler. FOC

Plain be the phrase, yet apt the verse. A Utilitarian View of the *Monitor's* Fight. Herman Melville. AmPP; NAAL-1; UnPo

Plain-Chant for America. Katherine Garrison Chapin. OPP

Plain Dealing. Alexander Brome. OBS

Plain Dealing's Downfall. *Unknown.* OBSV

Plain Fare. Daryl Hine. CoAP

Plain, Humble Letters. David Vogel, *tr. fr. Hebrew by* A. C. Jacobs. VWA

Plain Language from Truthful James ("I reside at Table Mountain"). Bret Harte. AA; BeLS; OBAL

Plain Language from Truthful James ("Which I wish to remark"). Bret Harte. AnAmPo; BeLS; BLPA; CTC; FaBoBe; NOBL; OBAL

(Heathen Chinee, The.) CenHV; FaBoCo

Plain Man's Dream, A. Frederick Keppel. AA

Plain of Adoration, The. *Unknown, tr. fr. Irish by* John Montague. BIrV

Plain of Heaven, The. Emperor Kogon, *tr. by* Steven D. Carter. WFTW

Plain of Heaven, think of it, The. Teika, *tr. fr. Japanese by* Hiroaki Sato. *Fr.* Eighty-four Tanka. FCEI

Plain of wild grasses, broad and tangled, A. Poem in the Form of a Coffin-Puller's Song ("A plain of wild grasses, broad and tangled"). T'ao Ch'ien, *tr. by* Burton Watson. CoBCP

Plain Sense of Things, The. Wallace Stevens. HCAP; NoAM

Plain Song. Benjamin Fondane, *tr. fr. French by* Matei Calinescu *and* Willis Barnstone. VWA

Plain Song. Craig Raine. TOF

Plain Song Talk. Richard Eberhart. PoA

Plain Tales from the Hills, *sels.* Kipling.

By the Hoof of the Wild Goat. OBNC

Look, You Have Cast Out Love! OxBSP

There Is a Tide. OxBSP

Plain Talk. William Jay Smith. FiBHP; MoAmPo

Plain truth would never serve. Take It from Me. Kenneth O. Hanson. CoAP

Plain was grassy, wild and bare, The. The Dying Swan. Tennyson. PBBP; WiR

Plainer Dubliners amaze us, The. On the Use of Jayshus. Oliver St. John Gogarty. FaBoEE

Plainly one's fears are never. The Orange Piano. David St. John. NAmP

Plainness. Jorge Luis Borges, *tr. fr. Spanish by* Norman Thomas Di Giovanni. NYBP

Plains Indians had a game, The. The Long Joke. R. T. Smith. STE

Plains of Heaven, The. Lorrie Goldensohn. NAmP

Plains of Waterloo, The. *Unknown.* OBET

Plaint. Ebenezer Elliott. OBD; OBEV

Plaint. Charles Henri Ford. EAS

Plaint has no melody. Asadullah Khan Ghalib, *tr. by* Ahmed Ali. GoT

Plaint of Flowers, A. Ernest Sandeen. CRP

Plaint of the Camel, The. Charles Edward Carryl. *Fr.* The Admiral's Caravan. BoTP; FaPON

(Camel's Complaint, The.) OBCA; OxBChV; RHPC

Plaint of the Wife, The. *Unknown, tr. fr. Russian by* W. R. S. Ralston. AWP

Plainview: 3. N. Scott Momaday. CDW

Plaits. Tabitha Tuckett. Mes

Plan for Understanding. Reinhard Priessnitz, *tr. fr. German by* Beth Bjorklund. CoAuP

Plan of Salvation, The. Milton. *See* Paradise Lost: O thou in heaven and earth the only place.

Plan to Live My Life Again, A. Diana O Hehir. NPGG

Plane: Earth, The. Sun-Ra. PoBA

Plane Geometer. David McCord. NYBP

Plane Geometry. Emma Rounds. ImOP

Plane leaves, The. Autumn Rain. D. H. Lawrence. BrPo

Plane tilts to Nashville, The. The Homecoming Singer. Jay Wright. PoBA

Plane Wreck at Los Gatos (Deportee). Woody Guthrie. PrIm; WTO

"Planet doesn't explode of itself, A," said drily. Earth ("A planet doesn't explode"). John Hall Wheelock. LiTM; OBD; SoSe

Planet is ours, The: and the blue and the desert spaces. The Jungle. Randolph Stow. *Fr.* Thailand Railway. CBAP

Planet of Descendance, A. William Frederick Stevenson. NOBVV

Planet of Nothing fills the sky, The. The Day You Are Reading This. William Stafford. PoA

Planet on the Table, The. Wallace Stevens. HAP; HCAP

Planet that we plant upon, The. Imagine Grass. Knute Skinner. SM

Planetarium. Adrienne Rich. CAPP; FaBoWP; HCAP; MoP; NAAL-2; NIP; NoAM; NOBA

Planetary Arc-Light, The. August Derleth. GoYe

Planets, the people, The. On Passing by Those Icy Stones (and Yes, Columbia!). Dave Calder. BWV

Planh, *sels.* Ray DiPalma. IAT

"Ceremony/ the triumph." *Fr.* VI.

"New world/ artful as monkeys, A." *Fr.* V.

"One deep in the dark."   *Fr.* X.
"Written granite."   *Fr.* I.
Plankton.   Ruth Miller.   PeSA
Planning the Perfect Evening.   Rita Dove.   MAYP
Plans.   Helen Morgan Brooks.   PoNe
Plans.   Dan Pagis, *tr. fr. Hebrew by* Warren Bargad *and* Stanley F. Chyet.
   IP
Plans for Altering the River.   Richard Hugo.   FYAP
Plant a Tree.   Lucy Larcom.   OHFP; WBLP
Plant the 'ahi'a and cause it to propagate.   The Crawlers.   Keaulumoku,
   tr. fr. Hawaiian by M. W. Beckwith.   *Fr.* Kumulipo, The; a Creation
   Chant.   WTO
"Plant the flower farms."   Wei Yüan, *tr. fr. Chinese by* Irving Lo.   *Fr.*
   Song of Chiang-nan, I.   WFTU
Plant without moisture sweet, A.   Rising in the Morning.   Hugh Rhodes.
   OxBChV
Plantation, The.   Seamus Heaney.   FaBCIP
Plantation Bitters.   *Unknown.*   FaBoUs
Plantation Ditty, A.   Frank Lebby Stanton.   AA
Planted Heel, The.   Sir Arthur Quiller-Couch.   EBVV
Planter.   Richard Murphy.   *Fr.* The Battle of Aughrim.   BIrV
Planter's Daughter, The.   Austin Clarke.   CIP; OxBTC
Planticru, The.   Robert Rendall.   OxBS
Planting, The.   Harley Elliott.   NeAC
Planting a Wood.   E. A. Baratynsky, *tr. fr. Russian by* Alan Myers.
   AAA
Planting Children: 1939.   Evan Zimroth.   ER
Planting Chrysanthemums.   Michizane, *tr. fr. Chinese by* Burton Watson.
   JLIC-1
Planting Flowers on the Eastern Embankment.   Po Chü-i, *tr. by* Arthur
   Waley.   BoNaP
Planting of the Apple-Tree, The.   Bryant.   AA; GN; OHIP
Planting Trees.   Violet Helen Friedlaender.   BoNaP
Planting Trout in the Chicago River.   Dennis Schmitz.   AnAn; NPGG
Plants don't talk, people say.   Rosalía de Castro, *tr. by* Doris Earnshaw.
   WPOW
Plaque.   Bruce Ruddick.   CaP
Plaque in the Reading Room for My Classmates Killed in Korea, The.   F.
   D. Reeve.   GOA
Plashes the Fountain.   Paul Celan, *tr. fr. German by* Michael Hamburger.
   OBVE
Plashes the tree-trunk lost in the river.   Remember Thou Me.   *Malay Oral
   Tradition, tr. by* R. J. Wilkinson *and* R. O. Winstedt.   WTO
Plasma.   Barrett Watten.   IAT
Plastic Airman.   Wrenne Jarman.   CN
Platform Goodbye.   Herbert B. Mallalieu.   WaP
Platform I stood upon began to move, The.   A Visit Home.   Joseph
   Glazer.   VWA
Plato, despair!   Meditation on Statistical Method.   James Vincent
   Cunningham.   CoAP; QFR; VGW
Plato to Theon.   Philip Freneau.   AA
Plato Told Him.   E. E. Cummings.   AmFN; AmPP; CTC; MoP; NoAM;
   NOBA; OxBA; PoE; WaP
Platonic[k] Love.   Abraham Cowley.   *Fr.* The Mistress.   NoP; SeCV-1
Platonick Love.   Lord Herbert of Cherbury.   OBS
Plato's Tomb.   *Unknown.*   *See* Eagle! why soarest thou above that tomb?
Platypus, The.   Oliver Herford.   FiBHP; NA
Plaudite, or End of Life, The.   Robert Herrick.   CaPo
Play.   A. R. Ammons.   PoA
Play.   Frank Asch.   NTCP
Play, The.   C. J. Dennis.   *Fr.* The Sentimental Bloke.   PoAu-1
Play-acting.   Frances Barber.   GoYe
Play I could once; but, gentle friend, you see.   To His Friend, on the
   Untunable.   Robert Herrick.   CaPo
Play is done, The; the curtain drops.   The End of the Play.   Thackeray.
   Fr. Dr. Birch and His Young Friends.   FaFP; GN
Play it once.   Saturday Night.   Langston Hughes.   MoAmPo
Play of the Four P.P., The, *sel.*   John Heywood.
   Palmer, The.   ACP
Play of the Weather, The, *sel.*   John Heywood.
   English Schoolboy, The.   ACP
Play on the seashore.   Shore.   Mary Britton Miller.   RAR
Play, Phoebus, on thy lute.   A Canticle to Apollo.   Robert Herrick.
   CaPo
Play Song.   Peter Clarke.   PBA
Play that thing.   Jazz Band in a Parisian Cabaret.   Langston Hughes.
   BANP; MoAmPo
Play their offensive and defensive parts.   Good Christians.   Robert
   Herrick.   LiTB
Play Time.   Blake.   *See* Songs of Innocence: Nurse's Song.

Play was done, The.   An Epilogue at Wallack's.   John Elton Wayland.
   AA
Play was each, pleasure each.   Cuchulain's Lament over Fardiad.
   Unknown, tr. by George Sigerson.   AnIL
Play Way, The.   Seamus Heaney.   NoP
Playboy.   Richard Wilbur.   FF; MoP; NIP; NoAM; NOBA; NoP; WeW
Playboy of the Demi-World: 1938, The.   William Plomer.   OxBTC;
   PeHV; TW
Player Piano, The.   Randall Jarrell.   MT; NAAL-2
Player Piano.   John Updike.   RR; WeW
Players.   Ruth Roston.   TSL
Playful monkey frisks with grand, A.   Retinue.   Paul Verlaine, *tr. by* C.
   F. MacIntyre.   ErPo
Playful Poem on a Chicken Egg, A.   Hsieh Chin, *tr. fr. Chinese by*
   Jonathan Chaves.   CoBLCP
Playgrounds.   L. Alma Tadema.   BoTP
Playhouse Key, The.   Rachel Field.   BoTP; FaPON
Playing at Cards.   Belle Randall.   CRP
Playing Bowl-and-Bead.   Tate Ryuwan, *tr. fr. Chinese by* Burton Watson.
   JLIC-2
Playing Cards, The.   Pope.   *Fr.* The Rape of the Lock, III.   ChTr
Playing hand after hand.   Full House.   Terry A. Garey.   BWV
Playing Horses.   Tadeusz Rozewicz, *tr. fr. Polish by* Czeslaw Milosz.
   PwPP
Playing House.   Jack Gilbert.   NPGG
Playing Pocahontas.   Lew Blockcolski.   VoR
Playing Solitaire.   Steven Fortney.   TSL
Playing the Game.   Barbara Goldowsky.   TSL
Playing the Game.   *Unknown.*   PWR
Playing the 7th.   48 Words for a Woman's Dance Song.   Jerome
   Rothenberg.   PoM
Playing Time.   Theresa Pappas.   TSL
Playing upon the hill three centaurs were!   The Centaurs.   James
   Stephens.   AmMo
Playing with Fire.   James Simmons.   CIP
Playing with friends one time.   What Her Girl Friend Said to Him (on Her
   Behalf) When He Came by Daylight.   *Unknown, tr. by* A. K.
   Ramanujan.   PLW
Playmates.   Lillian Everts.   GoYe
Plays.   Walter Savage Landor.   EnRP; NBLV; NoP; OxBoLi; OxBSP
Playthings.   William Cowper.   WaaP
Playwright, convict of public wrongs to men.   On Playwright.   Ben
   Jonson.   NoP
Plea.   John Ciardi.   OxBSP
Plea for a Captive.   W. S. Merwin.   NePoEA-2; NoAM; NYBP
Plea for a Plural, A.   Rudolph Chambers Lehmann.   CenHV
Plea for Flood Ireson, A.   Charles Timothy Brooks.   PAH
Plea for Hope.   Francis Carlin.   TrPWD
Plea for Mercy, A.   Kwesi Brew.   PBA
Plea for Peace.   Frank Prewett.   HATNAP
Plea for Trigamy, A.   Sir Owen Seaman.   NOBL
Plea of the Midsummer Fairies, The, *sels.*   Thomas Hood.   OBNC
   Fairy's Reply to Saturn, The.
   Green Dryad's Plea, The.
   Melodies of Time, The.
   Shakespeare: The Fairies' Advocate.
Plea to Boys and Girls, A.   Robert Graves.   GTBS-P; NAEL-2
Plea to My Sister, A.   James Cunningham.   JB
Plea to Those Who Matter.   James Welch.   AmPA
Plead for Me.   Emily Brontë.   PoEL-5
Pleaders, The.   Peter Davison.   NYBP
Pleading Voices.   Shalom Katav, *tr. fr. Arabic by* Yoffee Berkovitz.
   VWA
Pleasant and Delightful.   *Unknown.*   OBET, *with music;* OxBSS, *with
   music*
Pleasant Changes.   Jane Euphemia Browne.   OxBChV
Pleasant Comedy of Patient Grissell [*or* Grissel *or* Grissill], The, *sels.*
   Thomas Dekker *and others.*
   "Art thou poor, yet hast thou golden slumbers?"   HAP; InPS; UnPo
      (Basket-Maker's Song, The.)   OBSC; TrGrPo
      (Happy Heart, The.)   GTBS; GTBS-P; RB
      (Sweet Content.)   CH; EIL; OBEV
   Beauty, Arise!   EIL
      (Bridal Song, A ("Beauty arise, show forth thy glorious shining!").)
         OBSC; TrGrPo
   Golden Slumbers.   ELP
      (Cradle Song, A: "Golden slumbers kiss your eyes.")   OBSC;
         OxBChV; TrGrPo
      (Lullaby: "Golden slumbers kiss your eyes.")   EIL
Pleasant Delusion of a Sumpteous Citty.   Sarah Kemble Knight.   SCAP
Pleasant it looked.   This Newly Created World.   *Unknown.*   AiP

Pleasant Life in Newfoundland, The. Robert Hayman. NOBC

Pleasant Memories, *sel.* Charles Sangster.
Meadow-Field, The. OBCV

Pleasant New Ballad of Two Lovers, A. *Unknown.* CoMu

Pleasant New Court Song, A. *Unknown.* CoMu

Pleasant place I was at today, A. The Woodland Mass. Dafydd ap Gwilym, *tr. by* Gwyn Williams. OBWVE

Pleasant smell of frying sausages, A. Mixed Feelings. John Ashbery. HAP

Pleasant the House. *Unknown, tr. fr. Irish by* John Montague. BIrV

Please be silent, now my country, while I fill the speaker's place. The Negro Schools. Lizelia Augusta Jenkins Moorer. CBWP-3

Please, Chung Tzu. *Unknown, tr. fr. Chinese by* Burton Watson. CoBCP

Please do not die now. Listen. Unsent Message to My Brother in His Pain. Leon Stokesbury. MAYP

Please, everybody, look at me! Five Years Old. Marie Louise Allen. RAR

Please excuse me, Madam, if I constantly cough in your face. Prose behind the Insanity. Andreas Okopenko, *tr. by* Beth Bjorklund. CoAuP

Please excuse this letter. The Letter. Beatrice M. Murphy. PoNe

Please Excuse Typing. John Basil Boothroyd. FiBHP

Please Forward. James Welch. CDW

Please give me room, Howard! I've tried before. Trying to Separate. Robert Pack. KS

Please God, forsake your water and dry bread. To a Nun. John Ormond, *after the Welsh.* EBEV; FaBoTw

Please keep an eye on my house for a few moments. Vidya, *tr. by* Willis Barnstone. BoWoP

Please let my hair grow, mother. *Unknown, tr. by* Saduddin Shpoon. PBWP

Please Master. Allen Ginsberg. GLP; PeHV

Please Say Something. Tomioka Taeko, *tr. fr. Japanese by* Sato Hiroaki. FCEI; WPOW

Please tell me how you are not afraid. Departure. Genny Lim. BrSi

Please to remember. Gunpowder Plot Day. *Unknown.* FaBoPV; OxNR

Please you, draw near.—Louder the music there! Shakespeare. *Fr.* King Lear, IV, vii. EBEV

Please your Grace, from out your store. The Beggar to Mab, the Fairy [*or* Fairie] Queen. Robert Herrick. CaPo; WSC

Pleased am I, and more than willing. The Lay of the Honeysuckle. Marie de France, *tr. by* Robin Johnson. WPE

Pleasing Constraint, The. Aristaenetus, *tr. fr. Latin by* Richard Brinsley Sheridan *and* Nathaniel Brassey Halhed. ErPo

Pleasure and pride are not, as duty knows. A Vulgar Error. J. E. Thorold Rogers. FaBoEE

Pleasure-Boat, The. Richard Henry Dana. AnAmPo

Pleasure is so hard to remember. It goes. Santa Lucia II. Robert Hass. NAmP

Pleasure It Is. William Cornish. CH; MeEL
(Gratitude.) CTC; OBSC
(Spring.) BoNaP; ChTr

Pleasure me not, for love's pleasure drained me. In the Interstices. Ruth Stone. ErPo

Pleasure of Hope, The. Pope. *Fr.* An Essay on Man, Epistle I. ACP

Pleasure of Imagination, The, *sel.* Mark Akenside.
Love of Nature. *Fr.* III. NOEC

Pleasure of Ruins, The. J. D. McClatchy. PoA

Pleasure Reconciled to Virtue, *sels.* Ben Jonson. OAEL-1
Hymn to Comus. OAEL-1, *complete.*
(Hymn: "Room! room! make room for the bouncing belly.") NAEL-1
(Hymn to Comus.) ElL; SeCePo
(Hymn to the Belly.) SeCePo
"An eye of looking back were well." NAEL-1
"Come on, come on! and where you go." NAEL-1
"Great friend and servant of the good." NAEL-1
"It follows now you are to prove." NAEL-1
"O more, and more! this was so well." NAEL-1
"Ope, aged Atlas, open then thy lap." NAEL-1
"Wake, Hercules, awake: but heave up thy black eye." NAEL-1

Pleasures. Albert Goldbarth. GeTw

Pleasures. Denise Levertov. CAPP; NeAP; NoAM; NOBA; PoE

Pleasures among the Fields during the Four Seasons, *sels.* Li K'ai-hsien, *tr. fr. Chinese by* Jonathan Chaves. CoBLCP
"I've decided to study agriculture."
"I've followed the billowing dust as a traveler too long."
"Men plow, and know everything about "late" and "early", The."

Pleasures I took from life, The. The Ghost of a Ghost. Brad Leithauser. MAYP

Pleasures newly found are sweet. To the Same Flower. Wordsworth. EnRP

Pleasures of Darkness, The. Ahmad al-Safi al-Najafi, *tr. fr. Arabic by* Salma Khadra Jayyusi *and* John Heath-Stubbs. MAP

Pleasures of Hope, The, *sel.* Thomas Campbell.
"At summer eve, when Heaven's ethereal bow." EnRP

Pleasures of Imagination, The, *sels.* Mark Akenside.
Creative Process, The. *Fr.* II. NOEC
"Genius of ancient Greece! whose faithful steps." *Fr.* I. OBTV
Nature's Influence on Man. *Fr.* III. NOEC
(Love of Nature.) NOEC
Poetic Genius. *Fr.* IV. NOEC
That Delightful Time. SeCePo
"With what attractive charms this goodly frame." *Fr.* I. EnRP

Pleasures of Melancholy, The, *sels.* Thomas Warton the Younger.
"Beneath yon ruin'd abbey's moss-grown piles." NOEC
"Mother of musings, contemplation sage." EnRP

Pleasures of Merely Circulating, The. Wallace Stevens. LiTA; MAT; OBAL

Pleasures of Shinbashi. Liu E, *tr. fr. Chinese by* Jonathan Chaves. CoBLCP

Pleasures of the Door, The. Francis Ponge, *tr. fr. French by* Raymond Federman. RHTwFP

Pledge. N. M. Rashed, *tr. fr. Urdu by* Mahmood Jamal. PBMUP

Pledge. Avraham Shlonsky, *tr. fr. Hebrew by* Francis Landy. VWA

Pledge at Spunky Point, The. John Hay. OBAL

Pleiades, The. Mary Barnard. NYBP

Pleiades, The. Elizabeth Jane Coatsworth. ImOP

Pleiades are sinking calm as paint, The. Lesbos. Lawrence Durrell. EBEV

Plenary. *Unknown.* AmFP

Plenitude, oh what a plenitude. Song of Plenitude. Anna Swirszczynska, *tr. by* Czeslaw Milosz. PwPP

Plenteous place is Ireland for hospitable cheer, A. The Fair Hills of Ireland. *Unknown, tr. by* Sir Samuel Ferguson. FaBoPP; OBEV

Plentiful people went to the Cadillac drawing. Midweek. Josephine Miles. NoP

Plentiful snow deepens the path to the woods. Snow. Ruth Stone. NYBP

Plenty of Flowers. Two Songs about Flowers & Where I Was Walking. *Unknown, tr. by* Jerome Rothenberg *and* Johnny John. STP

Pliant the horn bow. *Unknown, tr. by* Arthur Waley. BoS

Plight, The. James W. Thompson. BPo

Plodder Seam, The. *Unknown.* ELP

Plop fall the plums; but there are still seven. *Unknown, tr. by* Arthur Waley. BoS

Plot against Proteus, The. Arthur James Marshall Smith. OBCV

Plot against the Giant, The. Wallace Stevens. CMoP; FF; OxBA

Plot to Assassinate the Chase Manhattan Bank, The. Carl Larsen. FF

Plough, The. Richard Henry Horne. OBEV

Plough-Hands' Song, The. Joel Chandler Harris. *Fr.* Uncle Remus and His Friends. AA

Ploughboy, The. John Clare. PoEL-4

Ploughed parallel as print the stony earth. Lines to My Grandfathers. Tony Harrison. *Fr.* The School of Eloquence. NoAM

Ploughing on Sunday. Wallace Stevens. FaPON; GoJo; RB; SOTW; TTTS

Ploughland has gone to bent, The. Gin the Goodwife Stint. Basil Bunting. CTC; TW

Ploughman, The. Karle Wilson Baker. WGRP

Ploughman. Patrick Kavanagh. TIRV

Ploughman, The. *Unknown.* GBP

Ploughman, The. *Unknown.* CoMu

Ploughman at the Plough. Louis Golding. OHIP

Ploughman he comes home at night, The. The Ploughman. *Unknown.* GBP

Ploughman he's a bonnie lad, The. The Ploughman. *Unknown.* CoMu

Ploughman, in Imitation of Milton, The. Samuel Jones. NOEC

Ploughman ploughing a level field. To a Schoolboy. *Unknown, tr. by* Anne Pennington. RB

Ploughman's Song, The. Nicholas Breton. *See* Honourable Entertainment Given to the Queen's Majesty in Progress at Elvetham, 1591, The: Phillida and Coridon.

Plovers on the Coast. Kenko, *tr. fr. Japanese by* Steven D. Carter. WFTW

Plovers over the evening waves of Lake Omi. Hitomaro. *Fr.* Manyo Shu. FCEI

Plow: "My beak is bent downward, I burrow below." *Unknown, formerly at. to* Cynewulf, *tr. fr. Anglo-Saxon. Fr.* Riddles (Exeter Book). AnOE

Plow, they say, to plow the snow, A. Plowmen. Robert Frost. SaC

Plowdens, Finns. Robert Hayden. *Fr.* Beginnings. CNA
Plower, The. Padraic Colum. MoBrPo
Plowman. Sidney Keyes. MoAB; PoRA
Plowman, The. Raymond Knister. OBCV
Plowman, The. *Unknown.* APAS
Plowman's Song. Raymond Knister. CaP
Plowmen. Robert Frost. SaC
Pluck the Fruit and Taste the Pleasure. Thomas Lodge. *Fr.* Robert, Second Duke of Normandy. ElL (Carpe Diem.) OBSC
Pluck Wins. *Unknown.* PWR
Plucking Out a Rhythm. Lawson Fusao Inada. AmPA
Plucking the Rushes. *Unknown, tr. fr. Chinese.* BoLoP; Mes; OBVE
Plucky as a postage stamp. Sport Items. Philippe Soupault, *tr. by* Joachim Neugroschel. POS
Plug. Edmund Vance Cooke. PWR
Plum, A. Mani Leib, *tr. fr. Yiddish by* John Hollander. PeBMYV
Plum-blossom, The. Akahito. *Fr.* Manyo Shu. AWP
Plum Blossoms. Chu Shu-chên, *tr. by* Kenneth Rexroth *and* Ling Chung. PBWP
Plum Blossoms. Michizane, *tr. fr. Chinese by* Burton Watson. JLIC-1
Plum blossoms are hard to make out. Teika, *tr. fr. Japanese by* Hiroaki Sato. *Fr.* A Compendium of Good Tanka. FCEI
Plum blossoms at their best. Basho, *tr. fr. Japanese by* Burton Watson. *Fr.* Seventy-six Hokku. FCEI
Plum Blossoms Late at Night. Shinkei, *tr. fr. Japanese by* Steven D. Carter. WFTW
Plum flowers/ blooming crimson. Kyogoku Tamekane, *tr. fr. Japanese by* Burton Watson. *Fr.* Twenty-three Tanka. FCEI
Plum fragrance startles me again and again. Lady Izumi, *tr. fr. Japanese by* Hiroaki Sato. *Fr.* Fifty-one Tanka. FCEI
Plum Scent through a Window closed against the Snow. Shotetsu, *tr. fr. Japanese by* Steven D. Carter. WFTW
Plum Tree, The. James Reaney. CaP
Plum tree breaks out in bees, The. April. Charles Wright. CAPP; MT
Plum Tree by the House, The. Oliver St. John Gogarty. OBEV; PoRA
Plum Tree Drops Its Fruit, The. *Unknown, tr. fr. Chinese by* Burton Watson. CoBCP
Plum Trees. Ranko, *tr. fr. Japanese.* FaPON
Plumber is icumen in. Murie Sing. Archibald Y. Campbell. FaBoPa
Plumber may be a poet, but a poet is not likely, A. The Difference. Stoddard King. OBAL
Plumes of love are black, The! Mad Sonnet 1. Michael McClure. PoM
Plump gold carp nudges a lily pad, A. The Humble Administrator's Garden. Vikram Seth. UAS
Plump servant of the spirit. The Flesh. Murano Shiro, *tr. by* Geoffrey Bownas *and* Anthony Thwaite. PeBJV
Plumpuppets, The. Christopher Morley. FaPON; RHPC
Plums already blooming. Yakamochi. *Fr.* Manyo Shu. FCEI
Plums are like blue pendulums, The. The Plum Tree. James Reaney. CaP
Plum's Heart, The. Gary Soto. NAmP
Plunging and labouring on in a tide of visions. In Front of the Landscape. Thomas Hardy. OBNC
Plunging downward through the slimy water. Death by Drowning. Elizabeth Brewster. NOBC
Plunging limbers over the shattered track, The. Dead Man's Dump. Isaac Rosenberg. BrPo; FaBoMo; GTBS-P; LiTM; MMA; NAEL-2; NoAM; NoP; OBWP; TrJP; VWA; WaP
Plunging towards Phrygia over violent water. Attis. Catullus, *tr. by* Peter Whigham. OBVE
Pluralist and Old Soldier, The. John Collier. NOEC
Plurality of Worlds. Washington Delgado, *tr. fr. Spanish by* Maureen Ahern *and* David Tipton. Per
+30[D]G/ C. Meir Wieseltier, *tr. fr. Hebrew by* Bernhard Frank. MHeP
Plutarch. Agathias, *tr. fr. Greek by* Dryden. AWP
Pluto's Council. Tasso, *tr. fr. Italian by* Edward Fairfax. *Fr.* Godfrey of Bulloigne; or, The Recoverie of Jerusalem. OBSC
Plymouth Women. Lyn Lifshin. ER
Po' Boy. *Unknown.* AS
Po' Boy Blues. Langston Hughes. BANP
Po Chu-i, balding old politician. As I Step over a Puddle at the End of Winter, I Think of an Ancient Chinese Governor. James Wright. CAPP; NaP
Po-hsia. Ku Yen-wu, *tr. fr. Chinese by* J. P. Seaton. WFTU
Po' lil' brack sheep dat strayed away. The Little Black Sheep. Paul Laurence Dunbar. WBLP
Poacher, The. *Unknown. See* When I was bound apprentice, in famous Lincolnshire.
Poaching *in Excelsis.* G. K. Menzies. FaBoCo

Pobble Who Has No Toes, The. Edward Lear. AmMo; FaBoCh; FaBoCo; FaBoNo; MoShBr; NA; OxBChV
Pocahontas. George Pope Morris. PAH
Pocahontas. Thackeray. AmFN; FaPON; GN; OnMSP; OPP; PAH "Wearied arm, and broken sword", *sel.* AiP
Pocahontas to Her English Husband, John Rolfe. Paula Gunn Allen. STE
Pock-marked player of the accordion, The. Wedding Party. Donald Hall. LCAP
Pocket Guide for Service Men. Hubert Creekmore. WaP
Pockets. Ernst Jandl, *tr. fr. German by* Beth Bjorklund. CoAuP
Pockets of our greatcoats full of barley, The. Requiem for the Croppies. Seamus Heaney. BIrV; CIP; FaBCIP; FaBoMo; OBWP
Pocomania. Philip Sherlock. PBCV
Pod of the Milkweed. Robert Frost. *See* Calling all butterflies of every race.
Poe. James Russell Lowell. *See* Fable for Critics, A: Poe and Longfellow.
Poe, a very sick man in Baltimore. The Poets of Hell. Karl Shapiro. NYBP
Poe and Longfellow. James Russell Lowell. *Fr.* A Fable for Critics. AmPP; NOBA; OxBA; TAP
Poe-'em of Passion, A. Charles Fletcher Lummis. BXAP
Poem/ (that flower of struggle most perfect lotus), The. On Hope. Lindolf Bell, *tr. by* William Jay Smith. CT
Poem, The/ that I chose for you. On the Margins of a Poem. Jiri Mordecai Langer, *tr. by* Gabriel Preil *and* Howard Schwartz. VWA
Poem: "About the size of an old-style dollar bill." Elizabeth Bishop. FYAP; HCAP; NoAM
Poem: "After your death." William Knott. EAS
Poem: "Ah, I know what happiness is!" Blanche Taylor Dickinson. CDC
Poem: "All the mirrors in the world." Frank O'Hara. CAPP
Poem: Alte Zachen. Abba Kovner, *tr. fr. Hebrew by* Warren Bargad *and* Stanley F. Chyet. IP
Poem: "And when I pay death's duty." Robin Blaser. NeAP
Poem: "As I traveled from the city." Salah Fa'iq, *tr. by* Patricia Alanah Byrne *and* Salma Khadra Jayyusi. MAP
Poem: "As the cat." William Carlos Williams. FaPON; InPS; InvP; NoP; PDV; RR; TTTS
Poem: "At night Chinamen jump." Frank O'Hara. NoAM; NOBA; SM
Poem: "At the edge of the window that limits space." Javier Sologuren, *tr. by* Maureen Ahern *and* David Tipton. Per
Poem: "At your light side trees shy." William Knott. EAS
Poem: "Atlantic is a sea of bones." Lucille Clifton. ER
Poem: "Beside the road the *wu t'ung* tree." Wu Chia-chi, *tr. fr. Chinese by* John E. Willis, Jr.. *Fr.* Miscellaneous Poems, I. WFTU
Poem: "Between rebellion as a private study and the public." Charles Donnelly. *See* Between rebellion as a private study and the public.
Poem: "By the road to the contagious hospital." William Carlos Williams. *See* By the road to the contagious hospital.
Poem: "Character of a landscape stands always in a mysterious relation, The." Charles Madge. EAS
Poem: "Clitoris is a kind of brain, A." Alice Notley. UL
Poem: "Come, brother, and tell me your life." Jorge Rebelo, *tr. by* Margaret Dickinson. WMBCH
Poem: "Country, The/ was back in the hands of the patriots." Fred Levinson. AmPA
Poem: "Disturbing to have a person." Barbara Guest. FaBoWP
Poem: "Eager note on my door said 'Call me,' The." Frank O'Hara. CAPP; EAS; NoAM; NoBA
Poem: "Every morning I forget how it is." Charles Simic. NNaP
Poem: "Face to face and in the face." Ray DiPalma. LP
Poem, A: "Father of all! in Death's relentless claim." Oliver Wendell Holmes. TrPWD
Poem: "For years I've heard." Robin Blaser. NeAP
Poem: "Form is the woods: the beast." Jim Harrison. VGW
Poem: "Geranium, houseleek, laid in oblong beds." John Gray. NOBVV
Poem: "Hail falls on the ocean, the night falls: "Have someone turn on the cowbeacons!" Max Jacob, *tr. by* Jerome Rothenberg. RHTwFP
Poem: "Hasten on your childhood to the hour when white." Pablo Picasso, *tr. by* David Gascoyne. EAS
Poem: "Hate is only one of many responses." Frank O'Hara. NeAP; SOTW
Poem: "He lying spilt like water from a bowl." Alison Boodson. ErPo
Poem: "He watched with all his organs of concern." W. H. Auden. PoA
Poem: "High on a ridge of tiles." Maurice James Craig. NeIP
Poem: "I believe the yellow flowers think with me." Alice Notley. UL
Poem: "I burn for England with a living flame." Gervase Stewart. *See* I Burn for England with a Living Flame.
Poem: "I cannot tell, not I, why she." Walter Savage Landor. GBL; OAEL-2

Poem: "I do not want only." Colleen Thibaudeau. NOBC

Poem, The: "I had never heard of the whiteness." David Schloss. PoA

Poem: "I have beaten my sword into an axe." Wu Chia-chi, *tr. fr. Chinese* by John E. Willis, Jr.. *Fr.* Miscellaneous Poems, II. WFTU

Poem: "I keep feeling all space as my image." Sanders Russell. EAS

Poem: "I knew a woman lovely in her bones." Theodore Roethke. *See* I Knew a Woman [Lovely in Her Bones].

Poem: "I know/ how fascinated we are with clarity." Salah Fa'iq, *tr. by* Patricia Alanah Byrne *and* Salma Khadra Jayyusi. MAP

Poem: "I lived in the first century of world wars." Muriel Rukeyser. UnPo

Poem: "I love the old melodious lays." Whittier. AA; AnAmPo; NoP; OxBA; TAP

Poem: "I loved my friend." Langston Hughes. ILY; NTCP

Poem, The: "I sing th' adventures of mine worthy wights." Thomas Morton. SCAP

Poem: "I take four devils with me when I ride." Gervase Stewart. WaP

Poem: "I walk at dawn across the hollow hills." Ruthven Todd. EAS

Poem: "I want to know today." Sargon Boulus, *tr. by* Sargon Boulus *and* Alistair Elliot. MAP

Poem: "I watched an armory combing its bronze bricks." Frank O'Hara. NoP

Poem: "I will always love you." Frank O'Hara. LLLT

Poem: "If I speak always of the dead." Salah Fa'iq, *tr. by* Patricia Alanah Byrne *and* Salma Khadra Jayyusi. MAP

Poem: "In its going down, the moon." Robert Hoggra. LLLT; MoCV

Poem: "In secret/ be quiet say nothing." Pablo Picasso, *tr. by* David Gascoyne. EAS

Poem, The: "In the beginning was the tune." A. Leyeles, *tr. by* Benjamin *and* Barbara Harshav. AYP

Poem: "In the corner a violet jug the bells the folds of paper." Pablo Picasso, *tr. by* David Gascoyne. EAS

Poem: "In the early evening, as now, a man is bending." Louise Glück. HCAP

Poem: "In the earnest path of duty." Charlotte Forten. BlSi

Poem: "In the stump of the old tree, where the heart has rotted out." Hugh Sykes Davies. EAS

Poem 4: "Irresponsible citizen." Abelardo Sanchez Leon, *tr. by* David Tipton. Per

Poem: "Is to love, this—to nurse a name." Rhoda Coghill. NeIP

Poem: "It doesn't look like a finger it looks like a feather of broken glass." Hugh Sykes Davies. EAS

Poem: "It's a dull poem." Steve Jonas. PeHV

Poem, The: "It's all in/ the sound. A song." William Carlos Williams. PCP

Poem: "Khrushchev is coming on the right day!" Frank O'Hara. NeAP; PoM

Poem: "Lana Turner has collapsed!" Frank O'Hara. CAPP; VGW

Poem: "Little brown boy." Helene Johnson. AmNP; BANP; CDC; PoBA

Poem: "Look at me 8th." Sonia Sanchez. PoBA

Poem: "My eyes have telescopes." João Cabral de Melo Neto, *tr. by* W. S. Merwin. TAP

Poem: "Night is beautiful, The." Langston Hughes. CDC

Poem: "Nothing is more cruel than to see." Salah Fa'iq, *tr. by* Patricia Alanah Byrne *and* Salma Khadra Jayyusi. MAP

Poem: "Nothing move thee." St. Theresa of Avila, *tr. by* Yvor Winters. CRP

Poem: "O men, walk on the hills." Maxwell Bodenheim. TrJP

Poem: "O sole mio, hot diggety, nix 'I wather think I can.'" Frank O'Hara. TTTS

Poem, A: "Of old, when Scarron his companions invited." Goldsmith. *Fr.* Retaliation. NOIV

Poem: "Oh who can ever praise enough." W. H. Auden. PoA

Poem: "Old man in the crystal morning after snow." Delmore Schwartz. PoA

Poem: "On getting a card." William Carlos Williams. VGW

Poem, The: "On this hill crossed." Galway Kinnell. NaP

Poem: "One whom I knew, a student and a poet." Alex Comfort. *See* One whom I knew, a student and a poet.

Poem: "Only response, The." William Knott. InPK

Poem: "Our eyes unlash slowly one." Bill Knott. PPR

Poem: "Our walls were thick." Venus Khoury-Gata, *tr. by* Carol Cosman. OV

Poem, The: "Painter of Dante's awful ferry-ride, The." Babette Deutsch. PoA

Poem: "Person who can do, The." Alan Dugan. ErPo

Poem: "Puriri moth's wing, A." Jan Kemp. ATNZ; PeNZ

Poem, The: "Rise Oedipus, and if thou canst unfold." Thomas Morton. SCAP

Poem: "So many pigeons at Columbus." Arthur Gregor. VGW

Poem: "So they begin. With two years gone." Boris Pasternak, *tr.* by C. M. Bowra. TrJP

Poem: "Some who are uncertain compel me." Art Lange. UL

Poem: "Something broke the dream." John Gill. NeAC

Poem: Spleen. John Gray. NOBVV

Poem: "There I could never be a boy." Frank O'Hara. NNaP

Poem: "There is a wailing baby under every stone." Norman MacCaig. EAS

Poem: "Thing, The/ To do/ Is organize." Kenneth Koch. CAPP

Poem: "This beauty that I see." James Schuyler. PoA

Poem: "This life like no other." Gregory Orr. AmPA

Poem: "This poem is not addressed to you." Donald Justice. CAPP

Poem: "This room is very old and very wise." Sam Harrison. NeIP

Poem: "Time and the weather wear away." Donald Justice. *See* Time and the weather wear away.

Poem: "To be sad in the morning." William Pillen. VWA

Poem: "Today I am like a." Judah Leib Teller, *tr. by* Benjamin *and* Barbara Harshav. AYP

Poem: "Upended, it crouches on broken limbs." Charles Tomlinson. CMoP

Poem: "Walls of the maelstrom are painted with trees, The." Charles Madge. EAS

Poem, The: "What ailes Pigmalion? Is it lunacy." Thomas Morton. SCAP

Poem 1: "What happens here happened to my grandfather and my father." Abelardo Sanchez Leon, *tr. by* David Tipton. Per

Poem: "What is hidden in the fruit of summer?" Teresa Torres, *tr. by* James Tipton. OV

Poem, A: "What is there that we can do or say." Ezekiel Mphahlele. WMBCH

Poem: "What's the balm." Alan Dugan. CAPP; SM

Poem: "When the dream departs leaving." Salah Fa'iq, *tr. by* Patricia Alanah Byrne *and* Salma Khadra Jayyusi. MAP

Poem: "While we were walking under the top." John Ashbery. EAS

Poem 2: "Why did that have to be the only answer? It's true." Abelardo Sanchez Leon, *tr. by* David Tipton. Per

Poem: "You are ill and so I lead you away." Alfred W. Purdy. NOBC

Poem: "You said./ don't write me/ a love poem." Pearl Cleage Lomax. CNA

Poem: "You sowed in me, not a child." Celia Dropkin, *tr. by* Adrienne Rich. OV

Poem 3: "You thought that I could help you out?" Abelardo Sanchez Leon, *tr. by* David Tipton. Per

Poem: "Your face,/so pale now it is blue." David St. John. AmPA

Poem about a Seashell. Ranice Henderson Crosby.

Poem about a Wolf Maybe Two Wolves, A. *Unknown, tr. fr. Seneca Indian by* Jerome Rothenberg *and* Richard Johnny John. STP

Poem about Beauty, Blackness, Poetry, A. Linda Brown Bragg. CNA

Poem about Breasts, A. James Wright. TAP

Poem about Breath. David Wagoner. NoAM

Poem about Fan the Fourth, A. Li K'ai-hsien, *tr. fr. Chinese by* Jonathan Chaves. CoBLCP

Poem about Morning. William Meredith. NYBP

Poem about My Rights. June Jordan. GLP; NoAM

Poem about People. Robert Pinsky. NPGG

Poem about Poems about Vietnam, A. Jon Stallworthy. NoAM

Poem about Your Face. Nathan Alterman, *tr. fr. Hebrew by* Ruth Nevo. VWA

Poem, after A. E. Housman. Hugh Kingsmill. *See* What, still alive at twenty-two.

Poem after Apollinaire. Ira Sadoff. AmPA

Poem after Leopardi. Mark Strand. AnAn

Poem against Catholics. James Fenton *and* John Fuller. OBSV

Poem against Rats, A. Fred Levinson. AmPA

Poem against the Rich. Robert Bly. NOBA

Poem and Message. Dannie Abse. TEP

Poem at Equinox. Hilary Corke. NYBP

Poem at Thirty. Sonia Sanchez. BlSi; BPo; CNA; NMM; PoBA

Poem before Departure. Jean Burden. WPE

Poem Beginning with a Line by Cavafy. Derek Mahon. FaBCIP

Poem Beginning with a Line by Pindar, A. Robert Duncan. NeAP; NNaP; PoM

Poem begins, The. Beginning. David Rokeah, *tr. by* Robert Mezey. VWA

Poem Begun in the Haro Strait When I Was 28 and Finished When I Was 38. Sandra McPherson. NAmP

Poem by a Perfectly Furious Academician. Shirley Brooks. FiBHP; NOBVV

Poem by an Unknown Poet from the Mid-Twentieth Century. László Benjámin, *tr. fr. Hungarian by* Edwin Morgan. MHuP

Poem by the Bridge at Ten-shin. Li Po, *tr. fr. Chinese by* Ezra Pound. OBVE

Poem by the Charles River. Robin Blaser. NeAP

Poem Called Poem. James Whitehead. GrPl

(Poem) (Chicago) (The Were-Age). William Knott. EAS

Poem Circling Hamtramck, Michigan All Night in Search of You, The. Philip Levine. NNaP

Poem Containing Some Remarks on the Present War, A. *Unknown.* PAH

Poem Ended by a Death. Fleur Adcock. PeNZ

Poem Entreating of Sorrow, A. Sir Walter Ralegh. SiPS

Poem exploded outside a, A. The Exploding Poem. E. G. Hallaman. SoTCo

Poem Expressing My Wife's Response to One I Sent Her, A. Li K'ai-hsien, *tr. fr. Chinese by* Jonathan Chaves. CoBLCP

Poem Following Discussion of Brain. Stan Rice. NPGG

Poem for a Marriage. Christine Craig. AIW

Poem for a Poet, A. Don L. Lee. PoBA

Poem for a Poet, A. Audre Lorde. NMM

Poem for a Singer. Milton Acorn. NeAC

Poem for Anton Schmidt, A. William Pillen. VWA

Poem for Aretha. Nikki Giovanni. BPo; PoBA

Poem for Ben Barney. Leslie Marmon Silko. CDW; VoR

Poem for Black Boys. Nikki Giovanni. BPo

Poem for Black Hearts, A. Imamu Amiri Baraka. IDB; PoBA; PoM; SOTW

Poem for Carroll, Descendant of Chiefs. Lance Henson. VoR

Poem for Diane Wakoski, A. Ray A. Young Bear. CDW

Poem for Dr. Spock. Ed Ochester. SoTCo

Poem for Easter. Robert Kelly. VGW

Poem for Ed "Whitey" Ford, A. Jonathan Holden. MAYP

Poem for Emily, A. Miller Williams. BLA; MT

Poem for Etheridge. Sonia Sanchez. BPo

Poem for Friends. Quincy Troupe. PoBA

Poem for Garcia Lorca. George Woodcock. NOBC

Poem for Half White College Students. Imamu Amiri Baraka. BPo; TAP; UnPo

Poem for Heroes, A. Julia Fields. CNA

Poem for Integration, A. Alvin Saxon. PoBA

Poem for J. Wendell Berry. GeTw

Poem for Jacqueline Hill. *Unknown.* BrRo

Poem for Jan. Joseph Bruchac. CDW

Poem for Peter Klappert. AmPA

Poem for Marc Chagall. Leonard Cohen. *See* Out of the Land of Heaven.

Poem for Museum Goers, A. John Wieners. NeAP

Poem for My Family: Hazel Griffin and Victor Hernandez Cruz. June Jordan. BPo

Poem for My Father, A. Sonia Sanchez. BPo; IHMS

Poem for My Father's Ghost. Mary Oliver. InPS

Poem for My Grandfather. A. C. Jacobs. VWA

Poem for My Little Boy. Li Shang-yin, *tr. fr. Chinese by* Burton Watson. CoBCP

Poem for My Mother. Siv Cedering Fox. TV

Poem for My Son. John Logan. DiL

Poem for My Twentieth Birthday. Kenneth Koch. PoA

Poem for My Wet Nurse, A. Cheng Hsieh, *tr. fr. Chinese by* Jonathan Chaves. CoBLCP

Poem for Myself and Mei: Abortion. Leslie Marmon Silko. VoR

Poem for Nana. June Jordan. BlSi

Poem for Otis Redding. Joyce Carol Thomas. CNA

Poem for Painters, A. John Wieners. NeAP; PoM

Poem for People Who Are Understandably Too Busy to Read Poetry. Stephen Dunn. GOYP

Poem for Positive Thinkers, A. Barbara Mahone. PoBA

Poem for Potential. Fanny Howe. PPR

Poem for Putzi Hanfstaengel. Evangeline Paterson. CN

Poem for Shane on Her Brother's Birthday. Donald T. Sanders. TTTS

Poem for Some Black Women. Carolyn M. Rodgers. BlSi

Poem for Speculative Hipsters, A. Imamu Amiri Baraka. NoAM; NOBA

Poem for the Creative Writing Class, Spring 1982. Merle Woo. BrSi

Poem for the Insane, A. John Weiners. NeAP; PoM

Poem for the Meeting of the American Medical Association, A. Oliver Wendell Holmes. PoEL-5

Poem for the Old Man, A. John Wieners. NeAP

Poem for the Sandman. James Tate. NAmP

Poem for the Year Twenty Twenty. Al Lee. AmPA

Poem for the Young White Man Who Asked Me How I, an Intelligent, Well-read Person, Could Believe in the War between Races. Lorna Dee Cervantes. CCP; WPOW

Poem for Thel—the Very Tops of Trees. Joseph Major. NBP

Poem for Trapped Things, A. John Wieners. GLP; NeAP; PoM

Poem for Unwed Mothers. Nikki Giovanni. OBAL

Poem for Valery Larbaud. "St.-John Perse", *tr. fr. French by* Richard Howard. RHTwFP

Poem for Viet Nam. Ray A. Young Bear. STE

Poem for You. Robert Pack. NePoEA

Poem from the Empire State. June Jordan. BPo

Poem from "The Revolution." Ilya Rubin, *tr. fr. Russian by* Linda Zisquit. VWA

Poem—Good or Bad—a Thing—with One Attribute—Flat, A. Melech Ravitch, *tr. fr. Yiddish by* Ruth Whitman. VWA

Poem H. Vincente Rodríguez Nietzche, *tr. by* Julio Marzán. InW

Poem in Black and White, A. Mongane Wally Serote. WMBCH

Poem in Defence of the Decent Ornaments of Christ-Church, Oxon, Occasioned by a Banbury Brother, Who Called Them Idolatries, A, *sels. Unknown.* OBS

  Beauty in Worship.

  Church-Windows, The.

Poem in May. John Hewitt. NeIP

Poem in Nueva York. Cyn Zarco. UL

Poem in October. Dylan Thomas. LiTB; NAEL-2; NAs; NoAM; PoA; PoRA; PrIm; RB; SeCePo; SoSe

Poem in Praise of Colum Cille, A. *At. to* Dallán Forgaill. NOIV

Poem in Progress, A. John Logan.

  First Prelude. Dream in Ohio; the Father. LCAP

  Second Prelude. Reality in Albuquerque: The Son. CAPP

Poem in Response. Liu Shih, *tr. fr. Chinese by* Irving Lo. WFTU

Poem in the Form of a Coffin-Puller's Song ("A plain of wild grasses, broad and tangled"). T'ao Ch'ien, *tr. fr. Chinese by* Burton Watson. CoBCP

Poem in the Form of a Coffin-Puller's Song ("In life I stroll the capital city"). Miu Hsi, *tr. fr. Chinese by* Burton Watson. CoBCP

Poem in the Form of a Coffin-Puller's Song ("In the old days I had no wine to drink"). T'ao Ch'ien, *tr. fr. Chinese by* Burton Watson. CoBCP

Poem in the Form of a Coffin-Puller's Song ("What has a life must have a death"). T'ao Ch'ien, *tr. fr. Chinese by* Burton Watson. CoBCP

Poem in the Matukituki Valley. James Keir Baxter. ATNZ

Poem in the Park, The. Peter Davison. GOYP

Poem in Three Parts. Robert Bly. CAPP; NaP; NOBA

Poem in Time of War. William Abrahams. WaP

Poem in Which My Legs Are Accepted. Kathleen Fraser. AmPA; LLLT; NMM

Poem in Yellow after Tristan Tzara, A. Jerome Rothenberg. PoM; RHTwFP

Poem Inscribed on a Landscape Painting, *sel.* Chu Yün-ming, *tr. fr. Chinese by* Jonathan Chaves.

  "Clouds are swept into the sunset—a sky beyond the sky." CoBLCP

Poem Intended to Incite the Utmost Depression, A. Samuel Hoffenstein. FaBoCo

Poem is something in the midst of a white plane, A. Poems. Jutta Schutting, *tr. by* Beth Bjorklund. CoAuP

Poem like a Grenade, A. John Haines. EAS

Poem like an object, A. Like an Object. Gerrit Kouwenaar, *tr. by* Koos Schuur. DuIn

Poem Made of Water. Nancy Willard. BLA

Poem makes truth a little more disturbing, The. Hands. Donald Finkel. CoAP; MAT

Poem Making Fun of Chi-ti for His Eye Illness, A. Yang Chi, *tr. fr. Chinese by* Jonathan Chaves. CoBLCP

Poem may boast bravado, A. Ar(chibald')s Poetica. Alan Ribback. BXAP

Poem must not charm us like a play, The. Against the False Magicians. Thomas McGrath. NePoEA

Poem near Midway Truck Stop. Lance Henson. STE

Poem near the sea. *Unknown.* WMBCH

Poem, Neither Hilláryous Norgay. Gardner E. Lewis. FiBHP

Poem, 1972. Syd Scroggie. PoSH

Poem Not about a Zebra, A. Pamela White Hadas. BLA

Poem No. 19 in the Old Manner. Li Po, *tr. fr. Chinese by* Burton Watson. CoBCP

Poem No. 21. Doughtry Long. CNA

Poem-Object. André Breton, *tr. fr. French by* Michael Benedikt. POS

Poem of A, The. Cathy Bernheim, *tr. fr. French by* Mary Ann Caws. DMF

Poem of a Maid Forsaken, A. *Unknown.* PBBP

Poem of Angela Yvonne Davis. Nikki Giovanni. PoBA

Poem of Distant Childhood. Noémia da Sousa, *tr. fr. Portuguese by* Kathleen Weaver *and* Allan Francovich. AIW

Poem of Explanations. Dahlia Ravikovich, *tr. fr. Hebrew.* BoWoP, *tr. by* Chana Bloch; IP, *tr. by* Warren Bargad *and* Stanley F. Chyet.

Poem of Holy Madness, *sel.* Ray Bremser.
"Let me lay it to you gently, Mr. Gone!" NeAP

Poem of João, The. Noémia da Sousa, *tr. fr. Portuguese by* Margaret Dickinson. WMBCH

Poem of Love. Roque Dalton, *tr. fr. Spanish by* Alejandro Murguía. Vol

Poem of Parting. Kyorai, *tr. fr. Japanese by* Burton Watson. *Fr.* Twenty Hokku. FCEI

Poem of Pathos. Tadeusz Rozewicz, *tr. fr. Polish by* Adam Czerniawski. FaBoPV

Poem of Prefectural Judge Yang T'ien-jui. Chao Meng-fu, *tr. fr. Chinese by* Jonathan Chaves. CoBLCP

Poem of the Conscripted Warrior. "Rui Nogar", *tr. fr. Portuguese by* Dorothy Guedes *and* Philippa Rumsey. TTY

Poem of the End, *sels.* Marina Tsvetayeva, *tr. fr. Russian by* Elaine Feinstein *and* Angela Livingstone.
"Blatant as factory buildings." PBWP
"I didn't want this, not." OBVE
"Last bridge I won't." *Fr.* VIII. OV
"Single post, a point of rusting, A." BrRo

Poem of the Forty-eight States, A. Kenneth Koch. NNaP; OBAL

Poem of the Frost and Snow. Lewis Morris, *tr. fr. Welsh by* Anthony Conran. OBWVE

Poem of the Future Citizen. José Craveirinha, *tr. fr. Portuguese by* Dorothy Guedes *and* Philippa Rumsey. TTY

Poem of the Intimate Agony. Julia de Burgos, *tr. by* Julio Marzán. InW

Poem of the mind in the act of finding, The. Of Modern Poetry. Wallace Stevens. InvP; MoP; NAAL-2; NoAM; OxBA; PrIm; TAP

Poem of the Universe, The. Charles Weldon. PWR

Poem of the Western Fields. Wu Wei-yeh, *tr. fr. Chinese by* Jonathan Chaves. CoBLCP

Poem of Towers, A. James Wright. CAPP

Poem on a Little Pine, A. Hsieh Chin, *tr. fr. Chinese by* Jonathan Chaves. CoBLCP

Poem on a Sleeping Butterfly. Liu Shih, *tr. fr. Chinese by* Irving Lo. WFTU

Poem on Azure. Anna de Noailles, *tr. fr. French by* Betty L. Schwimmer. WPOW

Poem on Buddha's Begging Bowl, A. Hsü Pen, *tr. fr. Chinese by* Jonathan Chaves. CoBLCP

Poem on Canada, *sels.* Patrick Anderson.
Cold Colloquy. *Fr.* V. CaP; NOBC
Coming of the White Man, The. MoCV
"Wide was the land." CaP

Poem on Drinking Wine with the Degree-Holder Ku. Ch'ien Ch'ien-i, *tr. fr. Chinese by* Jonathan Chaves. CoBLCP

Poem on Elijahs Translation, A. Benjamin Colman. SCAP

Poem on England's Happiness, A. Unknown. APAS

Poem on Falling Leaves. Liu E, *tr. fr. Chinese by* Jonathan Chaves. CoBLCP

Poem on His Birthday. Dylan Thomas. NAs

Poem on His Death-Bed. Cynddelw Brydydd Mawr, *tr. fr. Welsh by* Joseph P. Clancy. OBWVE

Poem on His Death-Bed. Meilyr Brydydd, *tr. fr. Welsh by* Joseph P. Clancy. OBWVE

Poem on Our Mother, Our Mother Rachel, The. Avot Yeshurun, *tr. fr. Hebrew by* Harold Schimmel. VWA

Poem on Passing by Hsin-k'ai Lake at Kao-yu, A. Yang Chi, *tr. fr. Chinese by* Jonathan Chaves. CoBLCP

Poem on Returning Home, A. Chang Wen-t'ao, *tr. fr. Chinese by* William Schultz. WFTU

Poem on the Guilt, The. Avot Yeshurun, *tr. fr. Hebrew by* Harold Schimmel. VWA

Poem on the Industry of the United States of Ame, A, *sel.* David Humphreys.
"Genius of Culture! thou, whose chaster taste." OPP

Poem on the Jews, The. Avot Yeshurun, *tr. fr. Hebrew by* Harold Schimmel. VWA

Poem on the Suicide of My Teacher. Joseph Stroud. NPGG

Poem on the Wandering Immortal. Kuo P'o, *tr. fr. Chinese by* Burton Watson. CoBCP

Poem on Theater, A. Sándor Weöres, *tr. fr. Hungarian by* Jascha Kessler. FOC

Poem, or Beauty Hurts Mr. Vinal. Edward Estlin Cummings. InPS; MoAB; MoAmPo; NAAL-2; OBAL; OxBA

Poem Out of Childhood. Muriel Rukeyser. NMM

Poem Put into My Lady Laiton's Pocket, A. Sir Walter Ralegh. SiPS

Poem quietly goes aside to weep, A. A Note on the Social Arts. Kendrick Smithyman. ATNZ

Poem Rocket. Allen Ginsberg. VGW

Poem should be palpable and mute, A. Ars Poetica. Archibald MacLeish. AmPP; AWP; CMoP; FPL; HAP; HeIP; HoPM; InPK; LiTA; LiTM; MoAB; MoAmPo; NAAL-2; NIP; NOBA; NoP; OxBA; PAL; PoA; PoRA; SoSe; TAP; WeW

Poem Some People Will Have to Understand, A. Imamu Amiri Baraka. BPo; NOBA

Poem That Took the Place of a Mountain, The. Wallace Stevens. LCAP

Poem Then, for Love, *sel.* Michael Harlow.
Anima Has a Predilection, The. *Fr.* I. PeNZ

Poem (3.11.66). Amiq Hanafi, *tr. fr. Urdu by* Mahmood Jamal. PBMUP

Poem to a Nigger Cop. Bobb Hamilton. TTY

Poem to a Redskin. Wendy Rose. CDW

Poem to a Young Man. Lindolf Bell, *tr. fr. Portuguese by* William Jay Smith. CT

Poem to al-Rahani. Maruf al-Rasafi, *tr. fr. Arabic by* Issa Boullata *and* Christopher Middleton. MAP

Poem to Be Read and Sung. César Vallejo, *tr. fr. Spanish by* James Wright *and* Robert Bly. EAS

Poem to Be Read at 3 A.M. Donald Justice. HoPM

Poem to Be Recited Every 8 Years While Eating Unleavened Tamales. *Unknown, tr. fr. Aztec Indian by* Anselm Hollo. STP

Poem to Be Said on Hearing the Birds Sing, A. Biddy Crummy, *tr. fr. Irish by* Douglas Hyde. AWP; WTO

Poem to Complement Other Poems, A. Don L. Lee. BPo

Poem to Ease Birth. *Unknown, tr. fr. Aztec Indian by* Anselm Hollo. BoWoP; STP

Poem to Explain Everything about a Certain Day in Vermont, A. Genevieve Taggard. NYBP

Poem to Galway Kinnell, A. Etheridge Knight. NNaP

Poem to Han-shan. Joseph Stroud. NPGG

Poem to Her Daughter, *sel.* Mwana Kupona Msham, *tr. fr. Swahili by* J. W. T. Allen.
"Daughter, take this amulet." AIW, *ad. by* Deirdre Lashgari; WPOW, *ad. by* Deirdre Lashgari.

Poem to His Grace the Duke of Marlborough, A. Joseph Addison. *Fr.* The Campaign. OBWP

Poem to Mary, A, *sel.* Bláthmac Mac Con Brettan.
"I call you with honest words." NOIV

Poem to My Death. Julia de Burgos, *tr. fr. Spanish by* Grace Schulman. BoWoP

Poem to My Father. Joseph Stroud. NPGG

Poem to My Sister, Ethel Ennis, Who Sang "The Star-spangled Banner" at the Second Inauguration of Richard Milhous Nixon. June Jordan. TAP

Poem to Negro and Whites. Maxwell Bodenheim. PoNe

Poem to Send to Friends in the Capital, A. Liu Tsung-yüan, *tr. fr. Chinese by* Burton Watson. CoBCP

Poem to Shout in the Ruins. Louis Aragon, *tr. fr. French by* Geoffrey Young. RHTwFP

Poem to Show the Trouble That Befell Him When He Was at Sea, A. Thomas Prys, *tr. fr. Welsh by* Gwyn Williams. OBTV; OBWVE

Poem to Some of my Recent Poems. James Tate. NAmP; NoAM

Poem to the Heart of Jesus, A. Teig Gaelach O'Sullivan, *tr. fr. Irish by* Thomas Kinsella. TIRV

Poem to the Memory of H. L. Mencken. Baron Wormser. MAYP

Poem to the Mother of the Gods, A. *Unknown, tr. fr. Aztec Indian by* Edward Kissam. STP

Poem to the Sun ("All the Cattle are resting in the fields"). *Ancient Egyptian Oral Tradition, tr. by* Christopher Wertz. TTTS

Poem to the Sun ("The boats sail upstream and downstream alike"). *Ancient Egyptian Oral Tradition, tr. by* Christopher Wertz. TTTS

Poem to the Tune of "Tsui hua yin." Li Ch'ing-chao, *tr. fr. Chinese by* Marsha Wagner. WPOW

Poem to the Tune of "Yi chian mei." Li Ch'ing-chao, *tr. fr. Chinese.* WPOW, *tr. by* Marsha Wagner

Poem to the Tune "Riverbank Willows." Yü Hsüan-chi, *tr. by* Geoffrey Waters. BoWoP

Poem Too Late, A. Natan Zach, *tr. fr. Hebrew by* Warren Bargad *and* Stanley F. Chyet. IP

Poem Touching the Gestapo. William Heyen. GeTw

Poem Unwritten, The. Denise Levertov. CAPP

Poem upon the Caelestial Embassy, A. Richard Steere. SCAP

Poem upon the Death of Oliver Cromwell, A, *sel.* Andrew Marvell.
(Upon the Death of His Late Highness the Lord Protector.)

"I saw him dead, a leaden slumber lyes [*or* lies]." JCP; OBS (Cromwell Dead.) ChTr

Poem upon the Imprisonment of Mr. Calamy in Newgate, A. Robert Wild. APAS

Poem upon the Triumphant Translation of. Mrs. Anne Eliot, A. John Danforth. SCAP

Poem with Capital Letters, A. Jane Cooper. FaBoWP

Poem with the Final Tune. Julia de Burgos, *tr. fr. Spanish* by Julio Marzán. InW

Poem without a Category. Liu Cheng, *tr. fr. Chinese* by Burton Watson. CoBCP

Poem without a Category ("Sun and moon refuse to slow their pace"). T'ao Ch'ien, *tr. fr. Chinese* by Burton Watson. CoBCP

Poem without a Category ("The brave man has ambitions wide as the four seas"). T'ao Ch'ien, *tr. fr. Chinese* by Burton Watson. CoBCP

Poem without a Main Verb. John Wain. NePoEA-2

Poem without a self is fit only to be excised, A. Chang Wen-t'ao, *tr. fr. Chinese* by Irving Lo. *Fr.* On Literature, VII. WFTU

Poem without a Title. Charles Simic. NNaP

Poem Wondering If I'm Pregnant. Kathleen Fraser. IHMS; NMM

Poem Written after Reading Wright's "American Hunger." Sonia Sanchez. ER

Poem Written during a Dream. Ch'ien Ch'ien-i, *tr. fr. Chinese* by Jonathan Chaves. CoBLCP

Poem Written in Time of Trouble by an Irish Priest Who Had Taken Orders in France, A. *Unknown, tr. fr. Irish* by Lady Gregory. OBMV

Poem You Asked For, The. Larry Levis. AmPA; GOYP

Poema Morale. Charles Gullans. NePoEA

Poem/Ditty-Bop. Carolyn M. Rodgers. JB

Poème Antipoème. Elio Pagliarani, *tr. fr. Italian* by Lawrence R. Smith. NItP

Poème de Terre; or, Love Song to a Potato. Jack Little. SoTCo

Poemlove (Fragment). José Luis Vega, *tr. fr. Spanish.* *Fr.* Erotic Suite. InW

Poems. Gary Gildner. Psk

Poems, *sels.* Antonio Machado, *tr. fr. Spanish* by John Dos Passos. AWP

"Figures in the fields against the sky!"

"Frail sound of a tunic trailing, A."

"Naked is the earth."

"We think to create festivals."

Poems (I-XI). Philip O'Connor. EAS

Poems. Jutta Schutting, *tr. fr. German* by Beth Bjorklund. CoAuP

Poems. Vittorio Sereni, *tr. fr. Italian* by Paul Vangelisti. PFI

Poems. Bruce Severy. NOVW

Poems about Playmates. Ronda Davis. JB

Poems about the Moon, *sels.* Vachel Lindsay.

Euclid. *Fr.* I. ImOP

Yet Gentle Will the Griffin Be. *Fr.* II. PDV

Poems after Beirut, *sels.* Mahmoud Darwish, *tr. fr. Arabic* by Lena Jayyusi *and* Christopher Middleton. MAP

Earth Scrapes Us. *Fr.* I.

We Move On to a Country. *Fr.* II.

We Travel like Other People. *Fr.* III.

Poems are bullshit unless they are. Black Art. Imamu Amiri Baraka. BPo

Poems Are Cheap. Amiq Hanafi, *tr. fr. Urdu* by Mahmood Jamal. PBMUP

Poems are my love, my romance now. New Romance. Nellie Wong. BrSi

Poems: Birmingham 1962–1964, *sels.* Julia Fields. PoBA; PoNe

Birmingham.

"I play the Masonic Funeral March."

Moths.

Poems by Women. Dacia Maraini, *tr. fr. Italian* by Muriel Kittel. DMI

Poems Come to Me in the Night. Alice Sadongei. HATNAP

Poems for My Brother Kenneth, *sel.* Owen Dodson.

"Sleep late with your dream." *Fr.* VII. IDB; PoBA; PoNe

Poems for My Daughter. Horace Gregory. MoAmPo

Poems for the Game of Silence, *sels. Unknown, tr. fr. Chippewa Indian* by Frances Densmore. STP

"It is hanging/ in the edge of sunshine."

"That/ that / whose/ track is it like?"

Poems for the New. Kathleen Fraser. IHMS; NMM

Poems for Yukiko of Tamba, *sels.* Liu E, *tr. fr. Chinese* by Jonathan Chaves. CoBLCP

"Last year, with jade hands, you offered cups of tea."

"Next year you must come again."

Poems from a Diary, *sels.* Abraham Sutskever, *tr. fr. Yiddish* by Cynthia Ozick. PeBMYV

1974.

1975.

1976.

1980.

1981.

Poems from a First Year in Boston, *sel.* George Starbuck. NePoEA-2

Aspects of Spring in Greater Boston. *Fr.* II. NYBP

Poems from Iowa City. Asher Reich, *tr. fr. Hebrew* by Vivian Eden. WCI

Poems from Mexico, *sels.* Ory Bernstein, *tr. fr. Hebrew* by Warren Bargad *and* Stanley F. Chyet. IP

Cuernavaca.

Mayan Ruins.

Small War, A.

Universal.

Poems from MSS. Blake

Poems from the Coalfields, *sels.* Ian Healy.

Advice from a Nightwatchman. *Fr.* II. PoAu-2

Air Shaft. *Fr.* I. PoAu-2

Poems in Praise of Practically Nothing, *sels.* Samuel Hoffenstein. FiBHP

"Only the wholesomest foods you eat." TrJP

"You buy some flowers for your table." FiBHP; TrJP

Poems Inscribed on Paintings, *sels.* T'ang Yin, *tr. fr. Chinese* by Jonathan Chaves. CoBLCP

"Among red leaves and green mountains, white clouds fly."

"Mountain pavilion is silent—few people visit me here, The."

"Pines and cedars, a hundred feet of green, clinging to the earth."

"Wind sighs in the reeds—autumn on the rustic shore, The."

Poems Inscribed on Paintings of Bamboo, *sels.* Wu Chen, *tr. fr. Chinese* by Jonathan Chaves. CoBLCP

"For action, I chant out loud, for quiet, I just think." *Fr.* 2.

"In leaf after leaf we seem to hear the sighing of the wind." *Fr.* 1.

"Leaning on clouds, hugging rocks, slanting every way." *Fr.* 3.

Poem's just a little thing, A. Toward a Poetic Art. Raymond Queneau, *tr. by* Teo Savory. RHTwFP

Poems of Li Po and Tu Fu, passed along by myriad voices, The. Chao Yi, *tr. fr. Chinese* by William Schultz. *Fr.* On Poetry, II. WFTU

Poems of Night. Galway Kinnell. NaP

Poems of Our Climate, The. Wallace Stevens. NoP; OxBA; TrGrPo; TwCP

Poems of Pain. Sirkka Turkka, *tr. fr. Finnish* by Aili Jarvenpa. SOP

Poems of Solitary Delights, *sels.* Tachibana Akemi, *tr. fr. Japanese* by Geoffrey Bownas *and* Anthony Thwaite. PeBJV; Mes

"What a delight it is/ When a guest you cannot stand."

"What a delight it is/ When, after a hundred days."

"What a delight it is/ when, borrowing."

"What a delight it is/ When everyone admits."

"What a delight it is/ When I blow away the ash."

"What a delight it is/ When I find a good brush."

"What a delight it is/ When, of a morning."

"What a delight it is/ When on the bamboo matting."

"What a delight it is/ When, skimming through the pages."

"What a delight it is/ When, spreading paper."

Poems of the Arabic. *Unknown, tr. fr. Arabic* by Sir Richard Burton. *Fr.* The Thousand and One Nights. ErPo

Poems of the End Wall, *sel.* Murray Edmond.

House. ATNZ

Poems of the Yellow Patch, *sel.* H. Leivick, *tr. fr. Yiddish* by Benjamin *and* Barbara Harshav.

Song of the Yellow Patch. AYP

Poems on the Ch'i-huai, *sels.* Wang Shih-chen, *tr. fr. Chinese* by Daniel Bryant. WFTU

"Over the years hearts have been broken on Mo-ling boats." *Fr.* I.

"When the tide ebbed in the Ch'in-huai, autumn after spring." *Fr.* XIV, *tr. by* Daniel Bryant.

Poems on Yi Garden: Written for Mr. Juan-t'ing, *sels.* Wu Wen, *tr. fr. Chinese* by Chang Yin-nan. WFTU

Bridge of Drifted Fragrance, The. *Fr.* III.

Crane Lodge. *Fr.* II.

Poems to a Brown Cricket. James Wright. NaP; NYBP

Poems We Can Understand. Paul Hoover. EOEF

Poe's Cottage at Fordham. John Henry Boner. AA

Poet. Ali Ja far al- Allaq, *tr. fr. Arabic* by Sharif Elmusa *and* Thomas G. Ezzy. MAP

Poet, The. Joel Benton. WGRP

Poet, The. Elizabeth Barrett Browning. WGRP

Poet, The. Bryant. AA; NAAL-1; TAP

Poet, The. Witter Bynner. WGRP

Poet, The. Paul Laurence Dunbar. BPo

Poet. Emerson. *Fr.* Quatrains. OxBA; PCP

Poet, The. Padraic Fiacc. CIP; NeIP
Poet, A. Thomas Hardy. NoAM
Poet. Donald Jeffrey Hayes. AmNP; PoNe
Poet, The. Amy Lowell. WGRP
Poet, The. George MacKay Brown. PoPo
Poet, The. Edwin Markham. WGRP
Poet, The. Cornelius Mathews. AA
Poet, The, *sel.* Angela Morgan. WGRP
  "Why hast thou breathed, O God, upon my thoughts." TrPWD
Poet, The. Edwin Morgan. PoPo
Poet, The. Yone Noguchi. WGRP
Poet. Karl Shapiro. CMoP; LiTM; MoAB; MoAmPo; NoAM
Poet. Peter Viereck. HoPM; MoAmPo
Poet, The. Sir William Watson. *Fr.* Two Epigrams. TrGrPo
Poet, The. Walt Whitman. *Fr.* By Blue Ontario's Shore, *sec.* IX–XVII.
  MoAmPo
Poet, A!—He Hath Put His Heart to School. Wordsworth. EnRP
Poet and Critic. Samuel Daniel. *Fr.* Musophilus; or, Defence of All
  Learning. OBSC
Poet and His Book, The. Edna St. Vincent Millay. MoAmPo
Poet and His Songs, The. Longfellow. AnAmPo
Poet and Lark. "Madeline Bridges." AA
Poet and Peasant. Richard Hoopell Long. PoAu-1
Poet and Saint! to thee alone are given. On the Death of Mr. Crashaw.
  Abraham Cowley. MeLP; MePo; OBS; SeCP; SeCV-1
Poet and the Child, The. Winifred Howells. AA
Poet and the Rose, The. John Gay. TEP
Poet and the World, The. Byron. *Fr.* Childe Harold's Pilgrimage, III.
  SeCePo
Poet as King of Gotham, The. Charles Churchill. *Fr.* Gotham. NOEC
Poet at Fifty, The. Laurence Lerner. PeSA
Poet at Night-Fall, The. Glenway Wescott. PoA
Poet at Seven, The. Robert Lowell. NaP, *ad. fr. the French of* Rimbaud
Poet at Seventeen, The. Larry Levis. NAmP
Poet at Seventy. Czeslaw Milosz, *tr. fr. Polish by the author.* AnAn
Poet at the Breakfast Table, The, *sel.* Oliver Wendell Holmes.
  Epilogue to the Breakfast-Table Series. AA
Poet at Twenty, A. Donald Hall. EAS
Poet, cast your careful eye. On Seeing a Poet of the First World War on
  the Station at Abbeville. Charles Causley. LiTM
Poet Confides, The. Herbert T. J. Coleman. CaP
Poet Defended, A. Paul Ramsey. InPK
Poet felt the rain, The. Rain. Margiad Evans. OBWVE
Poet G. B. says about himself, The. Socialism, I Say. Ute Erb, *tr. by*
  Susan L. Cocalis. DMG
Poet gathers fruit from every tree, The. The Poet. Sir William Watson.
  Fr. Two Epigrams. TrGrPo
Poet hath the child's sight in his breast, The. The Poet. Elizabeth Barrett
  Browning. WGRP
Poet homed, The. Lyric Barber. Liboria E. Romano. GoYe
Poet! I come to touch thy lance with mine. Wapentake. Longfellow.
  AA
Poet! I like not mealy fruit; give me. Walter Savage Landor. FaBoEE
Poet Imagines His Grandfather's Thoughts on the Day He Died, The.
  Wing Tek Lum. BrSi
Poet in his lone yet genial hour, The. Apologia Pro Vita Sua. Samuel
  Taylor Coleridge. EnRP; OxBSP
Poet in Old Age Fishing at Evening, The. Desmond O'Grady. CIP
Poet in Residence at a Country School. Don Welch. GOYP
Poet in Winter. Edward Lucie-Smith. TwCP
Poet Is Dead, The. William Everson. NoAM; NoP
Poet Is Not a Jukebox, A. Dudley Randall. NoAM
Poet is priest. Death to Van Gogh's Ear! Allen Ginsberg. NaP; VGW
Poet is the dreamer, The. Loneliness. Al Young. PoBA
Poet Laments the Coming of Old Age, The. Edith Sitwell. NAEL-2;
  NoAM
Poet, let passion sleep. Art, II. Alfred Noyes. OBEV
Poet lived in Galilee, A. The Poet. Witter Bynner. WGRP
Poet Lives, The. Jacob Glatstein, *tr. fr. Yiddish by* Ruth Whitman.
  VWA
Poet Loves a Mistress, but Not to Marry, The. Robert Herrick. CaPo;
  ErPo
Poet of Bray, The. John Heath-Stubbs. NOBL
Poet of Earth. Stephen Henry Thayer. AA
Poet of nature, thou hast wept to know. To Wordsworth. Shelley.
  EnRP; FiP; NoP; Son
Poet of Our Race. Maggie Pogue Johnson. CBWP-4
Poet of the Mountains, The. Thomas McCarthy. CIP
Poet of the pulpit, whose full-chorded lyre. Bartol. Amos Bronson
  Alcott. AA
Poet on the Island, The. Richard Murphy. CIP

Poet Prays, The. Grace Noll Crowell. TrPWD
Poet Questions Peace, The. George Chapman. *Fr.* Euthymiae Raptus;
  or, The Teares of Peace. JCP
Poet reads lines, The. The Record. Gabriel Preil, *tr. by* Grace
  Schulman. PeBMYV
Poet Recognizing the Echo of the Voice, A. Diane Wakoski. NIP
Poet Shadwell, The. Dryden. *See* MacFlecknoe; or, A Satire [*or* Satyr]
  upon the True-Blue [*or*-Blew] Protestant Poet T. S:
  All human[e] things are subject to decay.
Poet shrieks getting, The. The Poet. Edwin Morgan. PoPo
Poet Speaks, The. Georgia Douglas Johnson. AmNP
Poet Speaks from the Visitors' Gallery, A. Archibald MacLeish. NYBP
Poet spilled my gin, The. Tropisms on John Berryman. Gerald Vizenor.
  VoR
Poet Thinks, A. Lui Chi, *tr. fr. Chinese by* E. Powys Mathers. AWP
Poet to a Dancer, A. Auvaiyar, *tr. fr. Tamil by* A. K. Ramanujan. PLW
Poet to a Painter, A. Aubrey Thomas de Vere. Son
Poet to His Beloved, A. W. B. Yeats. BrPo
Poet to the Birds, The. Alice Meynell. FM
Poet to the Sleeping Saki, The. Goethe, *tr. fr. German by* John Weiss.
  PeHV
Poet to Tiger, *sels.* May Swenson. GLP
  Dream, The.
  Hair, The.
  Salt, The.
  Sand, The.
Poet told me if I was serious, The. Instruction from Bly. Cynthia
  MacDonald. ER; NMM
Poet-Tree. Earle Birney. OxBC
Poet vs. Parson. Ebenezer Elliott. Son
Poet was busted by a topless judge, A. Sermonette. Ishmael Reed.
  NIP; PoBA
Poet, what do we know today of our. Subjects and Arguments for an Act
  of Desperation. Elio Pagliarani, *tr. by* Lawrence R. Smith. NItP
Poet, whoe'er thou art, God damn thee. John Wilmot, 2nd Earl of
  Rochester. FaBoEE
Poet Wondering What He Is Up To. Dennis Joseph Enright. OxBC
Poet writ a song of May, A. The First Song. Richard Burton. AA
Poeta Fit, Non Nascitur. "Lewis Carroll." FaBoNo; OBSV
Poeta Loquitur. Swinburne. OAEL-2
Poetaster, The, *sels.* Ben Jonson.
  "O sacred poesie, thou spirit of artes." *Fr.* I, ii. PoEL-2
  "If I freely may discover." *Fr.* II, ii. EIL
  "There is no bountie to be shew'd to such." *Fr.* III, vi. PoEL-2
Poetaster, The. Samuel Rowlands. *Fr.* The Melancholy Knight. EIL
Poète Manqué. Ernest Sandeen. CRP
Poetess, The. Marta Fabiani, *tr. fr. Italian by* Muriel Kittel. DMI
Poetess Ko Ogimi, The. Helen Chasin. NMM
Poetess's Bouts-Rimés, The. *Unknown.* NOEC
Poeti-c Art ("The poetic cart"). Arudra, *tr. by* B. V. L. Narayana Row.
  PCP
Poetic Genius. Mark Akenside. *Fr.* The Pleasures of Imagination, IV.
  NOEC
Poetic Institution. Jotie T'Hooft, *tr. fr. Dutch by* James S. Holmes.
  DuIn
Poetic Pains. William Cowper. *Fr.* The Task, II. FiP
Poetic Thought. *Unknown.* FiBHP
Poetical Commandments. Byron. *Fr.* Don Juan, I. FiP; OxBoLi
  (Poet's Credo.) SeCePo
Poetical Economy. Harry Graham. CenHV; FaBoCo; Mes
Poetical Epistle, from the Island of Jamaica, to, A, *sel.* *Unknown.*
  "Our tropic fruits, nurs'd 'neath a torrid sky." PBCV
Poetical Numbers. Pope. *See* Essay on Criticism:
  But most by numbers judge a poet's song.
Poetical Philander only thought to love. Philander. Donald Hall. ErPo
Poetical Sketches, *sels.* Blake. PoE
  Mad Song.
  To the Evening Star.
Poetics. A. R. Ammons. NoP
Poetics. André Spire, *tr. fr. French by* Edouard Roditi. VWA
Poetics against the Angel of Death. Phyllis Webb. MoCV; NOBC
Poetry. Eleanor Farjeon. RHPC
Poetry. Lucius Harwood Foote. AA
Poetry. Yankev Fridman, *tr. fr. Yiddish by* Ruth Whitman. PeBMYV
Poetry. Nikki Giovanni. NIP
Poetry. Ella Heath. WGRP
Poetry. Greg Kuzma. PoA
Poetry. Edwin Markham. AA
Poetry. Marianne Moore. AmPP; BLPL; BoWoP; CMoP; FaBoWP; FF;
  HAP; HeIP; LiTA; LiTM; MoAB; MoAmPo; MoP; NAAL-2; NIP;
  NoAM; NOBA; NoP; OxBA; PoE; TAP; UnPo; ViBoPo

Poetry. Frank O'Hara. HCAP

Poetry. "Peter," *tr.* by Edmund Keeley *and* Philip Sherrard. Mes

Poetry. Abraham Sutskever, *tr. fr. Yiddish.* PeBMYV, *tr.* by Chana Bloch; VWA, *tr.* by Ruth Whitman.

Poetry. Claude Vigée, *tr. fr. French by* Anthony Rudolf. VWA

Poetry/ when she comes. Subversive. Ferreira Gullar, *tr.* by William Jay Smith. CT

Poetry, a Natural Thing. Robert Duncan. CAPP; NoAM; NOBA

Poetry, almost blind like a camera. Imaginary Elegies, I-IV. Jack Spicer. NeAP

Poetry and Learning. George Chapman. *Fr.* The Epistle Dedicatory to Chapman's Translation of the Iliad. OBS

Poetry and Philosophy. Thomas Randolph. *Fr.* An Eclogue to Mr. Johnson. OBS

Poetry and Politics. Lamberto Pignotti, *tr. fr. Italian by* Lawrence R. Smith. NItP

Poetry and Science. Walter James Turner. SeCePo

Poetry and the Poet. Henry Cuyler Bunner. OBAL

Poetry comes best. Babe. Maud Sulter. WS

Poetry Concert. Michael S. S. Harper. TAP

Poetry, cruel machine. Robot Poetry. Paul Rodenko, *tr.* by James S. Holmes. DuIn

Poetry Defined. John Holmes. GrPl

Poetry drives its lines into her forehead. A Young Highland Girl Studying Poetry. Iain Crichton Smith. NePoEA-2

Poetry, Emily. Brief History. Olga Hampel Briggs. GoYe

Poetry for Supper. R. S. Thomas. OxBC

Poetry has opened all my pores. After Reading Nelly Sachs. Linda Pastan. VWA

Poetry Is a Destructive Force. Wallace Stevens. AnAmPo; OxBA

Poetry is a projection across silence of cadences arranged to break the silence. Ten Definitions of Poetry. Carl Sandburg. MoAmPo

Poetry Is an Act. Remco Campert, *tr. fr. Dutch by* John Scott *and* Graham Martin. DuIn

Poetry Is Death Cast Out. Sydney Clouts. PeSA

Poetry Is in the Darkness. Aram Boyajian. NeAC

Poetry is like a swoon, with this difference. The Klupzy Girl. Charles Bernstein. IAT

Poetry is made in bed like love. On the Road to San Romano. André Breton, *tr.* by Charles Simic *and* Michael Benedikt. POS; RHTwFP

Poetry is motion graceful. Poetry. Nikki Giovanni. NIP

Poetry is poetry. Poetry. "Peter," *tr.* by Edmund Keeley *and* Philip Sherrard. Mes

Poetry is the supreme fiction, madame. A High-toned Old Christian Woman. Wallace Stevens. CMoP; MoP; NAAL-2; NoAM; NOBA; PPP; TAP

Poetry? It's a hobby. What the Chairman Told Tom. Basil Bunting. OxBTC

Poetry of Departures ("Sometimes you hear, fifth-hand"), *sel.* Philip Larkin. CMoP; FF; HeIP; NePoEA; OxBC; PoE; PrIm; TwCP

Ultimatum. FL

Poetry of earth is never dead, The. On the Grasshopper and [the] Cricket. Keats. BoTP; EnRP; FaBoBe; GN; LiTB; NIP; OAEL-2; Son; TrGrPo; TTTS

(Poetry of Earth, The.) WiR

Poetry of Gerard Manley Hopkins, The. Monk Gibbon. TIRV

"Poetry Ought to Have a Practical Purpose." Paul Eluard, *tr. fr. French by* Michael Benedikt. POS

Poetry Paper. Andrei Codrescu. EAS

Poetry Perpetuates the Poet. Robert Herrick. FaBoEE

Poetry Reading. Eileen Myles. UL

Poetry Reading. Vernon Scannell. NOBL

Poetry Reading in the Iowa City Railroad Station. Carlos Cortínez, *tr. fr. Spanish by* Miller Williams. WCI

Poetry's a gift wherein but few excell. Nathaniel Ward. SCAP

Poetry's a tree. Yes, the Secret Mind Whispers. Al Young. PoBA

Poetry's Buried. Meir Wieseltier, *tr. fr. Hebrew by* Warren Bargad *and* Stanley F. Chyet. IP

Poetry's Theme. Faiz Ahmad Faiz, *tr. fr. Urdu by* Mahmood Jamal. PBMUP

Poets. Kay Boyle. UL

Poets. Bozhidar Bozhilov, *tr. fr. Bulgarian by* Cornelia Bozhilova. WCI

Poets. Joyce Kilmer. WGRP

Poets, *sels.* Joseph Rolnik, *tr. fr. Yiddish by* Irving Feldman. PeBMYV Neighbors.

"We have such plain faces."

Poet's age is sad, The: for why? Robert Browning. *Fr.* Asolando. OAEL-2

Poets Agree to Be Quiet by the Swamp, The. David Wagoner. CoAP; VGW

Poets and Linnets. Tom Hood. CenHV

Poets and parents say he cannot die. Yet Another Poem about a Dying Child. Janet Frame. ATNZ; PeNZ

Poet's Arbour in the Birchwood, The. Edward Williams, *tr. fr. Welsh by* Kenneth Hurlstone Jackson. OBWVE

Poets at Tea, The, *sels.* Barry Pain.

"As the sin that was sweet in the sinning." *Fr.* III. Par

"Come, little cottage girl, you seem." *Fr.* VI. Par

"Cosy fire is bright and gay, The." *Fr.* IV. Par

"Here's a mellow cup of tea, golden tea!" *Fr.* VII. Par

"I think that I am drawing to an end." *Fr.* II. Par

Macaulay at Tea. *Fr.* I. CenHV; Par

Oh! Weary Mother. *Fr.* VIII. NA; Par

"One cup for my self-hood." *Fr.* X. Par

"Tut! Bah! We take as another case." *Fr.* V.

"Weel, gin ye speir, I'm no inclined." *Fr.* IX. Par

Poet's Call, The. Thomas Curtis Clark. WGRP

Poet's cat, sedate and grave, A. The Retired Cat. William Cowper. FM

Poets' Corner. Robert Graves. FaBoEE

Poet's Corner, The. Alexander Wilson. PF

Poet's Counsel, A ("You come from the line of a Cola king"). Kovur Kilar, *tr. fr. Tamil by* A. K. Ramanujan. PLW

Poet's Counsel, A ("Your enemy is not the kind who wears"). Kovur Kilar, *tr. fr. Tamil by* A. K. Ramanujan. PLW

Poet's Counsel, The. Philippe Soupault, *tr. fr. French by* Michael Benedikt. POS

Poet's Credo. Byron. *See* Don Juan: Poetical Commandments.

Poet's daily chore, The. Lens. Anne Wilkinson. MoCV; NOBC; OBCV

Poet's Day, The. Richard Weber. CIP

Poet's Dream, The. William Dunbar. *Fr.* The Golden [*or* Goldyn] Targe. PBBP; PoEL-1

Poet's Dream, The. Shelley. *See* Prometheus Unbound: On a poet's lips I slept.

Poet's Epitaph, A. Wordsworth. EnRP

Poet's Farewell to His Teeth, The. William Dickey. PoA

Poet's Fate, The. Thomas Hood. FaBoEE; FiBHP

Poet's Final Instructions, The. John Berryman. SM; Son; VGW

Poets Gathering, 1985. Charles A. Kortes. CowP

Poet's Grace, A. Burns. TrPWD

Poets have muddied all the little fountains, The. Abla. Antara, *tr.* by E. Powys Mathers. *Fr.* The Mu'allaqat. AWP

Poets Hitchhiking on the Highway. Gregory Corso. NeAP; PoM

Poet's Hope, A, *sel.* William Ellery Channing.

"Lady, there is a hope that all men have." AA

Poets, I want to follow them all. On Originality. Bill Manhire. PeNZ

Poet's Ideal, The. Henrietta Cordelia Ray. CBWP-3

Poets in Time of War. Bertram J. Warr. CaP

Poet's Journal, The, *sel.* Bayard Taylor.

"God, to whom we look up blindly." TrPWD

Poet's Lament on the Death of His Wife. Raage Ugaas. *See* Like the yu'ub wood bell tied to gelded camels that are running away.

Poets Light But Lamps, The. Emily Dickinson. HeIP

Poets like shepherds on green hills. The Shepherds. Beren Van Slyke. GoYe

Poet's Lot, The. Oliver Wendell Holmes. PoEL-5

Poets Love Nature. John Clare. OAEL-2

Poet's Loves, The. Hywel ab Owain Gwynedd, *tr. fr. Welsh by* Gwyn Williams. OBWVE

Poets make pets of pretty, docile words. Pretty Words. Elinor Wylie. NAAL-2

Poets may boast, as safely vain. Of English Verse. Edmund Waller. NAEL-1; OAEL-1; OBS; PoE; SeCP

Poets may sing of their Helicon streams. The Federal Constitution. William Milns. PAH

Poet's Memory Is Counsel, A. Kallil Attiraiyanar, *tr. fr. Tamil by* A. K. Ramanujan. PLW

Poet's Ministrants, The. Henrietta Cordelia Ray. CBWP-3

Poets, minor or major, should arrange to remain slender. Poets. Kay Boyle. UL

Poet's Mission, The. Ernest Charles Jones. PF

Poets of Hell, The. Karl Shapiro. NYBP

Poets of the Nineties, The. Derek Mahon. FaBCIP

Poet's Paradise, The. Michael Drayton. *See* Muses' Elysium [*or* Elizium]: Description of Elizium, The.

Poet's Photograph, The. Stephen E. Smith. SoTCo

Poet's Prayer. Adelaide Love. TrPWD

Poet's Prayer, The. Stephen Philipps. WGRP

Poet's Prayer, The. *Unknown.* OBSV

Poet's Progress, A. Michael Hamburger. NePoEA

Poet's Protest. Doris Hedges. CaP

Poet's Request, The. *Unknown, tr. fr. Irish by* John Montague. BIrV

Poet's Sabbath, The, *sel.* John Critchley Prince.
"Blest hour of peace, of poetry, and love!" PF

Poet's Secret, The. Elizabeth Stoddard. AA

Poets Seven Years Old. Rimbaud, *tr. fr. French by* Kenneth Koch *and* Georges Guy. SOTW

Poet's Simple Faith, The. Victor Hugo, *tr. fr. French by* Edward Dowden. WGRP

Poet's Song, The. Tennyson. EBVV; ELP; FiP

Poet's soul has sung its way to God, A. The Dead Singer. Mary Ashley Townsend. AA

Poets survive in fame. Lector Aere Perennior. James Vincent Cunningham. QFR

Poets tell us of an age of unalloyed felicity, The. The Golden Age. W. H. Auden. *Fr.* Man of La Mancha. AnAn

Poet's Terror at the Bailiffs of Exeter, The. Andrew Brice. *Fr.* Freedom; a Poem, Written in Time of Recess from the Rapacious Claws of Bailiffs. NOEC

Poet's thoughts are of the skies, The. Poet and Peasant. Richard Hoopell Long. PoAu-1

Poets to Come. Walt Whitman. FF; LiTA; TrGrPo

Poet's Voice, The. Blake. *See* Songs of Experience: Hear the Voice of the Bard!

Poet's Welcome to His Love-begotten Daughter, A. Burns. LiTB; NAs; NOEC; OxBoLi; PoEL-4

Poets, who in time of war. Poets in Time of War. Bertram J. Warr. CaP

Poet's Wish. Valery Larbaud, *tr. fr. French by* William Jay Smith. CT; GrPl

Poet's words are winged with fire, The. The Poet. Joel Benton. WGRP

Poet's yes obscenely seeing, The. Lawrence Ferlinghetti. *Fr.* A Coney Island of the Mind. LiTM

Poggio. Lawrence Durrell. OxBTC

Pogoing. Cynthia S. Pederson. RR

Pogroms. André Spire, *tr. fr. French by* Stanley Burnshaw. VWA

Poh! did ever one see such a troublesome bear? Delia Very Angry. *Unknown.* NOEC

Poietes Apoietes. Hartley Coleridge. OBNC

Poinsettia petal drops, A. The rain pastes twisted flowing drapery. Family Reunion. Hollis Spurgeon Summers. GoYe

Point, The. John Montague. IPY

Point, The. Gary Soto. MAYP

Point, greatly enlarged, The. Thomas Kinsella. *Fr.* A Technical Supplement. IPY

Point Grey. Daryl Hine. NOBC

Point Guard. Arnold Adoff. ASP

Point of No Return. Robert Graves. BIrV

Point of Origin. Dan Pagis, *tr. fr. Hebrew by* Bernhard Frank. MHeP

Point of rock. Kyorai, *tr. fr. Japanese by* Burton Watson. *Fr.* Twenty Hokku. FCEI

Point Shirley. Sylvia Plath. NIP; NoP

Point, the Line, the Surface and Sphere, The. Claude Bragdon. *Fr.* The Beautiful Necessity. ImOP

Point where beauty and intelligence meet, The. Gavin Ewart. WaP

Pointed Boots. Christopher Middleton. *Fr.* Herman Moon's Hourbook. NePoEA-2

Pointed clouds have become fixed in the heaven, The. A Stormy Day. *Unknown.* WTO

Pointed houses lean so you would swear, The. Amsterdam. Francis Jammes, *tr. by* Jethro Bithell. AWP; FaPON, *ll.* 1–20

Pointed People, The. Rachel Lyman Field. FaPON; WSC

Pointing, his face looked at the blackened windows. Black Fear. Elizabeth Woody. STE

Pointless Pride of Man, The. *Unknown.* MeEL

Poised between going on and back, pulled. The Base Stealer. Robert Francis. GoJo; NTCP; RHPC; SD; TSL

Poised, relaxed, as a cat that waits. Boxer. Joseph P. Clancy. SD

Poison Tree, A. Blake. *Fr.* Songs of Experience. AWP; EnRP; FaFP; HAP; HoPM; LiTB; NAEL-2; NoP; PoEL-4; PPP; RB; SCV; SoSe; TrGrPo; TW; WeW

Poke-Pole Fishing. Dennis Schmitz. AmPA

Poking with his ruler. *Unknown, tr. by* Burton Watson. FCEI

Poland/ 1931 "The Wedding." Jerome Rothenberg. PoM; Prf

Polar Bear. Gail Kredenser. RAR; RHPC

Polar DEW has just warned that, The. Your Attention Please. Peter Porter. OBWP; OxBTC

Polar Exploration. Stephen Spender. MoAB; NoAM
(The North.) FaBoMo

Polar Quest, The. Richard Burton. AA

Polarities. Kenneth Slessor. CBAP

Polaroid, *sel.* Clark Coolidge.
"Dial around forth enough means that there since." IAT

Pole Star, The. Coslett Coslett, *tr. fr. Welsh by* Kenneth Hurlstone Jackson. OBWVE

Pole Star for This Year. Archibald MacLeish. OxBA

Pole Vault. Murano Shiro, *tr. fr. Japanese by* Satoru Sato *and* Constance Urdang. SD

Pole Vaulter. David Allan Evans. ASP; TSL

Poles are flying where the two eyes set, The. Discoveries. Vernon Watkins. LiTM; WaP

Poles rode out from Warsaw against the German, The. The Abnormal Is Not Courage. Jack Gilbert. CoAP; NPGG

Police Manual, A. David Wagoner. AnAn

Police Station Ditties. Max Beerbohm. NOBL

Policeman, A/ is a pig. Definition for Blk/Children. Sonia Sanchez. PoBA

Policeman buys shoes slow and careful, The. Psalm of Those Who Go Forth before Daylight. Carl Sandburg. MoShBr; OxBA

Policeman Cleared in Jaywalking Case. Claire Harris. PBCV

Policeman, policeman, don't take me. I Stole Brass. *Unknown.* ChTr

Policeman walks with heavy tread, The. Action Rhyme. E. H. Adams. BoTP

Policeman's Lot, A. Wendy Cope. FaBoWP

Policeman's Lot, A [*or* The]. W. S. Gilbert. *Fr.* The Pirates of Penzance. NOBL; SaC; TrGrPo

Policemen Laughing. Ray Fraser. NeAC

Polishing the Porcelain Lamp. Park Je-chun, *tr. fr. Korean by* Koh Chang-soo. ACKP

Politeness. Una Marson. PVCV

Politest musician that ever was seen, The. The Music of the Future. Oliver Herford. CenHV

Political Activist Living Alone. Pat Arrowsmith. AIW; BrRo

Political Animal, A. Bruce Bennett. SoTCo

Political Customs. Roberto Roversi, *tr. fr. Italian by* Lawrence R. Smith. NItP

Political Despatch, A. George Canning. FaBoCo

Political Greatness. Shelley. EnRP

Political Intelligence. A. J. M. Smith. EAS

Political Meeting. A. M. Klein. MoCV; OBCV

Political Orlando, The. George MacBeth. NOBL

Political Poem. Amiri Baraka. CoAP; MoP; NAAL-2; NoAM

Political Prisoner, The. Mazisi Kunene. WMBCH

Political Relations. Audre Lorde. GLP

Politician, A. E. E. Cummings. InPK; TW
(Politician Is an Arse Upon, A.) FaBoEE; NBLV; OBAL

Politicians, heart and soul. Poll Star. Felicia Lamport. NBLV

Politics. Tom Marshall. NOBC

Politics. Marco Martos, *tr. fr. Spanish by* David Tipton. Per

Politics. Bob Perelman. BAP

Politics. W. B. Yeats. CMoP; FF; HeIP; InPS; OxBTC; PoE; SCV

Politics Kaiso. Roger McTair. PBCV

Politics of Rich Painters, The. Amiri Baraka. VGW

Politik. Tom Paulin. FaBCIP

Poll. Ed Roberson. PoBA

Poll Star. Felicia Lamport. NBLV

Polliwog, The. Arthur Guiterman. RHPC

Polly; an Opera, *sel.* John Gay.
Air. *Fr.* XLVIII. NOEC

Polly Be-en Upzides wi' Tom. William Barnes. NOBVV

Polly Oliver's Rambles. *Unknown.* OBET

Polly Perkins. *Unknown.* ELP; OxBoLi

Polly put the kettle on. Mother Goose. OxNR

Polly Vaughn. *Unknown.* AmFP

Polo Grounds. Rolfe Humphries. HoPM; SD

Polo Ponies Practicing. Wallace Stevens. ASP

Polonius' Advice to Laertes. Shakespeare. *Fr.* Hamlet, I, iii. OHFP
(Polonius to Laertes.) GN
(This Above All.) TrGrPo
(To Thine Own Self Be True.) FaFP; LiTB

Polwart on the Green. Allan Ramsay. NOEC

Polychromatic springtime's gay cadenza. Vernal Equinox. Martin Johnston. CBAP

Polyhymnia, *sels.* George Peele.
His Golden Lock[e]s [Time Hath to Silver Turned]. ElL; FaBoRV; HeIP; NoP
(Farewell to Arms, A.) NOBE; OBEV; OBWP; PoRA
(Old Knight, The.) ChTr; OBSC; TrGrPo
(Sonnet, A: "His golden locks time hath to silver turned.") ELP; InPS; PoEL-2

Polynesia. Allen Curnow. PeNZ

Polyolbion, *sels.* Michael Drayton.

"And, now that every thing may in the proper place." *Fr.* Fourteenth Song. FM

"Away yee barb'rous woods; how ever yee be plac't." *Fr.* Third Song. OBS

Charnwood Forest. *Fr.* Sixth and Twentieth Song. FaBoPP

"Duck, and Mallard first, the falconers onely sport, The." *Fr.* Five and Twentieth Song. FM
(Birds in the Fens.) ChTr

Dwindling Forest of Arden, The. *Fr.* Thirteenth Song. FaBoPP

"Earle Douglasse for this day doth with the Percies stand, The." *Fr.* Two and Twentieth Song. OBS

Fen-Men of Lincolnshire's Holland, The. *Fr.* Five and Twentieth Song. FaBoPP

Fools Gaze at Painted Courts. *Fr.* Eighteenth Song. ChTr

"Forest so much fallen from what she was before, The." *Fr.* Thirteenth Song. SeCePo

Hawking. *Fr.* Twentieth Song. SD

Lincolnshire's Holland Speaks of Her Waterfowl. *Fr.* Five and Twentieth Song. FM

"My various fleets for fowl, O who is he can tell." *Fr.* Fifth and Twentieth Song. PBBP

"Of all the beasts which we for our veneriall name." *Fr.* Thirteenth Song. OBS

Stonehenge. *Fr.* Third Song. FaBoPP

"To these, the gentle South, with kisses smooth and soft." *Fr.* Second Song. OBS

Trent Again, The. *Fr.* Sixth and Twentieth Song. FaBoPP

"When Phoebus lifts his head out of the winter's wave." *Fr.* Thirteenth Song. OBS; PBBP

"World of mightie kings and princes I could name, A." *Fr.* Twentieth Song. OBS

Wrestlers. *Fr.* First Song. SD

Pomade. Rita Dove. NAmP

Pomegranate, The. Louis Dudek. OBCV

Pomegranate. Gail N. Harada. BrSi

Pomegranate grows in the garden front, The. The Forsaken Wife. Ts'ao Chih, *tr. fr. Chinese by* Burton Watson. CoBCP

Pomegranate opened its mouth, A. Ozaki Hosai, *tr. fr. Japanese by* Hiroaki Sato. *Fr.* One Hundred Haiku in Free Form. FCEI

Pomegranate speaks, The. *Unknown, tr. fr. Egyptian Hieroglyphics by* Ezra Pound *and* Noel Stock. BoWoP

Pomegranate surprise was a New Deal, The. Fruit and Government. Mira Teru Kurka. UL

Pomegranate Tree in Jerusalem ("The pomegranate tree in my garden adorns itself"). Zerubavel Gilead, *tr. fr. Hebrew by* Dorothea Krook. VWA

Pomegranates. Paul Valéry, *tr. fr. French by* William Jay Smith. CT

Pomona. William Morris. NOBVV; WiR

Pomp of Egypt's elder day. An Egyptian Tomb. William Lisle Bowles. OBTV

Pompadour, The. George Walter Thornbury. BeLS

Pompeius, best of all my comrades, you and I. II, 7. "Pompeius, best of all my comrades, you and I" ("O saepe mecum"). Horace, *tr. fr. Latin. Fr.* Odes. WaaP, *tr. by* John Wight.
("Pompeius, chief of all my friends, with whom.") OBWP, *tr. by* James Michie.

Pompeius, chief of all my friends, with whom. Horace. *See* Odes: II, 7. "Pompeius, best of all my comrades, you and I" ("O saepe mecum").

Pomposo (insolent and loud). Charles Churchill. *Fr.* The Ghost. OBSV

Ponce de Leon. Edith M. Thomas. PAH

Ponce de León: A Morning Walk. Al Young. HoPM; NPGG

Pond, The. Anthony Thwaite. MAT; NYBP

Pond by the eastern gate, The. *Unknown, tr. by* Arthur Waley. BoS

Pond in a Jardiniere, A, *sels.* Han Yü, *tr. fr. Chinese by* Burton Watson. CoBCP
"My ceramic lake in dawn, water settled clear." *Fr.* 3.
"Old men are like little boys." *Fr.* 1.
"Pond shine and sky glow, blue matching blue." *Fr.* 5.

Ponder, Darling, These Busted Statues. E. E. Cummings. CMoP; NIP; PoE

Ponder thy cares, and sum them all in one. Sir David Murray. *Fr.* Caelia. EIL

Pond'rous projectiles, hurl'd by heavy hands. The Rejected "National Hymns." "Orpheus C. Kerr." OBAL

Pondy Woods. Robert Penn Warren. MoAmPo

Ponsonby/Remuera/My lai. David Mitchell. ATNZ

Pont and Blyth. *Unknown.* GBP

Pont Mirabeau. X. J. Kennedy, *from* Guillaume Apollinaire. BLA

Pont y Caniedydd. Alun Llywelyn-Williams, *tr. fr. Welsh by* Joseph R. Clancy. OBWVE

Pont-y-Wern. Arthur Hugh Clough. *Fr.* Ambarvalia. FaBoPP

Pontianak. Bee Bee Tan. ER

Pontoosuce. Herman Melville. NOBA

Pony, The. Rachel MacAndrew. BoTP

Pony air, wild wheat, The. The End of the Indian Poems. Stanley Plumly. GOA

Pony Express, The. Dorothy Brown Thompson. AmFN

Pooh! Walter de la Mare. FiBHP; HAP

Pool. Wanda Barford. Mes

Pool, The. Robert Creeley. CoAP

Pool, The. Hilda Doolittle ("H. D."). CMoP

Pool, A. Thomas Whitbread. NYBP

Pool & the Cow, The. Robert Phillips. SoTCo

Pool players, The. We Real Cool. Gwendolyn Brooks. CAPP; FF; HAP; HeIP; HoPM; IDB; InPK; NoP; PoA; PoBA; PoE; PrIm; SM; SoSe; TAP; TTY; WeW

Poor, The. John Langhorne. *Fr.* The Country Justice. NOEC

Poor, The. William Langland. *Fr.* The Vision of Piers Plowman. PoEL-1

Poor, The. Roberto Sosa, *tr. fr. Spanish by* Jack Hirschman. Vol

Poor, The. Emile Verhaeren, *tr. fr. French by* Ludwig Lewisohn. AWP

Poor, The. William Carlos Williams. MoAB; MoAmPo; NoP; PPP

Poor, and the dazed, and the idiots, the. Hurrying Away from the Earth. Robert Bly. NaP; PoA

Poor Angels. Edward Hirsch. MAYP

Poor are many, The. The Poor. Roberto Sosa, *tr. by* Jack Hirschman. Vol

Poor [*or* Poore] bird! I do not envy thee. The Robin. George Daniel. FaBoRV
(Ode: "Poor bird, I do not envy thee.") PBBP
("Poore bird! I doe not envie thee.") FM; OBS

Poor Brother. *Unknown.* NA

Poor But Honest. *Unknown. See* She Was Poor but She Was Honest.

Poor Can Feed the Birds, The. John Shaw Neilson. PoAu-1

Poor Children, The. Victor Hugo, *tr. fr. French by* Swinburne. AWP

Poor Christian Looks at the Ghetto, A. Czeslaw Milosz, *tr. fr. Polish by the author.* NIP; PwPP

Poor Cotton Weaver, The. *Unknown.* OBET

Poor crawlin' bodies, sair neglectit. John Learmont. *Fr.* An Address to the Plebeians. NOEC

Poor credulous and simple maid! Phyllis. Thomas Randolph. BoLoP

Poor Crow! Mary Mapes Dodge. OBCA

Poor Dad he got five years or more as everybody knows. Stir the Wallaby Stew. *Unknown.* FaBoBa

Poor dear dead have been laid out in vain, The. Thomas Hood. FaBoEE

Poor Dear Grandpapa. D'Arcy Wentworth Thompson. NA

Poor degenerate from the ape, A. First Philosopher's Song. Aldous Huxley. AWP

Poor devil that I am, being so attacked. Palladas, *tr. by* Tony Harrison. OBVE

Poor Dick! though first thy airs provoke. Dick Hairbrain Learns the Social Graces. John Trumbull. *Fr.* The Progress of Dulness. AmPP

Poor Doctor Blow went out of church. Queen Anne's Musicians. Thomas Hennell. FaBoTw

Poor drunkards, poor drunkards, take warning by me. John Adkins' Farewell. *Unknown.* AmFP

Poor Ellen Smith. *Unknown.* AmFP

Poor Estate, The. Robert Greene. *See* Farewell to Folly: Maesia's Song.

Poor fawn about to die. Image. Anna de Noailles, *tr. by* Carol Cosman. PBWP

Poor Fellow. Raymond Queneau, *tr. fr. French by* Teo Savory. RHTwFP

Poor fellow, what is it to you. Sir Charles Hanbury Williams. OBWVE

Poor Fool. Evan V. Shute. CaP

Poor for Our Sakes. Mary Brainerd Smith. BLRP

Poor French Sailor's Scottish Sweetheart, A. William Johnson Cory. EBVV

Poor George. George III. Robert Lowell. FaBoPV

Poor Ghost, The. Christina Rossetti. GBL

Poor Girl's Meditation, The. *Unknown, tr. fr. Irish by* Padraic Colum. BIrV; OBMV

Poor Hal caught his death standing under a spout. Fatal Love. Matthew Prior. FaBoCo; NBLV

Poor have hands, and feet, and eyes, The. The Poor Man and His Parish Church. Robert Stephen Hawker. EBVV

Poor heart, unsatisfied! Shadow and Sunrise. Henrietta Cordelia Ray. CBWP-3

Poor Hildegarde. The Singularity in Cygnus XI Viewed with Pity for HDE 226868. David Lunde. BWV

Poor humble roach. To a Humble Bug. Linda Lyon Van Voorhis. GoYe

Poor, impious Soul! that fixes its high hopes. Aspiration. Adah Isaacs Menken. CBWP-1

Poor in my youth, and in life's later scenes. On Late-acquired Wealth. *Unknown, tr. by* William Cowper. OBVE (Riches.) AWP

Poor in spirit on their rosary rounds, The. Lough Derg. Denis Devlin. BIrV; CIP; IPY

Poor is cold feet in the morning, cold floor. Linoleum: Breaking Down. Stanley Plumly. AnAn

Poor Is the Life That Misses. *Unknown.* EIL

Poor is the triumph o'er the timid hare. James Thomson. *Fr.* The Seasons: Autumn. EnRP; FM; PBBP

Poor Jack. Charles Dibdin. BeLS

Poor john, who joined in make of wrong. Welcome the Wrath. Stanley Kunitz. VGW

Poor Johnny was bended well nigh double. Apple-Seed John. Lydia Maria Child. OHIP

Poor Kid. William Cole. OBAL

Poor Kitty Popcorn. *Unknown.* AS

Poor lad once and a lad so trim, A. Jean Richepin's Song. Herbert Trench. OBMV

Poor Lil' Brack Sheep. Ethel M. C. Brazelton. BLPA

Poor little foal of an oppressèd race! To a Young Ass. Samuel Taylor Coleridge. EnRP

Poor Little Johnny. *Unknown.* AmFP

Poor little, pretty, fluttering [*or* flutt'ring] thing. Adriani Morientis ad Animam Suam. Emperor Hadrian, *tr. by* Matthew Prior. OBVE; OxBSP

Poor lone Hannah. Hannah Binding Shoes. Lucy Larcom. GN

Poor Lonesome Cowboy. *Unknown.* AS

Poor Lucy Lake was overgrown. Lucy Lake. Newton Mackintosh. BXAP

Poor Mailie's Elegy. Burns. FM

Poor Man and His Parish Church, The. Robert Stephen Hawker. EBVV

"Poor man, oh, poor man, come tell to me true." The Jolly Thresherman. *Unknown.* AmFP

Poor man's clothes—ragged and easy to get dirty, A. Shih-hou Pointed Out to Me That from Ancient Times There Had Never Been a Poem on the Subject of Li. Mei Yao-ch'en, *tr. by* Burton Watson. CoBCP

Poor Man's Hut. Masaoka Shiki, *tr. fr. Chinese by* Burton Watson. JLIC-2

Poor Man's Pig, The. Edmund Blunden. MoBrPo

Poor Man's Province, The. John Wright. NOEC

Poor man's sins are glaring, The. Rich and Poor; or, Saint and Sinner. Thomas Love Peacock. FaBoCo; NOBE; NOBL; OBSV

Poor Man's Sunday Walk, The. Charles MacKay. EBVV

Poor Man's Work Is Never Done, A. *Unknown.* OBET

Poor Matthias. Matthew Arnold. FM; PoEL-5

Poor Me. *Unknown, tr. fr. French by* Richard Beaumont. ErPo

Poor mortals that are clogged with earth below. Sir Robert Howard *and* John Dryden. *Fr.* The Indian Queen. TEP

Poor Movies. Will Bennett. UL

Poor naked wretches, wheresoe'er you are. Take Physic, Pomp. Shakespeare. *Fr.* King Lear, III, iv. TrGrPo

Poor nation, whose sweet sap and juice. The Jews. George Herbert. JCP

Poor North. Mark Strand. AnAn

Poor of London, The. William Forster. CBAP

Poor of the Borough, The; Peter Grimes. George Crabbe. *See* Borough, The: Peter Grimes.

Poor Old Fat Woman. Christine Donald. AIW

Poor Old Horse. David Holbrook. NePoEA-2

Poor Old Horse. *Unknown.* CH; OBET

Poor old Jonathan Bing. Jonathan Bing. Beatrice Curtis Brown. FaPON; OnMSP; PDV; RHPC

Poor Old Lady. *Unknown.* OBCA; RHPC

Poor old Mr. Bidery. Mr. Bidery's Spidery Garden. David McCord. RHPC

Poor Old Pilgrim Misery. Thomas Lovell Beddoes. *Fr.* The Bride's Tragedy. EnRP

Poor Old Prurient Interest Blues, The. John Hartford. MAT

Poor old Reuben Ranzo. Reuben Ranzo. *Unknown.* AmFP

Poor old Robinson Crusoe! Mother Goose. BoTP; OxNR

Poor old Widow in her weeds, A. A Widow's Weeds. Walter De la Mare. FaBV

Poor old woodman with a leafy load, A. Death and the Woodman. La Fontaine, *tr. by* Edward Marsh. OBD

Poor Omie. *Unknown.* PrIm

Poor Paddy Maguire, a fourteen-hour day. Patrick Kavanagh. *Fr.* The Great Hunger. IPY

Poor Paddy Works on the Railway. *Unknown.* AS

Poor painters oft with silly poets join. Cupid. Sir Philip Sidney. *Fr.* Arcadia. SiPS

Poor Parson, The. Chaucer. *Fr.* The Canterbury Tales: Prologue. ACP; NOCV; WGRP (Good Parson, The, *mod. by* H.C. Leonard) WGRP

Poor people use snare-nets, The. Song of the Painting "Catching Fish." Li Tung-yang, *tr. by* Jonathan Chaves. CoBLCP

Poor people who do not have the price of a fence ask son. Good Son Jim. Russell Edson. NAmP

Poor Poet-Ape, that would be thought our chief. On Poet-Ape. Ben Jonson. Son

Poor Poll. Robert Bridges. EBEV; OxBoLi; OxBTC

Poor Relations, The. Iain Crichton Smith. NPo

Poor restless dove, I pity thee. The Captive Dove. Anne Brontë. EBVV

Poor savage, doubting that a river flows. Watching the Dance. James Merrill. NIP

Poor Scholar. Cheng Hsieh. *tr. fr. Chinese by* Jan *and* Yvonne Walls. WFTU

Poor Scholar, The. Abraham Ibn Chasdai, *tr. fr. Hebrew by* J. Chotzner. TrJP

Poor Scholar of the 'Forties, A. Padraic Colum. AnIL; NOIV

Poor Shadow. Ilo Orleans. RAR

Poor Shammes of Berditchev, The. Rochelle Ratner. VWA

Poor silk-spinners. Song of the Venetian Silk-Spinners. *Unknown, tr. by* Muriel Kittel. DMI

Poor Snail, The. J. M. Westrup. BoTP

Poor song. The Tape. Myra Cohn Livingston. NTCP

Poor soul, in this thy flesh what dost thou know? John Donne. *Fr.* Of the Progresse of the Soule; the Second Anniversarie. OAEL-1 (Soules Ignorance in This Life and Knowledge in the Next, The.) OBS

Poor[e] soul[e] sat[e] sighing by a sycamore [*or* sicamore] tree, The. The Green Willow. *Unknown.* OBSC (Complaint of a Lover Forsaken of His Love, The.) CoMu

"Poor[e] soul[e], the centre of my sinful[l] earth." Shakespeare. *Fr.* Sonnets, CXLVI. AWP; EaLo; EIL; HAP; InPS; LiTB; NAEL-1; NIP; NOBE; NOCV; NoP; OAEL-1; OBEV; OBSC; PoE; PoEL-2; PPP; Son; TrGrPo (Soul and Body.) GTBS; GTBS-P

Poor South! Her books get fewer and fewer. J. Gordon Coogler. FaBoCo; FiBHP

Poor Swann, death, you know, is shy. Death says. The Duchess after the Burial. Norman Dubie. *Fr.* The Duchess' Red Shoes, IV. AnAn

Poor tired Tim! It's sad for him. Tired Tim. Walter De la Mare. BoTP; FaPON; MoShBr; NTCP; RHPC

Poor Tom. Charles Dibdin. NOEC; OxBoLi

Poor turtle, thou bemoans. William Drummond of Hawthornden. PBBP

Poor Uncle Joe. Sartorial Solecism. R. E. C. Stringer. FiBHP

Poor, varlet, pour the water. Macaulay at Tea. Barry Pain. *Fr.* The Poets at Tea, I. CenHV; Par

Poor vaunting earth, gloss'd with uncertain pride. George Alsop. SCAP

Poor Voter on Election Day, The. Whittier. OPP

"Poor wanderer," said the leaden sky. The Subalterns. Thomas Hardy. CMoP; MoAB; MoBrPo; MoP; NoAM; NOBVV; OAEL-2; PPP; TEP

Poor Wat. Shakespeare. *Fr.* Venus and Adonis. OBSC

Poor Wayfaring Stranger. *Unknown.* AmFP

Poor weaver, with the hopeless brow. How Different! Ebenezer Elliott. EBEV

Poor who begs with bated breath, The. The Price of Begging. Emmanuel ben David Frances, *tr. by* A. B. Rhine. TrJP

Poor Wolf Speaks. Poor Wolf. NU

Poor Women in a City Church. Seamus Heaney. TIRV

Poor Working Girl, The. *Unknown.* AS

Poore bird! I doe not envie thee. George Daniel. *See* Poor [*or* Poore] bird! I do not envy thee.

Poore [*or* Poor] Man Payes [*or* Pays] for All, The. *Unknown.* CoMu; OBET

Poore wench was sighing, and weeping amaine, A. The Bard. James Shirley. ErPo

Poore [*or* Povre] widwe [*or* widow], somdeel [*or* somedeal *or* somedel] stape in age, A. The Nun's Priest's Tale. Chaucer. *Fr.* The Canterbury Tales. FiP; NAEL-1; NoP; OAEL-1; PoEL-1; TrGrPo, *orig. and mod. vers. by* Frank Ernest Hill. (Cock and the Hen, The.) OBNV ("Once a poor widow, aging year by year.") NAWM-1, *mod. version by* Theodore Morrison. ("Once, long ago, set close beside a wood.") TrGrPo ("There liv'd, as authors tell, in days of yore.") OBVE "This Chauntecleer stood hye up-on his toos." Chauntecleer. FiP ("His comb was redder than the fine coral.") PBBP

Pop. David McFadden. NeAC

Pop bottles pop-bottles. Song of the Pop-Bottlers. Morris Bishop. FaPON; FiBHP

Pop Corn Song, A. Nancy Byrd Turner. FaPON

Pop Goes the Weasel! *at. to* W. R. Mardale. FaBoNo; OxNR

Pop Tune. Louis Aragon, *tr. fr. French by* Michael Benedikt. POS

Popcorn crunches. Crunch and Lick. Dorothy Aldis. RAR

Popcorn is greasy, and I forgot to bring a Kleenex, The. The James Bond Movie. May Swenson. FaBoWP

Popcorn peanuts clams and gum. Bar-Room Matins. Louis MacNeice. EaLo; NYBP

Pope from penance purgatorial, The. James Vincent Cunningham, *after the Latin of* George Buchanan. OBVE

Popish Plot, The. Dryden. *Fr.* Absalom and Achitophel, Pt. I. ACP

Poplar Field, The. William Cowper. CH; ChTr; ELP; FaBoPP; FaBoRV; FiP; GTBS; GTBS-P; HAP; NOBE; NOEC; PoEL-3; TrGrPo; WiR

Poplar is a French tree, The. The Trees. Christopher Morley. OHIP

Poplar is a lonely tree, The. Poplars. Edward Bliss Reed. OHIP

Poplar leaf was spiked upon a thorn, A. Temptation in Harvest. Patrick Kavanagh. FaBCIP

Poplar Tree. Padraic Colum. NePoAm

Poplars. Henryk Grynberg, *tr. fr. Polish by* Isaac Komem. VWA

Poplars. Helen Leuty. BoTP

Poplars. Edward Bliss Reed. OHIP

Poplars, The. Theodosia Garrison. OHIP

Poplars, The. Bernard Freeman Trotter. CaP

Poplars and Aspens. Jean-Paul de Dadelsen, *tr. fr. French by* Anselm Hollo. RHTwFP

Poplars are fell'd [*or* felled], farewell to the shade, The. The Poplar Field. William Cowper. CH; ChTr; ELP; FaBoPP; FaBoRV; FiP; GTBS; GTBS-P; HAP; NOBE; NOEC; PoEL-3; TrGrPo; WiR

Poplars are standing there still as death. Southern Mansion. Arna Bontemps. AiP; AmFN; AmNP; BANP; CNA; FB; FF; IDB; LiTM; PoBA; PoNe; TTY; WSC

Poplar's Shadow, The. May Swenson. NYBP

Popol Vuh, The, *sels. Unknown, tr. fr. Mayan by* Munro Edmonson. STP

 Alligator's Struggles with the 400 sons.

 Beginnings.

Poppies. Sandra McPherson. GeTw

Poppies. P. A. Ropes. BoTP

Poppies in July. Sylvia Plath. FaBoWP; LCAP; NaP; RB

Poppies in October. Sylvia Plath. FaBoWP; HCAP; LCAP; NoAM

Poppies in the Garden, The. ffrida Wolfe. BoTP

Poppies in the Wheat. Helen Hunt Jackson. AA

Poppy. Gerhard Fritsch, *tr. fr. German by* Beth Bjorklund. CoAuP

Poppy, The. Francis Thompson. MoBrPo

Poppy under a young. Necromance. Rae Armantrout. LP

Popular. Tennyson. NOBL

Popular Functionary, A. Charles Dibdin. NOEC

Popular leader, national hero. Finn's Wishes. Desmond O'Grady, *tr. by* the author. CIP

Popular Negro Song, A. *Unknown.* PVCV

Popular Personage at Home, A. Thomas Hardy. FM

Popular, popular, unpopular! Popular. Tennyson. NOBL

Popular Romance, A. Kevin Ireland. ATNZ; PeNZ

Popular Songs of Tuscany, *sels. Unknown, tr. fr. Italian by* John Addington Symonds. AWP

 "I see the dawn e'en now begin to peer."

 "I would I were a bird so free."

 "It was the morning of the first of May."

 "On Sunday morning well I knew."

 "Passing across the billowy sea."

 "Sleeping or waking, thou sweet face."

 "Strew me with blossoms when I die."

 "What time I see you passing by."

Popularity. Robert Browning. OAEL-2

Population. George Oppen. PoA

Population Drifts. Carl Sandburg. OxBA

"Porcelain is personal," he smiles. For His Ring and Watch on the Night Stand. Gladys Cardiff. HATNAP

Porch. Alden Nowlan. NeAC

Porch, The. Philip Pain. SCAP

Porch, The. R. S. Thomas. NOCV

Porch diminishes the fat men, The. The Fat Men. Cyril Dabydeen. PBCV

Porchlight coming on again, The. 1926. Weldon Kees. CoAP; NaP

Porcupine, The. Galway Kinnell. NaP; NOBA

Porgy, Maria, and Bess. DuBose Heyward. PoNe

Poring on Caesar's death with earnest eye. Julius Caesar and the Honey-Bee. Charles Tennyson Turner. FM

Poring over a book, or my sewing. The Gnomes. Beth Bentley. SaC

Porirua Friday Night. Sam Hunt. PeNZ

Pornoflicski is covered. X-Rated. F. F. Burch. SoTCo

Pornography Box, The. Dave Smith. DiL

Pornography, Nebraska. Sandra McPherson. MAYP

Porous. William Carlos Williams. NYBP

Porphyria's Lover. Robert Browning. AWP; BeLS; HAP; NAEL-2; OBEV; TEP; TrGrPo

Porpoise, The. Greg Pape. MAYP

Porson on German Scholarship. Richard Porson. FaBoCo; FaBoEE

Porson on His Majesty's Government. Richard Porson. FaBoCo

Porson's Visit to the Continent. Richard Porson. FaBoCo; FaBoEE

Port Admiral. Frederick Marryat. MOS

Port Bou. Stephen Spender. OBTV; TwCP

Port Jefferson. Louis Simpson. CAPP

Port Morazán. Carlos Martínez Rivas, *tr. fr. Spanish by* Alejandro Murguía *and* Walter Martínez. Vol

Port of Call: Brazil. Alun Lewis. OBTV

Port of Holy Peter. John Masefield. OBMV

Port of Many Ships. John Masefield. MOS; OBMV

Port of Spain. Derek Walcott. NoAM

Portent, The. AmPP; AnAmPo; InPK; NAAL-1; NOBA; NoP; OBWP; OxBA; PoE; PoEL-5; PrIm; TAP; WiR

Portents, The. Lucan, *tr. fr. Latin by* Christopher Marlowe. *Fr.* Pharsalia, I. OBSC

Porter to th' infernall gate is Sin, The. Sin, Despair, and Lucifer. Phineas Fletcher. *Fr.* The Locusts, or Appolyonists, I. OBS

Portia. Oscar Wilde. BrPo

Portion of this yew. Transformations. Thomas Hardy. PPP; RB; TEP

Portland County Jail. *Unknown.* AS

"Portland" Going Out, The. W. S. Merwin. NYBP

Portly he was, in carriage somewhat grand. The Bunch of Larks. Robert Leighton. EBVV

Portly prince, and goodly to the sight, A. Dryden. *Fr.* The Hind and the Panther, III. OBSV

Portly Roman Senator was sipping his Rock and Rye, A. A War Bird's Burlesque. *Unknown.* AS

Portola Valley. Amy Clampitt. EOEF

Portoncini dei Morti. Daniel Halpern. MAYP

Portrait. George Leonard Allen. CDC

Portrait. E. E. Cummings. *See* Buffalo Bill's.

Portrait, A. Walter de la Mare. NoAM

Portrait. John Lyle Donaghy. BIrV

Portrait, A. Caroline Duer. AA

Portrait. Kenneth Fearing. MoAmPo

Portrait. Gail Fox. NOBC

Portrait, The. Robert Graves. CMoP

Portrait, A. Keats. BXAP

Portrait, The. Stanley Kunitz. CAPP; DiL; Psk

Portrait. Adèle Naudé. PeSA

Portrait. Brenda Marie Osbey. MT

Portrait. Dahlia Ravikovich, *tr. fr. Hebrew by* Warren Bargad *and* Stanley F. Chyet. IP; OV

 ("She sits home many a day.") MHeP

Portrait, A. Robert Louis Stevenson. SeCePo

Portrait. Judith Wright. OxBSP

Portrait across a Room. Elizabeth Nannestad. ATNZ

Portrait by a Neighbor. Edna St. Vincent Millay. FaPON; MoShBr; OBCA; PDV

Portrait by Alice Neel. Aaron Kramer. EyDe

Portrait d'une Femme. Ezra Pound. CMoP; FF; InPS; MoAB; MoAmPo; MoP; NAAL-2; NoAM; NOBA; NoP; PPP; TAP; TwCP

Portrait in Georgia. Jean Toomer. NAAL-2; NoP

Portrait in the Guards, A. Laurence Whistler. GTBS-P

Portrait in Winter. Katherine Garrison Chapin. GoYe

Portrait is where you, The. Robert Creeley Also Watches. D. C. Berry. BXAP

Portrait: My Wife. John Holmes. UnAS

Portrait of a Cree. "Katherine Hale." CaP

Portrait of a Girl. Conrad Aiken. *See* Priapus and the Pool: This Is the Shape of the Leaf.

Portrait of a Jew Old Country Style. Jerome Rothenberg. NNaP

Portrait of a Lady. T. S. Eliot. TwCP

Portrait of a Lady. Elizabeth Nannestad. ATNZ; PeNZ

Portrait of a Lady. Michael Ryan. NAmP

Portrait of a Lady. William Carlos Williams. AmPP; CMoP; MoP; NAAL-2; NoAM; NOBA; OxBA

Portrait of a Lady in the Exhibition of the Royal Academy. Winthrop Mackworth Praed. *Fr.* Every-Day Characters. NOBL; PoEL-4

Portrait of a Machine. Louis Untermeyer. MoAmPo
Portrait of a Man. Alan Bernheimer. UL
Portrait of a Nun. Bobi Jones, *tr. fr. Welsh by* Joseph P. Clancy. OBWVE
Portrait of a Pregnant Woman. Bobi Jones, *tr. fr. Welsh by* Joseph P. Clancy. OBWVE
Portrait of a Very Old Man. Sara E. Carsley. CaP
Portrait of a Widow. Avner Strauss. VWA
Portrait of a Woman (and a Man). John Figueroa. PBCV
Portrait of a Young Girl Raped at a Suburban Party. Brian Patten. OxBTC
Portrait of an Artist. Barbara Howes. IHMS
Portrait of an Engine Driver. Bobi Jones, *tr. fr. Welsh by* Joseph P. Clancy. OBWVE
Portrait of an Ex-Young Bourgeois. Lindolf Bell, *tr. fr. Portuguese by* William Jay Smith. CT
Portrait of an Indian. R. E. Rashley. CaP
Portrait of an Old Man. Erika Mitterer, *tr. fr. German by* Beth Bjorklund. CoAuP
Portrait of Brutus. Shakespeare. *Fr.* Julius Caesar, V, v. TrGrPo (Noblest Roman, The.) FaFP
Portrait of Caesar. Shakespeare. *Fr.* Julius Caesar, I, ii. TrGrPo
Portrait of Cressida. Shakespeare. *Fr.* Troilus and Cressida, IV, v. TrGrPo
Portrait of Helen. Shakespeare. *Fr.* Troilus and Cressida, II, ii *and* IV, i. TrGrPo
Portrait of Henri III, A. Théodore Agrippa d' Aubigné, *tr. fr. French. Fr.* Tragiques, Les. PeHV
Portrait of Henry VIII, The. Earl of Surrey. ACP
Portrait of Hudibras. Samuel Butler. *See* Hudibras: Metaphysical Sectarian, The ("He was in logick a great critic").
Portrait of Malcolm X. Etheridge Knight. CNA; PoBA
Portrait of Milton, The. Dryden. *See* Three poets, in three distant ages born.
Portrait of Prince Henry, The. Sydney Clouts. VWA
Portrait of Rudy, A. James Cunningham. CNA
Portrait of Sidrophel. Samuel Butler. *Fr.* Hudibras, II, 3. PoEL-3
Portrait of the Artist as a Prematurely Old Man. Ogden Nash. BLPL; FaFP; InPS; LiTA; LiTM
Portrait of the Artist as an Old Man. Michael Dransfield. CBAP
Portrait of the Artist with Hart Crane. Charles Wright. GeTw
Portrait of the Autist as a New World Driver. Les A. Murray. CBAP
Portrait of the Boy as Artist. Barbara Howes. MoAmPo
Portrait of the Consort to Louis XIV. Blossom S. Kirschenbaum. SoTCo
Portrait of the Father. Lindy Hough. IHMS
Portrait of the Poet as Landscape. A. M. Klein. NoAM; NOBC
Portrait of the Pornographer. G. W. Jones. BXAP
Portrait Philippines. Alfred A. Duckett. PoNe
Portrait: The Freedom Fighter. George Jonas. NeAC; NOBC
Portrait with Background. Oliver St. John Gogarty. OBMV
Portraits, The. Anna Maria Lenngren, *tr. fr. Swedish by* C. W. Stork. WPOW
Portrait's All Feet, The. Rocco Scotellaro, *tr. fr. Italian by* Lawrence R. Smith. NItP
Portraits and Repetition, *sel.* Gertrude Stein.
  "How do you like what you have." AiP
Ports. István Vas, *tr. fr. Hungarian by* Jascha Kessler. FOC
Poseidon's Law. Kipling. MOS
Posing on the sloped rock. Horned Lizard. Charles Molesworth. GrPl
Position. Barrett Watten. IAT
Position is so well-known, The. Inside Diameter. Clarence Major. UL
Position is where you. The Window. Robert Creeley. CAPP; NoAM; NOBA; TAP; VGW
Positive. Otto Laaber, *tr. fr. German by* Beth Bjorklund. CoAuP
Positives. Jewel C. Latimore. PoBA
Positives for Sterling Plumpp. Don L. Lee. JB; PoBA
Positivists, The. Mortimer Collins. EBVV
Positivists ever talk in s-/Uch an epic style as Dawkins. John William Mackail. *Fr.* Balliol Rhymes. FaBoEE
Possessed shaman with the spear, The. Murukan, the Red One. Nakkiranar, *tr. by* A. K. Ramanujan. PLW
Possession. Richard Aldington. MoBrPo
Possession. Lynne Lawner. ErPo
Possession. Marie Ponsot. VGW
Possession. *Unknown.* BLRP
Possessions. Ivor Gurney. FaBoPP
Possessions. Ken Smith. EAS
Possessive Love. Tommy Tabermann, *tr. fr. Finnish by* Aili Jarvenpa. SOP
Possessor, The. Arthur Rex Dugard Fairburn. *Fr.* Album Leaves. PeNZ

Possessor. Things. W. S. Merwin. HAP
Possibilities. Peter Kane Dufault. NYBP
Possibilities of Snow. Cheng Wen-tao. WCI
Possibility That Has Been Overlooked Is the Future, The. Michael Hartnett. NOIV
Possible Landscape. Alfred Gesswein, *tr. fr. German by* Beth Bjorklund. CoAuP
Possible Salvation of Continuous Motion, The. Pattiann Rogers. MT
Possum lay on the tracks fully dead, The. The Lull. Molly Peacock. MAYP
Possum lies curled, The. Daydreamers. Norma L. Davis. PoAu-2
Post-Boy, The. William Cowper. *See* Task, The: Winter Evening, The ("Hark! 'tis the twanging horn o'er yonder bridge").
Post-boy drove with fierce career, The. Alice Fell; or, Poverty. Wordsworth. BeLS; OBNV
Post-Coitum Tristesse: A Sonnet. Brad Leithauser. EOEF
Post Early for Space. Peter J. Henniker-Heaton. AmFN
Post-horse bells are tinkling, The. *Unknown. Fr.* Manyo Shu. Ma
Post-Impressionist Susurration for the First of November, 1983, A. Hayden Carruth. BLA
Post-Meridian, *sels.* Wendell Phillips Garrison. AA
  Afternoon.
  Evening.
Post Mortem. Verna Loveday Harden. CaP
Post Mortem. Robinson Jeffers. MoAmPo; TrGrPo
Post Mortem. Arthur Munby. NOBVV
Post Mortem. Shakespeare. *See* If thou survive my well-contented day.
Post-Obits and the Poets. Martial, *tr. fr. Latin by* Byron. AWP; FaBoEE; OBVE
Post office automatic writing system, The. Health. Margo Lockwood. PPR
Post-Rail Song. *Unknown.* AS
Post-Roads. Kenneth Slessor. *Fr.* The Atlas. PoAu-2
Post That Fitted, The. Kipling. CenHV; OnMSP
Post-War. Libby Houston. CN
Post-War Christmas. Phoebe Hesketh. CN
Postcard. Margaret Atwood. NoAM
Postcard. Pamela Stewart. NAmP
Postcard from Mexico, 16.x.1973. Andrew Salkey. PBCV
Postcard from North Antrim, A. Seamus Heaney. FaBCIP; IPY
Postcard from the Garden. Marge Piercy. NoAM
Postcard from the Volcano, A. Wallace Stevens. HAP; HCAP; LiTA; NoAM; WeW
Postcard to Send to Sumer, A. William Bronk. VGW
Postcards from Kodai. Kevin Crossley-Holland. OBTV
Postcards of the Hanging: 1869. Andrew Hudgins. MOWH
Postcards to Athena. Michael Bishop. BWV
Posted. John Masefield. Son
Poster Girl, The. Carolyn Wells. BXAP
Poster of Our Dazzling Victory at Saarbrucken, A. Arthur Rimbaud, *tr. fr. French by* Robert Lowell. *Fr.* Eighteen-Seventy. FaBoPV; OBWP
Poster with my picture on it, The. Unwanted. Edward Field. GLP; Psk
Posterity. Cyril Dabydeen. BrSi
Posterity. Philip Larkin. OxBC
Posterity, thy name is Samuel Johnson. A Dream of Judgement. Douglas Dunn. OxBC
Posterity will ne'er survey. An Epitaph for Castlereagh. Byron. NIP (Epitaph: "Posterity will ne'er survey.") FaBoEE; TW
Posthumous. Henry Augustin Beers. AA
Posthumous Coquetry. Théophile Gautier, *tr. fr. French by* Arthur Symons. AWP; OBD
Posthumous Keats. Stanley Plumly. GeTw; SV
Posthumous Rehabilitation. Tadeusz Rozewicz, *tr. fr. Polish by* Adam Czerniawski. FaBoPV
Postilion Has Been Struck by Lightning, The. Patricia Beer. OxBC
Posting the Letter. John Welch. NPo
Postman, The. Buland al-Haidari, *tr. fr. Arabic by* Abdullah al-Udhari. MPAW
Postman, The. Gordon Challis. ATNZ
Postman, The. Clive Sansom. BoTP
Postman, The. Alice Todd. BoTP
Postman, The. *Unknown.* FaPON
Postman Cheval. André Breton, *tr. fr. French by* David Gascoyne. EAS; RHTwFP
Postman comes when I am still in bed, The. A Sick Child. Randall Jarrell. InPK; InvP; OxBC; SO; VGW
Postman's Bell Is Answered Everywhere, The. Horace Gregory. MoAmPo; NYBP

Postman's Fear, The. Muhammad al-Maghut, *tr. fr. Arabic by* Abdullah al-Udhari. MPAW
Postman's Knock. Rodney Bennett. BoTP
Postponement. André du Bouchet, *tr. fr. French by* Paul Auster. RHTwFP
Postscript. Henri Coulette. DiPo
Postscript. Sandra Hochman. NMM
Postscript. Mary Mills. NePoAm
Postscript. János Pilinszky, *tr. fr. Hungarian by* Edwin Morgan. MHuP
Postscript. R. S. Thomas. FaBoMo; OxBC
Postscript for Gweno. Alun Lewis. BoLoP; GTBS-P
Postscript to a Pettiness. A. S. J. Tessimond. OxBSP
Postscript to an Elegy. Gibbons Ruark. MT
Postscript to Verses on the History of France, A. *Unknown.* NOIV
Posture of the tree, The. Lovers in Winter. Robert Graves. FaBoEE; NYBP
Postures of Love, The, *sel.* Alex Comfort.
  "There is a white mare that my love keeps." ErPo
Posy of Thyme, The. *Unknown.* OBET
Posy Ring, The. Clément Marot, *tr. fr. French by* Ford Madox Ford. AWP
Pot of Earth, A. Jules Supervielle, *tr. fr. French by* Denise Levertov. RHTwFP
Pot of Flowers, The. William Carlos Williams. QFR
Pot of Tea. Susan Griffin. NPGG
Pot of wine among flowers, A. Drinking Alone in the Moonlight. Li Po, *tr. by* Amy Lowell *and* Florence Ayscough. AWP
Pot Poured Out, A. Samuel Menashe. Mes
Pot Shot. Padraic Fallon. CIP
Pot splits, and the night ice wakes me, A. Cold Nights. Basho, *tr. fr. Japanese by* Burton Watson. *Fr.* Seventy-six Hokku. FCEI
Potage au Petit Puss. Menu. Edward Lear. FaBoNo
Potato. Richard Wilbur. CAPP; LiTA; MoAB; TrGrPo
Potato Harvest, The. Sir Charles G. D. Roberts. CaP; NOBC
Potato was deep in the dark under ground, The. The Tryst. John Banister Tabb. OBAL
Potatoes. David Donnell. NIP; NOBC
Potatoes' Dance, The. Vachel Lindsay. FaPON
Potatoes of the corner store sing, The. At Kino Viejo, Mexico. Alberto Ríos. NoAM
Potchikoo Marries. Louise Erdrich. *Fr.* Old Man Potchikoo. HATNAP
Potpourri from a Surrey Garden. Sir John Betjeman. CenHV; FiBHP; NOBL
Potter,/ O potter. An Urn for Burial. *Unknown, tr. by* A. K. Ramanujan. PLW
Potter, The. *Unknown, tr. fr. Geez by* Halim El-Dabh. TTY
Potter at Mimaki in Kusuha, The. Emperor Go-Shirakawa, *tr. fr. Japanese by* Hiroaki Sato. *Fr.* Ryojin Hisho. FCEI
Potter's Song, The. Longfellow. *Fr.* Kéramos. PoEL-5
Poultries, The. Ogden Nash. CenHV
Poultry. Diana Der Hovanessian. GrPl
Pound at Spoleto. Lawrence Ferlinghetti. PoM
Pounded spise both tast and sent doth please, The. At Fotheringay. Robert Southwell. PoEL-2
Pour Commencer. Jon Stallworthy. NoAM
Pour demander le chemin. *Unknown.* *Fr.* A Lytell Treatyse for to Lerne Englysshe and Frens. OxBLMV
Pour l'Election de Son Sepulchre, I-V. Ezra Pound. *See* Hugh Selwyn Mauberley. (Life and Contacts):
  For three years, out of key with his time.
Pour O pour that parting soul in song. Song of the Son. Jean Toomer. AmNP; CDC; NIP; PoBA
Pour one for me, friend good and true. N. M. Yazykov, *tr. by* Alan Myers. AAA
Pour out your light, O stars. Ivor Gurney. FaBoEE; FaBoTw
Pour Us Wine. Ibn Kolthum. *Fr.* The Mu'allaqat. AWP
Pouring/ One sorrow, two sorrows. Yellow River. Fei Ma, *tr. by* Dominic Cheung. IFON
Pouring Out My Feelings after Parting from Yüan Chen. Po Chü-i, *tr. fr. Chinese by* Burton Watson. CoBCP
Pourquoi You Greased. *Unknown.* ChTr
Poussie, poussie, baudrons. *Unknown.* OxNR
Poussin. Louis MacNeice. EyDe
Poverty. Charles Simic. MAT
Poverty. Theognis, *tr. fr. Greek by* John Hookham Frere. AWP
Poverty. Thomas Traherne. Prf; TEP; TrCP
Poverty. *Unknown, tr. fr. Sanskrit by* Arthur Ryder. *Fr.* The Panchatantra. AWP
Poverty, in Imitation of Milton. Samuel Jones. NOEC

Poverty in London. Samuel Johnson. *See* London: A Poem in Imitation of the Third Satire of Juvenal:
  By numbers here from shame or censure free.
Poverty Knock. *Unknown.* OBET
Poverty, remorseless spectre. Christmas Eve, South, 1865. Mary E. Tucker. CBWP-1
Poverty? wealth? seek neither. Kassia, *tr. by* Patrick Diehl. WPOW
Povre Ame Amoureuse. Louise Labé, *tr. fr. French by* Robert Bridges. AWP
Pow Wow. Vickie Sears. GOS
Powder and scent and silence. The young dwarf. Clair de Lune. Anthony Hecht. NYBP
Powder of Sympathy, The. James Tate. AnAn
Power. Thomas Stephens Collier. AA
Power. Hart Crane. *See* Bridge, The: Cape Hatteras.
Power. Audre Lorde. GLP; NoAM
Power. Adrienne Rich. TAP
Power above powers, O heavenly Eloquence. English Poetry. Samuel Daniel. *Fr.* Musophilus; or, Defence of All Learning. OBSC (Heavenly Eloquence.) NOBE
Power and Light. James Dickey. NAAL-2
Power and Peace. Robert Herrick. CaPo
Power and the Glory, The. Siegfried Sassoon. OBMV
Power-Cut. Medbh McGuckian. FaBCIP
Power Failure. Michael Dennis Browne. AmPA
Power glides in the root. Root. Miklós Radnóti, *tr. by* Steven Polgar, Stephen Berg *and* S. J. Marks. VWA
Power-house, A. Classic Scene. William Carlos Williams. NAAL-2; OxBA
Power in the People, The. Robert Herrick. CaPo
Power lies in my hand. The Sibyl. Joan LaBombard. GoYe
Power of Fancy, The. Philip Freneau. AmPP
Power of Innocence, The. "C. G. H." NOEC
Power of Interval, The. John Byrne Leicester Warren, 3rd Baron De Tabley. NOBVV; OxBSP
Power of Love, The. Dryden. *Fr.* Cymon and Iphigenia. OBS
Power of Love He Wants Shih (Everything), The. Rochelle Owens. NMM
Power of Maples, The. Gerald Stern. NU
Power of Music, The. Thomas Lisle. NOBL
Power of Music, The. Shakespeare. *Fr.* The Merchant of Venice, V, i. GN
Power of my blood, your secret. Witches' Blood. Alma Villanueva. CCP
Power of Numbers, The. Abraham Cowley. *Fr.* Davideis, I. OBS
Power of Prayer, The. Samuel Johnson. *Fr.* Vanity of Human Wishes, The: The Tenth Satire of Juvenal Imitated. NOBE
Power of raven be thine. Good Wish. *Unknown, tr. by* Alexander Carmichael. FaBoCh
Power of Ridicule, The. Pope. *See* Epilogue to the Satires [*or* 1738]: Ask you what provocation I have had?
Power of Ridicule, The. *Unknown*
Power of Silence, The. W. H. Davies. BrPo
Power of Taste, The. Zbigniew Herbert, *tr. fr. Polish by* John Carpenter *and* Bogdana Carpenter. AnAn
Power of the celestial Lion is broken, The. The Lion. István Vas, *tr. by* Jascha Kessler. FOC
Power of the Dog, The. Kipling. BLPA; BLPL
Power of the Flowers. Ferenc Juhász, *tr. fr. Hungarian by* Kenneth McRobbie. MHuP
Power of Thought, The. Süsskind von Trimberg, *tr. fr. Middle High German.* TrJP
Power of Time, The. Swift. FaBoEE
Power speaks only out of sleep and blackness, The. Below Loughrigg. Fleur Adcock. PeNZ
Power, that gives with liberal hand, The. On the Religion of Nature. Philip Freneau. AmPP; NAAL-1
Power to Change Geography, The. Diana O Hehir. NPGG
Power to thine elbow, thou newest of sciences. Darwinity. Herman Charles Merivale. NA
Power Transformer. Ian Wedde. *Fr.* Earthly: Sonnets for Carlos, 26. ATNZ; PeNZ
Power was given at birth to me, The. One Token. W. H. Davies. BrPo
Powerful Eyes o' Jeremy Tait, The. Wallace Irwin. FiBHP
Powerful Officials. Cheng Hsieh, *tr. fr. Chinese by* Jan W. Walls. WFTU
Powerless emperor, The. The Hard Listener. William Carlos Williams. OxBSP
Powerless Frog. Saibara, *tr. fr. Japanese by* Hiroaki Sato. FCEI
Powerline Incarnation, The. Les A. Murray. CBAP

Powers of the Pen, The, *sel.* Evan Lloyd.
  Helen like the Rose. OBWVE
Powhatan's Daughter. Hart Crane. *Fr.* The Bridge, II. LiTA; NAAL-2
  Dance, The. LiTM; MoAB; MoAmPo; OxBA
  Harbor Dawn, The. AmPP; CMoP; FaBV; GOA; LiTM; MoAB;
    MoAmPo; NoAM; NOBA; OxBA; PrIm; TrGrPo
  River, The. AmPP; CMoP; GOA; MoAB; MoAmPo; NOBA; OxBA;
    PrIm
    "Down, down—born pioneers in time's despite," *sel.* TrGrPo
  Van Winkle. AmPP; FaBV; MoAB; MoAmPo
Powte's Complaint, The. *Unknown.* GBP
Powwow. W. D. Snodgrass. GrPl; NYBP
Powwow remnants. Lew Blockcolski. VoR
Powwow 79, Durango. Paula Gunn Allen. STE
Pox of this fooling and plotting of late, A. The Careless Good Fellow.
  John Oldham. APAS; SeCV-2
Pox on't, says Time to Thomas Hearne. *Unknown.* FaBoEE
Practical Concerns. William J. Harris. PoBA
Practical Poems. David Avidan, *tr. fr. Hebrew by* Warren Bargad *and*
  Stanley F. Chyet. IP
Practical Woman, A. Thomas Hardy. NAs
"Practically all you newspaper people." The Clown. Donald Hall.
  NYBP
Practice of Absence, The. Robert Friend. VWA
Practice of Magical Evocation, The. Diane di Prima. PoM
Practices/ silence, they way of wind. As a Possible Lover. Amiri
  Baraka. AmNP
Practicing calligraphy, not noticing night had come. Calligraphy Practice.
  Ou-yang Hsiu, *tr. by* Burton Watson. CoBCP
Præfatory Poem to the Little Book, A. Nicholas Noyes. SCAP
Prague is a famous, ancient, kingly seat. John Taylor. *Fr.* Taylor's
  Travels from London to Prague. OBTV
Prague, January 1964. Ingeborg Bachmann, *tr. fr. German by* Beth
  Bjorklund. CoAuP
Prague Spring. Tony Harrison. OBTV
Prairie. Herbert Bates. AA
Prairie, *sel.* Carl Sandburg.
  Look at Six Eggs. FaPON
Prairie Birth. Grace Stone Coates. OPP
Prairie child,/ Brief as dew. Nancy Hanks. Harriet Monroe. OHIP
Prairie-Dog Town. Mary Austin. FaPON
Prairie Fires. Hamlin Garland. OBCA
Prairie goes to the mountain. Open Range. Kathryn Jackson *and* Byron
  Jackson. FaPON
Prairie grass. Struggle for the Roads. Bruce Severy. NOVW
Prairie Graveyard. Anne Marriott. CaP; NOBC; OBCV
Prairie Water Colour, A. Duncan Campbell Scott. OBCV
Prairie Waters by Night. Carl Sandburg. NAAL-2
Prairie wind blew harder than it could, The. Swallows. Thomas Hornsby
  Ferril. RFM
Prairie women quilted. Bad Sport. Beth Kalikoff. TSL
Prairies, The. Bryant. AmPP; NAAL-1; NOBA; OPP; OxBA; PoEL-4;
  TAP
Praise. Mary Anderson. BoTP
Praise. Jane Cooper. TAP
Praise. Dinah Livingstone. AIW
Praise. William Matthews. AmPA
Praise. Rainer Maria Rilke, *tr. fr. German.* ChTr
Praise. Christopher Smart. OxBChV
Praise and Prayer. Sir William Davenant. *Fr.* Gondibert, II, vi. OBEV
Praise Doubt. Mark Van Doren. EaLo
Praise for an Urn. Hart Crane. AWP; CMoP; HAP; LiTM; MoAB;
  MoAmPo; NoAM; NOBA; OxBA; PPP; WeW
Praise for Mercies Spiritual and Temporal. Isaac Watts. NOEC
Praise for Sick Women. Gary Snyder. NeAP
Praise for the Fountain Opened. William Cowper. InPK
Praise-God Barebones. Ellen Mackay Hutchinson Cortissoz. AA
Praise Hearst, from whom all blessings flow! Doxology. Bert Leston
  Taylor. OBAL
Praise him for the place he picked. Death in the Aquarium. Richard
  Hugo. AnAn
Praise Him Who Makes Us Happy. Mark Van Doren. AH
Praise in Summer. Richard Wilbur. CAPP; NoP
Praise is devotion fit for mighty minds. Praise and Prayer. Sir William
  Davenant. *Fr.* Gondibert, II, vi. OBEV
Praise, my soul, the King of heaven. Bible, *O.T.* *See* Psalms: Psalm
  CIII ("Bless the Lord, O my soul. . .").
Praise Now Your God. H. P Brucker. AH
Praise, O my heart, with praise from depth and height. Adam's Song of
  the Visible World. Ridgely Torrence. TrPWD

Praise of a Child. *Yoruba Oral Tradition, tr. by* Ulli Beier *and* B.
  Gbadamosi. WTO
Praise of a Collie. Norman MacCaig. RB
Praise of a Train. *Zulu Oral Tradition, tr. by* B. W. Vilakazi. WTO
Praise of Amen Ra! Hymn to Amen Ra, the Sun God. *Unknown, tr. by*
  Frank Lloyd Griffith. WGRP
Praise of Ben Dorain, The. Duncan Ban MacIntyre, *tr. fr. Gaelic by*
  "Hugh MacDiarmid" (Christopher Murray Grieve). GoTS
Praise of Ceres. Thomas Heywood. *Fr.* The Silver Age. EIL
Praise of Created Things. Saint Francis of Assisi. FaPON
Praise of Dancing, The. Sir John Davies. *See* Orchestra; or, A Poem[e]
  of Da[u]ncing
Praise of Diseases. Jacopone da Todi, *tr. fr. Italian by* L. R. Lind. PFI
Praise of Dust, The. G. K. Chesterton. MoBrPo
Praise of Fionn, The. *Unknown, tr. fr. Irish by* Frank O'Connor. TIRV
Praise of God. *Unknown.* NOIV
Praise of His Lady, A. *At. to* John Heywood. EIL; OBEV
  (On the Princess Mary.) OBSC
Praise of His Love, Wherein He Reproveth Them That Compare Their
  Ladies with His, A. Surrey, Earl of. *See* Give [*or* Geve] Place, Ye
  Lovers.
Praise of Homer. George Chapman. OBS
Praise of Ibikunle. *Yoruba Oral Tradition, tr. by* B. Awe. WTO
Praise of Little Women. Juan Ruiz, Archpriest of Hita, *tr. fr. Spanish by*
  Longfellow. AWP
Praise of meaner wits this work like profit brings, The. Another of the
  Same. Sir Walter Ralegh. SiPS
Praise of New England. Thomas Caldecot Chubb. GoYe
Praise of New Netherland, The. Jacob Steendam. PAH
Praise of Philip Sparrow, The, *sel.* George Gascoigne.
  Of All the Birds That I Do Know. CH; PBBP
Praise of Poets. William Browne. *Fr.* Britannia's Pastorals, II, Songs 1
  and 2. OBS
Praise of Sailors, The. *Unknown.* OxBSS
Praise of Waterford, The, *sel.* *Unknown.*
  "God of his goodnes, praysed that he be." NOIV
Praise of Women. Robert Mannyng. OBEV
Praise Song for King Kalakaua. *Unknown, tr. fr. Hawaiian by* N. B.
  Emerson. WTO
Praise Song for My Mother. Grace Nichols. WS
Praise the day before night falls. Sometimes Believing. Jan G. Elburg,
  tr. by André Lefevere. DuIn
Praise the good angel doubt. Praise Doubt. Mark Van Doren. EaLo
Praise the Lord. Milton. *See* Let Us with a Gladsome Mind.
Praise the Lord for all the seasons. Praise. Mary Anderson. BoTP
Praise to my text, Water, which taught me writing. Poem Made of Water.
  Nancy Willard. BLA
Praise to the End! Theodore Roethke. InPS
  Mips and Ma the Mooly Moo, *sel.* NBLV; RB
Praise to the Holiest in the height. Chorus of Angels. Cardinal Newman.
  Fr. The Dream of Gerontius. NOCV; PoEL-5
  (Fifth Choir of Angelicals.) NOBVV
Praise we the Lord/ of Heaven's kingdom. Caedmon's Hymn. Caedmon.
  EBEV, *tr. by* Sally Purcell
Praise ye the Lord!/ For it is good to sing praises unto our God. Bible,
  O.T. Psalms, CXLVII.
  ("Hallelujah/ Praise ye the Lord.") TrJP
  (Psalm CXLVII: "Praise ye the Lord," *paraphrased by* Christopher
    Smart) NOCV
  (Psalm CXLVII: "Praise ye the Lord," *paraphrased by* the Countess of
    Pembroke) NOCV
  ("Sing unto the Lord with thanksgiving.") OHIP
  Who Maketh the Grass to Grow. FaPON, *greatly abr.*
Praise ye the Lord/ Praise ye the Lord. Bible, *O.T.* Psalms, CXLVIII.
  TrJP
  (Psalm CXLVIII: "Hallelujah! kneel and sing", *paraphrased by*
    Christopher Smart) OBVE, 1-10.
  (Song of Praise, A.) TrGrPo
Praise ye the Lord for the avenging of Israel. The Song of Deborah.
  Bible, *O.T.* Judges, V: 1-31. AWP; BoWoP; PBWP
  (Then Sang Deborah and Barak.) TrJP
  "Blessed above women/ shall Jael the wife of Heber the Kenite be."
    Fr. V:24-31.WPOW
Praise Ye the Lord. O Celebrate His Fame. Peleg Folger. AH
"Praise ye the Lord!" The psalm to-day. The Thanksgiving in Boston
  Harbor. Hezekiah Butterworth. AA; OHIP; PAH
Praise youth's hot blood if you will, I think that happiness. Age in
  Prospect. Robinson Jeffers. MoAB; MoAmPo
Praised be Diana's fair and harmless light. Diana. Sir Walter Ralegh.
  OBSC

(Homage to Diana.) WiR

(Shepherd's Praise of Diana, The.) SiPS

Praised be man, he is existing in milk. Jack Kerouac. *Fr.* Mexico City Blues, 228. NeAP

Praised be the name of the Lord, who created the wine. Five Arabic Verses in Praise of Wine. *Unknown, tr. by* Hartwig Hirschfeld. TrJP

Praised beyond all Enids be. In Morfudd's Arms. Dafydd ap Gwilym, *tr. by* Rolfe Humphries. OBWVE

Praisers of women in their proud and beautiful poems, The. "Not Marble nor the Gilded Monuments." Archibald MacLeish. BoLoP; CMoP; HoPM; MoAB; PoRA; TwCP

Praises, The. Charles Olson. VGW

Praises of a Country Life, The. Ben Jonson. OBVE; SeCP

Praises of God, The. *Unknown, tr. fr. Middle Irish by* Kenneth Jackson. AnIL

Praises of Henry Francis Fynn. *Zulu Oral Tradition, tr. by* T. Cope. WTO

Praises of King George VI. A. Z. Ngani, *tr. fr. Xhosa by* Jack Cope. PeSA

Praises of the King Dingana (Vesi). *Unknown, tr. fr. Zulu.* PeSA

Praises of the King of Oyo. *Yoruba Oral Tradition, tr. by* Ulli Beier. WTO

Praises of the King Tshaka. *Unknown, tr. fr. Zulu.* PeSA

Praises of the Train. Demetrius Segooa, *tr. fr. Sotho.* PeSA

Praises, Tamalpais. Song of the Turkey Buzzard. Lew Welch. PoM

Praises to those who can wait. Zealots of Yearning. David Rokeah, *tr. by* I. M. Lask. TrJP

Praising Spectacles. Yüan Mei, *tr. fr. Chinese by* Anthony C. Yu. WFTU

Praties, The. *Unknown.* WTO

(Famine Song.) WTO

Praxiteles and Phryne. William Wetmore Story. AA; BeLS

Pray! Irene Arnold. BLRP

Pray Billy Pitt explain thy rigs. On Mr. Pitt's Hair-Powder Tax. Burns. FaBoEE

Pray but one prayer for me 'twixt thy closed lips. Summer Dawn. William Morris. Mes; NOBE; NOBVV; OAEL-2; OBEV; OBNC

Pray for my soul. More things are wrought by prayer. Prayer. Tennyson. *Fr.* Idylls of the King: The Passing of Arthur. WGRP

Pray for the Dead. Arthur Wentworth Hamilton Eaton. AA

Pray—Give—Go. Annie Johnson Flint. BLRP

Pray how did she look? Was she pale, was she wan? On Lady Anne Hamilton. Sheridan. FaBoEE

Pray in the early morning. Pray! Irene Arnold. BLRP

Pray Remember the Poor. Christopher Smart. NOEC

Pray steal me not, I'm Mrs. Dingley's. On the Collar of Mrs. Dingley's Lap-Dog. Swift. FaBoEE; FM

Pray tell your querist if he may. Charm: Corns. *Unknown.* FaBoUs

Pray thee, take care, that tak'st my book[e] in hand. To the Reader. Ben Jonson. NoP; PoE; SeCV-1

Pray to What Earth Does This Sweet Cold Belong. Henry David Thoreau. UnPo

Pray, where are the little bluebells gone. About the Fairies. Jean Ingelow. BoTP

Pray where would lamb and lion be. Nature Be Damned. Anne Wilkinson. NOBC; OBCV

Pray who lies here? why don't you know. Original Epitaph on a Drunkard. Royall Tyler. OBAL

Pray why are you so bare, so bare. The Haunted Oak. Paul Laurence Dunbar. BANP; UnPo

Pray without Ceasing. Ophelia Guyon Browning. BLPA; BLPL

(Sometime, Somewhere.) BLRP

Prayer, A: "As I lie in bed." Joseph Seamon Cotter, Jr. BANP

Prayer: "As I walk through the streets." F. S. Flint. TrPWD

Prayer: "At life's most testing moment, when." Mikhail Yurevich Lermontov, *tr. by* Alan Myers. AAA

Prayer, A: "Be thou my vision, O Lord of my heart." *Unknown, tr. fr. Irish by* Eleanor Hull. TIRV

Prayer: "Bear with me, Master, when I turn from Thee." Edith Lovejoy Pierce. TrPWD

Prayer: "Clother of the lily, feeder of the sparrow." Christina Rossetti. *See* Clother of the lily. . .

Prayer: "Come let us also raise our hands to pray." Faiz Ahmad Faiz, *tr. by* Mahmood Jamal. PBMUP

Prayer, A: "Each day I walk with wonder." Clinton Scollard. TrPWD

Prayer: "Eternal God, our life is but." "Yehoash," *tr. by* Isidore Goldstick. TrJP

Prayer: "Fabric I must keep mended. Rend." Jorie Graham. NAmP

Prayer, A: "Father in Heaven! from whom the simplest flower." Felicia Dorothea Hemans. TrPWD

Prayer: "Fear of death disturbs me constantly, The." Gabrielle de Coignard, *tr. by* Raymond Oliver. WPOW

Prayer: "Forgive me, you whom they cast in a name." Avraham Shlonsky, *tr. by* Francis Landy. VWA

Prayer: "From your high bridge wave & wail." Lev Mak, *tr. by* Dan Jaffe. VWA

Prayer: "Give me a death like Buddha's. Let me fall." Stanley Moss. SM

Prayer: "God, although this life is but a wraith." Louis Untermeyer. WGRP

Prayer: "God, I need a job because I need money." Alan Dugan. CAPP; NoAM

Prayer, A: "God, is it sinful if I feel." Mary Dixon Thayer. TrPWD

Prayer: "God, listen through my words to the beating of my heart." Margueritte Harmon Bro. TrPWD

Prayer: "God of light and blossom." James P. Mousley. GoYe

Prayer: "God, though [or although] this life is but a wraith." Louis Untermeyer. MoAmPo; TrJP; WGRP

Prayer: "God who created me." Henry Charles Beeching. *See* God who created me.

Prayer: "Have pity on us, Power just and severe." John Hall Wheelock, *after* St. Theresa of Avila. EaLo; NePoAm

Prayer: "I ask good things that I detest." Robert Louis Stevenson. TrPWD

Prayer: "I ask you this." Langston Hughes. CDC; EaLo

Prayer: "I had thought of putting an/ altar." Isabella Maria Brown. PoNe

Prayer: "I kneel not now to pray that Thou." Harry Hibbard Kemp. WGRP

Prayer: "I know not by what methods rare." Eliza M. Hickock. BLRP

Prayer, A: "I pray not for the joy that knows." Marion Franklin Ham. TrPWD

Prayer, A: "I pray Thee O Lord." Julian Tuwim, *tr. by* Wanda Dynowska. TrJP

Prayer: "If I must of my senses lose." Theodore Roethke. TwCP

Prayer: "If, when I kneel to pray." Charles Francis Richardson. AA

Prayer: "In the bright bay of your morning, O God." Claire Goll, *tr. by* Babette Deutsch *and* Avram Yarmolinsky. TrJP

Prayer: "Inmost sense, The." Jacob Glatstein, *tr. by* Cynthia Ozick. PeBMYV

Prayer, A: "Let me do my work each day." Max Ehrmann. BLPA; BLPL; FaBoBe

Prayer: "Let me not know how sins and sorrows glide." James Elroy Flecker. TrPWD

Prayer, A: "Let me work and be glad." Theodosia Pickering Garrison. TrPWD

Prayer: "Let us leave our island woods grown dim and blue." "Æ." TIRV

Prayer: "Let us not look upon." Witter Bynner. EaLo

Prayer: "Lord, as thou wilt, bestow." Eduard Friedrich Mörike, *tr. by* John Drinkwater. TrPWD

Prayer, A: "Lord, for the erring thought." William Dean Howells. *See* Lord, for the erring thought.

Prayer: "Lord God of the oak and the elm." George Villiers. TrPWD

Prayer: "Lord I am not entirely selfish." Gavin Ewart. OxBC

Prayer, A: "Lord, let me live like a Regular Man." Berton Braley. BLPA

Prayer: "Lord, make me sensitive to the sight." Barbara Marr. TrPWD

Prayer, A: "Lord, not for light in darkness do we pray." John Drinkwater. TrPWD; WGRP

Prayer: "Lord, what a change within us one short hour." Richard Chenevix Trench. WBLP; WGRP

(Prevailing Prayer.) BLRP

(Sonnet.) TrPWD

Prayer: "Master, they say that when I seem." C. S. Lewis. TIRV; TrCP

Prayer: "Matthew, Mark, Luke, and John." *Unknown. See* Matthew, Mark, Luke, and John/ Bless the bed that I lie on.

Prayer: "More things are wrought by prayer." Tennyson, *Incorporated in* Idylls of the King *with changes, as* The Passing of Arthur. *Fr.* Morte d'Arthur. BLRP

("Pray for my soul.") WGRP

Prayer: "Mother of God, in this brazen sun." Denis Glover. *Fr.* Arawata Bill. ATNZ

Prayer, A: "My God (oh, let me call Thee mine)." Anne Brontë. TrPWD

Prayer: "O Christ, who in Gethsemane." Henrietta Cordelia Ray. CBWP-3

Prayer, A: "O Earth, O dewy mother, breathe on us." Archibald Lampman. TrPWD

Prayer, A: "O for one minute hark what we are saying!" Frederic William Henry Myers. TrPWD

Prayer: "O give us skulls of hot coals." Antonin Artaud, tr. by Michael Benedikt. POS

Prayer: "O God of goodness, forwardness, and fulness." Doris Hedges. GoYe

Prayer, A: "O God, our Father, if we had but truth!" Edward Rowland Sill. AA

Prayer, The: "O living will that shalt endure." Tennyson. See In Memoriam A. H. H.: O living will that shalt endure.

Prayer, A: "O Lord, the hard-won miles." Paul Laurence Dunbar. TrPWD

Prayer, A: "O Love, give me a passionate heart." Irene Rutherford McLeod. TrPWD

Prayer, A: "O that mine eyes might closed be." Thomas Elwood. PWR

Prayer, A: "Often the western wind has sung to me." Alfred Bruce Douglas. TrPWD

Prayer, A: "Oh, Lord! I lift my heart." Priscilla Jane Thompson. CBWP-2

Prayer: "Oh! that mine eye might closed be." Thomas Ellwood. WGRP

Prayer: "Omnipotent confederate of all good." Amos N. Wilder. TrPWD

Prayer, A: "Out of the deeps I cry to thee, O God!" Richard Le Gallienne. TrPWD

Prayer: "Pray for my soul. More things are wrought by prayer." Tennyson. Fr. Idylls of the King: The Passing of Arthur. WGRP

Prayer: "Prayer the church's [or churches] banquet, angels' age." George Herbert. Fr. The Temple. BLPL; EBEV; ELP; InPS; JCP; MePo; NAEL-1; NoP; OAEL-1; OBS; OBWVE; PoE; PoEL-2; SeCV-1; Son; TOF

Prayer, A: "Searcher of souls, you who in heaven abide." Samuel Butler. FaBoEE

Prayer: "Take from the earth its tragic hunger, Lord." Hazel J. Fowler. TrPWD

Prayer, A: "Teach me, Father, how to go." Edwin Markham. BoTP; TrPWD; WGRP

Prayer, A: "Teach me, teach me how." Abraham Reisen, tr. by Leonard Wolf. PeBMYV

Prayer, A: "Tend me my birds, and bring again." Norman Gale. TrPWD

Prayer: "These are the gifts I ask." Henry van Dyke. See These Are the Gifts I Ask.

Prayer, A: "Those who love Thee may they find." George F. Chawner. BLRP

Prayer, A: "Through every minute of this day." John Oxenham. BLRP

Prayer, A: "Throw me into a cloud o lord." Bogdan Czaykowski, tr. by Czeslaw Milosz. PwPP

Prayer: "Thy blessing on the boys—for time has come." Haim Guri, tr. by Ruth H. Lask. TrJP

Prayer, A: "To Thy continual Presence, in me wrought." William Ellery Channing. TrPWD

Prayer, A: "Until I lose my soul and lie." Sara Teasdale. TrPWD

Prayer unto Christ the Judge of the World, A. Michael Wigglesworth. SCAP

Prayer: "What a commanding power." Thomas Washbourne. WGRP

Prayer, The: "What do you say." Bill Manhire. ATNZ; PeNZ

Prayer: "What weight of ancient witness can prevail." Dryden. See Hind and the Panther, The: Private Judgement Condemned.

Prayer, A: "When I look back upon my life nigh spent." George Macdonald. TrPWD

Prayer, The: "Wilt Thou not visit me?" Jones Very. OxBA; TrCP; TrPWD

Prayer: "You may be right, divinity." Francis Sullivan. CRP

Prayer after Illness, A. Violet Alleyn Storey. TrPWD

Prayer after World War. Carl Sandburg. VGW

Prayer against Indifference. Joy Davidman. TrPWD

Prayer at Dawn. Edwin McNeill Poteat. TrPWD

Prayer before Birth. Louis MacNeice. FaBCIP; GTBS-P; LiTB; NAs; TIRV; TwCP

Prayer before Execution. Mary Queen of Scots, tr. fr. Latin by John Fawcett. WGRP

Prayer before Meat. Una W. Harsen. TrPWD

Prayer before Sleep. Alice Lucas. TrJP

Prayer before Study. Theodore Roethke. TrPWD

Prayer before Work. May Sarton. SaC

Prayer Brings Rain, A. Tasso, tr. fr. Italian by Edward Fairfax. Fr. Godfrey of Bulloigne; or, The Recoverie of Jerusalem. OBSC

Prayer by Moonlight. Roberta Teale Swartz. TrPWD

Prayer during Battle. Hermann Hagedorn. TrPWD

Prayer for a Happy New Year, A. Andrew Stuart Currie Clarke. BLRP

Prayer for a Little Home, A. Florence Bone. BLPA; FaBoBe; FaFP

Prayer for a Marriage, A. Mary Carolyn Davies. TrPWD

Prayer for a New House. Louis Untermeyer. See May nothing evil cross this door.

Prayer for a [or the] Pilot. Cecil Roberts. FaPON; TrPwD

Prayer for a Pilot. Cecil Roberts. See Prayer for the Pilot.

Prayer for a Play House. Elinor Lennen. TrPWD

Prayer for a Preacher, A. Edward Shillito. TrPWD

Prayer for a Second Flood. "Hugh MacDiarmid." EBEV

Prayer for a Sleeping Child, A. Mary Carolyn Davies. OHIP

Prayer for a Very New Angel. Violet Alleyn Storey. BLPA

Prayer for All Poets at This Time. Irwin Edman. TrPWD

Prayer for America. Peter Marshall. OPP

Prayer for Charity, A. Edwin O. Kennedy. TrPWD

Prayer for Contentment. Edwin McNeill Poteat. TrPWD

Prayer for Continuation. Susan Griffin. ER

Prayer for Dew. Eleazar ben Kalir, tr. fr. Hebrew by Israel Zangwill. TrJP

Prayer for Dreadful Morning. E. Merrill Root. TrPWD

Prayer for Every Day, A. Mary Carolyn Davies. BLPA; FaBoBe

Prayer for Every Day. Unknown, tr. fr. Fanti by Kweku Martin. PBA

Prayer for Faith, A. Alfred Norris. See I would not ask thee that my days.

Prayer for Forgiveness, A. Aengus the Culdee, tr. fr. Irish by Eoin Neeson. TIRV

Prayer for Gentleness to All Creatures. John Galsworthy. BoTP

Prayer for Guidance. Unknown, tr. fr. Tibetan by W. Y. Evans-Wentz. Fr. The Tibetan Book of the Dead. OBD

Prayer for Indifference, A ("Oft I've implored the gods in vain."), sel. Frances Greville. NOEC

"I ask no kind return of love." OBEV

Prayer for Kafka and Ourselves. Anthony Rudolf. VWA

Prayer for Light. Stanton A. Coblentz. TrPWD

Prayer for Living and Dying. Christopher La Farge. TrPWD

Prayer for Messiah. Leonard Cohen. OBCV

Prayer for My Daughter, A. W. B. Yeats. BLPL; CMoP; HAP; LiTB; LiTM; MoAB; MoP; NAEL-2; NAs; NoAM; NoP; OxBTC; PoA; PoLF; PoRA; PrIm; TEP

Prayer for My Son, A. Yvor Winters. TrPWD

Prayer for My Son, A. W. B. Yeats. EBEV; NAs; TIRV

Prayer for Pain. John G. Neihardt. TrPWD; WGRP

Prayer for Peace. Johnstone G. Patrick. TrPWD

Prayer for Peace, A. Edward Rowland Sill. TrPWD

Prayer for Peace: II. Léopold Sédar Senghor, tr. fr. French by John Reed and Clive Wake. TTY

Prayer for Pentecost, A. Catherine Bernard Brown. BLRP

Prayer for Purification, A. Buonarroti Michelangelo, tr. fr. Italian by John Addington Symonds. AWP

Prayer for Rain. Sheikh Aquib Abdullahi Jama, tr. fr. Somali by B. W. Andrzejewski. WTO

Prayer for Rain. Unknown, tr. fr. Finnish. WGRP

Prayer for Redemption. Unknown. TrJP

Prayer for Reptiles. Patricia Hubbell. PDV

Prayer for Rivers, A. Keith Wilson. GOYP

Prayer for Song. Fay Lewis Noble. TrPWD

Prayer for Thanksgiving, A. Joseph Auslander. TrPWD

Prayer for the Age. Myron H. Broomell. TrPWD

Prayer for the Great Family. Gary Snyder. HAP; OFD

Prayer for the Little Daughter between Death and Burial. Diana Scott. BrRo

Prayer for the New Year, A. Violet Alleyn Storey. TrPWD

Prayer for the New Year, A. Unknown. BLRP

Prayer for the Old Courage, A. Charles Hanson Towne. TrPWD

Prayer for the Pilot. Cecil Roberts. See Lord of sea and earth and air.

Prayer for the Self, A. John Berryman. Fr. Eleven Addresses to the Lord, VIII. PPP

Prayer for the Soul of My Country. Otto René Castillo, tr. fr. Spanish by Wilfredo Castaño. Vol

Prayer for the Speedy End of Three Great Misfortunes. Unknown, tr. fr. Irish by Frank O'Connor. OBMV

Prayer for the Useless Days. Edith Lovejoy Pierce. TrPWD

Prayer for This Day. Hildegarde Flanner. TrPWD

Prayer for This House. Louis Untermeyer. BLPL; FaPON; PoLF (Prayer for a New House.) TrPWD

Prayer from 1936, A. Siegfried Sassoon. TrPWD

Prayer in a Country Church. Ruth B. Van Dusen. TrPWD

Prayer in Affliction. Violet Alleyn Storey. TrPWD

Prayer in April. Sara Henderson Hay. TrPWD

Prayer in Darkness, A. G. K. Chesterton. FPL; MoBrPo; PoLF; TrGrPo

Prayer in Late Autumn, A. Violet Alleyn Storey. TrPWD

Prayer in Mid-Passage. Louis MacNeice. EaLo
Prayer in Spring, A. Robert Frost. TrCP; TrPWD
   (Oh, Give Us Pleasure in the Flowers Today.) AH
Prayer in the Prospect of Death, A. Burns. TrPWD; WGRP
Prayer in Time of Blindness, A. Clement Wood. TrPWD
Prayer in Time of War. Henry Treece. WaP
Prayer is the soul's sincere desire. What Is Prayer? James Montgomery.
   BLRP; WGRP
Prayer of a Beginning Teacher. Ouida Smith Dunnam. TrPWD
Prayer of a Little Hope. Jean Wahl, tr. fr. French. VWA, tr. by Charles
   Guenther
Prayer of a Pagan Woman. Cothrai Gogan. TIRV
Prayer of a Teacher. Dorothy Littlewort. TrPWD
Prayer of an Unbeliever. Lizette Woodworth Reese. TrPWD
Prayer of Columbus ("A batter'd, wrecked old man."), sel. Walt
   Whitman. AmPP; WGRP
   "Thou knowest my years entire, my life." TrPWD
Prayer of St. Francis of Assisi for Peace. St. Francis of Assisi, tr. fr.
   Latin. FPL; PoLF
Prayer of St. Francis Xavier. Pope. TrPWD
Prayer of the Arab Physician, The. Monk Gibbon. TIRV
Prayer of the Cat, The. Carmen Bernos de Gasztold, tr. fr. French by
   Rumer Godden. CRH; PDV
Prayer of the Donkey, The. Carmen Bernos de Gasztold. PChr
Prayer of the Fishing Net. Unknown, tr. fr. Hawaiian by N. B. Emerson.
   WTO
Prayer of the Goldfish, The. Carmen Bernos de Gasztold. PDV
Prayer of the Little Ducks, The. Carmen Bernos de Gasztold. PDV
Prayer of the Maidens to Mary. Rainer Maria Rilke, tr. fr. German by
   Jethro Bithell. AWP
Prayer of the Mouse, The. Carmen Bernos de Gasztold. PDV
Prayer of the Old Horse, The. Carmen Bernos de Gasztold. PDV
Prayer of the Old Woman, Villon's Mother. Villon, tr. fr. French by J.
   M. Synge. MoBrPo
Prayer of the Peoples, A, sel. Percy MacKaye. WGRP
   God of us who kill our kind! TrPWD, 3 sts.
Prayer of the Young Stoic. Stephen P. Dunn. TrPWD
Prayer on Making a Canoe. Unknown, tr. fr. Hawaiian by N. B.
   Emerson. WTO
Prayer-Poem, A. Mary S. Edgar. BLRP
Prayer Rug, The. Sara Beaumont Kennedy
Prayer Service in an English Church. Robert Bly. KS
Prayer the church's [or churches] banquet, angels' age. George Herbert.
   BLPL; EBEV; ELP; InPS; JCP; MePo; NAEL-1; NOBE; NoP;
   OAEL-1; OBS; OBWVE; PoE; PoEL-2; SeCV-1; TOF
Prayer the church's banquet, Angel's age. George Herbert. Fr. The
   Temple. Son
Prayer to Aphrodite. Timoshenko Aslanides. UAS
Prayer to Be Said When Thou Goest to Bed, A. Francis Seager.
   OxBChV
Prayer to Be Sung, sel. Miriam Yalan-Shteklis, tr. fr. Hebrew by
   Bernhard Frank.
   "Padlock your garden, my dear." MHeP
Prayer to Escape from the Market Place, A. James Wright. NaP
Prayer to Go to Paradise with the Asses. Francis Jammes, tr. fr. French.
   AWP, tr. by Jethro Bithell
Prayer to Go to Paradise with the Donkeys, A. Jammes Francis, tr. fr.
   French by Richard Wilbur. EaLo; RB
Prayer to God. "Placido", tr. fr. Spanish by Raoul Abdul. TTY
Prayer to Hermes. Robert Creeley. PoM
Prayer to Isis. Christina Walsh. BrRo
Prayer to Mother Mary. Padriac Pearse. TIRV
Prayer to My Mother. Pier Paolo Pasolini. PFI
Prayer to the Father of [or in] Heaven, A. John Skelton. HoPM;
   TrPWD
Prayer to the God Thot. Unknown, tr. fr. Egyptian by Ulli Beier. TTY
Prayer to the Holy Trinity, A. Richard Stanyhurst. EIl; PoEL-2
   (Prayer to the Trinity [or Trinitie], A.) EIL; TIRV
Prayer to the Hunting Star, Canopus. Unknown, tr. fr. Bushman by W.
   H. I. Bleek and Jack Cope. PeSA
Prayer to the Lord Ramakrishna, A. James Wright. NNaP
Prayer to the Mountain Spirit. Unknown, tr. by G. W. Cronyn.
   WGRP
Prayer to the Pacific. Leslie Silko. CDW; NoP; VoR
Prayer to the Sacrament of the Altar, A. Unknown. MeEL
Prayer to the Trinity, A. Unknown. MeEL
Prayer to the Trinity [or Trinitie], A. Richard Stanyhurst. See Prayer to
   the Holy Trinity, A.
Prayer to the Virgin. Saint Columcille, tr. fr. Irish by Kuno Meyer and
   John Strachan. TIRV

Prayer to the White Lady. László Nagy, tr. fr. Hungarian by George
   MacBeth. MHuP
Prayer to the Young Moon. Unknown, tr. fr. Bushman by W. H. I. Bleek
   and Jack Cope. PeSA
Prayer to Venus. Lucretius. See De Rerum Natura (On the Nature of
   Things): Address to Venus.
Prayer to Venus. Spenser. See Faerie Queene, The: Address to Venus.
Prayer to Venus. Spenser. Fr. The Faerie Queene.
Prayer under the Pressure of Violent Anguish. Burns. TrPWD
Prayer unsaid, and mass unsung. The Sea-Ritual. George Darley. Fr.
   Syren Songs, V. BIrV; OBNC; WiR; WSC
   (Deadman's Dirge.) CH
Prayerbooks return to Jerusalem. A Late Manuscript at the Schocken
   Institute. Gabriel Preil, tr. by Gabriel Levin. VWA
Prayers. Henry Charles Beeching. BoTP; OBEV
   (Boy's Prayer, A.) GN
   (Prayer: "God who created me.") SD
Prayers, The. Howard Schwartz. VWA
Prayers, Dorcas, Fellowship, and Children's Groups! Gwladys Rhys. W.
   J. Gruffydd, tr. by Myrddin Lloyd. OBWVE
Prayers I make will then be sweet indeed, The. For Inspiration.
   Buonarroti Michelangelo, tr. by Wordsworth. WGRP
   (To the Supreme Being.) AWP; PFI; TrPWD
Prayers in a Temple. Yusuf al-Khal, tr. fr. Arabic by Abdullah al-Udhari.
   MPAW
Prayers Must Have Poise. Robert Herrick. LiTB
Prayers of a Repentant Gentleman. Antonio Cisneros, tr. fr. Spanish by
   Maureen Ahern and David Tipton. Per
Prayers of Steel. Carl Sandburg. CMoP; FaPON; MoAmPo; PDV; TrCP;
   TrPWD
Prayers to Liberty. Anwar Shaul, tr. fr. Arabic by Yoffee Berkovitz.
   VWA
Prayerwheel: 2. David Meltzer. NeAP
Praying. P. J. Kavanagh. OxBSP
Praying Mantis. Mary Ann Hoberman. RHPC
Praying mantis doesn't pray, The. Mantis. David McCord. OBAL
Praying mantis drops with a thud, A. Ozaki Hosai, tr. fr. Japanese by
   Hiroaki Sato. Fr. One Hundred Haiku in Free Form. FCEI
Praying Mantis Visits a Penthouse, The ("The praying mantis with its
   length of straw"). Oscar Williams. FaFP; LiTM
Praying to the gods of heaven and earth. Otabe Aramimi. Fr. Manyo
   Shu. Ma
Pre-admonisheth the writer. The Flight of the Bucket. Kipling. BXAP
Pre-Columbian Sculpture, A. Adam Wazyk, tr. fr. Polish by Czeslaw
   Milosz. PwPP
Pre-dawn's pilot lights. Celebration for the Cold Snap. Carolyne Wright.
   NAmP
Pre Domina. Jean Lipkin. PeSA
Pre-Existence. Paul Hamilton Hayne. AnAmPo
Pre-Positions. Jose Isaacson, tr. fr. Spanish by Yishai Tobin. VWA
Pre-Raphaelite Notebook, A. Geoffrey Hill. NoAM
Preacher, The. Al-Mahdi, tr. fr. Arabic by A. J. Arberry. TTY
Preacher and the Slave, The. At. to Joe Hill. AS, with music; WTO
Preacher Sought to Find Out Acceptable Words, The. Richard Eberhart.
   WaP
Preacher's Mistake, The. William Croswell Doane. BLPA
Preacher's Vacation, The. Unknown. BLPA; BLPL
Preachment for Preachers. Alexander Barclay. Fr. The Ship of Fools.
   ACP
Preannual Poem. Yona Wallach, tr. fr. Hebrew by Warren Bargad and
   Stanley F. Chyet. IP
Preawd Tum's Prayer. Joseph Ramsbottom. PF
Precambrian [or Pre-Cambrian] Shield, The. E. J. Pratt. Fr. Towards
   the Last Spike. MoCV; NOBC; NoBC; OBCV
Precarious Ground. Leah Bodine Drake. GoYe
Precede me into this elusive country. The Caravan. Gwendolyn
   MacEwen. MoCV
Precedented. Marcy S. Powell. SoTCo
Precept of Silence, The. Lionel Johnson. MoBrPo
Precepts He Gave His Folk. Elijah ben Menahem Hazaken of Le Mans,
   tr. fr. Hebrew by Israel Zangwill. TrJP
Precinct Station, The. Louis Simpson. EOEF
Precincts at day, quiet leisure of spring, The. Written in the Office
   Precincts. Wang T'ing-hsiang, tr. by Jonathan Chaves. CoBLCP
Precious Bits of Family. Linda Belarde. GOS
Precious Child, So Sweetly Sleeping. Anna Hoppe. AH
Precious dry rose-geranium smell, The. Eilean Ni Chuilleanain. Fr. The
   Rose-Geranium, V. CIP
Precious in the Sight of the Lord. Unknown.
   BLRP

Precious Mettle. Lewis Warsh. UL

Precious Moments. Carl Sandburg. MoAmPo

Precious night-blooming cereus. Remembering Fannie Lou Hamer. Thadious M. Davis. BlSi

Precious, oh, how precious is that blessed sleep. Precious in the Sight of the Lord. *Unknown*. BLRP

Precious Pearl, The. Priscilla Jane Thompson. CBWP-2

Precious Pearl, The. Pat Wilson. ATNZ

Precious Things. *Unknown*. TTY

Precious thought, my Father knoweth. God Knoweth Best. *Unknown*. WBLP

(Your Father Knoweth.) BLRP

Precious to me—she still shall be. Emily Dickinson. PeHV

Precipitous point—river and lake. Climbing P'iao-miao Peak. Wu Wei-yeh, *tr. by* Jonathan Chaves. CoBLCP

Precipitous, rising beyond the purple clouds. The Natural Stockade at Bamboo Lake. Yang Shih-ch'i, *tr. fr. Chinese by* Jonathan Chaves. *Fr*. Ten Scenes at the Hsiao Family Stone Ridge. CoBLCP

Precise counterpart, The. The Orchestra. William Carlos Williams. HAP

Precisely down invisible threads these oak leaves. October Elegy. Margaret Gibson. FYAP

Precision, The. Yvor Winters. EAS

Precocious spring how beautiful you are! Ian Wedde. *Fr*. Earthly: Sonnets for Carlos, 27. ATNZ

Precursors. Louis MacNeice. OxBSP

Predestination and Free Will. Dryden. *Fr*. The State of Innocence. NOCV

Predicament: a corner of/ a room. Tenant at Number 9. John Blight. CBAP

Predicter of Famine, The. William Carlos Williams. VGW

Prediction, The. Mark Strand. EAS; LCAP

Predilections. Alfredo Giuliani, *tr. fr. Italian by* Lawrence R. Smith. NItP

Preface: "Aged catch their breath, The." W. H. Auden. *Fr*. The Sea and the Mirror. LiTA

Preface: "Artist is the creator of beautiful things, The." Oscar Wilde. *Fr*. The Picture of Dorian Gray. NAEL-2

Preface, The: "Infinity, when all things it beheld." Edward Taylor. *Fr*. God's Determinations. AmPP; HAP; NAAL-1; NOBA; OxBA; SCAP

Preface: "It's an old story." Ahmad Faraz, *tr. by* Mahmood Jamal. PBMUP

Preface: "Rigor of beauty is the quest. But how will you find beauty when it is locked." William Carlos Williams. *Fr*. Paterson. NoAM

Preface Shrink Lit: Elements of Style. Maurice Sagoff. NBLV

Preface: "Sonja Henie, the young girl." Theodore Weiss. VGW

Preface to a Twenty Volume Suicide Note. Amiri Baraka. AmNP; PoBA; PoM; PoNe; PPP; TTY

Preface to Dying. Gyorgy Raba, *tr. fr. Hungarian by* Jascha Kessler. FOC

Preface: "To make a start." William Carlos Williams. *Fr*. Paterson, I. CMoP; NoAM; NOBA

Preface to the Memoirs, A. James Merrill. NOBA

Preface to *The Progress of Learning*. Sir John Denham. OxBSP

Prefatory Poem, on. . . *Magnalia Christi Americana*. Nicholas Noyes. SCAP

Prefectural Engineer's Statement Regarding Clouds, The. Miyazawa Kenji, *tr. fr. Japanese by* Hiroaki Sato. FCEI

Prefer the cherry when the fruit hangs thick. Under the Boughs. Gene Baro. BoNaP

Preference. Langston Hughes. HCAP; NOBA

Preference Declared, The. Horace. *See* Odes: I, 38. Simplicity.

Preferring "resemblance to beauty." An Esthetic of Imitation. Donald Finkel. NePoEA

Prefix for "Ceylon trail" promises "main orange", The. "Oran" to "Ordain" for "J." Tina Darragh. LP

Prefontaine. Charles Ghigna. ASP

Pregnancy. Sandra McPherson. BoWoP; NMM

Pregnant girl, under sorrow's sign, A. Under Sorrow's Sign. Gofraidh Fionn O'Dalaigh, *tr. by* John Montague. BIrV

Pregnant Woman. Ingrid Jonker, *tr. fr. Afrikaans*. OV, *tr. by* Jack Cope *and* William Plomer; PeSA, *tr. by* Jack Cope *and* Uys Krige

Prehistoric Burials. Siegfried Sassoon. MoBrPo

Prehistory. David Avidan, *tr. fr. Hebrew by* Warren Bargad *and* Stanley F. Chyet. IP

Prehtys whilom dwelled in oure citee, A. The Cook's Tale. Chaucer. *Fr*. The Canterbury Tales. BXAP

Preiching of the Swallow, The. Robert Henryson. OxBS

Prejohn, The. Hunt Hawkins. KS

Prejudice. Georgia Douglas Johnson. AmNP; PoBA

Prejudice. Lizelia Augusta Jenkins Moorer. CBWP-3

Prejudice against the Past, The. Wallace Stevens. LiTM

Prelates, The. John Skelton. *Fr*. Colin Clout. TrGrPo

Preliminary Poem. John Heath-Stubbs. OxBC

Preliminary to Classroom Lecture. Josephine Miles. MoP; NoAM

Prelude: "Afterwards, afterwards the wind between two mountains." David Rosenmann-Taub, *tr. by* Charles Guenther. VWA

Prelude: "Along the roadside, like the flowers of gold." Whittier. *Fr*. Among the Hills. NAAL-1; OxBA; PoEL-4

Prelude: "And did those feet in ancient time." Blake. *See* Milton: And Did Those Feet in Ancient Time.

Prelude: "As one, at midnight, wakened by the call." W. W. Gibson. MoBrPo

Prelude VII: "Beloved, let us once more praise the rain." Conrad Aiken. *Fr*. Preludes for Memnon; or, Preludes to Attitude. LiTA; UnPo

Prelude: "England! awake! awake! awake!" Blake. *See* Jerusalem: England! awake! awake! awake!

Prelude: "Fields from Islington to Marybone, The." Blake. *See* Jerusalem: Fields from Islington to Marybone, The.

Prelude XXI: "First note, simple, The; the second note, distinct." Conrad Aiken. *Fr*. Preludes for Memnon; or, Preludes to Attitude. LiTA

Prelude: "Give us another poem, he said." Patrick Kavanagh. FaBCIP; IPY

Prelude: "Grace comes only after the long study of choice." Traise Yamamoto. BrSi

Prelude: "How could I love you more?" Richard Aldington. BrPo

Prelude: "I am the bird of the wayside." Christine Ama Ata Aidoo. PBWP

Prelude: "I saw the constellated matin choir." Edmund Clarence Stedman. AA

Prelude XLII: "Keep in the heart the journal nature keeps." Conrad Aiken. *Fr*. Preludes for Memnon; or, Preludes to Attitude. CMoP; OxBA

Prelude: "Lake loon paddles, A." Rokwaho. STE

Prelude: "Night and the hood." Conrad Kent Rivers. PoBA

Prelude: "Night was dark, though sometimes a faint star, The." Richard Watson Gilder. *Fr*. The New Day. PoLF

Prelude LIII: "Nothing to say? Then we'll say nothing." Conrad Aiken. *Fr*. Preludes for Memnon; or, Preludes to Attitude. LiTA

Prelude LVII: "One star fell and another as we walked." Conrad Aiken. *Fr*. Preludes for Memnon; or, Preludes to Attitude. MoAmPo

Prelude LVI: "Rimbaud and Verlaine, precious pair of poets." Conrad Aiken. *Fr*. Preludes for Memnon; or, Preludes to Attitude. FaBoMo; LiTA; LiTM; NoAM; TwCP

Prelude III: "Sleep: and between the closed eyelids of sleep." Conrad Aiken. *Fr*. Preludes for Memnon; or, Preludes to Attitude. LiTA

Prelude XX: "So, in the evening, to the simple cloister." Conrad Aiken. *Fr*. Preludes for Memnon; or, Preludes to Attitude. LiTA (Cloister.) MoAB; MoAmPo

Prelude: "Still south I went and west and south again." J. M. Synge. AWP; BoNaP; ChTr; FaBoPP; MoBrPo; OBMV

Prelude LII: "Stood, at the closed door." Conrad Aiken. *Fr*. Preludes for Memnon; or, Preludes to Attitude. LiTM

Prelude XXXIII: "Then came I to the shoreless shore of silence." Conrad Aiken. *Fr*. Preludes for Memnon; or, Preludes to Attitude. LiTA; OxBA

Prelude VI: "This is not you? These phrases are not you?" Conrad Aiken. *Fr*. Preludes for Memnon; or, Preludes to Attitude. MoAB; MoAmPo

Prelude: "This short straight sword." R. A. K. Mason. PeNZ

Prelude XXVIII: "Time has come, the clock says time has come, The." Conrad Aiken. *Fr*. Preludes for Memnon; or, Preludes to Attitude. LiTA; OxBA

Prelude II: "Two coffees in the Español, the last." Conrad Aiken. *Fr*. Preludes for Memnon; or, Preludes to Attitude. FYAP; LiTA; NoAM

Prelude XIX: "Watch long enough, and you will see the leaf." Conrad Aiken. *Fr*. Preludes for Memnon; or, Preludes to Attitude. CMoP; OxBA

Prelude XXIII: "We are those same children who amazed." Stefan George, *tr. fr. German by* C. F. MacIntyre. WaaP

Prelude: "What makes a plenteous harvest." Virgil, *tr. fr. Latin by* Dryden. *Fr*. Georgics, I. AWP

Prelude XXIX: "What shall we do—what shall we think—what shall we say?" Conrad Aiken. *Fr*. Preludes for Memnon; or, Preludes to Attitude. FaBoMo

Prelude I: "Winter for a moment takes the mind; the snow." Conrad Aiken. *Fr*. Preludes for Memnon; or, Preludes to Attitude. LiTA; LiTM; OxBA

Prelude: "Woman, Woman, let us say these things to each other." Conrad Aiken. NYBP

Prelude XIV: "You went to the verge, you say, and came back safely."
　Conrad Aiken. *Fr.* Preludes for Memnon; or, Preludes to Attitude.
　FaBoMo; LiTA; TwCP
Prelude [or, Growth of a Poet's Mind], The, *much abr.* Wordsworth.
　EnRP; OAEL-2
Sels.
　Books. *Fr.* V.
　　"He who in his youth." TOF
　　There Was a Boy ("There was a boy, ye knew him well"). ChER;
　　　FaBoCh; FaBoRV; OBNC; PoE; PoEL-4; RB
　　　(Winander Lake.) FiP
　Cambridge and the Alps. *Fr.* VI. FiP; ImOP; PoEL-4
　　"But 'twas a time when Europe was rejoiced." FaBoPV
　　Crossing the Alps. OBTV; RB
　　Imagination ("Imagination—here the power so called"). FiP
　　"'Tis told by one whom stormy waters threw." ImOP
　　"When from the Vallais we had turned." TOF
　Childhood and School-Time. *Fr.* I. CH; GN; HAP; NOBE; NoP; NU;
　　OBNC; PoE; SCV
　　"Dust as we are, the immortal spirit grows." SCV
　　"Fair seed-time had my soul, and I grew up." HAP; NoP
　　(Introduction—Childhood and School-Time.) PoEL-4
　　(On the Solitary Fells around Hawkshead.) FaBoPP
　　In Patterdale. FaBoRV
　　"Oh [*or* O] there is a blessing in this gentle breeze." EnRP;
　　　OAEL-2
　　On Ullswater. FaBoPP; RB
　　On Windermere; Bowness Bay and Belle Isle. FaBoPP
　　One Summer Evening ("One summer evening (led by her) I
　　　found"). FiP; NU
　　"So through the darkness and the cold we flew." CH; SD
　　　(On the Frozen Lake.) FaBoCh; GN
　　　(Skating.) TOF
　　"Wisdom and spirit of the universe!" NOBE
　　　(Influence of Natural Objects.) AWP
　　Was It for This. RB
　　Wordsworth Skates on Esthwaite Water. FaBoPP
　Conclusion ("It was a close, warm, breezeless summer night"). *Fr.*
　　XIV [XIII]. PoEL-4
　　Climb to Snowdon, The. FaBoRV
　　　(Snowdon Sunrise, The.) FaBoPP
　　"It was a summer's night, a close warm night." PoEL-4
　　"Oh! yet a few short years of useful life." EBEV; OBNC; PoEL-4
　France. *Fr.* XI [X *conclusion*].
　　"O pleasant exercise of hope and joy!" HAP; OBNC
　　　("France leered me forth; the realm that I had crossed.")
　　　FaBoPV
　　　(French Revolution, The.) FiP
　　　(Residence in France [Continued].) PoEL-4
　　One Christmas-Time. RB
　　To Coleridge in Sicily. OBNC
　Imagination and Taste, How Impaired and Restored. *Fr.* XII *and* XIII
　　[XI *and* XII]. PoE; PoEL-4, XII *abr.*; TOF
　　Imagination, How Impaired and Restored. *Fr.* XII *and* XIII.
　　　OBNC
　　Oh! Mystery of Man. *Fr.* XII. FiP
　"O there is blessing in this gentle breeze." NAEL-2, *Complete.*
　Residence at Cambridge. *Fr.* III. FaBoPP; HAP; ImOP
　　"Caverns there were within my mind, which sun." FaBoPP
　　"Evangelist St. John my patron was, The." HAP
　　　(Newton's Statue.) FaBoRV
　　Newton. ImOP
　Residence in France. *Fr.* IX.
　　"Among the band of Officers was one," *Oxford ed., incl.*
　　　Vaudracour and Julia ChER
　　"It was a beautiful and silent day." OBTV
　　Noble, The. ChTr
　Residence in France. *Fr.* X.
　　"Cheered with this hope, to Paris I returned." PoEL-4
　　"State, as if to stamp the final seal." FaBoPV
　　"When the proud fleet that bears the red-cross flag." FaBoPV
　Residence in London. *Fr.* VII. HAP, *short sel.;* PoEL-4
　　Fair below Helvellyn, The. FaBoPP
　　"From these sights/ Take one,—that ancient festival, the Fair."
　　　HAP
　　"Genius of Burke! forgive the pen seduced." FaBoPV
　　"Rise up, thou monstrous ant-hill on the plain." HAP
　　Young Wordsworth's London, The. FaBoPP
　Retrospect—Love of Nature Leading to Love of Mankind. *Fr.* VIII.
　　Shepherd, The. OBNC
　School-Time. *Fr.* II.

"Blest the infant Babe." TOF
"But who shall parcel out." TOF
　Intimations of Sublimity. OBNC
Summer Vacation. *Fr.* IV. PoEL-4
　Consummate Happiness. OBNC
　Dedicated Spirit, A. SeCePo
　"Favourite pleasure hath it been with me, A," *Oxford ed.*
　"In a throng,/ A festival company." EBEV
　"That heartless chase." TOF
Prelude for a Flower. Ruth Kim Chun-soo, *tr. fr. Korean by* Koh Chang-
　soo. ACKP
Prelude to Akwasidae. *Unknown, tr. fr. Twi by* Halim El-Dahb. TTY
Prelude to an Evening. John Crowe Ransom. EAS; MoAB; MoAmPo;
　OxBA
Prelude to Commencement. Marie De L. Welch. NYBP
Prelude to Memorial Song: 100 Years Later. Phillip William George.
　VoR
Prelude to this smooth scene—mark well!, The. After Jena. Thomas
　Hardy. *Fr.* The Dynasts, *pt.* II, Act I, sc. vii. WaaP
Preludes (I-IV), *sels.* T. S. Eliot. HeIP; LiTA; NoP; OBMV; PPP;
　SeCePo; SOTW; TwCP; UnPo; VGW; WeW
　"His soul stretched tight across the skies."
　"Morning comes to consciousness, The."
　"Winter evening settles down, The." MoShBr
　"You tossed a blanket from the bed."
Preludes for Memnon; or, Preludes to Attitude, *sels.* Conrad Aiken.
　"Beloved, let us once more praise the rain." LiTA; UnPo
　"First note, simple, The; the second note, distinct." LiTA
　"Keep in the heart the journal nature keeps." CMoP; OxBA
　"Nothing to say? Then we'll say nothing." LiTA
　"One star fell and another as we walked." MoAmPo
　"Rimbaud and Verlaine, precious pair of poets." FaBoMo; LiTA;
　　LiTM; NoAM; TwCP
　"Sleep: and between the closed eyelids of sleep." LiTA
　"So, in the evening, to the simple cloister." LiTA
　　(Cloister.) MoAB; MoAmPo
　"Stood, at the closed door." LiTM
　"Then came I to the shoreless shore of silence." LiTA; OxBA
　"This is not you? These phrases are not you?" MoAB; MoAmPo
　"Time has come, the clock says time has come, The." LiTA; OxBA
　"Two coffees in the Español, the last." FYAP; LiTA; NoAM
　"Watch long enough, and you will see the leaf." CMoP; OxBA
　"What shall we do—what shall we think—what shall we say?"
　　FaBoMo
　"Winter for a moment takes the mind; the snow." LiTA; LiTM; OxBA
　"You went to the verge, you say, and came back safely." FaBoMo;
　　LiTA; TwCP
Prelusive. Herman Melville. *Fr.* Clarel. AmPP
Premises we work from are not arbitrary, The. The Guests. Franco
　Fortini, *tr. by* Lawrence R. Smith. NItP
Premonition. Richard Hovey. AnAmPo
Premonition. Antonia Pozzi, *tr. fr. Italian by* Muriel Kittel. DMI
Premonition, The. Theodore Roethke. CAPP
Premonition. Tamura Ryuichi, *tr. fr. Japanese by* Hiroaki Sato. FCEI
Premonition. Laura Goodman Salverson. CaP
Premonition (in a Voice My Mother Called "Not Your Own"). Yvonne.
　See It was Mama who was partial.
'Prentice Boy, The. *Unknown.* AmFP
Preparation. Thomas Edward Brown. OBEV
Preparations. Leslie Silko. VoR
Preparations. *Unknown. See* Yet if his majesty, our sovereign [*or*
　soveraign] Lord.
Preparative, The. Thomas Traherne. PoEL-2
Preparatory Meditations before My Approach to the Lord's Supper, *sels.*
　Edward Taylor.
　"Am I thy gold? Or purse, Lord, for thy wealth." *Fr.* VI. LiTA;
　　OxBA; TAP
　"Apples of gold, in silver pictures shrined." *Fr.* XLII. NAAL-1
　"Deity of Love Incorporate, A." *Fr.* XI. TAP
　"I Kenning through astronomy divine." *Fr.* VIII. AmPP; LiTA;
　　NAAL-1; NOBA; NoP; OxBA; PoEL-3; SCAP; TAP
　"Leaf gold, Lord of thy golden wedge o'erlaid." *Fr.* XVI. NAAL-1
　"Like to the marigold, I blushing close." *Fr.* III. SCAP
　"Lord, art thou at the table head above." *Fr.* IV. AmPP; OxBA
　　(Reflexion, The.) AmPP; OxBA
　"Lord, can a crumb of dust the earth outweigh." NAAL-1
　"Methinks I spy Almighty holding in." *Fr.* LXVIII. HAP
　"My Blessed Lord, how doth thy Beautious Spouse." *Fr.* CL. SCAP
　"My gracious Lord, I would thee glory doe." *Fr.* IV. SCAP
　"My Lord, my life, can envy ever bee." *Fr.* XXIII. PoEL-3
　"My shattred phancy stole away from mee." *Fr.* XXIX. SCAP
　"My sin! my sin, my God, these cursed dregs." *Fr.* XXXIX. SCAP

"Oh! Golden Rose! Oh. Glittering Lilly White." *Fr.* II. SCAP
"Oh! Good, good, good, my Lord. What more love yet." *Fr.* CXII. NOBA
"Oh leaden heeld. Lord, give, forgive I pray." *Fr.* I. SCAP
"Oh, that I always breath'd in such an air." *Fr.* III. (Experience, The.) AmPP
"Oh that I was the Bird of Paradise!" *Fr.* LXIII. NOCV
"Oh! what a thing is man? Lord, who am I?" *Fr.* XXXVIII. NAAL-1; NOBA; OxBA
"Should I with silver tooles delve through the hill." *Fr.* LVI. OxBA; SCAP
"Still I complain; I am complaining still." *Fr.* XL. OxBA; PoEL-3
"Stupendious love! all saints astonishment." *Fr.* X. OxBA
"Thy grace, dear Lord's my golden wrack I find." *Fr.* XXXII. NoP; SCAP
"Thy human frame, my glorious Lord, I spy." *Fr.* VII. LiTA
"Unclean, unclean: my Lord, undone, all vile." *Fr.* XXVI. NAAL-1
"What love is this of thine, that cannot be." *Fr.* I. AmPP; NOCV; PoEL-3; SCAP
"What shall I say, my Lord? With what begin?." *Fr.* XXIX. HAP
"When thy bright beams, my Lord, so strike mine eye." *Fr.* XXII. NAAL-1
"Ye angells bright, pluck from your wings a quill." *Fr.* LX. PoEL-3
Prepare for death. But how can you prepare. Speculation. Howard Nemerov. TAP
Prepare for death, if here at night you roam. Samuel Johnson. *Fr.* London: A Poem in Imitation of the Third Satire of Juvenal. OAEL-1
Prepare for Songs; He's come, He's come. The New-Yeeres Gift, or Circumcisions Song, Sung to the King in the Presence at White Hall. Robert Herrick. SeCV-1
Prepare, prepare the iron helm of war. A War Song to Englishmen. Blake. *Fr.* King Edward the Third. CH; WaaP (War Song, A.) OHIP
"Prepare to meet the King of Terrors," cried. Ebenezer Elliott. NOBVV
Preparedness. Felicia Lamport. ASP
Preparedness. Edwin Markham. FaFP; MoAmPo
Preparing for Weather. Carole Oles. BLA
Preposterous. Jim Hall. MT
Presage and caveat not only seem. The Window Sill. Robert Graves. EnLoPo
Presaging. Rainer Maria Rilke, *tr. fr. German by* Jessie Lemont. AWP; TrJP
Presbyterian Church Government ("Synods are whelps of the Inquisition"). Samuel Butler. *Fr.* Hudibras, I, 3. OBS
Presbyterian Knight. Samuel Butler. *See* Hudibras: When civil fury first grew high.
Presbyterian Knight and Independent Squire. Samuel Butler. *See* Hudibras: Metaphysical Sectarian, The ("He was in logick a great critic").
Presbyterian Wedding, The. *Unknown.* CoMu; ErPo
Presbyterians, The. Dryden. *Fr.* The Hind and the Panther, I. OBS
Prescience. Thomas Bailey Aldrich. AA
Prescience. Donald Jeffrey Hayes. PoNe
Prescott, press my Ascot waistcoat. Ascot Waistcoat. David McCord. FiBHP; NBLV (Sportif.) NYBP
Prescription of Painful Ends. Robinson Jeffers. LiTA; MoAB; MoAmPo; OxBA
Presence, The. William Everson. ErPo
Presence, The. Maxine W. Kumin. RFM; WPE
Presence, The. Denise Levertov. NaP; NePoEA-2
Presence, The. Dana Naone. CDW
Presence, The. Jones Very. HAP
Presence of Snow. Melville Cane. GoYe
Presences. Donald Justice. CAPP
Presences. Zoé Karélli, *tr. fr. Modern Greek by* Kimon Friar. PBWP
Presences Perfected. Siegfried Sassoon. MoBrPo
Present, The. Franco Fortini, *tr. fr. Italian by* Lawrence R. Smith. NItP
Present, The. Adelaide Anne Procter. WGRP
Present. Sonia Sanchez. CNA; ER; WPOW
Present Age, The. Arthur Cleveland Coxe. BLPA
Present Age, The. Frances Ellen Watkins Harper. PWR
Present Crisis, The, *sels.* James Russell Lowell. OHFP
   "Count me o'er earth's chosen heroes—they were souls that stood alone." WGRP
   Once to Every Man and Nation. FaPoR
Present day we cannot spend, The. Isabella Whitney. *Fr.* Sweet Nosegay, A, or Pleasant Posy. WPE
Present from the Emperor's New Concubine, A. Lady Pan, *tr. fr. Chinese by* Kenneth Rexroth. BoWoP

Present in Absence. John Hoskyns. *See* Absence, hear thou my protestation.
Present of Butter, A. Tadhg Dall O'Huiginn, *tr. fr. Irish by* the Earl of Longford. BIrV
Present to a Lady, A. *Unknown.* ErPo
Present Winter. Murano Shiro, *tr. fr. Japanese by* Geoffrey Bownas *and* Anthony Thwaite. PeBJV
Presentation of Two Birds to My Son, A. James Wright. DiL; PPP
Presentation Piece. Marilyn Hacker. AmPA
Presented to a Mountain Dweller. Chao Chih-hsin, *tr. fr. Chinese by* Michael S. Duke. WFTU
Presented to Liu Ching-wen. Su Tung-p'o, *tr. fr. Chinese by* Burton Watson. CoBCP
Presented to Piao, the Prince of Pai-ma. Ts'ao Chih, *tr. fr. Chinese by* Burton Watson. CoBCP
Presented to Wang Lun. Li Po, *tr. fr. Chinese by* Burton Watson. CoBCP
Presented to Wang Wen-hsi. Ho Ching-ming, *tr. fr. Chinese by* Jonathan Chaves. CoBLCP
Presented to Wei Pa, Gentleman in Retirement. Tu Fu, *tr. fr. Chinese by* Burton Watson. CoBCP
Presentiment. Ambrose Bierce. AA
Presentiment, A. Bryant. AnAmPo
Presentiment—is that long shadow—on the lawn. Emily Dickinson. OxBA
Presently at our touch the teacup stirred. Voices from the Other World. James Merrill. TwCP
Preserve a respectful demeanor. To a Baked Fish. Carolyn Wells. FiBHP
Preserve that old kettle, so blackened and worn. My Dad's Dinner Pail. Edward Harrigan. BLPA
Preserve the red leaf of this burning winter. Pagan Prayer. Maria Luisa Spaziani, *tr. by* Muriel Kittel. DMI
Preserve thy sighs, unthrifty girl. The Soldier Going to the Field. Sir William Davenant. NOBE; OBWP (Souldier Going to the Field, The.) MePo
Preserves. Jack Butler. MT
Preserves. Michael Waters. GeTw
President caressed the mane of his favorite horse, The. Exiled from the Light. Sebastian Salazar Bondy, *tr. by* Ena Hollis *and* Maureen Ahern. Per
President Garfield. Longfellow. PAH
President has thus disclosed, The. The Door of Hope. Lizelia Augusta Jenkins Moorer. CBWP-3
President in His Country Residence, A. Remco Campert, *tr. fr. Dutch by* James Brockway. DuIn
President Lincoln's Grave. Caroline Atherton Briggs Mason. OHIP
President Ordains the Bee to Be, The. Wallace Stevens. *Fr.* Notes toward a Supreme Fiction. LiTA
President Parker. *Unknown.* OxBSS
President Roosevelt. Big Joe Williams. FaBoPV
President Slumming, The. James Tate. OBAL
Presidents, The. Lizelia Augusta Jenkins Moorer. CBWP-3
Presidents of the United States. *Unknown.* FaBoUs
Press, The. Ebenezer Elliott. PF
Press ahead, beloved children. Uncle Rube to the Young People. Clara Ann Thompson. CBWP-2
Press-Gang, The. *Unknown.* *See* Here's the Tender Coming.
Press [*or* Presse] me not to take more pleasure. The Rose. George Herbert. LiTB; PoEL-2
Press of the Spoon River *Clarion* was wrecked, The. Carl Hamblin. Edgar Lee Masters. *Fr.* Spoon River Anthology. CMoP; LiTA; LiTM; OBSV
Press often for, (nor, than at this time, more). Vox Oppressi, to the Lady Phipps. Richard Henchman. SCAP
Press Onward. *Unknown.* FaFP
Press'd by the moon, mute arbitress of tides. Sonnet Written in the Church-Yard at Middleton, in Sussex. Charlotte Smith. NOEC; WPE
Pressure. Anne Waldman. PoM
Pressure Drop. Oku Onuora. PBCV
Pressure of sun on the rockslide. Water. Gary Snyder. LCAP
Pressures, The. Amiri Baraka. BPo
Presto, pronto! Two boys, two horses. Boy Riding Forward Backward. Robert Francis. LCAP
Preston. *Unknown.* GBP
Pretences. Ibn Rashiq, *tr. fr. Arabic by* A. J. Arberry. TTY
Pretences, discontents. Ergo Sum. Charles Brasch. ATNZ
Pretend you are a dragon. Things to Do If You Are a Subway. Bobbi Katz. RHPC
Pretending. Bobbi Katz. RAR

Pretext. Stephen Rodefer. IAT; UL
Prettiest girl, The. Sucking Cider through a Straw. *Unknown.* AS; GBP
Prettiest lady that ever I've seen, The. Pretty Lady. Rose Fyleman. BoTP
Pretty. Stevie Smith. NAEL-2; NoAM; NoP; TEP
Pretty a Day, A. E. E. Cummings. CMoP
Pretty Ambition, A. Mary E. Wilkins Freeman. OBCA
Pretty Bonnie, you are quick as a rabbit. Giving Rabbit to My Cat Bonnie. Anne Stevenson. FaBoWP
Pretty Fair Maid, A. *Unknown.* AS
Pretty game, my girl, A. The Flirt. W. H. Davies. EnLoPo
Pretty Girl, A. J. Gordon Coogler. OBAL
Pretty Girls Just Are. ("Pretty girls don't talk"). Bunmi Ogunsiji. WS
Pretty girls of the fall, The. The Falls. F. D. Reeve. NYBP
Pretty John Watts. Mother Goose. OxNR
Pretty Lady. Rose Fyleman. BoTP
Pretty Lady Carenza. Tenson. Carenza *and* Iselda, *tr. by* Bridget Connelly *and* Doris Earnshaw. WPOW
Pretty lark, climbing the welkin clear. Joshua Sylvester. *Fr.* Du Bartas: His Divine Weeks and Works: The Fifth Day of the First Week. PBBP
Pretty little crocus, in your cosy bed. Waking Up. *Unknown.* BoTP
Pretty Maid, The. Paul Fort. *See* Pretty maid she died, she died, in love-bed as she lay, The.
Pretty maid both kind and fair, A. The Very Pretty Maid of This Town, and the Amorous 'Squire Not One Hundred Miles from the Place. *Unknown.* CoMu
Pretty Maid Marion. Ivy O. Eastwick. BoTP
Pretty maid, pretty maid,/ Where have you been? Gift for the Queen. *Unknown.* OxNR
Pretty maid she died, she died, in love-bed as she lay, The. Paul Fort, *tr. by* Frederick York Powell. AWP
(Pretty Maid, The.) OBMV
Pretty Maids Beware!!! *Unknown.* CoMu
Pretty Miss Apathy. Pooh! Walter de la Mare. FiBHP; HAP
Pretty party for people, A. And. Robert Creeley. LCAP
Pretty Ploughboy, The. *Unknown.* GBP
Pretty Polly ("Go get me some of your father's gold"). *Unknown.* AS
Pretty Polly ("Pretty Polly, Pretty Polly, come and go with me"). *Unknown.* AmFP
Pretty Polly of Topsham. *Unknown.* AmFP
Pretty prating poll. Little Miss and Her Parrot. John Marchant. OxBChV
Pretty red squirrel lives up in a tree, The. The Squirrel. Mary Howitt. BoTP
Pretty Redhead [*or* Red-Head], The. Guillaume Apollinaire, *tr. fr. French.* POS, *tr. by* Roger Shattuck; RHTwFP, *tr. by* James Wright.
Pretty Saro. *Unknown.* AmFP
Pretty sneaking knave I knew, A. Blake. FaBoEE
(Mr. Cromek.) ChTr
Pretty song, this coming spring, A. Miss Betty's Singing-Bird. John Winstanley. NOEC
Pretty Sport. William Habington. *See* Queen of Aragon, The: Fine Young Folly.
Pretty tint—what a splendid lotion. Advertisement. Oswald de Andrade, *tr. by* Jean R. Longland. ATCBP
Pretty Twinkling Starry Eyes. Nicholas Breton. *Fr.* The Passionate Shepherd. EIL
Pretty Vomit. Bob Rosenthal. UL
Pretty Wantons. *Unknown.* EIL
("Pretty wantons, sweetly sing.") PBBP
Pretty white city. Precious white city. The Idea of San Francisco. Jim Gustafson. UL
Pretty Woman, A. Simon J. Ortiz. CDW
Pretty Words. Elinor Wylie. NAAL-2
Pretty young actress, a stammerer, a. Eille Norwood. CenHV
Prevailing Prayer. Richard Chenevix Trench. *See* "Lord, what a change within us one short hour."
Prevailing west wind. Ernst David, *tr. by* Beth Bjorklund. CoAuP
Prevailing winds lied in intent, The. Statuary. John Ashbery. NoAM
Prevalent Poetry. Charles Follen Adams. CenHV
Prevaricator, The. Shirley Vogler Meister. SoTCo
Prevention of Stacy Miller, The. Peter Miller. MoCV
Previsioning death in advance, our doom is delayed. Foresight. Lincoln Kirstein. OBWP
Prewar Late October Sea Breeze. Robert Grenier. UL
Prey for us the Prince of Pees. A Song to John, Christ's Friend. *Unknown.* MeEL
Prey swooped up, the iron love seat shudders. Up and Down. James Merrill. GLP

Prey to Prey. David Rowbotham. CBAP
Priam and Achilles. Homer, *tr. fr. Greek by* George Chapman. *Fr.* The Iliad, XXIV. OBS
Priapus and the Pool, *sels.* Conrad Aiken.
This Is the Shape of the Leaf. *Fr.* IV [V]. CMoP; NOBA; OxBA; TrGrPo
(Portrait of a Girl.) GoJo; MoAB; MoAmPo
"When trout swim down Great Ormond Street." *Fr.* III [IV]. NoAM; NOBA
Price, The. John Davidson. EBVV
Price, The. Anne Stevenson. DiPo
Price He Paid, The. Ella Wheeler Wilcox. WBLP
Price of Begging, The. Emmanuel ben David Frances, *tr. fr. Hebrew by* A. B. Rhine. TrJP
Price of Disrespect, The. Lizelia Augusta Jenkins Moorer. CBWP-3
Price of Experience, The. Blake. *Fr.* Vala; or The Four Zoas. EnRP; Prf
(Night II (Enion's Lament).) PoE
Price of Giving Too Much, The. Vanparanar, *tr. fr. Tamil by* A. K. Ramanujan. PLW
Price of Rice, The, *sels.* Shu Wei, *tr. fr. Chinese by* Irving Lo. WFTU
"And so, wine and meat markets are proscribed." *Fr.* IV.
"Price of rice this year is so dear, The." *Fr.* I.
Price of Wildness, The. Judith Moffett. BLA
Price of Wisdom. Bible, *O.T. See* Job: "Surely there is a mine for silver."
Price seemed reasonable, location, The. Telephone Conversation. Wole Soyinka. SoSe; TTY
Priceless treasure it may be, A. Tabito. *Fr.* Manyo Shu. FCEI
Prices. Louis Ginsberg. TrJP
Prick a maiden nether holly. W. J. Webster. BXAP
Prickle a lamb. Conjuring Roethke. James Tate. OBAL
Pride. Violet Jacob. OxBS
Pride, The. John Newlove. MoCV; NOBC
Pride. Dahlia Ravikovich, *tr. fr. Hebrew by* Chana Bloch. OV
Pride cannot see itself by mid-day light. Barten Holyday. FaBoEE
Pride is his pity, artifice his praise. *Unknown.* FaBoEE
Pride Is the Canker. *Unknown. See* Do Not, Oh, Do Not Prize.
Pride, lust, ambition, and the people's hate. The Downfall of the Chancellor. *Unknown.* APAS
Pride of a Jew, The. Judah Halevi, *tr. fr. Hebrew by* Israel Cohen. TrJP
Pride of Ancestry. Robert Frost. OBAL
Pride of Cities. Akhtar-ul-Iman, *tr. fr. Urdu by* Mahmood Jamal. PBMUP
Pride of Kildare, The. *Unknown.* OBET
Pride of Ladies, A. Anne Halley. NMM
Pride of the peacock is the glory of God, The. Blake. *Fr.* The Marriage of Heaven and Hell. FF
Pride of wrights, the joy of smiths abide, The. The Junk Shop. Henri Coulette. NYBP
Pride of Youth. Dante Gabriel Rossetti. *Fr.* The House of Life, XXIV. OBNC
Pride of Youth, The. Sir Walter Scott. *See* Heart of Midlothian, The: Proud Maisie.
Priest and Pagan. Albert Durrant Watson. CaP
Priest and the Mulberry-Tree, The. Thomas Love Peacock. *Fr.* Crotchet Castle. BoTP; GN; OnMSP
Priest attending, found he spoke at times, The. George Crabbe. *Fr.* The Borough: Peter Grimes. PoE
Priest Lake. William Stafford. PoA
Priest of Felton. *Unknown.* OxNR
Priest of God, unto thee I come. Absolution. Edward Willard Watson. AA
Priest or Poet. Shane Leslie. WGRP
Priestcraft and Private Judgement. Dryden. *Fr.* Religio Laici. OBS
Priestin' of Father John, The. John D. Sheridan. TIRV
Priest's Chant, The. John Fletcher. *Fr.* The Faithful Shepherdess, II, i. OBS
(Evening Knell, The.) EIL
(Evening Song.) GN
(Folding the Flocks.) CH
Priest's Lament, The. Robert Hugh Benson. ACP
Priests of Apollo, sacred be the roome. The Sacrifice to Apollo. Michael Drayton. OBS
Priest's Prayer, A. Martha Gilbert Dickinson Bianchi. AA
Priest's Song, A. Thomas Dekker. *Fr.* Old Fortunatus. OBSC
Priests, the elders, and the scribes, The. Death and Resurrection. Priscilla Jane Thompson. CBWP-2
Prig offered Pig the first chance at dessert. Manners. Howard Nemerov. NBLV

Primacy of Dullness, The. Dryden. *See* MacFlecknoe; or, A Satire [*or* Satyr] upon the True-Blue [*or*-Blew] Protestant Poet T. S: All human[e] things are subject to decay.

Primaleon of Greece, *sel.* Anthony Munday.
  Beauty Sat Bathing by a Spring. EIL
    (Beauty Bathing.) NOBE; OBEV
    (Colin.) GTBS; GTBS-P
    (To Colin Clout.) OBSC

Primary Ground, A. Adrienne Rich. NNaP

Primary Lesson: The Second Class Citizens. Sun-Ra. PoBA

Prime. W. H. Auden. *Fr.* Horae Canonicae. CMoP; PoE

Prime. Donald Davie. *Fr.* Horae Canonicae. CRP

Prime. Langston Hughes. PoBA

Prime cantante! My Catbird. William Henry Venable. AA

Prime of my life has far declined, The. Tabito. *Fr.* Manyo Shu. Ma

Primer. Bob Perelman. LP

Primer for Schoolchildren, A. Richard Weber. CIP

Primer Lesson. Carl Sandburg. FaPON; MoAmPo; MoShBr

Primer of Plato. Jean Garrigue. NOBA

Primer of the Daily Round, A. Howard Nemerov. NYBP; SM; WeW

Primeval Forest, The. Longfellow. *See* Evangeline: This is the forest primeval. The murmuring pines and the hemlocks.

Primitive, The. Don L. Lee. BPo

Primitive like an Orb, A. Wallace Stevens. NOBA

Primitive Pithecanthropus erectus, The. Heredity. Arthur Guiterman. OBAL

Primitives. Dudley Randall. BPo

Primo Vere. Giosuè Carducci, *tr. fr. Italian by* John Bailey. AWP

Primrose, The. *At. to* Robert Herrick. FaBoUs; OBEV

Primrose Bed, The. Robert Graves. TEP

Primrose, Being at Montgomery Castle, upon the Hill, on Which It Is Situate, The. John Donne. FaBoPP; GBL

Primrose Hill. Rose Fyleman. BoTP

Primroses; salutations; the miry skull. A Pre-Raphaelite Notebook. Geoffrey Hill. NoAM

Prince Absalom and Sir Rotherham Redde. Evening. Edith Sitwell. MoBS

Prince Alfrid's Itinerary, *sel. Unknown, tr. fr. Middle Irish by* James Clarence Mangan.
  "I found in Munster, unfettered of any." BIrV

Prince, and bishop, and knight, and dame. The Pawns. William Young. *Fr.* Wishmakers' Town. AA

Prince Arthur. Spenser. *Fr.* The Faerie Queene, I, 7. OBSC

Prince Enters the Forest, The. Henri Cole. DiPo

Prince from Western Libya, A. C. P. Cavafy, *tr. fr. Greek by* Edmund Keeley *and* Philip Sherrard. VMG

Prince Hamlet thought Uncle a traitor. Hamlet. Stanley J. Sharpless. BXAP; NBLV

Prince Heathen. *Unknown.* ESPB, (A *and* B *vers.*)

Prince Henry the Navigator. Sydney Clouts. PeSA

Prince New Year, welcome to thy throne. To the New Year. Priscilla Jane Thompson. CBWP-2

Prince of Life, The. John Oxenham. TrPWD

Prince of Love, The. Blake. *See* "How sweet I roam'd from field to field."

Prince of Peace His Banner Spreads, The. Harry Emerson Fosdick. AH
  (Prince of Peace, The.) TrPWD

Prince of Wales' Marriage. *Unknown.* CoMu

Prince Robert. *Unknown.* AmFP; ESPB, (A *and* B *vers.*); OxBB

Prince Sumiya. *Mongol Oral Tradition, tr. by* C. R. Bawden. WTO

Prince William, of the Brunswick race. The Royal Adventurer. Philip Freneau. PAH

Prince, with wonder, sees the stately tow'rs, The. Virgil, *tr. fr. Latin by* Dryden. *Fr.* The Aeneid [*or* Eneados], I. OBVE

Princely Ditty in Praise of the English Rose, A. Thomas Deloney. BoTP

Princely eagle, and the soaring hawke, The. William Wood. SCAP

Princes and kings decay and die. Philip Freneau. GOA

Princes of Mercia were badger and raven, The. Geoffrey Hill. *Fr.* Mercian Hymns, VI. HAP; NAEL-2; NoAM; NoP; PoE

Prince's Progress, The, *sel.* Christina Rossetti.
  Bride Song. OBEV; WPE

Princes statue, or in marble carv'd, A. Poetry and Learning. George Chapman. *Fr.* The Epistle Dedicatory to Chapman's Translation of the Iliad. OBS

Princess, The. Muhammad al-Asad, *tr. fr. Arabic by* Lena Jayyusi *and* Charles Doria. MAP

Princess, The, *sels.* Tennyson.
  As thro' the Land at Eve. *Fr. Pt.* I. LiTB
  Ask Me No More [the Moon May Draw the Sea]. *Fr. Pt.* VI. GBL; LiTB; NAEL-2; OBNC; PoEL-5; TrGrPo

"Blame not thyself too much," I said, "nor blame."'' *Fr. Pt.* VII. NAEL-2

Come Down, O Maid, [from Yonder Mountain Height]. *Fr. Pt.* VII. EBVV; FF; GTBS-P; NAEL-2; NOBVV; OAEL-2; OBEV; OBNC (Idyl, An.) TrGrPo

Home They Brought Her Warrior Dead. *Fr. Pt.* V. TrGrPo

Now Sleeps the Crimson Petal. *Fr. Pt.* VII. BoLoP; ChER; ChTr; EBEV; EBVV; ELP; FiP; GBL; LLLT; NAEL-2; NIP; NOBE; NoP; OBNC; PoEL-5; PPP; SCV; TrGrPo
  (Song: "Now sleeps the crimson petal, now the white.") BLPL; FaBoBe
  (Summer Night.) OBEV; SeCePo

"Spirit haunts the year's last hours, A." InvP
  (Song: "Spirit haunts the last year's hours, A.") GTBS-P; HeIP; OBNC

Splendor Falls [on Castle Walls], The. *Fr. Pt.* III. AWP; CH; EBVV; ELP; FaBoCh; FaBV; FiP; GoJo; GTBS-P; HeIP; InPK; NAEL-2; NoP; OAEL-2; OBNC; PoEL-5; PrIm; TrGrPo; WSC
  (Blow, Bugle, Blow.) BLPL; ChTr; FaFP; LiTB; NOBE; OBEV; UnPo; UnS; WiR
  (Bugle Song.) FaPON; GN
  (He Hears the Bugle at Killarney.) FaBoPP

Sweet and Low [Sweet and Low]. *Fr. Pt.* II. BLPL; BoTP; FaBoBe; FaPON; MOS; NAEL-2; OxBChV; TrGrPo
  (Lullaby: "Sweet and low, sweet and low.") PoLF

Tears, Idle Tears [I Know Not What They Mean]. *Fr. Pt.* IV. AWP; EBVV; ELP; FaBoRV; FaFP; FaPoR; FiP; FPL; GTBS-P; HAP; InPS; InvP; LiTB; NAEL-2; NIP; NOBE; NoP; OAEL-2; OBNC; PoE; PoEL-5; PPP; TEP; TrGrPo; UnPo; WeW

"This world was once a fluid haze of light." *Fr. Pt.* IV. ImOP, 4 *ll.*

"Thy voice is heard through rolling drums." *Fr.* Interlude. TrGrPo

Princess Elizabeth of Bohemia, as Perdita. Frank O'Hara. PoA

Princess Ida, *sel.* W. S. Gilbert.
  Arac's Song. FiBHP

Princess of Scotland, The. Rachel Annand Taylor. GoTS

Princess Sabbath. Heine, *tr. fr. German by* Charles Godfrey Leland. TrJP

Princess Tatsuta's headband loosened. Teika, *tr. fr. Japanese by* Hiroaki Sato. *Fr.* A Compendium of Good Tanka. FCEI

Princess Vandora the thief. The Old Leader Complains. Moyshe-Leyb Halpern, *tr. by* Benjamin *and* Barbara Harshav *and* Kathryn Helle. AYP

Princess Who Fled to the Castle, The. Francis Landy. VWA

Principal and Principle. *Unknown.* FaBoUs

Principal British Writers. Edward B. Goodwin. FaBoUs

Principal pal of the principal, The. Principal and Principle. *Unknown.* FaBoUs

Principes portas tollite. The Harrowing of Hell. *Unknown.* ACP

Principle behind my nonconformist action, The. The Fugitive's Apologue. Nanni Balestrini, *tr. by* Lawrence R. Smith. NItP

Print of love could not, The. Asadullah Khan Ghalib, *tr. by* Ahmed Ali. GoT

Print of Your Hand, The. Sandor Csoori, *tr. fr. Hungarian by* Jascha Kessler. FOC

Print, with his hand, his eye, was more than print. Hiroshige. Mark Perlberg. NYBP

Printed English word quietly lies upon the desk, A. Glove and Love. Tu Yeh, *tr. by* Dominic Cheung. IFON

Printed Words. Liz Sohappy Bahe. CDW

Printer, The. Linda Pastan. KS

Printers. Denis Glover. PeNZ

Printer's Error. P. G. Wodehouse. FiBHP

Printing Jenny ("Printing Bibles is Jenny's daily chore"). Matthew Mitchell. OxBTC

Printing of these rhymes afflicts me more. A Panegyric on the Author of "Absalom and Achitophel." *Unknown.* APAS

Prioress, The. Chaucer. *Fr.* The Canterbury Tales: Prologue. CTC, *abr.*
  (Madam Eglantine.) NOBE
  ("There also was a nun, a Prioress," *mod. vers. by* Louis Untermeyer.) TrGrPo

Prioress's Tale, The. Chaucer. *Fr.* The Canterbury Tales. ACP, *mod. vers.*

Prior's Epitaph. Matthew Prior. *See* Nobles, and heralds by your leave.

Priory of St. Saviour, Glendalough, The. Donald Davie. OxBC

Pripet Marshes, The. Irving Feldman. VWA

Prisms. Philip Dacey. Psk

Prison fetters ate into our flesh, The. Against Negritude. Emanuel Corgo, *tr. by* Michael Wolfers. WMBCH

Prison House, The. Alan Paton. PeSA

Prison-house in which I live, The. Renewal of Strength. Frances Ellen Watkins Harper. PWR

Prison Song. Alan Dugan. PoA

Prisoned in Windsor, He Recounteth His Pleasure There Passed. Earl of Surrey. *Fr. Windsor Castle.* NAEL-1

Prisoner, A. *"Æ."* AnIL

Prisoner, The. Ai. ER

Prisoner, The, *sels.* Emily Brontë. NOBE; NoP; OBEV

"He comes with western winds, with evening's wandering airs." ELP

"In the dungeon-crypts, idly did I stray." NOBVV

"Still, let my tyrants know, I am not doomed to wear." ChER; NOBE; NoP; OBEV; OBNC

Prisoner. Marguerite George. GoYe

Prisoner, The. William Plomer. PeSA

Prisoner, The. Charles Spear. ATNZ

Prisoner/ rendered blind mute, The. Nelo Risi, *tr. fr. Italian by* Lawrence R. Smith. *Fr.* Variations on White. NItP

Prisoner, in whose tired bearing still I read. War Tribunal. Elizabeth Daryush. CN

Prisoner of Chillon, The. Byron. BeLS; EnRP; PoLF *Sels.*

"Kind of change came in my fate, A." NOBE

Sonnet on Chillon. FiP; LiTB; TrGrPo

(On the Castle of Chillon.) GTBS; GTBS-P

Prisoner of War. Gertrude May Lutz. GoYe

Prisoner of Zenda, The. Richard Wilbur. NBLV

Prisoners. Frederick William Harvey. MMA

Prisoners. Randall Jarrell. OxBA; WaP

Prisoners. Denise Levertov. NoAM

Prisoners, The. Stephen Spender. FaBoMo; MoAB; MoBrPo

Prisoners. *Unknown.* EIL

Prisoners everywhere. The Postman's Fear. Muhammad al-Maghut, *tr. by* Abdullah al-Udhari. MPAW

Prisoner's Song of Jerusalem, A. *Unknown.* ACP

Prisons. Lőrinc Szabó, *tr. fr. Hungarian by* Edwin Morgan. MHuP

Prison's Stream, The. Shauqi Abi Shaqra, *tr. fr. Arabic by* Abdullah al-Udhari. MPAW

Prithee die and set me free. Martial, *tr. by* Sir John Denham. OBVE

Prithee leave me, cratty hussy. The Cupbearer Speaks. Goethe, *tr. fr. German by* John Weiss. *Fr.* West-Easterly Divan, *Bk.* 9. PeHV

Prithee, let no raindrop fall. A. M. Sayers. BXAP

Prithee, no more, how can love sail? To Her Questioning His Estate. William Hammond. JCP

Prithee now, fond fool, give o'er. A Dialogue between Strephon and Daphne. John Wilmot, 2d Earl of Rochester. SeCV-2

Prithee, say aye or no. The Resolute Courtier. Thomas Shipman. ErPo; GBL

Private, A. Edward Thomas. GTBS-P; MMA

Private Acts. Leslie Ullman. NAmP

Private Blair of the Regulars. Clinton Scollard. PAH

Private Devotion. Phoebe Hinsdale Brown. *See* I Love to Steal Awhile Away.

Private Dining Room, The. Ogden Nash. NYBP

Private faces in public places. W. H. Auden. FaBoEE

Private Feast, A. Judson Jerome. SoTCo

Private Judgement Condemned. Dryden. *Fr.* The Hind and the Panther, I. OBS

Private Letter to Brazil, A. Gloria C. Oden. AmNP; PoNe

Private Life, A. Celia Gilbert. ER

Private madness has prevailed, A. O Virtuous Light. Elinor Wylie. MoAB; MoAmPo

Private Means Is Dead. Stevie Smith. OxBC

Private Meeting Place, The. James Wright. NYBP

Private of the Buffs; or, The British Soldier in China. Sir Francis Hastings Doyle. OBEV; OBTV

Private Pain in Time of Trouble. Kathleen Spivack. AmPA

Private Pantomime. Ruth Stone. PoA

Private Rooms. Diana O Hehir. NPGG

Private Theater, The. Nelo Risi, *tr. fr. Italian by* Lawrence R. Smith. NItP; PFI

Private Transport. Adrian Mitchell. FaBoEE

Private View, A. Dahlia Ravikovich, *tr. fr. Hebrew by* Warren Bargad *and* Stanley F. Chyet. IP

Privets Come into Season at High Tide. Ted Greenwald. LP

Privilege. Alejandra Pizarnik, *tr. fr. Spanish by* Yishai Tobin. VWA

Privilegium Minus. Reinhard Priessnitz, *tr. fr. German by* Beth Bjorklund. CoAuP

Privy-Love for My Landlady. George Farewell. NOEC

Prize Cat, The. E. J. Pratt. HeIP; MoP

Prize for Good Conduct. Kenneth Allott. OBWP

Prize-giving. Gwen Harwood. CBAP; PoAu-2

Prize of the *Margaretta,* The. Will M. Carleton. PAH

"Prize" Poem, A. Shirley Brooks. FaBoCo; FaBoNo

Prize-winning Limerick, A. R. Rhodes. FaBoUs

Prizefighter's Prayer, The. Menotti Vincent Caprani. TIRV

Pro Femina, *sels.* Carolyn Kizer.

"From Sappho to myself, consider the fate of women." *Fr.* I. NMM

"I take as my theme, 'The Independent Woman.'" *Fr.* II. MAT; NMM

"I will speak about women of letters, for I'm in the racket." *Fr.* III. CAPP; MAT; NMM

Pro Libra Mea. Joseph I. C. Clarke. TrPWD

Pro Patria. Constance Carrier. NYBP; WPE

Pro Patria. Adah Isaacs Menken. CBWP-1

Pro Patria Mori. Thomas Moore. GTBS; GTBS-P; HoPM

Pro Sua Vita. Robert Penn Warren. MoAmPo

Probability and Birds in the Yard. Russell Atkins. CNA; FB

Probably. Keith Preston. NBLV

Probably the Farmer. Laura Jensen. AnAn

Probatioun Officeres Tale, The. Gerard Benson. BXAP; NBLV

Probing my mouth as if searching for gold. Next. Tina Koyama. BrSi

Problem, The. Paul Blackburn. NeAP

Problem, The ("I like a church; I like a cowl"), *sel.* Emerson. AA; AmPP; AnAmPo; AWP; LiTA; NAAL-1; NOBA; NoP; OxBA; TAP; WGRP

"Hand that rounded Peter's dome, The." EyDe

Problem, The. Natan Zach, *tr. fr. Hebrew by* Warren Bargad *and* Stanley F. Chyet. IP

Problem in History, A. Robert Wallace. CRP

Problem in Morals, A. Howard Moss. ErPo

Problem in Social Geometry—the Inverted Square! Ray Durem. NBP; PoBA

Problem with black holes is, The. Collapsars. Sandra McPherson. LCAP

Problems. Alexander Scott. FF

Problems of a Journalist. Weldon Kees. NaP

Problems of a Writing Teacher, The. David Ray. NePoEA-2

Process, The. Tom Clark. UL

Process. John Montague. CIP

Process. Charles L. O'Donnell. TrPWD

Process in the Weather of the Heart, A. Dylan Thomas. MoAB

Process of Conception, The. Claude Quillet, *tr. fr. Latin by* George Sewell. *Fr.* Callipaedia; or, The Art of Getting Beautiful Children. FaBoUs

Process of time worketh such wonder. Sir Thomas Wyatt. SiPS

Processes of generation; deeds of settlement. Geoffrey Hill. *Fr.* Mercian Hymns, XXVIII. NoP

Procession. Philip Booth. BLA

Procession. Francisco Carrillo, *tr. fr. Spanish by* Maureen Ahern *and* David Tipton. Per

Procession. Dovid Hofshteyn, *tr. fr. Yiddish by* Robert Friend. PeBMYV

Procession: A New Protestant Ballad, The. *Unknown.* APAS

Procession at Candlemas, A. Amy Clampitt. FaBoWP; HCAP

Procession of honest men, A. Selah. R. S. Thomas. FaBoMo

Procession of the Flowers, The. Sydney Thompson Dobell. *See* Balder: Chanted Calendar, A.

Processionals. Alice Archer James. AA

Proclaim the Lofty Praise. Sarah Judson. AH

Proclamation, The. Longfellow. *Fr.* John Endicott. PAH

Proclamation, A. *Unknown.* PAH

Proclamation, The. Whittier. PAH

Proclamation/ From Sleep, Arise. Carolyn M. Rodgers. JB

Procne. Peter Quennell. LiTB; LiTM; MoBrPo

Procne, Philomela, and Itylus. Philomela. John Crowe Ransom. ChTr; CMoP; FaBoPP; NAAL-2; NoAM; NOBA; OBAL; OBSV; OxBA

Proconsul of Bithynia. To Petronius Arbiter. Oliver St. John Gogarty. OBMV

Procrastination. Martial, *tr. fr. Latin by* Abraham Cowley. AWP; FaBoEE; OBVE

Prodigal, The. Elizabeth Bishop. CoAP; InvP; LCAP; LiTM; MoAB; NYBP; PPP; TwCP

Prodigal of loves and barbecues. To the (Supposed) Patron. Geoffrey Hill. NePoEA-2

Prodigal Son, The. Christine Busta, *tr. fr. German by* Beth Bjorklund. CoAuP

Prodigal Son, The. Kipling. *Fr.* Kim. NoAM

Prodigal Son, The. E. A. Robinson. MoAmPo

Prodigal Son, The. Arthur Symons. BrPo

Prodiggus reptile! long and skaly kuss! Some Verses to Snaix. *Unknown.* NA

Prodigy. Charles Simic. GeTw

Produce the urn that Hannibal contains. Hannibal ("Produce the urn that Hannibal contains"). Juvenal, *tr. fr. Latin by* William Gifford. *Fr.* Satires, X. OBVE

Producify by exclusioness. Disinterment. James Sherry. UL

Product manager is deeply concerned, The. Economy, Convenience, Good Taste. Tom Disch. SoTCo

Proem: "If this little world to-nigh." Oliver Herford. *Fr.* The Bashful Earthquake. AA

Proem: "Lo, thus, as prostrate, 'In the dust I write.'" James Thomson ("B. V."). *Fr.* The City of Dreadful Night. GoTS; OxBS; ViBoPo

Proem: "Out of my own great woe." Heine, *tr. fr. German by* Elizabeth Barrett Browning. AWP

Proem: "There is no rhyme that is half so sweet." Madison Cawein. AA; BoNaP

Proem: To Brooklyn Bridge. Hart Crane. *See* Bridge, The: To Brooklyn Bridge.

Proem, A: "When in my walks I meet some ruddy lad." Samuel Ward. AA

Proem to "The Kid." Conrad Aiken. *Fr.* The Kid. MoAB

Profane, The. Horace. *See* Odes: III, 1. "Tread back—and back, the lewd and lay!" ("Odi profanum vulgus").

Professional, The. David Ignatow. NNaP

Professional dancer, Miss Fairleigh, A. Laurence Perrine. SoTCo

Professional Individual. Tom Riley. SoTCo

Professionals. Turner Cassity. MT

Professionals, The. Geoffrey Grigson. PoA

Professor at the Breakfast Table, The, *sels.* Oliver Wendell Holmes.
Lord of All Being, Throned Afar, *with music* AH
  (Sun-Day Hymn.) TrPWD; WGRP
O Love Divine, That Stooped to Share, *with music* Fr. 11. AH
  (Hymn of Trust.) AA; TrPWD
Under the Violets. AA

Professor Burke's symphony, "Colorado Vistas." Cultural Notes. Kenneth Fearing. CMoP; PoE

Professor Eisenbart, asked to attend. Prize-giving. Gwen Harwood. CBAP; PoAu-2

Professor Eisenbart, with grim distaste. Panther and Peacock. Gwen Harwood. CBAP; PoAu-2

Professor Gratt. Donald Hall. OBAL

Professor in Nirvana, The. Osman Edwards. *Fr.* Residential Rhymes, IV. OBTV

Professor Kelleher and the Charles River. Desmond O'Grady. CIP

Professor Noctutus. George MacDonald. NOBVV

Professor Palamedes parts down Westow Street. News from Norwood. Christopher Middleton. FaBoMo; NePoEA-2

Professor Robinson each summer beats. Don's Holiday. George Rostrevor Hamilton. FaBoCo

Professor Waking, The. James Tate. FF

Professor Y, my photographer friend. In the Field. Jung Han-mo, *tr. by* Koh Chang-soo. ACKP

Professor's Song, A. John Berryman. HeIP; MoP; NoAM; NOBA; OxBC

Proffered Love Rejected. Sir John Suckling. ErPo

Proffered to sun and moon. The Condemned. Enrique Gonzáles Martínez, *tr. by* Samuel Beckett. MexPo

Profile of Rose. Glyn Jones. OBWVE

Profile of the Lover of the Great Bear. Abdul Wahab al-Bayati, *tr. fr. Arabic by* Abdullah al-Udhari. MPAW

Profile on the Pillow, The. Dudley Randall. BPo; PoBA; TAP

Profiles of My Father. Rhyll McMaster. CBAP

Profit and Loss: An Elegy upon the Decease of Mrs. Mary Gerrish. John Danforth. SCAP

Profound, profound and brief. The Walk. Conrad Aiken. KS

Profound the radiance issuing. Eve. David Gascoyne. GTBS-P

Profoundly True Reflections on the Sea. A. E. Housman. *See* O Billows Bounding Far.

Profusely in confusion. Onitsura, *tr. fr. Japanese by* Hiroaki Sato. *Fr.* Twenty-three Hokku. FCEI

Prognosis. Louis MacNeice. CMoP; Mes; NOBE

Prognostication on Will Laud, Late Archbishop of Canterbury, A. *Unknown.* OxBoLi

Prognostication upon Cards and Dice, A. Sir Walter Ralegh. *See* Before the sixth day of the next new year.

Progress. Edith Agnew. AmFN

Progress. George Ella Lyon. MOWH

Progress. David McCord. ImOP

Progress. "Miraji", *tr. fr. Urdu by* Mahmood Jamal. PBMUP

Progress. Ella Wheeler Wilcox. BLPA; FPL

Progress is/ The law of life, man is not Man as yet. The Awakening of Man. Robert Browning. *Fr.* Paracelsus, V. WGRP

Progress of a Divine, The, *sel.* Richard Savage.
  "Now in the patron's mansion see the wight." OBSV

Progress of Dulness, The, *sels.* John Trumbull. AmPP
  Amorous Temper, An.
  Dick Hairbrain Learns the Social Graces.
  Harriet Simper Has Her Day.
  Tom Brainless as Student and Preacher at College.

Progress of Error, The, *sel.* William Cowper.
  "From school to Cam or Isis, and thence home." OBTV

Progress of Evening. Walter Savage Landor. OBNC

Progress of Faust, The. Karl Shapiro.
  MoAB; NYBP

Progress of Man, The, *sel.* George Canning.
  "Mark the dark rook, on pendent branches hung." FaBoNo

Progress of Poesy, The. Matthew Arnold. NOBVV

Progress of Poesy, The. Thomas Gray. AWP; EnRP; GTBS; GTBS-P; NOEC; OBEV

Progress of Poetry, The. "Christopher Caudwell." OxBTC

Progress of Poetry, The. Swift. InvP; NOIV

Progress of Sir Jack Brag, The. *Unknown.* PAH

Progress[e] of the Soul[e], The, *sels.* John Donne.
  "It quickned next a toyful Ape, and so." PoEL-2
  Whale, The. ChTr

Progress of the Soul, The ("Nothing could make me sooner to confess"). John Donne. *See* Of the Progresse of the Soule; the Second Anniversary.

Progress Report. Charles Simic. GeTw

Progression of the Species. Brian W. Aldiss. FF

Prohibition, The. John Donne. EIL; GBL; MeLP; OBS

Project, The. Gregory Orr. GeTw

Projection, A. Reed Whittemore. AiP; NePoEA

Proletarian Portrait. William Carlos Williams. AnAmPo; OBAL; TAP

Proletarian, unlikely bird, no monarch, A. On the Death of an Emperor Penguin in Regent's Park, London. David Wright. NYBP

Prolific. William Matthews. BLA

Prologue: "And the way goes on in the worn earth." Archibald MacLeish. *Fr.* Conquistador. NoAM

Prologue: "As needy gallants in the scriv'ners' hands." Dryden. *Fr.* Amboyna; or, The Cruelties of the Dutch to the English Merchants. OBSV

Prologue: "Borborygms! Borborygms!" Valery Larbaud, *tr. by* William Jay Smith. CT

Prologue: "By landscape reminded once of his mother's figure." W. H. Auden. MoP

Prologue: "Delusions of the days that once have been." Longfellow. *Fr.* Giles Corey of the Salem Farms. PAH

Prologue: "For who can longer hold? when every Press." John Oldham. *Fr.* Satires [*or* Satyrs] upon the Jesuits. SeCV-2

Prologue: "He says that woman speaks with nature." Susan Griffin. *Fr.* Woman and Nature. NPGG

Prologue: "He who writ this, not without pains and thought." Dryden. *Fr.* Secret Love; or, The Maiden Queen. SeCV-2

Prologue: "If yet there be a few that take delight." Nahum Tate. *Fr.* The Loyal General. SeCV-2

Prologue: "In a summer season, when soft was the sun." William Langland. *See* Vision of Piers Plowman, The: In a summer [*or* somer] season, when soft[e] was the sun [*or* sunne *or* sonne].

Prologue: "In your words." Lazer Eichenrand, *tr. by* Gabriel Preil *and* Howard Schwartz. VWA

Prologue: "Lord, can a crumb of dust the earth outweigh." Edward Taylor. *Fr.* Preparatory Meditations before My Approach to the Lord's Supper. NAAL-1

Prologue: Moments in a Glade. Alan Stephens. QFR

Prologue: "Musing upon the restless bisinesse." Thomas Hoccleve. *Fr.* De Regimine Principum. PoEL-1

Prologue: "Nothing has happened yet." Linda Pastan. KS

Prologue: "O love, the interest itself in thoughtless heaven." W. H. Auden. EBEV; FaBoMo
  Two Invocations of the Virgin, II. ACP

Prologue: "Of those few fools, who with ill stars are cursed." Congreve. *Fr.* The Way of the World. NAEL-1

Prologue: "Our author by experience finds it true." Dryden. *Fr.* Aureng-Zebe. FiP; OBS; OxBoLi; SeCV-2

Prologue: "Over! the sweet summer closes." Tennyson. *Fr.* Becket. GBL

Prologue: "Poet's age is sad, The: for why?" Robert Browning. *Fr.* Asolando. OAEL-2

Prologue: "See my lov'd Britons, see your Shakespeare rise." Dryden. *Fr.* Troilus and Cressida. SeCV-2

Prologue: The Wanderers. William Morris. *Fr.* The Earthly Paradise. EBVV

Prologue: "These alternate nights and days, these seasons." Archibald MacLeish. MoAmPo

Prologue: "To-night we strive to read, as we may best." Longfellow. *Fr.* John Endicott. PAH

Prologue, The: "To sing of wars, of captains, and of kings." Anne Bradstreet. BoWoP; NAAL-1; NOBA; OxBA; PoE; SCAP; TAP; WPE

Prologue: "We who with songs beguile your pilgrimage." James Elroy Flecker. *Fr.* The Golden Journey to Samarkand. BrPo; FaPoR; GoJo; OBMV; OxBTC

Prologue. Chaucer. *Fr.* The Canterbury Tales. NoP; OAEL-1; PPP, *abr.*

Clerk of Oxford, The. InPS; TrGrPo
   ("Student came from Oxford town also, A," *mod. vers. by* Louis Untermeyer) TrGrPo

"Good Wif [*or* Wyf] was ther of biside [*or* bisyde] Bathe, A." EBEV; InPS
   (Good Wyf was Ther of Bisyde Bathe, A.) TrGrPo
   ("There was a Wife from Bath, a well-appearing," *mod. vers. by* Louis Untermeyer.) TrGrPo

"Knyght ther[e] was, and that a worthy man, A." InPS
   ("Knight there was, and that a worthy man, A," *orig. and mod. version by* Louis Untermeyer.) TrGrPo

"Marchant was ther with a forked berd, A." CTC, *abr.*

"Miller was a stout carl, for the nones, The." TrGrPo
   ("Miller, stout and sturdy as the stones, The," *mod. vers. by* Louis Untermeyer) TrGrPo

"Monk ther was, a fair for the maistrye [*or* maistrie], A." CTC, *abr.*; TrGrPo
   ("Monk there was, a monk of mastery, A.") TrGrPo

Poor Parson, The. ACP; NOCV
   (Good Parson, The, *mod. vers. by* H.C. Leonard) WGRP

Prioress, The. CTC, *abr.*
   (Madam Eglantine.) NOBE
   ("There also was a nun, a Prioress," *mod. vers. by* Louis Untermeyer.) TrGrPo

"Sergeant of the Lawe, war and wys, A." CTC, *abr.*

Shipman, The. MOS

"This Pardoner had hair as yellow as wax," *mod. vers. by* Nevill Coghill SCV

"Whan that April[e] with his shoures [*or* shower] soote," *br. sels.* ChTr; CTC, *abr.*; FiP; InPS; NAEL-1; NIP; NoP; OAEL-1; PoE; SCV; TrGrPo
   (As soon as April pierces to the root, *mod. vers. by* Theodore Robinson) NAWM-1
   (When April with Its Sweet Showers.) PrIm
   (When in April the Sweet Showers Fall, *mod. vers. by* Nevill Coghill) TEP
   (When the Sweet Showers of April Follow March, *mod. vers. by* Louis Untermeyer) TrGrPo

"With him ther was his sone, a young Squyer." TrGrPo
   ("With him there was his son, a youthful Squire," *mod. vers. by* Louis Untermeyer.) TrGrPo

Prologue for a Bestiary. Ronald Perry. NePoEA-2

Prologue from "Legacy." Patricia Parker. GLP

Prologue in Heaven [*or* The Chorus of the Archangels]. Goethe, *tr. fr. German by* Shelley. *Fr.* Faust. AWP; OBVE

Prologue of the Prioress's Tale, The. Chaucer. *Fr.* The Canterbury Tales.

Prologue Spoken [by Mr. Garrick] [at the Opening of the Theatre in Drury-Lane, 1747]. Samuel Johnson. EBEV; NAEL-1; NOEC; NoP

Prologue to a Poem. Natan Zach, *tr. fr. Hebrew by* Warren Bargad *and* Stanley F. Chyet. IP

Prologue to Book VII, The. Virgil, *tr. into Middle English by* Gavin Douglas. *Fr.* The Aeneid [*or* Eneados], VII. OxBLMV; OxBS

Prologue to General Hamley, *sel.* Tennyson.
   Green Sussex. FaBoPP

Prologue to Hugh Kelly's "A Word to the Wise." Samuel Johnson. EBEV; FaPoR

Prologue to "London Nights." Arthur Symons. BrPo

Prologue to "Love Triumphant." Dryden. *Fr.* Love Triumphant. OxBoLi

Prologue to "Secret-Love; or, The Maiden-Queen." Dryden. SeCV-2

Prologue to Sir Thopas. Chaucer. *Fr.* The Canterbury Tales. Par

Prologue to the Avowis of Alexander. John Barbour. *Fr.* The Buik of Alexander. OxBS

Prologue to "The Boatman in the Moon." Sándor Weöres, *tr. fr. Hungarian by* Jascha Kessler. FOC

Prologue to the First Satire. Persius, *tr. fr. Latin by* Dryden. *Fr.* Satires. AWP

Prologue to "The Lakers; a Comic Opera", *sel.* James Plumptre.
   "Where Cumbria's mountains in the north arise." NOEC

Prologue to the Man of Law's Tale. Chaucer. *Fr.* The Canterbury Tales. FiP

Prologue to the Miller's Tale. Chaucer. *Fr.* The Canterbury Tales. NAWM-1

Prologue to the Second Nun's Tale, The. Chaucer. *Fr.* The Canterbury Tales.
   Two Invocations of the Virgin, I. ACP

Prologue to "The Tempest." Dryden. NoP

Prologue to the University of Oxford, 1673. Dryden. OBS

Prologue to the Wife of Bath's Tale, The. Chaucer. *See* Canterbury Tales, The: Wife of Bath's Prologue, The.

Prologues are over, The. It is a question, now. Asides on the Oboe. Wallace Stevens. FaBoMo; MoAB; MoAmPo

Prologues to the Aeneid, *sels.* Gawin Douglas.
   "As bryght Phebus, scheyn soverane hevynnys e." *Fr. Bk.* VII, Prologue. OxBS; SeCePo
   Difficulties of Translation, The, *abr.* *Fr. Bk.* I, Prologue. GoTS
   "Towart the evyn, amyd the symmyris heit." *Fr. Bk.* XIII, Prologue. OxBS

Prologues to What Is Possible. Wallace Stevens. LCAP

Prolonged Sonnet: In the Last Days of the Emperor Henry VII. Simone dall' Antella, *tr. fr. Italian by* Dante Gabriel Rossetti. AWP

Prolonged Sonnet: When the Troops Were Returning from Milan. Niccolò degli Albizzi, *tr. fr. Italian by* Dante Gabriel Rossetti. AWP; OBVE; PFI; WaaP

Promenade. David Ignatow. TrJP

Promenade of our waters. Epidermis of the Night-Time Growth. Tristan Tzara, *tr. by* Timothy Baum *and* Michael Benedikt. WGRP

Promenading their/ skirted galleons of sex. The Return to Work. William Carlos Williams. NYBP

Prometheus. Byron. EnRP; HeIP; InPS; NOBE; NoP; OAEL-2

Prometheus. Goethe, *tr. fr. German by* John S. Dwight. AWP

Prometheus. Jenny Mastoraki, *tr. fr. Modern Greek by* Nikos Germanakos. BoWoP

Prometheus. Egan Swift. FaBoPV

Prometheus Bound, *sel.* Aeschylus, *tr. fr. Greek by* Elizabeth Barrett Browning.
   Wail of Prometheus Bound, The. WGRP

Prometheus on His Crag, *sels.* Ted Hughes. AnAn
   "Now I know I never shall." *Fr.* IX.
   "Prometheus on his crag/ began to admire the vulture." *Fr.* X.
   "Prometheus on his crag/ heard the cry of the wombs." *Fr.* XIII.

Prometheus Unbound. A. D. Hope. OxBC

Prometheus Unbound, *sels.* Shelley. EnRP; OAEL-2
   "Canst thou imagine where those spirits live." *Fr.* II, ii. WSC
   "Eagle so caught in some bursting cloud, An." PBBP
   "I wandering went/ Among the haunts and dwellings of mankind." *Fr.* III. FiP
   Life of Life. *Fr.* II, v. CH; FiP; NOBE; PoE; PoEL-4
      (Hymn to the Spirit of Nature.) GTBS; GTBS-P
   "Loud deep calls me home even now to feed it, The." *Fr.* III, ii. ChER
   "Monarch of Gods and Dæmons, and all Spirits." *Fr.* I. FiP; NAEL-2
   "On a poet's lips I slept." *Fr.* I. ChER; ELP; FiP; TOF
      (Poet's Dream, The.) GTBS; GTBS-P
   "Soon as the sound had ceased whose thunder filled." *Fr.* III, iv. ChER
   "Sphere, which is as many thousand spheres, A." *Fr.* IV. ImOP
   "There the voluptuous nightingales." *Fr.* II, ii. PBBP
   "Thou, Earth, calm empire of a happy soul." *Fr.* IV. FaBoRV
   "Thou knowest that toads and snakes and loathly worms." *Fr.* III, iv. PoE
   Who Reigns? *Fr.* II, iv. SeCePo

Promiscuous lovers/ Pine to have. A Problem in Morals. Howard Moss. ErPo

Promise! Mafika Pascal Gwala. WMBCH

Promise, The. Johari M. Kunjufu. BlSi

Promise. Florence Lacey. BoTP

Promise, A. Sir Thomas Wyatt. *See* Once as methought/ Fortune me kissed.

Promise Made, A. *Unknown.* FaFP

Promise me no promises. Promises like Pie-Crust. Christina Rossetti. NOBVV

Promise of a Constant Lover, The. *Unknown.* EIL

Promise of our years was caught, The. Monody on a Century. Earle Birney. CaP

Promise of Peace. Robinson Jeffers. LiTA; LiTM; MoAB; MoAmPo

Promise of these fragrant flowers, The. With a Spray of Apple Blossoms. Walter Learned. AA

Promise was broken too freely, The. Galway Kinnell. *Fr.* The Avenue Bearing the Initial of Christ into the New World, VIII. NaP

Promised Land, The. Jessie E. Sampter. TrJP

Promised Land. Charles Spear. ATNZ

Promised Land, The. Samuel Stennett. AmFP

Promises. Ruth Forbes Sherry. GoYe

Promises, *sels.* Robert Penn Warren.
Founding Fathers, Nineteenth-Century Style. *Fr.* VIII. NoAM
"What was the promise that smiled from the maples at evening?." *Fr.* I. DiL

Promises like Pie-Crust. Christina Rossetti. NOBVV

Promises of Freedom. *Unknown.* BPo

Promises of the World, The. Moses Ibn Ezra, *tr. fr. Hebrew by* Solomon Solis-Cohen. *Fr.* The World's Illusion. TrJP

Promissory Note, The. Bayard Taylor. AnAmPo; BXAP; Par

Promontory Moment, The. May Swenson. NYBP

Promoted, kicked upstairs. The Chisizas I. Guy C. Z. Mhone. WMBCH

Prone couple still sleeps, A. First Light. Thomas Kinsella. BIrV; CMoP; PoE

Pronouncement on Returning Home. Narushima Ryuhoku, *tr. fr. Chinese by* Burton Watson. JLIC-2

Proof, The. W. H. Auden. OAEL-2

Proof. Bessie Calhoun Bird. BlSi

Proof. Brendan Kennelly. CIP

Proof. Czeslaw Milosz, *tr. fr. Polish by the author.* TOF

Proof, The. Richard Wilbur. CRP; EaLo; OxBSP

Proofs of Buddha's Existence. *Unknown.* WGRP

Propaganda Art. Väinö Kirstinä, *tr. fr. Finnish by* Aili Jarvenpa. SOP

Prope ripam fluvii solus. Malum Opus. James Appleton Morgan. FaBoCo; NA

Proper Clay. Mark Van Doren. PoRA; TrGrPo

Proper New Song, A, *sel.* Thomas Richardson.
Take Heed of Gazing Overmuch. EIL

Proper Pride. D. H. Lawrence. FaBoEE

Proper scale would pat you on the head, The. The Scales. William Empson. CMoP; FaBoMo; LiTM

Proper Song, Entitled: Fain Would I Have a Pretty Thing to Give unto My Lady, A. *Unknown.* CoMu; EIL; InvP

Proper Sonnet, How Time Consumeth All Earthly Things, A. *At. to* Thomas Proctor. FaBoRV; OBSC

Proper Study of Mankind, The. Pope. *See* Essay on Man, An: Know then thyself, presume not God to scan.

Proper way to eat a fig, The. Figs. D. H. Lawrence. OAEL-2

Proper way to leave a room, The. Nonsense Quatrains. Gelett Burgess. CenHV

Properte of every shire, The. The Properties of the Shires of England. *Unknown.* FaBoPP; GBP

Properties of a Good Greyhound, The. Dame Juliana Berners. RB

Properties of Breath, The. Jean Hanff Korelitz. NPo

Properties of the Shires of England, The. *Unknown.* FaBoPP; GBP

Property. Jacob Glatstein, *tr. fr. Yiddish by* Benjamin *and* Barbara Harshav. AYP

Property Is Theft. Gerhard Rühm, *tr. fr. German by* Beth Bjorklund. CoAuP

Prophecia Merlini Doctoris Perfecti. *Unknown.* OxBLMV

Prophecy. Aimé Césaire, *tr. fr. French by* Clayton Eshleman *and* Annette Smith. RHTwFP

Prophecy. Eileen Duggan. PeNZ

Prophecy, A. Allen Ginsberg. TAP

Prophecy. Donald Hall. BAP

Prophecy, A. Arthur Lee. PAH

Prophecy, A. Christopher Levenson. ErPo

Prophecy, The. Richard Ntiru. UAS

Prophecy. Luigi Pulci, *tr. fr. Italian.* *Fr.* Morgante Maggiore, II. PAH

Prophecy. Tennyson. *See* Locksley Hall: For I Dipped [*or* Dipt] into the Future.

Prophecy, A. Maurice Thompson. *Fr.* Lincoln's Grave. AA

"Prophecy." Gulian Verplanck. PAH

Prophecy. Elinor Wylie. BLPL; BoWoP; FaBoWP; PrIm; VGW

Prophecy in Flame. Frances Minturn Howard. AmFN

Prophecy of Cuauhtémoc, *sel.* Ignacio Rodríguez Galván, *tr. fr. Spanish by* Samuel Beckett.
"Space is azure and the mountains bathe." MexPo

Prophecy of Famine, The, *sels.* Charles Churchill.
"Oft have I heard thee mourn the wretched lot." OBSV
On His Own Poetry. NOEC
"Two boys, whose birth beyond all question springs." OBSV

Prophecy of King Tammany, The. Philip Freneau. GOA

Prophecy of the Winds. Ahmad Faraz, *tr. fr. Urdu by* Mahmood Jamal. PBMUP

Prophecy on Lethe. Stanley Kunitz. PoA

Prophecy Sublime, The. Frederick Lucian Hosmer. *See* Thy Kingdom Come, O Lord.

Prophet, The. Abraham Cowley. JCP; TrGrPo

Prophet, The, *sels.* Kahlil Gibran.
Of Love. PoLF
"Then Almitra spoke, saying, We would ask now of Death." DL

Prophet, The. Mikhail Yurevich Lermontov, *tr. fr. Russian by* Alan Myers. AAA

Prophet, The. Pushkin, *tr. fr. Russian.* AAA, *tr. by* Alan Myers; AWP, *tr. by* Babette Deutsch *and* Avrahm Yarmolisky; EaLo, *tr. by* Babette Deutsch; WGRP, *tr. by* Babette Deutsch.

Prophet, The. "Yehoash," *tr. fr. Yiddish by* Isidore Goldstick. TrJP

Prophet Bird. Alfred Corn. BLA

Prophet digs with iron hands, The. Transfiguration. Djuna Barnes. EAS

Prophet Jeremiah and the Personification of Israel, The. *At. to* Eleazar Ben Kalir, *tr. fr. Hebrew by* Nina Davis Salaman. TrJP

Prophet of the body's roving. Walt Whitman. Edwin Honig. TAP

Prophet, scourged by his own hand, progressed, The. John the Baptist. Louis Simpson. NePoEA

Prophet speaks, The. Saint Malcolm. Jewel C. Latimore. BPo

Prophetess, The. Dorothy Livesay. MoCV

Prophetess. Whittier. *Fr.* Snow-bound; a Winter Idyl. AA

Prophets, The. Richard Shelton. NYBP

Prophets at street corners, in neat grey suits. Saturday Night. Antigone Kefala. CBAP

Prophets for a New Day. Margaret Abigail Walker. BPo

Prophet's Warning or Shoot to Kill, The. Ebon Dooley. PoBA

Proportion. Amy Lowell. BoWoP

Proportion Poetry. Majken Johansson, *tr. fr. Swedish by* Joanna Bankier. OV

Proportions. Arto Melleri, *tr. fr. Finnish by* Aili Jarvenpa. SOP

Proportions. Joseph Stroud. NPGG

Proposition, The. Paul Blackburn. ErPo

Proposition. Nicolás Guillén, *tr. fr. Spanish by* Langston Hughes. FaPON; TTY

Proposition, The. Bill Manhire. ATNZ

Proposition. Robert Pinsky. *Fr.* Essay on Psychiatrists, III. HCAP; NoAM

Proposition II. Keith Waldrop. InPK

Propositions. Phyllis Webb. MoCV

Propped boughs are heavy with apples. In the Huon Valley. James McAuley. CBAP

Propped on a stick he viewed the August weald. The One-legged Man. Siegfried Sassoon. CMoP

Prorogued on prorogation—damned rogues and whores! On the Prorogation. *Unknown.* APAS

Prosaic miles of streets stretch all round. Seder-Night. Israel Zangwill. TrJP

Prose. Bernard Welt. EOEF

Prose behind the Insanity. Andreas Okopenko, *tr. fr. German by* Beth Bjorklund. CoAuP

Prose for Des Esseintes. Donald Davie, *after the French of* Stéphane Mallarmé. OBVE

Prose Poem. Humphrey Jennings. EAS

Proserpina. Thomas Campion. *See* Hark, All You Ladies.

Proserpina. Swinburne. *Fr.* The Garden of Proserpine. ChTr

Proserpine at Enna. Ronald Bottrall. SeCePo

Proserpine may pull her flowers. Song of the Stygian Naiades. Thomas Lovell Beddoes. EnRP; OAEL-2

Prospect Beach. Lou Lipsitz. VGW

Prospect of a Mountain. Andrew Young. PoSH

Prospect of Eden, The. Milton. *See* Paradise Lost: O for that warning voice, which he who saw.

Prospect of Heaven [Makes Death Easy], A. Isaac Watts. *See* There is a land of pure delight.

Prospect of the Future, The. Mrs. Henry Linden. CBWP-4

Prospect of the Future Glory of America. John Trumbull. AmPP

Prospect of the Wilds. Ch'en San-li, *tr. fr. Chinese by* Irving Lo. WFTU

Prospecting Dream. *Unknown.* AmFP

Prospective Immigrants Please Note. Adrienne Rich. AiP; GOA; VGW

Prospectus. Wordsworth. *Fr.* The Excursion. EnRP; NoP; OAEL-2

Prospectus [*incl. in* The Excursion]. Wordsworth. *See* Recluse, The: On Man, on Nature, and on Human Life.

Prosperity. Diane Ward. LP

Prosperity and decline have no fixed dwelling. T'ao Ch'ien, *tr. fr. Chinese by* Burton Watson. *Fr.* Drinking Wine, I. CoBCP

Prospero. Shakespeare. *Fr.* The Tempest, IV, i. FiP
Prospero Dreams of Arnaud Daniel Inventing Love in the Twelfth Century. Jack Gilbert. NPGG
Prospero on the Mountain Gathering Wood. Jack Gilbert. NPGG
Prospero without His Magic. Jack Gilbert. NPGG
Prosperous Villager, The. Li K'ai-hsien, *tr. fr. Chinese by* Jonathan Chaves. CoBLCP
Prospice. Robert Browning. BLPL; DL; FaBV; FiP; LiTB; NAEL-2; OBD; PoLF; PoRA; TrCP; TrGrPo; WGRP
Prosser. Raymond Carver. GeTw
Prostate Operation. Robert Pinsky. *Fr.* Three on Luck. AnAn
Prostitute, too, The. *Unknown, tr. by* Geoffrey Bownas *and* Anthony Thwaite. PeBJV
Prostration. David Semah, *tr. fr. Arabic by* Yoffee Berkovitz. VWA
Protagonist, The. Peter Hopegood. PoAu-2
Protea. Don Mattera. WMBCH
Protected by thick brick walls. International Ski-Flying Championship, Obersdorf. Elisavietta Ritchie. ASP
Protecting each other, right in the center. Burning a Book. William Stafford. BLA
Protection of Jehovah, The. Bible, *O.T. See* Psalms: Psalm XXIII ("The Lord is my shepherd.").
Protection of Plants, The. Erasmus Darwin. *Fr.* The Economy of Vegetation. FaBoUs
Protective Grigri, The. Ted Joans. PoBA
Protégés will come. The True Protocol of Poets. Kapilar, *tr. by* A. K. Ramanujan. PLW
Protest. Countee Cullen. CDC
Protest, A. Sir Thomas Wyatt. OBSC; SiPS
Protest from a Bushman (Masarwa), A. Albert G. T. K. Malikongwa. WMBCH
Protest in the Sixth Year of Ch'ien Fu, A. Ts'ao Sung, *tr. fr. Chinese by* Arthur Waley. FaBV
Protest of the Illiterate, The, *sel.* Gelett Burgess.
"I seen a dunce of a poet once, a-writin' a little book." FiBHP
Prothalamion, *sel.* Robert Hillyer.
"Hills turn hugely in their sleep, The." MoAmPo
Prothalamion. Maxine W. Kumin. NYBP; TSL
Prothalamion. Michael Ryan. AmPA
Prothalamion. Delmore Schwartz. OxBA
Prothalamion, *sels.* Spenser. AAS; AWP; ChTr; EBEV; EiL; FaBoPP; GoTL; GTBS; GTBS-P; HAP; LiTB; NIP; NoP; OBEV; OBSC; PPP; SeCePo
"Calm was the day, and through the trembling air." Mes
"With that I saw two swans of goodly hue." PBBP
Prothalamium. Donagh MacDonagh. BIrV; NeIP
Prothalamium. A. J. M. Smith. CaP
Protocols. Randall Jarrell. LCAP; OxBC; VGW
Proud and beaten we've passed the night. Our Dreams. Amir Gilboa, *tr. by* Warren Bargad *and* Stanley F. Chyet. IP
Proud and rest-ive Chim-pan-zee, The. Having a Wonderful Time. D. B. Wyndham Lewis. FiBHP
Proud as Apollo on his forked hill. Bufo. Pope. *Fr.* Epistle to Dr. Arbuthnot. OBSV
Proud Egyptian [*or* Aegyptian] queen, her Roman guest, The. And She Washed His Feet with Her Tear[e]s, and Wiped Them with the Hairs of Her Head. Sir Edward Sherburne, *after the Italian of* Giambattista Marina. ChTr; MeLP; OBS
(Magdalen, The.) ACP
(Proud Egyptian Queen, The.) OxBSP
Proud fountains, wave your plumes. Fountains. Sir Osbert Sitwell. MoBrPo
Proud freedom's noble inspiration. N. M. Yazykov, *tr. by* Alan Myers. AAA
Proud in Thy Love. *Unknown. Fr.* Zepheria, XIII. Son
Proud inclination of the flesh. Dilys Bennett Laing. ErPo
Proud King, The. Jacob Glatstein, *tr. fr. Yiddish by* Benjamin *and* Barbara Harshav. AYP
Proud Lady Margaret. (" 'T was on a night, an evening bright"). *Unknown.* ESPB
Proud Lady Margaret. *Unknown. See* Fair Margret was a young ladye.
Proud, languid lily of the sacred Nile. The Egyptian Lotus. Arthur Wentworth Hamilton Eaton. AA
Proud Little Spruce Fir. Jeannie Kirby. BoTP
Proud Maisie ("Proud Maisie is in the wood"). Sir Walter Scott. *Fr.* The Heart of Midlothian, *ch.* 38. CH; ChTr; EnRP; FaBoCh; FF; GoTS; Mes; NAEL-2; OAEL-2; OBEV; OxBS; PBBP; PoEL-4; SeCePo; TEP; TrGrPo; UnPo
(Madge Wildfire Sings.) OBNC
(Madge Wildfire's Death Song.) HAP
(Madge Wildfire's Song.) NOBE
(Pride of Youth, The.) GTBS; GTBS-P
Proud, majestic Southern sun, The. The Husband's Return. Priscilla Jane Thompson. CBWP-2
Proud Margret. *Unknown.* OxBB
Proud of my music, let me often make. Stéphane Mallarmé, *tr. fr. French by* Aldous Huxley. *Fr.* Après-midi d'un Faune, L'. ErPo
Proud of my pride. A Tale Told by a Head. Lois Moyles. NYBP
Proud Preston, poor people. Preston. *Unknown.* GBP
Proud Songsters. Thomas Hardy. MoP
Proud who never loved, The. Sublimation. Alex Comfort. ErPo
Proud with success, richly pleased. Alexander Jannai. Constantine P. Cavafy, *tr. by* Simon Chasen. TrJP
Proud word you never spoke, but you will speak. Walter Savage Landor. *Fr.* Ianthe. EnLoPo; GBL; OBEV
Proudest now is but my peer, The. The Poor Voter on Election Day. Whittier. OPP
Proudful and barefoot I stride the street. For a Man Who Walked Sideways. Martin Carter. PBCV
Proudly looking at the ruins of the conquered city. To the Germans. Antoni Slonimski, *tr. by* Czeslaw Milosz. PwPP
Proust on Noah. Eisig Silberschlag. VWA
Proust's Madeleine. Kenneth Rexroth. NoAM
Proverb. *Unknown.* FaBoBe; OxNR
Proverb reporteth, no man can deny, The. *Unknown. Fr.* Tom Tyler and His Wife. EIL
Proverbial Advice on Marriage. *Unknown. See* Who weds a sot to get his cot.
Proverbial Philosophy: Of Reading. Charles Stuart Calverley. FaBoCo
Proverbios Morales, *sel.* Santob de Carrion.
Friend, A. TrJP
Proverbs, *sels.* Bible, *O.T.*
Drunkard, The. *Fr.* XXIII: 29-35. TrJP
Fear of the Lord, The. *Fr.* I: 7. TrJP
Foolish Woman, A. *Fr.* IX: 13-18. TrGrPo
Go to the Ant [Thou Sluggard]. *Fr.* VI: 6-11. FaPON; TrJP
(Reproof, A.) TrGrPo
Happy Is the Man. *Fr.* III: 13-18. TrJP
Hay Appeareth, The. *Fr.* XXVII: 25. FaPON
He That Is Slow to Anger. *Fr.* XVI: 32. FaPON
House of Wisdom, The. *Fr.* IX: 1-6. TrGrPo
Legacy, The. *Fr.* IV: 13. TrJP
Lips of the Wise, The. *Fr.* XV: 1-5, 7-8, 15-17. TrGrPo
Neither Poverty nor Riches. *Fr.* XXX: 7-9. TrJP
Seven Evils. *Fr.* VI: 16-19. TrGrPo
She of the Impudent Face. *Fr.* VII: 6-27. TrJP
"Who can find a virtuous woman? for her price is far above rubies." *Fr.* XXXI: 10-31. SaC
(Good Wife, The.) TrGrPo
(Virtuous Woman, The.) TrJP
Word Fitly Spoken, A. *Fr.* XXV: 11. FaPON
Words of Agur, The. *Fr.* XXX: 4, 15-16, 18-19, 24-28.
Four Things. *Fr. ll.* 24-28.
Too Wonderful. *Fr. ll.* 18-19.TrJP
Proverbs. Samuel Ha-Nagid, *tr. fr. Hebrew by* Israel Abrahams. TrJP
Proverbs. Donald Hall. SoTCo
Proverbs of Alfred, The, *sels. At. to* Alfred, King of England. PoE
"Thus queth Alvred:/ 'Idelschipe and overprute, that lereth yong wif üvel thewes.'" *Fr.* XVI.
"Thus queth Alvred:/ 'If thu havest seorewe, ne seyethu hit than arewe.'" *Fr.* XIII.
"Thus queth Alvred:/ 'Ne schaltu nevere thi wif by hire wlyte cheose.'" *Fr.* XIV.
"Thus queth Alvred:/ 'Ne würth thu never so wod ne so wyn-drunke.'" *Fr.* XV.
"Thus queth Alvred:/ 'Nevre thu, bi thine lyve, the word of thine wyve.'" *Fr.* XVII.
Proverbs of Hell. Blake. *See* Marriage of Heaven and Hell, The: In seed time learn, in harvest teach, in winter enjoy.
Provide, Provide. Robert Frost. AmPP; CMoP; HAP; MoAB; MoP; NAAL-2; NIP; NoAM; NOBA; NoP; OPOP; PoE; PPP; TAP; TwCP; UnPo; WeW
Providence. Reginald Heber. GN; OHIP
Providence. David St. John. NAmP
Providential. Sándor Weöres, *tr. fr. Hungarian by* Jascha Kessler. FOC
Province has set up shrines, The. Parihaka. W. H. Oliver. PeNZ
Province I govern is humble and remote, The. To Li Chien. Po Chü-i, *tr. by* Arthur Waley. AWP
Province of Sanuki, renowned for lovely seaweed, The. Hitomaro. *Fr.* Manyo Shu. FCEI

Provincetown, *sels.* Louis Dudek. MoCV
  Avant Garde.
  Fishing Village.
  News.
  Ocean, The.
Provincetown, Mass. Harvey Shapiro. PoA
Provincia. Francisco Carrillo, *tr. fr. Spanish by* Maureen Ahern *and* David Tipton. Per
Provincia Deserta. Ezra Pound. OxBA
Proving. Georgia Douglas Johnson. CDC
Provisions. Margaret Atwood. IHMS
Prowling the Ridge. Judith Minty. GeTw
Prowling wolf, whose shaggy skin, A. The Wolf and the Dog. La Fontaine, *tr. by* Elizur Wright. OBVE
Prows o' Reekie, The. Lewis Spence. OxBS
Prudence. Emerson. OBAL
Prudent Simplicity. William Cowper. FaBoEE
Prue, my dearest maid, is sick. Upon Prudence Baldwin Her Sickness. Robert Herrick. JCP; SeCV-1
Pruned Tree, The. Howard Moss. NYBP
Pruners: Conca di Marini ("Pruners have come again among the vineyards"). Joseph Langland. NePoEA
Pruning. John Philips. *Fr.* Cyder. FaBoUs
Psalm CXXXVII: "As by the streams of Babylon." Bible, *O.T. See* Psalms: Psalm CXXXVII ("By the rivers of Babylon. . .").
Psalm XLII: "As the hart panteth after the water brooks." Bible, *O.T. Fr.* Psalms. AWP; TrJP
  (My Soul Thirsteth for God.) TrGrPo
  (Search, The, XLII *and* XLIII *Moulton, Modern Reader's Bible*) WGRP
Psalm: "Be silent with me, as all bells are silent!" Ingeborg Bachmann, *tr. by* Beth Bjorklund. CoAuP
Psalm CXXXIII: "Behold, how good and how pleasant. . ." Bible, *O.T. Fr.* Psalms. AWP
  (Psalm CXXXIII: "Beholde, how good and joyfull a thing it is.") OBVE, *tr. by* Miles Coverdale.
  (To Dwell Together in Unity.) TrJP
Psalm CXXXIII: "Beholde, how good and joyfull a thing it is." Bible, *O.T. See* Psalms: Psalm CXXXIII ("Behold, how good and how pleasant. . .").
Psalm CIII: "Bless the Lord, O my soul. . ." Bible, *O.T. Fr.* Psalms. AWP
  ("O Thou my soule, Jehovah blesse," *Bay Psalm Book*.) SCAP
  ("Praise, my soul, the King of heaven.")
  (Psalm CIII: "Praise the Lord, O my soul," *paraphrased by* Henry Francis Lyte) NOCV
Psalm CIV: "Bless the Lord, O my soul. . ." Bible, *O.T. Fr.* Psalms. NAWM-1; OHIP, *abr.;* TrJP
  (Hymn of the World Without, *Moulton Modern Reader's Bible*.) WGRP
  "So is this great and wide sea." *Fr.* 25-28. MOS
Psalm I: "Blessed is the man. . ." Bible, *O.T. Fr.* Psalms. AWP
  (Happy Is the Man.) TrJP
  ("O blessed man, that in th' advice," *Bay Psalm Book*) SCAP
  (Tree and the Chaff, The.) WGRP
Psalm CXXXVII: "By the rivers of Babel we sate." Bible, *O.T. See* Psalms: Psalm CXXXVII ("By the rivers of Babylon. . .").
Psalm CXXXVII: "By the rivers of Babylon. . ." Bible, *O.T. Fr.* Psalms. AWP; NAWM-1; OAEL-1; TrJP
  (Psalm CXXXVII: "As by the streams of Babylon," *paraphrased by* Thomas Campion.) OAEL-1
  (Psalm CXXXVII: "By the rivers of Babel we sate," *The Geneva Bible*.) OAEL-1
  (Psalm CXXXVII: "By the waters of Babylon we sat downe and weapte.") OBVE, *tr. by* Miles Coverdale.
  (Psalm CXXXVII: "Nigh seated where the river flows," *paraphrased by* the Countess of Pembroke.) OAEL-1
  (Psalm CXXXVII: "On the floodis of Babiloyne there we saten," *Second Wycliffite Version*.) OAEL-1
  (Psalm CXXXVII: "On the proud banks of great Euphrates' flood," *paraphrased by* Richard Crashaw.) OAEL-1
  (Psalm CXXXVII: "Sitting by the streams that glide," *paraphrased by* Thomas Carew.) OAEL-1
  (Psalm CXXXVII: "Upon the rivers of Babylon, there we sat and wept," *The Douay-Rheims Version*.) OAEL-1
  (Psalm CXXXVII: "When as we sat all sad and desolate," *paraphrased by* Francis Bacon.) OAEL-1
  (Psalm CXXXVII: "When on Euphrates' banks we sate," *paraphrased by* Sir John Denham.) OAEL-1
  (Psalm CXXXVII: "When we, our weary limbs to rest," *paraphrased by* Nahum Tate *and* Nicholas Brady.) OAEL-1

(Psalm CXXXVII: "Whenas we sat in Babylon," *paraphrased by* Thomas Sternhold *and* John Hopkins.) OAEL-1
(Psalme CXXXVII: "As on Euphrates shady banks we lay," *paraphrased by* George Sandys.) OBS
Song of Exile, A., TrGrPo 1-6.
Psalm CXXXVII: "By the waters of Babylon we sat downe and weapte." Bible, *O.T. See* Psalms: Psalm CXXXVII ("By the rivers of Babylon. . .").
Psalm CXXXIX. Countess of Pembroke. NOCV; OBSC; WPE
Psalm 3: "Day my poems, The." Mahmoud Darwish, *tr. by* Abdullah al-Udhari. MPAW
Psalm CIV: Deo Opt. Max. George Sandys. *Fr.* Paraphrase on the Psalms of David. OBS
Psalm LVIII: "Do ye indeed speak righteousness. . ." Bible, *O.T. Fr.* Psalms.
  (Psalm LVIII: "Do ye indeed speak righteousness, O congregation?" *paraphrased by* the Countess of Pembroke.) NOCV
  (Psalm LVIII: Si Vere Utique: "And call ye this to utter what is just," *paraphrased by* the Countess of Pembroke.) BoWoP; NAEL-1; WPE
Psalm LVIII: "Do ye indeed speak righteousness, O congregation?" Bible, *O.T. See* Psalms: Psalm LVIII ("Do ye indeed speak righteousness. . .").
Psalm CXXXIX: Domine, Probasti. Bible, *O.T. See* Psalms: Psalm CXXXIX ("O Lord, thou hast searched me. . .").
Psalm XXIV: "The Earth is the Lord's. . ." Bible, *O.T. Fr.* Psalms. AWP; EaLo; FaPON, (1-4); TrJP
  (Lift Up Your Heads.) TrGrPo
Psalm LV: Exaudi, Deus: "My God most glad to look, most prone to hear." Bible, *O.T. See* Psalms: Psalm LV ("Give ear to my prayer. . .").
Psalm CXXVII: "Except the Lord build the house. . ." Bible, *O.T. Fr.* Psalms. TrJP
Psalm: "Father/ You are the trunk." Howard Schwartz. VWA
  (Psalm CXXX: "Ffrom depth off sinn and from a diepe dispaire," *paraphrased by* Sir Thomas Wyatt) OBVE
Psalm CXXX: "Ffrom depth off sinn and from a diepe dispaire." Bible, *O.T. See* Psalms: Psalm CXXX ("Out of the depths. . .").
Psalm XIV: "Fool hath said in his heart . . ., The." Bible, *O.T. Fr.* Psalms. TrJP
Psalm CXIV: Fountain from Wilderness Stone, A. Bible, *O. T.* CRP
Psalm XXXVII: "Fret not thyself. . ." Bible, *O.T. Fr.* Psalms.
  (Trust in the Lord, 1-7 *paraphrased by* Charles Frederic Sheldon) BLRP
Psalm LXXVIII "Give ear, O my people, to my law. . ." Bible, *O.T. Fr.* Psalms.
  (Psalm LXXVIII: "There where the deepe did show his sandy flore," *paraphrased by* the Countess of Pembroke.) OBVE
Psalm LV: "Give ear to my prayer. . ." Bible, *O.T. Fr.* Psalms. AWP
  (Psalm LV: Exaudi, Deus: "My God most glad to look, most prone to hear," *paraphrased by* the Countess of Pembroke.) OBVE, (1-4); WPE
  Wings. FaPON, 6-7.
Psalm LXXII: "Give the king thy judgments. . ." Bible, *O.T. Fr.* Psalms.
  (Psalm LXXII: "Looke how the woods, where enterlaced trees", *paraphrased by* the Countess of Pembroke.) OBVE
Psalm XXIX: "Give unto the Lord. . ." Bible, *O.T. Fr.* Psalms. AWP
Psalm LXVII: "God be merciful unto us. . ." Bible, *O.T. Fr.* Psalms.
  (Let the Nations Be Glad.) FaPON
Psalm XLVI: "God is our refuge and strength. . ." Bible, *O.T. Fr.* Psalms. AWP
  (Though the Earth Be Removed.) TrGrPo
Psalm CXLVIII: "Hallelujah! kneel and sing." Bible, *O.T. See* Psalms: Psalm CXLVIII ("Praise ye the Lord. . .").
Psalm CXLVI: "Hallelujah./ Praise the Lord, O my soul." Bible, *O.T. Fr.* Psalms. TrJP
Psalm: "Happy is the man whom Thou hast set apart." "Yehoash," *tr. by* Isidore Goldstick. TrJP
Psalm XCI: "He that dwelleth. . ." Bible, *O.T. Fr.* Psalms. AWP
  (Everlasting Arms, The, *Moulton, Modern Reader's Bible*.) WGRP
  (Mighty Fortress, A.) TrGrPo
Psalm XVII: "Hear the right O Lord. . ." Bible, *O.T. Fr.* Psalms.
  (Psalm XVII: "My suite is just, just lord to my suite hark," *paraphrased by* Sir Philip Sidney.) OBVE
Psalm XIX: "Heavenly frame sets forth the fame, The." Bible, *O.T. See* Psalms: Psalm XIX ("The heavens declare the glory of God").

Psalm XIX: "Heavens declare the glory of God, The." Bible, *O.T.* *Fr.* Psalms. AWP; FaPON, 1-4; NAWM-1; OBVE, *tr. by* Miles Coverdale; WBLP

    God's Precepts Perfect. *Fr.* 7-9.BLRP

    (Glory of God, The.) TrJP

    (God's Glory.) TrGrPo

    (Heavens, The, 1-6.) ChTr

    (Heavens Above and the Law Within, The, *Moulton, Modern Reader's Bible.*) WGRP

    ("Heavens doe declare, The," *Bay Psalm Book)* SCAP

    (Psalm XIX: "Heavenly frame sets forth the fame, The", *paraphrased by* Sir Philip Sidney) OBVE

    (Psalm XIX: "Spacious firmament on high, The.") WGRP

Psalm 19: "Heavens doe declare/ The majesty of God, The." *Unknown.* *Fr.* The Bay Psalm Book. SCAP

Psalm LXXXIV: "How amiable are thy tabernacles. . ." Bible, *O.T.* *Fr.* Psalms. FaPON; TrJP

    (Psalm LXXXIV: "How lovely are thy dwellings fair!", *paraphrased by* Milton.) TrPWD

    Sparrow, The. *Fr.* 3.FaPON

How Lovely Are Thy Tabernacles. *Fr.* 1-5. TrJP

Psalm XIII: "How long, O Lord, shall I forgotten be?" Bible, *O.T.* *See* Psalms: Psalm XIII ("How long wilt thou forget me O Lord. . .").

Psalm XIII: "How long wilt thou forget me O Lord. . ." Bible, *O.T.* *Fr.* Psalms.

    (Psalm XIII: "How long, O Lord, shall I forgotten be?", *paraphrased by* Sir Philip Sidney) OBVE

Psalm LXXXIV: "How lovely are thy dwellings fair!" Bible, *O.T.* *See* Psalms: Psalm LXXXIV ("How amiable are thy tabernacles. . .").

Psalm LXXVII: "I cried unto God with my voice. . ." Bible, *O.T.* *Fr.* Psalms. AWP

"Waters saw thee, O God, The." *Fr.* 16-19. MOS

Psalm XXXIX: "I said: 'I will take heed to my ways.' " Bible, *O.T.* *Fr.* Psalms.

    (Lord, Make Me to Know Mine End.) TrJP

Psalm 121: 'I to the hills lift up mine eyes." *Unknown.* *Fr.* The Bay Psalm Book. OBCA

Psalm CXXI: "I will lift up mine eyes unto the hills." Bible, *O.T.* *Fr.* Psalms. AWP; FaPON

    ("I to the hills lift up mine eyes," *Bay Psalm Book.*) OBCA

    (Pilgrim's Song, The, *Moulton, Modern Reader's Bible.*) WGRP

    (Song of Trust, A.) TrGrPo

Psalm IX: "I will praise thee, O Lord. . ." Bible, *O.T.* *Fr.* Psalms.

    (I Will Sing Praise.) FaPON

Psalm XI: "In the Lord put I my trust. . ." Bible, *O.T.* *Fr.* Psalms.

    (Psalm XI: "Since I do trust Jehova still," *paraphrased by* Sir Philip Sidney.) OBVE

Psalm: "In the small beauty of the forest." George Oppen. NNaP

Psalm XCII: "Jehovah's Immovable Throne." Bible, *O.T.* *Fr.* Psalms. WGRP

Psalm XLIII: "Judge me, O God. . ." Bible, *O.T.* *Fr.* Psalms.

    (Search, The, XLII *and* XLIII *Moulton, Modern Reader's Bible.*) WGRP

Psalm LXXII: "Looke how the woods, where enterlaced trees." Bible, *O.T.* *See* Psalms: Psalm LXXII ("Give the king thy judgments. . .").

Psalm CII: "Lord here my prayre and let my crye passe." Bible, *O.T.* *Fr.* Psalms. OBVE

Psalm III: "Lord, how are they increased that trouble me!" Bible, *O.T.* *Fr.* Psalms.

    (Psalm III: "Lord how many are my foes," *paraphrased by* Milton.) OBVE

Psalm III: "Lord how many are my foes." Bible, *O.T.* *See* Psalms: Psalm III ("Lord, how are they increased that trouble me!").

Psalm XXVII: ("The Lord is my light. . ." Bible, *O.T.* *Fr.* Psalms.

    (Deliverance of Jehovah, The, *Moulton, Modern Reader's Bible.*) WGRP

    Serenity of Faith, The. *Fr.* 7-14. BLRP

Psalm XXIII: "Lord is my shepherd. . ., The." Bible, *O.T.* *Fr.* Psalms. AWP; BLPL; FaBoBe; FaPON; FPL; NAWM-1; NIP; OHIP; PoLF; TrGrPo; TrJP

    ("Lord to me a shepherd is, The," *Bay Psalm Book.*) OBCA

    (Lord's My Shepherd, The, *Scottish Psalter.*) AH, *with music;* WBLP, *ad. by* Francis Rous.

    (Protection of Jehovah, The, *Moulton, Modern Reader's Bible.*) WGRP

    (Psalm XXIII: "Lord my shepherd, me His sheep, The", *paraphrased by* George Sandys.) JCP

    (Psalm XXIII: "Lorde is my shepherde, The; therfore can I lack nothing.") OBVE, *tr. by* Miles Coverdale.

Psalm XXIII: "Lord my shepherd, me His sheep, The." Bible, *O.T.* *See* Psalms: Psalm XXIII ("The Lord is my shepherd. . .").

Psalm XXIII: "Lord my shepherd, me His sheep, The." George Sandys. *Fr.* Paraphrase on the Psalms of David. JCP

Psalm XC: "Lord, thou hast been our dwelling place in all generations." Bible, *O.T.* *Fr.* Psalms.

    (Lord, Thou Hast Been Our Dwelling Place.) AWP; DL; EaLo

Psalm 23: "Lord to me a shepherd is, The." *Unknown.* *Fr.* The Bay Psalm Book. OBCA

Psalm XXIII: "Lorde is my shepherde, The; therfore can I lack nothing." Bible, *O.T.* *See* Psalms: Psalm XXIII ("The Lord is my shepherd. . .").

Psalm C: "Make a joyful noise. . ." Bible, *O.T.* *Fr.* Psalms. BLRP; OFD; OHIP

    (Be Thankful unto Him.) FaPON

    ("Enter into His gates with thanksgiving.")

    (Giving Thanks, 4.) BLRP

    (Old Hundredth, *metrical vers. by* William Kethe.) FaPoR; NOCV

    (Scotch Te Deum.) WGRP

Psalm XXII: "My God, my God. . ." Bible, *O.T.* *Fr.* Psalms.

    (Cry in Distress, A, 1-15) TrGrPo

Psalm XVII: "My suite is just, just lord to my suite hark." Bible, *O.T.* *See* Psalms: Psalm XVII ("Hear the right O Lord. . .").

Psalm CXXXVII: "Nigh seated where the river flows." Bible, *O.T.* *See* Psalms: Psalm CXXXVII ("By the rivers of Babylon. . .").

Psalm: "No one kneads us again out of earth and clay." Paul Celan, *tr. by* Joachim Neugroschel. VWA

    ("No one moulds us again out of earth and clay.") CoAuP, *tr. by* Beth Bjorklund; OBVE, *tr. by* Michael Hamburger

Psalm CXV: "Not unto us, O Lord. . ." Bible, *O.T.* *Fr.* Psalms.

    (Psalm CXV: "Not unto us, O Lord, not unto us," *paraphrased by* the Countess of Pembroke.) NOCV

Psalm CXV: "Not unto us, O Lord, not unto us." Bible, *O.T.* *See* Psalms: Psalm CXV ("Not unto us, O Lord. . .").

Psalm 1: "O Blessed man, that in th'advice." *Unknown.* *Fr.* The Bay Psalm Book. SCAP

Psalm XCV: "O come let us sing unto the Lord." Bible, *O.T.* *Fr.* Psalms. AWP; BLRP, *abr.;* OHIP, *abr.*

Psalm CVII: "O give thanks. . ." Bible, *O.T.* *Fr.* Psalms.

    (O give yee thanks unto the Lord, *Bay Psalm Book.*) SCAP

    They That Go Down to the Sea. ChTr, 23-31; FaPON, 23-24; MOS, 23-30.

    (Ocean, The, *Moulton, Modern Reader's Bible.*) WGRP, (23-33).

Psalm CXVIII: "O give thanks unto the Lord. . ." Bible, *O.T.* *Fr.* Psalms. TrJP

Psalm CXXXVI: "O give thanks unto the Lord; for he is good." Bible, *O.T.* *Fr.* Psalms. AWP; OHIP, *abr.*

    ("Let us with a gladsome mind," *paraphrased by* Milton.) FL

Psalm 107: "O Give yee thanks unto the Lord." *Unknown.* *Fr.* The Bay Psalm Book. SCAP

Psalm, A: "O God, in whom my deepest being dwells." Edmund Blunden. TrPWD

Psalm LXXXIII: "O God, keep not Thou silence." Bible, *O.T.* *Fr.* Psalms.

    (Keep Not Thou Silence.) TrJP

Psalm LXXIX: "O God, the heathen are come into Thine inheritance." Bible, *O.T.* *Fr.* Psalms.

    (Heathen Are Come into Thine Inheritance, The.) TrJP

Psalm LXXIV: "O God, why hast thou cast us off. . ." Bible, *O.T.* *Fr.* Psalms.

    (Psalm LXXIV: "O God, why hast thou cast us off for ever?", *paraphrased by* the Countess of Pembroke.) NOCV

Psalm LXXIV: "O God, why hast thou cast us off for ever?" Bible, *O.T.* *See* Psalms: Psalm LXXIV ("O God, why hast thou cast us off. . .").

Psalm VI: "O lord, I dred, and that I did not dred." Bible, *O.T.* *See* Psalms: Psalm VI ("O Lord rebuke me not in thine anger. . .").

Psalm CXXXIX: "O Lord, in me there lieth nought." Bible, *O.T.* *See* Psalms: Psalm CXXXIX ("O Lord, thou hast searched me. . .").

Psalm VIII: "O Lord our Lord, how excellent is thy name. . ." Bible, *O.T.* *Fr.* Psalms. AWP; NAWM-1

    (How Glorious Is Thy Name.) TrJP

    (Psalm VIII: "O Lord, that rul'st the human heart", *paraphrased by* Christopher Smart) OBVE

    (Psalm VIII: "O Lorde oure governoure, howe excellent is thy name.") OBVE, *tr. by* Miles Coverdale.

    (What Is Man?.) TrGrPo

"Lord what is man, that he should find." *Fr.* 4-6 *paraphrased by* Christopher Smart.

When I Consider Thy Heavens. FaPON, 3-5; ImOP, 3-8.

Psalm VI: "O Lord rebuke me not in thine anger. . ." Bible, *O.T.* *Fr.*
Psalms.
(Psalm VI: "O lord, I dred, and that I did not dred".) OBVE, *freely*
ad. by Sir Thomas Wyatt.
Psalm VIII: "O Lord, that rul'st the human heart." Bible, *O.T.* *See*
Psalms: Psalm VIII ("O Lord our Lord, how excellent is thy
name. . .").
Psalm CXXXIX: "O Lord, thou hast searched me. . ." Bible, *O.T.* *Fr.*
Psalms.
(Psalm CXXXIX: Domine, Probasti.) WPE
(Psalm CXXXIX: "O Lord, in me there lieth nought," *paraphrased by*
the Countess of Pembroke.) NOCV; OBSC, 1-6; OBVE, 7-10.
Psalm VIII: "O Lorde oure governoure, howe excellent is thy name."
Bible, *O.T.* *See* Psalms: Psalm VIII ("O Lord our Lord, how
excellent is thy name. . .").
Psalm CL: "O praise God in his holiness. . ." Bible, *O.T.* *Fr.* Psalms.
(Laudate Dominum.) ChTr
Psalm XCVIII: "O sing unto the Lord. . ." Bible, *O.T.* *Fr.* Psalms.
TrJP
(Floods Clap Their Hands, The.) TrGrPo
(O Sing unto the Lord a New Song.) EaLo
(Sing unto Jehovah.) BLRP
Psalm 103: "O Thou my soule, Jehovah blesse." *Unknown.* *Fr.* The Bay
Psalm Book. SCAP
Psalm: "Oh Lord, I have been staring into a mirror." Eugene Heimler, *tr.*
by Anthony Rudolf. VWA
Psalm: "Old ones to the side." Charles Simic. AmPA; LCAP
Psalm CXXXVII: "On the floodis of Babiloyne there we saten." Bible,
O.T. *See* Psalms: Psalm CXXXVII ("By the rivers of Babylon. . .").
Psalm CXXXVII: "On the proud banks of great Euphrates' flood." Bible,
O.T. *See* Psalms: Psalm CXXXVII ("By the rivers of Babylon. . .").
Psalm CXXX: "Out of the depths. . ." Bible, *O.T.* *Fr.* Psalms. TrJP
(De Profundis.) BLRP; WGRP
(Song of Supplication, A.) TrGrPo
Psalm CIII: "Praise the Lord, O my soul." Bible, *O.T.* *See* Psalms:
Psalm CIII ("Bless the Lord, O my soul. . .").
Psalm CXLVII: "Praise ye the Lord." Bible, *O.T.* *See* Psalms: Psalm
CXLVII ("Praise ye the Lord").
Psalm CXLVIII: "Praise ye the Lord. . ." Bible, *O.T.* *Fr.* Psalms.
TrJP
(Psalm CXLVIII: "Hallelujah! kneel and sing," *paraphrased by*
Christopher Smart.) OBVE, 1-10.
(Song of Praise, A.) TrGrPo
Psalm CXLVII: "Praise ye the Lord," *paraphrased by* Christopher Smart.
NOCV
Psalm CXLVII: "Praise ye the Lord," *paraphrased by* Countess of
Pembroke. NOCV
Psalm CXLVII: "Praise ye the Lord." Bible, *O.T.* *Fr.* Psalms.
("Hallelujah/ Praise ye the Lord. . .") TrJP
(Psalm CXLVII: "Praise ye the Lord," *paraphrased by* Christopher
Smart.) NOCV
(Psalm CXLVII: "Praise ye the Lord," *paraphrased by* the Countess of
Pembroke.) NOCV
(Psalm CXLVII ("Sing unto the Lord with thanksgiving").)
("Sing unto the Lord with thanksgiving.") OHIP
Who Maketh the Grass to Grow. FaPON, *greatly abr.*
Psalm LVIII: Si Vere Utique: "And call ye this to utter what is just."
Bible, *O.T.* *See* Psalms: Psalm LVIII ("Do ye indeed speak
righteousness. . .").
Psalm XI: "Since I do trust Jehova still." Bible, *O.T.* *See* Psalms: Psalm
XI ("In the Lord put I my trust. . .").
Psalm CXLVII: "Sing unto the Lord with thanksgiving." Bible, *O.T.*
See Psalms: Psalm CXLVII ("Praise ye the Lord").
Psalm CXXXVII: "Sitting by the streams that glide." Bible, *O.T.* *See*
Psalms: Psalm CXXXVII ("By the rivers of Babylon. . .").
Psalm XIX: "Spacious firmament on high, The." Bible, *O.T.* *See*
Psalms: Psalm XIX ("The heavens declare the glory of God").
Psalm: "There are a very few moments when you." Avraham Ben-
Yitzhak, *tr.* by A. C. Jacobs. VWA
Psalm LXXVIII: "There where the deepe did show his sandy flore."
Bible, *O.T.* *See* Psalms: Psalm LXXVIII ("Give ear, O my people,
to my law. . .").
Psalm LXV: "Thou visitest the earth. . ." Bible, *O.T.* *Fr.* Psalms.
OHIP, *abr.*
Psalm III: "To God: to illuminate all men. Beginning with Skid Road."
Allen Ginsberg. CAPP
Psalm LXII: "Truly my soul waiteth. . ." Bible, *O.T.* *Fr.* Psalms.
(Psalm LXII: "Yet shall my soule in silence still", *paraphrased by* the
Countess of Pembroke.) PBWP
Psalm LII: "Tyrant, why swel'st thou thus." Bible, *O.T.* *See* Psalms:
Psalm LII ("Why boastest thou thyself in mischief. . .").

Psalm VI: Upon the Heavenly Scarp. Abraham Moses Klein. *Fr.* The
Psalter of Avram Haktani. PoA
Psalm CXXXVII: "Upon the rivers of Babylon, there we sat and wept."
Bible, *O.T.* *See* Psalms: Psalm CXXXVII ("By the rivers of
Babylon. . .").
Psalm: "Whale, says Jonah, is the war and its black-outs, The." Jean-Paul
de Dadelsen, *tr.* by Anselm Hollo. RHTwFP
Psalm: "What shall become of us, O Sun." József Tornai, *tr.* by Jascha
Kessler. FOC
Psalm CXXXVII: "When as we sat all sad and desolate." Bible, *O.T.*
See Psalms: Psalm CXXXVII ("By the rivers of Babylon. . .").
Psalm CXIV: "When Israel went out of Egypt. . ." Bible, *O.T.* *Fr.*
Psalms.
(Psalm CXIV: "When Israel came from Egypt's coast", *paraphrased*
by Christopher Smart.) OBVE
(When Israel Came Forth out of Egypt.) TrJP
Psalm CXXXVII: "When on Euphrates' banks we sate." Bible, *O.T.* *See*
Psalms: Psalm CXXXVII ("By the rivers of Babylon. . .").
Psalm CXXVI: "When the Lord brought back. . ." Bible, *O.T.* *Fr.*
Psalms.
(Like unto Them That Dream.) TrJP
Psalm CXXXVII: "When we, our weary limbs to rest." Bible, *O.T.* *See*
Psalms: Psalm CXXXVII ("By the rivers of Babylon. . .").
Psalm CXXXVII: "Whenas we sat in Babylon." Bible, *O.T.* *See* Psalms:
Psalm CXXXVII ("By the rivers of Babylon. . .").
Psalm, The: "While Northward the hot sun was sinking o'er the trees."
Robert Bridges. LiTB
Psalm LII: "Why boastest thou thyself in mischief. . ." Bible, *O.T.* *Fr.*
Psalms.
(Psalm LII: "Tyrant, why swel'st thou thus", *paraphrased by* the
Countess of Pembroke.) OBVE
Psalm II: "Why do the Gentiles tumult." Bible, *O.T.* *See* Psalms: Psalm
II ("Why do the heathen rage. . .").
Psalm II: "Why do the heathen rage. . ." Bible, *O.T.* *Fr.* Psalms.
NAAL-1, *paraphrased by* Edward Taylor.
(Psalm II: "Why do the Gentiles tumult", *paraphrased by* Milton.)
OBVE
Psalm LXII: "Yet shall my soule in silence still." Bible, *O.T.* *See*
Psalms: Psalm LXII ("Truly my soul waiteth. . .").
Psalm and Lament. Donald Justice. DiPo
Psalm Concerning the Castle. Denise Levertov. TwCP; WPE
Psalm of Battle. *Unknown, tr. fr. Arabic by* E. Powys Mathers. *Fr.* The
Thousand and One Nights. AWP
Psalm of Christ, The, *sels.* Chad Walsh. TrCP
My God, My God, Look upon Me.
There Is None to Help.
Why Hast Thou Forsaken Me?.
Psalm of Life, A. Andrew Lang. CenHV
Psalm of Life, A, *sels.* Longfellow. AA; AnAmPo; FaBoBe; FPL;
NAAL-l; OBCA; OHFP; PoLF; PrIm; PWR; TAP; WBLP
Life. GN
Tell Me Not in Mournful Numbers, *with music.* AH
"Psalm of Life" for thee is o'er, The. Longfellow. Henrietta Cordelia
Ray. CBWP-3
Psalm of Marriage. Phoebe Cary. PWR
Psalm of Montreal, A. Samuel Butler. *See* Stowed away in a Montreal
lumber room.
Psalm of Onan for Harp, Flute and Tambourine, A. Alden Nowlan.
NeAC
Psalm of Praise, A, *sel.* Richard Baxter.
"Ye holy Angels bright." NOCV
Psalm of St. The Priapus. James Richard Broughton. ErPo
Psalm of the Early Buddhist Sisters, A. *Unknown.* WGRP
Psalm of the Jealous God. Henry Abramovitch. VWA
Psalm of the West, *sels.* Sidney Lanier. PAH
Land of the Wilful Gospel.
Lexington.
Story of Vinland, The.
Triumph, The.
Psalm of Those Who Go Forth before Daylight. Carl Sandburg.
MoShBr; OxBA
Psalm C. William Kethe. *See* All people that on earth do dwell.
Psalm Praising the Hair of Man's Body, A. Denise Levertov. CAPP
Psalm to My Beloved. Eunice Tietjens. ErPo
Psalm to the Creatures. Gwilym R. Jones, *tr. fr. Welsh by* Joseph P.
Clancy. OBWVE
Psalm to the Holy Spirit. A. M. Sullivan. TrPWD
Psalm to the Son, A. Marguerite Wilkinson. TrPWD
Psalm 23 to the Singer's Nectar, *sel.* Ali al-Sharqawi, *tr. fr. Arabic by*
Lena Jayyusi *and* Naomi Shihab Nye.
"I shall knock three times at the door." MAP

Psalme CXXXVII: "As on Euphrates shady banks we lay." George Sandys. *Fr.* Paraphrase on the Psalms of David. OBS

Psalme CXXXVII: "As on Euphrates shady banks we lay." Bible, *O.T.* *See* Psalms: Psalm CXXXVII ("By the rivers of Babylon. . .").

Psalmodist. Mani Leib, *tr. fr.* Yiddish. VWA, *tr.* by David G. Roskies *and* Hillel Schwartz

Psalms. Yankev-Yitskhok Segal, *tr. fr.* Yiddish by Grace Schulman. PeBMYV

Psalms, *sels.* Bible, *O.T.*

Psalm I ("Blessed is the man. . ."). AWP
  (Happy Is the Man.) TrJP
  ("O blessed man, that in th' advice," *Bay Psalm Book*.) SCAP
  (Tree and the Chaff, The.) WGRP

Psalm II ("Why do the heathen rage. . ."). NAAL-1, *paraphrased by* Edward Taylor.
  (Psalm II: "Why do the Gentiles tumult," *paraphrased by* Milton.) OBVE

Psalm III ("Lord, how are they increased that trouble me!").
  (Psalm III: "Lord how many are my foes," *paraphrased by* Milton.) OBVE

Psalm VI ("O Lord rebuke me not in thine anger. . .").
  (Psalm VI: "O lord, I dred, and that I did not dred", *freely ad. and expanded by* Sir Thomas Wyatt.) OBVE

Psalm VIII ("O Lord our Lord, how excellent is thy name. . ."). AWP; NAWM-1
  (How Glorious Is Thy Name.) TrJP
  (Psalm VIII: "O Lord, that rul'st the human heart," *paraphrased by* Christopher Smart.) OBVE
  (Psalm VIII: "O Lorde oure governoure, howe excellent is thy name," *tr.* by Miles Coverdale.) OBVE
  (What Is Man?) TrGrPo
  "Lord what is man, that he should find." *Fr.* 4-6, *paraphrased by* Christopher Smart.
  When I Consider Thy Heavens. FaPON, (3-5); ImOP, (3-8).

Psalm IX ("I will praise thee, O Lord. . .").
  (I Will Sing Praise.) FaPON

Psalm XI ("In the Lord put I my trust. . .").
  (Psalm XI: "Since I do trust Jehova still," *paraphrased by* Sir Philip Sidney.) OBVE

Psalm XIII ("How long wilt thou forget me O Lord. . .").
  (Psalm XIII: "How long, O Lord, shall I forgotten be?" *paraphrased by* Sir Philip Sidney.) OBVE

Psalm XIV ("The fool hath said in his heart. . ."). TrJP

Psalm XVII ("Hear the right O Lord. . .").
  (Psalm XVII: "My suite is just, just lord to my suite hark," *paraphrased by* Sir Philip Sidney.) OBVE

Psalm XIX ("The heavens declare the glory of God"). AWP; FaPON, 1-4; NAWM-1; OBVE, *tr.* by Miles Coverdale; WBLP
  God's Precepts Perfect. *Fr.* 7-9.BLRP
    (Glory of God, The.) TrJP
    (God's Glory.) TrGrPo
    (Heavens, The, 1-6) ChTr
    (Heavens Above and the Law Within, The, *Moulton, Modern Reader's Bible*.) WGRP
    ("Heavens doe declare, The," *Bay Psalm Book*.) SCAP
    (Psalm XIX: "Heavenly frame sets forth the fame, The", *paraphrased by* Sir Philip Sidney.) OBVE
    (Psalm XIX: "Spacious firmament on high, The.") WGRP

Psalm XXII ("My God, my God. . .").
  (Cry in Distress, A, 1-15) TrGrPo

Psalm XXIII ("The Lord is my shepherd. . ."). AWP; BLPL; FaBoBe; FaPON; FPL; NAWM-1; NIP; OHIP; PoLF; TrGrPo; TrJP
  ("Lord to me a shepherd is, The," *Bay Psalm Book*.) OBCA
  (Lord's My Shepherd, The, *Scottish Psalter*.) AH, *with music;* WBLP, *ad.* by Francis Rous.
  (Protection of Jehovah, The, *Moulton, Modern Reader's Bible*.) WGRP
  (Psalm XXIII: "Lord my shepherd, me His sheep, The," *paraphrased by* George Sandys.) JCP
  (Psalm XXIII: "Lorde is my shepherde, The; therfore can I lack nothing.") OBVE, *tr.* by Miles Coverdale.

Psalm XXIV ("The Earth is the Lord's. . ."). AWP; EaLo; FaPON, (1-4); TrJP
  (Lift Up Your Heads.) TrGrPo

Psalm XXVII ("The Lord is my light. . .").
  (Deliverance of Jehovah, The, *Moulton, Modern Reader's Bible*.) WGRP
  Serenity of Faith, The. *Fr.* 7-14. BLRP

Psalm XXIX ("Give unto the Lord. . ."). AWP

Psalm XXXVII ("Fret not thyself. . .").

(Trust in the Lord, 1-7, *paraphrased by* Charles Frederic Sheldon.) BLRP

Psalm XXXIX ("I said: 'I will take heed to my ways' ").
  (Lord, Make Me to Know Mine End.) TrJP

Psalm XLII ("As the hart panteth after the water brooks"). AWP; TrJP
  (My Soul Thirsteth for God.) TrGrPo
  (Search, The, XLII *and* XLIII *Moulton, Modern Reader's Bible*.) WGRP

Psalm XLIII ("Judge me, O God. . .").
  (Search, The, XLII *and* XLIII *Moulton, Modern Reader's Bible*.) WGRP

Psalm XLVI ("God is our refuge and strength. . ."). AWP
  (Though the Earth Be Removed.) TrGrPo

Psalm LII ("Why boastest thou thyself in mischief. . .").
  (Psalm LII: "Tyrant, why swel'st thou thus," *paraphrased by* the Countess of Pembroke.) OBVE

Psalm LV ("Give ear to my prayer. . ."). AWP
  (Psalm LV: Exaudi, Deus: "My God most glad to look, most prone to hear," *paraphrased by* the Countess of Pembroke.) OBVE, 1-4; WPE
  Wings. FaPON, 6-7.

Psalm LVIII ("Do ye indeed speak righteousness. . .").
  (Psalm LVIII: "Do ye indeed speak righteousness, O congregation?" *paraphrased by* the Countess of Pembroke.) NOCV
  (Psalm LVIII: Si Vere Utique: "And call ye this to utter what is just," *paraphrased by* the Countess of Pembroke.) BoWoP; NAEL-1; WPE

Psalm LXII ("Truly my soul waiteth. . .").
  (Psalm LXII: "Yet shall my soule in silence still," *paraphrased by* the Countess of Pembroke.) PBWP

Psalm LXV ("Thou visitest the earth. . ."). OHIP, *abr.*

Psalm LXVII ("God be merciful unto us. . .").
  (Let the Nations Be Glad.) FaPON

Psalm LXXII ("Give the king thy judgments. . .").
  (Psalm LXXII: "Looke how the woods, where enterlaced trees," *paraphrased by* the Countess of Pembroke.) OBVE

Psalm LXXIV ("O God, why hast thou cast us off. . .").
  (Psalm LXXIV: "O God, why hast thou cast us off for ever?" *paraphrased by* the Countess of Pembroke.) NOCV

Psalm LXXVII ("I cried unto God with my voice. . ."). AWP
  "Waters saw thee, O God, The." *Fr.* 16-19. MOS

Psalm LXXVIII ("Give ear, O my people, to my law. . .").
  (Psalm LXXVIII: "There where the deepe did show his sandy flore," *paraphrased by* the Countess of Pembroke.) OBVE

Psalm LXXIX ("O God, the heathen are come into Thine inheritance").
  (Heathen Are Come into Thine Inheritance, The.) TrJP

Psalm LXXXIII ("O God, keep not Thou silence").
  (Keep Not Thou Silence.) TrJP

Psalm LXXXIV ("How amiable are thy tabernacles. . ."). FaPON; TrJP
  (Psalm LXXXIV: "How lovely are thy dwellings fair!," *paraphrased by* Milton.) TrPWD
  Sparrow, The. *Fr.* 3. FaPON
  How Lovely Are Thy Tabernacles. *Fr.* 1-5. TrJP

Psalm XC ("Lord, thou hast been our dwelling place in all generations").
  (Lord, Thou Hast Been Our Dwelling Place.) AWP; DL; EaLo

Psalm XCI ("He that dwelleth. . ."). AWP
  (Everlasting Arms, The, *Moulton, Modern Reader's Bible*.) WGRP
  (Mighty Fortress, A.) TrGrPo

Psalm XCII: "Jehovah's Immovable Throne." WGRP

Psalm XCV ("O come let us sing unto the Lord"). AWP; BLRP, *abr.;* OHIP, *abr.*

Psalm XCVIII ("O sing unto the Lord. . ."). TrJP
  (Floods Clap Their Hands, The.) TrGrPo
  (O Sing unto the Lord a New Song.) EaLo
  (Sing unto Jehovah.) BLRP

Psalm C ("Make a joyful noise. . ."). BLRP; OFD; OHIP
  (Be Thankful unto Him.) FaPON
  ("Enter into His gates with thanksgiving.")
  (Giving Thanks, 4.) BLRP
  (Old Hundredth, *metrical vers.* by William Kethe.) FaPoR; NOCV
  (Scotch Te Deum.) WGRP

Psalm CII ("Lord here my prayre and let my crye passe"). OBVE

Psalm CIII ("Bless the Lord, O my soul. . ."). AWP
  ("O Thou my soule, Jehovah blesse," *Bay Psalm Book*.) SCAP
  ("Praise, my soul, the King of heaven.")
  (Psalm CIII: "Praise the Lord, O my soul," *paraphrased by* Henry Francis Lyte.) NOCV

Psalm CIV ("Bless the Lord, O my soul. . ."). NAWM-1; OHIP, *abr.;* TrJP

(Hymn of the World Without, *Moulton Modern Reader's Bible*.) WGRP

"So is this great and wide sea." *Fr. 25-28.* MOS

Psalm CVII ("O give thanks. . .").
(O give yee thanks unto the Lord, *Bay Psalm Book*.) SCAP
They That Go Down to the Sea. ChTr, 23-31; FaPON, 23-24; MOS, 23-30.
(Ocean, The, *Moulton, Modern Reader's Bible*.) WGRP, 23-33.

Psalm CXIV ("When Israel went out of Egypt. . .").
(Psalm CXIV: "When Israel came from Egypt's coast," *paraphrased by* Christopher Smart.) OBVE
(When Israel Came Forth out of Egypt.) TrJP

Psalm CXV ("Not unto us, O Lord. . .").
(Psalm CXV: "Not unto us, O Lord, not unto us," *paraphrased by* the Countess of Pembroke.) NOCV

Psalm CXVIII (" 'O give thanks unto the Lord. . .' "). TrJP

Psalm CXXI ("I will lift up mine eyes unto the hills"). AWP; FaPON
("I to the hills lift up mine eyes," *Bay Psalm Book*.) OBCA
(Pilgrim's Song, The, *Moulton, Modern Reader's Bible*.) WGRP
(Song of Trust, A.) TrGrPo

Psalm CXXVI ("When the Lord brought back. . .").
(Like unto Them That Dream.) TrJP

Psalm CXXVII ("Except the Lord build the house. . ."). TrJP

Psalm CXXX ("Out of the depths. . ."). TrJP
(De Profundis.) BLRP; WGRP
(Psalm CXXX: "Ffrom depth off sinn and from a diepe dispaire," *paraphrased by* Sir Thomas Wyatt.) OBVE
(Song of Supplication, A.) TrGrPo

Psalm CXXXIII ("Behold, how good and how pleasant. . ."). AWP
(Psalm CXXXIII: "Beholde, how good and joyfull a thinge it is.") OBVE, *tr. by* Miles Coverdale.
(To Dwell Together in Unity.) TrJP

Psalm CXXXVI ("O give thanks unto the Lord; for he is good"). AWP; OHIP, *abr.*
("Let us with a gladsome mind," *paraphrased by Milton*.) FL

Psalm CXXXVII ("By the rivers of Babylon. . ."). AWP; NAWM-1; OAEL-1; TrJP
(Psalm CXXXVII: "As by the streams of Babylon," *paraphrased by* Thomas Campion.) OAEL-1
(Psalm CXXXVII: "By the rivers of Babel we sate," *The Geneva Bible*.) OAEL-1
(Psalm CXXXVII: "By the waters of Babylon we sat downe and weapte.") OBVE, *tr. by* Miles Coverdale.
(Psalm CXXXVII: "Nigh seated where the river flows," *paraphrased by* the Countess of Pembroke.) OAEL-1
(Psalm CXXXVII: "On the floodis of Babiloyne there we saten," *Second Wycliffite Version*.) OAEL-1
(Psalm CXXXVII: "On the proud banks of great Euphrates' flood," *paraphrased by* Richard Crashaw.) OAEL-1
(Psalm CXXXVII: "Sitting by the streams that glide," *paraphrased by* Thomas Carew.) OAEL-1
(Psalm CXXXVII: "Upon the rivers of Babylon, there we sat and wept," *The Douay-Rheims Version*.) OAEL-1
(Psalm CXXXVII: "When as we sat all sad and desolate," *paraphrased by* Francis Bacon.) OAEL-1
(Psalm CXXXVII: "When on Euphrates' banks we sate," *paraphrased by* Sir John Denham.) OAEL-1
(Psalm CXXXVII: "When we, our weary limbs to rest," *paraphrased by* Nahum Tate *and* Nicholas Brady.) OAEL-1
(Psalm CXXXVII: "Whenas we sat in Babylon," *paraphrased by* Thomas Sternhold *and* John Hopkins.) OAEL-1
(Psalme CXXXVII: "As on Euphrates shady banks we lay," *paraphrased by* George Sandys.) OBS
Song of Exile, A. *Fr. 1-6.* TrGrPo

Psalm CXXXIX ("O Lord, thou hast searched me. . .").
(Psalm CXXXIX: Domine, Probasti.) WPE
(Psalm CXXXIX: "O Lord, in me there lieth nought," *paraphrased by* the Countess of Pembroke.) NOCV; OBSC, (1-6); OBVE, (7-10).

Psalm CXLVI ("Hallelujah./ Praise the Lord, O my soul"). TrJP

Psalm CXLVII ("Praise ye the Lord").
("Hallelujah/ Praise ye the Lord. . .") TrJP
(Psalm CXLVII: "Praise ye the Lord," *paraphrased by* Christopher Smart.) NOCV
(Psalm CXLVII: "Praise ye the Lord," *paraphrased by* the Countess of Pembroke.) NOCV
(Psalm CXLVII ("Sing unto the Lord with thanksgiving").)

("Sing unto the Lord with thanksgiving.") OHIP
Who Maketh the Grass to Grow. FaPON, *greatly abr.*

Psalm CXLVIII ("Praise ye the Lord. . ."). TrJP
(Psalm CXLVIII: "Hallelujah! kneel and sing," *paraphrased by* Christopher Smart.) OBVE, 1-10.
(Song of Praise, A.) TrGrPo

Psalm CL ("O praise God in his holiness. . .").
(Laudate Dominum.) ChTr

Psalms of Love. Peter Baum, *tr. fr. German by* Jethro Bithell. AWP

Psalter of Avram Haktani, The, *sel.* A. M. Klein.
Upon the Heavenly Scarp. PoA

Pshytik. Nahum Bomze, *tr. fr. Yiddish by* Gabriel Preil. VWA

PSI. Melvin B. Tolson. PoBA

"Psittachus Eois Imitatrix Ales ab Indis." Sacheverell Sitwell. MoBrPo

Psss, the beard is a bit too long. Faces. D. C. Berry. BXAP

Psst, psst. Kitty Cornered. Eve Merriam. CRH

Psyche to Cupid: Her Ditty. James Richard Broughton. ErPo

Psyche with the Candle. Archibald MacLeish. PCP

Psychedelic Firemen. David Henderson. NBP

Psyche's Dream. Ann Lauterbach. BAP; EOEF

Psychiatrist. Peter De Vries. OBAL

Psycho. Peter Olds. PeNZ

Psychoanalysis. Gavin Ewart. NYBP

Psychoanalysis, *sels.* Judah Leib Teller, *tr. fr. Yiddish by* Benjamin *and* Barbara Harshav. AYP
Jud' Süss Oppenheimer on His First Visit with Professor Sigmund Freud.
Jud' Süss Tells about Them and about Himself.
Letter to Sigmund Freud.
Sigmund Freud at the Age of Eighty-Two.
Three.
Wilhelm Stekel Gives Up Life.

Psychologists, psychiatrists. Basic. Ray Durem. PoNe

Psycholophon. Gelett Burgess. CenHV; NA

Psychonaut Sonnets: Jones, The. Albert Goldbarth. SM

Psychopathology of Everyday Life, The. William Matthews. AnAn

Ptarmigan, The. *Unknown*. RHPC

Ptarmigan cries across the corrie, The. Silver in the Wind. Ian Strachan. PoSH

Ptarmigan is strange, The. The Ptarmigan. *Unknown*. RHPC

Pterodactyl, The. Philip José Farmer. BWV

Pub. Julian Symons. LiTB; WaP

Puberty Rite Dance Song (Traditional). *Unknown, tr. fr. Apache Indian by* Willis Barnstone. BoWoP

Puberty Tree, The. D. M. Thomas. TOF

Pubescence at 39. Vickie Sears. GLP

Public Aid for Niagara Falls. Morris Bishop. NBLV

Public Beach (Long Island Sound). Christopher Morley. NBLV

Public Garden, The. Robert Lowell. NoP; PoRA; TAP

Public haunt they found her in, A. A Girl of Pompeii. Edward Sandford Martin. AA

Public Holiday: Paris. Joyce Horner. GoYe

Public Journal. Phyllis McGinley. NBLV

Public Library. Dannie Abse. OxBC

Public Library. Candace Thurber Stevenson. GoYe

Public Nuisance, A. Reginald Arkell. SD

Public Schools. Robert Lloyd. *Fr.* A Familiar Epistle to J. B. Esq. NOEC

Public Television. Eileen Myles. BAP

Public Wash House, The. Alan Bold. NPo

Publication—is the auction. Emily Dickinson. AmPP; NAAL-1; NoP

Publisher's Party. Phyllis McGinley. OBAL

Publishing 2001. Bob Rosenthal. UL

Puck and the Fairy. Shakespeare. *See* Midsummer Night's Dream, A: Over Hill, over Dale.

Puck Goes to Court. Fenton Johnson. CDC

Puck of Pook's Hill, *sels.* Kipling.
Cities and Thrones and Powers. GoJo; NOBE; OBNC; OxBTC; PoEL-5
Harp Song of the Dane Women. HAP; OBNC; PoRA; SeCePo
Pict Song, A. NoAM
Puck's Song. FaBoCh; FaBV; OxBChV
Runes on Weland's Sword, The. NoAM
Smuggler's Song, A. OxBChV
Song to Mithras, A. NoAM

Puck's Song. Kipling. *Fr.* Puck of Pook's Hill. FaBoCh; FaBV; OxBChV

Puck's Song. Shakespeare. *See* Midsummer Night's Dream, A: Now the Hungry Lion Roars.
Pudden Tame. *Unknown.* ChTr
"Pudding and pie." Greedy Jane. *Unknown.* OxBChV
Pudding Charms. Charlotte Druitt Cole. BoTP
Puddy and the Mouse, The. *Unknown.* GBP
Puella Parvula. Wallace Stevens. HCAP; LCAP
Puer Aeternus. Kathleen Jessie Raine. NYBP
Puer ex Jersey. *Unknown.* NA
Puerperium. Edmund Waller. JCP
Puerto Rico Song. William Carlos Williams. NYBP
Puffed up with luring to her knees. The Flute. Joseph Russell Taylor. AA
Puffin, The. Robert Williams Wood. RHPC
Puk-Wudjies. Patrick Reginald Chalmers. BoTP
Pulitzer Prize Winning Refrigerator, The. Robert Funge. SoTCo
Pulkovo Meridian, The, *sel.* Vera Inber, *tr. fr. Russian by* Dorothea Prall Radin *and* Alexander Kaun. Leningrad: 1943. WaaP
Pull down the shades baby neighbors don want to see what you do. Crawl Blues. Vincent McHugh. ErPo
Pull in the net! Fishing Song. *Maori Oral Tradition, tr. by* A. Armstrong *and* R. Ngata. WTO
Pull me down, ladybug. Ladybug. Raymond Souster. MoCV
Pull My Daisy. Jack Kerouac. PoM
Pull my daisy. Song: Fie My Fum. Allen Ginsberg. ErPo
Pulley, The. George Herbert. AWP; EaLo; GTBS; GTBS-P; HAP; HeIP; InPK; InPS; LiTB; MePo; Mes; NAEL-1; NOBE; NOCV; NoP; OAEL-1; OBEV; OBS; PPP; PrIm; SeCP; SeCV-1; TEP; TrGrPo
Pullin me in off the corner to wash my face an. Black Jam for Dr. Negro. Mari E. Evans. BPo; PoBA
Pulling Out. Lyn Lifshin. NeAC
Pulling up flax after the blue flowers have fallen. The Linen Industry. Michael Longley. CIP; UAS
Pulling up in my car, I went into the cottage. After Five Years. Augustus Young. BIrV
Pulling Weeds. Eric Chock. BrSi
Pulpit to Be Let, A. *Unknown.* APAS
Pulse, The. Mark Van Doren. MoAmPo
Pult'ney, methinks you blame my breach of word. Epistle to the Right Honourable William Pulteney, Esq. John Gay. OBTV
Pulverized Screen, The. Edmond Jabès, *tr. fr. French by* Anthony Rudolf. VWA
Pumberly Pott's Unpredictable Niece. Jack Prelutsky. RHPC
Pumping Iron. Diane Ackerman. ASP
Pumpkin, The. Robert Graves. PDV; RHPC; WSC
Pumpkin. Robert Morgan. GeTw
Pumpkin, The. Whittier. OHIP
Pumpkin tendrils creep, The. Late Summer. Kinoshita Yuji, *tr. by* Geoffrey Bownas *and* Anthony Thwaite. PeBJV
Pumpkins. John Cotton. BoNaP
Puna's Fragrant Glades. Princess Lili'u-o-ka-lani, *tr. fr. Hawaiian by* S. H. Elbert *and* N. Mahoe. WTO
Punch, the Immortal Liar, *sel.* Conrad Aiken.
Puppet Dreams, The. MoAmPo
Punctilio. Mary Elizabeth Coleridge. OBEV
Punctual as bad luck. The Family Goldschmitt. Henri Coulette. CoAP; FF
Punctually at Christmas the soft plush. White Christmas. William Robert Rodgers. LiTM; MoAB; MoBrPo; SeCePo
Pundit, how can you be so dumb? Kabir, *tr. by* John Stratton Hawley *and* Mark Juergensmeyer. SSI
Pundit, so well-read, go ask God. Kabir, *tr. by* John Stratton Hawley *and* Mark Juergensmeyer. SSI
Pundits have taken, The. Kabir, *tr. by* John Stratton Hawley *and* Mark Juergensmeyer. SSI
Punishment. Seamus Heaney. FaBoPV; InPS; NAEL-2; NoAM; NoP
Punishment, The. Susan Ludvigson. MT
Punishment for a Wayward Train. Antonio Jacinto, *tr. fr. Portuguese by* Ron Rossner *and* Alexander Caskey. WMBCH
Punk Pantoum. Pamela Stewart. SM
Punkydoodle and Jollapin. Laura E. Richards. OBCA
Punting pole stuck in the reeds. Inscribed on a Painting of a Fisherman. T'ang Yin, *tr. by* Jonathan Chaves. CoBLCP
Puppet Dreams, The. Conrad Aiken. *Fr.* Punch, the Immortal Liar. MoAmPo
Puppet of the Wolf, The. Margaret Atwood. NoAM
Puppet Player, The. Angelina Weld Grimké. CDC
Puppeteers, The. Tadamichi, *tr. fr. Chinese by* Burton Watson. JLIC-1
Puppets. Patricia K. Page. MoCV

Puppets which perform before the curtains, The. Hsü Wei, *tr. fr. Chinese by* Jonathan Chaves. *Fr.* Inscribed on Paintings for the People of Hangchow. CoBLCP
Puppy and I. A. A. Milne. BoTP; FaPON; OnUR; PDV; PYC
Puppy Chased the Sunbeam, The. Ivy O. Eastwick. RAR
Purcell in many victories of his. Bounty. Josephine Miles. NoAM
Purchase of a Blue, Green, or Orange Ode. Josephine Miles. NoP
Pure air trembles, O pitiless God, The. Noon. Robinson Jeffers. MoAmPo
Pure blood domestic, guaranteed. The Prize Cat. E. J. Pratt. HeIP; MoP
Pure contralto sings in the organloft, The. Walt Whitman. *Fr.* Song of Myself, 15. TTTS
Pure cry sounds the alarum at midnight, A. Crane Lodge. Wu Wen, *tr. fr. Chinese by* Chang Yin-nan. *Fr.* Poems on Yi Garden: Written for Mr. Juan-t'ing, II. WFTU
Pure Death. Robert Graves. AWP; GTBS-P; MoAB
Pure fasted faces draw unto this feast. Easter Communion. Gerard Manley Hopkins. BrPo; OFD
Pure gold, bright sky about the sun. The Good Man. *Unknown, tr. by* Robin Flower. TIRV
Pure gold, they said in her praise. Around Thanksgiving. Rolfe Humphries. OFD
Pure in Heart Shall See God, The. Frances Ellen Watkins Harper. PWR
Pure is the body on the Earth. He Singeth in the Underworld. *Unknown, tr. fr. Egyptian by* Robert Hillyer. *Fr.* Book of the Dead. AWP
Pure is the sandalwood incense—a good place to live. Chang Wen-t'ao, *tr. fr. Chinese by* William Schultz. *Fr.* Moving to the Cottage of Pine and Bamboo, I. WFTU
Pure Notations. Steve Levine. UL
Pure poetry, programme of the living heart. The Network. Robert Finch. CaP
Pure products of America, The. To Elsie. William Carlos Williams. CMoP; InPS; NAAL-2; NOBA; OxBA; PoE
Pure Serene Music. Mao Hsi-chen, *tr. fr. Chinese by* Lois Fusek. ATF
Pure Serene Music. Sun Kuang-hsien, *tr. fr. Chinese by* Lois Fusek. ATF
Pure Serene Music. Wei Chuang, *tr. fr. Chinese by* Lois Fusek. ATF
Pure Serene Music. Wen T'ing-yün, *tr. fr. Chinese by* Lois Fusek. ATF
Pure Simple Love. Aurelian Townshend. SeCP
Pure Spirit of the always-faithful God. Hymn for Pentecost. James Clarence Mangan. TIRV
Pure stream, in whose transparent wave. To Leven Water. Tobias Smollet. OBEV
Pure sun dazzled, The. The Glazier. Stéphane Mallarmé. OBVE, *tr. by* Keith Bosley
Pure Thoughts. Washington Delgado, *tr. fr. Spanish by* David Tipton. Per
Pure were the thoughts that once were ours. The Friendly Wood. Paul Valéry, *tr. by* William Jay Smith. CT
Pure? What does it mean? Fever 103.° Sylvia Plath. CMoP; FaBoWP; NoAM; NOBA; VGW
Pure white bodies of my friends, The. Verigin 3. John Newlove. NeAC
Pure white, placeless. Pain. Herbert Zand, *tr. by* Beth Bjorklund. CoAuP
Pure with starlight. Emperor Fushimi, *tr. by* Steven D. Carter. WFTW
Pure woman is to man a crown. The Virtuous Wife. Süsskind von Trimberg. TrJP
Purer than Purest Pure. E. E. Cummings. AH
Purest soul that e'er was sent, The. Another [Epitaph on the Lady Mary Villiers]. Thomas Carew. CaPo; SeCV-1
Purgatorio. Dante, *tr. fr. Italian.* *Fr.* Divina Commedia.
"As the day stands when the Sun begins to glow." *Fr.* XXVII. NAWM-1, *tr. by* John Ciardi.
"At the hour when the heat of the day is overcome." *Fr.* XIX. NAWM-1, *tr. by* John Ciardi.
Celestial Pilot, The. *Fr.* II. WGRP
"Earnest to explore within and all around." *Fr.* XXVIII. OBVE
"For better waters now the little bark." *Fr.* I-II. NAWM-1, *tr. by* John Ciardi.
Lady Clothed in Flame, The. *Fr.* III. PFI
Oderisi D'Agobbio on Pride. *Fr.* IX. PFI
Virgil's Farewell to Dante. *Fr.* XXVII. FaBoTw
"When the Septentrion of the First Heaven." *Fr.* XXX-XXXI. NAWM-1, *tr. by* John Ciardi.
Purgatory. W. B. Yeats. CMoP
Purgatory of Hell, *sel.* Edoardo Sanguineti, *tr. fr. Italian by* Lawrence R. Smith.
"Barbed wire awaits you, the wasp, the viper, the bright, The." NItP

Purgatory of Suicides, The, *sel.* Thomas Cooper.
  "Methought, on this aspiring form I gazed." PF
Puriri moth's wing, A. Jan Kemp. ATNZ; PeNZ
Purist, The. Ogden Nash. FiBHP; GoJo; MoAmPo; MoShBr; NBLV;
  OBCA
Puritan, The. Karl Shapiro. MoAmPo
Puritan Lady, A. Lizette Woodworth Reese. MoAmPo
Puritan on His Honeymoon, The. Robert Bly. FF; NePoEA
Puritan Sonnet, IV. Elinor Wylie. *See* Wild Peaches:
  Down to the Puritan marrow of my bones.
Puritan Spring Beauties stood freshly clad for church, The. The Spring
  Beauties. Helen Gray Cone. AA
Purity. Hayim Lenski, *tr. fr. Hebrew by* Pearl Grodensky. VWA
Purity of Heart. John Keble. BLRP
Purple Chaos. Alistair Campbell. ATNZ
Purple cloud hangs half-way down, A. Before Sunrise in Winter.
  Edward Rowland Sill. AA
Purple Clover. Emily Dickinson. MoAmPo
Purple color, night's tribute, The. Lilac Garden. Yoshioka Minoru, *tr.*
  by Sato. FCEI
Purple Cow, The. Gelett Burgess. FaBoCo; FaBoNo; FaFP; FaPON;
  FiBHP; FPL; GrPl; NA; NBLV; NTCP; OBAL; OBCA; PDV; PoLF;
  RHPC
Purple Goatee. George Starbuck. SoTCo
Purple headland over yonder. Afternoon. Louisa S. Guggenberger.
  NOBVV
Purple Indians pas de bourrée. Lord Fluting Dreams of America on the
  Eve of His Departure from Liverpool. Paul Zimmer. VGW
Purple Island, The, *sels.* Phineas Fletcher.
  All-seeing Intellect, The. *Fr.* VI. JCP
  Desiderium. *Fr.* I. OBS
  Overthrow of Lucifer, The. *Fr.* XII. OBS
Purple Precincts touch Longevity Mountain. I Was Received in an
  Early Audience at Heaven-Gate. Yang Shih-ch'i, *tr. by* Jonathan
  Chaves. CoBLCP
Purple sky, the down's long spine, The. The Novice. Edward Davison.
  ErPo
Purple so deep, A. Masaoka Shiki, *tr. fr. Japanese by* Burton Watson.
  Fr. Thirty-nine Haiku. FCEI
Purple, White and Green, The. L. E. Morgan-Browne. BrRo
Purple, yellow, red and green. *Unknown.* OxNR
Purpose. Langdon Elwyn Mitchell. *Fr.* To a Writer of the Day. AA
Purpose. John James Piatt. AA
Purpose of Altar Boys, The. Alberto Ríos. MAYP; NAmP
Purpose of Fable-writing, The. Phaedrus, *tr. fr. Latin by* Christopher
  Smart. AWP
Purpose of Poetry, The. Jared Carter. MOWH
Purpose of the Chesapeake & Ohio Canal, The. Dave Smith. GeTw
Purse, dirk, cloak, night-cap, kerchief, shoeing-horn, buget, and shoes.
  Memorial Verses for Travellers. Sir Anthony Fitzherbert. *Fr.*
  Husbandry. FaBoUs
Purse-Seine, The. Robinson Jeffers. CMoP; HAP; NoAM; NOBA; NoP;
  OxBA; PrIm; WeW
Purse, who'll not know you have a poet's been. A Parley with His Empty
  Purse. Thomas Randolph. JCP; OBS
Pursuit. Hilda Doolittle ("H. D."). WPE
Pursuit. Julian Tuwim, *tr. fr. Polish by* Watson Kirkconnell. TrJP
Pursuit. Robert Penn Warren. HAP; LiTA; MoAmPo; TwCP
Pursuit from Under. James Dickey. HAP; PPP
Pursuit of an Ideal. Patrick Kavanagh. FaBCIP
Pursuit of Love. *Unknown, at. to* John Webster *and* William Rowley.
  See Thracian Wonder, The: Art Thou Gone in Haste?
Pursuit[e], The. Henry Vaughan. SeCP; TrCP; TrPWD
Push about the brisk bowl, 'twill enliven the heart. The Ass. Moses
  Mendes. *Fr.* The Chaplet. TrJP
Pushan, God of golden day. Pushan, God of Pasture. *Unknown, tr. fr.*
  Sanskrit by Romesh Dutt. *Fr.* Vedic Hymns. AWP
Pushan, God of Pasture. *Unknown, tr. fr. Sanskrit by* Romesh Dutt. *Fr.*
  Vedic Hymns. AWP
Pushing away last night violently. After Dawn. Lo Fu, *tr. by* Dominic
  Cheung. IFON
Pushing freely through the bush-clovers. Naga Okimaro. *Fr.* Manyo
  Shu. Ma
Pushing home at dawn. Narihira, *tr. fr. Japanese by* Burton Watson. *Fr.*
  Kokin Shu. FCEI
Pushkin. "Anna Akhmatova," *tr. fr. Russian by* Stanley Kunitz *with* Max
  Hayward. AnAn
Puss and the Boots, The, *sel.* Henry Duff Traill.
  "Put case I circumvent and kill him: good." BXAP; Par
Puss came dancing out of a barn. *Unknown.* OxNR
Pussicat, wussicat, with a white foot. *Unknown.* OxNR

Pussy and the Mice. *Unknown.* MoShBr
Pussy-Cat and Puppy-Dog. Lilian McCrea. BoTP
Pussy cat ate the dumplings. Pussycat. Mother Goose. OxNR
Pussy Cat Mole. *Unknown.* OxNR
Pussy Cat, Pussy Cat, where have you been? Mother Goose. BoTP;
  FaBoBe; FaFP; OxNR
"Pussy, Pussy Baudrons." Morley. CRH
Pussy sits beside the fire. By the Fire. Mother Goose. OxNR
Pussy Willows. Aileen Fisher. RAR
Pussycat. Mother Goose. OxNR
Put a sun in Sunday, Sunday. Yet Dish. Gertrude Stein. SOTW
Put case I circumvent and kill him: good. Henry Duff Traill. *Fr.* The
  Puss and the Boots. BXAP; Par
Put Down. Léon Damas, *tr. fr. French by* Seth L. Wolitz. TTY
Put-Down Come On, The. A. R. Ammons. NoP
Put down your weapons. Haka: The Blossoming. Pita Sharples, *tr. by*
  Pita Sharples. PeNZ
Put each step here. Mohammad Taqi Mir, *tr. by* Ahmed Ali. GoT
Put 'em up solid, they won't come down! Post-Rail Song. *Unknown.*
  AS
Put every tiny robe away! In Vain. Rose Terry Cooke. AA
Put Forth, O God, Thy Spirit's Might. Howard Chandler Robbins. AH,
  with music; TrPWD
Put forth thy leaf, thou lofty plane. Arthur Hugh Clough. EBEV
Put Hannibal i' th' scale. Hannibal ("Put Hannibal i' th' scale").
  Juvenal, *tr. fr. Latin by* Henry Vaughan. *Fr.* Satires, X. OBVE
Put his head. Odiham. John Gray. HAP
Put it this way, lovey, some people. Letter for a Daughter. Lorrie
  Goldensohn. PPR
Put It Through. Edward Everett Hale. PAH
Put my glad rags in a cardboard box. The Other Side of This World.
  Calvin Forbes. MAYP
Put Off Constricting Day. Mary Stanley. PeNZ
Put off the deference that this sea compels. Beach Talk. Norman
  MacCaig. PoA
Put off thy bark from shore, though near the night. Frederick Goddard
  Tuckerman. *Fr.* Sonnets. MOS
Put on your silks, and piece by piece. To His Mistresses. Robert
  Herrick. CaPo
Put out my eyes, and I can see you still. Rainer Maria Rilke, *tr. by*
  Babette Deutsch. UnAS
Put out to sea, if wine thou wouldest make. Sent from Egypt with a Fair
  Robe of Tissue to a Sicilian Vinedresser. T. Sturge Moore. OBEV
Put the pine tree in its pot by the doorway. Natalia M. Belting. ILY
Put the rubber mouse away. For a Dead Kitten. Sara Henderson Hay.
  CRH
Put them in print? Posthumous. Henry Augustin Beers. AA
Put things in their place. The Sky Is Blue. David Ignatow. FF; NNaP
Put this in your notebooks. The Last Class. Ellen Bryant Voigt. MT
Put your/ self out. Chasm. A. R. Ammons. OBAL
Put your finger in Foxy's hole. *Unknown.* OxNR
Put your hand in the creel. Marriage. *Unknown.* GBP
Put your hand on my heart, say that you love me as. A Betrothal. Edith
  Jay Scovell. GBL
Put your head, darling, darling, darling. Dear Black Head. *Unknown, tr.*
  by Sir Samuel Ferguson. BIrV
  (Cean Dubh Deelish.) GBL; SeCePo
Put your man down somewhere. After. Kendrick Smithyman. ATNZ
Put Your Mother on the Ceiling. Greg Pape. NAmP
Put Your Word to My Lips. Rachel Korn, *tr. fr. Yiddish by* Seymour
  Mayne *and* Rivka Augenfeld. VWA
Putta putta putt, A. Riding in a Motor Boat. Dorothy W. Baruch.
  FaPON
Putting a boat in the River of Eternal Heaven. Okura. *Fr.* Manyo Shu.
  FCEI
Putting facts by the thousands. Determinism. Lyn Hejinian. LP
Putting God in the nation's life. God in the Nation's Life. *Unknown.*
  BLRP; WBLP
Putting in below the dam, watching. Deliverance. Barbara Crooker.
  TSL
Putting in the Seed. Robert Frost. ErPo; NoAM; OxBA
Putting My Daughter to Bed. Li Nan, *tr. fr. Chinese by* Dominic Cheung.
  IFON
Putting my feet on the cool, cool wall. Later, Spending Some Time at
  Bokusetsu's Hut in Otsu. Basho, *tr. fr. Japanese by* Burton Watson.
  Fr. Seventy-six Hokku. FCEI
Putting On My Shoes I Hear the Floor Cry Out beneath Me. Michael
  Heffernan. BXAP
Putting On Nightgown. *Unknown.* OxNR
Putting out the candles. My Father after Work. Gary Gildner. Psk
Putting to Sea. Louise Bogan. LiTM; PoA

Puzzle. Arnold Spilka. ILY; RHPC
Puzzle faces in the dying elms. "Mystery Boy' Looks for Kin in Nashville." Robert Hayden. LCAP; NoAM; PoE
Puzzled. Langston Hughes. *See* Here on the edge of hell.
Puzzled. Carolyn Wells. OBCA
Puzzled Centipede, The. *Unknown*. *See* Centipede was happy quite, A.
Puzzled Game Birds, The. Thomas Hardy. PBBP
Pygmalion, *sels*. Hilda Doolittle ("H. D.").
"I made god upon god." WGRP
Pygmalion seeing these to spend their times. Ovid, *tr. fr. Latin*. *Fr.* Metamorphoses, X.
Pygmalion's Statue Comes to Life. Ovid, *tr. fr. Latin by* Arthur Golding. *Fr.* Metamorphoses, X. OAEL-1
"Pygmies Are Pygmies Still, Though Percht on Alps." Gwendolyn Brooks. PoNe
Pylon for some incomplete gateway. The Monadnock. John Gould Fletcher. PoA
Pylons, The. Stephen Spender. AWP; NoAM
Pyms Anarchy. *At.* to Thomas Jordan. OBS
Pyramids, first, which in Egypt were laid, The. The Seven Wonders of the Ancient World. *Unknown*. EyDe
Pyramis; or, The House of Ascent. A. D. Hope. PoAu-2
Pyramus and Thisbe. Abraham Cowley. FL
Pyramus and Thisbe, *sel*. Laurence Dakin.
"How sweetly sings this stream." *Fr.* III, iii. CaP
Pyramus and Thisbe. John Godfrey Saxe. OnMSP
Pyrargyrite Metal, 9. Cecília Meireles, *tr. fr. Portuguese by* James Merrill. ATCBP; PBWP
Pyre of My Indian Summer, The. Mani Leib, *tr. fr. Yiddish by* Keith Bosley. VWA
Pyrenees, The. Jacques Hamelink, *tr. fr. Dutch by* Scott Rollins. DuIn
Pyrography. John Ashbery. PoM
Pyrrha, what slender well-shap'd beau. Horace. *See* Odes: I, 5. "What slender youth bedewed with liquid odours" ("Quis multa gracilis").
Pythagoras planned it. Why did the people stare? The Statues. W. B. Yeats. AnIL; NoAM; OAEL-2; WeW
Python, The. Hilaire Belloc. NA; OxBChV
Python. *Yoruba Oral Tradition, tr. by* Ulli Beier. WTO
Python I should not advise, A. The Python. Hilaire Belloc. NA; OxBChV
Pythoness, The. Kathleen Jessie Raine. MoBrPo
Pyxidanthera, The. Augusta Cooper Bristol. AA

Q

Q:dwo. E. E. Cummings. OBAL
Qua Cursum Ventus. Arthur Hugh Clough. MOS; OBEV
Quack, Quack! "Dr. Seuss." RAR
Quack, quack, quack! Dumpy Ducky. Lucy Larcom. OBCA
Quaco Sam. *Unknown*. PBCV
Quadroon mermaids, Afro angels, black saints. A Ballad of Remembrance. Robert Hayden. AmNP; BPo; IDB; PoBA; PoNe
Quadrupedremian Song, A. Thomas Hood. AmMo; FaBoNo
Quaerè. George Farewell. NOEC
Quaerit Jesum Suum Maria. Richard Crashaw. ACP
Quail and rabbit hunters with tawny hounds. Hunters in the Snow: Brueghel. Joseph Langland. LiTM; NePoEA
Quail in Autumn. William Jay Smith. Psk
Quaint Mazes. Geoffrey Hill. *Fr.* An Apology for the Revival of Christian Architecture in England, 1. NoAM
Quaker Graveyard, The. S. Weir Mitchell. AA
Quaker Graveyard in Nantucket, The. Robert Lowell. CMoP; HAP; LiTM; MoAB; MoP; MOS; NAAL-2; NoAM; NOBA; NoP; OxBA; TAP; UnPo
Quaker Hill. Hart Crane. *Fr.* The Bridge, VI. LiTM; NAAL-2
Quaker Ladies. Ellen Mackay Hutchinson Cortissoz. AA
Quaker Widow, The. Bayard Taylor. AA
Quakeress Bride, The. Elizabeth Clementine Kinney. AA
Quaker's Meeting, The. Samuel Lover. CenHV
Quaker's Song, The. *Unknown*. CoMu
Quaker's wife got up to bake, The. *Unknown*. OxNR
Quaker's Wooing, The. *Unknown*. AS
Quality of Mercy [Is Not Strain'd], The. Shakespeare. *Fr.* The Merchant of Venice, IV, i. FaFP; LiTB
(Mercy.) OHFP; TrGrPo; WBLP
Quality of these trees, green height; of the sky, shining, The. Shine, Republic. Robinson Jeffers. FaBoPV

("Quality of these trees, green height, The.") AmFN; GOA
("Quality of these trees, green height; of the sky, The.") OPP
Quandoque bonus dormitat Homerus. Loosely from the Latin. David Galef. SoTCo
Quangle Wangle's Hat, The. Edward Lear. AmMo; EBEV; ILY; OnUR
Quantocks, The. Wordsworth. FaBoPP
Quantum. Martin Johnston. CBAP
Quantum Est Quod Desit. Thomas Moore. *See* Did Not.
Quarrel, The. Conrad Aiken. MoAB; MoAmPo
Quarrel, The. Diane DiPrima. NMM
Quarrel, The. Eleanor Farjeon. FaPON
Quarrel, The. Josephine D. Henderson Heard. CBWP-4
Quarrel, The. Karen Swenson. GrPl
Quarrel. *Yoruba Oral Tradition, tr. by* Ulli Beier. WTO
Quarrel of the sparrows in the eaves, The. The Sorrow of Love. W. B. Yeats. MoAB; MoBrPo; NoAM; NOBVV; OAEL-2; PoEL-5; TEP
Quarrel with Fortune, A. Benjamin Colman. SCAP
Quarrels have long been in vogue among sages. A Song from the Coptic. James Clarence Mangan. NOIV
Quarrelsome Bishop, A. Walter Savage Landor. FaBoEE; OBSV
Quarrelsome Trio, The. "L. G." WBLP
Quarries in Syracuse. Louis Golding. TrJP
Quarry, The. W. H. Auden. *See* O What Is That Sound [Which So Thrills the Ear].
Quarry, The. László Kálnoky, *tr. fr. Hungarian by* Jascha Kessler. FOC
Quarry, The. Vassar Miller. NePoEA-2; WPE
Quarry. Itamar Ya'oz-kest, *tr. fr. Hebrew by* Bernhard Frank. MHeP
Quarry Pool, The. Denise Levertov. VGW
Quarry whence thy form majestic sprung, The. Washington's Statue. Henry Theodore Tuckerman. AA
Quarry/Rock. Paul Mariah. GLP; PeHV
Quarter century ago, A. Wilberforce. Josephine D. Henderson Heard. CBWP-4
Quarter less four,/ Half twain. *Unknown*. AmFP
Quarto Centennial, The. Josephine D. Henderson Heard. CBWP-4
Quarts of ladybugs. Ladybugs. Peggy Shumaker. TDD
Quasimodo loomed. For Wilma. Don Johnson. GOYP
Quatorzain. Henry Timrod. AnAmPo
Quatrain: "At this remote village, I have no neighbors." Chang Yü, *tr. by* Jonathan Chaves. CoBLCP
Quatrain: "Dare I dislike the green pond for the reflection of my unkempt hair?" Ch'en Pao-shen, *tr. by* Irving Lo. WFTU
Quatrain: "East of the salt village, low and narrow." Wu Chia-chi, *tr. by* Jonathan Chaves. CoBLCP
Quatrain: "François am I, heavy my lot." Villon. OBD
Quatrain: "Golf links lie so near The mill." Sarah Norcliffe Cleghorn. *See* Golf Links, The.
Quatrain, A: "Hark at the lips of this pink whorl of shell." Frank Dempster Sherman. AA
Quatrain: "I am François to my great dismay." Villon, *tr. by* David Lunde. SoTCo
Quatrain: "I saw that thieves had burgled as they do." Ilyas Farhat, *tr. by* Salma Khadra Jayyusi *and* John Heath-Stubbs. MAP
Quatrain: "I've learnt to laugh now at adversity." Ilyas Farhat, *tr. by* Salma Khadra Jayyusi *and* John Heath-Stubbs. MAP
Quatrain: "Just life and death make up our worldly state." Ilyas Farhat, *tr. by* Salma Khadra Jayyusi *and* John Heath-Stubbs. MAP
Quatrain: "My bloodstream chokes on gall and spleen." Barend Toerien, *tr. by* author. PeSA
Quatrain: "My foolish heart keeps beckoning to me." Ilyas Farhat, *tr. by* Salma Khadra Jayyusi *and* John Heath-Stubbs. MAP
Quatrain: "O gold, a deep contempt for you I own." Ilyas Farhat, *tr. by* Salma Khadra Jayyusi *and* John Heath-Stubbs. MAP
Quatrain: "Oh! to be wafted away." *Unknown*. NA
Quatrain: "Old saltman, hair turned white, The." Wu Chia-chi, *tr. by* Jonathan Chaves. CoBLCP
Quatrain: Poet. Emerson. OxBSP
Quatrain: "Sarmèd, whom they intoxicated from the cup of love." Sarmèd the Yahud, *tr. by* David Shea. TrJP
Quatrain: "Seekers of peace, enough hypocrisy!" Ilyas Farhat, *tr. by* Salma Khadra Jayyusi *and* John Heath-Stubbs. MAP
Quatrain: "This existence has, without the azure sphere, no reality." Sarmèd the Yahud, *tr. by* David Shea. TrJP
Quatrain: "Three peaks beyond my pavilion show no human feelings, The." Ch'en Pao-shen, *tr. by* Irving Lo. WFTU
Quatrain: "Time promises, should I in that confide?" Ilyas Farhat, *tr. by* Salma Khadra Jayyusi *and* John Heath-Stubbs. MAP
Quatrain at Chen-chou. Wang Shih-chen, *tr. fr. Chinese by* Jonathan Chaves. CoBLCP
Quatrains. Gwendolyn B. Bennett. CDC
Quatrains, *sels*. Emerson.

Gardener. OxBA

Orator. OxBA

Poet. OxBA; PCP

Quatrains. Sidney Godolphin. *See* Song: "Noe more unto my thoughts appeare."

Quatrains. Salah Jahin, *tr. fr. Arabic by* Samir M. Zoghby. TTY

Quatrains. Omar Khayyám. *See* Rubáiyát of Omar Khayyám of Naishápúr, The: Book of verses underneath the bough, A.

Quatrains for Joy. Muhammad al-Ghuzzi, *tr. fr. Arabic by* May Jayyusi *and* John Heath-Stubbs. MAP

Quatrains on Peking's Western Suburb, *sels.* Chu Yi-tsun, *tr. fr. Chinese by* Irving Lo. WFTU

Brown Oxen Knoll. *Fr.* VI.

Chia Mountain Monastery. *Fr.* VIII.

Quatrains on Yung-chia, *sels.* Chu Yi-tsun, *tr. fr. Chinese by* Irving Lo. WFTU

Pine Pavilion Hill. *Fr.* I.

Southern Pavilion. *Fr.* VII.

Quatrina. Joseph Deericks Bennett. LiTA

Quavering cry, A. Screech-owl? Night, Death, Mississippi. Robert Hayden. CAPP; FF; LCAP; VGW

"Quay recedes, The. Hurrah! Ahead we go!" The Colonel's Soliloquy. Thomas Hardy. OBWP

Quebec. Henrietta Cordelia Ray. CBWP-3

Quebec Farmhouse. John Glassco. NOBC

Quebec Liquor Commission Store. Abraham Moses Klein. OBCV

Quebec, the grey old city on the hill. At Quebec. Jean Blewett. CaP

Queen. Dom Moraes. NePoEA-2

Queen, The. Kenneth Pitchford. NYBP

Queen[e] and huntress[e], chaste and fair. Hymn to Diana. Ben Jonson. *Fr.* Cynthia's Revels, V, vi. AWP; CH; ChTr; EiL; GTBS; GTBS-P; HAP; HeIP; NOBE; NoP; OAEL-1; OBEV; OBS; PoRA, QFR; SeCP; TrGrPo; WiR

(Hesperus' Hymn[e] to Cynthia.) JCP; SeCV-1

(Hesperus' Song.) GN

(Hymn: "Queen and huntress, chaste, and fair.") InPS

(Hymn to Cynthia.) PoE; PrIm; SeCePo

(Hymne, The: "Queene and huntress, chaste, and faire.") PoEL-2

(Queen and Huntress.) NAEL-1

Queen Anne. *Unknown.* ChTr

Queen Anne's Lace. June Jordan. TAP

Queen Anne's Lace. Mary Leslie Newton. FaPON; MoShBr

Queen Anne's Musicians. Thomas Hennell. FaBoTw

Queen-Ann's-Lace. William Carlos Williams. AmPP; BLPL; MoAB; MoAmPo; NAAL-2; NoAM; NOBA; NoP; PrIm; TAP

Queen Bee, The. Mary K. Robinson. BoTP

Queen Bess was Harry's daughter. Stand forward partners all! The Looking Glass. Kipling. FaBoTw; OBMV

Queen Charming. Pamela White Hadas. BLA

Queen declares, The: "The evening wears. Lullaby for an Emigrant. Benjamin Fondane, *tr. by* Keith Bosley. VWA

Queen Dido Rides Out Hunting. Virgil, *tr. into Middle English by* Gavin Douglas. *Fr.* The Aeneid [or Eneados], IV. OxBLMV

Queen Eleanor's Confession. *Unknown.* ESPB, (A *and* B *vers.*); OBET; PrIm

Queen has lately lost a part, The. Verses Said to Be Written on the Union. Swift. APAS

Queen is gone a-hunting in the royal wood, The. A-Hunting. Jennie Dunbar. BoTP

Queen is taking a drive today, The. The Queen's Last Ride. Ella Wheeler Wilcox. BLPA

Queen Jane sat at her window one day. The King's Dochter Lady Jean. *Unknown.* AmFP

Queen Jane was [or lay] in labor [or labour]. The Death of Queen Jane. *Unknown.* AmFP, 2 *vers.*; ESPB, (A *and* B *vers.*); OBET

("Queen Jeanie, Queen Jeanie, travel'd six weeks and more.") ESPB, B *vers.*

Queen Mab. Shakespeare. *See* Romeo and Juliet.

O [or Oh], then, I see Queen Mab hath been with you.

Queen Mab, *sels.* Shelley.

Magic Car Moved On, The. *Fr.* I. GN

War Is the Statesman's Game. *Fr.* IV. FF

Queen, mistress, crucified at the gates of the furthest city. Eve. Anne Hébert, *tr. by* Kathleen Weaver. OV

Queen Mother to New Queen. Robert Graves. OBSV

Queen Nefertiti. *Unknown.* RHPC

Queen of all Queens, oh! Wonder of the loveliness of women. Hymn to the Virgin Mary. Conor O'Riordan, *tr. by* Eleanor Hull. TIRV

Queen of Aragon, The, *sel.* William Habington.

Fine Young Folly. OBS

(Pretty Sport.) NOBE

(Song: "Fine young folly, though you were.") MePo

Queen of Cheese. James McIntyre. FiBHP

Queen of Corinth, The, *sel.* John Fletcher *and others.*

Weep No More. *At. to* John Fletcher, *fr.* III, ii. CH; EiL; OBEV

(Mourn No More.) TrGrPo

Queen of Courtesy, The. *Unknown.* Fr. Pearl. ACP

Queen of Elfan's [or Elfland's] Nourice [or Nourrice], The, *sel.* *Unknown.* ESPB

"I heard a cow low, a bonnie cow low." FaBoCh

Queen of fragrance, lovely rose. The Rose-Bud. William Broome. OBEV

Queen of Going. Roger Giroux, *tr. fr. French by* Anthony Barnett. RHTwFP

Queen of Hearts, The. Mother Goose. FaBoBe; OxNR

Queen of Hearts, The. *Unknown.* OBET

Queen of Heaven Mausoleum. Dennis Schmitz. LCAP

Queen of Heaven, of Hell eke Emperess. To the Virgin. John Lydgate. ACP

Queen of Lydia, The. C. H. Sisson. OxBC

Queen of Paphos, Erycine, The. *Unknown.* EiL; GBL

Queen of Scotland, The. *Unknown.* ESPB

Queen of the azure and the fool of the void go past you in a taxicab, The. Remarks from the Rocks. Robert Desnos, *tr. by* Michael Benedikt. POS

Queen of the Nile, The. William Jay Smith. GrPl

Queen of the River. Elizabeth Nannestad. ATNZ; PeNZ

Queen of the silver bow!—by thy pale beam. To the Moon. Charlotte Smith. Son

Queen Sabbath. Hayyim Nahman Bialik, *tr. fr. Hebrew by* Jessie Sampter. TrJP

Queen sat in her balcony, The. Gil, the Toreador. Charles Henry Webb. AA

Queen she sent to look for me, The. Grenadier. A. E. Housman. OBMV; OBWP

Queen Tatavane. Sándor Weöres, *tr. fr. Hungarian by* Edwin Morgan. MHuP

Queen Victoria. *Unknown.* CoMu

Queen Virtue's court, which some call Stella's face. Sir Philip Sidney. *Fr.* Astrophel and Stella, IX. NAEL-1

Queen was beloved by a jester, A. The Cap and Bells. W. B. Yeats. BrPo; ChTr; MoAB; MoBrPo; NoAM; NoP; OnMSP; WSC

Queen went from me while I slept, The. Queen. Dom Moraes. NePoEA-2

Queen Yang-Se-Fu/ Has seventy great castles. Yang-Se-Fu. "Yehoash," *tr. by* Isidore Goldstick. TrJP

Queenie. Mary Weston Fordham. CBWP-2

Queenie ("Queenie's strong and Queenie's tall"). Leland B. Jacobs. RHPC

Queens, The. Robert Fitzgerald. NYBP

Queens. J. M. Synge. ChTr; GBL; MoBrPo; OBMV

Queen's Chariot, The. Michael Drayton. *Fr.* Nymphidia. OBS

Queen's English, The. Tony Harrison. DiPo

Queen's Last Ride, The. Ella Wheeler Wilcox. BLPA

Queen's Marie, The. *Unknown.* OBEV

Queens of Hell had lissome necks to crane, The. The Tall Girl. John Crowe Ransom. Son

Queen's Song, The. James Elroy Flecker. BrPo

Queen's Speech, The. Arthur Mainwaring. APAS

Queen's Wake, The, *sel.* James Hogg.

Kilmeny. OBEV

(Bonny Kilmeny Gaed Up the Glen.) GoTS

Queer, The. Henry Vaughan. PoEL-2

Queer are the ways of a man I know. The Phantom Horsewoman. Thomas Hardy. CMoP; FaBoPP; NOBE; PoEL-5; WSC

Queer Assayers of the Frontier, The. Peter Porter. *Fr.* Baroque Quatrains. AnAn

Queer sights we every day do find. The Dandy Horse. *Unknown.* OBET

Queer thing about those waters: there are no, A. Across the Bay. Donald Davie. NoAM

Queer Things. Emanuel Carnevali. EAS

Queer Things. James Reeves. WSC

Queer's Song. Richard Howard. *Fr.* Gaiety. ErPo

Quentin Durward, *sel.* Sir Walter Scott.

Serenade. GTBS; GTBS-P

(Song: "Ah! County Guy, the hour is nigh.") CH

Quentin Matsys. Jaroslaw Iwaszkiewicz, *tr. fr. Polish by* Czeslaw Milosz. PwPP

Query. Ebon Dooley. PoBA

Query. Michael McTurk. PBCV

Query, a question, A.   The Water of Kane.   *Unknown, tr. by* N. B. Emerson.   WTO

Quesada, *sels.*   C. K. Stead.

"All over the plain of the world lovers are being hurt."   *Fr.* I.   ATNZ; PeNZ

"Dulcinea walks."   *Fr.* IV.   ATNZ

"He said God who gave the wound would give the cure."   *Fr.* VII. ATNZ

"Is there another poetry than the poetry of celebration?"   *Fr.* III. ATNZ

"Odysseus under wet snapping sheets."   *Fr.* X.   ATNZ; PeNZ

"Quesada on the dunes hurls himself at the elements."   *Fr.* II.   ATNZ

"That the balls of the lover are not larger than the balls of the priest." *Fr.* XVII.   ATNZ; PeNZ

Quest, The, *sels.*   W. H. Auden.   Son
City, The.
Door, The.

Quest.   Naomi Long Madgett.   BPo

Quest, The.   Eliza Scudder.   TrPWD

Quest.   Edmund Clarence Stedman.   *Fr.* Corda Concordia.   AA

Quest, The.   Harold Vinal.   GoYe

Quest, The.   James Wright.   NYBP

Quest of Silence, The, *sel.*   Christopher John Brennan.
"Fire in the heavens, and fire along the hills."   CBAP; PoAu-1

Quest of the Ideal, The.   Henrietta Cordelia Ray.   CBWP-3

Quest of the Sangraal, The, *sel.*   Robert Stephen Hawker.
"Land is lonely now, The: Anathema."   EBVV

Questing.   Anne Spencer.   CDC

Question, The.   James Beattie.   FaBoCo

?   E. E. Cummings.   FiBHP

Question, The.   Robert Duncan.   NeAP

Question, The.   Norman Gale.   FiBHP

Question, The.   Wilfrid Wilson Gibson.   MMA

Question, The.   Josephine D. Henderson Heard.   CBWP-4

Question, The.   David Ignatow.   CAPP

Question, The.   Karla Kuskin.   NTCP; PDV

Question, The.   Dennis Lee.   ILY

Question, A.   Edna Livingston.   GoYe

Question, The.   F. T. Prince.   BoLoP; GTBS-P; PeSA

Question, The.   Muriel Rukeyser.   IHMS; WPOW

Question, The.   Shelley.   CH; EnRP; FiP; OBEV

Question.   May Swenson.   HeIP; LiTM; NePoEA; PrIm; SM; VGW

Question, A.   J. M. Synge.   MoBrPo; NOIV; OBMV; OxBTC

Question Addressed to Liu Shih-chiu, A.   Po Chü-i, *tr. fr. Chinese by* Burton Watson.   CoBCP

Question and Answer.   Samuel Hoffenstein.   FiBHP

Question and Answer.   Langston Hughes.   BPo

Question and Answer.   Kathleen Jessie Raine.   MoBrPo

Question and the Answer, The.   Muhammad al-Faituri, *tr. fr. Arabic by* Sargon Boulus *and* Peter Porter.   MAP

Question Answered [*or* A Question Answered], The.   Blake.   *See* Several Questions Answered: What is it men in women do require?

Question ("Do you love me").   *Unknown.*   RHPC

Question ("If I really, really trust him").   *Unknown.*   BLRP

Question, The ("Were the whole world as good as you— —not an atom better").   *Unknown.*   WBLP

Question in a Field.   Louise Bogan.   NYBP

Question in the air, The.   Song for Luanda.   Luandino Vieira, *tr. by* Michael Wolfers.   WMBCH

Question is, The.   These Two.   Howard Schwartz.   VWA

Question is, The: how does one hold an apple.   The Gesture.   George Oppen.   *Fr.* Five Poems about Poetry.   NNaP

Question, lords and ladies, is, The.   Percy Shelley.   John Peale Bishop. ErPo

Question of Art, A.   Deborah Kendrick.   TSM

Question of Climate, A.   Audre Lorde.   NoAM

Question of Energy, A.   Amber Coverdale Sumrall.   TSM

Question of Form and Content, A.   Jon Stallworthy.   OxBC

Question of Libel, A.   Pope.   *Fr.* The First Satire of the Second Book of Horace.   PrIm, *abr.*

Question of Time.   Antonio Cisneros, *tr. fr. Spanish by* David Tipton. Per

Question the beauty of the earth.   Saint Augustine.   Joseph Mary Plunkett.   TIRV

Question, The ("I dream'd that, as I wander'd by the way").   Shelley. CH; EnRP; FiP; OBEV

Question then, to state it first, The.   Samuel Butler.   *Fr.* Hudibras, I, 3. NOBL

Question Time.   Thomas McCarthy.   CIP

Question to Life.   Patrick Kavanagh.   MoBrPo

Question to Lisetta, The.   Matthew Prior.   OBEV

Question was an academic one, The.   Tomorrows.   James Merrill. OBAL

Question Whither, The.   George Meredith.   WGRP

Question: Who am I?   A Woman Defending Herself Examines Her Own Character Witness.   Susan Griffin.   NPGG

Questioning.   Henrietta Cordelia Ray.   CBWP-3

Questioning Faces.   Robert Frost.   GrPl

Questionnaire.   Susan Saxe.   GLP

Questions.   Dagmar Hilarova, *tr. by* Ewald Osers.   VWA

Questions, The.   Robert Pinsky.   NoAM; NPGG

Questions.   Amber Coverdale Sumrall.   TSM

Questions & Answers.   A. L. Lazarus.   SoTCo

Questions and Answers.   Diana O Hehir.   NPGG

Questions at Night.   Louis Untermeyer.   FaPON

Questions My Son Asked Me, Answers I Never Gave Him.   Nancy Willard.   LCAP

Questions of Ethne Alba, The.   *Unknown, tr. fr. Irish by* James Carney. TIRV

Questions of Swimming, 1935.   Peter Davison.   DiPo

Questions of Travel.   Elizabeth Bishop.   NAAL-2; NOBA

Questions [1] ("Why do you love her").   Donald Hall.   FF

Questions [2] ("How is it now").   Donald Hall.   FF

Questions which have always been here, The.   New Age.   Keorapetse Kgositsile.   WMBCH

Quha Is Perfyte.   Alexander Scott.   OxBS

Quhen [*or* Qwhen *or* When] Alexander [*or* Alysandyr] our kynge [*or* King] was dede.   The Death of Alexander.   *Unknown.*   GoTS; OxBS
(When Alysandyr Our King Was Dede.)   FaBoCh

Quhen Flora Had O'erfret the Firth.   *Unknown.   See* When Flora had O'erfret the Firth.

Quhen he wes yung, and cled in grene.   Quhy Sowld Nocht Allane Honorit Be?   *Unknown.*   OxBS

Quhen Noye had maid his Sacrifyce.   After the Flood.   Sir David Lindsay.   *Fr.* The Monarche.   OxBS

Quhen Thai him fand. . . .   *See* When They him fand.

Quhen that I had oversene this regioun.   Of the Realme of Scotland.   Sir David Lindsay.   *Fr.* The Dreme.   OxBS

Quhen thou art careit to that cuntree.   Virgil, *tr. into Middle English by* Gavin Douglas.   *Fr.* The Aeneid [*or* Eneados], III.   OBVE

Quhy Sowld Nocht Allane Honorit Be?   *Unknown.*   OxBS

Quhy will ye, merchantis of renoun.   To the Merchantis of Edinburgh. William Dunbar.   FaBoPP; OxBS

Qui Bien Aime a Tard Oublie.   Chaucer.   *See* Parlement of Foules, The: Now Welcom[e], Somer [*or* Summer].

Qui Laborat, Orat.   Arthur Hugh Clough.   TrPWD

Qui nunc dancere vult modo.   A Holiday Task.   Gilbert Abbott À Beckett.   NA

Qui Perdiderit Animam Suam.   Richard Crashaw.   ACP

Quia Amore Langueo ("In a tabernacle").   *Unknown, tr. fr. Middle English by* Helen Gardner.   ACP; MeEL

Quia Amore Langueo ("In a valley [*or* the vale *or* the vaile] of this restless mind [*or* restles mind]").   *Unknown, tr. by* Helen Gardner.   NOBE; NOCV; OBEV; PoEL-1

Quick!/ Empty the offices.   Blue Alert.   Eve Merriam.   PCP

Quick! a last poem before I go.   On Rachmaninoff's Birthday.   Frank O'Hara.   PoM

Quick and Bitter.   Yehuda Amichai, *tr. fr. Hebrew.*   BoLoP, *tr. by* Assia Gutmann; IP, *tr. by* Warren Bargad *and* Stanley F. Chyet

Quick and the Dead, The.   Ilarie Voronca, *tr. fr. French.*   VWA, *tr. by* Edouard Roditi

Quick as shuttles the children move.   The Children's Party.   Eiluned Lewis.   CN

Quick climb to the Incense Terrace, A.   In the Mountains, Parting from Master Ning.   Kao Ch'i, *tr. by* Jonathan Chaves.   CoBLCP

Quick-falling dew.   Basho, *tr. by* Curtis Hidden Page.   AWP

Quick! Hoist the jib and cast us off, my son.   Over Bright Summer Seas. Robert Hillyer.   NYBP

Quick in spite I said unkind.   Brazen Tongue.   William Rose Benét. MoAmPo

Quick lunch! quick lunch! the neon cries, and I.   Essay on Lunch. Walker Gibson.   NYBP

Quick on my feet in those Novembers of my loneliness.   A Mad Fight Song for William S. Carpenter, 1966.   James Wright.   NoAM

Quick sparks on the gorse-bushes are leaping, The.   The Wild Common. D. H. Lawrence.   NoAM

Quick-Step.   Robert Creeley.   VGW

Quick, woman, in your net.   The Net.   W. R. Rodgers.   AnIL; BoLoP; CIP; ErPo

Quickening, The.   Stella Weston Tuttle.   GoYe

Quicker/ than that can't.   A Sight.   Robert Creeley.   NaP

Quickly, love, be lyrical & let.   La, La, La!   Thomas M. Disch.   NBLV

Quickness. Henry Vaughan. ELP; MeLP; MePo; NOBE; NOCV; OBS; SeCePo; SeCP; SeCV-1

Quicksands. William Zaranka. BXAP

Quid, omit, my simple friend. To an Ambitious Friend ("Quid bellicosus"). Horace, *tr. fr. Latin.* Fr. Odes, II, 11. AWP, *tr. by* Matthew Arnold.

Quid Restat. Lucius Beebe. RFM

Quid Sit Futurum Cras Fuge Quaerere. Matthew Prior. FaBoEE

Quid the Cynic's Song. Blake. *See* Island in the Moon, An: When old corruption first begun.

Quidditie, The. George Herbert. PoEL-2

Quiescent, a Person Sits Heart and Soul. Ring Lardner. OBAL

Quiet. Yves Bonnefoy, *tr. fr. French by* Paul Auster. RHTwFP

Quiet. Marjorie Pickthall. NOBC; OBCV

Quiet. Brian Swann. AmPA

Quiet. Giuseppe Ungaretti, *tr. fr. Italian by* Henry Taylor. PFI

Quiet as are the quiet skies. A Smiling Demon of Notre Dame. Sophie Jewett. AA

Quiet breeze stalks, A. Departure. Ory Bernstein, *tr. by* Bernhard Frank. MHeP

Quiet courtyard fills with greenery, The. Wen Cheng-ming, *tr. fr. Chinese by* Jonathan Chaves. *Fr.* What It's Like Living in My Studio Late in Spring. CoBLCP

Quiet deepens. You will not persuade, The. Farewell to Van Gogh. Charles Tomlinson. CMoP; GTBS-P; PoE

Quiet Desperation. Louis Simpson. SV

Quiet dreams interrupted. Traveling down the Yodo River on a Winter Night. Fujii Chikugai, *tr. by* Burton Watson. JLIC-2

Quiet Enemy, The. Walter De la Mare. BrPo

Quiet-eyed Cattle, The. Leslie Norris. PChr

Quiet Fog, The. Marge Piercy. UnPo

Quiet from Fear of Evil. "S. C. McK." BLRP

Quiet Glades of Eden, The. Robert Graves. BoLoP; ErPo

Quiet Glen, The. Douglas Fraser. PoSH

Quiet home had Parson Gray, A. Parson Gray. Goldsmith. NA

Quiet Hour, The. Louise Hollingsworth Bowman. BLRP

Quiet House, The. Charlotte Mew. BrRo; EBEV

Quiet House. Yoshioka Minoru, *tr. fr. Japanese by* Hiroaki Sato. FCEI

Quiet House in Ch'ang-lo Ward, A. Po Chü-i, *tr. fr. Chinese by* Burton Watson. CoBCP

Quiet Kingdom, The. Carl Busse, *tr. fr. German by* Ludwig Lewisohn. AWP

Quiet Life, The. *At. to* William Byrd. ElL

Quiet Life, The. Pope. *See* Happy The man whose wish and care.

Quiet Light of Flies, The. Natan Zach, *tr. fr. Hebrew by* Peter Everwine *and* Shula Starkman. VWA

Quiet Mind, The. *Unknown.* OBSC

Quiet moon, immaculate of face, The. William Baylebridge. *Fr.* Love Redeemed, CVII. CBAP

Quiet narrow river, life is winding, A. The Baron Tells of His Last Experience. Jacob Glatstein, *tr. by* Benjamin *and* Barbara Harshav. AYP

Quiet night is solemn and still, The. Sent to the Hsiu-ts'ai on His Entry into the Army. Hsi K'ang, *tr. by* Burton Watson. CoBCP

Quiet Normal Life, A. Wallace Stevens. LCAP; NAAL-2; NoAM

Quiet now, feel the kindly pressure of darkness. Winter Solstice Poem. Diana Scott. BrRo

Quiet of the Dead, The. Mary Morison Webster. PeSA

Quiet Pilgrim, The. Edith M. Thomas. AA

Quiet, quiet/ spring clouds float. Flower Shadows. Mo Shih-lung, *tr. by* Jonathan Chaves. CoBLCP

Quiet room, the flowers, the perfumed calm, The. Schumann's Sonata in A Minor. Celia Thaxter. AiP

Quiet Sitting. Wang Chiu-ssu, *tr. fr. Chinese by* Jonathan Chaves. CoBLCP

Quiet Soul, A. John Oldham. OBEV

Quiet Things. Grace Noll Crowell. PoLF

Quiet Tide near Ardossan, The. Charles Tennyson Turner. FaBoPP

Quiet Town. William Stafford. MAT

Quiet War in Leicester, A. Elaine Feinstein. CN

Quiet Waters. Blanche Shoemaker Wagstaff. BLPA

Quiet Work. Matthew Arnold. FaBoBe; TrGrPo

Quietly. Kenneth Rexroth. ErPo

Quietly/ just for himself. Peter Zumpf, *tr. by* Beth Bjorklund. CoAuP

Quietly/ So quietly. My Persecutor. Malka Heifetz Tussman, *tr. by* Kathryn Hellerstein. AYP

Quietly and while at rest on the trim grass I have gazed. The Air of June Sings. Edward Dorn. NeAP; PoM

Quietly as rosebuds. Love's Coming. John Shaw Neilson. PoAu-1

Quietly at our side the dead. The Dead Men. Sophia de Mello Breyner Andresen, *tr. by* Allan Francovich. PBWP

Quietly step onto a land. Kayenta Times Yet Dreaming On. Nia Francisco. HATNAP

Quietly the cloud cast its shadow. Story. Takenaka Iku, *tr. by* Geoffrey Bownas *and* Anthony Thwaite. PeBJV

Quietly the world lay sleeping. The Birth of Jesus. Josephine D. Henderson Heard. CBWP-4

Quietness: piercing the rocks. Basho, *tr. fr. Japanese by* Burton Watson. *Fr.* Seventy-six Hokku. FCEI

Quietude. Mihály Ladányi, *tr. fr. Hungarian by* Jascha Kessler. FOC

Quietude of a soft wind, The. The Creditor. Louis MacNeice. EaLo

Quijote. Marco Martos, *tr. fr. Spanish by* David Tipton. Per

Quilled Quilt, a Needle Bed, A. Brad Leithauser. MAYP; SM

Quilt, The. Larry Levis. MAYP

Quilt, The. Mary Effie Lee Newsome. CDC

Quilt, Dutch China Plate. Marvin Bell. BLA

Quilt Song. Mark Vinz. GOYP

Quilted silk from Tsukushi, The. Manzei. *Fr.* Manyo Shu. Ma

Quinnapoxet. Stanley Kunitz. AnAn; DiL

Quinquireme of Nineveh from distant Ophir. Cargoes. John Masefield. BLPL; CMoP; FaBV; FaPON; FaPoR; InPK; LiTM; MoAB; MoBrPo; MOS; NOBE; OBEV; OBMV; PoRA; PoRA; TEP

Quintana Lay in the Shallow Grave of Coral. Karl Shapiro. VGW

Quintina of Crosses, A. Chad Walsh. TrCP

Quip, The. George Herbert. JCP; LiTB; OBS; SeCP; SeCV-1

Quit now the town, and with a journeying dream. "George Eliot." *Fr.* The Spanish Gypsy. OBTV

Quite Apart from the Holy Ghost. Adrian Mitchell. OBSV

Quite for no reason. I've Been to a Marvelous Party. Noel Coward. NBLV

Quite Forsaken. D. H. Lawrence. BrPo

Quite horfen, fer a lark, coves on a ship. The Helbatrawss. Kingsley Amis. NOBL

Quite, quite./ Oh I agree. Restricted. Eve Merriam. TrJP

Quite rightly, we remained among the living. The Survivors. Adrienne Rich. NYBP

Quite spent with thoughts I left my cell, and lay. Vanity of Spirit. Henry Vaughan. TOF

Quite the Cheese. H. C. Waring. BXAP

Quite unexpectedly as Vasserot. The End of the World. Archibald MacLeish. BLPL; CMoP; HoPM; InPK; LiTM; MAT; MoAB; MoAMPo; NoAM; NOBA; OBAL; OxBA; Son; TAP; TrGrPo; VGW

Quite unimaginable, this blueness. The Color. Zsuzsa Beney, *tr. fr. Hungarian by* Jascha Kessler. *Fr.* A Broken Glass. FOC

Quits. Thomas Bailey Aldrich. AA

Quits. Matthew Prior. *See* To John I ow'd great obligation.

Quitter, The. *Unknown.* BLPA; WBLP

Quitting is out of the question yet. Dispatch Number Sixty. Doug Fetherling. NeAC

Quitting kickball, the gods. Warbler. Anzai Hitoshi, *tr. by* Sato. FCEI

Quivering/ in the heat waves. Kyotai, *tr. fr. Japanese by* Burton Watson. *Fr.* Sixteen Hokku. FCEI

Quivíra. Arthur Guiterman. PAH

Quo life, the warld is mine. The Flyting o' Life and Daith. Hamish Henderson. OxBS

Quod Dunbar to Kennedy. William Dunbar. OxBoLi

Quod Tegit Omnia. Yvor Winters. QFR

Quoich, the Ey, the Slugain, The. The Drunken Dee. Syd Scroggie. PoSH

Quoits. Mary Effie Lee Newsome. CDC

Quondam was I in my lady's grace. Sir Thomas Wyatt. GBL

Quoniam Ego in Flagella Paratus Sum. William Habington. ACP

Quotation from Shakespeare with Slight Improvements, A. "Lewis Carroll." FaBoNo

Quotations. George Oppen. NNaP

Quotella. Janet Fox. BWV

Quoth Cibber to Pope, tho' in verse you foreclose. Pope. FaBoEE

Quoth he, My faith as adamantine. Samuel Butler. *Fr.* Hudibras, II, 1. OBSV

Quoth he, to bid me not to love. Samuel Butler. *Fr.* Hudibras, II, 1. NOBL

Quoth John to Joan. *Unknown.* CH

Quoth Satan to Arnold: "My worthy good fellow." *Unknown.* PAH

Quoth she, I wish I could prescribe your help. Rachel Speght. *Fr.* A Dream. WPE

Quoth tongue of neither maid nor wife. Elena's Song. Sir Henry Taylor. *Fr.* Philip van Artevelde, II. OBEV

Qwhylum thair wes, as Esope can report. The Taill of the Wolf and the Wedder. Robert Henryson. OxBLMV

R

R. Alcona to J. Brenzaida. Emily Brontë. *See* Cold in the earth, and the deep snow piled above thee!
R-and-R Centre: An Incident from the Vietnam War. D. J. Enright. OxBC
R-E-M-O-R-S-E. George Ade. FiBHP; NBLV; OBAL
R-P-O-P-H-E-S-S-A-G-R. E. E. Cummings. AmPP; NoP; PoE; PPP
R the reviewer, reviewing my book. Hilaire Belloc. *Fr.* A Moral Alphabet. NoAM
Rabbi, The. Christian Morgenstern, *tr. fr. German by* W. D. Snodgrass *and* Lore Segal. OBD
Rabbi Ben Ezra, *sel.* Robert Browning. BLPL; FaBV; FaFP; FiP; NAEL-2; OBNC; TEP; WGRP
  Grow Old Along with Me. FaBV
Rabbi, if a child is born with two heads. Pilpul. Rodger Kamenetz. UL; VWA
Rabbi Levi Yitskhok's drayman—the one who wore. Sunday Shtetl. Jacob Glatstein, *tr. by* Cynthia Ozick. PeBMYV
Rabbi of condiments. The Garlic. Bert Meyers. VWA
Rabbi Pinhas:/ From true prayers. Expounding the Torah. Louis Zukofsky. VWA
Rabbi saw a Torah-scroll, The. The Long March. Joyce Peseroff. PPR
Rabbi Yom-Tob of Mayence Petitions His God. A. M. Klein. TrJP
Rabbi Yussel Luksh of Chelm. Jacob Glatstein, *tr. fr. Yiddish by* Nathan Halper. TrJP
Rabbit, The. Edith King. BoTP
Rabbit, The. Elizabeth Madox Roberts. OBCA; RHPC
Rabbit. Tom Robinson. FaPON
Rabbit, The. *Unknown.* FaBoCo; FiBHP
Rabbit as King of the Ghosts, A. Wallace Stevens. NoAM; SOTW; TTTS
Rabbit Cry. Edward Lucie-Smith. NePoEA-2
Rabbit has a charming face, The. The Rabbit. *Unknown.* FaBoCo; FiBHP
Rabbit Hunter, The. Robert Frost. ASP
Rabbit in the Moon, The. Ryokan, *tr. fr. Japanese by* Burton Watson. FCEI
Rabble of six arrived at my house, A. A Satire on the O'Haras. Tadhg Dall O'Huiginn. NOIV
Rabble Soldier. *Unknown.* AS
Rabid or dog-dull. Let me tell you how. A Profesor's Song. John Berryman. HeIP; MoP; NAAL-2; NoAM; NOBA; OxBC
Rabinal-Achí, *sel. Unknown, tr. fr. Mayan by* Nathaniel Tarn.
  "Cala-Achí! Ha! Aha! Yeha! Ahau! Wow! Achí!" *Fr.* IV. STP
Raccoon. Kenneth Rexroth. *Fr.* A Bestiary. NNaP
  (Racoon.) FiBHP
Raccoon on the Road. Joseph Payne Brennan. GoYe
Raccoon Poem. Miriam Palmer. NMM
Raccoon [*or* Racoon] wears a black mask, The. Raccoon. Kenneth Rexroth. *Fr.* A Bestiary. NNaP
  (Racoon.) FiBHP
Raccoons. Aileen Fisher. PDV
Raccoons are selectively polygamous. Raccoon Poem. Miriam Palmer. NMM
Race, The. Nuala Ni Dhomhnaill, *tr. fr. Irish by* Michael Hartnett. CIP
Race. Orkhan Muyassar, *tr. fr. Arabic by* Lena Jayyusi *and* Samuel Hazo. MAP
Race of the Kingfishers. Ray A. Young Bear. HATNAP
Race of the Oregon, The. John James Meehan. PAH
Race Question, The. Naomi Long Madgett. BPo
Race Riot, Tulsa, 1921. Sharon Olds. MAYP
Racer's Widow, The. Louise Glück. AmPA; ASP; GeTw; NYBP; SM
Rachel. Linda Pastan. TV
Rachel. Rachel, *tr. fr. Hebrew by* Naomi Nir. VWA
Rachel Goes to the Well for Water ("Rachel stands by the mirror and plaits"). Itzig Manger, *tr. fr. Yiddish by* Ruth Whitman. VWA
Rachel's Lament. Linda Zisquit. VWA
Rachmaninov. Martin Seymour-Smith. NPo
Racing Eight, A. James L. Cuthbertson. PoAu-1
Racing-Man, The. Sir A. P. Herbert. FiBHP
Racing, reckoning fingers flick. Palladas, *tr. by* Tony Harrison. OBVE
Rack upon rack of leaves all elbowing. Spring. W. R. Rodgers AnIL
Racoon. Kenneth Rexroth. *See* Raccoon [*or* Racoon] wears a black mask, The.

Racoon up the 'simmon tree. The Persimmon Tree. *Unknown.* GBP
Radar. Alan Ross. FF
Radha is lost to the onslaught of love. Surdas, *tr. by* John Stratton Hawley *and* Mark Juergensmeyer. SSI
Radiance, The. Kabir, *tr. fr. Hindi by* Robert Bly. LLLT
Radiance of Extinct Stars, The. Allan Kolski Horvitz. VWA
Radiance of that star that leans on me, The. Delay. Elizabeth Jennings. NePoEA; OxBTC
Radiant Is the World Soul. Rav Abraham Isaac Kook, *tr. fr. Hebrew by* Ben Zion Bokser. VWA
Radiant Ranks of Seraphim. Valery Yakovlevich Bryusov, *tr. fr. Russian by* Babette Deutsch *and* Avrahm Yarmolinsky. AWP
Radical, The. Waring Cuney. CDC
Radical Coherency. David Antin. UL
Radical Creed, A. Gelett Burgess. FaBoNo
Radical Song of 1786, A. St. John Honeywood. PAH
Radical War Song, A. Macaulay. OBSV
Radio. Frank O'Hara. PoA
Radio broadcast the news, The. Lovers in Fall. Yehuda Amichai, *tr. by* Warren Bargad *and* Stanley F. Chyet. IP
Radio glimmers, The. Paper Cities. Gjertrud Schnackenberg. AnAn
Radio Religion, The. William Ludlum. WBLP
Radio under the Bed, The. Reed Whittemore. NYBP
Radio's reality when. Monday, Monday. David Trinidad. UL
Radish-picker, The. Issa, *tr. by* Geoffrey Bownas *and* Anthony Thwaite. PeBJV
R.A.F. Sarah Churchill. CN
Rafts are moored to cherries. Kaya Shirao, *tr. fr. Japanese by* Hiroaki Sato. *Fr.* Twenty-one Hokku. FCEI
Rag Doll and Summer Birds. Owen Dodson. PoNe
Rag Rug. Rob Wilborn. SoTCo
Ragas, *sels.* David Meltzer. NeAP
  15th Raga: For Bela Lugosi.
  12th Raga: For John Wieners.
Ragged and Dirty. *Unknown.* AmFP
Ragged-and-Tough. Not Ragged-and-Tough. *Unknown.* ChTr; FaBoNo
Ragged block of rockets breaks up, A. Procession. Francisco Carrillo, *tr. by* Maureen Ahern *and* David Tipton. Per
Ragged Island. Edna St. Vincent Millay. NAAL-2; NoP
Ragged Robin. Elizabeth Godley. BoTP
Ragged, unheeded, stooping, meanly shod. The Poor Can Feed the Birds. John Shaw Neilson. PoAu-1
Ragged Wood, The. W. B. Yeats. GBL
Raggedy Dog, The. Sherman Ripley. RAR
Raggedy Man, The. James Whitcomb Riley. FaPON; OBCA; OxBChV
Raggle, Taggle Gipsies, The. *Unknown. See* There were three gypsies a-come to my door.
Raging Canawl. *Unknown.* AS
Raging Generation, The. Mbuyiseni Oswald Mtshali. WMBCH
Ragout. William Zaranka. BXAP
Ragoût Fin de Siècle (with Reference to Certain Cafés). Erich Kästner, *tr. fr. German by* Walter Kaufman. ErPo; PeHV
Rags. Edmund Vance Cooke. BLPA
Rags. Judith Thurman. TDD
Rags and tatters. Ragged Robin. Elizabeth Godley. BoTP
Rags and tatters, rags and tatters. Ryokan, *tr. by* Burton Watson. JLIC-2
  (Rags and Tatters.) FCEI
Ragwort, The. John Clare. ChTr
Rahab. Diane Glancy. CRP
Ráhat, The. John Jerome Rooney. AA
Raid, The. William Everson. MoP; NoAM; PrIm
Raid on the Market. Polycarp Chimedza. WMBCH
Raider, The. W. R. Rodgers. AnIL; MoBrPo
Rail on, poor feeble scribbler, speak of me. The Author's Reply. Sir Carr Scroope. APAS
Railing of crimson hue, A. A Ballad of a Springtime River: Presented to Wang the Elder. Hung Liang-chi, *tr. by* William Schultz. WFTU
Railroad, The. Henry David Thoreau. *See* What's the Railroad to Me?
Railroad Bill. *Unknown.* AS
Railroad Blues, The. *Unknown.* AmFP
Railroad bridge's, De. Homesick Blues. Langston Hughes. CDC; MoAmPo
Railroad Cars Are Coming, The. *Unknown.* AmFN, *with music;* AS, *with music;* FaPON, *with music*
Railroad look so pretty. Two Hoboes. *Unknown.* WTO
Railroad suddenly hops out of the, A. Machu Picchu, Peru. Fred Red Cloud. NOVW
Railroad Thieves. Berish Weinstein, *tr. fr. Yiddish by* Leonard Wolf. PeBMYV
Railroad track is miles away, The. Travel. Edna St. Vincent Millay. FaPON; MoShBr; OBCA; PDV; RHPC

Railroad yard in San Jose. In Back of the Real. Allen Ginsberg. AmPP; HeIP

Railroader for Me, A. *Unknown.* AmFP

Rails pause barely to tie the horizons, The. The Depot. Lewis Turco. GrPl

Railway car. Itamar Ya'oz-kest, *tr. fr. Hebrew by* Bernhard Frank. *Fr.* Ordeal by Fire. MHeP

Railway Junction, The. Walter de la Mare. OxBTC

Railway Station. John Hay. WaP

Railway Stationery, The. Kenneth Koch. NoP

Railway Train, The. Emily Dickinson. *See* I like to see it lap the miles.

Rain, The. Robert Creeley. CAPP; CoAP; PoE; VGW

Rain, The. Dafydd ap Gwilym, *tr. fr. Welsh by* Rolfe Humphries. OBWVE

Rain, The. W. H. Davies. BoTP; OxBTC

Rain. Emanuel diPasquale. InPK

Rain. Margiad Evans. OBWVE

Rain. Haim Guri, *tr. fr. Hebrew by* Mark Elliott Shapiro. VWA

Rain. Sam Harrison. NeIP

Rain. Lance Henson. VoR

Rain, The. Zbigniew Herbert, *tr. fr. Polish by* Czeslaw Milosz. PwPP

Rain. Anselm Hollo. PoM

Rain. Nishiwaki Junzaburo, *tr. fr. Japanese by* Sato. FCEI

Rain. Vachel Lindsay. CMoP

Rain. Lilian McCrea. BoTP

Rain. Howard Moss. ErPo

Rain, The. Muhammad al-Mahdi al-Majdhoub, *tr. fr. Arabic by* Matthew Sorenson. MAP

Rain. Paul Murray. BIrV

Rain. Vladimir Nabokov. GrPl

Rain. Nishiwaki Junzaburo, *tr. fr. Japanese by* Geoffrey Bownas *and* Anthony Thwaite. PeBJV

Rain. James Whitcomb Riley. *Fr.* Wet-Weather Talk. BoNaP

Rain. Gary Soto. *Fr.* The Elements of San Joaquin. NoAM

Rain. Robert Louis Stevenson. GoJo; NTCP

Rain. Adrien Stoutenburg. PDV

Rain. Edward Thomas. NAEL-2; OBWP; OxBTC

Rain. Hone Tuwhare. ATNZ

Rain, The. *Unknown.* BoTP; OxNR; RAR

Rain. Sándor Weöres, *tr. fr. Hungarian by* Jascha Kessler. FOC

Rain. James Wright. PoM

Rain/ drops/ spot/ they/ spit/ on/ rock. Rain Drops. Sallie Burrow Wood. RR

Rain:/ Grey, rat-grey rain. Rain on Castle Island. Kitahara Hakushu, *tr. by* Geoffrey Bownas *and* Anthony Thwaite. PeBJV

Rain. A heavy mane. Marina Tsvetayeva, *tr. fr. Russian by* Paul Schmidt. *Fr.* The Daughter of Jairus, XII. BoWoP

Rain after a Vaudeville Show. Stephen Vincent Benét. MoAmPo

Rain all over the cornfields. Butterfly Maidens. Lahpu, *tr. by* Natalie Curtis. WTO

Rain, and a flurry of wind shaking the pear's white blossom. C. K. Stead. *Fr.* Twenty-one Sonnets, II. PeNZ

Rain and sunlight and the boat between them. Leaving Inishmore. Michael Longley. FaBCIP

Rain and the Tyrants. Jules Supervielle, *tr. fr. French by* David Gascoyne. RHTwFP

Rain and wind, the rain and wind, raved endlessly, The. Melancholy. Edward Thomas. NoP

Rain at Wildwood. May Swenson. NYBP

Rain beating down. *Unknown, tr. by* Geoffrey Bownas *and* Anthony Thwaite. PeBJV

Rain beats on me, I make a shelter, The. *Unknown. Fr.* Manyo Shu. Ma

Rain before seven. *Unknown. Fr.* Weather Wisdom. FaBoBe; OxNR

Rain begins, The. This is no summer rain. Oregon Winter. Jeanne McGahey. AmFN

Rain came, The. The Black Angel. Katerina Anghelaki-Rooke, *tr. by* Gail Holst-Weirhaft. WCI

Rain came. Fog out of the slough and horses. Day after Chasing Porcupines. James Welch. NoAM

Rain Clouds. Elizabeth-Ellen Long. RHPC

Rain comes down through the alders. Seamus Heaney. *Fr.* Exposure. PoPo

Rain comes flapping through the yard, The. Gathering Mushrooms. Paul Muldoon. CIP

Rain-Crow, The. Madison Cawein. AA

Rain dampens Sung-ling, spring fills with mist. Hsiu-chou. T'ang Hsien-Tsu, *tr. by* Jonathan Chaves. CoBLCP

Rain. Dark night. My Street—Sheepshead Bay. Berysh Vaynshteyn, *tr. by* Benjamin *and* Barbara Harshav. AYP

Rain, do not fall. Mist. Andrew Young. PoSH

Rain Down. Mary Ellen Solt. BoWoP

Rain drifts forever in this place. The Falls of Glomach. Andrew Young. OxBS; PoSH

Rain-drops, The/ That fall this evening. *Unknown. Fr.* Manyo Shu. Ma

Rain Drops. Sallie Burrow Wood. RR

Rain falling over the land how sad this night dark great beast. No. 96. Lajos Kassák, *tr. by* Jascha Kessler. FOC

Rain falling, what things do you grow? River Winding. Charlotte Zolotow. RHPC

Rain Falls and Floods. Amir Gilboa, *tr. fr. Hebrew by* Warren Bargad *and* Stanley F. Chyet. IP

Rain falls and then vanishes, The. A Green Refrain. Avraham Huss, *tr. by* Mark Elliott Shapiro. VWA

Rain falls briskly on my worn shelter-half. Inner Brother. Stephen Stepanchev. WaP

Rain falls far in a realm unknown, The. Somewhat. Yang Mu, *tr. by* Dominic Cheung. IFON

Rain falls in Tel Aviv on a June morning. The Weather. Meir Wieseltier, *tr. by* Bernhard Frank. MHeP

Rain falls like knives, The. Another Life. Derek Walcott. PBCV

Rain fell like grass growing, The. Rain at Wildwood. May Swenson. NYBP

Rain Forest. Dave Smith. HCAP; MT

Rain Games. Tony Beyer. ATNZ

Rain had fallen, the Poet arose, The. The Poet's Song. Tennyson. EBVV; ELP; FiP

Rain has been reciting, The. Fishermen. Gabriel Preil, *tr. by* Betsy Rosenberg. VWA

Rain Has Fallen on the History Books. David Rosenberg. VWA

Rain has passed, The. Birth. Amir Gilboa, *tr. by* Stephen Mitchell. VWA

Rain Has Silver Sandals, The. May Justus. RHPC

Rain hits over and over. Rain. Adrien Stoutenburg. PDV

Rain in my ears: impatiently there raps. Robert David Fitzgerald. *Fr.* Essay on Memory. CBAP

Rain in Ohio. Mary Oliver. InPK

Rain in Summer. Longfellow. BoTP; GN

Rain in the Pine Grove, The. Gabriele D'Annunzio, *tr. fr. Italian by* William Giuliano. PFI

Rain in the Southwest. Reeve Spencer Kelley. AmFN

Rain is chronic, The. Dido's Farewell. Linda Pastan. GOYP

Rain is due to fall, The. A Poet Thinks. Lui Chi, *tr. by* E. Powys Mathers. AWP

Rain is good. April. Lucille Clifton. RAR

Rain is over, The. Birth. Amir Gilboa, *tr. by* Robert Mezey *and* Shula Starkman. OFD

Rain is raining all around, The. Rain. Robert Louis Stevenson. GoJo; NTCP

Rain It Raineth, The. Charles Synge Christopher Bowen, Baron Bowen. FiBHP; NBLV; NTCP ("Rain it raineth on the just, The.") CenHV

Rain it raineth every day, The. Pennsylvania Deutsch. Christopher Morley. NBLV

Rain it raineth on the just, The. Charles Synge Christopher Bowen, Baron Bowen. *See* Rain It Raineth, The.

Rain, it streams on stone and hillock, The. A. E. Housman. CMoP

Rain Journal: London: June 65. Lee Harwood. PeHV

Rain long and abrasive thickens the beard of summer. At Frost's Grave. Dave Smith. BLA

Rain Magic Song. *Unknown, tr. fr. Tewa Indian by* H. J. Spinden. WTO

Rain makes little cuts on the window, The. Dialogues 4 1 Voice Only. Doug Fetherling. NeAC

Rain, midnight rain, nothing but the wild rain. Rain. Edward Thomas. NAEL-2; OBWP; OxBTC

Rain Music. Joseph Seamon Cotter, Jr.. BANP; CDC

Rain of a winter storm. Ranko, *tr. by* Geoffrey Bownas *and* Anthony Thwaite. PeBJV

Rain of London pimples, The. London Rain. Louis MacNeice. HeIP; NoP

Rain of Rites, A. Jayanta Mahapatra. PoA

Rain on Castle Island. Kitahara Hakushu, *tr. fr. Japanese by* Geoffrey Bownas *and* Anthony Thwaite. PeBJV

Rain on Good Friday and Easter Day. *Unknown.* FaBoUs

Rain on the Cumberlands. James Still. GrPl

Rain on the Down. Arthur Symons. *Fr.* At Dieppe. BrPo; OBNC

Rain on the far tip of the grove. Scattered Leaves. Lance Henson. VoR

Rain on the green grass. *Unknown.* OxNR

Rain on the green grass. The Rain. *Unknown.* BoTP; RAR
Rain on the macadam quaver ticks. Lyn Hejinian. IAT
Rain on the Night of the Full Moon. Hsü Ts'an, *tr. fr. Chinese by* Irving Lo. WFTU
Rain on the Range. S. Omar Barker. CowP
Rain on the reservoir. Oracle. Donald Finkel. BLA
Rain on the Roof. Janet Frame. ATNZ
Rain on the West Side Highway. Adrienne Rich. *Fr.* Twenty-one Love Poems, XVIII. GLP; NAAL-2
Rain Passes. Yüan Mei, *tr. fr. Chinese by* J. P. Seaton. WFTU
Rain, rain. Sun after Rain. Norma Farber. RAR
Rain, rain, and sun! a rainbow in the sky. Merlin's Riddling. Tennyson. *Fr.* Idylls of the King: The Coming of Arthur. FaBoRV
Rain, rain, go away. Mother Goose. OxNR
Rain, rain, go to Spain. Mother Goose. OxNR
Rain Rain on the Splintered Girl. Ishmael Reed. PoBA
Rain rains sair on Duriesdyke, The. Duriesdyke. Swinburne. OxBB
Rain (Rapa Nui), The. Pablo Neruda, *tr. fr. Spanish by* Lynn C. Jarox. LPSS
Rain rins doun through Mirry-land toune, The. Sir Hugh; or, The Jew's Daughter. *Unknown.* ESPB (Hugh of Lincoln.) ACP; EnSB; OxBB
Rain, said the first, as it falls in Venice. Song Tournament: New Style. Louis Untermeyer. OBAL
Rain Says, The. Cheng Ch'ou-yu, *tr. fr. Chinese by* Dominic Cheung. IFON
Rain set early in to-night, The. Porphyria's Lover. Robert Browning. AWP; BeLS; HAP; NAEL-2; OBEV; TEP; TrGrPo
Rain smell comes with the wind. Leslie Marmon Silko. UnPo; VoR
Rain Song. Badr Shakir al-Sayyab, *tr. fr. Arabic by* Abdullah al-Udhari. MPAW
Rain Song. Badr Shakir al-Sayyab, *tr. fr. Arabic by* Lena Jayyusi *and* Christopher Middleton. MAP
Rain Song. Robert Loveman. *See* It isn't raining rain to me.
Rain Song, The. Alex Rogers. BANP
Rain Song of the Giant Society. *Unknown, tr. fr. Sia Indian by* Matilda Coxe Stevenson. AnAmPo
Rain stops, and a scent of lotus lingers in the air, The. Immortal at the River. Yen Hsüan, *tr. by* Lois Fusek. ATF
Rain-sunken roof, grown green and thin. The Barn. Edmund Blunden. MoBrPo; SeCePo
Rain That Fell upon the Height, The. Coventry Patmore. *See* Victories of Love, The: Your love lacks joy, your letter says.
Rain, The ("'twas in Koolau I met with the rain"). *Unknown, tr. fr. Hawaiian by* N. B. Emerson. WTO
Rain thunderstorms over the Potomac, in Georgetown. Rainscapes, Hydrangeas, Roses, and Singing Birds. Richard Eberhart. MoAmPo
Rain to the Tribe. Al-Khansa, *tr. fr. Arabic by* Willis Barnstone *and* Tony Nawfal. BoWoP
Rain was full of the freshness, The. The Dark and Falling Summer. Delmore Schwartz. NYBP
Rain was on the walls. Rain, Wind and a New City. Munir Niazi, *tr. by* Mahmood Jamal. PBMUP
Rain was raining cheerfully, The. The Vulture and the Husbandman. A. C. Hilton. CenHV; FaBoCo
Rain which in your most regrettable overflowings never forgets. Rains. Aimé Césaire, *tr. by* Michael Benedikt. POS
Rain, Wind and a New City. Munir Niazi, *tr. fr. Urdu by* Mahmood Jamal. PBMUP
Rain, with a silver flail. Whale. William Rose Benét. MoAmPo
Rain would fall on me, The. Watchful Wakeful. Amir Gilboa, *tr. by* Warren Bargad *and* Stanley F. Chyet. IP
Rainbow, The. W. H. Davies. BrPo
Rainbow, The. Gerard Manley Hopkins. FaBoPP; OxBSP
Rainbow. Robert Huff. NePoEA-2
Rainbow, The. David McCord. FaPON
Rainbow, The. Coventry Patmore. *Fr.* The Angel in the House, II, iii. GTBS-P
Rainbow, The. Christina Rossetti. *Fr.* Sing-Song. OxBChV
Rainbow, The. *Unknown, tr. fr. Hopi Indian by* Natalie Curtis. WTO
Rainbow, The. Wordsworth. *See* My Heart Leaps Up [When I Behold].
Rainbow and You. Tachihara Michizo, *tr. fr. Japanese by* Hiroaki Sato. FCEI
Rainbow arches in the sky, The. The Rainbow. David McCord. FaPON
Rainbow at night. *Unknown. Fr.* Weather Wisdom [*or* Weather Wise]. FaBoBe
Rainbow faded, the animals dispersed, The. Return to Ararat. Martyn Halsall. TrCP
Rainbow Fairies, The. *Unknown.* BoTP

Rainbow is the shape of god's desire, The. Colour-Scheme. Edward Baugh. PBCV
Rainbow on the ocean, The. So Slow to Die. George Edward Woodberry. *Fr.* Wild Eden, XXXVIII. AA
Rainbow stands red o'er the ocean, The. *Unknown, tr. by* N. B. Emerson. WTO
Rainbow Writing. Eve Merriam. GrPl
Rainbowesque dissonances of the Tower in its wireless, The. Sputterings. Blaise Cendrars, *tr. by* Ron Padgett. RHTwFP
Rainbows are lovely things. The Rainbow. W. H. Davies. BrPo
Raindrops. Aileen Fisher. RAR
Raindrops drip down, The. Teika, *tr. by* Steven D. Carter. WFTW
Raindrops fall. To a Man Who is Rob Southland. Nia Francisco. HATNAP
Raindrum. Niyi Osundare. UAS
Rainer,/ the man who was about to celebrate his 52nd birthday. The Death of Europe. Charles Olson. NeAP
Rainer Pichler always says the same thing. Important! Liesl Ujvary, *tr. by* Beth Bjorklund. CoAuP
Rainier. Jim Tollerud. VoR
Raining so much it's blackened fresh stubs of rice. By the Roadside in My Birthplace. Basho, *tr. fr. Japanese by* Burton Watson. *Fr.* Seventy-six Hokku. FCEI
Rainpoem. Michael Dransfield. CBAP
Rains. Aimé Césaire, *tr. fr. French by* Michael Benedikt. POS
Rains. Anna Hajnal, *tr. fr. Hungarian by* Jascha Kessler. FOC
Rain's all right. The boys who physic. Biography of Southern Rain. Kenneth Patchen. VGW
Rains, already old, The. The What She Said ("Rains, already old." Okkur Macatti, *tr. by* A. K. Ramanujan. PBWP
Rains for the Harvest. *Unknown, tr. fr. Tewa Indian by* H. J. Spinden. WTO
Rains have cleared above Wu Mountain, The. A Stretch of Cloud over Mount Wu. Mao Wen-hsi, *tr. by* Lois Fusek. ATF
Rains in season. What He Said to His Charioteer, on His Way Back. Cittalai Cattanar, *tr. by* A. K. Ramanujan. PLW
Rain's lovely gray daughter has lost her tall lover. Fog. Kenneth Patchen. NaP
Rains on the Island. Gabriel Preil, *tr. fr. Hebrew by* Robert Friend. VWA
Rains Pass. Yüan Mei, *tr. fr. Chinese by* Jonathan Chaves. CoBLCP
Rain's pounding away, The. Rain. Sándor Weöres, *tr. by* Jascha Kessler. FOC
Rain's unassuaging fountains multiply. The Waking Bird Refutes. Allen Curnow. ATNZ
Rainscapes, Hydrangeas, Roses, and Singing Birds. Richard Eberhart. MoAmPo
Rainstorm Has Dragged on for Ten Days Now, A, *sel.* T'ang Yin, *tr. fr. Chinese by* Jonathan Chaves.
"Ten days of wind and rain, depressing darkness!" CoBLCP
Rainuv; a Romantic Ballad from the Early Basque. Margaret Widdemer. BXAP
Rainwalkers, The. Denise Levertov. NePoEA-2; PPP
Rainy Day, The. Longfellow. AWP; FPL; PoLF
Rainy Day. William Wise. RAR
Rainy Midnight. Ivor Gurney. FaBoPP
Rainy Morning. Sotero Rivera-Avilés, *tr. fr. Spanish by* Julio Marzan. InW
Rainy morning. Don't get up. Don't even smoke. On the Hazards of Smoking. Leah Goldberg, *tr. by* Bernhard Frank. MHeP
Rainy Mountain Cemetery. N. Scott Momaday. CDW; HATNAP
Rainy Night. Ho Ching-ming, *tr. fr. Chinese by* Jonathan Chaves. CoBLCP
Rainy Night. Michizane, *tr. fr. Chinese by* Burton Watson. JLIC-1
Rainy night, A. Kyogoku Tamekane, *tr. fr. Japanese by* Burton Watson. *Fr.* Twenty-three Tanka. FCEI
Rainy Night at the Writers' Colony. Josephine Jacobsen. TAP
Rainy Nights. Irene Thompson. BoTP; RHPC
Rainy Pleiads Wester, The. A. E. Housman. BoLoP
Rainy Season, The. Linda Hogan. HATNAP
Rainy Season. Kan Sazan, *tr. fr. Chinese by* Burton Watson. JLIC-2
Rainy Season, The. William Meredith. NePoEA
Rainy Season, The. Wu Sheng, *tr. fr. Chinese by* Dominic Cheung. IFON
Rainy Season Love Song. Gladys May Casely Hayford. CDC
Rainy skies, misty mountains. Fifty. Kenneth Rexroth. TAP
Rainy Song. Max Eastman. FaBoBe
Rainy Summer, The. Alice Meynell. GoJo; OxBSP; OxBTC
Raise a "Rucus" To-Night. *Unknown.* BPo; TAP
Raise Me Up, Lord. Miguel de Guevara, *tr. fr. Spanish by* Samuel Beckett. MexPo

Raise the Cromlech high! The Lament of Maev Leith-Dherg. *Unknown*, *tr. by* Thomas W. H. Rolleston. OBWP
Raise the Shade. E. E. Cummings. VGW
Raised are the dripping oars. Matthew Arnold. *Fr.* The Youth of Nature: Wordsworth's Country. FaBoPP
Raisin, The. James Wright. TAP
Raising of Lazarus, The. Lucille Clifton. CNA
Raising of the Dead, The. Rosemary Dobson. PoAu-2
Raising the Flag. Gerald Vizenor. VoR
Raisins and Nuts. Charles Reznikoff. VWA
Raison d'Etre. Oliver Pitcher. AmNP
Raja, I wish I knew. To Raja Rao. Czeslaw Milosz. TOF
Raja, my heart is mad for you. My Heart Burns for Him. *Gond Oral Tradition, tr. by* V. Elwin *and* S. Hivale. WTO
Rajpoot Rebels. Sir Alfred Comyn Lyall. OBTV
Raking Leaves. Robert Pack. NYBP
Rakushisha. Basho, *tr. fr. Japanese by* Burton Watson. *Fr.* Seventy-six Hokku. FCEI
Ralegh's Prizes. Robert Pinsky. DiPo; MAYP
Raleigh Was Right. William Carlos Williams. NIP; NoAM; RB
Rally Song. Mary Weston Fordham. CBWP-2
Ralph Leech Believes. Ebenezer Elliott. *Fr.* The Year of Seeds. Son
Ralph Roister Doister, *sels.* Nicholas Udall. EIL
　　I Mun Be Married a Sunday.
　　Minion Wife, A.
Ram came last, The. Isaac. Haim Guri, *tr. by* Naomi Tauber *and* Howard Schwartz. VWA
Ram, the Bull, the Heavenly Twins, The. The Zodiac Rhyme. *Unknown.* GBP
Ram Time. William Heyen. GeTw
Rama ("Rama's a bunch of little shops"). Ivan Uriarte, *tr. fr. Spanish by* Jack Hirschman. Vol
Ramble. Anthony Howell. NPo
Ramble-eer, The. *Unknown.* PoAu-1
Ramble of the Gods through Birmingham, *sel.* James Bisset. Next day they rambled round the town, and swore. NOEC
Rambling Boy, The. *Unknown.* OBET
Rambling Sailor, The. Charlotte Mew. PoRA
Rambling Sailor, The. *Unknown.* OxBSS
Rambling Soldier, The. *Unknown.* OBET
Rambuncto. Margaret Widdemer. BXAP
Ramon. Bret Harte. BeLS
Ramon. E. A. Lacey. PeHV
Rampage, The. C. K. Williams. GeTw
Rampant rank reed, to repress it I try. Teika, *tr. fr. Japanese by* Hiroaki Sato. *Fr.* A Compendium of Good Tanka. FCEI
Ram's Horn, The. John Hewitt. BIrV
Ramshackles, archipelagoes, loose constellations. The Unifying Principle. A. R. Ammons. CAPP; NOBA
Ran against walls. Jackie Robinson. Lucille Clifton. ASP
Ran and caught up, in the wind. Ozaki Hosai, *tr. fr. Japanese by* Hiroaki Sato. *Fr.* One Hundred Haiku in Free Form. FCEI
Ran out of tear gas and became panicky. Kent State, May 4, 1970. Paul Goodman. MAT
Rana, I know you gave me poison. Mirabai, *tr. fr. Hindi by* Willis Barnstone *and* Usha Nilsson. BoWoP
Rana, why do you treat me as your enemy? Mirabai, *tr. by* Willis Barnstone *and* Usha Nilsson. BoWoP
Ranchers are selling their wheat early this year, The. Bunch Grass #37. Robert Sund. NU
Randal Groveling works where I work. Song from a Two-Desk Office. Byron Buck. NYBP
Random Feelings: Written in Japan. Ch'iu Chin, *tr. fr. Chinese by* Pao Chia-lin. WFTU
Random Generation of English Sentences; or, The Revenge of the Poets. William Jay Smith. OBAL
Random Poem, A. Cheng Hsiao-hsü, *tr. fr. Chinese by* Irving Lo. WFTU
Random Poem on the Lake. Sung Wan, *tr. fr. Chinese by* Yin-nan Chang. WFTU
Random Reflections on a Summer Evening. John Hall Wheelock. NYBP
Random Song on Approaching a River, A. Shih Jun-chang, *tr. fr. Chinese by* William Shultz. WFTU
Random Thoughts. Wang Kuo-wei, *tr. fr. Chinese by* Irving Lo. WFTU
Random Thoughts on Autumn. Liang Ch'i-ch'ao, *tr. fr. Chinese by* Cecile Chu-chin Sun. WFTU
Random Thoughts on the Love of God, *sel.* Simone Weil, *tr. fr. French by* Carol Cosman.
　　"Creatures speak in sounds." OV
Random Thoughts on the Skinkokinshu: Fujiwara no Teika. Anzai Hitoshi, *tr. fr. Japanese by* Hiroaki Sato. FCEI

Random Thoughts on the Writing of History, *sels.* Rai San'yo, *tr. fr. Chinese by* Burton Watson. JLIC-2
　　"I chastise the bones of an old villain of a thousand years ago." *Fr.* II.
　　"Twenty-some years and I've finished my book." *Fr.* VIII.
Random Thoughts upon Reading History, Hastily Composed, *sels.* Wang P'eng-yün, *tr. fr. Chinese by* Kang-i Sun Chang. WFTU
　　"Brilliant minds were legion by the gate of the ancestral kingdom."
　　"For thirty years the entire world has looked to *lung-men.*"
Random Verses from a Boat, *sels.* Fan Tseng-hsiang, *tr. fr. Chinese by* J. P. Seaton. WFTU
　　"Before dawn passing Chiang-k'ou town." *Fr.* IV.
　　"My good wife was born in the Capital." *Fr.* III.
　　"Within three days we've changed boats twice." *Fr.* II.
Rang'd on the line oppos'd, Antonius brings. Virgil, *tr. fr. Latin by* Dryden. *Fr.* The Aeneid [*or* Eneados], VIII. WaaP
Range. Rae Armantrout. LP
Range Cow in Winter. Vern Mortensen. CowP
Range-finding. Robert Frost. MoP; NIP; NoAM; NoP; OBWP; RB
Range in the Desert, The. Randall Jarrell. NOBA
Rank. Lincoln Kirstein. OBWP
Rank with the flesh of man and beast. The Lido. Edmund Wilson. ErPo
Rannoch, by Glencoe. T. S. Eliot. *Fr.* Landscapes, IV. FaBoPP; NAEL-2; PoSH; RB
Rannoch Moor. Malcolm MacGregor. PoSH
Ranolf and Amohia, *sel.* Alfred Domett.
　　"It was a wondrous realm beguiled." *Fr.* Canto I, iii. OBTV
Ransomed Spirit to Her Home, The. William Bingham Tappan. AH
Rant Block. Michael McClure. EAS
Rantin' Dog, the Daddie o't, The. Burns. OxBoLi; PPP
Rantin Laddie, The. *Unknown.* AmFP; ESPB; HAP; OxBA; TAP
Rantin, Rovin Robin. Burns. OxBS
Ranting Wanton's Resolution; 1672, The. *Unknown.* CoMu
Rapacious Spain/ Follow'd her hero's triumphs o'er the main. The Lust of Gold. James Montgomery. *Fr.* The West Indies. PAH
Rape. Joan Larkin. GLP
Rape. Tom Pickard. FaBoTw
Rape. Thomas Rabbitt. MAYP
Rape flowers: the moon in the east. Buson, *tr. fr. Japanese by* Hiroaki Sato. *Fr.* Eighty-seven Hokku. FCEI
Rape of Lucrece, The, *sels.* Thomas Heywood.
　　Pack, Clouds, Away. EIL; GBL; GTBS; GTBS-P; PBBP; SoSe
　　(Good Morrow.) CH
　　(Matin Song.) OBEV
　　Passing Bell, The. FaBoRV
　　She That Denies Me [I Would Have]. ErPo
Rape of Lucrece, The, *sels.* Shakespeare.
　　"Come, Philomele, that sing'st of ravishment." PBBP
　　Midnight. OBSC
　　"Mis-shapen Time, copesmate of ugly Night." OAEL-1
　　Opportunity. LiTB; OBSC; PoEL-2
　　(Outcry upon Opportunity, An.) NOBE
　　Time's Glory. ChTr
　　Troy Depicted. OBSC
Rape of Mensola, The. Boccaccio, *tr. fr. Italian by* Joseph Tusiani. *Fr.* Nymphs of Fiesole. PFI
Rape of the Lock, The. Pope. HAP; NoP; OAEL-1; OBNV; PoEL-3; TEP; TrGrPo
　　Sels.
　　"Close by those meads, for ever crowned with flow'rs." *Fr.* III. FiP; OxBoLi, *sl. abr.*
　　(Hampton Court.) FaBoPP, *shorter sel.; OBSV, shorter sel..*
　　"Not with more glories, in th' ethereal plain." *Fr.* II. EBEV; NOEC
　　(Voyage on the Thames, The.) NOBE
　　"On her white breast a sparkling cross she wore." *Fr.* II. ACP
　　Playing Cards, The. *Fr.* III. ChTr
　　Toilet, The. *Fr.* I. NOBE
　　"What dire offence from am'rous causes springs." *Fr.* I. NOEC
Rape of the Swan, The. Archibald MacLeish. AnAmPo
Rape Poem, The. Tommi Avicolli. GLP
Raper from Passenack, The. William Carlos Williams. TW
Raphael. Henrietta Cordelia Ray. CBWP-3
Raphael. Priscilla Jane Thompson. CBWP-2
Raphael, they're asking you to write a few lines. For Ammonis, Who Died at 29, in 610. C. P. Cavafy, *tr. by* Edmund Keeley *and* Philip Sherrard. VMG
Rapid, The. Charles Sangster. CaP
Rapid Transit. James Agee. MoAmPo
Rapidly cruising or lying on the air there is a bird. The Frigate Pelican. Marianne Moore. InvP
Rapids at Night. Duncan Campbell Scott. CaP

Rapier, lie there! and there, my hat and feather! Melancholy Conceit. Samuel Rowlands. OxBSP

Rapier, lie there! and there, my hat and feather! The Poetaster. Samuel Rowlands. *Fr.* The Melancholy Knight. EIL

Rapier of Treason, A. *Unknown, tr. fr. Arabic by* Willis Barnstone. BoWoP

Rapist's Villanelle, The. Thomas M. Disch. SM

Rapparees. Richard Murphy. *Fr.* The Battle of Aughrim. BIrV; NOIV

Rapping Along with Ronda Davis. James Cunningham. JB

Rapture, The. Henry Baker. NOEC

Rapture, A. Thomas Carew. CaPo; ErPo; JCP; NAEL-1; OAEL-1; SeCP; ViBoPo, *abr*

Rapture. Stefan George, *tr. fr. German by* Ludwig Lewisohn. AWP

Rapture, The. Thomas Traherne. OBS

Rapture Is Coming, The. Alice Golembiewski Phillips. KS

Rapunzel. Faye Kicknosway. UL

Rapunzel Rapunzel let down your hair. The After-Thought. Stevie Smith. OxBC

Rare medieval Spirit! brooding seer! Dante. Henrietta Cordelia Ray. CBWP-3

Rare Moments. Charles Henry Phelps. AA

Rare music! I would rather hear cat-courtship. The Dancing Bear. Robert Southey. FM

Rare News. Nicholas Breton. NIP

Rare Rhythms. Sara London. MOWH

Rare temples thou hast seen, I know. The Fairy Temple; or, Oberon's Chapel. Robert Herrick. CaPo

Rare Willie Drowned in Yarrow; or, The Water o Gamrie. *Unknown.* ESPB; GBP; GoTS

Rare Willy. *Unknown. See* Willy's rare, and Willy's fair.

Raree Show, A. Stephen College. APAS

Rarely, Rarely, Comest Thou. Shelley. EnRP; OBNC; TrGrPo
  ("Barely, rarely, comest thou.") CH; TEP
  (Invocation: "Rarely, rarely, comest thou.") GTBS; GTBS-P
  (Song: "Rarely, rarely comest thou.") Mes

Rash fading out fades in, The. Cure. Alan Brownjohn. PoPo

Raspberries. Laurence Lerner. EBEV

Raspberries they gave us for dessert, The. Going to Moscow. Lauris Edmond. ATNZ

Raspberry in the Pudding, The. Philip O'Connor. EAS

Rasping in his throat. *Unknown, tr. by* Burton Watson. FCEI

Rasping laughter of sunlight, The. Thule. Sándor Weöres, *tr. by* Jascha Kessler. FOC

Rassa, I rise. Bertrans de Born, *tr. by* Paul Blackburn. Pro

Rat, The. W. H. Davies. OBWVE; OxBTC

Rat, The. B. C. Leale. NPo

Rat-a-tat-tat, Rat-a-tat-tat. The Postman. Clive Sansom. BoTP

Rat and the Elephant, The. La Fontaine, *tr. fr. French by* Marianne Moore. OBVE

Rat at the Foot of the Cross. Vincent O'Sullivan. ATNZ

Rat claws, rat claws, rat claws, rat, rat claws, claws. Rats. Tu Kuo-ch'ing, *tr. by* Dominic Cheung. IFON

Rat has dropped into the water jar, A. Taigi, *tr. fr. Japanese by* Hiroaki Sato. *Fr.* Twenty-four Hokku. FCEI

Rat is in the trap, it is in the trap, The. Song of a Rat. Ted Hughes. CMoP; NoP

Rat Riddles. Carl Sandburg. SO

Rat says there is sugar or shit. Rat at the Foot of the Cross. Vincent O'Sullivan. ATNZ

Rat throws out all rattish thoughts, The. The Rat. B. C. Leale. NPo

Rat too has a skin (to tan), A. Sans Equity and sans Poise. Confucius, *tr. fr. Chinese by* Ezra Pound. *Fr.* Yung Wind. CTC

Rata blooms explode, the bow-legged tomcat, The. James Keir Baxter. *Fr.* Autumn Testament, 42. ATNZ; PeNZ

Ratcatcher's Daughter, The. *Unknown.* ChTr; GBP; OxBoLi

Ratcliffe Highway. *Unknown.* OxBSS

Rath in front of the oak wood, The. *Unknown.* NOIV

"Rather dead than spotted"; and/ believe it. Then the Ermine. Marianne Moore. PoA

Rather notice, mon cher. To a Solitary Disciple. William Carlos Williams. VGW

Rather than be a so-so human being. Tabito. *Fr.* Manyo Shu. FCEI

Rather than be wise. Tabito. *Fr.* Manyo Shu. PeBJV

Rather than Cry. Ishikawa Takuboku, *tr. fr. Japanese by* Geoffrey Bownas *and* Anthony Thwaite. PeBJV

Rather than have to serve. Voluntary Mutilation. Jean Follain, *tr. by* W. S. Merwin. RHTwFP

Rather than stay behind to languish. Princess Tajima. *Fr.* Manyo Shu. Ma

Rather than that I should remain at home. *The father of* Kusakabe Minaka. *Fr.* Manyo Shu. Ma

Rather than that I should thus pine. Yakamochi. *Fr.* Manyo Shu. Ma

Rather than worry. Tabito. *Fr.* Manyo Shu. PeBJV

Rather than your fine hotels. Sightseers in a Courtyard. Nicolás Guillén, *tr. by* Langston Hughes. TTY

Rather Too Good, Little Peggy! Adelaide O'Keeffe. FaBoUs

Rathers. Mary Austin. FaPON

Ratio. Lillian Morrison. UAS

Ration Card, The. Liz Sohappy Bahe. CDW

Ration Party. John Manifold. WaP

Rats. Tu Kuo-ch'ing, *tr. fr. Chinese by* Dominic Cheung. IFON

Rats, Ducks, Dogs, Cats, Pigs. *Unknown. See* Three young rats with black felt hats.

Rat's Legs, The. Russell Edson. NAmP

Rat's Tight Schedule, The. Russell Edson. AnAn

Rattan bed, paper netting. I wake from morning sleep. Li Ch'ing-chao, *tr. fr. Chinese by* Willis Barnstone *and* Sun Chu-chin. BoWoP

Rattat! Rattat! Postman's Knock. Rodney Bennett. BoTP

Rattle. Peter Blue Cloud. HATNAP

Rattle Bag, The. Dafydd ap Gwilym, *tr. fr. Welsh by* Joseph Clancy. NBLV; RB

Rattle creak very white. Sheep's Skull. Lucy Jane Simpson. OBD

Rattler, Alert. Brewster Ghiselin. HAP; WeW

Rattlesnake Band, The. Robert J. Conley. STE

Rattlesnake Country. Robert Penn Warren. NAAL-2

Rattlesnakes have begun to come out, The. Snakes. Peter Wild. AmPA

Rauf Coilyear, *sel. Unknown.*
  "Coilyear, gudlie in feir, tuke him be the hand, The." OxBS

Raura and Dali meet by chance in the. Surreal Appetite. George McWhirter. UAS

Rav, The/ of Northern White Russia declined. Illustrious Ancestors. Denise Levertov. AmPP; MoP; NAAL-2; NOBA; VGW

Ravaged Villa, The. Herman Melville. CTC; NOBA; PoEL-5

Ravel and Unravel. Jorie Graham. BLA

Ravel's Bolero. Gerrit Achterberg, *tr. fr. Dutch by* James Brockway. DuIn

Raven, The. Samuel Taylor Coleridge. WiR

Raven. Duane Niatum. STE

Raven, The. Poe. AA; AmPP; AnAmPo; BeLS; BLPA; CH; FaBoBe; FaBoCh; FaBV; FaFP; FPL; GN; GoJo; HeIP; LiTA; NAAL-1; NIP; NOBA; OBCA; OBNV; OHFP; OxBA; PoRA; PWR; TAP; WBLP

Raven, The. Adrienne Rich. NePoEA-2

Raven, The. E. A. Robinson, *after* Nicarchus. AWP; FaBoEE; OBAL

Raven/Moon. Anita Endrezze Probst. VoR

Raven croak'd as she sate at her meal, The. The Witch. Robert Southey. WiR

Raven Days, The. Sidney Lanier. AnAmPo; OxBA

Raven eyes blink. Raven is Two-Faced. Robert H. Davis. HATNAP

Raven, gather us to that dark breast. Raven Tells Stories. Robert H. Davis. HATNAP

Raven is Two-Faced. Robert H. Davis. HATNAP

Raven sat upon a tree, A. The Sycophantic Fox and the Gullible Raven. Guy Wetmore Carryl. BLPA; CenHV; FaFP; FiBHP; NBLV; OBCA

Raven Tells Stories. Robert H. Davis. HATNAP

Ravenglass Railway Station, Cumberland. Norman Nicholson. NYBP

Ravening Coyote comes. Three Songs of Mad Coyote. *Unknown, tr. by* Herbert J. Spinden. STP

Ravenna. Louis MacNeice. OBTV

Ravens. Ted Hughes. InPS; NAs

Ravens gnawing/ men's necks. Before the Last Battle. *Unknown, tr. fr. Irish by* Thomas Kinsella. *Fr.* The Táin. NOIV

Ravine, The. Yves Bonnefoy, *tr. fr. French by* Anthony Rudolf. RHTwFP

Raving warre, begot. Thomas Campion. AAS

Ravings. Tom Hood. BXAP; Par

Ravin's of Piute Poet Poe. C. L. Edson. BXAP

Ravished by all that to the eyes is fair. Buonarroti Michelangelo, *tr. fr. Italian by* George Santayana. *Fr.* Three Poems, III. AWP
  (Madrigal: "Ravished by all that to the eyes is fair.")

Raw and overwhelming danger, The. The Unpredictable. Thomas Blackburn. OPOP

Raw Cowardice. Bern Sharfman. SoTCo

Raw Honey. Lewis MacAdams. UL

Raw slopes of meat are stabbed with pikes, The. Norway. Norman Dubie. GeTw

Ray. Otto Orban, *tr. fr. Hungarian by* Emery George. VWA

Ray Charles. Sam Cornish. CNA

Ray Charles is the black wind of Kilimanjaro. Blues Note. Bob Kaufman. CNA; PoBA

Ray of light becomes the track, The. Asadullah Khan Ghalib, *tr. by* Ahmed Ali. GoT

Raya Brenner. Pinhas Sadeh, *tr. fr. Hebrew by* Gabriel Preil *and* Howard Schwartz. VWA

Raymond Chandler's Sentence. Tina Darragh. IAT

Raymondsville. Christine Busta, *tr. fr. German by* Beth Bjorklund. CoAuP

Rays of the autumn moon, The. Tsurayuki, *tr. fr. Japanese by* Burton Watson. *Fr.* Kokin Shu. FCEI

Rays of the sun, The. The Shepherd and His Flock. Mbuyiseni Oswald Mtshali. GrPl

Ray's third new car in half as many years. Family Reunion. Louise Erdrich. HATNAP; NoAM

Raziel. Iwan Goll, *tr. fr. French by* Anthony Rudolf. VWA

Razón de Amor, *sel.* Pedro Salinas, *tr. fr. Spanish by* Linda Gutierrez *and* Lawrence Pitkethly.

"Now I love you/ as the sea loves its water." LLLT

Razor blade rusted overnight, A. Boncho, *tr. fr. Japanese by* Hiroaki Sato. *Fr.* Twenty-one Hokku. FCEI

Razors pain you. Résumé. Dorothy Parker. AnAmPo; DL; HeIP; InPK; NAAL-2; NBLV; NoP; OBAL; TrJP

Razorsharp wind, A. Valentine. Len Gasparini. NeAC

Razzle dazzle maggots are summary, The. Easter. Frank O'Hara. EAS

RDA (Recommended Daily Addictions). Julia Older. SoTCo

Re-act for Action ("Re-act to Animals"). Don L. Lee. BPo; NBP

Re-birth. *Unknown, tr. fr. Bushman by* W. H. I. Bleek *and* Jack Cope. PeSA

Re-Birth of Venus, The. Geoffrey Hill. NePoEA

Re-education. Sybren Polet, *tr. fr. Dutch by* André Lefevere. DuIn

Re-forming the Crystal. Adrienne Rich. TAP

Re-plyed, extorted, oft transposed, and fleeting. Sea Voyage. William Empson. CMoP; MOS

Re: the question of poems. Memo from the Desk of X. Donald Justice. TwCP

Re your "Musée des Beaux Arts," Mr. Auden. Memo to Mr. Auden, 29/8/66. Alistair Campbell. ATNZ

Reach for arrows of falling light. A man once sang. Falling Moon. Roberta Hill. CDW

Reach like you never reached before past Night's somber robes. Tauhid. Askia Muhammad Touré. PoBA

Reach me down my Tycho Brahe, I would know him when we meet. The Old Astronomer to His Pupil. Sarah Williams. BLPA

Reach, with your whiter hands, to me. To the Water Nymphs, Drinking at the Fountain. Robert Herrick. CaPo; NAEL-1

Reaching down arm-deep into bright water. Shells. Kathleen Jessie Raine. ImOP

Reaching Forty. Abd al-Razzaq Abd al-Wahid, *tr. fr. Arabic by* Diana Der Hovanessian *and* Lena Jayyusi. MAP

Reaching the Horizon. Robert Mezey. NaP

Reaching to light my cigarette your hand. Jumping into Joy. Marg Yeo. DT

Reaching Yellow River. Roberta Hill Whiteman. HATNAP

Reactionary Poet, The. Ishmael Reed. CNA

Read a little Apollinaire and love it. French Desire. Keith Abbott. UL

Read about the Buddhist monk. Dilemma. Patricia Beer. OxBC

Read and committed to the flames, I call. On Not Being Milton. Tony Harrison. *Fr.* The School of Eloquence. NoAM

Read here,/ This is the story of Evarraman. Evarra and His Gods. Kipling. MoBrPo

Read here (sweet maid) the story of my woe. Michael Drayton. *Fr.* Idea's Mirrour, I. OBSC

Read me a lesson, Muse, and speak it loud. Written upon the Top of Ben Nevis. Keats. PoSH

Read me no moral, priest, upon my life. The Condemned. Edward Howland. AA

Read Me, Please! Robert Graves. NYBP

Read no more of cantos Pisan. To a Young Poet. Harry M. Meacham. GoYe

Read not Milton, for he is dry; no Shakespeare. Proverbial Philosophy: Of Reading. Charles Stuart Calverley. FaBoCo

"Read out the names!" and Burke sat back. The Fighting Race. Joseph I. C. Clarke. AA; AnAmPo; BLPA; BLPL; PAH

Read, sweet, how others strove. Emily Dickinson. AH, *with music;* NOCV

Read the Bible, it will tell. The Bible. Lizelia Augusta Jenkins Moorer. CBWP-3

Read This with Gestures. John Ciardi. RHPC

Read through another chapter of Ludwig's. If by Eternity. Riekus Waskowsky, *tr. by* André Lefevere. DuIn

Read up and down. *Unknown.* ILY

Read yr/ exile. A Poem for a Poet. Don L. Lee. PoBA

Readen ov a Head-Stwone. William Barnes. CH

Reader, The. Thomas Merton. CRP

Reader, behold! this monster wild. Infant Innocence. A. E. Housman. FaBoNo; NOBL

Reader, beneath this turf I lie. Thomas Brown. FaBoEE

Reader! I am no poet: but I grieve! To the Reader. Urian Oakes. SCAP

Reader, I was born and cried. Epitaph on the Fart in the Parliament House. John Hoskyns. FaBoEE

Reader, I would not have thee mistake. His Own Epitaph, When He Was Sick. John Hoskyns. FaBoEE

Reader over My Shoulder, The. Robert Graves. NAEL-2

Reader, pass on, nor idly waste [*or* don't waste] your time. In Peterborough Churchyard. Paulus Silentiarius. FaBoEE; NOBL

Reader, preserve thy peace: those busie eyes. An Elegie upon the Death of the Lord Hastings. Sir John Denham. SeCV-1

Reader, stay,/ And if I had no more to say. An Epitaph on Master Philip Gray. Ben Jonson. FaBoEE

Reader, we are getting ready to pull out. Epilogue: Author to Reader. Henri Coulette. *Fr.* The War of the Secret Agents, XII. NePoEA-2

Readers and the hearers like my books, The. Critics. Martial, *tr. by* Sir John Harington. AWP

Readers of the *Boston Evening Transcript*, The. The *Boston Evening Transcript*. T. S. Eliot. InPK

Reading. Elizabeth Barrett Browning. *Fr.* Aurora Leigh. GN

Reading, The. Hermann Jandl, *tr. fr. German by* Beth Bjorklund. CoAuP

Reading/ after your death. Upon Re-reading a Poem by Paul Celan. Erich Fried, *tr. by* Beth Bjorklund. CoAuP

Reading a Letter from Home. Michizane, *tr. fr. Chinese by* Burton Watson. JLIC-1

Reading a Medal. Terence Tiller. FaBoTw; GTBS-P

Reading about the Wisconsin Weeping Willow. Song. Ruth Krauss. LLLT

Reading an "Ode to a Widow." Natsume Seibi, *tr. fr. Japanese by* Hiroaki Sato. *Fr.* Twenty-seven Hokku. FCEI

Reading beside Ox Tail River, *sels.* Cheng Chen, *tr. fr. Chinese by* William Schultz. WFTU

"Dim, dim the light from the small window." *Fr.* II.

"I read books beside Ox Tail River." *Fr.* I.

Reading Books, *sels.* Rai San'yo, *tr. fr. Chinese by* Burton Watson.
"Eastern hills—dense and lush." *Fr.* VI.
"This morning, splendid breeze and sunlight." *Fr.* III.

Reading Books ("Eastern hills—dense and lush"). Rai San'yo, *tr. fr. Japanese by* Burton Watson. FCEI

Reading Books ("This morning, splendid breeze and sunlight"). Rai San'yo, *tr. fr. Japanese by* Burton Watson. FCEI

Reading how even the Swiss had thrown the sponge. Beyond the Alps. Robert Lowell. NOBA

Reading in bed, full of sentiment. The Bat. Ellen Bryant Voigt. MAYP

Reading in Fall Rain. Robert Bly. GrPl

Reading in Li Po. After the Last Dynasty. Stanley Kunitz. TAP

Reading in the Night. Roy Fuller. OxBC

Reading in the paper a summary. Larkinesque. Michael Ryan. NAmP

Reading in War Time. Edwin Muir. WaP

Reading Indian Poetry. Ramona Wilson. VoR

Reading Lesson, The. Richard Murphy. IPY

Reading Mother, The. Strickland W. Gillilan. BLPA

Reading Myself. Robert Lowell. HCAP; NAAL-2; TAP

Reading Plato. Jorie Graham. MAYP

Reading Pornography in Old Age. Howard Nemerov. NoAM

Reading Room, The New York Public Library. Richard Eberhart. GOYP

Reading the Analects. Natsume Seibi, *tr. fr. Japanese by* Hiroaki Sato. *Fr.* Twenty-seven Hokku. FCEI

Reading the Annals of Emperor Wu of the Han Dynasty. Wu Wei-yeh, *tr. fr. Chinese by* Jonathan Chaves. CoBLCP

Reading the Books Our Children Have Written. Dave Smith. HCAP

Reading the Brothers Grimm to Jenny. Lisel Mueller. NYBP

Reading The Classic of Hills and Seas. T'ao Ch'ien, *tr. fr. Chinese by* Burton Watson. CoBCP

Reading the headlines in the revolutionary. The Second Man. Julian Symons. WaP

Reading the Parable of the Cave. Living in the Cave. Adrienne Rich. AnAn

Reading the Poetry Collection of Lü Fang-ch'ing. Chang Yü, *tr. fr. Chinese by* Jonathan Chaves. CoBLCP

Reading through your work tonight. Negative Passage. Michael Newman. PoA

Reading Time: 1 Minute 26 Seconds. Muriel Rukeyser. PBWP

Reading Walt Whitman. Calvin Forbes. PoBA

Readings, Forecasts, Personal Guidance. Kenneth Fearing. MoAmPo

Ready. Phoebe Cary. PAH

Ready. Margaret Junkin Preston. PWR
Ready They Make Hauberks Sarrazinese. *Unknown, tr. fr. Old French by* C. K. Scott Moncrieff. *Fr.* The Song of Roland. WaaP
Ready to seek out death in my disgrace. Henry Constable. *Fr.* Diana. OBSC
Ready we stand in San Juan town. Rain Magic Song. *Unknown, tr. by* H. J. Spinden. WTO
Readymade. John Perreault. EAS
Reagan, The. Richard Quick. FaBoPa
Real duel of Apollo, The. Apollo and Marsyas. Zbigniew Herbert, *tr. by* Czeslaw Milosz. PwPP
Real Estate. Lorrie Goldensohn. NAmP
Real Estate. Carol Muske. PPR
Real Muse, The. Tom Scott. PoA
Real People. Merry Harris. GOS
Real People Loves One Another, The. Rob Penny. CNA; PoBA
Real poems are being written in outports, The. Without Benefit of Tape. Dorothy Livesay. NOBC
Real Presence. Ivan Adair. WGRP
Real Property. Harold Monro. BoNaP
Real Question Calling for a Solution, A. Robert Penn Warren. PPP
Real Talent. Sheryl L. Nelms. TDD
Real was always something that came out of streets, The. The Epiphany. George Strong. GoYe
Reality. Martha Gilbert Dickinson Bianchi. AA
Reality. Sir Aubrey De Vere. WGRP
Reality. Frances Ridley Havergal. WGRP
Reality. Angela Morgan. WGRP
Reality. Felix Pollak. TSM
Reality. Raymond Souster. CaP
Reality/ is like a contemporary string. Dazzled. Arthur Sze. BrSi
Reality gathers. Life Explains and Death Spies Out. Washington Delgado, *tr. by* Maureen Ahern *and* David Tipton. Per
Reality Is an Activity of the Most August Imagination. Wallace Stevens. NoAM
Reality of Autumn, The. Duane Niatum. HATNAP
Realization. Ananda Acharya. WGRP
Realm of Fancy, The. Keats. *Fr.* Fancy. GTBS; GTBS-P
Realm of truth: there dwells the Formless One, The. Nanak, *tr. by* John Stratton Hawley *and* Mark Juergensmeyer. SSI
Realpolitik. Blossom S. Kirschenbaum. SoTCo
Reaper, The. Leslie Holdsworth Allen. PoAu-1
Reaper, The. John Banister Tabb. ACP
Reaper, The. Wordsworth. *See* Behold her, single in the field.
"Reaper on the Suminoe fields." Hitomaro. *Fr.* Manyo Shu. Ma
Reapers. Mathilde Blind. WPE
Reapers. Jean Toomer. BPo; CDC; HAP; MoP; NoAM; PoBA; PPP; WeW
Reapers that with whetted sickles stand, The. Poetry and Philosophy. Thomas Randolph. *Fr.* An Eclogue to Mr. Johnson. OBS
Rear Guard, The. Irene Fowler Brown. PAH
Rear-Guard, The. Siegfried Sassoon. MoBrPo; NAEL-2; NoAM; OBWP; WaP
Rear Vision. William Jay Smith. NYBP
Rearmament. Robinson Jeffers. OxBA
Rearrange a wife's affection? Emily Dickinson. PoEL-5
Reason, A. Robert Creeley. NaP
Reason. Ralph Hodgson. *See* Reason has moons, but moons not hers.
Reason. Josephine Miles. InPK; NoAM; NoP; PoCH; TAP
Reason and Imagination. Blake. *Fr.* Milton, II. EnRP
Reason and Religion. Dryden. *See* Religio Laici: Dim, as the borrow'd beams of moon and stars.
Reason and Revelation. Dryden. *See* Religio Laici: Dim, as the borrow'd beams of moon and stars.
Reason for Poetry, The. Nancy Morejón, *tr. fr. Spanish by* Anita Whitney. WPOW
Reason for Skylarks, The. Kenneth Patchen. NaP
Reason for the Pelican, The. John Ciardi. PDV
Reason For Your Suffering. Tanikawa Shuntaro, *tr. fr. Japanese by* Hiroaki Sato. FCEI
Reason Has Moons. Ralph Hodgson. FaBoCh; OxBSP
(Reason.) MoBrPo
Reason I clobbered, The. With My Foot in My Mouth. Dennis Lee. ILY
Reason I Like Chocolate, The. Nikki Giovanni. RHPC
Reason I Stay on Job So Long. *Unknown.* GBP
"Reason, in faith thou art well served, that still." Sir Philip Sidney. *Fr.* Astrophel and Stella, X. NAEL-1
Reason, tell me thy mind, if here be reason. Love and Reason. Sir Philip Sidney. *Fr.* Arcadia. SiPS

Reason with them. Speak softly. Hide your stick. 13 Ways of Eradicating Blackbirds. Mark DeFoe. BXAP
Reasonable Affliction, A. Matthew Prior. NOEC; NoP; TrGrPo
(Cause and Effect.) NBLV
Reasonings of a Woman Poet. *Unknown, tr. fr. Spanish by* Robert L. Smith *and* Judith Candullo. DMH
Reasons. Thomas James. PoA
Reasons for and against Marrying Widows. Henricus Selyns. SCAP
Reawakening. Sharon A. Stern. TSM
Reb Hanina. Paul Raboff. VWA
Reb Moyshe Leyb of Sossov points to the heaps of ash. The "Lovers of Israel" at the Belzhets Death Camp. Itzig Manger, *tr. by* Leonard Wolf. PeBMYV
Reb of ruins my father. Zealot without a Face. Charles Dobzynski, *tr. by* Anita Barrows. VWA
Rebeca in a Mirror. Judith Rodriguez. CBAP
Rebecca. Joseph Eliyia, *tr. fr. Greek by* Rae Dalven. VWA
Rebecca, Who Slammed Doors for Fun and Perished Miserably. Hilaire Belloc. NOBL; SO
Rebecca's Hymn. Sir Walter Scott. *Fr.* Ivanhoe, *ch.* 39. EnRP
Rebecca's maid: a girl come from afar. Jacob and Esau. Else Lasker-Schüler, *tr. by* Rosemarie Waldrop. BoWoP
Rebel. Juana de Ibarbourou, *tr. fr. Spanish by* Kate Flores. DMH
Rebel, The. Mari E. Evans. AmNP; CRP; IDB; IHMS; PoBA
Rebel, A. John Gould Fletcher. MoAmPo
Rebel, *sel.* Irene Rutherford McLeod.
  "Beyond the murk that swallows me." WGRP
Rebel, The. Innes Randolph. NBLV; OBAL; OxBoLi
Rebel General, The. Chris Wallace-Crabbe. CBAP
Rebel [*or* Rebell] Scot, The, *sels.* John Cleveland.
  "Come keen iambicks with your badger's feet." OBS
  "Lord! what a goodly thing is want of shirts." OBSV
  Nature herself doth Scotchmen beasts confess. OBSV
Rebel Soldier, The. *Unknown. See* One Morning, one Morning, one Morning in May.
Rebellion Over, I See Off a Friend Who Is Returning North, The. Ssu-k'ung Shu, *tr. fr. Chinese by* Burton Watson. CoBCP
Rebellion shook an ancient dust. April Mortality. Léonie Adams. MoAB; MoAmPo
Rebellion was in her character. My Mother. Alistair Campbell. ATNZ
Rebellious Vine, The. Harold Monro. BrPo
"Rebels." Ernest Crosby. PAH
Rebels' cavalry are everywhere, The. Tsung Ch'en, *tr. fr. Chinese by* Jonathan Chaves. *Fr.* On Things Seen. CoBLCP
Rebels from Fairy Tales. Hyacinthe Hill. SO
Rebel's Progress. Tom Earley. OBWVE
Rebirth. Kipling. OBNC
Rebirth. Antonio Machado, *tr. fr. Spanish by* Robert Bly. NU
Rebirth. Catriona Stamp. BrRo
Rebolushinary X-mas. Carolyn M. Rodgers. JB
Reborn. Kingsley Amis. OxBC
Rebuke Me Not. John Addington Symonds. Son
Rec Room in Paradise. Tom Clark. UL
Recall. Reed Whittemore. NYBP
Recall the light. Eclipse. Bin Ramke. NAmP
Recalling War. Robert Graves. CMoP; LiTM; MMA; NoAM; OAEL-2; OBWP; WaP
Recapitulations, *sel.* Karl Shapiro.
  "We waged a war within a war." *Fr.* XI. PoNe
Receipt for Stewing Veal, A. *At. to* John Gay. FaBoUs
Receipt for the Vapours. Lady Mary Wortley Montagu. *See* Why will Delia thus retire.
Receipt to Cure a Love Fit, A. *Unknown.* NOEC
Receipt to Cure [*or* for] the Vapours, A. Lady Mary Wortley Montagu. NOEC; PBWP
(Receipt for the Vapours.) PBWP
Receive before you write, and write before you pay. How to Keep Accounts. *Unknown.* FaBoUs
Receive, dear friend, the truths I teach. II, 10. "Receive, dear friend, the truths I teach" ("Rectius vives"). Horace, *tr. fr. Latin. Fr.* Odes. AWP, *tr. by* William Cowper; OBVE, *tr. by* William Cowper.
  ("Of thy lyfe, Thomas, this compass well mark.") OBVE, *tr. by* Earl of Surrey.
  (To Licinius.) AWP, *tr. by* William Cowper.
  ("You better sure shall live, not evermore.") OBVE, *tr. by* Sir Philip Sidney.
Receiving Buddha. Ping-hsin, *tr. fr. Chinese by* K. C. Leung. OV
Receiving Communion. Vassar Miller. NePoEA-2
Receiving the Stigmata. Rita Dove. KS
Recent Status. Park Je-chun, *tr. fr. Korean by* Koh Chang-soo. ACKP

Recently cut she is unaccustomed. A Girl Combs Her Hair. Kimiko Hahn. BrSi
Reception, The. June Jordan. FaBoWP; NMM
Recessional. Georgia Douglas Johnson. CDC; PoNe
Recessional. Kipling. AWP; BLPA; BLPL; BLRP; BrPo; FaBoPV; FaBV; FaFP; GN; LiTB; MoBrPo; NoAM; NOBE; NOBVV; NoP; OBEV; OBNC; OHFP; PWR; TrGrPo; UnPo; WBLP; WGRP
Recessional. Thomas MacGreevy. CIP
Recessional. Isaac Watts. *See* O God, Our Help in Ages Past.
Recessional for the Class of 1959 of a School for Delinquent Negro Girls. Joseph R. Cowen. PoNe
Rechargeable Dry Cell Poem. Jim Wayne Miller. GOYP
Recipe. Albert Goldbarth. VWA
Recipe for a Pleasant Dinner-Party. *Unknown.* FaBoUs
Recipe for an Ocean in the Absence of the Sea. Richard Howard. TAP
Recipe for Sand. Barbara Brinson Curiel. ER
Recipe: Gourds. Nicander, *tr. fr. Greek.* FaBoUs
Recipe: Hare. Archestratus, *tr. fr. Greek.* FaBoUs
Recipe: Onions. Philemon, *tr. fr. Greek.* FaBoUs
Recipe: Sausage. Axionicus, *tr. fr. Greek.* FaBoUs
Reciprocity. John Drinkwater. PoA
Reciprocity. Vassar Miller. IHMS; MT; NePoEA
Recital. Muhammad Afifi Matar, *tr. fr. Arabic* by Ferial Ghazoul *and* Desmond O'Grady. MAP
Recital, The. Lloyd Schwartz. PPR
Recital. John Updike. OBAL; RR
Recitation for the Dismantling of a Hydrogen Bomb. Alan Williamson. BAP
Recitative. Hart Crane. FaBoMo
Recitative. Ronald McCuaig. PoAu-2
Recklessly/ I cast myself away. Izumi Shikibu, *tr.* by Edwin A. Cranston. PBWP
Reckoning, The. Alice R. Friman. KS
Reckoning, The. Theodore Roethke. PoA
Reckoning A.M. Thursday. Doris Turner. JB
Reclining Figure. Donald Hall. LCAP
Recluse. Aldo Camerino, *tr. fr. Italian* by Anita Barrows. VWA
Recluse, The, *sels.* Wordsworth.
  "On Man, on Nature, and on Human Life." OAEL-2
    (Prospectus [*incl. in* The Excursion].) EnRP; NoP; PoE
  Sunbeam Said, Be Happy, The. *Fr.* I. FaBoRV
Recluses, The. Stuart Z. Perkoff. NeAP
Recognition. John White Chadwick. AA
Recognition, The. Denise Levertov. VGW
Recognition of Eve, The. Karl Shapiro. *Fr.* Adam and Eve. MoAB
Recollection. Anne Reeve Aldrich. AA
Recollection. Duane Big Eagle. STE
Recollection, A. John Peale Bishop. LiTA; Son
Recollection. Amelia Walstien Carpenter. AA
Recollection, A. Frances Cornford. FaBoWP
Recollection. Donald D. Govan. NBP
Recollection, The. Shelley. *See* Now the last day of many days.
Recollection Long Ago: Sad Music. Robert Penn Warren. *See* Youthful Picnic Long Ago: Sad Ballad on Box.
Recollection of the Night of the Fourth, A, *sel.* Victor Hugo.
  "Is it children we are killing now? My God." OBD
Recollection of the Stone Circle near Keswick, A. Keats. *Fr.* Hyperion; a Fragment, II. FaBoPP
Recollections of a Day's Journey in Spain. Robert Southey. OBTV
Recollections of "Lalla Rookh." John Townsend Trowbridge. OBAL
Recollections of Love. Samuel Taylor Coleridge. ChER; NAEL-2
Recommend. Jackson MacLow. LP
Recompensed? Henrietta Cordelia Ray. CBWP-3
Reconcilement, The. John Sheffield. OBEV
Reconciliation. "Æ" OBMV; TrCP
Reconciliation. C. Day Lewis. TwCP
Reconciliation, *sel.* Elizabeth Doten.
  God of the Granite and the Rose! TrPWD
Reconciliation. Else Lasker-Schüler, *tr. fr. German* by Robert Alter. PBWP
Reconciliation, The. Archibald MacLeish. MoAmPo
Reconciliation. Caroline Atherton Briggs Mason. AA
Reconciliation. David Rosenmann-Taub, *tr. fr. Spanish* by Charles Guenther. VWA
Reconciliation. *Unknown, tr. fr. Late Middle Irish* by Kenneth Jackson. AnIL
Reconciliation. Walt Whitman. HAP; MoAmPo; NAAL-1; NoP; OBWP; OxBA; OxBSP; TrGrPo; WaaP; WeW
Reconciliation: A Modern Version, The. Horace. *See* Odes: III, 9. Dialogue between Horace and Lydia, A ("Donec gratus eram").
Reconnaissance. Arna Bontemps. AmNP; BPo

Record, A. Gyula Illyés, *tr. fr. Hungarian* by William Jay Smith. MHuP
Record, The. Gabriel Preil, *tr. fr. Yiddish* by Grace Schulman. PeBMYV
Record is nothing, and the hero great. Lord De Tabley. EBVV
Record of a Past Affair, A. Li K'ai-hsien, *tr. fr. Chinese* by Jonathan Chaves. CoBLCP
Record of My Trip to Mount She, A. Yüan Hung-tao, *tr. fr. Chinese* by Jonathan Chaves. CoBLCP
Recorded in time/ coming to be. Christine Busta, *tr.* by Beth Bjorklund. CoAuP
Recorder, tax collector, landlord, friends. Ode for the Burial of a Citizen. John Ciardi. LiTM
Recorders Ages Hence. Walt Whitman. MoAmPo
Recorders of Life. Paavo Haavikko, *tr. fr. Finnish* by Aili Jarvenpa. SOP
Recording a Dream. Yang Shih-ch'i, *tr. fr. Chinese* by Jonathan Chaves. CoBLCP
Recording a Weird Happening. Li K'ai-hsien, *tr. fr. Chinese* by Jonathan Chaves. CoBLCP
Recording My Happiness. Wang Chiu-ssu, *tr. fr. Chinese* by Jonathan Chaves. CoBLCP
Recording My Happiness upon Returning Home. Wen Cheng-ming, *tr. fr. Chinese* by Jonathan Chaves. CoBLCP
Records all agree, The. Against Te Rauparaha. Alistair Campbell. *Fr.* Sanctuary of Spirits, IX. PeNZ
Recovery, The. Edmund Blunden. MoBrPo
Recovery. F. R. Scott. CaP
Recovery. Patricia Y. Ikeda. BrSi
Recovery Room: Lying-in, The. Helen Chasin. IHMS
Recreation. Audre Lorde. NIP; NoP
Recreation. Jane Taylor. OxBoLi
Recrimination. Ella Wheeler Wilcox. AA
Recruit, The. A. E. Housman. FaPoR
Recruited Collier, The. *Unknown. See* Oh what's the matter with you, my lass.
Recruiting Drive. Charles Causley. NePoEA; OxBTC; PrIm
Recruiting Sergeant, The. *Unknown.* OBET
Recruiting Serjeant, The, *sel.* Isaac Bickerstaffe.
  "What a charming thing's a battle!" NOEC
Rectitude, and the terrible upstanding member. Washington in Love. John Berryman. LCAP
Rectors and parish priests complained to the bishop. William Langland. *Fr.* The Vision of Piers Plowman, Prologue. FaBoPV
Rector's pallid neighbor at The Firs, The. The Villagers and Death. Robert Graves. HeIP; OBD
Recuerdo. Paula Gunn Allen. STE
Recuerdo. Edna St. Vincent Millay. AmFN; FaFP; FPL; LiTA; LiTM; NAAL-2; NoAM; OxBA; PoA; TAP
Recurrences./ Coppery light hesitates. Measure. Robert Hass. GeTw
Recurring Opportunity. David Avidan, *tr. fr. Hebrew* by Warren Bargad *and* Stanley F. Chyet. IP
Red and blue and delicate green. Red and blue and delicate green. *Unknown.* GBP
Red and Blue Song, A. Amir Gilboa, *tr. fr. Hebrew* by Bernhard Frank. MHeP
Red and green neon lights, the jazz hysteria. Nuit Blanche: North End. Conrad Aiken. OxBA
Red and soft the grass rustles. Look in the Landscape. Gerhard Fritsch, *tr.* by Beth Bjorklund. CoAuP
Red and the Green, The. Anne Wilkinson. MoCV
Red Anger. R. T. Smith. STE
Red Ant Way, *sel. Unknown, tr. fr. Navajo Indian* by Jerome Rothenberg.
  "Red young men under the ground, The." STP
Red ants in a bamboo—the passion. *Malay Oral Tradition, tr.* by R. J. Wilkinson *and* R. O. Winstedt. WTO
Red as the guardroom lamp. Heartbreak Camp. Roy Campbell. OxBTC
Red Beard, A. A. Leyeles, *tr. fr. Yiddish* by Benjamin *and* Barbara Harshav. AYP
Red beast, The. Tasting the Wild Grapes. Mary Oliver. CAPP
Red Beauty. *Unknown, tr. fr. Gond Oral Tradition* by V. Elwin *and* S. Hivale. WTO
Red blossoms of mountain peach crowd the uplands. Bamboo Branch Song. Liu Yü-hsi, *tr.* by Burton Watson. CoBCP
Red Book of Hergest, The, *sel. Unknown, tr. fr. Middle Welsh* by Ernest Rhys.
  Lament for Urien, The. OBMV
Red bow is unstrung, The. *Unknown, tr.* by Arthur Waley. BoS
Red brick building. The Song of a Factory Worker. Ruth Collins. SaC

Red brick [or bricks] in the suburbs, white horse on the wall. Ballad to a Traditional Refrain. Maurice James Craig. BIrV; SeCePo; TIRV

Red brick monastery in, The/the suburbs. The Semblables. William Carlos Williams. FaBoMo; NOBA

Red-bud, the Kentucky tree, The. Christmas at Freelands. James Stephens. TIRV; TrCP

Red-capped egret rises high flying east of the city, A. Song of the River City. Niu Chiao, *tr. by* Lois Fusek. ATF

Red carpet-ing, The. While Cecil Snores: Mom Drinks Cold Milk. James Cunningham. JB

Red Cliff, The. Chao Yi, *tr. fr. Chinese by* Shirleen S. Wong. WFTU

Red cliffs arise. And up them service lifts. NW5 and N6. Sir John Betjeman. SCV

Red Corns. Ya Hsien, *tr. fr. Chinese by* Dominic Cheung. IFON

Red Cow Is Dead, The. E. B. White. NBLV; NYBP

Red crayon makes us, The. Red Horse. Bill Manhire. ATNZ

Red Cross Nurses. Gervase Stewart. WaP

Red Cuckatoo, The. Po Chü-i, *tr. fr. Chinese by* Arthur Waley. ChTr

Red dawn clouds coming up! the heavens proclaim you. Morning Light Song. Philip Lamantia. NeAP

Red days. Resonances. Cecilia Bustamante, *tr. by* David Tipton. Per

Red Dog, The. Laura Jensen. LCAP

Red Dust. Philip Levine. NNaP; NoAM

Red earth, The. What He Said ("The red earth"). Peyanar, *tr. fr. Tamil by* A. K. Ramanujan. *Fr.* Nine on Happy Reunion, 4. PLW

Red eyes of rabbits, The. The Springtime. Denise Levertov. CoAP

Red Flag, The. Michael Jackson. PeNZ

Red flag is up, The. We Meet in the Lives of Animals. Peter Everwine. NNaP

Red flame flowers bloom and die, The. Crosbie Garstin. CH

Red fool, my laughing comrade. To a Comrade in Arms. Alun Lewis. FaBoTw; MoBrPo

Red for Santa's fur-lined cloak. All in Red. Eileen Mathias. BoTP

Red fox, the vixen, The. Abnegation. Adrienne Rich. WPE

Red Fred exhumed the orangepeels. John Mason. IAT

Red from glory and fat from defeats. Ballad of a General. Paul Snoek, *tr. by* John Stevens Wade. DuIn

Red Geranium and Godly Mignonette. D. H. Lawrence. GTBS-P; NoAM

Red Geraniums. Martha Haskell Clark. BLPA

Red globes of light, the liquor-green, The. William Street. Kenneth Slessor. CBAP

Red Glow in the Sky, A. Aleksandr Aleksandrovich Blok, *tr. fr. Russian by* Jon Stallworthy *and* Peter France. OBVE

Red-Gold Rain, The. Sacheverell Sitwell. MoBrPo

Red granite and black diorite, with the blue. The Skeleton of the Future. "Hugh MacDiarmid." GoTS; MoBrPo; OBMV; OBTV

Red, green, yellow, pink. Antonina. Felix Mnthali. WMBCH

Red-haired Man's Wife, The. James Stephens. MoBrPo

Red Hanrahan's Song about Ireland. W. B. Yeats. CMoP; FaBoCh; NOIV

Red Harlaw. Sir Walter Scott. *Fr.* The Antiquary, *ch.* 40. OxBB

Red head, red head. Blackbird's Song. *Unknown.* GBP

Red-head swallows swoop and clip the waves in pairs, so light! Crossing the Yangtze in a Strong Wind. Wang Shih-chen, *tr. by* Jonathan Chaves. CoBLCP

Red Heart, The. James Reaney. CaP

Red Heart Station. Yang Shih-ch'i, *tr. fr. Chinese by* Jonathan Chaves. CoBLCP

Red Herring, The. George MacBeth. SO

Red Herring, The. *Unknown.* FaBoNo

Red Horse. Bill Manhire. ATNZ

Red hot needle, A. Hornet. Anne Sexton. AnAn

Red in Autumn. Elizabeth Gould. BoTP

Red Indian Corpse. Peter Redgrove. OxBC

Red inside, coal-black outside. *Unknown, tr. by* Hiroaki Sato. FCEI

Red Iron Ore,. *Unknown.* AS

Red is a sunset. What Is Red? Mary O'Neill. RHPC

Red is the battlefield. Tipputtolar, *tr. by* A. K. Ramanujan. PLW

Red is the down which is covering me. Ankotarinya. *Unknown, tr. by* T. G. H. Strehlow. CBAP

Red Jack. Mary Durack. PoAu-1

Red Jacket. Fitz-Greene Halleck. AA; AnAmPo

Red Leaves. Tameshige, *tr. fr. Japanese by* Steven D. Carter. WFTW

Red Leaves on a Buried Tree. Shotetsu, *tr. fr. Japanese by* Steven D. Carter. WFTW

Red Letters. Mekeel McBride. NAmP

Red Light. Amiri Baraka. SOTW

Red light/ Stop/ Green light. Traffic Lights. Mu'in Besseisso, *tr. by* Abdullah al-Udhari. MPAW

Red Lilies. Barbara Guest. PoM

Red lips are not so red. Greater Love. Wilfred Owen. BrPo; CMoP; EnLoPo; FaBoMo; FaBoRV; FaFP; GTBS-P; LiTB; LiTM; MoAB; MoBrPo; MoP; NoAM; WaaP; WaP

Red lotus incense fades on/ the jewelled curtain. Li Ch'ing-chao, *tr. by* Kenneth Rexroth. BoWoP

Red-Man, The. Frank Prewett. HATNAP

Red Man's Wife, The. *Unknown, tr. fr. Modern Irish by* Douglas Hyde. SeCePo

Red Men, The. Charles Sangster. CaP

Red Monkey. *Unknown, tr. fr. Yoruba by* Ulli Beier. *Fr.* Hunter Poems of the Yoruba. RB

Red o'er the forest glows the setting sun. John Keble. *See* Forest Leaves in Autumn: November.

Red of the dawn! The Dawn. Tennyson. NAEL-2

Red of the flaming rose, The. Mohammad Taqu', Mir, *tr. by* Ahmed Ali. GoT

Red on sun sky sail. Six Eagles. Thomas Peacock. VoR

Red oranges, white bamboo shoots, don't mention the cost! A Random Song on Approaching a River. Shih Jun-chang, *tr. by* William Shultz. WFTU

Red paths that wander through the gray, and cells. With God Conversing. Gene Derwood. LiTA; LiTM

Red pony cannot be fetched, The. Ujibe Kurome. *Fr.* Manyo Shu. Ma

Red, Red Rose, A. Burns. AWP; BoLoP; ChTr; FaBV; FaFP; FF; GBL; HAP; HeIP; InvP; NAEL-2; NIP; NOBE; NOEC; NoP; OAEL-1; OBEV; OxBS; PoEL-4; PoLF; PrIm; SoSe; TEP (My Luve.) FPL; TrGrPo

Red Ridinghood. Nathan Alterman, *tr. fr. Hebrew by* Bernhard Frank. MHeP

Red Right Returning. Louis O. Coxe. WaP

Red river, red river. Virginia. T. S. Eliot. *Fr.* Landscapes, II. InPK; RB

Red River Valley. *Unknown.* AS, *with music;* FaBoBe; FaFP

Red Road, The. Nila NorthSun. STE

Red Rock Canyon, Summer 1977, *sel.* Kitty Tsui. Vision, The. ER

Red Rock Ceremonies. Anita Endrezze-Danielson Probst. CDW; VoR

Red rock wilderness, The. Sidney Keyes. *Fr.* The Wilderness. OBWP; LiTB

Red Rose, proud Rose, sad Rose of all my days! To the Rose upon the Rood of Time. W. B. Yeats. NoAM; NoP; TEP

Red rose whispers of passion, The. A White Rose. John Boyle O'Reilly. AA; ACP; OBEV; SoSe

Red Roses. Gertrude Stein. *Fr.* Tender Buttons. TTTS

Red Sea. James Agee. *Fr.* Two Songs on the Economy of Abundance. MoAmPo

Red Sea Place in Your Life, The. Annie Johnson Flint. *See* Have you come to the Red Sea place in your life.

Red Seeds Opening in the Shade. Sandra McPherson. NAmP

Red Shift, *sel.* P. Inman. "Silos all by a stillness." LP

Red shoes on the ruined staircase. No Taker for the Small Shoes. Sue Roe. NPo

Red sky at night. *Unknown. Fr.* Weather Wisdom. OxNR

Red sky in the morning. Issa, *tr. by* Geoffrey Bownas *and* Anthony Thwaite. PeBJV

Red sky in the morning. *Unknown.* FaBoUs

Red smartweed flowers fill the ford in the autumn rains. Sand of the Silk-Washing Stream. Hsüeh Chao-yün, *tr. by* Lois Fusek. ATF

Red stockings, blue stockings. *Unknown.* OxNR

Red sumac presses. On the New Road. Lyn Lifshin. NeAC

Red swan, The. Leda and the Swan. Jerzy Harasymowicz, *tr. by* Czeslaw Milosz. PwPP

Red-tiled towers of the old Chateau, The. Chateau Papineau. Susan Frances Harrison. CaP

Red Wheelbarrow, The. William Carlos Williams. AnAmPo; BLPL; CMoP; GrPl; GrPl; HeIP; HoPM; InPK; LiTA; LiTM; MoAB; MoAmPo; MoP; NAAL-2; NIP; NoAM; NOBA; NoP; PoE; PrIm; SoSe; SOTW; TAP; TTTS; UnPo; WeW

Red Whiskey. *Unknown.* AmFP

Red, White and Blue. David T. Shaw. *See* O Columbia, the gem of the ocean.

Red, White and Red, The. *Unknown.* AmFP

Red Wig, The. *Unknown.* CoMu

Red young men under the ground, The. *Unknown, tr. fr. Navajo Indian by* Jerome Rothenberg. *Fr.* Red Ant Way. STP

Redbird, bluebird. They've All Gone South. Mary Britton Miller. RHPC

Redbreast, The, *sel.* Wordsworth. "Driven in by autumn's sharpening air." PBBP

Redbummed Sweeney bolts the gate. Sweeney, Old and Phthisic, among the Hippopotami. David Cummings. BXAP

Rededication. Emanuel Litvinoff. WaP

Redeemer, The. "Fiona Macleod." WGRP
Redeemer. Kizito Z. Muchemwa. WMBCH
Redeemer, The. Siegfried Sassoon. MMA; WGRP
Redemption. George Herbert. *Fr.* The Temple. EaLo; FF; HAP; InPK; InPS; JCP; LiTB; MeLP; MePo; NAEL-1; NOBE; NOCV; NoP; OBS; PoE; SCV; SeCP; SeCV-1; Son; SoSe; TEP; TrCP; WeW
Redeployment. Howard Nemerov. LiTM; OBWP; TrJP
Redesdale and Wise William. *Unknown.* ESPB
Redingote and the Vamoose, The. Richard Kendall Munkittrick. OBCA
Rediscovery. Kofi Awoonor. TTY
Redolent song, the sheaf-smell of dusk, A. The Dead of My Songs. István Agh, *tr. by* Alan Dixon. MHuP
Redoubted knights, and honorable Dames. Spenser. *Fr.* The Faerie Queene, III, 9–10. NoP
Redshanks, The. Julian Bell. OBMV
Reductions, *sel.* Lamberto Pignotti, *tr. fr. Italian by* Lawrence R. Smith.
"Here you get alarmed at the confusion." NItP
Redwings. James Wright. NNaP
Redwoods, The. Louis Simpson. AmFN; CoAP
Reed, The. Henry Bernard Carpenter. AA
Reed, The. Mikhail Yurevich Lermontov, *tr. fr. Russian by* J. J. Robbins. AWP
Reed, A. Osip Mandelstam, *tr. fr. Russian by* James Greene. VWA
Reed that sheds its, The. Eugenio Montale, *tr. fr. Italian by* Dana Gioia. *Fr.* The Motets, XIX. PFI
Reed-warbler, The. Mizuhara Shuoshi, *tr. by* Geoffrey Bownas *and* Anthony Thwaite. PeBJV
Reeds give, The. Small Song. A. R. Ammons. NoAM; NoP
Reeds in the Loch Sayis, The. *Unknown.* GoTS
Reeds of Innocence. Blake. *See* Songs of Innocence: Piping Down the Valleys Wild.
Reeking of unsolved crimes, the cop. Two Hookers. A. K. Redwing. VoR
Reever ryves at the gullie, The. Women's Wather. T. S. Law. OxBS
Refined Man, The. Kipling. *Fr.* Epitaphs of the War, 1914–1918. FaBoEE; FaBoTw; MMA
Refiner's Fire, The. *Unknown.* BLRP
Refiner's Gold, The. Frances Ellen Watkins Harper. PWR
Refining Fire. Lizelia Augusta Jenkins Moorer. CBWP-3
Reflected in a venetian mirror, heavy-framed. Soho. Joseph Brodsky, *tr. by* Alan Myers. VWA
Reflected in the pensioner's eye. Karoo Town. Robert Dederick. PeSA
Reflecting on the Aging-Process. Robert Peters. BXAP
Reflection. Michael Guttenbrunner, *tr. fr. German by* Beth Bjorklund. CoAuP
Reflection, A. Thomas Hood. FaBoEE
Reflection. Iain Crichton Smith. PoPo
Reflection. W. J. Turner. OBMV
Reflection: After Visiting Old Friends. John Allison. GrPl
Reflection and Advice. Ezra Pound. OBSV
Reflection by a Mailbox. Stanley Kunitz. TrJP; WaP
Reflection from Rochester. William Empson. PoA
Reflection from Sea and Sky. Walter Savage Landor. FaBoEE
Reflection in a Green Arena. Gregory Corso. VGW
Reflection in Red. Oku Onuora. PVCV
Reflection Kiss, one given, The. Some Kisses from *The Kama Sutra.* Hugo Williams. BoLoP
Reflection on Babies. Ogden Nash. FaBoUs; NBLV
Reflection on Ingenuity. Ogden Nash. RB
Reflections. Anita Barrows. NMM
Reflections. Zsuzsa Beney, *tr. fr. Hungarian by* Jascha Kessler. *Fr.* A Broken Glass. FOC
Reflections. Barbara Burford. DT
Reflections, *sel.* George Crabbe.
Late Wisdom. OBEV; TrGrPo
Reflections. Antoinette Deshoulières, *tr. fr. French by* Yvor Winters. PBWP
Reflections. Janet Dubé. DT
Reflections. Carl Gardner. PoBA
Reflections. Louis MacNeice. FaBCIP
Reflections. Vivian Smith. CBAP
Reflections. Constance E. Studer. TSM
Reflections at Dawn. Phyllis McGinley. FiBHP; NBLV; NOBL
Reflections by a Main Entrance, *sel.* Nikolai Alekseyevich Nekrasov, *tr. fr. Russian by* Alan Meyers.
"Do you know of just one habitation." AAA
Reflections in a Slum. "Hugh MacDiarmid." FaBoTw
Reflections in Bed. Julian Symons. WaP
Reflections in the river: trembling spring trees. Yang Chi, *tr. fr. Chinese by* Jonathan Chaves. *Fr.* Living in a Riverside Village — Miscellaneous Impressions. CoBLCP

Reflections of a Proud Pedestrian. Oliver Wendell Holmes. AnAmPo
Reflections on a Visit to the Burke Museum, University of Washington, Seattle. Gail Tremblay. HATNAP
Reflections on a Womb Which Is Called "Vacant." Jeanine Hathaway. IHMS
Reflections on Having Left a Place of Retirement. Samuel Taylor Coleridge. EnRP
Reflections on Ice-breaking. Ogden Nash. AiP; BLPL; FaBoCo; FaFP; LiTM; NBLV; NoP; OBAL
Reflections on Mirrors. Elder Olson. CRP
Reflections on the Death of a Parrot. Jaime Jacinto. BrSi
Reflections on the water catch the stirrings of dense trees. My Little Garden. Li Chien, *tr. by* Irving Lo. WFTU
Reflections Outside of a Gymnasium. Phyllis McGinley. SD
Reflections, Written on Visiting the Grave of a Venerated Friend. Ann Plato. BlSi
Reflections yet related light orange white to boom-boom. Prewar Late October Sea Breeze. Robert Grenier. UL
Reflective. A. R. Ammons. HCAP
Reflexion, The. Edward Taylor. *See* Preparatory Meditations before My Approach to the Lord's Supper:
Lord, art thou at the table head above.
Reflexions on suicide, & on my father, possess me. Of Suicide. John Berryman. NoAM
Reflexions on the Seizure of the Suez, and on a Proposal to Line the Banks of That Canal with Bill. Howard Nemerov. NBLV
Reformation of Manners, *sels.* Daniel Defoe.
London. NOEC
"Search all the Christian climes from pole to pole." OBSV
"Yet Ostia boasts of her regeneration." OBSV
Reformer to His Father, A. James Simmons. BIrV
Refracted Lights. Celia Parker Wooley. WGRP
Refrain. Mary Jo Salter. EOEF
Refrains. John Hollander. AnAn
Refreshing rest, ecstatic dream. In the Grass. Annette von Droste-Hülshoff, *tr. by* James Edward Tobin. PBWP
Refrigerator slams, The. Words from a Bottle. Deborah Lee. BrSi
Refrigerium. Cardinal Newman. OBNC
Refuge. Mabel E. McCartney. BLRP
Refuge. Lew Sarett. AA
Refuge, The. Marjorie Battcock. CN
Refugee. Naomi Long Madgett. PoNe
Refugee Blues. W. H. Auden. *See* Say this city has ten million souls.
Refugee in America. Langston Hughes. AmFN; GOA
(Words Like Freedom.) BPo
Refugee Room. Judah Leib Teller. *See* Late November evening in Vienna.
Refugees. Chaim Grade, *tr. fr. Yiddish by* Marc Kaminski. VWA
Refugees, The. Randall Jarrell. MoAB; MoAmPo
Refugees. Louis MacNeice. LiTB; WaP
Refugees, The. Edwin Muir. NoAM
Refugees, The. Sir Herbert Read. BrPo
Refusal. Lucie Delarue-Mardrus, *tr. fr. French by* Barbara Johnson. DMF
Refusal, A. Barnabe Googe. NoP
Refusal, A. Thomas Hardy. FaBoCo; LiTB
Refusal to Mourn the Death, by Fire, of a Child in London, A. Dylan Thomas. BLPL; CMoP; EBEV; FaBoMo; FaFP; FF; GTBS-P; HeIP; HoPM; LiTB; LiTM; MoAB; MoBrPo; MoP; NoAM; NOBE; NoP; OAEL-2; OBWVE; OxBTC; PoE; SeCePo; TEP; TwCP; UnPo; WaaP
Refusals. Jon Anderson. MAYP
Refuse to silence the light of this day and let us depart now with faces exposed. Millibars of Storm. Aimé Césaire, *tr. by* Michael Benedikt. POS
Refuses/ To refuse the racket. Old Tennis Player. Gwendolyn Brooks. SD
Refusing to fall in love with God, he gave. Didymus. Louis MacNeice. EaLo
Refuting the "Invitation to Hiding." Wang K'ang-chü, *tr. fr. Chinese by* Burton Watson. CoBCP
Regal realm with the sorrowless name, The. Ravidas, *tr. by* John Stratton Hawley *and* Mark Juergensmeyer. SSI
Regard her well—the austere face. Röntgen Photograph. Elisabeth Eybers, *tr. by* Jack Cope, Uys Krige *and* Ruth Miller. PeSA
Regard, O reader, how it is with me. Look, in the Labyrinth of Memory. Delmore Schwartz. TrJP
Regard the capture here, O Janus-faced. Recitative. Hart Crane. FaBoMo

Regard the little needle. The Needle. Grace Cornell Tall. GoYe

Regarding my infants as friends from old days. Teika, *tr. fr. Japanese by* Hiroaki Sato. *Fr.* Eighty-four Tanka. FCEI

Regardless: the devastated world. My Bird. Ingeborg Bachmann, *tr. by* Beth Bjorklund. CoAuP

Regeneration. Henry Vaughan. JCP; MeLP; MePo; NAEL-1; NoP; OBS; PoE

Regenesis. Ron Welburn. NBP

Regent of song! who bringest to our shore. To Rosina Pico. William Wilberforce Lord. AA

Regent's Park Terrace. Bernard Spencer. FaBoPP

Reggae Blue Sweater. Caroline Knox. SoTCo

Reggae fi Dada. Linton Kwesi Johnson. PBCV

Reginald Pugh, The Man Who Came from the Army. Emma Lee Warrior. HATNAP

Regine's Rebuke to Kierkegaard. Ruthann Robson. ER

Region desolate and wild, A. Hayeswater. Matthew Arnold. *Fr.* The Hayeswater Boat. FaBoPP

Region of life and light! The Life of the Blessed. Luís de León, *tr. by* Bryant. AWP

Regrat. William Drummond of Hawthornden. PoEL-2

Regret. *Malay Oral Tradition, tr. by* R. J. Wilkinson. WTO

Regret and Refusal. *Unknown, tr. fr. Tewa Indian by* H. J. Spinden. WTO

Regret for the Mourning Doves Who Failed to Mate. Bruce Weigl. NAmP

Regretful Thoughts. Yü Hsüan-chi, *tr. fr. Chinese by* Geoffrey Waters. BoWoP

Regretfully, I proffer my excuses. Lines Declining a Transatlantic Dinner Invitation. Marilyn Hacker. MAYP

Regrets, *sel.* Joachim Du Bellay, *tr. fr. French by* G. K. Chesterton. Hereux Qui, comme Ulysse, A Fait un Beau Voyage. *Fr.* XXXI. AWP

Regrets, The, *sel.* Charles Hubert Sisson.
"Beware of age." PoPo

Rehearsal. Cyril Dabydeen. BrSi; PBCV

Rehearsal. David Fisher. NPGG

Rehearsal, The. Horace Gregory. VGW

Rehearsing for Death. Angelos Sikelianos, *tr. fr. Greek by* Edmund Keeley *and* Philip Sherrard. VMG

Reid at Fayal. John Williamson Palmer. PAH

Reid in the Loch Sayis, The. *Unknown.* OxBS

Reign of Chaos, The. Pope. *See* Dunciad, The: Triumph of Dullness [*or* Dulness], The.

Reign of Peace, The. Mary Starck. WBLP

Rein your sorry nags, boys, buckle the polished saddle. Dance on Pushback. James Still. GrPl

Reincarnating Pythagoras, say. Decimus Magnus Ausonius. PeHV

Reincarnation. Mae Jackson. PoBA

Reincarnation. Wallace McRae. CowP

Reincarnation. David Banks Sickels. AA

Reincarnation (I) ("Still, passed through the spokes of an old wheel"). James Dickey. HoPM

Reindeer and Engine. Josephine Jacobsen. GrPl; WPE

Reindeer Report. U. A. Fanthorpe. OBCP

Reivers they stole Fair Annie, The. Fair Annie. *Unknown.* CH

Rejected Lover, The. *Unknown.* AmFP

Rejected "National Hymns, The." "Orpheus C. Kerr." OBAL

Rejecting a slanderous mind. Ozaki Hosai, *tr. fr. Japanese by* Hiroaki Sato. *Fr.* One Hundred Haiku in Free Form. FCEI

Rejoice. Joaquin Miller. PAH

"Rejoice holy bundles, sacred bundles." They Went to the Moon Mother. *Unknown, tr. by* Barbara Tedlock. STP

Rejoice in God. Christopher Smart. *Fr.* Jubilate Agno. PoE

Rejoice, Let Alleluias Ring. Sister M. Cherubim Schaefer. AH

Rejoice, O Bridegroom! *Unknown, tr. fr. Hebrew by* Israel Abrahams. TrJP

Rejoice, O youth, in the lovely hind. Moses Ibn Ezra, *tr. fr. Hebrew by* Solomon Solis-Cohen. *Fr.* Wedding Song in honor of R. Solomon ben Matir. TrJP

Rejoice, rejoice, brave patriots, rejoice! Reparation or War. *Unknown.* PAH

Rejoice you sots, your idol's come again. Upon the King's Return from Flanders. Henry Hall. APAS

Rejoicing/ because we had met again. The Good Dream. Denise Levertov. NNaP

Rejoicing at the Arrival of Chi'en Hsiung. Po Chü-i, *tr. fr. Chinese by* Arthur Waley. POB

Rejoicing That the Zen Master Pao Has Arrived from Dragon Mountain. Liu Ch'ang-ch'ing, *tr. fr. Chinese by* Burton Watson. CoBCP

Rekayi Tangwena. Mudereri Kadhani. WMBCH

Relapse, The. Thomas Stanley. OBEV

Relapse, The. Henry Vaughan. TrCP

Relating to Robinson. Weldon Kees. NaP

Relations. Orerulavanar, *tr. fr. Tamil by* A. K. Ramanujan. PLW

Relationship. The. Stephen Vincent. NeAC

Relatives are leaning over, staring expectantly, The. "The Dreadful Has Already Happened." Mark Strand. HCAP; NoAM

Relativities. Louis Untermeyer. BXAP

Relativity, *sel. Unknown, at. to* Arthur Buller. FaBoCo; FaFP; ImOP
"There was a young lady called Bright." OxBoLi
(Young Lady Named Bright, A.) FaPON

Relax. This won't last long. Poem for People Who Are Understandably Too Busy to Read Poetry. Stephen Dunn. GOYP

Relaxation. Dick Gallup. UL

Relaxed Abalone, The. Rosmarie Waldrop. InPK

Relaxed, nothing to do. Letting My Feelings Out. Yü Hsüan-chi, *tr. by* Geoffrey Waters. BoWoP

Relaxing all day in this tropical atmosphere. Foreign Aid. Lionel Kearns. NOBC

Relaxing among hanging plants. The Greenhouse in October. Peter Levi. PoPo

Relaxing in the Evening in My Study. Yang Wan-li, *tr. fr. Chinese by* Burton Watson. CoBCP

Relays. Barrett Watten. LP

Relearning the Alphabet. Denise Levertov. NOBA

Relearning the Language of April. Maxine W. Kumin. ER

Release. D. H. Lawrence. CMoP

Release, The. Adah Isaacs Menken. CBWP-1

Released [*or* Releas'd] from the noise of the butcher and baker. Jinny the Just. Matthew Prior. NOBE; NOEC; OBEV; PoEL-3

Relent, my dear yet unkind Coelia. William Percy. *Fr.* Coelia, XVII. AAS; Son

Relentless, black on white, the cable runs. T-Bar. Patricia K. Page. NoAM; NOBC; OBCV

Reliable Service, A. Allen Curnow. ATNZ

Reliance. Chang Ts'o, *tr. fr. Chinese by* Dominic Cheung. IFON

Reliance. Henry van Dyke. FaFP

Relic, The. John Donne. ElL; GBL; HAP; HeIP; LiTB; NOBE; NoP; OAEL-1; OBD, at. 1; PoEL-2; PPP
(Relique, The.) MeLP; MePo; OBS; PoEL-2; SeCP; SeCV-1

Relic, The. Robert Hillyer. GoYe; UnS

Relic. Ted Hughes. NAEL-2

Relief of putting fingers on the keyboard, The. Thanking My Mother for Piano Lessons. Diane Wakoski. NoAM

Religio Laici, *sels.* Dryden. SeCV-2
"But if there be a power too just and strong." NOCV
"Dim, as the borrow'd beams of moon and stars." OAEL-1
(Reason and Religion.) FiP
(Reason and Revelation.) OBS
Priestcraft and Private Judgement. OBS
Scriptures, The. OBS
"Thus man by his own strength to Heaven would soar." NOCV; WGRP
Tradition. OBS

Religio Medici, *sel.* Sir Thomas Browne.
Colloquy with God, A. OBS

Religion. John Donne. *See* Satires: Kind pity [*or* kinde pitty] chokes my spleen[e]; brave scorn forbids.

Religion. Henry Vaughan. NOCV; OAEL-1; OBS; TOF

Religion and Doctrine. John Milton Hay. WGRP

Religion and the Lower Classes. Evan Lloyd. *Fr.* The Methodist. NOEC

Religion Back Home. William Stafford. OBAL

Religion of Sweet Jesus, The. "Onward Christian Soldiers!" Frank Marshall Davis. FB

Religious faith is a most filling vapor. Innate Helium. Robert Frost. ImOP

Religious Musings, *sels.* Samuel Taylor Coleridge.
"Lovely was the death." EnRP
"There is one Mind, one omnipresent." WGRP

Religious Use of [Taking] Tobacco. Unknown, *at. to* Robert Wisdome. EIL; OBS
(Pipe and Can, I ("The Indian weed withered quite").) OBEV

Religious virgin of unspecific sex, A. Book Years. Bob Perelman. LP

Religious wars of Europe have been numbered with the past, The. The Peonage System. Lizelia Augusta Jenkins Moorer. CBWP-3

Reliquary. Hart Crane. PoA

Relique, The. John Donne. *See* Relic, The.

Reliques, *sel.* Edmund Blunden.
"And mathematics, fresh as May." ImOP

Relish honey. If you please. To a Swallow. John Peale Bishop, *after* Euenus. OBVE

Relished as cooler than usual tonight. Teika, *tr. fr. Japanese by* Hiroaki Sato. *Fr.* Eighty-four Tanka. FCEI

Relocation. David Mura. BrSi

Relocation. Simon J. Ortiz. NOVW

Reluctance. Robert Frost. CMoP; MoAB; MoAMPo; NOBA; OxBA

Relying on the disasters o' the war. March, 1941. Paul Goodman. LiTA

Remain, Ah Not in Youth Alone. Walter Savage Landor. *Fr.* Ianthe. HAP; OBNC

Remain apart,/ The world's yours. Waka on Seeing and Hearing Directly. Bunan, *tr. by* Lucien Stryk *and* Takashi Ikemoto. ZPCJ

Remain, Rata. Te Puea Herangi, *tr. fr. Maori by* Margaret Orbell. PeNZ

Remainder. Frederika Blankner. GoYe

Remained I all my life. Mohammad Taqi Mir, *tr. by* Ahmed Ali. GoT

Remains, The. Mark Strand. NYBP; PPP

Remains of an Indian Village. Alfred W. Purdy. NOBC

Remains of blue bog children, The. Blue Bog Children. Roger Weingarten. AmPA

Remark. Charles Spear. PeNZ

Remarks from the Rocks. Robert Desnos, *tr. fr. French by* Michael Benedikt. POS

Remarks of Soul to Body. Robert Penn Warren. NAs

Rembrandt's Late Self-Portraits. Elizabeth Jennings. EyDe

Remedy Worse than the Disease, The. Matthew Prior. FaBoEE; TrGrPo

Remeidis of Luve. *Unknown.* OxBS

Remember. Joy Harjo. STE

Remember. Georgia Douglas Johnson. PoNe

Remember. Christina Rossetti. AWP; BoLoP; CH; EnLoPo; FaBV; FPL; NOBE; NoP; OAEL-2; OBEV; OBNC; PoLF; PoRA; TrGrPo

Remember. *Unknown.* BXAP

Remember a season. A Symposium: Apples. Linda Pastan. NIP

Remember a while ago we happened to meet. My Neighbor to the South, the Office Clerk Hsiao, Came in the Evening to Say Good-bye. Mei Yao-ch'en, *tr. by* Burton Watson. CoBCP

Remember Barbara. Barbara. Jacques Prévert, *tr. by* Lawrence Ferlinghetti. RHTwFP

Remember Dear Mary. John Clare. WeW

Remember Eubolus, who lived and died sober? Leonidas of Tarentum, *tr. by* Fleur Adcock. OBD

Remember Haiti, Cuba, Vietnam. Andrew Salkey. PBCV

Remember how unimportant. Milkweed. Philip Levine. LCAP

Remember I am a garnet woman. If I Am Too Brown or Too White for You. Wendy Rose. HATNAP

Remember it, although you're far away. Remember. *Unknown.* BXAP

Remember me when I am dead. Simplify Me When I'm Dead. Keith Douglas. NePoEA; NoAM; OxBTC

Remember me when I am gone away. Remember [*or* Sonnet]. Christina Rossetti. AWP; BoLoP; CH; EnLoPo; FaBV; FPL; NOBE; NoP; OAEL-2; OBEV; OBNC; PoLF; PoRA; TrGrPo

Remember Medusa? Eunice De Souza. AIW

Remember Not. Helene Johnson. BANP; PoNe

Remember now, my Love, what piteous thing. A Carrion. Baudelaire, *tr. by* Allen Tate. AWP

Remember Now Thy Creator. Bible, *O.T. Fr.* Ecclesiastes, XII: 1-8. AWP; ChTr; OBVE

(Remember Then Thy Creator.) TrJP

(Youth and Age.) TrGrPo

Remember, Phyllis. Honeymoon. Samuel L. Albert. GoYe

Remember, poet, while gallivanting across the sky. Forget Me Not. Bob Kaufman. AmNP

Remember, remember/ The fifth of November. The Gunpowder Plot. *Unknown.* FaBoUs

("Please to remember.") OxNR

Remember Richard, lately king of price. The Tudor Rose. Alexander Barclay. *Fr.* The Ship of Fools. ACP

Remember, Ruapehu. A White Gentian. Sam Hunt. ATNZ

Remember Sabbath Days. Larry Eigner. VWA

Remember, Sinful Youth. *Unknown.* AH

Remember Suez? Adrian Mitchell. OxBTC

Remember that a soul can flower from a kiss. A Working-Class Woman. Louise Colet, *tr. by* Beth Archer. DMF

Remember That Country. Jean Garrigue. VGW

Remember that day on the beach, remember. Stitching in Time: Dorothy Ruddick. Richard Howard. KS

Remember that night. *Unknown, tr. by* Thomas Kinsella. NOIV

Remember that old love song, Daphne? Delfica. Gérard de Nerval, *tr. by* Andrew Hoyem. NU

Remember that Saturday morning. The Dirty-billed Freeze Footy. Judith Hemschemeyer. TV

Remember the covenant of our youth. A Dying Wife to Her Husband. Moses ibn Ezra. TrJP

Remember the Day of Judgement. *Unknown.* MeEL

Remember the day the sea turned red. Plankton. Ruth Miller. PeSA

Remember the Last Things. *Unknown.* MeEL

Remember the M. *Unknown.* ILY

Remember the Poor. Matilda Caroline Edwards. PWR

Remember the princess who kissed the frog. A Story Wet as Tears. Marge Piercy. NIP

Remember the sky that you were born under. Remember. Joy Harjo. STE

Remember the sun in the autumn, its rays. The Secret Town. Abraham Sutskever, *tr. by* Jacob Sonntag. TrJP

Remember the tree, Charlie? The Punishment. Susan Ludvigson. MT

Remember Thee! Remember Thee! Byron. BoLoP; OxBSP

Remember Then Thy Creator. Bible, *O.T. See* Ecclesiastes: Remember Now Thy Creator.

Remember this if wealth you have. Wealth; or Song Written for a Beggar. Vali Mohammad Nazir, *tr. by* Ahmed Ali. GoT

Remember those X-ray machines in shoe stores. On Hot Days. James Reiss. AmPA

Remember Thou Me. *Malay Oral Tradition, tr. by* R. J. Wilkinson *and* R. O. Winstedt. WTO

Remember, Though the Telescope Extend. George Dillon. ImOP

Remember Thy Creator Now. Peter Long. AH

Remember Times for Sandy. Carolyn M. Rodgers. JB

Remember us poor Mayers all. Song of the Mayers [*or* The Mayers' Song]. *Unknown.* CH; GBP

Remember when. Among Strangers. William Stafford. NNaP

Remember when I draped. Poem for My Mother. Siv Cedering Fox. TV

Remember when you hear them beginning to say Freedom. Notes for My Son. Alex Comfort. *Fr.* The Song of Lazarus, VI. LiTM; MoBrPo; SeCePo

Remember when you were the first one awake, the first. Little Girl Wakes Early. Robert Penn Warren. PoE

Remember, while you are sleeping here, offshore. Evolution. John Blight. CBAP

Remember Your Lovers. Sidney Keyes. WaP

Remembered Melody. Andrew Lang. *See* Three crests against the saffron sky.

Remembered Morning. Janet Lewis. WPE

Remembering. Akjartoq, *tr. fr. Eskimo.* WTO

Remembering. Clarisse Nicoïdski, *tr. fr. Judezmo by* Stephen Levy. VWA

Remembering. Judit Tóth, *tr. fr. Hungarian by* Emery George. VWA

Remembering Althea. William Stafford. NYBP

Remembering dark trees of home that keep. Pan in Battle. *Unknown.* PeNZ

Remembering England. Peter Bland. ATNZ

Remembering Fannie Lou Hamer. Thadious M. Davis. BlSi

Remembering Fire. Rodney Jones. MAYP

Remembering Golden Bells. Po Chü-i, *tr. fr. Chinese by* Arthur Waley. AWP

Remembering his taste for blood. Of Baiting the Lion. Sir Owen Seaman. NA

Remembering Lincoln. Frank Mundorf. GoYe

Remembering Lunch. Douglas Dunn. OxBC

Remembering Lutsky. Rayzel Zychlinska, *tr. fr. Yiddish by* Marc Kaminsky. VWA

Remembering macadam road rolls, The. The Macadam Road Remembers. István Csukás, *tr. by* Barbara Howes. MHuP

Remembering Mincemeat. George MacBeth. NPo

Remembering My Late Wife. Chu Yün-ming, *tr. fr. Chinese by* Jonathan Chaves. CoBLCP

Remembering Mykenai. Alfred Corn. SM

Remembering Nat Turner. Sterling A. Brown. PoBA; PoNe

Remembering Snow. Sandor Csoori, *tr. fr. Hungarian by* Jascha Kessler. FOC

Remembering Snow. Ralph Nixon Currey. PeSA

Remembering That Island. Thomas McGrath. NePoEA

Remembering the descriptions by Wilson. Passenger Pigeons. Robert Morgan. GeTw; MAYP; MT

Remembering the Past at Chin-ling. Wei Yüan, *tr. fr. Chinese by* Irving Lo. WFTU

Remembering the Strait of Belle Isle or. Large Bad Picture. Elizabeth Bishop. EyDe; NoP; NYBP; OxBC

Remembering the 'Thirties. Donald Davie. FaBoPV; NePoEA; OxBTC

Remembering what passed. Old Scent of the Plum Tree. Ietaka, *tr. by* E. Powys Mathers. AWP

Remembering with Feeling. Onitsura, *tr. fr. Japanese by* Hiroaki Sato. *Fr.* Twenty-three Hokku. FCEI

Remembering You. Maxine W. Kumin. ASP

Remembering you, I remember the horse you rode. John Douglas White. Mabel Ferrett. CN
Remembrance. John Henry Boner. AA
Remembrance. Emily Brontë. BLPL; BoLoP; BoWoP; CH; EBEV; EnLoPo; FaFP; HAP; LiTB; NAEL-2; NOBE; NoBWP; NoP; OBNC; PBWP; PoE; PoEL-5; TEP; TrGrPo; WeW; WPE (R. Alcona to J. Brenzaida.) BrRo; EBVV; OPOP
Remembrance, A. Willis Gaylord Clarke. AA
Remembrance. Mieczyslaw Jastrun, tr. fr. Polish by Czeslaw Milosz. PwPP
Remembrance. George Parsons Lathrop. AA
Remembrance. Shakespeare. See When to the sessions of sweet silent thought.
Remembrance. Antoni Slonimski, tr. fr. Polish by Frances Notley. TrJP
Remembrance. Prince P. A. Vyazemsky, tr. fr. Russian by Alan Myers. AAA
Remembrance. Sir Thomas Wyatt. See They Flee [or Fle] from Me That Sometime Did Me Seek [or Seke].
Remembrance. V. A. Zhukovsky, tr. fr. Russian by Alan Myers. AAA
Remembrance of a Color inside a Forest, A. Ray A. Young Bear. CDW
Remembrance of My Friend Mr. Thomas Morley, A. John Davies of Hereford. OxBSP
Remembrance of Pasternak: the earth of his forelock. 1976. Abraham Sutskever, tr. fr. Yiddish by Cynthia Ozick. Fr. Poems from a Diary. PeBMYV
Remembrancer of joys long passed away. To a Golden Heart, Worn round His Neck. Goethe, tr. by Margaret Fuller Ossoli. AWP
Remembrances, sel. John Clare.
  "When for school o'er Little Field with its brook and wooden brig." SaC
Remembrances, sel. H. Leivick, tr. fr. Yiddish by Benjamin and Barbara Harshav.
  Holiday. AYP
Remembrances of Guernica. Wieland Schmied, tr. fr. German by Beth Bjorklund. CoAuP
Rememorised, Maurice Devane. Austin Clarke. Fr. Mnemosyne Lay in Dust, XVIII. CMoP, (1970 ed.); IPY
Remind you, that there was darkness in my heart. Canticle of Darkness. Wilfred Watson. MoCV
Reminder, The. Thomas Hardy. CMoP; OBCP
Reminder. John D. Engle, Jr. SoTCo
Reminiscence. Thomas Bailey Aldrich. AA
Reminiscence, A. Anne Brontë. WPE
Reminiscence. Wallace Irwin. FiBHP; NOBL
Reminiscent Reflection. Ogden Nash. FaBoCo
Remittance Man. Judith Wright. NoAM
Remnant. Jung Han-mo, tr. fr. Korean by Koh Chang-soo. ACKP
Remnant Ghosts at Dawn. Oliver La Grone. FB
Remnants of a rainbow fall to the western bank at dawn, The. A Poem on Passing by Hsin-k'ai Lake at Kao-yu. Yang Chi, tr. by Jonathan Chaves. CoBLCP
Remodeling the Hermit's Cabin. Fred Chappell. MOWH
Remonstrance, A. John Gerrard. NOEC
Remonstrance, A. James Kenneth Stephen. NOBVV
Remonstrance to the King. William Dunbar. OxBS
Remorse. Sir John Betjeman. MoBrPo; OxBSP
Remorse, sel. Samuel Taylor Coleridge.
  Voice Sings, A. CH
Remorse. Richmond Lattimore. PoA
Remorse. Shelley. See Stanzas—April, 1814.
Remorse for Time, The. Howard Nemerov. Son
Remorse is memory awake. Emily Dickinson. NAAL-1; NOBA; NOCV; NoP
Remorse—is memory—awake. Remorse is memory awake. Emily Dickinson. NAAL-1; NOBA; NOCV; NoP
Remote and ineffectual Don. Lines to a Don. Hilaire Belloc. FaBoCo; MoBrPo; OBSV; TW
Remote from our sordid world. Purity. Hayim Lenski, tr. by Pearl Grodensky. VWA
Remote music of his swans, their long. His Swans. Geoffrey Grigson. FaBoRV
Remote, unfriended, melancholy, slow. Goldsmith. Fr. The Travel[l]er; or, A Prospect of Society. BIrV
Removal, The. Unknown, tr. fr. Seminole Indian by Frances Densmore. STP
Removal from Terry Street, A. Douglas Dunn. FaBoMo; OxBC
Removal: Last Part. Carroll Arnett. VoR
Remove me from this land of slaves. Ireland. Egan Swift. FaBoPV
Remove the Predicate. Clark Coolidge. UL
Removed from Europe's feuds, a hateful scene. A Warning to America. Philip Freneau. TAP

Remu. Wayne Brown. UAS
Renaissance. Robert Avrett. GoYe
Renaming, The. Valerie Sinason. BrRo
Renancing of Love, A. Sir Thomas Wyatt. See Sonnet: "Farewell, love, and all thy laws [or lawes] for ever."
Renascence, sel. Edna St. Vincent Millay. FaFP; MoAB; MoAmPo; OHFP
  "All I could see from where I stood." PDV
Rencontre. Jessie Redmond Fauset. CDC
Rend America asunder. The Ship Canal from the Atlantic to the Pacific. Francis Lieber. PAH
Renderings and Sunderings of Cobbett's "Rural Rides." B. C. Leale. NPo
Rendez-vous Manqué dans la Rue Racine. J. M. Synge. BIrV
Rendezvous, The. Alan Seeger. See I Have a Rendezvous with Death.
Rendezvous, The. Bernard Spencer. GTBS-P
Rendezvous in the Cave. Ahmad Abd al-Muti Hijazi, tr. fr. Arabic by Sargon Boulus and Peter Porter. MAP
Renegade Wants Words, The. James Welch. CDW
Renegado, The, sel. Philip Massinger.
  "Yet there's one scruple with which I am much." ACP
Renewal. Steve Kowit. UL
Renewal, The, sel. George MacBeth.
  "I needed somewhere with a flirt of grace." PoPo
Renewal, A. James Merrill. OxBSP; SM
Renewal, The. Theodore Roethke. VGW
Renewal, sels. Mustafa Zaidi, tr. fr. Urdu by Mahmood Jamal. PBMUP
  "Life!/ I came to your door like a beggar." Fr. I.
  "Lights were drowned in fog, The." Fr. II.
Renewal by Her Element. Denis Devlin. CIP
Renewal of Strength. Frances Ellen Watkins Harper. PWR
Renouncement. Alice Meynell. BoLoP; MoBrPo; NOBE; OBEV; OBMV; OBNC; Son; WPE
Renowned and gracious are those rulers, those sovereigns. Unknown, tr. by Arthur Waley. BoS
Renowned Generations, The. W. B. Yeats. OxBoLi
Renowned Spenser [or Spencer] lye [or lie] a thought more nye [or nigh]. Elegy on Shakespeare [or On Mr. Wm. Shakespeare]. William Basse. EiL; FaBoRV; OBS
Renowned was King Wên. Unknown, tr. by Arthur Waley. BoS
Rent. Jane Cooper. ER; FYAP; TAP
Renunciation. Wathen Mark Wilks Call. WGRP
Renunciation. Emily Dickinson. See There came a day at summer's full.
Renunciation, A. Edward de Vere, Earl of Oxford. See If Women Could Be Fair.
Renunciation, A. Henry King. OBEV
Renunciation. Padraic Pearse, tr. fr. Irish by the author. NOIV
Repairman in the doorway, The. Goodbye. Chana Bloch. MAYP
Reparation or War. Unknown. PAH
Repartée. Charles Follen Adams. OBAL
Repast. Gertrude Tiemer-Wille. GoYe
Repeat that, repeat. The Cuckoo. Gerard Manley Hopkins. MoAB; MoBrPo; OxBSP; PBBP; RB; TTTS
  (Fragment, The ("Repeat that, repeat").) FM
Repeated Journey, The. Thomas McGrath. NePoEA
Repeating fly, blueback, thumbthick—so gross, A. Harriet. Robert Lowell. NoP
Repent, O ye, predestinate to woe! The Conscience-Keeper. William Young. Fr. Wishmakers' Town. AA
Repentance. Brendan Behan, tr. fr. Irish by Ulick O'Conner. TIRV
Repentance. Chapman. Fr. Hero and Leander, Third Sestiad. OBSC
Repentance. George Alexander Stevens. NOEC
Repentance. Louis Untermeyer. NBLV
Repetition of Words and Weather. Ruth Stone. BoWoP
Repetitions of a Young Captain. Wallace Stevens. WaP
Repetitive Heart, The, sels. Delmore Schwartz.
  All Clowns Are Masked. LiTA; OxBA
  Calmly We Walk Through This April's Day. LiTM; PrIm
  (For Rhoda.) MoAB; MoAmPo; OxBA
  (Time Is the Fire.) LiTA
  "Heavy bear who goes with me, The." LiTA; LiTM; NoAM; NOBA; TAP; TrJP; TwCP; UnPo
Reply. Sidney Godolphin. OBS
Reply, The. Philip Levine. PoA
Reply, The. Theodore Roethke. NoP; NYBP
Reply, A. Unknown. FaBoCo; NBLV; NOBL
Reply from the Akond of Swat, A. Ethel Talbot Scheffauer. FiBHP
Reply of Socrates, The. Edith Thomas. WGRP
Reply to a Creditor. George Harding. FaBoUs

Reply to a Marriage Proposal. Irihapeti Rangi te Apakura, *tr. fr. Maori* by Roger Oppenheim *and* Allen Curnow. PBWZ
Reply to Dipsychus. Arthur Hugh Clough. FaBoCo
Reply to Her Daughter, IV. Madeleine Des Roches, *tr. fr. French by* Dorothy Backer. DMF
Reply to "In Flanders Fields." John Mitchell. BLPA
Reply to Lines by Thomas Moore, A, *sel.* Walter Savage Landor. "Will you come to the bower I have shaded for you?." ChTr
Reply to Mr. Wordsworth, *sel.* Archibald MacLeish. "Space-time, our scientists tell us, is impervious." ImOP
Reply to the Committed Intellectual. Francis Sparshott. NOBC
Reply to the Provinces. Galway Kinnell. NYBP
Reply to the Shade of Descartes. Anne de La Vigne, *tr. fr. French by* Dorothy Backer. DMF
Reply to the Verses of M. Lebrun Entitled: "My Last Word on Women Poets." Philippine de Vannoz, *tr. fr. French by* Beth Archer. DMF
Replying to a Poem from My Cousin Hui-lien. Hsieh Ling-yün, *tr. fr. Chinese by* Burton Watson. CoBCP
Report, The. Jon Swan. NYBP
Report after a Walk along the Avenue. Pyke Johnson, Jr.. SoTCo
Report for Isolda. Julio Ortega, *tr. fr. Spanish by* David Tipton. Per
Report from a Far Place. William Stafford. CAPP
Report from a Planet. Richmond Lattimore. FYAP
Report from California. Lois Moyles. NYBP
Report from K9 Operator Rover on the Motel at Grand Island. William Stafford. SoTCo
Report from Paradise. Zbigniew Herbert, *tr. fr. Polish by* Czeslaw Milosz. OBD
Report from the Besieged City. Zbigniew Herbert, *tr. fr. Polish by* John *and* Bogdana Carpenter. AnAn
Report from the Carolinas, *sel.* Helen Smith Bevington. "It's a debatable land. The winds are variable." AmFN
Report from the Correspondent They Fired. David McElroy. AmPA
Report on Experience. Edmund Blunden. FaBoTw; GTBS-P; NOBE; OBMV; OBWP
Report on Her Remains. Daniel David Moses. HATNAP
Report on the Poem. Otto Orban, *tr. fr. Hungarian by* Edwin Morgan. MHuP
Report on the Situation. Helga Novak, *tr. fr. German by* Susan L. Cocalis. DMG
Report Song [in a Dream], A. Nicholas Breton. GBL; OBSC; SeCePo
Report to Crazy Horse. William Stafford. AnAn; NoAM
Reportless subjects, to the quick. Emily Dickinson. NOBA
Reports Come In, The. J. D. Reed. NYBP
Reports of a Japanese surface presence have brought them speeding. Naval Photograph: 25 October 1942: What the Hand May Be Saying. David Bottoms. BLA
Reports of Midsummer Girls. Richmond Lattimore. PCP
Repose. Alfred Lichtenstein, *tr. fr. German by* Mary Zilzer. VWA
Repose. Una Marson. PBCV
Repose. Henrietta Cordelia Ray. CBWP-3
Repose in Calamity. Henri Michaux, *tr. fr. French by* W. S. Merwin. RHTwFP
Repose of Rivers. Hart Crane. AWP; CMoP; LiTM; MoAB; MoAmPo; NOBA; OxBA; PoE
Repose they know in storefronts, The. The Village of the Presents. James McMichael. AmPA
Representing nothing on God's earth now. Lines on the Back of a Confederate Note. Samuel Alroy Jonas. BLPA; OPP
Repression. Timothy Corsellis. WaP
Repression of War Experience. Siegfried Sassoon. BrPo; CMoP; MMA; NIP; NoAM; PoE
Reprieve. Barbara Villy Cormack. CaP
Reprisals. W. B. Yeats. OBWP
Reproach to Dead Poets. Archibald MacLeish. NAAL-2
Reproach to Julia. Robert Graves. FaBoEE
Reproachful eyes. Wrath to Sadness. Robert Grenier. UL
Reproduction of Life. Erasmus Darwin. *Fr.* The Temple of Nature; or, The Origin of Society, II. PBBP
Reproof, A. Bible, *O.T. See* Proverbs: Go to the Ant [Thou Sluggard].
Reptiles move like Navajo beadwork. Trench. Stephen Pett. GrPl
Reptilian green the wrinkled throat. Sir Gawaine and the Green Knight. Yvor Winters. MoP; NoAM; PoRA; QFR; VGW
Republic, The. Longfellow. *See* Thou, too, sail on, O Ship of State!
Republic of the West. On a Rhine Steamer. James Kenneth Stephen. *Fr.* England and America. NOBL; NOBVV; OBTV; TW
Republic to Republic. Witter Bynner. PAH
Repulse, The. Thomas Stanley. MeLP; MePo; OBS

Reputedly last of his kind. The Last Moriori. Kendrick Smithyman. ATNZ
Request for Meat and Drink. Sedulius Scottus, *tr. fr. Latin.* NOIV
Request Number. G. N. Sprod. FiBHP
Request of a Dying Child. Lydia Huntley Sigourney. OBCA
Request to a Year. Judith Wright. CBAP; FaBoWP; NoAM
Requests. Digby Mackworth Dolben. TrPWD
Requiem. Kenneth Fearing. CMoP
Requiem, A. Mary Weston Fordham. CBWP-2
Requiem. Sam Hunt. PeNZ
Requiem. Joseph Lee. OHIP
Requiem after Seventeen Years. Dahlia Ravikovich, *tr. fr. Hebrew.* IP, *tr. by* Warren Bargad *and* Stanley F. Chyet; VWA, *tr. by* Chana Bloch
Requiem: "Breathe, trumpets, breathe." George Lunt. AA
Requiem for a River. Kim Williams. RFM
Requiem for a Young Soldier. Florence Earle Coates. OHIP
Requiem for "Bird" Parker. Gregory Corso. PoNe
Requiem for My Mother. Keorapetse Kgositsile. WMBCH
Requiem for Soldiers Lost in Ocean Transports, A. Herman Melville. PoEL-5
Requiem for Sonora. Richard Shelton. Psk
Requiem for Sylvia Plath. Luciana Frezza, *tr. fr. Italian by* Muriel Kittel. DMI
Requiem for the Croppies. Seamus Heaney. BIrV; CIP; FaBCIP; FaBoMo; OBWP
Requiem for the Living, *sel.* C. Day Lewis. Offertorium. TIRV
Requiem for the Plantagenet Kings. Geoffrey Hill. NAEL-2; NoAM
Requiem For The Sumpul. Mercedes Durand, *tr. fr. Spanish by* Tina Alvarez Robles. Vol
Requiem for you, A. Requiem for Sylvia Plath. Luciana Frezza, *tr. by* Muriel Kittel. DMI
Requiem: "He tossed a life preserver to the young castaway in '55." Otto Orban, *tr. by* Jascha Kessler. FOC
Requiem: "I watch the roses float." Stephen Vincent. NeAC
Requiem: "Let the mountains stand forth!" Hamilton Warren. GoYe
Requiem: "Mother is gone. Bird songs wouldn't let her breathe." William Stafford. NaP
Requiem, A: "My father listening to opera, that's me." David Ignatow. DiL
Requiem 1935-1940 ("No, not under the vault of another sky."), *sels.* "Anna Akhmatova," *tr. fr. Russian by* Richard McKane. BoWoP "There I learned how faces fall apart." *Tr. by* D. M. Thomas. AIW "No, not under an alien sky." *Tr. by* Doris Earnshaw. OV
Requiem: "Pour out your light, O stars." Ivor Gurney. FaBoEE; FaBoTw
Requiem: "She wears, my beloved, a rose upon her head." John Frederick Matheus. CDC
Requiem: "There was a young belle of old Natchez." Ogden Nash. NoP
Requiem: "Under the wide and starry sky." Robert Louis Stevenson. BrPo; DL; EBVV; FaBV; FaPoR; FPL; GoTS; MoBrPo; NBLV; NOBE; NOBVV; OBD; OBEV; OBNC; OHFP; PoLF; PoRA; TrGrPo; WGRP
Requiem: "When the last voyage is ended." Joseph Lee. OHIP
Requiescant. Frederick George Scott. OHIP
Requiescat. Matthew Arnold. AWP; ELP; FiP; HeIP; InvP; LiTB; NOBE; OBD; OBEV; PoRA; TrGrPo
Requiescat. Oscar Wilde. BrPo; EBVV; FL; InvP; MoBrPo; OBNC; TrGrPo
Required Course. Frances Stoakley Lankford. GoYe
Required of You This Night. Peter Redgrove. PoE
Requirements. Niarchus, *tr. fr. Greek by* Wallace Rice. ErPo
Requirements ("Not too chary, not too fast."). Rufinus Domesticus, *tr. by* Wallace Rice. ErPo
Requirements ("Not too lean, and not too fat"). Rufinus Domesticus, *tr. by* Wallace Rice. ErPo
Requirements ("Not too old, and not too young"). Honestus, *tr. by* Wallace Rice. ErPo
Requirements ("Not too pallid, as if bleacht"). Xenos Palaestes, *tr. by* Wallace Rice. ErPo
Requiring something lovely on his arm. Labor Day. Louise Glück. NoAM
Rereading Old Writing. David Ferry. DiPo; PPR
Rescue, The. Robert Creeley. CAPP; CRP
Rescue. Olive Tilford Dargan. GoYe
Rescue, The. John Logan. CoAP; NYBP
Rescue. Dabney Stuart. NYBP
Rescue. Ellen Bryant Voigt. NoP

Rescue the Dead. David Ignatow. CAPP; PrIm; VGW
Rescued Year, The. William Stafford. LCAP
Rescuing gate is wide, The. Like a Mourningless Child. Kenneth Patchen. MoAmPo
Researchers will come to, The. Listening to the Music of Arsenio Rodríguez Is Moving Closer to Knowledge. Victor Hernandez Cruz. UL
Resemblance. *Unknown, tr. fr. Hawaiian by* N. B. Emerson. WTO
Resembles life what once was deem'd of light. What Is Life? Samuel Taylor Coleridge. FiP
Resenting all. No Regret. Rochelle Kraut. UL
Resentments Composed because of the Clamor of Town Topers Outside My Apartment. Sarah Kemble Knight. AiP; SCAP
Reservation Girls. Nila NorthSun. GOS
Reservation school is brown and bleak, The. Red Anger. R. T. Smith. STE
Reservation Special. Lew Blockcolski. VoR
Reserve. Richard Aldington. BrPo
Reserve. Lizette Woodworth Reese. AA
Reserve. Mary Ashley Townsend. AA
Reserved. Walter de la Mare. GTBS-P
Reserved beauty, restrained smile. The Taoist Nun. Wen T'ing-yün, *tr. by* Lois Fusek. ATF
Residence at Cambridge. Wordsworth. *Fr.* The Prelude [or, Growth of a Poet's Mind], III. FaBoPP; HAP; ImOP
   "Evangelist St. John my patron was, The." HAP
   (Newton's Statue.) FaBoRV
   "Caverns there were within my mind, which sun." FaBoPP
   Newton. ImOP
Residence in France. Wordsworth. *Fr.* The Prelude [or, Growth of a Poet's Mind], IX. EnRP; OAEL-2
   "Among the band of Officers was one," *Oxford ed., incl.* Vaudracour and Julia ChER
   "It was a beautiful and silent day." OBTV
   Noble, The, 3 *ll.* ChTr
Residence in France. Wordsworth. *Fr.* The Prelude [or, Growth of a Poet's Mind], X. EnRP; OAEL-2
   "Cheered with this hope, to Paris I returned." PoEL-4
   "State, as if to stamp the final seal." FaBoPV
   "When the proud fleet that bears the red-cross flag." FaBoPV
Residence in France [Continued]. Wordsworth. *See* Prelude [or, Growth of a Poet's Mind]; The: France.
Residence in London. Wordsworth. *Fr.* The Prelude [or, Growth of a Poet's Mind], VII. HAP, *short sel.*; PoEL-4
   Fair below Helvellyn, The. FaBoPP
   "From these sights/ Take one,—that ancient festival, the Fair." HAP
   "Genius of Burke! forgive the pen seduced." FaBoPV
   "Rise up, thou monstrous ant-hill on the plain." HAP
   Young Wordsworth's London, The. FaBoPP
Residence of the Emperors of Ch'en, The. Yang Wei-chen, *tr. fr. Chinese by* Jonathan Chaves. CoBLCP
Resident doctor said, The. Notice. Robert Lowell. NoAM
Residential Rhymes, *sels.* Osman Edwards. OBTV
   Merchant at Yokohama, The. *Fr.* I.
   Minister at Chiuzenji, The. *Fr.* III.
   Missionary at Karnizawa, The. *Fr.* II.
   Professor in Nirvana, The. *Fr.* IV.
Residue. Anthony McNeill. PBCV
Residue of Song. Marvin Bell. AmPA
Resign the rhapsody, the dream. To the Muse. Robert Louis Stevenson. EBEV
Resignation, *sel.* Matthew Arnold.
   If Birth Persists. FaBoRV
Resignation. Bliss Carman. AnAmPo
Resignation. Thomas Chatterton. TrCP
Resignation. Santob de Carrion, *tr. fr. Spanish by* George Ticknor. TrJP
Resignation. Wilhelm Szabo, *tr. fr. German by* Beth Bjorklund. CoAuP
Resignation. *Unknown.* OBSC
Resignation. Sir Thomas Wyatt. OBSC
Resignation; an Ode to the Journeyman Shoemakers, *sel.* "Peter Pindar."
   "Sons of Saint Crispin, 'tis in vain!" NOEC
Resign'd to live, prepar'd to die. Tom Southerne's Birth-Day Dinner at LD. Orrery's. Pope. NAs
Resigning from a Job in a Defense Industry. Sandra McPherson. LCAP
Resistance in the Ghetto. Jacob Glatstein, *tr. fr. Yiddish by* Benjamin *and* Barbara Harshav. AYP
Resistance marries faith, not faith. The Voyage of Life. Charles Bernstein. UL
Resisting poetry I am becoming a poem. Moon. Derek Walcott. MoP
Resolute Courtier, The. Thomas Shipman. ErPo; GBL

Resolution. Ted Berrigan. OFD
Resolution. Audrey Longbottom. UAS
Resolution, *sel.* Josefa Masanés, *tr. fr. Spanish by* Robert L. Smith *and* Judith Candullo.
   "That I be a writer? Absolutely not!" DMH
Resolution. W. S. Merwin. NYBP
Resolution. Charles L. O'Donnell. TrPWD
Resolution and Independence ("There was a roaring in the wind all night."), *sels.* Wordsworth. BoNaP; ChER; EBEV; EnRP; HAP; InPS; LiTB; MAT; NOBE; NOCV; NoP; OAEL-2; OBNC; PoEL-4; PPP; TEP
   "Now, whether it were by peculiar grace." Par
   We Poets in Our Youth. FaBoRV
Resolution in Four Sonnets, of a Poetical Question Put to Me by a Friend, Concerning Four Rural Sisters, *sels.* Charles Cotton. PoEL-3; Prf; Son
   Alice Is Tall and Upright as a Pine. *Fr.* I.
   (Alice.) TrGrPo
   (Two Rural Sisters.) BoLoP; EnLoPo
   Marg'ret of Humbler Stature by the Head. *Fr.* II.
   (Margaret.) TrGrPo
   (Two Rural Sisters.) BoLoP; EnLoPo
   Martha Is Not So Tall. *Fr.* IV.
   Mary Is Black. *Fr.* III.
Resolution of Dependence. George Barker. FaBoTw; LiTB; LiTM
Resolve, The. Alexander Brome. OBEV
Resolve, The. Mary Lee, Lady Chudleigh. WPE
Resolve. Charlotte Perkins Gilman. WGRP
Resolve, The. Denise Levertov. RFM
Resolve to make the best of life. Beyond the Beaten Way. George Sands Johnson. PWR
Resolved to dust, intombed here lieth Love. Here Lieth Love. Thomas Watson. *Fr.* Hecatompathia; or, Passionate Century of Love. ElL
   (Love's Grave.) OBSC
Resolved to Love. Henry Constable. *Fr.* Diana. Son
Resolving Doubts. William Dickey. ErPo
Resonances. Cecilia Bustamante, *tr. fr. Spanish by* David Tipton. Per
Resort, *sel.* Patricia Hampl.
   "August's dense astronomy fits itself, all stars." *Fr.* VII. NAmP
Resound my voyse [*or* voice], ye wodes [*or* woods] that here [*or* hear] me plain. Sir Thomas Wyatt. AAS; SiPS
Resounding Wall, The. Yip Wai-lim, *tr. fr. Chinese by* Dominic Cheung. IFON
Respect all surfaces. The skater is. In Defense of Superficiality. Elder Olson. NYBP
Respect for the Dead. Laura Riding. LiTA
Respect the dreams of old men, said the cricket. Song for September. Robert Fitzgerald. VGW
Respectabilities. Jon Silkin. NePoEA-2
Respectability. Robert Browning. EnLoPo
Respectable Burgher, The. Thomas Hardy. CMoP; NoAM
Respectable People. Austin Clarke. CMoP
Respected, Feared, and Somehow Loved. Marjorie Welish. BAP
Respice Finem. Edna Dean Proctor. OBSC
Respice Finem. Francis Quarles. *See* Epigram: "My soul, sit thou a patient looker-on."
Respite, The. Ingeborg Bachmann, *tr. fr. German by* Michael Hamburger. WPOW
Respite, The. Maria Gowen Brooks. *Fr.* Zophiël. AA
Resplendent studs of heaven's frame. *Unknown.* SCAP
Respondez! Walt Whitman. NoAM; PoEL-5
Responding to a Poem on T'ai-po Pavilion at Colored Stone. Chao Yi, *tr. fr. Chinese by* Irving Lo. WFTU
Responding to Yüan-ming's "Drinking Wine" Poems, *sels.* Cheng Chen, *tr. fr. Chinese by* Irving Lo. WFTU
   "Born to cling to this human road." *Fr.* XI.
   "Sad, sad is the bird in a cage." *Fr.* X.
Responding Voice. Francisco A. de Icaza, *tr. fr. Spanish by* Samuel Beckett. MexPo
Response. Mary Ursula Bethell. ATNZ; FaBoWP; PeNZ
Response of Telemachus, The. Sanford Pinsker. SoTCo
Response to Rimbaud's Later Manner. T. Sturge Moore. OBMV
Responses to Montale. Brian Turner. PeNZ
Responsibilities, *sel.* W. B. Yeats.
   "Pardon, old fathers, if you still remain." PoEL-5
Responsibility. *Unknown.* FaBoUs
Responsive to the tune of lawns and trees. Dogs in the Morning Light. Bruce Dawe. NoAM
Responsory, 1948, A. Thomas Merton. VGW
Ressaif My Saul. R. Crombie Saunders. OxBS
Rest. Miyazawa Kenji, *tr. fr. Japanese by* Sato. FCEI

Rest, The. Ezra Pound. *See* Lustra:
O helpless few in my country.
Rest. Christina Rossetti. NOBE; OAEL-2; OBEV; OBNC; TrGrPo
Rest. Jacob Isaac Segal, *tr. fr. Yiddish by* Seymour Mayne. VWA
Rest, and be thankful! On the verge. Adam Lindsay Gordon. *Fr.* Hippodromania; or, Whiffs from the Pipe. CBAP
Rest, Christ! from tireless war. See, it's midsummer. Derek Walcott. *Fr.* Midsummer. TOF
Rest from Loving and Be Living. C. Day Lewis. MoBrPo; OBMV
Rest in Peace. Wilfred J. Funk. PoLF
Rest Is Grace, The. János Pilinszky, *tr. fr. Hungarian by* William Jay Smith. MHuP
Rest is not quitting. True Rest. Goethe, *tr. by* John S. Dwight. WBLP
Rest lightly O Earth upon this wretched Nearchos. Epitaph of Nearchos. Ammianus, *tr. by* Dudley Fitts. WeW
Rest, little guest. After Annunciation. Anna Wickham. MoBrPo
Rest O Sun I Cannot. Joseph Tusiani. GoYe
Rest Only in the Grave. James Clarence Mangan. BIrV
Rest thee aged pilgrim, now thy toils are o'er. Death of a Grandparent. Mrs. Jennette Bonneau. Mary Weston Fordham. CBWP-2
Rest! This little Fountain runs. For a Fountain. "Barry Cornwall." OBEV
Rest ye in peace, ye Flanders dead. America's Answer. R. W. Lilliard. BLPA; OPP
Restaurant is empty, The. On Stopping Late in the Afternoon for Steamed Dumplings. Toi Derricotte. InPS
Restful place, reviver of my smart, The. Sir Thomas Wyatt. SiPS
Resting. Josephine D. Henderson Heard. CBWP-4
Resting my eyes on the bay of Miho. Masuhito. *Fr.* Manyo Shu. Ma
Resting Place. Jon Silkin. VWA
Restles mind, all night, A. Kaiseki, *tr. by* Lucien Stryk *and* Takashi Ikemoto. ZPCJ
Restless as a Wolf. Moyshe-Leyb Halpern, *tr. fr. Yiddish by* Jacob Sloan. TrJP
Restless he rolls about from whore to whore. John Wilmot, 2nd Earl of Rochester. *Fr.* A Satire on Charles II. OBSV
Restless Heart, The. Earl of Surrey. SiPS
Restless Heart, The. *Unknown, tr. fr. Marathi.* WGRP
Restless Night. Tu Fu, *tr. fr. Chinese by* Burton Watson. CoBCP
Restless she stirs as she reclines. The Sun and the Woman. Salah Abd al-Sabur, *tr. by* Lena Jayyusi *and* John Heath-Stubbs. MAP
Restless State of a Lover, The. Henry Howard, Earl of Surrey. AAS; SiPS
Restless, to-night, and ill at ease. In the Dark. Frances Louisa Bushnell. AA
Restoration. Woodridge Spears. GoYe
Restoration of Enheduanna to Her Former Station, The. Enheduanna, *tr. fr. Sumerian, ad. by* Aliki *and* Willis Barnstone. BoWoP
Restoration of slighted, by forecast thundering, The. Part Quake. Charles Bernstein. IAT
Restorative broth of trouts learne to make. Methods of Cooking Trout. Thomas Barker. *Fr.* The Art of Angling. FaBoUs
Restoring the Ancestral House. Katerina Te Hei Koko Mataira, *tr. fr. Maori by* Katerina Te Hei Koko Mataira. PeNZ
Restricted. Eve Merriam. TrJP
Restricted. Miriam Waddington. CaP
Results of Stealing a Pin, The. *Unknown.* FaBoUs
Résumé. Dorothy Parker. *Fr.* Some Beautiful Letters. AnAmPo; DL; HeIP; InPk; NAAL-2; NBLV; NoP; OBAL; TrJP
Resurgam. W. Nelson Bitton. BLRP
Resurgam. Emily Dickinson. WGRP
Resurgam. Marjorie Pickthall. OBCV; TrCP
Resurgam. Adah Isaacs Menken. CBWP-1
Resurgam. *Unknown.* WGRP
Resurge San Francisco. Joaquin Miller. PAH
Resurrection. R. P. Blackmur. PoA
Resurrection, The. Jonathan Henderson Brooks. AmNP; CDC; PoNe
Resurrection. John Donne. *Fr.* La Corona. OBS; Son
Resurrection. Margiad Evans. OBWVE
Resurrection. Kenneth Fearing. CMoP; PoE
Resurrection. Joy Harjo. ER; HATNAP
Resurrection. Frank Horne. OFD; PoBA
Resurrection. Marie Luise Kaschnitz, *tr. fr. German by* Michael Hamburger. WPOW
Resurrection. Sidney Lanier. PoEL-5
Resurrection. Robert Pack. NePoEA-2
Resurrection, The, *sels.* W. B. Yeats.
Two Songs from a Play. *Fr.* I. CMoP; FaBoTw; HAP; LiTB; NOBE; NoP; OAEL-2; PoE; PPP; PrIm
Two Songs from a Play. *Fr.* II. CMoP; FaBoTw; HAP; LiTB; NOBE; NoP; OAEL-2; PPP; PrIm

Resurrection. Sa'di Yusuf, *tr. fr. Arabic by* Abdullah al-Udhari. MPAW
Resurrection after the Rain. Alfredo Giuliani, *tr. fr. Italian by* Lawrence R. Smith. NItP
Resurrection: Fragments. Felix Mnthali. WMBCH
Resurrection of Arp. A. J. M. Smith. MoCV; NOBC
Resurrection of Chirst, The. William Dunbar. *See* Done Is a Battle.
Resurrection of the Dead. Aliza Shenhar, *tr. fr. Hebrew by* Linda Zisquit. VWA
Resurrection of the Right Side. Muriel Rukeyser. LCAP
Resurrection Song. Thomas Lovell Beddoes. FaBoEE
Resuscitation Team. U. A. Fanthorpe. FaBoWP
Retaining the colors of snow and moon. Teika, *tr. fr. Japanese by* Hiroaki Sato. *Fr.* Eighty-four Tanka. FCEI
Retaliation, *sels.* Goldsmith. LaA; OxBoLi
David Garrick. NOEC
"Here lies our good Edmund, whose genius was such." FaBoEE; FaBoPV
(Edmund Burke.) InVP; NOEC
Sir Joshua Reynolds. FaBoEE; NOEC; OBD; SeCePo
Retarded Children Find a World Built Just for Them, The. Diana O Hehir. NPGG
Retarded Class at F. A. O. Schwarz's Celebrates Christmas, The. David Fisher. NPGG
Reticent as the mouths of shells. The Sleeping Gods. Cees Nooteboom, *tr. by* Peter Nijmeijer. DuIn
Reticulations creep upon the slack stream's face. On Sturminster Foot-Bridge. Thomas Hardy. FaBoPP; OxBSP
Retinue. Paul Verlaine, *tr. fr. French by* C. F. MacIntyre. ErPo
Retired Ballerinas, Central Park West. Lawrence Ferlinghetti. NoAM
Retired Cat, The. William Cowper. FM
Retired Colonel, The. Ted Hughes. NePoEA-2
Retired Farmer. David Allan Evans. Psk
Retired gardener of solitudes. N.Y. to L.A. by Jet Plane. Sonya Dorman. GOA
Retired Lion by the Clothesline in the Cold Attic. Laura Jensen. AnAn
Retired this hour from wondering crowds. Walter Savage Landor. GBL
Retired thoughts enjoy their own delights. Look Home. Robert Southwell. NOCV
Retirement, The. Charles Cotton. *Fr.* To Mr. Izaak Walton. FaBoPP; OBS
Retirement, *sels.* William Cowper.
"I praise the Frenchman, his remark was shrewd." BLPA
London Suburbs. FaBoPP
Retirement, The. John Norris. OBS
Retirement. *Unknown, tr. fr. Irish by* Frank O'Connor. ErPo
Retirement of the Elephant, The. Russell Edson. AmPA
Retort, The. George Pope Morris. AnAmPo
Retreat, The. Sir Herbert Read. BrPo
Retreat from Paradise, The. Milton. *See* Paradise Lost: He ended; and thus Adam last replied.
Retreat of Ita Cagney, The. Michael Hartnett. CIP
Retreat of Liu Kuo-pao, The. Chang Yü, *tr. fr. Chinese by* Jonathan Chaves. CoBLCP
Retreat of Sun Ching-hsiang, The. Chang Yü, *tr. fr. Chinese by* Jonathan Chaves. CoBLCP
Retreat[e], The. Henry Vaughan. AWP; BLPL; FF; GTBS; GTBS-P; HAP; HeIP; InPK; InPS; InVP; JCP; LiTB; MeLP; MePo; NAEL-1; NIP; NOBE; NOCV; NoP; OAEL-1; OBEV; OBS; OBWVE; PoE; PoEL-2; PoRA; PPP; SeCePo; SeCP; SeCV-1; TOF; TrGrPo
Retribution. Friedrich von Logau, *tr. fr. German by* Longfellow. BLPA
Retribution. Lizelia Augusta Jenkins Moorer. CBWP-3
Retrieval System, The. Maxine W. Kumin. FaBoWP; WeW
Retrieval System. Peter Porter. AnAn
Retrievers run through the meadow. Exercise in a Meadow. Jean Elliot. GoYe
Retrospect. Josephine D. Henderson Heard. CBWP-4
Retrospect. Chidiock Tichborne. *See* My prime of youth is but a frost of cares.
Retrospect—Love of Nature Leading to Love of Mankind. Wordsworth. *Fr.* The Prelude [or, Growth of a Poet's Mind], VIII. EnRP; OAEL-2
Shepherd, The. OBNC
Retrospection. Sir Arthur Quiller-Couch. CenHV
Retrospection. Henrietta Cordelia Ray. CBWP-3
Return, The. John Peale Bishop. LiTA; OxBA; WaP
Return. Arna Bontemps. CDC; PoBA; PoNe
Return. Sterling A. Brown. CDC
Return, The. Alistair Campbell. ATNZ; PeNZ
Return. Constantine P. Cavafy, *tr. fr. Modern Greek by* John Mavrogordato. ErPo
Return, The. Eleanor Rogers Cox. PAH

Return. Seamus Deane. BIrV
Return, The. Emily Dickinson. MoAmPo
Return. Mary Dorcey. AIW
Return, The. Annie Fields. AA
Return. Michael Guttenbrunner, *tr. fr. German by* Beth Bjorklund. CoAuP
Return. Robinson Jeffers. GoYe
Return, The. Jessie Fauset. CDC
Return, The. Kipling. MoBrPo
Return. Johari M. Kunjufu. BlSi
Return. John Robert Lee. PBCV
Return, The. George MacBeth. NYBP
Return, The. Pittendrigh Macgillivray. GoTS; OxBS
Return, The, *sel. Margaret L. Woods.*
  "Father of Life, with songs of wonder." TrPWD
Return, The. Edna St. Vincent Millay. LiTA; MoAB; MoAmPo; MoP; NoAM; OxBA
Return. John Montague. FaBCIP
Return, The. Shmuel Moreh, *tr. fr. Arabic.* VWA, *tr. by* Yoffee Berkovitz
Return, The. Martha Ostenso. CaP
Return, The. Ezra Pound. AmPP; CMoP; HAP; MoAB; MoAmPo; MoP; NoAM; NoAM; NOBA; OxBA; PoE; RB; VGW; WeW
Return. Earl of Rochester. *See* Absent from thee, I languish still.
Return, The. Theodore Roethke. *Fr.* The Lost Son. NAAL-2; PoA
Return, The. Dennis Saleh. NeAC
Return, The. Jon Silkin. NePoEA-2
Return. Theodore Spencer. PoA
Return, The. Arthur Symons. *Fr.* Amor Triumphans. BrPo
Return. Richard Tillinghast. MAYP
Return. Mark Vinz. GOYP
Return. Wordsworth. *Fr.* The River Duddon. HAP
Return from Luluabourg. Michael Jackson. ATNZ; PeNZ; UAS
Return: Intensive Care, The. Sydney Lea. NAmP
Return Journey. Paul Henderson. ATNZ
Return, light of wing. The Cage. Avner Treinin, *tr. by* A. C. Jacobs. VWA
Return, my heart from wandering afar. Repose. Una Marson. PBCV
Return of a Popular Statesman. Vincent Buckley. CBAP
Return of a Reaper. Alan Creighton. CaP
Return of Astraea, The. Ben Jonson. NOBE
Return of Napoleon from St. Helena, The. Lydia Huntley Sigourney. AA
Return of Robinson Jeffers, The. Robert Hass. AmPA; AnAn
Return of the Children, The. Kipling. OBD
Return of the Dead, The, *sel.* Samar Attar.
  "And you came back." PBWP
Return of the Goddess Artemis. Graves. PoA
Return of the Greeks, The. Edwin Muir. *See* The veteran Greeks came home.
Return of the Native. Amiri Baraka. BPo
Return of the Native, The. Harley Matthews. PoAu-2
Return of the Proconsul, The. Zbigniew Herbert, *tr. fr. Polish by* Czeslaw Milosz. FaBoPV; PwPP
Return of the Prodigal Son, *sel.* Léopold Sédar Senghor, *tr. fr. French by* Ellen Conroy Kennedy.
  "Elephant of Moissel, hear my pious prayer." GrPl
Return of the Veil, The. Salah Niyazi, *tr. fr. Arabic by* Abdullah al-Udhari. MPAW
Return of the Wolves. Anita Endrezze-Danielson. HATNAP
Return often and take me. Return. C. P. Cavafy, *tr. by* John Mavrogordato. ErPo
Return, Return, O Shulammite. Bible, *O.T. Fr.* The Song of Solomon, VII: 1-10. TrJP
Return, Starting Out. Daniel Halpern. MAYP
Return, The ("The doors flapped open in Ulysses' house"). Edwin Muir. CMoP
Return, The ("The veteran Greeks came home.") Edwin Muir. CMoP
Return to a Place Lit by a Glass of Milk. Charles Simic. GeTw
Return to an Evil Domain. René Daumal, *tr. fr. French by* Michael Benedikt. POS
Return to Ararat. Martyn Halsall. TrCP
Return to Frankfurt, *sel.* Marie Luise Kaschnitz, *tr. fr. German by* Beatrice Cameron.
  "Girl thinks if I can only manage, The." OV
Return to Hinton. Charles Tomlinson. CMoP
Return to La Plata, Missouri. Jim Barnes. HATNAP
Return to Life. Abbie Huston Evans. NePoAm
Return to My Native Land, *sel.* Aimé Césaire, *tr. fr. French by* Emile Snyders.
  "I shall not regard my swelled head as a sign of real glory." TTY

Return to Solitude. Ad Zuiderent, *tr. fr. Dutch by* James S. Holmes. DuIn
Return to Spring. Florence Ripley Mastin. GoYe
Return to the most human, nothing less. Santos: New Mexico. May Sarton. EaLo
Return to the Tree of Time, A. Vesna Parun, *tr. fr. Croatian by* Vasa D. Mihailovich *and* Ronald Morgan. WPOW
Return to Work, The. William Carlos Williams. NYBP
Return we to the dangers of the night. Juvenal, *tr. fr. Latin by* Dryden. *Fr.* Satires, III. OAEL-1
Return'd from the opera, as lately I sat. A Bon Mot. *Unknown.* ErPo
Returned, a wraith from her defrauded tomb. Transformation Scene. Constance Carrier. FYAP; GoYe
Returned from California. Simon J. Ortiz. HATNAP
Returned from college R——gets a wife. The Discontented Student. St. George Tucker. OBAL
Returned from Mehiko he'll grab. A Hex on the Mexican X. David McCord. FiBHP
Returned to Say. William Stafford. NaP
Returned to the coastline of the continent. The Withinner. Ursula K. Le Guin. BWV
Returning, *sel.* Peter Porter.
  "It is time to recompose the face." PoPo
Returning. Kate Shanley. GOS
Returning/ to all the unsaid. The Charge. Denise Levertov. NePoEA-2
Returning after dark, I thought. Traditional Red. Robert Huff. HoPM; NePoEA-2
Returning at Night. Jim Harrison. VGW
Returning each morning from a timeless world. Autumn 1940. W. H. Auden. LiTA
Returning from Harvest. Vernon Watkins. NYBP
Returning from its daily quest, my Spirit. To Dante [*or* Sonnet: Guido Cavalcanti to Dante]. Guido Cavalcanti, *tr. by* Shelley. AWP; OBVE
Returning from the Seventy-Two Mountains. Hsü Wei, *tr. fr. Chinese by* Jonathan Chaves. CoBLCP
Returning Home. Rai San'yo, *tr. fr. Chinese by* Burton Watson. JLIC-2
Returning Home. Yüan Mei, *tr. fr. Chinese by* Jonathan Chaves. CoBLCP
Returning, I find her just the same. Passing Visit to Helen. D. H. Lawrence. CMoP
Returning Sails at a Distant Shore. Ma Chih-yüan, *tr. fr. Chinese by* Jonathan Chaves. *Fr.* Three Poems to the tune "Lo-mei Feng", 1. CoBLCP
Returning to Earth, *sel.* Jim Harrison.
  "She/ pulls the sheet of this dance." PPR
Returning to earth after his life. Home. John Witte. NIP
Returning to Goleufryn. Vernon Watkins. OBWVE
Returning to Granny. Shauqi Abi Shaqra, *tr. fr. Arabic by* Abdullah al-Udhari. MPAW
Returning to Lotus Village. Kao Ch'i, *tr. fr. Chinese by* Jonathan Chaves. CoBLCP
Returning to My Distant Home. Wei Chuang, *tr. fr. Chinese by* Lois Fusek. ATF
Returning to my Distant Home. Wen T'ing-yün, *tr. fr. Chinese by* Lois Fusek. ATF
Returning to my grandfather's house, after this exile. Returning to Goleufryn. Vernon Watkins. OBWVE
Returning to My Home in the Country ("I planted beans at the foot of the southern mountain"). T'ao Ch'ien, *tr. fr. Chinese by* Burton Watson. CoBCP
Returning to My Home in the Country ("In youth I couldn't sing to the common tune"). T'ao Ch'ien, *tr. fr. Chinese by* Burton Watson. CoBCP
Returning to My Home in the Country ("Out here in the fields, few social affairs"). T'ao Ch'ien, *tr. fr. Chinese by* Burton Watson. CoBCP
Returning to My Home in the Country ("So long since I've enjoyed the hills and ponds"). T'ao Ch'ien, *tr. fr. Chinese by* Burton Watson. CoBCP
Returning to Nanking. Cheng Hsiao-hsü, *tr. fr. Chinese by* Irving Lo. WFTU
Returning to Roots of First Feeling. Robert Duncan. PoA
Returning to Store Bay. Barbara Howes. Psk
Returning to that house. Birthplace; New Rochelle. George Oppen. DiL
Returning to the Alluvial Fields, *sel.* Wu Chia-chi, *tr. fr. Chinese by* Jonathan Chaves.
  "In the morning they build embankments against floods." CoBLCP
Returning to the room. Margaret Atwood. *Fr.* The Circle Game. MoCV

Returning to the Town Where We Used to Live. Susan Musgrave. NOBC
Returning to the World. Laura Chester. NPGG
Returning to Yin-ch'eng Early in the Year *Ting-ch'ou*. Tai Piao-yüan, *tr. fr. Chinese by* Jonathan Chaves. CoBLCP
Returning, We Hear the Larks. Isaac Rosenberg. BrPo; FaBoMo; MMA; NAEL-2; NoAM; OAEL-2; OBWP; VWA; WaaP
Returnings of Love in Vivid Landscapes. Rafael Alberti, *tr. fr. Spanish by* Perry Higman. LPSS
Reuben Bright. E. A. Robinson. AnAmPo; MoAB; MoAmPo; NOBA; NoP; Son; TAP; TrGrPo
Reuben James. James Jeffrey Roche. PAH
Reuben Ranzo. *Unknown*. AmFP
Reuben, Reuben. Michael S. Harper. GeTw; PoE
Reunion. Carolyn Forché. MAYP; NoAM
Reunion. Judith Herzberg, *tr. fr. Dutch by* Shirley Kaufman. BoWoP
Reunion. E. A. Robinson. NOBA
Reunion. Cyril Tawney. OBET
Reunion. Charles Wright. CAPP
Reunion: Swimming, The. William Meissner. TSL
Reunited. Sir Gilbert Parker. OBEV
Reunited. Henrietta Cordelia Ray. CBWP-3
Rev. Andrew Brown, over the Hill to Rest. Josephine D. Henderson Heard. CBWP-4
Rev. Homer Wilbur's "Festina Lente." James Russell Lowell. *Fr.* The Biglow Papers: 2d Series, No. IV. OBAL
Rev. Nicholas Noyes to the Rev. Cotton Mather, The. Nicholas Noyes. SCAP
Rev Owl. A. M. Klein. TrJP
Rev. Samuel Weston. Mary Weston Fordham. CBWP-2
Reveal Thy Presence now, O Lord. A Grace. Thomas Tiplady. TrPWD
Revealed. Harry Lyman Koopman. AA
Reveille, The. Bret Harte. GN; OHIP; PAH
Reveillé. Audrey Alexandra Brown. CaP
Reveille. John Godfrey. UL
Reveille. A. E. Housman. *Fr.* A Shropshire Lad, IV. CMoP; FaFP; FPL; LiTB; LiTM; MoAB; MoBrPo; NoP; PoLF; SoSe
Reveille. Ted Hughes. PPP
Reveille. Michael O'Connor. AA
Réveille. Lola Ridge. WPE
Revel, The. Bartholomew Dowling. BLPA
Revel, A. Donagh MacDonagh. NeIP
Revel pauses and the room is still, The. Pannyra of the Golden Heel. Albert Samain, *tr. by* James Elroy Flecker. AWP
Revelation. Verne Bright. BLRP; WBLP
Revelation. Alice Brown. *Fr.* The Road to Castaly. WGRP
Revelation. Warren F. Cook. BLRP
Revelation. Blanche Taylor Dickinson. CDC
Revelation. Sir Edmund William Gosse. OBEV
Revelation. Carole C. Gregory. BlSi
Revelation. Zbigniew Herbert, *tr. fr. Polish by* Czeslaw Milosz. PwPP
Revelation. Nancy Keesing. PoAu-2
Revelation. Edwin Markham. WGRP
Revelation, The. Coventry Patmore. *Fr.* The Angel in the House, I, viii. OxBSP
  ("Idle poet, here and there, An.") EnLoPo; GBL; GTBS-P; HAP; OBNC
Revelation, *sels*. Bible, *N.T.* TrGrPo
  New Jerusalem, The. *Fr.* XXI: 1-6, 10-12, 21, 23-25.
  There Shall Be No Night. *Fr.* XXII: 1-5.
Revelation. Robert Penn Warren. LiTA; NoAM
Revelation, The. James Wright. DiL
Revelations. David Meltzer. NeAP
Revenant. Kathleen Resch. VVA
Revenant, The. Robert Siegel. GeTw
Revenant, The. Walter de la Mare. GBL
Revenge. N. M. Rashed, *tr. fr. Urdu by* Mahmood Jamal. PBMUP
Revenge, The. Pierre de Ronsard, *tr. fr. French by* Thomas Stanley. AWP
Revenge, The, *sel*. Tennyson. BeLS; EBVV; FaBoCh; FaPoR; OnMSP; PoRA
  "At Flores in the Azores Sir Richard Grenville lay." OBWP
Revenge. Mary E. Tucker. CBWP-1
Revenge, The, *sel*. Edward Young. OBD
  "Life is the desert, life the solitude." OBD
Revenge Fable. Ted Hughes. TW
Revenge of America, The. Joseph Warton. OBTV
Revenge of Hamish, The. Sidney Lanier. PoEL-5
Revenge of Rain-in-the-Face, The. Longfellow. PAH
Revenge of the Hunted. R. A. D. Ford. MoCV

Revenge to Come. Sextus Propertius, *tr. fr. Latin by* Kirby Flower Smith. *Fr.* Elegies, III, 25. AWP
Revenger's Tragedy, The, *sels*. Cyril Tourneur.
  "Madame, his grace will not be absent long." *Fr.* III, v. PoEL-2
  "Thou sallow picture of my poison'd love." OBD
Revenue. Erich Fried, *tr. fr. German by* Beth Bjorklund. CoAuP
Reverberation. Maurice Kenny. HATNAP
Reverdure, *sel*. Wendell Berry.
  "One thing work gives." SaC
Reverence, reverence! *Unknown*, *tr. by* Arthur Waley. BoS
Reverend Butler came by. Madam and the Minister. Langston Hughes. NOBA
Reverend Henry Ward Beecher, The. Limerick [*or* An Eggstravagance *or* Henry Ward Beecher]. *At. to* Oliver Wendell Holmes. CenHV; ChTr; FaBoNo
Reverend Mr, The. Higginson. Edward Johnson. SCAP
Reverend William Winterbourne, The. Bishop Winterbourne. Walter de la Mare. FaBoNo
Reverie, A. Mary Weston Fordham. CBWP-2
Reverie. Don Marquis. FPL; PoLF
Reverie, The. Egan O'Rahilly, *tr. fr. Modern Irish by* Frank O'Connor. AnIL
Reverie, The. Egan O'Rahilly. *See* One morning before Titan thought of stirring his feet.
Reverie. Henrietta Cordelia Ray. CBWP-3
Reverie at Dawn. Egan O'Rahilly. *See* One morning before Titan thought of stirring his feet.
Reverie of a Mum. Nancy Keesing. CBAP
Reverie of Poor Susan, The. Wordsworth. CH; EnRP; GTBS; GTBS-P; OxBoLi; WiR
Reverse the flight of Lucifer. The Task. Ruth Pitter. MoBrPo
Reversion. Barry O. Higgs. PeSA
Reversionary. Stevie Smith. FaBoEE
Review from Staten Island. Gloria C. Oden. PoBA; PPP
Reviewing me without undue elation. A Choice of Weapons. Stanley Kunitz. LiTM; VGW
Reviewing Past Lives while Leaf-Burning. Anita Endrezze-Danielson. HATNAP
Reviewing the Troops at Kuei-lin. Yang Chi, *tr. fr. Chinese by* Jonathan Chaves. CoBLCP
Reviews are gaudy shows—allowed. On the Frequent Review of the Troops. "M." NOEC
Revised Notes for a Sonnet. Edward Pygge. BXAP
Revisionist, The, *sel*. Douglas Crase.
  "If I could raise rivers, I'd raise them." NAAL-2
Revisit. John Engels. BLA
Revisiting your marble-paved sea-perfumed town. Hardy's Plymouth. Geoffrey Grigson. FaBoPP
Revival. Steve Crow. HATNAP
Revival. George Garrett. MT
Revival, The. Henry Vaughan. NOCV; OBS; PoEL-2; TrGrPo
  (Unfold, Unfold.) ELP
Revivalist in Boston, A. Adrienne Rich. EaLo
Revocation, A. Sir Thomas Wyatt. *See* What should [*or* shulde] I say[e].
Revolt. Rachel, *tr. fr. Hebrew by* Robert Friend. VWA
Revolt. Adine Brabart Riom, *tr. fr. French by* Beth Archer. DMF
Revolt in Verse, A. Bogdan Czaykowski, *tr. fr. Polish by* Czeslaw Milosz. PwPP
Revolt of Islam, The, *sels*. Shelley.
  Child of Twelve, A. *Fr.* II. GN
  Ever as We Sailed. *Fr.* XII. SeCePo
  "I could not choose but gaze; a fascination." *Fr.* I. ChER
  "Islands and the mountains in the day, The." *Fr.* III. ChER
  "Lifting the thunder of their acclamation." *Fr.* V. ChER
  "Over the utmost hill at length I sped." *Fr.* V. OBWP
Revolution, The. Jack Gilbert. NPGG
Revolution. Lesbia Harford. PoAu-1
Revolution/ Damn you. Letter to the Revolution. Susan Griffin. NPGG
Revolution. Musaemura Bonus Zimunya. WMBCH
Revolution in Summertime. René Daumal, *tr. fr. French by* Michael Benedikt. POS
Revolutionaries, The. R. P. Lister. NOBL
Revolutionaries, The. *Unknown*. NOBL
Revolutionary, The/ element remained. Mrs. Hamer. Jane Stembridge. NMM
Revolutionary Dreams. Nikki Giovanni. CNA
Revolutionary Letter #19. Diane DiPrima. IHMS
Revolutionary Petunias. Alice Walker. BlSi
Revolutionary Poets. Mutabaruka. PBCV

Revolutions. Shakespeare. *See* Sonnets: LX. "Like as the waves make towards the pebbled shore."
Revving Up la Rêve. Joel Dailey. UL
Reward of Innocent Love, The. William Habington. *Fr.* Castara. ACP
Reward of Service. Elizabeth Barrett Browning. BLPA; FaBoBe
Rewards and Fairies, *sel.* Kipling.
  Way through the Woods, The. NoAM
Rewrite. E. A. Markham. PBCV
Rex regum, for whom praise flows freely. Poem on His Death-Bed. Meilyr Brydydd, *tr.* by Joseph P. Clancy. OBWVE
Reynard the Fox, *sels.* John Masefield.
  "Fox knew well, that before they tore him, The." OBNV
  "Meet was at "The Cock and Pye," The." OxBTC
  "Ock Gurney and old Pete were there." CMoP
Rhaicos was born amid the hills wherefrom. The Hamadryad. Walter Savage Landor. *Fr.* The Hellenics. EnRP
Rhapsodies. Cyril Dabydeen. BrSi
Rhapsodist cannot believe that maidens can make verse!, The. Verification of the Poetic Talents of Young Maidens. Susanna Elisabeth Zeidler, *tr.* by Susan L. Cocalis *and* Gerlinde Geiger. DMG
Rhapsody. William Stanley Braithwaite. AmNP; BANP
Rhapsody. Frank O'Hara. NoAM
Rhapsody, A. Henry Vaughan. NAEL-1
Rhapsody of Old Men, A, *sel.* Dimitris Tsaloumas, *tr. fr. Greek by* Margaret Carroll.
  "They brought him one morning." CBAP
Rhapsody on a Windy Night. T. S. Eliot. CMoP; HeIP; InPS; PoE
Rhapsody on Time. István Simon, *tr. fr. Hungarian by* Edwin Morgan. MHuP
Rhapsody, Written at the Lakes in Westmorland, A. John Brown. NOEC
Rhenish Carol, A. Robert Finch. NAs, *ad.* by Bernard de la Mannoye
Rhetoric of Langston Hughes, The. Margaret Danner. BlSi; FB
Rhino is a homely beast, The. The Rhinoceros. Ogden Nash. CenHV; FiBHP; MoAmPo; OBAL; OnUR
Rhinoceros, The. Hilaire Belloc. ChTr; FaPON
Rhinoceros, The. Herman de Coninck, *tr. fr. Dutch by* Theo Hermans. DuIn
Rhinoceros, The. Ogden Nash. CenHV; FiBHP; MoAmPo; OBAL; OnUR
Rhinoceros, your hide looks all undone. The Rhinoceros. Hilaire Belloc. ChTr; FaPON
Rhinos Purple, Hippos Green. Michael Patrick Hearn. RHPC
Rhodanthe. Agathias, *tr. fr. Greek by* Andrew Lang. AWP
Rhode Island. William Meredith. NoP
"Rhodesia, sweaty." Black and White. Leonard Adame. SoSe
Rhodora [On Being Asked Whence Is the Flower], The. Emerson. AA; AmPP; AnAmPo; AWP; BoNaP; GN; HeIP; LiTA; NAAL-1; NOBA; NoP; OHFP; OxBA; PoE; PWR; TAP; TrGrPo
Rhœcus, *sel.* James Russell Lowell.
  "Hear now this fairy legend of old Greece." AA
Rhotus on Arcadia. John Chalkhill. *Fr.* Thealma and Clearchus. OBS
Rhydcymerau. David Gwenallt Jones, *tr. fr. Welsh by* Anthony Conran. OBWVE
Rhyme-Beginning Fragment, A. *Unknown.* AnIL
Rhyme for Remembering How Many Nights There Are in the Month. Justin Richardson. FaBoUs
Rhyme for Remembering the Date of Easter. Justin Richardson. FaBoUs
Rhyme for the Child as a Wet Dog. Judith Johnson Sherwin. TAP
Rhyme for Washing Hands, A. Rodney. BoTP
Rhyme: "I like to see a thunder storm." Elizabeth Jane Coatsworth. RHPC
Rhyme of Joyous Garde, The, *sel.* Adam Lindsay Gordon.
  "We were glad together in gladsome meads." PoAu-1
Rhyme of My Inheritance. Joan Larkin. GLP
Rhyme of Rain. John Holmes. GrPl
Rhyme of the Antique Forest. Henrietta Cordelia Ray. CBWP-3
Rhyme of the Dead Self. A. R. D. Fairburn. ATNZ
Rhyme of the Dream-Maker Man, A. William Allen White. PoLF
Rhyme of the Fishermen's Children. *Unknown.* GBP
Rhyme of the Kipperling, The. Sir Owen Seaman. CenHV
Rhyme of the poet, The. The Merlin ("Rhyme of the poet. Emerson. *Fr.* Merlin, II. PoEL-4
Rhyme of the poet, The. Merlin, II. Emerson. NOBA; PoEL-4
Rhyme of the Rail[s]. John Godfrey Saxe. AnAmPo; MoShBr; PoLF
Rhyme of the Rain Machine, The. F. W. Clarke. BoNaP
Rhyme of the Sun-Dial, A. William Bell Scott. NOBVV
Rhyme of the Three Captains, The. Kipling. BeLS
Rhyme-Prose on the Desolate City. Pao Chao, *tr. fr. Chinese by* Burton Watson. CoBCP

Rhyme-Prose on the Goddess of the Lo. Ts'ao Chih, *tr. fr. Chinese by* Burton Watson. CoBCP
Rhyme-Prose on the Idle Life. P'an Yüeh, *tr. fr. Chinese by* Burton Watson. CoBCP
Rhyme-Prose on the Marriage of Man and Woman. Asatsuna, *tr. fr. Chinese by* Burton Watson. JLIC-1
Rhyme-Prose on the Owl. Chia Yi, *tr. fr. Chinese by* Burton Watson. CoBCP
Rhyme-Prose on the Sea. Mu Hua, *tr. fr. Chinese by* Burton Watson. CoBCP
Rhyme-Prose on the Small Hills. Yakatsugu, *tr. fr. Chinese by* Burton Watson. JLIC-1
Rhyme-Prose on the Snow. Hsieh Hui-lien, *tr. fr. Chinese by* Burton Watson. CoBCP
Rhyme Sheet of Other Lands, A. Hugh Chesterman. BoTP
Rhyme, the rack of finest wits. Ben Jonson. *See* Fit of Rime against Rime, A.
Rhymed Mnemonic of the Forty Counties of England. Donald Monat. FaBoUs
Rhymed Words Sent to My Eldest Son, *sels.* Yang Shih-ch'i, *tr. fr. Chinese by* Jonathan Chaves. CoBLCP
  "False words of the Buddhists and Taoists, The."
  "Li Hsü of Ch'ien-chou is an old friend of mine."
Rhymes. Charles Tomlinson. DiPo
Rhymes (?). Henry S. Leigh. NOBL
Rhymes for a Modern Nursery, *sels.* Paul Dehn.
  "Hey diddle diddle/ The physicists fiddle." FiBHP
  "In a cavern, in a canyon." FiBHP
  "Jack and Jill went up the hill/ To fetch some heavy water." FiBHP
  "Little Miss Muffet/ Crouched on a tuffet." FiBHP
  "Two blind mice." FiBHP
Rhymes for the Times. Janet Hamilton. PF
Rhymes on the Road, *sel.* Thomas Moore.
  "And is there then no earthly place." OBSV; OBTV
Rhyming a Friend's Poem. Yü Hsüan-chi, *tr.* by Geoffrey Waters. BoWoP
Rhyming Prophecy for a New Year. Leonard Cooper. FaBoCo
Rhyming Riddles, *sel.* Mary Austin.
  Snow. BoNaP; GrPl
Rhyming with a Friend. Yü Hsüan-chi, *tr. fr. Chinese by* Geoffrey Waters. BoWoP
Rhyming with Tzu-yu's "Treading the Green." Su Tung-p'o, *tr. fr. Chinese by* Burton Watson. CoBCP
Rhythm, The. Robert Creeley. LiTM
Rhythm. Ruth Kim Chun-soo, *tr. fr. Korean by* Koh Chang-soo. ACKP
Rhythm. Veijo Meri, *tr. fr. Finnish by* Aili Jarvenpa. SOP
Rhythm. Jean Percival Waddell. CaP
Rhythm and blues. The Blues Today. Mae Jackson. PoBA
Rhythm in the pulse of time. Rhythm. Jean Percival Waddell. CaP
Rhythm it is we. Spirits Unchained. Keorapetse Kgositsile. PoBA
Rib Sandwich. William J. Harris. CNA
Ribald and unbuttoned air, A. Back Lane. R. D. Murphy. PoAu-2
Ribald Romeos less and less berattle. Ribald Romeos Less and Less Berattle ("Parcius iunctas quatiunt fenestras"). Horace, *tr. fr. Latin.* Fr. Odes, I. 25. MAT, *tr.* by John Frederick Nims.
  ("Bloods and bucks of this lewd town, The.") OBVE, *tr.* by the Young Gentlemen of Mr. Rule's Academy at Islington.
  (To Lydia.) OBVE, *tr.* by Philip Francis.
  ("Wanton herd of rakes profest, The.")
  ("Young bloods come round less often now, The.") BoLoP, *tr.* by James Michie.
Ribbon-Fish, The. Robert Adamson. CBAP
Ribbons of iodine. Kelp. Nora Dauenhauer. HATNAP
Ribh Considers Christian Love Insufficient. W. B. Yeats. TW
Ribs and Terrors in the Whale, The. Herman Melville. *Fr.* Moby Dick, *ch.* 9. EaLo
  (Whale, The.) TrGrPo
Ribs of leaves lie in the dust, The. The Coming of the Cold. Theodore Roethke. OBCP
Rice. Carol Muske. AmPA
Rice-abounding Land of Reed Plains, The. Hitomaro. *Fr.* Manyo Shu. Ma
Rice and Rose Bowl Blues. Diane Mei Lin Mark. BrSi
Rice-Planting Song: Aomori Prefecture. *Unknown, tr. fr. Japanese by* Hiroaki Sato. FCEI
Rice this year ripens so late! Lament of the Farm Wife of Wu. Su Tung-p'o, *tr.* by Burton Watson. CoBCP
Rich and Poor; or, Saint and Sinner. Thomas Love Peacock. FaBoCo; NOBE; NOBL; OBSV
Rich blood disturbed my thought. Arrival. John Wain. EBEV

Rich damask roses in fair cheeks do bide. Robert Tofte. *Fr.* Laura.
EiL
Rich Days. W. H. Davies. BoNaP; BoTP
Rich earth has not pressed down. Epitaph for Mael Mhuru. *Unknown.*
NOIV
Rich folks 'cided to take a trip, De. De Titanic. *Unknown.* AS
Rich grass is flourishing, The. Song of the Fisherman. Sun Kuang-hsien,
tr. by Lois Fusek. ATF
Rich in the waning light she sat. Waiting. John Freeman. CH
Rich Irish Lady, A. *Unknown.* AmFP
Rich Is the Year with Much Millet and Rice. *Unknown, tr. fr. Chinese by*
Burton Watson. CoBCP
Rich king of a rainy country, The. The King in May. Michael Dennis
Browne. NYBP
Rich Lazarus! richer in those gems, thy teares. Upon Lazarus His Teares.
Richard Crashaw. SeCV-1
Rich man/ Poor man. *Unknown.* SaC
Rich Man, The. Franklin P. Adams. FiBHP; NBLV; OBAL
Rich man bought a swan and goose, A. The Swan and the Goose.
Aesop, *tr. by* William Ellery Leonard. AWP; FaPON
Rich man has his motorcar, The. The Rich Man. Franklin P. Adams.
FiBHP; NBLV; OBAL
Rich man lay on his velvet couch, The. Mag's Song. *Unknown.* AS
Rich men, trust not in wealth. Summer's Last Will and Testament.
Thomas Nashe. OBD
Rich Mine of Knowledge. George Chapman. SeCePo
Rich nights in another climate. Emblems. Douglas Dunn. FaBoMo
Rich Old Miser, A. *Unknown.* AmFP
Rich Statue, double-faced. To the New Yeere. Michael Drayton.
PoEL-2
Rich the peace of the elements tonight on the Land-of-Joy. The Path of
the Old Spells. Donald Sinclair. GoTS
Rich tuft of ivy, A. Suibne Geilt. NOIV
Rich, voluptuous languor of dim pain, A. Vanitas Vanitatum. Israel
Zangwill. TrJP
Rich Widow, The. *Unknown.* AmFP
Richard III's Speech. Sir John Beaumont. *Fr.* Bosworth Field. JCP
Richard Brought His Flute. Nancy Morejón, *tr. fr. Spanish by* Kathleen
Weaver. AIW
Richard Cory. Edwin Arlington Robinson. AmPP; AnAmPo; CMoP;
DL; FaFP; FF; FPL; HAP; InPK; LiTA; LiTM; MoAB; MoAmPo;
NAAL-2; NIP; NOBA; NoP; OxBA; PoLF; PoRA; PrIm; SoSe; TAP;
TrGrPo
Richard Cory. Paul Simon. InPK
Richard Dick upon a stick. *Unknown.* OxNR
Richard Hunt's Arachne. Robert Hayden. FB
Richard, may I ask a question? What is an episteme? Richard Howard.
Fr. Compulsive Qualifications. PoA
Richard on the cold roof screams, I'm the eye. In the Madness of Love.
Gary Soto. NPGG
Richard Roe and John Doe ("Richard Roe wished himself Solomon.").
Robert Graves. CMoP
Richard Somers. Barrett Eastman. AA
Richard, thah thou be ever trichard. Against the Baron's Enemies.
Unknown. MeEL
Richard Tolman's Universe. Leonard Bacon. ImOP
Richard, what will it be like when you ask the questions? Richard
Howard. *Fr.* Compulsive Qualifications. PoA
Richer now the body's juices. Lyall Tao Tschung Yu. OBD
Riches. Blake. TrGrPo
Riches. *Unknown. See* On Late-acquired Wealth *or* Riches.
Riches and honours Buckley layes aside. Onely the Reverend Grave and
Godly Mr. Buckly Remaines. Edward Johnson. SCAP
Riches I hold in light esteem. The Old Stoic. Emily Brontë. FaPoR;
FPL; NOBE; OBEV; OBNC; PoLF; TrGrPo
Richie Story. *Unknown.* ESPB
Rick De Travaille. Lewis Turco. *Fr.* Bordello. SM
Rick of Green Wood, The. Edward Dorn. NeAP; PoM
Rickety chimney suggests, A. Caravan. Michael Longley. CIP;
FaBCIP
Riddle: "As I went over London Bridge." *Unknown.* ChTr
Riddle: "As I went over Tipple Tyne." *Unknown.* ChTr
Riddle: "At the end of my yard there is a vat." *Unknown.* ChTr
Riddle, A: "Clothes make no sound when I tread ground." *Unknown.*
ChTr
Riddle: Cuckoo. *Unknown, formerly at. to* Cynewulf. *See* Riddles
(Exeter Book)
Riddle: Cuckoo. *Unknown.* PBBP
Riddle: "From Belsen a crate of gold teeth." William Heyen. SM
Riddle: "He went to the wood and caught it." *Unknown.* GBP; OxNR

Riddle: "Highty, tighty, paradighty, clothed [all] in green." *Unknown.*
ChTr; OxNR
Riddle: "House full, yard full." *Unknown.* NTCP
Riddle: "I am within as white as snow." *Unknown.* ChTr; GBP
Riddle: "I saw five birds all in a cage." *Unknown.* GBP
Riddle, A: "I walk on two legs." Cynthia Ozick. VWA
Riddle: I washed my face in water. *Unknown.* ChTr; GBP
Riddle, A: "I'm a strange contradiction; I'm new, and I'm old." Hannah
More. GN
Riddle: "In Mornigan's park there is a deer." *Unknown. See* In
Mornigan's park there is a deer.
Riddle: "It has a head like a cat, feet like a cat." *Unknown.* NTCP
Riddle: "It is in the rock, but not in the stone." *Unknown.* ChTr
Riddle: Jay: *Higora. Unknown, tr. fr. Anglo-Saxon.* PBBP
Riddle: "Land was white, The." *Unknown.* ChTr; OxNR
Riddle: "Limrick's writtn to plas, A." Laurence Perrine. SoTCo
Riddle: "Lives in winter." *Unknown.* NTCP
Riddle: Mute Swan. *Unknown, formerly at. to* Cynewulf. *See* Riddles
(Exeter Book): Wild Swan: "My attire is noiseless when I tread the
earth."
Riddle: Mute Swan. *Unknown.* PBBP
Riddle: Nightingale. *Unknown, tr. fr. Anglo-Saxon.* PBBP
Riddle, The: "No more, no more,/ We are already pin'd." Alexander
Brome. OBS
Riddle: "On yonder hill there is a red deer." *Unknown.* ChTr; GBP
Riddle, A: "Once when I was very scared." Charlotte Zolotow. NTCP
Riddle: "Shoemaker makes shoes without leather, A." *Unknown.* OxNR
Riddle: "Stiff standing on the bed." *Unknown.* GBL
Riddle: "Their tongues are knives, their forks are hands and feet." Adrian
Mitchell. FaBoEE; GBL; OxBSP
Riddle, A: "There is one that has a head without an eye." Christina
Rossetti. OxBChV
Riddle, A: "'Twas in heaven pronounced, and 'twas muttered in hell."
Catherine Fanshawe. ChTr
("'Twas whispered in Heaven, 'twas muttered in hell.") GN
Riddle 29: The Moon and the Sun. *Unknown, tr. fr. Anglo-Saxon by*
Burton Raffel. GoJo
Riddle: "Two legs sat upon three legs." Mother Goose. *See* Two legs sat
upon three legs.
Riddle, A: "We are little airy creatures." Swift. *See* We are little airy
creatures.
Riddle: "Wee man o' leather." *Unknown.* ChTr; GBP
Riddle: "White bird featherless/ Flew from Paradise." *Unknown.* ChTr;
GBP; OxNR
Riddle: "White bird floats down through the air, A." *Unknown.* ChTr;
GBP
Riddle, A: "Yon laddie wi' the gowdan pow." William Soutar. OxBS
Riddle, The. Georgia Douglas Johnson. PoBA
Riddle, A. Thomas Moore. *See* What's My Thought Like?
Riddle, a riddle, A/ As I suppose. Mother Goose. OxNR
Riddle, A; the Vowels. Swift. *See* On the Vowels—a Riddle.
Riddle cum diddle cum dido. Kindness to Animals. Laura Elizabeth
Richards. NTCP
Riddle in the Garden. Robert Penn Warren. NoAM
Riddle me, riddle me ree. Mother Goose. OxNR
Riddle of Night. Jiri Mordecai Langer, *tr. fr. Hebrew.* VWA, *tr. by*
Gabriel Preil *and* Howard Schwartz
Riddle of the World. Pope. *See* Essay on Man, An: Know then thyself,
presume not God to scan.
Riddle silently sees its image. It spins evening, The. Dusk in the Country.
Harry Edmund Martinson, *tr. by* Robert Bly. RB
Riddles (Exeter Book), *sels. Unknown, formerly at. to* Cynewulf, *tr. fr.*
Anglo-Saxon.
Anchor: "Oft I must strive with wind and wave." *Tr. by* Charles W.
Kennedy. AnOE
Book Moth: "A moth ate a word. To me it seemed." *Tr. by* Charles W.
Kennedy. AnOE
Cuckoo: "In former days my father and mother." *Tr. by* Charles W.
Kennedy. AnOE
Fish in River: "My house is not quiet, I am not loud." *Tr. by* Charles
W. Kennedy. AnOE
Honey-Mead: "I am valued by men, fetched from afar." *Tr. by* Charles
W. Kennedy. AnOE
Horn: "Time was when I was weapon and warrior." *Tr. by* Charles W.
Kennedy. AnOE
Plow: "My beak is bent downward, I burrow below." AnOE
Shield: "Lonely wanderer, wounded with iron, A." *Tr. by* Charles W.
Kennedy. AnOE
Swan, The: "Clothes make no sound when I tread ground." *Tr. by*
Geoffrey Grigson. RB

Weathercock, The: "I puff my breast out, my neck swells." *Tr. by* Geoffrey Grigson. RB

Wild Swan: "My attire is noiseless when I tread the earth." AnOE, *tr. by* Charles W. Kennedy.

Wind: "At times I resort, beyond man's discerning." AnOE

Riddles of Change, The. Felix Mnthali. WMBCH

Riddles Wisely Expounded. *Unknown.* ESPB, (3 *vers.*); FaBoBa; GBP

Riddling Knight, The. *Unknown.* FaBoCh; PoEL-1

"Riddling world, A!" one cried. The Two Questions. Alice Meynell. WPE

Ride. Josephine Miles. FaBoWP

Ride, The. Richard Wilbur. BLA; PPR

Ride a Cock Horse. Barry Pain. BXAP

Ride a cock-horse [*or* a-cock horse] to Banbury Cross,/ To see a fine lady upon a white horse. Mother Goose. BoTP; FaBoBe; FaFP; OxBoLi; OxNR

Ride a cock-horse to Banbury Cross/ To buy little Johnny a galloping horse. *Unknown.* OxNR

Ride a cock-horse to Banbury Cross/ To see what Tommy can buy. *Unknown.* OxNR

Ride away, ride away/ Johnny shall ride. Mother Goose. OxNR

Ride-by-Nights, The. Walter de la Mare. DuDa; FaPON; WSC

Ride in the swing. Tune: Crimson Lips Adorned. Li Ch'ing-chao. PBWP, *tr. by* C. H. Kwôck *and* Vincent McHugh ("After kicking on the swing.") BoWoP, *tr. by* Kenneth Rexroth *and* Ling Chung

Ride of Collins Graves, The. John Boyle O'Reilly. PAH

Ride round the Parapet, The. Friedrich Rueckert, *tr. fr. German by* James Clarence Mangan. AWP

Ride the Turtle's Back. Beth Brant. ER; STE

Ride to Cherokee, The. Amelia Walstien Carpenter. AA

Ride to the Lady, The. Helen Gray Cone. AA

Rider, The/ is fat. Horse & Rider. Wey Robinson. BXAP; SD

Rider at The Gate, The. John Masefield. BrPo

Rider Victory, The. Edwin Muir. CMoP; LiTM; WaP

Riders, The. Ann Stanford. WPE

Riders' Horses, The ("The riders' spears touched heaven"). Amir Gilboa, *tr. fr. Hebrew by* Bernhard Frank. MHeP

Rides. Gene Derwood. LiTM

Ridge, The, *sel.* John Cowper Powys. "Aye! What a thing is the passing of Cronos, the angular-minded." OBWVE

Riding. William Allingham. OxBChV

Riding. Harry Amoss. CaP

Riding a Boat on Wu-ling Stream. Tao-chi, *tr. fr. Chinese by* Jonathan Chaves. CoBLCP

Riding a One-eyed Horse. Henry Taylor. HeIP; InPK

Riding across John Lee's Finger. Stanley Crouch. PoBA

Riding bicycles up hills. Everywhere Pregnant Women Appear. Eric Nelson. SoTCp

Riding by there every day. Dog Hospital. Peter Wild. AmPA

Riding Double. Peter Wild. AmPA

Riding Down. Nora Perry. AA

Riding Down from Bangor. Louis Shreve Osborne. BLPA

Riding from Coleraine. Peg of Limavaddy. Thackeray. OBTV

Riding in a Motor Boat. Dorothy Walter Baruch. FaPON

Riding in an Airplane. Dorothy Walter Baruch. FaPON

Riding in the Rain. Maxine W. Kumin. RFM

Riding Lesson. Henry Taylor. ASP; NBLV

Riding on a Streetcar with My Father. Mary Ann Larkin. AiP

Riding rain, astride wind, my plain robe light. Crossing Lake Biwa. Geppa, *tr. by* Lucien Stryk *and* Takashi Ikemoto. ZPCJ

Riding the black express from heaven to hell. Lucifer in the Train. Adrienne Rich. EaLo; NePoEA; NePoEA-2

Riding the blue sapphire mountains. Mahadevi, *tr. by* A. K. Ramanujan. BoWoP; PBWP

Riding through Ruwu swamp, about sunrise. Bête Humaine. Francis Brett Young. CH

Riding Together. William Morris. NOBE; OAEL-2

Riding Westward. Harvey Shapiro. VWA

Riding with Kilpatrick. Clinton Scollard. PAH

Riding wooden horses from the hot Christmas Caves. The Bronze Rider, Wellington. Robin Hyde. ATNZ

Riesis the small. It Is a Lie. John Fowles. AnAn

Rifle barrel and a pair of eyes, A. A Meeting in the Forest. Yrjö Jylhä, *tr. by* Alli Jarvenpa. SOP

Rifled honeycomb, The. John Montague. *Fr.* The Cave of Night. CIP

"Rifleman, shoot me a fancy shot." Civil War. Charles Dawson Shanly. PAH

Rifleman's Song at Bennington. Joseph Rodman Drake. PAH

Rifles, The. *Unknown.* OBET

Rigadoon, rigadoon, now let him fly. *Unknown.* OxNR

Rigged poker-stiff on her back. All the Dead Dears. Sylvia Plath. IHMS

Right after her birth, they crowded in. Anaesthesia. Jean Valentine. TAP

Right Apprehension. Thomas Traherne. PoEL-2

Right Arm, The. Paul Muldoon. NoAM

Right as the star [*or* stern] of day began [*or* begouth] to s[c]hine. The Poet's Dream. William Dunbar. *Fr.* The Golden [*or* Goldyn] Targe. PBBP; PoEL-1 ("Ryght as the stern of day begouth to schyne.") OxBLMV; OxBS

Right at the height of the storm we crawled. Trusting Each Other. William Stafford. KS

Right before my eyes. The Moon. Gyoko, *tr. by* Steven D. Carter. WFTW

Right behind the leader slipped into the byway. The Art of Being Second. J. Bernlef, *tr. by* Peter Nijmeijer. DuIn

Right down the shocked street with a siren-blast. A Fire-Truck. Richard Wilbur. AiP

Right fresshe flowr, whos I ben have and shal. The Sorrow of Troilus. Chaucer. *Fr.* Troilus and Criseyde [*or* Criseide], V. PoEL-1

Right from the evening it burns. Mohammad Taqi Mir, *tr. by* Ahmed Ali. GoT

Right from the start he is dressed in his best—his blacks and his whites. A March Calf. Ted Hughes. NoP

Right hand winnows the sand, The. The Invention. Paul Éluard, *tr. by* Samuel Beckett. RHTwFP

Right Heart in the Wrong Place, The. James Joyce. FaBoPV

Right here I was nearly killed one night in February. Solitude. Tomas Tranströmer, *tr. by* Robert Bly. RB

"Right Here the Other Night Something." E. E. Cummings. NoAM

Right in the middle of the storm it was. The Storm. Elizabeth Jennings. NePoEA-2

Right in the morning appear the signs of the close of day. Asadullah Khan Ghalib, *tr. by* Ahmed Ali. GoT

Right Is Right. Frederick William Faber. WBLP

Right Kind of People, The. Edwin Markham. BLPA; FPL

Right Must Win, The. Frederick William Faber. PWR

Right next to a mud turtle a frog. Bunrin, *tr. by* Hiroaki Sato. FCEI

Right Now. William Stafford. NaP

Right now the elm seeds whisper to the ground. Ian Wedde. *Fr.* Earthly: Sonnets for Carlos, 39. ATNZ

Right On: White America. Sonia Sanchez. PoBA

Right or ruth. Susan Howe. *Fr.* Speeches at the Barriers, 2. LP

Rt. Rev. Richard Allen. Josephine D. Henderson Heard. CBWP-4

Right so this river storms. The Course of the Tavy. William Browne. *Fr.* Britannia's Pastorals, I, Song 2. FaBoPP

Right True End, The. *Gond Oral Tradition, tr. by* V. Elwin *and* S. Hivale. WTO

Right under the big sky. Ozaki Hosai, *tr. fr. Japanese by* Hiroaki Sato. *Fr.* One Hundred Haiku in Free Form. FCEI

Right under their noses, the green. The Dusk of Horses. James Dickey. LiTM; NYBP

Right up under our noses, roses. Intimacy. Al Young. NPGG

Right Use of Prayer, The. Sir Aubrey De Vere. TIRV; WGRP

Right well I wrote, most mighty soveraine. Spenser. *Fr.* The Faerie Queene, II *induction.* OAEL-1

Right Where He Left Off. Craig Weeden. ASP

Righteous Anger. James Stephens. *See* Glass of Beer, A.

Righteous Man, The. Samuel Butler. OBSV

Righteous or not, here comes an angry man. A View of the Burning. James Merrill. NePoEA-2

Right's fine, wrong's fine. Gudo, *tr. by* Lucien Stryk *and* Takashi Ikemoto. ZPCJ

Rights of Woman, The. Anna Laetitia Barbauld. NOEC

Rigid Body Sings. James Clerk Maxwell. FaBoCo; FaBoPa; Par

Rigid in their dead man's stare. Cripple in Sight. John Crosson. TSM

Rigoletto. Newman Levy. OBAL

Rigor of beauty is the quest. But how will you find beauty when it is locked. William Carlos Williams. *Fr.* Paterson. NoAM

Rigor Viris. Margaret Avison. CaP

Rigorists. Marianne Moore. NU

Rigs o' Barley, The. Burns. LiTB

Riley. Charles Causley. SO

Rilke, my river, I know your locked look of a poet. Visions. Kathleen Spivack. AmPA

Rilloby-Rill. Sir Henry Newbolt. BXAP

Rillons, Rillettes. Richard Wilbur. NYBP

Rim of a foot-wearying mountain hazy at dawn, The. Princess Shikishi, *tr. fr. Japanese by* Hiroaki Sato. *Fr.* Seventy-eight Tanka. FCEI

Rimbaud and Verlaine, precious pair of poets. Conrad Aiken. *Fr.* Preludes for Memnon; or, Preludes to Attitude. NoAM

Rimbaud and Verlaine, precious pair of poets. Conrad Aiken. *Fr.* Preludes for Memnon; or, Preludes to Attitude. FaBoMo; LiTA; LiTM; NoAM; TwCP

Rimbaud Fire Letter to Jim Applewhite. Fred Chappell. SM

Rime of the Ancient Feminist, The, *sel.* Stephanie Markman. "They lived out in a women's house." BrRo

Rime of the Ancient Mariner, The ("It is an ancient mariner."), *sels.* Samuel Taylor Coleridge. BeLS; CH; ChER; EBEV; EnRP; FaBoBe; FaBoCh; FaBV; FaFP; FiP; HAP; HeIP; HoPM; InPS; LiTB; MOS; NOBE; NoP; OAEL-2; OBEV; OBNC; OBNV; PoE; PoEL-4; PrIm; TEP; TOF, *abr.*; TrGrPo

"For when it dawn'd—they dropp'd their arms." UnS

He Prayeth Best.

(He Prayeth Well.) BoTP, *sl. longer sel..*

Rime of the Auncient Waggonere, The. William Maginn. BXAP

Rime, the rack of finest wits. A Fit of Rime against Rime. Ben Jonson. InvP; MAT; OAEL-1; PoEL-2; SeCP; SeCV-1

(Fit of Rhyme against Rhyme, A.) TEP

("Rhyme, the rack of finest wits.") TEP

Rimmed in by cypresses, tin water flashed. White Lake. James Applewhite. MT

Rimrock, Where It Is. Hayden Carruth. NNaP

Rin and rout, rin and rout. The Deevil's Waltz. Sydney Goodsir Smith. FaBoTw

Rinaldo. Henry Peterson. AA

Ring, The. Paul Mariani. GeTw

Ring, The. Pier Paolo Pasolini, *tr. fr. Italian by* Lawrence R. Smith. NItP

Ring, The. Diane Wakoski. PoA

Ring-a-Ring. Kate Greenaway. FaPON; MoShBr

Ring-a-ring o' roses, A. Mother Goose. OxNR, 2 *vers.*

Ring-a-ring of little boys. Ring-a-Ring. Kate Greenaway. FaPON; MoShBr

Ring and the Book, The, *sel.* Robert Browning. O Lyric Love. *Fr.* I. FiP

Ring around a rosey. Squat Down, Josey. *Unknown.* AmFP

Ring, arrows of honey, on the false smoking staffs. Tumult. Léon-Paul Fargue, *tr. by* Maria Jolas. RHTwFP

Ring Of, The. Charles Olson. NOBA; VGW

Ring of fear, A. My Daughter's Ring. Barbara Eve Reiss. TV

Ring of my true lover, The. V. A. Zhukovsky, *tr. by* Alan Myers. AAA

Ring of the moon, starshine, swept away as I watch. Traveler's Thoughts. Tu Hsün-ho, *tr. by* Burton Watson. CoBCP

Ring Out the Old, Ring In the New. Tennyson. *See* In Memoriam A. H. H.: Ring Out, Wild Bells.

Ring out to the stars the glad chorus! Our Nation Forever. Wallace Bruce. OHIP

Ring Out, Wild Bells. Tennyson. *Fr.* In Memoriam A. H. H., CVI. BLPL; EBVV; FaPON, 2 *sts.;* FaPoR; FiP, 7 *sts.;* LiTB; OFD; TrGrPo; WiR, 7 *sts., incl.* 2 *sts. fr.* CV.

(Ring Out the Old, Ring In the New.) WBLP

Ring out your bells, let mourning shows be spread. Sir Philip Sidney. TEP

(Litany, A: "Ring out your bells.") GBL; OBSC; UnPo

(Ring Out Your Bells.) EiL; NoP; SiPS

Ring Road. Sandra Mangini, *tr. fr. Italian by* Muriel Kittel. DMI

Ring round her! children of her glorious skies. The Foe at the Gates. John Dickson Bruns. PAH

Ring, so worn as you behold, The. A Marriage Ring. George Crabbe. BoLoP; EnLoPo; OBEV

(His Late Wife's Wedding-Ring.) NOBE

(His Mother's Wedding Ring.) OBNC; UnAS

Ring Taw? Ringer? Chasies? After Reading *The Great American Marble Book* and Reflecting on Life's Lessons Learned at An Early. Michael Cleary. TSL

Ring the bells, nor ring them slowly. Cedar Mountain. Annie Fields. PAH

Ring the bells, ring! The Dunce. *Unknown.* OxNR

Ring-ting! I wish I were a primrose. Wishing. William Allingham. BoTP; FaPON; OHIP; OxBChV

Ringed Plover by a Water's Edge. Norman MacCaig. OxBC

Ringers, The. John Peck, *tr. fr. Italian by* William Arrowsmith. AmPA; AnAn

Ringing the Bells. Anne Sexton. FF; HCAP; PoE; TAP; VGW

Ringing tire iron, A. Some Good Things to Be Said for the Iron Age. Gary Snyder. HoPM; TTTS

Ringless. Diane Wakoski. Prf

Ringleted Youth of My Love. *Unknown, tr. fr. Modern Irish by* Douglas Hyde. AnIL; WTO

Ringsend. Oliver St. John Gogarty. AnIL; OBMV; OxBTC

Rink Keeper's Sestina. George Draper. PrIm

Rino's Song. Lynne Lawner. IHMS

Rinsed fences dry themselves in the wind, The. Perets Markish, *tr. by* Leonard Wolf. PeBMYV

Rinsed with Gold, Endless, Walking the Fields. Robert Siegel. GeTw

Rintrah roars & shakes his fires in the burdend air. Blake. *Fr.* The Marriage of Heaven and Hell, *Argument.* NAEL-2

Rio Bravo—a Mexican Lament. José de Saltillo, *tr. fr. Spanish by* Charles Fenno Hoffman. PAH

Rio Bravo! Rio Bravo! Rio Bravo—a Mexican Lament. José de Saltillo, *tr. by* Charles Fenno Hoffman. PAH

Rio de Janeiro, Río de Enero. River of Oblivion. Alfonso Reyes, *tr. by* Samuel Beckett. MexPo

Rio Grande, The. Sacheverell Sitwell. SeCePo

Río Grande de Loíza. Julia de Burgos, *tr. fr. Spanish by* Grace Schulman. InW

Riot. Gwendolyn Brooks. BPo; PoBA; TAP

Riot, A. Mrs. Henry Linden. CBWP-4

Riot; or, Half a Loaf Is Better than No Bread, The. Hannah More. NOEC

Riots and Rituals. Richard W. Thomas. PoBA

Rioupéroux. James Elroy Flecker. OBEV; OBTV

Rip. Giancarlo Majorino, *tr. fr. Italian by* Lawrence R. Smith. NItP

Rip. James Wright. NaP

Rip-off #1: Hippie Capitalism. Geof Hewitt. NeAC

Ripe and Bearded Barley, The. *Unknown.* BoNaP; ChTr; GBP

Ripe apples were caught like red fish in the nets. The Great Scarf of Birds. John Updike. NYBP

Ripe, Being Plunged into Fire. Friedrich Hölderlin, *tr. fr. German by* James Blair Leishman. OBVE

Ripe cherries and ripe maidens. Cherries. Zalman Schneour, *tr. by* Joseph Leftwich. TrJP

Ripe Tack. Ray DiPalma. LP

Ripeness is all; her in her cooling planet. To an Old Lady. William Empson. FaBoTw; GTBS-P; MoAB; NoAM; NOBE

Ripley or not. A Street in Kaufman-ville. James Cunningham. JB

Ripperty! Kye! Ahoo! Henry Lawson. CBAP

Ripple of dust panicked across, A. Ghosts. Ethna MacCarthy. NeIP

Ripples. *Unknown, tr. fr. Japanese by* Hiroaki Sato. FCEI

Ripples! Karasaki in Shiga! Ripples. Kagura, *tr. by* Hiroaki Sato. FCEI

Ripples Sifting Sand. Huang-fu Sung, *tr. fr. Chinese by* Lois Fusek. ATF

Rippling, a wind from the Bay of Grebes. Teika, *tr. fr. Japanese by* Hiroaki Sato. *Fr.* Eighty-four Tanka. FCEI

Rippling in the ocean of that darkening room. Woman at the Piano. Marya Zaturenska. MoAmPo

Rippling waves of spring water drench the green moss. Sand of the Silk-Washing Stream. Mao Wen-hsi, *tr. by* Lois Fusek. ATF

Riprap. Gary Snyder. CAPP; HCAP; NAAL-2; NeAP; NoAM; NOBA; PoM

Rise, A. Ernest McGaffey. AA

Rise and hold up the curved glass. Pour Us Wine. Ibn Kolthum. *Fr.* The Mu'allaqat. AWP

Rise and Shine. Richmond Lattimore. NYBP

Rise! arise! arise! The Sunrise Call. *Unknown, tr. by* N. Barnes. WTO

Rise, Crowned with Light Imperial Salem Rise. Pope. *Fr.* Messiah. WGRP

Rise heart; thy Lord is risen. Sing his praise. Easter ("Rise, heart, thy Lord is risen. Sing his praise"). George Herbert. NAEL-1; SeCV-1; TrCP

Rise, Lady Mistress, Rise! Nathaniel Field. *Fr.* Amends for Ladies. EiL

(Song: "Rise Lady Mistresse, rise.") OBS

Rise, O earth, from out thy slumber. Prayer for Rain. *Unknown.* WGRP

Rise Oedipus, and if thou canst unfould. Thomas Morton. SCAP

Rise of capitalism parallels the advance of romanticism, The. Definition of Blue. John Ashbery. CAPP; NAAL-2

Rise of Man, The. John White Chadwick. AA

Rise of Shivaji, The. Zulfikar Ghose. MoBS

Rise, rise from sluggishness, fly fast my dear. The Verses of the Talkative Knight. Mary Sidney Wroth, Countess of Montgomery. *Fr.* Urania. WPE

Rise! Sleep no more! 'Tis a noble morn! The Hunter's Song. "Barry Cornwall." GN

Rise then, ere ruin swift surprize. John Trumbull. *Fr.* M'Fingal. GOA

Rise thou best and brightest morning. New Year's Day. Richard Crashaw. JCP

Rise, underground sleepers, rise from the grave. Ode against St. Cecilia's Day. George Barker. PoA

Rise up carcass and walk. Live Flesh. Pierre Reverdy, *tr. by* Kenneth Rexroth. RHTwFP

Rise Up, O Men of God. William Pierson Merrill. AH
(Festal Song.) WGRP

Rise up, rise up,/ And, as the trumpet blowing. The Trumpet. Edward Thomas. MMA; MoBrPo; OHIP

Rise up, rise up, Jack Spratt. And you, his wife. Sonnet XIII. Winfield Townley Scott. ErPo

"Rise up, rise up, my seven brave sons." Earl Brand (The Douglas Tragedy). *Unknown.* FaBoBa
(Douglas Tragedy, The.) NoP; OxBB, *with music;* TrGrPo
("Rise up, rise up, now, Lord Douglas," she says.) ESPB

"Rise up, rise up, now, Lord Douglas," she says. *Unknown. See* "Rise up, rise up, my seven brave sons."

Rise up, thou monstrous ant-hill on the plain. Wordsworth. *Fr.* The Prelude [or, Growth of a Poet's Mind]: Residence in London. HAP

Rise with the Lamb of Innocence. *Unknown.* MeEL

Rise, Ye Children. Justus Falckner, *tr. fr. German by* Emma Frances Bevan. AH

Rise You Up, My True Love. *Unknown.* AmFP

Risen above the uncertain. To Her. Robert Mezey. NaP

Risen from who knows what shadows. Awakening. Antonia Pozzi, *tr. by* Brenda Webster. OV

Risen Matters. Clark Coolidge. UL

Rises at five, just when a late moon. The Insomniac Sleeps Well for Once and. Hayden Carruth. NNaP

Risest thou thus, dim dawn, again. Tennyson. *Fr.* In Memoriam A. H. H., LXXII. OBNC; PoEL-5

Rising, The/ Let me proceed by this way. Canoe-hauling Chant. *Unknown, tr. by* Apirana Ngata. WTO

Rising, The. Thomas Buchanan Read. *Fr.* The Wagoner of the Alleghanies. PAH

Rising Early with My Son Chih to Leave Tung-ming Ch'an Monastery. Huang Tsung-hsi, *tr. fr. Chinese by* Lynn Struve. WFTU

Rising fondly before me. The Beloved's Image. *Unknown.* WTO, *tr. by* M. W. Beckwith

Rising from Sleep. Wang Chiu-ssu, *tr. fr. Chinese by* Jonathan Chaves. CoBLCP

Rising Glory of America, The, *sels.* Hugh Henry Brackenridge *and* Philip Freneau. AiP
Eugenio.
Leander.

Rising hills, the slopes, The. For the Children. Gary Snyder. NoP

Rising in lamplight dying at dawn. Voices Answering Back: The Vampires. Lawrence Raab. AmPA; VVA

Rising in the Morning. Hugh Rhodes. OxBChV

Rising in the North, The. *Unknown.* ACP; ESPB

Rising moon has hid the stars. Endymion. Longfellow. AA

Rising of the Session, The. Robert Fergusson. OxBS

Rising sun casts the same light, The. Teika, *tr. fr. Japanese by* Hiroaki Sato. *Fr.* Eighty-four Tanka. FCEI

Rising Village, The, *sels.* Oliver Goldsmith, the Younger.
"How sweet it is, at first approach of morn." OBCV
"Not fifty summers yet have passed thy clime." OBCV
"What noble courage must their hearts have fired." OBCV
(Lonely Settler, The.) NOBC
"While now the Rising Village claims a name." CaP

Rising without names today. The Survivor. Stephen Berg. *Fr.* Entering the Body. NaP

Risk, The. Anne Sexton. BoWoP

Risks. Malcolm Glass. SoTCo

Rite, The. Peter Dale. NAs

Rite, The. Dudley Randall. HoPM

Rite of Passage. Audre Lorde. CNA; PoBA

Rite of Passage. Sharon Olds. MAYP

Rite of Spring. Seamus Heaney. OxBC

Rite of Spring. Leo Kennedy. CaP

Rites for a Demagogue. Anthony Thwaite. NePoEA-2

Rites for Cousin Vit, The. Gwendolyn Brooks. InPK; SM; Son

Rites for Cousin Vit, The. Gwendolyn Brooks. *Fr.* The Womanhood, VI. BPo; HAP; WeW; WPE

Rites of Ancient Ripening. Meridel LeSueur. ER

Rites of Passage, *sel.* Robert Duncan.
"Something is taking place." *Fr.* II. NoAM

Rites of the Eastern Star. Janine Pommy-Vega. UL

Ritual, The. Edwin John Pratt. MoP

Ritual Not Religious. *Unknown, tr. fr. Telugu.* WGRP

Ritual of Departure. Thomas Kinsella. CIP; CMoP

Ritual of Memories, The. Tess Gallagher. GeTw

Ritualists, The. William Carlos Williams. NYBP

Rituals along the Arkansas. William Mills. MT

Rival, The. Sylvia Townsend Warner. MoAB; MoBrPo

Rival Curates, The. Sir William Schwenck Gilbert. CenHV

Rivals. *At. to* William Walsh *and* Sir George Etherege. OBEV

Rivals, The, *sel.* Sir William Davenant.
"My lodging it is on the cold ground." JCP

Rivals. *At. to* Sir George Etherege. OBEV

Rivals, The. James Stephens. BoTP; FaPON; InvP; OBEV; OBMV

Riven Doggeries. James Tate. MAYP

Riven Quarry, The. Gloria C. Oden. PoBA

River, The. Sam Cornish. PoBA

River, The. Hart Crane. *Fr.* The Bridge: Powhatan's Daughter. AmPP; CMoP; GOA; MoAB; MoAmPo; NOBA; OxBA; PrIm
("Down, down—born pioneers in time's despite.") TrGrPo

River. Ted Hughes. NAEL-2

River. Lawrence Locke. GrPl

River, The, *sels.* Pare Lorentz.
"Black spruce and Norway pine." AmFN
"Down the Yellowstone, the Milk, the White and Cheyenne." AmFN

River, The. Patrick MacDonogh. NeIP

River, The. Roy Macnab. PeSA

River. Philippe Soupault, *tr. fr. French by* Rosmarie Waldrop. POS

River, The. Dabney Stuart. NYBP

River, The. *Unknown.* PWR

River, The. Leo Vroman. VWA

River Afram. Andrew Amankwa Opoku. PBA

River Again and Again, The. Linda Gregg. NPGG

River and Death, The. Badr Shakir al-Sayyah, *tr. fr. Arabic by* Abdullah al-Udhari. MPAW

River and hills beyond the fog—I peer but can't make them out. *Keng-tzu* (1180), First Month, Fifth Day, Dawn. Yang Wan-li, *tr. by* Burton Watson. CoBCP

River bank I left in youth, The. Baby's Room. Jung Han-mo, *tr. by* Koh Chang-soo. ACKP

River bank—the evening tides have started to ebb. On the Fifteenth Day of the Ninth Month of the Year *Kuei-mao* of the *Chih-cheng* Period. Ni Tsan, *tr. by* Jonathan Chaves. CoBLCP

River Boats, The. Daniel Whitehead Hicky. AmFN

River brought down, The. How We Heard the Name. Alan Dugan. CoAP; NoAM

River Ching flows rapidly, The. Wu Wei-yeh, *tr. fr. Chinese by* Jonathan Chaves. CoBLCP

River Compared to an Oratorical Sentence, The. Luis de Góngora y Argote, *tr. fr. Spanish by* Edward Meryon Wilson. *Fr.* The First Solitude. OBVE

River Crossing, The. Denis Glover. *Fr.* Arawata Bill. ATNZ; PeNZ

River Dart, The. *Unknown.* GBP

River Don, The. *Unknown.* GBP

River Duddon, The, *sels.* Wordsworth.
"I thought of Thee, my partner and my guide." *Fr.* XXXIV. FaBoRV
(After-Thought.) EnRP; OBNC; SeCePo
(To the River Duddon: After-Thought.) FaBoPP
(Valediction to the River Duddon.) NOBE
(Valedictory Sonnet to the River Duddon.) OBEV
Return. HAP

River falls and over the walls the coffins of cold funerals, The. River in Spate. Louis MacNeice. FaBCIP

River Fight, The. Henry Howard Brownell. PAH

River-Fight, The, *sel.* Henry Howard Brownell.
Would you hear of the River-Fight?. AA

River flows before my door, The. Tennysonian Reflections at Barnes Bridge. Gavin Ewart. PoPo

River-Fog. Kiyowara Fukuyabu, *tr. fr. Japanese by* Arthur Waley. AWP; FaPON

River God, The. Sacheverell Sitwell. MoBrPo

River God, The. Stevie Smith. BrRo; FaBoNo; FaBoTw; FaBoWP; PBWP

River god cries far, The. Tâo. Alfred Goldsworthy Bailey. CaP

River God, The ("I am this fountain's god"). John Fletcher. *Fr.* The Faithful Shepherdess, III, i. TrGrPo

River God's Song. Anne Ridler. NYBP

River-God's Song, The ("Do not fear to put thy feet"). John Fletcher. *Fr.* The Faithful Shepherdess, III, i. FaPON; MoShBr
(Song: "Do not fear to put thy feet.") EIL; OBS

River gulls bob and toss in reed-flower autumn. Song of the Clear River. Huang T'ing-chien, *tr. by* Burton Watson. CoBCP

River, I am passing. River Afram. Andrew Amankwa Opoku. PBA

River in March, The. Ted Hughes. OxBC

River in Spate. Louis MacNeice. FaBCIP
River in the Meadows, The. Léonie Adams. MoAB; MoAmPo
River Is a Piece of Sky, The. John Ciardi. PDV
River is black—a single white flower lit on its breast, The. Dusk. Maruyama Kaoru, tr. by Hiroaki Sato. FCEI
River is calm, the moon reflected in its waters, The. A Noble Scholar Playing the Lute. Yang Chi, tr. by Jonathan Chaves. CoBLCP
River is so much mica, The. The River; North of Guelph. D. G. Jones. NOBC
River Lynher, The. Richard Carew. Fr. Survey of Cornwall. FaBoPP
River Man. Michael Jackson. ATNZ
River Mang has always been clear—not a trace of mud, The. Recording a Weird Happening. Li K'ai-hsien, tr. by Jonathan Chaves. CoBLCP
River-Mates. Padraic Colum. AWP
River Merchant's Wife; a Letter, The. Li Po, tr. fr. Chinese by Ezra Pound. AmPP; AWP; BoLoP; FYAP; HAP; HeIP; InPK; InPK; InPS; LiTA; MoAB; MoAmPo; MoP; NAAL-2; NIP; NIP; NoAM; NOAM; NOBA; NOBE; NoP; OBMV; OBVE; OxBA; PPP; PrIm; RB; SOTW; TAP; TTTS; TwCP; UnPo; WeW
River Messages. Chang Pi, tr. fr. Chinese by Lois Fusek. ATF
River Messages. Ku Hsiung, tr. fr. Chinese by Lois Fusek. ATF
River Messages. Li Hsün, tr. fr. Chinese by Lois Fusek. ATF
River Messages. Sun Kuang-hsien, tr. fr. Chinese by Lois Fusek. ATF
River Messages. Wei Chuang, tr. fr. Chinese by Lois Fusek. ATF
River Messages. Wen T'ing-yün, tr. fr. Chinese by Lois Fusek. ATF
River Messages. Yen Hsüan, tr. fr. Chinese by Lois Fusek. ATF
River moans, The. River. Lawrence Locke. GrPl
River Nile, The ("River Nile's/ length is 4,160 miles, The"). Joyce LaMers. SoTCo
River; North of Guelph, The. D. G. Jones. NOBC
River of autumn water, pale, cold mist, A. Ni Tsan, tr. fr. Chinese by Jonathan Chaves. Fr. Two Poems to the Tune "Hsiao-t'iao hung", I. CoBLCP
River of Bees, The. W. S. Merwin. HeIP; LCAP
River of Dart, O river of Dart. The Dart. Unknown. GBP
River of Heaven, The. Unknown. Fr. Manyo Shu. AWP
River of Life, The. Thomas Campbell. FaFP; GTBS; GTBS-P; LiTB
River of Oblivion. Alfonso Reyes, tr. fr. Spanish by Samuel Beckett. MexPo
River of Rivers in Connecticut, The. Wallace Stevens. HAP; HCAP; NOBA; VGW
River of Stars, The. Alfred Noyes. OnMSP
River of the gods, the act of recalling you. Tulsidas, tr. by John Stratton Hawley and Mark Juergensmeyer. SSI
River plovers, The. Empress Eifuku, tr. by Steven D. Carter. WFTW
River plovers crying. Yakamochi. Fr. Manyo Shu. FCEI
River Rhyme. William Carlos Williams. PoA
River Rhyme. Lila Zeiger. SoTCo
River Road. Stanley Kunitz. MoP; NoAM
River Road Studio. Barbara Guest. PoM
River Roads. Carl Sandburg. VGW
River Roses. D. H. Lawrence. BrPo; CMoP; GBL; OAEL-2; ViBoPo
River runs over, The. Trout. Brian Turner. ATNZ
River Skater. Winifred Welles. SD
River slopes, already into the midmonth of spring. On the Spur of the Moment. Tu Fu, tr. by Burton Watson. CoBCP
River Snow. Liu Tsung-yüan, tr. fr. Chinese by Burton Watson. CoBCP
River Song. Elizabeth Brewster. CaP
River Song. Weldon Kees. PPP
River Sound Remembered. W. S. Merwin. SM
River Swelleth More and More, The. Henry David Thoreau. NOBA
River takes the land, and leaves nothing, The. The Slip. Wendell Berry. NOCV
River that must turn full after I stop dying. "A 11" ("River that must turn full after I stop dying."). Louis Zukofsky. Fr. "A" (1–12), 11. VGW
River, that rollest by the ancient walls. Stanzas to the Po. Byron. OAEL-2
River turns, The. The Pike. Theodore Roethke. ASP
River used to store up in its mouth, The. The River. Roy Macnab. PeSA
River was announcing, The. The River Crossing. Denis Glover. Fr. Arawata Bill. ATNZ; PeNZ
River Water Music. Richard Eberhart. BLA
River waters ruffled in the west wind. By the River. Wang An-shih, tr. by Burton Watson. CoBCP
River, why in ceaseless flow. Maiden and River. Mary Weston Fordham. CBWP-2
River widens to a pathless sea, The. On a Ferry Boat. Richard Burton. AA
River Winding. Charlotte Zolotow. RHPC

River woods,/ dark made of owl hoots, in the crickets. The Wood House over the Wilia. Johannes Bobrowski, tr. by Don Bogen. AnAn
Riverbed for Damien. Gregory O'Brien. ATNZ
Riverman, The. Elizabeth Bishop. NYBP
Rivers. Thomas Storer. EIL; FaBoCh
Rivers and Mountains. John Ashbery. CoAP; NoAM; NOBA
Rivers Arise. Milton. See Rivers Arise; a Fragment.
Rivers Arise; a Fragment. Milton. ChTr
   (Rivers Arise.) FaBoPP
Rivers Come to the Hall of Proteus for the Marriage of the Thames and the Medway, The. Spenser. Fr. The Faerie Queene, IV, 2. FaBoPP
River's flow collects and forms a pool, The. Liang Family Pool. Yang Shih-ch'i, tr. fr. Chinese by Jonathan Chaves. Fr. Ten Scenes at the Hsiao Family Stone Ridge. CoBLCP
Rivers Remember, The. Nancy Byrd Turner. AmFN
Rivers rush into the sea, The. The Song of the Bird. Longfellow. BoTP
Rivers that flowed divided each from each. Chinese Poems: Arthur Waley. "C. A. Fair." PeSA
River's waves reflect a bent willow, The. Bent Willows. Li Chien, tr. by Hsin-sheng C. Kao. WFTU
Riverside willows sway their green mist, The. To the Retired Scholar Chang. Ni Tsan, tr. by Jonathan Chaves. CoBLCP
Riversongs of Arion, The, sels. Michael Anania. NoAM
   "Adrift on an oil-drum raft." Fr. I.
   "Among the provisions they carried." Fr. VII.
   "Which river is this." Fr. V.
Rivery field spread out below, A. Let All Things Pass Away. W. B. Yeats. ChTr
Riveter, The. Mabel Watts. RHPC
Rivulet with rush of sound, The. Midwinter Thaw. Lenore Pratt. CaP
Rizpah. Tennyson. PoEL-5
R.M.S. Titanic., sel. Anthony Cronin.
   "On the bog road the blackthorn flowers, the turf-stacks." BIrV
Roach, The. John Raven. BPo; HoPM
Roach/ came struttin, A. The Roach. John Raven. BPo; HoPM
Road, The. Conrad Aiken. MoAmPo
Road. David Chapman Berry. MT
Road, The. Helene Johnson. AmNP; BANP; BlSi; CDC; PoNe
Road, The. Herbert Morris. DiPo
Road, The. Edwin Muir. CMoP; FaFP; LiTB; LiTM; Mes
Road, The. Nikolay Platonovich Ogarev, tr. fr. Russian by P. E. Matheson. AWP
Road, The. Christine Orr. PoSH
Road, The. Zalman Schneour, tr. fr. Yiddish by Joseph Leftwich. TrJP
Road ahead, The. Seamus Heaney. Fr. Sweeney Redivivus. TOF
Road at My Door, The. W. B. Yeats. Fr. Meditations in Time of Civil War, V. BIrV; LiTB; NOBE; PoE
Road at the top of the rise, The. The Middleness of the Road. Robert Frost. LiTA; NOBA
Road Back, The. Anne Sexton. NYBP
Road beneath the giant original trees, The. Sanctuary. Judith Wright. WPE
Road can't be as sad as a shoe is sad, A. Shoe. John Perreault. EAS
Road climbs, villages, The. Going. Peter Everwine. NNaP
Road from Adonoi to I Don't Know, The. The Three Towns. Howard Nemerov. KS
Road goes ever on and on, The. The Old Walking Song. John R. R. Tolkien. RFM
Road in Kentucky, A. Robert Hayden. LCAP
Road is left that once was trod, The. The Old Road. Jones Very. AA
Road is so rough Severn is walking, The. Posthumous Keats. Stanley Plumly. GeTw; SV
Road is wide and the stars are out and the breath of the night is sweet, The. Roofs. Joyce Kilmer. BLPL; PoLF
Road Is Wider than Long, The, sel. Roland Penrose.
   "They breathe with the night." EAS
Road might lead to anywhere, A. Roads. Rachel Lyman Field. FaPON; PDV
Road Moves On, The. Dorothy Nash. Fr. Kinloch. PoSH
Road 1940. Sylvia Townsend Warner. CN
Road Not Taken, The. Robert Frost. AiP; AmPP; ChTr; CMoP; FaBoCh; FaFP; FPL; HAP; HeIP; LiTA; LiTM; MoAB; MoAmPo; MoP; NAAL-2; NIP; NoAM; NoP; OxBA; PoLF; RFM; SoSe; TAP; TwCP
Road of Life, The. William Morris. Fr. The Earthly Paradise. OBNC
Road runs straight with no turning, the circle, The. Black People: This Is Our Destiny. Imamu Amiri Baraka. CNA
Road that leads to Rannoch is the gangrel's royal way, The. For Summer's Here. Ratcliffe Barnett. PoSH
Road to Bologna, The. Roy Macnab. PeSA

Road to Castaly, The, *sel.* Alice Brown.
  Revelation. WGRP
Road to Eluela, The. Album. Haim Gouri, *tr. by* Warren Bargad *and* Stanley F. Chyet. IP
Road to France, The. Daniel Henderson. PAH
Road to Hate, The. Patrick Kavanagh. TW
Road to Hogan's Gap, The. Andrew Barton Paterson. CBAP
Road to Nijmegen, The. Earle Birney. OBCV
Road to Pengya, The. Tu Fu, *tr. fr. Chinese by* Rewi Alley *and* Edward Field. Prf
Road to Shinano, The. *Unknown. Fr.* Manyo Shu. FCEI
Road to the Bow, The. James David Corrothers. BANP
Road to the burn, The. Roads. George Mackay Brown. PoSH
Road to Town, The. H. M. Sarson. BoTP
Road to Vagabondia, The. Dana Burnet. PoLF
Road to Zoagli, The. Max Beerbohm. FaBoNo
Road turned out to be a cul-de-sac, The. Brother and Sisters. Judith Wright. FaBoWP
Road turns back, the desolate mountain parts, The. Passing by the Battlefield at Feng-k'ou. Kao Ch'i, *tr. by* Jonathan Chaves. CoBLCP
Road twisted through tongues of rock, The. The Vowels of Another Language. Tom Disch. PoA
Road was straight up to the last, The. Detour. Harold Bond. TSM
Road winds down through autumn hills, The. Tour 5. Robert Hayden. PPP
Roadmenders' Song, The. *Gond Oral Tradition, tr. by* V. Elwin *and* S. Hivale. WTO
Roads. George Mackay Brown. PoSH
Roads. Rachel Lyman Field. FaPON; PDV
Roads Also, The. Wilfred Owen. EBEV
Roads are now impassable, The. Spring Season of Muddy Roads. Joseph Brodsky, *tr. by* George L. Kline. AnAn
Road's End. Rolf Jacobsen, *tr. fr. Norwegian by* Robert Bly. NU
Road's End, The. John Montague. *Fr.* A Severed Head, I. IPY
Roads Go Ever On and On. J. R. R. Tolkien. FaPON
Roads have come to their end now, The. Road's End. Rolf Jacobsen, *tr. by* Robert Bly. NU
Roads were jammed, The. Snow in the City. Danny Siegel. VWA
Roadside forests here and there were touched with tawny gold, The. Mistress Hale of Beverly. Lucy Larcom. PAH
Roadside marsh mallow, The. Basho, *tr. fr. Japanese by* Burton Watson. *Fr.* Seventy-six Hokku. FCEI
Roadside thistle, eager, The. Basho, *tr. by* Curtis Hidden Page. AWP
Roadways. John Masefield. BoTP
Roam not from pole to pole, but enter here. Swift. *Fr.* Inscription for the Sign of *The Jolly Barber*, with a Razor in One Hand, and a Pot of Beer in the Other. FaBoUs
Roaming in Kan-chou. Mao Wen-hsi, *tr. fr. Chinese by* Lois Fusek. ATF
Roan galloped, The. The Corral. Earle Thompson. STE
Roan Hunter, The. Jana Harris. TSL
Roan Stallion. Robinson Jeffers. BeLS
Roar of welcome though the welkin, A. The Elk, The Whelk. Robert Williams Wood. NBLV
Roared her father, severest of men. Laurence Perrine. SoTCo
Roarers in a Ring. Ted Hughes. NePoEA-2
Roaring alongside he takes for granted, The. Sandpiper. Elizabeth Bishop. AiP; HeIP; NYBP; RB; TOF
Roaring Frost, The. Alice Meynell. EBVV; WPE
Roaring Lad and the Ranting Lass, The; or, A Merry Couple Madly Met. *Unknown.* CoMu
Roaring Mad Tom. *Unknown. See* From the hag and hungry goblin.
Roaring of the wheels has filled my ears, The. A Cry from the Ghetto. Morris Jacob Rosenfeld, *tr. by* Charles Weber Linn. TrJP
"Roast chestnuts, a shilling." Walking against the Wind. Jon Stallworthy. OxBC
Roast Potatoes. Gertrude Stein. IAT
Roasted Sucking Pig. *Unknown.* BXAP
Roasting alive of rabbis, The. In the Absence of Bliss. Maxine W. Kumin. NoAM
Rob me and maim me! Why, man, take such pains. To One Who Quotes and Detracts. Walter Savage Landor. FaBoEE
Rob Roy. *Unknown.* ESPB, (A *and* B *vers.*)
Robbed of our rights, and by such water-rats? In Defiance to the Dutch. *Unknown.* APAS
Robben Island. Robert Dederick. PeSA
Robber, The. "Hugh MacDiarmid." OBVE
Robber, The. W. J. Turner. MoBrPo
Robber of Kuan-shan, The, *sel.* Wang Chiu-ssu, *tr. fr. Chinese by* Jonathan Chaves.
  "Today I am a farmer in the fields." CoBLCP

Robbers came to our house, The. *Unknown.* GBP
Robbin, The. John Very. Son
Robe of Flame. Ali Sardar J'afri, *tr. fr. Urdu by* Mahmood Jamal. PBMUP
Robe of haze is wet at its hem, A. *Unknown, tr. fr. Japanese by* Hiroaki Sato. *Fr.* Inutsukuba Shu. FCEI
Robe of mist, The. Yukihira, *tr. by* Geoffrey Bownas *and* Anthony Thwaite. PeBJV
Robe too short, jacket too long. In High Spirits. Ryokan, *tr. by* Burton Watson. JLIC-2
Robene and Makyne. Robert Henryson. *See* Robin [*or* Robene] and Makyne.
Robens' Promised Land. George Purdom. WTO
Robert. Wendy Rose. HATNAP
Robert Barnes, fellow fine. Mother Goose. OxNR
Robert Bly Finds Something in New Jersey. Carol Poster. BXAP
Robert Bly Says Something Too. Henry Taylor. BXAP
Robert Creeley Also Watches. David Chapman Berry. BXAP
Robert Creeley Listens, Too. D. C. Berry. BXAP
Robert E. Lee. Stephen Vincent Benét. *Fr.* John Brown's Body. AmFN
Robert E. Lee. Julia Ward Howe. PAH
Robert Frost. Robert Lowell. *Fr.* Writers, VII. MoP; NAAL-2; NoAM; Son
Robert Frost's Left-leaning *Trespassers Will Be Shot* Sign. William Zaranka. BXAP
Robert G. Shaw. Henrietta Cordelia Ray. BlSi; CBWP-3; Son
Robert Gould Shaw. Paul Laurence Dunbar. Son
Robert Gould Shaw. William Vaughn Moody. *Fr.* An Ode in Time of Hesitation. AA
Robert Graves. Gavin Ewart. NoAM
Robert Lowell: His Death. Alan Williamson. PPR
Robert of Lincoln. Bryant. FaBoBe; FaPON; OBCA; WBLP, *abr*
Robert of Sicily, brother of Pope Urbane. King Robert of Sicily (The Sicilian's Tale). Longfellow. *Fr.* Tales of a Wayside Inn, *pt.* I. BeLS; OHIP
Robert Rowley rolled a round roll round. Mother Goose. OxNR
Robert, Second Duke of Normandy, *sel.* Thomas Lodge.
  Pluck the Fruit and Taste the Pleasure. EIL
  (Carpe Diem.) OBSC
Robert Sheridan Lowell. Robert Lowell. *Fr.* Marriage, *st.* 13. NAS
Robert the Bruce. Edwin Muir. OxBS
Robert Whitmore. Frank Marshall Davis. BPo; NoP; PoBA; PoNe
Robert, Who Is Often a Stranger to Himself. Gwendolyn Brooks. RAR
Robertin Tush. *Unknown.* GBP
Robes loosely flowing and aspect as free. Seeing Her Dancing. Robert Heath. OBS; OxBSP
Robespierre and Mozart as Stage. Robert Lowell. FaBoMo
Robespierre could live with himself: "The Republic." Robespierre and Mozart as Stage. Robert Lowell. FaBoMo
Robin, The. Laurence Alma-Tadema. BoTP
Robin, The. O. M. Bent. BoTP
Robin, The. John Clare. FL
Robin, The. George Daniel. FaBoRV
Robin, The. William Bell Scott. FM
Robin, A. Walter de la Mare. ChTr; CMoP; FaBoRV
Robin-a-bobin. Mother Goose. OxNR
Robin; a Pastoral Elegy. John Dobson. NOEC
Robin Adair. Caroline Keppel. FaBoBe
Robin and a robin's son, A. *Unknown.* OxNR
Robin and Gandelyn. *Unknown. See* Robyn and Gandeleyn.
Robin [*or* Robene] and Makyne. Robert Henryson. OBEV; PoEL-1
  (Robene and Makyne.) BoLoP; GoTS; OxBLMV; PoE
  ("Robene sat on gud grene [*or* green] hill.") BoLoP; GoTS
Robin and Richard. Mother Goose. OxBoLi; OxNR
Robin and Richard/ Were two pretty men. Robin and Richard. Mother Goose. OxBoLi; OxNR
Robin and the red-breast, The. Warning. *Unknown.* OxNR; PBBP
Robin and the wren, The. Greed. *Unknown.* OxNR
  (Four birds.) ChTr
  (Robin, Wren, Martin, Swallow.) GBP
Robin Burns, *sel.* Gerald Massey.
  "Hundred years ago this morn, A." PF
Robin chants when the thrush is dumb, The. To-Morrow. Florence Earle Coates. AA
Robin cries: *rain!*, The. Rain in Ohio. Mary Oliver. InPK
Robin dwelt in greenè wood. The Death of Robin Hood. *Unknown.* EnSB
Robin Friend has gone to bed. Bed-Time. L. Alma Tadema. BoTP
Robin Good-Fellow's Song: "Round about, little ones." *Unknown. Fr.* Robin Goodfellow, *Pt.* II. EIL
Robin Goodfellow. *Unknown.* FaBoCh

Robin Goodfellow, *sels.* *Unknown.*
And Can the Physician. *Fr. pt.* II. ELP
(Song: "And can the physician make sick men well?.") ElL
Robin Good-Fellow's Song: "Round about, little ones." *Fr. pt.* II. ElL
Robin he's gane to the wast. The Wife Wrapt [*or* Wrapped] in Wether's Skin. *Unknown.* AmFP; ESPB
Robin Hood. Keats. AWP; EnRP
Robin Hood. Rachel MacAndrew. BoTP
Robin Hood. Phyllis McGinley. *Fr.* Speaking of Television. OBSV
Robin Hood/ Has gone to the wood. Robin Hood. *Unknown.* OxNR
Robin Hood. *Unknown.* OxNR
Robin Hood and Allen [*or* Allin] -a-Dale. *Unknown.* ESPB; FaBoBe; GBP; MoShBr
Robin Hood and Guy of Gisborne. *Unknown.* ESPB
Robin Hood and Little John. *Unknown.* AmFP; ESPB
Robin Hood and Maid Marian. *Unknown.* ESPB
Robin Hood and Queen Katherine. *Unknown.* ESPB
Robin Hood and the Beggar, I. *Unknown.* ESPB
Robin Hood and the Beggar, II. *Unknown.* ESPB
Robin Hood and the Bishop. *Unknown.* ESPB
Robin Hood and the Bishop of Hereford. *Unknown.* ESPB
Robin Hood and the Butcher. *Unknown.* ESPB
Robin Hood and the Curtal Friar. *Unknown.* ESPB
Robin Hood and the Golden Arrow. *Unknown.* ESPB
Robin Hood and the Monk. *Unknown.* ESPB; FaBoBa; OBNV, *abr.*
Robin Hood and the Pedlars. *Unknown.* ESPB
Robin Hood and the Potter. *Unknown.* ESPB
Robin Hood and the Prince of Aragon. *Unknown.* ESPB
Robin Hood and the Ranger. *Unknown.* ESPB
Robin Hood and the Scotchman. *Unknown.* ESPB
Robin Hood and the Shepherd. *Unknown.* ESPB
Robin Hood and the Tanner. *Unknown.* ESPB
Robin Hood and the Three Squires. *Unknown.* *See* There are thirteen months in all the year.
Robin Hood and the Tinker. *Unknown.* ESPB
Robin Hood and the Valiant Knight. *Unknown.* ESPB
Robin Hood and the Widow's Three Sons. *Unknown.* *See* There are twelve months in all the year.
Robin Hood he was [*or* hee was] and a tall young man. Robin Hood's Progress to Nottingham. *Unknown.* ESPB; OBET
Robin Hood Newly Revived. *Unknown.* ESPB
Robin Hood Rescuing Three Squires. *Unknown.* ESPB, (A *and* B *vers.*)
Robin Hood Rescuing Three Squires. *Unknown.* ESPB
Robin Hood Rescuing Will Stutly. *Unknown.* ESPB
Robin Hood, Robin Hood,/ Is in the mickle wood. Mother Goose. BoTP; OxNR
Robin Hood's Barn. John Ashbery. AnAn
Robin Hood's Birth, Breeding, Valor, and Marriage. *Unknown.* ESPB
Robin Hood's Chase. *Unknown.* ESPB
Robin Hood's Death. *Unknown.* ESPB, (A *and* B *vers.*); FaBoBa; OBET; TrGrPo
Robin Hood's Delight. *Unknown.* ESPB
Robin Hood's End. *Unknown.* GoTL
Robin Hood's Funeral. Anthony Munday. *See* Death of Robert, Earl of Huntingdon: Weep, weep, ye woodmen! wail.
Robin Hood's Golden Prize. *Unknown.* ESPB
Robin Hood's Progress to Nottingham. *Unknown.* ESPB; OBET
Robin hurries through the quandrangle, A. Last Memo. Philip Hobsbaum. NPo
Robin is a lovely lad The Dance. *At. to* Thomas Campion. ElL; FaBoCh
Robin is the one, The. Emily Dickinson. FaBV
Robin laughed in the orange tree, The. Tampa Robins. Sidney Lanier. AnAmPo
Robin Red Breast. Lula Lowe Weeden. CDC
Robin Redbreast. William Allingham. FaBoBe; MoShBr; OxBChV; PBBP
Robin Redbreast. George Washington Doane. AA
Robin Redbreast. Stanley Kunitz. Prf
Robin Redbreast in a cage, A. Blake. *Fr.* Auguries of Innocence. OxBoLi, *sl. abr.*
Robin Redbreast's Testament. *Unknown.* GBP
Robin! Robin! call the Springtime. March. Henrietta Cordelia Ray. CBWP-3
Robin sang sweetly. *Unknown.* BoTP
Robin [*or* Robene] sat on gude green [*or* gud grene] hill. Robin [*or* Robene] and Makyne. Robert Henryson. OBEV; PoEL-1
(Robene and Makyne.) BoLoP; GoTS
("Robene sat on gud grene [*or* green] hill.") BoLoP; GoTS
Robin the Bobbin. *Unknown.* OxNR
Robin, Wren, Martin, Swallow. *Unknown.* *See* Greed.

Robinets and Jenny Wrens. *Unknown.* OxNR
Robin's call has stumbled on a rock, A. Shiba Sonome, *tr. fr. Japanese* by Hiroaki Sato. *Fr.* Fifteen Hokku. FCEI
Robin's Egg, The. Annie Charlotte Dalton. CaP
Robins in the treetop. Marjorie's Almanac. Thomas Bailey Aldrich. FaPON
Robin's Poem, A. Nikki Giovanni. AmNP
Robins sang in England. Robin's Song. Rodney Bennett. BoTP
Robin's Secret. Katharine Lee Bates. AA
Robin's Song. Rodney Bennett. BoTP
Robin's Song, The. C. Lovat Fraser. BoTP; MoShBr
Robinson. Alfred Gong, *tr. fr. German* by Beth Bjorklund. CoAuP
Robinson. Weldon Kees. MoP; NaP; NYBP
Robinson at cards at the Algonquin; a thin. Aspects of Robinson. Weldon Kees. CoAP; NaP; NYBP
Robinson at Home. Weldon Kees. CoAP; NYBP
Robinson Crusoe. Charles Edward Carryl. *Fr.* Davy and the Goblin, *ch.* 11. AA
(Robinson Crusoe's Story.) BeLS; FiBHP; PoRA
Robinson Crusoe breaks a plate on his way out. The Revolution. Jack Gilbert. NPGG
Robinson Crusoe Daniel Defoe. Maurice Sagoff. NBLV
Robinson Crusoe's Story. Charles Edward Carryl. *See* Davy and the Goblin: Robinson Crusoe.
Robot Poetry. Paul Rodenko, *tr. fr. Dutch* by James S. Holmes. DuIn
Robyn, A/ Joly Robyn. Sir Thomas Wyatt. AAS
Robyn and Gandeleyn. *Unknown.* EnSB; ESPB; OxBB
Roc, The. Richard Eberhart. CMoP
Roc, The. Edward Lowbury. AmMo
Rock, The, *sels.* T. S. Eliot.
Chorus from "The Rock." *Fr.* III. LiTB
"Eagle soars in the summit of heaven, The." OBMV, Chorus I.
"O Light Invisible, we praise Thee!" *Fr.* Chorus X. TrPWD
Rock, *sel.* Kathleen Jessie Raine.
"There is stone in me that knows stone." ImOP
Rock. Judah Leib Teller, *tr. fr. Yiddish* by Benjamin *and* Barbara Harshav. AYP
Rock, The. *Unknown, tr. fr. Welsh* by Geoffrey Grigson. ChTr; GBL
"Rock-a-by, baby, up in the tree-top!" In the Tree-Top. Lucy Larcom. OBCA
Rock-a-by Lady, The. Eugene Field. BoTP
Rock-a-bye, baby, thy cradle is green. Mother Goose. FaFP; OxNR
Rock, a leaf, mud, even the grass, A. The Concealment: Ishi, the Last Wild Indian. William Stafford. NaP
Rock among Bamboo. Hsü Wei, *tr. fr. Chinese* by Jonathan Chaves. *Fr.* A Kite. CoBLCP
Rock and Hawk. Robinson Jeffers. NoAM; NOBA; OxBA
Rock and precipice. Landscape. Octavio Paz. OBVE, *tr. by* Charles Tomlinson
Rock away, passenger, in the Third Class. *Unknown.* CenHV
Rock, Ball, Fiddle. *Unknown.* *See* He that lies at the stock.
Rock, Be My Dream. MacKnight Black. PoSH
Rock Carving. Douglas Stewart. SeCePo
Rock Climbing. Jane Cooper. NMM
Rock Crumbles, The. Else Lasker-Schüler, *tr. fr. German*. TrJP, *tr. by* Ralph Manheim
(My People.) WPOW, *tr. by* Michael Hamburger
Rock foundation of the fort was dread, The. Blockhouse. Olga Kirsch, *tr. by* Jack Cope. PeSA
Rock grows brittle, The. My People. Else Lasker-Schüler, *tr. by* Michael Hamburger. WPOW
Rock Island Line, The. *Unknown.* AmFP
Rock Leader. Dave Barthgate. PoSH
Rock-like the souls of men. Men Fade Like Rocks. Walter James Turner. OBMV
Rock-Lily. Roland Robinson. PoAu-2
Rock Lily's pale spay, The. Rock-Lily. Roland Robinson. PoAu-2
Rock Me to Sleep, [Mother]. (Elizabeth Chase Akers). AA; AnAmPo; BLPA; BLPL; FaBoBe; FaFP; OBCA; WBLP
Rock 'n' Roll. Lesley Frost. AiP
Rock of Ages. Augustus Montague Toplady. BLRP; FaFP; FaPoR; NOCV; WGRP
Rock of ages, cleft for me. A Living and Dying Prayer for the Holiest Believer in the World. Augustus Montague Toplady. NOEC
Rock of My Salvation. Mordecai, *tr. fr. Hebrew* by Solomon Solis-Cohen. TrJP
Rock of This Odd Coincidence, The. Penelope Scambly Schott. KS
Rock Painting. Carroll Arnett. VoR
Rock Painting. Jack Cope. PeSA
Rock Pilgrim. Herbert Edward Palmer. OxBTC
Rock, Rock, Sleep, My Baby. Clyde Watson. NTCP

Rock Thrown into the Water Does Not Fear the Cold, A. Audre Lorde.
 NAAL-2
Rock wrinkles, folds on the near. Monastery on Athos. Richmond
 Lattimore. EyDe
Rockaby, lullaby, bees in the clover! Josiah Gilbert Holland. *Fr.* The
 Mistress of the Manse. AA
Rocked in the Cradle of the Deep. Emma Hart Willard. AA; AnAmPo;
 BLPL; FaBoBe; FaFP; MOS; PWR; WBLP; WGRP
Rockefeller Collection of Primitive Art, The. Denis Johnson. NAmP
Rocket in My Pocket, A. *Unknown.* RHPC
Rockets bubble upward and explode, The. 14 July 1956. Laurence
 Lerner. PeSA
Rockferns. Norman Nicholson. MoBrPo
Rocking Chair, The. Abraham Moses Klein. CaP; HeIP; NoP
Rocking Hymn, A. George Wither. *See* Hallelujah; or, Britain's Second
 Remembrancer: Hymn L: Rocking Hymn, A.
Rocking My Child. Gabriela Mistral, *tr. fr. Spanish by* Perry Higman.
 LPSS
Rockland. Julia Randall. WPE
Rocks. Florence Parry Heide. NTCP
Rocks and Deals. Geoffrey Young. UL
Rocks flow and the mountain shapes flow, The. The Songs of the Birds.
 Edward Carpenter. WGRP
Rocks jagged in the morning mist. The Point. John Montague.
 IPY
Rocky Acres. Robert Graves. LiTB; NoAM; UnPo
Rocky Island, The. *Unknown.* AmFP
Rocky Mountains, The. *Unknown.* AmFP
Rocky path is sown with sombre cries, The. Gravida. Pierre Jean Jouve,
 tr. by David Gascoyne. RHTwFP
Rocky Road to Dublin, The. *Unknown.* FaBoBa
Rocky shore/ flocks of plovers. Kyorai, *tr. fr. Japanese by* Burton
 Watson. *Fr.* Twenty Hokku. FCEI
Rod light and taper, thy tackle fine, The. How to Catch Trout. Thomas
 Barker. *Fr.* The Art of Angling. FaBoUs
Rod of Jesse, The. Bible, *O.T. Fr.* Isaiah, XI: 1–11. AWP; OBVE;
 TrJP
Rod was but a harmless wand, The. The Virtues of Sid Hamet, the
 Magician's Rod. Swift. APAS
Rodney's Ride. *Unknown.* PAH
Rodomontade in the Menagerie. Eve Merriam. SoTCo
Rodomontade on His Cruel Mistress, A. John Wilmot, 2nd Earl of
 Rochester. OxBSP
Roe (and my joy to name) th'art now, to go. To William Roe. Ben
 Jonson. OAEL-1; OBS
Roe Deer. Ted Hughes. NoAM
Roebling, his life and mind reprieved enough. Raymond Henri. *Fr.* The
 Bridge from Brooklyn. EyDe
Roethke Plain. John Malcolm Brinnin. TAP
Rogation Days. Kenneth Rexroth. NaP
Roger and Dolly. Henry Carey. CoMu; NOEC; OxNR, *sl. diff. vers.*
Roger the Dog. Ted Hughes. RHPC
Roger Williams. Hezekiah Butterworth. PAH
Rogero's Song. George Canning , George Ellis and John Hookham Frere.
 Fr. The Rovers, I. NOEC
 (Song by Rogero.) FaBoNo
 (Song of One Eleven Years in Prison.) FiBHP
Róisín, have no sorrow for all that has happened you. Little Black Rose.
 Unknown, tr. by Thomas Kinsella. NOIV
Rokeby, *sels.* Sir Walter Scott.
 Allen-a-Dale. *Fr.* III. EnRP
 Brignall Banks. *Fr.* III. EnRP; OBEV
  (Edmund's Song.) PoRA
  (Outlaw, The.) GTBS; GTBS-P
 Man the Enemy of Man. *Fr.* III. WBLP
 Weary Lot Is Thine, A. *Fr.* III. CH
  (Rover, The.) GTBS; GTBS-P
  (Rover's Adieu [*or* Farewell], The.) NOBE; OBEV
  (Song: "Weary lot is thine, fair maid, A.") EnLoPo; OBNC
Rokeby Venus, The. Robert Conquest. MoP
Roll, *Alabama*, Roll. *Unknown.* OxBSS
Roll back, you fabulous animal. Carnal Knowledge. Gwen Harwood.
 CBAP
Roll Call: A Land of Old Folk and Children. Isaac J. Black. CNA
Roll forth, my song, like the rushing river. The Nameless One. James
 Clarence Mangan. ACP; BIrV; EnRP; NOIV; OBEV
Roll, Jordan, Roll. *Unknown.* AA; AH, *with music*
Roll on, sad world! Not Mercury or Mars. Frederick Goddard Tuckerman.
 Fr. Sonnets, II, xvii. QFR
Roll on the Ground. *Unknown.* AmFP
Roll on, thou ball, roll on! To the Terrestrial Globe. William Schwenck
 Gilbert. FaBoNo; NBLV; TrGrPo

Roll on, thou deep and dark blue ocean—roll! Byron. *Fr.* Childe
 Harold's Pilgrimage: The Ocean.
 (Roll On, Thou Deep and Dark Blue Ocean.) FaPON
 (To the Ocean.) GN; WGRP
Roll Out, O Song.) Frank Sewall. AA
Roll out ye drums, peal organs' loudest thunder. Elegy on Albert Edward
 the Peacemaker. *Unknown.* CoMu
Roll the Chariot. *Unknown.* AS
Roll the Cotton Down. *Unknown.* AmFP
Roll-Call. Nathaniel Graham Shepherd.
 AA; OHIP
Rolled down from some high mountain brow. Friendship. V. A.
 Zhukovsky, *tr. by* Alan Myers. AAA
Rolled off a side of mountains or. Serpent Country. A. R. Ammons.
 EOEF
Rolled over on Europe: the sharp dew frozen to stars. Stephen Spender.
 CMoP
Rolled umbrella on my wrist, The. Waterloo Bridge. Christopher
 Middleton. *Fr.* Herman Moon's Hourbook. NePoEA-2
Roller perched upon the wire, The. Driving Cattle to Casas Buenas. Roy
 Campbell. PeSA
Roller Rink. Betty Adcock. MT
Roller Skates. John Chipman Farrar. FaPON
Rollicking Mastodon, The. Arthur Macy. NA
Rolling and tossing out sparkles like roses. Night Landscape. Joan
 Aiken. DuDa
Rolling English Road, The. G. K. Chesterton. FaBoCh; NOBE; NOBL;
 OBEV; OBMV; OxBTC
Rolling from St. Patrick's, The. Burial of An Irish President. Austin
 Clarke. BIrV
Rolling Home. *Unknown.* OxBSS
Rolling John, *sel.* A. J. Wood.
 "Rolling John and night together." PoAu-2
Rolling John and night together. A. J. Wood. *Fr.* Rolling John.
 PoAu-2
Rolling Sailer, The. *Unknown.* OxBSS
Rolling the bamboo blind, I. Chokei, *tr. by* Lucien Stryk *and* Takashi
 Ikemoto. ZPCJ
Rolling the Lawn. William Empson. MoBrPo
Rolling Thunder. Phyllis Wolf. STE
Rollo says, "I can bring down rain." Rollo's Miracle. Paul Zimmer.
 GOYP
Rollo's Miracle. Paul Zimmer. GOYP
Rolly Trudum. *Unknown.* AmFP
Rom. Cap. 8 Ver. 19. Henry Vaughan. MeLP; OBS
Roma. Rutilius, *tr. fr. Latin by* Ezra Pound. CTC
Roma Aeterna. Adelaide Crapsey. QFR
Roman and Jew upon one level lie. In Galilee. Mary Frances Butts.
 AA
Roman Calendar, The. Benjamin Hall Kennedy. FaBoUs
Roman Earl, The. *Unknown, tr. fr. Irish by* Douglas Hyde.
 OBVE
Roman Epigram. Giovanni Giudici, *tr. fr. Italian by* Lawrence R. Smith.
 NItP
Roman Fountain. Louise Bogan. NoP; WPOW
Roman had an, A/ artist, a freedman. Marianne Moore. *Fr.* The Jerboa.
 CMoP
Roman History in Rhyme, *sel.* Edward B. Goodwin.
 "Aeneas built, in days of yore." FaBoUs
Roman in Libya, A. Ruth Evans. CN
Roman miniature urchin, A. Seeking an Explanation. Richard Emil
 Braun. NoAM
Roman Numerals. *Unknown.* *See* X shall stand for playmates Ten.
Roman Officer Writes, A. C. M. Doughty. *Fr.* The Dawn in Britain.
 FaBoTw
Roman Outposts. Derek Walcott. AnAn
Roman Presents. Martial, *tr. fr. Latin by* James Michie. OBCP
Roman Road, The. Thomas Hardy. BrPo; FaBoPP; GoJo; MoBrPo;
 NOBE
Roman Roman, A. Crescenzo del Monte, *tr. fr. Judeo-Romanesque by*
 Barbara Garvin. VWA
Roman Rooms. Paolo Volponi, *tr. fr. Italian by* Lawrence R. Smith.
 NItP
Roman soldiers come riding in full speed. "Sin-Killer" Griffin. *Fr.* The
 Man of Calvary. AmFP
Roman Stage, The. Lionel Johnson. BrPo; NOBVV
Roman Temple, A. Umar Abu Risha, *tr. fr. Arabic by* Issa Boullata *and*
 Thomas G. Ezzy. MAP
Roman Thank-You Letter, A. Martial, *tr. fr. Latin by* James Michie.
 OBCP
Roman threw us a road, a road, The. History. G. K. Chesterton. *Fr.*
 Songs of Education. OBSV

Roman Virgil [or Vergil], thou that singest Ilion's lofty temples robed in fire. To Virgil [or Vergil]. Tennyson. AWP; ChTr; GTBS-P; NoP; OAEL-2; PoEL-5

Roman Women, sel. Thomas Edward Brown.
"O Englishwoman on the Pincian." NOBVV; OBNC

Romance. Antonin Artaud, tr. fr. French by Michael Benedikt. POS

Romance. William Ernest Henley. Fr. In Hospital, XXI. BrPo; PAH

Romance, A. Chester Kallman. PoA

Romance. Poe. AmPP; AnAmPo; NAAL-1; OxBA

Romance. Gabriel Setoun. BoTP

Romance. Gerald Stern. CAPP

Romance. Robert Louis Stevenson. BLPL; BrPo; EBVV; GoTS; MoBrPo; OBEV; TrGrPo

Romance. Richard Stull. EOEF

Romance. Walter James Turner. CH; GoJo; MoBrPo; NOBE; OBMV; PoRA; TrGrPo

Romance, A. Bruce Weigl. NAmP

Romance of Citrus, The. Christy Sheffield Sanford. UL

Romance of Imprinting, The. Christy Sheffield Sanford. UL

Romance of the Living Corpse. Enrique Gonzáles Martínez, tr. fr. Spanish by Samuel Beckett. MexPo

Romance [or Romaunt] of the Rose, The, sels. Guillaume de Lorris and Jean de Meun, tr. fr. French.
Garden of Amour, The. Tr. by Chaucer. PoEL-1
"Short space my feet had traversed ere." Tr. by F. S. Ellis. OAEL-1
"There is no place in paradise." PBBP

Romance of the Swan's Nest. Elizabeth Barrett Browning. GN

Romance, who loves to nod and sing. Romance. Poe. AmPP; AnAmPo; NAAL-1; OxBA
(Introduction: "Romance, who loves to nod and sing.") NOBA

Romancer, far more coy than that coy sex. Hawthorne. Amos Bronson Alcott. AA

Romans Angry about the Inner World. Robert Bly. NOBA

Romans in England awhile did sway, The. The Chapter of Kings. John Collins. FaBoUs

Romans, rheumatic, gouty, came. La Condition Botanique. Anthony Hecht. NePoEA

Romantic. George Garrett. HoPM

Romantic to Burlesque. Byron. Fr. Don Juan, IV. EnRP; FiP; OAEL-2

Rome. Arthur Hugh Clough. See Amours de Voyage: Rome disappoints me still; but I shrink and adapt myself to it.

Rome. James Vincent Cunningham, after the Latin of Janus Vitalis Panormitanus. OBVE

Rome. Thomas Hardy. MoAB

Rome. Joachim du Bellay, tr. fr. French by Ezra Pound. AWP

Rome Araieth Stilico in Vesture of the Consul. Claudian, tr. fr. Latin by Osbern Bokenham. Fr. De Consulatu Stilichonis. OxBLMV

Rome: Building a New Street in the Ancient Quarter. Thomas Hardy. Son

Rome by Metella's Tomb. Byron. Fr. Childe Harold's Pilgrimage, IV. FaBoPP

Rome, Conqueror, Conquered. Joshua Sylvester. FaBoEE

Rome disappoints me much,—St. Peter's, perhaps, in especial. Rome ("Rome disappoints me much"). Arthur Hugh Clough. Fr. Amours de Voyage, Canto I, i. FaBoPP

Rome disappoints me still; but I shrink and adapt myself to it. Arthur Hugh Clough. Fr. Amours de Voyage, Canto I, ii. EBVV; OBTV (Rome.) FaBoPP

Rome never looks where she treads. A Pict Song. Kipling. Fr. Puck of Pook's Hill. NoAM

Rome Once Alone. Clark Coolidge. UL

Rome Remember. Sidney Keyes. MoAB

Rome ("Rome disappoints me much"). Arthur Hugh Clough. Fr. Amours de Voyage, Canto I, i. FaBoPP

Rome Sunday June 1960. John Hewitt. TIRV

Rome ("The City which thou seest no other deem"). Milton. Fr. Paradise Regained, bk. IV, ll. 44–108. OBS

Romeo and Juliet. H. Phelps Putnam. ErPo

Romeo and Juliet, sels. Shakespeare.
"Even or odd, of all days in the year." Fr. I, iii. SCV
"For here lies Juliet, and her beauty makes." Fr. V, iii. FaFP
(Thus with a Kiss I Die.) TrGrPo
"How oft when men are at the point of death." DL
(Romeo's Last Words.) FiP
Frost on the Flower. Fr. IV, v. FaBoRV
"Gallop apace, you fiery-footed steeds." Fr. III, ii. GBL
He Jests at Scars [That Never Felt a Wound]. Fr. II, ii. LiTB
(Living Juliet, The.) TrGrPo, II, i.
"If I profane with my unworthiest hand." Fr. I, v. Son; SoSe
Music's Silver Sound. Fr. IV, v. GN
"O my love, my wife!" Fr. V, iii. OBD

"O [or Oh], then, I see Queen Mab hath been with you." Fr. I, iv. WSC
(Mercutio's Queen Mab Speech.) LiTB
(Queen Mab.) FaPON; FiP
"She is the fairies' midwife, and she comes." RB
(Mercutio Describes Queen Mab.) TrGrPo

Romeo and Juliet in Central Park. Rose Ausländer, tr. fr. German by Beth Bjorklund. CoAuP

Romeo's Last Words. Shakespeare. See Romeo and Juliet: For here lies Juliet, and her beauty makes.

Rome's guns are spiked; and they'll stay so. Of Rome. Herman Melville. Fr. Clarel. OxBA

Romira, stay. The Call. John Hall. MeLP; MePo; OBS

Romp. Dave Etter. WeW

Ron Endaway, shepherd of the hills at Malvern, looked very sheepish. Come Live with Me. Naomi Marks. BXAP

Ron Mason. Hone Tuwhare. PeNZ

Ronald Wyn. Robert Bagg. TwCP

Ronas Hill. Hamish Brown. PoSH

Rondeau: "By two black eyes my heart was won." Unknown. FaBoCo

Rondeau: "Help me to seek, for I lost it here." Sir Thomas Wyatt. See Help Me to Seek.

Rondeau, A: "Jenny kissed me when we met." Leigh Hunt. See Jenny Kiss'd [or Kissed] Me.

Rondeau: "Lord, I'm done for: now Margot." Vincent Voiture, tr. by William Jay Smith. CT; FiBHP

Rondeau: "What no, perdy! ye may be sure!" Sir Thomas Wyatt. AAS; OBSC

Rondeau after a Transatlantic Telephone Call. Marilyn Hacker. NoAM; SM

Rondeau for You. Mário de Andrade, tr. fr. Portuguese by John Nist. TTY

Rondeau of My Life's Walk. A. Leyeles, tr. fr. Yiddish by Benjamin and Barbara Harshav. AYP

Rondeau of the Little Horses. Manuel Bandeira, tr. fr. Portuguese by Richard Wilbur. ATCBP

Rondel: "Beautiful snow falls on a bed, A." Philip Dacey. SM

Rondel: "Behold the works of William Morris." Unknown. BXAP; Par

Rondel: "Beside the idle summer sea." William Ernest Henley. OBNC

Rondel: "Good-by, the tears are in my eyes." Villon, tr. by Andrew Lang. AWP

Rondel: "Kissing her hair, I sat against her feet." Swinburne. BLPL; FaBoBe

Rondel: "Love, love, what wilt thou with this heart of mine?" Jean Froissart, tr. by Longfellow. AWP

Rondel: "Now that I am fifty-six." Muriel Rukeyser. FF

Rondel: "Strengthen, my Love, this castle of my heart." Charles d'Orléans, tr. by Andrew Lang. AWP

Rondel: "World is taking off her clothes, The." X. J. Kennedy. SM

Rondel of Luve [or Love], A. Alexander Scott. BoLoP; OBEV; OxBS

Rondel of Merciless Beauty, A. Chaucer. See Merciles[s] Beaute [or Beautée or Beauty]: Merciless Beauty.

Röntgen Photograph. Elisabeth Eybers, tr. fr. Afrikaans by Jack Cope, Uys Krige and Ruth Miller. PeSA

Roof, The. Jan Hanlo, tr. fr. Dutch by James S. Holmes. DuIn

Roof. Ishigaki Rin, tr. fr. Japanese by Hiroaki Sato. FCEI

Roof above "Jesus loves you" is loaded, The. Satellites. Gary Lenhart. UL

Roof comes down on Maruti's head, The. Heart of Ruin. Arun Kolatkar. UAS

Roof Garden, The. Howard Moss. MAT

Roof it has a lazy time, The. The Lazy Roof. Gelett Burgess. NA

Roof of the World, The. Michael Dennis Browne. AmPA

Roof repairman steps on dead leaves, The. Buson, tr. fr. Japanese by Hiroaki Sato. Fr. Eighty-seven Hokku. FCEI

Roof-tops, roof-tops, what do you cover? City Roofs. Charles Hanson Towne. BLPA

Roofs. Joyce Kilmer. BLPL; PoLF

Roofs are shining from the rain, The. April. Sara Teasdale. FaPON; PDV

Roofs of cars were crusted thick with frost, The. Citizen. Chris Wallace-Crabbe. CBAP

Roofs over the shops, The. Christmas Eve. Patricia Beer. OBCP

Roofs sizzle at the waking touch, The. Raindrum. Niyi Osundare. UAS

Rooftop, The. Thom Gunn. NoP

Roofwalker, The. Adrienne Rich. CoAP; NAAL-2; PPP

Rook he sells feathers, yet he still doth cry. Upon Rook: Epigram. Robert Herrick. CaPo

Rookery at Sunrise, The. "Fiona Macleod." *Fr.* Transcripts from Nature. FM

Rookhope Ryde ("Rookhope stands in a pleasant place"). *Unknown.* ESPB

Rooks, The. Jane Euphemia Browne. OxBChV

Rooks. Charles Hamilton Sorley. MoBrPo

Rooks, The. *Unknown.* GBP; OxNR

Rooks are alive, The. What the Weather Does. *Unknown.* BoTP

Rooks are building on the trees, The. The Rooks. Jane Euphemia Browne. OxBChV

Room, The. Conrad Aiken. LiTM; MoAmPo; NOBA

Room. Robert Finch. MoCV

Room, The. De Leon Harrison. PoBA

Room, The. Elizabeth Jennings. NePoEA-2

Room. Shirley Kaufman. NMM

Room, The. W. S. Merwin. NaP; NOBA

Room, The. Vladimir Nabokov. NYBP

Room, The. Gregory Orr. GeTw

Room, The. Lawrence Raab. BLA

Room, The. William Soutar. EBEV

Room. Ruth Stone. BoWoP

Room, The. Francis Webb. *Fr.* Leichhardt in Theatre. PoAu-2

Room, A. Sa'di Yusuf, *tr. fr. Arabic by* Abdullah al-Udhari. MPAW

Room a dying poet took, The. The Room. Vladimir Nabokov. NYBP

Room above the Square, The. Stephen Spender. NOBE

Room above the White Rose, The. Joseph Stroud. NPGG

Room after room/ I hunt the house through. Love in a Life. Robert Browning. InvP; NOBE; NOBVV; OBNC

Room after room, table after table. Public Library. Candace Thurber Stevenson. GoYe

Room beneath the Rafters, The. Ella Wheeler Wilcox. PWR

Room fills up with smoke, The. Their faces are. Paradiso Terrestre. Ian Wedde. *Fr.* Earthly: Sonnets for Carlos, 3. ATNZ

Room for a Jovial Tinker: Old Brass to Mend. *Unknown.* CoMu; OxBB

Room for a Soldier! lay him in the clover. Dirge for One Who Fell in Battle [*or* Dirge]. Thomas William Parsons. AA; GN; PAH

"Room for the leper! Room!" and as he came. The Leper. Nathaniel Parker Willis. WGRP

Room I Once Knew, A. Henry Birnbaum. GoYe

Room in Space. René Char, *tr. fr. French by* W. S. Merwin. RHTwFP

Room in the Villa, A. William Jay Smith. NYBP

Room is already white, The. Trim it in blue. Life in the City: In Memoriam Edward Gibbon. Philip Whalen. PoM

Room is full of gold, The. Jason. Anthony Hecht. DiL

Room is sparsely furnished, The. Thrall. Carolyn Kizer. ER

Room must be warmer than, The. How the Invalids Make Love. Susan Feldman. AmPA

Room on a Garden, A. Wallace Stevens. NoP

Room Poems. Eli Bachar, *tr. fr. Hebrew by* Jeremy Garber. VWA

Room, room for a blade of the town. The Bully. *At. to* John Wilmot, 2nd Earl of Rochester *and to* Thomas D'Urfey. InvP
(Song: Noble Name of Spark, The.) SeCePo

Room! room! make room for the bouncing belly. Hymn to Comus. Ben Jonson. *Fr.* Pleasure Reconciled to Virtue. OAEL-1, *complete.*
(Hymn: "Room! room! make room for the bouncing belly.") NAEL-1
(Hymn to Comus.) ElL; SeCePo
(Hymn to the Belly.) SeCePo

Room was a, The/ red glow. We Dance Like Ella Riffs. Carolyn M. Rodgers. CNA; PoBA

Room was dark, The. Something. The Vampire. Gregory Orr. VVA

Room was divided by a curtain, The. The Tailor's Wedding. Louis Simpson. NNaP

Room was suddenly rich and the great bay-window was, The. Snow. Louis MacNeice. CIP; CMoP; FaBCIP; FaBoMo; FPL; LiTM; MoP; NoAM; NOBE; OPOP; OxBSP; OxBTC

Room where someone, A. Avenue Y. Anita Barrows. VWA

Rooms. Charlotte Mew. PBWP

Room's Width, The. Elizabeth Stuart Phelps Ward. AA

Roosevelt and the Antinoe, The, sel. Edwin John Pratt. Burial at Sea. CaP

Rooster, The. Li Nan, *tr. fr. Chinese by* Dominic Cheung. IFON

Rooster crows like someone being sick, The. City Girl in the Country. Elizabeth Smither. PeNZ

Roosters. Elizabeth Bishop. LiTM

Roosters. Elizabeth J. Coatsworth. SO

Roosters Will Crow, The. Cecília Meireles, *tr. fr. Portuguese by* John Nist *and* Yolanda Leite. PBWP

Root. Miklós Radnóti, *tr. fr. Hungarian.* VWA, *tr. by* Steven Polgar, Stephen Berg *and* S. J. Marks

Root becomes him, the road ruts, The. Self-Portrait in 2035. Charles Wright. LCAP

Root Cellar. Theodore Roethke. AmPP; AnAmPo; BoNaP; HeIP; InPK; NoP; PPP

Root, Hog, or Die. *Unknown.* AmFP

Roots. Lucille Clifton. CAPP

Roots. Louis Ginsberg. TrJP

Roots. Seymour Mayne. NOBC

Roots and Branches. Robert Duncan. VGW

Roots around your soul and eyes, The. Sweating It Out on Winding Stair Mountain. Jim Barnes. CDW

Roots of Blue Bells. Nia Francisco. HATNAP

Roots of mankind are tangled in my hair, The. Epitaph. Wendy Rose. CDW

Rope, The. Tania Van Zyl. PeSA

Rope for Harry Fat, A. James Keir Baxter. MoBS

Ropero, so sad and so forlorn. El Ropero. Antonio di Montorio. TrJP

Ropes, pull them tight!, The. Fishermen's Song. *Unknown, tr. by* Margaret Orbell. PeNZ

Rory and Liam are dead and gone. In Memoriam. Padraig de Brun. WTO

Rosa Luxembourg. Eileen Duggan. PeNZ

Rosa Mystica. Gerard Manley Hopkins. ACP

Rosabelle. Sir Walter Scott. *Fr.* The Lay of the Last Minstrel, VI. BeLS; GTBS; GTBS-P
(Harold's Song: Rosabelle.) EnRP

Rosader's Sonnet. Thomas Lodge. *Fr.* Rosalynde; or Euphues' Golden Legacy. OBSC

Rosalie. Washington Allston. AA

Rosalind [*or* Rosalynde]. Thomas Lodge. *See* Rosalynde; or Euphues' Golden Legacy: Rosaline.

Rosalind, in a negligee. Early Unfinished Sketch. Austin Clarke. ErPo

Rosaline. Thomas Lodge. *Fr.* Rosalynde; or Euphues' Golden Legacy. GTBS; GTBS-P; LiTB; OBEV
(Rosalind [*or* Rosalynde].) ElL; TrGrPo
(Rosalind's Description.) OBSC

Rosalynde; or Euphues' Golden Legacy, *sels.* Thomas Lodge.
Fancy, A. ElL; OBSC
(Love's Protestation.) ACP
Montanus' Sonnet. PoEL-2
Rosader's Sonnet. OBSC
Rosalind's [*or* Rosalynd's] Madrigal[l]. ElL; InvP; NOBE; NoP; OBEV; OBSC; PoEL-2; SeCePo; TrGrPo
Rosaline. GTBS; GTBS-P; LiTB; OBEV
(Rosalind [*or* Rosalynde].) ElL; TrGrPo
(Rosalind's Description.) OBSC

Rosamond's Appeal. Samuel Daniel. *Fr.* The Complaint of Rosamond. OBSC

Rosane. Ida Hahn-Hahn, *tr. fr. German by* Susan L. Cocalis. DMG

Rosario, en la Cima. Angela de Hoyos. ER

Rosary, The. Robert Cameron Rogers. AA; FaBoBe; WBLP

Rosciad, The, *sel.* Charles Churchill.
Character of a Critic. NOEC

Rose, The. William Browne. *Fr.* Visions. CH; OBEV

Rose, The/ was not searching for the sunrise. Casida of the Rose. Federico García Lorca, *tr. by* Robert Bly. NU

Rose, A. Sir Richard Fanshawe, *after the Italian of* Giovanni Battista Guarini. *Fr.* Il Pastor Fido. OBEV; OBS; PoEL-2; SeCePo
(Rose of Life, The.) AWP

Rose, The. Mary R. Gaumond. TSM

Rose, The. Goethe, *tr. fr. German by* James Clarence Mangan. AWP

Rose, The. William Hammond. OBS

Rose, The. George Herbert. LiTB; PoEL-2

Rose, The. Thomas Howell. ElL; OBSC

Rose. Kathleen Raine. WPE

Rose, The. Thomas Lodge. *Fr.* The Life and Death of William Longbeard. OBSC
(Fancy, A.) ElL

Rose, The. Theodore Roethke. NOBA; NYBP

Rose, The. Pierre de Ronsard, *tr. fr. French by* Andrew Lang. AWP

Rose, The. William Carlos Williams. NOBA

Rose aloft in sunny air, The. Rose and Root. John James Piatt. AA

Rose and a Baby Ruth, A. Shelby Stephenson. SoTCo

Rose and Cushie. Charles Tennyson Turner. Mes

Rose and gold and violet, The. The Afterglow. Henrietta Cordelia Ray. CBWP-3

Rose and grape, pear and bean. *Unknown, tr. by* Willis Barnstone. BoWoP

Rose and Root. John James Piatt. AA

Rose and the Gauntlet, The. John Wilson. BeLS

Rose and the lily, the moon and the dove, The. Die Rose, die Lilie, die Taube, die Sonne. Heine, *tr. by* Richard Garnett. AWP

(Love's Resume.) TrJP, *tr. by* "J. F. C."

(Rose and the lily, the moon and the dove, The.) NAWM-2, *tr. by* P. G. L. Webb

Rose and the Thorn, The. Paul Hamilton Hayne. AA; FaBoBe

Rose-apple is in fruit, The. Show Me the Way. *Unknown, tr. by* U Win Pe. PBWP

Rose, as fair as ever saw the north, A. The Rose. William Browne. *Fr.* Visions. CH; OBEV

Rose Aylmer. Walter Savage Landor. AWP; BoLoP; CH; ELP; EnLoPo; EnRP; FaFP; GBL; HAP; HeIP; HoPM; LiTB; NAEL-2; NOBE; NoP; OAEL-2; OBEV; OBNC; PoEL-4; TEP; TrGrPo; UnPo; WeW

Rose-Bud, The. William Broome. OBEV

Rose, but one, none other rose had I, A. Tennyson. *Fr.* Idylls of the King: Pelleas and Ettarre. PoEL-5

Rose-cheeked [*or* cheekt] Laura, Come. Thomas Campion. EnLoPo; InPK; InPS; InvP; NAEL-1; NoP; OAEL-1; PoE; PoEL-2; TrGrPo (Laura.) EIL; NOBE; OBEV; OBSC; SeCePo; UnS ("Rose-cheekt Lawra, come.") AAS

Rose clings to her skull, A. Isis and the Animals: I. Hugo Claus, *tr. by* Theo Hermans. DuIn

Rose Connoley. *Unknown.* AmFP

Rose, die Lilie, die Taube, die Sonne, Die. Heine, *tr. fr. German by* Richard Garnett. AWP

Rose Family, The. Robert Frost. NIP; OBAL; OBCA; SoSe

Rose for a young head, A. The Watcher. James Stephens. MoBrPo; OBEV

Rose from al-Mutanabbi's Blood, A, *sel.* Abd-Allah al-Baraduni, *tr. fr. Arabic by* Diana Der Hovanessian *and* Sharif Elmusa. "His fame stole is real name." MAP

Rose-Geranium, The, *sels.* Eilean Ni Chuilleanain. CIP "A l'usage de M. et Mme. van Gramberen'." *Fr.* IV. "Precious dry rose-geranium smell, The." *Fr.* V.

Rose Growing into the House, The. Gibbons Ruark. InPK

Rose, harsh rose. Sea Rose. Hilda Doolittle ("H. D."). FaBoMo; HeIP; NoAM; NoP

Rose in October, A. James Whitcomb Riley. OBAL

Rose in the Afternoon. Jenny Joseph. BrRo

Rose in the breast. On Waking. Alida Carey Gulick. GoYe

Rose in the Garden. *Unknown.* AmFP

"Rose is a mystery, The"—where is it found? Rosa Mystica. Gerard Manley Hopkins. ACP

Rose is a rose, The. The Rose Family. Robert Frost. NIP; OBAL; OBCA; SoSe

Rose is not the rose unless thou see, The. Hafiz, *tr. fr. Persian by* Richard Le Gallienne. *Fr.* Odes, III. AWP

Rose is red, the grass is green, The. *Unknown.* OxNR

Rose is red, the rose is white, The. *Unknown.* OxNR

Rose is red, the violet's blue, The. *Unknown.* OxNR

"Rose, it is a royal flower, The." The Peace of the Roses. Thomas Philipps. ACP

Rose-Leaves ("Rose kissed me today."), *sel.* Austin Dobson. CenHV Urceus Exit. OBEV

Rose of Eden, The. Susan K. Phillips. BeLS

Rose of England, The. *Unknown.* ESPB

Rose of Life, The. Sir Richard Fanshawe, *after the Italian of* Giovanni Battista Guarini. *See* Il Pastor Fido: Rose, A.

Rose of Marble and the Rose of Iron, The. Robert Desnos, *tr. fr. French by* Michael Benedikt. POS

Rose of Sharon, The/ I lost in the tortured night. For the New Union Dead in Alabama. Edward Dorn. PoM

Rose of Stars, The. George Edward Woodberry. *Fr.* Wild Eden, IX. AA

Rose of that Garland! fairest and sweetest. To the Most Beautiful Lady, the Lady Bridget Manners. Barnabe Barnes. EnLoPo

Rose of the World, The. John Masefield. PoRA

Rose of the World, The. W. B. Yeats. BrPo; CMoP; MoAB; MoBrPo; NAEL-2

Rose, Oh Pure Contradiction. Rainer Maria Rilke, *tr. fr. German by* Stephen Mitchell. TTTS

Rose on My Cake, The. Karla Kuskin. ILY

Rose Red's hair is brown as fur. An Embroidery. Denise Levertov. NMM; NU

Rose Still Grows beyond the Wall, The. A. L. Frink. BLPA

Rose That Bore Jesu, The. *Unknown.* OxBLMV

Rose the Red and White Lil[l]y. *Unknown.* ESPB; OxBB

Rose Thieves, The. Vasco Popa, *tr. fr. Serbo-Croatian by* Anne Pennington. *Fr.* Games. RB

Rose to the roseburst break of day. The Cliff Rose. Ernest Fewster. CaP

Rose Tree, The. W. B. Yeats. CMoP; ELP; FaBoPV; OBMV

Rose was sick and smiling died, The. The Funeral Rites of the Rose. Robert Herrick. CaPo; OBEV

Roseberry to his lady says. Supper Is Na Ready. Burns. GBP

Rosebud. Jon Anderson. MAYP

Rosebud Morales, my friend. Pentecost. Ai. GeTw

Roselva says the only thing that doesn't change. Trying to Name What Doesn't Change. Naomi Shihab Nye. NAmP

Rosemary Lane. *Unknown.* OBET

Rosemary, Rosemary, let down your hair. A Nonsense Song. Stephen Vincent Benét. OBAL

Rosemary Spray, The. Luis de Góngora y Argote, *tr. fr. Spanish by* E. Churton. AWP

Rosemonde. Guillaume Apollinaire, *tr. fr. French by* Michael Benedikt. POS

Roses. Thomas Campion. *Fr.* Lord Hay's Mask. OBSC

Roses. George Eliot. BoTP

Roses. Pierre de Ronsard, *tr. fr. French by* Andrew Lang. AWP

Roses. Thomas Stanley, *after the Greek of* Anacreon. AWP

Roses and butterflies snared on a fan. A Painted Fan. Ellen Louise Chandler. AA

Roses and Revolutions. Dudley Randall. BPo; CNA; PoBA; TAP

Roses are red. Mother Goose. OxNR

Roses are red, diddle diddle, lavender's blue. The Lady's Song in Leap Year. *Unknown.* GBP

Roses at first were white. How Roses Came Red. Robert Herrick. CaPo; SoSe

Rose's crimson stain, A. Roses of Memory. A. C. Gordon. AA

Rose's Cup, The. Frank Dempster Sherman. AA

Roses every one were red, The. Spleen. John Gray. NOBVV

Roses in December. G. A. Studdert-Kennedy. BLPA

Roses (Love's delight) let's join. Roses. Thomas Stanley, *after the Greek of* Anacreon. AWP

Roses of Memory. A. C. Gordon. AA

Roses of Sa'adi, The. Marceline Desbordes-Valmore, *tr. fr. French.* BoWoP, *tr. by* Barbara Howes; WPOW, *tr. by* Deirdre Lashgari

Roses of yesteryear, The. At Twilight. Peyton Van Rensselaer. AA

Roses on the Breakfast Table. D. H. Lawrence. BrPo

Roses Only. Marianne Moore. LiTM

Roses Red. Arno Holz, *tr. fr. German by* Jethro Bithell. AWP

Roses red upon my neighbor's vine, The. My Neighbor's Roses. Abraham L. Gruber. BLPA

Roses, rose-red and white, and green. Alleluya. Rubén Darío, *tr. by* Lysander Kemp. TTY

Roses, roses, roses. June. Henrietta Cordelia Ray. CBWP-3

Rose's Scent, The. *Unknown. See* All Night by the Rose.

Roses, their sharp spines being gone. Bridal Song, A ("Roses, their sharp spines being gone"). John Fletcher *and* Shakespeare. *Fr.* The Two Noble Kinsmen, I, i. EIL; NOBE; OBSC

Roses with the scent bred out. In Lieu. Louis MacNeice. CMoP

Rosh Pina. Dovid Knut, *tr. fr. Russian.* VWA, *tr. by* Daniel Weissbort

Rosie-fingerd morne, no sooner shone, The. The Sacrifice. Homer, *tr. fr. Greek by* George Chapman. *Fr.* Odyssey, III. OBS

Rosie Nell. *Unknown.* AS

Rosin, tell me from the heart. Domna H., *tr. by* Meg Bogin. WT

Roslin and Hawthornden. Henry van Dyke. AA

Ross's Poems, *sels.* Geoffrey Lehmann. CBAP
   Auntie Bridge and Uncle Pat.
   I Was Born at a Place of Pines.
   Music Is Unevennesses.
   My Father's a Still Day.
   Some of Our Koorawatha Saints.
   There Are Some Lusty Voices Singing.

Rostov. G. S. Fraser. WaP

Rosy Apple, Lemon or Pear. *Unknown.* CH

Rosy Bosom'd Hours, The. Coventry Patmore. EnLoPo; NOBVV

Rosy Days Are Numbered, The. Moses Ibn Ezra, *tr. fr. Hebrew by* Solomon Solis-Cohen. *Fr.* Wine-Songs. TrJP

Rosy shield upon its back, A. The Dead Crab. Andrew Young. FaBoTw; FM; OBD; RB

Rotation. Julian Bond. FF

Rothiemurchus. Colin Lamont. PoSH

Rotten bale smouldering on a bonfire, A. The Squirrel. Anthony Howell. NPo

Rou-cou spoke the dove. Song of Fixed Accord. Wallace Stevens. InPS; NePoAm

Rouen. May Wedderburn Cannan. NAEL-2; OBWP; OxBTC

Rouge Bouquet. Joyce Kilmer. PAH

Rouge vendors come. Shiba Sonome, *tr. fr. Japanese by* Hiroaki Sato. *Fr.* Fifteen Hokku. FCEI

Rough fir, hauled from the hills. The Making of the Cross. William Everson. VGW

Rough Passage, *sel.* Rajagopal Parthasarathy.
   Exile: 2. UAS

Rough pasture where the blackberries grow! A Pasture. Frederic Lawrence Knowles. AA

Rough Ridge. Yüan Mei, *tr. fr. Chinese by* Jonathan Chaves. CoBLCP

Rough wind, that moanest loud. Shelley. ChTr; EnRP; NAEL-2; NOBE; PoRA; SoSe; TEP; TrGrPo; WiR

Rough Winds Do Shake. Louis Simpson. ErPo

Roughly estimated ones, who do not sort well, The. The Monuments of Hiroshima. Dennis Joseph Enright. OxBSP

Roughly figured, this man of moderate habits. Life Cycle of Common Man. Howard Nemerov. NBLV; NIP

Roughly-silvered leaves that are the snow. A Song from Armenia. Geoffrey Hill. FaBoMo

Roughly, so to say, you know. John William Mackail. *Fr.* Balliol Rhymes. CenHV

Round. Rachel Boimwall, *tr. fr. Yiddish by* Gabriel Preil *and* Howard Schwartz. VWA

Round, The: "Skunk cabbage, bloodroot." Philip Booth. BoNaP; GrPl

Round: "Wondrous life!" cried Marvell at Appleton House." Weldon Kees. CoAP; NaP

Round, A. *Unknown. See* Hey Nonny No!

Round a cleft in the cliffs to come upon. Venus of the Salty Shell. Denis Devlin. BlrV; NOIV

Round about in a fair ring-a. *Unknown.* BoTP

Round about, little ones. Robin Good-Fellow's Song: "Round about, little ones." *Unknown. Fr.* Robin Goodfellow, *pt.* II. EIL

Round about Me. Sappho, *tr. fr. Greek by* William Ellery Leonard. AWP

Round about, round about,/ Catch a wee mouse. *Unknown.* OxNR

Round about, round about,/ maggotty pie. *Unknown.* OxNR; PBBP

Round about, round about/ In a fair ring-a. The Elves' Dance. *At. to* John Lyly *and to* Thomas Ravenscroft. *Fr.* The Mayde's Metamorphosis. CH; FaPON

Round about, round about, here sits the hare. *Unknown.* OxNR

Round about the cauldron go! E. O. Parrott. BXAP

Round about the rosebush. *Unknown.* OxNR

Round about there/ Sat a little hare. *Unknown.* OxNR

Round among the quiet graves. Love's Resurrection Day. Louise Chandler Moulton. AA

Round and round. Private Transport. Adrian Mitchell. FaBoEE

Round and round our lavatory. The Thinker. Anthony Delius. PeSA

Round and round the garden. *Unknown.* OxNR

Round and round the rugged rock. *Unknown.* OxNR

Round and round time turns. Tamekane, *tr. by* Steven D. Carter. WFTW

Round and sad-eyed man puffed cigars as if, The. Song of the Round Man. Michael Palmer. NPGG

Round Barrow, The. Andrew Young. SeCePo

Round blazing sun, The. What She Said, Thinking of Him Crossing the Wilderness Alone. Auvaiyar, *tr. by* A. K. Ramanujan. PLW

Round dance of day has gone. Sitting Alone in Tulsa Three A.M. Lance Henson. VoR

Round of meadows am a-ringing. Massa's in de Cold Cold Ground. Stephen Collins Foster. AA

Round-head round-eyed Sebastian. Photograph of a Baby. Charles Brasch. ATNZ

Round her red garland and her golden hair. Of His Last Sight of Fiammetta. Boccaccio, *tr. fr. Italian by* Dante Gabriel Rossetti. *Fr.* Sonnets. AWP

Round moon hangs like a yellow lantern in the trees, The. The Ancient Thought. Watson Kerr. WGRP

Round of the Sidewalks. Benjamin Péret, *tr. fr. French by* James Laughlin. POS

Round, plain, Limerick boldness in her glance, The. A Founder of the Nation. Kevin Ireland. ATNZ

Round Quebec's embattled walls. Montgomery at Quebec. Clinton Scollard. PAH

Round Song, A. Rhyll McMaster. CBAP

Round Table, The. Robert Mannyng. ACP

Round table, holding eight, A. Recipe for a Pleasant Dinner-Party. *Unknown.* FaBoUs

Round the cape of a sudden came the sea. Parting at Morning. Robert Browning. AWP; FaBV; FF; FiP; HeIP; InPS; MOS; NAEL-2; NOBE; OBEV; OBNC; OxBSP; SoSe; UnPo; WiR

Round the house were lilacs and strawberries. Twenty Years Ago. D. H. Lawrence. Mes

Round the Year. Coventry Patmore. BoTP
(Year, The.) EBVV

Round Trip. Stan Rice. NPGG

Round Valley Reflections. William Oandasan. STE

Roundabout Turn, A. Robert E. Charles. MoShBr

"Rounded Catalogue Divine Complete, The." Walt Whitman. NAAL-1

Roundel: "Now welcom[e], somer, with thy sunne [*or* sonne] softe." Chaucer. *See* Parlement of Foules, The: Now Welcom[e], Somer [*or* Summer].

Roundel in the Rain. *Unknown.* FiBHP

Roundelay, A: "It fell upon a holy eve." Spenser. *See* Shepheardes [*or* Shepeards *or* Shepherd's] Calender, The: August.

Roundelay, A: "Tell me, thou skilful shepherd's swain." Michael Drayton. *Fr.* The Shepherd's Garland, Eclogue IX (1606 ed.). EIL

Roundhouse in Cheyenne is filled every night, The. The Dreary Black Hills. *Unknown.* AS

Roundhouse Voices, The. Dave Smith. GeTw; MAYP; MT; NoAM

Rounding a slip of the marsh, the boat skids. Looking for the Melungeon. Dave Smith. HCAP

Rounding the Cape. Roy Campbell. PeSA

Rounding the Horn. John Masefield. *Fr.* Dauber, VI. MoAB; MoBrPo

Rounding the Horn. *Unknown.* OxBSS

Rouse, Britons! at length. A New Ballad. *Unknown.* PAH

Rouse every generous, thoughtful mind. The Blasted Herb. Meshech Weare. PAH

Rouse for Stevens, The. Theodore Roethke. OBAL

Rousecastle. David Wright. MoBS

Rousing Canoe Song, The. Hermia Harris Fraser. CaP

Rousing to rein his pad's head back. Geoffrey Taylor. NeIP

Rousseau in His Day. Donald Davie. DiPo

Rousseau—Voltaire—our Gibbon—and De Staël. Sonnet to Lake Leman. Byron. Son

Rout of San Romano, The. Jon Manchip White. NePoEA

Route. Philippe Soupault, *tr. fr. French by* Michael Benedikt. POS

Route of evanescence, A. Emily Dickinson. NAAL-1; NoP; PoEL-5; SoSe

Routes. Peter Everwine. NNaP

Routine. Arthur Guiterman. RHPC

Rover, The. Sir Walter Scott. *See* Rokeby: Weary Lot Is Thine, A.

Rover. William Stafford. TDD

Rover killed the goat. Brave Rover. Max Beerbohm. NBLV

Rovers, The, *sel.* George Canning , George Ellis *and* John Hookham Frere.
  Rogero's Song. *Fr.* I. NOEC
  (Song by Rogero.) FaBoNo
  (Song of One Eleven Years in Prison.) FiBHP

Rover's Adieu [*or* Farewell], The. Sir Walter Scott. *See* Rokeby: Weary Lot Is Thine, A.

Rover's Song, A. Bliss Carman. AnAmPo

Roving breezes come and go, the reed-beds sweep and sway, The. The Travelling Post Office. Andrew Barton Paterson. CBAP

Roving Gambler, The. *Unknown.* AS

Roving Shanty Boy, The. *Unknown.* AmFP

Row after row. The Mule. Boynton Merrill, Jr.. CRP

Row after row with strict impunity. Ode to the Confederate Dead. Allen Tate. AiP; FaBoMo; HeIP; LiTA; LiTM; MoAB; MoAmPo; MoP; NAAL-2; NoAM; NOBA; NoP; OBD, *ll.* 1-9; OBWP; OxBA; PrIm; TAP; UnPo; ViBoPo

Row gently here, my gondolier; so softly wake the tide. Venetian Air. Thomas Moore. OxBSP

Row of pearls, A. Seeds. James Reeves. TSS

Row of Stalls, A, *sel.* Raymond Knister.
  Nell. NOBC; OBCV

Row of willow trees, almost green for the spring, A. Two Fish by a Willow Embankment. Hsü Wei, *tr. by* Jonathan Chaves. CoBLCP

Row, row, row your boat. *Unknown.* OxNR

Row us out from Desenzano, to your Sirmione row! "Frater Ave atque Vale." Tennyson. ChTr; EBVV; FaBoPP; GTBS-P; GTBS-P; HAP; InPS; NAEL-2; NoP; OBTV; OxBSP

Rowan, The. Violet Jacob. PoSH

Rowan County Crew, The. *At. to* James William Day. AmFP

Rowan like a lip-sticked girl, A. Seamus Heaney. IPY

Rowers, The. Laura Benét. GoYe

Rowing. Anne Sexton. BoWoP; CAPP

Rowing Early. John Peck. SM

Rowing, I reach'd a rock—the sea was low. Gerard Manley Hopkins. *Fr.* A Vision of the Mermaids. ChTr

Rowland's Rhyme. Michael Drayton. *Fr.* The Shepherd's Garland, Eclogue II (1606 ed.). OBSC

Rows of cells are unroofed, The. The Old Prison. Judith Wright. PoAu-2

Rows of Cold Trees, The. Yvor Winters. NOBA

Roxy's. Patrick Conrad, *tr. fr. Dutch by* Peter Nijmeijer. DuIn

Roy Bean. *Unknown.* AnAmPo; BeLS; OBAL

Royal Adventurer, The. Philip Freneau. PAH

Royal air comes from the east: hundreds of hard battles, A. Chang Hui-yen, *tr. by* Irving Lo. WFTU

Royal Angler, The, *sel. Unknown.*
  "Me thinks I see our mighty monarch stand." OBSV

Royal Charlie's now awa. Will He No Come Back Again? *Unknown.* OBEV

Royal Crown, The, *abr.* ("Wonderful are thy works, as my soul overwhelmingly knoweth."), *sel.* Solomon Ibn Gabirol, *tr. fr. Hebrew.* AWP, *tr. by* Israel Zangwill
    My God. *Tr. by* Alice Lucas *sel.* TrJP

Royal Education. Winthrop Mackworth Praed. OBSV

Royal feast was done, The; the King. The Fool's Prayer. Edward Rowland Sill. AA; BeLS; FaBoBe; OHFP; OnMSP; PoLF; WBLP; WGRP

Royal Fisherman, The. *Unknown.* ChTr; GBP

Royal George, The. William Cowper. *See* Toll for the brave.

Royal Guest, A. *Unknown. See* Yet if his majesty, our sovereign [*or* soveraign] Lord.

Royal Light Dragoon, The. *Unknown.* OBET

Royal Line, The. Leigh Hunt. FaBoUs

Royal Mummy to Bohemia, The. Charles Warren Stoddard. AA

Royal Palace of the Highest Heaven, The. *At. to* Alexander Montgomerie. GoTS

Royal Palm. Hart Crane. CMoP; MoAB; MoAmPo; MoP; NoAM; NoP; TrGrPo

Royal Pearl. Irena Klepfisz. ER

Royal [*or* Royall] Presents, *sel.* Nathaniel Wanley. OBS
    "Instead of Incense (Blessed Lord) if wee." TrPWD

Royal Princess, A. Christina Rossetti. BrRo

Royal Stag, The. "Hugh MacDiarmid." FaBoMo

Royal Tour, The. "Peter Pindar." OxBoLi

Royal Tour, and Weymouth Amusements, The, *abr., sel.* "Peter Pindar." OxBoli
    George III and the Sailor. NOEC

Royall Presents. Nathaniel Wanley. OBS

Royalties. D. J. Enright. NOBL

Royalty. Rimbaud, *tr. fr. French by* Enid Rhodes Peschal. SOTW

Roye Robert the Bruss the rayke he avowit, The. Sir Richard Holland. *Fr.* The Buke of the Howlat. OxBS
    (Douglas and the Bruce's Heart.) OxBLMV

Rrrrrrraaarghr/ We have paid you back. Fury against the Moslems at Uhud. Hind bint Utba, *tr. by* Bridget Connelly *and* Deirdre Lashgari. WPOW

Rt. Rev. Richard Allen. Josephine D. Henderson Heard. CBWP-4

Ruaumoko—the Earthquake God. Mohi Turei, *tr. fr. Maori by* A. Armstrong. WTO

Rub, A. John Banister Tabb. OBAL

Rub a dub dub,/ Three men in a tub. Mother Goose. NOBL; OxNR

Rubadub, rubadub, row-dow-dow! Whisperings for the Unwashed. William Thom. PF

Rubai: "How long, how long within this world will you remain." Mirza Mohammad Rafi Sauda, *tr. by* Ahmed Ali. GoT

Rubai: "In vain, in vain, my love, to the river bank you go." Khwaja Mir Dard, *tr. by* Ahmed Ali. GoT

Rubai Enlarged. Khwaja Mir Dard, *tr. fr. Urdu by* Ahmed Ali. GoT

Rubaiyat for Sue Ella Tucker. Miller Williams. SM

Rubáiyát of Omar Khayyám of Naishápúr, The. Omar Khayyám, *tr. fr. Persian by* Edward Fitzgerald. AWP; EBVV, *abr.;* FaBoBe; FaBoRV, *abr.;* FaFP; FaPoR, *abr.;* HAP, *abr.;* HeIP; LiTB; MaSP; NAEL-2; NoP; PoEL-5; PrIm, *abr.;* TrGrPo; WeW, *abr.* Sels.
    "Ah, with the grape my fading life provide." EBEV; GTBS-P
    "Awake! for morning in the bowl of night." Mes; NOBVV
    "Book of verses underneath the bough, A." HoPM; NOBE; OBEV (Quatrains.) SeCePo
    "Come, fill the cup, and in the fire of spring." FaBoRV; FaBV; TEP; WGRP
    "Iram indeed is gone with all his rose." OBVE
    "Myself when young did eagerly frequent." EaLo; WGRP
    "O Thou, who man of baser earth didst make." EaLo
    "They say the lion and the lizard keep." EBEV
    "Think, in this batter'd caravanserai." ChTr; OBD
    "Wake, for the sun, who scattered [*or* scatter'd] into flight." FF; OBNC; ViBoPo
    (Wake!) FaPON

Rubber. Donna Masini. ER

Rubber duck is paddling up the sky, A. It Is Nearly Summer. Bill Manhire. ATNZ

Rubber penis, the wig, false breasts, The. Poggio. Lawrence Durrell. OxBTC

Rubbing boats mark the twin churches, The. Tobacco Hole. Medbh McGuckian. FaBCIP

Rubbing her beads. *Unknown, tr. by* Geoffrey Bownas *and* Anthony Thwaite. PeBJV

Rubens, de Vos, Memling—room after room. Antwerp: Musée Des Beaux-Arts. Alan Ross. NYBP

Rubin. Charles Cooper. PoBA

Rubinstein Staccato Etude, The. Robert Nathaniel Dett. BANP

Ruby and amethyst eyes of anemones, The. Winter Anemones. Charles Brasch. *Fr.* Night Cries, Wakari Hospital. ATNZ; PeNZ

Ruby Tells All. Miller Williams. MT

Ruddigore, *sel.* W. S. Gilbert.
    Darned Mounseer, The. NOBL

Rude, The. Mark McCloskey. SoTCo

Rude Awakenings. Bob Rosenthal. UL

Rude Boreas. *Unknown.* OBET

Rude mass of earth, from which moilèd hands. On a Piece of Unwrought Pipeclay. John Frederick Bryant. NOEC

Rudely forced to drink tea, Massachusetts, in anger. *Unknown.* PAH

Rudely thou wrought my dear heart's desire. Spenser. *Fr.* Amoretti, V. EIL

Rudolph Is Tired of the City. Gwendolyn Brooks. PDV; RHPC

Rudolph Reed was oaken. The Ballad of Rudolph Reed. Gwendolyn Brooks. RB

Rue Ravignan, The. Max Jacob, *tr. fr. French by* John Ashbery. RHTwFP

Rueful Lamentation on the Death of Queen Elizabeth, A. Sir Thomas More. AAS; FaBoRV; LiTB; OBSC

Rufty and Tufty. Isabell Hempseed. BoTP

Rufus Mitchell's Confession. *Unknown.* AmFP

Rufus Prays. L. A. G. Strong. MoBrPo

Rug, The. Michael McClure. NeAP

Rug of Woven Magic. Nan Benally. GOS

Rugby Chapel. Matthew Arnold. PoEL-5; WGRP

Rugged forhead that with grave foresight, The. Spenser. *Fr.* The Faerie Queene, IV *proem.* OAEL-1
    (Love.) OBSC

Rugged Pyrrhus, he whose sable arm, The. Shakespeare. *Fr.* Hamlet, II, ii. Par

Rugged up for winter snow. Greenham Women. Wendy Poussard. AIW

Ruin, The. Richard Hughes. OBMV

Ruin, The. Charles Tomlinson. NePoEA-2

Ruin, The. *Unknown, tr. fr. Anglo-Saxon by* Gavin Bone. EBEV

Ruin, The. *Unknown, tr. fr. Anglo-Saxon by* Charles W. Kennedy. AnOE; PrIm

Ruin and death held sway. In Apia Bay. Sir Charles G. D. Roberts. PAH

Ruin, at least, was something; the yard, The. Late Return. E. A. Markham. PBCV

"Ruin seize thee, ruthless King!" The Bard a Pindaric Ode. Thomas Gray. EnRP; GTBS; GTBS-P; NOBE; NOEC; OAEL-1

Ruined and ill, a man of two score. Remembering Golden Bells. Po Chü-i, *tr. by* Arthur Waley. AWP

Ruined Cottage, The. Wordsworth. *See* Excursion, The: Wanderer, The.

Ruined House, A. Richard Aldington. BrPo

Ruined Maid, The. Thomas Hardy. BoLoP; BrPo; CMoP; ErPo; FiBHP; HeIP; LiTB; NAEL-2; NBLV; NOBL; NoP; NOP; OxBTC; SCV; TEP; WeW

Ruined Motel, The. Reginald Gibbons. MAYP

Ruined park is quiet behind serried doors of gold, The. Immortal at the River. Lu Ch'ien-i, *tr. by* Lois Fusek. ATF

Ruined, time ruined, all these once good things. Rimrock, Where It Is. Hayden Carruth. NNaP

Ruinous Rains. Fu Hsien, *tr. fr. Chinese by* Burton Watson. CoBCP

Ruins. Mark Strand. BLA

Ruins. Judah Leib Teller, *tr. fr. Yiddish by* Benjamin *and* Barbara Harshav. AYP

Ruins of a Great House. Derek Walcott. TwCP

Ruins of Rome, *sels.* Joachim Du Bellay, *tr. fr. French by* Spenser.
    "He that has seen a great oak dry and dead." FaBoPP
    "Hope ye, my verses, that posterity." PoE
    "Thou stranger, which for Rome in Rome here seekest." FaBoPP; OBVE
    "Thou that at Rome astonished doth behold." FaBoPP
    "Who list the Romane greatnes with to figure." OBVE

Ruins of the City of Hay. Randolph Stow. CBAP; PoAu-2

Ruins under the Stars, *sel.* Galway Kinnell. LCAP; NaP
    "Sometimes I see them." RFM

Rule, A. John Wesley. FaFP

Rule, Britannia! James Thomson *and* David Mallet. *Fr.* Alfred, A Masque, II, v. FaPoR; GTBS; GTBS-P; NOEC; OBWP; WBLP

Rule for Shooting, A. *Unknown.* FaBoUs

Rule of the Road, The. *Unknown.* FaBoUs

Ruler. Gyula Illyés, *tr. fr. Hungarian by* William Jay Smith. MHuP

Ruler and the Sparrow, The. Nizar Qabbani, *tr. fr. Arabic by* Abdullah al-Udhari. MPAW

Rulers: Philadelphia. Fenton Johnson. AmFN; PoNe

Rules. Karla Kuskin. RHPC
Rules and Regulations. "Lewis Carroll." FaBoUs; NoBVV
Rules break like a thermometer, The. Adrienne Rich. *Fr.* Twenty-one
    Love Poems, XIII. GLP
Rum Cove, a Stout Cove, A. Tom Paulin. FaBCIP
Rum Tum Tugger, The. T. S. Eliot. FaBoNo; FaBV; FaPON; PDV
Rumba. José Zacarías Tallet, *tr. fr. Spanish by* Sangodare Akanji. TTY
Rumble of guns, A—not earthly ones. Electric Storm. Michael C.
    Martin. WaP
Rumble of thunder brings evening rain, The. Chu Yün-ming, *tr. fr.*
    Chinese by Jonathan Chaves. *Fr.* Miscellaneous Poems Written in
    My Studio on an Autumn Day. CoBLCP
Rumble on, machines of the gold mines. In the Gold Mines. B. W.
    Vilakazi. TTY
    (On the Gold Mines.) PeSA
Rumble, rumble, rumble, goes the gloomy "L." Roller Skates. John
    Chipman Farrar. FaPON
Rumbling sound of man. Buzz. Jim Tollerud. VoR
Rumbling under blackened girders, Midland, bound for Cricklewood.
    Parliament Hill Fields. Sir John Betjeman. FaBoTw; NOBE;
    OPOP
Ruminant pillows! Gregarious soft boulders! The Black Faced Sheep.
    Donald Hall. LCAP; SV
Rumination. Richard Eberhart. LiTA; LiTM
Rummaging inside yourself. The Death of Fathers. Theodore Weiss.
    DiL; SV
Rummle an' dunt o' watter. Sumburgh Heid. George Bruce. OxBS
Rumor Verified. Robert Penn Warren. AnAn
Rumoresque Senum Severiorum. Marcus Argentarius, *tr. fr. Greek by*
    Dudley Fitts. ErPo
Rumors of the Turning Wheel. Anne Halley. PPR
Rumors open up. The Morning Star. Primus St. John. PoBA
Rumpled river, The. River Rhyme. William Carlos Williams. PoA
Rumpled sheet, A/ of brown paper. The Term. William Carlos
    Williams. InvP; LiTA
Rumpty-iddity, row, row, row. *Unknown.* OxNR
Run a Little. James Reeves. RAR
Run from Manassas Junction, The. *Unknown.* PAH
Run, Nigger, Run! *Unknown.* BPo
Run of is Jessy Watson fair. On Jessy Watson's Elopement. Marjory
    Fleming. Mes
Run out the boat, my broken comrades. Thalassa. Louis MacNeice.
    BIrV; FaBoMo; FaBoRV; NOBE
Run, shepherds, run where Bethlehem blest appears. The Angels.
    William, of Hawthornden Drummond. *Fr.* Flowers of Sion. GN
    (Nativitie, The.) OBS
Run toward the Nightland, *sel. Unknown, tr. fr. Cherokee Indian.*
    "Now! The Red Tobacco has come to strike your soul." STP
Runagate Runagate. Robert Hayden. BPo; CNA; IDB; InPS; LCAP;
    PoBA; PoNe
Runaway. Rhoda Coghill. NeIP
Runaway, The. Robert Frost. AWP; CH; FaBoCh; FaPON; GoJo;
    MoAB; MoAmPo; PDV; TwCP; VGW
Runaway, The. Bobbi Katz. RHPC
Runaway, The. William Wise. RAR
Runaway Slave, The. Walt Whitman. *Fr.* Song of Myself, X. PoNe
Runaway Slave at Pilgrim's Point, The. Elizabeth Barrett Browning.
    BrRo; PoNe
Runaways, The. Mark Van Doren. PoRA
Runaways Café II. Marilyn Hacker. NoAM
Rune. Muriel Rukeyser. SM
Rune for C, A. Barbara Howes. NYBP; SM
Rune of Riches, A. Florence Converse. BoTP
Runes for an Old Believer. Rolfe Humphries. NYBP
Runes on Weland's Sword, The. Kipling. *Fr.* Puck of Pook's Hill.
    NoAM; PoEL-5
Runnable Stag, A. John Davidson. BrPo; FaPoR; FM; GoTS; HAP;
    OBEV; OxBTC; PrIm; SD; WiR
Runner. W. H. Auden. SD
Runner, The. Gary Gildner. TAP
Runner, The. Alexandra Grilikhes. SD
Runner, The. Walt Whitman. ASP; InPK; InPS; SD
Runner in the Skies, The. James Oppenheim. TrJP
Running. Leslie Ullman. NAmP
Running. Richard Wilbur. ASP; CoAP
Running along a bank, a parapet. The Path. Edward Thomas. BrPo
Running from the rain. Summer Day. Kan Sazan, *tr. by* Burton Watson.
    JLIC-2
Running Lightly over Spongy Ground. Theodore Roethke. RB
Running on Empty. Robert Phillips. InPK
Running out of the nets. Buson, *tr. by* Hiroaki Sato. FCEI

Running rings. Susan Howe. LP
Running sweating hair wet from the shower. Captivity Narrative,
    September 1981. Adrian C. Louis. STE
Running the Batteries. Herman Melville. PAH
Running the Blockade. Nora Perry. PAH
Running the River Lines. David Baker. MAYP
Running through Sleep. Kathleen Norris. IHMS
Running through the thick wiry grasses to the pond. Shore. Jean
    Garrigue. TAP
Running to Paradise. W. B. Yeats. OxBoLi
Running yellow time. Yellow. Anna Hajnal, *tr. fr. Hungarian by* Jascha
    Kessler. *Fr.* Images. FOC
Runoff. A. R. Ammons. PPP
Runoff. William Everson. NoAM
Runs falls rises stumbles on from darkness into darkness. Runagate
    Runagate. Robert Hayden. BPo; CNA; IDB; InPS; LCAP; PoBA;
    PoNe
Runs the wind along the waste. Were-Wolf. Julian Hawthorne. AA
Rural. Erich Fried, *tr. fr. German by* Beth Bjorklund. CoAuP
Rural Carrier Stops to Kill a Nine-Foot Cottonmouth, The. T. R.
    Hummer. SM
Rural Colloquy with a Painter. Timothy Steele. CRP
Rural Dance about the Maypole, The. *Unknown.* GBP; OxBoLi; RR
Rural Dumpheap. Melville Cane. AmFN
Rural Lass, The. Catherine Jemmat. NOEC
Rural Life. George Crabbe. *Fr.* The Village. NOBE
Rural Mail, The. John Glassco. MoCV
Rural Poesy. Sir Philip Sidney. *Fr.* Arcadia. EIL
Rural Sights and Sounds. William Cowper. *See* Task, The: Sofa, The.
Rural Simplicity. H. J. Byron. NOBL
Rural Sports, *sels.* John Gay.
    Fly-fishing. SD
    "Nor less the spaniel, skillful to betray." PBBP
    "When a brisk gale against the current blows." FM
Ruses: A Coyote Tale, The. Diane di Prima. *Fr.* Loba. ER
"Rush hour." In the Subway ("Rush hour"). A. Leyeles, *tr. fr. Yiddish*
    by Benjamin *and* Barbara Harshav. *Fr.* New York. AYP
Rush of the *Oregon, The.* Arthur Guiterman. PAH
Rushes in a watery place. Christina Rossetti. ChTr; PDV
Rushing. Ray A. Young Bear. CDW
Rushing ax cools and bleeds; the ax drips, The. Executioners. Berish
    Weinstein, *tr. by* Leonard Wolf. PeBMYV
Rushing wind the Spirit came, A! A Prayer for Pentecost. Catherine
    Bernard Brown. BLRP
Rusia en 1931. Robert Hass. AnAn; MAYP
Rusia. Aleksandr Aleksandrovich Blok, *tr. fr. Russian by* Babette
    Deutsch *and* Avrahm Yarmolinsky. AWP
Russia. Nathan Haskell Dole. AA
Russia. Shmuel Halkin, *tr. fr. Yiddish by* Hillel Halkin. PeBMYV
Russia. William Carlos Williams. VGW
Russia 1812. Victor Hugo, *tr. fr. French by* Robert Lowell. OBWP
Russia! If my faith in you were any less great. Russia. Shmuel Halkin,
    tr. by Hillel Halkin. PeBMYV
Russia, 1927. Ai. NoAM
Russian and Turk. Robert J. Burdette. NA
Russian Asylum. Marilyn Bowering. NOBC
Russian Cathedral. Claude McKay. *See* Bow down my soul in worship
    very low.
Russian Cradle Song, A. David Nomberg, *tr. fr. Yiddish by* Alter Brody.
    TrJP
Russian Death. Leyb Kvitko, *tr. fr. Yiddish by* Allen Mandelbaum *and*
    Harold Rabinowitz. PeBMYV
Russian Doll, The. Jane Shore. PPR
Russian Fantasy, A. Nathan Haskell Dole. AA
Russian fields on winter evenings! In Winter's Dusk. Dovid Hofshteyn,
    tr. fr. Yiddish by Robert Friend. *Fr.* On Winter Evenings; 1912.
    PeBMYV
Russian God, The. Prince P. A. Vyazemsky, *tr. fr. Russian by* Alan
    Myers. AAA
Russian sailed over the blue Black Sea, A. "Soldier, Rest!" Robert
    Jones Burdette. OBAL
Russian Soul II, The. John Hollander. NBLV
Russians. Keith Douglas. OxBTC
Russia's Resentment. Lizelia Augusta Jenkins Moorer. CBWP-3
Rust, a little pile of western color, lies, The. We Continue. W. S.
    Merwin. CAPP
Rust destroys the wheat. New Wife. *Gond Oral Tradition, tr. by*
    V. Elwin *and* S. Hivale. WTO
Rusted Chain, The. Yosef Damana ben Yeshaq, *tr. fr. Amharic by*
    Ephraim Isaac. VWA
Rustic Childhood. William Barnes. OBNC

Rustic Landscape. Paul Snoek, *tr. fr. Dutch by* James S. Holmes. DuIn

Rustic Song, A. Anthony C. Deane. FiBHP

Rustily creak the crickets: Jack Frost came down last night. Jack Frost. Celia Thaxter. OBCA

Rustle among bones. Only wind, the bodiless angel. Emptiness. Ray. Otto Orban, *tr. by* Emery George. VWA

Rustle of each falling leaf, The. Love. Samuele Romanelli, *tr. by* A. B. Rhine. TrJP

Rustle of whispering wind over leaves, A. Kingfisher Flat. William Everson. PoM

Rustlers, The. Rocco Scotellaro, *tr. fr. Italian by* Lawrence R. Smith. NItP

Rustling of the silk is discontinued, The. Liu Ch'e. Ezra Pound. OBVE; VGW

Rustling of yellow leaves quickly wakens me from the wine, The. Dawn Journey. Yi Shun-ting, *tr. by* Timothy C. Wong. WFTU

Rusty spigot, The. Onomatopoeia. Eve Merriam. RR

Ruth. Thomas Hood. BoLoP; EnLoPo; EnRP; GN; NOBE; OBEV; OBNC

Ruth. Colleen J. McElroy. BlSi

Ruth. Pauli Murray. NMM

Ruth, *sels.* Bible, *O.T.*

  "And Ruth said, Intreat me not to leave." *Fr.* I: 16-17. FF

  (Ruth to Naomi.) TrGrPo

  Naomi and Ruth. *Fr.* I: 8-17. TrJP

Ruth; or, The Influences of Nature. Wordsworth. ChER; EnRP; GTBS; GTBS-P; PoEL-4

Ruth to Naomi. Bible, *O.T. See* Ruth: And Ruth said, Intreat me not to leave.

Rutherford McDowell. Edgar Lee Masters. *Fr.* Spoon River Anthology. EyDe; LiTA; OxBA

Ruthless unrest has urged slow feet. Rescue. Olive Tilford Dargan. GoYe

Ruyter the while, that had our ocean curbed. The Dutch in the Medway. Andrew Marvell. *Fr.* The Last Instructions to a Painter. OBS

Rwose in the Dark, The. William Barnes. NOBVV

Ryder. John Haines. LCAP

Rye Bread. William Stanley Braithwaite. CDC

Rye Whiskey. Rye Whiskey. *Unknown.* OxBoLi

  (Way Up on Clinch Mountain.) AS, A *and* B *vers., with music.*

Ryght as the stern of day begouth to schyne. William Dunbar. *See* Right as the star of day began to shine.

Ryojin Hisho, *sels.* Emperor Go-Shirakawa, *tr. fr. Japanese.*

  "Bamboo grass in front of the Oji Shrine, The." *Tr. by* Hiroaki Sato. FCEI

  "Brocade and rush hat you loved, The." *Tr. by* Hiroaki Sato. FCEI

  ("Brocade sedge-hat you loved, The.") PeBJV, *tr. by* Geoffrey Bownas *and* Anthony Thwaite.

  "Dance, dance, snail!" *Tr. by* Hiroaki Sato. FCEI

  ("Dance, dance, little snail!") PeBJV, *tr. by* Geoffrey Bownas *and* Anthony Thwaite.

  "Even if I had to sleep alone." *Tr. by* Hiroaki Sato. FCEI

  ("Hundred days, a hundred nights, A.") PeBJV, *tr. by* Geoffrey Bownas *and* Anthony Thwaite.

  "Even the moon." *Tr. by* Geoffrey Bownas *and* Anthony Thwaite. PeBJV

  "Head-lice make merry on my head." *Tr. by* Hiroaki Sato. FCEI

  "It's raining, but you say, "Go away!'" *Tr. by* Hiroaki Sato. FCEI

  "Let's make love. The night has turned." *Tr. by* Hiroaki Sato. FCEI

  "Listen, waves, tell of this, beach." *Tr. by* Hiroaki Sato. FCEI

  "Looking at you, my beauty." *Tr. by* Hiroaki Sato. FCEI

  "Lord Buddha is present everywhere." *Tr. by* Hiroaki Sato. FCEI

  "Lying awake quietly at daybreak." *Tr. by* Hiroaki Sato. FCEI

  "Much, much in love, you see her by chance." *Tr. by* Hiroaki Sato. FCEI

  "My daughter must be past ten by now." *Tr. by* Hiroaki Sato. FCEI

  "My son must be twenty by now." *Tr. by* Hiroaki Sato. FCEI

  ("My child is still not twenty.") PeBJV, *tr. by* Geoffrey Bownas *and* Anthony Thwaite.

  "Potter at Mimaki in Kusuha, The." *Tr. by* Hiroaki Sato. FCEI

  "Stay, stay, dragonfly!" *Tr. by* Hiroaki Sato. FCEI

  "Things a prostitute likes." *Tr. by* Hiroaki Sato. FCEI

  "Things a sage likes." *Tr. by* Hiroaki Sato. FCEI

  "Things a terrifying exorcist likes." *Tr. by* Hiroaki Sato. FCEI

  "Things exceedingly swift." *Tr. by* Hiroaki Sato. FCEI

  "Things hilariously bent." *Tr. by* Hiroaki Sato. FCEI

  "Things lately fashionable in the capital." *Tr. by* Hiroaki Sato. FCEI

  "Things that dance well, exquisitely." *Tr. by* Hiroaki Sato. FCEI

  "Things that pierce the heart." *Tr. by* Hiroaki Sato. FCEI

  "Was I born to play?." *Tr. by* Hiroaki Sato. FCEI

  "When my mirror clouds up." *Tr. by* Hiroaki Sato. FCEI

  "Women are at their best." *Tr. by* Hiroaki Sato. FCEI

  "You, a man who made me wait but didn't come." *Tr. by* Hiroaki Sato. FCEI

  ("May the man who gained my trust yet did not come.") PeBJV, *tr. by* Geoffrey Bownas *and* Anthony Thwaite.

  "You have no heart." *Tr. by* Hiroaki Sato. FCEI

  ("Oh, my man is so unfeeling.") PeBJV, *tr. by* Geoffrey Bownas *and* Anthony Thwaite.

  "Young man came to make you his wife, The." *Tr. by* Hiroaki Sato. FCEI

  ("Young man came to manhood, The.") PeBJV, *tr. by* Geoffrey Bownas *and* Anthony Thwaite.

S

S. L. A. B. S. for George Herbert. George Starbuck. SoTCo

s sz sz SZ sz SZ sz ZS zs Zs zs zs z. Siesta of a Hungarian Snake. Edwin Morgan. InPK

S. T. Coleridge Dismisses a Caller from Porlock. Gerard Previn Meyer. GoYe

Sa-cá-ga-we-a. Edna Dean Proctor. PAH

Saadabad. James Elroy Flecker. SeCePo

Saadi. Emerson. OxBA

Sabbath. John Berryman. *Fr.* Dream Songs. LCAP

Sabbath. Rivka Fried. VWA

Sabbath. Jacob Glatstein, *tr. fr. Yiddish by* Cynthia Ozick. PeBMYV

Sabbath. Jakov de Haan, *tr. fr. Dutch by* David Soetendorp. VWA

Sabbath. David Rosenmann-Taub, *tr. fr. Spanish.* VWA, *tr. by* Charles Guentheer

Sabbath Bells. Josephine D. Henderson Heard. CBWP-4

Sabbath Day Was By, The. Howard Chandler Robbins. AH

Sabbath day was ending in a village by the sea, The. The Last Hymn. "Marianne Farningham." BLPA

Sabbath Hours. A. Leyeles, *tr. fr. Yiddish by* Benjamin *and* Barbara Harshav. AYP

Sabbath, My Love. Judah Halevi, *tr. fr. Hebrew by* Solomon Solis-Cohen. TrJP

Sabbath of Rest, A. Isaac Luria, *tr. fr. Hebrew by* Nina Davis Salaman. TrJP

Sabbath Peal; or, Past, Present, and Future. A Moral Essay, The. Thomas Nicholson. PF

Sabbath Reflection. Denis Wrafter. NeIP

Sabbath Sonnet. Felicia Dorothea Hemans. Son

Sabbath, the pious carry no money. A Voice out of the Sabbaths. W. I. Derek Walcott. WeW

Sabbaths, *sels.* Wendell Berry.

  "Another Sunday morning comes." *Fr.* I. BLA

  "To sit and look at light-filled leaves." *Fr.* III. BLA

Sabbaths, W.I. Derek Walcott. WeW

Sabbatical. Linda Zisquit. VWA

Sable is my throat. Negro Spiritual. Perient Trott. PoNe

Sabrina Fair. Milton. *Fr.* Comus; a Masque Presented at Ludlow Castle. EBEV; ELP; FaBoCh, *much abr.;* GN; PoEL-3

  (Sabrina.) CH, *abr.;* NOBE; OBEV

Sacco-Vanzetti. Moyshe-Leyb Halpern, *tr. fr. Yiddish by* John Hollander. PeBMYV

  ("You can pull out.") AYP, *tr. by* Benjamin *and* Barbara Harshav

  ("You can tear a gray hair out of your head.") VWA, *tr. by* David G. Roskies *and* Hillel Schwartz

Sachem voices cloven out of the hills, The. Miramichi Lightning. Alfred Goldsworthy Bailey. OBCV

Sacheverell the learned. To the Tune of "Ye Commons and Peers Pray Lend Me Your Ears." *Unknown.* APAS

Sack of Deerfield, The. Thomas Dunn English. PAH

Sacrament of Gravity, The. Jorie Graham. NAmP

Sacrament of Sleep, The. John Oxenham. PoLF

Sacrament of the Altar, The. *Unknown.* MeEL

Sacramental Meditations. *See* Preparatory Meditations.

Sacramento. The Californian. *Unknown.* AmFP

Sacraments of Nature, The. Aubrey Thomas De Vere. ACP

Sacred, The. Stephen Dunn. MOWH

Sacred. Gertrude Stein. OBAL

Sacred and Profane Love, or, There's Nothing New Under the Moon Either. Peter De Vries. NBLV

Sacred Book, The. *At. to* Zoroaster, *tr. fr. Persian by* A. V. Williams Jackson. AWP

Sacred Ceremony, A. Louise Aston, *tr. fr. German by* Susan L. Cocalis. DMG

Sacred Children, The. H. R. Hays. EAS
Sacred Formula to Attract Affection. *Unknown, tr. fr. Cherokee Indian by* James Mooney. LiTA
Sacred Formula to Destroy Life. *Unknown, tr. by* James Mooney. LiTA
Sacred Grove, A. Edward Cracroft Lefroy, *after the Greek of* Theocritus. *Fr.* Echoes from Theocritus, XXIV. AWP
Sacred Grove, A. Fran Winant. BrRo
Sacred Hearth, The. David Gascoyne. FaBoTw
Sacred love for one's native land, The. Jeanne Manon Philipon-Roland. Kathinka Zitz-Halein, *tr. by* Susan L. Cocalis *and* Gerlinde Geiger. DMG
Sacred Mr. Hua, terrace of clouds. Seeing Off Han Ju-Ch'ing. Ho Ching-ming, *tr. by* Jonathan Chaves. CoBLCP
Sacred muse that first made love divine, The. Sir John Davies. *Fr.* The Gulling Sonnets. Son
Sacred Objects. Louise Glück. *Fr.* Dedication to Hunger, V. AnAn; GeTw
Sacred Objects. Louis Simpson. CAPP
Sacred Order, The. May Sarton. ImOP
Sacred Poetry. John Wilson. WBLP
Sacred to the Memory of Maria (To Say Nothing of Jane and Martha) Sparks. "Max Adeler." FaBoCo
Sacred Way, The. Angelos Sikelianos, *tr. fr. Greek by* Edmund Keeley *and* Philip Sherrard. VMG
Sacrifice, The. Frank Bidart. GLP; PPR
Sacrifice, The. Chana Bloch. VWA
Sacrifice, The. George Herbert. PoEL-2
Sacrifice, The. Homer, *tr. fr. Greek by* George Chapman. *Fr.* Odyssey, III. OBS
Sacrifice. Nana Issaia, *tr. fr. Modern Greek by* Helle Tzalopoulou Barnstone. BoWoP
Sacrifice. Thomas Kinsella. IPY
Sacrifice. H. Leivick, *tr. fr. Yiddish by* Robert Friend. PeBMYV
Sacrifice, The. Moshe Yungman, *tr. fr. Yiddish by* Marcia Falk. VWA
Sacrifice Bunt. Lucky Jacobs. ASP
Sacrifice of a Red Squirrel. Joseph Langland. NYBP
Sacrifice of a Virgin in the Mayan Ball Court. Norman Dubie. GeTw
Sacrifice to Apollo, The. Michael Drayton. OBS
Sacristans. Elizabeth Cook-Lynn. *Fr.* Journey, III. HATNAP
Sad. Nishiwaki Junzaburo, *tr. fr. Japanese by* Hiroaki Sato. FCEI
Sad, All Alone, Not Long I Musing Sat. Giles Fletcher the Elder. *Fr.* Licia, I. Son
Sad and forlorn: the shrike. Kato Shuson, *tr. by* Geoffrey Bownas *and* Anthony Thwaite. PeBJV
Sad and lonely, she shuts the vermilion door. Mountain Hawthorns. Sun Kuang-hsien, *tr. by* Lois Fusek. ATF
Sad and mournful history, A. The Cabin Creek Flood. *Unknown.* AmFP
Sad Boy, The. Laura Riding. RB
Sad Child's Song, The. Mark Van Doren. SO
Sad Day, The. Thomas Flatman. OBEV
Sad Day in Berlin. Sarah Kirsch, *tr. fr. German by* Gerda Mayer. PBWP
Sad Evenings. Iftiqar Arif, *tr. fr. Urdu by* Mahmood Jamal. PBMUP
Sad for those without sweet Anglo-Saxon. The Change. David O'Bruadair, *tr. by* Austin Clarke. BIrV
Sad Green. Sylvia Townsend Warner. MoBrPo
Sad guard/ Haven't you slept? Dialogue. Buland al-Haidari, *tr. by* Patricia Alanah Byrne *and* Salma Khadra Jayyusi. MAP
Sad heart, the gymnast of inertia, does not count. The Sad Indian. Hart Crane. PoA
Sad Hesper o'er the buried sun. Tennyson. *Fr.* In Memoriam A. H. H., CXXI. NoP
Sad Indian, The. Hart Crane. PoA
Sad Is the Seagull. Larin Paraske, *tr. fr. Finnish by* Jaakko A. Ahokas. PBWP
Sad Joke on a Marae. Apirana Taylor. PeNZ
Sad lagoons. Film Vermouth: Six o'Clock Show. Magda Portal, *tr. by* Allan Francovich *and* Kathleen Weaver. PBWP
Sad Little Round of Life. René Daumal, *tr. fr. French by* Kenneth Rexroth. RHTwFP
Sad, lost in thought, and mute I go. Norman Song, *tr. by* John Addington Symonds. AWP
Sad Lover, The. George Crabbe. *Fr.* Tales of the Hall. OBNC
Sad Memories ("They tell me I am beautiful: they praise my silken hair."), *sel.* Charles Stuart Calverley. FM
Cat, The. ChTr
Sad music from vermilion strings. Telling My Feelings. Yü Hsüan-chi, *tr. by* Geoffrey Waters. BoWoP
Sad Parting. Maruyama Kaoru, *tr. fr. Japanese by* Hiroaki Sato. FCEI

Sad, purple well! whose bubbling eye. Abel's Blood. Henry Vaughan. OBWVE
Sad Remembrance. Mei Yao-ch'en, *tr. fr. Chinese by* Burton Watson. CoBCP
Sad, sad is the bird in a cage. Cheng Chen, *tr. fr. Chinese by* Irving Lo. *Fr.* Responding to Yüan-ming's "Drinking Wine" Poems, X. WFTU
Sad seamstress, The. House Guest. Elizabeth Bishop. NYBP; TAP
Sad Shepherd, The, *sels.* Ben Jonson.
  Here She Was Wont to Go. OxBSP
    (Aeglamour's Lament.) CH
  Lincolnshire; from the Wolds to the Fens. *Fr.* II, vii. FaBoPP
  Mother Maudlin the Witch. ChTr
  Though I Am Young and Cannot Tell. *Fr.* I, v. ELP; NoP; TEP
    (Death and Love.) NOBE
    (Karolin's Song.) PoEL-2
    (Song: "Though I am young and cannot tell.") SeCP
Sad Shepherd, The. W. B. Yeats. MOS
Sad Song, The. Beaumont *and* Fletcher. *See* Captain, The: Away, Delights.
Sad Song, A. Philip Massinger. *See* Emperor of the East, The: Death Invoked.
Sad Song. *Unknown, tr. fr. Chinese by* Burton Watson. CoBCP
Sad Song about Greenwich Village, A. Frances Park. RHPC
Sad Steps. Philip Larkin. NoAM; NoP
Sad Strains of a Gay Waltz. Wallace Stevens. OxBA
Sad that in our growing. Robin Hood's Barn. John Ashbery. AnAn
Sad—the end that waits me. Komachi, *tr. fr. Japanese by* Burton Watson. *Fr.* Kokin Shu. FCEI
Sad Thyrsis weeps till his blue eyes are dim. Thyrsis. Edward Cracroft Lefroy, *after the Greek of* Theocritus. *Fr.* Echoes from Theocritus, XXVI. AWP
Sad winds rise in the middle of the night. A Miscellany. Wang Fu-chih, *tr. by* Irving Lo. WFTU
Saddest day will have an eve, The. Hope. Clara Ann Thompson. CBWP-2
Saddle and Cell. The Three Marias, *tr. fr. Portuguese by* Helen R. Lane. BoWoP
Saddle! saddle! saddle! After the Comanches. *Unknown.* PAH
Saddle Tramp. Buck Wilkerson. CowP
Saddled and bridled. Bonnie James Campbell. *Unknown.* ESPB
Saddled as everyone with karma. Tettsu, *tr. by* Lucien Stryk *and* Takashi Ikemoto. ZPCJ
Saddled Ass, The. La Fontaine, *tr. fr. French by* Deems Taylor. NBLV
Sadie. *Unknown. See* Frankie and Johnny [*or* Johnnie *or* Albert].
Sadie/ the cleaning lady. Personals. Leatrice W. Emeruwa. PCP
Sadie and Maud. Gwendolyn Brooks. InPK; MoP; NoAM; NOBA; TAP
Sadie went into the bar-room, and she ordered up a big glass of beer. Sadie. *Unknown.* AS
Sadie's Playhouse. Margaret Danner. PoBA
Sadly as some old medieval knight. My Books. Longfellow. AA
Sadly stars fall; two in love have side by side. Wakayama Bokusui, *tr. fr. Japanese by* Hiroaki Sato. *Fr.* Forty-four Tanka. FCEI
Sadly the dead leaves rustle in the whistling wind. The Church of a Dream. Lionel Johnson. OAEL-2; OBMV
Sadly unroll sleepingbag. 25:I:68. Philip Whalen. PoM
Sadness. Tennyson. FaBoEE
Sadness and Still Life. Bin Ramke. MAYP
Sadness, Glass, Theory. Roy Fuller. WaP
Sadness in Spring. *Unknown, tr. fr. Welsh by* Gwyn Jones. OBWVE
Sadness in the Autumn Chambers. Yün Shou-p'ing, *tr. fr. Chinese by* Jonathan Chaves. CoBLCP
Sadness in the human visage stares, The. At an Exhibition of Historical Paintings, Hobart. Vivian Smith. CBAP
Sadness of the Bare Copula. Dezsö Tandori, *tr. fr. Hungarian by* Kenneth McRobbie. MHuP
Sadness of the lifeless sand. Ishikawa Takuboku, *tr. fr. Japanese by* Hiroaki Sato. *Fr.* Forty-seven Tanka in Three Lines. FCEI
Sadomasochistic Satisfactions of Seafood, The. Gavin Ewart. NPo
Safari to Bwagamoyo. Bwagamoyo. Lebert Bethune. PoBA
Safari West. John A. Williams. NBP
Safe. James Walker. OBCP
Safe home, safe home in port. The Finished Course. Saint Joseph of the Studium, *tr. by* John Mason Neale. WGRP
Safe in His Keeping. Edgar Cooper Mason. BLRP
Safe in their alabaster chambers. Emily Dickinson. AmPP; NAAL-1; NAWM-2; NOBA; NoP, 2 *vers.*; OxBA; WPE
Safe Side, The. Norman Nicholson. PoPo
Safe sleeping on its mother's breast. The Baby. Ann Taylor. OHIP
Safed. Dovid Knut, *tr. fr. Russian by* Daniel Weissbort. VWA
Safed and I. Molly Myerowitz Levine. VWA
Safety. Rupert Brooke. *Fr.* 1914, II. BrPo; EnLoPo

Safety at Forty; or, An Abecedarian Takes a Walk. L. E. Sissman. Prf

Safety Lock. Louis Aragon, *tr. fr. French by* Michael Benedikt. POS

Safety of the king and's royal throne, The. The Tune to the Devonshire Cant. *Unknown.* APAS

Safety Pin. Moshe Dor, *tr. fr. Hebrew by* Bernhard Frank. MHeP

Safety Pin. Valerie Worth. TSS

Saffold's Cures. *At. to* Thomas Saffold. FaBoUs

Saffron. Guillaume Apollinaire, *trs. fr. French by* Roger Shattuck *and by* Michael Benedikt. POS

Sag' Mir Wer Einst die Uhren Erfund. Heine. *See* Who Was It, Tell Me.

Saga in daylight wilderness. Epos. Gyorgy Raba, *tr. by* Jascha Kessler. FOC

Saga of Gisli, The, *sels. Unknown, tr. fr. Icelandic by* George Johnston. OBVE

  "Goddess of threads gladly."

  "Wife, land of the wave fire'.".

Sagacity. William Rose Benét. MoAmPo

Sage and the ordinary man both have bodies, The. A Poem on Buddha's Begging Bowl. Hsü Pen, *tr. by* Jonathan Chaves. CoBLCP

Sage Counsel. Sir Arthur Quiller-Couch. *See* Lion is the [*or a*] beast to fight, The.

Sage desert: swept in the window by a snow-broom, The. On Being Told "You Have Stars in Your Eyes." Sandra McPherson. NAmP

Sage has the "Six Classics," The. Hsieh Chin, *tr. fr. Chinese by* Jonathan Chaves. *Fr.* What Does the Little Boy Love?, IV. CoBLCP

Sage nor saint nor soldier—these were not. At the Monument to Pierre Louÿs. Richard Howard. EOEF

Sage said: We are all books, The. The Word. D. J. Enright. PoPo

Sagesse, *sel.* Hilda Doolittle ("H. D.").

  "You look at me, a hut or cage contains." NOCV

Sagesse, *sels.* Paul Verlaine, *tr. fr. French.*

  "Sky is up above the roof, The." *Tr. by* Ernest Dowson. AWP; FaPON

  "Slumber dark and deep." *Tr. by* Arthur Symons. AWP

Sagest of women, even of widows, she. Byron. *Fr.* Don Juan, I. NOBL

Sagging Bough, The. Louis Untermeyer. BXAP

Sagimusume: The White Heron Maiden. Jonny Kyoko Sullivan. WPOW

Saginaw Song, The. Theodore Roethke. NBLV; RB

Sah gimme ah wuk nah. Wukhand. Paul Keens-Douglas. PBCV

Sahara. Coventry Patmore. *Fr.* The Angel in the House. EBVV

Said. George Starbuck. OBAL

Said/ a hip/ lip-ful. Leg-acy of a Blue Capricorn. James Cunningham. JB

Said a frog on a log. *Unknown.* BoTP

Said active priest, "My work has increased." There Is None to Help. Chad Walsh. *Fr.* The Psalm of Christ. TrCP

Said an ancient hermit, bending. The Olive Tree. Sabine Baring-Gould. GN

Said Burgoyne to his men, as they passed in review. The Progress of Sir Jack Brag. *Unknown.* PAH

Said Descartes, "I extol." Theological. Clifton Fadiman. FiBHP

Said Fading-leaf to Fallen-leaf. Fading-Leaf and Fallen-Leaf. Richard Garnett. EBVV

Said Folly to Wisdom. On the Road. Tudor Jenks. NA

Said God, "You sisters, ere ye go." Hope and Despair. Lascelles Abercrombie. OBMV

Said Hanrahan. P. J. Hartigan. PoAu-1

Said Henry VIII/ Accepting his fate. Edmund Conti. SoTCo

Said, I, Oh, give me simplicity. Rural Simplicity. H. J. Byron. NOBL

Said Jean Arp's wife to Mary Martin. Lila Zeiger. SoTCo

Said Jeremy Jonathan Joseph Jones. The Rhyme of the Rain Machine. F. W. Clarke. BoNaP

Said Jerome K. Jerome to Ford Madox Ford. Mutual Problem. William Cole. OBAL

Said Jim X. . . Ezra Pound. *Fr.* Cantos, XII. NAs

Said Life to Death: "Methinks, if I were you." Recrimination. Ella Wheeler Wilcox. AA

Said Maylard to Solly one day in Glen Brittle. Doing the Dubhs. *Unknown.* PoSH

Said Mr. Smith, "I really cannot. Bones. Walter de la Mare. FiBHP

Said my landlord, white-headed Gil Gomez. Battle of the King's Mill. Thomas Dunn English. PAH

Said Old Gentleman Gay, "On a Thanksgiving Day." A Good Thanksgiving. Annie Douglas Green Robinson. PoLF

Said one man to another. One Man to Another. Rita Anyiam–St. John. WS

Said Opie Read to E. P. Roe. To Be Continued. Julian Street *and* James Montgomery Flagg. FiBHP

Said Peter the Great to a Great Dane. Peterhof. Edmund Wilson. GoJo

Said, Pull her up a bit will you, Mac, I want to unload there. Reason. Josephine Miles. InPK; NoAM; NoP; PoCH; TAP

Said the archangels, moving in their glory. Voice. Harriet Prescott Spofford. AA

Said the bird in search of a cage. A Bird in Search of a Cage. Robert Pack. NePoEA

Said the Birds of America. The Birds of America. James Richard Broughton. AmFN

Said the Canoe. Isabella Valancy Crawford. NOBC

  (Canoe, The.) OBCV

Said the Captain: "There was wire." Our Modest Doughboys. Albert Charlton Andrews. PAH

Said the circus man, Oh what do you like. The Circus; or One View of It. Theodore Spencer. RR

Said the Duck to the Kangaroo. The Duck and the Kangaroo. Edward Lear. ILY; OxBChV

Said the Eagle. The Eagle's Song. Mary Austin. GOA

Said the Englishman: "W'at's all this bloomin' wow?" Foreigners at the Fair. Fred Emerson Brooks. OBAL

Said the father to the daughter. Our Ship She Lies in Harbour. *Unknown.* OBET

Said the first little chicken. Five Little Chickens. *Unknown.* PDV; RAR

  (Chickens, The.) FaPON; MoShBr

Said the first little chicken. Wishes. *Unknown.* BoTP

Said the grave Dean of Westminster. A Refusal. Thomas Hardy. FaBoCo; LiTB

Said the Lion: "On music I dote." The Musical Lion. Oliver Herford. OBCA

Said the Lion to the Lioness—"When you are amber dust." Heart and Mind. Edith Sitwell. OxBTC; TwCP

Said the little boy, "Sometimes I drop my spoon." The Little Boy and the Old Man. Shel Silverstein. RHPC

Said the little plaque in sober brass. This Tree. William Hathaway. NAmP

Said the monkey to the donkey. *Unknown.* FaFP

Said the Queen of the Nile. The Queen of the Nile. William Jay Smith. GrPl

Said the rabbit to the hop toad. The Toad and the Rabbit. John Martin. RAR

Said the Raggedy Man, on a hot afternoon. The Man in the Moon. James Whitcomb Riley. NA

Said the Robin to the Sparrow. Overheard in an Orchard. Elizabeth Cheney. BLRP

Said the Rose. George Henry Miles. BLPA

Said the shark to the flying fish over the phone. The Flattered Flying Fish. Emile Victor Rieu. PDV; RHPC; SO

Said the Sword to the Ax, 'twixt the whacks and the hacks. Ned Braddock. John Williamson Palmer. PAH

Said the trout to the fluke. Johnshaven. *Unknown.* GBP

Said the Wind to the Moon: "I will blow you out." The Wind and the Moon. George Macdonald. GoJo; MoShBr; OnMSP

Said Zwingli to Muntzer. How to Start a War. Phyllis McGinley. OBSV

Saies, "Come here, cuzen Gawaine so gay." King Arthur and King Cornwall. *Unknown.* ESPB

Saigon. Narushima Ryuhoku, *tr. fr. Chinese by* Burton Watson. JLIC-2

Saigon Bar Girls, 1975. Yusef Komunyakaa. MT

Sail, The [*or* A]. Mikhail Yurevich Lermontov, *tr. fr. Russian.* AAA, *tr. by* Alan Myers. AWP, *tr. by* Max Eastman. AAA

"Sail, A! a sail! Oh, whence away." Heart's Content. *Unknown.* PoLF

Sail and Oar. Robert Graves. MOS

Sail at the mast head dips from side to side, The. *Unknown, tr. by* C. H. Berndt. WTO

Sail Away. Robert Adamson. CBAP

Sail, Monarchs, rising and falling. Roots and Branches. Robert Duncan. VGW

Saîl of Claustra, Aelis, Azalais. The Alchemist. Ezra Pound. CMoP; LiTA; WSC

Sail On, O Ship of State. Longfellow. *See* Building of the Ship, The: Thou, too, sail on, O Ship of State!

Sail on the Lake after Rain, A. Huang Ching-jen, *tr. fr. Chinese by* Daniel Bryant. WFTU

Sail Peacefully Home. Simeon Grigoryevich Frug, *tr. fr. Yiddish.* TrJP

Sailboat, Your Secret. Robert Francis. SD

Sailing. Al Zolynas. TSL

Sailing close to shore. Shunzei, *tr. fr. Japanese by* Burton Watson. *Fr.* Thirty Tanka. FCEI

Sailing from the United States. Stanley Moss. VGW
Sailing Home from Rapallo. Robert Lowell. HCAP; TAP
Sailing Homeward. Chan Fang-sheng, *tr. fr. Chinese by* Arthur Waley. AWP; FaBoCh
Sailing in Crosslight. Anita Skeen. IHMS
Sailing in the boat when the tide runs high. Rose in the Garden. *Unknown.* AmFP
Sailing in the Rain. Hsiang Yang, *tr. fr. Chinese by* Dominic Cheung. IFON
Sailing of the Fleet, The. *Unknown.* PAH
Sailing on Lac d'Annecy. William Rossa Cole. *Fr.* A Mini-Samizdat of New River Rhymes. SoTCo
Sailing or Drowning. Allen Curnow. ATNZ
Sailing Pine, The; the Cedar, proud and tall. Kinds of Trees to Plant. Spenser. *Fr.* The Faerie Queene, I, 1. OHIP
Sailing, Sailing. Gray Burr. NYBP
Sailing, Sailing. Lillian Morrison. ASP
Sailing the Back River. Dave Smith. MT
Sailing to an Island. Richard Murphy. IPY
Sailing to Byzantium. W. B. Yeats. AnIL; CMoP; FaFP; FF; FPL; GTBS-P; HAP; HeIP; HoPM; InPK; InPS; InvP; LiTB; LiTM; MoAB; MoBrPo; MoP; NAEL-2; NAWM-2; NIP; NoAM; NOBE; NoP; OAEL-2; OBMV; OxBTC; PoE; PoRA; PPP; PrIm; SeCePo; SoSe; TEP; TIRV; TOF; UnPo; WeW
Sailing upon the River. George Crabbe. *Fr.* The Borough, Letter IX. OBNC
Sailor. Langston Hughes. PoA
Sailor, The. Goodridge MacDonald. CaP
Sailor, The. Sylvia Townsend Warner. OBMV
Sailor and His Bride, The. *Unknown.* AmFP
Sailor and the Shark, The. Paul Fort, *tr. fr. French by* Frederick York Powell. OBMV
Sailor at Midnight, A. Elizabeth Nancy Sargent. NMM
Sailor Boy, The. Tennyson. MOS
Sailor in his sailboat, homeward bound, The. Vacationer. Walker Gibson. SD
Sailor pops upon the Royal Pair, A. George III and the Sailor. "Peter Pindar." *Fr.* The Royal Tour, and Weymouth Amusements. NOEC
Sailor, we all stare at you. Wynyard Sailor. Ray Mathew. CBAP
"Sailorman, I'll give to you." The Silver Penny. Walter de la Mare. CMoP; OBMV
Sailors. Louis Simpson. NYBP
Sailors. Berysh Vaynshteyn, *tr. fr. Yiddish by* Benjamin *and* Barbara Harshav *and* Kathryn Helle. AYP
Sailors' Alphabet, The. *Unknown.* AmFP; OxBSS, *with music*
Sailor's Apology for Bow-Legs, A. Thomas Hood. MOS
Sailor's Carol. Charles Causley. OBCP
Sailor's Christmas Day, The. *Unknown.* OxBSS
Sailors come/ To the drum. Hornpipe. Dame Edith Sitwell. *Fr.* Façade. FaBoMo; GTBS-P; OAEL-2; SeCePo
Sailor's Complaint; or, The True Character of a Purser of a Ship, The. *Unknown.* OxBSS
Sailor's Consolation, The. *At. to* William Pitt. BeLS; FaBoCo
Sailors for My Money. Martin Parker. OxBSS
Sailor's Grave, The. *At. to* Eliza Cook. BLPA
Sailor's Harbor. Henry Reed. MoAB; MoBrPo; MOS
Sailors have hearts that yearn for trains and crowds and cities. Sailors. Berysh Vaynshteyn, *tr. by* Benjamin *and* Barbara Harshav *and* Kathryn Helle. AYP
Sailor's Lamentation, The. *Unknown.* OxBSS
Sailor's life is a merry life, A. Sweet William. *Unknown.* OBET (Sailor's Life, A, *with music.*) OxBSS
Sailor's Mother, The, *sel.* Wordsworth.
"And thus continuing, she said." Par
Sailors on Leave. Owen Dodson. AmNP
Sailor's Only Delight, The. *Unknown.* OxBSS
Sailor's Prayer, A. George Hornell Morris. TrPWD
Sailor's Return, The. *Unknown.* See As I Walked Out One Night.
Sailors there are of gentlest breed. Commemorative of a Naval Victory. Herman Melville. AiP; HAP; MOS; UnPo
Sailor's trade is a weary life, A. The Rocky Island. *Unknown.* AmFP
Sailor's Wife, A. Clara Bernhardt. CaP
Sailor's Wife, The. William Julius Mickle, *also at. to* Jean Adam. BeLS; GN; GTBS; GTBS-P
Sailors' Wives, The. *Unknown.* OxBSS
Sailor's Woman. Annette Patton Cornell. GoYe
Sailor's Yarn, A. James Jeffrey Roche. MOS; NA
Sails float on the margins of sunset. Switzerland 1938-1965. Judah Leib Teller, *tr. by* Benjamin *and* Barbara Harshav. AYP
Sainclaire's Defeat. *Unknown.* PAH
Saint. Robert Graves. CMoP

St. Agnes' Eve. Tennyson. LiTB; OBEV
St. Agnes' Eve—Ah, bitter chill it was! The Eve of St. Agnes. Keats. BeLS; ChER; EnRP; FiP; HAP; HoPM; NAEL-2; NIP; NoP; OAEL-2; OBNC; OBNV; PoE; PoEL-4; PoLF; TEP; TrGrPo; WeW
St. Andrew's Voyage to Mermedonia. *Unknown, tr. fr. Anglo-Saxon by* Charles W. Kennedy. *Fr.* Andreas. AnOE
Saint Anfaidh walked alone. Saint, Bird, Angel. *Unknown, tr. by* Brendan Kennelly. TIRV
St. Anthony and His Pig; a Cantata. Frederick Forrest. NOEC
St. Anthony's Township. Gilbert Sheldon. CH
St. Asaph's. Kingsley Amis. OxBTC
St. Aubin d'Aubigne. Paul Dehn. OBWP
Saint Augustine. Joseph Mary Plunkett. TIRV
St. Benedick. *Unknown.* FaBoUs
Saint Bernard's Hymn of Praise to the Virgin Mary. Dante, *tr. fr. Italian by* Dana Gioia. *Fr.* Divina Commedia: Paradiso, XXXIII. PFI
Saint Besht. Itzig Manger, *tr. fr. Yiddish by* Leonard Wolf. PeBMYV
Saint, Bird, Angel. *Unknown, tr. fr. Irish by* Brendan Kennelly. TIRV
Saint Bridget was/ A problem child. The Giveaway. Phyllis McGinley. PoRA
St. Bridget's Cross. Anne Hartigan. CIP
Saint Called "Truth," A. William Langland. *Fr.* The Vision of Piers Plowman. NOCV
Saint Cloud. Sir Walter Scott. OBTV
Saint Colm-Cille and the Cairn of Farewell. John Irvine. TIRV
Saint Columba. Lionel Johnson. TIRV
St. Columcille the Scribe. *At. to* Saint Columcille. AnIL, *tr. by* Kuno Meyer; BIrV, *tr. by* Flann O'Brien
St. Columcille's Island Hermitage. *Unknown, tr. fr. Middle Irish by* Kenneth Jackson. AnIL
Saint Coyote. Linda Hogan. STE
St. Crispin's Day. Shakespeare. *See* King Henry V: Henry V before Agincourt.
St. Dunstan, as the story goes. *Unknown.* OxNR
Saint Fiacre. John Irvine. TIRV
Saint Francis. John Peale Bishop. EaLo
Saint Francis and Saint Benedight. William Cartwright. *Fr.* The Ordinary, III, i. EaLo
(House Blessing, A.) ChTr
Saint Francis and the Birds. Seamus Heaney. TIRV
Saint Francis and the Sow. Galway Kinnell. CAPP; FYAP; InPK; NIP; RB
St. Francis of Assisi and the Miserable Jews. Josef Whittlin, *tr. by* Isaac Komem. VWA
St. Francis of the mountain cave and wattle hut. A Little Litany to St. Francis. Philip Murray. NePoAm
St. George. Charlie Walker. AmFP
St. Gervais. Michael Roberts. FaBoCh
St. Govan. A. G. Prys-Jones. OBWVE
Saint Harmony my patroness. Paul Goodman. VGW
St. Helena Lullaby, A. Kipling. EBEV; FaBoCh; OBMV; PoEL-5
Saint-Henri Spring. Milton Acorn. NeAC
Saint Hugh. Thomas Dekker. *See* Shoemaker's Holiday, The: Drinking Song.
St. Isaac's Church, Petrograd. Claude McKay. AmNP; PoBA
St. James Infirmary. *Unknown.* AmFP
Saint Jerome and his lion. Leonardo Da Vinci's. Marianne Moore. NYBP
Saint Jerome lived with a community. Elegy for Wright & Hugo. Norman Dubie. NoAM
St. John, *sels.* Bible, *N.T.*
"I am the true vine, and my Father is the husbandman." *Fr.* XV: 1-18. OBVE
Word, The. *Fr.* I: 1-5. TrGrPo
Saint John, The. George Frederick Clarke. CaP
St. John. Whittier. PAH
Saint John Baptist. William Drummond of Hawthornden. EaLo; GTBS; GTBS-P; NOBE; OBEV; TrCP
Saint John did lean on Jesus's breast. For Saint John's Day. Luke Wadding. TIRV
Saint Judas. James Wright. LCAP; NOBA; SM
St. Julien's Eve. James Cunningham. JB
Saint-Just 1767-93 ("Saint-Just: his name seems stolen from the Missal"). Robert Lowell. FaBoMo
St. Kevin. *At. to* Samuel Lover. WTO
St. Lawrence and the Saguenay, *sel.* Charles Sangster.
Thousand Islands, The. NOBC; OBCV
Saint Leger. Clinton Scollard. PAH
Saint-Lô. Samuel Beckett. NOIV

St. Louis/ such a colored town/ a whiskey. Nappy Edges (A Cross Country Sojourn). Ntozake Shange. BlSi
St. Louis Blues. William Christopher Handy. FF
St. Lucy's Day. Donald Revell. BAP
St. Luke, *sels*. Bible, *N.T.*
"And it came to pass in those days, that there went out a decree from Caesar Augustus." *Fr.* II. NAWM-1
"And there were in the same country shepherds abiding in the field." *Fr.* II: 8-14. PChr
"Feare not, litle flocke, for it is your fathers good pleasure to give you the kingdome." *Fr.* XII: 32-40. OBVE
Magnificat, The. *Fr.* I: 46-56. BoWoP; WGRP
("And Marie said, My soule doth magnifie the Lord.") OBVE
Nunc Dimittis. *Fr.* II: 29-32. WGRP
"Then drew near unto him all the publicans and sinners." *Fr.* XV. NAWM-1
St. McC. Charles Bernstein. IAT
St. Malachy. Thomas Merton. VGW
Saint Malcolm. Jewel C. Latimore. BPo
Saint Maria Maggiore. Gerhard Fritsch, *tr. fr. German by* Beth Bjorklund. CoAuP
St. Mark, *sels*. Bible, *N.T.*
"And as soon as it was morning the chief priests." *Fr.* XV: 1-39. DL
"And he said, So is the kingdome of God." *Fr.* IV: 26-32. OBVE
St. Martin and the Beggar. Thom Gunn. Mes; MoBS
Saint Mary Magdalene; or, The Weeper. Richard Crashaw. MeLP; SeCV-1
(Weeper,The.) MePo; OAEL-1, *abr*.; OBEV; SeCP
"And now where're he strayes," *sel*. FaBoCo; Par
St. Mary Virgine. A Cry to Mary. Saint Godric. MeEL
St. Mary's Loch. Geoffrey Faber. PoSH
St. Matthew, *sels*. Bible, *N.T.*
"And seeing the multitudes, he went up." *Fr.* V-VII. NAWM-1
"Blessed are the poor[e] in spirit for theirs is the kingdom[e] of heaven." *Fr.* V: 3-10. OBVE
(Beatitudes, The.) TrGrPo
God Provides. *Fr.* VI: 26-34. BLRP
"In the end of the sabbath, as it began to dawn toward the first day of the week." *Fr.* XXVIII. NAWM-1
"No man can serve two masters." *Fr.* VI: 24-29. OBVE
"Our Father which [*or* who] art in heaven." *Fr.* VI: 9-13. EaLo; PoLF; TrGrPo
Parable of the Good Seed, The. *Fr.* XIII: 24-30. InPK
"Then one of the twelve, called Judas Iscariot." *Fr.* XXVI: 14-XXVIII. NAWM-1
Treasures. *Fr.* VI: 19-21. TrGrPo
"When morning has come, all the chief priests and elders of the people." *Fr.* XXVII. NAWM-1
Saint Médard. István Vas, *tr. fr. Hungarian by* William Jay Smith. MHuP
Saint Nicholas. Marianne Moore. NYBP; WPE
St. Nicholas. Juliane Windhager, *tr. fr. German by* Beth Bjorklund. CoAuP
Saint Patrick. Sir Shane Leslie. TIRV
Saint Patrick for Ireland, *sel*. James Shirley.
Bard's Chant. ACP
Saint Patrick, slave to Milcho of the herds. The Proclamation. Whittier. PAH
Saint Patrick's Breastplate; or, The Deer's Cry. *At.* to Saint Patrick, *tr. fr. Irish*. FaBoCh, *tr. by* Frances Alexander; TIRV, *tr. by* Kuno Meyer; WGRP
Saint Patrick's Day, 1973. Wendy Rose. CDW
St. Patrick's Dean, your country's pride. To Dr. Swift on His Birthday, 30th November 1721. Esther Johnson. EnLoPo
St. Patrick's Hymn before Tara. James Clarence Mangan. EnRP
Saint Paul, *sel*. F. W. H. Myers.
Inner Light, The. WGRP
St. Peter. Christina Rossetti. NOCV
Saint Peter and the Bluestocking. Marie von Ebner-Eschenbach, *tr. fr. German by* Susan L. Cocalis *and* Gerlinde Geiger. DMG
St. Peter at the Gate. Joseph Bert Smiley. BLPA
St. Peter once: "Lord, dost Thou wash my feet?" St. Peter. Christina Rossetti. NOCV
Saint Peter sat by the celestial gate. The Vision of Judgment. Byron. EnRP; NAEL-2; OAEL-2; OBSV, *sts.* 1-23; OxBoLi, *sts.* 1-15; TEP
St. Peter stood guard at the golden gate. St. Peter at the Gate. Joseph Bert Smiley. BLPA

Saint Peter's Complaint, *sel*. Robert Southwell.
Stanzas from Saint Peter's Complaint. ACP
St. Peter's Day was celebrated by St. Brendan at sea. The Fish at Mass. *Unknown, tr. by* J. F. Webb. BIrV
St. Peter's Shadow. Richard Crashaw. ACP
St. Philip and St. James. Christopher Smart. *Fr.* Hymns and Spiritual Songs, XIII. NOCV; NOEC
Saint Pumpkin. Nancy Willard. LCAP
Saint Ras. Anthony McNeill. PBCV
St. Roach. Muriel Rukeyser. GLP
St. Simeon Stylites. Tennyson. NOBVV; OAEL-2
St. Simon and Jude, on you I intrude. *Unknown*. FaBoUs
St. Sophia. John Fuller. DiPo
St. Stephen and King Herod ("Seynt Stevene was a clerk"). *Unknown*. ESPB, *Middle English vers*.; NoP, *mod. vers*.; OxBoLi, *Middle English vers*.; TrGrPo, *mod. vers*.
(Carol for St. Stephen's Day, A.) CH
(Seynt Stevyn and Herowdes.) OxBB
Saint Stephen had an angel's face. For Saint Stephen's Day. Luke Wadding. TIRV
St. Stephen's cloistered hall was proud. Columbus. Lydia Huntley Sigourney. AA; PAH
St. Stephen's Day. Patric Dickinson. OBCP
St. Stephen's Day. John Hewitt. CIP
St. Swithin's Chair. Sir Walter Scott. WSC
St. Theresa's Book-Mark. St. Theresa of Avila. *See* Let nothing disturb thee.
St. Thomas Aquinas. Charles Simic. BAP
St. Thomas Aquinas thought. Vulture. Kenneth Rexroth. *Fr.* A Bestiary. NNaP
St. Thomas's Day is past and gone. *Unknown*. OxNR
St. Uncumber and St. Trunnion. The Palmer. John Heywood. *Fr.* The Play of the Four P.P. ACP
St. Ursanne. Michael Roberts. LiTM
St. Valentine. Marianne Moore. NYBP; OFD
St. Valentine. Tu Kuo-ch'ing, *tr. fr. Chinese by* Dominic Cheung. IFON
St. Valentine's Day. Wilfrid Scawen Blunt. *Fr.* The Love Sonnets of Proteus, LV. EnLoPo
Saint Valentine's Day. Coventry Patmore. *Fr.* The Unknown Eros, XLIII. OBNC
Saint Valentine's Day. Shakespeare. *See* Hamlet: Tomorrow Is Saint Valentine's Day.
Saint Wears a Halo, The. Robert Louis "Peter." BoTP
Saint, who overlaps. John Logan. *Fr.* A Cycle for Mother Cabrini. CRP
Sainte Marye Virgine. A Cry to Mary. Saint Godric. MeEL
Sainthood. Cristoir O'Flynn. TIRV
Saints. George Garrett. EaLo
Saints, and Their Care. Alberto Rios. UL
Saints are gathering at the real, The. The Confirmers. A. R. Ammons. TAP
Saint's Bridge. Lola Ridge. WPE
Saints have adored the lofty soul of you. Charles Hamilton Sorley. *Fr.* Two Sonnets, I. MMA; MoBrPo
Saints, I give myself up to thee. Jack Kerouac. *Fr.* Mexico City Blues, 219. NeAP
Saints in Glory, The. Dante, *tr. fr. Italian by* Henry F. Cary. *Fr.* Divina Commedia: Paradiso, XXXI. WGRP
Saints in Glory, We Together. Nehemiah Adams. AH
Saint's Parade. Robert Layzer. NePoEA
Sair Fyel'd, Hinny. *Unknown*. GBP
Saith the poet of nonsense. Scraps of Lear. Edward Lear. FaBoNo
Sakaki, or a Sacred Tree. *Unknown. tr. fr. Japanese by* Hiroaki Sato. FCEI
Sakhara. R. A. D. Ford. NOBC
Saki, for God's love, come and fill my glass. Hafiz, *tr. fr. Persian by* Richard Le Gallienne. *Fr.* Odes, I. AWP
Salaam Alaikum. *Unknown*. PoLF
Salad, *sels*. Mortimer Collins.
Salad: After Browning. Par
Salad: After Swinburne. Par
Salad: After Tennyson. CenHV; Par
Salad, A. Sydney Goodsir Smith. FaBoUs; NBLV
Salad: After Browning. Mortimer Collins. *Fr.* Salad. Par
Salad: After Swinburne. Mortimer Collins. *Fr.* Salad. Par
Salad: After Tennyson. Mortimer Collins. *Fr.* Salad. CenHV; FaBoCo; Par
(King Arthur Growing Very Tired Indeed.) FaBoCo
Salad Days. Susan Musgrave. NoAM

Salad La Raza. Janet Campbell Hale. VoR
Salad of greens! Salad of greens! The Universal Favorite. Carolyn Wells. NBLV
Salamanca Doctor's Farewell, The. *Unknown.* APAS
Salami. Philip Levine. NNaP; NOBA; TAP
Salamis. Aeschylus, *tr. fr. Greek by* G. M. Cookson. *Fr.* The Persians. WaaP
Salamis. Lawrence Durrell. NYBP
Salaziennes, Les, *sel.* Auguste Lacaussade, *tr. fr. French.* "My lips from this day forgot how to smile." TTY
Salcombe Seaman's Flaunt to the Proud Pirate, The. *Unknown.* ChTr
Sale. Josephine Miles. WPE
Sale. Miller Williams. WeW
Sale began—young girls were there, The. The Slave Auction. Frances Ellen Watkins Harper. BPo; PoNe; TTY
Sale of Smoke, A. Roberta Spear. AmPA
Sale of Souls. Adah Isaacs Menken. CBWP-1
Sale of the Pet Lamb, The. Mary Howitt. CH
Salem. Robert Lowell. AiP; NePoEA; Son
Salem. Edmund Clarence Stedman. AA; PAH
Salem, Massachusetts. Edwin Muir. OBTV
Salem Witch, A. Ednah Proctor Clarke. PAH
Sales Talk for Annie. Morris Bishop. NBLV
Salesman, A. E. E. Cummings. *See* Salesman Is an It That Stinks Excuse, A.
Salesman, The. Robert Mezey. NePoEA
Salesman Is an It That Stinks Excuse, A. E. E. Cummings. NoAM; OxBA; TW
(Salesman, A.) NIP
Salford Bridge—That Popular Resort of the Great Unwashed. William Billington. PF
Salient point, so first is call'd the heart, The. The Circulation of the Blood. Sir Richard Blackmore. *Fr.* Creation. FaBoUs
Salisbury Plain and Stonehenge. Wordsworth. *Fr.* Guilt and Sorrow. FaBoPP
Salisbury; the Cathedral Close. Coventry Patmore. *See* Angel in the House, The: Cathedral Close, The.
Sallow faces. Tokyo Imperial University Students. Nakano Shigeharu, *tr. by* Geoffrey Bownas *and* Anthony Thwaite. PeBJV
Sally. Paul Durcan. FaBCIP
Sally. Tom Mandel. IAT
Sally and Manda. Alice B. Campbell. RHPC
Sally Birkett's Ale. Julius Caeser Ibbetson. *See* O mortal man, that lives by bread.
Sally Brown. Thomas Hood. *See* Young Ben he was a nice young man.
Sally Brown. *Unknown.* AmFP
Sally Free and Easy. Cyril Tawney. OBET
Sally go round the sun. *Unknown.* OxNR
Sally Goodin. *Unknown.* AmFP
Sally, having swallowed cheese. Cruel, Clever Cat. Geoffrey Taylor. ChTr; FaBoEE
Sally in Our Alley. Henry Carey. AnAmPo; AWP; BLPL; BoLoP; CoMu; FaBoBe; FaFP; GTBS; GTBS-P; NOBE; OBEV
Sally is dead, and the children stand around. Death of a Dog. Peter Bland. ATNZ
Sally is gone that was so kindly. Ha'nacker Mill. Hilaire Belloc. FaPoR; MoBrPo; OxBTC; RB
Sally is the laundress, and every Saturday. The Dolls' Wash. Juliana Horatia Ewing. OxBChV
Sally Munro. *Unknown.* OxBSS
Sally, Sally Waters. *Unknown.* OxNR
Sally Simpkin's Lament. Thomas Hood. EnRP; MOS
Sally Sweetbread. Henry Carey. CoMu
Sally's Garden. *Unknown.* AmFP
Salma. Ilyas Farhat, *tr. fr. Arabic by* Salma Khadra Jayyusi *and* John Heath-Stubbs. MAP
Salman. Tawfiq Zayyad, *tr. fr. Arabic by* Sharif Elmusa *and* Charles Doria. MAP
Salmon. Jorie Graham. MAYP
Salmon, The. Christian Morgenstern, *tr. fr. German by* Geoffrey Grigson. FaBoNo
Salmon and red wine. Raisins and Nuts. Charles Reznikoff. VWA
Salmon Boy. David Wagoner. AnAn
Salmon Courage. Marlene Philip. PBCV
Salmon Cycle. Avner Treinin, *tr. fr. Hebrew by* Robert Friend. VWA
Salmon Drowns Eagle. Malcolm Lowry. MoCV; OBCV
Salmon Eggs. Ted Hughes. NAs

Salmon-fishing. Robinson Jeffers. ASP; SD
Salmon lying in the depths of Llyn Llifon, The. The Ancients of the World. R. S. Thomas. RB
Salmon were just down there, The. Salmon Eggs. Ted Hughes. NAs
Salome. Ai. NoAM
Salome was a dancer. *Unknown.* WTO
Salomon. Pierre Morhange, *tr. fr. French by* Edouard Roditi. VWA
Salon Chronicle. Rigoberto Paredes, *tr. fr. Spanish by* Walter Martínez. Vol
Saloon is gone up the creek, The. Hemmed-in Males. William Carlos Williams. *Fr.* A Folded Skyscraper. MAT; PoRA
Salt. Robert Francis. TSS
Salt. Anne Hartigan. CIP
Salt. Ruth Stone. NMM
Salt, The. May Swenson. *Fr.* Poet to Tiger. GLP
Salt and bread in our. H. C. Artmann, *tr. by* Beth Bjorklund. CoAuP
Salt and Memory. Zoltán Zelk, *tr. fr. Hungarian by* Barbara Howes. MHuP
Salt creek mouths unflushed by the sea. The South Coast. William Everson. NeAP
Salt Flats, The. Sir Charles G. D. Robert. CaP
Salt Garden, The. Howard Nemerov. NePoEA
Salt Gardens. Christine Busta, *tr. fr. German by* Beth Bjorklund. CoAuP
Salt Lake City. Hayden Carruth. AmFN
Salt of Pleasure. Pentti Saaritsa, *tr. fr. Finnish by* Aili Jarvenpa. SOP
Salt Peanuts. Riekus Waskowsky. DuIn
Salt Pork, The. Robert Clayton Casto. HeIP
Salt Statues. Tsfrirah Gar, *tr. fr. Hebrew by* Bernhard Frank. MHeP
Salt Water Story. Richard Hugo. NAAL-2; NoAM; NoP
Salt wave sings, The. Fingernail Sunrise. Vernon Watkins. NYBP
Salt worker always eats salty food, A. At the Ch'ang Family Well. Wu Chia-chi, *tr. fr. Chinese by* John E. Wills, Jr. *Fr.* Ten Miscellaneous Poems on Tung-t'ao, VIII. WFTU
Salted breams' gums are cold. Basho, *tr. fr. Japanese by* Burton Watson. *Fr.* Seventy-six Hokku. FCEI
Saltimbanques. Guillaume Apollinaire, *trs. fr. French by* Michael Benedikt *and by* Roger Shattuck. POS
Saltimbanques. Pierre Reverdy, *tr. fr. French.* CT, *tr. by* William Jay Smith; POS, *tr. by* Michael Benedikt.
Saltimbanques. Tristan Tzara, *tr. fr. French by* Michael Benedikt. POS
Saltmarsh on the horizon, The. The Estuarial Republic. Douglas Dunn. FaBoMo
Salts and Oils. Philip Levine. BLA
Salutamus. Sterling A. Brown. CDC
Salutation. Ezra Pound. HeIP; MoAB; MoAmPo; NOBA; OxBA; TAP; VGW
Salutation, The. Thomas Traherne. InVP; NOCV; NoP; OBS; SeCP; SeCV-2
Salutation of the Dawn, The. *Unknown.* PoLF
Salutation the Second. Ezra Pound. NOBA; OxBA
Salutation to Jesus Christ. John Calvin. WGRP
Salute. Moyshe-Leyb Halpern, *tr. fr. Yiddish.* AYP, *tr. by* Benjamin *and* Barbara Harshav; PeBMYV, *tr. by* John Hollander.
Salute. Oliver Pitcher. PoBA
Salute. James Schuyler. FYAP; NeAP
Salute the last and everlasting day. Ascension [*or* Ascention]. John Donne. *Fr.* La Corona. OBS; Son
Salute to the Elephant. Odeniyi Apolebieji, *tr. fr. Yoruba by* S. A. Babalola. WTO
Salute to the first earth, A. To Africa. Mazisi Kunene. WMBCH
Salute Your Partner. *Unknown.* AmFP
Salvador Dali. David Gascoyne. EAS; OxBTC
Salvation Army lass, The. Lola Ridge. *Fr.* Ward X. WPE
Salvation comes by Christ alone. An Evening Thought. Jupiter Hammon. PoNe
Salvation to all that will is nigh. Annunciation. John Donne. *Fr.* La Corona. TrCP
Salve! Thomas Edward Brown. OBEV
Sam. Walter de la Mare. FaBV; MoAB; MoBrPo; OnMSP
Sam Bass. *Unknown.* AmFP; AS, *with music;* BeLS
Sam had spirits naught could check. Impetuous Samuel. Harry Graham. NA

Sam [*or* Samuel] Hall. *Unknown.* AmFP; ChTr; TW; UnPo

Sam, Sam, the butcher man. *Unknown.* FaFP

Sam Speer, watching the black ball. The Last Man Killed by Indians in Kimble County, Texas. Mike Angelotti. MOWH

Samantabhadra Facing Westward. Ho Shao-chi, *tr. fr. Chinese by* Irving Lo. WFTU

Samba. Aimé Césaire, *tr. fr. French by* Michael Benedikt. POS

Sambo's Right to Be Kilt. Charles Graham Halpine. AA

Same, The. Wordsworth. *See* London, 1802 ("Milton! thou should'st be living at this hour").

Same But Different. Merle Collins. WS

Same Dream, The. Shlomit Cohen, *tr. fr. Hebrew by* Myra Glazer Schotz. VWA

Same Gesture, The. John Montague. BIrV

Same in Blues. Langston Hughes. *Fr.* Lenox Avenue Mural. InPS

Same Inside, The. Anna Swirszczynska, *tr. fr. Polish by* Czeslaw Milosz. PwPP

Same leaves over and over again, The! In Hardwood Groves. Robert Frost. HAP

Same Old Jazz, The. Philip Whalen. NeAP

Same old souvenirs, The. Niagara Falls Nocturne. Len Gasparini. NeAC

Same Side of the Canoe, The. Alda do Espírito Santo, *tr. fr. Portuguese by* Allan Francovich *and* Kathleen Weaver. PBWP

Same Voice, Still, The. Yves Bonnefoy, *tr. fr. French by* Paul Auster. RHTwFP

Samela. Robert Greene. *See* Menaphon: Doron's Description of Samela.

Sammy Lou of Rue. Revolutionary Petunias. Alice Walker. BlSi

Samos. James Merrill. *Fr.* Scripts for the Pageant. HCAP

Sampler from Haworth. Frances Minturn Howard. WPE

Sampson Imitated. Benjamin Franklin. *See* Jack, eating rotten cheese did say.

Sam's World ("Sam's mother has"). Sam Cornish. CNA

Samson. Amir Gilboa, *tr. fr. Hebrew by* Stephen Mitchell. VWA

Samson Agonistes ("A little onward lend thy guiding hand."), sels. Milton. OAEL-1; PoEL-3

  All Is Best. NOBE; OBEV; OBS; SeCePo

  Blindness of Samson, The. LiTB

    "I, dark in light, exposed," 5 *ll.* TrGrPo

  "But see here comes thy reverend Sire." EBEV

  "Come, come, no time for lamentation now." FiP

    (Death of Samson.) ChTr

    (No Time for Lamentation Now.) FaBoRV

  Delilah. SeCePo

  "Feast and noon grew high, and Sacrifice, The." EBEV

  Heroic Vengeance. OBS

  "Let me obtain forgiveness of thee, Samson." EBEV

  "Oh [*or* O], how comely it is, and how reviving." NOBE; NOCV; OBEV

    (Deliverer, The.) OBS

  Samson before the Prison in Gaza. FaBoPV

  "This, this is he; softly a while." UnPo

    (Samson Fallen.) OBS

  Transcendence of God, The. OBS

  Ways of God to Men, The. OBS

  "Wilt thou then serve the Philistines with that gift." EBEV

  Woman. OBS

Samson before the Prison in Gaza. Milton. *Fr.* Samson Agonistes. FaBoPV

Samson Fallen. Milton. *See* Samson Agonistes: This, this is he; softly a while.

Samson, Our Hero, *sels.* David Avidan, *tr. fr. Hebrew by* Warren Bargad *and* Stanley F. Chyet. IP

  First Date, The. *Fr.* 3.

  For Advanced Seminar Students Only. *Fr.* 6.

  General Truths. *Fr.* 1.

  Moral, The. *Fr.* 9.

  What Bothered Him. *Fr.* 2.

Samson Rends His Clothes. Anadad Eldan, *tr. fr. Hebrew by* Ruth Nevo. VWA

Samson to His Delilah. Richard Crashaw. TrGrPo

Samson wasn't the brightest. The Moral. David Avidan, *tr. fr. Hebrew by* Warren Bargad *and* Stanley F. Chyet. *Fr.* Samson, Our Hero, 9. IP

Samson's Hair. Natan Zach, *tr. fr. Hebrew by* Warren Bargad *and* Stanley F. Chyet. IP

Samuel. Bobbi Katz. RHPC

Samuel Allen. *Unknown.* AmFP

Samuel Brown. Phoebe Cary. OBAL

Samuel Hall. *Unknown. See* Sam Hall.

Samuel Hearne in Wintertime. John Newlove. NOBC

Samuel Hoar. Franklin Benjamin Sanborn. AA

Samuel Pepys. Allan M. Laing. FiBHP

Samuel, Samuel Palmer. In a Shoreham Garden. Laurence Lerner. NePoEA-2

Samuel Sewall. Anthony Hecht. LiTM; NBLV; NePoEA; PoRA; TwCP

Samurai and Hustlers. Joe Johnson. CNA

San Diego Poem, A. Simon J. Ortiz. CDW

San Francisco. John Vance Cheney. PAH

San Francisco. Joaquin Miller. PAH

San Francisco. Walter Adolphe Roberts. PoNe

San Francisco Company, The. *Unknown.* AmFP

San Francisco County Jail Cell B-6. Conyus. PoBA

San Francisco Poem. John Logan. NNaP

San Francisco remains in grave personal danger. Jeanne Dixon's America. Gerald Costanzo. MAYP

San Gloria, sel. Thomas MacDermot.

  "Dark foreboding haunts me lest I die, A." PBCV

San Luis/ with its soul of stone. Nocturnal Sunscape. Lucha Corpi. CCP

San Miniato. Oscar Wilde. TIRV

San Pedro Road. Robert Hass. GeTw

San Sepolcro. Jorie Graham. AnAn; HCAP

San Xavier Du Bac/ for Jon. Jorie Graham. NAmP

Sanary. Katherine Mansfield. ATNZ

Sanatorium. H. Leivick, *tr. fr. Yiddish by* Cynthia Ozick. PeBMYV

Sancho. William Edwin Collin. CaP

Sancho Panza's Dream. W. H. Auden. *Fr.* Man of La Mancha. AnAn

Sancho Panza's Homecoming. Ishihara Yoshiro, *tr. fr. Japanese by* Hiroaki Sato. FCEI

Sanct Christopher II ("Sanct Christopher's a muckle sanct and strang"). Robert Garioch, *after the Italian of* Giuseppe Belli. OBVE

Sancta Silvarum. Lionel Johnson. BrPo

Sanctification. Joseph Ibn Abithur, *tr. fr. Hebrew by* David Goldstein. TOF

Sanctimonious Poets, The. Friedrich Hölderlin, *tr. fr. German by* Robert Bly. NU

Sanctimony. *Malay Oral Tradition, tr. by* R. J. Wilkinson. WTO

Sanctity. Patrick Kavanagh. BIrV; NOIV

Sanctuary. John Basil Boothroyd. FiBHP

Sanctuary. Bruce Boyd. NeAP

Sanctuary. Clifford Dyment. PoA

Sanctuary, The. Ford Madox Ford. PoA

Sanctuary. Louise Imogen Guiney. AA

Sanctuary. Dorothy Hewett. CBAP

Sanctuary. Dorothy Parker. NBLV

Sanctuary, The. Howard Nemerov. NePoEA

Sanctuary. Judith Wright. WPE

Sanctuary. Elinor Wylie. BoWoP; MoAB; MoAmPo

Sanctuary of Spirits, *sel.* Alistair Campbell.

  Against Te Rauparaha. *Fr.* IX. PeNZ

Sanctum, The. T. A. Daly. TrPWD

Sand, The. May Swenson. *Fr.* Poet to Tiger. GLP

Sand birds fly east, they flee the spread net. Following the Rhymes of Bamboo Branch Songs. Yü Chi, *tr. by* Jonathan Chaves. CoBLCP

Sand Creek. Charles G. Ballard. UnPo; VoR

Sand Dunes. Robert Frost. MoAB; MoAmPo; RFM

Sand has the ants, clay ferny weeds for play. Possessions. Ivor Gurney. FaBoPP

Sand in the sun. Picnic at the Beach. Pyke Johnson, Jr. SoTCo

Sand is a fine grit, The. Dry Root in a Wash. Simon J. Ortiz. HATNAP

Sand Martin, The. John Clare. PBBP; TEP

Sand of Silk-Washing Stream. Chang Pi, *tr. fr. Chinese by* Lois Fusek. ATF

Sand of the Silk-Washing Stream. Hsüeh Chao-yün, *tr. fr. Chinese by* Lois Fusek. ATF

Sand of Silk-Washing Stream. Ku Hsiung, *tr. fr. Chinese by* Lois Fusek. ATF

Sand of Silk-Washing Stream. Li Hsün, *tr. fr. Chinese by* Lois Fusek. ATF

Sand of Silk-Washing Stream. Mao Hsi-chen, *tr. fr. Chinese by* Lois Fusek. ATF

Sand of the Silk-Washing Stream. Mao Wen-hsi, *tr. fr. Chinese by* Lois Fusek. ATF

Sand of Silk-Washing Stream. Ou-yang Chiung, *tr. fr. Chinese by* Lois Fusek. ATF

Sand of Silk-Washing Stream. Sun Kuang-hsien, *tr. fr. Chinese by* Lois Fusek. ATF
Sand of Silk-Washing Stream. Wei Chuang, *tr. fr. Chinese by* Lois Fusek. ATF
Sand of Silk-Washing Stream. Yen Hsüan, *tr. fr. Chinese by* Lois Fusek. ATF
Sand Painters, The. Ben Belitt. EyDe; GOA
Sand, sand; hills of sand. The Mermaids. Walter de la Mare. BrPo
Sand: the crystalline children. Kneeling Here, I Feel Good. Marge Piercy. NeAC
Sandal and garment of yellow and lotus garlands upon his body of blue. Jayadeva, *tr. fr. Sanskrit by* George Keyt. *Fr.* The Gita Govinda. ErPo
Sandal Mountain. Hsieh Chin, *tr. fr. Chinese by* Jonathan Chaves. CoBLCP
Sandalwood the hawser-ties, silk the puller ropes. Song to the Tune "Perching Crows." Wu Wei-yeh, *tr. by* Jonathan Chaves. CoBLCP
Sandbar egrets, sleeping, nestle close to my boat. Chu Yi-tsun, *tr. fr. Chinese by* Irving Lo. *Fr.* Mallard Lake Boating Songs, II. WFTU
Sandgate Girl's Lamentation, The. *Unknown.* CoMu; ELP
Sandhill People. Carl Sandburg. CMoP
Sandpaper kisses. Cat Kisses. Bobbi Katz. RAR
Sandpiper. Elizabeth Bishop. AiP; HeIP; NYBP; RB; TOF
Sandpiper, The. Witter Bynner. RHPC
Sandpiper, The. Frances Frost. RHPC
Sandpiper, The. Celia Thaxter. AA; FaBoBe; FaPON; GN; OBCA; OxBChV; PWR; WBLP
Sandpiper, The. Charlotte Zolotow. TSS
Sandpipers. Helen Merrill Egerton. CaP
Sandra: At the Beaver Trap. Michael S. Harper. NoAM
Sands of Dee, The. Charles Kingsley. *Fr.* Alton Locke, *ch.* 26. BeLS; CH; EBVV; FaBoPP; FaPON; FaPoR; GN; WBLP
Sandstone. Anne Marriott. CaP
Sandstone carriage, A. For Cal. James Cunningham. JB
Sandwich in Spain now, and the duke in love. The Third Advice to a Painter. Andrew Marvell. APAS
Sandwiches. David Donnell. NoAM
Sandy,/ Hi, got your letter a few days ago. Empty at the Heart of Things. Frank Polite. UL
Sandy Burial, A. Geoffrey Grigson. OBD
Sandy cat by the Farmer's chair, The. Summer Evening. Walter de la Mare. FM; MoAB; MoBrPo; MoShBr
Sandy he belongs to the mill. *Unknown.* OxNR
Sandy Hook. George Houghton. AA
Sandy Kildandy. *Unknown.* OxNR
Sandy Star and Willie Gee. William Stanley Braithwaite. BANP
Sane, Plain, and Tedious to Know. Jenny Morris. SoTCo
Sanford Barney. *Unknown.* AmFP
Sang a maiden in a meadow. Reunited. Henrietta Cordelia Ray. CBWP-3
Sang Solomon to Sheba. Solomon to Sheba. W. B. Yeats. CMoP; ELP
Sang: "There's a reid lowe in yer cheek." Robert MacLellan. OxBS
Sangaree Kill de Captain. *Unknown.* PBCV
Sanitary Message, A. Bret Harte. AnAmPo
Sanity be applicable something men. Matter of Fact. Bruce Andrews. LP
Sank through easeful. The Diver. Robert Hayden. AmPP; BPo; MOS
Sanquhar, whom this earth could scarce contain. William Drummond of Hawthornden. FaBoEE
Sans Equity and sans Poise. Confucius, *tr. fr. Chinese by* Ezra Pound. *Fr.* Yung Wind. CTC
Santa Anna *or* Ana came storming, as a storm might come. The Defense of the Alamo. Joaquin Miller. BeLS; FaBoBe; PAH (Defence of the Alamo.) OnMSP; PAH
Santa Barbara. Francis Fisher Browne. AA
Santa Barbara Earthquake, The. *Unknown.* AmFP
Santa Caterina. Myra Glazer Schotz. VWA
Santa Claus. Walter de la Mare. PChr
Santa Claus. Christopher Hassall. OxBTC
Santa Claus. Dom Moraes. NoAM
Santa Claus. Howard Nemerov. HAP
Santa Claus. *Unknown.* BoTP
Santa Fe Trail. Barbara Guest. NeAP; PoM
Santa Lucia II. Robert Hass. NAmP
Santa Maria del Fiore. George Herbert Clarke. CaP
Santa Maria, well thou tremblest down the wave. The Triumph. Sidney Lanier. *Fr.* Psalm of the West. PAH
Santiago. Thomas A. Janvier. PAH
Santorin. James Elroy Flecker. FaBoTw; GoJo; OBMV
Santos: New Mexico. May Sarton. EaLo

Sao Princess/ borrows a new robe of haze, The. Tamesada, *tr. by* Steven D. Carter. WFTW
Sao Princess/ has donned her new robe of haze, The. Tameuji, *tr. by* Steven D. Carter. WFTW
Saon of Acanthus. Callimachus, *tr. fr. Greek by* John Addington Symonds. AWP
Sap rises from the sodden ditch. For Jane Myers. Louise Glück. FaBoWP; GeTw
Sap weeps, The. Why the Wind Comes. Hirini Melbourne. PeNZ
Saphire (Metamorpho's Chick). Joe Rosenblatt. MoCV
Sapho and Phao, *sels.* John Lyly.
  Sapho's Song. OBSC
  Vulcan's Song. EBEV; ElL
  (Song in Making of the Arrows.) OBSC
Saplings of the green-tipped birch, The. Never Tell. *Unknown, tr. by* Anthony Conran. OBWVE
Sapphics. George Canning *and* John Hookham Frere. *See* Needy knife–grinder, whither are you going?
Sapphics. D. B. Wyndham Lewis. NOBL
Sapphics. Sir Philip Sidney. *Fr.* Arcadia. SiPS
Sapphics. Swinburne. PoEL-5
Sapphics against Anger. Timothy Steele. SM
Sapphics: At the Mohawk-Castle, Canada. Thomas Morris. NOEC
Sapphire, The. W. S. Merwin. PoA
Sappho. Catullus, *tr. fr. Latin by* William Ellery Leonard. AWP
Sappho. Jack Cope. PeSA
Sappho. Marie von Najmájer, *tr. fr. German by* Susan L. Cocalis *and* Gerlinde Geiger. DMG
Sappho. James Wright. NoAM
Sappho/ Sister/Mother. Invocation to Sappho. Elsa Gidlow. IHMS
"Sappho, if you do not come out." Sappho, *tr. by* Willis Barnstone. BoWoP
Sappho Lives Again. Renée Vivien, *tr. fr. French by* Beth Archer. DMF
Sappho to Eranna. Rainer Maria Rilke, *tr. fr. German by* Edward Snow. UnAS
Sappho's Last Song. Vittoria Aganoor Pompili, *tr. fr. Italian by* Muriel Kittel. DMI
Sappho's Reply. Rita Mae Brown. PeHV
Sappho's Tomb. Arthur Stringer. CaP
Sara in Her Father's Arms. George Oppen. NNaP
Saragossa. Henry Sambrooke Leigh. FaBoCo
Sarah. Edna Aphek, *tr. fr. Hebrew by* Yishai Tobin. VWA
Sarah. Delmore Schwartz. VWA
Sarah/ was a woman. Sarah. Edna Aphek, *tr. by* Yishai Tobin. VWA
Sarah Byng Who Could Not Read and Was Tossed into a Thorny Hedge by a Bull. Hilaire Belloc. CenHV; GoJo; NoAM
Sarah: Cherokee Doctor. Wendy Rose. STE
Sarah Cynthia Sylvia Stout Would Not Take the Garbage Out. Shel Silverstein. OBCA
Sarah Hazard's Love Letter. John Ellis. NOEC
Sarah they called you. The Noble Servant. Philippe Thoby-Marcelin, *tr. by* William Jay Smith. CT
Sarah T's husband shot her at the Tohatchi laundromat. The Shooting. Laura Tohe. STE
Sarai. Joseph Sherman. VWA
Sarajevo. Lawrence Durrell. GTBS-P; OBTV
Saratoga Ending. Weldon Kees. NaP
Saratoga Song. *Unknown.* PAH
Sarcophagi. Bernard Spencer. OBD
Sarcophagus. Paul Mariani. BLA
Sardanapalus. Earl of Surrey. *See* Assyrian king in peace, with foul desire, The.
Sargent's Portrait of Edwin Booth at "The Players." Thomas Bailey Aldrich. AA
Saris go by me from the embassies, The. The Woman at the Washington Zoo. Randall Jarrell. CAPP; CoAP; HAP; HCAP; LiTM; OxBC; TAP; TwCP; UnPo
Sark. Swinburne. *Fr.* The Garden of Cymodoce. FaBoPP
Sarmèd, whom they intoxicated from the cup of love. Sarmèd the Yahud, *tr. by* David Shea. TrJP
Sarolla's women in their picture hats. Lawrence Ferlinghetti. *Fr.* Pictures of a Gone World, *sec.* 8. NeAP; PoM
Sarpedon to Glaukos. Homer, *tr. fr. Greek by* Richard Lattimore. *Fr.* The Iliad, II. WaaP
Sarpedon's Speech. Homer, *tr. fr. Greek by* George Chapman. *Fr.* The Iliad, II. OBS
Sartorial Solecism. R. E. C. Stringer. FiBHP
Sarum Primer, *sel. Unknown.*
  God Be in My Head. EaLo
  (Hymnus: "God be in my hede.") ChTr; FaBoRV

Sarvent, Marster! Yes, sah, dat's me. Uncle Gabe's White Folks.
　　Thomas Nelson Page. AA
Sasha and the Poet ("Sasha: I dreamed you and he"). Jean Valentine.
　　VGW
Sassafras. Samuel Minturn Peck. AA
Sat a damsel on the hillside. The Messengers. Henrietta Cordelia Ray.
　　CBWP-3
Sat in the pub. The Diet. Maureen Burge. AIW; BrRo
Sat in the sun. Virginia. Elouise Loftin. PoBA
Sat up all night and lugged at the moon. Critter. W. M. Ransom.
　　CDW
Sat Will & Kate. Those Troublesome Disguises. Jonathan Williams.
　　NeAP
Satan and His Host. Milton. See Paradise Lost: But he his wonted pride.
Satan and Pilate's Wife. Unknown. ACP
Satan and the Fallen Angels. Milton. See Paradise Lost: He scarce had
　　ceas't when the superior Fiend.
Satan as Rebel-Liberator. Milton. See Paradise Lost: Is this the region,
　　this the soil, the clime.
Satan Beholds Adam and Eve. Milton. See Paradise Lost: O hell! what
　　do mine eyes with grief behold!
Satan ("He ceased; and Satan stayed not to reply"). Milton. See Paradise
　　Lost: He ceased; and Satan stayed not to reply.
Satan ("He scarce had ceas't when the superior Fiend"). Milton. See
　　Paradise Lost: He scarce had ceas't when the superior Fiend.
Satan ("His pride/ Had cast him out from Heaven, with all his host").
　　Milton. See Paradise Lost: His pride/ Had cast him out from Heaven,
　　with all his host.
Satan in Eden "was constrain'd." Error Pursued. Helen Pinkerton.
　　QFR
Satan is following me. Zulu Oral Tradition, tr. by H. Tracey.
　　WTO
Satan Is on Your Tongue. George Barker. Fr. Secular Elegies, III.
　　MoAB; MoBrPo
Satan Journey's to the Garden of Eden. Milton. See Paradise Lost:
　　How to th' ascent of that steep savage hill.
Satan's a Liah. Unknown. AS
Satan's Guile ("Whom thus answer'd th' Arch Fiend now undisguis'd").
　　Milton. Fr. Paradise Regained, bk. I, ll. 357-405. LiTB;
　　OBS
Satan's Legions and the Beech Leaves of the Casentino. Milton. See
　　Paradise Lost: He stood and call'd/ His legions, angel forms, who lay
　　intranced.
Satan's Soliloquy. Milton. See Paradise Lost: O thou that with
　　surpassing glory crown'd.
Satchmo. Melvin Beaunearus Tolson. BPo
　　(Lamda.) PoNe
Satellites. Gary Lenhart. UL
Sather Gate Illumination. Allen Ginsberg. NeAP
Satie. Jan G. Elburg, tr. fr. Dutch by André Lefevere. DuIn
Satie, at the End of Term. Simon Curtis. NOBL
Satin-clad. Stevie Smith. OxBC
Satin Doll. David Wojahn. NAmP
Satin of pages turned in books shapes a woman so beautiful, The. The
　　Writings Recede. André Breton, tr. by Michael Benedikt.
　　POS
Satire. Alexander Geddes. ACP
Satire, A, sel. John Oldham.
　　"On Butler who can think without rage." OBSV
Satire Addressed to a Friend, A. See Satyr Address'd to a Friend That Is
　　about to Leave the University, and Come Abroad in the World, A.
Satire against [Reason and] Mankind, A ("Were I, who to my cost already
　　am"). Earl of Rochester. LiTM; NoP; OAEL-1; OBSV; SCV
　　(Homo Sapiens.) NOBE
　　(Satyre against Mankind.) OBS; PoEL-3; SeCV-2
　　(Satyre against Reason and Mankind, A.) SCV
　　Wretched Man, sel. SeCePo
Satire, my friend ('twixt me and you). Satire. Alexander Geddes.
　　ACP
Satire on Charles II, A, sel. Earl of Rochester.
　　"Restless he rolls about from whore to whore." OBSV
Satire on London, A. Earl of Surrey. AAS; SiPS
Satire on Old Rowley. Unknown. APAS
Satire on the O'Haras, A. Tadhg Dall O'Huiginn. NOIV
Satire upon the French King, A. Thomas Brown. APAS
Satire upon the Heads. Thomas Gray. FaBoCo
Satire upon the Licentious Age of Charles II, sel. Samuel Butler.
　　"How silly were those sages heretofore." NOBL
Satires, sels. John Donne.
　　"Kind pity [or kinde pitty] chokes my spleen[e]; brave scorn forbids."
　　　Fr. III. EBEV; JCP; OAEL-1; OBS; PoEL-2; SeCV-1

(Religion.) NoP
(Satyre III.) MeLP
(Satyre III: On Religion.) NAEL-1; SeCP
(Satyre: Of Religion.) MePo; PoE
Seek True Religion! Fr. III. NOBE
"Seek true religion, O where? Mirreus." Fr. III. OBSV
　　(Truth.) SeCePo
　　"Though Truth and Falsehood be," sel. NOBE
"Sir: though (I thank God for it) I do hate." Fr. II. OBSV
"Thou shalt not laugh in this leaf, Muse, nor they." Fr. V.
　　OBSV
"Well, I may now receive, and die: my sin." Fr. IV. OBSV
Satires, sels. Juvenal, tr. fr. Latin.
"But of all the plagues, the greatest is untold." Fr. VI, tr. by Dryden.
　　OBSV
Celestial Wisdom. Fr. X, tr. by Samuel Johnson. AWP
Faggots in Ancient Rome. Fr. II. PeHV
"Give store of days, good Jove, give length of years." Fr. X, tr. by
　　Henry Vaughan. OBSV
Hannibal ("Produce the urn that Hannibal contains"). Fr. X, tr. by
　　William Gifford. OBVE
Hannibal ("Put Hannibal i' th' scale"). Fr. X, tr. by Henry Vaughan.
　　OBVE
Hannibal ("Throw Hannibal on the scales, how many pounds"). Fr. X,
　　tr. by Robert Lowell. OBVE
"Hear what Claudius suffered: When his wife knew he was asleep." Fr.
　　VI, tr. by Hubert Creekmore. ErPo
"In Saturn's reign, at Nature's early birth." Fr. VI, tr. by Dryden.
　　OAEL-1; OBSV; OBVE
" 'Life! length of life!' for this, with earnest cries." Fr. X, tr. by
　　William Gifford. OBVE
"Return we to the dangers of the night." Fr. III, tr. by Dryden.
　　OAEL-1
Sejanus ("How many men are killed by power, by power"). Fr. X, tr.
　　by Robert Lowell. OBVE
Sejanus ("Some ask for envy'd pow'r; which publick hate"). Fr. X, tr.
　　by Dryden. OBVE
Sejanus ("What crowds by envied power, the wish of all"). Fr. X, tr.
　　by William Gifford. OBVE
"What conscience has Venus drunk? Our inebriated beauties." Fr. VI,
　　tr. by Peter Green. PeHV
"When the last Flavius, drunk with fury, tore." Fr. IV, tr. by William
　　Gifford. OBVE
"Why do you look so gloomy, Naevolus?" Fr. IX. PeHV
Satires, sel. John Oldham, after the French of Boileau.
　　"Of all the creatures, in the world, that be." Fr. VIII. OBVE
Satires, sel. Persius, tr. fr. Latin by Dryden.
　　Prologue to the First Satire. AWP
Satires, sels. Sir Thomas Wyatt.
　　Mine Own John Poins [or Poyntz]. AAS; NoP; OBSV; OBVE;
　　　PoEL-1; SiPS
　　(Of the Courtier's Life.) OBSC
　　"My mother's maids [or maydes], when they did sew and spin [or sowe
　　　and spynne]." Fr. II. AAS; SiPS
　　"Spending hand that alway poureth out [or powreth owte], A." Fr. III.
　　　AAS
　　(To Sir Francis Brian.) SiPS
Satires of Circumstance, sels. Thomas Hardy.
　　At a Watering-Place. Fr. V. BrPo
　　At Tea. Fr. I. BrPo
　　At the Altar-Rail. Fr. IX. BrPo; MoAB; MoBrPo
　　At the Draper's. Fr. XII. BrPo; MoAB; MoBrPo
　　By Her Aunt's Grave. Fr. III. BrPo; MoAB; MoBrPo
　　In Church. Fr. II. BrPo; InPK; MoAB; MoBrPo; SCV
　　In the Cemetery. Fr. IV. BrPo; InPK
　　In the Moonlight. Fr. XV. BrPo
　　In the Nuptial Chamber. Fr. X. BrPo; InPK
　　In the Restaurant. Fr. XI. BrPo; MoAB; MoBrPo
　　In the Room of the Bride-Elect. Fr. IV. BrPo; InPK
　　In the Study. Fr. VIII. BrPo
　　On the Death-Bed. Fr. XIII. BrPo
　　Outside the Window. Fr. VII. BrPo
　　Over the Coffin. Fr. XIV. BrPo
Satires [or Satyrs] upon the Jesuits, sels. John Oldham.
　　"For who can longer hold? when every Press." SeCV-2
　　"Satyr III: "When shaven Crown, and hallow'd Girdle's Power.""
　　　SeCV-2
Satirical Elegy on the Death of a Late Famous General, A. Swift. FF;
　　HoPM; NBLV; NoP; OBSV; PoE; PoEL-3
Satirical Poem about Drink, A, sel. Chimedin Jigmed, tr. fr. Mongol
　　Oral Tradition by C. R. Bawden.
　　"There is drink fermented." WTO

Satirical Romance, A, *sels.* Sister Juana Inés de la Cruz, *tr. fr. Spanish* by Judith Thurman. PBWP
  "Critics: in your sight."
  "Ignorant men, who disclaim."
  "What humour can be so rare."
Satirist, The. Harry Lyman Koopman. AA
Satisfaction—is the agent. Emily Dickinson. NOBA
Satisfied. Samuel Valentine Cole. BLRP
Satisfied. Edgar Cooper Mason. BLRP
Satisfied this morning because I saw myself. Seeing the Scenery. Leslie Scalapino. *Fr.* Hmmmm. NPGG
Satisfying Portion, The. *Unknown.* BLRP
Satori. Gayl Jones. BlSi
Satori seekers make me sick! Kakua, *tr. by* Lucien Stryk *and* Takashi Ikemoto. ZPCJ
Satrapy, The. C. P. Cavafy, *tr. fr. Greek by* Edmund Keeley *and* Philip Sherrard. VMG
Saturday. Daniel Hoffman. SoTCo
Saturday Afternoon at the Movies. John Logan. NNaP
Saturday and nothing. Miracle in Milan. Kurt Klinger, *tr. by* Beth Bjorklund. CoAuP
Sat., Apr. 26, 1973. A Poem to Galway Kinnell. Etheridge Knight. NNaP
Saturday in the County Seat. Elijah L. Jacobs. AmFN
Saturday Market ("Bury your heart in some deep green hollow."), *sel.* Charlotte Mew. WPE
Saturday Market ("In Saturday Market, there's eggs a-plenty"). FaPON
Saturday Morning. Richard Howard. ErPo
Saturday morning. Mowing the Lawn. John Bensko. MAYP
Saturday Morning at the Laundry. Christopher Gilbert. MAYP
Saturday Night. A. P. Herbert. NBLV
Saturday Night. Langston Hughes. MoAmPo
Saturday Night. Antigone Kefala. CBAP
Saturday night in August when, A. Last Meeting. Robert Penn Warren. DiPo
Saturday Night in the Parthenon. Kenneth Patchen. EAS
Saturday Night in the Village. Giacomo Leopardi, *tr. fr. Italian by* Robert Lowell. OBVE
Saturday Night in Woody. Jesse Smith. CowP
Saturday night she comes in her little boat. Music on the Water. George Johnston. MoCV
Saturday on Seventh Street. The Fields. W. S. Merwin. CAPP; HCAP
Saturday Review, The. Dora Greenwell. EBVV
Saturday Sundae. F. R. Scott. CaP
Saturday Sunday Monday slow week and weak days. Behind Bars. Hugo Claus, *tr. by* Theo Hermans. DuIn
Saturday: The Small-Pox. Lady Mary Wortley Montagu. *Fr.* Six Town Eclogues. NOEC; WPE
Saturday under the Sky. Gary Soto. NAmP
Saturday's Child. Countee Cullen. LiTM; NAs; OFD; PoBA; SaC
Saturn. Keats. *See* Hyperion; a Fragment: Deep in the shady sadness of a vale.
Saturnian mother! why dost thou devour. Russia. Nathan Haskell Dole. AA
Saturninus. Katherine Eleanor Conway. AA
Satyr. Charles Gullans. PoA
Satyr, The, *sel.* Ben Jonson.
  Mab the Mistress-Fairy. ElL
  (Mab.) WiR
Satyr III: "When shaven Crown, and hallow'd Girdle's Power." John Oldham. *Fr.* Satires [*or* Satyrs] upon the Jesuits. SeCV-2
Satyr Address'd to a Friend That Is About to Leave the University, and Come Abroad in the World, A, *sel.* John Oldham.
  "If you for orders, and a gown design." *Fr.*
    "If you're so out of love with happiness." OBSV
Satyr against Mankind. Earl of Rochester. *See* Were I who to my cost....
Satyr on Elysium lights, A. The Tenth Nimphall. Michael Drayton. *Fr.* Muses' Elysium [*or* Elizium]. JCP
Satyre against Mankind, A. Earl of Rochester. *See* Were I, who to my cost already am.
Satyre against Reason and Mankind, A. Earl of Rochester. *See* Were I, who to my cost already am.
Satyre Entituled the Witch, A. *Unknown.* CoMu
Satyre: Of Religion. John Donne. *See* Satires: Kind pity [*or* kinde pitty] chokes my spleen[e]; brave scorn forbids.
Satyretericall Charracter of a Proud UpstartA. John Saffin. SCAP

Satyrs' Catch, The. Ben Jonson. *See* Oberon, the Fairy Prince: Buz, Quoth the Blue Fly.
Satyr's Farewell, The. John Fletcher. *Fr.* The Faithful Shepherdess, V, i. OBS
Satyr's Song. John Fletcher. *Fr.* The Faithful Shepherdess, IV, i. OBS
Satyrs upon the Jesuits. John Oldham. *See* Satires upon the Jesuits.
Satyrs used to fall for nymphs. Love-Songs, at Once Tender and Informative. Samuel Hoffenstein. OBAL
Satyrus Peregrinans, *sel.* William Rankins.
  "By this time long-gowned Lumen walked abroad." OBSV
Sauce thickens, The. I add more butter. Hollandaise. Sharon Bryan. MAYP
Saucer Station: Monday-Friday. Albert Goldbarth. BWV
Sauchs in the Reuch Heuch Hauch, The. "Hugh MacDiarmid." NoAM
Saucy Sailor, The. *Unknown.* OBET
Saul. Nathan Alterman, *tr. fr. Hebrew by* Dov Vardi. TrJP
Saul, *sels.* Robert Browning.
  "Oh, the wild joys of living! the leaping from rock up to rock." *Fr.* IX. FaBV; BoTP
  "Then I tuned my harp—took off the lilies we twine round its chords." *Fr.* V-IX. FiP
  "Yea, my King." *Fr.* XIII-XIX, *sl. abr.* WGRP
Saul. Amir Gilboa, *tr. fr. Hebrew by* Shirley Kaufman. VWA
Saul, *sels.* Charles Heavysege.
  Malzah's Song. OBCV
  "To hunt and to be hunted make existence." CaP
  Zaph Describes the Haunts of Malzah. OBCV
Saul. Else Lasker-Schüler, *tr. fr. German by* Joachim Neugroschel. VWA
Saul. Isaac Rosenberg. VWA
Saul, Afterward, Riding East. John Malcolm Brinnin. Prf
Saul did much care and diligence express. Rowland Watkyns. FaBoEE
Saul Re-enthroned. Meir Wieseltier, *tr. fr. Hebrew by* Warren Bargad *and* Stanley F. Chyet. IP
Saul! Saul! Saul. Amir Gilboa, *tr. by* Shirley Kaufman. VWA
Saul's Death: Two Sestinas. Joe W. Haldeman. BWV
Saul's Progress. Harvey Shapiro. DiL
Saul's Song of Love. Saul Tchernichowsky, *tr. fr. Hebrew by* Robert Friend. VWA
Sauntering home from church we lingered. Mary Ursula Bethell. *Fr.* By the River Ashley, IV. PeNZ
Sauntering in the orchard we bit the fruit. The Struggle with the Angel. Claude Vigée, *tr. by* Elizabeth Savage. VWA
Sauntering the pavement or riding the country by-road. Faces. Walt Whitman. PoEL-5
Sausage. Edgar A. Guest. OBAL
Savage, A. John Boyle O'Reilly. AA
Savage Beast, The. William Carlos Williams. TW
Savages, The. Josephine Miles. LiTM
Savage's romance, The. New York. Marianne Moore. NAAL-2
Savannah. Alethea S. Burroughs. PAH
Savannah, Sleepless. Richard Tillinghast. BLA
Savants. Lucien Stryk. KS
Save by the Old Road none attain the new. Coventry Patmore. FaBoEE
Save the Boys. Frances E. W. Harper. PWR
Save yourself. Run and leave me. I must go back. C. S. Lewis. *Fr.* Epigrams and Epitaphs, 6. EBEV
Saved. Maria Teresa Horta, *tr. fr. Portuguese by* Suzette Macedo. PBWP
Saved. Adah Isaacs Menken. CBWP-1
Saved. *Unknown.* FaBoUs
Saving the Harvest. Geoffrey Lehmann. CBAP
Savior [*or* Saviour]! I've no one else to tell. Emily Dickinson. TrCP; TrPWD
Savior looked on Peter, The. Ay, no word. The Look. Elizabeth Barrett Browning. TrCP
Saviour, bowed beneath his cross, climbed up the dreary hill, The. Why the Robin's Breast Was Red. James Ryder Randall. AA
Saviour! I've no one else to tell. *See* Savior! I've no one else to tell.
Saviour, Sprinkle Many Nations. Arthur Cleveland Coxe. AH
Saviour, Thy Dying Love. Sylvanus D. Phelps. AH
Saviour, Who Thy Flock Art Feeding. William Augustus Muhlenberg. AH
Saviour, Whose Love Is Like the Sun. Howard Chandler Robbins. TrPWD
Savonarola ("Savonarola looks more grim today"). Max Beerbohm. BXAP

Savonarola ("Savonarola/ Declined to wear a bowler"). E. C. Bentley. OxBoLi

Saw a home movie today. Uncle Carl. Uncle Carl: A Home Movie. J. Bernlef, tr. by Scott Rollins. DuIn

Saw a lamb being born. Lamb. Michael Dennis Browne. NU

Saw the Cloud Lynx. Samuel Makidemewabe, tr. fr. Cree Indian by Howard Norman. STP

Saw Ye Bonny Lesley. Burns. See O Saw Ye Bonnie Lesley.

Saw ye owt o' ma' lad. The Waggoner. Unknown. GBP

Saw You among Trees. Malka Heifetz-Tussman, tr. fr. Yiddish by Kathryn Hellerstein. AYP

Sawdust from the Scales. Hans Arp, tr. fr. French by Michael Benedikt. POS

Saws Were Shrieking, The. W. W. Eustace Ross. CaP

Saxon Legend of Language, The. Mary Weston Fordham. CBWP-2

Saxons of Flint, The. Unknown, tr. fr. Welsh by Mary C. Llewelyn. OBWVE

Saxophone turned into a dolphin, The. Albert Ayler: Eulogy for a Decomposed Saxophone Player. Stanley Crouch. PoBA

Saxophonetyx. Cyn Zarco. BrSi; UL

Say/ Did you see that magnificent blonde beast. Ski Trail. Samuel Allen. FB

Say, are you she that came to me last. The Second Vision. Tadhg Dall O'Huiginn, tr. by Earl of Longford. AnIL

"Say, bold but blessed Theefe." The Thief. Unknown. OBS

Say, bud, ya got a cigarette? Refugee. Naomi Long Madgett. PoNe

Say, but did you love so long? Sir Toby Matthews. Sir John Suckling. SeCV-1

Say, crimson rose and dainty daffodil. A Nosegay. John Reynolds. OBEV

Say, darkeys hab you seen de massa. The Year of Jubilee. Henry Clay Work. PAH

Say, dear Maria! is the modish life. A Familiar Epistle. Ann Murry. WPE

Say, did you go to Mae's rent party? Mae's Rent Party. Ernest J. Wilson, Jr. PoNe

Say, dwarf, for it seems to me. Unknown, tr. fr. Icelandic by W. H. Auden and Paul B. Taylor. Fr. The Words of the All-Wise. OBVE

Say, earth, why hast thou got thee new attire. Easter Morn. Giles Fletcher the Younger. Fr. Christ's Victory and Triumph: Christ's Triumph after Death, IV. EIL; NOCV

Say father, say mother. Dove's Song in Winter. Zulu Oral Tradition, tr. by B. W. Vilakazi. WTO

Say "flower," say it again. Rako, tr. by Hiroaki Sato. FCEI

Say, friend, if all is well still with the bowers. Vidya, tr. fr. Sanskrit by Daniel H. H. Ingalls. Fr. The Wanton. PBWP

Say good-by er howdy-do. Good-by er Howdy-do. James Whitcomb Riley. CTC

Say Goodbye to Big Daddy. Randall Jarrell. ASP; PoNe

Say goodbye to the help, the ranks. Dr. Joseph Goebbels. W. D. Snodgrass. Fr. The Führer Bunker.
("Stand back, make way, you mindless scum,." TW
"Say goodbye to the help, the ranks." CAPP

Say Hello to John. Sherley Anne Williams. BISi

Say Id Isn't So. Richard Armour. SoTCo

Say, in a hut of mean estate. The Soul of Man. Dora Read Goodale. AA

Say it and cry aloud. I Am a Negro. Muhammad al-Fituri, tr. by Halim El-Dabh. TTY

Say It Now. Unknown. See If You Have a Friend.

Say It with Music. Philippe Soupault, tr. fr. French by Eugene Jolas. RHTwFP

Say It with Vegetables. Paul Snoek, tr. fr. Dutch by Alasdair Mackinnon. DuIn

Say it's an important event like this. Off to Patagonia. Theodore Weiss. AnAn; TAP

Say language really does. The Tip of the Iceberg. Michael C. Blumenthal. BLA

Say life is the one-way trip, the one-way flight. Watchmaker God. Robert Lowell. HCAP

Say, lovely Tory, why the jest. To Miss Eleanor Ambrose on the Occasion of Her Wearing an Orange Lily at a Ball in Dublin Castle on July the 12th. Earl of Chesterfield. EnLoPo

"Say me, wight in the broom." Tell Me, Wight in the Broom. Unknown. NAEL-1

Say, mighty Love, and teach my song. Few Happy Matches. Isaac Watts. NOEC

Say Not. Arthur Hugh Clough. See Say Not the Struggle Nought Availeth.

Say not of beauty she is good. Beauty. Elinor Wylie. NAAL-2; OxBA

Say not of me that weakly I declined. Robert Louis Stevenson. EyDe; OBNC

Say not the age is hard and cold. The Present Age. Frances Ellen Watkins Harper. PWR

Say Not the Struggle Nought Availeth. Arthur Hugh Clough. AWP; EaLo; EBVV; FaBoRV; FaFP; FaPoR; GTBS-P; LiTB; NAEL-2; NOBE; NOBVV; OAEL-2; OBEV; OBNC; SoSe; TEP; TrGrPo; WaaP; WGRP
(Keeping On.) MoShBr
(Say Not.) FaBV

Say of them/ They knew no Spanish. To the Veterans of the Abraham Lincoln Brigade. Genevieve Taggard. OFD

Say over again, and yet once over again. Elizabeth Barrett Browning. Fr. Sonnets from the Portuguese, XXI. NAEL-2

Say Ram, say Ram, say Ram. Tulsidas, tr. by John Stratton Hawley and Mark Juergensmeyer. SSI

Say, sweet, my grief and I, we may not brook. Je ne veux de personne aupres de ma tristesse. Henri de Regnier, tr. by "Seumas O'Sullivan." AWP

Say (sweetest) whether thou didst use me well. To Cynthia on Her Being an Incendiary. Sir Francis Kynaston. HAP

Say that a ballad. Fr. Speeches at the Barriers. UL

Say that she couldn't forgive. Anna Margolin, tr. by Marcia Falk. PeBMYV

Say that the men of the old black tower. The Black Tower. W. B. Yeats. CMoP

Say there! P'r'aps. "Jim." (Francis Bret Harte). AA; AnAmPo

Say this city has ten million souls. W. H. Auden. LiTM
(Refugee Blues.) LiTA
(Song: "Say this city has ten million souls!") NYBP

Say This of Horses. Minnie Hite Moody. PoLF

Say, tyrant Custom, why must we obey. The Emulation. Sarah Fyge Egerton. NOEC

Say well and do well. Unknown. OxNR

Say, what is the spell, when her fledglings are cheeping. A Song of Love. "Lewis Carroll." GN

Say what slim youth, with moist perfumes. Horace. See Odes: I, 5. "What slender youth bedewed with liquid odours" ("Quis multa gracilis").

Say what you want about doctors or priests. The Lightning Rod Salesman. M. L. Hester. CRP

Say what you will in two. Air: Sentir avec Ardeur. Marie-Françoise-Catherine de Beauveau, Marquise de Boufflers, tr. by Ezra Pound. CTC; WPOW

"Say, where is the maiden sweet." Sag', wo ist dein schönes Liebchen. Heine, tr. by James Thomson. AWP

Say, who's going to win. The Cricket and the Machine Gun. Yu Kuang-chung, tr. by Dominic Cheung. IFON

Say why on this day, by the morn's first ray. The Vampire Bride. Henry Liddell. VVA

Say, wilt thou go with me, sweet maid. Invitation to Eternity. John Clare. PoEL-4
(Invite to Eternity.) OAEL-2; OBNC

Say, wilt thou more of scenes so sordid know? A Slum Dwelling. George Crabbe. Fr. The Borough, Letter XVIII. OBNC

Say, wouldst thou guard thy son. Of Caution. Francesco Da Barberini, tr. by Dante Gabriel Rossetti. AWP; PFI

Say you were the kid who could not sleep. The Actor. Thomas Snapp. NYBP

Sayes "Christ thee saue, good Child of Ell!" Earl Brand. Unknown. ESPB

Saying Dante Aloud. James Wright. InPK

Saying Goodbye to a Monk from Japan. Hsü Pen, tr. fr. Chinese by Jonathan Chaves. CoBLCP

Saying Good-bye to a Singing Girl. Mo Shih-lung, tr. fr. Chinese by Jonathan Chaves. CoBLCP

Saying Good-Bye to Feng the Hermit. Mo Shih-lung, tr. fr. Chinese by Jonathan Chaves. CoBLCP

Saying Goodbye. Suzanne Juhasz. IHMS

Saying Her Name. Brendan Galvin. KS

Saying nothing, asking nothing. Yosano Akiko, tr. fr. Japanese by Hiroaki Sato. Fr. Thirty-nine Tanka. FCEI

Saying, "There is no hope," he stepped. A Generous Creed. Elizabeth Stuart Phelps Ward. WGRP

Saying to himself. What Her Girl Friend Said ("Saying to himself"). Peyanar, tr. fr. Tamil by A. K. Ramanujan. Fr. Nine on Happy Reunion, 8. PLW

Saying, "What heat today!" Cooling Off in the Evening. Onitsura, tr. fr. Japanese by Hiroaki Sato. Fr. Twenty-three Hokku. FCEI

Sayings from the Northern Ice. William Stafford. NU

Saylors for My Money. Martin Parker. CoMu

Sayre. Lynn Strongin. IHMS

Says A, give me a good large slice. A Curious Discourse That Passed between the Twenty-five Letters at Dinner-Time. *Unknown.* FaBoUs

Says His Grace to Will Green, whom he found in his stall. Death and the Cobbler. *Unknown.* APAS

Says I to Myself. Edward Lear. FiBHP

Says Jack: "There is very good news; there is peace both by land and sea." Distressed Men of War. *Unknown.* OxBSS

Says my Uncle, I pray you discover. Molly Mog; or, The Fair Maid of the Inn. John Gay. CoMu

Says Robin to Jenny, "If you will be mine." *Unknown.* PBBP

Says-so is in a woe of shuddered. Irritable Song. Russell Atkins. AmNP

Says Stonewall Jackson to "Little Phil": "Phil, have you heard the news?" Joined the Blues. John Jerome Rooney. AA

Says the master to me, "Is it true, I am told." My Master and I. *Unknown.* CoMu; OBET

Says the Miner to the Mucker. *Unknown.* AmFP

Says the Pont to the Blyth. Pont and Blyth. *Unknown.* GBP

Says the window. Indoors. George Johnston. PoA

Says Tweed to Till. *Unknown.* BoNaP; ChTr; FaBoCh; FaBoPP; GBP; OBEV; OxBSP (Two Rivers, The.) ChTr; OBEV

Says William to Henry, "I cannot conceive." Henry's Secret. Dorothy Kilner. OxBChV

Says William to Phyllis, "How came you here so soon?" William and Phyllis. *Unknown.* OBET

Scaffold, The. Amal Dunqul, *tr. fr. Arabic by* Sharif Elmusa *and* Thomas G. Ezzy. MAP

Scaffolding. Seamus Heaney. GOYP

Scala Coeli. Kathleen Jessie Raine. NYBP

Scalded cat. Night Letter. Marge Piercy. NMM

Scales, The. William Empson. CMoP; FaBoMo; LiTM

Scales of pearly cloud inlay. Holiday at Hampton Court. John Davidson. EBVV

Scales of the Eyes, The. Howard Nemerov. CMoP

Scaling small rocks, exhaling smog. Central Park. Robert Lowell. LiTM

Scallion stands, gruel shops—half are run by ex-scholars! Inscribed on the Wall of a Rice Cake Shop. Chin Nung, *tr. by* Jonathan Chaves. CoBLCP

Scallions just washed white in this cold. Basho, *tr. fr. Japanese by* Burton Watson. *Fr.* Seventy-six Hokku. FCEI

Scalp Dance Song. *Unknown, tr. fr. Tewa Indian by* H. J. Spinden. WTO

Scampering over saucers. Buson, *tr. by* Geoffrey Bownas *and* Anthony Thwaite. PeBJV

Scandal among the Flowers, A. Charles S. Taylor. BLPA

Scandal or two, A. Tattle. Godfrey Turner. NOBL

Scandalous man, A. Mr. Tom Narrow. James Reeves. SO

Scant and straggling her yellow hair, from her lip. An Old Woman. David Gwenallt Jones, *tr. by* H. Idris Bell. OBWVE

Scaped. Stephen Crane. *Fr.* The Black Riders, LXV. AA

Scapegoat. W. R. Rodgers. CIP

Scapular of birds hung fast, A. Eclipses. Nancy Sullivan. TAP

Scar, The. John Hewitt. CIP

Scaramouche waves a threatening hand. Fantoches. Paul Verlaine, *tr. by* Arthur Symons. AWP; OBMV

Scarborough Fair. *Unknown.* OxBoLi

Scarce do I pass a day, but that I hear. Meditation 8. Philip Pain. NOBA; OxBSP; QFR

Scarce had I seen for the first time his eyes. To Luigi del Riccio, after the Death of Cecchino Bracci. Buonarroti Michelangelo, *tr. by* John Addington Symonds. PeHV

Scarce images of life, one here, one there. A Recollection of the Stone Circle near Keswick. Keats. *Fr.* Hyperion; a Fragment, II. FaBoPP

Scarcely. Alfonso Reyes, *tr. fr. Spanish by* Samuel Beckett. MexPo

Scarcely believe things shameful to utter which yet I shall speak of. Bernard of Cluny, *tr. fr. Latin by* John Mason Neale. *Fr.* De Contemptu Mundi. PeHV

Scare-Fire, The. Robert Herrick. HAP; NoP

Scarecrow, The. Michael Franklin. BoTP

Scarecrow, The. Walter de La Mare. MoBrPo; OxBTC

Scarecrow, The. Andrew Young. FaBoTw

Scarecrow doesn't worry him, The. *Unknown, tr. by* Geoffrey Bownas *and* Anthony Thwaite. PeBJV

Scarecrow in Capri, The. Karl Wawra, *tr. fr. German by* Beth Bjorklund. CoAuP

Scarecrow in the hillock. Waka on Zen Sitting. Dogen, *tr. by* Lucien Stryk *and* Takashi Ikemoto. ZPCJ

Scarecrow stood in a field one day, A. The Scarecrow. Michael Franklin. BoTP

Scared?/ are responsible negros running. Concerning One Responsible Negro with Too Much Power. Nikki Giovanni. BPo

Scarf, The. Ivy O. Eastwick. BoTP

Scaring Crows. *Unknown.* BoTP; OxNR; PBBP

Scarlet red flowers burst into flame everywhere. The Scarlet Red Tree. Liang Ch'i-ch'ao, *tr. by* Cecile Chu-chin Sun. WFTU

Scarlet Tanager, The. Joel Benton. AA

Scarlet Tanager, The. Mary Augusta Mason. AA

Scarlet tide of summer's life, The. To an Autumn Leaf. Albert Mathews. AA

Scarlet trees are spitting blood of leaves. Twelve Autumn Lines. Aaron Zeitlin, *tr. by* Robert Friend. PeBMYV

Scarlet Woman, The. Fenton Johnson. BANP; PoBA; PoNe

Scarlett O'Hara/ in time came to care a. Patricia Bunge. SoTCo

Scars Remaining, The. Samuel Taylor Coleridge. *Fr.* Christabel, *pt.* II. OBNC

Scars, touchable. Christine Busta, *tr. by* Beth Bjorklund. CoAuP

Scatter Seeds of Kindness. May Riley Smith. WBLP

Scattered Fog. Christy Sheffield Sanford. UL

Scattered Leaves. Lance Henson. VoR

Scattered like flotsam on the erupting sea. The Roc. Edward Lowbury. AmMo

Scattering blossoms. Empress Eifuku, *tr. by* Steven D. Carter. WFTW

Scazons. C. S. Lewis. EBEV

Scel Lem Duib. *Unknown. See* Here's a song.

Scenario. Barbara Eve Reiss. TV

Scene. Faiz Ahmad Faiz, *tr. fr. Urdu by* Mahmood Jamal. PBMUP

Scene, The. Denis Glover. *Fr.* Arawata Bill. ATNZ

Scene after Hunting at Swallowfield in Berkshire, A. Sneyd Davies. NOEC

Scene at Heaven Gate, The. T'ang Yin, *tr. fr. Chinese by* Jonathan Chaves. CoBLCP

Scene from a Dream. Janet Campbell Hale. STE

Scene from a Play, Acted at Oxford, Called "Matriculation." Thomas Moore. OBSV

Scene in Paradise, A. Milton. *See* Paradise Lost: Adam the goodliest man of men since born.

Scene is set now, The: in a silent room. Transfusion. Merrill Moore. PoA

Scene of a Summer Morning. Irving Feldman. NYBP

Scene on the Banks of the Hudson, A. Bryant. AnAmPo

Scene-Shifter Death. Mary Devenport O'Neill. NeIP

Scene, The: a public square in Ruritania. The Belle of the Balkans. Newman Levy. FiBHP

Scene with Figure. Babette Deutsch. TrJP

Scene within the paperweight is calm, The. The Paperweight. Gjertrud Schnackenberg. SM

Scenery. Ted Joans. PoBA

Scenes, *sel.* Yang Chi, *tr. fr. Chinese by* Jonathan Chaves. "Eastern neighbor, western neighbor." CoBLCP

Scènes de la Vie de Bohème, *sel.* Arthur Symons. Episode of a Night of May. BrPo; OBTV

Scenes from Carnac. Matthew Arnold. FaBoPP; OBTV

Scenes from the Life of the Peppertrees. Denise Levertov. LiTM; NeAP; NoP; PoM

Scenes in a Silver Mine. Tachibana Akemi, *tr. fr. Japanese by* Burton Watson. *Fr.* Thirty Tanka. FCEI

Scenes of Childhood. James Merrill. CoAP; DiL

Scenes of Childhood. Carl Morse. GLP

Scenes of my childhood, The, how oft I recall! My Infundibuliform Hat. Charles Follen Adams. OBAL

Scent is back, a bridal weave, The. Spring. Pamela Stewart. NAmP

Scent of beeswax, dust, A; the empty rooms. Meeting Myself. Edward Lucie-Smith. NePoEA-2

Scent of guava-blossoms and the smell, A. At Set of Sun. Mary Ashley Townsend. AA

Scent of plum flowers, The. Tamekane, *tr. by* Steven D. Carter. WFTW

Scent of ripeness from over a wall, A. Unharvested. Robert Frost. BoNaP

Scent of rotted apples, The. Late October. Sara King Carleton. GoYe

Scent of sage, The. Vision Song (Cheyenne). Lance Henson. STE

Scent of the plum blossoms, The. Teika, *tr. fr. Japanese by* Hiroaki Sato. *Fr.* Eighty-four Tanka. FCEI
Scent of the rose, the heart's lament, The. Asadullah Khan Ghalib, *tr. by* Ahmed Ali. GoT
Scent of unseen jasmine on the warm night beach, The. Malaga. Pearse Hutchinson. BIrV
Scented cloth and tooled flaps outfit his fine horse, A. Welcoming the Worthy Guest. Mao Wen-hsi, *tr. by* Lois Fusek. ATF
Scented, cool, and marble dark. Lemons. Ted Walker. NYBP
Scented Herbage of My Breast. Walt Whitman. NAAL-1
Scentless laurel a broad leaf displays, The. Walter Savage Landor. FaBoEE
Scheherazade. Barbara Burford. DT
Schemmelfennig. Bret Harte. OBAL
Scherzando. W. E. Henley. *Fr.* London Voluntaries, III. BrPo
Scherzo, A. Dora Greenwell. NOBVV
Scheveningen, Off Season. Valery Larbaud, *tr. fr. French by* William Jay Smith. CT
Schiehallion. Helen B. Cruickshank. PoSH
Schir, though your grace has put great order. Ane Supplication in Contemptioun of Syde Taillis. Sir David Lyndsay. GoTS
Schir William Wallace. Henry the Minstrel. *See* Wallace, The: Description of Wallace, A.
Schir, ye have mony servitouris. Remonstrance to the King. William Dunbar. OxBS
Schizophrenic. Patricia K. Page. HeIP
Schizophrenic, wrenched by two styles. Codicil. Derek Walcott. MoP; NoAM
Schizophrenics, The. Roy Fuller. AnAn
Schmaltztenor! M. W. Branch. FiBHP
Schoenberg Op. 11. Thomas W. Shapcott. *Fr.* Piano Pieces. CBAP
Scholar, The. Austin Clarke. RB
Scholar, The. Frances Cornford. BrRo
Scholar Complains, The. *Unknown.* MeEL
Scholar-Gipsy, The, *sel.* Matthew Arnold. ChTr; EBEV; EBVV; FiP; HAP; HeIP; NAEL-2; NOBE; NOBW; NoP; OAEL-2; OBEV; OBNC; PoE; PoEL-5; TEP
  "Go, for they call you, shepherd, from the hill." FaBoPP
Scholar I. Seamus Deane. NOIV
Scholar in the Narrow Street, The. Tso Ssu, *tr. fr. Chinese by* Arthur Waley. AWP
Scholar II. Seamus Deane. CIP; NOIV
Scholars. Walter De la Mare. NoAM
Scholars, The. W. B. Yeats. CMoP; NoP; OAEL-2; PoA
Scholars at the Orchid Pavilion. John Berryman. PoE
Scholar's Life, The. Samuel Johnson. *See* Vanity of Human Wishes, The: The Tenth Satire of Juvenal Imitated: When first the college rolls receive his name.
Scholar's Life, The. *Unknown, tr. fr. Irish by* Thomas Kinsella. NOIV
Scholar's Wife, The. Susan Mernit. VWA
Scholfield Huxley. Edgar Lee Masters. *Fr.* Spoon River Anthology. LiTA; TrPWD
School-Bell. Eleanor Farjeon. FaPON
School-bell rings, The. Nine o'Clock. Katharine Pyle. *Fr.* The Wonder Clock. OBCA
School Cadets. Anne Elder. CBAP
School Children, The. Louise Glück. AmPA; HCAP; WeW
School Creed. *Unknown.* BoTP
School Days. Maltbie Davenport Babcock. PWR
School Days. William Stafford. LCAP
School Days in New Amsterdam. Arthur Guiterman. FaPON
School for Objects, The. Paul Hoover. UL
School for Scandal, The, *sel.* Sheridan.
  Drinking Song. NOIV
  (Here's to the Maiden.) ELP
  (Song: "Here's to the maiden [*or* maid] of bashful fifteen.") NOEC; OxBoLi; PoRA
School Girl, The. William Henry Venable. AA
School Globe, The. James Reaney. NOBC
School greets me like a series, The. Poet in Residence at a Country School. Don Welch. GOYP
School Hockey Team in Amsterdam, The. Frank Ormsby. OBTV
School is over. It is too hot. The Lonely Street. William Carlos Williams. PoA; TwCP
School-Master and the Truants, The. "John Brownjohn." OBCA
School-Mistress, The. William Shenstone. LaA; NOEC
School of Beauty's a tavern now, The. A Street in Bronzeville: Southeast Corner. Gwendolyn Brooks. VGW
School of Eloquence, The, *sels.* Tony Harrison. NoAM
  Book Ends.
  Heredity.

  History Classes.
  Lines to My Grandfathers.
  Marked with D..
  Me Tarzan.
  On Not Being Milton.
  Self Justification.
  Timer.
  Turns.
School Of Night, The. A. D. Hope. PoA
School of Poetry. Lucebert, *tr. fr. Dutch by* James S. Holmes. DuIn
School of Sorrow, The. Harold Hamilton. BLRP
School Parted Us. "George Eliot." *Fr.* Brother and Sister, XI. Son
School Policy on Stickmen. Sam Hunt. ATNZ
School Report, A. Sam Hunt. ATNZ
School that looks like an army barracks, A. Ecole St. Luc. Ray Fraser. NeAC
School-Time. Wordsworth. *Fr.* The Prelude [or, Growth of a Poet's Mind], II. EnRP; OAEL-2
  "But who shall parcel out." TOF
  "Blest the infant Babe." TOF
  Intimations of Sublimity. OBNC
Schoolboy, The. Blake. *Fr.* Songs of Experience. BoNaP; CH; FaBoCh
Schoolboys in Winter. John Clare. InvP; PoEL-4
Schoolboy's Lament, The. *Unknown. See* Hay! Hay! By this day.
Schoolboys still their morning rambles take, The. Schoolboys in Winter. John Clare. InvP; PoEL-4
Schoolbus Comes before the Sun, The. Robert Currie. TDD
Schoolgirl on Speech-Day in the Open Air. Iain Crichton Smith. NePoEA-2
Schooling, A. Seamus Deane. CIP
Schoolmaster. George Rostrevor Hamilton. FaBoEE
Schoolmaster, The. *Unknown.* GBP
Schoolmaster Abroad, The. Sir Owen Seaman. OBTV
Schoolmaster Abroad with His Son, The. Charles Stuart Calverley. NOBL
Schoolmaster once known as, The. History Teacher in the Warsaw Ghetto Rising. Evangeline Paterson. CN
Schoolmaster's Admonition, A. *Unknown.* OxBChV
Schoolmaster's Precepts, A. John Penkethman. OxBChV
Schoolroom: 158– James E. Warren, Jr. GoYe
Schools. George Crabbe. *Fr.* The Borough, Letter XXIV CTC
Schools and Schoolmasters. Hilene Flanzbaum. PPR
Schools break up tonight, The. Lament for Fearghal Ruadh. Tadhg Og O'Huiginn. NePoEA-2
School's Out. W. H. Davies. OBMV
Schoolyard in April. Kenneth Koch. PoA
Schooner. Edward Kamau Brathwaite. PBCV
Schooner *Fred Dunbar*, The. Amos Hanson. AmFP
Schooner, noblest wood, nimble. Land and Sea. Luciano Erba, *tr. by* Lawrence R. Smith. NItP
Schooners with their pale green lights, The. A Dream within a Song. Henrietta Cordelia Ray. CBWP-3
Schreckhorn, The. Thomas Hardy. OAEL-2
Schubertiana. Tomas Tranströmer, *tr. fr. Swedish by* Robert Bly. NU
Schule Laddie's Lament on the Lateness o' the Season, A. James Logie Robertson. NOBVV
Schumann's Sonata in A Minor. Celia Thaxter. AiP
Schusssssssss. The Skibomber. Martin Steingesser. TSL
Science. Robinson Jeffers. NU; OxBA
Science/fiction. Adrienne Marcus. BWV
Science, Also the savants say. Emily Dickinson. ImOP
Science as Art. Hugh Seidman. AmPA
Science Fiction. Kingsley Amis. NePoEA-2; NoAM
Science Fiction. Nancy Willard. BLA
Science finds out ingenious ways to kill. The Modern World. Colin Ellis. FaBoEE
Science in God. Robert Herrick. ImOP
Science is what the world is, earth and water. The Laboratory Midnight. Reuel Denney. ImOP
Science long watched the realms of space. A World Beyond. Nathaniel Ingersoll Bowditch. AA
Science! meet daughter of old time thou art. Sonnet to Science. Poe. NAAL-1
Science of the Night, The. Stanley Kunitz. MoAmPo; TwCP
Science should work out a new deal for those Silent People in the boxes. On Passing by Those Icy Stones (and Yes, Columbia!). David R. Bunch. BWV
Science, that simple saint, cannot be bothered. Dr. Sigmund Freud Discovers the Sea Shell. Archibald MacLeish. SoSe

Science, the agile ape, may well. Coventry Patmore. FaBoEE
Science! thou fair effusive ray. Hymn to Science. Mark Akenside.
    PoEL-3
Science! true daughter of Old Time thou art! Sonnet to Science: Prologue.
    Poe. *Fr.* Al Aaraff. AmPP; NoP; OxBA; Aaraaf. TAP; TW
    (To Science.) AnAmPo; Son
Scientific Expedition in Siberia, 1913, A. Kelly Cherry. SM
Scientist, The. Janet Burroway. SoSe
Scientist has a test tube full of sheep, A. Counting Sheep. Russell
    Edson. LCAP
Scientist living at Staines, A. Genius. R. J. P. Hewison. FaFP
Scientists and technicians! An Arab Traveler in a Space Ship.
    Muhammad al-Maghut. MAP, *tr.* by Lena Jayyusi *and* John Heath-
    Stubbs; MPAW, *tr.* by Abdullah al-Udhari.
Scientists are in terror, The. Ezra Pound. *Fr.* Cantos, CXV. FaBoMo
Scientists Are Mistaken, The. Abba Kovner, *tr. fr. Hebrew by* Warren
    Bargad *and* Stanley F. Chyet. IP
Sicilian Muse, begin a loftier strain. The Messiah. Virgil, *tr. fr. Latin.*
    Fr. Eclogues, IV. AWP, *tr.* by Dryden.
Scilla's Metamorphosis, *sel.* Thomas Lodge.
    Earth, Late Choked with Showers, The. EiL
    (Melancholy.) OBSC
Scintilla. William Stanley Braithwaite. AmNP; BANP; CDC
Scissor-Man. George MacBeth. FaBoMo
Scissor-Man, The. Madeleine Nightingale. BoTP
Scissors and string, scissors and string. *Unknown.* OxNR
Scissors cut the long-grown hair, The. Upon Shaving Off One's Beard.
    John Updike. OxBSP
Scissors cut you? What tender ears! On Words and Concepts and Things.
    Paul Ramsey. CRP
Scobble for whoredom[e] whips his wife, and cries [or cryes]. Upon
    Scobble [Epigram]. Robert Herrick. CaPo; FaBoEE; NoP; TW
Scoffers, The. Blake. *See* Mock On, Mock On, Voltaire, Rousseau.
Scolded in a dream. On the Anniversary of My Father's Death. Natsume
    Seibi, *tr. fr. Japanese by* Hiroaki Sato. *Fr.* Twenty-seven Hokku.
    FCEI
Scolding Wives Vindication; or, An Answer to the Cuckold's Complaint,
    The. *Unknown.* CoMu
Scoop. Ernest Slyman. SoTCo
Scoops in the sea rock full of natural water. Bathtubs. Richmond
    Lattimore. NYBP
Scorched by the forest fire. Kabir, *tr.* by John Stratton Hawley *and* Mark
    Juergensmeyer. SSI
Scorching sun, enough to parch the Yangtze!, A. Tsung Ch'en, *tr. fr.*
    Chinese by Jonathan Chaves. *Fr.* Miscellaneous Words on the Lake.
    CoBLCP
Score of years had come and gone, A. John Underhill. Whittier. PAH
Scoring. Kent Cartwright. TSL
Scorn me as reason, who am always there. To a Friend. Charles
    Gullans. NePoEA
Scorn Not the Sonnet. Wordsworth. *See* Scorn not the sonnet; critic, you
    have frowned.
Scorn not the sonnet; critic. you have frowned. Wordsworth. EBEV
    (Scorn Not the Sonnet.) EnRP; HeIP; NIP; NoP; Son
    (Sonnet: "Scorn not the sonnet; critic, you have frowned.") OBEV;
    TrGrPo
"Scorn not the sonnet," though its strength is sapped. On a Magazine
    Sonnet. Russell Hillard Loines. OBAL
Scorne then their censure, who gave out thy wit. Jasper Mayne. *Fr.* To
    the Memory of Ben Johnson. OBS
Scorner, The. Felix TchiKaya U'Tamsi, *tr. fr. French by* Gerald Moore
    and Ulli Beier. TTY
Scorpion, The. William Plomer. OBMV
Scorpion. Stevie Smith. EBEV; FaBoWP; PoE
Scorpion's tails, silver hooks. Yün Shou-p'ing, *tr. fr. Chinese by*
    Jonathan Chaves. *Fr.* In the Tenth Month of the Year Jen-tzu.
    CoBLCP
Scot, a Welsh and an Irish Man, A. *Unknown.* GBP
Scotch Rhapsody. Edith Sitwell. TwCP
Scotch Te Deum. William Kethe. *See* All people on Earth that do dwell.
Scotch Te Deum. Bible, *O.T. See* Psalms: Psalm C ("Make a joyful
    noise. . .").
Scotish Feilde, *sel. Unknown.*
    Battle of Flodden, The. OxBLMV
Scotland. Sir Alexander Gray. GoTS; OxBS
Scotland. William Soutar. OxBS
Scotland 1941. Edwin Muir. OxBS
Scotland Small? "Hugh MacDiarmid." PoSH; RB
Scotland, when it is given to me. With a Lifting of the Head. "Hugh
    MacDiarmid." MoBrPo

Scotland's Winter. Edwin Muir. OxBS; OxBTC
Scots steel tempered wi' Irish fire. The Weapon. "Hugh MacDiarmid."
    RB
Scots Wha Hae [wi' Wallace Bled]. Burns. EnRP; FaPoR; NAEL-2;
    OAEL-1; OxBS; TEP
    (Before Bannockburn.) FaBoCh
Scott and I bent. Heaven. Gary Soto. NPGG
Scott-Moncrieff's Beowulf. Charles Spear. ATNZ
Scott, your last fragments I arrange tonight. On Editing Scott Fitzgerald's
    Papers. Edmund Wilson. NYBP
Scottish Bride, A. Bill Manhire. ATNZ
Scottish Mountaineering Club Song, The. John G. Stott. PoSH
Scottish Proverb, A. *Unknown.* FaBoUs
Scotts, Kerrs, and Murrays, and Deloraines all, The. A Border Ballad.
    Thomas Love Peacock. BXAP
Scottsboro. *Unknown.* InPK
Scottsboro, Too, Is Worth Its Song. Countee Cullen. PoBA
Scourge deep, and quick be done. Martyr. "E." CBAP
Scourge of Folly, The, *sel. John Davies of Hereford.*
    Author Loving These Homely Meats, The. EiL; FaBoNo; Son
    (Buttered Pippin-Pies.) ChTr
    (Homely Meats.) FaBoCh
Scourge of Villainy [or Villanie], The, *sels. John Marston.*
    To Detraction I Present My Poesie. OBSC; TW
    To Everlasting Oblivion. OBSC
Scourge of wind first, to flay, The. View from My Window. Alasdair
    Maclean. PoSH
Scrap Iron. Raymond Durgnat. PCP
Scrapbooks. Nikki Giovanni. CNA
Scrape no more your harmless Chins. Advice to the Old Beaux. Sir
    Charles Sedley. FaBoUs; SeCV-2
Scraping sound, A: The grasshopper. The Grasshopper's Song. H. N.
    Nachman, *tr.* by Jessie Sampter. FaPON
Scrapping Limits. Salma Khadra Jayyusi, *tr. fr. Arabic by the author and*
    Charles Doria. MAP
Scraps. Susannah Fried, *tr.* by Anthony Rudolf. VWA
Scraps. Rodger Kamenetz. UL
Scraps of Lear. Edward Lear. FaBoNo
Scraps of Time. Mrs. Henry Linden. CBWP-4
Scratch a Jew and you'll find a Wailing Wall. The Wall. Eve Merriam.
    TrJP
Scratching your eyebrows, sneezing. *Unknown. Fr.* Manyo Shu.
    FCEI
Scrawled in Pencil in a Sealed Railway Car. Dan Pagis, *tr. fr. Hebrew by*
    Anthony Rudolf. VWA
Scream, A. Dannie Abse. NPo
Scream, A. Muhammad al-Faituri, *tr. fr. Arabic by* Sargon Boulus *and*
    Peter Porter. MAP
Screamer Discusses Methods of Screaming, A. James Schevill.
    TAP
Screams round the Arch-druid's brow the sea-mew—white. Trepidation of
    the Druids. Wordsworth. *Fr.* Ecclesiastical Sonnets. Son
Screams that I screamed, despairing, aching. My White Book of Poems.
    "Rachel," *tr.* by "N. N." VWA
Scree empties down the mountain, The. One Way Down. David Craig.
    PoSH
Screech owl laughing alone?, A. Amused at My Own Figure while
    Traveling. Kikaku, *tr. fr. Japanese by* Hiroaki Sato. *Fr.* Thirty-
    three Hokku. FCEI
Screens are in dim shadows, The. Hatred of Distant Places. Ku Hsiung,
    tr. by Lois Fusek. ATF
Screw Spring. William M. Hoffman. FF
Scribblers, The. Walter Savage Landor. FaBoEE; OBSV
    ("Why should scribblers discompose.") FaBoEE
Scribe. Paul Auster. VWA
Scribe, The. *Unknown, tr. fr. Old Irish by* Kuno Meyer. AnIL
Scribe, The. *Unknown, tr. fr. Irish.* AnIL, *tr. fr.* by Kathleen Hoagland;
    TIRV, *tr.* by Robin Flower
Scribe, The. Walter de la Mare. CMoP; FaBoCh; OBMV; TrCP;
    TrPWD
Scribe's Prayer, The. Arthur Guiterman. TrPWD
Scribe's Prayer, The. Robert W. Service. TrPWD
Scripts for the Pageant, *sel.* James Merrill.
    Samos. HCAP
Scriptures, The. Dryden. *Fr.* Religio Laici. OBS
Scroll. Stanley Moss. VWA
Scrolls. Lotte Kramer. CN
Scrub woman for the old bank and jailhouse, The. Lamentations.
    Norman Dubie. NoAM
Scrubber. W. E. Henley. *Fr.* In Hospital, XIX. BrPo

Scruffy one, The. Hyena. *Unknown, tr. fr. Yoruba* by Ulli Beier. *Fr.* Hunter Poems of the Yoruba. RB

Scrut Gets Marty Crowe for Social Studies. George Roberts. TSL

Scrutiny [*or* Scrutinie], The. Richard Lovelace. BoLoP; CaPo; ELP; EnLoPo; GBL; MeLP; MePo; NoP; OBS; SeCP; TrGrPo

Scudamor in the Temple of Venus. Spenser. *Fr.* The Faerie Queene, IV, 10. PoE

Scudding cloud, A. Basho, *tr. fr. Japanese* by Burton Watson. *Fr.* Seventy-six Hokku. FCEI

Sculpting in the Imperial Presence. Takamura Kotaro, *tr. fr. Japanese* by Hiroaki Sato. *Fr.* A Brief History of Imbecility. FCEI

Sculptor, The. Russell Edson. NAmP

Sculptor first in breath and blood, A. With Metaphor. Sarah Wingate Taylor. GoYe

Sculptor musing sat one eve, A. The Sculptor's Vision. Henrietta Cordelia Ray. CBWP-3

Sculptor's Vision, The. Henrietta Cordelia Ray. CBWP-3

Sculpture. *Unknown.* BLPL; PoLF

Sculpture in a bare white gallery, A. The Field. Jean Valentine. LCAP

Scunner. "Hugh MacDiarmid." FaBoTw

Scurrilous Scribe, The. Philip Freneau. AA

Scurvy-grass creeps down the strand, The. January. Daniel James O'Sullivan. NeIP

Scuttle, scuttle little roach. Christopher Morley. *Fr.* Nursery Rhymes for the Tender-hearted, I. FaFP

Scylla and Charybdis. Homer, *tr. fr. Greek* by George Chapman. *Fr.* Odyssey, XII. OBS

Scylla and Charybdis. Thomas Kinsella. OxBTC

Scylla's Lament. Thomas Hood. *Fr.* Hero and Leander. EnRP

Scyros. Karl Shapiro. HoPM; LiTA; LiTM; WaP

Scythe, The. Henry Kanabus. UL

Scythe Song. Andrew Lang. GN

Scythians, The. Aleksandr Aleksandrovich Blok, *tr. fr. Russian* by Babette Deutsch *and* Avrahm Yarmolinsky. AWP; WaaP

Scything. Basil Dowling. ATNZ

Sè Stesso, A. Giacomo Leopardi, *tr. fr. Italian* by Lorna De' Lucchi. AWP

Sea, The. E. M. Adams. BoTP

Sea, The. Byron. *See* Childe Harold's Pilgrimage: Ocean, The.

Sea, The. "Barry Cornwall." GN

Sea, The. W. H. Davies. FaBoTw

Sea, The. Lloyd Frankenberg. MOS

Sea, The. Eugène Guillevic, *tr. fr. French* by John Montague. RHTwFP

Sea, The. D. H. Lawrence. BoNaP; MOS

Sea, The. Louis MacNeice. *Fr.* Nature Notes. FaBCIP

Sea, The. Ken Noyle. MOS

Sea. Shin Dong-jip, *tr. fr. Korean* by Koh Chang-soo. ACKP

Sea, The. Richard Henry Stoddard. AA

Sea, The. Swinburne. *See* Triumph of Time, The: I Will Go Back to the Great Sweet Mother.

Sea, The. *Unknown.* NA; RHPC

Sea, The. Francis Webb. CBAP; PoAu-2

Sea, The/ tore a rib from its side. Water without Sound. Malka Heifetz-Tussman, *tr.* by Marcia Falk. OV; PeBMyV; VWA

Sea and Land Victories. *Unknown.* PAH

Sea and Ourselves at Cape Ann, The. Lawrence Ferlinghetti. PoM

Sea and Shore. Harry Lyman Koopman. AA

Sea and the Canefield, The. João Cabral de Melo Neto, *tr. fr. Portuguese* by Louis Simpson. ATCBP

Sea and the Eagle, The. Sydney Clouts. PeSA

Sea and the Hills, The. Kipling. FaBV; MOS

Sea and the Mirror, The, *sels.* W. H. Auden.
Miranda. NoAM
Song of the Master and Boatswain. BoLoP; MOS
(Master and Boatswain.) FaBoTw

Sea and the Skylark, The. Gerard Manley Hopkins. FM; LiTB; OBMV

Sea and the Tiger, The. Laurence Collinson. PoAu-2

Sea at Evening, The. Christopher Laird. PBCV

Sea at evening moves across the sand, The. Soldiers Bathing. Frank Templeton Prince. GTBS-P; LiTB; LiTM; MoBrPo; NOCV; OBWP; OxBTC; PeSA; WaP

Sea at this town's neat threshold spills its gloss. At the Sea's Edge. Gwen Harwood. CBAP

Sea awoke at midnight from its sleep, The. The Sound of the Sea. Longfellow. MOS

Sea Battle, The. Dryden. *Fr.* Annus Mirabilis. FiP

Sea becomes light, a window is open, The. Ozaki Hosai, *tr. fr. Japanese* by Hiroaki Sato. *Fr.* One Hundred Haiku in Free Form. FCEI

Sea-Birds. Elizabeth Akers Allen. AA; FaBoBe

Sea Birds, The. Van K. Brock. NYBP; SM

Sea-bound landsman, looking back to shore, The. John Brown. Harry Lyman Koopman. AA

Sea Boy on the Giddy Mast, A. John Clare. PPP

Sea Burial from the Cruiser "Reve." Richard Eberhart. NYBP

Sea Cadences. Henrietta Cordelia Ray. CBWP-3

Sea Canes. Derek Walcott. HeIP

Sea Cathedral, The. E. J. Pratt. CaP

Sea Change. Mary Dorcey. *See* Your thighs, your belly.

Sea Change. John Masefield. FaBoTw; MOS; OBMV; RB

Sea-Change: For Harold, A. Joseph Langland. LiTM

Sea-Chantey, A, *sel.* Derek Walcott. RB
"In the middle of the harbour." TTY

Sea-Chaplain's Petition to the Lieutenants in the Ward-Room, for the Use of the Quarter-Gallery, A. "J. T." NOEC

Sea-Chill. Arthur Guiterman. BXAP; FaBoPa; MOS

Sea contains a destiny, The. The Sea and the Eagle. Sydney Clouts. PeSA

Sea-cow or grey manatee, The. The Manatee. Carey Blyton. AmMo

Sea cries with its meaningless voice, The. Pibroch. Ted Hughes. FaBoMo; NePoEA-2; OAEL-2; PoCH

Sea dark, The. Basho, *tr.* by Geoffrey Bownas *and* Anthony Thwaite. PeBJV

Sea darkens, and the voices of ducks, The. Basho, *tr. fr. Japanese* by Burton Watson. *Fr.* Seventy-six Hokku. FCEI

Sea Desires. Laila al-Saih, *tr. fr. Arabic* by Patricia Alanah Byrne *with* Salma Khadra Jayyusi. MAP

Sea Dialogue, A. Oliver Wendell Holmes. MOS; OBAL

Sea Dirge. Archias of Byzantium, *tr. fr. Greek* by Andrew Lang. AWP

Sea Dirge, A. "Lewis Carroll." CenHV; MOS

Sea Dirge, A. Shakespeare. *See* Tempest, The: Full fathom [*or* fadom] five thy father lies.

Sea-Distances. Alfred Noyes. MOS

Sea does not, The. Those Others. Ian Wedde. PeNZ

Sea Dreams, *sel.* Tennyson.
"What does little birdie say?." OxBChV

Sea-Elephant, The. William Carlos Williams. LiTA; NU

Sea Fairies. Eileen Mathias. BoTP

Sea Fever. John Masefield. FaBoBe; FaBV; FaPON; FaPoR; FPL; MoAB; MoBrPo; MOS; OBTV; OHFP; OxBTC; PDV; PoLF; TrGrPo

Sea Fight in '92, The. *Unknown.* OxBSS

Sea Flower. Mary Dorcey. BrRo
(Sea Change.) AIW

Sea Fog, The. Josephine Jacobsen. NYBP

Sea-Games. Aliza Shenhar, *tr. fr. Hebrew* by Linda Zisquit. VWA

Sea gleamed deep blue in the sunlight, The. Homage to Marcel Proust. Thomas MacGreevy. CIP

Sea go dark, dark with wind. Wild Iron. Allen Curnow. ATNZ; RB

Sea Gods. Hilda Doolittle ("H. D."). LiTA; MOS

Sea goes flick-flack or the light does, The. Sheep Dipping. Norman MacCaig. OxBC

Sea-Grape Tree and the Miraculous. William Pitt Root. GeTw

Sea-Grief. Dowell O'Reilly. PoAu-1

Sea guards warily its treasures, The. The Heart. Jakov Steinberg, *tr.* by Harry H. Fein. TrJP

Sea-Gull, The. Mary Howitt. BoTP; OxBChV

Sea-Gull, The. Ogden Nash. FaFP; FPL; MOS

Sea-Gull, The. *Unknown.* GBP

Sea gull/ who flaps his wings. Magic Words to Feel Better. Nakasuk, *tr.* by Jerome Rothenberg. STP

Sea gulls whiten and dip, The. In the Bay. Arthur Symons. *Fr.* Amorix Exsul, III. OBNC; PBBP

Sea Gypsy, The. Richard Hovey. AnAmPo; FaPON; PDV

Sea has its way, The: if you see. Cormorants. John Blight. CBAP

Sea has made a wall for its defence, The. Shoreline. Mary Barnard. PoA

Sea Hath Its Pearls, The. Heine, *tr. fr. German* by Longfellow. AWP

Sea Hath Many Thousand Sands, The. *Unknown.* ElL; LiTB; OBSC

Sea hath tempered it, The; the mighty sun. The Fountain. "Mustafa," *tr.* by Dulcie L. Smith. AWP

Sea-Hawk. Richard Eberhart. RB

Sea here used to look, The. At Darien Bridge. James Dickey. NoP

Sea Hold, The. Carl Sandburg. MOS

Sea Holly. Conrad Aiken. LiTM

Sea Horse, The. Robert Graves. FaBoMo

Sea in my mind, A. The Myrtle Tree. Nikos Gatsos, *tr. fr. Greek* by Edmund Keeley *and* Philip Sherrard. *Fr.* Four Songs. VMG

Sea Irony. John Langdon Heaton. AA

Sea is a circuit of holes, The. The Coral Reef. Laurence Lieberman. CoAP

Sea is a wilderness of waves, The. Long Trip. Langston Hughes. MOS

Sea is an acre of dull glass, the land is a table, The. Lusty Juventus. Charles Madge. FaBoMo

Sea is as green as you paint it, The. To Giovanni. Cesare Vivaldi, *tr. by* Lawrence R. Smith. NItP

Sea is calm tonight, The. Dover Beach. Matthew Arnold. AWP; BLPA; EaLo; EBVV; FaBoBe; FaBoPP; FaBoRV; FaBV; FaFP; FF; FiP; FPL; GTBS-P; HAP; HeIP; HoPM; InPK; InPS; InVP; InvP; LiTB; MAT; MOS; NAEL-2; NIP; NOBE; NOBVV; NoP; NU; OAEL-2; OBNC; OPOP; PoE; PoEL-5; PoRA; PPP; Prf; PrIm; SCV; SeCePo; TOF

Sea is flecked with bars of grey, The. Oscar Wilde. *Fr.* Impressions. MOS

    (Les Silhouettes.) BrPo; EBVV

Sea is large, The. The Sea Hold. Carl Sandburg. MOS

Sea is mighty, but a Mightier sways, The. A Hymn of the Sea. Bryant. MOS

Sea is never still, The. Young Sea. Carl Sandburg. MOS

Sea is obsidian, The. Fire Island. Rita Mae Brown. IHMS

Sea is ringed around with hills, The. Home. Jean Jaszi. RAR

Sea is rusted by the morning's carbon dioxide, The. Okhotsk Elegy. Miyazawa Kenji, *tr. by* Hiroaki Sato. FCEI

Sea its millions of waves, The. Rocking My Child. Gabriela Mistral, *tr. by* Perry Higman. LPSS

Sea-lashed coast outside the gate reaches to the hedge. Bamboo Branch Song of the Seacoast. Yang Wei-chen, *tr. by* Jonathan Chaves. CoBLCP

Sea Lavender. Louise Morey Bowman. CaP

Sea Legs. Susan Feldman. AmPA

Sea lies quieted beneath, The. After Sunset. Arthur Symons. *Fr.* At Dieppe. BrPo

Sea-Limits, The. Dante Gabriel Rossetti. MOS; NAEL-2; OAEL-2

Sea limps up here twice a day, The. Paphos. Lawrence Durrell. NYBP

Sea Love. Charlotte Mew. MoAB; MoBrPo; OxBTC; TrGrPo

Sea love song, The. Lilies for the Prophet. Nazik al-Mala'ika, *tr. by* Matthew Sorenson, *modified and abr. by* Christopher Middleton. MAP

Sea Lullaby. Elinor Wylie. BoNaP; MOS

Sea Marke, The. John Smith. SCAP

Sea Martyrs, The. *Unknown.* OxBSS

Sea Memories. Longfellow. *See* Often I think of the beautiful town.

Sea-Monster. Gertrud Kolmar, *tr. fr. German by* Henry A. Smith. VWA

Sea Monster. W. S. Merwin. WSC

Sea Monsters. Spenser. *Fr.* The Faerie Queene, II, 12. ChTr

Sea of Death, The. Thomas Hood. LiTB; OBNC; PoEL-4

Sea of Death, The. *Unknown.* CH

Sea of Silence Exhales Secrets, The. Hayyim Nahman Bialik, *tr. fr. Hebrew by* Gabriel Levin. VWA

Sea off Ise, The. Spring Sea. Tamemasa, *tr. by* Steven D. Carter. WFTW

Sea Offerings. Yu Kuang-chung, *tr. fr. Chinese by* Dominic Cheung. IFON

Sea Owl. Dave Smith. HCAP

Sea pearl, western star. On Leaving. Gertrudis Gomez de Avellaneda, *tr. by* Frederick Sweet. PBWP

Sea-preserved, heaped with sea-spoils. Picture of a Nativity. Geoffrey Hill. NoAM; OxBC

Sea Promenade, A. Pier Paolo Pasolini, *tr. fr. Italian by* Lawrence R. Smith. NItP

Sea retains such images, The. Louis Dudek. *Fr.* Europe, XCV. OBCV

Sea-Ritual, The. George Darley. *Fr.* Syren Songs, V. BIrV; OBNC; WiR; WSC

    (Deadman's Dirge.) CH

Sea Rose. Hilda Doolittle ("H. D."). FaBoMo; HeIP; NoAM; NoP

Sea-Ruck. Richard Eberhart. MOS

Sea-Sand and Sorrow. Christina Rossetti. *See* What Are Heavy?

Sea sang sweetly to the shore, The. Hymn Written for the Two Hundredth Anniversary of the Old South Church, Beverly, Massachusetts. Lucy Larcom. OHIP

Sea School. Barbara Howes. NYBP

Sea Serpant, The. Wallace Irwin. FiBHP

Sea-Serpent, The. James Robinson Planché. NA

Sea Serpent Chantey, The. Vachel Lindsay. AmMo; WSC

Sea Shell. Amy Lowell. BoTP; FaPON; RHPC

Sea-Shore. Emerson. LiTA; MOS; OxBA

Sea Shroud, The. (John Kerouac). PoM

Sea-Sleep. Thomas Lake Harris. AA

Sea-Song. A. Allan Cunningham. *See* Wet Sheet and a Flowing Sea, A.

Sea Song, A. Digby Mackworth Dolben. EBVV

Sea Song. Norah M. Holland. CaP

Sea Song, A: "Master, the swabber, the boatswain and I, The." Shakespeare. *See* Tempest, The: Master, the swabber, the boatswain and I, The.

Sea Song, A. *Unknown.* OxBSS

Sea-Song from the Shore, A. James Whitcomb Riley. BoTP

Sea Sonnet. Norma Lay. GoYe

Sea-Spell, A. Dante Gabriel Rossetti. WSC

Sea still plunges where as naked boys, The. The Grotto. Francis Scarfe. PoA

Sea sucks in the traveller, The. The Sea and the Tiger. Laurence Collinson. PoAu-2

Sea Surface Full of Clouds. Wallace Stevens. AmPP; CMoP; MoAB; MoAmPo; MOS; VGW

Sea swings owre the slants of sand, The. The Ballad of Dead Men's Bay. Swinburne. MOS

Sea tells something, but it tells not all, The. Reserve. Mary Ashley Townsend. AA

Sea, that problem Euclid never solved, The. Sutcliffe and Whitby. William Logan. MAYP

Sea, the last song. Sappho's Last Song. Vittoria Aganoor Pompili, *tr. by* Muriel Kittel. DMI

Sea, The! O the sea! *Unknown.* WTO

Sea, The—quick pugilist. Training. Herrera S. Demetrio, *tr. by* Dudley Fitts. TTY

Sea, The! the sea! the open sea! The Sea. "Barry Cornwall." GN

Sea Things. Gwendolyn MacEwen. FaBoWP

Sea touches sky, and now, moon down. Getsuo, *tr. by* Lucien Stryk *and* Takashi Ikemoto. ZPCJ

Sea-Turtle and the Shark, The. Melvin Beaunearus Tolson. *Fr.* Harlem Gallery. PoBA

Sea Violet. Hilda Doolittle ("H. D."). NoP

Sea Voyage. William Empson. CMoP; MOS

Sea-Voyage from Tenby to Bristol, A. Katherine Philips. WPE

Sea-ward, white gleaming through the busy scud. Samuel Taylor Coleridge. PBBP

Sea-Wash. Carl Sandburg. OBCA

Sea waves are green and wet. Sand Dunes. Robert Frost. MoAB; MoAmPo; RFM

Sea-Way. Ellen Mackay Hutchinson Cortissoz. AA

Sea-Weed, The. Elisabeth Cavazza Pullen. AA

Sea-Weed. D. H. Lawrence. BoNaP; MOS; RB

Sea-weed sways and sways and swirls. Sea-Weed. D. H. Lawrence. BoNaP; MOS; RB

Sea-Wind. Stéphane Mallarmé, *tr. fr. French by* Arthur Symons. AWP

Sea Wind, The. Harry Martinson, *tr. fr. Swedish by* Robert Bly. NU

Sea Wolf, The. Violet McDougal. FaPON

Sea would flow no longer, The. The Frozen Ocean. Viola Meynell. CH

Sea yes learns from the canefield, The. The Sea and the Canefield. João Cabral de Melo Neto, *tr. by* Louis Simpson. ATCBP

Seacoast late at night and a wheel of wind, A. On the Death of Her Mother. Muriel Rukeyser. SM

Seacoast wears you out with damp and heat. White Crane Hill. Su Tung-p'o, *tr. by* Burton Watson. CoBCP

Seaconk or Rehoboths Fate. Benjamin Tompson. SCAP

Seaconk Plain Engagement. Benjamin Thompson. SCAP

Seafarer. Archibald MacLeish. NoP

Seafarer, The. Earl of Surrey. *See* O happy dames that may embrace.

Seafarer. ("I will tell you a true tale of myself") *Unknown, tr. by* Kemp Malone. PoE

Seafarer, The ("May I for my own self song's truth reckon."), *Unknown, tr. fr. Anglo-Saxon by* Ezra Pound. CTC; FaBoTw; HeIP; LiTA; NoP; OxBA

    Sels.

    ("My purpose is to tell my own true tale.") EBEV, *tr. by* John Wain

    ("Song I sing of my sea adventure, A.") MOS, *tr. by* Charles W. Kennedy

    ("Tale I frame shall be found to tally, The.") OBVE, *tr. by* Michael Alexander

"I can sing of myself a true song." *Fr.* Pt. I, *tr. by* L. Iddings. PoRA

"Song I sing of my sea adventure, A." *Fr.* Pt. I, *tr. by* Charles W. Kennedy. AnOE

"That man cannot know." PBBP

Seafarer, The. ("My purpose is to tell my own true tale") *Unknown, tr. by* John Wain. EBEV

Seafarer, The. ("Shall I thus ever long, and be no whit the near?") *Unknown. See* Shall I thus. . .

Seafarer, The. ("Song I sing of my sea adventure, A"). *Unknown, tr. fr. Anglo-Saxon by* Charles W. Kennedy. AnOE; MOS

Seafarer, The. ("Tale I frame shall be found to tally") *Unknown, tr. by* Michael Alexander. OBVE

Seafarers tell of the Eastern Isle of Bliss, The. Li Po, *tr. fr. Chinese by* Shigeyoshi Obata. *Fr.* His Dream of the Sky-Land: A Farewell Poem. WSC
Seafarers tell of the Isles of Ying. Song of a Dream Visit to T'ien-mu. Li Po, *tr. by* Burton Watson. CoBCP
Seagull, The. Dafydd ap Gwilym, *tr. fr. Welsh by* Glyn Jones. OBWVE
Seagull, The. Siôn Phylip, *tr. fr. Welsh by* Joseph P. Clancy. OBWVE
Seagull flying from the sea. A Feather for My Cap. Ivy O. Eastwick. BoTP
Seagull raced in through the window, A. Wings. Maruyama Kaoru, *tr. by* Geoffrey Bownas *and* Anthony Thwaite. PeBJV
Seagull, spreadeagled, splayed on the wind, The. George Barker. *Fr.* Pacific Sonnets, V [*or* VII]. LiTM; MOS; WaP
Seagulls. Robert Francis. RFM
Seagulls. Patricia Hubbell. PDV
Seagulls. John Updike. Psk
Seagulls inland, The. The Natural Order of Things. Harley Elliott. NeAC
Seal. William Jay Smith. GrPl; RFM; RHPC
Seal at Stinson Beach. Roberta Hill. VoR
Seal Lullaby. Kipling. *Fr.* The Jungle Book. FaPON; SoSe
Seal of Fire. Mordecai Temkin, *tr. fr. Hebrew by* Jeremy Garber. VWA
Seal Rock. Katha Pollitt. MAYP
Seal thou the window! Yea, shut out the light. Cloistered. Alice Brown. AA
Seal up the book, all vision's at an end. On the Death of Mr. Pope. *Unknown.* NOEC
Sealed in rainlight one. The Magic Apple Tree. Elaine Feinstein. BrRo
Seals at High Island. Richard Murphy. CIP; IPY
Seals at play off Western Isle, The. Seals, Terns, Time. Richard Eberhart. LiTM; MoAB; MoAmPo
Seals in Penobscot Bay, The. Daniel Hoffman. TwCP
Seals of Love. Shakespeare. *See* Measure for Measure: Take, O Take Those Lips Away.
Seals, Terns, Time. Richard Eberhart. LiTM; MoAB; MoAmPo
Seaman, 1941. Molly Holden. CN; FaBoWP
Seaman's Compass, The. Laurence Price. OxBSS
Seaman's Confession of Faith, A. Harry Hibbard Kemp. TrPWD
Seamen and Soldiers' Last Farewell to Their Dearest Jewels, The. *Unknown.* OxBSS
Seamen Three. Thomas Love Peacock. *See* Nightmare Abbey: Wise Men of Gotham, The.
Seamen's Distress, The. *Unknown.* OxBSS
    (Mermaid, The.) ESPB
Seamen's Wives' Vindication, The. *Unknown.* OxBSS
Seamstress at St. Léon. Gillian Clarke. *Fr.* A Journal from France. OBTV
Seamus, Light-hearted and Loving Friend of My Breast, *sel.* Owen Roe O'Sullivan, *tr. fr. Irish by* Thomas Kinsella.
    "Seamus, light-hearted and loving friend of my breast." NOIV
Sean Spotted Wolf examined the yellow-tinted. Winter Count of Sean Spotted Wolf. Earle Thompson. STE
Séance. William Abrahams. NYBP
Séance. Francis King. PoA
Seance. Edouard Roditi. EAS
Search. Claribel Alegría, *tr. fr. Spanish by* Aliki *and* Willis Barnstone. BoWoP
Search, The. Kwesi Brew. PBA
Search, The. Thomas Curtis Clark. WGRP
Search, The. Ernest Crosby. AA
Search, The. Denis Glover. *Fr.* Arawata Bill. ATNZ
Search. Michael Hamburger. VWA
Search. Raymond Souster. OBCV
Search, The. Bible, *O.T. See* Psalms: Psalm XLII ("As the hart panteth after the water brooks").
Search, The. Bible, *O.T. See* Psalms: Psalm XLIII ("Judge me, O God.").
Search, The. Henry Vaughan. SeCP
Search, A. Adam Wazyk, *tr. fr. Polish by* Czeslaw Milosz. PwPP
Search. Margaret Widdemer. TrPWD
Search after Happiness, The, *sel.* Hannah More.
    Solitude. WBLP
Search all the Christian climes from pole to pole. Daniel Defoe. *Fr.* Reformation of Manners. OBSV
Search Party, The. William Matthews. GeTw
Search. Search. Seek. Seek. A Weary Song to a Slow Sad Tune. Li Ch'ing-chao, *tr. by* Kenneth Rexroth. BoWoP
Searcher of souls, you who in heaven abide. Samuel Butler. FaBoEE
Searching, The. Alice S. Cobb. BlSi
Searching for Herb Brazier and Cinnabar Well. Tao-chi, *tr. fr. Chinese by* Jonathan Chaves. CoBLCP

Searching for Lambs. *Unknown.* OBET
Searching for spring beyong the Five Ridges, I find spring's scenery strange. Written on a Boat in Canton, 1882. Wen T'ing-shih, *tr. by* Timothy C. Wong. WFTU
Searching for the Ruins of the Pavilion of the Drunken Old Man. Yang Shih-ch'i, *tr. fr. Chinese by* Jonathan Chaves. CoBLCP
Searching my heart for its true sorrow. Exiled. Edna St. Vincent Millay. MOS; PoRA
Searchlights, The. Sylvia Lynd. CN
Seas Are My Eyes, Birches My Voice. Tommy Tabermann, *tr. fr. Finnish by* Aili Jarvenpa. SOP
Seas are quiet when the winds give o'er, The. Edmund Waller. *Fr.* Of The Last Verses in the Book. NOCV
    (Old Age.) BLPL; NOBE; OBEV
Sea's Last Gift; 1961, The. Milton Kessler. DiL
Sea's Spell, The. Susan Marr Spalding. AA
Seascape. W. H. Auden. *See* Look , stranger, on this island now.
Seascape. Elizabeth Bishop. FaBoWP; MoAB; MOS; OxBC; PPP
Seascape. Stephen Spender. MOS; NoP
Seascape. Francis Brett Young. OxBTC
Seascape shifts, The. Distinctions. Charles Tomlinson. CMoP
Seashell. Israel Efrat, *tr. fr. Hebrew by* Bernhard Frank. MHeP
Seaside Golf. Sir John Betjeman. SD
Seaside: In and Out of the Season, The. Charles Tennyson Turner. Son
Season, ending, makes no sign, but the wind. Conserves. David Mus. *Fr.* The Joy of Cooking. PoA
Season greeter, The. Yomono Akara, *tr. by* Burton Watson. FCEI
Season has come, The. Yakamochi. *Fr.* Manyo Shu. FCEI
Season in Hell, A, *sel.* Rimbaud, *tr. fr. French by* Enid Rhodes Peschel.
    Dawn. TTTS
Season late, day late, sun just down, and the sky. Birth of Love. Robert Penn Warren. UnPo
Season of Beginning and End. Zuhur Dixon, *tr. fr. Arabic by* Patricia Alanah Byrne *and* Salma Khadra Jayyusi. MAP
Season of Blood. Arnaldo Santos, *tr. fr. Portuguese by* Michael Wolfers. WMBCH
Season of Loss, A. Jim Barnes. HATNAP
Season of mists and mellow fruitfulness. To Autumn. Keats. AWP; BoNaP; BoTP; CH; ChER; EBEV; EnRP; FaBoRV; FF; FiP; FPL; GTBS; HAP; HeIP; InPK; InPS; InvP; LiTB; Mes; NAEL-2; NAWM-2; NIP; NOBE; NOP; NU; OAEL-2; OBEV; OBNC; PoE; PoEL-4; PoLF; PPP; Prf; PrIm; RB; SCV; SoSe; TEP; UnPo; WeW (Ode to Autumn.) FaBV; GTBS-P; TrGrPo
Season of Phantasmal Peace, The. Derek Walcott. NoP
Season Song. *Unknown, tr. fr. Irish by* Flann O'Brien. RB (Scel Lem Duib.) BIrV
Season stalls, unseasonably fair, The. Indian Summer at Land's End. Stanley Kunitz. CAPP
Season, The? Not yet spring. The place? Beside. Rabbit Cry. Edward Lucie-Smith. NePoEA-2
Season Ticket. Gloria Frym. UL
Season 'Tis, My Lovely Lambs, The. E. E. Cummings. UnPo
Season when Nothing's in Place, A. Ory Bernstein, *tr. fr. Hebrew by* Warren Bargad *and* Stanley F. Chyet. IP
Seasoning. Paul Humphrey. SoTCo
Seasonless waves/ of the Izumi River, The. Teika, *tr. by* Steven D. Carter. WFTW
Seasons/ changes moods. A Common Poem. Carolyn M. Rodgers. CNA
Seasons, The. Thomas Holcroft. NOEC
Seasons, The. Rolfe Humphries. NYBP
Seasons, The. Kalidasa, *tr. fr. Sanskrit by* Arthur W. Ryder. AWP
Seasons, The. Spenser. *See* Faerie Queene, The: Mask of Mutability, The.
Seasons, The, *sels.* James Thomson.
    Autumn.
        Autumnal Moon, The. NOBE
        (Autumn ("Western sun withdraws the shorten'd day, The").) NOBE
        Autumn ("But see the fading many-colour'd woods"). EnRP
        "Here the rude clamour of the sportsman's joy." PBBP
        "Poor is the triumph o'er the timid hare." EnRP; FM; PBBP
    Hymn on the Seasons, A. EnRP
    Spring.
        "As rising from the vegetable World." PoEL-3
        Spring ("Behold yon breathing prospect bids the muse"). PoE
        "Lend me your song, ye nightingales! oh, pour." PBBP
        Spring Flowers. NOBE
        "Should I my steps turn to the rural seat." FM
    Summer.

Summer ("Home from his morning task the swain retreats"). FM
Happy Britannia. FaBoPP; SeCePo
  (Britannia.) FaBoPP
"Still let me pierce into the midnight depth." EnRP
"'Tis raging noon; and vertical, the sun." EBEV; OAEL-1
Winter.
  Winter ("See, Winter comes, to rule the varied year"). NOEC;
    TEP
  Winter ("As thus the snows arise, and foul and fierce"). SeCePo
  Winter ("Now, when the cheerless empire of the sky"). OxBA
  "Keener tempests come, The: and fuming dun." EBEV; EnRP;
    NoP
  Winter ("When from the pallid sky the sun descends"). OAEL-1;
    OxBS
  "Fowls of heaven, The." PBBP
  Winter ("Drooping, the labourer-ox"). FM
  Winter ("What art thou, frost? and whence are thy keen stores").
    OxBS
  Winter Night, A. NOBE
Seasons. Robert Penn Warren. KS
Seasons and Times. William Barnes. NOBVV
Season's anguish, crashing whirlwind, ice, The. Winter Garden. David
  Gascoyne. GTBS-P
Seasons burn, The. The wind is dry. Earthquake. R. A. D. Ford.
  NOBC
Seasons Greetings, Love and Revolution. Judy Miles. PVCV
Season's Lovers, The. Miriam Waddington. MoCV; OBCV
Seasons of the Soul. Allen Tate. OxBA
Seasons operate on ev'ry breast. About in London. John Gay. Fr.
  Trivia; or, The Art of Walking the Streets of London.
Seasons over there loam sifted. Logic. Alain Delahaye, tr. by Anthony
  Barnett. RHTwFP
Seasons Their Asterisks and Their Pawns. Hans Arp, tr. fr. French by
  Michael Benedikt. POS
Seasons waiting the miracle. Farmer. Lucien Stryk. CAPP
Seasons when the spring sun. Mushimaro. Fr. Manyo Shu. FCEI
Seat of the soul is where the inner world, The. Aphorism. "Novalis", tr.
  by Charles E. Passage. NU
Seated on a couch at the rear of my cabin. Thalassa. Valery Larbaud, tr.
  by William Jay Smith. CT
Seated on her bed legs spread open. Joyce Mansour, tr. by Willis
  Barnstone. BoWoP
Seated once by a brook, watching a child. The Brook. Edward Thomas.
  OAEL-2
Seated one day at the organ/ I was weary and ill at ease. A Lost Chord.
  Adelaide Anne Procter. FaFP; WBLP; WGRP
Seated, the harpist waits. Marble Statuette Harpist. Sara Van Alstyne
  Allen. GoYe
Seated there upon the floor. Fyodor Ivanovich Tyutchev, tr. by Alan
  Myers. AAA
Seattle weather: it has rained for weeks in this town. Homage to Arthur
  Waley. Weldon Kees. NaP
Seaward. Celia Thaxter. AA
Seaward. George Edward Woodberry. Fr. Wild Eden, XLI. AA
Seaward Bound. Alice Brown. TrPWD
Seaweed. Longfellow. MOS; OxBA; TAP
Seaweed, seaweed, drifting, drifting. Unknown, tr. by Barry Mitcalfe.
  WTO
Seaweeds. Sandra McPherson. AmPA; PoA
Sebastian. Yona Wallach, tr. fr. Hebrew by Warren Bargad and Stanley
  F. Chyet. IP
Secluded from domestic strife. The Double Transformation. Goldsmith.
  OBNV
Secluded within the women's quarters—that was sad enough. The Tomb
  of the Singing Girl Ch'iung-i. Hsü Pen, tr. by Jonathan Chaves.
  CoBLCP
Second Advice to a Painter, The. Andrew Marvell. APAS
Second after, A. The Settlers. Margaret Atwood. MoCV
2nd afternoon I come, The. A Poem for the Insane. John Weiners.
  NeAP; PoM
Second Air Force. Randall Jarrell. CMoP; LiTM; NAAL-2; WaP
Second and third month of sunny spring, The. Song of the Thoroughfare.
  Hsieh Shang, tr. by Burton Watson. CoBCP
Second Angel, The. Philip Levine. NaP
Second Anniversary, The. John Donne. See Of the Progresse of the
  Soule; the Second Anniversary.
Second Ascension of Christ, The. John Brooks Wheelwright. Fr. Forty
  Days. NOCV
Second Asgard, The. Matthew Arnold. Fr. Balder Dead. FiP
Second Best. Rupert Brooke. MoBrPo

Second Brother, The, sel. Thomas Lovell Beddoes.
  "Strew not earth with empty stars." OxBSP
Second Carolina Said-Song. A. R. Ammons. OBAL
Second class is the second grade, The. Primary Lesson: The Second Class
  Citizens. Sun-Ra. PoBA
Second Coming, The. Mohammad Bennis, tr. fr. Arabic by Sharif Elmusa
  and Charles Doria. MAP
Second Coming, The. Carl Clark. JB
Second Coming, The. John William Corrington. HoPM
Second Coming, The. W. B. Yeats. BIrV; BLPL; CMoP; EaLo;
  FaBoMo; FaBoPV; FF; GTBS-P; GTBS-P; HAP; HeIP; HoPM; InPK;
  InPS; LiTB; LiTM; MAT; MoAB; MoBrPo; MoP; NAEL-2;
  NAWM-2; NIP; NoAM; NOBE; NoP; OAEL-2; OxBTC; PoE; PPP;
  PrIm; SCV; SeCePo; SoSe; TEP; UnPo; WaP; WeW
Second Crucifixion, The. Richard Le Gallienne. WGRP
Second Cycle of Love Poems, sel. George Barker.
  O Tender under Her Right Breast. Fr. II. MoAB; MoBrPo
Second Dream, The. Jean Valentine. LCAP
Second Epistle of the Second Book of Horace Imitated, The, sels. Pope.
  TOF
  "Bred up at home, full early I begun."
  "But grant I may relapse, for want of grace."
Second Epitaph, A. Unknown. MeEL
Second Glance at a Jaguar. Ted Hughes. NoAM; NYBP; PrIm
Second Half. David McCord. SD
Second-hand platitudes like antique watches. Catching One Clear Thought
  Alive. Paula Gunn Allen. WPOW
Second-hand sights, like crumpled. Newark, for Now (68). Carolyn M.
  Rodgers. PoBA
Second Heart, The. Ellen Wittlinger. TV
Second Honeymoon. Unknown, tr. fr. Irish by Augustus Young. BIrV
Second Horn. W. S. Di Piero. MAYP
Second Hymn to Lenin. "Hugh MacDiarmid." OAEL-2
Second Hymn to the Night, The. "Novalis," prose poem version, tr. fr.
  German by Robert Bly. Fr. Hymns to the Night. NU
Second Iron Age, The. Michael Harrington. CaP
Second Life, The. Edwin Morgan. OxBS
Second Life of Lazarus, The. Gwen Harwood. CBAP
2nd Light Poem: For Diane Wakoski. Jackson MacLow. PoM
Second Madrigal, The. Anna Swirszczynska, tr. fr. Polish by Czeslaw
  Milosz. PwPP
Second Man, The. Julian Symons. WaP
Second man I love, The. Spring. Carole Gregory Clemmons. PoBA
Second Mate, The. Fitz-James O'Brien. AA
Second Molting, A. Ralph Salisbury. STE
Second Nature. Diana Chang. BrSi
Second Nature, sel. Paul Éluard, tr. fr. French by Samuel Beckett.
  "In honour of the dumb the blind the deaf." Fr. V. RHTwFP
Second Nimphall, The. Michael Drayton. Fr. Muses' Elysium [or
  Elizium]. PBBP
  "I have two sparrows white as snow," sel. PBBP
Second Ode to Persephone. Robert Kelly. Fr. The Book of Persephone.
  PoM
Second of August. Unknown. OxBSS
Second Poem. Peter Orlovsky. NeAP
Second Poem from Nicaragua Libre: War Zone. June Jordan. NoAM
Second Poem the Night-Walker Wrote, The. Goethe, tr. fr. German by
  Robert Bly. NU
Second Position. Mary Mackey. Fr. Arabesque: Five Poems for Women
  without Children. ER
Second Prelude. Reality in Albuquerque: The Son. John Logan. Fr.
  Poem in Progress. CAPP
Second Quest, The. Joseph Rodman Drake. Fr. The Culprit Fay. AA
Second Rapture, The. Thomas Carew. CaPo; OPOP
Second Review of the Grand Army, A. Bret Harte. PAH
Second Rose Motif. Cecília Meireles, tr. fr. Portuguese by James Merrill.
  ATCBP
Second Samuel, sel. Bible, O.T.
  "Beauty of Israel is slain [or slaine] upon thy high places, The."
    OBVE; OBWP
  (David's Lament.) ChTr, I: 19-27; FF, I: 19-27; TrGrPo, I: 19-27;
    TrJP, I: 19-27.
  (David's Lament for Saul and Jonathan.) AWP
  (How Are the Mighty Fallen.) WaaP
Second Satire of the First Book of Horace Imitated, The, sel. Pope.
  "With all a woman's virtues but the pox." OBSV
Second Seeing. Louis Golding. WGRP
2d Series. James Russell Lowell. Fr. The Biglow Papers.
  Courtin'. The, fr. Introduction. AA; AmPP; BeLS; NOBA; OBAL
  Jonathan to John. Fr. II. PAH

Mr. Hosea Biglow to the Editor of the Atlantic Monthly. *Fr.* X. AA, *abr.*
  ("Beaver roars hoarse with meltin' snows.") PoEL-5
Rev. Homer Wilbur's "Festina Lente." *Fr.* IV. OBAL
Sunthin' in the Pastoral Line. *Fr.* VI. AP
  (Spring.) FaBV
Second Sermon on the Warpland, The. Gwendolyn Brooks. BPo; NOBA; PoBA
Second Shadow. Theodore Roethke. PoA
Second Shaman Song. Gary Snyder. *Fr.* Myths and Texts: Burning, I. NeAP; NOBA; PoM
Second Shepherd's Play, The ("Lord, what these weders ar cold."), *sel. Unknown.* NAEL-1; PoEL-1
  (Wakefield Second Shepherd's Play.) OAEL-1, *mod. vers.*
  Hail, Comly and Clene. NAs
  (Haylle, Comly and Clene.) OBEV; OxBoli
  (Shepherds at Bethlehem, The.) ChTr
Second Sight. Michael Longley. FaBCIP
Second Skins—a Peyote Song. Joseph Bruchac. CDW
Second Stanza for Dr. Johnson, A. Donald Hall. FiBHP
Second Story, The. T. R. Hummer. KS; NAmP
Second Telegram ("Every evening when night retrieves the substance of our longings"). Abd al-Aziz al-Maqalih, *tr. fr. Arabic by* Lena Jayyusi *and* Christopher Middleton. *Fr.* Telegrams of Tenderness for Sanaa. MAP
Second Violinist's Son, The. Debora Greger. KS
Second Vision, The. Tadhg Dall O'Huiginn, *tr. fr. Late Middle Irish by* Earl of Longford. AnIL
Second Volume, The. Robert Mowry Bell. AA
Second Wife, The. Mririda n'Ait Attik, *tr. fr. Berber into French by* René Euloge, *English vers. by* Daniel Halpern *and* Paula Paley. OV
Second Wind. Fred Chappell. MT
Second Winery, The. Hsin Mu, *tr. fr. Chinese by* Dominic Cheung. IFON
Second Wisdom. Henry Morton Robinson. GoYe
Second Woman's Lament. Brenda Chamberlain. NeIP
Second Year, The. Marion Montgomery. KS
(Secondary experience, nouns). Zen Buddhism and Psychoanalysis/ Psychoanalysis and Zen Buddhism. Jackson MacLow. PoM
Seconds before I'm due to make. Writing, and Other Avenues. Sue Roe. NPo
Secrecy. Samuel Daniel. *See* Hymen's Triumph: Eyes Hide My Love.
Secrecy [*or* Secresie] Protested. Thomas Carew. CaPo; SeCP
Secret, The. "Æ" MoBrPo
Secret. Gwendolyn B. Bennett. BlSi; CDC
Secret, The. John Clare. GBL
Secret, The. Emily Dickinson. *See* I have not told my garden yet.
Secret, The. Elizabeth Fleming. BoTP
Secret. Maria Teresa Horta, *tr. fr. Portuguese by* Suzette Macedo. OV
Secret. Catherine Haydon Jacobs. GoYe
Secret. Raquel Jodorowsky, *tr. fr. Spanish by* Kate Flores. DMH
Secret, The. Lonny Kaneko. BrSi
Secret, The. Denise Levertov. NaP; NIP
Secret, The. James Stephens. WSC
Secret, A. *Unknown.* OBSC
Secret, The. Mary Morison Webster. PeSA
Secret, The. George Edward Woodberry. *Fr.* Wild Eden, VI. AA
Secret Affair Comes to Its End, A. Kenko, *tr. fr. Japanese by* Steven D. Carter. WFTW
Secret Ballgame. Ernst Schönwiese, *tr. fr. German by* Beth Bjorklund. CoAuP
Secret Cavern, The. Margaret Widdemer. FaPON
Secret Ceremony: The Sailboat. Susan Stewart. NAmP
Secret Garden, The. Rita Dove. NoAM
Secret Garden, The. Thomas Kinsella. IPY; TwCP
Secret Garden, The. Robert Nichols. WGRP
Secret Gratitude, A. James Wright. NoAM
Secret hidden thirty years, A. The Resounding Wall. Yip Wai-lim, *tr. by* Dominic Cheung. IFON
Secret in bed the lustful with soft cries. Sonnet against the Too-Facile Mystic. Elizabeth B. Harrod. NePoEA
Secret Joy, The. Mary Webb. BoTP
Secret Kept, A. Judah Al-Harizi, *tr. fr. Hebrew by* Robert Mezey. UnAS
Secret Laughter. Christopher Morley. FaBV
Secret Love. John Clare. FaBV; OBNC; PoE; PoEL-4; TrGrPo
  (Song: "I hid my love when young while I.) NOBVV; OAEL-2; RB
Secret Love; or, The Maiden Queen, *sels.* Dryden.
  "He who writ this, not without pains and thought." SeCV-2
  "I feed a flame within, which so torments me." AWP
  (Hidden Flame.) OBEV

Secret Love or Two I Must Confess[e], A. Thomas Campion. AAS; ErPo
Secret Muse, The. Roy Campbell. PeSA
Secret of Poetry, The. Jon Anderson. MAYP
Secret of the polar bear, The. Polar Bear. Gail Kredenser. RAR; RHPC
Secret of these hills was stone, and cottages, The. The Pylons. Stephen Spender. AWP; NoAM
Secret People, The. G. K. Chesterton. FaPoR; OxBTC
Secret Place, A. Judith W. Steinbergh. ILY
Secret Places. Irene Thompson. BoTP
Secret Pleasures. Robert Morgan. MAYP
Secret Rose, The. W. B. Yeats. NAEL-2
Secret Sits, The. Robert Frost. InPK
Secret Society of Failures. Lucha Corpi. CCP
Secret Song, The. Margaret Wise Brown. OBCA; PDV; RHPC
Secret Talk. Eve Merriam. ILY
Secret they are, sealed, annealed, and brainless. Oystering. Richard Howard. NoAM
Secret Thoughts. Ella Wheeler Wilcox. PWR
Secret Town, The. Abraham Sutskever, *tr. fr. Yiddish by* Jacob Sonntag. TrJP
Secret was the garden. The Mistress of Vision. Francis Thompson. BrPo; CH, *abr.*
Secret Woman. Meiling Jin. WS
Secretary. Ted Hughes. ErPo
Secretary, The. Peter Redgrove. OxBTC
Secrets. Ahmad Abd al-Muti Hijazi, *tr. fr. Arabic by* Sargon Boulus *and* Peter Porter. MAP
Secrets. Richard Hovey. AnAmPo
Secrets. Robert Pack. MOWH
Secrets of Angling, The, *sel.* John Dennys.
  Angler's Song, The. EIL
Secrets of the Earth, The. Blake. *Fr.* The Book of Thel. NOBE
Secretum, *sel.* Petrarch, *tr. fr. Latin by* W. H. Draper.
  Exchange between the Poet and St. Augustine, An. *Fr.* I. OxBLMV
Sects. Jack Gilbert. NPGG
Secular Elegies, *sels.* George Barker.
  O Golden Fleece ("O golden fleece she is where she lies tonight"). *Fr.* V. ErPo; LiTM; MoAB; MoBrPo
  Satan Is on Your Tongue. *Fr.* III. MoAB; MoBrPo
Secular Games. Richard Howard. PoA
Secular Masque, The ("Chronos, Chronos, mend thy ways"). Dryden. NAEL-1; PoE; PoEL-3; PrIm; SeCV-2
  Sels.
  All, All of a Piece Throughout. ChTr; ELP; HAP; InPS
    (Chorus to the Gods.) OxBSP
    (Song: "All, all of a piece throughout.") WeW
  Diana's Hunting-Song. NOBE; SeCePo
  Momus' Song to Mars. OxBSP
  "Sound the trumpet, beat the drum." FaBoRV
Security. Margaret E. Sangster. BLRP
Security. Charles L. O'Donnell. TrPWD
Seder-Night. Israel Zangwill. TrJP
Seder, 1944. Friedrich Torberg, *tr. fr. German by* Erna Baber Rosenfeld. VWA
Sedge of the marsh where irises bloom, The. *Unknown. Fr.* Manyo Shu. FCEI
Sediment. David Ignatow. NYBP
Seduced by Analogy. Bob Perelman. LP
Seduced Girl. Hedylos, *tr. fr. Greek by* Louis Untermeyer. BoLoP; ErPo
Seduction. Nikki Giovanni. NMM
Seduction. Jo Ann Hall-Evans. BlSi
Seduction, The. Suzanne Berger Rioff. NMM
Seduction of Engadu, The. *Unknown, tr. fr. Babylonian by* William Ellery Leonard. *Fr.* The Epic of Gilgamesh. ErPo
Seductive canopy, this visit I have paid. Desolation. E. A. Baratynsky, *tr. by* Alan Myers. AAA
See/ how they trace. Birds in Snow. Hilda Doolittle ("H.D."). PoA
See/ me. A Pair of Wings. Stephen Hawes. MeEL
See a man with sound eyes. James Berry. PBCV
See a pin and pick it up. *Unknown.* FaBoBe
See an old unhappy bull. The Bull. Ralph Hodgson. BrPo; LiTM; MoAB; MoBrPo; OBMV; OxBTC
See, and not see; and if thou chance t' espy. To the Generous Reader. Robert Herrick. CaPo
See, as the prettiest graves will do in time. Fame. Robert Browning. SoSe

See, Ben, the water. To Ben, at the Lake. Cilla McQueen. ATNZ; PeNZ

See, Chloris, how the clouds. To Chloris. William Drummond of Hawthornden. OxBSP

See columns rang'd in proud Palladian style! *Unknown.* FaBoEE

See commons, peers, and ministers of state. Edward Young. *Fr.* Love of Fame, the Universal Passion, Satire III. OBSV

See dear Pater with the bills. Christmas Bills. Joseph Hatton. OBCP

See! down the red road by the brown tree. The End of Exploring. David Campbell. SeCePo

See! from the brake the whirring Pheasant springs. Pope. *Fr.* Windsor Forest. FM; PoEL-3

See, from this counterfeit of him. On a Bust of Dante. Thomas William Parsons. AA

See her caught in the throb of a drum. Agbor Dancer. John Pepper Clark. PBA

See her come bearing down, a tidy craft! A Note on Wyatt. Kingsley Amis. WeW

See here an easy feast that knows no wound. On the Miracle of Multiplied Loaves. Richard Crashaw. OxBSP

See! Here, My Heart. *Unknown.* MeEL

See here, nice Death, to please his palate. Epitaph. *At.* to Pope. FaBoEE

See here she is pimply with cameras. Astronaut's Widow. Steve Sneyd. BWV

See, here's the grand approach. Verses on Blenheim. Martial, *tr. by* Swift. AWP

"See, here's the workbox, little wife." The Workbox. Thomas Hardy. InPK; NAEL-2; UnPo

See how Flora smiles to see. On Clarastella walking in Her Garden. Robert Heath. OBS

See how from far upon the eastern road. The Magi. Milton. *Fr.* On the Morning of Christ's Nativity, 2 *ll.* ChTr

See how he dives. Seal. William Jay Smith. GrPl; RFM; RHPC

See how it circles. *Ambo Oral Tradition. Fr.* Five Ghost Songs. TTTS

See how it flashes. In a Wine Cellar. Victor James Daley. PoAu-1

See, how like twilight slumber falls. Charles Cotton. OBS

See how she strips her lily for the sun. The Double Looking Glass. Alec Derwent Hope. CBAP

See how the brown kelp withers in air. Landed: A Valentine. Richard Howard. PoA

See how the flowers, as at parade. Andrew Marvell. *Fr.* Upon Appleton House, to My Lord Fairfax. TrGrPo

(Garden, A.) OBEV

See how the language listens up this spring. Poor Movies. Will Bennett. UL

See how the orient dew. On a Drop of Dew. Andrew Marvell. HAP; JCP; LiTB; MeLP; MePo; NIP; OBS; SeCP; SeCV-1; TEP

See How the Rising Sun. Elizabeth Scott. AH

See,—how the shining share. God Save the Plough. Lydia Huntley Sigourney. AnAmPo; OBAL

See how the sun has somewhat not of light. El Greco. Edward Leslie Mayo. HoPM

See how they hurry. At Luca Signorelli's Resurrection of the Body. Jorie Graham. HCAP

See how this trim girl. Artemis. Peter Davison. ErPo

See how this violet which before. On a Violet in Her Breast. Thomas Stanley. OBS

See how we produce. The Most-Age. Mihály Váci, *tr. by* Edwin Morgan. MHuP

See! I give myself to you, Beloved! A Gift. Amy Lowell. AnAmPo

See, I have climbed the mountain side. San Miniato. Oscar Wilde. TIRV

See, in the garden there, it hops and lurches about. On a Child with a Wooden Leg. Bertram J. Warr. OBCV

See in the Midst of Fair Leaves. Marianne Moore. MoAB

See! In the troubled glow of dawn. Environs of Vanholt II. Charles Spear. ATNZ

See, It Begins to Come Down. Wilhelm Szabo, *tr. fr.* German by Beth Bjorklund. CoAuP

See, Lord,/ my coat hangs in tatters. The Prayer of the Old Horse. Carmen Bernos de Gasztold. PDV

See me with all the terrors on my roads. The Face. Edwin Muir. GTBS-P

See, Mignonne, hath not the Rose. The Rose. Pierre de Ronsard, *tr. by* Andrew Lang. AWP

See my lov'd Britons, see your Shakespeare rise. Dryden. *Fr.* Troilus and Cressida. SeCV-2

See, neighbour,/ Washing morning greens in the river. *Unknown. Fr.* Manyo Shu. Ma

"See, nothing has happened to her," said my guide. Seeing Oloalok. Marilyn Bowering. NOBC

See now, dead friend. Duty to Death, LD. Dick Roberts. WaP

See on one hand. The Rainbow. Gerard Manley Hopkins. FaBoPP; OxBSP

See, one physician, like a sculler, plies. Joseph Jekyll. FaBoEE

See-saw, down in my lap. *Unknown.* OxNR

See-saw, Margery Daw,/ Jack[y] shall have a new master. Mother Goose. OxNR

See-saw, Margery Daw,/ The old hen flew over the malt house. Mother Goose. OxNR

See-saw, Margery Daw,/ Sold her bed and lay upon straw. *Unknown.* OxNR

See-saw, sacradown. Mother Goose. OxNR

See, see, mine own sweet jewel. Canzonet. *Unknown.* EIL

See, see, she wakes, Sabina wakes! Congreve. NOEC; OxBSP

See, see, what shall I see? Mother Goose. OxNR

See, she gathers white aster. *Unknown, tr. by* Arthur Waley. BoS

See! some strange comfort every state attend. Life's Poor Play. Pope. *Fr.* An Essay on Man, Epistle II. SeCePo

See that brave and trembling motorman. The Dying Mine Brakeman. Orville Jenks. AmFP

See that [*or* the] building which, when my mistress living. A Well-wishing to a Place of Pleasure. *Unknown.* GBL

See That One? Robert Bagg. ErPo

See the bunnies sitting there. Timid Bunnies. Jeannie Kirby. BoTP

See the chariot at hand here of Love. The Triumph of Charis. Ben Jonson. *Fr.* A Celebration of Charis in Ten Lyrick Peeces. CTC; EBEV; EIL; ELP; InvP; JCP; LiTB; NOBE; NoP; OBEV; OPOP; PoEL-2; PrIm; SeCP; SeCV-1

(Her Triumph.) CTC; EBEV; EIL; JCP; OPOP; PoEL-2; PrIm; SeCP; SeCV-1

See the day begins to break. Satyr's Song. John Fletcher. *Fr.* The Faithful Shepherdess, IV, i. OBS

See the dazzled stripling stand. Goliath and David. Louis Untermeyer. TrJP

See the fairies dancing in. The Fairies. Patricia Hubbell. WSC

See the fountain opened wide. Zion's Sons and Daughters. *Unknown.* AmFP

See the handsome hippopotamus. Hippopotamus. Joanna Cole. NTCP

See the happy moron. *Unknown.* CenHV

See the headlands yonder stand. Dirge Sung at Death. *Unknown, tr. by* John White. WTO

See the kitten on the wall. The Kitten at Play. Wordsworth. *Fr.* The Kitten and the Falling Leaves. FaPON

See the land, her Easter keeping. Easter Week. Charles Kingsley. OHIP

See the little maunderer. A Love for Patsy. John Thompson, Jr. LiTA; WaP

See the madly blowing dust. A Colorado Sand Storm. Eugene Fieldson, Jr. LiTA; WaP

See! the moon is smiling. Eliza in Uncle Tom's Cabin. Eloise Bibb. CBWP-4

See, the pretty planet! Blowing Bubbles. William Allingham. GN

See the Rat—at Least It's Got a Hide. *Unknown, tr. fr. Chinese by* Burton Watson. CoBCP

See the scaffold it is mounted. Life of the Mannings. *Unknown.* FaBoBa

See, the see, the Bishop's see, The. The Bishop's See. *Unknown.* CoMu

See, the smelle of my sone is as the smell of a feld. Bible, *O.T. Fr.* Genesis. OBVE

See [!] the smoking bowl before us. Burns. *Fr.* The Jolly Beggars. GoTS; NBLV

(Drinking Song.) TrGrPo

See the Spring herself discloses. Spring. Thomas Stanley, *after the Greek of* Anacreon. AWP

See the yellow catkins cover. A Spring Song. Mary Howitt. BoTP

See the young man I've laid out. Funeral Lament (Kommos) from Epiros. *Unknown, tr. by* Elene Kolb. BoWoP

See them joined by strings to history. Puppets. Patricia K. Page. MoCV

See! There he stands; not brave, but with an air. Brothers. James Weldon Johnson. BANP

See, they are clearing the sawdust course. Equestrienne. Rachel Field. *Fr.* A Circus Garland. OBCA

See, they return; ah, see the tentative. The Return. Ezra Pound. AmPP; CMoP; HAP; MoAB; MoAmPo; MoP; NoAM; NoAM; NOBA; OxBA; PoE; RB; VGW; WeW

See this air, how empty it is of angels. Five for the Grace of Man. Winfield Townley Scott. VGW

See this house, how dark it is. The Empty House. Walter de la Mare. BrPo

See those cherries, how they cover. The Cherries; a Parable. Thomas Moore. OBSV

See, though the oil be low, more purely still and higher. A Prisoner. "Æ" AnIL

See through four blocks. Pretty Vomit. Bob Rosenthal. UL

See two passenger trains, Lawd. Dey Got Each and de Udder's Man. *Unknown.* WTO

See what a clouded majesty, and eyes. To My Worthy Friend Master Peter Lely. Richard Lovelace. CaPo

See what a lovely shell. Tennyson. *Fr.* Maud, *pt.* II, ii. BoNaP; GoJo; PoEL-5
(Shell, The.) GN

See what a mass of gems the city wears. Impression de Nuit; London. Lord Alfred Bruce Douglas. OBEV

See what delights in sylvan scenes appear! Sylvan Delights. Pope. *Fr.* Pastorals. NOBE

See where Capella with her golden kids. Edna St. Vincent Millay. *Fr.* Epitaph for the Race of Man, VI. CMoP; MoAB; MoAmPo

See Where My Love a-Maying Goes. *Unknown.* EiL

See where she sits upon the grassie [*or* grassy] green[e]. Ditty, A: In Praise of Eliza, Queen of the Shepherds. Spenser. *Fr.* The Shepheardes [*or* Shepeards *or* Shepherd's] Calender: Aprill. OBEV (Ditty, A: "See where she sits upon the grassy green.") FaBoCh

See where the windows are boarded up. Where Are the Waters of Childhood? Mark Strand. HCAP; LCAP; WeW

See, Will, 'Ere's a Go. *Unknown.* ChTr; FaBoNo

See, Winter comes, to rule the varied year. Winter. James Thomson. *Fr.* The Seasons: Winter. NOEC; TEP

See with what constant motion. Gratiana Dancing [*or* Dauncing] and Singing. Richard Lovelace. CaPo; JCP; MeLP; MePo; OBEV, 2 *sts.*; OBS; SeCV-1, 2 *sts.*

See with what simplicity. The Picture of Little T. C. in a Prospect of Flowers. Andrew Marvell. JCP; LiTB; MeLP; MePo; NAEL-1; NOBE; NoP; OAEL-1; OBEV; OBS; PoE; PPP; PrIm; SeCP; SeCV-1

See! yonder hill the bitterns seek. Kisses. *Malay Oral Tradition, tr.* by R. J. Wilkinson *and* R. O. Winstedt. WTO

See yonder smoke, before it curls to heaven. Thomas Miller. *Fr.* Summer Morning. PF

See, yonder, the belfry tower. At Midnight. Frank Dempster Sherman. AA

See yonder, where a gem of night. Es fällt ein Stern herunter. Heine, *tr.* by Richard Garnett. AWP

See You Soon. Tomioka Taeko, *tr. fr. Japanese by* Hiroaki Sato. FCEI

See you the ferny ride that steals. Puck's Song. Kipling. *Fr.* Puck of Pook's Hill. FaBoCh; FaBV; OxBChV

See young John Sutton with his Kathaleen. Speaks the Whispering Grass. Jesse Stuart. FYAP

Seed. Herman Charles Bosman. PeSA

Seed, The. Aileen Fisher. OnUR

Seed, The. Vasco Popa, *tr. fr. Serbo-Croatian by* Anne Pennington. *Fr.* Games. RB

Seed Cutters, The. Seamus Heaney. *Fr.* Mossbawn: Two Poems in Dedication. FaBCIP

Seed Growing Secretly, The. Henry Vaughan. SeCV-1

Seed is dug under, A. Shekhinah. Karl Wolfskehl. TrJP, *tr. by* Carol North Valhope *and* Ernst Morwitz; VWA, *tr. by* Erna Baber Rosenfeld

Seed Journey. Gregory Corso. VGW

Seed Leaves. Richard Wilbur. BoNaP

Seed, Lord, falls on stony ground, The. Process. Charles L. O'Donnell. TrPWD

Seed of Nimrod, The. De Leon Harrison. PoBA

Seed-Picture, The. Medbh McGuckian. FaBCIP

Seed Shop, The. Muriel Stuart. BoNaP; GoTS

Seeded in the mud on turtle's back. Sweetgrass. Maurice Kenny. HATNAP

Seeds. John Oxenham. WGRP

Seeds. James Reeves. TSS

Seeds clutched in my hand. Hunting. Yehoash, *tr. by* Isidore Goldstick. TrJP

Seeds in a dry pod, tick, tick, tick. Petit, the Poet. Edgar Lee Masters. *Fr.* Spoon River Anthology. CMoP; MoAmPo; NoAM; NOBA; OxBA; TAP

Seeds of Lead. Amir Gilboa, *tr. fr. Hebrew.* VWA, *tr. by* Stephen Mitchell

Seeds of Love, The. *At. to* Mrs. Fleetwood Habergham. FaBoCh; GBP, *longer version;* OBET; OxBoLi, *sl. diff.;* WiR
(I Sowed the Seeds of Love.) ELP

Seeds of the pepper-plant, The. *Unknown, tr. by* Arthur Waley. BoS

Seedy Henry rose up shy in de world. John Berryman. *Fr.* Dream Songs. HCAP

Seeing. John Lyle Donaghy. NeIP

Seeing a Friend Off. Li Po, *tr. fr. Chinese by* Burton Watson. CoBCP

Seeing as the father saw the rosy morn. Ovid, *tr. fr. Latin by* Joseph Addison. *Fr.* Metamorphoses, II. OBVE

Seeing Auden Off. Philip Booth. PoA

Seeing Flowers I Remember My Late Daughter, Shu. Kao Ch'i, *tr. fr. Chinese by* Jonathan Chaves. CoBLCP

Seeing for a Moment. Denise Levertov. CAPP

Seeing good places/ for my hands. The Time We Climbed Snake Mountain. Leslie Marmon Silko. VoR

Seeing Her Dancing. Robert Heath. OBS; OxBSP

Seeing him in my bathtub. Spider. Saqi Farooqi, *tr. by* Mahmood Jamal. PBMUP

Seeing in flight along the lifting wind. Message. Dorothy M. Richardson. PoA

Seeing its corners, it is square. Benediction for the Felt. *Mongol Oral Tradition, tr. by* C. R. Bawden. WTO

Seeing love end. Cercamon, *tr. by* Paul Blackburn. Pro

Seeing means going far off, going off down the road. Recurring Opportunity. David Avidan, *tr. by* Warren Bargad *and* Stanley F. Chyet. IP

Seeing My Name in TV Guide. Gerald Costanzo. SoTCo

Seeing Off a Friend. Stephen Dobyns. AnAn

Seeing Off Commander-In-Chief Li. Li Meng-yang, *tr. fr. Chinese by* Jonathan Chaves. CoBLCP

Seeing off Editor Wang Chou-tz'u and Secretary Lin Shih-lai. Wang Shih-chen, *tr. fr. Chinese by* Jonathan Chaves. CoBLCP

Seeing Off Han Ju-Ch'ing. Ho Ching-ming, *tr. fr. Chinese by* Jonathan Chaves. CoBLCP

Seeing Off Mr. Yang, *sel.* Yün Shou-p'ing, *tr. fr. Chinese by* Jonathan Chaves.

"War ships, cold tides." CoBLCP

Seeing Off Sun Ling-hsiu. Wu Wei-yeh, *tr. fr. Chinese by* Jonathan Chaves. CoBLCP

Seeing Off Wang Yüan-chao—Reprise. Wu Wei-yeh, *tr. fr. Chinese by* Jonathan Chaves. CoBLCP

Seeing Oloalok. Marilyn Bowering. NOBC

Seeing Someone Off. Wang Wei, *tr. fr. Chinese by* Burton Watson. CoBCP

Seeing Spring Off. K'ang Yu-wei, *tr. fr. Chinese by* Eugene C. Eoyang. WFTU

Seeing such blooming beauty. Narihira, *tr. by* Geoffrey Bownas *and* Anthony Thwaite. PeBJV

Seeing the Bones. Maxine W. Kumin. NoAM

Seeing the Light. Tsfrirah Gar, *tr. fr. Hebrew by* Bernhard Frank. MHeP

Seeing the moon rise from the snowy land. Song of Moon and Snow. Koo Siu-sun. WCI

Seeing the movement of cowherds. An Attack, 1940. Pablo Guevara, *tr. by* Maureen Ahern *and* David Tipton. Per

Seeing the Plum Blossoms by the River. Lady Ise, *tr. fr. Japanese by* Etsuko Terasaki *and* Irma Brandeis. BoWoP

Seeing the Returning Geese. Lady Ise, *tr. by* Etsuko Terasaki *and* Irma Brandeis. BoWoP

Seeing the Scenery. Leslie Scalapino. *Fr.* Hmmmm. NPGG

Seeing the snowman standing all alone. Boy at the Window. Richard Wilbur. Mes; NoP

Seeing the stars through a willow. Miura Chora, *tr. fr. Japanese by* Hiroaki Sato. *Fr.* Sixteen Hokku. FCEI

Seeing them, I recognize the easy contempt. Unflushed Urinals. Donald Justice. AnAn

Seeing thou art faire, I barre not thy false playing. Ovid, *tr. fr. Latin by* Christopher Marlowe. *Fr.* Amores, III, 13. OBVE

Seeing through the Sun. Linda Hogan. ER; HATNAP

Seeing you/ in the laundromat. Thinking Twice in the Laundromat. Harley Elliott. NeAC

Seeing You Stand Once More before My Eyes. Amy Lowell. *Fr.* Eleanora Duse. Son

Seek Flowers of Heaven. Robert Southwell. TrCP

Seek not, Leuconöe, to know how long you're going to live yet. Horace, *tr. fr. Latin, by* Eugene Field. *Fr.* Odes, I, 11. AA

Seek not man to please, for that. Isabella Whitney. *Fr.* Sweet Nosegay, A, *or* Pleasant Posy. WPE

Seek not to know Love's full extent. The Ghost. W. H. Davies. BrPo

"Seek not to know" (the ghost replied with tears). Marcellus. Virgil, *tr. fr. Latin by* Dryden. *Fr.* The Aeneid [*or* Eneados], VI. OBS

Seek out a rill from the sound of its fall. Belmore. Anthony Howell. NPo

Seek Out Another Heart. Mikha'il Nu aima, *tr. fr. Arabic by* Sargon Boulus *and* Thomas G. Ezzy. MAP

Seek the Lord. Thomas Campion. TrCP

Seek True Religion! John Donne. *Fr.* Satires, III. NOBE (Truth.) SeCePo

"Though Truth and Falsehood be." NOBE

Seeke not to know my love, for shee. To One That Desired To Know My Mistris. Thomas Carew. SeCP

Seeker, The. Lascelles Abercrombie. *Fr.* The Fools' Adventure. WGRP

Seeker in the Marshes, The. Daniel Lewis Dawson. AA

Seeker in the Night, A. Florence Earle Coates. TrPWD

Seekers, The. John Masefield. WGRP

Seekers, The. Charles Hamilton Sorley. WGRP

Seekers, The. Victor Starbuck. WGRP

Seekers of peace, enough hypocrisy! Ilyas Farhat, *tr. by* Salma Khadra Jayyusi *and* John Heath-Stubbs. MAP

Seeking a Mooring. Wang Wei, *tr. fr. Chinese by* Kenneth Rexroth *and* Ling Chung. BoWoP; WPOW

Seeking an Explanation. Richard Emil Braun. NoAM

Seeking, earnestly seeking in the gloom. Creation of Man. *Maori Oral Tradition, tr. by* John White. WTO

Seeking God. Edward Dowden. WGRP

Seeking in my hut. Issa, *tr. by* Peter Beilenson. TSS

Seeking in squalor lean, elusive youth. Nightwood. William Jay Smith. PoA

Seeking out Hermit Hu. Kao Ch'i, *tr. fr. Chinese by* Jonathan Chaves. CoBLCP

Seeking Te Iwi-ika's death. Lament for Te Iwi-ika. *Unknown, tr. by* Margaret Orbell. PeNZ

Seeking the words. Poem for Jan. Joseph Bruchac. CDW

Seekonk Woods, The. Galway Kinnell. NoAM

Seele im Raum. Randall Jarrell. LCAP

Seemingly as other men, yet always. Momist. Amy Groesbeck. GoYe

Seems lak to me de stars don't shine so bright. Sence You Went Away. James Weldon Johnson. BANP

Seems like a long time. The Partial Explanation. Charles Simic. NoP

Seems Like We Must Be Somewhere Else. Denise Levertov. NePoEA-2

Seen, and yet not seen. Narihira, *tr. fr. Japanese by* Burton Watson. *Fr.* Kokin Shu. FCEI

Seen from above. Under the Mountain. Louis MacNeice. FaBCIP

Seen from the Quantocks. Samuel Taylor Coleridge. *Fr.* This Lime Tree Bower My Prison. FaBoPP

Seen my lady home las' night. A Negro Love Song. Paul Laurence Dunbar. BANP; PoNe

Seen through cat eyes, all problems become greater. The Cats. Kurt Klinger, *tr. by* Beth Bjorklund. CoAuP

Seepage of time rots judgment, makes it slip. Darkened Windows. Ronald Bottrall. PoA

Seer foretold that I would love one day, A. Louise Labé, *tr. by* Judith Thurman. PBWP

Seers have no monopoly. Communal. Mary Elizabeth Fullerton. PoAu-1

Sees the man. The Carver. Lucille Clifton. CAPP

Seesaw, The. Oscar Williams. LiTA

See'st thou not in clearest dayes. Philarete Praises Poetry. George Wither. *Fr.* The Shephe[a]rd's Hunting, Eclogue IV. OBS

See'st thou o'er my shoulders falling. Judah Halevi, *tr. by* Emma Lazarus. TrJP

Seferis. Lawrence Durrell. EBEV

Segovia and Madrid. Rose Terry Cooke. AA

Segregation. Carlos German Belli, *tr. fr. Spanish by* Maureen Ahern. Per

Sehnsucht. Anna Wickham. MoBrPo

Sehnsucht; or, What You Will. "Corinna." FiBHP

Seicheprey. *Unknown.* PAH

Seil o'yer face! the send has come. The Fleggit Bride. "Hugh MacDiarmid." OxBS

Seismograph. Ephraim Auerbach, *tr. fr. Yiddish by* Howard Schwartz. VWA

16 heures/ L'Etoile. Two X. E. E. Cummings. FaBoMo

Seize, O seize the sounding lyre. The Hero of Bridgewater. Charles L. S. Jones. PAH

Seized with a fancy for fresh meat. Hymn to Mercury. *Unknown, tr. fr. Greek by* Shelley. *Fr.* Homeric Hymns. OBVE

Seizure. Sappho, *tr. fr. Greek by* Willis Barnstone. LLLT

Sejanus ("How many men are killed by power, by power"). Juvenal, *tr. fr. Latin by* Robert Lowell. *Fr.* Satires, X. OBVE

Sejanus ("Some ask for envy'd pow'r; which publick hate"). Juvenal, *tr. fr. Latin by* Dryden. *Fr.* Satires, X. OBVE

Sejanus ("What crowds by envied power, the wish of all"). Juvenal, *tr. fr. Latin by* William Gifford. *Fr.* Satires, X. OBVE

Selah. R. S. Thomas. FaBoMo

Seldom a simmer passed but him an' me. In Lythe Strathdon. Charles Murray. PoSH

"Seldom we find," says Solomon Don Dunce. An Enigma. Poe. Son

Selected Epigrams. Mary Magdalene Kassia, *tr. fr. Byzantine Greek by* Patrick Diehl. PBWP

Selective Service. Carolyn Forché. MAYP; NAmP

Selenologist, The. Bill Manhire. PeNZ

Selestial apoley which Didest inspire. Odd to a Krokis. *Unknown.* NA

Self. N. H. Pritchard II. PoBA

Self Accuser, A. John Donne. FaBoEE

Self-Acquaintance. William Cowper. NOCV

Self-Analysis. Anna Wickham. MoBrPo

Self-Congratulatory Ode on Mr. Auden's Election to the Professorship of Poetry at Oxford. Ronald Mason. FaBoPa

Self-Consciousness Makes All Changes Happy; Ode. Jonathan Richardson. NOEC

Self-Criticism in February. Robinson Jeffers. AmPP

Self-Deceaver, The. *Tr. fr. Spanish by* Thomas Stanley. OBVE

Self-Defense. Santob de Carrion, *tr. fr. Spanish by* George Ticknor. TrJP

Self-Dependence. Matthew Arnold. WGRP

Self-Derision. Natsume Soseki, *tr. fr. Chinese by* Burton Watson. JLIC-2

Self Dirge. Wendy Rose. CDW

Self-Discipline. "Æ" MoBrPo

Self-employed. David Ignatow. NNaP

Self-Examination. *Unknown.* FaBoUs

Self-Hatred of Don L. Lee, The. Don L. Lee. BPo

Self, I want you now to be. The Thing is Violent. Gwendolyn MacEwen. MoCV; NOBC

Self in 1958. Anne Sexton. HCAP

Self-Judgment. Berta Lask, *tr. fr. German by* Susan L. Cocalis *and* Gerlinde Geiger. DMG

Self Justification. Tony Harrison. *Fr.* The School of Eloquence. NoAM

Self-Knowledge. Samuel Taylor Coleridge. SeCePo

Self-Made. Ilse Aichinger, *tr. fr. German by* Beth Bjorklund. CoAuP

Self-Mastery. Henrietta Cordelia Ray. CBWP-3

Self-Pity. D. H. Lawrence. OxBTC; RB

Self-Pity Is a Kind of Lying, Too. James Schuyler. PoM

Self-Portrait. Frank Bidart. HCAP

Self-Portrait. Cecil Bodker, *tr. fr. Danish by* Nadia Christensen. BoWoP

Self-Portrait. Nina Cassian, *tr. fr. Rumanian by* Herbert Kuhner. VWA

Self-Portrait. Robert Creeley. NoAM

Self-Portrait. Allen Curnow. ATNZ

Self-Portrait. Ugo Foscolo, *tr. fr. Italian by* William Jay Smith. CT; PFI

Self-Portrait. Moses Mendelssohn, *tr. fr. German.* TrJP

Self Portrait. Esther Raab, *tr. fr. Hebrew by* Bernhard Frank. MHeP

Self-Portrait. R. S. Thomas. NAs; PoPo

Self-Portrait. William Carlos Williams. *Fr.* Pictures from Brueghel, I. LCAP

Self Portrait II. Tove Ditlevsen, *tr. fr. Danish by* Ann Freeman. OV

Self-Portrait, as a Bear. Donald Hall. SO

Self Portrait as Both Parties. Jorie Graham. BLA

Self-Portrait as Felt. Miron Bialoszewski, *tr. fr. Polish by* Czeslaw Milosz. PwPP

Self-Portrait at Thirty. Miklós Veress, *tr. fr. Hungarian by* Richard Wilbur. MHuP

Self Portrait 4. Tove Ditlevsen, *tr. fr. Danish by* Ann Freeman. WPOW

Self-Portrait in a Convex Mirror. John Ashbery. HCAP; NAAL-2

Self-Portrait in 2035. Charles Wright. LCAP

Self-Portrait: Inscribed upon My Own Collection of Lyrics, A. Chu Yi-tsun, *tr. fr. Chinese by* Chang Yin-nan. WFTU

Self-Portrait of the Laureate of Nonsense. Edward Lear. *See* How Pleasant to Know Mr. Lear.

Self Portrait I. Tove Ditlevsen, *tr. fr. Danish by* Ann Freeman. OV

Self-Protection. D. H. Lawrence. NoP

Self-Ridicule. Yüan Mei, *tr. fr. Chinese by* Anthony C. Yu. WFTU

Self-slaved, The. Patrick Kavanagh. MoBrPo

Self to Self. Charles Brasch. ATNZ

Self Unsatisfied Runs Everywhere, The. Delmore Schwartz. PoA

Self-Unseeing, The. EBEV; HAP; MoBrPo; NOBE; NOBVV; OBNC; PrIm; RB; WeW

Selfe Banished, The. Edmund Waller. MePo; OBS

Self's the Man. Philip Larkin. NOBL

Selfsame Song, The. Thomas Hardy. CMoP; PBBP

Selfsame surface that billowed once with, The. Skin Flick. Fred Chappell. InPK

Selfsame toothless voice for death or bridal, The. Bell Speech. Richard Wilbur. MoAB; MoAmPo

Selichos. Francis Landy. VWA

Sell in May. Stock Exchange Wisdom. *Unknown.* FaBoUs

Sellin biscuit an salfish in de plantation shop at pie. Horse Weebles. Edward Kamau Brathwaite. PBCV

Selling My Official Robe. Yang Chi, *tr. fr. Chinese by* Jonathan Chaves. CoBLCP

Selling Ruined Peonies. Yü Hsüan-chi, *tr. fr. Chinese by* Geoffrey Waters. BoWoP

Semantic. Robert Conquest. TEP

Semblables, The. William Carlos Williams. FaBoMo; NOBA

Semele Recycled. Carolyn Kizer. CAPP; InPS

Semen. Martha Paley Francescato, *tr. fr. Spanish by* Willis Barnstone. BoWoP

Semi-Private Room. Alden Nowlan. NeAC

Semi-Revolution, A. Robert Frost. LiTM

Semichorus II: "There the voluptuous nightingales." Shelley. *Fr.* Prometheus Unbound, II, ii. PBBP

Semmes in the Garden. George Marion O'Donnell. NYBP

Semphill, his hat stuck full of hooks. Trout Fisher. George Mackay Brown. OxBC

Sempronius,/ Sends greeting, warden of this Roman shore. A Roman Officer Writes. C. M. Doughty. *Fr.* The Dawn in Britain. FaBoTw

Sempstress's linnet sings, The. The Blind Linnet. Robert Williams Buchanan. FM

Sen-Sen. Richard Frost. SoTCo

Senator Smoot (Republican, Ut.). Ogden Nash. OBAL

Sence You Went Away. James Weldon Johnson. BANP

Send cards send. Notes on a Long Evening. David Phillips. NeAC

Send down thy truth, O God! For the Gifts of the Spirit. Edward Rowland Sill. TrPWD

Send for Lord Timothy. John Heath-Stubbs. OxBC

Send Forth, O God, Thy Light and Truth. John Quincy Adams. AH

Send home my long-strayed [*or* strayd] eyes to me [e]. The Message. John Donne. ElL; MeLP; OBS

Send me no flowers, for they will die before they leave America. Junglegrave. S. E. Anderson. PoBA

Send me no messages, for they are lies. *Unknown, tr. by* Cecil Clifford Palmer. PFI

Send No Money. Philip Larkin. TW

Send-off, The. Wilfred Owen. BrPo; LiTB; MoAB; MoBrPo; OBWP; OBWVE; OxBTC; RB

Sending a Letter. Liu Shih, *tr. fr. Chinese by* Irving Lo. WFTU

Sending my dear brother. Princess Oku. *Fr.* Manyo Shu. PeBJV

Sending Spring Love to Tzu-An. Yü Hsüan-Chi, *tr. fr. Chinese by* Kenneth Rexroth *and* Ling Chung. UnAS

Sending Tzu-lung Off to a Post in Chi-chou. Lu Yu, *tr. fr. Chinese by* Burton Watson. CoBCP

Sending up billows. Tachibana Akemi, *tr. fr. Japanese by* Burton Watson. *Fr.* Thirty Tanka. FCEI

Senec. Traged. ex Thyeste Chor. 2. Seneca. *See* Thyestes: Stond [*or* Stand] who so list upon the slipper toppe.

Senex. Sir John Betjeman. RB

Senex to Matt. Prior. James Kenneth Stephen. *Fr.* Two Epigrams. CenHV; FiBHP

Senile. Pat Folk. PCP

Senior Members. Sean Lucy. CIP

Senior Poet. Robert Pinsky. *Fr.* Three on Luck. AnAn

Senlin; a Biography, *sel.* Conrad Aiken.
  "It is morning, Senlin says, and in the morning." LiTM, II, ii.
  ("It is morning, Senlin says, and in the morning.") LiTM; NoAM
  (Morning Song.) CMoP; MoAB; TrGrPo
  (Morning Song of Senlin.) LiTA; MoAmPo; OxBA

Señor Excellent. Daniel Halpern. NAmP

Señora, it is true the Greeks are dead. Invocation to the Social Muse. Archibald MacLeish. LiTM

Senryu. Robert Frazier. BWV

Senryu. Hakuin, *tr. fr. Japanese by* Lucien Stryk *and* Takashi Ikemoto. ZPCJ

Senryu. Pat Nolan. UL

Senryu: "Water mirror." *Unknown, tr. by* Geoffrey Bownas *and* Anthony Thwaite. PeBJV

Sensation. Rimbaud, *tr. fr. French.* SoTW; TTTS, *tr. by* Kenneth Koch; AWP, *tr. by* Jethro Bithell.

Sensationalism. Larry Levis. MAYP; NAmP

Sense and Spirit. George Meredith. WGRP

Sense of autumn grows daily more sparse and open, A. Musing beneath a Pine. P'eng Sun-yü, *tr. by* Daniel Bryant. WFTU

Sense of Coolness, A. Quincy Troupe. PoBA

Sense of danger must not disappear, The. Leap before You Look. W. H. Auden. NoAM

Sense of death is most in apprehension, The. Shakespeare. *Fr.* Measure for Measure, III, i. OBD

Sense of separation, The. Kabir, *tr. by* John Stratton Hawley *and* Mark Juergensmeyer. SSI

Sense of Smell, The. Louis MacNeice. NYBP

Sense of the Sleight-of-Hand Man, The. Wallace Stevens. HAP; LiTM; MoAB; MoAmPo; NoAM; NOBA; PoA; TwCP; WeW

Sense of the world is short, The. Eros. Emerson. FaBoBe

Sense with keenest edge unused. Pater Filio. Robert Bridges. CMoP; OBEV

Senseless school, where we must give, A. A Young Man's Epigram on Existence. Thomas Hardy. BrPo; MoP

Senses loving Earth or well or ill, The. Sense and Spirit. George Meredith. WGRP

Senses of Responsibility. Charles Bernstein. LP

Sensible Girl's Reply to Moore's, A. Walter Savage Landor. FaBoEE

Sensible Is the Label. Eldon Grier. MoCV

Sensitive Knife, The. Gerald Stern. DiL

Sensitive like hands. Madame. George McWhirter. UnAS

Sensitive Plant, The, *sel.* Shelley. EnRP; GoTL
  "Whether the sensitive plant, or that." OAEL-2

Sensitive, Seldom and Sad. Mervyn Laurence Peake. RHPC

Sensitive Sydney. Wallace Irwin. FiBHP; ILY

Sensitiveness. Cardinal Newman. TrCP

Sensualists, The. Theodore Roethke. ErPo

Sensuous/ sloe eyed. Seduction. Jo Ann Hall-Evans. BlSi

Sensuous Latin poet, now I will go off with a thermos, A. Lynn Strongin. *Fr.* First Aspen. IHMS

Sent as a present from Annam. The Red Cockatoo. Po Chü-i, *tr. by* Arthur Waley. ChTr

Sent away, I look at the banner above the gate. *Unknown, tr. by* Sato. FCEI

Sent from Egypt with a Fair Robe of Tissue to a Sicilian Vinedresser. T. Sturge Moore. OBEV

Sent from the Capital to Her Elder Daughter. Lady Otomo no Sakanoe, *tr. by* Geoffrey Bownas *and* Anthony Thwaite. AIW; BoWoP; WPOW

Sent in Parting. Tu Mu, *tr. fr. Chinese by* Burton Watson. CoBCP

Sent in Parting to Yen Kung-su. Shen Chou, *tr. fr. Chinese by* Jonathan Chaves. CoBLCP

Sent to a Lady, with a Seal. Robert Lloyd. FaBoUs

Sent to a Patient, with the Present of a Couple of Ducks. Edward Jenner. FaBoUs

Sent to a Woman. Shunzei, *tr. fr. Japanese by* Burton Watson. *Fr.* Thirty Tanka. FCEI

Sent to a Woman on a Rainy Day. Shunzei, *tr. fr. Japanese by* Burton Watson. *Fr.* Thirty Tanka. FCEI

Sent to All My Nephews and Nieces at Tung-ch'eng, *sel.* Yang Shih-ch'i, *tr. fr. Chinese by* Jonathan Chaves.
  "I've drawn a salary in the capital for forty years now." CoBLCP

Sent to Be Inscribed on the Temple of P'u-jun. Yü Chi, *tr. fr. Chinese by* Jonathan Chaves. CoBLCP

Sent to Liang-fen. Singde, *tr. fr. Chinese by* Julie Landau. WFTU

Sent to Miss Bell H——, with a Pair of Buckles. John Cunningham. FaBoUs

Sent to My Beloved Far Away. Chu Yi-tsun, *tr. fr. Chinese by* Irving Lo. WFTU

Sent to My Two Little Children in the East of Lu. Li Po, *tr. fr. Chinese by* Burton Watson. CoBCP

Sent to the Hsiu-ts'ai on His Entry into the Army. Hsi K'ang, *tr. fr. Chinese by* Burton Watson. CoBCP

Sent to the Master Physician, "Almond Orchard" Shih. Li K'ai-hsien, *tr. fr. Chinese.* CoBLCP

Sent to the Painter, Lu Hsiao-feng. Li K'ai-hsien, *tr. fr. Chinese by* Jonathan Chaves. CoBLCP

Sent to the Taoist Holy Man of Ch'üan-chiao. Wei Ying-wu, *tr. fr. Chinese by* Burton Watson. CoBCP

Sent to Wen T'ing-yün on a Winter Night. Yü Hsüan-chi, *tr. fr. Chinese by* Geoffrey Waters. BoWoP

Sent to Wu Tzu-lü Who Wished to See My Recent Lyrics. Hsiang Hung-tso, *tr. fr. Chinese by* Irving Lo. WFTU

Sent to Yü Te-fu upon His Receipt of an Official Commission, *sel.* Tsung Ch'en, *tr. fr. Chinese by* Jonathan Chaves.
  "When you enter Chin-hua Mountain." CoBLCP

Sent with a Rose to a Young Lady. Margaret Deland. AA

Sentence. Aimé Césaire, *tr. fr. French by* Clayton Eshleman *and* Annette Smith. RHTwFP
Sentence undulates, The. The End of the Parade. William Carlos Williams. NYBP
Sentences, *sel.* Tony Harrison.
    Brazil. OBTV
Sentences My Father Used. Charles Bernstein. LP
Sentences we studied are rungs upon the ladder Jacob saw, The. Luzzato. Charles Reznikoff. VWA
Sentences While Remembering Hiraethog. T. Glynne Davies, *tr. fr. Welsh by* R. Gerallt Jones. OBWVE
Sententiae. Vincent O'Sullivan. ATNZ
Sentence. Sandra McPherson. PoA
Sentiment. Thomas Chatterton. NOEC
Sentiment. Sa'di Yusuf, *tr. fr. Arabic by* Lena Jayyusi *and* Naomi Shihab Nye. MAP
Sentiment on a Journey. Basho, *tr. fr. Japanese by* Burton Watson. *Fr.* Seventy-six Hokku. FCEI
Sentimental blockade! Cargoes due from the East! The Coming of Winter. Jules Laforgue, *tr. by* William Jay Smith. CT
Sentimental Bloke, The, *sel.* C. J. Dennis.
    Play, The. PoAu-1
Sentimental Conversation. Paul Verlaine. *See* Colloque Sentimental.
Sentimental Lines to a Young Man Who Favors Pink Wallpaper While I Personally Lean to the Blue. Margaret Fishback. FiBHP
Sentimental Poem. Po Chü-i, *tr. fr. Chinese by* Burton Watson. CoBCP
Sentimentalist sends his mauve balloon, The. The Celebration in the Plaza. Adrienne Rich. NePoEA
Sentiments, The. *Unknown.* APAS
Sentiments are nice, "The Lonely Crowd." John Button Birthday. Frank O'Hara. NAs
Sentinel, The. *Unknown.* BLRP
Sentinel's Song, A. Rarawa Kerehoma, *tr. by* Barry Mitcalfe. WTO
Sentry, The. Wilfred Owen. MMA
Sentry and a ladder mark the wall, A. In Front of a Japanese Photograph. John Peck. SM
Sentry drums boom, The. Tune: Immortal at Magpie Bridge. Wang Kuo-wei, *tr. by* Li Chi *and* Michael Patrick O'Connor. WFTU
Senzangakhona. *Zulu Oral Tradition, tr. by* T. Cope. WTO
Separate Parties. Dabney Stuart. NYBP
Separate place between the thought and felt, A. The Corridor. Thom Gunn. NePoEA
Separate Time. Anna Hajnal, *tr. fr. Hungarian by* Edwin Morgan. MHuP
Separated Lovers. *Unknown. See* One I Love Is Gone Away, The.
Separately I still recall. Portrait. Adèle Naudé. PeSA
Separateness of the Fingers in Trance, The. Kit Robinson. IAT
Separating one by one. Island Waters. Tony Beyer. PeNZ
Separation. Martha Gilbert Dickinson Bianchi. AA
Separation, *sel.* Anne Bloch.
    Absent Friends. Mes
Separation. Alice Learned Bunner. *Fr.* Vingtaine, I. AA
Separation, A. William Johnson Cory. OBNC
Separation. W. S. Merwin. HAP; ILY; NoP; PCP
Separation. Derek S. Savage.
Separation from the Torah. Solomon Ibn Gabirol, *tr. fr. Hebrew by* David Goldstein. TOF
Separation on the River Kiang. Li Po, *tr. fr. Chinese by* Ezra Pound. InPS; SOTW; UnPo
Separations. Evan Zimroth. ER
Separations begin with placement. River Road Studio. Barbara Guest. PoM
Sephestia's Song to Her Child[e]. Robert Greene. *Fr.* Menaphon. ELP; PoEL-2; TrGrPo
    (Sephestia's Lullaby.) NOBE; OBEV
    (Sephestia's Song.) OBSC
    (Weep Not My Wanton.) ElL; SeCePo
Sepia Fashion Show. Maya Angelou. BlSi
September. K. O. Arvidson. *Fr.* The Four Last Songs of Richard Strauss at Takahe Creek above the Kaipara, II. ATNZ
September. Edwina Fallis. YeAR
September. Mary Howitt. BoTP
September. Ted Hughes. BoLoP
September. Aldous Huxley. EBEV
September. Joanne Kyger. UL
September. Robert Lowell. NaP
September. Linda Pastan. Psk
September. Henrietta Cordelia Ray. CBWP-3
September. Folgore Da San Gimignano, *tr. fr. Italian by* Dante Gabriel Rossetti. *Fr.* Sonnets of the Months. AWP
September. Cesare Vivaldi, *tr. fr. Italian by* Lawrence R. Smith. NItP

September Afternoon. Margaret Haley Carpenter. GoYe
September Afternoon at Four O'Clock. Marge Piercy. NIP
September Blue. Barbara Burford. DT
September [Days Are Here]. Helen Hunt Jackson. FaPON; FPL; GoJo; OBCA; PoLF
September eighth: I hear trains whistling. September. Cesare Vivaldi, *tr. by* Lawrence R. Smith. NItP
September Evening, 1938. William Plomer. SeCePo
September Gale, The, *sel.* Oliver Wendell Holmes.
    "It chanced to be our washing day." FiBHP
September Heath. Otto Laaber, *tr. fr. German by* Beth Bjorklund. CoAuP
September in Australia. Henry Clarence Kendall. PoAu-1
September: Last Day at the Beach. Richard Tillinghast. GOYP
September Midnight. Sara Teasdale. PoA
September 1913. W. B. Yeats. BrPo; CMoP; FaBoPV; GTBS-P; HAP; MoP; NAEL-2; NoAM; PoRA
September 1, 1939. W. H. Auden. CMoP; LiTA; MoAB; MoBrPo; OxBA; PoE; PrIm; WaP
September rain falls on the house. Elizabeth Bishop. InPK; LCAP; NoP; PoE; SM; WeW
September 7. Ellen Bass. NMM
September Song. Geoffrey Hill. NAEL-2; NoAM; NoP; OBWP
September sun, a little fog in the mornings. Calm. Robert Hass. NAmP
September, the First Day of School. Howard Nemerov. OxBC
September. The gypsy and the nightingale. Autumn. Itzig Manger, *tr. by* Ruth Whitman. TrJP; VWA
September 13, 1959 (Variation). Andrea Zanzotto, *tr. fr. Italian by* Lawrence R. Smith. NItP
September 30. Dick Lourie. NeAC
September twenty-second, Sir: today. After the Surprising Conversions. Robert Lowell. AmPP; HAP; NAAL-2; NePoEA; NoAM; NoP; PPP
September 2. Wendell Berry. PoA
September was when it began. The Coming of the Plague. Weldon Kees. NaP; VGW
September's here; delaying his first beams. Autumn. E. A. Baratynsky, *tr. by* Alan Myers. AAA
Septentrion. René Char, *tr. fr. French by* Thomas Merton. RHTwFP
Sepulchres, how thick they stand, The. Meditations on the Sepulchre in the Garden. Philip Doddridge. NOCV; NOEC
Sequaire. Godeschalk, *tr. fr. Latin by* Ezra Pound. CTC
Sequel, The. Theodore Roethke. NYBP
Sequel, The. Delmore Schwartz. LiTM
Sequel to the "Purple Cow." Gelett Burgess. *See* Ah, Yes, I Wrote the "Purple Cow."
Sequelula to "The Dynasts," A. Max Beerbohm. Par
Sequence. George Barker. PoA
Sequence. Edgar Daniel Kramer. BLRP
Sequence, A. Leslie Scalapino. *See* That They Were at the Beach.
Sequence for a Young Widow Passing. Deborah Munro. IHMS
Sequence for Saint Michael, A. Alcuin, *tr. fr. Irish by* Helen Waddell. TIRV
Sequence in Four Keys, A, *sel.* James Reaney.
    Baby, The. NAs
Sequence of Generations, The. Hayim Be'er, *tr. fr. Hebrew by* Stephen Mitchell. VWA
Sequence/ 28 Separate Poems, A, *sels.* Robert Grenier. IAT
    "Of life days like."
    "Snow covers the slopes, covers the slopes."
    Spring.
    "Yah gee."
Seraglio of the Sultan Bee! A Hollyhock. Frank Dempster Sherman. AA
Seraph and the Snob, The. May Kendall. CenHV
Seravezza. Hoyt W. Fuller. PoBA
Serenade: "Ah! Country Guy, the hour is nigh." Sir Walter Scott. *Fr.* Quentin Durward. GTBS; GTBS-P
Serenade: "Along the banks of the river." Federico García Lorca, *tr. fr. Spanish by* Perry Higman. LPSS
Serenade: "Come now, and let us wake them: time." *Unknown, tr. by* Jethro Bithell. AWP
Serenade, A: "Look out upon the stars, my love." Edward Coote Pinkney. AA; AnAmPo
Serenade, A: "Lullaby, O Lullaby." Thomas Hood. *Fr.* Domestic Poems. NBLV
Serenade: "Sleep, love sleep." Mary Weston Fordham. CBWP-2
Serenade: "Softly, O midnight Hours!" Aubrey Thomas De Vere. OBEV
Serenade: "Stars of the summer night!" Longfellow. *Fr.* The Spanish Student. AA; FaBoBe
Serenade at the Villa. Robert Browning. Mes
Serenade for Strings. Dorothy Livesay. NAs

Serenade for Two Poplars, A. Esther Raab, *tr. fr. Hebrew by* Robert Friend *and* Shimon Sandbank. VWA
Serenade of a Loyal Martyr. George Darley. *See* Song: "Sweet in her green cell the flower of beauty slumbers."
Serene and outraged in a trenchcoat. Severances. Aidan Carl Mathews. CIP
Serene descent, as a red leaf's descending. Sara Teasdale. PoA
Serene, I fold my hands [*or* arms] and wait. Waiting. John Burroughs. AA; AnAmPo; BLPA; FaBoBe; OHFP; WGRP
Serene, not as a prize for conflict won. On a Portrait of Mme. Rimsky-Korsakov. Kingsley Amis. NePoEA-2
Serene the silver fishes glide. At the Aquarium. Max Eastman. FaPON; WGRP
Serene, vast head, with silver cloud of hair. A Tribute of Grasses. Hamlin Garland. AA
Serenely I walked along my own. Mohammad Taqi Mir, *tr. by* Ahmed Ali. GoT
Serenely in the crystal jet. Ezra Pound. *Fr.* Cantos, LXXIV. PoE
Serenity in Stones, The. Simon J. Ortiz. CDW
Serenity of Faith, The. Bible, *O.T. Fr.* Psalms: Psalm XXVII ("The Lord is my light. . ."), 7-14. BLRP
Sereno. Sydney Lea. BLA
Serf, The. Roy Campbell. GTBS-P; LiTB; MoBrPo; OBMV
Sergeant, The. Don Johnson. MAYP
Sergeant Champe. *Unknown.* PAH
Sergeant, He Is the Worst of All, The. *Unknown.* AS
Sergeant-Major Money. Robert Graves. MMA; OBWP
Sergeant of the Lawe, war and wys, A. Chaucer. *Fr.* The Canterbury Tales: Prologue. CTC, *abr.*
Sgt. stands so fluently in leather, The. On a Photo of Sgt. Ciardi a Year Later. John Ciardi. AiP
Sergeant's Weddin', The. Kipling. OxBTC
Sergei's a flower. Ruth Herschberger. FF
Serials are all wound up now, The. Where Are You Now Superman? Brian Patten. FF
Serious and a Curious Night-Meditation, A. Thomas Traherne. SeCP
Serious Literary Slip, A. Kevin Ireland. ATNZ
Serious Merriment of Women, The. Patricia Goedicke. TAP
Serious over my cereals I broke one breakfast my fast. Breakfast with Gerard Manley Hopkins. Anthony Brode. BXAP; FaBoPa; FiBHP; NOBL; Par
Serious Poem, A. Ernest Walsh. ErPo
Serious Readers. Peter Redgrove. OxBC
Seriousness on the Rise. Wayne Hogan. SoTCo
Seriousness seems on. Seriousness on the Rise. Wayne Hogan. SoTCo
Sermon, The. Richard Hughes. OBMV
Sermon at Clevedon, A. T. E. Brown. NOBVV
Sermon in a Stocking. Ellen A. Jewett. BLPA
Sermon on Swift, A. Austin Clarke. BIrV; IPY
Sermon on the Mount. Jeff Wright. UL
Sermon on the Warpland, The. Gwendolyn Brooks. BPo; LiTM; NOBA; PoBA
Sermonette. Ishmael Reed. NIP; PoBA
Serpent, The. Theodore Roethke. AmMo; RHPC
Serpent Country. A. R. Ammons. EOEF
Serpent is shut out from paradise, The. Stanzas to Edward Williams. Shelley. OBNC
Serpent Knowledge. Robert Pinsky. *Fr.* An Explanation of America. NAAL-2; NPGG
Serpent Muses, The. Peggy Henderson. NMM
Serpent Sun. Aimé Césaire, *tr. fr. French by* Clayton Eshleman *and* Annette Smith. RHTwFP
Serpent with a voyce, so slie and fine, The. Samuel Gorton. SCAP
Serpents exploded, open balconies. Morvin. John Fuller. NePoEA-2
Serried hosts stood man to man, The. The Oranges. Abu Dharr, *tr. by* A. J. Arberry. OBAL
"Serva tibi minas!" The Judge with the Sore Rump. St. George Tucker. OBAL
Servant in Literature, The. Marjorie Welish. UL
Servant Man, The. *Unknown.* AmFP
Servant of Others, The. Kathleen Spivack. ER
Servant of Rosemary Lane, The. *Unknown.* OxBSS
Servant, taking leave, A. Taigi, *tr. fr. Japanese by* Hiroaki Sato. *Fr.* Twenty-nine Hokku. FCEI
Servant ("The gourd of wine"), The. Tachibana Akemi, *tr. fr. Japanese by* Burton Watson. *Fr.* Thirty Tanka. FCEI
Servant to Servants, A. Robert Frost. CMoP; NAAL-2
Servants, The. Richard Wightman. WGRP
Servants then (commanded) soone obaid, The. Nausicaa. Homer, *tr. fr. Greek by* George Chapman. *Fr.* Odyssey, VI. OBS
Serve Her Right. John Barford. PeHV
Service. Robert Browning. *Fr.* Pippa Passes, Introduction. TrGrPo

Service. Washington Gladden. *See* O Master, Let Me Walk with Thee.
Service. Georgia Douglas Johnson. CDC
Service for townsman, old sailor. Orchids. Judith Minty. GeTw
Service is joy, to see or swing. Allow. Tennis. Margaret Avison. MoP
Service Man, The. Kipling. Par
Service, or Latin *sorbus*, European. The Life of Service. Donald Davie. NYBP
Serving Girl, The. Gladys May Casely Hayford. CDC
Serving in endless bounty. What He Said after a Quarrel, Remembering His Wedding Night. Virrurru Muteyinanar, *tr. by* A. K. Ramanujan. PLW
Serving Maid, The. Arthur Munby. NOBVV
Serving man, A. Curled my hair. Thom Gunn. *Fr.* Misanthropos. OxBC
Serving Men's Song, A. John Lyly. *See* Alexander and Campaspe: O! [*or* Oh] for a bowl of fat canary.
Servitudes. Philippe Soupault, *tr. fr. French by* Michael Benedikt. POS
Sesostris. Lloyd Mifflin. AA
Session[s] of the Poets, A ("A session was held the other day"). Sir John Suckling. SeCV-1
(Wits, The.) CaPo
Sestina: Altaforte. Ezra Pound. CMoP; FaBoTw; LiTA; MoAB; MoAMPo; NOBA; SoSe; SOTW
Sestina: "Body of my love is a familiar country, The." Mary Stanley. PeNZ
Sestina: "Hang it all, Ezra Pound, there is only the one sestina!" Donald Hall. NePoEA
Sestina: Here in Katmandu. Donald Justice. SM
Sestina I: Of the Lady Pietra degli Scrovigni. Dante, *tr. fr. Italian by* Dante Gabriel Rossetti. AWP; OAEL-2; OBVE; PFI
Sestina: "I woke by first light in a wood." Donald Justice. NePoEA
Sestina: "Is this the object." Judith Kroll. AmPA; SM
Sestina: "September rain falls on the house." Elizabeth Bishop. InPK; LCAP; NoP; PoE; SM; WeW
Sestina d'Inverno. Anthony Hecht. NoAM; NoP
Sestina for My Dead in the First Snow. John Engels. AnAn
Sestina from the Home Gardener. Diane Wakoski. MoP
Sestina in a Cantina. Malcolm Lowry. MoCV
Sestina in Time of Winter. Patrick Anderson. PoA
Sestina of the Tramp-Royal. Kipling. BrPo; FPL; LiTB; MoBrPo; PrIm
Sestina on Her Portrait. Howard Nemerov. WaP
Sestina to the Common Glass of Beer: I Do Not Drink Beer. Diane Wakoski. SM
Sestina with Refrain. Thomas W. Shapcott. CBAP
"Set back your watches—this is Mountain Time." Continental Crossing. Dorothy Brown Thompson. AmFN
Set every stitch of canvas to woo the fresh'ning wind. The Slave Chase. *Unknown.* CoMu
"Set he that hat on his head?" Cardinal Fisher. John Heywood. ACP
Set Love in order, thou that lovest Me. Cantica: Our Lord Christ: Of Order. St. Francis of Assisi, *also at.* to Jacopone da Todi, *tr. by* Dante Gabriel Rossetti. AWP; OBVE; PFI
Set me as a seal upon your heart. Bible, *O.T. See* Song of Solomon, The: As a Seal upon Thy Heart.
Set me to sound for you. Ark Anatomical. Jay Macpherson. *Fr.* The Ark. NOBC
Set me where Phoebus' heat the flowers slayeth. The Last Trial. Petrarch, *tr. fr. Italian. Fr.* Sonnets to Laura: To Laura in Life, CXIII, *tr. unknown.* OBSC
Set me whereas the sun doth parch the green [*or* sonne dothe perche the grene]. Petrarch, *tr. fr. Italian by* the Earl of Surrey. *Fr.* Sonnets to Laura: To Laura in Life, CXIII. AAS; HAP; SiPS
(Love's Fidelity.) AWP
(To His Lady.) OBSC
(Vow to Love Faithfully, Howsoever He Be Rewarded, A.) TrGrPo
Set now,/ and I too will go below. Myoe, *tr. fr. Japanese by* Burton Watson. *Fr.* Ten Tanka. FCEI
Set of Romantic Hymns, A, *sel.* Robert Duncan.
"Fountain of forms! Life springs of unique being!" DiL
Set on this bubble of dead stone and sand. On an Engraving by Casserius. A. D. Hope. CBAP
Set silver cone to tulip flame! Inscription for a Mirror in a Deserted Dwelling. William Rose Benét. MoAmPo
Set up the drum. December. Maurice Kenny. HATNAP; STE
Set where the upper streams of Simois flow. Palladium. Matthew Arnold. GTBS-P; OAEL-2; OBNC; PPP
Seta/ colecc. David Melnick. IAT
Sète. Max Hölzer, *tr. fr. German by* Beth Bjorklund. CoAuP
Seth Compton. Edgar Lee Masters. *Fr.* Spoon River Anthology. LiTA
Settin' on de Fence. *Unknown.* WBLP
Setting, The/ had no special theme. Slow Riff for Billy. James Cunningham. JB

Setting a trotline after sundown. In the Deep Channel. William Stafford. NaP; RB

Setting down the bricks and her crane's-beak hoe. Bricks. Wang Jun-hua, *tr. by* Dominic Cheung. IFON

Setting of the Moon, The. Giacomo Leopardi, *tr. fr. Italian by* John Heath-Stubbs. PFI

Setting Off. Fu'ad Rifqa, *tr. fr. Arabic by* Abdullah al-Udhari. MPAW

Setting Out. W. D. Snodgrass. DiL

Setting Out at Dawn. Wu Wei-yeh, *tr. fr. Chinese by* Jonathan Chaves. CoBLCP

Setting Out from Hiroshima, Saying Goodby to My Father. Rai San'yo, *tr. fr. Japanese by* Burton Watson. FCEI; JLIC-2

Setting out on a journey. *Unknown, tr. by* Geoffrey Bownas *and* Anthony Thwaite. PeBJV

Setting out on the road. *Unknown, tr. by* Burton Watson. FCEI

Setting/ Slow Drag. Carolyn M. Rodgers. JB

Setting sun illuminates half the river, The. A Walk to the Eastern River Bank. Kao Ch'i, *tr. by* Jonathan Chaves. CoBLCP

Setting sun is molten gold, The. To The Tune "Eternal Happiness." Li Ch'ing-chao, *tr. by* Kenneth Rexroth *and* Ling Chung. AIW

Setting sun lingers lovingly among tall trees, A. Tao-wu Mountain. T'an Ssu-t'ung, *tr. by* Timothy C. Wong. WFTU

Setting the Table. Dorothy Aldis. FaPON

Settled Men, The. George M. Brady. NeIP

Settled on a temple bell and asleep. Buson, *tr. fr. Japanese by* Hiroaki Sato. *Fr.* Eighty-seven Hokku. FCEI

Settler. Stewart Lindh. PoA

Settler, The. Alfred Billings Street. AA; FaBoBe; PAH

Settler in the olden times went forth, A. Charles Harpur. *Fr.* The Creek of the Four Graves. PoAu-1

Settlers, The. Margaret Atwood. MoCV

Settlers, The. Judith Hemschemeyer. SO

Settlers. Tom Paulin. FaBCIP

Settlers abandoned our country long ago. Pauper Woodland. Ronald G. Everson. NOBC

Settler's Lament, The. *Unknown.* PoAu-1

Settling Some Old Football Scores. Morris Bishop. SD

Seumas Beg. James Stephens. FaPON; GrPl; OxBTC

Seven, The. *Unknown, tr. fr. Sumerian by* Jerome K. Rothenberg. RB
  Lament for the Two Brothers Slain by Each Other's Hand. AWP

Seven against Thebes, The, *sel.* Aeschylus, *tr. fr. Greek by* A. E. Housman.
  Lament for the Two Brothers Slain by Each Other's Hand. AWP

Seven ageing pine trees hide. Allen Curnow. *Fr.* A Small Room with Large Windows, II. PeNZ

Seven ages, first puking and mewling. "All the World's a Stage." Victor Gray. NBLV

Seven Ages of Elf-hood, The. Rachel Field. RHPC

Seven Ages of Man, The. Shakespeare. *See* As You Like It: All the World's a Stage.

Seven ancient women croak, "November." November. Itzig Manger, *tr. by* Leonard Wolf. PeBMYV

Seven around the moon go up. The Pinwheel's Song. John Ciardi. PDV; SO

Seven Black Friars sitting back to back. Blackfriars. Eleanor Farjeon. OxBChV

Seven candles in silver sticks. Planter. Richard Murphy. *Fr.* The Battle of Aughrim. BIrV

Seven continents, seven seas. Tropic Nightmare in Singapore. Melech Ravitch, *tr. by* Robert Friend. PeBMYV

7 Days in Another Town. Kit Robinson. IAT

Seven Days of the Sun, The, *sels.* W. J. Turner. OBMV
  "Beneath a thundery glaze."
  "Dian, Isis, Artemis, whate'er thy name."
  "I had watched the ascension and decline of the moon."
  "I have seen mannequins."
  "If God kept a terrarium."
  "Spirits walking everywhere."
  "This is the last time."
  "What is the meaning of this Ideal."
  "What is this tempest."

Seven dead men, Brigit. The Celtic Lyric. J. C. Squire. BXAP

Seven Deadly Sins, The. Stephen Hawes. *Fr.* The Pastime of Pleasure. PoEL-1

Seven dog-days we let pass. Queens. J. M. Synge. ChTr; GBL; MoBrPo; OBMV

Seven Dreams. John Clifford Bayliss. EAS

Seven Evils. Bible, *O.T. Fr.* Proverbs, VI: 16-19. TrGrPo

Seven Fiddlers, The. Sebastian Evans. EBVV; OnMSP

7:v:60 (an interesting *lapsus calami*). For Kai Snyder. Philip Whalen. PoM

Seven Forbidden Words. Michael Palmer. LP

747 (London-Chicago). Robert Conquest. OxBC

Seven Hells of Jigoku Zoshi, The, *sels.* Jerome Rothenberg. NNaP
  Fifth Hell, The.
  Sixth Hell, The.

Seven Houses, The. George Mackay Brown. NAs

700 years ago. Slim Man Canyon. Leslie Silko. VoR

Seven lang years I hae served the King. The Whummil Bore. *Unknown.* CH; ESPB

Seven-League Boots, The. Ilarie Voronca, *tr. fr. Rumanian by* Willis Barnstone *and* Matei Calinescu. VWA

Seven lean cows, The. Glimpse of an Open Dream. David Avidan, *tr. by* Warren Bargad *and* Stanley F. Chyet. IP

Seven Little Pigs. *Unknown.* BoTP

Seven Long Years in State Prison. *Unknown.* AS

Seven lovely poplars. Poplars. Helen Leuty. BoTP

Seven Metal Mountains. Bible, Pseudepigrapha. *Fr.* Enoch, LII: 6–9. TrJP

Seven Mexican Children. Tom Schmidt. NeAC

Seven Mysteries. Michael Jackson. ATNZ

7 o'clock, theater time, dinner time. Man. Margit Szécsi, *tr. by* Laura Schiff. MHuP

7 October, 1940. Valentine Ackland. CN

Seven of the Clock. Roy Macnab. PeSA

Seven Old Men, The. Baudelaire, *tr. fr. French by* Roy Campbell. OBVE

Seven One-Line Poems, *sel.* Harry Bose.
  M 13. BWV

Seven Poems on Living in the Mountains: Seeing Off, *sels.* Chang Yü, *tr. fr. Chinese by* Jonathan Chaves. CoBLCP
  Brewing Tea at Moon Pond.
  Cliff of the Ancient Tomb, The.
  Looking at Chrysanthemums.

Seven Rainy Months. William Plomer. OxBTC

Seven Sages, The. W. B. Yeats. NOIV

Seven Said by the Foster-Mother, *sels.* Peyanar, *tr. fr. Tamil by* A. K. Ramanujan. PLW
  "Embracing the young mother from behind." *Fr.* 2.
  "Embracing this woman." *Fr.* 5.
  "Evening in the yard." *Fr.* 7.
  "His heart swells." *Fr.* 3.
  "Like the red flame." *Fr.* 4.
  "Minstrels sing the jasmine songs." *Fr.* 6.
  "Way/ they lay together, The." *Fr.* 1.

Seven Seages, The, *sel.* John Rolland.
  "In haist ga hy thee to sum hoill." OxBS

Seven-Sided Poem. Carlos Drummond de Andrade, *tr. fr. Portuguese by* Elizabeth Bishop. ATCBP

Seven sights were veiled. Basho, *tr. by* Geoffrey Bownas *and* Anthony Thwaite. PeBJV

Seven Sleepers, The. Sir Herbert Read. SeCePo

Seven Sleepers, The. Mark Van Doren. FYAP

Seven Songs, *sels.* Cheng Hsieh, *tr. fr. Chinese by* Jonathan Chaves. CoBLCP
  "Master Cheng is thirty—and doesn't have a job!"
  "When I was three years old, my mother passed away."

Seven Songs Written During the Ch'ien-yüan Era, *sels.* Tu Fu, *tr. fr. Chinese by* Burton Watson. CoBCP
  "I have a sister, little sister, living in Chung-li." *Fr.* 4.
  "I have brothers, younger brothers in a place far away." *Fr.* 3.
  "Long hoe, long hoe, handle of white wood." *Fr.* 2.
  "To the south there is a dragon living in a mountain pool." *Fr.* 6.
  "Traveler, a traveler, Tzu-mei his name, A." *Fr.* 1.

Seven Sorrows, The. Ted Hughes. NAEL-2

Seven Sorrows, *sels.* Wang Ts'an, *tr. fr. Chinese by* Burton Watson. CoBCP
  "Tribes of Ching—that's not my home." *Fr.* II.
  "Western Capital in lawless disorder, The." *Fr.* I.

Seven South African Poems, *sels.* David Wright. PeSA
  "My countryman, the poet, wears a Stetson."
  "My grandfather was an elegant gentleman."

Seven Spiritual Ages of Mrs. Marmaduke Moore, The. Ogden Nash. MoAmPo

Seven Stanzas at Easter. John Updike. EaLo; TrCP

Seven stars in the still water. The Dole of the King's Daughter. *Unknown, tr. by* Oscar Wilde. AWP

Seven sweet singing birds up in a tree. The Dream of a Girl Who Lived at Sevenoaks. William Brighty Rands. OxBChV

Seven thousand acres of grass have faded yellow. Farmer, Dying. Richard Hugo. CAPP

Seven threads make the shroud. Shroud. George Mackay Brown. RB

Seven times hath Janus ta'en new year by hand. Upon the Author's First Seven Years' Service. Thomas Tusser. EIL
Seven Times One—Exultation. Jean Ingelow. *Fr.* Songs of Seven. BLPA; FaPON; OBNC
Seven times the centuple wheels of life have whirled. The Blessing of St. Francis. Sister Maura. CaP
Seven Times Three—Love. Jean Ingelow. *Fr.* Songs of Seven. PoLF
Seven Times Two—Romance. Jean Ingelow. *Fr.* Songs of Seven. GN
Seven treasures, The. Okura. *Fr.* Manyo Shu. PeBJV
Seven types of treasures, The. Okura. *Fr.* Manyo Shu. FCEI
Seven Virgins, The. *Unknown.* CH; ChTr; GBP; OBET; OBEV
Seven wealthy towns contend for Homer dead. A Cure for Poetry. *Unknown, after the Latin of* George Buchanan. FaBoEE
Seven weeks of sea, and twice seven days of storm. Gibraltar. Wilfrid Scawen Blunt. ACP; OBEV
Seven white peacocks against the castle wall, The. What the Orderly Dog Saw. Ford Madox Ford. CTC
Seven Wonders of England, The, *sel.* Sir Philip Sidney. Stonehenge. FaBoPP
Seven Wonders of North Wales, The. *Unknown, tr. fr. Welsh.* OBWVE
Seven Wonders of the Ancient World, The. *Unknown.* EyDe
Seven Woodland Crows. Gerald Vizenor. VoR
Seven years ago/ at forty five. Now or Never. Astra. AIW; BrRo
Seven years ago, almost to the month and day. Ramon. E. A. Lacey. PeHV
7 Years from Somewhere. Philip Levine. AnAn
Seven years I have kept him, dead. The Corpse-Keeper. *Unknown, tr. by* W. S. Merwin. BoWoP
Seven years I orbit around you. Sabbatical. Linda Zisquit. VWA
Seven years lived in Italy leave me convinced. The Oak and the Olive. George Barker. FaBoMo; OBTV
"Seven years ye shall be a stone." The Maid and the Palmer. *Unknown.* ESPB
Seventeen. Jonathan Holden. Psk
Seventeen Come Sunday. *Unknown.* OBET
1780 a.d. in the street they flung foam about and a young. Poems (I-XI). Philip O'Connor. EAS
17. IV. 71. Paul Blackburn. PoM
Seventeen Hokku, *sels.* Chiyojo, *tr. fr. Japanese by* Hiroaki Sato. FCEI
   At the Ferry in Kuwana.
   "Butterfly: now in front."
   "Butterfly: what's it dreaming of."
   "By its own wind, a small butterfly."
   "Clear water has no front or back."
   "Dandelion: from time to time."
   "From time to time, a butterfly."
   "Green willow's quiet, A."
   "I forget my lips are rouged."
   "I go on, and the clear water meets me again."
   "I raise my hands, and the clear water."
   "Mistaking birds for leaves."
   "Only over the river, darkness flows: fireflies."
   "To tangle or untangle a willow."
   "Touching the line from a fishing pole."
   "Willow flows away, The."
   "Wind spills plovers, picks them up, The."
1738. Pope. *See* Not twice a twelvemonth you appear in print.
Seventeen Warnings in Search of a Feminist Poem. Erica Jong. AmPA
Seventeen years ago you said. À Quoi Bon Dire. Charlotte Mew. OxBTC
Seventeenth day of the fourth month!, The. The Taoist Nun. Wei Chuang, *tr. by* Lois Fusek. ATF
Seventeenth stanza, The. My heart aches, my tears fall. Ts'ai Yen, *tr. fr. Chinese by* Kenneth Rexroth *and* Ling Chung. *Fr.* Eighteen Verses Sung to a Tatar Reed Whistle, XVII. WPOW
Seventeenth Telegram ("Your weeping gray streets"). Abd al-Aziz al-Maqalih, *tr. fr. Arabic by* Lena Jayyusi *and* Christopher Middleton. *Fr.* Telegrams of Tenderness for Sanaa. MAP
Seventh, The. Attila József, *tr. fr. Hungarian by* John Batki. RB
Seventh Answer. Erika Mitterer, *tr. fr. German by* Beth Bjorklund. CoAuP
Seventh Avenue. Muriel Rukeyser. NoAM
Seventh Day of the First Week, The, *sel.* Joshua Sylvester. *Fr.* Du Bartas: His Divine Weeks and Works.
   "There on his knee, behind a box tree shrinking." PBBP
Seventh dragon turned to his wife, The. Where Two o'Clock Came From. Kenneth Patchen. SO
Seventh Eclogue. Miklós Radnóti, *tr. fr. Hungarian by* Emery George. VWA
Seventh Garden, The. Sándor Weöres, *tr. fr. Hungarian by* Daniel Hoffman. MHuP

Seventh Month, Sixteenth Day. Ryokan, *tr. fr. Chinese by* Burton Watson. JLIC-2
Seventh Round, The. James Merrill. ASP
Seventh Son. Ed Roberson. PoBA
Seventh Street. Jean Toomer. NAAL-2
Seventh Telegram ("The day recedes"). Abd al-Aziz al-Maqalih, *tr. fr. Arabic by* Lena Jayyusi *and* Christopher Middleton. *Fr.* Telegrams of Tenderness for Sanaa. MAP
Seventies, The. Louis Johnson. PeNZ
Seventy-eight Tanka, *sels.* Princess Shikishi, *tr. fr. Japanese by* Hiroaki Sato. FCEI
   "Allured outside by someone's plum branches in bloom."
   " 'And still,' I say, and wait."
   "As I gaze, the moon dims."
   "As I grow used to the mattress of moss."
   "As I look, there's no place for my thoughts to go."
   "As I looked, winter came."
   "As I sleep somewhere near a mountain away from home."
   "As winter comes, the sound from the valley stream stops."
   "Autumn night grows late, The."
   "Away from home, in Fushimi village."
   "Away from home: over the dewdrops fragile on my pillow."
   "Be a guide—this is a boat rowing in the traceless waves."
   "Brocades left at the treetops ceased to be, The."
   "Calls of a clapper rail far into the night."
   "Clear-toned cicadas have exhausted their voices, The."
   "Clouds of May rain have closed into one, The."
   "Counting the dewdrops that vie in falling off."
   "Days accumulate; the more snow falls."
   "Deep in the mountains, the pine door isn't aware of spring."
   "Deep in the mountains, through the pine door closed."
   "Did the cuckoo pity me in the sky."
   "Does he not know how."
   "Dream broken by the sound of a mallet."
   "Evening mists in the depths of my heart."
   "Every day, throwing my heart down into the valley."
   "Faintly as a fisherman's bonfire way in the offing."
   "First day starts, and 'All's changed.', The"
   "For a moment we lay in the village of Fushimi."
   "Forgetting, I grieve this evening."
   "Frost that will not fall from the grebe's wings."
   "How could I possibly have lived until today."
   "I look far to the end of the haze."
   " 'I'm much in love, but look at me.' "
   "In spring too, what first stands out is Mount Otowa."
   "In the cold winds, leaves are cleared from the trees."
   "In the garden where no one comes."
   "I've grown used to the pine door unclosed."
   "Layers of eightfold kerria roses in such a glow."
   "Leaves of bamboo near my window stirring with the wind."
   "Moonlight is and is not, as of old, The."
   "Night deepens, the sound of water trickling, The."
   "No one to lose his way among the heaped up leaves."
   "Not even for a moment have we joined."
   "Not knowing the dream without beginning has been a dream."
   "October: as a storm sweeps down Mount Mimuro."
   "On the evening when, alone, I leave my village."
   "Only intermittent beads of water."
   "Opening on plum twigs in the unfaded snow."
   "Oppressing all, sunken in autumn sorrows."
   "Over the shingled roof the shower has passed."
   "Passing the cedar grove at Osaka Barrier."
   "Piercing to the marrow: beyond a garden fire."
   "Rim of a foot-wearying mountain hazy at dawn, The."
   "Shallow of me: I have grieved over this uncertain life."
   "Short night, A—outside the window bamboo rustles."
   "Since a wind over the rushes told me that autumn came."
   "Sleeping, wanting to have the past that does not return."
   "String of beads, if you must break, break."
   "Summer nights—little time to see the crescent moon decline."
   "Things I have seen, the future I have yet to see."
   "Though the shining sun is clearly of the summer sky."
   "Through the autumn night, quiet and dark."
   "Tumultuous winter sky all day."
   "Uji River boat piled with brushwood, An."
   "Voices of insects and a stag by the fence, The."
   "Waiting for you, I have not entered my bedroom."
   "Watching, I have grown lonely."
   "Water fragrant in my hands, I traced it upstream."
   "When I look around in the quiet before dawn."
   "Which peak do these blossoms come from?"

"Wild geese leave no trace in the citadel of water, The."
"Wind of heaven, the maidens cross the ice."
"Winter night, A: the moon, clear beyond a leafless tree."
"With plum blossoms from the fence visiting my sleeves."
"With spring manifest on moss-grown."
"Without a trace it has cleared on this side of the clouds."
"Would there were other means of consolation."
"Yet to be reconciled with the reality of the dark."
Seventy Feet Down. Philip Larkin. *Fr.* Livings. RB
Seventy-five feet hoed rows equals. Gary Snyder. *Fr.* Mountains and
    Rivers without End: The Market. NaP
Seventy-seven long years. Isan, *tr.* by Lucien Stryk *and* Takashi Ikemoto.
    ZPCJ
Seventy-six. Bryant. PAH
Seventy-six Hokku, *sels.* Basho, *tr. fr. Japanese by* Burton Watson.
    FCEI
"Ah, spring, spring!"
"Alive, sea cucumbers frozen in one lump."
"An old pond: a frog jumps in."
"As if touching a boil a willow bends."
"At my house small mosquitoes."
"At night secretly a worm."
At Saya-between-the-Hills.
At Takadachi in Oshu.
"Autumn's deep, The—my neighbor."
"Azaleas arranged, and by them."
"Bright moon: strolling around the pond all night long."
By the Roadside in My Birthplace.
"Chrysanthemum didn't spill a dewdrop, The."
Cold Nights.
"Coming by a mountain path."
Composed While Ill.
Congratulations on a New House.
"Cruel: under a helmet, a cricket."
"Cuckoo fades away, A."
"Cuckoo's voice lays itself over the water, A."
"Daybreak: a white fish."
"Departing spring: birds cry."
"Dragonfly—unable to get hold of a grass blade."
"Enfeebled: I've bitten on the sand in seaweed."
"First shower—even a monkey."
"First snow: luckily I find myself residing in my own hut."
"Fishermen's faces were seen first."
"Fleas, lice—a horse pisses right by my pillow."
"Gathering the May rains."
"Hair grown and face pale."
"Having planted a plantain."
Hozo Pass.
"I pluck my gray hair."
"I usually hate crows."
"I'd like to be called a traveler."
"If taken in hand, autumn frost."
"I'll make a fire tonight."
"In a fisherman's hut crickets mingle."
"In a rape field sparrows."
In Hatchobori.
"In mists and rains, the day."
"In morning dew, dirty and cool."
"In my hut, square light cast."
"In the middle of a plain."
"In the old village, no house without a persimmon tree."
"Iris looks exactly like the one in the water, The."
"It's spring! nameless mountains."
Later, Spending Some Time at Bokusetsu's Hut in Otsu.
"Lightning: going in the dark side."
"Lightning in my hand."
"Mistaken for a blind man."
"Mogami River has poured the hot sun into the sea, The."
"Month's last day, no moon, The."
"Moon as your guide, The."
Mottoes.
Nijiko.
"On dead branches crows remain."
On the Twenty-first of the Seventh Month of the Seventh Year of
    Genroku, at Bokusetsu's Hut.
"Only butterflies fly in the field."
"Pea crab crawls up my leg, A."
"People's voices: returning by this road as autumn ends."
"Pines of Karasaki, The."
"Plum blossoms at their best."
"Quietness: piercing the rocks."

Rakushisha.
"Roadside marsh mallow, The."
"Salted breams' gums are cold."
"Scallions just washed white in this cold."
"Scudding cloud, A."
"Sea darkens, and the voices of ducks, The."
Sentiment on a Journey.
"Skull exposed in a field in my mind."
"Sound of paddles slapping the waves."
Staying at Horai Temple.
Staying Overnight at Akashi.
Stopping by Saigyo's Willow.
"Summer clothes: I have yet to pick all the lice."
"This road: no one taking it as autumn ends."
"This snowy morning, alone."
"This white chrysanthemum doesn't have a speck of dust."
"Through the long day the skylarks."
"White fish clustering in seaweed."
"Whiter than the stones on Stone Mountain."
"Winter day, A: frozen on horseback, a shadow."
"With a young leaf may I wipe."
"With the morning-glories I eat my meal."
Seventy-six years. Tokken, *tr.* by Lucien Stryk *and* Takashi Ikemoto.
    ZPCJ
Several minutes each day I manage. Dishonorable Seaman's Grave.
    Hans Lodeizen, *tr.* by James S. Holmes. DuIn
Several months after we lost our way. The Natives. David Mura.
    BrSi
Several Questions Answered, *sels.* Blake.
    Eternity ("He who binds [*or* bends] to himself a joy"). AWP; EBEV;
       FaBoEE; NOBE; NoP; OBNC; OxBSP; RB; TrGrPo
    "What is it men in women do require?" OAEL-2
    (Question Answered [*or* A Question Answered], The.) ErPo;
       FaBoEE; GBL; NoP
Several years ago. A New Story. Simon J. Ortiz. STE
Severance. Kit Robinson. IAT
Severance of Connections, 1946. L. E. Sissman. *Fr.* In and Out.
    TwCP
Severances. Aidan Carl Mathews. CIP
Severe Figures. Charles Simic. KS
Severed hand flutters, The. The Persistence of Memory, the Failure of
    Poetry. Robert Phillips. GeTw
Severed Head, A, *sel.* John Montague.
    Road's End, The. *Fr.* I. IPY
Severed Selves. Dante Gabriel Rossetti. *Fr.* The House of Life, XL.
    BoLoP
Severn, The. Michael Drayton. *Fr.* The Baron's War, Canto I.
    ChTr
Severn sweeping smooth and broad, The. At Arley. Andrew Young.
    FaBoPP
Sew a Pocket. Jessie Welborn Smith. PWR
Sewanee Hills of dear delight. The Hills of Sewanee. George Marion
    McClellan. BANP
Sex. Jean Valentine. FaBoWP
Sex. Charles Wright. PPR
Sex, as they harshly call it. Adrienne Rich. *Fr.* Two Songs, I. NIP;
    NOBA; TAP
Sex Films. Vivienne Joseph. ATNZ
Sex fingers toes. Dear John, Dear Coltrane. Michael S. Harper.
    AmPA; GeTw; NIP
Sex floated like a moon. A Circle, a Square, a Triangle and a Ripple of
    Water. Jane Cooper. TAP
Sex Play in Four Acts. Doug Fetherling. NeAC
Sex without Love. Sharon Olds. MAYP; NIP; TSL
Sexes waking, now separate and sore, The. The Martyrs. Jay
    Macpherson. MoCV
Sext. W. H. Auden. *Fr.* Horae Canonicae. SaC
Sexton is opening up the grave, The. The Third Light. Michael
    Longley. FaBCIP
Sextus the Usurer. Martial, *tr. fr. Latin by* Kirby Flower Smith. AWP
Sexual intercourse began. Annus Mirabilis. Philip Larkin. NBLV; NIP;
    NOBL; OBAL
Sexual Privacy of Women on Welfare. Pinkie Gordon Lane. BlSi
Sexy Food Stamps. Jeffrey Miller. UL
Seyes, The. Raymond Queneau, *tr. fr. French by* Teo Savory. RHTwFP
Seynt Stevyn and Herowdes. *Unknown. See* Seynt Stevene was a clerk.
S.F. Southward. Allen Ginsberg. *Fr.* Continuation of a Long Poem of
    These States. NAAL-2
Sgoran Dhu. Nan Shepherd. PoSH
Sgurr Nan Gillean. Sorley MacLean. *Fr.* The Cuillin. PoSH
Sh-Ta-Ra-Dah-Dey. *Unknown.* AS

Sha-ch'eng, "Sand City" ("In former years I passed this city."). Yang Shih-ch'i, *tr. fr. Chinese by* Jonathan Chaves. CoBLCP

Sha-ch'eng, "Sand City" ("Overlooking the water, a desolate city"). Yang Shih-ch'i, *tr. fr. Chinese by* Jonathan Chaves. CoBLCP

Shabtai Tsvi lived, in fact, by the grace of the Turkish Sultan. King Shabtai Tsvi. Uri Zvi Greenberg, *tr. by* Robert Friend. PeBMYV

Shack. Murray Edmond. ATNZ

Shack and a few trees, The. After Work. Gary Snyder. HoPM; NNaP

Shack Poem. Robert Bly. CAPP

Shacked Up at the Ritz. Doug Fetherling. NeAC

Shackley-Hay. *Unknown.* GBP

Shadbush. Christina Rainsford. GoYe

Shade. Theodosia Pickering Garrison. OHIP

Shade. Charles Lynch. CNA

Shade and Noon Sun. Muhammad al-Maghut. *See* All the fields of the world.

Shade of His hand shall cover us, The. His Hand Shall Cover Us. Isaac ben Samuel of Dampière, *tr. by* Nina Davis Salaman. TrJP

Shade once swept about your boughs, The. The Fallen Tree. Andrew Young. BoNaP

Shade-Seller, The. Josephine Jacobsen. TAP

Shade, the light, the figures, the horizon as, The. October 1942. Roy Fuller. WaP

Shaded lamp and a waving blind, A. An August Midnight. Thomas Hardy. BrPo; NOBVV

Shades of Callimachus, Coan ghosts of Philetas. Ezra Pound. *Fr.* Homage to Sextus Propertius. CMoP; HAP; MoAB; NOBA; OBVE; OxBA

Shades of eve are quickly closing in, The. Night. Josephine D. Henderson Heard. CBWP-4

Shades of Night, The. A. E. Housman. BXAP; ChTr; FaBoNo; FiBHP; NBLV

Shades of night were falling fast, The. Excelsior. Longfellow. FaPON; FaPoR; NAAL-1; OBCA; OnMSP; PrIm; WBLP

Shades of Origin. Sebastian Salazar Bondy, *tr. fr. Spanish by* David Tipton. Per

Shadow. Guillaume Apollinaire, *tr. fr. French by* Jessie Degen *and* Richard Eberhart. WaaP

Shadow. Richard Bruce. CDC

Shadow. Anthony Delius. PeSA

Shadow, The. Ben Jonson. *See* Follow a shadow, it still flies.

Shadow. Ann Mars. GoYe

Shadow. Sybren Polet, *tr. fr. Dutch by* James S. Holmes. DuIn

Shadow, The. Richard Henry Stoddard. AA

Shadow, A. *Unknown. See* I Heard a Noise and Wishèd for a Sight.

Shadow, The. Walter de la Mare. OnUR

Shadow and Shade. Allen Tate. LiTA; VGW; ViBoPo

Shadow and Substance. *Unknown. See* I Heard a Noise and Wishèd for a Sight.

Shadow and Sunrise. Henrietta Cordelia Ray. CBWP-3

Shadow and the Light, The, *sel.* Whittier.
"All souls that struggle and aspire." TrPWD

Shadow become real; follower become leader. Yellow Woman Speaks. Merle Woo. BrSi

Shadow-Bride. John R. R. Tolkien. SO

Shadow Dance, The. Louise Chandler Moulton. AA

Shadow Evidence. Mary Mapes Dodge. AA

Shadow falls, the path I cannot trace, The. Satisfied. Samuel Valentine Cole. BLRP

Shadow his father makes with joined hands, A. Alphabets. Seamus Heaney. NoAM

Shadow is floating through the moonlight, A. The Bird of Night. Randall Jarrell. RFM

Shadow, killer of doves. Shadow. Anthony Delius. PeSA

Shadow-Love. Heine, *tr. fr. German by* Emma Lazarus. *Fr.* Songs to Seraphine. TrJP

Shadow me in, dark me in, disappear me. Small Night-Music. Jacob Glatstein, *tr. by* Benjamin *and* Barbara Harshav. AYP

Shadow of a Branch, The. Edith Marcombe Shiffert. WPE

Shadow of a fat man in the moonlight, The. Things to Come. James Reeves. OxBSP

Shadow of a summer tightly folded, The. Girls in the Plural. Medbh McGuckian. DT

Shadow of Cain, The. Dame Edith Sitwell. OxBTC

Shadow of Darkness. Aquah Laluah. PBA

Shadow of her profile lay stringent, The. Woman, Gallup, N. M. Karen Swenson. NYBP

Shadow of Himself, The. William Renton. NOBVV

Shadow of Night, The. George Chapman. PoEL-2

Shadow of Night, The, *sels.* George Chapman.

Hymnus in Noctem. PoEL-2

Night. OBSC

Shadow of Night, The. Coventry Patmore. *See* How strange it is to wake.

Shadow of the dwarf magnolia, The. The Magnolia's Shadow. Robert Lowell. NaP

Shadow of the little fishing launch, The. The Parrot Fish. James Merrill. NOBA

Shadow of the Night, A. Thomas Bailey Aldrich. AA

Shadow of the Old City. Yehuda Amichai, *tr. fr. Hebrew by* Shirley Kaufman. VWA

Shadow of the Venetian blind on the painted wall, The. Forties Flick. John Ashbery. NoAM

Shadow on the Stone, The. Thomas Hardy. QFR

Shadow Play. Ralph Angel. BAP

Shadow Replies to Substance. T'ao Ch'ien, *tr. fr. Chinese by* Burton Watson. *Fr.* Substance, Shadow, and Spirit. CoBCP

Shadow River. Pauline Johnson. CaP

Shadow Rose, The. Robert Cameron Rogers. AA

Shadow Shadow. Roger Weingarten. NAmP

Shadow Show. Ruth Dallas. ATNZ

Shadow streamed into the wall, The. Shadow and Shade. Allen Tate. LiTA; VGW; ViBoPo

Shadow through the room, a rising, A. Lord Myth. Norman Dubie. NAmP

Shadowboxing. James Tate. ASP

Shadowed by your dear hair, your dear kind eyes. The Sanctuary. Ford Madox Ford. PoA

Shadowgraphs, The. Richmond Lattimore. NYBP

Shadowless Man, The. Gordon Challis. ATNZ

Shadows. Samuel Daniel. *See* Tethys' Festival: Are They Shadows [That We See]?

Shadows. Patricia Hubbell. TDD

Shadows. D. H. Lawrence. OxBTC

Shadows. Linda Pastan. BLA

Shadows. Victor Plarr. NOBVV

Shadows, The. Frank Dempster Sherman. AA

Shadows. *Unknown, tr. fr. Tewa Indian by* H. J. Spinden. WTO

Shadows. "Yehoash," *tr. fr. Yiddish by* Elias Lieberman. TrJP

Shadows among the Ettrick Hills. William Addison. PoSH

Shadows are descending, The. Outgoing Sabbath. *Unknown, tr. by* Joseph Leftwich. TrJP

Shadows are long on Soldier's Field. Second Half. David McCord. SD

Shadows blown from trees, The. Vain Advice at the Year's End. James Wright. NYBP

Shadows do everywhere for substance pass. The Church-Windows. *Unknown. Fr.* A Poem in Defence of the Decent Ornaments of Christ-Church, Oxon, Occasioned by a Banbury Brother, Who Called Them Idolatries. OBS

Shadows grazing eastwards melt. Last Meeting. Gwen Harwood. PoAu-2

Shadows in the Water. Thomas Traherne. HAP; LiTB; MePo; NoP; OAEL-1; OBS; PoEL-2; SeCP

Shadows lay along Broadway, The. Two Women. Nathaniel Parker Willis. BeLS

(Unseen Spirits.) AA; AnAmPo

Shadows, like Navahoes, wear velvet. Tourist Country. William Stafford. NoAM

Shadows of bamboo hats beyond thousands of dikes. First Rain: Sent to Magistrate Mo-ch'ing. Sung Hsiang, *tr. by* Irving Lo. WFTU

Shadows of bars suggest perhaps. The Parakeet. Keith Sinclair. ATNZ

Shadows of His Lady. Jacques Tahureau, *tr. fr. French by* Andrew Lang. AWP

Shadows of Jaikur. Badr Shakir al-Sayyab, *tr. fr. Arabic by* Abdullah al-Udhari. MPAW

Shadows of late afternoon and the odors, The. Old Dominion. Robert Hass. MAYP

Shadows of night were a-comin' down swift, The. Higher. *Unknown.* FiBHP

Shadows; pillows; the garden sloping down. Refusal. Lucie Delarue-Mardrus, *tr. by* Barbara Johnson. DMF

Shadows, shadows,/ Hug me round. Escape. Georgia Douglas Johnson. PoBA

Shadows stand. At Sixty. Sándor Weöres, *tr. by* Jascha Kessler. FOC

Shadows steal/ past the window. Evening. Rose Ausländer, *tr. by* Beth Bjorklund. CoAuP

Shadows where the Mewlips dwell, The. The Mewlips. John R. R. Tolkien. AmMo; SO; WSC

Shadowy daughter of Urthona stood before red Orc, The. America a Prophecy. Blake. OAEL-2

Shadrach/ Shake the bed. *Unknown.* FaBoNo

Shadrach, Meshach, Abednego. Warm Babies. Keith Preston. FiBHP
Shadwell Stair. Wilfred Owen. FaBoTw
Shady, Shady. T'ao Ch'ien, *tr. fr. Chinese by* Arthur Waley. AWP
Shady Woods. E. M. Adams. BoTP
Shaemus. Conrad Aiken. OxBA
Shaft, The. Charles Tomlinson. DiPo
Shaftesbury. Dryden. *See* Absalom and Achitophel, Pt. I
Shag, The. Ellen Duggan. PeNZ
Shag Rock. Ruth France. PeNZ
Shaka, King of the Zulus ("He is Shaka the unshakable."), *sel. Unknown,
     tr. fr. Zulu by* A. C. Jordan. PBA; TTY
"Young viper grows as it sits, The." *Tr. by* T. Cope. WTO
Shake Hands with Your Bets, Friend. Lorenzo Thomas. UL
Shake, Mulleary, and Go-ethe. H. C. Bunner. FiBHP
Shake off your heavy trance! Francis Beaumont. *Fr.* The Masque of the
     Inner Temple and Gray's Inne, I. OBS; TrGrPo
     (Fit Only for Apollo.) ChTr
     (Song for a Dance.) EIL; FaBoCh
Shaken already, I know. Goodbye, Sally. James Simmons. BIrV
Shake'nbake Ballad. Peter Van Toorn. NOBC
Shakespeare. Matthew Arnold. FiP; HeIP; InvP; NoP; OBEV; Son;
     TrGrPo
Shakespeare. Henry Ames Blood. AA
Shakespeare. Longfellow. AWP
Shakespeare. Henrietta Cordelia Ray. CBWP-3
Shakespeare. Swinburne. TrGrPo
Shakespeare; an Epistle to David Garrick, Esq, *sel.* Robert Lloyd.
     True Genius. NOEC
Shakespeare and Milton—what third blazoned name. Tennyson. Thomas
     Bailey Aldrich. AA
Shakespeare Dead. Hugh Holland. ACP
Shakespeare Milton Keats are dead. Song of Allegiance. R. A. K.
     Mason. ATNZ
Shakespeare stand-ins, same string hair, gay, dirty. Ulysses. Robert
     Lowell. NAAL-2
Shakespeare: The Fairies' Advocate. Thomas Hood. *Fr.* The Plea of the
     Midsummer Fairies. OBNC
Shakespeare, whose heartfelt scenes shall ever give. To Shakespeare.
     Thomas Edwards. Son
Shakespearean Bear, The. Arthur Guiterman. CenHV
Shakespearean fish swam the sea, far away from land. Three Movements.
     W. B. Yeats. CMoP; FaBoEE
"Shakin like the." On a Country Road. Harley Elliot. NeAC
Shako, The. Robert Lowell. Son
Shakuhachi. Jim Mitsui. BrSi
Shalamouses. Moyshe-Leyb Halpern, *tr. fr. Yiddish by* Benjamin *and*
     Barbara Harshav. AYP
Shale. Anne Stevenson. BLA
Shall a Frown or Angry Eye. *Unknown.* EIL
Shall ancient worth, or ancient fame. True Genius. Robert Lloyd. *Fr.*
     Shakespeare; an Epistle to David Garrick, Esq. NOEC
Shall Dumpish Melancholy spoil my Joys. On Christmas-Day. Thomas
     Traherne. OBS; PoEL-2
Shall Earth No More Inspire Thee? Emily Brontë. ELP
Shall hearts that beat no base retreat. The Enthusiast. Herman Melville.
     NAAL-1
Shall hog with holy child converse? Hog at the Manger. Norma Farber.
     PChr
Shall I abide this jesting? *Unknown.* GBL
Shall I be false to friends. *Unknown. Fr.* Manyo Shu. Ma
Shall I begin at the beginning. Yiddish. Abraham Sutskever, *tr. by*
     Seymour Levitan. VWA.
Shall I begin by saying. Lafayette to Washington. Maxwell Anderson.
     Fr. Valley Forge. OPP
Shall I charge like a bull. Auvaiyar, *tr. by* A. K. Ramanujan. WPOW
Shall I come, if I swim? wide are the waves, you see. Thomas Campion.
     EnLoPo
Shall I Come, Sweet Love, to Thee? Thomas Campion. AAS; EBEV;
     EIL; GB2; HAP; OBSC; OxBoLi; PoEL-2
     (Lover's Plea, A.) NOBE
Shall I come there, or you here? Hafsa bint al-Hajj, *tr. fr. Arabic by*
     Michael Scott. WPOW
Shall I compare her to a summer play? Sonnet on Famous and Familiar
     Sonnets and Experiences. Delmore Schwartz. Son
Shall I Compare Thee to a Summer's Day? Howard Moss. InPK
Shall I compare thee to a summer's day? Shakespeare. *Fr.* Sonnets,
     XVIII. BoLoP; CTC; EIL; EnLoPo; FaBoBe; FaBV; FaFP; FiP; FPL;
     GBL; HAP; HeIP; InPK; InPS; InvP; LiTB; MAT; NIP; NOBE; NoP;
     OAEL-1; OBEV; OBSC; PoE; PoEL-2; PoLF; PoRA; PrIm; SCV;
     SeCePo; Son; TEP; TrGrPo; WeW
     (To His Love.) GTBS; GTBS-P

Shall I complain or not? Or shall I mask. Ovid, *tr. fr. Latin by* Henry
     Vaughan. *Fr.* De Ponto, Elegy IV, 3a. OBVE
Shall I connect for this world's eyes. The Dumb World. W. H. Davies.
     OxBTC
Shall I Do This. Swami Purohit. OBMV
Shall I embrace my disease. Monologue of a Dying Beast. Mark
     Ameen. GLP
Shall I equate thee with a summer's day? New Improved Sonnet XVIII.
     Peter Titheradge. FaBoPa
Shall I ever see it, the Queen's River. Fly fisherman in Wartime.
     Leonard Bacon. FYAP
Shall I expound "whore" to you? sure, I shall. An Execration against
     Whores. John Webster. *Fr.* The White Devil, III, ii. TW
Shall I get drunk or cut myself a piece of cake. Cairo Jag. Keith
     Douglas. NePoEA
Shall I have to spend the. Casablanca Time Again. Joy Howard. DT
Shall I, I wonder, ever find. Peace. Irwin Edman. TrJP
Shall I love God for causing me to be? The Proof. Richard Wilbur.
     CRP; EaLo; OxBSP
Shall I receive the spring rain dripping on swallow wings. Yosano Akiko,
     tr. fr. Japanese by Hiroaki Sato. *Fr.* Thirty-nine Tanka. FCEI
Shall I Repine. Swift. *See* If neither brass nor marble can withstand.
Shall I retire now. Nagachika, *tr. by* Steven D. Carter. WFTW
Shall I say how it is in your clothes? How It Is. Maxine W. Kumin.
     CAPP; NoAM
Shall I say that I love you. Of Disdainful Daphne. M. H. Nowell. EIL
Shall I sonnet-sing you about myself? House. Robert Browning.
     NAEL-2
Shall I strew on thee rose or rue or laurel. Ave atque Vale. Swinburne.
     NAEL-2; NOBE; OAEL-2; OBEV; OBNC
Shall I tell you the signs of a New Age coming? The New Age. Stevie
     Smith. NAEL-2
Shall I tell you who [*or* what] will come. Words from an Old Spanish
     Carol. *Unknown, tr. by* Ruth Sawyer. PChr
     (Christmas Morn.) OBCP
     (On Christmas Morn.) FaPON; PDV
Shall I Tell You Whom I Love? William Browne. *Fr.* Britannia's
     Pastorals, II, Song 2. EIL
Shall I then hope when faith is fled? Thomas Campion. AAS
Shall I then praise the heavens, the trees, the earth. Anne Bradstreet.
     Fr. Contemplations. PBWP
Shall I thus ever long, and be no whit the near? The Lady Prayeth the
     Return of Her Lover Abiding on the Seas. *Unknown.* EIL; GBL
     (Seafarer, The.) OBSC
     (To Her Sea-faring Lover.) OBEV
Shall I Wasting in Despair. George Wither. *Fr.* Fair Virtue, the Mistress
     of Philarete. EIL; LiTB; OBS
     (Author's Resolution, The.) AWP; OBEV
     (Lover's Resolution, A.) BoLoP; NOBE
     (Manly Heart, The.) FaBV; GTBS; GTBS-P
     (Sonnet: "Shall I, wasting in despair.") SeCV-1
     (What Care I.) TrGrPo
Shall Man, O God of Light. Timothy Dwight. AH
Shall one be sorrowful because of love. De Amore. Ernest Dowson.
     OBNC
Shall pride a heap of sculptur'd marble raise. Epitaph on Laurence Sterne.
     David Garrick. FaBoEE
Shall royal praise be rhym'd by such a ribald. On the Candidates for the
     Laurel. Pope. FaBoEE
Shall the Dead Praise Thee? George Macdonald. TrCP
Shall the water not remember Ember. Narcissus and Echo. Fred
     Chappell. MT
Shall we go along the hay? The hay? A Report Song [in a Dream].
     Nicholas Breton. GBL; OBSC; SeCePo
     (Country Song.) TrGrPo
     (Wooing in a Dream.) NOBE
Shall we go there, too? Whatever for? Another half-Gothic. Boccherini's
     Tomb. István Vas, *tr. by* William Jay Smith. MHuP
Shall we have a family born. For Walter Lowenfels. Wendy Rose.
     CDW
Shall we make love. *Unknown. Fr.* Manyo Shu. AWP
Shall we meet no more, my love, at the binding of the sheaves. Adonais.
     William Wallace Harney. AA
Shall we not open the human heart. Give Way! Charlotte Perkins
     Gilman. WGRP
Shall we send back the Johnnies their bunting. Those Rebel Flags. John
     H. Jewett. PAH
Shall we sit here some more. August at the Lake. David Young.
     AmPA
Shall we win at love or shall we lose. Hôtel Transylvanie. Frank
     O'Hara. NeAP; PoM

Shall you complain who feed the world? To Labor. Charlotte Perkins Gilman. PoLF

Shallow is the mountain well-pool. *Unknown*. *Fr.* Manyo Shu. Ma

Shallow of me: I have grieved over this uncertain life. Princess Shikishi, *tr. fr. Japanese by* Hiroaki Sato. *Fr.* Seventy-eight Tanka. FCEI

Shallow our union. Narihira, *tr. by* Geoffrey Bownas *and* Anthony Thwaite. PeBJV

Shallow river of tears, A. Narihira, *tr. fr. Japanese by* Burton Watson. *Fr.* Kokin Shu. FCEI

Shallow water, soft sand. Autumn Day Stroll in the Country. Kokan Shiren, *tr. by* Burton Watson. JLIC-2

Shallows, brighter, The. The Pier: Under Pisces. James Merrill. NoAM

Shalom Aleichem. *Unknown, tr. fr. Hebrew.* TrJP

Shaman. María Sabina, *tr. fr. Spanish by* Henry Munn. WPOW

Shaman Breaks. Gerald Vizenor. NOVW

Shaman Song. Luswat, *tr. fr. Tlingit Indian by* James Koller. STP

Shaman//Bear. Anita Endrezze-Danielson. NOVW

Shamans scurrying everywhere propagate ghostly teachings. Expelling Witches. Chiang Shih-ch'üan, *tr. by* Coy Harmon. WFTU

Shamash of the glade, The. The Venerable Bee. A. M. Klein. TrJP

Shame. Richard Wilbur. FaBoMo; OxBC

Shame checks our first attempts, but then 'tis proved. Sins Loathed, and Yet Loved. Robert Herrick. LiTB

"Shame it is," I say and sigh. Prince Toneri. *Fr.* Manyo Shu. Ma

Shame to all my thoughts now. On the Flightiness of Thought. *Unknown, tr. by* Brendan Kennelly. TIRV

Shamed have I been. Asadullah Khan Ghalib, *tr. by* Ahmed Ali. GoT

Shameful Death. William Morris. ChTr; GTBS-P

Shameful Impotence. Ovid. *See* Amores: Either she was foule, or her attire was bad.

Shameless thing, for ilka vileness able, A. The Octopus. "Hugh MacDiarmid." TW

Shampoo, The. Elizabeth Bishop. FaBoWP; OxBC

Shamrock, The. Maurice Francis Egan. AA

Shan Van Vocht, The. *Unknown*. AnIL; FaBoPV; GBP; NOIV; OxBoLi

Shancoduff. Patrick Kavanagh. BIrV; CIP; FaBCIP; FaBoTw; IPY; NoP

Shane O'Neill's Cairn. Robinson Jeffers. NoAM; NOBA

Shang ya! Oath of Friendship. Li Po, *tr. by* Arthur Waley. TTTS

Shango ("Shango is an animal like the gorilla"). *Unknown, tr. fr. Yoruba by* Gbadamosi *and* Ulli Beier. PBA, *st.* 1; TTY, *st.* 1

Shango ("Shango is the death who kills money with a big stick"). *Unknown, tr. fr. Yoruba by* Gbadamosi *and* Ulli Beier. TTY

Shankill. Eileen Shanahan. NeIP

Shannon and the *Chesapeake*, The. Thomas Tracy Bouvé. PAH

Shannon Estuary Welcoming the Fish, The. Nuala Ni Dhomhnaill, *tr. fr. Irish by* the author. CIP

Shantih shantih shantih. Edward Pygge. BXAP

Shanty Boys and the Pine, The. *Unknown*. AmFP

Shantyman's Life, A. *Unknown*. AmFP; AS, *with music*

Shao and the South, *sels*. Confucius, *tr. fr. Chinese by* Ezra Pound. CTC

"Chkk! chkk!" hopper-grass.

"Three stars, five stars rise over the hill."

Shapcot! To thee the Fairy State. Oberon's Feast. Robert Herrick. CaPo; SeCV-1; TrGrPo

Shape, like folded light, embodied air, A. Aishah Schechinah. Robert Stephen Hawker. OBNC

Shape of a Roethke, The? Theodore Roethke Foots It. D. C. Barry. BXAP

Shape of Autumn, The. Virginia Russ. GoYe

Shape of Death, The. May Swenson. TAP

Shape of the Fire, The. Theodore Roethke. CMoP; LCAP; LiTA; MoAB

Shape of the Heart, The. Louise Townsend Nicholl. ImOP

Shape-Shifter. Michael Jackson. ATNZ

Shape the lips to an *o*, say *a*. Ö. Rita Dove. HCAP; MAYP

Shaped and vacated. The Event. T. Sturge Moore. OBMV

Shaped new to your measure. Ark Articulate. Jay Macpherson. *Fr.* The Ark. NOBC

Shapelessness, The. Agnes Nemes Nagy, *tr. fr. Hungarian by* Alan Dixon. MHuP

Shapes of Death, The. Stephen Spender. OBMV

Shapes of swallows. Emperor Kogon, *tr. by* Steven D. Carter. WFTW

Shapes that frowned before the eyes, The. The Eclipse of Faith. Theodore Dwight Woolsey. AA

Shapes, Vanishings. Henry Taylor. MAYP

Shards. Perets Markish, *tr. fr. Yiddish by* Leonard Wolf. PeBMYV

Share-Croppers. Langston Hughes. SaC

Shared Sentences. Alan Davies. IAT; LP

Sharing Eve's Apple. Keats. ChER; ErPo; NBLV

Sharing Lodging with Hsieh Shih-hou. Mei Yao-ch'en, *tr. fr. Chinese by* Burton Watson. CoBCP

Shark, The. J. J. Bell. RHPC

Shark, The. Lord Alfred Bruce Douglas. RHPC

Shark, The. E. J. Pratt. NOBC

Sharks. Kaneko Mitsuharu, *tr. fr. Japanese by* Hiroaki Sato. FCEI

Sharks, The. Denise Levertov. NeAP

Sharks. Dick Lourie. NeAC

Sharks at the New York Aquarium. Charles Martin. SM

Sharks, Caloosahatchee River. Greg Pape. MAYP

Sharks in Shallow Water. Fred Levinson. AmPA

Shark's Parlor, The. James Dickey. MT; NYBP

Sharks tooth is perfect for biting, The. Canticle. Michael McClure. NeAP; PoM

Sharon Will Be No/Where on Nobody's Best-selling List. Sharon Scott. JB

Sharp air folds like giftwrap. Thirst of the Dragon. Dianne Hai-Jew. BrSi

Sharp Hour. Judah Leib Teller, *tr. fr. Yiddish by* Benjamin *and* Barbara Harshav. AYP

Sharp is the night, but stars with frost alive. Winter Heavens. George Meredith. NoP

Sharp Ridge, The. Robert Graves. FaBoEE

Sharp-Shin. David Wagoner. BLA

Sharp was the frost, the wind was high. Sly Dick. Thomas Chatterton. FL

Sharpbreasted Snake, The. Louis Oliver. STE

Sharpeville Inquiry. Anne Welsh. PeSA

Sharpie in a leisure suit, A. The Lease Hound. Wallace McRae. CowP

Sharpshooters. Wu T'e-Liang, *tr. fr. Chinese by* Dominic Cheung. IFON

Shash, The. *Unknown*. APAS

"Shatnes" or Uncleanliness. Eliezer Steinbarg, *tr. fr. Yiddish by* Seth L. Wolitz. VWA

Shatterday nite aucung lau town. My Deery Honey. *Unknown*. PBCV

Shattered water made a misty din, The. Once by the Pacific. Robert Frost. CMoP; HAP; HeIP; LiTA; LiTM; MoAB; MoAmPo; MOS; NAAL-2; NOBA; PrIm; Son; VGW; WeW

Shattering of Love, The. *Gond Oral Tradition, tr. by* V. Elwin *and* S. Hivale. WTO

Shavings, fall from the carved stick. Working Song. Buluguru, *tr. by* E. A. Worms. CBAP

Shawls, The. Monk Gibbon. NeIP

She. Zinaida Nikolayevna Gippius, *tr. fr. Russian by* Dianne Levitin. WPOW

She/ pulls the sheet of this dance. Jim Harrison. *Fr.* Returning to Earth. PPR

She/ not to be confused with she, a dog. Lady Tactics. Anne Waldman. PoM

She/ holds th mirror to her eye. My Lai/ Remuera/ Ponsonby. David Mitchell. PeNZ

She. Theodore Roethke. BoLoP; ErPo; NIP

She. Sista Roots. WS

She. Mark Strand. AnAn

She. Richard Wilbur. AmPP; NIP

She. Manfred Winkler, *tr. fr. Hebrew by* Mary Zilzer. VWA

She. A flower perhaps, a pool of fresh water. She (Marina Distant). Lucha Corpi, *tr. fr. Spanish by the author and* Catherine Rodríguez-Nieto. *Fr.* The Marina Poems, IV. CCP; OV

She acquired an eye. My Mother's Breakfront. Janet Sternburg. TV

She always leaned to watch for us. The Watcher. Margaret Widdemer. OHIP

She and I. Norman Cameron. OxBSP; RB

She appeared before me that night: the vanquished one. The Ancient Law. André Spire, *tr. by* Stanley Burnshaw. VWA

She, as a veil down to the slender waist. Milton. *Fr.* Paradise Lost, *Bk.* IV, *ll.* 304–311. ErPo

(Before the Fall). *NIP, fr. ll.* 304–355.

She asked brown eyes, "Burn me loose." Seal at Stinson Beach. Roberta Hill. VoR

She asked me twice. Pity. William Mills. MT

She Attempts to Refute the Praises That Truth, Which She Calls Passion, Inscribed on a Portrait of the Poet. Sister Juana Inés de la Cruz, *tr. fr. Spanish*. BoWoP

She bade me follow to her garden, where. Snap-Dragon. D. H. Lawrence. ErPo

She beat the happy pavement. Gratiana Dancing. Richard Lovelace. OBEV

She Being Brand. E. E. Cummings. ErPo; MoP; NOBA; OxBA

She Bewitched Me. Thomas Burbidge. EnLoPo

She beyond all others in deepest dreams comes. A Little Song. Charles O. Hartman. SM

She bites into the red skin. My Love Eats an Apple. Ralph Gustafson. MoCV

She bounded o'er the graves. Anna Playing in a Graveyard. Caroline Gilman. OBCA

She brings that breath, and music too. The Visitor. W. H. Davies. GBL; OBWVE

She brought a drinking-cup to him. Two. Hugo von Hofmannsthal, tr. by Jethro Bithell. TrJP.

She brought us a month noisy with rain. Full Moon in Malta. Asphodel. BrRo

She Called Him Mr. *Unknown.* FaPON

She called me the man of sands. The Gist of the Story. Salah Abd al-Sabur, tr. by Lena Jayyusi and John Heath-Stubbs. MAP

She calved in the ravine, beside. November Calf. Jane Kenyon. InPS

She came among the gathering crowd. Common Sense. Thomas Field. AA

She came among us from the south. Enrica, 1865. Christina Rossetti. TEP

She came and stood in the Old South Church. In the "Old South." Whittier. AA

She Came and Went. James Russell Lowell. AA; AnAmPo

She came and went as comes and goes. Under the Red Cross. Chauncey Hickox. AA

She Came, at First, Pure. Juan Ramón Jiménez, tr. fr. *Spanish* by Perry Higman. LPSS

She came every morning to draw water. A Drink of Water. Seamus Heaney. FaBCIP; OxBC

She came from distant Shiragi. Lady Otomo no Sakanoe. *Fr.* Manyo Shu. Ma

"She came home, my Lord, and smashed-in the television." Wife Who Smashed Television Gets Jail. Paul Durcan. CIP

She came home, smelling of another man. Kiss ("She came home, smelling of another man"). Tanikawa Shuntaro, tr. by Hiroaki Sato. FCEI

She came in from the snowing air. Ice. Stephen Spender. FaBoMo; GTBS-P; SeCePo

She came in reluctant. The dark shed. Teaching a Dumb Calf. Ted Hughes. AnAn

She came out of the field—low. Rover. William Stafford. TDD

She came through the room like an answer in long division. A Victorian Idyll. David Wagoner. NoAM

She came to him in dreams—her ears. Cowper's Tame Hare. Norman Nicholson. RB

She came to the village church. Tennyson. *Fr.* Maud, *Pt.* I, viii. EBVV; NAEL-2

She came walking. Parable. Bob Orr. PeNZ

She cannot read or write. Um Hakeem. Salah Niyazi, tr. by Lena Jayyusi and Charles Doria. MAP

She carefully regards her software. The amber. Nude Reclining at Word Processor, in Pastel. Carl Conover. GOYP

She carries it unsteadily, warily. A Young Girl with a Pitcher Full of Water. David Wagoner. NoAM

She clasps a jewel. Words. David Phillips. NeAC

She clasps the cup with both her hands. In a Café. Rosemary Dobson. CBAP

She cleaned house, and then lay down long. A Secret Gratitude. James Wright. NoAM

She climbs from the sea; moonlight. The Fish. Mary Oliver. CAPP

She coaxes her fat in front of her. New Day. Naomi Long Madgett. BlSi

She comes level with him at. Donahue's Sister. Thom Gunn. NoAM

She comes like the hush and beauty of the night. Poetry. Edwin Markham. AA

She Comes Majestic with Her Swelling Sails. Robert Southey. MOS

She Comes Not When Noon Is on the Roses. Herbert Trench. OBEV

She comes on drenched in a perfume called Self Satisfaction. Mae West. Edward Field. FYAP

She comes!—the spirit of the dance! Celeste Dancing. Frances Sargent Osgood. AnAmPo (Dancing Girl, A.) AA

She could die laughing. Minnie and Mrs. Hoyne. Kenneth Fearing. PoRA

She could not have made it. Madame Orchidée. Sherod Santos. AnAn

She could not remember anything about the voyage. The Migrant. A. L. Hendricks. PBCV

She coulda been somethin. Ho. Al Young. NPGG

She danced, near nude, to tom-tom beat. Zalka Peetruza. Ray Garfield Dandridge. BANP; PoBA

She dances,/ And I seem to be. Perdita. Florence Earle Coates. AA

She dealt her pretty words like blades. Emily Dickinson. HAP

"She did not climb the April hill." The April Hill. Janet Lewis. CRP

She did not love to love, but hated him. The End of It. Francis Thompson. NOBVV; OxBSP

She Didn't Even Wave. Ai. MAYP

She didn't know she was beautiful. On Getting a Natural. Dudley Randall. FB; PoBA

She died after the beautiful snow had melted. In Memorial. J. Gordon Coogler. OBAL

She died in the upstairs bedroom. Death in Leamington. Sir John Betjeman. NoP; RB

She died,—this was the way she died. Vanished. Emily Dickinson. AA

She died turning aside from the sink. Another Death. D. E. Borrell. FF

She does not know. No Images. Waring Cuney. AmNP; BANP; CDC; MAT; NIP; TTY

She Does Not Remember. Anna Swirszczynska, tr. fr. *Polish* by Czeslaw Milosz. PwPP

She does not talk. Floor: Five. Stephen Vincent. *Fr.* Elevator Landscapes. NeAC

She doesn't say a word, concentrating on one thing only. Balgu Song. *Unknown,* tr. by Clancy McKenna. CBAP

She doesn't want. Pumping Iron. Diane Ackerman. ASP

She dreamed along the beaches of this coast. Palo Alto; the Marshes. Robert Hass. NPGG

She dreamed they lived in Africa. Long History of the Short Poem. Paul Hoover. UL

She dreams her girl lover steals toward her. Dream. Stephen Dobyns. MAYP

She dreams of Love upon the temple stair. A Sleeping Priestess of Aphrodite. Robert Cameron Rogers. AA

She dressed his words in. Nuclear Unit. Valerie Sinason. DT

She drew back; he was calm. The Subverted Flower. Robert Frost. CMoP; HAP; MoP; NoAM; NOBA; OxBA; PoE; WeW

She dried her tears, and they did smile. Emily Brontë. NOBVV

She drove a green and black Mack. Matching Green Ribbon. Jim Hofer. CowP

She dwells, pale midnight sun, beyond the river. Une Idole du Nord. Francis Stuart. NeIP

She Dwelt among the Untrodden Ways. J. C. Squire. BXAP

She Dwelt among the Untrodden Ways. Wordsworth. *Fr.* Lucy. AWP; BLPA; BoLoP; ELP; EnLoPo; EnRP; FaBV; FF; FPL; HAP; HeIP; LiTB; NIP; NoP; OxBSP; PPP; PrIm; PWR; TEP; UnPo; WeW (Lost Love, The.) GTBS; GTBS-P

She Employed the Familiar "Tu" Form. Doug Fetherling. NeAC

She even thinks that up in heaven. For a Lady I Know. Countee Cullen. *Fr.* Four Epitaphs. AmNP; CDC; PoBA

She examines her hand, fingers spread wide. My Daughter Considers Her Body. Floyd Skloot. SM

She fears him, and will always ask. Eros Turannos. E. A. Robinson. CMoP; GBL; HAP; HeIP; LiTA; LiTM; MoAB; MoAmPo; MoP; NAAL-2; NoAM; NOBA; NoP; OxBA; PoA; PoE; QFR; TAP

She feels her presence as never. The Lost Carnival. Fred Chappell. GOYP

She fell asleep on Christmas Eve. My Sister's Sleep. Dante Gabriel Rossetti. NAEL-2

She fell away in her first ages spring. Spenser. *Fr.* Daphnaïda. OBEV

She felt, I think, but as a wild-flower can. An Irish Wild-flower. Sarah Morgan Bryan Piatt. AA

She finds grief, her meat. Hyena. Carol Muske. AmPA

She fled in anguish; he pursued desire. First Love. Charles Gullans. NePoEA

She floats/ in a white shell. Riddle of Night. Jiri Mordecai Langer, tr. by Gabriel Preil *and* Howard Schwartz. VWA

She flourished in the 'Twenties, "hectic" days of peace. Mews Flat Mona. William Plomer. FaBoTw

She fluted with her mouth as when one sips. Beauty and the Bird. Dante Gabriel Rossetti. FM

She Found Me Roots. R. W. Ransford. BXAP

She-Fox, The. Claire Goll, tr. fr. *French* by Mary Ann Caws. DMF

She frowned and called him Mr. She Called Him Mr. *Unknown.* FaPON

She gamboll'd on the greens. Olivia. Tennyson. *Fr.* The Talking Oak. GN

She gave it out as if it were. The Aphrodisiac. Medbh McGuckian. FaBCIP

She gets up. Her husband never wakes. A Night without Light. István Vas, tr. by Jascha Kessler. FOC

She goes but softly, but she goeth sure. Upon the [or a] Snail. Bunyan. ChTr; OxBSP

She goes out in the night again. The Wastrel-Woman Poem. Brenda Marie Osbey. ER; MT

She goes to the sun-bright palace. Sukunamaro. *Fr. Manyo Shu.* Ma

She goes with her pot for water. Who Can Tell? *Gond Oral Tradition, tr. by* V. Elwin *and* S. Hivale. WTO

She grew ninety years through sombre winter. Epitaph on a Fir-Tree. Richard Murphy. FaBoTw

She grew up in bedeviled southern wilderness. The Ballad of Sue Ellen Westerfield. Robert Hayden. AmPP; NoAM

She had a little time to think. Leda Reconsidered. Mona Van Duyn. NMM

She had a name among the children. A Cat. Edward Thomas. BrPo (She Had a Name.) OxBSP

She had corn flowers in her ear. Gipsy Jane. William Brighty Rands. BoTP; FaPON

She had looked for his coming as warriors come. Love's Coming. Ella Wheeler Wilcox. AnAmPo

She had no business doin' it, but she come o' the East. The Peeler's Lament. *Unknown.* WTO

She had not even known she was pregnant. Woman Has a Baby in Her Sleep. Jack Driscoll. SoTCo

She had not held her secret long enough. The Visitation. Elizabeth Jennings. MoBS

She Had Some Horses. Joy Harjo. ER; HATNAP; STE

She had thought the studio would keep itself. Living in Sin. Adrienne Rich. FF; IHMS; NePoEA; NoP; NYBP; SoSe; TAP; UnPo

She has been bleeding. Wounds. Judith Minty. GeTw

She has been condemned to death by hanging. Marrying the Hangman. Margaret Atwood. NOBC

She has begun to see men invite themselves. The Professional. David Ignatow. NNaP

She has calld to her her bower-maidens. Young Hunting. *Unknown.* ESPB

She has come next door to practice our piano. "The Wife Takes a Child." Ellen Bryant Voigt. SM

She has come, the stranger. The Second Wife. Mririda n'Ait Attik, *tr. by* René Euloge *into English vers. by* Daniel Halpern *and* Paula Paley. OV

She has decided that she no longer loves me. The Wind in the Tree. F. T. Prince. OxBSP

She has finished and sealed the letter. Parting, without a Sequel. John Crowe Ransom. MoAB; MoAmPo; OxBA; SoSe

She has gone,—she has left us in passion and pride. Brother Jonathan's Lament for Sister Caroline. Oliver Wendell Holmes. PAH

"She has gone to be with the angels." The Vision of the Snow. Margaret Junkin Preston. AA

She has gone to the bottom! the wrath of the tide. The *Alabama.* Maurice Bell. PAH

She has just reached sixteen, the age for marriage. Song of Ho Man-tzu. Ho Ning, *tr. by* Lois Fusek. ATF

She has kissed lips already grown inhuman. Cleopatra. "Anna Akhmatova," *tr. by* D. M. Thomas. AIW

She has laughed as softly as if she sighed. A Woman's Shortcomings. Elizabeth Barrett Browning. BLPA

She has left me, my pretty. Sylvia Townsend Warner. MoAB; MoBrPo

She has not found herself a hard pillow. To Clarissa Scott Delany. Angelina Weld Grimké. AmNP

She has taken a woman lover. Carol, in the Park, Chewing on Straws. Judy Grahn. *Fr.* The Common Woman, IV. PeHV; WPOW

She has that quality of innocence. Virgin Country. Roy McFadden. NeIP

She heard the sounds of a couple having intercourse and then. That They Were at the Beach. Leslie Scalapino. UL (Sequence, A.) NPGG

She heard with patience all unto the end. Prince Arthur. Spenser. *Fr.* The Faerie Queene, I, 7. OBSC

She hears, head empty. After a Photo. Judith Herzberg, *tr. by the author.* DuIn

She Hears the Storm. Thomas Hardy. NAEL-2

She hid herself in the soirée kettle. A Ballade of the Nurserie. John Twig. NA

She hissed in my ear. Lilith. Donald Finkel. VWA

She holds in memory this time last year. Song of the Wine Spring. Niu Chiao, *tr. by* Lois Fusek. ATF

She hovered hooded, blue-eyed. Catechism, 1958. W. M. Ransom. CDW

She Hugged Me and Kissed Me. *Unknown.* BPo

She hung away her years, her eyes grew young. Waiting for the Bus. D. J. Enright. OxBTC

She I loved so much will not appear again. Farewell and Good. Denis Devlin. IPY

She idly rests within the silken curtains. Song of the Wine Spring. Mao Hsi-chen, *tr. by* Lois Fusek. ATF

She, in dowdy dress and dumpy. Still Life: Lady with Birds. Quandra Prettyman. PoBA

She in whose lipservice. The Goddess. Denise Levertov. LiTM; NeAP; NOBA; PoM

She is a black crow being driven out of sight. Drinking the Wind. Tan Ying, *tr. by* Kenneth Rexroth *and* Ling Chung. WPOW

She is a reed swaying in blue. Earle Thompson. HATNAP

She is a rich and rare land. This Native Land. Thomas Davis. BoTP

She Is a Woman Impure. Fahmida Riaz, *tr. fr. Urdu by* Mahmood Jamal. PBMUP

She is about to awaken from a black and blue dream. Medusas. Paul Eluard, *tr. by* Michael Benedikt. POS

She is all so slight. After Two Years. Richard Aldington. MoBrPo

She is all there. For My Lover, Returning to His Wife. Anne Sexton. HCAP; IHMS; NMM; UnPo; WPE

She is as in a field a silken tent. The Silken Tent. Robert Frost. AmPP; BLPL; InPK; NOBA; Son; SoSe; TAP; TwCP

She is committed to the earth and the earth. Canaan. Muriel Spark. NYBP

She is dead. Birthdays. Hilde Domin, *tr. by* Tudor Morris. BoWoP

"She is dead!" they said to him. "Come away." He and She. Sir Edwin Arnold. BLPA

She is disconsolate that her youth is slipping away. Song of Ho Man-tzu. Mao Hsi-chen, *tr. by* Lois Fusek. ATF

She is even more old-fashioned than Mongkok, the market. An Old Woman in Mongkok. Yu Kuang-chung, *tr. by* Dominic Cheung. IFON

She is far away. Very far. Who Was Born Dead. Vicente Aleixandre, *tr. by* Perry Higman. LPSS

She Is Far from the Land. Thomas Hood. FaBoNo; WiR

She Is Far from the Land. Thomas Moore. AnIL; EnRP; FaBoNo; NOIV; OBNC; WiR

She is first seen dancing which is a figure. The Origin of Cities. Robert Hass. NPGG

She is free of the trap and the paddle. The Half-Breed Girl. Duncan Campbell Scott. CaP

She is gentil and al so wise. That Ever I Saw. *Unknown.* TrGrPo

She is gone, she is lost, she is found, she is ever fair. My Woe Must Ever Last. Sir Walter Ralegh. ElL

She is gone! The occasion for ever is past! Lines Written Immediately after Parting from a Lady. Sir Samuel Egerton Brydges. NOEC

She is in your painting the one you bought when the taxi. Framed. Claire Harris. PBCV

She is large and matronly. Lui et Elle. D. H. Lawrence. NoAM

She is like pearls, of course, and rubies, and other. Valentine. Hollis Spurgeon Summers. GoYe

She is like snow. My Youngest Daughter Getting Up in the Morning. Adèle Davide. Mes

She Is More to Be Pitied than Censured. William B. Gray. BeLS; BLPA

She is most fair. The Unknown. Edward Thomas. GBL

She Is No Liar. Robert Graves. OxBSP

She is not dead, but sleepeth. Mrs. Rebecca Weston. Mary Weston Fordham. CBWP-2

She Is Not Fair [to Outward View]. Hartley Coleridge. EnRP; FaBV; OBEV

She Is Not for Me. *Gond Oral Tradition, tr. by* V. Elwin *and* S. Hivale. WTO

She Is Not Mute. Chan Ch'e, *tr. fr. Chinese by* Dominic Cheung. IFON

She is not of the fireside. Revolution. Lesbia Harford. PoAu-1

She is not sure. An Old Thought for a New Couple. E. A. Markham. PBCV

She is not yet; but he whose ear. The Dominion of Australia. Brunton Stephens. PoAu-1

She is now water and air. Sea Burial from the Cruiser "Reve." Richard Eberhart. NYBP

She is older than the rocks among which she sits. Mona Lisa. Walter Pater. OBMV

She is purposeless as a cyclone; she must move. Cubist Portrait. Marjorie Allen Seiffert. PoA

She is shameless, despicable, vile. She. Zinaida Nikolayevna Gippius, *tr. by* Dianne Levitin. WPOW

She is so proper and so pure. My Sweet Sweeting. *Unknown.* CH

She is so young, and never never before. Edward Davison. ErPo

She is standing on my lids. Lady Love. Paul Eluard. OBVE, *tr. by* Samuel Beckett; RHTwFP (Beloved, The.) POS

She is still, she is cold. Shelley. *Fr.* Ginevra. ChER
She is teck'wi. The Taboo Woman. *Unknown, tr. by* K. Kennedy. WTO
She is the dark sister. Iscah. Howard Schwartz. VWA
She is the fairies' midwife, and she comes. Shakespeare. *Fr.* Romeo and Juliet: O [*or* Oh], then, I see Queen Mab hath been with you. RB
(Mercutio Describes Queen Mab.) TrGrPo
She is the finest banquet you could eat. Gastronomy. Adriaan Morriën, *tr. by* James S. Holmes. DuIn
She is the one you call sister. The Mirror in Which Two Are Seen as One. Adrienne Rich. NAAL-2; NNaP
She is the Rose, the glorie of the day. Lament for Daphnaida. Spenser. FiP
She is the woman hanging from the 13th floor. The Woman Hanging from the Thirteenth Floor Window. Joy Harjo. ER; GLP; HATNAP; NOVW
She is too young to eat. Defining It for Vanessa. Colleen J. McElroy. ER
She is touching the cycle—her tender tread. Tennessee. Virginia Fraser Boyle. PAH
She is tougher than me, harder. For My Mother. Iain Crichton Smith. OxBS
She is using. Persephone, 5, Outside. Keith Abbott. UL
She is very loving, very beautiful, and very easily hurt. Song of the River City. Wei Chuang, *tr. by* Lois Fusek. ATF
She is washed by white-water, white if she looked up. Fish. Daniel Halpern. AmPA
She issues radiant from her dressing-room. George Meredith. *Fr.* Modern Love, VII. NOBVV
She juliets him from a window in Soho. Short Time. Gavin Ewart. NoAM
She keeps the memory-game. The Net. Fleur Adcock. ATNZ; PeNZ
She kept her secret well, oh, yes. My Angeline. Harry B. Smith. NBLV
She kept her songs, they took so little space. Love Songs in Age. Philip Larkin. PPP
She kneads/ deep into the night. Don't Talk to Me about Bread. E. A. Markham. PBCV
She kneeled before me begging. Confession. Donald Jeffrey Hayes. CDC
She kneeled before the dead lamb weeping. Synekdechestai. Constance M. Schmid. GoYe
She knew that she was growing blind. Blind Louise. George Washington Dewey. AA
She laid it where the sunbeams fall. Motherhood. Charles Stuart Calverley. FM
She Lay All Naked in Her Bed. *Unknown.* BoLoP; ErPo
She lay, and serving-men her lithe arms took. Abishag. Rainer Maria Rilke, *tr. by* Jethro Bithell. AWP
She lay as if at play. Emily Dickinson. LiTA
She lay in her girlish sleep at ninety-six. Castoff Skin. Ruth Whitman. InPK
She Lay Wrapped. Gail Fox. NOBC
She Lays ("She lays each beautifully mooned finger"). Molly Peacock. EOEF
She leaned her back unto a thorn. The Cruel Mother. *Unknown.* ESPB
She leaned her cheek upon her hand. The Ballad of Oriskany. Obadiah Cyrus Auringer. AA
She leaned her head upon her hand. Vashti. Frances E. W. Harper. AIW; BlSi
She leans across a golden table. For Amy Lowell. Countee Cullen. PoA
She leans against the painted railing. Written on the Lake after a Shower, On the Sixteenth of the Seventh Month. Li E, *tr. by* Shirleen S. Wong. WFTU
She leans on a carved railing. Hatred of Distant Places. Wen T'ing-yün, *tr. by* Lois Fusek. ATF
She leaves the motor running. Shadow Play. Ralph Angel. BAP
She left me at the silent time. Lines Written in the Bay of Lerici. Shelley. OAEL-2
She let her golden ball fall down the well. The Frog and the Golden Ball. Robert Graves. NoP
She let him see it. Still completely bare. Among the Flowers. Rutger Kopland, *tr. by* James S. Holmes. DuIn
She lies at the side of the road, naked. Crime. Philip Dacey. NAmP
She lies by the man her husband. The Wife of Winter's Tale. Michael Dennis Browne. SM
She lies far inland, and no stick nor stone of her. Inland City. John Crowe Ransom. CMoP

She lies on her left side her flank golden. Landscape as a Nude. Archibald MacLeish. *Fr.* Frescoes for Mr. Rockefeller's City, I. AmPP; CMoP
She lies upon the cold stone of her cell. The Nun. Arthur Symons. BrPo
She, like the morning, is still fresh and fair. Her Praises. Anthony Scoloker. EIL
She liked mornings the best—Thomas gone. Weathering Out. Rita Dove. NoAM
She lived in storm and strife. That the Night Come. W. B. Yeats. PoEL-5
She lived there once where you were once. She Says. Bill Manhire. ATNZ
She Lives between Back Home and Home. Sindamani Bridglal. WS
She lives in a garret. A Sad Song about Greenwich Village. Frances Park. RHPC
She lives in light, not shadow. Of One Who neither Sees nor Hears. Richard Watson. AA
She lives in ming-blue daymares. Cinderella. Jan Kemp. ATNZ
She lives in the porter's room; the plush is nicotined. Bitter Sanctuary. Harold Monro. FaBoMo; LiTB; OBMV
She looked over his shoulder. The Shield of Achilles. W. H. Auden. EBEV; FaBoMo; FaBoPV; GTBS-P; HAP; NAEL-2; NoAM; NOBE; NOCV; NoP; PoA; PoE; WeW
She looked to east, she looked to west. Mater Dei. Katharine Tynan. TIRV
She looks closely at the color of the flowers. Offering Deep Affection. Ou-yang Chiung, *tr. by* Lois Fusek. ATF
She looks out in the blue morning. The Window. Conrad Aiken. CMoP
She looks so simple—a gardenia. Woman with Gardenia: A Sketch. Pamela White Hadas. BLA
She Lost Her Sheep. J. Moyr Smith. FaBoNo
She Loves. Olga Broumas. GLP
She loves, and she confesses too. Honour. Abraham Cowley. BoLoP
She loves him. . . and what small child could deny. Americanized. Bruce Dawe. CBAP
She loves the brown moles. The Woman Who Loves Old Men. Herbert Scott. NAmP
She loves the wind. The Old One and the Wind. Clarice Short. IHMS
She made a little shadow-hidden grave. The Dead Faith. Fanny Heaslip Lea. WGRP
She made her crossing. Miss Geeta. Margaret Reckord. AIW
She makes thee seek, yet fear to find. Love's Servile Lot. Robert Southwell. ACP
She (Marina Distant). Lucha Corpi, *tr. fr. Spanish.* *Fr.* The Marina Poems, IV. OV; CCP, *tr. by* Marta Ester Sánchez; OV, *tr. by the author and* Catherine Rodríguez-Nieto.
"She may have only one eye." *Unknown, tr. by* Geoffrey Bownas *and* Anthony Thwaite. PeBJV
She may not understand why it is that. Ms Understood. Sherma Springer. WS
She met a lion face to face. A Cautionary Tale. Anne Wilkinson. OBCV
She might have borne them had they come. Breaking Point. Sylvia Auxier. GoYe
She might have chosen cities, but the man. Droving Man. Thea Astley. PoAu-2
She might have known it in the earlier spring. Feminine. H. C. Bunner. AA
She might have stolen from his arms. Solitary Confinement. X. J. Kennedy. NePoEA-2
She might, so noble from head. A Thought from Propertius. W. B. Yeats. OAEL-2; OxBSP
She mixes blue and mauve and green. The Patchwork Quilt. Elizabeth Fleming. BoTP
She mocks the bones in you, as if it had. In Lombardy. Donald Revell. SM
She Moved through the Fair. Padraic Colum. BIrV; InvP; NOIV
She moves in tumult; round her lies. The Teresian Contemplative. Robert Hugh Benson. ACP
She must have been kicked unseen or brushed by a car. Dog's Death. John Updike. Psk
She naked lies asleep beside the wine. From Titian's "Bacchanal" in the Prado at Madrid. T. Sturge Moore. QFR
She never climbed a mountain. Farm Wife. John Hanlon Mitchell. CaP
She never could sleep in the earth, in the cold dark grave. Fire Burial. Edgar McInnis. CaP
She never told her love. Patience on a Monument. Shakespeare. *Fr.* Twelfth Night, II, iv. TrGrPo

She never was quite one of us. Sleep-Walking Child. Elisabeth Eybers, *tr. by* Jack Cope, Uys Krige *and* Adèle Naudé. PeSA

She of the Impudent Face. Bible, *O.T. Fr.* Proverbs, VII: 6-27. TrJP

She only knew the birth and death. At Dawn. Arthur Symons. OBNC

She packs the flower beds with leaves. For Fran. Philip Levine. FF; SM

She passed away like morning dew. Early Death. Hartley Coleridge. OBEV

She Plans Her Funeral. Louise Morey Bowman. CaP

She played me false, but that's not why. Our Photograph[s]. Frederick Locker-Lampson. NBLV; NOBL

She played upon her music-box a fancy air by chance. Her Polka Dots. Peter Newell. NA

She points to a star. The Fortune Teller. Fu'ad Rifqa, *tr. by* Sargon Boulus *and* Samuel Hazo. MAP

She practices a fugue, though it can matter. Suburban Sonnet. Gwen Harwood. CBAP

She Promised She'd Meet Me. *Unknown.* AS

She Proves the Inconsistency of the Desires and Criticism of Men Who Accuse Women of What They Themselves Cause. Sister Juana Inés de la Cruz, *tr. fr. Spanish by* Aliki *and* Willis Barnstone. BoWoP

She reads the paper. Two People. Eve Merriam. RHPC

She remembers the episode taking place at night. Night. Joyce Carol Oates. GeTw

She returned from the clinic. Unhappy Diary Days. Gerald Vizenor. VoR

She rides a broom and curses God. The Subversive. Merle Woo. BrSi

She rides the last few minutes. Squeal. Heather McHugh. GeTw

She rises clear to memory's eye. Red Jack. Mary Durack. PoAu-1

She roamed the meadows long in hope. Recompensed? Henrietta Cordelia Ray. CBWP-3

She rose among us where we lay. The Vampire: 1914. Conrad Aiken. VVA

She roves through shadowy solitudes. Tacita. James Benjamin Kenyon. AA

She Said. Jonathan Henderson Brooks. PoNe

She Said. Walter de la Mare. ELP

She said, "I cannot come." The Cenci's Curse upon His Daughter. Shelley. *Fr.* The Cenci. TW

She said, "I was not born to mope at home in loneliness." The Ride round the Parapet. Friedrich Rueckert, *tr. by* James Clarence Mangan. AWP

She said, "I will come back again." She Said. Walter de la Mare. ELP

She said, if tomorrow my world were torn in two. The 5:32. Phyllis McGinley. *Fr.* I Know a Village. NMM; WPE

She said: "I'm god and all." Against a Sickness: To the Female Double Principle God. Alan Dugan. NoAM

She said, "Not only music; brave men marching." She Said. Jonathan Henderson Brooks. PoNe

She said, "Now give me flesh to eat." Cherry. Gene Baro. ErPo

She said she don't love me anymore because I drink whiskey. *Unknown, tr. fr. Kiowa Indian. Fr.* "49" Songs. STP

She said she don't want no man. Faith. Lorenzo Thomas. UL

She said she forgave me. Parted. Clara Ann Thompson. CBWP-2

She said the Jehovah Witness man. 3-31-70. Gayl Jones. *Fr.* Journal. BlSi

She Said the Same to Me. *Unknown.* AS

She said: The world is empty that we loved. Eternal. Agnes Foley Macdonald. CaP

She said, "They gave me of their best." After Aughrim. Emily Lawless. OBEV

She said to one: "How glows." Subalterns. Elizabeth Daryush. OBWP

She said, Wear my leather jacket, a looser. How to Dress like a Scary Dyke. Jane Barnes. GLP

She sang beyond the genius of the sea. The Idea of Order at Key West. Wallace Stevens. CMoP; FF; HAP; HCAP; HeIP; MoAB; MoAmPo; MoP; MOS; NAAL-2; NAWM-2; NIP; NIP; NoAM; NOBA; NoP; OxBA; PoE; PPP; PrIm; TAP

She sat across from me and her eyes. Parting. Gabriel Preil, *tr. by* Laya Firestone. VWA

She sat and looked at a picture. Her Son. Ebba M. Leaf. PWR

She sat and sang alway. Christina Rossetti. GBL; NAEL-2

She sat and wept beside His feet; the weight. "Multum Dilexit." Hartley Coleridge. EnRP

She sat by me and eyed me craftily. Dinner at the Mongoloid's. Larry Rubin. MT

She sat down below a thorn. The Cruel Mother. *Unknown.* AmFP; ESPB (A, B, C *and* P *vers.*); FaBoBa; InPK; OBET; OxBB, *with music*

She sat on a shelf. Motherhood. May Swenson. CoAP

She sat on a willow-trunk. The Fly. Miroslav Holub, *tr. by* George Theiner. RB

She sate upon her Dobie. The Cummerbund. Edward Lear. CenHV; OBTV

She Saw Me in Church. *Unknown.* MeEL

She saw the bayonets flashing in the sun. Memorial Day. Richard Watson Gilder. OHIP

She saw the world from inside out, he saw it upside down. Reflections. Janet Dubé. DT

She Says. Bill Manhire. ATNZ

(She says)/ Not even listening. Game. Sándor Weöres, *tr. by* Jascha Kessler. FOC

She Says, Cocks Are Crowing! *Unknown, tr. fr. Chinese by* Burton Watson. CoBCP

She says how/ is it when you. John Knoepfle. *Fr.* The Ten-Fifteen Community Poems. MAT

She says "How was you?" Kissing. "Come on in." Unrecorded Speech. Anna Adams. BrRo

She says the coffin to be opened. Lady Alice ("She says the coffin to be opened"). *Unknown.* AmFP

She says, you are the negative. Michael Palmer. UL

She Schools the Flighty Pupils of Her Eyes. Gerard Manley Hopkins. OxBSP

She seemed an angel to our infant eyes! A Mother's Picture. Edmund Clarence Stedman. OHIP

She Sees Another Door Opening. Firman Houghton. Par

She sees her image in the glass. The Shadow Dance. Louise Chandler Moulton. AA

She Sent Him Away. Clara Ann Thompson. CBWP-2

She served love well. Elegy, Montreal Morgue. Goodridge MacDonald. CaP

She shakes in the take-off lounge. The Frightened Flier Goes North. Judith Kazantzis. BrRo

She sharpened her knife both sharp and keen. Young Hunting. *Unknown.* OxBoLi

She, she is dead; she's dead: when thou knowest this. John Donne. *Fr.* Anatomy [*or* Anatomie] of the World, An: The First Anniversary. JCP

She should have died hereafter. Shakespeare. *Fr.* Macbeth, V, v. DL; SoSe

(Out, Out, Brief Candle!) ChTr

(Tomorrow, and Tomorrow, and Tomorrow.) FaBoRV; FaFP; FF; LiTB; TrGrPo, *sl. shorter sel.*

("Wherefore was that cry?") FiP, *sl. longer sel.*

"She should have had. . .," I said, and there I stopped. After Speaking of One Dead a Long Time. Padraic Colum. GoYe

She shuts fast the red door. The Magnolia Flower. Mao Hsi-chen, *tr. by* Lois Fusek. ATF

She shuts out the city now. The Lonely Woman's Room. Ahmad Abd al-Muti Hijazi, *tr. by* Sargon Boulus *and* Peter Porter. MAP

She sinks/ into the tub of herself. A Life. Chana Bloch. MAYP

She sits home [*or* in the house] for days on end. Portrait. Dahlia Ravikovich, *tr. by* Warren Bargad *and* Stanley F. Chyet. IP; OV

("She sits home many a day.") MHeP

She sits in her glass garden. The One Whose Reproach I Cannot Evade. George Hitchcock. EAS

She sits in the park. Her clothes are out of date. In the Park. Gwen Harwood. CBAP

She sits in the tawny vapour. A Wife in London. Thomas Hardy. NOBVV; OBWP

She sits on a pattern called Temperance Tree. Mountain Soprano. Martha McFerren. KS

She sits on tumulus Savoor, and stares. Flax. Ivan Bunin, *tr. by* Babette Deutsch *and* Avrahm Yarmolinsky. AWP

She sits upon her Bulbul. Edward Lear. FaBoNo

She sits with one hand poised against her head. Dialogue. Adrienne Rich. TAP

She sits within the white oak hall. Helen. Edward A. U. Valentine. AA

She skimmed the yellow water like a moth. My Grandmother's Ghost. James Wright. Son

She skips on to the day's next blue radius. Maggie. Duane Niatum. HATNAP

She slept without the usual concerns. She. Mark Strand. AnAn

She slid past. And She Was Bad. Marvin Wyche, Jr. AmNP

She slipped. Heels over head she landed. Portrait. Gail Fox. NOBC

She smiled behind a lawny cloud. Fancy Dress. Dorothea MacKellar. PoAu-1

She Smiled like a Holiday. *Unknown.* OxBoLi

She sought him east, she sought him west. Rare Willie Drowned in Yarrow; or, The Water o Gamrie. Thomas Walsh. ESPB

She speaks always in her own voice. The Portrait. Robert Graves. CMoP

She speaks in a slight accent about her wild seas. Stranger. Gabriela Mistral, *tr. by* Langston Hughes. OV

She Speaks the Morning's Filigree. Philip Lamantia. VGW

She speaks with the accent of her savage seas. The Alien. Gabriela Mistral, *tr. by* Kate Flores. DMH

She spent her money with such perfect style. The Rapist's Villanelle. Thomas M. Disch. SM

She spent her time recalling. Play-acting. Frances Barber. GoYe

She spent the day counting how many birds came. Exactly. Roberta Metz. TSS

She spent three hundred and sixty four days a year. Grandmother Jackson. David Jackson. OBCP

She spoke to me gently with words of sweet meaning. Patrick MacDonogh. NeIP

She springs from the ground-clinging thicket, her face. Veneris Venefica Agrestis. Charles Tomlinson, *after* Lucio Piccolo. OBVE

She stands/ In the quiet darkness. Troubled Woman. Langston Hughes. PCP

She stands as pale as Parian statues stand. A Soul. Christina Rossetti. WPOW

She stands before the apple tree. Eve and the Apple Tree. Itzig Manger, *tr. by* Leonard Wolf. PeBMYV

She stands beside me, stands away. Like Rousseau. Imamu Amiri Baraka. PoA

She stands in the dead center like a star. The Mother. S. S. Gardons. NePoEA-2

She stands in the dead center like a star. The Mother. W. D. Snodgrass. CAPP

She stands under the white sun. The Scarecrow in Capri. Karl Wawra, *tr. by* Beth Bjorklund. CoAuP

She stirs on the pillow and cold mat. Song of the Wine Spring. Niu Hsi-chi, *tr. by* Lois Fusek. ATF

She stole my pencil-case, red leather. The Thief. Josephine Jacobsen. WPE

She stood/ apart from the grazing herd. The Death of an Elephant. Gianfranco Pagnucci. NU

She stood at the bar of justice. "Guilty or Not Guilty?" *Unknown*. BeLS; BLPA

She stood at the factory gate. The Shebeen Queen. Mafika Pascal Gwala. WMBCH

She stood breast high amid the corn. Ruth. Thomas Hood. BoLoP; EnLoPo; EnRP; GN; NOBE; OBEV; OBNC

She stood close to a tree and wrinkled. Tree Old Woman. Samuel Makidemewabe, *tr. by* Howard Norman. STP

She stood hanging wash before sun. Ghetto Lovesong—Migration. Carole Gregory Clemmons. NBP; NMM; PoBA (Migration.) PoBA

She Stoops to Conquer, *sel.* Goldsmith.
"Let school-masters puzzle their brain." *Fr.* I, ii. BIrV; NOIV
(Three Jolly Pigeons, The.) PoRA
(Three Pigeons, The.) ELP

She stops combing her hair. Tune: Dreaming of the South. Wen T'ing-yün, *tr. by* Burton Watson. CoBCP

She stroked molten tones. Yonosa House. R. T. Smith. STE

She strolls in the valley, alone. Madwoman at Rodmell. Michele Roberts. BrRo

She suckles her baby. *Unknown, tr. by* Geoffrey Bownas *and* Anthony Thwaite. PeBJV

She suffers like a red stone, small as a carat. Sisters. Sandra McPherson. AmPA; AnAn

She suns on grass, my dark, my gifted mistress. Nude. Harold Witt. ErPo

She swam smiling in the river. Waiting to Be Fed. Ray A. Young Bear. CDW

She sweeps the kitchen floor of the river bed her husband saw fit. Pomade. Rita Dove. NAmP

She sweeps with many-colored brooms. Emily Dickinson. SaC (Evening.) BoTP

She talks about the decimal point. Math Class. Myra Cohn Livingston. TSS

She talks not, plays not, visits not, in bed. *Unknown*. FaBoEE

She Tells Her Love while Half Asleep. Robert Graves. BoLoP; EBEV; FaBoTw; GBL; NOBE; OxBTC

She tells me with claret she cannot agree. Drinking Song. *Unknown*. NOBL

She tells us an interminable story, from television. The Somerset Dam for Supper. John Holmes. NYBP

She tests the curb with a chubby boot. For Heather, Entering Kindergarten. Roberta Hill Whiteman. HATNAP; NoAM

She that but little patience knew. On a Political Prisoner. W. B. Yeats. FaBoPV; OAEL-2; OBMV

She That Denies Me [I Would Have]. Thomas Heywood. *Fr.* The Rape of Lucrece. ErPo

She that holds me under the laws of love. Sir Arthur Gorges. GBL

She That Is Memory's Daughter. Vernon Watkins. NYBP

She, the mirror. Old Magic. Grace Nichols. PBCV

She, the mother, the sow, the soft sac. The Illegal Operation. Patrick Conrad, *tr. by* Peter Nijmeijer. DuIn

She, the sensual creature, the green singer. Slow Dancer That No One Hears but You. Duane Niatum. CDW

She threw a quince to me. *Unknown, tr. by* Arthur Waley. BoS

She thus; when I had great desire to prove. Homer, *tr. fr. Greek by* George Chapman. *Fr.* Odyssey, XI. OBVE

She Tied Up Her Few Things. John Clare. HAP

She, to Him ("When you shall see me in the toils of time."), *sel.* Thomas Hardy. OBEV; OxBTC
"This love puts all humanity from me." *Fr.* IV. TOF

She told how they used to form for the country dances. One We Knew. Thomas Hardy. NAEL-2

She told the story, and the whole world wept. Harriet Beecher Stowe. Paul Laurence Dunbar. BPo

She, too, the voyaging in doors and Keys. This Alice. Herbert Morris. PoRA

She took a last and simple meal when there were. The Lost Cat. Emile Victor Rieu. CRH

She took her name beneath according skies. The Ritual. Edwin John Pratt. MoP

She took the dappled partridge flecked [*or* fleckt] with blood. Tennyson. FM; NAEL-2

She tosses and rumples alone on the double bed. Flying Fox. Thomas W. Shapcott. CBAP

She touches me. Her fingers nibble gently. In Love. David Wevill. MoCV

She transplanted each spruce, blue as the. Spruce. Phillip William George. VoR

She tripped and fell against a star. Innocence. Anne Spencer. CDC

She trips across the meadows. April. Henrietta Cordelia Ray. CBWP-3

She truly needs good character. Women. *Yoruba Oral Tradition, tr. by* Ulli Beier. WTO

She turned her face to the wall. The Wall. Tadeusz Rozewicz, *tr. by* Czeslaw Milosz. PwPP

She turned in the high pew, until her sight. A Church Romance. Thomas Hardy. FaBoTw; NOBE; OxBTC

She turns and calls him by name. His Wife. Rachel, *tr. by* Sholom J. Kahn. WPOW

She turns the pillow, smoothes the rumpled bed. Rites for a Demagogue. Anthony Thwaite. NePoEA-2

She turns them over in her slow hands. A Mongoloid Child Handling Shells on the Beach. Richard Snyder. InPK

She Understands Me. Lucille Clifton. CAPP

She used to let her golden hair fly free. Petrarch, *tr. fr. Italian by* Morris Bishop. *Fr.* Sonnets to Laura: To Laura in Life, LXIX. NAWM-1

She views the clustered shrines by the river. The Spirit of the Yellow River. Wen T'ing-yün, *tr. by* Lois Fusek. ATF

She wadna bake, she wadna brew. The Wife Wrapt in Wether's Skin. *Unknown*. ESPB

She Waited. Tania Van Zyl. PeSA

She waited eagerly on a park bench. The Poem in the Park. Peter Davison. GOYP

She waited on the 7th floor. Frank Albert and Viola Benzena Owens. Ntozake Shange. BlSi

She wakes long before he does. A fierce shock. Mekeel McBride. MAYP

She walked along the crowded street. Revelation. Blanche Taylor Dickinson. CDC

She Walked Unaware. Patrick MacDonogh. BoLoP; ErPo; FaBoTw; NeIP

She walks down the road. Girl with the Green Skirt. Dana Naone. CDW

She Walks in Beauty. Byron. AWP; BLPA; BoLoP; ChER; ELP; EnRP; FaBoBe; FaFP; FF; FiP; FPL; GTBS; GTBS-P; HelP; InPS; LiTB; NAEL-2; NIP; NOBE; NoP; OBEV; OBNC; PoE; PoEL-4; PrIm; TrGrPo

She Walks in Ugly. Walter H. Kerr. SoTCo

She walks—the lady of my delight. The Shepherdess. Alice Meynell. ACP; AWP; MoBrPo; NOBVV; OBEV
(Lady of the Lambs, The.) OBEV

She wanders up and down the main. Derelict. Elisabeth Cavazza Pullen. AA

She wanted rain. Dust. Kathleen Spivack. BoWoP

She wants what no clerk in the city can bring her.   At the Millinery Shop.
Daniel Mark Epstein.   MAYP
She Warns Him.   Frances Cornford.   EnLoPo
She was a city of patience; of proud name.   Ypres.   Laurence Binyon.
MMA
She was a high-class bitch and a dandy.   Theodore Spencer.   LiTA
She was a lawyer, he a physician.   Career Women Who Marry Today.
Ned Pastor.   SoTCo
She was a maid of high degree.   He Took Her.   Tom Masson.   OBAL
She Was a Phantom of Delight.   Wordsworth.   BLPL; EnRP; FaBoBe;
FaBV; FaFP; GTBS; GTBS-P; HeIP; LiTB; NoP; OAEL-2; OHFP;
PoEL-4; PWR; TrGrPo
(Perfect Woman.)   OBEV
She Was a Pretty Little Girl.   Ramon Perez de Ayala, tr. fr. Spanish by
Alida Malkus.   FaPON
She was a small dog, neat and fluid.   Praise of a Collie.   Norman
MacCaig.   RB
She was a sweet country lassie.   Blackpool Breezes.   Unknown.
CoMu
She was a wet nurse, but I was afraid.   Terror.   Kitahara Hakushu, tr. by
Hiroaki Sato.   FCEI
She was a year younger.   Picture Bride.   Cathy Song.   AiP
She was able to kill herself.   The Way Down.   Ernest Sandeen.   CRP
She was afraid of men.   Chicken-Licken.   Maya Angelou.   FF
She was already lean when.   Parting.   A. R. Ammons.   NoAM
She was an evil stepmother.   She Does Not Remember.   Anna
Swirszczynska, tr. by Czeslaw Milosz.   PwPP
She was at work on a poem about breath.   Poem about Breath.   David
Wagoner.   NoAM
She was beautiful that evening and so gay.   An Escape.   Abu Nuwas, tr.
by E. Powys Mathers.   ErPo
She was careerish in a gentle way.   Domestic: Climax.   Merrill Moore.
ErPo
She was cleaning—there is always.   Black Silk.   Tess Gallagher.
FaBoWP; MAYP; NAmP
She was coming three, her hide was slick.   No Imposter.   Duane Reece.
CowP
She was cute, frizzled.   Vampire.   Ray Amorosi.   VVA
She was in love with the same danger.   Sandra McPherson.   SM
She was in terrible pain the whole day.   A Wedding.   James Tate.
NoAM
She was in the garden, sequestered behind bushes, as night came.   The
Garden.   Susan Griffin.   Fr. Woman and Nature.   NPGG
She was just a parson's daughter.   It's the Syme the Whole World Over.
Unknown.   AS, with music
(It's the Syme the Wide World Over.)   BeLS
She was lyin face down in her face.   William Knott.   MAT
She was my staff and I am blind.   Jana Bai, tr. by Willis Barnstone.
BoWoP
She was not as pretty as women I know.   My Kate.   Elizabeth Barrett
Browning.   OHFP; WBLP
She was oblivious the livelong day.   Feodor Tyutchev, tr. by Alan Myers.
AAA
She Was Poor but She Was Honest.   Unknown.   ErPo; FaBoCo; FiBHP;
GBP; NOBL
(Poor But Honest.)   NBLV; RB
She was so aesthetic and culchud.   The Cultured Girl Again.   Ben King.
FiBHP; OBAL
She was so little—little in her grave.   The Mother Who Died Too.   Edith
M. Thomas.   AA
She was so quiet.   His Half-Breed Wife.   Doris Seale.   GOS
She was so small and pretty.   Art's Variety.   David McFadden.   NeAC
She was urgent to speak of the moon: she offered delight.   An Old Woman
Speaks of the Moon.   Ruth Pitter.   WPE
She was wearing the coral taffeta trousers.   Full Moon.   V. Sackville-
West.   MoShBr
She wasn't the least bit pretty.   The Factory Girl.   J. A. Phillips.   SaC
She wears her middle age like a cowled.   From a Correct Address in a
Suburb of a Major City.   Helen Sorrells.   WPE
She wears, my beloved, a rose upon her head.   John Frederick Matheus.
CDC
She wears trousers.   Mary Ackerman, 1938.   Diane Glancy.   STE
She weaves away at the bower.   To-and-Fro of Saint Theresa.   Alfonso
Reyes, tr. by Samuel Beckett.   MexPo
She welcomes him with pretty impatience.   The Visit.   Ogden Nash.
FiBHP
She went along the road.   Hagar.   Francis Lauderdale Adams.   OxBS
She Went to Stay.   Robert Creeley.   OBAL
She went up the hill to pick angelica.   Old Poem.   Unknown.   AWP, tr.
by Arthur Waley; CoBCP, tr. by Burton Watson

She went up the mountain to pluck wild herbs.   Old and New ("She went
up the mountain to pluck wild herbs").   Unknown, tr. by Arthur
Waley.   AWP
She Wept, She Railed.   Stanley Kunitz.   ErPo; VGW
She, who could neither rest nor sleep.   Alas!   Sadi, tr. fr. Persian by L.
Cranmer-Byng.   Fr. The Gulistan.   AWP
She Who First Bore Our People.   Unknown, tr. fr. Chinese by Burton
Watson.   CoBCP
She who has no love for women.   Calliope in the Labour Ward.   Elaine
Feinstein.   BrRo
She who has power to call her man.   An Unsaid Word.   Adrienne Rich.
NMM
She who hath felt a real pain.   John Gay.   EnLoPo
She who in the beginning gave birth to the people.   Unknown, tr. by
Arthur Waley.   BoS
She who is always in my thoughts prefers.   Bhartrihari, tr. by John
Brough.   BoLoP
She who to Heaven more Heaven doth annex.   On a Virtuous Young
Gentlewoman That Died Suddenly.   William Cartwright.   HAP;
OBEV
She Who Understands.   Alfonsina Storni, tr. fr. Spanish by Kate Flores.
DMH
She who usually feeds us.   Teeth.   Susan Griffin.   NPGG
She who was burned more than half her body.   The Praises.   Charles
Olson.   VGW
She who was easy for any chance lover.   Effie.   Sterling Allen Brown.
BANP
She whose matchless beauty staineth.   Unknown.   OBSC
She will run to you for love whoever.   Children.   Sandra McPherson.
AnAn; FaBoWP
She woke at length, but not as sleepers wake.   The Death of Haidée.
Byron.   Fr. Don Juan, IV.   FiP
She Wolf, The.   Muriel Spark.   NYBP
She wore a cloche hat.   The Photo of Emily.   Lawrence Ferlinghetti.
CAPP
She wore a new "terra-cotta" dress.   A Thunderstorm in Town.   Thomas
Hardy.   BoLoP; EnLoPo; GBL; OxBSP
She Wore a Wreath of Roses.   Thomas Haynes Bayly.   BeLS
She wore lipstick and powder.   My Mother Was Always Dressed.
Abigail Luttinger.   TV
She Would Have Roses.   Nicholas Lloyd Ingraham.   PWR
She wouldn't believe.   Magical Eraser.   Shel Silverstein.   WSC
She wreaks such havoc in my library.   Minding Ruth.   Aidan Carl
Mathews.   CIP
She writes to him again.   Henri Michaux, tr. fr. French by Richard
Ellmann.   Fr. I Am Writing to You from a Far-Off Country, XI.
RHTwFP
She yearns for those times they came together in dreams.   Heaven's
Immortal.   Wei Chuang, tr. by Lois Fusek.   ATF
Sheaf, The.   Andrew Young.   ChTr
Sheaf-Tosser.   Eric Rolls.   PoAu-2
Sheafe of snakes used heretofore to be, A.   To Mr. George Herbert.   John
Donne.   OBVE
Shear your sheep in May.   Unknown.   FaBoUs
Shearer's Song, The.   Unknown.   PoAu-1
Shearer's Wife, The.   Louis Esson.   PoAu-1
Shearing, The.   Unknown, tr. fr. Welsh by Glyn Jones.   OBWVE
Shearing, as the gardener.   That's All?   Anna Hajnal, tr. by Jascha
Kessler.   FOC; PBWP
Shearing Grass.   Peter Redgrove.   NePoEA-2
Sheath and Knife.   Unknown.   CH; ESPB
Sheaves, The.   E. A. Robinson.   AWP; CMoP; FaBV; HAP; MoAB;
MoAmPo; MoP; NoAM; NOBA; OxBA; TAP
Sheaves of my love-thoughts, The.   Princess Hirokawa.   Fr. Manyo Shu.
Ma
Shebeen Queen, The.   Mafika Pascal Gwala.   WMBCH
Shechem.   David Shevin.   VWA
Shed a tear for Twickham Tweer.   Twickham Tweer.   Jack Prelutsky.
RHPC
She'd always been there.   Interface.   Gloria Anzaldúa.   GLP
Shed in blue-grey weatherboard with a high, A.   Hillside.   Alexander
Craig.   PoAu-2
Shed no tear! O, shed no tear!   Fairy Song.   Keats.   FaPON
(Faery Song.)   CH
She'd Say.   Frank Davey.   NOBC
Shee brought her to her joyous paradize.   The Garden of Adonis.
Spenser.   Fr. The Faerie Queene, III, 6.   PoEL-1
"In that same gardin all the goodly flowres."   NOBE
Shee is dead; and all which die.   The Dissolution.   John Donne.   SeCV-1
Shee with whom troopes of Bustuary slaves.   A Satyre Entituled the
Witch.   Unknown.   CoMu

Sheeny Mike. Jacob Glatstein, *tr. fr. Yiddish by* Benjamin *and* Barbara Harshav. AYP
Sheep. William Henry Davies. LiTM; MoBrPo; RB
Sheep. Robert Francis. LCAP
Sheep. Samuel Hoffenstein. TrJP
Sheep, *sel.* Ted Hughes.
    "When we sat his mother on her tail, he mouthed her teat." OBD
Sheep. Rochelle Kraut. UL
Sheep. Hal Porter. PoAu-2
Sheep, The. Ann Taylor. BoTP; OxBChV
Sheep!/ Unhappy connotation. Bleat of Protest. Mildred Weston. FiBHP
Sheep and Lambs. Katharine Tynan. BoTP; OBEV; TIRV
Sheep and the Goat, The. George Macdonald. EBVV
Sheep Child, The. James Dickey. CAPP; HCAP; MoP; MT; NoAM; NOBA; Prf; TAP
Sheep Dipping. Norman MacCaig. OxBC
Sheep Fair, A. Thomas Hardy. Prf
Sheep in Fog. Sylvia Plath. FaBoWP; HCAP; LCAP; NaP
Sheep in New York. Berysh Vaynshteyn, *tr. fr. Yiddish by* Benjamin *and* Barbara Harshav. *Fr.* New York Everywhere. AYP
Sheep in the Sheade. William Barnes. FM
Sheep is blind, The; a passing owl. The Blind Sheep. Randall Jarrell. NYBP; OBAL
Sheep Meadow. Samuel Menashe. Mes
Sheep Shearing. *Unknown.* OBET
Sheepbells. Edmund Blunden. BrPo
Sheepdog Trials in Hyde Park. Cecil Day Lewis. MoP; NoAM; NoP; OxBTC
Sheepfol', De. Sarah Pratt McLean Greene. AA
Sheepherder, The. Lew Sarett. AmFN; FaPON
Sheepherder Blues. Luci Tapahonso. STE
Sheeprancher Named John, A. Gretel Ehrlich. MAYP
Sheep's in the meadow, The. Bonny at Morn. *Unknown.* GBP
Sheep's Skull. Lucy Jane Simpson. OBD
Sheer cliff, far mountains. Inscribed on My Large Landscape Hanging Scroll "Listening to a Waterfall." Tao-chi, *tr. by* Jonathan Chaves. CoBLCP
Sheer fiction/ that autumn nights are longer. Komachi, *tr. fr. Japanese by* Burton Watson. *Fr.* Kokin Shu. FCEI
Sheer rock, four walls stand. Dragon Mouth Cliff. Chao Meng-fu, *tr. fr. Chinese by* Jonathan Chaves. *Fr.* Twenty-Eight Poems Inscribed on T'ien-kuan Mountai. CoBLCP
Sheet of paper, placed, A. Lakshmi. Padraic Fallon. NOIV
Sheet of writing paper, The. The Alchemist. Richard Church. OxBTC
Sheeted in steel, embedded face to face. At a Low Mass for Two Hot-Rodders. X. J. Kennedy. Psk
Sheets, The. Timothy Steele. DiPo
Sheets are exposed like film, The. Finding an Old Newspaper in the Woods. Robert Morgan. WeW
Sheets of night mist travel a long valley, The. Mist Forms. Carl Sandburg. CMoP
Sheets of rain, The. Tameko, *tr. by* Steven D. Carter. WFTW
Sheets on the floor, a stick. The Distance between Bodies. Bill Manhire. ATNZ
Sheets were frozen hard, and they cut the naked hand, The. Christmas at Sea. Robert Louis Stevenson. BLPL; BrPo; CH; EBVV; FaBoBe; FaBV; Mes; MOS; OBTV
Sheffield Apprentice, The. *Unknown.* OBET
Sheffield East End. Stanley Cook. NPo
Sheffield grinder's a terrible blade, The. The Grinders; or, The Saddle on the Right Horse. *Unknown.* GBP
Sheffield 'Prentice, The. *Unknown. See* I was brought up in Sheffield.
Sheiling, The. Edward Thomas. PoSH
Shekhina[h]. Karl Wolfskehl, *tr. fr. German.* TrJP, *tr. by* Carol North Valhope *and* Ernst Morwitz; VWA, *tr. by* Erna Baber Rosenfeld
Shekhina and the Kiddushim. Edouard Roditi. VWA
Shelf Is a Ledge, A. Gregory Orr. BLA
Shell, The. James Stephens. BoNaP; BoTP; CH; CMoP; MoAB; MoBrPo; MOS; MoShBr
Shell, The. Tennyson. *See* Maud: See what a lovely shell.
She'll Be Comin' 'Round. James Sherry. IAT
She'll Be Comin' Round the Mountain. *Unknown.* AS, A *and* B *vers., with music.*
Shell-less, on your slimey trail. After Tempest. Percy MacKaye. FYAP
Shell Secrets. *Unknown.* BoTP
Shell tears apart the door, A. He Steals Furs. Anna Swirszczynska, *tr. by* Magnus Jan Krynski *and* Robert A. Maguire. PwPP
Shellbrook. William Barnes. OBNC

Shelley and jazz and lieder and love and hymn-tunes. Louis MacNeice. *Fr.* Autumn Journal. NOBL
Shelley, madman, made his rhymes. Wiser Than the Children of Light. Monk Gibbon. NeIP
Shelley's "Arethusa" Set to New Measures. Robert Duncan. CMoP
Shelley's Skylark. Thomas Hardy. FaBV; PBBP
Shelling Jacobs Cattle Beans. Maxine W. Kumin. BLA
Shellpicker, The. Ronald Perry. NePoEA-2
Shells. Lorna Dee Cervantes. CCP
Shells. Thomas Sturge Moore. SeCePo
Shells. Kathleen Jessie Raine. ImOP
Shelly. James McIntyre. FiBHP
Shelly crawlers each returning year, The. William Diaper, *after the Greek of* Oppian. *Fr.* Halieutica. FM
Shelter Him in Milk and Meadow. Meridel LeSueur. ER
Shelter me from the myth, but gesture of. Gesture of Understanding. Ad Zuiderent, *tr. by* James S. Holmes. DuIn
Shelter, the old washhouse, The. A Quiet War in Leicester. Elaine Feinstein. CN
Sheltered from the spring wind by/ A silver screen. The Old Anguish. Chu Shu-chen, *tr. by* Kenneth Rexroth. BoWoP
Sheltered garden sleeps among the tall, The. Battledore. John Gray. NOBVV
Sheltering from rain. *Unknown, tr. by* Geoffrey Bownas *and* Anthony Thwaite. PeBIV
Sheltering Ground, The, *sels.* Sherod Santos. Son
    First Child, Born Out of Breach in Mid-May. *Fr.* I.
    I Bent to Touch a Damp Cloth to Your Mouth. *Fr.* IV.
Sheltering the Same Needs. Alex Kuo. UL
Shelving slimy river Don, The. The River Don. *Unknown.* GBP
Shema. Primo Levi, *tr. fr. Italian by* Ruth Feldman *and* Brian Swann. VWA
Shema Yisrael. *Unknown.* TrJP
Shen is very sick these days, he's fading away. On the Road through the Wu-i Mountains. Hsü Wei, *tr. by* Jonathan Chaves. CoBLCP
Shenandoah, *sel.* Delmore Schwartz.
    Let Us Consider Where the Great Men Are. MoAB; MoAmPo
Shenandoah. *Unknown.* AmFN
Shep lies long-bodied upon the auburn grass. February's Forgotten Mitts. Raymond Knister. NOBC
Shepeheards boye (no better doe him call), A. January Eclogue. Spenser. *Fr.* The Shepheardes [*or* Shepeards *or* Shepherd's] Calender. FiP
Shep'erd Bwoy, The. William Barnes. EBVV
Shephard loveth thow me vell? Jean Passerat, *tr. by* William Drummond of Hawthornden. OBVE
Shepheard and the Milkmaid, The. *Unknown.* CoMu
Shepheard Paris bore the Spartan bride, The. Theocritus, *tr. fr. Greek by* Dryden. *Fr.* Idylls, XXVII. OBVE
Shepheardes [*or* Shepeards *or* Shepherd's] Calender, The, *sels.* Spenser.
    Aprill. NAEL-1; PoEL-1
    ("Tell me, good Hobbinoll, what garres thee greete?") OBEV; OBSC; PoEL-1
    Elisa ("Ye dainty nymphs, that in this blessed brook"). OBSC
    (Lay to Eliza, The.) NOBE
    Ditty, A: In Praise of Eliza, Queen of the Shepherds. OBEV
    (Ditty, A: "See where she sits upon the grassy green.") FaBoCh
    August.
    It Fell upon a Holy Eve. InvP
    (Roundelay, A: "It fell upon a holy eve.") EIL
    February.
    Oak and the Brere, The. OBSC
    January Eclogue. FiP
    November. PoEL-1
    Dido My Dear, Alas, Is Dead. ChTr
    October. NAEL-1; OAEL-1
    (Contempt of Poetry, The.) OBSC
Shepheard's Daffodil, The. Michael Drayton. *Fr.* The Shepherd's Garland, Eclogue IX. EIL
Shepheard's Hunting, The. George Wither. *See* Shepherd's Hunting, The.
Shepherd, The. Blake. *Fr.* Songs of Innocence. BoTP; EnRP
Shepherd, The. Mary Gilmore. PoAu-1
Shepherd. William Stafford. PoA
Shepherd, The. Wordsworth. *Fr.* The Prelude [or, Growth of a Poet's Mind]: Retrospect—Love of Nature Leading to Love of Mankind. OBNC
Shepherd and His Flock, The. Mbuyiseni Oswald Mtshali. GrPl
Shepherd and Shepherdess. Nicholas Breton. *See* Passionate Shepherd, The: Merry Country Lad, The.
Shepherd and Shepherdess. Thomas Hennell. FaBoTw

Shepherd and the Nymph, The. Walter Savage Landor. *See* Gebir: Tamar's Wrestling.

Shepherd and the Shepherdess, The. *Unknown.* OBET

Shepherd Boy, The. John Clare. NOBVV

Shepherd Boy, The. Heine, *tr. fr. German.* BoTP

Shepherd-Boy and the Wolf, The. Aesop, *tr. fr. Greek by* William Ellery Leonard. AWP

Shepherd Boy Sings [in the Valley of Humiliation], The. Bunyan. *See* Pilgrim's Progress, The: He that is down needs fear no fall.

Shepherd Boys, The. Nicolas Saboly, *tr. fr. Provençal.* OHIP

Shepherd Boy's Song, The. Bunyan. *See* Pilgrim's Progress, The: He that is down needs fear no fall.

Shepherd: Echo, I ween, will in the wood reply. A Gentle Echo on Woman. Swift. FaBoCo; FiBHP; NU

Shepherd in Capri. Nishiwaki Junzaburo, *tr. fr. Japanese by* Hiroaki Sato. FCEI

Shepherd Kept Sheep on a Hill So High, A. Thomas D'Urfey. CoMu; ErPo

Shepherd Left Behind, The. Mildred Plew Meigs. TrCP

Shepherd, Ned Vaughan, A. Ned Vaughan. Walter de la Mare. FaBoEE

Shepherd plays his flute, The. Hollow Echo. Fazil Hüsnü Daglarca. CRP

Shepherd set him under a thorn, A. The Merry Bagpipes. *Unknown.* CoMu

Shepherd, Shepherd, Hark. Saint Teresa, *tr. fr. Spanish by* Arthur Symons. AWP

Shepherd, Show Me How to Go. Mary Baker Eddy. AH

Shepherd Song. Sir Philip Sidney. *Fr.* Arcadia. SiPS

Shepherd Speaks, The. John Erskine. TrCP

Shepherd stands at one end of the arena, A. Sheepdog Trials in Hyde Park. Cecil Day Lewis. MoP; NoAM; NoP; OxBTC

Shepherd to His Love, The. Christopher Marlowe. *See* Come live with me and be my love.

Shepherd, who can pass such wrong. Jorge de Montemayor, *tr. fr. Spanish by* Bartholomew Young. *Fr.* Diana. EIL

Shepherd Who Stayed, The. Theodosia Pickering Garrison. OHIP; PChr

Shepherd, wilt thou take counsel of the bird. Philomel to Corydon. William Young. AA

Shepherdess. Norman Cameron. *Fr.* Three Love Poems, III. GBL; OxBS

Shepherdess, The. Alice Meynell. ACP; AWP; MoBrPo; NOBVV; OBEV
   (Lady of the Lambs, The.) OBEV

Shepherdess—/ A fair one are you. Shakespeare. *Fr.* The Winter's Tale, IV, iv. PoE

Shepherdess and the Sailor, The. *Unknown.* OBET

Shepherdess' Valentine, *sel.* Francis Andrewes.
   "I bear, in sign of love." OFD

Shepherds, The. Beren Van Slyke. GoYe

Shepherds all, and maidens fair. The Priest's Chant. John Fletcher. *Fr.* The Faithful Shepherdess, II, i. OBS
   (Evening Knell, The.) EIL
   (Evening Song.) GN
   (Folding the Flocks.) CH

Shepherds armed with staff and sling. Carol of Patience. Robert Graves. OBCP

Shepherds at Bethlehem, The. *Unknown. See* Second Shepherd's Play, The: Hail, Comly and Clene.

Shepherd's [or Shepheards] Calendar, The, *sels.* John Clare.
   February. NOBE; OBNC
   "Or, trying simple charms and spells." FaBoUs

Shepherds' Carol. Norman Nicholson. OBCP

Shepherd's Complaint, A. Richard Barnfield. *See* My flocks feed not.

Shepherd's Complaint, The, *sel.* John Dickenson.
   Tityrus to His Fair Phyllis. EIL

Shepherd's daughter watching sheep, A. The Knight and the Shepherd's Daughter. *Unknown.* AmFP; ESPB, (A *and* B *vers.)*
   (Shepherd's Dochter, The.) OxBB

Shepherd's Dirge, The. George Peele. *See* Arraignment of Paris, The: Welladay, welladay, poor Colin, thou art going to the ground.

Shepherd's Dochter, The. *Unknown. See* There was a shepherd's dochter.

Shepherd's Dog, The. Leslie Norris. OBCP

Shepherd's Garland, The, *sels.* Michael Drayton.
   Cassamen and Dowsabell. *Fr.* Eclogue VIII (1593 ed.). OBSC
   "Late 'twas in June, the fleece when fully grown." *Fr.* Eclogue IX (1606 ed.). OBSC
   Rowland's Rhyme. *Fr.* Eclogue II (1606 ed.). OBSC
   Shepheard's Daffodil, The. *Fr.* Eclogue IX. EIL
   "O thou fair silver Thames." *Fr.* Eclogue III (1593 ed.). OBSC

"Tell me, thou skilful shepherd's swain." *Fr.* Eclogue IX (1606 ed.). EIL

Tenth Eclogue, The. JCP

Shepherd's Gift, A. Anytes, *tr. fr. Greek by* John William Burgon. AWP

Shepherd's Gratitude, The. Virgil, *tr. fr. Latin by* Charles Stuart Calverly. *Fr.* Eclogues, I. AWP

Shepherds Had an Angel, The. Christina Rossetti. OHIP

Shepherd's Home, The. William Shenstone. *See* My banks they are furnished with bees.

Shepherd's House, The, *sel.* Alfred de Vigny, *tr. fr. French by* Robert Bly.
   "Eva, I agree to love, among creation, all the creatures!" NU

Shephe[a]rd's Hunting, The, *sels.* George Wither.
   Fourth Eclogue, The. SeCV-1, *abr.*
   Philarete Praises Poetry. *Fr.* Eclogue IV. OBS

Shepherd's Hut, The. Andrew Young. GrPl; OxBTC

Shepherd's Hymn, The ("We saw Thee in Thy balmy nest"). Richard Crashaw. *Fr.* In the Holy Nativity of Our Lord God. ACP; NOBE; TrGrPo, 3 *sts.*
   (Verses from the Shepherd's Hymn.) OBEV

Shepherd's Lament, The. Goethe, *tr. fr. German by* Bayard Taylor. AWP

Shepherd's Ode, The. Robert Greene. *Fr.* Tullie's Love. OBSC

Shepherds on old hills, with robber. Gallery Shepherds. Patricia Beer. OxBC

Shepherd's Pipe, The, *sel.* William Browne.
   Dawn of Day. EIL

Shepherd's Play (Townley cycle), *sel. Unknown.*
   "It is sayde full ryfe." FaBoUs

Shepherd's Plea, The. Christopher Marlowe. *See* Come live with me and be my love.

Shepherd's Praise of Diana, The. Sir Walter Ralegh. *See* Praised be Diana's fair and harmless light.

Shepherd's Sirena, The, *sel.* Michael Drayton.
   Trent, The. FaBoPP; OBEV; PoEL-2
   (Jovial Shepheard's Song, The.) PoEL-2
   (Sirena.) OBEV

Shepherd's Song at Christmas. Langston Hughes. PChr

Shepherds' Song, Sung before Queen Anne, on the Wiltshire Downs, 11 June 1613, The, *sel.* George Ferebe.
   Houseless Downs, The. FaBoPP

Shepherd's star with trembling glint, The. En Bateau. Paul Verlaine, *tr. by* Arthur Symons. AWP

Shepherd's Tale, The. James Kirkup, *after the French of* Raoul Ponchon. OBCP

Shepherd's Tale, A. Sir Philip Sidney. *Fr.* Arcadia. SiPS

Shepherds that on this mountain ridge abide. Cleitagoras. Leonidas of Tarentum, *tr. by* William M. Hardinge. AWP

Shepherd's Week, The, *sels.* John Gay.
   Thursday; or, The Spell. PoEL-3
     "Last May-day fair I search'd to find a snail." FaBoUs
     "When first the year, I heard the cuckoo sing." PBBP
   Tuesday; or, the Ditty. NOEC
   Wednesday; or, The Dumps. OAEL-1

Shepherd's Wife's Song, The. Robert Greene. *Fr.* Greene's Mourning Garment. EIL; HAP; OBSC

Sher Imdad Ali's Tadpole. Saqi Farooqi, *tr. fr. Urdu by* Mahmood Jamal. PBMUP

Sheridan. Robert Lowell. DiL

Sheridan at Cedar Creek. Herman Melville. LiTA; PAH

Sheridan's Ride. Thomas Buchanan Read. AnAmPo; BeLS; FaBoBe; FaBV; FaFP; GN; OHFP; OHIP; PAH; WBLP

Sherman. Richard Watson Gilder. AA

Sherman Cyclone, The. *Unknown.* AmFP

Sherman's in Savannah. Oliver Wendell Holmes. PAH

Sherman's March to the Sea. Samuel H. M. Byers. PAH

Sherpa gasped out as they mounted the slope, The. Poem, Neither Hilláryous Norgay. Gardner E. Lewis. FiBHP

Sherwood in the twilight, is Robin Hood awake? A Song of Sherwood. Alfred Noyes. FaPON; MoBrPo
   (Sherwood.) MoBrPo

She's a copperheaded waitress. Ella, in a Square Apron, along Highway 80. Judy Grahn. *Fr.* The Common Woman, II. NMM

She's All My Fancy Painted Him. "Lewis Carroll." CenHV; FaBoNo; NA

She's dead—but in my grief. Tsurayuki, *tr. fr. Japanese by* Burton Watson. *Fr.* Kokin Shu. FCEI

She's found him, she has, but Radha disbelieves. Surdas, *tr. by* John Stratton Hawley *and* Mark Juergensmeyer. SSI

She's Free! Frances Ellen Watkins Harper. AIW; BlSi; Son

She's gone. She was my love, my moon or more. Complaint. James Wright. NOBA; TAP; VGW

She's had a Vassar education. An American Girl. Brander Matthews. AA

She's Hoy'd Me Out o' Lauderdale. *Unknown.* CoMu

She's in there all right. The New Lady Barber at Ralph's Barber Shop. Leo Dangel. MOWH

She's learned to hold her gladness lightly. A Lesson in Detachment. Vassar Miller. NePoEA-2

She's loveliest of the festal throng. The Rose and the Thorn. Paul Hamilton Hayne. AA; FaBoBe

She's not a faultless woman; no! After the Golden Wedding. James Kenneth Stephen. EBVV, *sel.*; NOBVV

She's small. Doll. Fahmida Riaz, *tr. by* Mahmood Jamal. PBMUP

She's somewhere in the sunlight strong. Richard Le Gallienne. OBEV

She's tall and gaunt, and in the hard, sad face. Scrubber. William Ernest Henley. *Fr.* In Hospital, XIX. BrPo

She's the camera. Judy-One. Don L. Lee. TAP

Shetland, Hill Dawn. Robin Munro. PoSH

Shi King, *sels. Unknown, tr. fr. Chinese.*
  Chou and the South. *Tr. by* Ezra Pound. CTC
  How Goes the Night? *Tr. by* Helen Waddell. AWP
  I Wait My Lord. *Tr. by* Helen Waddell. AWP
  Maytime. *Tr. by* L. Cranmer-Byng. AWP
  Morning Glory, The. *Tr. by* Helen Waddell. AWP
  Pear-Tree, The. *Tr. by* Allen Upward. AWP
  Under the Pondweed. *Tr. by* Helen Waddell. AWP
  Woman. *Tr. by* H. A. Giles. AWP
  You Will Die. *Tr. by* H. A. Giles. AWP

Shield from every dart, The. What Christ Is to Us. *Unknown.* BLRP

Shield: "Lonely wanderer, wounded with iron, A." *Unknown, formerly at.* to Cynewulf, *tr. fr. Anglo-Saxon by* Charles W. Kennedy. *Fr.* Riddles (Exeter Book). AnOE

Shield of Achilles, The. W. H. Auden. EBEV; FaBoMo; FaBoPV; GTBS-P; HAP; NAEL-2; NoAM; NOBE; NOCV; NoP; PoA; PoE; WeW

Shield of War, The. Thomas Sackville, *fr.* A Mirror [*or* Mirour] for Magistrates. *Fr.* Induction to "A Mirror for Magistrates." AAS; OBSC

Shift, here, in town, not meanest among squires. On Lieutenant Shift. Ben Jonson. OBSV

Shift of Emphasis, A. Lauris Edmond. *Fr.* Two Birth Poems, I. ATNZ

Shifting Colors. Robert Lowell. HCAP

Shifty-eyed, the frog. Ranran, *tr. by* Hiroaki Sato. FCEI

Shifty limpet on his rocky shore, The. Every Earthly Creature. John Malcolm Brinnin. LiTA

Shih Ching, *sels. Unknown, tr. fr. Chinese by* Arthur Waley.
  "Very handsome gentleman, A." BoWoP
  Widow's Lament. BoWoP

Shih-hou Pointed Out to Me That from Ancient Times There Had Never Been a Poem on the Subject of Li. Mei Yao-ch'en, *tr. fr. Chinese by* Burton Watson. CoBCP

Shillin' a Day. Kipling. NoAM

Shilling life will give you all the facts, A. Who's Who. W. H. Auden. MoAB; MoBrPo; MoP; NoAM; Son

Shiloh; a Requiem. Herman Melville. AmFN; AnAmPo; FF; LiTA; NOBA; NoP; OBWP; OxBA; SCV; WiR

Shimmering Pediment. John Yau. UL

Shine alone, shine nakedly, shine like bronze. Nuances of a Theme by Williams. Wallace Stevens. CMoP; LiTA

Shine forth into the night, O flame. Give Our Conscience Light. Aline B. Carter. TrPWD

Shine, O sun! tenderly on my skin. Love Dirge. *Unknown, tr. by* John White. WTO

Shine, O thou sacred shepherds' star. The Houseless Downs. George Ferebe. *Fr.* The Shepherds' Song, Sung before Queen Anne, on the Wiltshire Downs, 11 June 1613. FaBoPP

Shine, "O world!" don't weary the gulping Pole. Frank O'Hara. *Fr.* Life on Earth. UnPo

Shine on me, moon. A Sentinel's Song. Rarawa Kerehoma, *tr. by* Barry Mitcalfe. WTO

Shine on Me, Secret Splendor. Edwin Markham. TrPWD

Shine Out, Fair Sun, with All Your Heat. *At. to* George Chapman. *Fr.* The Masque of the Twelve Months. ChTr; ELP
  (Song: "Shine out, fair sun, with all your heat.") EiL

Shine, Perishing Republic. Robinson Jeffers. CMoP; FF; LiTA; LiTM; MAT; MoAB; MoP; NAAL-2; NoAM; NOBA; NoP; OxBA; PrIm; TAP; UnPo; VGW

Shine, Republic. Robinson Jeffers. FaBoPV

Shingle Beach Poem. James K. Baxter. ATNZ

Shining children in the fog. The Swimming Lesson. Robert Hershon. NeAC

Shining Eye of Horus cometh, The. He Kindleth a Fire. *Unknown, tr. fr. Egyptian by* Robert Hillyer. *Fr.* Book of the Dead. AWP

Shining in his stickiness and glistening with honey. The Friendly Cinnamon Bun. Russell Hoban. ILY

Shining like a star. Hunting Song. *Unknown, tr. by* Jerome Rothenberg. STP

Shining moon, A. Myoe, *tr. fr. Japanese by* Burton Watson. *Fr.* Ten Tanka. FCEI

Shining neutral summer has no voice, The. In Memoriam: Ernst Toller. W. H. Auden. NYBP

Shining Night or Dick Daring, the Poacher, A. *Unknown.* CoMu

Shining Thing. Gabriel Preil, *tr. fr. Hebrew by* Bernhard Frank. MHeP

Shining Things. Elizabeth Gould. BoTP

Shining waters rise and swell, The. The Drowning of Conaing. *Unknown, tr. by* Frank O'Connor. AnIL

Shiny beings come down out of the sky. The Compound Eye. Sandra McPherson. AnAn

Shiny Little House, The. Nancy M. Hayes. BoTP

Shiny record albums scattered over. As You Leave Me. Etheridge Knight. FF; MT; NNaP

Ship, The. Charles MacKay. BLPA

Ship, The. Lloyd Mifflin. AA

Ship, The. Sir John Collings Squire. CH

Ship, The. *Unknown.* PoLF

Ship, an Isle, a Sickle Moon, A. James Elroy Flecker. BrPo; FaBoRV

Ship-broken Men Whom Stormy Seas Sore Toss. William Fowler. GoTS

Ship-Building Emperors Commanded. Peter Levi. NePoEA-2

Ship Burning and a Comet All in One Day, A. Richard Eberhart. NYBP

Ship Canal from the Atlantic to the Pacific, The. Francis Lieber. PAH

Ship from Thames. Rex Ingamells. PoAu-2

Ship I have got in the North Country, A. The *Golden Vanity. Unknown.* FaBoCh

Ship in Distress, The. *Unknown.* OxBSS

Ship Is All Laden, The. *Unknown.* OxBSS

Ship, leaving or arriving, of my lover. After a Passage in Baudelaire. Robert Duncan. CMoP; PoA; PoE

Ship lowers its anchor, The. Estuary. Maruyama Kaoru, *tr. by* Hiroaki Sato. FCEI

Ship moves, The. 4th of July. William Carlos Williams. PoA

Ship of Death, The. D. H. Lawrence. CMoP; FaBoRV; FaBoTw; GTBS-P; LiTB; MoAB; MoBrPo; MoP; MOS; NAEL-2; NoAM; NoP; OAEL-2; PrIm

Ship of Earth, The. Sidney Lanier. MOS

Ship of Fools, The, *sels.* Alexander Barclay.
  Geographers. ACP
  Of Glotons and Dronkardes. OxBLMV
  Preachment for Preachers. ACP
  Star of the Sea. ACP
  Tudor Rose, The. ACP

Ship of Life, The. Ahmad al-Safi al-Najafi, *tr. fr. Arabic by* Salma Khadra Jayyusi *and* John Heath-Stubbs. MAP

Ship of Love, The. Salma Khadra Jayyusi, *tr. fr. Arabic by the author and* Charles Doria. MAP

Ship of Rio, The. Walter de la Mare. CenHV; MOS; PDV

Ship of State, The. Longfellow. *See* Building of the Ship, The: Thou, too, sail on, O Ship of State!

Ship Sails Up to Bideford, A. Herbert Asquith. BoTP

Ship That Never Returned, The. *Unknown.* AS

Ship That Never Returned, The. Henry Clay Work. BLPA

Ship That Went Down, The. Adah Isaacs Menken. CBWP-1

Ship! the White Ship!, The. Armando, *tr. fr. Dutch by* James S. Holmes. DuIn

Ship was large, The. Ode to a Lost Cargo in a Ship Called *Save.* José Craveirinha, *tr. by* Chris Searle. WMBCH

Ship with shields before the sun, A. Near Avalon. William Morris. OAEL-2

Shiperd-boy, what is yer trade? The Beggar-Laddie. *Unknown.* ESPB

Shipman, The. Chaucer. *Fr.* The Canterbury Tales: The Epilogue of the Man of Law's Tale. ACP

Shipman was ther, woning fer by weste, A. The Shipman. Chaucer. *Fr.* The Canterbury Tales: Prologue. MOS

Shipmates. Merle Collins. WS

Shipmen, The. William Hunnis. OBSC

Shipment to Maidanek. Ephim G. Fogel. OBWP; TrJP

Ships, The. J. J. Bell. BoTP

Ships are fitted, and the convoy sails, The. Convoy. William Jay Smith. WaP

Ship's Cook, a Captive Sings, The. Hugo von Hofmannsthal, *tr. fr. German by* Charles Wharton Stork. TrJP

Ship's master:/ before him, in the waist and before it. David Jones. *Fr.* The Anathemata. FaBoTw

Ships of Yule, The. Bliss Carman. CaP

Ships That Pass in the Night. Paul Laurence Dunbar. AnAmPo; BANP; CDC; MOS

Ships That Pass in the Night (The Theologian's Tale). Longfellow. *Fr.* Tales of a Wayside Inn, *pt.* III. MOS

Shipwreck, The, *sels.* William Falconer.
    "As the proud horse with costly trappings gay." *Fr.* II. MOS
    "But now Athenian mountains they descry." *Fr.* III. GoTL
    "Four hours the sun his high meridian throne." *Fr.* II. MOS
    Shortening Sail. *Fr.* II. MOS

Shipwreck. Mary Weston Fordham, *tr. by* Mary Ann Caws. CBWP-2

Shipwreck. Adriaan Morriën, *tr. fr. Dutch by* Ria Leigh-Loohuizen. DuIn

Shipwreck, The. E. Harriet Palmer. NA

Shir Ma'alot/ A Song of Degrees. Richard Flantz. VWA

Shira. Howard Schwartz. VWA

Shirt. Charles Simic. HCAP

Shirt of a Lad, The. *Unknown, tr. fr. Welsh by* Anthony Conran. OBWVE

Shirt Poem, The. Gerald Stern. CAPP

Shirt races in the meadow, A. Storm. Agnes Nemes Nagy, *tr. by* Laura Schiff. PBWP

Shirts, The. Tess Gallagher. MAYP

Shitty. Kingsley Amis. OxBC; TW

Shiva. Robinson Jeffers. NoAM; NOBA; Son

Shivering and hoping no one. Grandma's Bureau. Robert Morgan. EOEF

Shlomo Molkho Sings on the Eve of His Burning. A. Leyeles, *tr. fr. Yiddish by* Benjamin *and* Barbara Harshav. AYP

Shlup, shlup, the dog. Denise Levertov. *Fr.* Six Variations, III. HeIP; InPK

Sho Nuff. Nilene O. A. Foxworth. AIW

Sho-shó-ne Sa-cá-ga-we-a—captive and wife was she. Sa-cá-ga-we-a. Edna Dean Proctor. PAH

Shoal of idlers, from a merchant craft, A. Pelters of Pyramids. Richard Henry Horne. OBTV

Shoals of Herring, The. Ewan MacColl. OxBSS

Shoan Temple. Takamura Kotaro, *tr. fr. Japanese by* Hiroaki Sato. FCEI

Shocked that she missed the footbridge! The Suicide. V. R. Laing. PoA

Shocking Rape and Murder of Two Lovers. *Unknown.* CoMu

Shoe. John Perreault. EAS

Shoe a little horse. *Unknown.* OxNR

Shoe Shop. Barton Sutter. SM; SoSe

Shoe the colt, shoe the colt. Mother Goose. OxNR

Shoe the steed with silver. Sheridan at Cedar Creek. Herman Melville. LiTA; PAH

Shoe-tying, The. Robert Herrick. CaPo

Shoe with legs, A. Lobster. Anne Sexton. AnAn

Shoemaker, The. *Unknown.* FaPON

Shoemaker makes shoes without leather, A. *Unknown.* OxNR

Shoemaker Nikke. Arvo Turtiainen, *tr. fr. Finnish by* Aili Jarvenpa. SOP

Shoemaker's Holiday, The, *sels.* Thomas Dekker.
    Drinking Song. TrGrPo
    (Hey Derry Derry.) SeCePo
    (Saint Hugh.) OBSC
    (Troll the Bowl!) EIL
    O, the Month of May. *Fr.* III, v. EIL
    (May.) OBSC
    (Maytime.) TrGrPo
    (Song: "O the month of May, the merry month of May.") PBBP

Shoemakker, The. *Unknown.* OBET

Shoes. Valerie Worth. TDD

Shoes are made to fit the feet. *Gond Oral Tradition, tr. by* V. Elwin *and* S. Hivale. WTO

Shoes fall on their feet. How Things Fall. Donald Finkel. VWA

Shoes going over rocks have fins. Kikaku, *tr. fr. Japanese by* Hiroaki Sato. *Fr.* Thirty-three Hokku. FCEI

Shoes, secret face of my inner life. My Shoes. Charles Simic. CoAP; HCAP

Shoeshine for Louis Armstrong, A. Peter Goldsworthy. UAS

Shoichi brushed the black. Awakening. Lucien Stryk. CAPP; SV

Sholom Aleichem. Elias Lieberman. TrJP

Sholto Peach Harrison you are no son of mine. Correspondence between Mr. Harrison in Newcastle and Mr. Sholto Peach Harrison in Hull. Stevie Smith. FaBoNo; NBLV; OxBC

Shon a Morgan. *Unknown.* GBP; OxNR

Shoo over! *Unknown.* PBBP

Shoo stud besider her looms an' watch'd. The Factory Girl. "Bill o' th' Hoylus End." PF

Shoo the orioles, drive them away. Spring Grievance. Chin Ch'ang-hsü, *tr. by* Burton Watson. CoBCP

Shoofly, The. Felix O'Hare. AmFP

Shoot, comrades. Jacob Glatstein, *tr. by* Benjamin *and* Barbara Harshav. AYP

Shoot down the rebelsmen who dare. "Rebels." Ernest Crosby. PAH

Shoot, false Love, I care not. *Unknown.* OBSC

Shooter's Hill, *sel.* Robert Bloomfield.
    "Health! I seek thee; dost thou love." OBNC

Shooting. B. H. Fairchild. TDD

Shooting, The. Laura Tohe. STE

Shooting Crows. David Huddle. GOYP

Shooting Ducks in South Louisiana. Richard Tillinghast. MAYP

Shooting of Dan McGrew, The. Robert W. Service. BeLS; FaBoBe; FaFP; FPL; PoLF; PoRA; RB

Shooting of His Dear. *Unknown.* OxBoLi

Shooting of John Dillinger outside the Biograph Theater July 22, 1934, The. David Wagoner. CoAP; FYAP; RB; SM

Shooting of Werfel, The. Vernon Watkins. WaP

Shooting Script, A. Seamus Heaney. BAP

Shooting Script, *sels.* Adrienne Rich.
    "Mare's skeleton in the clearing: another sign of life, The." *Fr.* 11. FaBoWP
    Newsreel. *Fr.* 9. FaBoWP; HCAP
    "Of simple choice they are the villagers; their clothes come." *Fr.* 5. HCAP
    "Old blanket. The crumbs of rubbed wool turning up, The." *Fr.* 3. HCAP
    "They come to you with their descriptions of your soul." *Fr.* 10. HCAP
    "We are driven to odd attempts; once it would not have occurred." *Fr.* 13. HCAP
    "Whatever it was: the grains of the glacier caked in the." *Fr.* 14. FaBoWP; HCAP

Shooting Song, A. William Brighty Rands. OxBChV

Shooting the Horses. Pamela Mordecai. PVCV

Shooting the Loop. Michael Sheridan. NAmP

Shooting Whales. Mark Strand. CAPP; LCAP

Shop, The. Wu Sheng, *tr. fr. Chinese by* Dominic Cheung. IFON

Shop and Freedom. *Unknown.* PAH

Shop o' Meat-Weare. William Barnes. NOBVV

Shop Talk. Roy Fuller. OxBC

Shoplifters. Maura Stanton. MAYP

Shopping. Cees Buddingh', *tr. fr. Dutch by* James S. Holmes. DuIn

Shopping for Meat in Winter. Oscar Williams. LiTA; LiTM

Shopping for Midnight. G. E. Murray. MAYP

Shopping in Chicago. Ed Orr. SoTCo

Shopping in Ferney with Voltaire. Maxine W. Kumin. ER

Shops, the streets are full of old men, The. Talk. Roo Borson. NIP; NOBC

Shore. Jean Garrigue. TAP

Shore. Mary Britton Miller. RAR

Shore. Diana O Hehir. NPGG

Shore, The. David St. John. LCAP; MAYP

Shore Birds. Vi Gale. GoYe

Shore-lark soars to his topmost flight, The. Ecstasy. Duncan Campbell Scott. CaP

Shore looked wild, without a trace of man, The. Byron. *Fr.* Don Juan, II. HAP

Shore of Life, The. Robert Fitzgerald. VGW

Shore Scene. John Logan. SM

Shore seemed suddenly more distant. Or had the other slid close?, The. A Summer on the Lake. Otto Orban, *tr. by* Jascha Kessler. FOC

Shore Thing. Bernhard Hillila. SoTCo

Shore Tullye. Robert Rendall. OxBS

Shore wind is cold on my travel clothes, The. Abutsu the Nun, *tr. fr. Japanese by* Edwin O. Reischauer. *Fr.* The Diary of the Waning Moon. PBWP

Shoreham: Twilight Time. Samuel Palmer. OAEL-2

Shoreline. Mary Barnard. PoA

Shoreline Doesn't Change, The. Eddy van Vliet, *tr. fr. Dutch by* Theo Hermans. DuIn

Shores are crown'd with people, The. Luis de Camões, *tr. fr. Portuguese by* Sir Richard Fanshawe. *Fr.* The Lusiads. OBVE

Shores of anguish. Magda Portal, *tr. by* Allan Francovich *and* Kathleen Weaver. PBWP

Shores of my native land. Isaac Toussaint L'Ouverture, *tr. by* Edna Worthley Underwood. TTY

Shores of Styx are lone for evermore, The. Idle Charon. Eugene Lee-Hamilton. NOBVV

Shoriken. Charles Brasch. ATNZ; PENZ

Shoring up the ocean. A railroad track. Blood-Sister. Adrienne Rich. NAAL-2; NoP

Short, big-nosed men with nasty conical caps. The Hittites. Roy Fuller. OxBSP

Short Biography of a Washerwoman. Yolanda Ulloa. AIW

Short cut home lay through the cemetery, The. The Mistress. Joan Barton. OxBTC

Short day has grown, A. The Place of V. Ray A. Young Bear. VoR

Short Days, The. John Updike. AnAmPo

Short direction, A. Rules and Regulations. "Lewis Carroll." FaBoUs; NoBVV

Short Eulogy. Zali Gurevitch, *tr. fr. Hebrew by* Gabriel Levin. VWA

Short Fairy Tale, A. Stanislaw Grochowiak, *tr. fr. Polish by* Czeslaw Milosz. PwPP

Short History of British India, A. Geoffrey Hill. OxBC

Short Lay of Sigurd, The. *Unknown. See* Lay of Sigurd, The.

Short Life of the Hermit, A, *sel.* John Logan.
"He told the crowd 'The devils.'" CRP

Short night, A—outside the window bamboo rustles. Princess Shikishi, *tr. fr. Japanese by* Hiroaki Sato. *Fr.* Seventy-eight Tanka. FCEI

Short night: on a hairy caterpillar. Buson, *tr. fr. Japanese by* Hiroaki Sato. *Fr.* Eighty-seven Hokku. FCEI

Short Order. Charles Bukowski. HoPM

Short Prayer to Mary, A. *Unknown.* MeEL

Short service, to be sure, A. Lament for a Leg. John Ormond. OBWVE

Short Song of Congratulation [*or* To a Young Heir], A. Samuel Johnson. EBEV; ELP; HAP; InPK; InPS; InVP; NOBE; NOEC; NoP; OBSV; PoE; PoEL-3; TEP; UnPo

Short space my feet had traversed ere. Guillaume de Lorris *and* Jean de Meun, *tr. fr. French by* F. S. Ellis. *Fr.* The Romance [*or* Romaunt] of the Rose. OAEL-1

Short Story. Ellen Bryant Voigt. BLA; PPR

Short Time. Gavin Ewart. NoAM

Short Winter Tale, A. Natan Zach, *tr. fr. Hebrew by* Peter Everwine *and* Shula Starkman. VWA

Shortening Sail. William Falconer. *Fr.* The Shipwreck, II. MOS

Shorter American Memory of the American Character According to Santayana. Rosemarie Waldrop. EOEF

Shortest and Sweetest of Songs, The. George Macdonald. NOBVV

Shortest fight, The. The Knockout. Lillian Morrison. RHPC

Shortly after I Married, I Had to Go into Mourning, *sels.* Rai San'yo, *tr. fr. Chinese.*
"Fist like the mountain fern half unfurled." *Fr.* III, *tr. by* Burton Watson. FCEI; JLIC-2
"No fields, no house, one poor scholar." *Fr.* I, *tr. by* Burton Watson. FCEI; JLIC-2
"So stupid of me to hope you'll take to books." *Fr.* II, *tr. by* Burton Watson. FCEI; JLIC-2

Shortness and Misery of Life, The. Isaac Watts. NOCV

Shot. Itamar Ya'oz-kest, *tr. fr. Hebrew by* Bernhard Frank. *Fr.* Ordeal by Fire. MHeP

Shot at Random, A. D. B. Lewis. FaBoCo; FaFP; FiBHP

Shot? So Quick, So Clean an Ending? A. E. Housman. *Fr.* A Shropshire Lad, XLIV. PeHV

Shot Who? Jim Lane! Merrill Moore. MoAmPo

Should a horse-load of love. Yakamochi. *Fr.* Manyo Shu. Ma

Should all our churchmen foam in spite. At Farringford. Tennyson. *Fr.* To the Rev. F. D. Maurice. FaBoPP

Should all the world so wide to atoms fall. Our Insufficiency to Praise God Suitably for His Mercy. Edward Taylor. LiTA

Should any ask me on His form to dwell. He Hath No Parallel. Sadi, *tr. fr. Persian by* L. Cranmer-Byng. *Fr.* The Gulistan. AWP

Should auld acquaintance be forgot. Auld Lang Syne. Burns. AWP; BLPL; EnRP; FaFP; GoTS; LiTB; NAEL-2; NOBE; OBEV; OxBS; PoLF; TEP

Should Dennis print how once you robb'd your brother. On Dennis. Pope. FaBoEE

Should have a name. River Man. Michael Jackson. ATNZ

Should he upon an evening ramble fare. Shelley. *Fr.* Epistle to George Keats. ChER

Should I, a man, die in vain. Okura. *Fr.* Manyo Shu. Ma

Should I Be a Rabbi? Hayyim Nahman Bialik, *tr. fr. Hebrew by* Grace Goldin. TrJP

Should I be favoured with a happy lease of life. Hozumi Oyu. *Fr.* Manyo Shu. Ma

Should I believe you, e'en my oaths are witty. *Unknown.* FaBoEE

Should I get married? Should I be good? Marriage. Gregory Corso. CoAP; LiTM; MoP; NeAP; NoP; OBAL; PPP; PrIm; TAP

Should I know this room. Locale. Penelope Shuttle. BrRo

Should I my steps turn to the rural seat. James Thomson. *Fr.* The Seasons: Spring. FM

Should I not be ashamed. The Ending. Paul Engle. NYBP

Should I say, my people? I turned stone. Maratea Porto: Saying Goodbye to the Vitolos. Richard Hugo. MAT

Should I thee ranke with Radamanthus fell. A Satyretericall Charracter of a Proud Upstart. John Saffin. SCAP
(March 4th Anno 1698/9; a Charracteristicall Satyre.) SCAP

Should I with silver tooles delve through the hill. Edward Taylor. *Fr.* Preparatory Meditations before My Approach to the Lord's Supper, LVI. OxBA; SCAP

Should old acquaintance be forgot. Old-Long-Syne. *Unknown.* OBS

Should some ill painter, in a wild design. Horace, *tr. fr. Latin by* John Oldham. *Fr.* The Art of Poetry. OBVE

Should the building totter, run for an archway! The Fallen Tower of Siloam. Robert Graves. WaP

Should the cold Muscovit, whose furre and stove. To the Right Honourable the Countesse of C. William Habington. SeCP

Should the shade of Plato. On Installing an American Kitchen in Lower Austria. W. H. Auden. NYBP

Should the time come. Hitomaro. *Fr.* Manyo Shu. Ma

Should the wide world roll away. Stephen Crane. *Fr.* The Black Riders, X. AmPP

Should Thy Love Die. George Meredith. ELP

Should we go now a-wand'ring, we should meet. London in 1646. Henry Vaughan. FaBoPP

Should you ask me, whence these stories. Longfellow. *Fr.* The Song of Hiawatha. NOBA; PoE

Should you find no inn. Gesse Departing at Early Dusk. Kenko, *tr. by* Steven D. Carter. WFTW

Should You Go First. Albert K. Rowswell. BLPL; PoLF

Should you hide in the rock tomb. *Unknown. Fr.* Manyo Shu. FCEI

Should you love—be it a furnace. A. K. Tolstoy, *tr. by* Alan Myers. AAA

Should you, my lord, while you pursue my song. Phillis Wheatley. *Fr.* To the Right Honourable William, Earl of Dartmouth. BPo; TTY

Should you revisit us. New Approach Needed. Kingsley Amis. NoAM; OxBTC

Shoulder of rock, A. High Island. Richard Murphy. CIP; NOIV

Shouldered box has nested deep, The. Farewell to a Jovial Friend. Gloria Escoffery. PBCV

Shouldering firewood I climb down the green peak. Ryokan, *tr. by* Burton Watson. JLIC-2

Shouldering shapes of the skies of Broceliande. Taliessin's Song of the Unicorn. Charles Williams. FaBoTw

Shout came from the loquacious ones, A. A Welsh Ballad. Edmwnd Prys, *tr. by* Gwyn Williams. OBWVE

Shout for Joy. *Unknown.* AmFP

Shout, Little Lulu. *Unknown.* AmFP

Shout, shout, up with your song! The March of the Women. Cicely Hamilton. BrRo

Shouting Song. *Unknown.* AmFP

Shovel-gnats gnaw at the open wound, The. On the Edge of the Copper Pit. Pauline Henson. GoYe

Shovel Man, The. Carl Sandburg. HAP

Shovelling Iron Ore. *Unknown.* AS, *with music;* GBP

Show, The. Wilfred Owen. LiTB; LiTM; MoAB; MoBrPo; OBWVE; OxBTC; WaaP; WaP

Show for the Eyes. Pierre Reverdy, *tr. fr. French by* Michael Benedikt. POS

Show is not the show, The. Emily Dickinson. AmPP

Show me again the time. Lines: To a Movement in Mozart's E-Flat Symphony. Thomas Hardy. ELP; NoAM

Show me dear[e] Christ, thy spouse, so bright and clear. John Donne. *Fr.* Holy Sonnets, XVIII. MeLP; NAEL-1; NoP; OBS; PoE; Son

Show Me the Way. *Unknown, tr. fr. Burmese by* U Win Pe. PBWP

Show me thy feet: show me thy legs, thy thighs. To Dianeme. Robert Herrick. CaPo

Show Me Thyself. Margaret Sangster. TrPWD

Show of arrogant spirit fills the road, A. Light Furs, Fat Horses. Po Chü-i, *tr. by* Burton Watson. CoBCP

Show the runner coming through the shadows. The Runner. Gary Gildner. TAP

Shower, The. Linda Smukler. GLP

Shower [*or* Showre], The. Henry Vaughan. BoNaP; ChTr; FaBoPP; LiTB; MePo; OBS; SeCP
Shower, a sprinkle, A. Summer Rain. Eve Merriam. PDV
Shower and Sunshine. Maud Morin. BoTP
Shower comes up, A. Abutsu the Nun, *tr. by* Steven D. Carter. WFTW
Shower hath past, ere it hath well begun, The. After the Shower. Archibald Lampman. CaP
Shower of Cobwebs, A. Gilbert White, *tr. fr. Spanish.* TSS
Shower: on a raft the pole, A. Taigi, *tr. fr. Japanese by* Hiroaki Sato. *Fr.* Twenty-nine Hokku. FCEI
Shower passes, A. The Winter Moon after a Rain. Tamesada, *tr. by* Steven D. Carter. WFTW
Shower passes by, A. Crimson Leaves. Joben, *tr. by* Steven D. Carter. WFTW
Shower silently wets the roots, A. Buson, *tr. fr. Japanese by* Hiroaki Sato. *Fr.* Eighty-seven Hokku. FCEI
Showers. Marchette Chute. RAR
Showers are falling. Tameko, *tr. by* Steven D. Carter. WFTW
Showers go on, The. Tamesuke, *tr. by* Steven D. Carter. WFTW
Showers wet/ the orange blossoms. Shunzei, *tr. fr. Japanese by* Burton Watson. *Fr.* Thirty Tanka. FCEI
Showing it to the locum. *Unknown, tr. by* Geoffrey Bownas *and* Anthony Thwaite. PeBJV
Showre, The. Henry Vaughan. *See* Shower, The.
Shredded sunset, The. Night Interpreted. Everett Hoagland. NBP
Shreds of Our Webs, The. Charles Bernstein. LP
Shrew, The. Ogden Nash. CenHV
Shrewish, barren, bony, nosy servant, A. Daibhi O Bruadair, *tr. by* Thomas Kinsella. NOIV
Shriek said the saw smile said the mice. To the Age's Insanities. Marie Ponsot. VGW
Shrieks in dark leaves. The rumpled owl. Hunger and Thirst. John Peale Bishop. PoA
Shrike call takes a persimmon thief, A. Issa, *tr. fr. Japanese by* Hiroaki Sato. *Fr.* Forty-four Hokku. FCEI
Shrike calls when I kiss my infant's cheek, A. Kikaku, *tr. by* Hiroaki Sato. FCEI
Shrill, glass-clear notes—"Titmouse!" I sighed, enchanted. Tat for Tit. Walter de la Mare. FM
Shrill the fife, kettle the drum. Baldy Bane. William Sydney Graham. NePoEA
Shrilling locust slowly sheathes, The. James Whitcomb Riley. *Fr.* The Beetle. FaPON
Shrilly, the returning geese warn of the season's passing. Written in Response to Wei-yin's Rhymes. Wang Ts'ai-wei, *tr. by* Irving Lo. WFTU
Shrimp, The, *sel.* Moses Browne.
    "Shrimp, A! Black thing as widow's crape." NOEC
Shrimping boats are late today, The. Nocturne: Georgia Coast. Daniel Whitehead Hicky. AmFN
Shrine Festival. Wang Chia, *tr. fr. Chinese by* Burton Watson. CoBCP
Shrine of General Pien, The. Chu Yün-ming, *tr. fr. Chinese by* Jonathan Chaves. CoBLCP
"Shrink" is a misnomer. The religious. Some Terms. Robert Pinsky. *Fr.* Essay on Psychiatrists, II. HCAP
Shriving, The. Jared Carter. MOWH
Shropshire Lad, A. Sir John Betjeman. MoBS
Shropshire Lad, A, *sels.* A. E. Housman.
    Along the Field as We Came By. *Fr.* XXVI. HAP; MoAB; MoBrPo; WeW
    "Be still, my soul, be still; the arms you bear are brittle." *Fr.* XLVIII. MoAB; MoBrPo; NOBVV; OAEL-2; OBNC; TrGrPo
    Bredon Hill. *Fr.* XXI. BrPo; EBVV; FaBoPP; MoAB; MoBrPo; NAEL-2; SoSe
    Carpenter's Son, The. *Fr.* XLVII. MoAB; MoBrPo
    Could Man Be Drunk for Ever. LiTM; NAEL-2; OBMV; PPP
    Day of Battle, The. *Fr.* LVI. OHIP; WaaP
    1887. *Fr.* I. FaPoR; NIP; NOBVV; PrIm; UnPo
    Far In a Western Brookland. *Fr.* LII. AWP; PoEL-5
    Farewell to Barn and Stack and Tree. *Fr.* VIII. CMoP; MoAB; MoBrPo; SoSe; UnPo
    From Far, from Eve and Morning. *Fr.* XXXII. CMoP; HAP; HeIP; MoBrPo; NoP; PoEL-5; PrIm
    Hughley Steeple. *Fr.* LXI. FaBoPP
    I Hoed and Trenched and Weeded. *Fr.* LXIII. LiTM; MoBrPo; TrGrPo; UnPo; WeW
    Immortal Part, The. *Fr.* XLIII. MoBrPo; UnPo
    "In my own shire, if I was sad." *Fr.* XLI. BrPo
    Into My Heart [an Air That Kills]. *Fr.* XL. ChTr; CMoP; EBEV; LiTB; LiTM; Mes; MoAB; MoBrPo; NoAM; NoBE; NOBVV; OAEL-2; OxBTC

(Yon Far Country.) SeCePo
Is My Team Ploughing [*or* Plowing]. *Fr.* XXVII. CMoP; EBVV; LiTM; MoAB; MoBrPo; NoAM; NoP; OBD; OBEV; TrGrPo
Isle of Portland, The. *Fr.* LIX. MoBrPo
"It nods and curtseys and recovers." *Fr.* XVI. NOBVV
Lads in Their Hundreds, The. *Fr.* XXIII. MoBrPo; OxBTC
Lent Lily, The. *Fr.* XXIX. OHIP
Look Not in My Eyes, for Fear. *Fr.* XV. PeHV; PoEL-5
Loveliest of Trees [the Cherry Now]. *Fr.* II. AWP; BLPL; BoNaP; ChTr; CMoP; ELP; FaBoBe; FaBV; FaFP; FF; HAP; HeIP; InPK; LiTB; LiTM; MoAB; MoBrPo; MoP; NAs; NoAM; NoP; OAEL-2; OHIP; OxBTC; PoE; PoLF; PrIm; RB; SoSe; TEP; TrGrPo
New Mistress, The. *Fr.* XXXIV. MoBrPo
"Now hollow fires burn out to black." *Fr.* LX. NOBVV
Oh, See How Thick the Goldcup Flowers. *Fr.* V. FaBV; MoBrPo
Oh, When I Was in Love with You. *Fr.* XVIII. BoLoP; FaBV; LiTB; MoBrPo; TTTS
On Moonlit Heath and Lonesome Bank. *Fr.* IX. BrPo; CMoP; SoSe
On the idle hill of summer. *Fr.* XXXV. MoBrPo; NOBE; OAEL-2; OBNC; OBWP; SoSe
On Wenlock Edge [the Wood's in Trouble]. *Fr.* XXXI. BrPo; GTBS-P; LiTB; Mes; MoAB; MoBrPo; NAEL-2; NOBE; NoP; OBNC; OxBTC; PoEL-5; PoRA; PrIm; RB
"Others, I am not the first." *Fr.* XXX. CMoP; LiTB; MoBrPo; NOBVV; OxBTC; PoE; PPP
Reveille. *Fr.* IV. CMoP; FaFP; FPL; LiTB; LiTM; MoAB; MoBrPo; NoP; PoLF; SoSe
Shot? So Quick, So Clean an Ending? *Fr.* XLIV. PeHV
Terence, This Is Stupid Stuff. *Fr.* LXII. CMoP; HeIP; InPK; LiTB; LiTM; MoP; NAEL-2; NIP; NoAM; NoAM; NoP; PrIm
    (Epilogue: "Terence, this is stupid stuff.") MoAB; MoBrPo; TrGrPo
"'Tis spring; come out to ramble." *Fr.* XXIX. OHIP
To an Athlete Dying Young. *Fr.* XIX. BLPL; BrPo; CMoP; DL; HAP; HeIP; InPK; LiTB; LiTM; MoAB; MoBrPo; MoP; NAEL-2; NIP; NoAM; NoP; PoE; PoEL-5; PoRA; PrIm; SoSe; TEP; TrGrPo; UnPo; WeW
Wenlock Edge (" 'Tis time, I think; by Wenlock town"). *Fr.* XXXIX. FaBoPP
    (Wenlock.) SeCePo
When I was One-and-Twenty. *Fr.* XIII. CMoP; ELP; FaBV; FaFP; FPL; HeIP; InPK; LiTB; LiTM; MoAB; MoBrPo; NAEL-2; NoAM; PoE; PoLF; SoSe; TrGrPo
When I Watch the Living Meet. *Fr.* XII. CMoP; MoBrPo; NOBVV; NoP; TrGrPo
When Smoke Stood up from Ludlow. *Fr.* VII. MoBrPo
When the Lad for Longing Sighs. *Fr.* VI. MoBrPo
"White in the moon the long road lies." *Fr.* XXXVI. AWP; CMoP; ELP; LiTB
With Rue My Heart Is Laden. *Fr.* LIV. AWP; BLPL; CMoP; FaFP; HAP; HeIP; HoPM; InPK; LiTB; LiTM; MoAB; MoBrPo; NAEL-2; NoAM; NoP; PoE; PrIm; SoSe; TrGrPo; UnPo
Shropshire Lad, A. *Unknown.* ChTr
Shropshire Lad's Cousin, The. Samuel Hoffenstein. BXAP
Shroud. George Mackay Brown. RB
Shrouded Stranger, The. Allen Ginsberg. NeAP
Shrouding of the Duchess of Malfi, The. John Webster. *See* Duchess of Malfi, The: Hark, Now Everything Is Still.
Shrovetide's Countenance. Rabelais, *tr. fr. French by* Sir Thomas Urquhart. FaBoNo
Shrubbery, The. William Cowper. FaBoRV; NOBE
Shu Has Gone Hunting. *Unknown. See* Shu in the hunting-fields.
Shu in the hunting-fields. *Unknown, tr. by* Arthur Waley. BoS
    (Shu Has Gone Hunting.) CoBCP
Shu is away in the hunting-fields. *Unknown, tr. by* Arthur Waley. BoS
Shubble, The. Walter de la Mare. FaBoNo
Shudder, The. Donald Hall. NYBP
Shuddring the Spectre howls, his howlings terrify the night. Blake. *Fr.* Jerusalem, ch. I. OAEL-2
Shuffle and shudder of Autumn, The. Autumn Imagined. Donald Davie. PoA
Shui Shu, *sels. Unknown, tr. fr. Japanese by* Arthur Waley. AWP
    "Because river-fog." Kiyowara Fukuyabu.
    "Deer which lives, The." Onakatomi Yoshinobu.
    "If it were not for the voice." Nakatsukasa.
    "Time I went to see my Sister, The." Tsurayuki.
    "When,/ Halting in front of it, I look." Hitomaro.
    "Winter has at last come." Minamoto no Shigeyuki.
Shulamit in Her Dreams. Marcia Falk. VWA
Shulamite, The. Else Lasker-Schüler, *tr. fr. German by* Robert Alter. OV

Shun delays, they breed remorse. Loss in Delay. Robert Southwell. OBSC
Shurat Weaver's Song, The. Samuel Laycock. PF
Shut in behind the window, a glittering candle. Yang Chi, *tr. fr. Chinese by* Jonathan Chaves. *Fr.* Living in the Country at Kou-ch'ü in Autumn—Miscellaneous Impressions. CoBLCP
Shut in by spring showers. Saigyo, *tr. fr. Japanese by* Burton Watson. *Fr.* Sixty-four Tanka. FCEI
Shut in from all the world without. Whittier. *Fr.* Snow-bound; a Winter Idyl. OBCP
  (Firelight.) AA
Shut not so soon; the dull-eyed night. To Daisies, Not to Shut So Soon[e]. Robert Herrick. CaPo; CH; ELP; GBL; OBEV; OBS; OxBSP; SeCV-1; TrGrPo
Shut Not Your Doors. Walt Whitman. NOBA; OxBA
Shut Out That Moon. Thomas Hardy. BrPo; CMoP; NoAM; NOBE
Shut, shut the door, good John! Epistle from Mr. Pope to W. Arbuthnot. InPS; NoP; OAEL-1; PoE; PoEL-3
Shut the door against the setting sun. Tune: Full River Bed. Wu Tsao, *tr. by* Julie Landau. WFTU
Shut the gallery lock the door. Mouth. Dennis Scott. PBCV
Shut. The phantasmagoria. The Imagination of the Retina. S. R. Compton. BWV
Shut the Seven Seas against Us. George Barker. *Fr.* Third Cycle of Love Poems, II. MoAB; MoBrPo
Shut up. Shut up. There's nobody here. The Beast in the Space. William Sydney Graham. FaBoTw; PoA
Shutter of time darkening ceaselessly, The. August. Louis MacNeice. LiTM
Shutters closed. The Spiral Staircase. Liana Catri, *tr. by* Muriel Kittel. DMI
Shutters open, The. Taking the Cool to Forget Summer. Tamemasa, *tr. by* Steven D. Carter. WFTW
Shuttlecock:/ Smooth as oil. Takahama Kyoshi, *tr. by* Geoffrey Bownas *and* Anthony Thwaite. PeBJV
Shuttles of trains going north, going south, drawing threads of blue. Morning Sun. Louis MacNeice. MoAB; MoBrPo; TwCP
Shy and timid, Gloom to me. The Outcast. James Stephens. MoBrPo
Shy Geordie. Helen B. Cruickshank. GoTS; OxBS
Shy in their herding dwell the fallow deer. Deer. John Drinkwater. CH
Shy one, shy one. To an Isle in the Water. W. B. Yeats. AWP; TTTS
Shyly the silver-hatted mushrooms make. May. John Shaw Neilson. PoAu-1
Shyness and modesty, they said. Disillusionment. Virginia Graham. NBLV
Si Hubbard. *Unknown.* AS
Si Jeunesse Savait! Edmund Clarence Stedman. AA
Si Monumentum Requiris. Daryl Hine. EOEF
Si monumentum requiris. . .the church in which we are sitting. In Memory of George Whitby, Architect. Sir John Betjeman. EyDe
Si, señor, is halligators here, your guidebook say it. Sinalóa. Earle Birney. MoCV; OxBC
Siamese twins: one, maddened by. Twins. Robert Graves. FaBoEE
Siberia. James Clarence Mangan. BIrV; NOBVV; NOIV
Sibilla. Robert Herrick. *See* With paste of almonds Syb her hands doth scour.
Sibilla's Dirge. Thomas Lovell Beddoes. *See* Death's Jest Book: We Do Lie beneath the Grass.
Sibrandus Schafnaburgensis. Robert Browning. *Fr.* Garden Fancies, II. CTC; EBVV; TEP
Sibyl, The. Joan LaBombard. GoYe
Sibyl. Joseph Stroud. NPGG
Sibyl of the Waters. Ruth Fainlight. VWA
Sibyl's Song, The. Michele Roberts. BrRo
Sic a Wife as Willie Had. Burns. GoTS
Sic et Non. Sir Herbert Read. FaBoTw
Sic Itur. Arthur Hugh Clough. EBVV
Sic Transit. Joseph Mary Plunkett. ACP
Sic Transit. Thomas Proctor. *See* Ay me, ay me, I sigh to see the scythe afield.
Sic Transit Gloria Mundi. James Wreford Watson. CaP
Sic Transit Gloria Scotia. "Hugh MacDiarmid." CMoP
Sic Vita. William Stanley Braithwaite. BANP
Sic Vita. *At. to* Henry King. ELP; FF; FF; MePo; NOBE; OBS; OxBSP; SeCePo; SeCP
Sic Vita. Henry David Thoreau. *See* I Am a Parcel of Vain Strivings Tied.
Sicelides, *sel.* Phineas Fletcher. Woman's Inconstancy. EIL
Sicilian Airs. Leonard Wallace Robinson. SoTCo
Sicilian Cyclamens. D. H. Lawrence. NoAM

Sicilian Muse, I Would Try Now a Somewhat Grander Theme. Virgil. *See* Eclogues
Sicilian Muse, thy voice and subject raise. The Golden Age. *Unknown.* APAS
Sicilian Muses, sing we greater things. Virgil. *See* Eclogues
Sick Birds, The, *sel.* H. Leivick, *tr. fr. Yiddish.* "Do not wake the sick birds." *Tr. by* Benjamin *and* Barbara Harshav. AYP
Sick Child, A. Randall Jarrell. InPK; InvP; OxBC; SO; VGW
Sick Child, The. Stevenson. CH
Sick Face at the Base of the Earth. Hagiwara Sakutaro, *tr. fr. Japanese by* Geoffrey Bownas *and* Anthony Thwaite. PeBJV
Sick Image of My Father Fades, The. John Horder. TEP
Sick Love. Robert Graves. BoLoP; CMoP; EBEV; GTBS-P; HAP; NOBE; OAEL-2
Sick Nought, The. Randall Jarrell. OxBA
Sick of the day's heat, of noise. The Underground Gardens. Robert Mezey. NaP
Sick of my northern glooms, come, shepherd, seek. Philip Freneau. *Fr.* The Beauties of Santa Cruz. AmPP
Sick-room window. Ishida Hakyo, *tr. by* Geoffrey Bownas *and* Anthony Thwaite. PeBJV
Sick roots grope. The Knight Sings. Judah Leib Teller, *tr. by* Benjamin *and* Barbara Harshav. AYP
Sick Rose, The. Blake. *Fr.* Songs of Experience. AWP; BoLoP; ChER; ChTr; ELP; EnLoPo; HAP; HeIP; InPK; InPS; NAEL-2; NAWM-2; NIP; NOBE; NOEC; NoP; OAEL-2; OBNC; OxBSP; PoE; PoEL-4; PPP; PrIm; RB; SoSe; TrGrPo; WeW
Sick Stockrider, The. Adam Lindsay Gordon. CBAP; PoAu-1
Sick unto Death of Love. *Malay Oral Tradition, tr. by* R. J. Wilkinson *and* R. O. Winstedt. WTO
Sick, you said goodbye to me. Lamenting for My Wife. Wang Shih-chen, *tr. by* Jonathan Chaves. CoBLCP
Sickens my gut, Yellow Bittern. The Yellow Bittern. *Unknown, tr. by* Tom MacIntyre. CIP
Sickle maintained in the disordered heavens. The Assembled Whole. René Char, *tr. by* William Jay Smith. CT
Sickle Pears. Owen Dodson. AmNP
Sickles sound. Harvest Song. Ludwig Heinrich Christoph Hölty, *tr. by* Charles T. Brooks. AWP
Sickly Face at the Bottom of the Ground. Hagiwara Sakutaro, *tr. fr. Japanese by* Hiroaki Sato. FCEI
Sickness and death, you are but sluggish things. A Winged Heart. Henry Vaughan. *Fr.* Of Life and Death. FaBoRV
Sickness, intending my love to betray. Sir John Davies. *Fr.* Sonnets to Philomel. SiPS
Sickness is upon me, it will not leave! Beauty. "Badawi al-Jabal", *tr. by* Matthew Sorenson *and* John Heath-Stubbs. MAP
Sickness of Adam, The. Karl Shapiro. *Fr.* Adam and Eve. CRP; MoAB
Sickness of desire, that in dark days, The. Melancholia. Robert Bridges. CMoP
Sickness of Friends, The. Henri Coulette. NYBP
Side by side. Saigyo, *tr. fr. Japanese by* Burton Watson. *Fr.* Sixty-four Tanka. FCEI
Side by side in the crowded streets. The Cantelope. Bayard Taylor. AnAmPo
Side by side on the narrow bed. That Room. John Montague. CIP
Side by side, their faces blurred. An Arundel Tomb. Philip Larkin. NePoEA-2; PPP
Side by side, we ride out of the city. Tsung Ch'en, *tr. fr. Chinese by* Jonathan Chaves. *Fr.* An Excursion to the Suburbs. CoBLCP
Sidera Cadentia. Ford Madox Ford. OxBSP
Sideshow: Julia the Lion Woman. Wendy Rose. GOS
Sidewalk joins the concrete wall around the vacant lot, The. Where or When. Philip Whalen. PoM
Sidewalk Racer, The. Lillian Morrison. ASP
Sidewalk Racer; or, On the Skateboard, The. Lillian Morrison. NTCP; RHPC
Sidewalks of New York, The. James W. Blake. BLPA; FaBoBe
Siding near Chillicothe, A. Richmond Lattimore. AmFn
Sidney, according to report, was kindly hearted. Various Ends. Ruthven Todd. SeCePo
Sidney Godolphin. Clinton Scollard. AA
Sidonie. Jack Collom. UL
Sidrophel, the Rosicrucian Conjurer ("This said, he turned about his steed"). Samuel Butler. *Fr.* Hudibras, II, 3. OxBoLi
Siege. Sargon Boulus, *tr. fr. Arabic by* Sargon Boulus *and* Alistair Elliot. MAP

Siege. Muhammad al-Maghut, *tr. fr. Arabic* by Abdullah al-Udhari. MPAW

Siege. Dan Pagis, *tr. fr. Hebrew* by Warren Bargad *and* Stanley F. Chyet. IP

Siege of Belgrade, The. Alaric Alexander Watts. *See* Austrian Army, An.

Siege of Chapultepec, The. William Haines Lytle. PAH

Siege of Valencia, The, *sel.* Felicia Dorothea Hemans.
"Calm on the bosom of thy God." OBEV

Siena Mi Fe'; Disfecemi Maremma. Ezra Pound. *Fr.* Hugh Selwyn Mauberley. (Life and Contacts). MoAmPo

Sierra. Alfonsina Storni, *tr. fr. Spanish by* Rachel Benson. PBWP

Sierra Kid, *sel.* Philip Levine.
He Faces the Second Winter. PoA

Sierran Vigil. Ewart Milne. NeIP

Sierry Petes, The. Gail Gardner. CowP

Siesta, The. *Unknown, tr. fr. Spanish by* Bryant. AWP

Siesta of a Hungarian Snake. Edwin Morgan. InPK

" 'Sieurs et dames!" and the door slams. A Day in France. David Holbrook. OBTV

Sifting. Victor Emanuel Beck. GoYe

Sigh. Stéphane Mallarmé, *tr. fr. French by* Arthur Symons. AWP

Sigh, A. Harriet Prescott Spofford. AA

Sigh, The. Nathaniel Wanley. OBS

Sigh as It Ends. John Berryman. WeW

Sigh, heart, and break not; rest, lark, and wake not! Nuptial Song. Lord De Tabley. GTBS-P

Sigh, in the wind fall flowers, their petals dance. Selling Ruined Peonies. Yü Hsüan-chi, *tr. by* Geoffrey Waters. BoWoP

Sigh needs an age to have effect; who would, The. Asadullah Khan Ghalib, *tr. by* Ahmed Ali. GoT

Sigh no more, dealers, sigh no more. Much Ado about Nothing in the City. *Unknown.* FaBoPa

Sigh No More, Ladies [Sigh No More]. Shakespeare. *Fr.* Much Ado about Nothing, II, iii. AWP; CTC; EiL; ELP; FF; LiTB; TrGrPo

Sigh that heaves the grasses, The. A. E. Housman. NOBVV

Sigh, wind in the pine. Glencoe. Douglas Stewart. CBAP

Sighed a dear little shipboard divinity. Conrad Aiken. OBAL

Sighing, and sadly sitting by my Love. Richard Barnfield. *Fr.* Sonnets, XI. PeHV; Son

Sighing high and/ again a sigh! Weaving at the Window. Wang Chien, *tr. by* William H. Nienhauser. SaC

Sighing Time, The. Edmund Blunden. BrPo

Sighs and Grones. George Herbert. PoEL-2

Sighs Are My Food. Sir Thomas Wyatt. *See* Epigram: "Sighs are my food, drink are my tears."

Sighs are my food, drink are my tears. Sir Thomas Wyatt. SiPS
(Sighs Are My Food.) OxBSP

Sight, A. Robert Creeley. NaP

Sight. W. W. Gibson. MoBrPo

Sight and hearing finely tuned. When I Was Young, I Stopped by a Wine Shop in Chi-men. Yü Chi, *tr. by* Jonathan Chaves. CoBLCP

Sight and Insight. Eleanor Slater. TrPWD

Sight in Camp [in the Daybreak Gray and Dim], A. Walt Whitman. AA; AmPP; MoP; NAAL-1; NoAM; OFD; OxBA; PoE; PoEL-5; TAP

Sight of all these people in the street, The. Good People. Maura Stanton. NAmP; SM

Sight of his guests filled Lord Cray, The. Lord Cray. Edward Gorey. RHPC

Sight of our parents, The. Okura. *Fr.* Manyo Shu. Ma

Sight of the coffee was good for sore eyes, The. Upon Receipt of a Pound of Coffee in 1863. Mary E. Tucker. CBWP-1

Sight of the English is getting me down, The. Hiraeth in N.W.3. Wynford Vaughan-Thomas. NOBL

Sight Unseen. Kingsley Amis. ErPo; NePoEA-2; NoAM

Sighted a black tornado of. Comments. Peggy Susberry Kenner. JB

Sightseers, The. Paul Muldoon. CIP

Sightseers in a Courtyard. Nicolás Guillén, *tr. fr. Spanish by* Langston Hughes. TTY

Sigil. Hilda Doolittle ("H. D."). VGW
Sels.
"Are these ashes in my hand." *Fr.* XII. AnAn
"Are we unfathomable night." *Fr.* XVIII. AnAn
"But it won't be that way." *Fr.* XVI. AnAn
"I could say." *Fr.* XIII. AnAn
"I love you."" *Fr.* XIX. AnAn
"If you take the moon in your hands." *Fr.* XI. AnAn; FaBoWP
"Let me be." *Fr.* X. AnAn
"Now let the cycle sweep us here and there." *Fr.* XIV. AnAn; VGW
"So if you love me." *Fr.* XV. AnAn
"There is no signpost to say." *Fr.* VIII. AnAn

"Time breaks the barrier." *Fr.* XVII. AnAn
"You'll go on, talking away." *Fr.* IX. AnAn

Sigismonda and Guiscardo, *sel.* Dryden.
Ave atque Vale. OBS

Sigismundo. Linda Gregg. AmPA

Sigmund Freud. Howard Nemerov. PoA

Sigmund Freud at the Age of Eighty-Two. Judah Leib Teller, *tr. fr. Yiddish by* Benjamin *and* Barbara Harshav. *Fr.* Psychoanalysis. AYP

Sign for anger could be a felled pine tree, The. Learning to Type. Diana O Hehir. NPGG

Sign for My Father, Who Stressed the Bunt. David Bottoms. MAYP; MT

Sign of Saturn, The. Sharon Olds. InPS

Sign of the Bonny Blue Bell, The. *Unknown.* OBET

Sign on My Door Jamb. Agnes Gergely, *tr. fr. Hungarian by* Thomas Land. MHuP

Signal, The. David Ignatow. NNaP

Signal Fire, The. Aeschylus, *tr. fr. Greek by* Dallam Simpson. *Fr.* Agamemnon. CTC

Signal Gun, The. Mary E. Tucker. CBWP-1

Signal; or, A Satire against Modesty, The, *sel.* Francis Hawling.
Author Consults a Critic and Sells His Manuscript, The. NOEC

Signals. Jewel C. Latimore. PoBA

Signature. Hannah Kahn. IHMS

Signature. Dorothy Livesay. OBCV

Signature. Larry Mollin. NeAC

Signature for Tempo. Archibald MacLeish. CRP; VGW

Signature of All Things, The. Kenneth Rexroth. NNaP; NU

Signature of All Things, The ("My head and my shoulders, and my book."), *sel. Kenneth* Rexroth. NNaP; NU
"When I dragged the rotten log." BoNaP

Signature II ("All morning he lay in the tight, dark room"). Joseph Stroud. NPGG

Signature III ("Tsangyang Gyatso was twelve years old"). Joseph Stroud. NPGG

Signatures. Daniel Hoffman. VGW

Signatures. Candace Thurber Stevenson. AmFN

Significance of a Water Animal, The. Ray A. Young Bear. HATNAP

Significant Fevers. Alison Fell. BrRo

Signpost. Robinson Jeffers. GoYe

Signs, *sels. Ahmad al-Mushari al-Udwani, tr. fr. Arabic.* MAP
"Mysterious things within you, The." *Fr.* VI, *tr. by* Hilary Kilpatrick *and* Charles Doria.
"You I give no name to/ The mysterious things within you/ are an untrodden bower." *Fr.* III, *tr. by* Hilary Kilpatrick *and* Charles Doria.
"You I give no name to/ The mysterious things within you/ are fragrance, light and melody." *Fr.* IV, *tr. by* Hilary Kilpatrick *and* Charles Doria.

Signs. Charles Martin. SM

Signs. Gjertrud Schnackenberg. InPK; PoA

Signs of Christmas. Edwin Lees. OHIP

Signs of Love. Petrarch. Fr. Sonnets to Laura: To Laura in Life, CLXXXVIII, *tr. by* C. B. Cayley. AWP

Signs of Rain. Edward Jenner. BLPA; BoNaP; FaBoUs

Signs of the Times. Paul Laurence Dunbar. AnAmPo

Signs of the Zodiac, The. Ebenezer Cobham Brewer. FaBoUs

Signs of wear. Monogram 29. Martina Werner, *tr. by* Rosemarie Waldrop. BoWoP

Signs of Winter, *sel.* John Clare. BoNaP; WiR
"Cat runs races with her tail, The." OAEL-2

Sigurd of yore. The Lay [*or* Short Lay] of Sigurd. *Unknown, tr. fr. Old Norse by* William Morris *and* Eirikur Magnusson. *Fr.* The Elder Edda. AWP
"And now one prayer." OBVE

Sigurd Rideth to the Glittering Heath. William Morris. *Fr.* The Story of Sigurd the Volsung, II. PoEL-5

Siilenboor. *Mongol Oral Tradition, tr. by* C. R. Bawden. WTO

Sila. Robert Penn Warren. NoP

Silence/ falling/ the night comes. A Vampyre Legend. Kathleen Resch. VVA

Silence. Bella Akhmadulina, *tr. fr. Russian by* Daniel Halpern. BoWoP; OV

Silence. Alvin Aubert. MT

Silence. Robert Bly. NaP

Silence. E. E. Cummings. CMoP; PoE

Silence. Ghazi al-Gosaibi, *tr. fr. Arabic by* Sharif Elmusa *and* Charles Doria. MAP

Silence. Susan Griffin. *Fr.* Woman and Nature. NPGG

Silence. Avigdor Hame'iri, *tr. fr. Hebrew by* Bernhard Frank. MHeP

Silence. Thomas Hood. CH; EBEV; EnRP; NOBE; OBEV; PoEL-4; Son

Silence, The. Tomas Mac Siomoin, *tr. fr. Irish by the author. TIRV*

Silence. Edgar Lee Masters. MoAmPo

Silence. Marianne Moore. AnAmPo; CMoP; FaBoMo; FaBoWP; InPS; LiTA; NOBA; QFR

Silence. Thomas Sturge Moore. QFR

Silence. James Herbert Morse. AA

Silence. Gregory Orr. GeTw

Silence. John Lancaster Spalding. AA

Silence. Charles Hanson Towne. WGRP

Silence. Walter James Turner. MoBrPo

Silence. John Hall Wheelock. LiTM

Silence. William Carlos Williams. TDD

Silence all flesh, your selves prepare. A Judicious Observation of That Dreadful Comet. Ichabod Wiswall. SCAP

Silence, an Eloquent Applause. Leona Gregory. TrCP

Silence and solitude may hint. An Uninscribed Monument on One of the Battle-Fields of the Wilderness. Herman Melville. AA

Silence and Stealth of Day[e]s! Henry Vaughan. JCP; MePo; NAEL-1; SeCV-1

Silence augmenteth grief, writing increaseth rage. Epitaph on Sir Philip Sidney. *At.* to Fulke Greville *and* to Sir Edward Dyer. LiTB; OBSC; Prf

    (Epitaph Upon the Right Honorable Sir Philip Sidney.) Prf

Silence brought by the dark night: Eryri's. Nightfall. Walter Davies, *tr. by* Anthony Conran. OBWVE

Silence Concerning an Ancient Stone. Rosario Castellanos, *tr. fr. Spanish by* George D. Schade. PBWP

Silence here bears gunfire in its breath. Cozzo Grillo. Herbert B. Mallalieu. WaP

Silence in Court. "Lewis Carroll." *See* Alice's Adventures in Wonderland: Evidence Read at the Trial of the Knave of Hearts.

Silence in the classroom, The. Poem for the Creative Writing Class, Spring 1982. Merle Woo. BrSi

Silence, in truth, would speak my sorrow best. Tears at the Grave of Sir Albertus Morton. Sir Henry Wotton. SeCP

Silence instead of thy sweet song, my bird. Lament of a Mocking-Bird. Frances Anne Kemble. AA

Silence is harder, Una said. The Cup. Judith Wright. FaBoWP

Silence Is Nearer to Truth. Margot Jordan. WS

Silence of our watching, waiting springs, A. A View. Beverly Quint. NYBP

Silence on silence treads at each low morn. Philoctetes. John Byrne Leicester Warren, 3rd Baron De Tabley. NOBVV

Silence pelting down. Snow. Agnes Nemes Nagy, *tr. by* Jascha Kessler. FOC

Silence Plucks Chords, The. Ya'akov Beser, *tr. fr. Hebrew by* Bernhard Frank. MHeP

Silence rules in the home. The Convoy. Juan Antonio Corretjer, *tr. by* Julio Marzán. InW

Silence slipping around like death, A. A Winter Twilight. Angelina Weld Grimké. CDC; PoBA; PoNe

Silence, Spain, a silence and nothing, A. Spain. Eugène Guillevic, *tr. by* Denise Levertov. RHTwFP

Silence Spoke with Your Voice. Ryah Tumarkin Goodman. GoYe

Silence. The man defined. The Hand at Callow Hill Farm. Charles Tomlinson. NePoEA-2

Silence was envious of the only voice. Robert Underwood Johnson. *Fr.* The Voice of Webster. AA

Silence worsened the loss of a friend. Consolatrice. René Daumal, *tr. by* Michael Benedikt. POS

Silenced bells hang mutely in the towers, The. Oxford in Wartime. Mary Wilson. CN

Silences. E. J. Pratt. NOBC; OBCV

Silences. David Mitchell. PeNZ

Silences. Arthur William Edgar O'Shaughnessy. OBNC

Silences; a Dream of Governments. Jean Valentine. LCAP

Silent, about-to-be-parted-from house. Denise Levertov. PoA

Silent alone, where none or saw, or heard. Anne Bradstreet. *Fr.* Contemplations. PBWP

Silent amidst unbroken silence deep. India. Florence Earle Coates. AA

Silent and still: then. Basho, *tr. by* Geoffrey Bownas *and* Anthony Thwaite. PeBJV

Silent are the woods, and the dim green boughs are. On Eastnor Knoll. John Masefield. CH

Silent bivouac of the dead, we say, A. Decorating the Soldiers' Graves. Minot Judson Savage. OHIP

Silent, But. Tsuboi Shigeji, *tr. fr. Japanese by* Geoffrey Bownas *and* Anthony Thwaite. PeBJV

Silent Day, The. Luis G. Urbina, *tr. fr. Spanish by* Samuel Beckett. MexPo

Silent girl, The. In the Library. Ed Ochester. Psk

Silent girl at the spindle, The. The Spinning Girl. Nathan Alterman, *tr. by* Ruth Nevo. VWA

Silent Hill. Zilpha Keatley Snyder. WSC

Silent Hour. Rainer Maria Rilke, *tr. fr. German by* Jessie Lemont. AWP

Silent hush, the rusted hinges, The. Who Will Live in Our Houses When We Die? Michael C. Blumenthal. NoAM

Silent I gaze at the cataract. By the Waterfall. Friedrich Adler, *tr. by* Jethro Bithell. TrJP

Silent Icicles, The. Samuel Taylor Coleridge. *Fr.* Frost at Midnight. FaBoRV

Silent in America. Philip Levine. NaP

Silent Is the House. Emily Brontë. *See* Silent is the house: all are laid asleep.

Silent is the house: all are laid asleep. The Visionary. Emily Brontë. BLPL; LiTB; NOBE; NOBVV; OBNC; PBWP; SCV

    (Silent Is the House.) CH; ELP

    ("Silent is the house—all are laid asleep.") BrRo

Silent Love. John Clare. EnRP

Silent Love. Gabriela Mistral, *tr. fr. Spanish by* Perry Higman. LPSS

Silent Lover, The ("Passions are liken'd best to floods and streams."), *sels.* Sir Walter Ralegh. ElL; OBEV, *abr.*

Silent Lover, The. LiTB

Silent Lover, The. Sir Walter Ralegh. *Fr.* The Silent Lover. LiTB

Wrong Not, Sweete Empress of My Heart. *At.* to Sir Robert Ayton. OBS, *sl. diff. vers.*

    (Merit of True Passion, The.) LiTB

Silent Movies. Pedro Juan Pietri. InW

Silent, my jaws working, I knew. The Lesson. Paul Mariani. MAYP

Silent Night. The. Mrs. Henry Linden. CBWP-4

Silent Night! Holy Night! Joseph Mohr, *tr. fr. German.* FaFP

Silent Noon. Dante Gabriel Rossetti. *Fr.* The House of Life, XIX. HAP; NAEL-2; NoP; OBNC; PoEL-5; TrGrPo

Silent nymph, with curious eye! Grongar Hill. John Dyer. *Fr.* Looking Back. ChTr; EnRP; FaBoPP; GoTL; NOEC; NoP; PoEL-3

Silent Nymph, with curious eye. Grongar Hill. John Dyer. OBWVE

Silent, O Moyle, be the roar of thy water. The Song of Fionnuala. Thomas Moore. AnIL; BIrV

Silent One, The. Ivor Gurney. MMA; NAEL-2; OBWP

    "Who died on the wires, and hung there, one of two," *sel.* OBD

Silent Piano, The. Louis Simpson. CAPP

Silent Poem. Robert Francis. CRP; LCAP

Silent Pool, The. Harold Monro. BrPo

Silent Prayer of Peasants. Imre Csanádi, *tr. fr. Hungarian by* Edwin Morgan. MHuP

Silent Revolution. W. H. Oliver. ATNZ

Silent river village, bamboo wet with rain. Hearing the Cuckoo on the Nineteenth Day of the Third Month. Huang Tsung-hsi, *tr. by* Lynn Struve. WFTU

Silent Room, The. Kingsley Amis. OxBC

Silent room—gray with a dusty blight, A. Among His Books. Edith Nesbit. NOBVV

Silent room, the heavy creeping shade, The. Fabien Dei Franchi. Oscar Wilde. BrPo

Silent scream? The madrigal's top note?, A. Prague Spring. Tony Harrison. OBTV

Silent, silent evening passes. For My Love Rising Early. Ya'ir Hurvits, *tr. by* Bernhard Frank. MHeP

Silent Slain, The. Archibald MacLeish. *See* Too-late Born, The.

Silent Snake, The. *Unknown.* BoTP; FaPON

Silent Song. Ory Bernstein, *tr. fr. Hebrew by* Bernhard Frank. MHeP

Silent tepees stand like shocked corn, The. Always the Melting Moon Comes. Margot Osborn. CaP

Silent, thatched hut deep among the trees, A. A Little Landscape. Chu Yün-ming, *tr. by* Jonathan Chaves. CoBLCP

Silent, the autumn river, fishermen's fires sparse. Spending the Night on the River. T'ang Hsien-Tsu, *tr. by* Jonathan Chaves. CoBLCP

Silent the Forests. Tasso, *tr. fr. Italian by* Edwin Morgan. PFI

Silent Town, The. Richard Dehmel, *tr. fr. German by* Jethro Bithell. AWP

"Silent upon a peak in Darien." Darien. Sir Edwin Arnold. PAH

Silent Walls, The. Ian Strachan. PoSH

Silent was my lonely lodge among the mountain trees. Spring Day in a Mountain Lodge. Princess Uchiko, *tr. by* Burton Watson. JLIC-1

Silent, with her eyes. Blind Girl. W. S. Merwin. NePoEA-2

Silent Woman, The, *sel.* Ben Jonson.

    "Still to be neat, still to be dressed." OxBSP

Silent Wood, A. Elizabeth Siddal. NOBVV
Silent, you say, I'm grown of late. Walter Savage Landor. GBL
Silentium. Fyodor Ivanovich Tyutchev, tr. fr. Russian by Alan Myers. AAA
Silently my wife walks on the still wet furze. Berry Picking. Irving Layton. HeIP; MoCV; NoP
Silently she waits by the screen as he prepares to leave. Gazing after the Distant Traveler. Wei Chuang, tr. by Lois Fusek. ATF
Silently, slowly falls the snow from an ashen sky. Snowfall. Giosuè Carducci, tr. by Romilda Rendel. AWP
Silenus in Proteus. Thomas Lovell Beddoes. EnRP
Silet. Ezra Pound. MoAB; MoAmPo; Son
Silhouette. Marc Cohen. EOEF
Silhouette. Annette M'Baye, tr. fr. French by Kathleen Weaver. PBWP
Silhouette/ On the face of the moon. Shadow. Richard Bruce. CDC
Silhouette for its Rousseau, A. Bruce Andrews. IAT
Silhouettes, they lean against a ringed moon. Paiute Ponies. Jim Barnes. CDW
Silica Carbonate Rock. Fred Berry. NU
Silk,/ Satin. Unknown. OxNR
Silk and Silence. Haim Guri, tr. fr. Hebrew by Warren Bargad and Stanley F. Chyet. IP
Silk curtains will be fragrant as she sleeps, The. The Barbarian Chieftain. Mao Wen-hsi, tr. by Lois Fusek. ATF
Silk jacket, embroidered sleeves, a beautiful girl. The Joy of Meeting. Hsüeh Chao-yün, tr. by Lois Fusek. ATF
Silk Merchant's Daughter, The. Unknown. OxBSS, with music
Silk of flame composed his hair to fleck, A. Spastic Child. Vassar Miller. TSM
Silk Shearing Lake is half clogged by reeds and grass. Inscription for My Evergreen Pavilion. Ch'en Pao-shen, tr. by Yi-yu Cho Woo. WFTU
Silk Weaver's Daughter, The. Unknown. AmFP
Silken Snake, The. Robert Herrick. OxBSP
Silken Tent, The. Robert Frost. AmPP; BLPL; InPK; NOBA; Son; SoSe; TAP; TwCP
Silkweed. Philip Henry Savage. AA
Silkworm Song of Torchlit Fields. Kao Ch'i, tr. fr. Chinese by Jonathan Chaves. CoBLCP
Silkworms, The. Douglas Stewart. CBAP; PoAu-2
Silkworms my mother rears, The. Hitomaro. Fr. Manyo Shu. PeBJV
Silly boy, there is no cause. Thomas Pestel. EiL
Silly boy, 'tis full moon yet, thy night as day shines clearly. First Love. Thomas Campion. GBL; OxBoLi
Silly country maiden went, A. Leda in Stratford, Ont. Anne Wilkinson. MoCV
Silly Fool, The. W. H. Auden. OBMV
Silly girl! Yet morning lies. To a Pretty Girl. Israel Zangwill. TrJP
Silly Old Man, The. Unknown. CoMu; TW
Silly Song. Federico García Lorca, tr. fr. Spanish by M. D. Herter Norton. TTTS
Silly swain whose love breeds discontent, The. Tityrus to His Fair Phyllis. John Dickenson. Fr. The Shepherd's Complaint. EiL
Silly Sweetheart. Unknown. CH
Silos all by a stillness. P. Inman. Fr. Red Shift. LP
Silvana Goes A-Strolling. Unknown, tr. fr. Spanish by Kate Flores. DMH
Silver. A. R. Ammons. NoP
Silver/ War-lord. Barracuda. Joseph MacInnis. RR
Silver. Ferenc Juhász, tr. fr. Hungarian by David Wevill. MHuP
Silver. Walter de la Mare. BoNaP; BoTP; FaPON; MoAB; MoBrPo; PoRA; PYC; RHPC; TTTS
Silver Age, The, sel. Thomas Heywood.
  Praise of Ceres. EiL
Silver bark of beech, and sallow. Counting-out Rhyme. Edna St. Vincent Millay. GoJo; InPK; MoShBr; TTTS
Silver Bells. Hamish Hendry. BoTP
Silver Bells and Golden Spurs. Unknown. CowP
Silver birch is a dainty lady, The. Child's Song in Spring. Edith Nesbit. BOTP; OHIP; OxBChV
Silver birch-tree like a sacred maid, A. Recollection. Amelia Walstien Carpenter. AA
Silver Bowl, The, sel. Joseph Ezobi, tr. fr. Spanish by D. I. Friedmann. Barren Soul, A. TrJP
Silver Clasp. Unknown, tr. by Geoffrey Bownas and Anthony Thwaite. PeBJV
Silver Coin, The. Trish Reeves. PPR
Silver Dagger, The. Unknown. AmFP
Silver dust. Pear Tree. Hilda Doolittle ("H. D."). BoWoP; CMoP; MoAmPo; NOBA; PoE; UnPo
Silver Flask, The. John Montague. CIP; FaBCIP

Silver herring throbbed thick in my seine, The. Kenneth Leslie. Fr. By Stubborn Stars. ErPo; OBCV
  (Sonnet: "Silver herring throbbed thick in my seine, The.") NOBC
Silver House, The. John Lea. BoTP
Silver in the Wind. Ian Strachan. PoSH
Silver Jack. John P. Jones. CowP
Silver jet, A. Sitting Down, Looking Up. A. R. Ammons. PCP
Silver Jubilee. Llewelyn Wyn Griffith. OBWVE
Silver key of the fountain of tears. Music. Shelley. TrGrPo
Silver Leaf, The. John Hay. NePoAm
Silver Lucifer, A. Lunar Baedeker. Mina Loy. VGW
Silver Mouth, The. Shauqi Abi Shaqra, tr. fr. Arabic by Abdullah al-Udhari. MPAW
Silver Penny, The. Walter de la Mare. CMoP; OBMV
Silver Question, The. Oliver Herford. NA
Silver rain, the shining sun, The. The Harvest. Alice C. Henderson. BoTP
Silver Road, The. Hamish Hendry. BoTP
Silver-scaled Dragon with jaws flaming red, A. The Toaster. William Jay Smith. GrPl; RAR; RHPC
Silver shadow where the line falls grey, The. Upcountry. Adrienne Rich. ER
Silver Ships. Mildred Plew Meigs. FaPON
Silver Spirit of St. Louis, The. At the National Air and Space Museum. Janice Townley Moore. TSM
Silver Swan[ne], The. At. to Orlando Gibbons. ChTr; EiL; ELP; FaBoCh; HAP; HeIP; InPK; NAEL-1; NoP; OBD; OxBSP
Silver Tassie, The. Burns. GTBS; GTBS-P; NOBE; OBEV
Silver that shies off the silver-leaf maple, The. The Silver Leaf. John Hay. NePoAm
Silver Threads among the Gold. Eben Eugene Rexford. FaFP
Silver-vested monkey trips, A. Cortège. Paul Verlaine, tr. by Arthur Symons. AWP; OBVE
Silver Wedding. Ralph Hodgson. OxBTC; TrGrPo
Silverhill. Martin Seymour-Smith. NPo
Silverly. Dennis Lee. RAR
Silverthorn Bush. Robert Finch. NOBC
Silvery Fountain. Mary E. Tucker. CBWP-1
Silvery Tide, The. Unknown. AmFP
Silvery world, golden body. Shuzan, tr. by Lucien Stryk and Takashi Ikemoto. ZPCJ
Silvia. Shakespeare. See Two Gentlemen of Verona, The: Who Is Silvia [or Sylvia]?
Sim Ines. Jane Stubbs. FiBHP
Simchas Torah. Morris Jacob Rosenfeld, tr. fr. Yiddish. TrJP
Simhat Torah. Judah Leib Gordon, tr. fr. Hebrew by Alice Lucas and Helena Frank. TrJP
Similar Cases. Charlotte Perkins Gilman. PoLF
Similar people don't hear one another. Christine Lavant, tr. by Beth Bjorklund. CoAuP
Simile. N. Scott Momaday. CDW
Simile, A. Matthew Prior. NOEC
Simile for Her Smile, A. Richard Wilbur. HoPM; InPK
Similes for Two Political Characters of 1819. Shelley. FaBoPV; RB; TW
Simmer's a Pleasant Time. Burns. PoEL-4
  (Ay Waukin O.) NOEC
Simon and Susan. Unknown. OxBoLi
Simon and the Tarantula. James Wright. AnAn; NNaP
Simon Danz has come home again. A Dutch Picture. Longfellow. MoShBr
Simon Gerty. Elinor Wylie. OBAL
Simon Judson. Lewis Turco. Fr. Bordello. SM
Simon Lee. Wordsworth. EnRP; NAEL-2
Simon Lee the Old Huntsman. Wordsworth. See In the sweet shire of Cardigan.
Simon Legree—a Negro Sermon. Vachel Lindsay. Fr. The Booker Washington Trilogy, I. LiTA; TAP
Simon my son, son of my Nuptiall knot. A Lamentation on My Dear Son Simon. John Saffin. SCAP
Simon the Cyrenian Speaks. Countee Cullen. AmNP; BPo; HAP; MoAmPo; TrCP; TTY
Simón, we knew him as la Zorrauncouth but. Aquellos Vatos. Tino Villanueva. FIA
Simoom, The. Martin Farquhar Tupper. OBTV
Simple. Naomi Long Madgett. FB; PoBA
Simple Act (Story Two: My House), A, sel. Beth Brant.
  "I write because not to write is a breach of faith." ER
Simple as the attraction. The Name of God Is. Jeanine Hathaway. KS

Simple Autumnal. Louise Bogan. MoAB; MoAmPo; QFR; Son
Simple child, A. We Are Seven. Wordsworth. BLPA; BLPL; EnRP; GN; NAEL-2; OxBChV; TEP; WBLP
Simple child, A. Wordsworth. *Fr.* We Are Seven. OBD
Simple contact with a wooden spoon and the word, The. Words. Barbara Guest. BAP
Simple food, coarse clothing are all you need. The Bamboo Villa. Shen Chou, *tr. by* Jonathan Chaves. CoBLCP
Simple-hearted child was He, A. The Little Child. Albert Bigelow Paine. AA
Simple Matter, A. Gloria Rawlinson. PeNZ
Simple Minstrelsy. Elijah Ridings. PF
Simple, naked words. Again a Neighbor Died. H. Leivick, *tr. fr. Yiddish by* Benjamin *and* Barbara Harshav. *Fr.* Clouds behind the Forest. AYP
Simple nosegay! was that much to ask?, A. The Troll's Nosegay. Robert Graves. Son
Simple Ode. Kendrick Smithyman. ATNZ
Simple Pastoral, A. George Alexander Stevens. NOEC
Simple Ploughboy, The. *Unknown.* FaBoCh
Simple Poem. Anthony Thwaite. DiPo
Simple Purification, The. Kabir, *tr. fr. Hindi by* Robert Bly. NU
Simple Rituals. Dyan Sublett. KS
Simple Simon. Harriet S. Morgridge. AA
Simple Simon met a pieman. Mother Goose. BOTP; FaBoBe; OxNR
Simple Song. Marge Piercy. LLLT
Simple song, perchance may tell, A. Simple Minstrelsy. Elijah Ridings. PF
Simple Story, A. Gwen Harwood. FaBoWP
Simple Verses, *sels.* José Martí, *tr. fr. Spanish by* Seymour Resnick. TTY
  "I am a sincere man."
  "I grow a white rose."
Simple weight, as in "declarative bank buries words." Local Motions. Laurence Price. IAT
Simpler Thing, a Chair, A. Robert Mezey. NePoEA
Simplex Munditiis. Ben Jonson. *See* Epicoene; or, The Silent Woman: Still to Be Neat [Still to Be Drest (*or* Dressed)].
Simplicity. Louis Simpson. Prf
Simplicity Aims Circularly. Anna Walters. VoR
Simplicity sings it and 'sperience doth prove. Simplicity's Song. Robert Wilson. *Fr.* The Three Ladies of London. CTC; OBSC
Simplicity so graven hurts the sense. So Graven. Josephine Miles. NoAM
Simplicity yea even to write. Confections. Paul Éluard, *tr. by* Samuel Beckett. RHTwFP
Simplicity's Song. Robert Wilson. *Fr.* The Three Ladies of London. CTC; OBSC
Simplification, A. Richard Wilbur. CMoP
Simplify Me When I'm Dead. Keith Douglas. NePoEA; NoAM; OxBTC
Simply. Laura Chester. NPGG
Simply by sailing in a new direction. Landfall in Unknown Seas. Allen Curnow. ATNZ
Simply, it is a man who has died. Sordello, *tr. by* Paul Blackburn. Pro
Simply, one must imagine what has been lost. Letter to a Censor. Kelly Cherry. KS
Simply to breathe. An Emblem of Two Foxes. Barry Spacks. HoPM
Simulated Eden. Tropical Greenhouse. Dan Pagis, *tr. by* Warren Bargad *and* Stanley F. Chyet. IP
Simultaneous Equations. Anne French. ATNZ
Simultaneously. David Ignatow. GrPl; TwCP
Simultaneously, as soundlessly. Prime. W. H. Auden. *Fr.* Horae Canonicae. CMoP; PoE
Simultaneously, five thousand miles apart. Simultaneously. David Ignatow. GrPl; TwCP
Sin. George Herbert. NoP; OxBSP
Sin. János Pilinszky, *tr. fr. Hungarian by* Ted Hughes. MHuP
Sin against the Holy. though what, The. The Blasphemies. Louis MacNeice. FaBCIP
Sin and Death. Milton. *See* Paradise Lost: Meanwhile the adversary of God and man.
Sin, Despair, and Lucifer. Phineas Fletcher. *Fr.* The Locusts, or Appolyonists, I. OBS
Sin of Omission, The. Margaret Elizabeth Munson Sangster. *See* At Sunset.
"Sin [*or* Sinne] of self-love [*or* selfe-love] possesseth all mine eye [*or* eie]." Shakespeare. *Fr.* Sonnets, LXII. EBEV; PoEL-2
Sin-satiate, and haggard with despair. Tannhäuser. William Morton Payne. AA
Sin that I have a nounparall maistress. A Mistress without Compare . *At. to* Charles d'Orléans. MeEL

Sina. Alistair Campbell. ATNZ
Sinalóa. Earle Birney. MoCV; OxBC
Since/ Malcolm died. Aardvark. Julia Fields. CNA; OFD
Since. W. H. Auden. InPS
Since a harebrained Devil has changed the world. The Cats of Campagnatico. Peter Porter. OBTV
Since a wind over the rushes told me that autumn came. Princess Shikishi, *tr. fr. Japanese by* Hiroaki Sato. *Fr.* Seventy-eight Tanka. FCEI
Since Akkad Since Elam Since Sumer. Aimé Césaire, *tr. fr. French by* Michael Benedikt. POS
Since all living things die in the end. Tabito. *Fr.* Manyo Shu. FCEI
Since all our keys are lost or broken. An Art of Poetry. James McAuley. NOCV
Since all that beat anon at nature's range. Constancy to an Ideal Object. Samuel Taylor Coleridge. NAEL-2
Since all that I can ever do for thee. The Last Wish. Sir Edward Bulwer-Lytton. OxBSP
Since all the riches of this world. Blake. OAEL-2
Since all things must end. Tonna, *tr. by* Steven D. Carter. WFTW
Since Amaro died I cannot sleep at night. Dreaming of Amaro. Michizane, *tr. by* Burton Watson. JLIC-1
Since Amaro died I cannot sleep at night. Michizane, *tr. fr. Japanese by* Burton Watson. *Fr.* Kokin Shu. FCEI
Since Bonny-Boots Was Dead. *Unknown.* PoEL-2
  (Madrigal: "Since Bonny-boots was dead, that so divinely.") OxBoLi
Since born. Since beginning. Since dawn. Since When As Ever More. Lawson Fusao Inada. BrSi
Since brass, nor stone, nor earth, nor boundless sea." Shakespeare. *Fr.* Sonnets, LXV. AWP; FF; FiP; HAP; InPS; LiTB; NAEL-1; NOBE; NoP; PoRA; Son; UnPo
  (Since Brass, Nor Stone, Nor Earth.) FaFP
  (Time and Love, II.) GTBS; GTBS-P
Since Brunswick's smile has authoris'd my muse. Edward Young. *Fr.* The Instalment. FaBoCo
Since bundling very much abounds. A New Bundling Song. *Unknown.* ErPo
Since by just flames the guilty piece is lost. Advice to the Painter. Matthew Prior. APAS
Since by the imperial order to serve. Yakamochi. *Fr.* Manyo Shu. Ma
Since cast-iron has got all the rage. Humphrey Hardfeature's Descriptions of Cast-Iron Inventions. *Unknown.* OBET
Since Christmas they have lived with us. Balloons. Sylvia Plath. FaBoWP; PoE
Since clarity suggests simplicity. The Counterpart. Elizabeth Jennings. LiTM; TOF
Since Cleopatra Died. Thomas Wentworth Higginson. AA
Since counterfeit plots have affected this age. A Ballad upon the Popish Plot. John Gadbury. CoMu
Since Dew the Day. Hugues C. Pernath, *tr. fr. Dutch by* James S. Holmes. DuIn
Since early morning. Paracas. Antonio Cisneros, *tr. by* Maureen Ahern *and* David Tipton. Per
Since earnestly studying the Buddhist doctrine of emptiness. Idle Droning. Po Chü-i, *tr. by* Burton Watson. CoBCP
Since earth has put you away, O sons of Barmak. Abu Nowas for the Barmacides. *Unknown. tr. fr. Arabic by* E. Powys Mathers. *Fr.* The Thousand and One Nights. AWP
Since every quill is silent to relate. A Monumental Memorial of Marine Mercy. Richard Steere. SCAP
Since Feeling Is First. E. E. Cummings. MoAB; MoAmPo; NoP; PrIm
Since First I Saw Your Face. *Unknown.* ELP; LiTB; OBEV; OBSC; OxBSP
Since first the breast glowed with celestial fire. To the Memory of Ebenezer Elliott the Corn-Law Rhymer. Richard Furness. PF
Since first you knew my am'rous smart. Robert, Earl Nugent. NOEC
Since fortune's wrath envieth the wealth. Earl of Surrey. SiPS
Since Hanna Moved Away. Judith Viorst. RHPC
Since heaven and earth parted. Akahito. *Fr.* Manyo Shu. FCEI
Since his sharp sight has taught you. A Valediction. William DeWitt Snodgrass. PPR
Since honour from the honourer proceeds. Of Books. John Florio. EIL
Since I am coming [*or* comming] to that holy room[e]. Hymn[e] to God My God, In my Sickness[e]. John Donne. ChTr; EBEV; HeIP; InPS; MeLP; MePo; NAEL-1; NIP; NoP; OAEL-1; OBD; OBS; PoE; PoEL-2; PPP; SeCP; SeCV-1; TOF; TrPWD
Since I am convinced. Saigyo Hoshi, *tr. by* Arthur Waley. AWP
Since I believe in God the Father Almighty. Johannes Milton, Senex. Robert Bridges. CMoP; LiTB; PoEL-5
Since I, by My Good Fortune, Return to Look On. Veronica Gambara, *tr. fr. Italian by* Muriel Kittel. DMI

Since I came by chance into this life. Kanamura. *Fr.* Manyo Shu. Ma

Since I care naught for what is pale and cold. To a Brown Girl. Ossie Davis. PoNe

Since I do not hope to return ever. Last Song: from Exile. Guido Cavalcanti, *tr. by* G. S. Fraser. PFI

Since I emerged that day from the labyrinth. The Labyrinth. Edwin Muir. CMoP; MoBrPo

Since I entered the inner rooms. Written on a Leaf. *Unknown, tr. by* Geoffrey Waters. BoWoP

Since I find you will no longer love. Sway. Denis Johnson. SM

Since I got my cat Five White. An Offering for the Cat. Mei Yao-ch'en, *tr. by* Burton Watson. CoBCP

Since I had shut the gate. *Unknown. Fr.* Manyo Shu. Ma

Since I have given my whole life to you. Empty Promises. Chang Ts'o, *tr. by* Dominic Cheung. IFON

Since I have seen a bird one day. The Truth. W. H. Davies. FaBoTw

Since I have set my lips to your full cup, my sweet. More Strong Than Time. Victor Hugo, *tr. by* Andrew Lang. AWP

Since I heard. Mitsune, *tr. fr. Japanese by* Arthur Waley. *Fr.* Kokin Shu. AWP

Since I keep only what I give away. George Hetherington. NeIP

Since I left the loving hands of my mother. Hitomaro. *Fr.* Manyo Shu. Ma

Since I must love your north. To My Mountain. Kathleen Jessie Raine. OxBS

Since I must needs into thy school[e] return[e]. A Lady's Prayer to Cupid. Thomas Carew, *after* Giovanni Battista Guarini. CaPo (Ladies Prayer to Cupid, A.) OBVE

Since I need something else. In the Tent, Elche. Bill Manhire. ATNZ

Since I no longer speak I. Silent in America. Philip Levine. NaP

Since I no longer think. Saigyo, *tr. fr. Japanese by* Burton Watson. *Fr.* Sixty-four Tanka. FCEI

Since I noo mwore do zee your feace. The Wife a-Lost. William Barnes. BoLoP; EBVV; ELP; EnLoPo; HAP; OBEV

Since I parted from you, immortal bird. For Several Days I Have Not Visited the Garden Pavilion. Wang Chiu-ssu, *tr. by* Jonathan Chaves. CoBLCP

Since I was demoted and exiled and live in a shack. On Not Going Out the Gate. Michizane, *tr. by* Burton Watson. JLIC-1

Since I was in Syracuse is a month ago. Quarries in Syracuse. Louis Golding. TrJP

Since I was suddenly sent away. On a Snowy Night Thinking of the Bamboos at Home. Michizane, *tr. by* Burton Watson. *Fr.* Kokin Shu. FCEI; JLIC-1

Since I was ten I have not been unkind. The Final Word. Dom Moraes. NePoEA-2

Since I'm a girl. *Unknown, tr. by* Willis Barnstone. BoWoP

Since I'm completely drunk. *Unknown, tr. by* Peter Jay. PeHV

Since in a land not barren still. Love and Discipline. Henry Vaughan. TrPWD

Since in Karu lived my wife. Hitomaro. *Fr.* Manyo Shu. Ma

Since in religion all men disagree. To Caelia. *Unknown.* FaBoEE

Since it cannot be avoided. You Are Born Again and Again. Sirkka Turkka, *tr. by* Aili Jarvenpa. SOP

Since it was the eve of July 14. Phantom of the Clouds. Guillaume Apollinaire, *tr. by* Michael Benedikt. POS

Since I've assumed this form of life. Mohammad Taqi Mir, *tr. by* Ahmed Ali. GoT

Since I've felt this pain. Ono no Komachi, *tr. fr. Japanese by* Rob Swigart. WPOW

Since Juliet's on ice, and Joan. Carpe Diem. Christian Karlson Stead. ATNZ

Since last September I've been trying to describe. Edward Lear in February. Christopher Middleton. TwCP

Since last the tutelary hearth. Christmas Family Reunion. Peter De Vries. NBLV; NOBL

Since laws were made for ev'ry degree. John Gay. *Fr.* The Beggar's Opera, III, xiii. NOEC

Since life had brought us we had come. Sheikh Ibrahim Zauq, *tr. by* Ahmed Ali. GoT

Since life is nothing in your philosophy. Nothing. Julia de Burgos, *tr. by* Aliki *and* Willis Barnstone. BoWoP

Since long ago, a child at home. To an Island Princess. Robert Louis Stevenson. OBTV

Since, Lord, to thee/ A narrow way and little gate. Holy Baptisme. George Herbert. PoEL-2
(H. Baptisme.) SeCV-1

Since love and verse, as well as wine. A Letter to the Earl of Middleton. Sir George Etherege. OBTV

Since love is such that as ye wot. Sir Thomas Wyatt. SiPS

Since love will needs that I shall love. Sir Thomas Wyatt. SiPS

Since lovers' joys then leave so sick a taste. Henry King. *Fr.* Paradox: That Fruition Destroys Love. ErPo

Since man has been articulate. Every Thing. Harold Monro. MoBrPo

Since Man's a little world, to make it great. An Epigram on Woman. Philip Ayres. FaBoEE

Since men grow diffident at last. Youth Sings a Song of Rosebuds. Countee Cullen. BANP; PoLF; PoNe

"Since mountains sink to vales, and valleys die." The Bathos. Richard Porson. FaBoEE

Since my courage is clarified. Marcabrun, *tr. by* Paul Blackburn. Pro

Since my life's been spent. Côte d'Azur. Katherine Hoskins. NYBP

Since my Vivian left me. The Barrel Organ. Daniel Mark Epstein. *Fr.* Homage to Mallarmé. DiPo

Since my wife was born. Notes for the Legend of Salad Woman. Michael Ondaatje. NoAM

Since naturally black is naturally beautiful. Naturally. Audre Lorde. BlSi; CNA

Since Nature's works be good, and death doth serve. Why Fear to Die? Sir Philip Sidney. *Fr.* Arcadia. SiPS

Since Nine O'Clock. Constantine P. Cavafy, *tr. fr. Greek by* Edmund Keeley *and* Philip Sherrard. VMG

Since nought avails, let me arise and leave. Love's Last Resource. Sadi, *tr. fr. Persian by* L. Cranmer-Byng. *Fr.* The Gulistan. AWP

Since now I dare not ask. The Sharp Ridge. Robert Graves. FaBoEE

Since now in every public place. The Sea Horse. Robert Graves. FaBoMo

Since Oc-e-No has set the fire and drawn blood. Bertrans de Born, *tr. by* Paul Blackburn. Pro

Since o'er thy footstool here below. Heaven's Magnificence. William Augustus Muhlenberg. AA

Since of no creature living the last breath. Edna St. Vincent Millay. VGW

Since one anthologist put in his book. Anthologistics. Arthur Guiterman. NBLV

Since our ancestral gods. Yakamochi. *Fr.* Manyo Shu. Ma

Since our parting when the moon at dawn looked unfriendly. Teika, *tr. fr. Japanese by* Hiroaki Sato. *Fr.* A Compendium of Good Tanka. FCEI

Since Peter of Auvergne once sang. Monk of Montaudon, *tr. by* Paul Blackburn. Pro

Since Reverend doctors now declare. The Respectable Burgher. Thomas Hardy. CMoP; NoAM

Since she must go, and I must mourn, come Night. His Parting from Her. John Donne. *Fr.* Elegies, XII. EBEV
(Elegie: His Parting from Her.) OBS

Since she whom I lov'd hath paid [or payd] her last debt. John Donne. *Fr.* Holy Sonnets, XVII. JCP; MePo; NAEL-1; Son

Since Shylock's book has walk'd the circles here. To a Noisy Politician. Philip Freneau. TAP

Since, Sir, you have made it your study to vex. The Lady's Receipt for a Beau's Dress. *Unknown.* CoMu

Since sixteen, her name has drifted in the city. An Opera Songstress. Ya Hsien, *tr. by* Dominic Cheung. IFON

Since So Mine Eyes. Sir Philip Sidney. *Fr.* Arcadia. SiPS

Since so ye please to hear me plain. Sir Thomas Wyatt. SiPS

Since that afternoon when her girlfriend. Edith. Andreas Okopenko, *tr. by* Beth Bjorklund. CoAuP

Since that night/ I cannot know myself. Izumi Shikibu, *tr. by* Willis Barnstone. BoWoP

Since that night. Prague, January 1964. Ingeborg Bachmann, *tr. by* Beth Bjorklund. CoAuP

Since that parting. Mibu Tadamine, *tr. by* Geoffrey Bownas *and* Anthony Thwaite. PeBJV

Since that this thing we call the world. An Epicurean Ode. John Hall. MeLP; MePo

Since that time far off. Yakamochi. *Fr.* Manyo Shu. FCEI

Since the age of the gods it has always been said. Okura. *Fr.* Manyo Shu. Ma

Since the beginning of heaven and earth. Yakamochi. *Fr.* Manyo Shu. Ma

Since the Conquest none of us. The Conquest. Oliver St. John Gogarty. OBMV

Since the era of that sage sovereign. Hitomaro. *Fr.* Manyo Shu. Ma

Since the far beginning of heaven and earth. Yakamochi. *Fr.* Manyo Shu. Ma

Since the moon resides. Tameuji, *tr. by* Steven D. Carter. WFTW

Since the mountain cherries began to bloom. Teika, *tr. fr. Japanese by* Hiroaki Sato. *Fr.* A Compendium of Good Tanka. FCEI

Since the night is dark. *Unknown, tr. by* Willis Barnstone. BoWoP

Since the reign of Kashihara's sun-ruler. Hitomaro. *Fr.* Manyo Shu. FCEI

Since the rumor has been verified, you can, at least. Rumor Verified. Robert Penn Warren. AnAn

Since the sky started crying. Flood at the International Writing Program. Bogomil Gjuzel. WCI

Since the sparse bush clover began to flower. Teika, *tr. fr. Japanese by* Hiroaki Sato. *Fr.* A Compendium of Good Tanka. FCEI

Since the storm two nights ago. The Recognition. Denise Levertov. VGW

Since the time of the gods. Yakomochi. *Fr.* Manyo Shu. Ma

Since the wise men have not spoken, I speak that am only a fool. The Fool. Padraic Pearse. TIRV

Since the women. Roman Rooms. Paolo Volponi, *tr. by* Lawrence R. Smith. NItP

Since the world arose out of distances. A Walk. Ilse Aichinger, *tr. by* Beth Bjorklund. CoAuP

Since Then. Yehuda Amichai, *tr. fr. Hebrew by* Shlomo Vinner *and* Howard Schwartz. VWA

Since Then. D. J. Enright. OBSV

Since, then, constrain'd, we must expel the flock. How to Build a Ha-ha. William Mason. *Fr.* The English Garden. FaBoUs

Since then I was. The Significance of a Water Animal. Ray A. Young Bear. HATNAP

Since there's no help, come, let them kiss and part. The Limited. Robert Penn Warren. PoA

Since there's [*or* ther's] no help[e], come let us kiss[e] and part. Michael Drayton. *Fr.* Idea, LXI. AAS; AWP; BoLoP; EnLoPo; GBL; HAP; HeIP; InPS; JCP; NAEL-1; NOBE; NoP; OAEL-1; OBSC; PoEL-2; PrIm; SeCePo; Son; SoSe; TEP; TrGrPo
    (Farewell to Love.) BLPL
    (Love's Farewell.) GTBS; GTBS-P
    (Parting, The.) LiTB; OBEV; SCV
    (Sonnet: "Since there's no help. .") EIL

Since they were morose in August. The Branch. Stanley Moss. DiL

Since those bards. Ay: A Gift of Elephants. Mutamociyar, *tr. by* A. K. Ramanujan. PLW

Since Those We Love and Those We Hate. William Ernest Henley. OBMV

Since thou art gone, my friend, I seek in vain for peace. On Parting with Moses ibn Ezra. Judah Halevi, *tr. by* Solomon Solis-Cohen. TrJP

Since Thou Hast Given Me This Good Hope, O God. Robert Louis Stevenson. TrPWD

Since thou hast view'd some Gorgon, and art grown. Sonnet: The Double Rock. Henry King. SeCP

Since thou wou'dst [*or* wouldst] needs, bewitcht [*or* bewitched] with some ill charms. To One Married to an Old Man. Edmund Waller. FaBoEE; OxBSP; SeCP

Since through vertue encreaseth dignity. Good Counsel. James I, King of Scotland. ACP

Since thy reign is to endure. Emperor Junnin. *Fr.* Manyo Shu. Ma

Since thy third curing of the French infection. Against an Old Lecher. Sir John Harington. FaBoEE

Since Time began, such alphabets begin. From a Cheerful Alphabet. John Updike. FaBoCo

Since to obtaine thee, nothing me will sted. His Remedie for Love. Michael Drayton. *Fr.* Idea. AAS

Since Ventadorn and Comborn with Segur on one side. Bertrans de Born, *tr. by* Paul Blackburn. Pro

Since we agreed to let the road between us. No Road. Philip Larkin. EBEV; MoBrPo

Since we all say. Consecration of the Corn Tortilla. Ricardo Castorrivas, *tr. by* David Volpendesta. VoI

Since we can die but once, what matters it. Sentiment. Thomas Chatterton. NOEC

Since we had changed. Message. Allen Ginsberg. NeAP; VGW

Since we parted, spring half over. Tune: Pure Serene Music ("Since we parted, spring half over"). Li Yü, *tr. by* Burton Watson. CoBCP

Since we through war awhile must part. At Parting. Anne Ridler. CN

Since we'd always sky about. Can. Lit. Earle Birney. NOBC

Since we're not young, weeks have to do time. Adrienne Rich. *Fr.* Twenty-one Love Poems, III. GLP; UnAS

Since When As Ever More. Lawson Fusao Inada. BrSi

Since, when you die, delight. Modern Love Poems. *Somali Oral Tradition, tr. by* B. W. Andrzejewski *and* M. Laurence. WTO

Since without Thee we do no good. Elizabeth Barrett Browning. TrPWD

Since ye delight to know. Sir Thomas Wyatt. SiPS

Since you all will have singing, and won't be said nay. The King's Own Regulars. *Unknown.* PAH

Since you are this way and they are that. The Dreams of the One. Lörinc Szabó, *tr. by* Edwin Morgan. MHuP

Since you ask, most days I cannot remember. Wanting to Die. Anne Sexton. IHMS; MoP; NoAM; TAP

Since You Have Clipped the Wings of Fine Desire. Isabella di Morra, *tr. fr. Italian by* Muriel Kittel. DMI

Since you have turned unkind. To a Lady Friend. W. H. Davies. MoBrPo

Since you, my Lord, were gone. Empress Iwa no hime. *Fr.* Manyo Shu. Ma

Since You Seem Intent. Gerald Locklin. GOYP

Since you walked out on me. Lady of Miracles. Nina Cassian, *tr. by* Laura Schiff. AIW; WPOW

Since You Went Away. Wang K'ai-yün, *tr. fr. Chinese by* Jan *and* Yvonne Walls. WFTU

Since You Went Away. Wang Ts'ai-wei, *tr. fr. Chinese by* Irving Lo. WFTU

Since you will needs that I shall sing. Sir Thomas Wyatt. SiPS

Since you wrote a poem. What Color Is Lonely. Carolyn M. Rodgers. BPo

Since your voice like a soft vapour laps me. I Honour You in Dread. Ramón López Velarde, *tr. by* Samuel Beckett. MexPo

Since you're asking so many questions I'll be off to Tuia and seek ship. Song by a Woman Accused of Adultery. Kie Tapu, *tr. by* Margaret Orbell. PeNZ

Since youth is wise, and cannot comprehend. Inscription for Arthur Rackham's Rip Van Winkle. James Elroy Flecker. BrPo

Sincere Flattery of R. B. James Kenneth Stephen. FaBoPa; NOBL; Par

Sincere Flattery of W. W. (Americanus). James Kenneth Stephen. FiBHP; NOBL; Par

Sincere Praise, *sel.* Isaac Watts.
    "Almighty Maker God!" TrPWD

Sindhi Woman. Jon Stallworthy. OxBC

Sines. Raymond Queneau, *tr. fr. French by* Teo Savory. RHTwFP

Sinfonia Domestica. Jean Starr Untermeyer. MoAmPo

Sinfonia Eroica. Alice Archer James. AA

Sinful to Flirt. *Unknown.* AmFP

Sing a little as the feet unwearied. Voyageur. R. E. Rashley. CaP

Sing a song o' sixpence. Song of Sixpence. *Unknown.* OxBoLi

Sing a song of cobbler! Jeremy Hobbler. *Unknown.* BoTP

Sing a song of critics. Valentine. Ernest Hemingway. OBAL; TW

Sing a song of hollow logs. Song of Summer Days. J. W. Foley. BoTP

Sing a song of laughter. The Giraffe and the Woman. Laura E. Richards. PDV

Sing a song of mincemeat. Mincemeat. Elizabeth Gould. BoTP

Sing a Song of People. Lois Lenski. RHPC

Sing a song of picnics. Picnic Day. Rachel Lyman Field. RAR

Sing a song of pop corn. A Pop Corn Song. Nancy Byrd Turner. FaPON

Sing a song of Scissor-men. The Scissor-Man. Madeleine Nightingale. BoTP

Sing a song of sixpence. Mother Goose. FaBoBe; OxNR

Sing a Song of Subways. Eve Merriam. RHPC

Sing a song of washing-up. The Washing-Up Song. Elizabeth Gould. BoTP

Sing a song of winter. A Sledding Song. Norman C. Schlichter. FaPON

Sing, bird, on green Missouri's plain. The Death of Lyon. Henry Peterson. PAH

Sing, Brothers, Sing! William Robert Rodgers. MoAB; MoBrPo

Sing, cuccu, nu. Sing, cuccu. *Unknown. See* Summer [*or* Summer] is icumen [*or* y-comen] in.

Sing first the heroe in his goodly ship. *Unknown. Fr.* A Pindarique Ode on the Arrival of His Excellency. PBCV

Sing for the Garish Eye. W. S. Gilbert. NA

Sing hey! for bold George Washington. George Washington. Rosemary *and* Stephen Vincent Benét. FaPON

Sing, hey! Sing, hey!/ For Christmas Day. *Unknown.* ILY; PChr
    (An Old Christmas Greeting.) FaPON

Sing his praises that doth keep. John Fletcher. *Fr.* The Faithful Shepherdess, I, ii. OBS
    (Hymn to Pan.) NOBE; OBEV

Sing I for a brave and gallant barque, and a stiff and a rattling breeze. Ten Thousand Miles Away. *Unknown.* AS

Sing Ivy. *Unknown.* BoTP

Sing jigmijole the pudding-bowl. Kissing of My Dame. *Unknown.* GBP
    ("Sing jigmijole, the pudding bowl.") OxNR

Sing jigmijole, the pudding bowl. *Unknown. See* Kissing of My Dame.

Sing! Let us sing out. Songs That Cannot Be Silenced. Hien Luong, *tr. by* Chris Knipp *and* Mohammad Sadiq. OV

Sing Lullaby, as Women Do. George Gascoigne. *See* Lullaby [*or* Lullabie] of a Lover, The.

Sing lullaby [*or* lullabie] as women do[e]. The Lullaby [*or* Lullabie] of a Lover. George Gascoigne. AAS; EBEV; ElL; HAP; NAEL-1; QFR
(A Lover's Lullaby.)
(Gascoigne's Lullaby [*or* Lullabie].) NoP; PoEL-1; TrGrPo
(Sing Lullaby, as Women Do.) InvP
Sing, magnarello, merrily. The Leaf-picking. Frédéric Mistral, *tr. by* Harriet Waters Preston. AWP
Sing me a hero! Quench my thirst. Tray. Robert Browning. FM
Sing Me a New Song. John Henrik Clarke. PoBA
Sing me a song of a lad that is gone. Robert Louis Stevenson. BrPo; NOBE
(Over the Sea to Skye.) MOS
Sing Me a Song of Teapots and Trumpets. N. M. Bodecker. RHPC
Sing me a sweet, low song of night. Hildegarde Hawthorne. FaBoBe
Sing me the men ere this. He Would Have His Lady Sing. Digby Mackworth Dolben. EBEV
Sing, My Soul. *Unknown.* AH
Sing, my tongue, the Saviour's glory. Saint Thomas Aquinas. WGRP
Sing, O goddess, the wrath, the ontamable dander of Keitt. The Fight over the Body of Keitt. *Unknown.* PAH
Sing On, Blithe Bird. William Motherwell. GN
Sing out, my soul, thy songs of joy. Songs of Joy. W. H. Davies. MoBrPo
Sing out pent souls, sing cheerfully. The Vintage to the Dungeon. Richard Lovelace. CaPo; SeCV-1
Sing, sing,/ What shall I sing? Mother Goose. OxNR
Sing, Sing for Christmas. J. H. Egar. OHIP
Sing-Song, *sels.* Christina Rossetti.
   Caterpillar, The. BoTP; FaPON; GoJo; OxBChV; RHPC
   City Mouse and the Garden Mouse, The. BoTP; FaBoBe; FaPON; NTCP
   Ferry Me across the Water. ChTr; GoJo; OxBChV; PDV
   (Ferryman, The.) BoTP
   Flint. OxBChV; RHPC
   "Horses of the sea, The." FaPON; GoJo; NTCP
   Hurt No Living Thing. FaPON; FM; PDV; RHPC; TSS
   Let's Be Merry. FaPON
   Minnie and Mattie. GoJo; InvP
   Mix a Pancake. NTCP
   "O sailor, come ashore." FM
   Oh, Fair to See. FaPON; OHIP
   Rainbow, The. OxBChV
   Sound of the Wind, The. OnUR
   What Do They Do?. FaPON
   What Does the Bee Do?. OxBChV
   What Is Pink?. GoJo; OnUR; OxBChV; RHPC
   "When fishes set umbrellas up." FM
   Who Has Seen the Wind?. FaPON; GoJo; NTCP; PDV; RHPC
   (Wind, The.) BLPL; FaBoBe; OxBChV
Sing song/ Tag along. Tag Along. Nina Payne. RHPC
Sing-Song of Old Man Kangaroo, The. Kipling. FaPON
Sing to Apollo, God of Day. Song of Apollo. John Lyly. *Fr.* Midas. OBSC
Sing to Ashtaroth and Bel. To Ashtaroth and Bel. Saul Tchernichowsky, *tr. by* L. V. Snowman. TrJP
Sing to the Lord, for what can better be. Psalm CXLVII: "Praise ye the Lord." Countess of Pembroke. NoCV
Sing to the Lord Most High. Timothy Dwight. AH
Sing to whom a hallelujah? Whom endorse? The Umbrella, the Cane, and the Broom. Eliezer Steinbarg. VWA, *tr. by* Curt Leviant
Sing unto Jehovah. Bible, *O.T. See* Psalms: Psalm XCVIII ("O sing unto the Lord. . . .").
Sing unto the Lord with thanksgiving. Bible, *O.T. See* Psalms: Psalm CXLVII ("Praise ye the Lord").
Sing we all merrily. A Catch by the Hearth. *Unknown.* OHIP
Sing We and Chant It. *Unknown.* EBEV; OBSC
   (To Live in Pleasure.) TrGrPo
Sing we for love and idleness. An Immorality. Ezra Pound. CMoP; GoJo; GrPl; LiTM; MoAB; MoAmPo; NOBA; OBAL
Sing We Yule. *Unknown.* MeEL
Sing while you may, O bird upon the tree! Dark Wings. James Stephens. PoA
Sing! Why should I sing. Wayfaring. Francisco A. de Icaza, *tr. by* Samuel Beckett. MexPo
Sing with Your Body. Janice Mirikitani. WPOW
Singe we alle and say we thus. My Purse. *Unknown.* EBEV
Singed by a flight of scarlet ibises. I Will Enter. Grace Nichols. UAS
Singee a songee sick a pence. Song. *Unknown.* BXAP
Singer, The. Anna Wickham. MoBrPo
Singer has departed; and no more, The. To the Memory of William Billington. George Hull. PF

Singer in the Prison, The. Walt Whitman. BeLS
Singer of One Song, The. Henry Augustin Beers. AA
Singer within the little streets. Monk Gibbon. NeIP
Singers, The. George Bruce. OxBS
Singer's House, The. Seamus Heaney. EBEV
Singers in the Snow, The. *Unknown.* OHIP
Singers of serenades, The. Mandoline. Paul Verlaine, *tr. by* Arthur Symons. AWP; OBMV
Singers, sing! The hoary world. The Servants. Richard Wightman. WGRP
Singers to Come. Alice Meynell. WPE
Singing Aloud. Carolyn Kizer. IHMS
Singing & Doubling Together. A. R. Ammons. NAAL-2; NoAM
Singing Bones, The. Randolph Stow. CBAP
Singing Cat, The. Stevie Smith. CRH; OxBTC
Singing, dancing—handsome actors entertain. On the Cold Food Festival, Entertaining at the Southern Estate. Li K'ai-hsien, *tr. by* Jonathan Chaves. CoBLCP
Singing Death. Stan Rice. FYAP
Singing in the Dark. Irma Wassall. PoNe
Singing in the Spring. Ivy O. Eastwick. RAR
Singing is sweet; but be sure of this. James Thomson. *Fr.* Art. NOBVV
Singing Leaves, The. James Russell Lowell. GN
Singing Lesson, The. David Wagoner. NoAM
Singing Maid, The. *Unknown.* MeEL
Singing Maid, The. *Unknown. See* Now Springs the Spray.
Singing my days. Passage to India. Walt Whitman. AmPP; NAAL-1; PoEL-5
Singing, 1977. Roy Fuller. PoPo
Singing of the Moon. Emperor Mommu, *tr. fr.* Chinese by Burton Watson. JLIC-1
Singing of Thoughts, *sels.* Juan Chi, *tr. fr.* Chinese by Burton Watson. CoBCP
   "Beautiful trees make paths beneath themselves."
   "In North Ward they do many strange dances."
   "Long ago, at fourteen or fifteen."
   "This summer's burning heat."
   "Tung-ling melons—men say that long ago."
   "Years ago, when I was young."
Singing on the Moon. Ted Hughes. WSC
Singing School. Seamus Heaney. InPS
   Constable Calls, A, *sel.* FaBoPV; IPY; NOIV
Singing. Singing. Winter Song. Juan Ramón Jiménez, *tr. by* H. R. Hays. WSC
Singing the Reapers Homeward Come. *Unknown.* OHIP
Singing through the forests. Rhyme of the Rail[s]. John Godfrey Saxe. AnAmPo; MoShBr; PoLF
Singing-Time. Rose Fyleman. RAR
Singing, today I married my white girl. Dannie Abse. OBWVE
Single-eyed to child and sunbeam. Blue-eyed Mary. Mary E. Wilkins Freeman. OBCA
Single flow'r he sent me, since we met, A. One Perfect Rose. Dorothy Parker. FiBHP; NBLV; NIP; NoP; OBAL
Single Girl, The. *Unknown. See* I Wish I Was Single Again.
Single-handed, and surrounded by Lecompton's black brigade. Lecompton's Black Brigade. Charles Graham Halpine. PAH
Single illness has lasted three months, A. Written While Sick. Wen Cheng-ming, *tr. by* Jonathan Chaves. CoBLCP
Single man stands like a bird-watcher, A. The Mouth of the Hudson. Robert Lowell. AiP; AmFN; NaP
Single Most. Rae Armantrout. IAT
Single naked wire at ground level, A. George Jonas. *Fr.* To Christian Montpelier. NeAC
Single post, a point of rusting, A. Marina Tsvetayeva, *tr. fr.* Russian by Elaine Feinstein *and* Angela Livingstone. *Fr.* Poem of the End. BrRo
Single-Rhyme Alphabet, A. *Unknown.* FaBoUs
Single rock from Cinnabar Hill, A. On a Painting of Mushrooms. Yün Shou-p'ing, *tr. by* Jonathan Chaves. CoBLCP
Single rock, vast, A. Rock among Bamboo. Hsü Wei, *tr. fr.* Chinese by Jonathan Chaves. *Fr.* A Kite. CoBLCP
Single set of footsteps coming, A. Ozaki Hosai, *tr. fr.* Japanese by Hiroaki Sato. *Fr.* One Hundred Haiku in Free Form. FCEI
Single sleeper lying here, The. Epitaph for the Poet. George Barker. OxBSP
Single Sonnet. Louise Bogan. Son
Single story two bedroom dwelling across from. In the Orpheum Building. Kit Robinson. UL
Single Vision. Stanley Kunitz. CAPP

Singles. Michael Waters. GeTw; MAYP; NAmP

Sings Harry, *sels.* Denis Glover.
Casual Man, The. ATNZ
Once the Days. ATNZ; PeNZ
Song: "If everywhere in the street." *Fr.* II. PeNZ
(Sings Harry to an Old Guitar.) ATNZ
Song: "These songs will not stand." *Fr.* I. ATNZ; PeNZ
Song: "When I am old." *Fr.* III. PeNZ
Themes. ATNZ
Thistledown. ATNZ; PeNZ

Singular Indeed. David McCord. OBCA
Singular Sangfroid of Baby Bunting, The. Guy Wetmore Carryl. NA
Singular Singulars, Peculiar Plurals. Willard R. Espy. FaBoUs
Singularity in Cygnus XI Viewed with Pity for HDE 226868, The. David Lunde. BWV
Singularly and in pairs the decade has been ripped by bullets. Herbert Martin. PoBA
Sinister presence changed life in a twelvemonth, A. Mountain Convent. Laura Benét. GoYe
Sinkholes. Janet Reed McFatter. GrPl
Sinking of the *Graf Spee*, The. *Unknown.* OxBSS, *with music*
Sinking of the Mendi, The. S. E. K. Mqhayi, *tr. fr. Xhosa by* C. M. Mcanyangwa *and* Jack Cope. PeSA
Sinking of the *Merrimac*, The. Lucy Larcom. PAH
Sinking Rising. Dahlia Ravikovich, *tr. fr. Hebrew by* Warren Bargad *and* Stanley F. Chyet. IP
Sinks the sun below the desert. Cleopatra Dying. Thomas Stephens Collier. BLPA; BLPL; FaBoBe
Sinless Child, The, *sel.* Elizabeth Oakes Smith.
"Her ways were gentle while a babe." AA
Sinner, Is Thy Heart at Rest? Jared B. Waterbury. AH
Sinner man sat on the gates of hell, A. No Hiding Place Down There. *Unknown.* GBP
Sinner-Saint, The. Wilfrid Scawen Blunt. ACP
Sinners, abhor the Fiend. Charles Wesley. *Fr.* The Horrible Decree. NOCV
Sinner's Lament, A. Lord Herbert of Cherbury. SeCP
Sinners, Will You Scorn the Message? Jonathan Allen. AH
Sins Loathed, and Yet Loved. Robert Herrick. LiTB
Sins of Kalamazoo, The. Carl Sandburg. VGW
Sins of Youth, The. Thomas, 2d Baron Vaux of Harrowden Vaux. ACP
Sion lies [*or* Syon lyes] waste, and thy Jerusalem. Fulke Greville. *Fr.* Caelica, CIX [CX]. NoP; PoEL-1
Sioux, The. Eugene Field. FiBHP; GoJo
Sioux Indians. *Unknown.* AmFP
Sioux Metamorphoses, *sels. Unknown, tr. fr. Sioux Indian by* James Koller. STP
"He comes from the north."
"He was an old wolf, no teeth, his tail all but bare."
"I thought I saw buffalo."
"In wild flight."
Sip a little. Baby's Drinking Song. James Kirkup. NTCP
Sip of Coors makes children be, A. Booze Turns Men into Women. Bernadette Mayer. UL
Sipping a Schlitz. Bullfrogs. David Allan Evans. Psk
Sipping judiciously, he saw come near. Narcissus in a Cocktail Glass. Frances Minturn Howard. GoYe
Sipping whiskey and gin. Analysands. Dudley Randall. BPo
Sipsop's Song. Blake. *Fr.* An Island in the Moon. FaBoNo
Sir/ I read of late. Four Questions Addressed to His Excellency, the Prime Minister. James P. Vaughn. AmNP
Sir,/ Ere you pass this threshold, stay. To the King, at His Entrance into Saxham: By Master John Crofts. Thomas Carew. CaPo
Sir, after you have wip'd the eyes. A Consolatory Poem Dedicated unto Mr. Cotton Mather. Nicholas Noyes. SCAP
Sir Aldingar. *Unknown.* ESPB; ESPB, (A, B *and* C *vers.*); OxBB
Sir Andrew Bart[t]on. *Unknown.* AmFP, 2 *vers.;* EnSB; ESPB; OxBB
Sir, as your mandate did request. The Inventory, in Answer to the Usual Mandate Sent by a Surveyor of the Taxes, Requiring a Return of the Number of Horses, Servants, Carriages, etc., Kept. Burns. FaBoUs
Sir—awaiting you. Waiting for the Emperor Tenji. Princess Nukada. PBWP, *tr. by* Cid Corman *and* Susumu Kamaike
Sir Beelzebub. Dame Edith Sitwell. *Fr.* Façade. BoWoP; FaBoWP; HoPM; MoAB; MoBrPo; OxBTC; PrIm
Sir Bumper was a baron bold. The Lover's Leap; a Tale. Andrew Macdonald. NOEC
Sir Cawline. *Unknown.* ESPB
Sir Christopher Wren. Edmund Clerihew Bentley. *Fr.* Clerihews. CenHV; FaBoCo; FiBHP; MoShBr; NBLV
Sir Colin. *Unknown.* OxBB

Sir Dilberry Diddle, Captain of Militia. *Unknown.* NOEC
Sir Drake, whom well the world's end knew. Epigram: On Sir Francis Drake. *Unknown.* OBS; OBTV
Sir Eggnogg. Bayard Taylor. BXAP
Sir Eglamour. Samuel Rowlands. *Fr.* The Melancholy Knight. EIL; FaBoCh; FaBoNo; InvP
Sir Egrabell had sonnes three. Sir Lionel. *Unknown.* AmFP; ESPB
Sir Emperour, lorde of al the ground. *Unknown, tr. fr. French by* John Lydgate. *Fr.* The Dance of Death. OxBLMV
Sir Eustace Grey, *sels.* George Crabbe.
Frenzy. NOBE
"Peace, peace, my friend; these subjects fly." PoEL-4
"Then those ill-favour'd Ones, whom none." ELP
Sir Francis Drake, *sel.* Charles Fitz-Geffry.
Bee, The. EIL
Sir Francis Drake; or, Eighty-eight. *Unknown.* GBP; OxBSS
Sir Francis, Sir Francis, Sir Francis is come. Upon Sir Francis Drake's Return from His Voyage about the World, and the Queen's Meeting Him. *Unknown.* CoMu; EIL; FaBoCh; OxBSS
Sir Gawain and the Green Knight ("The siege and the assault being ceased at Troy."), *sels. Unknown, tr. fr. Middle English by* Brian Stone. OAEL-1
Gawain and the Lady of the Castle. EBEV
Passage of a Year, The. PoEL-1
Sir Gawayn Goes to Receive His Return Blow from the Green Knight. FaBoPP
Temptation of Sir Gawain, The. ACP
"This kyng lay at Camylot upon Krystmasse." PoE
Sir Gawain Encounters Sir Priamus. Tennyson, *Incorporated in* Idylls of the King *with changes, as* The Passing of Arthur. *Fr.* Morte d'Arthur. PoEL-1
Sir Gawaine and the Green Knight. Yvor Winters. MoP; NoAM; PoRA; QFR; VGW
Sir Gawayn Goes to Receive His Return Blow from the Green Knight. *Unknown, tr. fr. Middle English by* Brian Stone. *Fr.* Sir Gawain and the Green Knight. FaBoPP
Sir Geoffrey Chaucer. Robert Greene. *See* Greene's Vision: Description of Sir Geoffrey Chaucer, The.
Sir George Prevost, with all his host. The Battle of Plattsburg. *Unknown.* PAH
Sir Halewyn. Sir Alexander Gray. OxBB
Sir Henry Clinton's Invitation to the Refugees. Philip Freneau. PAH
Sir Hudibras, his passing worth. The Argument. Samuel Butler. *Fr.* Hudibras, I, 1. EBEV; NAEL-1; OAEL-1; SeCV-2
Sir Hudibras, His Passing Worth. Samuel Butler. *See* Hudibras: Metaphysical Sectarian, The ("He was in logick a great critic").
Sir Hudson Lowe, Sir Hudson *Low. To* Sir Hudson Lowe. Thomas Moore. OBSV
Sir Hugh; or, The Jew's Daughter. *Unknown.* CH; ESPB, A *and* C *vers.;* FaBoBa; AmFP
Sir Humphrey Gilbert. Longfellow. PAH
Sir Humphry Davy. Edmund Clerihew Bentley. *Fr.* Clerihews. CenHV; FaBoCo; ImOP
Sir, I admit your general [*or* gen'ral] rule,. Pope, *also at. to* Matthew Prior *and to* Samuel Taylor Coleridge. FaBoEE; FiBHP; LiTB (Fool and the Poet, The.) NBLV
Sir if one of the old proverbs. To Pope Julius II. Buonarroti Buonarroti Michelangelo, *tr. by* W. S. Merwin. PFI
Sir Isaac Newton. *Unknown.* WeW
Sir James the Rose. *Unknown.* ESPB
Sir John addressed the Snake-god in his temple. Robert Graves. *Fr.* Grotesques. CMoP
Sir John Barleycorn. *Unknown.* FaBoBa
Sir John Butler. *Unknown.* ESPB
Sir John Graeme and Barbara Allan. *Unknown. See* It was in and about the Martinmas time.
Sir John Suckling. Richard O'Connell. *Fr.* Lives of the Poets. SoTCo
Sir Josephs's Song. W. S. Gilbert. *Fr.* H. M. S. Pinafore. LiTB
Sir Joshua Reynolds. Blake. FaBoCo; FaBoEE; FiBHP; OxBoLi; TW
Sir Joshua Reynolds. Goldsmith. *Fr.* Retaliation. FaBoEE; NOEC; OBD; SeCePo
Sir knights, take heed hither in hie. The York Play of the Crucifixion. *Unknown.* NAEL-1
Sir Lark and King Sun; a Parable. George Macdonald. *Fr.* Adela Cathcart, *ch.* 16. GN
Sir Launfal and the Leper. James Russell Lowell. *Fr.* The Vision of Sir Launfal, *pt.* I. GN
Sir Lionel. *Unknown.* AmFP; ESPB
Sir Marmaduke's Musings. Theodore Tilton. AA
Sir Moses, Sir Aaron, Sir Jamramajee. A New Order of Chivalry. Thomas Love Peacock. CenHV

Sir Nameless, once of Athelhall, declared. The Children and Sir Nameless. Thomas Hardy. NoP

Sir Nicketty Nox. Hugh Chesterman. BoTP

Sir, no man's enemy, forgiving all. Petition. W. H. Auden. CMoP; LiTB; NAEL-2; Son

Sir, not that we did not hear the noise. What Her Girl Friend Said to Him. Kannan, *tr.* by A. K. Ramanujan. PLW

Sir, now unravelled is the Golden Fleece. To Dr. F. B. on His Book of Chess. Richard Lovelace. CaPo

Sir Olaf. Johann Gottfried von Herder, *tr. fr. German by* Elizabeth Craigmyle. AWP

Sir Oluf he rideth over the plain. The Elected Knight. *Unknown, tr. by* Longfellow. AWP

Sir Patient Fancy, *sel.* Aphra Behn.
   "What has poor Woman done, that she must be." *Fr.* Epilogue. WPOW

Sir Patrick Spens [*or* Spence]. *Unknown.* AmFP; AWP; CH; EBEV; ELP; EnRP; EnSB; ESPB, (A, B *and* G *vers.*); ESPB; FaBoBa; FaBoCh; FaPoR; FF; GN; GoJo; HAP; HoPM; HoPM; InPS; InvP; InVP; LiTB; MOS; NIP; NOBE; NoP, (A *vers.*); NoP; OAEL-1, *with music;* OAEL-1; OBEV; OxBB, (B *vers., with music);* OxBB; OxBS; PoEL-1; PPP; PrIm; TrGrPo; UnPo; WeW

Sir Rider Haggard. W. H. Auden. FaBoCo

Sir Robert Bolton had three sons. Sir Lionel. *Unknown.* ESPB

Sir Roland; a Fragment. Robert Merry. NOEC

Sir, say no more. Dramatic Fragment. Trumbull Stickney. OxBA
   (Sir, say no more.) InPK; OxBSP

Sir, since the last Elizabethan died. A Letter to a Live Poet. Rupert Brooke. BrPo

Sir Smasham Uppe. Emile Victor Rieu. RHPC

Sir, so suspicious. *Unknown, tr. by* Thomas Kinsella. NOIV

Sir T. J.'s Speech to His Wife and Children. *Unknown.* CoMu

Sir Thomas Armstrong's Last Farewell to the World. *Unknown.* APAS

Sir Thopas. Chaucer. *Fr.* The Canterbury Tales. Par

Sir Thopas's Tale. Chaucer. *See* Listeth lordes, in good entent.

Sir: though (I thank God for it) I do hate. John Donne. *Fr.* Satires, II. OBSV

Sir Toby Matthews. Sir John Suckling. SeCV-1

Sir Tristem, *sel. At. to* Thomas of Erceldoune.
   Tristrem and the Hunters. OxBS

Sir Walter, oh, oh, my own Sir Walter. Lady Ralegh's Lament. Robert Lowell. OxBSP

Sir Walter Ralegh to His Son. Sir Walter Ralegh. *See* Three Things [*or* Thinges] There Be[e] That Prosper All [*or* Up] Apace.

Sir Walter Raleigh. Edmund Clerihew Bentley. *Fr.* Clerihews. CenHV

Sir Walter Raleigh Sailing in the Lowlands ("Sir Walter Raleigh has built a ship"). *Unknown.* OxBoLi; OxBSS

Sir Walter Rauleigh His Lamentation. *Unknown.* CoMu

Sir Walter Scott at the Tomb of the Stuarts in St. Peter's. Richard Monckton Milnes. EBVV; OBTV

Sir Walter Scott's Tribute. Sir Walter Scott. *Fr.* The Monastery, *ch.* 12. WBLP

Sir, whatsoever you are pleas'd to do. To the Prince. Sir John Davies. *Fr.* Dedications [*of* Orchestra], II. SiPS

Sir, whatsoever you are pleas'd to do. Dedications, II: To the Prince. Sir John Davies. *Fr.* Orchestra; or, A Poem[e] of Da[u]ncing. SiPS

Sir! when I flew to seize the bird. Beau's Reply. William Cowper. FaBoCh

Sir, when you say. 15th Raga: For Bela Lugosi. David Meltzer. *Fr.* Ragas. NeAP

Sir William Dyer, Knight, *sel.* Lady Catherine Dyer.
   Epitaph on the Monument of Sir William Dyer at Colmworth, 1641. BoLoP; EnLoPo

Sir William of Deloraine at the Wizard's Tomb. Sir Walter Scott. *See* Lay of the Last Minstrel, The: Melrose Abbey.

Sir, you should notice me: I am the Man. Lascelles Abercrombie. MoBrPo

Sir, you were a credit to whatever. To a Teacher of French. Donald Davie. OxBC

Sire. W. S. Merwin. CoAP; NaP; VGW

Siren, The. Idea Vilariño, *tr. fr. Spanish by* Kate Flores. DMH

Siren Bird, The. Henrietta Cordelia Ray. CBWP-3

Siren Chorus. George Darley. *See* Syren Songs: Mermaidens' Vesper-Hymn, The.

Siren sang, and Europe turned away, A. To the Western World. Louis Simpson. CAPP; CoAP; GOA; LiTM; NePoEA-2; NOBA; SM; TAP

Siren Song. Margaret Atwood. *Fr.* Songs of the Transformed. HAP; PoA; WeW

Siren Song. Marg Yeo. DT

Sirena. Michael Drayton. *See* Shepherd's Sirena, The: Trent, The.

Sirens, The. Gordon Challis. PeNZ

Sirens, The. Donald Finkel. NePoEA

Sirens, The. John Manifold. LiTB; LiTM; MoBrPo; Son; WaP

Sirens in Bad Weather. Sherod Santos. MAYP

Sirens slice the afternoon air, The. Raid on the Market. Polycarp Chimedza. WMBCH

Sirens' Song, The. William Browne. *Fr.* The Inner Temple Masque. NOBE; OBEV

Sirius/ what mystery is this? Hilda Doolittle ("H. D."). *Fr.* The Walls Do Not Fall. PBWP

Sirmio. Catullus, *tr. fr. Latin by* Charles Stuart Calverley. AWP

Sirmio, thou dearest dear of strands. Catullus, *tr. by* Thomas Hardy. OBVE

Sirs—though we fail you—let us live. To Men. Anna Wickham. MoBrPo

Sirvente of the Linden Tree. Wesli Court. SoTCo

Sirventes. Paul Blackburn. NeAP; PoM

Sirventes against the Management of the Mammoth Supermarket in Toulouse, A. Chuck Wachtel. UL

Sister. Jerzy Harasymowicz, *tr. fr. Polish by* Czeslaw Milosz. PwPP

Sister. Gabriela Mistral, *tr. fr. Spanish by* Langston Hughes. BoWoP; OV

Sister. Mririda n'Ait Attik, *tr. fr. Berber into French by* René Euloge; *English vers.* by Daniel Halpern *and* Paula Paley. OV

Sister. Whittier. *Fr.* Snow-bound; a Winter Idyl. AA

Sister and mother and diviner love. To the One of Fictive Music. Wallace Stevens. MoAB; MoAmPo; NoP

Sister Anne, Sister Anne. Perspectives Are Precipices. John Peale Bishop. LiTA

Sister, Awake! *Unknown.* CH; EiL; NOBE; OBEV
   (Madrigal: "Sister, awake! close not your eyes.") BoTP

Sister darling, ope the window, let the balmy air once more. The Dying Girl. Mary Weston Fordham. CBWP-2

Sister Dolours hangs up her laundry. Sun Dance in St. Lucia. Joan Van Poznak. SoTCo

Sister, don't scold me. Sister. Mririda n'Ait Attik, *tr. by* René Euloge; *English vers.* by Daniel Halpern *and* Paula Paley. OV

Sister Helen. Dante Gabriel Rossetti. BeLS

Sister, I had a dream that I wed. Mirabai, *tr. by* John Stratton Hawley *and* Mark Juergensmeyer. SSI

Sister Johnson's Speech. Maggie Pogue Johnson. CBWP-4

Sister Lou. Sterling Allen Brown. AmNP; PoBA; PoNe

Sister Mary Appassionata Lectures the Journalism Class. David Citino. SoTCo

Sister Mother. Franca Maria Catri, *tr. fr. Italian by* Muriel Kittel. DMI

Sister Nell. *Unknown.* FaPON

Sister on the Tracks, A. Donald Hall. BLA

Sister once of weeds & a dark water that held still. Family Romance. Larry Levis. MAYP; NAmP

Sister Pharaoh. Ruth Whitman. MAT

Sister saying—"Soon you'll be back in the ward— In the Theatre. Dannie Abse. NoAM

"Sister, sister, go to bed!" Brother and Sister. "Lewis Carroll." ChTr; FaBoNo

Sister Songs, *sels.* Francis Thompson.
   "But lo! at length the day is lingered out." OBMV
   We Poets Speak. FaBV

Sister, the stars have no children. Mother of Nothing. Naomi Shihab Nye. NAmP

Sister! the sundering sea. Cuba. Thomas MacDermot. PBCV

Sister was wedged beside the wicker basket. The Burned Bridge. Ruth Stone. WPE

Sister Water. Robert Penn Warren. MT

Sister Zahava. Edith Bruck, *tr. fr. Italian by* Anita Barrows. VWA

Sisters, The. Roy Campbell. BoLoP; ErPo; FaBoTw; OBMV

Sisters, The. Alexis De Veaux. GLP

Sisters. Eleanor Farjeon. FaPON

Sisters, The. Nicki Jackowska. BrRo

Sisters. Sandra McPherson. AmPA; AnAn

Sisters. Adrienne Rich. IHMS

Sisters, The. Dorothy Roberts. CaP

Sisters, The. John Banister Tabb. AA

Sisters, The. Tennyson. InvP

Sisters, The. Whittier. AWP

Sisters are always drying their hair. Triolet against Sisters. Phyllis McGinley. OBCA

Sisters in Arms. Audre Lorde. ER

Sisterwoman sisterwoman. Woman Talk. a-dZiko Simba. WS

Sisyphus. Robert Garioch. PoSH

Sisyphus. Josephine Miles. NYBP

Sit/ Please sit down. Nostalgia. Wu T'e-Liang, *tr. by* Dominic Cheung. IFON

Sit as close to the stage as possible. How to Find Love in an Instant.
Michael Lassell. *Fr.* Times Square Poems. GLP
Sit down by the side of your mother, my boy. Mother's Advice.
Unknown. AmFP
Sit down with me awhile beside the heath-corner. Erica. Mary Ursula
Bethell. ATNZ; PeNZ
Sit here. A Secret Place. Judith W. Steinbergh. ILY
Sit in the car with the headlights off. Wingatui. Bill Manhire. ATNZ
Sit on the bed. I'm blind, and three parts shell. A Terre. Wilfred Owen.
LiTM; MMA; OxBTC; WaP
Sit quiet in my lap while solemnly. Evensong. Carleton Drewry. GoYe
Sit tight, little hills, little valleys. Dame Liberty Reports from Travel.
Dorothy Cowles Pinkney. GoYe
Sit too close. My Mother Spinning. Peter Olds. ATNZ; PeNZ
Site. Meir Wieseltier, *tr. fr. Hebrew by* Warren Bargad *and* Stanley F.
Chyet. IP
Site of Ambush, *sel.* Eiléan Ní Chuilleanáin.
"At alarming bell daybreak, before." CIP
Sith fortune favors not and all things backward go. A Refusal. Barnabe
Googe. NoP
Sith, in dark speech, Carvilios hymn unfolds. Hymn to the Sun. C. M.
Doughty. *Fr.* The Dawn in Britain. FaBoTw
Sith my life from life is parted. Marie Magdalens Complaint at Christs
Death. Robert Southwell. MePo
Sith sickles and the shearing scythe. Hawking for the Partridge. Thomas
Ravenscroft. OxBoLi
Sith Venus had her mole, Helen her stain. Against Proud Poor Phryna.
John Davies of Hereford. FaBoEE
Sits at the window, waits the threatened steel. Medusa. Vincent
O'Sullivan. ATNZ
Sits by a fireplace, the seducer talks. Leonard Wolf. ErPo
Sitter Bitter. Miss Bitter. N. M. Bodecker. NTCP
Sitters on the mead-bench, quaffing among questions. An Exeter Riddle.
Gavin Ewart. OxBC
Sitteth alle stille and herkneth to me. The Song of Lewes. *Unknown.*
OxBoLi
(Against the Baron's Enemies.) MeEL
Sitting. Susan Griffin. NPGG
Sitting alone (as one forsook). The Vision. Robert Herrick. CaPo;
ErPo; JCP; SeCP
Sitting Alone in the Courtyard. Yü Chi, *tr. fr. Chinese by* Jonathan
Chaves. CoBLCP
Sitting Alone in the Mountains. Tami No Kurohito, *tr. fr. Chinese by*
Burton Watson. JLIC-1
Sitting Alone in Tulsa Three A.M. Lance Henson. VoR
Sitting Around Waiting for Your Cat to Die. Bonnie Jacobson. SoTCo
Sitting at an edge. Buson, *tr. fr. Japanese by* Hiroaki Sato. *Fr.* Eighty-
seven Hokku. FCEI
Sitting at evening in the warm grass. For My Wife. Julian Symons.
WaP
Sitting at her table, she serves. Nani. A. A. Ríos. SM
Sitting at her [*or* a] window/ in her cloak and hat. Mother Tabbyskins.
Elizabeth Anna Hart. CenHV; OxBChV
Sitting at Night on the Front Porch. Charles Wright. LCAP
Sitting at Night on the Moonlit Terrace. Yang Wan-li, *tr. fr. Chinese by*
Burton Watson. CoBCP
Sitting back on both. Senryu. Hakuin, *tr. by* Lucien Stryk *and* Takashi
Ikemoto. ZPCJ
Sitting Bard, The. Sir Owen Seaman. NOBL
Sitting between the sea and the buildings. The Painter. John Ashbery.
HCAP; NOBA; NoP; PoE; SOTW
Sitting Bull's Will versus the Sioux Treaty of 1868 and Monty Hall. A.
K. Redwing. VoR
Sitting by a river['s] side. Robert Greene. *Fr.* Philomela, the Lady
Fitzwater's Nightingale. TEP
(Philomela's Ode in Her Arbour.) OBSC
Sitting by Myself. K'ang Hai, *tr. fr. Chinese by* Jonathan Chaves.
CoBLCP
Sitting by the riverside with a torn net. Li K'ai-hsien, *tr. fr. Chinese by*
Jonathan Chaves. *Fr.* Impromptu Poems. CoBLCP
Sitting Down, Looking Up. A. R. Ammons. PCP
Sitting down near him in the shade. The Smoker. Robert Huff.
NePoEA-2
Sitting in a Circle, Speaking Our Thoughts. Michizane, *tr. fr. Chinese by*
Burton Watson. JLIC-1
(Sitting in a tree-). E. E. Cummings. TSS
Sitting in an empty house. A Dog in San Francisco. Michael Ondaatje.
GOYP
Sitting in Meditation: A Random Thought. Ku T'ai-ch'ing, *tr. fr. Chinese*
by Pao Chia-lin. WFTU

Sitting in Meditation at Night, Facing Hui-shan. Wei Yüan, *tr. fr.*
Chinese by Irving Lo. WFTU
Sitting in the disorder of my silence. Fulfillment. Vassar Miller.
NePoEA-2
Sitting, legs crossed, copper-toned old man. My Song. King D. Kuka.
VoR
Sitting naked together. Rain Journal: London: June 65. Lee Harwood.
PeHV
Sitting on the toilet. 38 Main Street. Lyn Lifshin. TV
Sitting Outdoors. Lu Yu, *tr. fr. Chinese by* Burton Watson. CoBCP
Sitting Pretty. Margaret Fishback. PoLF
Sitting Quietly at Night. Kito, *tr. fr. Japanese by* Hiroaki Sato. *Fr.*
Twenty-four Hokku. FCEI
Sitting straightbacked, a modest Irish miss. A Lesson in Love. Philip
Hobsbaum. OxBTC
Sitting under the mistletoe. Mistletoe. Walter de la Mare. SO
Sitting Up at Night. Ku T'ai-ch'ing, *tr. fr. Chinese by* Pao Chia-lin.
WFTU
Sitting Up at Night. Lu Yu, *tr. fr. Chinese by* Burton Watson. CoBCP
Sitting Up with My Wife on New Year's Eve. Hsü Chün-ch'ien, *tr. fr.*
Chinese by Burton Watson. CoBCP
Situation. Langston Hughes. OBAL
Situation. Alois Vogel, *tr. fr. German by* Beth Bjorklund. CoAuP
Siwashing It Out Once in Siuslaw Forest. Gary Snyder. *Fr.* Four Poems
for Robin. NoAM
Six Badgers, The. Robert Graves. GoJo; GrPl; WSC
Six beds in a square room: you give your name. Wait. Timothy Steele.
PoA
Six children dear, God, died out in this waste. Beyond Feith Buidhe.
Hamish Brown. PoSH
Six days ago the water fell. A Peacock's Feather. Seamus Heaney.
DiPo
Six Dukes Went a-Fishing. *Unknown.* FaBoBa; OBET
Six Eagles. Thomas Peacock. VoR
Six Epigrams, *sel.* Gerard Manley Hopkins.
"No, they are come; their horn is lifted up." SeCePo
Six feet from my window the blackbirds. Amor Vacui. John Fowles.
AnAn
Six Feet of Earth. *Unknown.* BLPA
Six Feet Under. Janet Campbell Hale. VoR
Six-foot nest of the sea-hawk, The. Sea-Hawk. Richard Eberhart. RB
Six-forty-two Farm Commune Struggle Poem. Jay Leifer. MAT
Six Haiku for Graham V. Phillips Who First Said the First One. Robert
Phillips. GrPl
Six hundred dark feet from the cliffs. "But Still in Israel's Paths They
Shine." Carter Revard. VoR
Six hundred stalwart warriors of England's pride the best. Balaclava.
Unknown. OBET
Six Hundred Thousand Letters, The. Harvey Shapiro. VWA
Six inches tall, the Russian doll. The Russian Doll. Jane Shore. PPR
Six Jolly Wee Miners. *Unknown.* CoMu
Six Lines. Aaron Zeitlin, *tr. fr. Yiddish by* Robert Friend. PeBMYV
Six little mice sat down to spin. Mother Goose. BoTP; OxNR
Six month child, The. Slippery. Carl Sandburg. FaPON
Six Movements on a Theme. David Ignatow. NNaP
Six Nations Museum Onchiota, New York—January. Wendy Rose.
HATNAP
Six o'Clock. Owen Dodson. PoNe
Six o'Clock. Trumbull Stickney. AnAmPo; OxBA
Six o'clock and/ the sun rises. Miller Williams. MAT
Six o'clock. The cathedral blesses. Provincia. Francisco Carrillo, *tr. by*
Maureen Ahern *and* David Tipton. Per
Six o'clock, the morning still and. The Names. Lauris Edmond. ATNZ
Six of Ox Is. Lydia Tomkiw. BAP
Six of them, The. These Six. Sean Lucy. CIP
Six on the Desert Ways. Otalantaiyar, *tr. fr. Tamil by* A. K. Ramanujan.
PLW
Six or seven rows of waves struggle landward. On the Oregon Coast.
Galway Kinnell. NoAM
Six Periods of Creation. *Maori Oral Tradition, tr. by* Richard Taylor.
WTO
Six Poems on Remembering, *sels.* Shen Yüeh, *tr. fr. Chinese by* Burton
Watson. CoBCP
"I think of when she comes."
"I think of when she sits."
"I think of when she sleeps."
Six Poets in Search of a Lawyer. Donald Hall. NYBP
Six-Quart Basket, The. Raymond Souster. MoCV
Six Reasons for Drinking. Vernon Scannell. OxBC
Six Religious Lyrics, *sel.* Karl Shapiro.
"I sing the simplest flower." *Fr.* I. CMoP

Six Said by the Concubines to Him. Ammuvanar, *tr. fr. Tamil by* A. K. Ramanujan. PLW
Six street-ends come together here. Blue Island Intersection. Carl Sandburg. MoAmPo
Six Strings, The. Federico García Lorca, *tr. fr. Spanish by* Donald Hall. RB
Six Sunday. Hart Leroi Bibbs. NBP
Six Ten Sixty-nine. Conyus. PoBA
Six Things for Christmas. John May. Mes
Six times faster than the fool can weep. The Peasant. Leonard Wolf. NYBP
Six to Six. *Unknown, tr. fr. Xhosa by* A. C. Jordan. PBA
Six Town Eclogues, *sel.* Lady Mary Wortley Montagu. Saturday: The Small-Pox. NOEC; WPE
Six Variations. Denise Levertov. AmPP; LCAP
Six Variations ("We have been shown.") *sel.* Denise Levertov. AmPP; LCAP
"Shlup, shlup, the dog." *Fr.* III. HeIP; InPK
Six Ways of Eating Watermelons. Lo Ch'ing, *tr. fr. Chinese by* Dominic Cheung. IFON
Six Weeks Old. Christopher Morley. RHPC
Six Winter Privacy Poems. Robert Bly. LCAP
Six wives I've had and they're all dead. The Fox and the Hare. *Unknown.* OBET
Six Years. Alice Bloch. PeHV
Six years ago in Ohio we argued free will. On the Lawn at Ira's. Gregory Orr. GeTw
Six years the moon shone at mid-autumn. Mid-Autumn Moon. Su Tung-p'o, *tr. by* Burton Watson. CoBCP
Six Young Men. Ted Hughes. OBWP
"Sixpence a week," says the girl to her lover. By Her Aunt's Grave. Thomas Hardy. *Fr.* Satires of Circumstance, III. BrPo; MoAB; MoBrPo
Sixt Nimphall, The. Michael Drayton. *See* Muses' Elysium [*or* Elizium]: Clear [*or* Cleere] had the day been [*or* bin] from the dawn [*or* dawne].
Sixteen Dead Men. Dora Sigerson Shorter. ACP
Sixteen Dead Men. W. B. Yeats. FaBoPV; OBWP
16/53. Marge Piercy. NeAC
Sixteen Hokku, *sels.* Kyotai, *tr. fr. Japanese by* Burton Watson. FCEI
"Cold night/ pasania nuts rolling down."
"Column of mosquitoes, A."
"Day ending/ and again it starts."
"Daybreak/ whales trumpet."
"Falling leaves/ fall and pile up."
"Leaves falling/ on top of the smoke."
"Melting snow/ among deep mountains clouded over."
"Nights when the muddy river."
"Observing as I go along."
"On her way, the little nun."
"Quivering/ in the heat waves."
"Start of winter."
"Sun has set, The."
"Waves are hot, The."
"Winter shut in—/ a single fly."
Sixteen Hokku, *sels.* Miura Chora, *tr. fr. Japanese by* Hiroaki Sato. FCEI
"An insect spills its notes."
"As the evening shower clears."
"Brightness: not even a wind blowing."
"Brushing aside the clouds."
"Delightful at night, quiet during the day."
"Even the day with cherries."
"Glancing near the hands cutting."
"I broil shrimp and play with my illness."
"I first see the spring light."
"I think of flowers and birds."
"I turn to look: everything behind me."
"It's dark around the earth mortar."
"Moon in the cold, The."
"Mountain temple: no one comes, A."
"Out of the grass in a storm."
"Seeing the stars through a willow."
"White chrysanthemum, A."
16. ix. 65. James Merrill. NAs
Sixteen Songs of the Capital: Chicken Feather Shop. Chiang Shih-ch'üan, *tr. fr. Chinese by* Irving Lo. WFTU
Sixth Book of the Aeneis, The. Virgil, *tr. fr. Latin, tr. by* Dryden. *Fr.* The Aeneid [*or* Eneados]. SeCV-2
Sixth Hell, The. Jerome Rothenberg. *Fr.* The Seven Hells of Jigoku Zoshi. NNaP
Sixth-Month Song in the Foothills. Gary Snyder. HCAP

Sixth Song: "O you that hear this voice." Sir Philip Sidney. *Fr.* Astrophel and Stella. OBSC
Sixth was August, being rich arrayed, The. August. Spenser. *Fr.* The Faerie Queene, VII, 7. GN
Sixties brought a clash of arms, The. Emancipation Day. L. A. J. Moorer. CBWP-3
Sixties, I think, were not a total loss, The. January 15 as a National Holiday. Carter Revard. VoR
Sixty-eighth Birthday. James Russell Lowell. OxBSP; PCP; PoEL-5
Sixty-four Caprices for a Long-Distance Swimmer: Notes on Swimming 100 Miles, *sel.* Janice M. Lynch. TSL, *much abr.*
"Friend asks why I swim, A."
Sixty-four Tanka, *sels.* Saigyo, *tr. fr. Japanese by* Burton Watson. FCEI
"Across the face of the field."
After Entering Religious Life.
"As banked clouds."
"As I look at the moon."
"Butterflies darting."
"Cherry petals/ like the tears."
"Clear waters unchanged."
"Crickets—/ as the cold of the night."
"Cuckoo—/ I've yet to hear him."
"Deep snow that, The."
"Did I ever think."
"Did I hear you ask."
"Does the moon say 'Grieve.' "
"Drawing his/ sparrow-hunting bow."
"Even a person free of passion."
"Float-rigged strands, The."
"Garden that recalls the past, A."
"Gazing at them."
"How lonely, the light of the moon."
"I know/ how you must feel!"
"Ice wedged fast."
"If only there were."
"In a channel."
"In a hailstorm."
"In a mountain village."
"In Akishino/ is it raining."
"In some far-off."
In the little weeds.
"In the shade of a remote mountain."
"In willow shade."
"Leaves have fallen, The."
"Let me die in spring."
"Let me take a good look."
"Let us seek the past."
"Little boat with no treadboard."
"Moon-viewings in the capital."
"Mount Arachi so steep."
"Neglectful, we've yet."
"Now I understand."
Observing Children.
On the Impermanence of Life.
"On the road with not a soul."
"One lone pine tree."
"Pearls plucked,/ the oyster shells."
Perilous Love Affair, A.
"Shut in by spring showers."
"Side by side."
"Since I no longer think."
"Startled by the sound."
"To the dead."
"Today again/ I'll go to the hill."
"Trailing on the wind."
"Twilight cuckoo, The."
"Was it a dream."
"When you consider."
"Who lies here."
"Who lives here."
"Why does no one say, 'Pitiful!' "
"Why regret to leave."
"Why should my heart."
"Wild geese departing, The."
"With blooms of pampas grass."
Woman Forsaken in Love, A.
Sixty-nine years. Tomei, *tr. by* Lucien Stryk *and* Takashi Ikemoto. ZPCJ
"Sixty-seven years ago on Sunday," he said. The Survivor. Stanley Cook. NPo

Sixty-Six Poems for a Blackfoot Bundle. *Unknown, tr. fr. Blackfoot Indian by* Jerome Rothenberg. STP

Size of a cavern for men to crouch in, The. Dawn Hippo. Sydney Clouts. PeSA

Size of the human brain, The. Motorcycle Evolution. Peter Payack. BWV

Skaian Gate, The, *sel.* Geoffrey Scott.
  "Hector, the captain bronzed, from simple fight." OBMV

Skara Brae. Michael Longley. FaBCIP

Skate. Laurel Blossom. ASP

Skater, The. Sir Charles G. D. Roberts. NOBC

Skater in Blue. Jay Parini. ASP

Skaters, The. John Gould Fletcher. ASP; MoAmPo; SD

Skaters. Vern Rutsala. ASP

Skaters, The. John Williams. SD

Skaters upon thin ice. Black Water and Bright Air. Constance Carrier. SD

Skating. Herbert Asquith. FaPON

Skating. Philip Dacey. NAmP; TSL

Skating. Kipling. SD

Skating. Wordsworth. *Fr.* The Prelude [or, Growth of a Poet's Mind]: Childhood and School-Time. TOF

Skating after School. Barbara Crooker. TSL

Skating in Pleasant Hill, Ohio. Kathleen Iddings. ASP

'Skeeters am a hummin' on de honeysuckle vine. Kentucky Babe. Richard Henry Buck. AA

Skein, The. Carolyn Kizer. PrIm; VGW

Skeleton, The. G. K. Chesterton. FaBoTw

Skeleton at the Feast, The. James Jeffrey Roche. AA

Skeleton in Armor, The. Longfellow. AA; AmPP; AnAmPo; AWP; BeLS; BLPL; FaBoBe; PAH

Skeleton is hiding in the closet as it should, The. Everything in Its Place. Arthur Guiterman. NBLV; OBAL

Skeleton Key. John Hollander. NoP

Skeleton of the Future, The. "Hugh MacDiarmid." GoTS; MoBrPo; OBMV; OBTV

Skeleton of the Great Moa in the Canterbury Museum, Christchurch, The. Allen Curnow. ATNZ; PeNZ

Skeleton Parade. Jack Prelutsky. NTCP; RAR

Skeletons are out tonight, The. Skeleton Parade. Jack Prelutsky. NTCP; RAR

Skelton Laureate, Defender, against Lusty Garnesche, Well-beseen Christopher, Challenger. John Skelton. TW

Skeltoniad, A. Michael Drayton. PoEL-2

Skeptic, The. Clara Ann Thompson. CBWP-2

Skerryvore. Robert Louis Stevenson. EyDe

Sketch. Robert Farnsworth. GOYP

Sketch, A. Christina Rossetti. GTBS-P

Sketch for a Job Application Blank. Jim Harrison. AmPA; MoP

Sketch for a Memoir. Adam Wazyk, *tr. fr. Polish by* Czeslaw Milosz. PwPP

Sketch for a Modern Love Poem, A. Tadeusz Rozewicz, *tr. fr. Polish by* Czeslaw Milosz. PwPP

Sketch for a Morning in Muncie, Indiana. G. E. Murray. MAYP

Sketch from Private Life, A. Byron. OBNC

Sketch of Flower. Ruth Kim Chun-soo, *tr. fr. Korean by* Koh Chang-soo. ACKP

Sketch of Hands. Koh Chang-soo, *tr. fr. Korean by the author.* ACKP

Sketch of Lord Byron's Life, *sel.* Julia A. Moore. OBAL
  "Lord Byron was an Englishman."" FiBHP

Sketchbook, *sels.* Mihály Ladányi, *tr. fr. Hungarian by* Jascha Kessler. FOC
  Business.
  Entrance.
  Phalanstery.

Sketchbook Ashes of Jehoshaphat, The. Norman Dubie. NAmP

Sketches of Harlem. David Henderson. PoNe

Sketching from life. Masaoka Shiki, *tr. fr. Japanese by* Burton Watson. *Fr.* Thirty-nine Haiku. FCEI

Ski Song of the U.S. Army's Tenth Mountain Division. W. T. Levitt. ASP

Ski Trail. Samuel Allen. FB

Skibomber, The. Martin Steingesser. TSL

Skier. Robert Francis. RFM; SD; TSL

Skies are low, the winds are slow, The. Under the Blue. Francis Fisher Browne. AA

Skies contain still groves of silver clouds, The. Spring 1943. Roy Fuller. LiTB; LiTM; WaP

Skies o'ercast and fierce winds blow, The. December. Josephine D. Henderson Heard. CBWP-4

Skies they were ashen and sober, The. The Willows. Bret Harte. BXAP

Skies they were ashen and sober, The. Ulalume. Poe. AA; AmPP; AnAmPo; AWP; BLPL; LiTA; NOBA; OxBA; TAP (Ulalume—a Ballad.) NAAL-1

Skiing Home at Dusk. Jay Parini. BLA

Skiing on Russian Christmas. Nora Dauenhauer. HATNAP

Skiing the mountain alone. Remembering You. Maxine W. Kumin. ASP

Skilful Listener, The. John Vance Cheney. AA

Skilful Spearman! A. *Unknown, tr. fr. Hawaiian.* WTO

Skill originated in the West, The. Lines in Praise of a Self-Chiming Clock. Hsüan-yeh, *tr. by* Jonathan D. Spence. WFTU

Skill'd to deceive our ears and eyes. The County Member. Winthrop Mackworth Praed. *Fr.* The County Ball. OBNC

Skilled in each art that can adorn the fair. The Modern Fine Lady. Soame Jenyns. NOEC

Skilled to pull wires, he baffles Nature's hope. The Boss. James Russell Lowell. OBAL; SaC

Skilly Oogan. Russell Hoban. ILY

Skimbleshanks: The Railway Cat. T. S. Eliot. FaBoCo; NOBL

Skimmers. Ted Walker. NYBP

Skimming/ an asphalt sea. The Sidewalk Racer; or, On the Skateboard. Lillian Morrison. NTCP; RHPC

Skimming lightly, wheeling still. Shiloh; a Requiem. Herman Melville. AmFN; AnAmPo; FF; LiTA; NOBA; NoP; OBWP; OxBA; SCV; WiR

Skimming the waves, deep in the night. Sandal Mountain. Hsieh Chin, *tr. by* Jonathan Chaves. CoBLCP

Skin. Gerrit Achterberg, *tr. fr. Dutch by* James S. Holmes. DuIn

Skin-and-Bone Lady, The. *Unknown.* AmFP

Skin coarse, bird-shotted nose, the flesh loose. Encounter in a Glass. David Wright. NPo; PoPo

Skin Divers, The. George Starbuck. NYBP

Skin Diving in the Virgins. John Malcolm Brinnin. NYBP; TAP

Skin Flick. Fred Chappell. InPK

Skin like burnt glass or/ prepared leather, The. Eeva-Liisa Manner, *tr. by* Jaakko A. Ahokas. OV

Skin meeting skin, we want to think. Touching Each Other's Surfaces. Carol Jane Bangs. NIP

Skin of Light, The. René Daumal, *tr. fr. French by* Michael Benedikt. POS; RHTwFP

Skin of my mouth, chewed raw, tastes good, The. The Expectant Father. Ai. GeTw

Skin of the sea, The. In Sylvia Plath Country. Erica Jong. IHMS

Skin quickens to noises, The. One Eyed Black Man in Nebraska. Sam Cornish. PoBA

Skin ripples over my body like moon-wooed water, The. Prison Song. Alan Dugan. PoA

Skin-Teeth. Grace Nichols. AIW

Skin that is a closed curtain. Poll. Ed Roberson. PoBA

Skin the Goat's Curse on Carey. *Unknown.* BIrV; TW

Skinfull of bowls, he bowls them. Second Glance at a Jaguar. Ted Hughes. NoAM; NYBP; PrIm

Skinning-shops under the night's lead sky. Hides. Berysh Vaynshteyn, *tr. by* Benjamin *and* Barbara Harshav. AYP

Skinning-the-Cat. Dennis Schmitz. NPGG

Skinny Girl, The. Anne Hébert, *tr. fr. French by* Willis Barnstone. BoWoP

Skinny Mrs. Snipkin. Mrs. Snipkin and Mrs. Wobblechin. Laura E. Richards. OxBChV

Skinny red-haired girl gets up, The. A Romance. Bruce Weigl. NAmP

Skinny waterfalls, footpaths, The. Lastness. Galway Kinnell. NNaP

Skins. Elizabeth Spires. MAYP

Skins, *sels.* Charles Wright. HCAP
  "Under the rock, in the sand and the gravel run." *Fr.* 6.
  "You've talked to the sun and moon." *Fr.* 20.

Skip-Scoop-Anellie. Tom Prideaux. FiBHP

Skip to My Lou. *Unknown.* AmFP

Skipper Ireson's Ride. Whittier. AA; AnAmPo; BeLS; NOBA; OBAL; OBCA; OxBA; PAH; PoLF

Skippets, the Bad One. Christine E. Bradley. BoTP

Skirt Dance. Ishmael Reed. FF; UL

Skirting the river road, (my forenoon walk, my rest,). The Dalliance of the Eagles. Walt Whitman. AA; AmPP; FM; HAP; HeIP; NAAL-1; NoP; PPP; PrIm; TAP

Skreak and skritter of evening gone, The. Autumn Refrain. Wallace Stevens. LiTA

Skull, The. Ian Young. NeAC

Skull Changed to Glass, A. Stephen Spender, *tr. by* Jeffrey Fiskin *and* Erik Vestville. AnAn

Skull exposed in a field in my mind. Basho, *tr. fr. Japanese* by Burton Watson. *Fr.* Seventy-six Hokku. FCEI

Skull stark. The Strath of Kildonan. Betty Morris. PoSH

Skunk, The. Philip Dow. BXAP

Skunk, The. Seamus Heaney. FaBCIP; NAEL-2; OxBC; PoE

Skunk, The. Robert Tristram Coffin. FaPON

Skunk Cabbage. Mary Oliver. KS

Skunk cabbage, bloodroot. Philip Booth. BoNaP; GrPl

Skunk Hour. Robert Lowell. AmPP; CAPP; CMoP; CoAP; FaBoMo; HAP; HCAP; HeIP; InPK; InPS; LCAP; MoAmPo; MoP; NAAL-2; NIP; NoAM; NOBA; NoP; OPOP; OxBC; PoE; PPP; PrIm; SCV; TAP; WeW

Sky, The. Elizabeth Madox Roberts. MoAmPo

Sky, The. Richard Henry Stoddard. AA

Sky/ gains/ in significance, The. The Days Count Again. Alfred Gesswein, *tr.* by Beth Bjorklund. CoAuP

Sky, The. *Unknown, tr. fr. Ewe* by Ulli Beier. TTY

Sky a black sphere. The Lighthouse in the Night. Alfonsina Storni. BoWoP, *tr.* by Aliki *and* Willis Barnstone

Sky at night is like a big city, The. The Sky. *Unknown, tr.* by Ulli Beier. TTY

Sky blazing/ as I go down the gravel path. Masaoka Shiki, *tr. fr. Japanese* by Burton Watson. *Fr.* Thirty-nine Haiku. FCEI

Sky blooms cold and starry over Negro huts, The. Negro Village. Berysh Vaynshteyn, *tr. fr. Yiddish* by Benjamin *and* Barbara Harshav. *Fr.* Negroes. AYP

Sky can't get in, The. Room. Shirley Kaufman. NMM

Sky ceases. There is only. Michael Dransfield. *Fr.* Geography, VI. CBAP

Sky Clears, The. *Unknown, tr.* by Frances Densmore. OBVE

Sky-Conscious. Alice Coats. CN

Sky Diving. Ishmael Reed. UL

Sky extends upwards for ninety thousand miles, The. A Buddhist Monk Cut and Burned His Own Flesh to Make the Rains Stop. Hsü Wei, *tr.* by Jonathan Chaves. CoBLCP

Sky for the Sea, A. Mahmoud Darwish, *tr. fr. Arabic* by Abdullah al-Udhari. MPAW

Sky full of stars, The. Blue Night Road. Tanaka Fuyuji, *tr.* by Geoffrey Bownas *and* Anthony Thwaite. PeBJV

Sky grew darker with each minute, The. Before the Storm. Richard Dehmel, *tr.* by Ludwig Lewisohn. AWP

Sky hangs heavy tonight, The. Negro Woman. Lewis Alexander. CDC; PoBA

Sky has been dark, The. The Youngest Daughter. Cathy Song. MAYP; NoAM

Sky Has Wings, The. Tuomas Anhava, *tr. fr. Finnish* by Aili Jarvenpa. SOP

Sky in red mist. *Unknown.* FaBoUs

Sky is a dead fish, The. The Plaque in the Reading Room for My Classmates Killed in Korea. F. D. Reeve. GOA

Sky is a drinking-cup, The. The Sky. Richard Henry Stoddard. AA

Sky Is Blue, The. David Ignatow. FF; NNaP

Sky is cold as pearl, The. Ancient. "Æ." SeCePo

Sky is dark, and the hills are white, The. Norse Lullaby. Eugene Field. BoTP

Sky is dotted like th' unleavened bread, The. Haggadah. Abraham M. Klein. TrJP

Sky is full of night, The. 98 Fahrenheit. Judah Leib Teller, *tr.* by Benjamin *and* Barbara Harshav. AYP

Sky is gray with rain that will not fall, The. At the Zoo. Israel Zangwill. TrJP

Sky is heavy, it is raining stars, The. The Cannibal Hymn. *Unknown, tr.* by Samuel A. B. Mercer. TTY

Sky is high, The. Takahama Kyoshi, *tr.* by Geoffrey Bownas *and* Anthony Thwaite. PeBJV

Sky is low, the clouds are mean, The. Emily Dickinson. AA; BoNaP; FaBV; MoAmPo; OxBA; PoEL-5

Sky is only a white lens, The. Indian Summer. Nicolae Breban, *tr.* by Malinda Cox. WCI

Sky is overcast, The. A Night-Piece. Wordsworth. EnRP

Sky is such a softness, is such dark. No Moon, No Star. Babette Deutsch. NYBP

Sky is up above the roof, The. Paul Verlaine, *tr. fr. French* by Ernest Dowson. *Fr.* Sagesse. AWP; FaPON

Sky is washed with blue, the pond is like a mirror, The. Immortal at the River. Ku Hsiung, *tr.* by Lois Fusek. ATF

Sky-lark hath perceived his prison-door, The. On a Picture by J. M. Wright, Esq. Robert Southey. FM

Sky-Lark's Song, The. John Bennett. *Fr.* Master Sky-Lark. AA

Sky, lazily disdaining to pursue, The. Georgia Dusk. Jean Toomer. AmNP; BPo; CDC; NAAL-2; NoAM; NoP; PoBA

Sky links cloud waves, links dawn fog. Li Ch'ing-chao, *tr.* by Willis Barnstone *and* Sun Chu-chin. BoWoP

Sky low down in distant West, The. To Mary. Mary E. Tucker. CBWP-1

Sky of a hanged man, is it going to rain? Song in Time of Drought. Benjamin Péret, *tr.* by James Laughlin. POS; RHTwFP

Sky of gray is eaten in six places, The. Broken Sky. Carl Sandburg. PCP

Sky, out of reach, unexpected, The. Fossils, Metal, and the Blue Limit. Richard Tillinghast. NAmP

Sky over the waves, The. Pines along the Coast. Tameko, *tr.* by Steven D. Carter. WFTW

Sky Pair, A, *sels.* Robert Frost.
    Canis Major. MoAB; MoAmPo
    Peaceful Shepherd, The. MoAB; MoAmPo

Sky Picture. Henrietta Cordelia Ray. CBWP-3

Sky Pictures. Mary Effie Lee Newsome. CDC

Sky so pale, and the trees, such frail things, The. A la Promenade. Paul Verlaine, *tr.* by Arthur Symons. AWP; OBVE

Sky, stabbed by a rusty knife, bleeds midnight, The. Peru, 1955. Ai. *Fr.* He Kept On Burning, III. AnAn

Sky the color of a wren's [*or* wrens] breath, A. At Chadwicks Bar and Grill. Lance Henson. HATNAP; STE

Sky, The—like a lunatic's dream. Landscape. Abraham Sutskever. VWA, *tr.* by Ruth Whitman

Sky unfolding its blankets to free, The. Morning Workout. Babette Deutsch. SD

Sky unshaken, smokeless ashless, A. Of All My Loves. Abba Kovner, *tr.* by Warren Bargad *and* Stanley F. Chyet. IP

Sky was a bluey blue, The. Jerry Perm Poem. Carole Stewart. WS

Sky was battened down, The. On Galveston Beach. Barbara Howes. MoAmPo

Sky was blue, so blue, that day, The. For the Candle Light. Angelina Weld Grimké. BlSi; CDC; PoNe

Sky was gold in those days, The. In the Beginning. Valerie Sinason. BrRo

Sky was low, the sounding rain was falling dense and dark, The. The Late Passenger. C. S. Lewis. TrCP

Sky was on the hill, The. When You Reach the Hilltop the Sky Is on Top of You. Etta Blum. GoYe

Sky went before me wherever I went, The. Viljo Kajava, *tr.* by Aili Jarvenpa. SOP

Sky where the white clouds stand in prayer. Easter. Mary Carolyn Davies. OHIP

Sky widens to Cornwall, The. A sense of sea. In Memoriam: A. C., R.J.O., K.S. Sir John Betjeman. NYBP

Sky with clouds was overcast, The. Washing Day. *Unknown.* CoMu

Skycoast. Samuel Hazo. GrPl

Skydivers, The. Joseph Colin Murphy. ASP

Skye. John Gawsworth. PoSH

Skye, *sel.* W. W. Gibson.
    Witch, The. PoSH

Skye Summer ("Skye rasps the mind"). Islay Murray Donaldson. PoSH

Skyjacker, The. Stan Rice. NPGG

Skykomish River Running. Richard Hugo. PoA

Skylark, The. James Hogg. GN; PBBP

Skylark, The. Frederick Tennyson. GN

Skylark rises, A. Kaya Shirao, *tr. fr. Japanese* by Hiroaki Sato. *Fr.* Twenty-one Hokku. FCEI

Skylark rises through the dawn, A. Kito, *tr. fr. Japanese* by Hiroaki Sato. *Fr.* Twenty-four Hokku. FCEI

Skylarks. Ted Hughes. HAP

Skylarks are far behind that sang over the down, The. Good-Night. Edward Thomas. NoP

Skylark's Nest, The. R. H. Long. PoAu-1

Skylark's nest among the grass, The. Birds' Nests. *Unknown.* BoTP

Skylights. Tess Gallagher. MAYP

Skylike limpid eyes, The. Brennhaum. Ezra Pound. *Fr.* Hugh Selwyn Mauberley. (Life and Contacts). MoAmPo

Skyline of New York does not excite me, The. Review from Staten Island. Gloria C. Oden. PoBA; PPP

Sky's as blue and black as ink, The. Calligram, 15 May 1915. Guillaume Apollinaire, *tr.* by O. Bernard. OBWP

Sky's land and the sea's lip shut in peace, The. Lines on the Sea. Dilys Bennett Laing. NYBP

Sky's unresting cloudland, that with varying play, The. Robert Bridges. *Fr.* The Testament of Beauty, I. EBEV

Skyscraper. Dennis Lee. RAR

Skyscrapers. Rachel Lyman Field. FaPON

Skyscrapers are dancing by the river, The. The Skyscrapers of the Financial District Dance with Gasman. Marge Piercy. CAPP

Skyward mazes. A Look Askance. James Merrill. AnAn
Slack your rope, hangs—a—man. The Maid Freed from the Gallows. *Unknown.* AS, *with music*
   ("O good Lord Judge, and sweet Lord.") ESPB
Slag. C. D. Wright. MT
Slain. T. W. H. Crosland. OBWP
Slain Lamb of God. Nikolaus Ludwig, Graf von Zinzendorf, *tr. fr. German by* Sheema Z. Buehne. AH
Slant of Sun on Dull Brown Walls, A. Stephen Crane. *Fr.* War Is Kind, XIV. LiTM; NAAL-2, *sect.* 89.
Slant sheen/ wrinkled silver. Letters to Walt Whitman, II. Ronald Johnson. VGW
Slanting gables/ hang on the/ horizon. In the Chagall Village. Rose Ausländer, *tr. by* Beth Bjorklund. CoAuP
Slanting sun across the city wall clings to green trees, The. Chuang Yü, *tr. by* Shirleen S. Wong. WFTU
Slashed in a dream. Kikaku, *tr. fr. Japanese by* Hiroaki Sato. *Fr.* Thirty-three Hokku. FCEI
Slated for demolition. The Cathedral Is. John Ashbery. InPK
Slaughter-House, The. Alfred Hayes. LiTA
Slaughter of the Laird of Mellerstain, The. *Unknown.* ESPB
Slave. Langston Hughes. LiTM
Slave, The. James Oppenheim. TrJP
Slave, The. Jones Very. TAP
Slave and the Iron Lace, The. Margaret Danner. AmNP; BPo
Slave Auction, The. Frances Ellen Watkins Harper. BPo; PoNe; TTY
Slave-boat rides the open sea, The. *Unknown, tr. by* Geoffrey Bownas *and* Anthony Thwaite. PeBJV
Slave Chase, The. *Unknown.* CoMu
Slave Girl's Song. *Unknown, tr. fr. Maori by* Margaret Orbell. PeNZ
Slave, it seems, The. Yakamochi. *Fr.* Manyo Shu. PeBJV
Slave Marriage Ceremony Supplement. *Unknown.* BPo; TAP
Slave Quarters. James Dickey. NYBP
Slave Singing at Midnight, The. Longfellow. GOA
Slave Song. David Dabydeen. PVCV; UAS
Slave Story. Hodding Carter. PoNe
Slavery. Malka Heifetz-Tussman, *tr. fr. Yiddish by* Kathryn Hellerstein. AYP
Slaves/ Humming in the twilight by the shanty door. A. J. Seymour. PBCV
Slaves. James Grainger. *Fr.* The Sugar Cane. NOEC
Slaves. James Russell Lowell. *Fr.* Stanzas on Freedom. GN, 2 *sts.;* OHIP; PoNe
   (Stanza on Freedom, A.) AA
Slave's Dream, The. Longfellow. FaPoR; NAAL-1; PoNe
Slay fowl and beast; pluck clean the vine. Cavalier. Richard Bruce. CDC
Sled Burial, Dream Ceremony. James Dickey. CAPP
Sledburn Fair. *Unknown.* CH
Sledding Song, A. Norman C. Schlichter. FaPON
Sleep. Thomas Bailey Aldrich. AA
Sleep. Alice Brown. AA
Sleep, The. Elizabeth Barrett Browning. WGRP
Sleep. Abraham Cowley. ChTr
Sleep, *sel.* Robert Farren.
   "While now I lay me down to sleep." TIRV
Sleep. Bartholomew Griffin. *See* Fidessa, More Chaste than Kind: Care-Charmer Sleep.
Sleep. Bravig Imbs. EAS
Sleep. William Knott. EAS
Sleep. Dana Naone. CDW
Sleep. James Schuyler. GLP
Sleep ("Lock up, fair lids"). Sir Philip Sidney. *Fr.* Arcadia. OBSC; SiPS
   (Sonnet: "Lock up, fair lids, the treasure of my heart.") EIL
Sleep ("Come sleep! O sleep, the certain knot of peace"). Sir Philip Sidney. *Fr.* Astrophel and Stella, XXXIX. OBEV
Sleep. Charles Simic. CoAP
Sleep. Statius, *tr. fr. Latin by* W. H. Fyfe. AWP
Sleep, The. Mark Strand. CAPP
Sleep/ Now the charge is won. Taps. Lizette Woodworth Reese. OHIP
Sleep. Theophile de Viau, *tr. fr. French by* Sir Edmund Gosse. AWP
Sleep. Lewis Frank Tooker. AA
Sleep. Georg Trakl, *tr. fr. German by* Joachim Neugroschel. AnAn
Sleep after Toil. Spenser. *See* Faerie Queene, The: He there now does enjoy eternal rest.
Sleep: and between the closed eyelids of sleep. Conrad Aiken. *Fr.* Preludes for Memnon; or, Preludes to Attitude. LiTA
Sleep and His Brother Death. William Hamilton Hayne. AA
Sleep and Poetry ("What is more gentle than a wind in summer?") Keats. EnRP

Sels.
   "And can I ever bid these joys farewell?." TOF
   "Could all this be forgotten? Yes, a schism." ChER
   "O for ten years, that I may overwhelm." NAEL-2; OAEL-2
   "Stop and consider! life is but a day." SeCePo
Sleep, Angry Beauty. Thomas Campion. ErPo; OxBSP; TrGrPo
   (Sleep, Angry Beauty, Sleep.) FF
   ("Sleep, angry beauty, sleep and fear me not!") EIL
Sleep at Sea. Christina Rossetti. MOS
Sleep, Baby Boy. *Unknown.* FaPON
Sleep, Baby Mine, Desire. Sir Philip Sidney. OxBSP
Sleep, Baby, Sleep ("Sleep baby sleep!/ Thy father watches the sheep"). *Unknown.* FaPON
   (Cradle Song, A: ("Sleep baby sleep!/ Thy father watches the sheep").) BoTP
Sleep, baby, sleep. *Unknown, tr. by* Geoffrey Bownas *and* Anthony Thwaite. NOBE; PeBJV
Sleep Brought Me Vision. John Peale Bishop. Son
Sleep, calm winter sleep, the rides are woollen. Calm Winter Sleep. Hilary Corke. NYBP
Sleep, Christian warrior, sleep. To Rev. Thaddeus Saltus. Mary Weston Fordham. CBWP-2
Sleep Close to Me. Gabriela Mistral, *tr. fr. Spanish by* D. M. Pettinella. AIW; PBWP
Sleep, comrades, sleep and rest. Decoration Day. Longfellow. OHIP
Sleep in the Heat. Laura Jensen. AmPA; AnAn
Sleep in the Mojave Desert. Sylvia Plath. AiP; NoP
Sleep is a country of water. Country of Water. Bernice Ames. WPE
Sleep is a god too proud to wait in palaces. Sleep. Abraham Cowley. ChTr
Sleep Is a Reconciling. *Unknown. See* Weep [*or* Weepe] You No More [Sad Fountains].
Sleep is 20. 20. Barbara Guest. PoM
Sleep, King Jesus. Mary's Song. Charles Causley. OBCP
Sleep late with your dream. Owen Dodson. *Fr.* Poems for My Brother Kenneth, VII. IDB; PoBA; PoNe
Sleep-Learning. Ruth Fainlight. NMM
Sleep, Leopard, Sleep. David Avidan, *tr. fr. Hebrew by* Bernhard Frank. MHeP
Sleep, Leviathan, shouldering the Asian. Looking at Kapiti. Alistair Campbell. ATNZ
Sleep, little one, sleep. *Unknown, tr. by* Geoffrey Bownas *and* Anthony Thwaite. PeBJV
Sleep, little pigeon, and fold your wings. Japanese Lullaby. Eugene Field. AnAmPo
Sleep, love sleep. Mary Weston Fordham. CBWP-2
Sleep, love, sleep! Watching. "Fanny Forester." AA
Sleep, McKade. Evening Song. Kenneth Fearing. EAS
Sleep, Madame, Sleep. Annemarie Ewing. NePoAm
Sleep, Motley, with the great of ancient days. In Memory of John Lothrop Motley. Bryant. AA
Sleep, Mr. Speaker! it's surely fair. On Seeing the Speaker Asleep in His Chair. Winthrop Mackworth Praed. EnRP
   (Stanzas to the Speaker Asleep.) OBSV
Sleep, my babe, lie still and slumber. All through the Night. *Unknown.* FaPON
Sleep, My Child. Sholom Aleichem, *tr. fr. Yiddish by* Alter Brody. TrJP
Sleep my child. 1916. Mirko Lauer, *tr. by* David Tipton. Per
Sleep, my child, my little daughter. *Unknown, tr. by* Joseph Leftwich. TrJP
Sleep, my child—sleep, it is late! Lullaby for Miriam. Richard Beer-Hofmann. VWA, *tr. by* Jonathan Griffin
Sleep, my little baby, sleep. Samuel Hoffenstein. TrJP
Sleep, my sweet girl! and all the sleep. La Promessa Sposa. Walter Savage Landor. NOBVV
Sleep now. Shlomo Vinner, *tr. by* Laya Firestone. VWA
Sleep now, O sleep now. James Joyce. GBL
Sleep of the Brave, The. Odysseus Elytis, *tr. fr. Greek by* Edmund Keeley *and* Philip Sherrard. VMG
Sleep of this night deepens, The. Under Stars. Tess Gallagher. GeTw; InPK; MAYP
Sleep on, and dream of Heaven awhile. The Sleeping Beauty. Samuel Rogers. GTBS; GTBS-P
Sleep on, beloved, sleep and take thy rest. The Christian's "Good-Night." Sarah Doudney. BLPA
Sleep on, dear, now. The Dead Child. Ernest Dowson. BrPo
Sleep on, I lie at heaven's high oriels. Nirvana. John Hall Wheelock. MoAmPo
Sleep on, my love, in thy cold bed. Henry King. *Fr.* The Exequy. CH; OBD; TrGrPo
Sleep on the Fraser. Patrick Lane. NeAC

Sleep only with strangers. George Jonas. NeAC

Sleep, our lord, and for thy peace. Night Song for a Child. Charles Williams. OBEV

Sleep plays hide-and-seek with darkness. Night Blessing. Phil George. NOVW

Sleep-shatterer, uprooter. Since Akkad Since Elam Since Sumer. Aimé Césaire, *tr. by* Michael Benedikt. POS

Sleep, Silence' Child. William Drummond of Hawthornden. Son (Sonet to Sleepe.) OxBS

Sleep, sleep, beauty bright. Blake. EnRP; FPL; OBEV; PoLF

Sleep, sleep, sleep/ In thy folded waves, O Sea! Sea-Sleep. Thomas Lake Harris. AA

Sleep softly. eagle forgotten. under the stone. The Eagle That Is Forgotten. Vachel Lindsay. AWP; CMoP; LiTA; MoAB; MoAmPo; NOBA; OxBA

Sleep Sweet. Ellen M. Huntington Gates. BLPA; BLRP; FaBoBe

Sleep sweetly in your humble graves. Henry Timrod. GOA; NOBA; OxBA; TAP
(At Magnolia Cemetery.) AnAmPo
(Ode: "Sleep sweetly . . . ") GOA; NOBA; OxBA; TAP
(Sleep Sweetly.) AH, *with music*

Sleep the half-sleep. Mother Cat's Purr. Jane Yolen. RAR

Sleep, Thou little Child of Mary. Song of a Shepherd Boy at Bethlehem. Josephine Preston Peabody. OHIP

Sleep Upon the World. Alcman, *tr. by* Thomas Campbell. ChTr

Sleep-Walking Child. Elisabeth Eybers, *tr. fr. Afrikaans by* Jack Cope, Uys Krige *and* Adèle Naudé. PeSA

Sleep-walking vapor, like a visitant ghost. Still Life. Anthony Hecht. AnAn

Sleep was only a dream. Chicago: Near West-Side Renewal. Dennis Schmitz. AmPA

Sleep Watch. Lance Henson. VoR

Sleep, wayward thoughts, and rest you with my love. So Sleeps My Love. *Unknown.* TrGrPo

Sleep wrapped you in green leaves like a tree. George Seferis, *tr. fr. Greek by* Edmund Keeley *and* Philip Sherrard. *Fr.* Mythistorima, XV. VMG

Sleep, You hungry people, sleep! Lullaby for the Hungry. Muhammad Mahdi al-Jawahiri, *tr. by* Issa Boullata *and* John Heath-Stubbs. MAP

Sleeper, The. Sydney Clouts. PeSA; VWA

Sleeper, The. Edward Field. ASP

Sleeper, The. Poe. AA; AmPP; AnAmPo; LiTA; NAAL-1; NOBA; OxBA; PoEL-4; TAP; TrGrPo

Sleeper, The. *Unknown, tr. fr. Arabic by* E. Powys Mathers. *Fr.* The Thousand and One Nights. AWP

Sleeper, The. Walter de la Mare. MoAB; MoBrPo

Sleeper in the Valley, The. Rimbaud, *tr. fr. French by* Robert Lowell. *Fr.* Eighteen-Seventy. OBWP
("There's a green hollow where a river sings.") AWP, *tr. by* Ludwig Lewisohn.
("Through a green gorge the river like a fountain.") WaaP, *tr. by* Seldman Rodman.

Sleeper Rise. *Gond Oral Tradition, tr. by* V. Elwin *and* S. Hivale. WTO

Sleeper, the palm-trees drink the breathless noon. The Sleeper. *Unknown, tr. fr. Arabic by* E. Powys Mathers. *Fr.* The Thousand and One Nights. AWP

Sleepers, The. Frederick William Harvey. MMA

Sleepers, The. Peter Kocan. CBAP

Sleepers, The. Randolph Stow. *Fr.* Thailand Railway. CBAP

Sleepers, The. Walt Whitman. AmPP; NAAL-1

Sleepin' at the Foot o' the Bed. Luther Patrick. BLPA

Sleeping, The. Lynn Emanuel. AiP; MAYP

Sleeping at Last. Christina Rossetti. HeIP; NAEL-2; TrGrPo

Sleeping-bag, The. Herbert George Ponting. CenHV

Sleeping Beauty, The. Robert Layzer. NePoEA

Sleeping Beauty, The. Samuel Rogers. GTBS; GTBS-P

Sleeping Beauty, The, *sels.* Dame Edith Sitwell.
"In the great gardens, after bright spring rain." OxBTC
(Innocent Spring, The.) NOBE
"When we come to that dark house." OBMV

Sleeping Beauty: Variation of the Prince, The. Randall Jarrell. PoA

Sleeping butterfly. Kikaku, *tr. fr. Japanese by* Hiroaki Sato. *Fr.* Thirty-three Hokku. FCEI

Sleeping Fury, The. Louise Bogan. IHMS; LiTM

Sleeping Giant, The. Donald Hall. GrPl; NePoEA; NYBP; Psk; TwCP

Sleeping Gods, The. Cees Nooteboom, *tr. fr. Dutch by* Peter Nijmeijer. DuIn

Sleeping Heroes. Edward Shanks. OBMV

Sleeping House, The. Tennyson. *Fr.* Maud, *pt.* I, xiv. OBNC

Sleeping in fever, I am unfit. For God While Sleeping. Anne Sexton. NePoEA-2

Sleeping in the Forest. Mary Oliver. CAPP; InPS; NU

Sleeping in the grass, laying myself. Natsume Seibi, *tr. fr. Japanese by* Hiroaki Sato. *Fr.* Twenty-seven Hokku. FCEI

Sleeping Lord, The, *sel.* David Jones.
"Tawny-black sky-scurries." OBWVE

Sleeping on Fists. Alberto Ríos. DiL

Sleeping on Her Couch. Richard Leigh. *See* Thus Lovely Sleep.

Sleeping on the Ceiling. Elizabeth Bishop. TTTS

Sleeping on the Wing. Frank O'Hara. InPS; NAAL-2; SOTW

Sleeping or waking, thou sweet face. Popular Songs of Tuscany. *Unknown, tr. by* John Addington Symonds. AWP

Sleeping or waking, thou sweet face. *Unknown, tr. fr. Italian.* *Fr.* Popular Songs of Tuscany. AWP, *tr. by* John Addington Symonds

Sleeping Out with My Father. Gibbons Ruark. MT

Sleeping Outdoors. Marchette Chute. RAR

Sleeping Priestess of Aphrodite, A. Robert Cameron Rogers. AA

Sleeping They Bear Me. Alfred Mombert, *tr. fr. German by* Jethro Bithell. AWP

Sleeping, turning in turn like planets. Adrienne Rich. *Fr.* Twenty-one Love Poems, XII. GLP; PeHV

Sleeping, wanting to have the past that does not return. Princess Shikishi, *tr. fr. Japanese by* Hiroaki Sato. *Fr.* Seventy-eight Tanka. FCEI

Sleeping with Foxes. Roberta Hill. CDW

Sleeping with One Eye Open. Mark Strand. CAPP; NYBP; SM

Sleeping with Someone Who Came in Secret. Lady Ise. *See* Kokin Shu: Speak of this to no one.

Sleeping with Women. Kenneth Koch. PoM

Sleeping woman dreams she wakes, A. Nightmare. Isabella Gardner. CoAP

Sleeping Wrestler. Takahashi Mutsuo, *tr. fr. Japanese by* Hiroaki Sato. FCEI

Sleeping Youth, A. Keats. *Fr.* Endymion [a Poetic Romance]. SeCePo

Sleepless. Al-Khansa, *tr. fr. Arabic by* Willis Barnstone. BoWoP

Sleepless as Prospero back in his bedroom. Darwin in 1881. Gjertrud Schnackenberg. NoAM; SM

Sleepless at Crown Point. Richard Wilbur. InPK; WeW

Sleepless at the Fifth Watch. Chao Yi, *tr. fr. Chinese by* Shirleen S. Wong. WFTU

Sleepless ghost perpetually striving, The. Eros Out of the Sea. Dilys Bennett Laing. PoA

Sleepless hours who watch me as I lie, The. Hymn of Apollo. Shelley. EnRP; OAEL-2
(Song of Apollo.) NAEL-2

Sleepless I lay last night and watched the slow. The Men Who Wear My Clothes. Vernon Scannell. PoPo

Sleepless Night, A. Egan O'Rahilly, *tr. fr. Modern Irish by* Frank O'Connor. AnIL; KiLC

Sleepless Nights. Benjamin Péret, *tr. fr. French by* Michael Benedikt. POS

Sleepless on a Summer Night. Umberto Saba, *tr. fr. Italian.* VWA, *tr. by* Keith Bosley

Sleepless with longing for my love. Hitomaro. *Fr.* Manyo Shu. Ma

Sleepless, you hear the neighboring temple bell. A Poem Making Fun of Chi-ti for His Eye Illness. Yang Chi, *tr. by* Jonathan Chaves. CoBLCP

Sleeplessness. Yüan Mei, *tr. fr. Chinese by* J. P. Seaton. WFTU

Sleep's very dear to me, but being stone's. "Night" in the Medici Chapel. Michelangelo, *tr. by* William Jay Smith. PFI

Sleepwalker, The. Nelly Sachs, *tr. fr. German by* Michael Hamburger. BoWoP; NYBP

Sleepwalkers. Bella Akhmadulina, *tr. fr. Russian by* Barbara Einzig. BoWoP

Sleepwalkers' Ballad. Federico García Lorca, *tr. fr. Spanish by* John Frederick Nims. WeW

Sleepwalking. Gerrit Achterberg, *tr. fr. Dutch by* James Brockway. DuIn

Sleepy Betsy from her pillow. The Bedpost. Robert Graves. SO

Sleepy Giant, The. Charles Edward Carryl. OnUR

Sleepy vines on the chalk-white houses. Sancho. William Edwin Collin. CaP

Sleet. Norman MacCaig. OBCP

Sleet rattles on the leaves. Sanetomo, *tr. fr. Japanese by* Burton Watson. *Fr.* Twenty-four Tanka. FCEI

Sleet Storm on the Merritt Parkway. Robert Bly. NOBA

Sleeve of my dress, The. Lady Sanuki, *tr. by* Geoffrey Bownas *and* Anthony Thwaite. PeBJV

Sleighing Song. John Shaw. AA

Sleighride. Patrick Anderson. CaP; OBCV

Slender and fine, a lyric and tenuous. The Virtuous Sin. Luis Palés Matos, *tr. by* Perry Higman. LPSS

Slender boys run. Winter Evening. Judah Leib Teller, *tr. by* Benjamin *and* Barbara Harshav. AYP

Slender Fingers ("Slender, delicate, soft jade"). Chao Luan-luan, *tr. fr. Chinese by* Kenneth Rexroth *and* Ling Chung. BoWoP

Slender Lad, The. *Unknown, tr. fr. Welsh by* Kenneth Hurlstone Jackson. OBWVE

Slender Maid. Joseph Eliyia, *tr. fr. Modern Greek by* Rae Dalven. VWA

Slender, middle-aged woman. I Am Coming to You. Jacob Glatstein, *tr. by* Benjamin *and* Barbara Harshav. AYP

Slender pine skirts walls now silent, The. The Silent Walls. Ian Strachan. PoSH

Slender Ships. Anna Margolin, *tr. fr. Yiddish by* Marcia Falk. PeBMYV

Slender young blackbird built in a thorn-tree, A. The Blackbird. D. M. Mulock. BoTP

Slepynge Long in Greet Quiete Is Eek a Greet Norice to Leccherie. John Hollander. ErPo

Sliab Cua, dark and broken, is full of wolf packs. *Unknown. Fr.* Toward Winter. NOIV

Slice of Life, A. Lois Wickstrom. BWV

Slice of Wedding Cake, A. Robert Graves. BoLoP; NAEL-2; NOBE; OxBTC

Slicing my head off shaving I think of Charles I. Notes for a Revised Sonnet. Edward Pygge. BXAP

Slide, Kelly, Slide. John W. Kelly. FaFP

Slides. Jennifer Maiden. CBAP

Sliding down the banisters. On the Banisters. Margaret E. Gibbs. BoTP

Sliding down two feet of my gossamer sleeve. Yosano Akiko, *tr. fr. Japanese by* Hiroaki Sato. *Fr.* Thirty-nine Tanka. FCEI

Sliding Trombone. Georges Ribemont-Dessaignes, *tr. fr. French by* David Gascoyne. EAS

Slieve Gua. *Unknown, tr. fr. Old Irish.* ChTr

Slight as thou art, thou art enough to hide. To a Daisy. Alice Meynell. MoBrPo; Son; WGRP

Slight-boned animal, young, A. Small Colored Boy in the Subway. Babette Deutsch. PoNe

Slight Confusion, A. James Reiss. AmPA

Slight not these flowers! Hirotsugu. *Fr.* Manyo Shu. Ma

Slight unpremeditated words are borne. Love's Witness. Aphra Behn. BoWoP

Slightly before the middle of Congressman Pudd. E. E. Cummings. FaBoEE; OBAL

Slightly Old. Bob Rosenthal. UL

Sligo and Mayo. Louis MacNeice. FaBoPP

Slim and fine is the axle-pin of a coach. *Unknown, tr. by* Arthur Waley. BoS

Slim and singing copper girl, A. Early Copper. Carl Sandburg. HeIP

Slim Cunning Hands. Walter de la Mare. FaBoEE; NIP; SeCePo

Slim dragonfly/ too rapid for the eye. Arthur Mitchell. Marianne Moore. PoNe; RR

Slim Greer. Sterling Allen Brown. BANP

Slim in Hell ("Slim Greer went to heaven"). Sterling A. Brown. BPo; FB

Slim Man Canyon. Leslie Silko. VoR

Slim sentinels. Trees at Night. Helene Johnson. BlSi

Slimy obscene creatures, insane. The Nigga Section. Welton Smith. BPo

Sling me under the sea. Bones. Carl Sandburg. MOS

Slioch and Sgurr Mor. Loch Luichart. Andrew Young. PoSH

Slip, The. Wendell Berry. NOCV

Slip a little something. *Unknown, tr. by* Burton Watson. FCEI

Slip of loveliness, slim, seemly. In Praise of a Girl. Huw Morus, *tr. by* Gwyn Williams. OBWVE

Slipped it under a mothering. Beautiful Poultry. Ian Wedde. ATNZ

Slippery. Carl Sandburg. FaPON

Slippery Sam. Arnold Spilka. RAR

Slipping in blood, by his own hand, through pride. To an Artist, to Take Heart. Louise Bogan. GrPl; NYBP

Slipping in Orbit. Kathryn Rantala. BWV

Sliprails and the Spur, The. Henry Lawson. PoAu-1

Slips. Medbh McGuckian. FaBCIP

Slither Tither. Irene Warsaw. SoTCo

Slithergadee, The. Shel Silverstein. AmMo; NBLV; OnUR; RHPC (Not Me.) NTCP

("Slithergardee has crawled out of the sea, The.") WSC

Sloe Gin. Seamus Heaney. FaBCIP

Slog brute streets with rebel tramping! Our March. Vladimir Mayakovsky, *tr. by* Babette Deutsch *and* Avrahm Yarmolinsky. AWP

Slogan, The. Paul Blackburn. PoM

Sloops in the Bay. James Tate. AnAn; MAYP

Slope. Nishiwaki Junzaburo, *tr. fr. Japanese by* Hiroaki Sato. FCEI

Slopes/ of Mount Kugami. Taking Leave of Mount Kugami. Ryokan, *tr. by* Burton Watson. FCEI

Slopping like sphagnum, battered, baptised in cloud. Discomfort in High Places. Sydney Tremayne. PoSH

Sloth, The. Theodore Roethke. AnAmPo; FiBHP; NePoAm; OBAL; OBCA; RHPC

Sloth, The. George Romanes. FM

Slough. Sir John Betjeman. MoBrPo; NoAM

Slow bells at dawn. Bells. Duncan Campbell Scott. CaP

Slow bleak awakening from the morning dream. Living. Harold Monro. LiTB; SeCePo

Slow burn, A. Pit Viper. George Starbuck. NYBP

Slow, cold breathing, The. The Marsh, New Year's Day. Peter Everwine. NNaP

Slow Dance. David St. John. AmPA; AnAn; LCAP

Slow Dancer That No One Hears but You. Duane Niatum. CDW

Slow fall, a long unwinding, A. Desire and Revenge. Lawrence Raab. BLA

Slow freight wriggles along, The. The Freight Train. Rowena Bastin Bennett. PDV

Slow, groping giant, whose unsteady limbs. Doubt. Robert Cameron Rogers. AA

Slow, horses, slow. Night of Spring. Thomas Westwood. BoTP; SoSe

Slow is the heart. Nudes. Anthony Howell. NPo

Slow Movement. Louis MacNeice. FaBCIP

Slow Movement. William Carlos Williams. PoA

Slow moves the acid breath of noon. Field of Autumn. Laurie Lee. LiTM

Slow overture of rain, The. Mind. Jorie Graham. HCAP

Slow Oxen. Ilya Rubin, *tr. fr. Russian by* Linda Zisquit. VWA

Slow Pacific Swell, The. Yvor Winters. HeIP; MOS; NOBA; QFR

Slow pass the hours—ah, passing slow! Ballade Tragique à Double Refrain. Max Beerbohm. OBSV

Slow Rain. Gabriela Mistral, *tr. by* Gunda Kaiser *and* James Tipton. PBWP

Slow Riff for Billy. James Cunningham. JB

Slow sinks, more lovely ere his race be run. Sunset over the Aegean. Byron. *Fr.* The Corsair, III. OBNC

Slow, Slow, Fresh Fount. Ben Jonson. *Fr.* Cynthia's Revels, I, ii. ChTr; EiL; ELP; InPS; NoP; OAEL-1; OBS; PrIm (Echo's Lament for Narcissus.) (Echo's [*or* Eccho's] Song.) JCP; SeCV-1; TrGrPo (Song: "Slow, slow fresh fount, keep time with my salt tears.") OxBSP; PoEL-2; SeCP

Slow, slow, Melissima. Melissima's Waltz. Christopher Logue. NPo

Slow Spring. Katharine Tynan. BoTP

Slow Summer Twilight. John Hall Wheelock. LiTM

Slow the Kansas sun was setting o'er the wheat fields far away. Towser Shall Be Tied Tonight. *Unknown.* BLPA

Slow the moon rises, wraith of a moon long drowned. Fog-Horn. George Herbert Clarke. CaP

Slow to Come, Quick a-Gone. William Barnes. NOBVV

Slow to resolve, but in performance quick. King James II. Dryden. *Fr.* The Hind and the Panther, III. ACP

Slow to stir up the faded reds, tears soak my clothing. Thoughts upon Hearing a Singer. K'uang Chou-yi, *tr. by* Irving Lo. WFTU

Slow wand'ring came the sightless sire and she. Antigone and Oedipus. Henrietta Cordelia Ray. BlSi; CBWP-3

Slowest animals [*or* beasts] are, The. The Armchairs. Dan Pagis. IP, *tr. by* Warren Bargad *and* Stanley F. Chyet; MHeP, *tr. by* Bernhard Frank

Slowly/ the curtain flutters. Afternoon. Gerhard Fritsch, *tr. by* Beth Bjorklund. CoAuP

Slowly a hundred miles through the powerful rain. You Drive in a Circle. Ted Hughes. NYBP

Slowly, and flake by flake. At the drifted fond. Winter Night: Mount Royal. Abraham Moses Klein. NoAM

Slowly, as one who bears a mortal hurt. La Mort d'Arthur. William Edmonstoune Aytoun. FaBoPa

Slowly, by day, in the cold sun of autumn. The Stone Orchard. Joyce Carol Oates. GeTw

Slowly, by God's hand unfurled. Evening Hymn. William Henry Furness. AA; FaBoBe (Light of Stars, The.) TrPWD (Slowly, by God's Hand Unfurled.) AH, *with music*

Slowly England's sun was setting o'er the hilltops far away. Curfew Must Not Ring Tonight. Rose Hartwick Thorpe. BeLS; BLPA; BLPL; FaBoBe; FaPON

Slowly flutters the snow from ash-coloured heavens in silence. Snowfall. Giosuè Carducci. AWP, *tr. by* Romilda Rendel

Slowly he rode home at the end of day. The Captain. Jon Manchip White. NePoEA

Slowly he sways that head that cannot hear. Rattler, Alert. Brewster Ghiselin. HAP; WeW

Slowly he turns himself round and round. The Dancing Bear. Rachel Lyman Field. NTCP

Slowly I Begin to Play the Game. Lucebert, *tr. fr. Dutch by* Peter Nijmeijer. DuIn

Slowly I smoke and hug my knee. Ballade by the Fire. E. A. Robinson. AnAmPo

Slowly I walk the gully path alone. Painting. Chang Yü, *tr. fr. Chinese by* Jonathan Chaves. *Fr.* Twelve Miscellaneous Poems on the Fang Garden. CoBLCP

Slowly, O so slowly, longing rose up. Christ Walking on the Water. W. R. Rodgers. AnIL; MoAB

Slowly, silently, now the moon. Silver. Walter de la Mare. BoNaP; BoTP; FaPON; MoAB; MoBrPo; PoRA; PYC; RHPC; TTTS

Slowly sip the sweet thick brew. Written on Yün-lang's Nuptial Day. Ch'en Wei-sung, *tr. by* Madeline Chu. WFTU

Slowly, slowly, climb. Issa, *tr. by* Geoffrey Bownas *and* Anthony Thwaite. PeBJV

"Slowly, Slowly" Poem, The. Yüan Hung-tao, *tr. fr. Chinese by* Jonathan Chaves. CoBLCP

Slowly, slowly, swinging low. Swinging. Irene Thompson. BoTP

Slowly, Slowly Wisdom Gathers. Mark Van Doren. PoA

Slowly the mist o'er the meadow was creeping. Lexington. Oliver Wendell Holmes. PAH

Slowly the Moon her banderoles of light. A Battle. Isabella Valancy Crawford. NOBC

Slowly the moon is rising out of the ruddy haze. Aware. D. H. Lawrence. BoNaP; MoBrPo; NoAM

Slowly the muddy pool becomes a river. Let the Dead Depart in Peace. *Yoruba Oral Tradition, tr. by* Ulli Beier. WTO

Slowly the night blooms, unfurling. Flowers of Darkness. Frank Marshall Davis. AmNP; IDB; NoP; PoBA; PoNe

Slowly the ocean-liner. Ocean Liner. Koh Chang-soo, *tr. by the author.* ACKP

Slowly the poison the whole blood stream fills. Missing Dates. William Empson. CMoP; HAP; LiTB; LiTM; MoAB; MoBrPo; MoP; NoAM; NOBE; NoP; OAEL-2; PoE; UnPo

Slowly the ponderous doors of lead imponderous. Sleep. Bravig Imbs. EAS

Slowly the taste of bread rises into my life. Bread. Susan Mitchell. NAmP

Slowly the thing comes. Panic ("Slowly the thing comes"). Archibald MacLeish. *Fr.* Panic. MoAmPo

Slowly the vision grows. Lakeside Incident. Robin Skelton. NOBC

Slowly the women file to where he stands. Faith Healing. Philip Larkin. NoAM

Slowly the world contracts about my ears. The Flagpole Sitter. Donald Finkel. CoAP

Slowly thy flowing tide. The Ebb Tide. Robert Southey. OBNC

Slowly upwards past the girdles. The Escalator. Alex Glasgow. OBET

Slowly we learn; the oft repeated line. On National Vanity. J.E. Clare McFarlane. PBCV

Slowly with bleeding nose and aching wrists. The Hero. Robert Graves. PCP

Slowly, with intention to tempt, she sidles out. Egyptian Dancer. Terence Tiller. OBTV

Slowly, with the important carelessness. The Poets of the Nineties. Derek Mahon. FaBCIP

Slug in Woods. Earle Birney. CaP; NOBC; OBCV

Sluggard, The. Lucilius, *tr. fr. Greek by* Humbert Wolfe. SD

Sluggard, The. W. H. Davies. OBMV

Sluggard, The. Isaac Watts. CH; HAP; Mes; MoShBr; NOEC; OxBChV; OxBoLi; Par; PoEL-3

Sluggish morne as yet undrest, The. Upon Phillis Walking in a Morning before Sun-Rising. John Cleveland. MeLP

Sluice gates of sleep are open wide, The. Viaticum. Ethna MacCarthy. NeIP

Slum Dwelling, A. George Crabbe. *Fr.* The Borough, Letter XVIII. OBNC

Slum had been his home since he was born, The. Evacuee. Edith Pickthall. CN

Slumber dark and deep. Paul Verlaine, *tr. fr. French by* Arthur Symons. *Fr.* Sagesse. AWP

Slumber Did My Spirit Seal, A. Wordsworth. *Fr.* Lucy. AWP; BLPL; ELP; EnLoPo; EnRP; FaBoCh; GTBS; GTBS-P; HAP; HeIP; InPK; InPS; InvP; NoP; PoEL-4; PoRA; PPP; PrIM; SCV; TEP; UnPo; WeW

Slumber in Spring. Elizabeth Gould. BoTP

Slumber Song. Louis V. Ledoux. FaPON

Slumbering Passion. Josephine D. Henderson Heard. CBWP-4

Slump. Vassar Miller. BoWoP

Slung between the homely poplars at the end. Ursa Major. James Kirkup. ImOP

Slurped/ and waters moved. Lee-ers of Hew. James Cunningham. JB

Sly Dick. Thomas Chatterton. FL

Sly merchants plotted newer, greater gains. Renaissance. Robert Avrett. GoYe

Sly Mongoose. *Unknown (additional verses by* Knolly La Fortune). PBCV

Slyly, the sadness trickles down. Christine Lavant, *tr. by* Beth Bjorklund. CoAuP

Smacksman, The. Sam Larner. OxBSS

Small, The. Theodore Roethke. GrPl; SO

Small Aircraft. Bella Akhmadulina, *tr. fr. Russian by* Daniel Halpern. BoWoP

Small and Early. Tudor Jenks. AA

Small and emptied woman you lie here a thousand years dead. In the Museum. Isabella Gardner. CAPP; NYBP

Small babe, tell me. The Baby. James Reaney. *Fr.* A Sequence in Four Keys. NAs

Small bird/ tracks. Rain. Lance Henson. VoR

Small birds and turtle doves. Arise and Pick a Posy. *Unknown.* OBET

Small Bird's Nest Made of White Reed Fiber, A. Robert Bly. NNaP

Small birds swirl around, The. The Small. Theodore Roethke. GrPl; SO

Small black wedge, the shepherd, A. In the Cheviots. Maurice Lindsay. PoSH

Small block of granite, A. A Child's Grave Marker. Ted Kooser. GOYP

Small blond girl brings a dark haired woman, A. Trellis. Laura Chester. NPGG

Small Bones Ache. Moshe Dor, *tr. fr. Hebrew by* Ruth Fainlight. VWA

Small Boy, Dreaming, A. Albert Herzing. NYBP

Small boy drove the shaggy ass, The. Turf Carrier on Aranmore. John Hewitt. PoRA

Small boy has thrown a stone at a statue, A. The Statue. Robert Finch. OBCV

Small Boys. Anja Vammelvuo, *tr. fr. Finnish by* Aili Jarvenpa. SOP

Small bundles of rotting vines smoke beside. Evening Refrain. Sherod Santos. MAYP

Small, busy flames play through the fresh laid coals. To My Brothers. Keats. NAs; Son; ThB

Small child of a wind, A. Requiem for Sonora. Richard Shelton. Psk

Small Colored Boy in the Subway. Babette Deutsch. PoNe

Small Comment. Sonia Sanchez. NBP

Small Country. Claribel Alegría, *tr. fr. Spanish by* Aliki *and* Willis Barnstone. BoWoP

Small Craftsman. Imre Csanádi, *tr. fr. Hungarian by* Edwin Morgan. MHuP

Small dawn, sailor, A. First light glints. Here, but Unable to Answer. Richard Hugo. CAPP; DiL

Small dazzle of stained glass which, A. The Bedroom Window. Fleur Adcock. ATNZ

Small Dragon, A. Brian Patten. AmMo

Small dragon, phoenix, centaur, A. Monster Alphabet. Robert Fisher. AmMo

Small ears prick on the bushes, The. The Common Living Dirt. Marge Piercy. GeTw

Small Elegy, A. Richard Snyder. PCP

Small eyes water on the branch. Another Face. Ray A. Young Bear. CDW

Small fact and fingers and farthest one from me. A Poem for Emily. Miller Williams. BLA; MT

Small Faculty Stag for the Visiting Poet, A. Earle Birney. OxBC

Small Farm, A. Michael Hartnett. CIP

Small fists waving. The Baby Hilary, Sir Edmund. Kathleen Leland Baker. NBLV

Small foreign car full of farm ladies from Jones County, A. Double Semi-Sestina. George Starbuck. SM

Small Fountains. Lascelles Abercrombie. *Fr.* Emblems of Love: What shall we do for Love these days? CH

Small Frogs Killed on the Highway. James Wright. HCAP; NNaP; NoAM

Small girls hurried to the hill-top church, The. Whit Monday. John Hewitt. TIRV

Small girls on trikes. Christmas Day. Roy Fuller. OBCP
Small gnats that fly. Song: One Hard Look. Robert Graves. MoAB; MoBrPo
Small grey cloudy louse that nests in my beard, The. James Keir Baxter. *Fr.* Jerusalem Sonnets, I. ATNZ; NoP; PeNZ
Small hooves. The Loba Recovers the Memory of a Mare. Diane di Prima. *Fr.* Loba. ER
Small house with a pointed roof, A. Epiphany. Eileen Shanahan. NeIP
Small householder now comes out warily, The. Spring Voices. Louis MacNeice. Son
Small Is Beautiful. Liu K'o-hsiang, *tr. fr. Chinese by* Dominic Cheung. IFON
Small Lady, The. Stevie Smith. TEP
Small lights pirouette. Peterhead in May. Burns Singer. OxBS
Small Lizard, The. Linda Gregg. MAYP
Small Man. Alfonsina Storni, *tr. fr. Spanish by* Kate Flores. DMH
Small man suffers the indignities of childhood, The. Paul Klee. Ruthven Todd. EAS
Small mechanical, A. Oceanography. Bob Perelman. IAT
Small Moon. Howard Nemerov. PCP
Small moon. Prayer to the Young Moon. *Unknown, tr. by* W. H. I. Bleek *and* Jack Cope. PeSA
Small nests/ On branches up high. A Bird's Nest. Erez Biton, *tr. by* Judith Katz. VWA
Small Night-Music. Jacob Glatstein, *tr. fr. Yiddish by* Benjamin *and* Barbara Harshav. AYP
Small Park in East Germany: 1969. Gerda Mayer. OBTV
Small Paths. Henriëtte Roland-Holst, *tr. fr. Dutch by* Jonathan Crewe. WPOW
Small Pavilion. Hung Liang-chi, *tr. fr. Chinese by* Irving Lo. *Fr.* To Dispel the Cold: Two Poems on Spring, I. WFTU
Small Prayer. Weldon Kees. PoA; VGW
Small Registry of Births and Deaths, A, *sel.* C. K. Stead. All Night It Bullied You. NAs
Small rivulets ran about her feet. Cythera. Suniti Namjoshi. AIW
Small Room with Large Windows, A. Allen Curnow. ATNZ; PeNZ *Sels.*
   "In the interim, how the children should be educated." *Fr.* III.
   "Kingfisher's naked arc alight, A." *Fr.* IV.
   "Seven ageing pine tree hide." *Fr.* II.
   "What it would look like if really there were only." *Fr.* I.
Small room with one table and one chair, A. Poet in Winter. Edward Lucie-Smith. TwCP
Small rural newspaper, The. Ozaki Hosai, *tr. fr. Japanese by* Hiroaki Sato. *Fr.* One Hundred Haiku in Free Form. FCEI
Small Sad Song. Alastair Reid. NYBP
Small-scale Reflections on a Great House. A. K. Ramanujan. OxBC
Small service is true service while it lasts. To a Child. Wordsworth. OxBSP
   (In a Child's Album.) GN
   (Written in the Album of a Child.) OxBChV
Small Shoes (II), The. Sue Roe. NPo
Small Sieve. Jacques Roubaud, *tr. fr. French by* Neil Baldwin. RHTwFP
Small, Smaller. Russell Hoban. TDD; TSS
Small Song. A. R. Ammons. NoAM; NoP
Small space. Two Tile Beaks. Maria Amalia Fonte Boa, *tr. by* Willis Barnstone *and* Nelson Cerqueira. BoWoP
Small speckled visitor, A. Ladybug. Joan Walsh Anglund. RHPC
Small Square, The. Sophia de Mello Breyner Andresen, *tr. fr. Portuguese by* Alexis Levitin. WPOW
Small Talk in a Garden. O. B. Hardison, Jr. CRP
Small Towns. Alejandro Murguía. FIA
Small Towns of Ireland, The. Sir John Betjeman. OBTV
Small type of great ones, that do hum. A Fly Caught in a Cobweb. Richard Lovelace. CaPo; SeCP
Small vampire, gorger at your mother's teat. Last Child. X. J. Kennedy. OxBSP
Small vellum environment, A. Page from the Koran. James Merrill. KS
Small voice is fretting my house in the night, A. The Smallish Son. Hayden Carruth. DiL
Small War, A. Ory Bernstein, *tr. fr. Hebrew by* Warren Bargad *and* Stanley F. Chyet. *Fr.* Poems from Mexico. IP
Small war-chariot with its shallow body, The. *Unknown, tr. by* Arthur Waley. BoS
Small wax candles melt to light, The. Poor Women in a City Church. Seamus Heaney. TIRV
Small wheel, A. Watch Repair. Charles Simic. NoP

Small window opened. I asked for the six-pack, The. Visionary Oklahoma Sunday Beer. James Whitehead. SM
Small Woman on Swallow Street. W. S. Merwin. CoAP
Small Wonder. Brock. Paul Muldoon. NoAM
Smallest bark on life's tumultuous ocean, The. Influence. Sarah Knowles Bolton. PWR
Smallish Son, The. Hayden Carruth. DiL
Smart. Shel Silverstein. RHPC
Smart man was Bishop Colenso, A. Colenso Rhymes for Orthodox Children. Bret Harte. OBAL
Smear of blue peat smoke, The. The Shepherd's Hut. Andrew Young. GrPl; OxBTC
Smell. William Carlos Williams. MoAB; MoAmPo; TAP
Smell is tree blood, The Tonight. Three Drawings. Mihály Ladányi, *tr. by* Jascha Kessler. FOC
Smell of Blood, The. Faiz Ahmad Faiz, *tr. fr. Urdu by* Mahmood Jamal. PBMUP
Smell of cigar smoke, Sunday, after dinner. Cigar Smoke, Sunday, after Dinner. Louise Townsend Nicholl. FYAP
Smell of death is so powerful, The. Marguerite de Navarre, *tr. by* Aline Allard. PBWP
Smell of death was in the air, The. John Press. PoRA
Smell of Old Newspapers Is Always Stronger after Sleeping in the Sun, The. Mike Lowery. Psk
Smell of potatoes just taken out of the earth, The. Chilean Elegies: 5, The. The Interior. Tom Wayman. NOBC
Smell of sage, The. Church Poem. Joyce Carol Thomas. CNA
Smell of snow, stinging in nostrils as the wind lifts it from a beach, The. The Crystal Lithium. James Schuyler. PoM
Smell of woodyards in the rain is strong, The. Woodyards in the Rain. Anne Marriott. CaP
Smell the recorders buried here. Cedar. Robert Morgan. GeTw
Smelling or feeling of the several holes. Dishonor. Edwin Denby. ErPo
Smells. Kathryn Worth. RHPC
Smells—how many. The Sense of Smell. Louis MacNeice. NYBP
Smells of ordinariness, The. Night Drive. Seamus Heaney. FaBCIP
Smilax in our homes entwine, The. Christmas Eve. Lizelia Augusta Jenkins Moorer. CBWP-3
Smile/ to see the lake. Lorine Niedecker. VGW
Smile, The. Blake. RB
   ("There is a smile of love.") TEP
Smile, and the world smiles with you. Hustle and Grin. *Unknown.* WBLP
   (Smile.) BLPA
Smile at Me. Musa Moris Farhi. VWA
Smile at us, pay us, pass us; but do not quite forget. The Secret People. G. K. Chesterton. FaPoR; OxBTC
Smile, Death. Charlotte Mew. WPE; WPOW
Smile fell in the grass, A. The Night Dances. Sylvia Plath. LCAP
Smile is quite a funny thing, A. Growing Smiles. *Unknown.* PoLF
Smile, Massachusetts, smile. *Unknown.* PAH
Smile of the Goat, The. Oliver Herford. FiBHP
Smile of the Walrus, The. Oliver Herford. FiBHP
Smile, smile/ Blest isle! A Lilliputian Ode on Their Majesties' Accession. Henry Carey. NOEC
Smile then, children, hand in hand. James Elroy Flecker. BrPo
Smiles of the Bathers, The. Weldon Kees. NaP
Smiling Dawn, with diadem of dew, The. The Poet's Ministrants. Henrietta Cordelia Ray. CBWP-3
Smiling Demon of Notre Dame, A. Sophie Jewett. AA
Smiling girls, rosy boys. Mother Goose. OxNR
Smiling listlessly, I see a spray of blossoms and say. Listlessness. Ch'en Wei-sung, *tr. by* Madeline Chu. WFTU
Smiling Mouth and Laughing Eyen Grey, The. Charles d'Orléans. HAP; NoP
Smiling, sweet girl, this proffered toy approve. To a Lady, with a Present of a Fan. *At. to* Charles Brandling. FaBoUS; NOEC
Smiling, we set the testing tray before the hall. Wen Cheng-ming, *tr. fr. Chinese by* Jonathan Chaves. *Fr.* My Son's One-Year Test: Improvised. CoBLCP
Smith at the organ is like an anvil being. The Sound of Afroamerican History Chapt II. S. E. Anderson. PoBA
Smith makes me, A. The Runes on Weland's Sword. Kipling. *Fr.* Puck of Pook's Hill. NoAM; PoEL-5
Smithereens. Dante Gabriel Rossetti. NOBVV
Smithfield Ham. Dave Smith. HCAP
Smoke. Medbh McGuckian. FaBCIP
Smoke. Henry David Thoreau. *See* Walden: Light-winged Smoke, Icarian Bird.
Smoke. Charles Wright. NYBP

Smoke and Steel, *sels.* Carl Sandburg.
  "Bar of steel—it is only, A." AiP
  "Smoke of the fields in spring is one." MoAmPo
Smoke Animals. Rowena Bastin Bennett. PDV
Smoke beshags. History: Madness. Stan Rice. NPGG
Smoke contending with smoke which will be maddest. Portrait of an
  Engine Driver. Bobi Jones, *tr. by* Joseph P. Clancy. OBWVE
Smoke from the train-gulf hid by hoardings blunders upward.
  Birmingham. Louis MacNeice. CMoP; MoAB; MoBrPo
Smoke of the fields in spring is one. Carl Sandburg. *Fr.* Smoke and
  Steel. MoAmPo
Smoke over the city at dusk. Etude. Judah Leib Teller, *tr. by* Benjamin
  and Barbara Harshav. AYP
Smoke rising, The. Tamesada, *tr. by* Steven D. Carter. WFTW
Smoke snakes. Indian Camp. Janet Reed McFatter. GrPl
Smoke when the sun fell and when it rose. Peter Levi. *Fr.* Life Is a
  Platform. FaBoTw
Smoked Herring, The. Charles Cros, *tr. fr. French by* A. L. Lloyd.
  GrPl
Smoker, The. Robert Huff. NePoEA-2
Smokey the Bear Sutra. *Unknown.* MAT
Smoking Drugs with Strangers. George Bowering. NeAC
Smoking Flax. Mary Josephine Benson. CaP
Smoking in an Open Grave. David Bottoms. InPK
Smoking My Prayers. Simon J. Ortiz. NOVW
Smoking swamp before a cottage door, A. An Irish Picture. J. Stanyan
  Bigg. NOBVV
Smoky as peat your lank hair on my pillow. A Nest in a Wall. Richard
  Murphy. CIP
Smoky bar in Matamoros. Blind date. Scattered Fog. Christy Sheffield
  Sanford. UL
Smoky rain riddles the ocean plains, A. My Father Paints the Summer.
  Richard Wilbur. DiL; NOBA
Smoky sunset. I dab my eyes, A. Required of You This Night. Peter
  Redgrove. PoE
Smoldering dry fern. And What of Me? Liz Sohappy Bahe. CDW
Smooth-bottomed fellow named Fritz, A. *Unknown.* PeHV
Smooth Divine, The. Timothy Dwight. *Fr.* The Triumph of Infidelity:
  Here stood Hypocrisy, in sober brown. AA; WGRP
Smooth it feels. Driving. Myra Cohn Livingston. RR
Smooth smell of Manhattan taxis, The. Dance of the Infidels. Al Young.
  PoBA
Smooth was the water, calm the air. Sir Charles Sedley. SeCV-2
Smooth-worn coin and threadbare classic phrase, The. Andromeda.
  Thomas Bailey Aldrich. AA
Smothered Fires. Georgia Douglas Johnson. BlSi
Smothering dark engulfs relentlessly, The. A Child's Winter Evening.
  Gwen John. CH
Smudging. Diane Wakoski. AmPA; PrIm
Smuggler's Song, A. Kipling. *Fr.* Puck of Pook's Hill. OxBChV
Smuggler's Victory, The. *Unknown.* OxBSS
Snack, The. L. L. Zeiger. BXAP
Snacks. Ronald P. Tanaka. BrSi
Snail. ("To grass, or leaf, or fruit, or wall"). Vincent Bourne, *tr. fr.*
  Latin by William Cowper. BoTP; OBVE
Snail, The ("Frugal Snail. . ."). Vincent Bourne. *See* Frugal snail with
  forecast of repose, The.
Snail. John Drinkwater. GoJo; OnUR
Snail. Elisabeth Eybers, *tr. fr. Afrikaans by* Elisabeth Eybers. PeSA
Snail. Federico García Lorca, *tr. fr. Spanish by* William Jay Smith. *Fr.*
  Songs of Childhood. CT; TSS
Snail, The. Giuseppe Giusti, *tr. fr. Italian by* Nigel Dennis. PFI
Snail. Langston Hughes. FaPON
Snail, The. Richard Lovelace. CaPo; OAEL-1
  (Snayl, The.) PoEL-3
Snail, The. Mother Goose. *See* Four and twenty tailors.
Snail, The. James Reeves. TSS
Snail and the House, The. Laura Elizabeth Richards. RAR
Snail gives off stillness, The. Evening. Charles Simic. GeTw
Snail is climbing up the window-sill, A. For a Five-Year-Old. Fleur
  Adcock. ATNZ
Snail moves like a, The. Hedgehog. Paul Muldoon. BIrV; NoAM
Snail pushes through a green, The. Considering the Snail. Thom Gunn.
  GrPl; LiTM; NAEL-2; NePoEA-2; TwCP
Snail says, "Alas!", The. The Poor Snail. J. M. Westrup. BoTP
Snail, snail, put out your horns. *Unknown.* OxNR
Snail ("The snail crawls over blackness"). Takahashi Shinkichi, *tr. fr.*
  Japanese by Lucien Stryk *and* Takashi Ikemoto. NU
Snail upon the wall. Snail. John Drinkwater. GoJo; OnUR
Snail, who had a way, it seems, A. The Snail's Dream. Oliver Herford.
  RHPC

Snails. E. D. Blodgett. NOBC
Snails. Liagarang, *tr. fr. Dharlwangu dialect.* CBAP, *tr. by* Ronald M.
  Berndt; WTO, *tr. by* Ronald M. Berndt
Snail's Derby, A. Eugene Lee-Hamilton. FM
Snail's Dream, The. Oliver Herford. RHPC
Snails have made a garden of green lace, The. After Rain. Patricia K.
  Page. NOBC; PoE
"Snails lead slow idyllic lives." The Widow's Yard. Isabella Gardner.
  CAPP
Snail's Lesson, The. Priscilla Jane Thompson. CBWP-2
Snail's Pace. Aileen Fisher. RAR
Snake. Dannie Abse. NoAM
Snake, The. Wendell Berry. GeTw
Snake, The. Emily Dickinson. *See* Narrow fellow in the grass, A.
Snake ("A snake came to my water-trough."), *sel.* D. H. Lawrence.
  BrPo; CMoP; FaBoMo; HeIP; HoPM; LiTB; LiTM; MoAB; NoAM;
  NOBE; NoP; NU; OAEL-2; PoRA; PPP; PrIm; SoTW
  "He drank enough." RR
Snake. Theodore Roethke. NOBA; NYBP; RFM
Snake, The. Andrew Suknaski. NOBC
Snake-Charmer, The. Sarojini Naidu. PBWP
Snake emptied itself into the grass, A. Monsoon. David Wevill. NYBP
Snake Eyes. Imamu Amiri Baraka. VGW
Snake falls, A. Masaoka Shiki, *tr. by* Geoffrey Bownas *and* Anthony
  Thwaite. PeBJV
Snake fence—peace sign—"Poodle Pups." Learning to Count. Alberta
  Turner. LCAP
Snake fled, The. Takahama Kyoshi, *tr. by* Geoffrey Bownas *and* Anthony
  Thwaite. PeBJV
Snake-gourd in bloom. Masaoka Shiki, *tr. by* Geoffrey Bownas *and*
  Anthony Thwaite. PeBJV
Snake Hill. Jay Parini. MAYP
Snake, killed, A. Ozaki Hosai, *tr. fr. Japanese by* Hiroaki Sato. *Fr.*
  One Hundred Haiku in Free Form. FCEI
Snake sheds its skin, The. Snake Skin. Ya'akov Beser, *tr. by* Bernhard
  Frank. MHeP
Snake Skin. Ya'akov Beser, *tr. fr. Hebrew by* Bernhard Frank. MHeP
Snake snatched, The. The Horned Snake. Louis Oliver. HATNAP
Snake Star, The. Michael Guttenbrunner, *tr. fr. German by* Beth
  Bjorklund. CoAuP
Snake tooth pinches his own mail, The. Remorse. Richmond Lattimore.
  PoA
Snake Trying, The. W. W. E. Ross. MoCV; NOBC; OBCV
Snakebite. Thomas James. SM
Snakecharmer. Sylvia Plath. NePoEA-2
Snakes. Peter Wild. AmPA
Snakes, Mongooses, Snake-Charmers and the Like. Marianne Moore.
  CMoP
Snakes of September, The. Stanley Kunitz. AnAn; BLA
Snakeskin and Stone. Keith Douglas. NePoEA
Snap back the canopy. Parachute Descent. David Bourne. WaP
Snap-Dragon. D. H. Lawrence. ErPo
Snap, the thong broke. Ozaki Hosai, *tr. fr. Japanese by* Hiroaki Sato.
  Fr. One Hundred Haiku in Free Form. FCEI
Snapper, The. William Heyen. AmPA; MAYP; PCP
Snapping gunshot cold. The Women in Old Parkas. Mary TallMountain.
  AIW; STE
Snaps for Dinner, Snaps for Breakfast, and Snaps for Supper. George
  Moses Horton. OBAL
Snaps its twig-tethermounts. A Dove. Ted Hughes. OxBC
Snapshot. John Fuller. NePoEA-2
Snapshot. Lajos Kassák, *tr. fr. Hungarian by* Edwin Morgan. MHuP
Snapshot for Miss Bricka Who Lost in the Semi-final Round of the
  Pennsylvania Lawn Tennis Tournament, A. Robert Wallace. SD
Snapshot of a Crab-Picker among Barrels Spilling Over, Apparently at the
  End of Her Shift. Dave Smith. NoAM
Snapshot of Adam. James Merrill. EOEF
Snapshot of Hue. Daniel Halpern. MAYP
Snapshots, *sel.* X. J. Kennedy.
  Birth Report. NAs
Snapshots of a Daughter-in-Law. Adrienne Rich. FaBoWP; HCAP;
  NAAL-2; NIP; NMM; NoAM; NoP
Snapshots of the Cotton South. Frank Marshall Davis. PoBA
Snare, The. Patrick MacDonogh. NeIP
Snare, The. James Stephens. BoTP; CH; CMoP; PDV
Snarleyyow; or, The Dog Fiend, *sel.* Frederick Marryat.
  Captain Stood on the Carronade, The. MOS
Snatch the departing mood. To a Town Poet. Lizette Woodworth Reese.
  AA
Snatched from his wife's hand. *Unknown, tr. by* Burton Watson. FCEI
Snaw, snaw, coom faster. Snow. *Unknown.* GBP

Snayl, The. Richard Lovelace. *See* Snail, The.
Sneaked about here. By the Road. Geoffrey Grigson. OxBTC
Sneakers. Judith Herzberg, *tr. fr. Dutch by* Scott Rollins. DuIn
Sneaking in the State Fair. Kevin Fitzpatrick. RR
Sneaky Bill. William Cole. RHPC
Sneeze. Maxine W. Kumin. RAR
Sneeze on a Monday, You Sneeze for Danger. *Unknown.* NBLV
Sniff of the real, that's, The. Autobiography. Thom Gunn. NoAM
Sniffed, dilating my nostrils. Elvin's Blues. Michael S. S. Harper.
   BPo
Snipe in the Marshes, A. Tamemasa, *tr. fr. Japanese by* Steven D.
   Carter. WFTW
Snitterjipe, The. James Reeves. AmMo
Snore in the foam: the night is vast and blind. Tristan da Cunha. Roy
   Campbell. MoBrPo; PeSA
Snoring Bedmate, The. *Unknown, tr. fr. Irish.* BIrV, *tr. by* John V.
   Kelleher
Snorkeling in the Caribbean. Alixa Doom. TSL
Snorting his pleasure in the dying sun. Landscape, Deer Season. Barbara
   Howes. GoJo
Snot goes down. Pieces of Snot. *Unknown, tr. by* Franz Boas. STP
Snow/ blue/ eyes. Robert Grenier. IAT
Snow. Antonin Artaud, *tr. fr. French by* Michael Benedikt. POS
Snow. Mary Austin. *Fr.* Rhyming Riddles. BoNaP; GrPl
Snow. Margaret Avison. NOBC
Snow. Fay Chiang. BrSi
Snow. Ch'ü Ta-chün, *tr. fr. Chinese by* Paul W. Kroll. WFTU
Snow. Adelaide Crapsey. QFR
Snow. Walter de la Mare. OnUR
Snow, The. F. Ann Elliott. BoTP
Snow, The. Donald Hall. NePoEA-2
Snow. The June Jordan. GLP
Snow. Karla Kuskin. RAR
Snow. Longfellow. *See* Snow-Flakes.
Snow. Louis MacNeice. CIP; CMoP; FaBCIP; FaBoMo; FPL; LiTM;
   MoP; NoAM; NOBE; OPOP; OxBSP; OxBTC
Snow. David Malouf. CBAP
Snow. Agnes Nemes Nagy, *tr. fr. Hungarian by* Jascha Kessler. FOC
Snow. Ralph Pomeroy. Psk
Snow. Salvatore Quasimodo, *tr. fr. Italian by* William Weaver. PFI
Snow. W. R. Rodgers. LTM
Snow. Amelia Rosselli, *tr. fr. Italian by* Lawrence R. Smith. NItP
Snow. Anne Sexton. KS
Snow. Shin Dong-jip, *tr. fr. Korean by* Koh Chang-soo. ACKP
Snow. Javier Sologuren, *tr. fr. Spanish by* David Tipton. Per
Snow. Ruth Stone. NYBP
Snow. Edward Thomas. FaBoTw
Snow. *Unknown.* GBP
Snow. David Wevill. MoCV
Snow. Hubert Witheford. ATNZ
Snow. Charles Wright. CAPP; LCAP
Snow/ is an anthology. Snow Anthology. Arthur S. Bourinot. GoYe
Snow Anthology. Arthur S. Bourinot. GoYe
Snow-Ball, The. Soame Jenyns. OBVE
Snow-bound; a Winter Idyl, *sels.* Whittier. AmPP; GN, *sels.*; NOBA;
   OxBA; TAP; WiR
   Mother. AA; OHIP
   Prophetess. AA
   "Shut in from all the world without." OBCP
     (Firelight.) AA
   Sister. AA
   "Sun that brief December day, The." AiP
     (The Storm.) FaBV
     (Winter Day.) TrGrPo
   "Unwarmed by any sunset light." AiP
     (World Transformed, The.) AA
   Winter Night. TrGrPo
Snow-Bound; a Winter Idyl [*or* Idyll]. Whittier. AmPP; FaBV; GN;
   NAAL-1; NOBA; OxBA; TAP; TrGrPo; WiR
Snow-bound mountains, snow-bound valleys. Carol of the Russian
   Children. *Unknown.* OHIP
Snow by Morning. May Swenson. NYBP
Snow came down last night like moths, The. First Snow in Alsace.
   Richard Wilbur. NoP; OBWP
Snow cannot melt too soon for the birds left behind, The. Rag Doll and
   Summer Birds. Owen Dodson. PoNe
Snow Country. Dave Etter. AmFN
Snow Country Weavers. James Welch. CDW; HATNAP
Snow-covered and bleeding, he came home. Feeding Ground. Thomas
   McCarthy. CIP

Snow covers the slopes, covers the slopes. Robert Grenier. *Fr.* A
   Sequence/ 28 Separate Poems. IAT
Snow crept up overnight as we slept. The Vanishing Point. Peter
   Davison. DiPo
Snow Crystals on Meall Glas. Elizabeth A. Wilson. PoSH
Snow Curlew, The. Vernon Watkins. NYBP
Snow curls in on the cold wind. Courtyard in Winter. John Montague.
   IPY
Snow dances and the frost flies, The. Plum Blossoms. Chu Shu-chên, *tr.
   by* Kenneth Rexroth *and* Ling Chung. PBWP
Snow dissolv'd no more is seen. IV, 7. "The snow dissolv'd no more is
   seen" ("Diffugere nives"). Horace, *tr. fr. Latin. Fr.* Odes.
   NAEL-1, *tr. by* Samuel Johnson; OBVE, *tr. by* Samuel Johnson.
   (Diffugere Nives.) OBVE, *tr. by* A. E. Housman.
   ("Snows are fled away, leaves on the shaws, The.")
Snow fades into the river, The. Ozaki Hosai, *tr. fr. Japanese by* Hiroaki
   Sato. *Fr.* One Hundred Haiku in Free Form. FCEI
Snow Fall. Koh Chang-soo, *tr. fr. Korean by* the author. ACKP
Snow falling. Snowfall. Artis Bernard. NTCP
Snow falling and night falling fast, oh, fast. Desert Places. Robert Frost.
   AmPP; CMoP; InPK; MoAB; MoAmPo; MoP; NAAL-2; NoAM;
   NOBA; OxBA; PoE; PPP; RB; TAP; UnPo
Snow falling in quantities and the valley deep, The. Teika, *tr. fr.
   Japanese by* Hiroaki Sato. *Fr.* Eighty-four Tanka. FCEI
Snow falling outside, The. Written on a Paper Napkin. Len Gasparini.
   NeAC
Snow falls. +30° C. Meir Wieseltier, *tr. by* Bernhard Frank. MHeP
Snow falls deep, The; the forest lies alone. Gipsies ("The snow falls
   deep"). John Clare. CH; PoEL-4
   (Gipsy Camp, The.) ChTr
   (Gypsies.) NoP; PrIm
Snow falls in a hush under night lights, lampposts. Snow. Fay Chiang.
   BrSi
Snow falls on the cars in Doctors' Row and hoods the headlights.
   Doctors' Row. Conrad Aiken. HAP
Snow Fell. Timothy Holmes. UAS
Snow fell, and its power was multiplied, The. Russia 1812. Victor
   Hugo, *tr. by* Robert Lowell. OBWP
Snow fell as for Wenceslas. Roarers in a Ring. Ted Hughes.
   NePoEA-2
Snow fell slowly over the long sweep, The. Landscape. Alfred W.
   Purdy. CaP
Snow-filled Nest, The. Rose Terry Cooke. OBCA
Snow fills heaven and earth. On a Painting of a Knight-Errant. Cheng
   Hsieh, *tr. by* Jonathan Chaves. CoBLCP
Snow-Flakes. Longfellow. ChTr; FaBoRV; FPL; NOBA; NoP; PoEL-5;
   TAP; UnPo; WiR
   (Snow.) BoTP
Snow-Flakes, The. Priscilla Jane Thompson. CBWP-2
Snow Geese in the Wind. Philip Dow. NPGG
Snow-Girl. Yunna Moritz, *tr. fr. Russian by* Elaine Feinstein. VWA
Snow gone, the village fills up. Issa, *tr. fr. Japanese by* Hiroaki Sato.
   Fr. Forty-four Hokku. FCEI
Snow-Gum, The. Douglas Stewart. PoAu-2
Snow had begun in the gloaming, The. James Russell Lowell. *Fr.* The
   First Snowfall. FaPON
   (First Snowfall [*or* Snow-Fall].) AnAmPo; BLPA; BLPL; FaBoBe;
   TAP; WBLP
Snow had fallen many nights and days, The. The End of the World.
   Gordon Bottomley. BrPo; CH; MoBrPo
Snow Harvest. Andrew Young. BoNaP
Snow has cleared, The. Ozaki Hosai, *tr. fr. Japanese by* Hiroaki Sato.
   Fr. One Hundred Haiku in Free Form. FCEI
Snow has covered the next line of tracks. Looking at New-fallen Snow
   from a Train. Robert Bly. NaP
Snow has fallen all night. The Snow Curlew. Vernon Watkins.
   NYBP
Snow has left [*or* is gone from] the cottage top[s], The. February. John
   Clare. *Fr.* The Shepherd's [*or* Shepheards] Calendar. NOBE;
   OBNC
Snow has melted now, The. January. Douglas Gibson. OBCP
Snow-hills all about. Ice-Skaters. Elder Olson. SD
Snow hugs the mountain high. Winter Night, Reading Books. Kan
   Sazan, *tr. by* Burton Watson. JLIC-2
Snow in Iowa City. Jayanta Mahapatra. WCI
Snow in Jerusalem, A. Hayim Naggid, *tr. fr. Hebrew.* VWA, *tr. by*
   Shlomo Vinner *and* Howard Schwartz
Snow in October. Alice Dunbar Moore Nelson. BlSi; CDC
Snow in Spring. Ivy O. Eastwick. PDV
Snow in the City. Danny Siegel. VWA

Snow in the Suburbs. Thomas Hardy. BoNaP; CMoP; GoJo; MoAB; MoBrPo; OAEL-2; OBMV; OxBTC; PPP

Snow in Town. Rickman Mark. BoTP

Snow is a mind. Revival. Steve Crow. HATNAP

Snow is a piercing sleet, The. Flowers Fill the Palace. Wei Ch'eng-pan, *tr. by* Lois Fusek. ATF

Snow is a strange white word. On Receiving News of the War. Isaac Rosenberg. MMA; MoBrPo; OBWP

Snow is all gone, The. Tameshige, *tr. by* Steven D. Carter. WFTW

Snow Is Deep on the Ground, The. Kenneth Patchen, *tr. fr. Persian.* UnAS

Snow is falling. Monticello. Robert Hass. AnAn

Snow is fast descending, The. The Orphan Boy. *Unknown.* OBET

Snow is in the oak. The Snow. Donald Hall. NePoEA-2

Snow is sick. The pure. March Snow. Don McKay. NOBC

Snow is weaving a soft, white, shroud, The. The Dying Year. Clara Ann Thompson. CBWP-2

Snow-Leopard, The. Randall Jarrell. CAPP; LiTM; TwCP

Snow, less intransigent [*or* intransigeant] than their marble, The. At the Grave of Henry James. W. H. Auden. LiTA; NoP

Snow lies deep, The: nor sun nor melting shower. Winter at Tomi. Ovid, *tr. by* F. A. Wright. AWP

Snow Lies Sprinkled on the Beach, The. Robert Bridges. NoAM

Snow Light, The. May Sarton. NBLV

Snow makes whiteness where it falls. First Snow. Marie Louise Allen. RAR; RHPC

Snow-Man, The. "Marian Douglas." OBCA

Snow Man, The. Wallace Stevens. CMoP; GoJo; HAP; HCAP; HeIP; MAT; NAAL-2; NoAM; NoP; NU; PoE; PrIm; QFR; SoSe; WeW

Snow melting! Gyodai, *tr. by* Geoffrey Bownas *and* Anthony Thwaite. PeBJV

Snow melting and the dog. Tremayne. Donald Justice. BLA; MT

Snow melting when I left you, and I took. Holding a Raccoon's Jaw. Gjertrud Schnackenberg. PPR

Snow on Saddle Mountain, The. Miyazawa Kenji, *tr. fr. Japanese by* Gary Snyder. NoAM; NOBA

Snow on the Mountain at Dusk. Shotetsu, *tr. fr. Japanese by* Steven D. Carter. WFTW

Snow Owl. Dave Smith. AnAn

Snow Party, The. Derek Mahon. CIP; FaBCIP; FaBoPV; OxBC

Snow Print Two: Hieroglyphics. B. J. Ebensen. TSS

Snow Queen comes on dazzling feet, The. The North Wind. Dorothy Graddon. BoTP

Snow Signs. Charles Tomlinson. NoAM

Snow, snow faster. *Unknown.* OxNR; PBBP

Snow Song. Henrietta Cordelia Ray. CBWP-3

Snow Song. Zalman Shne'ur, *tr. fr. Hebrew by* Bernhard Frank. MHeP

Snow-Storm, A. Giosuè Carducci, *tr. fr. Italian by* G. L. Bickersteth. PFI

Snow-Storm, The. Emerson. AA; AmPP; AnAmPo; BLPL; BoNaP; FaBoBe; GN; LiTA; NAAL-1; NOBA; NoP; OHFP; OxBA; PoE; PoEL-4; PoLF; Prf; TAP; TrGrPo; UnPo; WiR

Snow Storm, The. Mary Weston Fordham. CBWP-2

Snow Storm, The. Edna St. Vincent Millay. NAAL-2; PoA

Snow Storm. Kenneth Rexroth. NaP

Snow-tanned: each night I blow. Lying Awake Endlessly in Old Age. Kaai Chigetsu, *tr. fr. Japanese by* Hiroaki Sato. *Fr.* Thirteen Hokku. FCEI

Snow That Falls on Chagall's Village. Ruth Kim Chun-soo, *tr. fr. Korean by* Koh Chang-soo. ACKP

Snow toward Evening. Melville Cane. PDV

Snow was red with patriot blood, The. Washington by the Delaware. Joaquin Miller. AnAmPo

Snow White and Rose Red. Debora Greger. BAP

Snow White and the Seven Deadly Sins. R. S. Gwynn. SoTCo

Snow White and the Seven Dwarfs. Anne Sexton. HCAP

Snow whiteness all around. Whiteness. A. Leyeles, *tr. by* Benjamin *and* Barbara Harshav. AYP

Snow wind-whipt to ice. Winter. Richard Hughes. OBMV; OBWVE

Snowbanks North of the House. Robert Bly. AiP; LCAP

Snowbound City, The. John Haines. EAS

Snowdon Sunrise, The. Wordsworth. *See* Prelude [*or*, Growth of a Poet's Mind], The: Conclusion ("It was a close, warm, breezeless summer night").

Snowdrift of the mountains. A Rover's Song. Bliss Carman. AnAmPo

Snowdrop. Anna Bunston de Bary. BoTP

Snowdrop, The. Mary Weston Fordham. CBWP-2

Snowdrop. Ted Hughes. FaBoMo

Snowdrop, A. Harriet Prescott Spofford. GN

Snowdrop of dogs, with ear of brownest dye. Sonnet: To Tartar, a Terrier Beauty. Thomas Lovell Beddoes. FM; NOBVV; OBNC

Snowdrop, who, in habit white and plain, The. The Poet as King of Gotham. Charles Churchill. *Fr.* Gotham. NOEC

Snowdrops. Margiad Evans. OBWVE

Snowdrops. George MacBeth. OBCP

Snowdrops. L. Alma Tadema. BoTP

Snowdrops. Mary Vivian. BoTP

Snowdrops, lift your timid heads. Easter Song. Mary Artemisia Lathbury. OHIP

Snowfall. Artis Bernard. NTCP

Snowfall. Giosuè Carducci, *tr. fr. Italian by* Romilda Rendel. AWP

Snowfall, The. Gwerfyl Mechain, *tr. fr. Welsh by* Kenneth Hurlstone Jackson. OBWVE

Snowfall, The. Donald Justice. CRP; NePoEA-2; VGW

Snowfall. W. S. Merwin. NNaP

Snowfall; a Poem about Spring. James Wright. LCAP; NoAM

Snowfall: Four Variations. George Amabile. NYBP

Snowfall in the Afternoon. Robert Bly. CAPP; EAS; NOBA

Snowfish, The. Edward Field. GrPl

Snowflake, The. Walter de la Mare. RHPC; TSS

Snowflake on asphodel, clear ice on rose. Conrad Aiken. CMoP

Snowflake Which Is Now and Hence Forever, The. Archibald MacLeish. NoP

Snowflakes. Ruth M. Arthur. BoTP

Snowflakes. Alice Behrend. GoYe

Snowflakes. Marchette Chute. PDV

Snowflakes. Mary Mapes Dodge. AA

Snowflakes. Howard Nemerov. HCAP; PCP

Snowflakes. Clive Sansom. OBCP

Snowflakes Sail Gently Down, The. Gabriel Okara. UAS

Snowing of the Pines, The. Thomas Wentworth Higginson. AA; GN

Snowman, The. E. M. Adams. BoTP

Snowman. David McCord. RAR

Snowman, The. Patricia K. Page. NOBC

Snowmelt pond warm granite. Bedrock. Gary Snyder. PoE

Snows, *sel.* "St.-John Perse", *tr. fr. French by* Denis Devlin.

"I, only accountant, from the height of this corner room surrounded by an." *Fr.* IV. RHTwFP

Snows are fled away, leaves on the shaws, The. Horace. *See* Odes: IV, 7. "The snow dissolv'd no more is seen" ("Diffugere nives").

Snows have joined the little streams and join the sea, The. One Morning When the Rain-Birds Call. Lloyd Roberts. CaP

Snows of Yester-year, The. Villon. *See* Ballad[e] of Dead Ladies.

Snowsong. Reinhard Priessnitz, *tr. fr. German by* Beth Bjorklund. CoAuP

Snowstorm. John Clare. BoNaP; WiR

Snowstorm: At a Gathering at Chang Chu-fu's House. Tsung Ch'en, *tr. fr. Chinese by* Jonathan Chaves. CoBLCP

Snowy Day, A. *Unknown, tr. fr. Welsh by* H. Idris Bell. OBWVE

Snowy day: the temple hall's. Issa, *tr. fr. Japanese by* Hiroaki Sato. *Fr.* Forty-four Hokku. FCEI

Snowy Egret. Bruce Weigl. MAYP

Snowy expanses. Storms and Towers. A. Leyeles, *tr. by* Benjamin *and* Barbara Harshav. AYP

Snowy Heron. John Ciardi. WeW

Snowy Morning, 1940. N. K. Cruikshank. CN

Snowy Mountains. Tsung Ch'en, *tr. fr. Chinese by* Jonathan Chaves. CoBLCP

Snowy Owl near Ocean Shores ("Snowy owl, storm cast from the arctic tundra"). Duane Niatum. HATNAP

Snowy path for squirrel and fox, A. The Brook in February. Sir Charles G. D. Roberts. BoNaP; OBCV

Snowy sky turns into a single crow, The. Ozaki Hosai, *tr. fr. Japanese by* Hiroaki Sato. *Fr.* One Hundred Haiku in Free Form. FCEI

Snub nose, the guts of twenty mules are in your cylinders/ and transmission. New Farm Tractor. Carl Sandburg. FaPON

Snuffed out imminence, the rising shadow recognizes it. The Old Man. Alfredo Giuliani, *tr. by* Lawrence R. Smith. NItP

Snug at hearthside, while heart of the backlog. Heart of the Backlog. Robert Penn Warren. MT

Snug at the club two fathers sat. The Fathers. Siegfried Sassoon. MoP

Snug—the robe sewn from coarse cotton. Lu Yu, *tr. fr. Chinese by* Burton Watson. *Fr.* Farm Families. CoBCP

So! Abraham Reisen, *tr. fr. Yiddish by* Leonard Wolf. PeBMYV

So/ I have time to wonder. There's Nothing to Do in New York. Tomioka Taeko, *tr. by* Hiroaki Sato. FCEI

So/ Went this little pig from the mainland to the market. Archibald MacLeish Suspends the Five Little Pigs. Louis Untermeyer. *Fr.* Mother Goose Up-to-Date. MoAmPo

So? James P. Vaughn. AmNP

So Abram rose, and clave the wood, and went. The Parable of the Old Man and the Young. Wilfred Owen. FaBoRV; OPOP

So active they seem passive, little sheep. Grace. Richard Wilbur. LiTA

So all day long the noise of battle rolled. Morte d'Arthur. Tennyson. *Incorporated in* Idylls of the King *with changes, as* The Passing of Arthur. DL; FaBoBe; FaBoRV; FiP; NIP; NOBVV; OAEL-2; OBNV; PoEL-5

So all day long the noise of battle rolled. The Passing of Arthur. J. C. Squire. BXAP

So all men come at last to their Explorer's Tree. Burke and Wills. Ken Barratt. PoAu-2

"So am I as the rich, whose blessed key." Shakespeare. *Fr.* Sonnets, LII. OBSC

So an age ended, and its last deliverer died. W. H. Auden. *Fr.* Sonnets from China, X. CMoP; PoE

So-and-So Reclining on Her Couch. Wallace Stevens. AmPP; LiTM; NOBA

"So are you to my thoughts as food to life." Shakespeare. *Fr.* Sonnets. PoEL-2

So as they travelled, the drouping night. Spenser. *Fr.* The Faerie Queene, IV, 5. OAEL-1

So, back again? To a Dog. Josephine Preston Peabody. BLPA; WGRP

So bandit-eyed, so undovelike a bird. Blue Jay [*or* Bluejay]. Robert Francis. LCAP; PCP

So be it. I am. Hayden Carruth. VGW

So beautiful—God himself quailed. The Woman. R. S. Thomas. OxBC

So Beautiful Is the Tree of Night. Pauline Hanson. TAP

So Big! Max Fatchen. AmMo

So, bored with dragons, he lay down to sleep. Beowulf. Kingsley Amis. FaBoCo; OxBC

"So careful of the type?" but no. Tennyson. *Fr.* In Memoriam A. H. H., LVI. FF; HAP; NoP; OBNC; TOF

So, circling about my head, a fly. For Mao Tse-tung; a Meditation on Flies and Kings. Irving Layton. NOBC

So Close Should Be Our Love. *Gond Oral Tradition, tr. by* V. Elwin *and* S. Hivale. WTO

So close, the poisonous berries. Just like That. Sam Hunt. ATNZ

So cold is the night. Ryoshun, *tr. by* Steven D. Carter. WFTW

So cold is the wind. Traveling past a Market Town. Shotetsu, *tr. by* Steven D. Carter. WFTW

So cold is this spring. Masayori, *tr. by* Steven D. Carter. WFTW

So cold the night. Sanetomo, *tr. fr. Japanese by* Burton Watson. *Fr.* Twenty-four Tanka. FCEI

So cool: brow laid on the green straw mat. Shiba Sonome, *tr. fr. Japanese by* Hiroaki Sato. *Fr.* Fifteen Hokku. FCEI

So cruel [*or* cruell *or* crewell] prison how could betide [*or* howe coulde betyde], alas. Earl of Surrey. AAS; SiPS
(In Windsor Castle.) NoBE; OBSC; SeCePo
(Prisoned in Windsor, He Recounteth His Pleasure There Passed.) NAEL-1
(So Cruel Prison.) HAP; NoP

So Davies wrote: "This leaves me in the pink." "In the Pink." Siegfried Sassoon. CMoP

So delicate, so airy. Pink Almond. Katharine Tynan. BoTP

So detached and cool she is. The Mask. Clarissa Scott Delany. CDC; PoNe

So died John So. On John So. *Unknown.* FaBoEE

So different, this man. Marriage. William Carlos Williams. PoA

So does the sun withdraw his beames. On His Mistress Going from Home. *Unknown.* OBS

So dream thy sails, O phantom bark. The Phantom Bark. Hart Crane. CMoP

So, each with special burdens, we poor singers. The City Singers. John L. Owen. PF

So earnest with thy God, can no new care. Of His Majesties Receiving the News of the Duke of Buckingham's Death. Edmund Waller. SeCV-1

So earth's inclined toward the one invisible. Winter Scene. Marguerite Young. NU; WPE

So, even with a severed tongue, Philomela recounted her tribulations. Philomela. Yannis Ritsos, *tr. by* Edmund Keeley. AnAn

So Fair, So Sweet, Withal So Sensitive. Wordsworth. EnRP; NoP

So faith is strong. The Tide of Faith. "George Eliot." *Fr.* A Minor Prophet. WGRP

So fallen! so lost! the light withdrawn. Ichabod. Whittier. AA; AnAmPo; LiTA; NAAL-1; NOBA; OxBA; PAH; PoEL-4; TAP

So far apart our meetings. Teika, *tr. fr. Japanese by* Hiroaki Sato. *Fr.* A Compendium of Good Tanka. FCEI

So far as I can see. Meditations of a Tortoise Dozing under a Rosetree Near a Beehive at Noon While a Dog Scampers About and a Cuckoo Calls from a Distant Wood. Emile Victor Rieu. FiBHP

So far from springlike. Emperor Hanazono, *tr. by* Steven D. Carter. WFTW

So Far, So Near. Christopher Pearse Cranch. TrPWD

So Far, So-So. Moyshe-Leyb Halpern, *tr. fr. Yiddish by* Benjamin *and* Barbara Harshav *and* Kathryn Helle. AYP

So far, your horse is a trough on four blocks. This I Said to My Only Son at Play—and to Nobody Else. Moyshe-Leyb Halpern, *tr. by* Benjamin *and* Barbara Harshav. AYP

So Fast Entangled. *Unknown.* TrGrPo

So few rays. Kyogoku Tamekane, *tr. fr. Japanese by* Burton Watson. *Fr.* Twenty-three Tanka. FCEI

So few, really. What Her Friend Said to Her, within the Lover's Hearing. Paranar, *tr. by* A. K. Ramanujan. PLW

So few the cicadas. Masaoka Shiki, *tr. by* Geoffrey Bownas *and* Anthony Thwaite. PeBJV

So fine, the boards of magnolia. Wrecked Boat on the River Shore. Chiang Lu, *tr. by* Burton Watson. CoBCP

So fleeting/ that dream of a night. Narihira, *tr. fr. Japanese by* Burton Watson. *Fr.* Kokin Shu. FCEI

So flies love's meteor to her shroud of winds. The Dead Words. Vernon Watkins. LiTM

So, forth issued the Seasons of the year. The Mask of Mutability. Spenser. *Fr.* The Faerie Queene, VII, 7. OBSC
(Seasons, The.) GN

So forth she comes, and to her coche does clyme. Spenser. *Fr.* The Faerie Queene, I, 4. NAEL-1; OAEL-1

So frisky and fit. Simchas Torah. Morris Jacob Rosenfeld. TrJP

So from the ground we felt that virtue branch. The Transfiguration. Edwin Muir. OxBS

So from the years their gifts were showered: each. W. H. Auden. *Fr.* Sonnets from China, I. CMoP

So from this life, male in its first motion. Vittoria Colonna. Roy Marz. PoA

So full of courtly reverence. Dudley North. OxBSP

So gay on your lovely head. Relaxation. Dick Gallup. UL

So gentle Ellen now no more. Samuel Taylor Coleridge. *Fr.* The Three Graves. ChER

So good luck came, and on my roof did light. The Coming of Good Luck. Robert Herrick. FaBoEE; JCP; OxBSP

So goodbye, Mrs. Brown. To-Day I Leave Mrs. Brown's Lodgings. Sir Walter Scott. FaBoEE

So grand, so tall. *Unknown, tr. by* Arthur Waley. BoS

So Graven. Josephine Miles. NoAM

So great the pain. On Love. Kyogoku Tamekane, *tr. fr. Japanese by* Burton Watson. *Fr.* Twenty-three Tanka. FCEI; LLLT

So hard for women to believe each other. Apron Strings. Marge Piercy. TAP

So hard to fall for. *Unknown, tr. by* Geoffrey Bownas *and* Anthony Thwaite. PeBJV

So hath been dawning another blue day. Today. Thomas Carlyle. PWR

So have I seen a little silly fly. A Quarrel with Fortune. Benjamin Colman. SCAP

"So Have I Spent on the Banks of Ysca Many a Serious Hour." Thomas Vaughan. FaBoPP

So having ended, silence long ensewed. Nature's Reply to Mutability. Spenser. *Fr.* The Faerie Queene, VII, 7 *and* VIII, 1. NOBE

So having said, Aglaura him bespake. Colin Clout at Court. Spenser. *Fr.* Colin Clout's Come Home Again. OBSC

So he came to write again. Burning Hills. Michael Ondaatje. NoAM; NOBC; NoP

So he sits down. His host will play for him. Concert Scene. John Logan. NePoEA-2

So he that saileth in this world of pleasure. Anne Bradstreet. *Fr.* Contemplations. WPOW

So he won't talk to me when we meet? Confucius, *tr. fr. Chinese by* Ezra Pound. *Fr.* Songs of Cheng. CTC

So here hath been dawning. To-Day. Thomas Carlyle. GN; WGRP

So here I sit behind my nasty desk. Any Man to His Secretary. Hilary Corke. ErPo

So here the great man stood. On the Porch at the Frost Place, Franconia, NH. William Matthews. MAYP

So hot the melons. Kyorai, *tr. fr. Japanese by* Burton Watson. *Fr.* Twenty Hokku. FCEI

So how is life with your new bloke? An Attempt at Jealousy. Craig Raine. NoAM

So, how was I to know, when he invited. Helen. James Harrison. NBLV

So Hrothgar's men lived happy in his hall. *Unknown, tr. fr. Anglo-Saxon by* Burton Raffel. *Fr.* Beowulf. PoE

So humble things thou hast borne for us, O God. Veni Creator. Alice Meynell. WPE

So I ask my dear wife. The End of the Book. Moyshe-Leyb Halpern, *tr. by* Benjamin *and* Barbara Harshav. AYP

So I came down the steps to Lenin. Dorothy Wellesley. *Fr.* Lenin. OBMV

So I cut my hair; so I'm shorn. Song of the Strange Young Duckling. Deborah Munro. IHMS

So I decided watching an old woman like her, who could rise so easily. Leslie Scalapino. *Fr.* Hmmmm. NPGG

So I have killed my black goat. I Have Got to Stop Loving You. Ai. GeTw

So I have known this life. Lollingdon Downs. John Masefield. LiTB

So, I have seen a man killed! Arthur Hugh Clough. *Fr.* Amours de Voyage, Canto II, vii. EBVV

So I Let Her Go. *Unknown.* AmFP

So I may gain thy death, my life I'll give. Qui Perdiderit Animam Suam. Richard Crashaw. ACP

So I possess a perfect thing. A Bed of Campanula. "John Crichton." CaP

So I refused to see them. Kurohito. *Fr.* Manyo Shu. Ma

So I Said I Am Ezra. A. R. Ammons. NAAL-2; NoAM; NOBA; NoP

So I, who love, with all this outward. The Meaning. Ralph Gustafson. OBCV

So I would hear out those lungs. Buckdancer's Choice. James Dickey. HeIP; NoAM; NOBA; NoP; NYBP; PoNe

So if you love me. Hilda Doolittle ("H. D."). *Fr.* Sigil, XV. AnAn

So I'm born a weaver. Kabir, *tr. by* John Stratton Hawley *and* Mark Juergensmeyer. SSI

So in Pieria, from the wedded bliss. In Memory of Bryan Lathrop. Edgar Lee Masters. PoA

So, in the evening, to the simple cloister. Conrad Aiken. *Fr.* Preludes for Memnon; or, Preludes to Attitude. LiTA (Cloister.) MoAB; MoAmPo

So, in the midst of Neptune's angry tide. The Halcyon's Nest. Giles Fletcher the Younger. *Fr.* Christ's Victory and Triumph: Christ's Triumph after Death, IV. FaBoPP

So intensely you had been waiting for lemon. Lemon Elegy. Takamura Kotaro, *tr. by* Sato. FCEI

"So is it not with me as with that muse." Shakespeare. *Fr.* Sonnets, XXI. InvP; OBSC

So is the child slow stooping beside him. Gardeners. David Ignatow. PCP

So is this great and wide sea. Bible, *O.T. Fr.* Psalms: Psalm CIV ("Bless the Lord, O my soul. "), 25-28. MOS

So it begins. Adam is in his earth. James Agee. *Fr.* Sonnets. OPOP

So it is. Coleman Barks. *Fr.* New Words. CRP

So it is, my dear. Even So. Dante Gabriel Rossetti. NOBE; NOBVV; OBNC

So it is, my dearest lover. *Unknown. Fr.* Manyo Shu. Ma

So It Shall Be. Moyshe-Leyb Halpern, *tr. fr. Yiddish by* Benjamin *and* Barbara Harshav *and* Kathryn Helle. AYP

So late in the 20th century. Au Bout du Temps. Andrei Codrescu. UL

So late, so late, so haunting. On the Threshold. Karl Kraus, *tr. by* Albert Bloch. TrJP

So lay the youth with Mary in his arms. J. C. Squire. *Fr.* Country Wooing. BXAP

So leave her, and cast care from thy heart. His Camel. Alqamah, *tr. fr. Arabic by* Sir Charles Lyall. *Fr.* The Mufaddaliyat. AWP

So Let Me Have My Fun. Aldo Palazzeschi, *tr. fr. Italian by* Felix Stefanile. PFI

So light no one noticed. Edward Dorn. VGW

So light the sleeves of this cicada-wing robe. Teika, *tr. fr. Japanese by* Hiroaki Sato. *Fr.* Eighty-four Tanka. FCEI

So like a flower or the flowing of the air. The Voice of Robert Desnos. Robert Desnos, *tr. by* Michael Benedikt. POS

So Little and So Much. John Oxenham. BLRP

So live, so love, so use that fragile hour. Robert Louis Stevenson. NOBVV

So lonely am I. Ono no Komachi, *tr. by* David Keene. BoWoP; PBWP

So Long. Jayne Cortez. BoWoP

So long. James Dickey. *Fr.* For the First Manned Moon Orbit. AiP

So long. Ross Knox. CowP

So Long Ago. Morris Jacob Rosenfeld, *tr. fr. Yiddish by* Elbert Aidline. TrJP

So long as lasts the span of life. Okura. *Fr.* Manyo Shu. Ma

So long as life remains. Khwaja Mir Dard, *tr. by* Ahmed Ali. GoT

So long as you live and move. Teach Us to Mark This, God. Franz Werfel, *tr. by* Jacob Sloan. TrJP

So long since I've enjoyed the hills and ponds. Returning to My Home in the Country ("So long since I've enjoyed the hills and ponds"). T'ao Ch'ien, *tr. by* Burton Watson. CoBCP

So Long Solon. Jack Myers. AmPA

So Long? Stevens. John Berryman. *Fr.* Dream Songs. HAP; HCAP; NOBA

So long was the road. Distant Love. Shotetsu, *tr. by* Steven D. Carter. WFTW

So long you wandered on the dusky plain. To His Friend in Elysium. Joachim Du Bellay, *tr. by* Andrew Lang. AWP

So Look the Mornings. Robert Herrick. ELP

So looks Anthea, when in bed she lyes. To Anthea Lying in Bed. Robert Herrick. SeCP

So loud the deer cries, calling to his mate. Yakamochi. *Fr.* Manyo Shu. Ma

So Love is dead that has been quick so long. Hic Jacet. Louise Chandler Moulton. AA

So low it used to seem almost. Full Moon, Rising. Jonathan Holden. GOYP

So luminous around them lay the air. Oystercatchers. Christopher Middleton. FaBoTw

So make your impassive passage to the act. Poem in Time of War. William Abrahams. WaP

So many books; A temple, whose thick walls are built of books. The Spirit Escapes. Pierre Reverdy, *tr. by* Michael Benedikt. POS

So many cares to vex the day. Summer Magic. Leslie Pinckney Hill. BANP

So many cats so often multiply. The Cats of Santa Anna. Tasso, *tr. by* Barbara Howes. PFI

So Many Cenotaphs. Peter Bland. ATNZ

So many churches against the sky. Star for a Glass. Michael Burkard. PPR

So many convolutions and not enough simplicity! To Marina. Kenneth Koch. NoAM

So many delights the excitement has no end. Sitting Up with My Wife on New Year's Eve. Hsü Chün-ch'ien, *tr. by* Burton Watson. CoBCP

So many evenings, on the red-tiled terrace. Lost Garden. "Katherine Hale." CaP

So Many Feathers. Jayne Cortez. BlSi

So many have lived here, who loved. House for Sale. André Frénaud, *tr. by* Keith Bosley. RHTwFP

So many little flowers. Cycle. Langston Hughes. FaPON

So many new crimes since then! Since Then. D. J. Enright. OBSV

So many nights. Emperor Fushimi, *tr. by* Steven D. Carter. WFTW

So many nights the solitary light had burned. Rousseau in His Day. Donald Davie. DiPo

So many of those I once knew. Villagers. Iain Crichton Smith. NPo

So many people. *Unknown, tr. by* Burton Watson. FCEI

So many, the Perfection of Snow. Andrea Zanzotto, *tr. by* Lawrence R. Smith. NItP

So many pigeons at Columbus. Arthur Gregor. VGW

So many things happen. The War of the Worlds. Vern Rutsala. Psk

So many thousands for a house! On a Certain Lord Giving Some Thousand Pounds for a House. David Garrick. FaBoEE

"So many unlived lives," she said; and idle. An Idyl in Idleness. Robert Pack. NePoEA

So many women, writing. Daughterly. Kathleen Spivack. TV

So many years I've seen the sun. The Mystery of Life. John Gambold. NOEC

So may the auspicious Queen of Love. I, 3. To the Ship on Which Virgil Sailed to Athens ("Sic te diva potens Cyri"). Horace, *tr. fr. Latin. Fr.* Odes. AWP, *tr. by* Dryden.

So me saary. Men and Women. David Dabydeen. PBCV

So Might is Right, you say; I fight in vain. "Might Is Right." Israel Zangwill. TrJP

So Might It Be. John Galsworthy. BLPL; PoLF

So Miss Myrtle is going to marry? The Charming Woman. Helen Selina Sheridan. WPE

So moping flat and low our valleys lie. Winter in the Fens. John Clare. BoNaP

So much bad food and worse liquor, friends. Guillaume de Poitiers, *tr. by* Paul Blackburn. Pro

So much depends. The Red Wheelbarrow. William Carlos Williams. AnAmPo; BLPL; CMoP; GrPl; GrPl; HeIP; HoPM; InPK; LiTA; LiTM; MoAB; MoAmPo; MoP; NAAL-2; NIP; NoAM; NOBA; NoP; PoE; PrIm; SoSe; SOTW; TAP; TTTS; UnPo; WeW

So much for the elves' wergild, the true governance. Geoffrey Hill. *Fr.* Mercian Hymns, V. NoAM

So much have I forgotten in ten years. Flame-Heart. Claude McKay. AmNP; BANP; CDC; PoNe

So much is parchment where I gloom. The Black Mesa. James Merrill. PoA

So much like an old couple on their nightly walk. Dusk: Mallards on the Charles River. Michael C. Blumenthal. BLA

So much like the flower and the current of air. The Voice of Robert Desnos. Robert Desnos, *tr. by* Bill Zavatsky. RHTwFP
So much more forlorn. Tamekane, *tr. by* Steven D. Carter. WFTW
So much of my early. Outhouse Blues. Sheryl L. Nelms. MOWH
So Much Suffering. Bertalicia Peralta, *tr. fr. Spanish by* Robert L. Smith *and* Judith Candullo. DMH
So much to ask. Narihira, *tr. fr. Japanese by* Burton Watson. *Fr.* Kokin Shu. FCEI
So much to tell you. 2 Variations: All About Love. Philip Whalen. NeAP
So—Murray to Byron in Italy. Kaleidoscope. G. K. Page. NoAM
So near to death yourself. For a Very Old Man, on the Death of His Wife. Jane Cooper. NePoEA-2
So neck to stubborn neck, and obstinate knee to knee. Antaeus; a Fragment. Wilfred Owen. PeHV
So nigh is grandeur to our dust. Duty. Emerson. *Fr.* Voluntaries, III. FaFP; GN
So Not Seeing I Sung. Arthur Hugh Clough. *See* Amours de Voyage: Tibur is beautiful, too, and the orchard slopes, and the Anio.
So nothing new from up here. Deportation Order. Franco Fortini, *tr. by* Lawrence R. Smith. NItP
So now, having fled into the stone world, I was slowly. Aleksander Wat, *tr. fr. Polish by* Czeslaw Milosz. *Fr.* Songs of a Wanderer, III. PwPP
"So now I have confessed that he is thine." Shakespeare. *Fr.* Sonnets, CXXXIV. InvP
So now I'm brooding moodily upon. A Simple Matter. Gloria Rawlinson. PeNZ
So now is come our joyful'st feast. George Wither. OBS
   (Our Joyful Feast.) OHIP
So now it's your turn. Instructions to the Double. Tess Gallagher. FaBoWP
So now just suppose that someone wanted to know. Surgery. Kenneth Pitchford. GLP
So now my summer task is ended, Mary. To Mary. Shelley. EnRP
So now the very bones of you are gone. Doricha. Poseidippus, *tr. by* E. A. Robinson. AWP; FaBoEE; OBVE
So now, this poet, who forsakes the stage. Prologue to "Love Triumphant." Dryden. *Fr.* Love Triumphant. OxBoLi
So oft as I her beauty do behold. Spenser. *Fr.* Amoretti, LV. Son; TrGrPo
So oft as I with state of present time. Spenser. *Fr.* The Faerie Queene, V *proem.* OAEL-1
So oft our hearts, belovèd lute. Dream and the Song. James David Corrothers. BANP
So often artists have painted a woman. January 18, 1979. John Yau. UL
So often, lady, I have asked you. Raimbaut de Vaqueiras, *tr. by* Paul Blackburn. Pro
So often we hear of the vacant chair. The Chair That Is Filled. Carrie Biggs. PWR
So on a night when a heavy full moon was low. On the Eve of a Birthday. Geoffrey Grigson. NAs
So on he pricked, and loe, he gan espy. Ride a Cock Horse. Barry Pain. BXAP
So on his Nightmare through the evening fog. Nightmare. Erasmus Darwin. *Fr.* The Botanic Garden: The Loves of the Plants. NOEC
So on she goes, and in her idle flight. Christopher Marlowe. *Fr.* Hero and Leander, Second Sestiad. PoE
So, on the bloody sand, Sohrab lay dead. Matthew Arnold. *Fr.* Sohrab and Rustum. GTBS-P
   (Sohrab Dead.) NOBE
So once again, hearing the tired aunts. In the House of the Dying. Jane Cooper. NMM
So open was his mind, so wide. The Independent. Phyllis McGinley. FaBoEE
So Orpheus stared, on passing the dog of hell. The Young Chess Player. Keith Sinclair. ATNZ
So Paradise was brightened, so 'twas blest. To Philomela. Benjamin Colman. SCAP
So passed they naked on, nor shunned the sight. Milton. *Fr.* Paradise Lost, *Bk.* IV, *ll.* 319–355.
   (Adam and Eve.) SeCePo
So Pleasant It Is To Have Money. Arthur Hugh Clough. *See* Dipsychus: As I sat at the café, I said to myself; *see also* Spectator ab Extra: As I Sat at the Café.
So prayis me as ye think caus quhy. Remedis of Luve. *Unknown.* OxBS
So proud in his furry robe. Baboon. *Unknown, tr. fr. Yoruba by* Ulli Beier. *Fr.* Hunter Poems of the Yoruba. RB
So proud she was to die. Emily Dickinson. NOBA; OBD

So prudent and so young a wife! To Geron. Hildebrand Jacob. NOEC
So, pure and dutiful, she sought that place. *Unknown, tr. fr. Sanskrit by* Franklin Edgerton. *Fr.* The Mahabharata. DL
So Quick, So Hot, So Mad is Thy Fond Sute. Thomas Campion. PoEL-2
So Quietly. Leslie Pinckney Hill. BANP; IDB; PoBA
So rare, so mere. Presence of Snow. Melville Cane. GoYe
So rending/ to come across a space. Tree-Felling, Upper Junction Road. Brian Turner. ATNZ
So runed on a rune-stick, and the rune-stick put. Gudveig. Francis Berry. OBTV
So sang he: and as meeting rose and rose. Willowwood ("So sang he: and as meeting rose and rose"). Dante Gabriel Rossetti. *Fr.* The House of Life, LII. NAEL-2; OAEL-2
So Sat the Muses. William Browne. *Fr.* Caelia, IV. Son
So Satan spake, and him Beëlzebub. Milton. *Fr.* Paradise Lost, *Bk.* I, *ll.* 271–669.
   (Council of Satan, The.) PoEL-3
So saying, light-foot Iris passed away. Homer, *tr. fr. Greek by* Tennyson. *Fr.* The Iliad, XVIII. OBVE
So seldom I come at night. Written in Autumn When Spending the Night Near the Grave of His Wife. Shunzei, *tr. fr. Japanese by* Burton Watson. *Fr.* Thirty Tanka. FCEI
So several factions from this first ferment. Achitophel: The Earl of Shaftsbury. Dryden. *Fr.* Absalom and Achitophel, Pt. I. NOBE
So shaken as we are, so wan with care. King Henry the Fourth, Pt. I. Shakespeare. NAEL-1
"So shall I live, supposing thou art true." Shakespeare. *Fr.* Sonnets, XCIII. InvP
So shall it ever be. As Thy Days. Grant Colfax Tullar. BLRP
So shalt thou come to a court as clear as the sun. The Palace of Truth. William Langland. *Fr.* The Vision of Piers Plowman. ACP
So she became a bird and bird-like danced. Procne. Peter Quennell. LiTB; LiTM; MoBrPo
So she went into the garden. The Great Panjandrum Himself. Samuel Foote. FaBoCh; FaBoCo; MoShBr; Par; PoLF
So shines the Earth in certain mornings' light. Yes to the Earth. Sibilla Aleramo, *tr. by* Muriel Kittel. DMI
So shoots a star as doth my mistress glide. John Davies of Hereford. EiL
So-shu dreamed. Ancient Wisdom, Rather Cosmic. Ezra Pound. NOBA
So shuts the marigold her leaves. William Browne. *Fr.* Britannia's Pastorals, III, Song 1. ChTr, *short sel.*
   (Memory.) OBEV
So, since your heart is set on those sweet fields. To Colman Returning. *At. to* Colman, *tr. by* Helen Waddell. BIrV
So sleep undoes itself and I arrive. For My Twenty-fifth Birthday in Nineteen Forty-one. John Ciardi. WaP
So Sleeps My Love. *Unknown.* TrGrPo
So Slow to Die. George Edward Woodberry. *Fr.* Wild Eden, XXXVIII. AA
So small are the flowers of Seamu. *Unknown, tr. by* Boris de Rachewiltz; *English vers. by* Ezra Pound *and* Noel Stock. BoWoP; PBWP; UnAS
So smell those odours that do rise. To the Most Fair and Lovely Mistress Anne Soame, Now Lady Abdie [*or* Abdy]. Robert Herrick. CaPo; NOBE
So smooth, so sweet, so silv'ry is thy voice. Upon Julia's Voice. Robert Herrick. InPK; JCP; NOBE; SeCePo; SeCP; SoSe
So, So. William Clerke. ELP
So, so, break[e] off this last lamenting kiss[e]. The Expiration. John Donne. EiL; MeLP; MePo; OxBSP; SeCP
So, So. It is an old man sleeping here. In the Forest. Pinhas Sadeh. VWA, *tr. by* Harris Lenowitz
So, so, spade and hoe. Baby's Baking. Evaleen Stein. RAR
So soft in the hemlock wood. Robert Hillyer. MoAmPo
So soft streams meet, so springs with gladder smiles. The Welcome to Sack. Robert Herrick. CaPo; SeCP; SeCV-1
So soon as day, forth dawning from the East. Artegall and Radigund. Spenser. *Fr.* The Faerie Queene, V, 5. OBSC
So soon grown old! Hast thou been six years dead. The Anniverse; an Elegy. Henry King. JCP
So soon my body will have gone. Immortal. Sara Teasdale. WGRP
So spake our Mother Eve, and Adam heard. Milton. *Fr.* Paradise Lost, *Bk.* XII, *ll.* 624–649.
   (Banishment, The.) NOBE; OBS
   (Exit from Eden, The.) FaBoRV
So spake th' archangel Michael; then paused. Milton. *Fr.* Paradise Lost, *Bk.* XII, *ll.* 466–649. FaBoPV, *fr. ll.* 466–551; NAEL-1; OAEL-1

So spake the enemy of mankind, enclosed. Milton. *Fr.* Paradise Lost, Bk. IX, *ll.* 494–526. FM

So spake the godlike power, and thus our sire. Milton. *Fr.* Paradise Lost, *Bk.* VIII, *ll.* 249–653. NAEL-1

So squeezed, wince you I scream? I love you & hate. John Berryman. *Fr.* Homage to Mistress Bradstreet. FF

So still the night swinging. Mariners' Carol. W. S. Merwin. EaLo

So stretched out huge in length the Arch-Fiend lay. Milton. *Fr.* Paradise Lost, *Bk.* I, *ll.* 209–238. TEP

So stupid of me to hope you'll take to books. Rai San'yo, *tr. fr. Chinese* by Burton Watson. *Fr.* Shortly after I Married, I Had to Go into Mourning, II. FCEI; JLIC-2

So summer comes in the end to these few stains. The Beginning. Wallace Stevens. VGW

So Sweet a Kiss. Shakespeare. *Fr.* Love's Labour's Lost, IV, iii. EIL; InvP

So Sweet Is She. Ben Jonson. *See* Devil Is an Ass, The: Have you seen but a bright lily grow.

So Sweet Love Seemed. Robert Bridges. FaBV

So sweet the plum trees smell! Plum Trees. Ranko. FaPON

So swete a kis yistrene fra thee I reft. To His Maistres [*or* Mistress]. Alexander Montgomerie. GBL; OxBS

So take a happy view. A Happy View. C. Day Lewis. CMoP

So tell me what you have. Tell Me. Pamela Mordecai. PBCV

So tender to the light it breaks them. Vampires. Lawrence Raab. VVA

So thank Mum for the book of poetry. 1916. R. S. Gwynn. MT

So that a colony will breed here. We Must Make a Kingdom of It. Gregory Orr. BLA; MAYP

So that each person may quickly find that. Johann Joachim Quantz's Five Lessons. William Sydney Graham. FaBoMo

So that no one will see. *Unknown. Fr.* Manyo Shu. FCEI

So that soldierly legend is still on its journey. Kearny at Seven Pines. Edmund Clarence Stedman. AA; AnAmPo; PAH

So that the vines burst from my fingers. Ezra Pound. *Fr.* Cantos, XVII. InPS; NAAL-2; OBMV

So That's Who I Remind Me Of. Ogden Nash. BLPL; PoLF

So the church Christ was hit and buried. Le Christianisme. Wilfred Owen. BrPo

So the committee met again, and again. The Committee. C. Day Lewis. CMoP

So the distances are Galatea. The Distances. Charles Olson. NAAL-2; NeAP; NoP

So the last day's come at last, the close of my fifteen year. The Old Place. Blanche Baughan. ATNZ; PeNZ

So the man spread his blanket on the field. A Tall Man Executes a Jig. Irving Layton. MoCV; NoAM; NOBC

So, the powder's low, and the larder's clean. The Last Cup of Canary. Helen Gray Cone. AA

So the sky wounded you, jagged at the heart. Daylights. Rosanna Warren. MAYP; NoAM

So the struck eagle, stretch'd upon the plain. Byron. OBD

So the tide forgets, as morning. The Shore. David St. John. LCAP; MAYP

So, the year's done with! Love. Robert Browning. EnLoPo

So then, at last, let me awake this sleep. Purpose. Langdon Elwyn Mitchell. *Fr.* To a Writer of the Day. AA

So then came his word here. Beginnings. *Unknown, tr. fr. Mayan* by Munro Edmonson. *Fr.* The Popol Vuh. STP

So Then, I Feel Not Deeply! Walter Savage Landor. EnRP

So then naturally/ This Count Rainuv I speak of. Rainuv; a Romantic Ballad from the Early Basque. Margaret Widdemer. BXAP

"So then you won't fight?" Dooley Is a Traitor. James Michie. NePoEA-2; OxBTC

So there stood Matthew Arnold and this girl. The Dover Bitch. Anthony Hecht. BXAP; MAT; NBLV; NePoEA-2; NIP; NOBA; NOBL; OBAL; PPP; UnPo; VGW

"So there we were stuck." The Life of. Theodore Weiss. NYBP

So, there, when sunset made the downs look new. Charles Hamilton Sorley. *Fr.* Marlborough. WGRP

So these are the hills of home. Hazy tiers. Double. Rae Armantrout. LP

So these then are the deeds of Alligator in turn. Alligator's Struggles with the 400 sons. *Unknown, tr. fr. Mayan* by Munro Edmonson. *Fr.* The Popol Vuh. STP

So these two faced each other there. A Portrait in the Guards. Laurence Whistler. GTBS-P

So they appeared before their lord the king. *Unknown, tr. by* Arthur Waley. BoS

So they begin. With two years gone. Boris Pasternak, *tr. by* C. M. Bowra. TrJP

So they came. The Animals' Arrival. Elizabeth Jennings. PBWP

So they carried the dead man out of the fighting. Patroclus' Body Saved. Homer, *tr. fr. Greek by* E. R. Dodds. *Fr.* The Iliad, XVII. WaaP

So they in Heav'n their odes and vigils tun'd. Messiah, The ("So they in Heav'n their odes and vigils tun'd"). Milton. *Fr.* Paradise Regained, *Bk.* I, *ll.* 182–293. OBS

So They Went Deeper into the Forest. Roy Daniells. Mes

So they went, leaving a picnic-litter of talk. The Party. William Robert Rodgers. BIrV

So, they will have it! Sumter. Henry Howard Brownell. PAH

So this bird comes, and under his wing is a crutch. The Bird. Moyshe-Leyb Halpern, *tr. by* John Hollander. PeBMYV; PPP

So this is Beirut. Beirut. Sami Mahdi, *tr. by* Abdullah al-Udhari. MPAW

So this is how I did myself in. The Will. Moyshe-Leyb Halpern, *tr. by* John Hollander. PeBMYV

So this is it. At the Western Wall. Barbara F. Lefcowitz. VWA

So this is life, the ranger said. Optimism. Blanaid Salkeld. NeIP

So this is love. Squid. Michael C. Blumenthal. MAYP

So this is Monday. The Art of Holding On. Dwight Okita. BrSi

So this is the dust that passes through porcelain. The Iron Lung. Stanley Plumly. AmPA; GeTw; LCAP

So this is the way it happens. Dreaded Road. Abd al-Razzaq Abd al-Wahid, *tr. by* Diana Der Hovanessian *and* Lena Jayyusi. MAP

So Thomas Edison. Lines to Be Embroidered on a Bib; or, The Child Is Father of the Man, but Not for Quite a While. Ogden Nash. FaBoUs

So thou art come again, old black-winged night. To Night. Thomas Lovell Beddoes. Son

So through that unripe day you bore your head. Philip Larkin. NoAM

So through the darkness and the cold we flew. Wordsworth. *Fr.* The Prelude [*or,* Growth of a Poet's Mind]: Childhood and School-Time. CH; SD

So thus he sorrowed till it was day. David Jones. *Fr.* In Parenthesis: King Pellam's Launde. NoAM

So tired! so weary. Catharine of Arragon. Eloise Bibb. CBWP-4

So tired, your footsteps drag. You Rise among Truths. Abd al-Razzaq Abd al-Wahid, *tr. by* Diana Der Hovanessian *and* Lena Jayyusi. MAP

So, to begin with, ghosts of rain arise. The Dance of Dust. Louis Untermeyer. BXAP

So to Tell the Truth. Janet Dubé. BrRo

So to the mud-bed. *Unknown. Fr.* Manyo Shu. Ma

So to the sea we came; the sea, that is. Her Heards Be Thousand Fishes. Spenser. *Fr.* Colin Clout's Come Home Again. ChTr

So to the sylvan lodge. Milton. *Fr.* Paradise Lost, *Bk.* V, *ll.* 377–512. NAEL-1

So Touch Our Hearts with Loveliness. Gail Brook Burket. AH

So unwarely was never no man caught. Sir Thomas Wyatt. SiPS

So very much having passed before our eyes. George Seferis, *tr. fr. Greek by* Edmund Keeley *and* Philip Sherrard. *Fr.* Mythistorima, XXII. VMG

So vile was poor Wat, such a miscreant slave. Burns. FaBoEE

So Wags the World. Ellen Mackay Hutchinson Cortissoz. AA

So warm I may melt. Sunday Morning. Christina Jenkins. BrRo

So was it even then. So soundlessly. A Trysting. Richard Dehmel, *tr. by* Jethro Bithell. AWP

So, we are ghosts of angels. Ghazal. Philip Dow. NPGG

So we are taking off our masks, are we, and keeping. Homosexuality. Frank O'Hara. PeHV; PoA; TAP

"So we diverted the river," he said. Requiem for a River. Kim Williams. RFM

So we must part, my body, you and I. Any Soul to Any Body. Cosmo Monkhouse. NOBVV

So we must say goodbye, my darling. Goodbye. Alun Lewis. BoLoP; NAEL-2; OBWP; OxBTC

So we ride, and ride through milked heaven. Rides. Gene Derwood. LiTM

So we were together. Hilda Doolittle ("H. D."). *Fr.* Winter Love. FaBoWP

So we, who've supped the self-same cup. After the Quarrel. Paul Laurence Dunbar. AnAmPo; CDC

So We'll Go No More a-Roving. Byron. AWP; BLPL; BoLoP; ELP; EnRP; FaFP; FiP; HAP; HeIP; LiTB; NAEL-2; NOBE; NoP; OAEL-2; OxBS; OxBSP; PoE; PoEL-4; PoRA; PrIm; TTTS; WeW (We'll Go No More a-Roving.) CH; FaBV; FaPoR; OBEV; PoLF; TrGrPo

So well I love thee, as without thee I. Michael Drayton. GBL (Verses Made the Night before He Died.) NOBE

So, we're estranged again—how it goes on! Drought. David Holbrook. OxBTC

So We've Come at Last to Freud. Alice Walker. IHMS

So What. Philip Appleman. BXAP

So what if I've been circumcised. Itsik Fefer, *tr. by* John Hollander. PeBMYV

So what if Lowry got spooked by sea-birds and volcanoes crossing. Imperfect Sestina. Phyllis Webb. NOBC

So what said the others and the sun went down. Mrs. Alfred Uruguay. Wallace Stevens. TwCP

So what shall we do about this angel. Lord, Forgive a Spirit. Gerald Stern. CAPP

So what's love? I'd watch my 2 older sisters. My Sisters. Bill Kushner. UL

So, When I Swim to the Shore. Molly Peacock. MAYP

So When the Hammers of the Witnesses of Heaven Are Raised All Together. Edward Brathwaite. *Fr.* Cherries. NAs

So white I was, he would have me cry. The Dead Bride. Geoffrey Hill. TW

So White, So Soft, So Sweet. Ben Jonson. *See* Devil Is an Ass, The: Have you seen but a bright lily grow.

So wild yet candle-calm. The Grave's Cherub. Sydney Clouts. PeSA

So Wily Are the Ways of Love. Florencia del Pinar, *tr. fr. Spanish by* Kate Flores. DMH

So winter closed its fist. Rite of Spring. Seamus Heaney. OxBC

So without sediment. The Hill Burns. Nan Shepherd. PoSH

So worn out with worry. Tameko, *tr. by* Steven D. Carter. WFTW

So ye're runnin' fer Congress, mister? Le' me tell ye 'bout my son. Whisperin' Bill. Irving Bacheller. PoLF

So you are married, girl. It makes me sad. Roy McFadden. NeIP

So you beg for a story, my darling, my brown-eyed Leopold. How He Saved St. Michael's. Mary A. P. Stansbury. BLPA

So you came/ with a hyacinth, a poem and a thousand kisses. Meeting. Sam Harrison. NeIP

So you have swept me back. Eurydice. Hilda Doolittle ("H. D."). VGW

So you keep looking back. Heat and Sweat. Mongane Wally Serote. WMBCH

So you said you'd go home to work on your father's farm. To a Young Poet Who Fled. John Logan. CAPP; SM

So, you want a lot of money.—The way. The Accountings. Albert Goldbarth. GeTw

So you'll know it—what annoys me most, and right. The Monk of Montaudon, *tr. by* Paul Blackburn. Pro

So Young Ane King. Sir David Lindsay. SeCePo

So you're playing. Identities. Al Young. NPGG

So you're twenty-five, three kids, on welfare and getting fat. Fat Blues. Charmaine Crowell. AIW

So, you've come to the tropics, heard all you had to do. Down and Out. Clarence Leonard Hay. BeLS; BLPA

So you've reached your thirty-eighth birthday. My Husband's Birthday. Josephine D. Henderson Heard. CBWP-4

So zestfully canst thou sing? The Blinded Bird. Thomas Hardy. CMoP; EaLo; LiTM

Soaked in sluices. Tachibana Akemi, *tr. fr. Japanese by* Burton Watson. *Fr.* Thirty Tanka. FCEI

Soap. Martin Gardner. RHPC

Soap Bubble: 3, A. Hans Warren, *tr. fr. Dutch by* James S. Holmes. DuIn

Soap (II). Jerome Rothenberg. NNaP

Soap Suds. Louis MacNeice. FaBCIP; FaBoMo; NAEL-2; NOIV; NoP; SCV

Soap, the Oppressor. Burges Johnson. PoLF

Soaping Down for Saint Francis of Assisi: The Canticle of Sister Soap. Gibbons Ruark. MAYP

Soapship went a-rocking, A. The Voyage of Jimmy Poo. James A. Emanuel. AmNP

Soar up, my soul, unto thy rest. Seek Flowers of Heaven. Robert Southwell. TrCP

Soaring. Cal Clother. PoSH

Soaring hawk from fist that flies, The. The Lover Compareth Himself to the Painful Falconer. *Unknown.* PBBP

Sob of fall, and song of forest, come you here on haunting quest. The Trail to Lillooet. Emily Pauline Johnson. CaP

Sober. Gabriel Preil, *tr. fr. Yiddish by* Grace Schulman. PeBMYV

Sober, he thinks of her; so he gets drunk. Man and Woman. Robert Conquest. OxBTC

Sober laverock, warbling wild, The. Burns. *Fr.* The Humble Petition of Bruar Water to the Noble Duke of Athole. PBBP

Soccer at the Meadowlands. Diane Ackerman. ASP

Social Glass, The. Lizelia Augusta Jenkins Moorer. CBWP-3

Social Life, The. Lizelia Augusta Jenkins Moorer. CBWP-3

Social Note. Dorothy Parker. *Fr.* Some Beautiful Letters. AnAmPo; FaBoUs

Socialism, I Say. Ute Erb, *tr. fr. German by* Susan L. Cocalis. DMG

Society has quite forsaken all her wicked courses. Anglicized Utopia. W. S. Gilbert. OBSV

Society upon the Stanislaus, The. Bret Harte. AA; AnAmPo; BeLS; OBAL
     (Plain Language from Truthful James.) FaBoCo

Sockeye Salmon. Ronald Hambleton. CaP; OBCV

Socrates' Death. Michael Jackson. PeNZ

Socrates' Ghost Must Haunt Me Now. Delmore Schwartz. LiTM

Socrates Snooks. Fitz Hugh Ludlow. BLPA

Socratic. Hilda Doolittle ("H. D."). HoPM

Sod-Breaker, The. Arthur Stringer. CaP

Soda Water with a Boyhood Friend. August Kleinzahler. BAP

Sodden with drink. Known. Joel Dailey. UL

Sodger laddie's socht a hoose, A. Under the Greenwood Tree. "Hugh MacDiarmid", *after the Cretan.* OBVE

Sodom. Chaim Grade, *tr. fr. Yiddish by* Joseph Leftwich. TrJP

Sodom. Herman Melville. *Fr.* Clarel. AmPP

Sodom; or The Quintessence of Debauchery, *sel.* At. to Earl of Rochester.
     "To Love and Nature all their rights restore." PeHV

Sodom's Sister City. Yehuda Amichai, *tr. fr. Hebrew by* Shirley Kaufman. VWA

Soe, Mistress Anne, faire neighbour myne. Salem. Edmund Clarence Stedman. AA; PAH

Sofa, The. William Cowper. *Fr.* The Task, *Bk.* I. EnRP
     (Rural Sights and Sounds.) NOEC

Sofa, The. Medbh McGuckian. FaBCIP

Soft/ The stars are melting. Sopranosound, Memory of John. Sharon Bourke. CNA

Soft answer turneth away wrath, A. The Lips of the Wise. Bible, *O.T. Fr.* Proverbs, XV: 1-5, 7-8, 15-17. TrGrPo

Soft Answers. Robert Bagg. FF

Soft Black Eyes. Priscilla Jane Thompson. CBWP-2

Soft-boiled Egg. Russell Hoban. NTCP
     (Egg Thoughts.) RHPC

Soft crying of the dawn while cockatoos. 'Morning, Morning. Ray Mathew. PoAu-2

Soft fall the February snows, and soft. Bereavement of the Fields. Wilfred Campbell. CaP

Soft falls the night. Evening Song. Edith King. BoTP

Soft falls the sweet evening. John Clare. NOBVV

Soft grasses, a plain of sedge fresh with passing rain. Tune: Sand of Silk-washing Stream ("Soft grasses, a plain of sedge fresh with passing"). Su Tung-p'o, *tr. by* Burton Watson. CoBCP

Soft gray hands of sleep, The. Forgotten Dreams. Edward S. Silvera. PoNe

Soft greens, deep reds, really fresh colors. On the Butterflies. T'ang Yin, *tr. by* Jonathan Chaves. CoBLCP

Soft grey of the distant hills, The. Dawn. Constance Ortmayer. SaC

Soft hangs the opiate in the brain. An Opium Fantasy. Maria White Lowell. AnAmPo; InPK

Soft Landings. Howard Sergeant. OnUR

Soft, lovely, rose-like lips, conjoined with mine. Barnabe Barnes. *Fr.* Parthenophil and Parthenophe. EnLoPo

Soft new grass is creeping o'er the graves, The. By the Potomac. Thomas Bailey Aldrich. PAH; Son

Soft on the sunset sky. Ashes of Roses. Elaine Goodale Eastman. AA

Soft on the wave the oars at distance sound. Netley Abbey; Midnight. William Sotheby. NOEC

Soft rainsqualls on the swells. Oil. Gary Snyder. LCAP

Soft sand under my feet, a whiteness of sun obscuring. A Roman in Libya. Ruth Evans. CN

Soft-sandalled twilight, handmaid of the night. Winter Twilight. George Tracy Elliot. AA

Soft she was, young. Dead Girl. Anna Hajnal, *tr. by* Jascha Kessler. FOC; VWA

Soft Snow. Blake. FF; SoSe; TEP
     ("I walked abroad on a snowy day.") TEP

Soft songs, like birds, die in poison air. Apology for Apostasy? Etheridge Knight. NeAC

Soft sounds and odours brim up through the night. Guided Missiles Experimental Range. Robert Conquest. OxBC

Soft spread the southern summer night. Saint Cloud. Sir Walter Scott. OBTV

Soft tanbark, cedar-dark falls. Sideshow: Julia the Lion Woman. Wendy Rose. GOS

Soft-throated South, breathing of summer's ease. South-Wind. George Parsons Lathrop. AA

Soft Warm Breeze, A. Natan Zach, *tr. fr. Hebrew by* Warren Bargad *and* Stanley F. Chyet. IP

Soft White. Lee Harwood. EAS

Soft Wood. Robert Lowell. LiTM

Soft you; a word or two before you go. Death of Othello. Shakespeare. *Fr.* Othello, V, ii. FiP

Softball Dreams. Karen Kevorkian. ASP

Softened by time's consummate plush. Emily Dickinson. NOBA

Softening of her face which comes, The. At Only That Moment. Alan Ross. ErPo

Softer my neighbor rocks his lover through the human night. The Rockefeller Collection of Primitive Art. Denis Johnson. NAmP

Softer than silence, stiller than still air. The Snowing of the Pines. Thomas Wentworth Higginson. AA; GN

Softly!/ She is lying/ With her lips apart. Dirge. Charles Gamage Eastman. AA

Softly along the road of evening. Nod. Walter de la Mare. BoTP; MoAB; MoBrPo; OxBTC

Softly and humbly to the Gulf of Arabs. Beach Burial. Kenneth Slessor. CBAP; PoAu-2

Softly blow lightly. Donald Jeffrey Hayes. CDC

Softly croons the radiogram, loudly hoot the owls. Invasion Exercise on the Poultry Farm. Sir John Betjeman. NOBL

Softly Fades the Twilight Ray. Samuel Francis Smith. AH

Softly, in the dusk, a woman is singing to me. Piano. D. H. Lawrence. BLPL; CMoP; GrPl; GTBS-P; HAP; HeIP; InPK; InvP; LiTB; MoAB; MoBrPo; MoP; NAEL-2; NIP; NoAM; NOBE; NoP; OAEL-2; OxBSP; PoE; PPP; RB; UnPo; WeW

Softly now the day is dawning. The Signal Gun. Mary E. Tucker. CBWP-1

Softly now the light of day. Evening Contemplation. George Washington Doane. AA; AH; BLPA; BLPL; FaBoBe

Softly, O midnight Hours! Aubrey Thomas De Vere. OBEV

Softly rustled the oaks, whispered low in my ear. The Graveyard. Hayyim Nahman Bialik, *tr.* by Bertha Beinkinstadt. TrJP

Softly sailing emerald lights. Fireflies. "Fiona Macleod." *Fr.* Transcripts from Nature. FM

Softly sighs the April air. Bel m'es quan lo vens m'alena. Arnaut Daniel, *tr.* by Harriet Waters Preston. AWP

Softly, softly, through the darkness. Christmas Night. B. E. Milner. BoTP

Softly the dead stir, call, through the afternoon. A Cemetery in New Mexico. Alfred Alvarez. VWA

Softly the Evening. William Hurrell Mallock. BXAP

Softly the Night. Unknown. OBET

Softly the waters ripple. Ares. Albert Ehrenstein, *tr.* by Babette Deutsch *and* Avram Yarmolinsky. TrJP

Softly through the Mellow Starlight. Unknown. OHIP

Soggarth Aroon. John Banim. TIRV

Soho. Joseph Brodsky, *tr. fr. Russian by* Alan Myers. VWA

Sohrab and Rustum ("And the first grey of morning filled the east."), *sels.* Matthew Arnold. OBNV

Death of Sohrab, The ("He spoke; and Sohrab smiled on him, and took"). FiP

"So, on the bloody sand, Sohrab lay dead." GTBS-P

(Sohrab Dead.) NOBE

"Then Sohrab with his sword smote Rustum's helm." OBWP

Soil and Flower. Hsiang Yang, *tr. fr. Chinese by* Dominic Cheung. IFON

Soil here is superbly rich, The. In Flanders Fields. Hugo Claus, *tr.* by Theo Hermans. DuIn

Soil is quick with dust of men, The. What Far Kingdom. Arthur Stanley Bourinot. CaP

Soil now gets a rumpling soft and damp, The. The Strong Are Saying Nothing. Robert Frost. CMoP

Soil of man's escape, The. Suburbia. Maurice Martinez. PoNe

Soil was deep and the field well-sited, The. A Failure. C. Day Lewis. NOBE

Soil ysowpit into water wak, The. Winter. Gawin Douglas. SeCePo

Sois sage o ma douleur. Baudelaire. *See* Peace, Be at Peace, O Thou My Heaviness.

Soissons. Keith Douglas. NoAM

Sojourner in Mika's plains, A. Kanamura. *Fr.* Manyo Shu. Ma

Sojourner Truth. Robert Hayden. *Fr.* Stars. CNA

Sokoya, I said, looking through. There Is No Word for Goodbye. Mary TallMountain. HATNAP; STE

Sol took his nightcap off and gazed. After the Storm. Henrietta Cordelia Ray. CBWP-3

Solace. Clarissa Scott Delany. AmNP; CDC; PoBA; PoNe

Solace. Josephine D. Henderson Heard. CBWP-4

Solace in Age. Sir Richard Maitland. OxBS

Solar Creation. Charles Madge. FaBoMo; OBMV; OxBTC

Solar Eclipse. József Tornai, *tr. fr. Hungarian by* Jascha Kessler. FOC

Solar Myth. Genevieve Taggard. MoAmPo

Soldier, The, *sels.* Conrad Aiken.

Unknown Soldier, The. *Fr.* II. WaaP; WaP

Wars, The. *Fr.* I. WaaP

Soldier, The. Rupert Brooke. *Fr.* 1914, V. BrPo; FaBV; FaFP; FaPoR; FF; FPL; HeIP; LiTB; LiTM; MoBrPo; NAEL-2; NOBE; NoP; OBEV; OBWP; OxBTC; PoA; PoLF; PoRA; Son; TEP; TrGrPo; WaP

Soldier, A. Robert Frost. OFD; OPP; WaaP; WaP

Soldier, The. Gerard Manley Hopkins. WaaP

Soldier, The. Uys Krige, *tr. fr. Afrikaans by author.* PeSA

Soldier, A. Sir John Suckling. PoE; SeCV-1

Soldier, The. J. Y. Watson. BXAP

"Soldier an' Sailor Too." Kipling. MOS

Soldier and a Sailor, A. Congreve. *Fr.* Love for Love. CoMu

Soldier and a Sailor, A. John Gay. *See* Beggar's Opera, The: Fox may steal your hens, sir, A.

Soldier and statesman, rarest unison. Washington. James Russell Lowell. *Fr.* Under the Old Elm. GN, *fr.* V; OHIP, *fr.* V.

Soldier Boy for Me. Unknown. AmFP

Soldier Boy's Dream, The. Mary E. Tucker. CBWP-1

Soldier brave, sailor true. Unknown. OxNR

Soldier from the Wars Returning. A. E. Housman. LiTB; OBMV

Soldier Going to the Field, The. Sir William Davenant. NOBE; OBWP

(Souldier Going to the Field, The.) MePo

Soldier in the Park, The. Elizabeth Riddell. CBAP

Soldier is, The/ all alone. Glove Glue. Ken Belford. NeAC

Soldier Is Home, The. John Shaw Neilson. CBAP

Soldier Loves His Rifle, The. W. H. Auden. TEP

Soldier maimed and in the beggars' list, A. The Pluralist and Old Soldier. John Collier. NOEC

Soldier of the Cromwell stamp, A. Heredity. Thomas Bailey Aldrich. AA

Soldier of the Legion lay dying in Algiers, A. Bingen on the Rhine. Caroline Elizabeth Norton. BeLS; BLPA; WBLP

Soldier passed me in the freshly fallen snow, A. To a Conscript of 1940. Sir Herbert Read. LiTB; LiTM; OBWP; WaP

Soldier Poet, A. Rossiter Johnson. AA

"Soldier, Rest!" Robert Jones Burdette. OBAL

Soldier Rest! [Thy Warfare O'er]. Sir Walter Scott. *Fr.* The Lady of the Lake, I. AWP; GN; MoShBr; NOBE; PoRA; TrGrPo

(Song: "Soldier rest! thy warfare o'er.") OBNC

Soldier (T. P.). Randall Jarrell. WaP

Soldier That Has Seen Service, The. Unknown. NOEC

Soldier, There Is a War between the Mind. Wallace Stevens. *Fr.* Notes toward a Supreme Fiction. LiTM; NoAM

Soldier: Twentieth Century. Isaac Rosenberg. MMA

Soldier Walks under the Trees of the University, The. Randall Jarrell. OxBA; WaP

Soldier, Won't You Marry Me? Unknown. AmFP; OxBoLi

Soldiers. Unknown. FaBoEE; GBP

Soldiers are citizens of death's grey land. Dreamers. Siegfried Sassoon. BrPo; MoBrPo; NoAM; Son

Soldiers are marching over the pontoon bridge. Nike. Adam Wazyk, *tr.* by Isaac Komem. VWA

Soldiers Bathing. Frank Templeton Prince. GTBS-P; LiTB; LiTM; MoBrPo; NOCV; OBWP; OxBTC; PeSA; WaP

Soldiers came, brewed tea in Snoddy's field, The. After the War. Douglas Dunn. OxBC

Soldier's Death, A. Cyril Tourneur. *Fr.* The Atheist's Tragedy: Walking next day upon the fatal shore. SeCePo

Soldier's Dove. James Forsyth. WaP

Soldier's Dream, The. Thomas Campbell. BeLS; EnRP; FaPoR; GTBS; GTBS-P

Soldier's Farewell to Manchester, The. Unknown. CoMu

Soldiers' Friend, The. George Canning *and* John Hookham Frere. Par

Soldier's Grave, A. John Albee. AA

Soldier's Grave, The. Henry D. Muir. OHIP

Soldiers have to fight and swear. Unequal Distribution. Samuel Hoffenstein. TrJP

Soldiers never do die well. Champs d'Honneur. Ernest Hemingway. AiP; PoA

Soldiers of Christ, arise. The Whole Armour of God. Charles Wesley. NOCV

Soldiers on the Platform. Frances Cornford. CN

Soldier's Prayer, A. Robert Freeman. TrPWD

Soldiers Returning, The. Richard Shelton. GOYP

Soldier's Song. Goethe, *tr. fr. German by* Bayard Taylor. *Fr.* Faust. AWP

Soldier's Song. *Unknown.* WiR
Soldiers suddenly struck by love, The. In Postures That Call. Oscar
   Williams. WaP
Soldiers who wish to be a hero. Soldiers. *Unknown.* FaBoEE; GBP
Soldier's Wife, The. George Canning *and* John Hookham Frere. Par
Soldier's Wife, The. Robert Southey. OxBSP
Soldier's Wooing, The. *Unknown.* AmFP
Soldier's Wound, The. Wallace Stevens. *See* Esthétique du Mal:
   How red the rose that is the soldier's wound.
Sole heir of virtue, and of beauty both. Sir John Davies. *Fr.* Orchestra;
   or, A Poem[e] of Da[u]ncing. NAEL-1
Sole Lord of Lords and very King of Kings. Sesostris. Lloyd Mifflin.
   AA
Sole positive of night. Ne Plus Ultra. Samuel Taylor Coleridge.
   OAEL-2
Sole true something—This! In Limbo's den, The. Limbo. Samuel Taylor
   Coleridge. OAEL-2
Sole watchman of the flying stars, guard me. John Berryman. *Fr.*
   Eleven Addresses to the Lord, III. UnPo
Soledad. Robert Hayden. CAPP
Solemn and slow they move. The Sod-Breaker. Arthur Stringer. CaP
Solemn Hour. Rainer Maria Rilke, *tr. fr. German by* C. F. MacIntyre.
   TrJP
Solemn Meditation, A. William Shenstone. NOEC
Solemn Noon of Night, The. Thomas Warton, the Younger. *See*
   Pleasures of Melancholy, The
Solemn pastors. The MJQ. Joyce Carol Thomas. CNA
Solemn plain-faced child stands gazing there, A. A Portrait. Walter de
   la Mare. NoAM
Solemn receptions given by death. Two of the Festivals of Death. João
   Cabral de Melo Neto, *tr. by* W. S. Merwin. ATCBP
Solemn the hallowed temple. *Unknown, tr. by* Arthur Waley. BoS
Solemn whip-poor-will, The. The Queens. Robert Fitzgerald. NYBP
Solemnly, mournfully,/ Dealing its dole. Curfew. Longfellow. AA;
   AnAmPo; OxBA
Solid citizens, The. Undertow. Langston Hughes. LiTM
Solid houses in the mist, The. New Year's. Charles Reznikoff. VGW
Solid Mountain. George Bowering. NeAC
Solid shimmer of his prose, The. Nabokov's Death. William Matthews.
   AnAn
Soliloquies. Denis Glover. *Fr.* Arawata Bill. ATNZ
Soliloquy. Frederick E. Laight. *See* Drought.
Soliloquy. Francis Ledwidge. HoPM
Soliloquy by the Shore. Martin Scholten. GoYe
Soliloquy from "Hamlet." Shakespeare. *See* Hamlet:
   To be, or not to be, that is the question.
Soliloquy I. Richard Aldington. BrPo
Soliloquy II. Richard Aldington. BrPo; MMA
Soliloquy in a Motel. Walker Gibson. GrPl
Soliloquy in an Air-Raid. Roy Fuller. PoA
Soliloquy in the Suburbs, A. *Unknown.* NOEC
Soliloquy of a Maiden Aunt. Dollie Radford. NOBVV
Soliloquy of a Turkey. Paul Laurence Dunbar. BPo
Soliloquy of One of the Spies Left in the Wilderness, A. Gerard Manley
   Hopkins. TrCP
Soliloquy of the Spanish Cloister. Robert Browning. FaBoCo; InPK;
   LiTB; NAEL-2; NIP; NOBL; NOBVV; NoP; OAEL-2; TEP; TOF;
   TrGrPo; TW
Soliloquy on a Southern Strand. John Montague. FaBCIP
Soliloquy on Death. F. K. Fiawoo. PBA
Soliloquy on Sleep. Shakespeare. *See* King Henry IV, Pt. II: Cares of
   Majesty, The.
Soliloquy: South Africa. Arthur Nortje. WMBCH
Soliloquy to Absent Friends. Douglas G. Jones. MoCV
Solitaire. Amy Lowell. MoAmPo
Solitaire. John Updike. SoTCo
Solitariness. Sir Philip Sidney. *Fr.* Arcadia. OBSC; SiPS
Solitary. Lance Henson. HATNAP
Solitary, The. Friedrich Wilhelm Nietzsche, *tr. fr. German by* Ludwig
   Lewisohn. AWP
Solitary, The. Rainer Maria Rilke, *tr. fr. German by* C. F. MacIntyre.
   TrJP
Solitary, The. Sara Teasdale. MoAmPo
Solitary, The. Wordsworth. *Fr.* The Excursion, II. EnRP
Solitary apartment house, the last one, A. Then. Philip Levine. PPR
Solitary bird crashing into the waves wings off in joy, A. Chu Hsiao-
   tsang, *tr. by* Irving Lo. WFTU
Solitary Canto to Chloris the Disdainful, A. John Smith. NOEC
Solitary Confinement. X. J. Kennedy. NePoEA-2
Solitary crow/ upward over the summit. Ernst David, *tr. by* Beth
   Bjorklund. CoAuP

Solitary invalid in a fuchsia garden, A. The Philosopher and the Birds.
   Richard Murphy. CIP
Solitary lamp glows in the dark room, A. An Earthen Stove. Sung Wan,
   tr. fr. Chinese by William Schultz. *Fr.* Songs Composed in Prison,
   VI. WFTU
Solitary Life, A. William Drummond of Hawthornden. *See* Thrice
   Happy He.
Solitary prospector, A. Sunstrike. Douglas Livingstone. PeSA
Solitary Reaper, The. Wordsworth. AWP; BLPL; CH; ChER; EnRP;
   FaBoCh; FaPoR; FiP; GN; HAP; HeIP; InPS; LiTB; NAEL-2; NOBE;
   NoP; OAEL-2; OBEV; OBNC; PoEL-4; PoRA; PPP; SCV; SoSe;
   TEP; TrGrPo; UnPo; WeW
   (Reaper, The.) GTBS; GTBS-P
Solitary Song. *Unknown, tr. fr. Eskimo.* WTO
Solitary Travel. Louis MacNeice. OBTV
Solitary Visions of a Kaufmanoid. James Cunningham. JB
Solitary wayfarer! George Darley. *Fr.* Nepenthe. PBBP
   (Hoopoe.) OBNC
Solitary Woodsman, The. Sir Charles G. D. Roberts. CaP; OBCV
Solitude. John Clare. *See* There is a charm in solitude that cheers.
Solitude. Walter de la Mare. CMoP
Solitude. Arthur Rex Dugard Fairburn. ATNZ
Solitude. Keats. EnRP
Solitude. Archibald Lampman. BoNaP; OBCV
Solitude, A. Denise Levertov. NePoEA-2
Solitude. Harold Monro. MoBrPo; TrGrPo
Solitude. Hannah More. *Fr.* The Search after Happiness. WBLP
Solitude. Frederick Peterson. AA
Solitude. Pope. *See* Ode on [*or* to] Solitude.
Solitude. Rainer Maria Rilke, *tr. fr. German by* C. F. MacIntyre.
   TrJP
Solitude. Philip Henry Savage. AA
Solitude. Thomas Traherne. OBS
Solitude. Tomas Tranströmer, *tr. fr. Swedish by* Robert Bly. RB
Solitude. Ella Wheeler Wilcox. AnAmPo; FaFP; FPL; OHFP; PoLF;
   PWR
   (Way of the World, The.) WBLP
Solitude and Reason, in the Village. Abraham Cowley. *Fr.* Of Solitude.
   FaBoPP
Solitude is like rain. Solitude. Rainer Maria Rilke, *tr. by* C. F.
   MacIntyre. TrJP
Solitude Late at Night in the Woods. Robert Bly. VGW
Solitude of Alexander Selkirk, The. William Cowper. *See* Verses
   Supposed to Be Written by Alexander Selkirk during His Solitary
   Abode on the Island of Juan Fernandez.
Solitude that unmakes me one of men. Compensation. Robinson Jeffers.
   MoAB; MoAmPo
Solo. Marcia Southwick. PPR
Solo for Bent Spoon. Donald Finkel. NePoEA-2
Solo for Ear-Trumpet. Dame Edith Sitwell. MoAB; MoBrPo
Solo Native. Thomas Lux. LCAP
Solomon. Heine, *tr. fr. German by* Emma Lazarus. TrJP
Solomon, *sels. Unknown, tr. fr. Greek by* J. Rendel Harris. WGRP
   Inspiration. *Fr.* VI.
   To Truth. *Fr.* XXXVIII.
Solomon and Morolph, Their Last Encounter. Oscar Levertin, *tr. fr.*
   Swedish by Richard Burns *and* Göran Printz-Pahlson. VWA
Solomon and the Bees. John Godfrey Saxe. GN
Solomon and the Witch. W. B. Yeats. NoAM
Solomon Grundy. Mother Goose. NBLV; OxBoLi; OxNR; RHPC
Solomon on the Vanity of the World, *sels.* Matthew Prior.
   "Fix thy corporeal, and internal eye." FM
   "Pass we the ills, which each man feels or dreads." *Fr. bk.* III.
   NOEC; PoEL-3
Solomon to Sheba. W. B. Yeats. CMoP; ELP
Solomon! where is thy throne? It is gone in the wind. Gone in the Wind.
   James Clarence Mangan, *after the German of* Friedrich Rückert.
   ACP; OnYI; SeCePo; TIRV
Solsequium, The. Alexander Montgomerie. GoTS; NoP; OxBS
Soluble Noughts and Crosses; or, California, Here I Come. Roger
   Roughton. EAS
Solution. Emerson. OBAL
Solution, The. Brian Merriman, *tr. fr. Modern Irish by* Arland Ussher.
   Fr. The Midnight Court. BIrV
Solway wind, The. On Ellson Fell. William Landles. PoSH
Som tyme this world was so stedfast and stable. Lak of Stedfastnesse.
   Chaucer. AWP
"Sombra?" The Shade-Seller. Josephine Jacobsen. TAP
Sombre [*or* Somber] and rich, the skies. By the Statue of King Charles at
   Charing Cross. Lionel Johnson. BrPo; FaBoRV; MoBrPo; NOBE;
   OBEV; OBMV; OBNC; PoEL-5

Sombre the night is. Returning, We Hear the Larks. Isaac Rosenberg. BrPo; FaBoMo; MMA; NAEL-2; NoAM; OAEL-2; OBWP; VWA; WaaP

Some-/ times I am/ a nigger/ myself. Hometown. Sam Cornish. PPR

Some act of love's bound to rehearse. Why I Write Not of Love. Ben Jonson. OxBSP

Some after a night of sex, some hungover. Fall Practice. Dabney Stuart. SM

Some ages hence, for it must not decay. Under a Lady's Picture. Edmund Waller. EnLoPo

Some angels were standing on the ground. The Angels. Richard Eberhart. BLA

Some are & are going to my howinouse. The 12th Horse Song of Frank Mitchell (Blue). Frank Mitchell, *tr. by* Jerome Rothenberg *and* David P. McAllester. STP

Some are bewildered in the maze of schools. Pope. *Fr.* Essay on Criticism, *pt.* I. OBSV

Some Are Born. Stevie Smith. FaBoCo

Some are home-sick—some two or three. The Delinquent Travellers. Samuel Taylor Coleridge. OBTV

Some are nights others stars. Ashes. Vasco Popa, *tr. fr. Serbo-Croatian by* Anne Pennington. *Fr.* Games. RB

Some are plain lucky we ourselves among them. A Lost Soul. Jay Macpherson. NOBC

Some are teethed on a silver spoon. Saturday's Child. Countee Cullen. LiTM; NAs; OFD; PoBA; SaC

Some are waiting, some can't wait. Heather McHugh. MAYP

Some ask for envy'd pow'r; which publick hate. Sejanus ("Some ask for envy'd pow'r; which publick hate"). Juvenal, *tr. fr. Latin by* Dryden. *Fr.* Satires, X. OBVE

Some autumn leaves a painter took. The Sumach Leaves. Jones Very. NOBA

Some beauties yet no precepts can declare. Pope. *Fr.* Essay on Criticism, *pt.* I. HAP

Some Beautiful Letters, *sels.* Dorothy Parker.
  Comment. OBAL
  News Item. FaBoUs; OBAL
  Observation. FiBHP
  Résumé. DL; HeIP; NoP; OBAL; TrJP
  Social Note. FaBoUs

Some beetle trilling. Continuum. Denise Levertov. LCAP

Some bite off the others'/ Arm. He. Vasco Popa, *tr. fr. Serbo-Croatian by* Anne Pennington. *Fr.* Games. RB

Some Blaze the Precious Beauties of Their Loves. John Davies of Hereford. *Fr.* Wit's Pilgrimage. Son

Some Blesseds. John Oxenham. WGRP

Some bloodied sea-bird's hovering decay. The Lie. Howard Moss. LiTM; MoAB; NePoAm

Some Bodies Are like Flowers. Luis Cernuda, *tr. fr. Spanish by* Perry Higman. LPSS

Some books are lies frae end to end. Death and Doctor Hornbook. Burns. OxBS

Some Boys. Chuck Ortleb. GLP; PeHV

Some Boys. John Penkethman. OxBChV

Some Brave, awake in you to-night. Fancy Dress. Siegfried Sassoon. BrPo

Some broken. A State of Nature. John Hollander. AiP

Some by their friends, more by themselves thought wise. Dryden. *Fr.* Absalom and Achitophel, Pt. I. OBSV

Some can gaze and not be sick. A. E. Housman. FaBoEE; NOBVV; OBSV

Some can leave the truth unspoken. Truth. Eileen Duggan. ATNZ; PeNZ

Some candle clear burns somewhere I come by. The Candle Indoors. Gerard Manley Hopkins. LiTB; LiTM; PoEL-5

Some, childless when they left. Tsurayuki, *tr. fr. Japanese by* Burton Watson. *Fr.* Kokin Shu. FCEI

Some clouds are rainclouds. On the Pole. Uri Zvi Greenberg, *tr. by* Robert Mezey *and* Ben Zion Gold. VWA

Some Contemplations of the Poor, and Desolate State of the Church at Deerfield. John Williams. SCAP

Some Cook. John Ciardi. PDV

Some cry up Haydn, some Mozart. Free Thoughts on Several Eminent Composers. Charles Lamb. FaBoCo; OxBoLi

Some curse that traitor Judas life and limb. On Judas Iscariot. Francis Quarles. FaBoEE

Some day. What Someone Said When He Was Spanked on the Day before His Birthday. John Ciardi. RHPC

Some day, all unawares, alone in the deep forest. My Death. Carl Zuckmayer, *tr. by* E. B. Ashton. TrJP

Some day I will go to Aarhus. The Tollund Man. Seamus Heaney. BIrV; CIP; EBEV; FaBCIP; FaBoMo; IPY; NoP; TEP

Some Day, Some Day. Cristobal de Castillejo, *tr. fr. Spanish by* Longfellow. AWP

Some day, some happy day. The Reign of Peace. Mary Starck. WBLP

Some day, when trees have shed their leaves. After the Winter. Claude McKay. BANP; IDB; PoBA; PoNe

Some days ago I remarried. Marrying Again. Mei Yao-ch'en, *tr. by* Burton Watson. CoBCP

"Some Days," Dorothy Parker Said, "It's Better Than Digging Ditches." Maureen Owen. UL

Some days, I'm sorely tempted to throw out the baby. Lamentations of an Au Pair Girl. Susan Feldman. AmPA

Some Days/ Out Walking Above. De Leon Harrison. PoBA

Some days, you say, are good days. Warp and Woof. Harry Halbisch. BLRP

Some die too late and some too soon. The Lost Occasion. Whittier. BLPL; NOBA

Some Dreams They Forgot. Elizabeth Bishop. NoAM

Some dreams we have are nothing else but dreams. The Haunted House. Thomas Hood. EBEV

Some Eyes Condemn. Edward Thomas. NoAM

Some few yards from the hut the standing beeches. Poem in the Matukituki Valley. James Keir Baxter. ATNZ

Some Flowers o' the Spring. Shakespeare. *Fr.* The Winter's Tale: Here's flowers for you. ChTr

Some folk like the chaffinch. The Robin. O. M. Bent. BoTP

Some folks are drunk, yet do not know it. An English Ballad, on the Taking of Namur by the King of Great Britain, 1695. Matthew Prior. PoEL-3

Some folks as can afford. Under a Wiltshire Apple Tree. Anna Bunston De Bary. CH

Some for everyone. Snow by Morning. May Swenson. NYBP

Some Foreign Letters. Anne Sexton. MoAmPo

Some fowls there be that have so perfect sight. How the Lover Perisheth in His Delight, As the Fly in the Fire. Petrarch, *tr. fr. Italian by* Sir Thomas Wyatt. *Fr.* Sonnets to Laura. Son

Some Frenchmen. John Updike. FaBoCo; NBLV

Some Futureplans. David Avidan, *tr. fr. Hebrew by* Warren Bargad *and* Stanley F. Chyet. IP

Some gain a universal fame. A Ballade of Lawn Tennis. Franklin P. Adams. SD

Some Geese. Oliver Herford. *Fr.* Child's Natural History. FiBHP; NA

Some gold lies veiled behind each evening cloud. Hidden Essence. Henrietta Cordelia Ray. CBWP-3

Some good people, daring and subtle voices. John Berryman. *Fr.* Dream Songs. HCAP

Some Good Things to Be Said for the Iron Age. Gary Snyder. HoPM; TTTS

Some Grand River Blues. Daniel David Moses. HATNAP

Some greek statue/ pick. The Statue. Alexandra Grilikhes. RR

Some hae meat and [*or* that] canna eat. A Child's Grace. Burns. FaBoCh; FaPON; MoShBr
  (Grace at Kirkudbright.) OxBSP
  (Two Graces: "Some hae meat that canna eat.") FaBoCh

Some hand, that never meant to do thee hurt. On Finding a Small Fly Crushed in a Book. Charles Tennyson Turner. FM

Some Harvard men, stalwart and hairy. Edward Gorey. OBAL

Some in the Godspeed, the Susan C. Enough. Marianne Moore. NOBA

Some in the Town go betimes to the Downs. The Hunt. *Unknown.* CoMu

Some in their harts their mistris colours bears. William Smith. *Fr.* Chloris, XXIX. AAS

Some Indian Uses of History on a Rainy Day. A. K. Ramanujan. OxBC

Some innocent girlish kisses by a charm. Wild Rose. William Allingham. GN

Some keep the Sabbath [*or* Sunday] going to church. Emily Dickinson. MoAB; MoAmPo; SoSe; WGRP

Some kinds of trees seem ever eager. The Mast Year. Medbh McGuckian. CIP

Some Kisses from *The Kama Sutra*. Hugo Williams. BoLoP

Some Lamb. Stan Rice. NPGG

Some lasses are nice and strange. The Innocent Country-Maid's Delight; or, A Description of the Lives of the Lasses of London. *Unknown.* CoMu

Some Last Questions. W. S. Merwin. CAPP; HCAP

Some leaders lead too far ahead. Leaders. *Unknown.* WBLP

Some leagues into that land I too have fared. Animae Superstiti. Charles Spear. ATNZ

Some like cats, and some like dogs. Cats and Dogs. N. M. Bodecker.
    RAR
Some like drink. Not I. Robert Louis Stevenson. NA; NOBL
Some like them gentle and sweet. I Like Them Fluffy. Sir Alan Patrick
    Herbert. NBLV
Some Litanies. Michael Benedikt. CoAP; TwCP
Some Little Bug. Roy Atwell. PoLF
Some Love. Peter Redgrove. NPo
"Some lovers speak, when they their muses entertain." Sir Philip Sidney.
    Fr. Astrophel and Stella, VI. NAEL-1; Son
Some lucky day each November great waves awake and are drawn.
    November Surf. Robinson Jeffers. NAAL-2; OxBA
Some Magic. James Koller. PoM
Some Magnetism in the Sea. Rodney Hall. Fr. The Owner of My Face.
    CBAP
Some Me of Beauty. Carolyn M. Rodgers. CNA
Some meanings move. Haying. Jorie Graham. KS
Some memories stand out. Precious Bits of Family. Linda Belarde.
    GOS
Some Men. Dazzly Anderson. AIW
Some men break your heart in two. Experience. Dorothy Parker.
    NAAL-2
Some men marriage do commend. De Se. John Weever. FaBoEE
Some men say there is a God. God? Cristoir O'Flynn. TIRV
Some men, 'tis said, prefer a woman fat. Nathaniel Parker Willis. Fr.
    Lady Jane, The; a Humorous Novel in Rhyme. OBAL
Some modest windfalls from the Tree. Vacation Trip. Donald G.
    Babcock. NePoAm
Some moralist or mythological poet. W. B. Yeats. Fr. Nineteen
    Hundred and Nineteen, III. PoE
Some morning, while you and I are dozing. Intruder. Susan Feldman.
    AmPA
Some must employ the scythe. The Dedicated. Philip Larkin. OxBC
Some names there are of telling sound. The *Cumberland.* Herman
    Melville. PAH
Some names there are that win the best applause. William Lloyd
    Garrison. Henrietta Cordelia Ray. CBWP-3
Some ne'er advance a judgment of their own. Pope. Fr. Essay on
    Criticism, pt. II. OBSV
Some Negatives: X. at the Chateau. James Merrill. NePoEA-2
Some newness of the heart I would discern. Mid Winter. Hubert
    Witheford, tr. by Sam Karetu. PeNZ
Some Night Again. William Stafford. GOYP
Some night I wish they'd knock. Because We Are Not Taken Seriously.
    Stephen Dunn. KS
Some nights. Hello. Naomi Shihab Nye. MT
Some nights it's bound to be your best way out. Insomnia I. Howard
    Nemerov. DiPo
Some nights the moon is the curve of a comb. The Window Frames the
    Moon. Laureen Mar. BrSi
Some nights when you're asleep. Dawn Walk. Edward Hirsch. MAYP;
    NAmP
Some nights when you're off. The Avenues. David St. John. MAYP
Some nine hundred fifty circlings of my moon. Birthday. Earle Birney.
    NAs
Some nineteen German planes, they say. Reprisals. W. B. Yeats.
    OBWP
Some Notes on Courage. Susan Ludvigson. MT
Some Notes on the Wind. Gábor Görgey, tr. fr. Hungarian by Jascha
    Kessler. FOC
Some of my best friends are white boys. Friends. Ray Durem. PoBA
Some of our dead are famous, but they would not care. W. H. Auden.
    Fr. In Time of War. GLP
Some of Our Koorawatha Saints. Geoffrey Lehmann. Fr. Ross's Poems.
    CBAP
Some of the cats I know about. My Cat Mrs. Lick-a-Chin. John Ciardi.
    CRH
Some of the girls are playing jacks. Narcissa. Gwendolyn Brooks.
    GrPl; NTCP
Some of their chiefs were princes of the land. Dryden. Fr. Absalom and
    Achitophel, Pt. I. EBEV; SCV
    (Zimri: "Some of their chiefs were princes of the land".) AWP
Some of us/ these days. Resurrection. Frank Horne. OFD; PoBA
Some of Us Are Exiles from No Land. Diana O Hehir. NPGG
Some of us stayed forever, under the lough. Frank Ormsby. Fr. A
    Northern Spring. CIP
Some of Wordsworth. Walter Savage Landor. ChTr
Some officers take them away: good guard. Lear and Cordelia.
    Shakespeare. Fr. King Lear, V, iii. FiP
Some "old Robin Down" they call me. Ibby Damsel. Unknown. AmFP
Some One. Walter de la Mare. PYC

Some One Liked Me when I Was Twelve. Peter Orlovsky. GLP
Some one started the whole day wrong—was it you? Was It You?
    Stewart I. Long. WBLP
Some Opposites. Richard Wilbur. OBCA
Some Painful Butterflies Pass Through. Tess Gallagher. MAYP
Some people,/ no matter what you give them. Adam's Complaint.
    Denise Levertov. BoWoP; NNaP
Some People. Rachel Lyman Field. FaPON; NTCP; PDV; RHPC
Some people admire the work of a fool. Blake. OAEL-2
Some people are incurably gentle. Portrait of a Lady. Elizabeth
    Nannestad. ATNZ; PeNZ
Some people cannot endure. Going the Rounds; a Sort of Love Poem.
    Anthony Hecht. BoLoP
Some people grow chalky dust on their skin. For My Mother, Feeling
    Useless. Paula Rankin. MAYP
Some people hang portraits up. A Likeness. Robert Browning. CTC
Some people have names like pitchforks, some people have names.
    Nomenclature. Stephen Vincent Benét. AnAmPo
Some People I Know. Jack Prelutsky. RHPC
Some people in the sky. Song for a Scalp Dance. Unknown, tr. by
    Jerome Rothenberg. STP
Some people know how to love. Poem of Explanations. Dahlia
    Ravikovich, tr. by Chana Bloch. BoWoP
Some people, now, like mountains, where the shafts. Horizontal World.
    Thomas Saunders. CaP
Some people say the world's all a stage. The Gate at the End of Things.
    Unknown. BLPA
Some people see only you. The Couple. Ana Blandiana, tr. by author
    and William M. Murray. WPOW
Some people talk and talk. People. Charlotte Zolotow. RHPC
Some people talk in a telephone. Thoughts on Talkers. Walter Rollin
    Brooks. RHPC
Some people think I think I'm good. Oh, If They Only Knew! Edith L.
    Mapes. BLRP; WBLP
Some people understand all about machinery. Up from the Wheelbarrow.
    Ogden Nash. FaBoBe
Some Pieces. Calvin Forbes. MAYP
Some pimps wear summer hats. What? Langston Hughes. NBLV;
    OBAL
Some primal termite knocked on wood. The Termite. Ogden Nash.
    CenHV; NBLV; OBCA
Some Questions to Be Asked of a Rajah, Perhaps by the Associated Press.
    Preston Newman. FiBHP
Some 're lovely N nawu nnnn but some 're & are at my hawuz nawu wnn.
    The 13th Horse Song of Frank Mitchell (White). Frank Mitchell, tr.
    by Jerome Rothenberg, and David P. McAllester. STP
Some rhythms must remain unbroken. Grande Jetée. Mary Mackey.
    Fr. Arabesque: Five Poems for Women without Children. AIW; ER
Some Ruthless Rhymes, sels. Harry Graham. CenHV
    "Auntie, did you feel no pain." Fr. III.
    "Bob was bathing in the Bay." Fr. V.
    "Father, chancing to chastise." Fr. IV.
    "O'er the rugged mountain's brow." Fr. VI.
    "Philip, foozling with his cheek." Fr. VII.
    Stern parent, The. Fr. I. ChTr
    Tender-heartedness. Fr. II. FaFP; NA; NBLV; RHPC
    (Billy.) FaBoCo
    "There's been an accident." Fr. VIII.
Some San Francisco Poems. George Oppen. NNaP
Some say/ it was a pear. Pears. Linda Pastan. VWA
Some say cavalry and others claim. Sappho, tr. by Willis Barnstone.
    BoWoP
Some say, compar'd to Bononcini. Epigram on the Feuds between Handel
    and Bononcini. John Byrom. FaBoEE; NOBL; NOEC
Some say kissin's ae sin. Kissin'. Unknown. FiBHP
Some say love. Menaphon's Song. Robert Greene. Fr. Menaphon.
    OBSC
Some say my love has proved unfaithful. The Weeping Willow.
    Unknown. AmFP
Some say that ever 'gainst that season comes. Shakespeare. Fr. Hamlet,
    I, i. OFD; PChr
    (Bird of Dawning, The.) FaBoRV
    (Christmas.) ChTr
    (Gracious Time, The.) GN
Some say the dead are lonely where they lie. Sonnets to My Mother.
    Arthur Stanley Bourinot. CaP
Some say the deil's deid. Unknown. FaBoCh
Some say the nightmare is. Nightmares. Siv Cedering Fox. WSC
Some say the Phoenix dwells in Aethiopia. The Phoenix. Siegfried
    Sasson. ChTr
Some say the sun is a golden earring. Natalia M. Belting. PDV

Some say the world will end in fire. Fire and Ice. Robert Frost.
AmPP; CMoP; FaBoEE; FaFP; FF; FPL; HeIP; HoPM; InPK; LiTA;
LiTM; MoAB; MoAmPo; MoP; NAAL-2; NIP; NoAM; NOBA;
OxBA; PPP; PrIm; SoSe; TAP; TrGrPo; TW

Some seek for ecstasies of joy. The One Thing Needful. Max Isaac
Reich. BLRP

Some seven score Bishops late at Lambeth sat. Lambeth Lyric. Lionel
Johnson. NOBVV

Some shapes cannot be seen in a glass. Holding the Mirror Up to Nature.
Howard Nemerov. PoA

Some silent movie star. The Flicker. Lew Blockcolski. VoR

Some sings of the lilly, and daisy, and rose. The Clover. James
Whitcomb Riley. AnAmPo

Some sit and stare. The Common Grave. James Dickey. CoAP

Some Small Shells from the Windward Islands. May Swenson. FYAP

Some sort of fire leaped out of the dirty and poor and merciless city. Otto
Orban, tr. by Emery George. VWA

Some Sound Advice from Singapore. John Ciardi. GrPl

Some sowe-dronke, swaloynge mete without mesure. Of Glotons and
Dronkardes. Alexander Barclay. Fr. The Ship of Fools. OxBLMV

Some space beyond the garden close. The Hollyhocks. Craven
Langstroth Betts. AA

Some starry head. not. Condition of Desire. Harry Mathews. EOEF

Some steerage. In a Dream Ship's Hold. Suzanne Bernhardt. VWA

Some Stories of the Beauty Wapiti. Ebbe Borregaard. NeAP

Some, striving knowledge to refine. A Thought on Human Life.
Unknown. OxBSP

Some Syrian rainmaker. Assumption. Padraic Fallon. BIrV; NOIV

Some talk of Alexander, and some of Hercules. The British Grenadiers.
Unknown. OxBoLi

Some talk of Ganymede th' Idalian boy. Richard Barnfield. Fr. Sonnets,
XII. PeHV

Some talk of trade as low and mean. Trade. Egbert Martin. PVCV

Some tell us 'tis a burnin' shame. Sambo's Right to Be Kilt. Charles
Graham Halpine. AA

Some Terms. Robert Pinsky. Fr. Essay on Psychiatrists, II. HCAP

Some that have deeper digged love's mine than [or myne then] I. Love's
Alchemy [or Alchemie]. John Donne. MePo; NAEL-1; NoP;
OAEL-1; PoE; SeCP

Some that reporte great Alexanders life. Thomas Watson. Fr.
Hecatompathia; or, Passionate Century of Love. AAS

Some, the great Adepts, found it. The Adepts. Lawrence Durrell. Fr.
Eight Aspects of Melissa. ErPo

Some—the ones with fish names—grow so north. Wildflower. Stanley
Plumly. AnAn; LCAP; NAmP

Some there are as fair to see to. Her Commendation. Francis Davison.
OBSC
(Madrigal.) EIL

Some there are who say that the fairest thing seen. Sappho, tr. by
Richmond Lattimore. WPOW

Some they will talk of bold Robin Hood. Robin Hood and the Bishop of
Hereford. Unknown. ESPB

Some thing is lost in me. Man Thinking about Woman. Don L. Lee.
CNA; MoP

Some Things. Amanda Eason. DT

Some Things. Gerhard Rühm, tr. fr. German by Beth Bjorklund.
CoAuP

Some things are truly lost. Think of a sun-hat. The Mind-Reader.
Richard Wilbur. NAAL-2; NoAM

Some Things Don't Make Any Sense at All. Judith Viorst. RHPC

Some things I do not profess. The Abduction. Stanley Kunitz. BLA;
CAPP; SV

Some things persist by suffering change, others. Homage to the
Philosopher. Babette Deutsch. ImOP; TrJP

Some Things That Easter Brings. Elsie Parrish. RAR

Some things that fly there be. Emily Dickinson. OxBA

Some things will never change although. Far Trek. June Brady. RHPC

Some think/ reft and light. Dilection. Ernst Jandl, tr. by Beth Bjorklund.
CoAuP

Some think that in the Christian scheme. Mutual Subjection. Christopher
Smart. Fr. Hymns for the Amusement of Children, XXVI. NOCV

Some thirty inches from my nose. W. H. Auden. FaBoEE

Some thousands in England are starving. An Appeal by Unemployed Ex-
Service Men. Unknown. OBET

Some three, or five, or seven, and thirty years. Lady-Probationer. W. E.
Henley. Fr. In Hospital, IX. BrPo

Some time ago, some time. Grampaw's Smoking Pipe. Hsiang Yang, tr.
by Dominic Cheung. IFON

Some Time at Eve. Elizabeth Clark Hardy. PoLF

Some time in the dark hours. Snowfall. W. S. Merwin. NNaP

Some time now past in the autumnal tide. Contemplations. Anne
Bradstreet. AmPP; NAAL-1; PoEL-3; SCAP; WPE

Some time there ben a lyttel boy. The Lyttel Boy. Eugene Field. AA

Some Time We'll Understand. Maxwell N. Cornelius. BLRP; WBLP

Some Tips on Watching Birds. Deatt Hudson. NYBP

Some to extinguish, others to prevent. The Dangers of Sexual Excess.
John Armstrong. Fr. The Art of Preserving Health. FaBoUs

Some Trees. John Ashbery. HCAP; NAAL-2; SM

Some tried to scratch the spot off the wall. The Spot Remained on the
Wall. David Avidan, tr. by Bernhard Frank. MHeP

Some tyme I fled the fyre that me brent. Sir Thomas Wyatt. AAS

Some Uses for Poetry. Eve Merriam. PCP

Some Verses to Snaix. Unknown. NA

Some Verses upon the Burning of Our House, July 10th, 1666. Anne
Bradstreet. NOBA; TAP
(Here Follow[e]s Some Verses upon the Burning of Our House.)
AIP; BoWoP; NAAL-1; NoP; SCAP
(Upon the Burning of Our House, July 10th, 1666.) AnAmPo;
OxBA; WPE

Some vex their souls with jealous pain. On One Who Died Discovering
Her Kindness. John Sheffield. OBEV

Some Walks with You. John Hollander. NoAM

Some were engirthed with a canopy. Era. Jaki Seroke. WMBCH

Some were for fires—not coal. Plague Sermon. William Heyen. KS

Some were for setting up a king. Samuel Butler. Fr. Hudibras, III, 2.
EBEV

Some whirled scythes through the thick oats. The Farm Hands. Dilys
Bennett Laing. SaC

Some who are uncertain compel me. Art Lange. UL

Some Who Do Not Go to Church. Unknown. WBLP

Some will tell. The Old Man Said. Carroll Arnett. STE

Some winters, taking leave. A Storm in April. Richard Wilbur. LCAP;
NoP

Some women marry houses. Housewife. Anne Sexton. NMM

Some women save their sanity with needles. Mr. McGregor's Garden.
Medbh McGuckian. CIP; FaBCIP

Some women think. Otis. Lorenzo Thomas. UL

Some words clink. Feelings about Words. Mary O'Neill. RHPC

Some Words Which, Up until Now, Had Remained Mysteriously
Forbidding for Me. Paul Eluard, tr. fr. French by Michael Benedikt.
POS

Some years ago, ere time and taste. The Vicar. Winthrop Mackworth
Praed. Fr. Every-Day Characters. EnRP; OBEV; OBNC; PoEL-4

Some years ago you heard me sing. Sarah Byng [Who Could Not Read
and Was Tossed into a Thorny Hedge by a Bull.] Hilaire Belloc.
CenHV; GoJo; NoAM

Some years back I worked a strip mine. Lester Tells of Wanda and the
Big Snow. Paul Zimmer. MOWH

Some years of late, in 'eighty-eight, as I do well remember-a. Sir Francis
Drake; or, Eighty-eight. Unknown. GBP
("Some years of late, in eighty-eight.") FaBoCh

Some young and saucy dandelions. The Dandelions. Unknown. BoTP

Somebodies walked the woods. The North. Barry McKinnon. NOBC

Somebody. Tennyson. FaBoEE; NOBL

Somebody. Unknown. OxBS

Somebody,/ Cut his hair. Young Poet. Myron O'Higgins. PoBA; PoNe

Somebody almost walked off wid alla my stuff. Ntozake Shange.
WPOW

Somebody being a nobody. Somebody. Tennyson. FaBoEE; NOBL
(Somebody Being a Nobody.) OxBSP

Somebody Call. Carolyn M. Rodgers. JB

Somebody did a golden deed. Somebody. Unknown. FaFP

Somebody has given my. Proust's Madeleine. Kenneth Rexroth.
NoAM

Somebody has got to tell me something real. Runaway. Rhoda Coghill.
NeIP

Somebody is hanging. A Wreath for the Suicide Heart. Anthony
McNeill. PVCV

Somebody loses whenever somebody wins. Crapshooters. Carl
Sandburg. VGW

Somebody loves you deep and true. Somebody ("Somebody loves you
deep and true"). RHPC

Somebody said that it couldn't be done. It Couldn't Be Done. Edgar
Albert Guest. BLPA; FaBoBe; FaFP; FPL; WBLP

Somebody Said That It Couldn't Be Done. Unknown. FiBHP

Somebody said wrecks. The Drowned. Norman MacCaig. OxBC

Somebody ("Somebody did a golden deed") Unknown. FaFP

Somebody ("Somebody loves you deep and true") Unknown. RHPC

Somebody ("Somebody's tall and handsome") Unknown. AS

Somebody threw away a piano. Street Music. Barbara Angell. AiP

Somebody told me I wouldn't know how to choose. Song: Paper. Keith Waldrop. MAT

Somebody up in the rocky pasture. The Ant Village. Marion Edey *and* Dorothy Grider. FaPON

Somebody, when I was young, stole my toy horse. The Toy Horse. Valentin Iremonger. NOIV

Somebody who should have been born. The Abortion. Anne Sexton. IHMS; MAT; NMM; SM; VGW

Somebody's Darling. Marie La Coste. BLPA; UnPo; WBLP

Somebody's Gone. Charles Henri Ford. EAS

Somebody's in there. Saint Pumpkin. Nancy Willard. LCAP

Somebody's knockin' at th' door. The Collier's Wife. D. H. Lawrence. OxBTC

Somebody's Mother. Mary Dow Brine. BeLS; BLPA; FaFP; WBLP

Somebody's tall and handsome. Somebody ("Somebody's tall and handsome"). *Unknown*. AS

Someday I'd like to climb the Puig. Balearic Idyll. Frederick Packard. FiBHP

Someday I'll announce on the radio. Women's Broadcast. Marie Luise Kaschnitz, *tr.* by Susan L. Cocalis. DMG

Somedays now/ I can squash a cockroach. Wendy G Rickert. NMM

Somehow/ I had come to the desert. Abraham in Egypt. Howard Schwartz. VWA

Somehow,/ I feel there are more people than I expect. Ishikawa Takuboku, *tr. fr. Japanese by* Hiroaki Sato. *Fr.* Forty-seven Tanka in Three Lines. FCEI

Somehow come to the calm of this present, a Sunday in summer. To Lighten My House. Alastair Reid. NePoEA

Somehow I can't help looking. Natsume Seibi, *tr. fr. Japanese by* Hiroaki Sato. *Fr.* Twenty-seven Hokku. FCEI

Somehow it should have been. Masks. Elizabeth Fenton. NMM

Somehow it sounds. Winter Bell. Shotetsu, *tr.* by Steven D. Carter. WFTW

Somehow my heart settles on the hill's rim. Teika, *tr. fr. Japanese by* Hiroaki Sato. *Fr.* Eighty-four Tanka. FCEI

Somehow the tutorial takes an unplanned direction. How Come the Truck-Loads? Judith Rodriguez. FaBoWP

Somehow We Survive. Dennis Brutus. WMBCH

Someone [*or* Some One]. Walter de la Mare. FaPON; MoBrPo; PDV; RHPC

Someone/ clinks/ a ring of keys. With a Ring. Veronica Porumbacu, *tr. by the author and* Kathleen Weaver. OV

Someone approaches to say his life is ruined. The Dream. David Ignatow. CoAP; MAT; NNaP; VWA

Someone Asked the Publisher. J. B. Morton. *Fr.* When We Were Very Silly. FaBoPa

Someone be a rose tree. The Rose Thieves. Vasco Popa, *tr. fr. Serbo-Croatian by* Anne Pennington. *Fr.* Games. RB

Someone Burning Firewood. Shin Dong-jip, *tr. fr. Korean by* Koh Chang-soo. ACKP

Someone came knocking. Someone [*or* Some One]. Walter de la Mare. FaPON; MoBrPo; PDV; RHPC

Someone comes knocking, he wants lodging. A Stranger. Sandor Csoori, *tr. by* Jascha Kessler. FOC

Someone Could Certainly Be Found. Anne Hébert, *tr. fr. French by* F. R. Scott. CaP

Someone doesn't like rubber bands. A Brickbat for Krazy Kat. K. Schippers, *tr.* by Peter Nijmeijer. DuIn

Someone drove a two-by-four. Child's Grave, Hale County, Alabama. Jim Simmerman. BLA

Someone else/ looked at the sky. Izumi Shikibu, *tr. by* Willis Barnstone. BoWoP

Someone else, I see. Man Missing. Charles Brasch. ATNZ

Someone fits a flute to his lips, and. Deception. Alfred Corn. PoA

Someone had been walking in and out. The Origin of Baseball. Kenneth Patchen. ASP

Someone has built a dirigible in my parlor. Zeppelin. Andrew Glaze. WeW

Someone has cut the grass. Someone has cut your your tall. Evening Prayer. Jorie Graham. NAmP

Someone has left a light on at the boathouse. Fishing on a Lake at Night. Robert Bly. LCAP

Someone has lived here where twin chimneys. The Grapevine. Zoe Kincaid Brockman. GoYe

Someone has opened and undone. Beyond the Tapestries. Norma Farber. GoYe

Someone has remembered to dry the dishes. Red Lilies. Barbara Guest. PoM

Someone has shut the shining eyes, straightened and folded. Beside the Bed. Charlotte Mew. MoAB; MoBrPo; OxBSP; TrGrPo; WPE

Someone hides from someone. Hide-and-Seek. Vasco Popa, *tr. fr. Serbo-Croatian by* Anne Pennington. *Fr.* Games. RB

Someone, I tell you,/ will remember us. Sappho, *tr.* by Willis Barnstone. BoWoP

Someone in a prayer-shawl is walking over your ramparts. Vilna. Moishe Kulbak, *tr.* by Joachim Neugroschel. VWA

Someone in a *tales* is walking your rooftops. Vilna. Moishe Kulbak. PeBMYV, *tr.* by Nathan Halper; VWA, *tr.* by Joachim Neugroschel

Someone in the next apartment. Room. Ruth Stone. BoWoP

Someone is breathing in the room. Waking. Hugh Maxton. BIrV; CIP

Someone is dead. Anne Sexton. WPE

Someone is glad that I, Theodorus, am dead. Simonides, *tr.* by Peter Jay. OBD

Someone is locking out the stars and the yellow flowers. Old Man in a Moon Loft. T. Glynne Davies, *tr.* by the author. OBWVE

Someone is upset. Evildoer. Gabriele Wohmann, *tr.* by Margaret Woodruff. DMG

Someone is walking through the snow. Hearing Steps. Charles Simic. HCAP

Someone Knocks. Peter Everwine. NNaP

Someone knocks at my window. That Very Night. Avigdor Hame'iri, *tr.* by Bernhard Frank. MHeP

Someone like No One Else. Forugh Farrokhzad, *tr. fr. Farsi by* Deirdre Lashgari. WPOW

Someone must be. Narihira, *tr. fr. Japanese by* Burton Watson. *Fr.* Kokin Shu. FCEI

Someone new has come to stay. Everett Anderson's Friend. Lucille Clifton. ILY

Someone next door is moving things about. Thin Partition. Gordon Challis. ATNZ

Someone painted pictures on my. Jack Frost. Helen Bayley Davis. RAR

Someone passes. Murasaki Shikibu, *tr.* by Kenneth Rexroth and Ikuko Atsomi. BoWoP

Someone passes on. Chikako, *tr.* by Steven D. Carter. WFTW

Someone runs about. Bullfight. Miroslav Holub, *tr.* by Ian *and* Jarmila Milner. RB

Someone said dead men make islands in the sea. Fishermen, Drowned beyond the West Coast. Vivian Smith. CBAP

Someone, somewhere—there's. Issa, *tr.* by Geoffrey Bownas *and* Anthony Thwaite. PeBJV

Someone sows someone. The Seed. Vasco Popa, *tr. fr. Serbo-Croatian by* Anne Pennington. *Fr.* Games. RB

Someone walks my father's way. On the Way. Mordechai Husid, *tr.* by Seymour Mayne *and* Rivka Augenfeld. VWA

Someone went playing a flute. Flute-Players. Michael Hoyland. NPo

Someone who well knew how she'd toss her chin. Loose Woman. X. J. Kennedy. WeW

Someone with skill juggles. Juggler. Lucien Stryk. CAPP

Someone would like to have you for her child. *Unknown*. TTTS

Someone's Face. John Ciardi. RAR

Someone's Knocking. Benjamin Péret, *tr. fr. French by* Michael Benedikt. POS

Someone's youngest daughter. The Vietnamese Girl in the Madhouse. David Fisher. NPGG

Someplace Else. Marge Piercy. NeAC

Somersaults. Jack Prelutsky. RAR

Somersby, Lincolnshire; after Leaving the Refectory. Tennyson. *See* In Memoriam A. H. H.: Unwatch'd [*or* unwatched], the garden bough shall sway.

Somerset Dam for Supper, The. John Holmes. NYBP

Somerset Maugham said a professional was someone who could do his best. Churchyard. Robert Hass. NAmP; NPGG

Somerset Wassail. *Unknown*. *See* Wassail! wassail! all round [*or* over] the town.

Somethin' Else and/ *Kind of Blue*. Cannon Arrested. Michael S. Harper. CNA

Something. Robert Creeley. NaP

Something/ holds up two or three leaves. In One Place. Robert Wallace. Psk

Something about Me. *Unknown*. RAR

Something about the closing evenings of winter. Midwinter Warm. Gillian Stone. NPo

Something about the idea. Abandonment of Autos. Bruce Dawe. CBAP

Something always remains a mystery. A Classical Idyll. Avraham Huss, *tr.* by Mark Elliott Shapiro. VWA

Something befell. At the Bottom of the Well. Louis Untermeyer. GoJo

Something broke the dream. John Gill. NeAC

Something broken something. Nightbreak. Adrienne Rich. IHMS

Something far off buried deep and free. The Flash. James Dickey. LCAP

Something for Jesus. Sylvanus D. Phelps. *See* Saviour, Thy Dying Love.

Something for My Russian Friends. Edmund Wilson. OBAL

Something for Supper. Carroll Arnett. VoR

Something forgotten for twenty years: though my fathers. A Map of the Western Part of the County of Essex in England. Denise Levertov. CoAP; NAAL-2

Something gnaws inside my head. Kirilov on a Skyscraper. Randall Jarrell. CAPP

Something goes wrong with my synthetic brain. The Case for the Miners. Siegfried Sassoon. SaC

Something hangs in back of me. The Wings. Denise Levertov. CAPP

Something happened the other day that never happened before. Shovelling Iron Ore. *Unknown.* AS, *with music;* GBP

Something has ceased to come along with me. Death of a Son. Jon Silkin. FF; GTBS-P; MoP; NePoEA; OxBTC; VWA

Something Has Fallen. Philip Levine. LCAP

Something has happened to my name. Catalogue Army. Naomi Shihab Nye. MAYP

Something Has Swept over Him. Elizabeth Smither. ATNZ

Something I saw or thought I saw. On the Heart's Beginning to Cloud the Mind. Robert Frost. CMoP

Something in the climate of a hammer. Because Going Nowhere Takes a Long Time. Kenneth Patchen. NaP

Something inspires the only cow of late. The Cow in Apple Time. Robert Frost. MoAB; MoAmPo; OxBSP; PoLF

Something is happening in the garden. The woman leans. The Sun. T. R. Hummer. NAmP

Something is taking place. Robert Duncan. *Fr.* Rites of Passage, II. NoAM

Something Is There. Lilian Moore. RHPC; WSC

Something Left to Say. Katherine Soniat. MOWH

Something like coasts clover-colored. Friederike Mayröcker, *tr. by* Beth Bjorklund. CoAuP

Something more than the lilt of the strain. Poetry. Lucius Harwood Foote. AA

Something occurred after the operation. Surgical Ward: Men. Robert Graves. FaBoMo

Something of a sauna for working women. The Public Wash House. Alan Bold. NPo

Something of glass about her, of dead water. Circe. Louis MacNeice. OBMV

Something of how the homing bee at dusk. Southern Gothic. Donald Justice. NIP

Something old and tyrannical burning there. A Coal Fire in Winter. Thomas McGrath. NU

Something one day occurr'd about a bill. George Crabbe. *Fr.* Tales of the Hall. Par

Something Precise. Bartolo Cattafi, *tr. fr. Italian by* Lawrence R. Smith. NItP

Something startles me where I thought I was safest. This Compost. Walt Whitman. AWP; LiTA; MoAmPo; NAAL-1

Something straight growing on the ground. Bamboo. Hagiwara Sakutaro, *tr. by* Hiroaki Sato. FCEI

Something that was not there before. The Beast. Brian Patten. AmMo

Something there is that doesn't love a wall. Mending Wall. Robert Frost. AmFN; AmPP; AnAmPo; CMoP; FaBoPV; FaBV; FaFP; FPL; HAP; HeIP; HoPM; InPS; LiTA; LiTM; MoAB; MoAmPo; MoP; NAAL-2; NoAM; NOBA; NoP; OHFP; OxBA; PoE; PrIm; SCV; SoSe; TAP; VGW; ViBoPo; WeW

Something this foggy day, a something which. Christina Rossetti. *Fr.* Later Life, XVII. NAEL-2

Something to Look Forward To. Marge Piercy. ER

Something Told the Wild Geese. Rachel Field. NTCP; OBCA; OnUR; PDV; RHPC

Something under the bones is calling. The Voices. Janine Pommy-Vega. UL

Something was whispered. Accusation. Utahania. WTO

Something went crabwise. The Presence. Maxine W. Kumin. RFM; WPE

Something Whispered in the *Shakuhachi.* Garrett Kaoru Hongo. InPS

Something you said—I found it written down. A Postcard to Send to Sumer. William Bronk. VGW

Sometime. May Riley Smith. BLPA

Sometime ago there was a rich old codger. Chaucer. *See* Canterbury Tales, The: Miller's [*or* Milleres] Tale, The.

Sometime during eternity. Lawrence Ferlinghetti. *Fr.* A Coney Island of the Mind. CAPP; NoAM

Sometime I sigh, sometime I sing. Sir Thomas Wyatt. SiPS

Sometime I sit and wonder long. Dis Time No Stan' Like befo' Time. James Martinez. PVCV

Sometime in the night I stir, rain. Loft. Michael Dransfield. CBAP

Sometime, Somewhere. Ophelia Guyon Browning. *See* Unanswered yet the prayer your lips have pleaded.

Sometime the Cow Kick Your Head. Andrew J. Grossman. SoTCo

Sometime the world seems sad and lonely. Lonely World. Mrs. Henry Linden. CBWP-4

Sometime, when all life's lessons have been learned. Sometime. May Riley Smith. BLPA

Sometimes. Hermann Hesse, *tr. fr. German by* Robert Bly. NU; WSC

Sometimes. Maggie Pogue Johnson. CBWP-4

Sometimes. Greg Kuzma. Psk

Sometimes. Jack Prelutsky. RAR

Sometimes/ I cool out. Spacin. Ronda Davis. JB

Sometimes/ I help my dad. Automobile Mechanics. Dorothy Walter Baruch. FaPON

Sometimes/ only in the reflection of. Alfred Gesswein, *tr. by* Beth Bjorklund. CoAuP

Sometimes/ the poems. Sharon Scott. JB

Sometimes/ you feel/ like/ a/ bottle. No Deposit. Earle Thompson. HATNAP

Sometimes a huge wave of thought. Francisco Arriví, *tr. fr. Spanish by* Julio Marzán. *Fr.* Song for a Day. InW

Sometimes a huge wave of thought. Song for a Day. Francisco Arriví, *tr. by* Julio Marzán. InW

Sometimes a lantern moves along the night. The Lantern out of Doors. Gerard Manley Hopkins. CMoP; LiTB; TrCP

Sometimes a light surprises. Joy and Peace in Believing. William Cowper. NOCV

Sometimes a rain comes. A Rain of Rites. Jayanta Mahapatra. PoA

Sometimes a right white mountain. Sky Pictures. Mary Effie Lee Newsome. CDC

Sometimes an effluence rises. Scarcely. Alfonso Reyes, *tr. by* Samuel Beckett. MexPo

Sometimes at night when the heart stumbles and stops. Caesura. Kenneth Mackenzie. CBAP

Sometimes, at Thirty-Six. Roger Weingarten. NAmP

Sometimes before great events a person will try. Things That Happen. William Stafford. NNaP

Sometimes Believing. Jan G. Elburg, *tr. fr. Dutch by* André Lefevere. DuIn

Sometimes, childishly watching a beetle, thrush or trout. Clarence Mangan. Thomas Kinsella. CIP

Sometimes goldfinches one by one will drop. Keats. *Fr.* I Stood Tiptoe [upon a Little Hill]. PBBP (Goldfinches.) GN

Sometimes he roars among the leafy trees. The Wind. W. H. Davies. SeCePo

Sometimes he was cool like an eternal. Lester Young. Ted Joans. AmNP

Sometimes Heaven Is a Mean Machine. William Pitt Root. MAYP

Sometimes I. Song of the Thunders. *Unknown, tr. by* Frances Densmore. OBVE

Sometimes I am a Tapster new. The Jolly Trades-Men. *Unknown.* CoMu

Sometimes I am an unseen. Cat. Alan Brownjohn. CRH

Sometimes I call X nostalgia. Little Ode for X. Maura Stanton. MAYP

Sometimes I catch a glimpse of it. The Presence. Dana Naone. CDW

Sometimes I feel like I will never stop. To Satch. Samuel Allen. AmNP; PoBA; PoNe; SD; SoSe; TTY (American Gothic.) IDB

Sometimes I feel so passionate a yearning. As by Fire. Ella Wheeler Wilcox. AnAmPo

Sometimes I get the feeling that I have been here before. Reincarnation. Mae Jackson. PoBA

Sometimes I Go to Camarillo and Sit in the Lounge. K. Curtis Lyle. PoBA

Sometimes I have supposed seals. Soft Wood. Robert Lowell. LiTM

Sometimes I have to cross the road. Bobby Blue. John Drinkwater. FaPON

Sometimes, I know not why, nor how, nor whence. Inspirations. William James Dawson. WGRP

Sometimes I know the way. Absence. Charlotte Mew. MoAB; MoBrPo

Sometimes I like to go. Memorandum. Rudy Bee Graham. PoNe

Sometimes I remember the poor relations. The Poor Relations. Iain Crichton Smith. NPo

Sometimes I see churches. Winter Walking. Alfred Wellington Purdy. NoAM

Sometimes I see reflections on bits of glass on sidewalks.   Wonder Woman.   Genny Lim.   BrSi

Sometimes I see them.   Galway Kinnell.   *Fr.* Ruins under the Stars.   RFM

Sometimes I see them coming.   Benediction.   Myra Sklarew.   VWA

Sometimes I seem to see gliding the green.   Nilotic Elegy.   George Sutherland Fraser.   WaP

Sometimes I stare into an awning of spirit.   Sometimes I Go to Camarillo and Sit in the Lounge.   K. Curtis Lyle.   PoBA

Sometimes I Think of Maryland.   Jodi Braxton.   CNA

Sometimes I think of those whose lives touch mine.   I Think of Those.   Paul Henderson.   ATNZ

Sometimes I think that nothing.   Small-scale Reflections on a Great House.   A. K. Ramanujan.   OxBC

Sometimes I visit the city.   Marco Martos, *tr. fr. Spanish by* David Tipton.   *Fr.* Casa Nuestra.   Per

Sometimes I walk in the shadow.   Walking with God.   *Unknown.*   BLRP

Sometimes I walk where the deep water dips.   Frederick Goddard Tuckerman.   *Fr.* Sonnets, III, x.   NOBA

Sometimes I Want to Go Up.   Rachel Korn, *tr. fr. Yiddish by* Ruth Whitman.   VWA

Sometimes I watch the moon at night.   The Moon and a Cloud.   W. H. Davies.   RB

Sometimes I wish that I his pillow were.   Richard Barnfield.   *Fr.* Sonnets, VIII.   PeHV

Sometimes I wish that I might do.   Patience.   Geoffrey Anketell Studdert-Kennedy.   TrPWD

Sometimes I write with the stub of a pencil.   The Poet Confides.   Herbert T. J. Coleman.   CaP

Sometimes I'd like to be a stone.   Devastation.   Peter Russell.   NPo

Sometimes—I'm sorry—but sometimes.   Yawning.   Eleanor Farjeon.   RHPC

Sometimes in bonnet that she.   Heart-summoned.   Jesse Stuart.   GoYe

Sometimes, in morning sunlights by the river.   Resurrection.   Sidney Lanier.   PoEL-5

Sometimes in some chance.   Friederike Mayröcker, *tr. by* Beth Bjorklund.   CoAuP

Sometimes in summer months, the gestate earth.   Summer Idyll.   George Barker.   FaBoMo

Sometimes, in the Evening.   Cees Buddingh', *tr. fr. Dutch by* Anthony Akerman.   DuIn

Sometimes in the hills.   Burma Hills.   Bernard Gutteridge.   WaP

Sometimes, in the middle of the lesson.   Music Lessons.   Mary Oliver.   CAPP

Sometimes in the over-heated house, but not for long.   Fame.   Charlotte Mew.   BrRo; InPK; PBWP

Sometimes in the winter mountains.   Buffalo Trace.   Robert Morgan.   GeTw

Sometimes in this summer of hydrangeas and blowzy.   A Dislike for Flowers.   Michael Cadnum.   KS

Sometimes in weariness I stop.   Years.   Jon Anderson.   AmPA

Sometimes it is like a beast.   A Trucker.   Thom Gunn.   PCP

Sometimes it seems.   The Children.   Susan MacDonald.   IHMS

Sometimes it seems as though some puppet player.   The Puppet Player.   Angelina Weld Grimké.   CDC

Sometimes it's only the square light.   When We Wake.   Gary Soto.   NAmP

Sometimes I've seen.   A Little Bird's Song.   Margaret Rose.   BoTP

Sometimes Love Poem, A.   George Leong.   BrSi

Sometimes Music Rises.   Wayne Dodd.   KS

Sometimes my daughter looks at me with an.   The Sign of Saturn.   Sharon Olds.   InPS

Sometimes, old pal, in the morning.   Is It Really Worth the While?   *Unknown.*   BLPA

Sometimes, riding in a car, in Wisconsin.   Three Kinds of Pleasures.   Robert Bly.   AiP

Sometimes Running.   John Ciardi.   RR

Sometimes she is a child within mine arms.   Heart's Haven.   Dante Gabriel Rossetti.   *Fr.* The House of Life, XXII.   Son

Sometimes she is like sherry, like the sun through a vessel of glass.   Polarities.   Kenneth Slessor.   CBAP

Sometimes the best move is not to.   Pac-Man.   Philip Dacey.   NAmP

Sometimes the celestial syrup slows.   Terminations.   A. R. Ammons.   AnAn

Sometimes the frugal matron seems in haste.   William King.   *Fr.* The Art of Making Puddings.   FaBoUs

Sometimes the light falls here too as at Florence.   The Old Age of Michelangelo.   Frank Templeton Prince.   PeSA

Sometimes the night echoes to prideless wailing.   John Berryman.   NoAM

Sometimes the night is not enough. I rise remembering.   The Biplane.   Steve Orlen.   GOYP

Sometimes the pencil, in cool airy halls.   James Thomson.   *Fr.* The Castle of Indolence.   PoEL-3, *fr.* I.

Sometimes the sea lays.   Dragging in Winter.   David McElroy.   AmPA

Sometimes the weather goes on for days.   The Mystery of Emily Dickinson.   Marvin Bell.   CAPP; LCAP; NIP

Sometimes there is a man.   John Clare.   Mark Halperin.   SM

Sometimes they cross an avenue at dusk.   Survivors.   Frank Ormsby.   CIP

Sometimes they smear the evening on the air.   Bat Angels.   Larry Levis.   AmPA

Sometimes this quiet settles in like a stone.   A Letter from a Friend.   Carolyn Maisel.   IHMS

Sometimes to think about age.   Age.   Rae Desmond Jones.   CBAP

Sometimes two people together.   Knockout.   John Skoyles.   NAmP

Sometimes up out of this land.   Bifocal.   William Stafford.   RB

Sometimes waking, sometimes sleeping.   Nestus Gurley.   Randall Jarrell.   HeIP; TwCP

Sometimes walking late at night.   Butcher Shop.   Charles Simic.   AmPA; InPK; LCAP; NNaP

Sometimes want makes touch too much.   Warmth.   Barton Sutter.   GOYP

Sometimes we get down to loneliness.   Refusals.   Jon Anderson.   MAYP

Sometimes we get up.   Resurrection.   Marie Luise Kaschnitz, *tr. by* Michael Hamburger.   WPOW

Sometimes we sit in Phil's.   My Care.   Peter Fallon.   CIP

Sometimes, what is most real shimmers, a dark.   To Speak of Chile.   Margaret Gibson.   MAYP

Sometimes, when a bird cries out.   Sometimes.   Hermann Hesse, *tr. by* Robert Bly.   WSC

Sometimes, when after spirited debate.   Change.   William Dean Howells.   AA

Sometimes when alone.   Outcast.   "Æ."   OxBSP

Sometimes when clouds float.   At the Edge of Town.   William Stafford.   NNaP

Sometimes when everything has become still.   Reflection.   Michael Guttenbrunner, *tr. by* Beth Bjorklund.   CoAuP

Sometimes when I have dropped to sleep.   The Room beneath the Rafters.   Ella Wheeler Wilcox.   PWR

Sometimes when I hold.   The School Globe.   James Reaney.   NOBC

Sometimes when I see the bare arms of trees in the evening.   The Bare Arms of Trees.   John Tagliabue.   Psk

Sometimes when I'm lonely.   Hope.   Langston Hughes.   ILY; OBAL; OBCA

Sometimes, when I'm tired of your dark beauty.   Natural Ice Cream.   Jack Myers.   NAmP

Sometimes when my eyes are red.   My Sad Self.   Allen Ginsberg.   UnPo

Sometimes, when Nature falls asleep.   Night Mists.   William Hamilton Hayne.   AA

Sometimes When Night.   Victoria Mary Sackville-West.   WPE

Sometimes when the boy was troubled he would go.   The Cave.   Glenn Ward Dresbach.   RFM

Sometimes, when the world.   The Faithful.   Michael Waters.   KS

Sometimes, when wearied eawt at neet.   A Warkin' Mon's Reflections.   William Baron.   PF

Sometimes when you are gone.   Suite from Catullus.   Vincent McHugh.   ErPo

Sometimes when you couldn't sleep it off.   Cows.   Stanley Plumly.   AnAn

Sometimes when you watch the fire.   Long Distance.   William Stafford.   SO; WSC

Sometimes, when you're away from home.   Away from Home.   *Unknown.*   PWR

Sometimes, when you're called a bastard.   When Something Happens.   James A. Randall, Jr.   BPo

Sometimes while I sleep.   1925.   Edwin Honig.   *Fr.* To Restore a Dead Child, I.   NoAM

Sometimes with One I Love.   Walt Whitman.   GBL; OxBSP

Sometimes you almost get a punch in.   Shadowboxing.   James Tate.   ASP

Sometimes you come on a whole.   Driving through Coal Country in Pennsylvania.   Jonathan Holden.   GOYP

Sometimes you feel/ alone within your ribs.   What Is Needed.   Marcos Rodríguez Frese, *tr. by* Julio Marzán.   InW

Sometimes you get tired of the dark, the humming.   Coming to the Surface.   Jack Myers.   NAmP

Sometimes you hear, fifth-hand.   Poetry of Departures.   Philip Larkin.   CMoP; FF; NePoEA; OxBC; PoE; PrIm; TwCP

Sometimes you take up the trap.   The Ruses: A Coyote Tale.   Diane di Prima.   *Fr.* Loba.   ER

Somewhat.   Yang Mu, *tr. fr. Chinese by* Dominic Cheung.   IFON

Somewhat apart from the village, and nearer the Basin of Minas. Evangeline in Acadie. Longfellow. *Fr.* Evangeline. AA
Somewhat back from the village street. The Old Clock on the Stairs. Longfellow. PWR; WBLP
Somewhat in the Kingdom of His Majesty, No. 2. Yang Tse, *tr. fr. Chinese by* Dominic Cheung. IFON
Somewhat Minimal. Roland Jooris, *tr. fr. Dutch by* James S. Holmes. DuIn
Somewhere. Robert Creeley. NoAM
Somewhere. Walter de la Mare. FaPON
Somewhere. Ezekiel Mphahlele. WMBCH
Somewhere/ a niche. Wish. Lance Henson. CDW
Somewhere a forest, every. These Leaves. William Stafford. NNaP
Somewhere a white horse gallops with its mane. Elsewhere. Derek Walcott. BAP
Somewhere afield here something lies. Shelley's Skylark. Thomas Hardy. FaBV; PBBP
Somewhere along the road. The Meeting. Gerald Costanzo. MAYP
Somewhere beneath that piano's superb sleek black. The Piano. D. H. Lawrence. WeW
Somewhere cities burn. April 68. Sam Cornish. CNA
Somewhere Else. Paula Rankin. MAYP
Somewhere Far Away. H. Leivick, *tr. fr. Yiddish by* Benjamin *and* Barbara Harshav. AYP
Somewhere he failed me, somewhere he slipt away. The Lost Shipmate. Theodore Goodridge Roberts. CaP
Somewhere his number must have been betrayed. The Common Man. A. J. M. Smith. NOBC
Somewhere I have travelled, gladly beyond. E. E. Cummings. BoLoP; InPS; LiTA; LiTM; MoAB; MoAmPo; NAAL-2; NoP; SOTW; TrGrPo; TwCP; UnAS; VGW
Somewhere I read how, long since. Parable of Two Talents. Kendrick Smithyman. ATNZ
Somewhere, I think in Dakota. A Sound from the Earth. William Stafford. NNaP; RFM
Somewhere in a hungry muzzle rooted. Design for Mediæval Tapestry. Abraham Moses Klein. CaP
Somewhere in Chelsea, early summer. Relating to Robinson. Weldon Kees. NaP
Somewhere, in deeps. Sport. Hamlin Garland. AnAmPo
Somewhere—in desolate wind-swept space. Identity. Thomas Bailey Aldrich. AA
"Somewhere in France," upon a brown hillside. The First Three. Clinton Scollard. PAH
Somewhere in his body a blood-clot is moving. Little Death. Gwyn Thomas, *tr. by* Joseph P. Clancy. OBWVE
Somewhere in India, upon a time. An Oriental Apologue. James Russell Lowell. PoEL-5
Somewhere in the House. Hanny Michaelis, *tr. fr. Dutch by* Marjolijn de Jager. DuIn
Somewhere in the next block. Early Sunday Morning. John Stone. MT
Somewhere in the night. At Midnight. Ted Kooser. GOYP
Somewhere in the night a mollusc is growing. Flesh of Terror. René Daumal, *tr. by* Michael Benedikt. POS
Somewhere in the world. Shekhina. Karl Wolfskehl, *tr. by* Erna Baber Rosenfeld. VWA
Somewhere inside me. Coming Back Home. Ray A. Young Bear. CDW
Somewhere Is Such a Kingdom. John Crowe Ransom. CMoP; LiTA
Somewhere it is about to snow. Weather Forecast. Linda Pastan. AnAn
Somewhere near here a new-loosed creek sloughs down. A Walk in March. Tim Reynolds. MAT
Somewhere near Phu Bai. Yusef Komunyakaa. MAYP
Somewhere near the end of a snowshoe trail. A Baby Ten Months Old Looks at the Public Domain. William Stafford. NYBP
Somewhere now she takes off the dress I am putting. Palindrome. Lisel Mueller. IHMS; WeW
Somewhere on his travels the strange child. Santa Claus. Howard Nemerov. HAP
Somewhere on the Coast of Maine. Robert Long. NAmP
Somewhere on the outskirts. New World in the Morning. Norman German. TSL
Somewhere or Other. Christina Rossetti. NOBE; NOBVV
Somewhere out on the blue seas sailing. When My Ship Comes In. Robert J. Burdett. FaFP
Somewhere outside your window. A Sense of Coolness. Quincy Troupe. PoBA
Somewhere she waits to make you win, your soul in her firm, white hands. The Woman Who Understands. Everard Jack Appleton. PoLF

Somewhere she was certain, but the sensation. Special Pleading. Charles Bernstein. UL
Somewhere someone is traveling furiously toward you. At North Farm. John Ashbery. HCAP; PoE
Somewhere, sometime, in an April twilight. Willa Cather. WPE
Somewhere, somewhen I've seen. The Parrots. W. W. Gibson. CH
Somewhere the Equation Breaks Down. Daniel Berrigan. NYBP
Somewhere there is Grace, Lord. Latter Day Psalms. Cliff Ashby. NOCV
Somewhere there must be music, and great swags of flowers. 1939 Somewhere in England. Virginia Graham. CN
Somewhere there waiteth in this world of ours. Destiny. Sir Edwin Arnold. PoLF
Somewhere we should sit down and rest. Just a While. Frantisek Gottlieb. VWA, *tr. by* Ewald Osers
Somewhere within me I've an id. Say Id Isn't So. Richard Armour. SoTCo
Somewhere you are always going home. The Sums. Lauris Edmond. ATNZ; FaBoWP
Somewhere You Exist. Manfred Winkler, *tr. fr. Hebrew by* Mary Zilzer. VWA
Somewhere you meet each other—fleeting. Love in the City. Mascha Kaléko, *tr. by* Susan L. Cocalis. DMG
Somewhile before the dawn I rose, and stept. A Memory. Rupert Brooke. BrPo
Somnambulist. John Russell Hervey. ATNZ
Somnia. Alfred Gong, *tr. fr. German by* Beth Bjorklund. CoAuP
Somnolent through landscapes and by trees. The Permanent Tourists. Patricia K. Page. LiTM; NOBC
Son, A. Lilian Bowes-Lyon. CN
Son, The. John Donne. *Fr.* The Litanie. NOCV
Son. James A. Emanuel. PoNe
Son, The. George Herbert. *Fr.* The Temple. Son
Son, A. Kipling. *Fr.* Epitaphs of the War, 1914–1918. FaBoEE
Son, The. R. S. Thomas. NAs
Son, The. Ridgely Torrence. InvP
"Son,"/ my father used to say. Father and I in the Woods. David McCord. SO
Son and Father. Cecil Day Lewis. EaLo
Son and Surf. Julia Hurd Strong. GoYe
"Son, come tell me 'bout the meetin." The Old and the New. Clara Ann Thompson. CBWP-2
Son Cotton! these light idle brooks. Izaac Walton, Cotton, and William Oldways. Walter Savage Landor. PoEL-4
Son David. *Unknown.* OxBB; OxBS
Son-Dayes. Henry Vaughan. SeCP
Son, my son! Lament of a Man for His Son. *Unknown, tr. by* Mary Austin. AWP
(Lament of a Young Man for His Son.) DL
Son of a Gambolier, The. *Unknown.* AS
Son of a mystic race, he came. Heinrich Heine. Ludwig Lewisohn. TrJP
Son of a Scots manse though you were. Curse. Robert Greacen. TW
Son of Enops, Thestor next he smote, The. Homer, *tr. fr. Greek by* William Cowper. *Fr.* The Iliad, XVI. OBVE
Son of God Goes Forth to War, The. Who Follows in His Train? Reginald Heber. WGRP
Son, of great fortune have I none. Christine to Her Son. Christine de Pisan, *tr. by* Barbara Howes. BoWoP
Son of Lamech let a black raven, The. Caedmon, *tr. fr. Anglo-Saxon. Fr.* Genesis. PBBP
Son of my mother. Tale of the Double Helix. György Somlyó, *tr. by* Daniel Hoffman. MHuP
Son of the King of Moy, The. *Unknown, tr. fr. Old Irish by* Myles Dillon. AnIL
Son of the righteous one, he who thunders on the ground. Praises of the King Tshaka. *Unknown.* PeSA
Son of the Romanovs, A. Louis Simpson. OxBC
Son of the Thundercloud. Song of the Thunder. *Unknown.* PeSA
Son replied, the, "For all your good advice." To His Father on Praising the Honest Life of the Peasant. Parvin E'tesami, *tr. by* Deirdre Lashgari. WPOW
"Son," said my mother. The Ballad of the Harp-Weaver. Edna St. Vincent Millay. WSC
Son who came forth on a winter's morning. Song for Te Hauapu. Noho-mai-te-Rangi, *tr. by* Margaret Orbell. PeNZ
Son with a Future, A. Charles Reznikoff. *Fr.* Five Groups of Verse. DiL
Son'ahchi. The Boy and the Deer. Andrew Peynetsa, *Zuni Oral Tradition, tr. by* Dennis Tedlock. STP
Sonata. John Fuller. DiPo

Sonatina in Yellow. Donald Justice. CAPP; DiL; LCAP

Sonet: "Fra bank [*or* banc] to bank [*or* banc], fra wood to wood I rin." Mark Alexander Boyd. *See* Fra Bank to Bank, Fra Wood to Wood I Rin.

Sonet to Sleepe. William Drummond of Hawthornden. *See* Sleep, Silence' Child.

Sonet Written in Prayse of the Browne Beautie, A. George Gascoigne. AAS

Sonetto XXXV: To Guido Orlando. Guido Cavalcanti, *tr. fr. Italian by* Ezra Pound. CTC

Song: "A ho! A ho!/ Love's horn doth blow." Thomas Lovell Beddoes. *Fr.* The Bride's Tragedy. ChER

Song, A: "Absent from thee, I languish still." John Wilmot, 2nd Earl of Rochester. BoLoP; ELP; EnLoPo; GBL; MePo; OBS; SeCePo; SeCV-2

(Return.) NOBE; OBEV

Song: "Adieu, farewell earth's blisse." Thomas Nashe. *See* Summer's Last Will and Testament: Adieu, Farewell, Earth's Bliss[e].

Song: "Ae fond kiss, and then we sever." Burns. *See* Ae Fond Kiss.

Song: "Afternoon cooking in the fall sun." Robert Hass. AmPA

Song: "Again rejoicing Nature sees." Burns. BoNaP

Song: "Age is when to a man." Samuel Beckett. NoAM

Song: "Ah Cloris! That I could now sit." Sir Charles Sedley. *See* Mulberry Garden, The: Child and Maiden.

Song: "Ah! County Guy, the hour is nigh." Sir Walter Scott. *See* Quentin Durward: Serenade.

Song: "Ah fading joy, how quickly art thou past!" Dryden. *See* Indian Emperor, The: Ah, Fading Joy.

Song: "Ah false Amyntas, can that hour." Aphra Behn. *Fr.* The Dutch Lover. WPE

Song: "Ah, vale of woe, of gloom and darkness moulded." Rachel Morpurgo, *tr. by* Nina Davis Salaman. TrJP

Song: "All, all of a piece throughout." Dryden. *See* Secular Masque, The: All, All of a Piece Throughout.

Song: "All joy to mortals, joy and mirth." Aphra Behn. *Fr.* Emperor of the Moon. WPE

Song: "And can the physician make sick men well?" *Unknown*. *See* Robin Goodfellow: And Can the Physician.

Song: "April, April,/ Laugh thy girlish laughter." Sir William Watson. OBEV; TrGrPo

(April.) BoTP; FaBV

(Song to April.) GN

Song: "Are they shadowes that we see?" Samuel Daniel. *See* Tethy's Festival: Are They Shadows [That We See]?

Song, A: "As Chloris [*or* Cloris] full of harmless thoughts." Earl of Rochester. ErPo; TEP

Song: "As I walked out one evening." W. H. Auden. *See* As I Walked Out One Evening.

Song: "Ask [*or* Aske] me no more where Jove bestows." Thomas Carew. *See* Ask Me No More Where Jove Bestows.

Song: "At the center of the earth." *Unknown*, *tr. by* Jerome Rothenberg. STP

Song: "Balkis was in her marble town." Lascelles Abercrombie. *Fr.* Judith. MoBrPo

Song: "Because I know deep in my own heart." Pauli Murray. BlSi

Song: "Before the barn-door crowing." John Gay. *Fr.* The Beggar's Opera, II, i. ErPo; OxBSP; PBBP; PoEL-3

Song: "Before we shall again behold." Sir William Davenant. *See* Before we shall again behold.

Song: "Bells of Sunday rang us down, The." John Ciardi. WaP

Song: "Bird in my bower, A." Francis Howard Williams. AA

Song: "Blow, blow, thou winter wind." Shakespeare. *See* As You Like It: Blow, Blow, Thou Winter Wind.

Song: "Boat is chafing at our long delay, The." John Davidson. OBEV

Song: "Bone-aged is my white horse." Brenda Chamberlain. NeIP

(Talysarn.) OBWVE

Song: "By the wayside." Edmond Jabès, *tr. fr. French by* Rosemarie Waldrop. *Fr.* Fall and Exile, IV. RHTwFP

Song, A: "Calm was the even, and clear [*or* cleer] was the sky." Dryden. *Fr.* An Evening's Love, IV, i. FF; SeCV-2

Song: "Can life be a blessing." Dryden. *See* Troilus and Cressida: Can Life Be a Blessing.

Song: "Can love be controlled by advice?" John Gay. *Fr.* The Beggar's Opera, I, viii. OxBSP

Song: "Care-charming sleep, thou easer of all woes." John Fletcher. *See* Tragedy of Valentinian, The: Care-charming Sleep [Thou Easer of All Woes].

Song: "Child, is thy father dead?" Ebenezer Elliott. PF; SaC

Song: "Chloris, forbear a while." Henry Bold. GBL

Song: "Chloris, it is not thy disdaine." Sidney Godolphin. *See* Chloris, it is not thy disdaine.

Song, A: "Chloris, when I to thee present." *Unknown*. OBS

Song: "Choose now among this fairest number." William Browne. GBL

Song: "Christ keep the Hollow Land." William Morris. *See* Hollow Land, The: Christ keep the Hollow Land.

Song: "Closes and courts and lanes." John Davidson. BrPo

Song: "Come away, come away, death." Shakespeare. *See* Twelfth Night: Come Away, Come Away, Death.

Song, A: "Come, cheer up, my lads, like a true British band." *Unknown*. PAH

Song: "Come down, O maid, from yonder mountain height." Tennyson. *See* Princess, The: Come Down, O Maid, [from Yonder Mountain Height].

Song: "Come into the garden, Maud." Tennyson. *See* Maud: Come into the garden, Maud.

Song: "Come, live with me and be my love." C. Day Lewis. *See* Two Songs: Come, live with me and be my love.

Song: "Come on, come on! and where you go." Ben Jonson. *Fr.* Pleasure Reconciled to Virtue. NAEL-1

Song: "Come unto these yellow sands." Shakespeare. *See* Tempest, The: Come unto these yellow sands.

Song: "Curse upon that faithless maid, A." Aphra Behn. *Fr.* Emperor of the Moon. WPE

Song: "Daughter of Egypt, veil thine eyes!" Bayard Taylor. AA

Song: "Day will rise and the sun from eastward." George Campbell Hay. OxBS

Song: "Deftly, admiral, cast your fly." W. H. Auden. GTBS-P

Song: "Delicious beauty that doth lie." John Marston. EIL

Song: "Desire for a woman took hold of me in the night." *Unknown*. LLLT

Song: "Dew on the bamboos." *Unknown*, *tr. by* E. Powys Mathers. LLLT

Song: "Did you see me walking by the Buick Repairs?" Frank O'Hara. TTTS

Song: "Distil not poison in mine ears." John Hall. OxBSP

Song: "Do I venture away too far." Keith Douglas. NePoEA

Song: "Do not fear to put thy feet." John Fletcher. *See* Faithful Shepherdess, The: River-God's Song, The ("Do not fear to put thy feet").

Song: "Donought would have everything." Ebenezer Elliott. NOBVV

Song: "Don't sing of crimson flowers or wings of the dragonfly." Nakano Shigeharu, *tr. by* Geoffrey Bownas *and* Anthony Thwaite. PeBJV

Song: "Don't Tell Me What You Dreamt Last Night." Franklin P. Adams. FiBHP

Song: "Dorinda's sparkling wit, and eyes." Charles Sackville. OBEV; OBS; SeCePo; SeCV-2

(On Dorinda.) OxBSP

(On the Countess of Dorchester.) APAS

Song: "Dressed up in my melancholy." M. Carl Holman. AmNP; PoNe

Song, The: "Drinke and be merry, merry, merry boyes." Thomas Morton. SCAP

Song: "Enchantment of my past existence." V. A. Zhukovsky, *tr. by* Alan Myers. AAA

Song: Endimion Porter and Olivia. Sir William Davenant. *See* Before we shall again behold.

Song: "Engine screams and Murphy, isolate, The." Thomas Kinsella. FaBCIP

Song: "Eye of looking back were well, The." Ben Jonson. *Fr.* Pleasure Reconciled to Virtue. NAEL-1

Song: "Fair Iris I love, and hourly I die." Dryden. *Fr.* Amphitryon. AWP

(Mercury's Song [to Phaedra].) OxBSP; PoEL-3; SeCV-2

Song, A: "Fair, sweet and young, receive a prize." Dryden. OBS

Song, A: "False though she be to me and love." Congreve. *See* False Though She Be.

Song, A: "Fame let thy trumpet sound." Joel Barlow. AmPP

Song, A: "Farewell, adieu, that court-like life!" John Pickering (or Pikerying). *See* Horestes: Haltersick's Song.

Song: Farewell before Dawn. Nakano Shigeharu, *tr. fr. Japanese by* Geoffrey Bownas *and* Anthony Thwaite. PeBJV

Song: "Farewell ungrateful[l] traytor [*or* traitor]." Dryden. *See* Spanish Friar [*or* Fryar], The: Farewell, Ungrateful Traitor.

Song: "Fear[e] no more the heat[e] o' the sun." Shakespeare. *See* Cymbeline: Fear No More the Heat o' the Sun.

Song: "Feathers of the willow, The." Richard Watson Dixon. BoNaP; CH; FaBoCh; GTBS-P; NOBE; OBNC

(Willow.) OBEV

Song: Fie My Fum. Allen Ginsberg. ErPo

Song: "Fine young folly, though you were." William Habington. *See*
    Queen of Aragon, The: Fine Young Folly.
Song: "Fire, fire." Henry Bold. GBL
Song: "First month of his absence, The." Alun Lewis. LiTM; NAEL-2;
    OBWP; WaaP
Song: "Fish in the unruffled lakes." W. H. Auden. BoLoP; CMoP;
    MoAB; MoBrPo; MoP
Song: "Flowers that in thy garden rise, The." Sir Henry Newbolt.
    FaBoTw
Song: "Fond affection, hence, and leave me!" Robert Parry. *Fr.* The
    Mirror of Knighthood. EIL
Song: "Fond men! whose wretched care the life soon ending." Phineas
    Fletcher. *Fr.* Brittain's Ida. EIL
Song: "Fool, take up thy shaft again." Thomas Stanley. EnLoPo
Song: "For A' That and A' That. Burns. *See* For A' That and A' That
    ("Is there, for honest poverty").
Song: "For her gait, if she be walking." William Browne. OBEV
Song, A: "For mercy, courage, kindness, mirth." Laurence Binyon.
    BoTP; MoBrPo
Song: "For the tender beech and the sapling oak." Thomas Love Peacock.
    See Maid Marian: For the Slender Beech and the Sapling Oak.
Song: "Four arms, two necks, one wreathing." *Unknown.* EIL
Song: "Fresh from the dewy hill, the merry year." Blake. EnRP
 . The Witch.
Song: "Full fathom [*or* fadom] five thy father lies." Shakespeare. *See*
    Tempest, The: Full fathom [*or* fadom] five thy father lies.
Song: "Give Isaac the nymph who no beauty can boast." Sheridan. *Fr.*
    The Duenna. NOIV
Song, A: "Glories, pleasures, pomps, delights, and ease." John Ford.
    Fr. The Broken Heart, V, iii. OBS
Song: "Go and catch a falling star." John Donne. AWP; EBEV; EIL;
    ELP; FaBV; FaFP; FPL; HAP; HeIP; InPK; InPS; JCP; LiTB;
    NAEL-1; NAWM-1; NBLV; NIP; NOBE; NoP; OBEV; PoE; SoSe;
    TrGrPo
    ("Goe and Catche a falling Starre.") HoPM; MeLP; MePo; PoEL-2;
    SeCP; SeCV-1
Song: Go and Catch a Falling Star. John Donne. PoE
Song: "Go [*or* Goe] lovely rose." Edmund Waller. *See* Go [*or* Goe,]
    Lovely Rose.
Song: "Goe, and catche a falling starre." John Donne. NBLV
Song: "Goe lovely rose." Edmund Waller. *See* Go lovely Rose.
Song: Good Counsel to a Young Maid. Thomas Carew. *See* When you
    the sunburnt pilgrim see.
Song, A: "Good neighbour, why do you look awry?" *Unknown.* TW
Song: "Great friend and servant of the good." Ben Jonson. *Fr.* Pleasure
    Reconciled to Virtue. NAEL-1
Song: Green Grow the Rashes. Burns. *See* Green Grow the Rashes, O.
Song: "Gross sun squats above, The." Dom Moraes. NePoEA-2
Song: "Hang sorrow, cast away care." *Unknown.* OBS
Song: "Hark, hark!/ Bow-wow./ The watch-dogs bark." Shakespeare.
    Fr. The Tempest. SoSe
Song: "Hark! hark! the lark at heaven's gate sings." Shakespeare. *See*
    Cymbeline: Hark! Hark! the Lark.
Song, A: "Hark! 'tis freedom that calls, come, patriots, awake!"
    Unknown. PAH
Song: "Hast thou seen the down i' th' air." Sir John Suckling. *See* Hast
    thou seen the down i' th' air.
Song: "He that will court a wench that is coy." *Unknown.* ErPo
Song: "He who offends a woman." Machiavelli, *tr. by* J. R. Hale. PFI
Song: "Heap cassia, sandal-buds and stripes." Robert Browning. *Fr.*
    Paracelsus. OBEV
Song: "Hear me, ye smokeless skies and grass-green earth." Charles
    Mair. *Fr.* The Last Bison. NOBC
Song: "Heare ye Ladies that despise." John Fletcher. *See* Tragedy of
    Valentinian, The: The Hear, Ye Ladies [That Despise].
Song: "Hears not my Phillis how the birds." Sir Charles Sedley.
    EnLoPo; SeCV-2
Song: "Help me now." Emmett Jarrett. NeAC
Song: "Hence all you vaine delights." John Fletcher. *See* Nice Valor,
    The: Melancholy.
Song: "Here's to the maiden [*or* maid] of bashful fifteen." Sheridan. *See*
    School for Scandal, The: Drinking Song.
Song: "Heron is harsh with despair." Brenda Chamberlain. NeIP
Song: "Hold back thy hours, dark night, till we have done." Francis
    Beaumont *and* Fletcher. *See* Maid's Tragedy, The
Song: "House is a cote for doves, The." Miguel Hernández, *tr. by* Perry
    Higman. LPSS
Song: How Can I Care? Robert Graves. GBL
Song: "How can that tree but withered be." *Unknown.* EIL
Song: "How many times do I love thee, dear?" Thomas Lovell Beddoes.
    Fr. Torrismond, Sc. iii. LiTB; NAEL-2; PoEL-4; TrGrPo

(How Many Times?.) ELP
(How Many Times Do I Love Thee, Dear?.) EnRP
Song: "How pleasant it is that always." Florence Smith. BLPA
Song: "How should I your true love know." Shakespeare. *See* Hamlet:
    How Should I Your True Love Know.
Song: "How sweet I roam'd from field to field." Blake. CH; ChER;
    ChTr; EnLoPo; EnRP; FL; LiTB; NAEL-2; NOEC; NoP; OAEL-2;
    OBNC; PoEL-4; SeCePo; TrGrPo
(Prince of Love, The.) NOBE
Song: Hunting Song. *Unknown, tr. fr.* Chippewa Indian by Jerome
    Rothenberg. STP
Song: Hunting Song ("There's my war club"). *Unknown, tr. fr.* Chippewa
    Indian by Jerome Rothenberg. STP
Song: Hunting Song ("This time I'll show up"). *Unknown, tr. fr.*
    Chippewa Indian by Jerome Rothenberg. STP
Song: "I am weaving a song of waters." Gwendolyn B. Bennett. BlSi
Song: "I can't be talkin' of love, dear." Esther Mathews. FaFP
Song: "I feed a flame within, which so torments me." Dryden. *Fr.*
    Secret Love; or, The Maiden Queen. AWP
(Hidden Flame.) OBEV
Song: "I had a bicycle called "Splendid." Arthur Waley. Mes
Song: I Had a Dove and the Sweet Dove Died. Keats. CH; FaPON; FM;
    PBBP
Song: "I had a dove, and the sweet dove died." Keats. *Fr.* I Had a
    Dove [and the Sweet Dove Died]. FaPON; PBBP
Song: "I hid my love when young while I. John Clare. *See* I hid my
    love. . .
Song: "I keep running around." *Unknown, tr. by* Jerome Rothenberg.
    STP
Song: "I know that any weed can tell." Louis Ginsberg. TrJP
Song: "I long for nothing more." György Petri, *tr. by* William Jay Smith.
    MHuP
Song: "I made another garden, yea." Arthur O'Shaughnessy.
    OBEV
Song: "I peeled bits of straw and I got switches too." John Clare.
    NAEL-2
(Bits of Straw.) WiR
Song: "I placed my dream in a boat." Cecília Meireles, *tr. by* Eloah F.
    Giacomelli. WPOW
Song: "I prithee send me back my heart." *At. to* Henry Hughes Suckling
    and also to Sir John Suckling. JCP
Song: "I promised Sylvia to be true." John Wilmot, 2nd Earl of
    Rochester. SeCePo
Song: "I walk'd in the lonesome evening." William Allingham. EnLoPo
Song: I Want a Witness. Michael S. S. Harper. CAPP
Song: "I want my dance." Yanette Delétang-Tardif, *tr. by* Martha Collins.
    DMF
Song: "I was so chill, and overworn, and sad." Anna Wickham.
    MoBrPo
Song: "I watered my horse at the Long Wall caves." Ch'en Lin, *tr. by*
    Burton Watson. CoBCP
Song: "I went my Sunday mornings round." John Clare. NOBVV
Song: "I went to her who loveth me no more." Arthur William Edgar
    O'Shaughnessy. OBNC
Song: "I wish I was where I would be." John Clare. NOBVV
Song: "I would not feign a single sigh." John Clare. GBL
Song, A: "I wrote a song shining as glass." P. Mustapää, *tr. by* Aili
    Jarvenpa. SOP
Song: "I'd much rather sit there in the sun." Ruth Krauss. RHPC; SO
Song: "If any wench Venus's girdle wear." John Gay. *Fr.* The Beggar's
    Opera, I, i. PoEL-3
Song: "If everywhere in the street." Denis Glover. *Fr.* Sings Harry, II.
    PeNZ
(Sings Harry to an Old Guitar.) ATNZ
Song: "If I freely may discover." Ben Jonson. *Fr.* The Poetaster, II, ii.
    EIL
Song: "If the scorn of your bright eyne." Shakespeare. *Fr.* As You Like
    It, IV, iii. CTC
Song: "If thou art sleeping, maiden." Gil Vicente, *tr. by* Longfellow.
    AWP; CTC
Song: "If words were nothing but signs." Tristan Tzara, *tr. by* Michael
    Benedikt. POS
Song: "If you love God, take your mirror between your hands and look."
    Mahmud Djellaladin Pasha, *tr. by* E. Powys Mathers. ErPo
Song: "If you're anxious for to shine in the high esthetic line as a man of
    culture." W. S. Gilbert. *Fr.* Patience: If You're Anxious for to
    Shine in the High Aesthetic Line. NBLV
Song: "I'm about to go shopping." James Schuyler. TTTS
Song: "I'm living in a cave." *Unknown, tr. by* Jerome Rothenberg. STP
Song: "In a maiden-time professed." Thomas Middleton. *Fr.* The Witch.
    OxBSP

Song: "In crystal towers and turrets richly set." Geffrey Whitney. *See* In crystal towers and turrets richly set.

Song: "In Ireland, in Ireland." Frederick Morgan. BLA

Song: "In mine own monument I lie." Richard Lovelace. OxBSP

Song, A: "In the air there are no coral-/ Reefs or ambergris." Duncan Campbell Scott

Song: "In the middle of the sea." *Unknown, tr.* by Jerome Rothenberg. STP

Song: In the Name of a Lover, to His Mistress; Who Said, She Hated Him for His Grey Hairs, Which He Had at Thirty, A. William Wycherley. SeCV-2

Song: "It Autumnne was, and on our hemispheare." William Drummond of Hawthornden. OBS

Song: "It follows now you are to prove." Ben Jonson. *Fr.* Pleasure Reconciled to Virtue. NAEL-1

Song: "It is all one in Venus' wanton school." John Lyly. SeCePo

Song, A: "It is not beauty I demand." George Darley. *See* It Is Not Beauty I Demand.

Song: "It was a lover and his lass." Shakespeare. *See* As You Like It: It Was a Lover and His Lass.

Song: "It was upon a Lammas night." Burns. *See* Rigs o' Barley, The.

Song: "Jog on, jog on, the footpath way." Shakespeare. *See* Winter's Tale, The: Jog On, jog on, the footpath way.

Song (2): "Keep the dream alive and growing always." Edwin Rolfe. TrJP

Song: "Kind lovers, love on." John Crowne. *Fr.* Calisto. OxBSP

Song: "Know then, my brethren, heaven is clear." *Unknown. Fr.* The Song of Anarchus. FaBoCo

Song: "Know what I'll promise you?" *Unknown, tr.* by Jerome Rothenberg. STP

Song: "Ladies, though to your conquering eyes." Sir George Etherege. *Fr.* The Comical Revenge, V, iii. OBS; OxBSP

Song: "Lady, you are with beauties so enriched." Francis Davison. EIL

Song: Landscape, The. William Shenstone. SeCePo

Song: "Lark now leaves his wat'ry [*or* watery] nest, The." Sir William Davenant. *See* Lark Now Leaves His Water [*or* Wat'ry] Nest.

Song: "Lay your sleeping head, my love." W. H. Auden. *See* Lay your sleeping head, my love.

Song: "Leave this gaudy gilded stage." Earl of Rochester. OxBSP

Song: "Leaves are still; not a breath is heard, The." William James Linton. PF

Song: "Let it be forgotten, as a flower is forgotten." Sara Teasdale. AnAmPo; MoAmPo; PoA; TrGrPo

Song: "Let not the sluggish sleep." *Unknown.* ACP; OxBSP

Song: "Let school-masters puzzle their brain." Goldsmith. *Fr.* She Stoops to Conquer, I, ii. BIrV; NOIV
(Three Jolly Pigeons, The.) PoRA
(Three Pigeons, The.) ELP

Song: "Let's sing a song together once." Louis Simpson. NePoAm

Song: "Light of spring, The." Alice Duer Miller. AA

Song: "Linnet in the rocky dells, The." Emily Brontë. HAP; OBNC

Song: "Little onion lay by the fireplace, A." Nicholas Moore. EAS

Song: "Living or dead, the one I love." Philippe Thoby-Marcelin, *tr.* by William Jay Smith. CT

Song: "Lo! here we come a-reaping, a-reaping." George Peele. *Fr.* The Old Wife's Tale. OBSC

Song: "Lo! here we come a-reaping, a-reaping." George Peele. *Fr.* The Old Wives' [*or* Wife's] Tale: Harvester's Song, 4 *ll.*.

Song, A: "Lord, when the sense of Thy sweet grace." Richard Crashaw. TrPWD

Song: "Love a Woman! y'are an ass." Earl of Rochester. *See* Love a woman! y'are an ass.

Song: Love Arm'd. Aphra Behn. *See* Abdelazer

Song: Love Charm, The. *Unknown, tr. fr. Chippewa Indian* by Jerome Rothenberg. STP

Song: "Love for such a cherry lip." Thomas Middleton. *Fr.* Blurt, Master Constable. EIL

Song: "Love in fantastic triumph sate." Aphra Behn. *See* Abdelazer: Love in fantastic [*or* fantastique] triumph sate [*or* satt].

Song: "Love is cruel, Love is sweet." Thomas MacDonagh. ACP

Song: "Love laid his sleepless head." Swinburne. TrGrPo

Song: "Love, love today, my dear." Charlotte Mew. MoBrPo

Song: "Love still has something of the sea." Sir Charles Sedley. GBL; NOBE; OBS; SeCV-2

Song: "Love thou thy dream." Ezra Pound. FL

Song: "Love was true to me." John Boyle O'Reilly. ACP

Song: "Lovely hill-torrents are." W. J. Turner. GoJo; MoBrPo

Song: "Lovers in ladies' magazines." Thomas McGrath. VGW

Song: "Lying is an occupation." Laetitia Pilkington. WPE

Song: "Make this night loveable." W. H. Auden. TW

Song: "Man's a poor deluded bubble." Robert Dodsley. OxBSP

Song: Mary Morison. Burns. *See* O Mary, at thy window be.

Song: "Master, the swabber, the boatswain and I, The." Shakespeare. *See* Tempest, The:
Master, the swabber, the boatswain and I, The.

Song: "Memory, hither come." Blake. NAEL-2; PoEL-4

Song: "Men of England", A. Shelley. *See* Men of England, wherefor plough.

Song: "Merchant, to secure his treasure, The." Matthew Prior. *See* Ode, An: "Merchant, to secure his treasure, The."

Song: "Methinks the poor town has been troubled too long." Charles Sackville. SeCV-2

Song: "Might have known it." *Unknown, tr.* by Jerome Rothenberg. STP

Song: "Mist rauk is hanging, The." John Clare. NOBVV

Song: "Misty and dim, a bush in the wilds of Kapa'a." Kaiama, *tr.* by N. B. Emerson. WTO

Song: "Mother Mother shave me." *Unknown, tr.* by Ulli Beier. BoWoP

Song: "Moth's kiss, first, The!" Robert Browning. *See* In a Gondola: Moth's kiss, first, The!

Song: Murdring Beautie. Thomas Carew. SeCP

Song, A: "Music, thou queen of souls, get up and string." Thomas Randolph. OxBSP

Song, The: "My body as an act of derision." Bill Manhire. ATNZ

Song: "My cabinets are oyster-shells." Margaret Cavendish, Duchess of Newcastle. *See* Convent of Pleasure, The: My Cabinets Are Oyster-Shells.

Song, A: "My dear mistress has a heart." Earl of Rochester. SeCV-2

Song, A: "My head on moss reclining." *Unknown.* NOEC

Song: "My love is the flaming sword." James Thomson

Song: My luve is like a red, red rose. Burns. EnRP; FaBoBe; HoPM

Song: "My silks and fine array." Blake. EnRP; OBNC; TrGrPo
(My Silks and Fine Array.) ChTr; ELP; GBL; TEP; UnPo

Song: "My straying thoughts, reduced stay." Anne Collins. WPE

Song: "My wife is far away." Prince Aki. *Fr.* Manyo Shu. FCEI

Song: "Nay but you, who do not love her." Robert Browning. TrGrPo

Song: "Never take her away." Vinícius de Moraes, *tr.* by Richard Wilbur. ATCBP

Song: "No, no, fair heretic[k], it needs must be." Sir John Suckling. *Fr.* Aglaura, IV, i. CaPo; OBS; PrIm

Song: "No, no, no, no, I cannot hate my foe." Sir Philip Sidney. SiPS

Song: "No, no, poor suff'ring Heart no Change endeavour." Dryden. *See* Cleomenes: No, No, Poor Suffering Heart.

Song: Noble Name of Spark, The. *At. to* Earl of Rochester *and to* Thomas D'Urfey. *See* Room, Room for a blade of the town.

Song: "Noe more unto my thoughts appeare." Sidney Godolphin. MeLP; MePo
(Quatrains.) OBS

Song: "Not from the whole wide world I chose thee." Richard Watson Gilder. *Fr.* The New Day. AA

Song: "Now and then there will arise." *Unknown, tr.* by Frances Densmore. OBVE

Song: "Now sleeps the crimson petal, now the white." Tennyson. *See* Princess, The: Now Sleeps the Crimson Petal.

Song: "Now that Fate is dead and gone." Dame Edith Sitwell. MoAB; MoBrPo

Song, A: "Nymph in vain bestows her pains, The." Anne Finch, Countess of Winchilsea. OxBSP

Song: "Nymphs and shepherds dance no more." Milton. *See* Arcades: Nymphs and Shepherds.

Song: "O Bird, thou dartest to the sun." Maria White Lowell. AA

Song, A: "O close of night, I would have you linger." "Adunis", *tr.* by Lena Jayyusi and John Heath-Stubbs. MAP

Song: "O fair! O sweet! when I do look on thee." Sir Philip Sidney. SiPS

Song: "O harmless feast." Barten Holyday. *Fr.* Technogamia. EIL

Song: "O lady, when the tipped cup of the moon blessed you." Ted Hughes. LLLT

Song: "O, let us howl some heavy note." John Webster. *See* Duchess of Malfi, The: Madman's Song, The.

Song: "O Love, how strangely sweet." John Marston. EIL

Song: "O lovely April, rich and bright." Gustave Kahn, *tr.* by Ludwig Lewisohn. TrJP

Song: "O mistress mine! where are you roaming?" Shakespeare. *See* Twelfth Night: O [*or* Oh] Mistress Mine [Where Are You Roaming?].

Song: "O more, and more! this was so well." Ben Jonson. *Fr.* Pleasure Reconciled to Virtue. NAEL-1

Song: "O once I loved a bonnie lass." Burns. FL

Song: "O ruddier than the cherry." John Gay. *See* Acis and Galatea: O ruddier than the cherry!

Song: "O sing into my roundelay." Thomas Chatterton. *See* Aella; a Tragycal Enterlude: Oh! sing unto my roundelay [*or* O! Synge untoe mie roundelaie].

Song: "O sweet, sad, singing river." Henrietta Cordelia Ray. CBWP-3

Song: "O the month of May, the merry month of May." Thomas Dekker. *See* Shoemaker's Holiday, The: O, the Month of May.

Song: " 'O Where Are You Going?' said reader to rider." W. H. Auden. *See* Orators, The: O Where Are You Going?

Song: "O whistle, and I'll come to ye, my lad. Burns. *See* Whistle, and I'll Come to YeMy Lad.

Song: "O'er the smooth enamelled green." Milton. *See* Arcades: O'er [*or* O're] the smooth enameled green.

Song: "O'er the waste of waters cruising." Philip Freneau. PAH

Song: "Oh, baby, baby, baby dear." Edith Nesbit. NOBVV

Song, A: "Oh do[e] not wanton with those eyes." Ben Jonson. OBS; SeCP; TEP

Song: "Oh [*or* O] fair[e] sweet face, oh [*or* O] eyes celestial[1] bright." John Fletcher. *Fr.* Women Pleased, III, iv. OBS; PoEL-2

Song, The: "Oh, foully slighted Ethiope maid!" Priscilla Jane Thompson. CBWP-2

Song: "Oh! Love, that stronger art than wine." Aphra Behn. *Fr.* The Lucky Chance. WPE; WPOW

Song: "Oh no more, no more, too late." John Ford. *See* Broken Heart, The: Oh [*or* O], no more, no more, too late.

Song: "Oh roses for the flush of youth." Christina Rossetti. ELP; GTBS-P; NOBVV

Song: "Oh the charming month of May!" Joseph Addison. NOEC

Song: "Old Adam, The carrion crow." Thomas Lovell Beddoes. *See* Death's Jest Book: Old Adam, the Carrion Crow.

Song: "Old England is eaten by Knaves." Alexander McLachlan. *Fr.* The Emigrant. NOBC; OBCV

Song: "Old Farmer Oats and his son Ned." John Jay Chapman. PoEL-5

Song: Old Rowley the King. *Unknown.* APAS

Song: "On the side of the road." Edmond Jabès, *tr. by* Anthony Rudolf. VWA

Song: "One day the god of fond desire." James Thomson. EnLoPo

Song: One Hard Look. Robert Graves. MoAB; MoBrPo

Song: "Only the wanderer." Ivor Gurney. FaBoPP

Song: "Ope, aged Atlas, open then thy lap." Ben Jonson. *Fr.* Pleasure Reconciled to Virtue. NAEL-1

Song: "Or love me less [*or* mee lesse], or love me more." Sidney Godolphin. JCP
("Or love me lesse, or love me more.") MePo
("Or love mee lesse, or love mee more.") OBS

Song: "Orpheus with his Lute made Trees." Shakespeare *and probably* John Fletcher. *See* King Henry VIII: Orpheus with His Lute [Made Trees].

Song: "Our sovereign familiar with the eight corners/ being a god, rules on high." Akahito. *Fr.* Manyo Shu. FCEI

Song: "Over hill, over dale." Shakespeare. *See* Midsummer Night's Dream, A: Over Hill, over Dale.

Song: "Palace of Yoshino where our sovereign, The." Akahito. *Fr.* Manyo Shu. FCEI

Song: Paper. Keith Waldrop. MAT

Song: "Pardon, goddess of the night." Shakespeare. *See* Much Ado about Nothing: Claudio's Lament: "Pardon, goddess of the night."

Song: "Peasant sun went crushing grapes, The." Laurence Dakin. *Fr.* Tancred, I, i. CaP

Song: Persuasions [*or* Persuasions] to Enjoy. Thomas Carew. *See* If the quick spirits in your eyes.

Song: "Phillis for shame let us improve." Charles Sackville. *See* Phillis for Shame Let Us Improve.

Song: "Phillis is my only joy." Sir Charles Sedley. EnLoPo; OBS; SeCP

Song: "Phillis, let's shun the common fate." Sir Charles Sedley. SeCV-2

Song: "Phoebus, Arise." William Drummond of Hawthornden. *See* Phoebus, Arise.

Song: "Pints and the pistols, the pike-staves and pottles, The." *At. to* Winthrop Mackworth Praed. SoSe

Song: "Pious Selinda goes to prayers." Congreve. *See* Pious Selinda [*or* Celinda].

Song: "Place in thy memory, dearest, A." Gerald Griffin. BLPA

Song: "Pour one for me, friend good and true." N. M. Yazykov, *tr. by* Alan Myers. AAA

Song: Promoting Women's Rights, A. Ch'iu Chin, *tr. fr. Chinese by* Pao Chia-lin. WFTU

Song: "Rarely, rarely comest thou." Shelley. *See* Rarely, Rarely, Comest Thou.

Song: "Reading about the Wisconsin Weeping Willow." Ruth Krauss. LLLT

Song: "Red young men under the ground, The." *Unknown, tr. fr. Navajo Indian by* Jerome Rothenberg. *Fr.* Red Ant Way. STP

Song: "Ring of my true lover, The." V. A. Zhukovsky, *tr. by* Alan Myers. AAA

Song: "Rise Lady Mistresse, rise." Nathaniel Field. *See* Amends for Ladies: Rise, Lady Mistress, Rise!

Song: "Rousing to rein his pad's head back." Geoffrey Taylor. NeIP

Song: "Rowan like a lip-sticked girl, A." Seamus Heaney. IPY

Song: "Say this city has ten million souls!" W. H. Auden. *See* Say this city has ten million souls.

Song: "See, how like twilight slumber falls." Charles Cotton. OBS

Song: "See, see, she wakes, Sabina wakes!" Congreve. NOEC; OxBSP

Song: "Sergei's a flower." Ruth Herschberger. FF

Song: "She has left me, my pretty." Sylvia Townsend Warner. MoAB; MoBrPo

Song: She Is Not Fair to Outward View. Hartley Coleridge. EnRP; OBEV
(She Is Not Fair.) FaBV

Song: "She sat and sang alway." Christina Rossetti. GBL; NAEL-2

Song: "She spoke to me gently with words of sweet meaning." Patrick MacDonogh. NeIP

Song: "She was lyin face down in her face." William Knott. MAT

Song: "Shephard loveth thow me vell?" Jean Passerat, *tr. by* William Drummond of Hawthornden. OBVE

Song: "Shepherd, who can pass such wrong." Jorge de Montemayor, *tr. fr. Spanish by* Bartholomew Young. *Fr.* Diana. EIL

Song: "She's somewhere in the sunlight strong." Richard Le Gallienne. OBEV

Song: "Shine out, fair sun, with all your heat." *At. to* George Chapman. *See* Masque of the Twelve Months, The: Shine Out, Fair Sun, with All Your Heat.

Song: "Sigh no more, ladies, sigh no more." Shakespeare. *See* Much Ado about Nothing: Sigh No More, Ladies.

Song: "Silly boy, there is no cause." Thomas Pestel. EIL

Song, A: "Sing me a sweet, low song of night." Hildegarde Hawthorne. FaBoBe

Song: "Singer within the little streets." Monk Gibbon. NeIP

Song: "Slow, slow fresh fount, keep time with my salt tears." Ben Jonson. *See* Cynthia's Revels: Slow, Slow, Fresh Fount.

Song, A: "Smile, Massachusetts, smile." *Unknown.* PAH

Song: "Smooth was the water, calm the air." Sir Charles Sedley. SeCV-2

Song, The: "So light no one noticed." Edward Dorn. VGW

Song: "Soft falls the sweet evening." John Clare. NOBVV

Song: "Soldier rest! thy warfare o'er." Sir Walter Scott. *See* Lady of the Lake, The: Soldier Rest! [Thy Warfare O'er].

Song, A: "Song, A/ That seemed so brief at first." Howard Schwartz. VWA

Song: Song for a Scalp Dance. *Unknown, tr. fr. Chippewa Indian by* Jerome Rothenberg. STP

Song, A: "Song of grass, A,/ A song of earth." "Yehoash", *tr. by* Isidore Goldstick. TrJP

Song: Song of Starvation. *Unknown, tr. fr. Chippewa Indian by* Jerome Rothenberg. STP

Song, The: "Song, The! the song!" Hemda Roth, *tr. by* Mariana Potasman. VWA

Song: "Soules joy, now I am gone." *at. to* Earl of Pembroke. OBS

Song: "Sound is fading out." *Unknown, tr. by* Jerome Rothenberg. STP

Song: "Spirit haunts the last year's hours, A." Tennyson. *See* Princess, The: Spirit haunts the year's last hours, A.

Song: "Stay Phoebus, stay." Edmund Waller. SeCP

Song: "Still to be neat, still to be dressed [*or* drest]." Ben Jonson. *See* Epicoene; or, The Silent Woman: Still to Be Neat [Still to Be Drest (*or* Dressed)].

Song: Stop All the Clocks. W. H. Auden. *See* Stop All the Clocks, Cut Off the Telephone.

Song: "Stranger, you who hide my love." Stephen Spender. FaBoTw

Song: "Strew not earth with empty stars." Thomas Lovell Beddoes. *Fr.* The Second Brother. OxBSP

Song IV: Sudden light. Dante Gabriel Rossetti. *See* I have been here before.

Song: "Sunny shaft did I behold, A." Samuel Taylor Coleridge. *See* Zapolya: Glycine's Song.

Song: "Sure thing/ I'm a spirit!" *Unknown, tr. by* Jerome Rothenberg. STP

Song: "Sweet are the thoughts that savour of content." Robert Greene. *See* Farewell to Folly: Maesia's Song.

Song: "Sweet beast, I have gone prowling." William DeWitt Snodgrass. LLLT; MoAmPo; NYBP; SM

Song: "Sweet in her green cell the flower of beauty slumbers." George Darley. OBEV
(Serenade of a Loyal Martyr.) NOBE; OBNC
Song: "Sweetest love, I do not go[e]." John Donne. AWP; BoLoP; ElL; ELP; HeIP; InPS; InvP; JCP; MeLP; MePo; NOBE; NoP; OAEL-1; OBS; PoEL-2; SeCP; SeCV-1
(Sweetest Love, I Do Not Go.) TEP; TrGrPo
Song: "Sylvia the fair, in the bloom of fifteen." Dryden. EBEV; ErPo
Song: "Take, oh take those Lips away." Robert H. Fletcher *and others.* *See* Bloody Brother, The: Take, Oh, Take Those Lips Away.
Song: "Take, O take those lips away." Shakespeare. *See* Measure for Measure: Take, O Take Those Lips Away.
Song: "Tell me where is fancy bred." Shakespeare. *See* Merchant of Venice, The: Tell Me Where Is Fancy [*or* Fancie] Bred.
Song, The: "That day, in the slipping of torsos and straining flanks." Lola Ridge. WPE
Song: That Women Are but Men's Shadows. Ben Jonson. *See* Follow a shadow, it still flies you.
Song: Willing Prisoner to His Mistress, The. Thomas Carew. CaPo
Song, A: "There is ever a song somewhere, my dear." James Whitcomb Riley. AnAmPo
Song: "There is no joy in water apart from the sun." Ralph Nixon Currey. PeSA
Song: "There stands a lonely pine-tree." Heine, *tr. by* Emma Lazarus. TrJP
Song: "There was a Knight of Bethlehem." Henry Neville Maughan. *Fr.* The Husband of Poverty. BoTP
Song: "There's a barrel of porter at Tammany Hall." Fitz-Greene Halleck. OBAL
Song: "There's no more talk and ease." Audrey Beecham. CN
Song: "There's nothing in this gardenous world more delightful." Gerald Stern. CAPP
Song: "These songs will not stand." Denis Glover. *Fr.* Sings Harry, I. ATNZ; PeNZ
Song: "Think of dress in every light." John Gay. *See* Achilles: Think of dress in every light.
Song: "This is the song of those who live alone." William Justema. NYBP
Song, A: "Those rivers run from that land." Robert Creeley. VGW
Song, A: "Thou art the soul of a summer's day." Paul Laurence Dunbar. AmNP
Song: "Though I am young and cannot tell." Ben Jonson. *See* Sad Shepherd, The: Though I Am Young and Cannot Tell.
Song: "Though regions farr divided." Aurelian Townshend. *See* Though Regions Far [*or* Farr] Divided.
Song: Thoughts of a Traveler on the Chikuma River. Shimazaki Toson, *tr. fr. Japanese by* Burton Watson. FCEI
Song: "Three little maidens they have slain." Maurice Maeterlinck, *tr. by* Jethro Bithell. AWP
Song: "Thus when the swallow, seeking prey." John Gay. *Fr.* The Beggar's Opera, II, ii. PoEL-3
Song: "Thy face I have seen as one seeth." Sophie Jewett. AA
Song: "Thy fingers make early flowers of all things." E. E. Cummings. MoAmPo; NAAL-2
Song: "Time drawes neere." Anne Waldman. UL
Song: "'Tis affection but dissembled." Sidney Godolphin. JCP
Song: "'Tis said that absence conquers love!" Frederick William Thomas. AA
Song: "'Tis true our life is but a long dis-ease." Katherine Philips. OxBSP
Song: To Amarantha, that She Would Dishevel Her Hair. Richard Lovelace. *See* Amarantha sweet and fair.
Song: To Celia. Ben Jonson. *See* To Celia ("Drink to me only with thine eyes").
Song: To Her Againe, She Burning in a Feaver. Thomas Carew. SeCP
Song: To Lucasta, Going to the Wars. Richard Lovelace. *See* Tell me not, sweet, I am unkind.
Song: To My Inconstant Mistress. Thomas Carew. *See* When thou, poor excommunicate.
Song: To One That Desired To Know My Mistris. Thomas Carew. SeCP
Song: "To the old, long life and treasure." Ben Jonson. *Fr.* The Gypsies Metamorphosed. OxBSP
Song: "Tomorrow is Saint Valentine's Day." Shakespeare. *See* Hamlet: Tomorrow Is Saint Valentine's Day.
Song: "Trip it Gipsies, Trip it Fine." Thomas Middleton *and* William Rowley. *Fr.* The Spanish Gipsy [*or* Gypsy]. OBS
Song: "Turn, turn thy beauteous face away." Francis Beaumont *and* Fletcher. *Fr.* Love's Cure. PoEL-2
Song: "Under the greenwood tree." Shakespeare. *See* As You Like It: Under the Greenwood Tree.

Song: "Virtue's branches wither, virtue pines." Thomas Dekker. *See* Old Fortunatus: Priest's Song, A.
Song: Voice Speaks from the Well, A. George Peele. *Fr.* The Old Wive's Tale. OBSC
Song: "Wake, Hercules, awake: but heave up thy black eye." Ben Jonson. *Fr.* Pleasure Reconciled to Virtue. NAEL-1
Song: "Wake not, but hear me, love!" Lew Wallace. *Fr.* Ben Hur. AA
Song: Wanderers, The. Robert Browning. OBEV
Song: "Water's flowing." *Unknown, tr. by* Jerome Rothenberg. STP
Song: "We break the glass, whose sacred wine." Edward Coote Pinkney. AA
Song: "We have bathed, where none have seen us." Thomas Lovell Beddoes. *See* Death's Jest Book: Bridal Song to Amala.
Song: "We raise de wheat." *Unknown.* BPo; TAP
Song: "We sail toward evening's lonely star." Celia Thaxter. AA
Song: "Weary lot is thine, fair maid, A." Sir Walter Scott. *See* Rokeby: Weary Lot Is Thine, A.
Song: "Weep, weep, ye woodmen, wail." Anthony Munday. *See* Death of Robert, Earl of Huntingdon: Weep, weep, ye woodmen! wail.
Song: "We'll, placed in Love's triumphant chariot high." William Cavendish, Duke of Newcastle. *Fr.* The Humorous Lovers. OxBSP
Song: "Were I laid on Greenland's coast." John Gay. *Fr.* The Beggar's Opera, I, i. EnLoPo; NAEL-1; OxBoLi; PoEL-3
(Macheath and Polly.) NOEC
(Over the Hills and Far Away.) NOBE; PrIm
Song: "What binds the atom together." Philip Dow. NPGG
Song: "What bird so sings." John Lyly. *See* Alexander and Campaspe: Trico's Song.
Song: "What I took in my hand." Robert Creeley. NoP; PoA
Song: "What is there hid in the heart of a rose." Alfred Noyes. CH
Song: "What shall he have that kill'd the dear?" Shakespeare. *See* As You Like It: Amien's Song.
Song: "What think you of this age now." *Unknown.* APAS
Song: "Whaur yon broken brig hings owre." William Soutar. GoTS; OxBS
Song: "When as [*or* whenas] the rye [*or* rie] reach to the chin." George Peele. *See* Old Wives' [*or* Wife's] Tale, The: Whenas [*or* When as] the Rye [Reach to the Chin].
Song: "When daffodils begin to peer." Shakespeare. *See* Winter's Tale, The: When daffodils begin to peer.
Song: "When daisies pied and violets blue." Shakespeare. *See* Love's Labour's Lost: When Daisies Pied [and Violets Blue].
Song: "When, dearest, I but think on [*or* of] thee." *at. to* Sir John Suckling *and to* Owen Feltham. MePo
(When, Dearest, I but Think on [*or* of] Thee.) JCP; OBEV; OBS
Song: "When I am dead, my dearest." Christina Rossetti. AWP; BoLoP; CH; DL; EBEV; FaFP; FF; FPL; GBL; InPS; NAEL-2; NOBE; NOBVV; NoP; OAEL-2; OBD; OBEV; PoLF; PoRA; SCV; SoSe; ViBoPo; WPE
(When I Am Dead My Dearest.) ELP LiTB; TrGrPo
Song: "When I am old." Denis Glover. *Fr.* Sings Harry, III. PeNZ
Song: "When I show up." *Unknown, tr. by* Jerome Rothenberg. STP
Song: "When I was a greenhorn and young." Charles Kingsley. NOBVV
Song: "When icicles hang by the wall." Shakespeare. *See* Love's Labour's Lost: When Icicles Hang by the Wall.
Song: "When love on time and measure makes his ground." John Lilliat. *See* When love on time and measure makes his ground.
Song: "When lovely woman, prone to folly." *Unknown.* FaBoPa
Song: "When lovely woman stoops to folly." Goldsmith. *See* Vicar of Wakefield, The: When Lovely Woman Stoops to Folly.
Song: "When maidens are young, and in their spring." Aphra Behn. *Fr.* Emperor of the Moon. FF
Song: "When o'er the wold the heedless lamb." Thomas Holcroft. NOEC
Song: "When that I was and a little tiny boy." Shakespeare. *See* Twelfth Night: When That I Was and a Little Tiny Boy.
Song: "When the echo of the last footstep dies." E. W. Mandel. MoCV; OBCV
Song: "When the heart's feeling." Thomas Moore. OxBSP
Song: "When the water's calm." *Unknown, tr. by* Jerome Rothenberg. STP
Song: "When thy beauty appears." Thomas Parnell. OBEV
Song: "When working blackguards come to blows." Ebenezer Elliott. EBEV
Song: "When your boyfriend writes you a letter." Ruth Krauss. RR
Song: "Whenever, Chloe, I begin." Earl of Chesterfield. NOEC
Song: "Where did you borrow that last sigh." Sir William Berkeley. *Fr.* The Lost Lady. OxBSP
Song: "Where in blind files." Eavan Boland. CIP
Song: "Where is the nymph, whose azure eye." Thomas Moore. EnLoPo
Song: "Where shall Celia fly for shelter." Christopher Smart. EnLoPo

Song: "Where shall the lover rest." Sir Walter Scott. *See* Marmion: Where shall the lover rest.

Song, A: "While a thousand fine projects are planned ev'ry day." *Unknown.* NOEC

Song: "While Morpheus thus doth gently lay." Henry Killigrew. CH

Song: "Whilst Alexis lay pressed." Dryden. *See* Marriage à la Mode: Whil'st Alexis Lay Prest [*or* Press'd].

Song: "Whilst landmen wander, though controlled." *Unknown.* OxBSS

Song: "Whipped by sorrow now." Miklós Radnóti, *tr. by* Steven Polgar *and* Stephen Berg *and* S. J. Marks. VWA

Song: "Who can say." Tennyson. FaBoCh

Song: "Who has robbed the ocean cave." John Shaw. AA

Song: Who Hath His Fancy [*or* Fancie] Pleased. Sir Philip Sidney. EIL; PoEL-1; QFR (Immortality.) OBSC

Song: "Why fadest thou in death." R. W. Dixon. ChTr

Song: "Why should a foolish marriage vow." Dryden. *See* Marriage à la Mode: Why Should a Foolish Marriage Vow.

Song: Why So Pale and Wan, Fond Lover? Sir John Suckling. NAEL-1; NBLV; NIP; OPOP

Song: "Why so pale and wan, fond lover?" Sir John Suckling. *See* Aglaura: Why So Pale and Wan, Fond Lover?

Song, A: "Widow bird sate mourning for her love, A." Shelley. *See* Charles the First: Widow bird sate mourning for her love, A.

Song: "With a basket, a lovely basket." Emperor Yuryaku. *Fr.* Manyo Shu. FCEI

Song, A: "With Love among the haycocks." Ralph Hodgson. GoJo

Song: "Woman sits on her porch." Earle Thompson. HATNAP; STE

Song: "Woman's beauty is like a white, A." W. B. Yeats. *Fr.* The Only Jealousy of Emer. MoAB

Song: "Woman's face is full of wiles, A." Humphrey Gifford. EIL

Song, A: "World is young today, The." Digby Mackworth Dolben. NOBVV; OBNC ("To all you ladies now at land.") SeCV-2

Song: "Year's at the Spring, The." Robert Browning. *See* Pippa Passes: Year's at the Spring, The.

Song: "Years have flown since I knew thee first." Richard Watson Gilder. *Fr.* The New Day. AA

Song: "You are as gold." Hilda Doolittle ("H. D."). LiTA; LiTM; MoAmPo

Song, A: "You charm'd me not with that fair face." Dryden. *Fr.* An Evening's Love, II, i. MoAB

Song: "You spotted snakes with double tongue." Shakespeare. *See* Midsummer Night's Dream, A: You Spotted Snakes [with Double Tongue].

Song: "You virgins that did late despair." James Shirley. *See* Imposture, The: Piping Peace.

Song: "You wear the morning like your dress." Hilaire Belloc. OBEV

Song: "Young flowers were whispering in melody." Poe. *Fr.* Al Aaaraff. NOBA

Song: "Young Philander woo'd me long." *Unknown.* ErPo

Song: "Your hay it is mow'd, and your corn is reap'd." Dryden. *See* King Arthur: Harvest Home.

Song: "Your heart is a music-box, dearest!" Frances Sargent Osgood. AA

Song, A: "Your song comes to me in little pieces." Jacob Glatstein, *tr. by* Benjamin *and* Barbara Harshav. VWA

Song: "You're wondering if I'm lonely." Adrienne Rich. InPK; PBWP

Song, A/ That seemed so brief at first. Howard Schwartz. VWA

Song, a poem of itself—the word itself a dirge, A. Yonnondio. Walt Whitman. NAAL-1

Song, A! What songs have died. A Song for the Asking. Francis Orrery Ticknor. AA

Song about a Dead Person—or Was It a Mole?, A. *Unknown, tr. fr. Seneca Indian by* Jerome Rothenberg *and* Richard Johnny John. STP

Song about Charleston, A. *Unknown.* PAH

Song about Great Men, A. Michael Hamburger. NePoEA

Song about Major Eatherly, A. John Wain. OxBTC

Song about Myself, A. Keats. *See* There Was a Naughty Boy.

Song about Singing, A. Anne Reeve Aldrich. AA

Song about the Moon, A. Bill Manhire. ATNZ

Song about Whiskers. P. G. Wodehouse. FiBHP

Song against Grocers, The. G. K. Chesterton. CenHV; FaBoCo

Song and Poetry. *Unknown, tr. fr. Welsh by* Gwyn Jones. OBWVE

Song and Science. Milicent Washburn Shinn. AA

Song as Yet Unsung, A. "Yehoash", *tr. fr. Yiddish by* Isidore Goldstick. TrJP

Song at Easter, A. Charles Hanson Towne. BLRP

Song at Morning, A. Edith Sitwell. CMoP

Song at Night. Norman Nicholson. FaBoTw

Song at the Beginning of Autumn. Elizabeth Jennings. OxBTC

Song at the Feast of Brougham Castle. Wordsworth. EnRP

Song at the Moated Grange, A. Shakespeare. *See* Measure for Measure: Take, O Take Those Lips Away.

Song at the Ruin'd Inn. Tennyson. *Fr.* The Vision of Sin. PoEL-5

Song at the Skirts of Heaven. Uri Zvi Greenberg, *tr. fr. Hebrew by* Zvi Jagendorf. VWA

Song Ballet (I Was Sixteen Years of Age). *Unknown.* AmFP

Song Be Delicate. John Shaw Neilson. PoAu-1

Song before Grief, A. Rose Hawthorne Lathrop. AA

Song-birds, The? are they flown away? Flight. Madison Cawein. AA

Song by a Woman Accused of Adultery. Kie Tapu, *tr. fr. Maori by* Margaret Orbell. PeNZ

Song by Isbrand. Thomas Lovell Beddoes. *See* Death's Jest Book: Squats on a toad-stool under a tree.

Song by Mr. Cypress. Thomas Love Peacock. *Fr.* Nightmare Abbey, *ch.* 11. OAEL-2; OBNC; Par

Song by Rogero. George Canning , George Ellis *and* John Hookham Frere. *See* Rovers, The: Rogero's Song.

Song Called "His Hide Is Covered with Hair," The. Hilaire Belloc. FaBoNo; FM

Song Encountered in the Landscape. H. C. ten Berge, *tr. fr. Dutch by* Theo Hermans. DuIn

Song for a Ball-Game. Wilfrid Thorley. BoTP

Song for a Birth or a Death. Elizabeth Jennings. EBEV

Song for a Blue Roadster. Rachel Lyman Field. FaPON

Song for a Country Wedding. William Jay Smith. GrPl

Song for a Dance. Francis Beaumont. *See* Masque of the Inner Temple and Gray's Inne, The: Shake off your heavy trance!

Song for a Dance. Abraham Sutskever, *tr. fr. Yiddish by* Ruth Whitman. VWA

Song for a Dancer. Kenneth Rexroth. TAP

Song for a Dark Girl. Langston Hughes. AmPP; CDC; IDB; NAAL-2; PoBA

Song for a Day. Francisco Arriví, *tr. by* Julio Marzán. InW

Song for a Day, *sel.* Francisco Arriví, *tr. fr. Spanish by* Julio Marzán. "Sometimes a huge wave of thought." InW

Song for a Departure. Elizabeth Jennings. GOYP

Song for a Girl. Dryden. ELP; ErPo

Song for a Girl on Her First Menstruation. *Unknown, tr. fr. Boikin by* Joe Prentuo. BoWoP; OV

Song for a Jewess. Iwan Goll, *tr. fr. French by* Joseph T. Shipley. TrJP

Song for a Little Bit of Breath. Marvin Bell. BLA

Song for a Little House. Christopher Morley. BoTP; FaPON

Song for a Lyre. Louise Bogan. LiTA

Song for a Suicide. Langston Hughes. PoNe

Song for a Transformation, *sel.* Francisco Arriví, *tr. fr. Spanish by* Julio Marzán. "This tree/ growing out of me." InW

Song for a Young Girl's Puberty Ceremony. *Unknown, tr. fr. Papago Indian by* Frances Densmore. OV

Song for All Seas, All Ships. Walt Whitman. CH; FaBoBe; MOS

Song for Apollo. Matthew Arnold. *See* Empedocles on Etna: Song of Callicles, The ("Through the black, rushing smoke-burst").

Song for Autumn. Andrew Young. GBL

Song for Bringing a Child into the World. *Unknown, tr. fr. Seminole Indian by* Frances Densmore. OV

Song for "Buvez les Vins du Postillion"—Advt. Jean Garrigue. TAP

Song for Dov Shamir. Dannie Abse. VWA (Song of a Hebrew.) WTO

Song for England, A. Andrew Salkey. PBCV

Song for February. Tom Paulin. FaBCIP

Song for Fine Weather. Constance Lindsay Skinner. *Fr.* Three Songs from the Haida. AWP

Song for Fine Weather. *Unknown, tr. fr. Haida Indian by* Constance Lindsay Skinner. AWP

Song for Healing. Roberta Hill. CDW

Song for Healing, A. Margot LeBrasseur. GOS

Song for Ireland. Phil *and* June Colclough. OBET

Song for Ishtar. Denise Levertov. MoP; NaP; NMM; NoAM; PoM

Song for Joseph. *Unknown, tr. fr. Maori by* Margaret Orbell. PeNZ

Song for Lexington, A. Robert Kelley Weeks. AA

Song for Luanda. Luandino Vieira, *tr. fr. Portuguese by* Michael Wolfers. WMBCH

Song for Memorial Day. Clinton Scollard. OHIP

Song for My Father. Jessica Hagedorn. BrSi; ER

Song for My Lady. A. Godwin. OxBoLi (Now Wolde.) CH (Song in His Lady's Absence, A.) MeEL

Song for My Little Friends. Leonard Adame, *tr. fr. Spanish by* Toni Empringham. FIA

Song for My Mother, A: Her Hands.   Anna Hempstead Branch.   *Fr.*
  Songs for My Mother.   OHIP
Song for My Mother, A: Her Stories.   Anna Hempstead Branch.   *Fr.*
  Songs for My Mother.   OHIP
Song for My Mother, A: Her Words.   Anna Hempstead Branch.   *Fr.*
  Songs for My Mother.   FaPON
Song for My Name.   Linda Hogan.   STE
Song for My Son.   Marilyn Davis.   TSM
Song for New Orleans, A.   George Keithley.   NPGG
Song for Our Flag, A.   Margaret E. M. Sangster.   FaFP
Song for Past Midnight.   Geoffrey Lehmann.   CBAP
Song for St. Cecilia's Day.   W. H. Auden.   FaBoTw; TwCP
Song for St. Cecilia's Day, 1687, A.   Dryden.   AWP; FaBoTw; GTBS;
  GTBS-P; HAP; InPS; LiTB; OAEL-1; OBEV; OPOP; PoEL-3; PPP;
  SeCV-2; TEP; TrGrPo; UnS
  Fife and Drum, 8 *ll.* GN
Song for September.   Robert Fitzgerald.   VGW
Song for Simeon, A.   T. S. Eliot.   EaLo; LiTB; NAs; NOCV
Song for Susannah: A Lullaby.   Doris Hardie.   TDD
Song for Te Hauapu.   Noho-mai-te-Rangi, *tr. fr. Maori by* Margaret
  Orbell.   PeNZ
Song for the Asking, A.   Francis Orrery Ticknor.   AA
Song for the Burial of my Mother.   Shimazaki Toson, *tr. fr. Japanese by*
  Burton Watson.   FCEI
Song for the Clatter-Bones.   F. R. Higgins.   AnIL; LiTB; OBMV
Song for the Dead, III.   *Unknown, tr. by* Frances S. Herskovits.   TTY
Song for the free—the brave and the free, A.   Thomas Cooper.   *Fr.* Two
  Chartist Songs.   PF
Song for the Greenwood Fawn.   I. L. Salomon.   GoYe
Song for the Head.   George Peele.   *See* Old Wives' [*or* Wife's] Tale,
  The: Gently Dip.
Song for the Heroes.   Alex Comfort.   MoBrPo
Song for the Infant Judas.   Thomas Blackburn.   NAs
Song for the Last Act.   Louise Bogan.   NePoAm; NoP; NYBP; UnPo;
  WPE
Song for the Middle of the Night, A.   James Wright.   SM; WeW
Song for the Moon.   Nazik al-Mala'ika, *tr. fr. Arabic by* Matthew
  Sorenson *and* Christopher Middleton.   MAP
Song for the Newborn.   *Unknown, tr. fr. Grande Pueblo Indian by* Mary
  Austin.   OFD; WPE
Song for the Old Ones.   Maya Angelou.   SaC
Song for the Passing of a Beautiful Woman.   *Unknown, tr. fr. Paiute
  Indian by* Mary Austin.   LiTA
Song for the Richest Woman in Wrangell.   Guxnawu, *tr. fr. Tlingit Indian
  by* James Koller.   STP
Song for the Squeeze-Box.   Theodore Roethke.   NBLV; NePoAm
Song for the Sun That Disappeared behind the Rainclouds.   *Hottentot Oral
  Tradition, tr. by* Ulli Beier.   TTTS; TTY
Song for the unsung heroes who rose in the country's need, A.   The
  Unsung Heroes.   Paul Laurence Dunbar.   BPo
Song for Unbound Hair.   Genevieve Taggard.   PoRA
Song Form.   Imamu Amiri Baraka.   SOTW; TTTS
Song from a Country Fair.   Léonie Adams.   GoJo; GrPl
Song from a Drama.   Edmund Clarence Stedman.   AA
Song from a Two-Desk Office.   Byron Buck.   NYBP
Song from "Al Aaraaf."   Poe.   *Fr.* Al Aaaraff.   AmPP; AnAmPo;
  OxBA
Song from Armenia, A.   Geoffrey Hill.   FaBoMo
Song from Chartivel.   Marie de France, *tr. fr. French by* Arthur
  O'Shaughnessy.   AWP; EnLoPo; WPOW
Song from Sylvan, A.   *At. to* Elizabeth Barrett Browning *and to* Louis
  Imogen Guiney.   *See* Little cares that fretted me, The.
Song from the Bride of Smithfield.   Sylvia Townsend Warner.   MoBrPo
Song from the Coptic, A.   James Clarence Mangan.   NOIV
Song from the Italian, A.   Dryden.   *Fr.* The Kind Keeper.   SeCV-2
Song from the Maker of Totems [*or* Totem Maker.]   Duane Niatum.
  NOVW; STE
Song from the Waters.   Thomas Lovell Beddoes.   *See* Death's Jest Book:
  Dirge: "Swallow leaves her nest, The."
Song gives birth to.   In the chipped and tattered.   Round Valley
  Reflections.   William Oandasan.   STE
Song gives birth to.   The woman with white hair.   The Song of Ancient
  Ways.   William Oandasan.   HATNAP; STE
Song, *Hamlet.*   John Poole.   BXAP
Song I sing of my sea-adventure, A.   The Seafarer.   *Unknown, tr. by*
  Charles W. Kennedy.   AnOE; MOS
Song I sing of my sea adventure, A.   *Unknown, tr. fr. Anglo-Saxon by*
  Charles W. Kennedy.   *Fr.* The Seafarer, Pt. I.   AnOE
Song I sing of sorrow unceasing, A.   The Wife's Lament.   *Unknown.*
  AnOE, *tr. by* Charles W. Kennedy
  (Wife's Complaint, The.)   BoLoP, *tr. by* Michael Alexander
Song in a Siege.   Robert Heath.   OBS

Song in August.   Badr Shakir al-Sayyab, *tr. fr. Arabic by* Lena Jayyusi
  and Christopher Middleton.   MAP
Song in His Lady's Absence, A.   A. Godwin.   *See* Now wolde I fayne
  sum merthis make.
Song in Making of the Arrows.   John Lyly.   *See* Sapho and Phao:
  Vulcan's Song.
Song in March.   William Gilmore Simms.   AA
Song in Passing, A.   Yvor Winters.   CRP; VGW
Song in Praise of a Beggar's Life, A.   "A. W."   *See* Bright shines the
  sun.
Song in Praise of a Favourite Humming-Top, A.   Hone Tuwhare.   PeNZ
Song in Praise of Paella.   C. W. V. Wordsworth.   FiBHP
Song in Space.   Adrian Mitchell.   PoPo
Song in the Cold Season.   Samuel French Morse.   PoA
Song in the Dell, The.   Charles Edward Carryl.   AA
Song in the Front Yard, A.   Gwendolyn Brooks.   CAPP; IDB; NAAL-2;
  NoAM; NOBA; PoBA
Song in the valley of Nemea, A.   Nemea.   Lawrence Durrell.   FaBoTw;
  GTBS-P
Song in the Wood.   John Fletcher.   *Fr.* The Little French Lawyer.   ElL
Song in Three Characters, A.   Ou-yang Chiung, *tr. fr. Chinese by* Lois
  Fusek.   ATF
Song in Time of Drought.   Benjamin Péret, *tr. fr. French by* James
  Laughlin.   POS; RHTwFP
Song in Time of Plague.   Thomas Nashe.   *See* Summer's Last Will and
  Testament: Adieu, Farewell, Earth's Bliss[e].
Song is gone; the dance, The.   Bora Ring.   Judith Wright.   NoAM
Song Longs to Be Light.   Federico García Lorca, *tr. fr. Spanish by*
  William Jay Smith.   CT
Song-Maker.   Anita Endrezze-Danielson.   HATNAP; STE
Song-Maker, The.   Anna Wickham.   MoBrPo
Song Making.   Sara Teasdale.   WGRP
Song My.   Susan Griffin.   NMM; WPOW
Song My Paddle Sings, The.   E. Pauline Johnson.   CaP; FaPON
Song (October 1969).   Kath Fraser.   AIW; PeHV
Song of a blackbird in my ears.   Eino Leino, *tr. by* Aili Jarvenpa.   SOP
Song of a Common Lover.   Flavien Ranaivo, *tr. fr. French by* Alan
  Ryder.   TTY
Song of a Dandy.   Sun Kuang-hsien, *tr. fr. Chinese by* Lois Fusek.
  ATF
Song of a Dream, The.   *Unknown, tr. fr. Aztec Indian by* John Bierhorst.
  ILY
Song of a Dream Journey over the Vast Sea.   Yang Wei-chen, *tr. fr.
  Chinese by* Jonathan Chaves.   CoBLCP
Song of a Dream Visit to T'ien-mu.   Li Po, *tr. fr. Chinese by* Burton
  Watson.   CoBCP
Song of a Factory Worker, The.   Ruth Collins.   SaC
Song of a Fisherman, A.   Sung Wan, *tr. fr. Chinese by* William Schultz.
  WFTU
Song of a Girl Journeying to the Country of the Dead.   *Unknown, tr. fr.
  Kiriwina.*   OV
Song of a Happy Rising, The.   John Thewlis.   ACP
Song of a Heathen, The.   Richard Watson Gilder.   AA; AnAmPo;
  WGRP
Song of a Hebrew.   Dannie Abse.   *See* Working is another way of
  praying.
Song of a Jewish Boy.   "M. J.", *tr. fr. Polish by* A. Glanz-Leyeless
  TrJP
Song of a Lady from Mie.   *Unknown, tr. fr. Japanese by* Hiroaki Sato.
  Fr. The Kojiki.   FCEI
Song of a Man about to Die in a Strange Land.   *Unknown, tr. fr.
  Chippewa Indian by* Mary Austin.   DL
Song of a Man Who Has Come Through.   D. H. Lawrence.   CMoP;
  FaBoMo; GTBS-P; InPS; LiTM; OxBTC; PoE
Song of a Prison Guard.   Lupenga Mphande.   WMBCH
Song of a Rat.   Ted Hughes.   CMoP; NoP
Song of a Second April.   Edna St. Vincent Millay.   CMoP; OxBA
Song of a Shepherd Boy at Bethlehem.   Josephine Preston Peabody.
  OHIP
Song of a Sick Child.   *Malay Oral Tradition, tr. by* R. J. Wilkinson *and*
  R. O. Winstedt.   WTO
Song of a Silesian Weaver.   Louise Aston, *tr. fr. German by* Susan L.
  Cocalis *and* Gerlinde Geiger.   DMG
Song of a Train.   John Davidson.   BrPo
Song of a Traveller, The.   Robert Louis Stevenson.   *See* I will make you
  brooches and toys for your delight.
Song of a Woman Abandoned by the Tribe.   *Unknown, tr. fr. Shoshone
  Indian by* Mary Austin.   AIW; WPE
Song of a Woman in Labor.   *Unknown, tr. fr. Papago Indian by* Frances
  Densmore.   OV
Song of a Young Lady to Her Ancient Lover, A.   2nd Earl of Rochester.
  BoLoP; EBEV; ErPo; GBL; MePo; OPOP

Song of Abuse. *Yoruba Oral Tradition, tr. by* Ulli Beier *and* B. Gbadamosi. WTO

Song of Accius and Silena. John Lyly. *See* Mother Bombie: O Cupid! Monarch over Kings.

Song of Agony. Gouveia de Lemos, *tr. fr. Portuguese by* Margaret Dickinson. WMBCH

Song of Albert Graeme. Sir Walter Scott. *Fr.* The Lay of the Last Minstrel, VI. EnRP

Song of Ale, A. *At. to* William Stevenson *and also to* John Still. *See* Gammer Gurton's Needle: Back and Side Go Bare, Go Bare.

Song of Allegiance. R. A. K. Mason. ATNZ

Song of an Autumn Night. Chao Meng-fu, *tr. fr. Chinese by* Jonathan Chaves. CoBLCP

Song of Anarchus, The, *sel. Unknown.*
"Know then, my brethren, heaven is clear." FaBoCo

Song of Ancient Ways, The. William Oandasan. HATNAP; STE

Song of Apelles. John Lyly. *See* Alexander and Campaspe: Cupid and my Campaspe played.

Song of Apollo. John Lyly. *Fr.* Midas. OBSC

Song of Apollo. Shelley. *See* Sleepless Hours who watch me as I lie, The.

Song of Battle. Bertrans de Born. *See* Well Pleaseth Me the Sweet Time of Easter.

Song of Bekotsidi, The. *Unknown, tr. fr. Navajo Indian by* Washington Matthews. OBVE

Song of Bitter Drought, A. Cha Shen-hsing, *tr. fr. Chinese by* William Schultz. WFTU

Song of Black Cubans. Federico García Lorca, *tr. fr. Spanish by* William B. Logan. SOTW

Song of Bliss. Spenser. *See* Faerie Queene, The: Whiles someone did chant this lovely lay, The.

Song of Braddock's Men, The. Stephen Tilden. PAH

Song of Breath. Peire Vidal, *tr. fr. French by* Ezra Pound. AWP

Song of Bullets, The. Jessica Hagedorn. ER

Song of Callicles, The ("Far, far from here"). Matthew Arnold. *See* Empedocles on Etna: Far far from here.

Song of Callicles, The ("Through the black, rushing smoke-burst"). Matthew Arnold. *Fr.* Empedocles on Etna, II. NOBE; OAEL-2; OBEV
(Callicles' Song.) ChTr
(Not Here, O Apollo.) FaBoRV
(Song for Apollo.) FiP
(Song of the Muses, The.) WiR

Song of canaries, The. The Canary. Ogden Nash. FiBHP; RHPC

Song of Caribou, Musk Oxen, Women, and Men Who Would Be Manly ("Glorious it is to see/ The caribou flocking down from the forests."), *sel. Unknown, tr. fr. Eskimo.* WTO
"Glorious it is/ to see long-haired winter caribou." RFM

Song of Catching Tigers, *sel.* Hsü Chung-hsing, *tr. fr. Chinese by* Jonathan Chaves.
"How brave the peasant who lives beside the lake." CoBLCP

Song of Chess, The. *At. to* Abraham ibn Ezra, *tr. fr. Hebrew by* Nina Davis Salaman. TrJP

Song of Chiang-nan, *sel.* Tsung Ch'en, *tr. fr. Chinese by* Jonathan Chaves.
"On the spring river, you depart." CoBLCP

Song of Chiang-nan, *sels.* Wei Yüan, *tr. fr. Chinese by* Irving Lo. WFTO
"Ah-fu-jung, ah-fu-jung!" *Fr.* VIII.
"Plant the flower farms.'" *Fr.* I.

Song of Childbirth, The. *Unknown, tr. fr. Irish by* Eleanor Hull. TIRV

Song of Choyong, The, *sel.* Ruth Kim Chun-soo, *tr. fr. Korean by* Koh Chang-soo.
"It was raining in winter." *Fr.* I. ACKP

Song of Clover, A. Helen Hunt Jackson. GN

Song of Coridon and Melampus. George Peele. *Fr.* The Hunting of Cupid. OBSC

Song of Cove Creek Dam, The. *Unknown.* AmFP

Song of Cradle-making. Constance Lindsay Skinner. CaP

Song of Crede, The. *Unknown, tr. fr. Middle Irish by* Alfred Perceval Graves. BIrV

Song of Crows Gleaning the Grain, A. Cha Shen-hsing, *tr. fr. Chinese by* William Schultz. WFTU

Song of Cursive Calligraphy. Hsieh Chin, *tr. fr. Chinese by* Jonathan Chaves. CoBLCP

Song of Dalliance, A. William Cartwright. ErPo; JCP

Song of Daphne to the Lute, A. John Lyly. *See* Midas: Daphne.

Song of Deborah, The. Bible, *O.T. Fr.* Judges, V: 1-31. AWP; BoWoP; PBWP
(Then Sang Deborah and Barak.) TrJP
"Blessed above women/ shall Jael the wife of Heber the Kenite be." *Fr.* V:24-31.WPOW

Song of Degrees. Paul Auster. VWA

Song of Degrees, A. W. P. Ker. PoSH

Song of Dejection. W. H. Auden. *Fr.* Man of La Mancha. AnAn

Song of Delight. Shao Yung, *tr. fr. Chinese by* Burton Watson. CoBCP

Song of Derivations, A. Alice Meynell. WGRP

Song of Despair. Rangiaho, *tr. fr. Maori by* Barry Mitcalfe. WTO

Song of Diana's Nymphs, A. John Lyly. *See* Galathea: Cupid's Indictment.

Song of Doubt, A. Josiah Gilbert Holland. WGRP

Song of Duke William. Hilaire Belloc. FaBoNo

Song of Dust, A. John Byrne Leicester Warren, 3rd Baron De Tabley. EnLoPo

Song of Ecstasy, *sel.* Abu al-Qasim al-Shabbi, *tr. fr. Arabic by* Sargon Boulus *and* Christopher Middleton.
"Cupbearer, take your wine away." MAP

Song of Egla. Maria Gowen Brooks. AA

Song of Emptiness to Fill up the Empty Pages Following, A. Michael Wigglesworth. SCAP

Song of Enitharmon. Blake. *Fr.* Vala; or The Four Zoas, The Four Zoas. OAEL-2

Song of Eros. George Edward Woodberry. *Fr.* Agathon. AA

Song of Exile, *sel.* Antônio Gonçalves Dias, *tr. fr. Portuguese by* Frances Ellen Buckland.
"There are palm trees in my homeland." TTY

Song of Exile, A. Bible, *O.T. Fr.* Psalms: Psalm CXXXVII ("By the rivers of Babylon. "), 1-6. TrGrPo

Song of Expectancy. George Hitchcock. EAS

Song of Faith, A. Josiah Gilbert Holland. WGRP

Song of Farewell. Nellie Wong. BrSi

Song of Finis, The. Walter de la Mare. MoBrPo

Song of Fionnuala, The. Thomas Moore. AnIL; BIrV

Song of Fixed Accord. Wallace Stevens. InPS; NePoAm

Song of Four Priests Who Suffered Death at Lancaster, A. *Unknown.* ACP

Song of Granny Smith. Mary McArthur. SoTCo

Song of grass, A,/ A song of earth. "Yehoash", *tr. by* Isidore Goldstick. TrJP

Song of Greatness, A. *Unknown, tr. fr. Chippewa Indian by* Mary Austin. AmFN; FaPON

Song of Greece, The. Chiang Hsun, *tr. fr. Chinese by* Dominic Cheung. IFON

Song of Hannah, The. Bible, *O.T. See* First Samuel: Hannah's Song of Thanksgiving.

Song of Hate. Jacob ben David Frances, *tr. fr. Hebrew by* A. B. Rhine. TrJP

Song of Hate for Eels. Arthur Guiterman. OBAL

Song of Hiawatha, The, *sels.* Longfellow.
Death of Minnehaha, The. AA, XX.
"From his pouch he took his colors." EyDe
"From his wanderings far to eastward." *Fr.* XXI. GOA
"Give me of your bark, O Birch-tree!" Mes
(Hiawatha's Canoe.) OHIP
Hiawatha's Brothers. BoTP
Hiawatha's Childhood. *Fr.* III. FaPON; OHFP; WBLP
("At the door on summer evenings.") BoTP
("Downward through the evening twilight.") FaBV
Hiawatha's Wooing. *Fr.* X. BeLS
Little Hiawatha, The. *Fr.* III. OnUR
"When he heard the owls at midnight." *Fr.* III. FM

Song of History: Peter the Great. Sakuma Shozan, *tr. fr. Chinese by* Burton Watson. JLIC-2

Song of Ho Man-tzu. Ho Ning, *tr. fr. Chinese by* Lois Fusek. ATF

Song of Ho Man-tzu. Mao Hsi-chen, *tr. fr. Chinese by* Lois Fusek. ATF

Song of Ho Man-tzu. Mao Wen-hsi, *tr. fr. Chinese by* Lois Fusek. ATF

Song of Ho Man-tzu. Sun Kuang-hsien, *tr. fr. Chinese by* Lois Fusek. ATF

Song of Honor [*or* Honour], The. Ralph Hodgson. LiTB; MoBrPo

Song of Hope. Mary Artemisia Lathbury. BLPA

Song of Hope. Daisy Yamora, *tr. fr. Spanish by* James Black *and* Bernardo Garcia-Pandavenes. AIW

Song of Impossibilities, A. Winthrop Mackworth Praed. NA

Song of Instruction, A. Te Kooti Rikirangi, *tr. fr. Maori by* Margaret Orbell. PeNZ

Song of Jed Smith, The, *sel.* John G. Neihardt.
"One more rendezvous." FYAP

Song of Jehane du Castel Beau, The. William Morris. *Fr.* Golden Wings. ChTr

Song of Job, A. Khalil Touma, *tr. fr. Arabic by* Lena Jayyusi *and* Samuel Hazo. MAP

Song of Joy. *Unknown. See* Uvavnuk.

Song of Kan-chou. Ku Hsiung, *tr. fr. Chinese* by Lois Fusek. ATF

Song of Kuk-ook, the Bad Boy, The. *Eskimo Oral Tradition.* TTTS

Song of Labour, A, *sel.* Alexander Anderson.
  "Heart! But this grand world rolls onward through the shadows of the years." PF

Song of Lazarus, The, *sel.* Alex Comfort.
  Notes for My Son. *Fr.* VI. LiTM; MoBrPo; SeCePo

Song of Lewes, The. *Unknown.* OxBoL
  (Against the Baron's Enemies.) MeEL

Song of Liberty, A. Blake. EnRP

Song of Life, A. Franz Werfel, *tr. fr. German* by Edith Abercrombie Snow. TrJP

Song of Lin Liang's Painting "Two Horned Falcons." Li Meng-yang, *tr. fr. Chinese* by Jonathan Chaves. CoBLCP

Song of Lo-fu, The. *Unknown, tr. fr. Chinese* by Arthur Waley. AWP

Song of Loneliness. Judah Halevi, *tr. fr. Hebrew* by Nina Davis Salaman. TrJP

Song of Longing. *Gond Oral Tradition*, tr. by V. Elwin *and* S. Hivale. WTO

Song of Longing. *Unknown, tr. fr. Maori* by John White. WTO

Song of Love, A. "Lewis Carroll." GN

Song of Love, The. Rainer Maria Rilke, *tr. fr. German* by Ludwig Lewisohn. AWP

Song of Love and Death, The. Tennyson. *Fr.* Idylls of the King: Lancelot and Elaine. OBNC

Song of Love for Jesus, A. Richard Rolle. MeEL

Song of Lung-hsi. Ch'en Tao, *tr. fr. Chinese* by Burton Watson. CoBCP

Song of Man Chipping an Arrowhead. W. S. Merwin. InPK

Song of Marion's Men. Bryant. AnAmPo; PAH

Song of Meeting. Tsung Ch'en, *tr. fr. Chinese* by Jonathan Chaves. CoBLCP

Song of Mehitabel, The. Don Marquis. *Fr.* Archy and Mehitabel. FiBHP

Song of Milkanwatha, The, *parody, sel.* George A. Strong.
  Modern Hiawatha, The. FaBoCo; FaBoPa; FaFP; FaPON; FiBHP; MoShBr; NA; Par; RHPC
  (Hiawatha Revisited.) BXAP

Song of Moon and Snow. Koo Siu-sun. WCI

Song of Mr. Toad, The. Kenneth Grahame. *Fr.* The Wind in the Willows. FaPON; FiBHP; GoJo; NOBL

Song of My Song, in Three Parts, A. *Unknown, tr. fr. Seneca Indian* by Jerome Rothenberg *and* Richard Johnny John. STP

Song of My Soul. Ralph Chubb. PeHV

Song of Myself. Walt Whitman. AmPP; LiTA; MoAmPo, *abr.*; NoBA; OxBA; SOTW, *much abr.*
 Sels.
  Battle of the *Bonhomme Richard* and the *Serapis*. *Fr.* XXXV-XXXVI. MOS; RB; UnPo
  "Child said, A, *What is the grass?*." *Fr.* VI. NoP
    (Grass.) BLPL
    (Leaves of Grass, VI *and* XX) AA
  Drayman, The. *Fr.* XIII. PoNe
    "Oxen that rattle the yoke and chain or halt in the leafy shade," *sel.* FM
  "Flaunt of the sunshine I need not your bask." *Fr.* XL. TrGrPo
  "Gigantic beauty of a stallion, fresh and responsive to my caresses, A." *Fr.* XXXII. PDV
  Has Any One Supposed It Lucky to Be Born?. *Fr.* VII. NAs
  Heroes. *Fr.* XXXIII *and* XXXV. AA
  "Houses and rooms are full of perfumes." *Fr.* II. TrGrPo; UnPo
  Hub to the Universe, A. *Fr.* XLVIII. FaFP
  "I am the poet of the Body and I am the poet of the Soul." *Fr.* XXI. WeW
    I Am He That Walks with the Tender and Growing Night, *sel.* ChTr
  "I believe a leaf of grass is no less than the journey-work of the stars." *Fr.* XXXI. PDV
  "I believe in the flesh and the appetites." *Fr.* XXIV. Prf
  "I believe in you my soul." *Fr.* V. Prf
    Swiftly Arose, *sel.* TrCP, *abr.*
  "I celebrate myself, and sing myself." *Fr.* I. AA; NAWM-2; NoAM; NoP; PoE
    (Myself.) BLPL; FaBoBe
  "I hear and behold God in every object, yet understand God not in the least." *Fr.* XLVIII. WGRP
  "I know I have the best of time and space." *Fr.* XLVI. NoAM
  "I think I could turn and live with animals." *Fr.* XXXII. HAP; NU; PDV; TrGrPo; WeW; WGRP
    (Animals.) FaFP
  Infinity. *Fr.* XLIV–XLV. AA

  "Little one sleeps in its cradle, The." *Fr.* VIII. TrGrPo
  "My signs are a rain-proof coat, good shoes, a staff cut from the woods." *Fr.* XLVI. Prf
  "Now I will do nothing but listen." *Fr.* XXVI. HoPM
  "Pure contralto sings in the organloft, The." *Fr.* XV. TTTS
  Runaway Slave, The. *Fr.* X. PoNe
  "Spotted hawk swoops by and accuses me, The." *Fr.* LII. NoP
  Stallion, The. *Fr.* XXXII. PDV
  "Trippers and askers surround me." *Fr.* IV. UnPo
  "Twenty-eight young men bathe by the shore." *Fr.* XI. HAP; NoP
  "Walt Whitman, a kosmos, of Manhattan the son." *Fr.* XXIV. NoP; SCV
  "Who goes there? hankering, gross, mystical, nude." *Fr.* XX. TrGrPo
  "With music strong I come, with my cornets and my drums." *Fr.* XVIII. TrGrPo
  Wounded Person, The. *Fr.* XXXIII. PoNe

Song of Napalm. Bruce Weigl. MAYP

Song of Nezahualcoyotl. *Unknown.* DL

Song of Nu-Numma-Kwiten, The. *Unknown, tr. fr. Bushman.* PeSA

Song of Nuns, A. James Shirley. *See* Imposture, The: O Fly My Soul.

Song of Occident. Claude Vigée, *tr. fr. French* by Anthony Rudolf. VWA

Song of Oenone and Paris. George Peele. *See* Arraignment of Paris, The: Fair and Fair.

Song of One Eleven Years in Prison. George Canning, George Ellis *and* John Hookham Frere. *See* Rovers, The: Rogero's Song.

Song of Panama, A. Damon Runyon. PAH

Song of Parents Who Want to Wake Up Their Son. *Unknown, tr. fr. Kwakiutl Indian.* TTTS

Song of Peach Blossom Retreat. T'ang Yin, *tr. fr. Chinese* by Jonathan Chaves. CoBLCP

Song of P'eng-ya. Tu Fu, *tr. fr. Chinese* by Burton Watson. CoBCP

Song of Plenitude. Anna Swirszczynska, *tr. fr. Polish* by Czeslaw Milosz. PwPP

Song of Poverty. *Gond Oral Tradition*, tr. by V. Elwin and S. Hivale. WTO

Song of Praise, A. Bible, *O.T. See* Psalms: Psalm CXLVIII ("Praise ye the Lord. ").

Song of Praise for an Ox. Abraham Sutskever, *tr. fr. Yiddish* by Ruth Whitman. VWA

Song of Quoodle, The. G. K. Chesterton. GoJo

Song of Reasons. Robert Pinsky. AnAn; HCAP

Song of Regret. Lady Pan, *tr. fr. Chinese* by Burton Watson. CoBCP

Song of Renunciation, A. Sir Owen Seaman. CenHV

Song of Resignation. Yehuda Amichai, *tr. fr. Hebrew* by Assia Gutmann. NYBP

Song of Returnings. William Pitt Root. GeTw

Song of Riches, A. Katharine Lee Bates. AA

Song of Roland, The ("Charles the King, our Emperor, the Great."). *Unknown, tr. fr. Old French.* NAWM-1, *abr.*, tr. by Frederick Goldin.
 Sels.
  "In wrath and grief away the Paynims fly." *Tr.* by Dorothy L. Sayers. OBWP
  Ready They Make Hauberks Sarrazinese. *Tr.* by C. K. Scott Moncrieff. WaaP

Song of Sack, A. *At. to* Charles Cotton. OBS

Song of Samuel Sweet, The. Charles Causley. OBNV

Song of Selling Flowers. Tsung Ch'en, *tr. fr. Chinese* by Jonathan Chaves. CoBLCP

Song of Seyd Nimetollah of Kuhistan. Emerson. NOBA

Song of shadows: never glory was, A. Shadows. Victor Plarr. NOBVV

Song of Sherman's Army, The. Charles Graham Halpine. PAH

Song of Sherwood, A. Alfred Noyes. FaPON; MoBrPo

Song of Sickness, A. Hine Tangikuku, *tr. fr. Maori* by Barry Mitcalfe. WTO

Song of Sitting Bull. *Unknown.* GOA

Song of Sixpence. *Unknown.* OxBoLi

Song of Slaves in the Desert. Whittier. OxBA

Song of Snohomish, The. William S. Wallace. ASP

Song of Snow-white Heads. Cho Wen-chün, *tr.* by Arthur Waley. BoWoP

Song of Solomon, The ("Let him kiss me with the kisses of his mouth."), *sels. Bible, O.T.*
  (Song of Songs, The.) AWP; TrGrPo
  As a Seal upon Thy Heart. *Fr.* VIII: 6-7. TrJP
  ("Set me as a seal on your heart.") BoWoP, *ad.* by Willis Barnstone.
  Awake! *Fr.* IV: 16. FaPON
  "Behold, thou art fair." *Fr.* IV: 1-7. TrJP
  "For, lo, the winter is past." *Fr.* II: 11–12. PDV
    (Lo, the Winter Is Past.) FaPON

Hark! My Beloved! *Fr.* II: 8-13. TrJP
("Voice of my darling, The.") BoWoP, *ad.* by Willis Barnstone, 8–14.
"I am come into my garden, my sister, my spouse." *Fr.* V. OBVE; TOF
I Am My Beloved's. *Fr.* VII: 11–14. TrJP
("I am my lover's and he desires me.") BoWoP, *ad.* by Willis Barnstone.
"I am the rose of Sharon, and the lily of the valleys." *Fr.* II. BoLoP; FF; GBL; LLLT; OBVE
(I Am the Rose of Sharon.) ChTr
I Sleep, but My Heart Waketh. *Fr.* V: 2-16; VI: 1-3. TrJP
("I sleep but my heart is awake.") BoWoP, *ad.* by Willis Barnstone, 2–18.
"My love has gone down to his garden." BoWoP, *ad.* by Willis Barnstone.
"My love is white and ruddy." BoWoP, *ad.* by Willis Barnstone.
On My Bed I Sought Him. *Fr.* III: 1-5. TrJP
("In my bed at night.") BoWoP, *ad.* by Willis Barnstone.
Return, Return, O Shulammite. *Fr.* VII: 1-10. TrJP
"Song of songs, which is Solomon's, The." *Fr.* I. OBVE
"Turning to him, who meets me with desire." *Fr.* VII: 10–13, tr. by Marcia Falk. PBWP
"Under the quince tree." *Fr.* VIII: 5, tr. by Marcia Falk. PBWP
"Yes, I am black! and radiant." *Fr.* I: 5–6, tr. by Marcia Falk. PBWP
Song of Songs, The. Bible, *O.T. See* Song of Solomon, The.
Song of songs, which is Solomon's, The. Bible, *O.T. Fr.* The Song of Solomon, I. OBVE
Song of Sorrow. *Unknown, tr. fr. Chinese* by Burton Watson. CoBCP
Song of Spring. Keats. BoTP
Song of Spring. Wu Chün, *tr. fr. Chinese* by Burton Watson. CoBCP
Song of Sukkaartik, the Assistant Spirit. Ajukutooq, *tr. fr. Eskimo.* WTO
Song of Summer Days. J. W. Foley. BoTP
Song of Sungbuk. Jung Han-mo, *tr. fr. Korean* by Koh Chang-soo. ACKP
Song of sunshine through the rain, A. Calvary and Easter. Susan Coolidge. WBLP
(An Easter Song.) BLRP
Song of Supplication, A. Bible, *O.T. See* Psalms: Psalm CXXX ("Out of the depths. ").
Song of Surfing on the Bore. Cheng Hsieh, *tr. fr. Chinese* by Jonathan Chaves. CoBLCP
Song of Texas. William Henry Cuyler Hosmer. PAH
Song of Thanks, A. Edward Smyth Jones. BANP
Song of the Ancient People, The. Edna Dean Proctor. AA
Song of the Angels. Lizelia Augusta Jenkins Moorer. CBWP-3
Song of the Arrow, The. Isabella Valancy Crawford. *Fr.* Gisli, the Chieftain. OBCV
Song of the Autumn Wind. Liu Ch'e, *tr. fr. Chinese* by Burton Watson. CoBCP
Song of the Bald Eagle. *Unknown, tr. fr. Crow Indian* by Lewis Henry Morgan. STP
Song of the Ballet. J. B. Morton. FiBHP
Song of the Bamboo Branches. Sun Kuang-hsien, *tr. fr. Chinese* by Lois Fusek. ATF
Song of the Banana Man, The. Evan Jones. PVCV
Song of the Banjo, The. Kipling. FaBoCh; PrIm
Song of the Barber. W. H. Auden. *Fr.* Man of La Mancha. AnAn
Song of the Bath, The. Margaret Gibbs. BoTP
Song of the Beautiful Ladies. Tu Fu, *tr. fr. Chinese* by Burton Watson. CoBCP
Song of the Bird, The. Longfellow. BoTP
Song of the Blue-Corn Dance. *Unknown, tr. fr. Hopi Indian* by Natalie Curtis. WTO
Song of the Boat-Pullers. Pien Kung, *tr. fr. Chinese* by Jonathan Chaves. CoBLCP
Song of the Boat Trackers, The. Ch'en Wei-sung, *tr. fr. Chinese* by Madeline Chu. WFTU
Song of the Bomber. Ethel Mannin. CN
Song of the Borderguard, The. Robert Duncan. NeAP; PoM
Song of the Bowmen of Shu. Ezra Pound, *after the Chinese.* OBVE
Song of the Breaking of the Willow. *Unknown, tr. fr. Chinese* by Burton Watson. CoBCP
Song of the Breed. Carroll Arnett. STE
Song of the Bride. Susan Mernit. VWA
Song of the Brightness of Water. Karol Wojtyla. CRP
Song of the Broad-Ax, *sel.* Walt Whitman.
Broad-Ax, The. MoAmPo
Song of the Builders. Jessie Wilmore Murton. AmFN

Song of the Bush-Shrike. *Unknown, tr. fr. Zulu.* PeSA
Song of the Butterflies. Chang Pi, *tr. fr. Chinese* by Lois Fusek. ATF
Song of the Camels. Elizabeth Jane Coatsworth. FaPON
Song of the Camp, The. Bayard Taylor. AA; AnAmPo; BeLS; GN; WBLP
Song of the Cannibals, A. Countess of Winchilsea. PoE
Song of the Cape of Good Hope. Christian Schubart, *tr. fr. German* by Alfred Baskerville. NU, *ad.* by Robert Bly
Song of the Captured Woman. James Devaney. PoAu-1
Song of the Cauld Lad of Hylton. *Unknown. See* Wae's me! wae's me.
Song of the Chattahooche. Sidney Lanier. AnAmPo
Song of the Chattahoochee. Sidney Lanier. AA; AmFN; BoNaP; FaBoBe; FaBV; LiTA; OHFP
Song of the Ch'in-Dynasty Mirror. Wang Shih-chen, *tr. fr. Chinese* by Jonathan Chaves. CoBLCP
Song of the Christmas Tree, The. Blanche Elizabeth Wade. OHIP
Song of the Clear River. Huang T'ing-chien, *tr. fr. Chinese* by Burton Watson. CoBCP
Song of the Closing Service. Aliza Shenhar, *tr. fr. Hebrew* by Linda Zisquit. VWA
Song of the Clouds. Aristophanes, *tr. fr. Greek* by Oscar Wilde. *Fr.* The Clouds. AWP
Song of the Crab Medicine-Bag. *Unknown, tr. fr. Chippewa Indian* by Jerome Rothenberg. STP
Song of the Cricket. Lo Fu, *tr. fr. Chinese* by Dominic Cheung. IFON
Song of the Darkness. John Bricuth. SM
Song of the Dew. *Unknown, tr. fr. Hebrew* by Solomon Solis-Cohen. TrJP
Song of the Dragon's Daughter, The. Ursula K. Le Guin. BWV
Song of the Duck Hunters. Kao Ch'i, *tr. fr. Chinese* by Jonathan Chaves. CoBLCP
Song of the Elfin Steersman. George Hill. AA
Song of the Emigrants [in Bermuda]. Andrew Marvell. *See* Where the remote Bermudas ride.
Song of the Enchanters. W. H. Auden. AnAn
Song of the Engine, The. H. Worsley-Benison. BoTP
Song of the Evil Spirit of the Woods. Thomas Moore. OBTV
Song of the Exile. Huang Tsun-hsien, *tr. fr. Chinese* by J. D. Schmidt. WFTU
Song of the Exposition, *sel.* Walt Whitman.
Muse in the New World, The. MoAmPo
Song of the Factory Girls. *Unknown.* SaC
Song of the Fallen Deer. *Unknown, tr. fr. Pima Indian* by Frank Russell. OBVE
Song of the Fire-Charm. *Unknown, tr. fr. Chippewa Indian* by Frances Densmore; *English vers.* by Jerome Rothenberg. STP
Song of the Fisherman. Ku Hsiung, *tr. fr. Chinese* by Lois Fusek. ATF
Song of the Fisherman. Li Hsün, *tr. fr. Chinese* by Lois Fusek. ATF
Song of the Fisherman. Sun Kuang-hsien, *tr. fr. Chinese* by Lois Fusek. ATF
Song of the Fisherman. Wei Ch'eng-pan, *tr. fr. Chinese* by Lois Fusek. ATF
Song of the Fisherman's Lover. Roseann Lloyd. TSL
Song of the Flags, The. Silas Weir Mitchell. PAH
Song of the Flea. Judah Al-Harizi, *tr. fr. Hebrew.* TrJP
Song of the Flood. *Unknown, tr. fr. Navajo Indian.* TTTS
Song of the Forest Ranger, The. Herbert Bashford. OHIP
Song of the Four Winds, The. Thomas Love Peacock. *Fr.* The Misfortunes of Elphin. WiR
Song of the Fucked Duck. Marge Piercy. BoWoP; NMM
Song of the Full Catch. Constance Lindsay Skinner. CaP
Song of the Galley, The. *Unknown, tr. fr. Spanish* by John Gibson Lockhart. AWP
Song of the Galley-slaves. Kipling. ChTr; GTBS-P; HAP; PoEL-5
Song of the Good Samaritan, The. Vernon Watkins. LiTM
Song of the GPO, A. Gerry Hamill. NOBL
Song of the Grass, The. Leigh Hunt. BoTP
Song of the Graves, The. *Unknown, tr. fr. Welsh* by Ernest Rhys. *Fr.* The Black Book of Carmarthen. OBMV
Song of the Gull. Maruyama Kaoru, *tr. fr. Japanese* by Hiroaki Sato. FCEI
Song of the Hammer. Armanda Guiducci, *tr. fr. Italian* by Muriel Kittel. DMI
Song of the Hanged. Eléni Vakaló, *tr. fr. Modern Greek* by James Damaskos. PBWP
Song of the Happy Shepherd, The. W. B. Yeats. NoAM
Song of the Harlot. Bible, *O.T. Fr.* Isaiah, XXIII: 16. TrJP
Song of the Harvest. Henry Stevenson Washburn. OHIP
Song of the Highest Tower. Rimbaud, *tr. fr. French* by Edgell Rickword. AWP
Song of the Hill. Edith Lodge. GoYe

Song of the Horse. *Unknown, tr. fr. Navajo Indian* by Natalie Curtis. AWP

Song of the Hunt, The. John Bennett. *Fr. Master Sky-Lark.* AA

Song of the Ill-Married. *Unknown, tr. fr. French* by Patricia Terry. BoWoP

(Weaving Song.) DMF

Song of the Indian Maid ("O Sorrow,/ Why dost borrow"). Keats. *Fr. Endymion [a Poetic Romance]*, IV. NOBE; OBEV

(O Sorrow!, *abr.*) CH

Song of the Indian Maid, The ("Beneath my palm-trees, by the riverside"). Keats. *Fr. Endymion [a Poetic Romance].* NOBE

Song of the Invisible Corpse in the Field. Gregory Orr. AnAn

Song of the Jade Tower in Spring. Ku Hsiung, *tr. fr. Chinese* by Lois Fusek. ATF

Song of the Jade Tower in Spring. Niu Chiao, *tr. fr. Chinese* by Lois Fusek. ATF

Song of the Jade Tower in Spring. Wei Ch'eng-pan, *tr. fr. Chinese* by Lois Fusek. ATF

Song of the Jellicles, The. T. S. Eliot. FaBoCh; FaBoNo; OxBChV

Song of the King of the Eboes. *Unknown.* PBCV

Song of the Knight of the Mirrors. W. H. Auden. *Fr. Man of La Mancha.* AnAn

Song of the Lamp. Maruyama Kaoru, *tr. fr. Japanese* by Hiroaki Sato. FCEI

Song of the Last Jewish Child. Edmond Jabès, *tr. fr. French* by Anthony Rudolf. VWA

Song of the Lilies, The. Lucy Wheelock. OHIP

Song of the Lioness for Her Cub. *Unknown, tr. fr. Hottentot* by Thomas Hahn. BoWoP

Song of the Lotus-Eaters. Tennyson. See Lotos-Eaters, The: There Is Sweet Music Here.

Song of the Love of Jesus, A ("Luf es lif that lastes ay, thar it in Christe es feste."), *sel.* Richard Rolle of Hampole. PoEL-1

Love is Life. ACP

Song of the Low, The. Ernest Charles Jones. NOBVV; PF

Song of the Lower Classes, The. Ernest Charles Jones. CoMu

Song of the Lute. Po Chü-i, *tr. fr. Chinese* by Burton Watson. CoBCP

Song of the Mad Prince, The. Walter de la Mare. EBEV; FaBoCh; GoJo; MoP; NoAM; NOBE; OxBChV

Song of the Man of Green Hill, The. Kao Ch'i, *tr. fr. Chinese* by Jonathan Chaves. CoBLCP

Song of the Man Who Succeeded. *Unknown, tr. fr. Chippewa Indian* by Jerome Rothenberg *from* Frances Densmore. STP

Song of the Master and Boatswain. W. H. Auden. *Fr. The Sea and the Mirror.* BoLoP; MOS

(Master and Boatswain.) FaBoTw

Song of the Mayers [*or* The Mayers' Song]. *Unknown.* CH; GBP

Song of the Merchant's Wife. Yang Shih-ch'i, *tr. fr. Chinese* by Jonathan Chaves. CoBLCP

Song of the Merchant's Wife. Yang Wei-chen, *tr. fr. Chinese* by Jonathan Chaves. CoBLCP

Song of the Mermaids and Mermen. Sir Walter Scott. *Fr. The Pirate, ch. 16.* WSC

Song of the Micmac, The. Joseph Howe. CaP

Song of the Militant Romance, The. Wyndham Lewis. FaBoTw; OxBTC

Song of the Mischievous Dog, The. Dylan Thomas. FaFP; FL; FPL; GrPl

Song of the Moderns. John Gould Fletcher. AWP

Song of the Moon, A. Claude McKay. PoNe

Song of the Moon. Priscilla Jane Thompson. CBWP-2

Song of the Murdered Child. *Unknown.* GBP

(Milk-white Dove.) ChTr

Song of the Muses, The. Matthew Arnold. See Empedocles on Etna: Song of Callicles, The ("Through the black, rushing smoke-burst").

Song of the Narcissus, The. *Unknown, tr. fr. Arabic* by E. Powys Mathers. *Fr. The Thousand and One Nights.* AWP

Song of the Negro Boatman. Whittier. *Fr. At Port Royal.* GN

Song of the Negro on the Ferry. José Craveirinha, *tr. fr. Portuguese* by Chris Searle. WMBCH

Song of the Night at Daybreak. Alice Meynell. CH

Song of the Ogres. W. H. Auden. MoBrPo

Song of the Old Mother, The. W. B. Yeats. MoBrPo

Song of the Old Oak. Chang Yü, *tr. fr. Chinese* by Jonathan Chaves. CoBLCP

Song of the Old Woman. *Unknown, tr. fr. Eskimo in French.* AIW, *tr. by* Paul-Emile Victor; *English vers.* by Armand Schwerner; BoWoP, *tr. by* Paul-Emile Victor; *English vers.* by Armand Schwerner; OV, *tr. by* Paul-Emile Victor; *English vers.* by Armand Schwerner

Song of the Open Road. Ogden Nash. AnAmPo; FaBoCo; FPL; OBAL

Song of the Open Road, A. *Unknown, tr. fr. Latin* by John Addington Symonds. AWP

Song of the Open Road, *sel.* Walt Whitman. FaFP; NOBA

"Afoot and light-hearted I take to the open road." RFM

Song of the Owl, The. Richard Kendall Munkittrick. OBCA

Song of the Painting "Catching Fish." Li Tung-yang, *tr. fr. Chinese* by Jonathan Chaves. CoBLCP

Song of the Painting of the Long-Life Star. Wang Chiu-ssu, *tr. fr. Chinese* by Jonathan Chaves. CoBLCP

Song of the Painting "River and Mountains," by Wu Wei. Ho Ching-ming, *tr. fr. Chinese* by Jonathan Chaves. CoBLCP

Song of the Palm. Tracy Robinson. AA

Song of the Pen, The. Judah al-Harizi, *tr. fr. Hebrew* by J. Chotzner. TrJP

Song of the Pike. Sato Haruo, *tr. fr. Japanese* by Geoffrey Bownas *and* Anthony Thwaite. PeBJV

Song of the Pilgrims, The, *sel.* Rupert Brooke. "O Thou/ God of all long desirous roaming." TrPWD

Song of the Pilgrims. Thomas Cogswell Upham. PAH

Song of the Plain. Anna Hajnal, *tr. fr. Hungarian* by William Jay Smith. MHuP

Song of the Poor Man. *Unknown, tr.* by Anselm Hollo. TTY

Song of the Pop-Bottlers. Morris Bishop. FaPON; FiBHP

Song of the Precious Knife, A. Ch'iu Chin, *tr. fr. Chinese* by Pao Chia-lin. WFTU

Song of the Queen Bee. E. B. White. NYBP

Song of the Quest. W. H. Auden. *Fr. Man of La Mancha.* AnAn

Song of the Rabbits outside the Tavern, The. Elizabeth Jane Coatsworth. OBCA

Song of the Rain. Hugh McCrae. CBAP; PoAu-1

Song of the Rain Chant. *Unknown, tr. fr. Navajo Indian* by Natalie Curtis. AWP

Song of the Red & Green Buffalo, A. *Unknown, tr. fr. Oto Indian* by William Whitman. STP

Song of the Redwood-Tree. Walt Whitman. AmPP

Song of the Reed Sparrow, The. *Unknown.* OxBChV

Song of the Reim-Kennar, The. Sir Walter Scott. *Fr. The Pirate, ch. 6.* OAEL-2; OBNC

Song of the Rejected Woman. Kibkarjuk, *tr. fr. Eskimo into Danish* by Knud Rasmussen; *into English* by Tom Lowenstein. WPOW

Song of the Rice Workers. *Unknown, tr. fr. Italian* by Muriel Kittel. DMI

Song of the Riders. Stephen Vincent Benét. *Fr. John Brown's Body.* MoAmPo

Song of the Ringing in the Ear. Ishihara Yoshiro, *tr. fr. Japanese* by Hiroaki Sato. FCEI

Song of the River City. Chang Pi, *tr. fr. Chinese* by Lois Fusek. ATF

Song of the River City. Niu Chiao, *tr. fr. Chinese* by Lois Fusek. ATF

Song of the River City. Ou-yang Chiung, *tr. fr. Chinese* by Lois Fusek. ATF

Song of the River City. Wei Chuang, *tr. fr. Chinese* by Lois Fusek. ATF

Song of the Road, A. Robert Louis Stevenson. BrPo

Song of the Round Man. Michael Palmer. NPGG

Song of the Sabbath. Kadya Molodowsky, *tr. fr. Yiddish* by Jean Valentine. PBWP; WPOW

Song of the Sacred Strings. Li Ho, *tr. fr. Chinese* by Burton Watson. CoBCP

Song of the Sail. Maruyama Kaoru, *tr. fr. Japanese* by Hiroaki Sato. FCEI

Song of the Screw. *Unknown.* NA

Song of the Seamen and Land Soldiers, A. *Unknown.* OxBSS

Song of the Seaweed, *sel.* Eliza Cook. "Many a lip is gaping for drink." FiBHP

Song of the Seeress. *Unknown, tr. fr. Norse* by Paul B. Taylor *and* W. H. Auden. NAWM-1

Song of the Self-Made Orphans. David Avidan, *tr. fr. Hebrew* by Warren Bargad *and* Stanley F. Chyet. IP

Song of the Settlers. Jessamyn West. FaPON

Song of the Shadows, The. Walter de la Mare. CMoP; MoBrPo; TrGrPo

Song of the Sheet. *Unknown.* BXAP

Song of the Shepherd Boy. Bunyan. See Pilgrim's Progress, The: He that is down needs fear no fall.

Song of the Shepherd in the Valley of Humiliation, The. Bunyan. See Pilgrim's Progress, The: He that is down needs fear no fall.

Song of the Shirt, The. Thomas Hood. EBVV; EnRP; FaPoR; SaC; TEP; WBLP

Song of the Shirt, The, *sel.* Thomas Hood. "Work—work—work." RR

Song of the Silent Land. Johann Gaudenz von Salis-Seewis, *tr. fr. German* by Longfellow. AWP

Song of the Sirens. William Browne. *See* Inner Temple Masque, The: Sirens' Song, The.

Song of the Ski, The. Wilson MacDonald. CaP

Song of the Sky Loom. *Unknown, tr. fr. Tewa Indian by* Herbert J. Spinden. WTO

Song of the Smoke, The. W. E. B. DuBois. PoBA; UnPo

Song of the Son. Jean Toomer. AmNP; CDC; NIP; PoBA

Song of the Soul That Knows God by Faith. Saint John of the Cross, *tr. fr. Spanish by* Seamus Heaney. TIRV

Song of the Soul that Rejoices in Knowing God through Faith. Saint John of the Cross, *tr. fr. Spanish by* K. Kavanagh *and* O. Rodrigues. TOF

Song of the Southern Country. Li Hsün, *tr. fr. Chinese by* Lois Fusek. ATF

Song of the Southern Country. Ou-yang Chiung, *tr. fr. Chinese by* Lois Fusek. ATF

Song of the spheres in their revolutions, The. Jalal ed-Din Rumi, *tr. by* E. H. Whinfield. TOF

Song of the Springbok Does. *Unknown, tr. fr. Hottentot by* W. H. I. Bleek. PeSA

Song of the Strange Young Duckling. Deborah Munro. IHMS

Song of the Stygian Naiades. Thomas Lovell Beddoes. EnRP; OAEL-2

Song of The Suffering Servant, The. Bible, *O.T. Fr.* Isaiah, LII: 13-LIII: 12. NAWM-1

Song of the Syrens. William Browne. *See* Inner Temple Masque, The: Sirens' Song, The.

Song of the Tailless Ox. Shitago. *See* I have an ox but its tail is missing.

Song of the Tart. Kaneko Mitsuharu, *tr. fr. Japanese by* Geoffrey Bownas *and* Anthony Thwaite. PeBJV

Song of the Taste. Gary Snyder. CAPP; LCAP

Song of the Thoroughfare. Hsieh Shang, *tr. fr. Chinese by* Burton Watson. CoBCP

Song of the Three Minstrels. Thomas Chatterton. *See* Aella; a Tragycal Enterlude: Budding floweret blushes at the light [Boddynge flourettes bloshes atte the lyghte], The.

Song of the Thunder. *Unknown, tr. fr. Hottentot.* PeSA

Song of the Thunders. *Unknown, tr. fr. Chippewa Indian by* Frances Densmore. OBVE

Song of the Toad, The. John Burroughs. FaPON

Song of the Tortured Girl, The. John Berryman. CAPP; CoAP

Song of the Train. David McCord. FaPON; NTCP

Song of the Transport Workers. Pien Kung, *tr. fr. Chinese by* Jonathan Chaves. CoBLCP

Song of the Trees. *Unknown, tr. fr. Chippewa Indian by* Frances Densmore. OBVE

Song of the Trees of the Black Forest. Edmond Jabès, *tr. fr. French by* Anthony Rudolf. VWA

Song of the Trout Fisher, The. Ikinilik, *tr. fr. Eskimo.* WTO

Song of the Truck. Doris Frankel. AmFN

Song of the Turkey Buzzard. Lew Welch. PoM

Song of the Turnkey, The. Harry Bache Smith. AA

Song of the Turtle and the Flamingo, The. James Thomas Fields. GN (Turtle and Flamingo, The.) AnAmPo

Song of the Ungirt Runners, The. Charles Hamilton Sorley. MoBrPo; OBEV

Song of the Unloved. *Unknown, tr. fr. Sotho by* Jack Cope *and* Dan Kunene. PeSA

Song of the Unsuccessful, The. Richard Burton. WGRP

Song of the Valkyries, The. *Unknown, tr. fr. Norse by* Lee M. Hollander. WaaP

Song of the Venetian Silk-Spinners *Unknown, tr. fr. Italian by* Muriel Kittel. DMI

Song of the Virgin Mother, A. Lope de Vega, *tr. fr. Spanish by* Ezra Pound. AWP

Song of the Wanderer. Wang T'ing-hsiang, *tr. fr. Chinese by* Jonathan Chaves. CoBLCP

Song of the Water Clock at Night. Ku Hsiung, *tr. fr. Chinese by* Lois Fusek. ATF

Song of the Water Clock at Night. Mao Hsi-chen, *tr. fr. Chinese by* Lois Fusek. ATF

Song of the Water Clock at Night. Mao Wen-hsi, *tr. fr. Chinese by* Lois Fusek. ATF

Song of the Water Clock at Night. Niu Chiao, *tr. fr. Chinese by* Lois Fusek. ATF

Song of the Water Clock at Night. Sun Kuang-hsien, *tr. fr. Chinese by* Lois Fusek. ATF

Song of the Water Clock at Night. Wei Chuang, *tr. fr. Chinese by* Lois Fusek. ATF

Song of the Water Clock at Night. Wen T'ing-yün, *tr. fr. Chinese by* Lois Fusek. ATF

Song of the Waterfall at Mount Lu. Yang Wei-chen, *tr. fr. Chinese by* Jonathan Chaves. CoBLCP

Song of the Weaving Woman. Yüan Chen, *tr. fr. Chinese by* Wu-chi Liu. SaC

Song of the Well. Bible, *O.T. Fr.* Numbers, XXI: 17–18. TrJP

Song of the West Stream. Li Hsün, *tr. fr. Chinese by* Lois Fusek. ATF

Song of the West Stream. Mao Wen-hsi, *tr. fr. Chinese by* Lois Fusek. ATF

Song of the West Stream. Niu Chiao, *tr. fr. Chinese by* Lois Fusek. ATF

Song of the Western Men, The. Robert Stephen Hawker. EnRP; FaPoR; OBNC

Song of the Wild Crane: Presented to a Friend, A. Singde, *tr. fr. Chinese by* William Schultz. WFTU

Song of the Wild Dove, The. Cassiano Ricardo, *tr. fr. Portuguese by* Jean R. Longland. ATCBP

Song of the Wind. Munir Niazi, *tr. fr. Urdu by* Mahmood Jamal. PBMUP

Song of the Wind and the Rain. Solomon Ibn Gabirol, *tr. fr. Hebrew by* Solomon Solis-Cohen. TrJP

Song of the Wine Spring. Chang Pi, *tr. fr. Chinese by* Lois Fusek. ATF

Song of the Wine Spring. Ku Hsiung, *tr. fr. Chinese by* Lois Fusek. ATF

Song of the Wine-Spring. Li Hsün, *tr. fr. Chinese by* Lois Fusek. ATF

Song of the Wine Spring. Mao Hsi-chen, *tr. fr. Chinese by* Lois Fusek. ATF

Song of the Wine Spring. Mao Wen-hsi, *tr. fr. Chinese by* Lois Fusek. ATF

Song of the Wine Spring. Niu Chiao, *tr. fr. Chinese by* Lois Fusek. ATF

Song of the Wine Spring. Niu Hsi-chi, *tr. fr. Chinese by* Lois Fusek. ATF

Song of the Wine Spring. Sun Kuang-hsien, *tr. fr. Chinese by* Lois Fusek. ATF

Song of the Wine Spring. Wei Chuang, *tr. fr. Chinese by* Lois Fusek. ATF

Song of the Wine Spring. Wen T'ing-yün, *tr. fr. Chinese by* Lois Fusek. ATF

Song of the Witches. Shakespeare. *Fr.* Macbeth: Thrice the Brinded Cat Hath Mewed. RHPC

Song of the Woman, The. *Unknown, tr. fr. Old Irish by* Kuno Meyer. *Fr.* The Voyage of Bran. TIRV

Song of the Woman-Drawer, The. Mary Gilmore. PoAu-1

Song of the Woman with Her Parts Coming Out, The. Susan Griffin. GLP

Song of the Woodcutter of the Sea. Pien Kung, *tr. fr. Chinese by* Jonathan Chaves. CoBLCP

Song of the Yellow Cedar Face, A. George Clutesi. HATNAP

Song of the Yellow Patch. H. Leivick, *tr. fr. Yiddish by* Benjamin *and* Barbara Harshav. *Fr.* Poems of the Yellow Patch. AYP

Song of the Zambra Dance. Dryden. *Fr.* The Conquest of Granada, *pt.* I, Act III, sc. i. ErPo; PoEL-3 (Zambra Dance, The.) SeCV-2

Song of This House, The. Stephen Vincent. NeAC

Song of Those Who Died, A. Donald McDonald. PVCV

Song of Three Smiles. W. S. Merwin. CoAP; NOBA; VGW

Song of Thyrsis. Philip Freneau. *Fr.* Female Frailty. AA; LiTA

Song of Travel on the Chikuma River. Shimazaki Toson, *tr. fr. Japanese by* Geoffrey Bownas *and* Anthony Thwaite. PeBJV

Song of Troylus, The. Chaucer. *See* Troilus and Criseyde [*or* Criseide]: If no love is, O God, what fele I so.

Song of Trust, A. Bible, *O.T. See* Psalms: Psalm CXXI ("I will lift up mine eyes unto the hills").

Song of Two Angels, A. Laura E. Richards. AA

Song of Venus. Dryden. *Fr.* King Arthur. OxBoLi; PoEL-3

Song of Victory: the Battle of Port Authur. Nogi Maresuke, *tr. fr. Chinese by* Burton Watson. JLIC-2

Song of Waking, A. Katharine Lee Bates. OHIP

Song of Wandering Aengus, The. W. B. Yeats. BrPo; CH; CMoP; FaBoCh; GoJo; MAT; MoAB; MoBrPo; PoEL-5; PoRA; SOTW; TTTS; UnAS; WSC

Song of Wandering Times. Rosario Murillo, *tr. fr. Spanish by* Magaly Fernández. Vol

Song of Welcome. Hermia Harris Fraser. CaP

Song of Winter, A. Emily Jane Pfeiffer. OBWVE

Song of Winter, A. *Unknown, tr. fr. Middle Irish by* Kuno Meyer. AnIL; CH

Song of Wu-ch'eng, *sel.* Wang T'ing-hsiang, *tr. fr. Chinese by* Jonathan Chaves. "Don't ask about the Six Dynasties of the Sui Palace." CoBLCP

Song of Yearning, A. Kohine Whakarua Ponika, *tr. fr. Maori by the author*. PeNZ

Song of Yüan-yüan, The. Wu Wei-yeh, *tr. fr. Chinese by* John D. Coleman *and* Gloria Shen. WFTU

Song on a Pine on Yellow Mountain. Shen Te-ch'ien, *tr. fr. Chinese by* Irving Lo. WFTU

Song on Beholding an Enlightenment. Matías de Bocanegra, *tr. fr. Spanish by* Samuel Beckett. MexPo

Song on Being Too Lazy to Get Up. Shao Yung, *tr. fr. Chinese by* Burton Watson. CoBCP

Song on Climbing Yu-chou Gate Tower. Ch'en Tzu-ang, *tr. fr. Chinese by* Burton Watson. CoBCP

Song on Enduring the Cold. Susan Ts'ao Ts'ao, *tr. fr. Chinese by* Burton Watson. CoBCP

Song on King William III, A. *Unknown. See* As I Walked [*or* Walk'd] by Myself.

Song on [*or* of] May Morning. Milton. BoNaP; CH; GN; TrGrPo

Song on the Duke's Late Glorious Success over the Dutch, A. *Unknown. See* One day as I was sitting still.

Song on the End of the World, A. Czeslaw Milosz, *tr. fr. Polish by the author*. PwPP

Song on the South Sea, A. Countess of Winchilsea. NOEC

Song on the Water. Thomas Lovell Beddoes. *Fr.* Death's Jest Book. FaBoCh

Song on the Way to Jail. Kakayek, *tr. fr. Tlingit Indian by* James Koller. STP

Song seizes me, but my own vers gives me dolor. Guillaume de Poitiers, *tr. by* Paul Blackburn. Pro

Song Sequence, *sels.* Ben-Zion Tomer, *tr. fr. Hebrew by* Bernhard Frank. MHeP
　Copy.
　Heartfelt Pity.

Song Set by John Farmer. *Unknown.* CTC; OBSC

Song Set by Nicholas Yonge. *Unknown. See* Brown Is My Love.

Song Sung, A. Federico García Lorca, *tr. fr. Spanish by* William Jay Smith. *Fr.* Songs of Childhood. CT

Song that I'm going to sing, The. The Crafty Farmer. *Unknown.* ESPB

Song that she sang was all written, The. The Moon of Mobile. Thomas Holley Chivers. OBAL

Song the Body Dreamed in the Spirit's Mad Behest, The. William Everson. ErPo

Song—the Owl. Tennyson. *See* When cats run home and light is come.

Song, The! the song! Hemda Roth, *tr. by* Mariana Potasman. VWA

Song thumbed down a cruiser for a ride, A. James Cunningham. *Fr.* The Narrator's Trance. JB

Song, 'tis my will that thou do seek out Love. Dante, *tr. fr. Italian by* Dante Gabriel Rossetti. *Fr.* Vita Nuova, La, V. AWP

Song to a Fair Young Lady, Going Out of the Town in the Spring. Dryden. OBEV; OBS

Song to a Lover. *Unknown, tr. fr. Amharic (Ethiopia) by* Willis Barnstone. BoWoP

Song to a LuteA. Sir John Suckling. CaPo; TrGrPo
　(Song: "Hast thou seen the down i' th' air.") EnLoPo

Song to a Tree. Edwin Markham. FaPON

Song to April. Sir William Watson. *See* Song: "April, April,/ Laugh thy girlish laughter."

Song to be Sung by the Father of Infant Female Children. Ogden Nash. MoAmPo

Song to Beta: "O thou fair silver Thames." Michael Drayton. *Fr.* The Shepherd's Garland, Eclogue III (1593 ed.). OBSC

Song to Celia. Ben Jonson. *See* Volpone: Come, my Celia, let us prove.

Song to Celia. Sir Charles Sedley. *See* Not, Celia, that I juster am.

Song to Cloris, A. John Wilmot, 2nd Earl of Rochester. ErPo

Song to David, A. Christopher Smart. ChTr; EBEV; LaA; NAEL-1; NOBE; OAEL-1; PoEL-3; TrGrPo

Song to David, A, *sels.* Christopher Smart. ChTr; EBEV; LaA; NAEL-1; NOBE, *abr.*; OAEL-1; PoEL-3; TrGrPo, *abr.*
　Beauteous, Yea Beauteous More than These. EaLo
　"Glorious the sun in mid career." FaBoCh
　Man of Prayer, The, 3 *Sts.* LiTB
　"O David, highest in the list," 38 *Sts.* NOEC
　"O thou, that sitst upon a throne." OBWVE; PoE
　"Strong is the lion—like a coal." HAP
　"Sublime—invention ever young." OBEV
　"Tell them, I AM, Jehovah said." WGRP

Song to Erin. Mary Weston Fordham. CBWP-2

Song to His Purse for the King, A. Chaucer. *See* To you my purse. . .

Song to Imogen. Shakespeare. *See* Cymbeline: Hark! Hark! the Lark.

Song to Imogen [in Basic English]. Richard L. Greene. BXAP

Song to John, Christ's Friend, A. *Unknown.* MeEL

Song to Mary, A. *At. to* William of Shoreham. MeEL

Song to Mithras, A. Kipling. *Fr.* Puck of Pook's Hill. NoAM

Song to Promote Growth. *Unknown, tr. by* Washington Matthews. OBVE

Song to Silvia. Shakespeare. *See* Two Gentlemen of Verona, The: Who Is Silvia [*or* Sylvia]?

Song to Sleep. John Fletcher. *See* Tragedy of Valentinian, The: Care-charming Sleep [Thou Easer of All Woes].

"Song to the Gods, Is Sweetest Sacrifice." Annie Fields. AA

Song to the Masquers. James Shirley. *Fr.* The Triumph of Peace. OxBSP

Song to the Men of England. Shelley. EnRP; FiP; InPS; SaC; TrGrPo
　(Song: "Men of England", A.) NAEL-2

Song to the Most Holy Name of Jesus. Fernando de Córdova y Bocanegra, *tr. fr. Spanish by* Samuel Beckett. MexPo

Song to the Mountains. *Unknown, tr. fr. Pawnee Indian by* Alice C. Fletcher. AWP

Song To the New Day, *sel.* Giaconda Belli, *tr. fr. Spanish by* Angel Flores.
　"I rise up." DMH

Song to the oak, the brave old oak, A. The Brave Old Oak. Henry Fothergill Chorley. FaBoBe

Song to the Runaway Slave. *Unknown.* BPo

Song to the Tune "Perching Crows." Wu Wei-yeh, *tr. fr. Chinese by* Jonathan Chaves. CoBLCP

Song to the Wind, A. Taliesin, *tr. fr. Welsh by* A. P. Graves. FaBoCh

Song Tournament: New Style. Louis Untermeyer. OBAL

Song Turning Back into Itself, The, *sel.* Al Young.
　"Ocean Springs Mississippy." *Fr.* 3. CNA; NPGG

Song unto liberty's brave buccaneer, A. Paul Jones. *Unknown.* PAH

Song (We Sing). Cosmo Pieterse. WMBCH

Song went to the garden, The. Where the Song Went Where She Went & What Happened When They Met. *Unknown, tr. by* Jerome Rothenberg *and* Richard Johnny John. STP

Song will deceive you, the scent will incite you to sing, The. You Cannot Go Down to the Spring. John Shaw Neilson. CBAP

Song with a Discord, A. Authur Colton. AA

Song with Words. James Agee. MoAmPo

Song Written at Sea in the First Dutch War (1665), the Night before an Engagement. Charles Sackville. CoMu; EnLoPo; NOBE; OBEV; OBS; OBWP

Song you sang you will not sing again, The. Local Places. Howard Moss. NePoEA-2

Song, Youth, and Sorrow. William Cranston Lawton. AA

Songe betwene the Quenes Majestie and Englande, A. William Birche. CoMu

Songhous, The: Love Was Rising between Us. Miguel Hernández, *tr. fr. Spanish by* Perry Higman. LPSS

Songs. The. Martin Bell. FF

Songs, *sel.* Steve Crow.
　"They say a man dies." *Fr.* XIV. HATNAP

Songs. Petrarch. *Fr.* Sonnets to Laura.
　I Saw a Phoenix in the Wood Alone. AWP, *tr. by* Spenser; ChTr, *tr. by* HelenLee Peabody.
　Visions, The. *Fr.* Canzone VIII, *tr. by* Edmund Spenser. AWP; PFI

Songs. Richard Henry Stoddard. AA

Songs, The. *Unknown, tr. fr. Zuni Indian by* K. Kennedy. WTO

Songs, *sels. Unknown.* PBCV
　"New-come buckra/ He get sick." *Fr.* I.
　"One, two, tree/ All de same." *Fr.* II.

Songs about Life and Brighter Things Yet, *sels.* Samuel Hoffenstein. NBLV
　"Nothing from a straight line swerves."
　"Of all the birds that sing and fly."

Songs Composed in Prison, *sels.* Sung Wan, *tr. fr. Chinese by* William Schultz. WFTU
　Earthen *K'ang,* An. *Fr.* II.
　Earthen Stove, An. *Fr.* VI.
　Piece of Rush Matting, A. *Fr.* I.
　Stool with a Broken Leg, A. *Fr.* III.

Song's Eternity. John Clare. FaBoCh

Songs Exchanged between Prince Okuninushi and Princess Nunakawa ("Divine prince of eight thousand spears"). *Unknown, tr. fr. Japanese by* Hiroaki Sato. *Fr.* The Kojiki. FCEI

Songs Exchanged between Prince Okuninushi and Princess Nunakawa ("The divine prince of eight thousand spears/ great ruler of our land"). *Unknown, tr. fr. Japanese by* Hiroaki Sato. *Fr.* The Kojiki. FCEI

Songs Exchanged between Prince Okuninushi and Princess Nunakawa ("When, having carefully put on"). *Unknown, tr. fr. Japanese by* Hiroaki Sato. *Fr.* The Kojiki. FCEI

Songs for a Colored Singer, *sel.* Elizabeth Bishop. PoNe; RB
"Washing hangs upon the line, A." FaBoWP

Songs for a Three-String Guitar. Léopold Sédar-Senghor, *tr. fr. French by* Miriam Koshland. PBA

Songs for My Mother, *sels.* Anna Hempstead Branch. OHIP
Song for My Mother, A: Her Hands.
Song for My Mother, A: Her Stories.
Song for My Mother, A: Her Words. FaPON

Songs for the Cisco Kid; or, Singing for the Face. K. Curtis Lyle. PoBA

Songs for the Four Parts of the Night. Owl Woman (Juana Manwell), *tr. fr. Papago Indian by* Frances Densmore. PBWP

Songs for the Old New Jersey Shelling the Shouf. George Starbuck. BLA

Songs for the People. Frances Ellen Watkins Harper. PWR

Songs from Cyprus, *sels.* Hilda Doolittle ("H. D."). MoAmPo
"Gather for festival." *Fr.* I.
"Where is the nightingale." *Fr.* II.

Songs from Living in the Mountains, *sels.* Huang Tsung-hsi, *tr. fr. Chinese by* Lynn Struve. WFTU
"For fifty years I followed an "overturned cart."" *Fr.* III.
"I've come again to Yen Bend and built a hut of thatch." *Fr.* V.
"Who says that in the mountains everything is grand?" *Fr.* II.

Songs in Absence, *sel.* Arthur Hugh Clough.
Where Lies the Land [to Which the Ship Would Go?]. *Fr.* VII. FaBoRV; MOS

Songs in Flight, *sel.* Ingeborg Bachmann, *tr. fr. German by* Daniel Huws.
"Instructed in love." WPOW

Songs in the Garden of the House God. *Unknown, tr. fr. Navajo Indian by* Washington Matthews. AnAmPo

Songs in the Turtle Dance at Santa Clara. *Unknown, tr. fr. Tewa Indian by* H. J. Spinden. WTO

Songs of a Poor Man, *sel.* Moishe Kulbak, *tr. fr. Yiddish by* Leonard Wolf.
"In the attic, at night, a poor man sits." PeBMYV

Songs of a Wanderer, *sels.* Aleksander Wat, *tr. fr. Polish by* Czeslaw Milosz. PwPP
"Disgusted by everything alive I withdrew into the." *Fr.* II.
"So now, having fled into the stone world, I was slowly." *Fr.* III.

Songs of Ch'ang-kan. Ts'ui Hao, *tr. fr. Chinese by* Burton Watson. CoBCP

Songs of Ch'en, *sels.* Confucius, *tr. fr. Chinese by* Ezra Pound. CTC Aliter.
"Marsh bank, lotus rank."

Songs of Cheng, *sels.* Confucius, *tr. fr. Chinese by* Ezra Pound. CTC
"Be kind, good sir, and I'll lift my sark."
"Hep-Cat Chung, 'ware my town."
"In chariot like an hibiscus flower at his side."
"So he won't talk to me when we meet?."

Songs of Chiang-nan, *sels.* Wang T'ing-hsiang, *tr. fr. Chinese by* Jonathan Chaves. CoBLCP
"I am a man of Chiang-nan."
"I pluck *heng*-herbs at the Chin-ling riverside."

Songs of Childhood, *sels.* Federico García Lorca, *tr. fr. Spanish by* William Jay Smith. CT
Chinese Song.
Landscape.
Little Song of Seville.
Snail.
Song Sung, A.

Songs of Divorce. Jane Green, *tr. fr. Ojibwa Indian by* Frances Densmore. WPOW

Songs of Education, *sels.* G. K. Chesterton.
For the Crèche. FaBoCo
Geography. OBSV
History. OBSV

Songs of Experience, *sels.* Blake.
Ah! Sun-Flower ("Ah! Sun-flower, weary of time"). AWP; EBEV; ELP; EnRP; FaBoRV; HAP; NAEL-2; NIP; NOEC; NoP; OAEL-2; OBNC; PoE; PoEL-4; PPP; PrIm; RB; TEP; TOF; UnPo; WeW
Angel, The. CH; EnRP; LiTB
Chimney Sweeper ("A little black thing among the snow"), The. NAEL-2; NAWM-2; NOEC; OAEL-2; PPP; RB; SaC; TEP
Clod and the Pebble, The. EnLoPo; EnRP; FaBV; InPS; NAEL-2; NOBE; NoP; OBNC; OxBSP; PoE; PrIm; RB; SCV; TEP; TrGrPo
Divine Image, A ("Cruelty has a human heart"). ChTr; NAEL-2; NoP; OBNC; RB; TEP

Earth's Answer. EnRP; InPS; NAEL-2; NAWM-2; NOEC; OAEL-2; PoE
Garden of Love, The. AWP; EnLoPo; EnRP; FaBV; GBL; HAP; LiTB; MAT; NAEL-2; NoP; PoE; RB; SoSe; TEP
Hear the Voice of the Bard!, *Introd.* EBEV; ELP; NAEL-2; NAWM-2; NOBE; NU; PoE; RB
(Bard, The.) WGRP
(Hear the Voice.) OBEV
(Introduction: "Hear the voice of the bard!") NOEC; NoP; OAEL-2; PoEL-4; TEP
(Poet's Voice, The.) ChTr
Holy Thursday ("Is this a holy thing to see"). EnRP; FF; InPS; NAEL-2; NOEC; NoP; OAEL-2; TEP
Human Abstract, The. EnRP; NAEL-2; NOEC; OAEL-2; PoE; PoEL-4; PPP
Infant Sorrow. InPS; NAEL-2; NAs; OBNC; OxBSP; PoEL-4; RB
Little Boy Lost, A ("Nought loves another as itself"). EnRP
"Little Fly,/ Thy summers play." NAEL-2; NBLV
(Fly, The.) FM; TrGrPo
Little Vagabond, The. NBLV; OBSV
London ("I wander through each chartered street"). AWP; ChER; ChTr; EnRP; FaBoPP; FaBoPV; FF; HAP; HeIP; InPK; InPS; LiTB; MAT; Mes; NAEL-2; NAWM-2; NIP; NOBE; NOEC; NoP; OAEL-2; OBNC; PoE; PoEL-4; PrIm; RB; SCV; SeCePo; TEP; UnPo; WeW
My Pretty Rose Tree. BoLoP; NAEL-2
Nurse's Song. EnRP; FF; NAEL–2
Poison Tree, A. AWP; EnRP; FaBoPV; HAP; HoPM; LiTB; NAEL-2; NoP; PoEL-4; PPP; RB; SCV; SoSe; TrGrPo; TW; WeW
Schoolboy, The. BoNaP; CH; FaBoCh
Sick Rose, The. AWP; BoLoP; ChER; ChTr; ELP; EnLoPo; HAP; HeIP; InPK; InPS; NAEL-2; NAWM-2; NIP; NOBE; NOEC; NoP; OAEL-2; OBNC; OxBSP; PoE; PoEL-4; PPP; PrIm; RB; SoSe; TrGrPo; WeW
Tiger [or Tyger], The. AWP; BoTP; CH; ChTr; EaLo; EnRP; FaBoBe; FaBoCh; FaBoPV; FaBV; FaFP; FaPON; FaPoR; FF; FM; FPL; GN; HAP; HeIP; HoPM; InPK; InPS; LiTB; Mes; NAWM-2; NIP; NOBE; NOEC; NoP; OAEL-2; OBEV; OBNC; PoE; PoEL-4; PoLF; PoRA; PPP; PrIm; RB; SCV; SeCePo; SoSe; TEP; TTTS; UnPo; WGRP
To Tirzah. EnRP; NAEL-2; NOBE; OAEL-2

Songs of Innocence, *sels.* Blake.
Blossom, The. GoJo; PBBP
Chimney Sweeper, The ("When my mother died I was very young"). CH; EnRP; FaBoPV; FF; HeIP; InPK; NAEL-2; NAWM-2; NOEC; OAEL-2; OxBChV; PoE; PPP; SaC; SoSe; TEP
Divine Image, The ("To mercy, pity, peace, and love"). BoTP; EnRP; NAEL-2; NOBE; NOEC; NoP; OAEL-2; OBNC; PoE; PoEL-4; PPP; TEP; WGRP
Dream, A. CH; EnRP
Echoing [or Ecchoing] Green, The. BoTP; CH; NAEL–2; PoE; UnPo; WiR
Holy Thursday (" 'Twas on a Holy Thursday, their innocent faces clean"). CH; EnRP; InPS; NAEL-2; NAWM-2; NOBE; NOEC; NoP; OAEL-2; OFD; PoE; SCV; TEP; TrCP
Infant Joy. FaPON; GoJo; NAEL-2; NAs; OxBSP; PoLF; TEP
Lamb, The. BLPL; BoTP; CH; EaLo; EnRP; FaBoBe; FaBoCh; FaPON; GoJo; HeIP; InPS; LiTB; NAEL-2; NAWM-2; NIP; NOEC; NoP; OAEL-2; OxBChV; PoE; SoSe; TEP; TrCP; TrGrPo; UnPo; WGRP
Laughing Song. BoTP; NAEL-2
(When the Green Woods Laugh.) CH; EnRP; GoJo; NBLV; OxBChV
Little Black Boy, The. AWP; CH; EnRP; HeIP; NAEL-2; NAWM-2; NOEC; NoP; OAEL-2; OBEV; OBNC; OxBChV; PoE; PoEL-4; PoNe; TrGrPo
Little Boy Found, The. EnRP; NoP
Little Boy Lost, The ("Father, father, where are you going?"). EnRP; NoP
Night. BLPL; BoNaP; BoTP; CH; EnRP; FaBoBe; FaPON; OBEV; OxBChV; PoLF; WiR
Nurse's Song. AWP; BLPL; CH; EnRP; FaBoBe; NAEL-2; OxBChV
(Play Time.) FaPON
On Another's Sorrow. AWP; EnRP; FaBV; PoEL-4
Piping Down the Valleys Wild. FaBoCh; FaBV; HeIP; InvP; NAEL-2; NAWM-2; NIP; NOBE; OnUR; PoE
(Introduction to "Songs of Innocence.") EnRP; FaBoBe; GoJo; InPS; NOEC; NoP; OAEL-2; OBNC; PoEL-4; RHPC; SoSe; TEP; TrGrPo
(Piper, The.) AWP; OxBChV; PDV
(Reeds of Innocence.) LiTB; OBEV
Shepherd, The. BoTP; EnRP
Spring. BoTP; FaBoCh; FaPON; MoShBr; TTTS

Songs of Joy. W. H. Davies. MoBrPo

Songs of Kabir. Kabir, *tr. fr. Hindi* by Rabindranath Tagore. WGRP
Songs of Labor, *sel.* Whittier.
"I would the gift I offer here." OxBA
Songs of Lake Tung-t'ing, *sels.* Yang Wei-chen, *tr. fr. Chinese* by Jonathan Chaves. CoBLCP
"Man of Tao-his iron flute plays music, The." *Fr.* II.
"Sun sets on Tung-t'ing's waves." *Fr.* I.
Songs of Maximus. Charles Olson. *Fr.* The Maximus Poems. NeAP
"This morning of the small snow." *Fr.* III. PPP
(All/ wrong.) NoAM, II.
"Colored pictures/ of all things to eat: dirty." *Fr.* I. NeAP; NoAM
Songs of Satsuma, *sel.* Rai San'yo, *tr. fr. Chinese* by Burton Watson.
"On the road I meet descendants of the Korean prisoners." *Fr.* II. JLIC-2
Songs of Seven, *sels.* Jean Ingelow.
Longing for Home. WGRP
Maternity. OHIP
Seven Times One—Exultation. BLPA; FaPON; OBNC
Seven Times Three—Love. PoLF
Seven Times Two—Romance. GN
Songs of shepherds and rustical roundelays. The Hunting of the Gods. *Unknown.* OxBoLi
Songs of Sorrow (Spring 1918), *sel.* Viljo Kajava, *tr. fr. Finnish* by Aili Jarvenpa.
"Torn widow's veil." SOP
Songs of T'ang, *sel.* Confucius, *tr. fr. Chinese* by Ezra Pound.
Alba. CTC
Songs of the Birds, The. Edward Carpenter. WGRP
Songs of the Common Day, *sels.* Sir Charles G. D. Roberts.
Herring Weir, The. NOBC
Pea-Fields, The. NOBC; OBCV
Songs of the Frontier, *sels.* Li K'ai-hsien, *tr. fr. Chinese* by Jonathan Chaves. CoBLCP
"Crack soldiers get no sleep, The."
"Flying sand darkens the air, the moon is a dull yellow."
Songs of the Ghost Dance. *Unknown, tr. fr. Paiute Indian.* WSC
Songs of the Greenwood. Shakespeare. *See* As You Like It: Under the Greenwood Tree.
Songs of the Greenwood: "Blow, blow, thou winter wind." Shakespeare. *See* As You Like It: Blow, Blow, Thou Winter Wind.
Songs of the Land of Zion Jerusalem, *sels.* Yehuda Amichai, *tr. fr. Hebrew* by Warren Bargod *and* Stanley F. Chyet. IP
"All these stones, all this sadness, all." *Fr.* 37.
"And in spite of it all I must." *Fr.* 38.
"I have nothing to say about the war." *Fr.* 4.
Songs of the People, *sels.* Hayyim Nahman Bialik, *tr. fr. Hebrew* by Maurice Samuel. AWP
"On a hill there blooms a palm." *Fr.* II.
"Two steps from my garden rail." *Fr.* I.
Songs of the Priestess. Malka Heifetz-Tussman, *tr. fr. Yiddish* by Marcia Falk. PeBMYV; VWA
Songs of the Priestess. Malka Heifetz Tussman, *tr. fr. Yiddish* by Marcia Falk. VWA
Songs of the Psyche, *sel.* Thomas Kinsella.
"Character, indistinct, entered, A." *Fr.* I. NoAM
Songs of the Sea-Children, *sels.* Bliss Carman. OBCV
"I see the golden hunter go." *Fr.* LIV.
"What is it to remember?." *Fr.* LXVI.
Songs of the Squatters. Robert Lowe. PoAu-1
Songs of the Transformed, *sel.* Margaret Atwood.
Siren Song. HAP; PoA; WeW
Songs of Travel, *sels.* Robert Louis Stevenson. OBNC
"Bright is the ring of words."
If This Were Faith.
To S. R. Crockett.
Songs of Yen-ching, *sels.* Hsü Wei, *tr. fr. Chinese* by Jonathan Chaves. CoBLCP
"In the northwestern pond there is a dragon-ox."
"Where does the dragon-ox display its imposing form."
Songs on Accompanying the Governor-General, *sels.* Shih Jun-chang, *tr. fr. Chinese* by William Shultz. WFTU
"Drums and horns rouse the river town." *Fr.* I.
"On the battlefield, the spring wind is harsh." *Fr.* II.
Songs on the Death of Children, *sel.* Friedrich Rückert.
"Sun is soon to rise as bright, The." OBD
Songs on the Voices of Birds, *sel.* Jean Ingelow.
Child and Boatman. FM
Songs, so old and bitter, The. The Coffin. Heine, *tr. by* Louis Untermeyer. AWP
Songs That Cannot Be Silenced. Hien Luong, *tr. fr. Vietnamese* by Chris Knipp *and* Mohammad Sadiq. OV

Songs to a Lady Moonwalker. Abraham Sutskever, *tr. fr. Yiddish* by Ruth Whitman. VWA
Songs to Seraphine, *sels.* Heine, *tr. fr. German* by Emma Lazarus. TrJP
Shadow-Love.
Waves Gleam in the Sunshine, The.
Songs to Survive the Summer. Robert Hass. AmPA
Songs to Welcome the Society of the Mystic Animals. *Unknown, tr. fr. Seneca Indian* by Jerome Rothenberg *and* Richard Johnny John. STP
Songs without Words. John Ashbery. NAAL-2
Song's Worth, A. Susan Marr Spalding. AA
Sonic Flowerfall of Primes, The. Andrew Joron. BWV
Sonja Henie Sonnet. Edward Field. ASP
"Sonja Henie," the young girl." Theodore Weiss. VGW
Sonne, The. George Herbert. SeCP
Sonne, with his beams of brightnesse, The. Balade and Roundel to Master Somer. Thomas Hoccleve. OxBLMV
Sonnet XVI: "After an age when thunderbolts and hail." Louise Labé, *tr. by* Willis Barnstone. BoWoP
Sonnet: "After dark vapours. . ." Keats. *See* After Dark Vapours.
Sonnet XIX: "After having slain very many beasts." Louise Labé, *tr. by* Willis Barnstone. BoWoP
Sonnet: "Afternoon sun on her back." Robert Pinsky. BLA
Sonnet: "Afterwards there are dogends in." Maureen Duffy. PeHV
Sonnet: "Ah, sweet Content! where is thy mild abode." Barnabe Barnes. *See* Parthenophil and Parthenophe: Ah, sweet Content! where is thy mylde abode?
Sonnet: "Alexis, here she stayed; among these pines." William Drummond of Hawthornden. EiL; OBS
(Spring Bereaved.) OBEV
Sonnet: All That's to Others Pleasing, I Dislike. Cino da Pistoia, *tr. fr. Italian* by Barbara Howes. PFI
Sonnet: "All we were going strong last night this time." John Berryman. FaBoMo
Sonnet XIV: "Although I cry and though my eyes still shed." Louise Labé. BoWoP, *tr. by* Willis Barnstone
Sonnet, A: "Amazing thing happened to me, An." Daniil Kharms, *tr. by* George Gibian. FaBoNo
Sonnet: "And then I sat me down, and gave the rein." Gustav Rosenhane, *tr. by* Sir Edmund Gosse. AWP
Sonnet: And You as Well Must Die, Beloved Dust. Edna St. Vincent Millay. FPL; PoLF; PoRA; TAP
Sonnet: Annunciation. Giuseppe Gioacchino Belli, *tr. fr. Italian* by Anthony Burgess. PFI
Sonnet: "As in a duskie and tempestuous night." William Drummond of Hawthornden. OBS
Sonnet: "As long as I continue weeping." Louise Labé, *tr. by* Joan Keefe *and* Richard Terdiman. PBWP
Sonnet IX: "As soon as I lie down in my soft bed." Louise Labé, *tr. by* Willis Barnstone. BoWoP
Sonnet: "As when, to one who long hath watched, the morn." John Codrington Bampfylde. NOEC
Sonnet: At Ostend. William Lisle Bowles. *See* Sonnet: "How sweet the tuneful bells' responsive peal!"
Sonnet: Autumn Garden. Dino Campana, *tr. fr. Italian* by Charles Wright. PFI
Sonnet: "Avenge, O Lord, thy slaughtered saints, whose bones." Milton. *See* On the Late Massacre *or* Massacher in Piedmont *or* Piemont.
Sonnet: "Azured [*or* Azur'd] vault, the crystal circles bright, The." James I, King of England. EiL; SeCePo
(Heaven and Earth.) ChTr
Sonnet: Beauty on a Western Balcony. Luis de Sandoval y Zapata, *tr. fr. Spanish* by Samuel Beckett. MexPo
Sonnet: "Beauty, sweet love, is like the morning dew." Samuel Daniel. *See* To Delia: Beauty, sweet Love, is like the morning dew.
Sonnet: "Because my grief seems quiet and apart." Robert Nathan. TrJP
Sonnet: "Beckie, my luve!—What is't, ye twa-faced tod?" George Campbell Hay. OxBS
Sonnet: "Bible says Sennacherib's campaign was spoiled, The." C. S. Lewis. TrCP
Sonnet: "Caelica, I overnight was finely used." Fulke Greville. *See* Caelica: Caelica, I overnight was finely used.
Sonnet: "Captain or colonel or knight in arms." Milton. *See* Captain or colonel. . .
Sonnet: "Care-charmer sleep[e], son[ne] of the sable night." Samuel Daniel. *See* To Delia:
Care-charmer sleep[e], son[ne] of the sable night.
Sonnet: Cell, The. John Thelwall. NOEC
Sonnet: "Cleare moving cristall, pure as the Sunne beames." William Alexander, Earl of Stirling. *Fr.* Aurora, XXV. OxBS

Sonnet, A: "Cold are the crabs that crawl on yonder hills." Edward Lear. *See* Cold Are the Crabs.

Sonnet: Comes Often to My Memory. Dante, *tr. fr. Italian*. PFI, *tr. by* Frederick Morgan

Sonnet VI: "Coming of that limpid star is twice, The." Louise Labé, *tr. by* Willis Barnstone. BoWoP

Sonnet: Composed after a Journey across the Hamilton Hills, Yorkshire. Wordsworth. ChER

Sonnet: Composed while the Author Was Engaged in Writing a Tract Occasioned by the Convention of Cintra. Wordsworth. ChER

Sonnet: Content and Resolute. William Drummond of Hawthornden. JCP

Sonnet: "Crumbled rock of London is dripping under, The." Roy Fuller. PoA

Sonnet: "Cry, crow." Hayden Carruth. NNaP; Son

Sonnet: "Cyriack, whose grandsire, on the royal bench." Milton. *See* Cyriack, whose grandsire. . .

Sonnet: Dante Alighieri to Guido Cavalcanti. Dante. *See* Guido I would that Lapo. . . .

Sonnet: "Daughter to that good Earl, once president." Milton. *See* Daughter to that good Earl. . .

Sonnet: "Dead men of 'ninety-two, also of 'ninety-three." Rimbaud, *tr. by* Norman Cameron. WaaP

Sonnet, A: "Dear, if you love me, hold me most your friend." Alice Duer Miller. AA

Sonnet: "Dear to my soul! then leave me not forsaken!" Henry Constable. *See* Diana: Dear to my soul! then leave me not forsaken!

Sonnet: "Dear [*or* Deere], why should you command me to my rest." Michael Drayton. *See* Deare [*or* Dear], why should you command [*or* commaund] me to my rest.

Sonnet: Death Is Not without but within Him. Cino da Pistoia, *tr. fr. Italian by* Dante Gabriel Rossetti. AWP

Sonnet: The Death of Virgil. Angelo di Costanzo, *tr. fr. Italian by* David Wright. PFI

Sonnet: Death Warnings. Francisco de Quevedo y Villegas, *tr. fr. Spanish by* John Masefield. AWP

Sonnet: Death's Last Will. William Drummond of Hawthornden. JCP

Sonnet: "Deep in a vale where rocks on every side." Gustav Rosenhane, *tr. by* Sir Edmund Gosse. AWP

Sonnet: Dolce Stil Novo. Gavin Ewart. GrPl

Sonnet XXIV: "Don't blame me, ladies, if I've loved. No sneers." Louise Labé. BoWoP, *tr. by* Willis Barnstone
(Sonnet: "Don't scold me, ladies, if I have loved"). PBWP, *tr. by* Carol Cosman

Sonnet: "Do'st see how unregarded now." Sir John Suckling. CaPo; ELP

Sonnet: Double Rock, The. Henry King. SeCP

Sonnet: "Downe in the depth of mine iniquity." Fulke Greville. *See* Caelica: Down in the depth of mine iniquity.

Sonnet: "Dream not, poor poet, that th' ephemeral breath." Henry F. Lott. PF

Sonnet: "Each man me telleth I change most my devise." Sir Thomas Wyatt. SiPS

Sonnet: "Earth with thunder torn, with fire blasted, The." Fulke Greville. *See* Caelica: Earth with thunder torn[e], with fire blasted, The.

Sonnet XVIII: "Kiss me again, rekiss, kiss me more." Louise Labé. *See* Sonnet XVIII: "Kiss me again, re-kiss and kiss me whole."

Sonnet: England in 1819. Shelley. *See* Old, mad, blind, despised, and dying King.

Sonnet: "England! the time is come when thou shouldst wean." Wordsworth. Son

Sonnet: Equality of the Sexes. Gavin Ewart. Son

Sonnet: "Eternall Truth, almighty, infinite." Fulke Greville. *See* Caelica: Eternall Truth, almighty, infinite.

Sonnet: "Evening, as slow thy placid shades descend." William Lisle Bowles. NOEC

Sonnet: Fable. James Facos. NBLV

Sonnet: "Fair is my love, and cruel as she's fair." Samuel Daniel. *See* To Delia: Fair is my love, and cruel as she's fair.

Sonnet: "Fair is my love that feeds among the lilies." Bartholomew Griffin. *See* Fidessa, More Chaste than Kind: Faire Is My Love.

Sonnet: "Farewell, love, and all thy laws [*or* lawes] for ever." Sir Thomas Wyatt. AAS; LiTB; NAEL-1; OAEL-1; SiPS
(Lover Renounceth Love, The.) TrGrPo
(Renancing of Love, A.) GBL; Son

Sonnet: French and the Spanish Guerrillas, The. Wordsworth. *See* Hunger and sultry heat. . .

Sonnet IV: "From that first flash when awful Love took flame." Louise Labé, *tr. by* Willis Barnstone. BoWoP

Sonnet: "Go, thou that vainly dost mine eyes invite." Henry King. OxBSP

Sonnet: "Go you, O winds that blow from north to south." Alexander Craig. EIL
(To Pandora.) Son

Sonnet: Good Spiritual Father, The. Giuseppe Gioacchino Belli, *tr. fr. Italian by* Miller Williams. PFI

Sonnet: Grievous Peril of a Gallant in Moth Metaphor. Luis de Sandoval y Zapata, *tr. fr. Spanish by* Samuel Beckett. MexPo

Sonnet: "Guido, I wish that you and Lapo and I." Dante, *tr. by* Kenneth Koch. RB; TTTS

Sonnet: He Argues His Case with Death. Cecco Angiolieri da Siena, *tr. fr. Italian by* Dante Gabriel Rossetti. AWP

Sonnet: "He came in silvern armor, trimmed with black." Gwendolyn B. Bennett. AmNP; CDC; PoBA; PoNe

Sonnet: He Compares All Things with His Lady, and Finds Them Wanting. Guido Cavalcanti, *tr. fr. Italian by* Dante Gabriel Rossetti. AWP

Sonnet: He Craves Interpreting of a Dream of His. Dante da Maiano, *tr. fr. Italian by* Dante Gabriel Rossetti. AWP

Sonnet: He Is Out of Heart with His Time. Guerzo di Montecanti, *tr. fr. Italian by* Dante Gabriel Rossetti. AWP

Sonnet: He Is Past All Help. Cecco Angiolieri da Siena, *tr. fr. Italian by* Dante Gabriel Rossetti. AWP

Sonnet: He Jests Concerning His Poverty. Bartolomeo di Sant' Angelo, *tr. fr. Italian by* Dante Gabriel Rossetti. AWP

Sonnet: He Rails against Dante, Who Had Censured His Homage to Becchina. Cecco Angiolieri da Siena, *tr. fr. Italian by* Dante Gabriel Rossetti. AWP

Sonnet: He Speaks of a Third Love of His. Guido Cavalcanti, *tr. fr. Italian by* Dante Gabriel Rossetti. AWP

Sonnet: He Will Not Be Too Deeply in Love. Cecco Angiolieri da Siena, *tr. fr. Italian by* Dante Gabriel Rossetti. AWP

Sonnet: He Will Praise His Lady. Guido Guinicelli, *tr. fr. Italian by* Dante Gabriel Rossetti. AWP; PFI

Sonnet: "Here in the self is all that men can know." John Masefield. *Fr.* Lollingdon Downs. AWP

Sonnet: "High on the wall that holds Jerusalem." G. K. Chesterton. OBTV

Sonnet, A: "His golden locks time hath to silver turned." George Peele. *See* Polyhymnia: His Golden Lock[e]s [Time Hath to Silver Turned].

Sonnet: "How many faults you might accuse me of." Elinor Wylie. NAAL-2

Sonnet: "How many paltry. . ." Michael Drayton. *See* Idea: How many paltry, foolish, painted things.

Sonnet: "How sweet the tuneful bells' responsive peal!" William Lisle Bowles. OBTV
(Bells of Ostend, The.) EnRP
(Sonnet: At Ostend.) NOEC

Sonnet: "How that vast heaven intitled First is rolled." William Drummond of Hawthornden. EIL

Sonnet: "I abide and abide and better abide." Sir Thomas Wyatt. BoLoP; EnLoPo; SiPS

Sonnet: "I am in love, but am not so in love." Cecco Angiolieri da Siena, *tr. by* Felix Stefanile. PFI

Sonnet: "I am not moved to love thee, my Lord God." Miguel de Guevara, *tr. by* Samuel Beckett. MexPo

Sonnet: "I, being born a woman and distressed." Edna St. Vincent Millay. *See* I, Being Born a Woman and Distressed.

Sonnet: "I dreamed that I was thrown from a crag." Francisco de Terrazas, *tr. by* Samuel Beckett. MexPo

Sonnet: "I envy not Endymion now no more." William Alexander, Earl of Stirling. *See* Aurora: I Envy Not Endymion.

Sonnet: "I feel I am;—I only know I am." John Clare. *See* I Feel I Am.

Sonnet XVII: "I flee the city, temples, and each place." Louise Labé, *tr. by* Willis Barnstone. BoWoP

Sonnet: "I had no thought of violets of late." Alice Dunbar Moore Nelson. BANP; BlSi; CDC; PoBA; PoNe; Son

Sonnet: "I have not spent the April of my time." Bartholomew Griffin. *See* Fidessa, More Chaste than Kind: I have not spent the April of my time.

Sonnet: "I hereby swear that to uphold your house." Elinor Wylie. *Fr.* One Person, XVI. LiTA; MoAB; NAAL-2; OxBA; Son
(Sonnet from "One Person.") LiTA; MoAmPo

Sonnet: "I know that all beneath the moon decays." William Drummond of Hawthornden. JCP; Son

Sonnet VIII: "I live, I die, I burn myself and drown." Louise Labé, *tr. by* Willis Barnstone. BoWoP

Sonnet: "I must not grieve my love, whose eyes would read." Samuel Daniel. *See* To Delia: I must not grieve my love, whose eyes would read.

Sonnet: "I saw magic on a green country road." Michael Hartnett. BIrV

Sonnet: "I saw the object of my pining thought." Thomas Watson. EIL

Sonnet: "I want you to come rushing in the wind." Yang Mu, *tr. by* Dominic Cheung. IFON

Sonnet XX: "I was foretold that on a certain day." Louise Labé. BoWoP, *tr. by* Willis Barnstone
(Sonnet: "Seer foretold that I would love one day, A.") PBWP, *tr. by* Joan Keefe *and* Richard Terdiman.

Sonnet: "Ice over time." David Shapiro. UL

Sonnet: "Idly she yawned, and threw her heavy hair." George Moore. ErPo

Sonnet: "If ever Sorrow spoke from soul that loves." Henry Constable. *Fr. Diana.* EIL

Sonnet XIII: "If I could linger on his lovely chest." Louise Labé, *tr. by* Aliki *and* Willis Barnstone. BoWoP

Sonnet I: "If it must be; if it must be, O God!" David Gray. *Fr. In the Shadows.* OxBS

Sonnet: "If 'twere not for the dignity inborn." Henry F. Lott. PF

Sonnet: "Ile give thee leave my love, in beauties field." William Alexander, Earl of Stirling. *Fr. Aurora, XXVI.* OxBS

Sonnet: In Absence from Becchina. Cecco Angiolieri da Siena, *tr. fr. Italian by* Dante Gabriel Rossetti. AWP

Sonnet: "In every dream thy lovely features rise." William Barnes. BoLoP

Sonnet: "In minds pure glasse when I my selfe behold." William Drummond of Hawthornden. OBS

Sonnet: "Ingratitude, how deadly is the smart." Anna Seward. NOEC

Sonnet: "Innumerable Beauties, thou white haire." Herbert of Cherbury. PoEL-2

Sonnet XI: "Is God invisible? This very room." Adele Greeff. GoYe

Sonnet: "It is as true as strange, else trial feigns." John Davies of Hereford. EIL

Sonnet: "It is not death, that sometime in a sigh." Thomas Hood. OBNC

Sonnet: "It shall be said [*or* sayd] I died [*or* dy'de] for Coelia." William Percy. *Fr. Coelia, XIX.* EIL

Sonnet 7: "I've found out why, that day, that suicide." John Berryman. PoE

Sonnet IV: "If I should pray this lady pitiless." Guido Cavalcanti, *tr. by* Ezra Pound. PFI

Sonnet: Kamikaze. Bernadette Mayer. UL

Sonnet: Keen, Fitful Gusts. Keats. EnRP; PoEL-4; Son; TEP

Sonnet XVIII: "Kiss me again, re-kiss and kiss me whole." Louise Labé. WPOW, *tr. by* Raymond Oliver
(Sonnet XVIII: "Kiss me again, rekiss, kiss me more.") BoWoP, *tr. by* Willis Barnstone

Sonnet: Ladies Home Journal, The. Sandra M. Gilbert. NIP

Sonnet: Lady Laments for Her Lost Lover, by Similitude of a Falcon, A. *Unknown, tr. fr. Italian by* Dante Gabriel Rossetti. AWP

Sonnet: "Lamp of heaven's crystal hall that brings the hours." William Drummond. JCP

Sonnet: "Lawrence of virtuous father." Milton. *See* Lawrence of virtuous father. . .

Sonnet: "Leave me, all sweet refrains my lip hath made." Luis de Camões, *tr. by* Richard Garnett. AWP

Sonnet: Leaves. William Barnes. BoNaP; ChTr; FaBoRV; OBNC

Sonnet: "Let others of the world's decaying tell." William Alexander, Earl of Stirling. *Fr. Aurora.* EIL

Sonnet: "Let others sing of knights and paladin[e]s." Samuel Daniel. *See* To Delia: Let others sing of knights and paladins [*or* palladines].

Sonnet: "Let us leave talking of angelic hosts." Elinor Wylie. *Fr. One Person.* OxBA

Sonnet: "Lift not the painted veil which those who live." Shelley. EnRP; OBNC; Son

Sonnet: "Like Memnon's rock, touched with the rising sun." Giles Fletcher the Elder. *See* Licia: Like [*or* Lyke] Memnons rock, touched [*or* rocke toucht] with the rising sun[ne].

Sonnet: "Like to an hermit poor, in place obscure." *At. to* Sir Walter Ralegh. EIL
(Like to a Hermit Poor.) GBL

Sonnet: "Lock up, fair lids, the treasure of my heart." Sir Philip Sidney. *See* Arcadia: Sleep.

Sonnet: "Long time a child." Hartley Coleridge. *See* Long Time a Child.

Sonnet: "Look, Delia, how we esteem the half-blown rose." Samuel Daniel. *See* To Delia: Look, Delia, how we esteem the half-blown rose.

Sonnet: "Lord, what a change. . ." Richard Chenevix Trench. *See* Prayer: "Lord, what a change within us one short hour."

Sonnet: "Love is the peace, whereto all thoughts do strive." Fulke Greville. *See* Caelica: Love is the peace, whereto all thoughts do[e] strive.

Sonnet XII: "Lute, companion of my calamity." Louise Labé, *tr. by* Aliki *and* Willis Barnstone. BoWoP

Sonnet: "Madam, 'tis true, your beauties move." Sidney Godolphin. JCP

Sonnet: "Man, dream[e] no more of curious mysteries." Fulke Greville. *See* Caelica:
Man, dream[e] no more of curious mysteries.

Sonnet: "Men call you fair, and you do credit it." Spenser. *See* Amoretti: LXXIX. "Men call you fair [*or* fayre], and you do[e] credit it."

Sonnet: "Men, that delight to multiply desire." Fulke Greville. *See* Caelica:
Men, that delight to multiply desire.

Sonnet: "Methought I saw my late espoused saint." Milton. *See* Methought I saw. . .

Sonnet: "Month of January has flown Past, The." Joseph Brodsky, *tr. by* George L. Kline. AnAn

Sonnet: Most Men Know Love But as a Part of Life. Henry Timrod. AA
(Most Men Know Love.) Son

Sonnet: "My duchess was the werst she laffed she bitte." Ernest Walsh. ErPo

Sonnet: My Friend's Library. Henry F. Lott. PF

Sonnet: "My God, where is that ancient heat towards Thee." George Herbert. FL; OAEL-1

Sonnet: "My lady's presence makes the roses red." Henry Constable. *Fr. Diana.* EIL; NIP; OBSC

Sonnet: "My Love, I cannot thy rare beauties place." William Smith. *Fr. Chloris.* EIL; InvP

Sonnet: "My love took scorn my service to retain." Sir Thomas Wyatt. SiPS

Sonnet: "My lute, be as thou wast [*or* wert] when thou didst grow." William Drummond of Hawthornden. EIL; OBS; Son; ViBoPo
(To His Lute.) GTBS; GTBS-P

Sonnet: "My soul surcharged with grief now loud complains." Rachel Morpurgo, *tr. by* Nina Davis Salaman. TrJP

Sonnet: "My true love hath my heart." Sir Philip Sidney. *See* Arcadia: My True Love Hath My Heart [and I Have His].

Sonnet: "No worst, there is none." Gerard Manley Hopkins. *See* No Worst, There Is None.

Sonnet: "Not, I'll not, carrion comfort, Despair, not feast on thee." Gerard Manley Hopkins. *See* No, I'll not.

Sonnet I: "Not Ulysses, no, nor any other man." Louise Labé, *tr. by* Willis Barnstone. BoWoP

Sonnet: "Not with vain tears, when we're beyond the sun." Rupert Brooke. BrPo

Sonnet: "Not wrongly moved by this dismaying scene." William Empson. LiTM; WaP

Sonnet: "Now keep that long revolver at your side." George Hetherington. NeIP

Sonnet: "Now the bat circles on the breeze of eve." Anne Radcliffe. WPE

Sonnet: "Nuns fret not at their convent's narrow room." Wordsworth. *See* Nuns Fret Not at Their Convent's Narrow Room.

Sonnet: "Nurse-life wheat within his green husk growing, The." Fulke Greville. *See* Caelica: Nurse-life wheat, within his greene huske growing, The.

Sonnet XXII: "O blazing Sun, how happy you are there." Louise Labé, *tr. by* Willis Barnstone. BoWoP

Sonnet XI: "O eyes clear with beauty, O tender gaze." Louise Labé, *tr. by* Willis Barnstone. BoWoP

Sonnet: "O false and treacherous Probability." Fulke Greville. *See* Caelica: O false and treacherous Probability.

Sonnet II: "O handsome chestnut eyes, evasive gaze." Louise Labé, *tr. by* Willis Barnstone. BoWoP

Sonnet: "O! how my poet's-spirit doth it vex." Henry F. Lott. PF

Sonnet III: "O interminable desires, O futile hope." Louise Labé, *tr. by* Willis Barnstone. BoWoP

Sonnet, A: "O lovely O most charming pug." Marjory Fleming. *See* O lovely, O most charming pug.

Sonnet: "O shady vales, O fair enriched meads." Thomas Lodge. *Fr. A Margarite of America.* EIL; OBSC

Sonnet: "O thou who never harbored fear." Eloise Bibb. CBWP-4

Sonnet: Of All He Would Do. Cecco Angiolieri da Siena, *tr. fr. Italian by* Dante Gabriel Rossetti. AWP; PFI

Sonnet: Of an Ill-Favored Lady. Guido Cavalcanti, *tr. fr. Italian by* Dante Gabriel Rossetti. AWP

Sonnet: Of Beatrice de' Portinari, on All Saints' Day. Dante, *tr. fr. Italian by* Dante Gabriel Rossetti. AWP

Sonnet: Of Beauty and Duty. Dante, *tr. fr. Italian by* Dante Gabriel Rossetti. AWP

Sonnet: Of Becchina in a Rage. Cecco Angiolieri da Siena, *tr. fr. Italian by* Dante Gabriel Rossetti. AWP

Sonnet: Of Becchina, the Shoemaker's Daughter. Cecco Angiolieri da Siena, *tr. fr. Italian by* Dante Gabriel Rossetti. AWP

Sonnet: Of Caution. Francesco Da Barberini, *tr. fr. Italian by* Dante Gabriel Rossetti. AWP; PFI; PFI

Sonnet: Of His Lady in Heaven. Jacopo da Lentino, *tr. fr. Italian by* Dante Gabriel Rossetti. AWP; PFI

Sonnet: Of His Lady's Face. Jacopo da Lentino, *tr. fr. Italian by* Dante Gabriel Rossetti. PFI
  (Sonnet: Of His Lady's Face.) AWP

Sonnet: Of His Lady's Face. Jacopo da Lentino. *See* Her face has made my life. . .

Sonnet: Of His Pain from a New Love. Guido Cavalcanti, *tr. fr. Italian by* Dante Gabriel Rossetti. AWP

Sonnet: Of Love, in Honor of His Mistress Becchina. Cecco Angiolieri da Siena, *tr. fr. Italian by* Dante Gabriel Rossetti. AWP

Sonnet: Of Love in Men and Devils. Cecco Angiolieri da Siena, *tr. fr. Italian by* Dante Gabriel Rossetti. AWP

Sonnet: Of Moderation and Tolerance. Guido Guinicelli, *tr. fr. Italian by* Dante Gabriel Rossetti. AWP

Sonnet: Of the Eyes of a Certain Mandetta. Guido Cavalcanti, *tr. fr. Italian by* Dante Gabriel Rossetti. AWP

Sonnet: Of the Grave of Selvaggia, on the Monte della Sambuca. Cino da Pistoia, *tr. fr. Italian by* Dante Gabriel Rossetti. AWP

Sonnet: Of the Making of Master Messerin. Rustico di Filippo, *tr. fr. Italian by* Dante Gabriel Rossetti. AWP; PFI

Sonnet: Of the 20th of June 1291. Cecco Angiolieri da Siena, *tr. fr. Italian by* Dante Gabriel Rossetti. AWP

Sonnet: "Of thee (kind boy) I ask no red and white." Sir John Suckling. CaPo; MeLP; MePo; NoP; OBS; OxBoLi; SeCP; SeCV-1

Sonnet: "Of two fair virgins, modest, though admired." Jacopo Vittorelli. *See* Of two fair virgins. . .

Sonnet: Of Virtue. Folgore da San Geminiano, *tr. fr. Italian by* Dante Gabriel Rossetti. AWP

Sonnet: Of Why He Is Unhanged. Cecco Angiolieri da Siena, *tr. fr. Italian by* Dante Gabriel Rossetti. AWP; PFI

Sonnet: Of Why He Would Be a Scullion. Cecco Angiolieri da Siena, *tr. fr. Italian by* Dante Gabriel Rossetti. AWP; PFI

Sonnet: Ofto'er My Brain. Samuel Taylor Coleridge. *See* Composed on a Journey Homeward; the Author Having Received Intelligence of the Birth of a Son.

Sonnet: "Oh! Death will find me, long before I tire." Rupert Brooke. MoBrPo; Son
  (Oh! Death Will Find Me.) PoRA

Sonnet: Oh for a Poet—for a Beacon Bright. Edwin Arlington Robinson. OxBA

Sonnet: "Oh! [*or* O!] for some honest lover's ghost." Sir John Suckling. BXAP; JCP; MeLP; MePo; OBS; Par; PoEL-3; SeCP; SeCV-1
  (Doubt of Martyrdom, A.) BoLoP; CaPo; NOBE; OBEV

Sonnet: "Oh, if thou knew'st how thou thyself dost harm." William Alexander, Earl of Stirling. *See* Aurora: Oh, If Thou Knew'st How Thou Thyself Dost Harm.

Sonnet: Oh, Think Not I Am Faithful to a Vow! Edna St. Vincent Millay. FaBV

Sonnet: On a Picture of Leander. Keats. EnRP

Sonnet: On First Looking into Chapman's Homer. Keats. *See* Much have I travelled in the realms of gold.

Sonnet: On the 9th of June 1290. Dante, *tr. fr. Italian by* Dante Gabriel Rossetti. AWP

Sonnet: On the Detection of a False Friend. Guido Cavalcanti, *tr. fr. Italian by* Dante Gabriel Rossetti. AWP

Sonnet: On the Late Massacre in Piedmont. Milton. *See* Avenge, O Lord, thy slaughtered Saints.

Sonnet: On the Religious Memorie of Mrs. Catherine Thomason My Christian Freind Deceas'd Decem. 1646. Milton. OBS

Sonnet: On the Sea. Keats. *See* It keeps eternal whisperings around.

Sonnet: "Open wound which has been healed anew, An." Richard Chenevix Trench. TrPWD

Sonnet: "Orgasm completely, The." Tom Clark. CoAP

Sonnet: "Patience, hard thing! the hard thing but to pray." Gerard Manley Hopkins. NOBVV; OBNC
  (Patience, Hard Thing!) Prf; Son

Sonnet XXIX: Pity Me Not [Because the Light of Day]. Edna St. Vincent Millay. CMoP; FaBoWP; MoAB; MoAmPo; OxBA; TrGrPo

Sonnet: "Poet at Seven, The." Donald Justice. MT

Sonnet: "Point where beauty and intelligence meet, The." Gavin Ewart. WaP

Sonnet: "Ponder thy cares, and sum them all in one." Sir David Murray. *Fr. Caelia.* EIL

Sonnet: Poor Drooping Flowers and Pallid Violets. Matteo Maria Boiardo, *tr. Italian by* Peter Russell. PFI

Sonnet: Rapture Concerning His Lady, A. Guido Cavalcanti, *tr. fr. Italian by* Dante Gabriel Rossetti. AWP; PFI

Sonnet: "Record is nothing, and the hero great." Lord De Tabley. EBVV

Sonnet: Remember [*or* Sonnet]. Christina Rossetti. AWP; BoLoP; CH; EnLoPo; FaBV; FPL; NOBE; NoP; OAEL-2; OBEV; OBNC; PoLF; PoRA; TrGrPo

Sonnet: Saturday Evening in the Village. Giacomo Leopardi, *tr. fr. Italian by* John Heath-Stubbs. PFI

Sonnet: "Scorn not the sonnet; critic, you have frowned." Wordsworth. *See* Scorn not the sonnet; critic, you have frowned.

Sonnet: "Seer foretold that I would love one day, A." Louise Labé, *tr. by* Judith Thurman. PBWP

Sonnet: "Seer foretold that I would love one day, A." Louise Labé. *See* Sonnet XX: "I was foretold that on a certain day."

Sonnet: September, 1815. Wordsworth. ChER

Sonnet: September 1, 1802. Wordsworth. ChER

Sonnet: "Shall I, wasting in despair." George Wither. *See* Fair Virtue, the Mistress of Philarete: Shall I Wasting in Despair.

Sonnet: "She is so young, and never never before." Edward Davison. ErPo

Sonnet: "She took the dappled partridge flecked [*or* fleckt] with blood." Tennyson. FM; NAEL-2

Sonnet: Silence. Thomas Hood. *See* There is a silence. . .

Sonnet: "Silver herring throbbed thick in my seine, The." Kenneth Leslie. *See* By Stubborn Stars: Silver herring throbbed thick in my seine, The.

Sonnet: "Since I keep only what I give away." George Hetherington. NeIP

Sonnet: "Since there's no help. . ." Michael Drayton. *See* Idea: Since there's [*or* ther's] no help[e], come let us kiss[e] and part.

Sonnet: "Sits by a fireplace, the seducer talks." Leonard Wolf. ErPo

Sonnet: "So shoots a star as doth my mistress glide." John Davies of Hereford. EIL

Sonnet: "Sometimes the night echoes to prideless wailing." John Berryman. NoAM

Sonnet, A [*or* The]: "Sonnet is a moment's monument." Dante Gabriel Rossetti. *Fr.* The House of Life, *introd..* HeIP; NAEL-2; NoP; Son

Sonnet: Sounds of the Day. Norman MacCaig. RB

Sonnet: Supernatural Beings. Gavin Ewart. Son

Sonnet: Suppos'd to Be Written at Lemnos. Thomas Russell. NOEC

Sonnet: "Sure, Lord, there is enough in Thee to dry." George Herbert. FL

Sonnet: "Sweet semi-circled Cynthia played at maw." John Taylor. *Fr.* Odcomb's Complaint. EIL
  (Mockado, Fustian, and Motley.) FaBoNo

Sonnet: "Sweet soul, which in the April of thy years." William Drummond of Hawthornden. JCP

Sonnet: "Sweet spring, thou turnst. . ." William Drummond of Hawthornden. *See* Sweet spring, thou turnst. . .

Sonnet, A: "Take all of me, I am thine own, heart, soul." Amélie Rives. AA

Sonnet: "Tell me[e] no more how fair[e] she[e] is." Henry King. EnLoPo; MeLP; MePo; OBS; SeCP
  (That Distant Bliss.) TrGrPo

Sonnet: "That learned Graecian (who did so excell)." William Drummond of Hawthornden. OBS

Sonnet: There Is a Bondage Worse. Wordsworth. ChER

Sonnet: "There, on the darkened deathbed, dies the brain." John Masefield. EBEV
  (There, on the Darkened Deathbed.) DL; LiTB

Sonnet: "There was an Indian, who had known no change." J. C. Squire. CH; FaPON
  (Discovery, The.) OFD
  (There Was An Indian.) AmFN

Sonnet: "They may suppose, because I would not cloy your ear." John Berryman. NoP

Sonnet: "They say that shadow[e]s of deceased ghosts." Joshua Sylvester. EIL; OBS
  (They Say that Shadows of Deceased Ghosts.) Son

Sonnet: "This is the garden: colours come and go." E. E. Cummings. *See* This Is the Garden.

Sonnet: "This world is too much with us: late and soon." Wordsworth. *See* World Is Too Much with Us, The.

Sonnet XV: "This is the way we say it in our time." Winfield Townley Scott. ErPo

Sonnet: Thought of a Briton on the Subjugation of Switzerland. Wordsworth. *See* Two voices are there. . .

Sonnet: "Three colours have I known the Deep to wear." Wilfred Owen. FL

Sonnet: "Three silences made him a single word." R. P. Blackmur. PoA

Sonnet: "Three things there be in mans opinion deare." Fulke Greville. *See* Caelica: Three things there be in man's opinion dear[e].

Sonnet: Time and Account. Miguel de Guevara, *tr. fr. Spanish by* Samuel Beckett. MexPo

Sonnet: "Time and the mortal will stand never fast." Luis de Camões, *tr. by* Richard Garnett. AWP

Sonnet: To——— Wordsworth. ChER

Sonnet: To a Friend. Hartley Coleridge. *See* Where we were idlers. . .

Sonnet: To a Friend Who Does Not Pity His Love. Guido Cavalcanti, *tr. fr. Italian by* Dante Gabriel Rossetti. AWP

Sonnet: To a Young Lady Who Sent Me a Laurel Crown. Keats. EnRP

Sonnet: To an American Painter Departing for Europe. Bryant. *See* Thine eyes shall see the light. . .

Sonnet: To Brunetto Latini. Dante, *tr. fr. Italian by* Dante Gabriel Rossetti. AWP

Sonnet: To Certain Ladies; When Beatrice Was Lamenting Her Father's Death. Dante, *tr. fr. Italian by* Dante Gabriel Rossetti. AWP

Sonnet: To Crucify the Son. Miguel de Guevara, *tr. fr. Spanish by* Samuel Beckett. MexPo

Sonnet: To Dante Alighieri (He Commends the Work of Dante's Life). Giovanni Quirino, *tr. fr. Italian by* Dante Gabriel Rossetti. AWP

Sonnet: To Dante Alighieri (He Writes to Dante, Then in Exile at Verona, Defying Him as No Better Than Himself). Cecco Angiolieri da Siena, *tr. fr. Italian by* Dante Gabriel Rossetti. AWP

Sonnet: To Dante Alighieri on the Last Sonnet of the Vita Nuova. Cecco Angiolieri da Siena, *tr. fr. Italian by* Dante Gabriel Rossetti. AWP

Sonnet: To Guido Cavalcanti. Dante, *tr. fr. Italian by* Shelley. AWP
(Sonnet: Dante Alighieri to Guido Cavalcanti.) OBVE
(To Guido Cavalcanti.) PFI

Sonnet: To His Lady Joan, of Florence. Guido Cavalcanti, *tr. fr. Italian by* Dante Gabriel Rossetti. AWP

Sonnet: To Homer. Keats. *See* Standing aloof in giant ignorance.

Sonnet XV: "To honor the return of sparkling sun." Louise Labé, *tr. by* Willis Barnstone. BoWoP

Sonnet: To Love, In Great Bitterness. Cino da Pistoia, *tr. fr. Italian by* Dante Gabriel Rossetti. AWP

Sonnet: To Mr. H. Lawes, on His Aires. Milton. *See* Harry, whose tuneful. . .

Sonnet: To Mr. Lawrence. Milton. AWP; GTBS; GTBS-P; OBEV; PoE (Sonnet.) OBS

Sonnet: To One Who Has Been Long in City Pent. Keats. BLPA; EnRP; FaBoBe; FPL; LiTB; TrGrPo

Sonnet: To Primal Matters. Luis de Sandoval y Zapata, *tr. fr. Spanish by* Samuel Beckett. MexPo

Sonnet: "To rail or jest, ye know I use it not." Sir Thomas Wyatt. SiPS

Sonnet: To Tartar, a Terrier Beauty. Thomas Lovell Beddoes. FM; NOBVV; OBNC

Sonnet: To That Fair Kingdom, O My Gentle Lord. Boccaccio, *tr. fr. Italian by* T. G. Bergin. PFI

Sonnet: To the Admirable Transubstantiation of the Roses into the Marvellous Image of Our Lady of Guadalupe. Luis de Sandoval y Zapata, *tr. fr. Spanish by* Samuel Beckett. MexPo

Sonnet: To the Asshole. Rimbaud *and* Paul Verlaine, *tr. fr. French by* J. Murat *and* W. Gunn. PeHV

Sonnet: To the Departing Spirit of an Alienated Friend. Anna Seward. PeHV

Sonnet: To the Lady Beaumont. Wordsworth. ChER

Sonnet: To the Lady Pietra degli Scrovigni. Dante, *tr. fr. Italian by* Dante Gabriel Rossetti. AWP

Sonnet: To the River Lodon. Thomas Warton, the Younger. NOEC

Sonnet: To the River Otter. Samuel Taylor Coleridge. ChER; OAEL-2 (To the River Otter.) Son

Sonnet: To the Same Ladies; With Their Answer. Dante, *tr. fr. Italian by* Dante Gabriel Rossetti. AWP

Sonnet: Trance of Love. A. Cino da Pistoia, *tr. by* Dante Gabriel Rossetti. AWP

Sonnet, A: "Two voices are there: one is of the deep." James Kenneth Stephen. BXAP; FaBoCo; FaBoPa; FiBHP; NOBL; Par (Sonnet on Wordsworth, A.) CenHV

Sonnet: Verses Expressing the Feelings of a Lover. Sister Juana Inés de la Cruz, *tr. fr. Spanish by* Samuel Beckett. MexPo

Sonnet VII: "We see each living thing finally die." Louise Labé, *tr. by* Willis Barnstone. BoWoP

Sonnet: Wall, The. Donald Justice. CRP

Sonnet: "We will not whisper, we have found the place." Hilaire Belloc. MoBrPo

Sonnet, A: "Weeping, murmuring, complaining." Goldsmith. NOIV

Sonnet: "Were I as base as is the lowly plain." Joshua Sylvester. *See* Were I as Base as Is the Lowly Plain.

Sonnet: "What doth it serve to see sun's burning face." William Drummond of Hawthornden. ElL

Sonnet XXIII: "What good is it to me if long ago." Louise Labé, *tr. by* Willis Barnstone. BoWoP

Sonnet XXI: "What grandeur makes a man seem venerable?" Louise Labé, *tr. by* Willis Barnstone. BoWoP

Sonnet, The: "What is a sonnet? 'Tis the pearly shell." Richard Watson Gilder. AA

Sonnet: "When as man's life, the light of human lust." Fulke Greville. *See* Caelica: Whenas [*or* When as] man's life, the light of human[e] lust.

Sonnet: "When from the tower whence I derive love's heaven." *Unknown*. *Fr.* Zepheria. ElL

Sonnet: "When I catch sight of your fair head." Louise Labé. *See* Sonnet X: "When I perceive your blond and graceful head."

Sonnet: "When I have fears that I may cease to be." Keats. *See* When I Have Fears [That I May Cease to Be].

Sonnet X: "When I perceive your blond and graceful head." Louise Labé. BoWoP, *tr. by* Willis Barnstone
(Sonnet: "When I catch sight of your fair head.") PBWP, *tr. by* Joan Keefe *and* Richard Terdiman.

Sonnet: "When I was marked for suffering, Love forswore." Cervantes, *tr. by* Sir Edmund Gosse. AWP

Sonnet: "When men shall find thy flower, thy glory, pass." Samuel Daniel. *See* To Delia: When men shall find thy flower [*or* flow'r], thy glory, pass.

Sonnet: "When Phoebe formed a wanton smile." William Collins. EnLoPo; OxBSP

Sonnet: When She Walks by Here. Petrarch, *tr. fr. Italian by* Nicholas Kilmer. PFI

Sonnet XXVIII: "When we are old and these rejoicing veins." Edna St. Vincent Millay. ErPo; VGW

Sonnet: "Where are we to go when this is done?" Alfred A. Duckett. AmNP; PoBA; PoNe

Sonnet: Where Lies the Land. Wordsworth. *See* Where Lies the Land to Which Yon Ship Must Go ?

Sonnet: White Lily. Luis de Sandoval y Zapata, *tr. fr. Spanish by* Samuel Beckett. MexPo

Sonnet V: "White Venus limpid wandering in the sky." Louise Labé, *tr. by* Aliki *and* Willis Barnstone. BoWoP

Sonnet: Whoso List to Hunt [I Know Where Is an Hind]. Sir Thomas Wyatt. AAS; BoLoP; EBEV; GBL; HAP; InvP; NAEL-1; NoP; OAEL-1; OBVE; PoE; PoEL-1; PrIm
(Sonnet: "Whoso list to hunt, I know where is an hind.") SiPS

Sonnet: "Whoso list to hunt, I know where is an hind." Sir Thomas Wyatt. *See* Sonnet: Whoso List to Hunt [I Know Where Is an Hind].

Sonnet: Wild Duck's Nest, The. Wordsworth. *See* Imperial consort of the fairy king, The.

Sonnet: "Wind has blown the rain away and blown, A." E. E. Cummings. MoAB; MoAmPo

Sonnet: "Women have loved before as I love now." Edna St. Vincent Millay. PoA

Sonnet: World Is Too Much with Us, The. Wordsworth. *See* World Is Too Much with Us, The.

Sonnet: "World's bright comforter, whose beamsome light, The." Barnabe Barnes. *See* Divine Century of Spiritual Sonnets, A: God's Virtue.

Sonnet: Written at the End of "The Floure and the Lefe." Keats. EnRP

Sonnet: Written in a Blank Leaf of Dugdale's "Monasticon." Thomas Warton the Younger. SeCePo
(Written in a Blank Leaf of Dugdale's "Monasticon.") Son

Sonnet: Written in London, September, 1802. Wordsworth. *See* O friend! I know not which way I must look.

Sonnet: Written on the Day That Mr. Leigh Hunt Left Prison. Keats. ChER
(Written on the Day That Mr. Leigh Hunt Left Prison.) Son

Sonnet: You Have in You the Flowers and the Green Grass. Guido Cavalcanti, *tr. fr. Italian by* G. S. Fraser. PFI

Sonnet: "You that in love find[e] luck[e] and abundaunce [*or* habundance]." Sir Thomas Wyatt. AAS; SiPS
(May Time.) OBSC

Sonnet: "You waken slowly. In your dream you're straying." William Bell. NePoEA

Sonnet: Zone ("You're weary of this ancient world at last"). Guillaume Apollinaire, *tr. fr. French by* Louis Simpson. POS

Sonnet [*or* Sonetto] VII. Guido Cavalcanti, *tr. by* Ezra Pound. CTC; OBVE

Sonnet against the Too-Facile Mystic. Elizabeth B. Harrod. NePoEA

Sonnet and Limerick. Morris Bishop. FiBHP

Sonnet Composed upon Westminster Bridge, September 3, 1802.
Wordsworth. *See* Earth has not anything to show more fair .
Sonnet Ending with a Film Subtitle. Marilyn Hacker. MAYP; SM
Sonnet for a Picture. Swinburne. *Fr.* The Heptalogia. BXAP; FaBoNo;
OAEL-2
Sonnet for My Son. Melanie Gordon Barber. GoYe
Sonnet Found in a Deserted Madhouse. *Unknown.* FaBoCo; FaBoNo;
InvP; NA
Sonnet, Freely Adapted, for J. R. S. Bernice Zamora. CCP
Sonnet from Below the Age Gap. Keith Sinclair. PeNZ
Sonnet from "One Person." Elinor Wylie. *See* One Person:
I hereby swear that to uphold your house.
Sonnet in Autumn. Donald Petersen. NePoEA-2
Sonnet in the Mail Coach. Henry Taylor. TEP
Sonnet in Which I Say My Son Is a Long Way Off and Has Been for More
Than a Year, A. Antonio Cisneros, *tr. fr. Spanish by* Ena Hollis *and*
David Tipton. Per
Sonnet is a moment's monument, A. Sonnet, A [*or* The: "Sonnet is a
moment's monument"]. Dante Gabriel Rossetti. *Fr.* The House of
Life, *introd..* HeIP; NAEL-2; NoP; Son
Sonnet Made on Isabella Markham, A. John Harington. EIL; OBSC
Sonnet Made upon the Groves near Merlou Castle. Lord Herbert of
Cherbury. JCP
Sonnet Manqué. Sándor Weöres, *tr. fr. Hungarian by* Jascha Kessler.
FOC
Sonnet No. 21. Mark Ameen. GLP
Sonnet No. 22. Mark Ameen. GLP
Sonnet of Black Beauty. Lord Herbert of Cherbury. MePo
Sonnet of Brotherhood. R. A. K. Mason. ATNZ; PeNZ
Sonnet of Fishes. George Barker. FaBoMo; Son
Sonnet of Intimacy. Vinícius de Moraes, *tr. fr. Portuguese by* Elizabeth
Bishop. ATCBP
Sonnet of the Moon, A. Charles Best. CH
(Moon, The.) OBSC
(Of the Moon.) EIL
Sonnet of the Mountain, The. Mellin de Saint-Gelais, *tr. fr. French by*
Austin Dobson. AWP
Sonnet on a Family Picture. Thomas Edwards. NOEC
Sonnet on a Monkey, A. Marjory Fleming. FaBoCo; FaFP; FiBHP
(Sonnet, A: "O lovely O most charming pug.") FaBoCo; NBLV
Sonnet on a Still Night. J. V. Cunningham. PoA
Sonnet on Chillon. Byron. *Fr.* The Prisoner of Chillon. FiP; LiTB;
TrGrPo
(On the Castle of Chillon.) GTBS; GTBS-P
Sonnet on Famous and Familiar Sonnets and Experiences. Delmore
Schwartz. Son
Sonnet on Fidelity. Vinícius de Moraes, *tr. fr. Portuguese by* Ashley
Brown. ATCBP
Sonnet on Hearing the *Dies Irae* Sung in the Sistine Chapel. Oscar Wilde.
TrPWD
Sonnet on Passing the Bridge of Alcantra, near Lisbon. William Mickle.
OBTV
Sonnet on Separation. Vinícius de Moraes, *tr. fr. Portuguese by* Ashley
Brown. ATCBP
Sonnet on Sir William Alexander's Harsh Verses after the English Fashion,
A. James I, King of England. Son
Sonnet on the Crimean War. William Forster. CBAP
Sonnet on the Death of Mr. Richard West. Thomas Gray. EnRP; NOEC;
NoP; OBD; PeHV; PoE; PoEL-3; SeCePo
(On the Death of Mr. Richard West.) NOBE; Son; TrGrPo
Sonnet on the Sea. Keats. *See* On the Sea.
Sonnet on Wordsworth, A. James Kenneth Stephen. *See* Two voices are
there: one is of the deep.
Sonnet Reversed. Rupert Brooke. NOBL
Sonnet September, 1802. Wordsworth. *See* Inland, within a hollow vale.
Sonnet—Silence. Poe. NOBA
Sonnet XIII. Winfield Townley Scott. ErPo
Sonnet to a Clam. John Godfrey Saxe. AnAmPo
Sonnet to a Friend Who Asked, How I Felt When the Nurse First Presented
My Infant to Me. Samuel Taylor Coleridge. EnRP
Sonnet to a Negro in Harlem. Helene Johnson. AmNP; BANP; CDC;
NIP
Sonnet to Ailsa Rock. Keats. *See* Harken thou, craggy. . .
Sonnet to Be Written from Prison. Robert Adamson. CBAP
Sonnet to Britain. William Edmonstoune Aytoun. FaBoCo
Sonnet to Eurydice. Sophia de Mello Breyner Andresen, *tr. fr.*
Portuguese by Ruth Fainlight. OV
Sonnet to Gath. Edna St. Vincent Millay. BoWoP; CMoP; MoAB;
MoAmPo
Sonnet to Heavenly Beauty, A. Joachim du Bellay, *tr. fr. French by*
Andrew Lang. AWP; CTC
Sonnet to Lake Leman. Byron. Son

Sonnet to My Father. Donald Justice. DiL
Sonnet to My First Born. Mary Weston Fordham. CBWP-2
Sonnet to My Friend, with an Identity Disc. Wilfred Owen. PeHV
Sonnet to My Mother. George Barker. FaFP; LiTB; MoAB; SeCePo;
WaP
(To My Mother.) FaBoMo; FF; LiTM; OxBTC; Son; TwCP
Sonnet to My Mother, A. Heine. *See* In fond delusion once I left thy
side.
Sonnet to Negro Soldiers. Joseph Seamon Cotter, Jr.. PoBA
Sonnet to Opium; Celebrating Its Virtues, A. "Orestes." NOEC
Sonnet to Poesy. James Waddington. PF
Sonnet to Science [Prologue]. Poe. *Fr.* Al Aaraaf. AmPP; NAAL-1;
NoP; OxBA; TAP; TW
Sonnet to Sleep. Keats. *See* O soft embalmer. . .
Sonnet to Vauxhall. Thomas Hood. PoEL-4
Sonnet XX. Louise Labé, *tr. by* Willis Barnstone. BoWoP
Sonnet 21. Paul Goodman. VGW
Sonnet upon a Swedish Cottage. Sir John Carr. OBTV
Sonnet upon Sonnets, A. Burns. Son
Sonnet Variations, *sels.* Peyton Houston. Son
"Love, which is least sure and most dared, the pure, keen." *Fr.* CVI,
ii.
Doll, The. *Fr.* XVII.
The/ Quick Gold, Slant Blue, Sharp Scarlet. *Fr.* CV.
Time's Mirror. *Fr.* LXXVII.
Sonnet with a Different Letter at the End of Every Line. George Starbuck.
OBAL
Sonnet with her Mona Lisa smile, The. Sonnet and Limerick. Morris
Bishop. FiBHP
Sonnet Written in the Church-Yard at Middleton, in Sussex. Charlotte
Smith. NOEC; WPE
Sonnet Written in Tintern Abbey, Monmouthshire. Edmund Gardner.
NOEC
Sonnet (You were born; must die; were loved; must love). Stephen
Spender. *See* You were born; must die; were loved; must love.
Sonneteering Made Easy. S. B. Botsford. NYBP
Sonnets, *sels.* James Agee. MoAmPo
"Now stands our love on that still verge of day." *Fr.* XX.
"Our doom is in our being. We began." *Fr.* II.
"So it begins. Adam is in his earth." *Fr.* I. OPOP
"Those former loves wherein our lives have run." *Fr.* XIX.
Sonnets, *sels.* Richard Barnfield. PeHV
"Ah no; nor I myselfe: though my pure love." *Fr.* XIX.
"But now my Muse toyled with continuall care." *Fr.* XX.
"Cherry-lipt Adonis in his snowie shape." *Fr.* XVII.
"Here hold this glove (this milk-white cheveril glove)." *Fr.* XIV.
"Sighing, and sadly sitting by my Love." *Fr.* XI.
"Some talk of Ganymede th' Idalian boy." *Fr.* XII.
"Sometimes I wish that I his pillow were." *Fr.* VIII.
"Sporting at fancie, setting light by love." *Fr.* I.
"Sweet corrall lips, where Nature's treasure lies." *Fr.* VI.
"Sweet Thames I honour thee, not for thou art." *Fr.* VII.
"Thus was my love, thus was my Ganymed." *Fr.* X.
"Two stars there are in one faire firmament." *Fr.* IV.
Sonnets, *sels.* John Berryman. Son
Great Citadels whereon the Gold Sun Falls. *Fr.* IX.
Marble Nor Monuments whereof Then We Spoke. *Fr.* XL.
What Was Ashore, Then. *Fr.* XV.
Sonnets, *sels.* Boccaccio, *tr. fr. Italian by* Dante Gabriel Rossetti.
Inscription for a Portrait of Dante. AWP
Of Fiammetta Singing. AWP
Of His Last Sight of Fiammetta. AWP
Of Three Girls and of Their Talk. AWP; PFI
To Dante in Paradise, after Fiammetta's Death. AWP
To One Who Had Censured His Public Exposition of Dante. AWP
Sonnets, *sel.* George Henry Boker.
To My Lady. AA
Sonnets, *sels.* John Masefield.
Flesh, I Have Knocked at Many a Dusty Door. LiTM
How Many Ways ("How many ways, how many times"). LiTB; WGRP
"I never see the red rose crown the year." GoYe
"If I could get within this changing I." WGRP
"Is there a great green commonwealth of Thought." LiTM; MoBrPo
"O little self, within whose smallness lies." WGRP
"There is no God, as I was taught in youth." CMoP; WGRP
What Am I, Life?. ImOP
Sonnets, *sels.* George Santayana.
After Grey Vigils. *Fr.* XLIX. AnAmPo
"Among the myriad voices of the spring." AnAmPo
"As in the midst of battle there is room." AnAmPo
"Deem not, because you see me in the press." *Fr.* XI. TrGrPo
"Dreamt I today the dream of yesternight." AnAmPo

"Have I the heart to wander on the earth." AnAmPo

"I sought on earth a garden of delight." AnAmPo

"Mightier storms than this are brewed on earth." AnAmPo

"O world, thou choosest not the better part!" *Fr*. III. AnAmPo;
TrGrPo

(Faith.) WGRP

(O World.) FPL

On the Death of a Metaphysician. AnAmPo

"Perfect love is nourished by despair, A." AnAmPo

"Sweet are the days we wander with no hope." AnAmPo

"There may be chaos still around the world." AnAmPo

"'Tis love that moveth the celestial spheres." AnAmPo

"What riches have you that you deem me poor?" *Fr*. XXIV. TrGrPo

Sonnets, *sels*. Shakespeare.

I. "From fairest creatures we desire increase." CTC; LiTB; OBSC;
TrGrPo

II. "When forty winters shall besiege thy brow." BLPL; FF; LiTB;
OBSC; Son; TEP

III. "Look in thy glass, and tell the face thou viewest." LiTB; NAEL-1;
OBSC

V. "Those hours, that with gentle work did frame." TEP

VIII. "Music[k] to hear[e], why hear'st thou music[k] sadly?" PoEL-2

XII. "When I do count the clock that tells the time." AWP; EiL; InPS;
NAEL-1; NoP; OAEL-1; OBSC; Son; TEP

(When I Do Count the Clock.) FaFP

XIII. "Oh [*or* O]! that you were yourself! but, love, you are." TEP

XIV. "Not from the stars do I my judgement pluck." Son

XV. "When I consider everything that grows." AWP; BLPL; NAEL-1;
OBSC; Son; TEP; TrGrPo

XVII. "Who will believe my verse in time to come." OBSC

XVIII. "Shall I compare thee to a summer's day?" BoLoP; CTC; EiL;
EnLoPo; FaBoBe; FaBV; FaFP; FiP; FPL; GBL; HAP; HeIP; InPK;
InPS; InvP; LiTB; MAT; NIP; NOBE; NoP; OAEL-1; OBEV; OBSC;
PoE; PoEL-2; PoLF; PoRA; PrIm; SCV; SeCePo; Son; TEP; TrGrPo;
WeW

(To His Love.) GTBS; GTBS-P

XIX. "Devouring Time, blunt thou the lion's paws [lyons pawes]."
AWP; ChTr; EBEV; MAT; NAEL-1; OAEL-1; OBSC; PoE; PoEL-2;
TrGrPo

XX. "Woman's face with nature's own hand painted, A." ErPo; InvP;
NAEL-1; OAEL-1; PeHV

XXI. "So is it not with me as with that muse." InvP; OBSC

XXII. "My glass shall not persuade me I am old." OBSC; Son

XXIII. "As an unperfect actor on the stage." InvP; Son

XXIV. "Mine eye hath play'd the painter, and hath steel'd." EyDe

XXV. "Let those who are in favour with their stars." OBSC

XXVII. "Weary with toil, I haste me to my bed." OBSC

XXVIII. "How can I then return in happy plight." OBSC

XXIX. "When, in disgrace with fortune and men's eyes." AWP; CTC;
EBEV; EiL; FaBoRV; FaBV; GBL; HAP; HeIP; InPS; InvP;
LiTB; NAEL-1; NOBE; NoP; OAEL-1; OBEV; OBSC; OPOP; PeHV;
PoEL-2; Son

(Consolation, A.) GTBS; GTBS-P

XXX. "When to the sessions of sweet silent thought." AWP; CTC;
EBEV; EiL; FaBoRV; FaBV; FF; FPL; GBL; HAP; InPS; LiTB;
NAEL-1; NOBE; NoP; OAEL-1; OBEV; OBSC; PoE; PoEL-2; PoLF;
PoRA; PPP; PrIM; TEP; TrGrPo

(Remembrance.) FaFP; GTBS; GTBS-P

XXXI. "Thy bosom is endeared with all hearts." NOBE; OBEV;
OBSC; PoEL-2

XXXII. "If thou survive my well-contented day." EiL; OBSC

(Post Mortem.) GTBS; GTBS-P

XXXIII. "Full many a glorious morning have I seen[e]." AWP; EBEV;
EiL; HAP; LiTB; NoP; OAEL-1; OBSC; PoRA; PPP; SeCePo; Son;
TEP; TrGrPo; WeW

(Full Many a Glorious Morning.) FaFP

XXXIV. "Why didst thou promise such a beauteous day." OBSC

XXXV. "No more be grieved at that which thou hast done." NAEL-1;
PeHV; PoE; TEP; UnPo

XXXVI. "Let me confess that we two must be twain." PeHV

XL. "Take all my loves, my Love, yea, take them all." InvP; OBSC

XLI. "Those petty wrongs that liberty commits." InvP

XLII. "That thou hast her, it is not all my grief." InvP

XLIV. "If the dull substance of my flesh were thought." Son

XLVI. "Mine eye and heart are at a mortal war." EyDe

XLVII. "Betwixt mine eye and heart a league is took." EyDe

XLIX. "After grey vigils, sunshine in the heart." AnAmPo

LII. "So am I as the rich, whose blessed key." OBSC

LIII. "What is your substance, whereof are you made." CTC; EBEV;
EiL; FaFP; LiTB; NOBE; NoP; OBEV; OBSC; PeHV

LIV. "O [*or* Oh], how much more doth beauty beauteous seem." AWP;
EiL; OBEV; OBSC; PoE

LV. "Not marble, nor the gilded monuments." AWP; BLPL; CTC;
FaFP; FF; HeIP; LiTB; NAEL-1; NIP; NOBE; NoP; OAEL-1; OBSC;
PeHV; PoE; PoEL-2; PoRA; Son; TEP; TrGrPo

LVI. "Sweet love, renew thy force, be it not said." PoLF

LVII. "Being your slave, what should I do[e] but tend." HAP; OBEV;
PeHV; PoEL-2

(Absence.) GTBS; GTBS-P

LX. "Like as the waves make towards the pebbled shore." ChTr;
EBEV; EiL; FPL; LiTB; NIP; NOBE; OBSC; PeHV; PoRA; Son;
TEP; UnPo

(Like as the Waves.) FaFP

(Revolutions.) GTBS; GTBS-P

LXI. "Is it thy wil, thy Image should keepe open." PoEL-2

LXII. "Sin [*or* Sinne] of self-love [*or* selfe-love] possesseth all mine eye
[*or* eie]." EBEV; PoEL-2

LXIII. "Against my Love shall be, as I am now." OBSC

LXIV. "When I have seen by Time's fell hand defaced." AWP; BLPL;
EiL; EnLoPo; FaFP; HAP; HeIP; LiTB; NOBE; NoP; OAEL-1;
OBSC; PoE; PoRA; Son

(Time and Love, I.) GTBS; GTBS-P

LXV. "Since brass, nor stone, nor earth, nor boundless sea." AWP;
FF; FiP; HAP; InPS; LiTB; NAEL-1; NOBE; NoP; PoRA; Son; UnPo

(Since Brass, Nor Stone, Nor Earth.) FaFP

(Time and Love, II.) GTBS; GTBS-P

LXVI. "Tired [*or* Tyr'd] with all these, for restful death I cry." AWP;
CTC; EBEV; FaBoPV; FaFP; HAP; InPS; LiTB; NOBE; OAEL-1;
OBSC; PoEL-2; TrGrPo; WeW

(World's Way, The.) GTBS; GTBS-P

LXVII. "Ah wherefore with infection should he live." PeHV

LXVIII. "Thus is this cheek the map of days outworn." OBSC

LXXI. "No longer mourn for me when I am dead." AWP; EBEV; EiL;
FaBoRV; GBL; HAP; LiTB; NAEL-1; NoP; OBSC; PoRA; Son; TEP;
TrGrPo

(Triumph of Death, The.) GTBS; GTBS-P

LXXIII. "That time of year thou may'st [*or* maist] in me behold."
AWP; BoLoP; ChTr; CTC; EBEV; EiL; EnLoPo; FaBoRV; FaBV; FF;
FiP; GBL; GTBS; GTBS-P; HAP; HeIP; HoPM; InPS; InvP;
LiTB; NAEL-1; NIP; NOBE; NoP; OAEL-1; OBD; OBEV; OBSC;
OHFP; PoE; PoEL-2; PoRA; PPP; PrIm; QFR; Son; SoSe; TEP;
TrGrPo; UnPo; WeW

LXXIV. "But be contented: when that fell arrest." NAEL-1; OBSC;
Son

LXXV. "So are you to my thoughts as food to life." PoEL-2

LXXVI. "Why is my verse so barren of new pride." EBEV; InvP

LXXVII. "Thy glass will show thee how thy beauties wear." QFR

LXXXI. "Or I shall live your epitaph to make." OBSC

LXXXV. "My tongue-tied muse in manners holds her still." Son

LXXXVI. "Was it the proud full sail of his great verse." InvP;
OAEL-1; Son; TEP

LXXXVII. "Farewell! Thou art too dear [*or* deare] for my possessing."
EBEV; EiL; GTBS; GTBS-P; InPS; InvP; LiTB; NAEL-1; NOBE;
OAEL-1; OBEV; OBSC; PeHV; PoEL-2; QFR; Son; TrGrPo

XC. "Then hate me when thou wilt; if ever, now." AWP; EBEV; EiL;
NOBE; OBEV; OBSC; PoEL-2

XCIII. "So shall I live, supposing thou art true." InvP

XCIV. "They that have power to hurt, and will do none." BLPL; EiL;
InPS; LiTB; NAEL-1; NOBE; NoP; OAEL-1; OBEV; PeHV; PoE;
PoEL-2; PPP; SCV; Son; TEP; TrGrPo

(Life without Passion.) GTBS; GTBS-P

XCV. "How sweet and lovely dost thou make the shame." TrGrPo

XCVII. "How like a winter hath my absence been[e]." AWP; EiL;
EnLoPo; EyDe; GTBS; GTBS-P; NAEL-1; NOBE; OAEL-1; OBEV;
OBSC; PoRA; Son; TEP; TrGrPo

XCVIII. "From you have I been absent in the spring." AWP; ChTr;
EBEV; EiL; LiTB; NAEL-1; NOBE; OBEV; OBSC; TEP

XCIX. "Forward violet thus did I chide, The." OBSC

C. "Where art thou, Muse, that thou forget'st so long." OBSC

CII. "My love is strengthen'd, though more weak in seeming." AWP;
EiL; OBEV; OBSC

CIV. "To me, fair[e] friend, you never can be old." EiL; FPL; GBL;
GTBS; GTBS-P; HeIP; OBEV; OBSC; Prf

CVI. "When in the chronicle of wasted time." AWP; BLPL; CTC; EiL;
EnLoPo; FaBoCh; FaBV; FiP; LiTB; NAEL-1; NOBE; NoP; OBEV;
OBSC; PoRA; Son; TEP; TrGrPo

(To His Love.) GTBS; GTBS-P

CVII. "Not mine own fears nor the prophetic soul." AWP; CTC;
EBEV; FiP; HAP; LiTB; NAEL-1; NoP; OAEL-1; OBSC

CIX. "O [*or* Oh]! Never say that I was false of heart." EiL; NOBE;
OBEV; OBSC

(Unchangeable, The.) GTBS; GTBS-P

CX. "Alas, 'tis true I have gone here and there." EBEV; OBSC;
PeHV

CXVI. "Let me not to the marriage of true minds." AWP; EIL; EnLoPo; FaBV; FaFP; FPL; GBL; HAP; HeIP; InPS; InvP; LiTB; NAEL-1; NIP; NOBE; NoP; OAEL-1; OBEV; OBSC; PeHV; PoE; PoEL-2; PoRA; PPP; PrIm; SCV; SeCePo; Son; SoSe; TEP; TrGrPo; UnPo; WeW
(True Love.) GTBS; GTBS-P

CXX. "That you were once unkind befriends me now." InvP

CXXI. " 'Tis better to be vile than vile esteemed." InvP; OAEL-1; PoEL-2

CXXIII. "No, Time, thou shalt not boast that I do change!" OBSC; Son; TrGrPo

CXXVI. "O thou, my lovely boy, who in thy power." NAEL-1

CXXVII. "How oft, when thou, my music, music play'st." EIL; NAEL-1; PoE

CXXIX. "Expense of spirit in a waste of shame, The [or Th']." AWP; EBEV; ErPo; GBL; HAP; HeIP; InPS; LiTB; NAEL-1; NIP; NOBE; NoP; OAEL-1; OBEV; OBSC; PoE; PoEL-2; PPP; QFR; SCV; SeCePo; Son; TEP; TrGrPo; UnPo; WeW

CXXX. "My mistress' eyes are nothing like the sun." AWP; BoLoP; EBEV; FF; HAP; HoPM; InPK; InPS; InvP; LiTB; NAEL-1; NIP; NoP; OAEL-1; PoE; PPP; PrIm; Son; SoSe; TEP; WeW

CXXXII. "Thine eyes I love, and they, as pitying me." OBSC

CXXXIII. "Beshrew that heart that makes my heart to groan." InvP

CXXXIV. "So now I have confessed that he is thine." InvP

CXXXV. "Whoever hath her wish, thou hast thy Will." NAEL-1; OAEL-1

CXXXVII. "Thou blind fool, Love, what dost thou to mine eyes." WeW

CXXXVIII. "When my love swears [or sweares] that she is made of truth." AWP; EBEV; NAEL-1; NoP; OAEL-1; PoEL-2; PPP; SoSe; TEP; TrGrPo

CXLI. "In faith, I do[e] not love thee with mine eyes." PoEL-2; TrGrPo

CXLIV. "Two loves I have of comfort and despair." EBEV; InvP; NAEL-1; NIP; OAEL-1; PeHV; PoEL-2; Son

CXLV. "Those lips that love's own hand did make." Son

CXLVI. "Poor[e] soul[e], the centre of my sinful[l] earth." AWP; EaLo; EIL; HAP; InPS; LiTB; NAEL-1; NIP; NOBE; NOCV; NoP; OAEL-1; OBEV; OBSC; PoE; PoEL-2; PPP; Son; TrGrPo
(Soul and Body.) GTBS; GTBS-P

CXLVII. "My love is as a fever [or feaver], longing still." EBEV; HoPM; NAEL-1; PoEL-2; TEP

CXLVIII. "O me! what eyes hath love put in my head." (Blind Love.). GTBS; GTBS-P

CLI. "Love is too young to know what conscience is." EBEV; HeIP; PoE; PoEL-2

Sonnets, sels. Frederick Goddard Tuckerman.
"And change with hurried hand has swept these scenes." Fr. II, xviii. HAP; NOBA; QFR; TAP
"And faces, forms and phantoms, numbered not." Fr. II, xix. QFR
"And me my winter's task is drawing over." Fr. V, xiv. QFR
"But we are set to strive to make our mark." Fr. III, xv. TrCP
"Gertrude and Gulielma, sister-twins." Fr. II, xv. HAP; QFR
"Hast thou seen reversed the prophet's miracle." Fr. IV, x. NOBA
"Here, where the red man swept the leaves away." Fr. IV, ix. NOBA; TAP
"Not the round natural world, not the deep mind." Fr. I, xxviii. NoP
"O hard endeavor, to blend in with these." Fr. II, xx. QFR
"Put off thy bark from shore, though near the night." MOS
"Roll on, sad world! Not Mercury or Mars." Fr. II, xvii. QFR
"Sometimes I walk where the deep water dips." Fr. III, x. NOBA
"Still pressing through these weeping solitudes." Fr. II, xi. NOBA
"Thin little leaves of wood fern, ribbed and toothed." Fr. III, iv. TAP
"Under the mountain, as when first I knew." Fr. II, xvi. HAP; QFR; TAP
"Upper chamber in a darkened house, An." Fr. I, x. NOBA; NoP; TAP
"Yes: though the brine may from the desert deep." Fr. II, iii. HAP

Sonnets—Actualities, sel. E. E. Cummings.
I Like My Body When It Is With Your Body. BoLoP; ErPo; LLLT; VGW

Sonnets are full of love, and this my tome. To My First Love, My Mother. Christina Rossetti. OHIP

Sonnets at Christmas, sels. Allen Tate. HAP; LiTA; LiTM; NOBA; OxBA; VGW
Ah, Christ. Fr. II. PoNe; Son
This Is the Day. Fr. I. Son
"This is the day His hour of life draws near." NAAL-2

Sonnets at Christmas, II. Allen Tate. HAP; LiTA; LiTM; PoNe; VGW

Sonnets Attempted in the Manner of Contemporary Writers. sels. Samuel Taylor Coleridge. Son
On a Ruined House in a Romantic Country.

Pensive at Eve.
To Simplicity.

Sonnets for a Dying Man, sels. Burns Singer. NePoEA-2
"Christ comes to mind and comes across the mind." Fr. XXXIX.
"I promise you by the harsh funeral." Fr. XLVIII.
"Old man dozed, The. The hospital quietened." Fr. XV.
"Those flaming Christians with their hygienic rose." Fr. XXXIII.
"To see the petrel cropping in the farmyard." Fr. XXX.

Sonnets for Roseblush, sel. John Hollander.
"Why drink, why touch you now? If it will be." SM

Sonnets from China, sels. W. H. Auden.
"Chilled by the present, its gloom and its noise." Fr. XVIII. PPP
"Far from a cultural centre he was used." Fr. XIII. CMoP; NoAM
"He stayed, and was imprisoned in possession." Fr. IV. CMoP
"He was their servant (some way he was blind)." Fr. VII. CMoP
"He watched the stars and noted birds in flight." Fr. VI. CMoP
"Here war is harmless like a monument." Fr. XII. OBWP
"His care-free swagger was a fine invention." Fr. V. CMoP
"So an age ended, and its last deliverer died." Fr. X. CMoP; PoE
"So from the years their gifts were showered: each." Fr. I. CMoP
"They wondered why the fruit had been forbidden." Fr. II. CMoP

Sonnets from Greece, sel. Trumbull Stickney.
Mount Lykaion. OxBA; Son; TrGrPo

Sonnets from the Portuguese, sels. Elizabeth Barrett Browning.
"And wilt thou have me fashion into speech." Fr. XIII. BrRo
"Belovéd, my Belovéd, when I think." Fr. XX. Son; WPE
"Belovéd, thou hast brought me many flowers." Fr. XLIV. EBVV; OBNC; WPE
"Can it be right to give what I can give?." Fr. IX. CTC; Son
"Face of all the world is changed, I think, The." Fr. VII. CTC
"First time he kissed me, he but only kissed." Fr. XXXVIII. BLPA; BLPL; CTC; FaBoBe
"First time that the sun rose on thine oath, The." Fr. XXXII. NAEL-2; WPE
"Go from me. Yet I feel that I shall stand." Fr. VI. BLPL; OBEV; TrGrPo
"How do I love thee? Let me count the ways." Fr. XLIII. BoLoP; CTC; EBVV; FaBoBe; FaBV; FaFP; FF; FPL; HeIP; HoPM; InPK; LiTB; NAEL-2; NIP; NoP; PoE; PoLF; PoRA; Son; TEP; TrGrPo; UnPo; WPE
"I never gave a lock of hair away." Fr. XVIII. EBVV; HAP
"I thought once how Theocritus had sung." Fr. I. EBVV; GBL; NOBE; NoP; OBEV; OBNC; WPE
"If I leave all for thee, wilt thou exchange." Fr. XXXV. Son
"If thou must love me, let it be for nought." Fr. XIV. CTC; FaFP; HeIP; InPS; LiTB; OBEV; OBNC; TrGrPo
"Let the world's sharpness, like a clasping knife." Fr. XXIV. NOBVV
"My letters! all dead paper, mute and white." Fr. XXVIII. HAP
"My poet, thou canst touch on all the notes." Fr. XVII. BrRo
"Say over again, and yet once over again." Fr. XXI. NAEL-2
"Thou hast thy calling to some palace floor." Fr. IV. Son
"Unlike are we, unlike, O princely heart!" Fr. III. OBEV; TrGrPo
"When our two souls stand up erect and strong." Fr. XXII. BoWoP; NAEL-2; NOBE; OBEV; TrGrPo; WPE
"Yet, love, mere love, is beautiful indeed." Fr. X. CTC

Sonnets from the Series Relating to Edgar Allan Poe, sels. Sarah Helen Whitman. AA
"If thy sad heart, pining for human love." Fr. VI.
"Oft since thine earthly eyes have closed on mine." Fr. III.
"On our lone pathway bloomed no earthly hopes." Fr. V.
"When first I looked into thy glorious eyes." Fr. II.

Sonnets in Quaker Language, sels. Hildegarde Flanner. WPE
"Hearing a sound that may be thy return." Fr. VI.
"Thee sets a bell to swinging in my soul." Fr. II.

Sonnets of English Dramatic Poets, sels. Swinburne. Son
Ben Jonson.
Christoper Marlowe.
John Webster.

Sonnets of Michelangelo, The, sel. Elizabeth Jennings.
"I wish, God, for some end I do not will." Fr. LXXV. TOF

Sonnets of the Blood, sels. Allen Tate. PoA
"Fire I praise was once perduring flame, The." Fr. VII.
"Near to me as my flesh, my flesh and blood." Fr. II.
"Not power nor the storied hand of God." Fr. IX.
"Times have changed, there is not left to us, The." Fr. IV.
"What is this flesh and blood compounded of." Fr. I.

Sonnets of the Months ("Unto the blithe and lordly fellowship."), sels. Folgore Da San Gimignano, tr. fr. Italian by Dante Gabriel Rossetti. AWP
April. PFI
August. CTC
Conclusion AwP

December. PFI
Dedication. AWP
February. AWP
January. PFI
July. AWP
June. AWP
March. AWP
May. AWP; PFI
November. AWP
October. AWP; PFI
September. AWP
Sonnets of the Triple-headed Manichee, *sel.* George Barker.
"Keelhauled across the star-wrecked death of God." *Fr.* II. PoA
Sonnets—Realities, *sel.* E. E. Cummings.
Cambridge Ladies Who Live in Furnished Souls, The. AmPP; HeIP; MoP; NAAL-2; NoAM; NoAM; NOBA; NoP; OBAL; OxBA; TAP
Sonnets to Aurelia, *sels.* Robert Nichols. OBMV
"But piteous things we are—when I am gone."
"Come, let us sigh a requiem over love."
"Though to your life apparent stain attach."
"When the proud World does most my world despise."
Sonnets to Karl Theodore German, *sels.* August, Graf von Platen. PeHV
"How shall I still mankind's good will retrieve." *Fr.* XXII.
"When shall I master this anxiety." *Fr.* I.
Sonnets to Laura, *sels.* Petrarch, *tr. fr. Italian.*
Songs.
I saw a Phoenix in the Wood Alone. AWP, *tr. by* Spenser; ChTr, *tr. by* Helen Lee Peabody.
Visions, The. *Fr.* Canzone VIII, *tr. by* Edmund Spenser. AWP; PFI
To Laura in Death.
"Eyes that drew from me such fervent praise, The." *Fr.* XXIV, *tr. by* Edwin Morgan. NAWM-1
"First day she passed up and down through the Heavens, The." *Fr.* LXXV, *tr. by* J. M. Synge. OBMV
"Go, grieving rimes of mine, to that hard stone." *Fr.* LX, *tr. by* Morris Bishop. NAWM-1
"Great is my envy of you, earth, in your greed." *Fr.* XXXII, *tr. by* Edwin Morgan. NAWM-1
(Translation from Petrarch, A.) MoBrPo
How the Lover Perisheth in His Delight, As the Fly in the Fire. *Tr.* Sir Thomas Wyatt. Son
"In the years of her age the most beautiful." OBMV
"My flowery and green age was passing away." *Fr.* XLVII, *prose tr. by* J. M. Synge. OBMV
(He Understands the Great Cruelty of Death.) BIrV
"What a grudge I am bearing the earth." *Fr.* XXXIII, *tr. by* J. M. Synge.
To Laura in Life.
Alas! So All Things Now Do Hold Their Peace. *Fr.* CIX, *tr. by* Sir Thomas Wyatt. NAEL-1; NoP; OAEL-1; OBVE
(Lover for Shamefastnesse Hideth His Desire within His Faithfull Hart, The.) AAS, 2 *versions.*
"Blest be the day, and blest the month and year." *Fr.* XLVII, *tr. by* Joseph Auslander. NAWM-1
("Father in heaven, after each lost day," *tr. by* Bernard Bergonzi) NAWM-1
Heart on the Hill, The. *Fr.* CCV, *tr. by* C. B. Cayley. AWP
"I find [*or* fynde] no peace and all my war[r] is done." *Fr.* CIV, *tr. by* Sir Thomas Wyatt. AAS; LiTB; OAEL-1; OBVE; SiPS
(Description of the Contrarious Passions in a Lover.) FF; Son; TrGrPo
If It Be Destined. *Fr.* XI, *tr. by* Edward FitzGerald. AWP; SiPS
"It was the morning of that blessed day." *Fr.* III, *tr. by* Joseph Auslander. NAWM-1
Last Trial, The. *Fr.* CXIII, *tr. unknown.* OBSC
Love, That Doth Reign [*or* Raine] and Live Within My Thought. AAS; HeIP; NAEL-1; NoP; OAEL-1; OBVE
(Complaint of a Lover Rebuked.) AWP; Son; TrGrPo
("Love that liveth and reigneth in my thought.") SiPS
My Galley ("My galley charged with forgetfulness"). *Fr.* CLVI, *tr. by* Sir Thomas Wyatt. AAS; HAP; MOS; NoP; OAEL-1; OBVE; PPP; SiPS; Son
(Galley, The.) OBSC
(Lover Comparath His State to a Ship in Perilous Storm Tossed on the Sea, The.) EIL; GBL; HeIP; PoEL-1
"Set me whereas the sun doth parch the green [*or* sonne dothe perche the grene]." *Fr.* CXIII, *tr. by* the Earl of Surrey. AAS; HAP; SiPS

(Love's Fidelity.) AWP
(To His Lady.) OBSC
(Vow to Love Faithfully, Howsoever He Be Rewarded, A.) TrGrPo
"She used to let her golden hair fly free." *Fr.* LXIX, *tr. by* Morris Bishop. NAWM-1
Signs of Love. *Fr.* CLXXXVIII, *tr. by* C. B. Cayley. AWP
Sonnets to Miranda, *sel.* Sir William Watson.
"If I had never known your face at all." *Fr.* VIII. FaBoBe
Sonnets to My Mother. Arthur Stanley Bourinot. CaP
Sonnets to Orpheus, *sels.* Rainer Maria Rilke, *tr. fr.* German.
"Full, ripe apple, a pear and banana." *Tr. by* Christopher Hawthorne. SOTW
"Mirrors, no one yet has really described." *Tr. by* Christopher Hawthorne. SOTW
"Spring has come again. The earth." *Tr. by* Christopher Hawthorne. SOTW
"This is the creature there has never been." *Tr. by* James Blair Leishman. OBVE
"Tree ascending there. O pure transcension, A." *Tr. by* James Blair Leishman. TOF; UnS
"Wait. that tastes good. already it is on the wing." *Tr. by* Christopher Hawthorne. SOTW
"Where in what ever-blissfully watered gardens." *Tr. by* James Blair Leishman. OBVE
("Where, in whatever happily watered garden, on what trees.") SOTW, *tr. by* Christopher Hawthorne.
Sonnets to Philomel, *sels.* Sir John Davies. SiPS
"If you would know the love which I you bear."
"Oft did I hear our eyes the passage were."
"Once did my Philomel reflect on me."
"Sickness, intending my love to betray."
Sonnets to the Seasons, *sels.* Hartley Coleridge.
November. *Fr.* XII. OBNC
Sonnets—Unrealities, *sel.* E. E. Cummings.
It May Not Always Be So. BoLoP; FaBV
Sonnets Written in the Fall of 1914. George Edward Woodberry. PAH
Sonnets Written in the Orillia Woods, *sel.* Charles Sangster.
"Our life is like a forest, where the sun." *Fr.* VII. NOBC
Sons. Jack Cope. PeSA
Sons and Fathers. Larry Mitchell. GLP
Sons, my sons. Black Star Line. Henry Dumas. PoBA
Sons of freedom, listen to me, and ye daughters, too, give ear. James Bird. *Unknown.* AmFP
Sons of Levi, The. *Unknown.* AmFP
Sons of Martha. Kipling. WGRP
The sons of Mary seldom bother, for they have inherited that good part. The Sons of Martha. Kipling. WGRP
Sons of New England, in the fray. Treason's Last Device. Edmund Clarence Stedman. PAH
Sons of Our Sons, The. Ilya Grigoryevich Ehrenburg, *tr. fr. Russian by* Babette Deutsch. TrJP
Sons of Saint Crispin, 'tis in vain! "Peter Pindar." *Fr.* Resignation; an Ode to the Journeyman Shoemakers. NOEC
Sons of the King. Joan Agnew. BoTP
Sons of the prophet are hardy and bold, The. Abdul, the Bulbul Ameer. *Unknown.* AS, *with music*
(Abdullah Bulbul Amir; or, Ivan Petrofsky Skovar.) FPL
("Sons of the prophet are valiant and bold, The.") FPL
Sons of valor, taste the glories. Off from Boston. *Unknown.* PAH
Sons of War. Samih al-Qasim, *tr. fr. Arabic by* Abdullah al-Udhari. MPAW
Sons of War sometimes are known, The. Evan Lloyd. *Fr.* The Methodist. OBSV
Sonsito. Victor Hernandez Cruz. RR
"Sooeep!" Walter de la Mare. BoTP
Soon. Jacob Glatstein, *tr. fr. Yiddish by* Benjamin *and* Barbara Harshav. AYP
Soon as/ you stop. Cleavage. A. R. Ammons. OBAL
Soon as the Azure-colored Gates. Richard Lynche. *Fr.* Diella, II. Son
Soon as the general broke Hsüan-chou's seige. Ballad of the Girl from Lan-ling. Chin Ho, *tr. by* J. D. Schmidt. WFTU
Soon as the harvest hath laid bare the plains. Stephen Duck. *Fr.* The Thresher's Labour. NOEC
Soon as the sound had ceased whose thunder filled. Shelley. *Fr.* Prometheus Unbound, III, iv. ChER
Soon as the sun forsook the eastern main. An Hymn to the Evening. Phillis Wheatley. WPE

Soon at Last My Sighs and Moans. Louis Ginsberg. TrJP
Soon Autumn. Tachihara Michizo, *tr. fr. Japanese* by Hiroaki Sato. FCEI
Soon I shall be in tears this birthday morning. A Birthday in Hospital. Elizabeth Jennings. NAs
Soon I will climb the hill to the sunlight. From the Rain Forest. Desirée Flynn. BrRo
Soon it will die. Basho, *tr.* by Geoffrey Bownas *and* Anthony Thwaite. PeBJV
Soon, summer's drum will shake the earth no longer. Fall of Leaves. Derek S. Savage. PoA
Soon the night in mantle dark. The Ploughboy. John Clare. PoEL-4
Soon they will come riding. Evening Jews. Jacob Glatstein, *tr.* by Benjamin *and* Barbara Harshav. AYP
Soon to die. Masaoka Shiki, *tr.* by Geoffrey Bownas *and* Anthony Thwaite. PeBJV
Soon we entered in the woods. The Arrival. Alexander McLachlan. *Fr.* The Emigrant. NOBC
Soon we'll have lost all the words. Soon. Jacob Glatstein, *tr.* by Benjamin *and* Barbara Harshav. AYP
Sooner I may some fixed statue be. On the Duke of Buckingham, Slain by Felton, the 23rd August, 1628. Owen Felltham. JCP
Sooner or Later. Sam Cornish. CNA
Sooner or Later. John Digby. EAS
Sooner or later they will go in. Ernst Nowak, *tr.* by Beth Bjorklund. CoAuP
Sooner tears than sleep this midnight. The Wind's Lament. John Morris-Jones, *tr.* by Anthony Conran. OBWVE
Sooner be a man. Tabito, *tr.* by Geoffrey Bownas *and* Anthony Thwaite. *Fr.* Manyo Shu. PeBJV
Soonest Mended. John Ashbery. HCAP; NAAL-2; Prf
Soot-black as she is, like the shed. *Unknown. Fr.* Manyo Shu. Ma
Soot on the cassies, The. And Happy Am I. Syd Scroggie. PoSH
Soote Season, The. Henry Howard, Earl of Surrey, *after* Petrarch. AAS; HeIP; InPS; NAEL-1; NoP; Son
   (Description of Spring, Wherein Each Thing Renews Save Only the Lover.) EIL; OBEV; SeCePo
Sooth-Sayer, The. Sadi, *tr. fr. Persian* by Sir Edwin Arnold. *Fr.* The Gulistan. AWP
Soothsayer. Mary Ursula Bethell. ATNZ
Sooty, swart smiths, smattered with smoke. The Blacksmiths. *Unknown.* TW
   (Swarte-smeked Smithes.) HAP
Sophia, her age between. Wisdom of the Gazelle. George P. Solomos. GoYe
Sopolis. Callimachus, *tr. fr. Greek* by William M. Hardinge. AWP
Sopping lies the dew. *Unknown, tr.* by Arthur Waley. BoS
Sopranosound, Memory of John. Sharon Bourke. CNA
Soraidh Slan Don Oidhche Areir. Niall Mor MacMuireadach, *tr. fr. Irish.* BIrV, *tr.* by Maire Cruise O'Brien
Sorcerer, Mr. Wells, The, *sel.* William Schwenck Gilbert.
   Oh! my name is John Wellington Wells. WSC
Sorcerers, they've turned. Living with Children. Jim Wayne Miller. GOYP
Sorceress, The! Vachel Lindsay. PDV; WSC
Sorceress, The. Eugène Marais, *tr. fr. Afrikaans* by Jack Cope *and* Uys Krige. PeSA
Sorcery. René Daumal, *tr. fr. French* by Michael Benedikt. POS
Sore this dere strykyn ys. Blow Thy Horn, Hunter. *Unknown.* OxBLMV
Sorrow. Chu Shu-chen, *tr. fr. Chinese* by Kenneth Rexroth. BoWoP
Sorrow. D. H. Lawrence. CMoP; GTBS-P; OBD; OBMV
Sorrow. Samuel Daniel. *See* Hymn's Triumph: Had Sorrow Ever Fitter Place.
Sorrow. Aubrey Thomas De Vere. BLPA; WGRP; WiR
Sorrow. Emily Dickinson. WGRP
Sorrow. T. R. Hummer. MT
Sorrow. Noshiwaki Junzaburo, *tr. fr. Japanese* by Hiroaki Sato. FCEI
Sorrow. Marie Tello Phillips. GoYe
Sorrow. George Santayana. WGRP
Sorrow. Shin Dong-jip, *tr. fr. Korean* by Koh Chang-soo. ACKP
Sorrow. Katrina Trask. AA
Sorrow. *Unknown, tr. fr. Russian* by W. R. S. Ralston. AWP
Sorrow has a harp of seven strings. The Harp of Sorrow. Ethel Clifford. WGRP
Sorrow heaped on sorrow, ruin on disaster. On My Sorrowful Life. Moses ibn Ezra, *tr.* by Solomon Solis-Cohen. TrJP
Sorrow how high it is. Dark Song. A. R. Ammons. MAT
Sorrow Humanize Our Race. Jean Ingelow. WGRP
Sorrow is my own yard. The Widow's Lament in Springtime. William Carlos Williams. CMoP; HAP; LiTM; MoP; NAAL-2; NoAM; NOBA; PoE; TAP

Sorrow is my stock in trade. Reunion. Cyril Tawney. OBET
Sorrow Is the Only Faithful One. Owen Dodson. AmNP
Sorrow lay upon my breast more heavily than winter clay. "Desolation Is a Delicate Thing." Elinor Wylie. MoAmPo
Sorrow, mute, a guitar. Luzumiyya. Abd al-Wahhab al-Bayyati, *tr.* by Salma Khadra Jayyusi *and* Christopher Middleton. MAP
Sorrow, my friend. A Song before Grief. Rose Hawthorne Lathrop. AA
Sorrow My Love. Ya'ir Hurvits, *tr. fr. Hebrew* by Bernhard Frank. MHeP
Sorrow of Kodio, The. *Unknown, tr. fr. Baule* by Miriam Koshland. PBA
Sorrow of Love, The. W. B. Yeats. MoAB; MoBrPo; NoAM; NOBVV; OAEL-2; PoEL-5; TEP
Sorrow of Mydath. John Masefield. MoBrPo
Sorrow of Parting. Maruyama Kaoru, *tr. fr. Japanese* by Geoffrey Bownas *and* Anthony Thwaite. PeBJV
Sorrow of parting, unfulfilled, The. Mohammad Taqi Mir, *tr.* by Ahmed Ali. GoT
Sorrow of Troilus, The. Chaucer. *Fr.* Troilus and Criseyde [*or* Criseide], V. PoEL-1
Sorrow of Unicume, The. Sir Herbert Read. BrPo
Sorrow on Gazing at the River. Niu Chiao, *tr. fr. Chinese* by Lois Fusek. ATF
Sorrowin.' Joseph Ramsbottom. PF
Sorrowing nymph, oh why display. On a Statue of Sir Arthur Sullivan. G. Rostrevor Hamilton. FaBoCo
Sorrows of my heart enlarged are, The. Some Contemplations of the Poor, and Desolate State of the Church at Deerfield. John Williams. SCAP
Sorrows of Sunday; an Elegy, The, *sel.* "Peter Pindar."
   "Susan, the constant slave to mop and broom." NOEC
Sorrows of Werther, The. Thackeray. BLPA; CenHV; FaBoCo; FiBHP; FPL; NA; NBLV; NOBL; NOBVV; OBD
Sorry world is sighing now, The. Fin de Siècle. Newton Mackintosh. NA
Sort of a Song, A. William Carlos Williams. HoPM; NAAL-2; NoP; OxBSP; TAP
Sort of extra hunger, A. Poet Wondering What He Is Up To. D. J. Enright. OxBC
Sort of girl I like to see, The. The Olympic Girl. Sir John Betjeman. SD
Sorting It Out. Philip Booth. PPR
Sorting out letters and piles of my old. W. D. Snodgrass. FF; HeIP; MoAmPo; NePoEA-2; UnPo
Sory beuerech it is and sore it is abouth, A. Christ's Prayer in Gethsemane. *Unknown.* SeCePo
SOS. Imamu Amiri Baraka. BPo; CNA; PoBA
Sospetto d'Herode. Giovanni Battista Marino, *tr. fr. Italian* by Richard Crashaw. *Fr.* Strage degli innocenti, La, II. SeCV-1
Soufrière. Andrew Salkey. PBCV
Soufrière (79). "Shake" Keane. *Fr.* Volcanoe Suite, I. PBCV
Sought by the world, and hath the world disdained. Love's Ending. *Unknown.* OBSC
Soul. Austin Black. NBP
Soul, The. Madison Cawein. AA
Soul, The. Richard Henry Dana. AnAmPo
Soul. D. L. Graham. PoBA
Soul, A. Randall Jarrell. CMoP
Soul, A. Christina Rossetti. WPOW
Soul and Body. Margaret Cavendish, Duchess of Newcastle. OxBSP
Soul and Body. Shakespeare. *See* Sonnets: CXLVI. "Poor[e] soul[e], the centre of my sinful[l] earth."
Soul and Body of John Brown, The. Muriel Rukeyser. MoAmPo
Soul and race. Here Where Coltrane Is. Michael S. Harper. CAPP; CNA; PoBA
Soul and Sense. Hannah Parker Kimball. AA
Soul and the Body, The. Sir John Davies. *See* Nosce Teipsum: In What Manner the Soule Is United to the Body.
Soul-blind, behind the ashes. Paul Celan, *tr.* by Beth Bjorklund. CoAuP
Soul, do you hear the trumpets down in the valley. Reveillé. Audrey Alexandra Brown. CaP
Soul in the Body, The. Edith Matilda Thomas. AA
Soul Incense. Henrietta Cordelia Ray. CBWP-3
Soul is lonely, The. La Selva. Cid Corman. VGW
Soul Lifted. Albert Durrant Watson. CaP
Soul lonely comes and goes; for each our theme. Lachesis. Kathleen Jessie Raine. NYBP
Soul Longs to Return Whence It Came, The. Richard Eberhart. CMoP

Soul must have, for its great need, The. Neoplatonic Soliloquy. Donald Campbell Babcock. NePoAm

Soul of a coconut can't live, The. Coconut. Mario Satz. VWA, *tr. by* Willis Barnstone

Soul of a tree ungrown, new life out of God's life proceeding. Yosemite. Milicent Washburn Shinn. *Fr.* The Washington Sequoia. AA

Soul of Jesus Is Restless, The. Cyprus R. Mitchell. TrCP

Soul of Man, The. Dora Read Goodale. AA

Soul of my child, Princess Splendid! Invocation before the Rice Harvest. *Malay Oral Tradition, tr. by* R. O. Winstedt. WTO

Soul of the World, The. Ernest Crosby. AA

Soul of Time, The. Trumbull Stickney. LiTA

Soul, Remember This! Eduard Friedrich Mörike. OBD

Soul Remembers, The. Richard Burdick Eldridge. GoYe

Soul selects her own society, The. Emily Dickinson. AmPP; AWP; BLPL; BoWoP; CMoP; InPK; InPS; MoAB; MoAmPo; NAAL-1; NAWM-2; NoAM; NOBA; NoP; OxBA; PoE; PoEL-5; TAP; TrGrPo; UnPo; WPE

Soul-Severance. St. John Emile Clavering Hankin. FaBoPa

Soul-soothing drug! your virtues let me laud. A Sonnet to Opium; Celebrating Its Virtues. "Orestes." NOEC

Soul that's fed on Nature is content, The. Nature's Uplifting. Henrietta Cordelia Ray. CBWP-3

Soul, thou must seek thyself in Me. St. Theresa of Avila, *tr. by* E. Allison Peers. TOF

Soul unto Soul Glooms Darling. Charles Leonard Moore. AA

Soul was cold, too; we headed south, The. Here Is No Southern Island. László Nagy, *tr. by* Jascha Kessler. FOC

Soul, Wherefore Fret Thee? "Stuart Sterne." AA

Soul wherein God dwells, The. The Cherubic Pilgrim. "Angelus Silesius." WGRP

Souldier Going to the Field, The. Sir William Davenant. *See* Preserve thy sighs, unthrifty girl.

Souldiers Farewel to His Love, The. *Unknown.* CoMu

Soules Ignorance in This Life and Knowledge in the Next, The. John Donne. *See* Of the Progresse of the Soule; the Second Anniversarie: Poor soul, in this thy flesh what dost thou know?

Soules joy, now I am gone. At. to Earl of Pembroke. OBS

Soulfolk, think a minute. To Soulfolk. Margaret Goss Burroughs. BlSi

Souling Song. *Unknown. See* "God bless the master of this house."

Soulless matchmaking of lunar moths, The. Champagne. Medbh McGuckian. FaBCIP

Souls. Paul Wertheimer, *tr. fr. German by* Jethro Bithell. TrJP

Soul's a tiny woman, The. Suppose. William Trowbridge. SoTCo

Soul's Beauty. Dante Gabriel Rossetti. *Fr.* The House of Life, LXXVII. OBEV

Soul's Bitter Cry, The. *Unknown, tr. fr. Tamil.* WGRP

Soul's Calm Sunshine, The. Pope. *Fr.* An Essay on Man, IV. FaBoRV

Soul's Courts, The. Henrietta Cordelia Ray. CBWP-3

Soul's Dark Cottage, The. Edmund Waller. *Fr.* Of The Last Verses in the Book. ChTr; OBD

Soul's Defiance, The. Lavinia Stoddard. AA

Soul's Desire, The. *Unknown, tr. fr. Irish by* Eleanor Hull. TIRV

Soul's Errand, The. Sir Walter Ralegh. *See* Go, soul, the body's guest.

Soul's Garment, The. Margaret Cavendish, Duchess of Newcastle. SeCePo; WPE

Soul's Groan to Christ for Succo[u]r, The. Edward Taylor. *Fr.* God's Determinations. NAAL-1; PoEL-3

"Soul's joy, bend not those morning stars from me." Sir Philip Sidney. *Fr.* Astrophel and Stella, XLVIII. NoP

Souls joy, when thou art gone. George Herbert. OBS

Soul's Kiss. Samuel Greenberg. LiTA

Souls Lake. Robert Fitzgerald. TwCP

Soul's Liberty. Anna Wickham. MoBrPo; OxBSP

Souls of drunks bob in the rafters, The. Blues' Body. Richard Katrovas. NAmP

Souls of men! why will ye scatter. God Our Father. Frederick William Faber. WGRP

Souls of poets dead and gone. Lines on the Mermaid Tavern. *Unknown.* EnRP; PoRA

     (Mermaid Tavern, The.) BLPL; FaBoBe; GTBS; GTBS-P

Souls of the patriot dead. The Kidnapping of Sims. John Pierpont. PAH

Souls of the Slain, The. Thomas Hardy. CMoP; LiTB; PoEL-5

Souls of Women at Night, The. Wallace Stevens. CMoP

Soul's Soliloquy, A. Wenonah Stevens Abbott. BLPA

Sound. Jim Harrison. VGW

Sound, The. Robert Kelly. PoM

Sound, A. Gertrude Stein. *Fr.* Tender Buttons. TTTS

Sound Advice. *Unknown.* FaBoUs; NBLV

Sound and Sense. Pope. *See* Essay on Criticism: True ease in writing comes from art, not chance.

Sound came booming through the air, A. The Philosopher and Her Father. Shirley Brooks. CenHV

Sound Country Lass, The. *Unknown.* CoMu; ErPo

Sound from the Earth, A. William Stafford. NNaP; RFM

Sound is fading out. *Unknown, tr. by* Jerome Rothenberg. STP

Sound is in the Pyrenees!, A. Murder of a Spanish Lady by a Pirate. Richard Henry Dana. AnAmPo

"Sound, majestic wind!" From an old notebook. Some Notes on the Wind. Gabór Görgey, *tr. by* Jascha Kessler. FOC

Sound of Afroamerican History Chapt II, The. S. E. Anderson. PoBA

Sound of Afroamerican History Chapt I, The ("The history of blacklife is put down in the motions"). S. E. Anderson. PoBA

Sound of Breaking. Conrad Aiken. AWP

Sound of casting a net downstream. Taigi, *tr. fr. Japanese by* Hiroaki Sato. *Fr.* Twenty-nine Hokku. FCEI

Sound of happy laughter leap with shadows on the walls. Taos Winter. Patty L. Harjo. VoR

Sound of Matter, The. J. Bernlef, *tr. fr. Dutch by* James S. Holmes. DuIn

Sound of Morning in New Mexico, The. Reeve Spencer Kelley. AmFN

Sound of My Sneezing Nose, The. Te Whetu, *tr. fr. Maori by* Margaret Orbell. PeNZ

Sound of Night, The. Maxine W. Kumin. BoNaP; WPE

Sound of paddles slapping the waves. Basho, *tr. fr. Japanese by* Burton Watson. *Fr.* Seventy-six Hokku. FCEI

Sound of pine winds and their color are one, The. Teika, *tr. fr. Japanese by* Hiroaki Sato. *Fr.* Eighty-four Tanka. FCEI

Sound of Rain, The. Bella Akhmadulina, *tr. fr. Russian by* Daniel Halpern *and* Albert Todd. BoWoP

Sound of Rain, The. David Allan Evans. GOYP

Sound of rain dripping, The. Tonan, *tr. by* Frogs. FCEI

Sound of rain on the roof was too loud, The. The Gold Country, The; Hotel Leger, Mokelumne Hill, Revisited. Joseph Stroud. NPGG

Sound of snails—crying. Snails. Liagarang. CBAP, *tr. by* Ronald M. Berndt; WTO, *tr. by* Ronald M. Berndt

Sound of the Drum, The. *Unknown.* OBET

Sound of the florist's scissors, The. Ozaki Hosai, *tr. fr. Japanese by* Hiroaki Sato. *Fr.* One Hundred Haiku in Free Form. FCEI

Sound of the Horn, The. Alfred de Vigny, *tr. fr. French by* Wilfred Thorley. AWP

Sound of the rain, The. Taigi, *tr. fr. Japanese by* Hiroaki Sato. *Fr.* Twenty-nine Hokku. FCEI

Sound of the Sea, The. Longfellow. MOS

Sound of the Trees, The. Robert Frost. *See* Sound of Trees, The.

Sound of the Wind, The. Christina Rossetti. *Fr.* Sing-Song. OnUR

Sound of the Wind That Is Blowing, The, *sel.* J. Kitchener Davies, *tr. fr. Welsh by* Joseph P. Clancy.

     "Today,/ there came a breeze thin as the needle of a syringe." OBWVE

Sound of thy sweet name, my dearest treasure, The. Francis Davison. ElL

Sound of Trees, The. Robert Frost. NoAM

Sound of Water. Mary O'Neill. NTCP

Sound of Water. Julio Ortega, *tr. fr. Spanish by* David Tipton. Per

Sound of water running, The. Civilization. Tom Schmidt. NeAC

Sound of your lips beating, The. Thoughts for My Grandmother. Laya Firestone. VWA

Sound, Sound the Clarion. At. to Thomas Osbert Mordaunt. *Fr.* Verses Written during the War, 1756-1763. EBEV; FaBoEE; FaPoR; NOBE

     (Call, The.) OBEV

     (One Crowded Hour.) TrGrPo

     (To a Lady on Reading Sherlock "Upon Death.") NOEC

Sound the deep waters. Sleep at Sea. Christina Rossetti. MOS

Sound the flute! Spring. Blake. *Fr.* Songs of Innocence. BoTP; FaBoCh; FaPON; MoShBr; TTTS

Sound the trumpet, beat the drum. Dryden. *Fr.* The Secular Masque. FaBoRV

Sound variegated through beneath lit. Gyre's Galax. Norman Henry Pritchard, II. PoBA

Sounding, The. Conrad Aiken. AnAmPo

Sounding. Doris Ferne. CaP

Sounding cataract, The/ Haunted me like a passion. Wordsworth. *Fr.* Lines Composed a Few Miles above Tintern Abbey [on Revisiting the Banks of the Wye during a Tour, July 13, 1798]. WGRP

Sounding Fog, The. Susan Nichols Pulsifer. PDV

Sounding Portage, The. Annie Charlotte Dalton. CaP

Soundings. Paula Gunn Allen. HATNAP

Soundless, The/ light drifts over. The Light of the World. B. Alquit. VWA, *tr. by* Howard Schwartz

Soundless dusk was growing dim, The. The Caress. Juana de Ibarbourou, *tr. by* Perry Higman. LPSS

Soundlessly, a tide at the ear. Awakening. John Haines. EAS
Sounds. Tanikawa Shuntaro, *tr. fr. Japanese by* Hiroaki Sato. FCEI
Sounds are heard too high for ears. Watching Television. Robert Bly.
 CoAP
Sounds Begin Again, The. Dennis Brutus. WMBCH
Sounds like big. Waking from a Nap on the Beach. May Swenson.
 NTCP; PCP; RFM
Sounds of freight trains, the old, The. Conversation. Rutger Kopland,
 tr. by Ria Leigh-Loohuizen. DuIn
Sounds of Ireland, The. Windharp. John Montague. CIP; FaBCIP
Sounds that shapes make in the air, The. Death of a Ceiling. Medbh
 McGuckian. DT
Soup. Carl Sandburg. NOBA; NOBE; OBCA
Soup, The. Charles Simic. AnAn
Soup Jar, The. Dabney Stuart. MT
Soup of Venus, The. James Tate. AmPA
Sour daylight cracks through my sleep-caked lids, The. The Distant
 Winter. Philip Levine. VGW
Sour fiend, go home and tell the Pit. Ghoul Care. Ralph Hodgson.
 MoBrPo
Sour smell, The. Getting in the Wood. Gary Snyder. NoAM
Source, The. Jon Stallworthy. NoP
Source immaterial of material naught. The Rejected "National Hymns."
 "Orpheus C. Kerr." OBAL
Sources of Good Counsel. Peter Idley. OxBChV
Sources of My Being, The. Moses Ibn Ezra, *tr. fr. Hebrew by* David
 Goldstein. TOF
Sourdough french bread and pinot chardonnay. Maps. Robert Hass.
 NPGG
Sourdough mountain called a fire in. Gary Snyder. *Fr.* Myths and Texts:
 Burning, XVII. NAAL-2; NaP; NoP
Sourdough Mountain Lookout. Philip Whalen. NeAP; PoM
Sourwood Mountain. *Unknown.* AS, *with music;* GBP
Sourwood Mountain. *Unknown.* AmFP
Sourwood sprouts are long, The. Secret Pleasures. Robert Morgan.
 MAYP
Sous-Entendu. Anne Stevenson. OxBSP
Souster. Ray Fraser. NeAC
South, The. Wang Chien, *tr. fr. Chinese by* Arthur Waley. AWP
South African Bloodstone. Quincy Troupe. CNA
South African Broadsheets, *sel.* David Wright.
 "Under the African lintel, Table Mountain." PeSA
South Afrikan/ Brothers and sisters. Guess Who! Sista Roots.
 WS
South Atlantic clouds rode low, The. Safari West. John A. Williams.
 NBP
South Carolina, The. *Unknown.* PAH
South Carolina to the States of the North. Paul Hamilton Hayne.
 PAH
South Coast, The. William Everson. NeAP
South Country, The. Hilaire Belloc. ACP; MoBrPo
South Country. Kenneth Slessor. CBAP
South End. Conrad Aiken. CMoP; HoPM; OxBA
South-Folk in Cold Country. Ezra Pound, *after the Chinese.* OBVE
South is green with coming spring, The. The Trial. Muriel Rukeyser.
 PoNe
South Lake in the Rain. Li E, *tr. fr. Chinese by* Shirleen S. Wong.
 WFTU
South of Boston, south of Washington. Robert Lowell. *Fr.* Mexico, 4.
 HCAP
South of Mount Sumeru. Ikkyu, *tr. by* Lucien Stryk *and* Takashi
 Ikemoto. ZPCJ
South of My Days. Judith Wright. FaBoWP; PoAu-2; WPE
South of Nan-yang, north of Yi Mountain. A Song of a Fisherman.
 Sung Wan, *tr. by* William Schultz. WFTU
South of Sokipo port. Painter Jung-sup Lee. Ruth Kim Chun-soo, *tr. by*
 Koh Chang-soo. ACKP
South of success and east of gloss and glass are. Gwendolyn Brooks.
 Fr. Two Dedications: The Wall. PoNe
South of the Bridge. Shen Chou, *tr. fr. Chinese by* Jonathan Chaves.
 Fr. The Stone Bridge. CoBLCP
South of the fabled pillars of Hercules. Volubilis, North Africa. Ralph
 Nixon Currey. PeSA
South of the house, north of the house. Tai Piao-yüan, *tr. fr. Chinese by*
 Jonathan Chaves. *Fr.* Following His Rhymes and Answering the
 Poems of My Friend Next Door, VI. CoBLCP
South of the Line, inland from far Durban. A Christmas Ghost-Story.
 Thomas Hardy. OBWP
South Seas. Cesare Pavese, *tr. fr. Italian by* William Arrowsmith.
 AnAn
South Street. Edward S. Silvera. CDC
South Texas Summer Rain. Rebecca Gonzales. AiP

South-west wind is blowing, The. Autumn Morning. Adeline White.
 BoTP
South-Wind. George Parsons Lathrop. AA
South Wind. Siegfried Sassoon. BoTP
South Wind. Nathan Yonathan, *tr. fr. Hebrew by* Richard Flantz. VWA
South wind blows day and night across rivers and lakes, The. Sent to My
 Beloved Far Away. Chu Yi-tsun, *tr. by* Irving Lo. WFTU
South-wind brings, The. Emerson. AA
South wind brings wet weather, The. *Unknown. Fr.* Weather Wisdom
 [*or* Weather Wise]. FaBoUs
South wind has brought gentle goddesses, The. Rain. Nishiwaki
 Junzaburo, *tr. by* Sato. FCEI
South Wind laid his moccasins aside, The. Isabella Valancy Crawford.
 Fr. Malcolm's Katie. OBCV
South-wind strengthens to a gale, The. Low Barometer. Robert Bridges.
 CMoP; LiTB; MoP; NoAM; NOCV; OBNC; QFR
South wind's molded by a spine of hill, The. Another Kind of Burning.
 Ruth Fox. NYBP
Southbound. Betty Adcock. MT
Southbound on the Freeway. May Swenson. AmFN; NTCP; NYBP
Southeast, and storm, and every weathervane. Hatteras Calling. Conrad
 Aiken. BoNaP; NOBA; TAP
Southeast Arkansia. Maya Angelou. SaC
Southeast at low tide. Skiing on Russian Christmas. Nora Dauenhauer.
 HATNAP
Southeast Ramparts of the Seine, The. Judit Tóth, *tr. by* Emery George.
 VWA
Southeast the Peacock Flies. *Unknown, tr. fr. Chinese by* Burton Watson.
 CoBCP
Souther, wind, souther! Rhyme of the Fishermen's Children. *Unknown.*
 GBP
Southern Cop. Sterling Allen Brown. NIP; SoSe
Southern Cross. Hart Crane. *Fr.* The Bridge. NAAL-2
Southern Cross. Herman Melville. LiTA
Southern Girl, A. Samuel Minturn Peck. AA
Southern Gothic. Donald Justice. NIP
Southern Mansion. Arna Bontemps. AiP; AmFN; AmNP; BANP; CNA;
 FB; FF; IDB; LiTM; PoBA; PoNe; TTY; WSC
Southern Pacific. Carl Sandburg. AnAmPo
Southern Pavilion. Chu Yi-tsun, *tr. fr. Chinese by* Irving Lo. *Fr.*
 Quatrains on Yung-chia, VII. WFTU
Southern Pines. John Peale Bishop. GOA
Southern Press, The. Lizelia Augusta Jenkins Moorer. CBWP-3
Southern Pulpit, The. Lizelia Augusta Jenkins Moorer. CBWP-3
Southern Road. Sterling Allen Brown. BANP; BPo; FB; PoBA
Southern Road, The. Dudley Randall. CNA; PoBA; SM
Southern Scene, A. Priscilla Jane Thompson. CBWP-2
Southern Ships and Settlers. Rosemary *and* Stephen Vincent Benét.
 AmFN
Southern Snow-Bird, The. William Hamilton Hayne. AA
Southern Song, A. Chang Pi, *tr. fr. Chinese by* Lois Fusek. ATF
Southern Song, A. Mao Hsi-chen, *tr. fr. Chinese by* Lois Fusek.
 ATF
Southern Song, A. Wen T'ing-yün, *tr. fr. Chinese by* Lois Fusek.
 ATF
Southern Summer. Francis Stuart. NeIP
Southern Work of Dr. and Mrs. L. M. Dunton. Lizelia Augusta Jenkins
 Moorer. CBWP-3
Southerner, The. Karl Shapiro. NYBP; PoNe
Southey and Wordsworth. Byron. *See* Don Juan: Bob Southey! You're a
 poet—poet-laureate.
Southey Looks out of the Window at Greta Hill. Robert Southey. *Fr.* A
 Vision of Judgement. FaBoPP
Southpaw. Lisel Mueller. KS
Southrons, hear your country call you! Dixie. Albert Pike. AA; PAH
Southward Bound. J. F. A. Burt. PoSH
Southward with fleet of ice. Sir Humphrey Gilbert. Longfellow. PAH
Southwest Passage. Dudley Fitts. PoA
Southwest wind blows in from the sea unceasing, The. Return to Life.
 Abbie Huston Evans. NePoAm
Souvenir. Alfred de Musset, *tr. fr. French by* George Santayana. AWP
Souvenir, The. Dan Pagis, *tr. fr. Hebrew by* Warren Bargad *and* Stanley
 F. Chyet. IP
Souvenir. Edwin Arlington Robinson. NoAM
Souvenirs. Dudley Randall. BPo
Sou'wester whips the day awake, The. Bruce Beaver. *Fr.* Letters to
 Live Poets, X. CBAP
Sovereign and Transforming Grace. Frederic Henry Hedge. AH
Sovereign poet, The. Sir William Watson. WGRP
Sovereign Poets. Lloyd Mifflin. *See* Sovereigns, The.
Sovereign Queen. Padeshah Khatun, *tr. fr. Farsi by* Deirdre Lashgari.
 WPOW

Sovereign soul, The/ Of him who lives self-governed and at peace.
  Unknown, tr. fr. Sanskrit by Sir Edwin Arnold. *Fr.* The Bhagavad-
  Gita. TOF
Sovereigns, The. Lloyd Mifflin. AA
Sovereignty, His. Kalonymos ben Moses of Lucca, *tr. fr. Hebrew by*
  Nina Davis Salaman. TrJP
Soviet Union, The. John Berryman. FaBoPV
Sow came in with the saddle, The. Mother Goose. OxNR
Sow had pigged, and went running to the house, A. The Manure Book.
  Russell Edson. AnAn
Sow of Feeling, The. Robert Fergusson. NOEC
Sow thin. *Unknown.* FaBoUs
Sower, The. Laurence Binyon. MMA
Sower, The. Mathilde Blind. WPE
Sower, The. William Cowper. SaC
Sower, The. R. Olivares Figueroa, *tr. fr. Spanish by* Dudley Fitts.
  FaPON
Sower, The. Sir Charles G. D. Roberts. CaP; OBCV
Soweto. Sipho Sepamla. WMBCH
Sowing of Tears, A. Philippe Jaccottet, *tr. fr. French by* W. S. Merwin.
  RHTwFP
Sowing Seeds. Ursula Cornwall. BoTP
Soy Sauce. Gary Snyder. CAPP
Soyer is gone! Then be it said. On the Death of the Great Chef Alexis
  Soyer. *Unknown.* FaBoEE
Sozzled, Mo-tsu, after a silence, vouchsafed. Scholars at the Orchid
  Pavilion. John Berryman. PoE
Space. William Hart-Smith. *Fr.* Christopher Columbus. PoAu-2
Space. Edward Rowland Sill. AnAmPo
Space and Time. Syd Scroggie. PoSH
Space beats the ruddy freedom of their limbs. Daughters of War. Isaac
  Rosenberg. BrPo
Space Being (Don't Forget to Remember) Curved. E. E. Cummings.
  NoAM
Space Burial. Brian W. Aldiss. BWV
Space Child's Mother Goose, The, *sel.* Frederick Winsor.
  "This little pig built a spaceship." RHPC
Space Fiction. Norman MacCaig. TEP
Space in the Air, A. Jon Silkin. NePoEA; TrJP
Space Invaders Machine, The. Pita Sharples, *tr. fr. Maori by the author.*
  PeNZ
Space is azure and the mountains bathe. Ignacio Rodríguez Galván, *tr. fr.
  Spanish by* Samuel Beckett. *Fr.* Prophecy of Cuauhtémoc. MexPo
"Space Is Not Merely a Background for Events, But Possesses an
  Autonomous Structure." A. Einstein. Alan Dugan. CAPP
Space is too full. Did nothing happen here? American Farm, 1934.
  Genevieve Taggard. VGW
Space-man, space-man. Soft Landings. Howard Sergeant. OnUR
Space of wrinkled gold where I passed the time, The. Clear Winter.
  Pierre Reverdy, *tr. by* John Ashbery. POS; RHTwFP
Space Shuttle. Diane Ackerman. MAYP
Space-Suit Sammy. Going Up. John Travers Moore. RHPC
Space-time, our scientists tell us, is impervious. Archibald MacLeish.
  Fr. Reply to Mr. Wordsworth. ImOP
Space we feel inside us, The. After. Michael Ryan. MAYP
Spacepoem 3: Off Course. Edwin Morgan. BWV
Spaces await their people. Homage to Robert Bresson. Jon Anderson.
  MAYP
Spaces inside Sleep, The. Robert Desnos, *tr. fr. French by* Michael
  Benedikt. POS
Spacin. Ronda Davis. JB
Spacious firmament on high, The. Joseph Addison. BLPA; EaLo; ELP;
  FaBoBe; FaPoR; FPL; GN; HeIP; NOCV; NOEC; PoEL-3; TOF
Spacious Land of Yamato, The. Empress Koken. *Fr.* Manyo Shu. Ma
Spade, A! a rake! a hoe! The Lay of the Labourer. Thomas Hood. SaC
Spade-bearded grandfather, squat Lenin. Summer Pogrom. Fay Zwicky.
  CBAP
Spade Is Just a Spade, A. Walter Everette Hawkins. PoBA
Spade Scharnweber. Don Welch. Psk
Spades take up leaves. Gathering Leaves. Robert Frost. RB; VGW
Spading earth. Animal Kingdom. Sydney Clouts. PeSA
Spads Krags battleships howitzers those were the good old days. Songs
  for the Old New Jersey Shelling the Shouf. George Starbuck. BLA
Spaewife, The. Robert Louis Stevenson. BrPo; OxBS
Spain. W. H. Auden. *See* Yesterday all the past. The language of size.
Spain. Eugène Guillevic, *tr. fr. French by* Denise Levertov. RHTwFP
Spain. Dorothy Livesay. NOBC
Spain. Arthur Symons. OBTV
Spain drew us proudly from the womb of night. Full Cycle. John White
  Chadwick. PAH
Spain frightened you. Spain. You Hated Spain. Ted Hughes. OBTV
Spain 1937. W. H. Auden. FaBoPV; LiTB; NAEL-2; OBWP; WaP

Spain, 1929. Ai. *Fr.* He Kept On Burning, I. AnAn
Spain. The wild dust, the whipped corn, earth easy for. Teresa of Avila.
  Elizabeth Jennings. NePoEA-2; TOF
Spain's Last Armada. Wallace Rice. PAH
Spake the Lord Christ—"I will arise." An Easter Hymn. Richard Le
  Gallienne. OHIP
Span of Life, The. Robert Frost. HoPM; LiTM; SoSe
Spangled Pandemonium, The. Palmer Brown. AmMo; RHPC
Spaniel, Beau, that fares like you, A. On a Spaniel Called Beau Killing a
  Young Bird. William Cowper. FaBoCh
Spanish Blue. Herbert Morris. NYBP
Spanish Curate, The, *sel.* John Fletcher.
  "Let the bells ring, and let the boys sing." *Fr.* III, ii. OBS
Spanish Descent, The ("Long had this nation been amused in vain"), *sel.*
  Daniel Defoe. APAS
  "Word's gone out, and now they spread the main, The." OBWP
Spanish expression, The, *Cuando yo era muchacho. Habla Usted
  Español?* James Reiss. AmPA
Spanish Folk Songs, *sels.* Antonio Machado, *tr. fr. Spanish by* Havelock
  Ellis. AWP
  "Let the rich man fill his belly."
  "My father was a sailor."
Spanish Friar [*or* Fryar], The, *sels. Dryden.*
  Farewell, Ungrateful Traitor. *Fr.* V, i. BoLoP; ELP; EnLoPo; HAP;
  LiTB; NOBE
  (Love's Despair.) ACP
  (Song: "Farewell ungrateful[l] traytor [*or* traitor].") FiP; OBS;
  SeCV-2
  "'Twere well your judgments but in plays did range," *prologue* OBSV
Spanish Gipsy [*or* Gypsy], The, *sel. Thomas* Middleton *and* William
  Rowley.
  "Trip it Gipsies, Trip it Fine." OBS
Spanish Girls, The. Iván Argüelles. FIA
Spanish Gypsy, The, *sels.* "George Eliot."
  I Am Lonely. GN
  Plaça Santiago, The. OBTV
  "Quit now the town, and with a journeying dream." OBTV
Spanish Gypsy, The. Thomas Middleton *and* William Rowley. *See* Trip
  it, gipsies, trip it fine.
Spanish Johnny. Willa Cather. AiP; FaPON
Spanish Ladies. *Unknown.* FaBoCh; OxBSS, *with music*
Spanish Lions, The. Phyllis McGinley. NYBP
Spanish noon is a blaze of azure fire, and the dusty pilgrims, The. The
  Exodus (August 3, 1492). Emma Lazarus. *Fr.* By the Waters of
  Babylon. WPE
Spanish Student, The, *sel.* Longfellow.
  "Stars of the summer night!" AA; FaBoBe
Spanish War, The. "Hugh MacDiarmid." CMoP; NOBC
Spanish Waters. John Masefield. BeLS; FaPON; OnMSP
Sparafucile fought his peasant war. Dead Fly. Eiléan Ní Chuilleanáin.
  CIP
Spare, gen'rous victor, spare the slave. To a Lady: She Refusing to
  Continue a Dispute with Me, and Leaving Me in the Argument.
  Matthew Prior. NoP
Spare Professor, grave and bald, The. At a Reading. Thomas Bailey
  Aldrich. AnAmPo; OBAL
Spare Quilt, The. John Peale Bishop. GOA
Spare then the person, and expose the vice. Pope. *Fr.* Epilogue to the
  Satires [*or* 1738], Dialogue II. OBSV
Spare Us, O Lord, Aloud We Pray. Isaac Watts. AH
"Spare us of dying beauty," cries out Youth. Of Dying Beauty. Louis
  Zukofsky. PoA
Spare us this silence after the guns. Map Reference T994724. John
  Pudney. WaP
Spared by a car- or airplane-crash or. Accidents of Birth. William
  Meredith. NoP
Sparhawk [*or* Sparrow-hawk] proud did hold in wicked jail, A. A
  Sparrow-Hawk. *Unknown.* CH; EBEV; PBBP
Spark, The. Joseph Mary Plunkett. AWP
Sparkles from the Wheel. Walt Whitman. InPS; NAAL-1
Sparkling and Bright. Charles Fenno Hoffman. AA
Spark's Farewell to Its Clay, The. R. A. K. Mason. ATNZ; PeNZ
Sparks from a stonemason. Buson, *tr. fr. Japanese by* Hiroaki Sato. *Fr.*
  Eighty-seven Hokku. FCEI
Sparks showering off the paint, The. Second Horn. W. S. Di Piero.
  MAYP
Sparrow. Shin Dong-jip, *tr. fr. Korean by* Koh Chang-soo. ACKP
Sparrow, The. Bible, *O.T. Fr.* Psalms: Psalm LXXXIV ("How amiable
  are thy tabernacles. "), 3. FaPON
Sparrow, The. William Carlos Williams. DiL; InPS; LCAP; PrIm; VGW
Sparrow and Diamond, The. Matthew Green. FM; PBBP
Sparrow Bathing. Ono Tozaburo, *tr. fr. Japanese by* Hiroaki Sato. FCEI

Sparrow dips in his wheel-rut bath, The. The Five Students. Thomas Hardy. CMoP; GTBS-P; PoEL-5

Sparrow Flock. Ono Tozaburo, *tr. fr. Japanese by* Hiroaki Sato. FCEI

Sparrow goes in and out of jail, A. Issa, *tr. fr. Japanese by* Hiroaki Sato. *Fr.* Forty-four Hokku. FCEI

Sparrow Hawk, The. Russell Hoban. RHPC

Sparrow-Hawk, A. *Unknown.* CH; EBEV; PBBP

Sparrow Hills. Robert Lowell. NaP, *ad. fr. the Russian of* Boris Pasternak

Sparrow in the Dust, A. Ruth Domino, *tr. fr. Italian by* Daniel Hoffman *and* Jerre Mangione. BoWoP

Sparrow in the Zoo, The. Howard Nemerov. MoP

Sparrow in Winter. Takahashi Shinkichi, *tr. fr. Japanese by* Lucien Stryk *and* Takashi Ikemoto. NU

Sparrow lights, A. Abandoned House in Late Light. Chase Twichell. MAYP

Sparrow told it to the robin, The. Early News. Anna Maria Pratt. AA

Sparrows. Remco Campert, *tr. fr. Dutch by* John Scott *and* Graham Martin. DuIn

Sparrows, The. Peter Cooley. NAmP

Sparrows all at once are gone, The. Ozaki Hosai, *tr. fr. Japanese by* Hiroaki Sato. *Fr.* One Hundred Haiku in Free Form. FCEI

Sparrows among Dry Leaves ("The sparrows/ by the iron fence post"). William Carlos Williams. NYBP

Sparrow's Dirge, The. John Skelton. *See* Phyllyp Sparowe [*or* Philip Sparrow]: When I remember again.

Sparrow's Fall, The. Frances Ellen Watkins Harper. PWR

Sparrow's Feather, A. George Barker. NYBP

Sparrows' friendship breaks up. Issa, *tr. fr. Japanese by* Hiroaki Sato. *Fr.* Forty-four Hokku. FCEI

Sparrows, mating. Kaya Shirao, *tr. fr. Japanese by* Hiroaki Sato. *Fr.* Twenty-one Hokku. FCEI

Sparrow's Nest, The. Wordsworth. EnRP

Sparrows quarreled outside our window. Waking an Angel. Philip Levine. NaP

Sparrows scurrying. Ishida Hakyo, *tr. by* Geoffrey Bownas *and* Anthony Thwaite. PeBJV

Sparrow's Skull, The. Ruth Pitter. EaLo; FaBoWP

Sparrows twitter, The. Emperor Hanazono, *tr. by* Steven D. Carter. WFTW

Sparrows were feeding in a freezing drizzle. Because You Asked about the Line between Prose and Poetry. Howard Nemerov. WeW

Sparse mists of moonlight hurt our eyes. Festubert: The Old German Line. Edmund Blunden. MMA

Sparta. Angelos Sikelianos, *tr. fr. Greek by* Edmund Keeley *and* Philip Sherrard. VMG

Spastic Child. Vassar Miller. TSM

Spate in Winter Midnight. Norman MacCaig. GTBS-P; PoSH

Spatial depths of being survive. The Lost Dancer. Jean Toomer. PoBA

Spawn of fantasies. Love Songs. Mina Loy. VGW; WPE, *abr*

Spawn of Slums, The. James W. Thompson. BPo

Spawning in Northern Minnesota. David McElroy. AmPA

S.P.C.A. Sermon. Stuart Hemsley. FiBHP

Speak. N. M. Rashed, *tr. fr. Urdu by* Mahmood Jamal. PBMUP

Speak! Wordsworth. OBEV

Speak. James Wright. HAP; SM; TAP; WeW

Speak and tell us, our Ximena, looking northward far away. The Angels of Buena Vista. Whittier. BeLS; PAH

Speak earth and bless me with what is richest. Audre Lorde. GLP; NoAM

Speak for us, great sea. Great Sea. Charles Brasch. ATNZ

Speak Gently. David Bates. Par; PWR

Speak gently, Spring, and make no sudden sound. Four Little Foxes. Lew Sarett. FaPON; PDV; RFM; RHPC

Speak gently to the herring and kindly to the calf. Kindness to Animals. Joseph Ashby-Sterry. NA

Speak, Gracious Lord, oh speak; thy Servant hears. Pope. *Fr.* A Paraphrase on Thomas à Kempis. TrPWD

Speak like Rain. Jerred Metz. VWA

Speak no evil today, for we honour Cornutus' birth. Dicamus Bona Verba. Albius Tibullus, *tr. by* Constance Carrier. NAs

Speak not ill of womankind. Against Blame of Woman. Gerald Fitzgerald, 4th Earl of Desmond, *tr. by* the Earl of Longford. AnIL; BIrV

"Speak not of niceness, when there's chance of wreck,." Sir Walter Scott. *See* Peveril of the Peak: Speak not of niceness, when there's chance of wreck.

Speak of our love. Colophon Written on the Flyleaf of a Book Sent to My Several Friends at Hsi-ling. Wu Hsi-ch'i, *tr. by* Frederick P. Brandauer. WFTU

Speak of this to no one. Lady Ise, *tr. fr. Japanese by* Burton Watson. *Fr.* Kokin Shu. FCEI

(Sleeping with Someone Who Came in Secret.) LLLT

Speak Out. *Unknown. See* If You Have a Friend.

Speak [*or* Speke], Parrot, *sel.* John Skelton.

"My name is Parrot, a byrd of paradise." OxBoLi

(Parrot, The.) ACP

(Parrot's Soliloquy.) PoEL-1

Speak roughly to your little boy. "Lewis Carroll." *Fr.* Alice's Adventures in Wonderland, *ch.* 6. FaBoCh; FaBoCo; NBLV; Par

(Duchess's Lullaby, The.) FaBoNo

(Lullaby, A.) RHPC

Speak, Satire, for there's none can tell like thee. The True-born Englishman. Daniel Defoe. APAS

"Speak! speak! thou fearful guest!" The Skeleton in Armor. Longfellow. AA; AmPP; AnAmPo; AWP; BeLS; BLPL; FaBoBe; PAH

Speak, thou jaded heart, defective heart. To a Bad Heart. Tim Reynolds. TW

Speak to her heart! Ars Amoris. J. V. Cunningham. QFR

Speak to Her Tenderly. Mary E. Tucker. CBWP-1

Speak to me. Take my hand. What are you now? Effort at Speech between Two People. Muriel Rukeyser. FYAP; MoAB; MoAmPo; TrGrPo; TrJP; TwCP; WeW

Speak to the Sun. Dedie Huffman Wilson. GoYe

Speak to us who. Tiresias. George Garrett. SM

Speak when you're spoken to,/ Come for one call. Mother Goose. OxNR

Speak when you're spoken to,/ Do as you're bid. *Unknown.* CenHV

Speak with the Sun. David Campbell. SeCePo

Speake gentle heart, where is thy dwelling place? Thomas Watson. *Fr.* Hecatompathia; or, Passionate Century of Love. AAS

Speaker, The. Charles G. Ballard. VoR

Speakers, Columbus Circle. Raymond Souster. CaP

Speakin' in general, I 'ave tried 'em all. Sestina of the Tramp-Royal. Kipling. BrPo; FPL; LiTB; MoBrPo; PrIm

Speaking. Michael Ryan. AmPA

Speaking in storm language. Whale Songs. Diane Ackerman. BWV

Speaking like wind. Swimmer. Gladys Cardiff. CDW

Speaking My Mind. Chung-ch'ang T'ung, *tr. fr. Chinese by* Burton Watson. CoBCP

Speaking My Thoughts. Prince Otomo, *tr. fr. Chinese by* Burton Watson. JLIC-1

Speaking of Gabriel. Rosario Castellanos, *tr. fr. Spanish by* Kate Flores. DMH

Speaking of Loss. Lucille Clifton. CAPP

Speaking of Love. Ku Hsiung, *tr. fr. Chinese by* Lois Fusek. ATF

Speaking of Love. Mao Wen-hsi, *tr. fr. Chinese by* Lois Fusek. ATF

Speaking of Love. Wei Ch'eng-pan, *tr. fr. Chinese by* Lois Fusek. ATF

Speaking of Love. Wei Chuang, *tr. fr. Chinese by* Lois Fusek. ATF

Speaking of Love. Wen T'ing-yün, *tr. fr. Chinese by* Lois Fusek. ATF

Speaking of marvels, I am alive. Alive Together. Lisel Mueller. IHMS

Speaking of Poetry. John Peale Bishop. LiTA; OxBA

Speaking of Television, *sel.* Phyllis McGinley.

Robin Hood. OBSV

Speaking Tree, The. Muriel Rukeyser. VGW

Speaks the Whispering Grass. Jesse Stuart. FYAP

Speargrass crackles under the billy and overhead is the winter sun, The. While the Billy Boils. David McKee Wright. PeNZ

Spearmen heard the bugle sound, The. Beth Gêlert. William Robert Spencer. BeLS

(Beth Gêlert; or, The Grave of the Greyhound.) BLPA; OBNV

Special Bulletin. Langston Hughes. PoBA

Special Delivery. John Montague. IPY

Special Jurymen of England! who admire your country's laws. Damages, Two Hundred Pounds. Thackeray. OBSV

Special Pleading. Charles Bernstein. UL

Special Preference. Louis Aragon, *tr. fr. French by* Michael Benedikt. POS

Special Rider Blues. *Unknown.* AmFP

Specimen of an Induction to a Poem. Alan Bernheimer. UL

Speck of protoplasm in a finch's egg, The. Birdsong. Burns Singer. FaBoTw

Speck of Sand, A. Paul Celan, *tr. fr. German by* Joachim Neugroschel. VWA

Speck that would have been beneath my sight, A. A Considerable Speck. Robert Frost. MoAB; MoAmPo; OBAL; PPP

Speckle-black Toad and freckle-green Frog. George Darley. *Fr.* Thomas à Becket, a Dramatic Comedy. FM

Speckled bird sings in the tree, The. The Nightingale. Katharine Tynan. BoTP

Speckled cat and a tame hare, A. Two Songs of a Fool. W. B. Yeats. CMoP; RB

Speckled horse is bucking, The. *Mongol Oral Tradition, tr. by* C. R. Bawden. WTO

Speckled sky is dim with snow, The. Midwinter. John Townsend Trowbridge. AA; AnAmPo; GN

Speckled with glints of star and moonshine. Mr. Walter de la Mare Makes the Little Ones Dizzy. Samuel Hoffenstein. Par

Spectacular Blossom. Allen Curnow. ATNZ; PeNZ

Spectator ab Extra, *sels.* Arthur Hugh Clough. FaBoCo; OxBoLi

  As I Sat at the Café, *also in* Dipsychus ELP; FiBHP; GTBS-P, 3 *sts.*; NBLV

  (How Pleasant It Is to Have Money.) NOBE; OAEL-2

  (So Pleasant It Is to Have Money.) SeCePo

  "Come along, 'tis the time, ten or more minutes past." OBSV

Spectator's Guide to Contemporary Art, *sels.* Phyllis McGinley.

  On the Farther Wall, Marc Chagall. OBSV

  Squeeze Play. FaBoEE; OBSV

Spectators lurk everywhere. Madhouse. Mustafa Zaidi, *tr. by* Mahmood Jamal. PBMUP

Spectators only on this bustling stage. Charles Churchill. *Fr.* Night; an Epistle to Robert Lloyd. OBSV

Specter, The. Ernst Hardt, *tr. fr. German by* Jethro Bithell. AWP

Spectral Attitudes, The. André Breton, *tr. fr. French by* David Gascoyne. EAS

Spectral Lovers. John Crowe Ransom. GBL; HeIP

Spectre is haunting America—the spectre of hoodooism, A. Black Power Poem. Ishmael Reed. BPo

Spectrum. Mari E. Evans. BPo

Speculation. Eeva-Liisa Manner, *tr. fr. Finnish by* Aili Jarvenpa. SOP

Speculation. Howard Nemerov. TAP

Speculative Evening. Marguerite Young. LiTA

Speculators, The. Thackeray. OBSV

Speech. Henry Taylor. MAT; NBLV

Speech after long silence; it is right. After Long Silence. W. B. Yeats. BoLoP; CMoP; EnLoPo; HeIP; HoPM; LiTM; NAEL-2; OAEL-2; OBMV; PPP; PrIm; UnPo

Speech and Silence. Richard Hovey. AnAmPo

Speech for the Repeal of the McCarran Act. Richard Wilbur. CMoP; GOA

Speech of the Salish Chief. Earle Birney. *Fr.* Damnation of Vancouver. OBCV

Speech, or dark cities screaming. Johnie Scott. *Fr.* The American Dream. NBP

Speech that has conceived poetry, The. Bare Tree and Poetry. Ruth Kim Chun-soo, *tr. by* Koh Chang-soo. ACKP

Speech to a Crowd. Archibald MacLeish. MoAB; MoAmPo

Speech to Those Who Say Comrade. Archibald MacLeish. OxBA

Speech Warts. Myra Sklarew. CRP

Speeches at the Barriers, *sels.* Susan Howe.

  "Right or ruth." *Fr.* 2. LP

  "Say that a ballad." UL

  "Torn away from number weight." *Fr.* 5. LP

Speechless. Erich Fried, *tr. fr. German by* Beth Bjorklund. CoAuP

Speechless Sorrow sat with me. The Guest. Harriet McEwen Kimball. AA

Speechless tree and animal and bird. A Lesson from Van Gogh. Howard Moss. MoAB

Speechless [upon the Marriage of Two Deaf and Dumb Persons]. Philip Bourke Marston. EBVV

Speed of Darkness, The. Muriel Rukeyser. GLP; LCAP

Speed Track, The. "Peter." BoTP

Speke, Parrot. John Skelton. *See* Speak, Parrot.

Spell, A. Dryden. *See* Oedipus: Incantation to Oedipus.

Spell, The. Robert Herrick. CaPo; WSC

Spell, A. George Peele. *Fr.* The Old Wives' [*or* Wife's] Tale. ChTr

Spell against Sorrow. Kathleen Jessie Raine. PBWP

Spell against Spelling, The. George Starbuck. FYAP

Spell before Winter, A. Howard Nemerov. LiTM

Spell for Making the First Man. *Unknown, tr. fr. Maori by* Margaret Orbell. PeNZ

Spell o' the Hills, The. Douglas Fraser. PoSH

Spell of Creation. Kathleen Jessie Raine. FaBoCh; OxBS

Spell of Invisibility, A. *At. to.* Christopher Marlowe. ChTr

Spell of the Yukon, The. Robert W. Service. BLPA; BLPL; FaBoBe; FaFP

Spell, treasure-bearing spell, prop up the sky standing above. *Unknown, tr. by* Margaret Orbell. PeNZ

Spellbound. Emily Brontë. *See* Night Is Darkening round Me.

Spelling. Margaret Atwood. NoAM; NoP

Spelling of Elliot, The. *Unknown.* FaBoUs

Spelling reformer indicted, A. Ambrose Bierce. *Fr.* The Devil's Dictionary. OBAL

Spelt from Sibyl's Leaves. Gerard Manley Hopkins. BrPo; CMoP; FaBoMo; LiTM; NOBVV; OAEL-1; OAEL-2; PrIm; TOF

Spencer the Rover. *Unknown.* OBET

Spencers were coming, but have to delay, The. Can We Make It Next Weekend Instead? Willard R. Espy. SoTCo

Spend the years of learning squandering. Gnome. Samuel Beckett. BIrV; OxBSP

Spending beyond their income on gifts for Christmas. Christmas Shopping. Louis MacNeice. OBCP

Spending hand that alway poureth out [*or* powreth owte], A. Sir Thomas Wyatt. *Fr.* Satires, III. AAS

  (To Sir Francis Brian.) SiPS

Spending the Night. Maxine W. Kumin. CAPP

Spending the Night at Monk Ch'ao Yün's Retreat on Mount Lung-men. Li E, *tr. fr. Chinese by* Shirleen S. Wong. WFTU

Spending the Night in a Rundown Temple. Takeuchi Unto, *tr. fr. Chinese by* Burton Watson. JLIC-2

Spending the Night on the River. T'ang Hsien-Tsu, *tr. fr. Chinese by* Jonathan Chaves. CoBLCP

Spendthrift, disinherited and graceless, The. Remittance Man. Judith Wright. NoAM

Spenser's Ireland. Marianne Moore. FaBoWP; LiTA; LiTM; NoAM; NOBA; OxBA; TAP

Spent purpose of a perfectly marvellous, The. In Favor of One's Time. Frank O'Hara. NeAP; PoA

Sperrins surround it, the Faughan flows by, The. Claudy. James Simmons. CIP

Sphere, *sels.* A. R. Ammons.

  "I don't know about you,/ but I'm sick of good poems." *Fr.* 138-145. HCAP

  "I was pulling Veronica out of the lawn when this hornet came." *Fr.* 115-120. NoAM

  "There is a faculty or knack, smallish, in the mind that can turn." *Fr.* 71-72. NoAM

Sphere of pure chance, free agent of no cause. Calvin in the Casino. Turner Cassity. NIP

Sphere, which is as many thousand spheres, A. Shelley. *Fr.* Prometheus Unbound. ImOP, *fr.* IV.

Sphinx, The. Henry Howard Brownell. AA

Sphinx, The. Emerson. AmPP; NOBA; OxBA

Sphinx. Robert Hayden. HCAP

Sphinx, The, *sel.* Oscar Wilde.

  "How subtle-secret is your smile! Did you love none then? Nay, I know." MoBrPo

Sphinx Speaks, The. Francis Saltus Saltus. AA

Sphinxes Inclined to Be. Olga Orozco, *tr. fr. Spanish by* Leslie Keffer. WPOW

Spicewood. Lizette Woodworth Reese. MoAmPo

Spicy smell of tall shadowy eucalyptuses. Sabbath Hours. A. Leyeles, *tr. by* Benjamin *and* Barbara Harshav. AYP

Spider. Basho, *tr. fr. Japanese.* TTTS

Spider, The. Robert Peter Tristram Coffin. ImOP

Spider. Thomas Cole. PoA

Spider, The. Richard Eberhart. NoAM; PoA

Spider. Norma Farber. PChr

Spider. Saqi Farooqi, *tr. fr. Urdu by* Mahmood Jamal. PBMUP

Spider, The. Hannah Flagg Gould. OBCA

Spider, The. Edward Littleton. NOEC

Spider, The. Michizane, *tr. fr. Chinese by* Burton Watson. JLIC-1

Spider, The. Robert Penn Warren. MT

Spider and the Fly, The. Mary Howitt. BeLS; FaFP; FaPON; OHFP; OnUR; OxBChV; Par; PWR; WBLP

Spider and the Ghost of the Fly, The. Vachel Lindsay. VGW

Spider bite the size of a dinner plate, A. Into the Dark. Paul Monette. AmPA

Spider crouching on the ledge above the sink, The. James Keir Baxter. *Fr.* Autumn Testament, 48. ATNZ; PeNZ

Spider Crystal Ascension. Charles Wright. GeTw; HCAP; LCAP

Spider Dream. Elaine Hall. GOS

Spider expects the cold of winter, The. The Spider. Richard Eberhart. NoAM; PoA

Spider holds a silver ball, The. Emily Dickinson. FM; WPOW

Spider in the bath, A. The image noted. The Image. Roy Fuller. GTBS-P; OxBTC

Spider, juiced crystal and Milky Way, drifts on his web through the night sky, The. Spider Crystal Ascension. Charles Wright. GeTw; HCAP; LCAP

Spider Reeves. Henry Carlile. Psk
Spider sewed at night, A. Emily Dickinson. NAAL-1
Spider! thou need'st not run in fear about. To a Spider. Robert Southey. FM
Spider weaves his silver wire, The. Of a Spider. Wilfred Thornley. FaPON; PDV
Spider Web. Stephen Dobyns. BLA; PPR
Spider, World-Spinner. Elaine Hall. GOS
Spiders. Diane Ackerman. MAYP
Spiders. David Wevill. MoCV
Spiders crawling up the wall. The Vampire's Love Song. Margaret G. Keyes *and* Jeanne Youngson. VVA
Spiders started out to go with the wind on its pilgrimage, The. The Broken. W. S. Merwin. LCAP
Spider's web, The. Special Delivery. John Montague. IPY
Spiderwebs on the casement. Old Times. Daniel Mark Epstein. DiPo
Spiel. Halvard Johnson. TSL
Spiel of the Three Mountebanks. John Crowe Ransom. MoAB; MoAmPo
Spies, you are lights in state, but of base stuff. On Spies. Ben Jonson. NoP; OxBSP
Spike of Green, A. Barbara Baker. RAR
Spiked thorns all over, and a thirty-foot wall. Ballad of the Government Granary Clerk. Ho Ching-ming, *tr. by* Jonathan Chaves. CoBLCP
Spikenard. Laurence Housman. TrPWD
Spikes of new smell driven up nostrils. Gary Snyder. *Fr.* Myths and Texts: Burning, XIII. NaP
Spilled from a tree-searing wind. Shiba Sonome, *tr. fr. Japanese by* Hiroaki Sato. *Fr.* Fifteen Hokku. FCEI
Spilled into the cup. Bubbling Wine. Abu Zakariya, *tr. by* A. J. Arberry. TTY
Spilt Milk. W. B. Yeats. OxBSP
Spin a coin, spin a coin. Queen Nefertiti. *Unknown.* RHPC
Spin, a hardy spin, and here's the globe, A. A Small Boy, Dreaming. Albert Herzing. NYBP
Spin cheerfully. Leave the Thread with God. *Unknown.* BLRP
Spin Control. George Starbuck. SoTCo
Spin, Dame, spin. *Unknown.* OxNR
Spin the ball! I reel, I burn. Song of Seyd Nimetollah of Kuhistan. Emerson. NOBA
Spinal Guard. Alan Bernheimer. IAT
Spindrift. Galway Kinnell. NaP; NYBP
Spine has been tingled; the horn has been swoggled, The. Woolly Words. Robert N. Feinstein. NBLV
Spinner, The. "Madeline Bridges." AA
Spinner's lights from house to house brighten the deep night. Sitting Up at Night. Lu Yu, *tr. by* Burton Watson. CoBCP
Spinning. Alfred W. Purdy. NoAM; NoBC
Spinning Girl, The. Nathan Alterman, *tr. fr. Hebrew by* Ruth Nevo. VWA
Spinning Song. Edith Sitwell. MoAB; MoBrPo
Spinning Wheel, The. A. M. Klein. CaP
Spinning-Wheel, The. John Francis Waller. ChTr
Spinning Woman, The. Leonidas of Tarentum, *tr. fr. Greek by* Andrew Lang. AWP
Spinning Yarns, Relatively Speaking. Peter Payack. BWV
Spinoza/ Collected curiosa. *Unknown.* NOBL
Spinoza Was a Bee. Jaroslaw Marek Rymkiewicz, *tr. fr. Polish by* Czeslaw Milosz. PwPP
Spinster. Sylvia Plath. FaBoWP
Spinsterish/ silver/ Before the shuttered window. Men Walked To and Fro. Blanaid Salkeld. NeIP
Spinster's Lullaby. Vassar Miller. BoWoP; NMM
Spiral Staircase, The. Liana Catri, *tr. fr. Italian by* Muriel Kittel. DMI
Spiralwise it spins. Time. Ralph Hodgson. BrPo; GTBS-P
Spire, The. Ellen Bryant Voigt. NoAM
Spire cranes, The. Its statue is an aviary. Dylan Thomas. PoA
Spires, firm on their monster feet rose light and thin, The. Denis Devlin. *Fr.* The Heavenly Foreigner. CIP
Spires of Oxford, The. Winifred M. Letts. FaFP; OHFP; OnYI; PoLF; PoRA; WGRP
Spirit Craft, The. Charles G. Ballard. VoR
Spirit Epiloguizes, The. Milton. *See* Comus; a Masque Presented at Ludlow Castle: To the ocean now I fly.
Spirit Escapes, The. Pierre Reverdy, *tr. fr. French by* Michael Benedikt. POS
Spirit Expounds. T'ao Ch'ien, *tr. fr. Chinese by* Burton Watson. *Fr.* Substance, Shadow, and Spirit. CoBCP
Spirit Flowers. Della Burt. BiSi

Spirit from Perfecter Ages. Arthur Hugh Clough. *See* Amours de Voyage: Is it illusion? or does there a spirit from perfecter ages.
Spirit from Whom Our Lives Proceed. Howard Chandler Robbins. TrPWD
Spirit haunts the year's last hours, A. Tennyson. *Fr.* The Princess. InvP
(Song: "Spirit haunts the last year's hours, A.") GTBS-P; HeIP; OBNC; PoEL-5
Spirit in Our Hearts, The. Henry Ustic Onderdonk. AH
Spirit Land, The. Jones Very. HAP
Spirit-like before Light. Arthur Gregor. VWA
Spirit moves, The. A Light Breather. Theodore Roethke. NoP
Spirit of Earth with still, restoring hands, The. The Last Furrow. Edwin Markham. AA
Spirit of "Fire and dew." To O. S. C. Annie Eliot Trumbull. AA
Spirit of Life, in This New Dawn. Earl Bowman Marlatt. AH
Spirit of Night, The. Thomas Rogers. EiL
Spirit of Plato. Spirit of Plato. *Unknown, tr. by* Shelley. AWP; OBVE
Spirit of Plato. *Unknown, tr. fr. Greek by* Shelley. AWP; OBVE
Spirit of romance dies not to those, The. Pictures of the Rhine. George Meredith. OBTV
Spirit of song, whose shining wings have borne. Song and Science. Milicent Washburn Shinn. AA
Spirit of the Birch, The. Arthur Ketchum. OHIP
Spirit of the *Bluenose,* The. Claire Harris MacIntosh. CaP
Spirit of the Cairngorms, The. Axel Firsoff. PoSH
Spirit of the Fall, The. Danske Bedinger Dandridge. AA
Spirit of the *Maine,* The. Tudor Jenks. AA; PAH
Spirit of the Wheat, The. Edward A. U. Valentine. AA
Spirit of the Yellow River. Chang Pi, *tr. fr. Chinese by* Lois Fusek. ATF
Spirit of the Yellow River. Sun Kuang-hsien, *tr. fr. Chinese by* Lois Fusek. ATF
Spirit of the Yellow River, The. Wen T'ing-yün, *tr. fr. Chinese by* Lois Fusek. ATF
Spirit of Wrath, The. William Heyen. AmPA
Spirit Pool ("Spirit pool is never polluted."). Chao Meng-fu, *tr. fr. Chinese by* Jonathan Chaves. *Fr.* Twenty-Eight Poems Inscribed on T'ien-kuan Mountain. CoBLCP
Spirit seems to pass, A. Lausanne. Thomas Hardy. FaBoRV; FaBoTw; OBTV
Spirit, Silken Thread. Margot Ruddock. OBMV
Spirit Song. *Unknown, tr. fr. Eskimo.* WTO
Spirit that breathest through my lattice, thou. The Evening Wind. Bryant. AA
Spirit that walked upon the face of the waters, The. Passage. Denise Levertov. CAPP
Spirit! What art thou erecting. The Poet's Ideal. Henrietta Cordelia Ray. CBWP-3
Spirit who sweepest the wild Harp of Time! Ode to the Departing Year. Samuel Taylor Coleridge. EnRP
Spirit Whose Work Is Done. Walt Whitman. NAAL-1
Spirit world we may not see, The. Day and Night. Fyodor Ivanovich Tyutchev, *tr. by* Alan Myers. AAA
Spirits. Robert Bridges. *See* Angel Spirits of Sleep.
Spirits. Victor Hernandez Cruz. PoBA; WSC
Spirits and illusions have died. Life from the Lifeless. Robinson Jeffers. CMoP
Spirits, Dancing. Arthur Gregor. NYBP; VGW
Spirit's Epochs, The. Coventry Patmore. *Fr.* The Angel in the House, I, viii. EBEV; GBL; OxBSP
Spirits Everywhere. Ludwig Uhland, *tr. fr. German by* James Clarence Mangan. AWP
Spirit's Odyssey, The. M. Krishnamurti. InPK
Spirits of the heights, I must face up to you. The Pyrenees. Jacques Hamelink, *tr. by* Scott Rollins. DuIn
Spirits of well-shot woodcock, partridge, snipe. "New King Arrives in His Capital by Air." —Daily Newspaper. Sir John Betjeman. NOBE; OxBoLi
(Death of King George V.) NOBE; OxBS
Spirit's Song. Louise Bogan. NYBP
Spirits Unchained. Keorapetse Kgositsile. PoBA
Spirits walking everywhere. W. J. Turner. *Fr.* The Seven Days of the Sun. OBMV
Spiritual, A. Paul Laurence Dunbar. BPo
Spiritual Isolation. Isaac Rosenberg. TrJP
Spiritual, the carnal, are one, The. Dorothy Wellesley. *Fr.* Matrix. OBMV
Spirituality. Samuel Greenberg. LiTA
Spirk Troll-Derisive. James Whitcomb Riley. *See* Craqueodoom.
Spit. Charles Kenneth Williams. CAPP; NAmP; VWA

Spit in my face you Jew[e]s, and pierce my side. John Donne. *Fr.* Holy Sonnets, IX. JCP; OBS; Son; TOF

Spite hath no power to make me sad. Sir Thomas Wyatt. SiPS

Spite o' the tempests a-blowin.' "Tollable Well!" Frank Lebby Stanton. FaFP

Spits of glitter in lowgrade ore. Conserving the Magnitude of Uselessness. A. R. Ammons. NoAM

Spittal wives are no' very nice. The Wives of Spittal. *Unknown.* GBP

Spitting on Ira Rosenblatt. Robert Hershon. NeAC

Spiv Song. Royston Ellis. PeHV

Splash, that falling spring. *Unknown, tr. by* Arthur Waley. BoS

Splashing along the boggy woods all day. Together. Siegfried Sassoon. BrPo

Splashing hot water over my navel. Ozaki Hosai, *tr. fr. Japanese by* Hiroaki Sato. *Fr.* One Hundred Haiku in Free Form. FCEI

Splat of bare feet on wet tile, The. Women's Locker Room. Marilyn Nelson Waniek. MAYP

Spleen. Ernest Dowson. BrPo; MoBrPo; NOBVV

Spleen, The, *sels.* Matthew Green.
    "But now more serious let me grow." PoEL-3
    "First know, my friend, I do not mean." NOEC
    In Praise of Water-Gruel. FaBoUs

Spleen. Paul Verlaine, *tr. fr. French by* Ernest Dowson. AWP

Spleen LXXVI ("I have more memories than if I had lived a thousand years."). Baudelaire, *tr. by* Anthony Hecht

Splendid burns the huge house with bronze. An Armoury. Alcaeus, *tr. by* Gilbert Highet. WaaP

Splendid fellow in the grass, A. Feathered Friends. Robert Peters. BXAP

Splendid paper palace, The. The Mask and the Poem. Alejandra Pizarnik, *tr. by* Alina Rivero. VWA

Splendid Shilling, The, *sels.* John Phillips. BXAP; OAEL-1, *abr.*; Par
    "Happy the man, who, void of cares and strife." NOEC
    "Thus while my joyless hours I lingring spend." FaBoPa

Splendid Village, The, *sel.* Ebenezer Elliott.
    "Village! thy butcher's son, the steward now." OBSV

Splendid woman and upstanding, A. *Unknown, tr. by* Arthur Waley. BoS

Splendidis Longum Valedico Nugis. Sir Philip Sidney. *See* Astrophel and Stella: CX. "Leave me, O Love, which reachest but to dust."

Splendor. Shin Shalom, *tr. fr. Hebrew by* Abraham Birman. VWA

Splendor Falls [on Castle Walls], The. Tennyson. *Fr.* The Princess, *pt.* III. AWP; CH; EBVV; ELP; FaBoCh; FaBV; FiP; GoJo; GTBS-P; HeIP; InPK; NAEL-2; NoP; OAEL-2; OBNC; PoEL-5; PrIm; TrGrPo; WSC
    (Blow, Bugle, Blow.) BLPL; ChTr; FaFP; LiTB; NOBE; OBEV; UnPo; UnS; WiR
    (Bugle Song.) FaPON; GN
    (He Hears the Bugle at Killarney.) FaBoPP

Splendor of Thine Eyes, The. Moses ibn Ezra, *tr. fr. Hebrew by* Solomon Solis-Cohen. TrJP

Splendour of life so splendidly contained. The Masque of Blackness. Geoffrey Hill. *Fr.* Lachrimae, II. NoAM

Splendour of my Spring I destroy here, The. Not knowing. Abishag. Jacob Fichman, *tr. by* Sholom J. Kahn. TrJP

Splendour recurrent. Fraternitas. Confucius, *tr. fr. Chinese by* Ezra Pound. *Fr.* Deer Sing. CTC; OBVE

Splinter. Carl Sandburg. FaPON; OBCA; SoSe

Splinter, The. James Kenneth Stephen. CenHV

Splinter of a broken mirror lies, A. Suburbs on Spring Day. Shin Dong-jip, *tr. by* Koh Chang-soo. ACKP

Splinters of information, stones of information. Minerals of Cornwall, Stones of Cornwall. Peter Redgrove. FaBoMo

Splish splosh, February-fill-the-dike. February. John Heath-Stubbs. OBCP

Splitting birches, spiky thicket, kinship. Black Bread. Tom Paulin. CIP

Splitting the Infinite. Yona Wallach, *tr. fr. Hebrew by* Warren Bargad *and* Stanley F. Chyet. IP

Splitting Wood Near Morris, Oklahoma on Robbie and Lesa McMurtry's Farm. Lance Henson. HATNAP

Splittings. Adrienne Rich. CAPP

Spoil. Malka Heifetz Tussman, *tr. fr. Yiddish by* Marcia Falk. OV

Spoilers and the Spoils, The. Judith Johnson Sherwin. SM

Spoiler's Return, The. Derek Walcott. PBCV

Spoiling daylight inched along the bar-top, The. The Mill. Richard Wilbur. Psk; SoSe

Spoils. Robert Graves. HAP; Son; WeW

Spoils of Love, The. Robert Graves. *See* When all is over and you march for home.

Spoils of War, The. Vernon Watkins. WaP

Spokane Falls. Phillip William George. VoR

Spoken by Venus on Seeing Her Statue Done by Praxiteles. *Unknown, tr. fr. Greek.* EyDe; FaBoEE

Spoken Extempore. Earl of Rochester. SeCePo

Spoken Extempore on the Death of Mr. Pope. *Unknown.* NOEC

Spontaneous Me. Walt Whitman. NAAL-1; OxBA

Spontaneous Requiem for the American Indian. Gregory Corso. MAT; PoM

Spool of Thread, A. Sophie E. Eastman. PAH

Spoon, The. Charles Simic. NNaP

Spoon River Anthology, *sels.* Edgar Lee Masters.
    Aaron Hatfield. LiTA
    Amanda Barker. NoAM
    Anne Rutledge. AmFN; CMoP; FaFP; HAP; LiTA; LiTM; MoAmPo; MoP; NoAM; NOBA; NoBA; OFD; OHFP; OxBA; TrGrPo
    Arlo Will. LiTA
    "Butch" Weldy. SaC
    Carl Hamblin. CMoP; LiTA; LiTM; OBSV
    Cassius Hueffer. OxBA
    Circuit Judge, The. FaBoEE
    Cooney Potter. SaC
    Daisy Fraser. CMoP; HAP; PoE
    Davis Matlock. LiTA; LiTM
    Dora Williams. HAP
    Editor Whedon. CMoP; FaBoEE; NOBA; OBSV; OxBA
    Edmund Pollard. ErPo
    Elliott Hawkins. OxBA
    Elsa Wertman. MoP; NoAM; OxBA
    English Thornton. OxBA
    Father Malloy. OxBA
    Franklin James. OBD
    Hamilton Greene. MoP; NoAM; OxBA
    Henry C. Calhoun. LiTA; LiTM
    Herman Altman. OxBA
    Hill, The. CMoP; FYAP; LiTA; LiTM; NoAM; NOBA; OxBA; TAP
    Jacob Godbey. LiTA
    Jonathan Houghton. OxBA
    Jonathan Swift Somers. OBAL
    Judge Somers. FaBoEE; OBSV
    Knowlt Hoheimer. OxBA
    Lucinda Matlock. CMoP; FaBV; FF; HAP; LiTA; LiTM; MoAmPo; MoP; NoAM; NOBA; OxBA
    Petit, the Poet. CMoP; MoAmPo; NoAM; NOBA; OxBA; TAP
    Rutherford McDowell. EyDe; LiTA; OxBA
    Scholfield Huxley. LiTA; TrPWD
    Seth Compton. LiTA
    Spooniad, The. OBAL
    Village Atheist, The. EaLo; LiTA
    William Jones. ImOP

Spooniad, The. Edgar Lee Masters. *Fr.* Spoon River Anthology. OBAL

Spoonmeat at Bill Porter's in the Hall. After Tennyson. Edward Lear. FaBoNo

Sport. Hamlin Garland. AnAmPo

Sport, an adventitious sprout, A. Perspective. Margaret Avison. OBCV

Sport Items. Philippe Soupault, *tr. fr. French by* Joachim Neugroschel. POS

Sportif. David McCord. *See* Prescott, press my Ascot waistcoat.

Sporting a sword. Sword. Kagura, *tr. by* Hiroaki Sato. FCEI

Sporting Acquaintances. Siegfried Sassoon. OxBTC

Sporting at fancie, setting light by love. Richard Barnfield. *Fr.* Sonnets, I. PeHV

Sporting Goods. Philippe Soupault, *tr. fr. French by* Rosemarie Waldrop. RHTwFP; TTTS

Sports and gallantries, the stage, the arts, the antics of dancers. Boats in a Fog. Robinson Jeffers. MOS; NAAL-2; NoP; OxBA

Sportsman in the Zuider Zee, A. River Rhyme. Lila Zeiger. SoTCo

Sportsmen keep hawks, and their quarry they gain, The. Air. John Gay. *Fr.* Polly; an Opera, XLVIII. NOEC

Sporus. Pope. *See* Epistle to Dr. Arbuthnot:
    Let Sporus tremble—"What? That thing of silk."

Spot-Check at Fifty. Vernon Scannell. NAs

Spot on the Sun, A. Tsfrirah Gar, *tr. fr. Hebrew by* Bernhard Frank. MHeP

Spot Remained on the Wall, The. David Avidan, *tr. fr. Hebrew by* Bernhard Frank. MHeP

Spot the Ball. Frank Ormsby. CIP
Spotless curtain. The garden has. Note apropos the Neighbor's Garden. Abba Kovner, *tr. by* Bernhard Frank. MHeP
Spotlights had you covered, The. A Poem about Poems about Vietnam. Jon Stallworthy. NoAM
Spots of Blood. Phyllis Webb. NOBC
Spots on black skin. Blind Old Woman. Clarence Major. PoBA
Spotted Flycatcher, The. Walter de la Mare. OxBSP
Spotted hawk swoops by and accuses me, The. Walt Whitman. *Fr.* Song of Myself, LII. NoP
Spouse! Sister! Angel! Pilot of the Fate. Shelley. *Fr.* Epipsychidion. ChER
Spouse to the Beloved, The. William Baldwin. *See* Christ, My Beloved.
Spouse to the Younglings, The. William Baldwin. *See* Christ, My Beloved.
Spouting Whale. Takamura Kotaro, *tr. fr. Japanese by* Hiroaki Sato. FCEI
Sprawled/ on our faces in the spring. The Hen Flower. Galway Kinnell. NNaP
Sprawled in the pigsty. For a Young Artist. Robert Hayden. NoAM
Sprawled, like park derelicts, about. The Sleepers. Peter Kocan. CBAP
Sprawled on the crates [*or* bags] and sacks [*or* crates] in the rear of the truck. Green, Green Is El Aghir. Norman Cameron. MoBS; OBWP; OxBTC
(El Aghir.) FaBoTw
Spray. D. H. Lawrence. BoNaP
Spray of Honeysuckle, A. Mary Emily Bradley. AA
Spray rises from those waters. *Unknown, tr. by* Arthur Waley. BoS
Spray sprang up across the cusps of the moon, The. Once at Swanage. Thomas Hardy. FaBoPP
Sprayed with strong poison. Paul Goodman. InPK
Spraying of the waters, The. *Unknown, tr. by* Arthur Waley. BoS
Spraying the Potatoes. Patrick Kavanagh. BIrV; FaBCIP; IPY; NoP
Sprays of frost flowers form. Ping-hsin, *tr. by* Kenneth Rexroth *and* Ling Chung. OV
Sprays of wisteria, The/ arranged in the vase/ are so short. Masaoka Shiki, *tr. fr. Japanese by* Burton Watson. *Fr.* Fifteen Haiku. FCEI
Sprays of wisteria/ arranged in a vase—/ one cluster. Masaoka Shiki, *tr. fr. Japanese by* Burton Watson. *Fr.* Fifteen Haiku. FCEI
Sprays of wisteria/ arranged in a vase—/ the blossoms hang down. Masaoka Shiki, *tr. fr. Japanese by* Burton Watson. *Fr.* Fifteen Haiku. FCEI
Spread on the roadway. The Cyclists. Amy Lowell. WPE
Spread the board with linen snow. Invitation to the Dance. Apollinaris, *tr. by* Howard Mumford Jones. AWP
Spreading and low, unwatered, concentrate. The California Oaks. Yvor Winters. GOA
Spreading clouds of mist. On the Road at Dusk. Emperor Hanazono, *tr. by* Steven D. Carter. WFTW
Spreading our winged arms before the flames, we offered. In the Beginning. Sándor Weöres, *tr. by* Jascha Kessler. FOC
Spreading Wings on Wind. Simon J. Ortiz. HATNAP
Spree. Maxine W. Kumin. NoAM
Sprig of Karo, A. Murray Edmond. PeNZ
Sprig of Lime, The. Robert Nichols. GTBS-P
Sprig of Rosemary, A. Amy Lowell. PeHV; UAS; UnAS
Sprigs of Blossoms. Tamemasa, *tr. fr. Japanese by* Steven D. Carter. WFTW
Sprin' Fevah. Ray Garfield Dandridge. BANP
Spring:/ A hill without a name. Basho, *tr. by* Geoffrey Bownas *and* Anthony Thwaite. PeBJV
Spring, The. William Barnes. BoNaP
Spring. Blake. *Fr.* Songs of Innocence. BoTP; FaBoCh; FaPON; MoShBr; TTTS
Spring. Reed Bye. TTTS
Spring, The. Thomas Carew. CaPo; GN; NoP; PoE; PoEL-3; SeCV-1; TEP; TrGrPo; WiR
Spring. Chang Yü, *tr. fr. Chinese by* Jonathan Chaves. *Fr.* The Four Seasons in the Mountains. CoBLCP
Spring. Christina Rossetti. OBNC
Spring. Carole Gregory Clemmons. PoBA
Spring. William Cornish. *See* Pleasure It Is.
Spring, The. Abraham Cowley. *Fr.* The Mistress. HAP; JCP; MeLP; OBS
Spring. Aubrey Thomas De Vere. *Fr.* A Year of Sorrow. OBNC
Spring, The. Rose Fyleman. FaPON
Spring. Thomas Gisborne. *Fr.* Walks in a Forest. PBBP
Spring. Robert Grenier. *Fr.* A Sequence/ 28 Separate Poems. IAT
Spring. Giovanni Battista Guarini, *tr. fr. Italian by* Leigh Hunt. AWP
Spring. Michael Hogan. InPK

Spring. Gerard Manley Hopkins. BoNaP; BrPo; EBVV; FaBV; HAP; InvP; LiTM; MoAB; MoBrPo; NAEL-2; NoAM; NOBE; NOBVV; OAEL-2; OBMV; OBNC; RB; SoSe; TrCP
Spring. Louis Johnson. *Fr.* Four Poems from the Strontium Age, III. ATNZ
Spring. Moishe Kulbak, *tr. fr. Yiddish by* Ruth Whitman. VWA
Spring. Karla Kuskin. PDV; RHPC
Spring. Philip Larkin. MoBrPo
Spring. James Russell Lowell. *Fr.* The Biglow Papers: 2d Series, No. VI.
Spring, The. John Lyly. *See* Alexander and Campaspe: Trico's Song.
Spring. Meleager, *tr. fr. Greek by* William M. Hardinge. AWP
Spring. W. S. Merwin. NaP
Spring. Edna St. Vincent Millay. BoWoP; MoAB; MoAmPo; NoP
Spring. Richard Moore. SoTCo
Spring. Thomas Nashe. *See* Summer's Last Will and Testament: Spring, the Sweet Spring.
Spring. Charles, Duc d' Orléans, *tr. fr. French by* Andrew Lang. AWP; CTC
Spring. Vess Quinlan. CowP
Spring. Lola Ridge. WPE
Spring. William Robert Rodgers. AnIL
Spring. Isaac Rosenberg. TrJP
Spring. Shakespeare. *See* Love's Labour's Lost: When Daisies Pied [and Violets Blue].
Spring. Princess Shikishi, *tr. fr. Japanese by* Hiroaki Sato. PBWP
Spring. André Spire, *tr. fr. French by* Jethro Bithell. AWP
Spring. Thomas Stanley, *after the Greek of* Anacreon. AWP
Spring. Pamela Stewart. NAmP
Spring. James Still. GrPl; MT
Spring. James Thomson. *Fr.* The Seasons.
  "As rising from the vegetable World." PoEL-3
  Spring ("Behold yon breathing prospect bids the muse"). PoE
  "Lend me your song, ye nightingales! oh, pour." PBBP
  "Should I my steps turn to the rural seat." FM
  Spring Flowers. NOBE
Spring. Mary E. Tucker. CBWP-1
Spring. V. Sackville-West. *Fr.* The Land. PeHV
Spring. Paul Verlaine, *tr. fr. French by* Roland Grant *and* Paul Archer. ErPo; PeHV
Spring, The. Ellen Bryant Voigt. MAYP
Spring. Ruth Whitman. IHMS
Spring. Oscar Williams. LiTA
Spring. Nathaniel Parker Willis. AnAmPo
Spring; a Formal Ode. Fyodor Tyutchev, *tr. fr. Russian by* Charles Tomlinson. FaBoRV
Spring Air. Gene Derwood. FaFP
Spring all the Graces of the age. Ben Jonson. *Fr.* Neptune's Triumph. OBS
Spring, and a new pair of moccasins! Sunflower Moccasins. Phillip William George. VoR
Spring and All. William Carlos Williams. CMoP; HAP; InPK; InPS; LiTM; MoP; NAAL-2; NoAM; NOBA; OxBA; PoE; QFR; TAP
Spring & Asura. Miyazawa Kenji, *tr. fr. Japanese by* Sato. FCEI
Spring and Autumn. William James Linton. EBVV
Spring and Death. Gerard Manley Hopkins. BrPo
Spring and Fall. Gerard Manley Hopkins. BrPo; CMoP; EBEV; ELP; FaBoUs; FF; GTBS-P; HAP; HeIP; HoPM; InPK; InPS; LiTM; MAT; NAEL-2; NIP; NoAM; NOBE; NoP; OBD; PoE; PoEL-5; PPP; RB; SCV; SOTW; TEP; TOF; WeW
Spring and Fall: To a Young Child. Gerard Manley Hopkins. *See* Margaret, are you grieving.
Spring, and the Blind Children. Alfred Noyes. OxBTC
Spring appears, in which the earth, The. The Vigil of Venus. *Unknown, tr. by* Thomas Stanley. AWP
Spring Arithmetic. *Unknown.* FiBHP
Spring at Arm's Length. Charles Vandersee. KS
Spring at dusk. Buson, *tr. fr. Japanese by* Hiroaki Sato. *Fr.* Eighty-seven Hokku. FCEI
Spring at Fort Okanogan. Ramona Wilson. VoR
Spring at Nant Dywelan. Bobi Jones, *tr. fr. Welsh by* Joseph P. Clancy. OBWVE
Spring Beauties, The. Helen Gray Cone. AA
Spring ("Behold yon breathing prospect bids the muse"). James Thomson. *Fr.* The Seasons. PoE
Spring Bereaved. William Drummond of Hawthornden. *See* Sonnet: "Alexis, here she stayed; among these pines."
Spring Bereaved. William Drummond of Hawthornden. OBEV
Spring Bereaved 2. William Drummond of Hawthornden. OBEV
Spring Betrayed. Marjorie Boulton. CN

Spring bird—thinking of what?, A. Natsume Seibi, *tr. fr. Japanese by* Hiroaki Sato. *Fr.* Twenty-seven Hokku. FCEI

Spring breeze. Raizan, *tr. by* Geoffrey Bownas *and* Anthony Thwaite. PeBJV

Spring breeze is a loafer, The. Chang Hui-yen, *tr. fr. Chinese by* An-yan Tang. *Fr.* Composed on a Spring Day and Shown to Yang Tzu-sha. WFTU

Spring breezes waft along the avenue. The Horseman at the Roadside. Yang Wei-chen, *tr. by* Jonathan Chaves. CoBLCP

Spring Burning. Patrick Roland. PeSA

Spring bursts to-day. Christina Rossetti. OHIP

Spring, but the day was dark with rain and sleet. An Adage Concerning a Man and an Old Book. Yisroel Shtern, *tr. by* Robert Friend. PeBMYV

Spring came earlier on, The. A Song for Lexington. Robert Kelley Weeks. AA

Spring came, with orioles singing. A Farmer's Thoughts. Ch'u Kuang-hsi, *tr. by* Burton Watson. CoBCP

Spring came with tiny lances thrusting. Blossom Time. Wilbur Larremore. AA

Spring Cellar. Gladys McKee. GoYe

Spring Cleaning. Phillip William George. VoR

Spring come again, after moody. Ryokan, *tr. by* Lucien Stryk *and* Takashi Ikemoto. ZPCJ

Spring comes/ and the night sadly wanes away. Yakamochi. *Fr.* Manyo Shu. FCEI

Spring comes early to the gardens. Green Jade Plum Trees in Spring. Ou-yang Hsiu, *tr. by* Kenneth Rexroth. NaP

Spring comes in with all her hues and smells, The. A Spring Morning. John Clare. GBL

Spring comes: the flowers learn their coloured shapes. A Vision. Maria Konopnicka, *tr. by* Jerzy Peterkiewicz *and* Burns Singer. WPOW

Spring Comes to Murray Hill. Ogden Nash. FiBHP

Spring comes to the pond in a ripple of shallow waves. Song of the Jade Tower in Spring. Niu Chiao, *tr. by* Lois Fusek. ATF

Spring Coming. A. R. Ammons. HeIP; InPK

Spring covers the mountains like the sea. Prospect of the Wilds. Ch'en San-li, *tr. by* Irving Lo. WFTU

Spring Cricket. Frances Rodman. FaPON

Spring Dawn. Ietaka, *tr. fr. Japanese by* Steven D. Carter. WFTW

Spring Dawn by the River. Emperor Saga, *tr. fr. Chinese by* Burton Watson. JLIC-1

Spring Day. John Ashbery. NOBA

Spring day: a sparrow sand-bathing in my garden. Onitsura, *tr. fr. Japanese by* Hiroaki Sato. *Fr.* Twenty-three Hokku. FCEI

Spring Day in a Mountain Lodge. Princess Uchiko, *tr. fr. Chinese by* Burton Watson. JLIC-1

Spring day in the weeds, A. Dog Yoga. Charles Wright. LCAP

Spring day is slowly ending, her thoughts are lonely, The. Gazing After the Distant Traveler. Li Hsün, *tr. by* Lois Fusek. ATF

Spring Day—Remembering Living on the River, A. Kao Ch'i, *tr. fr. Chinese by* Jonathan Chaves. CoBLCP

Spring day the teen on his bike slanted his caucasian eyes, The. Woodtick. Joy Kogawa. BrSi

Spring Days in My Home Town, *sel.* Yang Chi, *tr. fr. Chinese by* Jonathan Chaves.
    "Thousands of flowers, thousands of petals." CoBLCP

Spring Doggerel. Rhoda Coghill. NeIP

Spring Drawing II. Robert Hass. MAYP

Spring dream—that I don't go mad is what I resent, A. Raizan, *tr. fr. Japanese by* Hiroaki Sato. *Fr.* Thirteen Hokku. FCEI

Spring Dreams. Yang Chi, *tr. fr. Chinese by* Jonathan Chaves. CoBLCP

Spring Ecstasy. Lizette Woodworth Reese. MoAmPo

Spring Equinox. Peter Blue Cloud. *Fr.* Within the Seasons. HATNAP

Spring Festival on the River, The. John Peck. AmPA

Spring fills the palace, and the sun sets beyond the hills. Willow Branches. Huang-fu Sung, *tr. by* Lois Fusek. ATF

Spring Fiord. *Unknown, tr. fr. Eskimo by* Armand Schwerner. STP

Spring Floods. Gregory Orr. GeTw

Spring Flowers. James Thomson. *Fr.* The Seasons: Spring. NOBE

Spring flowers and autumn moon enter poems. For Hidden Mist Pavilion. Yü Hsüan-chi, *tr. by* Geoffrey Waters. BoWoP

Spring Flowers from Ireland. Denis Florence MacCarthy. ACP

Spring, for Julian, was amber in the hand. In the Henry James Country. William Abrahams. WaP

Spring garden, The. Yakamochi. *tr. by* Burton Watson. *Fr.* Manyo Shu. FCEI

Spring-gazing Song. Hsüeh T'ao, *tr. fr. Chinese by* Carolyn Kizer. BoWoP

Spring Goeth All in White. Robert Bridges. BoNaP; BoTP; ChTr

Spring Grass. Carl Sandburg. FaPON

Spring grasses grow luxuriantly on Pa-ling's shores. A Toast to the Traveler. Wei Chuang, *tr. by* Lois Fusek. ATF

Spring Grievance. Chin Ch'ang-hsü, *tr. fr. Chinese by* Burton Watson. CoBCP

Spring Has Come. *Unknown.* BoTP

Spring has come again, The. Asadullah Khan Ghalib, *tr. by* Ahmed Ali. GoT

Spring has come again. The earth. Rainer Maria Rilke, *tr. fr. German by* Christopher Hawthorne. *Fr.* Sonnets to Orpheus. SOTW

Spring has come, and the grass by Ch'ang-men grows green. Manifold Little Hills. Hsüeh Chao-yün, *tr. by* Lois Fusek. ATF

Spring has come and the snow has gone. Captive. Peretz Hirshbein, *tr. by* Joseph Leftwich. TrJP

Spring has come to the pass. Two Springs. Li Ch'ing-chao, *tr. by* Kenneth Rexroth. BoWoP

Spring has darkened with activity, The. Time and the Garden. Yvor Winters. MoAmPo; NoAM; QFR; VGW

Spring has passed. Empress Jito. *Fr.* Manyo Shu. FCEI

Spring has passed [away]. Empress Jito. *Fr.* Manyo Shu. FCEI; Ma

Spring having passed. Tamesada, *tr. by* Steven D. Carter. WFTW

Spring here in Tien-nan, The. To the Tune "Chiang ch'eng tzu." Yang Shen, *tr. by* Jonathan Chaves. CoBLCP

Spring I remember wild canaries. Saint-Henri Spring. Milton Acorn. NeAC

Spring in his death abounds among the lily islands. Elegy on My Father. Allen Curnow. ATNZ

Spring in its tall towers, flower-viewing banquets. Moon over the Ruined Castle. Tsuchii Bansui, *tr. by* Geoffrey Bownas *and* Anthony Thwaite. PeBJV

Spring in New Hampshire. Claude McKay. BANP; BPo; PoNe

Spring in the Land. Tuvia Rübner, *tr. fr. Hebrew by* Bernhard Frank. MHeP

Spring in the Moon Palace. Mao Wen-hsi, *tr. fr. Chinese by* Lois Fusek. ATF

Spring in the Park. Dorothy Wellesley. CN

Spring in the Phoenix Tower. Ou-yang Chiung, *tr. fr. Chinese by* Lois Fusek. ATF

Spring in the Students' Quarter. Henry Murger, *tr. fr. French by* Andrew Lang. AWP

Spring in the Woods. Marguerite Clerbout, *tr. fr. French by* Kathleen Weaver. OV

Spring in Tien is fine! To the Tune "Spring in Tien Is Fine." Yang Shen, *tr. by* Jonathan Chaves. CoBLCP

Spring in Virginia. Ramona Wilson. VoR

Spring in War-Time. Sara Teasdale. OHIP

Spring in Wartime. Phoebe Hesketh. CN

Spring in Westend. Helga Novak, *tr. fr. German by* Susan L. Cocalis. DMG

Spring Is. Bobbi Katz. RHPC

Spring is a juice, a rejoicing, forcing. Bertrans de Born, *tr. by* Paul Blackburn. Pro

Spring Is a Looping-free Time. Martin Robbins. SD

Spring is a recurring astonishment—like poetry. C. K. Stead. *Fr.* The Yellow Sonnets. ATNZ

Spring is a requiem rehearsed. Spring Song. Leroy Smith, Jr.. NePoAm

Spring is almost at an end. Jade Butterflies. Sun Kuang-hsien, *tr. by* Lois Fusek. ATF

Spring is almost over. Returning to My Distant Home. Wei Chuang, *tr. by* Lois Fusek. ATF

Spring Is at Work with Beginnings of Things. Greta Leora Rose. CaP

Spring is coming by a many signs, The. Young Lambs. John Clare. TrGrPo

Spring is coming, spring is coming. *Unknown.* BoTP

Spring is coming to an end. A Song in Three Characters. Ou-yang Chiung, *tr. by* Lois Fusek. ATF

Spring is hard on us. *Unknown.* ErPo

Spring is here, and everywhere they pursue the sweet fragrance. Butterflies. Chang Yü, *tr. fr. Chinese by* Jonathan Chaves. *Fr.* Twelve Miscellaneous Poems on the Fang Garden. CoBLCP

Spring is here—the delicate-footed May, The. Spring. Nathaniel Parker Willis. AnAmPo

Spring is in her eyes. A Little Girl. Charles Angoff. GoYe

Spring is like a perhaps hand. E. E. Cummings. AmPP; NoP; SOTW; TAP; VGW

Spring is over, and flowers fall in the small court. Lotus Leaf Cup. Ku Hsiung, *tr. by* Lois Fusek. ATF

Spring is passing and. Empress Jito, *tr. by* Cid Corman *and* Susumu Kamaike. PBWP

Spring is past and over these many days. September. Aldous Huxley. EBEV

Spring is short. Yosano Akiko, *tr. by* Geoffrey Bownas *and* Anthony Thwaite. BoWoP; PBWP; PeBJV

"Spring is short! Who says our life's immortal?" I said. Yosano Akiko, *tr. fr. Japanese by* Hiroaki Sato. *Fr.* Thirty-nine Tanka. FCEI

Spring is showery, flowery, bowery. *Unknown.* FaBoUs (Four Seasons.) RHPC

Spring is the morning of the year. The Golden Rod. Frank Dempster Sherman. FaPON

Spring is the period. Emily Dickinson. TAP

Spring is when. Spring Is. Bobbi Katz. RHPC

Spring is when the grass turns green and glad. Lines Written for Gene Kelly to Dance To. Carl Sandburg. AiP

Spring-Joy Praising God; Praise of the Sun. Catharina Regina von Greiffenberg, *tr. fr. German by* George C. Schoolfield. WPOW

Spring Landscape. Melvin Walker La Follette. NePoEA-2

Spring light, soft bank mist. Fisherman. Setcho, *tr. by* Lucien Stryk *and* Takashi Ikemoto. ZPCJ

Spring made little promise. Portrait of an Indian. R. E. Rashley. CaP

Spring Memorandum, A. Robert Duncan. PoA

Spring Moon Concealed, The. Tamemasa, *tr. fr. Japanese by* Steven D. Carter. WFTW

Spring Moon in Lingering Cold. Shotetsu, *tr. fr. Japanese by* Steven D. Carter. WFTW

Spring moon it is that brings the buds, The. We Women. Klara Müller-Jahnke, *tr. by* Susan L. Cocalis. DMG

Spring Morning, A. John Clare. GBL

Spring Morning. Frances Cornford. BoTP

Spring Morning. D. H. Lawrence. BrPo; CMoP; MoAB; MoBrPo

Spring Morning. Lin Huan-ch'ang, *tr. fr. Chinese by* Dominic Cheung. IFON

Spring Mountain Climb. Richard Eberhart. GoYe

Spring, my dear, The. Out of Tune. W. E. Henley. MoBrPo

Spring Night. Chang Yü, *tr. fr. Chinese by* Jonathan Chaves. *Fr.* Twelve Miscellaneous Poems on the Fang Garden. CoBLCP

Spring Night. Hagiwara Sakutaro, *tr. fr. Japanese by* Hiroaki Sato. FCEI

Spring night. Shunzei, *tr. fr. Japanese by* Burton Watson. *Fr.* Thirty Tanka. FCEI

Spring Night. Su Tung-p'o, *tr. fr. Chinese by* Burton Watson. CoBCP; Prf

Spring Night. Sara Teasdale. BLPL; FaBoBe; LiTA; MoAmPo

Spring night: a neighbor comes. Reading the Analects. Natsume Seibi, *tr. fr. Japanese by* Hiroaki Sato. *Fr.* Twenty-seven Hokku. FCEI

Spring night: I frighten a woman, A. Taigi, *tr. fr. Japanese by* Hiroaki Sato. *Fr.* Twenty-nine Hokku. FCEI

Spring Night in Lo-Yang—Hearing a Flute. Li Po, *tr. fr. Chinese by* Burton Watson. CoBCP; TTTS

Spring Night in Shokoku-ji, A. Gary Snyder. *Fr.* Four Poems for Robin. NNaP; NoAM; NOBA; NoP; SOTW; VGW

Spring night—one hour worth a thousand gold coins. Spring Night. Su Tung-p'o, *tr. by* Burton Watson. CoBCP; Prf

Spring 1940. Prudence Macdonald. CN

Spring 1943. Roy Fuller. LiTB; LiTM; WaP

Spring 1942. Roy Fuller. LiTM; OxBTC; WaaP

Spring Nocturne. Abraham Liessin, *tr. fr. Yiddish.* TrJP

Spring Oak. Galway Kinnell. BoNaP

Spring of Cities, The. David Rokeah, *tr. fr. Hebrew by* Bernhard Frank. MHeP

Spring of Joy Is Dry, The. *Unknown.* EiL

Spring of life is only a wink, The. Mohammad Taqi Mir, *tr. by* Ahmed Ali. GoT

Spring of the Thief. John Logan. CAPP; NNaP

Spring Offensive. Wilfred Owen. BrPo; GTBS-P; LiTB

Spring Offensive, 1941. Maurice Biggs. PoAu-2

Spring Offensive of the Snail, The. Marge Piercy. TAP

Spring omnipotent goddess thou dost. E. E. Cummings. *Fr.* Tulips & Chimneys. NBLV; OxBA

Spring once said to the nightingale. The Birds' Ball. Charles William Bardeen. BLPA

Spring over the City. Anne Hébert, *tr. fr. French by* Kathleen Weaver. PBWP

Spring overflows the garden. Paying Homage at the Golden Gate. Hsüeh Chao-yün, *tr. by* Lois Fusek. ATF

Spring passed, and summer it seems has come. Teika, *tr. fr. Japanese by* Hiroaki Sato. *Fr.* A Compendium of Good Tanka. FCEI

Spring Poem, A. Chikako, *tr. fr. Japanese by* Steven D. Carter. WFTW

Spring Pools. Robert Frost. AmPP; MoAB; NAAL-2; NoAM; NOBA; NoP; OxBA

Spring Prayer. Emerson. BoTP

Spring Prospect. Tu Fu, *tr. fr. Chinese by* Burton Watson. CoBCP

Spring Quiet. Christina Rossetti. BoNaP; BoTP; CH; GTBS-P; InPS; PoE; PoEL-5; WPE

Spring Rain. Marchette Chute. RHPC

Spring Rain. William Hawkins. MoCV

Spring Rain. Li Shang-yin, *tr. fr. Chinese by* Burton Watson. CoBCP

Spring rain:/ A man lives here. Buson, *tr. by* Geoffrey Bownas *and* Anthony Thwaite. PeBJV

Spring rain:/ In our sedan. Buson, *tr. by* Geoffrey Bownas *and* Anthony Thwaite. PeBJV

Spring rain:/ Soaking on the roof. Buson, *tr. by* Geoffrey Bownas *and* Anthony Thwaite. PeBJV

Spring rain:/ Telling a tale as they go. Buson, *tr. by* Geoffrey Bownas *and* Anthony Thwaite. PeBJV

Spring rain:/ The uneaten ducks. Issa, *tr. by* Geoffrey Bownas *and* Anthony Thwaite. PeBJV

Spring rain. Kaga no Chiyo, *tr. by* R. H. Blyth. PBWP

Spring rain: a child's hands. Torai, *tr. by* Hiroaki Sato. FCEI

Spring rain falling on my bed, The. Momin Khan Momin, *tr. by* Ahmed Ali. GoT

Spring rain falls, unknown to the cow's eyes. Raizan, *tr. fr. Japanese by* Hiroaki Sato. *Fr.* Thirteen Hokku. FCEI

Spring rain: I put my foot out of the footwarmer. Raizan, *tr. fr. Japanese by* Hiroaki Sato. *Fr.* Thirteen Hokku. FCEI

Spring rain isn't even enough, The. Boncho, *tr. fr. Japanese by* Hiroaki Sato. *Fr.* Twenty-one Hokku. FCEI

Spring rain: small clams. Buson, *tr. fr. Japanese by* Hiroaki Sato. *Fr.* Eighty-seven Hokku. FCEI

Spring rain: telling stories. Buson, *tr. fr. Japanese by* Hiroaki Sato. *Fr.* Eighty-seven Hokku. FCEI

Spring rains beat at the window, The. Song of the Wine Spring. Chang Pi, *tr. by* Lois Fusek. ATF

Spring rains weaving. Lady Ise, *tr. fr. Japanese by* Burton Watson. *Fr.* Kokin Shu. FCEI

Spring rides down, The; from Judith and the Larb. A Missouri Traveller Writes Home: 1830. Robert Bly. NePoEA

Spring River. Po Chü-i, *tr. fr. Chinese by* Burton Watson. CoBCP

Spring—River—Flower—Moon—Night, *sel.* T'ang Yin, *tr. fr. Chinese by* Jonathan Chaves.

"Fog of night envelops the flowering trees, The." CoBLCP

Spring scene is splendid, The. Roaming in Kan-chou. Mao Wen-hsi, *tr. by* Lois Fusek. ATF

Spring scenery is luxuriant, The. Delight in the High-Flying Orioles. Mao Wen-hsi, *tr. by* Lois Fusek. ATF

Spring Sea. Tamemasa, *tr. fr. Japanese by* Steven D. Carter. WFTW

Spring sea sloshes, The. Buson, *tr. fr. Japanese by* Hiroaki Sato. *Fr.* Eighty-seven Hokku. FCEI

Spring Season of Muddy Roads. Joseph Brodsky, *tr. fr. Russian by* George L. Kline. AnAn

Spring shakes the windows; doors whang to. A Spring Wind. Bernard Spencer. GTBS-P

Spring shall rouse my buried Lord, The. Easter Poem. Kathleen Jessie Raine. LiTB

Spring Snow. Chugan Engetsu, *tr. fr. Chinese by* Burton Watson. JLIC-2

Spring Snow. William Matthews. AnAn

Spring Snow and Tui. Mary Ursula Bethell. PeNZ

Spring Song. Bliss Carman. AnAmPo

Spring Song. Peter Fallon. CIP

Spring Song. Donald Finkel. NYBP

Spring Song. Hermann Hesse, *tr. fr. German by* Ludwig Lewisohn. AWP

Spring Song, A. Mary Howitt. BoTP

Spring Song. Nahum, *tr. fr. Hebrew by* Emma Lazarus. TrJP

Spring Song. Katharine O'Brien. GoYe

Spring Song. George Brandon Saul. GoYe

Spring Song. Leroy Smith, Jr. NePoAm

Spring Song ("As my eyes search the prarie"). *Unknown, tr. fr. Chippewa Indian by* Frances Densmore. OBVE

Spring Song, A ("Old mother earth woke up from her sleep"). *Unknown.* PoLF

Spring Song—1834, A. John Bethune. PF

Spring Song of the Birds. James I, King of Scotland. OBEV

Spring Song of Tzu-yeh, A. Hsiao Yen, *tr. fr. Chinese by* Jan W. Walls. LLLT

Spring Storm. Jim Wayne Miller. GOYP

Spring Street Bar. Mei-Mei Berssenbrugge. WPOW

Spring Sun. Wang K'ai-yün, *tr. fr. Chinese by* Jan *and* Yvonne Walls. WFTU

Spring that I was six I found in the woods, The. Paul Smyth. *Fr.* A Frame for the Angels. CRP

Spring: the first morning when that one true block of sweet. From My Window. C. K. Williams. CAPP; SV

Spring: The Lover and the Birds. William Allingham. OBNC

Spring, the Sweet Spring. Thomas Nashe. *Fr.* Summer's Last Will and Testament. CH; HeIP; LiTB; NAEL-1; NoP

(Spring.) BoNaP; EIL; GTBS; GTBS-P; NOBE; OBEV; OBSC; OnUR; TrGrPo; WiR

Spring, the Travelling Man. Winifred M. Letts. BoTP

Spring Thoughts. Huang-fu Jan, *tr. fr. Chinese* by Witter Bynner. OFD

Spring Thoughts Sent to Tzu-an. Yü Hsüan-chi, *tr. by* Geoffrey Waters. BoWoP

Spring thunder. Story Tellers Summer, 1980. Nia Francisco. STE

Spring-Tide. *Unknown. See* Lenten Is [*or* Ys] Come [with Love to Toune].

Spring to Winter. George Crabbe. *Fr.* The Ancient Mansion. ChTr (In Suffolk.) FaBoPP

Spring Training. Robert Polito. PPR

Spring under a Thorn, The. *Unknown.* MeEL

Spring up, O well—sing ye unto it. Song of the Well. Bible, *O.T. Fr.* Numbers, XXI: 17–18. TrJP

Spring Vacation, The. Derek Mahon. FaBCIP

Spring Variation. Miyazawa Kenji, *tr. fr. Japanese* by Hiroaki Sato. FCEI

Spring Vista from the Tower of Illuminated Distance. Li Meng-yang, *tr. fr. Chinese* by Jonathan Chaves. CoBLCP

Spring Voices. Louis MacNeice. Son

Spring Was Begging to Be Born. James Tate. NAmP

Spring water flows through the mountainless land. Buson, *tr. fr. Japanese* by Hiroaki Sato. *Fr.* Eighty-seven Hokku. FCEI

Spring water flows, wetting violets. Buson, *tr. fr. Japanese* by Hiroaki Sato. *Fr.* Eighty-seven Hokku. FCEI

Spring Waters, *sels.* "Ping Hsin," *tr. fr. Chinese* by Kai-yu Hsu.

"Falling Star, The." PBWP

"In shaping the snow into blossoms." BoWoP; WPOW

"O, Lord/If in life eternal." WPOW

Spring waters flow by the gate. Song of the Bamboo Branches. Sun Kuang-hsien, *tr. by* Lois Fusek. ATF

Spring water's visible here and there, The. Onitsura, *tr. fr. Japanese* by Hiroaki Sato. *Fr.* Twenty-three Hokku. FCEI

Spring we went into the heat of lilacs. For My Father. Philip Schultz. DiL

Spring—where has it come from. Song of Spring. Wu Chün, *tr. by* Burton Watson. CoBCP

Spring Whistles. Lucy Larcom. OBCA

Spring Will Come, The. H. D. Lowry. BoNaP

Spring Wind, A. Bernard Spencer. GTBS-P

Spring Wind, The. Charlotte Zolotow. RAR

Spring wind on the Bowery, A. Spring. Lola Ridge. WPE

Spring wind: over the river bank comes a bull's voice. Raizan, *tr. fr. Japanese* by Hiroaki Sato. *Fr.* Thirteen Hokku. FCEI

Spring wind, proud rider! To the Tune "Shui hsien-tzu." Ma Chih-yüan. CoBLCP

Spring Work at the Farm. Thirza Wakley. BoTP

Spring Workman. Alan Creighton. CaP

Spring Worm I. Tu Yeh, *tr. fr. Chinese* by Dominic Cheung. IFON

Spring Worm II. Tu Yeh, *tr. fr. Chinese* by Dominic Cheung. IFON

Springboard, The. Louis MacNeice. PoA

Springboard, The. Adrienne Rich. ASP

Springbok. *Unknown, tr. fr. Hottentot.* PeSA

Springbok doe mothers sang, The. Song of the Springbok Does. *Unknown,* tr. by W. H. I. Bleek. PeSA

Springfield Mountain. *Unknown.* AmFP

Spring's Arrival. *Unknown.* FaPON

Spring's Delights. Joseph Ashby-Sterry. CenHV

Spring's sadness lines the south road. Pure Serene Music. Wei Chuang, *tr. by* Lois Fusek. ATF

Spring's second month. Things Seen on Spring Days. Yüan Mei, *tr. by* Jonathan Chaves. CoBLCP

Spring's Welcome. John Lyly. *See* Alexander and Campaspe: Trico's Song.

Springtime, The. Denise Levertov. CoAP

Springtime—and the green willow catkins. To the Tune "Bamboo at West Lake." Shen Chou, *tr. by* Jonathan Chaves. CoBLCP

Springtime Embroidery. Yang Chi, *tr. fr. Chinese* by Jonathan Chaves. *Fr.* Paintings of Ladies Engaged in Four Springtime Occupations. CoBLCP

Springtime hurries to its end. Paying Homage at the Golden Gate. Wei Chuang, *tr. by* Lois Fusek. ATF

Springtime of low walls and flowery darkness. In Harmony with Kao "The Second" Ch'i's Poem "On Hearing a P'i-p'a Played Next Door." Hsü Pen, *tr. by* Jonathan Chaves. CoBLCP

Springtime of the earth has come, The. Isaiah Shembe, *tr. by* B. G. M. Sundkler. WTO

Springtime, Summer and Fall: days to behold a world. In Due Season. W. H. Auden. Prf

Sprinkler twirls, the. August. John Updike. *Fr.* A Child's Calendar. OBCA; RHPC

Sprinklers spray the still lawns. Summer in Academia (Sumerian Academia). Kirby Olson. SoTCo

Sprinters, The. Lee Murchison. SD

Spritely Dead, The. Oscar Williams. *Fr.* Variations on a Theme, II. LiTA; Son

Spruce. Phillip William George. VoR

Spruce and limber yellow-hammer, The. Samuel Taylor Coleridge. FM; PBBP

Spruce Macaronis, and pretty to see. The Maryland Battalion. John Williamson Palmer. AA; PAH

Sprung from a race that had long till'd the soil. The Adventures of Simon Swaugum, a Village Merchant. Philip Freneau. PoEL-4

Spry, wry, and gray as these March sticks. Among the Narcissi. Sylvia Plath. FaBoMo; RB; SCV

Spur, The. W. B. Yeats. WeW

Spur is red upon the briar, The. An Outdoor Litany. Louise Imogen Guiney. TrPWD

Spurt of Literary Criticism, A. W. R. Moses. SoTCo

Sputterings. Blaise Cendrars, *tr. fr. French* by Ron Padgett. RHTwFP

Spy bears his bald intent like a maniac, The. John Tranter. *Fr.* Crying in Early Infancy. CBAP

Spyglass Conversations. *Unknown, tr. fr. Tule Indian* by Frances Densmore. STP

Squadron-blue the hemp-yellow drink of triumph, The. Friederike Mayröcker, *tr. by* Beth Bjorklund. CoAuP

Squalid, empty-headed hen, A. Hen under Bay-Tree. Ruth Pitter. OxBTC

Squalid village set in wintry mud, A. Born without a Chance. Edmund Vance Cooke. BLPA

Squalid with wounds, and many a gaping sore. The Wounded Man and the Swarm of Flies. William Somervile. FM

Squall. Stanley Moss. CoAP

Square as a House, *sel.* Karla Kuskin.

"If you could be small." TSS

Square as a seed-box, in their attic stands. The Handloom. Judith Rodriguez. InVP

Square figures climb off and on. On the "Sievering" Tram. Bernard Spencer. NAs

Square-heeled boat sets off for the Statue, The. To the Statue. May Swenson. GOA

Square sheets—they saw the marble into. Island Quarry. Hart Crane. PPP

Square, squat room (a cellar on promotion), A. Waiting. W. E. Henley. *Fr.* In Hospital, II. NAEL-2

Square-toed Princes. Robert Peter Tristram Coffin. AmFN

Squared/ within the vast. Watchers and Seekers. Amryl Johnson. WS

Squared by Walls. László Nagy, *tr. fr. Hungarian* by Tony Connor. MHuP

Squares. Michael Hamburger. FF

Squaring the Circle. Louis O. Coxe. NYBP

Squash in Blossom. Robert Francis. FYAP

Squat Down, Josey. *Unknown.* AmFP

Squat in swamp shadows. Second Shaman Song. Gary Snyder. *Fr.* Myths and Texts: Burning, I. NeAP; NOBA; PoM

Squats on a toad-stool under a tree. Thomas Lovell Beddoes. *Fr.* Death's Jest Book, III, ii. InVP; OBD

(Song by Isbrand.) InVP; NOBVV; OBNC; PrIM

Squatter's Children. Elizabeth Bishop. NoP

Squatting a day in the sun. Fire in the Hole. Gary Snyder. NAAL-2

Squeak the fife, and beat the drum. Independence Day. Royall Tyler. PAH

Squeal. Heather McHugh. GeTw

Squeal. Louis Simpson. BXAP; FiBHP; Par; UnPo

Squealing under city stone. Rapid Transit. James Agee. MoAmPo

Squeeze Play. Phyllis McGinley. *Fr.* Spectator's Guide to Contemporary Art. FaBoEE; OBSV

Squeezing it slender, I slip it in quickly. *Unknown, tr. by* Hiroaki Sato. FCEI

Squelch and squirt and squiggle. Showers. Marchette Chute. RAR

Squid. Michael C. Blumenthal. MAYP

Squinting against neon signs. Eclipse. Anita Endrezze Probst. CDW

Squire, a squire, he lived in the woods, A. The Broomfield Wager. *Unknown.* OBET

Squire and Milkmaid; or, Blackberry Fold. *Unknown.* CoMu; OBET; OxBB
   (Blackberry Fold.) OBET
Squire he had whose name was Ralph, A. Independent Squire. Samuel Butler. *Fr.* Hudibras, I, 1. NOBE
Squire her hent in arms two, The. Medieval Mirth. *Unknown. Fr.* The Squire of Low Degree. ACP
Squire is in his library, The. He is rather worried. Send for Lord Timothy. John Heath-Stubbs. OxBC
Squire Meldrum at Carrickfergus. Sir David Lindsay. *Fr.* The Historie of Squyer William Meldrum. OxBS
Squire of Low Degree, The, *sels. Unknown.*
   Medieval Mirth. ACP
   "On every branch sat birdes three." PBBP
Squire sat alone beside the board, The. Little Fay's Thanksgiving. Henrietta Cordelia Ray. CBWP-3
Squirrel, The. Saleem Barakat, *tr. fr. Arabic by* Lena Jayyusi *and* Naomi Shihab Nye. MAP
Squirrel, The. Anthony Howell. NPo
Squirrel, The. Mary Howitt. BoTP
Squirrel, The. Ogden Nash. CenHV
Squirrel, The ("Whisky, Frisky, hippity hop"). *Unknown.* FaPON; PDV
Squirrel, The ("Winds they did blow, The"). *Unknown.* BoTP; OxNR
Squirrel in his shirt, The. Ground-Squirrel Song. *Navajo Indian Oral Tradition.* TTTS
Squirrel in the Rain. Frances Mary Frost. RAR
Squirrel is the curliest thing, The. The Curliest Thing. *Unknown.* BoTP
Squirrel near Library. Genevieve Taggard. WPE
Squirrel Stand. Jim Wayne Miller. MT
Squirrel to some is a squirrel, A. The Squirrel. Ogden Nash. CenHV
Sri Rama's Raiment. *Malay Oral Tradition, tr. by* R. O. Winstedt. WTO
S.S.R., Lost at Sea—*The Times.* Ralph Gustafson. OBCV
St Enda. Laurence Lerner. PeSA
Stab, The. William Wallace Harney. AA
Stab incision below nipple. Debridement: Operation Harvest Moon: On Repose. Michael S. Harper. GeTw
Stabat Mater. Sam Hunt. ATNZ
Stabat Mater. *At. to* Jacopone da Todi, *tr. fr. Latin.* WGRP
Stable Cat, The. Leslie Norris. PChr
Stable-lamp is lighted, A. A Christmas Hymn. Richard Wilbur. OBCP; OFD; PChr; TrCP
Stable Straw. Robert Farren. TIRV
Stable-Talk. Raymond Knister. CaP
Stable yields a stercoraceous heap, The. How to Grow Cucumbers. William Cowper. *Fr.* The Task, III. FaBoUs
Stabled horse bearing a thousand weights, A. Leaving My Post to Retire at the Sui Garden. Yüan Mei, *tr. by* Anthony C. Yu. WFTU
Stacademia. George Barlow. NAmP
Staccato! Staccato! The Rubinstein Staccato Etude. Robert Nathaniel Dett. BANP
"Stack Arms!" Joseph Blynth Alston. PAH
Stacked houses on either side, The. The Languages We Are. Frederick Bryant, Jr.. NBP
Stacking countless lights of relief. Sancho Panza's Homecoming. Ishihara Yoshiro, *tr. by* Hiroaki Sato. FCEI
Staff is now greased, The. The Hag. Robert Herrick. CaPo
Staff-Nurse: New Style. W. E. Henley. *Fr.* In Hospital, X. BrPo
Staff-Nurse: Old Style. W. E. Henley. *Fr.* In Hospital, VIII. BrPo
Staff of Aesculapius, The. Marianne Moore. ImOP
Staff slips from the hand, The. Outward. Louis Simpson. NYBP
Stafford in Kansas. James Baker Hall. BXAP
Stag of the Ogura Mountain, The. Emperor Jomei. *Fr.* Manyo Shu. Ma
Stag that calls on Mount Ogura when the evening comes, The. Emperor Jomei. *Fr.* Manyo Shu. FCEI
Stage is about to be swept of corpses, The. Horatian Epode to the Duchess of Malfi. Allen Tate. FaBoMo
Stage is burned, The. Nizar Qabbani, *tr. fr. Arabic by* Diana Der Hovanessian *and* Lena Jayyusi. *Fr.* The Actors, X. MAP
Stage-lit streets. S.F. Southward. Allen Ginsberg. *Fr.* Continuation of a Long Poem of These States. NAAL-2
Stage Love. Swinburne. PoEL-5
Stages on a Journey Westward. James Wright. LCAP; NaP
Stagger of the Wind That I Think Is Your Turning, The. Jane Miller. KS
Staggering down the road at midnite. The Encounter. Paul Blackburn. NeAP
Stagolee. *Unknown.* MAT; OxBoLi, *sl. diff. vers.;* TTY
Stags. William Montgomerie. PoSH

Staid schizophrenic named Struther, A. *Unknown.* NIP
Stains. Theodosia Garrison. WGRP
Staircase, The. Samuel Allen. PoBA
Staircase with a Hundred Steps, The. Benjamin Péret, *tr. fr. French by* David Gascoyne. EAS
Stairs. Oliver Herford. FiBHP
Stairs. W. S. Merwin. KS
Stairs, echoes. Last Year in Capricorn. Eeva-Liisa Manner, *tr. by* Aili Jarvenpa. SOP
Stairs mount to his eternity, The. The Staircase. Samuel Allen. PoBA
Stairway is not, The. The Jacob's Ladder. Denise Levertov. AmPP; CAPP; PoM; PPP
Stairway up to heaven, The. *Unknown. Fr.* Manyo Shu. PeBJV
Stalagmites and Stalactites. *Unknown.* FaBoUs
Stalin. Robert Lowell. HCAP
Stalin Epigram, The. Osip Mandelstam, *tr. fr. Russian by* W. S. Merwin *and* Clarence Brown. FaBoPV
Stalin stood committed to peasant hunger. Reply to the Committed Intellectual. Francis Sparshott. NOBC
Stalking your being, land never revealed. What I Owe Iowa. Tomislav Longinovic. WCI
Stalks of rice. Tsurayuki, *tr. fr. Japanese by* Burton Watson. *Fr.* Kokin Shu. FCEI
Stalks of Wild Hay. H. L. Davis. PoA
Stalky Jack. William Brighty Rands. BoTP
Stall so tight he can't raise heels or knees, The. Bronco Busting, Event #1. May Swenson. ASP; RR
Stalled before my metal shaving mirror. Notes for a Sonnet. Edward Pygge. BXAP
Stalling ox, shuffling, swirls up dust, A. Teika, *tr. fr. Japanese by* Hiroaki Sato. *Fr.* Eighty-four Tanka. FCEI
Stallion, The. Tudur Aled, *tr. fr. Welsh by* Joseph P. Clancy. OBWVE
Stallion, The. Walt Whitman. *Fr.* Song of Myself, XXXII. ASP; PDV
Stalwart was Liu the Duke. *Unknown, tr. by* Arthur Waley. BoS
Stamm'ring cuckoo, whose lewd voice doth grieve, The. Ingratitude. Francis Thynne. PBBP
Stand back, bright morning. Black Song. Amin Nakhla, *tr. by* Matthew R. Sorenson. MAP
Stand back, make way, you mindless scum. W. D. Snodgrass. *Fr.* The Führer Bunker: Dr. Joseph Goebbels. TW
Stand by the Flag. John Nichols Wilder. GN
Stand close around, ye Stygian set. Dirce. Walter Savage Landor. *Fr.* Pericles and Aspasia, CCXXX. AWP; CTC; EBEV; EnRP; FaBoEE; GBL; HAP; LiTB; NOBE; NoP; OAEL-2; OBEV; OBNC; OxBSP; PoEL-4; PoRA; TrGrPo; WeW
   (Stand Close Around.) ChTr
Stand here, you can see the hill. A Memory of the Hill. Kapilar, *tr. by* A. K. Ramanujan. PLW
Stand: knees slightly. Dance Instructions for a Young Girl. Kimiko Hahn. BrSi
Stand not uttering sedately. Epitaphium Citharistriae. Victor Plarr. EnLoPo; NBLV
   (Stand Not Uttering Sedately.) PoRA
Stand of winter trees, A. Kito, *tr. fr. Japanese by* Hiroaki Sato. *Fr.* Twenty-four Hokku. FCEI
Stand on the highest pavement of the stair. La Figlia Che Piange. T. S. Eliot. FaBoTw; GBL; HeIP; LiTA; MAT; OPOP; OxBTC; PoA; UnPo; VGW
Stand out, maids, and look on the land of Cynddylan. *Unknown, tr. fr. Welsh by* Kenneth Hurlstone Jackson. *Fr.* The Elegy on Cynddylan. OBWVE
Stand, Stately Tavie. *Unknown.* ErPo
Stand still, and I will read to thee. A Lecture upon the Shadow. John Donne. AWP; NAEL-1; OBS; SeCP; TEP; UnPo
Stand still. The trees ahead and bushes beside you. Lost. David Wagoner. PoA
Stand still, true poet that you are! Popularity. Robert Browning. OAEL-2
Stand still, you floods, do[e] not deface. On Sight of a Gentlewoman's Face in the Water. Thomas Carew. CaPo; SeCV-1
Stand! the ground's your own, my braves! Warren's Address at Bunker Hill [*or* to the American Soldiers]. John Pierpont. AA; AnAmPo; FaBoBe; GN; GOA; PAH; WBLP
Stand-to, The. C. Day Lewis. OBWP
Stand-to: Good Friday Morning. Siegfried Sassoon. FaBoTw
"Stand to your guns, men!" Morris cried. On Board the *Cumberland.* George Henry Boker. PAH
Stand up, but not for Jesus. Stand Up! D. H. Lawrence. OxBTC
Stand Up! Stand Up for Jesus. George Duffield, Jr.. AH
Stand with thy nose against. Of One That Had a Great Nose. George Turberville, *after the Greek of* Trajan. FaBoEE

Standard model of reality comes to me in the mail, A. Assembling the Model. Peter Payack. BWV
Standin' on the Walls of Zion. *Unknown.* AS
Standing, The. Medbh McGuckian. FaBCIP
Standing aloof in giant ignorance. To Homer. Keats. EBEV; NAEL-2; NoP; Son
  (Sonnet: To Homer.) ChER
Standing at the gate before the service started. Inishkeel Parish Church. Tom Paulin. FaBCIP
Standing at the portal. At the Portal. Frances Ridley Havergal. BLRP
Standing before the bar. And the Fete Continues. Jacques Prévert, *tr. by* Lawrence Ferlinghetti. RHTwFP
Standing Broad Jump, The. Richard Frost. ASP
Standing by a plum, a penniless poet. Natsume Seibi, *tr. fr. Japanese by* Hiroaki Sato. *Fr.* Twenty-seven Hokku. FCEI
Standing corn is green, the wild in flower, The. Nunc Viridant Segetes. Sedulius Scottus, *tr. by* Helen Waddell. BIrV
Standing guests, a grotesque glade, The. The Party. Margaret Avison. PoA
Standing high on the shoulders of all things, all things. The Place at Albert Bay. Muriel Rukeyser. PoA
Standing high to see tidal dawn. Cockcrow. Ted Hughes. AnAn
Standing in the hall against the/ wall. Listening to Grownups Quarreling. Ruth Whitman. NTCP
Standing, in the shadow. Paul Celan, *tr. by* Beth Bjorklund. CoAuP
Standing in the shower stall. Thermodynamics. Adrianne Marcus. BWV
Standing on a stepladder. Soy Sauce. Gary Snyder. CAPP
Standing on Earth ("Standing on Earth, not rapt above the Pole"). Milton. *Fr.* Paradise Lost, *bk.* VII, *ll.* 23–39. ChTr
Standing on 127th the. Langston. Mari E. Evans. CNA
Standing on the Corner. Philip Levine. NNaP
Standing on the little Bluefields pier. Pier. Ivan Uriarte, *tr. by* Jack Hirschman. Vol
Standing on the mountaintop. Lost Silvertip. J. D. Reed. NYBP
Standing on Tiptoe. George Frederick Cameron. CaP; OBCV
Standing on top of the hay. The Farm. Donald Hall. LiTM
Standing or sitting/ I know not what to do. *Unknown. Fr.* Manyo Shu. Ma
Standing there. Ito Sachio, *tr. by* Geoffrey Bownas *and* Anthony Thwaite. PeBJV
Standing there they began to grow skins. Pilgrims. Jean Valentine. LCAP; TAP
Standing under the fobbed. Send No Money. Philip Larkin. TW
Standing up on lifted, folded rock. By Frazier Creek Falls. Gary Snyder. GOA; InPS
Standing upon the margent of the Main. The Tempest. Charles Cotton. SeCePo
Standing While We Die, *sel.* Qasim Haddad, *tr. fr. Arabic by* Sharif Elmusa *and* Charles Doria.
  "Book of the defeated man." MAP
Standing Woman, The. Peter Rosei. CoAuP
Stands for Gnu, whose weapons of Defense. G. Hilaire Belloc. FiBHP
Stands in a corner of my kitchen, its gleaming white façade. The Pulitzer Prize Winning Refrigerator. Robert Funge. SoTCo
Stane-chack! Malison of the Stone-chat. *Unknown.* GBP
Stanes. Duncan Glen. PoSH
Stanley Matthews. Alan Ross. OxBTC
Stanley Meets Mutesa. James D. Rubadiri. PBA
Stanza. Emily Brontë. *See* Often rebuked, yet always back returning.
Stanza from an Early Poem. Christopher Pearse Cranch. *See* Thought is deeper than all speech.
Stanza on Freedom, A. James Russell Lowell. *See* Stanzas on Freedom: Slaves.
Stanza Put on Westminster Hall Gate, A. *Unknown.* APAS
Stanzas: "Black absence hides upon the past." John Clare. EnLoPo; NOBVV
Stanzas: "How smooth that lake expands its ample breast!" Anne Radcliffe. WPE
Stanzas: "I don't want to pay down the last penny of my soul." Osip Mandelstam, *tr. by* W. S. Merwin *and* Clarence Brown. AnAn
Stanzas: "I thought I woke: the midnight sun." Paul Goodman. PoA
Stanzas: "I'll not weep that thou art going to leave me." Emily Brontë. WPE
Stanzas: "In a drear-nighted December." Keats. *See* In a Drear-nighted December.
Stanzas: "Mighty thought of an old world, The." Thomas Lovell Beddoes. *See* Ivory Gate, The: Mighty Thoughts of an Old World, The.
Stanzas: "My life is like the summer rose." Richard Henry Wilde. *See* My Life Is like the Summer Rose.

Stanzas: "Often rebuked, yet always back returning." *At. to* Emily Brontë, *also at. to* Charlotte Brontë. ChER; LiTB; NoBVV; OAEL-2; OBNC; PBWP
  (Stanza.) OBEV
Stanzas: On Prayer. Czeslaw Milosz, *tr. fr. Polish by* Robert Hass. AnAn
Stanzas: On Seeing the Speaker Asleep in His Chair. Winthrop Mackworth Praed. EnRP
  (Stanzas to the Speaker Asleep.) OBSV
Stanzas: "Passing of a dream, The." John Clare. NOBVV
Stanzas: "Princes and kings decay and die." Philip Freneau. GOA
Stanzas: "When a man hath no freedom to fight for at home." Byron.
  See When a man hath no freedom to fight for at home.
Stanzas: "With tears thy grief thou dost bemoan." Solomon Ibn Gabirol, *tr. by* Emma Lazarus. TrJP
Stanzas, *sel.* Charles Newton.
  Wild Nature. NOEC
Stanzas—April, 1814. Shelley. ChER; EnRP; FiP; OBNC
  (Remorse.) OBEV
Stanzas Concerning an Ecstasy Experienced in High Contemplation. Saint John of the Cross, *tr. fr. Spanish by* K. Kavanaugh *and* O. Rodrigues. TOF
Stanzas Concerning Love. Stefan George, *tr. fr. German by* Ludwig Lewisohn. AWP
Stanzas for Music. Byron. AWP; ChER; ELP; EnRP; FiP; GTBS; HAP; LiTB; NAEL-2; NoP; OAEL-2; PoRA; TrGrPo
Stanzas from "Child Harold." John Clare. *Fr.* Child Harold. OBNC
  (In Epping Forest.) FaBoPP
Stanzas from Saint Peter's Complaint. Robert Southwell. *Fr.* Saint Peter's Complaint. ACP
Stanzas from the Grande Chartreuse. Matthew Arnold. EBVV; NAEL-2; OAEL-2; PoE; PoEL-5; TEP
Stanzas from "The Ivory Gate." Thomas Lovell Beddoes. *See* Ivory Gate, The: Mighty Thoughts of an Old World, The.
Stanzas in Meditation, *sels.* Gertrude Stein.
  "Full well I know that she is there." PoA
  "How I wish I were able to say what I think." PBWP
Stanzas Occasioned by the Ruins of a Country Inn *or* On the Ruins of a Country Inn. Philip Freneau. AnAmPo; OxBA
  (On the Ruins of a Country Inn.) AA
Stanzas of the Graves, The, *sel. Unknown, tr. fr. Welsh by* Gwyn Jones.
  "Graves the rain makes wet and sleek, The." OBWVE
Stanzas of the Soul that Suffers with Longing to See God. Saint John of the Cross, *tr. fr. Spanish by* K. Kavanaugh *and* O. Rodrigues. TOF
Stanzas on Freedom, *sel.* James Russell Lowell. GN, 2 *sts.;* OHIP; PoNe
  Slaves, *last st.*
  (Stanza on Freedom, A.) AA
Stanzas on Mutability. Hugo von Hofmannsthal, *tr. fr. German by* Jethro Bithell. AWP; TrJP
Stanzas on Woman. Goldsmith. *See* Vicar of Wakefield, The: When Lovely Woman Stoops to Folly.
Stanzas Subjoined to the Yearly Bill of Mortality of the Parish of All Saints, Northampton; for the Year 1787. William Cowper. NOCV
Stanzas to— — —. Emily Brontë. WPE
Stanzas to a Lady, with the Poems of Camoëns. Byron. FaBoUs
Stanzas to Augusta. Byron. EnRP
Stanzas to Edward Williams. Shelley. OBNC
Stanzas to Mr. Bentley. Thomas Gray. NoP
Stanzas to the Po. Byron. OAEL-2
Stanzas to the Speaker Asleep. Winthrop Mackworth Praed. *See* Stanzas: On Seeing the Speaker Asleep in His Chair.
Stanzas Written in Dejection [–December 1818,] near Naples. Shelley. ChER; EnRP; FaBV; FiP; GTBS; GTBS-P; NAEL-2; NAWM-2; NoP; PoRA; TEP
Stanzas Written in Great Haste in Reply to Some Proposing That Women Are Fickle. Marcia Belisarda, *tr. fr. Spanish by* Kate Flores. DMH
Stanzas Written in My Pocket Copy of Thomson's "Castle of Indolence." Wordsworth. EnRP
Stanzas Written on the Road between Florence and Pisa. Byron. EnRP; NAEL-2
  (All for Love.) GTBS; GTBS-P
Staoineag. Leen Volwerk. PoSH
Star, A. Philippe Denis, *tr. fr. French by* Paul Auster. RHTwFP
Star, A. George MacBeth. NYBP
Star, The. Beatrice Redpath. CaP
Star, The. Marion Couthouy Smith. PAH
Star, The. Jane Taylor. BoTP; FaBoBe; FaFP; FaPON; NTCP; OxBChV; OxNR; Par; PYC; RAR; RHPC
Star,/ If you are. A Christmas Tree. William Burford. SoSe

Star and Dead Leaves. Tsuboi Shigeji, *tr. fr. Japanese by* Geoffrey Bownas *and* Anthony Thwaite. PeBJV

Star & Garter Theater. Dennis Schmitz. LCAP; NPGG

Star Blanket. Ray A. Young Bear. CDW

Star Boys. Richard Katrovas. NAmP

Star crashes in a small plaza and a bird loses its eyes, A. The Things I Say Are True. Blanca Varela, *tr. by* Donald Yates. BoWoP

Star-crowned cliffs seem hinged upon the sky, The. Glencoe. G. K. Chesterton. PoSH

Star Drifter Grounded, The. Bruce Boston. BWV

Star Drill. Tom Inglis Moore. PoAu-2

Star-dust and vaporous light. Noel. Richard Watson Gilder. AA

Star-filled seas are smooth tonight, The. The Isle of Portland. A. E. Housman. *Fr.* A Shropshire Lad, LIX. MoBrPo

Star for a Glass. Michael Burkard. PPR

Star-Gazer. Louis MacNeice. NAEL-2; NoP

Star-gazing. Microcosmos. Peter Payack. BWV

Star is gone, A! a star is gone! The Fallen Star. George Darley. OBEV

Star Journey. Naomi Long Madgett. BPo

Star light, star bright. Wishing Poem. *Unknown.* NTCP; OxNR

Star looks down at me, A. Waiting Both. Thomas Hardy. MoAB; MoBrPo; OxBoLi; TTTS

Star Morals. Friedrich Wilhelm Nietzsche, *tr. fr. German by* Ludwig Lewisohn. AWP

Star Motel. Bill Berkson. UL

Star must cease to burn with its own light, The. Et Mori Lucrum. John Lancaster Spalding. *Fr.* God and the Soul. AA

Star of Calvary, The. Nathaniel Hawthorne. AA

Star of Ethiopia. Lucian B. Watkins. BANP

Star of my mishap imposed this pain, The. Samuel Daniel. *Fr.* To Delia. OBSC

Star of the Evening. James M. Sayles. Par

Star of the North! though night winds drift. The Fugitive Slave's Apostrophe to the North Star. John Pierpont. AA

Star of the Sea. Alexander Barclay. *Fr.* The Ship of Fools. ACP

Star of the sea, surest point of brightness. Stella Maris. O. B. Hardison, Jr. CRP

Star over all. Christmas Tree. Laurence Smith. OBCP

Star Quilt. Roberta Hill. CDW; NoAM; NOVW

Star Song. Henrietta Cordelia Ray. CBWP-3

Star-Song; a Carol to the King; Sung at White-Hall, The. Robert Herrick. GN

Star Song of the Bushman Women. *Unknown, tr. fr. Bushman by* W. H. I. Bleek. PeSA

Star-Sown. Eli Netser, *tr. fr. Hebrew by* Bernhard Frank. MHeP

Star-spangled Banner, The. Francis Scott Key. AA; AiP; AnAmPo; BLPA; FaBoBe; FAFP; FaPON; FaPoR; OPP; PAH; TAP; WBLP

Star-Splitter, The. Robert Frost. ImOP

Star Struck. Sandra Inskeep-Fox. SoTCo

Star System, The. Richard Wilbur. NBLV

Star-Talk. Robert Graves. BoNaP; GoJo; MoBrPo; OxBTC

Star that bids the shepherd fold, The. Milton. *Fr.* Comus; a Masque Presented at Ludlow Castle. FaBoCh; OBEV
  (Comus' Invocation to His Readers.) TrGrPo
  (Comus Speaks.) NOBE
  (Invocation of Comus, The.) OBS, *longer sel.*
  (Mask, A.) FiP

Star that bringest home the bee. To the Evening Star. Thomas Campbell. GTBS; GTBS-P

Star Trek III. Richard Harteis. GLP

Star was talking with the withered leaves, A. Star and Dead Leaves. Tsuboi Shigeji, *tr. by* Geoffrey Bownas *and* Anthony Thwaite. PeBJV

Star Watcher, The. Peter Davison. TwCP

Starbirth. Albert Goldbarth. BWV

Starchart. Jan Kuijper, *tr. fr. Dutch by* Jacob Lowland. DuIn

Stare at the monster: remark. Famous Poet. Ted Hughes. LiTM; PoPo

Stare at the stars, the stars say. Look at me. Ego. Norman MacCaig. GTBS-P

Stared, astonied all. È, the Feasting Florentines. Daniel Hoffman. VGW

Stared Story, A. William Stafford. Son

Stare's Nest by My Window, The. W. B. Yeats. *Fr.* Meditations in Time of Civil War, VI. BIrV; GTBS-P; InPS; LiTB; NOBE
  ("Bees in the crevices, The.") FaBoPV

Starfish. Lorna Dee Cervantes. CCP

Starfish, The. Robert Peter Tristram Coffin. ImOP

Starfish. Winifred Welles. FaPON

Stargazer, The. *Unknown.* OxBChV

Staring at an Empty Space. Hans Faverey, *tr. fr. Dutch by* J. M. Coetzee. DuIn

Staring at the mud turtle's eye. Concepts and Their Bodies (The Boy in the Field Alone). Pattiann Rogers. MAYP; MT

Staring corpselike at the ceiling. Suicide. W. E. Henley. *Fr.* In Hospital, XXIV.

Stark naked. Tachibana Akemi, *tr. fr. Japanese by* Burton Watson. *Fr.* Thirty Tanka. FCEI

Starless and chill is the night. A Night by the Sea. Heine, *tr. fr. German by* Howard Mumford Jones. *Fr.* The North Sea. AWP

Starlight. John White Chadwick. AA

Starlight. Freda Downie. FaBoWP

Starlight. Philip Levine. CAPP

Starlight. William Meredith. NePoEA

Starlight Night, The. Gerard Manley Hopkins. ACP; BrPo; GTBS-P; InPS; LiTM; MoAB; MoBrPo; NAEL-2; PoE; PPP; SeCePo; WSC

Starlight Scope Myopia. Yusef Komunyakaa. MAYP

Starlight Thought. Henrietta Cordelia Ray. *Fr.* A Group of Musings. CBWP-3

Starling, The. Robert Buchanan. FM

Starling and a Willow-Wren, A. W. H. Auden. FaBoMo

Starling didn't loaf around, The. Marcabrun, *tr. by* Paul Blackburn. Pro

Starling Lake, The. "Seumas O'Sullivan." AWP

Starling, take wing and go. Marcabrun, *tr. by* Paul Blackburn. Pro

Starling thatch watches, and sudden swallow. October Thought. Seamus Heaney. FL

Starlings slander in the fall, The. Village Path. Ilse Aichinger, *tr. by* Beth Bjorklund. CoAuP

Starman, The. Diane Ackerman. BWV

Starre, The. Henry Vaughan. MePo

Starry frost descends, The. *Att. to* Suibne Geilt. NOIV

Starry Host, The. John Lancaster Spalding. *Fr.* God and the Soul. AA

Starry hosts whose far-flung cohorts gleam, The. Human Greatness. Edwin Barclay. PBA

Starry Night, The. Anne Sexton. NoAM; PoE

Starry Night, The. George Starbuck. NYBP

Starry Sky. *Unknown, tr. fr. Old Irish by* Sean O'Faolain. AnIL

Stars. Sara Boyes. DT

Stars. Emily Brontë. *See* Ah! Why, because the Dazzling Sun.

Stars. George Mackay Brown. OxBS

Stars, The. Mary Mapes Dodge. AA

Stars. Robert Hayden. LCAP

Stars ("Stood there then among."), *sel.* Robert Hayden. LCAP
  Sojourner Truth. CNA

Stars. Langston Hughes. GLP

Stars. Howard Moss. AnAn

Stars, The, *sel.* "Ping Hsin," *tr. fr. Chinese by* Kai-yu Hsu. WPOW
  Builder of Continents, The.

Stars, The, *sel.* Christopher Smart.
  "Stars of the superior class." ChTr

Stars. Gary Soto. TDD

Stars. Takenaka Iku, *tr. fr. Japanese by* Geoffrey Bownas *and* Anthony Thwaite. PeBJV

Stars. Sara Teasdale. FaPON

Stars. Hans Verhagen, *tr. fr. Dutch by* Peter Nijmeijer. DuIn

Stars above the peaks. Mizuhara Shuoshi, *tr. by* Geoffrey Bownas *and* Anthony Thwaite. PeBJV

Stars all fell out of the sky, The. Guy Fawkes '58. Fiona Kidman. PeNZ

Stars and atoms have no size. Measurement. A. M. Sullivan. RHPC

Stars and Planets. Norman MacCaig. OxBSP

Stars and Stripes. Mary Weston Fordham. CBWP-2

Stars and trouble, stars and trouble. Walk out. One Reason for Stars. Jack Butler. MT

Stars are circles of children. Everything Is Round. Gabriela Mistral, *tr. by* D. M. Pettinella. PBWP

Stars are dropping thick as stones into the twiggy. Stars over the Dordogne. Sylvia Plath. PoA

Stars are everywhere to-night, The. Daisies. Andrew Young. GoJo

Stars are forth, the moon above the tops, The. Byron. *Fr.* Manfred: A Dramatic Poem, III, iv. OAEL-2

Stars Are Glittering in the Frosty Sky, The. Charles Heavysege. CaP
  (Winter Galaxy.) NOBC; OBCV

Stars are gone out spark by spark, The. At Cockcrow. Lizette Woodworth Reese. TrPWD

Stars Are Lit, The. Hayyim Nahman Bialik, *tr. fr. Hebrew by* Florence L. Friedman. TrJP

Stars are old, that stood for me, The. Emily Dickinson. PeHV

Stars are only a backdrop for, The. Notes on a Life to Be Lived. Robert Penn Warren. NYBP

Stars are pale, The. Break of Day. John Shaw Neilson. PoAu-1

Stars are pinned against the sky, The. It Is the Stars That Govern Us. Michael Magee. PoA

Stars are shining/ the eyes of men are closed. Rabi'a al-Adawiyya, tr. by Margaret Smith. WPOW

Stars are thundering in the sky, The. Gond Oral Tradition, tr. by V. Elwin and S. Hivale. WTO

Stars Are Twinkling, The. Joseph Skipsey. PF

Stars Are with the Voyager, The. Thomas Hood. EnRP

Stars at night, The. Ode to Bohemians. Ron Padgett. UL

Stars at their zenith, more tranquil than you, The. The Stars on Shabbat. Avraham Shlonsky, tr. by Francis Landy. VWA

Stars Begin to Fall. Unknown. AA

Stars beyond the railing, a thin thread of moon. Sleepless at the Fifth Watch. Chao Yi, tr. by Shirleen S. Wong. WFTU

Stars catch my eyes, The. A Thought for My Love. Bruce Williamson. NeIP

Stars Climb Girders of Light. Bert Meyers. MAT

Stars Dance, The. Thomas Campion. Fr. The Lord's Mask[e]. OBSC

Stars Fade. Peretz Hirshbein, tr. fr. Yiddish by Joseph Leftwich. TrJP

Stars glowed red in leaf-still weather, The. A. A. Fet, tr. by Alan Myers. AAA

Stars Go over the Lonely Ocean, The. Robinson Jeffers. LiTA; LiTM; WaP

Stars had the look of dogs to him sometimes. The Star Watcher. Peter Davison. TwCP

Stars have given me a hard fate, The. Gaspara Stampa, tr. fr. Italian by Lynne Lawner. PBWP

Stars Have Not Dealt Me, The. A. E. Housman. OxBoLi ("Stars have not dealt me the worst they could do, The.") EBEV; GTBS-P

Stars have not yet retired, and the sky is still dark, The. Women Transport Corps. Unknown, tr. by Kai-yu Hsu. WPOW

Stars Heng and Chi never halt their courses, The. Fulling Cloth for Clothes. Hsieh Hui-lien, tr. by Burton Watson. CoBCP

Stars, I Have Seen Them Fall. A. E. Housman. ChTr; NoP; OxBSP

Stars in Apple Cores. Luci Shaw. TrCP

Stars in the great sky fall in confusion. Wakayama Bokusui, tr. fr. Japanese by Hiroaki Sato. Fr. Forty-four Tanka. FCEI

Stars in the sky are as big as coins. Turkish Love Songs. Unknown, tr. by Reza Baraheni and Zahra-Soltan Shokoohtaezeh. BoWoP

Stars in your face, The. In Missing. Ray A. Young Bear. CDW

Stars know a secret, The. Force. Edward Rowland Sill. AA; AnAmPo

Stars must make an awful noise, The. One Blackbird. Harold Monro. BoTP

Stars of night contain the glittering day, The. The Dying Words of Stonewall Jackson. Sidney Lanier. PAH

Stars of the summer night! Longfellow. Fr. The Spanish Student. AA; FaBoBe

Stars of the superior class. Christopher Smart. Fr. The Stars. ChTr

Stars on Shabbat, The. Avraham Shlonsky, tr. fr. Hebrew by Francis Landy. VWA

Stars over snow. Night. Sara Teasdale. FaPON

Stars over the Dordogne. Sylvia Plath. PoA

Stars rest cold by shoals of cloud. Li Ho, tr. fr. Chinese by Burton Watson. Fr. For the Examination at Ho-nan-fu: Songs of the Twelve Months. CoBCP

Stars rise on high as the moon crests. The Taoist Nun. Li Hsün, tr. by Lois Fusek. ATF

Stars Sang in God's Garden, The. Joseph Mary Plunkett. TIRV

Stars shine down, The. Rosh Pina. Dovid Knut, tr. by Daniel Weissbort. VWA

Stars slowly fade from view, The. Song of the Water Clock at Night. Niu Chiao, tr. by Lois Fusek. ATF

Stars Stand Up in the Air, The. Unknown, tr. fr. Irish by Thomas Macdonagh. BIrV

Stars threatened you into feeling. Terrestrial Magnetism. Alice Fulton. NAmP

Stars walk downhill. Concert. Robert Sward. VGW

Stars wheel in purple, yours is not so rare. Hilda Doolittle ("H. D."). Fr. Let Zeus Record. MoAmPo; NOBA; TAP

Stars Which See, Stars Which Do Not See. Marvin Bell. LCAP

Starscape, A. John Bellenden. ACP

Starscraping monuments of human pride. Philosophiae Consolationis. Paul Scarron, tr. by G. N. Gabbard. SoTCo

Starshine on the Arch is silver white, The. Villanelle of Washington Square. Walter Adolphe Roberts. PoNe

Starships. Jotie T'Hooft, tr. fr. Dutch by Scott Rollins. DuIn

Start, The. Unknown. SD

Start anywhere. "X." Barrett Watten. LP

Start here: something has exhaled this marble and moved. Monuments. John Hollander. KS

Start like pieces of string. Advice to the Orchestra. David Wagoner. NoAM

Start of summer, grass and trees grown tall. Reading The Classic of Hills and Seas. T'ao Ch'ien, tr. by Burton Watson. CoBCP

Start of winter. Kyotai, tr. fr. Japanese by Burton Watson. Fr. Sixteen Hokku. FCEI

Start to think of progress. Ambitious. Jim Gustafson. UL

Start with a simple room. Plucking Out a Rhythm. Lawson Fusao Inada. AmPA

Starting a Pasture. Walter McDonald. MT

Starting again. A Dark Country. Derek Mahon. BIrV

Starting at Dawn. Sun Yün-feng, tr. by Kenneth Rexroth and Ling Chung. PBWP

Starting Early from the Ch'u-ch'êng Inn. Po Chü-i, tr. fr. Chinese by Arthur Waley. OBVE

Starting from some point in a circle these. The Blocks. Clark Coolidge. IAT

Starting in the morning from the sea of Suzu. Yakamochi. Fr. Manyo Shu. Ma

Starting Out on a Journey in a Windstorm, sels. Wu Wen, tr. fr. Chinese by Irving Lo. WFTU
　"All day I fret over wind and sand." Fr. I.
　"Heart that yearns for fame never dies, A." Fr. II.

Starting out on my travels. Unknown. Fr. Manyo Shu. Ma

Starting Over. Shirley Kaufman. VWA

Starting, then stopping. Tamekane, tr. by Steven D. Carter. WFTW

Starting. Words which begin, A. Zoetropes. Bill Manhire. ATNZ; PeNZ

Startled/ By a single scream. Saigyo Hoshi, tr. by Arthur Waley. AWP

Startled awake, back from a dream. Ni Tsan, tr. fr. Chinese by Jonathan Chaves. Fr. Two Poems to the Tune "Jen-yüeh yüan." CoBLCP

Startled by the sound. Saigyo, tr. fr. Japanese by Burton Watson. Fr. Sixty-four Tanka. FCEI

Startled salamander freezes, The. Place of the Salamander. Yves Bonnefoy, tr. by Galway Kinnell. RHTwFP

Startled stag, the blue-grey night, A. The Dark Stag. Isabella Valancy Crawford. NOBC

Startled traveler wakes to the thunder by his pillow, The. Niagara Falls. Narushima Ryuhoku, tr. by Burton Watson. JLIC-2

Starvation and Blues. Edward Kamau Brathwaite. PBCV

Starvation Camp near Jaslo. Wislawa Szymborska, tr. fr. Polish by Jan Darowski. WPOW

Starved old gelding, blind and lamed, A. An Irish Marriage Night. Brian Merriman, tr. fr. Modern Irish by Frank O'Connor. Fr. The Midnight Court. BIrV

Starved, scarred, lenten, amidst ash of air. The Sugaring. A. M. Klein. OBCV

Starving, savage, I aspire. The Tiger of Desire. Tom MacInnes. OBCV

Starving to Death on a Government Claim. Unknown. AmFP; OBAL

Stasis in darkness. Ariel. Sylvia Plath. CMoP; HCAP; HeIP; LCAP; MoP; NAAL-2; NoAM; NOBA; NoP; PBWP; PoE

State, The. Randall Jarrell. LiTM

State, as if to stamp the final seal. Wordsworth. Fr. The Prelude [or, Growth of a Poet's Mind]: Residence in France. FaBoPV

State Funeral. Thomas McCarthy, tr. fr. Irish. CIP

State of Fever, A. Sa'di Yusuf, tr. fr. Arabic by Lena Jayyusi and Naomi Shihab Nye. MAP

State of Innocence, The, sels. Dryden. NOCV
　Death the Consequence of the Fall.
　Predestination and Free Will.

State of Nature, A. John Hollander. AiP

State Street is lonely today. Aunt Jane Allen. Fenton Johnson. IDB; PoBA; PoNe

State with the prettiest name, The. Florida. Elizabeth Bishop. TwCP

Stately Homes of England, The. Noel Coward. FaBoPa

Stately homes of England, The. The Homes of England. Felicia Dorothea Hemans. FaPoR; WPE

Stately Lady, The. Flora Sandstrom. BoTP

Stately rainbow came and stood, A. The Rainbow. Coventry Patmore. Fr. The Angel in the House, II, iii. GTBS-P

Stately Southerner, The. Unknown. See 'Tis of a gallant Yankee ship that flew the stripes and stars.

Stately state that wise men count their good, The. Barmenissa's Song. Robert Greene. FaBoRV

Stately Structure of This Earth, The. Martha Brewster. AH

Stately the feast, and high the cheer. The Grave of King Arthur. Thomas, the Younger Warton. EnRP
Stately Verse. *Unknown.* FaPON
Statement on Our Higher Education. W. M. Ransom. CDW
States. Tom Paulin. FaBCIP
States when they black out and lie there rolling, The. Falling. James Dickey. LCAP; MT; NoAM; NYBP
Statesman, The. Hilaire Belloc. NOBE
Statesman's Holiday, The. W. B. Yeats. CMoP; OxBTC
Statesmen bicker about the non-essential, The. Vital Statistics. William Rose Benét. AnAmPo
Static. Judith Kazantzis. DT
Static Autumn. Yvor Winters. PoA
Station Island, *sels.* Seamus Heaney.
"Black water. White waves. Furrows snowcapped." *Fr.* VII. NoAM
"I had come to the edge of the water." *Fr.* VII. FaBCIP
"Like a convalescent, I took the hand." *Fr.* XII. NAEL-2; NoAM; TOF
"My brain dried like spread turf, my stomach." *Fr.* IX. CIP
Station Master, The. Arun Kolatkar. UAS
Station nameplate creaks in the wind, The. Posting the Letter. John Welch. NPo
Stationmaster is garrulous in, The. Daphne Stillorgan. Denis Devlin. CIP
Stations. Ted Hughes. NoAM
Statistically. Limited Access. Mary Pierce Brosmer. ER
Statistics. Stephen Spender. MoBrPo
Statuary. John Ashbery. NoAM
Statue. Gerrit Achterberg, *tr. fr. Dutch by* Adrienne Rich. DuIn
Statue, The. Kenneth Allott. EAS
Statue, The. Hilaire Belloc. ACP
Statue, The. Robert Creeley. LCAP
Statue, The. Robert Finch. OBCV
Statue, The. John Fuller. NePoEA-2; NOBE
Statue, The. Alexandra Grilikhes. RR
Statue, The. Orkhan Muyassar, *tr. fr. Arabic by* Lena Jayyusi *and* Samuel Hazo. MAP
Statue, The. Edith Roseveare. Mes
Statue against a Clear Sky. Wallace Stevens. *Fr.* New England Verses. EyDe
Statue and Birds. Louise Bogan. EyDe; MoAB; MoAmPo
Statue and the Bust, The, *sel.* Robert Browning.
"There's a palace in Florence, the world knows well." Mes
Statue of a rich industrialist, The. In the City of Bogotá. Greg Pape. MAYP
Statue of Lautréamont, The. Lethal Relief. André Breton, *tr. by* Samuel Beckett. RHTwFP
Statue of Liberty, The. Thomas Hardy. LiTB
Statue of Lorenzo de' Medici, The. James Ernest Nesmith. AA
Statue of Medusa, The. William Drummond of Hawthornden. EyDe
Statue of Shadow, The. John Peale Bishop. LiTA
Statue stood of Newton, The. Newton. Wordsworth. *Fr.* The Prelude [or, Growth of a Poet's Mind]: Residence at Cambridge. ImOP
Statues, The. Laurence Binyon. OBEV
Statues. Agnes Nemes Nagy, *tr. fr. Hungarian by* Daniel Hoffman. MHup
Statues. Kathleen Jessie Raine. NYBP
Statues. Richard Wilbur. EyDe
Statues, The. W. B. Yeats. AnIL; NoAM; OAEL-2; WeW
Statues in the Public Gardens, The. Howard Nemerov. EyDe
Status Quo. Binga Dismond. PoNe
Status Symbol. Mari E. Evans. IDB
Stavrogin's Farewell. János Pilinszky, *tr. fr. Hungarian by* Jascha Kessler. *Fr.* Three Poems. FOC
Stavrogin's Return. János Pilinszky, *tr. fr. Hungarian by* Jascha Kessler. *Fr.* Three Poems. FOC
Stavro's dead. A truant vine. Lawrence Durrell. FaBoCo
Stay All Night, Stay a Little Longer. *Unknown.* AmFP
Stay Beautiful. Jeff Wright. UL
Stay beautiful/ but dont stay down underground too long. For Poets. Al Young. CNA; PoBA; RFM
Stay! Beneath your feet is a wonder of women. On a Woman. Robert Williams, *tr. by* H. Idris Bell. OBWVE
Stay here, fond youth, and ask no more, be wise. Against Fruition. Sir John Suckling. CaPo
"Stay here with us, you can have our name, be our son." Then. The Little Jesus of the Barren. László Nagy, *tr. by* Jascha Kessler. FOC
Stay me with Winesap. Song of Granny Smith. Mary McArthur. SoTCo
Stay near me—do not take thy flight! To a Butterfly. Wordsworth. EnRP; FM

Stay now with me, and listen to my sighs. Dante, *tr. fr. Italian by* Dante Gabriel Rossetti. *Fr.* Vita Nuova, La, XX. AWP
Stay, O sweet, and do not rise! Break of Day. *Unknown, at. to* John Donne. EIL; TrGrPo
(Aubade.) BoLoP; NOBE
(Daybreak.) OBEV
Stay Phoebus, stay. Edmund Waller. SeCP
Stay, shade of my shy treasure! Oh, remain. Sister Juana Inés de la Cruz, *tr. by* Alice Stone Blackwell. WPOW
Stay, ship from Thames, with fettered sails. Ship from Thames. Rex Ingamells. PoAu-2
Stay silent/ keep away from sharks. Anticipation of Sharks. Diane Wakoski. MAT
Stay, speedy time; behold, before thou pass. Michael Drayton. *Fr.* Idea, XVII (*also given as* VII *in* Idea's Mirrour). OBSC
Stay, Spring. Andrew Young. FaBoTw
Stay, stay at home, my heart, and rest. Home Song. Longfellow. GN
Stay, stay, dragonfly! Emperor Go-Shirakawa, *tr. fr. Japanese by* Hiroaki Sato. *Fr.* Ryojin Hisho. FCEI
Stay, Thames, to heare my Song, thou great and famous Flood. Michael Drayton. *Fr.* The Third Eclogue. PoEL-2
Stay, Time. James Wreford Watson. CaP
Stay weary traveler, stay! The Fountain at the Tomb. Nicias, *tr. by* Charles Merivale. AWP
Stay yet, pale flower, though coming storms will tear thee. On a Rose in December. Ebenezer Elliott. FaBoEE
Stay your rude steps, or e'er your feet invade. John Hookham Frere. *Fr.* The Loves of the Triangles. FaBoNo
Stayed late in town, sped home in my boat. On the Fifteenth Day of the Seventh Month I Came Home Late from the City. Shen Chou, *tr. by* Jonathan Chaves. CoBLCP
Staying Alive. David Wagoner. BoNaP; CoAP; InPK; NYBP; RFM; SM; WeW
Staying at Horai Temple. Basho, *tr. fr. Japanese by* Burton Watson. *Fr.* Seventy-six Hokku. FCEI
Staying here at home. *The father of* Kusakabe Omininaka. *Fr.* Manyo Shu. PeBJV
Staying here, we turn inflexible. Setting Out. W. D. Snodgrass. DiL
Staying in a Mountain Pavilion on a Summer Night. Ma Chih-yüan, *tr. fr. Chinese by* Jonathan Chaves. *Fr.* Two Poems to the Tune "Po pu tuan." CoBLCP
Staying in the Mountains in Summer. Yü Hsüan-chi, *tr. fr. Chinese by* Geoffrey Waters. BoWoP
Staying Overnight at Akashi. Basho, *tr. fr. Japanese by* Burton Watson. *Fr.* Seventy-six Hokku. FCEI
Staying Overnight at Blue Cloud Temple. Mo Shih-lung, *tr. fr. Chinese by* Jonathan Chaves. CoBLCP
Staying Overnight at Spirit-Source Temple. Wen Cheng-ming, *tr. fr. Chinese by* Jonathan Chaves. CoBLCP
Staying Overnight at T'ien-ning Ch'an Temple. Chang Yü, *tr. fr. Chinese by* Jonathan Chaves. CoBLCP
Staying Overnight on the Banks of Embroidered River. Li K'ai-hsien, *tr. fr. Chinese by* Jonathan Chaves. CoBLCP
Stays shut. My Mouth. Arnold Adoff. RHPC
Steadfast a lamp burns sheltered from the wind. *Unknown, tr. fr. Sanskrit by* Sir Edwin Arnold. *Fr.* The Bhagavad-Gita. TOF
Steadfastness. Sir Thomas Wyatt. *See* Forget Not Yet.
Steady heart, which in its steadiness, The. Angina Pectoris. W. R. Moses. LiTA
Steady time of being unknown, The. Consider a Move. Michael Ryan. MAYP; SM
Steak tartare and sushi are fun. Raw Cowardice. Bern Sharfman. SoTCo
Steal Away to Jesus. *Unknown.* BPo
(Steal Away.) TrGrPo
Steal into the Prayerbook. Jacob Glatstein, *tr. fr. Yiddish by* Benjamin *and* Barbara Harshav. *Fr.* Variations on a Theme. AYP
Steal not this book for fear of shame. *Unknown.* FaBoUs
Stealing. Ono Tozaburo, *tr. fr. Japanese by* Hiroaki Sato. FCEI
Stealing along in this eyelighter city. Rome Once Alone. Clark Coolidge. UL
Stealing Trout. Ted Hughes. NYBP
Stealing white from the withered moon. Halloween. Myra Cohn Livingston. OFD
Steam at Sheffield. Ebenezer Elliott. PF
Steam Engine; or, The Power of the Flame, The, *sels.* Thomas Baker.
Electric Telegraph, The. FaBoUs
"I dream'd I walk'd in raptures high." BXAP
Means of Propulsion for Steam-Ships. FaBoUs
Watt's Improvements to the Steam Engine. FaBoUs
Steam in Sacrifice. Robert Herrick. CaPo

Steam King, The. Edward P. Mead. PF
Steam Power. Erasmus Darwin. *Fr.* The Botanic Garden: The Economy of Vegetation. NOEC
Steam Shovel. Charles Malam. NTCP; PYC; RHPC
Steam Threshing-Machine, The. Charles Tennyson Turner. OBNC
Steamboats, Viaducts, and Railways. Wordsworth. NAEL-2
Steaming hunk of meat, A. Hero's Portion. John Montague. NOIV
Steddefast [*or* Steadfast] cross[e], inmong [*or* among] alle [*or* all] other. Holy Cross. *Unknown.* ACP
  (A Hymm to the Cross.) MeEL
Stedes ther stumbelyd in that stownde. *Unknown.* OxBLMV
Steed, a steed of matchlessespeed, A! The Cavalier's Song. William Motherwell. GN
Steed bit his master, The. On a Clergyman's Horse Biting Him. *Unknown.* FaBoCo; FaBoEE; NBLV; OxBoLi
Steed of life is galloping fast, The. Asadullah Khan Ghalib, *tr. by* Ahmed Ali. GoT
Steeds the prince of Minu keeps, The. *Unknown. Fr.* Manyo Shu. Ma
Steekit, consecrat, fou o fire but fuel. Douglas Young, *after the French of* Paul Valéry. *Fr.* The Kirkyaird by the Sea. OBVE
Steel anchors with thick ropes lie on stone floors. In the Port. Berish Weinstein, *tr. by* Leonard Wolf. PeBMYV
Steel doors—guillotine gates. The Prisoners. Robert Hayden. CAPP
Steel fibrous slant & ribboned glint, The. The Turncoat. Amiri Baraka. NeAP; PoE
Steel voice of a steel god. Pans at Carnival. Henry Beissel. PVCV
Steel worker on the girder, The. The Building of the Skyscraper. George Oppen. GOA
Steele Glas, The. George Gascoigne. AAS
Steely train in the stupid green, The. Train: Abstraction. Genevieve Taggard. WPE
Steep mountain-road of Ashigara, The. Shidoribe Karamaro. *Fr.* Manyo Shu. Ma
Steep valley overhung by trees, A. Plea for Peace. Frank Prewett. HATNAP
Steeped in ecstasies of perfume. Spring Nocturne. Abraham Liessin. TrJP
Steepies for the bairnie. Supper. William Soutar. OxBS
Steeple-Jack, The. Marianne Moore. *Fr.* Part of a Novel, Part of a Poem, Part of a Play. BoWoP; CMoP; FaBoMo; FaBoWP; HAP; InPS; NoAM; NOBA; NoP; OxBA; PBWP; WeW; WPE
Steer, Bold Mariner, On! Schiller, *tr. fr. German.* PAH
Steer hither, steer your wingéd pines. The Sirens' Song. William Browne. *Fr.* The Inner Temple Masque. NOBE; OBEV
  (Song of the Sirens.) ElL
  (Song of the Syrens.) ChTr; OBS
  (Syrens' Song, The.) GBL
Steer on, courageous sailor! Columbus. Schiller, *tr. by* Erika Gathmann Koessler. OFD
Stele. Robert Marteau, *tr. fr. French by* Anne Winters. RHTwFP
Stella. Charles Henry Crandall. AA
Stella at Wood-Park. Swift. BIrV
Stella Maris. O. B. Hardison, Jr. CRP
"Stella oft sees the very face of woe." Sir Philip Sidney. *Fr.* Astrophel and Stella, XLV. InPS; NAEL-1; PoE
"Stella! since thou so right a princess art." Sir Philip Sidney. *Fr.* Astrophel and Stella, CVII. NoP
"Stella, the only planet of my light." Sir Philip Sidney. *Fr.* Astrophel and Stella, LXVIII. OBSC
"Stella, think not that I by verse seek fame." Sir Philip Sidney. *Fr.* Astrophel and Stella, XC. OBSC
Stella this day is thirty-four. Stella's Birth-day, 1718/19. Swift. EnLoPo; NAs
  (On Stella's Birthday (1719).) InPK; NIP; NOIV; OAEL-1
"Stella, while now by honour's [*or* honor's] cruel might." Sir Philip Sidney. *Fr.* Astrophel and Stella, XCI. NAEL-1; PoE
Stella's Birthday; March 13, 1726/27. Swift. NAs; NoP; OAEL-1; PoE; PoEL-3
Stella's Birth-day, 1718/19. Swift. EnLoPo; NAs
  (On Stella's Birthday (1719).) InPK; NIP; NOIV; OAEL-1
Stella's Birthday, 1725. Swift. NOEC
Stella's Birthday, 1721 ("All travelers at first incline"). Swift. NAEL-1; PoEL-3
Stellenbosch. Sir Alfred Kipling. OBTV
Stem heaped up, heaped, heaped up. Spell for Making the First Man. *Unknown, tr. by* Margaret Orbell. PeNZ
Stenographers, The. Patricia K. Page. CaP; HeIP; LiTM; NoAM; NoP; OBCV
Step aside, you ornery tenderfeet. I'm an Old Cowhand. Johnny Mercer. OBAL

Step Away from Them, A. Frank O'Hara. HCAP; InPS; NAAL-2; VGW
Step by Step. Cees Buddingh', *tr. fr. Dutch by* James S. Holmes. DuIn
Step in, young man, I know your face. The Gaol Song. *Unknown.* GBP
Step into my room tonight. People Trying to Love. Stephen Berg. NaP
Step on His Head. James Laughlin. VGW
"Step on it," said Aunt Alice, "for God's sake." The Ascension: 1925. John Malcolm Brinnin. InPK
Step on the path, A. Ireland Lake. Robert Hershon. NeAC
Step to the garden from the cool-roomed house. Weekend Stroll. Frances Cornford. BoNaP
Stepfathers. David Donnell. NOBC
"Stephen Smith, University of Iowa sophomore, burned what he said was his draft card." Of Late. George Starbuck. VGW
Stephen's Vampire Poem. James Joyce. *Fr.* Ulysses. VVA
Stepney Green. John Singer. WaP
Steppe in the Nazas Country, A. Manuel José Othón, *tr. fr. Spanish by* Samuel Beckett. MexPo
Stepping about on the beach of Koyorogi. Koyorogi. *Unknown, tr. by* Hiroaki Sato. FCEI
Stepping gingerly. Cat in the Snow. Aileen Fisher. NTCP
Stepping on a tendril. Hara Sekitei, *tr. by* Geoffrey Bownas *and* Anthony Thwaite. PeBJV
Stepping on violets. Kito, *tr. fr. Japanese by* Hiroaki Sato. *Fr.* Twenty-four Hokku. FCEI
Stepping Outside. Tess Gallagher. AmPA
Stepping-stone. Ruth Kim Chun-soo, *tr. fr. Korean by* Koh Chang-soo. ACKP
Stepping through the sleet. Tachibana Akemi, *tr. fr. Japanese by* Burton Watson. *Fr.* Thirty Tanka. FCEI
Stepping Westward. Denise Levertov. CAPP; NMM; VGW
Stepping Westward. Wordsworth. CH; EnRP; PoEL-4
Steps. Roberta Hill. VoR
Steps. Frank O'Hara. CAPP
Steps are saucered in the trodden parts, The. The Old Provincial Council Buildings, Christchurch. Allen Curnow. ATNZ
Steps out/ from a lily. Woman. Carl Rakosi. TAP
Steps step into light, The. Draining the Ornamental Lake. Simon Rae. NPo
Stereo. Don L. Lee. AmNP
Sterile these stones. The Corner Stone. Walter de la Mare. BrPo
Sterility in Metamorphosis. Adriano Spatola, *tr. fr. Italian by* Lawrence R. Smith. NItP
Sterkfontein. Ruth Miller. PeSA
Stern be the pilot in the dreadful hour. To Abraham Lincoln. John James Piatt. AA
Stern daughter of the voice of God! Ode to Duty. Wordsworth. AWP; EnRP; FPL; GTBS; GTBS-P; NAEL-2; NoP; OAEL-2; OBEV; WGRP
Stern eagle of the far north-west. The Song of the Reim-Kennar. Sir Walter Scott. *Fr.* The Pirate, *ch.* 6. OAEL-2; OBNC
Stern Master Munchem, rod in hand, stole out of school one day. The School-Master and the Truants. "John Brownjohn." OBCA
Stern parent, The. Harry Graham. *Fr.* Some Ruthless Rhymes, I. ChTr
Stethoscope tells what everyone fears, The. Academic. Theodore Roethke. FaBoEE; OBAL
Stevedore. Leslie Morgan Collins. AmNP
Steveston, *sel.* Daphne Marlatt.
  Imagine: A Town. NOBC
Sticheron for Matins, Wednesday of Holy Week. Mary Magdalene Kassia, *tr. fr. Greek by* Patrick Diehl. WPOW
Stick around now and I'll tell ya one more. "Bueno," Which in Spanish Means Good. Nyle A. Henderson. CowP
Stick in the Forest, The. William Stafford. CAPP
Stick the finger inside. Black Mail. Alice Walker. AmPA
Stick to It. Edgar A. Guest. FaFP
Stick was almost a staff, The. Hebrew Letters in the Trees. J. Rutherford Willems. VWA
Stick your patent name on a signboard. The River. Hart Crane. *Fr.* The Bridge: Powhatan's Daughter. AmPP; CMoP; GOA; MoAB; MoAmPo; NOBA; OxBA; PrIm
  ("Down, down—born pioneers in time's despite.") TrGrPo
Stickball. Virginia Schonborg. RHPC
Sticking out my head from. Kato Shuson, *tr. by* Geoffrey Bownas *and* Anthony Thwaite. PeBJV
Sticks-in-a-drowse droop over sugary loam. Cuttings. Theodore Roethke. HCAP; LCAP; MoP; NAAL-2; NoAM; NOBA; TAP; UnPo
Sticky Fingers. Robert Grenier. IAT
Sticky inside their winter suits. Thaw. Margaret Avison. FaBoWP; NOBC

Stiff in a white coat. A Child's Visit to the Biology Lab. Kathleen Spivack. AmPA

Stiff spokes of this wheel, The. July in Washington. Robert Lowell. LCAP; NAAL-2; NaP; Prf

Stiff standing on the bed. *Unknown.* GBL

Stiff wind off the channel, A. Wet Thursday. Weldon Kees. NaP; NYBP

Stigmata. Patrick Lane. NOBC

Stigmata. Charles Warren Stoddard. TrPWD

Stiles. John Pudney. NYBP

Still. Lucille Clifton. InPS

Still. Tony Harrison. OBD

Still. Aila Meriluoto, *tr. fr. Finnish by* Jaakko A. Ahokas. PBWP

Still. Lisa Zeidner. SM

Still,/ I would leap too. Small Frogs Killed on the Highway. James Wright. HCAP; NNaP; Prf

Still/ it was nice. Still. Lucille Clifton. InPS

Still a bare, silent, solitary glen. Thalaba and the Banquet. Robert Southey. *Fr.* Thalaba the Destroyer. SeCePo

Still a bit dazed. Saul, Afterward, Riding East. John Malcolm Brinnin. Prf

Still, after all, the kelp remain. At the Western Shore. Sarah Youngblood. IHMS

"Still alive" the message ran. The Emergency Maker. David Wagoner. NePoEA-2

Still am I haunting. Come Down. George Macdonald. TrPWD

Still and All. Burns Singer. NePoEA-2; OxBS

Still and blanched and cold and lone. The Mountains. Walter de la Mare. BrPo

Still and dark along the sea. Twilight on Sumter. Richard Henry Stoddard. PAH

Still are there wonders of the dark and day. To Keep the Memory of Charlotte Forten Grimké. Angelina Weld Grimké. BlSi

Still as I move thou movest. Her Shadow. Elisabeth Cavazza Pullen. AA

Still asleep his body wakes from sleep. Day. Khairi Mansour, *tr. by* Lena Jayyusi *and* Charles Doria. MAP

Still baking down. Basho, *tr. by* Geoffrey Bownas *and* Anthony Thwaite. PeBJV

Still-born silence, thou that art. Invocation of Silence. Richard Flecknoe. OxBSP

Still Century. Tom Paulin. FaBCIP

Still, Citizen Sparrow. Richard Wilbur. AmPP; CMoP; HoPM; LiTM; MoAB; MoP; NoAM

Still, Dear, it is incredible to me. Her Second Husband Hears Her Story. Thomas Hardy. OBD

"Still Do I Keep My Look, My Identity." Gwendolyn Brooks. PoA

Still do the stars impart their light. Falsehood. William Cartwright. OBEV

Still drifting together. The Unpossessed. Adèle Naudé. PeSA

Still explosions on the rocks, The. The Shampoo. Elizabeth Bishop. FaBoWP; OxBC

Still Falls the Rain. Edith Sitwell. BoWoP; CN; LiTM; MoAB; MoBrPo; MoP; NAEL-2; NoAM; NOBE; OBWP; SeCePo; TEP; TrGrPo; TwCP; WaaP

Still fettered, still unconquered, still in pain. Prometheus Unbound. A. D. Hope. OxBC

Still for the world he lives, and lives in bliss. Written on the Anniversary of Our Father's Death. Hartley Coleridge. Son

Still green on the limbs o' the woak wer the leaves. Which Road? William Barnes. NOBVV

Still Growing. *Unknown. See* Trees They Do Grow High, The.

Still hanging back. Snow on the Mountain at Dusk. Shotetsu, *tr. by* Steven D. Carter. WFTW

Still He Sings. Allan Taylor. OBET

Still-Heart. Frank Pearce Sturm. OBMV

Still Here. Langston Hughes. BPo

Still Hunting. Don Welch. TSL

Still I complain; I am complaining still. Edward Taylor. *Fr.* Preparatory Meditations before My Approach to the Lord's Supper, XL. OxBA; PoEL-3

Still I do think he's losing. That the Sun Will Rise Tomorrow. Riekus Waskowsky, *tr. by the author.* DuIn

Still I Rise. Maya Angelou. BlSi

Still in an amorphous world she moves. The Idiot. Adèle Naudé. PeSA

Still in October, the woodcock. On the Mountain. Ruth Stone. BoWoP

Still in one body, locked and barred? Prisons. Lörinc Szabó, *tr. by* Edwin Morgan. MHuP

Still in sleeping bags, the promised delivery. Bats. Dave Smith. NoAM

Still, in some hidden towns of our Dispersion. The Talmud Student. Hayyim Nahman Bialik, *tr. by* Helena Frank. TrJP

Still in the countryside among the lowly. Graveyard in Norfolk. Sylvia Townsend Warner. OBD

Still, it is dear defiance now to carry. Flags. Gwendolyn Brooks. AmNP

Still it is raining lightly. A Love Medicine. Louise Erdrich. HATNAP

Still let me pierce into the midnight depth. James Thomson. *Fr.* The Seasons: Summer. EnRP

Still, let my tyrants know, I am not doomed to wear. Emily Brontë. *Fr.* The Prisoner. ChER; NOBE; NoP; OBEV; OBNC

Still let us go the way of beauty; go. A Prayer for the Old Courage. Charles Hanson Towne. TrPWD

Still Life. Mike Angelotti. MOWH

Still Life. Rose Ausländer, *tr. fr. German by* Beth Bjorklund. CoAuP

Still Life. Roy Blount, Jr. SoTCo

Still-Life. Elizabeth Daryush. FaBoWP; QFR; WPE

Still Life. Walter de la Mare. EyDe

Still Life. William Hathaway. NAmP

Still Life. Anthony Hecht. AnAn

Still-Life. Ted Hughes. NYBP

Still Life. Yoshioka Minoru, *tr. fr. Japanese by* Hiroaki Sato. FCEI

Still-Life. Ronald Perry. NePoEA-2

Still Life, *sel.* Anne Ridler.

"Night passed and the fog froze." PoPo

Still Life. Francis Sullivan. CRP

Still Life. C. K. Williams. NAmP

Still Life. Reed Whittemore. CoAP

Still Life: Lady with Birds. Quandra Prettyman. PoBA

Still night. The old clock ticks. Last Night in Calcutta. Allen Ginsberg. NoAM

Still Night Thoughts. Li Po, *tr. fr. Chinese by* Burton Watson. CoBCP; TTTS

Still on my cheeks I feel their fondling breath. Stanzas on Mutability. Hugo von Hofmannsthal, *tr. by* Jethro Bithell. AWP; TrJP

Still on the spot Lord Marmion stay'd. Edinburgh from the Pentland Hills. Sir Walter Scott. *Fr.* Marmion, IV. FaBoPP

Still, passed through the spokes of an old wheel. Reincarnation (I). James Dickey. HoPM

Still playing... In the Cabinet. Shlomo Vinner, *tr. by* Laya Firestone *and* Howard Schwartz. VWA

Still Poem 9. Philip Lamantia. NeAP

Still Pond, No More Moving. Howard Moss. NYBP

Still Pool, The. Kathleen Raine. MoAB

Still pressing through these weeping solitudes. Frederick Goddard Tuckerman. *Fr.* Sonnets, II, xi. NOBA

Still round thy towers descend the fertile rain! Cordova. Ibn Zaydun, *tr. by* H. A. R. Gibb. AWP

Still salt pool locked in with bars of sand, A. Lincolnshire Shores ("A still salt pool locked in with bars of sand"). Tennyson. *Fr.* The Palace of Art. FaBoPP

Still shall the tyrant scourge of Gaul. Ode to the Inhabitants of Pennsylvania. Longfellow. PAH

Still Shines When You Think of It. Vincent O'Sullivan. PeNZ

Still sits the school-house by the road. In School-Days. Whittier. AA; AnAmPo; BLPA; FaBoBe; FaPON; FPL; OBCA; OxBChV

Still Small Voice, The. A. M. Klein. OBCV

Still south I went and west and south again. J. M. Synge. AWP; BoNaP; ChTr; FaBoPP; MoBrPo; OBMV

Still sparkles here the glory of the west. M. J. Chapman. *Fr.* Barbadoes. PBCV

Still, still my eye will gaze long fixed on thee. The Columbine. Jones Very. NOBA

Still, still, stillness. Loneliness. Felice Holman. ILY

Still, Still, with Thee. Harriet Beecher Stowe. AH, *with music;* BLRP (When I Awake I Am Still with Thee.) TrPWD

Still tell me no, my God, and tell me no. Though He Slay Me. Vassar Miller. NePoEA-2

Still the ghost of Joseph Alston. Theodosia Burr. Myra Burnham Terrell. GoYe

Still the mighty mountains stand. Epilogue to Alun Mabon. John Ceiriog Hughes, *tr. by* H. Idris Bell. OBWVE

Still the Mind Smiles. Robinson Jeffers. CMoP

Still things moving. Earthquake. Kokan Shiren, *tr. by* Burton Watson. FCEI; JLIC-2

Still thirteen years: 'tis autumn now. Palinode. James Russell Lowell. AA

Still this, still that I would! all I surmise. William Lithgow. OBTV

Still Though the One I Sing. Walt Whitman. AA

Still to Be Neat [Still to Be Drest (*or* Dressed)]. Ben Jonson, *tr. fr. the Latin of* Jean Bonnefons. *Fr.* Epicoene; or, The Silent Woman, I, i. EIL; FF; GBL; HAP; HeIP; JCP; NoP; OxBSP; PrIm; SeCePo; TEP; WeW

   (Clerimont's Song.) InPS; OAEL-1; PoE; PPP; SeCP; SeCV-1; TrGrPo

   (Simplex Munditiis.) AWP; HoPM; NOBE; OBEV

   (Song: "Still to be neat, still to be dressed [*or* drest].") OBS

Still to one end they both so justly drew. David and Jonathan. Abraham Cowley. *Fr.* Davideis, II. PeHV

Still unable to pronounce the months. Ice Cream. Peter Wild. Psk

Still Voice of Harlem, The. Conrad Kent Rivers. CNA; IDB; PoBA

Still was the night, serene and bright. The Day of Doom. Michael Wigglesworth. SCAP

Still, when evening comes in October. The English Cemetery. Franco Fortini, *tr. by* Lawrence R. Smith. NItP

Still Your Footprint Delicate as an Animal's. Giancarlo Marmori, *tr. fr. Italian by* Lawrence R. Smith. NItP

Still your people and mine were tearing each other to pieces when we. Letter to the Actor Charles Laughton concerning the Work on the Play "The Life of Galileo." Bertolt Brecht, *tr. by* Michael Hamburger. AnAn

Stillborn (Domesticity # three), The. Bill Knott. PPR

Stilled is the quarrel over his bones. At Dante's Grave. Ezra Zussman, *tr. by* D. Shnayorson. VWA

Stillness. James Elroy Flecker. BrPo; CH; GoJo; MoBrPo

Stillness, The/ of the wood. The Figures. Robert Creeley. UnPo

Stillness and moonlight, with. Loneliness. Hayden Carruth. SM

Stillness and splendour of the night. Canticle. James McAuley. PoAu-2

Stillness of the Austral noon, The. The Bell-Bird. "Fiona MacLeod." *Fr.* Australian Transcripts. FM

Stillness of the jungle, The. The Stillness of the Poem. Ron Loewinsohn. NeAP; PoM

Stillness of the rose, The. The Rose. William Carlos Williams. NOBA

Stillness whispers from afar. Summer Night. Nathan Alterman, *tr. by* Bernhard Frank. MHeP

Stimulus beyond the Grave, The. Emily Dickinson. OxBSP

Sting of Death, The. Frederick George Scott. OBCV

Stingier your suppers, The. Karl Marx. Al Lee. AmPA

Stinging/ gold swarms. Sunset. E. E. Cummings. MoAmPo

Stingo! to thy bar-room skip. Anacreontic to Flip. Royall Tyler. OBAL

Stings. Sylvia Plath. AnAn; NaP

Stink stink stink. Louis XVI Goes to the Guillotine. Benjamin Péret, *tr. by* Charles Simic. POS; RHTwFP

Stinking drunk from morning to night, a thousand times over now. A Note to My Friends, While Slightly Ill. Huang Ching-jen, *tr. by* Daniel Bryant. WFTU

Stir not the sand too much, for there lies Stuyvesant. Epitaph for Peter Stuyvesant. Henricus Selyns. SCAP

Stir not, whisper not. The River. Patrick MacDonogh. NeIP

Stir the Wallaby Stew. *Unknown.* FaBoBa

Stirling's Hotel. *Unknown.* AmFP

Stirring as among, A/ cattle. Snow. David Malouf. CBAP

Stirring of a feathering cloud, The. Nature's Minor Chords. Henrietta Cordelia Ray. CBWP-3

Stirring suddenly from long hibernation. Mid-Winter Waking. Robert Graves. MoAB

Stirrings in his chest, The. The Man Who Would Be a Mother. Herbert Scott. NAmP

Stirrings of love alone were here, The. Silent Song. Ory Bernstein, *tr. by* Bernhard Frank. MHeP

Stirrup Cup, The. Douglas Ainslie. GoTS

Stirrup-Cup, The. John Hay. AA

Stirrup-Cup, The. Sidney Lanier. AA; AmPP; AnAmPo

"Stirrups, leggings, a stainless." Love Medley: Patrice Cuchulain. Michael S. S. Harper. GeTw

Stirs its ashes and embers, its burnt sticks. Old Age Gets Up. Ted Hughes. NoAM

Stitch in the side. Want of Ᵽ Want of ♁. Anne Szumigalski. FaBoWP

Stitching in Time: Dorothy Ruddick. Richard Howard. KS

Stock Exchange Wisdom. *Unknown.* FaBoUs

Stockdove, The. Ruth Pitter. SeCePo

Stockholm. Eddy van Vliet, *tr. fr. Dutch by* Theo Hermans. DuIn

Stocking and Shirt. *Unknown.* OnUR

Stocking Fairy. Winifred Welles. FaPON

Stocking Song on Christmas Eve. Mary Mapes Dodge. OHIP

Stocky, cocky little man, A. Instamatic. Edwin Morgan. FF

Stocky woman at the door, The. The Last Day and the First. Theodore Weiss. TwCP; VGW

Stockyard, The. J. C. Squire. OxBTC

Stoic. Lawrence Durrell. NYBP

Stoic; for Laura von Courten, The. Edgar Bowers. CoAP; MT; NePoEA; QFR

Stoklewath; or, The Cumbrian Village, *sel.* Susanna Blamire. "From where dark clouds of curling smoke arise." NOEC

Stolen Child, The. W. B. Yeats. CMoP; NAEL-2; NoP; WSC

Stolen Fifer, The. Padraic Fiacc. NeIP

Stolen kisses, wary eyes. Strato, *tr. by* Sydney Oswald. PeHV

Stolen Pleasure. William Drummond of Hawthornden. EnLoPo

Stomach. Kathleen Norris. OBAL

Stomach: lonely. Through Walls. Rae Armantrout. LP

Stomach of goat, crushed. Salami. Philip Levine. NNaP; NOBA; TAP

"Stond well, moder, under Rode." The Mother and Her Son on the Cross. *Unknown.* MeEL

Stond [*or* Stand] who so list upon the slipper toppe. Seneca, *tr. fr. Latin by* Sir Thomas Wyatt. *Fr.* Thyestes, II. AAS; NoP; OBVE; PoEL-1; SiPS

   ("Climb at court for me that will.") OBVE, *tr. by* Andrew Marvell.

   ("Let him that will, ascend the tottering seat.") OBVE, *tr. by* Sir Matthew Hale.

   ("Let who so lyst with might mace to raygne.") OBVE, *tr. by* Jasper Heywood.

   (Senec. Traged. ex Thyeste Chor. 2.) SeCV-1, *tr. by* Andrew Marvell.

   ("Upon the slippery tops of humane state.") OBVE, *tr. by* Abraham Cowley.

Stone. Aharon Amir, *tr. fr. Hebrew by* Bernhard Frank. MHeP

Stone, The. Paul Blackburn. NYBP

Stone, The. W. W. Gibson. MoBrPo

Stone. Donald Justice. TDD

Stone. Kusano Shimpei, *tr. fr. Japanese by* Geoffrey Bownas *and* Anthony Thwaite. PeBJV

Stone. Charles Simic. InPS; NU

Stone, The. Thomas Vaughan. OBS; OBWVE

Stone, A. Richard Wilbur. *Fr.* Two Voices in a Meadow. CRP

Stone./ The stone in the air, which I followed, The. Flower. Paul Celan, *tr. by* Michael Hamburger.

Stone/ cold/ daylight. Poem for Etheridge. Sonia Sanchez. BPo

Stone, The/ would like to be. Evolution. May Swenson. TrGrPo *tr. by* Beth Bjorklund. CoAuP

Stone Age. Pat Nolan. UL

Stone and Rock. Webster Ross. Naomi Mitchison. PoSH

Stone and the Blade of Grass in the Warsaw Ghetto, The. David Scheinert, *tr. fr. French by* Edouard Roditi. VWA

Stone Angel. Anne Ridler. EaLo

Stone bounces off the water, The. Wetness. Paul Eluard, *tr. by* Michael Benedikt. POS

Stone Bridge, The, *sel.* Shen Chou, *tr. fr. Chinese by* Jonathan Chaves. "South of the Bridge." CoBLCP

Stone, bronze, stone, steel, stone, oakleaves, horses' heels. Triumphal March. T. S. Eliot. *Fr.* Coriolan. OBWP; WaaP

Stone Canyon Nocturne. Charles Wright. HCAP; LCAP

Stone Castle Music. *Unknown, tr. fr. Chinese by* Burton Watson. CoBCP

Stone cliffs, no clouds. Early Summer in the Year *Jen-tzu*. Yün Shou-p'ing, *tr. by* Jonathan Chaves. CoBLCP

Stone cries from the wall, The. *Unknown.* TrJP

Stone-cutters fighting time with marble, you foredefeated. To the Stone-Cutters. Robinson Jeffers. AmPP; MoAB; MoAmPo; NAAL-2; NOBA; NoP; OxBAP; PoRA; PrIm; TrGrPo

Stone Diary, A. Pat Lowther. NOBC

Stone Face is the likeness of all lovers. Buster Keaton & the Cops. George Keithley. NPGG

Stone-flake and salmon. Gary Snyder. *Fr.* Myths and Texts: Burning, XV. NaP

Stone found me in bright sunlight, The. The Stone. Paul Blackburn. NYBP

Stone from the Gods. Irma Wassall. GoYe

Stone from which I carved you. A Speck of Sand. Paul Celan, *tr. by* Joachim Neugroschel. VWA

Stone Gentleman, The. James Reeves. OxBSP

Stone Giant. Joseph Bruchac. CDW

Stone God, The. Aila Meriluoto, *tr. fr. Finnish by* Aili Jarvenpa. SOP

Stone goes straight, The. Washington Monument by Night. Carl Sandburg. CMoP; FaPON; OFD; OHIP

Stone Hammer Poem. Robert Kroetsch. NOBC

Stone-Hitter, The. Medbh McGuckian. DT

Stone Horse Shoals. Malcolm Cowley. NYBP

Stone Man Peak. Chao Meng-fu, *tr. fr. Chinese* by Jonathan Chaves. *Fr.* Twenty-Eight Poems Inscribed on T'ien-kuan Mountai. CoBLCP

Stone mortar rushes through the air, The. Yooku, *tr.* by Lucien Stryk *and* Takashi Ikemoto. ZPCJ

Stone on the Hilltop, The. Lu Yu, *tr. fr. Chinese* by Burton Watson. CoBCP

Stone Orchard, The. Joyce Carol Oates. GeTw

Stone Song (Zen Rock) the Seer & the Unbeliever. Karoniaktatie. STE

Stone speaks. The stone becomes bread, The. Prayers in a Temple. Yusuf al-Khal, *tr.* by Abdullah al-Udhari. MPAW

Stone stark naked. Winter. Shmu'el Shatal, *tr.* by Bernhard Frank. MHeP

Stone Stars. Jack Dann. BWV

Stone Too Can Pray. Conrad Aiken. EaLo

Stone Trees. John Freeman. BoNaP

Stone Troll, The. J. R. R. Tolkien. SO

Stone Walls. Julie Mathilde Lippmann. AA

Stone went out, dressed as a man, The. Concerning the Stone. Gregory Orr. AnAn

Stoned cheek turned again. March. Roy McFadden. TIRV

Stoned dogs crawl back through the blood, The. The Contours of Fixation. Weldon Kees. NaP

Stonehenge. Michael Drayton. *Fr.* Polyolbion, Third Song. FaBoPP

Stonehenge. Sir Philip Sidney. *Fr.* The Seven Wonders of England. FaBoPP

Stonehouse. Jeff Tagami. BrSi

Stonemason cools his chisels, The. Buson, *tr. fr. Japanese* by Hiroaki Sato. *Fr.* Eighty-seven Hokku. FCEI

Stones. William Jeffrey. OxBS

Stones. Maxine W. Kumin. CAPP

Stones, The. Sylvia Plath. SM

Stones (a miracle to mortal view), The. Ovid, *tr. fr. Latin* by Dryden. *Fr.* Metamorphoses, I. OBVE

Stones are stomachs. Domesticated Stones. Hans Arp, *tr.* by Michael Benedikt. POS

Stones: Avesbury. Daisy Aldan. PoA

Stones huddled together on the ramparts, The. Faction du Muet. René Char, *tr.* by Thomas Merton. RHTwFP

Stones in Jordan's stream, The. Stones. William Jeffrey. OxBS

Stones must form a circle first not a wall. First Rule. Maurice Kenny. HATNAP

Stones no longer interest me. Forum Romanum. István Vas, *tr.* by Jascha Kessler. FOC

Stones of Time, The. Kenneth Koch. *Fr.* Days and Nights, II. NoAM

Stones only, the *disjecta membra* of this Great House. Ruins of a Great House. Derek Walcott. TwCP

Stonetalk. Jacques Hamelink, *tr. fr. Dutch* by Ria Leigh-Loohuizen. DuIn

Stonewall Jackson. Henry Lynden Flash. AA; PAH

Stonewall Jackson's Way. John Williamson Palmer. AA; PAH

Stoney Ridge Dance Hall. Alden Nowlan. MoCV

Stony Brook Tavern. Ken Belford. NeAC

Stony contours coil round, descending from halcyon heights. Written upon Coming Again to the Tu-hsü Taoist Temple. Ch'ü Ta-chün, *tr.* by Paul W. Kroll. WFTU

Stony Grey Soil. Patrick Kavanagh. CIP

Stony Lonesome. Langston Hughes. NOBA

Stood, at the closed door. Conrad Aiken. *Fr.* Preludes for Memnon; or, Preludes to Attitude. LiTM

Stood on the top of a spur once. Still Shines When You Think of It. Vincent O'Sullivan. PeNZ

Stood straight/ holding the choker high. Gary Snyder. *Fr.* Myths and Texts: Logging, III. NaP; NOBA

Stood there then among. Stars. Robert Hayden. LCAP

Stool at the Head of My Bed, A. Kadya Molodovsky, *tr. fr. Yiddish* by Irving Feldman. PeBMYV

Stool Ball. *Unknown.* CH

Stool with a Broken Leg, A. Sung Wan, *tr. fr. Chinese* by William Schultz. *Fr.* Songs Composed in Prison, III. WFTU

Stoop on the log-house is brown with sweet rain-rot, The. Joan Finnigan. *Fr.* May Day Rounds: Renfrew County. WPE

Stop. Richard Wilbur. LCAP

Stop All the Clocks, Cut Off the Telephone. W. H. Auden. RB (Song: Stop All the Clocks.) MoBrPo

Stop and consider! life is but a day. Keats. *Fr.* Sleep and Poetry. SeCePo

Stop, Christian passer-by!—Stop, child of God. Samuel Taylor Coleridge. EnRP; FiP; NAEL-2; NOCV; NoP; OAEL-2 (O, Lift One Thought.) FP

"Stop!" cried the kinght. "No more of this good sir!" Chaucer. *See* Canterbury Tales, The: Nun's Priest's Prologue, The.

Stop! don't swat the fly. Issa, *tr.* by Geoffrey Bownas *and* Anthony Thwaite. PeBJV

Stop! Don't touch me. *Unknown*, *tr.* by Willis Barnstone. BoWoP

Stop! for thy tread is on an empire's dust! Byron. *Fr.* Childe Harold's Pilgrimage, III. InPS

Stop-Go. Dorothy W. Baruch. FaPON

Stop, let me have the truth of that! Dîs Aliter Visum; or, Le Byron de Nos Jours. Robert Browning. NAEL-2

Stop look listen. Crossing. Philip Booth. AmFN; GOA

Stop on the Appian Way. On the Campagna. Elizabeth Stoddard. AA

Stop playing with your melancholy. Goethe, *tr. fr. German* by Walter Kaufmann. *Fr.* Faust. DL

Stop Press. Blaise Cendrars, *tr. fr. French* by Anselm Hollo. RHTwFP

Stop, Science—Stop! A. P. Herbert. FiBHP

Stop, Shadow of My Elusive Beloved. Sister Juana Inés de la Cruz, *tr. fr. Spanish* by Perry Higman. LPSS

Stop, stop and listen for the bough top. The Blackbird of Derrycairn. *Unknown*, *tr.* by Austin Clarke. BIrV; NeIP

Stop that Alabama bus I don't wanna ride. Alabama Bus. Will Hairston. FaBoPV

Stop there, old one, within your haven. Lament for Apirana Ngata. Arnold Reedy, *tr.* by Barry Mitcalfe. WTO

Stoplights edged the licorice street with ribbon. Leap in the Dark. Roberta Hill. WPOW

Stopover, The. Brian Turner. ATNZ

Stopped to piss. *Unknown*, *tr.* by Burton Watson. FCEI

Stopped to talk. Make Way. Steven Lavoie. UL

Stopping at an otel with an Ibernian. Dropping Your Aitches. Joseph Warren Beach. NYBP

Stopping by Home. David Huddle. GOYP

Stopping by Saigyo's Willow. Basho, *tr. fr. Japanese* by Burton Watson. *Fr.* Seventy-six Hokku. FCEI

Stopping by Shadows. Robin Fulton. PoSH

Stopping by Woods on a Snowy Evening. Robert Frost. AmPP; BoNaP; CMoP; FaBoCh; FaBV; FaFP; FaPON; FF; FPL; GoJo; GrPl; HAP; HeIP; HoPM; InPK; InPS; LiTA; LiTM; MoAB; MoAmPo; MoP; MoShBr; NAAL-2; NIP; NoAM; NOBA; NoP; NTCP; OBCA; OxBA; PDV; PoE; PoRA; PrIm; PYC; RB; RHPC; SCV; SoSe; TAP; TOF; TTTS

Stopping on the Green. The Stories in the Light. Michael Waters. GeTw

Stopping Overnight at Black Dragon River. Singde, *tr. fr. Chinese* by William Schultz. WFTU

Stopping the diary. Forget What Did. Philip Larkin. NoAM

Stopping Wine. T'ao Ch'ien, *tr. fr. Chinese* by Burton Watson. CoBCP

Stopwatch and an Ordnance Map, A. Stephen Spender. MoBS

Store cattle from Nelanjie! The mob goes feeding past. From the Gulf. Will H. Ogilvie. PoAu-1

Store-House, A. Louis Dudek. CaP

Store in Havana, The. José Kozer, *tr. fr. Spanish* by David Unger. VWA

Stores and filling stations prefer a roof. Christmas Tree. Stanley Cook. OBCP

Stories from Kansas. William Stafford. RFM

Stories from the Res. Nila NorthSun. GOS

Stories in the Light, The. Michael Waters. GeTw

Stories of Snow. Patricia K. Page. NOBC; NoP; OBCV; PoA

Stork questioned the swan whose moving song, The. Aria Senza da Capo. Robert Finch. MoCV

Storks like elbows had a fit of falling, The. There's No Place to Sleep in This Bed, Tanguy. Charles Henri Ford. EAS

Storm, The. Shauqi Abi Shaqra, *tr. fr. Arabic* by Abdullah al-Udhari. MPAW

Storm, The. Alcaeus, *tr. fr. Greek* by John Hermann Merivale. AWP

Storm, The. Elizabeth Jane Coatsworth. OBCA

Storm, The. Robert David Cohen. NYBP

Storm. Emily Dickinson. *See* It sounded as if the streets were running.

Storm, The. John Donne. *See* Storme, The.

Storm, The. Heine, *tr. fr. German* by Louis Untermeyer. AWP

Storm, The. Elizabeth Jennings. NePoEA-2

Storm. Agnes Nemes Nagy, *tr. fr. Hungarian* by Laura Schiff. PBWP

Storm. Mary Oliver. CAPP

Storm, The. Coventry Patmore. EnLoPo

Storm, The. Edward Shanks. BoNaP

Storm, The. Henry Vaughan. FaBoPP

Storm, The. Ellen Bryant Voigt. BLA

Storm, The. Robert Wallace. NYBP

Storm, The. Whittier. *See* Snow-bound; a Winter Idyl: Sun that brief December day, The.

Storm, The. William Carlos Williams. PCP

Storm. Judith Wright. PoAu-2; WPE
Storm and unconscionable winds once cast. The Wreck. Walter de la Mare. MOS
Storm at a House in the Hills, A. Yoshimoto, *tr. fr. Japanese by* Steven D. Carter. WFTW
Storm at Sea. *Malay Oral Tradition, tr. by* R. O. Winstedt. WTO
Storm at Sea, A. John Donne. *Fr.* The Storme. NOBE
Storm at Sea, A. *Unknown, tr. fr. Irish by* Robin Flower. AnIL
Storm at Sea. *Malay Oral Tradition, tr. by* R. O. Winstedt. WTO
Storm-Beaten. Clara Ann Thompson. CBWP-2
Storm-beaten old watch-tower, A. Symbols. W. B. Yeats. OBMV
Storm breaks in the bureau-drawer, The. Round of the Sidewalks. Benjamin Péret, *tr. by* James Laughlin. POS
Storm came up so very quick, The. Spring Rain. Marchette Chute. RHPC
Storm-Cock's Song, The. "Hugh MacDiarmid." OxBTC
Storm Cone, The. Kipling. NoAM; OxBTC
Storm cries every night, The. Spring Song. Hermann Hesse, *tr. by* Ludwig Lewisohn. AWP
Storm-dances of gulls, the barking game of seals, The. Divinely Superfluous Beauty. Robinson Jeffers. HeIP; MoAmPo
Storm Fear. Robert Frost. CMoP; OxBA
Storm from the East, A. Reed Whittemore. NYBP
Storm House, The. Elizabeth Jennings. WPE
Storm in April, A. Richard Wilbur. LCAP; NoP
Storm in Summer, A. Wilfrid Scawen Blunt. FaBoTw
Storm in the Distance, A. Paul Hamilton Hayne. AA
Storm is over, the land hushes to rest, The. Robert Bridges. BrPo; GTBS-P
(Storm is over, The.) LiTB; LiTM; OBMV
Storm lasted all night, The. The Complaisant Friend. Pierre Louÿs, *tr. fr. French. Fr.* Chansons de Bilitis. PeHV
Storm not, brave Friend, that thou hast never yet. To Scilla. Sir Charles Sedley. FaBoEE
Storm of Love, A. Hilary Corke. NYBP
Storm of wind and rain suddenly whips up, autumn talking with itself, A. Burning Incense. Yu T'ung, *tr. by* Paul W. Kroll. WFTU
Storm-song/ Gather ye silently, A. The Gathering of the People. William James Linton. PF
Storm that needed a mountain, A. Found in a Storm. William Stafford. RFM
Storm Tide on Mejit. *Unknown, tr. fr. Micronesian by* Augustin Kramer *and* Willard Trask. RFM
Storm Warning. Howard Moss, *tr. fr. Italian by* William Arrowsmith. AnAn
Storm Warnings. Adrienne Rich. AiP; GOYP; NAAL-2; NIP
Storm was coming, that was why it was dark, A. Sudden Things. Donald Hall. EAS
Storm-Wind, The. William Barnes. NOBE
Storm Windows. Howard Nemerov. InPK
Storm winds carry snow. Deer Song. Leslie Silko. VoR
Storme, The ("Thou which art I, ('Tis nothing to be soe)"), *sel.* John Donne. MOS
Storm at Sea, A. NOBE
Storming of Stony Point, The. Arthur Guiterman. PAH
Stormpetrel. Richard Murphy. IPY
Storms and Towers. A. Leyeles, *tr. fr. Yiddish by* Benjamin *and* Barbara Harshav. AYP
Storms are past, the clouds are overblown, The. Bonum Est Mihi Quod Humiliasti Me. Earl of Surrey. SiPS
Storms come and sorrows come. Security. Margaret E. Sangster. BLRP
Storms lend you wings, destroyer of the lands. Inanna and Enlil. Enheduanna. BoWoP
Stormy are the waters of Waiapu. The Waters of Waiapu. Paraire Henare Tomoana, *tr. by* Margaret Orbell. PeNZ
Stormy Day. W. R. Rodgers. LiTB
Stormy Day, A. *Unknown, tr. fr. Hawaiian.* WTO
Stormy Hebrides, The. William Collins. *Fr.* An Ode on the Popular Superstitions of the Highlands of Scotland [Considered as the Subject of Poetry]. NOBE
Stormy March is come at last, The. March. Bryant. GN
Stormy Night in Autumn. Chu Shu-chen, *tr. fr. Chinese by* Kenneth Rexroth. BoWoP
Stormy Nights. Robert Louis Stevenson. BrPo
Stormy Scenes of Winter, The. *Unknown.* AmFP
Stormy sea, A! Waves dashing high! He Shall Speak Peace unto the Nations. Lila V. Walters. WBLP

Stormy Weather, Boys. *Unknown.* OxBSS
Story, A. Margaret Avison. MoCV
Story, A. Susan Mitchell. NAmP
Story, The. Muhammad al-Faituri, *tr. fr. Arabic by* Sargon Boulus *and* Peter Porter. MAP
Story. Dennis Saleh. NeAC
Story, The. Charles Simic. NNaP
Story, The. Iain Crichton Smith. NPo
Story, A. William Stafford. NNaP; RFM
Story, The. Mark Strand. AnAn
Story. Takenaka Iku, *tr. fr. Japanese by* Geoffrey Bownas *and* Anthony Thwaite. PeBJV
Story, A. Yusuf al-Sa'igh, *tr. fr. Arabic by* Diana Der Hovanessian *with* Salma Khadra Jayyusi. MAP
Story, a story, A! Rowing. Anne Sexton. BoWoP; CAPP
Story, a story, a story anon, A. The Bishop of Canterbury. *Unknown.* AmFP
Story, a story to you I will tell, A. The Cunning Cobbler Done Over. *Unknown.* CoMu
Story about Chicken Soup, A. Louis Simpson. LCAP; NNaP; PoE; TAP
Story about Indians, A. The Climate of Paradise. Louis Simpson. NOBA
Story about the Body, A. Robert Hass. GeTw; NPGG
Story, as now we see, was over-written, The. Thermopylae. Michael Thwaites. PoAu-2
Story from Bear Country. Leslie Silko. STE
Story from Russian Author. Peter Redgrove. NePoEA-2
Story haunts this tribe that cannot wipe from its eyes, The. Isaac. Stanley Burnshaw. VWA
Story I shall tell today, The. The Nightingale. Marie de France, *tr. by* Patricia Terry. BoWoP
Story in Poetic Form: The Androgyne. Marguerite Grépon, *tr. fr. French by* Barbara Johnson. DMF
Story of a Hotel Room. Rosemary Tonks. AIW; OxBTC
Story of a Well-made Shield, The. N. Scott Momaday. CDW; GrPl; HATNAP
Story of Abraham and Hagar, The. Edna Aphek, *tr. fr. Hebrew by* Yishai Tobin. VWA
Story of Augustus, Who Would Not Have Any Soup, The. Heinrich Hoffmann, *tr. fr. German.* FaBoUs; GoJo; MoShBr; NBLV; OxBChV; RHPC
Story of Bitter Tea, The. Lo Ch'ing, *tr. fr. Chinese by* Dominic Cheung. IFON
Story of Cruel Psamtek, The. *Unknown.* NA
Story of Fidgety Philip, The. Heinrich Hoffmann, *tr. fr. German.* OxBChV
Story of Frederick Gowler, The. The King of Canoodle-Dum. W. S. Gilbert. CenHV
Story of Good, The. Phyllis Janik. IHMS
Story of How a Wall Stands, A. Simon J. Ortiz. HATNAP; MAYP
Story of Isaac. Leonard Cohen. VWA
Story of Johnny Head-in-Air, The. Heinrich Hoffmann, *tr. fr. German.* OxBChV
Story of Lava, The. David Allan Evans. Psk
Story of Lovers Leap, The. Maggie Pogue Johnson. CBWP-4
Story of Marie, The. Michael Burkard. NAmP
Story of My Life, The. Carroll Arnett. NOVW; VoR
Story of Phoebus and Daphne Applied [*or* Applyed], etc., The. Edmund Waller. InvP; NAEL-1; OBS
Story of Ponce de Leon, A. The Fountain of Youth. Hezekiah Butterworth. PAH
Story of Prince Agib, The. W. S. Gilbert. FaBoCo; NA
Story of Pyramid Thothmes, The. *Unknown.* NA
Story of Rimini, The, *sel.* Leigh Hunt.
"Noble range it was, of many a rood, A." *Fr.* III. EnRP
Story of Sigurd the Volsung, The, *sels.* William Morris.
Brooding of Sigurd, The. SeCePo
Sigurd Rideth to the Glittering Heath. *Fr.* II. PoEL-5
Story of the Ashes and the Flame, The. E. A. Robinson. AnAmPo
Story of the Corn. K. Fisher. BoTP
Story of the Eaters, A. Santiago Mendes Zapata, *tr. fr. Tzeltal Indian by* W. S. Merwin. STP
Story of the Flowery Kingdom. James Branch Cabell. OnMSP
Story of the Gadsbys, The, *sel.* Kipling.
Winners, The. BLPA; FaPoR; FPL
(L'Envoi: "What is the moral? Who rides may read.") MoBrPo; TrGrPo
Story of the Pot and the Kettle, The. Charles Montagu. APAS
Story of the Shepherd, "The. *Unknown, tr. fr. Spanish.* OHIP

Story of the Unknown Man, The. Samih al-Qasim, *tr. fr. Arabic by* Abdullah al-Udhari. MPAW
Story of the Wild Huntsman, The. Heinrich Hoffman, *tr. fr. German.* NA
Story of the World, The. Moyshe-Leyb Halpern, *tr. fr. Yiddish by* Benjamin *and* Barbara Harshav *and* Kathryn Helle. AYP
Story of the Zeros, The. Victor Hernandez Cruz. PoBA
Story of Uriah, The. Kipling. BrPo; NOBVV; SCV
Story of Vinland, The. Sidney Lanier. *Fr.* Psalm of the West. PAH
Story of Wildflowers, The. Yip Wai-lim, *tr. fr. Chinese by* Dominic Cheung. IFON
Story of Your Life, The. Bruce Bennett. RR
Story Tellers Summer, 1980. Nia Francisco. STE
Story That Could Be True, A. William Stafford. GOYP; NTCP
Story to you I'll tell of little Omie Wise, A. Poor Omie. *Unknown.* PrIm
Story We Know, The. Martha Collins. SM
Story went that once someone, an unbeliever, The. Face. Robert Morgan. GeTw
Story Wet as Tears, A. Marge Piercy. NIP
Story You Know, A. Mark Strand. KS
Storys to rede ar delitabill. John Barbour. *Fr.* The Bruce. OxBS
Storyteller, The. Ree Young. MOWH
Stout and strong our stallions. *Unknown, tr. by* Arthur Waley. BoS
Stout seamen, come away, never be daunted. The Boatswain's Call. *Unknown.* OxBSS
Stove. Ken Belford. NeAC
Stove. Philip Booth. FYAP
Stove was grey, the coal was gone, The. Into Laddery Street. Laura Riding. *Fr.* Forgotten Girlhood. RB
Stove's Out. Charles Bernstein. LP
Stowaway in a fold. The Witnesses. X. J. Kennedy. PChr
Stowed away in a Montreal lumber room. O God! O Montreal! Samuel Butler. FaBoCo; OBSV; OxBoLi
  (Psalm of Montreal, A.) OBTV
Strage degli Innocenti, La, *sel.* Giovanni Battista Marino, *tr. fr. Italian by* Richard Crashaw.
  Sospetto d'Herode. SeCV-1
Stragglers. Pietro Aretino, *tr. fr. Italian by* Samuel Putnam. ErPo
Strahan, Tonson, Lintot of the times. To Mr. Murray. Byron. FaBoCo
Straight flagged road, laid on the rough earth, A. Field Ambulance in Retreat. May Sinclair. OBTV
Straight-jacketing sprang to every lock. Austin Clarke. *Fr.* Mnemosyne Lay in Dust, II. CMoP; IPY
Straight up against the clouds above the ridge, stands the awesome pass alone. Crossing Ta-yü Mountain Ridge. Chu Yi-tsun, *tr. by* Irving Lo. WFTU
Straight up away from this road. Achieving Perspective. Pattiann Rogers. MAYP; MT
Strain, strain thine eyes, this parting is for aye! Lohengrin. William Morton Payne. AA
Strained daybreak breaks in past the blinds. Lorenzo Thomas. UL
Strains of Sight. Robert Duncan. CMoP; PoE
Strampin' the bent, like the Angel o' Daith. Molecatcher. Albert D. Mackie. GoTS
Strand at Lough Beg, The. Seamus Heaney. AnAn; CIP; NoAM; NoP; OBWP
Strand Hotel, Rosslare, The. James Liddy. CIP
Strand on the Green. *Unknown.* GBP
Strand-Thistle. Gustav Falke, *tr. fr. German by* Jethro Bithell. AWP
Stranded in My Ontario. Ronald G. Everson. NOBC
Stranded on the moon. Moon-Man. Dorothy Hewett. CBAP
Stranded Whales, The. Geoffrey Dutton. CBAP
Strange. Stanley Burnshaw. TrJP
Strange. Kirby Doyle. NeAP
Strange,/ That in this nigger place. Esthete in Harlem. Langston Hughes. BANP; BPo
Strange, All-absorbing Love. Digby Mackworth Dolben. TrPWD
Strange and unnatural! lets stay and see. Destinie. Abraham Cowley. MeLP
Strange appears the garden. Mohammad Taqi Mir, *tr. by* Ahmed Ali. GoT
Strange are the feelings arising within me. The Love of Hell. Abraham Burstein. TrJP
Strange—as I sat brooding here. Lucy. Walter de la Mare. CMoP
Strange as it seems, the smallest mammal. The Shrew. Ogden Nash. CenHV

Strange atoms unto ourselves. Lovelight. Georgia Douglas Johnson. AmNP
Strange beauty, eight-limbed and eight-handed. Octopus. A. C. Hilton. BXAP; CenHV; FaBoCo; FaBoPa; Par
Strange bed, whose recurrent dream we are, The. Hotel de l'Univers et Portugal. James Merrill. MoAB; NePoEA-2; PoA
Strange bird/ His song remains secret. Youth. James Wright. DiL; NaP; NoP
Strange, bright dancers, The. Poppies. P. A. Ropes. BoTP
Strange, but he cheats his master. Man of the World. Michael Hamburger. NePoEA-2
Strange but true is the story. The Sea-Turtle and the Shark. Melvin Beaunearus Tolson. PoBA
Strange Case, The. Michael Ondaatje. NIP
Strange church smelled a bit "high," of censers, The. Geoffrey Hill. *Fr.* Mercian Hymns, IX. PoE
Strange City, A. Sándor Weöres, *tr. fr. Hungarian by* Jascha Kessler. FOC
Strange creeper. The Creeper. Tom Schmidt. NeAC
Strange Fits of Passion Have I Known. Wordsworth. EBEV; EnRP; FiP; GBL; LiTB; NAEL-2; NOBE; OAEL-2; OBEV; OBNC; PoE; PPP; TEP; TrGrPo
Strange Fortunes of Two Excellent Princes, The, *sel.* Nicholas Breton. "I would thou wert not fair, or I were wise." ElL; InvP
  (His Wisdom.) OBSC
Strange Fruit. Randolph Stow. PoAu-2
Strange grows the river on the sunless evenings! Vesperal. Ernest Dowson. OBMV
Strange Guest, The. Itzig Manger, *tr. fr. Yiddish by* Stephen Garrin. VWA
Strange Hells. Ivor Gurney. OxBTC
Strange how/ socks pulled over plastic toes. On Forgetting to Cry. Norma Thomas Colvin. TSM
Strange how the mind will stand outside. Chopping Wood. Dave Smith. SM
Strange land is hard to live in, A. Sanu Chigami. *Fr.* Manyo Shu. Ma
Strange Legacies. Sterling A. Brown. CNA; PoBA; TTY
Strange light, one thread falling from the blue, A. Atomic Bomb. Tsuchiya Kyutai, *tr. by* Burton Watson. JLIC-2
Strange Love. Moses Ibn Ezra, *tr. fr. Hebrew by* Solomon Solis-Cohen. TrJP
Strange Man, The. *Unknown.* FaPON
Strange Meeting. Wilfred Owen. BrPo; CMoP; FaBoMo; FaBoRV; GTBS-P; HeIP; HoPM; LiTB; MMA; MoAB; MoBrPo; MoP; NAEL-2; NoAM; NOBE; NoP; OAEL-2; OBWP; PoE; RB; SCV; TrGrPo; WaaP; WaP
Strange Meetings, *sels.* Harold Monro.
  Birth. PoA
  Flower Is Looking, A. MoBrPo
  If Suddenly a Clod of Earth. MoBrPo
  You Live There; I Live Here. Mes
Strange Monsters. Rowland Watkyns. FaBoEE
Strange now to think of you, gone without corsets & eyes. Kaddish. Allen Ginsberg. HCAP; NAAL-2; NeAP; NOBA; PoM; VWA
Strange People, The. Louise Erdrich. NOVW; TSL
Strange people we. Sad Evenings. Iftiqar Arif, *tr. by* Mahmood Jamal. PBMUP
Strange pie that is almost a passion. A Melton Mowbray Pork Pie. Richard Le Gallienne. BXAP; Par
Strange plants are much written about. Beware, My Successor. Loren C. Eiseley. BWV
Strange spirit with inky hair. The Lion. W. J. Turner. MoBrPo
Strange Talk. L. E. Yates. BoTP
Strange that I did not know him then. An Old Story. E. A. Robinson. AnAmPo; MoAmPo; OxBSP
Strange, that such horror and such grace. To a Fair Lady Playing with a Snake. Edmund Waller. EBEV; HoPM; PoE
  (Of a Fair Lady Playing with a Snake.) PoEL-3
Strange the formation of the eely race. William Diaper, *after the Greek of* Oppian. *Fr.* Halieutica. OBVE
  (Eels and Tortoises.) NOEC
Strange to be torn away from your embrace. Strange. Stanley Burnshaw. TrJP
Strange to feel this sun again. Free Country: July 19, 1979. Giaconda Belli, *tr. by* Magaly Fernández. Vol
Strange to step straight into the beautiful dawn. Miraculous Dawn. R. Williams Parry, *tr. by* Joseph P. Clancy. OBWVE
Strange to think what solvents. Flood. William Matthews. KS
Strange Tree. Elizabeth Madox Roberts. BoNaP; FaPON; GrPl; WSC
Strange Visitor, The. *Unknown.* ChTr; FaBoCh; GBP

Strange walkers! See their professional. The Mushroom Gatherers. Donald Davie. NePoEA-2

Strange was the manner of my life and wondrous were its ways. My Father. Hayyim Nahman Bialik, *tr. by* Bernhard Frank. MHeP

Strange Western town at the round edge of night. Western Town. Karl Shapiro. NYBP

Strange, what I thought last night, waking. The Teaching Staff Disbanded. György Rónay, *tr. by* Michael Hamburger. MHuP

Strange wind off the night, A. The Face. Philip Levine. DiL

Strange years, these years. 1975. Remco Campert, *tr. by* James S. Holmes. DuIn

Strangely/ my mother's sad eyes. X-Ray. David Ray. NePoEA-2

Strangely assorted, the shape of song and the bloody man. The Military Harpist. Ruth Pitter. FaBoTw

Strangely Insane. Michael Burkard. NAmP

Strangeness of Heart. Siegfried Sassoon. TrJP

Stranger, A. Sandor Csoori, *tr. fr. Hungarian by* Jascha Kessler. FOC

Stranger, The. Walter de la Mare. BrPo; OxBTC

Stranger, The. William Everson. FF

Stranger, The. Jean Garrigue. LiTA; LiTM; NOBA; TwCP

Stranger, The. Juan Gelman, *tr. fr. Spanish by* Yishai Tobin. VWA

Stranger, A. Lionel Johnson. NOBVV

Stranger. Thomas Merton. EaLo

Stranger. Gabriela Mistral, *tr. fr. Spanish by* Langston Hughes. OV

Stranger, The. Adrienne Rich. NNaP

Stranger. Elizabeth Madox Roberts. MoAmPo

Stranger! Approach this spot with gravity! A Dentist. *Unknown.* FaBoCo; FaBoEE

(Epitaph on a Dentist.) OxBoLi

Stranger arrived, A. The Minaret. "Adunis," *tr. by* Abdullah al-Udhari. MPAW

Stranger arrives at her door, A. The Widow. Susan Ludvigson. MAYP; MT

Stranger asked me what my country was, The. An Answer. Ahmad al-Mushari al-Udwani, *tr. by* Hilary Kilpatrick *and* Charles Doria. MAP

Stranger came one night to Yussouf's tent, A. Yussouf. James Russell Lowell. BeLS; BLPA; BLPL; BoTP; FaBoBe

Stranger came to the door at eve, A. Love and a Question. Robert Frost. MoBS

Stranger died for me, A. The Infinite Debt. Rachael Bates. CN

Stranger from Rakahanga, A. Alistair Campbell. ATNZ

Stranger here, as all my fathers were, A. John Amner. OxBSP

Stranger, if thou hast learned a truth which needs. Inscription for the Entrance to a Wood. Bryant. AmPP; OxBA; TAP

Stranger in his own element. Penguin on the Beach. Ruth Miller. PeSA

Stranger in my gates, The—lo! that am I. Omnia Exeunt in Mysterium. George Sterling. WGRP

Stranger in the Pumpkin, The. John Ciardi. NTCP

Stranger in This Land, A. Cliff Ashby. NOCV

Stranger it was never meant for, A. Mine. Frank Polite. NYBP

Stranger Not Ourselves, The. William Stafford. NNaP

Stranger, pause and drop a tear. Sacred to the Memory of Maria (To Say Nothing of Jane and Martha) Sparks. "Max Adeler." FaBoCo

Stranger! Tell the people of Spoon River two things. Unknown Soldiers. Edgar Lee Masters. *Fr.* The New Spoon River. NoAM; TAP

Stranger than the Worst. Babette Deutsch. WPE

Stranger, the bark you see before you says. The Yacht. Catullus, *tr. by* John Hookham Frere. AWP; OBVE

Stranger walks into the dark room, The. Seance. Edouard Roditi. EAS

Stranger walls, that shall no violent presence. Zimbabwe. F. D. Sinclair. PeSA

Stranger, when you come to/ Lakedaimon. Simonides, *tr. by* Kenneth Rexroth. OBVE

Stranger, whoe'er thou art, whose ling'ring feet. Sonnet Written in Tintern Abbey, Monmouthshire. Edmund Gardner. NOEC

Stranger with the pile of luggage proudly labelled for Portree. At Euston. A. M. Harbord. PoSH

Stranger, wond'ring, stalks, and stares upon, The. Rome, Conqueror, Conquered. Joshua Sylvester. FaBoEE

Stranger, you freeze to this: there ain't no kinder gin-palace. Home, Sweet Home, with Variations, II. H. C. Bunner. CenHV

Stranger, you who hide my love. Stephen Spender. FaBoTw

Strangers. Mani Leib, *tr. fr. Yiddish by* John Hollander. PeBMYV

Strangers. William Stafford. NNaP

Strangers, The. Jones Very. AnAmPo; OxBA

Strangers Are We All upon the Earth. Franz Werfel, *tr. fr. German by* Edith Abercrombie Snow. TrJP

"Strangers are we and pilgrims here!" At a Friends' Meeting. Mary Elizabeth Coleridge. WPE

Strangers ask. The Tower. Philip Booth. NePoEA-2

Strangers' eyes don't see. Memorial Poem. Jacob Glatstein, *tr. by* Ruth Whitman. VWA

Strangers in a Hostile Landscape. Meiling Jin. WS

Strangers on a train. Travels with the Band-Aid Army. Lance Henson. VoR

Stranger's Song, The. Thomas Hardy. BrPo

Strangers! your eyes are on that valley fixed. The Field of the Grounded Arms. Fitz-Greene Halleck. PoEL-4

Strangling women in the suburban bush. Das Kapital. Imamu Amiri Baraka. PoM

Strappado for the Devil, A, *sel.* Richard Brathwaite. Of Maids' Inconstancy. EIL

Strapped helpless, monarchs and prelates, round they swung. The Wheel of Fortune. Thom Gunn. OxBC

Strapped to my seat, I turn. Above It All. Philip Levine. NOBA

Strapping young stockman lay dying, A. The Dying Stockman. *Unknown.* PoAu-1

Strategies. Welton Smith. NBP; PoBA

Strategy for a Marathon. Marnie Mueller. ASP

Strath of Kildonan, The. Betty Morris. PoSH

Stratis Thalassinos among the Agapanthi. George Seferis, *tr. fr. Greek by* Edmund Keeley *and* Philip Sherrard. VMG

Stratton Water. Dante Gabriel Rossetti. OxBB

Straunge Passion of a Lover, A. George Gascoigne. AAS

Straw, The. Robert Graves. OxBTC

Straw, and figures of moulded clay. Stable Straw. Robert Farren. TIRV

Straw-coat vendor saw the frog last year, The. Rika, *tr. by* Hiroaki Sato. FCEI

Straw Mat. Fu'ad Rifqa, *tr. fr. Arabic by* Abdullah al-Udhari. MPAW

Straw matting/ to sleep on. *Unknown. Fr.* Manyo Shu. FCEI

Straw mattress: the Bridge Princess of Uji. Teika, *tr. fr. Japanese by* Hiroaki Sato. *Fr.* Eighty-four Tanka. FCEI

Straw sandals worn through, soles blistered. Taiko, *tr. by* Lucien Stryk *and* Takashi Ikemoto. ZPCJ

Straw shoe was found buried in his grave, A. Dong Jin. Park Je-chun, *tr. by* Koh Chang-soo. ACKP

Strawberries. Edwin Morgan. BoLoP; LLLT

Strawberries in Mexico. Ron Padgett. EAS

Strawberries in November. John Shaw Neilson. PoAu-1

Strawberries that in gardens grow. Wild Strawberries. Robert Graves. FaBoCh

Strawberry, The. Maggie Pogue Johnson. CBWP-4

Strawberry Fair. *Unknown.* OBET

Strawberry Jam. May Justus. FaPON

Strawberry Moon. Mary Oliver. InPS

Strawberry Roan, The. Curley W. Fletcher. CowP

Strawberry Shrub, The. Edna St. Vincent Millay. CMoP; FaBoWP

Strawberrying. Maurice Kenny. HATNAP

Straws. Elizabeth J. Coatsworth. AmFN

Straws like tame lightnings lie about the grass. Summer Farm. Norman MacCaig. OxBTC

Stray, The. Barbara Euphan Todd. CRH

Stray Animals. James Tate. NoAM

Stray Bird's Homeland, A. Liu K'o-hsiang, *tr. fr. Chinese by* Dominic Cheung. IFON

Stray cat, A. Masaoka Shiki, *tr. fr. Japanese by* Burton Watson. *Fr.* Thirty-nine Haiku. FCEI

Stray Dog. Charlotte Mish. PoLF

Stray Dog. Sándor Weöres, *tr. fr. Hungarian by* Jascha Kessler. FOC

Stray Dog, near Ecully. Margaret Avison. OBCV; PoA

Stray Prostrations. Kaifi A'Zmi, *tr. fr. Urdu by* Mahmood Jamal. PBMUP

Strayed Reveller, The ("Faster, Faster/ O Circe, Godess."), *sel.* Matthew Arnold. OAEL-2

Strayed Reveller to Ulysses, The. OBEV

Straying Student, The. Austin Clarke. AnIL; BIrV; CIP; IPY; MoAB; NeIP; NOIV

Streak of Sappho, it is said, A. Mould of Castile. Jack R. Clemo. NOCV

Streaked and fretted with effort, the thick. The Street. Robert Pinsky. MAYP

Stream, The. Lula Lowe Weeden. CDC

Stream, The/ piles out of the pile. The Crossing. Paul Blackburn. NYBP

Stream flowing steadily over a stone does not wet its core, A. An Elder's Reproof to his Wife. 'Abdillaahi Muuse, *tr. by* B. W. Andrzjewski *and* I. M. Lewis. TTY; WTO

Stream is frozen hard, The. Going by. Antenora. "Hugh MacDiarmid." SeCePo

Stream of Faith, The. William Channing Gannett. *See* From Heart to Heart.

Stream of tender gladness, A. Shadow River. Pauline Johnson. CaP

Stream sorrow, eyes. Elegy for Her Brother Sakhr. Al-Khansa. BoWoP, *tr.* by Willis Barnstone; WPOW, *tr.* by Bridget Connelly

Stream swirls, The. The wind moans in. Jade Flower Palace. Tu Fu, *tr.* by Kenneth Rexroth. NaP

Stream to mingle with your favorite Dee, A. To Lady Eleanor Butler and the Honourable Miss Ponsonby, Composed in the Grounds of Plas-Newydd, Llangollen. Wordsworth. PeHV

Stream was swift, and so cold, The. Captivity. Louise Erdrich. HATNAP; NoAM

Streamful of flowing water, A. A Spring Day—Remembering Living on the River. Kao Ch'i, *tr.* by Jonathan Chaves. CoBLCP

Stream's clear: five inches, The. Taigi, *tr. fr. Japanese* by Hiroaki Sato. *Fr.* Twenty-nine Hokku. FCEI

Streams fall down and through the darkness bear, The. Spate in Winter Midnight. Norman MacCaig. GTBS-P; PoSH

Streams of Bunclody, The. *Unknown.* BIrV

Streams of Lovely Nancy, The. *Unknown.* FaBoBa; OBET; OxBoLi

Stream's Song, The. Lascelles Abercrombie. OBMV

Street, The. Gene Baro. NYBP

Street, The. James Russell Lowell. AnAmPo; Son

Street, The. Octavio Paz, *tr. fr. Spanish* by Willis Knapp Jones. FF

Street, The. Robert Pinsky. MAYP

Street, The. Gary Soto. NPGG

Street belongs, The. Fata Morgana. Juliane Windhager, *tr.* by Beth Björklund. CoAuP

Street blood throbbing. Disco Chinatown. Yuri Kageyama. BrSi

Street climbs upward steeply, The. The Street. Gene Baro. NYBP

Street Corner College. Kenneth Patchen. MoAmPo

Street Cries. Marjorie Welish. EOEF

Street Demonstration. Margaret Abigail Walker. BPo; CNA

Street Drummer, The. Moyshe-Leyb Halpern, *tr. fr. Yiddish* by John Hollander. PeBMYV

Street Fight. Harold Monro. FaBoTw

Street Fire. Daniel Halpern. AmPA

Street in April, A. Louis Dudek. OBCV

Street in Bronzeville, A, *sels.* Gwendolyn Brooks.
   Kitchenette Building. CAPP; NAAL-2
   Mother, The. CAPP
   Of De Witt Williams on His Way to Lincoln Cemetery. CAPP
   Song in the Front Yard, A. CAPP

Street in Bronzeville: Southeast Corner, A. Gwendolyn Brooks. VGW

Street in Kaufman-ville, A. James Cunningham. JB

Street in our town, A. The Watchmaker's Shop. *Unknown.* BoTP

Street is no river, The. For slouching. The Dogchain Gang. Stan Rice. NPGG

Street is soon there, The. To Ride. Paul Eluard, *tr.* by Kenneth Koch. TTTS

Street is very long and filled with silence, The. The Street. Octavio Paz, *tr.* by Willis Knapp Jones. FF

Street Kid. Duane Niatum. STE

Street Lanterns. Mary Elizabeth Coleridge. BoTP; PoRA

Street Music. Barbara Angell. AiP

Street Musicians. John Ashbery. CAPP; HCAP

Street of Named Houses, The. Robert David Cohen. NYBP

Street of Nectar, Street of Contingency. Address. Bruce Smith. *Fr.* In My Father's House. Son

Street Performers, 1851. Terence Tiller. GTBS-P

Street puddle. Suburb. Abraham Chalfi, *tr.* by Bernhard Frank. MHeP

Street Scene. W. E. Henley. BoTP

Street Scene. Robert Mezey. LiTM

Street Scene. A. Lizette Woodworth Reese. OBCA

Street Scene—1946. Kenneth Porter. PoNe

Street, shade, a tree, a house, a door, The. Scene. Faiz Ahmad Faiz, *tr.* by Mahmood Jamal. PBMUP

Street Song. Thom Gunn. HeIP; NoP; OxBC

Street Song. Edith Sitwell. CMoP

Street Sounds to the Soldiers' Tread, The. A. E. Housman. PPP

Street there is in Paris famous, A. The Ballad of Bouillabaisse. Thackeray. OBEV; OBTV

Street Window. Carl Sandburg. PCP

Streets. Bob Perelman. LP

Streets also have eyes, The. The Messiah. Moshe Yungman, *tr.* by David G. Roskies *and* Hillel Schwartz. VWA

Streets are a bit confused, The. Drunken Streets. Malka Locker, *tr.* by Jeremy Garber. VWA

Streets are full of people moving, The. Reality. Felix Pollak. TSM

Streets are good, The. We're Satisfied. Ilse Tielsch, *tr.* by Beth Björklund. CoAuP

Streets at Their Leisure Rise, The. David Avidan, *tr. fr. Hebrew by* Bernhard Frank. MHeP

Streets of Air, The. Malcolm Cowley. *Fr.* Blue Juniata. PoA

Streets of Baltimore. *Unknown.* BLPA

Streets of Ch'ang-an, The. Ch'u Kuang-hsi, *tr. fr. Chinese by* Burton Watson. CoBCP

Streets of Forbes, The. *Unknown.* CBAP

Streets of Laredo, The. Louis MacNeice. ChTr; MoBS; OBWP

Streets of Laredo, The. *Unknown. See* As I Walked Out in the Streets of Laredo.

Streets of the roaring town. On a Soldier Fallen in the Philippines. William Vaughn Moody. AnAmPo; NOBA; PAH

Streets that slept all afternoon in sun, The. Camptown. John Ciardi. WaP

Strength for To-Day. *Unknown.* PWR

Strength leaves the hand I lay on this beech bole. The Beech. Andrew Young. BoNaP

Strength, Love, Light. Robert II, King of France. WGRP

Strength, of Fate, The. Euripides, *tr. fr. Greek by* A. E. Housman. *Fr.* Alcestis. AWP

Strength through Joy. Kenneth Rexroth. FYAP; VGW

Strength to War. Stephen Stepanchev. WaP

Strengthen, my Love, this castle of my heart. Charles d'Orléans, *tr.* by Andrew Lang. AWP

Strengthened to live, strengthened to die for. In Distrust of Merits. Marianne Moore. EaLo; LiTA; LiTM; MoAB; MoAmPo; NAAL-2; OBWP; OxBA; TrGrPo; WaaP; WaP

Stress of his anger set me back. The Revelation. James Wright. DiL

Stretch of Cloud over Mount Wu, A. Li Hsün, *tr. fr. Chinese by* Lois Fusek. ATF

Stretch of Cloud over Mount Wu, A. Mao Wen-hsi, *tr. fr. Chinese by* Lois Fusek. ATF

Stretched in the shadow of the broad beech. The Shepherd's Gratitude. Virgil, *tr. fr. Latin by* Charles Stuart Calverly. *Fr.* Eclogues, I. AWP

Stretcher to stretcher still they came. Bomb Incident. Barbara Catherine Edwards. CN

Strew lightly o'er the soldier's grave. The Soldier's Grave. Henry D. Muir. OHIP

Strew me with blossoms when I die. *Unknown. Fr.* Popular Songs of Tuscany, *tr. fr. Italian by* John Addington Symonds. AWP

Strew not earth with empty stars. Thomas Lovell Beddoes. *Fr.* The Second Brother. OxBSP

Strew on her roses, roses. Requiescat. Matthew Arnold. AWP; ELP; FiP; HeIP; InvP; LiTB; NOBE; OBD; OBEV; PoRA; TrGrPo

Strewn out in the smog. Ernst David, *tr.* by Beth Björklund. CoAuP

Stricken Average, The. William Rose Benét. AnAmPo

Stricken Deer, The. William Cowper. *See* Task, The: Garden, The.

Stricken South to the North, The. Paul Hamilton Hayne. PAH

Strict hairshirt of circumstance tears the flesh. The Veterans. Donagh MacDonagh. CIP

Strictly Bucolic. Charles Simic. PPR

Strictly for Posterity. Charles Simic. NNaP

Strictly Germ-proof. Arthur Guiterman. BLPA; TrJP

Strictly speaking for my sylph. Now and Then. Eileen Blacker Peterson. SoTCo

Strictures on the Economy of Nature. George Outram. FaBoCo

"Strife is grown between Virtue and Love, A." Sir Philip Sidney. *Fr.* Astrophel and Stella, LII. NAEL-1; NoP

Strike. Giaconda Belli, *tr. fr. Spanish by* David Volpendesta. Vol

Strike, The. *Unknown.* OBET

Strike among the Poets, A. *Unknown.* FaBoCo; FiBHP

Strike down into my breast, O sun, and cleanse my soul. Hymn to the Sun. William Alexander Percy. TrPWD

Strike the Bell. *Unknown.* OxBSS

Strike the Blow. *Unknown.* PAH

Strike the concertina's melancholy string! The Story of Prince Agib. W. S. Gilbert. FaBoCo; NA

Strike up, you lusty gallants, with music [*or* musick] and sound of drum. Captain Ward and the *Rainbow. Unknown.* ESPB; OBET; OxBSS

Striking. Charles Stuart Calverley. CenHV

Striking a Pose. Kevin Ireland. ATNZ

Striking Times. *Unknown.* OBET

Strikover Rabbi, The. Zishe Landau, *tr. fr. Yiddish by* Irving Feldman. PeBMYV

Strikover Rabbi's Wife, The. Zishe Landau, *tr. fr. Yiddish by* Irving Feldman. PeBMYV

String. Dennis Schmitz. LCAP

String-chewing bass players. Mingus. Bob Kaufman. PoBA

String of beads, if you must break, break. Princess Shikishi, *tr. fr. Japanese by* Hiroaki Sato. *Fr.* Seventy-eight Tanka. FCEI

String of Pearls. Katri Vala, *tr. fr. Finnish by* Aili Jarvenpa. SOP
String vibrates, The. The steel string vibrates. The skin. The calfskin. Acoustics. Susan Griffin. *Fr.* Woman and Nature. NPGG
Strings/Himo. Yuri Kageyama. BrSi
Strings' Excitement, The. W. H. Auden. MoAB; MoBrPo
Strings lay all about. The Disconnection. Rita Mae Brown. IHMS
Strip Me Naked, or Royal Gin for Ever; a Picture. *Unknown.* NOEC
Strip of Blue, A. Lucy Larcom. AA; WGRP
Strip off your clothes and give them to a man. The Visiting Hour. David Wagoner. HoPM
Striped blouse in a clearing by Bazille, A. Ceremony. Richard Wilbur. CoAP; MoP; NAAL-2; NoAM
Striped Canvas. Robert Grenier. IAT
Striped equilateral sails. Choosing Craft. May Swenson. ASP
Striped Shell, A. Ruth Dallas. ATNZ
Stripped/ you're beginning to float free. November 1968. Adrienne Rich. CAPP; NMM
Stripped almond of the plane is gone, The. Between Two Worlds. Rosemary Thomas. NYBP
Stripped of its leaves. Trees on a Frosty Night. Mairtin O Direain, *tr. by the author.* TIRV
Stripper, The. Anita Endrezze Probst. CDW
Stroke. Mike Lowery. Psk
Stroke. Stroke/ Time that turn. The Swimmer's Chant. Carol D. Spelius. RR
Stroke Units. Frederike Frei, *tr. fr. German by* Susan L. Cocalis. DMG
Strokes. William Stafford. PCP
Strolling in a Nearby Village. Tani Rokkoku, *tr. fr. Chinese by* Burton Watson. JLIC-2
Strolling in Simplicity Garden for the First Time. Chin Ho, *tr. fr. Chinese by* J. D Schmidt. WFTU
Strolling in the Moonlight. Ch'en San-li, *tr. fr. Chinese by* Irving Lo. WFTU
Strolling Player, The. Rimbaud, *tr. fr. French by* William Jay Smith. CT; GrPl
Strolling under the Moon. Li Chien, *tr. fr. Chinese by* Irving Lo. WFTU
Strolling vaguely after luncheon through the streets of Amsterdam. Belle de Jour. George Melly. FaBoPa
Strong, The. John Vance Cheney. AA
Strong and slippery, built for the midnight grass-party confronted by four cats. Peter. Marianne Moore. CMoP; NAAL-2; NoP; OxBA
Strong ankled, sun burned, almost naked. Vitamins and Roughage. Kenneth Rexroth. NoAM
Strong Are Saying Nothing, The. Robert Frost. CMoP
Strong Bond, The. Juana de Ibarbourou, *tr. fr. Spanish by* Linda Scheer. PBWP
Strong, but with gentleness. Variations on a Medieval Theme. Geoffrey Dutton. PoAu-2
Strong grow the reeds. *Unknown, tr. by* Arthur Waley. BoS
Strong Heroic Line, The. Oliver Wendell Holmes. AA
Strong hot breath of the land is lashing, The. A Night in the Red Sea. Sir Alfred Comyn Lyall. OBTV
Strong in a dream of perfect bloom. To the Brave Soul. Wilbur Underwood. WGRP
Strong in thy steadfast purpose, be. Purpose. John James Piatt. AA
Strong is the horse upon his speed. The Man of Prayer. Christopher Smart. *Fr.* A Song to David. LiTB
Strong is the lion—like a coal. Christopher Smart. *Fr.* A Song to David. HAP
Strong man, a fair woman, A. Sun and Moon. Jay Macpherson. SoSe
Strong man as I am. Hitomaro. *Fr.* Manyo Shu. Ma
Strong Men. Sterling A. Brown. BANP; BPo; CNA; FB; PoBA; TTY
Strong men keep coming on, The. Upstream. Carl Sandburg. MoAB; MoAmPo
Strong Men, Riding Horses. Gwendolyn Brooks. PoBA
Strong rods for scepters to bear sway. On the Decease of the Religious and Honourable Jno Haynes Esqr. John James. SCAP
Strong-shouldered mole. A Dead Mole. Andrew Young. FM; GTBS-P; OxBSP
Strong sob of the chafing stream, The. Orara. Henry Clarence Kendall. CBAP; PoAu-1
Strong Son of God. Tennyson. *Fr.* In Memoriam A. H. H., Proem. EaLo; HAP; LiTB; NAWM-2; TrCP; TrGrPo; TrPWD; WGRP
Strong song tows, A. Coda. Basil Bunting. *Fr.* Briggflatts [An Autobiography]. OAEL-2
Strong sun across the sod can make. Song for the Passing of a Beautiful Woman. *Unknown, tr. by* Mary Austin. LiTA
Strong Swimmer, The. William Rose Benét. PoNe
Strong Thighs astride My Chest. Caroline Griffin. DT
Strong Wind, A. Austin Clarke. BoNaP; RB

Strong women told the faggots that there are two important, The. Women Wisdom. Larry Mitchell. GLP
Stronger than alcohol, more great than song. Ted Berrigan. EAS
Strongest, The. "Yehoash," *tr. fr. Yiddish by* Marie Syrkin. TrJP
Strongest and the noblest argument, The. Sir John Davies. *Fr.* Nosce Teipsum. SiPS
Strophes. O. V. de L. Milosz, *tr. fr. French by* Ezra Pound. RHTwFP
Struck with huge Love, of what to be possest. Prefatory Poem, on. . . *Magnalia Christi Americana.* Nicholas Noyes. SCAP
Structural Study of Myth, The. Jerome Rothenberg. PoM
Structure of process, The. Process. John Montague. CIP
Struggle. Sidney Lanier. LiTA; OxBA
Struggle, The. Sully-Prudhomme, *tr. fr. French by* Arthur O'Shaughnessy. AWP
Struggle for the Roads. Bruce Severy. NOVW
Struggle is strong and splendid, The. Sounding. Doris Ferne. CaP
Struggle with the Angel, The. Claude Vigée, *tr. fr. French by* Elizabeth Savage. VWA
Struggles of Words, The. Pierre Reverdy, *tr. fr. French by* Michael Benedikt. POS
Strut for Roethke, A. John Berryman. NOBA
Stuart's gallantry. I recall how once. Wild Honey. Alistair Campbell. ATNZ
Stubborn Back—And Nothing More, A. H. Leivick, *tr. fr. Yiddish by* Robert Friend. PeBMYV
Stuck each summer at Bible camp. Constipation. Ronald Wallace. MOWH
Stud. Michael Lassell. *Fr.* Times Square Poems. GLP
Stud Groom. John Glassco. OBCV
Student. The. Shauqi Abi Shaqra, *tr. fr. Arabic by* Sargon Boulus *and* Peter Porter. MAP
Student. Cheng Min, *tr. by* Kenneth Rexroth *and* Ling Chung. PBWP
Student, The. Peter Meinke. SoTCo
Student, The. Josephine Miles. NoP
Student, The. Marianne Moore. NAAL-2; TwCP
Student, The. *Unknown, tr. fr. Early Modern Irish by* Frank O'Connor. AnIL; OBMV
Student came from Oxford town also, A. Chaucer. *See* Canterbury Tales, The: Prologue.
Student, do the simple purification. The Simple Purification. Kabir, *tr. by* Robert Bly. NU
Student's life is pleasant, The. The Student. *Unknown, tr. by* Frank O'Connor. AnIL; OBMV
Students, like students, form and fly. "When the Students Resisted, a Minor Clash Ensued." David Knight. MoCV
Students of Justice, The. W. S. Merwin. NaP
Student's Tale, The. Longfellow. *Fr.* Tales of a Wayside Inn, *Pt.* III. AmPP
Studied poverty of a moon roof, The. Slips. Medbh McGuckian. FaBCIP
Studies at Delhi, 1876. Sir Alfred Comyn Lyall. OBTV
Studio, The. Derek Mahon. FaBCIP
Studio for Listening to the Snow, The. Yang Chi, *tr. fr. Chinese by* Jonathan Chaves. CoBLCP
Studio Poem. Cilla McQueen. PeNZ
Studium Generale. Alfred Gong, *tr. fr. German by* Beth Bjorklund. CoAuP
Study: A Hand. Gyorgy Raba, *tr. fr. Hungarian by* Jascha Kessler. FOC
Study in Aesthetics, A. Robert Peters. BXAP
Study in Aesthetics, The. Ezra Pound. CMoP; NOBA; NoP
Study in Terror, A. Tamura Ryuichi, *tr. fr. Japanese by* Hiroaki Sato. FCEI
Study of a Spider, The. Lord De Tabley. NOBVV
Study of Geography, or History, The. Lauris Edmond. UAS
Study of Reading Habits, A. Philip Larkin. InPK; NOBL; PoPo; PPP; SoSe; TW
Study of the Object. Zbigniew Herbert, *tr. fr. Polish by* Czeslaw Milosz. PwPP
Study of Two Pears. Wallace Stevens. InPS; NAAL-2; NoAM; NU; OxBA
Study Peace. Imamu Amiri Baraka. PoBA
Stuff of Dreams, The. Shakespeare. *See* Tempest, The: Our Revels Now Are Ended.
Stuff of the moon. Nocturne in a Deserted Brickyard. Carl Sandburg. MoAmPo
Stuffed Owl, The, *sel.* Wordsworth.
"While Anna's peers and early playmates tread." Par
Stuffed owls drum in my heart. Fear. Thomas Love Peacock. VoR
Stuffy chill of clouded Summer, crowdsmell, booksmell. Supervising Examinations. Sean Lucy. CIP
Stumbling. Dick Lourie. NeAC

Stump, The. Robert Bly. PPR
Stumpfoot on 42nd Street. Louis Simpson. NNaP; UnPo; VGW
Stun. James Schuyler. MAT
Stuntman. Lionel Kearns. MoCV
Stupendious love! all saints astonishment. Edward Taylor. *Fr.* Preparatory Meditations before My Approach to the Lord's Supper, X. OxBA
Stupid Old Body, The. Edward Carpenter. WGRP
Stupid Old Myself. Russell Hoban. RHPC
Stupidity. "E." CBAP
Stupidity achieves the crime. Martyr. Mary Elizabeth Fullerton. CBAP
Stupidity Street. Ralph Hodgson. BrPo; CH; LiTM; MoAB; MoBrPo; OBD; OxBTC; PDV
Sturdiest of forest trees, The. The Holly. Walter de la Mare. CMoP
Sturdy Conq'ror, politic, severe, The. The Royal Line. Leigh Hunt. FaBoUs
Sturdy in Me, The. H. Leivick, *tr. fr. Yiddish by* Benjamin *and* Barbara Harshav. *Fr.* My Father. AYP
Sturdy ploughman doth the soldier see, The. Joseph Hall. *Fr.* Virgidemiarum, *bk.* IV, Satire VI. OBSV
Stutterer. Alan Dugan. NYBP
Stwonen Steps, The. William Barnes. NOBVV
Stwuns that built Gaarge Ridler's oven, The. George Ridler's Oven. *Unknown.* OBET
Stygian council thus dissolved; and forth, The. Milton. *Fr.* Paradise Lost, *Bk.* II, *ll.* 506–870. OAEL-1
Style. Charles Bukowski. HoPM
Style. Howard Nemerov. NoAM
Style is the answer to everything. Style. Charles Bukowski. HoPM
Suave and paltry man, my enemy, A. In the Tail of the Scorpion. Genevieve Taggard. VGW
Suave Mari Magno. Lucretius, *tr. fr. Latin by* W. H. Mallock. *Fr.* De Rerum Natura (On the Nature of Things). AWP
Sub-average *Time* Reader, The. Ernest Wittenberg. FiBHP
Sub Rosa. Susan Prospere. AnAn
Sub Specie Aeternitatis. Robert Hayden. AmPP
Subalterns. Elizabeth Daryush. OBWP
Subalterns, The. Thomas Hardy. CMoP; MoAB; MoBrPo; MoP; NoAM; NOBVV; OAEL-2; PPP; TEP
Subaltern's Love-Song, A. Sir John Betjeman. BoLoP; HAP; NoAM; NOBL; OxBTC; TwCP
Subject. Marie Ponsot. VGW
Subject chosen for tonight's discussion, The. An Evening of Russian Poetry. Vladimir Nabokov. NYBP
Subject of Heroic Song, The. Milton. *See* Paradise Lost: No more of talk where God or Angel Guest.
Subject to All Pain. *Unknown.* MeEL
Subject was put to bed at midnight, The. Operative No. 174 Resigns. Kenneth Fearing. NYBP
Subjection of Women, The. Austin Clarke. CIP
Subjectivity at Sestos. P. M. Hubbard. NYBP
Subjects and Arguments for an Act of Desperation. Elio Pagliarani, *tr. fr. Italian by* Lawrence R. Smith. NItP
Sublimation. Alex Comfort. ErPo
Sublime—invention ever young. Christopher Smart. *Fr.* A Song to David. OBEV
Submarine Bed, The. John Peale Bishop. LiTA
Submerged city, The. Cologne. Hilde Domin, *tr. by* Tudor Morris. VWA
Submerged, silent, rooted in water. Foetus. Phyllis Haring. PeSA
Submission. George Herbert. JCP
Submission. Clara Ann Thompson. CBWP-2
Submission. *Unknown, tr. fr. Siamese by* E. Powys Mathers. ErPo
Submission and Rest. Anna Temple Whitney. *See* Camel at the close of day, The.
Submission to Afflictive Providences. Isaac Watts. NOCV
Submit. The Young Writer Smells a Rat. Bonnie Jacobson. SoTCo
Submit to you. Komachi, *tr. fr. Japanese by* Burton Watson. *Fr.* Kokin Shu. FCEI
Submitting a Memorial Requesting Permission to Return Home and Care for My Parents. Yang Chi, *tr. fr. Chinese by* Jonathan Chaves. CoBLCP
Submitting to a sentry's fate. Common Dawn. Guy Butler. PeSA
Subnarcosis. Andrea Zanzotto, *tr. fr. Italian by* Lawrence R. Smith. NItP
Subplot. Jack Butler. MT
Substance Addresses Shadow. T'ao Ch'ien, *tr. fr. Chinese by* Burton Watson. *Fr.* Substance, Shadow, and Spirit. CoBCP
Substance, Shadow, and Spirit, *sels.* T'ao Ch'ien, *tr. fr. Chinese by* Burton Watson. CoBCP
  Shadow Replies to Substance.

  Spirit Expounds.
  Substance Addresses Shadow.
Substantiations, *sel.* Vidya, *tr. fr. Sanskrit by* Daniel H. H. Ingalls. "One born to hardship in his place and station." PBWP
Substitute for Time, The. John Koethe. EOEF
Substitution. Elizabeth Barrett Browning. WGRP
Substitution. Anne Spencer. BlSi; CDC
Subterfuge. Vassar Miller. TSM
Subtle almost beyond thought are these dim colours. Dun-Colour [*or* Dun-Color]. Ruth Pitter. FM; PoRA
Subtle chain of countless rings, A. Nature. Emerson. AWP
Subtlest strain a great musician weaves, The. Limitations. Henrietta Cordelia Ray. CBWP-3
Subtlety. Bruce St. John. PBCV
Suburb. Abraham Chalfi, *tr. fr. Hebrew by* Bernhard Frank. MHeP
Suburb, The. Anne Stevenson. NMM
Suburb ("A woodland of silent oak trees"). Buson, *tr. fr. Japanese by* Hiroaki Sato. *Fr.* Eighty-seven Hokku. FCEI
Suburb ("Cold moon: amidst dead trees"). Buson, *tr. fr. Japanese by* Hiroaki Sato. *Fr.* Eighty-seven Hokku. FCEI
Suburb ("Heat haze: a bug I don't know"). Buson, *tr. fr. Japanese by* Hiroaki Sato. *Fr.* Eighty-seven Hokku. FCEI
Suburb Hilltop. Richard Moore. NYBP
Suburban. John Ciardi. NBLV
Suburban. H. R. Coursen. GOYP
Suburban Dreams. Edwin Muir. OxBTC
Suburban Dusk. Bert Meyers. EAS
Suburban Garden a Nature Reserve. W. G. Shepherd. NPo
Suburban Song. Elizabeth Riddell. CBAP
Suburban Sonnet. Gwen Harwood. CBAP
Suburban Swamp. Jay Parini. BLA
Suburban villas, highway-side retreats. London Suburbs. William Cowper. *Fr.* Retirement. FaBoPP
Suburban Wife's Song. Robert Hutchinson. NYBP
Suburbia. Maurice Martinez. PoNe
Suburbs is a Fine Place, The. *Unknown.* CoMu
Suburbs on a Hazy Day. D. H. Lawrence. OBMV
Suburbs on Spring Day. Shin Dong-jip, *tr. fr. Korean by* Koh Chang-soo. ACKP
Subversive. Ferreira Gullar, *tr. fr. Portuguese by* William Jay Smith. CT
Subversive, The. Merle Woo. BrSi
Subverted Flower, The. Robert Frost. CMoP; HAP; MoP; NoAM; NOBA; OxBA; PoE; WeW
Subway, The. Allen Tate. NOBA
Subway messes me up, The. Tubes. Larry Mollin. NeAC
Subway Rush Hour. Langston Hughes. InPK
Subway Wind. Claude McKay. PBCV
Subway Witnesses, The. Lorenzo Thomas. PoBA
Succeeding to the Celestial Throne. Yakamochi. *Fr.* Manyo Shu. Ma
Success! Berton Braley. WBLP
Success. Rupert Brooke. OxBTC
Success. Emily Dickinson. *See* Success is counted sweetest.
Success. William Empson. OxBTC
Success. *Unknown.* FaFP
Success and failure are not our affairs. Seeing Off Sun Ling-hsiu. Wu Wei-yeh, *tr. by* Jonathan Chaves. CoBLCP
Success is counted sweetest. Emily Dickinson. CMoP; FPL; GoJo; InPS; LiTM; LiTM; MoAB; MoAmPo; NAAL-1; NOBA; OxBA; PoRA; TAP; WaaP; WPE
  (Success.) AnAmPo; AWP
Success is like some horrible disaster. After Publication of *Under the Volcano.* Malcolm Lowry. FaBoTw
Success is speaking words of praise. Success. *Unknown.* FaFP
Success Story. Terence Winch. UL
Successful Attempt. Hermann Jandl, *tr. fr. German by* Beth Bjorklund. CoAuP
Succession, The. Frances Laughton Mace. AA
Succubi. John Newlove. NeAC
Succubus, The. Robert Graves. OAEL-2
Succubus, The. Harriet Rose. BrRo
Succulent flower bleeds molasses, The. Sugar Cane. Faustin Charles. PBCV
Succumbing. Paul Eaton Reeve. ErPo
Such a beast is the Hipporhinostricow. Hipporhinostricow. Spike Milligan. AmMo
Such a Blustery Day! Elizabeth Gould. BoTP
Such a calmness. Rest. Jacob Isaac Segal, *tr. by* Seymour Mayne. VWA
Such a fleeting life though we shared together. Yakamochi. *Fr.* Manyo Shu. Ma

Such a fool as I am you had better ignore. The Usk. C. H. Sisson. NOCV

Such a hubbub in the nests. Freaks of Fashion. Christina Rossetti. FM

Such a morning it is when love. Day of These Days. Laurie Lee. BoNaP

Such a Parcel of Rogues in a Nation. Burns. OxBS

Such a peculiar lot. Fantasy of an African Boy. James Berry. PVCV

Such a prelate, I trow. John Skelton. *Fr.* Why Come Ye Not to Court. OBSV

Such a sad celebration. A Grain of Moonlight. Asya, *tr.* by Gabriel Preil *and* Howard Schwartz. VWA

Such a simple desire. Poem Written after Reading Wright's "American Hunger." Sonia Sanchez. ER

Such a strange girl. Chiqui and Terra Nova. Jessica Hagedorn. UL

Such a strong color on the late chrysanthemums. T'ao Yuan-ming. *Fr.* Two Drinking Songs, 2. NU

Such a time of it they had. Stanley Meets Mutesa. James D. Rubadiri. PBA

Such a wide, still landscape, all cold and white! A Greenland Winter. Lucy Diamond. BoTP

Such a wizened creature. Old Age. E. Keary. NOBVV

Such an easy phrase. Confused. Chang Ts'o, *tr.* by Dominic Cheung. IFON

Such as in God the Lord Do Trust. William Kethe. AH

Such as it is. Such as two men. The Clothing's New Emperor. Donald Finkel. NePoEA

Such as, retired from sight of men, like thee. To Saint Mary Magdalen. Henry Constable. Son

Such cats are useful to calm the horses. Throwing the Racetrack Cats at Saratoga. David Ray. SM

Such Comfort as the Night Can Bring to Us. Peter Cooley. MAYP; NAmP

Such darkness as when Jesus died! San Francisco. Joaquin Miller. PAH

Such easy, easy hours. Moon as Medusa. Vinnie-Marie D'Ambrosio. IHMS

Such fame as I have drops from me in a flash. The Perturbations of Uranus. Roy Fuller. ErPo

Such hap as I am happed in. Sir Thomas Wyatt. SiPS

Such hints as untaught Nature yields! Nature: The Artist. Frederic Lawrence Knowles. AA

Such ills attend. Advice to Lovers. John Armstrong. *Fr.* The Oeconomy of Love; a Poetical Essay. NOEC

Such Instance. Byron Herbert Reece. KS

Such Is the Death the Soldier Dies. Robert Burns Wilson. AA

Such is the Mode of these censorious Days. On Mr. Hobbs, and His Writings. John Sheffield. PoEL-3

Such is the secret union, when we feel. The Creative Process. Mark Akenside. *Fr.* The Pleasures of Imagination, II. NOEC

Such Is the Sickness of Many a Good Thing. Robert Duncan. CAPP

Such is the way of the world. "St.-John Perse," *tr. fr. French by* T. S. Eliot. *Fr.* Anabasis, IV. OBVE

Such is the wood-pigeon's song when the shower approaches. Room in Space. René Char, *tr.* by W. S. Merwin. RHTwFP

Such light is in sea-caves. Musica No. 3. Richard Duerden. NeAP

Such loneliness! If I could carve in stone. Wakayama Bokusui, *tr. fr. Japanese by* Hiroaki Sato. *Fr.* Forty-four Tanka. FCEI

Such marvellous ways to kill a man! The Bofors A. A. Gun. Gavin Ewart. WaP

Such moving sounds from such a careless touch. Of My Lady Isabella Playing on the Lute. Edmund Waller. HAP; MePo
(On My Lady Isabella Playing on the Lute.) SeCP

Such natural debts of love our Oxford knows. Martyr's Memorial. Louise Imogen Guiney. AA

Such pictures of the heavens were never seen. The Invisible. Richard Watson Gilder. WGRP

Such poor folk as to law do go. Isabella Whitney. *Fr.* Sweet Nosegay, A, or Pleasant Posy. WPE

Such power there is in drawing breath. Backing into the Fan Mail (Unreceived). Dick Gallup. UL

Such pungent odors the old synagogues dispel. Odors. Mani Leib, *tr.* by John Hollander. PeBMYV

Such shameless bards we have; and yet 'tis true. Pope. *Fr.* Essay on Criticism, Pt. III. OBSV

Such should this day be, so the sun should hide. On the Marriage of T. K. and C. C., the Morning Stormy. Thomas Carew. BoLoP

Such skill, matcht with such courage as he had. Spenser. *Fr.* Astrophel. OBWP

Such soft ideas all my pains beguile. Lady Mary Wortley Montagu. OBTV

Such splendid icecaps and hard rills, such weights. Piano Practice. Howard Moss. NYBP

"Such Stuff as Dreams." Franklin P. Adams. FiBHP

Such Stuff as Dreams are Made Of. Thomas Wentworth Higginson. AA

Such Stuff as Dreams Are Made On. Shakespeare. *See* Tempest, The: Our Revels Now Are Ended.

Such subtile filigranity and nobless of construccion. "Wellcome, to the Caves of Artá!" Robert Graves. NBLV; NOBL; NYBP

Such, such is Death: no triumph: no defeat. Charles Hamilton Sorley. *Fr.* Two Sonnets, II. MMA; MoBrPo

Such times as windy moods do stir. The Spirit of the Wheat. Edward A. U. Valentine. AA

Such Tophet was; so looked the grinning fiend. Tophet. Thomas Gray. FaBoEE; NOEC; OxBSP

Such was he, our Martyr-Chief. Our Martyr-Chief. James Russell Lowell. OHIP

Such was old Chaucer. Such the placid mien. For a Statue of Chaucer at Woodstock. Mark Akenside. SeCePo

Such[e] wayward[e] ways [*or* wais] hath love, that most[e] part[e] in discord[e]. Earl of Surrey. AAS; SiPS

Sucked into the hillside darkness. Wakayama Bokusui, *tr. fr. Japanese by* Hiroaki Sato. *Fr.* Forty-four Tanka. FCEI

Sucking Cider through a Straw. *Unknown.* AS; GBP

Sucking the dandelion roots. A Sandy Burial. Geoffrey Grigson. OBD

Suction's Anthem. Blake. *Fr.* An Island in the Moon. FaBoNo

Sudbury Fight, The. Wallace Rice. PAH

Sudden amid the slush and rain. In the City. Israel Zangwill. WGRP

Sudden autumn winds, like hounds, The. Mary Gilmore. *Fr.* The Disinherited. PoAu-1

Sudden bad news—reading, I couldn't believe it. Mourning for My Younger Sister. Rai San'yo, *tr.* by Burton Watson. JLIC-2

Sudden blow, A: the great wings beating still. Leda and the Swan. W. B. Yeats. AnIL; CMoP; EBEV; ErPo; FF; FPL; GTBS-P; HAP; HeIP; InPK; LiTM; MoAB; MoBrPo; MoP; NAEL-2; NAWM-2; NIP; NoAM; NOBE; NoP; OAEL-2; PBBP; PoE; PPP; PrIm; SCV; Son; SoSe; SoSe; TEP; TEP; TrGrPo; WeW

Sudden crocuses start up, erupt, The. Spring in the Park. Dorothy Wellesley. CN

Sudden Inspiration on a Summer Day. Michizane, *tr. fr. Chinese by* Burton Watson. JLIC-1

Sudden, it comes for you. Ode to Garlic. William Stafford. CAPP

Sudden Light. Dante Gabriel Rossetti. BoLoP; CTC; ELP; FPL; NOBE; NOBVV; NoP; OAEL-2; OBNC; OPOP; PoLF; TrGrPo

Sudden nightfall around us. The Terrace. Vittorio Sereni, *tr.* by Henry Taylor. PFI

Sudden refreshment came upon the school. Physical Geography. Louise Townsend Nicholl. ImOP

Sudden shower. Buson, *tr.* by Geoffrey Bownas *and* Anthony Thwaite. PeBJV

Sudden Shower. Okubo Shibutsu, *tr. fr. Chinese by* Burton Watson. JLIC-2

Sudden snowfall comes in darkness, A. Snowy Mountains. Tsung Ch'en, *tr.* by Jonathan Chaves. CoBLCP

Sudden the desert changes. Bridge-Guard in the Karroo. Kipling. OBWP

Sudden Things. Donald Hall. EAS

Sudden thrust of speech is no mean test, The. The Fire i' the Flint. Lucy Catlin Robinson. AA

Sudden upriseth from her stately palace. Spenser. *Fr.* The Faerie Queene, I, 4. PPP

Sudden wakin', a sudden weepin', A. Man's Days. Eden Phillpotts. OBEV; OxBTC

Suddening one day by myself. The Fence. Heather McHugh. GeTw

Suddenly. Yusuf al-Sa'igh, *tr. fr. Arabic by* Diana Der Hovanessian *with* Salma Khadra Jayyusi. MAP

Suddenly. Robin Blaser. PoM

Suddenly,/ out of the faint gray smother. White Fox. Elizabeth Alsop Shepard. GoYe

Suddenly/ a flash of thought strikes. Telephone Booth in the Rain. Tu Yeh, *tr.* by Dominic Cheung. IFON

Suddenly/ there towers. Vanity. Giuseppe Ungaretti, *tr.* by Charles Tomlinson. PFI

Suddenly/ in middle age. Icons. Miriam Waddington. NOBC

Suddenly a squeal. Itamar Ya'oz-kest, *tr. fr. Hebrew by* Bernhard Frank. *Fr.* Ordeal by Fire. MHeP

Suddenly, after the quarrel, while we waited. The Quarrel. Conrad Aiken. MoAB; MoAmPo

Suddenly as the riot squad moved in. Belfast Confetti. Ciaran Carson. CIP

Suddenly darkening, the sky beyond my eaves. Teika, *tr. fr. Japanese by* Hiroaki Sato. *Fr.* Eighty-four Tanka. FCEI

Suddenly drawn through the thick glass plate. Sharks at the New York Aquarium. Charles Martin. SM

Suddenly everything stops. Slump. Vassar Miller. BoWoP

Suddenly half in jest. Album Leaf. Stéphane Mallarmé, *tr. by* Keith Bosley. OBVE

Suddenly her breast has never been larger. Impotence. Marvin Bell. AmPA

Suddenly his mouth filled with sand. Death of a Poet. Charles Causley. OxBTC

Suddenly his poor body. Stations. Ted Hughes. NoAM

Suddenly horizons clouded. The Vision. Muhammed al-Faituri, *tr. by* Sargon Boulus *and* Peter Porter. MAP

Suddenly I remember the holes. The Holes. Stephen Berg. NaP; NYBP

Suddenly I saw the cold and rook-delighting heaven. The Cold Heaven. W. B. Yeats. AWP; CTC; GTBS-P; HAP; NoAM; OAEL-2; OxBSP; RB; TEP; WeW

Suddenly in the dark wood. Her Voice Could Not Be Softer. Austin Clarke. NOIV

Suddenly in the midnight on mortal men. The Last Judgment. *Unknown, tr. fr. Anglo-Saxon by* Charles W. Kennedy. *Fr.* Christ 3. AnOE

Suddenly it was quiet as a Sunday. The Wave. Daryl Hine. Prf

Suddenly it's autumn, I think, as I look in the garden. Last Sheet. Roy Fuller. TEP

Suddenly laughter became sobbing. Sonnet on Separation. Vinícius de Moraes, *tr. by* Ashley Brown. ATCBP

Suddenly leaves struck the street. Allenby. Meir Wieseltier, *tr. by* Warren Bargad *and* Stanley F. Chyet. IP

Suddenly night crushed out the day and hurled. The Unreturning. Wilfred Owen. MoBrPo

Suddenly, out of my darkness, shines Thy beauty, O Brother. A Psalm to the Son. Marguerite Wilkinson. TrPWD

"Suddenly she slapped me, hard across the face." Elizabeth in Italy. Richard Weber. BoLoP
(In Memoriam, II.) ErPo

Suddenly the evening touched us. They Walk on Cat's Paws. Rocco Scotellaro, *tr. by* Lawrence R. Smith. NItP

Suddenly the sky turned gray. Snow toward Evening. Melville Cane. PDV

Suddenly there stirs in you the image of parks in polaroid colors like. To the Things That Are Immortal. Abba Kovner, *tr. by* Warren Bargad *and* Stanley F. Chyet. IP

Suddenly there was a dress. White Notes. Donald Justice. LCAP

Suddenly there were forms there. Horses. Gwyn Thomas, *tr. by* Joseph P. Clancy. OBWVE

Suddenly they came flying, like a long scarf of smoke. The Thing. Theodore Roethke. CMoP

Suddenly they change the calendar, spring coming much earlier. End of Winter in a Mountain Village. Yaguchi Kensai, *tr. by* Burton Watson. JLIC-2

Suddenly things have changed, my soul. Bahadur Shah Zafar, *tr. by* Ahmed Ali. GoT

Suddenly tonight we must say goodby. At a Farewell Party for Fujiwara no Yoshino. Emperor Junna, *tr. by* Burton Watson. JLIC-2

Suddenly, warm weather, I change to lighter clothes. Yang Chi, *tr. fr. Chinese by* Jonathan Chaves. *Fr.* Living in a Riverside Village— Miscellaneous Impressions. CoBLCP

Suddenly with intense. The Runner. Alexandra Grilikhes. SD

Sue Ella Tucker was barely in her teens. Rubaiyat for Sue Ella Tucker. Miller Williams. SM

Suelick is the greatest Indian power. The Origin of the Skagit Indians. Lucy Williams, *tr. by* Carl Cary. STP

Suet Dumpling, The. *Unknown.* BXAP

Suez Crisis. *Somali Oral Tradition, tr. by* B. W. Andrezjewski. WTO

Suffenus, whom so well you know [*or* whom you know]. To Varus. Catullus, *tr. by* Walter Savage Landor. AWP
(Carmina XXII.) OBVE, *tr. by* Matthew Prior

Suffer, Poor Negro! David Diop, *tr. fr. French by* Langston Hughes. PBA

Suffer the Children. Audre Lorde. PoBA

Sufferance of her race is shown, The. "Formerly a Slave." Herman Melville. PoNe; TAP

Suffering. Albert Ehrenstein, *tr. fr. German by* Babette Deutsch. TrJP

Suffering. Maria Guacci Nobile, *tr. fr. Italian by* Muriel Kittel. DMI

Suffering. P. K. Page. NoAM

Suffering has settled like a sly disguise. A Korean Woman Seated by a Wall. William Meredith. NePoEA

Sufficed not, madame, that you did tear. Sir Thomas Wyatt. SiPS

Sufficeth it to you [*or* yow] my joys [*or* joyes] interred. The Ocean's Love to Cynthia. Sir Walter Ralegh. SiPS, *sl. abr*
(Ocean to Cynthia, The.) OBSC, *sl. abr*

Sufficient unto the Day. Cees Buddingh', *tr. fr. Dutch by* Elizabeth Willems-Treeman. DuIn

Suffocation. Linda Pastan. BLA

Suffolk. Swinburne. *Fr.* By the North Sea, III. FaBoPP

Suffolk Miracle, The. *Unknown.* AmFP

Suffolk Miracle, The. *Unknown.* ESPB

Suffolk Shore, The. George Crabbe. *Fr.* The Borough, Letter XXIII. FaBoPP

Sufi Quatrain. Rabi'a bint Isma'il of Syria, *tr. fr. Arabic by* Deirdre Lashgari. WPOW

Sugar-Candy Bird, A. Ian Young. NeAC

Sugar Cane. Faustin Charles. PVCV

Sugar Cane, The, *sels.* James Grainger.
  Compost. NOEC
  (How to Fertilize Soil.) FaBoUs
  How to Exterminate Rats. FaBoUs
  "On festal days; or when their work is done." PBCV
  Slaves. NOEC
  "Then earthquakes, nature's agonizing pangs." PBCV

Sugar-cane is just a cubit high, The. Love Songs (Dadaria). *Gond Oral Tradition, tr. by* V. Elwin *and* S. Hivale. WTO

Sugar dripping into your vein, The. Firstborn. Charles Wright. DiL

Sugar in the Cane. Tennessee Williams. OBAL

Sugar Lady, The. Frank Asch. RHPC

Sugar-Plum Tree, The. Eugene Field. FaFP; NBLV; OxBChV

Sugar Weather. Peter McArthur. CaP

Sugarfields. Barbara Mahone. CNA; PoBA

Sugaring, The. Abraham Moses Klein. OBCV

Suggestion Made by the Posters of the *Globe*, A. J. E. Thorold Rogers. FaBoEE

Suicide. W. E. Henley. *Fr.* In Hospital, XXIV.

Suicide, A. Tom Kryss. NeAC

Suicide, The. V. R. Laing. PoA

Suicide. Robert Lowell. PoE

Suicide, The. Louis MacNeice. FaBCIP

Suicide, The. Joyce Carol Oates. Psk

Suicide. Anne Stevenson. FaBoWP

Suicide. Alice Walker. FF

Suicide in [the] Trenches. Siegfried Sassoon. BrPo; MMA

Suicide of Atzesivano Disciple of Buddha, The. Angelos Sikelianos, *tr. fr. Greek by* Edmund Keeley *and* Philip Sherrard. VMG

Suicide of the night—ah, flotsam. Strange Fruit. Randolph Stow. PoAu-2

Suicide off Egg Rock. Sylvia Plath. PPP

Suicide Pond. Kathy McLaughlin. PoA

Suicided by Night. Robert Desnos, *tr. fr. French by* Michael Benedikt. POS

Suicide's Note. Langston Hughes. CDC

Suilven. Andrew Young. OxBS

Suilven and the Eagle, *sel.* Gordon Bottomley.
  Eagle Song. MoBrPo

Suit of Nettles, A, *sels.* James Reaney.
  Branwell's Sestina. MoCV
  January. OBCV
  November. OBCV

Suitable for a gentleman with medals. War Lord in the Early Evening. P. K. Page. NoAM

Suitcases, The. Abd al-Karim Kassid, *tr. fr. Arabic by* Lena Jayyusi *and* Anthony Thwaite. MAP

Suite for Celery and Blind Date. Philip Dow. BXAP

Suite for Marriage, A. David Ignatow. NNaP

Suite from Catullus. Vincent McHugh. ErPo

Suite of Six Pieces for Siskind, A. John Logan. LCAP

Suite to Fathers. Jim Harrison. AmPA; DiL

Suitor, The. Jane Kenyon. InPK

Suits hang half a year in. Tyburn and Westminster. John Heywood. ACP

Suk, suk go the bustard's plumes. *Unknown, tr. by* Arthur Waley. BoS

Sukey, you shall by my wife. *Unknown.* OxNR

Sukkot. Sol Lachman. VWA

Sulk. Felice Holman. RHPC

Sulk when you're spoken to. *Unknown.* CenHV

Sulkily the sticks burn, and though they crackle. Under the Pot. Robert Graves. FaBoEE

Sulky old gray brute!, The. The Bristol Channel. Thomas Edward Brown. NOBVV

Sullen and dark [*or* dull], in the September day. The Last Reservation. Walter Learned. AA; PAH

Sullen Sullom Voe. Ronas Hill. Hamish Brown. PoSH
Sullivan arrived at the very lowest Heaven. John L. Sullivan Enters
    Heaven. Robert Frost. BXAP
Sulphur-yellow chord of the eleventh, A. On Hearing Prokofieff's
    Grotesque for Two Bassoons, Concertina and Snare-Drums. Louis
    Untermeyer. BXAP
Sultry air, the smoke of shavings. A Night in a Village. Ivan Savvich
    Nikitin, tr. by P. E. Matheson. AWP
Sum, Es, Est ("Sum—I am a gentleman"). Unknown. ChTr
Sum of Life, The. Ben King. CTC
Sum speiks of lords, sum speiks of lairds. Johnie Armstrang. Unknown.
    ESPB; OxBB
Suma fisherman/ may know the ring of the sea breeze, A. Teika, tr. by
    Steven D. Carter. WFTW
Sumach Leaves, The. Jones Very. NOBA
Sumburgh Heid. George Bruce. OxBS
Sumer Is Icumen In. Unknown. See Summer [or Summer] is icumen [or
    y-comen] in.
Summa is i-cumen in. Baccalaureate. David McCord. BXAP; NBLV;
    OBAL
Summah night an' sighin' breeze. Lover's Lane. Paul Laurence Dunbar.
    BANP
Summary. Sonia Sanchez. BPo
Summary of the Distance between the Bomber and the Objective. Walter
    Benton. WaP
Summer. Conrad Aiken. NoAM
Summer. Frank Asch. NTCP; RHPC
Summer. John Ashbery. NAAL-2
Summer. Robert Bloomfield. Fr. The Farmer's Boy. PBBP
Summer. Chang Yü, tr. fr. Chinese by Jonathan Chaves. Fr. The Four
    Seasons in the Mountains. CoBLCP
Summer. John Clare. BoNaP
Summer. Douglas Crase. NoP
Summer. John Davidson. BoNaP
Summer. Javier Heraud, tr. fr. Spanish by Maureen Ahern. Per
Summer. Moishe Kulbak, tr. fr. Yiddish. PeBMYV, tr. by Leonard
    Wolf; VWA, tr. by Ruth Whitman
Summer. Tom Marshall. NOBC
Summer. Josephine Miles. FaBoWP; WPE
Summer. Christina Rossetti. BoNaP; ELP
Summer. Gary Soto. WeW
Summer. Spenser. Fr. The Faerie Queene, VII, 7. GN
Summer. Lucien Stryk. CAPP
Summer. James Thomson. Fr. The Seasons.
    Summer ("Home from his morning task the swain retreats"). FM
    Happy Britannia. FaBoPP; SeCePo
    (Britannia.) FaBoPP
    "Still let me pierce into the midnight depth." EnRP
    "'Tis raging noon; and vertical, the sun." EBEV; OAEL-1
Summer. Diane Wakoski. VGW
Summer/ Ramona Wilson. VoR
Summer/ The earth is warm, the sun's ablaze. The Four Seasons. Jack
    Prelutsky. RHPC
Summer!/ the painting is organized. The Corn Harvest. William Carlos
    Williams. Fr. Pictures from Brueghel, VII. PPP
Summer Acres. Anne Wilkinson. CaP
Summer, adieu. Ode to the End of Summer. Phyllis McGinley. NBLV
Summer Afternoon. Elizabeth B. Harrod. NePoEA
Summer Afternoon. Raymond Souster. BoNaP
Summer again. Margaret Atwood. Fr. The Circle Game. MoCV
Summer and autumn had been so wet, The. God's Judgment on a Wicked
    Bishop. Robert Southey. ChTr; EnRP; OBNV; OnMSP
    (Bishop Hatto.) ChTr; OBNV
Summer and Winter. Shelley. BoNaP
Summer Anniversaries, The. Donald Justice. AnAn
Summer Band Concert. Vivian Smith. CBAP
Summer Beach. Frances Cornford. BrRo
Summer, betray this tree again! Misericordia. Margaret Mead. PoA
Summer Breeze. Unknown. BoTP
Summer brings out the girls in their green dresses. Summer 1967. James
    Keir Baxter. ATNZ
Summer Christmas in Australia, A. Douglas Sladen. OBCP
Summer clothes: I have yet to pick all the lice. Basho, tr. fr. Japanese by
    Burton Watson. Fr. Seventy-six Hokku. FCEI
Summer Cloud, A. Waldo Williams, tr. fr. Welsh by Joseph P. Clancy.
    OBWVE
Summer come soon and turn the sickness from my house. Entreaty.
    Robert Fitzgerald. OxBSP
Summer comes/ The ziczac hovers. Magalu. Helene Johnson. BlSi;
    CDC; PoBA; PoNe

Summer comes October, the green becomes the brown. The Long and
    Lonely Winter. Dave Goulder. OBET
Summer Commentary, A. Yvor Winters. LiTM; QFR
Summer Concert. Reed Whittemore. AmFN
Summer Countries, The. Henry Rago. VGW
Summer darkening along walls crept in among, A. The Flears. John
    Hollander. AnAn
Summer Dawn. William Morris. Mes; NOBE; NOBVV; OAEL-2;
    OBEV; OBNC
Summer Day, A. Florence Harrison. BoTP
Summer Day. Kan Sazan, tr. fr. Chinese by Burton Watson. JLIC-2
Summer Day in the Mountains. Li Po, tr. fr. Chinese by Burton Watson.
    CoBCP
Summer day is full of ease, A. Joyful. Rose Burgunder. RAR; RHPC
Summer day suffocates, smothers, pants, The. Poem on Azure. Anna de
    Noailles, tr. by Betty L. Schwimmer. WPOW
Summer Days. Wathen Mark Wilks Call. EBVV
Summer Days. Roy Daniells. CaP
Summer delights the scholar. The Scholar. Austin Clarke. RB
Summer Ending, The. Glenway Wescott. PoA
Summer ends now; now, barbarous in beauty, the stooks arise. Hurrahing
    in Harvest. Gerard Manley Hopkins. BoNaP; BrPo; ChTr; CMoP;
    FaBoPP; InvP; MoAB; MoBrPo; NAEL-2; PoE; TOF
Summer Evening. John Clare. BoTP
Summer Evening. Charles Cotton. See The Day's grown old, the
    fainting Sun.
Summer Evening. Walter de la Mare. FM; MoAB; MoBrPo; MoShBr
Summer Evening. Emperor Kogon, tr. fr. Japanese by Steven D. Carter.
    WFTW
Summer Farm. Norman MacCaig. OxBTC
Summer Fragments, sels. Andreas Okopenko, tr. fr. German by Beth
    Bjorklund. CoAuP
    Brooding Afternoon in July. Fr. III.
    End of a Summer Sunday. Fr. I.
    July Morning. Fr. II.
Summer Garden. "Anna Akhmatova," tr. fr. Russian by Stephen
    Stepanchev. BoWoP
Summer Gone, A. Howard Moss. NePoEA
Summer, goodbye. October. Donald Justice. BLA
Summer grass/ way in the distance. Masaoka Shiki, tr. fr. Japanese by
    Burton Watson. Fr. Thirty-nine Haiku. FCEI
Summer grass: where the warriors used to dream. At Takadachi in Oshu.
    Basho, tr. fr. Japanese by Burton Watson. Fr. Seventy-six Hokku.
    FCEI
Summer grasses. Basho, tr. by Geoffrey Bownas and Anthony Thwaite.
    PeBJV
Summer Grasses in the Fields at Dusk. Gyoko, tr. fr. Japanese by Steven
    D. Carter. WFTW
Summer grows old, cold-blooded mother. Frog Autumn. Sylvia Plath.
    OxBSP
Summer Haloed. Sandor Csoori, tr. fr. Hungarian by Jascha Kessler.
    FOC
Summer hangs. The Death of the Bronx. Chana Bloch. MAYP
Summer Harvest Spreads the Fields, The. Nathan Strong. AH
Summer has doft his latest green. Winter. W. D. Landor. BoTP
Summer holds, The: upon its glittering lake. W. H. Auden. Fr. The
    Dog beneath the Skin. OxBTC
Summer Holiday. Robinson Jeffers. MoAmPo; OxBA
Summer Holidays. W. R. Rodgers. LiTB
Summer Home. Seamus Heaney. FaBCIP; IPY
Summer ("Home from his morning task the swain retreats"). James
    Thomson. Fr. The Seasons: Summer. FM
Summer Idyll. George Barker. FaBoMo
Summer Images. John Clare. ChTr; OBNC
Summer in a Small Town. Linda Gregg. MAYP
Summer in Academia (Sumerian Academia). Kirby Olson. SoTCo
Summer in England, 1914. Alice Meynell. BrRo; WPE
Summer in the Tehachapi Mountains. Naming. Joseph Stroud. NPGG
Summer Interlude. Lionel Stevenson. CaP
Summer is a chartreuse hell in the mountains. Old Roadside Resorts.
    Molly Peacock. MAYP
Summer is come, and evening spreads its gold. Return. Theodore
    Spencer. PoA
"Summer is coming, summer is coming." The Throstle. Tennyson.
    BoNaP; FaPON; PBBP
Summer Is Ended. Christina Rossetti. NOBVV
Summer is fading; the broad leaves that grew. Farewell to Summer.
    George Arnold. AA
Summer Is Gone ("My titdings for you: the stag bells"). Unknown, tr. by
    Sean O'Faolain. AnIL

Summer Is Gone ("May's the merriest month of all"). *Unknown, tr. fr. Old Irish* by Kuno Meyer. FaBoCh
Summer is gone, The. Your Hair. Ruth Kim Chun-soo, *tr.* by Koh Chang-soo. ACKP
Summer is gone and all the merry noise. Autumn ("Summer is gone and all the merry noise"). John Clare. SaC
Summer is gone with all its roses. Bitter for Sweet. Christina Rossetti. GBL
Summer is here now. Summer Wisteria. Shotetsu, *tr.* by Steven D. Carter. WFTW
Summer [*or* Sumer] is icumen [*or* y-comen] in. Cuckoo [*or* Cuccu] Song. *Unknown.* AWP; EBEV; FF; HAP; HeIP; InPS; InvP; NIP; PBBP; TEP
(Cuckoo.) ChTr; NBLV; NOBE; NoP; OBEV; TrGrPo
("Sing, cuccu, nu. Sing, cuccu.") MeEL; NoP; OAEL-1
Summer Is Nigh. *Unknown.* BoTP
Summer is over, the old cow said. Moo! Robert Hillyer. OBAL
Summer Island. William Logan. MAYP
Summer Journey. W. R. Rodgers. OBTV
Summer journeys. Manhattan. Lorenz Hart. OBAL
Summer Killer. T. Alan Broughton. MOWH
Summer Landscape; or, The Dragon's Teeth, The. Rolfe Humphries. NYBP
Summer Letters. Michael Davidson. IAT
Summer Lightning. Thomas Sturge Moore. BrPo
Summer, like a dread disease. Thredbo River. Sydney Jephcott. PoAu-1
Summer Lullaby, A. Eudora S. Bumstead. BoTP
Summer Magic. Leslie Pinckney Hill. BANP
Summer Malison, The. Gerard Manley Hopkins. CMoP; PoEL-5
Summer Matures. Helene Johnson. BlSi; CDC; PoNe
Summer Moon. Tamemasa, *tr. fr. Japanese* by Steven D. Carter. WFTW
Summer Morning, A. Rachel Lyman Field. PDV
Summer Morning, *sel.* Thomas Miller.
"See yonder smoke, before it curls to heaven." PF
Summer Morning, A. Richard Wilbur. FaBoMo; NBLV
Summer morning. Fig-leaves. Leaves of the Fig-Tree. Nakahara Chuya, *tr.* by Geoffrey Bownas *and* Anthony Thwaite. PeBJV
Summer morning—five o'clock. In the Courtyard. Miriam Ulinover, *tr.* by Seth L. Wolitz. VWA
Summer mountains: across the span of Kyoto. Buson, *tr. fr. Japanese* by Hiroaki Sato. *Fr. Eighty-seven Hokku.* FCEI
Summer near the River. Carolyn Kizer. CoAP; VGW
Summer nests uncovered by autumn wind, The. Birds' Nests. Edward Thomas. HeIP
Summer night. Moritake, *tr.* by Geoffrey Bownas *and* Anthony Thwaite. PeBJV
Summer night/ I close my eyes. Tsurayuki, *tr.* by Geoffrey Bownas *and* Anthony Thwaite. PeBJV
Summer Night. Nathan Alterman, *tr. fr. Hebrew* by Bernhard Frank. MHeP
Summer Night, A. Matthew Arnold. SeCePo
Summer Night, A. W. H. Auden. FaBoRV
Summer Night. Hayyim Nahman Bialik, *tr. fr. Hebrew* by Robert Friend. VWA
Summer Night. Emperor Kogon, *tr. fr. Japanese* by Steven D. Carter. WFTW
Summer Night, A. Elizabeth Stoddard. AA
Summer Night. Tennyson. *See* Now Sleeps the Crimson Petal.
Summer Night at the Pond Pavillion. Chang Yü, *tr. fr. Chinese* by Jonathan Chaves. *Fr. Twelve Miscellaneous Poems on the Fang Garden.* CoBLCP
Summer night has turned to dawn, The. Natsume Seibi, *tr. fr. Japanese* by Hiroaki Sato. *Fr. Twenty-seven Hokku.* FCEI
Summer Night in the Beehive, A. Charles Tennyson Turner. FM
Summer Nights. Daniel Halpern. NAmP
Summer Nights. James Tate. AnAn; NAmP
Summer nights—little time to see the crescent moon decline. Princess Shikishi, *tr. fr. Japanese* by Hiroaki Sato. *Fr. Seventy-eight Tanka.* FCEI
Summer, 1970. Daniel Halpern. AmPA
Summer 1970. Lindiwe Mabuza. WPOW
Summer 1969. Seamus Heaney. CIP
Summer 1967. James Keir Baxter. ATNZ
Summer noon/ I passed under a large *kihada* tree. Broadax. Nishiwaki Junzaburo, *tr.* by Hiroaki Sato. FCEI
Summer of nineteen eighteen, The. The Bad Old Days. Kenneth Rexroth. NNaP; NoAM
Summer of sixty-eight. A Day in a Long Hot Summer. Yuri Kageyama. BrSi

Summer of 'sixty-three, sir, and Conrad was gone away. Kentucky Belle. Constance Fenimore Woolson. BeLS; BLPA; FaBoBe; PAH
Summer on the Lake, A. Otto Orban, *tr. fr. Hungarian* by Jascha Kessler. FOC
Summer Oracle. Audre Lorde. BlSi; PoBA
Summer Palace burnt, the Winter Palace, wherever it was, The. 10:X:57, 45 Years Since the Fall of the Ch'ing Dynasty. Philip Whalen. PoM
(Forty-five Years Since the Fall of the Ch'ing Dynasty.) NeAP
Summer pipers have flickered, The. In the Rut. Hamish Brown. PoSH
Summer Pogrom. Fay Zwicky. CBAP
Summer Rain. Eve Merriam. PDV
Summer Rain. Sir Herbert Read. LiTM
Summer Rain ("Summer rain and the voices of children"). Richard Tillinghast. MAYP; MT
Summer Rain in Mountains. Robert Penn Warren. AnAn
Summer rain isn't here yet, The. The Language of Weather. Ray A. Young Bear. HATNAP
Summer Reflection. Cyril Cusack. TIRV
Summer Rentals, The. Daniel Halpern. DiL; MAYP; NAmP
Summer Report. Paul Celan, *tr. fr. German* by Beth Bjorklund. CoAuP
Summer Report. Klaus Demus, *tr. fr. German* by Beth Bjorklund. CoAuP
Summer Resort. P. K. Page. CaP
Summer Sabbath. Jessie E. Sampter. TrJP
Summer Sanctuary, A. John Hall Ingham. AA
Summer set lip to earth's bosom bare. The Poppy. Francis Thompson. MoBrPo
Summer Shower, A. *Unknown.* BoTP
Summer slams the tropic sun, The. A Country Club Romance. Derek Walcott. OxBC
Summer Solstice. Peter Blue Cloud. *Fr. Within the Seasons.* HATNAP
Summer Solstice, *sel.* George Bowering.
"I am slowly dying, water evaporating." NOBC
Summer Solstice. P'eng Sun-yü, *tr. fr. Chinese* by William H. Nienhauser, Jr. WFTU
Summer Solstice. George Seferis, *tr. fr. Greek* by Edmund Keeley *and* Shilip Sherrard. AnAn
Summer Song, A. George Peele. *See* Whenas [*or* When as] the Rye [Reach to the Chin].
Summer Song. W. W. Watt. FiBHP
Summer Spinning. Saibara, *tr. fr. Japanese* by Hiroaki Sato. FCEI
Summer Stars. Carl Sandburg. RFM
Summer still plays across the street. Dying: An Introduction. L. E. Sissman. NYBP
Summer Storm, A. Anne French. ATNZ
Summer Storm. Lionel Johnson. BrPo
Summer Storm. John Montague. IPY
Summer Storm. Louis Simpson. ErPo; OxBC
Summer storm/ all the sheets of blank paper. Masaoka Shiki, *tr. fr. Japanese* by Burton Watson. *Fr. Thirty-nine Haiku.* FCEI
Summer Sun. Robert Louis Stevenson. MoBrPo; PWR
Summer sun is sinking low, The. Sunset. Longfellow. BoTP
Summer Sunday morning, A. A Battle Ballad. Francis Orrery Ticknor. PAH
Summer Term had just begun, The. Mamzelle. Mary Wilson. AIW
Summer that I was ten, The. The Centaur. May Swenson. FaBoWP; GrPl; NMM; SO; TwCP
Summer, this is our flesh. Seasons of the Soul. Allen Tate. OxBA
Summer. Time to leave. Time to Leave. Ory Bernstein, *tr.* by Warren Bargad *and* Stanley F. Chyet. IP
Summer Vacation. Wordsworth. *Fr. The Prelude [or, Growth of a Poet's Mind], IV.* PoEL-4
Consummate Happiness. OBNC
Dedicated Spirit, A. SeCePo
"Favourite pleasure hath it been with me, A," *Oxford ed.*
"In a throng,/ A festival company." EBEV
"That heartless chase." TOF
Summer voice. Musketaquit, The. Two Rivers. Emerson. AmPP
Summer was killed with the first drop of rain. Helen. Odysseus Elytis, *tr.* by Edmund Keeley *and* Philip Sherrard. VMG
Summer was over, the season unkind, The. The Colliers' March. John Freeth. OBET
Summer was sauntering by. Austin Clarke. *Fr. Mnemosyne Lay in Dust, XVII.* IPY
Summer wasn't over yet, The. The Way to the Lighthouse. Nishiwaki Junzaburo, *tr.* by Hiroaki Sato. FCEI

Summer Wind. Bryant. PoEL-4
Summer wind, The. The Spring Wind. Charlotte Zolotow. RAR
Summer wind, The. What Her Girl Friend Said before the Elopement. Kutavayir Kirattanar, *tr.* by A. K. Ramanujan. PLW
Summer Wish, A. Christina Rossetti. OBNC
Summer Wisteria. Shotetsu, *tr. fr. Japanese by* Steven D. Carter. WFTW
Summer Words of [*or* for] a Sistuh [*or* Sister] Addict. Sonia Sanchez. BlSi; BPo; TV; UnPo
Summerhouse. Melvin Walker La Follette. NePoEA
Summers Ago. Isabella Gardner. CAPP
Summers and summers have come, and gone with the flight of the swallow. The Tantramar Revisited. Sir Charles G. D. Roberts. CaP; NOBC; OBCV
Summer's Cold, The. Max Hölzer, *tr. fr. German by* Beth Bjorklund. CoAuP
Summer's Day, A. Alexander Hume. CH
Summer's Day, A. James Whitcomb Riley. AnAmPo
Summer's Dream, A. Elizabeth Bishop. OxBC
Summer's Early End at Hudson Bay. Hayden Carruth. NYBP
Summer's End. Paolo Volponi, *tr. fr. Italian by* Lawrence R. Smith. NItP
Summer's Farewell. Thomas Nashe. *Fr.* Summer's Last Will and Testament. PoEL-2
Summer's gone brown, and, with it. Me to You. Alastair Reid. NYBP
Summer's last half moon waning high. 16. ix. 65. James Merrill. NAs
Summer's Last Will and Testament, *sels.* Thomas Nashe.
  Adieu, Farewell, Earth's Bliss[e]. CH; EBEV; EIL; ELP; HAP; HeIP; InvP; QFR; TEP; WeW
  (Dust Hath Closed Helen's Eye.) SeCePo
  (In a Time of Pestilence.) HoPM; OBEV; TrGrPo
  (In Plague Time.) FaBoCh; FaPoR; OBSC
  (In Time of Pestilence.) NOBE
  (Litany in Time of Plague, A.) DL; NAEL-1; NoP; OAEL-1; PoRA; PPP; PrIm
  (Lord, Have Mercy on Us.) ChTr
  (Song: "Adieu, farewell earth's blisse.") PoEL-2
  (Song in Time of Plague.) SCV
  Autumn. EIL; OAEL-1; OBSC; QFR; TrGrPo
  Fair Summer Droops. EIL
  (Waning Summer.) OBSC; OxBSP
  Harvest. OBSC
  "Rich men, trust not in wealth." OBD
  Spring, the Sweet Spring. CH; HeIP; LiTB; NAEL-1; NoP
  (Spring.) BoNaP; EIL; GTBS; GTBS-P; NOBE; OBEV; OBSC; OnUR; TrGrPo; WiR
  Summer's Farewell. PoEL-2
Summer's morning sun creeps up the blue, The. Sunrise in Summer. John Clare. FaBoPP
Summer's put the idy in, The. A Summer's Day. James Whitcomb Riley. AnAmPo
Summer's residue, The. Lines with a Gift of Herbs. Janet Lewis. QFR
Summer's sun is warm and bright. Pleasant Changes. Jane Euphemia Browne. OxBChV
Summers were spent in a fog that rains. Like Plump Birds along the Shore. Lyn Hejinian. LP
"Summertime and the Living." Robert Hayden. PoBA; PPP; TwCP
Summing-up, The. Stanley Kunitz. OBAL
Summing Up, A. Gabriel Preil, *tr. fr. Hebrew by* Jeremy Garber. VWA
Summit, The. Kathleen Jessie Raine. *Fr.* Beinn Naomh, IV. OxBS
Summit gain'd how glorious the reward, The. Robert Dunbar. *Fr.* The Cruise. PBCV
Summit of Delight. Jorge Guillén, *tr. fr. Spanish by* Perry Higman. LPSS
Summits and vales, slim cypresses and pines. Santa Maria del Fiore. George Herbert Clarke. CaP
Summoned. Diana O Hehir. NPGG
Summoned by Bells, *sels.* Sir John Betjeman.
  "Afternoons/ Brought coconut smell of gorse." FaBoPP
  Back Again for the Holidays. FaBoPP
  "My dear deaf father, how I loved him then." OxBTC
Summoned by love and heat and God knows what. News from the Court. David Wagoner. NePoEA-2
Summoned by the frantic powers. Summoned. Diana O Hehir. NPGG
Summonee's Tale, The. Stanley J. Sharpless. BXAP; FaBoPa
Summons, The. James Laughlin. LiTA
Summons, The. Elizabeth Roberts MacDonald. CaP
Summons, The. W. W. Eustace Ross. CaP
Summons to Love. William Drummond of Hawthornden. *See* Phoebus, Arise.
Summum Bonum. Robert Browning. OHFP

Sumo Wrestlers. James Kirkup. OBTV
Sums, The. Lauris Edmond. ATNZ; FaBoWP
Sumter. Henry Howard Brownell. PAH
Sumter. Edmund Clarence Stedman. PAH
Sumter—a Ballad of 1861. *Unknown.* PAH
Sumter's Band. J. W. Simmons. PAH
Sun, The. John Davis. NA
Sun, The. John Drinkwater. FaPON; NTCP
Sun, The. T. R. Hummer. NAmP
Sun, The. Andrew Oerke. PoA
Sun. Henry Rowe. OBEV
Sun, The. Anne Sexton. NYBP; PBWP
Sun, The. Francis Thompson. *Fr.* Ode to the Setting Sun. MoAB; MoBrPo
Sun, The. W. J. Turner. MoBrPo
Sun, The, *sel.* Vidya, *tr. fr. Sanskrit by* Daniel H. H. Ingalls. "I praise the disk of the rising sun." PBWP; WPOW
Sun/ proud Bessemer. World Winter. Earle Birney. GrPl
Sun, The/ Is warm to-day. Roma Aeterna. Adelaide Crapsey. QFR
Sun a shine but tings noh bright. Dutty Tough. Louise Bennett. PVCV
Sun after Rain. Norma Farber. RAR
Sun and Moon. Charlotte Druitt Cole. BoTP
Sun and Moon. Jay Macpherson. SoSe
Sun and moon lusterless, heaven and earth grow dark, The. Random Feelings: Written in Japan. Ch'iu Chin, *tr.* by Pao Chia-lin. WFTU
Sun and moon refuse to slow their pace. Poem without a Category ("Sun and moon refuse to slow their pace"). T'ao Ch'ien, *tr.* by Burton Watson. CoBCP
Sun and Moon So High and Bright, The. *Unknown.* AH
Sun and moon, that ceaselessly obey, The. Immortal Israel. Judah Halevi, *tr.* by Solomon Solis-Cohen. TrJP
Sun and Rain and Dew from Heaven. Adam Lindsay Gordon. *Fr.* Ye Wearie Wayfarer. PoLF
Sun and rain at work together. The Red-Gold Rain. Sacheverell Sitwell. MoBrPo
Sun and Shadow. Oliver Wendell Holmes. AnAmPo
Sun and softness. Sun Song. Langston Hughes. CNA
Sun and the Moon and Fear of Loneliness, The. *Unknown, tr. fr. Eskimo.* WTO
Sun and the Woman, The. Salah Abd al-Sabur, *tr. fr. Arabic by* Lena Jayyusi *and* John Heath-Stubbs. MAP
Sun appeared so smug and bright, The. The Silver Question. Oliver Herford. NA
Sun appearing, The: a pendant. Plainview: 3. N. Scott Momaday. CDW
Sun as zenith; the sun-cross is hoisted. Ants and the Sun. Khalil Khouri, *tr.* by Sharif Elmusa *and* Christopher Middleton. MAP
Sun at noon to higher air, The. March. A. E. Housman. FaBoCh
Sun-beames in the East are spred, The. Epithalamion Made at Lincolnes Inne. John Donne. OBS; SeCP
Sun became a small round moon, The. Climbing in Glencoe. Andrew Young. SD
Sun blazed while the thunder yet, The. The Mill-Pond. Edward Thomas. RB
Sun blazing slowly in its last hour, The. An Evening. Robert Mezey. NaP
Sun blooms in our bodies. Summer. Tom Marshall. NOBC
Sun, bronze voice, and holy etesian wind. Odysseus Elytis, *tr. fr. Greek by* Edmund Keeley *and* Philip Sherrard. *Fr.* Heroic and Elegiac Song for the Lost Second Lieute, X. VMG
Sun burns out, The. The Last Fire. Moishe Steingart, *tr.* by Gabriel Preil. VWA
Sun Came, The. Etheridge Knight. NeAC; PoBA
Sun Came Out in April, The. Cecil Day Lewis. MoBS
Sun came up, The. Rain Rain on the Splintered Girl. Ishmael Reed. PoBA
Sun cheers us for a pin-point, flicks, then westers. Mating Answer. Ronald Bottrall. PoA
Sun Children. Leslie Marmon Silko. VoR
Sun comes up. The Sun: Day. Bert Schierbeek, *tr.* by Charles McGeehan. DuIn
Sun comes up: a day in June. Time sinks, The. Memory of Dust and Light. Julio Ortega, *tr.* by David Tipton. Per
Sun comes up and the sun goes down, The. The Fallow Field. Julia Caroline Ripley Dorr. AA
Sun comes up, wind starts to ripple, The. Going to the Ministry with Chao Tzu-ch'i. Yü Chi, *tr.* by Jonathan Chaves. CoBLCP
Sun Dance in St. Lucia. Joan Van Poznak. SoTCo
Sun: Day, The. Bert Schierbeek, *tr. fr. Dutch by* Charles McGeehan. DuIn

Sun-Day Hymn. Oliver Wendell Holmes. *See* Lord of All Being, Throned Afar.

Sun dazzle and black shadow. Mending the Adobe. Hayden Carruth. EyDe; Psk

Sun descending in the west, The. Night. Blake. *Fr.* Songs of Innocence. BLPL; BoNaP; BoTP; CH; EnRP; FaBoBe; FaPON; OBEV; OxBChV; PoLF; WiR

Sun-Dial, The. Thomas Love Peacock. *Fr.* Melincourt. OBNC

Sun doth arise, The. The Echoing [*or* Ecchoing] Green. Blake. *Fr.* Songs of Innocence. BoTP; CH; NAEL–2; PoE; UnPo; WiR

Sun drew off at last his piercing fires, The. Witchcraft: New Style. Lascelles Abercrombie. MoBrPo

Sun drops below the elms. Routes. Peter Everwine. NNaP

Sun falls perpendicularly west, The. Gateway Arch. Cheng Ch'ou-yu, *tr. by* Dominic Cheung. IFON

Sun fine old fellow. Greenland Fossil an Icy Poet. H. C. ten Berge, *tr. by* Theo Hermans. DuIn

Sun-Flower, The. Dora Greenwell. WPE

Sun frets, a fat wafer falling like a trap of failed mesh, The. Hole, Where Once in Passion We Swam. Dave Smith. NoAM

Sun from the east tips the mountains with gold, The. Hunting Song. Paul Whitehead. *Fr.* Apollo and Daphne. OxBoLi

Sun God, The. Aubrey Thomas De Vere. ACP

Sun-god was reclining on a couch of rosy shells, The. Sunset Picture. Henrietta Cordelia Ray. CBWP-3

Sun, God's eye, The. The Nature of Love. James Kirkup. EaLo

Sun goes down, The. Midsummer Night. Elizabeth Gould. BoTP

Sun goes down. Thu Sun: Night. Bert Schierbeek, *tr. by* Charles McGeehan. DuIn

Sun goes down, and over all, The. Low Tide on Grand Pré. Bliss Carman. CaP; NOBC; OBCV

Sun goes down for hours, taking more of her along, The. The Lady in the Pink Mustang. Louise Erdrich. HATNAP; NOVW

Sun Going Down upon Our Wrath, The. Denise Levertov, *tr. fr. Japanese*. AIW

Sun had begun in the gloaming, The. The First Snow-fall. James Russell Lowell. AA

Sun had clos'd the winter-day, The. The Vision. Burns. OxBS

Sun had long since in the lap, The. Godly Casuistry. Samuel Butler. *Fr.* Hudibras, II, 2. OBS

Sun had set, The;/ The leaves with dew. Keenan's Charge. George Parsons Lathrop. AA; PAH

Sun had sunk beneath the west, The. The Ocean-Fight. *Unknown*. PAH

Sun has come, I know, The. The Sun. W. J. Turner. MoBrPo

Sun has gone from the shining skies, The. A Summer Lullaby. Eudora S. Bumstead. BoTP

Sun has kissed the violet sea, The. Betrayal. Sidney Lanier. *Fr.* The Jaquerie. AA

Sun has long been set, The. A Night in June. Wordsworth. BoTP

Sun has risen on the eastern brim of the world, The. The Song of Lo-fu. *Unknown*, *tr. by* Arthur Waley. AWP

Sun Has Set, The. Emily Brontë. UnPo

Sun has set, The. Kyotai, *tr. fr. Japanese by* Burton Watson. *Fr.* Sixteen Hokku. FCEI

Sun has sunk 'neath yonder distant hill, The. Belshazzar's Feast. Eloise Bibb. CBWP-4

Sun hath twice brought forth[e] the tender green, The. The Restless State of a Lover. Henry Howard, Earl of Surrey. AAS; SiPS

Sun Heals, A. Jewel C. Latimore. JB

Sun Held in Tender Hands, The. Manfred Winkler, *tr. fr. Hebrew by* Bernhard Frank. MHeP

Sun, his journey ending in the west, The. Henry Constable. *Fr.* Diana. OBSC

Sun in Capricorn, The. Joyce Mansour, *tr. fr. French*. PBWP, *tr. by* Carol Cosman

Sun, in clownish yellow, but not a clown, The. Wallace Stevens. *Fr.* Esthétique du Mal. NOBA

Sun in the east! *Unknown*, *tr. by* Arthur Waley. BoS

Sun is a gold coin slipping into, The/ an envelope of sea. Mediterranean. Ruth Whitman. VWA

Sun is a huntress young, The. An Indian Summer Day on the Prairie. Vachel Lindsay. RFM

Sun is almost down, The. Tamekane, *tr. by* Steven D. Carter. WFTW

Sun is black, is black today, The. The Black Sun. Nikos Gatsos, *tr. fr. Greek by* Edmund Keeley *and* Philip Sherrard. *Fr.* Four Songs. VMG

Sun is blue and scarlet on my page, The. Falling Asleep over the Aeneid. Robert Lowell. MoAmPo; OxBA

Sun is bright,—the air is clear, The. It Is Not Always May. Longfellow. PWR

Sun is down, The. What the Passersby Said to the Lover Eloping with the Girl. Uraiyur Mutukorran, *tr. by* A. K. Ramanujan. PLW

Sun is folding, cars stall and rise, The. The New World. Imamu Amiri Baraka. NoAM; NoP

Sun is going down, The. Aranda Song. *Unknown*, *tr. by* T. G. H. Strehlow. CBAP

Sun Is Good, The. Mani Leib, *tr. fr. Yiddish by* John Hollander. PeBMYV

Sun is gray and without a rim, The. Father Fisheye. Peter Balakian. MAYP

Sun is in the west. Fishing boats, The. Drinking at Night with Yen Kung-mou. Shen Chou, *tr. by* Jonathan Chaves. CoBLCP

Sun is just appearing, The. Lyn Hejinian. UL

Sun is lord and god, sublime, serene, The. The Lake of Gaube. Swinburne. NAEL-2; OAEL-2

Sun is low, to say the least, The. The Sunset. Gelett Burgess. FaBoNo

Sun is nigh the verge, The. Soon we must part. A Walk. Hedwig Lachmann, *tr. by* Jethro Bithell. TrJP

Sun is not abed, when I, The. The Sun's Travels. Robert Louis Stevenson. FaPON

Sun is not in love with us, The. The Isles of Greece. Demetrios Capetanakis. GTBS-P

Sun is red. It naps, The. Silence. Avigdor Hame'iri, *tr. by* Bernhard Frank. MHeP

Sun is rising, The. Healing Song. *Unknown*, *tr. by* Frances Densmore. OBVE

Sun is shining in my backdoor, The. Myself When I Am Real. Al Young. CNA; PoBA

Sun is sinking over hill and sea, The. At Night. George Edgar Montgomery. AA

Sun is soon to rise as bright, The. Friedrich Rückert. *Fr.* Songs on the Death of Children. OBD

Sun is the blind eyes of statues gilded, The. The Sun. Andrew Oerke. PoA

Sun is warm, the sky is clear, The. Stanzas Written in Dejection [– December 1818,] near Naples. Shelley. ChER; EnRP; FaBV; FiP; GTBS; GTBS-P; NAEL-2; NAWM-2; NoP; PoRA; TEP

Sun like a sleepy giant, The. Narcolepsy. Maureen Owen. TTTS

Sun like an orange mousse through the trees. Dog Day Vespers. Charles Wright. LCAP

Sun looked from his everlasting skies, The. My Old Counselor. Gertrude Hall. AA

Sun made diamonds on the white sidewalk, The. Rubber. Donna Masini. ER

Sun makes music as of old, The. Prologue in Heaven [*or* The Chorus of the Archangels]. Goethe, *tr. fr. German by* Shelley. *Fr.* Faust. AWP; OBVE

Sun [*or* Sunne] may set and rise, The. Sir Walter Ralegh, *after the Latin of* Catullus. FaBoEE; OBVE
(Lines from Catullus.) SiPS
(Sun May Set, The.) FaBoRV

Sun Moon Kelp Flower or Goat. Linda Gregg. NPGG

Sun must be setting, The. Tamesuke, *tr. by* Steven D. Carter. WFTW

Sun Noise. Jacques Roubaud, *tr. fr. French by* Robert Kelly. RHTwFP

Sun now darts his fervid rays, The. Lines Written in the Dog-Days. William Woty. NOEC

Sun Now Risen, The. Johann Conrad Beissel. AH

Sun of Our Existence, The. Mrs. Henry Linden. CBWP-4

Sun of the moral world; effulgent source. Freedom. Joel Barlow. OPP

Sun of the stately day. The National Ode. Bayard Taylor. PAH

Sun, of whose terrain we creatures are, The. Solar Creation. Charles Madge. FaBoMo; OBMV; OxBTC

Sun on hillsides, wind on seas. Desolation. *Unknown*, *tr. by* Aneirin Talfan Davies. OBWVE

Sun on his face wakes him. Morning Song. Gregory Orr. MAYP

Sun on his back, sun on its stomach. Pig. Paul Eluard, *tr. by* Michael Benedikt. MAYP

Sun on the tree-tops no longer is seen, The. Queen Sabbath. Hayyim Nahman Bialik, *tr. by* Jessie Sampter. TrJP

Sun on the walls, the roofs. Tarma. Antonio Cisneros, *tr. by* Maureen Ahern *and* David Tipton. Per

Sun raging like a battle. Rock. Judah Leib Teller, *tr. by* Benjamin *and* Barbara Harshav. AYP

Sun reveals the galaxy of dust, The. Parallel Bars. Jeffrey Stockwell. TSL

Sun revolves in its red flames, The. Winter-Night Sonnet. A. Leyeles, *tr. by* Benjamin *and* Barbara Harshav. AYP

Sun revolving on his axis turns, The. The Copernican System. Thomas Chatterton. FaBoUs

Sun rises, The. In Fields of Summer. Galway Kinnell. BoNaP; RFM; VGW

Sun [or Sunne] Rising, The. John Donne. BoLoP; FF; GBL; HAP; HeIP; InPS; InvP; JCP; LiTB; MeLP; MePo; NAEL-1; NIP; NOBE; NoP; OAEL-1; PoE; PoEL-2; PPP; SCV; SeCePo; SeCP; SeCV-1; SoSe; TEP; TrGrPo; WeW

Sun rose over a mound of corpses, The. I Hear a Voice. H. Leivick, tr. by David G. Roskies. VWA

Sun rushed up the sky, The; the taxi flew. Parting as Descent. John Berryman. LiTA; MoAmPo

Sun scanned the river with its lidless, The. The Breakdown. Sherod Santos. MAYP; SM

Sun set, but set not his hope, The. Character. Emerson. AA; LiTA; OxBSP

Sun set over Acrocorinth, The. On Acrocorinth. Angelos Sikelianos, tr. by Edmund Keeley and Philip Sherrard. VMG

Sun sets in the cold without friends, The. Dusk in Winter. W. S. Merwin. NaP

Sun sets on a bright blameless wall a barrage of rays. In Impressions of Hawk Feathers Willow Leaves Shadow. Elizabeth Woody. STE

Sun sets on Tung-t'ing's waves. Yang Wei-chen, tr. fr. Chinese by Jonathan Chaves. Fr. Songs of Lake Tung-t'ing, I. CoBLCP

Sun Sets, Sun Rises, The. Pentti Saarikoski, tr. fr. Finnish by Aili Jarvenpa. SOP

Sun sets, the pagoda is darkened, The. Evening Bell from a Misty Temple. Wen Cheng-ming, tr. by Jonathan Chaves. CoBLCP

Sun sets, The. The wind moans. Ts'ai Yen, tr. fr. Chinese by Kenneth Rexroth and Ling Chung. Fr. Eighteen Verses Sung to a Tatar Reed Whistle, VII. BoWoP; WPOW

Sun shines, The. Tommies in the Train. D. H. Lawrence. MMA

Sun shines bright, but sadly, The. Autumn ("The sun shines bright, but sadly"). Priscilla Jane Thompson. CBWP-2

Sun shines bright in the old Kentucky home, The. My Old Kentucky Home, [Good Night]. Stephen Collins Foster. AA; AnMPo; FaBoBe; FaBV; FaFP; PoLF; TrGrPo

Sun shines center stage, The. History. Bob Perelman. IAT

Sun shines high on yonder hill, The. The False Lover Won Back. Unknown. ESPB; OxBB

Sun shines in Heng Chor's eyes. Cambodia Witness. Lisa Vice. ER

Sun Shines over the Mountain, The. Unknown. AmFP

Sun shone in my hut, The. He Who Has Lost All. David Diop, tr. by Anne Atik. TTY

Sun sinks softly to his ev'ning post, The. The Rejected "National Hymns. "Orpheus C. Kerr." OBAL

Sun Song. Langston Hughes. CNA

Sun sought thy dim bed and brought forth light, The. Africa. Claude McKay. Son

Sun Spirit, The, sel. Ralph Chubb.
    "At the time of puberty I had obsessions." PeHV

Sun strikes gold the dirty street, The. Brest Left Behind. John Chipman Farrar. PAH

Sun struts over the asphalt world, The. Noon of the Sunbather. Marge Piercy. NMM

Sun, stun me, sustain me. On Looking into Henry Moore. Dorothy Livesay. OBCV

Sun-tanned men and women, toiling there together. Reapers. Mathilde Blind. WPE

Sun, that brave man, The. The Brave Man. Wallace Stevens. SOTW

Sun that brief December day, The. Whittier. Fr. Snow-bound; a Winter Idyl [or Idyll]. AiP; AmPP; FaBV; GN; NAAL-1; NOBA; OxBA; TAP; TrGrPo; WiR
    (Storm, The.) FaBV
    (Winter Day.) TrGrPo

Sun that shines all day so bright, The. Night. Unknown. BoTP

Sun, the moon, the stars, the seas, the hills and the plains, The. The Higher Pantheism. Tennyson. WGRP

Sun, the rose, the lily, the dove, The. Love's Résumé. Heine, tr. by J. F. C.. TrJP

Sun, the Sun, The. Pier Paolo Pasolini, tr. fr. Italian by Lawrence R. Smith. NItP

Sun through the window, The. The Mullins Farm. Richard H. W. Dillard. MT

Sun-up in March. Abbie Huston Evans. NePoAm

Sun upon the lake is low, The. Datur Hora Quieti. Sir Walter Scott. GTBS; GTBS-P

Sun upon the Weirdlaw Hill, The. The Dreary Change. Sir Walter Scott. FaBoPP; NAEL-2; OAEL-2; OBNC

Sun Used to Shine, The. Edward Thomas. FaBoTw

Sun was bright when we went in, The. At the Theater. Rachel Lyman Field. FaPON

Sun was down, and twilight grey, The. In the Room. James Thomson. NOBVV

Sun was hanging in the west, The. On the Way Back. A. Leyeles, tr. by Benjamin and Barbara Harshav. AYP

Sun was now withdrawn, The. Damon and Cupid. John Gay. EnLoPo

Sun was shining on the sea, The. The Walrus and the Carpenter. "Lewis Carroll." Fr. Through the Looking-Glass, ch. 4. BeLS; BLPA; FaBoBe; FaBoCo; FaBoNo; FaBV; FaFP; FaPON; FiBHP; FPL; GN; LiTB; NA; NAEL-2; NoAM; NOBL; NOBVV; OxBChV; PoRA; TEP

Sun was sinking when we reached the glen, The. On Walking Back to the Bus. Alan Gardner. PoSH

Sun was Slumbering in the West, The. Thomas Hood. FiBHP

Sun-Watchers. Abba Kovner, tr. fr. Hebrew by Warren Bargad and Stanley F. Chyet. IP

Sun went down behind yon hill, The. The Farmer's Boy. Unknown. OBET

Sun which doth the greatest comfort bring[e], The. Mr. Francis Beaumont's Letter to Ben Johnson. Francis Beaumont. OBS (Francis Beaumont's Letter from the Country to Jonson.) SeCP

Sun Wields Mercy, The. Charles Bukowski. MAT

Sun-Witch to the Sun, The. George Howe. NYBP

Sun, with his great eye, The. Daisy's Song. Keats. BoNaP

Sun Witness, The. Nurunnessa Choudhury, tr. fr. Bengali by Nurunnessa Choudhury and Paul Joseph Thompson. AIW

Sun woke me this morning loud, The. A True Account of Talking to the Sun at Fire Island. Frank O'Hara. HCAP; NNaP; RB; SOTW; TTTS

Sun, yon glorious orb of day, The. The Sun. John Davis. NA

Sunbeam, The. Unknown. NA

Sunbeam Said, Be Happy, The. Wordsworth. Fr. The Recluse, I. FaBoRV

Sunbeams. Avner Trainin, tr. fr. Hebrew by Bernhard Frank. MHeP

Sunbeams Diagonally. Dov Khomsky, tr. fr. Hebrew by Bernhard Frank. MHeP

Sunbeams streamed without, The. In the Morgue. Israel Zangwill. TrJP

Sunburst cabbage in grey light. Return. Richard Tillinghast. MAYP

Sunday. Elizabeth J. Coatsworth. AmFN

Sunday. George Herbert. OBS; SeCV-1; TrCP

Sunday. Josephine Miles. PoA

Sunday. James Schuyler. TTTS

Sunday. Philippe Soupault, tr. fr. French by Michael Benedikt. POS

Sunday Afternoon. Carol Jane Bangs. NIP

Sunday Afternoon. Denise Levertov. IHMS

Sunday Afternoon. Philip Levine. NaP

Sunday afternoon/ and couples walk the breakwater. Veracruz. Robert Hayden. AmNP

Sunday Afternoon in Italy. D. H. Lawrence. BrPo

Sunday Afternoon Service in St. Enodoc Church, Cornwall. Sir John Betjeman. NOCV

Sunday Afternoons. Anthony Thwaite. OxBTC

Sunday and sunlight ashen on the Square. The Self Unsatisfied Runs Everywhere. Delmore Schwartz. PoA

Sunday at Hampstead, sel. James Thomson ("B. V.").
    In the Train. OBEV

Sunday at the End of Summer. Howard Nemerov. BoNaP

Sunday at the State Hospital. David Ignatow. CAPP

Sunday before Christmas, The. Sandor Csoori, tr. fr. Hungarian by Jascha Kessler. NPo

Sunday, Boswell, and you visit me. David Hume, Dying, Talks to Boswell. Alan Bold. NPo

Sunday Dreamer's Guide to Yarrow, Missouri, A. Jim Barnes. HATNAP

Sunday Evening. Barbara Guest. NeAP

Sunday Evening. Sam Hunt. PeNZ

Sunday Evening in the Common. John Hall Wheelock. MoAmPo

Sunday Evenings. John Hollander. NYBP

Sunday Graveyard. Maura Stanton. NAmP

Sunday heavy lid on the boiling of blood. Approximate Man. Tristan Tzara, tr. by Paul Auster. RHTwFP

Sunday in Cambridge, A. Eddie Linden. PeHV

Sunday in Old England. Kearsarge. Silas Weir Mitchell. PAH

Sunday in the Park. William Carlos Williams. See Paterson: Outside/ outside myself/ there is a world.

Sunday is the dullest day, treating. "Myra Buttle." Fr. The Sweeniad. FaBoPa
    (Sweeney in Articulo.) BXAP; Par

Sunday, July 14th; a Fine Day at the Baths. Julian Symons. WaP

Sunday lamb cracks in its fat, The. Mary's Song. Sylvia Plath. CAPP; FaBoMo; FaBoWP

Sunday Morning. Christina Jenkins. BrRo

Sunday Morning. Louis MacNeice. FaBCIP; FaBoMo; HeIP; LiTB; MoAB; MoBrPo; NAEL-2; NIP; Son

Sunday Morning. Wayne Moreland. PoBA
Sunday Morning. Wallace Stevens. AmPP; AmPP; BLPL; CMoP; HAP; HCAP; HeIP; InPS; LiTA; LiTM; MoAB; MoAmPo; MoP; NAAL-2; NAWM-2; NIP; NoAM; NOBA; NoP; OxBA; PoA, *early version*; PoA; PoE; QFR; TAP; WeW
Sunday morning and her mother's hands. Birmingham 1963. Raymond R. Patterson. CNA; PoBA
Sunday Morning in the Park. Hermann Gail, *tr. fr. German by* Beth Bjorklund. CoAuP
Sunday Morning, King's Cambridge. Sir John Betjeman. EaLo
Sunday: New Guinea. Karl Shapiro. AmFN
Sunday News, The. Dana Gioia. GOYP
Sunday Night in Santa Rosa. Dana Gioia. GrPl
Sunday Night Walk. Raymond Souster. CaP
Sunday on Riverside Drive. Rose Ausländer, *tr. fr. German by* Beth Bjorklund. CoAuP
Sunday: Outskirts of Knoxville, Tennessee. James Agee. ErPo
Sunday Piece. Jules Laforgue, *tr. fr. French by* William Jay Smith. CT
Sunday ran away from a priest like a nannygoat. My Arms Became the Month of October. Shauqi Abi Shaqra, *tr. by* Abdullah al-Udhari. MPAW
Sunday Review Section. Baron Wormser. MAYP
Sunday Service. Michael Heffernan. BXAP
Sunday Shtetl. Jacob Glatstein, *tr. fr. Yiddish by* Cynthia Ozick. PeBMYV
Sunday shuts down on this twentieth-century evening. Boy with His Hair Cut Short. Muriel Rukeyser. LiTM; MoAB; NoAM; TwCP; VGW; WPE
Sunday solid lid above the boilings of bubbling blood. Tristan Tzara, *tr. fr. French by* Michael Benedikt. *Fr.* The Approximate Man, I. POS
Sunday Stroll. Michael Pettit. MAYP
Sunday strollers along a sewage-choked Schuylkill. To Some Millions Who Survive Joseph E. Mander, Sr. Sarah E. Wright. PoBA
Sunday the only day we don't work. A Walk. Gary Snyder. NOBA
Sunday the sea made morning worship, sang. Half-Tide Ledge. Richard Palmer Blackmur. MOS
Sunday up the River, *sels.* James Thomson ("B. V.").
  Gifts. *Fr.* XV. OBEV
  "Wine of Love is music, The." *Fr.* XVIII. OBEV
Sundays too my father got up early. Those Winter Sundays. Robert Hayden. CAPP; CNA; DiL; FF; GrPl; HAP; HCAP; IDB; InPK; LCAP; MoP; NIP; NoAM; NoP; PoBA; PPP; SoSe; UnPo; WeW
Sunder me from my bones, O sword of God. The Sword of Surprise. Gilbert Keith Chesterton. MoBrPo
Sundered. John Barford. PeHV
Sundered. Israel Zangwill. TrJP
Sundered from this beauty is this fond lover. Elegy in the Orongorongo Valley. Hubert Witheford. ATNZ
Sundew, The. Swinburne. ELP; NoP; OBNC
Sundial. Jorie Graham. NAmP
Sundown. Léonie Adams. MoAB; MoAmPo; TrGrPo
Sundown at Darlington 1878. Lance Henson. VoR
Sundowner, The. Shaw Neilson. CBAP; PoAu-1
Sundry Christian Passions Contained in Two Hundred, *sels.* Henry Lok.
  Son
    It Is Not, Lord, the Sound of Many Words, *preface*
    Words May Well Want, *conclusion*
Sunfish Races. James Preston. InPK
Sunflakes. Frank Asch. NTCP
Sunflower, The. Blake. *See* Songs of Experience
Sunflower. André Breton, *tr. fr. French by* Edouard Roditi. RHTwFP
Sunflower. Rolf Jacobsen, *tr. fr. Norwegian*. NU, *tr. by* Robert Bly
Sunflower, The. Eugenio Montale, *tr. fr. Italian by* Maurice English. PFI
Sunflower. Tuvia Rübner, *tr. fr. Hebrew by* Bernhard Frank. MHeP
Sunflower. John Updike. BoNaP; GrPl
Sunflower ain't de daisy, De. Doan't You Be What You Ain't. Edwin Milton Royle. BLPA
Sunflower Moccasins. Phillip William George. VoR
Sunflower, of flowers. Sunflower. John Updike. BoNaP; GrPl
Sunflower Sonnet Number One. June Jordan. SM; Son
Sunflower Sonnet Number Two. June Jordan. SM; Son
Sunflower Sutra. Allen Ginsberg. AmPP; CoAP; HCAP; InPS; MAT; NAAL-2; NeAP; NOBA
Sunflower to the Sun, The. Mary Elizabeth DeWitt Stebbins. AA
Sunflowers and Saturdays. Melba Joyce Boyd. BlSi
Sunflowers in October. Gerhard Fritsch, *tr. fr. German by* Beth Bjorklund. CoAuP
Sung-ling road in setting sunlight. Feelings Come As I Pass through Wu-chiang. Wu Wei-yeh, *tr. by* Jonathan Chaves. CoBLCP

Sung on a Sunny Morning. Jean Starr Untermeyer. TrPWD
Sunglare and sea pale as tears. Blackfish Poem. Milton Acorn. NeAC
Sunk earlier in the silence of gray cashmere. Slepynge Long in Greet Quiete Is Eek a Greet Norice to Leccherie. John Hollander. ErPo
Sunk Lyonesse. Walter de la Mare. FaBoCh; LiTM
Sunken Evening [in Trafalgar Square]. Laurie Lee. LiTM; NYBP
Sunken Gold. Eugene Lee-Hamilton. NOBVV
Sunken Temple. Tamura Ryuichi, *tr. fr. Japanese by* Hiroaki Sato. FCEI
Sunlight still on me, you row'd in clood, The. At My Father's Grave. "Hugh MacDiarmid." GTBS-P
Sunlight. Seamus Heaney. *See* Mossbawn: Mossbawn Sunlight.
Sunlight: A Sequence for My Daughter, *sels.* David Ignatow. CAPP
  "I am proud of your soft, brown eyes."
  "My infinite child, hold me to sleep."
Sunlight and Sea. Alfred Noyes. MOS
Sunlight and summer wind are never sure. The Attic. Charles Bruce. *Fr.* The Flowing Summer. CaP
Sunlight drawing from shadow, up and down the street. Passages. Larry Eigner. NeAP
Sunlight in the house. Maritimes. Penelope Shuttle. BrRo
Sunlight lies along my table. The Weather of Six Mornings. Jane Cooper. IHMS; NYBP
Sunlight on the Garden, The. Louis MacNeice. CMoP; EBEV; GTBS-P; HAP; InPS; LiTB; NAEL-2; NOBE; NOIV; NoP; OxBTC; PrIm; TwCP
Sunlight pillars through glass, probes each desk. The Play Way. Seamus Heaney. NoP
Sunlight quivers on crater and cone. A Drive on the Peninsula. Brian Turner. ATNZ
Sunlight Shining of Red Leaves. Masayori, *tr. fr. Japanese by* Steven D. Carter. WFTW
Sunlight speaks, and its voice is a bird, The. The Hummingbird. Harry Hibbard Kemp. FaPON
Sunlight streaming on Incense Stone kindles violet smoke. Viewing the Waterfall at Mount Lu. Li Po, *tr. by* Burton Watson. CoBCP; TTTS
Sunlight that pulls itself over the rooftops looks vacant, The. Inertia. Kirti Chaudhari, *tr. by* Leonard Nathan. WPOW
Sunlight the tall women may never have seen. Children, the Sandbar, That Summer. Muriel Rukeyser. LCAP
Sunlit sea. Comparatives. N. Scott Momaday. SM
Sunne Rising, The. John Donne. *See* Busy old fool, unruly sun.
Sunning. James Sterling Tippett. RHPC
Sunny Bank. *Unknown*. *See* As I Sat on a Sunny Bank.
Sunny Prestatyn. Philip Larkin. NoAM
Sunny shaft did I behold, A. Glycine's Song. Samuel Taylor Coleridge. *Fr.* Zapolya. CH; OBEV
  (Song: "Sunny shaft did I behold, A.") PBBP
Sunny Spring. Hagiwara Sakutaro, *tr. fr. Japanese by* Hiroaki Sato. FCEI
Sunrise. Frank Asch. RHPC
Sunrise. Ben King. AnAmPo
Sunrise. Sidney Lanier. *Fr.* Hymns of the Marshes. AA; PoEL-5
Sunrise. Henrietta Cordelia Ray. *Fr.* Idyl. CBWP-3
Sunrise. Jim Tollerud. VoR
Sunrise. Robert Wells. NPo
Sunrise Call, The. *Unknown, tr. by* N. Barnes. WTO
Sunrise I look to the source of the sun. In T'ang China Longing for Home. Bensho, *tr. by* Burton Watson. JLIC-1
Sunrise in Summer. John Clare. FaBoPP
Sunrise of the Poor, The. Robert Burns Wilson. AA
Sunrise on Rydal Water. John Drinkwater. LiTM
Sunrise on the Sea. Shakespeare. *Fr.* A Midsummer Night's Dream, III, ii. ChTr
Sunrise. The weedy rubblefield turns pink. Hear Now the Fable of the Missing Link. Judith Moffett. BLA
Sunrise Thought. Henrietta Cordelia Ray. *Fr.* A Group of Musings. CBWP-3
Sunrise Trumpets. Joseph Auslander. TrJP
Sunrise. & toward the sunrise stands the village of the Bow People. Muu's Way; or Pictures from the Uterine World. *Unknown, tr. by* Jerome Rothenberg. STP
Sun's Darling, The, *sel.* Thomas Dekker.
  Haymakers, Rakers. ELP
  (Country Glee.) OBSC
Sun's going down. Which is nothing new, The. "Heaven in Ordinarie." Daniel Wolff. SM
Suns have set and suns will rise. Keep Cool. Marcus Garvey. PVCV
Sun's high, I've slept enough, still too lazy to get up, The. Writing Again on the Same Theme. Po Chü-i, *tr. by* Burton Watson. CoBCP

Suns in a skein, the uncut stones of night. Roy Fuller. *Fr.* Mythological Sonnets, VIII. GTBS-P

Sun's light and the water's light muddy one color, The. Wakayama Bokusui, *tr. fr. Japanese by* Hiroaki Sato. *Fr.* Forty-four Tanka. FCEI

Sun's low light splinters in a plastic gleam, The. On a Scooter. Desmond A. Greig. PeSA

Sun's noon throne is hid in hazy cloud, The. A View of the Present State of Ireland. Edmund Blunden. BrPo

Sun's Perpendicular Rays, The. William Lort Mansel. ChTr; FaBoEE

Suns, planets, stars, in glorious array. Victor James Daley. *Fr.* Night. PoAu-1

Sun's rays that shoot up, stretched out, The. An Old Song of Rejoicing. *Unknown, tr. by* Margaret Orbell. PeNZ

Sun's snow, conversing, lowly slides from limbs. To a Young Lady Swinging Upside Down on a Birch Limb over a Winter-swollen Creek. James H. Koch. GoYe

Sun's Travels, The. Robert Louis Stevenson. FaPON

Sunscape. Lucha Corpi. CCP

Sunset. Arthur Bayldon. PoAu-1

Sunset. Hayyim Nahman Bialik, *tr. fr. Hebrew by* Helena Frank. TrJP

Sunset, The. Gelett Burgess. FaBoNo

Sunset, A. Samuel Taylor Coleridge. OxBSP

Sunset. E. E. Cummings. MoAmPo

Sunset. Mary Weston Fordham. CBWP-2

Sunset. Mafika Pascal Gwala. WMBCH

Sunset, A. Victor Hugo, *tr. fr. French by* Francis Thompson. *Fr.* Feuilles d'Automne. AWP

Sunset. Longfellow. BoTP

Sunset. John Montague. *Fr.* Félire Oengus. FaBCIP

Sunset. Lilian Moore. TDD

Sunset. Henrietta Cordelia Ray. *Fr.* Idyl. CBWP-3

Sunset. Ella Wheeler Wilcox. AnAmPo

Sunset/ molten bronze. Tune: Endless Union. Li Ching-chao. PBWP, *tr. by* C. H. Kwôck *and* Vincent McHugh

Sunset, a huge flower, wilts on the horizon, The. Flowers. Roo Borson. NOBC

Sunset after Rain. W. S. Merwin. PoA

Sunset and evening star. Crossing the Bar. Tennyson. BLRP; DL; EBVV; FaBoRV; FaBV; FaFP; FaPoR; FF; FiP; FPL; HeIP; LiTB; MOS; NAEL-2; NOBE; NOBVV; NoP; OAEL-2; OBEV; OBNC; OHFP; PoLF; PoRA; PWR; SoSe; TEP; TrCP; TrGrPo; WBLP; WGRP

Sunset and silence! A man: around him earth savage, earth broken. The Plower. Padraic Colum. MoBrPo

Sunset at Les Éboulements, A. Archibald Lampman. OBCV

Sunset at Twin Lake. Anita Endrezze-Danielson. HATNAP

Sunset from Omaha Hotel Window. Carl Sandburg. AiP

Sunset—God's face from which grief radiates. Sodom. Chaim Grade, *tr. by* Joseph Leftwich. TrJP

Sunset grew bold: it insisted on staying, The. Deer at the Red Sea. Abraham Sutskever, *tr. by* Chana Bloch. PeBMYV

Sunset Horn. Myron O'Higgins. AmNP; PoNe

Sunset in the Sea. Tom Hood. FaBoNo

Sunset is always disturbing. Afterglow. Jorge Luis Borges, *tr. by* Norman Thomas di Giovanni. NYBP

Sunset of the City, A. Gwendolyn Brooks. FaBoWP; PBWP

Sunset on Calvary. *Unknown. See* Now Goeth [*or* goth *or* goothe] Sun [*or* Sunne] under Wood.

Sunset over icy blue roads. Sweet sleepy. In the Hamlet. Abraham Sutskever, *tr. by* Chana Bloch. PeBMYV

Sunset over the Aegean. Byron. *Fr.* The Corsair, III. OBNC

Sunset over the Ægean. Byron. OBNC

Sunset Picture. Henrietta Cordelia Ray. CBWP-3

Sunset Song. *Unknown, tr. fr. Pueblo Indian by* N. Barnes. WTO

Sunset: the blaze of evening burns. Hospital Evening. Gwen Harwood. FaBoWP

Sunset, the cheapest of all picture-shows. Frederiksted, Dusk. Derek Walcott. NoAM

Sunset Thought. Henrietta Cordelia Ray. *Fr.* A Group of Musings. CBWP-3

Sunset Wings. Dante Gabriel Rossetti. FM

Sunsets. Carl Sandburg. MoAmPo

Sunset's mounded cloud, A. An Evening. William Allingham. EnLoPo; NOBVV

Sunshade, The. Thomas Hardy. OxBTC

Sunshine after Cloud. Josephine D. Henderson Heard. CBWP-4

Sunshine after rain, rain after sunshine. After the Rain. Liang Ch'i-ch'ao, *tr. by* Cecile Chu-chin Sun. WFTU

Sunshine and shadow play amid the trees. July. Henrietta Cordelia Ray. CBWP-3

Sunshine, come softly here. Prayer for a Play House. Elinor Lennen. TrPWD

Sunshine let it be or frost. After St. Augustine. Mary Elizabeth Coleridge. TrPWD

Sunshine of the Gods, The, *sel.* Bayard Taylor.
"Ah, moment not to be purchased." AA

Sunshine of Thine Eyes, The. George Parsons Lathrop. AA

Sunshiny shower, A. *Unknown. Fr.* Weather Wisdom [*or* Weather Wise]. FaBoBe; OxNR

Sunstrike. Douglas Livingstone. PeSA

Sunt Leones. Stevie Smith. NoAM

Sunthin' in the Pastoral Line. James Russell Lowell. *Fr.* The Biglow Papers: 2d Series, No. VI. AP (Spring.)

Super-cool/ ultrablack. But He Was Cool; or, He Even Stopped for Green Lights. Don L. Lee. AmNP; BPo; MoP; PoBA

Super Flumina Babylonis. Swinburne. PoEL-5

Super-suburbia of the Southern Seas. Farewell to New Zealand. Wynford Vaughan-Thomas. NOBL; OBTV

Superb and sole, upon a plumëd spray. The Mocking Bird. Sidney Lanier. AA

Superb Lily, The. Robert Pinsky. AnAn

Superballs. Tom Clark. EAS

Supercilious nabob of the East, A. A Modest Wit. Selleck Osborn. BLPA

Supererogatory divinations one is. The Unknown. Denise Levertov. NAAL-2

Superfluous Were the Sun. Emily Dickinson. AnAmPo

Superintindint wuz Flannigan. Finnigin to Flannigan. Strickland W. Gillilan. FaBoBe

Superior Nonsense Verses. *Unknown.* NA

Superliminare. George Herbert. SeCP

Supermarket in California, A. Allen Ginsberg. AmPP; CoAP; HAP; HCAP; HeIP; InPK; InPS; LiTM; NAAL-2; NaP; NeAP; NoAM; NOBA; PoM; PrIm; SOTW; TAP; TwCP; UnPo

Supermarket in Guadalajara, Mexico, A. Denise Levertov. RR

Supernatural Love. Gjertrud Schnackenberg. DiPo; NoAM

Superscription, A. Dante Gabriel Rossetti. *Fr.* The House of Life, XCVII. EBVV; GTBS-P; NAEL-2; NoP; OAEL-2; OBNC; PoEL-5; SeCePo

Supersensual. Evelyn Underhill. WGRP

Superstition. Minji Karibo. WPOW

Superstitions. Maggie Pogue Johnson. CBWP-4

Supervising Examinations. Sean Lucy. CIP

Supervisor, Han Chün-mei, Has Shown Me Five Poems He Has Written, The. Tai Piao-yüan, *tr. fr. Chinese by* Jonathan Chaves. CoBLCP

Supper. Walter De la Mare. NYBP

Supper. George Keithley. SoTCo

Supper. William Soutar. OxBS

Supper after the Last, The. Galway Kinnell. NOBA

Supper eaten, still blessed. Ozaki Hosai, *tr. fr. Japanese by* Hiroaki Sato. *Fr.* One Hundred Haiku in Free Form. FCEI

Supper Is Na Ready. Burns. GBP

Supper is over, the hearth is swept, The. Sermon in a Stocking. Ellen A. Jewett. BLPA

Supplement, A. Benjamin Tompson. SCAP

Suppliant. Florence Earle Coates. TrPWD

Suppliant, The. Georgia Douglas Johnson. CDC; PoBA; PoNe

Suppliant. Alan Sullivan. CaP

Supplication, A. Nicholas Breton. OBSC

Supplication, A. Abraham Cowley. *Fr.* Davideis. GTBS, *fr.* III; GTBS-P, *fr.* III.

Supplication. Josephine Johnson. TrPWD

Supplication. Joseph Seamon Cotter, Jr.. BANP; CDC; PoNe

Supplication. Edgar Lee Masters. TrCP; TrPWD

Supplication. Edith Lovejoy Pierce. TrPWD

Supplication, A. Sir Thomas Wyatt. *See* Forget Not Yet.

Supplication of the Black Aberdeen. Kipling. BLPA

Support Your Local Police Dog. Carter Revard. VoR

Suppose. Phoebe Cary. BLPA; BLPL

Suppose. William Trowbridge. SoTCo

Suppose he had been tabled at thy teats. Luke XI: Blessed Be the Paps Which Thou Hast Sucked. Richard Crashaw. BXAP; JCP

Suppose his body was the meticulous layering. Suppose Your Father Was a Redbird. Pattiann Rogers. MT

Suppose it, for the last time, in that moment. The Coming of the White Man. Patrick Anderson. *Fr.* Poem on Canada. MoCV
"Wide was the land." CaP

Suppose it is nothing but the hive. Davis Matlock. Edgar Lee Masters. *Fr.* Spoon River Anthology. LiTA; LiTM

Suppose me dead; and then suppose. Swift. *Fr.* Verses on the Death of Doctor Swift [D.S.P.D., Occasioned by Reading a Maxim in Rochefoucauld]. NOBE; NOEC; OxBoLi, *abr.*; PoEL-3; TEP

Suppose, my little lady. Suppose. Phoebe Cary. BLPA; BLPL

Suppose one thing. For Those Who Always Fear the Worst. *Unknown.* NBLV

Suppose some peddler offered. The Market Economy. Marge Piercy. GeTw

Suppose that you have seen. Shakespeare. *Fr.* King Henry V, III. MOS

Suppose the ceiling went outside. The Ceiling. Theodore Roethke. EyDe

Suppose the dead could crown their wit. A Responsory, 1948. Thomas Merton. VGW

Suppose they had cheated me out of my. Remember Times for Sandy. Carolyn M. Rodgers. JB

Suppose This Moment Some Stupendous Question. Alden Nowlan. NOBC

Suppose those/ who made/ wars. Nigerian Unity/ or Little Niggers Killing Little Niggers. Don L. Lee. NeAC

Suppose we are standing together a minute. April. Jean Valentine. TAP

Suppose You Met a Witch, *sel.* Ian Serraillier.
  "Suppose you met a witch. There's one I know." WSC

Suppose you screeve? or go cheap-jack? Villon's Straight Tip to All Cross Coves. W. E. Henley, *after* Villon. AWP; CenHV; FaBoCo; InvP; NA; SeCePo

Suppose you were dreaming about your family. Benign Neglect/ Mississippi, 1970. Primus St. John. PoBA

Suppose Your Father Was a Redbird. Pattiann Rogers. MT

Suppose your parents had called you Dirk. A Name. Maxine Chernoff. UL

Suppose your whole life. An Everlasting Once. Theodore Weiss. AnAn

Suppose you're a solo native here. Solo Native. Thomas Lux. LCAP

Supposing we could just go on and on as two. Sunflower Sonnet Number Two. June Jordan. SM; Son

Supremacy. E. A. Robinson. NoAM

Supreme Death. Douglas Dunn. FaBoMo

Supreme Fortune Falls Soonest. Robert Herrick. CaPo

Supreme my holdings, greater yet my need. John Berryman. *Fr.* Dream Songs. CRP

Supreme Sacrifice, The. John S. Arkwright. WGRP

Supremer Sacrifice, The. "Furnley Maurice." CBAP

Supremes, The. Mark Jarman. NAmP

Supremes done gone, The. Memorial. Sonia Sanchez. BlSi

Surcease. Patrick Lane. NeAC

Surcharged with discontent. *Unknown.* PBBP

Sure. Naomi Shihab Nye. MT

Sure a Poor Man. *Unknown, tr. fr. Hawaiian by* M. K. Pukui *and* A. L. Korn. WTO

Sure an' twas a/ fine st. patrick's day. Saint Patrick's Day, 1973. Wendy Rose. CDW

Sure and exact, the master's quiet touch. The Dead Player. Burns. AA

Sure as hell. Blueline. Ken Belford. NeAC

Sure, It was so. Man in those early days. Corruption. Henry Vaughan. JCP; NAEL-1; NOCV; OAEL-1; OBS; Prf; SeCP; SeCV-1

Sure, Lord, there is enough in Thee to dry. George Herbert. FL

Sure never was picture drawn more to the life. The Virginia Song. *Unknown.* PAH

"Sure," Said Benny Goodman. Hayden Carruth. BLA

Sure there are poets which did never dream. Cooper's Hill. Sir John Denham. SeCP; SeCV-1

Sure thing/ I'm a spirit! *Unknown, tr. by* Jerome Rothenberg. STP

Sure, this world is full of trouble. Ain't It [*or* It's] Fine Today. Douglas Malloch. BLPA; WBLP

Sure thou didst flourish once! and many springs. The Timber. Henry Vaughan. FaBoRV, *abr.*; NoP; OBEV; SeCP; SeCV-1

Sure You Can Ask Me a Personal Question. Diane Burns. STE

Surely a dead moth's. Funeral. Bert Meyers. PCP

Surely among a rich man's flowering lawns. Ancestral Houses. W. B. Yeats. *Fr.* Meditations in Time of Civil War, I. LiTB; OAEL-2

Surely in my eyes that light is now lost. The Photograph of Myself. Jon Anderson. AmPA

Surely it is death to come here. Tlanusi' Yi, the Leech Place. Gladys Cardiff. CDW; STE

Surely My Soul. Jacob Cohen, *tr. fr. Hebrew by* I. M. Lask. TrJP

Surely one of my finest days, I'd just. Extract from Memoirs. Howard Nemerov. OxBC

"Surely there is a mine for silver." Bible, *O.T.* *Fr.* Job, XXVIII: 1–11. SaC
  (Price of Wisdom.) TrGrPo

Surely this is the moon. Narihira, *tr. fr. Japanese by* Burton Watson. *Fr.* Kokin Shu. FCEI

Surely you paused at this roadside oasis. A Garage in Co. Cork. Derek Mahon. DiPo; FaBCIP

Surely You Remember. Dahlia Ravikovich, *tr. fr. Hebrew.* IP, *tr. by* Warren Bargad *and* Stanley Chyet; MHeP, *tr. by* Bernhard Frank; VWA, *tr. by* Chana Bloch.

Surely you would not ask me to have known. Question to Life. Patrick Kavanagh. MoBrPo

Surf. Lillian Morrison. NTCP

Surf-casting. W. S. Merwin. NOBA

Surf is a partial deafness islanders. Polynesia. Allen Curnow. PeNZ

Surface. Roger Giroux, *tr. fr. French by* Anthony Barnett. RHTwFP

Surface dreams are easily remembered, The. Mornings After. Fleur Adcock. ATNZ

Surface of the earth displays, The. Primer. Bob Perelman. LP

Surface of the pond was mostly green, The. The Lotus Flowers. Ellen Bryant Voigt. BLA; MAYP; MT

Surfer, The. Judith Wright. RR; WPE

Surfers at Santa Cruz. Paul Goodman. ASP; FF

Surgeons must be very careful. Emily Dickinson. ImOP; TAP

Surgery. Kenneth Pitchford. GLP

Surgical Ward: Men. Robert Graves. FaBoMo

Surging over the reef. Akaotu. Alistair Campbell. ATNZ

Surging sea of human life forever onward rolls, The. A Hundred Years from Now. Mary A. Ford. BLPA

Surnames to Be Avoided in Marriage. *Unknown.* FaBoUs

Surpise. Jean Conder Soule. RHPC

Surprise at Ticonderoga, The. Mary A. P. Stansbury. PAH

Surprise in the Peninsula, A. Fleur Adcock. ATNZ

Surprise Surprise. Rachel McAlpine. ATNZ

Surprise with which one performs, The. Found Subjects. Gerrit Kouwenaar, *tr. by* Peter Nijmeijer. DuIn

Surprised by Evening. Robert Bly. CAPP; NaP; VGW

Surprised by Joy [Impatient as the Wind]. Wordsworth. BoLoP; EnRP; HAP; LiTB; NAEL-2; NOBE; NoP; OAEL-2; OBD; PoE; Son; TEP (Desideria.) BLPL; GTBS; GTBS-P; OBEV

Surprised by Me. Walter Darring. NYBP

Surprised by Winter. Michizane, *tr. fr. Chinese by* Burton Watson. JLIC-1

Surprised Pen, The. Gabriel Preil, *tr. fr. Yiddish by* Grace Schulman. PeBMYV

Surprises are round. Surpise. Jean Conder Soule. RHPC

Surprising my dupe by his egg of Oedipus. Dirge for Three Trumpets. *Unknown.* EAS

Surreal Appetite. George McWhirter. UAS

Surrealism in the Middle Ages. Philip Lamantia. UL

Surrender. Angelina Weld Grimké. CDC

Surrender, The. Henry King. BoLoP; EBEV; JCP; MePo; TrGrPo

Surrender at Appomattox, The. Herman Melville. PAH

Surrender of Cornwallis, The. *Unknown.* PAH

Surrender of New Orleans, The. Marion Manville. PAH

Surrender of Spain, The. John Milton Hay. AA

Surrendered Names. Gerald Vizenor. HATNAP

Surrounded by beakers, by strange coils. The Naked World. Sully-Prudhomme, *tr. by* William Dock. ImOP

Surrounded by scientists in a faculty. Homage to the New World. Michael S. Harper. LCAP

Surrounded by tigers. The Life of the Wolf. Gary Gildner. AmPA

Surrounded by unnumbered foes. His Banner over Me. Gerald Massey. WGRP

Surrounded with tall board fences. Yoshiwara. Hagiwara Sakutaro, *tr. by* Hiroaki Sato. FCEI

Suruga Dance. *Unknown, tr. fr. Japanese by* Geoffrey Bownas *and* Anthony Thwaite. PeBJV

Suruga Dance. *Unknown, tr. fr. Japanese by* Sato. FCEI

Surveillances. Tom Paulin. CIP

Survey, A. William Stafford. RB

Survey of Cornwall, *sel.* Richard Carew.
  River Lynher, The. FaBoPP

Survey of Literature. John Crowe Ransom. FaBoCh; LiTA; NBLV; OBAL; TAP; TwCP; VGW

Survey of the Amphitheatre, A. Moses Browne. NOEC

Surveyor. Guy Butler. PeSA

Survival, The. Edmund Blunden. OBEV; OBMV

Survival. Florence Earle Coates. AA

Survival This Way ("Survival, I know how this way"). Simon J. Ortiz. CDW; STE

Surviving. Maureen Ismay. WS
Surviving. James Welch. CDW; HATNAP; STE
Surviving the Journey, *sel.* Tony Beyer.
    Word of Snow. ATNZ
Survivor, The. Stephen Berg. *Fr.* Entering the Body. NaP
Survivor, The. Stanley Cook. NPo
Survivor, The. Katherine Gallagher. AIW
Survivor, The. Robert Graves. CMoP
Survivor. Roger McGough. PoPo
Survivor. Archibald MacLeish. PrIm
Survivor. Judy Dothard Simmons. CNA
Survivor, The. R. S. Thomas. FaBoTw
Survivor sole, and hardly such, of all. Yardley Oak. William Cowper.
    LaA; NOEC
Survivors. Elaine Feinstein. VWA
Survivors, The. Judith Hemschemeyer. TV
Survivors, The. Daryl Hine. TwCP
Survivors. Frank Ormsby. CIP
Survivors, The. Adrienne Rich. NYBP
Survivors, The. Miriam Waddington. VWA
Susan. Robin Magowan. EAS
Susan is eating a mandarin orange Eiffel Tower. The Good Ship.
    Michael Stephens. UL
Susan ("Susan poisoned her grandmother's tea"). *Unknown.* NA
Susan, the constant slave to mop and broom. "Peter Pindar." *Fr.* The
    Sorrows of Sunday; an Elegy. NOEC
Susan, we meet in late fall. The Meeting. Kathleen Spivack. NMM
Susanna and the Elders. Adelaide Crapsey. WPE
Susanna and the Elders. Jack Gilbert. NPGG
Susanna: girl and bride. The Man-Fate. William Everson. NoAM
Susannah and the Elders. *Unknown.* ErPo
Susannah Prout. Walter de la Mare. FaBoEE
Susannah the fair. Susannah and the Elders. *Unknown.* ErPo
Susano-o's Song. *Unknown, tr. fr. Japanese by* Hiroaki Sato. *Fr.* The
    Kojiki. FCEI
Sushi. Paul Muldoon. CIP
Sushi-Okashi and Green Tea with Mitsu Yashima. Al Robles. BrSi
Susie Asado. Gertrude Stein. NoAM; SOTW; TAP
Susie Wong Doesn't Live Here. Diane Mei Lin Mark. BrSi
Susie's galoshes. Galoshes. Rhoda Warner Bacmeister. NTCP
Suspended Moment. Mariana B. Davenport. GoYe
Suspense. Emily Dickinson. *See* Elysium is as far as to.
Suspense. D. H. Lawrence. MoBrPo
Suspension. Constance E. Studer. TSM
Suspicious Truth, The, *sel.* Juan Ruiz de Alarcón, *tr. fr. Spanish by*
    Samuel Beckett.
    Feast by the Manzanares. *Fr.* I. MexPo
Suspiria. *Unknown.* OBEV
Sussex Legend, A. Charles Dalmon. BoTP
Sussyissfriin, *sel.* Philip Dow.
    "My son & I, between *Fu-Sang* and/ Cathay." NPGG
Susuki, growing along the way to my beloved. *Unknown. Fr.* Manyo
    Shu. Ma
Sutcliffe and Whitby. William Logan. MAYP
Suthun Accent. Leonard Trawick. SoTCo
Sutra is sour, The. Yosano Akiko, *tr. by* Geoffrey Bownas *and* Anthony
    Thwaite. PeBJV
Suttee, The. Thomas Skinner. OBTV
Suzanne. John Logan. CAPP
Suzanne Takes You Down. Leonard Cohen. NIP; NoP
Swaggering prince. Python. *Yoruba Oral Tradition, tr. by* Ulli Beier.
    WTO
Swahili Love Song. *Unknown, tr. by* Jan Knappert. LLLT
Swain, give o'er your fond pretension. Hildebrand Jacob. FaBoEE
Swallow, The. Lucy Aikin. OxBChV
Swallow, The. Abraham Cowley. EBEV; FM; OBEV; PBBP
Swallow, The, *sel.* J. C. Squire.
    "Birds, trees and flow'rs they bring to me." BXAP
Swallow, The. Ogden Nash. RAR
Swallow, The. Thomas Stanley. AWP
Swallow, for a moment seen, The. Thomas Warton, the Younger. *Fr.*
    Ode: The First of April. PBBP
Swallow has come again, The. The Children's Song. *Unknown.*
    FaPON
Swallow has erased a rainbow, A. Kikaku, *tr. fr. Japanese by* Hiroaki
    Sato. *Fr.* Thirty-three Hokku. FCEI
Swallow is flying over, The. Tears in Spring. William Ellery Channing.
    AA
Swallow leaves her nest, The. Dirge. Thomas Lovell Beddoes. *Fr.*
    Death's Jest Book, I. PoEL-4
    (Song from the Waters.) NOBE

(Voice from the Waters, A.) OBNC
("We do lie beneath the grass.") ELP; NOBE; OBNC; WiR
Swallow, mud in its beak, A. Dreaming of the South. Niu Chiao, *tr. by*
    Lois Fusek. ATF
Swallow, my sister, O sister swallow. Itylus. Swinburne. ChTr
Swallow-shell that eases birth, The. Gary Snyder. *Fr.* Myths and Texts:
    Hunting, IV. NaP
Swallow sings "Dawn," The. *Unknown, tr. by* Ezra Pound and Noel
    Stock. BoWoP
Swallow Song. Marjorie Pickthall. CaP
Swallow, swallow on your flight. *Unknown, tr. by* Arthur Waley. BoS
Swallow, swallow, swooping free. The Swallow. Ogden Nash. RAR
Swallow Tails. Tom Robinson. FaPON
Swallow, that on rapid wing. The Swallow. Lucy Aikin. OxBChV
Swallow the Lake. Clarence Major. PoBA
Swallowing every river there is. Watching the Sea. Lo Men, *tr. by*
    Dominic Cheung. IFON
Swallowing of the Earth, The. Gust Gils, *tr. fr. Dutch by* James S.
    Holmes. DuIn
Swallows. Thomas Hornsby Ferril. RFM
Swallows. Wu Tsao, *tr. fr. Chinese by* Irving Lo. WFTU
Swallows flap in waves against the house, The. Late Spring: A Heaving,
    a Turning. John Gill. NeAC
Swallows flew in the curves of an eight, The. Overlooking the River
    Stour. Thomas Hardy. FaBoPP
Swallow's Flight, The. Louis Levy, *tr. fr. Danish by* Martin S. Alwood
    and Sanford Kaufman. TrJP
Swallows hide, The. From Life. Lazer Eichenrand, *tr. by* Gabriel Preil
    and Howard Schwartz. VWA
Swallows over the Camp. Uys Krige, *tr. fr. Afrikaans. PeSA, tr. by* the
    author [*and*] Jack Cope
Swallows reel in the winds. River Messages. Ku Hsiung, *tr. by* Lois
    Fusek. ATF
Swallows return in the freshness of spring, The. Feeling Regret at the Silk
    Window. Mao Wen-hsi, *tr. by* Lois Fusek. ATF
Swallows travel to and fro. Robert Louis Stevenson. EBVV
Swallows, when your wings are full grown. *Unknown, tr. by* Hiroaki
    Sato. FCEI
Swam too far out: the swell took him. Elegy for a School-Friend.
    Augustus Young. BIrV
Swamp. Roberta Hill. VoR
Swamp at the end of our cozy county road, The. Suburban Swamp. Jay
    Parini. BLA
Swamp Fox, The. William Gilmore Simms. AA; BeLS; FaBoBe; PAH
Swamp Nocturne. Aimé Césaire, *tr. fr. French by* Michael Benedikt.
    POS
Swamp reeds murmur the song, The. Marsh Leaf. David Wagoner.
    PoA
Swamp unrolling its lasso which had previously been kept, The. Swamp
    Nocturne. Aimé Césaire, *tr. by* Michael Benedikt. POS
Swampland Mulberries Are Lovely. *Unknown, tr. fr. Chinese by* Burton
    Watson. CoBCP
Swampstrife and spatterdock. The Marsh. William DeWitt Snodgrass.
    BoNaP; NePoEA
Swampy State of Illinois, The. Excelsior. *Unknown.* BXAP
Swan. Donald Hall. LCAP
Swan. D. H. Lawrence. CMoP; PoE
Swan. Edward Lowbury. GTBS-P
Swan, The. Theodore Roethke. VGW
Swan, The. *Unknown. See* Swan swam over the sea.
Swan and Shadow. John Hollander. InPK; NoP; PoA
Swan and the Goose, The. Aesop, *tr. fr. Greek by* William Ellery
    Leonard. AWP; FaPON
Swan Bathing, The. Ruth Pitter. MoBrPo
Swan bears on its neck the initial of sleep, The. Entreaty to the Cloud.
    Amado Nervo, *tr. by* Samuel Beckett. MexPo
Swan Song. Morton Marcus. NAmP
Swan Song of Parson Avery, The. Whittier. AA
Swan swam over the sea. *Unknown.* OxNR
    (Swan, The.) ChTr; FaPON
Swan Swims So Bonny, The. *Unknown.* OBET
Swan, The: "Clothes make no sound when I tread ground." *Unknown,
    formerly at.* to Cynewulf, *tr. fr. Anglo-Saxon by* Geoffrey Grigson.
    Fr. Riddles (Exeter Book). RB
Swank, The. V. C. Vickers. AmMo
Swann had gone to the estate that afternoon to tell his. Norman Dubie.
    Fr. The Duchess' Red Shoes, III. AnAn
Swann has visited the Duc and Duchess de Guermantes. Norman Dubie.
    Fr. The Duchess' Red Shoes, I. AnAn
Swans. Lawrence Durrell. MoBrPo; SeCePo
Swans, The. Edith Sitwell. CMoP; WPE

Swans. Leonora Speyer. FYAP

Swans at Night, *sel.* Mary Gilmore.
  "Within the night, above the dark." PoAu-1

Swan's Feet, The. Edith Jay Scovell. FaBoWP; OxBTC

Swans in Flight. Miroslav Holub, *tr. fr. Czech by* Ewald Osers.
  FaBoPV

Swans Mating. Michael Longley. FaBCIP

Swans of Vadstena, The. Ralph Gustafson. MoCV

Swans rise up with their wings in day, The. The Boy and the Geese.
  Padraic Fiacc. NeIP

Swans sing before they die: 't were no bad thing. On a Bad Singer.
  Samuel Taylor Coleridge. FaBoCo; FaBoEE; RHPC

Swansong. Carol Muske. AmPA

Swarm of bees in May, A. Proverb. *Unknown.* FaBoBe; OxNR
  ("Swarm of bees in May, A.") FaBoBe; OxNR

Swarm of flies is drumming on, A. The Tannery. Francisco Carrillo, *tr.
  by* Maureen Ahern *and* David Tipton. Per

Swarming, A. A Sheeprancher Named John. Gretel Ehrlich. MAYP

Swarming Bees, The. James Laughlin. VGW

Swarming over the damp ground with pocket lenses. Sweet Everlasting.
  Ellen Bryant Voigt. AnAn; MT

Swarms of minnows show their little heads. Minnows. Keats. FaPON;
  GN

Swart Italian with his breast of fur, The. Public Beach (Long Island
  Sound). Christopher Morley. NBLV

Swart swarthy smiths besmattered with smoke. The Blacksmiths.
  Unknown. RB; TW, *mod. vers. by* Wesli Court; WiR

Swarte-smeked Smithes. *Unknown. See* Blacksmiths, The.

Swarthy bee is a buccaneer, The. A More Ancient Mariner. Bliss
  Carman. AnAmPo; OBAL

Swarthy little statue, The. Naked War. Michael Heffernan. BXAP

Swarthy youth rambled, A. Pushkin. "Anna Akhmatova," *tr. by* Stanley
  Kunitz *with* Max Hayward. AnAn

Swathe of violet at break of day, A. Joachim of Flora. Charles Spear.
  ATNZ

Swathe Uncut, The. John Hewitt. NeIP

Sway. Denis Johnson. SM

Sway. Louis Simpson. NoAM

Sway song. Eye of God. Jim Tollerud. VoR

Swear by what the sages spoke. Under Ben Bulben. W. B. Yeats.
  CMoP; HAP; LiTM; MoP; NAEL-2; NoAM; NoP; OxBTC

Swearing. Henry Fitzsimon. ACP

Sweat, The. Nila NorthSun. STE

Sweat dripping down. Moto Mokuami, *tr. by* Geoffrey Bownas *and*
  Anthony Thwaite. PeBJV

Sweat-House Ritual No. 1. *Unknown, tr. fr. Omaha Indian by* Jerome
  Rothenberg *from* Alia Fletcher *and* Francis La Flesche. STP

Sweat is a style of the body. John Tranter. *Fr.* Crying in Early Infancy,
  XCIII. NoAM

Sweat like drops of blood run down, The. Dark Was the Night.
  Unknown. AmFP

Sweat Song. Peter Blue Cloud. STE; VoR

Sweating It Out on Winding Stair Mountain. Jim Barnes. CDW

Sweatshop, The. Morris Jacob Rosenfeld, *tr. fr. Yiddish by* Aaron
  Kramer. PeBMYV

Swedes. Edward Thomas. BrPo; OAEL-2; RB

Swedish Angel. Winfield Townley Scott. LiTM

Swedish Lesson. Barton Sutter. SM

Swedish Organs. Paul Snoek, *tr. fr. Dutch by* James S. Holmes. DuIn

Sweeney Agonistes, *sels.* T. S. Eliot. UnPo
  "Under the bamboo."
  "You'll be my little seven stone missionary!"

Sweeney among the Nightingales. T. S. Eliot. AmPP; AnAmPo; CMoP;
  FaBoMo; HAP; HeIP; InvP; LiTA; LiTM; MoP; NAAL-2; NAEL-2;
  NoAM; NOBA; NOBE; NoP; OBMV; OxBA; PPP; WeW

Sweeney Astray, *sels.* Seamus Heaney.
  "I perched for rest, and imagined." *Fr.* 23. PPR
  "Sweeney kept going until he reached the church at/ Swim-two-birds."
  Fr. 22. PPR

Sweeney Erect. T. S. Eliot. OxBTC; VGW

Sweeney in Articulo. "Myra Buttle." *See* Sweeniad, The:
  Sunday is the dullest day, treating.

Sweeney kept going until he reached the church at/ Swim-two-birds.
  Seamus Heaney. *Fr.* Sweeney Astray, 22. PPR

Sweeney, Old and Phthisic, among the Hippopotami. David Cummings.
  BXAP

Sweeney Praises the Trees. *Unknown, tr. fr. Irish by* Seamus Heaney.
  RB

Sweeney Redivivus, *sels.* Seamus Heaney.
  "I stirred wet sand and gathered myself." NoAM
  "Road ahead, The." TOF

Sweeney the Mad, *sel. Unknown, tr. fr. Middle Irish by* J. G. O'Keefe.
  "Man by the wall snores, The." AnIL

Sweeney to Mrs. Porter in the Spring. L. E. Sissman. NYBP

Sweeniad, The, *sel.* "Myra Buttle."
  "Sunday is the dullest day, treating." FaBoPa
  (Sweeney in Articulo.) BXAP; Par

Sweep. Rodney Jones. MT

Sweep Me through Your Many-Chambered Heart. Diane Ackerman. NIP

Sweep the house. The Dead Baby. William Carlos Williams. NAAL-2

Sweep the house clean. William Carlos Williams. MoAB; MoAmPo

Sweep thy faint strings, Musician. The Song of the Shadows. Walter de
  la Mare. CMoP; MoBrPo; TrGrPo

Sweeper, The. Agnes Lee. QFR

Sweeper of Ways, The. Howard Nemerov. HCAP

Sweepers, The. William Whitehead. NOEC

Sweeping Leaves. Ryushu Shutaku, *tr. fr. Japanese by* Burton Watson.
  FCEI

Sweeping the Skies. Elizabeth Anna Hart. CenHV

Sweeping the sky our willow tree has thrown. Willow in a Gale. Jane
  Wilson. NPo

Sweet, a delicate white mouse, A. The Waltzer in the House. Stanley
  Kunitz. ErPo; NYBP; RHPC

Sweet, acidulous, down-reaching thrill, A. Ode on [*or* to] a Jar of
  Pickles. Bayard Taylor. BXAP; FaBoPa

Sweet Adon, darest not glance thine eye. Infida's Song. Robert Greene.
  Fr. Never Too Late. OBSC

Sweet after showers, ambrosial air. Tennyson. *Fr.* In Memoriam A. H.
  H., LXXXVI. EBVV

Sweet Afton. Burns. *See* Flow Gently, Sweet Afton.

Sweet Amarillis, by a spring's. Upon Mistress Elizabeth Wheeler under
  the Name of Amarillis. Robert Herrick. CaPo; PBBP

Sweet and calm the breezes stealing. Sabbath Bells. Josephine D.
  Henderson Heard. CBWP-4

Sweet and lovely, dimly in my dreams. An Oriole at Dawn. Li Meng-
  yang, *tr. by* Jonathan Chaves. CoBLCP

Sweet and Low [Sweet and Low]. Tennyson. *Fr.* The Princess, *pt.* II.
  BLPL; BoTP; FaBoBe; FaPON; MOS; NAEL-2; OxBChV; TrGrPo
  (Lullaby: "Sweet and low, sweet and low.") PoLF

Sweet-and-Twenty. Shakespeare. *See* Twelfth Night: O [*or* Oh] Mistress
  Mine [Where Are You Roaming?].

Sweet antidote to sorrow, toil and strife. To a Segar. Samuel Low.
  OBAL

Sweet Apple. James Stephens. CMoP

Sweet are the days we wander with no hope. George Santayana. *Fr.*
  Sonnets. AnAmPo

Sweet are the thoughts that savo[u]r of content. Maesia's Song. Robert
  Greene. *Fr.* Farewell to Folly. CTC; OBSC; UnPo
  (Mind Content, A.) EIL; ViBoPo
  (Poor Estate, The.) TrGrPo
  (Song: "Sweet are the thoughts that savour of content.") PoEL-2

Sweet are the ways of death to weary feet. Lord De Tabley. *Fr.* Medea.
  OBEV

Sweet are the whispers of yon pine that makes. The Death of Daphnis.
  Theocritus, *tr. fr. Greek by* Charles Stuart Calverley. *Fr.* Idylls, I.
  AWP

Sweet Armida tooke this charge on hand, The. Tasso, *tr. fr. Italian by*
  Edward Fairfax. *Fr.* Godfrey of Bulloigne; or, The Recoverie of
  Jerusalem, IV. OBVE

Sweet as violets to a weary heart. The Pleiades. Elizabeth Jane
  Coatsworth. ImOP

Sweet, at this morn I chanced. Buen Matina. Sir John Salusbury. EIL

Sweet Auburn! loveliest village of the plain. Auburn. Goldsmith. *Fr.*
  The Deserted Village. SeCePo
  (Sweet Auburn.) LiTB; NOBE
  (Village, The.) TrGrPo

Sweet Auburn! parent of the blissful hour. Goldsmith. *Fr.* The Deserted
  Village. EBEV

Sweet baby sleep: What ail[e]s my dear? A Hymn L: Rocking Hymn.
  George Wither. *Fr.* Hallelujah; or, Britain's Second Remembrancer.
  SeCV-1
  (Rocking Hymn, A.) OxBChV

Sweet baked apple dappled cinnamon speckled sin of mine. Love Child—
  a Black Aesthetic. Everett Hoagland. BPo

Sweet basil. Having Replaced Love with Food and Drink. Diane
  Wakoski. NAs

Sweet, be not proud of those two eyes. To Dianeme. Robert Herrick.
  CaPo; GTBS; GTBS-P; JCP; NOBE; OBEV; OBS; SeCV-1; TrGrPo

Sweet beast, I have gone prowling. William DeWitt Snodgrass. LLLT;
  MoAmPo; NYBP; SM

Sweet beats of jazz impaled on slivers of wind. Walking Parker Home.
  Bob Kaufman. PoBA

Sweet bell of Stratford, tolling slow. The Passing Bell at Stratford. William Winter. AA

Sweet Be'mi'ster, that bist a-bound. Be'mi'ster. William Barnes. EBVV

Sweet Benedict, whilst thou art young. To His Little Son Benedict from the Tower of London. John Hoskyns. OxBChV

Sweet Bets[e]y from Pike. Unknown. AmFP; AS, with music; FaBoBa; OBAL; OxBoLi

Sweet bird that shunn'st the noise of folly. Milton. Fr. Il Penseroso. CH

Sweet bird, that sing'st away the early howres. To a Nightingale. William, of Hawthornden Drummond. OBS

Sweet birds! that sit and sing amid the shady valleys. Phyllis. Nicholas Breton. OBSC; TrGrPo
    (Pastoral, A: "Sweet Bird! that sit and sing amid the shady valleys.") EIl

Sweet blackbird is silenced with chaffinch and thrush. Winter. Christina Rossetti. BoTP

Sweet boy, gentle boy. Pushkin, tr. by Valery Pereleshin. PeHV

"Sweet boy," she says, "this night I'll waste in sorrow." Shakespeare. Fr. Venus and Adonis. ErPo

"Sweet" breath that you move. Eclogue IV. Andrea Zanzotto, tr. by Lawrence R. Smith. NItP

Sweet-breathed and young. A Woman's Execution. Edward King. AA

Sweet Chance, that led my steps abroad. A Great Time. W. H. Davies. LiTB; MoBrPo

Sweet child of April, I have found thy place. The Pyxidanthera. Augusta Cooper Bristol. AA

Sweet children amid the apple boughs. On the Picture of a Child. Henrietta Cordelia Ray. CBWP-3

Sweet Content. Thomas Dekker and others. See Pleasant Comedy of Patient Grissell [or Grissel or Grissill], The:
    Art thou poor, yet hast thou golden slumbers?

Sweet corrall lips, where Nature's treasure lies. Richard Barnfield. Fr. Sonnets, VI. PeHV

Sweet Country Life, A. Unknown. OBET

Sweet creatures, did you truly understand. To All Those Worthy Women, Who Have Any Desire to live in Newfound-land. Robert Hayman. OBTV

Sweet Cupid, Ripen Her Desire. Unknown. OBSC; OxBSP

Sweet cyder is a great thing. Great Things. Thomas Hardy. GTBS-P; NOBE

Sweet Cynthia, take the book away. To Cynthia, Not to Let Him Read the Ladies' Magazines. P. M. Hubbard. FiBHP

Sweet day, so cool, so calm, so bright. Virtue. George Herbert. AWP; CH; ELP; HAP; HeIP; InPS; InvP; JCP; NAEL-1; NOBE; NOCV; NoP; OAEL-1; OBD; OBEV; PoE; PoRA; PPP; SoSe; TEP; TrGrPo; WGRP
    (Vertue.) FaBoRV; MeLP; MePo; OBS; SeCP; SeCV-1

Sweet, deep sense of mystery filled the wood, A. In Cool, Green Haunts. Mahlon Leonard Fisher. WeW

Sweet Diane. George Barlow. CNA

Sweet Disorder. Robert Herrick. See Delight in Disorder.

Sweet disorder in the dress, A. Delight in Disorder. Robert Herrick. CaPo; EBEV; EnLoPo; ErPo; FaBV; FF; GTBS; GTBS-P; HAP; HeIP; InPK; InPS; JCP; LiTB; NAEL-1; NIP; NOBE; NoP; OAEL-1; OBEV; OBS; PoE; PoRA; PPP; PrIm; SeCePo; SeCP; SeCV-1; TEP; TrGrPo; WeW
    (Sweet Disorder.) AWP; BLPL

Sweet Dreams. Ogden Nash. OnUR

Sweet dreams, form a shade. Blake. Fr. Songs of Innocence. EnRP; OBCP

Sweet dreams, sweet memories, sweet taste of earth. Cemetery Nights. Stephen Dobyns. NAmP; SV

Sweet earth, he ran and changed his shoes to go. Arrangements with Earth for Three Dead Friends. James Wright. NIP

Sweet earth of Palestine. To Those Palestinians Martyred in Foreign Lands. Faiz Ahmad Faiz, tr. by Mahmood Jamal. PBMUP

Sweet Echo, sweetest Nymph, that livest unseen. Echo. Milton. Fr. Comus; a Masque Presented at Ludlow Castle. ELP; OBEV; OBS
    (Lady Sings, The.) NOBE
    (Lady's Song.) TrGrPo

Sweet elfin music comes to me. A Dream of Elfland. Henrietta Cordelia Ray. CBWP-3

Sweet Ethel. Linda Piper. BlSi

Sweet Everlasting. Ellen Bryant Voigt. AnAn; MT

Sweet eyes by sorrow still unwet. Wonderland. Harry Thurston Peck. AA

Sweet Father. Malka Heifetz-Tussman, tr. fr. Yiddish by Kathryn Hellerstein. AYP

Sweet father I have shrunk a bit. Father Father Son and Son. Jon Swan. NYBP

Sweet flower, that art so fair and gay. Medieval Norman Song. Unknown, tr. by John Addington Symonds. AWP

Sweet floweret, pledge o' meikle love. On the Birth of a Posthumous Child, Born in Peculiar Circumstances of Family Distress. Burns. NAs

Sweet for a little even to fear, and sweet. Erotion. Swinburne. PoEL-5

Sweet gem of infant fairy-flowers! To an Infant Daughter. John Clare. NAs

Sweet gentle angel, not that I aspire. To Miss M———, Written by Moonlight, July 18, 1782. Sir Samuel Egerton Brydges. Son

Sweet girl graduate, lean as a fawn, A. Nancy Hanks, Mother of Abraham Lincoln. Vachel Lindsay. CMoP

Sweet Grass Is around Her. Salli Benedict. GOS

Sweet hand! the sweet yet cruel bow thou art. Love's Franciscan. Henry Constable. ACP

Sweet handsome friend, I can tell you truly. Tibors, tr. by Meg Bogin. WT

Sweet heart,/ A morning, climbing in its brass. Letter from an Island. John Malcolm Brinnin. TAP

Sweet Highland Girl, a very shower. To the [or a] Highland Girl of Inversneyde. Wordsworth. EnRP; GTBS; GTBS-P

Sweet Hour of Prayer. William W. Walford. BLRP; WBLP

Sweet if thou wilt be. Come Turn to Mee, Thou Pretty Little One. Unknown. CoMu

Sweet, if you like and love me still. His Farewell to His Unkind and Unconstant Mistress. Francis Davison. EIl; OBSC

Sweet in goodly fellowship. There's No Lust like to Poetry. Unknown, tr. by John Addington Symonds. AWP

Sweet in her green cell the flower of beauty slumbers. George Darley. OBEV
    (Serenade of a Loyal Martyr.) NOBE; OBNC

Sweet in your antique body, not yet young. To a Child. Wilfred Owen. Son

Sweet in your sight the fiery stride. Unknown, tr. fr. Irish by Thomas Kinsella. Fr. Exile of the Sons of Uisliu. NOIV

Sweet infancy! The Rapture. Thomas Traherne. OBS

Sweet Innisfallen. Thomas Moore. OBNC

Sweet is the breath of Morn, her rising sweet. Milton. Fr. Paradise Lost, IV.

Sweet is the scholar's life. The Scholar's Life. Unknown, tr. by Thomas Kinsella. NOIV

Sweet is the time for joyous folk. Hora Christi. Alice Brown. TrPWD; WGRP

Sweet is true love tho' given in vain, in vain. The Song of Love and Death. Tennyson. Fr. Idylls of the King: Lancelot and Elaine. OBNC

Sweet it is to see the sun. Every Day Thanksgiving Day. Harriet Prescott Spofford. OHIP

Sweet Jane. Unknown. AmFP

Sweet land of song, thy harp doth hang. The War Ship of Peace. Samuel Lover. PAH

Sweet, Let Me Go! Unknown. EIl; InvP; OxBSP; TrGrPo

Sweet, let us love enjoy. Love Play. William Cavendish, Duke of Newcastle. ErPo

Sweet Levinsky. Allen Ginsberg. NBLV

Sweet little bell. Unknown. NOIV
    (Church Bell in the Night, The.) AnIL, tr. by Kuno Meyer, sl. diff. vers.

Sweet little bird in russet coat. The Autumn Robin. John Clare. BoTP

Sweet little maid with winsome eyes. The Other One. Harry Thurston Peck. AA

Sweet love, everything/ closes its eyes now to sleep. Lullaby. Steve Kowit. TDD

Sweet love, mine only treasure. Where His Lady Keeps His Heart. "A. W." CTC; EIl; OBSC

"Sweet love, renew thy force, be it not said." Shakespeare. Fr. Sonnets, LVI. PoLF

Sweet Loving Friendship. Peter Bellamy. OBET

Sweet Lullaby, A. Nicholas Breton. See Cradle Song, A: "Come, little babe, come, silly soul."

Sweet maid, if thou wouldst charm my sight. A Persian Song of Hafiz. Hafiz, tr. by Sir William Jones. AWP

Sweet maiden of Passamaquoddy. Lines to Miss Florence Huntingdon. At. to James De Mille. NA

Sweet Mary was a servant girl. Edwin in the Lowlands Low. Unknown. AmFP

Sweet Meat Has Sour Sauce; or, The Slave-Trader in the Dumps. William Cowper. NOEC; OBSV

Sweet mermaid of the incomparable eyes. The Mermaid. Ben King. AnAmPo; OBAL

Sweet Mother! rare in gifts of tenderness! To My Mother. Henrietta Cordelia Ray. CBWP-3

Sweet Mouth, The. Luis de Góngora y Argote, tr. fr. Spanish by Perry Higman. LPSS

Sweet mouth, that send'st a musky-rosed breath. Joshua Sylvester. EnLoPo

Sweet Muse, Descend. Isaac Watts. NOBE

Sweet Music's Power. Shakespeare and probably John Fletcher. See King Henry VIII: Orpheus with His Lute [Made Trees].

Sweet my musings used to be. Mot eran dous miei cossir. Arnaut Daniel, tr. by Harriet Waters Preston. AWP

Sweet 'n Sour. Genny Lim. BrSi

Sweet names, the rosary of my evening prayer. Love's Rosary. George Edward Woodberry. AA

Sweet nature, give me holy dreams. At Nature's Shrine. Henrietta Cordelia Ray. CBWP-3

Sweet "No! no!" with a sweet smile beneath, A. A Love-Lesson. Clément Marot, tr. by Leigh Hunt. AWP

Sweet Nosegay, A, or Pleasant Posy, sels. Isabella Whitney. WPE
  "Do not account that for thine own."
  "Gold savours well, though it be got."
  "In loving, each one hath free choice."
  "Little gold in law will make, A."
  "Present day we cannot spend, The."
  "Seek not man to please, for that."
  "Such poor folk as to law do go."

Sweet-numbered poet, proudly we thy name. Gerald Massey. William Billington. PF

Sweet nymph, come to thy lover. Unknown. PBBP

Sweet o' the Year, The. George Meredith. BoNaP

Sweet peace, where dost thou dwell? I humbly crave. Peace. George Herbert. AWP; ChTr; ELP; NOCV; TEP

Sweet Peas. Keats. Fr. I Stood Tiptoe [upon a Little Hill]. GN

Sweet Peril. George Macdonald. BLPA; FaBoBe

Sweet Phillis, if a silly swain. A Supplication. Nicholas Breton. OBSC

Sweet Philomel in groves and deserts haunting. Unknown. PBBP

Sweet Phosphor tricks to a smile the brow of heaven. All's Right with the World. Gerald Massey. EBVV

Sweet Pity, Wake. Unknown. EiL

Sweet poems. The Death of Poetry. Livia Candiani, tr. by Muriel Kittel. DMI

Sweet Polycaste, Nestor's youngest daughter. The Bath in Pylos. Gábor Devecseri, tr. by Robert Graves. MHuP

Sweet procession, rose-blue. Seems Like We Must Be Somewhere Else. Denise Levertov. NePoEA-2

Sweet rains of summer. Sweetgrass. Peter Blue Cloud. NOVW

Sweet Reader. E. B. White. ImOP

Sweet Rivers of Redeeming Love. John A. Granade. AH

Sweet Robin, I have heard them say. Robin Redbreast. George Washington Doane. AA

Sweet Robinette. Unknown. CoMu

Sweet rois of vertew and of gentleness. William Dunbar. See To a Lady[e].

Sweet Rose, Fair Flower. At. to Shakespeare. Fr. The Passionate Pilgrim, X. EiL

Sweet sadness, you were never far to seek. The Last Betrayal. Guido Gozzano, tr. by Michael Palma. PFI

Sweet Saint, thou better canst declare to me. To Saint Mary Magdalen ("Sweet Saint, thou better canst declare to me"). Henry Constable. ACP

Sweet saint! whose rising dawned upon the sight. Ariana. Franklin Benjamin Sanborn. AA

Sweet semi-circled Cynthia played at maw. John Taylor. Fr. Odcomb's Complaint. EiL
  (Mockado, Fustian, and Motley.) FaBoNo

Sweet September. George Arnold. GN

Sweet serene sky-like Flower. To Lucasta: The Rose. Richard Lovelace. SeCV-1

Sweet she was, as kind a love. She Smiled like a Holiday. Unknown. OxBoLi

Sweet Slug-a-Bed. Unknown. FaBoCo

Sweet smell of earth and easy rain on. Sleeping Out with My Father. Gibbons Ruark. MT

Sweet smiling village, loveliest of the lawn. Goldsmith. Fr. The Deserted Village. NOIV

Sweet softness with which love serves me often, The. Guilhem de Cabestanh, tr. by Paul Blackburn. Pro

Sweet Solitude, thou placid queen. Solitude. Hannah More. Fr. The Search after Happiness. WBLP

Sweet soul, which in the April of thy years. William Drummond of Hawthornden. JCP

Sweet sounds, oh, beautiful music, do not cease! On Hearing a Symphony of Beethoven. Edna St. Vincent Millay. LiTA; LiTM; MoAB; MoAmPo; TrGrPo

Sweet spouse, you must presently troop and be gone. Imitation of Martial, Book II Ep, An 105. "Captain H—" NOEC

Sweet Spring. William Drummond of Hawthornden. See Spring Bereaved 2.

Sweet Spring, thou turn'st with all thy goodly train. Spring Bereaved 2. William Drummond of Hawthornden. OBEV
  (Sonnet.) EiL
  (Sweet Spring.) Son

Sweet Stay-at-Home. W. H. Davies. CH

Sweet stream, that dost with equal pace. On His Mistress Drown'd. Thomas Spratt. EnLoPo

Sweet stream, that winds through [or thro'] yonder glade. To a Young Lady. William Cowper. GTBS; GTBS-P
  (Addressed to a Young Lady.) EnRP

Sweet Suffolk Owl. At. to Thomas Vautor. CH; ChTr; EBEV; EiL; FaBoRV; PBBP

Sweet Surprises. Sarah Doudney. BoTP

Sweet Swan of Avon! what a sight it were. Ben Jonson. Fr. To the Memory of My Beloved Master William Shakespeare [and What He Hath Left Us]. ChTr

Sweet sweet Robinette all the shepherds do declare. Sweet Robinette. Unknown. CoMu

Sweet, sweet, sweet,/ Is the wind's song. Harvest. Ellen Mackay Hutchinson Cortissoz. AA

Sweet, sweet, sweet, let me go. Unknown. GBL

Sweet sweet sweet sweet sweet tea. Susie Asado. Gertrude Stein. NoAM; SOTW; TAP

Sweet, sweet wine. Circumstance. Alice Bowen. GOS

Sweet Teviot! on thy silver tide. A Father's Notes of Woe. Sir Walter Scott. Fr. The Lay of the Last Minstrel, IV. OBNC

Sweet Thames I honour thee, not for thou art. Richard Barnfield. Fr. Sonnets, VII. PeHV

"Sweet, thou art pale." The Three Enemies. Christina Rossetti. TrCP

Sweet, though short, our. The Silver Flask. John Montague. CIP; FaBCIP

Sweet timber land. Homing. Arna Bontemps. CDC

Sweet to the morning traveller. The Traveller's Return. Unknown. BoTP

Sweet trees who shade this mould. Unknown, tr. by James Mabbe. GBL

Sweet Trinity, The. Unknown. AmFP

Sweet Trinity; or, The Golden Vanity, The. Unknown. OBET

Sweet Trinity, The. Unknown. See I have a ship in the north country.

Sweet Unsure. Sir Walter Raleigh. SiPS

Sweet upland, to whose walks, with fond repair. To Hampstead. Leigh Hunt. EnRP

Sweet Violets. Unknown. NoP
  (Sweet Violets, Love's Paradise.) EiL
  (Violets and Roses.) OBSC

Sweet Violets, Love's Paradise. Unknown. See Sweet Violets.

Sweet voice of the Garb. Suibne Geilt. NOIV

Sweet waft their rounds those tuneful brothers five. Balsham Bells. Kenrick Prescot. NOEC

Sweet Was the Song. Unknown. NOCV

Sweet were the dayes, when thou didst lodge with Lot. Decay. George Herbert. SeCP; SeCV-1

Sweet were the joys that both might like and last. Sweet Unsure. Sir Walter Raleigh. SiPS

Sweet [or Swete] were the sauce would please e[a]ch kind of tast[e]. In Commendation of George Gascoigne's Steel Glass. Sir Walter Ralegh. SiPS
  (Walter Rawley of the Middle Temple, in Commendation of the Steele Glasse.) AAS

Sweet western wind, whose luck it is. To the Western Wind. Robert Herrick. CaPo; OBEV; SeCV-1

Sweet Will. Philip Levine. BLA

Sweet William ("A sailor's life is a merry life"). Unknown. OBET

Sweet William and May Margaret. Unknown. See Sweet William's Ghost.

Sweet William he married [him] a wife. The Wife Wrapt in Wether's Skin. Unknown. AmFP; ESPB, F vers.

Sweet William he would a-wooing ride. Fair Margaret and Sweet William ("Sweet William he would a-wooing ride"). Unknown. ESPB, B vers.; OBET

Sweet William rode up to the old man's gate. Earl Brand. Unknown. AmFP

Sweet William would [or he would] a wooing ride. Fair Margaret and Sweet William. Unknown. ESPB, B vers.; OBET

Sweet William's Farewell to Black-eyed Susan. John Gay. AmFP, (*folk version*); BeLS; BoLoP; NOEC
    (Black-eyed Susan.) GTBS; GTBS-P; MOS
Sweet William's Ghost ("There comes a ghost to Margret's door").
    Unknown. ESPB, (A, B, F *and* G *vers.*)
Sweet William and May Margaret. *Unknown.* CH
Sweet William's gone over seas. Lord William; or, Lord Lundy.
    Unknown. ESPB
Sweet Willie. *Unknown.* OxBB
Sweet Willie was a widow's son. Willie and Lady Margerie [*or* Maisry].
    Unknown. ESPB; OxBB
Sweet Willie's ta'en him o'er the faem. Sweet Willie. *Unknown.*
    OxBB
Sweet, winsome May, coy, pensive fay. May. Henrietta Cordelia Ray.
    CBWP-3
Sweet wooded way in life, forgetful Sleep! To Sleep. Maybury Fleming.
    AA
Sweet World, if you will hear me now. Sarah Morgan Bryan Piatt.
    AA
Sweeter Far than the Harp, More Gold than Gold. "Michael Field."
    OBMV
Sweeter Saint I Serve, A. Sir Philip Sidney. *Fr.* Arcadia. SiPS
Sweeter than sour apples flesh to boys. Ted Berrigan. EAS
Sweetes' Li'l' Feller. Frank Lebby Stanton. FaFP
Sweetest lives are those to duty wed, The. Reward of Service. Elizabeth
    Barrett Browning. BLPA; FaBoBe
Sweetest Love, I Do Not Go. John Donne. *See* Song: "Sweetest love, I
    do not go[e]."
Sweetest love, I do not go[e]. John Donne. AWP; BoLoP; EIL; ELP;
    HeIP; InPS; InvP; JCP; MeLP; MePo; NOBE; NoP; OAEL-1; OBS;
    PoEL-2; SeCP; SeCV-1
    (Sweetest Love, I Do Not Go.) TEP; TrGrPo
Sweetest of all childlike dreams. The Vanishers. Whittier. AA;
    AnAmPo
Sweetest of sweets, I thank you: when displeasure. Church-Music[k].
    George Herbert. OxBSP; SeCV-1; UnS
Sweetest Saviour, if my soul. A Dialogue. George Herbert. MePo;
    OBEV; OBS; SeCV-1
Sweetest Thing, The. *Unknown, tr. fr. Susu by* Ulli Beier. TTY
Sweetgrass. Peter Blue Cloud. NOVW
Sweetgrass. Maurice Kenny. HATNAP
Sweetheart. Phil Hey. GOYP
Sweetheart, another summer's gone. Both of Us Together and Each
    Apart. Yehuda Amichai, *tr. by* Bernhard Frank. MHeP
Sweetheart, remember those small hours when time's. Wilderness.
    Martin Seymour-Smith. NPo
Sweetly-favored face, The. Canzonetta: Of His Lady in Absence.
    Giacomino Pugliesi, *tr. by* Dante Gabriel Rossetti. AWP
Sweetly (my Dearest) I left thee asleep. John Saffin. SCAP
Sweetness. *Unknown, tr. fr. Irish by* John Montague. BIrV
Sweetness of Nature, The. *Unknown, tr. fr. Irish by* Frank O'Connor.
    TIRV
Sweetness of poverty like this, The. Aspiration. Mário de Andrade, *tr.
    by* John Nist. TTY
Sweet rose [*or* Sweit rois] of virtue [*or* vertew] and of gentleness [*or*
    gentilnes]. To a Lady[e]. William Dunbar. EBEV; GBL; MeEL;
    OxBS
    ("Sweet rois of vertew and of gentleness.") OBEV
Sweets That Die. Langdon Elwyn Mitchell. AA
Swell foams where they float and crawl, The. Girls Bathing, Galway
    1965. Seamus Heaney. InPS
Swell Idea, A. Steve Kowit. UL
Swell My Net Full. *Unknown.* OxBSS
Swell the Anthem, Raise the Song. Nathan Strong. AH
Swell'd with our late successes on the foe. Dryden. *Fr.* Annus
    Mirabilis. EBEV
Swell's Soliloquy. *Unknown.* FiBHP
Swept by the hot wind, stark, untrackable. Mohammed and Seid.
    Harrison Smith Morris. AA
Swerve, The. William Stafford. SM
Swerving east, from rich industrial shadows. Here. Philip Larkin.
    CMoP; PoE
Swet Jesus. Friar Michael of Kildare. NOIV
Swet Jesus/ Is cum to us. Welcome! Our Messiah. *Unknown.* MeEL
Swete were the sauce would please ech kind of tast. *See* Sweet were the
    sauce would please each kind of taste.
Swetnam, the Woman-Hater, *sel. Unknown.*
    Ding Dong. EIL
Swich fyn hath, lo, this Troilus for love! Chaucer. *Fr.* Troilus and
    Criseyde [*or* Criseide]. NOCV
Swift, *sel.* Thomas Caulfield Irwin.
    "It was a dim October day." BIrV

Swift. Delmore Schwartz. PoA
Swift across the palace floor. Little Guinever. Annie Fields. AA
Swift as a spirit hastening to his task. The Triumph of Life. Shelley.
    ChER; NAEL-2; OAEL-2; PoEL-4
Swift fleet the billowy clouds along the sky. Charlotte Smith. *Fr.*
    Montalbert. BoWoP; WPE
Swift Floods. Kata Szidónia Petröczi, *tr. fr. Hungarian by* Laura Schiff.
    WPOW
Swift had pains in his head. January 1940. Roy Fuller. LiTM; SeCePo;
    WaP
    (War Poet.) HoPM
Swift had sailed into his rest. Swift's Epitaph. W. B. Yeats. CMoP;
    OBVE
Swift Is That Falcon. *Unknown, tr. fr. Chinese by* Burton Watson.
    CoBCP
Swift is't in pace, light poiz'd, to look in clear. Description of a New
    England Spring. John Josselyn. SCAP
Swift Love, Sweet Motor. Hildegarde Flanner. WPE
Swift o'er the sunny grass. Shadow Evidence. Mary Mapes Dodge.
    AA
Swift over the plains of Shimotsuke. *Unknown. Fr.* Manyo Shu.
    Ma
Swift rapids, The. Emperor Sutoku, *tr. by* Geoffrey Bownas *and* Anthony
    Thwaite. PeBJV
Swift red flash, a winter king, The. The Dance. Hart Crane. *Fr.* The
    Bridge: Powhatan's Daughter. LiTM; MoAB; MoAmPo; OxBA
Swift shot the curlew 'thwart the rising blast. Ode on Lord Macartney's
    Embassy to China. William Shepherd. NOEC
Swift through some trap mine eyes have never found. The Harlequin of
    Dreams. Sidney Lanier. AA
Swift through the yielding air I glide. The Lark. *Unknown.* OBS
Swift to the western bounds of this wide land. On the Completion of the
    Pacific Telegraph. Jones Very. TAP
Swiftly Arose. Walt Whitman. *Fr.* Song of Myself: I believe in you my
    soul. TrCP
Swiftly flows the emerald Potomac River. Visiting Mount Vernon and
    Paying Homage at George Washingon's Burial Vault. K'ang Yu-wei,
    tr. by Chang-fang Chen. WFTU
Swiftly those warriors of Yin. *Unknown, tr. by* Arthur Waley. BoS
Swiftly walk o'er the western wave. To Night. Shelley. AWP; ChER;
    EnRP; FPL; NAEL-2; NoP; OAEL-2; OBNC; PoLF; PoRA; TEP;
    TrGrPo; WiR
    (Night.) OBEV
    (To the Night.) CH; GTBS; GTBS-P
Swift's Epitaph. W. B. Yeats. CMoP; OBVE
Swim in Ohuira Bay, A. Robert Peterson. NeAC
Swimmer. Gladys Cardiff. CDW
Swimmer. Robert Francis. NePoAm; TSL; WeW
Swimmer, The. John Crowe Ransom. SD
Swimmer, The. Philippe Soupault, *tr. fr. French by* Paul Auster.
    RHTwFP
Swimmer, The. Philippe Soupault, *tr. fr. French by* Michael Benedikt.
    POS
Swimmers, The. Allen Tate. InPS; MoAmPo; NoAM; NOBA
Swimmers, *sel.* Louis Untermeyer.
    "Then, the quick plunge into the cool, green dark." SD
Swimmer's Chant, The. Carol D. Spelius. RR
Swimmer's Moment, The. Margaret Avison. NOBC
Swimming. Byron. *Fr.* The Two Foscari. GN
Swimming. Alice Higgins. RAR
Swimming. Clinton Scollard. FaPON
Swimming. Swinburne. *Fr.* Tristram of Lyonesse. GN
Swimming/ an asphalt sea. The Sidewalk Racer. Lillian Morrison.
    ASP
Swimming, a frog looks as if. Buson, *tr. fr. Japanese by* Hiroaki Sato.
    Fr. Eighty-seven Hokku. FCEI
Swimming by Night. James Merrill. NYBP; SM; VGW
Swimming Chenango Lake. Charles Tomlinson. FaBoMo; MoP; NoAM
Swimming in the Pacific. Robert Penn Warren. ASP
Swimming Lady; or, A Wanton Discovery, The. *Unknown.* ErPo
Swimming laps/ Is such. Greg Hoffman. Mel Glenn. RR
Swimming Lesson, The. Robert Hershon. NeAC
Swimming Lesson, The. Mary Oliver. CAPP
Swimming Pool, The. Jonathan Holden. MAYP
Swimming Pool. Maria Teresa Horta, *tr. fr. Portuguese by* Suzette
    Macedo. PBWP
Swine com jingling doun Pelton Ionin, The. Pigs o' Pelton. *Unknown.*
    GBP
Swineherd. Eiléan Ni Chuilleanáin. BIrV; CIP; FaBoWP; WPOW
Swing, The. Mary I. Osborn. BoTP
Swing, The. Robert Louis Stevenson. FaBoBe; FaFP; GoJo; NTCP;
    PDV; TEP

Swing dat hammer—hunh. Southern Road. Sterling Allen Brown. BANP; BPo; FB; PoBA

Swing Low, Sweet Chariot ("I ain't never been to heaven"). *Unknown*. GBP

Swing Low, Sweet Chariot ("I looked over Jordan. . ."). *Unknown*. AmFN; FaPON; UnPo

Swing Low, Sweet Chariot ("Oh de good ole' chariot swing so low"). *Unknown*. AA; AnAmPo

Swing Song, A. William Allingham. FaPON; MoShBr

Swing your honey like swinging on a gate. Dance Calls. *Unknown*. RR

Swinging. Irene Thompson. BoTP

Swinging mill bell changed its rate, The. A Lone Striker. Robert Frost. SaC

Swirl of water dominated the plain, The. The Blue-Hole. Charles G. Bell. GrPl

Swirl sleeping in the waterfall! Chomei at Toyama. Basil Bunting. OxBTC

Swirling in circles I see. Mohammad Taqi Mir, *tr. by* Ahmed Ali. GoT

Swirling spring. Young Girl. Ricarda Huch, *tr. by* Janine Canan *and* Deirdre Lashgari. WPOW

Swirls of dust. *Unknown, tr. by* Burton Watson. FCEI

Swiss Air. Bret Harte. NA

Switch Blade; or, John's Other Wife, The. Jonathan Williams. NeAP

Switchback. Dame Edith Sitwell. PBWP

Switzerland, *sels*. Matthew Arnold.
Isolation: To Marguerite. *Fr*. IV. EBVV; TEP
Meeting. *Fr*. I. ELP
To Marguerite—Continued. *Fr*. V. BoLoP; EBEV; EBVV; ELP; FiP; GTBS-P; MOS; NOBE; NoP; OAEL-2; OBEV; OBNC; PoEL-5; PPP; PrIM; TEP

Switzerland. Alfred Denis Godley. OBTV

Switzerland. Anthony Thwaite. OBTV

Switzerland 1938-1965. Judah Leib Teller, *tr. fr. Yiddish by* Benjamin *and* Barbara Harshav. AYP

Swollen river sang through the green hole, The. The Sleeper in the Valley. Arthur Rimbaud, *tr. fr. French by* Robert Lowell. *Fr*. Eighteen-Seventy. OBWP
("There's a green hollow where a river sings.") AWP, *tr. by* Ludwig Lewisohn.
("Through a green gorge the river like a fountain.") WaaP, *tr. by* Seldman Rodman.

Swooning swim to less and less. Buddha. Herman Melville. HeIP

Swoop flies that falcon. *Unknown, tr. by* Arthur Waley. BoS

Sword, The. Abu Bakr, *tr. fr. Arabic by* A. J. Arberry. TTY

Sword, The. Mir Babbar Ali Anis, *tr. fr. Urdu by* Ahmed Ali. GoT

Sword, A. Karin Boye, *tr. fr. Swedish by* Joanna Bankier. OV; WPOW

Sword. *Unknown, tr. fr. Japanese by* Hiroaki Sato. FCEI

Sword and the Sickle, The. Blake. *See* Gnomic Verses:
Sword sang on the barren heath, The.

Sword fell down, The: I heard a knell. The Leader. Hilaire Belloc. ACP

Sword of Li Ling, The. Lo Ch'ing, *tr. fr. Chinese by* Dominic Cheung. IFON

Sword of Lies, The. Jacob Glatstein. *See* Baron Tells of His Last Experience.

Sword of light is unsheathed from the cloud, A. Parting. Shlomo Vinner, *tr. by* Laya Firestone *and* Howard Schwartz. VWA

Sword of Surprise, The. G. K. Chesterton. MoBrPo

Sword sang on the barren heath, The. Blake. *Fr*. Gnomic Verses. FaBoEE; TrGrPo
(Sword and the Sickle, The.) ChTr

Sword was sheathed, The: in April's sun. The Vow of Washington. Whittier. PAH

Swords crossed, but not in strife! The Crossed Swords. Nathaniel Langdon Frothingham. AA

Swordscape, tombscape, flame ploughed. After the Fall. Gloria Escoffery. PVCV

Sycamore Tree, The. *Unknown*. AmFP

Sycophantic Fox and the Gullible Raven, The. Guy Wetmore Carryl. BLPA; CenHV; FaFP; FiBHP; NBLV; OBCA

Sydney and the Bush. Les A. Murray. DiPo

Sydney Cove, 1788. Peter Porter. NoAM

Syllables disintegrate ingrate alphabets. Phyllis Webb. *Fr*. The Kropotkin Poems. NOBC

Syllogism. Bin Ramke. KS

Sylph, The. Paul Valéry. CT

Sylphs! on each oak-bud wound the wormy galls. The Protection of Plants. Erasmus Darwin. *Fr*. The Economy of Vegetation. FaBoUs

Sylvae, *sel*. Statius, *tr. fr. Latin*.
"Too harsh the man who setting bounds to grief." PeHV

Sylvan Delights. Pope. *Fr*. Pastorals. NOBE

Sylvan Muses, can ye sing. Aglaia. Nicholas Breton. *Fr*. The Passionate Shepherd. OBSC

Sylvan Revel, A. Edward Cracroft Lefroy, *after the Greek of* Theocritus. *Fr*. Echoes from Theocritus, XXV. AWP

Sylvester's Dying Bed. Langston Hughes. NoAM; UnPo

Sylvia. Samuel Croxall. NOEC

Sylvia. Robert Lowell. NaP, *ad. by* the Italian of Giacomo Leopardi

Sylvia, do you remember the minutes. Sylvia. Robert Lowell. NaP

Sylvia the fair, in the bloom of fifteen. Dryden. EBEV; ErPo

Sylvia's Death. Anne Sexton. NAAL-2

Sylvie and Bruno, *sel*. "Lewis Carroll."
Mad Gardener's Song, The. BLPL; FaBoCo; FaBoNo; FiBHP, 6 *sts*.; NA; OnUR, , 4 *sts*.; OxBChV; WiR

Sylvie and Bruno Concluded, *sels*. "Lewis Carroll."
King-Fisher Song, The. FaBoNo
Little Birds ("Little birds are playing"). FaBoNo; OxBoLi
Pig-Tale, A. WiR
(Melancholy Pig, The.) FaPON

Sylvius, your hands near my mouth are heady flowers. Marguerite Burnat-Provins, *tr. by* Cassia Berman. BoWoP

Sym of Lyntoun, be the ramis horn. King Berdok. *Unknown*. OxBS

Symbiosis. James Sherry. LP

Symbol from the first, of mastery, A. The Staff of Aesculapius. Marianne Moore. ImOP

Symbols. Vance Thompson. AA

Symbols. W. B. Yeats. OBMV

Symbols of Gross Experience. C. Day Lewis. *Fr*. Oh Dreams, Oh Destinations. Son

Symbolum. Goethe, *tr. fr. German by* Tom Paulin. FaBoPV

Symmetrical Poem. Michael Palmer. NPGG

Symmetry. A. Leyeles, *tr. fr. Yiddish by* Benjamin *and* Barbara Harshav. AYP

Symon's Lesson of Wisdom for All Manner of Children. *Unknown*. OxBChV

Sympathy. Paul Laurence Dunbar. AmNP; CDC; IDB; PoBA; PoNE

Sympathy. Reginald Heber. BeLS

Sympathy. Lizelia Augusta Jenkins Moorer. CBWP-3

Sympathy, a Welcome, A. John Berryman. GrPl; NYBP

Symphony. Frank Horne. AmNP

Symphony, The. Sidney Lanier. AmPP; LiTA

Symphony in Yellow. Oscar Wilde. EBVV; FaBoPP; MoBrPo; NoAM; NoBVV; OxBSP

Symphony No. 3, in D Minor. Jonathan Williams. *Fr*. Mahler. VGW

Symposium, The, *sel*. Leah Goldberg, *tr. fr. Hebrew by* Robert Alter.
"Outside the cats are wailing." PBWP

Symposium: Apples, A. Linda Pastan. NIP

Symptoms of Love. Robert Graves. BoLoP

Synekdechestai. Constance M. Schmid. GoYe

Synods are whelps of the Inquisition. Presbyterian Church Government ("Synods are whelps of the Inquisition"). Samuel Butler. *Fr*. Hudibras, I, 3. OBS

Syntax of lightning! O pure speech of exile! Far is that other shore where. "St.-John Perse", *tr. fr. French by* Denis Devlin. *Fr*. Exile, VII. RHTwFP

Synthesizing Several Abstruse Concepts with an Experience. Carol Poster. BXAP

Syon lyes waste, and thy Jerusalem. *See* Sion lies waste.

Syren Songs, *sels*. George Darley.
Mermaidens' Vesper-Hymn, The. *Fr*. VI. GBL; NAEL-2; OBNC; PoEL-4
(Siren Chorus.) BIrV; FaBoRV; WSC
Sea-Ritual, The. *Fr*. V. BIrV; OBNC; WiR; WSC
(Deadman's Dirge.) CH

Syrens' Song, The. William Browne. *See* Inner Temple Masque, The: Sirens' Song, The.

Syringa. John Ashbery. HCAP; NoAM

Syrinx. John Lyly. *See* Midas: Pan's Syrinx.

Syrinx. James Merrill. HCAP

Syrup. Steve Rasnic Tem. BWV

System. Robert Louis Stevenson. PWR; TEP

T

T. A. H. Ambrose Bierce. AA

T-Bar. Patricia K. Page. NoAM; NOBC; OBCV

T. E. Lawrence Poems, The, *sels.* Gwendolyn MacEwen. NOBC
  There Is No Place to Hide.
  Void, The.

T. H. Blake. *See* To William Hayley.

T. R. Donald Hall. PoA

T. S. Eliot. W. H. Auden. OBAL

T. S. Eliot. Robert Lowell. NoAM; NOBA

T.V. (1). Anselm Hollo. UL

Tabernacle of Peace. Hayim Be'er, *tr. fr. Hebrew by* Stephen Mitchell.
  VWA

Tabernacle Thought, A. Israel Zangwill. TrJP

Table, The. Ray DiPalma. LP

Table, The. Carlos Drummond de Andrade, *tr. fr. Portuguese by*
  Elizabeth Bishop. ATCBP

Table, The. Michael Heffernan. PoA

Table-Birds. Kenneth Mackenzie. PoAu-2

Table Manners. Gelett Burgess. OBCA; RAR; RHPC

Table Manners. *Unknown.* OxBLMV

Table Richly Spread, A. Milton. *Fr.* Paradise Regained, *Bk.* II, *ll.* 340–
  365. FaBoCh

Table Rules for Little Folk[s]. *Unknown.* FaBoUs; OxBChV

Table Talk. Derek Mahon. DiPo

Table Talk. Donald Mattam. FiBHP

Table Talk. Wallace Stevens. NoP

Table was filled with many objects, The. The "Utopia." Lee Harwood.
  EAS

Tableau. Countee Cullen. AmFN; BANP; PoBA

Tableau. Judith Wright. CBAP

Tableau at Twilight. Ogden Nash. FiBHP

Tableau Mourant. Gerrit Achterberg, *tr. fr. Dutch by* James S. Holmes.
  DuIn

Tableau Vivant. Tess Gallagher. GeTw

Table's long and gleaming, The. The Board Meets. John Gloag.
  FiBHP

Tables Turned, The. Wordsworth. EnRP; NAEL-2; OAEL-2; TOF

Taboo to Boot. Ogden Nash. FiBHP; RB

Taboo Woman, The. *Unknown, tr. fr. Zuni Indian by* K. Kennedy.
  WTO

Taborer beat/ Your little drum. Jig for Sackbuts. D. B. Wyndham
  Lewis. ErPo

Tabula Rasa. Bartolo Cattafi, *tr. fr. Italian by* Lawrence R. Smith.
  NItP

Tabula Rasa? Luciano Erba, *tr. fr. Italian by* Lawrence R. Smith.
  NItP

Taches Jaunes, Les, *sel.* Théophile Gautier, *tr. fr. French by* Lafcadio
  Hearn.
  Clarimonde. VVA

Tacita. James Benjamin Kenyon. AA

Tacking Ship Off Shore. Walter Mitchell. AA; FaBoBe; GN

Tact. Emerson. AnAmPo

Tact. Paul Pascal. WeW

Tact. E. A. Robinson. NoAM

Taddeo Gaddi built me. I am old. The Old Bridge at Florence.
  Longfellow. EyDe

Tadhg sat up on his hills. Senior Members. Sean Lucy. CIP

Tadlow. Abel Evans. FaBoCo

Tadoussac. Charles Bancroft. BLPA

Tadpole, The. E. E. Gould. BoTP

Tae be wan o them Kings. Stars. George Mackay Brown. OxBS

Tae titly. *Unknown.* OxNR

Taffy, the topaz-coloured cat. In Honour of Taffy Topaz. Christopher
  Morley. CRH

Taffy was a Welshman, Taffy was a thief. Mother Goose. GBP; OxNR;
  RB

Taffy was born. *Unknown.* OxNR

Tag Along. Nina Payne. RHPC

Taghore. Muhammad al-Ghuzzi, *tr. fr. Arabic by* May Jayyusi *and* John
  Heath-Stubbs. MAP

Tagus, Farewell. Sir Thomas Wyatt. QFR
  ("Tagus, fare well, that westward with thy stremes [*or* streams].")
  AAS; OBTV

Tahiti. Louis Johnson. PeNZ

Tahiti, Tahiti. Vor a Gauguin Picture zu Singen. Kurt M. Stein.
  FiBHP

Taiaha Haka Poem. Apirana Taylor. PeNZ

Tail behind, a trunk in front, A. The Elephant, or the Force of Habit.
  A. E. Housman. NOBL
  (Elephant, The.) FaBV

Tail of the See, A. Elizabeth T. Corbett. OBCA

Tail toddle, tail toddle. Tommie Makes My Tail Toddle. Burns. ErPo

Taill of the Foxe, That Begylit the Wolf, in the Schadow of the Mone,
  The. Robert Henryson. OxBS

Taill of the Wolf and the Wedder, The. Robert Henryson. OxBLMV,
  ad. fr. Aesop

Tailor, The. "S. Ansky," *tr. fr. Yiddish by* Joseph Leftwich. TrJP

Tailor, The. Thomas Lovell Beddoes. WiR

Tailor. Eleanor Farjeon. OxBChV

Tailor, The. Joseph Leftwich. TrJP

Tailor Called Sorrow, A. Betti Alver, *tr. fr. Estonian by* Willis Barnstone
  and Felix Oinas. BoWoP

Tailor of Bicester. *Unknown.* OxNR

Tailor's Wedding, The. Louis Simpson. NNaP

Tails and Heads. Suzanne Knowles. RB

Tailspinning from the shelves of sky. Jubilo. Allen Tate. WaP

Táin, the, *sels. Unknown, tr. fr. Irish by* Thomas Kinsella. NOIV
  Armies Enter Cuailnge, The.
  Before the Last Battle.

Taint. Liz Socolow. PPR

Taisigh Agat Fein Do Phog. *Unknown, tr. fr. Irish by* Maire Cruise
  O'Brien. BIrV

Taj, The. H. G. Keene. OBTV

Tajo, tajo, tajo! tajo, my mackey massa! *Unknown. Fr.* Dancing Songs,
  II. PBCV

Tak for Sidst. Babette Deutsch. PoA

Tak tyme in tym, or tym will not be tane. A Description of Tyme.
  Alexander Montgomerie. OxBS

Tak' Your Auld Cloak about Ye. *Unknown.* OxBS

Takamura Kotaro/ speaks. On Writing Asian-American Poetry.
  Geraldine Kudaka. BrSi

Takase Mountain:/ I push along. Kyogoku Tamekane, *tr. fr. Japanese by*
  Burton Watson. *Fr.* Twenty-three Tanka. FCEI

Take a chair. The Witness Chair. Michael Harlow. ATNZ

Take a father's admonition, from a heart disturbed. A Father's Testament.
  Judah Ibn Tibbon, *tr. by* Israel Abrahams. TrJP

Take a golden comb. This Earthen Body. Gond Oral Tradition, *tr. by* V.
  Elwin *and* S. Hivale. WTO

Take a Gun. Nancy Price. CN

Take a harp. Song of the Harlot. Bible, *O.T. Fr.* Isaiah, XXIII: 16.
  TrJP

Take a knuckle of veal. A Receipt for Stewing Veal. *At. to* John Gay.
  FaBoUs

Take a large olive, stone it and then stuff it. A Dish for a Poet.
  Unknown. OBCP

Take a little back-ache. The Soup. Charles Simic. AnAn

Take a Look at My Rebels. Meir Wieseltier, *tr. fr. Hebrew by* Warren
  Bargad *and* Stanley F. Chyet. IP

Take a look, i/ sd. For Kelley. Ken Belford. NeAC

Take a model of the world so big. The Rescued Year. William Stafford.
  LCAP

Take a pen in your uncertain fingers. The Pen. Muhammad al-Ghuzzi,
  tr. by May Jayyusi *and* John Heath-Stubbs. MAP

Take a statement: the same as yesterday's dictation. Vowel Movements.
  Daryl Hine. PoA

Take a strip of white paper, turn. Farolita. Mei-Mei Berssenbrugge.
  BrSi

Take a Whiff on Me. *Unknown.* NOBA

"Take all my loves, my Love, yea, take them all." Shakespeare. *Fr.*
  Sonnets, XL. InvP; OBSC

Take all of me, I am thine own, heart, soul. Amélie Rives. AA

Take as a gift. Giving and Taking. James Kirkup. EaLo

Take Away. Margot Ruddock. OBMV

Take away the stuff! Dry. Samuel Hoffenstein. BXAP

Take Back the Virgin Page. Thomas Moore. OBNC

Take Down the Fiddle, Karl! Shaw Neilson. CBAP

Take for the sake of example. Credo. Jean Lipkin. AIW

Take fortune as it falls, as one adviseth. The Author, of His Own
  Fortune. Sir John Harington. FaBoEE

Take Frankincense, O God. Charles Fitz-Geffry. *Fr.* Holy
  Transportations. ChTr

Take from my palms, to soothe your heart. Osip Mandelstam, *tr. by*
  Clarence Brown *and* W. S. Merwin. UnAS

Take from the earth its tragic hunger, Lord. Hazel J. Fowler. TrPWD

Take, gentle marble, to thy trust. An Elegy upon His Tomb in Herndon-
  Hill Church, Erected by His Wife, Who Speaks. James Howell.
  OBWVE

Take heart, monsieur, four-fifths of this province. For Jean Vincent d'Abbadie, Baron St.-Castin. Alden Nowlan. NOBC

Take heart, Prytherch. Aside. R. S. Thomas. OxBC

Take heart, the journey's ended. In the Town. *Unknown, tr.* by Eleanor Farjeon. OBCP; PChr

Take heed betime, lest ye be spied. Sir Thomas Wyatt. SiPS

Take Heed of Gazing Overmuch. Thomas Richardson. *Fr.* A Proper New Song. EIL

Take heed of loving me[e]. The Prohibition. John Donne. EIL; GBL; MeLP; OBS

Take heed of this small child of earth. The Poor Children. Victor Hugo, *tr.* by Swinburne. AWP

Take Him away, he's dead as they die. Obituary. Kenneth Fearing. VGW

"Take him to the Gulley! Take him to the Gulley!" A Popular Negro Song. *Unknown.* PVCV

Take him up tendahly. Parody on Thomas Hood's "The Bridge of Sighs." *Unknown.* FiBHP

Take hold of them. Words for You. Hans Andreus, *tr.* by James S. Holmes. DuIn

Take home Thy prodigal child, O Lord of Hosts! Birthday Sonnet. Elinor Wylie. MoAB; MoAmPo

Take in hand the cup of delusion. Drink On. Mary E. Tucker. CBWP-1

Take it as a pledge: a dewdrop on a lotus leaf. Teika, *tr. fr. Japanese* by Hiroaki Sato. *Fr.* Eighty-four Tanka. FCEI

Take It from Me. Kenneth O. Hanson. CoAP

Take it from me kiddo. Poem, or Beauty Hurts Mr. Vinal. E. E. Cummings. InPS; MoAB; MoAmPo; NAAL-2; OBAL; OxBA

Take it not back! the priceless gift. Invocation to the Muse. Henrietta Cordelia Ray. CBWP-3

Take me as I drive alone. White Blossoms. Robert Mezey. NaP; VWA

Take me for example: I am no dumb belle. The Case of Ample Ora: Sweetness and Light. Pamela White Hadas. BLA

Take Me Out to the Ball Game. Jack Norworth. ASP; OBAL

Take me to the distant northlands. Tirzah and the Wide World. Dahlia Ravikovich, *tr.* by Warren Bargad *and* Stanley F. Chyet. IP

Take Me under Your Wing. Hayyim Nahman Bialik, *tr. fr. Hebrew* by Bernhard Frank. MHeP

Take my hand. There are two of us in this cave. The Blind Leading the Blind. Lisel Mueller. IHMS

Take My Life and Let It Be. Frances Ridley Havergal. BLRP

Take my share of Soul Food. High on the Hog. Julia Fields. CNA

Take my song of love to heart. *Unknown, tr.* by Thomas Kinsella. NOIV

Take my tunic, woman. Goll Mac Morna Parts from His Wife. *Unknown.* NOIV

Take note, passers-by, of the sharp erosions. The Circuit Judge. Edgar Lee Masters. *Fr.* Spoon River Anthology. FaBoEE

Take, O take the cream away. Breakfast Song in Time of Diet. Stoddard King. OBAL

Take, O Take Those Lips Away. Shakespeare. *Fr.* Measure for Measure, IV, i. AWP; EBEV; EIL; ELP; EnLoPo; FaBV; GBL; HeIP; InPS; LiTB; NoP; OAEL-1; OBEV
  (At the Moated Grange.) NOBE
  (Seals of Love.) TrGrPo
  (Song at the Moated Grange, A.) OBSC
  (Song: "Take, O take those lips away.") FiP; PoEL-2

Take of me what is not my own. Kathleen Jessie Raine. NOBE

Take off your hat. Pass Office Song. *Unknown.* PBA, *tr.* by Peggy Rutherford. TTY, *tr.* by Peggy Rutherford
  ("Take off your hat.") WTO, *tr.* by H. Tracey

Take, Oh, Take Those Lips Away. Robert H. Fletcher *and others.* *Fr.* The Bloody Brother, V, ii, *st.* 1 *also in* Shakespeare's Measure for Measure. NoP
  (Song: "Take, oh take those Lips away.") PoEL-2

Take I, 4:11:58. Philip Whalen. NeAP

Take 1 green pepper and 2 tomatoes. Pour Commencer. Jon Stallworthy. NoAM

Take One Home for the Kiddies. Philip Larkin. OBD; OxBTC

Take our broken lives. Duct Tape Psalm. Greg Keeler. SoTCo

Take Physic, Pomp. Shakespeare. *Fr.* King Lear, III, iv. TrGrPo

Take pity on me! Prince Munenaga, *tr.* by Steven D. Carter. WFTW

Take Poems, but Don't Read. Meir Wieseltier, *tr. fr. Hebrew* by Bernhard Frank. MHeP

Take poems, but don't read them. Meir Wieseltier, *tr.* by Warren Bargad *and* Stanley F. Chyet. IP

Take *quantum sufficit* of meadows and trees. To Make a Pastoral; a Receipt. *Unknown.* FaBoUs

Take the apple from the bowl or bough. Apple Poem. Vernon Scannell. NPo

Take the back off the watch. Time Piece. William Cole. GrPl

Take the cloak from his face, and at first. After. Robert Browning. TrGrPo

Take the cloak of all my love. Song for a Jewess. Iwan Goll, *tr.* by Joseph T. Shipley. TrJP

Take the Crust. Sadi, *tr. fr. Persian* by L. Cranmer-Byng. *Fr.* The Gulistan. AWP

Take, then your paltry Christ. To the Christians. Francis Lauderdale Adams. OxBS; WGRP

Take these who will as may be: I. Permit Me Voyage. James Agee. MoAmPo

Take this blessing. Benediction. William Freedman. VWA

Take this kiss upon the brow! A Dream within a Dream. Poe. AmPP; AnAmPo; BLPL; ChTr; GBL; NOBA; OxBA; TAP; TrGrPo

Take this old man with the soldierly straight back. Louis MacNeice. *Fr.* The Kingdom. LiTM

Take Thou Our Minds, Dear Lord. William H. Foulkes. AH

Take Thy Bliss, O Man. Blake. *Fr.* Visions of the Daughters of Albion. EnRP

Take time, my dear, ere Time takes wing. Fading Beauty. *Unknown.* FaBoEE

Take Time to Be Holy. W. D. Longstaff. BLRP

Take time while time doth last. Song Set by John Farmer. *Unknown.* CTC; OBSC

Take Tools Our Strength. Gerald L. Simmons, Jr.. NBP

Take two-o coo, Taffy! *Unknown.* PBBP

Take two photographs. King Kong Meets Wallace Stevens. Michael Ondaatje. HeIP

Take up the pen and write a text. *Malay Oral Tradition, tr.* by R. J. Wilkinson *and* R. O. Winstedt. WTO

Take up the White Man's burden. The White Man's Burden. Kipling. FaBoPV

Take what is at hand. Ode on a Decision to Settle for Less. William Pillen. VWA

Take Who Takes You. Fred Gardner. ASP

Take Your Accusation Back! Kittaararter, *tr. fr. Eskimo.* WTO

Take your bucket, and take your spade. The Sea. E. M. Adams. BoTP

Taken from the. The Primitive. Don L. Lee. BPo

Taking a Captive/ 1984. Barney Bush. HATNAP

Taking away/ writing is. Writing. Roland Jooris, *tr.* by Peter Nijmeijer. DuIn

Taking between them/ A specially straight willow tree. Eulogy to the Bow and Arrow. *Mongol Oral Tradition, tr.* by C. R. Bawden. WTO

Taking Care of It. Deborah Lee. BrSi

Taking Ford's dictation on Samuel Butler. Ford Madox Ford. Robert Lowell. OxBC

Taking, giving back their lives. The Field Hospital. Paul Muldoon. CIP

Taking In Wash. Rita Dove. PPR

Taking Leave of a Friend. Li Po, *tr. fr. Chinese* by Ezra Pound. RB; SOTW

Taking Leave of Mount Kugami. Ryokan, *tr. fr. Japanese* by Burton Watson. FCEI

Taking Long Views. May Kendall. CenHV

Taking me into your body. The Source. Jon Stallworthy. NoP

Taking Off. Ron Rogers. NOVW

Taking Off My Clothes. Carolyn Forché. AmPA; AnAn; NoAM

Taking off my gloves, my hands stop. Ishikawa Takuboku, *tr. fr. Japanese* by Hiroaki Sato. *Fr.* Forty-seven Tanka in Three Lines. FCEI

Taking one's head off. The Wonderful Tangerines. John Ash. NPo

Taking pity on this scrag-end of the city. One Kingfisher and One Yellow Rose. Eileen Brennan. NeIP

Taking the air rifle from my son's hand. Cain. Irving Layton. MoCV

Taking the Cool in the Shade of the Trees. Tamemasa, *tr. fr. Japanese* by Steven D. Carter. WFTW

Taking the Cool to Forget Summer. Tamemasa, *tr. fr. Japanese* by Steven D. Carter. WFTW

Taking the Milk to Grandmother. William Kloefkorn. KS

Taking the Train Home. William Matthews. GeTw

Taking this painting at an appropriate distance. Art Market: Leopoldville. Michael Jackson. ATNZ

Taking to the Woods. Henry Taylor. MAYP; MT

Taking your pocket calculator, consider. Amortization. Nancy G. Westerfield. SoTCo

Taku Skanskan. Paula Gunn Allen. HATNAP

Talbragar. Henry Lawson. PoAu-1

Tale, A. Edward Thomas. ChTr

Tale about a Flower. György Somlyó, *tr. fr. Hungarian* by Daniel Hoffman. MHuP

Tale about a/an. György Somlyó, *tr. fr. Hungarian by* Daniel Hoffman. MHuP

Tale for Husbands, A. Sir Philip Sidney. *Fr.* Arcadia. SiPS

Tale I frame shall be found to tally, The. The Seafarer. *Unknown, tr. by* Michael Alexander. OBVE

Tale is every time the same, The. Maurice James Craig. NeIP

Tale is told of long ago, A. A Song of the Yellow Cedar Face. George Clutesi. HATNAP

Tale of a Dog and a Bee, The. *Unknown.* BoTP

Tale of a Pony, The. Bret Harte. OBNV

Tale of Custard the Dragon, The. Ogden Nash. FaPON; OBCA; PoRA; PYC

  (Custard the Dragon.) OnUR

Tale of Drury Lane, A. Horace Smith. FaBoCo

Tale of Genji, The, *sels.* Murasaki Shikibu, *tr. fr. Japanese by* Kenneth Rexroth *and* Ikuko Atsumi.

  "Lady Murasaki says." BoWoP

  "Troubled waters, The/ are frozen fast." WPOW

Tale of Genji. Hugh Seidman. AmPA

Tale of Italy, A. Eloise Bibb. CBWP-4

Tale of Jorkyns and Gertie; or, Vice Rewarded, The. Richard Percival Lister. NYBP

Tale of Last Stands, A. Fred Red Cloud. NOVW

Tale of Lord Lovell, The. *Unknown.* NOBL

Tale of Sigemund, The. *Unknown, tr. fr. Anglo-Saxon by* Charles W. Kennedy. *Fr.* Beowulf. AnOE

Tale of Sir Thopas. Chaucer. *See* Canterbury Tales, The: Sir Thopas.

Tale of Sunlight, The. Gary Soto. NoAM

Tale of the Airly Days, A. James Whitcomb Riley. AnAmPo

Tale of the Assyrian Statue. Mahmoud al-Buraikan, *tr. fr. Arabic by* Lena Jayyusi *and* Naomi Shihab Nye. MAP

Tale of the Double Helix. György Somlyó, *tr. fr. Hungarian by* Daniel Hoffman. MHuP

Tale of the Fly, The. Moyshe-Leyb Halpern, *tr. fr. Yiddish by* John Hollander. PeBMYV

Tale of the times of old, A! The deeds of days of other years! Carthon; a Poem. James Macpherson. EnRP

Tale of the Upland Mouse and the Burgess Mouse, The. Robert Henryson. OBNV

Tale the Hermit Told, The. Alastair Reid. NePoEA-2

Tale Told by a Head, A. Lois Moyles. NYBP

Talent is what they say. For the Young Who Want To. Marge Piercy. Psk

Talented Man, The. Winthrop Mackworth Praed. EnRP; FiBHP; NOBL

Tales, *sel.* George Crabbe.

  Frank Courtship, The.

    Jonas Kindred's Household. OBNC

Tales about My Father. Abd al-Karim Kassid, *tr. fr. Arabic by* Lena Jayyusi *and* Anthony Thwaite. MAP

Tales from a Family Album. Donald Justice. NePoEA-2

Tales of a Wayside Inn, *sels.* Longfellow.

  Birds of Killingworth, The (The Poet's Tale). *Fr. pt.* I. OnMSP; OxBA

    "Do you ne'er think what wondrous beings these?." *Fr.* 2 *sts.*.WBLP

  King Robert of Sicily (The Sicilian's Tale). *Fr. pt.* I. BeLS; OHIP

  Monk of Casal-Maggiore, The (The Sicilian's Tale). *Fr. pt.* III. AmPP; OxBA

  Paul Revere's Ride (The Landlord's Tale). *Fr. pt.* I. BeLS; BLPA; FaBoBe; FaBoTw; FaBV; FaFP; FaPON; FaPoR; FPL; OBAL; OBCA; OBNV; OHFP; PAH; PWR; TrGrPo; WBLP

  Ships That Pass in the Night (The Theologian's Tale). *Fr. pt.* III. MOS

  Student's Tale, The. *Fr. pt.* III. AmPP

Tales of Shatz. Dannie Abse. OxBC; VWA

Tales of the Hall, *sels.* George Crabbe.

  East Anglian Fen. FaBoPP

  Sad Lover, The. OBNC

  "Something one day occurr'd about a bill." Par

Tales of the Islands. Derek Walcott. OxBTC

Tales Told of the Fathers. John Hollander. DiL

Taliesin, *sel.* Richard Hovey.

  "Here falls no light of sun nor stars." AA

Taliessin's Song of the Unicorn. Charles Williams. FaBoTw

Talis of the Fyve Bestis, The, *sel. Unknown.*

  Unicornis Tale, The. OxBLMV

Talisman, A. Marianne Moore. GoJo; MoAB; MoAmPo

Talisman 18. Sharon A. Stern. TSM

Talk. Roo Borson. NIP; NOBC

Talk. Philip A. Stalker. FiBHP

Talk about the mother tongue. Swedish Lesson. Barton Sutter. SM

Talk about the shade of the sheltering palms. Under the Anheuser Bush. Andrew B. Sterling. OBAL

Talk about your harbor girls around the corner, Sally. Haul Away, My Rosy. *Unknown.* AmFP

Talk happiness. The world is sad enough. Optimism. Ella Wheeler Wilcox. BLPA; BLPL; FaBoBe

Talk no more of the lucky escape of the head. On a Stone Thrown at a Very Great Man, But Which Missed Him. "Peter Pindar." NBLV

Talk of chocolate! Bacchus on Beverages. Francesco Redi, *tr. fr. Italian by* Leigh Hunt. *Fr.* Bacchus in Tuscany. PFI

Talk of knifed bodies in the canals, The. The School Hockey Team in Amsterdam. Frank Ormsby. OBTV

Talk of passion is a winter thing. The Kiss. Ned O'Gorman. FYAP

"Talk of pluck!" pursued the sailor. Romance. W. E. Henley. *Fr.* In Hospital, XXI. BrPo; PAH

Talk of the Greeks at Thermopylae! A Ballad of Redhead's Day. Richard Butler Glaenzer. PAH

Talk of the Town, The. Ed Fisher. FiBHP

Talk to Me. Margaret Randall. ER

Talk to Me, Talk to Me. Hedva Harkavi, *tr. fr. Hebrew by* Tova Weizman. VWA

Talk was of that lovely one, The. Asadullah Khan Ghalib, *tr. by* Ahmed Ali. GoT

Talk was of too much, too, The. Zürich, zum Storchen. Paul Celan, *tr. by* Joachim Neugroschel. VWA

Talk with a Poet. Helen Smith Bevington. SaC

Talk with My Cousin Alone, A. Hone Tuwhare. PeNZ

Talked to my father again in a dream he seemed happy. Le Jazz Hot. Anselm Hollo. PoM

Talker, The. Benjamin Appel. TrJP

Talkers in a Dream Doorway. Judy Grahn. ER; GLP

Talking Designs. Liz Sohappy Bahe. CDW

Talking Drums, The. Kojo Gyinaye Kyei. PBA

Talking Fish, The. Ruth Stone. BoWoP

Talking his cock, talking. Mr. Muscle-On. Faye Kicknosway. GeTw

Talking in Bed. Philip Larkin. BoLoP; NAEL-2; NoP

Talking in Their Sleep. Edith Matilda Thomas. BoNaP; OHIP

Talking Myself to Sleep in the Mountain. Gibbons Ruark. MAYP

Talking oak, The/ To the ancients spoke. Be Different to Trees. Mary Carolyn Davies. FaPON; OHIP

  (Be Deferent to Trees.) OHIP

Talking Oak, The, *sel.* Tennyson.

  Olivia. GN

Talking of Ezra Pound and long-dead pantos. Robert Nichols. *Fr.* Fisbo. OBSV

Talking of houses, cars and kids. Ladder-Climbing and Grocery. Cheng Ch'ou-yu, *tr. by* Dominic Cheung. IFON

Talking of sects quite late one eve. No Sects in Heaven. Elizabeth H. Jocelyn Cleaveland. BLPA

Talking to Animals. Barbara Howes. GrPl

Talking to emptiness. Hollow of Light. Hans Andreus, *tr. by* James S. Holmes. DuIn

Talking to her, he knew it was the end. Hector. Valentin Iremonger. CIP; NeIP

Talking to Myself. W. H. Auden. OBD

Talking to Myself, *sel.* Vincent McHugh.

  "I am very fond of the little ribs of women." ErPo

Talking to strange men on the subway. My Mother. John Wieners. GLP

Talking to the Mule. Laura Jensen. AmPA

Talking to the Townsfolk in Ideal, Georgia. Isaac J. Black. CNA

Talking Union: 1964. L. E. Sissman. TW

Talking with Soldiers. W. J. Turner. MoBrPo

Tall Ambrosia. Henry David Thoreau. PoEL-4

Tall and clothed in samite. A White Iris. Pauline B. Barrington. PoLF

Tall and great-bearded: black and white. Anachronism. Oliver St. John Gogarty. FYAP

Tall as a foxglove spire, on tiptoe. Fox Dancing. Suzanne Knowles. RB

Tall Braunighrindas left her bed. A Legend of Camelot. George Du Maurier. CenHV

Tall camels of the spirit, The. "A World without Objects Is a Sensible Emptiness." Richard Wilbur. LiTM; MoAmPo; MoP; NAAL-2; NoAM; NOBA; PoA

Tall dancer dances, The. The Dancer. Joseph Campbell. OBMV

Tall Girl, The. John Crowe Ransom. Son

Tall grows that pear-tree. *Unknown, tr. by* Arthur Waley. BoS

Tall, handsome, tweeded Dr. Leeper. Austin Clarke. *Fr.* Mnemosyne Lay in Dust, IV. IPY

Tall Hat. Victor Daley. CBAP

Tall is the pear-tree. *Unknown, tr. by* Arthur Waley. BoS

Tall Man Executes a Jig, A. Irving Layton. MoCV; NoAM; NOBC

Tall Nettles. Edward Thomas. BoTP; BrPo; ChTr; FaBoTw; MoAB; MoBrPo; OxBSP

Tall Oaks from Little Acorns Grow. David Everett. FaFP
　(Boy Reciter, The.) BLPA

Tall palm tree sixty feet high, The. Prayer to the God Thot. *Unknown, tr. by* Ulli Beier. TTY

Tall people, short people. People. Lois Lenski. FaPON

Tall pines enveloped my thatched roof. Encountering Fire in Early Spring, 1662. Huang Tsung-hsi, *tr. by* Lynn Struve. WFTU

Tall pines pine, The. The Cow Slips Away. Ben King. AnAmPo

Tall Sky, The. Arthur Ball. PoSH

Tall, somber, grim, against the morning sky. Aspects of the Pines. Paul Hamilton Hayne. AA

Tall stand the peaks. Staying in a Mountain Pavilion on a Summer Night. Ma Chih-yüan, *tr. fr. Chinese by* Jonathan Chaves. *Fr.* Two Poems to the Tune "Po pu tuan." CoBLCP

Tall stands that pear-tree. *Unknown, tr. by* Arthur Waley. BoS

Tall Tale; or, A Moral Song, A. Phyllis Webb. OBCV

Tall tall, the hundred foot tower. Imitating the Old Poems. T'ao Ch'ien, *tr. by* Burton Watson. CoBCP

Tall terrace crumbled long ago, The. Dragon-Tiger Terrace. Yang Shih-ch'i, *tr. by* Jonathan Chaves. CoBLCP

Tall timber stood here once. Improved Farm Land. Carl Sandburg. RFM

Tall-topped acacia, you, full of branches. Elephant ("Tall-topped acacia"). *Unknown.* PeSA

Tall Trees. Eileen Mathias. BoTP

Tall Trees by Still Waters. James Tate. MAYP

Tall unpopular men. Oliver St. John Gogarty. OBMV

Tall willows canopy the thrashing ground with their shade. Cheng Chen, *tr. fr. Chinese by* Irving Lo. *Fr.* Miscellaneous Poems Composed While Drinking Wine, IV. WFTU

Tall Wind, The. K. O. Arvidson. ATNZ; PeNZ

Tall Windows. Robert Hass. NPGG

Tall winter oak, A. Morden Lecture, 1978. Ursula K. Le Guin. BWV

Talla ly li oh/ Freedom a come oh! Freedom a Come Oh! *Unknown.* PVCV

Tallahassee, *sel.* Andrew Merkel.
　"Ann stood and watched the combers race to shore." CaP

Taller than the Stair of Qtub Minar. Howrah Bridge. James Keir Baxter. ATNZ

Taller to-day, we remember similar evenings. W. H. Auden. CMoP

Tallest poet for his height. Arroyo. Tom Weatherly. PoBA

Tallulah at the Schubert. Bruce Berger. SoTCo

Tally. Josephine Miles. NoAM

Tally Stick, The. Jarold Ramsey. NIP

Talmud, The. Simeon Grigoryevich Frug, *tr. fr. Yiddish by* Alice Stone Blackwell. TrJP

Talmud, The, *sels. Unknown, tr. fr. Hebrew.* TrJP
　God to Man.
　Good Man, The.
　Why?

Talmud Student, The. Hayyim Nahman Bialik, *tr. fr. Hebrew by* Helena Frank. TrJP

Talmudist. Stanley Burnshaw. DiPo; VWA

Talysarn. Brenda Chamberlain. *See* Song: "Bone-aged is my white horse."

Tam Cari Capitis. Louis MacNeice. OBD

Tam Glen. Burns. AWP; OxBS

Tam i' the Kirk. Violet Jacob. GBL; GoTS

Tam Lin. *Unknown.* ESPB; FaBoBa; NOBE; OBEV; OBNV; OxBB; OxBS
　(Tamlane.) WSC

Tam o' Shanter. Burns. BeLS; EnRP; GoTS; NAEL-2; NoP; OAEL-1; OBNV; OxBS; SeCePo; TrGrPo, *sl. abr.*

Tam o' the linn cam up the gait. *Unknown.* FaBoCh

Tam Samson's Elegy. Burns. PoEL-4

Tamaki of a Hundred Lovers. Hirini Melbourne. PeNZ

Tamaki of a Hundred Lovers. Merimeri Penfold, *tr. fr. Maori by* Margaret Orbell. PeNZ

Tamarack. Eugene McCarthy. GrPl

Tamaracks swing light away. Swamp. Roberta Hill. VoR

Tamarindo Puppy, The. Charlotte Pomerantz. ILY

Tamar's Wrestling. Walter Savage Landor. *Fr.* Gebir, I. EnRP
　(Shepherd and the Nymph, The.) OBNC

Tamborillo. Mario Payeras, *tr. fr. Spanish by* Barbara Paschke. Vol

Tambour. István Vas, *tr. fr. Hungarian by* Jascha Kessler. FOC; VWA

Tambourine. James Cunningham. JB

Tambourine song for Soldiers Going into Battle. Hind bint Utba, *tr. fr. Arabic by* Bridget Connelly *and* Deirdre Lashgari. WPOW

Tamburlaine the Great, *sels.* Christopher Marlowe.
　"Ah, fair Zenocrate, divine Zenocrate." *Fr. pt.* I, Act V, sc. ii. EBEV; PoEL-2
　(Fair Is Too Foul an Epithet.) LiTB
　And Ride in Triumph through Persepolis. *Fr. pt.* I, Act II, sc. v. TrGrPo
　Beauty. *Fr. pt.* I, Act V. TrGrPo
　Bloody Conquests of Mighty Tamburlaine, The. *Fr. pt.* II, Act IV, sc. iii. ChTr
　(Emperor of the Threefold World.) TrGrPo
　If All the Pens That Ever Poets Held. *Fr. pt.* I, Act V, sc. ii. ChTr; TrGrPo
　Nature That Framed Us of Four Elements. *Fr. pt.* I, Act II, sc. vii. PoEL-2; TrGrPo
　(Perfect Bliss and Sole Felicity.) SeCePo
　Now Clear the Triple Region of the Air. *Fr. pt.* I, Act IV, sc. ii. TrGrPo
　Overreacher, The. *Fr. pt.* I, Act I. NIP
　To Entertain Divine Zenocrate. *Fr. pt.* II, Act II, sc. iii. ChTr
　("Virgins, in vain you labour to prevent.") OBD

Tame Cat. Ezra Pound. OBAL

Tamed by Miltown, we lie on Mother's bed. Man and Wife. Robert Lowell. AmPP; BoLoP; CAPP; NAAL-2

Tameless in his stately pride, along the lake of islands. The Loon. Alfred Billings Street. AA

Tamer and Hawk. Thom Gunn. FaBoTw; NePoEA

Tamerlane. Victor James Daley. PoAu-1

Tamerton Church-Tower or First Love, *sel. Coventry Patmore.* Devonshire Scenes. FaBoPP

Tamlane. *Unknown. See* Tam Lin.

Tammuz. Nathan Alterman, *tr. fr. Hebrew.* VWA, *tr. by* Robert Friend

Tammuz. Rayner Heppenstall. WaP

Tammuz dies on the skyline. Song in August. Badr Shakir al-Sayyab, *tr. by* Lena Jayyusi *and* Christopher Middleton. MAP

Tammy Messer. *Unknown.* FaBoEE

Tampa Robins. Sidney Lanier. AnAmPo

Tamping Ties ("Tamp 'em up solid"). *Unknown.* AmFP

Tan like young mango leaf. What Her Girl Friend Said, Seeing Her Friend Suffer in Silent Dignity over Her Husband's Infidelity. Kayamanar, *tr. by* A. K. Ramanujan. PLW

Tanagra! think not I forget. Corinna, from Athens, to Tanagra. Walter Savage Landor. *Fr.* Pericles and Aspasia, XLIV. OBEV
　(Corinna to Tanagra.) OBNC
　(Corinna, to Tanagra, from Athens.) NOBE; OBTV

Tancred, *sels.* Laurence Dakin. CaP
　"All night I raced the moon." *Fr.* II, i.
　"How gently sings my soul and whets its wings." *Fr.* III, i.
　"Peasant sun went crushing grapes, The." *Fr.* I, i.

Tang! tang! went the gong's wild roar. Night Quarters. Henry Howard Brownell. GN

Tangi. Hone Tuwhare. ATNZ

Tangier. Stephen Dunn. SM

Tangier: Hotel Rif. Donald Thomas. OBTV

Tangle of iron rods and spluttered beams, A. Les Halles d'Ypres. Edmund Blunden. MMA

Tangled [*or* Tanglid] I was [*or* was I] in Love's snare. The Lover Rejoiceth. Sir Thomas Wyatt. SiPS; TrGrPo
　(Liberty.) OBSC
　("Tanglid I was yn love's snare.") AAS

Tangled web indeed we weave, A. Women's Degrees. Alfred Denis Godley. NOBL

Tanglid I was yn love's snare. Sir Thomas Wyatt. *See* Lover Rejoiceth, The.

Tangmalangaloo. Patrick Joseph Hartigan. PoAu-1

Tango. Elena Jordana, *tr. fr. Spanish by* William M. Davis. DMH

Tania died/ with the fever of the task still waiting. Ita. Yolanda Ulloa, *tr. by* Margaret Randall. AIW

Tank, The. Roland Robinson. PoAu-2

Tank Town. John Atherton. NYBP

Tanka (I–VIII). Lewis Alexander. CDC

Tanks. Mirko Lauer, *tr. fr. Spanish by* David Tipton. Per

Tanks. Rhyll McMaster. CBAP

Tanned blonde, The. The Once-over. Paul Blackburn. ErPo; NeAP; PoM

Tanned young men about to dive. An Imagined Description of Myself, in Another Scene. Ory Bernstein, *tr. by* Warren Bargad *and* Stanley F. Chyet. IP

Tannery, The. Francisco Carrillo, *tr. fr. Spanish by* Maureen Ahern *and* David Tipton. Per

Tannhäuser, *sel.* Heine, *tr. fr. German by* Emma Lazarus.
  Best Religion, The. TrJP
Tannhäuser. Newman Levy. OBAL
Tannhäuser. William Morton Payne. AA
Tant' Amare. *Unknown, tr. fr. Mozarabe by* Paul Blackburn. ErPo
Tantalos. Paulus Silentiarius, *tr. fr. Greek by* Dudley Fitts. ErPo
Tantanoola Tiger, The. Max Harris. MoBS; PoAu-2
Tantramar Revisited, The. Sir Charles G. D. Roberts. CaP; NOBC;
  OBCV
Tâo. Alfred Goldsworthy Bailey. CaP
Tao. A. Leyeles, *tr. fr. Yiddish by* Benjamin *and* Barbara Harshav.
  AYP
Tao and Unfitness at Inistiogue on the River Nore. Thomas Kinsella.
  FaBCIP
Tao Te Ching. Lao Tzu, *tr. fr. Chinese by* Witter Bynner. OBD
Tao-wu Mountain. T'an Ssu-t'ung, *tr. fr. Chinese by* Timothy C. Wong.
  WFTU
Taoist Huang Has Died of Alcoholism, The. Shen Chou, *tr. fr. Chinese
  by* Jonathan Chaves. CoBLCP
Taoist Nun, The. Chang Pi, *tr. fr. Chinese by* Lois Fusek. ATF
Taoist Nun, The. Hsüeh Chao-yün, *tr. fr. Chinese by* Lois Fusek. ATF
Taoist Nun, The. Li Hsün, *tr. fr. Chinese by* Lois Fusek. ATF
Taoist Nun, The. Lu Ch'ien-i, *tr. fr. Chinese by* Lois Fusek. ATF
Taoist Nun, The. Mao Hsi-chen, *tr. fr. Chinese by* Lois Fusek. ATF
Taoist Nun, The. Niu Chiao, *tr. fr. Chinese by* Lois Fusek. ATF
Taoist Nun, The. Sun Kuang-hsien, *tr. fr. Chinese by* Lois Fusek. ATF
Taoist Nun, The. Wei Chuang, *tr. fr. Chinese by* Lois Fusek. ATF
Taoist Nun, The. Wen T'ing-yün, *tr. fr. Chinese by* Lois Fusek. ATF
Taos Winter. Patty L. Harjo. VoR
Tape, The. Myra Cohn Livingston. NTCP
Tape Mark. Nanni Balestrini, *tr. fr. Italian by* Lawrence R. Smith. NItP
Taped to the wall of my cell are 47 pictures: 47 black. The Idea of
  Ancestry. Etheridge Knight. BPo; CNA; NIP; NNaP; PoBA; SV
Tapering stars glint cool. Challengers. Alfred Dorn. GoYe
Tapestries. Colleen J. McElroy. ER
Tapestry, The. Howard Nemerov. Prf
Tapestry. Charles Simic. LCAP
Tapestry of the Great Fear. Louis Aragon, *tr. fr. French by* Malcolm
  Cowley. RHTwFP
Tapestry Trees. William Morris. BoNaP; FaPON; OHIP
Tapestry Weavers, The. Anson G. Chester. BLPA; BLRP; WBLP
Taps. Lizette Woodworth Reese. OHIP
Tapu. Arthur Rex Dugard Fairburn. ATNZ; PeNZ
Tapwater. Laura Jensen. LCAP
Tar. Charles Kenneth Williams. CAPP; GeTw; NAmP
Tara Is Grass. *Unknown, tr. fr. Irish by* Padraic Pearse. AnIL
Tarahumara Herbs ("Tarahumara Indians have come down, The").
  Alfonso Reyes, *tr. fr. Spanish by* Samuel Beckett. MexPo
Tarantella. Hilaire Belloc. CH; FaBoCh; MoBrPo; MoShBr; OBMV;
  RB; RR
Taranto. James Wright. AnAn
Tarantula. Diana O Hehir. NPGG
Tarantula, The. Reed Whittemore. CoAP
Tarantula or the Dance of Death. Anthony Hecht. CoAP; OBD
Tarantula rattling at the lily's foot, The. O Carib Isle! Hart Crane.
  NoAM; PoA; VGW
Tardy Epithalamium for E. and N., A. Ralph Pomeroy. GLP; PeHV
Tardy George. *Unknown.* PAH
Target of the hunting shepherd boys. Zebra Stallion. *Unknown.* PeSA
Target Practice. Donald Finkel. NePoEA-2
Target shudders in the layered heat, The. Technique on the Firing Line.
  Turner Cassity. PoA
Tarkib-Bund, *sel.* Khwaja Mir Dard, *tr. fr. Urdu by* Ahmed Alli.
  "Waiting for the morning breeze am I." *Fr.* II-IV. GoT
Tarma. Antonio Cisneros, *tr. fr. Spanish by* Maureen Ahern *and* David
  Tipton. Per
Tarn, how delightful wind thy willowed waves. Verses Written at
  Montauban in France, 1750. Joseph Warton. OBTV
Tarpauling Jacket. *Unknown.* OxBoLi
Tarquin and Tullia. Arthur Mainwaring. APAS
Tarragona Wine. George McWhirter. UAS
Tarry a moment, happy feet. The Statues. Laurence Binyon. OBEV
Tarry Flynn, *sel.* Patrick Kavanagh.
  "On an apple-ripe September morning." FaBCIP; IPY
Tarry, Shadow of My Scornful Treasure. Sister Juana Inés de la Cruz, *tr.
  fr. Spanish by* Samuel Beckett. MexPo
Tarry with Me, O My Saviour. Caroline Sprague Smith. AH
Tars of the *Blanche*, The. *Unknown.* OxBSS
Tarsier worked as a waiter, A. The Contrary Waiter. Edgar Parker.
  RHPC

Tartar. Solyman Brown. *Fr.* Dentologia; a Poem on the Diseases of the
  Teeth and Their Proper Remedies. FaBoUs
Tartary. Walter de la Mare. OxBChV
Tartuffe. Molière, *tr. fr. French by* Richard Wilbur. NAWM-2
Tarye no lenger; toward thyn herytage. Vox Ultima Crucis. John
  Lydgate. OBEV
Tarzan Once More. Rutger Kopland, *tr. fr. Dutch by* Ria Leigh-
  Loohuizen. DuIn
Tashkent Breaks into Bloom. "Anna Akhmatova," *tr. fr. Russian by*
  Richard McKane. BoWoP
Tashlich. Abba Kovner, *tr. fr. Hebrew by* Warren Bargad *and* Stanley F.
  Chyet. IP
Task, The, *sels.* William Cowper.
  "Come evening once again, season of peace." *Fr.* IV. NAEL-1
  Ease. *Fr.* I. TEP
  England. *Fr.* II. FiP
  Garden, The. *Fr.* III. PoE
  Garden, The. *Fr.* III. EnRP; FaBoRV; NAEL-1
    (Stricken Deer, The.) FiP
  God Made the Country. *Fr.* I. FiP; PoEL-3
  "Groans of nature in this nether world, The." *Fr.* VI. NoP
  Hatred and Vengeance, My Eternal Portion. FaBoRV
  How to Grow Cucumbers. *Fr.* III. FaBoUs
  "Lord of all, himself through all diffused, The." *Fr.* VI. OAEL-1
  "Night was winter in his roughest mood, The." *Fr.* VI. EnRP; TEP
  Poetic Pains. *Fr.* II. FiP
  Sofa, The. *Fr. bk.* I. EnRP
    (Rural Sights and Sounds.) NOEC
  "Thou knowest my praise of nature most sincere." *Fr.* I. NAEL-1
  Time-Piece, The. *Fr.* II. EnRP
    (Against Slavery.) NOEC
  "Tis morning; and the sun with ruddy orb." *Fr.* V. PoEL-3
    (Frosty Morning, A.) NOEC
  "Whose freedom is by suff'rance, and at will." *Fr.* V. EnRP
  Winter Evening ("Just when our drawing-rooms begin to blaze").
    NOEC
  Winter Evening, The ("Hark! 'tis the twanging horn o'er yonder
    bridge"). *Fr.* IV. SeCePo
    (Post-Boy, The.) FiP
  Winter Walk at Noon, A. *Fr.* VI. EnRP; TEP
    "No noise is here, or none that hinders thought." PBBP
Task, The. Ruth Pitter. MoBrPo
Task That Is Given to You, The. Edwin Markham. WBLP
Taste. Christopher Smart. *Fr.* Hymns for the Amusement of Children,
  XV. NOCV
Taste in my mouth, The. East Texas. Leon Stokesbury. SM
Taste now, dear Teresa, the living poison of the ivy. Carmelite.
  Raymond Murray, *tr. by the author.* TIRV
"Taste of Honey, A." King D. Kuka. NOVW
Taste of peaked champagne. This Night. Dianne Hai-Jew. BrSi
Taste of Prayer, The. Ralph W. Seager. TrPWD
Taste of Purple. Leland B. Jacobs. RHPC
Tasting the Wild Grapes. Mary Oliver. CAPP
Tat for Tit. Walter de la Mare. FM
Tatar chief forced me to become his wife, A. Ts'ai Yen, *tr. fr. Chinese
  by* Kenneth Rexroth *and* Ling Chung. *Fr.* Eighteen Verses Sung to a
  Tatar Reed Whistle, II. WPOW
Tatiana Kalatschova. William Logan. SM
Tatsuta River/ carries its red autumn leaves. Emperor Hanazono, *tr. by*
  Steven D. Carter. WFTU
Tattle. Godfrey Turner. NOBL
Tattoo, The. Muhammad al-Maghut, *tr. fr. Arabic by* May Jayyusi *and*
  John Heath-Stubbs. MAP
Tattoo. Wallace Stevens. LiTA
Tattooed Man, The. Robert Hayden. CAPP; NoAM
Tattoos. Charles Wright. HCAP
Taught early that his mother's skin was the sign of error. Mr. Z. M.
  Carl Holman. SoSe
Tauhid. Askia Muhammad Touré. PoBA
Taunt. *Malay Oral Tradition, tr. by* R. J. Wilkinson *and* R. O.
  Windstedt. WTO
Taut as a tent the heavenly dome is blue. March Day, 1941. Joyce
  Grenfell. CN
Taut bow, The. A Vague Dream. Munir Niazi, *tr. by* Mahmood Jamal.
  PBMUP
Taut on the leash, at last I have my way. Moving: New York—New
  Haven Line. Alfred Corn. MAYP
Tautology. Nelo Risi, *tr. fr. Italian by* Lawrence R. Smith. NItP
Tavern, The. E. A. Robinson. AnAmPo
Tavern is closed for the night, The. The Closed Door. Muhammad al-
  Faituri, *tr. by* Sargon Boulus *and* Peter Porter. MAP

Tavernkeeper, The. Cheng Hsieh, *tr. fr. Chinese* by Jan W. Walls. WFTU

Tawny are the leaves turned, but they still hold. Antique Harvesters. John Crowe Ransom. MoAB; MoAmPo; NoP; OxBA

Tawny-black sky-scurries. David Jones. *Fr.* The Sleeping Lord. OBWVE

Tawny gleam in the sunlight, A. The First Robin. Lilian Leveridge. CaP

Tax-Gatherer, The. John Banister Tabb. GN

Tax not the royal Saint with vain expense. Inside of King's College Chapel, Cambridge. Wordsworth. *Fr.* Ecclesiastical Sonnets, *pt.* III, XLIII. EnRP; OBNC

Tax Return. *Unknown.* FaBoUs

Taxi, The. Amy Lowell. BoWoP; MoAmPo

Taxi-cab whore out at Iver, A. Victor Gray. NOBL

Taxi halts before a pale museum, The. Letter to Statues. John Malcolm Brinnin. EyDe

Taxi Suite, *sel.* Lew Welch. After Anacreon. NeAP; PoM

Taxicabs scuttle by on the wet streets. Whaddaya Do for Action in This Place? George Starbuck. NePoEA-2

Taxiing to 71 via Tijuana. Seasons Greetings, Love and Revolution. Judy Miles. PVCV

Taxis. Rachel Lyman Field. FaPON

Taxis, The. Louis MacNeice. FaBCIP; OxBTC

Taxonomical Note. David Sutton. Mes

Taylor's Travels from London to Prague, *sels.* John Taylor.
"I come from Bohem, yet no news I bring." OBTV
"Prague is a famous, ancient, kingly seat." OBTV

Tcheliabtraktrostroi Waltz, *sel.* Louis Aragon, *tr. fr. French.*
"This is an ancient waltz." *Tr.* by Nancy Cunard. RHTwFP

Te Atairangikaahu. Kingi M. Ihaka, *tr. fr. Maori* by Kingi M. Ihaka. PeNZ

Te Deum. Charles Reznikoff. TrJP; VWA

Te Deum, The. *Unknown, tr. fr. Latin* by Dryden. AWP

Te Deum Laudamus. *Unknown, tr. fr. Latin.* WGRP

Te Kaha. Rachel McAlpine. PeNZ

Te Martyrum Candidatus. Lionel Johnson. ACP; OBMV; TIRV

Te Rangi Hiroa/ Buck. Kendrick Smithyman. ATNZ

Te Whetu Plains. Edward Tregear, *tr.* by Alan Myers. ATNZ; PeNZ

Tea at the Palaz of Hoon. Wallace Stevens. FaBoMo; PoA

Tea for Two. Pat Nolan. UL

Tea garden shows you how, A. Bridge. A. R. Ammons. CoAP; NAAL-2

Tea party at Le Cannet, The. Bonnard; a Novel. Richard Howard. CoAP; NYBP

Tea Poems. George Mackay Brown. OxBC

Tea-rose tea-gown, etc., The. Ezra Pound. *Fr.* Hugh Selwyn Mauberley. (Life and Contacts), III. MoAmPo; NOBE

Tea-shop, A. Hugh Dallas. ATNZ

Tea Shop, The. Ezra Pound. HeIP

Teach me, Father, how to go. Edwin Markham. BoTP; TrPWD; WGRP

Teach me, life. Only the Heart. Marjorie Freeman Campbell. CaP

Teach me, my God and King. The Elixir. George Herbert. BoTP; FaBoCh; GN; NoP; OHIP; SeCV-1; TrGrPo; WGRP

Teach me, teach me how. Abraham Reisen, *tr.* by Leonard Wolf. PeBMYV

Teach me the ritual that runs beyond. Worship. Robert Whitaker. TrPWD

Teach me the secret of thy loveliness. To a Wind-Flower. Madison Cawein. AA

Teach me to live! 'Tis easier far to die. The Harder Task. *Unknown.* BLRP

Teach me to love? Go, teach thyself more wit. The Prophet. Abraham Cowley. JCP; TrGrPo

Teach Us to Mark This, God. Franz Werfel, *tr. fr. German* by Jacob Sloan. TrJP

"Teach Us to Number Our Days." Rita Dove. NoAM

Teacher, The. David Fisher. NPGG

Teacher, The. Leslie Pinckney Hill. BANP; PoNe; TrPWD

Teacher, The. Virginia Brady Young. GoYe

Teacher, Jimmie's toe is bleedin.' Johnny's Pet Superstition. Clara Ann Thompson. CBWP-2

Teacher Taught Me, A. Anna Walters. VoR

Teachers, The. Nicanor Parra, *tr. fr. Spanish* by William Jay Smith. CT

Teacher's Dream, The. William Henry Venable. BeLS

Teacher's Prayer, A, *sel.* Frances Ridley Havergal.
For Every Day, *1 st.* BLRP

Teacher's Prayer, A. Frances Ridley Havergal. *See* Lord, speak to me, that I may speak.

Teachers, really. Fording. Shih Shan-chi, *tr.* by Dominic Cheung. IFON

Teaching a Dumb Calf. Ted Hughes. AnAn

Teaching My Students Prosody. Jay Rogoff. KS

Teaching Poetry. Cyn Zarco. BrSi

Teaching Staff Disbanded, The. György Rónay, *tr. fr. Hungarian* by Michael Hamburger. MHuP

Teaching Swift to Young Ladies. William Dickey. PoA

Teaching the Children. Myra Sklarew. CRP

Teahouse at Hoshioka, A. Liu E, *tr. fr. Chinese* by Jonathan Chaves. CoBLCP

Teak Forest, The, *sel.* "Laurence Hope."
For This Is Wisdom. PoLF

Team, The. "Furnley Maurice." CBAP

Team of Budweiser horses, The. 8-Ball at the Twilite. David Baker. MAYP

Team of crushed tree shadows, A. A Night Song: How to Defend against Tree Shadows. Yang Mu, *tr.* by Dominic Cheung. IFON

Teams, The. Henry Lawson. CBAP; PoAu-1

Teapots and Quails. Edward Lear. GoJo

The Tear. Byron. PoM

Tear [*or* The Teare], The. Richard Crashaw. LiTB; SeCP

Tear. Thomas Kinsella. IPY; NOIV

Tear, The. Ramón López Velarde, *tr. fr. Spanish* by Samuel Beckett. MexPo

Tear, The. Prince P. A. Vyazemsky, *tr. fr. Russian* by Alan Myers. AAA

Tear down the Ivory Tower! Bring Torches. Alexander Maitland Stephen. CaP

Teare, The. Richard Crashaw. *See* Tear, The.

Tearing at my package like a child. Eczema. David R. Slavitt. TW

Tearing away from the black. Title Lost. Wan Kin-lau. WCI

Tearless oblivion in an expanse, The. In Mutual Time. Steven Lavoie. UL

Tears. Elizabeth Barrett Browning. WPE

Tears. Khansa, *tr. fr. Arabic* by R. A. Nicholson. AWP

Tears. Ruth Kim Chun-soo, *tr. fr. Korean* by Koh Chang-soo. ACKP

Tears. "Owen Meredith." *Fr.* Glenaveril. EBVV

Tears. Lizette Woodworth Reese. AA; AnAmPo; MoAmPo; WGRP

Tears. Dame Edith Sitwell. CMoP

Tears. Edward Thomas. GTBS-P; LiTB; NAEL-2

Tears. Prince P. A. Vyazemsky, *tr. fr. Russian* by Alan Myers. AAA

Tears at evening?—not infrequent. Inscribed on a Plantain Leaf to Show to a Certain Person. Liu Ling-hsien, *tr.* by Burton Watson. CoBCP

Tears at the Grave of Sir Albertus Morton. Sir Henry Wotton. SeCP

Tears, ere thy death, for many a one I shed. Tears. Khansa, *tr.* by R. A. Nicholson. AWP

Tears fall within mine heart. Il Pleut Doucement sur la Ville. Paul Verlaine, *tr.* by Ernest Dowson. AWP; BrPo

Tears, Flow No More. Herbert of Cherbury. EllL; OBS; SeCP

Tears from long ago. A Wish. Jenny Joseph. NPo

Tears, Idle Tears [I Know Not What They Mean]. Tennyson. *Fr.* The Princess. AWP; EBVV; ELP; FaBoRV; FaFP; FaPoR; FiP; FPL; GTBS-P; HAP; InPS; InvP; LiTB; NAEL-2; NIP; NOBE; NoP; OAEL-2; OBNC; PoE; PoEL-5; PPP; TEP; TrGrPo; UnPo; WeW

Tears in Spring. William Ellery Channing. AA

Tears in the eyes of the surgeon. To My Friends. Peter De Vries. FiBHP

Tears of Fancy, The, *sels.* Thomas Watson.
Go Idle Lines. Son
I Saw the Object. Son

Tears of Pearl, The. Chang Ts'o, *tr. fr. Chinese* by Dominic Cheung. IFON

Tears of Scotland, The. Tobias Smollett. NOEC

Tears of Shame. Ali Sardar J'afri, *tr. fr. Urdu* by Mahmood Jamal. PBMUP

Tears of the Excavator, The. Pier Paolo Pasolini, *tr. fr. Italian* by Norman Macafee *and* Luciano Martinengo. PFI

Tears of the Poplars, The. Edith M. Thomas. AA

Tears of the widower, when he sees. Tennyson. *Fr.* In Memoriam A. H. H., XIII. PeHV

Tears of the World. Mu'tamid, King of Seville, *tr. fr. Arabic* by Dulcie L. Smith. AWP

Tears of wild geese crying, The. Teika, *tr. fr. Japanese* by Hiroaki Sato. *Fr.* A Compendium of Good Tanka. FCEI

Teasers, The. William Empson. OxBTC

Teasing Song. Princess Magogo, *tr. fr. Zulu* by D. K. Rycroft. WTO

Teatime Variations: After A. E. Housman. Peter Titheradge. FaBoPa
Teatime Variations: After a Thirties Poet. Peter Titheradge. FaBoPa
Teatime Variations: After Algernon Charles Swinburne. Peter Titheradge. FaBoPa
Teatime Variations: After John Keats. Peter Titheradge. FaBoPa
Teatime Variations: After Robert Herrick. Peter Titheradge. FaBoPa
Teatime Variations: After W. B. Yeats. Peter Titheradge. FaBoPa
Teatime Variations: After Walter de la Mare. Peter Titheradge. FaBoPa
Technical Supplement, A, *sels.* Thomas Kinsella.
  "It is hard to beat a good meal." CIP
  "Point, greatly enlarged, The." IPY
Technicalities for Jack Spicer. Philip Whalen. PoM
Technique. Burnham Eaton. GoYe
Technique. Langdon Elwyn Mitchell. *Fr.* To a Writer of the Day. AA
Technique on the Firing Line. Turner Cassity. PoA
Technogamia, *sel.* Barten Holyday.
  "O harmless feast." EIL
Technologies. George Starbuck. NYBP
Technology of Inspiration, The. Lynn Emanuel. SoTCo
Tecumseh, *sels.* Charles Mair.
  "I love you better than I love my race." NOBC
  "Tell me more of those unrivalled wastes." *Fr.* IV, vi. CaP
  "There was a time on this fair continent." NOBC; OBCV
  "We left/ The silent forest." OBCV
Ted & marge had been married eight years. Wasp Sex Myth (Two). Anselm Hollo. PoM
Teddy Bear. Alan Alexander Milne. OnUR
Teddy bear is a faithful friend, A. My Teddy Bear. Marchette Chute. RAR
Teddy bear is nice to hold, A. My Teddy Bear. Margaret Hillert. RAR
Teddy Bear, Teddy Bear. *Unknown.* NTCP; RAR
Tedium. Giuseppe Ungaretti, *tr. fr. Italian by* Charles Tomlinson. PFI
Teen-Ager, A. W. D. Snodgrass. TW
Teeth. Susan Griffin. NPGG
Teeth Mother Naked at Last, The. Robert Bly. NNaP
Teeth of clogs, carriage wheels, the hooves of horses. Walking in the Country outside T'ai-yüan on a Spring Day. Yang Chi, *tr. by* Jonathan Chaves. CoBLCP
Teeth of flowers, coif of dew. I'm Going to Sleep. Alfonsina Storni, *tr. by* Perry Higman. LPSS
Teeth of flowers, hairnet of dew. I Am Going to Sleep (Suicide Poem). Alfonsina Storni, *tr. by* Aliki *and* Willis Barnstone. BoWoP
Teeth on the saw. Piney Woods. Malcolm Cowley. NYBP
Teevo cheevo cheevio chee. The Woodlark. Gerard Manley Hopkins. RB
Tefillin: phylacteries. The Journey with Hands and Arms. Benjamin Saltman. VWA
Teika, a No Play. *at. to* Komparu Zenchiku, *tr. fr. Japanese by* Hiroaki Sato. FCEI
Telegram. Dick Lourie. NeAC
Telegrams of Tenderness for Sanaa, *sels.* Abd al-Aziz al-Maqalih, *tr. fr. Arabic by* Lena Jayyusi *and* Christopher Middleton. MAP
  Fifteenth Telegram ("Birds that migrated, The").
  First Telegram ("As I retire, each day, with myself").
  Nineteenth Telegram ("Love has changed the face of distances").
  Ninth Telegram ("Trains roll over my heart, The").
  Second Telegram ("Every evening when night retrieves the substance of our longings").
  Seventeenth Telegram ("Your weeping gray streets").
  Seventh Telegram ("The day recedes").
  Tenth Telegram ("I wish I had a boat").
  Thirteenth Telegram ("Faces that stab the eye are familiar, The").
  Twentieth Telegram ("Ah my city, my lady").
Telemachus with a Transistor. Ruth Dallas. PeNZ
Telemann to A.C. Helen Chasin. TV
Telephone, The. Robert Frost. SO; SoSe
Telephone, The. Li Nan, *tr. fr. Chinese by* Dominic Cheung. IFON
Telephone Booth in the Rain. Tu Yeh, *tr. fr. Chinese by* Dominic Cheung. IFON
Telephone Conversation. Wole Soyinka. SoSe; TTY
Telephone Directory. Harry Crosby. EAS
Telephone-installer was interested, The. Moving In. Josephine Miles. NoP
Telephone is a house without doors. The Telephone. Li Nan, *tr. by* Dominic Cheung. IFON
Telephone line goes cold, A. The Farm on the Great Plains. William Stafford. HAP; VGW

Telephone Poles. John Updike. FYAP; Psk; SaC
Telephone poles, The. Crossing Kansas by Train. Donald Justice. AiP; NYBP
Telephonist. Janet Frame. WPE
Telescope. Sydney Lea. BLA
Teletype-music. OK, Maestro, hit it. The New Republic Is Infuriated at the News Coverage. George Starbuck. BLA
Television. Fei Ma, *tr. fr. Chinese by* Dominic Cheung. IFON
Television/ radio sunday benevolent sunday. They Are Killing All the Young Men. David Henderson. PoBA
Television aerials, Chinese characters. On Roofs of Terry Street. Douglas Dunn. OxBTC
TELEX FOR JIX RE SUNDAY. Vincent O'Sullivan. ATNZ
Tell a wise person, or else keep silent. The Holy Longing. Goethe, *tr. by* Robert Bly. NU
Tell all my mourners. Wake. Langston Hughes. OBAL
Tell all the truth but tell it slant. Emily Dickinson. AmPP; HeIP; LiTA; NAAL-1; NAWM-2; NoAM; NOBA; NoP; PPP; TAP; UnPo; WeW
Tell Freedom, *sel.* Peter Abrahams.
  Me, Colored. PBA
Tell her I love. Poems for My Daughter. Horace Gregory. MoAmPo
Tell Her So. Mrs. Henry Linden. CBWP-4
Tell Him, O Night. *Unknown, tr. fr. Arabic by* E. Powys Mathers. *Fr.* The Thousand and One Nights. AWP
Tell Him So. J. A. Egerton. PWR
Tell Him So. *Unknown.* BLPA; BLPL; WBLP
Tell him the tale is a lie! A Learned Mistress. *Unknown, tr. by* Frank O'Connor. OBMV
Tell just this one thing. Prince Munenaga, *tr. by* Steven D. Carter. WFTW
Tell Me. Jayne Cortez. ER
Tell Me. Pamela Mordecai. PBCV
Tell Me. Edith Matilda Thomas. *Fr.* The Inverted Torch. AA
Tell me. What She Said Her Lover within Earshot. Kapilar, *tr. by* A. K. Ramanujan. PLW
Tell me,/ Was Venus more beautiful. Venus Transiens. Amy Lowell. PoA
Tell me,/ you visited. Peter Zumpf, *tr. by* Beth Bjorklund. CoAuP
Tell me a riddle, I said, that has no answer. Winter Birds. Linda Gregg. NAmP
"Tell me a story." Bedtime Story. Lilian Moore. NTCP; RAR
Tell Me a Story. Robert Penn Warren. MT
"Tell me a story, father, please." The Natives of America. Ann Plato. BlSi
Tell me a story, Father, please do. Request Number. G. N. Sprod. FiBHP
Tell me, abandoned miscreant, prithee tell. Upon the Author of a Play Called *Sodom.* John Oldham. TW
Tell me about that harvest field. Real Property. Harold Monro. BoNaP
Tell me about yourself they. A Word in Edgeways. Charles Tomlinson. NOBL
Tell Me Again. Niğâr Hanim, *tr. fr. Turkish by* Tâlat S. Halman. PBWP
Tell Me Again. Paul Keens-Douglas. PVCV
Tell Me Dearest, What is Love? Francis Beaumont *and* Fletcher. *Fr.* The Captain. EIL
Tell me, Dorinda, why so gay. On the Countess of Dorchester. Charles Sackville. APAS
"Tell me, good dog, whose tomb you guard so well." The Tomb of Diogenes. *Unknown, tr. by* John Addington Symonds. AWP
Tell me good Hobbinoll, what garres thee greete? Aprill. Spenser. *Fr.* The Shepheardes [*or* Shepeards *or* Shepherd's] Calender. NAEL-1; PoEL-1
  ("Tell me, good Hobbinoll, what garres thee greete?") OBEV; OBSC; PoEL-1
  Ditty, A: In Praise of Eliza, Queen of the Shepherds. OBEV
  (Ditty, A: "See where she sits upon the grassy green.") FaBoCh
  Elisa ("Ye dainty nymphs, that in this blessed brook"). OBSC
  (Lay to Eliza, The.) NOBE
Tell me if it is too far for you. Elegy for N. N. Czeslaw Milosz. SV
Tell me, is it right if I stop being afraid. Third Letter. Erika Mitterer, *tr. by* Beth Bjorklund. CoAuP
Tell me is there anything lovelier. Greenness. Angelina Weld Grimké. CDC
Tell me, is there sovereign cure. Tell Me. Edith Matilda Thomas. *Fr.* The Inverted Torch. AA
Tell me it was just a dream. Julia. Wendy Rose. STE
Tell Me Little Woodworm. Spike Milligan. RAR
Tell me, lovely, loving pair! On the Friendship betwixt Two Ladies. Edmund Waller. PeHV

Tell me, men with wisdom gifted. Hiraeth. *Unknown, tr. by* Aneirin Talfan Davies. OBWVE

Tell me more of those unrivalled wastes. Charles Mair. *Fr.* Tecumseh, IV, vi. CaP

Tell me (my love) since Hymen ty'de. An Hymeneall Dialogue. Thomas Carew. SeCP

Tell me, my patient friends, awaiters of messages. Speech to a Crowd. Archibald MacLeish. MoAB; MoAmPo

Tell Me News. Sipho Sepamla. WMBCH

Tell Me No More. William Drummond of Hawthornden. TrGrPo

Tell me[e] no more how fair[e] she[e] is. Henry King. EnLoPo; MeLP; MePo; OBS; SeCP
  (That Distant Bliss.) TrGrPo

Tell me no more of constancy. Against Constancy. Earl of Rochester. GBL

Tell me no more of minds embracing minds. No Platonic Love. William Cartwright. ErPo; GBL; InvP; JCP; LiTB; OAEL-1
  (No Platonique Love.) PoEL-2

Tell me no secret, friend. The Burden. Francesca Yetunde Pereira. PBA

Tell Me Not Here [It Needs Not Saying]. A. E. Housman. ELP; GTBS-P; LiTM; NoAM; NOBE; OAEL-2; OBNC; OxBTC; SCV

Tell me not in idle jingle. Psalm of Marriage. Phoebe Cary. PWR

Tell me not in joyous numbers. Stephen Crane. OBAL

Tell me not, in mournful numbers. A Psalm of Life. Longfellow. AA; AH, *sel., with music;* AnAmPo; FPL; NAAL-1; OBCA; OHFP; PoLF; PrIm; PWR; TAP; WBLP

Tell me not, O Soul that slumbers. A Psalm of Life. Andrew Lang. CenHV

Tell me not of a face that's fair. The Resolve. Alexander Brome. OBEV

Tell me not of joy; there's none. The Dead Sparrow. William Cartwright. CH

Tell me not, Sweet, I am unkind. Lines Where Beauty Lingers. Franklin P. Adams. OBAL

Tell me not, Sweet, I am unkind. To Lucasta, Going to the Wars [*or* Warres]. Richard Lovelace. AWP; CaPo; ELP; EnLoPo; FaBV; FaFP; FF; FPL; GBL; GTBS; GTBS-P; HAP; HeIP; HoPM; InPS; JCP; LiTB; MeLP; MePo; NAEL-1; NIP; NOBE; NoP; OAEL-1; OBEV; OBS; OBWP; OxBSP; PoEL-3; PoRA; SCV; SeCePo; SeCP; SeCV-1; TrGrPo; WeW
  (Song: To Lucasta, Going to the Wars.) PoE
  (To Lucasta.) InPK

Tell me not what too well I know. On Catullus. Walter Savage Landor. OBEV

Tell Me Now. Wang Chi, *tr. fr. Chinese by* Arthur Waley. FaBoCh

Tell me now in what hidden way is. Ballad[e] of Dead Ladies. Villon, *tr. by* Dante Gabriel Rossetti. AWP; CTC; FaFP; OBVE; PoRA; PrIm
  (Snows of Yester-year, The.) WiR

"Tell me now, what should a man want." Tell Me Now. Wang Chi, *tr. by* Arthur Waley. FaBoCh

"Tell me, O Muse of the shifty, the man who wandered afar." Jubilee before Revolution. Andrew Lang. BXAP

Tell me, O Octopus, I begs. The Octopus. Ogden Nash. MOS; RB

Tell me, O Swan, your ancient tale. Songs of Kabir. Kabir, *tr. by* Rabindranath Tagore. WGRP

Tell me, O tell, what kind[e] of thing is wit. Ode: Of Wit. Abraham Cowley. MeLP; MePo; NAEL-1; OAEL-1; SeCP; SeCV-1
  (Of Wit.) OBS

Tell me of a brother. Tell Me News. Sipho Sepamla. WMBCH

Tell me of thy heart's devotion. Whisper Words of Love to Me. Lizelia Augusta Jenkins Moorer. CBWP-3

Tell me, Oh Muse (for thou, or none canst tell). The Power of Numbers. Abraham Cowley. *Fr.* Davideis, I. OBS

Tell me, Perigot, what shalbe the game. August. Spenser. *Fr.* The Shepheardes [*or* Shepeards *or* Shepherd's] Calender.
  It Fell upon a Holy Eve. InvP
  (Roundelay, A: "It fell upon a holy eve.") EIL

Tell me, Pyrrha, what fine youth. Horace. *See* Odes: I, 5. "What slender youth bedewed with liquid odours" ("Quis multa gracilis").

Tell me, Ram: what will happen to me? Kabir, *tr. by* John Stratton Hawley *and* Mark Juergensmeyer. SSI

Tell me, shepherd, tell me, pray. Country Gods. Cometas, *tr. by* T. F. Higham. FaBoCh

Tell Me, Tell Me. Marianne Moore. LiTM; NYBP

"Tell me, tell me,/ Unknown stranger." The Galliass. Walter de la Mare. FaBoTw

Tell me, tell me, gentle Robin. The Cat and the Bird. George Canning. ChTr

Tell me, tell me, smiling child. Emily Brontë. TEP

Tell me that the plutonium sludge. Tell Me. Jayne Cortez. ER

Tell me the auld, auld story. The Parrot Cry. "Hugh MacDiarmid." OxBS

Tell me, thou skilful shepherd's swain. Michael Drayton. *Fr.* The Shepherd's Garland, Eclogue IX (1606 ed.) EIL

Tell me, thou Star, whose wings of light. The World's Wanderers. Shelley. TTTS

Tell me though safest end of all our woe. On Death. Anne Killigrew. BoWoP

Tell me today, when all my tides are gone. Sea Sonnet. Norma Lay. GoYe

Tell me what sail the seas. Under the Stars. Wallace Rice. AA; OHIP

"Tell me what you're doing over here, John Gorham." John Gorham. E. A. Robinson. MoAB; MoAmPo

Tell me whaur, in whit countrie. Ballat o the Leddies o Langsyne. Villon, *tr. by* Tom Scott. OBVE

Tell Me Where Is Fancy [*or* Fancie] Bred. Shakespeare. *Fr.* The Merchant of Venice, III, ii. CH; EIL; ELP; LiTB; NAEL-1; OAEL-1
  (Casket Song, A.) OBSC
  (Fancy.) FaPON; TrGrPo
  (Love.) OBEV
  (Madrigal: "Tell me where is fancy bred.") GTBS; GTBS-P
  (Song: "Tell me where is fancy bred.") GTBS; GTBS-P

Tell me, where is your home? Songs of Ch'ang-kan. Ts'ui Hao, *tr. by* Burton Watson. CoBCP

Tell me where thy lovely love is. Heine, *tr. fr. German by* Ezra Pound. *Fr.* Heimkehr, Die. AWP

Tell me whither, maiden June. The Reaper. John Banister Tabb. ACP

Tell me, wide wandering soul, in all thy quest. But Once. Theodore Winthrop. AWP

Tell Me, Wight in the Broom. *Unknown.* NAEL-1

Tell me, you anti-saints, why glass. Upon Fairford Windows. Richard Corbett. EyDe

Tell Me You Wandering Spirits. *Unknown.* OBS

Tell me your secrets, pretty shell. Shell Secrets. *Unknown.* BoTP

Tell Our Daughters. Besmilr Brigham. IHMS

Tell the random pilgrims. Eve's Advice to the Children of Israel. Joachim Neugroschel. VWA

Tell the story to your sons. The Fight of the *Armstrong* Privateer. James Jeffrey Roche. PAH

Tell them/ I was a persimmon eater. After I'm Dead. Masaoka Shiki, *tr. fr. Japanese by* Burton Watson. *Fr.* Thirty-nine Haiku. FCEI

Tell them, I AM, Jehovah said. Christopher Smart. *Fr.* A Song to David. WGRP

Tell Them I'm Struggling to Sing with Angels. David Meltzer. VWA

Tell them in Lacedaemon [*or* Lakedaimon], passer-by. At Thermopylae. Simonides. WaaP
  (On the Army of Spartans, Who Died at Thermopylae.) ChTr; FaBoEE

Tell them to go away. Insomnia. Ethna MacCarthy. NeIP

Tell this poem. Daily Delights. Hameed Said, *tr. by* Lena Jayyusi *and* Naomi Shihab Nye. MAP

Tell this to ladies: how a hero man. Man without Sense of Direction. John Crowe Ransom. LiTM; OxBA

Tell thou the world, when my bones lie whitening. The Nameless One. James Clarence Mangan. ACP

Tell us/ how we'll be together in that time. When/Then. Adrienne Rich. ER

"Tell us, streaming lady." History. James Liddy. CIP

Tell us, thou clear and heavenly tongue. The Star-Song; a Carol to the King; Sung at White-Hall. Robert Herrick. GN

Tell us! ye dead! Will none of you in pity. Robert Blair. *Fr.* The Grave. OBD

Tell Us, Ye Servants of the Lord. William Staughton. AH

Tell you? ha! who. Maximus, to Gloucester, Letter 2. Charles Olson. *Fr.* The Maximus Poems. NoAM

Tell you I chyll. The Tunnyng [*or* Tunning] of Elynour [*or* Elinour] Rummyng [*or* Rumming]. John Skelton. AAS; TrGrPo

Tell you what I like the best. Knee-deep in June. James Whitcomb Riley. OHFP

Tell your son, my son. Message. Renata Pallottini, *tr. by* Monique *and* Carlos Altschul. WPOW

Telling about Coyote. Simon J. Ortiz. STP

Telling It. Nancy Sullivan. TAP

Telling My Feelings. Yü Hsüan-chi, *tr. by* Geoffrey Waters. BoWoP

Telling the Bees. Lizette Woodworth Reese. AA

Telling the Bees. Whittier. AnAmPo; AWP; BLPL; NOBA; TAP

Tellus. William Reed Huntington. AA

Tèma con Variazióni. "Lewis Carroll." FaBoNo

Temagami. Archibald Lampman. OBCV

Temari. Ryokan, *tr. fr. Chinese by* Burton Watson. JLIC-2

Temeraire, The. Herman Melville. WaaP

Temper. Rose Fyleman. OxBChV

Temper, The. George Herbert. MePo; NOCV; NoP; OBS; PoEL-2

Temper my spirit, O Lord. The Passionate Sword. Jean Starr Untermeyer. TrJP; TrPWD

Temper of Aristippus, The. John Gilbert Cooper. *Fr.* Epistles to His Friends in Town. PBBP

Temperament. Martial, *tr. fr. Latin by* Joseph Addison. AWP

Temperaments, The. Ezra Pound. BoLoP; ErPo; NoAM; NOBA

Temperance. *Unknown.* ACP

Temperance and Virginity. Milton. *Fr.* Comus; a Masque Presented at Ludlow Castle. OBS

Temperance Billiards Rooms, The. P. J. Kavanagh. OxBTC

Temperance Note: and Weather Prophecy. James Agee. *Fr.* Two Songs on the Economy of Abundance. MoAmPo

Temperance or the Cheap Physitian upon the Translation of Lessius. Richard Crashaw. SeCV-1

Temperance Song. *Unknown.* FaBoUs

Temperature. Gerard Malanga. NYBP

Temperature/ Cruises down, slides, The. Storm. Mary Oliver. CAPP

Tempered, annealed, the hard essence of autumn metals. Needle and Thread. Pan Chao, *tr. by* Richard Mather *and* Rob Swigart. WPOW

Tempest, The. Charles Cotton. SeCePo

Tempest, The ("Boatswain!"), *sels.* Shakespeare. OAEL-1, *with music*
   Be Not Afeard: The Isle is Full of Noises. *Fr.* III, ii. RB
   (Caliban.)
   (To Dream Again.) TrGrPo
   Brave New World. *Fr.* V, i. TrGrPo
   "Come unto these yellow sands." *Fr.* I, ii. BoTP; CH; EIL; HeIP; OBEV; OBSC; TTTS
   (Ariel's Song: "Come unto these yellow sands.") CTC; FaBoCh; GN; GoJo; NOBE; TEP
   (Song: "Come unto these yellow sands.") PoEL-2
   "Full fathom [*or* fadom] five thy father lies." *Fr.* I, ii. AWP; ChTr; EBEV; EIL; ELP; FaBoCh; HAP; HeIP; HoPM; InPK; InPS; LiTB; MOS; NAEL-1; NoP; OBEV; OxBSP; PoE; PoRA; TEP
   (Ariel's Dirge.) GoJo
   (Ariel's Song: "Full fathom five thy father lies.") GN; NOBE; OBSC; SeCePo
   (Sea Dirge, A.) GTBS; GTBS-P; TrGrPo
   (Song: "Full fathom [*or* fadom] five thy father lies.") PoEL-2
   "I saw him beat the surges under him." *Fr.* I, i. MOS
   "If by your art, my dearest father, you have." *Fr.* I, ii. MOS
   "Master, the swabber, the boatswain and I, The." *Fr.* II, ii. MOS
   (Sea Song, A: "Master, the swabber, the boatswain and I, The.") NBLV
   (Song: "Master, the swabber, the boatswain and I, The.") FF; NOBL; OxBSP
   Our Revels Now Are Ended. *Fr.* IV, i. LiTB; RB
   (Stuff of Dreams, The.) FaBV
   (Such Stuff as Dreams Are Made On.) TrGrPo
   Prospero. *Fr.* IV, i. FiP
   "Hark, hark!/ Bow-wow./ The watch-dogs bark." SoSe
   "Where the bee sucks, there suck I." *Fr.* V, i. AWP; BoTP; CH; CTC; EIL; FaBV; HeIP; NAEL-1; NBLV; NoP; OBEV; OxBSP; TTTS
   (Ariel's Song: "Where the bee sucks, there suck I.") GN; NOBE; OBSC; PDV
   "Ye elves of hill, brooks, standing lakes, and groves." *Fr.* V, i. EBEV; SCV
   (Magic.) AWP

Tempest, The. William Jay Smith. MoAmPo

Tempest, The. *Unknown.* AmFP

Tempest, The. Marya Zaturenska. MoAmPo

Tempest cracked on the theatre, A. Quickly. Repetitions of a Young Captain. Wallace Stevens. WaP

Tempest on the great seaborders! A Storm at Sea. *Unknown, tr. by* Robin Flower. AnIL

Temple. John Donne. *Fr.* La Corona. OBS; Son

Temple, The, *sels.* George Herbert. Son
   Love ("Immortal heat, O let thy greater flame").
   Love ("Immortal love, author of this great flame").
   Redemption.
   Son, The.

Temple, The. Robert Herrick. CaPo

Temple, The. Gustave Kahn, *tr. fr. French by* Edouard Roditi. VWA

Temple, A. Kenneth Patchen. EAS

Temple, The. Po Chü-i, *tr. fr. Chinese by* Arthur Waley. OBMV

Temple, The. C. H. Sisson. OxBTC

Temple in the Hills, A. Yao Nai, *tr. fr. Chinese by* Daniel Bryant. WFTU

Temple is full of blood, The. Salvador Villanueva, *tr. by* Julio Marzán. InW

Temple of Bequeathed Love, The. Po Chü-i, *tr. fr. Chinese by* Burton Watson. CoBCP

Temple of Infamy, The, *sel.* Charles Harpur.
   "But hark! What hubbub now is this that comes." PoAu-1

Temple of Nature; or, The Origin of Society, The, *sels.* Erasmus Darwin.
   " 'How few,' the Muse in plaintive accents cries." *Fr.* IV. FM
   Reproduction of Life. *Fr.* II. PBBP

Temple of the Animals, The. Robert Duncan. NOBA

Temple of the Muses. Beth Bentley. EyDe

Temple of the Ocean of Awakening. Shen Chou, *tr. fr. Chinese by* Jonathan Chaves. CoBLCP

Temple of Venus, The. Soame Jenyns. NOEC

Temple of Venus, The. Spenser. *Fr.* The Faerie Queene, IV, 10. EIL

Temple stands on the edge of a valley, A. Festival in Fishing Village No. 19. Park Je-chun, *tr. by* Koh Chang-soo. ACKP

Temple to Friendship, A. Thomas Moore. BeLS

Temple tree grew in our garden in Ceylon, A. Coppersmith. Richard Murphy. IPY

Templeogue. Blanaid Salkeld. NeIP

Temples of Mount T'ai greeted the sun in the east, The. Reading the Annals of Emperor Wu of the Han Dynasy. Wu Wei-yeh, *tr. by* Jonathan Chaves. CoBLCP

Tempora Mutantur. Charles Brasch. *Fr.* Night Cries, Wakari Hospital. ATNZ

Tempora Mutantur. James Russell Lowell. HAP

Temporal. George Jonas. NOBC

Temporary Facts. William Stafford. CAPP

Tempt Me No More. C. Day Lewis. *Fr.* The Magnetic Mountain, XXIV. MoAB; MoBrPo; OBMV; PoA

Temptation. Robert Herrick. LiTB

Temptation and Fall of Man, The. Caedmon, *tr. fr. Anglo-Saxon by* C. W. Kennedy. *Fr.* Genesis. AnOE

Temptation in Harvest. Patrick Kavanagh. FaBCIP

Temptation of Saint Anthony, The. Arthur Symons. BrPo

Temptation of Sir Gawain, The. *Unknown, tr. fr. Middle English by* Brian Stone. *Fr.* Sir Gawain and the Green Knight. ACP

Temptations of Saint Anthony, The. Phyllis McGinley. OxBSP

Temptations of St. Antony by His Housekeeper. Elizabeth Smither. ATNZ; PeNZ

Temptations still nest in it like basilisks. Dead Hand. W. S. Merwin. CAPP; InPK

Tempted. Edward Rowland Sill. AA; AnAmPo

Ten bloody years with this quill lying. Valentin Iremonger. BIrV

Ten Commandments, The. Bible, *O.T. Fr.* Exodus, XX: 3-17. WBLP

Ten Commandments. Moishe Kulbak, *tr. fr. Yiddish by* Leonard Wolf. PeBMYV

Ten Commandments, The. *Unknown.* FaBoUs; OxBChV

Ten Commandments, Seven Deadly Sins, and Five Wits. *Unknown.* ChTr; FaBoEE

Ten cuckolds slain without confession. Ballad of Don Juan Tenorio and the Statue of the Comendador. Roy Campbell. PeSA

Ten dancers glide. Ballad of the Ten Casino Dancers. Cecília Meireles, *tr. by* James Merrill. ATCBP; BoWoP; OV

Ten days ago, he sold a son. Flight from Famine: A Ballad. Cheng Hsieh, *tr. by* Jan *and* Yvonne Walls. WFTU

Ten Days Leave. W. D. Snodgrass. MoAmPo; Psk; UnPo

Ten days of wind and rain, depressing darkness! T'ang Yin, *tr. fr. Chinese by* Jonathan Chaves. *Fr.* A Rainstorm Has Dragged on for Ten Days Now. CoBLCP

Ten Definitions of Poetry. Carl Sandburg. MoAmPo

Ten-Fifteen Community Poems, The, *sel.* John Knoepfle.
   "She says how/ is it when you." MAT

Ten Fingers. *Unknown.* RAR

Ten Groschen. Aaron Zeitlin, *tr. fr. Yiddish by* Robert Friend. PeBMYV

Ten heads and twenty hearts! so that this me. Perhaps. Sydney Thompson Dobell. NOBVV

Ten Heawrs a Day. Joseph Burgess. PF

Ten Kinds. Mary Mapes Dodge. RHPC

Ten Lines: Autumn. Hsiang Yang, *tr. fr. Chinese by* Dominic Cheung. IFON

Ten Lines: On Seed. Hsiang Yang, *tr. fr. Chinese by* Dominic Cheung. IFON

Ten little children. Dancing on the Shore. M. M. Hutchinson. BoTP

Ten Little Christmas Trees. Rodney Bennett. BoTP

Ten Little Dicky-Birds. A. W. I. Baldwin. BoTP

Ten Little Indian Boys. M. M. Hutchinson. BoTP

Ten Little Injuns. Septimus Winner. OBAL

Ten little nigger boys went out to dine. *Unknown.* OxNR

Ten Little Rembrandts. Theodore Weiss. NoAM

Ten longstemmed purple tulips. Mimesis. György Somlyó, *tr. by* Jascha Kessler. FOC

Ten men will dress in white, The. The Hunters of the Deer. Dale Zieroth. NOBC

Ten Miscellaneous Poems on Tung-t'ao, *sel.* Wu Chia-chi, *tr. fr. Chinese by* John E. Wills, Jr..
    At the Ch'ang Family Well. *Fr.* VIII. WFTU

Ten Miscellaneous Poems Written as a Member of the Imperial Retinue, *sel.* Yang Shih-ch'i, *tr. fr. Chinese by* Jonathan Chaves.
    "Forty *li* through Chü-yang Pass." CoBLCP

Ten months after Florimel happen'd to wed. Another True Maid. Matthew Prior. FaBoEE

Ten O'Clock News. Simon J. Ortiz. NOVW

Ten o'clock train to New York, The. Winter. Ruth Stone. BoWoP

10:X:57, 45 Years Since the Fall of the Ch'ing Dynasty. Philip Whalen. PoM
    (Forty-five Years Since the Fall of the Ch'ing Dynasty.) NeAP

Ten of the night is Talavera tolling. The Field of Talavera. Thomas Hardy. *Fr.* The Dynasts, *pt.* II, Act IV, sc. iv. CMoP

Ten Poems on Almond Blossoms, *sel.* K'ang Hai, *tr. fr. Chinese by* Jonathan Chaves.
    "When I have chanted my new poems." CoBLCP

Ten Poems on the Tuan-yang Festival, *sel.* Yang Chi, *tr. fr. Chinese by* Jonathan Chaves.
    Pitch-Ball. CoBLCP

Ten Poems Recording Things that Happened at the Ye, *sel.* Liu-K'o-chuang, *tr. fr. Chinese by* Burton Watson.
    "Beggar in patched robe stands in my doorway, A." CoBCP

Ten Scenes at the Hsiao Family Stone Ridge, *sels.* Yang Shih-ch'i, *tr. fr. Chinese by* Jonathan Chaves. CoBLCP
    Blue Mud Shoal.
    Liang Family Pool.
    Natural Stockade at Bamboo Lake, The.

Ten South Sea Island boys. Fun with Fishing. Eunice Tietjens. FaPON

Ten Tanka, *sels.* Myoe, *tr. fr. Japanese by* Burton Watson. FCEI
    "Because fog engulfs."
    "Bright bright!/ bright bright bright!"
    "Floating cloud, A."
    "How they sting!"
    "Night deepening."
    "Set now,/ and I too will go below."
    "Shining moon, A."
    "Under the pines."
    "While I, with no guide."
    "Winter moon."

10.30 AM Mass, June 16, 1985. Paul Durcan. CIP

Ten thousand bees in the backyard. Bees inside Me. Laura Chester. NPGG

Ten thousand flakes about my window blow. Walter Savage Landor. FaBoEE

Ten thousand heaps of fragrant snow fallen in the dust. Rai San'yo, *tr. fr. Chinese by* Burton Watson. *Fr.* Mount Yoshino, II. JLIC-2

Ten Thousand Miles. *Unknown.* AmFP

Ten Thousand Miles Away from Home. *Unknown.* AS

Ten Thousand Nations. József Tornai, *tr. fr. Hungarian by* Jascha Kessler. FOC

Ten thousand things wound my heart when you're be fore my eyes. In Illness, Dismissing My Singing Girl. Ssu-k'ung Shu, *tr. by* Burton Watson. CoBCP

Ten tired tortoises. Ten to One. Ivy O. Eastwick. RAR

Ten to One. Ivy O. Eastwick. RAR

Ten Tom-Toms. *Unknown.* RR

Ten Types of Hospital Visitor. Charles Causley. OxBC

Ten years/ and will you be/ a footnote. Return to Hinton. Charles Tomlinson. CMoP

Ten years ago I was a visitor at the wine jar. Tune: Song of Picking Mulberry ("Ten years ago I was a visitor at the wine jar"). Ou-yang Hsiu, *tr. by* Burton Watson. CoBCP

Ten years ago it seemed impossible. In Progress. Christina Rossetti. BoWoP; NAEL-2; WPE

Ten Years and More. Miriam Waddington. NOBC

Ten years! and to my waking eye. The Terrace at Berne. Matthew Arnold. OBTV

Ten years being enough of copra, he souvenired a. Trader's Return. Sylvia Lawson. PoAu-2

Ten years—dead and living dim and draw apart. Tune: Song of River City. Su Tung-p'o, *tr. by* Burton Watson. CoBCP

Ten years in the brothels—hard to wear out desire. Ikkyu Sojun, *tr. by* Burton Watson. FCEI

Ten years into memory, a house. Things Past. Richard Tillinghast. PPR

Ten years of honing my sword. A Self-Portrait: Inscribed upon My Own Collection of Lyrics. Chu Yi-tsun, *tr. by* Chang Yin-nan. WFTU

Ten years of my life, spent at the window or beneath the lamp. Song of Cursive Calligraphy. Hsieh Chin, *tr. by* Jonathan Chaves. CoBLCP

Ten years older in an hour. In the Ward. Robert Lowell. NAAL-2; PPR

Ten years together without yet a cloud. Firelight. E. A. Robinson. NoAM

Ten years Villon lived in a small village. Exile. Joseph Stroud. NPGG

Tenancy, The. Mary Gilmore. CBAP; PoAu-1

Tenant at Number 9. John Blight. CBAP

Tend me my birds, and bring again. Norman Gale. TrPWD

Tended by Faustina. Faustina, or Rock Roses. Elizabeth Bishop. FaBoMo

Tender and pretty are the yellow orioles. *Unknown, tr. by* Arthur Waley. BoS

Tender Arc. Diane Ward. LP

Tender Buttons, *sels.* Gertrude Stein.
    Blue Coat, A. PBWP
    Colored Hats. TTTS
    Dog, A. TTTS
    More. PBWP
    New Cup and Saucer, A. TTTS
    Nothing Elegant. PBWP
    Petticoat, A. TTTS
    Piano, A. PBWP
    Red Roses. TTTS
    Sound, A. TTTS
    Umbrella, An. TTTS
    Water Raining. PBWP

Tender each to the other, gentle. Imperialists in Retirement. Edward Lucie-Smith. PVCV

Tender fingers ran up my ankle. "Can I Tempt You to a Pond Walk?" James Schuyler. PoA

Tender-handed stroke a nettle. Written on a Window. Aaron Hill. OxBSP

Tender-heartedness. Harry Graham. *Fr.* Some Ruthless Rhymes, II. FaFP; NA; NBLV; RHPC
    (Billy.) FaBoCo

Tender mulberry leaves fill the basket-racks. Poem Written during a Dream. Ch'ien Ch'ien-i, *tr. by* Jonathan Chaves. CoBLCP

Tender, semi-/ articulate flickers. For My Mother: Genevieve Jules Creeley. Robert Creeley. PoM

Tender, Slow. *Unknown, tr. fr. Greek by* Wallace Rice. ErPo

Tender softness, infant mild. To an Infant Expiring the Second Day of Its Birth. Hetty Wright. NOEC

Tender, the young auburn woman. Spring. Paul Verlaine, *tr. by* Roland Grant *and* Paul Archer. ErPo; PeHV

Tender willow. Haiku of a Day. José Juan Tablada, *tr. by* Samuel Beckett. MexPo

Tenderfoot, The. D. J. O'Malley. AS
    (D-2 Horse Wrangler.) CowP, *diff. vers.*

Tenderly, day that I have loved, I close your eyes. Day That I Have Loved. Rupert Brooke. FPL; PoLF

Tenderness, ache on me, and lay your neck. James Dickey. *Fr.* The Zodiac. TAP

Tenderness and resolution! Reliquary. Hart Crane. PoA

Tenderness Closed like a Flower. Sirkka Turkka, *tr. fr. Finnish by* Aili Jarvenpa. SOP

Tenderness of dignity of souls, The. Peter Viereck. *Fr.* Crass Times Redeemed by Dignity of Souls. HoPM

Tending a bare hill takes no small talent. Kung Tzu-chen, *tr. fr. Chinese by* Shirleen S. Wong. *Fr.* Miscellaneous Poems of the Year *Chi-hai*, CCII. WFTU

Tending the Garden. Eric Pankey. MOWH

Tending the hallowed tomb. Princess Nukada. *Fr.* Manyo Shu. Ma

Tendril in the Mesh, *sel.* William Everson.
    "Daughter of earth and child of the wave be appeased." *Fr.* IV. NoAM

Tenebrae. Paul Celan, *tr. fr. German.* VWA, *tr. by* Joachim Neugroschel

Tenebrae. Austin Clarke. AnIL; BIrV; CIP; IPY; NeIP; NOIV

Tenebrae. Denise Levertov. NoP

Tenebris. Angelina Weld Grimké. CDC; PoBA; PoNe

Tenebris Interlucentem. James Elroy Flecker. MoBrPo

Tennessee. Virginia Fraser Boyle. PAH

Tennessee. Francis Brooks. *Fr.* Intaglios. AA

Tennessee. *Unknown.* AmFP

Tennis. Margaret Avison. MoP

Tennis, The. E. B. White. ASP

Tennis Court Oath, The. John Ashbery. NoAM; TAP

Tennis in San Juan. Reuel Denney. SD

Tennis in the City. F. R. Higgins. ASP

Tennyson. Thomas Bailey Aldrich. AA

Tennyson. Alan Ansen. CoAP

Tennyson. Florence Earle Coates. AA

Tennyson. Henry van Dyke. AA

Tennysonian Reflections at Barnes Bridge. Gavin Ewart. PoPo

Tennyson's Poems. Josephine D. Henderson Heard. CBWP-4

Tenor of your madness, The. Up Early. Kit Robinson. UL

Tension in the tendons of her wing, The. Soldier's Dove. James Forsyth. WaP

Tenson. Carenza *and* Iselda, *tr. fr. Provençal by* Bridget Connelly *and* Doris Earnshaw. WPOW

Tent-lights glimmer on the land, The. At Port Royal. Whittier. PAH

Tent stitch is repeated in the blue and red, The. Oh, Nothing. John Ashbery. NAAL-2

Tent that is pitched at the base, A. War. Edgar Wallace. OBWP

Tentacled for food. In the Sea of Tears. Naomi Replansky. BrRo

Tenth Eclogue, The. Michael Drayton. *Fr.* The Shepherd's Garland. JCP

Tenth Nimphall, The. Michael Drayton. *Fr.* Muses' Elysium [*or* Elizium]. JCP

Tenth Reunion. Edward Steese. GoYe

Tenth Symphony. John Ashbery. NOBA

Tenth Telegram ("I wish I had a boat"). Abd al-Aziz al-Maqalih, *tr. fr. Arabic by* Lena Jayyusi *and* Christopher Middleton. *Fr.* Telegrams of Tenderness for Sanaa. MAP

Tenuous and Precarious. Stevie Smith. FaBoNo; OxBTC

Tenzone. Ezra Pound. *Fr.* Contemporania. PoA

Tepehua Thought-Songs, *sels. Unknown, tr. fr. Tepehua Indian by* Charles Boilès. STP

  "Knowing that the music knows." *Fr.* I.

  "Thought was/ & though it had been." *Fr.* II.

  "When they play like that where everyone is." *Fr.* III.

Tequila. Elizabeth Spires. MAYP

Terce. James McMichael. PoA

Tercets. Louis Aragon, *tr. fr. French by* Michael Benedikt. POS

Terence, if I could return. To Myself, after Forty Years. T. H. White. NYBP

Terence McDiddler. *Unknown.* OxNR

Terence, This Is Stupid Stuff. A. E. Housman. *Fr.* A Shropshire Lad, LXII. CMoP; HeIP; InPK; LiTB; LiTM; MoP; NAEL-2; NIP; NoAM; NoAM; NoP; PrIm

  (Epilogue: "Terence, this is stupid stuff.") MoAB; MoBrPo; TrGrPo

Terenure. Blanaid Salkeld. NeIP

Teresa. Richard Wilbur. NoAM

Teresa of Avila. Elizabeth Jennings. NePoEA-2; TOF

Teresa was God's familiar. She often spoke. Conversation in Avila. Phyllis McGinley. EaLo

Teresa's Red Adidas. Paul B. Janeczko. TDD

Teresian Contemplative, The. Robert Hugh Benson. ACP

Tergvinder's Stone. W. S. Merwin. CAPP

Term, The. William Carlos Williams. InvP; LiTA

Term of Death, The. Sarah Morgan Bryan Piatt. AA

Terminal Vision. Diana O Hehir. NPGG

Terminations. A. R. Ammons. AnAn

Terminus. Emerson. AA; AmPP; AWP; FPL; NOBA; OxBA; PoEL-4; PoLF; TAP

Termite, The. Ogden Nash. CenHV; NBLV; OBCA

Termites. Eric Chock. BrSi

Terms. Lorrie Goldensohn. NAmP

Terms of all kinds mellow with time, growing. Their Speech, Compared with Wisdom and Poetry. Robert Pinsky. *Fr.* Essay on Psychiatrists, XIV. NoAM; PoA

Terms of Appointment. Arthur Rex Dugard Fairburn. PeNZ

Terms of Surrender. Michael Bachstein. TSM

Ternarie of Littles, upon a Pipkin of Jellie [*or* Jelly] Sent to a Lady, A. Robert Herrick. BoTP, *sel.*, FaBoCh; FaBoUs; GoJo; PoEL-3

Ternissa! You Are Fled. Walter Savage Landor. *Fr.* The Hellenics. PoEL-4

  (On Ternissa's Death.) ELP

  (Ternissa.) NOBE; OBNC

Terpsichore looks kindly on me. Korinna, *tr. by* John Dillon. PBWP

Terra Cotta. K. Curtis Lyle. CNA

Terra cotta girl, The. In the Counselor's Waiting Room. Bettie M. Sellers. InPK

Terra-cotta house in the moonlight, The. Birth of a Country. Agnes Gergely, *tr. by* Emery George. VWA

Terra Incognita. Sherod Santos. AnAn

Terrace, The. Vittorio Sereni, *tr. fr. Italian by* Henry Taylor. PFI

Terrace at Berne, The. Matthew Arnold. OBTV

Terrace in the Snow, The. Su Tung-p'o, *tr. fr. Chinese by* Kenneth Rexroth. NaP

Terrace is empty, which shows how flat it is, The. Heron Weather. Douglas Crase. NoP

Terracotta Flower Pot, The. Jenny Morris. SoTCo

Terrapin, The. Elizabeth Smither. PeNZ

Terrapin War. *Unknown.* PAH

Terre, A. Wilfred Owen. LiTM; MMA; OxBTC; WaP

Terre Promise. Ernest Dowson. NOBVV

Terrestrial Cuckoo, A. Frank O'Hara. SOTW

Terrestrial Magnetism. Alice Fulton. NAmP

Terribilis Est Locus Iste. John Engels. AnAn

Terrible/ a horse at night. Lawrence Ferlinghetti. HoPM

Terrible are the ocean billows. *Unknown. Fr.* Manyo Shu. Ma

Terrible Beauty. Kingsley Amis. *See* Evans Country, The: Aldport (Mystery Tour).

Terrible childbed hast thou had, my dear, A. Shakespeare. *Fr.* Pericles, III, i. EBEV

Terrible Door, The. Harold Monro. BoLoP; EnLoPo; FaBoTw

Terrible in his power was King Wu. *Unknown, tr. by* Arthur Waley. BoS

Terrible Infant, A. Frederick Locker-Lampson. FiBHP

Terrible is my plight this night. Wolves for Company. *Unknown.* BIrV

Terrible is the price. The Price. John Davidson. EBVV

Terrible lodgings. In the frightful lodgings. Lodgers. Julian Tuwim, *tr. by* Isaac Komem. VWA

Terrible Sonnets. Gerard Manley Hopkins. *See* Carrion Comfort; I wake and feel the fell of dark; No worst, there is none.

Terrible Sons, The. Eleazar Ben Kalir, *tr. fr. Hebrew by* Israel Zangwill. TrJP

Terrible sons of the mighty race, The. The Terrible Sons. Eleazar Ben Kalir, *tr. by* Israel Zangwill. TrJP

Terrible Thought, A. Eliezer Steinbarg, *tr. fr. Yiddish by* Joseph Leftwich. TrJP

Terribly for mystery or glory my dawns have arisen. Dawns I Have Seen. Ivor Gurney. FaBoPP

Terrifying are the attent sleek thrushes on the lawn. Thrushes. Ted Hughes. FaBoMo; GoYe; NePoEA-2

Territory. Jean Chapman. CRH

Terror. Kitahara Hakushu, *tr. fr. Japanese by* Hiroaki Sato. FCEI

Terror. Denise Levertov. PoE

Terror. Thomas O'Brien. NeIP

Terror. Robert Penn Warren. PoA; WaP

Terror. "Yehoash," *tr. fr. Yiddish by* Isidore Goldstick. TrJP

Terror and dream. The Rest Is Grace. János Pilinszky, *tr. by* William Jay Smith. MHuP

Terror Conduction. Philip Lamantia. NeAP

Terror does not belong to open day. Counterpoint. Owen Dodson. PoNe

Terror sculpted. Salt Statues. Tsfrirah Gar, *tr. by* Bernhard Frank. MHeP

Terror strikes lightly your stillness. Spider. Thomas Cole. PoA

Terror swoops down on his heart like a vulture. Ezekiel. A. N. Stencl, *tr. by* Joseph Leftwich. VWA

Terrorist Smiles, The. Anselm Hollo. UL

Terrorless, I awake. To a Wasp Caught in the Storm Sash at the Advent of the Winter Solstice. Peter Cooley. MAYP

Terry. Albert Rowe. CRH

Terry is sitting in the kafeneion writing letters to all his friends. Human Relations. Emmett Jarrett. NeAC

Terse Elegy for J.V. Cunningham. X. J. Kennedy. DiPo

Tess's Lament. Thomas Hardy. FaBoTw; TEP

Test, The. Emerson. AA; OBAL

Test, The. Michael Guttenbrunner, *tr. fr. German by* Beth Bjorklund. CoAuP

Test of Manhood, The, *sel.* George Meredith.

  "In fellowship Religion has its founts." WGRP

Test of Men, The. Bible, Apocrypha. *Fr.* Ecclesiasticus, XXXVI: 5-8. TrJP

Testament. Sebastian Salazar Bondy, *tr. fr. Spanish by* David Tipton. Per

Testament. Lucille Clifton. GeTw

Testament. Mikhail Yurevich Lermontov, *tr. fr. Russian by* Alan Myers. AAA

Testament. Nizar Qabbani, *tr. fr. Arabic by* Diana Der Hovanessian *and* Lena Jayyusi. MAP

Testament, A. *Unknown.* OBSC

Testament. Bill Zavatsky. UL

Testament of Beauty, The, *sels.* Robert Bridges.
　Ethick. *Fr.* IV. OxBTC
　"Sky's unresting cloudland, that with varying play, The." *Fr.* I.
　　EBEV

Testament of Cresseid, The. Robert Henryson. GoTS; OxBLMV; OxBS
　Sels.
　Assembly of the Gods, The. PoEL-1
　Cresseid's Complaint against Fortune. MeEL
　Cressida's Leprosy. SeCePo
　"I mend the fyre and beikit me about." EBEV; PoE

Testament of John Davidson, The, *sel.* John Davidson.
　Last Journey, The. GoTS
　"Oh, long before the bere was steeped for malt." PoSH

Testament of Mr. Andro Kennedy, The. William Dunbar. OxBS

Testament of Perpetual Change, The. William Carlos Williams. GOA

Testaments, *sels.* James Weigel, Jr. TSM
　"Egg grew human, The." *Fr.* I.
　"I should quit this craft." *Fr.* XXVI.
　"Mouth should launch words gracefully, A." *Fr.* XXX.
　"Out of my sleeves ten bones protrude." *Fr.* XXVIII.
　"Translated once." *Fr.* V.

Testimonies. Yehuda Amichai, *tr. fr. Hebrew by* Warren Bargad *and* Stanley F.Chyet. IP

Testimony, A. George Ella Lyon. GOYP

Testimony. Dan Pagis, *tr. fr. Hebrew by* Warren Bargad *and* Stanley F. Chyet. IP

Testimony. Carolyn M. Rodgers. BPo

Testimony in trials that never got heard. A Woman Is Talking to Death. Judy Grahn. GLP

Testing-Tree, The. Stanley Kunitz. FYAP; MAT; UnPo

Testubicles spill blood across the page. Crossedroads. Martin Staples Shockley. FF

Tête-à-Tête. Edwin Honig. NoAM

Tetélestai. Conrad Aiken. LiTA; LiTM; MoAB; MoAmPo; PrIm

Tethy's Festival, *sel.* Samuel Daniel.
　Are They Shadows [That We See]? CH; EiL; InvP; NoP
　　(Shadows). NOBE; OBSC
　　(Song: "Are they shadowes that we see?") PoEL-2

Tewkesbury Road. John Masefield. BoTP

Texas. Amy Lowell. AmFN

Texas. Whittier. PAH

Texas Cowboy, The. *Unknown.* AmFP

Texas Cowboy [lay down] on a barroom floor, A. The Hell-bound Train. *Unknown.* BeLS; BLPA

Texas Ranger, The. Margie B. Boswell. AiP

Text. Audrey Wurdemann. FYAP

Text. Aaron Zeitlin, *tr. fr. Yiddish by* Ruth Whitman. VWA

Text for These Distracted Times, A. Rodney Hall. CBAP

Th' have left thee naked, Lord, O that they had. On Our Crucified Lord, Naked and Bloody. Richard Crashaw. HoPM; NAEL-1; OAEL-1; SeCV-1; TrCP
　(Upon the Body of Our Blessed Lord Naked and Bloody.) ACP; InvP; OBS; SeCP

Th' other way Satan went down. Milton. *Fr.* Paradise Lost, *bk.* X, *ll.* 414–584. NAEL-1

Th Wundrfulness uv th Mountees Our Secret Police. Bill Bissett. NOBC

Thaba Bosio. S. D. R. Sutu, *tr. fr. Sotho by* Dan Kunene *and* Jack Cope. PeSA

Thack church and a wooden steeple, A. Legsby, Lincolnshire. *Unknown.* GBP

Thaddeus Stevens. Phoebe Cary. PAH

Thai passit in thare pilgramage. *Unknown. Fr.* Golagros and Gawane. OxBS

Thailand Railway, *sels.* Randolph Stow. CBAP
　Jungle, The.
　Sleepers, The.

Thair is a knichte rydis through the wood. The Vampyre. James Clerk Maxwell. VVA

Thair is nocht ane Winche. *Unknown.* OxBS

Thaïs. Newman Levy. FiBHP

Thalaba and the Banquet. Robert Southey. *Fr.* Thalaba the Destroyer. SeCePo

Thalaba and the Magic Thread. Robert Southey. SeCePo

Thalaba the Destroyer, *sels.* Robert Southey. SeCePo
　"Night of darkness and of storms!, A." VVA
　Thalaba and the Banquet. SeCePo

Thalamos. Peter Kane Dufault. ErPo

Thalassa. Valery Larbaud, *tr. fr. French by* William Jay Smith. CT

Thalassa. Louis MacNeice. BIrV; FaBoMo; FaBoRV; NOBE

Thalatta! Thalatta! Joseph Brownlee Brown. AA

Thalero. Angelos Sikelianos, *tr. fr. Greek by* Edmund Keeley *and* Philip Sherrard. VMG

Thalia. Thomas Bailey Aldrich. AA

Thalia, you will remember that recently I made. Mlle de– – –, *tr. fr. French by* Dorothy Backer. *Fr.* The Fair Sex Avenged by the Fair Sex, or a New Satire on Husbands. DMF

Thames, The. M. M. Hutchinson. BoTP

Thames from Cooper's Hill, The. Sir John Denham. *See* Cooper's Hill: My eye descending from the Hill, surveys.

Thames Head Wassailers' Song. *Unknown.* OBET

Thames nocturne of blue and gold, The. Impression du Matin. Oscar Wilde. BrPo; EBVV; MoBrPo; NAEL-2; NoAM

Thamuris Marching. Robert Browning. OAEL-2

Than (By Yon Sunset's Wintry Glow). E. E. Cummings. VGW

Than in your mynde Dydo ye shall espy. The Letter of Dydo to Eneas. Chaucer. OxBLMV

Than mind a child/ That yelps like this/ I'd all day work. *Unknown, tr. by* Geoffrey Bownas *and* Anthony Thwaite. Mes; PeBJV

Than this great universe no less. Rowland's Rhyme. Michael Drayton. *Fr.* The Shepherd's Garland, Eclogue II (1606 ed.). OBSC

Thanaton Melein. Alfred Gong, *tr. fr. German by* Beth Bjorklund. CoAuP

Thanatopsis. Bryant. AA; AmPP; AnAmPo; AWP; BLPL; BoNaP; DL; FaBoBe; FaFP; LiTA; NAAL-1; NOBA; OBEV; OHFP; OxBA; PWR; TAP; TrGrPo; WBLP; WGRP

Thank God. Joseph Rolnik, *tr. fr. Yiddish by* Joseph Leftwich. TrJP

Thank God, bless God, all ye who suffer not. Tears. Elizabeth Barrett Browning. WPE

Thank God for Little Children. Frances Ellen Watkins Harper. PWR

Thank God for sleep! The Sacrament of Sleep. John Oxenham. PoLF

Thank God for sleep in the long quiet night. Morning Thanksgiving. John Drinkwater. BoTP

Thank God for the Country! Irene Arnold. WBLP

Thank God my brain is not inclined to cut. The Menagerie. William Vaughn Moody. AnAmPo

Thank God our liberating lance. The Road to France. Daniel Henderson. PAH

Thank God, thank God, we do believe. Christina Rossetti. PChr

Thank God that God shall judge my soul, not man. The Eternal Justice. Anne Reeve Aldrich. AA

Thank God they're all gone. Nazis. Ira Sadoff. BLA

Thank Goodness, the moving is over. "When the World Was in Building." Ford Madox Ford. CTC

Thank Heaven! the crisis. For Annie. Poe. AmPP; AnAmPo; BLPL; LiTA; NOBA; OBEV; OxBA

Thank heav'n! I'm safely landed frae Ostend. To the Memory of Gavin Wilson (Boot, Leg and Arm Maker). George Galloway. NOEC

Thank Thee, O Giver of life, O God! Thanksgiving. Angela Morgan. TrPWD

Thank You. Geoffrey Grigson. PoPo

Thank You. Kenneth Koch. NeAP; PoM

Thank You/ for all my hands can hold. Thanksgiving. Ivy O. Eastwick. RHPC

Thank You: A Poem in Seventeen Parts. *Unknown, tr. fr. Seneca Indian by* Richard Johnny John and Jerome Rothenberg. STP

Thank You, America. Joanna Salamon, *tr. fr. Polish by* Christopher Wertz. WCI

Thank You for Friends, A. Rodney Bennett. BoTP

Thank you for leaving the bar of soap. Note to the Previous Tenants. John Updike. GOYP

Thank You for the Valentine. Diane Wakoski. HoPM

Thank You for Your Letter. Ch'ao Li-houa, *tr. fr. Chinese by* Kenneth Rexroth. ILY

Thank you for your recent letter. Dear Mother. Emmett Jarrett. NeAC

Thank you, my dear. Sappho, *tr. by* Mary Barnard. UnAS

Thank you, pretty cow, that made. The Cow. Ann Taylor. OxBChV
　(Thank You, Pretty Cow.)

Thank your engines. Swinburne. *Fr.* The Unhappy Revenge. FL

Thankful Acknowledgment of God's Providence, A. John Cotton. SCAP

Thankful Country Lass, The; or, The Jolly Batchelor Kindly Entertained. *Unknown.* CoMu

Thankfulness. Adelaide Anne Procter. TrPWD

Thanking Doctor Jen. Li K'ai-hsien, *tr. fr. Chinese by* Jonathan Chaves. CoBLCP

Thanking My Mother for Piano Lessons. Diane Wakoski. NoAM

Thanking Prince Chen-chi, *sel.* Hsü Chung-hsing, *tr. fr. Chinese by* Jonathan Chaves.
　"This metal is engraved with Shang-style markings." CoBLCP

Thankless for favours from on high. On a Similar Occasion for the Year 1792. William Cowper. NOCV

Thanks. Nina Cassian, *tr. fr. Rumanian* by Laura Schiff. AIW
Thanks and a Plea to Mary. *Unknown.* MeEL
Thanks, fair Urania; to your scorn. The Indifference. Sir Charles Sedley. SeCV-2
Thanks for Everything. Helen Isabella Tupper. *See* For all that God in mercy sends.
Thanks from Earth to Heaven, *sel.* John Hall Wheelock.
  "Holy Poet, I have heard." TrPWD
Thanks, I will. Phono, at the Boar's Head. Henri Coulette. *Fr.* The War of the Secret Agents, IX. NePoEA-2
Thanks Just the Same. *Unknown.* PoLF
Thanks to Industrial Essex. Donald Davie. OxBTC
Thanks to Saint Matthew, who had been. Comrade Jesus. Sarah Norcliffe Cleghorn. WGRP
Thanks to Spring. Mary Anderson. BoTP
Thanks to the latest technology. Blimps and Nightingales. Richard Moore. SoTCo
Thanksgibin' day am now at han.' De Day befo' Thanksgibin.' Maggie Pogue Johnson. CBWP-4
Thanksgiving. Susie Montgomery Best. TrPWD
Thanksgiving. Florence Earle Coates. TrPWD
Thanksgiving. Ivy O. Eastwick. RHPC
Thanksgiving. Robert Herrick. LiTB; OFD
Thanksgiving, A, *sel.* William Dean Howells. TrPWD
  "Lord, for the erring thought." WGRP
Thanksgiving. Kenneth Koch. VGW
Thanksgiving, A, *sel.* Lucy Larcom. OHIP
  "For the rosebud's break of beauty." TrPWD
Thanksgiving. David Abenatar Melo, *tr. fr. Spanish* by Henry Hart Milman. TrJP
Thanksgiving. Lizelia Augusta Jenkins Moorer. CBWP-3
Thanksgiving. Angela Morgan. TrPWD
Thanksgiving. John N. Morris. OFD
Thanksgiving, A. Cardinal Newman. TrPWD
Thanksgiving. Robert Nichols. MMA
Thanksgiving. John Oxenham. BLRP; WBLP
Thanksgiving. Margaret Elizabeth Munson Sangster. BLRP
Thanksgiving. N. M. Yazykov, *tr. fr. Russian* by Alan Myers. AAA
Thanksgiving. "Yehoash," *tr. fr. Yiddish* by Isidore Goldstick. TrJP
Thanksgiving after Communion. *Unknown, tr. fr. Gaelic* by Douglas Hyde. WTO
Thanksgiving at Snake Butte. James Welch. AiP; STE
Thanksgiving Day. John Kendrick Bangs. TrPWD
Thanksgiving Day. Robert Bridges. OHIP
Thanksgiving Day. Lydia Maria Child. FaPON; NTCP; OHIP; RHPC
  (New-England Boy's Song about Thanksgiving Day, The.) OBCA
Thanksgiving Day. Jannick Storm, *tr. fr. Danish* by the author. WCI
Thanksgiving Day. Annette Wynne. OHIP
Thanksgiving Day I like to see. Thanksgiving Magic. Rowena Bastin Bennett. RHPC
Thanksgiving Dinner during Pelting Season. Mary Moran. GOS
Thanksgiving for a former, doth invite. Thanksgiving. Robert Herrick. LiTB; OFD
Thanksgiving for a Habitat, *sel.* W. H. Auden. NYBP
  "From gallery-grave and the hunt of a wren-king." EyDe
Thanksgiving for America, The. Hezekiah Butterworth. PAH
Thanksgiving for the Body. Thomas Traherne. ImOP
Thanksgiving, Growing Older. William Doreski. KS
Thanksgiving Hymn. *Unknown.* PAH
Thanksgiving in Boston Harbor, The. Hezekiah Butterworth. AA; OHIP; PAH
Thanksgiving Magic. Rowena Bastin Bennett. RHPC
Thanksgiving (1956). E. E. Cummings. FaBoPW
Thanksgiving to God for His House, A. Robert Herrick. BLPL; ChTr; FaBoBe; HAP; OBS; OFD; OHIP; PoRA; SeCP; SeCV-1; TrCP; TrPWD; ViBoPo; WGRP
Thanksgiving to the gods! The Seeker in the Marshes. Daniel Lewis Dawson. AA
Thanksgivings for the Beauty of His Providence. Thomas Traherne. FaBoCh
Thar's More in the Man than Thar Is in the Land. Sidney Lanier. NOBA
Thass a funny title, Mr. Bones. April Fool's Day, or St. Mary Egypt. John Berryman. *Fr.* Dream Songs. NaP
Thassyryans king, in peas with fowle desyre. Earl of Surrey. *See* Assyrian King in peace, with foul desire, The.
That/ that / whose/ track is it like? *Unknown, tr. fr. Chippewa Indian* by Frances Densmore. *Fr.* Poems for the Game of Silence. STP
That Act. Tanikawa Shuntaro, *tr. fr. Japanese* by Hiroaki Sato. FCEI
That afternoon where the yellow light. Farewell, My Latin Master. Stephen Plaice. NPo

That all things should be mine. Amendment. Thomas Traherne. SeCV-2
That August afternoon the family. State Funeral. Thomas McCarthy. CIP
That August the birds kept away from the village, afraid. For the Last Time, Fire. Dennis Scott. PBCV; UAS
That autumn day suddenly broken into. Ian Wedde. *Fr.* Losing the Straight Way, II. ATNZ
That balmy eve, within a trellised bower. The Marriage of Pocahontas. Mary Morison Webster. PAH
That bird that bears our branchy future flies. Anzac Ceremony. Kendrick Smithyman. ATNZ
That blue/ and unwithdrawing. Até. Claude Royet-Journoud, *tr. by* Keith Waldrop. RHTwFP
That boat has killed three people. Building her. Unlucky Boat. George Mackay Brown. NePoEA-2
That bony potbellied arrow, wing-pumping along. The Cormorant in His Element. Amy Clampitt. InPK
That boy was hungry. His mother gave him Dog Salmon. Salmon Boy. David Wagoner. AnAn
That bridge from the city, that was Waimakariri. Mary Ursula Bethell. *Fr.* By the River Ashley, V. PeNZ
That Bright Chimeric Beast. Countee Cullen. AmNP
That Broad and Spreading Sweet Pear. *Unknown, tr. fr. Chinese* by Burton Watson. CoBCP
That broken star. David McCord. *Fr.* A Christmas Package. PChr
That bull-necked blotch-faced farmer from Drumlore. Ghosts' Stories. Alastair Reid. NePoEA-2
That calm above those trees in the gray spaces. A Colloquy of Silences. Michael Heffernan. SM
That Cat. Ben King. AnAmPo; CRH; FiBHP
That child I was. Beginning Speech. "Adunis," *tr. by* Lena Jayyusi *and* John Heath-Stubbs. MAP
That child will never lie in me, and you. The Unknown Child. Elizabeth Jennings. PBWP
That Chinese restaurant was a joke. The Will to Change. Adrienne Rich. NMM
That circle/ when full/ is blinding. A Spot on the Sun. Tsfrirah Gar, *tr. by* Bernhard Frank. MHeP
That civilisation may not sink. Long-legged Fly. W. B. Yeats. CMoP; FaBoMo; FaBoTw; InPS; LiTM; MoP; NAEL-2; NoAM; NOBE; NOP; NoP; OPOP; PoE; TEP
That cock-pheasant in its flight. *Unknown, tr. by* Arthur Waley. BoS
That comes to pieces in your hand. Shale. Anne Stevenson. BLA
That conversation we were always on the edge. Adrienne Rich. *Fr.* Twenty-one Love Poems, XX. BoWoP; GLP; NoAM
"That cop was powerful mean." The Idiot. Dudley Randall. BPo
That corner of the earth. Aware Aware. Tram Combs. TwCP
That crackle is well worth hearing. Mr. T. S. Eliot Cooking Pasta. József Tornai, *tr. by* Richard Wilbur. GrPl; MHuP
That crafty cat, a buff-black Siamese. Double Dutch. Walter de la Mare. CRH
That "Craning of the Neck." Isabella Gardner. WPE
That crazed girl improvising her music. The Crazed Girl. W. B. Yeats. InPS; Son
That creepy feeling you have. Ishikawa Takuboku, *tr. fr. Japanese* by Hiroaki Sato. *Fr.* Forty-seven Tanka in Three Lines. FCEI
That creepycrawly traversing the stone. Close-ups of Summer. Norman MacCaig. OxBC
That cuckoo who sang. *Unknown, tr. fr. Japanese* by Burton Watson. *Fr.* Kokin Shu. FCEI
That Cypress Boat Is Drifting. *Unknown, tr. fr. Chinese* by Burton Watson. CoBCP
That dandy black-and-white gentleman doodling notes. Magpie and Pines. Louis Johnson. ATNZ; PeNZ
That dark brown rabbit, lightness in his ears. John Berryman. *Fr.* Dream Songs. TwCP
That Dark Other Mountain. Robert Francis. CRP; SD
That Day. David Kherdian. SaC
That Day. John Leax. TrCP
That Day. Anne Sexton. BoWoP
That day. To a Detainee. Musaemura Bonus Zimunya. WMBCH
That Day. Mark Van Doren. WaP
That day all the slaves were freed. Brazilian Fazenda. Patricia K. Page. FaBoWP
That day everything went wrong. Poetry Defined. John Holmes. GrPl
That day in the Interpreter's house, in one of his Significant Rooms. Christiana. Peter Redgrove. OxBC
That day, in the slipping of torsos and straining flanks. Lola Ridge. WPE

That Day Is Not So Far, My Love. Faiz Ahmad Faiz, *tr. fr. Urdu by* Mahmood Jamal. PBMUP

That day she threw the goose over the roof. Grandma's Man. James Welch. NoAM

That day, so innocent appeared. Picnic Remembered. Robert Penn Warren. NAAL-2

That day, someone died down the beach. Hard Strain in a Delicate Place. Janet Sylvester. MAYP

That day the/ words. That Day. John Leax. TrCP

That day the eggshell of appearance split. Transfigured Bird. James Merrill. MoAB

That day the huge water drowned all voices until. River Sound Remembered. W. S. Merwin. SM

That day the sails of the ship were torn. Lament for Tadhg Cronin's Children. Michael Hartnett. RB

That day the sunlight lay on the farms. On Heaven. Ford Madox Ford. CTC

That day when oats were reaped, and wheat was ripe. When Oats Were Reaped. Thomas Hardy. OxBTC

That death might not be casual. Burns Singer. FaBoTw

That Death should thus from hence our Butler catch. In Obitum Promi. Henry Parrot. FaBoCo

That decade with Rimbaud I don't regret. Rimbaud Fire Letter to Jim Applewhite. Fred Chappell. SM

That Delightful Time. Mark Akenside. *Fr.* The Pleasures of Imagination. SeCePo

That desire is quite over. Thinking of Love. Elizabeth Jennings. GOYP

That dignified old woman. Mothers. Maturaipputan Ilanakanar, *tr. by* A. K. Ramanujan. PLW

That Distant Bliss. Henry King. *See* "Tell me[e] no more how fair[e] she[e] is."

That dog with daisies for eyes. The Dog of Art. Denise Levertov. MoP; NoAm

That dolphin-torn, that gong-tormented face. The Death of Yeats. George Barker. LiTB

That duck, bobbing up. Joso, *tr. by* Harry Behn. WSC

That Each Thing Is Hurt of Itself. *Unknown.* EIL

That eternal spring is hidden. Song of the Soul that Rejoices in Knowing God through Faith. Saint John of the Cross, *tr. by* K. Kavanagh *and* O. Rodrigues. TOF

That Eureka of Archimedes out of his bath. Voluptuaries and Others. Margaret Avison. MoCV

That evening/ faces faded around us. In the Flux. Fadwa Tuqan, *tr. by* Patricia Alanah Byrne, Salma Khadra Jayyusi, *and* Charles Doria. MAP

That evening all in fond discourse was spent. The Sad Lover. George Crabbe. *Fr.* Tales of the Hall. OBNC

That Ever I Saw. *Unknown.* TrGrPo

That every county in this developed state. Manifest Destiny. Pearse Hutchinson. CIP

That every night my father. My Father. Tuvia Rübner, *tr. by* Bernhard Frank. MHeP

That Everything Moves Its Bowels. David R. Slavitt. BXAP

That Fabulous Nebula. Alastair Fowler. NPo

That face so faintly colored. Violets in Saint Mark's Square. Diego Valeri, *tr. by* I. L. Salomon. PFI

That face which no man ever saw. Sargent's Portrait of Edwin Booth at "The Players." Thomas Bailey Aldrich. AA

That famous old pederast, Wilde. *Unknown.* PeHV

That final newsreel of the war. A Welcoming Party. John Montague. FaBCIP; IPY

That first September day was blue and warm. The Artist on Penmaenmawr. Charles Tennyson Turner. FaBoPP; OBNC

That flattering glass whose smooth face wears. A Looking-Glass. Thomas Carew. CaPo

That flower unseen, that gem of purest ray. In a Churchyard. Richard Wilbur. HeIP

That for seven lustres [*or* lusters] I did never come. To the Reverend Shade of His Religious Father. Robert Herrick. CaPo; JCP; OBS; SeCV-1

That force is lost. Snake Eyes. Imamu Amiri Baraka. VGW

That fording place in the Saho. Yakamochi. *Fr.* Manyo Shu. FCEI

That forest/ has too much verdigris poured on it. The Landscape Inspector. Miyazawa Kenji, *tr. by* Hiroaki Sato. FCEI

That frantic error I adore. The Apostasy of One and But One Lady. Richard Lovelace. CaPo

That Gentle Man from Boston Town. Joaquin Miller. AnAmPo

That girl/ lovely as the little oaks. *Unknown.* *Fr.* Manyo Shu. FCEI

That girl from the sun is bathing in the creek. The Dosser in Springtime. Douglas Stewart. ErPo

That Glove. Mary E. Tucker. CBWP-1

That God of ours, the Great Geometer. Grace to Be Said at the Supermarket. Howard Nemerov. SoSe

That Harp You Play So Well. Marianne Moore. MoAB; MoAmPo; PoA

That haughty tyranny of thine. Luís de León, *tr. by* Thomas Walsh. TrJP

That He Findeth Others as Fair, but Not So Faithful as His Friend. George Turberville. EIL

That he to his unmeasur'd mightie acts. Praise of Homer. George Chapman. OBS

That he was born it cannot be denied. On a Certain Alderman. John Cunningham, *after the Greek of* Simonides. FaBoEE

That he was ugly we have no doubt. Socrates' Death. Michael Jackson. PeNZ

That heartless chase. Wordsworth. *Fr.* The Prelude [*or,* Growth of a Poet's Mind]: Summer Vacation. TOF

That Heaven. Park Je-chun, *tr. fr. Korean by* Koh Chang-soo. ACKP

That her serene influence should spread. Two Loves. Richard Eberhart. CMoP

That Hill. Blanche Taylor Dickinson. CDC

That hill is too high. *Unknown, tr. by* Geoffrey Bownas *and* Anthony Thwaite. PeBJV

That hill where. Tsurayuki, *tr. fr. Japanese by* Burton Watson. *Fr.* Kokin Shu. FCEI

That history is an event. Taku Skanskan. Paula Gunn Allen. HATNAP

That hobnailed goblin, the bobtailed Hob. Country Dance. Edith Sitwell. MoP; NoAM

That Holy Thing. George Macdonald. *Fr.* Paul Faber, Surgeon. OBEV; TrPWD; WGRP

That hopes are never fulfilled. Portrait of an Old Man. Erika Mitterer, *tr. by* Beth Bjorklund. CoAuP

That horse whose rider fears to jump will fall. Masters. Kingsley Amis. NePoEA

That hour-glass, which there ye see. The Hour-Glass. Robert Herrick. CaPo

That house, a stone's throw from the shell-strewn shore. Boat-Haven, Co. Mayo. Geoffrey Taylor. NeIP

That houses forme within was rude and strong. The House of Richesse. Spenser. *Fr.* The Faerie Queene, II, 7. CH

That hump of a man bunching chrysanthemums. Old Florist. Theodore Roethke. OxBSP; PCP; SaC

That Hypocrite. *Unknown.* BPo

That I am living. Insects near a Hut in the Fields. Masayori, *tr. by* Steven D. Carter. WFTW

That I be a writer? Absolutely not! Josefa Masanés, *tr. fr. Spanish by* Robert L. Smith *and* Judith Candullo. DMH

That I have felt the rushing wind of Thee. The Poet's Prayer. Stephen Philipps. WGRP

That I have often been in love, deep love. "Peter Pindar." NOEC

That I went to warm my self in Lady Betty's Chamber. To Their Excellencies the Lords Justices of Ireland, the Humble Petition of Frances Harris, Who Must Starve, and Die a Maid if It Miscarries. Swift. NOEC; Par; PoEL-3

That I who thought myself a strong man. Tabito. *Fr.* Manyo Shu. Ma

That ill-faur'd lump of mossy stane. The Mossy Stane. Robert Nicoll. PF

That I'm Ill Married. *Unknown, tr. fr. Spanish by* William M. Davis. DMH

That insect, without antennae, over its. The Crane. Charles Tomlinson. MoBrPo

That Is All I Heard. "Yehoash," *tr. fr. Yiddish by* Isidore Goldstick. TrJP

That is certainly a sensitive man. Stroke Units. Frederike Frei, *tr. by* Susan L. Cocalis. DMG

That is her lover lying there. Illumination. Jeffrey Wainwright. DiPo

That is no country for old men. The young. Sailing to Byzantium. W. B. Yeats. AnIL; CMoP; FaFP; FF; FPL; GTBS-P; HAP; HeIP; HoPM; InPK; InPS; InvP; LiTB; LiTM; MoAB; MoBrPo; MoP; NAEL-2; NAWM-2; NIP; NoAM; NOBE; NoP; OAEL-2; OBMV; OxBTC; PoE; PoRA; PPP; PrIm; SeCePo; SoSe; TEP; TIRV; TOF; UnPo; WeW

That is the glebe and this is the glissando. The future is nothing. Codex. Stephen Rodefer. IAT; UL

That is what they say, who were broken off from love. Children's Elegy. Muriel Rukeyser. *Fr.* Eighth Elegy. LCAP

That it might be so always. Sanetomo, *tr. by* Geoffrey Bownas *and* Anthony Thwaite. PeBJV

That it should end in an Albert Pick hotel. At the End of the Affair. Maxine W. Kumin. TAP

That it will never come again. Emily Dickinson. NOBA

That jolly little fellow who sang without stopping. The Broken Mirror. Jacques Prévert, *tr.* by Michael Benedikt. POS

That June before the judge gave. Seventeen. Jonathan Holden. Psk

That just one of you. Tameyo, *tr.* by Steven D. Carter. WFTW

"That just reminds me of a yarn," he said. The Jester in the Trench. Leon Gellert. PoAu-1

That Justice is a blind goddess. Justice. Langston Hughes. BPo

That kiss from the past. Ishikawa Takuboku, *tr. fr. Japanese* by Hiroaki Sato. *Fr.* Forty-seven Tanka in Three Lines. FCEI

That knife/ has stabbed me in the eye a long time. Ernst Nowak, *tr.* by Beth Bjorklund. CoAuP

That knight of the city. *Unknown*, *tr.* by Arthur Waley. BoS

That knot in the wood if wood. The Man with the Hollow Breast. Tania Van Zyl. PeSA

That labor/ a face to remember in wonder. Sappho, *tr.* by Guy Davenport. OBVE

That lady of all gentle memories. Dante, *tr. fr. Italian* by Dante Gabriel Rossetti. *Fr.* Vita Nuova, La, XXII. AWP

That lamb. Some Lamb. Stan Rice. NPGG

That learned Graecian (who did so excell). William Drummond of Hawthornden. OBS

That leaven of my soul is like. Mohammad Taqi Mir, *tr.* by Ahmed Ali. GoT

That leviathan tanker. Ports. István Vas, *tr.* by Jascha Kessler. FOC

That lifted blade transformed our jangling clans. James Russell Lowell. *Fr.* Under the Old Elm, VII. GOA

That Little Black Cat. D'Arcy Wentworth Thompson. OxBChV

That Little Blue Roan. Bruce Kiskaddon. CowP

That little grey-haired lady. The Little Old Lady. Rodney Bennett. BoTP

That Little Lump of Coal. *Unknown*. AmFP

That look you had, Agnes, was a temporary fact. Temporary Facts. William Stafford. CAPP

That love is all there is. Emily Dickinson. NOBA

That love which once was nearest to my heart. Vetus Flamma. Robert Mezey. PoA

That Love,—whose power and sovranty we own. The Creation of My Lady. Francesco Redi, *tr.* by Sir Edmund Gosse. AWP

That lovely spot which thou dost see. Upon a Mole in Celia's Bosom. Thomas Carew. CaPo

That lover of a night. Crazy Jane on God. W. B. Yeats. CMoP; EBEV; MoAB; OxBTC

That mad boy. *Unknown*, *tr.* by Arthur Waley. BoS

That man. Night Song for Two Mystics. Paul Blackburn. NeAP

That man at arms. *Unknown*, *tr.* by Arthur Waley. BoS

That man cannot know. *Unknown*, *tr. fr. Anglo-Saxon* by Ezra Pound. *Fr.* The Seafarer. PBBP

That man entered through my eyes. Dream of the Forgotten Lover. Lucia Fox, *tr.* by R. Maghan. BoWoP

That man over there say. Ain't I a Woman? Sojourner Truth. AIW; BlSi

That man walks along weeping. Narration. George Seferis, *tr.* by Edmund Keeley *and* Philip Sherrard. VMG

That master weaver, whose skills. Kabir, *tr.* by John Stratton Hawley *and* Mark Juergensmeyer. SSI

That matter of the murder is hushed up. The Cenci. Shelley. EnRP

That May Morning. Leland B. Jacobs. RHPC

That me alone you lov'd, you once did say. Catullus, *tr.* by Richard Lovelace. OBVE

That meadow which my heart loved. *Unknown*. *Fr.* Manyo Shu. Ma

That melancholy that inhabited me once has died. Autumn Leaves Are Virgin Mary. Unsi al-Haj, *tr.* by Patricia Alanah Bryne *and* Salma Khadra Jayyusi. MAP

That Memory. Pierre Reverdy, *tr. fr. French* by John Ashbery. POS

That memory like a derelict plane. Payments. Diana O Hehir. NPGG

That Men Should Fear. Shakespeare. *See* Julius Caesar: Cowards die many times before their deaths.

That mirror/ Which makes of men a transparency. Moments of Vision. Thomas Hardy. OAEL-2

That Moment. Ted Hughes. *Fr.* Crow. FF; PoE

That Month. *The daughter of* Pari, *tr. fr. Tamil* by A. K. Ramanujan. PLW

That month he was broke. Whiplash. William Matthews. MAYP

That morn which saw me made a bride. Upon a Maid That Died [*or* Dyed] the Day She Was Married [*or* Marryed]. Meleager, *tr.* by Robert Herrick. AWP; OBD; OBVE

That morning, after the storm. After the Storm. Elizabeth Bartlett. GoYe

That morning I set off. *Unknown*. *Fr.* Manyo Shu. FCEI

That morning their sighs. Heaven and Hell. Pablo Guevara, *tr.* by Maureen Ahern *and* David Tipton. Per

That mountain I crossed. Kyorai, *tr. fr. Japanese* by Burton Watson. *Fr.* Twenty Hokku. FCEI

That mountain there. Pilgrimage Song. *Unknown*, *tr.* by Mary Austin. WPE

That Mulberry Wine. Janet Sylvester. MAYP

That my old bitter heart was pierced in this black doom. A Grey Eye Weeping. Egan O'Rahilly, *tr.* by Frank O'Conner. AnIL; FaBoPV; OBMV

That Nature Is a Heraclitean Fire and of the Comfort of the Resurrection. Gerard Manley Hopkins. BrPo; FaBoMo; GTBS-P; LiTB; MoAB; NoP; OAEL-2; PoE; PoEL-5; TEP

That neither fame nor love might wanting be. To Sir Henry Cary. Ben Jonson. NoP

That Night. Oliver Bernard. PoPo

That Night. John Welch. NPo

That night I think that no one slept. The Last Fight. Lewis Frank Tooker. AA; FaBoBe

That night, I was a clockwork doll. Clockwork Doll. Dahlia Ravikovich, *tr.* by Chana Bloch. OV

("That night I was a mechanical doll.") MHeP, *tr.* by Bernhard Frank

That night I was not there. Something Left to Say. Katherine Soniat. MOWH

That night my angel stooped and strained. My Angel. Jonathan Henderson Brooks. PoNe

That night she felt those searching hands. Mary, Mother of Christ. Countee Cullen. PChr

That night the moon drifted over the pond. The Prediction. Mark Strand. EAS; LCAP

That night, when I woke suddenly, was sweet. Conversation with Rain. Louise D. Gunn. GoYe

That Night When Joy Began. W. H. Auden. OxBTC; SoSe

That night, when storms were spent and tranquil heaven. John Addington Symonds. *Fr.* Ithocles. PeHV

That night, when through the mooring-chains. The Ballad of Fisher's Boardinghouse. Kipling. PoRA

That night your great guns, unawares. Channel Firing. Thomas Hardy. BrPo; CMoP; EBEV; HAP; HeIP; LiTB; MoP; NAEL-2; NIP; NoAM; NoP; OAEL-2; OxBTC; PoE; PoEL-5; PoRA; PrIm; RB; SoSe; UnPo; WaaP

That no fair woman will, wonder not why. Catullus, *tr.* by Richard Lovelace. OBVE

That none beguiled be by time's quick flowing. That None Beguiled Be. Sir John Suckling. PoEL-3

(Love's Clock.) CaPo

That nose is out of drawing. With a gasp. Sonnet for a Picture. Swinburne. *Fr.* The Heptalogia. BXAP; FaBoNo; OAEL-2

That note comes clear, like water running clear. The Piano Tuner's Wife. Karl Shapiro. NoAM

That Nova was a moderate star like our good sun. Nova. Robinson Jeffers. CMoP; HAP

That nude kneeling so sad-seeming. Touching the River. Thomas Kinsella. FaBCIP

That ocean you of late surveyed. To Mr. Newton on His Return from Ramsgate. William Cowper. NOEC

That odyssey? We three left Amherst late. To My Fellow-Mariners, March, '53. Thomas Whitbread. NYBP

That of which many large varieties are found in the major. Nothing. James Sherry. LP

That "old last act"! Adrienne Rich. *Fr.* Two Songs, II. NIP; NOBA; TAP

That old man at the corner. In January. Lorna Dee Cervantes. CCP

That old man at the farm near Norman's Lane. The Farm near Norman's Lane. Olive Mary Finnin. PoAu-2

That Old Sauna High. Anselm Hollo. PoM

That on her lap she casts her humble eye. On the Blessed Virgin's Bashfulness. Richard Crashaw. HAP; OxBSP

That once this life was really mine. A Song of Life. Franz Werfel, *tr.* by Edith Abercrombie Snow. TrJP

That once which pained to think of. The Forgiven Past. Laura Riding. PBWP

That one small boy with a face like pallid cheese. Incendiary. Vernon Scannell. OxBC

That Orpheus Calliops sonne who stayde the running brooke. Seneca, *tr. fr. Latin* by John Studley. *Fr.* Medea, III. OBVE

That other time, spirits so high I seemed to soar over the clouds. Crossing Hakone Pass. Rai Mikisaburo, *tr.* by Burton Watson. JLIC-2

That our earth mother may wrap herself. Our Earth Mother. *Unknown*, *tr.* by R. Bunzel. WTO

That path through the azaleas. *Unknown*. *Fr.* Manyo Shu. Ma

That Poem. Juan Sáez Burgos, *tr. fr. Spanish* by Julio Marzán. InW

That poets are far rarer births than kings. To Elizabeth, Countess of Rutland. Ben Jonson. NoP

That praying mantis over there. Praying Mantis. Mary Ann Hoberman. RHPC

That Priapus with his big divining rod. To Bellinus. *Unknown.* PeHV

That prudent Prince who ends Shakespearian plays. Elizabethan Tragedy; a Footnote. Howard Moss. NePoEA

That Pull from the Left. Louise Erdrich. NoAM

That ragged/ leaking raft held. Ireland. Richard Ryan. CIP

That Rama whom the Indian sung. Of Rama. Herman Melville. LiTA

That Reminds Me. Ogden Nash. FiBHP

That resigned look! Here I am. Self-Portrait. Ronald Stuart Thomas. NAs; PoPo

That Room. John Montague. CIP

That row of icicles along the gutter. Beyond Words. Robert Frost. TW; WeW

That ruthless little tyrant can trifle, flirt, and fling. Anti-Cupid. Catharina Regina von Greiffenberg, *tr. by* Susan L. Cocalis *and* Gerlinde Geiger. DMG

That same look. Leslie. Marvin Wyche, Jr. AmNP

That scream from the street erased all content. A Scream. Dannie Abse. NPo

That sculptor we know, the passionate-eyed son of a quarryman. An Artist. Robinson Jeffers. VGW

That scything wind has cut the rich corn down. John Knox. Iain Crichton Smith. OxBS

That sea was greater than we knew. The Voyage. Edwin Muir. LiTM

That season when the leaf deserts the bole. October 1. Karl Shapiro. MoAB; MoAmPo; PoA

That seat of Science, Athens. Free America. Joseph Warren. PAH

That second time they hunted me. The Italian in England. Robert Browning. FaBoPV; OBNV

That selfsame tongue which first did thee entreat. The Constancy of a Lover. George Gascoigne. QFR

That shaman, owl man. The Deadly Dance. *Unknown, tr. by* Edward Kissam. STP

That she adored me as the most. Elegy on Any Lady by George Moore. Max Beerbohm. FaBoEE

That she hath gone to Heaven suddenly. Dante, *tr. fr. Italian by* Dante Gabriel Rossetti. *Fr.* Vita Nuova, La, III. CTC

That she may know I love her and miss her. Elegies for Her Daughter, Ko-Shikibu. Lady Izumi, *tr. fr. Japanese by* Hiroaki Sato. *Fr.* Fifty-nine Tanka. FCEI

That Sleepless Flame. Roberto Obregón, *tr. fr. Spanish by* Tina Alvarez Robles. VoI

That smoke/ would remain. If It All Went Up in Smoke. George Oppen. VWA

That soldier with a machinegun bolted. Two Summers in Moravia. Roger McDonald. CBAP

That somebody, my own special one. Shadows. *Unknown, tr. by* H. J. Spinden. WTO

That song there I borrow. Take Your Accusation Back! Kittaararter. WTO

That sort of place where you stop. Colville 1964. Kendrick Smithyman. PeNZ

(Colville.) ATNZ

That sound like the scratch. One, The Other, And. Wendy Wieber. NMM

That sovereign thought obscured? That vision clear. On a Great Man Whose Mind Is Clouding. Edmund Clarence Stedman. AA

That spot of blood on the drawing room wall. The Conversation in the Drawing Room. Weldon Kees. EAS

That spring day. My Happiness. Greg Pape. MAYP; MOWH

That story which the bold Sir Bedivere. The Passing of Arthur. Tennyson. *Fr.* Idylls of the King. NAEL-2; OBNC

(Morte d'Arthur, *incorporated in the* Idylls *with changes, as* The Passing of Arthur.) DL; FiP; OAEL-2

"And answer made King Arthur, breathing hard." EBEV

"But now farewell. I am going a long way." FaBoRV

Prayer ("Pray for my soul. More things are wrought by prayer"). WGRP

That Strain Again. Ronald Hambleton. CaP

That strange flower, the sun. Gubbinal. Wallace Stevens. NAAL-2; SOTW

That Street of Mine. Yekhi'el Mar, *tr. fr. Hebrew by* Bernhard Frank. MHeP

That stretch of water, it's always. States. Tom Paulin. FaBCIP

That such have died enables us. Emily Dickinson. AA

That Summer. Henry Treece. NYBP

That Summer I did not go crazy. To the Bone. Dorothy Allison. GLP

That summer it just appeared. Roller Rink. Betty Adcock. MT

That summer, the red may and the white may made. That Summer. Henry Treece. NYBP

That summer we saw the Blue Horse. The Blue Horse. Melvin Walker La Follette. NePoEA

That Summer's Shore. John Ciardi. ErPo

That sun that breathed love's fire into my youth. Dante, *tr. fr. Italian by* John Ciardi. *Fr.* Divina Commedia: Paradiso, III. NAWM-1

That Sunday morning, at half past ten. The Ballad of Longwood Glen. Vladimir Nabokov. NYBP

That Sunday was like an unfinished dream. A Sunday in Cambridge. Eddie Linden. PeHV

That swollen paunch you are doomed to bear. Heredity. William Dean Howells. AnAmPo

That tea is not the most benign of Latter-day beverages. After Algernon Charles Swinburne. Peter Titheradge. *Fr.* Teatime Variations. FaBoPa

That teacher gave me a new name. again. Name Giveaway. Phillip William George. VoR

That teenage boy. Into Fish. Sheryl L. Nelms. GOYP

That Texan Cattle Man. Joaquin Miller. AnAmPo

That the autumn has come. Buson, *tr. fr. Japanese by* Hiroaki Sato. *Fr.* Eighty-seven Hokku. FCEI

That the balls of the lover are not larger than the balls of the priest. C. K. Stead. *Fr.* Quesada, XVII. ATNZ; PeNZ

That the glass would melt in heat. The Glass of Water. Wallace Stevens. MoAB; MoAmPo; OxBA; TAP

That the high sheen of death could blot. Midsummer. James Scully. NYBP; TwCP

That the mere glimpse of a plain cap. *Unknown, tr. by* Arthur Waley. BoS

That the neighborhood might be covered. Larry Eigner. PoM

That the Night Come. W. B. Yeats. PoEL-5

That the poet "does not number the streaks of the tulip." To Hugh MacDiarmid. Edwin Morgan. FaBoTw

That the Sun Will Rise Tomorrow. Riekus Waskowsky, *tr. fr. Dutch by the author.* DuIn

That the Traylee's the best cigarette. A Prize-winning Limerick. R. Rhodes. FaBoUs

That the war would be over before they got to you. When You Have Forgotten Sunday: The Love Story. Gwendolyn Brooks. WPOW

That the world will never be quite—what a cliché—the same again. Tam Cari Capitis. Louis MacNeice. OBD

That there is falsehood in his looks. The Parson's Looks. Burns. OxBoLi

That There Should Be Laughter. Innocent Banda. WMBCH

That these we take for granted. Hitchcock Blue. Lucie Brock-Broido. EOEF

That They Were at the Beach. Leslie Scalapino. UL

That thief has gone thieving, careening around the world. Kabir, *tr. by* John Stratton Hawley *and* Mark Juergensmeyer. SSI

That Things Are No Worse, Sire. Helen Hunt Jackson. OHIP

That things in the Colony aren't what they should be. In a Large Greek Colony, 200 B.C. C. P. Cavafy, *tr. by* Edmund Keeley *and* Philip Sherrard. VMG

That Thou Art Nowhere to Be Found. George Macdonald. *Fr.* Diary of an Old Soul. TrCP

"That thou hast her, it is not all my grief." Shakespeare. *Fr.* Sonnets, XLII. InvP

That thou mayst injure no man, dove-like be. Prudent Simplicity. William Cowper. FaBoEE

That time/ we all heard it. Paul Robeson. Gwendolyn Brooks. CNA; PoBA

That time/ in the sun. When Sun Came to Riverwoman. Leslie Marmon Silko. VoR

That Time in Tangier. Marvin Bell. AnAn

That time of drought the embered air. Drought Year. Judith Wright. NoAM

That time of evening, weightless and disparate. Blackwater Mountain. Charles Wright. CAPP; GeTw

That time of revolution being come. Reflections in Bed. Julian Symons. WaP

"That time of year thou may'st [*or* maist] in me behold." Shakespeare. *Fr.* Sonnets, LXXIII. AWP; BoLoP; ChTr; CTC; EBEV; EiL; EnLoPo; FaBoRV; FaBV; FF; FiP; GBL; GTBS; GTBS-P; HAP; HeIP; HoPM; InPK; InPS; InvP; LiTB; NAEL-1; NIP; NOBE; NoP; OAEL-1; OBD; OBEV; OBSC; OHFP; PoE; PoEL-2; PoRA; PPP; PrIm; QFR; Son; SoSe; TEP; TrGrPo; UnPo; WeW

That time of year you may in me behold. The Winter Twilight, Glowing Black and Gold. Delmore Schwartz. NoAM

That time stands up vertically. Elegies, or the Stations of the Other Time. Ahmad Abd al-Muti Hijazi, *tr. by* May Jayyusi *and* Naomi Shihab Nye. MAP

That Time, That Country. Susan Donnelly. PPR

That time that mirth did steer my ship. Sir Thomas Wyatt. SiPS

That time when/ the senator noticed that the tornado had been napping. The Tornado. Aimé Césaire, *tr. by* Michael Benedikt. POS

That transitory moment between. A Moment Ago. David Avidan, *tr. by* Warren Bargad *and* Stanley F. Chyet. IP

That tremor rising. Snow Geese in the Wind. Philip Dow. NPGG

That trumpet tongue which taught a nation. The Demagogue. Phyllis McGinley. FaBoEE

"That turn'll get her," I said. Toujours la Politesse. Ezra Pound, *after the Chinese.* OBVE

That vengeaunce I ask and cry. O Cat of Carlishkind. John Skelton. *Fr.* Phyllyp Sparowe [*or* Philip Sparrow]. ChTr

That very day I saw that is we saw. Amir Gilboa, *tr. by* Warren Bargad *and* Stanley F. Chyet. IP

That Very Night. Avigdor Hame'iri, *tr. fr. Hebrew by* Bernhard Frank. MHeP

That very time I saw, but thou couldst not. Love-in-Idleness. Shakespeare. *Fr.* A Midsummer Night's Dream, II, i. TrGrPo

That war should bankrupts make of merchants is no wonder. Upon the Bankruptcy of a Physician. Henricus Selyns. SCAP

That was a brave old epoch. The Battle of La Prairie. William Douw Schuyler-Lighthall. PAH

That was I, you heard last night. A Serenade at the Villa. Robert Browning. Mes

That Was Summer. Marci Ridlon. NTCP

That was the coldest of mornings. Bait-Gathering. Angus Martin. NPo

That was the proverb. Let my mistress be. Long and Lazy. Robert Herrick. FaBoEE

That was the religion of the realm of religion. Nanak, *tr. by* John Stratton Hawley *and* Mark Juergensmeyer. SSI

That Was Then. Isabella Gardner. CAPP

That Way. Anne Welsh. PeSA

That wayward train. Punishment for a Wayward Train. Antonio Jacinto, *tr. by* Ron Rossner *and* Alexander Caskey. WMBCH

That We Head Towards. Stephany Fuller. BPo

That well you drew from is the coldest drink. The Cottage at Chigasaki. Edmund Blunden. OBTV

That wet gravelly sound is rain. The Drought Breaks. Fleur Adcock. ATNZ

That we've broken their statues. Ionic. C. P. Cavafy, *tr. by* Edmund Keeley *and* Philip Sherrard. VMG

That which her slender waist confined. On a Girdle. Edmund Waller. AWP; BLPL; FF; GTBS; GTBS-P; HeIP; InPK; LiTB; NAEL-1; NoP; OBEV; OBS; PoE; PoRA; SeCePo; SeCV-1; TrGrPo

That which is, being the only answer. Question and Answer. Kathleen Jessie Raine. MoBrPo

That which is, for example. The Bicycle. Stan Rice. NPGG

That which my fault has made me, o paint not. A Poet to a Painter. Aubrey Thomas de Vere. Son

That which shall last for aye can have no birth. Or Ever the Earth Was. Charles Leonard Moore. AA

That Which We Call a Rose. Michael Dransfield. CBAP

That which we dare invoke to bless. Tennyson. *Fr.* In Memoriam A. H. H., CXXIV. NOCV; TOF; WGRP

That white whiteness—snowy mountain snow, cold in my eyes. In India, Deeply Moved. Mokurai, *tr. by* Burton Watson. JLIC-2

That Whitsun, I was late getting away. The Whitsun Weddings. Philip Larkin. FaBoMo; HeIP; MoP; NePoEA-2; NoAM; NoP; OxBTC

That whole morning we were full of joy. Interlude of Joy. George Seferis, *tr. by* Edmund Keeley *and* Philip Sherrard. VMG

That widowed crow. Emperor Kogon, *tr. by* Steven D. Carter. WFTW

That wife of mine. Wakayama Mimaro. *Fr.* Manyo Shu. PeBJV

That Wind. Emily Brontë. CH

That wind's still there that I remember afire. The Agrigentum Road. Salvatore Quasimodo, *tr. by* Richard Wilbur. PFI

That wine-millet bends under its weight. *Unknown, tr. by* Arthur Waley. BoS

That winter, the dead could not be buried. Leningrad Cemetery, Winter of 1941. Sharon Olds. NIP

That with this bright believing band. The Impercipient. Thomas Hardy. EBVV; NAEL-2; PrIm; TrGrPo; WGRP

That wolf, shivering by the palisade. Colonial Set. Alfred Goldsworthy Bailey. OBCV

That woman down there beneath the sea. *Unknown.* WSC

"That woman there is almost dead." The Rat. W. H. Davies. OBWVE; OxBTC

That woman, vacuum in her mouth. The Great Nebula in Andromeda. Hugh Seidman. AmPA

That woman who to me seems most a woman. Sonnet: Dolce Stil Novo. Gavin Ewart. GrPl

That Women Are but Men's Shadows. Ben Jonson. ElL; OBS (Shadow, The.) NOBE; OBEV (Song: That Women Are but Men's Shadows.) OxBSP; SeCP (Women Men's Shadows.) WBLP

That wondrous instant of our meeting. K***. Pushkin, *tr. by* Alan Myers. AAA

That wooded face of cliffs and shadows. Remembering Lincoln. Frank Mundorf. GoYe

That year, for the poet awakening from his slumber. The Tears of Pearl. Chang Ts'o, *tr. by* Dominic Cheung. IFON

That year no wondering shepherds came. Christmas, the Year One, A.D. Sara Henderson Hay. PoRA

That year of the cloud, when my marriage failed. River Road. Stanley Kunitz. MoP; NoAM

That year spring came very late. A Walk. Eeva-Liisa Manner, *tr. by* Aili Jarvenpa. SOP

That year spring snowmelt. Arrows. William Heyen. SM

That year the doves sounded autumn early. Nothing Happened. Betty Adcock. KS

That year the end of winter stood under a sign. The Comet. Michael Palmer. NPGG

That year they fought in the snow. Rostov. George Sutherland Fraser. WaP

That year we hardly slept, waking like inmates. Getting Out. Cleopatra Mathis. MAYP

That year? Yes, doubtless I remember still. The World Well Lost. Edmund Clarence Stedman. AA

That you came back, that your plans. Changing the Tire. Lorrie Goldensohn. NAmP

That you like me not. *Unknown. Fr.* Manyo Shu. Ma

"That you were once unkind befriends me now." Shakespeare. *Fr.* Sonnets, CXX. InvP

That young beanpole was maybe six feet tall. I've Been Waiting These Thirty Years. Anna Swirszczynska, *tr. by* Magnus Jan Krynski *and* Robert A. Maguire. PwPP

That your honour's petitioners (dealers in rhymes). To the Right Hon. Henry Pelham. Edward Moore. OBSV

That zephyr every year. Spring Bereaved. William Drummond of Hawthornden. OBEV

Thatch gate works all right but I never open it. Idle Thoughts. Lu Yu, *tr. by* Burton Watson. CoBCP

Thatched Cottage, The. Hung Sheng, *tr. fr. Chinese by* Paul W. Kroll. WFTU

Thatched hut among the pines, door open near a cliff. Inscribed on a Painting ("Thatched hut among the pines, door open near a cliff"). T'ang Yin, *tr. by* Jonathan Chaves. CoBLCP

Thatched temple, leaning toward collapse, The. The Monk. Cheng Hsieh, *tr. by* Jan W. Walls. WFTU

Thatcher. Seamus Heaney. FaBCIP; IPY

Thatcher, The. Brendan Kennelly. CIP

Thatcher of Thatchwood went to Thatchet a-thatching, A. *Unknown.* OxNR

That's/ your son? the brother. A Man's Song, about His Daughter. *Unknown, tr. by* Armand Schwerner. STP

That's a rich man coming. *Unknown, tr. by* James Koller. STP

That's All? Anna Hajnal, *tr. fr. Hungarian by* Jascha Kessler. FOC; PBWP

That's All. Lawrence Joseph. EOEF

That's enough of that, Mr. Bones. Some lady you make. John Berryman. NAAL-2

That's Ethan Allen on the monument. Green Mountain Boy. Florida Watts Smyth. GoYe

That's his saddle across the tie-beam, an' them's his spurs up there. My Mate Bill. George Herbert Gibson. PoAu-1

That's his specialty. *Unknown, tr. by* Burton Watson. FCEI

That's how life is. Tsurayuki, *tr. fr. Japanese by* Burton Watson. *Fr.* Kokin Shu. FCEI

That's It. A. Leyeles, *tr. fr. Yiddish by* Benjamin *and* Barbara Harshav. AYP

That's Jack. Jack. Charles Henry Ross. OxBChV; RHPC

That's Life? Alan Bold. FF

That's me, second from the left. Perpetuum Immobile. Bruce Dawe. CBAP

That's my house with the red door, and all those steps. Taking Care of It. Deborah Lee. BrSi

That's my last duchess painted on the wall. My Last Duchess. Robert Browning. AWP; BeLS; EBVV; FaBoPV; FaFP; FF; FiP; FPL;

GTBS-P; HAP; HeIP; HoPM; InPK; InPS; LiTB; MAT; NAEL-2; NIP; NOBE; NOBVV; NoP; OAEL-2; OBNC; PoE; PoEL-5; PoLF; PPP; PrIm; SCV; SoSe; TEP; TrGrPo; WeW

That's my star. Orion. Blaise Cendrars, *tr.* by John Dos Passos. RHTwFP

That's Not a Tiger. Pertti Nieminen, *tr. fr. Finnish by* Aili Jarvenpa. SOP

That's Our Lot. Moyshe-Leyb Halpern, *tr. fr.* Yiddish. VWA, *tr. by* Kathryn Hellerstein

That's the cuckoo, you say. I cannot hear it. The Cuckoo. Edward Thomas. BrPo; OBD

That's the only image. A Wall. Charles Simic. HCAP

That's the queer life *said the chair.* Chair, Dog, and Clock. Hilary Corke. NYBP

That's what love is like. The whole river. Crossing Over. William Meredith. NoAM

That's what misery is. Poetry Is a Destructive Force. Wallace Stevens. AnAmPo; OxBA

That's What We'd Do. Mary Mapes Dodge. OBCA

That's you—the eternal Jew. Jud' Süss Oppenheimer on His First Visit with Professor Sigmund Freud. Judah Leib Teller, *tr. fr.* Yiddish by Benjamin *and* Barbara Harshav. *Fr.* Psychoanalysis. AYP

Thaw. Margaret Avison. FaBoWP; NOBC

Thaw. Edward Thomas. EBEV; FaBoTw; FM; GTBS-P; MoAB; MoBrPo; OxBSP; OxBTC

Thaw in the City. Lou Lipsitz. MAT

Thay walkit furth so derk oneith they wist. The Entrance to Hell. Virgil, *tr. into Middle English by* Gavin Douglas. *Fr.* The Aeneid [*or* Eneados], VI. GoTS

The Cumberland. Herman Melville. PAH

The/ Quick Gold, Slant Blue, Sharp Scarlet. Peyton Houston. *Fr.* Sonnet Variations, CV. Son

Thealma and Clearchus, *sel.* John Chalkhill. *Fr.* Thealma and Clearchus. Rhotus on Arcadia. OBS

Thease stwonen steps a-zet so true. The Stwonen Steps. William Barnes. NOBVV

Theatre, The. Horace Smith *and* James Smith. Par

Theaw God above, alone to-day. Preawd Tum's Prayer. Joseph Ramsbottom. PF

Thebes of the Seven Gates. Sophocles, *tr. fr.* Greek by Dudley Fitts *and* Robert Fitzgerald. *Fr.* Antigone. WaaP

Thee finds me in the garden, Hannah. The Quaker Widow. Bayard Taylor. AA

Thee for my recitative. To a Locomotive in Winter. Walt Whitman. AmPP; FaBV; InPK; MoAmPo; MoP; NAAL-1; NoAM; NoP; PoEL-5; TAP

Thee Pompey thy past deeds by turns infest. Lucan, *tr. fr. Latin by* Nicholas Rowe. *Fr.* Pharsalia, I. OBVE

Thee sets a bell to swinging in my soul. Hildegarde Flanner. *Fr.* Sonnets in Quaker Language, II. WPE

Thee, Sovereign God, our grateful accents praise. The Te Deum. *Unknown, tr. by* Dryden. AWP

Thee, Thee, Only Thee. Thomas Moore. GBL; OBNC

Thee too, modest tressèd maid. Moon. Henry Rowe. OBEV

Thefts of the Morning. Edith Matilda Thomas. AA

Theh Thet Hi Can Wittes Fule-Wis. *Unknown.* HAP

Their ardour kindles all the Grecian pow'rs. Homer, *tr. fr. Greek by* Pope. *Fr.* The Iliad, XII. OBVE

Their attendant nuns spare the tourists well. Bathing the Aged. Paul Monette. AmPA

Their auburn or black hair, curly hair. Just This. István Vas, *tr. by* Jascha Kessler. FOC; VWA

Their Banishment. Milton. *See* Paradise Lost:
    For now too nigh/ The archangel stood, and from the other hill.

Their barbarism did not assuage the grief. The Retreat of Ita Cagney. Michael Hartnett. CIP

Their Beginning. C. P. Cavafy, *tr. fr.* Greek. AnAn, *tr. by* Edmund Keeley *and* Philip Sherrard; PeHV, *tr.* by John Mavrogordato

Their belongings were buried side by side. The Drawer. George MacBeth. NePoEA-2

Their black truck rattled up the dusty hill. The Diviners. Mary Oliver. WPE

Their bodies lined up against the walls. Waiting for Truth. Susan Griffin. GLP

Their calendars are based on rice. Rice. Carol Muske. AmPA

Their Cone-like Cabins. Charles G. Ballard. VoR

Their duffle-bags sprawl like a murder. Words without Music. Irving Layton. CaP

Their eyelids are drooping, no tears lie beneath. Weavers. Heine. TrJP

Their eyes had known the quiet color blue. Prisoner of War. Gertrude May Lutz. GoYe

Their faces, safe as an interior. The Middle-aged. Adrienne Rich. HCAP; NePoEA-2

Their feet on London, their heads in the grey clouds. Whit Monday. Louis MacNeice. NYBP; OAEL-2

Their fingers numb in thimbles. You Owe Them Everything. John Allman. SaC

Their footless dance. Love and Knowledge. Robert Penn Warren. *Fr.* Audubon, VI.

Their ground they stil made good. Homer, *tr. fr.* Greek by George Chapman. *Fr.* The Iliad, V. OBVE

Their hair, pomaded, faces jaded. Sepia Fashion Show. Maya Angelou. BlSi

Their heels slapped their bumping mules. Merchants from Cathay. William Rose Benét. MoAmPo

Their hour had come. Savants. Lucien Stryk. KS

Their house faces east, is protected by trees. A Storm from the East. Reed Whittemore. NYBP

Their illicit pleasure has been fulfilled. Their Beginning. C. P. Cavafy. AnAn, *tr.* by Edmund Keeley *and* Philip Sherrard; PeHV, *tr.* by John Mavrogordato

Their lips upon each other's lips are laid. Speechless [upon the Marriage of Two Deaf and Dumb Persons]. Philip Bourke Marston. EBVV

Their little room grew light with cries. Proper Clay. Mark Van Doren. PoRA; TrGrPo

Their Lonely Betters. W. H. Auden. GoJo; NAEL-2; NoAM

Their many children each reading. Ozaki Hosai, *tr. fr. Japanese by* Hiroaki Sato. *Fr.* One Hundred Haiku in Free Form. FCEI

Their meetings were so few. Mountain Hawthorns. Chang Pi, *tr.* by Lois Fusek. ATF

Their midst mix power. Letters. Bruce Andrews. IAT

Their minds are so frail the least squeak upsets them. Dismissing Progress and Its Progenitors. George Reavey. EAS

Their mockery brought him double force. Blind Samson. William Plomer. PeSA

Their mouths blur like leaves caught. A House. Steve Orlen. BLA; NAmP

Their noonday never knows. Fame. John Banister Tabb. AA

Their Party, Our House. Jon Swan. NYBP

Their Patients. Robert Pinsky. *Fr.* Essay on Psychiatrists, XVII. NoAM

Their Philistinism Considered. Robert Pinsky. *Fr.* Essay on Psychiatrists, XI. NoAM

Their Plan. Sista Roots. WS

Their rugs are sodden, their heads are down. Gun Teams. Gilbert Frankau. OxBTC

Their scrape and clink together of musical coin. Some Small Shells from the Windward Islands. May Swenson. FYAP

Their sense is with their senses all mixed in. George Meredith. *Fr.* Modern Love, XLVIII. NAEL-2; NoP; OAEL-2

Their Seriousness, with Further Comparisons. Robert Pinsky. *Fr.* Essay on Psychiatrists, VI. NoAM

Their shoulders you shook. The Preacher. Al-Mahdi, *tr.* by A. J. Arberry. TTY

Their song is almost painful the way it. Against Starlings. Stanley Plumly. BLA

Their spades grafted through the variably-resistant. Geoffrey Hill. *Fr.* Mercian Hymns, XII. PoE

Their spare, fanatic sentry comes. Ants and Others. Adrien Stoutenburg. FYAP; NYBP

Their Speech, Compared with Wisdom and Poetry. Robert Pinsky. *Fr.* Essay on Psychiatrists, XIV. NoAM; PoA

Their thoughts are night gulls. Old People Dozing. Denise Levertov. AIW

Their throats glittering like blue sapphire. What Her Girl Friend Said to Her. Maturai Marutan Ilanakanar, *tr.* by A. K. Ramanujan. PLW

Their time past, pulled down. Burning the Christmas Greens. William Carlos Williams. LiTM; MoP; NAAL-2; NoAM; NOBA

Their tongues are knives, their forks are hands and feet. Adrian Mitchell. FaBoEE; GBL; OxBSP

Their verdure dare not show. Louis MacNeice. AnIL; FaBCIP

Their voices heard, I stumble suddenly. One More New Botched Beginning. Stephen Spender. CMoP; NoAM; NYBP

Their war-boots said big shots to the plank floor. Behold, One of Several Little Christs. Kenneth Patchen. NaP

Their Wedded Love. Milton. *See* Paradise Lost:
    Hail wedded love, mysterious law, true source.

Their wings beat the floor. Angels in the House. Jerred Metz. VWA

Theirs is a gesture of sorrow, infinite and taut. Snails. E. D. Blodgett. NOBC

Theirs is a white and a green life, a smooth. Red Cross Nurses. Gervase Stewart. WaP

Theirs is the house whose windows—every pane. On the Asylum Road. Charlotte Mew. MoBrPo

Theirs was a language within ours, a loge. The Parnassians. James Merrill. BLA

Thekla's Song. Schiller, tr. fr. German by Samuel Taylor Coleridge. Fr. The Piccolomini. AWP

Thel's Motto. Blake. Fr. The Book of Thel, 4 ll.. ChTr

Them. Vincent O'Sullivan. ATNZ

Them. Hugo Williams. Fr. Calling Your Name in the Zoo. NPo

Them Decade, The. Terence Winch. UL

Them ez wants, must choose. A Baker's Duzzen uv Wize Sawz. Edward Rowland Sill. FaBoBe; FaFP

Them Gar'n Town People. Unknown. PBCV

Theme and Variation. Peter De Vries. NYBP

Theme and Variations. Ingeborg Bachmann, tr. fr. German by Beth Bjorklund. CoAuP

Theme and Variations. W. P. Ker. PoSH

Theme Brown Girl. Elton Hill. NBP

Theme for English B. Langston Hughes. HCAP; MoP; NIP; NoAM; NOBA; NoP

Theme no poet gladly sung. Prudence. Emerson. OBAL

Theme of morning was the sound of rain, The. Rain. Sam Harrison. NeIP

Theme One: The Variations. August Wilson. PoBA

Theme tune occurs again, The! Das Liebesleben. Thom Gunn. ErPo

Themes. Denis Glover. Fr. Sings Harry. ATNZ

Themes of love and death I have rehearsed, The. Judges, Judges. Gene Baro. NePoEA-2

Then. Philip Levine. PPR

Then. Edwin Muir. CMoP; PoA; PoE

Then. David Rokeah, tr. fr. Hebrew by Bernhard Frank. MHeP

Then. Muriel Rukeyser. GLP; LCAP

Then a partridge-shaped cloud over dust storm. Ezra Pound. Fr. Cantos, CXIII. NYBP

Then after Eden. New World. Derek Walcott. OxBC

Then all became silent. White Bird. Matti Megged, tr. by Howard Schwartz. VWA

Then all the nations of birds lifted together. The Season of Phantasmal Peace. Derek Walcott. NoP

Then Almitra spoke, saying, We would ask now of Death. Kahlil Gibran. Fr. The Prophet. DL

Then and Now. Frances Ellen Watkins Harper. PWR

Then and Now. Charles Frederick Johnson. AA

Then and Now. Kapilar, tr. fr. Tamil by A. K. Ramanujan. PLW

Then and Now. Anne B. Murray. PoSH

Then and Now. Kath Walker. IHMS

Then, blessing all, "Go, children of my care!" The Triumph of Dulness. Pope. Fr. The Dunciad. NOEC

Then bold Robin Hood to the north he would go. Robin Hood and the Scotchman. Unknown. ESPB

Then both ourselves and seed at once to free. Milton. Fr. Paradise Lost, Bk. X, ll. 999–1006. OBD

Then call me traitor if you must. To Certain Critics. Countee Cullen. BPo

Then came fair May, the fairest maid on ground. May. Spenser. Fr. The Faerie Queene, VII, 7. GN

Then came I to the shoreless shore of silence. Conrad Aiken. Fr. Preludes for Memnon; or, Preludes to Attitude. LiTA; OxBA

Then came jolly Summer, being dight. Summer. Spenser. Fr. The Faerie Queene, VII, 7. GN

Then came the Autumn all in yellow clad. Autumn. Spenser. Fr. The Faerie Queene, VII, 7. GN

Then came the cry of "Call all hands on deck!" Rounding the Horn. John Masefield. Fr. Dauber, VI. MoAB; MoBrPo

Then Constantine, mindful of the Holy Cross. Helena Embarks for Palestine. Cynewulf, tr. fr. Anglo-Saxon by Charles W. Kennedy. Fr. Elene. AnOE

Then, day by day, her broidered gown. The Earth in Spring. Judah Halevi, tr. by Edward G. King. TrJP

Then drew near unto him all the publicans and sinners. Bible, N.T. Fr. St. Luke, XV. NAWM-1

Then earthquakes, nature's agonizing pangs. James Grainger. Fr. The Sugar Cane. PBCV

Then fire burned my body to a clear shell. A Clear Shell. Frances Bellerby. FaBoWP

Then first he form'd th' immense and solid shield. Homer, tr. fr. Greek by Pope. Fr. The Iliad, XVIII. OBVE

Then fled, O brethren, the wicked juba. The Ballad of Nat Turner. Robert Hayden. BPo; SM; VGW

Then forth issewed (great goddesse) great Dame Nature. Dame Nature. Spenser. Fr. The Faerie Queene, VII, 7. PoEL-1

Then from the sea the dawning 'gan arise. Dido's Hunting. Virgil, tr. fr. Latin by the Earl of Surrey. Fr. The Aeneid [or Eneados], IV. OBSC

Then from their poverty they rose. The Ordinary Women. Wallace Stevens. OxBA

"Then hate me when thou wilt; if ever, now." Shakespeare. Fr. Sonnets, XC. AWP; EBEV; EIL; NOBE; OBEV; OBSC; PoEL-2

Then Hrothgar's minstrel rehearsed the lay. The Lay of Finn. Unknown, tr. fr. Anglo-Saxon by Charles W. Kennedy. Fr. Beowulf. AnOE

Then I heard a voice celestial. John Lydgate. Fr. Devotions of the Fowls. PBBP

Then I said to the elegant ladies. Sappho, tr. by Willis Barnstone. BoWoP

Then I Saw What the Calling Was. Muriel Rukeyser. FaBoWP

Then I stand up on my hassock and say sing that. Pretext. Stephen Rodefer. IAT; UL

Then I tuned my harp—took off the lilies we twine round its chords. Robert Browning. Fr. Saul, V-IX. FiP

Then I was one long curve, from. The Hard Summer. Medbh McGuckian. FaBCIP

Then I was young. Karma. Pierre Kemp, tr. by Fred van Leeuwen. DuIn

Then, if you say you do not know. Unknown. FaBoUs

Then I'll Believe. B. W. Vilakazi, tr. fr. Zulu by Jack Cope. PeSA

Then, in the form of a white rose, the host. Dante, tr. fr. Italian. Divina Commedia: Paradiso, XXXI-XXXIII. NAWM-1, tr. by John Ciardi.

Then is our charter, Pollexfen, quite lost? The Great Despair of the London Whigs. Unknown. APAS

Then it came to pass that a pestilence fell on the city. The Finding of Gabriel. Longfellow. Fr. Evangeline. AA

Then it was dusk in Illinois, the small boy. First Song. Galway Kinnell. CAPP; GoJo; GOYP; GrPl; LiTM; NoP; TwCP

Then it was still called hard rubber. The Melmac Year. David Hilton. UL

Then it's a hooraw, and a hooraw. Standin' on the Walls of Zion. Unknown. AS

Then it's collar 'im tight. Police Station Ditties. Max Beerbohm. NOBL

Then Job answered and said. Not Flesh of Brass. Bible, O.T. Fr. Job, X: 1–22. TrJP

Then, land!—then, England! oh, the frosty cliffs. Elizabeth Barrett Browning. Fr. Aurora Leigh. FaBoPP; NAEL-2

Then Laugh. Bertha Adams Backus. BLPA; PWR; WBLP

Then lay I lax. Circe. William Gibson. PoA

Then leave old regret. A Moral Poem. J. V. Cunningham. VGW

Then Lelex rose, an old experienced man. Ovid, tr. fr. Latin by Arthur Golding. Fr. Metamorphoses: Philemon and Baucis. AWP, tr. by Dryden; OBVE, tr. by Dryden.

Then let us boast of ancestors no more. Daniel Defoe. Fr. The True-born Englishman, conclusion. OBSV

Then Lose in Time Thy Maidenhead. Unknown. ErPo

Then loudly cried the bold Sir Bedivere. Tennyson, incorporated in Idylls of the King with changes, as The Passing of Arthur. Fr. Morte d'Arthur. TOF

Then Mahoney, standing in the surf. Mahoney. Sean Jennett. NeIP

Then Margery [or Marjorie] Milkduck. John Skelton. Fr. The Tunnyng [or Tunning] of Elynour [or Elinor] Rummyng [or Rumming]. EBEV; OAEL-1; PoE

Then Milton rose up from the heaven of Albion ardorous! Blake. Fr. Milton, I. OAEL-1

Then next a merry Woodsman, clad in green. The Green Dryad's Plea. Thomas Hood. Fr. The Plea of the Midsummer Fairies. OBNC

Then one of the twelve, called Judas Iscariot. Bible, N.T. Fr. St. Matthew, XXVI: 14-XXVII. NAWM-1

Then out-streamed a Light/ Brightest that of beaming pillars! Death of Saint Guthlac. Cynewulf, tr. fr. Anglo-Saxon. Fr. Guthlac. ACP

Then Petra flashed by in a wink. Air Travel in Arabia. Sir Charles Johnston. OBTV

Then rising in his rage above the shores. Homer, tr. fr. Greek by Pope. Fr. The Iliad, XXI. OBVE

Then roll the swag and blanket up. The Golden Gullies of the Palmer. Unknown. PoAu-1

Then said Almitra, Speak to us of Love. Of Love. Kahlil Gibran. Fr. The Prophet. PoLF

Then said that royall Pere in sober wise. Spenser. Fr. The Faerie Queene, I, 12. OAEL-1

Then saith the timid Fay—"Oh, mighty Time!" The Fairy's Reply to Saturn. Thomas Hood. Fr. The Plea of the Midsummer Fairies. OBNC

Then Sang Deborah and Barak. Bible, *O.T. See* Judges: Song of Deborah, The.

Then sang Moses and the children of Israel this song. Bible, *O.T. Fr.* Exodus, XV: 1-18. OBWP

Then Saturn thus: "Sweet is the merry lark." The Melodies of Time. Thomas Hood. *Fr.* The Plea of the Midsummer Fairies. OBNC

Then saw I, with gray eyes fulfilled of rest. In Hades. Anna Callender Brackett. AA

Then, say, was I or nature in the wrong. *Unknown. Fr.* Don Leon. PeHV

Then Shall We See. Charles Leonard Moore. AA

Then Sings My Soul. Paul Mariani. GeTw; MAYP

Then Sohrab with his sword smote Rustum's helm. Matthew Arnold. *Fr.* Sohrab and Rustum. OBWP

Then sprang up first the golden age, which of itself maintained. Ovid, *tr. fr. Latin by* Arthur Golding. *Fr.* Metamorphoses, I. NAEL-1 (Golden Age, The.) OAEL-1

Then step by step walks Autumn. Autumn's Processional. Dinah Maria Mulock Craik. GN

Then strip, lads, and to it, though sharp be the weather. Football Song. Sir Walter Scott. SD

Then that dread angel near the awful throne. Fiat Lux. Lloyd Mifflin. AA

Then the air was perfect. And his descent. The Parachutist. Jon Anderson. AmPA; NYBP

Then the Brother of the Wind. Charles Kenneth Williams. CAPP

Then the Ermine. Marianne Moore. PoA

Then the golden hour. Length of Moon. Arna Bontemps. CDC; LiTM; PoNe

Then the knee of the wave. Reclining Figure. Donald Hall. LCAP

Then the little Hiawatha. The Little Hiawatha. Longfellow. *Fr.* The Song of Hiawatha. OnUR, *fr.* III.

Then the little Hiawatha. Hiawatha's Brothers. Longfellow. *Fr.* The Song of Hiawatha. BoTP

Then the long sunlight lying on the sea. The Insusceptibles. Adrienne Rich. HeIP; SM; Son

Then the Lord Answered ("Who is this that darkeneth counsel by words without knowledge?"). Bible, *O.T. Fr.* Job, XXXVIII: 2–XXXIX. AWP

    God Replies, XXXVIII: 2–41. TrGrPo

    Hast Thou Given the Horse Strength. *Fr.* XXXIX: 19–25. ChTr (Horse, The.) FaPON, *abr.*; TrGrPo

    "Knowest thou the time when the wild goates of the rocke bring forth?" *Fr.* XXXIX. OBVE

    "Then the Lord answered Job out of the whirlewind, and sayd." *Fr.* XXXVIII. AWP; OBVE

    "Where wast thou when I laid the foundations of the earth?" *Fr.* XXXVIII: 4–38. ImOP, *abr.*

    "Wilt thou hunt the prey for the lion?." *Fr.* XXXVIII: 38–XXXIX. FM

Then the Lord God spoke and said unto Noah. Noah's Flood. Caedmon, *tr. fr. Anglo-Saxon by* C. W. Kennedy. *Fr.* Genesis. AnOE

Then the Master. Longfellow. *Fr.* The Building of the Ship. NAAL-1; OHFP

Then the Northmen fled in their nailed ships. *Unknown, tr. fr. Anglo-Saxon by* Tennyson. *Fr.* Battle of Brunanburh. PBBP

Then the Provost he uprose. William Edmonstoune Aytoun. *Fr.* Edinburgh after Flodden. OBWP

Then, the quick plunge into the cool, green dark. Louis Untermeyer. *Fr.* Swimmers. SD

Then the Skin Falls Apart. Dara Wier. TV

Then the son of Weohstan, stalwart in war. The Funeral Pyre. *Unknown, tr. fr. Anglo-Saxon by* Charles W. Kennedy. *Fr.* Beowulf. AnOE

Then the sun full soone shott under the clouds. The Battle of Flodden. *Unknown. Fr.* Scotish Feilde. OxBLMV

Then there is this civilising love of death, by which. Ignorance of Death. William Empson. CMoP; LiTM; NoAM; OBD

Then there shall be signs in Heaven. The Fifteen Days of Judgment. Sebastian Evans. NOBVV

Then they paraded Pompey's urn. Jenny Mastoraki, *tr. by* Nikos Germanakos. BoWoP; PBWP

Then they saw/ Forth and forward faring. The Approach of Pharaoh. Caedmon, *tr. fr. Anglo-Saxon by* C. W. Kennedy. *Fr.* Genesis. ACP; WaaP

Then they took whole stones according to the law. Bible, Apocrypha. *Fr.* First Maccabees, IV: 47-59. OFD

Then thick as locusts black'ning all the ground. Carnations and Butterflies. Pope. *Fr.* The Dunciad. NOEC

Then those ill-favour'd Ones, whom none. George Crabbe. *Fr.* Sir Eustace Grey. ELP

Then thus the sire of gods, with look serene. Ovid, *tr. fr. Latin by* Dryden. *Fr.* Metamorphoses, VIII. OBD

Then thus we have beheld. Samuel Daniel. *Fr.* Cleopatra. OBSC

Then to the bar, all they drew near. Michael Wigglesworth. *Fr.* The Day of Doom. OBCA

Then tooke they seate, and forth our passage strooke. Homer, *tr. fr. Greek by* George Chapman. *Fr.* Odyssey, XII. MOS

Then Trystan and Gwalchmai went to Arthur. Trystan and Esyllt. *Unknown, tr. by* Gwyn Jones. OBWVE

Then turn on the music, Marcia. Rock 'n' Roll. Lesley Frost. AiP

Then up I rose, and made no more delay. Elizabeth Melvill, Lady Culross. *Fr.* A Godly Dream. WPE

Then Urizen wept & thus his lamentation poured forth. Urizen's Curse upon His Children. Blake. *Fr.* Vala; or The Four Zoas. TW

Then was I cast from out my state. Frenzy. George Crabbe. *Fr.* Sir Eustace Grey. NOBE

Then was there heard a most celestial sound. The Rivers Come to the Hall of Proteus for the Marriage of the Thames and the Medway. Spenser. *Fr.* The Faerie Queene, IV, 2. FaBoPP

Then watching the unposed beggars pose. Et Quid Amabo Nisi Quod Aenigma Est. Stephen Sandy. NYBP

Then we descended, as into a labyrinth. Fear. Aldo Camerino, *tr. by* Anita Barrows. VWA

"Then, we'll go through with the journey." Jansenist Journey. Denis Devlin. IPY

Then we'll sing of Lydia Pinkham. Lydia Pinkham. *Unknown.* AS

Then what is the answer?—Not to be deluded by dreams. The Answer. Robinson Jeffers. CMoP; GoYe

Then, when I'd seen them leave the bay. And Back. Rodney Bennett. BoTP

Then, when the child was gone. The Empty House. Stephen Spender. NYBP; PCP

Then will a quiet gather round the door. Beyond Wars. David Morton. PAH

Thence forward by that painfull way they pas. Spenser. *Fr.* The Faerie Queene, I, 10. OAEL-1

Thence passing forth, they shortly did arriue. Spenser. *Fr.* The Faerie Queene: The Bower of Bliss. FiP

Theobald James. J. B. Morton. *Fr.* When We Were Very Silly. FaBoPa

Theocritus. Annie Fields. AA

Theocritus. Oscar Wilde. NOBE

Theodor Herzl. Israel Zangwill. TrJP

Theodore Roethke Foots It. D. C. Barry. BXAP

Theodosia Burr. Myra Burnham Terrell. GoYe

Theodosia Burr: The Wrecker's Story. John Williamson Palmer. PAH

Theodotos. C. P. Cavafy, *tr. fr. Greek by* Edmund Keeley *and* Philip Sherrard. VMG

Theologians. Walter de la Mare. EaLo

Theological. Clifton Fadiman. FiBHP

Theological Limerick. T. Lindsay. FaBoCo

Theology. Ted Hughes. FaBoMo; NAEL-2; NoAM

Theology and a Patchwork Absolute. Heather McPherson. PeNZ

Theology of Bongwi, the Baboon, The. Roy Campbell. PeSA

Theology of Jonathan Edwards, The. Phyllis McGinley. MoAmPo

Theophany. Evelyn Underhill. WGRP

Theophilus Thistledown, the successful thistle sifter. *Unknown.* OxNR

Theoretikos. Oscar Wilde. BrPo

Theory, A. Charles Simic, *tr. fr. Czech by* Jeffrey Fiskin *and* Erik Vestville. AnAn

Theory of the Flower, The. Michael Palmer. NPGG

Theory of Wind, A. Albert Goldbarth. MAYP

Ther is no rose of swych vertu. The Rose That Bore Jesu. *Unknown.* OxBLMV

Ther was a frier of order gray. The Friar and the Nun. *Unknown.* OxBLMV

Ther was a knight, a worthy for the chaffre. Portrait of the Pornographer. G. W. Jones. BXAP

Ther was a lady fair an rear. The Kitchie-Boy. *Unknown.* ESPB

Ther was also a povre closet queane. Lost Lines from Chaucer's Prologue to "The Canterbury Tales." *Unknown.* PeHV

There. Rodney Bennett. BoTP

There/ I take off all my human clothes. End of Solitude. Kim Hyun-sung, *tr. by* Koh Chang-soo. ACKP

There. Robert Mezey. NaP

There/ is someone I can bear. W. S. Landor. Marianne Moore. OBAL

There. Franz Wright. PPR

There Actually Stood. Roy Fuller. *Fr.* Mythological Sonnets, II. Son

There ain' no liars there. In My Father's House. *Unknown.* AS

There aince was a very pawky duke. The Pawky Duke. David Rorie. GoTS

There all the dirty laundry lay. News from the Basement Laundromat. G. N. Gabbard. SoTCo

There all the golden codgers lay. News for the Delphic Oracle. W. B. Yeats. CMoP; FaBoMo; LiTB; LiTM; NoAM

There also was a nun, a Prioress. Chaucer. *See* Canterbury Tales, The: Prologue.

There always is a noise when it is dark! In the Night. James Stephens. OBMV

There among the plum twigs. Waka. *Unknown, tr. by* Lucien Stryk *and* Takashi Ikemoto. ZPCJ

There ance was a may, and she lo'ed na men. Werena My Heart Licht I Wad Dee. Lady Grisel Baillie. OBEV

There are/ two methods. In the Case of Lobsters. Petra von Morstein, *tr. by* Rosemarie Waldrop. BoWoP

There are a very few moments when you. Avraham Ben-Yitzhak, *tr. by* A. C. Jacobs. VWA

There are abandoned corners of our Exile. The Mathmid. Hayyim Nahman Bialik, *tr. by* Maurice Samuel. AWP

There are all kinds of men. A Thank You for Friends. Rodney Bennett. BoTP

There are always shadows among the hills. Shadows among the Ettrick Hills. William Addison. PoSH

There are angels on the road from San Sepulcro. Walking in the 15th Century. Daniel Halpern. NAmP

There Are Bad Times Just around the Corner. Noel Coward. NOBL

There Are Big Waves. Eleanor Farjeon. BoTP; OnUR

There Are Black. Jimmy Santiago Baca. InPS

There are blind eyes. A Prayer in Time of Blindness. Clement Wood. TrPWD

There are brightest apples on those trees. The Fertile Muck. Irving Layton. NoAM; NOBC; OBCV

There are butterflies! Song of the Butterflies. Chang Pi, *tr. by* Lois Fusek. ATF

There are caverns/ under our feet. Shirley Kaufman. BoWoP

There are cemeteries that are lonely. Nothing but Death. Pablo Neruda, *tr. by* Robert Bly. EAS

There are certain things—as, a spider, a ghost. A Sea Dirge. "Lewis Carroll." CenHV; MOS

There are constantly, she told him further, lions in the village. Henri Michaux, *tr. fr. French by* Richard Ellmann. *Fr.* I Am Writing to You from a Far-Off Country, VII. RHTwFP

There are cool breezes. Pow Wow. Vickie Sears. GOS

There are days when housework seems the only. Coast to Coast. Adrienne Rich. NIP

There are dealers in pictures named Agnew. Tom Agnew, Bill Agnew. Dante Gabriel Rossetti. ChTr; FaBoEE

There Are Delicacies. Earle Birney. NoP

There are depths even in a household. The Whale in the Blue Washing Machine. John Haines. AnAn

There are different ways of dying without. After the Revolution. Marilyn Hacker. AmPA

"There are dreams that need rest." Okay. Sharon Scott. JB

There are fairies at the bottom of our garden! Fairies. Rose Fyleman. FaPON; OxBChV

There are flowers of Zait in the garden. *Unknown, tr. by* Boris de Rachewiltz; *English vers. by* Ezra Pound and Noel Stock. BoWoP; PBWP

There are four men mowing down by the Isar. A Youth Mowing. D. H. Lawrence. HmPK; MoAB; MoBrPo; NoAM; TrGrPo

There are four vibrators, the world's exactest clocks. Four Quartz Crystal Clocks. Marianne Moore. AmPP; ImOP; TwCP

There Are Gains for All Our Losses. Richard Henry Stoddard. AnAmPo
(Flight of Youth, The.) AA
(Never Again.) PWR

There Are Gods. C. L. Riley. PoSH

There are gold ships. *Unknown.* ILY

There are half-naked men who stand. The Glass Eaters. George Jonas. NeAC

There are harps that complain to the presence of the night. Music of the Night. John Neal. AA

There are hermit souls that live withdrawn. The House by the Side of the Road. Sam Walter Foss. AnAmPo; BLPA; BLPL; FaBoBe; FaFP; OHFP; WBLP; WGRP

There are hours I imagine. Romance of the Living Corpse. Enrique Gonzáles Martínez, *tr. by* Samuel Beckett. MexPo

There are (I scarce can think it, but am told.). The First Satire of the Second Book of Horace. Pope. OAEL-1; OBSV; PPP; PrIm

There are important matters on the agenda. Important Matters. Charles Mungoshi. WMBCH

There are in our existence spots of time. Imagination and Taste, How Impaired and Restored. Wordsworth. *Fr.* The Prelude [or, Growth

of a Poet's Mind], XII *and* XIII [XI *and* XII]. PoE; PoEL-4, XII *abr.;* TOF

Imagination, How Impaired and Restored. *Fr.* XII *and* XIII.OBNC

Oh! Mystery of Man. *Fr.* XII.FiP

There are in Paradise. The Shepherd Who Stayed. Theodosia Pickering Garrison. OHIP; PChr

There are liberators. Tupac Amaru Relegated. Antonio Cisneros, *tr. by* David Tipton. Per

There are lions and roaring tigers, and enormous camels and things. At the Zoo. A. A. Milne. FaPON

There are lonely hearts to cherish. While the Days Are Going By. George Cooper. BLRP; WBLP

There are loved ones who are missing. The Blessings That Remain. Annie Johnson Flint. BLRP

There are loyal hearts, there are spirits brave. Life's Mirror. "Madeline Bridges." BLPA; FaBoBe; PWR; WBLP

There are many cumbersome ways to kill a man. Five Ways to Kill a Man. Edwin Brock. DL

There are many dead in the brutish desert. First Elegy for the Dead in Cyrenaica. Hamish Henderson. OxBS

There are many like him here, without epitaph, without a mound. Saul Tchernichowsky. *See* Grave in Ukraine, A.

There are many like him there—unsymbolled heap. A Grave in Ukraine. Saul Tchernichowsky. TrJP, *tr. by* L. V. Snowman
(Grave, The.) VWA, *tr. by* Robert Mezey *and* Shula Starkman.
("There are many like him here, without epitaph, without a mound.") VWA, *tr. by* Robert Mezey *and* Shula Starkman.

There are many monsters that a glassen surface. The Octopus. James Merrill. CAPP; CoAP

There are many souls which are neither music nor voice. The Ear. Louis MacNeice. OxBSP

There are many tonight and the rink. Skaters. Vern Rutsala. ASP

There are many Washingtons. Which Washington? Eve Merriam. NTCP

There are many ways to die. History among the Rocks. Robert Penn Warren. *Fr.* Kentucky Mountain Farm. GOA; MoAmPo

There are many who say that a dog has his day. The Song of the Mischievous Dog. Dylan Thomas. FaFP; FL; FPL; GrPl

There are men in the village of Erith. Erith, on the Thames *or* The Village of Erith. *Unknown.* ChTr; FaBoPP; GBP; WSC

There are men making death together in the wood. The Delta. Michael Dennis Browne. NYBP

There are miracles that happen. Breaking Silence. Janice Mirikitani. BrSi

There are moments. Snow Crystals on Meall Glas. Elizabeth A. Wilson. PoSH

There are no angels yet. Gabriel. Adrienne Rich. VGW

There are no asphodels, violets, or hyacinths. Stratis Thalassinos among the Agapanthi. George Seferis, *tr. by* Edmund Keeley *and* Philip Sherrard. VMG

There are no crocodiles or hippos here. Bullrush Basket. Jan Kuijper, *tr. by* Jacob Lowland. DuIn

There are no crosses. A Death in the Desert. Charles Tomlinson. FF

There are no dry bones. The Bones of My Father. Etheridge Knight. DiL

There are no fairy-folk in our Southwest. Western Magic. Mary Austin. AmFN

There Are No Gods. Euripides, *tr. fr. Greek by* John Addington Symonds. *Fr.* Bellerophon. EaLo

There are no heroes. Dead Heroes. Karoniaktatie. STE

There are no hollows any more. Ironic: LL.D. William Stanley Braithwaite. BANP

There are no more shopping days to Christmas. Eve. Howard Nemerov. CRP

There are no more tears for the body to weep with. Milk Boy. Dorothy Wellesley. CN

There are no nightmares now. Only when memory settles. Seravezza. Hoyt W. Fuller. PoBA

There Are No People Song. *Navajo Indian Oral Tradition.* TTTS

There are no roads but the frost. Old Age Compensation. James Wright. NNaP

There are no signs. The sky is entirely bland. Augury. W. H. Oliver. PeNZ

There are no stars to-night. My Grandmother's Love Letters. Hart Crane. BLPL; CMoP; FaBoBe; HeIP; InPK; MoAB; NoAM; NOBA; NoP

There are no stars which fell on Alabama. Elements of Grammar. Calvin C. Hernton. NBP

There are no trenches dug in the park, not yet. Nightmare at Noon. Stephen Vincent Benét. OxBA

There are no upper hands in love. After You, Madam. Alex Comfort. ErPo

There are notes to lightning in my bedroom. Star Quilt. Roberta Hill Whiteman. CDW; NoAM

There are on the earth 50,000 dead whom no one. Fourth Poem. Costa Andrade, *tr.* by Michael Wolfers. WMBCH

There are one or two things I should just like to hint. To His Countrymen. James Russell Lowell. *Fr.* A Fable for Critics. AA

There are only two things now. New Year's Eve. D. H. Lawrence. BoLoP; ErPo

There are palm trees in my homeland. Antônio Gonçalves Dias, *tr. fr. Portuguese by* Frances Ellen Buckland. *Fr.* Song of Exile. TTY

There are people go to Carmel. At Carmel. Mary Austin. AmFN

There are people, I know, to be found. Drinking Song. James Kenneth Stephen. NOBL

"There are people so dumb," my father said. Plain Talk. William Jay Smith. FiBHP; MoAmPo

There are people who know how to love. Poem of Explanations. Dahlia Ravikovich, *tr.* by Warren Bargad *and* Stanley F. Chyet. IP

There are people who maybe go on bragging. I Shall Never Go On Bragging. Moyshe-Leyb Halpern, *tr.* by Benjamin *and* Barbara Harshav. AYP

There are people whom I meet every dozen years or so. A Search. Adam Wazyk, *tr.* by Czeslaw Milosz. PwPP

There are, perhaps, whom passion gives a grace. The Aged Lover Discourses in the Flat Style. J. V. Cunningham. NoAM; SM

There are pines that are tall enough. An Elegy Is Preparing Itself. Donald Justice. CRP; HoPM

There Are Places. Myra von Riedemann. OBCV

There are portraits and still-lifes. Paring the Apple. Charles Tomlinson. CMoP; NePoEA-2; OxBTC; PoE

There are questions that must be asked. Incidents in Playfair House. Nicholas Moore. ErPo

There are rare moments. Oboe. Eugenio Montale, *tr. fr. Italian by* Jonathan Galassi. *Fr.* Chords, V. PFI

There are records. Do not. Buying a Record. Robert Peters. BXAP

There are rivers. Wilderness Rivers. Elizabeth Jane Coatsworth. AmFN

There are rock-rooted ranges to dominate. Rex Ingamells. *Fr.* Memory of Hills. CBAP

There Are Roughly Zones. Robert Frost. CMoP; PPP

There are seas, there are mountains. Hurrah, Hurrah. Remco Campert, *tr.* by Greta Kilburn. DuIn

There are seeds within the tide. City. Joseph Bruchac. CDW

There are seven hills. The Windy Bishop. Wilfred Watson. OBCV

There are seventy times seven kinds of loving. Veterans. George Johnston. NOBC

There are several attitudes towards Christmas. The Cultivation of Christmas Trees. T. S. Eliot. OFD

"There are sixteen lang miles, I'm sure." The Bent Sae Brown. *Unknown.* ESPB

There are sixty-five miles. "Are You Still There." Joy Harjo. NOVW

There are so many crosses. Crosses. Faiz Ahmad Faiz, *tr.* by Mahmood Jamal. PBMUP

There Are So Many Fatherless Children Around. John Wieners. PPR

There are so many ideas of heaven. Heaven. Howard Moss. BLA

There are so many lies in nature. Degas. Paul Monette. AmPA

There are so many things to do to-day. Every Day. Mary Osborn. BoTP

There Are So Many Ways of Going Places. Leslie Thompson. FaPON

There are some/ secrets. July 31. Norman Jordan. PoBA

There are some birds in these valleys. The Decoys. W. H. Auden. CMoP; PoE

There are some days the happy ocean lies. Seascape. Stephen Spender. MOS; NoP

There are some heights in Wessex, shaped as if by a kindly hand. Wessex Heights. Thomas Hardy. CMoP; EBVV; FaBoPP; OAEL-2; OBNC; PoEL-5

There Are Some Lusty Voices Singing. Geoffrey Lehmann. *Fr.* Ross's Poems. CBAP

There are some qualities—some incorporate things. Sonnet—Silence. Poe. NOBA

There are some questions one should know by heart. Postscript. Henri Coulette. DiPo

There are some quiet crossings in his city. Water Color. Stephen Mooney. NYBP

There are some quiet ways. The Wayside. James Herbert Morse. AA

There are some that love the Border-land and some the Lothians wide. The Road. Christine Orr. PoSH

There are some tiny obvious details in human life. Against Surrealism. James Wright. LCAP

There are songs too wide for sound. There are quiet. Answerers. William Stafford. CAPP

There are spaces. Old Maps and New. Norman MacCaig. OxBC

There are statues moving into a war. The War. W. S. Merwin. LCAP

There are stories that unwind themselves as simply. Spider Web. Stephen Dobyns. BLA; PPR

There are strange hells within the minds war made. Strange Hells. Ivor Gurney. OxBTC

There are strange things done in the midnight sun. The Cremation of Sam McGee. Robert W. Service. BLPL; FaFP; NOBC; OBNV; PoLF

There are sunsets who whisper a good-by. Sunsets. Carl Sandburg. MoAmPo

There Are Sweet Flowers. Walter Savage Landor. EnRP

There are the Alps. What is there to say about them? On the Fly-Leaf of Pound's Cantos. Basil Bunting. FaBoTw; NoAM; OxBTC

There are the fair-limbed nymphs o' the woods. Leigh Hunt. *Fr.* The Nymphs. OBNC

There are the local orchard boughs. Hart Crane. AnAn

There are the many red birds holding a document. Sacrifice of a Virgin in the Mayan Ball Court. Norman Dubie. GeTw

There are things a man does. Being with Men. Linda Gregg. NPGG

There are things in this country too. Salute. Moyshe-Leyb Halpern, *tr.* by Benjamin *and* Barbara Harshav. AYP

There are things to be said. No doubt. Cid Corman. VGW

There are things you have words for. Two Words; a Wedding. B. P. Nichol. NOBC

There are thirteen months in all the year. Robin Hood and the Three Squires. *Unknown.* EnSB

There are those fish that swim ever in the dim. Pearl Perch. John Blight. CBAP

There are those to whom place is unimportant. The Rose. Theodore Roethke. NOBA; NYBP

There are those who think. Prologue from "Legacy." Patricia Parker. GLP

There Are Three Bones in the Human Ear. Anita Endrezze-Danielson. STE

There are three names. National Security. Archibald MacLeish. GOA

There are three plenties. The Fort of Ard Ruide. *Unknown.* NOIV

There are three preachers, ever preaching. The Three Preachers. Charles MacKay. EBVV

There are three things which are too wonderful for me. Too Wonderful. Bible, *O.T. Fr.* Proverbs: The Words of Agur, *ll.* 18-19. TrJP

There are three valleys where the warm sun lingers. The Long Harbour. Mary Ursula Bethell. ATNZ; PeNZ

There are three who await my death. *Unknown, tr.* by Thomas Kinsella. NOIV

There are times in one's life which one cannot forget. Mr. Billings of Louisville. Eugene Field. NBLV

There are times that falter. Solo. Marcia Southwick. PPR

There are too many waterfalls here. Questions of Travel. Elizabeth Bishop. NAAL-2; NOBA

There are trails that a lad may follow. Silver Ships. Mildred Plew Meigs. FaPON

There are truths you Americans need to be told. James Russell Lowell. *Fr.* A Fable for Critics. OBSV

There are twelve months in all the year. Robin Hood Rescuing Three Squires. *Unknown.* ESPB
    (Robin Hood and the Three Squires.) NAEL-1
    (Robin Hood and the Widow's Three Sons.) OnMSP

There are twelve months throughout the year. September. Mary Howitt. BoTP

There are twenty dead who're sleeping near the slopes of Bud Dajo. The Fight at Dajo. Alfred E. Wood. PAH

There are two angels, messengers of light. Peace and Love. Ella Wheeler Wilcox. PWR

There are two bends in the road, and an unexpected dip. Pont y Caniedydd. Alun Llywelyn-Williams, *tr.* by Joseph R. Clancy. OBWVE

There are two different kinds, I believe, of human attraction. Arthur Hugh Clough. *Fr.* Amours de Voyage, Canto II, xi. GTBS-P

There are two drinking places in Iowa where I go with him. Captain Michael. Park Je-chun. WCI

There are two kinds of people on earth today. Lifting and Leaning. Ella Wheeler Wilcox. BLPA; WBLP

There are two Mays. Emily Dickinson. NOBA

There are two miseries in human life. Walter Savage Landor. FaBoEE

There are two sorrows to be proud of. Between. Tomioka Taeko, *tr. by* Sato. FCEI

There are two ways now. Progress. Edith Agnew. AmFN

There are two women; one I love, and one. Twins. "Owen Meredith." ErPo

There are voices, voices. Light's dying. Birds have quit. John Berryman. *Fr.* Dream Songs. CAPP

There are wolves in the next room waiting. The Wolves. Allen Tate. LiTA; LiTM; NOBA; OxBA; PoA

There are words like freedom. Refugee in America. Langston Hughes. AmFN; GOA
(Words Like Freedom.) BPo

There are words that can only be said on paper. Words. Robert Finch. PoA

There are wrongs done in the fair face of heaven. The Deeds That Might Have Been. Wilfrid Scawen Blunt. *Fr.* In Vinculis. TrGrPo

There are youngsters now. Furniture. Phyllis Harris. NYBP

There arent. Untitled Requiem for Tomorrow. Conyus. PoBA

There, as she sewed, came floating through her head. Past. Winifred Howells. AA

There, at the other side. The Unasked For. Peter Cooley. NAmP

There at the top of the world. Harlem in January. Julia Fields. CNA

There at the watershed I turned. Ba Cottage. Andrew Young. OxBSP

There be four things which are little upon the earth. Four Things . Bible, *O.T. Fr.* Proverbs: The Words of Agur, *ll.* 24-28.

There be many kinds of parting—yes, I know. Separation. Martha Gilbert Dickinson Bianchi. AA

There be none of Beauty's daughters. Stanzas for Music. Byron. AWP; ChER; ELP; EnRP; FiP; GTBS; GTBS-P; LiTB; NAEL-2; NoP; OAEL-2; PoRA; TrGrPo

There be three badgers on a mossy stone. The Three Badgers. "Lewis Carroll." FaBoNo

There be three hundred different ways and more. Tears. "Owen Meredith." *Fr.* Glenaveril. EBVV

There be three things seeking my death. Prayer for the Speedy End of Three Great Misfortunes. *Unknown, tr.* by Frank O'Connor. OBMV

There between the riverbank. Angel. Brad Leithauser. DiPo; FYAP; MAYP

There Blooms No Bud in May. Walter De la Mare. MoAB; MoBrPo

There calleth me ever a marvelous horn. Home-Sickness. Justinus Kerner, *tr.* by James Clarence Mangan. AWP

There cam' seven Egyptians on a day. The Gypsy Countess. *Unknown.* OBET

There came a bird out o' a bush. Lady Isabel and the Elf-Knight. *Unknown.* ESPB

There came a day at summer's full. Emily Dickinson. NAAL-1; NOBA
(Renunciation.) MoAmPo

There came a dove, an Easter dove. My Easter Dove. Henrietta Cordelia Ray. CBWP-3

There came a ghost to Margret's door. Sweet William's Ghost *or* Sweet William and May Margaret. *Unknown.* AWP; CH; ESPB

There came a gray owl at sunset. *Unknown.* WSC

There came a knocking at the front door. A Person from Porlock. R. S. Thomas. TOF

There came a whisper from the night to me. God's Remembrance. Francis Ledwidge. TIRV

There came a wind like a bugle. Emily Dickinson. CMoP; MoAB; NAAL-1; NAWM-2; NOBA; OPOP; OxBA; RB

There came an earl a-riding by. The Gypsy Countess. *Unknown.* OBET

There came from Normandy an old. The Two Lovers. Marie de France, *tr.* by Patricia Terry. BoWoP

There came this bright young thing. As for the Quince. Nuala Ni Dhomhnaill, *tr.* by Paul Muldoon. CIP

There came three men from out of the west. Sir John Barleycorn. *Unknown.* FaBoBa

There came to port last Sunday night. The New Arrival. George Washington Cable. AA

There came two gentlemen. The Cock. Ewa Lipska, *tr.* by Peter Jay *and* Geri Lipschultz. VWA

There can be no songs for dead children. Kindertotenlieder. Michael Longley. CIP

There chanced to be a pedlar bold. The Bold Pedlar and Robin Hood. *Unknown.* AmFP; ESPB

There Charon stands, who rules the dreary coast. Virgil, *tr. fr. Latin by* Dryden. *Fr.* The Aeneid [*or* Eneados], VI. OBVE

There cloud moves in front of cloud, and above, suggesting. Range. Rae Armantrout. LP

There comes a moment when to believe is not enough. Action. James Oppenheim. TrJP

There Comes a Time. Ella Wheeler Wilcox. PWR

There comes a time when everything is laced. The Imagination of Necessity. Andrei Codrescu. EAS

There comes a wail of anguish. A Cry for Light. *Unknown.* BLRP

There comes Emerson first, whose rich words, every one. James Russell Lowell. *Fr.* A Fable for Critics. NAAL-1
(Emerson.) AmPP; NOBA; OxBA; TAP

There comes Poe, with his raven, like Barnaby Rudge. Poe and Longfellow. James Russell Lowell. *Fr.* A Fable for Critics. AmPP; NOBA; OxBA; TAP
(Poe.) TAP

There comes the time. Moving. Darrell Gray. UL

There died a myriad. Ezra Pound. *Fr.* Hugh Selwyn Mauberley. (Life and Contacts), V. FF; MoAmPo; NOBE; PoE; WaaP

There dwelt a fair maid in the West. James Harris (The Daemon Lover). *Unknown.* ESPB

There dwelt a man in fair[e] Westmoreland [*or* Westmerland]. Johnie Armstrong. *Unknown.* ESPB, (A *vers.*); FaBoBa; HoPM, *cond.*; NoP, (A *vers.*); TrGrPo

There dwelt a miller, hale and bold. The Miller of Dee. *Unknown.* GBP

There dwelt the Man, the flower of human kind. Mount Vernon, the Home of Washington. William Day. OHIP

There exists no proof as. E. C. Bentley. *Fr.* Clerihews. NOBL

There falls with every wedding chime. Walter Savage Landor. *Fr.* The Last Fruit Off an Old Tree. SeCePo

There fared a mother driven forth. The House of Christmas. G. K. Chesterton. MoBrPo

There Faunus and Sylvanus keep their courts. Sir John Denham. *Fr.* Cooper's Hill. JCP

There fell red rain of spears athwart the sky. Last Judgment. John Gould Fletcher. AWP

There flourished once a potentate. The King of Yvetot. Pierre Jean de Béranger, *tr.* by William Toynbee. AWP

There goes the dog of the mind. Soliloquy by the Shore. Martin Scholten. GoYe

There goes the grandson, run off to the beach! The Grandson. James Scully. NYBP

There goes the Wapiti. The Wapiti. Ogden Nash. MoShBr

There Gowans Are Gay. *Unknown.* GBP

There grew a goodly tree him faire beside. Balme. Spenser. *Fr.* The Faerie Queene, I, 11. CH

There grew an aged tree on the green. The Oak and the Brere. Spenser. *Fr.* The Shepheardes [*or* Shepeards *or* Shepherd's] Calender: February. OBSC

There grew two olives, closest of the grove. Homer, *tr. fr. Greek by* Pope. *Fr.* Odyssey, V. OBVE

There grows no rootless flower. The First Reader. Winfield Townley Scott. PoA

There had been multitudes, yea, multitudes, O God. They. Mani Leib, *tr.* by John Hollander. PeBMYV

There had been rain in the morning and a chaffinch. All Possession Is Theft. Lauris Edmond. PeNZ

There had been years of passion—scorching, cold. "And There Was a Great Calm." Thomas Hardy. ChTr; CMoP; FaBoRV; LiTM; OAEL-2

There hartes ware so roted in the popes lawes. Fragment of an Anti-Papist Ballad. *Unknown.* CoMu

There has been. To W. C. W. M. D. Alfred Kreymborg. PoA

There has been a light snow. In a Train. Robert Bly. CAPP; NaP; TTTS

There has been a play on T.V. Lesbian Play on T.V. Caroline Gilfillan. PeHV

There has been no change. Autumn. Princess Shikishi, *tr.* by Hiroaki Sato. PBWP

There has something gone wrong. Keep a Stiff Upper Lip. Phoebe Cary. FaFP

There Has to Be a Jail for Ladies. Thomas Merton. VGW

There have been poets that in verse display. To Wordsworth. Hartley Coleridge. Son

There have been three storms in my heart. Summerhouse. Melvin Walker La Follette. NePoEA

There have been times when I well might have passed and the ending have come. Thomas Hardy. *Fr.* In Tenebris, III. OAEL-2

There he comes, armed and fierce. The Guerrilla. *Unknown, tr.* by Philippa Rumsey. WMBCH

There he is, woman! The Seduction of Engadu. *Unknown, tr. fr. Babylonian by* William Ellery Leonard. *Fr.* The Epic of Gilgamesh. ErPo

There he moved, cropping the grass at the purple canyon's lip. The Horse Thief. William Rose Benét. MoAmPo; OnMSP

There he stands. see? Two Jazz Poems. Carl Wendell Hines, Jr.. AmNP

There he was—having spent. "Yes, But. . ." Theodore Weiss. TAP

There I buried the wishfulness and the watchfulness that was in me. Tideline. Marvin Bell. BLA

There I could never be a boy. Frank O'Hara. NNaP

There I learned how faces fall apart. "Anna Akhmatova", *tr. fr. Russian by* D. M. Thomas. *Fr.* Requiem 1935-1940. AIW

There. I set you free. Manumission. Barbara Burford. DT

There I was, hunched over office desk. Seiken, *tr. by* Lucien Stryk *and* Takashi Ikemoto. ZPCJ

There in a bare place, in among the rocks. The Little Lough. John Hewitt. NeIP

There in Fiesole it was always fresh. Basil. Gibbons Ruark. MT

There in his room, whene'er the moon looks in. Ode for a Master Mariner Ashore. Louise Imogen Guiney. AA

There in midnight water. Waka on the Correct-Law Eye Treasury. Dogen, *tr. by* Lucien Stryk *and* Takashi Ikemoto. ZPCJ

There in the bracken was the ominous spoor mark. The Tantanoola Tiger. Max Harris. MoBS; PoAu-2

There, in the corner, staring at his drink. Docker. Seamus Heaney. HeIP; MoP; NOIV; TW

There, in the earliest and chary spring, the dogwood flowers. Sunday: Outskirts of Knoxville, Tennessee. James Agee. ErPo

There in the flower garden. *Unknown, tr. by* Willis Barnstone. BoWoP

There in the hard light. An Irish Lake. William Robert Rodgers. BIrV

There, in the market, with Mrs. Peters. Journal of the Storm. Greg Kuzma. AmPA

There in the oozy ground by the Fen. *Unknown, tr. by* Arthur Waley. BoS

There, in the very middle. Mothers. Auvaiyar, *tr. by* A. K. Ramanujan. PLW

There is/ A welcome at the door to which no one comes? Angel Surrounded by Paysans. Wallace Stevens. HCAP; LCAP; PPP

There Is. Guillaume Apollinaire, *tr. fr. French by* Michael Benedikt. POS

There is/ One great society alone on earth. The Noble. Wordsworth. *Fr.* The Prelude [or, Growth of a Poet's Mind]: Residence in France, 3 *ll.*. ChTr

There is a bale of hay. Beside the Road. Ken Belford. NeAC

There is a bar I go to when I'm in Chicago. A Story. Susan Mitchell. NAmP

There is a big artist named Val. Dante Gabriel Rossetti. FaBoEE

There is a bird bath on our grass. The Bird Bath. Florence Hoatson. BoTP

There is a bird in the poplars. Metric Figure. William Carlos Williams. MoAB; MoAmPo

There is a bird who, by his coat. The Jackdaw. Vincent Bourne, *tr. by* William Cowper. PBBP

There is a birth. Cold Night. A. Leyeles, *tr. by* Benjamin *and* Barbara Harshav. AYP

There is a black dog in my painting. Joan Brown, about Her Painting. Kathleen Fraser. NPGG

There is a blue star, Janet. Baby Toes. Carl Sandburg. FaPON

There is a bondage worse, far worse, to bear. There Is a Bondage Worse. Wordsworth. ChER

There Is a Box. Uri Zvi Greenberg, *tr. fr. Hebrew by* Robert Mezey *and* Ben Zion Gold. VWA

There is a change—and I am poor. A Complaint. Wordsworth. NOBE; PoEL-4

There is a charm in solitude that cheers. John Clare. NOBVV (Solitude.) EnRP; OxBSP

There Is a Charming Land. Adam Oehlenschläger, *tr. fr. Danish by* Robert Hillyer. AWP; FaPON

There Is a City. "The Jewish Sibyl", *tr. fr. Greek by* Bohn. *Fr.* The Fourth Book of Sibylline Oracles. TrJP

There is a city, builded by no hand. Paradisi Gloria. Thomas William Parsons. AA

There is a clouded city, gone to rest. The Aztec City. Eugene Fitch Ware. AA

There is a club for boys where they. To G. R. Samuel Elsworth Cottam. PeHV

There is a coarseness. Jungle Taste. Edward S. Silvera. CDC

There is a Coke bottle on the roof. Kissing Game. Bob Rosenthal. UL

There is a concert in the trees. A Spring Song—1834. John Bethune. PF

There is a connection between us. Connection. Caroline Halliday. DT

There is a cool river. Detroit. Donald Hall. AmFN

There is a country Lost. Ice, Eden. Paul Celan, *tr. by* Michael Hamburger. OBD

There is a creator named God. On the Painter Val Prinsep. Dante Gabriel Rossetti. FaBoEE

There is a crying in the world. End of the World. Else Lasker-Schüler, *tr. by* Willis Barnstone *and* Michael Gillespie. BoWoP

There is a dark planet striking against us. Invisible. The Dark Planet. John Heath-Stubbs. OAEL-2

There is a darkness, dark. Lost Moments. Glover Davis. SM

There is a day when elaborate weathers ease down. Vincent O'Sullivan. *Fr.* Brother Jonathan, Brother Kafka, 43. ATNZ

There is a dead part of the day. Late Naps. Marvin Bell. AnAn

There is a dear and lonely tract of hell. Supremacy. E. A. Robinson. NoAM

There is a deep brooding. My Arkansas. Maya Angelou. BlSi

There is a destiny that makes us brothers. A Creed. Edwin Markham. BLPA; BLPL; FaBoBe; FaFP

There is a dish to hold the sea. Imagination. John Davidson. *Fr.* New Year's Eve. MoBrPo

There is a distance in the heart. Ancestor of the Hunting Heart. John Haines. BLA

There Is a Dream Dreaming Us. Norman Dubie. GeTw

There is a drought, the farmers have a hard time finding food. Following the Rhymes of Shao-pao Huang's Poem on Being Moved While Visiting the Farmers. Yang Shih-ch'i, *tr. by* Jonathan Chaves. CoBLCP

There is a drunk on Main Avenue, slumped. Song-Maker. Anita Endrezze-Danielson. HATNAP; STE

There is a faculty or knack, smallish, in the mind that can turn. A. R. Ammons. *Fr.* Sphere, 71-72. NoAM

There is a far country where there is a hall for dreams. The Far Country. Robert Greacen. NeIP

"There is a fashion in this land." The Knight's Ghost. *Unknown*. ESPB

"There is a feast in your father's house." Leesome Brand. *Unknown*. ESPB

There is a fever of the spirit. Song by Mr. Cypress. Thomas Love Peacock. *Fr.* Nightmare Abbey, ch. 11. OAEL-2; OBNC; Par

There is a fine stuffed chavender. A False Gallop of Analogies. Warham St. Leger. CenHV; FaBoCo; FiBHP

There is a flower, a little flower. James Montgomery. *Fr.* The Daisy. BoTP

There is a flower blossoming out of season. Flower Ensnarer of Psalms. Rossana Ombres, *tr. by* I. L. Salomon. BoWoP

There is a flower I wish to wear. Hearts-Ease. Walter Savage Landor. EnRP

There is a flower in my cell. A Flower. Carlos José Guadamuz, *tr. by* David Volpendesta. Vol

There is a flower that bees prefer. Purple Clover. Emily Dickinson. MoAmPo

There is a flower, the Lesser Celandine. A Lesson. Wordsworth. GTBS; GTBS-P

There is a fountain filled with blood. Praise for the Fountain Opened. William Cowper. InPK

There is a fox dragging along. *Unknown, tr. by* Arthur Waley. BoS

There Is a Garden in Her Face. Thomas Campion. AAS; ElL; GoJo; HeIP; InPK; NAEL-1; NIP; NoP; OAEL-1; OBSC; OPOP; PoE; PoEL-2; PrIm; TrGrPo

(There Is a Garden.) ELP

There is a garden where lilies. Eutopia. Francis Turner Palgrave. EBVV

There is a gentle nymph not far from hence. Sabrina. Milton. *Fr.* Comus; a Masque Presented at Ludlow Castle. OBS

There is a ghost. Ghost. Christian Morgenstern, *tr. by* W. D. Snodgrass *and* Lore Segal. WSC

There is a girdle in the east. *Unknown, tr. by* Arthur Waley. BoS

There Is a Girl Inside. Lucille Clifton. CAPP

There is a girl you like so you tell her. Courtship. Mark Strand. HCAP

There is a golden rule in life. Do As You Would Be Done By. Matilda Caroline Edwards. PWR

There is a gray enameled sky. Private Rooms. Diana O Hehir. NPGG

There is a great amount of poetry in unconscious/ fastidiousness. Critics and Connoisseurs. Marianne Moore. AmPP; CMoP; FaBoWP; NoAM; NOBA; OxBA

There is a great river this side of Stygia. The River of Rivers in Connecticut. Wallace Stevens. HAP; HCAP; NOBA; VGW

There Is a Green Hill Far Away. Cecil Frances Alexander. BLRP; OxBChV; TIRV; WGRP

There is a grey thing that lives in the tree-tops. Stephen Crane. WSC

There is a growth that hurts the child. An Age. Laura Jensen. LCAP

There is a halo around the moon. Debt. *Gond Oral Tradition, tr. by* V. Elwin *and* S. Hivale. WTO

There is a hawk that is picking the birds out of our sky. Shiva. Robinson Jeffers. NoAM; NOBA; Son

There is a heigh-ho in these glowing coals. Heigh-ho on a Winter Afternoon. Donald Davie. NePoEA-2; OxBTC

There Is a High Place. Edwin Markham. AH

There is a hill and on that hill is a stone. The Heart of the World. Rabbi Nahman of Bratzlav, *tr. by* Joseph Leftwich. TrJP

There is a hill beside the silver Thames. Robert Bridges. BrPo

There is a hornet in the room. Buried at Springs. James Schuyler. CoAP; PoM

There is a house with ivied walls. Architectural Masks. Thomas Hardy. EyDe

There is a hush this golden afternoon. Classroom in October. Elias Lieberman. GoYe

There is a joyful night in which we lose. When the Dumb Speak. Robert Bly. NOBA

There is a kind of lace laid over the city, a lightness. The Serious Merriment of Women. Patricia Goedicke. TAP

There is a kind of loss. Exile. Dennis Scott. UAS

There is a king, and a ruthless king. The Steam King. Edward P. Mead. PF

There Is a Lady ("There is a lady conquering with glances"). Walther von der Vogelweide, *tr. fr. German by* Jethro Bithell. AWP

There Is a Lady Sweet and Kind. *At. to* Thomas Ford. CH; EBEV, EIL; ELP; FaFP; GBL; HeIP; LiTB; NoP; OBEV; OBS; TrGrPo
  (Passing By.) NOBE

There Is a Land. James Montgomery. OPP

There Is a Land. Isaac Watts. *See* There is a land of pure delight.

There is a land called Lost. Two Chorale-Preludes. Geoffrey Hill. OxBC

There Is a Land Mine Eye Hath Seen. Gurdon Robins. AH

There is a land of Dream. Dream Fantasy. "Fiona Macleod." WGRP

There is a land, of every land the pride. There Is a Land. James Montgomery. OPP

There is a land of pure delight. Isaac Watts. TOF
  (A Prospect of Heaven.) OBD
  (Heaven.) WGRP
  (Prospect of Heaven Makes Death Easy, A.) NOCV; NoP
  (There Is a Land.) ELP

There is a language in a naval log. E. J. Pratt. *Fr.* Behind the Log. MoCV

There is a languor of the life. Emily Dickinson. BoWoP

There is a little lightning in his eyes. Of Robert Frost. Gwendolyn Brooks. MoP; NoAM; NOBA

There is a lonely mountain-top. Jephthah's Daughter. "Yehoash", *tr. by* Alter Brody. TrJP

There is a long journey to be made. The Journey. Vivienne Finch. TSM

There is a loud noise of Death. To Dear Daniel. Samuel Greenberg. LiTA

There is a magic melting pot. The Melting Pot. Dudley Randall. BPo

There is a Maker. Wizards. Alonzo Gonzales Mó, *tr. by* Allan F. Burns. STP

There is a meadow. Last Light. Robert Kelly. VGW

There is a middleaged man, Tim Flanagan. The Middleaged Man. Louis Simpson. NNaP

There is a moment country children know. Village before Sunset. Frances Cornford. BoNaP

There is a monstrous garden in the sky. Garden in the Sky. Margery Lawrence. CN

There is a morn by men unseen. Emily Dickinson. OxBA

There is a mountain everyone must climb. The Mountain. Robert Finch. CaP

There is a mystery too deep for words. Silence. John Hall Wheelock. LiTM

There is a mystic borderland that lies. The Mystic Borderland. Helen Field Fischer. WBLP

There is a niland on a river lying. Collusion between a Alegaiter and a Water-Snaik. J. W. Morris. NA

There is a pain—so utter. Emily Dickinson. BoWoP; NAAL-1; NOBA

There is a painted bus. The Bus. "Peter." BoTP

There is a panther caged within my breast. The Black Panther. John Hall Wheelock. FF; LiTM

There is a parrot imitating spring. The Cane Fields. Rita Dove. *Fr.* Parsley, I. ER; HCAP; NAmP; NoAM

There is a people mighty in its youth. Tribute to America. Shelley. AiP; OPP

There is a perfect. Moving. P. J. Kavanagh. PoPo

There is a place,/ List, daughter! in a black and hollow vault. John Ford. *Fr.* 'Tis Pity She's a Whore. OBD

There is a place in Montana where the grass stands up two feet. Rosebud. Jon Anderson. MAYP

There is a place that some men know. The Cross. Allen Tate. AWP; MoAmPo; OxBA

There is a place where contrarieties are equally true. Vision of Beulah, The ("There is a place where contrarieties are equally true"). Blake. *Fr.* Milton, II. OAEL-2

There is a place where goblins dwell. Where Goblins Dwell. Jack Prelutsky. RHPC

There is a place where, wisdom won, right recorded. Elegy for Our Dead. Edwin Rolfe. WaP

There is a plan far greater than the plan you know. There Is No Death. *Unknown.* BLPA; FPL

There is a pleasure in poetic pains. Poetic Pains. William Cowper. *Fr.* The Task, II. FiP

There is a pleasure in the pathless woods. Byron. *Fr.* Childe Harold's Pilgrimage: The Ocean. MOS
  (Apostrophe to the Ocean.) OHFP; WBLP
  (Deep and Dark Blue Ocean.) ChTr
  (Ocean, The.) FaBV; TrGrPo
  (Roll On, Thou Deep and Dark Blue Ocean.) FiP
  (Sea, The.) BLPL; FaBoBe; LiTB

There is a poor sneak called Rossetti. On Himself. Dante Gabriel Rossetti. FaBoEE

There is a precise instant in time. Midway. Robert Desnos, *tr. by* George Quasha. RHTwFP

There is a precise moment in time. Half Way. Robert Desnos, *tr. by* Michael Benedikt. POS

There is a pretty piece of work. The Naughty Lord and the Gay Young Lady—Damages, $10,000. *Unknown.* CoMu

There is a private tension that endears. The Crack. Michael Goldman. NYBP

There is a quest that calls me. The Mystic. Cale Young Rice. WGRP

There is a quiet kingdom's strand. The Quiet Kingdom. Carl Busse, *tr. by* Ludwig Lewisohn. AWP

There is a record. Prayer for Continuation. Susan Griffin. ER

There is a ring which shines brightly. Circle of Thorns. Amryl Johnson. WS

There is a river. No End of No-Story. George MacDonald. NOBVV

There is a river clear and fair. Fragment in Imitation of Wordsworth. Catherine Fanshawe. FaBoNo; FaBoPa
  (Fragment: "There is a river clear and fair.") Par
  (Fragments.) BXAP
  (Imitation of Wordsworth, An.) NA

There is a road that turning always. The Road. Edwin Muir. CMoP; FaFP; LiTB; LiTM; Mes

There is a rumour. Forecast. Howard Fergus. PBCV

There is a sad carnival up the valley. Are They Dancing. Edward Dorn. NeAP; PoM

There is a secret laughter. Secret Laughter. Christopher Morley. FaBV

There is a secret room. The Same Gesture. John Montague. BIrV

There is a sentinel before the gate. The City Church. "E. H. K." WGRP

There is a serpent in perfection tarnished. True Vine. Elinor Wylie. LiTA

There is a shattered palm. Egypt, Tobago. Derek Walcott. AnAn

There is a silence where hath been no sound. Silence. Thomas Hood. CH; EBEV; EnRP; NOBE; OBEV; PoEL-4; Son
  (Sonnet: Silence.) OBNC

There is a singer everyone has heard. The Oven Bird. Robert Frost. AmPP; AWP; HeIP; MoP; NAAL-2; NoAM; NOBA; NoP; OxBA; PoE; PPP; Son; TAP

There is a small store-house of knowledge in which I sit sometimes on hard wooden cases. A Store-House. Louis Dudek. CaP

There is a smile of love. The Smile. Blake. RB
  ("There is a smile of love.") TEP

There is a soldier on the battlefield. *Unknown, tr. by* Geoffrey Waters. BoWoP

There is a sound I would not hear. Fear. Langdon Elwyn Mitchell. AA

There is a special privacy on stage. Gig at Big Al's. Heather McHugh. GeTw

There is a sphere, a secret sphere. The Inner Realm. Priscilla Jane Thompson. CBWP-2

There is a spot where all our hopes. Home. Matilda C. Edwards. PWR

There is a stane in yon water. Burd Isabel and Earl Patrick. *Unknown.* ESPB

There is a story so true, so becoming, so full of duty. Window. Bruce Smith. DiL

There is a stream. Bach. Eeva-Liisa Manner, *tr. by* Aili Jarvenpa. SOP

There is a stream, I name not its name. Arthur Hugh Clough. *Fr.* The Bothie of Tober-na-Vuolich, *bk.* III. FaBoPP
  (Highland Glen near Loch Ericht, A.) FaBoPP

There is a stream that flowed before the first beginning. Kathleen Jessie Raine. *Fr.* Water. ImOP

There is a stream which rises. Joseph Bruchac. CDW

There is a Supreme God in the ethnological section. Homage to the British Museum. William Empson. CMoP; FaBoMo; LiTM; MoAB; MoBrPo; PoE

There is a tall long-sided dame. Samuel Butler. *Fr.* Hudibras, II, 1. OBSV

There is a tall tower by the river. Kung Tzu-chen, *tr.* by Shirleen S. Wong. WFTU

There Is a Tavern in the Town. *Unknown.* FaFP

There is a thing which in the light. A Candle. Sir John Suckling. ErPo

There is a Thorn—it looks so old. The Thorn. Wordsworth. EnRP

There is a three-cornered stone, white even in the dark. Thinking Stone. Takenaka Iku, *tr.* by Geoffrey Bownas *and* Anthony Thwaite. PeBJV

There Is a Tide. Kipling. *Fr.* Plain Tales from the Hills. OxBSP

There is a time, we know not when. The Hidden Line. Joseph Addison Alexander. BLPA

There is a time when the dead, not yet fully fallen from. The Sculptor. Russell Edson. NAmP

There is a tiny car on a tiny bureau by a tiny pink comb. 3 More Things. Elinor Nauen. UL

There is a tiny wind in our room. Loving. Shirley Kaufman. VWA

There is a train inside this iris. Iris. David St. John. LCAP

There is a tree, by day. Tenebris. Angelina Weld Grimké. CDC; PoBA; PoNe

There is a tree native in Turkestan. Note on Local Flora. William Empson. EBEV; FaBoMo

There Is a Tree That Stands. Itzig Manger, *tr. fr. Yiddish by* Leonard Wolf. PeBMYV

There is a two-headed goat, a four-winged chicken. Believe It. John Logan. AnAn; CAPP; LCAP

There is a wailing baby under every stone. Norman MacCaig. EAS

There is a walled garden where the flowers never pale or turn dark. Paradise. E. N. Sargent. NYBP

There is a warm mist by the pond, and the grass is lush. Melody in C. Wei Ch'eng-pan, *tr.* by Lois Fusek. ATF

There is a way of seeing that is not seeing. Trompe L'Œil. Daryl Hine. MoCV

There is a way to enter a field. Receiving the Stigmata. Rita Dove. KS

There is a white mare that my love keeps. Alex Comfort. *Fr.* The Postures of Love. ErPo

There is a willow grows aslant a brook. Shakespeare. *Fr.* Hamlet, V, i. RB
(Ophelia's Death.) ChTr

There is a wind where the rose was. Autumn. Walter de la Mare. OxBTC

There is a window stuffed with hay. The Hay Hotel. Oliver St. John Gogarty. BIrV

There is a woman climbing a glass hill. Two Women. Naomi Replansky. NMM

There is a woman in our town. William Carlos Williams. *Fr.* Paterson, V, ii. CMoP; PoE

There Is a Woman in This Town. Patricia Parker. BlSi

There is a woman running. The Joining. Gerda Norvig. VWA

There is a word at heart for the next of death. Written in Exile. Kathleen Jessie Raine. TrCP; WPE

There is a yew tree, pride of Lorton Vale. Yew Trees. Wordsworth. EnRP; UnPo

There is a young lady, whose nose. Edward Lear. OxBChV

There is a young Muslim Chinese. Taunt. *Malay Oral Tradition, tr. by* R. J. Wilkinson *and* R. O. Windstedt. WTO

There is about these autumn evenings bright. F. I. Tyutchev, *tr.* by Alan Myers. AAA

There is always a first flinging. Variations on a Theme. Anne Wilkinson. MoCV

There is always a lonely farm on the prairie. In America. Michael Sheridan. NAmP

There is an aggression of fact. After Jericho. R. S. Thomas. OxBC

There is an aggressive ring at my door. I'm Taking Off. Barbro Backberger, *tr.* by Joanna Bankier. OV

There is an air for which I would disown. An Old Tune. Gérard de Nerval, *tr.* by Andrew Lang. AWP

There is an ancient story. My Father's Story. Priscilla Jane Thompson. CBWP-2

There is an emptiness that fills. Stove's Out. Charles Bernstein. LP

There is an end of joy and sorrow. Ilicet. Swinburne. NOBVV

There is an evening coming in. Going. Philip Larkin. CMoP

There is an exquisite torture in living with dull people. Always Battling. Thomas O'Brien. NeIP

There is an eye in the stone. The Emperor. Tamura Ryuichi, *tr.* by Hiroaki Sato. FCEI

There is an Eye that never sleeps. God the Omniscient. James Cowden Wallace. BLRP
(God.) WGRP

There is an eye, there was a slit. Sabbath. John Berryman. *Fr.* Dream Songs. LCAP

There Is an Hour of Peaceful Rest. William Bingham Tappan. *See* Hour of Peaceful Rest, The.

There is an inevitability. Norman Harris. NYBP

There is an island in a far-off sea. Where the Single Men Go in Summer. Nina Bourne. FiBHP

There is an old and very cruel god. Vicarious Atonement. Richard Aldington. MoBrPo; WGRP

There Is an Old City. Karl Bulcke, *tr. fr. German by* Ludwig Lewisohn. AWP

There is an old he-wolf named Gambart. Dante Gabriel Rossetti. CenHV; FaBoEE

There is an old lady who lives down the hall. The Sugar Lady. Frank Asch. RHPC

There is an olden story. The Flowers' Ball. Ben King. AnAmPo

There is another world above this one. Gary Snyder. *Fr.* Through the Smoke Hole. PoA; PoM

There is blood on thy desolate shore. Apostrophe to the Island of Cuba. James Gates Percival. PAH

There is bright light. Its Name Is Known. Daniel Lawrence Kelleher. NeIP

There is Bryant, as quiet, as cool, and as dignified. Bryant. James Russell Lowell. *Fr.* A Fable for Critics. NOBA; TAP

There is but one great sorrow. The Shadow. Richard Henry Stoddard. AA

There is but one May in the year. May-Time. *Unknown.* BoTP

There is (conveniently) a hollow space. Shingle Beach Poem. James K. Baxter. ATNZ

There is craft in this smallest insect. The Spider. Michizane, *tr.* by Burton Watson. JLIC-1

There is death enough in Europe without these. Dead Ponies. Brenda Chamberlain. OBWVE; WPE

There is death in this river. To the Spirit of Monahsetah. Charlotte DeClue. GOS; STE

There is delight in singing, though none hear. To Robert Browning. Walter Savage Landor. EnRP; NoP

There is drink fermented. Chimedin Jigmed, *tr. fr. Mongol Oral Tradition by* C. R. Bawden. *Fr.* A Satirical Poem about Drink. WTO

There is enjoyment in a wilderness of trees. K. N. Bathushkov, *tr.* by Alan Myers. AAA

There is ever a song somewhere, my dear. James Whitcomb Riley. AnAmPo

There is fear in/ Turning the mind away. The Sun and the Moon and Fear of Loneliness. *Unknown.* WTO

There is, for me, now, in my life. Éric Clémens. WCI

There is frost in the air. Schoenberg Op. 11. Thomas W. Shapcott. *Fr.* Piano Pieces. CBAP

There is great mystery, Simone. Hair. Remy de Gourmont, *tr.* by Jethro Bithell. AWP; ErPo

There is Hawthorne, with genius so shrinking and rare. Hawthorne. James Russell Lowell. *Fr.* A Fable for Critics. AmPP; NOBA; OxBA; TAP

There is health in thy gray wing. To a Marsh Hawk in Spring. Henry David Thoreau. PoEL-4

There is in human closeness a sacred boundary. "Anna Akhmatova", *tr.* by Dianne Levitin. WPOW

There is in the dog's mind. The Dog. Li Nan, *tr.* by Dominic Cheung. IFON

There is in this world something. The Sweetest Thing. *Unknown, tr.* by Ulli Beier. TTY

There is interest in being able to feel what you see. Symmetrical Poem. Michael Palmer. NPGG

There is joy in/ Feeling the warmth. Eskimo Chant. *Unknown, tr.* by Knud Rasmussen. RFM

There is little in afternoon tea. On Drawing-Room Amenities. Gelett Burgess. FaBoNo

There is Lowell, who's striving Parnassus to climb. Lowell. James Russell Lowell. *Fr.* A Fable for Critics. AmPP; NOBA; OxBA; TAP
(On Himself.) AA

There is much to be said for the portrait painted in winter. Portrait in Winter. Katherine Garrison Chapin. GoYe

There is music in me, the music of a peasant people. The Banjo Player. Fenton Johnson. BANP; PoNe

There is my country under glass. At the Tourist Center in Boston. Margaret Atwood. NoP

There is naught for thee by thy haste to gain. The Created. Jones Very. NOCV; QFR

There Is Never a Day So Dreary. Lilla M. Alexander. BLRP

There is never an open door to the wild beasts' home. The Uninvited. William D. Mundell. NYBP

There Is No. Faye Kicknosway. GeTw

There is no answer. We do here what we will. The Usurpers. Edwin Muir. CMoP

There is no balm on earth. Gilbert Thomas. TrPWD

There is no bountie to be shew'd to such. Ben Jonson. Fr. The Poetaster, III, vi. PoEL-2

There is no cattle brand. Cattle Brand. János Pilinszky, tr. by William Jay Smith. MHuP

There is no chance, no destiny, no fate. Will. Ella Wheeler Wilcox. BLPA; FPL

There is no chapel on the day. Oscar Wilde. Fr. The Ballad of Reading Gaol. EBVV; NoAM; TIRV

There Is No Country. Julian Tuwim, tr. fr. Polish by Watson Kirkconnell. TrJP

There is no cross to mark. Missing, Presumed Killed. Pamela Holmes. CN

There is no cut rock. Climbing Zero Gully. David J. Morley. PoSH

There is no dearer lover of lost hours. Idleness. Weir Mitchell. AA

There Is No Death. John Luckey McCreery. BLPA; FaBoBe; PWR; WBLP

There Is No Death. Unknown. BLPA; FPL

There is no death, O child divine. The Great Victory. R. V. Gilbert. BLRP

There is no death! The stars go down. There Is No Death. John Luckey McCreery. BLPA; FaBoBe; PWR; WBLP

There is no end to the/ Deception of quiet things. The Chinese Banyan. William Meredith. NePoEA

There is no fire of the crackling boughs. Glenaradale. Walter Chalmers Smith. OBEV

There is no fitter end than this. In Memoriam S.C.W., V.C. Charles Hamilton Sorley. MMA

There is no form but shape! Rant Block. Michael McClure. EAS

There is no frigate like a book. Emily Dickinson. FPL; GoJo; MoAmPo; NIP; OBCA; PoLF; SoSe; TAP; TrGrPo

Book, A ("There is no frigate like a book"). FaPON

There Is No God. Arthur Hugh Clough. See Dipsychus: "There Is No God," the wicked saith.

There is no God, as I was taught in youth. John Masefield. Fr. Sonnets. CMoP; WGRP

"There is no God," the foolish saith. Convinced by Sorrow. Elizabeth Barrett Browning. Fr. The Cry of the Human. BLRP; WBLP

"There is no God," the wicked saith. Arthur Hugh Clough. Fr. Dipsychus, pt. I, sc. v. NAEL-2; NOBVV

(There Is No God.) BLPL; NOBE

There is no great and no small. The Informing Spirit. Emerson. AWP

There is no happy life. Love's Matrimony. William Cavendish. SeCePo

There is no hope or light. Asadullah Khan Ghalib, tr. by Ahmed Ali. GoT

There is no impeding. Sailing, Sailing. Lillian Morrison. ASP

There is no Job but cries to God and hopes. A Copy of Verses. John Wilson. SCAP

There is no joy in water apart from the sun. Ralph Nixon Currey. PeSA

There is no limit to the number of times. From Father to Son. Emyr Humphreys. OBWVE

There is no lover for hee or shee. A Paradox. Aurelian Townshend. SeCP

There is no mercy anywhere. Tenderness Closed like a Flower. Sirkka Turkka, tr. by Aili Jarvenpa. SOP

There is no music now in all Arkansas. Variations for Two Pianos. Donald Justice. NYBP

There Is No Name So Sweet on Earth. George W. Bethune. AH

(Blessed Name, The.) BLRP

There is no one among men that has not a special failing. Madly Singing in the Mountains. Po Chü-i, tr. by Arthur Waley. Mes

There Is No Opera like "Lohengrin." John Wheelwright. NYBP

There Is No Paradise. André Frénaud, tr. fr. French by Serge Gavronsky. RHTwFP

There is no passion that torments our life. Agnodicia, or Ignorance Banished from the Presence of Women. Catherine Des Roches, tr. by Dorothy Backer. DMF

There is no peace with you. Enigma. Jessie Redmond Fauset. PoNe

"There is no permanence," you sagely said. Samuel A. DeWitt. Fr. Two Sonnets for a Lost Love, I. GoYe

There is no place. Kenko, tr. by Steven D. Carter. WFTW

There Is No Place. Aleksander Wat, tr. fr. Polish by Isaac Komem. VWA

There is no place for me in any heart. Asadullah Khan Ghalib, tr. by Ahmed Ali. GoT

There is no place in paradise. Guillaume de Lorris and Jean de Meun, tr. fr. French. Fr. The Romance [or Romaunt] of the Rose. PBBP

There is no place like home. Here and There. Ralph Meredith. Mes

There Is No Place to Hide. Gwendolyn MacEwen. Fr. The T. E. Lawrence Poems. NOBC

"There is no place to turn," she said. The Sensualists. Theodore Roethke. ErPo

There is no point in work. Work. D. H. Lawrence. OBMV

There is no portrait. Robert Creeley Listens, Too. D. C. Berry. BXAP

There is no quenching of the other thirst. Hagar. Elisabeth Eybers, tr. by the author. PeSA

There is no rest for her, and sleep has left her bed. Gond Oral Tradition, tr. by V. Elwin and S. Hivale. WTO

There is no rhyme that is half so sweet. Madison Cawein. AA; BoNaP

There Is No Riot. Martin Carter. PBCV

There is no rose of such virtue. Two Carols to Our Lady. Unknown. ACP

There is no siding for the brain. Listening to a Broadcast. John Manifold. WaP

There is no signpost to say. Hilda Doolittle ("H. D.") Fr. Sigil, VIII. AnAn

There is no silence in the earth—so silent. Emily Dickinson. FaBoEE

There is no silence upon the earth or under the earth like the silence under the sea. Silences. E. J. Pratt. NOBC; OBCV

There is no silk nor worm to spin it. There Is No. Faye Kicknosway. GeTw

"There is no sky in Tokyo," Chieko said. Artless Talk. Takamura Kotaro, tr. by Geoffrey Bownas and Anthony Thwaite. PeBJV

There is no sky today. Echoes of birds. Counterparts. Stephen Dobyns. PoA

There is no sorrow. Away. Walter de la Mare. NoP

There is no sound of guns here, nor echo of guns. The Evacuees. Freda Laughton. CN

There is no sweeter sight, I swear, in Heaven. The Crimson Cherry Tree. Henry Treece. WaP

There is no thing in all the world but love. The Camel-Rider. Unknown, tr. by Wilfrid Scawen Blunt. AWP

There Is No Unbelief. Elizabeth York Case. WBLP; WGRP

There Is No Word for Goodbye. Mary TallMountain. HATNAP; STE

There Is None like Her. Tennyson. Fr. Maud, pt. I, xviii. OBNC

There Is None, O None but You. Thomas Campion. EiL; OBSC

There Is None to Help. Chad Walsh. Fr. The Psalm of Christ. TrCP

There is not a poem in sight. Writing while My Father Dies. Linda Pastan. PCP

There is not half so warm a fire. Against Fulfillment of Desire. Unknown. TrGrPo

There is not in the wide world a valley so sweet. The Meeting of the Waters. Thomas Moore. AnIL; NOIV; OxBoLi; PoEL-4

There Is Nothin' like a Dame. Oscar Hammerstein II. OBAL

There is nothing as sweet as independence. Independence. Adebayo Faleti, tr. by Bakare Gbadamosi and Ulli Beier. PBA

There is nothing between. Between You and Me. Fahmida Riaz, tr. by Mahmood Jamal. PBMUP

There is nothing I can do. Nizar Qabbani, tr. by Lena Jayyusi and W. S. Merwin. MAP

There is nothing to save, now all is lost. Nothing to Save. D. H. Lawrence. SOTW

There is one flower. Fleshflower. William Pitt Root. GeTw

There is one grief worse than any other. Daughter. Ellen Bryant Voigt. MT

There is one Mind, one omnipresent. Samuel Taylor Coleridge. Fr. Religious Musings. WGRP

There is one sin: to call a green leaf grey. Ecclesiastes. G. K. Chesterton. MoBrPo; OxBSP

There is one story and one story only. To Juan at the Winter Solstice. Robert Graves. CMoP; EBEV; FaBoMo; LiTB; LiTM; MoBrPo; MoP; NAEL-2; NoAM; OAEL-2; PoE; TwCP

There is one that has a head without an eye. Christina Rossetti. OxBChV

There is one who sits in his room. The Ancestors. Anita Barrows. VWA

There Is Only One of Everything. Margaret Atwood. NOBC

There is pleasure in the wet, wet clay. The Lie. Kipling. NOBL

There is red/ on the clown-lady's lips. Toulouse Lautrec. Astrid Tollefsen, tr. by Nadia Christensen. PBWP

There is room up in the sky. Hawk. Aaro Hellaakoski, tr. by Aili Jarvenpa. SOP

There Is Snowdrift on the Mountain. W. P. Ker. PoSH

There is so much blossom and naked dawn. Mountain Girl. Rafaela Chacón Nardi, *tr. by* Margaret Randall. AIW

There is so much good in the worst of us. Charity. *Unknown.* BLPA

There is so much loveliness gone out of the world. The Triumph of Doubt. John Peale Bishop. EaLo

There is some beauty in sorrow. Placing a $2 Bet for a Man Who Will Never Go to the Horse Races Any More. Diane Wakoski. UnPo

There is some demon turning me into an old man. The Banjo. Robert Winner. FF

There is some will talk of lords and knights. Robin Hood's Delight. *Unknown.* ESPB

There is someone naked flying alongside the airplane. Centerfold Reflected in a Jet Window. Sandra McPherson. GeTw; MAYP

There is something. I Sing to Myself. Alma Villanueva. CCP

There is something between us. Breasts. Donald Hall. OBAL

There Is Something I Want to Say. Alex Kuo. BrSi

There is something in the autumn that is native to my blood. A Vagabond Song. Bliss Carman. AnAmPo; FaPON; GN

There is something so sad in the wise eyes of hogs. Elegy of the Hogs. H. H. ter Balkt, *tr. by* Scott Rollins. DuIn

There is somewhere a Secret Garden, which none hath seen. The Secret Garden. Robert Nichols. WGRP

There is sorrow enough in the natural way. The Power of the Dog. Kipling. BLPA; BLPL

There is stone in me that knows stone. Kathleen Jessie Raine. *Fr.* Rock. ImOP

There Is Strength in the Soil. Arthur Stringer. OHIP

There Is Sweet Music Here. Tennyson. *Fr.* The Lotus-Eaters. FaBV
(Choric Song of the Lotus-Eaters.) FaFP
(Choric Song: "There is sweet music here that softer falls.") HeIP; OBNC
(Song of the Lotus-Eaters.) NOBE; OBEV

There is that sound like the wind. Summer. John Ashbery. NAAL-2

There is the cab driver root and elevator. I Am Listening: A Lyric of Roots. Anita Valerio. GOS

There is the caw of a crow. Jonathan Houghton. Edgar Lee Masters. *Fr.* Spoon River Anthology. OxBA

There is the moon, there is the sun. The Universe. Mary Britton Miller. RHPC

There is the morning shuffle of traffic confined. City Walk-up, Winter 1969. Carolyn Forché. MAYP

There is the one who turns. Chiapas. Gary Soto. NoAM

There is the poverty of children shy with child. After Rilke. Stanley Plumly. NAmP

There is the prayer of the father. The Prayers. Howard Schwartz. VWA

There is the sleep of my tongue. The Sleep. Mark Strand. CAPP

There is the star bloom of the moss. Forest. Jean Garrigue. LiTM; NOBA

There is this cave. The Jewel. James Wright. CAPP; CoAP; NAAL-2

There is this distance between me and what I see. Still Poem 9. Philip Lamantia. NeAP

There is this photograph of you dancing. Last Sonnet. Bill Manhire. ATNZ

There is unfeminine, (but oh, so Female). Questionnaire. Susan Saxe. GLP

There is unknown dust that is near us. Surprised by Evening. Robert Bly. CAPP; NaP; VGW

There is Whittier, whose swelling and vehement heart. Whittier. James Russell Lowell. *Fr.* A Fable for Critics. AmPP; NOBA; OxBA

There is wonder past all wonder. The Ways of Living Things. Jack Prelutsky. RHPC

There is yet some elastic. Ulysses. Claude Clayton Smith. TSL

There Isn't Time. Eleanor Farjeon. BoTP; FaPON

"There it is!/ You play beside a death-bed like a child." Elizabeth Barrett Browning. *Fr.* Aurora Leigh. BrRo

There it is on a kitchen chair. How a Guitar Can Lie on a Chair. K. Schippers, *tr. by* Peter Nijmeijer. DuIn

There it is, the jagged sprawl of the familiar. Return, Starting Out. Daniel Halpern. MAYP

There it lies. The Foundered Tram. Harold Monro. BrPo

There it was/ the temple of Durga. Two White Women in the Sun. Munir Niazi, *tr. by* Mahmood Jamal. PBMUP

There it was, my face. Ozaki Hosai, *tr. fr. Japanese by* Hiroaki Sato. *Fr.* One Hundred Haiku in Free Form. FCEI

There it was, word for word. The Poem That Took the Place of a Mountain. Wallace Stevens. LCAP

There lay in an album. Unparalleled Severity. Jules Laforgue, *tr. by* William Jay Smith. CT

There leeft a may, an a weel-far'd may. Katharine Jaffray. *Unknown.* ESPB

There leeved a wee man at the fit o yon hill. Get Up and Bar the Door. *Unknown.* ESPB

There Let Thy Bleeding Branch Atone. Emily Brontë. SeCePo

There Leviathan/ Hugest of living creatures, on the deep. Milton. *Fr.* Paradise Lost, *Bk.* VII, *ll.* 412–416. (Leviathan.) AmMo

There lies a city inaccessible. The Unknown City. Sir Charles G. D. Roberts. CaP

There lies a cold corpse upon the sands. Death Song. Robert Stephen Hawker. OBNC

There lies a lone isle in the tropic seas. Easter Island. Frederick George Scott. OBCV

There lies a somnolent lake. In the Past. Trumbull Stickney. AnAmPo; NOBA; OxBA

There lies afar behind a western hill. The Town without a Market. James Elroy Flecker. MoBrPo

There! little girl, don't cry! A Life-Lesson. James Whitcomb Riley. AA; FPL; PoLF

There liv'd a lady in Lauderdale. She's Hoy'd Me Out o' Lauderdale. *Unknown.* CoMu

There livd a laird down into Fife. The Wife Wrapt in Wether's Skin. *Unknown.* ESPB

There liv'd a lass in yonder dale. Katharine Jaffray. *Unknown.* ESPB

There livd a lord on yon sea-side. Fair Annie. *Unknown.* ESPB

There liv'd a man in yonder glen. Johnie Blunt. *Unknown.* OxBB, *with music.*

There liv'd, as authors tell, in days of yore. Chaucer. *Fr.* The Canterbury Tales: The Nun's Priest's Tale. OBVE

There liv'd of late in Luteners Lane. A Westminster Wedding; or, Like unto Like, Quoth the Devil to the Collier. *Unknown.* CoMu

There lived a carl in Kellyburnbraes. Kellyburnbraes. *Unknown.* OxBB

There lived a fat old lady, in London she did dwell. The Old Lady of London. *Unknown.* AmFP

There Lived a King. W. S. Gilbert. *Fr.* The Gondoliers. FiBHP

There lived a maiden Tamana. Mushimaro. *Fr.* Manyo Shu. Ma

There lived a man at the foot of a hill. Get Up and Bar the Door. *Unknown.* EnSB

There lived a Puddy in a well. The Puddy and the Mouse. *Unknown.* GBP

There lived a sage in days of yore. A Tragic Story. Adelbert von Chamisso, *tr. by* Thackeray. BOTP; FaPON; MoShBr; OnMSP

There lived a small hermaphrodite beside the silver Brent. The Waif. Walter de la Mare. FaBoNo

There lived a wife at Usher's Well. The Wife of Usher's Well. *Unknown.* AmFP; AWP; CH; ChTr; EBEV; EnRP; EnSB; ESPB, (A, B, C *and* D *vers.*); FaBoBa; GoTS; LiTB; NAAL-1; NOBE; NoP; OAEL-1, *with music;* OBEV; OnMSP; OxBB, *with music;* OxBS; PoEL-1; PrIm; RB; TrGrPo

There Lived among the Untrodden Ways. Hartley Coleridge. BXAP

There lived an old man in the Kingdom of Tess. The New Vestments. Edward Lear. NOBVV; RHPC

There lived an old woman at Lynn. *Unknown.* OxBChV

There lived in a laburnum tree. The Yellow Fairy. Charlotte Druitt Cole. BoTP

There lived in ancient Scribbletown a wise old writer-man. Puzzled. Carolyn Wells. OBCA

There lives a celibate of the hill at home. The Dwarf of the Hill Caves. Lupenga Mphande. WMBCH

There lives a good-for-nothing cat. The Lazy Pussy. Palmer Cox. OBCA

There lives a land beside the western sea. On the South Coast of Cornwall. John Gray. NOBVV

There lives a maid down under yon brae. Katherine Jaffray. *Unknown.* OxBB

There lives a man in Rynie's land. Lang Johnny More. *Unknown.* ESPB

There lives in/ my childhood street. Self Portrait 4. Tove Ditlevsen, *tr. by* Ann Freeman. WPOW

There may be a basement to the Atlantic. Somebody's Gone. Charles Henri Ford. EAS

There may be agony in furnished rooms. The Room. Francis Webb. *Fr.* Leichhardt in Theatre. PoAu-2

There may be chaos still around the world. George Santayana. *Fr.* Sonnets. AnAmPo

There mighte men the royal eagle find. Chaucer. *Fr.* The Parlement of Foules. PBBP

There mounts in squalls a sort of rusty mire. The Exile's Return. Robert Lowell. AmPP; OxPA

There mournful cypress grew in greatest store. The Garden of Proserpina. Spenser. *Fr.* The Faerie Queene, II, 7. ChTr

There must be fairy miners. Buttercups. Wilfrid Thorley. FaPON

There,—my blessing with you! Polonius' Advice to Laertes.
Shakespeare. *Fr.* Hamlet, I, iii. OHFP
(Polonius to Laertes.) GN
(This Above All.) TrGrPo
(To Thine Own Self Be True.) FaFP; LiTB

There, my lad, lie the Articles. Scene from a Play, Acted at Oxford,
Called "Matriculation." Thomas Moore. OBSV

There never breathed a man who, when his life. Gabriello Chiabrera, *tr.*
by Wordsworth. *Fr.* Epitaphs. AWP

There never was yet a boy or a man. Tinker Man. *Unknown.* RR

There never yet was honest man. Loving and Beloved. Sir John
Suckling. CaPo; NAEL-1; OBS

There never yet was woman made. Woman's Constancy. Sir John
Suckling. CaPo

There on his knee, behind a box tree shrinking. Joshua Sylvester. *Fr.*
Du Bartas: His Divine Weeks and Works: The Seventh Day of the
First Week. PBBP

There, on the darkened deathbed, dies the brain. John Masefield. EBEV
(There, on the Darkened Deathbed.) DL; LiTB

"There, on the left!" said the colonel. Marthy Virginia's Hand. George
Parsons Lathrop. PAH

There on the sea sails wandered. The Names of Georgian Women. Bella
Akhmadulina. BoWoP, *tr. by* Stanley Noyes *and* Olga Carlisle

There on the top of the down. June Bracken and Heather. Tennyson.
EnLoPo

There once/ Was a green. The Frog on the Log. Ilo Orleans. RAR

There once the walls. A Tale. Edward Thomas. ChTr

There once was a cobbler. The Kind Mousie. Natalie Joan. BoTP

There once was a cow with a double udder. The Cow. Theodore
Roethke. FiBHP; OBAL; OBCA

There Once Was a Dove. Haim Guri, *tr. fr. Hebrew by* Bernhard Frank.
MHeP

There once was a girl of New York. Cosmo Monkhouse. NA

There once was a girl of Pitlochry. *Unknown.* CenHV

There once was a man of Bengal. *Unknown.* CenHV
(Bengal.) OnUR

There once was a man [*or* There was a young man] who said, "Damn!"
Maurice Evan Hare. CenHV; NOBL; OxBoLi
(Determinism.) FaBoCo

There once was a man who said, "God." Idealism. Ronald Arbuthnott
Knox. FaBoCo; NBLV
(Limerick: "There once was a man who said "God.") NOBL

There once was a man who said, "How," *Unknown.* NA

There once was a Marquis de Sade. De Sade. John Fuller. NBLV

There once was a painter named Scott. Dante Gabriel Rossetti. CenHV

There once was a person of Benin. Cosmo Monkhouse. NA

There Once Was a Pious Young Priest. *Unknown.* NIP

There Once Was a Puffin. Florence Page Jaques. NTCP

There once was a Renaissance man. *Unknown.* PeHV

There Once Was a Spinster of Ealing. *Unknown.* NIP

There once was a time. *Unknown.* NOIV

There once was a warden of Wadham. *Unknown.* PeHV

There once was a wicked young minister. Conrad Aiken. OBAL

There once was a Willow, and he was very old. The Willow-Man.
Juliana Horatia Ewing. OxBChV

There once was a wonderful wizard. Conrad Aiken. FaBoNo

There once was an old man of Blackheath. *Unknown.* CenHV

There once was an old man of Lyme. *At. to* Edward Lear *and* Cosmo
Monkhouse. NA

There once was an old sailor my grandfather knew. The Old Sailor. A.
A. Milne. CenHV

There once were some people called Sioux. The American Indian.
Unknown. FaBoCo; FiBHP; NBLV

There once were three brothers from merry Scotland. Sir Andrew Barton.
Unknown. AmFP

There or Elsewhere. Pierre Reverdy, *tr. fr. French by* Michael Benedikt.
POS

There ought to be capital punishment for cars. Thoughts on Capital
Punishment. Rod McKuen. InPK

There our murdered brother lies. The Wake of William Orr. William
Drennan. TIRV

There out of hell the Old One bellows. Lamentations of the Fallen
Angels. *Unknown, tr. fr. Anglo-Saxon by* Charles W. Kennedy. *Fr.*
Christ and Satan. AnOE

There, pay it, James! 'tis cheaply earned. Vers de Société. H. D. Traill.
Par

There, perched mugwump-style he. Quotella. Janet Fox. BWV

There piped a piper in the wood. The Magic Piper. E. L. Marsh.
BoTP

There pipes the wood-lark, and the song thrush there. Thomas Gray. FM

There remain/ imprinted. Inventory. Otto Laaber, *tr. by* Beth Bjorklund.
CoAuP

There Rolls the Deep. Tennyson. *Fr.* In Memoriam A. H. H., CXXIII.
FaBoRV; HAP; NOBE; SeCePo

There sat a happy fisherman. The Reed. Mikhail Yurevich Lermontov,
tr. by J. J. Robbins. AWP

There sat an old man on a rock. Too Late. Fitz Hugh Ludlow. PoLF

There sat down, once, a thing on Henry's heart. John Berryman. *Fr.*
Dream Songs. CAPP; HAP; HCAP; NoP; PoE

There sat two glasses filled to the brim. The Two Glasses. Ella Wheeler
Wilcox. BLPA; BLPL

There sate the seniors of the Trojan Race. Homer, *tr. fr. Greek by* Pope.
Fr. The Iliad, III. OBVE

There seems to be, about certain lives. Mistral. John Koethe. BAP

There seems to be someone. The Mountain Spirit. *Unknown, tr. fr.*
Chinese by Burton Watson. *Fr.* Nine Songs. CoBCP

There set out, slowly, for a different world. A War. Randall Jarrell.
OxBSP

There shall be no more songs. Black Power. Alvin Saxon. PoBA

There Shall Be No Night. Bible, *N.T. Fr.* Revelation, XXII: 1-5.
TrGrPo

There She Is. Linda Gregg. NPGG

There she sits a'-smokin'. Motorcycle Irene. Skip Spence. MAT

There She Stands a Lovely Creature. *Unknown.* AmFP

There Should Have Been. Sydney Lea. SM

There sits a fair couple courting. The Jealous Brothers. *Unknown.* AmPF

There smiled the smooth Divine, unused to wound. The Smooth Divine.
Timothy Dwight. *Fr.* The Triumph of Infidelity: Here stood
Hypocrisy, in sober brown. AA; WGRP

There souls of men are bought and sold. London ("There souls of men are
bought and sold"). Blake. *Fr.* The Human Image. ChTr

There, spring lambs jam the sheepfold. In air. Watercolor of Grantchester
Meadows. Sylvia Plath. LCAP; NYBP; SM

There stand three mills on Manor Water. Manor Water. *Unknown.*
GBP

There stands a lady on a mountain. Kiss in the Ring. *Unknown.*
OxBoLi

There stands a lonely pine-tree. Heine, *tr. by* Emma Lazarus. TrJP

There stood a hill not far whose grisly top. Milton. *Fr.* Paradise Lost,
bk. I, *ll.* 670–798. OBEL-1

There stood an unsold captive in the mart. Parrhasius. Nathaniel Parker
Willis. AA

There the ash-tree leaves do vall. Leaves a-Vallen. William Barnes.
NOBVV

There the black river, boundary to hell. The Southern Road. Dudley
Randall. CNA; PoBA; SM

There the companions of his fall, o'erwhelmed. Milton. *Fr.* Paradise
Lost, *bk.* I, *ll.* 76–124.
(Immortal Hate.) NOBE

There the most daintie Paradise on ground. Spenser. *Fr.* The Faerie
Queene, II, 12. EBEV

"There the Parthenon, & there." Slides. Jennifer Maiden. CBAP

There the sea spoke to us. Anatolia. Christine Busta, *tr. by* Beth
Bjorklund. CoAuP

There the voluptuous nightingales. Shelley. *Fr.* Prometheus Unbound,
II, ii. PBBP

There, there is no mountain within miles. Nebraska. Jon Swan. RFM

There, there where those black spruces crowd. Ragged Island. Edna St.
Vincent Millay. NAAL-2; NoP

There they are. The Blackstone Rangers. Gwendolyn Brooks. NoAM;
PoBA

There they are. The Fury of Cocks. Anne Sexton. CAPP

There they are, my fifty men and women. One Word More. Robert
Browning. FiP; PoEL-5

There they are now. Three Sentences for a Dead Swan. James Wright.
NaP; NOBA

There they dismounting, drew their weapons bold. Britomart in the House
of Busirane. Spenser. *Fr.* The Faerie Queene: The Legend of
Britomartis, or of Chastitie, III, 11–12. FiP

There they go. Seed Journey. Gregory Corso. VGW

There they go, down to the fatal ship. Cythera. David Ferry. DiPo

There they stand, on their ends, the fifty faggots. Fifty Faggots. Edward
Thomas. BrPo; MoAB; MoBrPo

There they were many, O God, so many. They. Mani Leib, *tr. by* David
G. Roskies *and* Hillel Schwartz. VWA

There though where they/ were regardless. Degree Four. Nathaniel
Mackey. BAP

There 'tis the shepherd's task the winter long. Retrospect—Love of
Nature Leading to Love of Mankind. Wordsworth. *Fr.* The Prelude
[*or*, Growth of a Poet's Mind], VIII. EnRP; OAEL-2
Shepherd, The. OBNC

There, truly they said in this house. The Hidden People and the Star People. *Unknown, tr. fr. Osage Indian by* Barbara Tedlock. *Fr.* Ceremony of Sending. STP

There.xx. thousande met in fere. Capystranus. *Unknown.* OxBLMV

There used to be a long silent end of hall. You Smell like Grandma's Beads. Elizabeth Woody. GOS

There used to be a picket fence. The Picket Fence. Christian Morgenstern, *tr. by* Max Knight. GrPl

There used to be a rich old oaf who made. Chaucer. *See* Canterbury Tales, The: Miller's [*or* Milleres] Tale, The.

There used to be gods in everything, and now they're gone. The Companions. Howard Nemerov. NYBP

There walked on Plover's shady banks. Driving Saw-Logs on the Plover. *Unknown.* AS

There wanders many a lighted star. The North Star. John Morris-Jones, *tr. by* Anthony Conran. OBWVE

There wanders through the world, a knee. The Knee. Christian Morgenstern, *tr. by* W. D. Snodgrass *and* Lore Segal. RB

There wanst was [*or* once were] two cats of [*or* in] Kilkenny. The Kilkenny Cats. *Unknown.* CRH; FaFP
   (Limerick: "There once were two cats of Kilkenny.") CenHV

There was a bad poet named Clough. On Arthur Hugh Clough. Swinburne. FaBoEE

There was a battle in her face. The Battle. W. H. Davies. BrPo

There was a battle in the north. Geordie. *Unknown.* ESPB; FaBoBa; OxBB

There was a big bear. Honey Bear. Elizabeth Lang. BoTP

There was a blacksmith in my breast. The Dead Sheep. Andrew Young. FM

There was a bond between you and me. Momin Khan Momin, *tr. by* Ahmed Ali. GoT

There Was a Boy. Wordsworth. *Fr.* Prelude, V. ChER; FaBoCh; FaBoRV; FiP; OBNC; PoE; PoEL-4; RB

There was a boy bedded in bracken. John Short. FaBoCh; FaBoTw

There was a boy in a village who made. Saw the Cloud Lynx. Samuel Makidemewabe, *tr. by* Howard Norman. STP

There was a boy of other days. Lincoln. Nancy Byrd Turner. FaPON; RHPC

There was a boy whose name was Jim. Jim, Who Ran Away from His Nurse, and Was Eaten by a Lion. Hilaire Belloc. CenHV; ChTr; OxBChV
   (Jim.) CenHV; ChTr; NoAM

There was a boy whose name was Phinn. A Fishing Song. William Brighty Rands. CenHV

There was a boy, ye knew him well. Wordsworth. *Fr.* The Prelude [*or,* Growth of a Poet's Mind]: Books. ChER; FaBoCh; FaBoRV; FiP; OBNC; PoE; PoEL-4; RB
   (Winander Lake.) FiP

There was a bridge that Rozinante would not cross. The Bridge of Heraclitus. George Reavey. BIrV

There was a bright and happy tree. The Happy Tree. Gerald Gould. WGRP

There was a captain-general who ruled in Vera Cruz. El Capitan-General. Charles Godfrey Leland. AA

There was a certain assistant minister. A Record of a Past Affair. Li K'ai-hsien, *tr. by* Jonathan Chaves. CoBLCP

There was a chap—I forget his name. The Gemlike Flame. R. P. Lister. FiBHP

There was a child. Courage, a Tale. Thom Gunn. GLP

There Was a Child Went Forth. Walt Whitman. *Fr.* Autumn Rivulets. AmPP; AWP; InPS; NAAL-1; OxBA; SoSe; TAP
   "There was a child went forth every day." RFM

There was a clever skipper, in Akron he did dwell. The Clever Skipper. *Unknown.* AmFP

There was a company of young folk living. Chaucer. *See* Canterbury Tales, The: Pardoner's Tale, The.

There Was a Crimson Clash of War. Stephen Crane. UnPo

There was a crooked man, and he went [*or* walked] a crooked mile. Mother Goose. BoTP; FaBoBe; FaFP; OxBoLi; OxNR; PYC

There was a dark and awful wood. Wood. Thomas Hornsby Ferril. PoRA

There was a darkness in this man. John Gould Fletcher. *Fr.* Lincoln, II. OFD

There was a dear lady of Eden. *Unknown.* NA

There was a devil and his name was I. Malzah's Song. Charles Heavysege. *Fr.* Saul. OBCV

There was a duck egg as green as the evening sky. Ulinda. David Campbell. CBAP

There was a duke's daughter lived in York. The Cruel Mother. *Unknown.* ESPB

There was a fair maiden who lived on the shore. The Fair Maid by the Shore. *Unknown.* AmFP

There was a fair young creature who lived by the seaside. The Silvery Tide. *Unknown.* AmFP

There was a faith-healer of Deal. *Unknown.* CenHV
   (Faith-Healer.) FaFP
   (Mind and Matter.) FaBoCo

There was a famous landowner. The Landowner. Samuel Bamford. PF

There was a farmer's son kept sheep upon a hill. Blow Away the Morning Dew. *Unknown.* OBET

There Was a Frog. *Unknown.* NA

There was a frozen tree that I wanted to paint. Vegas. Charles Bukowski. NoP

There was a gallant lady all in her tender youth. Canada-I-O. *Unknown.* AmFP

There was a gallant ship, and a gallant ship was she. The Golden Vanity. *Unknown.* CH
   (Sweet Trinity (The Golden Vanity), The.) ESPB, B *vers.*

There was a gay damsel of Lynn. *Unknown.* NA

There was a gay maiden lived down by the mill. The Ferry. George Henry Boker. AA

There was a giant by the orchard wall. In the Orchard. James Stephens. SO; WSC

There was a giant in times of old. The Dorchester Giant. Oliver Wendell Holmes. FaPON; OnMSP

There was a girl in our town. *Unknown.* OxNR

There was a girl with us in our carriage. *Unknown, tr. by* Arthur Waley. BoS

There was a good Canon of Durham. William Ralph Inge. CenHV

There was a graveyard once—or cemetery. Evening Hour. Robert Penn Warren. MT

There was a gray rat looked at me. Rat Riddles. Carl Sandburg. SO

There was a great battle Saturday morning. The Battle of Argoed Llwyfain. Taliesin, *tr. by* Anthony Conran. OBWVE

There was a great swimmer named Jack. On Being Much Better Than Most and Yet Not Quite Good Enough. John Ciardi. GOYP

There was a great white man—bare, bare, bare. The Smoked Herring. Charles Cros, *tr. by* A. L. Lloyd. GrPl

There was a hag who kept two chambermaids. The Hag and the Slavies. Jean de la Fontaine, *tr. by* Edward Marsh. AWP; OBVE

There was a jolly beggar, and a begging he was born. The Jolly Beggar. *At. to* James V, King of Scotland. CoMu; OxBB

There was a jolly frog that did in the river swim O. The Frog and the Crow. *Unknown.* GBP

There was a jolly miller once. Isaac Bickerstaffe. *Fr.* Love in a Village, *st.* 1. OxNR

There was a jovial beggar. The Jovial Beggar. *Unknown.* BoTP

There was a jury sat at Perth. The Earl of Errol. *Unknown.* ESPB

There was a kind curate of Kew. *Unknown.* CenHV

There was a kind lady called Gregory. James Joyce. FaBoEE

There Was a King. *Unknown.* NBLV; OxBoLi

There was a king, and a very great king. Lady Diamond. *Unknown.* ESPB

There was a king met a king. *Unknown.* OxNR

There was a knicht riding frae the east. Riddles Wisely Expounded. *Unknown.* ESPB, (3 *vers.*); FaBoBa; GBP
   (Jennifer Gentle and Rosemary.) OxBoLi
   (There Was a Knight.) CH; Mes

There was a knight, an he had a daughter. Erlinton. *Unknown.* ESPB

There was a knight and a lady bright. The Broomfield Hill. *Unknown.* ESPB; OxBB, *with music*

There Was a Knight [and He Was Young]. *Unknown*
   ("Baffled Knight, The.") ESPB
   ("Courteous Knight, The.") OxBB, *with music.*

There was a knight, in a summer's night. The Bonny Birdy. *Unknown.* ESPB

There was a Knight of Bethlenem. Henry Neville Maughan. *Fr.* The Husband of Poverty. BoTP

There was a lad was born in Kyle. Rantin, Rovin Robin. Burns. OxBS

There was a lady all skin and bone. The Skin-and-Bone Lady. *Unknown.* AmFP

There was a lady fair and gay. The Wife of Usher's Well. *Unknown.* ESPB

There was a lady fine and gay. Willie o [*or* of] Winsbury. *Unknown.* AmFP; ESPB, (A *and* D *vers.*)

There was a lady in this land. The Tinker. *Unknown.* CoMu

There was a lady lived in a hall. Two Red Roses across the Moon. William Morris. EBVV

There was a lady lived in York. The Cruel Mother. *Unknown.* AmFP; OBET

There Was a Lady Loved a Swine. *Unknown.* GBP; OxNR

There was a lady of beauty rare. The Wife of Usher's Well. *Unknown.* AmFP

There was a lady of the North Country. Riddles Wisely Expounded. *Unknown.* ESPB

There was a Lass of Islington. The Lass of Islington. *Unknown.* CoMu (Fair Lass of Islington, The.) OxBB, *with music*

There was a light pig from Montclair. Arnold Lobel. ILY

There was a little Baby once. A Child's Christmas Carol. Christine Chaundler. BoTP

There was a little boy and a little girl. Mother Goose. OxNR

There was a little boy went into a barn. *Unknown.* OxNR

There was a little dog, and he had a little tail. *Unknown.* BoTP

There was a little, Elvish man. The Man Who Hid His Own Front Door. Elizabeth MacKinstry. FaPON

There Was a Little Girl. Mother Goose, *st.* 1; *sts.* 2 *and* 3, *unknown, at. to* Longfellow. BLPA, *st.* 1; FaFP, *st.* 1; NA; OxBChV, *st.* 1; OxNR; RHPC, *st.* 1 (Jemima.) FaBoCh

There was a little guinea-pig. The Guinea-Pig. *Unknown.* NA; OxNR (Guinea-Pig Song, A.) OxBChV

There was a little maid, and she was afraid. *Unknown.* OxNR

There was a little man,/ And he had a little gun. Mother Goose. FaFP; OxNR

There was a little man,/ and he wooed a little maid. Mother Goose. OxNR

There was a little man and he had a little can. No More Booze. *Unknown.* OBAL (Fireman Save My Child.) AS, *with music*

There was a little one-eyed gunner. *Unknown.* OxNR

There was a little rabbit sprig. *Unknown.* BoTP

There was a little rill of water, near the den. The Coyote. Carter Revard. NOVW; VoR

There was a little ship in South Amerikee. The Sweet Trinity. *Unknown.* AmFP

There was a little turtle. The Little Turtle. Vachel Lindsay. FaPON; GoJo; NTCP; OBAL; OBCA; PDV; RAR

There was a little woman, as I've heard tell. Mother Goose. *See* There was an old [*or* little woman], as I've heard tell.

There was a lord of worthy fame. The Lady Isabella's Tragedy. *Unknown.* GBP

There was a maid come out of Kent. A Maid of Kent. *Unknown.* OxBoLi (There Was a Maid.) EIL

There was a maid, richly arrayd. Blancheflour and Jellyflorice. *Unknown.* ESPB

There Was a Maid Went to the Mill. *Unknown.* GBP

There was a man/ who collected facts. Introduction of the Shopping Cart. Gerald Costanzo. MAYP

There was a man/ Whose name was Pete. The Tragedy of Pete. Joseph S. Cotter, Sr. CDC

There was a man,/ And his name was Dob. *Unknown.* OxNR

There was a man a-coming from the south. Trooper and Maid. *Unknown.* AmFP

There was a man and he had nought. Mother Goose. OxNR

There Was a Man and He Was Mad. *Unknown.* GBP; RB

There was a man from Singapore. Some Sound Advice from Singapore. John Ciardi. GrPl

There was a man, he went mad. *Unknown.* OxNR

There was a man here, Samian born, but he. Ovid, *tr. fr. Latin by* Rolfe Humphries. *Fr.* Metamorphoses, XV. NAWM-1

There was a man in Arkansaw. Tuscaloosa Sam. "Orpheus C. Kerr." OBAL

There was a man in olden times. Dives and Lazarus ("There was a man in olden times"). *Unknown.* AmFP

There was a man lived in the moon. Aiken Drum. *Unknown.* FaBoCh; FaBoNo; OxNR

There was a man lived quite near us. The Man with the Wooden Leg. Katherine Mansfield. ATNZ

There was a man made a thing. *Unknown.* GBP

There was a man named Johnny Sands, who married Betty Hague. Johnny Sands ("There was a man named Johnny Sands, who married Betty Hague"). *Unknown.* AmFP

There was a man named Jooseppi Kirvesmies. Holy Night. Yrjö Jylhä, *tr. by* Aili Jarvenpa. SOP

There was a man, now please take note. The Goat. *Unknown.* BLPL; OnUR; PoLF

There was a man of double deed. *Unknown.* GBP; OxNR; RB

There was a man of our town. Mother Goose. FaFP

There was a man of Thessaly. The Man of Thessaly. *Unknown.* FaBoCo; FaBoNo; OxNR

There was a man rode through our town. *Unknown.* OxNR

There was a man who drove his mule. Cool Mule. Dale A. Schreiber. SoTCo

There was a man who dwelt alone. Shadow-Bride. J. R. R. Tolkien. SO

There was a man who found two leaves. The Fall. Russell Edson. LCAP

There was a man who had no eyes. *Unknown.* OxNR

There was a man who married a maid. She laughed as he led her home. I Love My Love. Helen Adam. NeAP; NMM; WPOW

There was a man who studied the art of disappearing. A Parable. Li K'ai-hsien, *tr. by* Jonathan Chaves. CoBLCP

There was a man who watched the river flow. The Cranes of Ibycus. Emma Lazarus. AA

There was a man who would marry his mother. The Having to Love Something Else. Russell Edson. AnAn

There was a man whom Sorrow named his friend. The Sad Shepherd. W. B. Yeats. MOS

There Was a Man with a Tongue of Wood. Stephen Crane. *Fr.* War Is Kind, XVI. LiTA; MoAmPo

There was a man within our tenement. The Spritely Dead. Oscar Williams. *Fr.* Variations on a Theme, II. LiTA; Son

"There was a marriage in Cana of Galilee. And both." The Bridegroom of Cana. Marjorie Pickthall. TrCP

There was a monkey climbed a tree. *Unknown.* OxNR (There Was a Monkey.) NA

There Was a Naughty Boy. Keats. *Fr.* A Song about Myself. BoTP, *sts.* 1 *and* 2; FaBoCh; FaBoCo, *st.* 4; LiTB; MoShBr; OnUR; OxBChV, *sts.* 1 *and* 4. (Song about Myself, A.) InvP; PoEL-4 (Verses from a Letter.) EBEV

There was a person. Revenge Fable. Ted Hughes. TW

There was a Pig that sat alone. A Pig-Tale. "Lewis Carroll." *Fr.* Sylvie and Bruno Concluded. WiR (Melancholy Pig, The.) FaPON

There was a piper had a cow. Mother Goose. OxNR

There was a poet whose untimely tomb. Shelley. *Fr.* Alastor; or, The Spirit of Solitude. TOF

There was a poor chap called Rossetti. Dante Gabriel Rossetti. CenHV

There was a Presbyterian cat. *Unknown.* FaBoCh (Auld Seceder Cat, The.) FaBoCo

There was a princess of Bengal. *At. to* Walter Parke. NA

There was a professor of Beaulieu. Materialism. C. E. M. Joad. FaBoCo

There was a queen that fell in love with a jolly sailor. The Sailor and the Shark. Paul Fort, *tr. by* Frederick York Powell. OBMV

There was a queer fellow named Woodin. "Cuthbert Bede." CenHV

There was a rat, for want of stairs. *Unknown.* OxNR

There was a rich lady, from London she came. A Rich Irish Lady. *Unknown.* AmFP

There was a rich lord, and lived in Forfar. Bonnie Annie. *Unknown.* ESPB

There was a rich merchant in London did right. The Silk Merchant's Daughter. *Unknown.* OxBSS, *with music*

There was a road ran past our house. The Unexplorer. Edna St. Vincent Millay. MoShBr; PoA

There was a roof over our heads. Lost on September Trail, 1967. Alberto Ríos. FYAP

There was a rover from a western shore. Mother England. Edith M. Thomas. AA

There was a Russian came over the sea. Russian and Turk. Robert J. Burdette. NA

There Was a Saviour. Dylan Thomas. NAEL-2

There was a serpent who had to sing. The Serpent. Theodore Roethke. AmMo; RHPC

There was a shepherd's dochter [*or* daughter]. The Knight and Shepherd's Daughter. *Unknown.* ESPB (Shepherd's Dochter, The.) OxBB

There was a shepherd's son. Blow the Winds, I-Ho. *Unknown.* GBP; OxBoLi

There was a ship and a ship of fame. Captain Glen's Unhappy Voyage to New Barbary. *Unknown.* OxBSS

There was a ship called *The Golden Vanitie.* The Golden Vanitie. *Unknown.* EnSB

There was a ship of Rio. The Ship of Rio. Walter de la Mare. CenHV; MOS; PDV

There was a ship sailed from the North Countree. The *Golden Vanity.* *Unknown.* WiR

There was a sick man of Tobago. *Unknown.* OxBChV

There was a small maiden named Maggie. Maggie. *Unknown.* OnUR

There Was a Small Pig Who Wept Tears. Arnold Lobel. RAR

There was a sound of hunting in the mountains. Incident on a Front Not Far from Castel di Sangro. Harry Brown. NYBP

There was a sound of revelry by night. Byron. *Fr.* Childe Harold's
Pilgrimage, III. EBEV; OBWP
  (Battle of Waterloo, The.) FaFP
  (Eve of Waterloo, The.) BeLS; FaBoBe; FaBoCh; FaBV; NOBE;
OBNC
  (Night before the Battle of Waterloo, The.) WBLP
  (Night before the Battle of Waterloo, The.) GN
  (Waterloo.) FiP; TrGrPo; WaaP
There was a strange and unknown race. The New World. Paul Engle.
AmFN
There was a stunted handpost just on the crest. Near Lanivet, 1872.
Thomas Hardy. AWP; CMoP; NoAM
There was a sudden croon of lilies. The Martyrdom of St. Theresa. A.
D. Hope. CBAP
There was a sunlit absence. Mossbawn Sunlight. Seamus Heaney. *Fr.*
Mossbawn: Two Poems in Dedication, I. BIrV
  (Sunlight.) FaBCIP; NoP
There was a thing a full month old. *Unknown.* OxNR
There Was a Time. Edward Thomas. MMA
There was a time for discoveries. Voyage West. Archibald MacLeish.
VGW
There was a time in former years. She Hears the Storm. Thomas Hardy.
NAEL-2
There was a time on this fair continent. Charles Mair. *Fr.* Tecumseh.
NOBC; OBCV
There was a time (such songs begin this way). Inflation. Charles O.
Hartman. PoA
There was a time when Death and I. Beyond Recall. Mary Emily
Bradley. AA
There was a time when death was terror. New Fashions. George Moses
Horton. OBAL
There was a time when I was very small. Childhood. Jens Baggesen, *tr.*
by Longfellow. AWP
There was a time when I would magnify. Elegy for an Unknown Soldier.
James K. Baxter. ATNZ
There was a time when meadow, grove and stream. Wordsworth. *Fr.*
Ode: Intimations of Immortality from Recollections of Early
Childhood. NAEL-2; TOF
There was a time when the stars fell like rain. Tauhindauli. STE
There was a time when this poor frame was whole. There Was a Time.
Edward Thomas. MMA
There was a tinker liv'd of late. The Jovial Tinker; or, The Willing
Couple. *Unknown.* CoMu
There was a tree stood in the ground. The Green Grass Growing All
Around. *Unknown.* MoShBr
There was a troop of merry gentlemen. The Broom of Cowdenknows.
Unknown. ESPB
There was a tumult in the city. Independence Bell—July 4, 1776.
Unknown. BLPA; FaBoBe; FPL; OPP
There was a way out of here. The Elaboration. Bill Manhire. ATNZ
There was a wealthy merchant/ in London still did dwell. The Wars of
Santa Fe. *Unknown.* AmFP
There was a weasel lived in the sun. The Gallows. Edward Thomas.
FM; InPS; LiTB; MoAB; MoBrPo; MoP; NoAM; UnPo
There Was a Wee Bit Mousikie. *Unknown.* MoShBr
  (Cheetie-Poussie-Cattie, O.) FaBoCh
There was a wee bit wifie. *Unknown.* OxNR
There was a whispering in my hearth. Miners. Wilfred Owen. BrPo;
MoAB; MoBrPo; NAEL-2; NOBE; OBWVE
There was a widow-woman lived in far Scotland. The Wife of Usher's
Well. *Unknown.* ESPB
There was a Wife from Bath, a well-appearing. Chaucer. *See* Canterbury
Tales, The: Prologue.
There was a winter. Alba after Six Years. Christopher Middleton.
NePoEA-2
There was a witch. Two Witches. Alexander Resnikoff. RHPC
There was a wood, a witches' wood. The Witches' Wood. Mary
Elizabeth Coleridge. PBWP
There Was a Wyly Ladde. *Unknown.* ErPo
There was a young bard of Japan. *Unknown.* CenHV
There was a young belle of old Natchez. Ogden Nash. NoP
There was a young boy [*or* man] of Quebec. *At. to* Kipling. FaBoCo
  (Boy of Quebec, The.) FaBoNo
There was a young critic of King's. Arthur Clement Hilton. CenHV
There was a young curate of Hants. E. V. Knox. CenHV
There was a young curate of Salisbury. *Unknown.* FaBoCo
There was a young doctor, from London he came. The Fair Damsel from
London. *Unknown.* AmFP
There was a young fellow called Crouch. Victor Gray. NOBL
There was a young fellow called Green. *Unknown.* CenHV
There was a young fellow named Nutz. *Unknown.* PeHV

There was a young Fellow of Caius. *Unknown.* NOBL
There was a young fellow of Ceuta. *Unknown.* CenHV
There was a young Fellow of King's. *Unknown.* NOBL
There was a young Fellow of Wadham. *Unknown.* NOBL
There was a young fellow went by. Trinity Brethren Attend. I. A.
Richards. CRP
There was a young fir-tree of Bosnia. The Fir-Tree of Bosnia. Dante
Gabriel Rossetti. FaBoNo
There was a young genius of Queens'. Arthur Clement Hilton. CenHV
There was a young gourmand of John's. Arthur Clement Hilton. CenHV
There was a young lady called Bright. *See* There was a young lady named
Bright.
There was a young lady called Starky. *Unknown.* CenHV
There was a young lady named [*or* called] Bright. *At. to* Arthur Buller.
CenHV; NOBL; OxBoLi
  (Relativity.) FaBoCo; FaFP; ImOP
  (Young Lady Named Bright, A.) FaPON
There was a young lady of Corsica. Edward Lear. CenHV; ChTr;
FaBoNo
There Was a Young Lady of Crete. *Unknown.* OnUR
There was a young lady of Ealing. *Unknown.* CenHV
There was a young lady of Flint. *Unknown.* CenHV
There was a young lady of Hull. Edward Lear. MoShBr
There was a young lady of Kent. *Unknown.* CenHV; ILY
There was a young lady of Limerick. Andrew Lang. CenHV
There was a young lady of Milton. *Unknown.* NA
There Was a Young Lady of Niger. *Unknown, also at. to* Cosmo
Monkhouse. FaPON; InvP; NBLV; PDV
  (Limerick: "There was a young lady of Niger.") NA
  (Not Just for the Ride.) FaFP
There Was a Young Lady of Norway. Edward Lear. EBEV
  (Young Lady of Norway, A.) FaPON
There was a young lady of Portugal. Edward Lear. OxBoLi
There was a young lady of Rheims. Moonshine. Walter de la Mare.
FiBHP
There was a young lady of Riga. *Unknown.* CenHV; FaBoCo
There was a young lady of Russia. Edward Lear. MoShBr
There was a young lady of Ryde/ Whose shoe-strings were seldom untied.
Edward Lear. OxBoLi
There was a young lady of Spain. Monica Raymond. SoTCo
There was a young lady of Spain. *Unknown.* FaBoCo
There Was a Young Lady of Station. "Lewis Carroll." FaBoNo
  (Limerick: "There was a young lady of station.") CenHV
There was a young lady of Sweden. Edward Lear. EBEV
There was a young lady of Tottenham. *Unknown.* WeW
There was a young lady of Wales. *Unknown.* NA
There was a young lady whose bonnet. Edward Lear. EBEV
There was a young lady whose eyes. Edward Lear. EBEV
  (Limerick: "There was a young lady whose eyes.") NOBVV
There Was a Young Lady Whose Nose. Edward Lear. EBEV; FaPON
There was a young maid who said, "Why." *Unknown.* NA; SoSe
There was a young man from Port Jervis. At the Tennis Club. I. L.
Martin. SD
There Was a Young Man from Trinity. *Unknown.* ImOP
There was a young man of Bengal. *Unknown.* OxBoLi
There was a young man of Cohoes. Robert J. Burdette. NA
There was a young man of Devizes. *At. to* Archibald Marshall. CenHV
There was a young man of Japan. *Unknown.* FaBoCo
There was a young man of Mauritius. Theological Limerick. T.
Lindsay. FaBoCo
There was a young man of Montrose. Arnold Bennett. CenHV; FaBoNo;
OxBoLi
  (It Pays.) FaFP
There was a young man of Quebec. *See* There was a young boy of
Quebec.
There was a young man of St. Bees. *Unknown.* FaBoCo
There was a young man of the Clyde. Just for the Ride. *Unknown.*
FaFP
There was a young man who said "Damn!" *See* There once was a man
who said "Damn!"
There was a young man who was bitten. *At. to* Walter Parke. NA
There was a young man who was famed among. Momin Khan Momin, *tr.*
by Ahmed Ali. GoT
There was a young person of Crete. Edward Lear. FaBoNo
There was a young person of Smyrna. Edward Lear. OxBoLi; TEP
There was a young poet of Thusis. *Unknown.* OxBoLi
There was a young woman, and what do you think? A Lost Illusion.
George Du Maurier. CenHV
There was a young woman, as I've heard tell. Ripperty! Kye! Ahoo!
Henry Lawson. CBAP

There was a young woman called Starkie. Mendelian Theory. *Unknown.* FaBoCo
  (Limerick: "There was a young woman called Starky.") NOBL
There was a young woman from Aenos. The Young Woman from Aenos. *Unknown.* OBAL
There was a young woman named Plunnery. Edward Gorey. OBAL
There was a youth[e], and a well belovd [*or* well-belovéd] youth[e]. The Bailiff's Daughter of Islington. *Unknown.* ESPB; FaBoBa; GN; OBET; OxBB; OxBoLi
There was airy music and sport at the fair. The Fair at Windgap. Austin Clarke. OxBTC; SeCePo
There [*or* Ther] was also a nun [*or* Nonne], a Prioress[e]. The Prioress. Chaucer. *Fr.* The Canterbury Tales: Prologue. CTC, *abr.*
  (Madam Eglantine.) NOBE
  ("There also was a nun, a Prioress," *mod. vers. by* Louis Untermeyer.) TrGrPo
There was always the river or the train. Grandmother Watching at Her Window. W. S. Merwin. PrIm; VGW
There was an ancient craftsman once, who made. The Leaf-Makers. Harold Stewart. PoAu-2
There was an ancient Grecian boy. A Tiger Tale. John Bennett. OBCA
There was an ancient spring inside the glacier. Found. Carol Muske. AmPA
There was an archbishop named Tait. Archbishop Tait. *Unknown.* ChTr; FaBoNo
There was an archdeacon who said. *Unknown.* OxBoLi
There was an Auchtergaven mouse. A Whigmaleerie. William Soutar. OxBS
There was an auld birkie ca'ed Milton. Andrew Lang. CenHV
There was an earthquake. The Earthquake. *Unknown, tr. by* K. Kennedy. WTO
There was an ease of mind that was like being alone in a boat at sea. Prologues to What Is Possible. Wallace Stevens. LCAP
There was an emptiness. The Day You Are Born. Cathy Song. BrSi
There was an end to hearts and rhymes. John Hollander. EOEF
There was an Indian, who had known no change. J. C. Squire. CH; FaPON
  (Discovery, The.) OFD
  (There Was An Indian.) AmFN
There was an old bear that lived near a wood. The Bear and the Squirrels. Christopher Pearse Cranch. OBCA
There was an old crow. *Unknown.* OxNR
There was an old dragon under grey stone. The Dragon's Hoard. J. R. R. Tolkien. AmMo
There was an old farmer in Sussex did dwell. The Farmer's Curst Wife. *Unknown.* ESPB
There was an old fellow of Trinity. *At. to* Arthur Clement Hilton. CenHV
There was an old Fox. The Owl and the Fox. *Unknown.* BLPA
There was an old grocer of Goring. Green. Walter de la Mare. FaBoNo
There was an old lady/ Who had three faces. Godmother. Phyllis B. Morden. RHPC
There was an old lady of Chertsey. Edward Lear. OxBChV
There was an old man,/ And he had a calf. *Unknown.* OxNR
There was an old-man and a jolly old-man. The Old Man and Young Wife. *Unknown.* CoMu
There was an old man and he lived [out] in a wood. Broom, Green Broom. *Unknown.* LiTB; OxBoLi; PoRA
  (Green Broom.) CH, *diff. vers.*
There was an old man at the bank today. Fourth Street, San Rafael. Bill Berkson. UL
There was an old man at the foot of the hill. The Farmer's Curst Wife. *Unknown.* AmFP
There was an old man from Darjeeling. Old Man from Darjeeling. *Unknown.* NTCP
There Was an Old Man from Peru. *Unknown. See* There was an old man of [*or* from] Peru/ Who dreamt he was eating his shoe.
There was an old man in a Barge. Edward Lear. EBEV
There was an old man in a boat. Edward Lear. EBEV; FaBoNo
  (Floating Old Man, The.) WiR
There was an old man in a tree. Edward Lear. InvP; NoP
  (Limerick: "There was an old man in a tree.") FaBoNo; MoShBr; OxBChV; TEP
There was an old man in a trunk. Ogden Nash. CenHV
  (Ultimate Reality.) FaBoCo
There was an old man in a velvet coat. Mother Goose. OxNR
There was an old man in the North Countrie. The Two Sisters. *Unknown.* PrIm
There was an old man lived under the hill/ As you may plainly see, see. Father Grumble. *Unknown.* AmFP

There was an old man of Bengal. "F. Anstey." CenHV
There was an old man of Blackheath. *Unknown.* PDV
There was an old man of Boulogne. *Unknown.* FaBoCo; OxBoLi
  (Limerick: "There was an old man of Boulogne.") CenHV
There was an old man of Calcutta. Arthur. Ogden Nash. FiBHP; NoP
There was an old man of Cape Horn. Edward Lear. EBEV
There was an old man of Cape Race. *Unknown.* FaBoCo
There Was an Old Man of Dumbree. Edward Lear. OxBChV
There was an old man of Dunblane. Edward Lear. EBEV
There was an old man of Dundee. Edward Lear. FaBoNo
There was an old man of El Hums. Edward Lear. FaBoNo
There was an old man of Girgenti. Edward Lear. FaBoNo
There was an old man of Hong Kong. Edward Lear. FaBoCo
There was an old man of Ibreem. Edward Lear. EBEV
There was an old man of Kamschatka. Edward Lear. NA; NOBL
There was an old man of Khartoum. *At. to* William Ralph Inge. OxBoLi
  (Limerick: "There Was an old man of Khartoum.") NOBL
There was an old man of Leghorn. Edward Lear. NA
There was an old man of Madras. Edward Lear. FaBoNo
There was an old man of Peru/ Who never knew what he should do. Edward Lear. EBEV
There was an old man of Peru/ Who watched his wife making a stew. Edward Lear. EBEV
There was an old man of Peru/ Who dreamt he was eating his shoe. *Unknown.* CenHV; PDV; SoSe
  (Old Man from Peru, An.) FaFP; NTCP
  (There Was an Old Man from Peru.) OnUR
There Was an Old Man of St. Bees. W. S. Gilbert. InvP
There was an old man of Spithead. Edward Lear. FaBoNo
There was an old man of the coast. Edward Lear. CenHV; MoShBr
There was an old man of the Dargle. Edward Lear. ChTr
There was an old man of the Dee. Edward Lear. FaBoNo
There was an old man of the East. Edward Lear. EBEV
There was an old man of the West. Edward Lear. EBEV
There was an old man of Thermopylae. Edward Lear. EBEV; FaBoNo; NA; NOBL
There was an old man of Three Bridges. Edward Lear. FaBoNo
There was an old man of Vesuvius. Edward Lear. FaBoNo
There was an old man of West Dumpet. Edward Lear. EBEV
There was an old man of Whitehaven. Edward Lear. EBEV
There was an old man on some rocks. Edward Lear. NOBVV
There was an old man on the Border. Edward Lear. CenHV; EBEV
There was an old man said, "I fear." The Shubble. Walter de la Mare. FaBoNo
There was an old man who had a kite for a son. An Old Man's Son. Russell Edson. LCAP
There was an old man who lived [*or* liv'd] in Middle Row. The Five Hens. *Unknown.* GBP
  ("There was an old man who lived in Middle Row.") OxNR
There was an old man who [*or* that] lived in the [*or* a] wood [*or* woods]. Father Grumble. *Unknown.* AmFP
  (Old Man Who Lived in a Wood, The.) MoShBr
  (Old Man Who Lived in the Woods, The.) OnUR
There was an old man who lived on a common. The Wonderful Old Man. *Unknown.* NA
There was an old man who made his will. The Dishonest Miller. *Unknown.* NA
There Was an Old Man Who Said, "Do." *Unknown.* FaPON; ImOP
  (Limerick: "There was an old man who said 'Do.' ") NA
There was an old man who said: "How." Edward Lear. OxBChV
There was an old man who said, "Hush!" Edward Lear. FaBoCo; GoJo; NA; NOBL; OxBChV; OxBoLi; TEP
There was an old man who screamed out. Edward Lear. EBEV; NOBVV
There was an old man who supposed. Edward Lear. NA; NAEL-2; NOBVV
  (There Was an Old Man Who Supposed.) NoP
There was an old man whose despair. Edward Lear. FaBoNo
There was an old man with a beard. Edward Lear. ChTr; FaBoCo; FaBoNo; NOBL; OxBChV; PDV; PYC; TEP
  (Old Man with a Beard.) FaPON; NTCP
There was an old man with a gong. Edward Lear. GoJo
There was an old man with a gun. Miss Pheasant. Walter de la Mare. FaBoNo
There was an old man with a ribbon. Edward Lear. FaBoNo
There was an old miser at Reading. *Unknown.* OxBChV
There was an old Monk of great renown. The Monk of Great Renown. *Unknown.* CoMu
There was an old owl. The Owl and the Crow. Ben King. AnAmPo
There was an old owl lived in an oak. *Unknown.* CenHV

There was an old party called Pennycomequick. Mr. Pennycomequick. P. M. Stone. BoTP

There was an old party of lyme. *At. to* Edward Lear. FaBoCo; FF; OxBoLi
    (Limerick: "There once was an old man of Lyme.") NA

There was an old person of Anerley. Edward Lear. FaBoCo

There was an old person of Bar. Edward Lear. FaBoNo

There was an old person of Basing. Edward Lear. EBEV

There was an old person of Blythe. Edward Lear. EBEV

There was an old person of Bow. Edward Lear. EBEV

There was an old person of Brussels. Edward Lear. FaBoNo

There was an old person of Burton. Edward Lear. EBEV

There was an old person of Cassel. Edward Lear. EBEV

There was an old person of Crowle. Edward Lear. FaBoNo

There was an old person of Dean. Edward Lear. MoShBr; TSS

There was an old person of Diss. Edward Lear. GoJo

There was an old person of Dover. Edward Lear. FaBoNo

There was an old person of Dutton. Edward Lear. EBEV

There was an old person of Grange. Edward Lear. FaBoNo

There was an old person of Gretna. Edward Lear. ChTr; OxBChV

There was an old person of Harrow. Edward Lear. FaBoNo

There was an old person of Hove. Edward Lear. FaBoNo

There was an old person of Lear. Edward Lear. CenHV

There was an old person of Philae. Edward Lear. FaBoNo

There was an old person of Prague. Edward Lear. EBEV

There was an old person of Rhodes. Edward Lear. EBEV

There was an old person of Skye. Edward Lear. ChTr

There was an old person of Twickenham. Edward Lear. FaBoNo

There was an old person of Ware. Edward Lear. NA
    (Old Person of Ware, An.) RAR

There was an old person of Wick. Edward Lear. FaBoNo; NA

There was an old person of Woking. Edward Lear. NA

There was an old person whose habits. Edward Lear. FaBoNo

There was an old poop from Poughkeepsie. John Updike. *Fr.* Two Limericks after Lear. SoTCo

There was an old skinflint of Hitching. Buttons. Walter de la Mare. FaBoNo

There Was an Old Soldier. *Unknown.* AS

There was an old soldier of Bicester. *Unknown.* FaBoNo; OxBChV

There was an old stupid who wrote. *At. to* Walter Parke. NA

There was an old tailor of Bicester. *Unknown.* CenHV

There was an old vicar of Sinder. J. J. Walter de la Mare. FaBoNo

There was an old wife and she lived all alone. The Old Wife and the Ghost. James Reeves. PDV

There was an old woman/ Went blackberry picking. Berries. Walter de la Mare. MoBrPo

There was an old woman/ Lived under a hill/ She put a mouse in a bag. Mother Goose. OxNR

There was an old woman/ Lived down in a dell. Was She a Witch? Laura E. Richards. PDV

There was an old woman/ And nothing she had. *Unknown.* OxNR

There was an old woman/ Lived under a hill/ And if she's not gone. *Unknown.* OxNR

There was an old woman/ Sold puddings and pies. *Unknown.* OxNR

There was an old woman/ Who lived in Dundee. *Unknown.* OxNR

There was an old woman and she lived in a shoe. Mother Goose. *See* There was an old woman who lived in a shoe.

There was an old woman, and what do you think? Mother Goose. FaBoCh

There was an old [*or* little woman], as I've heard tell. Mother Goose. MoShBr; OnMSP
    ("There was a little woman, as I've heard tell.") InvP; OxNR

There was an old woman as ugly as sin. An Old Woman. Charles Henry Ross. OxBChV

There was an old woman called Nothing-at-all. Mother Goose. OxNR

There was an old woman had three cows. *Unknown.* OxNR

There was an old woman, her name was Peg. *Unknown.* OxNR

There was an old woman in Surrey. Mother Goose. OxBChV

There was an old woman lived on the seashore. The Two Sisters. *Unknown.* AmFP
    (Cruel Sister, The.) OxBB, *with music*

There was an old woman lived under the hill. The Trooper's Horse. *Unknown.* OBET

There was an old woman named Towl. *Unknown.* OxBChV
    (Mistress Towl.) FaBoNo

There was an old woman of Harrow. Old Woman of Harrow. *Unknown.* FaBoNo

There was an old woman sat spinning. Mother Goose. OxNR

There was an old woman tossed up in a basket [*or* blanket]. Mother Goose. OxNR; PDV

There was an old woman who lived in a shoe. Mother Goose. FaBoBe; FaFP; OxNR
    ("There was an old woman and she lived in a shoe.") OxBoLi

There was an old woman who never was wed. Ballad of an Old Woman. Frank A. Collymore. PBCV

There was an owd yowe wi' only one horn. The One-horned Ewe. *Unknown.* GBP

There was an owl lived in an oak. *Unknown.* OxNR

There was an unwanted child. End, Middle, Beginning. Anne Sexton. PoE

There was an young lady of Corsica. Edward Lear. ChTr

There was Dai Puw. He was no good. On the Farm. R. S. Thomas. OxBTC

There was debtor's prison before inmates. Empty Pitchforks. Thomas Lux. NAmP

There was fire & the people were yelling. running crazy. Urban Dream. Victor Hernandez Cruz. NBP

There was great beauty by the Tree. Eve. Arthur J. Bull. UnPo

There was heat lightning out west. Last Night in Sisseton, S. D. Mary Goose. STE

There was her name, printed on the poster. The Brooch. Chang Hsian-hua, *tr. by* Valeria Doran. WCI

There was in Asia, in a great city. The Prioress's Tale. Chaucer. *Fr.* The Canterbury Tales. ACP, *mod. vers.*

There was in danger desperate delight. The Aging Poet, on a Reading Trip to Dayton, Visits the Air Force Museum and Discovers There a Plane He Once Flew. Richard Snyder. Psk

There was little important. An American Boyhood. Jonathan Holden. Psk

There was monie a braw noble. Glenlogie. *Unknown.* GN

There was movement at the station, for the word had passed around. The Man from Snowy River. A. B. Paterson. CBAP; PoAu-1

There was music in the air. Music in the Air. Ronald McCuaig. ErPo

There was never a leaf on bush or tree. A Winter Morning. James Russell Lowell. *Fr.* The Vision of Sir Launfal, II. GN

There was never a sound beside the wood but one. Mowing. Robert Frost. AnAmPo; BLPL; CMoP; HoPM; LiTA; NAAL-2; NOBA; OxBA; PPP; VGW

There was never nothing more me pained [*or* payned]. Sir Thomas Wyatt. AAS; GBL; SiPS

There was no beauty. A Wartime Maternity Ward. Barbara Catherine Edwards. CN

There was no ceremony. Lion. Mary Elizabeth Fullerton. PoAu-1

There was no change in the summer wind. In the Flowering Season. Michael Roberts. FaBoTw

There was no fire. The Blue Flame. Amryl Johnson. WS

There was no hole in the universe to fit him. Suicide. Anne Stevenson. FaBoWP

There was no hunted one. The Baying Hounds. Mary Gilmore. PoAu-1

There was no one. The water—no one? Galente Garden: II. Juan Ramón Jiménez, *tr. by* H. R. Hays. WSC

There was no reason to expect sadness. Wen Cheng-ming, *tr. fr. Chinese by* Jonathan Chaves. *Fr.* Lines Written on New Year's Day. CoBLCP

There was no reason whatever for the critique of pure reason to come. Love Poem No. 2. Yona Wallach, *tr. by* Warren Bargad *and* Stanley F. Chyet. IP

There was no road at all to that high place. The Grove. Edwin Muir. LiTM

There was no song nor shout of joy. The Ship. J. C. Squire. CH

There was no such man in my house. There Wasn't. Moyshe-Leyb Halpern, *tr. by* Benjamin *and* Barbara Harshav. AYP

There was no union in the land. Gettysburg. James Jeffrey Roche. PAH

There was once a boat on a billow. Longing for Home. Jean Ingelow. *Fr.* Songs of Seven. WGRP

There was once a considerate crocodile. The Considerate Crocodile. Amos R. Wells. OBCA

There was once a Filipino hombre. A Filipino Hombre. *Unknown.* AS

There was once a high wall, a bare wall. The Red Herring. George MacBeth. SO

There was once a hog theater where hogs performed. A Performance at Hog Theater. Russell Edson. AmPA

There was once a little animal. Similar Cases. Charlotte Perkins Gilman. PoLF

There was once a maiden who loved a cheese. Quite the Cheese. H. C. Waring. BXAP

There was once a man with a beard. Edward Lear. NA

There was once a swing in a walnut tree. The Walnut Tree. David McCord. OBCA

There was once a young lady of Ryde. *Unknown.* CenHV; PDV

There was once a young man of Oporta. "Lewis Carroll." FaBoNo

There was once two Irish labouring men; to England they came over. How Paddy Stole the Rope. *Unknown.* BLPA

There was once upon a time a little owl. The Owl's Bedtime Story. Randall Jarrell. ILY

There was once upon a time a man who lost the. Doctor Bill Williams. Ernest Walsh. InvP

There was one among us who rose. Death of a Friend. Pauli Murray. PoBA

There Was One I Met upon the Road. Stephen Crane. EaLo

There was peace in the cell. A Night in Prison. Sibilla Aleramo, *tr. by* Muriel Kittel. DMI

There was rebellion, Father, and the door was slammed. Father. Robert Lowell. DiL

There was six jovial tradesmen, they all sat down to drinking. When Jones's Ale Was New. *Unknown.* AmFP

There was such speed in her little body. Bells for John Whiteside's Daughter. John Crowe Ransom. CMoP; FF; HAP; HeIP; HoPM; InPK; InPS; LiTA; LiTM; MoAB; MoAmPo; MoP; NAAL-2; NIP; NoAM; NOBA; NoP; OxBA; PoE; PPP; PrIm; RB; SoSe; TAP; UnPo; VGW; WeW

There was that business in Siberia, in '19. The Soviet Union. John Berryman. FaBoPV

There was that fall the fall of desire. Two. Winfield Townley Scott. NYBP

There was the buffalo blowing. Composition. Peter Blue Cloud. VoR

There was the chiropodist. Plain Song. Craig Raine. TOF

There was the sonne of Ampycus of great forecasting wit. Meleager. Ovid, *tr. fr. Latin by* Arthur Golding. *Fr.* Metamorphoses, VIII. CTC

There was this. Imperfections Is the Summit. Yves Bonnefoy, *tr. by* Anthony Rudolf. RHTwFP

There was this empty bird cage in the garden. A Sparrow's Feather. George Barker. NYBP

There was this gym-teacher. Strato, *tr. by* Teddy Hogge. PeHV

There was this road. The Legs. Robert Graves. LiTB; LiTM; RB

There was this time in Boston. The Wedding Night. Anne Sexton. PoA

There was three Kings into the east. Burns. RB
(John Barleycorn.) FaBoCh

There was three ladies play'd at the ba'. The Cruel Brother. *Unknown.* ESPB; OxBB

There was three worms on yonder hill. Died of Love. *Unknown.* OBET

There was, 'tis said, and I believe, a time. Burials. George Crabbe. *Fr.* The Parish Register, *pt.* III. OAEL-1, *abr.*

Ancient Virgin, An. OBNC

Lady of the Manor, The. NOBE; OBNC

There was [*or* were] twa sisters sat in a bow'r [*or* bower]. The Twa Sisters. *Unknown.* ESPB; FaBoBa; NoP; OxBS
(Binnorie; or, The Twa Sisters.) OBVE; PoE; TrGrPo
(Cruel Sisters, The.) OxBB, *with music.*

There was two little boys going to the school. The Twa Brothers. *Unknown.* CH; EBEV; ESPB, (A *and* B *vers.*); OxBB

There was your voice, astonishment. May Sarton. UAS

There Wasn't. Moyshe-Leyb Halpern, *tr. fr. Yiddish by* Benjamin *and* Barbara Harshav. AYP

There went most passionately to life, impellance. Life and Impellance. William Frederick Stevenson. NOBVV

There went out in the dawning light. *Unknown, tr. by* John Addington Symonds. AWP

There went three children down to the shore. The Black Pebble. James Reeves. PDV

There Were an Old and Wealthy Man. *Unknown.* AmFP

There were bees about. From the start I thought. Shore Scene. John Logan. SM

There were blood spots on the skirt. James Cunningham. *Fr.* The Narrator's Trance. JB

There were bonfires on the hillsides. Ohakune Fires. Lauris Edmond, *tr. by* Margaret Orbell. PeNZ

There were cities here in the hills. Before the Day of Wrath. Louis Johnson. *Fr.* Four Poems from the Strontium Age, I. ATNZ

There were five of us within the room. I Come to Bury Caesar. Sydney Justin Harris. PoA

There were four of us about that [*or* the] bed. Shameful Death. William Morris. ChTr; GTBS-P

There were four red apples on the bough. August. Swinburne. WiR

There were ghosts that returned to earth to hear his phrases. Large Red Man Reading. Wallace Stevens. HAP; LCAP

There were ladies, they lived in a bower. Mary [*or* Marie] Hamilton. *Unknown.* ESPB, B *vers.*

There were many sounds I was raised with. The Story of Marie. Michael Burkard. NAmP

There were miners from Bisbee. Tramp Miner's Song. *Unknown.* AmFP

There were never strawberries. Strawberries. Edwin Morgan. BoLoP; LLLT

There Were Ninety and Nine. Elizabeth C. Clephane. WGRP

There were no antelope on the balcony. Midnight Special. Kenneth Patchen. VGW

There were no hidden motives to his life. David Ignatow. CAPP

There were no men and women then at all. Then. Edwin Muir. CMoP; PoA; PoE

There were no undesirables or girls in my set. Commander Lowell. Robert Lowell. DiL; VGW

There were once two cats of Kilkenny. The Cats of Kilkenny. *Unknown.* RHPC

There were only Adam and Eve. From the Dust. Elaine Dallman. VWA

There were saddened hearts in Mudville for a week or even more. Casey's Revenge. James Wilson. BLPA; OnMSP

There were some dirty plates. The Last Words of My English Grandmother. William Carlos Williams. RB; SOTW

There were some pines, a canal, a piece of sky. Landscape with Little Figures. Donald Justice. CAPP; LCAP

There Were Some Summers. Thomas Lux. LCAP

There were the roses, in the rain. The Act. William Carlos Williams. SOTW; VGW

There were the whales, six of them. The Stranded Whales. Geoffrey Dutton. CBAP

There were thirty-six streets between us. Secret Ceremony: The Sailboat. Susan Stewart. NAmP

There were three brethren come from Spain. Three Knights from Spain. *Unknown.* CH
(We Are Three Brethren Come from Spain.) GBP
("We are three brethren out of Spain.") OxNR

There were three cherry trees once. The Three Cherry Trees. Walter de la Mare. CMoP

There were three cooks of Colebrook. *Unknown.* OxNR

There were three crows sat on a tree. *Unknown.* *See* There were three ravens sat on a tree.

There were three gipsies a-come to my door. The Wraggle Taggle Gipsies. *Unknown.* BoTP; CH; FaPON; WiR
(Black Jack Davey.) MAT
(Raggle, Taggle Gipsies, The.) FaPON

There were three in the meadow by the brook. The Code. Robert Frost. OBNV; PoA; UnPo

There were three jovial huntsmen. Three Jovial Huntsmen. *Unknown.* NA

There were three jovial Welshmen. The Three Welshman. *Unknown.* MoShBr

There were three kings cam' frae the East. The Kings from the East. Heine, *tr. by* Alexander Gray. GoTS

There were three ladies [*or* maids] lived in a bower [*or* barn]. Babylon; or, The Bonnie Banks o' Fordie. *Unknown.* AmFP; ESPB; OxBB
(Baby Lon; or, The Bonnie Banks o' Fordie.) SeCePo

There were three maidens who loved a king. Three Loves. Lucy H. Hooper. BeLS

There were three maids lived in a barn. *See* There were three ladies lived in a bower.

There were three men came out of the west. John Barleycorn. *Unknown.* OBET

There were three men of Gotham. The Three Wise Men of Gotham. *Unknown.* FaBoNo

There were three ravens [*or* rauens *or* crows] sat on a tree. The Three Ravens. *Unknown.* ChTr; ESPB; FaBoBa; GBP; HeIP; InPK; Mes; NAEL-1; NoP; OAEL-1, *with music;* OBD; OBET; OBEV; OxBB, *with music;* PoE; PoEL-1; TrGrPo; UnPo
("There were three crows sat on a tree.") AmFP

There were three sailors of Bristol city. Little Billee. Thackeray. CenHV; FaBoCh; FaBoCo; MOS; NA; NOBL
(Three Sailors, The.) OxBB

There were three sisters fair and bright. The Riddling Knight. *Unknown.* FaBoCh; PoEL-1

There were three sisters in a hall. *Unknown.* OxNR

There Were Times. Alma Villanueva. CCP

There were twa brethren in the North. The Twa Brothers. *Unknown.* CH; EBEV; ESPB, (A *vers.*); OxBB

There were twa knights in fair Scotland. The Twa Knights. *Unknown.* ESPB

There were twa sisters sat in a bower [*or* bour *or* bowr]. Binnorie; or,

The Two Sisters. *Unknown*. OBEV; PoE; TrGrPo
(Twa Sisters of Binnorie.) CH; EnSB

There were two birds sat on a stone. Mother Goose. OxNR

There were two great trees. Laly, Laly. Mark Van Doren. SO

There were two of you in the dream, you. Betrayal. Sherod Santos.
NAmP

There were two sisters sat in a bower. *See* There was twa sisters. . .

There were two sisters, they went playing. The Twa Sisters. *Unknown*.
ESPB

There were two wrens upon a tree. *Unknown*. OxNR

There were years when I knew. The Falcons. W. S. Merwin.
CAPP

There where adventure stays clear-sighted. Prophecy. Aimé Césaire, *tr.
by* Clayton Eshleman *and* Annette Smith. RHTwFP

There where he sits, in the cold, in the gloom. The Hidden Weaver.
Odell Shepard. WGRP

There, where it was, we never noticed how. The Sagging Bough. Louis
Untermeyer. BXAP

There where the course is. At Galway Races. W. B. Yeats.
SD

There where the Kulo Saari bridge. Arvo Turtiainen, *tr. fr. Finnish by*
Aili Jarvenpa. *Fr.* Ballad of Herman's Rose, I. SOP

There where the rusty iron lies. Rooks. Charles Hamilton Sorley.
MoBrPo

There where the sun first dwelt. Odysseus Elytis, *tr. fr. Greek by* Edmund
Keeley *and* Philip Sherrard. *Fr.* Heroic and Elegiac Song for the
Lost Second Lieutenant of the Albanian Campaign, I. VMG

There, where the sun shines first. The Azalea. Coventry Patmore. *Fr.*
The Unknown Eros. ELP; GBL

There will be a rusty gun on the wall, sweetheart. A. E. F. Carl
Sandburg. CMoP; MoAB; MoAmPo; WaaP

There will be bluebells growing under the big trees. Bluebells for Love.
Patrick Kavanagh. FaBCIP; IPY

There will be bread no matter what. Bread. Stephen Corey. KS

There will be no Holyman crying out this year. Jitterbugging in the
Streets. Calvin C. Hernton. PoBA

There will be no more cats. Mort aux Chats. Peter Porter. OxBC

There will be no speech from. No Speech from the Scaffold. Thom
Gunn. OxBTC

There will be rose and rhododendron. Elegy before Death. Edna St.
Vincent Millay. CMoP; LiTA; LiTM

There Will Come Soft Rains. Sara Teasdale. LiTA

There, with ten Rembrandts. Ten Little Rembrandts. Theodore Weiss.
NoAM

There Won't Be Another. Diane Glancy. STE

There, wrapped in his own roars, the lone airman. The Raider. W. R.
Rodgers. AnIL; MoBrPo

There you are again. To Marie Osmond. Jack Skelley. UL

There you are once more near me. Shadow. Guillaume Apollinaire, *tr.
by* Jessie Degen *and* Richard Eberhart. WaaP

There . . . you are revealing your secret to me alone. Secrets. Ahmad
Abd al-Muti Hijazi, *tr. by* Sargon Bonlus *and* Peter Porter.
MAP

There you go, it's everywhere. Shopping for Midnight. G. E. Murray.
MAYP

There you were in my dreams last night. Stepfathers. David Donnell.
NOBC

There'd be an orchestra. F. Scott Fitzgerald. *Fr.* Thousand-and-First
Ship. AiP; GoJo

There'd ha'e to be nae warnin'. Times ha'e changed. Prayer for a Second
Flood. "Hugh MacDiarmid." EBEV

Therefore all seasons shall be sweet to thee. All Seasons Shall Be Sweet.
Samuel Taylor Coleridge. BoTP

Therefore he no more troubled the pool of silence. The Poet. George
MacKay Brown. PoPo

Therefore I Must Tell the Truth. Torlino, *tr. fr.* Navajo Indian *by*
Washington Matthews. STP

Therefore Is the Name of It Called Babel. Sir Osbert Sitwell. MMA

Therefore let pass, as they are transitory. Milton. *Fr.* Paradise Regained,
bk. IV, *ll.* 209-364. OAEL-1

Therefore Philippi saw once more the Roman battalions. We Have Paid
Enough Long Since in Our Own Blood. Virgil, *tr. fr. Latin by*
Richmond Lattimore. *Fr.* Georgics. WaaP

Therefore We Preserve Life. Shen Ch'üan, *tr. fr. Chinese by* William C.
White. TrJP

Therefore, We Thank Thee, God. Reuben Grossman, *tr. fr. Hebrew by* L.
V. Snowman. TrJP

Therefore, when thou wouldst pray, or dost thine alms. The Right Use of
Prayer. Sir Aubrey De Vere. TIRV; WGRP

There'll Be No Better. Gerda Mayer. DT

There'll be no war. No War. Judith Kazantzis. AIW

There's/ A/ Little/ Light. Little Light. Jim Brodey. UL

There's a/ sort of a/ tickle. Sneeze. Maxine W. Kumin. RAR

There's a band of men who roam this land. Ballad of Badmen. Owen
Dodson. FB

There's a barrel of porter at Tammany Hall. Fitz-Greene Halleck.
OBAL

There's a barrel-organ caroling across a golden street. The Barrel-Organ.
Alfred Noyes. BLPA; FaBV; MoBrPo; PoRA

There's a bear in the Truro woods. The Truro Bear. Mary Oliver.
SoSe

There's a beautiful island away in the West. The Land of the Evening
Mirage. *Unknown, tr. by* A. M. Bede. WGRP

There's a bird perched on my shoulder. Bird. Agnes Nemes Nagy, *tr.
by* Bruce Berlind. BoWoP

There's a bit of sky across the street. My "Patch of Blue." Mary
Newland Carson. BLPA

There's a black fog hiding London. Promise. Florence Lacey.
BoTP

There's a breathless hush in the Close tonight. Vitaï Lampada. Sir
Henry Newbolt. BLPA; FaPoR; OBWP

There's a brief spring in all of us and when it finishes. To S. T. C. on
His 179th Birthday, October 12th, 1951. Maurice Carpenter.
FaBoTw

There's a buzz in my ears crying: "Is there a point in these." Song of
Dejection. W. H. Auden. *Fr.* Man of La Mancha. AnAn

There's a Certain Difference in the Air. Moshe Dor, *tr. fr. Hebrew by*
Bernhard Frank. MHeP

There's a certain slant of light. Emily Dickinson. AmPP; BLPL;
BoWoP; CMoP; HAP; HeIP; LiTM; MoAB; MoAmPo; MoP;
NAAL-1; NAWM-2; NoAM; NOBA; NoP; OxBA; PoE; PoEL-5; PPP;
QFR; RB; TOF; WPE
(Certain Slant of Light, A.) LiTA

There's a certain young lady. A Certain Young Lady. Washington
Irving. FaBoBe

There's a combative artist named Whistler. Dante Gabriel Rossetti.
CenHV; FaBoEE

There's a comforting thought at the close of the day. Touching Shoulders.
Unknown. BLPA

There's a cow in Dick Wilbur's swimming pool. The Pool & the Cow.
Robert Phillips. SoTCo

There's a craze among us mortals that is cruel hard to name. The Other
Fellow's Job. Strickland W. Gillilan. WBLP

There's a dead pig hanging above his place. Annemarie Fischer: Portrait
of Robbert. Jan Kuijper, *tr. by* Jacob Lowland. DuIn

There's a deep secret place, dark in the hold of this ship. Down Below.
Joan Aiken. WSC

There's a fabulous story. The Place Where the Rainbow Ends. Paul
Laurence Dunbar. PWR

There's a faerie at the bottom of my garden. My Garden. Janice
Appleby Succorsa. HoPM

There's a fairmer up in Cairnie. Drumdelgie. *Unknown*.
GBP

There's a family nobody likes to meet. The Grumble Family. *Unknown*.
PWR; WBLP

There's a famous seaside place called Blackpool. The Lion and Albert.
Marriott Edgar. OBNV

There's a feeling that comes with the daze of joy. Undertones. George
R. Sims. NOBVV

There's a fortune to be made in just about everything. My Great Great
etc. Uncle Patrick Henry. James Tate. OBAL

There's a Friend for little children. Albert Midlane. *Fr.* Above the
Bright Blue Sky. OxBChV

There's a game much in fashion—I think it's called Euchre. The Game of
Life. John Godfrey Saxe. BLPA; BLPL

There's a gathering in the village, that has never been outdone. The
Country Doctor. Will M. Carleton. BLPA

There's a glade in Aghadoe, Aghadoe, Aghadoe. Aghadoe. John
Todhunter. AnIL

There's a good old war-cry sounding, it hangs on every lip. Waitekauri
Every Time! Edwin Edwards. PeNZ

There's a Grandfather's Clock in the Hall. Robert Penn Warren. NoAM;
NoP

There's a graveyard near the White House. The Unknown Soldier. Billy
Rose. BLPA; FPL; OPP

There's a great divinity. For Windows. Robert Grenier. UL

There's a green hollow where a river sings. Arthur Rimbaud. *See*
Eighteen-Seventy: Sleeper in the Valley, The.

There's a grey wind wails on the clover. Numerous Celts. J. C. Squire.
BXAP

There's a half hour towards dusk when flies. In the Attic. Donald
Justice. SM

There's a haven of sure rest. Forgetfulness. James Russell Lowell.
AnAmPo

There's a knack in living with you. Living with You. Angela Langfield. FF

There's a little black train a-coming. The Little Black Train. *Unknown.* AmFP

There's a little grey friar in yonder green bush. The Grey Linnet. James McCarroll. CaP

There's a little sun still, the cables creak. Between the Quay of San Nicolas and the Sea. Antonio Cisneros, *tr. by* David Tipton. Per

There's a lonely stretch of hillocks. Anzac Cove. Leon Gellert. PoAu-1

There's a long-legged girl. Pickin Em Up and Layin Em Down. Maya Angelou. NBLV

There's a lot of music in 'em—the hymns of long ago. The Old Hymns. Frank Lebby Stanton. BLRP

There's a lot of tales in history about the American West. Tribute to Freckles and Tornado. Jon Bowerman. CowP

There's a machine. The Fat Boy. Mark Vinz. TDD

There's a man goin' 'round takin' names. The Angel of Death. *Unknown.* AmFP

There's a man I really believe's in heaven. Sappho, *tr. by* John Frederick Nims. WeW

There's a man with a nose. Ambrose Bierce. *Fr.* The Devil's Dictionary. OBAL

There's a memory keeps a-runnin. The Old Apple-Tree. Paul Laurence Dunbar. AnAmPo

There's a merry brown thrush sitting up in the [or a] tree. The Brown Thrush. Lucy Larcom. BoTP; FaPON; OBCA

There's a mouse house. I Wouldn't. John Ciardi. TDD

There's a nice green little gully on the Numerella shore. The Numerella Shore. "Cockatoo Jack." PoAu-1

There's a notable family named Stein. *Unknown.* NOBL

There's a one-eyed yellow idol to the north of Khatmandu. The Green Eye of the Yellow God. J. Milton Hayes. BLPA

There's a palace in Florence, the world knows well. Robert Browning. *Fr.* The Statue and the Bust. Mes

There's a part o' the sun in an apple. Each a Part of All. Augustus Wright Bamberger. WBLP

There's a patch of old snow in a corner. A Patch of Old Snow. Robert Frost. CMoP; OxBSP; WeW

There's a path that leads to Nowhere. The Path that Leads to Nowhere. Corinne Roosevelt Robinson. BLPA

There's a piping wind from a sunrise shore. Off to the Fishing Ground. Lucy Maud Montgomery. CaP

There's a place the man always say. Where? Kenneth Patchen. LiTM

There's a Portuguese person named Howell. *At. to* Dante Gabriel Rossetti. CenHV

There's a pretty fuss and bother both in country and in town. A New Song on the Birth of the Prince of Wales. *Unknown.* CoMu; FaBoBa; NOBVV

There's a puckle lairds in the auld house. The Auld House. William Soutar. OxBS

There's a quaint little place they call Lullaby Town. Lullaby Town. John Irving Diller. BLPA

There's a race of men that don't fit in. The Men That Don't Fit In. Robert W. Service. BLPA; BLPL

There's a ragged old man in the garden to-day. Mr. Scarecrow. Sheila Braine. BoTP

There's a red light on the track for Bolsum Brown. Bolsum Brown. *Unknown.* AS

There's a reid lowe in yer cheek. Robert MacLellan. OxBS

There's a Sampson lying, sleeping in the land. The Black Sampson. Josephine D. Henderson Heard. CBWP-4

There's a saucy, wild packet and a packet of fame. The *Dreadnought.* *Unknown.* AmFP

There's a sea beneath a sea beneath a sea. Marine Biology. Israel Efrat, *tr. by* Bernhard Frank. MHeP

There's a serpent, namely, drinking. The Social Glass. Lizelia Augusta Jenkins Moorer. CBWP-3

There's a silver house in the lovely sky. The Silver House. John Lea. BoTP

There's a Silvery Lining to Every Cloud. Matilda Caroline Edwards. PWR

There's a small café off the avenue. Wardour Street. Humbert Wolfe. OxBTC

There's a snake on the western wave. The Sea Serpent Chantey. Vachel Lindsay. AmMo; WSC

There's a song in the air! Josiah Gilbert Holland. AA; GN; OHIP

There's a stir among the trees. The Christmas Trees. Mary Frances Butts. OHIP

There's a stone deer in that garden, plus two or three nude. A Floridian Museum of Art. Reed Whittemore. EyDe

There's a strange frenzy in my head. Jalal ed-Din Rumi, *tr. by* John Moyne *and* Coleman Barks. UnAS

There's a street in Trieste where I see my reflection. Three Streets. Umberto Saba, *tr. by* Anita Barrows. VWA

There's a sweet old story translated for man. The Gospel According to You. *Unknown.* BLRP

There's a three-penny Lunch on Dover Street. Eat and Walk. James Norman Hall. BLPA

There's a time yes a time. Home. Sipho Sepamla. WMBCH

There's a town called Don't-You-Worry. The Town of Don't-You-Worry. I. J. Barlett. BLPA; WBLP

There's a trade you all know well. The Overlander. *Unknown.* PoAu-1

There's a tramping of hoofs in the busy street. The Troop of the Guard. Hermann Hagedorn. OHIP

"There's a tree in father's garden, lovelye William," says she. Lovelye William. *Unknown.* AmFP

There's a tree out in our garden which is very nice to climb. The Tree in the Garden. Christine Chandler. BoTP

There's a very funny insect that you do not often spy. The Triantiwontigongolope. C. J. Dennis. AmMo

There's a vile old man. Limeraiku. Ted Pauker. NOBL

There's a whisper down the field where the year has shot her yield. Kipling. OBEV
  (Long Trail, The.) FaBV; MOS

There's a whisper down the line at 11:39. Skimbleshanks: The Railway Cat. T. S. Eliot. FaBoCo; NOBL

There's a whisper of life in the grey dead trees. The White Canoe. Alan Sullivan. CaP

There's a wideness in God's mercy. The All-embracing. Frederick William Faber. BLRP
  (There's a Wideness.) WBLP

There's a woman like a dew-drop, she's so purer than the purest. Earl Mertoun's Song. Robert Browning. *Fr.* A Blot in the 'Scutcheon. OBEV

There's a wonderful story. The Angel's Message. Clara Ann Thompson. CBWP-2

There's all of pleasure and all of peace. A Friend of Two. Wilbur Dick Nesbit. PoLF

There's all sorts of fowl and fish. An Invitation to Lubberland. *Unknown.* FaBoNo; GBP

There's always something in our land, too. Salute. Moyshe-Leyb Halpern, *tr. by* John Hollander. PeBMYV

There's an ancient party. Old Brown's Daughter. *Unknown.* OBET

There's an Irishman, Arthur O'Shaughnessy. Dante Gabriel Rossetti. CenHV

There's an Unknown River in Soweto. Zindzi Mandela. WMBCH

There's antimony, arsenic, aluminium, selenium. The Elements. Tom Lehrer. FaBoUs

There's Asia on the avenue. Manhattan. Morris Abel Beer. AmFN

There's beauty in the azure skies. The World Is Full of Beauty. Matilda Caroline Edwards. PWR

There's beauty in the deep. The Deep. John Gardiner Calkins Brainard. AA

There's been a death in the opposite house. Emily Dickinson. InPS; SoSe

"There's been an accident," they said. Mr. Jones. Harry Graham. *Fr.* Some Ruthless Rhymes, VIII. CenHV; FaBoCo; FaFP; FiBHP
  (Common Sense.) FiBHP

There's blood between us, love, my love. The Convent Threshold. Christina Rossetti. NoP

There's dazzle/ in the western sky. Sunset. Lilian Moore. TDD

There's definitely been a mistake. An Unraveled Thought. Shlomit Cohen, *tr. by* Myra Glazer Schotz. VWA

There's even someone combing her hair. Kaya Shirao, *tr. fr. Japanese by* Hiroaki Sato. *Fr.* Twenty-one Hokku. FCEI

There's folks that like the good dry land, an' folks that like the sea. When the Drive Goes Down. Douglas Malloch. AmFN

There's four square miles of timber, mostly oak. Wild Pigs. Ted Kooser. SM

There's half a god in many a man. Inspiration. Mary Elizabeth Fullerton. PoAu-1

There's heaven above, and night by night. Johannes Agricola in Meditation. Robert Browning. TOF

There's Holmes, who is matchless among you for wit. Holmes. James Russell Lowell. *Fr.* A Fable for Critics. NOBA

There's in my mind a woman. In Mind. Denise Levertov. NMM

"There's just one Book!" cried the dying sage. Just One Book. *Unknown.* BLRP

There's Life in a Mussel; a Meditation. George Farewell. NOEC

"There's light ahead!" Hope ever cries. Hope Deferred. Clara Ann Thompson. CBWP-2

There's little joy in life for me. On the Death of Anne Brontë. Charlotte Brontë. WPE

There's little wildness in my city head. The Wind Blows. Donagh MacDonagh. NeIP

There's lots of things I'd like to be. The Hurdy-Gurdy Man. Elizabeth Fleming. BoTP

"There's machinery in the butterfly." The Horrid Voice of Science. Vachel Lindsay. PoA

There's Many a Man Killed on the Railroad. *Unknown*. AS

There's many types and sizes. The Old Cowman. Dick Gibford. CowP

There's moaning somewhere in the dark. Voice in Darkness. Richard Dehmel, *tr. by* Margarete Münsterberg. AWP

There's Money in Mother and Father. Morris Bishop. FiBHP

There's more in words than I can teach. Loving and Liking. Dorothy Wordsworth. OxBChV

There's More Pretty Girls than One. *Unknown*. AmFP

There's much afoot in heaven and earth this year. The Rainy Summer. Alice Meynell. GoJo; OxBSP; OxBTC

There's Music in a Hammer. *Unknown*. RAR

There's my war club. Hunting Song ("There's my war club"). *Unknown*, *tr. by* Jerome Rothenberg. STP

There's Nae Luck about the House. William Julius Mickle. *See* And are ye sure the news is true?

There's naught (thou say'st) but one eternal flux. The Infidel Reclaimed. Edward Young. *Fr.* Night Thoughts, Night VII. NOEC

There's never enough whiskey or rain. Wishing Africa. Marilyn Bowering. NOBC

"There's no a bird in a' this foreste." Johnie Cock. *Unknown*. ESPB

There's no accounting for. Clayfeld's Anniversary Song. Robert Pack. BLA

There's no Avenging Angel. The Tree of Life Is Also a Tree of Fire. Gerda Norvig. VWA

There's no color called love in this world. Lady Izumi, *tr. fr. Japanese by* Hiroaki Sato. *Fr.* Fifty-one Tanka. FCEI

There's no comfort inside me, only a small. Beehive Cell. Richard Murphy. CIP

There's no dew left on the daisies and clover. Seven Times One— Exultation. Jean Ingelow. *Fr.* Songs of Seven. BLPA; FaPON; OBNC

There's no end to wisdom, no mask for folly. To the Elephants. Nathan Alterman, *tr. by* Ruth Nevo. VWA

There's no fleeing the cry-bird. This evening. The Cry-Bird Journey. Stan Rice. NPGG

There's no history in the past. Streets. Bob Perelman. LP

There's no horse this time. To the Coast. Denis Glover. *Fr.* Arawata Bill. ATNZ

There's No Lust like to Poetry. *Unknown*, *tr. by* John Addington Symonds. AWP

There's no more talk and ease. Audrey Beecham. CN

There's no past. History of Peru. Washington Delgado, *tr. by* David Tipton. Per

There's No Place to Sleep in This Bed, Tanguy. Charles Henri Ford. EAS

There's no salvation in elsewhere. Tangier. Stephen Dunn. SM

There's no smoke in the chimney. The Deserted House. Mary Elizabeth Coleridge. BoTP; CH

There's no such thing as death everybody. Then the Brother of the Wind. C. K. Williams. CAPP

There's no track. NN 616410. Bill Tulloch. PoSH

There's no way out. In the Suburbs. Louis Simpson. CAPP; MAT

There's Nobody. Idea Vilariño, *tr. fr. Spanish by* Kate Flores. DMH

There's nobody here. A Woman. Denis Johnson. MAYP

There's not a chance now that I might recover. The Scar. John Hewitt. CIP

There's not a joy the world can give like that it takes away. Stanzas for Music. Byron. EnRP; HAP
(Youth and Age.) GTBS; GTBS-P

There's not a nook within this solemn Pass. The Trosachs. Wordsworth. OBEV; SeCePo

There's not a spider in the sky. A Love-Song by a Lunatic. *Unknown*. NA

There's not a tear that brims thine eye unshed. Faithless. Louis Lavater. PoAu-1

There's nothing gentle where Aphrodite was. Trying to Believe. Linda Gregg. NPGG

There's nothing grieves me, but that age should haste. Michael Drayton. *Fr.* Idea, VIII. AAS; OAEL-1

There's nothing happening that you hate. Leave Them Alone. Patrick Kavanagh. OxBSP

There's nothing in this gardenous world more delightful. Gerald Stern. CAPP

There's Nothing like the Sun. Edward Thomas. FaBV

"There's nothing mysterious about the skull." The Scientist. Janet Burroway. SoSe

There's Nothing to Do in New York. Tomioka Taeko, *tr. fr. Japanese by* Hiroaki Sato. FCEI

There's nothing you can say to a man who drinks. The Drunken Man. Steve Orlen. MAYP

There's old Molly Hogan who cooks from a book. Stirling's Hotel. *Unknown*. AmFP

There's one rides very sagely on the road. Upon the Horse and His Rider. Bunyan. OxBChV

There's panic in Paris. Bicycalamity. Edmund W. Peters. SD

There's pleasure, sure, in being clad in green. A Scene after Hunting at Swallowfield in Berkshire. Sneyd Davies. NOEC

There's raw meat for the tiger cub. Song for the Infant Judas. Thomas Blackburn. NAs

There's recompense to balm your spirit's ire. Da Silva Gives the Cue. Walter Hart Blumenthal. TrJP

There's room in the bus. Jittery Jim. William Jay Smith. RHPC

There's snakes on the mountain. Wanderin'. *Unknown*. AS, B *vers.*

There's snow in every street. Winter. J. M. Synge. NOIV; OBMV; OxBTC

There's Snow on the Fields. Christina Rossetti. BoTP

There's some is born with their legs straight by natur. A Sailor's Apology for Bow-Legs. Thomas Hood. MOS

There's some magic influential. Song of the Barber. W. H. Auden. *Fr.* Man of La Mancha. AnAn

There's some really good work. The Cream Song. Apirana Ngata, *tr. by* Margaret Orbell. PeNZ

There's some who say she put death up her dress. Ellie Mae Leaves in a Hurry. Peter Klappert. SM

There's somebody who's dying. They Warned Him Then They Threw Him Away. C. K. Williams. CAPP

"There's someone at the door," said gold candlestick. Green Candles. Humbert Wolfe. MoBrPo; RHPC; SO

There's Someone I Think Of. *Unknown, tr. fr. Chinese by* Burton Watson. CoBCP

There's Somethin'. Adam Small, *tr. fr. Afrikaans.* PeSA

There's something about me. Something about Me. *Unknown*. RAR

There's something in a noble boy. The Torn Hat. Nathaniel Parker Willis. AA

There's something in a noble tree. The Trees. Samuel Valentine Cole. OHIP

There's something in a stupid ass. Byron. Par

There's something in the air. The Coming of Spring. Nora Perry. PWR

"There's something in the air," he said. Two Voices. Edmund Blunden. OBWP

There's something to love in each thing in the world. Money. Yüan Mei, *tr. by* J. P. Seaton. WFTU

There's somewhat on my breast, father. The Confession. "Thomas Ingoldsby." FiBHP

There's such a tiny little mouse. The Mouse. Thirza Wakley. BoTP

There's Tap o' Noth, the Buck, Ben Newe. Bennachie. Charles Murray. PoSH

There's teuch sauchs growin' i' the Reuch Heuch Hauch. The Sauchs in the Reuch Heuch Hauch. "Hugh MacDiarmid." NoAM

There's the field. I can see it. The Word. Neil Weiss. NYBP

There's the Irishman Arthur O'Shaughnessy. On the Poet O'Shaughnessy. Dante Gabriel Rossetti. ChTr

There's the story of me sitting in the grass in the dark. In the Dead of the Night. Norman Dubie. AmPA

There's the wonderful love of a beautiful maid. Love. *Unknown*. SoSe

There's This That I Like about Hockey, My Lad. John Kieran. ASP

There's three fair maids went to play at ball. The Cruel Brother. *Unknown*. AmFP

There's trampling of hoofs in the busy street. A Troop of the Guard. Hermann Hagedorn. OHIP

There's wonderful things in this world to do. Grey's River Roundup. Howard Norskog. CowP

Therese. Alden Nowlan. NeAC

Theresienstadt Poems, *sel.* Robert Mezey.
"In your watercolor, Nely Silvínová." NaP; VWA

Theris the old, the waves that harvested. The Fisherman. Leonidas of Tarentum, *tr. by* Andrew Lang. AWP

Thermal Stair, The. W. S. Graham. FaBoMo

Thermodynamics. Adrianne Marcus. BWV

Thermopylae. C. P. Cavafy, *tr. fr. Greek by* Edmund Keeley *and* Philip Sherrard. VMG

Thermopylae. Simonides, *tr. fr. Greek by* William Lisle Bowles. AWP; OBVE; OBWP

Thermopylae. Michael Thwaites. PoAu-2

Thermopylae Ode, The. Simonides, *tr. fr. Greek by* Richmond Lattimore. WaaP

Thermostatic Man, The. Gordon Challis. ATNZ

These. William Carlos Williams. MoAB; MoAmPo; MoP; NOBA; NoP; OxBA

These acres, always again lost. Lost Acres. Robert Graves. NoAM

These acres breathe my family. Summer Acres. Anne Wilkinson. CaP

These all their care expend on outward show. Edward Young. *Fr.* Love of Fame, the Universal Passion, Satire II. OBSV

These alternate nights and days, these seasons. Archibald MacLeish. MoAmPo

These Apple Trees. Valentin Iremonger. NeIP

These are also/ The war victims. "O. D." Zack Gilbert. CNA

These are amazing: each. Some Trees. John Ashbery. HCAP; NAAL-2; SM

These are men! the gaunt, unforesold, the vocal. Ol' Bunk's Band. William Carlos Williams. NOBA

These are my legs. I don't have to tell them, legs. Walter Jenks' Bath. William Meredith. HoPM

These are my murmur-laden shells that keep. On Some Shells Found Inland. Trumbull Stickney. LiTA; Son

These are my scales to weigh reality. Reality. Martha Gilbert Dickinson Bianchi. AA

These are my thoughts on realising. Anniversary. John Wain. NePoEA-2; TwCP

These are not dewdrops, these are tears. Epitaph on a Free but Tame Redbreast. William Cowper. PBBP

These are not my own hills. My Own Hills. Robert Story. PF

These are not words set down for the rejected. A Communication to Nancy Cunard. Kay Boyle. PoNe

These are notes to lightning in my bedroom. Star Quilt. Roberta Hill. CDW; NOVW

These are the arrows that kill sleep. Créide's Lament for Dínertech. *Unknown.* NOIV

These are the arrows that murder sleep. The Song of Crede. *Unknown, tr. by* Alfred Perceval Graves. BIrV

These are the beds. Sylvia Plath. *Fr.* The Bed Book. RHPC

These Are the Chosen People. Robert Nathan. TrJP

These are the clothes your dainty girl. Sanu Chigami. *Fr.* Manyo Shu. Ma

These are the days of our youth, our days of glory and honor. The Days of Our Youth. *Unknown, tr. by* Wilfrid Scawen Blunt. AWP

These are the days when birds come back. Emily Dickinson. FF; NAAL-1

(Indian Summer.) MoAmPo

These are the days whose fingers. Ninth of Av. Myra Sklarew. CRP

These are the desolate, dark weeks. These. William Carlos Williams. MoAB; MoAmPo; MoP; NOBA; NoP; OxBA

These are the dog days. Songs to Survive the Summer. Robert Hass. AmPA

These are the fellows who smell of salt to the prairie. Words Are Never Enough. Charles Bruce. CaP; OBCV

These are the fields of light, and laughing air. The Pea-Fields. Sir Charles G. D. Roberts. *Fr.* Songs of the Common Day. NOBC; OBCV

These are the first citizens of contingency. Proposition. Robert Pinsky. *Fr.* Essay on Psychiatrists, III. HCAP; NoAM

These are the first days of fall. The wind. How to Like It. Stephen Dobyns. BLA

These are the gardens of the Desert, these. The Prairies. Bryant. AmPP; NAAL-1; NOBA; OPP; OxBA; PoEL-4; TAP

These Are the Gifts I Ask. Henry van Dyke. FaBoBe

(Prayer.) WGRP

These are the green paths trodden by patience. The Rural Mail. John Glassco. MoCV

These are the lumps, these the scars. In This Manner. Nanni Balestrini, *tr. by* Lawrence R. Smith. NItP

These are the middle years. The Middle Years. Anthony Cronin. CIP

These are the mornings and evenings. Ozaki Hosai, *tr. fr. Japanese by* Hiroaki Sato. *Fr.* One Hundred Haiku in Free Form. FCEI

These are the names of the idols. The Names of the Idols. József Tornai, *tr. by* Jascha Kessler. FOC

These are the original monies of the earth. A Cabinet of Seeds Displayed. Howard Nemerov. CRP; KS

These are the saddest of possible words. Baseball's Sad Lexicon. Franklin P. Adams. FaFP; SD

These are the signs in which my days endure. Museum Piece. Lawrence P. Spingarn. GoYe

These are the small hours when. Michael Longley. CIP

These are the voices of the pastors calling. The Old Lutheran Bells at Home. Wallace Stevens. NoAM

These are the words. Stone from the Gods. Irma Wassall. GoYe

These are thy glorious works, Parent of good. Milton. *Fr.* Paradise Lost, *Bk.* V.

(Adam's Morning Hymn.) WGRP, *ll.* 153–210.

(Morning Hymn of Adam.) TrPWD, *ll.* 153–165, 195–208.

These, as they change, Almighty Father, these. A Hymn on the Seasons. James Thomson. *Fr.* The Seasons. EnRP

These as they clack in the wind. In the Pea Patch. Maxine W. Kumin. CAPP

These baby chicks do not leave their mother. Paintings of Various Subjects by Fang Jih-sheng. Pien Kung, *tr. by* Jonathan Chaves. CoBLCP

These barbarians, laying wood aside, and brick, and clay, build in rock so as to build forever! To the Ten Thousand Years. Victor Segalen, *tr. by* Nathaniel Tarn. RHTwFP

These barrows of the century-darkened dead. Prehistoric Burials. Siegfried Sassoon. MoBrPo

These be/ Three silent things. Triad. Adelaide Crapsey. WPE

These beds of bracken, climax of the summer's growth. Bracken Hills in Autumn. "Hugh MacDiarmid." NoP

These being the haunts of those. The Death of Friends. Adele Levi. GoYe

These birds frequent the rolling plains. The Moon Bird. V. C. Vickers. AmMo

These birds were born singing for joy. Another Song of the Same Woman, to Some Partridges, Sent to Her Alive. Florencia del Pinar, *tr. by* Julie Allen. BoWoP

These blue and yellow balloons. Mohajir. Fahmida Riaz, *tr. by* Mahmood Jamal. PBMUP

These Bones. T. H. Parry-Williams, *tr. fr. Welsh by* H. Idris Bell. OBWVE

These bottle-washer trees that give no shade. Palm Trees. Rex Warner. OBTV

These buildings are too close to me. Rudolph Is Tired of the City. Gwendolyn Brooks. PDV; RHPC

These butterflies, in twos and threes. Flying Blossoms. W. H. Davies. BrPo

These carved and glowing crowds. Chartres. Raymond Henri. *Fr.* View of the Cathedral. EyDe

These caverns yield. The Bats. Robert Hillyer. GoYe

These cherries are not wine-filled bowls for thirsty birds. The Flowering Cherry. Janet Frame. PeNZ

These children nowadays—she says. The Castillian Mother Speaks. Baldomero Fernández Moreno, *tr. by* Perry Higman. LPSS

These children playing at statues fill. Statues. Richard Wilbur. EyDe

These chill pillars of fluted stone. Winter Homily on the Calton Hill. Douglas Young. OxBS

These city streets, the labyrinthine black roads. Words and Truth. Yasin Taha Hafiz, *tr. by* Sharif Elmusa *and* Christopher Middleton. MAP

These Colors This Tune. Eli Netser, *tr. fr. Hebrew by* Bernhard Frank. MHeP

These conquered kings pass furiously away. End of a Year. Robert Lowell. HCAP

These country folk dancing a schottische. Country Dance. Edward Baugh. PBCV

These Damned Trees Crouch. Jim Barnes. CDW

These daughters are bone. God's Mood. Lucille Clifton. CAPP

These Days. Otto Laaber, *tr. fr. German by* Beth Bjorklund. CoAuP

These Days. Andrew Motion. DiPo

These Days. William Stafford. NNaP

These days I get up with the birches. Days in White. Ingeborg Bachmann. BoWoP, *tr. by* Daniel Huws; CoAuP, *tr. by* Beth Bjorklund

These days in prison seem a decayed time where. Decayed Time. Jean Wahl, *tr. by* Charles Guenther. VWA

These days of disinheritance, we feast. Cuisine Bourgeoise. Wallace Stevens. LiTA

These Days the Papers in the Street. Charles Reznikoff. VGW

These days we're advised. The Night. Rodolfo Hinostroza, *tr. by* Maureen Ahern *and* David Tipton. Per

These days you keep on meeting. The Seventies. Louis Johnson. PeNZ

These dream meetings. Yakamochi. *Fr.* Manyo Shu. FCEI

These dried-out paint brushes which fell from my lips have been removed. Sestina from the Home Gardener. Diane Wakoski. MoP

These drifting leaves, for instance. The Old Man's Example. Bill Manhire. ATNZ

These eighty-four years. Kangan, *tr. by* Lucien Stryk *and* Takashi Ikemoto. ZPCJ

These emotional dive-bombers. Nervous Miracles. Jim Gustafson. UL

These errors loved no less than the saint loves arrows. Elegy V: Separation of Man from God. George Barker. FaBoTw; LiTB

These eyes, [deare Lord,] once brandons of desire. For the Magdalene. William Drummond of Hawthornden. PoEL-2

These faces are true. Back to Hometown Kingston. James Berry. PBCV

These fallen boughs now never more will weave. The Fallen Tree. Patrick Maybin. NeIP

These fat cassia trees. What Her Girl Friend Said to Her. Kovatattan, *tr. by* A. K. Ramanujan. PLW

These fell miasmic rings of mist, with ghoulish menace bound. Prejudice. Georgia Douglas Johnson. AmNP; PoBA

These flowering fields you love so much. Rubai Enlarged. Khwaja Mir Dard, *tr. by* Ahmed Ali. GoT

These flowers are I, poor Fanny Hurd. Voices from Things Growing in a Churchyard. Thomas Hardy. OBD; OxBTC

"These foreigners with strange and avid faces." Immigrants. Nancy Byrd Turner. AmFN

These fought in any case. Ezra Pound. *Fr.* Hugh Selwyn Mauberley (Life and Contacts), IV. FF; HeIP; MoAmPo; NOBE; OBWP; PoE; VGW; WaaP

These fresh beauties, we can prove. Why Flowers Change Color. Robert Herrick. HAP

These going home at dusk. French Peasants. Monk Gibbon. NeIP; TIRV

"These Gothic windows, how they wear me out." The Young Glass-Stainer. Thomas Hardy. CTC; EyDe; SaC

These grand and fatal movements toward death. Rearmament. Robinson Jeffers. OxBA

These great brown hills move in herds, humped like bison. Among the Finger Lakes. Robert Wallace. GrPl

These Green-going-to-Yellow. Marvin Bell. CAPP; FYAP; LCAP

These green painted park benches are. In a Season of Unemployment. Margaret Avison. MoCV; NOBC

These had been together from the first. Leolin and Edith. Tennyson. *Fr.* Aylmer's Field. GN

These hands all chapped. *Unknown. Fr.* Manyo Shu. FCEI

These have forsaken other lives and ways. The Monks at Ards. Patrick Maybin. NeIP

These have no Christ to spit and stoop. Black Magdalens. Countee Cullen. BANP

These hearts were woven of human joys and cares. The Dead ("These hearts were woven"). Rupert Brooke. *Fr.* 1914, IV. BrPo; CH; LiTB; MMA; PoA

These hemp-clothes which you take. *Unknown. Fr.* Manyo Shu. Ma

These hips are big hips. Homage to My Hips. Lucille Clifton. CAPP

These Horses Came. Ray A. Young Bear. CDW

These I have loved with passion, loved them long. Quiet Things. Grace Noll Crowell. PoLF

These I: hidden plants that grow by the river's edge. West Creek at Ch'u-chou. Wei Ying-wu, *tr. by* Burton Watson. CoBCP

These Indians once imitated life. The Only Bar in Dixon. James Welch. AmPA; FF

These insects, golden. Insect Heads. Robert Bly. CAPP

These jewel-coloured walls, gemmed Salomè. "L'Apparition" of Gustave Moreau. Gordon Bottomley. BrPo

These Labdanum Hours. Kathleen Fraser. NPGG

These labor days, when shirking hardly looks like working. Back to Town. John Hollander. NoAM

These labouring wits, like paviours, mend our ways. Edward Young. *Fr.* Epistles to Mr. Pope. OBSV

These Lacustrine Cities. John Ashbery. HCAP; PoM; UnPo

These Leaves. William Stafford. NNaP

These light-footed, celebrated cats, created. The Tigers of Nanzen-ji. Brad Leithauser. DiPo

These little firs to-day are things. A Young Fir-Wood. Dante Gabriel Rossetti. GN

These little limbs [*or* limmes]. The Salutations. Thomas Traherne. InvP; NOCV; NoP; OBS; SeCP; SeCV-2

These locks on doors have brought me happiness. Locks. Kenneth Koch. CoAP

These locusts by day, these crickets by night. Wallace Stevens. PoA

These lodge in London in Lent and at other times too. The Civil Service. William Langland. *Fr.* The Vision of Piers Plowman. NOCV

These London wenches are so stout. The Sound Country Lass. *Unknown.* CoMu; ErPo

These lovely groves of fountain-trees that shake. Golden Bough. Elinor Wylie. MoAmPo; PBWP

These lover's inklings which our loves enmesh. Counsel to Unreason. Léonie Adams. PoA

These lusty plants, complete with blaring sex. Marrows. Louis Johnson. PeNZ

These magnificent senses. A Hymn of Touch. Gordon Bottomley. BrPo

These male descendants of the Queen. The Laureate's Complaint. Gavin Ewart. SoTCo

These market-dames, mid-aged, with lips thin-drawn. Former Beauties. Thomas Hardy. *Fr.* At Casterbridge Fair, II. NoAM; OBMV; OBNC

These Men. Leon Gellert. PoAu-1

These men were kings, albeit they were black. Black Majesty. Countee Cullen. PoBA; VGW

These messages are secret, the initials. Personal Column. Tom Paulin. FaBCIP

These Mornings. Marcelin Pleynet, *tr. fr. French by* Harry Mathews. RHTwFP

These native angles of decay. Deserted Buildings under Shefford Mountain. John Glassco. OBCV

These new night. Ivory Masks in Orbit. Keorapetse Kgositsile. PoBA

These nights when the wind blows. 0°. Elizabeth Spires. DiPo

These nostrils of bone and skin. Invocation to the Mummy. Antonin Artaud, *tr. by* Michael Benedikt. POS

These Obituaries of Rattlesnakes Being Eaten by the Hogs. Roger Weingarten. AmPA

These ornaments as we pass. Facades for Norma Cole. Michael Palmer. LP

These panting damsels, dancing for their lives. The Mother's Choice. *Unknown.* OxBoLi

These pearls of thought in Persian gulfs were bred. In a Copy of Omar Khayyám. James Russell Lowell. AA

These people have not heard your name. In a Cathedral City. Thomas Hardy. EnLoPo; FaBoPP

These people, with their illegible diplomas. Metamorphoses. Howard Nemerov. EyDe; HCAP

These pines, these fall oaks, these rocks. After Drinking All Night with a Friend, We Go Out in a Boat at Dawn to See Who Can Write the Best Poem. Robert Bly. NaP

These plaintive verse, the posts [*or* postes] of my desire. Samuel Daniel. *Fr.* To Delia. AAS; OBSC

These Poems, She Said ("These poems, these poems"). Robert Bringhurst. NOBC

"These poems were anticipations." Alfred Kolleritsch, *tr. by* Beth Bjorklund. CoAuP

These pools that, though in forests, still reflect. Spring Pools. Robert Frost. AmPP; MoAB; NAAL-2; NoAM; NOBA; NoP; OxBA

These populous slopes. The Quantocks. Wordsworth. FaBoPP

These pretty little birds see how. Humaine Cares. Nathaniel Wanley. OBS

These Purists. William Carlos Williams. OBAL

These retroactive small. First Rain. Robert Creeley. CAPP

These rioteres three of which I tell. Death and the Three Revellers. Chaucer. *Fr.* The Canterbury Tales: The Pardoner's Tale. OBNV

These rock stars amaze me. Out of Sight. R. C. Shebelski. SoTCo

These royall kinges, that reare up to the skye. Thomas Sackevyll in Commendation of the Worke to the Reader. Thomas Sackville. AAS

These Rumours of Hexagonal Rooms in Gone Bee City. David Eggleton. PeNZ

These set a crown of glory on their land. On the Lacedaemonian Dead at Plataea. Simonides, *tr. by* Richard Eberhart. WaaP

These seven houses have learned to face one another. On a Painting by Patient B of the Independence State Hospital for the Insane. Donald Justice. CoAP; NePoEA-2; NoAM

These sheets primeval doctrines yield. On Barclay's Apology for the Quakers. Matthew Green. NOEC

These Six. Sean Lucy. CIP

These six things doth the Lord hate. Seven Evils. Bible, *O.T. Fr.* Proverbs, VI: 16-19. TrGrPo

These songs will not stand. Song: "These songs will not stand." Denis Glover. *Fr.* Sings Harry, I. ATNZ; PeNZ

These souls, my lord, assembled at the bar. The Parish Poor-Officers. Edward Ward. *Fr.* Journey to Hell, A; or, A Visit Paid to the Devil. NOEC

These spectres resting on plastic stools. Cafe in Warsaw. Allen Ginsberg. HAP

These sticks I am holding. This Preparation. Simon J. Ortiz. NOVW

These suggestions by Asians are not taken seriously. Asian Peace Offers Rejected without Publication. Robert Bly. NaP

These summer-birds did with thy master stay. To His Maid Prew. Robert Herrick. OBS

These sweeter far than lilies are. Thanksgivings for the Beauty of His Providence. Thomas Traherne. FaBoCh
These tall lilies, color. The Lilies. Richard Emil Braun. NoAM
These ten-year-olds all want other names. Lunch with Girl Scouts. Sharon Bryan. MAYP
These the assizes: here the charge, denial. Epigraph from *The Judge Is Fury*. J. V. Cunningham. QFR
These the dread days which the seers have foretold. The Death of Justice. Walter Everette Hawkins. PoBA
These Things I Do Remember. Solomon Ephraim ben Aaron of Lenczicz, *tr. fr. Hebrew by* Nina Davis Salaman. TrJP
These tiny Mexican mosquitoes are like lost souls. Baja. Gerald Stern. SV
These tracings from a world that's dead. To Violet [with Prewar Poems]. Basil Bunting. FaBoMo; PoA
These Trees Are No Forest of Mourners. Douglas G. Jones. NOBC
These Trees Stand. W. D. Snodgrass. MoP; NIP; PPP
These trees that fling their leafy boughs aloft. London Trees. Beryl Netherclift. BoTP
These triangulations on thirsty water. Love without a Truce. Antonin Artaud, *tr. by* Michael Benedikt. POS
These truly are the Brave. The Negro Soldiers. Roscoe Conkling Jamison. BANP
These Two. Howard Schwartz. VWA
These two, dissimilar, understood. Pain. Jack Hand. TSM
These two meet for dinner once a week. Imaginary Translation. Marilyn Hacker. DiPo
These umbered cliffs and gnarls of masonry. Rome: Building a New Street in the Ancient Quarter. Thomas Hardy. Son
These unshaped islands, on the sawyer's bench. New Zealand. James Keir Baxter. NoP
These walls, so full of monument and bust. The Abbey Church at Bath. Henry Harington. FaBoEE
These walls they knew those shadows. Wall Shadows. Carl Sandburg. WSC
These were contemporaries of the mammoth. The Death of Floyd Collins. Clark Coolidge. LP
These were our fields. Dust Bowl. Robert A. Davis. IDB
These were the sounds that dinned upon his ear. Dream of Winter. George Mackay Brown. FaBoTw
These white-clay pits of Byfield. The Byfield Rabbit. Katherine Hoskins. SaC
These winds bully me. Foreigner. Fleur Adcock. PoPo
These wisterias. Masaoka Shiki, *tr. fr. Japanese by* Burton Watson. *Fr.* Fifteen Haiku. FCEI
These women all. Women. ― ― ―Heath. CTC; FaBoCo; OBSC
These women have no language and so they chatter. Lines for Those to Whom Tragedy Is Denied. Joyce Carol Oates. IHMS
These wonderful things. A Last World. John Ashbery. PoM
These woods are one of my great lies. The Owl. W. S. Merwin. PPP
These words are dedicated to those who died. Irena Klepfisz. *Fr.* Bashert. ER
These words spake Don Henriquez. The Last Words of Don Henriquez. Zalman Schneour, *tr. by* Joseph Leftwich. TrJP
These words the poet heard in Paradise. President Garfield. Longfellow. PAH
These words were composed by Spencer the Rover. Spencer the Rover. *Unknown.* OBET
Theseus: A Trilogy. Yvor Winters. NOBA
Theseus and Ariadne. Robert Graves. HAP
Theseus and Ariadne. Lloyd Mifflin. AA
Thesis. Edward Dorn. NOBA
Thesis, Antithesis and Nostalgia. Alan Dugan. PCP
Thespian in Jerusalem. Myra Glazer Schotz. VWA
Thespians at Thermopylae, The. Norman Cameron. GTBS-P
Thespius had fifty daughters. M 13. Harry Bose. *Fr.* Seven One-Line Poems. BWV
Thessalian. Winifred Bryher. PoA
They. Marvin Bell. CAPP
They. Mani Leib, *tr. fr. Yiddish.* PeBMYV, *tr. by* John Hollander; VWA, *tr. by* David G. Roskies *and* Hillel Schwartz.
"They." Siegfried Sassoon. CMoP; NAEL-2; OBSV; OBWP
They. R. S. Thomas. OxBTC
They/ say/ you/ went/ abroad. Incidental Pieces to a Walk. James Cunningham. JB
They, after the slow building of the house. Asmodai. Geoffrey Hill. NePoEA
　　(Asmodeus.) FaBoTw
They aint no use a-telling, boy, what's for you to do. Dan Ellis's Boys. *Unknown.* AmFP

They all are riders: Spring on a two-year-old. The Seasons. Rolfe Humphries. NYBP
They all arrived, and them with generous show. The Wedding Feast. Luis de Góngora y Argote, *tr. fr. Spanish by* Edward Meryon Wilson. *Fr.* The First Solitude. OBVE
They all climbed up on a high board-fence. The Nine Little Goblins. James Whitcomb Riley. OBCA
They All Must Fall. Muhammad Ali. ASP
They all see the same movies. Powwow. W. D. Snodgrass. GrPl; NYBP
They All Want to Play Hamlet. Carl Sandburg. NOBA
They all were looking for a king. That Holy Thing. George Macdonald. *Fr.* Paul Faber, Surgeon. OBEV; TrPWD; WGRP
They alone are left me; they alone still faithful. My Dead. Rachel, *tr. by* Robert Mezey. VWA
They always put a large crimson sheet. Parakeet. Leonard Clark. Mes
They amputated/ Your thighs off my hips. A Pity; We Were Such a Good Invention. Yehuda Amichai, *tr. by* Assia Gutmann. BoLoP
They Answer Back. "Francis." FiBHP
They are a gift I have wanted again. Horses in Snow. Roberta Hill Whiteman. NoAM
They are able, with science, to measure. C Stands for Civilization. Kenneth Fearing. TrJP
They are all dying. Death as History. Jay Wright. PoBA
They Are All Gone. Henry Vaughan. *See* They Are All Gone into the World of Light.
They are all gone away. The House on the Hill. E. A. Robinson. AA; FaPON; GoJo; MoAmPo; NAAL-2; PrIm; TrGrPo
They Are All Gone into the World of Light. Henry Vaughan. ChTr; FaBoRV; InPS; JCP; MePo; NAEL-1; NOBE; NoP; OAEL-1; OBS; PoEL-2; SeCP; SeCV-1
　　(Ascension Hymn.) MeLP; NOCV
　　(Friends Departed.) OBEV
　　(They Are All Gone.) BLPL; HeIP; LiTB; SeCePo
　　(World of Light, The.) CH; WGRP
They are all outline, uniformly gray. Those before Us. Robert Lowell. LCAP
They Are All Too Kind. Susan L. Dunn. TSM
They are at rest. Refrigerium. Cardinal Newman. OBNC
They are at table. The Last Supper. Jacques Prévert, *tr. by* Lawrence Ferlinghetti. RHTwFP
They are at their places, straining. The Boat Race. Virgil, *tr. fr. Latin by* Rolfe Humphries. *Fr.* The Aeneid [*or* Eneados], V. SD
They are beating up a man in the bar. A Man Is Beaten Up. Gábor Garai, *tr. by* Edwin Morgan. MHuP
They are born in the swamps of sleeplessness. Mosquitoes. José Emilio Pacheco, *tr. by* Alastair Reid. TSS
They are bringing him down. Casualty. Robert Nichols. MMA
They are by nature lonely things. Ideal Angels. John Robert Colombo. MoCV
They are chanting now the service of All the Dead. All Souls. D. H. Lawrence. FaBoRV
They Are Coming? Josephine D. Henderson Heard. CBWP-4
They are cutting down the great plane-trees at the end of the gardens. The Trees Are Down. Charlotte Mew. BoNaP; BrRo; MoAB; MoBrPo; TrCP; WPE; WPOW
They are disturbed even by my hair. My Strawlike Hair. Asya, *tr. by* Gabriel Preil *and* Howard Schwartz. VWA
They are dreaming of children. Torrential. Nocturne in the Women's Prison. Maria Beneyto, *tr. by* Catherine Rodriguez-Nieto. WPOW
They are 18 inches long. Trees at the Arctic Circle. Alfred W. Purdy. NoP
They are formidable under any feather. The Murmurers. Josephine Jacobsen. GrPl
They are gathered, astounded and disturbed. The Last Supper. Rainer Maria Rilke, *tr. by* M. D. Herter Norton. OFD
They are gathering round. Concert Party. Siegfried Sassoon. MMA
They are heard as a choir of seven. The Pleiades. Mary Barnard. NYBP
They are his planets. Marbles. Joan LaBombard. TDD
They are immortal, voyagers like these. Flight. Harold Vinal. FaPON
They are in the forest. In the Forest. George Bowering. NOBC
They are inspecting hearts again. A Glimpse of the Body Shop. Stephen Berg. NaP
They Are Killing All the Young Men. David Henderson. PoBA
They are lang deid, folk that I used to ken. Robert Garioch. OxBS
They are left alone in the dear old home. They Two. Mrs. Frank A. Breck. WBLP
They are light as flakes of dandruff with scrawny legs. Crabs. Marge Piercy. NBLV

They are like figures held in some glass ball. Children Walking Home from School through Good Neighborhood. Donald Justice. DiPo

They are making a crèche at the Saturday morning classes. The Crib. Robert Finch. OBCP

They are moving inwards; the circle is closing. Man Meeting Himself. Howard Sergeant. EAS

They are my laddie's hounds. My Laddie's Hounds. Marguerite Elizabeth Easter. AA

They are my secret food. The Children's Letters. Dorothy Livesay. NOBC

They are not automobiles. The Cherokee Dean. Norman H. Russell. STE

They are not dead, they are not dead! The Argonauts. D. H. Lawrence. NoAM

They are not given much to laughter. Hill People. Harriet Gray Blackwell. AmFN

They are not here. And we, we are the Others. The Absent. Edwin Muir. NoAM

They are not long, the weeping and the laughter. Vitae Summa Brevis Spem Nos Vetat Incohare Longam. Ernest Dowson. AWP; BrPo; ChTr; EBVV; FaBoRV; HAP; NOBE; NoP; OBEV; OxBSP; TrGrPo; WGRP
   (Envoy: "They are not long, the weeping and the laughter.") MoBrPo; NOBVV; PCP
   (They Are Not Long.) NAEL-2; PoRA

They are not those who used to feed us. The Puzzled Game Birds. Thomas Hardy. PBBP

They Are Ours. A. B. Magil. PoNe

They are picking off all my friends, one by one. A Credential. Philip Hobsbaum. NPo

They are pounded into the earth. It Is This Way with Men. C. K. Williams. CAPP

They are rattling breakfast plates in basement kitchens. Morning at the Window. T. S. Eliot. AWP; PoA

They are rebuilding/ the old bridge, the Nagara. Lady Ise, tr. fr. Japanese by Etsuko Terasaki and Irma Brandeis. BoWoP

They are rhymes rudely strung with intent less. Adam Lindsay Gordon. CBAP; PoAu-1

They are riding away from whatever might have been. A Shooting Script. Seamus Heaney. BAP

They are riding bicycles on the other side. Snapshot of Hue. Daniel Halpern. MAYP

They are 7 in number, just 7. The Seven. Unknown, tr. by Jerome K. Rothenberg. RB

They are slaves who fear to speak. Slaves. James Russell Lowell. Fr. Stanzas on Freedom. GN, 2 sts.; OHIP; PoNe
   (Stanza on Freedom, A.) AA

They are so alike. Dolls. David St. John. LCAP

They are so moving in. The Love of Older Men. James Kirkup. PeHV

They are so persistent, that give them a few stones. Czesław Miłosz, tr. fr. Polish by the author and Peter Dale Scott. Fr. Throughout Our Lands, IX. PwPP

They are sprouting, those wayside reeds. Unknown, tr. by Arthur Waley. BoS

They are taking us beyond Miami. The Removal. Unknown, tr. by Frances Densmore. STP

They are terribly white. Cyclamens. "Michael Field." NOBVV

They are the angels of that watery world. Goldfish. Harold Monro. BrPo

They are the flesh we feed upon come from the depths. The Ribbon-Fish. Robert Adamson. CBAP

They are the last romantics, these candles. Candles. Sylvia Plath. NMM

They are the oldest living captive race. Ginkgoes in Fall. Howard Nemerov. HCAP

They are the real spirits of the place. The Hospital Kangaroos. Peter Kocan. UAS

They Are the Same. Priscilla Jane Thompson. CBWP-2

They are the slums of great cities, with narrow streets. In the Ghetto. Hugo Sonnenschein, tr. by Edouard Roditi. VWA

They are the spit of virtue now. Austin Clarke. Fr. Civil War. NOIV

They are weighing the babies again on color television. Video Cuisine. Maxine W. Kumin. NoAM

They Are Wicked. Ernest Sandeen. CRP

They are without memory, making. Crickets. David Rigsbee. KS

They argued on till dead of night. Theologians. Walter de la Mare. EaLo

They Ask: Is God, Too, Lonely. Carl Sandburg. ILY

They ask me to handle bronzes. Bronzes. Carl Sandburg. EyDe

They asked for bread. For Our Soldiers Who Fell in Russia. Franco Fortini, tr. by Ruth Feldman. VWA

They bade me cast the thing away. Doubt. Helen Hunt Jackson. WGRP

They bear no laurels on their sunless brows. Failures. Arthur W. Upson. WGRP

They beat their drums with a loud noise. Unknown, tr. by Arthur Waley. BoS

They become fragrant, and the Spring ends. Teika, tr. fr. Japanese by Hiroaki Sato. Fr. Eighty-four Tanka. FCEI

They belong here in their own quenched country. By the Boat House, Oxford. Anne Stevenson. FaBoWP

They bide their time off serpentine. Ancient Monuments. John Ormond. OBVVE

They bloom and then. Onitsura, tr. by Geoffrey Bownas and Anthony Thwaite. PeBJV

They borrowed a bed to lay His head. The Cross Was His Own. Unknown. BLPA
   ("Borrowed.") BLRP

They bowed to him: "O man of God." The Prophet. "Yehoash," tr. by Isidore Goldstick. TrJP

They breathe with the night. Roland Penrose. Fr. The Road Is Wider than Long. EAS

They bring me gifts, they honour me. If They Honoured Me, Giving Me Their Gifts. "Michael Field." OBMV

They brought a bouquet of thistles. Thistle. Nikolai Alekseevich Zabolotsky, tr. by Daniel Weissbort. RB

They brought him in on a stretcher from the world. Grandfather. Derek Mahon. FaBCIP; OxBC

They brought him one morning. Dimitris Tsaloumas, tr. fr. Greek by Margaret Carroll. Fr. A Rhapsody of Old Men. CBAP

They brought in the brine-crusted drift-wood. Drift-Wood. Clara Ann Thompson. CBWP-2

They brought me ambrotypes. Rutherford McDowell. Edgar Lee Masters. Fr. Spoon River Anthology. EyDe; LiTA; OxBA

They built the front, upon my word. The Building of a New Church. Unknown. EyDe
   (On the Building of a New Church.) FaBoEE

They buried him today. My Father Today. Sam Hunt. PeNZ

They burn:/ The bones like tinder. Kabir, tr. by John Stratton Hawley and Mark Juergensmeyer. SSI

They burn the radio and listen to the blues. John Tranter. Fr. Crying in Early Infancy, V. NoAM

They burn you. The Hitchhikers. Diane Wakoski. NoAM

They call it love; but it's the lover's distress. Nawab Mirza Khan Dagh, tr. by Ahmed Ali. GoT

They call it regional, this relevance. Lake Chelan. William Stafford. NaP

They call me and I go. Complaint. William Carlos Williams. QFR

They call me cruel. Do I know if mouse or songbird feels? The Cat. Charles Stuart Calverley. Fr. Sad Memories. ChTr

They call me Hanging Johnny. Hanging Johnny. Unknown. GBP

They call thee rich; I deem thee poor. Treasure. Lucilius, tr. by William Cowper. AWP

They call them Wet and Dry. Passage Rite. John Caddy. TSL

They call us aliens, we are told. On Behalf of Some Irishmen Not Followers of Tradition. "Æ." AnIL

They call your name in vain. St. Francis of Assisi and the Miserable Jews. Josef Whittlin, tr. by Isaac Komem. VWA

They called him Bill, the hired man. William Brown of Oregon. Joaquin Miller. AnAmPo

"They called it Annandale—and I was there." How Annandale Went Out. E. A. Robinson. MoAB; MoAmPo; NoAM; NOBA

They called my love a poor blind maid. On a Blind Girl. Baha Ad-din Zuhayr, tr. by E. H. Palmer. AWP

They called the place Lookout Farm. Memoirs of a Spinach-Picker. Sylvia Plath. GrPl

They came by water. The Dead Conquerors. Antonio Cisneros, tr. by David Tipton. Per

They came from Persia to the sacred way. Peacocks. Walter Adolphe Roberts. PBCV

They came hurrying across the mountain highway. Monkeys on Mt. Hiei. Edith Marcombe Shiffert. WPE

They came in to the little town. We Are Going. Kath Walker. CBAP

They came into the wilderness, clichés in suitcases. Tourists. Kizito Z. Muchemwa. WMBCH

They came on ponies, barefoot. Bolsheviks. Aba Shtoltsenberg, tr. by Stanley Kunitz. PeBMYV

They came on to fish-hook Gettysburg in this way, after this fashion. The Battle of Gettysburg. Stephen Vincent Benét. Fr. John Brown's Body. BeLS

They came out of the sun undetected. The Raid. William Everson. MoP; NoAM; PrIm

They came running over the perilous sands. 1945. Sir Herbert Read. OxBTC

They Came This Evening. Léon Damas, *tr. fr. French by* Seth L. Wolitz. TTY

They Came to Me and Said, "There Is a Child." Muriel Rukeyser. *Fr.* Nine Poems for the Unborn Child, II. Son

They came to the lodge door. Wolf "Aunt." Maurice Kenny. HATNAP

They came when the Czar banned the Yiddish. Yiddish Speaking Socialists of the Lower East Side. Ed Sanders. UL

They can have your thighs. M. A. P. Calvin Forbes. MAYP

They cannot speak who have no words to say. Green Hammock, White Magnolia Tree. Ruth Gilbert. PeNZ

They cannot wholly pass away. The Departed. John Banister Tabb. AA

They Can't Do That. *Unknown.* WTO

They cared for nothing but the days and hours. The Disinherited. Charles Spear. ATNZ; PeNZ

"They carry on." Floodtide. Askia Muhammad Touré. PoBA; PoNe

They cast lots on the day of Azazel. Lament for Azazel. Francis Landy. VWA

They Cast Their Nets in Galilee. William A. Percy. AH

They catch your eye early, those rising black. For Stephen Drawing Birds. Pattiann Rogers. MAYP

They chained her fair young body to the cold and cruel stone. Andromeda. James Jeffrey Roche. AA

They change/ though you can't see it. Komachi, *tr. fr. Japanese by* Burton Watson. *Fr.* Kokin Shu. FCEI

They changed her name. Nechama. Shirley Kaufman. LCAP

They Clapped. Nikki Giovanni. WPOW

They clear away the grass, the trees. *Unknown, tr. by* Arthur Waley. BoS

They Closed Her Eyes. Gustavo Adolfo Bécquer, *tr. fr. Spanish by* John Masefield. AWP

They come as a boon and a blessing to men. The Waverley Pen. *Unknown.* FaBoUs

They come, beset by riddling hail. Albuera. Thomas Hardy. *Fr.* The Dynasts, *Pt.* II, Act VI, sc. iv. WaaP

They come down. Deer in the Bush. Chana Bloch. MAYP

They come from beds of lichen green. The Assembling of the Fays. Joseph Rodman Drake. *Fr.* The Culprit Fay. GN

They come into. Feeding the Lions. Norman Jordan. NBP; PoBA

They come into this room while the quail are crying to huddle up. Reading the Books Our Children Have Written. Dave Smith. HCAP

They come not within the tall woods. To One Elect. S. I. Hayakawa. PoA

They come!—they come!—the heroes come. Evacuation of New York by the British. *Unknown.* PAH

They come, they come, with fife and drum. The Palace. Charles Stuart Calverley. EBVV

They come to the door, usually carrying or leading. Pilgrims. William Stafford. BLA

They come to you with their descriptions of your soul. Adrienne Rich. *Fr.* Shooting Script, 10. HCAP

They come with, ah, fell footfall. Fêtes, Fates. John Malcolm Brinnin. LiTA

They cross from Glasgow to a black city. Settlers. Tom Paulin. FaBCIP

They cross the frontier as their names cross your pages. The New Emigration. Kay Boyle. WPE

They cross the yard. Dedication to Hunger. Louise Glück. AnAn; FaBoWP; GeTw

They crucified my Lord, an' He never said a mumbalin' word. Crucifixion. *Unknown.* BPo; TAP; TrGrPo

"They cut it in squares." Socratic. Hilda Doolittle ("H. D."). HoPM

They deployed military troops. White Weekend. Quincy Troupe. NBP

They did it George. They did it. Conversation with Washington. Myra Cohn Livingston. OFD

They did not come to claim you back. Helen Todd: My Birthname. Sandra McPherson. NAmP

They did not know this face. Job. Elizabeth Sewell. EaLo

They did the deed of darkness. You and I Saw Hawks Exchanging the Prey. James Wright. NAAL-2; NoAM

They Didn't Hire Him. Gary Snyder. *Fr.* Hitch Haiku. LCAP; SM

They didn't recognize me. The Passport. Mahmoud Darwish, *tr. by* Abdullah al-Udhari. MPAW

They dither softly at her bedroom door. Cover Her Face. Thomas Kinsella. CIP; IPY

They do it with knives. Alistair Paterson. *Fr.* The Toledo Room, I, ix. PeNZ

They do little interminable things. Christina. Yona Wallach, *tr. by* Warren Bargad *and* Stanley F. Chyet. IP

They do me wrong who say I come no more. Opportunity. Walter Malone. BLPA; BLPL; FaBoBe; PWR; WBLP

They do move with grace. Dressed to Kill. Clarence Major. UL

They do not care, the dying, whether it be dawn or dusk or daylight full and clear. Illi Morituri. Mary Morison Webster. PeSA

They do not come with furred caps. Barbarians. John Fowles. AnAn

They do not live in the world. The Animals. Edwin Muir. CMoP; CRP; EBEV; HeIP; MoBrPo; NoP

They do not speak but into their empty mood. Two Old Men Look at the Sea. J. R. Hervey. ATNZ

They do zay that a travellen chap. The Leane. William Barnes. EBVV

They dogged him all one afternoon. On the Way to the Mission. Duncan Campbell Scott. CaP; NOBC

They done took Cordelia. Stony Lonesome. Langston Hughes. NOBA

They don't build houses like that any more. Verandahs. Robert Francis Brissenden. CBAP

They don't get anywhere. The Couple Overheard. William Meredith. HoPM; TW

They don't hold grudges. First Monday Scottsboro Alabama. Tom Weatherly. PoBA

They don't like strangers. Stoney Ridge Dance Hall. Alden Nowlan. MoCV

They don't nail down. Why the Many Words? Gerhard Fritsch, *tr. by* Beth Bjorklund. CoAuP

They Don't Speak English in Paris. Ogden Nash. OBAL

They dragged you from [the] homeland. Strong Men. Sterling A. Brown. BANP; BPo; CNA; FB; PoBA; TTY

They Dream Only of America. John Ashbery. CAPP; EAS

They dressed us up in black. The Funeral. Walter de la Mare. CMoP

They drop with periodic regularity. The Preacher Sought to Find Out Acceptable Words. Richard Eberhart. WaP

They dropped like flakes, they dropped like stars. Emily Dickinson. AA; OHIP

They eat beans mostly, this old yellow pair. The Bean Eaters. Gwendolyn Brooks. AIW; BlSi; GrPl; HAP; HeIP; MAT; NoP; PoBA; PoE; PrIm; TAP; TTY; WeW

They Eat Out. Margaret Atwood. NeAC; NoAM; NoP

They ended parle, and both addressed for fight. Milton. *Fr.* Paradise Lost, *Bk.* VI, *ll.* 296–353. OBWP

They enter the bare wood, drawn. The Novices. Denise Levertov. NaP

They erect gallows in the prison yard. The Condemned. Edmond Jabès, *tr. by* Jack Hirschman. VWA

They expanded. McDonald's, New Hartford, NY. Valerie Worth. AiP

They feed on shadows. The Wall of Tomorrow. Orkhan Muyassar, *tr. by* Lena Jayyusi *and* Samuel Hazo. MAP

They Feed They Lion. Philip Levine. CAPP; LCAP; MAT; MoP; NNaP; NoAM; NOBA; Prf

They feel the calm delight, and thus proceed. The Suffolk Shore. George Crabbe. *Fr.* The Borough, Letter XXIII. FaBoPP

They Fell on the Stairway. Mercedes Durand, *tr. fr. Spanish by* Barbara Paschke. Vol

They fished and they fished. The Fish with the Deep Smile. Margaret Wise Brown. PDV

They Flee from Me That Sometime Did Me Seek. Gavin Ewart. OxBC

They Flee [*or* Fle] from Me That Sometime Did Me Seek [*or* Seke]. Sir Thomas Wyatt. BLPL; EnLoPo; FaBoPV; FF; HAP; HeIP; InPK; LiTB; NAEL-1; NoP; OAEL-1; OPOP; OxBC; PoE; PPP; PrIm; SiPS; TEP; WeW

  (Lover Showeth How He Is Forsaken of Such as He Sometime Enjoyed, The.) AAS, 2 *versions;* EIL; ELP; HoPM; InPS; PoEL-1; PoRA; TrGrPo

  (Remembrance.) BoLoP; NOBE; OBSC; QFR

  (Vixi Puellis Nuper Idoneus.) OBEV

They fling their flags upon the morn. Spain's Last Armada. Wallace Rice. PAH

They fly up in front of you. Ground Birds in Open Country. Stanley Plumly. NAmP

They formed the ritual circle. A Local Man Goes to the Killing Ground. James Whitehead. MT

They fought last year by the upper valley of Son-Kan. The Long War. Li Po, *tr. by* Cheng Yu Sun. WaaP

They fought south of the Castle. Fighting South of the Castle. *Unknown, tr. by* Arthur Waley. AWP; WaaP

They fought south of the ramparts. Fighting South of the Ramparts. *Unknown, tr. by* Arthur Waley. OBD

They Fought South of the Wall. *Unknown, tr. fr. Chinese by* Burton Watson. CoBCP

They found a taxi. He took her home. The Moral Taxi Ride. Erich Kästner, *tr. by* Jerome Rothenberg. ErPo

They found him looking north. In Mosa's Time. Roberta Hill
　Whiteman. ER
They Found Him Sitting in a Chair. Horace Gregory. MoAmPo
They framed him once. The Hills of *Tsa la gi*. Robert J. Conley.
　STE
They fuck you up, your mum and dad. This Be the Verse. Philip
　Larkin. NoAM
They gamble on you. The Greyhound. Saleem Barakat, *tr.* by Lena
　Jayyusi *and* Naomi Shihab Nye. MAP
They gathered around and told him not to do it. Noah. Roy Daniells.
　Mes
They gave him an overdose. Loyal. William Matthews. MAYP
They gave me in my kindergarten year. Now or Never. Judith Moffett.
　SM; Son
They gave me the wrong name, in the first place. Her Story. Naomi
　Long Madgett. IHMS; PoBA
They gave my father a television. Death. Howard Byatt. FF
They gave us the mysterious deep warehouse. The Ajax Samples. Laura
　Jensen. LCAP
They give me a bad. Crows. Marge Piercy. CAPP
They glare—those stony eyes! The Sphinx. Henry Howard Brownell.
　AA
They glued me into time, they dressed me up. Map. Murilo Mendes, *tr.*
　by W. S. Merwin. ATCBP
They go by, go by, love, the days and the hours. Teresa de Jesús, *tr. fr.*
　Spanish by Maria A. Proser, Arlene Scully *and* James Scully.
　WPOW
They got him in the end, of course. Walt Whitman at the Reburial of
　Poe. Nicholas Christopher. MAYP
They grew in beauty side by side. The Graves of a Household. Felicia
　Dorothea Hemans. FaPoR; WBLP; WPE
They Grow Up Too Fast, She Said. Diana O Hehir. NPGG
They guided birds and came to hear their story. Of History More Like
　Myth. Jean Garrigue. NYBP
They had agreed, walking into the delicatessen on 6th Avenue. Vintage.
　Robert Hass. AnAn
They had been there a month; the water had begun to tear them apart. A
　Negro Soldier's Viet Nam Diary. Herbert Martin. PoBA
They had brought in such sheafs of hair. The Last Bowstrings. Edward
　Lucas White. AA
They had dragged for hours. These Trees Are No Forest of Mourners.
　Douglas G. Jones. NOBC
They had me laid out in a white. April Fools' Day. Yusef Komunyakaa.
　MAYP
They had questioned him for hours. Campaign. Ciaran Carson.
　CIP
They had secured their beauty to the dock. The Crowd. John Masefield.
　OxBTC
They had warned him so often: "Play it." Essay. Riekus Waskowsky, *tr.*
　by James S. Holmes. DuIn
They hanged him on a clement morning, swung. Dennis Scott.
　PBCV
They hanged Jeff Buckner from a sycamore tree. Jeff Buckner. Frank
　Beddo. WTO
They hanged the King of Ai at eventide. The King of Ai. Hyam Plutzik.
　LiTM; VWA
They have a certain beauty, those wheeled. Over the Field. May
　Swenson. RR
They have been with us a long time. Telephone Poles. John Updike.
　FYAP; Psk; SaC
They have brought me a snail. Snail. Federico García Lorca, *tr. by*
　William Jay Smith. *Fr.* Songs of Childhood. CT; TSS
They have carried the mahogany chair and the cane rocker. Mourning
　Picture. Adrienne Rich. CoAP
They have chiseled on my stone the words. Cassius Hueffer. Edgar Lee
　Masters. *Fr.* Spoon River Anthology. OxBA
They have come by carloads. Surfers at Santa Cruz. Paul Goodman.
　ASP; FF
They have connived at those jewelled fascinations. Auspice of Jewels.
　Laura Riding. LiTA
They have dreamed as young men dream. Old Black Men. Georgia
　Douglas Johnson. CDC; PoBA; PoNe
They have fenced in the dirt road. Burial. Alice Walker. AmPA;
　PrIm
They have gone/ into the green hill. Apples. Donald Hall.
　LCAP
They have laid the penthouse scenes away. Elegy in a Theatrical
　Warehouse. Kenneth Fearing. NYBP
They have left bread on the table. Bread. Gabriela Mistral, *tr. by* Allan
　Francovich *and* Kathleen Weaver. WPOW

They have [*or* They've *or* Th' have] left Thee naked, Lord, O that they
　had! Upon the Body of Our Blessed Lord, Naked and Bloody.
　Richard Crashaw. ACP; InvP; SeCP
　(On Our Crucified Lord, Naked and Bloody.) HoPM; OAEL-1; OBS;
　OxBSP; SeCV-1; TrCP
They have lived in each other so long. The Demolition. Anne
　Stevenson. OxBSP
They have met at last—as storm-clouds. Manassas. Catherine Anne
　Warfield. PAH
They have met here before: five old women. At Nuclear Medicine.
　Dixie Partridge. TSM
They have no word for conscience. Carrier Indians. Ken Belford.
　NOBC
They have not gone from us. O no! they are. Our Dead. Robert Nichols.
　WGRP
They have put my bed beside the unpainted screen. Last Poem. Po Chü-
　i, *tr. by* Arthur Waley. OBD
They have said evil of my dear. Medieval Norman Song. *Unknown, tr.*
　by John Addington Symonds. AWP
They have sed. Hospital/Poem. Sonia Sanchez. BPo; PoBA
They have stopped drilling since yesterday. Panic on the Oil Rig. Paul
　Snoek, *tr. by* Alasdair MacKinnon. DuIn
They Have Taken It from Me. Timothy Corsellis. WaP
They have taken the gable from the roof of clay. Swedes. Edward
　Thomas. BrPo; OAEL-2; RB
They have taken the maps and spread them out. Still Pond, No More
　Moving. Howard Moss. NYBP
They have turned, and say that I am dying. That. I Substitute for the
　Dead Lecturer. Amiri Baraka. NAAL-2; NOBA; PoE
They have yarns. *Fr.* The People, Yes, *sec.* 45.
　AmFN; LiTA; MoAmPo
They haven't got no noses. The Song of Quoodle. G. K. Chesterton.
　GoJo
They heard the south wind sighing. The Crocuses. Frances E. W.
　Harper. BlSi
They heated hatchet blades over gas fires in roadside workshops and.
　While the Record Plays. Gyula Illyés, *tr. by* William Jay Smith.
　MHuP
They heaved the stone; they heaped the cairn. Aideen's Grave. Samuel
　Ferguson. NOIV
They held her south to Magellan's mouth. The Rush of the *Oregon*.
　Arthur Guiterman. PAH
They hire you for the silk to line their budgets. Advice from Euterpe.
　Carter Revard. VoR
They hold their hands over their mouths. The Poets Agree to Be Quiet by
　the Swamp. David Wagoner. CoAP; VGW
They hounded us like dogs. Like Dogs. Amryl Johnson. WS
They howled 'til Pilate. Crucifixion. Waring Cuney. BANP
They huddle over garbage fires. Houston Street. Lisa Vice. ER
They hunt chameleon worlds with cameras. Adina. Harold Milton
　Telemaque. TTY
They hunt, the velvet tigers in the jungle. India. W. J. Turner.
　MoBrPo; PDV
They hurt no one. They rove the North. In Fur. William Stafford.
　RFM
They ignore me now, but there have been. Where Are the Snows?
　Leonard Trawick. SoTCo
They journeyed,/ When the darkness of night. Ibn al-Arabi, *tr. by* R. A.
　Nicholson. AWP
They kept it all level. And low. Even. The Early Ones. William
　Stafford. CAPP
They kill me for the death within them. Mihailovich. Roy McFadden.
　NeIP
They knew. Workers of the Sun's Land. Antonio Cisneros, *tr. by*
　Maureen Ahern *and* David Tipton. Per
They knew the conjugations of the flesh. Emeritus, n. Henri Coulette.
　FF
They knew they were fighting our war. As the months grew to years.
　Pershing at the Tomb of Lafayette. Amelia Josephine Burr. PAH
They Know. Tawfiq Zayyad, *tr. fr. Arabic by* Sharif Elmusa *and* Charles
　Doria. MAP
They knew not of their mission from above. Cowper's Three Hares.
　Charles Tennyson Turner. FM
They know the time to go! Time to Go. "Susan Coolidge." GN
They laughed at one I loved. Innocence. Patrick Kavanagh. FaBCIP;
　RB
They lean against the cooling car, backs pressed. The Discovery of the
　Pacific. Thom Gunn. HeIP
They lean over the path. Orchids. Theodore Roethke. CMoP
They leave from positions of strength, like all baroque. Friends Who
　Have Failed. Alan Williamson. PPR

They leave us—artists, singers, all. When London Calls. Victor James Daley. CBAP

They leave us so to the way we took. In Neglect. Robert Frost. OxBSP; VGW

They led him to the guillotine. February 1. A. Leyeles, *tr. fr. Yiddish* by Benjamin *and* Barbara Harshav. *Fr.* Fabius Lind's Diary. AYP

They left the primrose glistening in its dew. Spring, and the Blind Children. Alfred Noyes. OxBTC

They left the vine-wreathed cottage and the mansion on the hill. The Women of the West. G. Essex Evans. PoAu-1

They left their Babylon bare. The Destruction of Jerusalem by the Babylonian Hordes. Isaac Rosenberg. VWA

They lie at rest, our blessed dead. Christina Rossetti. NOBVV

They lie in the Sunday street. The Dead. C. Day Lewis. TwCP

They lie on beaches and are proud to tan. Summer Resort. P. K. Page. CaP

They lie on mattresses. Evening at the Merrills. Hans Lodeizen, *tr. by* James Brockway. DuIn

They lie, the men who tell for reasons of their own. Faces in the Street. Henry Lawson. CBAP

They lie unwatched, in waste and vacant places. The Dwellings of Our Dead. Arthur H. Adams. ATNZ

They lie who say that love must be. No Sufferer for Her Love. *Unknown, tr. by* Robin Flower. AnIL

They lied, those lying traitors all. Medieval Norman Song ("They lied, those lying traitors all"). *Unknown, tr. by* John Addington Symonds. AWP

They like to come here. Pleasant sidestreets pave. The Visitors. Richard Moore. DiPo

They Live. Randall Swingler. WaP

They live alone. Neighbors. David Allan Evans. Psk

They live by the Lakes, an appropriate quarter. On the Lake Poets. Charles Townsend. FaBoEE

They Live in Parallel Worlds. William J. Harris. CNA

They live in their country. Restricted. Miriam Waddington. CaP

They live 'neath the curtain. Puk-Wudjies. Patrick Reginald Chalmers. BoTP

They lived in places tourists don't care to visit. The Other Great Composers. John Ash. NPo

They lived out in a women's house. Stephanie Markman. *Fr.* The Rime of the Ancient Feminist. BrRo

They look/ like newlyweds. Ryota. TTTS

They look at me. Self-Portrait as Felt. Miron Bialoszewski, *tr. by* Czeslaw Milosz. PwPP

They look like big dogs badly drawn, drawn wrong. Wolves in the Zoo. Howard Nemerov. NoAM

They look up with their pale and sunken faces. Elizabeth Barrett Browning. *Fr.* The Cry of the Children. OBD

They looked at me all ghosts. Mellisandra. Harriet Rose. BrRo

They looked so good. The Young Fenians. Padraic Fallon. BIrV

They made a myth of you, professor. Mr. Attila. Carl Sandburg. ImOP

"They made her a grave too cold and damp." The Lake of the Dismal Swamp. Thomas Moore. BLPA

They made her bed of the softest clay. Marina Mother. Lucha Corpi, *tr. fr. Spanish by the author and* Catherine Rodríguez-Nieto. *Fr.* The Marina Poems, I. CCP; OV

They made impudent inspection of our coast. Rex Ingamells. *Fr.* The Great South Land. CBAP

They Made Me Erect and Lone. Henry David Thoreau. OxBSP

They made them idols in the elder days. Idols. Richard Burton. TrPWD

They made them ready and we saw them go. The Travellers. Mark A. de Wolfe Howe. AA

They make a fake tiger, and hope it will seem real. The Artemisia Tiger. Chang Yü, *tr. fr. Chinese by* Jonathan Chaves. *Fr.* Four Poems On the Ch'ung-wu Festival. CoBLCP

They make in the twining tide the motions of birds. The Bathers. W. S. Merwin. PoE

They May Rail at This Life. Thomas Moore. PoEL-4

They may suppose, because I would not cloy your ear. John Berryman. NoP

They meet but with unwholesome Springs. Against Them Who Lay Unchastity to the Sex of Women. William Habington. *Fr.* Castara, II. JCP; MePo; OBS; SeCP

They met in passion; Satyrs of the glade. Once. George Ives. PeHV

They met inside the gateway that gives the view. Wind and Mist. Edward Thomas. BrPo

They might have hurled stones. Ishikawa Takuboku, *tr. by* Geoffrey Bownas *and* Anthony Thwaite. PeBJV

They more than we are what we are. Statues. Kathleen Jessie Raine. NYBP

They mouth love's language. Gnash. A Memory of the Players in a Mirror at Midnight. James Joyce. InvP

They move on tracks of never-ending light. The Master Singers. Rhys Carpenter. WGRP

They moved like rivers in their mended stockings. The Grandmothers. Mary Oliver. WPE

They must be shown as about to taste of the tree. Adam and Eve. C. H. Sisson. FaBoTw

They must to keep their certainty accuse. The Leaders of the Crowd. W. B. Yeats. EBEV; MoAB; MoBrPo

They mutilate their torment each other. A Voice. Tadeusz Rozewicz, *tr. by* Czeslaw Milosz. PwPP

They named it Aultgraat—Ugly Burn. Black Rock of Kiltearn. Andrew Young. FaBoTw; RB

They named the huge one Grendel. Grendel. *Unknown, tr. fr. Anglo-Saxon by* Burton Raffel. *Fr.* Beowulf. NU

They Never Quite Leave Us. Margaret E. M. Sangster. WBLP

They never seem to be far away. Within the Veil. Margaret E. M. Sangster. BLRP

They nicknamed me Mririda. Mririda. Mririda n'Ait Attik, *tr. by* René Euloge; *English vers. by* Daniel Halpern *and* Paula Paley. AIW; WPOW

They nod at me and I at stems. Open. Larry Eigner. NeAP

They often begin by saying, "Paris! How I wish I were there!" What People Say about Paris. Kenneth Koch. BAP

They often haunt me, these substantial ghosts. The Hymn Tunes. Edward Lucie-Smith. PBCV

They opn our mail petulantly. Th Wundrfulness uv th Mountees Our Secret Police. Bill Bissett. NOBC

They, our everyday enemies. The Other Death. Roberto Sosa, *tr. by* Alejandro Murguía. Vol

They paddled the street as fast as rowboats can. The Flood Viewed by the Tourist from Iowa. James Whitehead. SM

They paper the walls of their world. The Recluses. Stuart Z. Perkoff. NeAP

They pass like a warning of snow. The Insects. Nancy Willard. LCAP

They pass me by like shadows, crowds on crowds. The Street. James Russell Lowell. AnAmPo; Son

They pass too fast. Ships, and there's time for sighing. Earth Has Shrunk in the Wash. William Empson. CMoP

They pat the sick man on the head. Albumen. Tadeusz Rozewicz, *tr. by* Czeslaw Milosz. PwPP

They pity me./ "Look at him, see." Lonely. André Spire, *tr. by* Jethro Bithell. AWP; TrJP

They played till the dusk of summer in the wood. Coogan's Wood. Francis Stuart. NeIP

They pointed me out on the highway, and they said. The Traveller. John Berryman. PoA; VGW

They possessed nothing. The Inheritors. Gary Geddes. NOBC

They Pray the Best Who Pray and Watch. Edward Hopper. AH

They put him here because God came at night. Dementia Praecox. Morris Bishop. PoA

They put up big wooden gods. Manufactured Gods. Carl Sandburg. WGRP

They ran through the streets of the seaport town. A Greyport Legend. Bret Harte. AnAmPo; GN; MOS

They ranged themselves in facing lines. Poem by an Unknown Poet from the Mid-Twentieth Century. László Benjámin, *tr. by* Edwin Morgan. MHuP

They really scheme for millet and grain. A Modern Poem in Response to "Wild Geese on the Lake" by Shen Yüeh. Li Chien, *tr. by* Irving Lo. WFTU

They Return. Jay Macpherson. *Fr.* The Way Down. NOBC; PoA

They rise like sudden fiery flowers. Fireworks. James Reeves. OnUR

They rise to mastery of wind and snow. Pioneers. Hamlin Garland. AA

They rode from the camp at morn. Sidney Godolphin. Clinton Scollard. AA

They rode north. Blackie Thinks of His Brothers. Stanley Crouch. PoBA

They roused him with muffins—they roused him with ice. The Baker's Tale. "Lewis Carroll." *Fr.* The Hunting of the Snark. EBEV; NAEL-2

They said a while ago that the fuzz were coming to take us away. Moment of Truth. Rowley Habib. PeNZ

They said it was you. Shape-Shifter. Michael Jackson. ATNZ

They said reality was all there was. For the Shadow. Jacques Hamelink, *tr. by* Paul Vincent. DuIn

They said, "The Master is coming." Unawares. Emma A. Lent. PoLF
They said the moon wasn't going to rise no no. August 18. Joanne Kyger. PoM
They said this mystery shall never cease. Blake. *Fr.* Gnomic Verses. TrGrPo
They said to me: Smile. Portrait of an Ex-Young Bourgeois. Lindolf Bell, *tr. by* William Jay Smith. CT
They said, "Wait." Well, I waited. Alabama Centennial. Naomi Long Madgett. BPo
They said, "You are no longer a lad." Battle Won Is Lost. Phil George. GrPl; NOVW
They sat by the water. The fine women. Stars Which See, Stars Which Do Not See. Marvin Bell. LCAP
They sat. They stood about. Of Commerce and Society. Geoffrey Hill. NePoEA-2
They sat upon a hill. The Munition Workers. Diana James. CN
They sate to meat, and Satyrane his chaunce. Spenser. *Fr.* The Faerie Queene, III, 9. OAEL-1
They saw you behind your muzzle much more clearly. To a Farmer Who Hung Five Hawks on His Barbed Wire. David Wagoner. NoAM
They Say. Ella Wheeler Wilcox. WBLP
They say a maiden conceived. Christmas Carols. Patricia Beer. OxBC
They say a man dies. Steve Crow. *Fr.* Songs, XIV. HATNAP
They say, God wot! On the Death of the Giraffe. Thomas Hood. FaBoEE; OBD
They say he became deaf—but it isn't true. Beethoven. Zbigniew Herbert, *tr. by* John Carpenter *and* Bogdana Carpenter. AnAn
They say: He lives with colours. Sons. Jack Cope. PeSA
They say, his strange, large eyes. Father. Margit Kaffka, *tr. by* Laura Schiff. PBWP
They say I am excitable! How could. The King of Owls. Louise Erdrich. NoAM
They say I am harsh and haughty. Uncle Sam's Soliloquy. George Sands Johnson. PWR
They say I am your enemy. To Julia de Burgos. Julia de Burgos, *tr. by* William M. Davis. DMH
They say in my village. Coda. Shafiq al-Kamali, *tr. by* Sargon Boulus *and* Christopher Middleton. MAP
They say, in other days. John Gray. NOBVV
They say it is waiting for more, the snow. Snow Signs. Charles Tomlinson. NoAM
They say it's better to be poor. Rain Has Fallen on the History Books. David Rosenberg. VWA
They say La Jac Brite Pink Skin Bleach avails not. Government Injunction. Josephine Miles. PoNe
They say my love is going far away. Stone Castle Music. *Unknown, tr. by* Burton Watson. CoBCP
They Say My Verse Is Sad: No Wonder. A. E. Housman. NoAM
They say no one died. Celebration 1982. Terri Meyette. GOS
They say, old man, your horse will die. The Dead Horse. *Unknown.* AS
They say Revis found a flatrock. Mountain Bride. Robert Morgan. GeTw; MAYP; MOWH; MT
They Say She Is Veiled. Judy Grahn. UL
They say "Son." Old Black Men Say. James A. Emanuel. PoBA
They say that, afar in the land of the west. The Green Isle of Lovers. Robert Charles Sands. AA
They say that Byron, though lame. Anacreontic. Austin Clarke. NOIV
They say that every idle word. Idle Words. Walter Savage Landor. OBSV
They say that God lives very high! A Child's Thought of God. Elizabeth Barrett Browning. FaPON
They Say That Hope Is Happiness. Byron. OxBSP
They say that I was in my youth. *Unknown.* CenHV
They Say That in the Unchanging Place. Hilaire Belloc. *Fr.* Dedicatory Ode. PoLF
They say that man is mighty. What Rules the World. William Ross Wallace. OHIP
They say that once it mirrored palace ladies. The Well of the King of Wu. Kao Ch'i, *tr. by* Jonathan Chaves. CoBLCP
They say that plants don't talk, nor do. Rosalía de Castro, *tr. by* Aliki *and* Willis Barnstone. BoWoP
They say that Richard Cory owns. Richard Cory. Paul Simon. InPK
They say that shadow[e]s of deceased ghosts. Joshua Sylvester. EIL; OBS
   (They Say that Shadows of Deceased Ghosts.) Son
They say that "Time assuages." Emily Dickinson. OxBSP
   (Sorrow.) WGRP
They say that when they burned young Shelley's corpse. The Fishes and the Poet's Hands. Frank Yerby. AmNP; PoNe
They Say the Butterfly Is the Hardest Stroke. Paul Durcan. FaBCIP

They say the experimental. Nothing. Burns Singer. OxBS
They say "the lighthouse keeper's world is round." Requiem. Sam Hunt. PeNZ
They say the lion and the lizard keep. Omar Khayyám, *tr. fr. Persian by* Edward Fitzgerald. *Fr.* The Rubáiyát of Omar Khayyám of Naishápúr. EBEV
They say the men are. The Men Are Coming Back! Barry Cole. OxBTC
They say the Phoenix is dying, some say dead. News of the Phoenix. A. J. M. Smith. MoCV
They say the plan to build Jerusalem. On the Job. Felix Munso. SoTCo
They say the rose garden. Khwaja Mir Dard, *tr. fr. Urdu by* Ahmed Ali. GoT
They say the sea is cold, but the sea contains. Whales Weep Not! D. H. Lawrence. CMoP; MOS; NoAM; NU
They Say the Sea Is Loveless. D. H. Lawrence. MOS
They say the Spanish ships are out. The Dragon of the Seas. Thomas Nelson Page. PAH
They say the war is over. But water still. Redeployment. Howard Nemerov. LiTM; OBWP; TrJP
They say the world is round, and yet. Life's Scars. Ella Wheeler Wilcox. BLPA
They say there is a land. Idaho. *Unknown.* GBP
They say there is a sweeter air. A Carriage from Sweden. Marianne Moore. HAP; LiTA; LiTM; MoAB; TwCP; WeW
They say there is no hope. Sea Gods. Hilda Doolittle ("H. D."). LiTA; MOS
They say there's a high windless world and strange. Mutability. Rupert Brooke. BrPo
They say 'tis sinful to flirt. Sinful to Flirt. *Unknown.* AmFP
They say Tom Starr. Tom Starr. Robert J. Conley. STE
They Say You're Staying in a Mountain Temple. Tu Fu, *tr. fr. Chinese by* Burton Watson. CoBCP; TTTS
They see Gods wonders that are call'd. Roger Williams. SCAP
They seem hundreds of years away. Breughel. The Seed Cutters. Seamus Heaney. *Fr.* Mossbawn: Two Poems in Dedication. FaBCIP
They seem to be tiny insects celebrating. Snow. Amelia Rosselli, *tr. by* Lawrence R. Smith. NItP
They sell good beer at Haslemere. West Sussex Drinking Song. Hilaire Belloc. MoBrPo
They sent him back to her. The letter came. Not to Keep. Robert Frost. CMoP; OxBA
They serve revolving saucer eyes. The Ex-Queen among the Astronomers. Fleur Adcock. FaBoWP
They served tea in the sandpile, together with. The Party. Reed Whittemore. CoAP
They Set Out in Fog. Carole Oles. PPR
They set the fish upon the table. Pesci Misti. Leonard Aaronson. FaBoTw
They set the slave free, striking off his chains. The Slave. James Oppenheim. TrJP
They set the whins on fire along the road. Smoke. Medbh McGuckian. FaBCIP
They settle like dew. The Riddles of Change. Felix Mnthali. WMBCH
They shall go down unto life's borderland. Sonnet to Negro Soldiers. Joseph Seamon Cotter, Jr. PoBA
"They shall not die in vain," we said." Ralph Gustafson. CaP
They shall not return to us, the resolute, the young. Mesopotamia. Kipling. MMA
They shall see Him in the crimson flush. The Pure in Heart Shall See God. Frances Ellen Watkins Harper. PWR
They shall sink under water. The Cities. "Æ." OBMV
They shook the green leaves down. Magic Fox. James Welch. CDW; HATNAP; NoAM
They shot him on the Nine-Stane Rig. Barthram's Dirge. *Unknown.* FaBoRV
They should never have built a barn there, at all. The Barn. Edward Thomas. EyDe
They shout no stranger, troublous news. Waifs. Vivian Virtue. PBCV
They shut me up in prose. Emily Dickinson. InPS; NOBA
They shut the road through the woods. The Way Through the Woods. Kipling. *Fr.* Rewards and Fairies. CH; FaBoCh; FaPON; NoAM; NOBE; OBEV; OBNC; OxBChV; OxBTC; RFM
They sin who tell us love can die. Love Indestructible. Robert Southey. *Fr.* The Curse of Kehama. OBNC
They Sing. Theodore Roethke. NYBP
They sing their dearest songs. During Wind and Rain. Thomas Hardy. CMoP; ELP; GTBS-P; HAP; Mes; NAEL-2; NIP; OAEL-2; OxBTC; PoE; PPP; QFR; TEP; TOF

They sit and smoke on the esplanade. At a Watering-Place. Thomas Hardy. *Fr.* Satires of Circumstance, V. BrPo; CMoP

They sit at table. The Last Supper. Jacques Prévert, *tr. by* Michael Benedikt. POS

They sit in a glass egg. Dead Embryos. Judit Tóth, *tr. by* Laura Schiff. MHuP; WPOW

They sit in the roots. The Lost Tribe. Robert Finch. CaP

They sit on the wall at the square. The Old Men. Cid Corman. PCP

They sit with necks under the lights. Industrial Landscape. Giancarlo Majorino, *tr. by* Lawrence R. Smith. NItP

They slept on the field which their valor had won. Beyond the Potomac. Paul Hamilton Hayne. PAH

They slew by night. The Pentecost Castle. Geoffrey Hill. HAP

They slip on to the bus, hair piled up high. The Young Ones. Elizabeth Jennings. OxBTC

They sneaked into the limbo of time. Ancestral Faces. Kwesi Brew. PBA

They Sometimes Call Me. Wendy Rose. CDW

They sound like howling wolves from here. Song on the Way to Jail. Kakayek, *tr. by* James Koller. STP

They spat on the poet. Poem of Pathos. Tadeusz Rozewicz, *tr. by* Adam Czerniawski. FaBoPV

They speak not of torment. Flowers in the Ward. John Shaw Neilson. CBAP

They speak of time, as if the hour were split. Madaket Beach. Isabel Harriss Barr. GoYe

They spent my life plotting against me. Possessions. Ken Smith. EAS

They spoke/ of the queen at night growing. Short Eulogy. Zali Gurevitch, *tr. by* Gabriel Levin. VWA

They spoke of the horse alive. The Horse. Philip Levine. CoAP

They spoke the loveliest of languages. History of World Languages. D. J. Enright. OxBC

They sprint eight feet and. Ringed Plover by a Water's Edge. Norman MacCaig. OxBC

They stand confronting, the coffin between. Over the Coffin. Thomas Hardy. *Fr.* Satires of Circumstance, XIV. BrPo

They stand in a row like chimneys. Poplars. Henryk Grynberg, *tr. by* Isaac Komem. VWA

They stand like penitential Augustines. Gothic Landscape. Irving Layton. TrJP

They stare:/ a woman about my age. Questions. Amber Coverdale Sumrall. TSM

They still seem G.I., the uniform lines. G. I. Graves in Tuscany. Richard Hugo. CAPP

They still smell of incense, and their faces are burnt by their. The Sleep of the Brave. Odysseus Elytis, *tr. by* Edmund Keeley *and* Philip Sherrard. VMG

They still vibrate with the sound. The Drowned. Stephen Spender. MOS

They stole little Bridget. Up the Airy Mountain. William Allingham. FaFP

They stood among many others. The Window of the Tobacco Shop. C. P. Cavafy, *tr. by* Edmund Keeley *and* Philip Sherrard. PeHV

They stood at the foot of the figure. At a Pause in a Country Dance. Thomas Hardy. Mes

They stood looking four stories high on the roof. The Roof. Jan Hanlo, *tr. by* James S. Holmes. DuIn

They stood—rain pelting at window, shrouded sea. In the Local Museum. Walter de la Mare. HAP

They stuck pigs in the throat. Might I not have done. Work. Gyula Illyés, *tr. by* William Jay Smith. MHuP

They suck and whisper it in mercury. The Break-up. A. M. Klein. NOBC

They sucked at the sweat on his forehead. Motive for Mercy. Ken Milburn. PoSH

They sucked me to their satisfaction. *Unknown, tr. fr. Japanese by* Hiroaki Sato. FCEI

They sung how God spoke out the worlds vast ball. The Creation. Abraham Cowley. *Fr.* Davideis, I. OBS

They swathed me in. Capes. Frederica Goldsmith. TSM

They swore to wipe out the nomads, no thought for themselves. Song of Lung-hsi. Ch'en Tao, *tr. by* Burton Watson. CoBCP

They take their stand, each rising. The Boxing Match. Virgil, *tr. fr. Latin, by* Rolfe Humphries. *Fr.* The Aeneid [*or* Eneados], V. SD

They teeter with an inane care among the skewbald stones. Sheep. Hal Porter. PoAu-2

They tell me I am beautiful: they praise my silken hair. Sad Memories. Charles Stuart Calverley. FM

They Tell Me I Am Lost. Maurice Kenny. HATNAP; STE

They tell me, Liberty! that in thy name. Liberty for All. William Lloyd Garrison. AA

They Tell Me That Over There. André Breton, *tr. fr. French by* Michael Benedikt. POS

They tell that I must not love. Love Unsought. Emma Catherine Embury. AA

They tell us/ That our skin is black. Politeness. Una Marson. PBCV

They tell us of an Indian tree. To My Mother. Thomas Moore. OHIP

They tell you Lincoln was ungainly, plain? His Face. Florence Earle Coates. OHIP

They tell you of the horny carapace. Of Growing Old. D. J. Enright. AnAn

They tell you that Death's at the turn of the road. The Unillumined Verge. Robert Bridges. AA

They that eat the uncrushed grape. Distillation. Richard Hovey. AnAmPo

They That Go Down to the Sea. Bible, *O.T. Fr.* Psalms: Psalm CVII ("O give thanks.") ChTr, (23-31); FaPON, (23-24); MOS, (23-30). (Ocean, The, *Moulton, Modern Reader's Bible*) WGRP, (23-33).

"They that have power to hurt, and will do none." Shakespeare. *Fr.* Sonnets, XCIV. BLPL; EiL; InPS; LiTB; NAEL-1; NOBE; NoP; OAEL-1; OBEV; PeHV; PoE; PoEL-2; PPP; SCV; Son; TEP; TrGrPo (Life without Passion.) GTBS; GTBS-P

They that in play can do the thing they would. Robert Bridges. *Fr.* The Growth of Love, I. NoAM

They that never had the use. An Apologie for Having Loved Before. Edmund Waller. MePo

They that wash on Monday. Mother Goose. FaBoBe (They That Wash on Monday.) NBLV

They think it's easy to be dead, those. Tableau Vivant. Tess Gallagher. GeTw

They throw in Drummer Hodge, to rest. Drummer Hodge. Thomas Hardy. AWP; BrPo; EBEV; GTBS-P; HAP; InPS; MoP; NAEL-2; NoAM; NOBVV; NoP; OBWP; WeW

They tied my mother's legs when I was born. Years Later. Laurence Lerner. NAs; PeSA

They Toil Not neither Do They Spin. Christina Rossetti. TrPWD

They told me/ I smile prettier with my mouth closed. Witch. Jean Tepperman. AIW; NMM

They told me/ This summer. To a Painter. Yu Kuang-chung, *tr. by* Dominic Cheung. IFON

They told me first she was a tree. Girl. Dom Moraes. NePoEA-2

They told me, Heraclitus, they told me you were dead. Heraclitus. William Johnson Cory, *paraphrased fr. the Greek of* Callimachus. AWP; EBVV; FaBoEE; FaPoR; InPK; NOBE; OBEV; OBNC; OxBSP; PeHV; PoRA; SeCePo

They told me that Life could be just what I made it. Life. Nan Terrell Reed. BLPA

They told me the water was lovely. It's Great When You Get In. Eugene O'Neill. ASP

They told me you had been to her. Evidence Read at the Trial of the Knave of Hearts. "Lewis Carroll." *Fr.* Alice's Adventures in Wonderland, *ch.* 12. FaBoNo; FaFP; GTBS-P; NoBVV; OxBoLi (Silence in Court.) FaBoCo

They told us/ Our mothers told us. Cornfields in Accra. Ama Ata Aidoo. WPOW

They told us that the King was coming up to see the base. The Inspection. Frederick B. Watt. CaP

They took a tire tool to his head. An Ex-Deputy Sheriff Remembers the Eastern Oklahoma Murderers. Jim Barnes. HATNAP

They took John Henry to the steep hillside. If I Die a Railroad Man. *Unknown.* AS

They took me out. Ku Klux. Langston Hughes. BPo

They took their time to die, this dynasty. The Last of the Princes. A. K. Ramanujan. OxBC

They tore down the toll-gate. The Toll-Gate Man. Wilson Pugsley MacDonald. CaP

They travelled like a blue pencil against the stars. In Praise of Antonioni. Stephen Holden. NYBP

They tried to evolve a sphere. Succumbing. Paul Eaton Reeve. ErPo

They try to say what you are, spiritual or sexual? Jalal ed-Din Rumi, *tr. by* John Moyne *and* Coleman Barks. UnAS

They Two. Mrs. Frank A. Breck. WBLP

They unfold before the sky. Doors. Thérèse Plantier, *tr. by* Willis Barnstone *and* Elene Kolb. BoWoP

They unfold like a snake. Young Ukrainians. Aba Shtoltsenberg, *tr. by* Dennis Silk. PeBMYV

They use everything they've got to putrify a man alive. Freehand Sketch. Roberto Sosa, *tr. by* David Volpendesta. Vol

They used to meet one night a week at a place on top of Telegraph Hill. The Harbor at Seattle. Robert Hass. NPGG; SV

They used to tell me I was building a dream. Brother, Can You Spare a Dime? E. Y. Harburg. SaC

They visit me often now. Mothers: A Meditation. Mary Pierce Brosmer. ER

They wait all day unseen by us, unfelt. The Stars. Mary Mapes Dodge. AA

They wait like darkness not becoming stars. The New Pietà: For the Mothers and Children of Detroit. June Jordan. PoBA

They wake like opening sea anemones. By-Blows. Mark Jarman. NAmP

They walk dangerously. The Home. Susan Axelrod. NMM

They Walk on Cat's Paws. Rocco Scotellaro, tr. fr. Italian by Lawrence R. Smith. NItP

They walked black Bible streets and piously tilled. Salem, Massachusetts. Edwin Muir. OBTV

They walked in straitened ways. The Old Ladies. Colin Ellis. OxBTC

They Warned Him Then They Threw Him Away. C. K. Williams. CAPP

They was twenty men on the Cabbage Rose. The Fate of the Cabbage Rose. Wallace Irwin. FiBHP

They wear air. Naked in Borneo. May Swenson. NYBP

They wear white scarves and shawls. The Madwomen of the Plaza de Mayo. Eli W. Mandel. NOBC

They went/ along the Camino Real. O California. Alejandro Murguía, tr. by Toni Empringham. FIA

They Went Forth to Battle but They Always Fell. Shaemas O'Sheel. WaaP; WGRP

They Went Home. Maya Angelou. AIW; IHMS

They went to sea in sieve, they did. The Jumblies. Edward Lear. BLPL; ChTr; EBEV; FaBoBe; FaBoNo; FaFP; GoJo; LiTB; MOS; NA; NAEL-2; OnMSP; OxBChV; OxBoLi; PoRA; TEP; WiR

They Went to the Moon Mother. Unknown, tr. fr. Zuni Indian by Barbara Tedlock. STP

They went with axe and rifle, when the trail was still to blaze. Western Wagons. Rosemary and Stephen Vincent Benét. AiP

They were a close family of giant otters. Giant Otters. Jackson Mac Low. LP

They were a man's words, a ballad of an old time. James Still. MT

They Were All like Geniuses. Horace Gregory. Fr. The Passion of M'Phail. NYBP

They were alone once more; for them to be. Byron. Fr. Don Juan, IV. EBEV

They were at play, she and her cat. Femme et Chatte. Paul Verlaine, tr. by Arthur Symons. AWP; OBVE

They were beautiful, the old books, beautiful I tell you. The Old Books. Vernon Scannell. OxBC

They were both still. Lamentations. Louise Glück. BoWoP; HCAP; MAYP

They were coming across the prairie, they were galloping hard and fast. The Cattle Thief. Emily Pauline Johnson. WPOW

They were dancing as if. Glass. Takako Uchino Lento, tr. by the author. BoWoP

They were hopeful of a curtain raiser. Because in This Sorrowing Statue of Flesh. Kenneth Patchen. NaP

They were human, they suffered. Founding Fathers, Nineteenth-Century Style. Robert Penn Warren. Fr. Promises, VIII. NoAM

They were introduced in a grave glade. Louis MacNeice. FaBCIP

They were just meant as covers. My Mother Pieced Quilts. Teresa Palma Acosta. FIA; WPOW

They were like fish meal. Lead. Jayne Cortez. PoBA

They were lovely in the quartz and jasper sand. Starfish. Lorna Dee Cervantes. CCP

They were parted then at last? Winter Song. George MacDonald. NOBVV

They Were Pure Gold. Pertti Nieminen, tr. fr. Finnish by Aili Jarvenpa. SOP

They were six. Bull-Fights. H. Leivick, tr. by Benjamin and Barbara Harshav. AYP

They were still young, younger than I am now. I Remember the Room Was Filled with Light. Judith Hemschemeyer. SM

They were the local Ohio palm, tropic in the heat of trains. Tree Ferns. Stanley Plumly. SM

They Were the Lucky Ones. Faiz Ahmad Faiz, tr. fr. Urdu by Mahmood Jamal. PBMUP

They were the people, those who. The Broken String. Unknown, tr. by W. H. I. Bleek. PeSA

They were there falling. Hart Crane. AnAn

They were walking in the woods along the coast. The Apple Trees at Olema. Robert Hass. NAmP; NPGG

They were women then. Women. Alice Walker. GOA; WPOW

They who create rob death of half its stings. The Sovereigns. Lloyd Mifflin. AA
(Sovereign Poets.) WGRP

They who have best succeeded on the stage. Dryden. Fr. The Conquest of Granada, pt. II. FiP; SeCV-2

They who in folly or mere greed. Where Are the War Poets? C. Day Lewis. FaBoMo; OBWP; OxBSP; OxBTC

They whose life is given utterly over to valor. Epitaph: Inscription from Anticyra. Unknown, tr. by Richmond Lattimore. WaaP

They will be telling you soon who you are. Arsenic. Howard Moss. CoAP; NYBP

They will blow from your mouth one morning. For the Mute. Lucille Clifton. CAPP

They will bury that fair body and cover you. Epitaph on a Young Child. Ivor Gurney. FaBoEE

They will bury you at last. At Last. Syd Scroggie. PoSH

They will catch me. On Hearing the Airlines Will Use a Psychological Profile to Catch Potential Skyjackers. Stephen Dunn. AmPA

They will come for you in morning. Whispers. Roberta Hill. CDW

They Will Look for a Few Words. Nancy Byrd Turner. AmFN

They will never die on that battlefield. Uccello. Gregory Corso. FF; NeAP; PoM

They will wash all my kisses and fingerprints off you. Poem Ended by a Death. Fleur Adcock. PeNZ

They will win, I thought once. Politics. Tom Marshall. NOBC

They wished [or whisted] all, with fixèd face attent. Virgil, tr. fr. Latin by the Earl of Surrey. Fr. The Aeneid [or Eneados], II. LiTB; SiPS

They Wondered Why. W. H. Auden. Fr. In Time of War, II. Son

They wondered why the fruit had been forbidden. W. H. Auden. Fr. Sonnets from China, II. CMoP

They won't come to you. These nights, you could sit for a year. Seal Rock. Katha Pollitt. MAYP

They wore it walking Sunday, three small men. Spanish Blue. Herbert Morris. NYBP

They wore light dresses and their arms were bare. A Pride of Ladies. Anne Halley. NMM

They would be shamed to see back at us. The Shirts. Tess Gallagher. MAYP

They'd learn more playing stickball in the street. Ghetto Summer School. Douglas Worth. FF

They'll all get up. I know I see them. Amir Gilboa, tr. by Warren Bargad and Stanley F. Chyet. IP

They'll be priestin' him the morra. The Priestin' of Father John. John D. Sheridan. TIRV

They'll Tell You about Me. Ian Mudie. PoAu-2

They'll tell you, after the rain, the sun comes out. The Great Book. Jean-Paul de Dadelsen, tr. by Anselm Hollo. RHTwFP

They'll walk no longer to Mass on Sunday. The Shawls. Monk Gibbon. NeIP

They're altogether otherworldly now. Grandparents. Robert Lowell. LiTM

They're building a skyscraper. Building a Skyscraper. James S. Tippett. OnUR

They're Calling. Felice Holman. RHPC

They're changing guard at Buckingham Palace. Buckingham Palace. A. A. Milne. OxBChV; PDV

They're checking the Ping-Pong ball. Unsound Condition. Richard Armour. ASP

They're collapsing, the ancestors. Cannibal Future. Gyula Illyés, tr. by Jascha Kessler. FOC

They're determined to have fun. They Set Out in Fog. Carole Oles. PPR

They're Dying Just the Same in Station Homesteads. Rodney Hall. Fr. Black Bagatelles. CBAP

They're dying off, the kerchiefed. Elegy for Bella, Sarah, Rosie, and All the Others. Sonya Dorman. GOA

They're hiding by the pebbles. Sea Fairies. Eileen Mathias. BoTP

They're like the valentines from old schoolmates. Butchery. Sandra McPherson. LCAP

They're more beautiful than the angels of heaven. Lennox Island. David McFadden. NOBC

They're mouthing things down in the dark street at the far end. At the World's Last Outpost. Robert Desnos, tr. by Michael Benedikt. POS

They're nice—one would never dream of going over. A Healthy Spot. W. H. Auden. AiP

They're of lime and brine. Old since the beginning of time. Market Women. Angela Figueroa-Aymerich, tr. by Kate Flores. DMH

They're out of sorts in Sunderland. There Are Bad Times Just around the Corner. Noel Coward. NOBL

They're out of the dark's ragbag, these two. Blue Moles. Sylvia Plath. NePoEA-2

They're putting Man-Fix on my hair. Wanting Out. Gavin Ewart. EAS

They're richer who diminish their desires. The Truly Rich. T. Urchard. PWR

They're selling tickets to the sundance. Indian America. Mah-do-ge Tohee. STE

They're Shifting Father's Grave. *Unknown.* CoMu

They're taking down a tree at the front door. Learning by Doing. Howard Nemerov. HAP; TwCP; WeW

They're waiting to be murdered. Old Couple. Charles Simic. HCAP

They's a predjudice allus twixt country and town. Town and Country. James Whitcomb Riley. AnAmPo

They've advertised for whalermen, five hundred brave and true. Blow Ye Winds. *Unknown.* OxBSS

They've All Gone South. Mary Britton Miller. RHPC

They've Come. Alfonsina Storni, *tr. fr. Spanish.* BoWoP, *tr. by* Aliki *and* Willis Barnstone; WPOW, *tr. by* Marti Moody

They've cut down the willow. Masaoka Shiki, *tr. fr. Japanese by* Burton Watson. *Fr.* Thirty-nine Haiku. FCEI

They've found a coelacanthus in the sea. Ichthyology. Gerrit Achterberg, *tr. by* James S. Holmes. DuIn

They've got a brand-new organ, Sue. The New Church Organ. Will M. Carleton. PoLF

They've killed you. Martyrdom. Richard W. Thomas. PoBA

They've left thee naked, Lord, O that they had! *See* They have left thee naked, Lord, O that they had!

They've opened up a road in the jungle and found. 2976. Julia Uceda, *tr. by* Willis Barnstone. BoWoP

They've paid the last respects in sad tobacco. Padraic O'Conaire—Gaelic Storyteller. F. R. Higgins. OBMV

They've putten her into prison strang. Sir Aldingar. *Unknown.* ESPB

They've turned at last! Good-by, King George. Haarlem Heights. Arthur Guiterman. PAH

Th' have left thee naked, Lord, O that they had! *See* They have left thee naked, Lord, O that they had!

Thick grow the oak clumps. *Unknown, tr. by* Arthur Waley. BoS

Thick grow the rush leaves. *Unknown, tr. by* Arthur Waley. BoS

Thick grows that southernwood. *Unknown, tr. by* Arthur Waley. BoS

Thick grows that tarragon. *Unknown, tr. by* Arthur Waley. BoS

Thick grows the cocklebur. *Unknown, tr. by* Arthur Waley. BoS

Thick grows the plantain. *Unknown, tr. by* Arthur Waley. BoS

Thick grows the star-thistle. *Unknown, tr. by* Arthur Waley. BoS

Thick grows the tarragon. *Unknown, tr. by* Arthur Waley. BoS

Thick lids of night closed upon me, The. The Souls of the Slain. Thomas Hardy. CMoP; LiTB; PoEL-5

Thick now with sludge from the years of suburbs, with toys. The Purpose of the Chesapeake & Ohio Canal. Dave Smith. GeTw

Thick sea-pine, The. Hitomaro. *Fr.* Manyo Shu. PeBJV

Thick thick the woods in front of my house. Matching a Poem by Secretary Kuo. T'ao Ch'ien, *tr. by* Burton Watson. CoBCP

Thick woods lead to a long embankment. Walking to Mou-chou at Dawn. Chu Yi-tsun, *tr. by* Chang Yin-nan. WFTU

Thick wool is muslin to-night, and the wire. A Cold Night. Bernard Spencer. WaP

Thickening, The. Russell Edson. NAmP

Thickness of paint or flesh cannot deface. Sestina on Her Portrait. Howard Nemerov. WaP

Thief, The. Abraham Cowley. *Fr.* The Mistress. JCP

Thief, The. Josephine Jacobsen. WPE

Thief, The. Stanley Kunitz. MoAmPo; VGW

Thief, The. Irene F. Pawsey. BoTP

Thief, The. *Unknown.* OBS

Thief became the rabbi, The. The Structural Study of Myth. Jerome Rothenberg. PoM

Thief in me is running a, The/ round in circles. Zapata & the Landlord. Alfred B. Spellman. PoBA

Thief is dying in the moonlit night, The. Dying Thief. Itzig Manger, *tr. by* Stephen Garrin. VWA

Thief's Niece, The. George Keithley. NPGG

Thiepval Wood. Edmund Blunden. MMA

Thieves, The. Robert Graves. BoLoP; CMoP; GTBS-P; LiTM; OAEL-2

Thieves' Anthology, The. *sel.* Theodore Martin.
 "I met a cracksman coming down the Strand." FaBoPa

Thieves gave more to blue. Detroit City. Jill Witherspoon Boyer. CNA

Thieving hands poke around where. Mother. Aldo Camerino, *tr. by* Anita Barrows. VWA

Thigh-deep in sedge and marigolds. The Other Side. Seamus Heaney. CIP; FaBCIP

Thin Air. Robert Hass. BAP

Thin and transparent. Old Age. Jacob Glatstein, *tr. by* Benjamin *and* Barbara Harshav. AYP

Thin are, oh Mind!—the colours which delight. Charles Swain. *Fr.* The Mind. PF

Thin, erect and silent. Alone. Elsie Laurence. CaP

Thin Façade for Edith Sitwell, A. John Malcolm Brinnin. FiBHP; NYBP

Thin feet are caught. The Wanderer. Claude Vigée. VWA, *tr. by* Anthony Rudolf

Thin fox, A/ sidled by with his stingy shadow. Dead Center. Ruth Whitman. NYBP

Thin ill-natured ghost that haunts the king, A. The Nine. John Sheffield. APAS

Thin in beard, and thick in purse. On Tom-o-Combe. *Unknown.* FaBoEE

Thin-legged, thin chested, slight unspeakably. Apparition. W. E. Henley. *Fr.* In Hospital, XXV. BrPo; TrGrPo

Thin little frog. Issa, *tr. by* Geoffrey Bownas *and* Anthony Thwaite. PeBJV

Thin little leaves of wood fern, ribbed and toothed. Frederick Goddard Tuckerman. *Fr.* Sonnets, III, iv. TAP

Thin Man, The. Donald Justice. SM

Thin mask of my sleep, The. Lament for the European Exile. A. L. Strauss, *tr. by* A. C. Jacobs. VWA

Thin Partition. Gordon Challis. ATNZ

Thin Places. Clark Coolidge. LP

"Thin Rain, whom are you haunting." Wraith. Edna St. Vincent Millay. WSC

Thin snow, and the first small pools of dusk. Faeryland. Robert Pinsky. MAYP

Thin steel in paired lines, forever mated, cuts. North Philadelphia, Trenton, and New York. Richmond Lattimore. NYBP

Thin under the arc lights. Tennis in San Juan. Reuel Denney. SD

Thin warmth toward which the body turns. Sunrise. Robert Wells. NPo

Thin wet sky, that yellows at the rim, A. Marshlands. Pauline E. Johnson. NOBC

Thin wickedly intricate, The. Dark Area. Russell Atkins. FB

Thin women woo each other, The. Christine Donald. AIW

Thine be the praise, good Lord. Canticle of Created Things. Saint Francis of Assisi, *tr. by* Henry Taylor. PFI

Thine be those motions strong and sanative. To Coleridge in Sicily. Wordsworth. *Fr.* The Prelude [or, Growth of a Poet's Mind]: France. OBNC

Thine elder that I am, thou must not cling. Sweeter Far than the Harp, More Gold than Gold. "Michael Field." OBMV

"Thine eyes I love, and they, as pitying me." Shakespeare. *Fr.* Sonnets, CXXXII. OBSC

Thine eyes shall see the light of distant skies. To Cole, the Painter, Departing for Europe. Bryant. AiP; AmPP; TAP
 (Sonnet: To an American Painter Departing for Europe.) NAAL-1

Thine Eyes Still Shined. Emerson. NOBA

Thine is a happy name. Emperor Shomu. *Fr.* Manyo Shu. Ma

Thine is a strain to read amongst the hills. To the Poet Wordsworth. Felicia Dorothea Hemans. BrRo

Thine old-world eyes—each one a violet. On a Miniature. Henry Augustin Beers. AA

Thine Own. Josephine D. Henderson Heard. CBWP-4

Thine was a brain of nature's finest mould. Charles Sumner. Henrietta Cordelia Ray. CBWP-3

Thing, The/ To do/ Is organize. Kenneth Koch. CAPP

Thing, The. Theodore Roethke. CMoP

Thing about a shark is—teeth, The. About the Teeth of Sharks. John Ciardi. OBCA

Thing could barely stand. Yet taken, The. The Bull Calf. Irving Layton. InPK; OBCV

Thing Dylan Thomas once said, A. Talk with a Poet. Helen Smith Bevington. SaC

Thing Is Sex, Ben, The. Edgar Lee Masters. *Fr.* Tomorrow Is My Birthday. NAs

Thing is Violent, The. Gwendolyn MacEwen. MoCV; NOBC

Thing itself was rough and crudely done, The. The Knight in the Wood. Lord De Tabley. NOBVV

Thing, loved one, A. The 29th Month. Stan Rice. NPGG

Thing Made Real, The. Ron Loewinsohn. NeAP

Thing of beauty is a joy forever, A. Keats. *Fr.* Endymion [a Poetic Romance], I. BLPL; CTC; EnRP; FaBV; FaFP; FiP; LiTB; NIP; OBNC; PrIm

Thing Poem. Petra von Morstein, *tr. fr. German by* Rosemarie Waldrop. BoWoP

Thing Remembered, A. Kendrick Smithyman. ATNZ

Thing Remembered, A. *Unknown, tr. fr. Arabic by* E. Powys Mathers. ErPo

Thing split Good Friday in two, The. Soufrière (79). "Shake" Keane. *Fr.* Volcanoe Suite, I. PBCV

Thing that arrests me is, The. Waking in the Dark. Adrienne Rich. FaBoWP

Thing that brought you among my people, The. Homage to John Millington Synge. Mairtin O Direain, *tr. by* Thomas Kinsella. NOIV

Thing that goes the farthest toward making life worth while, The. Let Us Smile. Wilbur Dick Nesbit. WBLP

Thing to do is try for that sweet skin, The. Catch What You Can. Jean Garrigue. VGW

Thing which fades, A. Komachi, *tr. fr. Japanese by* Arthur Waley. *Fr.* Kokin Shu. AWP; BoWoP; PBWP

Things, The. Conrad Aiken. HAP; WeW

Things, *sel.* Donald Justice. "Hard, but you can polish it." CRP

Things. Walter de la Mare. PoA

Things. W. S. Merwin. HAP

Things. Louis Simpson. OxBC

Things/ do not know their collective name. Workaday Morning. Astrid Tollefsen, *tr. by* Nadia Christensen. PBWP

Things a prostitute likes. Emperor Go-Shirakawa, *tr. fr. Japanese by* Hiroaki Sato. *Fr.* Ryojin Hisho. FCEI

Things a sage likes. Emperor Go-Shirakawa, *tr. fr. Japanese by* Hiroaki Sato. *Fr.* Ryojin Hisho. FCEI

Things a terrifying exorcist likes. Emperor Go-Shirakawa, *tr. fr. Japanese by* Hiroaki Sato. *Fr.* Ryojin Hisho. FCEI

Things are the mind's mute looking-glass. Things. Walter de la Mare. PoA

Things begin again. Return. Johari M. Kunjufu. BlSi

Things come from nothing. Metaphysical Shock while Watching a TV Cartoon. Stan Rice. NPGG

Things concentrate at the edges; the pond-surface. Marginalia. Richard Wilbur. CMoP; PoA

Things Dead. Marcel Schwob, *tr. fr. French by* William Brown Meloney. TrJP

Things disappear. Debts. Robert Long. NAmP

Things exceedingly swift. Emperor Go-Shirakawa, *tr. fr. Japanese by* Hiroaki Sato. *Fr.* Ryojin Hisho. FCEI

Things Experienced upon Withdrawal from Court, *sel.* Hsieh Chin, *tr. fr. Chinese by* Jonathan Chaves. "Government wine of Peking is sweeter than honey, The." CoBLCP

Things Going out of My Life. Robert Adamson. CBAP

Things hard to say. *Unknown, tr. by* Burton Watson. FCEI

Things have their own lives here. The hall chairs. Dispossessions. Jane Cooper. FaBoWP

Things hilariously bent. Emperor Go-Shirakawa, *tr. fr. Japanese by* Hiroaki Sato. *Fr.* Ryojin Hisho. FCEI

Things I did, I did because of trees, The. Long Island. Marvin Bell. BLA; CAPP

Things I Didn't Know I Loved. Nazim Hikmet, *tr. fr. Turkish by* Randy Blasing *and* Mutlu Konuk. LLLT

Things I have seen, the future I have yet to see. Princess Shikishi, *tr. fr. Japanese by* Hiroaki Sato. *Fr.* Seventy-eight Tanka. FCEI

Things I Like. Marjorie H. Greenfield. BoTP

Things I Miss, The. Thomas Wentworth Higginson. TrPWD

Things I Say Are True, The. Blanca Varela, *tr. fr. Spanish by* Donald Yates. BoWoP

Things I Used to Do. *Unknown.* AS

Things I'm told, I could raise your hair, The. The Old Man's Tale. Brian Merriman, *tr. fr. Modern Irish by* David Marcus. *Fr.* The Midnight Court. BIrV

Things Keep Dawning on President Joshua. George Starbuck. SoTCo

Things Kept. William Dickey. NYBP

Things lately fashionable in the capital. Emperor Go-Shirakawa, *tr. fr. Japanese by* Hiroaki Sato. *Fr.* Ryojin Hisho. FCEI

Things like littlenecks. Spring Night. Hagiwara Sakutaro, *tr. by* Hiroaki Sato. FCEI

Things live there, held still in glass cases, The. Reflections on a Visit to the Burke Museum, University of Washington, Seattle. Gail Tremblay. HATNAP

Things Lovelier. Humbert Wolfe. TrJP

Things Men Have Made. D. H. Lawrence. PCP

Things Not of This Union. Linda Gregg. NPGG

Things of every day are all so sweet, The. Life's Common Things. Alice E. Allen. WBLP

Things of Late. David Phillips. NeAC

Things of René Magritte, The. Wieland Schmied, *tr. fr. German by* Beth Bjorklund. CoAuP

Things of the Earth. Ferreira Gullar, *tr. fr. Portuguese by* William Jay Smith. CT

Things of the North, The. Rennie McOwan. PoSH

Things of the Spirit. Mason Jordan Mason. PoNe

Things on a Microscope Slide. X. J. Kennedy. TSS

Things Past. Richard Tillinghast. PPR

Things remember me. A Field Poem. Laura Valaitis. GOYP

Things seem empty. On Vacation. Robert Creeley. CAPP

Things Seen. Wang Shih-chen, *tr. fr. Chinese by* Jonathan Chaves. CoBLCP

Things Seen. Yüan Mei, *tr. fr. Chinese by* Jonathan Chaves. CoBLCP

Things Seen on Spring Days. Yüan Mei, *tr. fr. Chinese by* Jonathan Chaves. CoBLCP

Things that are going out of my life remain, The. Things Going out of My Life. Robert Adamson. CBAP

Things that are good and great my land has given. The Great Land. William Rose Benét. OPP

Things That Are More Excellent, The. Sir William Watson. OHFP

Things That Are Worse than Death. Sharon Olds. MAYP

The Things That Cause a Quiet Life. Martial. *See* Happy Life, The.

Things that dance well, exquisitely. Emperor Go-Shirakawa, *tr. fr. Japanese by* Hiroaki Sato. *Fr.* Ryojin Hisho. FCEI

Things That Endure. Ted Olson. WBLP

Things That Go Bump in the Night. *Unknown. See* From ghoulies and ghosties.

Things That Happen. William Stafford. NNaP

Things That Happen to You. Alonzo Gonzales Mó, *tr. fr. Mayan by* Allan F. Burns. STP

Things That Happen Where There Aren't Any People. William Stafford. CAPP

Things that make a life to please, The. A Happy Life. Martial, *tr. by* Sir Richard Fanshawe. OBVE

Things that Make a Soldier Great, The. Edgar Albert Guest. NIP

Things that make the happier life, are these, The. Martial, *tr. by* Ben Jonson. FaBoEE; OBVE

Things That Matter, The. Edith Nesbit. OxBTC

Things that pierce the heart. Emperor Go-Shirakawa, *tr. fr. Japanese by* Hiroaki Sato. *Fr.* Ryojin Hisho. FCEI

Things that Will Not Die, The. Edward Rowland Sill. AnAmPo

Things the way they are. Saturday Morning at the Laundry. Christopher Gilbert. MAYP

Things they did together, no one knew, The. 1904. Frederick Morgan. BLA

Things to Come. James Reeves. OxBSP

Things to Do around a Lookout. Gary Snyder. NaP; TAP

Things to Do around Kyoto. Gary Snyder. NaP

Things to Do If You Are a Subway. Bobbi Katz. RHPC

Things to Do in Providence. Ted Berrigan. UL

Things to Say When You Quit Smoking. Laurel Blossom. SoTCo

Things We Dreamt We Died For. Marvin Bell. CoAP

Things we'll donate to the world. Poem H. Vincente Rodríguez Nietzche, *tr. by* Julio Marzán. InW

Think as I Think. Stephen Crane. *Fr.* The Black Riders, XLVII. WeW

Think from how many trees. The Compost Heap. Vernon Watkins. NYBP

Think how a peacock in a forest of high trees. Peacock. D. H. Lawrence. TTTS

Think how some excellent, lean torso hugs. The Cost. Anthony Hecht. OxBC

Think, in this batter'd caravanserai. Omar Khayyám, *tr. fr. Persian by* Edward Fitzgerald. *Fr.* The Rubáiyát of Omar Khayyám of Naishápúr. ChTr; OBD

Think it's your snow. Kikaku, *tr. fr. Japanese by* Hiroaki Sato. *Fr.* Thirty-three Hokku. FCEI

Think me not unkind and rude. The Apology. Emerson. AmPP; AnAmPo

Think no more, lad; laugh, be jolly. A. E. Housman. CMoP

Think not by rigorous judgment seized. Pope. *Fr.* Three Epitaphs on John Hewet and Sarah Drew, I. NIP

Think not 'cause men flattering say. To A. L. Thomas Carew. CaPo; SeCP

Think not my Phebe, cause a cloud. To His Mistris Confined. James Shirley. OBS

Think not, nor for a moment let your mind. Edna St. Vincent Millay. VGW

Think not of these as dead, the brave young souls. A Song of Those Who Died. Donald McDonald. PVCV

Think not this paper comes with vain pretense. Epistle from Mrs. Yonge to Her Husband. Lady Mary Wortley Montagu. NAEL-1; NoP

Think Not When You Gather to Zion. Eliza R. Snow. AH

Think now about all the things which made up. And Forgetful of Europe. Geoffrey Grigson. OBTV

Think, now: if you have found a dead bird. Advice to a Discarded Lover. Fleur Adcock. PeNZ

Think of—/ Stepping on shore and finding it heaven! Heaven. *Unknown*. PoLF

Think of a child who goes out. Some Notes on Courage. Susan Ludvigson. MT

Think of a tree-lined city street. Parade: Liberation Day. Kevin Ireland. ATNZ

Think of dress in every light. John Gay. *Fr*. Achilles. InvP
(Song: "Think of dress in every light.") OxBSP

Think of it little, a fib. The Lie. Al Lee. AmPA

"Think of it this way," the doctor tells him. Inner Ear. T. R. Hummer. MT

Think of only now, and how this pencil. The Promontory Moment. May Swenson. NYBP

Think of sweet and chocolate. The Anniad. Gwendolyn Brooks. BlSi

Think of the shark's tiny brain. In a Museum in the Capital. William Stafford. LCAP

Think of the storm roaming the sky uneasily. Little Exercise at 4. A.M. Elizabeth Bishop. CoAP; MoAB; MoAmPo; NYBP; UnPo

Think Small. Elaine Equi. UL

Think that this world against the wind of time. Signature for Tempo. Archibald MacLeish. CRP; VGW

Think this. The first modern. The first striker of. Fault/line. Vincent O'Sullivan. ATNZ

Think thou and act; to-morrow thou shalt die. The Choice. Dante Gabriel Rossetti. *Fr*. The House of Life, LXXIII. GTBS-P; OBEV

Think upon Death. Hartley Coleridge. Son

Think what you like, but. You and It. Mark Strand. NYBP

Think you I am not fiend and savage too? To the White Fiends. Claude McKay. BANP; PoBA

Think you the dead are lonely in that place? The Dead. David Morton. PAH

Thinke not cause men flatt'ring say. To A. L.: Perswasions to Love. Thomas Carew. SeCP
("Think not 'cause men flattering say.") CaPo
(To A. L.: Persuasions to Love.) CaPo

Thinke then, my soule, that death is but a groome. Contemplation of Our State in Our Deathbed. John Donne. *Fr*. Of the Progresse of the Soule; the Second Anniversarie. OBS

Thinker, The. Berton Braley. BLPA; WBLP

Thinker, The. Anthony Delius. PeSA

Thinker, The, *sel.* Salah Niyazi, *tr. fr. Arabic by* Abdullah al-Udhari.
"Within my bolted infernal gates." MPAW

Thinkers and airmen—all such. To Poets and Airmen. Stephen Spender. WaP

Thinking. Walter D. Wintle. WBLP
(Man Who Thinks He Can, The.) PoLF; SoSe

Thinking about something. Ozaki Hosai, *tr. fr. Japanese by* Hiroaki Sato. *Fr*. One Hundred Haiku in Free Form. FCEI

Thinking about the Past. Donald Justice. MT

Thinking about you. Ratio. Lillian Morrison. UnAS

Thinking hard, hunting rhymes, humming by my lamp. Sent to Wen T'ing-yün on a Winter Night. Yü Hsüan-chi, *tr. by* Geoffrey Waters. BoWoP

Thinking I'm after them. Joso, *tr. fr. Japanese by* Hiroaki Sato. *Fr*. Fifteen Hokku. FCEI

Thinking in the Dark. Amiq Hanafi, *tr. fr. Urdu by* Mahmood Jamal. PBMUP

Thinking is not a smile. For Mattie and Eternity. Sterling Plumpp. CNA

Thinking it sinful, he doesn't dip it. *Unknown, tr. by* Hiroaki Sato. FCEI

Thinking myself in a warm country. Six Movements on a Theme. David Ignatow. NNaP

Thinking of Constantin Brancusi. Wieland Schmied, *tr. fr. German by* Beth Bjorklund. CoAuP

Thinking of East Mountain. Li Po, *tr. fr. Chinese by* Burton Watson. CoBCP; TTTS

Thinking of her had saddened me at first. Celandine. Edward Thomas. OxBTC

Thinking of Hölderlin. Christopher Middleton. NePoEA-2

Thinking of Iceland. Tom Paulin. FaBCIP

Thinking of Love. Elizabeth Jennings. GOYP

Thinking of Mr. D. Thomas Kinsella. NoAM

Thinking of My Friends at Kou-jung Subprefecture, *sel.* Yang Chi, *tr. fr. Chinese by* Jonathan Chaves.
Wu Shan-yang. CoBLCP

Thinking of My Wife. P'an Yüeh, *tr. fr. Chinese by* Burton Watson. CoBCP

Thinking of painters, musicians, poets. Orgy. Norman MacCaig. OxBC

Thinking of Tents. Reed Whittemore. TAP

Thinking of "The Autumn Fields." Robert Bly. NNaP

Thinking of the Lost World. Randall Jarrell. NoAM; NOBA

Thinking of the past. Nagachika, *tr. by* Steven D. Carter. WFTW

Thinking of the past I wake. Teika, *tr. fr. Japanese by* Hiroaki Sato. *Fr*. Eighty-four Tanka. FCEI

Thinking of the Past on an Autumn Night at Tz'u-jen Temple. Wang Shih-chen, *tr. fr. Chinese by* Jonathan Chaves. CoBLCP

Thinking of the tall triumphant horsemen. Granada the Last City. M. K. Joseph. *Fr*. The Tourist in Seat 29. ATNZ

Thinking of those who walked here long ago. On the Ridgeway. Andrew Young. FaBoPP

Thinking of words that would save him, slanting. Finding Them Lost. Howard Moss. CoAP; NYBP; SM

Thinking of You. Dick Lourie. NeAC

Thinking of you, I think of the *coureurs de bois*. Coureurs de Bois. Douglas Le Pan. CaP; MoCV; NOBC

Thinking of your vocation, I am filled. To a Friend with a Religious Vocation. Elizabeth Jennings. TOF

Thinking on my life under. It Says. Jon Silkin. VWA

Thinking sad thoughts over and over. Yakamochi, *tr. fr. Japanese*. *Fr*. Manyo Shu. Ma

Thinking Stone. Takenaka Iku, *tr. fr. Japanese by* Geoffrey Bownas *and* Anthony Thwaite. PeBJV

Thinking that it was a toy. My Daughter. Habib Jalib, *tr. by* Mahmood Jamal. PBMUP

Thinking to take on the power. The Wives of Mafiosi. Erica Jong. AmPA

Thinking "Today! Today!" I wait for you. Yosami. *Fr*. Manyo Shu. FCEI

Thinking Twice in the Laundromat. Harley Elliott. NeAC

Thinking we were safe—insanity! Story of a Hotel Room. Rosemary Tonks. AIW; OxBTC

Think'st Thou that this Love can stand. Ametas and Thestylis Making Hay-Ropes. Andrew Marvell. InvP; SeCP

Think'st Thou to Seduce Me Then. Thomas Campion. ElL; NAEL-1; OxBSP

Thinly covered with snow, the leaves look brighter along this mountain path. Three Poets at Yuyama. Shohaku *and others, tr. by* Hiroaki Sato. FCEI

Thinner now/ we are together. Air Is. John Michael Brennan. MAT

Thinnest Shadow, The. John Ashbery. TTTS

Thir Lenterne Dayis Ar Luvely Lang. *At. to* William Stewart. OxBS

Thir riveris and thir watteris kepit war. Virgil, *tr. into Middle English by* Gavin Douglas. *Fr*. The Aeneid [*or* Eneados], VI. OBVE

Third Advice to a Painter, The. Andrew Marvell. APAS

Third Avenue in Sunlight. Anthony Hecht. CoAP; NePoEA-2; PPP

Third Century, The, *sel.* Thomas Traherne.
News. MePo; NOBE; OBEV; SeCV-2
(On News.) QFR

Third Cycle of Love Poems, *sel.* George Barker.
Shut the Seven Seas against Us. *Fr*. II. MoAB; MoBrPo

Third day I went into the kitchen, The. Words of the Newly Wed Wife. Wang Chien, *tr. by* Burton Watson. CoBCP

Third Degree. Langston Hughes. BPo

Third Dimension, The. Denise Levertov. NeAP

Third Eclogue, The, *sel.* Michael Drayton.
"Stay, Thames, to heare my Song, thou great and famous Flood." PoEL-2

Third Enemy Speaks. C. Day Lewis. *Fr*. The Magnetic Mountain, XXI. EaLo

Third Eye, The. Jay Macpherson. MoCV

Third House, The, *sels.* Amy Károlyi, *tr. fr. Hungarian*.
"Coffee-stained, knife-cut tablecloth." *Fr*. V, *tr. by* Laura Schiff. OV
"Jewel towers relay to jewel towers." *Fr*. VI, *tr. by* Laura Schiff. OV
"Like a cloud haunted by the moon." *Fr*. I, *tr. by* Laura Schiff. OV
("Like moon-hunted clouds, the two.") MHuP, *tr. by* Edwin Morgan. OV

Third in our Borough's last appears the sign. The Caroline. George Crabbe. *Fr*. The Borough, Letter XI. SeCePo

Third Letter. Erika Mitterer, *tr. fr. German by* Beth Bjorklund. CoAuP

Third Light, The. Michael Longley. FaBCIP

Third Month, Night of the Seventeenth, Written While Drunk. Lu Yu, *tr. fr. Chinese by* Burton Watson. CoBCP

Third month, the thirtieth day. The Last Night of the Third Moon. Chia Tao, *tr. by* Burton Watson. CoBCP

Third month, third day, in the air a breath of newness. Song of the Beautiful Ladies. Tu Fu, *tr. by* Burton Watson. CoBCP

Third Ode to Persephone. Robert Kelly. *Fr.* The Book of Persephone, 14. PoM
Third Person, The. Lauris Edmond. ATNZ
Third Sermon on the Warpland, The. Gwendolyn Brooks. BPo
Third Song: "If Orpheus voyce had force to breathe such musickes love." Sir Philip Sidney. *Fr.* Astrophel and Stella. PoEL-1
Third Wonder, The. Edwin Markham. FYAP
Third World. Salah Niyazi, *tr. fr. Arabic by* Abdullah al-Udhari. MPAW
Third World Snapshots. John Robert Lee. PBCV
Third-World Theme. Angela de Hoyos. ER
Thirsis a youth of the inspired train. The Story of Phoebus and Daphne Applyed. Edmund Waller. OBS
Thirst. Emily Dickinson. *See* We thirst at first—'tis nature's act.
Thirst. Jacques Dupin, *tr. fr. French by* Auster. RHTwFP
Thirst. Musa Moris Farhi. VWA
Thirst of the Dragon. Dianne Hai-Jew. BrSi
Thirsty earth soaks up the rain, The. Drinking. Abraham Cowley, *after the Greek of* Anacreon. BLPL; FF; MePo; NOBE; OBEV; OBVE; SeCP; SeCV-1; TrGrPo
   (Anacreontic: Drinking.) HeIP
   (Anacreontic on Drinking.) SeCePo
   (Thirsty Earth, The.) WiR
Thirsty Island. Jim Tollerud. VoR
Thirsty—that's how Mount Fuji makes you feel. *Unknown, tr. by* Hiroaki Sato. FCEI
Thirteen black and white witches. The Bird Mertsyfint. Moyshe-Leyb Halpern, *tr. by* Benjamin *and* Barbara Harshav. AYP
Thirteen gentlemen in top hats hard as tin. A Funeral. Yisroel Rabon, *tr. by* Robert Friend. PeBMYV
Thirteen Hokku, *sels.* Kaai Chigetsu, *tr. fr. Japanese by* Hiroaki Sato. FCEI
   "Cricket chirps in a scarecrow's sleeve, A."
   "Despite myself I become so childish."
   "Each morning a wren comes."
   Fifteenth of the Eighth Month, The.
   "I know and I don't know what I am."
   "I sleep alone; throughout the night."
   "In a wide garden peonies open amply."
   "In autumn a dove looks as if loneliness."
   Loving My Grandchild.
   Lying Awake Endlessly in Old Age.
   On the Anniversary of Basho's Death I Visited His Grave in Kiso.
   "Today's moon—if there were another."
   "Unaware I'm growing old."
Thirteen Hokku, *sels.* Raizan, *tr. fr. Japanese by* Hiroaki Sato. FCEI
   "Blossoms bloom, I don't wanna die, but this illness."
   "Both have whiskers—I mean, the cat's wife, too."
   "Green, green, the young herbs are green in the snowy field."
   "How many autumns? unable to soothe myself."
   "I hug myself and again it's hard to breathe."
   "I pluck, I pluck and throw away spring grasses."
   "I turn to look: cold in the evening dusk, mountain cherries."
   "Mosquitoes came in, and while the two."
   "Spring dream—that I don't go mad is what I resent, A."
   "Spring rain falls, unknown to the cow's eyes."
   "Spring rain: I put my foot out of the footwarmer."
   "Spring wind: over the river bank comes a bull's voice."
   "White fish graphically move in the water's color."
Thirteen pieces of silver means bad luck. Digging Out the Roots. Duane Niatum. STE
13 Ways of Eradicating Blackbirds. Mark DeFoe. BXAP
Thirteen Ways of Looking at a Blackbird. Wallace Stevens. BLPL; CMoP; HCAP; HeIP; InPK; InPS; LiTM; MoP; NAAL-2; NoAM; NOBA; NoP; PoE; RB; SOTW; TAP
Thirteen White Chrysanthemums. Chou Meng-tieh, *tr. fr. Chinese by* Dominic Cheung. IFON
Thirteen Years. Ilse Aichinger, *tr. fr. German by* Beth Bjorklund. CoAuP
13th Horse Song of Frank Mitchell (White), The. Frank Mitchell, *tr. fr. Navajo Indian by* Jerome Rothenberg *and* David P. McAllester. STP
Thirteenth Telegram ("Faces that stab the eye are familiar, The"). Abd al-Aziz al-Maqalih, *tr. fr. Arabic by* Lena Jayyusi *and* Christopher Middleton. *Fr.* Telegrams of Tenderness for Sanaa. MAP
Thirteenth Year of *Genroku* [1700], the Year My Boy Toshiaki Died, The. Onitsura, *tr. fr. Japanese by* Hiroaki Sato. *Fr.* Twenty-three Hokku. FCEI
Thirti dayes hath Novembir. The Months. Chaucer. OxBLMV
Thirtieth Anniversary Report of the Class of '41. Howard Nemerov. HCAP

Thirtieth of November, The. Toward the Solstice. Adrienne Rich. NAAL-2; NoP
Thirtieth of November last, eighteen hundred and thirty, The. The Owslebury Lads. *Unknown.* OBET
Thirty Bob a Week. John Davidson. EBEV; EBVV; FaBoPV; FaBoTw; FaFP; LiTB; NoAM; NOBE; NOBVV; OAEL-2; OBNC; OxBS; OxBTC
Thirty candles and one. The Birthday. Philip Dacey. AmPA
Thirty days hath November. The Months of the Year. Richard Grafton. FaBoUs
Thirty days hath September. Mother Goose. FaBoBe; FaBoUs; OxNR
Thirty-eight. Charlotte Smith. WPOW
38 Main Street. Lyn Lifshin. TV
.38, The. Ted Joans. WeW
Thirty eighth year, The. Lucille Clifton. AmPA
31st day of August 1914, The. The Little Car. Guillaume Apollinaire, *tr. by* Ron Padgett *and others.* RHTwFP; SOTW
34 Blues. Charlie Patton. FaBoPV
Thirty Miles West of Chicago. Lyn Lifshin. ER
Thirty-nine Haiku, *sels.* Masaoka Shiki, *tr. fr. Japanese by* Burton Watson. FCEI
   After I'm Dead.
   "Airing books."
   "Always someone resting there."
   "Clog with a broken thong."
   "Country road—/ boys whacking at a snake."
   "Cricket singing, A."
   "Crickets/ in the corner of the garden."
   "Daily routine."
   "Dead squid, A."
   "Fall rains/ scum collecting on."
   "Fluttering, fluttering."
   "For eating persimmons, too."
   "Forsythia blossoms gone."
   "From the firefly."
   "Getting lazy."
   "Home alone/ my mother off cherry-viewing."
   "I checked/ three thousand haiku."
   "I pulled on a creeper."
   In a Strong Wind at the Suma Seashore.
   "Lonely sound—/ simmering in the firepit."
   "Long night/ when the waterfall."
   "Morning fog/ one man's got a fire going."
   "Peeling pears/ sweet juice drips."
   "People going home."
   "Purple so deep, A."
   "Sketching from life."
   "Sky blazing/ as I go down the gravel path."
   "Stray cat, A."
   "Summer grass/ way in the distance."
   "Summer storm/ all the sheets of blank paper."
   "They've cut down the willow."
   "This year/ I took sick with the peonies."
   "Twilight cicadas."
   Written when Sick in Bed ("I keep on asking").
   Written when Sick in Bed ("I'm trying to sleep").
Thirty-nine Tanka, *sels.* Yosano Akikò, *tr. fr. Japanese by* Hiroaki Sato. FCEI
   "After throwing a parasol to the grass."
   "Another look like his mixed me up again."
   "As I wait for you in the grass with lilies."
   "At least, at least in his dreams"—so thinking."
   "At least let it burn just as it burns!"—that way I feel."
   "Black hair, a thousand strands of hair."
   "Camellia, yes, and plum, yes."
   "Can't say that now, you have little spring."
   "For some reason I thought you'd be waiting for me."
   "Girl, twenty—her black hair, The."
   "Hair, five feet long."
   "Having changed my tangled hair into Shimada style."
   "Hugging my breasts I lightly kick."
   "I bathe and step out of the Spring."
   " 'I don't want to take a beautiful bud,' said the god."
   " 'I must go now, goodbye,' said the god of night."
   "I won't let you go, this spring evening turns dark."
   "In the spring dusk I find our next-door painter."
   "Just one room away, from time to time you sighed."
   "Not even trying to touch the hot blood-tide."
   "Not speaking of the Way."
   "Our friend's feet were cold the morning we set out."
   "Saying nothing, asking nothing."

"Shall I receive the spring rain dripping on swallow wings."
"Sliding down two feet of my gossamer sleeve."
" 'Spring is short! Who says our life's immortal?' I said."
"The three of us are relatives not doing well."
"This evening rainfall is merciful."
"To Kiyomizu, through Gion."
"To smear poisoned honey on my lips."
"Way morning looks in the plum valley, The."
"When I reflect on it now."
"Who shall I tell of the color rouge?"
"With your other hand support me."
"Wondering, I touched it with my young lips."
"Yesterday feels like a thousand years ago."
"You are ill; let me put my slender arm."
"You picked a white chrysanthemum and smiled."
"You think of him, and so do I; our hearts."
Thirty-one Camels, The.   Rachel Korn, *tr. fr. Yiddish by* Howard
    Schwartz.   VWA
Thirty-one nights hath December.   Rhyme for Remembering How Many
    Nights There Are in the Month.   Justin Richardson.   FaBoUs
Thirty Poems of Longing for People, *sel.*   Chin Nung, *tr. fr. Chinese by*
    Jonathan Chaves.
    "I get so drunk, I could be called the Earl of Dissipation!"
      CoBLCP
Thirty Tanka, *sels.*   Shunzei, *tr. fr. Japanese by* Burton Watson.
    FCEI
"As evening comes."
Congratulations.
"Cuckoo, what are you."
Dawn.
"Glowing moon, The."
"In my grass hut."
"In this world."
"Journey is a short one, The."
"Kibune River—/ the rocky waves of its rapids."
Looking over Poems by Persons of Long Ago.
"Mountain stream, The."
"Old though I am."
"On the Fushimi hills."
One-Sided Love.
"Sailing close to shore."
Sent to a Woman.
Sent to a Woman on a Rainy Day.
"Showers wet/ the orange blossoms."
"Spring night."
"This world/ no road that takes us out of it."
"We hearing them."
"When spring comes."
"Where the water."
"While I gaze far off."
"Who'd have thought it?."
"Will someone/ at the scent of orange blossom."
Written in Autumn When Spending the Night Near the Grave of His
    Wife.
Written when He Was Well Over Eighty.
Written when the Poet Was Seventy-six.
Thirty Tanka, *sels.*   Tachibana Akemi, *tr. fr. Japanese by* Burton Watson.
    FCEI
"Deafening noise!"
Happiness Is When.
"Ingots of silver."
Scenes in a Silver Mine.
"Sending up billows."
Servant ("The gourd of wine"), The.
"Soaked in sluices."
"Stark naked."
"Stepping through the sleet."
"Thirty," the doctor said, "three grains, each one."   Felo de Se.   Thomas
    Blackburn.   OxBTC
33, *sels.*   Julia Alvarez.   Son
He: Age Doesn't Matter When You're Both in Love.
Mother Asks What I'm Put To.
33 Is the Year That Jesus Christ.
33.   David St. John.   NAmP
Thirty-three, goodbye.   Happy Birthday.   Frank Bidart.   HCAP
Thirty-three Hokku, *sels.*   Kikaku, *tr. fr. Japanese by* Hiroaki Sato.
    FCEI
"Against the morning glories."
Amused at My Own Figure while Traveling.
"An evening shower."
"At a grass hut I eat smartweed."

"Autumn sky has detached itself, The."
"Began drinking sake at fifteen."
Bosho's Old Hut.
"Bright moon: on the straw mat."
"Darkening mountains are distant."
"Even on the bridge."
"Even swallows seem to have no time."
"Evening dusk: flying in the middle."
"Evening shower has washed, The."
"Haziness is the blackness of pines."
"He goes, his horse as his shield."
"In an evening shower ducks walk around."
"In the sleet too, the heron."
"In the tree-searing wind."
"Lightning: again the sky's morning glow."
"Lightning: in the east yesterday."
"On charcoal dust."
"Shoes going over rocks have fins."
"Slashed in a dream."
"Sleeping butterfly."
"Swallow has erased a rainbow, A."
"Think it's your snow."
"Voice hoarse, the monkey's teeth."
"Winter comes, and a crow perches."
"Winter river: a raft sits, A."
"Woman on a spring night, A."
Yearly Regret.
"Year's first day, The."
"Young woman plants seedlings, A."
33 Is the Year That Jesus Christ.   Julia Alvarez.   *Fr.* 33.   Son
Thirty today, I saw.   A Birthday Candle.   Donald Justice.   NYBP
Thirty-two times have I entered life.   For My Birthday.   Yehuda Amichai,
    tr. by Bernhard Frank.   MHeP
Thirty-two years since, up against the sun.   Zermatt: To the Matterhorn.
    Thomas Hardy.   OBNC
Thirty white horses upon a red hill.   Mother Goose.   NTCP; OxNR
Thirty years ago I climbed to the top of this pavilion.   The Pavilion of the
    Infinite Heavens.   Yao Nai, *tr. by* Daniel Bryant.   WFTU
Thirty years ago we stood in rows.   Invitation to a Dance.   Susan
    Wallbank.   AIW
Thirty years from now, you might.   Photograph of My Room.   Carolyn
    Forché.   NAmP
This/ Long/ Night!   Memory.   Unsi al-Haj, *tr. by* Abdullah al-Udhari.
    MPAW
This.   Anne Stevenson.   ER
This Above All.   Shakespeare.   *See* Hamlet: Polonius' Advice to Laertes.
This above All Is Precious and Remarkable.   John Wain.   LiTM
This act reminds me, ge'men, under favour.   Four Epigrams on the
    Naturalization Bill.   John Byrom.   NOBL
This admirable gadget, when it is.   Gyroscope.   Howard Nemerov.
    NoAM
This ae nighte [*or* ean night], this ae nighte.   Lyke-Wake Dirge, The.
    Unknown.   CH; ChTr; EaLo; FaBoCh; FaBoRV; GBP; HAP; HoPM;
    NOBE; NoP; OBEV; PoEL-1; WeW
    (Cleveland Lyke Wake Dirge, The.)   EnSB
    (Final Dirge.)   ACP
This Afternoon.   Juan Sáez Burgos, *tr. fr. Spanish by* Julio Marzán.   InW
This afternoon as I sat.   Elegy for Jack Bowman.   Joseph Bruchac.
    CDW
This afternoon I swam with a school of fish.   Sea School.   Barbara
    Howes.   NYBP
This afternoon, my love, speaking to you.   In Which She Satisfies a Fear
    with the Rhetoric of Tears.   Sister Juana Inés de la Cruz, *tr. by* Aliki
    and Willis Barnstone.   BoWoP
This ain't Torquemada.   Dialect Quatrain.   Marcus B. Christian.   AmNP
This Alice.   Herbert Morris.   PoRA
This almost bare tree is racing.   November through a Giant Copper Beech.
    Edwin Honig.   NoAM; NYBP
This Amber Sunstream.   Mark Van Doren.   GoYe; LiTA
This America is an ancient land.   Edgar Lee Masters.   *Fr.* The New
    World.   AmFN
This anchorage will do.   A Diary of the Sailors of the North.   David
    Shulman, *tr. by the author*.   VWA
This ancient hag.   Mexican Market Woman.   Langston Hughes.   SaC
This ancient silver bowl of mine, it tells of good old times.   On Lending a
    Punch-Bowl.   Oliver Wendell Holmes.   AA
This and That.   Florence Boyce Davis.   FaPON
This angel, who mediates between us.   The Angel.   Galway Kinnell.
    NoAM
This animal, this sleek and beautiful ox ambling along the pleasant road.
    The Ox.   Mary Morison Webster.   PeSA

This apartment full of books could crack open. Adrienne Rich. *Fr.*
Twenty-one Love Poems, V. GLP
This autumn day a noble man has died. Lamenting Noble Scholar Chu.
Ni Tsan, *tr. by* Jonathan Chaves. CoBLCP
This autumn, why do I get old? Sentiment on a Journey. Basho, *tr. fr.*
Japanese by Burton Watson. *Fr.* Seventy-six Hokku. FCEI
This autumn, without my son in my lap. The Thirteenth Year of *Genroku*
[1700], the Year My Boy Toshiaki Died. Onitsura, *tr. fr. Japanese*
by Hiroaki Sato. *Fr.* Twenty-three Hokku. FCEI
This bamboo I painted a long time ago. I Once Did a Bamboo Painting
for Somebody. Hsü Wei, *tr. by* Jonathan Chaves. CoBLCP
This Be Our Revenge. Saul Tchernichowsky, *tr. fr. Hebrew by* Shalom
Spiegel. TrJP
This Be the Verse. Philip Larkin. NoAM
This bears the seal of immortality. The Living Book. Charlotte Fiske
Bates. AA
This Beast That Rends Me. Edna St. Vincent Millay. PrIm
("This beast that rends me in the sight of all.") VGW
This beauty, is it yours or is it mine? You or I? Ilyas Abu Shabaku, *tr.*
by Adnan Haydar *and* Michael Beard. MAP
This beauty that I see. James Schuyler. PoA
This began somewhere. Essay on Language. Wanda Coleman. BAP
"This beginning of miracles did." Cana. Thomas Merton. TrCP
This being a fair and peaceful day. Benediction for the Tent. *Mongol*
Oral Tradition, tr. by C. R. Bawden. WTO
This being a minimum security facility, it feels more like being on a
reservation. Visiting Day. Al Young. NPGG
This being a place over which. Tabito. *Fr.* Manyo Shu. Ma
This biplane is the shape of human flight. The Wrights' Biplane. Robert
Frost. WeW
This bird that a cat sprang loose in the house. More Joy in Heaven.
Howard Nemerov. NoAM
This black life. Spring Rain. William Hawkins. MoCV
This black scrap from Viet Nam. Nocturn at the Institute. David
McElroy. Psk
This black "Yeyhoo" said he's Seminole. Indian Macho. Louis Oliver.
STE
This Blatant Beast was finally overcome. Saint. Robert Graves. CMoP
This Blessed Plot. This England. Shakespeare. *See* King Richard II:
John of Gaunt's Dying Speech.
This Blood. Ali Sardar J'afri, *tr. fr. Urdu by* Mahmood Jamal. PBMUP
This blue-washed, old, thatched summerhouse. The Old Summerhouse.
Walter de la Mare. CMoP; FaBoPP; FaBoRV; GTBS-P
This bodily world is a difficult road—hilly, overgrown. Ravidas, *tr. by*
John Stratton Hawley *and* Mark Juergensmeyer. SSI
This body of my mother, pierced by me. Leo Kennedy. OBCV
This body offers to carry us for nothing—as the ocean. Finding the
Father. Robert Bly. DiL
This bond of the prelates I pray you revoke. Now God Stand Up for
Bastards. Brian Merriman, *tr. fr. Modern Irish by* Arland Ussher.
Fr. The Midnight Court. BIrV
This book, by a woman writ. For the Christian Reader. Anna Owena
Hoyers, *tr. by* Susan L. Cocalis. DMG
This book is all that's left me now. My Mother's Bible. George Pope
Morris. AA; AnAmPo; BLRP; WBLP
This book is mine. *Unknown.* FaBoUs
This book is one thing. *Unknown.* FaBoUs
This book was written in order to change the world. Foreword to New
Numbers. Christopher Logue. OxBTC
This bough here in my vase. Faint Echo. Zelda, *tr. by* Bernhard Frank.
MHeP
This Bouillabaisse a noble dish is. Thackeray. *Fr.* The Ballad of
Bouillabaisse. FaBoUs
This brand of soap has the same smell as once in the big. Soap Suds.
Louis MacNeice. FaBCIP; FaBoMo; NAEL-2; NOIV; NoP; SCV
This Bread I Break Was Once the Oat. Dylan Thomas. FaBoTw
This bread is rock, not wheat. The Bread of Our Affliction. Martin
Grossman. VWA
This bright burning pyre. Auvaiyar, *tr. by* A. K. Ramanujan. PLW
This bronze doth keep the very form and mold. On the Life-Mask of
Abraham Lincoln. Richard Watson Gilder. AA
This brown woman's voice. Nina Simone. Lance Jeffers. CNA
This burly son of a bitch. Not Just Yet. Carter Revard. VoR
This calls for a toast. She hates. Jane Seagrim's Party. Leonard Nathan.
GOYP
This can be seen as placing a mirror against the page. Book of the Yellow
Castle. Michael Palmer. LP
This cankered earth, this murrain'd patch of land. King Ethelred the
Unready. Bill Greenwell. BXAP
This cannon cannot shoot again; but sits, a relic in the park. Cannon
Park. Mark St. Germain. PCP

This cargo of confessions, messages. The Postman. Gordon Challis.
ATNZ
This cat was bought upon the day. The Family Cat. Roy Fuller.
OxBC; TEP
This celestial seascape, with white herons got up as angels. Seascape.
Elizabeth Bishop. FaBoWP; MoAB; MOS; OxBC; PPP
This Chauntecleer stood hye up-on his toos. Chaucer. *Fr.* The
Canterbury Tales: The Nun's Priest's Tale. FiP
This Child Is the Mother. Gloria C. Oden. BISi
This Child ("This child, exile of hope"). Norman Rosten.
TrJP
This, children, is the famed mon-goos. The Mon-Goos. Oliver Herford.
Fr. Child's Natural History. AA
This Christmas Day you pray me sing. For Christmas Day. Luke
Wadding, *tr. by* Thomas Kinsella. TIRV
This city and this country has brought forth many mayors. Good English
Hospitality. Blake. *Fr.* An Island in the Moon. CoMu
(Mayors, The.) CH
This city has even got the machine. In This City. Salvatore Quasimodo,
tr. by Allen Mandelbaum. PFI
This city is made of stone, of blood, and fish. Anchorage. Joy Harjo.
HATNAP; STE
This city is the child of France and Spain. Vieux Carré. Walter Adolphe
Roberts. PoNe
This clerk-work, this first January chore. A New Diary. Dannie Abse.
NoAM
This cold night bamboos stir. Hearing the Snow. Kido, *tr. by* Lucien
Stryk *and* Takashi Ikemoto. ZPCJ
This Cold Nothing Else. Dara Wier. MAYP
This coloured counterfeit that thou beholdest. Sister Juana Inés de la
Cruz, *tr. fr. Spanish by* Samuel Beckett. MexPo; PBWP
This Compost. Walt Whitman. AWP; LiTA; MoAmPo; NAAL-1
This conduit stream that's tangled here and there. Zillebeke Brook.
Edmund Blunden. MMA
This consciousness that is aware. Emily Dickinson. NAAL-1
This cool night is strange. Gwendolyn B. Bennett. BANP
This Corruptible. Elinor Wylie. MoAB; MoAmPo
This country might have. Right On: White America. Sonia Sanchez.
PoBA
This Country's Needs ("This country needs more noble men"). Mrs.
Henry Linden. CBWP-4
This crab—where does it come from? Emperor Ojin. *Fr.* Manyo Shu.
PeBJV
(Emperor Ojin's Song.) *Tr. by* Hiroaki Sato. FCEI
This crazy man has escaped the world. Wang Chiu-ssu, *tr. fr. Chinese by*
Jonathan Chaves. *Fr.* After Reading the Poems of Master Han Shan.
CoBLCP
This creature kneeling. November. Margaret Atwood. NOBC
This Cross-Tree Here. OFD
This crowded night my people's kindling pride. The Hour. Vivian
Virtue. PVCV
This Cruel Age Has Deflected Me. "Anna Akhmatova," *tr. fr. Russian by*
Stanley Kunitz *with* Max Hayward. AnAn
This darkest of ages has destroyed. Tulsidas, *tr. by* John Stratton Hawley
and Mark Juergensmeyer. SSI
This darkness has a quality. Composition for Words and Paint. Fleur
Adcock. ATNZ
This darksome burn, horseback brown. Inversnaid. Gerard Manley
Hopkins. ACP; BLPL; BrPo; CMoP; FaBoPP; GTBS-P; LiTB;
LiTM; MoAB; MoBrPo; NoAM; OAEL-2; PoRA; PoSH; RB; RR;
UnPo
This dawn he rose early again. Shooting the Horses. Pamela Mordecai.
PVCV
This dawn that's marked and wounded. Freedom's Dawn. Faiz Ahmad
Faiz, *tr. by* Mahmood Jamal. PBMUP
This Day. Hildegarde Flanner. WPE
This Day. Lawrence Raab. BLA; NoP
This Day after Yesterday. Philip Booth. KS
This day at least. At Least. Don Mattera. WMBCH
This Day Be with Me. George Macdonald. *Fr.* Diary of an Old Soul.
TrCP
This day day dawes. The Lily-white Rose. *Unknown.* MeEL
This day for our new navigation. The New Navigation. John Freeth.
OBET
This day is called the Feast of Crispian. Henry V before Agincourt.
Shakespeare. *Fr.* King Henry V, IV, iii. FaPoR
(St. Crispin's Day.) FF
This day is for Israel light and rejoicing. A Sabbath of Rest. Isaac
Luria, *tr. by* Nina Davis Salaman. TrJP
This Day is Thine. Verna Whinery. BLRP
This day of all our days has done. Byron. FaBoEE

This day relenting God. Lines Written after the Discovery by the Author of the Germ of Yellow Fever. Sir Ronald Ross. ImOP

This day the children of Speakthunder. In My Lifetime. James Welch. CDW; STE

This day, twice as long as the same day in Sheffield, Vermont. December Day in Honolulu. Galway Kinnell. AnAn

This Day, under My Hand. David Malouf. CBAP

This day upon the bitter tree. Good Friday. A. J. M. Smith. CaP

This day, whate'er the Fates decree. Stella's Birthday; March 13, 1726/27. Swift. NAs; NoP; OAEL-1; PoE; PoEL-3

This day when I lay my hope aside. This Day. Hildegarde Flanner. WPE

This day will be remembered by America's noble sons. The Battle of Bull Run. *Unknown.* AmFP

This day writhes with what? The Ultimate Poem Is Abstract. Wallace Stevens. PoA

This daylit doll, this dim divinity. Neo-Classical Poem. William Jay Smith. WaP

This Decoration. Hayden Carruth. NNaP

This definition poetry doth fit. Thomas Randolph. FaBoEE

This delightful young man. Heine, *tr. fr. German by* Ezra Pound. *Fr. Heimkehr, Die.* AWP

This desert is a plateau of light. The Language of Fossils. Anita Endrezze-Danielson. HATNAP

This Dim and Ptolemaic Man. John Peale Bishop. ImOP; LiTA; LiTM

This dirty little heart. Emily Dickinson. PoEL-5

This divine October afternoon I would like. Pain. Alfonsina Storni, *tr. by* Merrilee Antrim. WPOW

This Do in Remembrance of Me, *sel.* Horatius Bonar. "Here, O my Lord, I see Thee face to face." TrPWD

This dread is like a calm. Winter Holding off the Coast of North America. N. Scott Momaday. CDW

This dreadful, dark and dismal day. Frankie Silvers. Frances Silvers. AmFP

This dream the world is having about itself. Vocation. William Stafford. CAPP

This drop of ink chance leaves upon my pen. A Drop of Ink. Joseph Ernest Whitney. AA

This dry night nothing unusual. The War Horse. Eavan Boland. BIrV; CIP

This dust was Timas. The Dust of Timas. Sappho, *tr. by* E. A. Robinson. AWP

This Earth. Phillip Yellowhawk Minthorn. STE

This earth is not the steadfast place. William Vaughn Moody. *Fr.* Gloucester Moors. WGRP

This earth Pythonax and his brother hides. On Two Brothers. Simonides, *tr. by* W. H. D. Rouse. AWP

This Earthen Body. *Gond Oral Tradition, tr. by* V. Elwin *and* S. Hivale. WTO

This Easter, Arthur Winslow, less than dead. Death from Cancer. Robert Lowell. *Fr.* In Memory of Arthur Winslow. TwCP

This Edward in the Aprill of his age. Michael Drayton. *Fr.* Piers Gaveston. PeHV

This endless gray-roofed city, and each heart. London Despair. Frances Cornford. OBMV

This Endris Night. *Unknown.* EBEV; NOCV

This endsaying—moon pried loose. The Goodbye. Myra Sklarew. GOYP

This England. Shakespeare. *Fr.* King Richard II, II, i. BoTP; TrGrPo

This Englishwoman is so refined. Stevie Smith. FaBoEE

This Evening. Zishe Landau, *tr. fr. Yiddish by* Irving Feldman. PeBMYV

This evening. Nadia Tuéni, *tr. by* Carol Cosman. OV

This evening. Summer's End. Paolo Volponi, *tr. by* Lawrence R. Smith. NItP

This evening holds her breath. Winter Night. Cecil Day Lewis. PoA

This evening I prepared Wardance Soup. Wardance Soup. Phillip William George. VoR

This evening, my love, even as I spoke vainly. Sister Juana Inés de la Cruz, *tr. by* Judith Thurman. PBWP

This evening on my journey far from home. *Unknown. Fr.* Manyo Shu. Ma

This evening rainfall is merciful. Yosano Akiko, *tr. fr. Japanese by* Hiroaki Sato. *Fr.* Thirty-nine Tanka. FCEI

This evening so cold and chill. Prince Shiki. *Fr.* Manyo Shu. Ma

This evening the cuckoo and the corncrake. Seamus Heaney. *Fr.* Glanmore Sonnets, III. IPY

This Evening When I Spake with Thee, Beloved. Sister Juana Inés de la Cruz, *tr. fr. Spanish by* Samuel Beckett. MexPo

This Excellent Machine. John Lehmann. OxBTC

This existence has, without the azure sphere, no reality. Sarmèd the Yahud, *tr. by* David Shea. TrJP

This face had no use for light, took none of it. Made Shine. Josephine Miles. NoAM

This fairest lady, who, as well I wot. Sonnet: Death Is Not without but within Him. Cino da Pistoia, *tr. by* Dante Gabriel Rossetti. AWP

This fairest one of all the stars, whose flame. Ballata: One Speaks of the Beginning of His Love. *Unknown, tr. by* Dante Gabriel Rossetti. AWP

This fall you will taste carrots. Digging In. Marge Piercy. CAPP

This far out in the country no one is talking. Starting a Pasture. Walter McDonald. MT

This father, mother and son, trapped in the lens. What Became of the Family? Louis Johnson. ATNZ

This feast-day of the sun, his alter there. The Hill Summit. Dante Gabriel Rossetti. *Fr.* The House of Life, LXX. NoP

This Feast of the Law. *Unknown, tr. fr. Hebrew by* Israel Zangwill. TrJP

This festival links these lakes. Nocturnal Festival. Antonin Artaud, *tr. by* Michael Benedikt. POS

This fever dances. Weaponry. Wendy Rose. ER

This field-grass brushed our legs. In the Field. Richard Wilbur. NAAL-2; NYBP

This field of stones, he said. In a Christian Churchyard. James Thomson. NOBVV

This first day of the year. On the Circumsision: New Year's Day. Luke Wadding. NOIV

This flattering glass, whose smooth face wears. On His Mistress Looking in a Glass. Thomas Carew. CaPo

This flickering at night. Little Testament. Eugenio Montale, *tr. by* William Arrowsmith. AnAn

This floating life—a grain of millet on a boundless sea! Chang Wen-t'ao, *tr. fr. Chinese by* William Schultz. *Fr.* Moving to the Cottage of Pine and Bamboo, II. WFTU

This Flock So Small, *with music.* Anna Nitschmann, *tr. fr. German by* Sheema Z. Buehne. AH

This flying angel's torrent cry. Eastern Tempest. Edmund Blunden. MoBrPo

This Form of Life Needs Sex. Allen Ginsberg. NNaP

This fountain sheds her flowery spray. The Fountain. A. J. M. Smith. CaP

This Fresshe Flour. Chaucer. *Fr.* Legend of Good Women, The: Prologue. SeCePo

This from that soul incorrupt whom Athens had doomed to the death. The Reply of Socrates. Edith Thomas. WGRP

This Fugitive Beauty. Eli Netser, *tr. fr. Hebrew by* Bernhard Frank. MHeP

This fugue must be hummed, found. Dumb Dick. Leslie A. Fiedler. ErPo

This garden does not take my eyes. The Garden. James Shirley. OBS

This garden is outlandish. The Women's Jail. Miriam Waddington. NOBC

This garden of Paradise. Asadullah Khan Ghalib, *tr. by* Ahmed Ali. GoT

This garden too pleasant. Concert. Helen G. Quigless. NBP

This gentle and half melancholy breeze. An Autumn Breeze. William Hamilton Hayne. AA

This gentleman the charming duck. A Trueblue Gentleman. Kenneth Patchen. SO

This girl/ Waits at the corner for. Girl, Boy, Flower, Bicycle. M. K. Joseph. ATNZ; PeNZ

This girlchild was born as usual. Barbie Doll. Marge Piercy. CAPP; NIP

This glacier that creaks. The Light of the Blade. André du Bouchet, *tr. by* Paul Auster. RHTwFP

This god who has gaped ever since we created him. Lost. Orkhan Muyassar, *tr. by* Lena Jayyusi *and* Samuel Hazo. MAP

This golden head has wit in it. I live. George Meredith. *Fr.* Modern Love, XXXI. NOBVV

This Golden Summer. Robert Lowell. NoP

This "good plan, fleshed in childhood"; these fruits. Jerusalem. Jon Silkin. VWA

This grandson of fishes holds inside him. Evolution from the Fish. Robert Bly. MoP; NoAM; NOBA

This grasped, all's dust. Seigensai, *tr. by* Lucien Stryk *and* Takashi Ikemoto. ZPCJ

This great liquid silence. Landscape of a Child on His Way to the Place of the Regents. Jean Follain, *tr. by* W. S. Merwin. RHTwFP

This ground once was consecrated. Cry for a Disused Synagogue in Booysens. Mannie Hirsch. VWA

This grove is too secret: one thinks of murder. The Grove Beyond the Barley. Alden Nowlan. MoCV

This guy is an animal. A pig? Squealing sinus breathing. Wrestling The Beast. Arnold Adoff. ASP

This guy on t.v. The Electric Cop. Victor Hernandez Cruz. PoBA

This handless clock stares blindly from its tower. A Clock in the Square. Adrienne Rich. HeIP

This Happened Everywhere. Remco Campert, *tr. fr. Dutch by* John Scott *and* Graham Martin. DuIn

This harpie with dry red curls. Red Dust. Philip Levine. NNaP; NoAM

This has little to do with the flower. The Night-blooming Cactus. John Bensko. MAYP

This having learnt, thou hast attaind the summe. Milton. *Fr.* Paradise Lost, *bk.* XII, *ll.* 575–649. SCV

This He was then. The Carpenter. Mary Brent Whiteside. TrCP

This head/ The eye distinct. The Invasion. Pierre Reverdy, *tr. by* John Ashbery. RHTwFP

This heaven is too clear and bright. Macrocosm. Philip Child. CaP

This helmet, I suppose. Arac's Song. W.S. Gilbert. *Fr.* Princess Ida. FiBHP

This high-caught hooded Reason broods upon my wrist. The Falcon and the Dove. Sir Herbert Read. BrPo; FaBoMo

This high-way. March of the Three Kings. *Unknown.* OHIP

This hill indents my soul. Champ de Manœuvres. Sir Herbert Read. BrPo

This holy night in open forum. Office Party. Phyllis McGinley. OBSV

This Hour. Oliver La Grone. PoNe

This hour was set the time for heaven's descent. Twilit Revelation. Léonie Adams. MoAB; MoAmPo

This Houre Her Vigill. Valentin Iremonger. CIP; NOIV; OxBTC (Elizabeth.) NeIP

This House. Ray A. Young Bear. CDW

This house cannot be handed down. Usufruct. Austin Clarke. IPY

This house has been far out at sea all night. Wind. Ted Hughes. NAEL-2; SoSe

This house is built within a sheltering. Back Road Farm. Charles Bruce. CaP

This house is closed to neighbors. The Wayfarers. Yusuf al-Khal, *tr. by* Sargon Boulus *and* Samuel Hazo. MAP

This house is floored with water. The Water Below. Fleur Adcock. ATNZ

This house is haunted, this house is haunted. Calliope. *Unknown.* AS

This house that has been our home has been condemned. Packing a Photograph from Firenze. William H. Matchett. NePoEA

This house was built beside the emerald bamboo. The Moon Window. Chang Yü, *tr. fr. Chinese by* Jonathan Chaves. *Fr.* Twelve Miscellaneous Poems on the Fang Garden. CoBLCP

This huge and purged trust I have. My Love behind Walls. Heather Spears. OBCV

This *Humanist* Whom No Beliefs Constrained. J. V. Cunningham. InPK (Epigram: "This *Humanist* Whom No Beliefs Constrained.") RB; VGW

This I admit, Death is terrible to me. Pure Death. Robert Graves. AWP; GTBS-P; MoAB

This I ask Thee—tell it to me truly, Lord! The Sacred Book. *At. to* Zoroaster, *tr. by* A. V. Williams Jackson. AWP (Zoroaster Devoutly Questions Ormazd.) WGRP

This I beheld, or dreamed it in a dream. Opportunity. Edward Rowland Sill. AnAmPo; BLPA; GN; OHFP; WGRP

This I Said to My Only Son at Play—and to Nobody Else. Moyshe-Leyb Halpern, *tr. fr. Yiddish by* Benjamin *and* Barbara Harshav. AYP

This I would like to be—braver and bolder. Lord, Make a Regular Man out of Me. Edgar A. Guest. BLPA; BLPL

This, if Japanese. Thyme Flowering among Rocks. Richard Wilbur. EOEF; LCAP

This ignorance upon my tongue. On Reading Aloud My Early Poems. John Williams. WeW

This Imperial city. Vienna. Peter Porter. OBTV

This indecent procession of the undead. Mannequins. Daniel Mark Epstein. MAYP

This Indian weed, that once did grow. Tobacco. Philip Freneau. TAP

This institution,/ perhaps one should say enterprise. Marriage. Marianne Moore. NOBA

This is a breath of summer wind. On Reading a Poet's First Book. H. C. Bunner. AA

This is a common plantain, the simple weed. Ground Hog Lock. Gerald Stern. AnAn

This is a corner of heaven here. In Carpenter's Woods. Gerald Stern. CAPP

This is a country where there are no mountains. Morning on the St. John's. Jane Cooper. NYBP

This is a damned inhuman sort of war. Unseen Fire. R. N. Currey. OBWP; OxBTC

This is a day to celebrate can-openers. The Cast Off. Marge Piercy. NoAM

This is a fair in Magh Eala of the king. The Headless Phantoms. *Unknown, tr. by* Eoin MacNeill. AnIL

This is a fearful thing to bear. Horror. Peter Baum, *tr. by* Jethro Bithell. AWP

This is a fervent time. The Skydivers. Joseph Colin Murphy. ASP

This is a glove. The Village of Reason. Michael Palmer. NPGG

This is a hard life you are living. Album. Josephine Miles. FaBoWP

This is a lie. Adam and Eve at the Garden Gate. Marsha Pomerantz. VWA

This is a marine cemetery. Cemetery in Pernambuco. João Cabral de Melo Neto, *tr. by* Jane Cooper. ATCBP

This is a morning to say something. Morning to Remember, A; or, E Pluribus Unum. Edward Dorn. NoAM

This is a new sort of poem. Buy One Now. D.J. Enright. NOBL

This is a nice vase that's so very Greek. Ode on a Grecian Urn. E. O. Parrott. BXAP

This Is a Photograph of Me. Margaret Atwood. NoAM; NoP

This is a place of ease. Marion Strobel. PoA

This is a place where a door might be. A Door. W. S. Merwin. CAPP

This is a poem for a woman doing dishes. Three Poems for Women. Susan Griffin. NPGG

This is a poem for my daughter. For Alissa. Peter Cooley. NAmP

This Is a Poem for the Dead. Michael Ryan. AmPA; DiL

This Is a Poem for the Fathers and for Michael Ryan. Thomas Lux. AmPA; DiL

This Is a Poem of Love. Ory Bernstein, *tr. fr. Hebrew by* Warren Bargad *and* Stanley F. Chyet. IP

This is a poem. Take it. Pack it up. Notes to the Reader. Robert Bringhurst. NOBC

This is a pool which bears deep looking into. A Pool. Thomas Whitbread. NYBP

This is a prayer. On the Marshes at Dawn. David Weiss. KS

This is a quiet sector of a quiet front. A Letter from Aragon. John Cornford. OBWP

This is a request, a realization. Hugues C. Pernath, *tr. fr. Dutch by* James S. Holmes. *Fr.* Index, 31. DuIn

This is a rune I ravelled in the still. The Cow. Bernard O'Dowd. PoAu-1

This is a silence. Arabesque. Fred Johnson. PoBA

This is a small pool of water after the morning rain. A Car. Lan Ling, *tr. by* Dominic Cheung. IFON

This is a song to be sung at night. The Middle of the Night. Karla Kuskin. RHPC

This is a song to celebrate banks. Bankers Are Just like Anybody Else, except Richer. Ogden Nash. LiTA

This is a spray the bird clung to. Misconceptions. Robert Browning. OBEV

This is a story Jung would understand. Candelaria and the Sea Turtle. Gladys Cardiff. HATNAP

This is a story my father told to me. *Tsa'lagi* Council Tree. Gladys Cardiff. HATNAP

This is a strange museum. In one square yard see. In a Country Museum. Patricia Beer. FaBoWP

This is a tale that the coachman told. The Coachman's Yarn. Edwin James Brady. PoAu-1

This is a theme for muted coronets. The Plot against Proteus. A. J. M. Smith. OBCV

This is a white. Imperial Thumbprint. Tom Weatherly. PoBA

This is a wild land, country of my choice. Rocky Acres. Robert Graves. LiTB; NoAM; UnPo

This is a word we use to plug. Variations on the Word *Love*. Margaret Atwood. NoAM

This is about about, until now a subject reference. About. James Sherry. LP

This is about the summer and the wheels of sleep. The Salt Pork. Robert Clayton Casto. HeIP

This is about the women of that country. The Women in Vietnam. Grace Paley. NMM

This is an accidental couple like millions. The Back Seat Dodge '38. Patrick Conrad, *tr. by* Peter Nijmeijer. DuIn

This Is an African Worm. Margaret Danner. BPo

This is an ancient pattern on these hills. American Vineyard. Mildred Cousens. GoYe

This is an ancient waltz. Louis Aragon, *tr. fr. French by* Nancy Cunard. *Fr.* Tcheliabtraktrostroi Waltz. RHTwFP

This is the day of the night it began to turn. By the Sea. Cynthia Macdonald. ER

This is the day the circus comes. Parade. Rachel Lyman Field. *Fr.* A Circus Garland. OBCA

This is the day when all through the town. Sunday. Elizabeth J. Coatsworth. AmFN

This is the day when the fairy kind. Friday. Sir Walter Scott. BoTP

This is the dead fiddle. Look where the wood. The Dead Fiddle. Humbert Wolfe. TrJP

This is the death by water. This is dying. Dead Marine. Louis O. Coxe. WaP

This is the debt I pay. The Debt. Paul Laurence Dunbar. AmNP; BANP; CDC; SoSe

This is the desk I sit at. That Day. Anne Sexton. BoWoP

This is the dragon's country, and these his own streams. Dragon Country: To Jacob Boehme. Robert Penn Warren. PPP

This is the easy time, there is nothing doing. Wintering. Sylvia Plath. NMM

This is the end of him, here he lies. Amy Levy. NOBVV; TrJP

This is the end of the book. Written at the End of a Book. Langdon Elwyn Mitchell. AA

This is the face of him, whose quick resource. On Seeing a Little Child Spin a Coin of Alexander the Great. Charles Tennyson Turner. NOBVV

This is the feast-time of the year. The Feast-Time of the Year. *Unknown.* OHIP

This is the female form. Walt Whitman. *Fr.* I Sing the Body Electric. ErPo

This is the field where the battle did not happen. At the Un-National Monument along the Canadian Border. William Stafford. HAP; HeIP

This is the first year. The Poet Imagines His Grandfather's Thoughts on the Day He Died. Wing Tek Lum. BrSi

This is the football hero's moment of fame. Settling Some Old Football Scores. Morris Bishop. SD

This is the forest primeval. The murmuring pines and the hemlocks. Longfellow. *Fr.* Evangeline. BeLS, *complete.* (Primeval Forest, The.) WBLP

This is the form my passion takes. A Form of Passion. David McFadden. NOBC

This is the foul fiend Flibbertigibbet: he begins at. Shakespeare. *Fr.* King Lear, III, iii. WSC

This is the future, what we feared. Another Small Town in Georgia. Bin Ramke. NAmP

This Is the Garden. E. E. Cummings. MoAmPo (Sonnet: "This is the garden: colours come and go.") MoAB

This is the gay cliff of the nineteenth century. Brooklyn Heights. John Wain. LiTM; OBTV; OxBTC

This is the gospel of labor. The Gospel of Labor. Henry Van Dyke. WBLP

This is the grave of Mike O'Day. On Mike O'Day. *Unknown.* FaBoEE

This is the green wherein a river chants. The Sleeper in the Valley. Rimbaud. CT, *tr. by* William Jay Smith; OBWP, *tr. by* Robert Lowell; WaaP, *tr. by* Selden Rodman

This Is the Hay That No Man Planted. Elizabeth Jane Coatsworth. OBCA

This is the highest learning. Turn from Self. George Macdonald. PWR

This is the horror that, night after night. Gerald Gould. OxBTC

This is the hour of magic, when the Moon. The Hour of Magic. William Henry Davies. MoBrPo

This is the hour of reckoning. The Mistake. Sami Mahdi, *tr. by* May Jayyusi. MAP

This is the hour that we must mourn. Tenebrae. Austin Clarke. AnIL; BIrV; CIP; IPY; NeIP; NOIV

This is the house of Bedlam. Visits to St. Elizabeths. Elizabeth Bishop. CoAP; VGW

This is the house that Jack built. The House That Jack Built. Mother Goose. BoTP; FaBoBe; OxBoLi; OxNR

This is the house we used to know so well. I. M. H. Maurice Baring. ACP

This is the house where Jesse White. Lowery Cot. L. A. G. Strong. MoBrPo

This is the huge dream of us that we are heroes. The Flowers of Politics, I. Michael McClure. NeAP

This Is the Key. *Unknown.* CH; FaBoCh; FaFP; MoShBr; OxBoLi; Prf ("This is the key of the kingdom.") BoTP; OxNR

This is the key to the playhouse. The Playhouse Key. Rachel Field. BoTP; FaPON

This is the kind/ of marriage they live in. The Way Sun Keeps Falling Away from Every Window. Lyn Lifshin. NeAC

This is the knife with a handle of horn. The House That Jack Built. *Unknown.* NBLV; OxBoLi

This is the land where hate should die. The Land Where Hate Should Die. Denis Aloysius McCarthy. OPP

This is the landscape of the Cambrian age. Coastline. Elaine Feinstein. BrRo

This is the last day of the world. On the river docks. Downwards. C. K. Williams. GeTw

This is the last hotel. Irish Hotel. David Wevill. NYBP

This is the last stroke my toungs clock must strike. Summer's Farewell. Thomas Nashe. *Fr.* Summer's Last Will and Testament. PoEL-2

This is the last time. W. J. Turner. *Fr.* The Seven Days of the Sun. OBMV

This is the law of the Yukon, and ever she makes it plain. The Law of the Yukon. Robert W. Service. CaP

This is the lay of Ike. The Lay of Ike. John Berryman. *Fr.* Dream Songs. LCAP

This is the letter of Hobbes the kilted and corpulent hero. Arthur Hugh Clough. *Fr.* The Bothie of Tober-na-Vuolich, *bk.* IX. FaBoPV

This Is the Life. Louis MacNeice. NoAM

This is the light of the mind, cold and planetary. The Moon and the Yew Tree. Sylvia Plath. CoAP; FaBoMo; FaBoWP; NaP; NYBP; PPP; VGW; WPE; WPOW

This is the light we dream in. Negatives. Charles Wright. PoA

This is the loggia Browning loved. Browning at Asolo. Robert Underwood Johnson. AA

This is *The Making of America in Five Panels.* Empire Builders. Archibald MacLeish. OxBA

This is the meadow of the mind. A Way of Keeping. Nancy Willard. IHMS

This is the metre Colombian. The Metre Colombian. *Unknown.* BXAP; Par

This is the midnight—let no star. The Storm Cone. Kipling. NoAM; OxBTC

This is the month the nightingale, clod-brown. The Nightingale. John Clare. EBVV

This is the morning. The Charge. Jay Wright. DiL; FB

This is the most audacious landscape. The gangster's. Alloy. Muriel Rukeyser. NoAM

This is the most ridiculous womb! Womb Song. Susan Fromberg Schaeffer. IHMS

This is the mountain souvenir. Empress Gensho. *Fr.* Manyo Shu. Ma

This is the mouth-filling song of the race/ that was run by a Boomer. The Sing-Song of Old Man Kangaroo. Kipling. FaPON

This is the naked rock. Right here. From here. Lookout on a Rock on the Heights of Mount Hermon. Abba Kovner, *tr. by* Warren Bargad *and* Stanley F. Chyet. IP

This is the night mail crossing the border. The Night Mail. W. H. Auden. ChTr; GrPl; OxBTC

This is the old way. New Year. Gail N. Harada. BrSi

This is the one song everyone. Siren Song. Margaret Atwood. *Fr.* Songs of the Transformed. HAP; PoA; WeW

This is the only thing that clarifies my life. Days of 1978. Gerald Stern. CAPP

This is the pathway where she walked. Amy. James Matthew Legaré. AA

This is the place/ Where far from the unholy populace. In a Meadow. John Swinnerton Phillimore. OBEV

This is the place/ you would rather not know about. Notes towards a Poem That Can Never Be Written. Margaret Atwood. NOBC

This is the place: be still for a while, my high-pressure steamboat! Nauvoo. Bayard Taylor. OBAL

This is the place I love. Here I belong. Mountain Creed. Medora Addison Nutter. GoYe

This Is the Place to Wait. Horace Gregory. *Fr.* The Passion of M'Phail. MoAmPo

This is the poetry reading. Before the Poetry Reading. Louis Simpson. OxBC

This is the point when we are innocent. In Perfect Time. Dinah Livingstone. DT

This is the prettiest motion. To a Lady That Desired Me I Would Bear My Part with Her in a Song. Richard Lovelace. CaPo

This is the realm no man dares. The World Looks On. Louis I. Newman. PoNe

This is the river that had to be dammed. Pentagonia. G. E. Bates. NYBP

This is the road I tread today. The Death of Moses. *Unknown, tr. by* Alice Lucas. TrJP

This is the room where summer ends. Ararat. Peter Cooley. KS

This is the shack where the old man died. Post Mortem. Verna Loveday Harden. CaP

This Is the Shape of the Leaf. Conrad Aiken. *Fr.* Priapus and the Pool, IV [V]. CMoP; NOBA; OxBA; TrGrPo (Portrait of a Girl.) GoJo; MoAB; MoAmPo

This is the ship of pearl, which, poets feign. The Chambered Nautilus. Oliver Wendell Holmes. *Fr.* The Autocrat of the Breakfast Table, *Ch.* 4. AA; AmPP; FaBoBe; FaFP; FPL; GN; HoPM; LiTA; MOS; NOBA; NoP; OHFP; PoEL-5; PoLF; PrIm; WGRP

This is the silence known, a place. Twentieth Anniversary. Betty Adcock. MT

This is the sin against the Holy Ghost. The Unpardonable Sin. Vachel Lindsay. CMoP

This is the song I rested with. Mammy Hums. Carl Sandburg. PoNe

This is the song of Kuk-ook, the bad boy. The Song of Kuk-ook, the Bad Boy. *Eskimo Oral Tradition.* TTTS

This is the song of Mehitabel. The Song of Mehitabel. Don Marquis. *Fr.* Archy and Mehitabel. FiBHP

This is the song of those who live alone. William Justema. NYBP

This is the song that the truck drivers hear. Song of the Truck. Doris Frankel. AmFN

This is the sorrowful story. The Legends of Evil, I. Kipling. MoShBr

This is the south. I look for evidence. New Orleans. Joy Harjo. HATNAP; STE

This is the southeast section of town now. The Southeast Ramparts of the Seine. Judit Tóth, *tr. by* Emery George. VWA

This is the stagnant hour. Drunken Lover. Owen Dodson. AmNP

This is the story/ of a beautiful. Reading Plato. Jorie Graham. MAYP

This is the story that I've always loved. The Story. Iain Crichton Smith. NPo

This is the sugar. At the Long Island Jewish Geriatric Home. Jorie Graham. NPGG

This is the surest death. Mortality. Naomi Long Madgett. PoBA; PoNe

This is the tale of the man. Ticonderoga; a Legend of the West Highlands. Robert Louis Stevenson. OBNV

This is the tale that Cassidy told. The Mornin's Mornin. Gerald Brennan. BLPA

This is the tale that was told to me. A Sailor's Yarn. James Jeffrey Roche. MOS; NA

This is the terminal: the light. At the San Francisco Airport. Yvor Winters. AiP; HeIP; InPK; NIP; NOBA; QFR

This Is the Time. Josina Machel. WMBCH

This is the time lean woods shall spend. Sundown. Léonie Adams. MoAB; MoAmPo; TrGrPo

This is the time of the crit, the creeple, and the makeiteer. Five Men against the Theme "My Name Is Red Hot. Yo Name Ain Doodley Squat." Gwendolyn Brooks. CNA

This is the time of wonder, it is written. It Rolls On. Morris Bishop. ImOP

This is the time of year. The Armadillo[—Brazil]. Elizabeth Bishop. CAPP; HCAP; MoP; NAAL-2; NoAM; NOBA; NoP; NYBP; SM; TAP; VGW

This is the time when fresh, green leaves. Mohammad Taqi Mir, *tr. by* Ahmed Ali. GoT

This is the time when larks are singing loud. The End of April. Robert Fuller Murray. CenHV

This is the true end of desire. The Ballad of the Frozen Field. Dabney Stuart. MT

This is the truth sent from above. The Truth from Above. *Unknown.* OBET

This is the truth what I now tell you. The Miramichi Fire. *Unknown.* AmFP

This is the urgency: Live! The Second Sermon on the Warpland. Gwendolyn Brooks. BPo; NOBA; PoBA

This is the voice of high midsummer's heat. The Mowing. Sir Charles G. D. Roberts. NOBC; OBCV

This is the way. Overture. Linda Pastan. BLA

This is the way a tree: from the rain down. From the Rain Down. Rhina P. Espaillat. GoYe

This is the way I always like you to sit. For Ch'iao. Ya Hsien, *tr. by* Dominic Cheung. IFON

This is the way it is. We see. Ingmar Bergman's "Seventh Seal." Robert Duncan. CAPP; PoE

This is the way it must have been in the first dusk. Invisible Landscape. Charles Wright. LCAP

This is the way the baby slept. The Way the Baby Slept. James Whitcomb Riley. AA

This is the way the ladies ride. Mother Goose. OxNR

This is the way we come. Riding in the Rain. Maxine W. Kumin. RFM

This is the way we do it dear. The Old Whore Speaks to a Young Poet. Dave Smith. SM

This is the way we make our hay. Haymaking. A. P. Graves. BoTP

This is the way we say it in our time. Winfield Townley Scott. ErPo

This is the way we wash our clothes. Wash-Day. Lilian McCrea. BoTP

This is the weather the cuckoo likes. Weather[s]. Thomas Hardy. BoTP; CH; FaBoCh; FaBV; MoAB; MoBrPo; OBMV; RB; SeCePo

This is the week when Christmas comes. In the Week When Christmas Comes. Eleanor Farjeon. PChr; PDV

This is the Wheel of Dreams. Carriers of the Dream Wheel. N. Scott Momaday. CDW

This is the Wild Huntsman that shoots the hares. The Story of the Wild Huntsman. Heinrich Hoffman. NA

This is the wind, the wind in a field of corn. Wind. James Fenton. NAEL-2

This is the wisdom of the ape. The Theology of Bongwi, the Baboon. Roy Campbell. PeSA

This is the Word whose breaking heart. Mathematics or the Gift of Tongues. Anna Hempstead Branch. ImOP

This is the world we wanted. Gretel in Darkness. Louise Glück. AmPA; NoAM

This is the year Europe looks up in sublime disregard. Berlin Interior with Jews, 1939. Lynn Emanuel. MAYP

This is their image: the desert and the wild. Pyramis; or, The House of Ascent. A. D. Hope. PoAu-2

This is their third parting. Now she goes. The Adventurers. John Thompson. PoAu-2

This is Thomas Jones's book. Thomas Jones. FaBoUs

This is thy hour O Soul, thy free flight into the wordless. A Clear Midnight. Walt Whitman. HAP; OxBSP

This is to say, my dear Augusta. King William's Dispatch to Queen Augusta. Coventry Patmore. FaBoEE

This is to say we remember. Not that remembering saves us. For Victor Jara. Miller Williams. SM

This Is Today. David W. Martinez. NOVW

This is too good for words. I lie here naked. Fritz. Gerald Stern. AnAn

This is true Love, by that true Cupid got. The Dance of Love. Sir John Davies. *Fr.* Orchestra; or, A Poem[e] of Da[u]ncing. EiL; SeCePo

This is what/ the villagers told me. *Unknown. Fr.* Manyo Shu. FCEI

This is what I want to happen. Offering. Robert Bly. NU

This is what it was like? God on a donkey. The Palms. David Knight. MoCV

This Is What the Watchbird Sings, Who Perches in the Lovetree. Bruce Boyd. NeAP

This is what we really want. By Fiat of Adoration. Oscar Williams. LiTM

This is what you changed me to. Pig Song. Margaret Atwood. NoP

This is where he finds you. February. Over the phone. Over the Phone. Mekeel McBride. MAYP

This is where I wanted to be. 33. David St. John. NAmP

This is where I yank the old roots. Change. Ellen Bass. ER

This is where the scarlet lords-and-ladies. Under the Cliff. Geoffrey Grigson. WaP

This is where the serpent lives, the bodiless. Wallace Stevens. *Fr.* The Auroras of Autumn, I. CMoP; PoE

This is where we're at the gate. Photograph at the Cloisters: April 1972. Helen Chasin. NMM

This is Willy Walker, and that's Tam Sim. *Unknown.* OxNR

This island, garlanded with wild woods. Archilochus, *tr. by* Guy Davenport. OBVE

This island is the world's end. The Island. Sean Jennett. NeIP; SeCePo

This Island Mopsy. Victor Questel. PBCV

This isn't what I want to write I. Amir Gilboa, *tr. by* Warren Bargad *and* Stanley F. Chyet. IP

This Italian square. Dancers at the Moy. Paul Muldoon. BIrV

This? it's my Lounge Lizard look, very. Up. Bill Kushner. GLP; UL

This jar of roses and carnations on the window-sill. Decoration. Mary Ursula Bethell. ATNZ; PeNZ

This Journey. Ingrid Jonker, *tr. fr. Afrikaans by* Jack Cope *and* William Plomer. BoWoP

This journey through another world, beyond bad dreams. Sacristans. Elizabeth Cook-Lynn. *Fr.* Journey, III. HATNAP

This Kampuchea. Jay Parini. BLA

This Kansas boy who never knew the sea. Kansas Boy. Ruth Lechlitner. AmFN

This kind o' sogerin' ain't a mite like our October trainin'. Letter, A. James Russell Lowell. *Fr.* The Biglow Papers: 1st Series, No. II. OxBA

This knot I knit. To Know Whom One Shall Marry. *Unknown.* GBP

This kyng lay at Camylot upon Krystmasse. *Unknown, tr. fr. Middle English by* Brian Stone. *Fr.* Sir Gawain and the Green Knight. PoE

This lady, curled like a shell. The Shellpicker. Ronald Perry. NePoEA-2
This Lady She Wears a Dark Green Shawl. *Unknown.* AmFP
This land grows the oldest living things. Karl Shapiro. *Fr.* California Winter. AmFN
This Land Is Your Land. Woody Guthrie. OPP
This land like a mirror turns you inward. Dark Pines under Water. Gwendolyn MacEwen. NOBC
This landscape demands: open vowels. Campi Flegrei. Barend Toerien, *tr. by the author.* PeSA
This landscape, masterpiece of modern terror. Tapestry of the Great Fear. Louis Aragon, *tr. by* Malcolm Cowley. RHTwFP
This Last Pain. William Empson. CMoP; EBEV; FaBoMo; GTBS-P; LiTM; MoAB; MoBrPo; NoAM; OAEL-2; SeCePo
This late in our century. Sheltering the Same Needs. Alex Kuo. UL
This lay, a favorite of mine. Honeysuckle (Chevrefoil). Marie de France, *tr. by* Patricia Terry. BoWoP
This legend is told of me. Actaeon. Rayner Heppenstall. FaBoTw
This legendary house, this dear enchanted tomb. Monticello. May Sarton. GOA
This let me further add, that nature knows. Ovid, *tr. fr. Latin by* Dryden. *Fr.* Metamorphoses: Of the Pythagorean Philosophy. OBVE
This Life. Rita Dove. AmPA
This Life. William Drummond of Hawthornden. *See* This life which seems so fair.
This Life. *Unknown.* FaBoRV
This Life a Theater. Palladas, *tr. fr. Greek by* Robert Bland. NIP
This Life Is All Chequer'd with Pleasures and Woes. Thomas Moore. ELP
This life is but a game of cards. Life's a Game. *Unknown.* BLPA
This Life Is Full of Numbness. Christina Rossetti. *Fr.* Later Life, XXVI. Son
This life is not a circus where. Lawrence Ferlinghetti. *Fr.* A Coney Island of the Mind. PPP
This life like no other. Gregory Orr. AmPA
This life, which seems [*or* seemes] so fair [*or* faire]. Madrigal. William Drummond of Hawthornden. CH; ElL; GTBS; GTBS-P; OAEL-1; OBS; SeCePo; TrGrPo
(This Life.) CH; TrGrPo
This life's a hollow bubble. Fin de Siècle. Edmund Vance Cooke. BLPA
This lilac loses its leaves. Vertigos or Contemplation of Something That Is Over. Alejandra Pizarnik, *tr. by* Yishai Tobin. VWA
This Lime-Tree Bower My Prison. Samuel Taylor Coleridge. EnRP; FaBoPP, *br. sel.*; HeIP; NAEL-2; NIP; PoE; PoEL-4; TOF
This Little Bride and Groom Are. E. E. Cummings. AmPP
This little bunny said, "Let's play." Finger Play. Maud. BoTP
This little courtyard—the wind is pure. Wen Cheng-ming, *tr. fr. Chinese by* Jonathan Chaves. *Fr.* The Chung-i Temple. CoBLCP
This little flag to us so dear. The Union Jack. Jeannie Kirby. BoTP
This little flower from afar. With a Pressed Flower. James Russell Lowell. AnAmPo
This Little House Is Sugar. Langston Hughes. NTCP
(Winter Sweetness.) RAR
This little house swallows. Ray A. Young Bear. STP
This little old lady I meet. One That Got Away. Jenny Joseph. NPo
This little pig built a spaceship. Frederick Winsor. *Fr.* The Space Child's Mother Goose. RHPC
This little pig had a rub-a-dub. *Unknown.* OxNR
This little pig went to market. Mother Goose. OxNR
This little residence is far from any village. Hermit Li's Herb Garden Retreat at T'ung-ch'uan. Hsü Pen, *tr. by* Jonathan Chaves. CoBLCP
This little vault, this narrow room. An Epitaph on the Lady Mary Villiers. Thomas Carew. SeCP
(Another [Epitaph on Lady Mary Villiers].) CaPo
(Epitaph, An.) OBEV
(Other, An.) SeCV-2
This Living Hand, Now Warm and Capable. Keats. BoLoP; InPK; InPS; NoP; OAEL-2
(This Living Hand.) HAP; OxBSP
(To Fanny Brawne.) NOBE
This Loneliness for You Is like the Wound. Dunstan Thompson. WaaP; WaP
This lonely following in the old town. Lines for a Young Wanderer in Mexico. John Logan. PoA
This, Lord, was an anxious brother, and. Funeral Oration for a Mouse. Alan Dugan. HAP; NIP; OBD, *st.* 1; PPP
This Love. Judith Hemschemeyer. GOYP
This love, I canna' bear it. Love's Pains. John Clare. NOBVV

This love is a rich cry over. A Black Wedding Song. Gwendolyn Brooks. CNA
This love puts all humanity from me. Thomas Hardy. *Fr.* She, to Him, IV. TOF
This lovely flower fell to seed. For My Grandmother. Countee Cullen. *Fr.* Four Epitaphs. MoAmPo; VGW
This lovely little life whose toes. With the Shell of a Hermit Crab. James Wright. NoP; SM
This loving attention to the details. At a Private Showing in 1982. Maxine W. Kumin. SV
This Lunar Beauty. W. H. Auden. MoAB; MoBrPo; OBMV; OxBTC; RB; SOTW
This luxury they call the Flesh. Phineas Pratt. Gloria MacArthur. GoYe
This lyfe, I see, is but a cheyre feyre. *Unknown.* *Fr.* Farewell, This World. ChTr
This mad carnival of loving. Heine, *tr. fr. German by* Emma Lazarus. *Fr.* To Angélique. TrJP
"This making of bastards great." Song: Old Rowley the King. *Unknown.* APAS
This man escaped the dirty fates. Flyer's Fall. Wallace Stevens. MoAB
This man is o so. Item. E. E. Cummings. MoAB; MoAmPo
This man likes to dive. Cold Logic. Barney Hutchinson. SD
This man, this stranger in my arms. Indian Summer. Barbara Howes. IHMS
This man was generous not because he wanted to see himself as generous. Convergence of the Many. René Char, *tr. by* Thomas Merton. RHTwFP
This Man Was Strong. C. Day Lewis. Son
This man, who his own fatherland forgets. He Is My Countryman. Antoni Slonimski, *tr. by* Frances Notley. TrJP
This man whose homely face you look upon. Abraham Lincoln. Richard Henry Stoddard. GN; OHIP
This man's poems are unusable. Verdict. Ernst Jandl, *tr. by* Beth Bjorklund. CoAuP
This mast, new-shaved, through whom I rive the ropes. Choosing a Mast. Roy Campbell. FaBoTw; PeSA
This May Be Your Captain Speaking. Christian Karlson Stead. ATNZ
This meadow is sickly but pretty in the fall. Saffron. Guillaume Apollinaire, *tr. by* Michael Benedikt. POS
This Measure. Léonie Adams. MoAB; MoAmPo
This Memory. Roger Giroux, *tr. fr. French by* Anthony Barnett. RHTwFP
This menopause of mine. Bloody Pause. Astra. BrRo
This metal is engraved with Shang-style markings. Hsü Chung-hsing, *tr. fr. Chinese by* Jonathan Chaves. *Fr.* Thanking Prince Chen-chi. CoBLCP
This midnight breathing. A House Divided. Michael Ondaatje. MoCV
This midnight brings a moonless. Is This All That Remains of Love? Yusuf al-Sa'igh, *tr. by* Diana Der Hovanessian *with* Salma Khadra Jayyusi. MAP
This midnight dream whispered to me. The Dream about Our Master, William Shakespeare. Hyam Plutzik. Mes; RB
This might have been a place for sleep. Thistledown. Harold Monro. BrPo; OxBTC
This mighty empire hath but feet of clay. Theoretikos. Oscar Wilde. BrPo
This mighty god is tall as heaven. Stone Man Peak. Chao Meng-fu, *tr. fr. Chinese by* Jonathan Chaves. *Fr.* Twenty-Eight Poems Inscribed on T'ien-kuan Mountai. CoBLCP
This mild September mist recalls the soul. The Origin of Centaurs. Anthony Hecht. NePoEA
This miracle in me I scan. William Baylebridge. *Fr.* Life's Testament, VIII. PoAu-1
This Moment. Annie Johnson Flint. BLRP
This moment is precious. Urgency. Sarah E. Wright. PoNe
This month of May, one pleasant eventide. Medieval Norman Song. *Unknown, tr. by* John Addington Symonds. AWP
This monument will outlast. This Monument Will Outlast ("Exegi monumentum aere perennius.") Horace, *tr. fr. Latin. Fr.* Odes, III, 30. CTC, *tr. by* Ezra Pound.
This moonlit evening. Kimpu, *tr. by* Hiroaki Sato. FCEI
This morn a young squire shall be made a knight. On Knighthood. Folgore da San Geminiano, *tr. by* John Addington Symonds. AWP
This morn, ere yet had rung the matin peal. On a Frightful Dream. John Codrington Bampfylde. NOEC
This morn my friend Al mentioned his wife had taken a job. The Day of the Pancreas. David McFadden. NeAC
This Morning. Javier Gálvez. FF
This Morning. Muriel Rukeyser. BoWoP; NMM
This Morning. Jon Stallworthy. NoP

This morning/ My child dances naked. Variations on a Theme. Mark Vinz. Psk

This morning/ With a class of girls outdoors. In a Spring Still Not Written Of. Robert Wallace. BoNaP

This morning a cat got. Dad and the Cat and the Tree. Kit Wright. OnUR

This morning after breakfast. Sufficient unto the Day. Cees Buddingh', tr. by Elizabeth Willems-Treeman. DuIn

This morning blue vast clarity of March sky. Birth of Rainbow. Ted Hughes. AnAn; NAs

This morning gathering wood. Sunday Evening. Sam Hunt. PeNZ

This morning I am ready if you are. A Note to the Difficult One. William Sydney Graham. AnAn

This morning I argued with a friend. Listening to Baseball in the Car. Gail Mazur. ASP

This morning I can't seem to get out of bed. Han Yü, tr. fr. Chinese by Burton Watson. Fr. Autumn Thoughts, 6. CoBCP

This morning I clipped my fingernails. Dino. Michael Lassell. Fr. Times Square Poems. GLP

This morning I come to the water again. Going to the Water. Geary Hobson. STE

This morning I feel dreams dying. Overcast Dawn. Roberta Hill Whiteman. NOVW

This morning I fight against the silence. Against the Silences to Come. Ron Loewinsohn. PoM

This morning I found a hare gaoled alive in a gin. The Trapped Hare. Basil Dowling. ATNZ

This morning I have decided not to write. A Midsummer's Rose. Eeva Kilpi, tr. by Aili Jarvenpa. SOP

This morning I held Harriet in my head. True Love. Joe Johnson. CNA

This Morning I Wakened among Loud Cries of Seagulls. Patrick MacDonogh. NeIP

This morning I wanted to bring you roses. The Roses of Saadi. Marceline Desbordes-Valmore, tr. by Deirdre Lashgari. WPOW

This morning I will not. Hitomaro, tr. by Kenneth Rexroth. UnAS

This morning I woke/ to an impatient scratching on the window. Apricot Tree. Magda Isanos, tr. by Willis Barnstone and Matei Calinescu. BoWoP

This morning, in Assisi, I woke. In Assisi. Michael C. Blumenthal. MAYP

This morning, in the faint light of dawn a pheasant called, lords. Unknown, tr. by Hiroaki Sato. FCEI

This morning it was cold in my office study. Sent to the Taoist Holy Man of Ch'üan-chiao. Wei Ying-wu, tr. by Burton Watson. CoBCP

This morning kelp is drying on the dockside. Homage to Hart Crane. Peter Balakian. MAYP

This morning of the small snow. Charles Olson. Fr. The Maximus Poems: Songs of maximus, III. PPP
(All/ wrong.) NoAM, II.

This morning, on the opposite shore of the river. Fire. William Carpenter. Psk

This morning saw I, fled the shower. Contemplation. Francis Thompson. BrPo

This morning, splendid breeze and sunlight. Rai San'yo, tr. fr. Chinese by Burton Watson. Fr. Reading Books, III. FCEI; JLIC-2

This morning the air is fine for Ch'ing-ming. Yang Wei-chen, tr. fr. Chinese by Jonathan Chaves. Fr. Impromptu Inspirations, II. CoBLCP

This morning, the memory of you. Inertia. Vivienne Finch. BrRo

This morning the overhanging clouds are piecrust. Overhanging Cloud. Robert Lowell. Fr. Marriage, st. 14. NAS

This morning the rose wallpaper in my hotel room was replaced. Homeless. Louis Aragon, tr. by Joachim Neugroschel. POS

This morning, there flew up the lane. Lady Lost. John Crowe Ransom. MoAB; MoAmPo; TrGrPo; UnPo

This morning they are putting away the whales. Autumn. William Carpenter. Psk

This morning, timely rapt [or wrapt] with holy fire. On Lucy Countesse of Bedford. Ben Jonson. OBS; SeCP; SeCV-1

This Morning Tom Child, the Painter, Died. Samuel Sewall. SCAP

This morning we found him. Bushed. Charles Lillard. NOBC

This morning we shall spend a few minutes. Money. Howard Nemerov. OxBC; WeW

This morning, when he looked at me. Black All Day. Raymond R. Patterson. PoBA

This morning, when I had to kill. Circle of Struggle. William Pitt Root. NYBP

This morning, when I heard the crows. The Crows. David McCord. MoAmPo.

This morning with a blue flame burning. A Poem for Trapped Things. John Wieners. GLP; NeAP; PoM

This morning, with the rain tapping. Saturday under the Sky. Gary Soto. NAmP

This mossie [or mossy] bank they prest [or press'd or pressed]. A Pastorall Dialogue. Thomas Carew. CaPo; GBL; SeCP

This motel room. Motel. William Mills. MT

This moth caught in the room tonight. Lying Awake. W. D. Snodgrass. HoPM; MoAmPo; NYBP

This mound the Achaeans reared—Achilles' tomb. Epitaph on Achilles. Unknown, tr. by William M. Hardinge. AWP

This much, O heaven—if I should brood or rave. A Prayer in Darkness. G. K. Chesterton. FPL; MoBrPo; PoLF; TrGrPo

This must be a bad dream. We will wake up. On Leaving Town. Alan Dugan. CAPP

This my father taught. Four Things Choctaw. Jim Barnes. HATNAP; STE

This my heart, so flowing and so simple. Poem of the Intimate Agony. Julia de Burgos, tr. by Julio Marzán. InW

This Native Land. Thomas Davis. BoTP

This never-ended searching for the eyes. Egg-and-Dart. Robert Finch. OBCV

This new Daks suit, greeny-brown. Metamorphosis. Peter Porter. OxBTC

This New Day. Vail Read. AH

This new kind of metal will not suffer. Christianite. William Stafford. NoAM

This Newly Created World. Unknown, tr. fr. Winnebago Indian. AiP

This Night. Nathan Alterman, tr. fr. Hebrew by Ruth Nevo. VWA

This Night. Dianne Hai-Jew. BrSi

This Night. William Heyen. MAYP

This Night. Osip Mandelstam, tr. fr. Russian by Daniel Weissbort. VWA

This night cast iron over flat land. The Unreal Song of the Old. James Koller. PoM

This night is pure and clear as thrice refinèd silver. Fountains ("This night is pure and clear as thrice refinèd silver"). Sacheverell Sitwell. MoBrPo

This night last year, attending at the Seiryo Palace. Ninth Month, Tenth Day. Michizane, tr. by Burton Watson. JLIC-1

This night of no moon. Ono no Komachi, tr. by Donald Keene. PBWP

This night presents a play, which publick rage. Prologue to Hugh Kelly's "A Word to the Wise." Samuel Johnson. EBEV; FaPoR

This Night Sees Ireland [or Eire] Desolate. Aindrais MacMarcuis, tr. fr. Irish by Robin Flower. BIrV
(Flight of the Earls, The.) AnIL

"This night shall thy soul be required of thee." Scorpion. Stevie Smith. EBEV; FaBoWP; PoE

This night talk is godless. From Which War. Phillip Yellowhawk Minthorn. STE

This night there is a child born. Unknown. Fr. Three Christmas Carols, III. ACP

This noiseless ball and top so round. Philocles. Leonidas of Tarentum, tr. by F. A. Wright. AWP

This, O my stomach, is a painting. American Heritage. Robert Sward. OBAL

This Octopus Exploits Women. James Fenton. NoAM

This old crabbed man, with his wrinkled, fusty clothes. Old Crabbed Men. James Reeves. ErPo

This Old Hammer. Unknown. RR

This old man grazed thirty head of cattle. The Purpose of Poetry. Jared Carter. MOWH

This old woman. A Warning. Elizabeth Smart. PoPo

This olde man gan looke in his visage. Chaucer. Fr. The Canterbury Tales: The Pardoner's Tale. OBD

This on thy posy-ring I've writ. The Posy Ring. Clément Marot, tr. by Ford Madox Ford. AWP

This once protected flesh the war-god uses. Casualties. Frances Cornford. CN

This one arrived on time. Twins. Gloria Escoffery. PVCV

This One Goes and That One Goes. Rosalía de Castro, tr. fr. Spanish by Kate Flores. DMH

This one, said the sculptor, is the last of the biblical figures. David. Linda Pastan. CRP

This 1,000 lira bill. Doubly Employed. Giancarlo Majorino, tr. by Lawrence R. Smith. NItP

This one was put in a jacket. Counting the Mad. Donald Justice. CAPP; FF; NePoEA; NIP; UnPo

This one's for you, Uncle Bill. Papio. Eric Chock. BrSi

This One's on Me. Phyllis Gotlieb. MoCV; NOBC

This onion-dome holds all intricacies. Greenwich Observatory. Sidney Keyes. MoAB; MoBrPo
This only grant me, that my means may lye. Abraham Cowley. Fr. A Vote.
(Of Myself.) OBS
This oriental country, year after year. A Fan from Korea. Chu Yün-ming, tr. by Jonathan Chaves. CoBLCP
This Our Life. Harold Monro. Mes
This Pacific ocean. This Earth. Phillip Yellowhawk Minthorn. STE
This page I send you, sir, your Newgate fate. Poem upon the Imprisonment of Mr. Calamy in Newgate, A. Robert Wild. APAS
This pagoda penetrates the clouds. The Pagoda of Master Chih. Wang T'ing-hsiang, tr. fr. Chinese by Jonathan Chaves. Fr. Miscellaneous Poems on Spirit-Valley Temple. CoBLCP
This Palace Standeth in the Air. Michael Drayton. Fr. The Fairy Palace. Mes
This Pardoner had hair as yellow as wax. Chaucer. Fr. The Canterbury Tales: Prologue. SCV
This Paris sky, cleaner than winter sky lucid with cold. In the World's Heart. Blaise Cendrars, tr. by Anselm Hollo. RHTwFP
This park is public property and should. Signs. Charles Martin. SM
This perspex model is what you might call a perfect replica. Naming of Private Parts. John Lloyd Williams. BXAP; FaBoPa
This phantom who is always with me. Phantom. Tawfiq Sayigh, tr. by Anne Royal and Thomas G. Ezzy. MAP
This picnic tea. After Walter de la Mare. Peter Titheradge. Fr. Teatime Variations. FaBoPa
This pig got in the barn. Unknown. OxNR
This pit is Hell where through thou now must go. Elizabeth Melvill, Lady Culross. Fr. A Godly Dream. WPE
This Place in the Ways. Muriel Rukeyser. AiP
This place is cold. Three Poems for the Indian Steelworkers. Joseph Bruchac. CDW
This place is near Hua-yang Mountain. Yang Chi, tr. fr. Chinese by Jonathan Chaves. Fr. Living in the Country at Kou-ch'ü in Autumn—Miscellaneous Impressions. CoBLCP
This place is not ours. The New House. Vern Rutsala. GOYP
This place is white. From the Salt Lake City Airport—82. Joy Harjo. GOS
This place moves from me. Poem before Departure. Jean Burden. WPE
This place (quoth she) they say's enchanted. Samuel Butler. Fr. Hudibras, II, 1. NOBL
This Place Rumord to Have Been Sodom. Robert Duncan. NeAP; NOBA; PoM; PPP
This pleasant tale is like a little copse. Sonnet: Written at the End of "The Floure and the Lefe." Keats. EnRP
This ploughman dead in battle slept out of doors. A Private. Edward Thomas. GTBS-P; MMA
This poem by Rupert Brookeborough. A Written Answer. Tom Paulin. FaBCIP
This poem has a door, a locked door. The House. Philip Levine. CAPP
This poem I write to teach the reader. Writing in England Now. Philip O'Connor. OxBTC
This poem is a letter to tell you that I. Transformations. Joy Harjo. HATNAP
This poem is a poem about people. Prologue to a Poem. Natan Zach, tr. by Warren Bargad and Stanley F. Chyet. IP
This poem is about the strength and sadness of potatoes. Potatoes. David Donnell. NIP; NOBC
This poem is an erection. Poemlove (Fragment). José Luis Vega, tr. fr. Spanish. Fr. Erotic Suite. InW
This poem is concerned with language on a very plain level. Paradoxes and Oxymorons. John Ashbery. CAPP; HeIP; NoAM; NoP
This Poem Is for Bear. Gary Snyder. Fr. Myths and Texts: Hunting, VI. NoBA; NU
This Poem is for Deer. Gary Snyder. Fr. Myths and Texts: Hunting, VIII. NaP; NOBA
This Poem Is for Nadine. Paul B. Janeczko. GOYP
This poem is not addressed to you. Donald Justice. CAPP
This poem is written in an ancient form. Poem Called Poem. James Whitehead. GrPl
This Poem Should Have Etc. Yona Wallach, tr. fr. Hebrew by Warren Bargad and Stanley F. Chyet. IP
This Poem Will Never Be Finished. Raymond Souster. CaP
This poem's about somebody else, not me. Symbiosis. James Sherry. LP
This poet describes carbon paper, how it lies flat. Salad Days. Susan Musgrave. NoAM
This poet is. Meeting Mick Jagger. Robert Peters. BXAP

This poet loves mountains like his own flesh and blood. I Love Mountains. Ho Shao-chi, tr. by J. D. Schmidt. WFTU
This poetry gets bored of being alone. Living Poetry. Hugo Margenat, tr. by Julio Marzán. InW
This points through place. Canoe. Patrick Anderson. SD
This pool, the quiet sky. March Evening. L. A. G. Strong. MoBrPo
This Poor Man. W. J. Gruffydd, tr. fr. Welsh by Gwyn Jones. OBWVE
This poore damoseyll with chylde is grete. Disposing of a Pregnant Daughter. Unknown. Fr. The Fyftene Joyes of Maryage. OxBLMV
This poring over your Grand Cyrus. On a Romantic Lady. Mary Monck. NOEC
This porthole overlooks a sea. Bendix. John Updike. AnAmPo; NYBP
This portrait which I treasure so. Epigram: The Likeness. Martial, tr. by Brian Hill. PeHV
This precarious peak commands a view. A Trip to Yüeh-lu Temple. Li Tung-yang, tr. by Jonathan Chaves. CoBLCP
This Preparation. Simon J. Ortiz. NOVW
This pretty bird, oh, how she flies and sings! Upon the Swallow. Bunyan. OxBChV
This prince of a former dynasty. A Little Landscape by Chao Ch'ien-li. Yü Chi, tr. by Jonathan Chaves. CoBLCP
This prophecy came by mail. Requiem for "Bird" Parker. Gregory Corso. PoNe
This queen of prey (now prey to you). A Lady with a Falcon on Her Fist. Richard Lovelace. CaPo
This Quiet Dust. John Hall Wheelock. MoAmPo
This quiet dust was gentlemen and ladies. Emily Dickinson. CMoP; DL; OxBA
(Cemetery, A.) MoAB; MoAmPo
This quiet morning light. To Mark Anthony in Heaven. William Carlos Williams. NOBA
This quiet mound beneath. Corporal Pym. Walter de la Mare. FaBoEE
This Quintus, Corydon, for whom you lust. "Panormitanus." PeHV
This, quoth the Eskimo master. Latter-day Geography Lesson. R. A. K. Mason. ATNZ; PeNZ
This racer of the watry plain. Catullus. OBVE
This Rage. Silvia Batisti, tr. fr. Italian by Muriel Kittel. DMI
This rain like silver corn, this northern rain. Count Orlo in England. Jon Manchip White. NePoEA
This ration card, once shocking pink. The Ration Card. Liz Sohappy Bahe. CDW
This realm is sacred to the silent past. In a Garret. Elizabeth Akers Allen. AA
This red/ Italian hand. For My Daughter. John Logan. CRP
This red nun on my left hand leans away. Red Right Returning. Louis O. Coxe. WaP
This region, surely, is not of the earth. Naples. Samuel Rogers. OBTV
This revelation, the retreat of tide. Liberation. Diane Mei Lin Mark. BrSi
This reverend shadow cast that setting sun. Upon Bishop Andrewes His Picture before His Sermons. Richard Crashaw. OBS
This rich marble doth enter. An Epitaph on the Marchioness of Winchester. Milton. OBS
This road ends in a field of grain. Documentation. Michael Palmer. NPGG
This road I'm taking is long and bright. Artemis. Rita Boumi-Pappas, tr. by Eleni Fourtouni. AIW
This road is like a tomb. On Passing Two Negroes on a Dark Country Road Somewhere in Georgia. Conrad Kent Rivers. IDB
This road is so fuzzy. Cinéma Vérité. Dorothy Walters. IHMS
This road: no one taking it as autumn ends. Basho, tr. fr. Japanese by Burton Watson. Fr. Seventy-six Hokku. FCEI
This road winds smooth. The Belly of the Land. Luci Tapahonso. STE
This Rocky Land. Väinö Kirstinä, tr. fr. Finnish by Aili Jarvenpa. SOP
This room, how well I know it. The Afternoon Sun. C. P. Cavafy, tr. by Edmund Keeley and Philip Sherrard. VMG
This room I know so well becomes. The Room. Elizabeth Jennings. NePoEA-2
This room is not for staying. Demon-Lover. Sylvia Paskin. DT
This room is very old and very wise. Sam Harrison. NeIP
This root of bog-oak the sea dug up she found. Trouvaille. Richard Murphy. IPY
This rose tree is not made to bear. Envy. Charles and Mary Lamb. OxBChV
This Royal Infant. Shakespeare. Fr. King Henry VIII, V, iv. NAs
This royal throne of kings, this sceptred isle. John of Gaunt Speaks. Shakespeare. Fr. King Richard II: John of Gaunt's Dying Speech. FaBoPP; FaPoR
(This Blessed Plot. This England.) FaBV

This rudely sculptured porter-pot. Undying Thirst. Antipater of Sidon, *tr. by* Robert Bland. AWP

This rule in gardening ne'er forget. *Unknown.* FaBoUs

This Runner. Francis Webb. CBAP

This rusty mound of cans. Rural Dumpheap. Melville Cane. AmFN

This sad world we inhabit. *Unknown. Fr.* The Calendar of Oengus. NOIV

This sadness could only be a color. When You Leave. Kimiko Hahn. BrSi

This said; he (begging) gather'd clouds from land. Ulysses in the Waves. Homer, *tr. fr. Greek by* George Chapman. *Fr.* Odyssey, V. OBS

This said; he high Olympus reacht, the king then left his coach. Priam and Achilles. Homer, *tr. fr. Greek by* George Chapman. *Fr.* The Iliad, XXIV. OBS

This said, he reacht to take his sonne. Homer, *tr. fr. Greek by* George Chapman. *Fr.* The Iliad, VI. OBVE

This said, he turned about his steed. Sidrophel, the Rosicrucian Conjurer. Samuel Butler. *Fr.* Hudibras, II, 3. OxBoLi

This sailor knows of wondrous lands afar. The Child and the Mariner. W. H. Davies. CH

This saying good-by on the edge of the dark. Good-by and Keep Cold. Robert Frost. CMoP

This sea will never die, neither will it ever grow old. Middle of the World. D. H. Lawrence. HAP; NoAM

This seems, in a world where love must take its chances. Mona Van Duyn. *Fr.* Footnotes to "The Autobiography of Bertrand Russell," II. HAP

This sentence have I left behind. A Nameless Epitaph. Matthew Arnold. FaBoEE

This shade-bestowing pear-tree, thou. The Pear-Tree. *Unknown, tr. fr. Chinese by* Allen Upward. *Fr.* Shi King. AWP

This shadow at my shoulder doesn't shed. Climbing. Jennifer Maiden. CBAP

This shall be called the laying on of hands. A Necessary Miracle. Eda Lou Walton. NYBP

This sheepskin coat may be worn out. Wearing a Worn-Out Coat. Chin Nung, *tr. by* Jonathan Chaves. CoBLCP

This shepherdess. Christmas Hymn. Sister Juana Inés de la Cruz, *tr. by* Samuel Beckett. MexPo

This ship is the ship of butchery and increase. Songs for the Cisco Kid; or, Singing: Song #2. K. Curtis Lyle. PoBA

This Shirt. Arturo Trías, *tr. fr. Spanish by* Julio Marzán. InW

This short straight sword. R. A. K. Mason. PeNZ

This silken wreath, which circles in mine arm. Upon a Ribband. Thomas Carew. CaPo; OAEL-1
(Upon a Ribband.) PoE

This sky is to be opened. Hermetic Bird. Philip Lamantia. VGW

"This small lodge is now." Old Man, the Sweat Lodge. Phil George. GrPl; NOVW

This Smoking World. Graham Lee Hemminger. *See* Tobacco is a dirty weed.

This snowy morning, alone. Basho, *tr. fr. Japanese by* Burton Watson. *Fr.* Seventy-six Hokku. FCEI

This Solitude of Cataracts. Wallace Stevens. LCAP

This song of late autumn. Autumn. Itzig Manger, *tr. by* Joseph Leftwich. TrJP

This song of mine sets my soul free. Vusumzi's Song. L. T. Manyase, *tr. by* C. M. Mcanyangwa *and* Jack Cope. PeSA

This song of mine will wind its music around. My Song. Rabindranath Tagore. OHIP

This Song Shows Me Pictures; Morningside Drive, New York City 1950-1960. Richard Oyama. BrSi

This soup is cold. The Soup of Venus. James Tate. AmPA

This sparrow/ who comes to sit at my window. The Sparrow. William Carlos Williams. DiL; InPS; LCAP; PrIm; VGW

This speech all Trojans did applaud; who from their traces loos'd. The Trojans Outside the Walls. Homer, *tr. fr. Greek by* George Chapman. *Fr.* The Iliad, VIII. OBVE

This spiritual man left the world behind. Sent to Be Inscribed on the Temple of P'u-jun. Yü Chi, *tr. by* Jonathan Chaves. CoBLCP

This spoke, a huge wave tooke him by the head. Homer, *tr. fr. Greek by* George Chapman. *Fr.* Odyssey, V. MOS; OBVE

This spoonful of chocolate tapioca. Thinking of the Lost World. Randall Jarrell. NoAM; NOBA

This spot is the sweetest I've seen in my life. *Unknown.* FiBHP

This spring as it comes bursts up in bonfires green. The Enkindled Spring. D. H. Lawrence. NoAM

This spring night. Teika, *tr. by* Geoffrey Bownas *and* Anthony Thwaite. PeBJV

This Spring of Love. Shakespeare. *Fr.* The Two Gentlemen of Verona, I, iii. ChTr

This spring, the sky is leaking. Finding Serenity. Yüan Mei, *tr. by* Jonathan Chaves. CoBLCP

This spring, you'd swear it actually gets dark earlier. Turning Thirty. Katha Pollitt. InPS; WeW

This square. The Moments-of-Past-Happiness Quilt. Kathleen Spivack. ER

This star is only an augury of the morning. And in the 51st Year of That Century, While My Brother Cried in the Trench, While My Enemy Glared from the Cave. Hyam Plutzik. RB

This starry world, and I in it. Death. James Oppenheim. WGRP

This statue of Liberty, busy man. The Statue of Liberty. Thomas Hardy. LiTB

This steaming night in Vientiane. A filthy room. The Room above the White Rose. Joseph Stroud. NPGG

This Stone. *Unknown, tr. fr. Greek by* Goldwin Smith. AWP

This stone. Stone Hammer Poem. Robert Kroetsch. NOBC

This stone commemorates his name. Epitaph on a Dwarf. Immanuel Frances, *tr. by* Hyam Maccoby. OBD

This story's strange, but altogether true. "R. B." SCAP

This strange thing must have crept. Fork. Charles Simic. AmPA; HCAP; LCAP; PCP

This stream that. Lady Ise, *tr. fr. Japanese by* Burton Watson. *Fr.* Kokin Shu. FCEI

This string upon my harp was best beloved. Harmonics. William Vaughn Moody. AnAmPo

This sudden cockerel who stood. Cock-Crow. Ralph Nixon Currey. PeSA

This sudden flare of light you've become. Lighting the Colony. Steve Rasnic Tem. BWV

This Summer and Last. Thomas Hardy. OxBTC

This summer is your perfect summer. Never will the skies. To a Child before Birth. Norman Nicholson. NAs

This summer, most friends out of town. Missoula Softball Tournament. Richard Hugo. TSL

This summer's burning heat. Juan Chi, *tr. fr. Chinese by* Burton Watson. *Fr.* Singing of Thoughts. CoBCP

This Sun Is Hot. *Unknown.* BPo

This sun was mine and yours; we shared it. Our Sun. George Seferis, *tr. by* Edmund Keeley *and* Philip Sherrard. VMG

This sun wears a live chemise of blood. Recital. Muhammad Afifi Matar, *tr. by* Ferial Ghazoul *and* Desmond O'Grady. MAP

This sunken-eyed moment wobbling. Christmas in Biafra (1969). Chinua Achebe. UAS

This sunlight shames November where he grieves. Autumn Idleness. Dante Gabriel Rossetti. *Fr.* The House of Life, LXIX. GBL; OAEL-2

This sweet sadness. A Snipe in the Marshes. Tamemasa, *tr. by* Steven D. Carter. WFTW

This table/ this chair. What Belongs to Me. Ilse Tielsch, *tr. by* Beth Bjorklund. CoAuP

This tempest sweeps the Atlantic!—Nevasink. Night Storm. William Gilmore Simms. MOS

This terror in whose thrall I am. Interrogation. Qasim Haddad, *tr. by* Lena Jayyusi *and* Christopher Middleton. MAP

This that I give you now. Bread. Stanley Burnshaw. TrJP

This that is washed with weed and pebblestone. The Figurehead. Léonie Adams. WPE

This thatched hut, its master returned. Yang Chi, *tr. fr. Chinese by* Jonathan Chaves. *Fr.* Living in the Country at Kou-ch'ü in Autumn—Miscellaneous Impressions. CoBLCP

This the house of Circe, queen of charms. Circe. Lord De Tabley. NOBVV

This the house that Jack built. The House That Jack Built. *Unknown.* FaBoBe

This, the last ornament among the peers. Hilaire Belloc. OBSV

This the quick halibut's so rusty. All These Examples. Tom Mandel. IAT

This the true sign of ruin to a race. The Decay of a People. William Gilmore Simms. AA

This, the twentieth day of March. A Letter to Three Irish Poets. Michael Longley. BIrV

This, then, is the grave of my son. The Nettles. Thomas Hardy. OxBSP

This they know well: the Goddess yet abides. In Her Praise. Robert Graves. BIrV

This thing called parting. Tsurayuki, *tr. fr. Japanese by* Burton Watson. *Fr.* Kokin Shu. FCEI

This Thing Only. Anna Rydstedt-Dannstedt, *tr. fr. Swedish by* Joanna Bankier. OV

This thing the night flashes. Little Testament. Eugenio Montale, *tr. by* Robert Lowell. PFI

This, this is he; softly a while. Milton. *Fr.* Samson Agonistes. UnPo (Samson Fallen.) OBS

This time/ in the darkness. Stuntman. Lionel Kearns. MoCV

This time, I mean it. A Little Tumescence. Jonathan Williams. ErPo; NeAP; PoM

This time I will. To My Mothers. Sigrid Ammer, *tr. by* Susan L. Cocalis. DMG

This time I'll show up. Hunting Song. *Unknown, tr. by* Jerome Rothenberg. STP

This time of pause is as though. Shag Rock. Ruth France. PeNZ

This time the snow came fiercely down. Of Snow. Norman Brick. WaP

This time we have not returned from a trip. Alfred Kolleritsch, *tr. by* Beth Bjorklund. CoAuP

This time you're with me. Barbara's Land Revisited—August 1978. Geary Hobson. STE

This to the crown and blessing of my life. A Letter to Daphnis. Anne Finch, Countess of Winchilsea. EnLoPo

This Tokyo. Gary Snyder. NeAP

This told, strange Teras touched her lute, and sung. The Wedding of Alcmane and Mya. Chapman. *Fr.* Hero and Leander, Fifth Sestiad. OBSC

This too is an experience of the soul. Isis Wanderer. Kathleen Jessie Raine. OxBS

This Too Is Ars Poetica. István Vas, *tr. fr. Hungarian by* Jascha Kessler. FOC

This, Too, Shall [*or* Will] Pass Away. Lanta Wilson Smith. BLPA

This torch, still burning in my hand. From the Greek Anthology. Robert Krinagoras, *tr. by* Kenneth Rexroth. SD

This torment of love. Describes Rationally the Irrational Effects of Love. Sister Juana Inés de la Cruz, *tr. by* Samuel Beckett. MexPo

This town has docks where channel boats come sidling. Arrivals, Departures. Philip Larkin. MoBrPo

This tragical tale, which, they say, is a true one. Pyramus and Thisbe. John Godfrey Saxe. OnMSP

This Train ("This train is bound for glory, this train"). *Unknown.* OxBoLi
(This Train Don't Carry No Gamblers.) AmFP

This Tree. William Hathaway. NAmP

This tree/ growing out of me. Francisco Arriví, *tr. fr. Spanish by* Julio Marzán. *Fr.* Song for a Transformation. InW

This tree and its trembling. Tree. Antonin Artaud, *tr. by* Michael Benedikt. POS

This tree, here fall'n, no common birth or death. On the Site of a Mulberry-Tree Planted by William Shakespeare, Felled by the Rev. F. Gastrell. Dante Gabriel Rossetti. TW

This tree outside my window here. On Not Saying Everything. C. Day Lewis. NoP

This tree which surprised me. Apple Trees Apple Trees Apple Trees. Nelo Risi, *tr. by* Lawrence R. Smith. NItP

This trip shall take me through hills to the north and east. Kung Tzu-chen, *tr. fr. Chinese by* Shirleen S. Wong. *Fr.* Miscellaneous Poems of the Year Chi-hai, IV. WFTU

This Troilus [*or* Troylus], with blisse [*or* Blysse] of that supprysed [*or* supprised]. Chaucer. *Fr.* Troilus and Criseyde [*or* Criseide], III. EBEV; PoE

This truly wonderful steed. Title of a Swift Horse. *Mongol Oral Tradition, tr. by* C. R. Bawden. WTO

This truth-telling is well enough. Visited. Fleur Adcock. PeNZ

This tuft that thrives on saline nothingness. The Air Plant. Hart Crane. MoAB; MoAmPo; NoP

This twilight of two yeares, not past nor next. To the Countesse of Bedford, on New-Yeares Day. John Donne. OBS

This Tzu-hsia of Hsi-ho. An Inkstone Inscription for the Blind Scholar Ho Yung-kuang. Chin Nung, *tr. by* Jonathan Chaves. CoBLCP

This ultimate austerity. Desert Claypan. Frederick Macartney. PoAu-1

This unheated star is not the kind to take in pious babble. Computer. Otto Orban, *tr. by* Emery George. VWA

This Unimportant Morning. Lawrence Durrell. BoLoP; OxBTC

This urge, wrestle, resurrection of dry sticks. Cuttings. Theodore Roethke. CAPP; HCAP; LCAP; MoP; NAAL-2; NoAM; NOBA; TAP; UnPo

This Urn Contains Earth from German Concentration Camps. Audre Lorde. ER

This vale of teargas. Unlawful Assembly. D. J. Enright. OxBTC

This valley wood is hedged. An English Wood. Robert Graves. BrPo

This vanishing old road. The New Direction. Emerson Blackhorse Mitchell. NOVW

This vast web, of Nature's weaving. The Cosmic Fabric. Yakov Petrovich Polonsky, *tr. by* Avrahm Yarmolinsky *and* Cecil Cowdery. EaLo

This verandah is fixed. Clouds' Work. Ferreira Gullar, *tr. by* Paul Blackburn. ATCBP

This vers I make. Gavaudan, *tr. by* Paul Blackburn. Pro

This Version of Love. Dorothy Hewett. CBAP

This very day, a little while ago, you lived. Dead on the War Path. *Unknown, tr. by* H. J. Spinden. OBD; WTO

This very remarkable man. On Monsieur Coué. Charles Cuthbert Inge. FaFP

This votive pledge of fond esteem. Stanzas to a Lady, with the Poems of Camoëns. Byron. FaBoUs

This wailing in the wind, this heartless dark. Before Suicide. "Sahir Ludhianvi," *tr. by* Mahmood Jamal. PBMUP

This wall-paper has lines that rise. Missing My Daughter. Stephen Spender. GTBS-P

This warning, Gallus, for thy love I send. Hylas. Sextus Propertius, *tr. fr. Latin by* F. A. Wright. *Fr.* Elegies, I, 20. AWP

This was a love in which there was always. Brief Farewell. Anthony Delius. PeSA

This was a man of mighty mould. On a Bust of Lincoln. Clinton Scollard. OHIP

This was a poet—It is that. Emily Dickinson. AmPP; NAAL-1; NOBA

This Was a Wonderful Night. Gerald Stern. BLA

"This was Mr. Bleaney's room. He stayed." Mr. Bleaney. Philip Larkin. HoPM; InPS; NePoEA-2; OxBC; PoE

"This was Mr. Strugnell's room," she'll say. Mr. Strugnell. Wendy Cope. FaBoPa

This Was My Brother. Mona Gould. CaP

This was my dream! I saw a forest. Robert Browning. *Fr.* Bad Dreams, III. OAEL-2

This was my dream: Nature stood nigh me. A View from Middle-Earth. William Langland. *Fr.* The Vision of Piers Plowman. Mes

This was not to be expected. Seaman, 1941. Molly Holden. CN; FaBoWP

This was our first line of defense. It held. Ferniehirst Castle. Richard Hugo. NoAM

This was sanity—of star and snowflake. Quilt, Dutch China Plate. Marvin Bell. BLA

This was that mystery of clearest light. The Statue of Shadow. John Peale Bishop. LiTA

This was the brown bull of Cuailnge. The Two Bulls. *Unknown, tr. fr. Irish by* Thomas Kinsella. *Fr.* How the Bulls Were Begotten. NOIV

This was the color of coolness. Spring Cellar. Gladys McKee. GoYe

This was the crucifixion on the mountain. Dylan Thomas. *Fr.* Altarwise by Owl-Light, VIII. CMoP

This was the end and yet, another start. Merlin in the Cave: He Speculates without a Book. Thom Gunn. NePoEA

This was the first world, where the wild dove cries. Creation. Louise Townsend Nicholl. GoYe

This was the hawk's way. This was the hawk. Hawk's Way. Ted Olson. HoPM

This was the man God gave us when the hour. George Washington. John Hall Ingham. AA; OHIP; PAH

This was the moment when Before. BC:AD. U. A. Fanthorpe. OBCP

This was the noblest Roman of them all. Portrait of Brutus. Shakespeare. *Fr.* Julius Caesar, V, v. TrGrPo
(Noblest Roman, The.) FaFP

This was the summer when the tired girls. Now Kindness. Peter Viereck. LiTA

This was the time of their heaviest migration. No Matter What, after All, and That Beautiful Word So. Hayden Carruth. BLA

This Was the Woman. George Meredith. *Fr.* Modern Love, III. Son

This was your butterfly, you see. After Wings. Sarah Morgan Bryan Piatt. AA

This was your very first wall, your crib against. Comes Winter, the Sea Hunting. Norman Dubie. MAYP

This water is so clear. The Fisherman Writes a Letter to the Mermaid. Joan Aiken. WSC

This water, sad and fearful. Slow Rain. Gabriela Mistral, *tr. by* Gunda Kaiser *and* James Tipton. PBWP

This way from the north. Corn-grinding Song. *Unknown, tr. by* N. Barnes. WTO

This way I salute you. City Johannesburg. Mongane Wally Serote. WMBCH

This Way Only. Lesbia Harford. PoAu-1

This Way, This Way. Abba Kovner, *tr. fr. Hebrew by* Bernhard Frank. MHeP

This way, this way, come and hear. Song in the Wood. John Fletcher. *Fr.* The Little French Lawyer. EIL

This wayward virgin girl of my thought. Inhibition. Fahmida Riaz, *tr. by* Mahmood Jamal. PBMUP

This weighty machine. The Army. Hagiwara Sakutaro, *tr. by* Hiroaki Sato. FCEI

This wet sack, wavering slackness. MacDuff. Charles Tomlinson. NAs; OxBC

This while we are abroad. An Ode Written in the Peak[e]. Michael Drayton. FaBoPP; OBS

This white chrysanthemum doesn't have a speck of dust. Basho, *tr. fr. Japanese by* Burton Watson. *Fr.* Seventy-six Hokku. FCEI

This white sedge hat came from Kyoto yesterday. *Unknown, tr. by* Hiroaki Sato. FCEI

This whole land belongs to me sleeping and awake I see. Amir Gilboa, *tr. by* Warren Bargad *and* Stanley F. Chyet. IP

This wight all mercenary projects tries. Sir Samuel Garth. *Fr.* The Dispensary. OBSV

This wild carriage hurtles at a wild canter. If My Bones Must Be Handed Over. Milán Füst, *tr. by* Edwin Morgan. MHuP

This wild night, gathering the washing as if it were flowers. From the Roof. Denise Levertov. NoP

This will I do for my true love, Craig. The Vampire's Tryst. Wade Wellman. VVA

This will really try you. Mamma! Frank Horne. BPo

This Wind. Tom Kryss. NeAC

This Wind That Loiters. Odysseus Elytis, *tr. fr. Greek by* Edmund Keeley *and* Philip Sherrard. VMG

This window frames an alien climate. The Documentary on Brazil. Alfred Corn. MAYP

This wine I have brewed for you. Tabito. *Fr.* Manyo Shu. Ma

This wine-press is call'd war on earth. Blake. *Fr.* Milton, I. EBEV (Wine-Press of Los, The.) EnRP

This winter's morning, turning the other way. Turning. Robert Finch. MoCV; OBCV

This Winter's Weather It Waxeth Cold. *Unknown.* InvP

This woman had a number of beautiful lovers. Disfigurement. Yannis Ritsos, *tr. by* Edmund Keeley. AnAn

This woman is getting on her last bus. Poem for Jacqueline Hill. *Unknown.* BrRo

This Woman That I Am Becoming. Marcie Rendon. GOS

This woman vomiten [*or* vomiting] her. Present. Sonia Sanchez. CNA; ER; WPOW

This woman with a dead face. A Cold Front. William Carlos Williams. NAs

This wondrous art in the human realm. To a Pyrotechnist. Chao Meng-fu, *tr. by* Jonathan Chaves. CoBLCP

This worker is a fearless one. The Riveter. Mabel Watts. RHPC

This world/ is amazingly flat. Natalya Gorbanyevskaya, *tr. by* Barbara Einzig. BoWoP

This world—/ call it an image. Sanetomo, *tr. fr. Japanese by* Burton Watson. *Fr.* Twenty-four Tanka. FCEI

This world/ no road that takes us out of it. Shunzei, *tr. fr. Japanese by* Burton Watson. *Fr.* Thirty Tanka. FCEI

This world a-hunting is. William Drummond of Hawthornden. OxBSP

This world a vale of soul-making. In Cemeteries. Dennis Joseph Enright. OxBC

This world and this life are so scattered, they try me. Zu fragmentarisch ist Welt und Leben. Heine, *tr. by* Charles Godfrey Leland. AWP

This World I'd Wish to Leave and God to Serve. Compiuta Donzella, *tr. fr. Italian by* Muriel Kittel. DMI

This world is gradually becoming a place. John Berryman. *Fr.* Dream Songs. MoP; NoAM; NOBA

This world is not, as you may think. Mohammad Taqi Mir, *tr. by* Ahmed Ali. GoT

This world is not conclusion. Emily Dickinson. EaLo; NAAL-1

This world is so full. Princess Takata. *Fr.* Manyo Shu. Ma

This world is very odd we see. Reply to Dipsychus. Arthur Hugh Clough. FaBoCo

This World Lives Because. Ilam Peruvaluti, *tr. fr. Tamil by* A. K. Ramanujan. PLW

This world was not. The Golden Age. Ernest Francisco Fenollosa. AA

This world was once a fluid haze of light. Tennyson. *Fr.* The Princess, 4 *ll.* ImOP

This worlde is full of variaunce. The Duplicity of Women. John Lydgate. MeEL

This worthy lymytour, this noble Frere. The Friar's Prologue. Chaucer. *Fr.* The Canterbury Tales. PoE

This would be spring, if seasons could be found. Perhaps the Best Time. William Meredith. NePoEA

This would not be the war we fought in. See, the foliage. Newsreel. Adrienne Rich. *Fr.* Shooting Script, 9. FaBoWP; HCAP

This year/ I took sick with the peonies. Masaoka Shiki, *tr. fr. Japanese by* Burton Watson. *Fr.* Thirty-nine Haiku. FCEI

This year,/ I'm raising the emotional ante. These Green-going-to-Yellow. Marvin Bell. CAPP; FYAP; LCAP

This year,/ Next year. *Unknown.* OxNR

This year again the bruise-colored oak. Seeing the Bones. Maxine W. Kumin. NoAM

This year I intended children. Margaret Atwood. NeAC

This year I traveled far. Yehuda Amichai, *tr. fr. Hebrew by* Warren Bargad *and* Stanley F. Chyet. *Fr.* Jerusalem 1967, 1. IP

This year of famine, old and young suffer many strange diseases. Pien Kung, *tr. fr. Chinese by* Jonathan Chaves. *Fr.* Mooring at K'ou-ch'üeh, II. CoBLCP

"This year she has changed greatly"—meaning you. Change. Robert Graves. OxBTC

This year, till late in April, the snow fell thick and light. The Nineteenth of April. Lucy Larcom. PAH

This year turning sixty-four, elements. Nangaku Gentai, *tr. by* Lucien Stryk *and* Takashi Ikemoto. ZPCJ

This year's ice age is half gone. February. Leo Vroman, *tr. by the author and* Peter Nijmeijer. DuIn

This yellow velvet visitor. Caterpillar. R. E. Rashley. CaP

This Yonder Night I Sawe a Sighte. *Unknown.* NAs

This yonge fresshe wenche, wel loking honey-swete. The Hicche-Hykeres Tale. W. F. N. Watson. BXAP

This, you were sure, whatever happened. A Pair of Shoes. Theodore Weiss. NoAM

Thisbe. Helen Gray Cone. AA

Thise olde gentil Britons in hir dayes. The Franklin's Prologue. Chaucer. *Fr.* The Canterbury Tales. NAEL-1; OAEL-1

Thistle, The. Jerzy Harasymowicz, *tr. fr. Polish by* Czeslaw Milosz. PwPP

Thistle. Eeva Kilpi, *tr. fr. Finnish by* Aili Jarvenpa. SOP

Thistle. Nikolai Alekseevich Zabolotsky, *tr. fr. Russian by* Daniel Weissbort. RB

Thistle and darnel and dock grew there. Nicholas Nye. Walter de la Mare. BoTP

Thistle, briar, thorn. Charles Brasch. *Fr.* The Estate, XXX. ATNZ

Thistle-Down. Clara Doty Bates. AA

Thistle whips spitefully across brown thigh. Judean Summer. Fay Lipshitz. VWA

Thistledown. Denis Glover. *Fr.* Sings Harry. ATNZ; PeNZ

Thistledown. James Merrill. UnPo

Thistledown. Harold Monro. BrPo; OxBTC

Thistledown blows over the poisoned fields. The Martyred Earth. Ewart Milne. BIrV

Thistledown's flying, though the winds are all still, The. Autumn ("The thistledown's flying."). John Clare. BoNaP; HAP; NU; PoEL-4; WeW

Thistles. Ted Hughes. NoAM; OxBSP; OxBTC

Tho' [*or* Though] grief and fondness in my breast rebel. London. Samuel Johnson. PoEL-3; TEP

Tho he is young. The Red Road. Nila NorthSun. STE

Tho' I can not your cruelty constrain. Sir Thomas Wyatt. SiPS

Tho' I my party long have chose. Moderation. Christopher Smart. *Fr.* Hymns for the Amusement of Children, IX. NOCV

Tho' ill at ease, a stranger and alone. Thoughts on Pausing at a Cottage near the Paukataug River. Sarah Kemble Knight. SCAP

Tho' I'm no Catholic. The Catholic Bells. William Carlos Williams. CMoP; NOBA; OxBA

Tho' my verse is exact. Hence These Rimes. Bert Leston Taylor. FiBHP

Tho' unfit to tak' part i' loife's battles. Homely Advice to the Unemployed. Samuel Laycock. PF

Tho when as chearelesse night ycovered had. Spenser. *Fr.* The Faerie Queene, III, 12. OAEL-1

Tho' You May Boast You're Fairer. *Unknown.* OBS

Thocht raging stormes movis us to schaik. The Reid in the Loch Sayis. *Unknown.* OxBS

Thocht that this warld be verie strange. Solace in Age. Sir Richard Maitland. OxBS

Thoeisu. David Melnick. IAT

Thomas à Becket, a Dramatic Comedy, *sel.* George Darley. "Speckle-black Toad and freckle-green Frog." FM

Thomas à Kempis. Richard Rogers Bowker. AA

Thomas à Kempis. Lizette Woodworth Reese. AA

Thomas and Charlie. Peter Wild. AmPA

Thomas at Chickamauga. Kate Brownlee Sherwood. PAH

Thomas Carlyle. *Unknown.* FiBHP

Thomas Cromwell. *Unknown.* ESPB

Thomas Dudley, Ah! Old Must Dye. *Unknown.* SCAP

Thomas Gray's View of Nature. William Mason. *Fr.* The English Garden, III. NOEC

Thomas Hardy. Walter de la Mare. NoAM

Thomas Hardy and A. E. Housman. Max Beerbohm. NBLV

Thomas Hardy Considers the Newly-Published Special Theory of Relativity. Brian W. Aldiss. BWV

Thomas in the Fields. Lois Moyles. NYBP

Thomas Iron-Eyes. Marnie Walsh. WPOW

Thomas Jefferson [1743-1826]. Rosemary *and* Stephen Vincent Benét. FaPON

Thomas lay on the Huntlie bank. Thomas the Rhymer. *Unknown.* ELP; FaBoCh; GoTS; InPS; LiTB; NOBE; OAEL-1, *with music;* OBEV; OnMSP; OxBB, *with music;* Prf
    (Thomas Rhymer [and the Queen of Elfland].) CH; ChTr; ESPB, A *and* C *vers.;* FaBoBa; HAP
    (Thomas Rymer.) ESPB
    (Thomas The Rimer.) EnSB; InPK
    (True Thomas.) OxBS; TrGrPo

Thomas Logge. Walter de la Mare. FaBoEE

Thomas MacDonagh. Francis Ledwidge. *See* He shall not hear the bittern cry.

Thomas o Yonderdale. *Unknown.* ESPB

Thomas Rhymer [and the Queen of Elfland]. *Unknown. See* Thomas the Rhymer.

Thomas Rymer. *Unknown. See* Thomas lay on the Huntlie bank.

Thomas Sackevyll in Commendation of the Worke to the Reader. Thomas Sackville. AAS

Thomas Shadwell the Poet. Dryden *and* Nahum Tate. *Fr.* Absalom and Achitophel: Part II. ChTr

Thomas Stuart was a lord. Lord Thomas Stuart. *Unknown.* ESPB

Thomas the Rhymer [*or* Rimer]. *Unknown.* ELP; EnSB; FaBoCh; GoTS; InPK; InPS; LiTB; NOBE; OAEL-1, *with music;* OBEV; OnMSP; OxBB, *with music;* OxBS; PoE; Prf; RB; TrGrPo

Thomas, the vagrant piper's son. John Masefield Relates the Story of Tom, Tom, the Piper's Son. Louis Untermeyer. *Fr.* Mother Goose Up-to-Date. MoAmPo

Thoralf and Synnöv. Hjalmar Hjorth Boyesen. AA

Thoreau. Amos Bronson Alcott. AA

Thoreau. Rodney Jones. MAYP

Thoreau,/ grabbing on, hard. The Distances to the Friend. Jonathan Williams. NeAP

Thoreau's Flute. Louisa May Alcott. AA

Thorn, The, *sel.* Wordsworth. EnRP
    "High on a mountain's highest ridge." Par

Thorn Leaves in March. W. S. Merwin. TwCP

Thorn Piece. Amy Lowell. PeHV

Thorn tree, pale and sharp, The. The Tree of Hatred. Shmuel Moreh, *tr. by the author.* VWA

Thorn Vine on the Wall. *Unknown, tr. fr. Chinese by* Burton Watson. CoBCP

Thorns. Haim Gouri, *tr. fr. Hebrew by* Warren Bargad *and* Stanley F. Chyet. IP

Thorns have whitened along the way, The. Do Not Accompany Me. Shimon Halkin. VWA, *tr. by* Ruth Nevo

Those animals that follow us in dream. Lupus in Fabula. Malcolm Lowry. OBCV
    (Xochitepec.) NOBC

Those at garage sales. Garage Sales. Paul Sawyer. SoTCo

Those awful words "Till death do part." Early Thoughts of Marriage. Nathaniel Cotton. FaBoUs; OxBChV
    (Marriage.) FaBoUs

Those Beauteous Maids. Moses ibn Ezra, *tr. fr. Hebrew by* Solomon Solis-Cohen. TrJP

Those before Us. Robert Lowell. LCAP

Those Being Eaten by America. Robert Bly. CoAP; NaP

Those Betrayed at Dawn. Stanislaw Wygodski, *tr. fr. Polish by* Isaac Komem. VWA

Those bitter feelings. Tamekane, *tr. by* Steven D. Carter. WFTW

Those blessed structures, plot and rhyme. Robert Lowell. CAPP; HCAP; NAAL-2; NoAM; NoP

Those Boys That Ran Together. Lucille Clifton. CNA; PoBA

Those calm swamp-green eyes. Pisces Child. Sandra McPherson. NMM

Those Cambridge generations, Russell's, Keynes'. On Bertrand Russell's "Portraits from Memory." Donald Davie. FaBoTw

Those charming eyes within whose starry sphere. On the Death of Catarina de Attayda. Luis de Camões, *tr. by* R. F. Burton. AWP

Those cherry blossoms. Ietaka, *tr. by* Steven D. Carter. WFTW

Those city states staked out. The Hyperboreans. Tom Paulin. FaBCIP

Those clarities detached us, gave us form. The Tourist and the Town. Adrienne Rich. NePoEA-2

Those creatures that live forever, the fossils. Fossils. Dan Pagis, *tr. by* Bernhard Frank. MHeP

Those dabbing hens I ferociously love. Cock before Dawn. Norman MacCaig. OxBC

Those dark mountains face to face. Dark Mountains. Milton Lockyer, *tr. by* Frank Wordick. CBAP

Those days I didn't even notice. Ishikawa Takuboku, *tr. fr. Japanese by* Hiroaki Sato. *Fr.* Forty-seven Tanka in Three Lines. FCEI

Those days we spent on Lebanon. On Lebanon. David Gray. AA

Those days when it was all right. Letter to E. Franklin Frazier. Imamu Amiri Baraka. BPo; PoBA

Those dreams that on the silent night intrude. On Dreams. Swift. BIrV

Those—dying then. Emily Dickinson. NoP; OBD

Those earlier men that owned our earth. The After-Comers. Robert Traill Spence Lowell. AA

Those early-rice paddies by the hill. Teika, *tr. fr. Japanese by* Hiroaki Sato. *Fr.* A Compendium of Good Tanka. FCEI

Those eyes (dear Lord) once brandons of desire. On Mary Magdalene. William Drummond of Hawthornden. OAEL-1

Those eyes that [*or* which] set my fancy on a fire. Conquest [*or* His Lady's Might]. Philippe Desportes. AWP
    (His Lady's Might.) OBSC
    ("Those eyes which set my fancy on a fire.") OBSC

Those famous men of old, the Ogres. Ogres and Pygmies. Robert Graves. CMoP; FaBoMo; LiTB; LiTM; MoP; NoAM; SeCePo

"Those fantastic forms, fang-sharp." City without Walls. W. H. Auden. NYBP

Those flaming Christians with their hygienic rose. Burns Singer. *Fr.* Sonnets for a Dying Man, XXXIII. NePoEA-2

Those Flapjacks of Brown's. Bert Leston Taylor. OBAL

Those flaxen locks, those eyes of blue. To My Son. Byron. NAs

Those former loves wherein our lives have run. James Agee. *Fr.* Sonnets, XIX. MoAmPo

Those four black girls blown up. American History. Michael S. S. Harper. BPo; HCAP; NoAM

Those Gambler's Blues. *Unknown.* AS

Those gathered by heartache in alien lands. Beyond Memory. Monny De Boully. VWA, *tr. by* Aleksander Nejgebauer

Those good students who only loved working. Led by the Hebrew School Rabbi. Judith Baumel. ASP

Those graves, with bending osier bound. A Night-Piece on Death. Thomas Parnell. SeCePo

Those great rough ranters, Branns. A Simplification. Richard Wilbur. CMoP

Those great sweeps of snow that stop suddenly six feet from the house. Snowbanks North of the House. Robert Bly. AiP; LCAP

Those groans men use. The Mutes. Denise Levertov. IHMS; NaP; NOBA

Those hands which you so clapt [*or* clapped], go now and wring. Upon the Lines and Life of the Famous Scenic Poet, Master William Shakespeare. Hugh Holland. OBWVE
    (Shakespeare Dead.) ACP

Those high floating clouds. Love Likened to Clouds. Tamesada, *tr. by* Steven D. Carter. WFTW

"Those hours, that with gentle work did frame." Shakespeare. *Fr.* Sonnets, V. TEP

Those Hours When Happy Hours Were My Estate. Edna St. Vincent Millay. PrIm

Those houses haunt in which we leave. Ghosts. Elizabeth Jennings. NePoEA-2

Those I vainly wish to meet are like the whales. Poem Begun in the Haro Strait When I Was 28 and Finished When I Was 38. Sandra McPherson. NAmP

Those Images. W. B. Yeats. CMoP

Those in the vegetable rain retain. Stories of Snow. Patricia K. Page. NOBC; NoP; OBCV; PoA

Those Last, Late Hours of Christmas Eve. Lou Ann Welte. PChr

Those lathered horses galloping past. The Horsemen. Gene Baro. NePoEA-2

"Those lips that love's own hand did make." Shakespeare. *Fr.* Sonnets, CXLV. Son

Those long black tresses. Teika, *tr. by* Steven D. Carter. WFTW

Those long days measured by my little feet. "George Eliot." *Fr.* Brother and Sister. NOBVV

Those long uneven lines. MCMXIV. Philip Larkin. EBEV; NAEL-2; NoAM; OBWP

Those lumbering horses in the steady plough. Horses. Edwin Muir. CMoP; FaBoCh; OAEL-2; SeCePo

Those Makheta Nights. Frank Mkalawile Chipasula. WMBCH

Those many children running in your space. The Children. Qasim Haddad, *tr.* by Sharif Elmusa *and* Charles Doria. MAP

Those Mathura people, they're rife with vice. Surdas, *tr.* by John Stratton Hawley *and* Mark Juergensmeyer. SSI

Those Men, So Powerful. Stanislaw Baranczak, *tr. fr. Polish by* Magnus Jan Krynski *and* Robert A. Maguire. PwPP

Those men who love the *crwth* and harp. Song and Poetry. *Unknown*, *tr.* by Gwyn Jones. OBWVE

Those men whom the gods wish. Rec Room in Paradise. Tom Clark. UL

Those men with dollars on the mind. Gamble. Linda Hogan. HATNAP

Those moon-gilded dancers. The Gay. "Æ" OBMV

Those most assailed trees. Macrocarpas. Michael Jackson. PeNZ

Those mothers down there off the hill. Seventh Son. Ed Roberson. PoBA

Those my friendships most obtain. Contentment. Nathaniel Cotton. OxBChV

Those nights lit by the moon and the moon's nimbus. Nights in Hackett's Cove. Mark Strand. GeTw

Those occasions involving the veering of axles. Munich Elegy No. 1. George Barker. SeCePo; WaP

Those of Pure Origin. Roy Fuller. FaBoMo

Those old letters have turned. History of Lit: A Communication. István Vas, *tr.* by Jascha Kessler. FOC

Those old tunes take me back. I used to go. Her Dancing Days. Anna Adams. BrRo

Those old Winnebago men. Beautiful Ohio. James Wright. CAPP

Those Others. Ian Wedde. PeNZ

Those paths on the mountainside. Circumambulation of Mt. Tamalpais. Andrew Hoyem. PoA

"Those petty wrongs that liberty commits." Shakespeare. *Fr.* Sonnets, XLI. InvP

Those pines standing in rows. Mononobe Mashima. *Fr.* Manyo Shu. Ma

Those poems that once I wrote for you. Market Place. "Sahir Ludhianvi," *tr.* by Mahmood Jamal. PBMUP

Those quaint old worn-out words! Antiques. Walter de la Mare. PoA

Those ravens black that rested. Heavy-hearted. Judah al-Harizi. TrJP

Those Rebel Flags. John H. Jewett. PAH

Those reckless hosts rush to the wells. Baruch of Worms. TrJP

Those red men you offended were my brothers. In My First Hard Springtime. James Welch. AmPA; CDW

Those rivers run from that land. Robert Creeley. VGW

Those roman stones. Dan, the Dust of Masada Is Still in My Nostrils. Ruth Whitman. VWA

"Those Romans tagged it right." A Literary Tag. Kevin Ireland. ATNZ

Those scraps of paper. Scraps. Susannah Fried, *tr.* by Anthony Rudolf. VWA

Those sedges in light-flooded Naniwa. Lady Otomo no Sakanoe. *Fr.* Manyo Shu. FCEI

Those seven wise men of the past. Tabito. *Fr.* Manyo Shu. FCEI

Those ships which left. Saigyo Hoshi, *tr.* by Arthur Waley. AWP

Those snooty boys in all their purple drag! Strato, *tr.* by Tony Harrison. PeHV

Those speckled trout we glimpsed in a pool last year. Two Fish. Katha Pollitt. DiPo

Those stopped by the barrage. Dirge; for the Barrel-Organ of the New Barbarism. Louis Aragon, *tr.* by Selden Rodman. WaaP

Those tender feelings. Emperor Fushimi, *tr.* by Steven D. Carter. WFTW

Those that can give, open their hands this day. A New Year's Sacrifice: To Lucinda. Thomas Carew. CaPo

Those times I have you when my flesh. For Eyes to Bless You. Pamela Mordecai. PVCV

Those tiny black chips that corrected my breath. Sen-Sen. Richard Frost. SoTCo

Those Troublesome Disguises. Jonathan Williams. NeAP

Those two bad shepherds, hunched above their sheep. Buachaille Etive Mor and Buachaille Etive Beag. Naomi Mitchison. PoSH

Those Two Boys. Franklin P. Adams. FiBHP; TrJP

Those two chairs were not really. Chairs above the Danube. Szabolcs Várady, *tr.* by William Jay Smith. MHuP

Those two young men, dancing quietly together in a corner. Gay Boys. James Kirkup. PeHV

Those upon whom Almighty doth intend. The Frowardness of the Elect in the Work of Conversion. Edward Taylor. SCAP

Those upturned leaves. Cool beneath the Summer Moon. Shotetsu, *tr.* by Steven D. Carter. WFTW

Those village children. On a Journey. Shohaku, *tr.* by Steven D. Carter. WFTW

Those villages stricken with the melancholia of Sunday. Sabbaths, W.I. Derek Walcott. WeW

Those we have loved the dearest. The Fallen. Duncan Campbell Scott. TrPWD

Those we love die like birds. Mai Sayigh, *tr.* by Charles Doria *with* Salma Khadra Jayyusi. MAP

Those we love truly never die. Forever. John Boyle O'Reilly. WGRP

Those were countries simple to observe, difficult. Report from a Planet. Richmond Lattimore. FYAP

Those were good times, in olden days. Written on a Fly-Leaf of Theocritus. Maurice Thompson. AA

Those were the conquered, still too proud to yield. The Battle-Field. Lloyd Mifflin. PAH

Those Were the Days. *Zulu Oral Tradition, tr.* by H. Tracey. WTO

Those who cannot love the heavens or the earth. The Chaff. W. S. Merwin. PPP

Those Who Died for Their Country. *Unknown, tr. fr. Chinese by* Burton Watson. *Fr.* Nine Songs. CoBCP

Those who favor our plan to alter the river. Plans for Altering the River. Richard Hugo. FYAP

Those who fling off, toss head. Meeting Together of Poles & Latitudes: In Prospect. Margaret Avison. NOBC; OBCV

Those who have chosen to pass the night. Violent Storm. Mark Strand. NYBP

Those who have laid the harp aside. To Wordsworth. Walter Savage Landor. OAEL-2

Those who lift the sword. Shinkei, *tr.* by Steven D. Carter. WFTW

Those who lived here are gone. A Ruined House. Richard Aldington. BrPo

Those Who Lost Everything. David Diop, *tr. fr. French by* Langston Hughes. PBA

Those who love Thee may they find. George F. Chawner. BLRP

Those who loved me. Memento Vivendi. Eva Brudne. VWA

Those who piously/ Those who copiously. Attempt at a Description of a Supper of Various Heads in Paris, France. Jacques Prévert, *tr.* by Michael Benedikt. POS

Those who said God is praised. For the New Railway Station in Rome. Richard Wilbur. NePoEA

Those who think the word "terrace" unusable. The Moon. Howard Moss. EOEF

Those who were here are gone. Komachi, *tr. fr. Japanese by* Burton Watson. *Fr.* Kokin Shu. FCEI

Those whose time. The Candle of Brief Times. Anadad Eldan, *tr.* by Bernhard Frank. MHeP

Those Winter Sundays. Robert Hayden. CAPP; CNA; DiL; FF; GrPl; HAP; HCAP; IDB; InPK; LCAP; MoP; NIP; NoAM; NoP; PoBA; PPP; SoSe; UnPo; WeW

Those with experience look for a special kind. Going for Peaches, Fredericksburg, Texas. Naomi Shihab Nye. MT

Those years, I was a green-youthed wanderer. Arriving in Lo-yang Again. Shao Yung, *tr.* by Burton Watson. CoBCP

Those Zionists. Crescenzo Del Monte, *tr. fr. Judeo-Romanesque by* Barbara Garvin. VWA

Thothmes, who loved a pyramid. The Story of Pyramid Thothmes. *Unknown.* NA

Thou alive on earth, sweet boy. Francis Davison. OBSC

Thou art as a lone watcher on a rock. England. Richard Edwin Day. AA

Thou Art Coming! Frances Ridley Havergal. WGRP

Thou Art Indeed Just, Lord, If I Contend. Gerard Manley Hopkins. AWP; BrPo; CMoP; EaLo; EBVV; GTBS-P; HAP; HoPM; InPK; LiTM; MoAB; MoBrPo; NAEL-2; NoAM; NOBE; NOBVV; NoP; OAEL-2; TOF; TrPWD; UnPo
(Justus Quidem Tu Es, Domine.) EBEV

Thou art King of Israel and of Davides kunne. A Palm-Sunday Hymn. William Herebert. MeEL

Thou art like to a flower. The Translated Way. Franklin P. Adams. FiBHP

Thou art lost to me forever!—I have lost thee, Isadore! The Widowed Heart. Albert Pike. AA

Thou art love's victim; and must die. Richard Crashaw. *Fr.* A Hymn to the Name and Honour [*or* Honor] of the Admirable Saint[e] T[h]eresa. OBD

Thou art mine, thou hast given thy word. Song from a Drama. Edmund Clarence Stedman. AA

Thou art my God, sole object of my love. Prayer of St. Francis Xavier. Pope. TrPWD

Thou art not dead, although the spoiler's hand. Africa. Lewis Alexander. CDC

Thou art not dead, my Prote! thou art flown. To Prote. Simmias of Thebes, *tr. by* John Addington Symonds. AWP

Thou Art Not Fair. Thomas Campion. EIL; InvP
("Thou art not fair for all thy red and white.") AAS; EnLoPo; OBSC

Thou art not near me, but I see Thine eyes. I Love Thee. Josephine D. Henderson Heard. CBWP-4

Thou art not, Penshurst, built to envious show. To Penshurst. Ben Jonson. FaBoPP; FaBoPV; JCP; NAEL-1; NIP; NoP; OAEL-1; OBS; PoE; PoEL-2; PPP; SeCP; SeCV-1; TEP

Thou art not so black as my heart. A Jet Ring Sent. John Donne. OxBSP
(Jet [*or* Jeat] Ring Sent, A.) PoEL-2

Thou Art, O God, the God of Might. Emily Swan Perkins. AH

Thou art, O God, the life and light. The Glory of God in Creation *or* Thou Art, O God. Thomas Moore. OHIP; TrPWD
(Thou Art, O God.) TrPWD; PWR

Thou Art of All Created Things. Pedro Calderón de la Barca, *tr. fr. Spanish.* WGRP

Thou art present in my shadowiness. Venus Poised. Rafael López, *tr. by* Samuel Beckett. MexPo

Thou art so fair, and young [*or* yong] withal [*or* withall]. Youth and Beauty. Aurelian Townshend. GBL; MePo; SeCP

Thou art the essence of all created things. Thou Art of All Created Things. Pedro Calderón de la Barca. WGRP

Thou Art the Sky. Rabindranath Tagore. *Fr.* Gitanjali, LXVII. OBMV

Thou art the soul of a summer's day. Paul Laurence Dunbar. AmNP

Thou art the Star, blazing with beames bright. Star of the Sea. Alexander Barclay. *Fr.* The Ship of Fools. ACP

Thou Art the Tree of Life. Edward Taylor. AH

Thou Art the Way. George Washington Doane. AH

Thou art the Way. "I Am the Way." Alice Meynell. ACP; NOBVV; OBMV; OxBSP

Thou art to all lost love the best. To the Willow-Tree. Robert Herrick. CaPo; OBEV

Thou, att whose feete I waste mie soule in sighes. To Mie Tirante. George Darley. Son

Thou barren waste; unprofitable strand. Winter in Lower Canada. Standish O'Grady. *Fr.* The Emigrant. NOBC; OBCV

Thou beauteous off-spring of a syre as fair. On a Sunbeam. Thomas Heyrick. MePo

Thou Beautiful Sabbath. *Unknown, tr. fr. Yiddish* by Isidore Myers. TrJP

Thou bleedest, my poor heart! and thy distress. On a Discovery Made Too Late. Samuel Taylor Coleridge. EnRP; Son

"Thou blind fool, Love, what dost thou to mine eyes." Shakespeare. *Fr.* Sonnets, CXXXVII. WeW

Thou Blind Man's Mark. Sir Philip Sidney, *sometimes considered Sonnet CIX of* Astrophel and Stella; *also in* Certain Sonnets. ErPo; HeIP; NAEL-1; PPP; Son
(Desire.) LiTB; NOBE; OBSC; SiPS; TrGrPo

Thou blossom bright with autumn dew. To the Fringed Gentian. Bryant. AA; AnAmPo; AWP; FaBoBe; FPL; GN; NoP; PoLF; TAP

Thou booby, say'st thou nothing but cuckoo? Of the Cuckoo. Bunyan. PBBP

Thou, born to sip the lake or spring. On a Honey Bee [*or* To a Honey Bee]. Philip Freneau. TAP
(To a Honey Bee.) AA; AnAmPo

Thou, burning Topaz. Invocation and Proposition. Carlos de Sigüenza y Góngora, *tr. fr. Spanish by* Samuel Beckett. *Fr.* Eastern Evangelic Planet. MexPo

Thou canst not die whilst any zeal abound. Samuel Daniel. *Fr.* To Delia. OBSC; Son

Thou canst not prove that thou art body alone. The Ancient Sage. Tennyson. WGRP

Thou cheat'st us Ford, mak'st one seem two by art. Upon Ford's Two Tragedies, "Loves Sacrifice" and "The Broken Heart." Richard Crashaw. OBS

Thou Christ, my soul is hurt and bruised! The Doubter. Richard Watson Gilder. TrPWD

Thou comest, much wept for: such a breeze. Tennyson. *Fr.* In Memoriam A. H. H., XVII. EBVV

Thou comest to me, thou exultest, seeing my beauty. Hymn of Victory: Thutmose III. Amon-Re, *tr. by* James Henry Breasted. WaaP

Thou cursed cock, with thy perpetual noise. On a Cock at Rochester. Sir Charles Sedley. FaBoEE; OPOP; TW

Thou dancer of two thousand years. The Dancing Faun. Robert Cameron Rogers. AA

Thou dear and mystic semblance. Lines to the Blessed Sacrament. *Unknown, tr. by* Jeremiah J. Callanan. TIRV

Thou Didst Delight My Eyes. Robert Bridges. ELP; MoAB; MoBrPo

Thou Didst Say Me. Miriam Waddington. OBCV

Thou divinest, fairest, brightest. The Satyr's Farewell. John Fletcher. *Fr.* The Faithful Shepherdess, V, i. OBS

Thou, Earth, calm empire of a happy soul. Shelley. *Fr.* Prometheus Unbound, IV. FaBoRV

Thou ever young! Persephone but gazes. To Demeter. Maybury Fleming. AA

Thou fair-hair'd [*or* fair-haired] angel of the evening. To the Evening Star. Blake. *Fr.* Poetical Sketches. BoNaP; CH; ChER; ChTr; EnRP; FaBoRV; FaBV; FPL; NAEL-2; NOEC; NoP; OAEL-2; PoE; PoLF; TEP; TrGrPo; WiR

Thou fool profane, be silent! *Unknown, tr. fr. Hebrew.* *Fr.* Duel with Verses over a Great Man. TrJP

Thou for whose birth the whole creation yearned. The Rise of Man. John White Chadwick. AA

Thou from th' enthroned martyrs blood-stain'd line. Henry King. *Fr.* An Elegy upon the Most Incomparable King Charles the First. OBS

Thou gallant Chief whose glorious name. Washington. Denis O'Crowley. OHIP

Thou gav'st me leave to kiss. Chop-Cherry. Robert Herrick. EnLoPo

Thou glorious mocker of the world! I hear. To the Mocking-Bird. Albert Pike. AA

Thou God of all, whose presence dwells. John Haynes Holmes. TrPWD

Thou God of This Great Vast, Rebuke These Surges. Shakespeare. *Fr.* Pericles, III, i. MOS; NAs

Thou God, whose high, eternal Love. Wedding-Hymn. Sidney Lanier. TrPWD

Thou Grace Divine, Encircling All. Eliza Scudder. AH

Thou Great God. *Unknown, tr. fr. Xhosa* by A. C. Jordan. PBA

Thou great Supreme, whom angel choirs adore. Unseen. Fanny Crosby. TrPWD

Thou green and blooming, cool and shaded hill. The Heart on the Hill. Petrarch, *tr. fr. Italian by* C. B. Cayley. *Fr.* Sonnets to Laura: To Laura in Life, CCV. AWP

Thou grimmest far o grusome tykes. To a Hedgehog. Samuel Thompson. BIrV

Thou Guide to doubt, be silent evermore. *Unknown, tr. fr. Hebrew.* *Fr.* Duel with Verses over a Great Man. TrJP

Thou half-unfolded flower. The Blossom of the Soul. Robert Underwood Johnson. AA

Thou happiest thing alive. To the Boy. Elizabeth Clementine Kinney. AA

Thou happy, happy elf! A Parental Ode to My Son, Aged Three Years and Five Months. Thomas Hood. FiBHP, *abr.*; PoLF
(To My Son, Aged Three Years and Five Months.) FaPON, *abr.*

Thou has come from the old city. The Old City. Ruth Manning-Sanders. CH

Thou Has Wounded the Spirit That Loved Thee. Mrs. David Porter. BLPA

Thou hast been very tender to the Moon. Malvolio. Walter Savage Landor. Par

Thou Hast Diamonds. Heine, *tr. fr. German by* Emma Lazarus. *Fr.* Homeward Bound. TrJP

Thou hast done evil. The Judgment. Dora Read Goodale. AA

Thou hast made me, and shall thy work[e] decay? John Donne. *Fr.* Holy Sonnets, I. EBVV; MeLP; NAEL-1; NOBE; NOCV; NoP; OBS; PoEL-2; SeCP; Son; TEP

Thou hast not drooped thy stately head. Savannah. Alethea S. Burroughs. PAH

Thou hast not left the rough-barked tree to grow. I Was Sick and in Prison. Jones Very. NOBA

Thou hast not rais'd, Ianthe, such desire. Walter Savage Landor. *Fr.* Ianthe. GBL

Thou hast on earth a Trinity. To the Christ. John Banister Tabb. TrPWD

Thou hast stirred. Song of Cradle-making. Constance Lindsay Skinner. CaP

Thou hast thy calling to some palace floor. Elizabeth Barrett Browning. *Fr.* Sonnets from the Portuguese, IV. Son

Thou hearest the nightingale begin the song of spring. Blake. *Fr.* Milton, II. PBBP
(Choir of Day, The.) EnRP
(Lark's Song, The.) WiR
(Vision of Beulah, The. ("Thou hearest the nightingale begin the song of spring").) NOBE
(Vision of the Lamentation of Beulah, A.) OBNC

Thou heaven-threat'ning Rock, gentler then she! Echo to a Rock. Lord Herbert of Cherbury. PoEL-2

Thou heavenly quivering beneath the deathlike above! To a Lark in War-Time. Franz Werfel, *tr. by* Edith Abercrombie Snow. TrJP

Thou hermit, haunter of the lonely glen. The Sand Martin. John Clare. PBBP; TEP

Thou hidden love of God, whose height. John Wesley. NOEC

Thou ill-formed offspring of my feeble brain. The Author to Her Book. Anne Bradstreet. AnAmPo; AmPP; InPK; NAAL-1; NOBA; NoP; OxBA; PoE; SCAP; TAP

Thou inmost, ultimate. To the Body. Alice Meynell. ACP

"Thou jestedst when thou swor'st that thou bettothedst." Tudor Aspersions. R. A. Piddington. FiBHP

Thou king of terrors with thy gastly eyes. A Fig for Thee, Oh! Death. Edward Taylor. NAAL-1

Thou Knowest. Katharine Lee Bates. TrPWD

Thou knowest, love, I know that thou dost know. Michelangelo, *tr. by* John Addington Symonds. PeHV
(Love's Entreaty.) AWP

Thou knowest my praise of nature most sincere. William Cowper. *Fr.* The Task, I. NAEL-1

Thou knowest my years entire, my life. Walt Whitman. *Fr.* Prayer of Columbus. TrPWD

Thou knowest that toads and snakes and loathly worms. Shelley. *Fr.* Prometheus Unbound, III, iv. PoE

Thou knowest, Thou who art the soul of all. Thou Knowest. Katharine Lee Bates. TrPWD

Thou knowest what is best. Trust and Obedience. *Unknown.* BLRP

Thou know'st, my Julia, that it is thy turn. To Julia, the Flaminica Dialis, or Queen-Priest. Robert Herrick. CaPo

Thou large-brained woman and large-hearted man. To George Sand: A Desire. Elizabeth Barrett Browning. BoWoP; NAEL-2; TEP

Thou leanest to the shell of night. James Joyce. EBEV

Thou Light of Ages. Rolland W. Schloerb. TrPWD

Thou Ling'ring Star. Burns. EnRP

Thou little bird, thou dweller by the sea. The Little Beach-Bird. Richard Henry Dana. AA; AnAmPo

Thou Livest, O Soul! Charles Leonard Moore. AA

Thou Long Disowned, Reviled, Oppressed. Eliza Scudder. AH

Thou, Lord, Hast Been Our Sure Defense. John Hopkins. AH

Thou Lord of Hosts, Whose Guiding Hand. Octavius Brooks Frothingham. AH

Thou lovely and belovèd, thou my love. Mid-Rapture. Dante Gabriel Rossetti. *Fr.* The House of Life, XXVI. BLPL; FaBoBe

Thou Lovest Me. Josephine D. Henderson Heard. CBWP-4

Thou mercenary renagade, thou slave. To Mr. Bays. Charles Sackville. APAS

Thou mighty gulf, insatiate cormorant. To Everlasting Oblivion. John Marston. *Fr.* The Scourge of Villainy [*or* Villanie]. OBSC

Thou mighty Mars, the god of soldiers brave. An Epitaph on Sir Philip Sidney. James I, King of England. Son

Thou monstrous gilt and rainbow-tinted thing. The New Organ. Josephine D. Henderson Heard. CBWP-4

Thou Moon, that aidest us with thy magic might. A Charm. Dryden. ChTr

Thou more than most sweet glove. The Glove. Ben Jonson. *Fr.* Cynthia's Revels, IV. EIL; GBL

Thou most absurd of all absurdities. The Sloth. George Romanes. FM

Thou mother dear and thou my father's shade. For Erotion's Grave. Martial, *tr. by* F. A. Wright. OBD

Thou must be true thyself. Be True [*or* Be True Thyself]. Horatius Bonar. FaBoBe; GN; PWR

Thou need'st not flutter from thy half-built nest. The Robbin. John Very. Son

Thou ne're wutt [*or* nere wilt] riddle, neighbour Jan [*or* John]. A Devonshire Song. *At. to* William Strode. OBS; PoEL-2, *sl. diff. vers.*

Thou noblest monument of Albion's isle! Written at Stonehenge. Thomas Warton the Younger. Son

Thou One in All, Thou All in One. Seth Curtis Beach. AH

Thou, paw-paw-paw; thou, glurd; thou, spotted. Adam's Task. John Hollander. NIP; NoP; PPP

Thou perceivest the flowers put forth their precious odors. The Wild Thyme. Blake. *Fr.* Milton, II. WiR

Thou pleasant island, whose rich garden-shores. Corfou. Richard Monckton Milnes. *Fr.* The Ionian Islands. OBTV

Thou Pleiad of the lyric world. Adelina Patti. Adah Isaacs Menken. CBWP-1

Thou, proud man, look upon yon starry vault. Man's Littleness in Presence of the Stars. Henry Kirke White. WBLP

Thou Remainest. Annie Johnson Flint. BLRP

Thou rob'st [*or* robb'st] my days of bus'ness [*or* business] and delights. The Thief. Abraham Cowley. *Fr.* The Mistress. JCP

Thou saidst that I alone thy heart cou'd move. Catullus, *tr. by* William Walsh. OBVE
(To His False Mistress.) OxBSP

Thou saist Love's dart. To Oenone. Robert Herrick. CaPo

Thou saist my lines are hard. To My Ill Reader. Robert Herrick. CaPo

Thou sallow picture of my poison'd love. Cyril Tourneur. *Fr.* The Revenger's Tragedy. OBD

Thou Seemest Like a flower. Heine. *See* Homeward Bound: Du bist wie eine Blume.

Thou seest me, Lucia, this year droop. Crutches. Robert Herrick. CaPo

Thou seest the hills candied with snow. Horace. *See* Odes: I, 9. "Behold yon mountain's hoary height." ("Vides ut alta")

Thou seest the under side of every leaf. Omniscience. Blanche Mary Kelly. TrPWD

Thou sent to me [*or* mee] a heart was crowned [*or* crown'd]. Upon a Diamond Cut in Form[e] of a Heart. Sent in a New Year's [*or* New-yeares] Gift. Sir Robert Ayton. EIL; OBS

Thou shalt have no other gods before me. The Ten Commandments. Bible, *O.T. Fr.* Exodus, XX: 3-17. WBLP

Thou shalt have one God only; who. The Latest Decalogue. Arthur Hugh Clough. ChTr; EBEV; EBVV; FaBoCo; FaBoEE; FF; GTBS-P; HAP; HoPM; NAEL-2; NIP; NOBE; NOBVV; OAEL-2; OBNC; OBSV; OPOP; PPP; WeW; WGRP

Thou Shalt Not. Malka Heifetz-Tussman, *tr. fr. Yiddish by* Marcia Falk. AWP; VWA

Thou shalt not laugh in this leaf, Muse, nor they. John Donne. *Fr.* Satires, V. OBSV

Thou shalt say to the eye of the strange woman: Be the water. In Egypt. Paul Celan, *tr. by* Joachim Neugroschel. VWA

Thou shalt seek the beach of sand. The Fay's Sentence. Joseph Rodman Drake. *Fr.* The Culprit Fay. GN

Thou Ship of Earth, with Death, and Birth, and Life, and Sex aboard. The Ship of Earth. Sidney Lanier. MOS

Thou should'st be living at this hour. Heathcote William Garrod. CenHV

Thou, Sibyl rapt! whose sympathetic soul. Margaret Fuller. Amos Bronson Alcott. AA

Thou simple bird what mak'st thou here to play? Upon the Lark and the Fowler. Bunyan. CH; PBBP

Thou Sleepest Fast. *Unknown.* EIL; OxBSP

Thou snowy farm with thy five tenements! Elinda's [*or* Ellinda's] Glove. Richard Lovelace. CaPo; OBS

Thou, so far, we grope to grasp thee. So Far, So Near. Christopher Pearse Cranch. TrPWD

Thou sorrow, venom elfe. Upon a Spider Catching a Fly. Edward Taylor. AmPP; NOBA; NoP; OxBA; PoEL-3; SCAP; TAP

Thou spark of life that wavest wings of gold. Ode to a Butterfly. Thomas Wentworth Higginson. AA; FaBoBe

Thou speakest always ill of me. To an Acquaintance. *Unknown.* FaFP

Thou stately stream that with the swelling tide. The Lover to the Thames of London, to Favour [*or* Favor] His Lady Passing Thereon. George Turberville. ChTr; EIL; NoP; OBSC

Thou still unravished [*or* unravish'd] bride of quietness. Ode on a Grecian Urn. Keats. AWP; ChER; EBEV; EnRP; FaBoBe; FaFP; FF; FiP; FPL; HAP; HeIP; HoPM; InPS; LiTB; NAEL-2; NAWM-2; NIP; NOBE; NoP; OAEL-2; OBEV; OBNC; OHFP; PoE; PoEL-4; PPP; PrIm; SoSe; TEP; TOF; TrGrPo; UnPo

Thou strainest through the mountain fern. Robert Louis Stevenson. NOBVV

Thou stranger, which for Rome in Rome here seekest. Joachim Du Bellay, *tr. fr. French by* Spenser. *Fr.* Ruins of Rome. FaBoPP; OBVE

Thou swear'st thou'lt drink no more; kind Heaven send. To Julius. Martial, *tr. by* Sir Charles Sedley. FaBoEE

Thou sweetly-smelling fresh red rose. Dialogue: Lover and Lady. Ciullo d'Alcamo, *tr. by* Dante Gabriel Rossetti. AWP

Thou that art by Fates degree. New Canaans Genius; Epilogus. Thomas Morton. SCAP

Thou that art wise, let wisdom minister. Sonnet: He Craves Interpreting of a Dream of His. Dante da Maiano, *tr. by* Dante Gabriel Rossetti. AWP

Thou that at Rome astonished doth behold. Joachim Du Bellay, *tr. fr. French by* Spenser. *Fr.* Ruins of Rome. FaBoPP

Thou that didst grant the wise King his request. The Sins of Youth. Thomas, 2d Baron Vaux of Harrowden Vaux. ACP

Thou that didst leave the ninety and the nine. Missing. John Banister Tabb. TrPWD

Thou that from the heavens art. Goethe, *tr. fr. German.* *Fr.* Wanderer's Night-Songs, I. AWP

Thou that in prayeres hes bene lent. Rise with the Lamb of Innocence. *Unknown.* MeEL

Thou the faint beams of reason's scattered light. Solitude and Reason, in the Village. Abraham Cowley. *Fr.* Of Solitude. FaBoPP

Thou, to whom my name bears witness. Be Not Silent. David ben Meshullam. TrJP

Thou, to whom the World unknown. Ode to Fear. William Collins. NOEC; TrGrPo, *abr.*

Thou too art gone, thou loved and lovely one! To Eddleston. Byron. *Fr.* Childe Harold's Pilgrimage, II. PeHV

Thou, too, sail on, O Ship of State! Longfellow. *Fr.* The Building of the Ship. MOS; PWR
  (O Ship of State.) FaFP
  (Republic, The.) AA; OPP; PAH; WGRP
  (Sail On, O Ship of State.) FaPON
  (Ship of State, The.) FaBoBe; OHIP

Thou tool of faction, mercenary scribe. Upon the Anonymous Author of Legion's Humble Address to the Lords. Thomas Brown. APAS

Thou tryant, whom I will not name. Wedlock; a Satire. Hetty Wright. NOEC

Thou two-faced year, Mother of Change and Fate. 1492. Emma Lazarus. WPE

Thou unrelenting Past! The Past. Bryant. AA

Thou vague dumb crawler with the groping head. To My Tortoise Chronos. Eugene Lee-Hamilton. FM

Thou visitest the earth, and waterest it. Psalm LXV ("Thou visitest the earth."). Bible, *O.T.* *Fr.* Psalms. OHIP, *abr.*

Thou wast all that [*or* that all] to me, love. To One in Paradise. Poe. *Fr.* The Assignation. AA; AmPP; AnAmPo; BLPL; BoLoP; LiTA; OBEV; OxBA; PoLF; TAP; TrGrPo

Thou wast not born for death, immortal Bird! Magic Casements. Keats. *Fr.* Ode to a Nightingale. FaBV

Thou water turn'st to Wine (faire friend of Life). To Our Lord, upon the Water Made Wine. Richard Crashaw. MePo

Thou wert the morning star among the living. To Stella. Plato, *tr. by* Shelley. EnLoPo; FaBoEE; OBVE
  (Morning and Evening Star.) AWP

Thou who art clothed in silk, who drawest on. Man Is a Weaver. Moses ibn Ezra, *tr. by* Emma Lazarus. TrJP

Thou who art Lord of the wind and rain. A Hymn of Thanksgiving. Wilbur D. Nesbit. OHIP

Thou Who Createdst Everything. *Unknown, tr. fr. Middle English by* Donald Davie. NOCV

Thou who didst hang upon a barren tree. Long Barren. Christina Rossetti. PBWP; TrCP

Thou, who didst lay all other bosoms bare. To Shakespeare. Richard Edwin Day. AA

Thou, who dost dwell alone. Desire. Matthew Arnold. WGRP

Thou, who dost feel Life's vessel strand. Edmund Clarence Stedman. *Fr.* The Ordeal by Fire. WGRP

Thou who hast slept all night upon the storm. To the Man-of-War-Bird. Walt Whitman. AA; AmPP; FaBoBe; FM

Thou who, like death's deceiving stroke. The Vampire. Baudelaire, *tr. by* Arthur Symons. VVA

Thou who on Sin's wages starvest. Barnfloor and Winepress. Gerard Manley Hopkins. ACP

Thou, who on some dark mountain's brow. Captain Jones' Invitation. Philip Freneau. MOS

Thou who ordainest, for the land's salvation. God Save the Nation. Theodore Tilton. AA

Thou who, when fears attack. Ode to Tobacco. C. S. Calverley. FaBoCo; FiBHP

Thou who wilt not love, do this. Upon Some Women. Robert Herrick. CaPo

Thou who wouldst see the lovely and the wild. Monument Mountain. Bryant. BeLS

Thou, who wouldst wear the name. The Poet. Bryant. AA; NAAL-1; TAP

Thou, Whom rich and poor adore. An Offer. Arthur Guiterman. TrJP

Thou, whom the former precepts have. Superliminare. George Herbert. SeCP

Thou whose birth on earth. Swinburne. *Fr.* Christmas Antiphones. TrPWD

Thou whose chaste song simplicity inspires. To Mrs. Smith, Occasioned by the First of Her Sonnets. William Hayley. Son

Thou, whose diviner soul hath caus'd thee now. To Mr. Tilman after He Had Taken Orders. John Donne. EBEV

Thou, whose endearing hand once laid in sooth. Edmund Clarence Stedman. AA

Thou, whose unmeasured temple stands. Bryant. BLRP
  (How Amiable Are Thy Tabernacles!) TrPWD

"Thou wilt forget me." "Love has no such word." Spring and Autumn. William James Linton. EBVV

Thou wilt remember. Thou art not more dear. Robert Browning. *Fr.* Pauline. OAEL-2

Thou, with thy looks, on whom I look full oft. The Looks of a Lover Enamoured. George Gascoigne. EIL; SeCePo

Thou wommon boute fere. The Devout Man Prays to His Relations. William Herebert. MeEL

Thou wonder of the Atlantic shore. To Aaron Burr, under Trial for High Treason. Sarah Wentworth Morton. PAH

Thou wouldst be greate and to such height wouldst rise. Greatness. *Unknown.* OBS

Thou youngest virgin-daughter of the skies. To the Pious Memory of the Accomplished [*or* Accomplisht] Young Lady, Mrs. Anne Killigrew, [Excellent in the Two Sister-Arts of Poesie and Painting]. Dryden. NAEL-1; OAEL-1; PoEL-3; SeCV-2
  (Ode to the Pious Memory of the Accomplished Young Lady, Mrs. Anne Killigrew.) OBEV

Thou, Zion, old and suffering. David Levi, *tr. fr. Italian by* Mary A. Craig. *Fr.* The Bible. TrJP

Though a seeker since my birth. A Garland of Precepts. Phyllis McGinley. NBLV

Though a time come. Sanetomo, *tr. fr. Japanese by* Burton Watson. *Fr.* Twenty-four Tanka. FCEI

Though All the Fates Should Prove Unkind. Henry David Thoreau. HAP

Though all thy gestures and discourses be. The Innocent Ill. Abraham Cowley. OPOP

Though Amaryllis Dance in Green. *Unknown.* EIL; NAEL-1; NIP

Though authors are a dreadful clan. I Missed His Book, I Read His Name. John Updike. OBAL

Though aware of our rank and alert to obey orders. Ode: To My Pupils. W. H. Auden. MoBrPo

Though beauty be the mark of praise. Ben Jonson. NoP; OBEV; QFR
  (Elegie, An: "Though beautie be the marke of praise.") SeCV-1

Though Bodies Are Apart. C. Day Lewis. *Fr.* From Feathers to Iron. NAs

Though buds still speak in hints. Field-Glasses. Andrew Young. GTBS-P; RB

Though clasp'd and cradled in his nurse's arms. William Cowper. *Fr.* Hope. PoEL-3

Though clear and bright. *Unknown.* *Fr.* Manyo Shu. Ma

Though clock,/ To tell how night drawes hence, I've none. His Grange, or Private Wealth. Robert Herrick. CaPo; FM; GoJo; SeCV-1

Though conscience void of all offence. Praise. Christopher Smart. OxBChV

Though countless as the grains of sand. Boethius, *tr. fr. Latin by* Samuel Johnson. *Fr.* The Consolation of Philosophy, II, 2. OBVE

Though critics may bow to art, and I am its own true lover. Art and Heart. Ella Wheeler Wilcox. AnAmPo

Though cuckoos call across the kyle. Prospect of a Mountain. Andrew Young. PoSH

Though days do gain upon the night. The Vierzide Chairs. William Barnes. NOBVV

Though divorced, she steps. Buson, *tr. fr. Japanese by* Hiroaki Sato. *Fr.* Eighty-seven Hokku. FCEI

"Though dusty wits dare scorn astrology." Sir Philip Sidney. *Fr.* Astrophel and Stella, XXVI. OAEL-1; Son

Though Earth has full many a beautiful spot. The Land Which No Mortal May Know. Bernard Barton. PWR

Though earthworms are so cunningly contrived. Wet Morning. Janet Frame. ATNZ

Though false rumors pop up as at a fair. Teika, *tr. fr. Japanese by* Hiroaki Sato. *Fr.* A Compendium of Good Tanka. FCEI

Though fast youth's glorious fable flies. Lone Founts. Herman Melville. LiTA

Though Fatherland Be Vast. Allen Eastman Cross. AH

Though frost and snow locked [*or* lock'd] from mine eyes. To Saxham. Thomas Carew. JCP; NoP; OBS

Though gifts like thine the fates gave not to me. To Hafiz. Thomas Bailey Aldrich. AA

Though good things answer many good intents. Crosses. Robert Herrick. CaPo

Though he hung dumb upon her wall. And One Shall Live in Two. Jonathan Henderson Brooks. PoNe

Though he lives in the same town. What She Said. Palaipatiya Perunkatunko, *tr. by* A. K. Ramanujan. PLW

Though He Slay Me. Vassar Miller. NePoEA-2

Though he that, ever kind and true. Verses Written in 1872. Robert Louis Stevenson. BLPA; BLPL

Though heart grows faint and spirits sink. The Word of God. Annie Johnson Flint. BLRP

Though her mother told her/ Not to go a-bathing. Leda and the Swan. Oliver St. John Gogarty. AnIL; HAP

Though I am chidden like a horse. *Unknown. Fr.* Manyo Shu. Ma

Though I am dark. *Unknown, tr. by* Willis Barnstone. BoWoP

Though I am humble, slight me not. The Moss Supplicateth for the Poet. Richard Henry Dana. AA

Though I am Laila of the Persian romance. Princess Zeb-un-Nissa, *tr. by* Willis Barnstone. BoWoP

Though I am native to this frozen zone. Reminiscence. Thomas Bailey Aldrich. AA

Though I Am Young and Cannot Tell. Ben Jonson. *Fr.* The Sad Shepherd, I, v. ELP; NoP; TEP
  (Death and Love.) NOBE
  (Karolin's Song.) PoEL-2
  (Song: "Though I am young and cannot tell.") SeCP

Though I be now a grey, grey friar. The Friar. Thomas Love Peacock. *Fr.* Maid Marian. SD

Though I be wooden Priapus (as thou see'st). Epigrams on Priapus. *Unknown.* ErPo

Though I close my eyes. Ishikawa Takuboku, *tr. fr. Japanese by* Hiroaki Sato. *Fr.* Forty-seven Tanka in Three Lines. FCEI

Though I get home how late, how late! The Return. Emily Dickinson. MoAmPo

Though I had [*or* have] twice been at the doors [*or* doores] of death. To Sir William Alexander. William Drummond of Hawthornden. OBS
  (To Sir W. A.) PoEL-2

Though I have an admiration for your charming resignation. Not Tonight, Josephine. Colin Curzon. ErPo

Though I have given. Lines Written in a Mausoleum. Lillian Grant. GoYe

Though I have silks. *Unknown. Fr.* Manyo Shu. Ma

Though I know in time. Tsurayuki, *tr. fr. Japanese by* Burton Watson. *Fr.* Kokin Shu. FCEI

Though I lie here. Ryokan, *tr. by* Burton Watson. FCEI

Though I must live here, and by force. To My Mistresse in Absence. Thomas Carew. CaPo

Though I only/ saw you dimly. Lady Kasa. *Fr.* Manyo Shu. FCEI

Though I regarded not. Earl of Surrey. AAS; SiPS

Though I see the white azaleas on the shore. *Unknown. Fr.* Manyo Shu. Ma

Though I Should Seek. Henry Ustic Onderdonk. AH

Though I Speak with the Tongues of Men and Angels. Bible, *N.T. Fr.* First Corinthians, XIII: 1–13. OAEL-1
  (Greatest of These, The, *abr.*) TrGrPo

Though I think I'd like to go to France. On a Trip. Hagiwara Sakutaro, *tr. by* Hiroaki Sato. FCEI

Though I Thy Mithridates Were. James Joyce. MoP; NoAM

Though I tried to forget, as I came. Akino Osamaro. *Fr.* Manyo Shu. Ma

Though I try to calm down my soul. Sanu Chigami. *Fr.* Manyo Shu. Ma

Though I with strange desire. Kisses Desired. William Drummond of Hawthornden. EnLoPo

Though I would take comfort against sorrow. The Cry of the Daughter of My People. Bible, *O.T. Fr.* Jeremiah, VIII: 18-23. TrJP

Though I'm old now. *Unknown. Fr.* Manyo Shu. FCEI

Though I'm thinking of you ceaselessly. Beginning of Love. Tanikawa Shuntaro, *tr. by* Hiroaki Sato. FCEI

Though, in the land where rules our sovereign. Hitomaro. *Fr.* Manyo Shu. Ma

Though it be the night when I make. *Unknown. Fr.* Manyo Shu. Ma

Though it will die soon. Basho, *tr. by* Anne Pennington. OBD

Though it's true we were young girls when we met. For Jan, in Bar Maria. Carolyn Kizer. VGW

Though I've a Clever Head. *Unknown.* HAP

Though joy is better than sorrow, joy is not great. Joy. Robinson Jeffers. CMoP

Though knowledge must be got with pain. For Scholars and Pupils. George Wither. OxBChV

Though leaves are many, the root is one. The Coming of Wisdom with Time. W. B. Yeats. FaBoEE; SoSe

Though loath to grieve. Ode Inscribed to W. H. Channing. Emerson. AmPP; HAP; NAAL-1; NOBA; NoP; OxBA; TAP

"Though logic-choppers rule the town." Tom O'Roughley. W. B. Yeats. CMoP

Though love's my daily and my nightly theme. To Emma, Extempore; Hyaena, off Gambia, June 4, 1779. Edward Thompson. NOEC

Though many are the lofty mountains. Tajihi Kunihito. *Fr.* Manyo Shu. Ma

Though many were the hot springs. Akahito. *Fr.* Manyo Shu. Ma

Though marriage by some folks. My Three Wives. *Unknown, after* Etienne Pasquier. FaBoEE

Though men say/ An autumn night is long. *Unknown. Fr.* Manyo Shu. Ma

Though Mine Eye Sleep Not. *Unknown, tr. fr. Hebrew, tr. by* Theodor H. Gaster. *Fr.* The Dead Sea Scrolls. TrJP

Though much a little map unfolds, more still. The River Compared to an Oratorical Sentence. Luis de Góngora y Argote, *tr. fr. Spanish by* Edward Meryon Wilson. *Fr.* The First Solitude. OBVE

Though my eyes could see your spirit soar. Empress Yamato-hime. *Fr.* Manyo Shu. Ma

Though my heart isn't a summer field. Elegies for Prince Atsumichi. Lady Izumi, *tr. fr. Japanese by* Hiroaki Sato. *Fr.* Fifty-one Tanka. FCEI

Though my love, long standing at the gate. *Unknown. Fr.* Manyo Shu. Ma

Though My Thoughts. Francis Daniel Pastorius, *tr. fr. German by* Sheema Z. Buehne. AH

Though my thoughts of her. Hitomaro. *Fr.* Manyo Shu. Ma

Though my wanderings are many. Suibne Geilt. NOIV

Though naked trees seem dead to sight. Hopeless Desire Soon Withers and Dies. "A. W." OBSC

Though naughty flesh will multiply. No Mean City. Patrick MacDonogh. BIrV; OxBSP

Though never in the wards of the hospital for/ Disabled servicemen at Erskine. Warriors. Douglas Dunn. OxBC

Though no blossoms cluster. Mrs. Mary Furman Weston Byrd. Mary Weston Fordham. CBWP-2

Though no kin to those fine glistening. Christening-Day Wishes for My God-Child. Robert P. Tristram Coffin. OFD

Though not commanded. Okura. *Fr.* Manyo Shu. PeBJV

Though not sure of the tale of old. *Unknown. Fr.* Manyo Shu. Ma

Though now in factory wombs. Human Remains. Bruce Boston. BWV

Though once a puppy, and though Fop by name. Epitaph on Fop. William Cowper. OBD

Though one with all that sense or soul can see. Transcendence. Richard Hovey. WGRP

Though only your name still shines. Sappho. Marie von Najmájer, *tr. by* Susan L. Cocalis *and* Gerlinde Geiger. DMG

Though other lands may boast of skies. No Land like Ours. J. R. Barrick. OPP

Though pleasures still can touch my soul. How Singular. Tom Hood. FaBoNo

Though prejudice perhaps my mind befogs. I Think I Know No Finer Things than Dogs. Hally Carrington Brent. BLPA

Though raging stormes movis us to shake. The Reeds in the Loch Sayis. *Unknown.* GoTS

Though Regions Far [*or* Farr] Divided. Aurelian Townshend. JCP; PoEL-2
  (Song: "Though regions farr divided.") MePo

Though riders be thrown in black disgrace. *Unknown, tr. by* Douglas Hyde. BIrV

Though rudely blows the wintry blast. The Charcoalman. John Townsend Trowbridge. AnAmPo

Though Shakespeare asks us, "What's in a name?" Her Christening. Thomas Hood. *Fr.* Miss Kilmansegg and Her Precious Leg. NOBVV

Though short her strain nor sung with mighty boast. Erinna. Antipater of Sidon, *tr. by* A. J. Butler. AWP

Though skilled in Latin and in Greek. To a New England Poet. Philip Freneau. NAAL-1

Though somewhat large, exuberant, and truculent. Byron. *Fr.* Don Juan, IX. OAEL-2

Though spacious lands and oceans and far skies. Through a Glass, Darkly. Basil Dowling. ATNZ

Though the Asuka River. Lady Ise, *tr. fr. Japanese by* Burton Watson. *Fr.* Kokin Shu. FCEI

Though the bee. In Him. James Vila Blake. WGRP

Though the cover is worn. My Old Bible. *Unknown.* BLRP

Though the cunning of the Indian and the Zulu's thirst for blood. Claflin's Alumni. Lizelia Augusta Jenkins Moorer. CBWP-3

Though the day of my destiny's over. Stanzas to Augusta. Byron. EnRP

Though the Earth Be Removed. Bible, *O.T. See* Psalms: Psalm XLVI ("God is our refuge and strength. . .").

Though the glow. Kyogoku Tamekane, *tr. fr. Japanese by* Burton Watson. *Fr.* Twenty-three Tanka. FCEI

Though the great song return no more. The Nineteenth Century and After. W. B. Yeats. FaBoEE

Though the great waters sleep. Emily Dickinson. EaLo

Though the hemp you've spun. *Unknown. Fr.* Manyo Shu. FCEI

Though the land of wave-bright Naniwa. Kanamura. *Fr.* Manyo Shu. Ma

Though the mills of God grind slowly. Retribution. Friedrich von Logau, *tr. by* Longfellow. BLPA

Though the moon beaming matronly and bland. To Lucia at Birth. Robert Graves. NAs

Though the music of love is Schubérty. *Unknown.* PeHV

Though the New Teacher Is a Trifle Odd. Richard Moore. *Fr.* Word from the Hills, XXXVII. Son

Though the nightingale sings. Emperor Gotoba, *tr. by* Geoffrey Bownas *and* Anthony Thwaite. PeBJV

Though the road turn at last. Prisoners. Denise Levertov. NoAM

Though the rough, bitter-sweet haw of pioneering. American History. W. R. Moses. LiTA

Though the roving bee, as lightly. The Bridal Pair. William Young. *Fr.* Wishmakers' Town. AA

Though the shining sun is clearly of the summer sky. Princess Shikishi, *tr. fr. Japanese by* Hiroaki Sato. *Fr.* Seventy-eight Tanka. FCEI

Though the space may be short. Teika, *tr. fr. Japanese by* Hiroaki Sato. *Fr.* A Compendium of Good Tanka. FCEI

Though the spirit seldom moves us. No Regrets. Ned Pastor. SoTCo

Though the tough cough and hiccough plough me through. Ways of Pronouncing "Ough." *Unknown.* FaBoUs

Though the world has slipped and gone. Dame Edith Sitwell. CMoP; LiTM; WaP

Though there are distances between us. Desert Warfare. Michael Longley. CIP

Though there are men without number. *Unknown. Fr.* Manyo Shu. Ma

Though there are wild dogs. Orpheus and Eurydice. Geoffrey Hill. NePoEA-2

Though there was nothing final then. The Parting. Elizabeth Jennings. NePoEA-2

Though they have loved me as the gentle roebuck. Deirdre and the Poets. Ewart Milne. NeIP

Though they say her tomb is here. Akahito. *Fr.* Manyo Shu. Ma

Though this body, I know. Kino Sadamaru, *tr. by* Hiroaki Sato. FCEI

Though this the port, and I thy servant true. Sir Thomas Wyatt. SiPS

Though thou, indeed, hast quite forgotten ruth. Ballata: Of a Continual Death in Love. Guido Cavalcanti, *tr. by* Dante Gabriel Rossetti. AWP

Though thou, my ring, be small. To His Ring, Given to His Lady, Wherein Was Graven This Verse, "My Heart Is Yours." George Turberville. EIL

"Though three men dwell on Flannan Isle." Flannan Isle. W. W. Gibson. CH; PoRA

Though thy constant love I share. To M. T. Bayard Taylor. AA

Though to good breeding she made no pretence. On a Gentleman Marrying His Cook. Colin Ellis. FaBoEE

Though to strangers' approach. Paired Lives. W. R. Rodgers. CIP

Though to think/ Rejoiceth me. Margot Ruddock. OBMV

Though to your life apparent stain attach. Robert Nichols. *Fr.* Sonnets to Aurelia. OBMV

Though Truth and Falsehood be. Seek True Religion! John Donne. *Fr.* Satires, III. NOBE

Though tuneless, stringless, it lies there in dust. The Old Violin. Maurice Francis Egan. AA

Though Virtue be the same when low she stands. To the Lady Lucy, Countess of Bedford. Samuel Daniel. OBSC

Though, waiting for you to come. Okura. *Fr.* Manyo Shu. Ma

Though we lived in the same lane. Answering Li Ying Who Showed Me His Poems about Summer Fishing. Yü Hsüan-chi. BoWoP, *tr. by* Geoffrey Waters

Though we may waver, He remaineth steadfast. The Everlasting Love. Annie Johnson Flint. BLRP

Though we thought it, Doña Carolina did not die. A Dream of Husbands. Alberto Ríos. NoAM

Though winds blow. Narihira, *tr. fr. Japanese by* Burton Watson. *Fr.* Kokin Shu. FCEI

Though Winter come with dripping skies. A Song with a Discord. Authur Colton. AA

Though with the North we sympathize. Shop and Freedom. *Unknown.* PAH

Though wolves against the silver moon do bark. To the Detracted. John Andrews. *Fr.* The Anatomy of Baseness. EIL

Though Ye Suppose. John Skelton. OxBSP

Though you are a continent and two seasons away. Cape Coast Castle Revisted. Jo Ann Hall-Evans. BlSi

Though you are young and I am old. Thomas Campion. OBSC

Though you be absent here, I needs must say. The Spring. Abraham Cowley. *Fr.* The Mistress. HAP; JCP; MeLP; OBS

Though you desire me I will still feign sleep. Reserve. Richard Aldington. BrPo

Though you Diana-like have liv'd still chaste. Lutea Allison. Sir John Suckling. ErPo

Though you say, "Do not grieve!" Yosami. *Fr.* Manyo Shu. Ma

Though you tear the medals. Nightmare Inspection Tour for American Generals. Gibbons Ruark. TW

Though you'll forgive, I think, my sweet. Postscript to a Pettiness. A. S. J. Tessimond. OxBSP

Though your prerogative is to disdain. To His Coy Mistress. Peter Scupham. BXAP

Though your season is not over. *Unknown. Fr.* Manyo Shu. Ma

Though your strangenesse frets my hart. Thomas Campion. AAS

Though you're not exactly blue. When They've Finished Shipping Cattle in the Fall. Bruce Kiskaddon. CowP

Thought. Christopher Pearse Cranch. WGRP

Thought. Fazil Hüsnü Daglarca. CRP

Thought, A. William Henry Davies. MoShBr

Thought. Emerson. AmPP

Thought, The. Herbert of Cherbury. InvP

Thought, A. Mikhail Yurevich Lermontov, *tr. fr. Russian by* Max Eastman. AWP

Thought, The. William Brighty Rands. OBEV

Thought, A. Abram Joseph Ryan. PWR

Thought, A. James Kenneth Stephen. FiBHP

Thought at Walden, A. Henrietta Cordelia Ray. CBWP-3

Thought beneath so slight a film, The. Emily Dickinson. AmPP; OxBA

Thought Eternal, The. Goethe, *tr. fr. German by* Ludwig Lewisohn. AWP

Thought flashed 'cross a kindly mind, A. A Kindly Deed. Priscilla Jane Thompson. CBWP-2

Thought for My Love, A. Bruce Williamson. NeIP

Thought-Fox, The. Ted Hughes. FaBoMo; HeIP; InPS; MoP; NePoEA-2; NoAM; NoP; NYBP; SCV

Thought from Propertius, A. W. B. Yeats. OAEL-2; OxBSP

Thought I heard the wind. Spring at Fort Okanogan. Ramona Wilson. VoR

Thought in Time, A. Robert Hillyer. NYBP

Thought is deeper than all speech. Thought. Christopher Pearse Cranch. WGRP

(Stanza from an Early Poem.) AA

Thought is false happiness: the idea. Crude Foyer. Wallace Stevens. LiTM

Thought [*or* Thoughts] of a Briton on the Subjugation of Switzerland. Wordsworth. EnRP

(England and Switzerland 1802.) GTBS; GTBS-P

(Sonnet: Thought of a Briton on the Subjugation of Switzerland.) ChER

Thought of Death, A. Thomas Flatman. OBS

Thought of dropping bust of Socrates. Underwater Lake Michigan Socrates. "Antler." SoTCo

Thought of Lake Ontario, A. Henrietta Cordelia Ray. CBWP-3

Thought of Marigolds, A. Janice Farrar. GoYe

Thought of Paradise. Wen T'ing-yün, *tr. fr. Chinese by* Lois Fusek. ATF

Thought of what America would be like, The. Cantico del Sole. Ezra Pound. OBAL

Thought of writing came to me today, The. W. H. Auden. *Fr.* Letter to Lord Byron. NOBL

Thought on Human Life, A. *Unknown.* OxBSP

Thought on June 26. Mazisi Kunene. WMBCH

Thought rattles along the empty railings. Respectable People. Austin Clarke. CMoP

Thought-resembling moonlight at a cloud's edge, The. Roman Outposts. Derek Walcott. AnAn

Thought Suggested by the New Year, A. Thomas Campbell. *See* More we live, more brief appear, The.

Thought that in a single day, The. Firth Park Road: 9:30 A.M. Stanley Cook. NPo

Thought was/ & though it had been. *Unknown, tr. fr. Tepehua Indian by* Charles Boilès. *Fr.* Tepehua Thought-Songs, II. STP

Thought went up my mind today, A. Emily Dickinson. AmPP

Thought While Dressing to Meet the "Girls." Alma Denny. SoTCo

Thought: Zero. Fell at his feet wanted to eat him right up. The Knife.
Jean Valentine. LCAP
Thoughts. Maggie Pogue Johnson. CBWP-4
Thoughts about My Daughter before Sleep. Sandra Hochman. TV
Thoughts about the Person from Porlock. Stevie Smith. FaBoCo;
NAEL-2; NoAM; NoP
Thoughts after Ruskin. Elma Mitchell. FaBoWP
Thoughts after Work. David Rubadiri. WMBCH
Thoughts are broken in my memory, The. Dante, *tr. fr. Italian by* Dante
Gabriel Rossetti. *Fr.* Vita Nuova, La, VIII. AWP
Thoughts at the End of Spring—A Farewell Poem for, *sels.* Liang Ch'i-
ch'ao, *tr. fr. Chinese by* Cecile Chu-chin Sun. WFTU
"Trying to stay the departing spring is of no avail." *Fr.* II.
"What is it that troubles you?." *Fr.* I.
Thoughts during an Air Raid. Stephen Spender. MoBrPo
Thought's End. Léonie Adams. MoAB; MoAmPo
Thoughts for a Cold Day. *Unknown.* BoTP
Thoughts for My Grandmother. Laya Firestone. VWA
Thoughts for You (When She Came Back from the Mountains). Ranice
Henderson Crosby. NMM
Thoughts from a Bottle. Carl Clark. JB
Thoughts from Abroad. Patrick Maybin. NeIP
Thoughts in a Garden. Andrew Marvell. *See* How vainly men
themselves amaze.
Thoughts in Separation. Alice Meynell. ACP
Thoughts in the Cold. Li Shang-yin, *tr. fr. Chinese by* Burton Watson.
CoBCP
Thoughts of a Little Girl. María Enriqueta, *tr. fr. Spanish by* Emma
Gutiérrez Suárez. FaPON
Thoughts of a Young Girl. John Ashbery. TAP; VGW
Thoughts of Chairman Mao. David Young. AmPA
Thoughts of God. *Unknown, tr. fr. Gaelic by* Douglas Hyde. WTO
Thoughts of him stalk me even in my dreams. Surdas, *tr. by* John
Stratton Hawley *and* Mark Juergensmeyer. SSI
Thoughts of Home. Arthur Hugh Clough. FL
Thoughts of Jack Kerouac—& Other Things. Peter Olds. ATNZ; PeNZ
Thoughts of Loved ones appear. Margaret Fishback. FiBHP
Thoughts of Men appear, The. Consummation. Thomas Traherne.
SeCV-2
Thoughts of Paradise. Sun Kuang-hsien, *tr. fr. Chinese by* Lois Fusek.
ATF
Thoughts of Paradise. Wei Chuang, *tr. fr. Chinese by* Lois Fusek. ATF
Thoughts of Phena [at News of Her Death]. Thomas Hardy. EBVV;
NOBVV; NoP; OxBTC
Thoughts of the Yüeh Beauty. Chang Pi, *tr. fr. Chinese by* Lois Fusek.
ATF
Thoughts of the Yüeh Beauty. Lu Ch'ien-i, *tr. fr. Chinese by* Lois Fusek.
ATF
Thoughts of the Yüeh Beauty. Sun Kuang-hsien, *tr. fr. Chinese by* Lois
Fusek. ATF
Thoughts on a Pore Joke. James Whitcomb Riley. AnAmPo
Thoughts on Capital Punishment. Rod McKuen. InPK
Thoughts on Climbing the Swept-Leaves Pavilion on the Third Day before
the Double-Ninth Festival. Ching An, *tr. fr. Chinese by* Irving Lo.
WFTU
Thoughts on One's Head. William Meredith. HAP
Thoughts on Pausing at a Cottage near the Paukataug River. Sarah
Kemble Knight. SCAP
Thoughts on Schoolchildren. Ahmad Shauqi, *tr. fr. Arabic by* M. Mustafa
Badawi *and* John Heath-Stubbs. MAP
Thoughts on Talkers. Walter Rollin Brooks. RHPC
Thoughts on the Commandments. George Augustus Baker. AA
Thoughts on the Shape of the Human Body. Rupert Brooke. BrPo
Thoughts on the Sight of the Moon. Sarah Kemble Knight. SCAP
Thoughts on the Works of Providence. Phillis Wheatley. NAAL-1
Thoughts on T'ien-chin Bridge. Shao Yung, *tr. fr. Chinese by* Burton
Watson. CoBCP
Thoughts South of the Yangtze. Yü Hu, *tr. fr. Chinese by* Burton
Watson. CoBCP
Thoughts That Move the Heart of Man, The. Ebenezer S. Oakley.
TrPWD
Thoughts upon Hearing a Singer. K'uang Chou-yi, *tr. fr. Chinese by*
Irving Lo. WFTU
Thou'lt fight, if any man call Thebe whore. To Sergius. Sir Charles
Sedley. FaBoEE
Thou'rt more inconstant than the wind or sea. The Hypocrite. John
Caryll. APAS
Thou's welcome, wean! Mischanter fa' me. A Poet's Welcome to His
Love-begotten Daughter. Burns. LiTB; NAs; NOEC; OxBoLi;
PoEL-4

Thousand-and-First Ship, *sel.* F. Scott Fitzgerald.
"There'd be an orchestra." AiP; GoJo
Thousand and One Nights, The, *sels. Unknown, tr. fr. Arabic by* E.
Powys Mathers.
Abu Nowas for the Barmacides. AWP
Birds. AWP
Dates. AWP; FaPON
Death ("Once he will miss, twice he will miss"). AWP
Haroun Al-Rachid for Heart's-Life. AWP
Haroun's Favorite Song. AWP
Her Rival for Aziza. AWP
Inscription on a Chemise. ErPo
Inscriptions at the City of Brass. AWP; WaaP, 3 *sts.*
Love ("Love was before the light began"). AWP
"O sons of men." OBD
Of Women. ErPo
Poems of the Arabic. *Tr. by* Sir Richard Burton. ErPo
Psalm of Battle. AWP
Sleeper, The. AWP
Song of the Narcissus, The. AWP
Tell Him, O Night. AWP
To Lighten My Darkness. AWP
Tumadir al-Khansa for Her Brother. AWP
(For Her Brother.) PBWP
Wazir Dandan for Prince Sharkan, The. AWP
Thousand and Second Night, The. James Merrill. NYBP
Thousand bird calls, A. The Swimmer. Philippe Soupault, *tr. by* Paul
Auster. RHTwFP
Thousand deaths a day, A. Resurrection of the Dead. Aliza Shenhar, *tr.*
by Linda Zisquit. VWA
Thousand-foot snow dragon, The. Flying Snow Rock. Zetsuzo, *tr. by*
Lucien Stryk *and* Takashi Ikemoto. ZPCJ
Thousand guileless sheep have bled, A. Song from the Bride of
Smithfield. Sylvia Townsend Warner. MoBrPo
Thousand Hairy Savages, A. Spike Milligan. NBLV; OnUR; RHPC
Thousand Islands, The. Charles Sangster. *Fr.* St. Lawrence and the
Saguenay. NOBC; OBCV
Thousand Killed, A. Bernard Spencer. OBWP
Thousand Martyrs I Have Made, A. Aphra Behn. OPOP
Thousand men then came thronging together, A. A Saint Called "Truth."
William Langland. *Fr.* The Vision of Piers Plowman. NOCV
Thousand miles of pure river water, A. On the Road to Pyongyang—An
Improvisation. Liu E, *tr. by* Jonathan Chaves. CoBLCP
Thousand Nights and Days, A. Cees Nooteboom, *tr. fr. Dutch by* Peter
Nijmeijer. DuIn
Thousand paces long, the flying arch leaps the river, A. Toasting the
Moon at Ten-Thousand-Year Bridge. Chiang Shih-ch'üan, *tr. by* Coy
Harmon. WFTU
Thousand silent years ago, A. Praxiteles and Phryne. William Wetmore
Story. AA; BeLS
Thousand sounds, and each a joyful sound, A. Omnipresence. Edward
Everett Hale. WGRP
Thousand streets of London gray, The. The Sheep and the Goat. George
Macdonald. EBVV
Thousand Things, The. Christopher Middleton. NePoEA-2
Thousand threads, ten-thousand strands, A. The Hundred-Fold Cord.
Chang Yü, *tr. fr. Chinese by* Jonathan Chaves. *Fr.* Four Poems On
the Ch'ung-wu Festival. CoBLCP
Thousand Times, A. Benjamin Péret, *tr. fr. French by* Michael Benedikt.
POS
Thousand times a day, A. *Unknown. Fr.* Manyo Shu. Ma
Thousand times you've seen that scene, A. Country Burying (1919).
Robert Penn Warren. LiTM
Thousand words lie under the dust, A. Mohammad Taqi Mir, *tr. by*
Ahmed Ali. GoT
Thousand years from now, A. The Extermination of the Jews. Marvin
Bell. CAPP; VWA
Thousand Years Have Come, A. Thomas T. Lynch. BLRP
Thousand years now had his breed, A. Edwin John Pratt. *Fr.* The
Cachalot. MoCV; OBCV
Thousand years, you said, A. Lady Heguri, *tr. by* Geoffrey Bownas *and*
Anthony Thwaite. *Fr.* Manyo Shu. BoLoP; PeBJV
Thousands and Three. Paul Verlaine, *tr. fr. French by* François Pirou.
PeHV
Thousands of cries birds. The Swimmer. Philippe Soupault, *tr. by*
Michael Benedikt. POS
Thousands of flowers, thousands of petals. Yang Chi, *tr. fr. Chinese by*
Jonathan Chaves. *Fr.* Spring Days in My Home Town. CoBLCP
Thousands of miles away—the Fu-sang tree. Saying Goodbye to a Monk
from Japan. Hsü Pen, *tr. by* Jonathan Chaves. CoBLCP

Thousands of mountains, tens of thousands of mountains. Wang T'ing-hsiang, *tr. by* Jonathan Chaves. CoBLCP
Thousands of white wings wheel in the morning wind. Wakayama Bokusui, *tr. fr. Japanese by* Hiroaki Sato. *Fr.* Forty-four Tanka. FCEI
Thracian Wonder, The, *sels. Unknown, at. to* John Webster *and* William Rowley.
  Art Thou Gone in Haste?. *Fr.* I, i. ElL; ELP; OxBoLi
    (Chase, The.) CH
    (Love Pursued.) GBL
    (Pursuit of Love.) ChTr
  Love Is a Law. *Fr.* I, i. ElL; GBL
  "Whither shall I go." *Fr.* II, i. GBL
Thraldome, The. Abraham Cowley. *Fr.* The Mistress. SeCV-1
Thrall. Carolyn Kizer. ER
Thrash away, you'll hev to rattle. Letter, A ("Thrash away, you'll hev to rattle"). James Russell Lowell. *Fr.* The Biglow Papers: 1st Series, No. I. AmPP; OxBA
    (Mr. Hosea Biglow Speaks.) PAH
Thraw oot your shaddaws. Moonlight among the Pines. "Hugh MacDiarmid." OAEL-2
Thrawn water? Aye, owre thrawn to be aye thrawn! By Wauchopeside. "Hugh MacDiarmid." EBEV
Thre Prestis of Peblis, The, *sel. At. to* John Reid of Stobo.
  "In Peblis town sum tyme, as I heard tell." OxBS
Thread of Life, The, *sel.* Christina Rossetti.
  "Irresponsive silence of the land, The." NOBE; OBNC
    (Aloof.) OBEV, I; TrGrPo, I.
Thread of red ants, A. Ants. Yusuf al-Sa'igh, *tr. by* Diana Der Hovanessian *with* Salma Khadra Jayyusi. MAP
Thread of silver marks along the sand, A. The Lost Continent. Jenny Joseph. BrRo
Thread suns/ above the gray-black [*or* grey-black] wasteland [*or* wilderness]. Paul Celan, *tr. by* Beth Bjorklund. CoAuP
    (Thread Suns.) OBVE, *tr. by* Michael Hamburger
Thread the nerves through the right holes. Resurrection Song. Thomas Lovell Beddoes. FaBoEE
Threading the palm, a web of little lines. Signs. Gjertrud Schnackenberg. InPK; PoA
Threads of rain weave lambent light. To the Tune "Yellow Oriole" ("Threads of rain weave lambent light"). Yang Shen, *tr. by* Jonathan Chaves. CoBLCP
Threads spiral toward a center. Notes for Albuquerque. Roberta Hill Whiteman. STE
Threat, The. Andrei Codrescu. UL
Threat'ning clouds of yesternight, The. While the Choir Sang. Priscilla Jane Thompson. CBWP-2
Thredbo River. Sydney Jephcott. PoAu-1
Three. Elizabeth Jane Coatsworth. ILY
Three. Marilyn Kitchell. UL
Three. Judah Leib Teller, *tr. fr. Yiddish by* Benjamin *and* Barbara Harshav. *Fr.* Psychoanalysis. AYP
3 A.M. John Updike. AnAmPo
Three a.m.—a far bell. December. Gary Snyder. InPS
Three ancient men in Bethlehem's cave. The Mystic Magi. Robert Stephen Hawker. ChTr; OBCP
Three, and/ There is no past for me. Growing Up. Tanikawa Shuntaro, *tr. by* Geoffrey Bownas *and* Anthony Thwaite. PeBJV
Three angels came to the red red clay. From the Coptic. Stevie Smith. Mes
Three Animals, *sels.* Ron Padgett. TTTS
  Butterfly, The.
  Electric Eel, The.
  Giraffe, The.
Three anti-depressants and one diuretic a day. Bruce Beaver. *Fr.* Letters to Live Poets, XII. CBAP
Three Badgers, The. "Lewis Carroll." FaBoNo
Three Ballate, *sels.* Angelo Poliziano, *tr. fr. Italian by* John Addington Symonds. AWP
  "He who knows not what thing is Paradise." *Fr.* II.
  "I found myself one day all, all alone." *Fr.* I.
  "I went a roaming, maidens, one bright day." *Fr.* III.
Three Best Things, The, *sel.* Henry van Dyke.
  Zest of Life, The. WBLP
Three black boys. Panther. Sam Cornish. PoBA
Three blind mice, see how they run! Mother Goose. OxNR
Three blind mice, three blind mice,/ Dame Julian, Dame Julian. *Unknown.* FaBoNo; OBS
Three bold brothers of merrie Scotland. Henry Martyn. *Unknown.* ESPB

Three boys, American, in dungarees. February 22. John Updike. GOA
Three Bushes, The, *sel.* W. B. Yeats.
  Lady's Third Song, The. FaBoTw
Three Captains, The. *Unknown, tr. fr. French by* Andrew Lang. AWP
Three Cherry Trees, The. Walter de la Mare. CMoP
Three Children. John Gay. *See* Three children sliding on the ice.
Three children dash in the dim dooryard. Tree Tag. Mary E. Caragher. GoYe
Three children sliding on the ice. *At. to* John Gay. OxNR
    (Three Children.) NA; NOBL
Three Christmas Carols, *sels. Unknown.* ACP
  "Babe is born all of a May, A." *Fr.* I.
  "Man, be merry, I thee rede." *Fr.* II.
  "This night there is a child born." *Fr.* III.
Three City Cantos. Charles Wagner. GoYe
Three clear days. January. Robert Hass. NPGG
Three colours have I known the Deep to wear. Wilfred Owen. FL
Three 'coons come at his garbage. He be cross. John Berryman. *Fr.* Dream Songs. LCAP
Three counties blacken and vanish. L'Aurore Grelottante. Peter Levi. NePoEA-2
Three crests against the saffron sky. Twilight on Tweed. Andrew Lang. EBVV
    (Remembered Melody.) PoSH
Three crooked cripples went through Cripplegate. Mother Goose. OxNR
Three cups of wine a prudent man may take. The Benefits and Abuse of Alcohol. Eubulus, *tr. by* Richard Cumberland. FaBoUs; NBLV
Three dark buds for the Trinity. James Keir Baxter. *Fr.* Jerusalem Sonnets, XXVII. ATNZ
Three dark maids, I loved them when. Villancico. *Unknown, tr. by* Thomas Walsh. AWP
Three Darks Come Down Together. Robert Francis. CRP; LCAP
Three days and still the slow fogged rain. Kumara God. Peter Bland. ATNZ
Three days of rain: indoors. Rainpoem. Michael Dransfield. CBAP
Three days of rest. The Sun in Capricorn. Joyce Mansour. PBWP, *tr. by* Carol Cosman
Three days through sapphire seas we sailed. The Bay Fight. Henry Howard Brownell. PAH
Three Dead and the Three Living, The. George Barker. LiTB
Three Dispositions Regarding One Woman, *sels.* Sa'di Yusuf, *tr. fr. Arabic by* Sargon Boulus *and* Naomi Shihab Nye. MAP
  "As though you never lived." *Fr.* III.
  "Last train to Barcelona, The." *Fr.* II.
  "Why does your name continue." *Fr.* I.
Three Dogs. E. C. Brereton. BoTP
Three Dostoievskian Masks. Sándor Rákos, *tr. fr. Hungarian by* Jascha Kessler. FOC
Three Drawings. Mihály Ladányi, *tr. fr. Hungarian by* Jascha Kessler. FOC
Three Dreams. James Michie. NePoEA-2
Three drunks, a leg on one quite gone, bereft. My Iambic Pentameter Lines. Robert Crawford. InPK
Three Elements. Stephen Vincent Benét. *Fr.* John Brown's Body. EaLo
Three Enemies, The. Christina Rossetti. TrCP
Three Epigrams, *sels.* J. V. Cunningham.
  "Here lies New Critic who would fox us." MoAmPo; OBAL
  "I had gone broke, and got set to come back." MoAmPo
  "I married in my youth a wife." MoAmPo; TW
Three Epigrams, *sels.* Paul Ramsey. CRP
  Consolations.
  Exiles, The.
  Modern Theologian, A.
Three Epigrams, *sels.* Theodore Roethke. NBLV
  Mistake, The. *Fr.* 2.
  Pipling. *Fr.* 1.
Three Epitaphs on John Hewet and Sarah Drew, *sels.* Pope. NIP
  "Here lie two poor lovers, who had the mishap." *Fr.* III. FaBoEE
  "Think not by rigorous judgment seized." *Fr.* I.
  "When Eastern lovers feed the fun'ral fire." *Fr.* II.
Three excellent qualities in narration. Triads. *Unknown, tr. fr. Old Irish by* Thomas Kinsella. *Fr.* The Triads of Ireland. BIrV
Three-faced, The. Robert Graves. FaBoEE
Three faces. . ./mirrored in the muddy streams of living. For Andy Goodman—Michael Schwerner—and James Chaney. Margaret Walker. BPo
Three Fates, The. Rosemary Dobson. BoWoP

Three feet of mud in this narrow alley. Yang Chi, *tr. fr. Chinese by* Jonathan Chaves. *Fr.* Living in a Riverside Village—Miscellaneous Impressions. CoBLCP

Three fellows were marching over the Rhine. The Hostess' Daughter. Ludwig Uhland, *tr. by* Margarete Münsterberg. AWP

Three Fishers, The. Charles Kingsley. BeLS; EBVV; FaPoR; OnMSP; PoLF; PWR; WBLP

Three Flights Up. Hanny Michaelis, *tr. fr. Dutch by* Manfred Wolf. DuIn

Three Floors. Stanley Kunitz. SM

Three flutes, two oboes, English horn, violins. Guide to the Symphony. Weldon Kees. VGW

Three folds in cloth, yet there is but the one cloth. To the Holy Trinity. *Unknown, tr. by* Thomas Kinsella. NOIV

3 for 25. William Jay Smith. WaP

Three Found Poems. George Hitchcock. OBAL

Three Foxes, The. A. A. Milne. GoJo; GrPl; MoShBr; OxBChV

Three Friends. *Unknown, tr. fr. Yoruba by* Ulli Beier. BoWoP; PBA

Three Gates. *After the Arabian.* BLPA

Three Ghostesses. *Unknown.* OxNR; RHPC

Three ghosts on the lonesome road, The. Stains. Theodosia Garrison. WGRP

Three Girls on a Buttress. Eilidh Nisbet. PoSH

Three grand arcs. Nine Triads. Lillian Morrison. ASP

Three Graves, The, *sel.* Samuel Taylor Coleridge.
"So gentle Ellen now no more." ChER

Three Green Windows. Anne Sexton. NYBP

Three grey boys tracked us to an old house. In One Battle. Amiri Baraka. BPo

Three grey geese in a green field grazing. *Unknown.* OxNR; PBBP

Three halves of you are elsewhere. How to Reach the Moon. Marsha Pomerantz. VWA

Three-handed Fugue. Phyllis Gotlieb. NOBC

Three ha'pence worth. Issa, *tr. by* Geoffrey Bownas *and* Anthony Thwaite. PeBJV

Three Helpers in Battle. Mary Elizabeth Coleridge. EaLo

Three Hermits, The. W. B. Yeats. CMoP

Three Holy Kings from Morgenland. Heine, *tr. fr. German by* Herman Eichenthal. PChr

Three horsemen galloped the dusty way. On the Road to Chorrera. Arlo Bates. AA

Three hours ago he blundered up the trench. A Working Party. Siegfried Sassoon. CMoP; MMA

Three hugest dinosaurs do not outweigh. The Blue Whale. Robert Watson. MAT

Three hundred bridges. Tropic Circle. Reinhard Priessnitz, *tr. by* Beth Bjorklund. CoAuP

300,000,000. What Happened Here Before. Gary Snyder. NNaP

Three Hundred Thousand More. James Sloan Gibbons. PAH

.303. Keith Douglas. FL

Three images of dying stick in my mind like morbid transfers. Bruce Beaver. *Fr.* Letters to Live Poets, V. CBAP

Three inch wide streamlet, The. On the North Side of Suilven. Norman MacCaig. NPo

Three Jewish Boys Write to an Ancient Chinese Poet. Judd Teller, *tr. fr. Yiddish by* Grace Schulman. PeBMYV

Three Jolly Fishermen. *Unknown.* OxBSS

Three jolly gentlemen. The Huntsmen. Walter de la Mare. CenHV; RAR

Three Jolly Pigeons, The. Goldsmith. *See* She Stoops to Conquer: Let school-masters puzzle their brain.

Three Journeys. Edward Hirsch. NAmP

Three Jovial Gentlemen. Daniel Hoffman. MoBS

Three Jovial Huntsmen. *Unknown.* NA

Three Kinds of Pleasures. Robert Bly. AiP

Three Kingdoms of Nature, The. Gotthold Ephraim Lessing, *tr. fr. German.* NU, *tr. by* Alfred Baskerville, *ad. by* Robert Bly

Three Kings, The. Rubén Darío, *tr. fr. Spanish by* Lysander Kemp. PChr

Three Kings, The. Eugene Field. GN

Three Kings, The. Longfellow. GN; OnMSP

Three Kings. James P. Vaughn. PoNe

Three Kings Came. Thomas W. Shapcott. PoAu-2

Three Kings came riding from far away. The Three Kings. Longfellow. GN; OnMSP

Three kings embark on a long journey. Starlight. Freda Downie. FaBoWP

Three kings stood before the manger. The Gifts. John Heath-Stubbs. OxBC

Three kings went down to the soul of the sea. Three Kings. James P. Vaughn. PoNe

Three Knights from Spain. *Unknown.* CH
(We Are Three Brethren Come from Spain.) GBP
("We are three brethren out of Spain.") OxNR

Three Ladies, The. Robert Creeley. NeAP

Three Ladies of London, The, *sels.* Robert Wilson.
New Brooms. EIl
(Conscience's Song.) OBSC
Simplicity's Song. CTC; OBSC

Three limbs, three seasons smashed; well, one to go. John Berryman. *Fr.* Dream Songs. HCAP

Three lines of "clerk script" calligraphy. Chin Nung, *tr. fr. Chinese by* Jonathan Chaves. *Fr.* Inscribed on a Lichen-Covered Wall in My Hut. CoBLCP

Three little chickens. A Tug-of-War. M. M. Hutchinson. BoTP

Three little children sitting on the sand. All, All a-Lonely. *Unknown.* ChTr; OxBoLi

Three little fellows sing to the wind. Tohub. Jakov van Hoddis, *tr. by* Charles Guenther. VWA

Three little ghostesses. Three Ghostesses. *Unknown.* OxNR; RHPC

Three Little Girls. Richard Aldington. BrPo

Three Little Kittens, The. *At. to* Eliza Lee Follen *and to* Eliza Cook. BOTP; FaPON; OBCA; OxNR

Three little maidens they have slain. Maurice Maeterlinck, *tr. by* Jethro Bithell. AWP

Three Little Men in a Boat. Rodney Bennett. BoTP

Three little mice sat down to spin. Pussy and the Mice. *Unknown.* MoShBr

Three little mice walked into town. Three Mice. Charlotte Druitt Cole. BoTP

Three Little Pigs, The. Sir Alfred Scott Gatty. BoTP; OxBChV

Three little words you often see. The Parts of Speech. *Unknown.* FaBoUs

Three lonely months and more without news. Michizane, *tr. fr. Japanese by* Burton Watson. *Fr.* Kokin Shu. FCEI
(Reading a Letter from Home.) JLIC-1

Three long nights, an' three long days. Walk, Mary, down de Lane. *Unknown.* BoAN-2

Three Love Poems, *sels.* Norman Cameron. FaBoTw; GTBS-P
From a Woman to a Greedy Lover. *Fr.* I. FaBoEE
In the Queen's Room. *Fr.* II. OxBTC
Shepherdess. *Fr.* III. GBL; OxBS

Three lovely notes he whistled, too soft to be heard. The Unknown Bird. Edward Thomas. RB

Three lovely sisters working were. The Parcae; or, Three Dainty Destinies: The Armillet. Robert Herrick. CaPo

Three Loves. Lucy H. Hooper. BeLS

Three magnolias, identical. Yüan Mei, *tr. fr. Chinese by* Jonathan Chaves. *Fr.* Moments of Fullfillment—Writing Down Miscellaneous. CoBLCP

Three Maids a-Milking Would Go. *Unknown.* CoMu

Three men came talking up the road. Night Piece. John Manifold. LiTM; MoBrPo; WaP

Three men coming down the winter hill, The. Winter Landscape. John Berryman. LiTA; LiTM; MoAmPo; TwCP

Three men in a limousine travelling westward. The Three Dead and the Three Living. George Barker. LiTB

Three Men of Gotham. Thomas Love Peacock. *See* Nightmare Abbey: Wise Men of Gotham, The.

Three Mice. Charlotte Druitt Cole. BoTP

Three Migrations. Ralph Salisbury. STE

Three Mile Island. Maureen Owen. UL

Three miles extended around the fields of the homestead. Frithiof's Homestead. Esaias Tegnér, *tr. fr. Swedish by* Longfellow. *Fr.* Frithiof's Saga. AWP

Three Mirrors, The. Edwin Muir. NoAM

"Three months," they said in July. The Noh Plays. Lauris Edmond. ATNZ

Three Moral Tales. Emmanuel Hocquard, *tr. fr. French by* Michael Palmer. RHTwFP

3 More Things. Elinor Nauen. UL

Three Movements, The. Donald Hall. NePoEA-2

Three Movements. W. B. Yeats. CMoP; FaBoEE

Three Moves. John Logan. CAPP

Three Musicians, The. Aubrey Beardsley. NOBVV; OBTV

Three of a Kind. Richard Hovey. AnAmPo

Three of us/ in the bar. Jazz. Carolyn M. Rodgers. JB

Three of us afloat in the meadow by the swing. Pirate Story. Robert Louis Stevenson. BeLS; FaPON

"The three of us are relatives not doing well." Yosano Akiko, *tr. fr. Japanese by* Hiroaki Sato. *Fr.* Thirty-nine Tanka. FCEI

Three of us went to the top of the city. Poem from the Empire State. June Jordan. BPo

Three of us without a care. Three of a Kind. Richard Hovey. AnAmPo

3 of Washingtons heads. George Washington Goes to a Girlie Movie. Aram Boyajian. NeAC

Three old hermits took the air. The Three Hermits. W. B. Yeats. CMoP

Three on Luck, *sels.* Robert Pinsky. AnAn
  Late Child.
  Prostate Operation.
  Senior Poet.

Three outas from the bleak Karoo. D. J. Opperman, *tr. by* Anthony Delius. PeSA

Three Pagoda Dragon Pond. To the Tune "Chiu-ch'üan tzu." Wu Chen, *tr. by* Jonathan Chaves. CoBLCP

Three peaks beyond my pavilion show no human feelings, The. Ch'en Pao-shen, *tr. by* Irving Lo. WFTU

Three Phases of Africa. Francis Ernest Kobina Parkes. PBA

Three Pigeons, The. Goldsmith. *See* She Stoops to Conquer: Let school-masters puzzle their brain.

Three pigeons down-swing. Possibilities. Peter Kane Dufault. NYBP

Three places most loved I have left. Saint Columcille. NOIV

Three Plum Buns. Christina Rossetti. BoTP

3 pm/ sunless. Paki Go Home. Himani Bannerji. AIW

Three Poems, *sels.* Michelangelo, *tr. fr. Italian by* George Santayana. AWP
  "Haven and last refuge of my pain, The." *Fr.* II. AWP
  "I know not if from uncreated spheres." *Fr.* I. AWP
  "Ravished by all that to the eyes is fair." *Fr.* III. AWP
    (Madrigal: "Ravished by all that to the eyes is fair.")

Three Poems, *sels.* János Pilinszky, *tr. fr. Hungarian by* Jascha Kessler. FOC
  "Bow down. (Prostrates himself.)."
  Stavrogin's Farewell.
  Stavrogin's Return.

Three Poems, *sel.* "Ping Hsin," *tr. fr. Chinese by* Julia C. Lin.
  "Fishing boats have returned, The!" PBWP

Three Poems about Children. Austin Clarke. CIP

Three Poems for Kaddish. Robert Lowell. PPR

Three Poems for the Indian Steelworkers. Joseph Bruchac. CDW

Three Poems for the New Year, *sel.* Charles Wright.
  "I have nothing to say about the way the sky tilts." CAPP

Three Poems for Women. Susan Griffin. NPGG

Three Poems in Black and White, *sels.* Chamutal Reich. WCI
  "And the rain came. And the water came." *Fr.* 3.
  "At twilight amidst the currents of water." *Fr.* 2.
  "Other days on another continent." *Fr.* 1.

Three Poems of Nightmare, *sels.* Judah Leib Teller, *tr. fr. Yiddish by* Benjamin *and* Barbara Harshav. AYP
  Flood.
  Midnight.

Three Poems of the Atomic Bomb, *sel.* Dame Edith Sitwell.
  Dirge for the New Sunrise. CMoP; EaLo; MoAB; MoBrPo; SeCePo

Three Poems on Ch'ang-sha, *sel.* Yang Shih-ch'i, *tr. fr. Chinese by* Jonathan Chaves. CoBLCP
  Palace of Prince Ma, The.

Three Poems to the tune "Lo-mei Feng", *sels.* Ma Chih-yüan, *tr. fr. Chinese by* Jonathan Chaves. CoBLCP
  "Dew on roses." *Fr.* 3.
  Evening Bell from Misty Temple. *Fr.* 2.
  Returning Sails at a Distant Shore. *Fr.* 1.

Three Poems to the Tune "Ssu-k'uai yü", *sels.* Ma Chih-yüan, *tr. fr. Chinese by* Jonathan Chaves. CoBLCP
  Enjoying Retirement ("Beside green water"). *Fr.* 2.
  Enjoying Retirement ("The wine just purchased"). *Fr.* 1.
  Lamenting Life. *Fr.* 3.

Three Poets at Yuyama. Shohaku *and others, tr. fr. Japanese by* Hiroaki Sato. FCEI

Three poets, in three distant ages born. Lines Printed under the Engraved Portrait of Milton [in Tonson's Folio of the "Paradise Lost"]. Dryden. HeIP; InPK; SeCV-2
  (Epigram on Milton.) TrGrPo
  (Lines on Milton.) OAEL-1
  (Portrait of Milton, The.) ACP

Three Portraits. George Hitchcock. VGW

Three practical farmers from back of the dale. Shepherds' Carol. Norman Nicholson. OBCP

Three Preachers, The. Charles MacKay. EBVV

Three Presidents. Robert Bly. LCAP

Three Ravens, The. *Unknown.* ChTr; ESPB; FaBoBa; GBP; HeIP; InPK; Mes; NAEL-1; NoP; OAEL-1, *with music;* OBD; OBET; OBEV; OxBB, *with music;* PoE; PoEL-1; TrGrPo; UnPo
  ("There were three crows sat on a tree.") AmFP

Three red foxes on my head, come down. False Youth: Autumn: Clothes of the Age. James Dickey. CAPP; MT

Three roads were shadowy and the sky over. Vanessa Vanessa. Ewart Milne. BIrV; NeIP

Three Roses, The. Walter Savage Landor. NAEL-2

Three rounded flanks I loved. *Unknown.* NOIV

Three Roundels of Love Unreturned. Chaucer. *See* Merciles[s] Beauty [*or* Beaute[e]].

Three rubberbands on a thin tin pot. What Do We Know, Dear Brothers? Moyshe-Leyb Halpern, *tr. fr. Yiddish by* Benjamin *and* Barbara Harshav. *Fr.* Zarkhi on the Sea Shore. AYP

Three Sailors, The. Thackeray. *See* Little Billee.

Three sang of love together. A Triad. Christina Rossetti. NAEL-2; PBWP

Three Sayings from Highlands, North Carolina. Jonathan Williams. OBAL

Three Score and Ten "Three score and ten, the life and age of man." *Unknown.* OxBSS

Three score and ten! The tumult of the world. Life's Evening. Dudley Foulke. WGRP

Three Seamstresses, The. Isaac Leibush Peretz, *tr. fr. Yiddish by* Joseph Leftwich. TrJP

Three Seasons. Francis Sparshott. NOBC

Three Secret Poems, *sels.* George Seferis, *tr. fr. Greek by* Edmund Keeley *and* Philip Sherrard. VMG
  "Flame is healed by flame." *Fr.* I: 7.
  "Now/ with the lead melted for divination." *Fr.* III: 14.
  "When will you speak again?." *Fr.* II: 6.
  "Years ago you said." *Fr.* I: 4.

Three secrets that never were said. Secrets. Richard Hovey. AnAmPo

Three Self-Plagiarisms. David Avidan, *tr. fr. Hebrew by* Warren Bargad *and* Stanley F. Chyet. *Fr.* Traveling in the City, 4. IP

Three Sentences for a Dead Swan. James Wright. NaP; NOBA

Three Sermons to the Dead, *sels.* Laura Riding. LiTA
  Nor Is It Written. *Fr.* III.
  Not All Immaculate. *Fr.* II.
  Way of the Air, The. *Fr.* I.

Three Shades of Light on the Windowsill. Susan Griffin. NPGG

Three ships of war had Preble when he left the Naples shore. Reuben James. James Jeffrey Roche. PAH

Three silences made him a single word. R. P. Blackmur. PoA

Three Singing Birds, The. James Reeves. PDV

Three Sisters. Walter de la Mare. FaBoEE

Three small towns. Three Towns. Leopold Staff, *tr. by* Czeslaw Milosz. PwPP

Three Songs. Hart Crane. *Fr.* The Bridge, V. LiTA; NAAL-2
  National Winter Garden. ErPo; InPS; LiTM; NAAL-2; OxBA

Three Songs. William Dickey. BLA

Three Songs, *sels.* Thom Gunn. AnAn
  Baby Song.
  Encolpius.
  Hitching into Frisco.

Three Songs from the Haida, *sels.* Constance Lindsay Skinner.
  Bear's Song, The. AWP
  Love Song. AWP
  Song for Fine Weather. AWP

Three Songs from the Temple. Don Domanski. NOBC

Three Songs of Mad Coyote. *Unknown, tr. fr. Nez Percé Indian by* Herbert J. Spinden. STP

Three Songs of Mary, *sel.* Madeleine L'Engle.
  O Simplicitas. OBCP; PChr

Three Sonnets for Iva. Marilyn Hacker. GLP

Three spirits came to me. April. Ezra Pound. CMoP

Three Spring Notations on Bipeds. Carl Sandburg. AWP

3 Stanzas about a Tree. Marvin Bell. Prf

Three Star Final. Conrad Aiken. OxBA

Three stars, five stars rise over the hill. Confucius, *tr. fr. Chinese by* Ezra Pound. *Fr.* Shao and the South. CTC

Three steps and I reach the door. Fate. Louis James Block. AA

Three strange men came to the inn. A Lady Comes to an Inn. Elizabeth J. Coatsworth. MoAmPo; SO

Three Streets. Umberto Saba, *tr. fr. Italian by* Anita Barrows. VWA

Three strings, a neck of almond, and the heart. Balalaika. Norman Dubie. AmPA

Three students once tarried over the Rhine. From the German of Uhland. James Weldon Johnson. CDC

Three summers since I chose a maid. The Farmer's Bride. Charlotte Mew. BoLoP; ErPo; FaBoWP; MoAB; MoBrPo; OxBTC; TrGrPo; WPE

Three Tall Men, The. *Unknown.* OBET

Three tall poplars. Evening. Federico García Lorca, *tr. by* William Jay Smith. CT

Three Testimonies of Ayacucho. Antonio Cisneros, *tr. fr. Spanish by* Maureen Ahern *and* David Tipton. Per

Three then came forward out of darkness, one. The Road. Conrad Aiken. MoAmPo

Three thinges there bee that prosper up apace. *See* Three things there be that prosper up apace.

Three Things. Joseph Auslander. TrJP

Three Things. W. B. Yeats. OBMV

Three Things Enchanted Him. "Anna Akhmatova", *tr. fr. Russian by* Stanley Kunitz *with* Max Hayward. AiP

Three things filled this day for me. Three Things. Joseph Auslander. TrJP

Three Things Jeame Lacks. *Unknown.* MeEL

Three Things [*or* Thinges] There Be[e] That Prosper All [*or* Up] Apace. Sir Walter Ralegh. NoP; PoEL-2
   (Sir Walter Ralegh to His Son.) NAEL-1; RB; Son
   (To His Son.) InPS; OxBSP
   (Wood, the Weed, the Wag, The.) SiPS

Three things remind me of you. Meditation. Carl Rakosi. VWA

Three things seek my death. Inheritance. *Unknown, tr. by* Frank O'Connor. TW

Three things the Master hath to do. Pray—Give—Go. Annie Johnson Flint. BLRP

Three things there be in man's opinion dear[e]. Fulke Greville. *Fr.* Caelica, CV [CVI]. LiTB; NOCV; PoEL-1
   (Sonnet: "Three things there be in mans opinion deare.") OBS

Three Things to Remember. Blake. *See* Auguries of Innocence: Robin Redbreast in a cage, A.

Three Tickles. Dennis Lee. RAR

Three times a day my prayer is. *Unknown.* OBSC

Three times he crossed our way where with me went. Old Man Pondered. John Crowe Ransom. MoAmPo

Three times round the cuckoo waltz. Cuckoo Waltz. *Unknown.* AS

Three times we heard it calling with a low. The Ground-Swell. E. J. Pratt. CaP

Three Tiny Songs, *sel.* Cid Corman.
   "I have come far to have found nothing." VGW

Three Towns, The. Howard Nemerov. KS

Three Towns. Leopold Staff, *tr. fr. Polish by* Czeslaw Milosz. PwPP

Three Trees. C. H. Crandall. OHIP

Three Troopers, The. George Walter Thornbury. BeLS

Three turkeys fair their last have breathed. A Melancholy Lay. Marjory Fleming. FaBoCh; FiBHP; NBLV

Three Variations. Boris Pasternak, *tr. fr. Russian by* Babette Deutsch. TrJP

Three viands in three different courses served. Oyster-Crabs. Carolyn Wells. BXAP

Three Voices, The. "Lewis Carroll." BXAP

Three Voices. Tamura Ryuichi, *tr. fr. Japanese by* Geoffrey Bownas *and* Anthony Thwaite. PeBJV

Three Warnings, The. Hester Lynch Thrale. BeLS

Three Ways to Screw Up on Your Way to The Doings Three Ways. *Unknown, tr. fr. Seneca Indian by* Jerome Rothenberg *and* Richard Johnny John. STP

Three weeks, and now I hear! My Olson Elegy. Irving Feldman. Prf

Three weeks gone and the combatants gone. Vergissmeinnicht. Keith Douglas. FaBoMo; GTBS-P; InPS; NAEL-2; NePoEA; NoAM; OBD; OBWP; OxBTC; RB; SoSe

Three Welshman, The. *Unknown.* MoShBr

Three Wise Couples, The. Elizabeth T. Corbett. BLPA

Three wise men looked equivocally, The. The Magi. Ramon Guthrie. PoE

Three wise men of Gotham. Mother Goose. FaBoBe; FaBoNo; FaFP; OxNR

Three Wise Men of Gotham, The. *Unknown.* FaBoNo

Three Wise Monkeys, The. Florence Boyce Davis. WBLP

Three Wise Old Women. Elizabeth T. Corbett. BLPA; OBCA; OxBChV

Three Women. Alan Dienstag. ErPo

Three Women ("I am slow as the world. I am very patient."), *sel.* Sylvia Plath. NAs

"I see her in my sleep, my red, terrible girl." TV

Three words fall sweetly on my soul. Mother, Home, Heaven. William Goldsmith Brown. FaBoBe

Three years ago I left these city walls. Returning to Yin-ch'eng Early in the Year *Ting-ch'ou.* Tai Piao-yüan, *tr. by* Jonathan Chaves. CoBLCP

Three Years She Grew in Sun and Shower. Wordsworth. *Fr.* Lucy. EnRP; FiP; GN; HAP; NoP; PoEL-4
   (Education of Nature, The.) GTBS; GTBS-P

Three yellow wasps belly crawl by slow feel. Still Life. William Hathaway. NAmP

Three Young Rats. *Unknown.* ChTr; FaBoNo; InvP; OxBoLi; OxNR
   (Rats, Ducks, Dogs, Cats, Pigs.) GBP

Three youths went a-fishing. The Banished Duke of Grantham. *Unknown.* EnSB

Threes. Carl Sandburg. AnAmPo; CMoP; OxBA; PoLF

Threnode for Young Soldiers Killed in Action. Juliette de Bairacli-Levy. CN

Threnody. Thomas Lovell Beddoes. EnRP

Threnody: "Let happy throats be mute." Donald Jeffrey Hayes. AmNP

Threnody: "Only quiet death." Waring Cuney. AmNP; BANP

Threnody: "South-wind brings, The." Emerson. AA

Threnody: "Truth is a golden sunset far away." I. O. Scherzo. HoPM

Threnody, A: "What, what, what/ What's the news from Swat?" George Thomas Lanigan. AA; FiBHP; NA; NBLV
   (Ahkoond of Swat, The.) AnAmPo; CaP
   (Threnody on the Ahkoond of Swat, A.) CenHV

Threnody for a Poet. Bliss Carman. CaP

Threnody for Berlin—1945. Wrenne Jarman. CN

Threnody on the Ahkoond of Swat, A. George Thomas Lanigan. *See* Threnody, A: "What, what, what/ What's the news from Swat?"

Threshed corn lay piled like grit of ivory. The Barn. Seamus Heaney. HAP

Thresher motor stops, The. The Threshing. Rocco Scotellaro, *tr. by* Paul Vangelisti. PFI

Thresher's Labour, The, *sel.* Stephen Duck.
   "Soon as the harvest hath laid bare the plains." NOEC

Threshing, The. Rocco Scotellaro, *tr. fr. Italian by* Paul Vangelisti. PFI

Threshing Machine, The. Alice Meynell. SeCePo; WPE

Threshing Machine. Wilhelm Szabo, *tr. fr. German by* Beth Bjorklund. CoAuP

Threshold, The. Fu'ad Rifqa, *tr. fr. Arabic by* Sargon Boulus *and* Samuel Hazo. MAP

Threw a woman's shoe. My Atlas Poet. George Bowering. NeAC

Thrice, and above, blest, my soul's half [*or* my soules halfe], art thou. A Country Life: To His Brother, Master Thomas Herrick. Robert Herrick. CaPo; SeCP; SeCV-1

Thrice Blest the Man. John Barnard. AH

Thrice-cruel maid, may Heaven frown on thee. The Elusive Maid. Abraham ibn Chasdai, *tr. by* J. Chotzner. TrJP

Thrice happy authors, who with little skill. A Soliloquy in the Suburbs. *Unknown.* NOEC

Thrice Happy He. William Drummond of Hawthornden. BoNaP
   (Solitary Life, A.) OBS

Thrice happy, who free from ambition and pride. Isaac Hawkins Browne. *Fr.* The Foundling Hospital for Wit.

Thrice he came. Malacoda. Samuel Beckett. CIP

Thrice Holy. Reginald Heber. *See* Holy, Holy, Holy.

Thrice the age of a dog is that of a horse. The Age of Animals. *Unknown.* FaBoUs

Thrice the Brinded Cat Hath Mewed. Shakespeare. *Fr.* Macbeth, IV, i. InvP; OFD; RB; WSC
   (Charm, The.) EiL
   Song of the Witches. RHPC

Thrice Toss [*or* Tosse] These Oaken Ashes in the Air [*or* Ayre]. Thomas Campion. EBEV; EiL; EnLoPo; FaBoCh; HAP; MAT; OAEL-1; OBSC; OxBSP; PoEL-2; PoRA; WeW; WSC
   (Love-Charms.) NOBE

Thrice Welcome First and Best of Days. Isaac Chanler. AH

Thriftles thred which pampred beauty spinnes, The. A Sonet Written in Prayse of the Browne Beautie. George Gascoigne. AAS

Thrifty Elephant, The. John Holmes. NYBP

Thrippsy pillivinx. A Letter to Evelyn Baring. Edward Lear. FaBoNo

Thro elm and maple and syringa branches. Commencement. Constance Carrier. WPE

Thro' the night of doubt and sorrow. Pilgrim's Song. Bernard S. Ingemann, *tr. by* Sabine Baring-Gould. WGRP

Thro' the night Thy angels kept. A Child's Prayer. William Canton. BoTP

Throat of thunder, a tameless heart, A.   A Cyclone at Sea.   William Hamilton Hayne.   AA

Throat Song: The Whirling Earth.   Wendy Rose.   HATNAP

Throb, throb, throb. the tall ship.   Night Boat.   Audrey Alexandra Brown.   CaP

Throbbing—all I can hear!   Drums.   Martha Chosa.   NOVW

Throbs the Night with Mystic Silence.   Hayyim Nahman Bialik, *tr. fr. Hebrew by* Bertha Beinkinstadt.   TrJP

Throne of the Lily-King, The.   Joseph Rodman Drake.   *Fr.* The Culprit Fay.   GN

Throne was reared upon the grass, The.   The Throne of the Lily-King.   Joseph Rodman Drake.   *Fr.* The Culprit Fay.   GN

Throng of eyes.   Covenant.   Paul Auster.   VWA

Throstle, The.   Tennyson.   BoNaP; FaPON; PBBP

Through a bend in the hillside.   *Unknown, tr. by* Arthur Waley.   BoS

Through a dull tract of woe, of dread.   My Birthday.   George Crabbe.   OxBSP

Through a Glass, Darkly.   Basil Dowling.   ATNZ

Through a Glass Eye, Lightly.   Carolyn Kizer.   BoWoP

Through a green gorge the river like a fountain.   Arthur Rimbaud.   *See* Eighteen-Seventy: Sleeper in the Valley, The.

Through a long night.   Issa, *tr. fr. Japanese by* Hiroaki Sato.   *Fr.* Forty-four Hokku.   FCEI

Through a mist an army marches.   It Happened Before.   Wrenne Jarman.   CN

Through a rift in evening rainclouds.   Teika, *tr. fr. Japanese by* Hiroaki Sato.   *Fr.* Eighty-four Tanka.   FCEI

Through a square sealed-off with.   A Word about Freedom and Identity in Tel Aviv.   Jon Silkin.   VWA

Through a wild midnight all my mountainous past.   The Monster.   Henry Rago.   PoA

Through a window in the attic.   Burglar Bill.   "F. Anstey."   CenHV; FiBHP

Through all the frozen winter.   Smells.   Kathryn Worth.   RHPC

Through All Your Abstract Reasoning.   Brian Patten.   FaBoTw

Through Alpine meadows soft-suffused.   Stanzas from the Grande Chartreuse.   Matthew Arnold.   EBVV; NAEL-2; OAEL-2; PoE; PoEL-5; TEP

Through and through the inspired leaves.   The Book-Worms.   Burns.   ChTr; FaBoEE; FiBHP

Through autumn fields of bush clover.   *Unknown, tr. fr. Japanese by* Burton Watson.   *Fr.* Kokin Shu.   FCEI

Through Baltimore.   Bayard Taylor.   PAH

Through Binoculars.   Charles Tomlinson.   OAEL-2

Through brush and love-vine, well blooded by blackberry thorn.   Boy Wandering in Simms' Valley.   Robert Penn Warren.   SoSe

Through bushes and through briars I lately took my way.   Bushes and Briars.   *Unknown.*   OBET

Through calm and storm the years have led.   Centennial Hymn.   Bryant.   PAH

Through Dangly Woods the aimless Doze.   The Doze.   James Reeves.   AmMo

Through darkening pines the cavaliers.   The Legend of Waukulla.   Hezekiah Butterworth.   PAH

Through every age, eternal God.   Isaac Watts.   AmFP

Through every minute of this day.   John Oxenham.   BLRP

Through every night we hate.   Mothers, Daughters.   Shirley Kaufman.   BoWoP; NMM; TV

Through Fire in Mobile Bay.   *Unknown.*   PAH

Through frost and snow locked from mine eyes.   To Saxham.   Thomas Carew.   CaPo; JCP; NoP; OBS

Through grass, through amber'd cornfields, our slow Stream.   Meadowsweet.   William Allingham.   OBNC

Through grief and through danger thy smile hath cheered my way.   The Irish Peasant to His Mistress.   Thomas Moore.   ACP; TIRV

Through his million veins are poured.   William Bull Wright.   *Fr.* The Brook.   AA

Through holes in a wall, as it were.   Exile: 2. Rajagopal Parthasarathy.   *Fr.* Rough Passage.   UAS

Through jaggedy cliffs of snow, along sidewalks of glass.   Party in Winter.   Karl Shapiro.   PCP

Through Jane's village.   Jane's Village.   Koh Chang-soo, *tr. by the author.*   ACKP

Through lane or black archway.   The Young Woman of Beare.   Austin Clarke.   MoP; NoAM

Through lenses the world opens.   Microscope.   Gwyn Thomas, *tr. by* Joseph P. Clancy.   OBWVE

Through life's dull road, so dim and dirty.   On My Thirty-third Birthday.   Byron.   FaBoEE; NAs

Through love to light! O, wonderful the way.   After-Song.   Richard Watson Gilder.   AA; TrPWD

Through me the way is to the city of woe.   The Gates of Hell.   Dante, *tr. fr. Italian by* Laurence Binyon.   *Fr.* Divina Commedia: Inferno, III.   PFI

Through me you enter the city of lament.   Dante, *tr. fr. Italian by* Ronald Bottrall.   *Fr.* Divina Commedia: Inferno, III.   OBD

Through moonlight's milk.   White Cat in Moonlight.   Douglas Gibson.   CRH

Through most that sets the hills on fire.   Dundonnel Mountains.   Andrew Young.   PoSH

Through Nurseryland.   *Unknown.*   BoTP

Through our laced and latticed windows.   Shacked Up at the Ritz.   Doug Fetherling.   NeAC

Through pearly deeps of sky, cloud-mountains rose.   Sky Picture.   Henrietta Cordelia Ray.   CBWP-3

"Through pleasures and palaces."   Nostalgia.   Amy Lowell.   AnAmPo

Through rain falling on us no faster.   Goodbye to Serpents.   James Dickey.   NYBP

Through random doors we wandered.   Exits and Entrances.   Naomi Long Madgett.   BlSi

Through reason Russia can't be known.   F. I. Tyutchev, *tr. by* Alan Myers.   AAA

Through reedy banks.   The Nima.   Jorge Isaacs, *tr. by* Alice Jane McVan.   TrJP

Through Ruddy Orchards.   Mary Oliver.   WPE

Through salt marsh, grassy channel where the shark's.   Tide Turning.   John Frederick Nims.   DiPo; FYAP

Through sepia air the boarders come and go.   The Landlady.   P. K. Page.   CaP; SoSe

Through some strange sense of sight or touch.   Death.   Madison Cawein.   AA

Through storm and fire and gloom, I see it stand.   The Celtic Cross.   Thomas D'Arcy Magee.   TIRV

Through storm and wind.   *Unknown.*   OxNR

Through storms you reach them and from storms are free.   The Enviable Isles.   Herman Melville.   AA; FaBoBe

Through swamps and alligators I wend my weary way.   On the Lakes of Ponchartrain.   *Unknown.*   AmFP

Through that pure virgin-shrine.   The Night.   Henry Vaughan.   EBEV; LiTB; MeLP; MePo; NAEL-1; NOBE; NOCV; NoP; OAEL-1; OBEV; OBS; OBWVE; PoEL-2; SeCV-1; TOF

Through that window—all else being extinct.   The Room.   Conrad Aiken.   LiTM; MoAmPo; NOBA

Through the ample open door of the peaceful country barn.   A Farm Picture.   Walt Whitman.   InPS

Through the autumn night, quiet and dark.   Princess Shikishi, *tr. fr. Japanese by* Hiroaki Sato.   *Fr.* Seventy-eight Tanka.   FCEI

Through the Barber Shop Window.   Violet Anderson.   CaP

Through the black, rushing smoke-burst.   Song of Callicles, The ("Through the black, rushing smoke-burst").   Matthew Arnold.   *Fr.* Empedocles on Etna, II.   NOBE; OAEL-2; OBEV
   (Callicles' Song.)   ChTr
   (Not Here, O Apollo.)   FaBoRV
   (Song for Apollo.)   FiP
   (Song of the Muses, The.)   WiR

Through the blue, blue moonless night.   Wakayama Bokusui, *tr. fr. Japanese by* Hiroaki Sato.   *Fr.* Forty-four Tanka.   FCEI

Through the bound cable strands, the arching path.   Atlantis.   Hart Crane.   *Fr.* The Bridge, VIII.   LiTM

Through the bright gleaming.   Yakamochi.   *Fr.* Manyo Shu.   FCEI

Through the chinks.   *Unknown, tr. fr. Japanese by* Geoffrey Bownas *and* Anthony Thwaite.   *Fr.* Koka Shu.   PeBJV

Through the clangor of the cannon.   Defeat and Victory.   Wallace Rice.   PAH

Through the cracks.   Ray A. Young Bear.   STP

Through the Dark the Dreamers Came.   Earl Bowman Marlatt.   AH

Through the deep night a magic mist led me.   A Magic Mist.   Owen Roe O'Sullivan, *tr. by* Thomas Kinsella.   NOIV

Through the deep woods, at peep of day.   The Canadian Herd-Boy.   Susanna-Strickland Moodie.   OBCV

Through the drought we flew now we're singing of April.   No. 42.   Lajos Kassák, *tr. by* Jascha Kessler.   FOC

Through the dusky purple glimmer.   Anita and Giovanni.   Henrietta Cordelia Ray.   CBWP-3

Through the Eye of the Needle.   Mani Leib, *tr. fr. Yiddish by* John Hollander.   PeBMYV

Through the fault the last earthquake just exposed.   Just Now.   Benjamin Péret, *tr. by* Michael Benedikt.   POS

Through the fierce fever I nursed him, and then he said.   Little Wild Baby.   "Margaret Vandegrift."   AA

Through the first days of Lent. The Street. Gary Soto. NPGG
Through the Forest Have I Gone. Shakespeare. *Fr.* A Midsummer
    Night's Dream, II, ii. CTC
Through the forest the boy wends all day long. The Boy and the Flute.
    Björnstjerne Björnson, *tr.* by Sir Edmund Gosse. AWP
Through the garden of shadow-/ flowers. The Boy and the Lantern.
    Evaristo Ribera Chevremont, *tr.* by Julio Marzán. InW
Through the green tassels of the weeper tree. Triumphal Ode
    MCMXXXIX. George Barker. LiTB; WaP
Through the House. Shakespeare. *Fr.* A Midsummer Night's Dream, V,
    ii. CTC
    (Oberon and Titania to the Fairy Train.) GN
Through the house what busy joy. The First Tooth. Charles *and* Mary
    Lamb. OxBChV; RHPC
Through the larch forest. Larches. Kitahara Hakushu, *tr.* by Geoffrey
    Bownas *and* Anthony Thwaite. PeBJV
Through the light rain I think I see them going. The Burial in Flanders.
    Robert Nichols. PeHV
Through the long day the skylarks. Basho, *tr. fr. Japanese by* Burton
    Watson. *Fr.* Seventy-six Hokku. FCEI
Through the long death of the moon. The Death of the Moon. David
    Wagoner. PoA
Through the Long Night. Edward Carpenter. *Fr.* Towards Democracy.
    PeHV
Through the Looking-Glass, *sels.* "Lewis Carroll."
    "I'll tell thee everything I can." *Fr. ch.* 8. InVP; Par
    (A-Sitting on a Gate.) PoRA
    (Aged, Aged Man, The.) BXAP; FaBoPa; OxBChV
    (Ways and Means.) FiBHP; NA
    (White Knight's Ballad, The.) FaBoNo; HAP
    (White Knight's Song, The.) FaBoCh; FaBoCo; InPS; NAEL-2;
      NOAM; NOBE; NOBL; NoP; OAEL-2
    "In winter, when the fields are white." *Fr. ch.* 6. EBEV; NOBVV
    (Humpty Dumpty's Poem.) Mes
    (Humpty Dumpty's Recitation.) ChTr; FaBoCo; FaBoNo; FiBHP
    (Humpty Dumpty's Song.) GTBS-P; OnMSP; OxBChV; OxBoLi
    Jabberwocky. *Fr. ch.* 1. AmMo; EBEV; EBVV; FaBoBe; FaBoCo;
      FaBoNo; FaBV; FaFP; FaPON; FF; FiBHP; FPL; GoJo; HeIP; HoPM;
      InPK; InPS; LiTB; NA; NAEL-2; NBLV; NIP; NoAM; NOBE;
      NOBL; NOBVV; NoP; NTCP; OAEL-2; OPOP; OxBChV; PoRA;
      PPP; RB; RHPC; TEP; TTTS
    "To the Looking-Glass world it was Alice that said." *Fr. ch.* 9.
    Par
    Walrus and the Carpenter, The. *Fr. ch.* 4. BeLS; BLPA; FaBoBe;
      FaBoCo; FaBoNo; FaBV; FaFP; FaPON; FiBHP; FPL; GN; LiTB;
      NA; NAEL-2; NoAM; NOBL; NOBVV; OxBChV; PoRA; TEP
Through the Maze. *Unknown.* BLRP
Through the new wound that fate had opened in me. The Sacred Way.
    Angelos Sikelianos, *tr.* by Edmund Keeley *and* Philip Sherrard.
    VMG
Through the night on fire with my blood. She Speaks the Morning's
    Filigree. Philip Lamantia. VGW
Through the night, through the night. The Sea. Richard Henry Stoddard.
    AA
Through the open french window the warm sun. Still-Life. Elizabeth
    Daryush. FaBoWP; QFR; WPE
Through the Parklands, through the Parklands. The Parklands. Stevie
    Smith. MoBS
Through the plain of Miyake. *Unknown. Fr.* Manyo Shu. Ma
Through the Porthole. Marjorie Wilson. BoTP
Through the pregnant universe rumbles life's terrific thunder. Exhortation:
    Summer, 1919. Claude McKay. CDC
Through the rain forests, up a long river. The Deceptive Grin of the
    Gravel Porters. Gavin Ewart. FaBoMo
Through the revolving door. Alligator on the Escalator. Eve Merriam.
    SO
Through the shrubs as I can crack[e]. Doron's Jigge. Robert Greene.
    Fr. Menaphon. PoEL-2
    (Jig, A.) EiL
Through the singing of birds I rise. Morning in Christchurch. Lauris
    Edmond. UAS
Through the small door of a hut. The Collector of the Sun. Dave Smith.
    SM
Through the Smoke Hole ("There is another world above this one"), *sel.*
    Gary Snyder. PoM
    "There is another world above this one." PoA
Through the Snow to Early Duty at the Office. Michizane, *tr. fr. Chinese
    by* Burton Watson. JLIC-1
Through the strait pass of suffering. Emily Dickinson. TOF
Through the stricken air, through the buttonwood balls. Rain on the
    Cumberlands. James Still. GrPl

Through the sunny garden. Chillingham. Mary Elizabeth Coleridge.
    BoTP
Through the technology of science. MC²-E. Lois Wickstrom. BWV
Through the thick morning steam they took shape. A Papuan Shepherd.
    Francis Webb. *Fr.* A Drum for Ben Boyd. PoAu-2
Through the train window. Ishikawa Takuboku, *tr.* by Geoffrey Bownas
    and Anthony Thwaite. PeBJV
Through the trees, with the moon underfoot. The Call. James Dickey.
    NePoEA-2
Through the vague morning, the heart preoccupied. Bombers. C. Day
    Lewis. CMoP; MoAB
Through the Valley. Ella Wheeler Wilcox. AnAmPo
Through the viridian (and black of the burnt match). Virgo Descending.
    Charles Wright. LCAP
Through the walls. The Walls of My House. Ilse Tielsch, *tr.* by Beth
    Bjorklund. CoAuP
Through the Whole Long Night. H. Leivick, *tr. fr. Yiddish by* Ruth
    Whitman. VWA
Through the windy valley. Yün Shou-p'ing, *tr. fr. Chinese by* Jonathan
    Chaves. *Fr.* Inscribed on a Painting by Shih-ku. CoBLCP
Through the Year. Julian S. Cutler. BLPA
Through these glassy afternoons. Christine Lavant, *tr.* by Beth Bjorklund.
    CoAuP
Through These Pale Cold Days. Isaac Rosenberg. TrJP
Through this toilsome world, alas! I Shall Not Pass This Way Again.
    Unknown. BLPA; FPL
Through throats where many rivers meet, the curlews cry. In the White
    Giant's Thigh. Dylan Thomas. LiTB
Through torrid entrances, past icy poles. To Shakespeare. Hart Crane.
    Son
Through Unknown Paths. Frederick L. Hosmer. TrPWD
Through verdant banks where Thames's branches glide. The Assault on
    the Fortress. Timothy Dwight. PAH
Through Walls. Rae Armantrout. LP
Through Warmth and Light of Summer Skies. Austin Faricy. AH
Through water, his own waterfall. Cold Fire. George Starbuck. NYBP
Through what long heaviness, assayed in what strange fire. Carthusians.
    Ernest Dowson. NAEL-2
Through what obscure, half-comprehending night. Candlemas Day.
    Sister Mary Madeleva. CRP
Through Willing Heart and Helping Hand. Frederick Lucian Hosmer.
    AH
Through winter-time we call on spring. The Wheel. W. B. Yeats.
    GTBS-P
Through woods, Mme Une Telle, a trifle ill. Autumn Chapter in a Novel.
    Thom Gunn. FaBoMo; OxBTC
Through years of Irish history. Mr. Gunman. Vin Garbutt. OBET
Through You. Edwin Honig. TAP
Through your eyes' round and perfect pupils. Narrative. Louis Dudek.
    CaP
Through your love words became clear. The Word "Silk." Thomas
    McCarthy. CIP
Throughe a forest as I can ryde. Crow and Pie. *Unknown.* ESPB
Throughout a garden greene and gay. The Rose of England. *Unknown.*
    ESPB
Throughout Australian history no tongue or pen can tell. The Death of
    Morgan. *Unknown.* FaBoBa
Throughout Our Lands, *sels.* Czeslaw Milosz, *tr. fr. Polish by the author
    and* Peter Dale Scott. PwPP
    "Cabeza, if anyone knew all about civilization, it was you." *Fr.* XIV.
    "If I had to tell what the world is for me." *Fr.* III.
    "Paulina, her room behind the servants' quarters." *Fr.* XI.
    "They are so persistent, that give them a few stones." *Fr.* IX.
    "With their chins high, girls come back from the tennis courts.'" *Fr.*
    VII-VIII.
Throughout the day our sweet bells chime. Bluebells. P. A. Ropes.
    BoTP
Throughout the day we are able to ban the voices. Henriëtte Roland-
    Holst, *tr.* by Manfred Wolf. PBWP
Throughout the field I find no grain. Winter in Durnover Field. Thomas
    Hardy. MoBrPo
Throughout the land, blossoms are in their prime. Teika, *tr. fr. Japanese
    by* Hiroaki Sato. *Fr.* A Compendium of Good Tanka.
    FCEI
Throughout the soft and sunlit day. The Pines. Julie Mathilde
    Lippmann. AA
Throughout the World, If It Were Sought. Sir Thomas Wyatt. MAT;
    OxBSP
    (Honesty.) OBSC
Throw Away the Flowers. Elizabeth Daryush. PBWP

Throw away Thy rod. Discipline. George Herbert. FPL; LiTB; MeLP; MePo; NAEL-1; NOBE; NOCV; NoP; OBEV; OBS; PoLF; SeCePo; TrGrPo

Throw away your old ball! Secret Ballgame. Ernst Schönwiese, *tr. by* Beth Bjorklund. CoAuP

Throw-Back, The. Waddie Mitchell. CowP

Throw Hannibal on the scales, how many pounds. Hannibal ("Throw Hannibal on the scales, how many pounds"). Juvenal, *tr. fr. Latin by* Robert Lowell. *Fr.* Satires, X. OBVE

Throw him into the river. Kasenduaxtc, *tr. by* James Koller. STP

Throw me into a cloud o lord. Bogdan Czaykowski, *tr. by* Czeslaw Milosz. PwPP

Throw on rouge and powder, watch the governor pass! Tune: Sand of Silk-washing Stream ("Throw on rouge and powder, watch the governor pass!"). Su Tung-p'o, *tr. by* Burton Watson. CoBCP

Throw something to the gulls, any old scrap. Writing on the Wall. Padraic Fallon. NeIP

Throwing a bomb is bad. Ethics for Everyman. Roger Woddis. NOBL

Throwing the Racetrack Cats at Saratoga. David Ray. SM

Thrown suddenly into a corner of the world. Exodus 1940. Alfred Wolfenstein, *tr. by* Erna Baber Rosenfeld. VWA

Thrush, The. Alfred Austin. TEP

Thrush, The. Timothy Corsellis. WaaP; WaP

Thrush before Dawn, A. Alice Meynell. MoBrPo; WPE

Thrush in February, The. George Meredith. OBNC

Thrush is tapping a stone, A. Dawn. Gordon Bottomley. BoTP; MoBrPo

Thrush, linnet, stare and wren. In Glencullen. J. M. Synge. FM; OBMV

Thrush Relinquished, The. Allen Grossman. PPR

Thrushes. Ted Hughes. FaBoMo; GoYe; NePoEA-2

Thrushes flying under the lake. Nightingales singing underground. Pewter. Jack Gilbert. NPGG

Thrushes sing as the sun is going, The. Proud Songsters. Thomas Hardy. MoP

Thrush's Nest, The. John Clare. BoTP; GoJo

Thrush's Song, The. *Unknown, tr. fr.* Gaelic *by* William MacGillivray. CH

Thrust in life between heaven and earth, I can't but feel cramped. Random Thoughts. Wang Kuo-wei, *tr. by* Irving Lo. WFTU

Thrust of the dragon's tight bone, The. The Dream Feast (Three Poems). Anita Endrezze-Danielson. VoR

Thrusting glance grows dim, The. Portrait of a Very Old Man. Sara E. Carsley. CaP

Thrusting halfway up into the sky—the two pagodas. Viewing Nara from a Distance in Wind and Rain. Fujii Chikugai, *tr. by* Burton Watson. JLIC-2

Thrusting its armoury of hot delight. Descartes and the Stove. Charles Tomlinson. FaBoMo

Thu sikest sore. Christ's Tear Breaks My Heart. *Unknown.* MeEL

Thu Sun: Night. Bert Schierbeek, *tr. fr. Dutch by* Charles McGeehan. DuIn

Thule. Sándor Weöres, *tr. fr.* Hungarian *by* Jascha Kessler. FOC

Thule, The Period of Cosmography. *Unknown. See* Wonders.

Thumb, The. Dennis Saleh. MAT; NeAC

Thumb bold. *Unknown.* OxNR

Thumb, for a summer's promise, The. The Sand Painters. Ben Belitt. EyDe; GOA

Thumb he. *Unknown.* OxNR

Thumb, loose tooth of a horse. Bestiary for the Fingers of My Right Hand. Charles Simic. AmPA; LCAP

Thumbikin, Thumbikin, broke the barn. *Unknown.* OxNR

Thumbing Old Magazines. Gerald Vizenor. VoR

Thumbkin says, I'll dance. *Unknown.* OxNR

Thumbprint. Celeste Turner Wright. Psk

Thumbs. Shel Silverstein. TSS

"Thumbs in the thumb-place." The Mitten Song. Marie Louise Allen. NTCP; RAR

Thump I leap you shake. Dance a Ghost. "Chrystos." GOS

Thumping old tunes give a voice to its whereabouts. Fairground. W. H. Auden. NYBP

Thunder/ The Gallop of innumerable Walkyrie. Barrage. Richard Aldington. BrPo

Thunder. Walter de la Mare. BoNaP

Thunder. Wang Chiu-ssu, *tr. fr. Chinese by* Jonathan Chaves. CoBLCP

Thunder clouds are sweeping, shrouding. A Russian Cradle Song. David Nomberg, *tr. by* Alter Brody. TrJP

Thunder God rouses sleeping dragons, The. Thunder God Cliff. Chao Meng-fu, *tr. fr. Chinese by* Jonathan Chaves. *Fr.* Twenty-Eight Poems Inscribed on T'ien-kuan Mountain. CoBLCP

Thunder in the southern mountains, the third month of the year. Thunder. Wang Chiu-ssu, *tr. by* Jonathan Chaves. CoBLCP

Thunder Moth. Miyoshi Tatsuji, *tr. fr. Japanese by* Geoffrey Bownas *and* Anthony Thwaite. PeBJV

Thunder mutters louder & more loud, The. John Clare. NOBVV

Thunder My Brother. Malka Heifetz-Tussman, *tr. fr. Yiddish by* Kathryn Hellerstein. AYP

Thunder of riotous hoofs over the quaking sod. The Maid. Theodore Goodridge Roberts. MoShBr

Thunder of the Rain God. A House in Taos. Langston Hughes. CDC

Thunder of waves out of the dying west. Oreti Beach. Charles Brasch. ATNZ

Thunder our thanks to her—guns, hearts, and lips. *Mayflower.* John Boyle O'Reilly. AA; PAH

Thunder, rain falling, falling. Inscribed on a Painting. Hsü Wei, *tr. by* Jonathan Chaves. CoBLCP

Thunder-Storm, A. Emily Dickinson. *See* Wind begun to rock the grass, The.

Thunder: the flesh quails, and the soul bows down. John Webster. Swinburne. *Fr.* Sonnets of English Dramatic Poets. InvP; Son

Thunderer, The. Phyllis McGinley. EaLo

Thunderhead. Archibald MacLeish. AnAmPo

Thunderlight on the split logs: big raindrops. Seamus Heaney. *Fr.* Glanmore Sonnets, VII. IPY

Thunder's Son, The. Aimé Césaire, *tr. fr.* French *by* Michael Benedikt. POS

Thunderstorm, A. Archibald Lampman. CaP; NOBC

Thunderstorm in South Dakota. Kay Boyle. WPE

Thunderstorm in Town, A. Thomas Hardy. BoLoP; EnLoPo; GBL; OxBSP

Thurn, A. John Berryman. NOBA

Thursday. Edna St. Vincent Millay. PoA

Thursday in the morn, the Ides of May. The Sea Fight in '92. *Unknown.* OxBSS

Thursday; or, The Spell. John Gay. *Fr.* The Shepherd's Week. PoEL-3

"Last May-day fair I search'd to find a snail." FaBoUs

"When first the year, I heard the cuckoo sing." PBBP

Thus Adam himself lamented loud. Milton. *Fr.* Paradise Lost, bk. X, ll. 845–1104. OAEL-1

Thus all is here in motion, all is life. The Wool Trade. John Dyer. *Fr.* The Fleece, III. SeCePo

Thus at the panting dove a falcon flies. Homer, *tr. fr. Greek by* Pope. *Fr.* The Iliad, XXII. OBVE

Thus been they parted, Arthur on his way. The Cave of Despair. Spenser. *Fr.* The Faerie Queene, I, 9. OBNV

"Ere long they come, where that same wicked wight." NOBE; OAEL-1

Thus began/ Outrage from lifeless things; but Discord first. Milton. *Fr.* Paradise Lost, bk. X, ll. 706–1104. NAEL-1

Thus being entered, they behold around. Spenser. *Fr.* The Faerie Queene, II, 12. OAEL-1

Thus Belial with words clothed in reason's garb. Milton. *Fr.* Paradise Lost, bk. II, ll. 226–378. FaBoPV

Thus briefly sketched [*or* sketch'd] the sacred rights of man. On Mr. Paine's Rights of Man. Philip Freneau. NAAL-1
(To a Republican.) AmPP

Thus, brother theologian, here you are. Poet at Seventy. Czeslaw Milosz, *tr. by the author.* AnAn

Thus by himself compelled to live each day. George Crabbe. *Fr.* The Borough: Peter Grimes. NOBE; OBNC; SeCePo

Thus charg'd he; nor Argicides denied. Homer, *tr. fr. Greek by* George Chapman. *Fr.* Odyssey, V. OBVE

Thus chydand with her drery desteny. Cressida's Leprosy. Robert Henryson. *Fr.* The Testament of Cresseid. SeCePo

Thus Crosslegged on Round Pillow Sat in Space. Allen Ginsberg. NNaP

Thus deaths hand clos'd his eyes. The Death of Hector. Homer, *tr. fr. Greek by* George Chapman. *Fr.* The Iliad, XXII. OBS

Thus down a lone valley with cedars o'er spread. Columbia. *Unknown.* AmFP

Thus dullness, the safe opiate of the mind. On Dullness. Pope. OxBSP

Thus ends my Love, but this doth grieve me most. Loves End. Lord Herbert of Cherbury. SeCP

Thus ere another noon they emerged from the shades. The Lakes of the Atchafalaya. Longfellow. *Fr.* Evangeline. PoEL-5

Thus Eve to Adam. Milton. *See* Paradise Lost: My author and disposer, what thou biddest.

Thus far the Lord hath led us on[ ]in darkness and in day. Light Shining Out of Darkness. Jane Borthwick. BLRP

Thus far, with rough and all-unable pen. Shakespeare. *Fr.* King Henry V. CTC

Thus fell the King, who yet surviv'd the state. Virgil, *tr. fr. Latin by* Sir John Denham. *Fr.* The Aeneid [*or* Eneados], II. OBVE

Thus glory hath her being! thus she stands. Glory and Enduring Fame. William Gilmore Simms. Son

Thus Harriet, rising on the stage. Harriet Simper Has Her Day. John Trumbull. *Fr.* The Progress of Dulness. AmPP

Thus has he forsaken me, the god unknown. Heat Spell in Venice. Leah Goldberg, *tr. by* Bernhard Frank. MHeP

Thus have I back again to thy bright name. An Apology for the Foregoing Hymn. Richard Crashaw. JCP

Thus have I shunned the fire for fear of burning. Shakespeare. *Fr.* The Two Gentlemen of Verona, I, iii. GBL

Thus having passed all peril, I was come. Happy Isle. Spenser. *Fr.* The Faerie Queene, IV, 10. OBSC

Thus I/ Pass by. Upon His Departure Hence. Robert Herrick. FaBoRV; QFR

Thus I awaked and wrote what I had dreamed. The Vision of Jesus. William Langland. *Fr.* The Vision of Piers Plowman. ACP

Thus I come to you. Author Unknown. William Montgomerie. OxBS

Thus I heard a poet say. The Expected Ship. John Godfrey Saxe. AnAmPo

Thus I Resolve. Thomas Campion. OxBSP

Thus I would walk abroad when gentle night. Walking at Night. Henry Treece. WaP

"Thus is this cheek the map of days outworn." Shakespeare. *Fr.* Sonnets, LXVIII. OBSC

Thus laykes this lorde by lynde-wodes eves. Gawain and the Lady of the Castle. *Unknown, tr. fr. Middle English by* Brian Stone. *Fr.* Sir Gawain and the Green Knight. EBEV

Thus let us drink and be merry! Lady Otomo no Sakanoe. *Fr.* Manyo Shu. Ma

Thus Lovely Sleep. Richard Leigh. ELP
(Sleeping on Her Couch.) MePo

Thus man by his own strength to Heaven would soar. Dryden. *Fr.* Religio Laici. NOCV; WGRP

Thus much be sung of picking—next succeeds. How to Cure Hops and Prepare Them for Sale. Christopher Smart. *Fr.* The Hop-Garden. FaBoUs

Thus much the fates have allotted me. Turning Aside from Battles. Sextus Propertius, *tr. by* Ezra Pound. WaaP

Thus, near the gates conferring as they drew. Ulysses and His Dog. Homer, *tr. fr. Greek by* Pope. *Fr.* Odyssey, XVII. FiP

Thus piteously Love closed what he begat. George Meredith. *Fr.* Modern Love, L. EBEV; EnLoPo; GTBS-P; HAP; NOBE; NOBVV; NoP; OAEL-2; OBNC; PoE; PoEL-5; SeCePo; Son; TrGrPo
(Dusty Answer, A.) SeCePo

Thus pressed to the edge. Alfred Kolleritsch, *tr. by* Beth Bjorklund. CoAuP

Thus queth Alvred:/ "Idelschipe and overprute, that lereth yong wif üvel thewes." *at. to* Alfred, King of England. *Fr.* The Proverbs of Alfred, XVI. PoE

Thus queth Alvred:/ "If thu havest seorewe, ne seyethu hit than arewe." *at. to* Alfred, King of England. *Fr.* The Proverbs of Alfred, XIII. PoE

Thus queth Alvred:/ "Ne schaltu nevere thi wif by hire wlyte choese." *at. to* Alfred, King of England. *Fr.* The Proverbs of Alfred, XIV. PoE

Thus queth Alvred:/ "Ne würth thu never so wod ne so wyn-drunke." *at. to* Alfred, King of England. *Fr.* The Proverbs of Alfred, XV. PoE

Thus queth Alvred:/ "Nevre thu, bi thine lyve, the word of thine wyve." *at. to* Alfred, King of England. *Fr.* The Proverbs of Alfred, XVII. PoE

Thus re-inforc'd, against the adverse fleet. The Fourth Day's Battle. Dryden. *Fr.* Annus Mirabilis. OBS

Thus reader, by our astrologick art. Almanac Verse. *Unknown.* SCAP

Thus said The Lord in the Vault above the Cherubim. The Last Chantey. Kipling. FaBoCh; MoBrPo; MOS

Thus said the rushing raven. A Croon on Hennacliff. Robert Stephen Hawker. NOBVV

Thus saith my Chloris bright. Giovanni Battista Guarini. GBL

Thus saith the great god Thoth. He Is Declared True of Word. *Unknown, tr. fr. Egyptian by* Robert Hillyer. *Fr.* Book of the Dead. AWP

Thus saith the Ruler of the Skies. The Passion and Exaltation of Christ. Isaac Watts. NOCV

Thus say the famished she-devils. "Ikeda." *Fr.* Manyo Shu. Ma

Thus saying, from her husband's hand her hand. Milton. *Fr.* Paradise Lost, *bk.* IX, *ll.* 385–1189.
(Fall, The.) PoEL-3

Thus saying, from her side the fatal key. Milton. *Fr.* Paradise Lost, *bk.* II, *ll.* 871–1055. EBEV

Thus she had lain. Africa. Maya Angelou. NIP

Thus should have been our travels. Over 2000 Illustrations and a Complete Concordance. Elizabeth Bishop. HCAP; LCAP; NAAL-2; NoAM

Thus, some tall tree that long hath stood. On the Death of Benjamin Franklin. Philip Freneau. PAH

Thus spake the Lord. The Word of the Lord from Havana. Richard Hovey. PAH

Thus Spake the Saviour. Jeremy Belknap. AH

Thus spoke Priam's shining son with words supplicating. Achilles to Lycaon. Homer, *tr. fr. Greek by* Richmond Lattimore. *Fr.* The Iliad, XXI. WaaP

Thus spoke the lady underneath the tree. Colonel Fantock. Dame Edith Sitwell. MoAB; MoBrPo; OBMV

Thus spoke the Lord to Israel. Amalek. Friedrich Torberg, *tr. by* Erna Baber Rosenfeld. VWA

Thus Sung Orpheus to His Strings. *Unknown.* GBL

Thus talking hand in hand alone they pass'd. Milton. *Fr.* Paradise Lost, *bk.* IV, *ll.* 689–775. EBEV

Thus the Mayne Glideth. Robert Browning. *Fr.* Paracelsus, V. OBEV

Thus the old men lamented. Pogroms. André Spire, *tr. by* Stanley Burnshaw. VWA

Thus the rains came (waking and bird-song). Of a Sea-Born Aphrodite. Emmanuel Hocquard, *tr. by* Michael Palmer. RHTwFP

Thus the Trees Change Places. Sirkka Turkka, *tr. fr. Finnish by* Aili Jarvenpa. SOP

Thus they in Heav'n, above the starry sphear. Milton. *Fr.* Paradise Lost, *bk.* III, *ll.* 416–515. EBEV

Thus, thus, begin the yearly rites. Pans Anniversarie. Ben Jonson. OBS

Thus to Glaucus spake/ Divine Sarpedon. Homer, *tr. fr. Greek by* Sir John Denham. *Fr.* The Iliad, XII. OBVE

Thus was my love, thus was my Ganymed. Richard Barnfield. *Fr.* Sonnets, X. PeHV

Thus when the swallow, seeking prey. John Gay. *Fr.* The Beggar's Opera, II, ii. PoEL-3

Thus while my joyless hours I lingring spend. John Phillips. *Fr.* The Splendid Shilling. FaBoPa

Thus will despair/ In ecstasy of nightmare. The Succubus. Robert Graves. OAEL-2

Thus with a Kiss I Die. Shakespeare. *See* Romeo and Juliet: For here lies Juliet, and her beauty makes.

Thus with Hermetic art the adept combines. The Action of Invisible Ink. Erasmus Darwin. *Fr.* The Economy of Vegetation. FaBoUs

Thus with imagin'd wing our swift scene flies. Shakespeare. *Fr.* King Henry V, *Prologue to* III. EBEV

Thwarted. Priscilla Jane Thompson. CBWP-2

Thy arms with bracelets I will deck. Homage. Gustave Kahn, *tr. by* Jethro Bithell. TrJP

Thy azure robe, I did behold. Julia's Petticoat. Robert Herrick. CaPo

Thy beauty haunts me heart and soul. The Moon. W. H. Davies. BrPo; MoBrPo

Thy Best. Henry Cole. PWR

Thy blessing on the boys—for time has come. Haim Guri, *tr. by* Ruth H. Lask. TrJP

Thy blue waves, Patapsco, flow'd soft and serene. Fort McHenry. *Unknown.* PAH

"Thy bosom is endeared with all hearts." Shakespeare. *Fr.* Sonnets, XXXI. NOBE; OBEV; OBSC; PoEL-2

Thy braes were bonny, Yarrow stream. The Braes of Yarrow. John Logan. GTBS; GTBS-P

"Thy breath is far sweeter than honey." Far Sweeter than Honey. Abraham Ibn Ezra, *tr. by* Israel Abrahams. TrJP

Thy byrth, thy beautie, nor thy brave attyre. Farewell with a Mischeife. George Gascoigne. AAS

Thy copp's, too, nam'd of Gamage, thou hast there. Ben Jonson. *Fr.* To Penshurst. FM

Thy country, Wilberforce, with just disdain. To William Wilberforce, Esq. William Cowper. Son

Thy cruise is over now. Mr. Merry's Lament for "Long Tom." John Gardiner Calkins Brainard. AA

Thy dawn, O Ra, opens the new horizon. Adoration of the Disk by King Akhnaten and Princess Nefer Neferiu Aten. *Unknown, tr. fr. Egyptian by* Robert Hillyer. *Fr.* Book of the Dead. AWP

"Cattle roam again across the field, The." FaPON

Thy error, Frémont, simply was to act. To John C. Frémont. Whittier. PAH

Thy eyes and eyebrows I could spare. *Unknown.* FaBoEE

Thy eyes are sparks, Lycines, god-like made. Strato, *tr. by* Sydney Oswald. PeHV

Thy face I have seen as one seeth. Sophie Jewett. AA

Thy Faithful Sons. Eleazar, *tr. fr. Hebrew.* TrJP

Thy fingers make early flowers of all things. E. E. Cummings. MoAmPo; NAAL-2

Thy flattering picture, Phryne, is like thee. Phryne. John Donne. FaBoEE

Thy forests, Windsor! and thy green retreats. Pope. *Fr.* Windsor Forest. NOEC

Thy [*or* Your] friendship oft has made my heart to ache [*or* ake]. To William Hayley. Blake. FaBoCo
(T. H.) FF
(To Hayley.) FaBoEE; TrGrPo

Thy Garden. "Mustafa", *tr. fr. Arabic by* Dulcie L. Smith. AWP

Thy garden, orchard, fields. Francis Daniel Pastorius. SCAP

"Thy glass will show thee how thy beauties wear." Shakespeare. *Fr.* Sonnets, LXXVII. EnRePo; QFR

Thy grace, dear Lord's my golden wrack I find. Edward Taylor. *Fr.* Preparatory Meditations before My Approach to the Lord's Supper, XXXII. NoP; SCAP

Thy Heart ("Thy heart is like some icy lake"). *Unknown.* NA

Thy Heaven. Thomas Moore. TIRV

Thy hue, dear pledge, is pure and bright. To a Lock of Hair. Sir Walter Scott. GTBS; GTBS-P

Thy human frame, my glorious Lord, I spy. Edward Taylor. *Fr.* Preparatory Meditations before My Approach to the Lord's Supper, VII. LiTA

Thy Kingdom Come, O Lord. Frederick Lucian Hosmer. WGRP
(Prophecy Sublime, The.) TrPWD

Thy Kingdom Come ("Thy kingdom come—on bended knee"). Frederick Lucian Hosmer. WGRP

Thy kingdom come: yea, bid it come. Holy Family. Katharine Tynan. TIRV

Thy Kingdom, Lord, We Long For. Vida Scudder. WGRP

Thy laugh's a song an oriole trilled. Kitty's Laugh. Arlo Bates. *Fr.* Conceits. AA

Thy leopard legs and python thighs. The Zoo of You. Arthur Freeman. ErPo

Thy life has touched the edges of my life. My Spirit's Complement. Henrietta Cordelia Ray. CBWP-3

Thy little footsteps on the sands. To William Shelley. Shelley. ChER

Thy Loving Kindness, Lord, I Sing. George Barrell Cheever. AH

Thy lovingkindness, Lord!—Who, sin to quell. Occasions of Grace at a Poetry Performance. John Frederick Nims. SoTCo

Thy Mercies, Lord, to Heaven Reach. William Kethe. AH

Thy merits, Wolfe, transcend all human praise. The Death of Wolfe. *Unknown.* PAH

Thy Mother Was like a Vine. Bible, *O.T. Fr.* Ezekiel, XIX: 10-14. TrJP

Thy nags (the leanest things alive). Matthew Prior. FaBoEE

Thy Name We Bless and Magnify. John Power. BLRP

Thy nature, immortality! who knows? Edward Young. *Fr.* Night Thoughts, Night VI. OBD

Thy need is great. For the Earth God. *Unknown, tr. by* Frances Herskovits. EaLo

Thy nights moan into my days. Psalms of Love. Peter Baum, *tr. by* Jethro Bithell. AWP

Thy one white leaf is open to the sky. To a Cherokee Rose. William Hamilton Hayne. AA

Thy Praise, O God, in Zion Waits. Jacob Kimball. AH

Thy praise, O Lord, will I proclaim. Palms and Myrtles. Eleazar Ben Kalir, *tr. by* Alice Lucas. TrJP

Thy praise or dispraise is to me alike. To Fool, or Knave. Ben Jonson. FaBoEE; NoP; SoSe

Thy restless feet now cannot go. Christ Crucified. Richard Crashaw. OBEV

Thy Sea So Great ("Thy sea, O God, so great"). Winfred Ernest Garrison. TrPWD

Thy sooty godhead I desire. To Vulcan. Robert Herrick. CaPo

Thy soul/ Grown delicate with satieties. O Atthis. Ezra Pound. PoA

Thy soul within such silent pomp did keep. A Quiet Soul. John Oldham. OBEV

Thy span of life was all too short. To a Withered Rose. John Kendrick Bangs. AA

Thy stricken daughter, now, O Lord, prepares. Hymn for the Eve of the New Year. Abraham Gerondi, *tr. by* Solomon Solis-Cohen. TrJP

Thy summer voice, Musketaquit. Two Rivers. Emerson. AmPP; NOBA; OxBA; PoE; TrGrPo

Thy Sun Posts Westward. William Drummond of Hawthornden. SeCePo

Thy sword within the scabbard keep. Momus' Song to Mars. Dryden. *Fr.* The Secular Masque. OxBSP

Thy thoughts, dear Keats, are like fresh-gathered leaves. To Keats: On Reading His Sonnet Written in Chaucer. John Hamilton Reynolds. Son

Thy trivial harp will never please. Merlin ("Thy trivial harp will never please"). Emerson. *Fr.* Merlin, I. AA; OxBA

Thy trivial harp will never please. Merlin. Emerson. AA; AmPP; NAAL-1; NOBA; OxBA

Thy various works, imperial queen, we see. On Imagination. Phillis Wheatley. AmPP; BlSi; PoNe

Thy voice, as tender as the light. To a Friend. James Fenimore Cooper. PeHV

Thy voice is heard through rolling drums. Tennyson. *Fr.* The Princess, Interlude. TrGrPo

Thy voice is hovering o'er my soulit lingers. To Constantia Singing. Shelley. EnRP

Thy voice is on the rolling air. Tennyson. *Fr.* In Memoriam A. H. H., CXXX. HeIP; NoP; PeHV

Thy Way, Not Mine. Horatius Bonar. TrPWD

Thy weary feet have pressed once more thy native soil. Welcome Home. Josephine D. Henderson Heard. CBWP-4

Thy Will Be Done. John Milton Hay. *See* Not in Dumb Resignation.

Thy Will Be Done. Hugh Thomson Kerr. BLRP

Thy Will is best for me. God's Will Is Best. *Unknown.* BLRP

Thy will, O God, is best. Thy Will Be Done. Hugh Thomson Kerr. BLRP

Thy wisdom speaks in me, and bids me dare. Shelley. *Fr.* Epipsychidion. OAEL-2

Thy words are compounded of sweet-smelling myrrh. Words Wherein Stinging Bees Lurk. Judah Halevi, *tr. by* Nina Davis Salaman. TrJP

Thyestes, *sels.* Seneca, *tr. fr. Latin.*
"O yee, whome lorde of lande and waters wyde." *Fr.* III, *tr. by* Jasper Heywood. OBVE
"Stond [*or* Stand] who so list upon the slipper toppe." *Fr.* II, *tr. by* Sir Thomas Wyatt. AAS; NaP; OBVE; PoEL-1; SiPS
("Climb at court for me that will.") OBVE, *tr. by* Andrew Marvell.
("Let him that will, ascend the tottering seat.") OBVE, *tr. by* Sir Matthew Hale.
("Let who so lyst with might mace to raygne.") OBVE, *tr. by* Jasper Heywood.
(Senec. Traged. ex Thyeste Chor. 2.) SeCV-1, *tr. by* Andrew Marvell.
("Upon the slippery tops of humane state.") OBVE, *tr. by* Abraham Cowley.

Thyme. *Unknown.* AmFP

Thyme carpet, by-passed, The. Summer Report. Paul Celan, *tr. by* Beth Bjorklund. CoAuP

Thyme Flowering among Rocks. Richard Wilbur. EOEF; LCAP

Thyrsis, *sel.* Matthew Arnold. FiP; NAEL-2; NOBE; NoP; OBEV; OBNC
"How changed is here each spot man makes or fills!" FaBoPP; Mes

Thyrsis. Edward Cracroft Lefroy, *after the Greek of* Theocritus. *Fr.* Echoes from Theocritus, XXVI. AWP

Thyrsis, a youth of the inspired train. The Story of Phoebus and Daphne Applied, etc. Edmund Waller. InvP; NAEL-1; OBS

Thyrsis and Milla, arm in arm together. *Unknown.* GBL

Thyrsis, Sleep'st Thou? *Unknown.* InvP; OBSC; OxBSP

Thys ender nyght. *Unknown.* TrGrPo, *abr*

Thys Endris Nyght. *Unknown. See* This Endris Night.

Ti-ch'ü Song Words. *Unknown, tr. fr. Chinese by* Burton Watson. CoBCP

Tiare Tahiti. Rupert Brooke. BrPo

Tibetan Book of the Dead, The, *sel. Unknown, tr. fr. Tibetan by* W. Y. Evans-Wentz.
Prayer for Guidance. OBD

Tibur is beautiful, too, and the orchard slopes, and the Anio. Arthur Hugh Clough. *Fr.* Amours de Voyage, Canto III, xi. GTBS-P
(So Not Seeing I Sung.) OBNC
(Valley and Villa of Horace, The.) FaBoPP

Tichborne's Elegy. Chidiock Tichborne. EiL; FaBoRV; FF; HAP; HeIP; InPS; NoP; OAEL-1
(Elegy for Himself.) RB
(Elegy: "My prime of youth is but a frost of cares.") ChTr; EBEV; NOBE; OBSC; WeW
(Elegy, Written with His Own Hand in the Tower before His Execution.) DL; InPK
(On the Eve of His Execution.) TrGrPo
(Retrospect.) ACP
(Written on the Eve of Execution.) LiTB
(Written the Night before His Execution.) SCV

Tick-a-lock rock-a-bye. Child's Game. Judson Jerome. DuDa

Tick Picking in the Quetico. Don Johnson. MAYP

Tick tick tick tick tick tick tick. Toaster Time. Eve Merriam. RAR

Tickle Rhyme, The. Ian Serraillier. NTCP; OnUR; PYC; RHPC

Tickled,/ my thoughts wander. Celebration for My Mother. Wendy Rose. CDW

Tickly, tickly, on your knee. *Unknown.* OxNR

Ticonderoga; a Legend of the West Highlands. Robert Louis Stevenson. OBNV

Tidal throughway from a distance, The. Lyn Hejinian. IAT

Tidal wave entered the room, The. The Brothers Lacôte. Louis Aragon, *tr. by* Michael Benedikt. POS

Tiddle liddle lightum. *Unknown.* OxNR

Tide, The. Longfellow. *See* Tide Rises, the Tide Falls, The.

Tide and Time. Roger McGouch. TDD

Tide be runnin' the great world over. Sea Love. Charlotte Mew. MoAB; MoBrPo; OxBTC; TrGrPo

Tide of Faith, The. "George Eliot." *Fr.* A Minor Prophet. WGRP

Tide of Life, The, *sel.* Watson Kirkconnell.
"Ah, Flood of Life on which I am a wave." CaP

Tide Rises, the Tide Falls, The. Longfellow. AA; AmPP; BLPL; ChTr; FaFP; MOS; NOBA; OxBA; PoE; PoRA; TAP
(Tide, The.) WiR

Tide slips up the silver sand, The. Sea-Way. Ellen Mackay Hutchinson Cortissoz. AA

Tide That from the West Washes Africa to the Bone, The. David Rubadiri. WMBCH

Tide Turning. John Frederick Nims. DiPo; FYAP

Tideline. Marvin Bell. BLA

Tides, The. Paul Blackburn. PoM

Tides, The. Bryant. TAP

Tides. William Stafford. KS

Tides carry the haze, The. Kaya Shirao, *tr. fr. Japanese by* Hiroaki Sato. *Fr.* Twenty-one Hokku. FCEI

Tides Run up the Wairau, The. Eileen Duggan. ATNZ; PeNZ

Tides shape the sides of the agate mountain. On Visiting My Son, Port Angeles, Washington. Duane Niatum. CDW

Tidewash. Memories. Lament of the Flutes. Christopher Okigbo. PBA

Tidewater born he was, and ever. The Rivers Remember. Nancy Byrd Turner. AmFN

Tie a bandage over his eyes. A Rebel. John Gould Fletcher. MoAmPo

Tie me haan up. Slave Song. David Dabydeen. PVCV; UAS

Tie one end of a rope fast over a beam. A Receipt to Cure a Love Fit. *Unknown.* NOEC

Tie the moccasin, bind the pack. Young Washington. Arthur Guiterman. FaPON; OHIP

Tie the strings to my life, my Lord. Emily Dickinson. PoE; TrCP

Tie your own noose if you want to be. The Advice of an Efficiency Expert. Augustus Young. CIP

Tiempo Muerto. Ricardo Alonso. SaC

T'ien Kuang has grown old. On a Historical Topic. Ts'ao Chen-chi, *tr. by* William H. Nienhauser, Jr.. WFTU

T'ien-t'ai Mountain is tall. Ballad of Peach Blossom Spring. Yüan Mei, *tr. by* Jonathan Chaves. CoBLCP

Ties. Raymond Souster. MoCV; OBCV

Ties. Dabney Stuart. GrPl

Tiger, The. Hilaire Belloc. MoBrPo

Tiger [*or* Tyger], The. Blake. *Fr.* Songs of Experience. AWP; BoTP; CH; ChTr; EaLo; EnRP; FaBoBe; FaBoCh; FaBoPV; FaBV; FaFP; FaPON; FaPoR; FF; FM; FPL; GN; HAP; HeIP; HoPM; InPK; InPS; LiTB; Mes; NAWM-2; NIP; NOBE; NOEC; NoP; OAEL-2; OBEV; OBNC; PoE; PoEL-4; PoLF; PoRA; PPP; PrIm; RB; SCV; SeCePo; SoSe; TEP; TTTS; UnPo; WGRP

Tiger. Alec Derwent Hope, *tr. fr. Russian.* OxBC; RB

Tiger, The. Kuramakal Ilaveyini, *tr. fr. Tamil by* A. K. Ramanujan. PLW

Tiger. Claude McKay. BPo

Tiger. *Yoruba Oral Tradition, tr. by* B. King. WTO

Tiger Bay. *Unknown.* OxBSS

Tiger Christ unsheathed his sword. For the One Who Would Take Man's Life in His Hands. Delmore Schwartz. LiTA; LiTM; MoAB; MoAmPo; VGW; WaP

Tiger in the tiger-pit, The. Lines for an Old Man. T. S. Eliot. FaBoTw; RB; TW

Tiger-Lilies. Thomas Bailey Aldrich. GN

Tiger of Desire, The. Tom MacInnes. OBCV

Tiger, on the other hand, is kittenish and mild, The. The Tiger. Hilaire Belloc. MoBrPo

Tiger People. Geary Hobson. STE

"Tiger, strolling at my side." Triumph of Sensibility. Sylvia Townsend Warner. MoAB; MoBrPo

Tiger, Sunflowers, King of Cats. The Marmalade Man Makes a Dance to Mend Us. Nancy Willard. ILY

Tiger Tale, A. John Bennett. OBCA

Tiger! Tiger! [*or* Tyger! Tyger!] burning bright. The Tiger [*or* Tyger]. Blake. *Fr.* Songs of Experience. AWP; BoTP; CH; ChTr; EaLo; EnRP; FaBoBe; FaBoCh; FaBoPV; FaBV; FaFP; FaPON; FaPoR; FF; FM; FPL; GN; HAP; HeIP; HoPM; InPK; InPS; LiTB; Mes; NAWM-2; NIP; NOBE; NOEC; NoP; OAEL-2; OBEV; OBNC; PoE; PoEL-4; PoLF; PoRA; PPP; PrIm; RB; SCV; SeCePo; SoSe; TEP; TTTS; UnPo; WGRP

Tigers of Nanzen-ji, The. Brad Leithauser. DiPo

Tiggady Rue. David McCord. WSC

Tight,—proof, unavailable. Falling Out. Helen Chasin. IHMS

Tight Rope. Imamu Amiri Baraka. CNA

Tight scrimmage of blankets in the dark. Ward Two. Francis Webb. CBAP

Tight-sphinctered and inhibited. Peace Delegate. Douglas Livingstone. PeSA

Tightly-folded bud. Born Yesterday. Philip Larkin. NAs

Tihei Mauriora I called. Sad Joke on a Marae. Apirana Taylor. PeNZ

Till as ye ought your barren lands. Cultivate Your Men. Edwin Waugh. PF

Till Christ ("Till Christ, quhome I am haldin for to lufe"). *Unknown.* *Fr.* The Gude and Godlie Ballatis. OxBS

Till Death Do Us Part. Leila Miccolis, *tr. fr. Portuguese by* Willis Barnstone *and* Nelson Cerqueira. BoWoP

Till I shall come again, let this suffice. A Panegyric to Sir Lewis Pemberton. Robert Herrick. CaPo

Till my black hair be white. "Takahashi." *Fr.* Manyo Shu. Ma

Till my hair is white like the falling snow. Tachihana Moroe. *Fr.* Manyo Shu. Ma

Till now the doubtful dusk reveal'd. Tennyson. *Fr.* In Memoriam A. H. H., XCV. GTBS-P

Till now your indiscretion sets us free. Eves Apologie. Emilia Lanier. BoWoP

Till the laughter dies down. *Unknown, tr. by* Geoffrey Bownas *and* Anthony Thwaite. PeBJV

Till the Sea Runs Dry. *Malay Oral Tradition, tr. by* R. J. Wilkinson. WTO

Till the slow daylight pale. The Sun-Flower. Dora Greenwell. WPE

Till they see it. *Unknown.* *Fr.* Manyo Shu. FCEI

Till they tangled and seemed to trip and lie down. His Legs Ran About. Ted Hughes. LLLT

Till thinking had worn out my enterprise. Spring Mountain Climb. Richard Eberhart. GoYe

Till you've earned. Mahádéviyakka, *tr. by* A. K. Ramanujan. PBWP

Tilly. James Joyce. RB

Tilt. Wilt. Snow. Ralph Pomeroy. Psk

Tilth. Robert Graves. FaBoEE; OBSV

Tilting Sail. Gyula Illyés, *tr. fr. Hungarian by* William Jay Smith. MHuP

Tim. John Montague. FaBCIP

Tim Finnegan [*or* Finnigin *or* Finigan] liv'd in Walkin [*or* lived in Walker] Street. Finnegan's Wake. *Unknown.* FaBoBa; NBLV
(Finigan's Wake.) BLPA

Tim, the Fairy. Florence Randal Livesay. CaP

Tim tryeth truth convicting all that strive. T. Street. SCAP

Tim Turpin. Thomas Hood. WiR

Timarista and Krito. Rosanna Warren. *Fr.* Funerary Portraits, III. NOAM

Timber. *Unknown.* AS

Timber, The. Henry Vaughan. FaBoRV, *abr.*; NoP; OBEV; SeCP; SeCV-1

Timbers heaving to heaven we sailed at seven. Crabbing. Norman Levine. CaP; OBCV

Time. Mary Ursula Bethell. FaBoWP

Time. Bhartrihari, *tr. fr. Sanskrit by* Paul Elmer More. AWP

Time. Amy Clampitt. NIP

Time. Thomas Stephens Collier. AA

Time. Robert Creeley. LCAP

Time. Allen Curnow. ATNZ

Time, The. George Sutherland Fraser. WaP

Time. Giles Fletcher the Elder. *See* Licia: In time [*or* tyme] the strong and stately [*or* statelie] turrets fall.

Time. Robert Graves. LiTM

Time. George Herbert. NAEL-1; TEP

Time. Ralph Hodgson. BrPo; GTBS-P

Time. Avraham Huss, *tr. fr. Hebrew by* Mark Elliott Shapiro. VWA

Time. Juana de Ibarbourou, *tr. fr. Spanish by* Perry Higman. LPSS

Time. Jasper Mayne. OBEV

Time. Jacques Roubaud, *tr. fr. French by* Robert Kelly. RHTwFP

Time. Shelley. FaBoRV; FPL; MOS; Par; PoLF

Time. William Stafford. Son

Time. Allan Taylor. OBET

Time. Thomas Watson. *Fr.* Hecatompathia; or, Passionate Century of Love. FaBoRV; OBSC

Time. John Huddlestone Wynne. OxBChV

Time after time, afraid of the chilly spring weather. Hsü Pen, *tr. fr. Chinese by* Jonathan Chaves. *Fr.* Five Things Sought For——In the Manner of Han Wo. CoBLCP

Time after time you're placed at the imagined. Yehuda Amichai, *tr. fr. Hebrew by* Warren Bargad *and* Stanley F. Chyet. *Fr.* Achziv, 4. IP

Time allowed for sleep at length elapsed, The. Thomas Cole. *Fr.* The Life of Hubert. NOEC

Time and again. Theology and a Patchwork Absolute. Heather McPherson. PeNZ

Time and Eternity. Bunyan. WiR

Time and Eternity. Fulke Greville. *See* Caelica: You that seek what life is in death.

Time and Eternity. Stephen Hawes. *Fr.* The Pastime of Pleasure. PoEL-1

Time and Grief. William Lisle Bowles. OBEV

Time and Love, I. Shakespeare. *See* Sonnets: LXIV. "When I have seen by Time's fell hand defaced."

Time and Love, II. Shakespeare. *See* Sonnets: LXV. "Since brass, nor stone, nor earth, nor boundless sea."

Time and the changing passions played them tricks. The Early Rebels. Mervyn Morris. PVCV

Time and the Child. Hone Tuwhare. ATNZ

Time and the Garden. Yvor Winters. MoAMPo; NoAM; QFR; VGW

Time and the mortal will stand never fast. Luis de Camões, *tr. by* Richard Garnett. AWP

Time and the weather wear away. Houses. Donald Justice. EyDe (Poem: "Time and the weather wear away.") PoA

Time and the World, whose magnitude and weight. Robert Southey. OBNC

Time and Tide. Hazel Washington Lamarre. PoNe

Time & time again the laughter after the footsteps. The Jungle. Diane DiPrima. PoM

Time breaks the barrier. Hilda Doolittle ("H. D."). *Fr.* Sigil, XVII. AnAn

Time can [*or* will] say nothing but I told you so. W. H. Auden. LiTA; MoAB; MoBrPo

Time cannot age thy sinews, nor the gale. Albatross. Charles Warren Stoddard. AA

Time cannot break the bird's wing from the bird. To a Young Poet. Edna St. Vincent Millay. OxBSP

Time Caught in a Net. Dahlia Ravikovich, *tr. fr. Hebrew by* Warren Bargad *and* Stanley F. Chyet. IP

Time comes when, A. Komachi, *tr. fr. Japanese by* Burton Watson. *Fr.* Kokin Shu. FCEI

Time, cruel time, come and subdue that brow. Samuel Daniel. *Fr.* To Delia. OBSC

Time demands a rolling eye, The. The Time. George Sutherland Fraser. WaP

Time Does Not Bring Relief. Edna St. Vincent Millay. FaBV

Time does not burn you. In the Zoo. Solomon Mahaka. WMBCH

Time drawes neere. Anne Waldman. UL

Time draws near the birth of Christ, The. Tennyson. *Fr.* In Memoriam A. H. H., XXVIII. FaBoRV; NOCV; PChr

Time drops in decay. The Moods. W. B. Yeats. CTC

Time ends when vision sees its lapse in/ liberty. Beata l'Alma. Sir Herbert Read. FaBoMo

Time Exposures. Muriel Rukeyser. PoA

Time: first day of the eighth month. Ryokan, *tr. by* Burton Watson. JLIC-2

Time flees time, time is like a larva. Time. Jacques Roubaud, *tr. by* Robert Kelly. RHTwFP

Time flits away, time flits away, lady. Variation on Ronsard. T. Sturge Moore. OBMV

Time folds you in. Skin. Gerrit Achterberg, *tr. by* James S. Holmes. DuIn

Time for Building, A. Myra Cohn Livingston. PDV

Time for Everything, A. Bible, *O.T. See* Ecclesiastes: To Everything There Is a Season.

Time for rain! for your long hot dry autumn. Piano di Sorrento. Robert Browning. *Fr.* The Englishman in Italy. FaBoPP; SeCePo (Englishman in Italy, The ["Time for rain! for your long hot dry autumn"].) SeCePo

Time for the brave would be algebra, terminal. Spring Betrayed. Marjorie Boulton. CN

Time goes, you say? Ah, no! The Paradox of Time. Pierre de Ronsard, *tr. by* Austin Dobson. AWP

Time gone. Blue Mason Jars. Keith Abbott. UL

Time has a certain rhythm. Sound of Water. Julio Ortega, *tr. by* David Tipton. Per

Time has a magic wand! On an Old Muff. Frederick Locker-Lampson. CenHV

Time has an end, they say. Hilda Doolittle ("H. D."). *Fr.* Good Frend. NOBA; VGW

Time has been that these wild solitudes, The. A Winter Piece. Bryant. AmPP; OxBA

Time has been when I longed for this safety. The Elegy of a Bronze Age Man. Zoltán Jékely, *tr. by* Edwin Morgan. MHuP

Time has brought about great changes. Scraps of Time. Mrs. Henry Linden. CBWP-4

Time has come for us to part, The. I'm Through with You. *Unknown.* WTO

Time has come, the clock says time has come, The. Conrad Aiken. *Fr.* Preludes for Memnon; or, Preludes to Attitude. LiTA; OxBA

Time has come to devote myself to my hiker's stick, The. On Receiving My Letter of Termination. Yüan Hung-tao, *tr. by* Jonathan Chaves. CoBLCP

Time has no flight—'tis we who speed along. Time. Thomas Stephens Collier. AA

Time has pulled up a chair, dashed. Ron Mason. Hone Tuwhare. PeNZ

Time hath, my Lord, a wallet at his back. Ulysses Advises Achilles. Shakespeare. *Fr.* Troilus and Cressida, III, iii. LiTB

Time heals not: it extends a sorrow's scope. J. V. Cunningham. VGW

Time holds no purring hour-glass to your face. The Day. George M. Brady. NeIP

Time I dropped your almost body down, The. The Lost Baby Poem. Lucille Clifton. BlSi; CAPP; WPE

Time I went to church I sat, The. Mr. Rockefeller's Hat. Helen Smith Bevington. OBAL

Time I went to see my Sister, The. Tsurayuki, *tr. fr. Japanese by* Arthur Waley. *Fr.* Shui Shu. AWP

Time in the Rock [or, Preludes to Definition], *sels.* Conrad Aiken. VGW

"Bird flying past my head said previous previous, The." *Fr.* LXII.

"But no, the familiar symbol, as that the." *Fr.* XCII.

"Mysticism, but let us have no words." *Fr.* XI.

"What face she put on it, we will not discuss." *Fr.* LXXXIV.

"Where we were walking in the day's light, seeing." *Fr.* XXXVII.

Time is, The. Anger. Robert Creeley. NaP

Time is a fox on quick, velvet feet. Earthly Illusion. Louise Leighton. GoYe

Time is a thief who leaves his tools behind him. The Angel-Thief. Oliver Wendell Holmes. AnAmPo

Time is a thing. Stephen Spender. MoBrPo

Time is a treasure. New Time. *Unknown.* BLRP

Time is after dinner, The. Cigarettes. The Boarder. Louis Simpson. InPK; SM

Time is at the end, The. Ox-Bow. Donald Davie. DiPo

Time is come to speak, I think, The. Mrs. Golightly. Gertrude Hall. AA

Time is divided into. Time Is the Mercy of Eternity. Kenneth Rexroth. VGW

Time is engraved on the pale green faces. Written in the Sunset. Hsiung-hung, *tr. by* Kenneth Rexroth *and* Ling Chung. OV

Time is gold in the Golden Land. "Watch Your Step!" Moyshe-Leyb Halpern, *tr. by* Benjamin *and* Barbara Harshav *and* Kathryn Helle. AYP

Time is mainly a fiction here. There are. New Guinea Time. Louis Johnson. ATNZ; PeNZ

Time is moving, people move up and down. The Parade. Ashton Greene. NePoAm

Time is never wasted, listening to the trees. The Trees. Lucy Larcom. OHIP

Time is not remote when I, The. Swift. *Fr.* Verses on the Death of Doctor Swift [D.S.P.D., Occasioned by Reading a Maxim in Rochefoucauld]. EBEV; Mes; NOBE; NOBL; NOIV

Time is of the essence. This is a highly skilled. Polo Grounds. Rolfe Humphries. HoPM; SD

Time is ripe and I repent, The. Oengus Céile Dé. NOIV

Time Is Swiftly Rolling On, The. Berryman Hicks. AH, *with music* (Dying Father's Farewell, The.) AmFP

Time is the feather'd thing. Time. Jasper Mayne. OBEV

Time Is the Fire. Delmore Schwartz. *See* Repetitive Heart, The: Calmly We Walk Through This April's Day.

Time Is the Mercy of Eternity. Kenneth Rexroth. VGW

Time is the root of all this earth. Time. Bhartrihari, *tr. by* Paul Elmer More. AWP

Time Is Today, The. John Chipman Farrar. GoYe

Time it took he could have, The. The Invention of the Telephone. Peter Klappert. AmPA

Time I've Lost in Wooing, The. Thomas Moore. EnRP; HoPM; NAEL-2

Time like an Ever-rolling Stream. P. G. Wodehouse. FiBHP

Time like the receptions of a child's piano. The Reconciliation. Archibald MacLeish. MoAmPo

Time Machine, The. Jon Anderson. AnAn; NAmP

Time of Change, A. Egan O'Rahilly, *tr. fr. Irish.* BIrV, *tr. by* Eavan Boland; FaBoPV, *tr. by* Eavan Boland

Time of coppersun, of hot withering. Jud' Süss Tells about Them and about Himself. Judah Leib Teller, *tr. fr. Yiddish by* Benjamin *and* Barbara Harshav. *Fr.* Psychoanalysis. AYP

Time of Creation Has Come, The. *Yoruba Oral Tradition, tr. by* Ulli Beier. WTO

Time of Day. Selden Rodman. PoA

Time of Fish Dying. Gabriela Melinescu, *tr. fr. Rumanian by* Stavros Deligiorgis. BoWoP

Time of grease beginneth at Midsummer day. Julians Barnes. *Fr.* Book of Hunting. WPE

"The Time of Man." Phyllis Webb. MoCV

Time of Roses. Thomas Hood. *See* It Was Not in the Winter.

Time of the Barmecides, The. James Clarence Mangan. EnRP

Time of the Sea. Pierre Reverdy, *tr. fr. French by* Michael Benedikt. POS

Time of Waiting. Geoffrey Dutton. CBAP

Time of Waiting in Amsterdam. Ingrid Jonker, *tr. fr. Afrikaans by* Jack Cope *and* William Plomer. BoWoP; OV

Time; or, How the Line about Chagall's Lovers Disappears. Jane Miller. SM

Time Out. Frances Westgate Butterfield. GoYe

Time Out. Donald Finkel. HoPM

Time Out. Oliver Jenkins. GoYe

Time out of mind I have stood. The Old Grey Wall. Bliss Carman. CaP

Time Passes. Kitahara Hakushu, *tr. fr. Japanese by* Hiroaki Sato. FCEI

Time Passes. Richard Percival Lister. NYBP

Time Passing, Beloved ("Time passing, and the memories of love"). Donald Davie. BoLoP; NePoEA-2

Time Past, A. Denise Levertov. NoAM

Time Piece. William Cole. GrPI

Time-Piece, The. William Cowper. *Fr.* The Task, II. EnRP

Time pleats dark flesh. Faces and Skulls. Jan Carew. PVCV

Time Poem. Quentin Hill. NBP

Time present and time past. Burnt Norton. T. S. Eliot. *Fr.* Four Quartets. CMoP; LiTM; MoAB; MoAmPo; NAAL-2; PoE
"Words move, music moves." *Fr.* V. UnS

Time promises, should I in that confide? Ilyas Farhat, *tr. by* Salma Khadra Jayyusi *and* John Heath-Stubbs. MAP

Time quietly compiling us like sheaves. Seferis. Lawrence Durrell. EBEV

Time, Real and Imaginary. Samuel Taylor Coleridge. EnRP; NOBE; OBEV; OxBSP

Time Recover'd. Thomas Stanley, *after the Italian of* Girolamo Casone. OBVE

Time Reminded Me. Julia Uceda, *tr. fr. Spanish by* Willis Barnstone. BoWoP

Time requires me to give account. Time and Account. Miguel de Guevara, *tr. by* Samuel Beckett. MexPo

Time rolls his ceaseless course. The race of yore. The Gathering. Sir Walter Scott. *Fr.* The Lady of the Lake. OBNC

Time seems not now beneath his years to stoop. Dryden. *Fr.* To His Sacred Majesty, a Panegyrick on His Coronation, 1661. OBS

Time-Servers. Judah Halevi, *tr. fr. Hebrew by* Solomon Solis-Cohen. TrJP

Time shall come when wrong shall end, The. Thomas Cooper. *Fr.* Two Chartist Songs. PF

Time sitting on the throne of Memory. October XXIX, 1795. William Stanley Braithwaite. CDC

Time spirals upright this unflowing river. The Well. A. J. Seymour. PVCV

"Time stands still." The Unbeseechable. Frances Cornford. MoBrPo

Time stands still, with gazing on her face! *Unknown.* EnLoPo

Time, sweeping, desolates. To Be Absent without Leave. Kendrick Smithyman. ATNZ

Time taken by the forelock as he flies. Bluebell. Geoffrey Taylor. NeIP

Time that bringes all things to light. Thomas Morton. SCAP

Time that is moved by little fidget wheels. Five Bells. Kenneth Slessor. CBAP; PoAu-2; PoRA; SeCePc

Time there was—as one may guess. Before Life and After. Thomas Hardy. FaBoRV

Time ticks away the centre of my pride. The Empty Glen. R. Crombie Saunders. OxBS

Time time said old King Tut. Don Marquis. FiBHP

Time to Die. Ray Garfield Dandridge. BANP; PoBA

Time to Die, The. Matilda Caroline Edwards. PWR

Time to get. It's Nation Time. Imamu Amiri Baraka. NoP

Time to Go. "Susan Coolidge." GN

Time to Leave. Ory Bernstein, *tr. fr. Hebrew by* Warren Bargad *and* Stanley F. Chyet. JP

Time to Myself. Paulette Jiles. NOBC

Time to put off the world and go somewhere. Beggar to Beggar Cried. W. B. Yeats. CMoP; NoAM

Time to Rise. Robert Louis Stevenson. OxBChV

Time to Stay, a Time to Go, A. Baxter Black. CowP

Time to Talk, A. Robert Frost. ILY

Time to tell you things are well, A. Snow Country Weavers. James Welch. CDW; HATNAP

Time to Tickle a Lizard, The. The Lizard. Theodore Roethke. GrPI; RHPC

Time to Trust, The. *Unknown.* BLRP

Time transcribes its passage on seashell piles. Down There. Robert Marteau, *tr. by* John Montague. RHTwFP

Time was, an Englishman would join. James Cawthorn. *Fr.* Of Taste; an Essay. NOEC

Time was, and that was termed the time of Gold. Joseph Hall. *Fr.* Virgidemiarum, *bk.* III, Satire I. OBSV (Olden Days, The.) OBSC

Time was away and somewhere else. Meeting Point. Louis MacNeice. FaBCIP

Time was he sang the British brute. Ballade of Expansion. Hilda Johnson. PAH

Time was he went for weeks without. The Elk on Mutability. John Bensko. MT

Time was, I shrank from what was right. Sensitiveness. John Henry, Cardinal Newman. TrCP

Time was I was a plowman driving. Plowman. Sidney Keyes. MoAB; PoRA

Time Was the Trail Went Deep. Charles G. Ballard. NOVW

Time was upon/ The wing, to flie away. Upon Time. Robert Herrick. OBS

Time was when his half million drew. Bewick Finzer. E. A. Robinson. CMoP; MoAB; MoAmPo; NAAL-2; PPP

Time was when I was free as air. On a Goldfinch Starved to Death in His Cage. William Cowper. OBD

Time was when I was weapon and warrior. Horn: "Time was when I was weapon and warrior." *Unknown, formerly at. to* Cynewulf, *tr. fr. Anglo-Saxon by* Charles W. Kennedy. *Fr.* Riddles (Exeter Book). AnOE

Time was when once upon a time, such toys. Glaukos, *tr. by* Peter Jay. PeHV

Time wasted and time spent. The Times. Charles Madge. OBMV

Time wasteth years, and months, [and days], and hours. Time. Thomas Watson. *Fr.* Hecatompathia; or, Passionate Century of Love. FaBoRV; OBSC

Time We Climbed Snake Mountain, The. Leslie Marmon Silko. VoR

Time When the Day Ended. Michael Burkard. NAmP

Time will assuage. To the Reader. J. V. Cunningham. QFR

Time will come when, looking in a glass, The. The Frailty of Beauty. "J. C." *Fr.* Alcilia. EIL

Time will not be mastered, he will do just as he please. Time. Allan Taylor. OBET

Time Will Not Grant. Sidney Keyes. SeCePo

Time will say nothing but I told you so. *See* Time can say nothing but I told you so.

Time Will Surely Come, The. Robert T. Daniel. AH

Time will surely not be in the least evil anymore then. Moment of Calm. Aimé Césaire, *tr. by* Michael Benedikt. POS

Time with his scythe honed fine. Hay Fever. Alec Derwent Hope. NoAM

Time would not wait on me. Time and Tide. Hazel Washington Lamarre. PoNe

Time wounds all heals, spills through. You. Charles Bernstein. LP

Time, You Old Gypsy Man. Ralph Hodgson. BoTP; BrPo; CH; FaPON; LiTM; MoAB; MoBrPo; MoShBr; TrGrPo

Time you won your town the race, The. To an Athlete Dying Young. A. E. Housman. *Fr.* A Shropshire Lad, XIX. BLPL; BrPo; CMoP; DL; HAP; HeIP; InPK; LiTB; LiTM; MoAB; MoBrPo; MoP; NAEL-2; NIP; NoAM; NoP; PoE; PoEL-5; PoRA; PrIm; SoSe; TEP; TrGrPo; UnPo; WeW

Time Zones for Forty-four. Donald A. Stauffer. WaP
Timely blossom, infant fair. To Miss Charlotte Pulteney in Her Mother's Arms [*or* To Charlotte Pulteney]. Ambrose Philips. ELP; GTBS; GTBS-P; NOEC
Timepiece, A. James Merrill. HoPM; NePoEA-2
Timer. Tony Harrison. *Fr.* The School of Eloquence. NoAM
Timers. Flora J. Arnstein. GoYe
Times, The, *sels.* Charles Churchill.
   "Go where we will, at ev'ry time and place." PeHV
   "Is a son born into this world of woe?." OBSV
Times, The. Charles Madge. OBMV
Times, The. *Unknown.* PAH
Time's a circumference. The Soul of Time. Trumbull Stickney. LiTA
Time's an hand's-breadth; 'tis a tale. Time. John Huddlestone Wynne. OxBChV
Times are good, there's no cruel government, The. Along the River, Seeing the Home of Absconded Farmers. Kao Ch'i, *tr. by* Jonathan Chaves. CoBLCP
Times are right for the organ, The. Organ and Sulphur. Antonin Artaud, *tr. by* Michael Benedikt. POS
Times are swiftly drawing nigh. When You and I Must Part. *Unknown.* AmFP
Time's Bright Sand. Robert Finch. CaP
Time's Changes. James Bramston. *Fr.* The Art of Politics. NOEC
Times come round again, The. To a Military Rifle, 1942. Yvor Winters. MoAmPo; WaP
"Time's Conscience!" cried the allerion. For-ever Morning. Laura Riding. LiTA
Time's Dedication. Delmore Schwartz. VGW
Time's Fool. Ruth Pitter. MoBrPo; OxBTC; PoRA; WPE
Time's fool, but not heaven's: yet hope not for any return. Time's Fool. Ruth Pitter. MoBrPo; OxBTC; PoRA; WPE
Times Gettin' Hard, Boys. *Unknown.* AS
Time's Glory. Shakespeare. *Fr.* The Rape of Lucrece ChTr
Times Go [*or* Goe] By Turns [*or* Turnes]. Robert Southwell. ACP; EIL; LiTB; OBSC; PoEL-2
Times Have Altered, The. *Unknown.* CoMu
Times have changed. Anything Goes. Cole Porter. OBAL
Times have changed, there is not left to us, The. Allen Tate. *Fr.* Sonnets of the Blood, IV. PoA
Time's Mirror. Peyton Houston. *Fr.* Sonnet Variations, LXXVII. Son
Time's No Grammar. Márton Kalász, *tr. fr. Hungarian by* Jascha Kessler. FOC
Times o' Year. William Barnes. BoNaP
Time's Revenges. Sir Owen Seaman. FaBoUs
Times she'll sit quiet by the hearth, and times. The Woodcutter's Wife. William Rose Benét. AWP
Time's Song. Winthrop Mackworth Praed. EnRP
Times Square Poems, *sels.* Michael Lassell.
   Dino. GLP
   Going Rate, The. GLP
   How to Find Love in an Instant. GLP
   Stud. GLP
Times-Square-Shoeshine-Composition. Maya Angelou. RR
Times stir in me uncalendrically, chaotically. Amir Gilboa, *tr. by* Warren Bargad *and* Stanley F. Chyet. IP
Times wherein old Pompion was a Saint, The. New-Englands Crisis. Benjamin Tompson. SCAP
Time's winged chariot (poets say). To His Not-so-coy Mistress. Wynford Vaughan-Thomas. BXAP; NOBL
Timid Bunnies. Jeannie Kirby. BoTP
Timid child with heart oppressed, A. Buffalo Creek. John Le Gay Brereton. PoAu-1
Timid corn-poney's heart fluttered, The. The Corn-Pone-y. Carolyn Wells. *Fr.* A Baker's Dozen of Wild Beasts. OBCA
Timid Gazelle, The. Kasmuneh, *tr. fr. Arabic.* TrJP
Timid Hortense. Peter Newell. NA
Timid Lover. Countee Cullen. BANP
Timon Curses Athens and Mankind. Shakespeare. *Fr.* Timon of Athens, IV, i. TW
Timon of Archimedes. Charles Battell Loomis. NA
Timon of Athens, *sels.* Shakespeare.
   Timon Curses Athens and Mankind. *Fr.* IV, i. TW
   Timon's Epitaph. *Fr.* V, iv. AWP
   "Warr'st thou 'gainst Athens?" *Fr.* IV, iii. EBEV
Timon Speaks to a Dog. Philip Hobsbaum. TW
Timon's Epitaph. Shakespeare. *Fr.* Timon of Athens, V, iv. AWP
Timon's Villa. Pope. *Fr.* Epistles to Several Persons, to Richard Boyle, Earl of Burlington: Of the Use of Riches. PoE
Timor Mortis. *Unknown.* FF; NoP
   ("In what state that ever I be.") PBBP

Timor Mortis Conturbat Me. William Dunbar. *See* I that in heill wes and gladness.
Timoshenko. Sidney Keyes. OBWP
Timothy. Timothy Steele. InPK
Timothy Titus took two ties. *Unknown.* OxNR
Timothy Tompkins had turnips and tea. The Meal. Karla Kuskin. RAR
Timothy Winters. Charles Causley. RB
Tin Frog, The. Russell Hoban. RHPC; TSS
Tin-Ore. *Malay Oral Tradition, tr. by* W. W. Skeat. WTO
Tin shack, where my baby sleeps on his back. Everything: Eloy, Arizona, 1956. Ai. AmPA; FF
Tin Toys. Tsfrirah Gar, *tr. fr. Hebrew by* Bernhard Frank. MHeP
Tin Woodsman, The. Paulette Jiles. NOBC
Tina and Seth met in the midst of an overcrowded militarism. Histoire. Harry Mathews. BAP
Tinder, The. Thomas Carew. CaPo
Ting-star is in the middle of the sky, The. *Unknown, tr. by* Arthur Waley. BoS
Ting, ting goes the woodman's axe. *Unknown, tr. by* Arthur Waley. BoS
Tinged with the blood of Aztec lands. El Vaquero. Lucius Harwood Foote. AA
Tingle, The. Norman Andrew Kirk. TSM
Tiniest of Lives, The. Chin Jen-Jui, *tr. fr. Chinese by* Irving Lo. WFTU
Tiniest of turtles! Ladybird. Clive Sansom. GrPl
Tink dere is a God in a top. *Unknown. Fr.* Work-Songs, I. PBCV
Tinker,/ Tailor. *Unknown.* OxNR; SaC
Tinker, The. *Unknown.* CoMu
Tinker Man. *Unknown.* RR
Tinker, The ("There was a lady in this land"). *Unknown.* CoMu
Tinker's Wife. Patrick Kavanagh. CIP; InPS; MoP; NoAM
"Tinkle, tinkle, tinkle": 'tis the muffin-man you see. The Muffin-Man's Bell. Ann Hawkshawe. BoTP
Tins fixed to stakes. Western Civilization. Agostinho Neto, *tr. by* Marga Holness. WMBCH
Tint I cannot take is best, The. Emily Dickinson. MoAmPo
Tintern Abbey. Edward Davies. *Fr.* Chepstow: A Poem. OBWVE
Tintock. *Unknown.* GBP
Tiny ant at night you would be seeking, The. The Disdainful Mistress. *Malay Oral Tradition, tr. by* R. J. Wilkinson *and* R. O. Winstedt. WTO
Tiny baby, you're ugly. King D. Kuka. VoR
Tiny Catullus. Steve Levine. UL
Tiny children. Yityangu Ejong, *tr. by* Frank Wordick. CBAP
Tiny fish enjoy themselves, The. Little Fish. D. H. Lawrence. OxBTC; RB; SOTW; TTTS
Tiny fly fell down on my page, A. A Death to Us. Jon Silkin. NePoEA
Tiny green birds skate over the surface of the room. Saturday Night in the Parthenon. Kenneth Patchen. EAS
Tiny island, A. Ladybug. François Dodat, *tr. by* Bert *and* Odette Meyers. TSS
Tiny light, A. Central Heating. Pierre Reverdy, *tr. by* Michael Benedikt. POS
Tiny little pine tree, still shorter than the fence, A. A Poem on a Little Pine. Hsieh Chin, *tr. by* Jonathan Chaves. CoBLCP
Tiny moon as small and white as a single jasmine flower, A. A White Blossom. D. H. Lawrence. MoBrPo
Tiny nut, a bit of tasteless betel, A. Carved on an Areca Nut. Ho Xuan Huong, *tr. by* Nguyen Ngoc Bich *and* Burton Raffel. PBWP
Tiny shoes so trim and neat. The Fairy Shoemaker. Phyllis L. Garlick. BoTP
Tiny slippers of gold and green. To a Pair of Egyptian Slippers. Sir Edwin Arnold. OBTV
Tiny snow of the stunningly cold black day. In the Snowfall. Gwerfyl Mechain. BoWoP, *tr. by* Willis Barnstone
Tiny spill of bird-things in a swirl, A. The Finches. Thomas William Shapcott. PoAu-2
Tiny structure with one entry, A. The Land of Look Beyond. Michelle Cliff. ER
Tiny, tiny/ Open window. Insect Eyes. Ruth Kim Chun-soo, *tr. by* Koh Chang-soo. ACKP
Tip, The. Albert Goldbarth. HCAP
Tip of my existence, the soldering iron of wet hot flesh, The. Myself in an Anatomical Chart of Sexual Intercourse. Takahashi Mutsuo, *tr. by* Hiroaki Sato. FCEI
Tip of the Iceberg, The. Michael C. Blumenthal. BLA
Tip-of-the-Single-Feather. Velema, *tr. fr. Fijian by* B. H. Quain. WTO
Tip-Toe Tail. Dixie Willson. NTCP
Tippecanoe and Tyler Too. Alexander Coffman Ross. AnAmPo

Tipperty-toes, the smallest elf. Red in Autumn. Elizabeth Gould.
   BoTP
Tips Tongueless. Robert Herrick. CaPo
Tiptoe. Karla Kuskin. PDV
Tired. Fenton Johnson. BANP; IDB; PoBA; PoLF; PoNe; TTY
Tired air groans as the heavies swing over, The. Thiepval Wood.
   Edmund Blunden. MMA
Tired and bloodshot. Abraham Sutskever. Seymour Mayne. VWA
Tired and thirsty, weary of the way. After the Hunt. Detlev, Freiherr
   von Liliencron, tr. by Ludwig Lewisohn. AWP
Tired and Unhappy, You Think of Houses. Delmore Schwartz. LiTM;
   MoAB; MoAmPo
Tired heart sleeps well through the night, The. Twilight Room.
   Hagiwara Sakutaro, tr. by Hiroaki Sato. FCEI
Tired Lovers They Are Machines, The. Lucebert, tr. fr. Dutch by Peter
   Nijmeijer. DuIn
Tired nature's sweet restorer, balmy Sleep! Edward Young. Fr. Night
   Thoughts, Night I. EnRP; NOEC
   (Night.) SeCePo, much abr..
Tired of Eating Kisses. Edward Vincent Swart. PeSA
Tired of sitting indoors all day long. Yakamochi. Fr. Manyo Shu. Ma
Tired of Towns. Andrew Lang. EBVV
Tired of walking in the red dust. The Retreat of Sun Ching-hsiang.
   Chang Yü, tr. by Jonathan Chaves. CoBLCP
Tired Petitioner, The, sel. George Wither.
   "It may be 'tis observ'd, I want relations." SeCV-1
Tired Tim. Walter de la Mare. BoTP; FaPON; MoShBr; NTCP; RHPC
"Tired [or Tyr'd] with all these, for restful death I cry." Shakespeare.
   Fr. Sonnets, LXVI. AWP; CTC; EBEV; FaBoPV; FaFP; HAP; InPS;
   LiTB; NOBE; OAEL-1; OBSC; PoEL-2; TrGrPo; WeW
   (World's Way, The.) GTBS; GTBS-P
Tired with books and rolling on the bed. The New River Head, a
   Fragment. E. Dower. NOEC
Tired with dull grief, grown old before my day. 1916 Seen from 1921.
   Edmund Blunden. MMA
Tired with its dogs and doves. Summer Band Concert. Vivian Smith.
   CBAP
Tired with the noisome follies of the age. Earl of Rochester. Fr.
   Farewell to the Court. TrGrPo
Tired with too long a chase, though stout. On the Death of Squire
   Christopher. John Wigson. OxBSP
Tired Woman, The. Anna Wickham. MoBrPo
Tired Worker, The. Claude McKay. BANP; BPo
Tireles Sculptor, The. Henrietta Cordelia Ray. CBWP-3
Tirelessly the stream licks the world until. Elk Ghosts: A Birth Memory.
   Dave Smith. GeTw
Tires on my bike are flat, The. Since Hanna Moved Away. Judith
   Viorst. RHPC
Tiresias, sel. Austin Clarke.
   "My mother wept loudly." CIP
Tiresias. George Garrett. SM
Tiresias' Lament. Ellen de Young Kay. NePoEA
Tirocinium; or, A Review of Schools, sels. William Cowper. OBSV
   "Father, who designs his babe a priest, The."
   "To you, then, tenants of life's middle state."
   "Would you your son should be a sot or dunce."
Tirumal. Katuvan Ilaveyinanar, tr. fr. Tamil by A. K. Ramanujan. PLW
Tirzah and the Wide World. Dahlia Ravikovich, tr. fr. Hebrew by Warren
   Bargad and Stanley F. Chyet. IP
'Tis a dull sight. Old Song. Edward Fitzgerald. GN; OBEV
'Tis a lesson you should heed. Try, Try Again. At. to T. H. Palmer.
   FaFP; FaPON
'Tis a moon-tinted primrose, with a well. Another. Thomas Lovell
   Beddoes. Son
'Tis a new life;—thoughts move not as they did. The New Birth. Jones
   Very. NOBA
'Tis a puzzlement. Pie Are Square. Pearl Bloch Segall. SoTCo
'Tis a soft Rogue, this Lycias. Lycias. John Wilmot, 2nd Earl of
   Rochester. ErPo
'Tis a stern and startling thing to think. Her Death. Thomas Hood. Fr.
   Miss Kilmansegg and Her Precious Leg. NOBVV
'Tis a time for much rejoicing. Emancipation. Priscilla Jane Thompson.
   CBWP-2
'Tis a world of silences. I gave a cry. Silences. Arthur William Edgar
   O'Shaughnessy. OBNC
'Tis advertised in Boston, New York and Buffalo. Blow Ye Winds in the
   Morning. Unknown. AmFP
'Tis affection but dissembled. Sidney Godolphin. JCP
'Tis all a myth that Autumn grieves. Autumn's Mirth. Samuel Minturn
   Peck. GN

'Tis all the way to Toe-town. Foot Soldiers. John Banister Tabb.
   OBAL
'Tis an act of the priest to give patience a test. Matrimony. John
   Williams. NOEC
'Tis bad enough in man or woman. On Inclosures. Unknown. FaBoCo
   (Epigram: On Inclosures.) OxBoLi
   (On Enclosures.) FaBoEE
" 'Tis better to be vile than vile esteemed." Shakespeare. Fr. Sonnets,
   CXXI. InvP; OAEL-1; PoEL-2
'Tis braul I cudgel, ranters, Quakers braul. Claudius Gilbert. John
   Wilson. SCAP
'Tis But a Little Faded Flower. Ellen Clementine Howarth. AA
'Tis But a night, a long and moonless night. The Grave. Robert Blair.
   OBD
'Tis but a phantom of the weary brain. Life for a Life. Mary E. Tucker.
   CBWP-1
'Tis Christmas weather, and a country house. George Meredith. Fr.
   Modern Love, XXIII. NAEL-2; NOBVV
Tis clear, Great Dane, thy barque's worse than thy bite. King Canute.
   Stanley J. Sharpless. BXAP
'Tis day, my crystal Usk: now the sad night. "So Have I Spent on the
   Banks of Ysca Many a Serious Hour." Thomas Vaughan. FaBoPP
'Tis daylight still, but now the golden cross. The Plaça Santiago.
   "George Eliot." Fr. The Spanish Gypsy. OBTV
'Tis dead night round about: Horror [or Horrour] doth creep[e]. The
   Lamp[e]. Henry Vaughan. QFR
'Tis "Done"—the wondrous thoroughfare. The Pacific Railway. C. R.
   Ballard. PAH
'Tis down in the valley my father does dwell. The Only Daughter.
   Unknown. OBET
'Tis easy enough to be twenty-one. Responsibility. Unknown. FaBoUs
'Tis eight o'clock—a clear March night. The Idiot Boy. Wordsworth.
   OBNV
'Tis evening, the black snail has got on his track. Evening. John Clare.
   NOBVV
'Tis fine to see the Old World, and travel up and down. America for Me.
   Henry Van Dyke. BLPA; BLPL; FaFP; OHFP; OPP; SoSe; WBLP
'Tis God that girds our armor on. The American Soldier's Hymn.
   Unknown. PAH
'Tis gone, that bright and orbèd blaze. Evening. John Keble. TrPWD
'Tis goodbye then to last night. Soraidh Slan Don Oidhche Areir. Niall
   Mor MacMuireadach. BIrV, tr. by Maire Cruise O'Brien
'Tis Hard to Find God. Robert Herrick. LiTB
'Tis hard to find in life. True Friendship. Unknown, tr. fr. Sanskrit by
   Arthur Ryder. Fr. The Panchatantra. AWP
'Tis hard to say, if greater want of skill. An Essay on Criticism. Pope.
   NAEL-1; PoEL-3
'Tis hard to say, if greater want of skill. Pope. Fr. Essay on Criticism,
   pt. I. FiP; HAP; OAEL-1
'Tis in the spirit that attire. Elegance. Christopher Smart. Fr. Hymns
   for the Amusement of Children, XIII. NOCV
'Tis known, at least it should be, that throughout. Beppo; a Venetian
   Story. Byron. NOBL; OBNV; OBSV
'Tis late and cold; stir up the fire. The Dead Host's Welcome. John
   Fletcher. Fr. The Lover's Progress, III, i. TrGrPo
'Tis Lent, the holy time of fast and prayer. The Easter Light. Clara Ann
   Thompson. CBWP-2
'Tis like stirring living embers when, at eighty, one remembers.
   Grandmother's Story of Bunker-Hill Battle. Oliver Wendell Holmes.
   PAH
'Tis love that moveth the celestial spheres. George Santayana. Fr.
   Sonnets. AnAmPo
'Tis May, and yet the skies are overcast. Lines Written on a Very
   Boisterous Day in May, 1844. John Clare. OxBSP
Tis Merry in Greenwood. Sir Walter Scott. Fr. Harold the Dauntless.
   FaPON; OHIP
'Tis Midnight. Unknown. NA; NTCP
'Tis Midnight, and the setting sun. 'Tis Midnight. Unknown. NA;
   NTCP
'Tis mirth that fills the veins with blood. Mirth. Francis Beaumont and
   Fletcher. Fr. The Knight of the Burning Pestle, II, viii. ElL
   (Laugh and Sing.) TrGrPo
Tis morning; and the sun with ruddy orb. William Cowper. Fr. The
   Task, V. PoEL-3
   (Frosty Morning, A.) NOEC
'Tis mute, the word they went to hear on high Dodona mountain. The
   Oracles. A. E. Housman. HAP
'Tis Nancy's birth-day[]raise your strains. On My Wife's Birth-Day.
   Christopher Smart. NAs
'Tis never or but seldom known. Power and Peace. Robert Herrick.
   CaPo

'Tis nigh two thousand years. Sir Lewis Morris. *Fr.* Christmas 1898. TrPWD

" 'Tis no sin for a man to labour in his vocation." The Ballad of Villon and Fat Madge. Villon, *tr.* by Swinburne. OBVE

'Tis noonday by the buttonwood, with slender-shadowed bud. The Minute-Men of Northboro.' Wallace Rice. PAH

'Tis not by brooding on delight. Marcus Curtius. Oliver St. John Gogarty. OBMV

'Tis not by guilt the onward sweep. Edward Rowland Sill. *Fr.* The Fool's Prayer. TrPWD

'Tis not enough for one that is a wife. Lady Elizabeth Carey. *Fr.* Mariam, III. WPE

'Tis not ev'ry day that I. Not Every Day Fit for Verse. Robert Herrick. PoRA

'Tis not for the unfeeling, the falsely refined. The Farmer of Tilsbury Vale. Wordsworth. EBEV

'Tis not how witty, nor how free. Upon Kinde and True Love. Aurelian Townshend. MeLP; MePo; OBS

'Tis not my ladies face that makes me love her. Love's without Reason. Alexander Brome. OBS

'Tis not on the face displayed. The Bedlamite. Thomas Mozeen. NOEC

'Tis not that both my eyes are black. The Penalties of Baldness. Sir Owen Seaman. FiBHP

'Tis not that dying hurts us so. Emily Dickinson. BoWoP

'Tis not that I am weary grown. Upon [His] Leaving His Mistress. John Wilmot, 2nd Earl of Rochester. EnLoPo; GBL; TEP (Upon Leaving His Mistress.) NBLV; TrGrPo

'Tis not that I design to rob. An Epistle to Robert Lloyd, Esq. William Cowper. FiP

'Tis not the gaudy stream of rosy flame. Self-Consciousness Makes All Changes Happy; Ode. Jonathan Richardson. NOEC

'Tis not the President alone. McKinley. *Unknown.* PAH

'Tis now clear[e] day: I see a rose. The Search. Henry Vaughan. SeCP

'Tis now since I began to dy. Upon Absence. Katherine Philips. PBWP

'Tis Now, Since I Sat[e] Down Before. Sir John Suckling. PoEL-3; SeCV-1 (Love's Siege.) CaPo; JCP

'Tis of a blind beggar who a long time was blind. The Blind Beggar. *Unknown.* AmFP

'Tis of a brisk young Farmer, in——shire did dwel. The Frolicsome Farmer. *Unknown.* CoMu

'Tis of a gallant Yankee ship that flew the stripes and stars. The Yankee Man-of-War. *Unknown.* AA; FaBoBe; OxBSS; PAH (Stately Southerner, The.) AmFP

'Tis of a jolly soldier that lately came from war. The Jolly Soldier. *Unknown.* AmFP

'Tis of a lady both fair and handsome. The Servant Man. *Unknown.* AmFP

'Tis of a little drummer. The Little Drummer. Richard Henry Stoddard. AmFP; PAH

'Tis of a pedlar, a pedlar trim. The Bold Pedlar and Robin Hood. *Unknown.* AmFP

'Tis of a sad and dismal story that happened off the fatal rock. The Loss of the *New Columbia. Unknown.* AmFP

'Tis of a wild Colonial boy, Jack Doolan was his name. The Wild Colonial Boy. *Unknown.* FaBoBa; PoAu-1

'Tis of just a cabin home. Whispering Wind. Catherine Braan Layne. PWR

'Tis of my country that I would endite. Ezra Pound. *Fr.* L'Homme Moyen Sensuel. OBSV

'Tis oft I'm tired of an old man. An Old Man He Courted Me. *Unknown.* OBET

'Tis on October thirty-first. Hallowe'en. Lizelia Augusta Jenkins Moorer. CBWP-3

'Tis only a half truth the poet has sung. Crowded Ways of Life. Walter S. Gresham. BLPA

'Tis Pity She's a Whore, *sel.* John Ford.
  "There is a place,/ List, daughter! in a black and hollow vault." OBD

'Tis queer, it is, the ways o' men. The Ways o' Men. Angelina Weld Grimké. CDC

'Tis raging noon; and vertical, the sun. James Thomson. *Fr.* The Seasons: Summer. EBEV; OAEL-1

'Tis religion that can give. The Satisfying Portion. *Unknown.* BLRP

'Tis sad to see the sons of learning. He That Never Read a Line. *Unknown, tr.* by Robin Flower. AnIL

'Tis said, as Cupid danced among. How Roses Came Red. Robert Herrick. CaPo; ChTr; SoSe

'Tis said but a name is friendship. Lines to Mrs. Isabel Peace. Mary Weston Fordham. CBWP-2

'Tis said that absence conquers love! Frederick William Thomas. AA

'Tis Said That Some Have Died for Love. Wordsworth. EnRP

'Tis said that the gods on Olympus of old. The Mint Julep. Charles Fenno Hoffman. AA

'Tis said the Gods lower down that chain above. George Alsop. SCAP

'Tis said there were no thought of hell. Heaven and Hell. Francis Thompson. OxBSP

'Tis so appalling—it exhilirates. Emily Dickinson. PoE

'Tis so much joy! 'tis so much joy! Emily Dickinson. NOCV

'Tis solemn darkness; the sublime of shade. Night. Charles Heavysege. OBCV

'Tis something from that tangle to have won. Icarus. Harry Lyman Koopman. AA

'Tis Sorrow Builds the Shining Ladder Up. James Russell Lowell. WGRP

'Tis spring; come out to ramble. A. E. Housman. *Fr.* A Shropshire Lad, XXIX.

'Tis spring, warm glows the south. Birds' Nests. John Clare. OAEL-2; OxBSP

'Tis still observ'd, that Fame ne'er sings. Fame. Robert Herrick. FaBoEE

'Tis strange how my head runs on! 'tis a puzzle to understand. The City Clerk. Thomas Ashe. EBVV

'Tis strange, the miser should his cares employ. To Richard Boyle, Earl of Burlington: Of the Uses of Riches. Pope. *Fr.* Moral Essays, Epistle IV. NOEC; OAEL-1; OBSV; PoEL-3; PPP
"At Timon's villa let us pass a day." NOEC; OBSV

'Tis summer time on Bredon. Hugh Kingsmill. FaBoCo; NOBL

'Tis Sweet to Rest in Lively Hope. *Unknown.* AmFP

'Tis Sweet to Roam. *Unknown.* NA

'Tis sweet to view, from half-past five to six. The Theatre. Horace Smith *and* James Smith. Par

'Tis the Arabian bird alone. The Chaste Arabian Bird. John Wilmot, 2nd Earl of Rochester. ErPo

'Tis the blithest, bonniest weather for a bird to flirt a feather. Robin's Secret. Katharine Lee Bates. AA

'Tis the Gift To Be Simple. *Unknown.* AH

'Tis the great art of life to manage well. Madness. John Armstrong. *Fr.* The Art of Preserving Health. NOEC

'Tis the hour of fairy ban and spell. Fairy Dawn. Joseph Rodman Drake. *Fr.* The Culprit Fay. GN

'Tis the hour when white-horsed Day. Morning. Charles Stuart Calverley. FiBHP

'Tis the human touch in this world that counts. The Human Touch. Spencer Michael Free. BLPA; FaBoBe

'Tis the Last Rose of Summer. Thomas Moore. BLPA; BoNaP; ELP; FPL; NOIV; PoEL-4; WBLP
(Last Rose of Summer, The.) FaBoBe; FaFP; OxBoLi

'Tis the laughter of pines that swing and sway. The Phantom Light of the Baie des Chaleurs. Arthur Wentworth Hamilton Eaton. CaP

'Tis the middle of night by the castle clock. Christabel. Samuel Taylor Coleridge. CH; EnRP; FiP; GoTL; NAEL-2; OAEL-2; SeCePo

'Tis the middle watch of a summer's night. The Culprit Fay. Joseph Rodman Drake. AnAmPo

"Tis the Octoroon ball! And the halls are alight!" Ballade des Belles Milatraisses. Rosalie Jonas. BlSi

'Tis the season when Nature awakes from her sleep. Easter; or, Spring-Time. Lizelia Augusta Jenkins Moorer. CBWP-3

'Tis the terror of tempest. The rags of the sail. A Vision of the Sea. Shelley. MOS

'Tis the voice of a sluggard; I heard him complain. *See* 'Tis the voice of the sluggard; I heard him complain.

'Tis the voice of the Lobster: I heard him declare. Alice's Recitation. "Lewis Carroll." *Fr.* Alice's Adventures in Wonderland, *ch.* 10. FaBoCo; FaBoNo; NOBL; Par
(Lobster, The, *sl. diff.*) OxBChV

'Tis the voice of the [*or* a] sluggard; I heard him complain. The Sluggard. Isaac Watts. CH; HAP; Mes; MoShBr; NOEC; OxBChV; OxBoLi; Par; PoEL-3

'Tis the week before Christmas and every night. For the Children or the Grown-ups? *Unknown.* OBCP

'Tis the white anemone, fashioned so. "Owen Meredith." *Fr.* The White Anemone. GN

'Tis the White Plum Tree. John Shaw Neilson. PoAu-1

'Tis the witching hour of night. Keats. TEP

'Tis the year's [*or* yeares] midnight, and it is the day's [*or* dayes]. A Nocturnal[l] upon Saint Lucy's [*or* S. Lucies] Day, Being the Shortest Day. John Donne. EBEV; GBL; JCP; LiTB; MeLP; MePo; NAEL-1; NOBE; NoP; OAEL-1; OBS; PoE; PoEL-2; PPP; SeCP; SeCV-1; TEP

'Tis these that free the small entangled fly. Shakespeare: The Fairies' Advocate. Thomas Hood. *Fr.* The Plea of the Midsummer Fairies. OBNC

'Tis thus with people in an open boat. Byron. *Fr.* Don Juan, II. FaBoPV

'Tis time, I think; by Wenlock town. Wenlock Edge (" 'Tis time, I think; by Wenlock town"). A. E. Housman. *Fr.* A Shropshire Lad, XXXIX. FaBoPP (Wenlock.) SeCePo

'Tis time this heart should be unmoved. On This Day I Complete My Thirty-sixth Year. Byron. EnRP; FiP; NAs; NoP; OAEL-2; OBWP; PoE

'Tis to yourself I speak; you cannot know. Yourself. Jones Very. AA; NOBA; OxBA; PoEL-4; Son

'Tis told by one whom stormy waters threw. Wordsworth. *Fr.* The Prelude [or, Growth of a Poet's Mind]: Cambridge and the Alps. ImOP

'Tis true, dear[e] Ben, they chastising [or chastizing] hand. To Ben Jonson [or Johnson]. Thomas Carew. CaPo; MePo; NAEL-1

'Tis true, fair Celia, that by thee I live. Against Platonick Love. *Unknown.* OBS

'Tis true no human eye can penetrate. Eugenio. Hugh Henry Brackenridge *and* Philip Freneau. *Fr.* The Rising Glory of America. AiP

'Tis true, one half of woman's life is hope. Her Horoscope. Mary Ashley Townsend. AA

'Tis true our life is but a long dis-ease. Katherine Philips. OxBSP

'Tis true—then why should I repine. In Sickness Written Soon after the Author's Coming to Live in Ireland, upon the Queen's Death, October 1714. Swift. NOEC

'Tis true, 'tis day; what though it be? Break[e] of Day. John Donne. ErPo; LiTB; NAEL-1

'Tis well, 'tis something; we may stand. Tennyson. *Fr.* In Memoriam A. H. H., XVIII. EBVV

'Tis well you think me truly one of those. To John Keats. Leigh Hunt. Son

'Tis what they say. The Red Man's Wife. *Unknown, tr. by* Douglas Hyde. SeCePo

'Tis Winter Now. Samuel Longfellow. AH

'Tis years, soubrette, since last we met. To a Soubrette. Eugene Field. AnAmPo

Tissue. Susan Griffin. NPGG

Tit for Tat; a Tale. John Aikin. OxBChV

Tit, tat, toe. *Unknown.* OxNR (Baby Verse, A.) BoTP

Titan! to whose immortal eyes. Prometheus. Byron. EnRP; HeIP; InPS; NOBE; NoP; OAEL-2

Titanic, The, *sel.* Edwin John Pratt. Final Moments, The. NOBC

Titanic , The. *Unknown.* AmFP

Titans, The. Betti Alver, *tr. fr. Estonian by* Willis Barnstone *and* Felix Oinas. BoWoP

Tithe: To The Bride, The. Robert Herrick. CaPo

Tithonus. Tennyson. HAP; LiTB; NAEL-2; NAWM-2; NOBE; NOBVV; NoP; OAEL-2; OBNC; PoE; PoEL-5; PPP; TEP

Titicaca. Cees Nooteboom, *tr. fr. Dutch by* Scott Rollins. DuIn

Title divine—is mine! Emily Dickinson. NOBA

Title Lost. Wan Kin-lau. WCI

Title of a Swift Horse. *Mongol Oral Tradition, tr. by* C. R. Bawden. WTO

Titmouse. Walter de la Mare. BrPo

Tittery-Irie-Aye. *Unknown.* AmFP

Titty cum tawtay. *Unknown.* OxNR

Titus and Berenice. John Heath-Stubbs. GTBS-P

Titus reads neither prose nor rhyme. The Writer. Hildebrand Jacob. FaBoCo

Titwillow. William Schwenck Gilbert. *See* Mikado, The: Ko-Ko's Winning Song.

Tityrus to His Fair Phyllis. John Dickenson. *Fr.* The Shepherd's Complaint. ElI

Tlanusi' Yi, the Leech Place. Gladys Cardiff. CDW; STE

To———: "Half in the dim light from the hall." William Stanley Braithwaite. PoBA

To ———: "I fear thy kisses, gentle maiden." Shelley. GTBS; GTBS-P

To———?: "I have baptized thee Withey." Richard Dehmel, *tr. fr. German by* Jethro Bithell. AWP

To———: "I gaze upon a city." Thomas Hood. OBTV

To———: "Let those with cost deck their ill-fashioned clay." Thomas Rymer. OxBSP

To———: "Music, when soft voice die". Shelley. *See* Music, When Soft Voices Die.

To———: "One word is too often profaned." Shelley. BoLoP; ELP; EnRP; FaBV; GTBS; NOBE; OBEV; OBNC; OPOP; PoLF; PPP; TrGrPo (Love.) FiP ("One word is too often profaned.") BLPL; GTBS-P; LiTB

To———: "What can I do to drive away." Keats. OAEL-2

To———: "When I loved you, I can't but allow." Thomas Moore. EnLoPo; OxBSP

To———: "You have been my love for so many years." René Char, *tr. by* Michael Hamburger. RHTwFP

To———, with an Ivory Hand-Glass. Lord Alfred Bruce Douglas. FaBoUS

To. William Carlos Williams. OBAL

To/ clean/ over. Ludicrous Stick. Tina Darragh. LP

To a Bad Heart. Tim Reynolds. TW

To a Baked Fish. Carolyn Wells. FiBHP

To a Barrage Balloon. May Morton. CN

To a Beautiful Pear Tree. James Wright. HAP

To a Bed of Tulips. Robert Herrick. CaPo

To a Bicycle. *Unknown.* BXAP

To a Blind Student Who Taught Me to See. Samuel Hazo. GOYP

To a Blockhead. Pope. *See* You beat your pate, and fancy wit will come.

To a Blue Flower. John Shaw Neilson. PoAu-1

To a Blue Hippopotamus. Ellen de Young Kay. NePoEA

To a Book. Elinor Wylie. LiTA

To a Boon Companion. Oliver St. John Gogarty. OBMV

To a Boy. Nancy Morejón, *tr. fr. Spanish by* Kathleen Weaver. AIW

To a Boy-Poet of the Decadence. Sir Owen Seaman. CenHV; FiBHP

To a Bride-to-Be. Natalie Clifford Barney, *tr. fr. French by* Barbara Johnson. DMF

To a Brown Girl. Ossie Davis. PoNe

To a Bull-Dog. Sir John Collings Squire. FM

To a Butterfly. William Henry Davies. FM

To a Butterfly. Wordsworth. EnRP; FM

To a Cactus Seller. Anwar Shaul, *tr. fr. Arabic by* Yoffee Berkovitz. VWA

To a Calvinist in Bali. Edna St. Vincent Millay. NoAM

To a Candle. Walter de la Mare. ELP

To a Captious Critic. Paul Laurence Dunbar. BPo

To a Cat. Hartley Coleridge. FM

To a Cat. Keats. FaBoCh (On Mrs. Reynolds's Cat.) FM

To a Caty-did. Philip Freneau. AA; TAP

To a Certain Lady, in Her Garden. Sterling A. Brown. CDC

To a Certain Most Certainly Certain Critic. David McCord. OBAL

To a Chameleon. Marianne Moore. GoYe

To a Cherokee Rose. William Hamilton Hayne. AA

To a Child. S. S. Gardons. NePoEA-2

To a Child. George Edgar Montgomery. AA

To a Child. Wilfred Owen. Son

To a Child. Wordsworth. OxBSP

To a Child before Birth. Norman Nicholson. NAs

To a Child Born in Time of Small War. Helen Sorrells. WPE

To a Child Five Years Old. Nathaniel Cotton. OxBChV

To a Child in Death. Charlotte Mew. MoAB; MoBrPo

To a Child of Quality [Five Years Old, the Author Supposed Forty]. Matthew Prior. GN; LiTB; NIP; NOBE; NOEC; OBEV; PoEL-3

To a Child Running with Outstretched Arms in Canyon de Chelly. N. Scott Momaday. CDW; HATNAP

To a Child Trapped in a Barber Shop. Philip Levine. CAPP; InPK; MoP; NoAM; NOBA; TAP; VGW

To a Child Who Inquires. Olga Petrova. BLPA

To a Christian Woman. Judah Leib Teller, *tr. fr. Yiddish by* Benjamin *and* Barbara Harshav. AYP

To a Christmas Two-Year-Old. Luci Shaw. TrCP

To a Common Prostitute. Walt Whitman. MoAmPo

To a Comrade in Arms. Alun Lewis. FaBoTw; MoBrPo

To a Conscript of 1940. Sir Herbert Read. LiTB; LiTM; OBWP; WaP

To a Contemporary Bunkshooter. Carl Sandburg. WGRP

To a Courtesan a Thousand Years Dead. Paul Eldridge. PoA

To a Covetous Churl. Edward May. FaBoEE

To a Cricket. William Cox Bennett. BoTP; GN

To a Crow. Robert Burns Wilson. AA

To a Crucifix. Anna Wickham. MoBrPo

To a Daisy. Alice Meynell. MoBrPo; Son; WGRP

To a Dark Girl. Gwendolyn B. Bennett. BANP; BlSi; CDC; PoBA

To a Dark Moses. Lucille Clifton. CAPP

To a Daughter at Fourteen Forsaking the Violin. Carole Oles. BLA

To a Daughter Leaving Home. Linda Pastan. ER
To a Daughter with Artistic Talent. Peter Meinke. Psk
To a Dead Actress. Luis de Sandoval y Zapata, tr. fr. Spanish by Samuel Beckett. MexPo
To a Dead Childhood. Rodolfo Hinostroza, tr. fr. Spanish by Maureen Ahern and David Tipton. Per
To a Dead Elephant. Douglas Livingstone. PeSA
To a Dead Journalist. William Carlos Williams. QFR
To a Deaf and Dumb Little Girl. Hartley Coleridge. PoEL-4
To a Deceased Friend. Priscilla Jane Thompson. CBWP-2
To a Defeated Saviour. James Wright. NePoEA
To a Detainee. Musaemura Bonus Zimunya. WMBCH
To a Dictatorial Sultan. Somali Oral Tradition, tr. by B. W. Andrzejewski. WTO
To a Dog. Josephine Preston Peabody. BLPA; WGRP
To a Dog Injured in the Street. William Carlos Williams. LCAP; LiTM; MoAB
To a Fair Lady Playing with a Snake. Edmund Waller. EBEV; HoPM; PoE
To a Faithless Friend. Salaan Arrabey, tr. fr. Somali by M. Laurence. WTO
To a Farmer Who Hung Five Hawks on His Barbed Wire. David Wagoner. NoAM
To a Fat Lady Seen from the Train. Frances Cornford. BLPA; FaBoWP; GoJo; MoBrPo; OBMV; WeW
To a Field Mouse. Burns. See Wee, sleekit, cow'nn, tim'rous beastie.
To a Fine Young Woman. William Wycherley. TW
To a Fish. Leigh Hunt. NBLV
To a Flea in a Glass of Water. Desmond A. Greig. PeSA
To a Fly, Taken out of a Bowl of Punch. "Peter Pindar." NOEC
To a Friend. Matthew Arnold. NAEL-2; Son
To a Friend. William Lisle Bowles. Son
To a Friend. Hartley Coleridge. PoLF
To a Friend. James Fenimore Cooper. PeHV
To a Friend. Grace Stricker Dawson. BLPA
To a Friend. Charles Gullans. NePoEA
To a Friend. Amy Lowell. FPL; PoLF
To a Friend Concerning Several Ladies. William Carlos Williams. VGW
To a Friend Going on a Journey. Mahammed Abdille Hassan, tr. fr. Somali by M. Laurence. WTO
To a Friend in Love during the Riots. William Parsons. NOEC
To a Friend, on Her Examination for the Doctorate in English. James Vincent Cunningham. VGW
To a Friend on His Marriage. F. T. Prince. LiTM
To a Friend Shot on a Mexican Bus. Daniel Halpern. NAmP
To a Friend Who Wouldn't Bother to Strain His Noodleboard because Even So It Is Hard to Go Hunting When Your Rifle Is Blunt and Love Is Soft as an Old blanket. Jacob Glatstein, tr. fr. Yiddish by Benjamin and Barbara Harshav. AYP
To a Friend Whose Work Has Come to Nothing. W. B. Yeats. AWP; InPK; LiTM; MoAB; MoBrPo; OAEL-2; OBMV; PoA
To a Friend Whose Work Has Come to Triumph. Anne Sexton. InPK
To a Friend with a Religious Vocation. Elizabeth Jennings. TOF
To a Friend's Child. Aliki Barnstone. BoWoP
To a Gentleman and Lady on the Death of the Lady's Brother and Sister, and a Child of the Name Avis, Aged One Year. Phillis Wheatley. BlSi
To a Gentleman, Who Desired Proper Materials for a Monody. Unknown. NOEC
To a Gentlewoman Objecting to Him His Grey Hairs. Robert Herrick. CaPo; JCP
To a Girl. Horace. See Odes: I, 5. "What slender youth bedewed with liquid odours" ("Quis multa gracilis").
To a Girl. Edmund Waller. See Why came I sountimely forth.
To a God Unknown. David Eller. VWA
To a Golden-haired Girl in a Louisiana Town. Vachel Lindsay. MoAmPo
To a Golden Heart, Worn round His Neck. Goethe, tr. fr. German by Margaret Fuller Ossoli. AWP
To a Gone Era. Irma McClaurin. BlSi
To a Good Friend Who Would Prove the Fickleness of Women with the Example of Queen Anne. Margaretha Susanna von Kuntsch, tr. fr. German by Susan L. Cocalis and Gerlinde Geiger. DMG
To a Good Physician. William Wycherley. ACP
To a Goose [ITor Gosse]. Robert Southey. BXAP; FM; NOBL; Son
To a Greek Ship in the Port of Dublin. William Bedell Stanford. NeIP
To a Hedgehog. Samuel Thompson. BIrV
To a Hermit in the Mountains. Hsü Pen, tr. fr. Chinese by Jonathan Chaves. CoBLCP
To a Hero Dead at al-Safra. Hind bint Uthatha, tr. fr. Arabic by Bridget Connelly and Deirdre Lashgari. WPOW

To a Honey Bee. Philip Freneau. See On a Honey Bee or To a Honey Bee.
To a Humble Bug. Linda Lyon Van Voorhis. GoYe
To a Hurt Child. Grace Denio Litchfield. AA
To a Husband. Maya Angelou. IHMS
To a Japanese Poet. Lucien Stryk. CAPP
To a Jewish Dancer, sel. Perets Markish, tr. fr. Yiddish. "My homeless one, will you ever fly again?." Tr. by Leonard Wolf. PeBMYV
To a Jilt. Martin Armstrong. FaBoEE
To a June Breeze. Henry Cuyler Bunner. AA
To a Junior Waiter. A. P. Herbert. FiBHP
To a Korean Percussion Ensemble. Koh Chang-soo, tr. fr. Korean by the author. ACKP
To A. L. Thomas Carew. CaPo; SeCP
To A. L.: Perswasions to Love. Thomas Carew. SeCP
To a Lady. Franklin Pierce Adams. FiBHP
To a Lady. John Gay. OBEV
To a Lady. Stanislaw Grochowiak, tr. fr. Polish by Czeslaw Milosz. PwPP
To a Lady. Thomas William Parsons. AA
To a Lady. John James Piatt. AA
To a Lady Asking Him How Long He Would Love Her. Sir George Etherege. OBEV
To a Lady Friend. W. H. Davies. MoBrPo
To a Lady Holding the Floor. Mildred Weston. FiBHP
To a Lady, in a Wartime Queue. Ruth Pitter. CN
To a Lady Lately Married. Walter Savage Landor. FL
To a Lady on Her Marriage. William Bell. NePoEA
To a Lady on Her Passion for Old China. John Gay. FaFP; LiTB
To a Lady on Reading Sherlock "Upon Death." Earl of Chesterfield. See Mistaken fair, lay Sherlock by.
To a Lady on Reading Sherlock "Upon Death." At. to Thomas Osbert Mordaunt. See Verses Written during the War, 1756-1763: Sound, Sound the Clarion.
To a Lady on the Death of Her Husband. Phillis Wheatley. TAP
To a Lady: She Refusing to Continue a Dispute with Me, and Leaving Me in the Argument. Matthew Prior. NoP
To a Lady That Desired I Would Love Her. Thomas Carew. CaPo; MeLP; MePo; OBS; SeCV-1
To a Lady That Desired Me I Would Bear My Part with Her in a Song. Richard Lovelace. CaPo
To a Lady That Forbade to Love before Company. Sir John Suckling. CaPo
To a Lady to Answer Directly with Yea or Nay. Sir Thomas Wyatt. See Madame, withouten Many Wordes.
To a Lady Who Did Sing Excellently. Herbert of Cherbury. OBS; SeCP
To a Lady, with a Compass. George Napier. FaBoUs
To a Lady, with a Guitar. Shelley. See With a Guitar, to Jane.
To a Lady, with a Present of a Fan. At. to Charles Brandling. FaBoUs; NOEC
To a Lady, with a Present of a Walking-Stick. John Hookham Frere. FaBoUs
To a Lady[e]. William Dunbar. EBEV; GBL; MeEL; OxBS ("Sweet rois of vertew and of gentilness.") OBEV
To a Lark in War-Time. Franz Werfel, tr. fr. German by Edith Abercrombie Snow. TrJP
To a Lily. James Matthew Legaré. AA
To a Little Boy, Who Had Destroyed a Nest of Young Birds. Unknown. FaBoUs
To a Little Colored Boy. Priscilla Jane Thompson. CBWP-2
To a Little Girl, One Year Old, in a Ruined Fortress, sel. Robert Penn Warren. Colder Fire. LiTM
To a Living Author. Unknown. NBLV
To a Lock of Hair. Sir Walter Scott. GTBS; GTBS-P
To a Locomotive in Winter. Walt Whitman. AmPP; FaBV; InPK; MoAmPo; MoP; NAAL-1; NoAM; NoP; PoEL-5; TAP
To a Lost Sweetheart, sels. Don Marquis. "I oft stand in the snow at dawn." FiBHP "When Whistler's Mother's Picture's frame." FiBHP
To a Loudmouth Pontificator. Ray Mizer. TW
To a Louse [on Seeing One on a Lady's Bonnet at Church]. Burns. BLPA; EnRP; FaFP; InvP; LiTB; NAEL-2; NOEC; OxBS; PrIm
To a Loved One. Mary Weston Fordham. CBWP-2
To a Loved One of Other Days. Matilda Caroline Edwards. PWR
To a Magnolia Flower in the Garden of the Armenian Convent at Venice. Silas Weir Mitchell. AA
To a Maid Demure. Edward Rowland Sill. AnAmPo
To a Man. Susana March, tr. fr. Spanish by Kate Flores. DMH

To a man eating a pear. Please Say Something. Tomioka Taeko, *tr. by* Sato Hiroaki. FCEI; WPOW

To a Man I Met Only Briefly. Lady Izumi, *tr. fr. Japanese by* Hiroaki Sato. *Fr.* Fifty-one Tanka. FCEI

To a Man of the World. Betty Paoli, *tr. fr. German by* Susan L. Cocalis *and* Gerlinde Geiger. DMG

To a Man Who is Rob Southland. Nia Francisco. HATNAP

To a Man Who Left Me Early in My Life. Lady Izumi, *tr. fr. Japanese by* Hiroaki Sato. *Fr.* Fifty-one Tanka. FCEI

To a Man Who Said, "You've forgotten me." Lady Izumi, *tr. fr. Japanese by* Hiroaki Sato. *Fr.* Fifty-one Tanka. FCEI

To a Maori Figure Cast in Bronze outside the Chief Post Office, Auckland. Hone Tuwhare. ATNZ

To a Maple Seed. Lloyd Mifflin. AA

To a Marsh Hawk in Spring. Henry David Thoreau. PoEL-4

To a Mayflower. William E. Marshall. CaP

To a' men living be it kend. The Rising of the Session. Robert Fergusson. OxBS

To a Midge. Eilidh Nisbet. PoSH

To a Military Rifle, 1942. Yvor Winters. MoAmPo; WaP

To a Millionaire. Archibald Lampman. NOBC

To a Monk Departing for Mid Stream. Seigan, *tr. fr. Chinese by* Lucien Stryk *and* Takashi Ikemoto. ZPCJ

To a Mountain Daisy. Burns. EnRP; GN; PoLF; WBLP

To a Mouse on Turning Her Up in Her Nest with the Plough, November, 1785 *or* To a Mouse. Burns. EnRP; FaFP; FF; FM; GoTS; HAP; HeIP; InPS; NAEL-2; NOEC; NoP; OAEL-1; OxBS; PoE; PoLF; PPP; PrIM; TEP; TrGrPo

To a Negro Boy Graduating. Eugene T. Maleska. PoNe

To a New England Poet. Philip Freneau. NAAL-1

To a Nightingale. William Drummond, of Hawthornden. OBS

To a Nightingale. Keats. *See* Ode to a Nightingale.

To a Noisy Politician. Philip Freneau. TAP

To a Nude Walking. Raymond Radiguet, *tr. fr. French by* William Jay Smith. CT

To a Nun. John Ormond, *after the Welsh.* EBEV; FaBoTw

To a Painter. Yu Kuang-chung, *tr. fr. Chinese by* Dominic Cheung. IFON

To a Pair of Egyptian Slippers. Sir Edwin Arnold. OBTV

To a Persistent Phantom. Frank Horne. AmNP; BANP; CDC

To a Plagiarist. Moses ibn Ezraa, *tr. fr. Hebrew by* Solomon Solis-Cohen. TrJP

To a Poet. Pushkin, *tr. fr. Russian by* Alan Myers. AAA

To a Poet a Thousand Years Hence. James Elroy Flecker. ChTr; FaBoRV; MoBrPo; PoRA

To a Poet a Thousand Years Hence. John Heath-Stubbs. OxBC

To a Poet I Knew. Jewel C. Latimore. PoBA

To a Poet, Who Would Have Me Praise Certain Bad Poets, Imitators of His and Mine. W. B. Yeats. CTC; FaBoEE

To a Political Poet. Heine, *tr. fr. German by* Tom Paulin. FaBoPV

To a Poor Old Woman. William Carlos Williams. AnAmPo; OBAL; SOTW; TAP; TTTS

To a Pope. Pier Paolo Pasolini, *tr. fr. Italian by* James Kirkup. PeHV

To a Portrait of Lermontov. Margarita Aliger, *tr. fr. Russian by* Elaine Feinstein. VWA

To a Post-Office Inkwell. Christopher Morley. PoLF

To a President. Witter Bynner. OBAL

To a President. Walt Whitman. NAAL-1

To a Pretty Girl. Israel Zangwill. TrJP

To a Print of Queen Victoria. James Keir Baxter. OxBC

To a Publisher. Cut-out. Imamu Amiri Baraka. NeAP

To a Pyrotechnist. Chao Meng-fu, *tr. fr. Chinese by* Jonathan Chaves. CoBLCP

To a Red-headed Do-good Waitress. Alan Dugan. CAPP; Son

To a Republican. Philip Freneau. *See* Thus briefly sketch'd the sacred rights of man.

To a Republican Friend, 1848. Matthew Arnold. Son

To a Reviewer Who Admired My Book. John Ciardi. OBAL

To a River in the South. Sir Henry Newbolt. CH

To a Rose. Frank Dempster Sherman. AA

To a Rose, Brought from Near Alloway. Burns. Fitz-Greene Halleck. AnAmPo

To a Sacred Cow. *Unknown, tr. fr. Toda by* W. E. Mashiel. WGRP

To a Sad Daughter. Michael Ondaatje. GOYP; NoAM

To a Sage in Harima. Lady Izumi, *tr. fr. Japanese by* Hiroaki Sato. *Fr.* Fifty-one Tanka. FCEI

To a Salesgirl, Weary of Artificial Holiday Trees. James Wright. NYBP

To a School-Girl. Neilson. PoAu-1

To a Schoolboy. *Unknown, tr. fr. Serbian by* Anne Pennington. RB

To a Sea Eagle. "Hugh MacDiarmid." MoBrPo

To a Seagull. Gerald Griffin. TIRV

To a Seaman Dead on Land. Kay Boyle. PoA

To a Segar. Samuel Low. OBAL

To a Shade. W. B. Yeats. AnIL; LiTB; NAEL-2; PoEL-5

To a Sicilian Boy. Theodore Wratislaw. PeHV

To a Single Shadow without Pity. Sam Cornish. NBP; PoBA

To a Skeleton. Anna Jane Vardhill. BLPA

To a Skull. Joshua Henry Jones. BANP

To a Skylark. Shelley. EnRP; FaBoBe; FaBV; FaFP; FaPON; FPL; GN; GTBS; GTBS-P; HAP; InPS; InvP; LiTB; NAEL-2; NoP; OAEL-2; OBEV; OBNC; OHFP; PBBP; PoLF; TEP; TrGrPo (Ode to a Skylark.) NOBE

To a Skylark ("Ethereal minstrel! pilgrim of the sky"). Wordsworth. EnRP; FPL; PBBP; TrGrPo (To the Skylark.) FaFP; GTBS; GTBS-P

"Up with me! up with me into the clouds!" TTTS

To a Sleeping Friend. Jean Cocteau, *tr. fr. French.* PeHV

To a Small Boy Standing on My Shoes While I Am Wearing Them. Ogden Nash. FiBHP

To a Snail. Marianne Moore. CMoP; FaBoMo; FaBoWP; NAAL-2

To a Snowflake. Francis Thompson. BoNaP; FaBV; ImOP; MoAB; MoBrPo; SeCePo; TrGrPo

To a Solitary Disciple. William Carlos Williams. VGW

To a Soubrette. Eugene Field. AnAmPo

To a Spaniel. Walter Savage Landor. FM

To a Spider. Robert Southey. FM

To a Squirrel at Kyle-na-no. W. B. Yeats. FaPON; FM; PDV; RHPC

To a Steam Roller. Marianne Moore. BoWoP; CMoP; FaBoMo; MoAB; MoAmPo; OxBA; VGW

To a Stranger. Walt Whitman. NOBA

To a Swallow. John Peale Bishop, *after* Euenus. OBVE

To a Teacher of French. Donald Davie. OxBC

To a "Tenting" Boy. Charles Tennyson Turner. OBNC

To a Thesaurus. Franklin P. Adams. BLPL; NBLV

To a thirteen-year-old sleeping. The Last Thing I Say. Marvin Bell. CAPP

To a Town Poet. Lizette Woodworth Reese. AA

To a Traveler. Lionel Johnson. MoBrPo

To a Traveler [*or* Traveller]. Lionel Johnson. MoBrPo

To a Traveler. Su Tung-p'o, *tr. by* Kenneth Rexroth. HoPM

To a Troubled Friend. James Wright. Son

To a Tyrant. Joseph Brodsky, *tr. fr. Russian by* Alan Myers. VWA

To a Vagabond. Constance Davies Woodrow. CaP

To a Very Wise Man. Siegfried Sassoon. BrPo

To a Very Young Lady. Edmund Waller. OBS; SeCP; TrGrPo

To a Vine-clad Telegraph Pole. Louis Untermeyer. MoAmPo

To a Visiting Poet in a College Dormitory. Carolyn Kizer. PoA

To a Wall of Flame in a Steel Mill, Syracuse, New York, 1969. Larry Levis. DiL; MAYP

To a Wanton. William Habington. SeCP

To a Wasp Caught in the Storm Sash at the Advent of the Winter Solstice. Peter Cooley. MAYP

To a Waterfowl. Bryant. AA; AmPP; AnAmPo; AWP; BLPL; CH; FaBoBe; FaFP; GN; HoPM; LiTA; NAAL-1; NOBA; NoP; OHFP; OxBA; PoEL-4; PoLF; PrIm; PWR; SoSe; TAP; TrGrPo; WBLP; WGRP

To a Waterfowl. Donald Hall. OBAL

To a Weak Gamester in Poetry. Ben Jonson. JCP

To a Wind-Flower. Madison Cawein. AA

To a Withered Rose. John Kendrick Bangs. AA

To a Witty Man of Wealth and Quality; Who, after His Dismissal from Court, Said, He Might Justly Complain of It. William Wycherley. SeCV-2

To a Woman Socialist. Abraham Reisen, *tr. fr. Yiddish by* Leonard Wolf. PeBMYV

To a woman that I knew. Her Eyes. John Crowe Ransom. LiTM; OBAL

To a Woman Who Wants Darkness and Time. Gerald Barrax. PoBA

To a Worm. Mikha'il Nu aima, *tr. fr. Arabic by* Sargon Boulus *and* Thomas G. Ezzy. MAP

To a Worm Which the Author Accidentally Trode Upon. William Hawkins. FM

To a Worthy Friend Who Often Objects the Coldness of the Winter in Newfoundland. Robert Hayman. OBTV

To a Writer of the Day, *sels.* Langdon Elwyn Mitchell. AA Purpose. Technique.

To a Young Ass. Samuel Taylor Coleridge. EnRP

To a Young Beauty. W. B. Yeats. CMoP

To a Young Brother. Maria Jane Jewsbury. OxBChV

To a Young Child. Eliza Scudder. AA

To a Young Friend, *sel.* Samuel Taylor Coleridge.
  "And haply, bason'd in some unsunn'd cleft." ChER
To a Young Gentle-Woman, Councel Concerning Her Choice. Richard
  Crashaw. OBS
To a Young Gentlemen in Love; a Tale. Matthew Prior. TEP
To a Young Girl. David Rosenmann-Taub, *tr. fr. Spanish by* Charles
  Guenther. VWA
To a Young Girl. W. B. Yeats. EBEV
To a Young Girl Dying. Thomas William Parsons. AA
To a Young Girl Leaving the Hill Country. Arna Bontemps. CDC
To a Young Lady. William Cowper. GTBS; GTBS-P
To a Young Lady. Wordsworth. EnRP
To a Young Lady Swinging Upside Down on a Birch Limb over a Winter-
  swollen Creek. James H. Koch. GoYe
To a Young Lady, with Some Lampreys. John Gay. FaBoUs;
  NOEC
To a Young Leader of the First World War. Stefan George, *tr. fr.*
  German by E. B. Ashton. WaaP
To a Young Poet. Harry M. Meacham. GoYe
To a Young Poet. Edna St. Vincent Millay. OxBSP
To a Young Poet Who Fled. John Logan. CAPP; SM
To a Young Wretch. Robert Frost. OFD
To Aaron Burr, under Trial for High Treason. Sarah Wentworth Morton.
  PAH
To Aberdein. William Dunbar. FaBoPP
To Abraham Lincoln. John James Piatt. AA
To Adam, His Scribe. Chaucer. OAEL-1
  (To His Scribe Adam.) NAEL-1
  (Unto Adam, His Own Scriveyn.) OxBSP
To Adhiambo. Gabriel Okara. PBA
To Africa. Mazisi Kunene. WMBCH
To Age. Walter Savage Landor. EnRP
To Ailsa Rock. Keats. EnRP; OBNC
To Akashi's strand/ I came in hope of finding. Tameie, *tr. by* Steven D.
  Carter. WFTW
To Alan. Douglas Fraser. PoSH
To Alexander Meiklejohn, *sel.* John Beecher.
  "I read your testimony and I thought." GOA
To Alexander Neville. Barnabe Googe. NoP
To All Angels and Saints. George Herbert. SeCV-1
To All Brothers. Sonia Sanchez. BPo
To All Sisters. Sonia Sanchez. PoBA
To all the humble beasts there be. Prayer for Gentleness to All Creatures.
  John Galsworthy. BoTP
To All Those Worthy Women, Who Have Any Desire to Live in
  Newfound-land. Robert Hayman. OBTV
To all who carve their love on a picnic table. Open Letter from a
  Constant Reader. Mona Van Duyn. PoA
To all you ladies now at Bath. Farewell to Bath. Lady Mary Wortley
  Montagu. WPE
"To all you ladies now at land." Charles Sackville. SeCV-2
  (Song Written at Sea in the First Dutch War (1665), the Night before
  an Engagement.) CoMu; EnLoPo; NOBE; OBEV; OBS; OBWP
To all young men that love to wooe. To Chuse a Friend, but Never
  Marry. *At. to* John Wilmont, 2nd Earl of Rochester.
  CoMu
To Allegra Florence in Heaven, *sel.* Thomas Holley Chivers.
  "As an egg, when broken, never." BXAP
To Althea, from Prison. Richard Lovelace. AWP; BLPA; CaPo;
  FaBoBe; FPL; GBL; GTBS; GTBS-P; HAP; HeIP; InPS; JCP; LiTB;
  MeLP; MePo; NAEL-1; NOBE; NoP; OBEV; OBS; PoE; PoRA;
  SeCP; SeCV-1; SoSe; TEP; TrGrPo
To Amarantha, That She Would Dishevel Her Hair. Richard Lovelace.
  HoPM; MePo; NIP; NoP; OBEV; SeCP; SeCV-1; TrGrPo
  (Song: To Amarantha, that She Would Dishevel Her Hair.) CaPo;
  PoE
To America. Alfred Austin. GN
To America. H. Leivick, *tr. fr. Yiddish by* Benjamin *and* Barbara
  Harshav. AYP
To America, on Her First Sons Fallen in the Great War. E. M. Walker.
  PAH
To Amine. James Clarence Mangan. ObEV
To Amoret. Henry Vaughan. EnLoPo; SeCP
To Amoret. Edmund Waller. SeCV-1
To Amoret Gone from Him. Henry Vaughan. EnLoPo; MeLP; OBS;
  SeCP
To Amy. J. Gordon. OBAL
To an Acquaintance. *Unknown.* FaFP
To an Adolescent Weeping Willow. Marvin Bell. DiL
To an Alcoholic. Sandra McPherson. MAYP
To an American Poet Just Dead. Richard Wilbur. HCAP; NBLV; NoP

To an Angry God. X. J. Kennedy. CRP
To an Araucaria. Salvador Díaz Mirón, *tr. fr. Spanish by* Samuel Beckett.
  MexPo
To an Artful Theatre Manager. Lorenzo da Ponte, *tr. fr. Italian by* John
  Mazzinghi. *Fr.* Capriccio Dramatico, II. TrJP
To an Artist. Burns. EyDe
To an Artist, to Take Heart. Louise Bogan. GrPl; NYBP
To an Athlete Dying Young. A. E. Housman. *Fr.* A Shropshire Lad,
  XIX. BLPL; BrPo; CMoP; DL; HAP; HeIP; InPK; LiTB; LiTM;
  MoAB; MoBrPo; MoP; NAEL-2; NIP; NoAM; NoP; PoE; PoEL-5;
  PoRA; PrIm; SoSe; TEP; TrGrPo; UnPo; WeW
To an Author. Philip Freneau. AmPP; NOBA; OxBA
To an Autumn Leaf. Albert Mathews. AA
To an Avenue Sport. Helen Johnson Collins. PoNe
To an Aviator. Daniel Whitehead Hicky. RHPC
To an Early Primrose. Henry Kirke White. OBNC
To an Elder Poet. William Carlos Williams. PoA
To an Elderly Virgin. Mael Ísu O Brolcháin, *tr. fr. Old Irish by* Thomas
  Kinsella. NOIV
To an Enemy. Maxwell Bodenheim. TrJP
To an Expatriate Friend. Mervyn Morris. PBCV
To an Icicle. Blanche Taylor Dickinson. CDC
To an Imaginary Father. Wendy Rose. CDW
To an Imperilled Traveller. Nathan Haskell Dole. AA
To an impervious nothingness they're thinned. Paul Valéry, *tr. fr. French
  by* C. Day Lewis. *Fr.* The Graveyard by the Sea. OBD
To an Inconstant One. Sir Robert Ayton. *See* I loved thee once, I'll love
  no more.
To an Indian Poet. Patty L. Harjo. VoR
To an Indian Skull, *sel.* Alexander McLachlan.
  "And art thou come to this at last." CaP
To an Infant. Mary Weston Fordham. CBWP-2
To an Infant Daughter. John Clare. NAs
To an Infant Expiring the Second Day of Its Birth. Hetty Wright.
  NOEC
To an Insect. Oliver Wendell Holmes. AnAmPo
To an Island Princess. Robert Louis Stevenson. OBTV
To an Isle in the Water. W. B. Yeats. AWP; TTTS
To an Oak Tree. Sir Walter Scott. *Fr.* Waverley, 29. OBNC
To an Obscure Poet Who Lives on My Hearth. Charles Lotin Hildreth.
  AA
To an Old Gentlewoman That Painted Her Face. George Turberville.
  OxBSP
To an Old Lady, William Empson. FaBoTw; GTBS-P; MoAB; NoAM;
  NOBE
To an Old Philosopher in Rome. Wallace Stevens. MoP; NoAM;
  NOBA
To an Old Rebel. Lauris Edmond. ATNZ
To an Old San Francisco Poet. Keith Abbott. UL
To an open house in the evening. Home at Last. G. K. Chesterton.
  WGRP
To an Unborn Pauper Child. Thomas Hardy. FaBoRV; GTBS-P; LiTB;
  NAs; ViBoPo
To and fro in the city I go. A City Flower. Austin Dobson. TEP
To-and-Fro of Saint Theresa. Alfonso Reyes, *tr. fr. Spanish by* Samuel
  Beckett. MexPo
To Angélique, *sel.* Heine, *tr. fr. German by* Emma Lazarus.
  "This mad carnival of loving." TrJP
To Annie. Mary E. Tucker. CBWP-1
To Anthea. Robert Herrick. CaPo
To Anthea Lying in Bed. Robert Herrick. SeCP
To Anthea ("Now is the time, when all the lights wax dim"). Robert
  Herrick. OBS; PoEL-3
To Anthea, Who May Command Him Anything. Robert Herrick. CaPo;
  GTBS; GTBS-P; JCP; NOBE; OAEL-1; OBEV; OBS; SeCP; SeCV-1;
  TrGrPo
To Any Member of My Generation. George Barker. LiTM; Son; WaP
To Archaeanassa, on whose furrow'd brow. On Archaeanassa. Plato, *tr.*
  by Thomas Stanley. AWP
To Archangel. Jan Hanlo, *tr. fr. Dutch by* James S. Holmes. DuIn
To Archinus. Callimachus, *tr. fr. Greek by* F. A. Wright. AWP
To Ariadne. Sylvia Plath. FL
To Ariake Kambara. Norman Rosten. NYBP
To Aristius Fuscus. Horace. *See* Odes: I, 22. "Virtue, dear friend, needs
  no 'defence' " ("Integer vitae").
To Arms. Park Benjamin. PAH
To arms, to arms! my jolly grenadiers. The Song of Braddock's Men.
  Stephen Tilden. PAH
To arrive in front of large video screen. Manifest Destiny. Anselm
  Hollo. UL

To Arthur's court, when men began. A Scot, a Welsh and an Irish Man. *Unknown*. GBP

To Ashtaroth and Bel. Saul Tchernichowsky, *tr. fr. Hebrew by* L. V. Snowman. TrJP

To Ask for All Thy Love. *Unknown*. EiL

To assassinate the Chase Manhattan Bank. The Plot to Assassinate the Chase Manhattan Bank. Carl Larsen. FF

To Auden on His Fiftieth. Richard Eberhart. NAs

To Aunt Rose. Allen Ginsberg. LiTM, *ad. by* NoAM; NAAL-2, *ad. by* NoAM; NoP, *ad. by* NoAM; PoE, *ad. by* NoAM; VGW, *ad. by* NoAM

To Aurora. William Alexander, Earl of Stirling. *See* Aurora: Oh, If Thou Knew'st How Thou Thyself Dost Harm.

To Ausonius. Paulinus of Nola, *tr. fr. Latin by* Helen Waddell. PeHV

To Autumn. Blake. BoNaP; NAEL-2; WiR

To Autumn. Keats. AWP; BoNaP; BoTP; CH; ChER; EBEV; EnRP; FaBoRV; FF; FiP; FPL; GTBS; HAP; HeIP; InPK; InPS; InvP; LiTB; Mes; NAEL-2; NAWM-2; NIP; NOBE; NOP; NU; OAEL-2; OBEV; OBNC; PoE; PoEL-4; PoLF; PPP; Prf; PrIm; RB; SCV; SoSe; TEP; UnPo; WeW

To 'ave a garden in fettle. Michael Hyde. BXAP

To Avisa. Henry Willoby. *Fr.* Willobie His Avisa. EiL

To B. C. Sir John Suckling. CaPo

To banish your shape from my mind. Exorcism. Oliver St. John Gogarty. AnIL

To Barba. Edward May. FaBoEE

To Bary Jade. Charles Follen Adams. OBAL

To Be. Manuel Gutiérrez Nájera, *tr. fr. Spanish by* Samuel Beckett. MexPo

To be a birth there must be a begetting. Begetting. Dorothea Spears. PeSA

To be a giant and keep quiet about it. Trees. Howard Nemerov. BoNaP; Psk

To Be a Jew. Aaron Zeitlin, *tr. fr. Yiddish by* Robert Friend. PeBMYV

To Be a Jew in the Twentieth Century. Muriel Rukeyser. *Fr.* Letter to the Front, VII. TrJP

To be a marionette. Marionette. Dahlia Ravikovich, *tr. by* Warren Bargad *and* Stanley F. Chyet. IP

To Be a Master in Your House. Natan Zach, *tr. fr. Hebrew by* Peter Everwine *and* Shula Starkman. VWA

To be a mistress. Kiyoko Tsuda, *tr. by* Edith Marcombe Shiffert *and* Yuki Sawa. BoWoP

To Be a Mouse. Aleksander Wat, *tr. fr. Polish by* Czeslaw Milosz. PwPP

To be a Negro in a day like this. At the Closed Gate of Justice. James David Corrothers. BANP

To Be a Pilgrim. Bunyan. *See* Pilgrim's Progress, The: Who would true valour see.

To Be a Pilgrim. Robert Conquest. OxBC

To be a poet and not know the trade. Sanctity. Patrick Kavanagh. BIrV; NOIV

To be a poet is to be vanquished. Ars Poetica. Victor van Vriesland, *tr. by* Adriaan J. Barnouw. TrJP

To Be a Top Hand. Georgie Sicking. CowP

To be a whore, despite of grace. Madrigal. Charles Cotton. FaBoEE

To be a writer and write things. John Ashbery. CAPP

To be able/ and not to do it. To an Elder Poet. William Carlos Williams. PoA

To be able to see every side of every question. Editor Whedon. Edgar Lee Masters. *Fr.* Spoon River Anthology. CMoP; FaBoEE; NOBA; OBSV; OxBA; PoE

To Be Absent without Leave. Kendrick Smithyman. ATNZ

To be alive in such an age! Today. Angela Morgan. BLPA

To be an orphan. The Orphan. *Unknown, tr. by* Arthur Waley. PoA

To Be Answered in Our Next Issue. *Unknown*. RHPC

To Be Black, to Be Lost. Hannah Kahn. GoYe

To Be Born Male. Adela Zamudio, *tr. fr. Spanish by* Robert L. Smith *and* Judith Candullo. DMH

To be brave enough to make noise, and to make it. At the Five Corners. Blaise Cendrars, *tr. by* Anselm Hollo. RHTwFP

To Be Carved on a Stone at Thoor Ballylee. W. B. Yeats. FaBoEE; NoAM; NoP

To be chosen. Jeanne d'Arc. Susan Ludvigson. MT

To Be Continued. Benjamin Péret, *tr. fr. French by* Michael Benedikt. POS

To Be Continued. Julian Street *and* James Montgomery Flagg. FiBHP

To Be Engraven on a Dial. Samuel Sewall. SCAP

To be forever young. Immortality. Frank Horne. BANP

To be free is my desire. Nocturne for Freedom. Tirso Canales, *tr. by* Juan Felipe Herrera. Vol

To be grumpy, grouchy, petulant, paranoid, and mean: to hit out. If I Ever Grow Old: Grim and Gleeful Resolutions. Elinor Nauen. UL

To be homeless is a pride. A Jealous Man. Robert Graves. CMoP

To Be Honest, to Be Kind. Robert Louis Stevenson. *Fr.* A Christmas Sermon. PoLF

To be in a place for spring and not have lived its winter. Vincent O'Sullivan. *Fr.* Brother Jonathan, Brother Kafka, 13. ATNZ; PeNZ

To Be in Love. Gwendolyn Brooks. IHMS

To be in love. Cheese. Mark Irwin. SoTCo

To be in love is like going outside. The Business. Robert Creeley. CAPP

To be like the water. "Transients Welcome." Gregory Orr. AnAn

To be male, always. Eros. Louise Glück. *Fr.* Dedication to Hunger, III. AnAn; GeTw

To be married. The Relationship. Stephen Vincent. NeAC

To be moved comes of want, though want be complete. 1892-1941. Louis Zukofsky. PoA

To be my own Messiah to the. The Rows of Cold Trees. Yvor Winters. NOBA

To Be of Use. Marge Piercy. CAPP; GeTw

To be or not to be. Descartes. Mark Insingel. DuIn

To Be or Not to Be. William H Edmunds. FaBoPa

To Be or Not to Be. *Unknown*. FaBoCo; FaFP; MoShBr; RHPC

To Be or Not to Be ("I sometimes think I'd rather crow"). *Unknown.* FaBoCo; FaFP; MoShBr; RHPC

To be, or not to be, that is the question./ Whether to suffer with mental anguish. Plantation Bitters. *Unknown*. FaBoUs

To be, or not to be, that is the question. Shakespeare. *Fr.* Hamlet, III, i. FaFP; FF; FiP; HoPM; LiTB; OBD; TrGrPo (Hamlet's Soliloquy.) WBLP (Soliloquy from "Hamlet.") OHFP

To Be Poor. Otto Orban, *tr. fr. Hungarian by* Edwin Morgan. MHuP

To be put on the train and kissed and given my ticket. Observation Car. Alec Derwent Hope. MoP; NoAM

To Be Quicker. Don L. Lee. JB

To Be Recited to Flossie on Her Birthday. William Carlos Williams. VGW

To be sad in the morning. William Pillen. VWA

To Be Said at the Seder. Karl Wolfskehl, *tr. fr. German by* Carol North Valhope *and* Ernst Morwitz. TrJP

To be solitary is shameful. All day long. Daily Round of the Spinster. Rosario Castellanos, *tr. by* Kate Flores. DMH

To Be Sung. Peter Viereck. FaBV

To Be Sung on the Water. Louise Bogan. PrIm; VGW

To be sure the cantonal seagulls. La Belle Dame Sans Merci. Eugenio Montale, *tr. by* G. Singh. PFI

To be ten and skinny. Exodus. Anita Endrezze Probst. CDW

To be unloved brings sweet relief. Lovers. Mary Elizabeth Fullerton. PoAu-1

To be wiped out to the last man would mean missing. The Art of Surrender. David Wagoner. KS

To Bear Bryant, Somewhere on That Taller Tower. Don Welch. TSL

To bear the label of disabled is as dull. Crip. Norman Andrew Kirk. TSM

To Begin. Fran Winant. BrRo

To begin I cut fine silk of Ch'i. Song of Regret. Lady Pan, *tr. by* Burton Watson. CoBCP

To Begin the Day. *Unknown*. BLRP

To begin with she wouldn't have fallen in. Our Silly Little Sister. Dorothy Aldis. FaPON

To Bellinus. *Unknown, tr. fr. Latin*. PeHV

To Ben, at the Lake. Cilla McQueen. ATNZ; PeNZ

To Ben Jonson [*or* Johnson]. Thomas Carew. CaPo; MePo; NAEL-1

To Bethlehem's silly shed, methinks I see. The Bee. Henry Hawkins. ACP

"To Bethlem did they go, the shepherds three." Masters, in This Hall. William Morris. ChTr

To better the condition of humanity. Our Club Work. Mrs. Henry Linden. CBWP-4

To Billy, My Son. Vera Bax. CN

To Blok/ words that had stuck together. Blok: Let Me Learn the Poem. Aram Boyajian. NeAC

To Blossoms. Robert Herrick. BoNaP; CaPo; GTBS; GTBS-P; JCP; NAEL-1; OBEV; OBS; SeCP; SeCV-1

To Bobby Seale. Lucille Clifton. CNA; PoBA

To Borglum's Seated Statue of Abraham Lincoln. Charlotte Brewster Jordan. OHIP

To Boris Pasternak. Aleksander Kushner, *tr. fr. Russian*. VWA, *tr. by* Dimitry Pospielovsky *and* Keith Bosley

To brave and to know the unknown. The Unknown. John Davidson. MoBrPo

To bring forth and rear a son is my duty. A Mother's List of Duties. Ponmutiyar, *tr. by* A. K. Ramanujan. PLW
To Bring Spring. George Keithley. NPGG
To Bring the Dead to Life. Robert Graves. MoBrPo
To Brooklyn Bridge. Hart Crane. *Fr.* The Bridge. AiP; AmPP; BLPL; CMoP; EyDe; HAP; HeIP; InPS; LiTA; LiTM; MoAB; MoAmPo; NoAM; NOBA; NoP; OxBA; PoE; PrIm; TAP; WeW
   (Proem: To Brooklyn Bridge.) AmFP; AmPP; CMoP; HAP; HeIP; NoAm; NoP; TAP; WeW
To Build a Poem. Christine E. Hemp. GOYP
To Bülow. August, Graf von Platen, *tr. fr. German by* Reginald Bancroft Cooke. PeHV
To buy, or not to buy; that is the question. Investor's Soliloquy. Kenneth Ward. FaFP; FPL
To C. F. H. on Her Christening-Day. Thomas Hardy. NAs
To C——— her lover. Love-Letter One. *Unknown.* PeHV
To Caelia. *Unknown.* FaBoEE
To call our sight Vision. I Am Not a Camera. W. H. Auden. EyDe
To Calliope. Robert Graves. CMoP
To Carry on Living. Yehuda Amichai, *tr. fr. Hebrew by* the author. LLLT
To Carry the Child. Stevie Smith. MoP; NoAM; NYBP
To Castara, upon Beautie. William Habington. *Fr.* Castara, II. SeCP
To catch the spirit in its wayward flight. Self-Mastery. Henrietta Cordelia Ray. CBWP-3
To Cattraeth's vale in glitt'ring row. Aneirin, *tr. fr. Welsh by* Thomas Gray. *Fr.* The Gododdin. OBVE
To cause accord or to agree [*or* aggre]. Sir Thomas Wyatt. AAS; SiPS
To Celia. Ben Jonson. AWP; EiL; JCP; OAEL-1; OBVE; SeCP; SeCV-1
To Celia. Sir Charles Sedley. *See* Not, Celia, that I juster am.
To Celia ("Drink to me only with thine eyes"). Ben Jonson. BoLoP; EnLoPo; FaBoBe; FaBV; FaFP; FPL; GTBS; GTBS-P; InPK; LiTB; NOBE; OBEV; OBS; OBVE; PoLF; TEP; TrGrPo
To Celia Pleading Want of Merit. Thomas Stanley. *See* To One That Pleaded Her Own Want of Merit.
To Certain Critics. Countee Cullen. BPo
To Chaadaev. Pushkin, *tr. fr. Russian by* Alan Myers. AAA
To change the name, and not the letter. Surnames to Be Avoided in Marriage. *Unknown.* FaBoUs
To Charles Cowden Clarke, *sel.* Keats. EnRP
   "Oft have you seen a swan superbly frowning." PBBP
To Chaucer. Thomas Hoccleve. *Fr.* De Regimine Principum. ACP
To Cheer Our Minds. William Ronksley. OxBChV
To Ch'eng Fei-t'ao. Wu Chia-chi, *tr. fr. Chinese by* Jonathan Chaves. CoBLCP
To Cherry-Blossomes. Robert Herrick. SeCV-1
To "Chick." Frank Horne. *Fr.* Letters [*or* Notes] Found near a Suicide. BPo
To Children. Lawrence McGaugh. PoBA
To Chin Nung. Cheng Hsieh, *tr. fr. Chinese by* Jonathan Chaves. CoBLCP
To Chloe, [who for His Sake Wished Herself Younger]. William Cartwright. *See* Chloe, why wish you that your years.
To Chloe, Who Wished Herself Young Enough for Me. William Cartwright. JCP; LiTB; MePo; OBS
To Chloris. William Drummond, of Hawthornden. OxBSP
To Chloris. Sir Charles Sedley. *See* Mulberry Garden, The: Child and Maiden.
To Chloris, upon a Favour Received. Edmund Waller. OxBSP
To Christ. Fadwa Tuqan, *tr. fr. Arabic by* Abdullah al-Udhari. MPAW
To Christ Our Lord. Galway Kinnell. NIP; PrIm; RFM; SM; TwCP
To Christian Montpelier, *sel.* George Jonas.
   "Single naked wire at ground level, A.". NeAC
To Christopher North. Tennyson. FaBoEE; FiBHP
To Christopher Smart. Joseph Stroud. NPGG
To church! I heard a sermon once in spring. God. Harold Monro. *Fr.* Dawn. WGRP
To Chuse a Friend, but Never Marry. *At. to* John Wilmont, 2nd Earl of Rochester. CoMu
To claim, at a dead party, to have spotted a grackle. Lying. Richard Wilbur. BLA; DiPo; HCAP; SV
To Clarastella on St. Valentines Day Morning. Robert Heath. OBS
To Clarissa. Robert, Earl Nugent. NOEC
To Clarissa Scott Delany. Angelina Weld Grimké. AmNP
To Clements' Ferry. Josephine D. Henderson Heard. CBWP-4
To climb a hill that hungers for the sky. Fulfillment. Helene Johnson. CDC; PoNe
To Clio, from Rome. John Dyer. NOEC

To Cloe. George Granville. FaBoEE (*at. to* Charles Sackville); NBLV
To Cloe. Hildebrand Jacob. NOEC
To Cloe. Martial, *tr. fr. Latin by* Thomas Moore. AWP; NBLV
To Cloris. Sir Charles Sedley. BoLoP
To clothe the fiery thought. Poet. Emerson. *Fr.* Quatrains. OxBA; PCP
   (Poet.) OxBSP
To Coelia. Charles Cotton. OBEV
To Cole, the Painter, Departing for Europe. Bryant. AiP; AmPP; TAP
   (Sonnet: To an American Painter Departing for Europe.) NAAL-1
To Coleridge in Sicily. Wordsworth. *Fr.* The Prelude [*or*, Growth of a Poet's Mind]: France. OBNC
To Colin Clout. Anthony Munday. *See* Primaleon of Greece: Beauty Sat Bathing by a Spring.
To Colman Returning. *At. to* Colman, *tr. by* Helen Waddell. BIrV
To Columbus. Rubén Darío, *tr. fr. Spanish by* Lysander Kemp. TTY
To come back from the sweet South, to the North. Italia, Io Ti Saluto. Christina Rossetti. OBTV; WPE
To Come Back Home. Samuel Chimsoro. WMBCH
To come free to a city under siege. Amir Gilboa, *tr. by* Warren Bargad *and* Stanley F. Chyet. IP
To come to the river. The Resolve. Denise Levertov. RFM
To Comfort My Little Son and Daughter. Michizane, *tr. fr. Chinese by* Burton Watson. JLIC-1
To condone rotten rubbish is to deny the miraculous. Chang Wen-t'ao, *tr. fr. Chinese by* Irving Lo. *Fr.* On Literature, I. WFTU
To Conquer Variety. Hart Crane. AnAn
To Constantia Singing. Shelley. EnRP
To Cordelia. Joseph Stansbury. CaP; NOBC
To Corinth came a solitary stranger. The Bride of Corinth. Goethe, *tr. by* Christopher Middleton, W. E. Aytoun *and* Theodore Martin. VVA
To countries far from here, beneath an alien heaven. Remembrance. Prince P. A. Vyazemsky, *tr. by* Alan Myers. AAA
To Creuzer. Karoline von Günderode, *tr. fr. German by* Susan L. Cocalis. DMG
To Crinog. *Unknown. tr. fr. Middle Irish by* Kuno Meyer. AnIL
To Critics. Robert Herrick. CaPo
To Critics. Walter Learned. AA
To Crown It. Robert Herrick. CaPo
To cry that the *gabacho. Notes from a Chicana "COED."* Bernice Zamora. CCP
To Cupid. Francis Davison. OBSC
To Cupid. Michael Drayton. EiL
To Cynthia. *At. to* Sir Walter Ralegh *and to* George Clifford. *See* My thoughts are winged with hopes.
To Cynthia, Not to Let Him Read the Ladies' Magazines. P. M. Hubbard. FiBHP
To Cynthia, on Concealment of Her Beauty. Sir Francis Kynaston. MeLP; MePo; NOBE; OBS
To Cynthia on Her Being an Incendiary. Sir Francis Kynaston. HAP
To Cynthia. On Her Changing. Sir Francis Kynaston. MePo
To Cynthia, on Her Embraces. Sir Francis Kynaston. GBL
To Cyriack Skinner ("Cyriack, this three years' day"). Milton. *See* To Mr. Cyriack Skinner upon His Blindness.
To Cyriack Skinner ("Cyriack, whose grandsire"). Milton. GTBS; GTBS-P; NoP; OBEV; Son
To D——, Dead by Her Own Hand. Howard Nemerov. PoA
To Daffodils [*or* Daffadills]. Robert Herrick. AWP; BoNaP; CaPo; ELP; FaBoCh; GN; GoJo; GTBS; GTBS-P; InPS; JCP; LiTB; NOBE; NoP; OBEV; OBS; PoEL-3; PoRA; PPP; QFR; SeCP; SeCV-1; TrGrPo; TTTS; UnPo
To Daisies, Not to Shut So Soon[e]. Robert Herrick. CaPo; CH; ELP; GBL; OBEV; OBS; OxBSP; SeCV-1; TrGrPo
To dance, at a dark party, to old tunes. What a Time! Michael C. Blumenthal. BLA
To D'Annunzio: Lines from the Sea. Robert Nichols. OBMV
To Dante. Vittorio Alfieri, *tr. fr. Italian by* Lorna De' Lucchi. AWP
To Dante [*or* Sonnet: Guido Cavalcanti to Dante]. Guido Cavalcanti, *tr. fr. Italian by* Shelley. AWP; OBVE
To Dante Alighieri. Guido Cavalcanti, *tr. fr. Italian by* Dante Gabriel Rossetti. AWP
To Dante Alighieri: He Conceives of Some Compensation in Death. Cino da Pistoia, *tr. fr. Italian by* Dante Gabriel Rossetti. AWP
To Dante Alighieri: He Interprets Dante Alighieri's Dream. Dante da Maiano, *tr. fr. Italian by* Dante Gabriel Rossetti. AWP
To Dante Alighieri: He Interprets Dante's Dream. Cino da Pistoia, *tr. fr. Italian by* Dante Gabriel Rossetti. AWP
To Dante Alighieri: He Mistrusts the Love of Lapo Gianni. Guido Cavalcanti, *tr. fr. Italian by* Dante Gabriel Rossetti. AWP

To Dante Alighieri: He Reports, in a Feigned Vision, the Successful Issue of Lapo Gianni's Love. Guido Cavalcanti, *tr. fr. Italian by* Dante Gabriel Rossetti. AWP

To Dante in Paradise, after Fiammetta's Death. Boccaccio, *tr. fr. Italian by* Dante Gabriel Rossetti. *Fr.* Sonnets. AWP

To Dark Eyes Dreaming. Zilpha Keatley Snyder. RHPC

To David, about His Education. Howard Nemerov. DiL; HCAP

To-Day. Thomas Carlyle. GN; WGRP

To-Day. Lessie M. Drown. PWR

To-day a rude brief recitative. Song for All Seas, All Ships. Walt Whitman. CH; FaBoBe; MOS

To-Day a Shepherd. St. Theresa of Avila, *tr. fr. Spanish by* Arthur Symons. AWP

To-day a wind from the West out over the hills came blowing. A Wind from the West. Lauchlan MacLean Watt. PoSH

To-day, all day, I rode upon the Down. St. Valentine's Day. Wilfrid Scawen Blunt. *Fr.* The Love Sonnets of Proteus, LV. EnLoPo

To-day as I went out to play. The Brown Frog. Mary K. Robinson. BoTP

To-Day I Leave Mrs. Brown's Lodgings. Sir Walter Scott. FaBoEE

To-day, I saw the catkins blow. February. Dorothy Una Ratcliffe. BoTP

To day old Janus opens the new yeare. A New-Yeares-Gift Sung to King Charles, 1635. Ben Jonson. SeCP

To-day, taking my last sight of the mallards. Prince Otsu. *Fr.* Manyo Shu. Ma

To-day the lot caved in upon me. Page from a Diary. Desmond O'Grady. NoAM

To-day they laid him in the earth's cold colour. For Angus MacLeod. Iain Crichton Smith. OxBS

To-day, when people in China, it is said. Yakamochi. *Fr.* Manyo Shu. Ma

To-day's house makes to-morrow's road. The Survival. Edmund Blunden. OBEV; OBMV

To Dean-bourn, a Rude River in Devon, by which Sometimes He Lived. Robert Herrick. *See* Dean-bourn, a Rude River in Devon, by Which Sometimes He Lived ("Dean-bourn, farewell; I never look to see").

To Dear Daniel. Samuel Greenberg. LiTA

To Death. Oliver St. John Gogarty. FaBoEE; OBD; OBMV

To Death, of His Lady. Villon, *tr. fr. French by* Dante Gabriel Rossetti. AWP

To deities of gauds and gold. Ad Patriam. Clinton Scollard. PAH

To Delia. Samuel Daniel. OBSC

To Delia, *sels.* Samuel Daniel.

"And yet I cannot reprehend the flight." OBEV

Beauty, sweet Love, is like the morning dew. NOBE; OBEV; OBSC

(Sonnet: "Beauty, sweet Love, is like the morning dew.") EiL

"But love whilst that thou mayst be loved again." EiL; NoP; OBSC

"Care-charmer sleep[e], son[ne] of the sable night." AAS; GTBS; GTBS-P; InPS; NAEL-1; NOBE; NoP; OBSC; TrGrPo

(Care-charmer Sleep.) LiTB; NiP; OAEL-1; Son

(Sonnet: "Care-charmer sleep[e], son[ne] of the sable night.") EiL; PoEL-2

"Fair is my love, and cruel as she's fair." AAS; NOBE; NoP; OBSC; TEP; TrGrPo

(Beauty, Time and Love.) OBEV

(Fair Is My Love.) LiTB

(Sonnet: "Fair is my love, and cruel as she's fair.") EiL; HoPM

"I must not grieve my love, whose eyes would read." OBEV

("Sonnet: "I must not grieve my love, whose eyes would read.'") EiL

"I once may see when yeares shall wreck my wrong." AAS

"If it so hap, this of-spring of my care." AAS

"If this be love, to draw [*or* drawe] a weary [*or* wearie] breath." AAS; GBL; OBSC; TrGrPo

"Let others sing of knights and paladins [*or* palladines]." AAS; NOBE; NoP; OBEV; OBSC

(Sonnet: "Let others sing of knights and paladin[e]s.") EiL

"Look, Delia, how we esteem the half-blown rose." HeIP; NoP; OBSC

(Half-blown Rose, The.) SeCePo

(Sonnet: "Look, Delia, how we esteem the half-blown rose.") EiL

"My cares draw on mine everlasting night." OBSC

"My spotless love hovers, with purest wings." OBEV; OBSC

(Most Unloving One, The.) SeCePo

"None other fame mine unambitious muse." AAS

"Star of my mishap imposed this pain, The." OBSC

"These plaintive verse, the posts [*or* postes] of my desire." AAS; OBSC

"Thou canst not die whilst any zeal abound." OBSC; Son

"Time, cruel time, come and subdue that brow." OBSC

"Unto the boundless ocean of thy beauty." OBSC

"When men shall find thy flower [*or* flow'r], thy glory, pass." NAEL-1; NOBE; NoP; OBEV; OBSC; Son; TrGrPo

(Sonnet: "When men shall find thy flower, thy glory, pass.") EiL

"When winter snows upon thy sable hairs." CTC; OBSC; Son; TEP

Why Should I Sing in Verse. Son

To Demeter. Maybury Fleming. AA

To demolish it. All Splendor on Earth. Karin Kiwus, *tr. by* Almut McAuley. BoWoP

To deny what we know. Nelo Risi, *tr. fr. Italian by* Gavin Ewart. *Fr.* Elementary Thoughts, XX. PFI

To Desi as Joe as Smoky the Lover of 115th Street. Audre Lorde. CNA

To Destiny. *Unknown, tr. fr. Dahomean song by* Frances Herskovits. EaLo

To destroy in order to perceive. In Memory of Reinhold Koehler. Wieland Schmied, *tr. by* Beth Bjorklund. CoAuP

To destroy or deride Creation's task. Kashrut. Edouard Roditi. VWA

To Detraction I Present My Poesie. John Marston. *Fr.* The Scourge of Villainy [*or* Villanie]. OBSC; TW

To Dianeme. Robert Herrick. CaPo; FaBoBe; GTBS; GTBS-P; JCP; NOBE; OBEV; OBS; SeCV-1; TrGrPo

To Dianeme ("Dear, though to part it be a hell"). Robert Herrick. CaPo

To Die for Something. József Tornai, *tr. fr. Hungarian by* William Jay Smith. MHuP

To die like Rachel. Like Rachel. Dahlia Ravikovich, *tr. by* Warren Bargad *and* Stanley F. Chyet. IP

To die like thirsty larks. Agony. Giuseppe Ungaretti, *tr. by* Patrick Creagh. PFI

To die old. Ancient of Days. Anthony Rudolf. VWA

To die with a forlorn hope, but soon to be raised. The Survivor. Robert Graves. CMoP

To Dinah Washington. Etheridge Knight. PoBA

To Dispel the Cold: Two Poems on Spring, *sels.* Hung Liang-chi, *tr. fr. Chinese by* Irving Lo. WFTU

Small Pavilion. *Fr.* I.

Winding Pond. *Fr.* II.

To Disraeli. Shirley Brooks. NOBL

To dive for the nimbus on the sea-floor. Nimbus. Douglas Le Pan. MoCV; OBCV

To Dives. Hilaire Belloc. OBSV

To Doctor Empiric[k]. Ben Jonson. FaBoEE; NoP; SeCP

To Don at Salaam. Gwendolyn Brooks. CAPP

To Don Juan Baz. Mary E. Tucker. CBWP-1

To Dorothy. Marvin Bell. CAPP; Psk

To Dorothy on Her Exclusion from the *Guinness Book of World Records*. X. J. Kennedy. Psk

To Dr. Arbuthnot. Pope. *See* Epistle to Dr. Arbuthnot.

To Dr. F. B. on His Book of Chess. Richard Lovelace. CaPo

To Dr. Kipling. Richard Porson. FaBoCo

To Dr. Swift on His Birthday, 30th November 1721. Esther Johnson. EnLoPo

To draw no envy, Shakespeare, on thy name. To the Memory of My Beloved Master [*or* the Author, Mr.] William Shakespeare and What He Hath Left Us. Ben Jonson. HeIP; JCP; LiTB; NoP; OAEL-1; OBS; PoEL-2; SeCP; SeCV-1; TrGrPo

To Dream Again. Shakespeare. *See* Tempest, The: Be Not Afeard: The Isle is Full of Noises.

To dream of love, and, waking, to remember you. Dreams. Arthur Symons. PoA

To dreamy languors and the violet mist. Dogwood Blossoms. George Marion McClellan. BANP

To drift with every passion till my soul. Hélas! Oscar Wilde. BrPo; MoBrPo; NAEL-2; Son; TEP; TIRV

To Drink. Gabriela Mistral, *tr. fr. Spanish by* Gunda Kaiser. NU

To drink in moderation, and to smoke. Party Knee. John Updike. FiBHP

To drink, no fine wines, to eat, no fish. Li K'ai-hsien, *tr. fr. Chinese by* Jonathan Chaves. *Fr.* Impromptu Poems. CoBLCP

To Drink to Friends. André Frénaud, *tr. fr. French by* Keith Bosley. RHTwFP

To drive the kine one summer's morn. The Cow-Chace. John André. PAH

To drum-beat and heart-beat. Nathan Hale. Francis Miles Finch. PAH

To Duty. Thomas Wentworth Higginson. AA

To Dwell Together in Unity. Bible, *O.T.* *See* Psalms: Psalm CXXXIII ("Behold, how good and how pleasant.").

To E. Fitzgerald. Tennyson. NOBVV; PoEL-5

To each one is given a marble to carve for the wall. The Task That Is Given to You. Edwin Markham. WBLP

To Earth. James Applewhite. PoA

To Earthward. Robert Frost. BLPL; LiTA; MoAB; MoAmPo; MoP; NoAM; NOBA; NoP; OxBA; TAP

To eastward ringing, to westward winging, o'er mapless miles of. When the Great Gray Ships Come In. Guy Wetmore Carryl. AnAmPo; FaBoBe; PAH

"To eat a green fig, my dear." Green Figs at Table. James Keir Baxter. ATNZ

To eat pain like bread is a condition. Ruth Miller. *Fr.* Cycle. PeSA

To Eddleston. Byron. *Fr.* Childe Harold's Pilgrimage, II. PeHV

To Edom. Heine, *tr. fr. German.* TrJP

To Edward Allen (Alleyne). Ben Jonson. OBS

To Edward Fitzgerald. Robert Browning. NAEL-2; OxBSP; TW

To Edward Thomas. Alun Lewis. WaP

To Egypt. Gloria Davis. NBP

To E.L., on His Travels in Greece. Tennyson. SeCePo

To Electra. Robert Herrick. BLPL; CaPo; HoPM; OBEV; OBS; SeCV-1

To Eliza, Duchess of Dorset. Joseph Deericks Bennett. LiTA

To Elsie. William Carlos Williams. CMoP; InPS; NAAL-2; NOBA; OxBA; PoE

To Emily Dickinson. Hart Crane. CMoP; NIP; NoAM; NOBA; NoP; Son; TAP

To Emily Dickinson. Yvor Winters. Son

To Emma, Extempore; Hyaena, off Gambia, June 4, 1779. Edward Thompson. NOEC

To End Her Fear. John Freeman. OBMV

To end it all, the people elected a thumb. The Thumb. Dennis Saleh. MAT; NeAC

To end this day. Celestial. Michael Pettit. MOWH

To England. George Henry Boker. AA

To England. Charles Leonard Moore. AA

To English Connoisseurs. Blake. OxBoLi

To enter the dark. Winter Moon. Philippe Jaccottet, *tr. by* Charles Tomlinson. RHTwFP

To Entertain Divine Zenocrate. Christopher Marlowe. *Fr.* Tamburlaine the Great, *pt.* II, Act II, sc. iii. ChTr

To Ernest Hemingway. Abdul Wahab al-Bayati, *tr. fr. Arabic by* Abdullah al-Udhari. MPAW

To Evening. William Collins. *See* Ode to Evening.

To Everlasting Oblivion. John Marston. *Fr.* The Scourge of Villainy [*or* Villanie]. OBSC

To every Form of being is assigned. Discourse of the Wanderer, and an Evening Visit to the Lake. Wordsworth. *Fr.* The Excursion, IX. EnRP

To every heart which the sweet pain doth move. Dante, *tr. fr. Italian by* Dante Gabriel Rossetti. *Fr.* Vita Nuova, La, I. AWP

To every hearth a little fire. A Christmas Wish. Rose Fyleman. BoTP

To every man. The Treehouse. James A. Emanuel. AmNP; BPo; PoBA

To every man there openeth. The Ways. John Oxenham. PoLF

To Everything There Is a Season. Bible, *O.T. Fr.* Ecclesiastes, III: 1-8. FF; OBVE

("For everything there is a season.") DL

(Time for Everything, A.) TrGrPo

To explain the nature of fishes in craft of verse. Unknown, *tr. fr. Anglo-Saxon by* Gavin Bone. *Fr.* Physiologus: The Whale. EBEV

To F. C. Mortimer Collins. NOBVV

To fair Fidele's grassy tomb. A Fidele. William Collins. EnRP; NOEC

(Dirge in "Cymbeline.") ELP; Mes; NOBE; SeCePo

(Fidele.) OBEV

To fall in love, though classically human. Advice to Colonel Valentine. Robert Graves. NYBP

To fall, like an apple, no mind. In the Emptied Rest Home. Bella Akhmadulina. BoWoP, *tr. by* Jean Valentine *and* Olga Carlisle

To Fannie. Mary E. Tucker. CBWP-1

To Fanny. Keats. BoLoP; EBEV; EnRP; PPP; Son; TrGrPo

To Fanny Brawne. Keats. *See* This Living Hand Now Warm and Capable.

To farther this, Achitophel unites. The Malcontents. Dryden. *Fr.* Absalom and Achitophel, Pt. I. OBS

To Father. Mary E. Tucker. CBWP-1

To Favonius. Edmund Bolton. OBSC

To feel and speak the astonishing beauty of things. The Beauty of Things. Robinson Jeffers. PoA

To Female Duties Clorinda Scorned. Petronilla Paolini Massimi, *tr. fr. Italian by* Muriel Kittel. DMI

To Fido, His Horse. Vittorio Alfieri, *tr. fr. Italian by* Barbara Howes. PFI

To fight aloud is very brave. Emily Dickinson. LiTA; WPE

To find the Western path. Morning. Blake. FaBoCh; OAEL-2

To Finde God. Robert Herrick. WGRP

To Fine Grand. Ben Jonson. JCP

To Fine Lady Would-Be. Ben Jonson. FaBoEE; JCP; NoP; OxBSP

To fish for pearls in Lethe. The Great Magicians. C. Day Lewis. EaLo

To fix attention on the dead. The Last Rebirth. Coleman Barks. KS

To Flaxman. Blake. FaBoEE; OxBoLi

To flee from memory. Emily Dickinson. FaBoEE

To fleece the Fleece from golden sheep. The Scales of the Eyes. Howard Nemerov. CMoP

To Fletcher Reviv'd. Richard Lovelace. OBS

To fling my arms wide. Dream Variation [*or* Variations]. Langston Hughes. AmNP; CDC; HAP; IDB; NAAL-2; NOBA; PoBA; PoNe; WeW

To Flood Stage Again. James Wright. NOBA; Prf

To flow is a verb. Water. Lo Fu, *tr. by* Dominic Cheung. IFON

To fly off, a ripe pear in a storm. Definition of the Soul. Boris Pasternak, *tr. by* Babette Deutsch. TrJP

To Fool, or Knave. Ben Jonson. FaBoEE; NoP; SoSe

To Ford Madox Ford in Heaven. William Carlos Williams. AmPP; NOBA

To Forget Me. Theodore Weiss. CoAP

To Forget Self and All. Allen Curnow. ATNZ

To forgive enemies Hayley does pretend. Blake. FaBoEE

To Form a Just and Finish'd Piece. Swift. *Fr.* Directions for Making a Birth-Day Song. NAs

To Fortune. Robert Herrick. OxBSP; SeCV-1

To Fortune. Sir Thomas More. ACP

To Francis Beaumont. Ben Jonson. OBS

To Frankfort I on *Schobbas* came. The Best Religion. Heine, *tr. fr. German by* Emma Lazarus. *Fr.* Tannhäuser. TrJP

To free me from domestic strife. At Hadleigh, Suffolk. *Unknown.* FaBoCo

To free the ball the chief now turns his mind. Victory on the Last Green. Thomas Mathison. *Fr.* The Goff; an Heroi-comical Poem. NOEC

To freight cars in the air. The Descent of Winter (Section 10/300). William Carlos Williams. InPK

To fret at the times, bewail the age—how pointless! In the Army. Fujita Koshiro, *tr. by* Burton Watson. JLIC-2

To Friend and Foe. *Unknown.* CoMu

To Friend-Tree of Counted Days. René Char, *tr. fr. French by* William Carlos Williams. RHTwFP

To Friends. Franco Fortini, *tr. fr. Italian by* Lawrence R. Smith. NItP

To Friends Who Have Also Considered Suicide. Phyllis Webb. NOBC

To Frighten a Storm. Gladys Cardiff. CDW; STE

To Fuscus Aristus. Horace, *tr. fr. Latin by* Abraham Cowley. *Fr.* Epistles, I, 10. AWP

To G. H. B. James Bayard Taylor. Son

To G, her one and only rose. Love-Letter Two. *Unknown.* PeHV

To G. R. Samuel Elsworth Cottam. PeHV

To gallop off to town post-haste. Friar Lubin. Clément Marot, *tr. by* Longfellow. AWP

To "Garryowen" upon an organ ground. In the Dials. W. E. Henley. BrPo

To gather flowers Sappha went. The Apron of Flowers. Robert Herrick. CaPo; SeCV-1

To gather hope. Revenue. Erich Fried, *tr. by* Beth Bjorklund. CoAuP

To gather the wave-borne pearls. *Unknown. Fr.* Manyo Shu. Ma

To George Pulling Buds. Adelaide O'Keeffe. FaBoUs

To George Sand. Ida von Reinsberg-Düringsfeld, *tr. fr. German by* Susan L. Cocalis *and* Gerlinde Geiger. DMG

To George Sand: A Desire. Elizabeth Barrett Browning. BoWoP; NAEL-2; TEP

To George Sand: A Recognition. Elizabeth Barrett Browning. BoWoP; NAEL-2; TEP

To Germany. Charles Hamilton Sorley. MoBrPo

To Geron. Hildebrand Jacob. NOEC

To get a fix on it. What Is Happening Now? Hubert Witheford. PeNZ

To get betimes in Boston town I rose this morning early. A Boston Ballad. Walt Whitman. OBAL

To get into it/ As it lies. Shirt. Charles Simic. HCAP

To Gild Refinèd Gold. Shakespeare. *Fr.* King John, IV, ii. LiTB

To Giotto. W. Wesley Trimpi. NePoEA

To Giovanni. Cesare Vivaldi, *tr. fr. Italian by* Lawrence R. Smith. NItP

To Giovanni da Pistoia on the Painting of the Sistine Chapel, 1509. Michelangelo, *tr. fr. Italian by* John Addington Symonds. PFI

To Giulia Grisi. Nathaniel Parker Willis. AA

To give up everything. Huck Finn at Ninety, Dying in a Chicago Boarding House Room. James Schevill. TAP

To go along dying and singing. And to baptize the darkness. Pagan Woman. César Vallejo, *tr. by* Robert Bly. AnAn

To go to Rome. The Pilgrim at Rome. *Unknown.* AnIL

To go up to the sun-lit Imperial City. Okura. *Fr.* Manyo Shu. Ma

To Go with Shih K'o's Painting of an Old Man Tasting Vinegar. Huang T'ing-chien, *tr. fr. Chinese by* Burton Watson. CoBCP

To go with the horses over this hill and down into the shadowy. The Sacrament of Gravity. Jorie Graham. NAmP
To God. Blake. OAEL-2
To God. Robert Herrick. TrPWD; WGRP
To God alone, the only donour. Francis Daniel Pastorius. SCAP
To God Our Strength Shout Joyfully. Henry Ainsworth. AH
To God, the Architect. Harry Hibbard Kemp. *See* God the Architect.
To God, the everlasting, who abides, *sel.* John Addington Symonds. WGRP
"O God, unknown, invisible, secure." TrPWD
To God the highest glory. Song of the Angels. Lizelia Augusta Jenkins Moorer. CBWP-3
To God the Son. Henry Constable. OBSC
To God: to illuminate all men. Beginning with Skid Road. Allen Ginsberg. CAPP
To Graham and Anna: from the Arctic Gate. Letter to Graham and Anna. Louis MacNeice. OBTV
To Grandmother on Her Going. Gail Tremblay. HATNAP
To grass, or leaf, or fruit, or wall. The Snail. Vincent Bourne, *tr. by* William Cowper. BoTP; OBVE
To Greet a Letter-Carrier. William Carlos Williams. OBAL
To Grosphus. Godfrey the Satirist, *tr. fr. Latin.* PeHV
To Groves. Robert Herrick. CaPo
To grow unguided at a time when none. A Tough Generation. David Gascoyne. LiTM
To Guido Cavalcanti. Dante. *See* Guido, I would that Lapo, thou, and I.
To Guillaume Apollinaire. Jim Brodey. UL
To H. C. Wordsworth. ChER; EnRP; PoEL-4
To Hafiz. Thomas Bailey Aldrich. AA
To Hampstead. Leigh Hunt. EnRP
To have/ red mouth and green shanks. Moorhen. William Logan. DiPo
To Have a Child These Days. Gloria Fuertes, *tr. fr. Spanish by* Kate Flores. DMH
To have been a little ill. Convalescence. Noël Coward. TTTS
To have been loved once by someone—surely. When the Sun Went Down. John Ashbery. NAAL-2
To have been one. Aspects of Eve. Linda Pastan. CRP
To have grown old. Teika, *tr. by* Steven D. Carter. WFTW
To have it out or not? that is the question. "C. A. W." BXAP
To have known him, to have loved him. Monody. Herman Melville. LiTA; NAAL-1; OxBSP; PoEL-5
To have liv'd eminent in a degree. Upon the Death of My Ever Desired Friend Doctor Donne Dean of Pauls. Henry King. SeCP
To Have Taken the Trouble. C. P. Cavafy, *tr. fr. Greek by* Edmund Keeley *and* Philip Sherrard. VMG
To Have without Holding. Marge Piercy. NIP
To Haydn. Thomas Holcroft. NOEC
To Hayley. Blake. *See* Thy Friendship oft has made my heart to ache.
To heal you Hieronymus I had brought you. Bear's Blood. Ileana Malancioiu, *tr. by* Stavros Deligiorgis. BoWoP
To hear a dripping water tap in a house. Betweens. Norman MacCaig. EAS
To hear an oriole sing. Emily Dickinson. PoEL-5
To Hear My Head Roar. Henry Taylor. MAYP
To Heaven. Ben Jonson. HAP; JCP; LiTB; NAEL-1; NOCV; OBS; QFR; SeCP; TrPWD; UnPo
To Helen. Poe. AA; AmPP; AnAmPo; AWP; BoLoP; CH; ChTr; FaBoBe; FaBV; FaFP; FL; FPL; GBL; HAP; HeIP; HoPM; InPS; InvP; LiTA; NAAL-1; NIP; NOBA; NOBE; NoP; OBEV; OxBA; PoE; PoEL-4; PoLF; PoRA; PrIm; TAP; TrGrPo; WeW
To Helen. Winthrop Mackworth Praed. NOBVV
To Helen in a Huff. Nathaniel Parker Willis. AnAmPo; OBAL
To Helen of Troy (N.Y.). Peter Viereck. WeW
To Hell with Commonsense. Patrick Kavanagh. FaBoTw
To Hell with It. Frank O'Hara. NeAP
To Hell with Your Fertility Cult. Gary Snyder. NAs; TW
To Henrietta, on Her Departure for Calais. Thomas Hood. OBTV; OxBChV
To Henry Constable and Henry Keir. Alexander Montgomerie. OxBS
To Henry Reynolds, of Poets and Poesy, *sel.* Michael Drayton. Christopher Marlowe. ChTr
To Henry Vaughan. A. J. M. Smith. OBCV
To Henry Wright of Mobberley, Esq. on Buying the Picture of Father Malebranche. John Byrom. NOEC
To Her. Robert Mezey. NaP
To Her Dead Mate: Montana, 1966. Elizabeth Libbey. AmPA
To Her Eyes. Lord Herbert of Cherbury. JCP; OBS
To Her in Absence; a Ship. Thomas Carew. CaPo
To Her Little Son Rinaldo When Sick. Faustina Maratti Zappi, *tr. fr. Italian by* Muriel Kittel. DMI
To Her Love. Edward May. FaBoEE

To Her Lover's Complaint. Jane Barker. OxBSP
To Her Questioning His Estate. William Hammond. JCP
To Her Sea-faring Lover. *Unknown. See* Shall I thus ever long, and be no whit the near.
To herald in another year. January. Henrietta Cordelia Ray. CBWP-3
To Hero nightly, wet and rather cold. Subjectivity at Sestos. P. M. Hubbard. NYBP
To hide her ordure, claws the cat. A Quarrelsome Bishop. Walter Savage Landor. FaBoEE
To him who in the love of Nature holds. Thanatopsis. Bryant. AA; AmPP; AnAmPo; AWP; BLPL; BoNaP; DL; FaBoBe; FaFP; LiTA; NAAL-1; NOBA; OBEV; OHFP; OxBA; PWR; TAP; TrGrPo; WBLP; WGRP
To Him Who Is Feared. Eleazar Ben Kalir, *tr. fr. Hebrew by* Lady Katie Magnus. TrJP
To Himself. Catullus, *tr. fr. Latin by* William Ellery Leonard. AWP
To Himself. Pierre Jean Jouve, *tr. fr. French by* Keith Bosley. RHTwFP
To Himself. Giacomo Leopardi, *tr. fr. Italian by* John Heath-Stubbs. PFI
To Himselfe and the Harpe. Michael Drayton. OBS
To His Book. Robert Herrick. CaPo; OxBSP
To His Book. Leon Stokesbury. SM
To His Book[e]. Robert Herrick. FaBoUs; JCP
To His Book[e]. Martial, *tr. fr. Latin by* Robert Herrick. AWP; OBVE
To His Books. Henry Vaughan. QFR
To his book's end this last line he'd have placed. Robert Herrick. CaPo; NAEL-1
To His Chi Mistress. George Starbuck. NYBP
To His Child. William Bullokar. OxBChV
To His Children in Darkness. James Dickey. DiL
To His Conscience. Robert Herrick. NAEL-1; NoP; PoEL-3
To His Countrymen. James Russell Lowell. *Fr.* A Fable for Critics. AA
To His Coy Mistress. Edward Bird. BXAP; FaBoPa
To His Coy Mistress. John Flood. BXAP; FaBoPa
To His Coy Mistress. Gerry Hamill. BXAP
To His Coy Mistress. Andrew Marvell. AWP; BoLoP; EBEV; ELP; EnLoPo; ErPo; FaBV; FaFP; FF; FPL; GBL; HAP; HeIP; HoPM; InPK; InPS; InvP; JCP; LiTB; MAT; MeLP; MePo; NAEL-1; NIP; NOBE; NoP; OAEL-1; OBD; OBEV; OBS; OPOP; PoE; PoEL-2; PoLF; PoRA; PPP; PrIm; SCV; SeCePo; SeCP
To His Coy Mistress. Peter Scupham. BXAP
To His Coy Mistress. Stanley J. Sharpless. BXAP
To His Coy Mistress. W. J. Webster. BXAP
To His Darrest Freind. John Stewart of Baldynneis. OxBS
To His Dead Body. Siegfried Sassoon. NoAM
To His Dear Friend, Bones. Jay Parini. MAYP
To His Dying Brother, Master William Herrick. Robert Herrick. CaPo; SeCV-1
To His Ever-loving God. Robert Herrick. TrPWD
To His Ever-worshipped Will from W. H. "Francis." *See* Whenas-methinks that is a pretty way.
To His Excellency, General Washington. Phillis Wheatley. NAAL-1; OFD; WPE
(His Excellency General Washington.) PoNe
To His Excellency Joseph Dudley. John Saffin. SCAP
To His False Mistress. Catullus. *See* Thou saidst that I alone thy heart cou'd move. OBVE
To His Father. Robinson Jeffers. DiL
To His Father on Praising the Honest Life of the Peasant. Parvin E'tesami, *tr. fr. Persian by* Deirdre Lashgari. WPOW
To His Flocks. *At. to* Henry Constable *and to* Henry Chettle. FM
To His Forsaken Mistress. Sir Robert Ayton. EIL; ErPo; OBEV; OBS; SeCePo
(Inconstancy Reproved.) GBL
To His Friend. George Turberville. *See* I wot full well that beauty cannot last.
To His Friend in Absence. Walafrid Strabo, *tr. fr. Latin by* Helen Waddell. PeHV
To His Friend in Elysium. Joachim Du Bellay, *tr. fr. French by* Andrew Lang. AWP
To His Friend Master R.L., In Praise of Music and Poetry. Richard Barnfield. AAS; EIL; Son; UnS
To His Friend, on the Untunable. Robert Herrick. CaPo
To His Friend, Promising That Though Her Beauty Fade, Yet His Love Shall Last. George Turberville. CTC; OBSC
To His Good Friend, Sir Anthony Cooke. Sir John Davies. *Fr.* The Gulling Sonnets. Son
To His Heart. Sir Thomas Wyatt. OBSC; SiPS
To His Honoured and Most Ingenious Friend, Master Charles Cotton. Robert Herrick. CaPo

To His Importunate Mistress. Peter De Vries. NBLV
To His Inconstant Mistress. Thomas Carew. *See* When thou, poore excommunicate.
To His Kinsman, Master Thomas Herrick, Who Desired to Be in His Book. Robert Herrick. CaPo
To His Kinswoman, Mistress Penelope Wheeler. Robert Herrick. CaPo
To His Lady. Sir John Davies. SiPS
To His Lady. Fulke Greville. *See* Caelica: More than most fair, full of that heavenly fire.
To His Lady. Henry VIII, King of England. CTC; EBEV; OBSC
To His Lady. Petrarch. *See* Sonnets to Laura: To Laura in Life.
To His Lady. Sir Thomas Wyatt. *See* Madame, withouten Many Wordes.
To His Lady, Who Had Vowed Virginity. Walter Davison. OBSC
To His Late Majesty Concerning the True Form of English Poetry. Sir John Beaumont. JCP; OBS
To His Little Son Benedict from the Tower of London. John Hoskyns. OxBChV
To His Love. John Dowland. *See* Come Away, Come, Sweet Love.
To His Love. Ivor Gurney. MMA; NAEL-2; OBWP
To His Love. Shakespeare. *See* Sonnets: XVIII. "Shall I compare thee to a summer's day?"
To His Love. Shakespeare. *See* Sonnets: CVI. "When in the chronicle of wasted time."
To His Lovely Mistresses. Robert Herrick. CaPo; CTC; SeCP
To His Lute. William Drummond of Hawthornden. *See* Sonnet: "My lute, be as thou wast [*or* wert] when thou didst grow."
To His Lute. Sir Thomas Wyatt. *See* My lute, awake! Perform the last.
To His Maid Prew. Robert Herrick. OBS
To His Maistres [*or* Mistress]. Alexander Montgomerie. GBL; OxBS
To His Mistress. Earl of Rochester. OBEV
To His Mistress. Robert Herrick. OFD
To His Mistress. Ovid, *tr. fr. Latin by* Dryden. *Fr.* Amores, I, 4. BoLoP; ErPo
To His Mistress. Sir Walter Ralegh. SiPS
To His Mistress, Dead and Darkly Return'd. Roger Johnson. VVA
To His Mistress Desiring to Travel with Him as His Page. John Donne. *See* Elegies: On His Mistress [*or* Mistris].
To His Mistress for Her True Picture. Lord Herbert of Cherbury. SeCP
To His Mistress [*or* Mistris] Going to Bed. John Donne. *See* Elegies: Going to Bed.
To His Mistress in Absence. Tasso, *tr. fr. Italian by* Thomas Stanley. AWP
To His Mistress Objecting to Him neither Toying or Talking. Robert Herrick. FaBV
To His Mistresses. Robert Herrick. CaPo; ErPo; SeCP
To His Mistris Confined. James Shirley. OBS
To his Mother. John Banister Tabb. *Fr.* The Child. AA
To His Muse. Nicholas Breton. OBSC
To His Not-so-coy Mistress. Wynford Vaughan-Thomas. BXAP; NOBL
To His Pandora, from England. Alexander Craig. Son
To His Pen. Sir Thomas Wyatt. *See* My Pen, Take Pain a Little Space.
To His Reader. Samuel Daniel. *See* Behold, once more with serious labour here.
To His Retired Friend, an Invitation to Brecknock, *sels.* Henry Vaughan.
"Come then! and while the slow icicle hangs." FaBoRV
Winter's Frosty Pangs. FaBoRV
To His Ring, Given to His Lady, Wherein Was Graven This Verse, "My Heart Is Yours." George Turberville. EIL
To His Sacred Majesty, a Panegyrick on His Coronation, 1661, *sel.* Dryden.
"Time seems not now beneath his years to stoop." OBS
To His Saviour, a Child; a Present, by a Child. Robert Herrick. OHIP; SeCP; TrCP
(Child's Present, A.) OxBChV
To His Scribe Adam. Chaucer. *See* Adam scrivein, if ever it thee bifalle.
To His Son. Sir Walter Ralegh. *See* Three Things [*or* Thinges] There Be[e] That Prosper All [*or* Up] Apace.
To His Son Bennet. John Hoskyns. FaBoEE
To His Son [*or* Sonne], Vincent Corbet[t]. Richard Corbet. FaBoCh; OBS; OxBChV; TrGrPo
To his studio Pablo Picasso. People. X. J. Kennedy. SoTCo
To His Tomb-Maker. Robert Herrick. SeCV-1
To His Valentine. Michael Drayton. PoEL-2
To His Very Friend, Master Richard Martin. Sir John Davies. *Fr.* Dedications [*of* Orchestra], I. SiPS
To His Watch. Gerard Manley Hopkins. MoAB; MoBrPo
To His Watch, When He Could Not Sleep. Lord Herbert of Cherbury. JCP; MePo; NOBE; PoEL-2
To His Wife. Ausonius, *tr. fr. Latin by* Terrot Reaveley Glover. AWP

To His Wife, for Striking Her Dog. Sir John Harington. OxBSP
To His Young Mistress. Pierre de Ronsard, *tr. fr. French by* Andrew Lang. AWP
To Homer. Keats. EBEV; NAEL-2; NoP; Son
(Sonnet: To Homer.) ChER
To honor the return of sparkling sun. Louise Labé, *tr. by* Willis Barnstone. BoWoP
To hope is good, but with such wild applause. Hope. Sir Richard Fanshawe, *after the Italian of* Giovanni Battista Guarini. *Fr.* Il Pastor Fido. OBS
To hope, to fear, remember, suffer pain. On His Life. Vittorio Alfieri, *tr. by* Barbara Howes. PFI
To Houston at Gonzales town, ride, Ranger, for your life. The Men of the Alamo. James Jeffrey Roche. PAH
To Hsiao Shih-ying. Hsieh Chin, *tr. fr. Chinese by* Jonathan Chaves. CoBLCP
To Hsü Shih-t'ing. Hsü Wei, *tr. fr. Chinese by* Jonathan Chaves. CoBLCP
To Hugh MacDiarmid. Edwin Morgan. FaBoTw
To Hunt. Blake. OxBoLi
To hunt and to be hunted make existence. Charles Heavysege. *Fr.* Saul. CaP
To hurt the Negro and avoid the Jew. University. Karl Shapiro. LiTA; OxBA
To I. Lavrentevaya. Natalya Gorbanyevskaya, *tr. fr. Russian by* Daniel Weissbort. BoWoP
To Ianthe. Walter Savage Landor. *See* Past Ruined Ilion Helen Lives.
To Ibn Zaidun. Wallada, *tr. fr. Arabic by* James Monroe *and* Deirdre Lashgari. WPOW
To Imagination. Edith M. Thomas. AA
To increase your hold. Keepsake. Lawrence Durrell. PoPo
To Inez Milholland. Edna St. Vincent Millay. AiP; WPE
To Inscribe on a Picture of a Skull I Painted. Ryokan, *tr. fr. Japanese by* Burton Watson. FCEI; JLIC-2
To Inscribe on My Portrait. Ema Saiko, *tr. fr. Chinese by* Burton Watson. JLIC-2
To Insure Survival. Simon J. Ortiz. CDW
To invoke rhymes and verse in vain I try. Suffering. Maria Guacci Nobile, *tr. by* Muriel Kittel. DMI
To Ireland in the Coming Times. W. B. Yeats. NoAM; NOIV
(Apologia Addressed to Ireland in the Coming Days.) BrPo
To Iron-Founders and Others. Gordon Bottomley. OBEV; OBMV
To Italy. Giacomo Leopardi, *tr. fr. Italian by* Romilda Rendel. AWP
To James. Frank Horne. *Fr.* Letters [*or* Notes] Found near a Suicide. BPo
To James Smith. Burns. HoPM
To Jane. Shelley. Mes; NoP
To Jane: The Invitation. Shelley. *See* Best and Brightest, Come Away
To Jane: The Recollection ("Now the last day of many days."), *sel.* Shelley. ChER; OBNC
(Recollection, The.) GTBS; GTBS-P
"We wandered to the pine forest." CH
To Janet. Ralph Pomeroy. NYBP
To Jann, in Her Absence. C. J. Driver. PeSA
To Jessie's Dancing Feet. William De Lancey Ellwanger. AA
To Jesus of Nazareth. Frederic Lawrence Knowles. TrPWD
To Jesus on His Birthday. Edna St. Vincent Millay. TrCP; TrGrPo
To Jesus Villanueva, with Love. Alma Villanueva. CCP
To Joan. Lucille Clifton. GeTw
To John Ashbery. Frank O'Hara. CAPP
To John C. Frémont. Whittier. PAH
To John Clare. John Clare. Son
To John Donne. Ben Jonson. JCP; NAEL-1; NoP; OBS; SeCP; SeCV-1
To John Greenleaf Whittier. William Hayes Ward. AA
To John I ow'd great obligation. Matthew Prior. FaBoCo; FaBoEE; FaFP; OBVE
(Quits.) AWP
To John Keats. Leigh Hunt. Son
To John Keats. Amy Lowell. Son
To John Keats, Poet, at Springtime. Countee Cullen. BANP; CDC
To John Lamb, Esq.: Of the South-Sea House. Charles Lamb. Son
To Johnny a box. Johnny. Marci Ridlon. RAR
To Joshua. Alice Thomas Ellis. OBD
To Juan at the Winter Solstice. Robert Graves. CMoP; EBEV; FaBoMo; LiTB; LiTM; MoBrPo; MoP; NAEL-2; NoAM; OAEL-2; PoE; TwCP
To Judith Asleep. John Ciardi. LiTM
To Julia. Robert Herrick. CaPo
To Julia de Burgos. Julia de Burgos, *tr. fr. Spanish.* BoWoP, *tr. by* Grace Schulman; PBWP, *tr. by* Grace Schulman; DMH, *tr. by* William M. Davis; OV, *tr. by* Maria Arrillaga.
To Julia in Shooting Togs. Sir Owen Seaman. BXAP

To Julia, the Flaminica Dialis, or Queen-Priest. Robert Herrick. CaPo
To Julia under Lock and Key. Sir Owen Seaman. BXAP; FaBoPa
To Julius. Martial, *tr. by* Sir Charles Sedley. FaBoEE
To K. H. Thomas Edward Brown. OBNC
To Kalon. Ezra Pound. PoA
To Kate, Skating Better than Her Date. David Daiches. ASP; FiBHP; NYBP; SD
To K[atharine de M]attos. Robert Louis Stevenson. OBNC
To Keats: On Reading His Sonnet Written in Chaucer. John Hamilton Reynolds. Son
To Keep a True Lent. Robert Herrick. TrCP
   (True Lent, A.) OFD; OHIP
To keep my health! Resolve. Charlotte Perkins Gilman. WGRP
To keep silent and act wise. Tabito. *Fr.* Manyo Shu. FCEI
To Keep the Memory of Charlotte Forten Grimké. Angelina Weld Grimké. BlSi
To kill a bat is easy. Easy as a Bat. *Gond Oral Tradition, tr. by* V. Elwin *and* S. Hivale. WTO
To kill its enemies and cheat its friends. International Conference. Colin Ellis. FaBoEE
To kiss my Celia's fairer breast. On Snow-Flakes Melting on His Lady's Breast. William Martin Johnson. AA
To Kiyomizu, through Gion. Yosano Akiko, *tr. fr. Japanese by* Hiroaki Sato. *Fr.* Thirty-nine Tanka. FCEI
To Know All Is to Forgive All. Nixon Waterman. BLPA
To know how not to hang on any more song. Black. Marcelin Pleynet, *tr. by* John Ashbery. RHTwFP
To know just how He suffered would be dear. Emily Dickinson. InvP
To know the inhabiting reasons. For the Rebuilding of a House. Wendell Berry. EyDe
To know there are rhododendrons on the slopes of the Himalayas. Nearer. Judith Herzberg, *tr. by* Shirley Kaufman. BoWoP; VWA
To know thy bent and then pursue. Ella Wheeler Wilcox. CenHV
To Know Whom One Shall Marry. Unknown. GBP
To Krishna Haunting the Hills. Andal, *tr. fr. Tamil by* Willis Barnstone. BoWoP
To Kuvos. Theognis, *tr. fr. Greek by* G. Lowes Dickinson. PeHV
To Kyris. Strato, *tr. fr. Greek by* Teddy Hogge. PeHV
To L. Julianne Perry. PoBA
To L. H. B. Katherine Mansfield. ATNZ
To Labor. Charlotte Perkins Gilman. PoLF
To lace my shoes. Unusual Shoelaces. X. J. Kennedy. TDD
To Ladies' Eyes. Thomas Moore. OxBoLi; PoEL-4
To Lady Anne Fitzpatrick, When about Five Years Old, with a Present of Shells, 1772. Horace Walpole. NOEC
To Lady Eleanor Butler and the Honourable Miss Ponsonby, Composed in the Grounds of Plas-Newydd, Llangollen. Wordsworth. PeHV
To Lake Aghmoogenegamook. The American Traveller. "Orpheus C. Kerr." FaBoCo; OBAL
To Larr [*or* Lar]. Robert Herrick. CaPo; SeCV-1
To Laura. Henrietta Cordelia Ray. CBWP-3
To Laura in Death. Petrarch *Fr.* Sonnets to Laura.
To Laura in Life. Petrarch *Fr.* Sonnets to Laura.
   Alas! So All Things Now Do Hold Their Peace. *Fr.* CIX, *tr. by* Sir Thomas Wyatt. NAEL-1; OAEL-1; OBVE; NoP
      (Lover for Shamefastnesse Hideth His Desire within His Faithfull Hart, The.) AAAS, 2 *versions*.
   My Galley ("My galley charged with forgetfulness.") *Fr.* Sonnets to Laura: To Laura in Life, CLVI, *tr. by* Sir Thomas Wyatt. AAS; HAP; MOS; NoP; OAEL-1; OBVE; PPP; SiPS; Son
      (Galley, The.) OBSC
      (Lover Comparath His State to a Ship in Perilous Storm Tossed on the Sea, The.) EIL; GBL; HeIP; PoEL-1
To Laura Phelan: 1880-1906. Leon Stokesbury. MAYP; MT
To Laurels. Robert Herrick. CaPo; SeCV-1
To learn silence. Wish. Ilse Aichinger, *tr. by* Beth Bjorklund. CoAuP
To learn the massrock's lesson, leave your car. Penal Rock: Altamuskin. John Montague. FaBCIP
To learn the transport by the pain. Emily Dickinson. NOCV
To learn to be without desire, you must desire that. Mad Words. Yüan Mei, *tr. by* J. P. Seaton. WFTU
To leave the earth was my wish, and no will stayed my rising. A Temple. Kenneth Patchen. EAS
To leave the world and serve God. Compiuta Donzella, *tr. by* Laura Stortoni. WPOW
To Leigh Hunt, Esq. Keats. EnRP; Son
   (Dedication: To Leigh Hunt, Esq.) OBNC
To Lesbia. Thomas Campion. *See* My Sweetest Lesbia [Let Us Live and Love].
To Let. D. Newey-Johnson. BoTP
To Leven Water. Tobias Smollet. OBEV

To Li Chien. Po Chü-i, *tr. fr. Chinese by* Arthur Waley. AWP
To Licinius. Horace. *See* Odes: II, 10. "Receive, dear friend, the truths I teach" ("Rectius vives").
To lie at the edge of the forest. In Memory of François Rabelais. Yunna Moritz, *tr. by* Elaine Feinstein. VWA
To lie in shadow on the lawn. The Wall. Eugenio Montale, *tr. by* Maurice English. PFI
To Liebig. August, Graf von Platen, *tr. fr. German by* Reginald Bancroft Cooke. PeHV
To Life I Said Yes. Chaim Grade, *tr. fr. Yiddish by* Joseph Leftwich. TrJP
To Light. Linda Hogan. ER; HATNAP
To Lighten My Darkness. Unknown, *tr. fr. Arabic by* E. Powys Mathers. *Fr.* The Thousand and One Nights. AWP
To Lighten My House. Alastair Reid. NePoEA
To Like, to Love. Anne Sexton. AnAn
To Live. Philippe Denis, *tr. fr. French by* Paul Auster. RHTwFP
To live a life, free from gout, pain, and phthisic. Athletic Employment. Unknown. SD
To live and not to be thine own. Thine Own. Josephine D. Henderson Heard. CBWP-4
To Live at the Speed of Biography. Yona Wallach, *tr. fr. Hebrew by* Warren Bargad *and* Stanley F. Chyet. IP
To Live Here. Paul Eluard, *tr. fr. French by* Michael Benedikt. POS
To live illusionless, in the abandoned mine. Double Monologue. Adrienne Rich. NePoEA-2
To live in/ myself. Drifting. Kathleen Spivack. IHMS
To live in hell, and heaven to behold. Henry Constable. *Fr.* Diana. AAS; OBSC; Son
To Live in Pleasure. Unknown. *See* Sing We and Chant It.
To live in Wales is to be conscious. Welsh Landscape. R. S. Thomas. FaBoMo
To Live Merrily, and to Trust to Good Verses. Robert Herrick. AWP; CaPo; InvP; OBS; SeCP; SeCV-1
To live within a cave—it is most good. Salve! Thomas Edward Brown. OBEV
To live's a gift, to dye's a debt that we. The Porch. Philip Pain. SCAP
To Lizbie Browne. Thomas Hardy. ELP; NOBVV
To London once my stepps [*or* steps] I bent. London Lickpenny. Unknown. CoMu; FaBoPP; OBSV
      (London Lackpenny.) ChTr
      (London Lyckpeny.) OxBLMV
To Look at Any Thing. John Moffitt. RFM
To look from the Acrocorinth. Mycenae. David Fisher. NPGG
To look in my son's eyes. Address. William Carlos Williams. DiL
To loosen with all ten fingers held wide and limber. Moss-gathering. Theodore Roethke. RFM; VGW
To lose it all at once. Marina Tsvetayeva, *tr. fr. Russian by* Paul Schmidt. *Fr.* The Daughter of Jairus, XI. BoWoP
To Lou Gehrig. John Kieran. SD
To love a man without return. Lady Kasa. *Fr.* Manyo Shu. PeBJV
To Love and Nature all their rights restore. At. to John Wilmot, 2nd Earl of Rochester. *Fr.* Sodom; or The Quintessence of Debauchery. PeHV
To Love and to Remember. Christina Rossetti. *Fr.* Later Life, VII. Son
"To love is to give," said the crooked old man. Cupidon. William Jay Smith. NePoEA
To love love and not its meaning. The Rape of the Swan. Archibald MacLeish. AnAmPo
To love, My Lord, I do knight's service owe. Sir John Davies. *Fr.* The Gulling Sonnets. Son
To love November, a turned joy. Late in Fall. Ramona Wilson. VoR
To love one woman, or to sit. Woman and Tree. Robert Graves. ErPo
To love some one more dearly ev'ry day. My Task. Maude Louise Ray. PWR
To love somebody/ Who doesn't love you. Lady Kasa, *tr. by* Kenneth Rexroth. WPOW
To love someone/ Who does not return that love. Lady Kasa, *tr. by* Harold P. Wright. PBWP
To love thee brings me sadness, for I know. The Waning of Love. "Arthur Lyon Raile." PeHV
To love you who love me not. Lady Kasa. *Fr.* Manyo Shu. Ma
To Lovers of Earth: Fair Warning. Countee Cullen. CDC
To Lucasta, from Prison. Richard Lovelace. CaPo
To Lucasta, Going to the Wars [*or* Warres]. Richard Lovelace. AWP; CaPo; ELP; EnLoPo; FaBV; FaFP; FF; FPL; GBL; GTBS; GTBS-P; HAP; HeIP; HoPM; InPS; JCP; LiTB; MeLP; MePo; NAEL-1; NIP; NOBE; NoP; OAEL-1; OBEV; OBS; OBWP; OxBSP; PoEL-3; PoRA; SCV; SeCePo; SeCP; SeCV-1; TrGrPo; WeW

(Song: To Lucasta, Going to the Wars.) PoE

(To Lucasta.) InPK

To Lucasta: Her Reserved Looks. Richard Lovelace. CaPo; SeCV-1

To Lucasta, [on] Going beyond the Seas. Richard Lovelace. CaPo; GTBS; GTBS-P; LiTB; MeLP; MOS; OBEV; OBS; SeCP; SeCV-1

To Lucasta: The Rose. Richard Lovelace. SeCV-1

To Lucia at Birth. Robert Graves. NAs

To Lucy, Countesse of Bedford, with Mr. Donnes Satyres. Ben Jonson. OBS; SeCV-1

To Luigi del Riccio, after the Death of Cecchino Bracci. Michelangelo, *tr. fr. Italian by* John Addington Symonds. PeHV

To Luve Unluvit. Alexander Scott. GoTS; OxBS

To Lydia. Horace. *See* Odes: I, 25. Ribald Romeos Less and Less Berattle ("Parcius iunctas quatiunt fenestras").

To Lydia, with a Coloured Egg, on Easter Monday. John Jones. FaBoUs

To M———: "What? Dorval, me you applaud." Constance-Marie de Salm-Dyck, *tr. by* Dorothy Backer. DMF

To M. T. Bayard Taylor. AA

To Mackinnon of Strath. Iain Lom, *tr. fr. Gaelic.* GoTS

To Madame A. V. Pletneff. Karolina Pavlova, *tr. fr. French by* Paul Schmidt. PBWP

To Maecenas. Horace. *See* Odes: III, 29. "Descended of an ancient line" ("Tyrrhena regum progenies").

To Mainz! Ursula Krechel, *tr. fr. German by* Susan L. Cocalis. DMG

To make a final conquest of all me. The Fair Singer. Andrew Marvell. EnLoPo; MeLP; MePo; NOBE; NoP; PoEL-2

To make a Juju of my own. A Juju of My Own. Lebert Bethune. PoBA; PoNe

To Make a Pastoral; a Receipt. *Unknown.* FaBoUs

To make a prairie it takes a clover and one bee. Emily Dickinson. BoWoP; HeIP; Mes; NBLV; OBCA; OxBA

To make a resurrection there must be a death. Twin. Phyllis Haring. PeSA

To make a start. William Carlos Williams. *Fr.* Paterson, I. CMoP; NoAM; NOBA

To make me do the thing I will, I won't. The Human Animal. Jane Mayhall. TAP

To make quick way I'll leap o'er heavy blocks. John Dryden *and* Nahum Tate. *Fr.* Absalom and Achitophel: Part II. OBSV

To make reparation for love so blindly rejected. No Reparation. Charles Brasch. ATNZ

To make some bread you must have dough. One, Two, Three—Gough! Eve Merriam. NTCP

To make the vapor bath. That Old Sauna High. Anselm Hollo. PoM

To make this condiment, your poet begs. A Salad. Sydney G. Smith. FaBoUs; NBLV

To make your candles last for aye. Mother Goose. OxNR

To man, my friend, whose conscious heart. Horace. *See* Odes: I, 22. "Virtue, dear friend, needs no 'defence' " ("Integer vitae").

To Man Who Goes Seeking Immortality. Adelaide Crapsey. QFR

To Margot Heinemann. John Cornford. *See* Heart of the heartless world.

To Marguerite—Continued. Matthew Arnold. *Fr.* Switzerland, V. BoLoP; EBEV; EBVV; ELP; FiP; GTBS-P; MOS; NOBE; NoP; OAEL-2; OBEV; OBNC; PoEL-5; PPP; PrIM; TEP

To Maria Gisborne in England, from Italy. Shelley. *Fr.* Letter to Maria Gisborne. NOBE

To Marie. *Unknown.* NA

To Marie Osmond. Jack Skelley. UL

To Marina. Kenneth Koch. NoAM

To Mark Anthony in Heaven. William Carlos Williams. NOBA

To market, to market/ To buy a plum bun. Mother Goose. OxNR

To market, to market, to buy a fat pig. *Unknown.* BoTP; FaBoBe; FaFP; OxNR

To Mary. John Clare. *See* To Mary: I Sleep with Thee, and Wake with Thee.

To Mary. William Cowper. EnLoPo; EnRP; FiP; NOEC

(My Mary.) OBEV

(To the Same.) GTBS; GTBS-P

To Mary. Shelley. EnRP

To Mary. Mary E. Tucker. CBWP-1

To Mary. Charles Wolfe. OBEV

To Mary: I Sleep with Thee, and Wake with Thee. John Clare. GBL

(To Mary.) EnLoPo

To Mary: It Is the Evening Hour. John Clare. BoLoP; ChTr; GBL; Mes

(Mary.) EnLoPo

To Mary Lady Wroth. Ben Jonson. OBS

To Mary our Queen, that flower so sweet. The Marigold. William Forrest. ACP

To Mary Unwin [or Sonnet to Mrs. Unwin]. William Cowper. GTBS; GTBS-P; OBEV; TrGrPo

To Marygolds. Robert Herrick. NAEL-1

To Master Davenant for Absence. Sir John Suckling. CaPo

To Master Henry Lawes, the Excellent Composer, of His Lyrics. Robert Herrick. CaPo

To Match the Prince of Lang-yeh's Poem in the Old Style. Wang Seng-ta, *tr. fr. Chinese by* Burton Watson. CoBCP

To Max Jacob. Rosanna Warren. DiPo

To Maystres Jane Blenner-Haiset. John Skelton. *Fr.* The Garlande [*or* Garlands] of Laurell. AAS

To Me. William Barnes. PoEL-4

"To me, fair[e] friend, you never can be old." Shakespeare. *Fr.* Sonnets, CIV. EIL; FPL; GBL; GTBS; GTBS-P; HeIP; OBEV; OBSC; PeHV; Prf

To me he seems like a god. Sappho, *tr. by* Willis Barnstone. BoWoP

To me, one silly task is like another. Cassandra. Louise Bogan. HAP; MoAmPo; PBWP; VGW

To me that man equals a god. Seizure. Sappho, *tr. by* Willis Barnstone. LLLT

To me the earth once seemed to be. Then and Now. Charles Frederick Johnson. AA

To me, whom in their lays the shepherds call. Inscription for a Grotto. Mark Akenside. NOEC; PoEL-3

(For a Grotto.) SeCePo

To Meadows. Robert Herrick. AWP; CaPo; CH; JCP; NOBE; OBEV; QFR

(To Meddowes.) OBS; PoEL-3; SeCP; SeCV-1

To Meath of the pastures. A Drover. Padraic Colum. AnIL; AWP; MoBrPo; OBMV; RB

To Meddowes. Robert Herrick. *See* Ye have been fresh and green.

"To meet and then to part," and that is all. The Close of Day. Wesley Curtright. CDC

To meet my love. *Unknown. Fr.* Manyo Shu. PeBJV

To Meet, or Otherwise. Thomas Hardy. OBNC

To meet the fountain of true life I run. Longing. Judah Halevi, *tr. by* Nina Davis Salaman. TrJP

To Melancholy. Countess of Winchilsea. WPE

To Melody. George Leonard Allen. CDC

To Men. Anna Wickham. MoBrPo

To mend their every hurt, to heal all their ills. Mountain Medicine. Elizabeth-Ellen Long. AmFN

To Mercy, Pity, Peace, and Love. Divine Image, The ("To mercy, pity, peace, and love"). Blake. *Fr.* Songs of Innocence. BoTP; EnRP; NAEL-2; NOBE; NOEC; NoP; OAEL-2; OBNC; PoE; PoEL-4; PPP; TEP; WGRP

To Michael. Norman Dubie. AnAn

To Mie Tirante. George Darley. Son

To Miguel de Cervantes Saavadra. Richard Kendall Munkittrick. AA

To Military Progress. Marianne Moore. AnAmPo

To Milk in the Valley Below. *Unknown.* OBET

To Milton. Oscar Wilde. BrPo

To Milton. Wordsworth. *See* London, 1802 ("Milton! thou should'st be living at this hour").

To Mind. Clark Coolidge. UL

To Minerva. Thomas Hood. ChTr; FaBoCo; FaBoNo; FiBHP; NBLV; NOBL; OxBoLi

To Miss———: "With woman's form and woman's tricks." Thomas Moore. OxBSP

To Miss B. John Clare. NOBVV

To Miss Charlotte Pulteney in Her Mother's Arms [*or* To Charlotte Pulteney]. Ambrose Philips. ELP; GTBS; GTBS-P; NOEC

To Miss Eleanor Ambrose on the Occasion of Her Wearing an Orange Lily at a Ball in Dublin Castle on July the 12th. Earl of Chesterfield. EnLoPo

To Miss L. F. on the Occasion of Her Departure for the Continent. J. C. Squire. BXAP

To Miss Laetitia Van Lewen. Constantia Grierson. WPE

To Miss Lucy F——, with a New Watch. George Lyttelton. FaBoUs

To Miss M———, Written by Moonlight, July 18, 1782. Sir Samuel Egerton Brydges. Son

To Miss———on the Death of Her Goldfish. Mr. Meredyth. FM

To Mistress Anne Cecil, upon Making Her a New Year's Gift, January 1, 1567-8. William Cecil, Lord Burghley. EIL; OBSC

To Mistress [*or* Maystres] Isabell Pennell. John Skelton. *Fr.* The Garlande [*or* Garlands] of Laurell. AAS; InPS; NAs; NOBE; OBEV; OBSC; OxBoLi; PoEL-1; TrGrPo; TTTS

(In Praise of Isabel Pennell.) CH

To Mistress Katherine Bradshaw, the Lovely, That Crowned Him with Laurel. Robert Herrick. CaPo

To Mistress [*or* Maystres] Margaret Hussey. John Skelton. *Fr.* The Garlande [*or* Garlands] of Laurell. AAS; ACP; EBEV; EnLoPo; GN;

GoJo; HeIP; HoPM; InPS; NAEL-1; NBLV; NOBE; NoP; OAEL-1; OBEV; OBSC; OPOP; PoE; PoEL-1; PoRA; PPP; SCV; TrGrPo (Mistress Margaret Hussey.) FaBoCh

To Mistress Margaret Tilney. John Skelton. *Fr.* The Garlande [*or* Garlands] of Laurell. MeEL

To Mistress Margery Wentworth. John Skelton. *Fr.* The Garlande [*or* Garlands] of Laurell. EBEV; EnLoPo; NOBE; OAEL-1; OBEV; OBSC; TrGrPo

To Modigliani to Prove to Him That I Am a Poet. Max Jacob, *tr. fr. French by* Wallace Fowlie. TrJP

To Mollidusta. James Robinson Planché. NA

To Monsieur de la Mothe le Vayer. Molière, *tr. fr. French by* Austin Dobson. AWP

To Morfydd. Lionel Johnson. MoBrPo; OAEL-2; OBMV

To Morning. Blake. EnRP

To-Morrow. Florence Earle Coates. AA

To-Morrow. Félix Lope de Vega Carpio, *tr. fr. Spanish by* Longfellow. AWP; TrPWD

To-morrow shall be my dancing day. My Dancing Day. *Unknown.* OxBoLi; PoEL-1

To mortal men Peace giveth these good things. Peace on Earth. Bacchylides, *tr. by* John Addington Symonds. AWP

To Mother. Lessie M. Drown. PWR

To Mother. Frank Horne. *Fr.* Letters [*or* Notes] Found near a Suicide. BPo

To Mother and Steve. Mari E. Evans. BPo; PoBA

To Mother Fairie. Alice Cary. OBCA

To move over shifting borders. Eeva-Liisa Manner, *tr. fr. Finnish by* Jaakko A. Ahokas. *Fr.* Cambrian, I. PBWP

To Mr. Alexander Ross. James Beattie. OxBS

To Mr. ———, an Unlettered Poet, on Genius Unimproved. Ann Yearsley. NOEC

To Mr. Bays. Charles Sackville. APAS

To Mr. C., St. James's Place, London, October 22nd. Pope. OxBSP

To Mr. Cyriack Skinner upon His Blindness. Milton. OBS; Son (To Cyriack Skinner ("Cyriack, this three years' day").) TrGrPo

To Mr. Gay, Who Wrote Him a Congratulatory Letter on the Finishing His House. Pope. NOEC

To Mr. George Herbert. John Donne. OBVE

To Mr. Gray. Thomas Warton the Younger. Son

To Mr. H. Lawes on His Airs. Milton. AWP; NoP (Sonnet: To Mr. H. Lawes, on His Aires.) OBS

To Mr. Henry Lawes. Katherine Philips. WPE

To Mr. Henry Lawes, Who Had Then Newly Set a Song of Mine in the Year 1635. Edmund Waller. CTC; SeCP; SeCV-1

To Mr. Hobs. Abraham Cowley. SeCV-1

To Mr. Hsiao Ch'ien. Lo Fu, *tr. fr. Chinese by* Dominic Cheung. IFON

To Mr. I. L. John Donne. SeCP

To Mr. Izaak Walton, *sel.* Charles Cotton. Retirement, The. FaBoPP; OBS

To Mr. Murray. Byron. FaBoCo

To Mr. Newton on His Return from Ramsgate. William Cowper. NOEC

To Mr. Punchinello. *Unknown.* OxNR

To Mr. Rowland Woodward. John Donne. MePo

To Mr. S. T. Coleridge. Anna Laetitia Barbauld. NOEC

To Mr. Tilman after He Had Taken Orders. John Donne. EBEV

To Mr. William Long, On His Recovery from a Dangerous Illness, 1785. William Hayley. Son

To Mrs. M. B. on Her Birthday. Pope. EnLoPo

To Mrs. Smith, Occasioned by the First of Her Sonnets. William Hayley. Son

To Mrs. Thrale [on Her Thirty-fifth Birthday]. Samuel Johnson. FaBoEE; NaS

To Mrs. Will H. Low. Robert Louis Stevenson. NOBVV

To Music ("Begin to charm and as thou strik'st mine ears"). Robert Herrick. CaPo

To Musick ("Musick, thou Queen of Heaven, Care-charming-spel"). Robert Herrick. UnS

To Music Bent Is My Retired Mind. Thomas Campion. AAS; NOCV; UnS (To Musicke Bent.) TrPWD

To Music, to Becalm a Sweet-sick Youth. Robert Herrick. CaPo

To Music, to Becalm his Fever, *sel.* Robert Herrick. CaPo; GoJo; OBEV; OBS; QFR; SeCV-1 "Charm me asleep, and melt me so." UnS

To Musicke Bent. Thomas Campion. *See* To Music Bent Is My Retired Mind.

To mute and to material things. Nelson, Pitt, Fox. Sir Walter Scott. *Fr.* Marmion, I. OBEV, *fr. Introd. to* I.

To My Body. Nancy Sullivan. TAP

To My Book. Ben Jonson. NAEL-1; SeCV-1

To My Brother. Louise Bogan. AiP; NYBP

To My Brother George. Keats. EnRP

To My Brother Hanson. W. S. Merwin. NAAL-2

To My Brothers. Keats. NAs; Son; TEP

To My Child. Abraham Sutskever, *tr. fr. Yiddish by* David G. Roskies *and* Hillel Schwartz. VWA

To My Child Carlino. Walter Savage Landor. NoP

To My Children. Rosanna Guerrini, *tr. fr. Italian by* Muriel Kittel. DMI

To My Children Unknown, Produced by Artificial Insemination. James Kirkup. NAs

To My Cosen Mrs. Ellinor Evins. George Alsop. SCAP

To My Country. "Rahel," *tr. fr. Hebrew by* Diane Mintz. PBWP

To My Cousin (C.R.) Marrying My Lady (A.). Thomas Carew. SeCP

To My Cousin Mary, for Mending My Tobacco Pouch. Francis Scott Key. OBAL

To My Daughter. James Michie. OxBSP

To My Daughter Betty. Thomas Michael Kettle. TIRV

To My Daughter Riding in the Circus Parade. Joan Labombard. GOYP

To My Daughter the Junkie on a Train. Audre Lorde. CNA

To My Daughters. Martin Seymour-Smith. NPo

To My Dead Brother. Clara Ann Thompson. CBWP-2

To My Dead Father. Frank O'Hara. CAPP; DiL

To My Dead Friend Ben: Johnson. Henry King. SeCP

To My Dear and Loving Husband. Anne Bradstreet. AmPP; AnAmPo; BLPL; BoWoP; FF; HAP; HeIP; NAAL-1; NIP; NOBA; NOCV; OPOP; OxBA; OxBSP; PoE; PoEL-3; PoLF; PrIm; SCAP; TAP; WeW; WPE

To My Dear Friend Mr. Congreve [on His Comedy Called "The Double-Dealer"]. Dryden. EBEV; FiP; OAEL-1; OBS; PoEL-3; SeCV-2

To my dear wife. A Last Will and Testament. John Winstanley. OBSV

To My Distaff. Catherine Des Roches, *tr. fr. French by* Dorothy Backer. DMF

To My Distant Beloved. Alois Jeitteles, *tr. fr. German by* the Reverend Dr. Troutbeck. TrJP

To My Dog "Blanco." Josiah Gilbert Holland. PoLF

To My Ever-honoured Cousin W. R. Esquire, *sel.* Phineas Fletcher. Lines Written at Cambridge, to W. R., Esquire. EiL

To My Excellent Lucasia, on Our Friendship. Katherine Philips. MeLP; OBS; PeHV; WPE; WPOW

To My Father. Dinah Butler. AIW

To My Father. Blaga Dmitrova, *tr. fr. Bulgarian by* J. Bossolova *and* Guillevic *into French*; Joanna Bake *from French to English.* OV

To My Father. Susannah Fried, *tr. fr. Slovak by* Anthony Rudolf. VWA

To My Father. William Sydney Graham. FaBoTw

To My Father. Henrietta Cordelia Ray. BlSi; CBWP-3; Son

To My Fellow-Mariners, March, '53. Thomas Whitbread. NYBP

To My First Love, My Mother. Christina Rossetti. OHIP

To my firstborn land, in the south. The Firstborn Land. Ingeborg Bachmann, *tr. by* Daniel Huws. BoWoP

To My Four-Year-Old Daughter. Gail Todd. TV

To My Friend. Francis Thompson. PoA

To My Friend Butts I Write. Blake. EnRP

To My Friend, Dr. Charleton, on His Learned and Useful Works; and More Particularly This of Stone-Heng, by Him Restored to the True Founders. Dryden. SeCV-2

To my Friend G.N. from Wrest. Thomas Carew. CaPo

To My Friends. Konstantin Nikolayevich Batyushkov, *tr. fr. Russian by* Alan Myers. AAA

To My Friends. Stephen Berg. NaP; NYBP

To My Friends. Peter De Vries. FiBHP

To My Friends. Peter Levi. NePoEA-2

To My Friends. Schiller, *tr. fr. German by* James Clarence Mangan. AWP

To My Generation. Benyamin Galai, *tr. fr. Hebrew by* Jacob Sonntag. TrJP

To My God. George Macdonald. TrPWD

To My God in His Sickness. Philip Levine. NNaP

To My Grandmother. Medbh McGuckian. FaBCIP

To My Hairdresser. Warham St. Leger. CenHV

To My Honour'd Kinsman, John Driden, of Chesterton, *sel.* Dryden. OBS, *abr.* "No porter guards the passage of your door." EBEV

To My Honoured Patron Humphery Davie. Benjamin Tompson. SCAP

To my hut overgrown with burdocks. Teika, *tr. fr. Japanese by* Hiroaki Sato. *Fr.* A Compendium of Good Tanka. FCEI

To My Ill Reader. Robert Herrick. CaPo

To My Inconstant Mistress [*or* Mistris]. Thomas Carew. EnLoPo; MeLP; MePo; NOBE; OBS; SeCePo; SeCV-1; TrGrPo (Song: To My Inconstant Mistress.) CaPo; GBL; JCP; NoP; SeCP (To His Inconstant Mistress.) OBEV

To My Infant Daughter. Yvor Winters. VGW

To My Ingenious and Worthy Friend William Lowndes, Esq. John Gay. OBSV

To My Lady. George Henry Boker. *Fr.* Sonnets. AA

To My Lady. E. S. Miller. Son

To My Lady Rogers, the Authors Wives Mother, How Doctor Sherwood Commended Her House in Bathe. Sir John Harington. EyDe

To My Least Favorite Reviewer. Howard Nemerov. TW

To My Lucasia, in Defence of Declared Friendship. Katherine Phillips. MeLP

To My Mistress Sitting by a River's Side; an Eddy. Thomas Carew. CaPo

To My Mistresse in Absence. Thomas Carew. CaPo

To My Mistris, I Burning in Love. Thomas Carew. SeCP

To My More Than Meritorious Wife. John Wilmot, 2nd Earl of Rochester. OxBSP

To My Most Dearly-loved Friend, Henry Reynolds, Esquire, of Poets and Poesy. Michael Drayton. OBS
    (First Steps Up Parnassus.) NOBE, *abr.*

To My Mother. George Barker. *See* Sonnet to My Mother.

To My Mother. Giuseppina Turrisi Colonna, *tr. fr. Italian by* Muriel Kittel. DMI

To My Mother. Mary Weston Fordham. CBWP-2

To My Mother. Heine, *tr. fr. German by* Matilda Dickson. AWP
    (Sonnet to My Mother, A.) TrJP, *tr. by* Emma Lazarus

To My Mother. Thomas Moore. OHIP

To My Mother. Poe. OxBA

To My Mother. Henrietta Cordelia Ray. CBWP-3

To my mother, and to my mother's monument. Rosario Ferré, *tr. by the author.* DMH

To My Mother at 73. Elizabeth Jennings. NAs

To My Mothers. Sigrid Ammer, *tr. fr. German by* Susan L. Cocalis. DMG

To My Mountain. Kathleen Jessie Raine. OxBS

To My Mouse-colored Mare. Tristan Corbière, *tr. fr. French by* C. F. MacIntyre. ErPo

To My Native Land. James Clarence Mangan. AnIL

To My Nephew, J. B. Clement Barksdale. OxBSP

To My Ninth Decade I Have Tottered On. Walter Savage Landor. EnRP; NAs
    (On His Ninth Decade.) TrGrPo

To My Noble Kinsman, Thomas Stanley, Esquire, on His Lyric Poems Composed by Master John Gamble. Richard Lovelace. CaPo

To My Nose. Alfred A. Forrester. BLPA

To My Now Distant But Once Much Loved Friend, Mr. Michael White. Christopher Logue. NPo

To My Old Schoolmaster. Whittier. NOBA

To my parents I am/ a thick layer of innovation. Houses, Past and Present. Eli Bachar, *tr. by* Jeremy Garber. VWA

To My People. Edwin Seaver. TrJP

To my people it's as though he gave them a sacrifice. Eadwacer. *Unknown, tr. by* Willis Barnstone *and* Elene Kolb. WPE
    (Wulf and Eadwacer.) BoWoP; CIP; TrGrPo

To my prowd foe thus, sister, humblie saye. Virgil, *tr. fr. Latin by* the Earl of Surrey. *Fr.* The Aeneid [*or* Eneados], II. OBVE

To my revenge and to her desperate fears. The Bubble; a Song. Robert Herrick. CaPo

To My Reverend Dear Brother, M. Samuel Stone. John Cotton. SCAP

To My Setter, Scout. Frank H. Seldon. BLPA

To My Sister. Olga Berggolts, *tr. fr. Russian.* BoWoP, *tr. by* Daniel Weissbort

To My Sister. Wordsworth. EnRP; OAEL-2
    (Change in the Year, A.) BoTP

To My Son, *sel.* George Barker.
    "My darkling child the stars have obeyed." *Fr.* I. TwCP

To My Son. Byron. NAs

To My Son. Margaret Johnston Grafflin. SoSe
    (Like Mother, like Son.) BLPA

To My Son. *Unknown.* PoLF

To My Son, Aged Three Years and Five Months. Thomas Hood. *See* Thou happy, happy elf!

To My Son Parker, Asleep in the Next Room. Bob Kaufman. PoBA; TwCP; VGW

To My Tortoise Chronos. Eugene Lee-Hamilton. FM

To my true king I offered free from stain. A Jacobite's Epitaph. Macaulay. FaPoR; NOBE; OBEV; OBNC
    (Epitaph on a Jacobite.) EBEV; NOBVV

To My Truly Valiant, Learned Friend, Who in His Book Resolved the Art Gladiatory into the Mathematics. Richard Lovelace. CaPo; PoEL-3

To my twin who lives in a cruel country. The Dual Site. Michael Hamburger. NePoEA-2; TwCP

To My Unborn Son. Cyril Morton Thorne. BLPA

To My Unknown Friend. Irina Ratushinskaya, *tr. fr. Russian by* David McDuff. AIW

To My Very Loving and Discreet Friend, Master Peter Miller of Bristol. Robert Hayman. OBTV

To my village fair no lass can compare. The Lovely Village Fair; or, I Dont Mean to Tell You Her Name. *Unknown.* CoMu

To My Wife. James Forsyth. WaP

To my wife. To the mailman. Report after a Walk along the Avenue. Pyke Johnson, Jr.. SoTCo

To My Worthy Friend Master George Sands [*or* Sandys], on His Translation of the Psalms. Thomas Carew. CaPo; JCP; MeLP; MePo; OBS; SeCV-1

To My Worthy Friend Master Peter Lely. Richard Lovelace. CaPo

To My Worthy Friend, Mr. James Bayley. Nicholas Noyes. SCAP

To My Young Lady, Lucy Sidney. Edmund Waller. *See* Why came I so untimely forth.

To My Youngest Kinsman, R. L. Abraham Chear. OxBChV

To Myra. Fulke Greville. *See* Caelica:
    I, with whose colors [*or* colours] Myra dressed [*or* dress'd] her head.

To Myself, after Forty Years. T. H. White. NYBP

To Myself, Late, in a Myrtle Grove. Robert Peterson. NeAC

To N. V. de G. S. Robert Louis Stevenson. BrPo

To Naples. Herbert B. Mallalieu. WaP

To Naso. Catullus, *tr. fr. Latin by* Jack Lindsay. ErPo

To Natalia Nikolaevna Pushkina. Prince P. A. Vyazemsky, *tr. fr. Russian by* Alan Myers. AAA

To Nature. Samuel Taylor Coleridge. OAEL-2

To Nature, in her shop one day, at work compounding simples. Filling an Order. John Townsend Trowbridge. AnAmPo; OBAL

To Nature Seekers. Robert W. Chambers. MoShBr

To Ned. Herman Melville. MOS; NAAL-1; NOBA; PoEL-5

To New York. Léopold Sédar-Senghor, *tr. fr. French by* Ulli Beier. PBA

To Night. Thomas Lovell Beddoes. Son

To-Night. Louise Chandler Moulton. AA

To Night. Shelley. AWP; ChER; EnRP; FPL; NAEL-2; NoP; OAEL-2; OBNC; PoLF; PoRA; TEP; TrGrPo; WiR
    (Night.) OBEV
    (To the Night.) CH; GTBS; GTBS-P

To Night. Joseph Blanco White. EBEV; OBEV; Son; WGRP

To-night he makes his one journey of the year. *Unknown. Fr.* Manyo Shu. Ma

To-night I am coming. *Unknown. Fr.* Manyo Shu. Ma

To-night I do not come to conquer thee. Anguish. Stéphane Mallarmé, *tr. by* Arthur Symons. AWP

To-night I saw three maidens on the beach. Ibant Obscuræ Thomas Edward Brown. OBNC

To-night retir'd the queen of heaven. Ode to the Evening Star *or* The Nightingale *or* To the Evening Star. Mark Akenside. PBBP
    (Nightingale, The.) OBEV
    (To the Evening Star.) PoEL-3

To-night, the gaudy auditorium. After the Show. Sam Harrison. NeIP

To Night, the Mother of Sleep and Death. John Addington Symonds. Son

To-night the very horses springing by. Winter Evening. Archibald Lampman. NOBC; OBCV

To-night the Winds Begin. Tennyson. *Fr.* In Memoriam A. H. H., XV. GTBS-P; LiTB; NOBE; OBNC; PoEL-5

To-night this sunset spreads two golden wings. Sunset Wings. Dante Gabriel Rossetti. FM

To-night we strive to read, as we may best. Longfellow. *Fr.* John Endicott. PAH

To no one Muse does she her glance confine. On a Squinting Poetess. Thomas Moore. FaBoCo

To Nobodaddy. Blake. OAEL-2

To Noel. Gabriela Mistral, *tr. fr. Spanish by* Doris Dana. PChr

To Noël Coward. Noel Coward. FaBoPa

To nothing fitter can I thee compare. Michael Drayton. *Fr.* Idea, X. ElL; OBSC; Son; TrGrPo

To Nysus. Sir Charles Sedley. FaBoEE; OBSV

To O. E. A. Claude McKay. BANP; BPo

To O. S. C. Annie Eliot Trumbull. AA

To Oenone. Robert Herrick. CaPo; OBEV

To Olive. Lord Alfred Douglas. OBEV

To Olivia. Francis Thompson. MoBrPo

To One Being Old. Langdon Elwyn Mitchell. AA

To One Elect. S. I. Hayakawa. PoA

To one fair Lady out of Court. The Challenge. Pope. PoEL-3

To One in Bedlam. Ernest Dowson. ACP; BrPo; MoBrPo; OBMV; Son

To One in Paradise. Poe. *Fr.* The Assignation. AA; AmPP; AnAmP; BLPL; BoLoP; LiTA; OBEV; OxBA; PoLF; TAP; TrGrPo

To one kneeling down no word came. In a Country Church. R. S. Thomas. FaBoMo; TOF

To One Married to an Old Man. Edmund Waller. FaBoEE; OxBSP; SeCP

To one of the ears. Ozaki Hosai, *tr. fr. Japanese by* Hiroaki Sato. *Fr.* One Hundred Haiku in Free Form. FCEI

To One Persuading a Lady to Marriage. Katherine Philips. *See* Forbear, bold youth; all's heaven here.

To One Put to Death in a Gas Chamber. Erica Marx. CN

To One That Pleaded Her Own Want of Merit. Thomas Stanley. OBS (To Celia Pleading Want of Merit.) MeLP

To One Who Had Censured His Public Exposition of Dante. Boccaccio, *tr. Italian by* Dante Gabriel Rossetti. *Fr.* Sonnets. AWP

To One Who Hankers after Buddhahood. Bunan, *tr. fr. Japanese by* Lucien Stryk *and* Takashi Ikemoto. ZPCJ

To one who has been long in city pent. To One Who Has Been Long in City Pent. Keats. BLPA; EnRP; FaBoBe; FPL; LiTB; TrGrPo

To One Who Quotes and Detracts. Walter Savage Landor. FaBoEE

To One Who Reveres Buddhism. Bunan, *tr. fr. Japanese by* Lucien Stryk *and* Takashi Ikemoto. ZPCJ

To One Who Sleepeth. Mary E. Tucker. CBWP-1

To onpreise women[e] it were a shame. A Woman Is a Worthy Thing. *Unknown.* FaBoCo; GBP (Women Are Worthy.) MeEL

To Open. Antonio Porta, *tr. fr. Italian by* Lawrence R. Smith. NItP

To orisons, the midnight bell. William Beckford. OBTV

To other eyes and ears you are a great. Bernard O'Dowd. *Fr.* The Bush. CBAP

To Our Blessed Lady. Henry Constable. ACP; OBSC

To Our Blessed Lord upon the Choice of His Sepulchre. Richard Crashaw. ACP (Upon Our Saviour's Tomb Wherein Never Man Was Laid.) OAEL-1

To Our Daughter. Jennifer Armitage. BrRo

To Our Friends. Lucian B. Watkins. BANP

To Our House-Dog Captain. Walter Savage Landor. PoEL-4

To Our Ladies of Death. James Thomson. GoTS

To Our Lady. Robert Henryson. ACP

To Our Lord, upon the Water Made Wine. Richard Crashaw. MePo

To our theme.—The man who has stood on the Acropolis. Byron. *Fr.* Don Juan, XI. InPS; OBSV

To own nothing, but to be. Words Spoken Alone. Dannie Abse. NYBP

To Oxford. Gerard Manley Hopkins. BrPo; FaBoPP

To Oxford. Thomas Russell. Son

To Paint the Portrait of a Bird. Jacques Prévert, *tr. fr. French by* Michael Benedikt. POS

To paint without a palette. Some Uses for Poetry. Eve Merriam. PCP

To Pan. John Fletcher. *See* Faithful Shepherdess, The: God of Sheep, The.

To Pandora. Alexander Craig. *See* Sonnet: "Go you, O winds that blow from north to south."

To Paris that was once her owne though now it be not so. Ovid, *tr. fr. Latin by* George Turberville. *Fr.* Heroides. OBVE

To Parker. George Turberville. OBTV

To Pass the Place Where Pleasure Is. *Unknown.* CoMu

To Pass the Time. Benjamin Péret, *tr. fr. French by* Michael Benedikt. POS

To Patrice Lumumba. Roberto Armijo, *tr. fr. Spanish by* David Volpendesta. Vol

To Penshurst ("Thou art not, Penshurst, built to envious show."), *sel.* Ben Jonson. AWP; FaBoPP; FaBoPV; JCP; NoP; OAEL-1; OBS; PoE; PoEL-2; PPP; SeCP; SeCV-1; TEP

"Thy copp's, too, nam'd of Gamage, thou hast there." FM

To people who allege that we. The Uses of Ocean. Sir Owen Seaman. FiBHP

To Percy Shelley: On the Degrading Notions of Deity. Leigh Hunt. Son

To Perilla. Robert Herrick. CaPo; OBS; SeCP; SeCV-1

To Pertinax Cob. Ben Jonson. JCP

To Pete Atkin: A Letter from Paris, *sel.* Clive James. "Weather's cleared, The. We're filming at Versailles." OBSV

To Petronius Arbiter. Oliver St. John Gogarty. OBMV

To Phillis. Edmund Waller. SeCP

To Philomela. Benjamin Colman. SCAP

To Phyllis. Edmund Waller. TrGrPo

To Phyllisto Love and Live with Him. Robert Herrick. CaPo

To Phylocles, Inviting Him to Friendship. "Ephelia." WPE

To Pius IX. Whittier. TW

To place one's little boy—just so. Archery. Walter de la Mare. FaBoNo

To plant plum-flowers. *Unknown, tr. fr. Japanese by* Geoffrey Bownas *and* Anthony Thwaite. *Fr.* Kokin Shu. PeBJV

To plant three roses for you each one only a dollar. Third Ode to Persephone. Robert Kelly. *Fr.* The Book of Persephone, 14. PoM

To Poem. Lyn Lifshin. NeAC

To Poesy. John Critchley Prince. PF

To Poets. George Darley. Son

To Poets. Walter Savage Landor. FaBoEE

To Poets and Airmen. Stephen Spender. WaP

To Pope Julius II. Michelangelo, *tr. fr. Italian by* W. S. Merwin. PFI

To popularize the mule, its neat exterior. The Labors of Hercules. Marianne Moore. OxBA

To Praise. Ellen Bass. ER

To praise the blue whale's crystal jet. The Whale, His Bulwark. Derek Walcott. OxBC; TTY

To praise thy life or wail thy worthy death. Epitaph on Sir Philip Sidney . *At. to.* Sir Walter Ralegh. SiPS

To pray for an easy heart is no prayer at all. James Keir Baxter. *Fr.* Autumn Testament, 22. ATNZ

To pray you open your whole self. Eagle Poem. Joy Harjo. HATNAP

To Primroses Filled with Morning Dew. Robert Herrick. OBS; SeCV-1; ViBoPo

To Prink Me Up. George Gascoigne. *Fr.* Gascoigne's Memories. Son

To prinke me up and make me higher plaste. George Gascoigne. AAS

To print, or not to print—that is the question. Hamlet's Soliloquy Imitated. Richard Jago. BXAP; FaBoCo; FaBoPa

To print our poems the propulsive cause. Fame Makes Us Forward. Robert Herrick. CaPo

To Professor Byrd Prillerman. Maggie Pogue Johnson. CBWP-4

To Prote. Simmias of Thebes, *tr. fr. Greek by* John Addington Symonds. AWP

To prove himself no plagiary, Moore. On J. M. S. Gent. Pope. FaBoEE

To Purity and Truth. *Unknown, tr. fr. Chinese by* William C. White. TrJP

To put new shingles on old roofs. A Little Brother of the Rich. Edward Sandford Martin. AA

To put off a decision. No Easy Harbour. Anne Hartigan. CIP

To Pyrrha. Horace. *See* Odes: I, 5. "What slender youth bedewed with liquid odours" ("Quis multa gracilis").

To Queen Elizabeth. Sir John Davies. *Fr.* Nosce Teipsum. OBSC (Dedication I: "To that clear majesty which in the north.")

To R. B. Gerard Manley Hopkins. CMoP; GTBS-P; InvP; OAEL-2

To R. Hudson. Alexander Montgomerie. OxBS

To R. K. James Kenneth Stephen. BXAP; CenHV; FaBoCo; FaBoEE; FaBoPa; NBLV; NOBL; Par

To rack and torture thy unmeaning brain. On the Supposed Author of a Late Poem "In Defense of Satire." Earl of Rochester. APAS

To rage I/ gravitate. Field. Susan Griffin. NPGG

To rail or jest, ye know I use it not. Sir Thomas Wyatt. SiPS

To Raise a Chimney. Gary Young. MOWH

To raise an iron tree. A Calder. Karl Shapiro. EyDe

To Raja Rao. Czeslaw Milosz. TOF

To reach it. Waterfall. Anne Welsh. PeSA

To read my book[e], the virgin shy [or shie]. To His Book[e]. Martial, *tr. by* Robert Herrick. AWP; OBVE

To Redouté. John Ashbery. PoA

To Remain. C. P. Cavafy, *tr. fr. modern Greek.* BoLoP, *tr. by* Nikos Stangos *and* Stephen Spender; ErPo, *tr. by* John Mavrogodato.

To remember is not always to go back to what was. Time Reminded Me. Julia Uceda, *tr. by* Willis Barnstone. BoWoP

To remember you in the next world. To Someone, when I Was Distressed. Lady Izumi, *tr. fr. Japanese by* Hiroaki Sato. *Fr.* Fifty-one Tanka. FCEI

To remember. To forgive. To have loved. Manuel Gutiérrez Nájera, *tr. fr. Spanish by* Samuel Beckett. *Fr.* Pax Anima. MexPo

To reply, in face of a bad season. The Ill Wind. Jay Macpherson. MoCV

To Restore a Dead Child, *sel.* Edwin Honig. 1925. *Fr.* I. NoAM

To Retirement. Luis de León, *tr. fr. Spanish by* Thomas Walsh. TrJP

To Retreat into Myself, to Accept. Maria Luisa Spaziani, *tr. fr. Italian by* Muriel Kittel. DMI

To Rev. Thaddeus Saltus. Mary Weston Fordham. CBWP-2

To Richard Boyle, Earl of Burlington: Of the Uses of Riches. Pope. *Fr.* Moral Essays, Epistle IV. NOEC; OAEL-1; OBSV; PoEL-3; PPP
"At Timon's villa let us pass a day." NOEC; OBSV
To Richard, My Son. Vera Bax. CN
To Richard Wright. Conrad Kent Rivers. AmNP; IDB; PoBA
To Ride. Paul Eluard, *tr. fr. French by* Kenneth Koch. TTTS
To ride piggy-back. Slave. Langston Hughes. LiTM
To Rimbaud. Mu'in Besseisso, *tr. fr. Arabic by* Abdullah al-Udhari. MPAW
To Rise, So Suddenly. Robin Behn. KS
To robbers furious, and to lovers tame. Samuel Johnson, *after the Latin of* Joachim du Bellay. FaBoEE
To Robert Browning. Walter Savage Landor. EnRP; NoP
To Robert Louis Stevenson. W. E. Henley. MoBrPo
To Robin Redbreast. Robert Herrick. OBS; PBBP; PoE; TrGrPo
To Rosamond. Chaucer. NoP
(Ballade to Rosamund.) MeEL
(To Rosamound.) OAEL-1; PoE
To Rosamound. Chaucer. *See* To Rosamond.
To Roses in the Bosom[e] of Castara. William Habington. *Fr.* Castara, *pt.* I. EnLoPo; MeLP; OBEV; SeCP
To Rosina Pico. William Wilberforce Lord. AA
To Rotenham. August, Graf von Platen, *tr. fr. German by* Reginald Bancroft Cooke. PeHV
To run a night's distance, distances by night, nothing's easier than traveling distances. Amir Gilboa, *tr. by* Warren Bargad *and* Stanley F. Chyet. IP
To run a thousand miles from a thousand men. Open the Heart. Charles Brasch. ATNZ
To Russia. Cincinnatus Hiner Miller. AA
To S. A. Thomas Edward Lawrence. PeHV
To S. R. Crockett. Robert Louis Stevenson. *Fr.* Songs of Travel. OBNC
To S. T. C. on His 179th Birthday, October 12th, 1951. Maurice Carpenter. FaBoTw
To safeguard man from wrongs, there nothing must. Distrust. Robert Herrick. CaPo
To Saffold's Customers. *At. to* John Case. FaBoUs
To Saint Margaret. Henry Constable. ACP
To Saint Mary Magdalen ("Such as, retired from sight of man, like thee"). Henry Constable. Son
To St. Mary Magdalen. Benjamin Dionysius Hill. AA
To Saint Mary Magdalen ("Blessed Offendour: who thyself haist try'd"). Henry Constable. PoEL-2
To Saint Mary Magdalen ("Sweet Saint, thou better canst declare to me"). Henry Constable. ACP
To St. Peter and St. Paul. Henry Constable. Son
To Sally. John Quincy Adams, *after* Horace. AA; AWP; OBAL
To Sally. Horace. *See* Odes: I, 22. "Virtue, dear friend, needs no 'defence' " ("Integer vitae").
To San Francisco. S. J. Alexander. PAH
To Satch. Samuel Allen. AmNP; PoBA; PoNe; SD; SoSe; TTY (American Gothic.) IDB
To save your world, you asked this man to die. Epitaph for the Unknown Soldier. W. H. Auden. FaBoCo
To save yourself. The Reunion: Swimming. William Meissner. TSL
To Saxham. Thomas Carew. CaPo; JCP; NoP; OBS
To say it once held daisies and bluebells. The Broken Bowl. James Merrill. PoA
To say no. The Siren. Idea Vilariño, *tr. by* Kate Flores. DMH
To Schmidlein. August, Graf von Platen, *tr. fr. German by* Reginald Bancroft Cooke. PeHV
To School! Stevie Smith. FaBoEE
To school till five! and then again we fly. Elizabeth Barrett Browning. FL
To Science. Poe. AnAmPo; Son
To Scilla. Sir Charles Sedley. FaBoEE
To Scott. Winifred M. Letts. PoLF
To Scream. Aimé Césaire, *tr. fr. French by* Michael Benedikt. POS
To Sea. Thomas Lovell Beddoes. *Fr.* Death's Jest Book, I, i. CH
To see a strange [*or* quaint] outlandish fowl. The Bounty of Our Age. Henry Farley. FaBoCh; FaBoEE; SeCePo
To see a [*or* the] world in a grain of sand. Blake. *Fr.* Auguries of Innocence. BLPL; EBEV; EnRP; FaBoCh; FaBV; FaFP; FaPoR; FM; ImOP; InPk; LiTB; OAEL-2; OBNC; PoEL-4; RB; RHPC; TrGrPo; WGRP
To see both blended in one flood. Upon the Infant Martyrs. Richard Crashaw. NoP; OAEL-1
To see her is a picture. Emily Dickinson. PeHV

To See Long like El Greco. Yona Wallach, *tr. fr. Hebrew by* Warren Bargad *and* Stanley F. Chyet. IP
To see my coat hanging there limp as a scarecrow's. On the Couch. Oscar Williams. WaP
To see my father. Golden State. Frank Bidart. DiL; NoAM
To See Ol' Booker T. Maggie Pogue Johnson. CBWP-4
To see such dainty ghosts as you appear. On Meeting a Gentlewoman in the Dark. *Unknown.* FaBoEE
To see the anemones, urchins, and crabs. Open Casket. Sandra McPherson. GeTw
To See the Cross at Christmas. Roger Cooper. TrCP
To see the lizard there. Jerome in Solitude. James Wright. AnAn
To See the Minstrels. Sue Roe. NPo
To see the petrel cropping in the farmyard. Burns Singer. *Fr.* Sonnets for a Dying Man, XXX. NePoEA-2
To see them coming headstrong. In Love with the Bears. Greg Kuzma. NYBP
To see them go by drowning in the river. Eli, Eli. Judith Wright. CBAP
To seek each where where man doth live. Sir Thomas Wyatt. SiPS
To Seem the Stranger Lies My Lot. Gerard Manley Hopkins. BrPo
To Seneca Lake. James Gates Percival. BoTP
To Send to Li Tan and Yüan Hsi. Wei Ying-wu, *tr. fr. Chinese by* Burton Watson. CoBCP
To Sergius. Sir Charles Sedley. FaBoEE
To Sextus. Martial, *tr. fr. Latin by* Sir Charles Sedley. FaBoEE
To Shades of Underground. Thomas Campion. *See* When Thou Must Home to Shades of Underground.
To shaggy Pan, and all the Wood-Nymphs fair. A Shepherd's Gift. Anytes, *tr. by* John William Burgon. AWP
To Shakespeare. Hart Crane. Son
To Shakespeare. Richard Edwin Day. AA
To Shakespeare. Thomas Edwards. Son
To Shakespeare. Frances Anne Kemble. Son
To shave, or not to shave? that is the question. T. F. Dillon Crocker. BXAP
To Shelley. John Banister Tabb. AA
To Shimá Sání. Laura Tohe. STE
To shoot, to shoot, would be my delight. A Shooting Song. William Brighty Rands. OxBChV
To Show How Humble. *Unknown.* AH
To Show My Sons. Lu Yu, *tr. fr. Chinese by* Burton Watson. CoBCP
To show the laboring [*or* lab'ring] bosom's deep intent. To S.M. a Young African Painter, on Seeing His Works. Phillis Wheatley. BlSi; NAAL-1
To shred them: a narrow labor, and simply toss. Destruction of Letters. Babette Deutsch. WPE
To Sidmouth and Castlereagh. Shelley. *See* As from an ancestral oak.
To Silence. Thomas Lovell Beddoes. Son
To Silence. T. S. Moore. BrPo
To Simplicity. Samuel Taylor Coleridge. *Fr.* Sonnets Attempted in the Manner of Contemporary Writers. Son
To sin, unshamed, to lose, unthinking. Russia. Aleksandr Aleksandrovich Blok, *tr. by* Babette Deutsch *and* Avrahm Yarmolinsky. AWP
To Sing in the Darkness. Doris Mühringer, *tr. fr. German by* Beth Bjorklund. CoAuP
To sing of wars, of captain[e]s, and of kings. Anne Bradstreet. BoWoP; NAAL-1; NOBA; OxBA; PoE; SCAP; TAP; WPE
To sin's a vice in nature, and we find. Daniel Defoe. *Fr.* More Reformation. OBSV
To Sir Edward Herbert at Julyers. John Donne. SeCV-1
To Sir Francis Brian. Sir Thomas Wyatt. *See* Satires: Spending hand that alway poureth out [*or* powreth owte], A.
To Sir H. W. at His Going Ambassador to Venice. John Donne. MeLP (Letter to Sir H. Wotton at His Going Ambassador to Venice.) OBS
To Sir Henrie Savile upon His Translation of Tacitus. Ben Jonson. OBS; SeCV-1
To Sir Henry Cary. Ben Jonson. NoP
To Sir Henry Vane the Younger. Milton. OBS; Son
To Sir Hudson Lowe. Thomas Moore. OBSV
To Sir Philip Sidney's Soul. Henry Constable. *See* Give pardon blessed soul, to my bold cries.
To Sir Robert Wroth. Ben Jonson. SeCV-1
To Sir Thomas Egerton. Samuel Daniel. OBSC
To Sir Toby. Philip Freneau. NAAL-1; NoP; TAP
To Sir W. A. William Drummond of Hawthornden. *See* Though I have twice been at the Doores of Death.
To Sir William Alexander. William Drummond of Hawthornden. OBS
To Sir William Davenant, Upon His Two First Books of Gondibert. Abraham Cowley. SeCV-1

To sit and look at light-filled leaves. Wendell Berry. *Fr.* Sabbaths, III. BLA

To sit composing like a sunlit ghost. The Table. Michael Heffernan. PoA

To sit in Solemn Silence. W. S. Gilbert. *Fr.* The Mikado. FiBHP

To sit on a shelf in the cabin across the lake. What Good Poems Are For. Tom Wayman. NoP

To Siva, the Unmaker. Ursula K. Le Guin. BWV

To Sleep. Maybury Fleming. AA

To Sleep. John Fletcher. *See* Tragedy of Valentinian, The: Care-charming Sleep [Thou Easer of All Woes].

To Sleep. Giovanni della Casa, *tr. fr. Italian by* John Addington Symonds. AWP

To Sleep. Keats. ChTr; EnRP; FaBoRV; NIP; OBEV; PoEL-4; PrIm; Son; TEP

(Sonnet to Sleep.) NAEL-2

To Sleep. Frances Sargent Osgood. AA

To Sleep. Sir Philip Sidney. *See* Astrophel and Stella, XXXIX: "Come sleep! O sleep, the certain knot of peace."

To Sleep. Charlotte Smith. Son; WPE

To Sleep. Wordsworth. EnRP; GTBS; GTBS-P; TrGrPo

To sleep easy all night. *Unknown.* OxNR

To Sleep ("Fond words have oft been spoken to thee, sleep!"). Wordsworth. Son

To sleep here, I play dead. Ia Drang Valley. Yusef Komunyakaa. MT

To Sleep ("O gentle sleep! do they belong to thee"). Wordsworth. Son

To S.M., a Young African Painter, on Seeing His Works. Phillis Wheatley. BlSi; NAAL-1

To smash the simple atom. Atomic Courtesy. Ethel Jacobson. FaFP

To smear poisoned honey on my lips. Yosano Akiko, *tr. fr. Japanese by* Hiroaki Sato. *Fr.* Thirty-nine Tanka. FCEI

To So-kin of Rakuyo, ancient friend, Chancellor of Gen. Exile's Letter. Li Po, *tr. by* Ezra Pound. CTC; FaBoMo; OxBA

To Soar in Freedom and in Fullness of Power. Walt Whitman. RFM

To Some Millions Who Survive Joseph E. Mander, Sr. Sarah E. Wright. PoBA

To Some Supposed Brothers. Essex Hemphill. GLP

To some, the pattering raindrops on the roof. Reprieve. Barbara Villy Cormack. CaP

To Someone. Takamura Kotaro, *tr. fr. Japanese by* Hiroaki Sato. FCEI

To Someone, when I Was Distressed. Lady Izumi, *tr. fr. Japanese by* Hiroaki Sato. *Fr.* Fifty-one Tanka. FCEI

To Song. Olga Berggolts, *tr. fr. Russian by* Daniel Weissbort. BoWoP

To Soulfolk. Margaret Goss Burroughs. BlSi

To Spain—a Last Word. Edith M. Thomas. PAH

To Speak I Know Not Where. Angèle Vannier, *tr. fr. French by* Barbara Johnson. DMF

To speak in a flat voice. Speak. James Wright. HAP; SM; TAP; WeW

To speak in summer in a lecture hall. Lecture Hall. Patrick Kavanagh. FaBoTw

To Speak of Chile. Margaret Gibson. MAYP

"To Speak of Woe That Is in Marriage." Robert Lowell. CAPP; MoP; NAAL-2; NoAM

To speak out clean. Telling It. Nancy Sullivan. TAP

To speak with the blind alleys. Paul Celan, *tr. by* Beth Bjorklund. CoAuP

To speed my brother. Princess Oku. *Fr.* Manyo Shu. Ma

To Spencer. George Turberville. OBTV

To spend uncounted years of pain. Arthur Hugh Clough. NOBVV; OBNC; OxBSP

To Spenser. John Hamilton Reynolds. Son

To Spring. Blake. BLPL; BoNaP; BoTP; EnRP; NAEL-2; NOEC; OAEL-2; OBEV; PoEL-4; PoLF; PPP; WiR

To Spring. Charlotte Smith. WPE

To spring belongs the violet, and the blown. A Petition. Thomas Bailey Aldrich. AA

To stand here in the wings of Europe. On a Return from Egypt. Keith Douglas. NePoEA

To stand on common ground. A Common Ground. Denise Levertov. PoM

To Stand Up Straight. A. E. Housman. OAEL-2

To stand within a gently gliding boat. The Haunts of the Halcyon. Charles Henry Lüders. AA

To Stanislaw Wyspianski. Katherine Mansfield. ATNZ

To starve, or not to starve? that is the question. W. H. Ireland. BXAP

To state each horror. From the Monkey House and Other Cages: Monkey II. Irena Klepfisz. GLP

To stave off disaster, or bring the devil to heel. Tapu. Arthur Rex Dugard Fairburn. ATNZ; PeNZ

To Stay. Doris Mühringer, *tr. fr. German by* Beth Bjorklund. CoAuP

To Stay Alive. Elizabeth McKim. ER

To Stay Alive. Paul Snoek, *tr. fr. Dutch by* Claire Nicolas White. DuIn

To Stella. Plato, *tr. fr. Greek by* Shelley. EnLoPo; FaBoEE; OBVE (Morning and Evening Star.) AWP

To Stella. Sir Philip Sidney. *See* Astrophel and Stella: Doubt you to whom my Muse these notes intendeth.

To Stella. Swift. NOEC

To step over the low wall that divides. To the Sea. Philip Larkin. AnAn

To Stephen Spender. Timothy Corsellis. WaP

To Stew a Rump-Steak. *Unknown.* FaBoUs

To stones trust not your monument. To W. B. Yeats Who Says That His Castle of Ballylee Is His Monument. Oliver St. John Gogarty. AnIL

To stop time, a twig spinning. A Juggle of Myrtle Twigs. Edward Codish. VWA

To Strike for Night. Lebert Bethune. NBP

To Sultan Murad II. James Clarence Mangan, *tr. fr. Turkish.* NOIV

To Summer. Blake. WiR

To sup with thee thou didst me home invite. The Invitation. Robert Herrick. CaPo

To Swim, to Believe. Maxine W. Kumin. TSL

To Switzerland, right up the Rhine. The Salmon. Christian Morgenstern, *tr. by* Geoffrey Grigson. FaBoNo

To Sycamores. Robert Herrick. CaPo

To T. A. R. H. Stephen Spender. PeHV

To T. H., a Lady Resembling My Mistress. Thomas Carew. CaPo

To T. S. Eliot. Emanuel Litvinoff. VWA

To-ta Ti-om. Peter Blue Cloud. HATNAP; STE

To Tan Ch'iu. Li Po, *tr. fr. Chinese by* Arthur Waley. AWP

To tangle or untangle a willow. Chiyojo, *tr. fr. Japanese by* Hiroaki Sato. *Fr.* Seventeen Hokku. FCEI

To Taufiq Sayigh. Riad al-Rayyes, *tr. fr. Arabic by* Abdullah al-Udhari. MPAW

To tell strange feats of deamons, here I am. To the Much Honoured R. F. Esq. Richard Chamberlain. SCAP

To tell the truth, I really am. The All-Night Waitress. Maura Stanton. AmPA

To tell you from the start, I have lost him whose hand and eye are gentle. He Whose Hand and Eye Are Gentle. *Unknown, tr. by* Kenneth Hurlstone Jackson. OBWVE

To Teresa. Iván Silén, *tr. fr. Spanish by* Julio Marzán. InW

To Terraughty, on His Birth-Day. Burns. NAs

To Thaliarchus ("Behold yon mountains"). Horace, *tr. fr. Latin by* Dryden. *Fr.* Odes, I, 9. OBVE

To that clear majesty which in the north. To Queen Elizabeth. Sir John Davies. *Fr.* Nosce Teipsum. OBSC

(Dedication I: "To that clear majesty which in the north.") SiPs

To That Most Senseless Scoundrel, the Author of Legion's Humble Address to the Lords. Thomas Brown. APAS

To That Person. Victor Segalen, *tr. fr. French by* Nathaniel Tarn. RHTwFP

To: The Access Committee. H. N. Beckerman. TSM

To the Accuser Who Is the God of This World. Blake. *See* Gates of Paradise, The: Truly, my Satan, thou art but a dunce.

To the Age's Insanities. Marie Ponsot. VGW

To the Animal Lover. Sándor Rákos, *tr. fr. Hungarian by* Jascha Kessler. *Fr.* Bear Song. FOC

To the Anxious Mother. Valente Malangatana, *tr. fr. Portuguese by* Dorothy Guedes *and* Philippa Rumsey. PBA

To the Archbishop of Tuam. *Unknown.* FaBoEE

To the Archdeacon. George Farewell. NOEC

To the Atoyac. Ignacio Manuel Altamirano, *tr. fr. Spanish by* Samuel Beckett. MexPo

To the Author of Clarissa. Thomas Edwards. Son

To the Avon River above Stratford, Canada. James Reaney. MoCV

To the banks of the Moldau River. How They Made the Golem. John Robert Colombo. MoCV

To the Bat. Edith King. BoTP

To the Bear. Sándor Rákos, *tr. fr. Hungarian by* Jascha Kessler. *Fr.* Bear Song. FOC

To the Beloved Grown Past Youth. Amin Nakhla, *tr. fr. Arabic by* Matthew R. Sorenson. MAP

To the Blessed Sacrament. Henry Constable. ACP

To the Blessed Virgin Mary. Gerald Griffin. TIRV

To the Body. Alice Meynell. ACP

To the Body. Coventry Patmore. *Fr.* The Unknown Eros, XL. OAEL-2; PoEL-5

To the Bone. Dorothy Allison. GLP

To the Borrower of This Book. Samuel Showell, Jr. FaBoUs

To the Boston Women. *Unknown.* PAH

To the Boy. Elizabeth Clementine Kinney. AA

To the boy who comes in summer the country. The Goat God. Cesare Pavese, *tr. by* William Arrowsmith. AnAn

To the brave all homage render. Ashby. John Reuben Thompson. AA

To the Brave Soul. Wilbur Underwood. WGRP

To the Cambro-Britons and Their Harp, His Ballad of Agincourt. Michael Drayton. *See* Fair [*or* Faire] stood the wind for France.

To the Canary Bird. Jones Very. AnAmPo

To the Carter's Daughter. Rocco Scotellaro, *tr. fr. Italian by* Paul Vangelisti. PFI

To the Child Jesus. Henry van Dyke. TrPWD

To the Christ. John Banister Tabb. TrPWD

To the Christians. Francis Lauderdale Adams. OxBS; WGRP

To the Christians. Blake. *Fr.* Jerusalem, IV, Prologue. EnRP; WGRP (Epigraph.) OBNC

To the Cicada. James Wright. KS

To the City of London [*or* In Honour of the City of London]. William Dunbar. ChTr; EBEV; FaBoPP; OBEV

To the Coast. Denis Glover. *Fr.* Arawata Bill. ATNZ

To the cold peak without their careful women. The Climbers. Elizabeth Jennings. NePoEA

To the Conference. Mrs. Henry Linden. CBWP-4

To the Countesse of Bedford. John Donne. MeLP

To the Countesse of Bedford, on New-Yeares Day. John Donne. OBS

To the Countesse of Salisbury. Aurelian Townshend. MePo; OBS; SeCP (Loves Victory.) MeLP

To the Cowpens riding proudly, boasting loudly, rebels scorning. The Battle of the Cowpens. Thomas Dunn English. PAH

To the Cuckoo. Michael Bruce, *revised by* John Logan. OBEV (Ode: To the Cuckoo.) NOEC; PBBP

To the Cuckoo. F. H. Townsend. ChTr; FaBoNo

To the Cuckoo. Wordsworth. BoTP; ELP; EnRP; FaFP; FiP; GTBS; GTBS-P; PoLF; TrGrPo

To the Daisy ("Bright Flower! whose home is everywhere"). Wordsworth. EnRP

To the Daisy ("In youth from rock to rock I went"). Wordsworth. EnRP

To the Daisy ("With little here to do or see"). Wordsworth. GTBS; GTBS-P (To the Same Flower.) EnRP

To the Dandelion. James Russell Lowell. AnAmPo; NAAL-1 "Dear common flower, that grow'st beside the way," *sel.* FaPON, 2 *sts.;* GN

To the Dead. Frank Bidart. EOEF

To the dead. Saigyo, *tr. fr. Japanese by* Burton Watson. *Fr.* Sixty-four Tanka. FCEI

To the Defenders of New Orleans. Joseph Rodman Drake. PAH

To the Detracted. John Andrews. *Fr.* The Anatomy of Baseness. EiL

To the dim light and the large circle of shade. Of the Lady Pietra degli Scrovigni. Dante, *tr. by* Dante Gabriel Rossetti. AWP; OAEL-2; OBVE; PFI

To the Divine Neighbor. Judah Leib Teller, *tr. fr. Yiddish by* Gabriel Preil *and* Howard Schwartz. VWA

To the Driving Cloud. Longfellow. ChTr; FaBoRV; PoEL-5

To the Eagle. Mary Weston Fordham. CBWP-2

To the Earl of Oxford, Late Lord Treasurer. Swift, *after the Latin of* Horace. OBVE

To the Earl of Warwick, on the Death of Mr. Addison. Thomas Tickell. NOEC

To the Editor of Mr. Pope's Works. Thomas Edwards. Son

To the Elephants. Nathan Alterman, *tr. fr. Hebrew by* Ruth Nevo. VWA

To the End. John E. Bode. BLRP

To the end of the alley sloshing through new mud. Coming Home. Rai San'yo, *tr. by* Burton Watson. FCEI; JLIC-2

To the Eternal Feminine. Tristan Corbière, *tr. fr. French by* C. F. MacIntyre. ErPo

To the Etruscan Poets. Richard Wilbur. OxBC

To the Evening. John Codrington Bampfylde. NOEC

To the Evening Star. Mark Akenside. *See* To-night retir'd the queen of heaven.

To the Evening Star. Blake. *Fr.* Poetical Sketches. BoNaP; CH; ChER; ChTr; EnRP; FaBoRV; FaBV; FPL; NAEL-2; NOEC; NoP; OAEL-2; PoE; PoLF; TEP; TrGrPo; WiR

To the Evening Star. Thomas Campbell. GTBS; GTBS-P; OBNC

To the Evening Star: Central Minnesota. James Wright. NaP

To the Fates. Friedrich Hölderlin, *tr. fr. German by* Michael Hamburger. OBD

To the Federal Convention. Timothy Dwight. PAH

To the fence posts leaning. Go Home. Janet Reed McFatter. GrPl

To the Field Goal Kicker in a Slump. Linda Pastan. ASP

To the Filial Son, Ts'ui. Hsü Pen, *tr. fr. Chinese by* Jonathan Chaves. CoBLCP

To the Film Industry in Crisis. Frank O'Hara. NOBA; OBAL; SOTW

To the First of August. Ann Plato. BlSi

To the first of my lovers. The First of My Lovers. Sydney Carter. OBET

To the fishers of Gjendin the bold Skipper spoke. Ode to the Last Pot of Marmalade. "John." OBTV

To the Foot from Its Child. Pablo Neruda, *tr. fr. Spanish by* Alistair Reid. RB

To the Fortuneteller Hsüeh T'ieh-yai. Hsieh Chin, *tr. fr. Chinese by* Jonathan Chaves. CoBLCP

To the Four Courts, Please. James Stephens. BIrV; MoAB; MoBrPo; UnPo

To the French of the Second Empire. Arthur Rimbaud, *tr. fr. French by* Robert Lowell. *Fr.* Eighteen-Seventy. FaBoPV; OBWP

To the Fringed Gentian. Bryant. AA; AnAmPo; AWP; FaBoBe; FPL; GN; NoP; PoLF; TAP

To the Gardener at Nuneham. Horace Walpole. FaBoEE

To the gaunt House of Art which lacks for naught. Athanasia. Oscar Wilde. BrPo

To the Generous Reader. Robert Herrick. CaPo

To the Gentile Poet. Mani Leib, *tr. fr. Yiddish by* John Hollander. PeBMYV

To the Gentlewoman of Llanarth Hall. Evan Thomas, *tr. fr. Welsh by* Gwyn Jones. OBWVE

To the Germans. Antoni Slonimski, *tr. fr. Polish by* Czeslaw Milosz. PwPP

To the Ghost of a Kite. James Wright. NePoEA

To the Girls of My Graduating Class. Irving Layton. ErPo

To the go-between. *Unknown, tr. by* Geoffrey Bownas *and* Anthony Thwaite. PeBJV

To the God of all sure mercies let my blessing rise to-day. Cassandra Southwick. Whittier. AnAmPo; PAH

To the God of Love. E. V. Knox. NOBL

To the Good Thief. Saunders Lewis, *tr. fr. Welsh by* Gwyn Morgan. OBWVE

To the Grasshopper and the Cricket. Leigh Hunt. EnRP; GN; OBNC; Son

To the Greek Anthologists. G. Rostrevor Hamilton, *after the Greek of* Satyros. FaBoEE

To the Hand. W. S. Merwin. EAS

To the Harbormaster. Frank O'Hara. CoAP; CRP; MOS; NAAL-2; PoM

To the hard-working miner whose dangers are great. The Hard-working Miner. *Unknown.* AmFP

To the Health of the Serpent. René Char, *tr. fr. French by* Jackson Mathews. RHTwFP

To the Heart. Tadeusz Rozewicz, *tr. fr. Polish by* Czeslaw Milosz. PwPP

To the Heavens above us. An Astrologer's Song. Kipling. MoBrPo

To the [*or* a] Highland Girl of Inversneyde. Wordsworth. EnRP; GTBS; GTBS-P

To the hill of Kasuga where *kuzu* vines creep. *Unknown. Fr.* Manyo Shu. Ma

To the Holy Spirit. Yvor Winters. MoAmPo; QFR; VGW

To the Holy Trinity. *Unknown, tr. fr. Irish by* Thomas Kinsella. NOIV

To the Hosts: A Reply. Chang Ts'o, *tr. fr. Chinese by* Dominic Cheung. IFON

To the house on the grassy hill. The Presence. Denise Levertov. NaP; NePoEA-2

To the houses, to our crops. We Must Return. Agostinho Neto, *tr by* Marga Holness. WMBCH

To the Hunter. Sándor Rákos, *tr. fr. Hungarian by* Jascha Kessler. *Fr.* Bear Song. FOC

To the Immortal Memory of the Halibut on Which I Dined This Day, Monday, April 26, 1784. William Cowper. MOS; SeCePo

To the Immortal[l] Memory [*or* Memorie] and Friendship of That Noble Pair[e], Sir Lucius Cary and Sir Henry Morrison ("Brave infant of Saguntum, clear."), *sel.* Ben Jonson. NAEL-1; NOBE; NoP; OAEL-1; OBS; PoEL-2; SeCP; SeCV-1

It Is Not Growing Like a Tree. ChTr; HeIP; LiTB (Noble Nature, The.) GN; GTBS; GTBS-P (Oak and Lily.) TrGrPo (Part of an Ode, A.) OBEV

To the Infant Martyrs. Richard Crashaw. NAEL-1; NoP; OxBSP; SeCV-1

To the Innkeeper at Five Rivers, Sun Pen. Chang Yü, *tr. fr. Chinese by* Jonathan Chaves. CoBLCP

To the Islands. Howard Moss. SM

To the Jews in Poland. Jozef Wittlin, *tr. fr. Polish by* Isaac Komem. VWA

. . . to the King./ Thou art the wall-stone rejected. *Unknown, tr. fr. Anglo-Saxon. Fr.* Christ 1: Advent Lyrics, I. AnOE, *tr. by* Charles W. Kennedy

To the King, at His Entrance into Saxham: By Master John Crofts. Thomas Carew. CaPo

To the King, upon His Coming with His Army into the West. Robert Herrick. CaPo

To the King's Most Excellent Majesty. Phillis Wheatley. TAP

To the Lacedemonians. Allen Tate. NAAL-2; NoAM

To the Ladies. Mary Lee, Lady Chudleigh. NOEC; WPE; WPOW

To the Lady in the Chemisette with Black Buttons. Nathaniel Parker Willis. OBAL

To the Lady Lucy, Countess of Bedford. Samuel Daniel. OBSC

To the Lady Margaret, Countess of Cumberland. Samuel Daniel. OBSC

To the Lady Margaret Ley. Milton. GTBS; GTBS-P; OBEV
(Sonnet: "Daughter to that good Earl, once president.") OBS

To the Lady May. Aurelian Townshend. GBL; MePo

To the Lady Portrayed by Margaret Dumont. John Hollander. OBAL; PoA
(For the Passing of Groucho's Pursuer.) PoA

To the Laggards. Joseph Bovshover, *tr. fr. Yiddish by* Joseph Bovshover. TrJP

To the Last Wedding Guest. Horace Gregory. NYBP

To the Learned and Reverend Mr. Cotton Mather, on His Excellent Magnalia. Grindall Rawson. SCAP

To the legion of the lost ones, to the cohort of the damned. Gentlemen-Rankers. Kipling. NOBVV

To the Liffey with the Swans. Oliver St. John Gogarty. AnIL

To the Looking-Glass world it was Alice that said. "Lewis Carroll." *Fr.* Through the Looking-Glass, *ch.* 9. Par

To the Lord General Cromwell. Milton. FaBoPV; NAEL-1; NoP; OBS; Son; TrGrPo

To the Lord Love. "Michael Field." OBMV

To the Lords of Convention 'twas Claver'se who spoke. Bonny [*or* Bonnie] Dundee. Sir Walter Scott. *Fr.* The Doom of Devorgoil, II, ii. EnRP; FaBoCh; OxBoLi; OxBS; Par

To the Maiden in the East. Henry David Thoreau. AnAmPo; OxBA

To the Maids Not to Walk in the Wind. Oliver St. John Gogarty. AnIL; ErPo

To the Man after the Harrow. Patrick Kavanagh. CIP; FaBCIP; GTBS-P

To the Man I Live With. Ann Menebroker. IHMS

To the man-in-the-street, who, I'm sorry to say. Note on Intellectuals. W. H. Auden. FiBHP

To the Man-of-War-Bird. Walt Whitman. AA; AmPP; FaBoBe; FM

To the Man Who Sidled Up to Me and Asked: "How Long You In Fer, Buddy?" Etheridge Knight. NeAC

To the Marchesana of Pescara. Michelangelo. *See* Yes! hope may with my strong desire keep pace.

To the Marquis of Graham on His Marriage. *Unknown.* OBSV

To the Memory of a Pre-Incaic Wiseman. Mirko Lauer, *tr. fr. Spanish by* David Tipton. Per

To the Memory of Abraham Lincoln. Bryant. *See* Oh, slow to smite and swift to spare.

To the Memory of Ben Johnson, *sel.* Jasper Mayne.
"Scorne then their censure, who gave out thy wit." OBS

To the Memory of Ebenezer Elliott the Corn-Law Rhymer. Richard Furness. PF

To the Memory of Gavin Wilson (Boot, Leg and Arm Maker). George Galloway. NOEC

To the Memory of J. Horace Kimball. "Ada." BlSi

To the Memory of Lord Halifax, *sel.* Ambrose Philips.
"Weeping o'er the sacred urn." FaBoCo

To the Memory of Mr. Oldham. Dryden. AWP; EBEV; FiP; HAP; HeIP; InPK; InPS; NIP; NOBE; NoP; OAEL-1; OBS; PoE; PoEL-3; PPP; Prf; SeCV-2

To the Memory of My Beloved Master William Shakespeare [and What He Hath Left Us] ("To draw no envy, Shakespeare, on thy name."), *sels.* Ben Jonson. TrGrPo
"I, therefore, will begin. Soul of the age!" NOBE
"Sweet Swan of Avon! what a sight it were." ChTr

To the Memory of My Dear and Ever Honored Father Thomas Dudley Esq. Anne Bradstreet. NAAL-1

To the Memory of Sir Isaac Newton, *sel.* James Thomson.
"All–intellectual eye, our solar round." ImOP; NOEC

To the Memory of the Brave Americans. Philip Freneau. AiP; AmPP; PoLF

To the Memory of the Learned and Reverend, Mr. Jonathan Mitchell. Francis Drake. SCAP

To the Memory of William Billington. George Hull. PF

To the Men of Kent. Wordsworth. OBWP

To the Men Who Lose. George L. Scarborough. BLPA

To the Merchantis of Edinburgh. William Dunbar. FaBoPP; OxBS

To the Mercy Killers. Dudley Randall. DL

To the Milkweed. Lloyd Mifflin. AA

To the Minister Liu. Yu Hsüan-chi, *tr. fr. Chinese by* Geoffrey Waters. BoWoP

To the Mock-Bird. Mary Weston Fordham. CBWP-2

To the Mocking-Bird. Albert Pike. AA

To the Mocking-Bird. Richard Henry Wilde. AA

To the Monk Wu-hsia. Mo Shih-lung, *tr. fr. Chinese by* Jonathan Chaves. CoBLCP

To the Moon. Thomas Hardy. BoNaP; ChTr

To the Moon. Giacomo Leopardi, *tr. fr. Italian.* PFI, *tr. by* John Heath Stubbs; TTTS, *tr. by* Kenneth Koch.
Koch; PFI, *tr. by* John Heath Stubbs.

To the Moon. Pierre de Ronsard, *tr. fr. French by* Andrew Lang. AWP

To the Moon. Shelley. BoNaP; ChER; GTBS; GTBS-P; PPP; TrGrPo; TTTS

To the Moon. Charlotte Smith. Son

To the Moon. Yvor Winters. HeIP

To the Moonflower. Craven Langstroth Betts. AA

To the Most Beautiful Lady, the Lady Bridget Manners. Barnabe Barnes. EnLoPo

To the Most Excellent and Learned Shepherd, Colin Clout. William Smith. *Fr.* Chloris. AAS; Son

To the Most Excellent Lady Veronica Gambara. Laura Terracina, *tr. fr. Italian by* Muriel Kittel. *Fr.* The Discourse on the Principle in All the Cantos. DMI

To the Most Fair and Lovely Mistress Anne Soame, Now Lady Abdie [*or* Abdy]. Robert Herrick. CaPo; NOBE

To the Most Learned, Wise, and Arch-Antiquary, M. John Selden. Robert Herrick. SeCV-1

To the Most Virtuous Mistress Pot, Who Many Times Entertained Him. Robert Herrick. CaPo

To the Mothers. Ernst Toller, *tr. fr. German by* E. Ellis Roberts. TrJP

To the Mountains. Henry David Thoreau. PoEL-4

To the Much Honoured R. F. Esq. Richard Chamberlain. SCAP

To the much-tossed Ulysses, never done. Ulysses. Robert Graves. CMoP; FaBoTw; MoP; NoAM; PrIm

To the Muse. Robert Louis Stevenson. EBEV

To the Muse. Philip Whalen. PoM

To the Muse. James Wright. NAAL-2; NNaP; NoP

To the Muse ("Is it for long you deign to visit my seclusion"). Afanasi Afanasievich Fet, *tr. fr. Russian by* Alan Myers. AAA

To the Muse ("You came, were seated. Happy and uplifted"). Afanasi Afanasievich Fet, *tr. fr. Russian by* Alan Myers. AAA

To the Muses. Blake. ChER; ChTr; EnRP; HAP; HeIP; LiTB; NAEL-2; NOBE; NOEC; NoP; OAEL-2; OBEV; TrGrPo

To the music of the guzla. Attic Dance. Joan Drew Ritchings. RR

To the Mutable Fair. Edmund Waller. SeCP

To the Name above Every Name, the Name of Jesus, a Hymn. Richard Crashaw. SeCV-1

To the Nativity. Fernán Gonzáles de Eslava, *tr. fr. Spanish by* Samuel Beckett. MexPo

To the New Annex to the Detroit County Jail. Richard W. Thomas. PoBA

To the New Ordained. John D. Sheridan. TIRV

To the new wick/ Of freedom's torch. My Thread. Dovid Hofstein, *tr. by* Joseph Leftwich. TrJP

To the New World. Randall Jarrell. CAPP

To the New Year. Thomas Carew. CaPo

To the New Year. Priscilla Jane Thompson. CBWP-2

To the New Yeere. Michael Drayton. PoEL-2

To the Newborn. Judit Tóth, *tr. fr. Hungarian by* Laura Schiff. MHuP; WPOW

To the Night. Shelley. *See* Swiftly walk over the western wave.

To the Nightingale. Countess of Winchilsea. WPE

To the Nightingale. Sir John Davies. *Fr.* Hymns of Astraea. OBSC; PBBP; TrGrPo

To the Noble Sir Francis Drake. Thomas Beedome. OxBSP

To the Noblest and Best of Ladies, the Countess of Denbigh. Richard Crashaw. JCP; MeLP

To the north, the bright tower, the town square, the eternal meeting. Map. Marcos Konder Reis, *tr. by* Mark Strand. ATCBP

To the Oaks of Glencree. J. M. Synge. MoBrPo; NOIV

To the Ocean. Byron. *See* Childe Harold's Pilgrimage: Ocean, The.

To the ocean now I fly. Milton. *Fr.* Comus; a Masque Presented at Ludlow Castle. OBEV; OBS
(Farewell of the Attendant Spirit.) TrGrPo
(Spirit Epiloguizes, The.) NOBE

To the old, long life and treasure. Ben Jonson. *Fr.* The Gypsies Metamorphosed. OxBSP

To the Old Masters. Wing Tek Lum. BrSi

To the One I Love Most. *Unknown.* MeEL

To the One of Fictive Music. Wallace Stevens. MoAB; MoAmPo; NoP

To the Palmetto State, in the year seventy three. Southern Work of Dr. and Mrs. L. M. Dunton. Lizelia Augusta Jenkins Moorer. CBWP-3

To the Parted One. Goethe, *tr. fr. German by* Christopher Pearse Cranch. AWP

To the Pending Year. Walt Whitman. OxBSP

To the People of England, the humble Petition. The Petition of the Orangemen of Ireland. Thomas Moore. NOIV

To the Pines. *Unknown.* WTO

To the pines, to the pines. To the Pines. *Unknown.* WTO

To the Pious Memory of the Accomplished [*or* Accomplisht] Young Lady, Mrs. Anne Killigrew, [Excellent in the Two Sister-Arts of Poesie and Painting]. Dryden. NAEL-1; OAEL-1; PoEL-3; SeCV-2

To the pit of my heart I pine. Yakamochi. *Fr.* Manyo Shu. PeBJV

To the Poem. Frank O'Hara. SM

To the Poet Wordsworth. Felicia Dorothea Hemans. BrRo

To the Poets. *Unknown.* PeNZ

To the Poets in New York. James Wright. NAAL-2

To the Prince. Sir John Davies. *Fr.* Dedications [*of* Orchestra], II. SiPS

To the Queen. Blake. *See* Door of Death is made of Gold, The.

To the Queen. Lord Darnley. OxBS

To the Queen of Hearts is the Ace of Sorrow. The Queen of Hearts. *Unknown.* OBET

To the Queen of Sweden, on Her Contempt for Women's Minds. Mlle Certain, *tr. fr. French by* Dorothy Backer. DMF

To the Queen of the British Government. Mrs. Henry Linden. CBWP-4

To the Queene, Entertain'd at Night by the Countesse of Anglesey. Sir William Davenant. MeLP; MePo; OBS

To the quick brow Fame grudges her best wreath. The Guerdon. John James Piatt. AA

To the Reader. J. V. Cunningham. QFR

To the Reader. Samuel Daniel. OBSC (To His Reader.) OBSC

To the Reader. Mark Jarman. NAmP

To the Reader. Ben Jonson. NoP; PoE; SeCV-1

To the Reader. Denise Levertov. AmPP; PoM; VGW

To the Reader. Urian Oakes. SCAP

To the reader of Master William Davenant's Play, The Wits. Thomas Carew. CaPo

To the Reader of These Sonnets. Michael Drayton. *See* Idea: Into these loves, who but for passion looks.

To the Redbreast. John Codrington Bampfylde. Son

To the Respective Judges. *Unknown.* APAS

To the Retired Scholar Chang. Ni Tsan, *tr. fr. Chinese by* Jonathan Chaves. CoBLCP

To the Returning Brave. Robert Underwood Johnson. PAH

To the Rev. F. D. Maurice, *sel.* Tennyson. GTBS-P; NOBVV At Farringford. FaBoPP

To the Rev. Mr. Powell. Christopher Smart. OBWVE

To the Rev'd Mr. Jno. Sparhawk on the Birth of his Son. Samuel Sewall. SCAP

To the Revd. Mr. ———on His Drinking Sea-Water. John Winstanley. NOEC

To the Reverend Shade of His Religious Father. Robert Herrick. CaPo; JCP; OBS; SeCV-1

To the Reverend W. L. Bowles. Samuel Taylor Coleridge. EnRP; Son

To the Reviewers. Thomas Hood. *See* What is a [*or* the] modern Poet's fate?

To the Right Hon. Henry Pelham. Edward Moore. OBSV

To the Right Honourable the Countesse of C. William Habington. SeCP

To the Right Honourable William, Earl of Dartmouth ("Hail happy day, when smiling like the morn"), *sels.* Phillis Wheatley. AmPP "No more, America, in mournful strain." WPOW "Should you, my lord, while you pursue my song." BPo; TTY

To the right, the sky, to the left, the sea. Lying Down. Robert Desnos, *tr. by* Bill Zavatsky. RHTwFP

To the River Duddon: After-Thought. Wordsworth. *See* River Duddon, The: I thought of Thee, my partner and my guide.

To the River Isca. Henry Vaughan. FaBoPP

To the River Itchin, near Winton. William Lisle Bowles. OAEL-2

To the River Otter. Samuel Taylor Coleridge. *See* Dear native Brook! Wild Streamlet of the West!

To the Rose. Sir John Davies. *Fr.* Hymns of Astraea. OBSC

To the Rose; a Song. Robert Herrick. SeCP (To the Rose: Song.) OBS

To the Rose upon the Rood of Time. W. B. Yeats. NoAM; NoP; TEP

To the Royal Society, *sel.* Abraham Cowley. "Philosophy, the great and only heir." JCP

To the Rulers. Howard Nemerov. OxBC

To the Sad Moon. Sir Philip Sidney. *See* Astrophel and Stella: XXXI. "With how sad steps, O [*or* Oh] Moon, thou climb'st the skies!"

To the sagging wharf. A Summer's Dream. Elizabeth Bishop. OxBC

To the Same. William Cowper. *See* To Mary.

To the Same Flower. Wordsworth. *See* With little here to do or see.

To the Same Purpos[e]. Thomas Traherne. NoP; SeCV-2

To the Sea. Philip Larkin. AnAn

To the sea-shell's spiral round. Appreciation. Thomas Bailey Aldrich. AA

To the ship I carried statues. I Carried Statues. Agnes Nemes Nagy. BoWoP, *tr. by* Bruce Berlind; MHuP, *tr. by* Daniel Hoffman

To the Skylark. Wordsworth. *See* Ethereal minstrel! pilgrim of the sky.

To the Small Celandine. Wordsworth. EnRP

To the Snake. Denise Levertov. AmPP; LiTM; NePoEA-2; NMM; PoA

To the Snipe. John Clare. FaBoPV; OBNC

To the Soul. John Collop. TrGrPo

To the sound of the wind. Tameko, *tr. by* Steven D. Carter. WFTW

To the Sour[e] Reader. Robert Herrick. NBLV; NoP; SeCP

To the South. Brewster Ghiselin. LiTA

To the south there is a dragon living in a mountain pool. Tu Fu, *tr. fr. Chinese by* Burton Watson. *Fr.* Seven Songs Written During the Ch'ien-yüan Era, 6. CoBCP

To the spectral garden to the silent laurel. Autumn Garden. Dino Campana, *tr. by* Charles Wright. PFI

To the Spider. Thomas Russell. Son

To the Spider in the Crevice behind the Toilet Door. Janet Sutherland. DT

To the Spirit Great and Good. Leigh Hunt. TrPWD

To the Spirit of Keats. James Russell Lowell. Son

To the Spirit of Monahsetah. Charlotte DeClue. GOS; STE

To the Spring. Sir John Davies. *Fr.* Hymns of Astraea. EiL

To the Spring Sun. Freda Laughton. NeIP

To the State of Love; or, The Senses' Festival. John Cleveland. MePo

To the state of West Virginia. The Story of Lovers Leap. Maggie Pogue Johnson. CBWP-4

To the States. Walt Whitman. CTC; NAAL-1

To the Statue. May Swenson. GOA

To the Stone-Cutters. Robinson Jeffers. AmPP; MoAB; MoAmPo; NAAL-2; NOBA; NoP; OxBA; PoRA; PrIm; TrGrPo

To the Street Piano, *sel.* John Davidson. Labourer's Wife, A. EBVV

To the Summer Sweethearts. Sydney Lea. NAmP

To the Sun. Ingeborg Bachmann, *tr. fr. German.* BoNaP, *tr. by* Michael Hamburger; CoAuP, *tr. by* Beth Bjorklund

To the Sun. Roy Campbell. *Fr.* Mithraic Emblems. EaLo

To the Sun/ Who has shone. Last Song. James Guthrie. PDV

To the Sun from a Flower. Guido Gezelle, *tr. fr. Flemish by* Jethro Bithell. FaPON

To the sun's path. Basho, *tr. by* Geoffrey Bownas *and* Anthony Thwaite. PeBJV

To the (Supposed) Patron. Geoffrey Hill. NePoEA-2

To the Supreme Being. Michelangelo. *See* Prayers I make will then be sweet indeed, The.

To the Swallow. William Cowper, *after the Greek of* Euenus. OBVE

To the Swallows of Viterbo. Gibbons Ruark. SM

To the Ten Thousand Years. Victor Segalen, *tr. fr. French by* Nathaniel Tarn. RHTwFP

To the Terrestrial Globe. W. S. Gilbert. FaBoNo; NBLV; TrGrPo

To the Thawing Wind. Robert Frost. OxBA

To the Things That Are Immortal. Abba Kovner, *tr. fr. Hebrew by* Warren Bargad *and* Stanley F. Chyet. IP

To the Thirty-ninth Congress. Whittier. PAH

To the Thoughtful Reader. William Meredith. NoAM

To the tin toys there was. Tin Toys. Tsfrirah Gar, *tr. by* Bernhard Frank. MHeP

To the Translator of Lucan's Pharsalia (1614). Sir Walter Ralegh. SiPS

To the Tune "A Floating Cloud Crosses Enchanted Mountain." Huang Ho, *tr. fr. Chinese by* Kenneth Rexroth *and* Ling Chung. AIW; BoWoP

To the Tune "Bamboo at West Lake." Shen Chou, *tr. fr. Chinese by* Jonathan Chaves. CoBLCP

To the Tune "Chao-chün's Sorrow." Yang Shen, *tr. fr. Chinese by* Jonathan Chaves. CoBLCP

To the Tune "Chiang ch'eng tzu. Yang Shen, *tr. fr. Chinese by* Jonathan Chaves. CoBLCP

To the Tune "Chieh san ch'eng" ("I love the autumn moon"). Yang Shen, *tr. fr. Chinese by* Jonathan Chaves. *Fr.* Four Poems from the Sequence "Singing of the Moon," III. CoBLCP

To the Tune "Chieh san ch'eng" ("I love the spring moon"). Yang Shen, *tr. fr. Chinese by* Jonathan Chaves. *Fr.* Four Poems from the Sequence "Singing of the Moon," I. CoBLCP

To the Tune "Child at Play." Yang Shen, *tr. fr. Chinese* by Jonathan Chaves. CoBLCP

To the Tune, "Ch'ing-p'ing Yüeh." Yang Shen, *tr. fr. Chinese* by Jonathan Chaves. CoBLCP

To the Tune "Chiu-ch'üan tzu." Wu Chen, *tr. fr. Chinese* by Jonathan Chaves. CoBLCP

To The Tune "Eternal Happiness." Li Ch'ing-chao, *tr. fr. Chinese* by Kenneth Rexroth *and* Ling Chung. AIW

To the Tune "Flowers in the Rain." Yang Shen, *tr. fr. Chinese* by Jonathan Chaves. CoBLCP

To the Tune "Glittering Sword Hilts." Liu Yü Hsi, *tr. fr. Chinese* by Kenneth Rexroth. UnAS

To the Tune "Heavenly Immortal" ("I remember those years when we shared the joy of love"). Yang Shen, *tr. fr. Chinese* by Jonathan Chaves. CoBLCP

To the Tune "Heavenly Immortal" ("Waves wash off the peach blossoms"). Yang Shen, *tr. fr. Chinese* by Jonathan Chaves. CoBLCP

To the Tune "Moon Over West River." Yang Shen, *tr. fr. Chinese* by Jonathan Chaves. CoBLCP

To the Tune "Nan-hsiang-tz." Shen Chou, *tr. fr. Chinese* by Jonathan Chaves. CoBLCP

To the Tune "New Moon." Yang Shen, *tr. fr. Chinese* by Jonathan Chaves. CoBLCP

To the Tune of, In Fayth I Cannot Keepe My Father's Sheepe. Sidney Godolphin. OBS

To the Tune of the Coventry Carol. Stevie Smith. FaBoTw; OPOP

To the Tune of "Ye Commons and Peers Pray Lend Me Your Ears." *Unknown.* APAS

To the Tune "Partridge Sky." Yang Shen, *tr. fr. Chinese* by Jonathan Chaves. CoBLCP

To the Tune "Red Embroidered Shoes." Huang O, *tr. fr Chinese* by Kenneth Rexroth *and* Ling Chung. PBWP; WPOW

To the Tune "Shui hsien-tzu." Ma Chih-yüan, *tr. fr. Chinese.* CoBLCP

To the Tune "Soaring Clouds." Huang O, *tr. fr. Chinese* by Kenneth Rexroth *and* Ling Chung. BoWoP; PBWP; WPOW

To the Tune "Song of the Plum Blossom at the River Town." Yang Shen, *tr. fr. Chinese* by Jonathan Chaves. CoBLCP

To the Tune "Spring in Tien Is Fine." Yang Shen, *tr. fr. Chinese* by Jonathan Chaves. CoBLCP

To the Tune "Stopping My Horse to Listen." Yang Shen, *tr. fr. Chinese* by Jonathan Chaves. CoBLCP

To the Tune "The Fall of a Little Wild Goose." Huang O, *tr. fr. Chinese* by Kenneth Rexroth *and* Ling Chung. AIW; WPOW

To the Tune "The Phoenix Hairpin." T'ang Wan, *tr. fr. Chinese* by Kenneth Rexroth *and* Ling Chung. WPOW

To the Tune "The River Is Red." Ch'iu Chin, *tr.* by Kenneth Rexroth *and* Ling Chung. AiP; BoWoP; PBWP

To the Tune "The Southerner." Yang Shen, *tr. fr. Chinese* by Jonathan Chaves. CoBLCP

To the Tune "T'ien ching sha," *sel.* Autumn Thoughts. Ma Chih-yüan, *tr. fr. Chinese* by Jonathan Chaves. CoBLCP

To the Tune "Yellow Oriole" ("Threads of rain weave lambent light"). Yang Shen, *tr. fr. Chinese* by Jonathan Chaves. CoBLCP

To the Tune "Yellow Oriole" ("Willows weave spring sorrow"). Yang Shen, *tr. fr. Chinese* by Jonathan Chaves. CoBLCP

To the Tune "Yu hu-lu" ("I love the summer moon"). Yang Shen, *tr. fr. Chinese* by Jonathan Chaves. *Fr.* Four Poems from the Sequence "Singing of the Moon," II. CoBLCP

To the Tune "Yu hu-lu" ("I love the winter moon"). Yang Shen, *tr. fr. Chinese* by Jonathan Chaves. *Fr.* Four Poems from the Sequence "Singing of the Moon," IV. CoBLCP

To the Unborn and Waiting Children. Lucille Clifton. InPK

To the United States of America. Robert Bridges. InPK

To the University of Cambridge, in New-England. Phillis Wheatley. AmPP; NAAL-1; TAP

To the Unknown Eros. Coventry Patmore. *Fr.* The Unknown Eros. PoEL-5

To the Unknown Light. Edward Shanks. TrPWD

To the Unknown Warrior. G. K. Chesterton. MMA

To the Veterans of the Abraham Lincoln Brigade. Genevieve Taggard. OFD

To the Virgin. John Lydgate. ACP

To the Virginian Voyage. Michael Drayton. Aip, *abr.*

To the Virgins, to Make Much of Time. Robert Herrick. AWP; BLPA; BoLoP; CaPo; ChTr; ELP; EnLoPo; ErPo; FaBV; FaFP; FPL; GBL; HAP; HeIP; InPK; InPS; JCP; LiTB; NAEL-1; NBLV; NIP; NOBE; NoP; OAEL-1; OBEV; OBS; PoE; PoEL-3; PrIm; QFR; SeCP; SeCV-1; SoSe; TEP; TrGrPo

To the Vision-Seekers: Remember This. Wendy Rose. ER

To the Wagoner's Daughter. Rocco Scotellaro, *tr. fr. Italian* by Lawrence R. Smith. NItP

To the Waitress at the Hickory Pit. Lisa Vice. ER

To the Water Nymphs, Drinking at the Fountain. Robert Herrick. CaPo; NAEL-1

To the Western Wind. Judah Halevi, *tr. fr. Hebrew* by Solomon Solis-Cohen. TrJP

To the Western Wind. Robert Herrick. CaPo; OBEV; SeCV-1

To the Western World. Louis Simpson. CAPP; CoAP; GOA; LiTM; NePoEA-2; NOBA; SM; TAP

To the Wheel of Progress. Mrs. Henry Linden. CBWP-4

To the White Fiends. Claude McKay. BANP; PoBA

To the white-mantled maidens. Korinna, *tr.* by Richmond Lattimore. WPOW

To the wild wild beat of a tom tom tom. Reversion. Barry O. Higgs. PeSA

To the Willow-Tree. Robert Herrick. CaPo; OBEV

To the Wind. Vicente Riva Palacio, *tr. fr. Spanish* by Samuel Beckett. MexPo

"To the winds give our banner!" St. John. Whittier. PAH

To the Woman in Bond Street Station. Edward Weismiller. LiTA; WaP

To the Woman in the Office. "Kim." DT

To the Woodville Depot. David Chapman Berry. MT

To the World. Andrea Zanzotto, *tr. fr. Italian by* Lawrence R. Smith. NItP

To the World; a Farewell for a Gentlewoman, Virtuous and Noble. Ben Jonson. JCP; QFR; SeCP

To the World; the Perfection of Love. William Habington. JCP

To the Yew and Cypress to Grace His Funeral. Robert Herrick. QFR

To the young man I would say. I'm Older than You, Please Listen. Arthur Rex Dugard Fairburn. ATNZ; PeNZ

To the Young Man Jesus. Annie Charlotte Dalton. CaP

To thee, dear Henry Morison. Fynes Moryson. OBTV

To Thee, Eternal Soul, Be Praise. Richard Watson Gilder. AH

To thee, fair freedom! I retire. Written at [*or* in] an Inn at Henley. William Shenstone. AWP; NOBE; OBEV

To thee now, Christes dere derling. A Song to John, Christ's Friend. *Unknown.* MeEL

To Thee, O God. Abiel Holmes. AH

To Thee, O God, the Shepherd Kings. John Gardiner Calkins Brainard. AH

To thee obeyeth all the East as far as Ganges goes. Ovid, *tr. fr. Latin by* Arthur Golding. *Fr.* Metamorphoses, IV. OBVE

To thee, sweet Fop, these lines I send. Bounce to Fop; an Heroick Epistle from a Dog at Twickenham to a Dog at Court. Pope. FM

To Thee the Tuneful Anthem Soars. Mather Byles. AH

To Thee, Then, Let All Beings Bend. Nathaniel Evans. AH

To thee, whose cautious step and specious air. Annabella Plumptre. *Fr.* Ode to Moderation. NOEC

To Their Excellencies the Lords Justices of Ireland, the Humble Petition of Frances Harris, Who Must Starve, and Die a Maid if It Miscarries. Swift. NOEC; Par; PoEL-3

To their long home the greatest princes go. Upon a Funeral. Sir John Beaumont. FaBoRV

To them who crossed the flood. Inscription for Marye's Heights, Fredericksburg. Herman Melville. UnPo

To Theodora. *Unknown.* OxBChV

To these I turn, in these I trust. The Kiss. Siegfried Sassoon. MMA

To these, the gentle South, with kisses smooth and soft. Michael Drayton. *Fr.* Polyolbion, Second Song. OBS

To these whom death again did wed. An Epitaph upon Husband and Wife Who Died and Were Buried Together. Richard Crashaw. EBEV; NOBE; OBEV; OBS; TrGrPo

(Epitaph upon a Young Married Couple Dead and Buried Together, An.) ELP; FaBoEE; SeCePo; SeCP

To Thine Eternal Arms, O God. Thomas Wentworth Higginson. AH

To Thine Own Self Be True. Shakespeare. *See* Hamlet: Polonius' Advice to Laertes.

To think/ I must be alone. Moonshine. Richard Murphy. PoPo

To think of it! He knows me. And Yet. Arthur B. Rhinow. BLRP

To Think of Time. Walt Whitman. BLPL; LiTA

To think that this meaningless thing was ever a rose. Summer Is Ended. Christina Rossetti. NOBVV

To Think That Two and Two Are Four. A. E. Housman. ImOP

To think to know the country and not know. A Hillside Thaw. Robert Frost. CMoP

"To this day no one knows." Mayan Ruins. Ory Bernstein, *tr. fr. Hebrew by* Warren Bargad *and* Stanley F. Chyet. *Fr.* Poems from Mexico. IP

To this day, no one knows who he was or she was. The Dog Poisoner. Keith Wilson. MOWH

To This Hill Again. James Macmillan. PoSH
To this land of Tsukushi. Okura. *Fr. Manyo Shu.* Ma
To this the Panther, with a scornful smile. Dryden. *Fr.* The Hind and the Panther, III. SeCV-2
To this world, farewell. Chikamatsu Monzaemon, *tr. fr. Japanese by* Geoffrey Bownas *and* Anthony Thwaite. *Fr.* The Love Suicides at Sonezaki. PeBJV
   ("Farewell to the world, and to the night farewell.") DL
To Thomas Lord Chancellor. Ben Jonson. OBS
To Thomas Moore. Byron. EnRP
To Thoreau on Rereading Walden. Isabella Gardner. CAPP
To those fair isles where crimson sunsets burn. Toussaint L'Ouverture. Henrietta Cordelia Ray. CBWP-3
To Those Palestinians Martyred in Foreign Lands. Faiz Ahmad Faiz, *tr. fr. Urdu by* Mahmood Jamal. PBMUP
To those who await. Ietaka, *tr. by* Steven D. Carter. WFTW
To those who look to Hanuman. Tulsidas, *tr. by* John Stratton Hawley *and* Mark Juergensmeyer. SSI
To Those Who Sing America. Frank Marshall Davis. FB
To throw away the key and walk away. The Walking Tour. W. H. Auden. *Fr.* Paid on Both Sides. CMoP
   (Chorus: "To throw away the key and walk away.") MoBrPo
To Thy continual Presence, in me wrought. William Ellery Channing. TrPWD
To thy lover. Out of the Italian; a Song. Richard Crashaw. SeCV-1
To Time. "A. W." EIL
To Tirzah. Blake. *Fr.* Songs of Experience. EnRP; NAEL-2; NOBE; OAEL-2
To Tommaso de' Cavalieri. Michelangelo, *tr. fr. Italian by* John Addington Symonds. PeHV
To touch all points in the past. Reflection: After Visiting Old Friends. John Allison. GrPl
To touch the cup with eager lips and taste, not drain it. Living. *Unknown.* BLPA; FaBoBe
To Toussaint L'Ouverture. Wordsworth. EnRP; FaBoPV; InPK; NOBE; OBNC; PoNe; PoRA; PPP; TrGrPo
To trap them is almost impossible. Neutrinos. Georgette Perry. BWV
To travel like a bird, lightly to view. Cecil Day Lewis. *Fr.* O Dreams, O Destinations. GTBS-P
To treat the thing directly, Ezra Pound. A High-toned Old Fascist Gentleman. William Zaranka. BXAP
To tremble, when I touch her hands. Divine Awe. George Edward Woodberry. *Fr.* Wild Eden, XVI. AA
To true roses uplifted on the bilious tide of evening. To Redouté. John Ashbery. PoA
To Trust. Antonia Pozzi, *tr. fr. Italian by* Lynne Lawner. PBWP
To Truth. *Unknown, tr. fr. Greek by* J. Rendel Harris. *Fr.* Solomon, XXXVIII. WGRP
To Turn Back. John Haines. BoNaP
To Turn from Love. Sarah Webster Fabio. BlSi
To turn my volume o'er nor find. How to Read Me. Walter Savage Landor. NOBVV
To Two Bereaved. Thomas Ashe. NOBVV
To Tzu-an. Yü Hsüan-chi, *tr. by* Geoffrey Waters. BoWoP
To understand everything. Painted Words. Paul Eluard, *tr. by* Michael Benedikt. POS
To Urania. Joseph Brodsky. BAP
To Urania. Benjamin Colman. SCAP
To Usward. Gwendolyn B. Bennett. BlSi
To Vanity. Darwin T. Turner. PoNe
To Varus. Catullus, *tr. fr. Latin by* Walter Savage Landor. AWP
To Vera Thompson. John Haines. LCAP
To Verse Let Kings Give Place. Ovid, *tr. fr. Latin by* Christopher Marlowe. *Fr.* Elegies, XV. ChTr
To Vietnam. Charlie Cobb. PoBA
To Vineyarders in cold Korea. Pinkletinks. Grace Elisabeth Allen. GoYe
To Violet [with Prewar Poems]. Basil Bunting. FaBoMo; PoA
To Violets. Robert Herrick. CaPo; JCP; OBEV; OBS; SeCP; TrGrPo
To Virgil [or Vergil]. Tennyson. AWP; ChTr; GTBS-P; NoP; OAEL-2; PoEL-5
To Virgins. Robert Herrick. CaPo
To Virgins, to Make Much of Time. Robert Herrick. *See* Gather ye rose-buds while ye may.
To Vittoria Colonna. Buonarroti Michelangelo, *tr. fr. Italian by* Longfellow. AWP; PFI
To Vulcan. Robert Herrick. CaPo
To Vyazemsky. Pushkin, *tr. fr. Russian by* Alan Myers. AAA
To W. B. Yeats Who Says That His Castle of Ballylee Is His Monument. Oliver St. John Gogarty. AnIL
To W. C. W. M. D. Alfred Kreymborg. PoA

To W. J. M. "G. G." PeHV
To W. L. G. on Reading His "Chosen Queen." Charlotte Forten. BlSi
To W. P, *sel.* George Santayana.
   "With you a part of me hath passed away." TrGrPo
To W. R. W. E. Henley. *See* Madam Life's a Piece in Bloom.
"To wade the sea mist, then to wade the sea." Stone Horse Shoals. Malcolm Cowley. NYBP
To wake up with a back sore from the hard mattress. James Keir Baxter. *Fr.* Autumn Testament, 7. ATNZ
To Waken a Small Person. Donald Justice. NYBP
To Waken an Old Lady. William Carlos Williams. HAP; InPK; NoP; QFR; WeW
To Walk Abroad. Thomas Traherne. ELP
   (Walking.) EBEV; SD; TrGrPo
To walk in the Sun. The Curfew Breakers. Samuel Chimsoro. WMBCH
To Walk in Warm Rain. David McCord. RHPC
To Walk on Hills. Robert Graves. SD
To Walt Whitman. Tom MacInnes. CaP
To warm life passing singing with the grace. Ants. Ramón López Velarde, *tr. by* Samuel Beckett. MexPo
To watch the tipsy cripples on the beach. After Tennyson. Edward Lear. FaBoNo
To wear the arctic fox. The Arctic Ox. Marianne Moore. NYBP
To weary hearts, to mourning homes. The Angel of Patience. Whittier. WGRP
To Wed or Not to Wed. Una Marson. PVCV
To wed, or not to wed? That is the question. *Unknown.* BXAP
To western woods and lonely plains. On the Emigration to America [and Peopling the Western Country]. Philip Freneau. NAAL-1; PAH; TAP
To wet your eye withouten tear. Sir Thomas Wyatt. SiPS
To W.H. Auden at 63. Michael Jackson. UAS
To what intent or purpose was Man made. As Concerning Man. Alexander Radcliffe. OBSV
To what new fates, my country, far. Unmanifest Destiny. Richard Hovey. AA; WGRP
To what purpose, April, do you return again? Spring. Edna St. Vincent Millay. BoWoP; MoAB; MoAmPo; NoP
To what shall I compare this world? Manzei. *Fr. Manyo Shu.* FCEI
To What Strangers, What Welcome, *sel.* J. V. Cunningham. Miramar Beach. PoA
To what unfriendly lands. Mirza Mohammad Rafi Sauda, *tr. by* Ahmed Ali. GoT
To Which I Never Wanted. Charles Bernstein. IAT
To Whistler, American. Ezra Pound. AiP; NAAL-2; PoA
To White South Africa. Cosmo Pieterse. WMBCH
To Whittier. Josephine D. Henderson Heard. CBWP-4
To Whom Else? Robert Graves. FaBoMo
To whom I owe the leaping delight. A Dedication to My Wife. T. S. Eliot. BoLoP; FF
To Whom It May Concern. J. V. Cunningham. FYAP
To Whom It May Concern. Adrian Mitchell. OBWP
To whom now, Pyrrha, art thou kind? Horace. *See* Odes: I, 5. "What slender youth bedewed with liquid odours" ("Quis multa gracilis").
To whom our Saviour calmly thus reply'd. True and False Glory ("To whom our Saviour calmly thus reply'd"). Milton. *Fr.* Paradise Regained, *bk.* III, *ll.* 43–107. LiTB; OBS
To whom shall I this dancing poem send. Dedications [of Orchestra], I: To His Very Friend, Master Richard Martin. Sir John Davies. SiPS
To Whom Shall the World Henceforth Belong? John Oxenham. WBLP
To whom should I speak today? A Dispute over Suicide. *Unknown, tr. by* T. Eric Peet. TTY
To Whom This May concern. Leo Vroman, *tr. fr. Dutch by the author and* Peter Nijmeijer. DuIn
To whom thus also th' angel last replied. Milton. *Fr.* Paradise Lost, *bk.* XII, *ll.* 574–649. FiP
To whom thus Michael. Justly thou abhorr'st. Milton. *Fr.* Paradise Lost, *bk.* XII, *ll.* 79–104. FaBoPV
To whom thus Michael. Those whom last thou saw'st. Milton. *Fr.* Paradise Lost, *bk.* XI, *ll.* 782–835. FaBoPV
To William Camden. Ben Jonson. AWP; JCP; NAEL-1; OBS; SeCV-1
To William Carlos Williams. Galway Kinnell. NePoAm; NOAM; SM
To William Earle of Pembroke. Ben Jonson. SeCP
To William Hayley. Blake. FaBoCo
   (T. H.) FF
   (To Hayley.) FaBoEE; TrGrPo
To William Hayley, Esq.: In Reply to His Solicitation to Write with Him in a Literary Work. William Cowper. Son
To William Lloyd Garrison. Whittier. PAH

To William Roe. Ben Jonson. OAEL-1; OBS; SeCV-1
To William Shelley. Shelley. ChER
To William Simpson, Ochiltree. Burns. OxBS
To William (Whom We Have Missed). P. G. Wodehouse. NOBL
To William Wilberforce, Esq. William Cowper. Son
To William Wordsworth. Samuel Taylor Coleridge. EnRP; NAEL-2; OAEL-2
To William Wordsworth from Virginia. Julia Randall. NMM; WPE
To win the love of women one should first discover. Kenneth Koch. Fr. The Art of Love. NNaP
To Winter. Blake. WiR
To wish/ for the moon. You Can't Go to the Moon There's No Trains. Joy Howard. DT
To wish, and want, and not obtain. Sir Thomas Wyatt. SiPS
To wish to climb a ladder to the loft. James Keir Baxter. Fr. Autumn Testament, 12. PeNZ
To Women. Richard Hugo. NIP
To Women, as Far as I'm Concerned. D. H. Lawrence. InPS; OxBSP; WeW
To Women, to Hide Their Teeth, if They Be Rotten or Rusty. Robert Herrick. FaBoUs
To Wordsworth. John Clare. OAEL-2; Son
To Wordsworth. Hartley Coleridge. Son
To Wordsworth. Walter Savage Landor. OAEL-2
To Wordsworth. Shelley. EnRP; FiP; NoP; Son
To work. To my own office, my own job. Louis MacNeice. Fr. Autumn Sequel, IV. FaBCIP
To write down a word late at night. Late at Night. Rudolf Bayer, tr. by Beth Bjorklund. CoAuP
To Wystan Auden. Geoffrey Grigson. NAs
To Xanadu, Which Is Beth Shaul. Arye Sivan, tr. fr. Hebrew by Anthony Rudolf and Natan Zach. VWA
To yon fause stream that, by the sea. The Mermaid. Unknown. CH
To You. Frank Horne. Fr. Letters [or Notes] Found near a Suicide. BPo
To You, sels. Huda Na mani, tr. fr. Arabic by Lena Jayyusi. MAP
"Blind man asked me, A." Fr. III.
"Why do the sun rays laugh across the swamp?" Fr. I.
"You sever a hand." Fr. II.
To you, brave warrior, starting for the Land of Kara. Tajihi Takanushi. Fr. Manyo Shu. Ma
To You Building the New House. Nelly Sachs, tr. fr. German by Keith Bosley. VWA
To you, morning and evening. Prayers to Liberty. Anwar Shaul, tr. by Yoffee Berkovitz. VWA
To you, my lordis, that standis by. So Young Ane King. Sir David Lindsay. SeCePo
To you, my purse [or purs], and to non [or no or noon] other wight. The Complaint [or Compleint or Compleinte] of Chaucer to His Empty Purse. Chaucer. NAEL-1
(Complaint of Chaucer to His Purse, The.) OAEL-1
(Complaint to His Purse.) NoP
(Compleinte of Chauser to His Empty Purs, The Chaucer's Complaint to His Empty Purse.) TrGrPo, 2 vers.
(Song to His Purse for the King, A.) MeEL
To you, then, tenants of life's middle state. William Cowper. Fr. Tirocinium; or, A Review of Schools. OBSV
To you this little village is dear as the moon. Dear as the Moon. Gond Oral Tradition, tr. by V. Elwin and S. Hivale. WTO
To you, troop so fleet. Hymn to the Winds. Joachim Du Bellay, tr. by Andrew Lang. AWP
To you, vague aspirations; enthusiasms. Alma Perdida. Valery Larbaud, tr. by Ron Padgett and Bill Zavatsky. RHTwFP
To You Who Wait. John Pudney. WaP
To you whose groves protect the feathered choirs. The Goldfinches. Richard Jago. PBBP
To you, whose temperate pulses flow. On the Fly-Leaf of Manon Lescaut. Walter Learned. AA
To Your Question. Duane Niatum. CDW
To Youth. Josephine D. Henderson Heard. CBWP-4
To Youth. Walter Savage Landor. EnRP
To youths, who hurry thus away. On a Painted Woman. Shelley. FaBoCo; NBLV
To Yung-erh. Li Tung-yang, tr. fr. Chinese by Jonathan Chaves. CoBLCP
To Yvor Winters, 1955. Thom Gunn. GTBS-P
To zig-zag with the ant. Summer Afternoon. Raymond Souster. BoNaP
To Zion. Judah Halevi, tr. fr. Hebrew by Maurice Samuel. AWP
Toad, A. Elizabeth Akers Allen. OBCA

Toad, The. Elizabeth Jane Coatsworth. RAR
Toad, The. Robert S. Oliver. RHPC
Toad and the Rabbit, The. John Martin. RAR
Toad beneath the harrow knows, The. Pagett, M. P. Kipling. BrPo
Toad-Eater, The. Burns. TW
Toad Song. D. Brennan. NPo
Toad that lived on Albury Heath, A. A Roundabout Turn. Robert E. Charles. MoShBr
Toad the power mower caught, A. The Death of a Toad. Richard Wilbur. CMoP; LiTM; MoP; NAAL-2; NoAM; NoP; PoA
Toad the Tailor. N. E. Hussey. BoTP
Toads. Philip Larkin. CMoP; NePoEA; NoAM; NOBL; OxBTC; PoE; SoSe
Toads Revisited. Philip Larkin. CMoP; NOBL; SaC
Toadstool Wood, The. James Reeves. DuDa; TSS; WSC
Toadstools. Elizabeth Fleming. BoTP
Toast. Olivia FitzRoy. CN
Toast. Frank Horne. BANP; PoNe
Toast for the Original Survivors. Kathryn Rantala. BWV
Toast to Our Native Land, A. Robert Bridges. OPP; PAH
Toast to the Flag, A. John Jay Daly. OPP; PoLF
Toast to the Traveler, A. Sun Kuang-hsien, tr. fr. Chinese by Lois Fusek. ATF
Toast to the Traveler, A. Wei Chuang, tr. fr. Chinese by Lois Fusek. ATF
Toaster, The. William Jay Smith. GrPl; RAR; RHPC
Toaster Time. Eve Merriam. RAR
Toasting the Moon at Ten-Thousand-Year Bridge. Chiang Shih-ch'üan, tr. fr. Chinese by Coy Harmon. WFTU
Tobacco. Philip Freneau. TAP
Tobacco fields lie fallow the migrant pickers, The. Adrienne Rich. Fr. Contradictions: Tracking Poems, 20. ER
Tobacco Hole. Medbh McGuckian. FaBCIP
Tobacco is a filthy weed. Unknown. FaBoEE
Tobacco Plant. Ivor Gurney. OBTV
Tobacco ("Tobacco is a dirty weed"). Graham Lee Hemminger. FPL; PoLF
(This Smoking World.) NBLV
Tobias and the Angel. John Gray. NOBVV
Tobias, journeying to Ecbatane. Tobias and the Angel. John Gray. NOBVV
Tobit, sel. Bible, Apocrypha, tr. fr. Greek by D. C. Simpson.
Blessed Is God. Fr. XIII. TrJP
Toccata of Galuppi's, A. Robert Browning. EBVV; GTBS-P; HAP; LiTB; Mes; NAEL-2; NOBE; NOBVV; NoP; OAEL-2; TEP
Today. Thomas Carlyle. PWR
Today. Langston Hughes. GLP; VGW
Today. Jung Han-mo, tr. fr. Korean by Koh Chang-soo. ACKP
Today. Angela Morgan. BLPA
Today. Frank O'Hara. TTTS
Today. György Somlyó, tr. fr. Hungarian by Jascha Kessler. FOC
Today. Jones Very. TAP
Today. Margaret Abigail Walker. FB
Today/ the clocks strike. Lever de Rideau. Mary Ursula Bethell. ATNZ
Today,/ there came a breeze thin as the needle of a syringe. J. Kitchener Davies, tr. fr. Welsh by Joseph P. Clancy. Fr. The Sound of the Wind That Is Blowing. OBWVE
Today/ the west/ burns down. The Coup-clock Clicks. Brian Meeks. PBCV
Today:/ Hark! Heaven sings! On Christmas Day to My Heart. Clement Paman. OBS
Today/ I lost my temper. For Witches. Susan Sutheim. NMM
Today/ August 6, the sun. We Must Shed our Illusions. Jukka Vieno, tr. by Aili Jarvenpa. SOP
Today, a candle in a glass. Poem for My Grandfather. A. C. Jacobs. VWA
Today a silver coffin guards St. Agnes'. Catacombs. István Vas, tr. by Jascha Kessler. VWA
Today above the gull's call. Louise Glück. AnAn
Today again/ I'll go to the hill. Saigyo, tr. fr. Japanese by Burton Watson. Fr. Sixty-four Tanka. FCEI
Today again, quietly and leisurely I make my ablutions. Lady Izumi, tr. fr. Japanese by Hiroaki Sato. Fr. Fifty-one Tanka. FCEI
Today, Again, the Jagged Black Line. Susan L. Dunn. TSM
Today as I hang out the wash I see them again, a code. The Geese. Jorie Graham. HCAP
Today as the news from Selma and Saigon. Monet's "Waterlilies." Robert Hayden. CAPP
Today at dawn. For the Record. Mihály Ladányi, tr. by Edwin Morgan. MHuP

Today at the Farmer's Market. Ithaca. Katharyn Machan Aal. ER
Today at the Gateway. Butter. Tom Schmidt. NeAC
Today, because I am not dead. Vincent O'Sullivan. ATNZ
Today beneath Benignant Skies. Denis Wortman. AH
Today between skirmishes. For Alan Blanchard. John Oliver Simon. NeAC
Today Black Hair. Rosalía de Castro, tr. fr. Spanish by Kate Flores. DMH
Today Blackness. For Muh' Dear. Carolyn M. Rodgers. CNA
Today, Day of the Dead, procession of shadows. Pentachromatic. Julia de Burgos, tr. by Julio Marzán. InW
Today, dear heart, but just today. Her Answer. John Bennett. AA; BLPA
Today ees com' from Eetaly. Boy from Rome, Da. Thomas Augustin Daly. FaPON
Today for the first time. A New Dress. Rachel Korn, tr. by Ruth Whitman. VWA
Today has it all, sunshine. Gwyn Williams. Fr. Aspects of Now. OBWVE
Today, having turned 83. To the Reader. Mark Jarman. NAmP
Today I am a farmer in the fields. Wang Chiu-ssu, tr. fr. Chinese by Jonathan Chaves. Fr. The Robber of Kuan-shan. CoBLCP
Today I Am Envying the Glorious Mexicans. Michael C. Blumenthal. MAYP
Today I am like a. Judah Leib Teller, tr. by Benjamin and Barbara Harshav. AYP
Today I Am Modest as a Beast. Esther Raab, tr. fr. Hebrew by Bernhard Frank. MHeP
Today/ I am 24. January 3, 1970. Mae Jackson. PoBA
Today I am walking alone in a bare place. Late November in a Field. James Wright. CAPP; NAAL-2; NNaP
Today I cleared out the kitchen with Dougie so Hedley could sand the kitchen floor. A Day in the Life. Stef Pixner. BrRo
Today I found myself in the failing light looking in. Sundial. Jorie Graham. NAmP
Today I get this letter from you and the sun. Tom Clark. Fr. You, III. EAS
Today I have grown taller from walking with the trees. Good Company. Karle Wilson Baker. FaPON; WGRP
Today I Have Touched the Earth. William Jay Smith. WaP
Today I put on. Saint Patrick's Breastplate. Unknown. NOIV
Today, I responded in my way. Mourning a Lost Poem. Ed Coletti. SoTCo
Today I saw a picture of the cancer cells. The Cancer Cells. Richard Eberhart. HAP; LiTM
Today I saw a place no one has seen. Iron Heaven. Betti Alver, tr. by Willis Barnstone and Felix Oinas. BoWoP
Today I saw a thing of arresting poignant beauty. Snow in October. Alice Dunbar Moore Nelson. BlSi; CDC
Today I saw a woman plowing a furrow. Sister. Gabriela Mistral, tr. by Langston Hughes. BoWoP; OV
Today I saw a woman wrapped in rags. At the Slackening of the Tide. James Wright. MOS; UnPo; VGW
Today I saw the arrogant truth. A Red Beard. A. Leyeles, tr. by Benjamin and Barbara Harshav. AYP
Today I think. Digging. Edward Thomas. BrPo; MoAB; MoBrPo; OxBTC
Today I think of a boy in the Transvaal. Remembering Snow. Ralph Nixon Currey. PeSA
Today I thought I'd call home. Cuento. Carlos Cumpian. FIA
Today I was awakened by the moon. Remembering Lutsky. Rayzel Zychlinska, tr. by Marc Kaminsky. VWA
Today I wear my boots. Woman '77. Vivienne Joseph. ATNZ
Today, I will see some empty spaces. Today: The Idea Market. Michael Nicholas. NBP
Today I wrote the ending of all poems. Discreet. Maria Flook. EOEF
Today I'll draw/ A line in the dust. Adam's Death. Gabriel Levin. VWA
Today in Peru, this first day of summer. Lawrence Raab. AmPA
Today in the field I saw. Sacred Objects. Louise Glück. Fr. Dedication to Hunger, V. AnAn; GeTw
Today in the middle of Missouri. The Porpoise. Greg Pape. MAYP
Today Is a Day of Great Joy. Victor Hernandez Cruz. TTY
Today is a holiday in the Western heart. Today Is Armistice, a Holiday. Delmore Schwartz. TrJP
Today is a thought, a fear is tomorrow. Dirge Written for a Drama. Thomas Lovell Beddoes. EnRP
Today Is Armistice, a Holiday. Delmore Schwartz. TrJP
Today is execution day for the pacifists. Ascension. Kaneko Mitsuharu, tr. by Geoffrey Bownas and Anthony Thwaite. PeBJV
Today Is Friday. Ramon Guthrie. PoE

Today Is Ours. Abraham Cowley. See Fill the bowl with rosie wine.
Today Is Saturday. Zilpha Keatley Snyder. ILY
Today it rained vengefully and hard. Barquisimeto, Venezuela, October 27, 1561. Ai. Fr. The Gilded Man, II. AnAn
Today it's going to cost us twenty dollars. How Things Work. Gary Soto. NoAM
Today, lonely for my father, I saw. My Father's Wedding. Robert Bly. CAPP; DiL; InPS; NoAM
Today, my friends seemed. Ishikawa Takuboku, tr. by Geoffrey Bownas and Anthony Thwaite. PeBJV
Today my heart is paying for past joy. Elegy on the Death of His Mistress Hoor Tal'at. Momin Khan Momin, tr. by Ahmed Ali. GoT
Today my mother and sisters. They've Come. Alfonsina Storni. BoWoP, tr. by Aliki and Willis Barnstone; WPOW, tr. by Marti Moody
Today now at this moment the world flies against me. Rossana Ombres, tr. by Muriel Kittel. DMI
Today on the lip of a bowl in the backyard. The Caterpillar. Miller Williams. MT
Today she parades her shape like swellings of song. Portrait of a Pregnant Woman. Bobi Jones, tr. by Joseph P. Clancy. OBWVE
Today, should you let fall a glass it would. Tramontana at Lerici. Charles Tomlinson. GTBS-P
Today six slender fruit trees stand. Planting Trees. Violet Helen Friedlaender. BoNaP
Today, ten thousand people will die. Choosing to Think of It. Stephen Dunn. AnAn
Today, the first dead leaf in the hall. A Dead Leaf. Howard Moss. NYBP
Today: The Idea Market. Michael Nicholas. NBP
Today the jailbird maple in the yard. For My Son on the Highways of His Mind. Maxine W. Kumin. MAT
Today the journey is ended. A Soul's Soliloquy. Wenonah Stevens Abbott. BLPA
Today the leaves cry, hanging on branches swept by wind. The Course of a Particular. Wallace Stevens. HCAP; QFR
Today the peace of autumn pervades the world. Autumn. Rabindranath Tagore. WGRP
Today the self-destroying anger. Bruce Beaver. Fr. Letters to Live Poets, XXX. CBAP
Today the skies are clear and blue. Now. Sarah Knowles. PWR
Today the sky hangs just above my brows. Reflections. Barbara Burford. DT
Today the trees are only blazed with paint. The Wilderness. Maura Stanton. MAYP
Today, the Twenty-sixth of February. George Barker. Fr. The True Confession of George Barker. NAs
Today, the world unwrapped itself [or was unfurled] again [or once more]. Summer. Moishe Kulbak. PeBMYV, tr. by Leonard Wolf; VWA, tr. by Ruth Whitman
Today, today,/ I wait for him. Yosami. Fr. Manyo Shu. PeBJV
Today Was Not. Michael Rosen. PYC
Today we have naming of parts. Naming of Parts. Henry Reed. Fr. Lessons of the War, I. FF; GoJo; HoPM; InPS; MoAB; MoBrPo; NOBE; NoP; OxBTC; PoRA; PrIm; SeCePo; SoSe; TrGrPo; UnPo; WaP
Today we went to see the summer rentals. The Summer Rentals. Daniel Halpern. DiL; MAYP; NAmP
Today we will speak in megatons. How Do You Spell "Missile"?: Preliminary Instructions in the Nuclear Age. George Uba. BrSi
Today you rain on me from every corner of the sky. Sure. Naomi Shihab Nye. MT
Today you were supposed to come. I Waited for Chuang Hsüan-yüan. Mo Shih-lung, tr. by Jonathan Chaves. CoBLCP
Today your Hari is coming. Mirabai, tr. by John Stratton Hawley and Mark Juergensmeyer. SSI
Today your oid golf clubs arrived. Last Game. Cary Waterman. TSL
Today's American car. Emergency Poem 1973. Cyn Zarco. UL
Today's Ferns. Ono Tozaburo, tr. fr. Japanese by Hiroaki Sato. FCEI
Today's landowner planted stacks of paddies. Unknown, tr. by Hiroaki Sato. FCEI
Today's modern runway is straight as an arrow. Uneasy Riders. Robert N. Feinstein. SoTCo
Today's moon—if there were another. Kaai Chigetsu, tr. fr. Japanese by Hiroaki Sato. Fr. Thirteen Hokku. FCEI
Today's my birthday. Poem (3.11.66). Amiq Hanafi, tr. by Mahmood Jamal. PBMUP
Today's News. Ted Berrigan. UL
Todlen Butt, and Todlen Ben. Unknown. OBS
Tod's Hole, The. Unknown. GBP

Toe after toe, a snowing flesh. *See* Toe upon toe, a snowing flesh.
Toe sticking out from under the hem, The. On a Fifteenth-Century
 Flemish Angel. David Ray. CRP; NePoEA-2
Toe tipe. *Unknown.* OxNR
Toe, trip and go. *Unknown.* OxNR
Toe upon [*or* after] toe, a snowing flesh. Nude Descending a Staircase.
 X. J. Kennedy. CoAP; HoPM; NePoEA; NePoEA-2; NIP; OxBSP;
 PoA; SM
Toe'osh; a Laguna Coyote Story. Leslie Marmon Silko. CDW; NoAM;
 STE; VoR
Together. Paul Engle. RHPC
Together. Maxine W. Kumin. BoWoP; NMM
Together. Ludwig Lewisohn. TrJP
Together. Siegfried Sassoon. BrPo
Together Again. William Stafford. LCAP
Together, fourteen years older. In the Cathedral. Patricia Beer.
 OxBC
Together how many hours. Tant' Amare. *Unknown, tr. by* Paul
 Blackburn. ErPo
Together in infinite shade. Too Much Coffee. E. A. Robinson.
 MoAmPo
Together with my wife I passed. Tabito. *Fr.* Manyo Shu. Ma
Tohub. Jakov van Hoddis, *tr. by* Charles Guenther. VWA
Toil, brothers, toil; sing and toil. Labour Song. James Syme.
 PF
Toil on, poor muser, to attain that goal. The Ideal. Francis Saltus
 Saltus. AA
"Toil! toil! toil!" The Wandering Jew. Eloise Bibb. CBWP-4
Toiler's Wife, The. George Hull. PF
Toilet, The. Pope. *Fr.* The Rape of the Lock, I. NOBE
Toiling fisher here is tewing of his net, The. The Fen-Men of
 Lincolnshire's Holland. Michael Drayton. *Fr.* Polyolbion, Five and
 Twentieth Song. FaBoPP
Toiling of Felix, The, *sels.* Henry Van Dyke.
 Angler's Reveille, The. GN
 "Legend of Felix is ended, the toiling of Felix is done, The." BLPA
Toils Are Pitched, The. Sir Walter Scott. *Fr.* The Lady of the Lake, IV.
 EnRP
Token, A. Robert Creeley. VGW
Token, The. F. T. Prince. FaBoTw; OxBTC
Tokens. William Barnes. PoEL-4
Tokens of Love, The. *Unknown.* GBP
Tokyo Imperial University Students. Nakano Shigeharu, *tr. fr. Japanese*
 by Geoffrey Bownas *and* Anthony Thwaite. PeBJV
Told from age to age. Yakamochi. *Fr.* Manyo Shu. Ma
Toledo. Roy Campbell. MoBrPo
Toledo Room, The, *sel.* Alistair Paterson.
 "They do it with knives." *Fr.* I, ix. PeNZ
Tolerance of Crows, The. Charles Donnelly. CIP
Toleration. John Barford. PeHV
Toll for the brave! On the Loss of the *Royal George.* William Cowper.
 EBEV; FiP; GN; NOBE; TrGrPo
 (Loss of the *Royal George.*) GTBS; GTBS-P
 (*Royal George*, The.) FaPoR
Toll-Gate Man, The. Wilson Pugsley MacDonald. CaP
Toll no bell for me, dear Father, dear Mother. The Changeling.
 Charlotte Mew. CH
Toll! Roland, toll! The Great Bell Roland. Theodore Tilton.
 PAH
Toll the bell, fellow. The Red Cow Is Dead. E. B. White. NBLV;
 NYBP
"Tollable Well!" Frank Lebby Stanton. FaFP
Tolling. Lucy Larcom. OHIP
Tolling from St. Patrick's, The. Burial of an Irish President. Austin
 Clarke. BIrV; IPY
Tollund Man, The. Hugo Claus, *tr. fr. Dutch by* Theo Hermans. DuIn
Tollund Man, The. Seamus Heaney. BIrV; CIP; EBEV; FaBCIP;
 FaBoMo; IPY; NoP; TEP
Tom. Victor Questel. PBCV
Tom. James Schuyler. GLP
Tom Agnew, Bill Agnew. Dante Gabriel Rossetti. ChTr; FaBoEE
Tom Brainless as Student and Preacher at College. John Trumbull. *Fr.*
 The Progress of Dulness. AmPP
Tom Brainless, at the close of last year. An Amorous Temper. John
 Trumbull. *Fr.* The Progress of Dulness. AmPP
Tom Brown's two little Indian boys. *Unknown.* OxNR
Tom-Cat, The. Don Marquis. PoRA
Tom Child had often painted Death. This Morning Tom Child, the
 Painter, Died. Samuel Sewall. SCAP
Tom Dooley. *Unknown.* AmFP
Tom Farley. Colin Thiele. PoAu-2

Tom Fool at Jamaica. Marianne Moore. NYBP
Tom Gage's Proclamation. *Unknown.* PAH
Tom—garlanded with squat and surely steel. Tom's Garland: Upon the
 Unemployed. Gerard Manley Hopkins. BrPo; FaBoPV; Son
Tom, He Was a Piper's Son. *Unknown.* GBP; OxNR
Tom Joanides. Lloyd Schwartz. EOEF
Tom Jones's Plum Tree. *Unknown.* AmFP
Tom o' Bedlam's Song. *Unknown.* ChTr; InvP; LiTB; Mes; PoEL-2;
 TrGrPo
Tom O'Roughley. W. B. Yeats. CMoP
"Tom Pearse, Tom Pearse, lend me your gray mare." Widdecombe [*or*
 Widdicombe] Fair. *Unknown.* CH; MoShBr
Tom Potts. *Unknown.* ESPB
Tom Southerne's Birth-Day Dinner at LD. Orrery's. Pope. NAs
Tom Starr. Robert J. Conley. STE
Tom Sucklebat, in dressing-gown, without his teeth. An Administrator.
 Geoffrey Grigson. FaBoEE
Tom the Porter. John Byrom. NOEC
Tom Thomson. Arthur Stanley Bourinot. CaP
Tom Thumbkin. *Unknown.* OxNR
Tom Tigercat is noted. Feline Fine. J. Patrick Lewis. TDD
Tom Tiler; or, The Nurse. *Unknown.* APAS
Tom-tom, c'est moi. The blue guitar. Wallace Stevens. *Fr.* The Man
 with the Blue Guitar, XII. CMoP
Tom, Tom, the piper's son. Mother Goose. OxNR
Tom Tyler and His Wife, *sel. Unknown.*
 "Proverb reporteth, no man can deny, The." EIL
Tom Wedgwood Tells. Brian W. Aldiss. NOBL
Tom, working thirty storeys up. The Fall. Leonard Nathan. BLA
Tomarata. Kendrick Smithyman. PeNZ
Tomb. David Semah, *tr. fr. Arabic by* Yoffee Berkovitz. VWA
Tomb/ A hollow hateful word. Agamemnon's Tomb. Sacheverell
 Sitwell. LiTB; OBMV
Tomb of an Ancestor. Allen Curnow. ATNZ
 "Oldest of us burst into tears and cried, The," *sel. Fr.* I.
 PeNZ
Tomb of Crethon, The. Leonidas of Tarentum, *tr. fr. Greek by* John
 Hermann Merivale. AWP
Tomb of Diogenes, The. *Unknown, tr. fr. Greek by* John Addington
 Symonds. AWP
Tomb of Lt. John Learmonth, A.I.F., The. John Manifold. CBAP;
 PoAu-2
Tomb of the Brave, The. Joseph Hutton. PAH
Tomb of the Kings, The. Anne Hébert. BoWoP, *tr. by* Aliki *and* Willis
 Barnstone, PBWP, *tr. by* Kathleen Weaver.
Tomb of the Singing Girl Ch'iung-i, The. Hsü Pen, *tr. fr. Chinese by*
 Jonathan Chaves. CoBLCP
Tombe, The. Thomas Stanley. OBS
Tombstone. Lucia M. *and* James L. Hymes, Jr.. RHPC
Tombstone told when she died, The. Dylan Thomas. OxBTC
Tombstones in the Starlight: The Fisherwoman. Dorothy Parker. NIP
Tomlinson. Kipling. BeLS
Tommie Makes My Tail Toddle. Burns. ErPo
Tommies in the Train. D. H. Lawrence. MMA
Tommorow. Amal Dunqul, *tr. fr. Arabic by* Sharif Elmusa *and* Thomas
 G. Ezzy. MAP
Tommy. Kipling. BrPo; EBEV; FaBV; FaPoR; MoBrPo; NoP; OBWP;
 OxBTC
Tommy kept a chandler's shop. *Unknown.* OxNR
Tommy O'Linn was a Scotsman born. *Unknown.* OxNR
Tommy Tibule. *Unknown.* OxNR
Tommy Trot, a man of law. *Unknown.* OxNR
Tommy Tucker. Mother Goose. OxNR
"Tommy" you was when it began. The Service Man. Kipling. Par
Tomorrow. John Collins. GTBS; GTBS-P
Tomorrow. Kenneth Fearing. CMoP
Tomorrow. John Masefield. MoBrPo; TrGrPo
Tomorrow. Henri Michaux, *tr. fr. French by* Armand Schwerner.
 RHTwFP
Tomorrow. Mark Strand. GOYP
Tomorrow/ will be/ different. Resolution. Audrey Longbottom.
 UAS
"Tomorrow, a body of youth." Tulsidas, *tr. by* John Stratton Hawley *and*
 Mark Juergensmeyer. SSI
Tomorrow, and Tomorrow, and Tomorrow. Shakespeare. *See* Macbeth:
 She should have died hereafter.
Tomorrow I Will Heat the Sauna. Eeva Kilpi, *tr. fr. Finnish by* Aili
 Jarvenpa. SOP
Tomorrow I'll come again to this wild path. Teika, *tr. fr. Japanese by*
 Hiroaki Sato. *Fr.* A Compendium of Good Tanka. FCEI

Tomorrow Is a Birthday. Gwendolen Haste. GoYe

Tomorrow Is March Already. Paolo Volponi, *tr. fr. Italian by* Lawrence R. Smith. NItP

Tomorrow Is My Birthday, *sel.* Edgar Lee Masters. Thing Is Sex, Ben, The. NAs

Tomorrow Is Saint Valentine's Day. Shakespeare. *Fr.* Hamlet. EnLoPo; OFD

(Saint Valentine's Day.) CH; LiTB

(Song: "Tomorrow is Saint Valentine's Day.") FaPON; NTCP

Tomorrow, Julia, I betimes must rise. The Perfume. Robert Herrick. CaPo

Tomorrow let loveless, let lover tomorrow make love. The Vigil of Venus. *Unknown, tr. by* Allen Tate. GBL

"Tomorrow morn I'll be sixteen, and Billy Grimes the rover." Billy Grimes. *Unknown.* AmFP

Tomorrow morning, some poet will wake up. Modern Poetry. Anita Skeen. IHMS

Tomorrow shall be my dancing day. *Unknown.* OxBOLi; PoEL-1

Tomorrow the Heroes. Alfred B. Spellman. CNA; PoBA

Tomorrow we'll meet again. Over and Over Again. Norman MacCaig. NPo

Tomorrow when the farm boys find this. The Two-headed Calf. Laura Gilpin. FYAP

Tomorrow you will live, you always cry. Procrastination. Martial, *tr. by* Abraham Cowley. AWP; FaBoEE; OBVE

Tomorrows. James Merrill. OBAL

Tomorrow's Ideas. Sybren Polet, *tr. fr. Dutch by* James S. Holmes. DuIn

Tomorrow's the Fair. *Unknown.* GBP; RHPC

Tom's Angel. Walter de la Mare. Mes

Tom's Garland: Upon the Unemployed. Gerard Manley Hopkins. BrPo; FaBoPV; Son

Tom's sickness did his morals mend. Matthew Prior. FaBoEE

Tomtit, The. Walter de la Mare. FM

Tone. Rae Armantrout. IAT

Tongue, The. Zbigniew Herbert, *tr. fr. Polish by* Czeslaw Milosz. PwPP

Tongue. Morton Marcus. NAmP

Tongue, The. Phillips Burrows Strong. WBLP

Tongue,/ wild meat rose. Tongue. Morton Marcus. NAmP

Tongue-Doughty Pedant. Thomas Edwards. Son

Tongue of the waves roll in the earth's bell, The. The Want Bone. Robert Pinsky. BLA; EOEF

Tongue that mothered such a metaphor, The. Hogwash. Robert Francis. LCAP

Tongue-tied. Carlos German Belli, *tr. fr. Spanish by* Maureen Ahern. Per

Tongue-tied in Black and White. Michael S. Harper. HCAP

Tongues of Dying Men, The. Shakespeare. *Fr.* King Richard II, II, i. FaBoRV

Tongues of Fire. Jorge Plescoff, *tr. fr. Spanish by* Yishai Tobin. VWA

Tonic. Tristan Tzara, *tr. fr. French by* Michael Benedikt. POS

Tonight. Franklin P. Adams. FiBHP

Tonight. Nathan Alterman, *tr. fr. Hebrew by* Bernhard Frank. MHeP

Tonight. Ada Negri, *tr. fr. Italian by* Brenda Webster. OV

Tonight/ when the moon comes out. Proposition. Nicolás Guillén, *tr. by* Langston Hughes. FaPON; TTY

Tonight a blackout. Twenty years ago. Christmas Eve under Hooker's Statue. Robert Lowell. CAPP; FF; OxBA

Tonight and forever I shall be yours so says the oleo king. Some Stories of the Beauty Wapiti. Ebbe Borregaard. NeAP

Tonight, as hail falls on bamboo leaves. Lady Izumi, *tr. fr. Japanese by* Hiroaki Sato. *Fr.* Fifty-one Tanka. FCEI

Tonight, at Least, My Sinner. *Gond Oral Tradition, tr. by* V. Elwin *and* S. Hivale. WTO

Tonight, at the bar. The Leather Bar. Ralph Pomeroy. PeHV

Tonight, Autumn. Autumn, Again Grass. José Hidalgo, *tr. by* Brady Earnhart. WCI

Tonight Everyone in the World Is Dreaming the Same Dream. Susan Litwack. VWA

Tonight, grave sir, both my poor[e] house and I. Inviting a Friend to Supper. Ben Jonson, *after* Martial. AWP; JCP; LiTB; NOBE; NoP; OAEL-1; OBS; OxBoLi; PoEL-2; PPP; SeCP; SeCV-1

Tonight I am told. Juan Rulfo Moved Away. Alberto Rios. UL

Tonight I can write the saddest line. Pablo Neruda, *tr. fr. Spanish by* W. S. Merwin. BoLoP

Tonight I could die as easily as the grass. In the Soul Hour. Robert Mezey. AmPA; NaP

Tonight I disentangle. Wakepick I. Kristjana Gunnars. NOBC

Tonight I have a date. A Serenade for Two Poplars. Esther Raab, *tr. by* Robert Friend *and* Shimon Sandbank. VWA

Tonight I have taken all that I was. Rhyme of the Dead Self. A. R. D. Fairburn. ATNZ

Tonight I looked at the pale northern sky. Back. Robert Mezey. AmPA

Tonight I may die. Rain, wind, sun. The Impossible. Jules Laforgue, *tr. by* William Jay Smith. CT

Tonight I run past the city limit. Night Runner's Prayer. Mykie Silz Reidy. TSL

Tonight I Stood Looking. Susan L. Dunn. TSM

Tonight I think again. Yehuda Amichai, *tr. by* Warren Bargad *and* Stanley F. Chyet. IP

Tonight I thought of you as I smoked a cigar. Havana Blues. Henry Carlile. SM

Tonight I want to say something wonderful. For the Sleepwalkers. Edward Hirsch. FYAP; MAYP

Tonight I watch my father's hair. Two Postures beside a Fire. James Wright. HCAP

Tonight, if they came, I'd be mute. Saucer Station: Monday-Friday. Albert Goldbarth. BWV

Tonight, I'll pull your limbs through. The Mulatta as Penelope. Lorna Goodison. PVCV

Tonight I'll walk the razor along your throat. Punk Pantoum. Pamela Stewart. SM

Tonight in Chicago. *Unknown.* AmFN

Tonight in our secret town. Right Now. William Stafford. NaP

Tonight in the hills there was a light. Hawktree. Dave Smith. HCAP

Tonight is the night. Hallowe'en. Harry Behn. FaPON; PDV

Tonight is 'he one. A Way of Speaking. Gretel Ehrlich. MAYP

Tonight my children hunch. "It Out-Herods Herod. Pray You, Avoid It." Anthony Hecht. CoAP; NiP; NoAM; NOBA; OxBC

Tonight my mother, dinner over. The Last Gift. Peter Cooley. NAmP

Tonight no one takes fish. Tattered pennants. Sailing the Back River. Dave Smith. MT

Tonight, not far from where Jefferson Davis. Night Fishing for Blues. Dave Smith. GeTw

Tonight, on a bank line strung. Running the River Lines. David Baker. MAYP

Tonight, on the balcony. Historical Materialism. Cees Buddingh', *tr. by* James S. Holmes. DuIn

Tonight, on the deck, the lights. Two Stories. Charles Wright. FYAP

Tonight our cat, Tahi, who lately lost. The Buried Stream. James Keir Baxter. OxBC

Tonight, precisely at that wall. Midnight. Arthur Nortje. WMBCH

Tonight the Famous Psychiatrist. Louis Simpson. OxBC

Tonight, the first snow. November Song. Mark Vinz. Psk

Tonight the Moon Fell. Abraham Chalfi, *tr. fr. Hebrew by* Bernhard Frank. MHeP

Tonight the moon is high, to summon all. William Bell. FaBoTw

Tonight the moths. Tyranny of Moths. Gerald Vizenor. VoR

Tonight the Sabbath dreams stalk. Sabbath. Rivka Fried. VWA

Tonight the schools disperse. On the Breaking-up of a School. Tadhg O'g O'Huiginn, *tr. by* Osborn Bergin. AnIL

Tonight the spirit of an elder. Havdolah. Susan Litwack. VWA

Tonight the waves march. Moonlight Night: Carmel. Langston Hughes. MOS

Tonight the wind gnaws. Christmas Landscape. Laurie Lee. OBCP

Tonight they need to be both host and stranger. Familiar Story. Alan Shapiro. DiFo

Tonight we sat,/ telly dead. Old Man. Alan J. Carr

Tonight when the hoar frost falls on the wood. Christmas in the Wood. Frances Mary Frost. TrCP

Tonight you broke into my dreams. For Anne, Who Doesn't Know. Gail Fox. IHMS

Tonio told me at catechism. The Purpose of Altar Boys. Alberto Ríos. MAYP; NAmP

Tonite I walked out of my red apartment door on East tenth street's dusk. Allen Ginsberg. *Fr.* Mugging. NoAM

Tonite, thriller was. Beware: Do Not Read This Poem. Ishmael Reed. BPo; CNA; NIP; NoP; PoBA; WSC

Tons of snow have fallen in my village. Emperor Temmu. *Fr.* Manyo Shu. FCEI

Tonversation with Baby, A. Morris Bishop. FiBHP

Tony/ To be casual and have the wish to heal. The Book of Gawain. Jack Spicer. *Fr.* The Holy Grail. PoM

Tony Baloney ("Tony Baloney is fibbing again"). Dennis Lee. RHPC

Tony Get the Boys. D. L. Graham. PoBA

Tony O! Colin Francis. CH; FaBoCo

Tony said: "Boys are better!" Girls Can, Too! Lee Bennett Hopkins. RHPC

Tony the Turtle ("Tony was a turtle"). Emile Victor Rieu. SO

Too aware of endings, I search among. Child in a Blue Linen Dress. Helen Sorrells. MOWH

Too Bad for Me. Louis Aragon, tr. fr. French by Joachim Neugroschel. POS

Too bad that, cut out as you are. The Satrapy. C. P. Cavafy, tr. by Edmund Keeley and Philip Sherrard. VMG

Too beautiful for me, but I have to cleave in. Unknown, tr. fr. Japanese by Hiroaki Sato. Fr. Inutsukuba Shu. FCEI

Too Bright a Day. Norman MacCaig. GTBS-P

Too Busy. Paul Laurence Dunbar. See Get Somebody Else.

Too close/ to call. Love. Carol Sue Muth. RR

Too cold this night for Hugh Maguire. Hugh Maguire. Eochy O'Hussey, tr. by Frank O'Connor. AnIL

Too Dark. Mark McCloskey. PoA

Too dark to tell the gate. Kyorai, tr. fr. Japanese by Burton Watson. Fr. Twenty Hokku. FCEI

Too dearly had I bought my green and youthful years. Earl of Surrey. SiPS

Too far afield thy search. Nay, turn. Nay, turn. To Man Who Goes Seeking Immortality. Adelaide Crapsey. QFR

Too foraging to blue-print or deploy! Naomi. Gwendolyn Brooks. NAAL-2

Too frail to soar—a feeble thing. The Sparrow's Fall. Frances Ellen Watkins Harper. PWR

Too green the springing April grass. Spring in New Hampshire. Claude McKay. BANP; BPo; PoNe

Too happy time dissolves itself. Emily Dickinson. NOBA

Too harsh the man who setting bounds to grief. Statius, tr. fr. Latin. Fr. Sylvae. PeHV

Too Late. Rachel Korn, tr. fr. Yiddish by Seymour Mayne and Rivka Augenfeld. VWA

Too Late? Longfellow. See Morituri Salutamus: It Is Too Late.

Too Late. Fitz Hugh Ludlow. PoLF

Too Late. Philip Bourke Marston. OBNC

Too-late Born, The. Archibald MacLeish. GoJo; MoAB; MoAmPo; OxBA; WaP

(Silent Slain, The.) CMoP; LiTM

Too late for love, too late for joy. Bride Song. Christina Rossetti. Fr. The Prince's Progress. OBEV; WPE

Too lazy to wave the white plume fan. Summer Day in the Mountains. Li Po, tr. by Burton Watson. CoBCP

Too Lazy to Write Poetry. Chu Yün-ming, tr. fr. Chinese by Jonathan Chaves. CoBLCP

Too little/ has been said. The Door. Charles Tomlinson. PoA

Too Long I Followed. William Drummond of Hawthornden. Fr. Urania, or Spiritual Poems. Son

Too long outside your door I have shivered. The Terrible Door. Harold Monro. BoLoP; EnLoPo; FaBoTw

Too Many Daves. "Dr. Seuss." OBCA; RHPC

Too many of the dead, some I knew well. In the Backs. Frances Cornford. BrRo

Too many splashes, too many gashes. Lone Kauri Road ("Too many splashes, too many gashes"). Allen Curnow. Fr. Trees, Effigies, Moving Objects, XVII. ATNZ; PeNZ

Too many summers out of the way of a trowel. The Lawn Roller. Robert Layzer. NePoEA

Too many tumbleweeds on 66. Oklahoma Rt. 66. Nora Naranjo-Morse. GOS

Too momentary/ to be called evanescent. Teika, tr. by Steven D. Carter. WFTW

Too Much. Edwin Muir. LiTB

Too much/ at one time. Sanetomo, tr. fr. Japanese by Burton Watson. Fr. Twenty-four Tanka. FCEI

Too Much Coffee. E. A. Robinson. MoAmPo

Too much good luck no less than misery. Joy May Kill. Michelangelo, tr. by John Addington Symonds. AWP

Too Much Sex. Unknown. MeEL

Too much to drink these days, late getting up each morning. Late Rising on Spring Days. Wei Chuang, tr. by Burton Watson. CoBCP

Too new in town, we're told. Being Refused Local Credit. Paula Rankin. MAYP

Too often you keep so near me, where I do not want to stand. You. Michel Deguy, tr. by Anthony Rudolf. RHTwFP

Too old to carry arms and fight like the others. Report from the Besieged City. Zbigniew Herbert, tr. by John Carpenter and Bogdana Carpenter. AnAn

Too powerful a drug is Hope. "Bottle Should Be Plainly Labeled 'Poison.'" Sara Henderson Hay. GoYe

Too proud, too delicate to tell her wants. With a China Chamberpot, to the Countess of Hillsborough. Lord Holland. FaBoUs

Too restless to sleep. Teika, tr. by Steven D. Carter. WFTW

Too sad is the grief in my heart. Elegy for His Daughter Ellen. Goronwy Owen, tr. by George Borrow. OBWVE

Too Short. Meir Wieseltier, tr. fr. Hebrew by Warren Bargad and Stanley F. Chyet. IP

Too Slow. Lillian Morrison. ILY

Too solemn for day, too sweet for night. William Sidney Walker. OBEV

Too soon to be out of me bed. On a Monday Morning. Cyril Tawney. OBET

"Too tame, too pretty," you said. At Staufen. Michael Hamburger. VWA

Too tight, it is running over. Fence Wire. James Dickey. NYBP; VGW

Too tired to move fast. Teika, tr. by Steven D. Carter. WFTW

Too Wonderful. Bible, O.T. Fr. Proverbs: The Words of Agur, ll. 18-19. TrJP

Took Bladyn then his crowth, anew, and toucht. Bladyn's Song of Cloten. C. M. Doughty. Fr. The Dawn in Britain. PoEL-5

Tool of Fate. The. "Yehoash", tr. fr. Yiddish by Isidore Goldstick. TrJP

Toot! Toot! Unknown. RHPC

Toothsome. Norah Smaridge. RAR

Top and the Tip, The. Charlotte Zolotow. RAR

Topcliffe's horses shake. John Logan. Fr. The Death of Southwell. CRP

Tophet. Thomas Gray. FaBoEE; NOEC; OxBSP

Topic for a Painting, A. Natsume Seibi, tr. fr. Japanese by Hiroaki Sato. Fr. Twenty-seven Hokku. FCEI

Toplight hammered down by shadowless noon. Fire: The People. Alfred Corn. Fr. A Call in the Midst of the Crowd. MAYP; NAAL-2

Topographies, sel. Riemke Ensing.

"Already 5 drownings 32." ATNZ

Topography. Mark A.R. Facknitz. KS

Topper's a splendid kind of hat, A. O, Shmuel My Brother! Moyshe-Leyb Halpern, tr. by John Hollander. PeBMYV

Tops of the spruces here have always done, The. Jefferson Valley. John Hollander. PPP

Topsy-Turvy Land. Phyllis M. Stone. BoTP

Topsy-turvy Land. H. E. Wilkinson. BoTP

Topsy-turvy World. William Brighty Rands. OxBChV

Torch, The. Theodosia Pickering Garrison. BLPA

Torch-Bearers, The, sel. Arlo Bates.

America. AA

Torch-Light in Autumn. John James Piatt. AA

Torches surrounded by butterflies, The. The Mutilated Soldier. David Fisher. NPGG

Tories' flag is deepest blue, The. The Blue Flag. Chris Miller. FaBoPa

Torment wanders into the light beyond the roof. The Struggles of Words. Pierre Reverdy, tr. by Michael Benedikt. POS

Tormented Mystic. Al-Tijani Yusuf Bashir, tr. fr. Arabic by Matthew Sorenson and Patricia Alanah Byrne. MAP

Tormented with incessant pains. To Stella. Swift. NOEC

Torn away from number weight. Susan Howe. Fr. Speeches at the Barriers, 5. LP

Torn between griefs, which grief shall I lament. Sophocles, tr. fr. Greek by Ezra Pound. Fr. Women of Trachis. OBVE

Torn Hat, The. Nathaniel Parker Willis. AA

Torn into light, you woke wriggling. How Much Earth. Philip Levine. NNaP

Torn Mountain. René Char, tr. fr. French by William Jay Smith. CT

Torn remains of a cobweb. On Something Observed. Kokan Shiren, tr. by Burton Watson. JLIC-2

Torn upon Thy wheel. Out of the Depths. Frederic Lawrence Knowles. TrPWD

Torn widow's veil. Viljo Kajava, tr. fr. Finnish by Aili Jarvenpa. Fr. Songs of Sorrow (Spring 1918). SOP

Torn Windows, No Paper. Keijo Shurin, tr. fr. Japanese by Burton Watson. FCEI

Torn-Word. Joan McGavin. NPo

Torn-word dozes at the root of the tongue, The. Torn-Word. Joan McGavin. NPo

Tornado, The. Aimé Césaire, tr. fr. French by Michael Benedikt. POS

Tornado, The. Norman H. Russell. STE

Tornado. William Stafford. NaP

Tornado Soup. A. K. Redwing. VoR

Toroi Bandi. Mongol Oral Tradition, tr. by C. R. Bawden. WTO

Torrent, A/ of cobalt bullets. Lacrimas or There Is a Need to Scream. K. Curtis Lyle. PoBA

Torrismond, sel. Thomas Lovell Beddoes.

"How many times do I love thee, dear?." Fr. Sc. iii. LiTB; PoEL-4; TrGrPo

(How Many Times?.) ELP

(How Many Times Do I Love Thee, Dear?.) EnRP

Torso: Passages 18, The. Robert Duncan. CAPP

Tortoise, The. Cid Corman. InPK; SM; VGW

Tortoise Family Connections. D. H. Lawrence. BrPo

Tortoise Gallantry. D. H. Lawrence. CMoP; MoP

Tortoise in Eternity, The. Elinor Wylie. FaPON; ImOP

Tortoise-Shell. D. H. Lawrence. CMoP; FM; NAEL-2; OAEL-2

Tortoise Shout. D. H. Lawrence. LiTM; NAEL-2

Torture. Margaret Atwood. PoE

Torture chamber is not like anything, The. Footnote to the Amnesty Report on Torture. Margaret Atwood. NoAM

Torture scene developed under a glass bell, The. Heirloom. Leonard Cohen. NOBC

Torture, that we pray it may be mild. The Beanstalk, Meditated Later. Judith Wright. NoAM

Tortured body, lie at rest alone. Unknown Man in the Morgue. Merrill Moore. MoAmPo

Tortured Heart, The. Rimbaud, tr. fr. French. PeHV

Tortured mullet served the Roman's pride, The. On a Vase of Gold-Fish. Charles Tennyson Turner. NOBVV

Tory Pledges. Thomas Moore. FaBoCo; OBSV

Toss your gay heads. At April. Angelina Weld Grimké. BlSi

Tossed in a troubled sea of griefs, I float. To Her in Absence; a Ship. Thomas Carew. CaPo

Tossed is that cypress boat. Unknown, tr. by Arthur Waley. BoS

Tossed night between us, A. Schooner. Edward Kamau Brathwaite. PBCV

Tossed on the stormy waves of time. "I Was a Stranger and Ye Took Me In." Mary E. Tucker. CBWP-1

Tossing his mane of snows in wildest eddies and tangles. Earliest Spring. William Dean Howells. OBEV

(In Earliest Spring.) AA; FaBoBe

Tossing in my bed. Narihira, tr. by Geoffrey Bownas and Anthony Thwaite. PeBJV

Tossing, turning—this poor man can't fall asleep. For My Wife: A Poem Written in Sickness. Yüan Mei, tr. by Anthony C. Yu. WFTU

Total Eclipse. Michael J. Rosen. DiPo

Total failure—Master Han Shan, A. Wang Chiu-ssu, tr. fr. Chinese by Jonathan Chaves. Fr. Miscellaneous Poems on Living in the Woods. CoBLCP

Total Influence or Outcome of the Matter: The Sun, The. Marge Piercy. WPOW

Totem. Nissim Ezekiel. VWA

T'other eb'ning eb'ryting was still, Oh! babe. Mister Johnson. Ben Harney. OBAL

Toto has a goat's nose and the foot of a pig. Poor Fellow. Raymond Queneau, tr. by Teo Savory. RHTwFP

Toto Merumeni. Guido Gozzano, tr. fr. Italian by J. G. Nichols. PFI

Tottering and elastic, middle name of Groan. Pedestrian. Thomas Lux. NAmP

Toucan, The. Pyke Johnson, Jr.. NTCP

Toucannery. Jack Prelutsky. OnUR

Touch/ is what the eyes do, sometimes. From a Brother Dreaming in the Rye. James Cunningham. JB

Touch. Thom Gunn. CMoP

Touch. Octavio Paz, tr. fr. Spanish. BoLoP, tr. by Charles Tomlinson

Touch but thy lyre, my Harry, and I hear. To Master Henry Lawes, the Excellent Composer, of His Lyrics. Robert Herrick. CaPo

Touch Football. Jack Driscoll. TSL

Touch from my hands brings you strength, A. A Song for Healing. Margot LeBrasseur. GOS

Touch It. Robert Mezey. NaP

Touch it: it won't shrink like an eyeball. A Life. Sylvia Plath. NOBA

Touch me, touch me. Grass Fingers. Angelina Weld Grimké. CDC

Touch my hand as though it were an old coin. Sailing in Crosslight. Anita Skeen. IHMS

Touch of cold in the autumn night, A. Autumn. T. E. Hulme. FaBoMo; SeCePo

Touch of red left on your lip, A. Out Early One Morning, I Met an Old Acquaintance. Shen Yüeh, tr. by Burton Watson. CoBCP

Touch of the Hand, A. Allen Curnow. ATNZ

Touch of the Master's Hand, The. Myra Brooks Welch. BLPA

Touch Thou Mine Eyes. Marion Franklin Ham. AH

Touché. Jessie Redmond Fauset. BlSi; CDC

Touched. Roger Giroux, tr. fr. French by Anthony Barnett. RHTwFP

Touching. Christopher Gilbert. MAYP

Touching books. For Gabriel. Laya Firestone. VWA

Touching Each Other's Surfaces. Carol Jane Bangs. NIP

Touching Ezekiel his workman's hand. Jesus. James McAuley. CBAP

Touching Heartsease. Janet Sutherland. DT

Touching Shoulders. Unknown. BLPA

Touching the leg of a girl. Spiel. Halvard Johnson. TSL

Touching the line from a fishing pole. Chiyojo, tr. fr. Japanese by Hiroaki Sato. Fr. Seventeen Hokku. FCEI

Touching the River. Thomas Kinsella. FaBCIP

Touching the tulips was a shyness. Tulips. Medbh McGuckian. FaBCIP

Touching your goodness, I am like a man. The Illiterate. William Meredith. NoP

Touchstone, The, sels. Kalonymos ben Kalonymos, tr. fr. Hebrew by J. Chotzner. TrJP

Hypocrite, The.

Unfortunate Male, The.

Yoke, The.

Touchy old gent from Cohasset, A. John Updike. Fr. Two Limericks after Lear. SoTCo

Tough Captain Spud and his First Mate, Spade. Captain Spud and His First Mate, Spade. John Ciardi. OBCA

Tough Generation, A. David Gascoyne. LiTM

Tough hand closes gently on the load, The. Man Carrying Bale. Harold Monro. BrPo; MoBrPo

Tough strong men from foreign lands. Foreign Agents. "Sahir Ludhianvi", tr. by Mahmood Jamal. PBMUP

Toughest gal I ever did see. Kissie Lee. Margaret Abigail Walker. BlSi; NMM

Toughs walk by in groups explosive. David Kirby. SoTCo

Toujours la Politesse. Ezra Pound, after the Chinese. OBVE

Toulouse Lautrec. Astrid Tollefsen, tr. fr. Norwegian by Nadia Christensen. PBWP

Tour de Force. Peter Kane Dufault. ErPo

Tour 5. Robert Hayden. PPP

Tour of Duty, sels. David Huddle. Son

Nerves.

Words.

Touring. David Morton. TrPWD

Touring the old miles again. Baldpate Pond. E. F. Weisslitz. NYBP

Touris, white man, wipin his face. The Song of the Banana Man. Evan Jones. PVCV

Tourist. Muhammad al-Maghut, tr. fr. Arabic by May Jayyusi and John Heath-Stubbs. MAP

Tourist and the Town, The. Adrienne Rich. NePoEA-2

Tourist came in from Orbitville, A. Southbound on the Freeway. May Swenson. AmFN; NTCP; NYBP

Tourist Country. William Stafford. NoAM

Tourist dame, A. Miss Tourist. "Lord Kitchener." PBCV

Tourist Death. Archibald MacLeish. NAAL-2

Tourist from Syracuse, The. Donald Justice. CAPP; NoAM; TwCP

Tourist in Seat 29, The, sel. M. K. Joseph.

Granada the Last City. ATNZ

Tourist Japan. Takenaka Iku, tr. fr. Japanese by Geoffrey Bownas and Anthony Thwaite. PeBJV

Tourist, spare the avid glance. The Attic Landscape. Herman Melville. AnAmPo; NOBA; OBAL

Tourists, The. C. Day Lewis. OBTV

Tourists. Howard Moss. FiBHP; NYBP

Tourists. Kizito Z. Muchemwa. WMBCH

Tourists on Paros. Michael Ryan. NAmP

Tournament of Tottenham, The. Unknown. OxBoLi

Tours. C. D. Wright. MT

Toussaint L'Ouverture. E. A. Robinson. PoNe

Toussaint L'Ouverture. Henrietta Cordelia Ray. CBWP-3

Toussaint, the most unhappy man of men! To Toussaint L'Ouverture. Wordsworth. EnRP; FaBoPV; InPK; NOBE; OBNC; PoNe; PoRA; PPP; TrGrPo

Toward a Better Love. Roque Dalton, tr. fr. Spanish by Jack Hirschman. Vol

Toward a Poetic Art. Raymond Queneau, tr. fr. French by Teo Savory. RHTwFP

Toward dusk last night. Love in Spring. Shotetsu, tr. by Steven D. Carter. WFTW

Toward evening on an ancient plain. Evening Prospect. Cheng Chen, tr. by Chang Yin-nan. WFTU

Toward evening, the weather turns cold. Night Rain beneath the City Walls of P'i-chou. Yang Shih-ch'i, tr. by Jonathan Chaves. CoBLCP

Toward evening whither shall I go? Thoughts on Climbing the Swept-Leaves Pavilion on the Third Day before the Double-Ninth Festival. Ching An, tr. by Irving Lo. WFTU

Toward Lesbos. Renée Vivien, tr. fr. French by Sandia Belgrade. PeHV

Toward morning/ an impatient, breathless. Oceanic World. Friederike Mayröcker, tr. by Beth Bjorklund. CoAuP

Toward Myself. Leah Goldberg, *tr. fr. Hebrew by* Robert Friend. VWA
Toward the dawn. Blanche Baughan. *Fr.* Maui's Fish. PeNZ
Toward the end. On the Death of Ho Chi Minh. Eli W. Mandel. NIP
Toward the end of her life she said that the. Berthe Morisot. Anne Waldman. UL
Toward the Other. Alain Veinstein, *tr. fr. French by* Rosmarie Waldrop. RHTwFP
"Toward the person who has died." Dying Away. William Meredith. NoAM
Toward the sea turning my troubled eye. The Huge Leviathan. Spenser. *Fr.* Visions of the World's Vanity. ChTr
Toward the Solstice. Adrienne Rich. NAAL-2; NoP
Toward the Verrazano. Stephen Dunn, *tr. by* Joachim Neugroschel. AnAn
Toward Winter, *sels. Unknown.* NOIV
  "Night is cold on the Great Bog, The."
  "Sliab Cua, dark and broken, is full of wolf packs."
  "Want and winter are upon us."
  "We are shattered and battered, engulfed."
Toward world's end, through the bare. The Magi. Louise Glück. PoA
Towards Democracy, *sel.* Edward Carpenter.
  Through the Long Night. PeHV
Towards Lillers. Ivor Gurney. NAEL-2
Towards nightfall when the wind. Winter Mask. Allen Tate. OxBA; Prf
Towards not being/ anyone else's center. Movement. Denise Levertov. LLLT
Towards the altar sober-paced I went. Keats. *Fr.* The Fall of Hyperion, I. TOF
Towards the east it is still dark. *Unknown, tr. by* Arthur Waley. BoS
Towards the end he sailed into an extraordinary mildness. Herman Melville. W. H. Auden. LiTA; OxBA
Towards the end the fortunes of the king. Of Kings and Dukes. Roy Fuller. AnAn
Towards the Last Spike, *sels. E. J. Pratt.*
  Gathering, The. MoCV; OBCV
  Precambrian [*or* Pre-Cambrian] Shield, The. MoCV; NOBC; NoBC; OBCV
Towards the latter days of the evening. Shared Sentences. Alan Davies. IAT; LP
Towards the Source, *sels. Christopher Brennan.* PoAu-1
  I Saw My Life as Whitest Flame.
  Let Us Go Down, the Long Dead Night Is Done.
Towards the sun, towards the south-west. D. H. Lawrence. *Fr.* Eagle in New Mexico. RB
Towards the Vanishing Point. David Lehman. SM
Towart the evyn, amyd the symmyris heit. Gawin Douglas. *Fr.* Prologues to the Aeneid, *Bk.* XIII, Prologue. OxBS
T'owd pig's got mezzles an' she's deead, poor thing. The Dead Pig. *Unknown.* FaBoNo
Tower, The. Philip Booth. NePoEA-2
Tower, The. Dan Pagis, *tr. fr. Hebrew by* Stephen Mitchell. VWA
Tower, The. W. B. Yeats. CMoP; LiTB; LiTM; NoAM; PoE
Tower, The ("What shall I do with this absurdity."), *sel.* W. B. Yeats. CMoP; LiTB; LiTM; NoAM
  "Now shall I make my soul." OBD
Tower of Babel, The. Nathaniel Crouch. OxBChV
Tower of Refuge is our God, A! Ein feste Burg ist unser Gott. Martin Luther, *tr. by* M. Woolsey Stryker. CTC
Tower of Saint-Jacques in Paris totters, The. Vigilance. André Breton, *tr. by* Michael Benedikt. POS
Tower of the Dream, The, *sel.* Charles Harpur.
  "Yes, wonderful are dreams: and I have known." PoAu-1
Towering life of the towering city, The. H. Leivick, *tr. fr. Yiddish by* Benjamin *and* Barbara Harshav. *Fr.* Here Lives the Jewish People. AYP
Towering Rocks. Song of a Woman in Labor. *Unknown, tr. by* Frances Densmore. OV
Towery city and branchy between towers. Duns Scotus's Oxford. Gerard Manley Hopkins. EBEV; EyDe; FaBoPP; GTBS-P; NAEL-2; NoAM; OBMV; PoEL-5
Town, The. David Rowbotham. PoAu-2
Town and Country. James Whitcomb Riley. AnAmPo
Town Betrayed, The. Edwin Muir. CMoP
Town Called Providence, Its Fate, The. Benjamin Tompson. SCAP
Town Child, The. Irene Thompson. BoTP
Town Clerk's Views, The. Sir John Betjeman. CMoP
Town does not exist, The. The Starry Night. Anne Sexton. NoAM; PoE
Town Dump, The. Howard Nemerov. CMoP; MAT

Town fire-watcher in his tower, The. *Unknown, tr. by* Burton Watson. FCEI
Town has opened to the sun, The. Bombardment. D. H. Lawrence. MMA
Town I Left. Helen Sorrells. IHMS
Town I Was Born In, The. Yehuda Amichai, *tr. fr. Hebrew by* A. C. Jacobs. VWA
Town is tilted toward the stream, The. A Sunday Dreamer's Guide to Yarrow, Missouri. Jim Barnes. HATNAP
Town lies in the valley, A. The Silent Town. Richard Dehmel, *tr. by* Jethro Bithell. AWP
Town might abort, A. How the Death of a City Is Never More than the Sum of the Deaths of Those Who Inhabit Its Spaces. Victor Coleman. NOBC
Town Mouse and the Country Mouse, The. Matthew Prior. BXAP
Town of Don't-You-Worry, The. I. J. Barlett. BLPA; WBLP
Town of Hay, The. Sam Walter Foss. AA
Town of Hill, The. Donald Hall. CAPP; TAP
Town of Nogood, The. W. E. Penny. BLPA
Town of Passage, The. *Unknown.* OxBoLi
Town of Passage is both large and spacious, The. The Attractions of a Fashionable Irish Watering-Place. Francis Sylvester Mahony. FaBoPP
Town or poem, I don't care how it looks. Old woman. White Center. Richard Hugo. NAAL-2; NoP
Town-Rakes, The. *At. to* P. A. Motteux. CoMu
Town remembers no such plenty, The. Lancashire Winter. Tony Connor. OxBTC
Town smells of things, The. Boncho, *tr. fr. Japanese by* Hiroaki Sato. *Fr.* Twenty-one Hokku. FCEI
Town to take is in a room. The enemy's plunder isn't heavy, The. My Life. Max Jacob, *tr. by* Ron Padgett. RHTwFP
Town was aflutter on rodeo week, The. Two of a Kind. Bob Schild. CowP
Town Window, A. John Drinkwater. BoTP
Town without a Market, The. James Elroy Flecker. MoBrPo
Townsman on his yielding bed, The. Michael Hamburger. *Fr.* The Note-Book of a European Tramp. NePoEA
Townspeople peer out of their windows, The. The Wind Carol. Lewis Turco. SM
Tow'rds the lofty walls of Balbi, lo! Durand of Blonden hies. Durand of Blonden. Ludwig Uhland, *tr. by* James Clarence Mangan. AWP
Towser Shall Be Tied Tonight. *Unknown.* BLPA
Toy Band, The. Sir Henry Newbolt. BoTP
Toy Bone, The. Donald Hall. CAPP
Toy Horse, The. Valentin Iremonger. NOIV
Toy-Maker, The. Padraic Colum. SaC
Toy of the Titans. Ebenezer Elliott. *Fr.* The Year of Seeds. Son
Toys, The. Coventry Patmore. *Fr.* The Unknown Eros, I, x. ACP; BeLS; EBEV; EBVV; FaFP; NoBVV; OBEV; SoSe; TrGrPo; TrPWD
Toys. Abraham Sutskever, *tr. fr. Yiddish by* PBMYV, *tr. by* Chana Bloch; VWA, *tr. by* Seymour Levitan.
Toys I bought for you, The. Gill Boy. Dennis Schmitz. NPGG
Toys Talk of the World, The. Katharine Pyle. OBCA
"Tra la la la — See me dance the polka." Neptune — Polka. Dame Edith Sitwell. NOBE
Trace of flowers, a streak of moonlight, A. Sending a Letter. Liu Shih, *tr. by* Irving Lo. WFTU
Track, The. Nicholas Christopher. MAYP
Track. Tomas Tranströmer, *tr. fr. Swedish by* Robert Bly. EAS; RB
Track-lining Song. *Unknown.* AmFP
Track of a broad rattler, dragged over dust at dawn, The. The Catch. Brewster Ghiselin. HAP
Tracking Rabbits: Night. Jim Barnes. CDW
Tracking the Siuslaw Man. Jim Barnes. HATNAP
Tracks. John Montague. CIP; FaBCIP
Tracks diverge from each other. I don't know, The. A Letter. Dan Pagis, *tr. by* Warren Bargad *and* Stanley F. Chyet. IP
Tract. William Carlos Williams. BLPL; DL; FF; LiTA; LiTM; MoAB; MoAMPo; MoP; NoAM; NOBA; TAP; TrGrPo; TwCP; VGW
Tractatus. Derek Mahon. *See* World Is Everything That Is the Case, The.
Traction Engine, The. W. H. Auden. FL
Traction: November 22, 1963. Howard Moss. AmFN
Tractor now is an essential, A. Horatian Variation. Leonard Bacon. NYBP
Tracy & Co. Hugo Williams. *Fr.* Calling Your Name in the Zoo. NPo
Trade. Egbert Martin. PVCV
"Trade" Rat. Eleanor Glenn Wallis. NePoAm
Trade Winds. John Masefield. FaBoCh; OBMV

Trader I am to the African shore, A. Sweet Meat Has Sour Sauce; or, The Slave-Trader in the Dumps. William Cowper. NOEC; OBSV
Trader's Return. Sylvia Lawson. PoAu-2
Trading Post—Winslow, Arizona. Terri Meyette. GOS
Tradition. Dryden. Fr. Religio Laici. OBS
Tradition of Conquest. Sarah Morgan Bryan Piatt. AA
Traditional Funeral Songs. Unknown, tr. fr. Modern Greek by Willis Barnstone and Elene Kolb. BoWoP
Traditional Red. Robert Huff. HoPM; NePoEA-2
Traditions. Seamus Heaney. FaBoMo
Trafalgar. Thomas Hardy. See Dynasts, The: Night of Trafalgar, The.
Trafalgar. Francis Turner Palgrave. BeLS; FaBoBe
Traffic Lights. Mu'in Besseisso, tr. fr. Arabic by Abdullah al-Udhari. MPAW
Traffic Lights. Lina Kasdaglis, tr. fr. Modern Greek. BoWoP, tr. by Edmund and Mary Keeley; BoWoP, tr. by Edmund Keeley and Mary Keeley
Trafique Is Earth's Great Atlas. George Alsop. SCAP
Tragedie of Philotas, The, sel. Samuel Daniel.
  "How dost thou wear and weary out thy days." OBSC
Tragedy. "Æ" MoBrPo
Tragedy, A. Tom Masson. OBAL
Tragedy. Howard Moss. NePoEA
Tragedy. Jill Spargur. BLPA
Tragedy of Charles Duke of Byron, The. George Chapman. OBD
Tragedy of Dido, The, sel. Christopher Marlowe.
  I Have an Orchard. Fr. IV, v. ChTr
Tragedy of Leaves, The. Charles Bukowski. HoPM
Tragedy of Pete, The. Joseph S. Cotter, Sr.. CDC
Tragedy of Pompey the Great, The, sel. John Masefield.
  "Man is a sacred city built of marvelous earth." WGRP
Tragedy of Valentinian, The, sels. John Fletcher.
  Care-charming Sleep [Thou Easer of All Woes]. Fr. V, ii. ELP; FaBoRV; OxBSP; TrGrPo
  (Into Slumbers.) SeCePo
  (Song: "Care-charming sleep, thou easer of all woes.") OBS; PoEL-2
  (Song to Sleep.) OxBoLi
  (To Sleep.) PoRA
  God Lyaeus, Ever Young. Fr. V, viii. OBEV
  Hear, Ye Ladies [That Despise]. EIL; ELP; NOBE; OBEV
  (Mighty Love.) TrGrPo
  (Song: "Heare ye Ladies that despise.") PoEL-2
  Now the Lusty Spring [Is Here]. Fr. II, iv. ELP; ErPo; FF
  (Love's Emblems.) BoLoP; EIL; NOBE
Tragi-Comedy of Titus Oates, The. Unknown. APAS
Tragic Condition of the Statue of Liberty, The. Bernadette Mayer. UL
Tragic Guilt. Keidrych Rhys. WaP
Tragic Love. Walter James Turner. OBMV
Tragic Mary Queen of Scots, The. "Michael Field." EnLoPo; OBMV
Tragic Mary Queen of Scots, II, The. "Michael Field." OBMV
Tragic, said I. Oh, Tragicker, says she. Noël Tragique. Ramon Guthrie. ErPo
Tragic Story, A. Adelbert von Chamisso, tr. fr. German by Thackeray. BOTP; FaPON; MoShBr; OnMSP
Tragic Verses. Unknown. CoMu
Tragical History of the Life and Death of Doctor Faustus, The. Christopher Marlowe. See Doctor Faustus.
Tragiques, Les, sel. Théodore Agrippa d' Aubigné, tr. fr. French. Portrait of Henri III, A. PeHV
Trail, The. Edward Weismiller. WaP
Trail All Your Pikes. Countess of Winchilsea. WPE
Trail beside the River Platte, The. William Heyen. GOA
Trail Breakers. James Henry Daugherty. AmFN
Trail climbing/ you have to watch your footing. Finding a Poem. Eve Merriam. RFM
Trail climbs in zig-zags, The. The Trail up Wu Gorge. Sun Yün-feng, tr. by Kenneth Rexroth and Ling Chung. BoWoP; PBWP
Trail Crew Camp at Bear Valley. 9000 Feet. Gary Snyder. HCAP
Trail dust settled behind him. Saddle Tramp. Buck Wilkerson. CowP
Trail into Kansas, The. W. S. Merwin. GOA
Trail to Lillooet, The. Emily Pauline Johnson. CaP
Trail to Mexico, The, diff. versions. Unknown. AmFP; AS
Trail up Wu Gorge, The. Sun Yün-feng, tr. fr. Chinese by Kenneth Rexroth and Ling Chung. BoWoP; PBWP
Trailing her father, bearing his hand axe. Goose. Richard Emil Braun. NoAM
Trailing on the wind. Saigyo Hoshi, tr. by Geoffrey Bownas and Anthony Thwaite. PeBJV
Trailing on the wind. Saigyo, tr. fr. Japanese by Burton Watson. Fr. Sixty-four Tanka. FCEI
Train, The. Alan Brownjohn. OxBTC

Train, The. Mary Elizabeth Coleridge. BoTP
Train, The. Antonio Machado, tr. fr. Spanish by Perry Higman. LPSS
Train. Ken Smith. EAS
Train, The. Unknown, tr. by D. F. van der Merwe. TTY
Train: Abstraction. Genevieve Taggard. WPE
Train at night, A. Night Train. Adrien Stoutenburg. PDV
Train Butcher, The. Thomas Hornsby Ferril. GoYe
Train from out the castle drew, The. Marmion and Douglas. Sir Walter Scott. Fr. Marmion, VI. OHFP
Train has come to rest and ceased its creaking, The. La Máquina a Houston. Edward Dorn. PoM
Train has stopped for no apparent reason, The. En Route. Duncan Campbell Scott. NOBC; OBCV
Train is a dragon that roars through the dark, A. A Modern Dragon. Rowena Bastin Bennett. PDV; RAR
Train is hounded, like an exile's heart, The. In the Train. Itzig Manger, tr. by Leonard Wolf. PeBMYV
Train Is Off the Track, The. Unknown. AmFP
Train Journey. Judith Wright. PBWP
Train of Religion, The, sel. Martin Farquhar Tupper. "How beautiful their feet." FaBoCo
Train Out, The. Sydney Lea. MAYP
Train Ride. John Wheelwright. VGW
Train Runs Late to Harlem, The. Conrad Kent Rivers. IDB; PoBA
Train shot through the dark, The. Return. Seamus Deane. BIrV
Train Song. Fiona Kidman. PeNZ
Train Song. Diane Siebert. RHPC
Train, The! The twelve o'clock for paradise. Harold Monro. Fr. Week-End, I. MoBrPo
Train to Dublin. Louis MacNeice. FaBCIP
Train to Glasgow, The. Wilma Horsburgh. OnUR
Train to Hell, The. Monique Buri, tr. fr. French by Serge Gavronsky. DMF
Train track distances reflect with the chill light of signals. Railroad Thieves. Berish Weinstein, tr. by Leonard Wolf. PeBMYV
Train Tune. Louise Bogan. RR
Train Will Be at Least an Hour Late, The. Sandro Penna, tr. fr. Italian by W. S. Di Piero. PFI
Train will come tomorrow year, The. The Train. Alan Brownjohn. OxBTC
Train Window. Robert Finch. OBCV
Train Wreck, The. Marcia Southwick. PPR
Training. Herrera S. Demetrio, tr. fr. Spanish by Dudley Fitts. TTY
Training for the Apocalypse. Gloria Frym. UL
Training I received did not apply because. Nerves. David Huddle. Fr. Tour of Duty. Son
Training on the Shore. Shlomo Vinner, tr. fr. Hebrew by Laya Firestone and Howard Schwartz. VWA
Trains. Amal Dunqul, tr. fr. Arabic by Sharif Elmusa and Thomas G. Ezzy. MAP
Trains. James S. Tippett. FaPON
Trains, The. "Seumas O'Sullivan." BoTP
Trains. Hope Shepherd. BoTP
Train's french horn sighs, sheds a few tears, The. To I. Lavrentevaya. Natalya Gorbanyevskaya, tr. by Daniel Weissbort. BoWoP
Trains Made of Stone. Ray A. Young Bear. CDW
Trains ran through the eleven, The. The Dance of the Elephants. Michael S. S. Harper. LCAP
Trains roll over my heart, The. The Ninth Telegram ("Trains roll over my heart.") Abd al-Aziz al-Maqalih, tr. fr. Arabic by Lena Jayyusi and Christopher Middleton. Fr. Telegrams of Tenderness for Sanaa. MAP
Trains travel on a two-railed course. Trains. Amal Dunqul, tr. by Sharif Elmusa and Thomas G. Ezzy. MAP
Trala Trala Trala Le-la. William Carlos Williams. OFD
Tram-car full, The. Unknown, tr. by Geoffrey Bownas and Anthony Thwaite. PeBJV
Tramontana at Lerici. Charles Tomlinson. GTBS-P
Tramp. Richard Hughes. MoBrPo
Tramp, The. Ben King. AnAmPo
Tramp Miner's Song. Unknown. AmFP
Tramp, Tramp, Tramp, Keep on a-Tramping. Unknown. AS
Trample! trample! went the roan. The Cavalier's Escape. George Walter Thornbury. FaBoBe; GN
Trampwoman's Tragedy, A. Thomas Hardy. BeLS; NAEL-2; OBNC; OBNV
Tramway climbs from Merthyr to Dowlais, The. The Deluge 1939. Saunders Lewis, tr. by Gwyn Morgan. OBWVE
Tramways run away. Late Evening. Judah Leib Teller, tr. by Benjamin and Barbara Harshav. AYP
Trance. Mary Ursula Bethell. ATNZ

Tranquil above the rapids, rocks, and shoals. Richard Monckton Milnes. *Fr.* The Burden of Egypt. OBTV

Tranquil waters slept 'neath nature's smile, The. Noonday Thought. Henrietta Cordelia Ray. *Fr.* A Group of Musings. CBWP-3

Tranquility as his breath, his eye a camera. Observation Car and Cigar. William Stafford. LCAP

Transaction. A. R. Ammons. HCAP; PoA

Transcendence. Richard Hovey. WGRP

Transcendence of God, The. Milton. *Fr.* Samson Agonistes. OBS

Transcendentalism. *Unknown.* NA

Transcripts from Nature, *sels.* "Fiona Macleod." FM
    Eagle, The.
    Fireflies.
    Rookery at Sunrise, The.
    Wasp, The.

Transfiguration. Djuna Barnes. EAS

Transfiguration, The. Robert Herrick. CaPo

Transfiguration, The. Edwin Muir. OxBS

Transfiguration of Beauty, The. Michelangelo, *tr. fr. Italian by* John Addington Symonds. AWP

Transfigured. Sarah Morgan Bryan Piatt. AA

Transfigured Bird. James Merrill. MoAB

Transfigured Night. Ralph Gustafson. MoCV

Transfixing muscles and blood. Judgment of the Light. Aimé Césaire, *tr. by* Michael Benedikt. POS

Transformation. Lewis Alexander. CDC; PoNe

Transformation. Quincy Troupe. CNA

Transformation Scene. Constance Carrier. FYAP; GoYe

Transformations. Thomas Hardy. PPP; RB; TEP

Transformations. Joy Harjo. HATNAP

Transformations. Orkhan Muyassar, *tr. fr. Arabic by* Lena Jayyusi *and* Samuel Hazo. MAP

Transformations. Tadeusz Rozewicz, *tr. fr. Polish by* Czeslaw Milosz. PwPP

Transfusion. Merrill Moore. PoA

Transience. John Armstrong. *Fr.* The Art of Preserving Health. NOEC

Transient Americans. Gifts. Karen Snow. FYAP

Transient as a Rose. John Lydgate. MeEL

Transient city, marvellously fair, A. Buffalo. Florence Earle Coates. PAH

"Transients Welcome." Gregory Orr. AnAn

Transit. Margaret Avison. FaBoWP

Transit. John Berryman. AnAn

Transit. Adrienne Rich. NoP

Transit. Richard Wilbur. DiPo; LCAP

Transition. May Sarton. NePoAm

Translated into language it is something like this. The Voice. Judith Herzberg, *tr. by* Shirley Kaufman. VWA

Translated once. James Weigel, Jr. *Fr.* Testaments, V. TSM

Translated Way, The. Franklin P. Adams. FiBHP

Translating. Ruth Whitman. VWA

Translation. Roy Fuller. NOBE; OxBTC

Translation. Rika Lesser. PoA

Translation. Howard Nemerov. CRP

Translation. Anne Spencer. BANP

Translation From, A. Fred Levinson. AmPA

Translation from Petrarch. Petrarch, *tr. fr. Italian by* Sir Thomas Wyatt. SiPS

Translation from Petrarch, A. Petrarch. *See* Sonnets to Laura: To Laura in Death.

Translation from Walter von der Vogelweide, A. Walther von der Vogelweide, *tr. fr.* by J. M. Synge. MoBrPo

Translation into the Original. Jack Gilbert. NPGG

Translation is man's deep, continual task. Required Course. Frances Stoakley Lankford. GoYe

Translation of a South American Ode. Goldsmith. NOIV

Translation of Lines by Benserade. Samuel Johnson, *after the French of* Isaac Benserade. FaBoEE

Translations. Patricia Y. Ikeda. BrSi

Translations. Wing Tek Lum. BrSi

Translations. Adrienne Rich. WPOW

Translations from the English. George Starbuck. VGW

Translator attempted to bare things unsaid, The. A Lesson in Translation. Gabriel Preil, *tr. by* Howard Schwartz. VWA

Translator to Translated. Ezra Pound. FaBoEE

Translucent green on the wall, a dance of leaves. The Green Afternoon. Henry Rago. VGW

Transmigration. Mekeel McBride. NAmP

Transmissions. Shin Dong-jip, *tr. fr. Korean by* Koh Chang-soo. ACKP

Transparent Man, The. Anthony Hecht. BLA; FYAP

Transport. William Meredith. WaP

Transubstantiation. Gary Geddes. NOBC

Trapped Fly, A. Robert Herrick. *See* Amber Bead, The.

Trapped Hare, The. Basil Dowling. ATNZ

Trapped me in ice. No, not one chink is gaping. Ennui. Peter Viereck. NYBP

Trapped Mouse. Julia Cunningham. TSS

Trappers have collected their rabbit traps, The. Meeting Trappers on the Road in Heavy Snow. Li K'ai-hsien, *tr. by* Jonathan Chaves. CoBLCP

Trapping fairies in West Virginia. Gelett Burgess. FaBoNo

Trappists. Antonin Artaud, *tr. fr. French by* Michael Benedikt. POS

Tras Os Montes, *sel.* L. E. Sissman.
    "Whether the rivals for a wife and mother can." DiL

Trash Men, The. Charles Bukowski. NoP

Traubel, Traubel, boil and bubble. I Like to Sing Also. John Updike. FiBHP

Trauma. Brad Leithauser. InPK

Travail of Passion, The. W. B. Yeats. TrCP

Travel. Gyoko, *tr. fr. Japanese by* Steven D. Carter. WFTW

Travel. Edna St. Vincent Millay. FaPON; MoShBr; OBCA; PDV; RHPC

Travel. Robert Louis Stevenson. BrPo; FaBoCh; FaPON; MoShBr

Travel Poem, A. Teika, *tr. fr. Japanese by* Steven D. Carter. WFTW

Travel Song. Hugo von Hofmannsthal, *tr. fr. German by* Charles Wharton Stork. TrJP

Travel was homespun, The. Distance of a City. James Berry. PBCV

Traveler, The. Mir Babbar Ali Anis, *tr. fr. Urdu by* Ahmed Ali. GoT

Traveler. Miyazawa Kenji, *tr. fr. Japanese by* Hiroaki Sato. FCEI

Traveler, The. Vachel Lindsay. MoAmPo

Traveler, The. Cleopatra Mathis. PPR

Traveler, The. Duane Niatum. HATNAP

Traveler, The. *Unknown.* AmFP

Traveler, a traveler, Tzu-mei his name, A. Tu Fu, *tr. fr. Chinese by* Burton Watson. *Fr.* Seven Songs Written During the Ch'ien-yüan Era, 1. CoBCP

Traveler at Night Writes His Thoughts, A. Tu Fu, *tr. fr. Chinese by* Burton Watson. CoBCP

Traveler has come from south of the Yangtze, A. The Traveler's Moon. Po Chü-i, *tr. by* Burton Watson. CoBCP

Traveler I saw yesterday, The. Natsume Seibi, *tr. fr. Japanese by* Hiroaki Sato. *Fr.* Twenty-seven Hokku. FCEI

Traveler, I've been through a thousand changes, A. Chin Nung, *tr. fr. Chinese by* Jonathan Chaves. *Fr.* On New Year's Eve of the Year Hsin-wei. CoBLCP

Traveler journeys through the Wu-hsia Gorge, A. A Stretch of Cloud over Mount Wu. Li Hsün, *tr. by* Lois Fusek. ATF

Traveler on a dusty road, A. Little and Great. Charles MacKay. PoLF

Travel[l]er; or, A Prospect of Society, The, *sels.* Goldsmith.
    Britain. NOEC
    First, Best Country, The. GN
    On Freedom and Ambition. NOIV
    "Remote, unfriended, melancholy, slow." BIrV
    "Turn we to survey." OBTV

Traveler stands in the freezing cold, The. Silver. Ferenc Juhász, *tr. by* David Wevill. MHuP

Travel[l]er take heed for journeys undertaken in the dark of the year. October Journey. Margaret Abigail Walker. AmNP; IDB; PoBA; PoNe

Traveler who wants to stay, The. Inscribed on the Wall at the Temple of the Auspicious Talisman. Tao-chi, *tr. by* Jonathan Chaves. CoBLCP

Traveler will rise at midnight, The. Presented to Wang Wen-hsi. Ho Ching-ming, *tr. by* Jonathan Chaves. CoBLCP

Travelers/ are all up and on their way, The. Abutsu the Nun, *tr. by* Steven D. Carter. WFTW

Travel[l]er's Curse after Misdirection. Robert Graves, *tr. fr. Welsh.* BrPo; CMoP; FiBHP; HoPM; LiTM; MoAB; MoBrPo; NBLV; TW

Traveler's heart has a hundred thoughts already, The. At Parting. Ho Sun, *tr. by* Burton Watson. CoBCP

Traveler's homesickness, sad and lonely. Thinking of the Past on an Autumn Night at Tz'u-jen Temple. Wang Shih-chen, *tr. by* Jonathan Chaves. CoBLCP

Traveler's life is full of difficulties, The. The Traveler. Mir Babbar Ali Anis, *tr. by* Ahmed Ali. GoT

Traveler's Moon, The. Po Chü-i, *tr. fr. Chinese by* Burton Watson. CoBCP

Traveler's Night, A. P'eng Sun-yü, *tr. fr. Chinese by* William H. Nienhauser, Jr.. WFTU

Traveler's pillow,/ bundled up, undone, A. Kyogoku Tamekane, *tr. fr. Japanese by* Burton Watson. *Fr.* Twenty-three Tanka. FCEI

Traveler's sleeves fluttered by an autumn wind, A. Teika, tr. fr. Japanese by Hiroaki Sato. Fr. Eighty-four Tanka. FCEI
Traveler's Thoughts. Tu Hsün-ho, tr. fr. Chinese by Burton Watson. CoBCP
Travelers who came that day to Pisa's Baptistry. Echo. Elizabeth Stanton Hardy. GoYe
Traveling America. "Jan Struther." AmFN
Traveling by Boat, sel. Wang T'ing-hsiang, tr. fr. Chinese by Jonathan Chaves.
   "At Arrow Rapids, the water splashes foam." CoBLCP
Traveling by Boat at Shun-ch'ang. Hsü Chung-hsing, tr. fr. Chinese by Jonathan Chaves. CoBLCP
Traveling down the Yodo River on a Winter Night. Fujii Chikugai, tr. fr. Chinese by Burton Watson. JLIC-2
Traveling Early through a Snowy Valley. Yü Chi, tr. fr. Chinese by Jonathan Chaves. CoBLCP
Traveling fair pitched by our pasture gate, A. One-Night Fair. Nancy Price. GOYP
Traveling for days to reach you. Journey. Diane Wakoski. IHMS
Traveling in the City, sels. David Avidan, tr. fr. Hebrew by Warren Bargad and Stanley F. Chyet. IP
   Another Catalogue Item. Fr. 12.
   End of the Trip. Fr. 19.
   Not Allowed to Make a Movie in This Country. Fr. 18.
   Three Self-Plagiarisms. Fr. 4.
Traveling Light. Alice Fulton. NAmP
Traveling Onion, The. Naomi Shihab Nye. MT
Traveling past a Market Town. Shotetsu, tr. fr. Japanese by Steven D. Carter. WFTW
Traveling sky goes landward, the blind mass, The. Headland. Brewster Ghiselin. PoA
Traveling theatres of the seasons will have played out my life, The. Curtain Curtain. André Breton, tr. by Michael Benedikt. POS
Traveling through Ports That Begin with "M." Christy Sheffield Sanford. UL
Traveling through the Dark. William Stafford. CAPP; CoAP; GrPl; HAP; HeIP; InPK; LCAP; LiTM; NIP; NoAM; NoP; SM; SoSe; WeW
Traveling to Town. Duane Big Eagle. AiP
Traveller, The. John Berryman. PoA; VGW
Traveller, A. J. R. Rowland. CBAP
Traveller, The. Allen Tate. LiTM
Traveller, A. Unknown. WGRP
Traveller for many long years I have been, A. The Widow That Keeps the Cock Inn. Unknown. CoMu
Traveller Has Regrets, The. G. S. Fraser. OBTV
Traveller in bed, The. Unknown, tr. by Geoffrey Bownas and Anthony Thwaite. PeBJV
Traveller on the skirt of Sarum's Plain, A. Salisbury Plain and Stonehenge. Wordsworth. Fr. Guilt and Sorrow. FaBoPP
Traveller wended the wilds among, A. The Quaker's Meeting. Samuel Lover. CenHV
Traveller who crossed Les Halles at summer's end, The. Sunflower. André Breton, tr. by Edouard Roditi. RHTwFP
Traveller who walks a temperate zone, A. Against Romanticism. Kingsley Amis. NePoEA; NoAM
Travellers. Arthur St. John Adcock. BoTP
Travellers, The. Mark A. de Wolfe Howe. AA
Travellers, The. Elizabeth Spires. KS
Traveller's Guide to Antarctica. Adrien Stoutenburg. NYBP
Traveller's Return, The. Unknown. BoTP
Travellers Turning Over Borders. Basil Ransome. BXAP
Travelling. Dorothy Graddon. BoTP
Travelling. Denis Johnson. NAmP
Travelling,/ where darkness hauls the world. Tanks. Rhyll McMaster. CBAP
Travelling Backward. Gene Baro. NYBP
Travelling Companions. Richard Armour. GrPl
Travelling eye has seen its many birds, The. Many Birds. Anne Welsh. PeSA
Travelling in the Family. Carlos Drummond de Andrade, tr. fr. Portuguese by Elizabeth Bishop. ATCBP
Travelling Out, The. Lucile Adler. IHMS; NYBP
Travelling Post Office, The. Andrew Barton Paterson. CBAP
Travelling south, leaves overflow the farms. The Puritan on His Honeymoon. Robert Bly. FF; NePoEA
Travelogue. Ernst Jandl, tr. fr. German by Beth Bjorklund. CoAuP
Travelogue. Nishiwaki Junzaburo, tr. fr. Japanese by Hiroaki Sato. FCEI
Travelogue for Exiles. Karl Shapiro. MoAmPo; TrJP
Travels with the Band-Aid Army. Lance Henson. VoR
Travis Licked Me. Bruce Bennett. SoTCo
Travis, the Kid Was All Heart. Terry Stokes. AmPA

Tray. Robert Browning. FM
Tray, The. Thomas Cole. NePoAm
Treacherous monster is the shark, A. The Shark. Lord Alfred Bruce Douglas. RHPC
Treacherous words,—tearing my thought across. Nowhere. John Berryman. AnAn
Tread back—and back, the lewd and lay ("Odi profanum vulgus"). Horace, tr. fr. Latin. Fr. Odes, III, 1. OBVE, tr. by Gerard Manley Hopkins.
   ("Hence ye prophane; I hate ye all.") OBVE, tr. by Abraham Cowley, 2 sts.
   (Profane, The.) AWP, tr. by Abraham Cowley.
Tread lightly here, for here, 'tis said. An Epitaph on a Robin Redbreast. Samuel Rogers. FaBoEE; FM; PBBP
Tread lightly, she is near. Requiescat. Oscar Wilde. BrPo; EBVV; FL; InvP; MoBrPo; OBNC; TrGrPo
Tread not the earth where lies her youthful form. Mrs. E. Cohrs Brown. Mary Weston Fordham. CBWP-2
Tread not the snow. Mikata Shami. Fr. Manyo Shu. Ma
Tread softly; bid a solemn music sound. Epitaph. J. B. Morton. FaBoEE
Treading a field I saw afar. Death on a Live Wire. Michael Baldwin. MoBS
Treading mid-river. Unknown, tr. by Geoffrey Bownas and Anthony Thwaite. PeBJV
Treading pigeon arcs his wings, The. The Ivory Bed. Winfield Townley Scott. ErPo
Treadmill prisoner of that century, The. Scene with Figure. Babette Deutsch. TrJP
Treason doth never prosper [or Treason never prospers]; what's the reason? Of Treason. Sir John Harington. FaBoEE; FF; InPK; OxBoLi
   (On Treason.) FiBHP
   (Treason.) FaBoCo
   ("Treason never prospers; what's the reason?") InvP
Treason of Sand. Hemda Roth, tr. fr. Hebrew by Mariana Potasman. VWA
Treason's Last Device. Edmund Clarence Stedman. PAH
Treasure. Lucilius, tr. fr. Greek by William Cowper. AWP
Treasure, A. Reed Whittemore. NePoEA
Treasure Hunt. Robert Penn Warren. NoP
Treasure Island, sel. Robert Louis Stevenson.
   Pirate Ditty. NOBVV
Treasure-like, I found her in a field. The Meeting. Pierre Louÿs, tr. fr. French. Fr. Chansons de Bilitis. PeHV
Treasures. Bible, N.T. Fr. St. Matthew, VI: 19-21. TrGrPo
Treaties. A. R. Ammons. HCAP
Treatise of the Subtle Body, A. Salamis. Lawrence Durrell. NYBP
Treatment by old Mr. Mears, The. Unknown. PeHV
Treaty-Trip from Shulus Reservation. Patrick Lane. NeAC
Trebetherick. Sir John Betjeman. CMoP
Tree. Antonin Artaud, tr. fr. French by Michael Benedikt. POS
Tree, The. Björnstjerne Björnson, tr. fr. Norwegian. FaPON; OHIP
Tree, The. Ilya Grigoryevich Ehrenburg, tr. fr. Russian by Babette Deutsch. TrJP
Tree, The. John Freeman. BoTP
Tree, The. Ezra Pound. CMoP
Tree, The. Joel Sloman. VGW
Tree, The. Jones Very. GN; OHIP
Tree, The. Pat Wilson. ATNZ
Tree ages in the tree, it is summer, The. The Tree, the Lamp. Yves Bonnefoy, tr. by Anthony Rudolf. RHTwFP
Tree and Boulder. Yün Shou-p'ing, tr. fr. Chinese by Irving Lo. WFTU
Tree and the Bird: A Duet, The. Lo Men, tr. fr. Chinese by Dominic Cheung. IFON
Tree and the Chaff, The. Bible, O.T. See Psalms: Psalm I ("Blessed is the man.").
Tree and the Lady, The. Thomas Hardy. MoAB; MoBrPo
Tree ascending there. O pure transcension, A. Rainer Maria Rilke, tr. fr. German by James Blair Leishman. Fr. Sonnets to Orpheus. TOF; UnS
Tree at My Window. Robert Frost. BLPL; BoNaP; FaBoBe; MoAB; MoAmPo; NoAM; OxBA; TAP; TrGrPo
Tree beside the synagogue atones, A. Yom Kippur. Linda Pastan. VWA
Tree Birthdays. Mary Carolyn Davies. OHIP
Tree by the river, A. The Mirror. Chan Ch'e, tr. by Dominic Cheung. IFON
Tree Celebrates the River, The. Leah Goldberg, tr. fr. Hebrew by Bernhard Frank. MHeP
Tree Design, A. Arna Bontemps. CDC
Tree earth and sky. Time and the Child. Hone Tuwhare. ATNZ

Tree-Felling, Upper Junction Road. Brian Turner. ATNZ

Tree Ferns. Stanley Plumly. SM

Tree Frog, The. John Travers Moore. RHPC

Tree has entered my hands, The. A Girl. Ezra Pound. MoAB; MoAmPo

Tree I know where a love-bird's lighted, A. Open the Door. *Malay Oral Tradition, tr. by* R. J. Wilkinson *and* R. O. Winstedt. WTO

Tree in December. Melville Cane. MoAmPo

Tree in the Garden, The. Christine Chandler. BoTP

Tree in the Wood, The. *Unknown.* AmFP

Tree is more than a shadow, A. A Tree Design. Arna Bontemps. CDC

Tree leaves flutter, and autumn begins. Early Autumn. Onitsura, *tr. fr. Japanese by* Hiroaki Sato. *Fr.* Twenty-three Hokku. FCEI

Tree let your arms fall. No Ordinary Sun. Hone Tuwhare. ATNZ; PeNZ

Tree Marriage. William Meredith. GLP

Tree of Death, The. Claude Vigée, *tr. fr. French by* J. R. Le Master *and* Kenneth L. Beaudoin. VWA

Tree of deepest root is found, The. The Three Warnings. Hester Lynch Thrale. BeLS

Tree of Diana, The. Alejandra Pizarnik, *tr. fr. Spanish by* Yishai Tobin. VWA

Tree of Faith its bare dry boughs must shed, The. Adjustment. Whittier. WGRP

Tree of Hatred, The. Shmuel Moreh, *tr. fr. Arabic by the author.* VWA

Tree of intense, The. Ode to the Watermelon. Pablo Neruda, *tr. by* Robert Bly. EAS; NU

Tree of Knowledge. Edward Lowbury. VWA

Tree of Knowledge, The. Lizelia Augusta Jenkins Moorer. CBWP-3

Tree of Liberty, The. Burns. FaBoPV

Tree of Life Is Also a Tree of Fire, The. Gerda Norvig. VWA

Tree of roses. The water crashed headlong. Peter Levi. TOF

Tree of Silence, The. Vassar Miller. NePoEA-2

Tree Old Woman. Samuel Makidemewabe, *tr. fr. Cree Indian by* Howard Norman. STP

Tree, paddock, river: plan. Inheritance. Kendrick Smithyman. ATNZ

Tree Party. Louis MacNeice. FaBCIP; OxBTC

Tree-planting. Samuel Francis Smith. OHIP

Tree Planting. *Unknown.* OHIP

Tree reddens in the frost; the setting sun chills, A. Sent to Wu Tzu-lü Who Wished to See My Recent Lyrics. Hsiang Hung-tso, *tr. by* Irving Lo. WFTU

Tree, says good Swedenborg, is a close relative of man, The. Into the Tree. Czeslaw Milosz, *tr. by* Robert Hass. AnAn

Tree-searing wind: wrinkles of age. Taigi, *tr. fr. Japanese by* Hiroaki Sato. *Fr.* Twenty-nine Hokku. FCEI

Tree Sleeps in the Winter, The. Norman H. Russell. STE

Tree still bends over the lake, The. Winter. Sheila Wingfield. EnLoPo

Tree Surgeon. Judith Herzberg, *tr. fr. Dutch by* Ria Leigh Loohuizen. DuIn

Tree Tag. Mary E. Caragher. GoYe

Tree, the Lamp, The. Yves Bonnefoy, *tr. fr. French by* Anthony Rudolf. RHTwFP

Tree the tempest with a crash of wood, The. On a Tree Fallen across the Road. Robert Frost. RB

Tree to Flute. Anna Hajnal, *tr. fr. Hungarian by* Jascha Kessler. FOC; VWA

Tree Toad, The ("The tree Toad is a creature neat"). Monica Shannon. FaPON

Tree Toad ("A tree toad loved a she-toad"). *Unknown.* NTCP, *ad. by* Stephanie Calmenson

Tree, too, wants to bend over, The. 3 Stanzas about a Tree. Marvin Bell. Prf

Tree-topped Hill. *Unknown.* NOEC

Tree turned yellow all over, The. Images from the Midwest. Georgi Belev. WCI

Treefrog winks without springing. Drawings of the Song Animals. Duane Niatum. HATNAP

Treehouse, The. James A. Emanuel. AmNP; BPo; PoBA

Trees. Bliss Carman. OHIP

Trees, The. Samuel Valentine Cole. OHIP

Trees. Sara Coleridge. BOTP; OHIP; OxBChV; RHPC

Trees. Walter de la Mare. OHIP

Trees. Ted Hughes. NYBP

Trees. Joyce Kilmer. BLPA; FaBoBe; FaFP; FaPON; FPL; OHFP; WBLP; WGRP

Trees, The. Lucy Larcom. OHIP

Trees, The. Philip Larkin. AnAn; Mes; NoAM

Trees, The. Bill Manhire. PeNZ

Trees, The. Christopher Morley. OHIP

Trees. Howard Nemerov. BoNaP; Psk

Trees, The. Adrienne Rich. CoAP; NOBA; WPE

Trees. Jutta Schutting, *tr. fr. German by* Beth Bjorklund. CoAuP

Trees/ and the wind. The Hand. Brian Fawcett. NOBC

Trees across the street have loved me, The. Midwinter Stars. Roberta Hill Whiteman. STE

Trees along the River, The. Luci Tapahonso. GOS

Trees along this city street, The. City Trees. Edna St. Vincent Millay. FaPON

Trees and Cattle. James Dickey. NePoEA-2

Trees and Evening Sky. N. Scott Momaday. CDW

Trees, and What They Raise, The. Lorrie Goldensohn. NAmP

Trees are afraid to put forth buds, The. A Backward Spring. Thomas Hardy. PPP

Trees are a'ivied, the leaves they are green, The. The Bonnie Laddie's Lang a-Growin.' *Unknown.* OxBS

Trees are ancient, thick with patterns of moss, The. Hsü Chung-hsing, *tr. fr. Chinese by* Jonathan Chaves. *Fr.* Following the Rhymes of Magistrate Liu's Poems. CoBLCP

Trees are cages for them: water holds its breath. Stars and Planets. Norman MacCaig. OxBSP

Trees are coming into leaf, The. The Trees. Philip Larkin. AnAn; Mes; NoAM

Trees are dead, The. Mood. David Gascoyne. FL

Trees Are Down, The. Charlotte Mew. BoNaP; BrRo; MoAB; MoBrPo; TrCP; WPE; WPOW

Trees are God's great alphabet, The. A B C's in Green. Leonora Speyer. OHIP

Trees are green in the late spring, The. Song of the Wine Spring. Mao Wen-hsi, *tr. by* Lois Fusek. ATF

Trees are growing, The. The Princess Who Fled to the Castle. Francis Landy. VWA

Trees are in their autumn beauty, The. The Wild Swans at Coole. W. B. Yeats. ChTr; CMoP; FaBoPP; FaBoRV; FM; HeIP; InPS; MoAB; MoBrPo; MoP; NAEL-2; NoAM; NoAM; NoP; PBBP; PPP; SoSe; SOTW; TEP; UnPo

Trees are not made of bluebirds, The. Late Fall. René Altmann, *tr. by* Beth Bjorklund. CoAuP

Trees are tall, but the moon small, The. Hide and Seek. Robert Graves. NTCP

Trees are tracing in the waning haze, The. Evening. Victor van Vriesland, *tr. by* Adrian J. Barnouw. TrJP

Trees are uncurling their first, The. Married Love. Liz Rosenberg. NIP

Trees are waving to and fro, The. Just Like This. D. A. Olney. BoTP

Trees ask me, The. Who Am I? Felice Holman. RFM; TSS

Trees at Night. Helene Johnson. BlSi

Trees at the Arctic Circle. Alfred W. Purdy. NoP

Trees both in hills and plaines, in plenty be. William Wood. SCAP

Trees break their silence, The. Let the Roots Speak. Yusuf al-Khal, *tr. by* Abdullah al-Udhari. MPAW

Tree's early leaf-buds were bursting their brown, The. The Tree. Björnstjerne Björnson. FaPON; OHIP

Trees, Effigies, Moving Objects, *sels.* Allen Curnow. PeNZ
    Family Matter, A. *Fr.* VII.
    Lone Kauri Road ("First time I looked seaward, westward"). *Fr.* I.
    Lone Kauri Road ("Too many splashes, too many gashes"). *Fr.* XVII.

Tree's green explains what a light means, The. Notes for Echo Lake 5. Michael Palmer. NPGG

Trees have been born. In Memoriam Paul Celan. Gad Hollander. VWA

Trees in groves,/ Kine in droves. Saadi. Emerson. OxBA

Trees in the Garden. D. H. Lawrence. CMoP; MoAB; MoBrPo; NoP

Trees in the Garden Rained Flowers, The. Stephen Crane. *Fr.* War Is Kind, XXVI. LiTM; PrIm

Trees in the old days used to stand. Carentan O Carentan. Louis Simpson. CoAP; MoBS; NOBA; OBWP; PoE; PrIm; RB

Trees in the Road, The. James Still. GrPl

Trees inside are moving out into the forest, The. The Trees. Adrienne Rich. CoAP; NOBA; WPE

Trees learn music from the birds they hold, The. Wood Music. Ethel King. GoYe

Tree's leaves may be ever so good, A. Leaves Compared with Flowers. Robert Frost. NOBA

Trees, like great jade elephants, The. John Gould Fletcher. *Fr.* Irradiations, III *or* VII [X]. MoAmPo

Trees Lose Parts of Themselves Inside a Circle of Fog. Francis Ponge, *tr. fr. French by* Robert Bly. NU

Trees of Life, The. Jones Very. NOBA

Trees of the elder lands, The. St. Anthony's Township. Gilbert Sheldon. CH

Trees of the same age. Masayori, *tr. by* Steven D. Carter. WFTW

Trees on a Frosty Night. Mairtin O Direain, *tr. fr. Irish by the author.* TIRV

Trees on the Calais Road. Edmund Blunden. BrPo

Trees on the hospital lawn, The. University Hospital, Boston. Mary Oliver. CAPP

Trees Once Walked and Stood. Joshua Tan Pai, *tr. fr. Hebrew by* Yishai Tobin. VWA

Trees shake gentle skaters out. Cadenza. Miriam Waddington. CaP

Trees So High, The. *Unknown.* OxBoLi

Trees They Do Grow High, The. *Unknown.* OBET
(Still Growing.) FaBoBa

Trees were taller than the night, The. The Robber. W. J. Turner. MoBrPo

Trees, Who Are Distant. Bertram J. Warr. CaP

Treetalk and windsong are. Sugarfields. Barbara Mahone. CNA; PoBA

Treetops. Marvin Bell. AmPA; DiL

Tregardock. Sir John Betjeman. FaBoPP

Treizane. Sir Thomas Wyatt. *See* If in the World There Be More Woe.

Trekking back along the high trail. The Vision. Kitty Tsui. *Fr.* Red Rock Canyon, Summer 1977. ER

Trellie. Lance Jeffers. CNA; FB

Trellis. Laura Chester. NPGG

Trellis, shorn of grapes, The. Song of an Autumn Night. Chao Meng-fu, *tr. by* Jonathan Chaves. CoBLCP

Tremayne. Donald Justice. BLA; MT

Trembling. Aliza Shenhar, *tr. fr. Hebrew by* Linda Zisquit. VWA

Trembling before Thine Awful Throne. Augustus Hillhouse. AH
(Forgiveness of Sins a Joy Unknown to Angels.) AA

Trembling I write my dream, and recollect. Philip Freneau. *Fr.* The House of Night. NAAL-1, *much abr..*

Trembling November winds. Nocturnal Sounds. Kattie M. Cumbo. BlSi

Trembling old men are stamm'ring. Lines on Carmen Sylva. Emma Lazarus. TrJP

Trembling, sand-dollar. Grunion. Wendy Rose. CDW

Trembling the spectres glide, and plaintive vent. Homer, *tr. fr. Greek by* Pope. *Fr.* Odyssey, XXIV. OBVE

Trembling train clings to the leaning wall, The. Moonrise in the Rockies. Ella Higginson. AA

Tremolo. Joan Shaddox Isom. GOS

Tremor, like magnitude, shook the world, A. Coup d'Etat. Ruth Herschberger. LiTA

Tremors at Balvano, The. Norman Williams. KS

Trench. Stephen Pett. GrPl

Trenchtown Rock. Bob Marley. PBCV

Trent, The. Michael Drayton. *Fr.* The Shepherd's Sirena. FaBoPP; OBEV; PoEL-2
(Jovial Shepheard's Song, The.) PoEL-2
(Sirena.) OBEV

Trent Again, The. Michael Drayton. *Fr.* Polyolbion, Sixth and Twentieth Song. FaBoPP

Trenton and Princeton. *Unknown.* PAH

Trepidation of the Druids. Wordsworth. *Fr.* Ecclesiastical Sonnets. Son

Tresco. Geoffrey Grigson. FaBoPP

Trespass. Robert Frost. FaBV

Tretis of the Tua Mariit Wemen and the Wedo, The ("Apon the midsummer evin, mirriest of Michtis."), *sel.* William Dunbar. GoTS; OxBS
"Bot of ane bowrd in to bed I sall yow breif yit." EBEV

Tri-colored flower. Leave-Taking. Giosuè Carducci, *tr. by* William Jay Smith. CT; PFI

Tri tri tri. So Let Me Have My Fun. Aldo Palazzeschi, *tr. by* Felix Stefanile. PFI

Triad. Adelaide Crapsey. WPE

Triad, A. Christina Rossetti. NAEL-2; PBWP

Triads. *Unknown, tr. fr. Irish by* Thomas Kinsella. BIrV

Triads of Ireland, The, *sel. Unknown, tr. fr. Old Irish.*
Triads ("Three excellent qualities in narration"). *Tr. by* Thomas Kinsella. BIrV

Trial, The. Longfellow. *Fr.* Giles Corey of the Salem Farms. PAH

Trial, The. Muriel Rukeyser. PoNe

Trial, The. Gershom Scholem, *tr. fr. German.* VWA, *tr. by* Jonathan Griffin

Trial by Jury, *sel.* W. S. Gilbert.
When I, Good Friends, Was Called to the Bar. NAEL-2

Trials of a Tourist. Anne Tibble. FaBoCo; NBLV

Trials that the Saviour bore have paved the golden way, The. Benefits of Sorrow. Lizelia Augusta Jenkins Moorer. CBWP-3

Triangles are commands of God. The Starfish. Robert Peter Tristram Coffin. ImOP

Triangular Field, The. Stephen Dobyns. MAYP

Triangular Legs. A. P. Herbert. NBLV

Triantiwontigongolope, The. C. J. Dennis. AmMo

Tribal Cemetery. Janet Campbell Hale. NOVW

Tribal Memories. Robert Duncan. *Fr.* Passages. NOBA

Tribe Searching, A. Shlomo Reich, *tr. fr. French.* VWA, *tr. by* Mira Reich

Tribes, The. Roy Fuller. LiTM

Tribes of Ching—that's not my home. Wang Ts'an, *tr. fr. Chinese by* Burton Watson. *Fr.* Seven Sorrows, II. CoBCP

Tribulations of an Uneducated Poet in the 1760's, The. James Woodhouse. *Fr.* The Life and Lucubrations of Crispinus Scriblerus. NOEC

Tribute. Eloise Bibb. CBWP-4

Tribute, The. Coventry Patmore. *Fr.* The Angel in the House, I, iv. EBEV; OBNC

Tribute of Grasses, A. Hamlin Garland. AA

Tribute to a Lost Steamer. Mary Weston Fordham. CBWP-2

Tribute to America. Shelley. AiP; OPP

Tribute to Capt. F. W. Dawson. Mary Weston Fordham. CBWP-2

Tribute to Chief Joseph, A. Duane Niatum. NOVW

Tribute to Freckles and Tornado. Jon Bowerman. CowP

Tribute to Grass. John James Ingalls. WBLP

Tribute to Kafka for Someone Taken. Alan Dugan. CAPP

Tribute to Nervous. Kit Robinson. IAT

Tribute to the Angels, *sels.* Hilda Doolittle ("H. D.").
"Ah (you say), this is Holy Wisdom." NoAM
"Every hour, every moment." NoAM
"Invisible, indivisible Spirit." BoWoP
"Not in our time, O Lord." NOBA
"This is no rune nor riddle." InPS
"We have seen her/ the world over." CRP; VGW

Tribute to the Bride and Groom, A. Priscilla Jane Thompson. CBWP-2

Tribute to the Founder, A. Kingsley Amis. NePoEA-2

Tribute to the Memory of the Same Dog. Wordsworth. FM

Tribute to Washington. *Unknown.* OHIP

Trick for Tyburn; or, A Prison Rant, A. *Unknown.* APAS

Trick is, to live your days, The. Advice to My Son. Peter Meinke. Psk

Trick that everyone abhors, A. Rebecca, Who Slammed Doors for Fun and Perished Miserably. Hilaire Belloc. NOBL; SO

Tricked Again. Ridhiana. NBP

Trickle Drops. Walt Whitman. NAAL-1

Tricks. Sharon Olds. TV

Tricks, the wonders of nature, The. Is It Right to Move to the Country? Giovanni Giudici, *tr. by* Lawrence R. Smith. NItP

Trico's Song. John Lyly. *Fr.* Alexander and Campaspe, V, i. EIL; OBSC; PBBP; TrGrPo

Trifle. Georgia Douglas Johnson. AmNP

Trifle for Trafalgar Day, A. Ted Pauker. NOBL

Trifling Women. *Unknown.* AmFP

Trilby. Alice Brown. AA

Trilby, *sel.* George Du Maurier.
Little Work, A. *Fr. pt.* VIII. FaBoBe; PoLF

Trilogy for X, *sels.* Louis MacNeice.
"And love hung still as crystal over the bed." *Fr.* II. CIP; GBL
(And Love Hung Still.) MoBrPo
"When clerks and navvies fondle." *Fr.* I. ErPo
(For X.) BoLoP; EnLoPo

Trim the lamp; polish the lens; draw, one by one, rare coins. Geoffrey Hill. *Fr.* Mercian Hymns, XIII. FaBoMo

Trimdon Grange Explosion, The. Thomas Armstrong. OBET

Trimming the Sails. Vassar Miller. NMM

Trim's Song: The Fair Kitchen-Maid. Sir Richard Steele. *Fr.* The Funeral. OxBSP

Trinità dei Monti. Nelo Risi, *tr. fr. Italian by* Lawrence R. Smith. NItP

Trinity, The. Marian Osborne. CaP

Trinity. Pattiann Rogers. NAmP

Trinity, The. *Unknown.* ACP

Trinity [*or* Trinitee] blessed, deity [*or* deitee] coequal. A Prayer to the Holy Trinity. Richard Stanyhurst. EIL; PoEL-2
(Prayer to the Trinity [*or* Trinitie], A.) EIL; TIRV

Trinity Brethren Attend. I. A. Richards. CRP

Trinity Place. Phyllis McGinley. MoAmPo; OxBSP; SaC

Trinity Sunday. George Herbert. OxBSP

Trinket. Marvin Bell. AnAn

Trio for Two Cats and a Trombone. Dame Edith Sitwell. *Fr.* Façade. NAEL-2; PBWP

Triolet: "All women born are so perverse." Robert Bridges. SeCePo;
   TW
Triolet: "Child Is father to the man, The." Gerard Manley Hopkins. *See*
   "Child Is Father to the Man, The."
Triolet: "She was in love with the same danger." Sandra McPherson.
   SM
Triolet: "When first we met we did not guess." Robert Bridges. BrPo;
   OxBSP
Triolet against Sisters. Phyllis McGinley. OBCA
Trip, The. Emmett Jarrett. NeAC
Trip. Reinhard Priessnitz, *tr. fr. German by* Beth Bjorklund. CoAuP
Trip, The. William Stafford. PCP
Trip it Gipsies, Trip it Fine. Thomas Middleton *and* William Rowley.
   Fr. The Spanish Gipsy [*or* Gypsy]. OBS
Trip on the Staten Island Ferry, A. Audre Lorde. CNA
Trip: San Francisco. Langston Hughes. AmFN
Trip to a Mountain Village, A. Li K'ai-hsien, *tr. fr. Chinese by* Jonathan
   Chaves. CoBLCP
Trip to Four or Five Towns, A. John Logan. CoAP; NNaP
Trip to Hua-yang Mountain, A. Tao-chi, *tr. fr. Chinese by* Jonathan
   Chaves. CoBLCP
Trip to Mountain West Village, A. Lu Yu, *tr. fr. Chinese by* Burton
   Watson. CoBCP
Trip to Paris and Belgium, A, *sel.* Dante Gabriel Rossetti.
   Antwerp to Ghent. OBTV
Trip to the Grand Banks, A. Amos Hanson. AmFP
Trip to the Village of the River of White Sand, A. Tao-chi, *tr. fr.*
   Chinese by Jonathan Chaves. CoBLCP
Trip to Yüeh-lu Temple, A. Li Tung-yang, *tr. fr. Chinese by* Jonathan
   Chaves. CoBLCP
Trip trap in a gap. *Unknown.* GBP
Trip upon trenchers, and dance upon dishes. Mother Goose. NOBL;
   OxNR
Trip with Knives. Armando, *tr. fr. Dutch by* James S. Holmes. DuIn
Tripart. Gayl Jones. BlSi
Triphammer Bridge. A. R. Ammons. NAAL-2; NOBA
Triple Bension, The. Henrietta Cordelia Ray. CBWP-3
Triple-decker and the double-cone, The. Saturday Sundae. Francis
   Reginald Scott. CaP
Triple Feature. Denise Levertov. FF; NoP
Triple Fool, The. John Donne. GBL
Triple Mirror, The. Gloria C. Oden. IHMS
Triple Trouble. Assotto Saint. GLP
Triplets. Michael Brownstein. UL
Trippers and askers surround me. Walt Whitman. *Fr.* Song of Myself,
   IV. UnPo
Trips to Farmington were a special treat. It Was a Special Treat. Luci
   Tapahonso. STE
Triptych. Frank A. Collymore. PBCV
Tristan da Cunha. Roy Campbell. MoBrPo; PeSA
Tristan und Isolt. Gottfried von Strassburg, *tr. fr. German.* OBD
Tristesse d'animal. Lauris Edmond. ATNZ
Tristium, *sels.* Ovid, *tr. fr. Latin.*
   "And here I wish my soul died with my breath." *Fr.* III, 3a, *tr. by*
     Henry Vaughan. OBVE
   "And on this day, which poets unto thee." *Fr.* V, 3, *tr. by* Henry
     Vaughan. OBVE
   "Look, he is superfluous—for of what use was it to be born?." *Fr.*
     XIII, *tr. by* L. R. Lind. NAs
Tristram lies sick to death. Tristram's End. Laurence Binyon. OBMV
Tristram of Lyonesse, *sel.* Swinburne.
   Swimming. GN
Tristram's End. Laurence Binyon. OBMV
Tristram's Song. Tennyson. *Fr.* Idylls of the King: The Last
   Tournament. FaBoRV
Tristrem and the Hunters. *At. to* Thomas of Erceldoune. *Fr.* Sir Tristem.
   OxBS
Trit trot to market to buy a penny doll. *Unknown.* OxNR
Triumph, The. Sidney Lanier. *Fr.* Psalm of the West. PAH
Triumph, The. William Gilmore Simms. Son
Triumph. L. D. Stearns. BLRP
Triumph is at hand, The. The Ladies to Mademoiselle de Scudéry: Ode.
   Anne de La Vigne, *tr. by* Dorothy Backer. DMF
Triumph of Bacchus and Ariadne. Lorenzo de' Medici, *tr. fr. Italian.*
   Fr. Carnival Songs. CTC, *tr. by* Richard Aldington; PFI, *tr. by*
   Lorna de' Lucchi.
Triumph of Beautie Song, The, *sel.* James Shirley.
   "Heigh-ho, what shall a shepheard doe." ErPo
Triumph of Charis, The. Ben Jonson. *Fr.* A Celebration of Charis in
   Ten Lyrick Peeces. CTC; EBEV; EiL; ELP; InvP; JCP; LiTB;
   NOBE; NoP; OBEV; OPOP; PoEL-2; PrIm; SeCP; SeCV-1

(Her Triumph.) CTC; EBEV; EiL; JCP; PoEL-2; PrIm; SeCP;
   SeCV-1
Triumph of Death, The. Shakespeare. *See* Sonnets: LXXI. "No longer
   mourn for me when I am dead."
Triumph of Doubt, The. John Peale Bishop. EaLo
Triumph of Dullness [*or* Dulness], The. Pope. *Fr.* The Dunciad, IV.
   EBEV; FaBoPV; FiP; NOBE; NOEC; NoP; SCV
   (Reign of Chaos, The.) FiP
Triumph of Infidelity, The, *sel.* Timothy Dwight.
   "Here stood Hypocrisy, in sober brown." NOCV
   (Smooth Divine, The.) AA; WGRP
Triumph of Life, The. Shelley. ChER; NAEL-2; OAEL-2; PoEL-4
Triumph of Love. John Hall Wheelock. MoAmPo
Triumph of Peace, The, *sel.* James Shirley.
   Song to the Masquers. OxBSP
Triumph of Sensibility. Sylvia Townsend Warner. MoAB; MoBrPo
Triumph of the Muses over Love, The, *sel.* Pernette Du Guillet, *tr. fr.*
   French by Dorothy Backer.
   Maiden's Lament, A. DMF
Triumph of the Whale, The, *sel.* Charles Lamb.
   "Io! Paean! Io! sing." ImOP
Triumph of Time, The, *sel.* Swinburne.
   I Will Go Back to the Great Sweet Mother. NAEL-2
   (Sea, The.) TrGrPo
Triumph of Vice, The. Pope. *See* Epilogue to the Satires [*or* 1738]:
   Virtue may choose the high or low degree.
Triumphal Chant. Bible, *O.T. Fr.* Exodus, XV: 1-13, 18. TrGrPo
Triumphal March. T. S. Eliot. *Fr.* Coriolan. OBWP; WaaP
Triumphal Ode MCMXXXIX. George Barker. LiTB; WaP
Triumphant Demons stand, and Angels start. The Heart's Abysses.
   Walter Savage Landor. FaBoEE; OBSV
Triumphs. Petrarch, *tr. fr. Italian by* Morris Bishop. OBD
Triumphs of Owen, The. Thomas Gray. EnRP; PoEL-3
Trivia; or, The Art of Walking the Streets of London, *sels.* John Gay.
   About in London. FaBoPP
   Dangers of Foot-ball, The. SD
   "Experienced men, inured to city ways." *Fr.* II. OAEL-1
   Great Frost, The. SeCePo
   "Let due civilities be strictly paid." *Fr.* II. OAEL-1
   London at Night. FaBoPP
   "Where the mob gathers, swiftly shoot along." *Fr.* III. OAEL-1
   "Who can the various city frauds recite." *Fr.* III. OAEL-1
   "Winter my theme confines; whose nitry wind." *Fr.* II. NOEC
Triviality, A. Waring Cuney. CDC
Troades, *sel.* Seneca, *tr. fr. Latin by* the Earl of Rochester.
   "After death nothing is, and nothing, death." *Fr.* II. EBEV; OBD;
    OBVE
Trochee trips from long to short. Metrical Feet. Samuel Taylor
   Coleridge. FaBoUs; NIP; OxBChV; SoSe
Troika, The. Louis Simpson. NOBA
Troilus and Cressida, *sels.* Dryden.
   Can Life Be a Blessing. SeCePo
   (Song: "Can life be a blessing.") NoP; SeCV-2
   "See my lov'd Britons, see your Shakespeare rise." SeCV-2
Troilus and Cressida, *sels.* Shakespeare.
   "Heavens themselves, the planets and this center, The." *Fr.* I, iii.
    ImOP
   Portrait of Cressida. *Fr.* IV, v. TrGrPo
   Portrait of Helen. *Fr.* II, ii *and* IV, i. TrGrPo
   Ulysses Advises Achilles. *Fr.* III, iii. LiTB
Troilus and Criseyde [*or* Criseide], *sels.* Chaucer.
   At the Gate. SeCePo
   Complaint of Troilus, The. *Fr.* V. NOBE; OBEV
   Go, Little Book ("Go, litel book, go litel myn tragedy"). *Fr.* V.
    OAEL-1; ViBoPo
   (Envoy, The.) FiP
   "If no love is, O God, what fele I so." *Fr.* I. FF; OAEL-1
   (Song of Troylus, The.) AWP
   Love Unfeigned. *Fr.* V. NOBE; OBEV
   Sorrow of Troilus, The. *Fr.* V. PoEL-1
   "Swich fyn hath, lo, this Troilus for love!" NOCV
   "This Troilus [*or* Troylus], with blisse [*or* Blysse] of that supprysed [*or*
    supprised]." *Fr.* III. EBEV; PoE
   "Whan they unto the paleys were yoemen." *Fr.* V. PoE
   Wooing of Criseide, The. III. PoEL-1
Trojan Horse, The. William Drummond of Hawthornden. EyDe
Trojans. C. P. Cavafy, *tr. fr. Greek by* Edmund Keeley *and* Philip
   Sherrard. VMG
Trojans Outside the Walls, The. Homer, *tr. fr. Greek by* George
   Chapman. *Fr.* The Iliad, VIII. OBVE
Troll, The. Jack Prelutsky. RHPC

Troll Chanting. Anselm Hollo. *Fr.* Out of the "Kalevala." WSC

Troll sat alone on his seat of stone. The Stone Troll. John R. R. Tolkien. SO

Troll the Bowl! Thomas Dekker. *See* Shoemaker's Holiday, The: Drinking Song.

Trolling for Blues. Richard Wilbur. BAP

Trolling for love. The Compleat Anglers. Dennis Scott. UAS

Troll's Nosegay, The. Robert Graves. Son

Trombone blurts plumply. Holiday-Afternoon Rhapsody. Imre Csanádi, *tr. by* Edwin Morgan. MHuP

Trombone Solo. Stoddard King. NBLV

Trompe L'Œil. Daryl Hine. MoCV

Troop home to silent grots and caves. The Mermaidens' Vesper-Hymn. George Darley. *Fr.* Syren Songs, VI. GBL; NAEL-2; OBNC; PoEL-4
(Siren Chorus.) BlrV; FaBoRV; WSC

Troop of the Guard, The. Hermann Hagedorn. OHIP

Troop Train. Karl Shapiro. OxBA; WaaP; WaP

Trooper and Maid. *Unknown.* AmFP

Trooper's Horse, The. *Unknown.* OBET

Troops, The. Siegfried Sassoon. CMoP

Troops brought enough suffering to the people, The. On Hearing That the Sea-Barbarians Are about to Attack Hu-chou. Tsung Ch'en, *tr. by* Jonathan Chaves. CoBLCP

Troops exulting sate in order round, The. Homer, *tr. fr. Greek by* Pope. *Fr.* The Iliad, VIII. OBVE

Troopship, The. Lionel Johnson. EBVV

Troopship in the Tropics. Alun Lewis. WaP

Trope Market. Jackson MacLow. LP

Trophy, The. Edwin Muir. LiTM

Tropic Circle. Reinhard Priessnitz, *tr. fr. German by* Beth Bjorklund. CoAuP

Tropic Nightmare in Singapore. Melech Ravitch, *tr. fr. Yiddish by* Robert Friend. PeBMYV

Tropic of ice. Cape Ann; a View. John Malcolm Brinnin. NYBP

Tropic Rain. Robert Louis Stevenson. OBTV

Tropic tonight, burning, filled with fast trains. At the Band Concert. John Malcolm Brinnin. PoA

Tropical Greenhouse. Dan Pagis, *tr. fr. Hebrew by* Warren Bargad *and* Stanley F. Chyet. IP

Tropics. Ellen Bryant Voigt. SM

Tropics in New York, The. Claude McKay. AmNP; NoAM; PoBA; PoNe; TTY

Tropisms on John Berryman. Gerald Vizenor. VoR

Trosachs, The. Wordsworth. OBEV; SeCePo

Trot, and a canter, a gallop, and over, A. *Unknown.* OxNR

Troubadour of God, The. Charles Wharton Stork. WGRP

Trouble. David Keppel. FaFP; FPL; PoLF; WBLP

Trouble. James Wright. FF

Trouble at the Farm. Ivy O. Eastwick. BoTP

Trouble has done her good. Charity. Connie Bensley. FaBoWP

Trouble in the "Amen Corner." Thomas Chalmers Harbaugh. BLPA

Trouble is, it's getting harder. Wild West. Mark Vinz. Psk

Trouble, not of clouds, or weeping rain, A. On the Departure of Sir Walter Scott from Abbotsford, for Naples. Wordsworth. EBEV; EnRP

Trouble Oh. *Unknown.* PBCV

Trouble was too much, The. Indian Love Song. Lew Blockcolski. VoR

Trouble with a kitten is, The. The Kitten. Ogden Nash. CRH; FaPON; MoShBr

Trouble With In, The. Heather McHugh. NAmP

Trouble with you is, The. Denunciation; or, Unfrock'd Again. Philip Whalen. NeAP

Trouble with you is, The. Love in a Warm Room in Winter. James Wright. OBAL

Troubled Jesus. Waring Cuney. BANP

Troubled Soldier, The. *Unknown.* AS

Troubled throughout the year. Teika, *tr. fr. Japanese by* Hiroaki Sato. *Fr.* Eighty-four Tanka. FCEI

Troubled was a house in Ealing. The Widow's Plot; or, She Got What Was Coming to Her. William Plomer. MoP

Troubled waters, The/ are frozen fast. Murasaki Shikibu, *tr. fr. Japanese by* Kenneth Rexroth *and* Ikuko Atsumi. *Fr.* The Tale of Genji. WPOW

Troubled Woman. Langston Hughes. PCP

Troubles are many in the path of a little boat. *Unknown. Fr.* Manyo Shu. Ma

Troubles of the Day. William Barnes. GTBS-P

Trousers first of ancient fabric. Sri Rama's Raiment. *Malay Oral Tradition, tr. by* R. O. Winstedt. WTO

Trousers of Wind. *Unknown, tr. fr. Amharic by* Sylvia Pankhurst. PBA; TTY

Trout, The. Daryl Hine. CoAP

Trout, The. John Montague. FaBCIP; IPY; PoE

Trout. Brian Turner. ATNZ

Trout Fisher. George Mackay Brown. OxBC

Trout leaping. Onitsura, *tr. by* Geoffrey Bownas *and* Anthony Thwaite. PeBJV

Trouvaille. Richard Murphy. IPY

Troy. Robin Flower. SeCePo

Troy. Edwin Muir. CMoP

Troy. Thomas Sackville. *Fr.* Induction to "A Mirror for Magistrates." SeCePo

Troy Depicted. Shakespeare. *Fr.* The Rape of Lucrece. OBSC

Troynovant ("Troynovant is now no more a city"). Thomas Dekker. *Fr.* Entertainment to James. ChTr; OBSC

Truant, The. E. J. Pratt. NOBC; NoP; OBCV

Truants, The. Walter de la Mare. MoBrPo

Truce, gentle love, a parley now I crave. Michael Drayton. *Fr.* Idea, LXIII. NoP

Truck put me off on Fell. Hitching into Frisco. Thom Gunn. *Fr.* Three Songs. AnAn

Trucker, A. Thom Gunn. PCP

Trucks. James S. Tippett. FaPON

Trudge, Body. Robert Graves. MoAB

True/ The first messenger angel may arrive. Message. Fred Chappell. BLA

True Account of Talking to the Sun at Fire Island, A. Frank O'Hara. HCAP; NNaP; RB; SOTW; TTTS

True and Faithful Inventory of the Goods Belonging to Dr. Swift, Vicar of Laracor, A; upon Lending His House to the Bishop of Meath, till His Palace Was Rebuilt. Swift. FaBoUs

True and False Glory ("To whom our Saviour calmly thus reply'd"). Milton. *Fr.* Paradise Regained, *bk.* III, *ll.* 43–107. LiTB; OBS

True and Joyful News. *Unknown.* APAS

True Apostolate, The. Ruby T. Weyburn. BLRP

True Aristocrat, The. W. Stewart. WBLP

True Ballad of the Great Race to Gilmore City, The. Phil Hey. Psk

True Beauty. Francis Beaumont. EIL

True-blue the salmon—from his sally. No Place Like Home. Llawdden, *tr. by* Gwyn Jones. OBWVE

True-born Englishman, The ("Speak, Satire, for there's none can tell like thee.") *sels.* Daniel Defoe. APAS
"Breed's described, The: Now, Satire, if you can." *Fr.* II. OBSV
"In their religion they are so unev'n." *Fr.* II. OBSV
"Labouring poor, in spite of double pay, The." *Fr.* II. NOBL; SaC
"Then let us boast of ancestors no more." *Fr. conclusion.* OBSV
"Wherever God erects a house of prayer." *Fr.* I. NOBL; OBSV

True Brahmin, in the morning meadows wet. Gardener. Emerson. *Fr.* Quatrains. OxBA

True Brotherhood. Ella Wheeler Wilcox. WBLP

True Christian hearts cease to lament. The Song of a Happy Rising. John Thewlis. ACP

True Confession of George Barker, The, *sels.* George Barker.
"I see the young bride move among." ErPo
"I sent a letter to my love." FaBoTw
"Today, the Twenty-sixth of February." NAs

True Confessional. Lawrence Ferlinghetti. NAs

True daughters of Lilith, night demons. Summer Night. Hayyim Nahman Bialik, *tr. by* Robert Friend. VWA

True ease in writing comes from art, not chance. Pope. *Fr.* Essay on Criticism, *pt.* II. HAP; InPK; PrIm; TrGrPo
(Sound and Sense.) SoSe; UnPo

True Encounter, The. Edna St. Vincent Millay. OxBSP

True Englishmen, drink a good health to the miter. A New Catch in Praise of the Reverend Bishops. *Unknown.* APAS

True Facts of the Case, The. Anthony Euwer. OBAL

True faith discovered was, The. Wisdom. W. B. Yeats. TrCP

True faith, he claims, has the most doubt. A Modern Theologian. Paul Ramsey. *Fr.* Three Epigrams. CRP

True feelings come from my innermost heart. On a Painting "Ancient Trees and Flowing Stream." Yün Shou-p'ing, *tr. by* Jonathan Chaves. CoBLCP

True Friendship. *Unknown, tr. fr. Sanskrit by* Arthur Ryder. *Fr.* The Panchatantra. AWP

True friendship unfeigned. Of Perfect Friendship. Henry Cheke. EIL

True Genius. Robert Lloyd. *Fr.* Shakespeare; an Epistle to David Garrick, Esq. NOEC

True genius, but true woman! dost deny. To George Sand: A
  Recognition. Elizabeth Barrett Browning. BoWoP; NAEL-2; TEP
True Heaven, The. Paul Hamilton Hayne. WGRP
True Hymn, A. George Herbert. InvP; NOCV
True Import of Present Dialogue, Black vs. The Negro. Nikki Giovanni.
  BPo; PoBA
True Knight [or True Knighthood], The. Stephen Hawes. Fr. The
  Pastime of Pleasure, 27. ACP; OBEV; TrGrPo
True knight, worthy of the name, A. Don Quixote's Credo. W. H.
  Auden. Fr. Man of La Mancha. AnAn
True Knowledge. Panatattu, tr. fr. Sanskrit. WGRP
True Lent, A. Robert Herrick. See It this a fast, to keep.
True Life Romance. Lindsay MacRae. DT
True Love. Waring Cuney. CDC
True Love, A. Nicholas Grimald. EiL; OBEV
True Love. Joe Johnson. CNA
True Love. Shakespeare. See Let me not to the marriage of true minds.
True Love. Sir Philip Sidney. See Arcadia: My True Love Hath My
  Heart [and I Have His].
True Love. Unknown, tr. fr. German by Jethro Bithell. AWP
True Love. Robert Penn Warren. BLA
True love/ warms my heart. Cercamon, tr. by Paul Blackburn. Pro
True love, come O come to me. True Love. Unknown, tr. by Jethro
  Bithell. AWP
True Love Ditty, A. Thomas Middleton. Fr. Blurt, Master Constable.
  EiL
True Love in this differs from gold and clay. Shelley. Fr.
  Epipsychidion. OBNC
True love is sweet and true love is pleasant. William Hall. Unknown.
  AmFP
True love, true love, what have I done. In the Pines. Unknown.
  AmFP
True Lovers Bold, The. Unknown. AmFP
True Lover's Farewell, The. Unknown. AS
True love's own talisman, which here. A Footnote to a Famous Lyric.
  Louise Imogen Guiney. AA
True Maid, A. Matthew Prior. ErPo; FaBoCo; FaBoEE; NAEL-1; NIP;
  NOEC
True Marriage Is True Love. William Ellery Leonard. Fr. Two Lives.
  Son
True Master, The. Kabir, tr. by John Stratton Hawley and Mark
  Juergensmeyer. SSI
True Mexican or not, let's open our shirts. Kearney Park. Gary Soto.
  NPGG
True mirth resides not in the smiling skin. Mirth. Robert Herrick.
  LiTB
True Name. Yves Bonnefoy, tr. fr. French by Galway Kinnell.
  RHTwFP
True name is not the one that gilds portals, illustrates proceedings, The.
  Hidden Name. Victor Segalen, tr. by Nathaniel Tarn. RHTwFP
True, nature is wonderful. The Music Makers. Cees Buddingh', tr. by
  James S. Holmes. DuIn
True: nor love or loving is ultimate. "A Taste of Honey." King D.
  Kuka. NOVW
True, one must read ten thousand volumes until threadbare. Sung Hsiang,
  tr. fr. Chinese by Irving Lo. Fr. On Poetry, VIII. WFTU
True or False. Catullus, tr. fr. Latin by Walter Savage Landor. AWP;
  OBVE
True path is shadowy and still, far away and hard to find, The. Natsume
  Soseki, tr. fr. Japanese by Burton Watson. JLIC-2
True, pleasures, self-reliance. Truth. Fahmida Riaz, tr. by Mahmood
  Jamal. PBMUP
True poesy is not in words. Pastoral Poesy. John Clare. OAEL-2
True poetry sometimes likes to ride. Poetry. Yankev Fridman, tr. by
  Ruth Whitman. PeBMYV
True Protocol of Poets, The. Kapilar, tr. fr. Tamil by A. K. Ramanujan.
  PLW
True Rest. Goethe, tr. fr. German by John S. Dwight. WBLP
True Son of God, Eternal Light. P. J. Cormican. AH
True Story, A. Marvin Bell. SV
True Story of Snow White, The. Bruce Bennett. SM
True Tale of Robin Hood, A. Unknown. ESPB
True Thomas lay o'er yond grassy [or on Huntlie] bank. Thomas the
  Rhymer. Unknown. ELP; FaBoCh; GoTS; InPS; LiTB; NOBE;
  OAEL-1; OBEV; OnMSP; OxBB; OxBS; PoE; Prf; RB
  (Thomas Rhymer [and the Queen of Elfland].) CH; ChTr; ESPB;
  (A and C vers.); FaBoBa; HAP
  (Thomas the Rimer.) EnSB; InPK
  (True Thomas.) OxBS; TrGrPo
True to a Dream. Donald Petersen. NePoEA-2

True to your might [or Truth to your mighty] winds on dusky shores. On
  the Death of William Edward Burghardt Du Bois by African
  Moonlight and Forgotten Shores. Conrad Kent Rivers. NBP; PoBA
True Vine. Elinor Wylie. LiTA
True, we must tame our rebel will. Courage. Matthew Arnold.
  OAEL-2
True Weather for Women, The. Louis Simpson. NePoAm
True worth is in being, not seeming. Nobility. Alice Cary. OHFP;
  WBLP
True young woman, yes, for midnight, A. Unknown, tr. by Hiroaki Sato.
  FCEI
Trueblue Gentleman, A. Kenneth Patchen. SO
Truelove, A. Nicholas Grimald. See What sweet relief the showers to
  thirsty plants we see.
Truest Poetry Is the Most Feigning; or, Ars Poetica for Hard Times, The.
  W. H. Auden. NYBP
Truganinny. Wendy Rose. HATNAP
Truisms, The. Louis MacNeice. FaBCIP; NOBE; OBSV
Truly. Ingeborg Bachmann, tr. fr. German by Susan L. Cocalis. DMG
Truly buzzards/ Around my sky are circling! Glyph. Unknown, tr. by
  Mary Austin. LiTA
Truly do we live on earth? Unknown, tr. by Jack Emory Davis. OBD
Truly Great. W. H. Davies. OBMV
Truly in the East. Songs in the Garden of the House God. Unknown, tr.
  by Washington Matthews. AnAmPo
Truly in the east/ The white bean. Song to Promote Growth. Unknown,
  tr. by Washington Matthews. OBVE
Truly, my Satan, thou art but a dunce. Epilogue. Blake. Fr. The Gates
  of Paradise. HAP; OAEL-2; OBNC; PoE; WeW
  (To the Accuser Who Is the God of This World.) NoP; OxBSP;
  TrGrPo
Truly my soul waiteth upon God. Psalm LXII ("Truly my soul waiteth.")
  Bible, O.T. Fr. Psalms.
  (Psalm LXII: "Yet shall my soule in silence still," paraphrased by the
  Countess of Pembroke) PBWP
Truly Rich, The. T. Urchard. PWR
Truly the light is sweet. The Light Is Sweet. Bible, O.T. Fr.
  Ecclesiastes, XI: 7. FaPON
Truly, those southern hills. Unknown, tr. by Arthur Waley. BoS
Truly Wise Man, The. Margarita Hickey, tr. fr. Spanish by Kate Flores.
  DMH
Trump hath blown, The. The Lonely Bugle Grieves. Grenville Mellen.
  Fr. Ode on the Celebration of the Battle of Bunker Hill, June 17,
  1825. AA
Trumpet, The. Ilya Grigoryevich Ehrenburg, tr. fr. Russian by Y.
  Hornstein. TrJP
Trumpet, The, sel. Robinson Jeffers.
  Grass on the Cliff. Fr. V. PoA
Trumpet, The. Edward Thomas. MMA; MoBrPo; OHIP
Trumpet, A/ A trumpet. Lewis Has a Trumpet. Karla Kuskin. PDV
Trumpet hath sounded, its voice is gone forth, The. The Fairies'
  Farewell. Charlotte Brontë. FL
Trumpet of Liberty, The. John Taylor. NOEC
Trumpet Player. Langston Hughes. NAAL-2; TTY
Trumpet Voluntary. Paul Hoover. UL
Trumpeter, The. Unknown. CoMu
Trumpeter of Fyvie, The. Unknown. OxBB
Trumpets. A valley opens and beyond. Drums in Scotland. Richard
  Hugo. LCAF
Trumpet's loud clangor, The. Fife and Drum. Dryden. Fr. A Song for
  St. Cecilia's Day, 1687, 8 ll. GN
Trumpets sound and steeples ring. A Trick for Tyburn; or, A Prison Rant.
  Unknown. APAS
Trundled from/ the strangeness of the sea. The Sea-Elephant. William
  Carlos Williams. LiTA; NU
Trunk of cherry-tree without bark or flowers. Materia Nupcial. Pablo
  Neruda, tr. by Clayton Eshleman. ErPo
Truro Bear, The. Mary Oliver. SoSe
Trus' an' Smile. Bertye Young Williams. BLRP
Trust. Lizette Woodworth Reese. AA
Trust and Obedience. Unknown. BLRP
Trust in God and Do the Right, sel. Norman Macleod.
  Trust in God. BLRP
Trust in Me. Unknown. AH
Trust in the Lord. Bible, O.T. See Psalms: Psalm XXXVII ("Fret not
  thyself.").
Trust in Women ("When nettles in winter bring forth roses red."), sel.
  Unknown. NA
  "When sparrows build churches and steeples high." PBBP
Trust me from here to there. Jacob Glatstein, tr. fr. Yiddish by Chana
  Bloch. Fr. Kleine Nachtmusik. PeBMYV

Trust me. The world is run on a shoestring. Hard Times. John Ashbery. NoAM

Trust not his wanton tears. Aeliana's Ditty. Henry Chettle. *Fr.* Piers Plainness' Seven Years' Prenticeship. OBSC (Of Cupid.) EIL

Trust not that thing called woman: she is worse. A Rodomontade on His Cruel Mistress. John Wilmot, 2nd Earl of Rochester. OxBSP

Trust not too much, fair youth, unto thy feature. White Primit Falls. *Unknown.* ChTr

Trust Only Yourself. *Unknown.* MeEL

Trust-Song, A. Eben Eugene Rexford. BLRP

Trust the Great Artist. Thomas Curtis Clark. WBLP

Trust Thou Thy Love. John Ruskin. OBEV

Trustful curator has left me alone, The. Museum of Man. Earle Birney. OxBC

Trusting Each Other. William Stafford. KS

Truth. "Æ." AnIL; MoBrPo

Truth. Chaucer. *See* Flee from [*or* Fle fro] the press [*or* prees *or* pres] and dwelle with soothfastnesse [*or* sothefastnesse.]

Truth, *sel.* William Cowper. "Man on the dubious waves of error toss'd." NOCV

Truth, The. W. H. Davies. FaBoTw

Truth. John Donne. *See* Satires: Seek true religion, O where? Mirreus.

Truth. Eileen Duggan. ATNZ; PeNZ

Truth. Josephine D. Henderson Heard. CBWP-4

Truth, The. Randall Jarrell. DiL; OxBC

Truth, The. Ted Joans. AmNP; TTY

Truth, The. Archibald Lampman. CaP

Truth. Cecil Francis Lloyd. CaP

Truth. Claude McKay. BPo

Truth. John Masefield. WGRP

Truth. Howard Nemerov. HoPM; LiTM

Truth. Coventry Patmore. *See* Unknown Eros, The: Here, in This Little Bay.

Truth. Fahmida Riaz, *tr. fr. Urdu* by Mahmood Jamal. PBMUP

Truth. Susan Fromberg Schaeffer. IHMS

Truth about Horace, The. Eugene Field. AnAmPo

Truth about My Sister and Me, The. Anita Endrezze Probst. CDW

Truth and Consequences. Edward Baugh. PBCV

Truth and right are my bases. Peire Cardenal, *tr.* by Paul Blackburn. Pro

Truth, be more precious to me than the eyes. Max Eastman. WGRP

Truth, Beauty, Love, in these are formed a ring. The Trinity. Marian Osborne. CaP

Truth Brought to Light, or Murder Will Out. Stephen College. APAS

Truth from Above, The. *Unknown.* OBET

Truth Has Perished. Ulma Seligman, *tr. fr. Yiddish* by Joseph Leftwich. TrJP

Truth I pursued, as Fancy sketch'd the way. Samuel Taylor Coleridge. FaBoEE

Truth in Poetry. George Crabbe. *Fr.* The Village. SeCePo

Truth in Two Halves, A. Norman MacCaig. PoPo

Truth Is, The. Linda Hogan. HATNAP

Truth is a golden sunset far away. I. O. Scherzo. HoPM

Truth is a native, naked beauty; but. Roger Williams. SCAP

Truth is as old as God. Emily Dickinson. MoAmPo

"Truth Is Blind, The." David Gascoyne. EAS

Truth is love and love is truth. Mendacity. A. E. Coppard. OBMV

Truth is that there comes a time, The. Sad Strains of a Gay Waltz. Wallace Stevens. OxBA

Truth like the Belly of a Woman Turning, The. Gary Synder. NNaP

Truth-loving Persians do not dwell upon. The Persian Version. Robert Graves. CMoP; FaBoCo; LiTB; LiTM; MoP; NoAM; NOBL; OBWP; WeW

Truth Made Breakfast, The. Jeffrey Miller. UL

Truth Never Dies. *Unknown.* WBLP

Truth Shall Set You Free. Chaucer. *See* Flee from [*or* fle fro] the press [*or* prees *or* pres] and dwelle with soothfastnesse [*or* sothefastnesse.]

Truth, so far, in my book; the truth which draws. Elizabeth Barrett Browning. *Fr.* Aurora Leigh. WGRP

Truth Suppressed, The. Lizelia Augusta Jenkins Moorer. CBWP-3

Truth the Dead Know, The. Anne Sexton. MoAmPo; NePoEA-2; NoAM; PBWP; TAP

Truth to your mighty winds on dusky shores. *See* True to your might winds on dusky shores.

Truthful James. Bret Harte. *See* Do I sleep? do I dream?

Truth's Complaint over England. Thomas Lodge. ACP

Truth's the Best. Elizabeth Turner. OxBChV

Truxton's Victory. *Unknown.* PAH

Try. Philip Appleman. BXAP

Try Again. Eliza Cook. BoTP

Try first this figure 2. A Lesson in Handwriting. Alastair Reid. NYBP

Try it out with a bird or a fish. Though a woman would do. Silent Revolution. W. H. Oliver. ATNZ

Try Smiling. *Unknown.* BLPA; FaFP; PWR; WBLP

Try the Uplook. *Unknown.* BLRP

Try This Once. *Unknown.* WBLP

Try to detain joy, and alas, it will not remain. Falling Teeth. Shih Jun-chang, *tr.* by William Shultz. WFTU

Try Topic. Genevieve Taggard. MoAmPo

Try, Try Again. *At. to* T. H. Palmer. FaFP; FaPON

Try wading in sand. Try. Philip Appleman. BXAP

Trying On for Size. Mary Dorcey. AIW

Trying to Believe. Linda Gregg. NPGG

Trying to chop mother down is like. She Went to Stay. Robert Creeley. OBAL

Trying to fall asleep. Night Thought. Gerald Jonas. NYBP

Trying to hide her nestlings, a skylark cries. Issa, *tr.* by Hiroaki Sato. FCEI

Trying to Name What Doesn't Change. Naomi Shihab Nye. NAmP

Trying to Say, #15. Susan Griffin. *Fr.* Nineteen Pieces for Love. LLLT

Trying to scrape the burned soup from my only pot. The Lives of Famous Men. Jack Gilbert. NPGG

Trying to Separate. Robert Pack. KS

Trying to stay the departing spring is of no avail. Liang Ch'i-ch'ao, *tr. fr. Chinese* by Cecile Chu-chin Sun. *Fr.* Thoughts at the End of Spring—A Farewell Poem for II. WFTU

Trying to Talk with a Man. Adrienne Rich. HCAP

Tryptych for Jan Bockelson, A. John Oliver Simon. NeAC

Tryst, The. E. V. Knox. CenHV

Tryst. Eve Merriam. NMM

Tryst, The. William Soutar. EBEV; ErPo; GoTS; OxBS

Tryst, The. John Banister Tabb. OBAL

Tryst, The. Mary E. Tucker. CBWP-1

Tryst, The. *Unknown, tr. fr. Welsh* by Joseph P. Clancy. OBWVE

Tryst in Brobdingnag, A. Adrienne Rich. NYBP

Trystan and Esyllt. *Unknown, tr. fr. Welsh* by Gwyn Jones. OBWVE

Trysting, A. Richard Dehmel, *tr. fr. German* by Jethro Bithell. AWP

Trysting Bush, The. Joanna Baillie. WPE

Trysting Place, The. William Soutar. *See* O luely, luely, cam she in.

Ts'ai Chi'h. Ezra Pound. NoP

Tsa'lagi Council Tree. Gladys Cardiff. HATNAP

Tsangyang Gyatso was twelve years old. Signature III ("Tsangyang Gyatso was twelve years old"). Joseph Stroud. NPGG

Ts'eekkaayah. Mary TallMountain. STE

Tseutsuki Pass. Ishigaki Rin, *tr. fr. Japanese* by Hiroaki Sato. FCEI

Tsigane's Canzonet, The. Edward King. AA

Ts'in Chi Huang Ti (Divus Augustus) who. The Great Wall. Lucebert, *tr.* by James S. Holmes. DuIn

Tu-lu Poem ("Tu-lu, Tu-lu, evil waters running muddy."). Yang Wei-chen, *tr. fr. Chinese* by Jonathan Chaves. CoBLCP

"Tu Non Se' in Terra, Si Come Tu Credi." Kathleen Jessie Raine. WPE

Tu-Whit To-Who. Shakespeare. *See* Love's Labour's Lost: When Icicles Hang by the Wall.

"Tu-whitt, Tu-whitt, Tu-whoo, Tu-whoo." "Good Night," Says the Owl. Lady Erskine Crum. BoTP

Tua Mariit Wemen and the Wedo, The, *sel.* William Dunbar. Widow Has Buried Her Second Husband, The. OxBLMV

Tuba. Morton Marcus. NAmP

Tubal Cain. Charles MacKay. WBLP

Tubby or not tubby—there's the rub. F. C. Burnand. BXAP

Tuberculosis. Dannie Abse. NPo

Tuberose. Louis James Block. AA

Tubes. Larry Mollin. NeAC

Tucking in yellow curls, she poises, set. The Diver. Leonard E. Nathan. ErPo

Tudor Aspersions. R. A. Piddington. FiBHP

Tudor indeed is gone and every rose. Ezra Pound. *Fr.* Cantos, LXXX. FaBoTw

Tudor Portrait. Richmond Lattimore. EyDe

Tudor Rose, The. Alexander Barclay. *Fr.* The Ship of Fools. ACP

Tuesday. Zishe Landau, *tr. fr. Yiddish* by Ruth Whitman. VWA

Tuesday afternoons in the cave of our basement. Making Music. Judith Minty. GeTw

Tuesday; or, the Ditty. John Gay. *Fr.* The Shepherd's Week. NOEC

Tuft by Tuft. Remco Campert, *tr. fr. Dutch* by James S. Holmes. DuIn

Tuft of Flowers, The. Robert Frost. AWP; GoYe; LiTA; MoAB; MoAmPo; NAAL-2; OxBA

Tuft of Kelp, The. Herman Melville. ChTr; FaBoEE; FaBoRV; MOS

Tug-of-War, A. M. M. Hutchinson. BoTP

Tug pulls, tightening the steel strand, The. From Le Havre. Charles G. Bell. NePoAm

Tugging my forelock fathoming Xenophon. Still. Tony Harrison. OBD
Tugs. James S. Tippet. FaPON
Tulip. Humbert Wolfe. MoBrPo
Tulip Tree. Sacheverell Sitwell. MoBrPo
Tulips. Padraic Colum. ImOP
Tulips. Medbh McGuckian. FaBCIP
Tulips. Sylvia Plath. HAP; NaP; NoP; NYBP; PPP; WeW; WPE
Tulips and Addresses. Edward Field. NYBP; Psk
Tulips & Chimneys, *sel.* E. E. Cummings.
  "Spring omnipotent goddess thou dost." NBLV
Tulips are too excitable, it is winter here, The. Tulips. Sylvia Plath.
  HAP; NaP; NoP; NYBP; PPP; WeW; WPE
Tulips charge the grazing dikes, and I walk. Dutch April. Daniel
  Halpern. GrPl
Tulips from Their Blood. Edwin Brooks. NBP
Tullie's Love, *sels.* Robert Greene.
  Mars and Venus. OBSC
  Shepherd's Ode, The. OBSC
Tullochgorum. John Skinner. GoTS; OxBS
Tully, the queen of beauty's boast. Molly Moor. George Farewell.
  NOEC
Tumadir al-Khansa for Her Brother. *Unknown, tr. fr. Arabic by* E. Powys
  Mathers. *Fr.* The Thousand and One Nights. AWP
Tumble, fall, crash, then silence, A. Kito, *tr. fr. Japanese by* Hiroaki
  Sato. *Fr.* Twenty-four Hokku. FCEI
Tumble me down, and I will sit. To Fortune. Robert Herrick. OxBSP;
  SeCV-1
Tumbled out of heaven. The Blue Day Journey. Gwyn Jones. OBWVE
Tumbleweed. Ramona Carden. NOVW
Tumbleweed. David Wagoner. BoNaP
Tumbling. *Unknown.* OxBChV
Tumbling among its stones. The Ladder. Gene Baro. NePoEA-2
Tumbling Mustard. Malcolm Cowley. AmFN
Tumbling, pausing, leaping, knocking together. Metaphysic of Snow.
  Donald Finkel. PoA
Tumbling water breaks upon the rocks, The. *Unknown. Fr.* Manyo Shu.
  Ma
Tumult. Léon-Paul Fargue, *tr. fr. French by* Maria Jolas. RHTwFP
Tumult. Charles Enoch Wheeler. PoNe
Tumult in a Syrian town had place, A. The Great Physician. Sadi, *tr. fr.*
  Persian by Sir Edwin Arnold. *Fr.* The Bustan. AWP
Tumult of death, dizziness hath seized me, The. Elegy (for Himself).
  Moses Rimos of Majorca, *tr. by* Israel Abrahams. TrJP
Tumult of my fretted mind, The. Self-Analysis. Anna Wickham.
  MoBrPo
Tumult, weeping, many new ghosts. Snow Storm. Kenneth Rexroth.
  NaP
Tumultuous clamor of voices, A. Delight in the High-Flying Orioles.
  Wei Chuang, *tr. by* Lois Fusek. ATF
Tumultuous sea, whose wrath and foam are spent. Eumares.
  Asclepiades, *tr. by* Richard Garnett. AWP
Tumultuous winter sky all day. Princess Shikishi, *tr. fr. Japanese by*
  Hiroaki Sato. *Fr.* Seventy-eight Tanka. FCEI
Tunbridge Wells. Earl of Rochester. FaBoPP; OBSV
Tune, A. Arthur Symons. BoLoP; OBNC
Tune: A Song to Induce Laughter. Wu Hsi-ch'i, *tr. fr. Chinese by*
  Frederick P. Brandauer. WFTU
Tune: As in a Dream ("Always I recall the river arbor at twilight"). Li
  Ch'ing-chao, *tr. fr. Chinese by* Burton Watson. CoBCP
Tune beyond us as we are, A. Wallace Stevens. *Fr.* The Man with the
  Blue Guitar, VI. CMoP
Tune: Bitter Longing. Wu Tsao, *tr. fr. Chinese by* Julie Landau. WFTU
Tune: Crimson Lips Adorned. *See* After Kicking on the swing.
Tune: Crows Crying at Night. Li Yü, *tr. fr. Chinese by* Burton Watson.
  CoBCP
Tune: Cuckoo Sky. Singde, *tr. fr. Chinese by* Julie Landau. WFTU
Tune: Deva-like Barbarian ("Blossoms bright, the moon dark, shadowed in
  thin mist"). Li Yü, *tr. fr. Chinese by* Burton Watson. CoBCP
Tune: Deva-like Barbarian ("In her ornate tower by bright moonlight
  always she thinks of him"). Wen T'ing-yün, *tr. fr. Chinese by*
  Burton Watson. CoBCP
Tune: Deva-like Barbarian ("On the many-leafed bedscreens, gold flickers
  and fades"). Wen T'ing-yün, *tr. fr. Chinese by* Burton Watson.
  CoBCP
Tune: Deva-like Barbarian ("People all say the southland's better"). Wei
  Chuang, *tr. fr. Chinese by* Burton Watson. CoBCP
Tune: Dreaming of the South, *sels.* Ch'ü Ta-chün, *tr. fr. Chinese by*
  Irving Lo. WFTU
  "Lament the falling leaves:/ The falling leaves, let them fall in spring."
  "Lament the falling leaves:/ The falling leaves sever the date of return."

Tune: Dreaming of the South. Wen T'ing-yün, *tr. fr. Chinese by* Burton
  Watson. CoBCP
Tune: Drunk among the Flowers. Mao Wen-hsi, *tr. fr. Chinese by* Burton
  Watson. CoBCP
Tune: Endless Union. Li Ching-chao, *tr. fr. Chinese by* C. H. Kwôck *and*
  Vincent McHugh. PBWP
Tune: Eternal Longing ("He was a traveler west of the river,/ only he knew
  how lonely he was"). *Unknown, tr. fr. Chinese by* Burton Watson.
  Fr. Four *Tz'u* from Tun-huang, II. CoBCP
Tune: Eternal Longing ("He was a traveler west of the river,/ then he took
  sick, lay an inch away from death"). *Unknown, tr. fr. Chinese by*
  Burton Watson. *Fr.* Four *Tz'u* from Tun-huang, III. CoBCP
Tune: Eternal Longing ("He was a traveler west of the river,/ with wealth
  and eminence rare in this world"). *Unknown, tr. fr. Chinese by*
  Burton Watson. *Fr.* Four *Tz'u* from Tun-huang, I. CoBCP
Tune: Flirtatious Laughter. Wei Ying-wu, *tr. fr. Chinese by* Burton
  Watson. CoBCP
Tune for a Lonesome Fife. Donald Justice. *See* Merry the green, the
  green hill shall be merry.
Tune: Fragrant Wandering: A Song. Wu Tsao, *tr. fr. Chinese by* Julie
  Landau. WFTU
Tune: Full River Red. Ch'iu Chin, *tr. fr. Chinese by* Pao Chia-lin.
  WFTU
Tune: Full River Bed. Wu Tsao, *tr. fr. Chinese by* Julie Landau. WFTU
Tune: Gazing at the South. Li Yü, *tr. fr. Chinese by* Burton Watson.
  CoBCP
Tune: Immortal at Magpie Bridge. Wang Kuo-wei, *tr. fr. Chinese by* Li
  Chi *and* Michael Patrick O'Connor. WFTU
Tune: Immortal at the River. Su Tung-p'o, *tr. fr. Chinese by* Burton
  Watson. CoBCP
Tune is cowboy, The; the words, sentimental crap. D-Y Bar. James
  Welch. CDW; STE
Tune: Joy at Meeting, *sels.* Chang Hui-yen, *tr. fr. Chinese.* WFTU
  "Year after year, I've missed the season of flowers." *Fr.* I, *tr. by*
  Irving Lo.
  "Young warbler crying through the Festival of Tombs." *Fr.* II, *tr. by*
  Michael Duke.
Tune: Lotus-leaf Cup. Wei Chuang, *tr. fr. Chinese by* Burton Watson.
  CoBCP
Tune: Magnolia Blossom. Li Ch'ing-chao, *tr. by* C. H. Kwôck *and*
  Vincent McHugh. PBWP
Tune: Magpie on the Branch. *Unknown, tr. fr. Chinese by* Burton
  Watson. *Fr.* Four *Tz'u* from Tun-huang, IV. CoBCP
Tune me for life again, oh, quiet Musician. A Prayer after Illness.
  Violet Alleyn Storey. TrPWD
Tune Me, O Lord, into One Harmony. Christina Rossetti. TrPWD
Tune on my pipe the praises of my Love. Of His Mistress. Robert
  Greene. *Fr.* Menaphon. EIL
Tune on my pipe the praises of my Love. In Praise of His Daphnis. Sir
  John Wotton. EIL
Tune: Palace of Night Revels. Chou Pang-yen, *tr. fr. Chinese by* Burton
  Watson. CoBCP
Tune: Partridge Sky. Su Tung-p'o, *tr. fr. Chinese by* Burton Watson.
  CoBCP
Tune: Phoenix Hairpin. Lu Yu, *tr. fr. Chinese by* Burton Watson.
  CoBCP
Tune: Prelude to Water Music. Su Tung-p'o, *tr. fr. Chinese by* Burton
  Watson. CoBCP
Tune: Pure Serene Music ("Since we parted, spring half over"). Li Yü, *tr.*
  fr. Chinese by Burton Watson. CoBCP
Tune: Pure Serene Music ("Year after year in the snow"). Li Ch'ing-chao,
  tr. fr. Chinese by Burton Watson. CoBCP
Tune: Remembering the South. Singde, *tr. fr. Chinese by* William
  Schultz. WFTU
Tune: Ripples Sifting Sand. Li Yü, *tr. fr. Chinese by* Burton Watson.
  CoBCP
Tune: Sand of Silk-washing Stream ("Flutter flutter on clothes and cap,
  jujube flowers fall"). Su Tung-p'o, *tr. fr. Chinese by* Burton Watson.
  CoBCP
Tune: Sand of Silk-washing Stream ("Layer on layer of hemp leaves, jute
  leaves shining"). Su Tung-p'o, *tr. fr. Chinese by* Burton Watson.
  CoBCP
Tune: Sand of Silk-washing Stream ("Soft grasses, a plain of sedge fresh
  with passing"). Su Tung-p'o, *tr. fr. Chinese by* Burton Watson.
  CoBCP
Tune: Sand of Silk-washing Stream ("Throw on rouge and powder, watch
  the governor pass!"). Su Tung-p'o, *tr. fr. Chinese by* Burton
  Watson. CoBCP
Tune: Song of Picking Mulberry ("Evening comes with an onslaught of
  wind and rain."). Li Ch'ing-chao, *tr. fr. Chinese by* Burton Watson.
  CoBCP

Tune: Song of Picking Mulberry ("Ten years ago I was a visitor at the wine jar"). Ou-yang Hsiu, *tr. fr. Chinese by* Burton Watson. CoBCP
Tune: Song of River City. Su Tung-p'o, *tr. fr. Chinese by* Burton Watson. CoBCP
Tune: Song of Tzu-yeh. Li Yü, *tr. fr. Chinese by* Burton Watson. CoBCP
Tune: Telling of Innermost Feelings ("Long nights when he neglects me—where's he gone?"). Ku Hsiung, *tr. fr. Chinese by* Burton Watson. CoBCP
Tune: Telling of Innermost Feelings ("Night comes and, drowsy with drink, I'm slow to shed my ornaments."). Li Ch'ing-chao, *tr. fr. Chinese by* Burton Watson. CoBCP
Tune: The Butterfly Woos the Blossoms. Li Ching-chao, *tr. by* C. H. Kwock *and* Vincent McHugh. PBWP
Tune: The Fisherman. Li Yü, *tr. fr. Chinese by* Burton Watson. CoBCP
Tune: The Taoist Priestess. Wei Chuang, *tr. fr. Chinese by* Burton Watson. CoBCP
Tune thy music[ke]to thy heart [*or* hart]. Heart's Music. At. *to* Thomas Campion. AAS; OBEV
Tune to the Devonshire Cant, The. *Unknown.* APAS
Tune: Treading on Grass. Ou-yang Hsiu, *tr. fr. Chinese by* Burton Watson. CoBCP
Tune: Ugly Rogue. Hsin Ch'i-chi, *tr. fr. Chinese by* Burton Watson. CoBCP
Tune: Willow Branch. Cheng Wen-cho, *tr. fr. Chinese by* William Schultz. WFTU
Tuneful Hipponax rests him here. Epitaph of Hipponax. Theocritus, *tr. by* Charles Stuart Calverley. FaBoEE
Tuneful poet, Britain's glory. The Mutual Congratulations of the Poets Anna Seward and Hayley. Richard Porson. FaBoEE; OBSV
Tunes fainter on winds waywarder than others. Graves Are Made to Waltz On. Peter Viereck. PoA
Tunes for Bears to Dance To. Ronald Wallace. GOYP
Tung, Chü, Ni, Huang—I've never laid eyes on them. Inscribed on Landscapes I Painted Myself. Rai San'yo, *tr. by* Burton Watson. JLIC-2
T'ung-ch'uan is a beautiful place. As My Way Passed through T'ung-ch'uan. Tai Piao-yüan, *tr. by* Jonathan Chaves. CoBLCP
Tung-ling melons—men say that long ago. Juan Chi, *tr. fr. Chinese by* Burton Watson. *Fr.* Singing of Thoughts. CoBCP
T'ung Pass. T'an Ssu-t'ung, *tr. fr. Chinese by* Timothy C. Wong. WFTU
Tuning myself by morning coffee. May Morn. Michael McClure. EAS
Tunnel, The. Hart Crane. *Fr.* The Bridge, VII. CMoP; MAT; MoAB; MoAmPo; OxBA
Tunnel, The. Russell Edson. NAmP
Tunnel, The. Mark Strand. HeIP; TwCP; WeW
Tunnel Visions, *sels.* Felix Pollak. TSM
  "Another transparent skin has grown." *Fr.* IV.
  "First the light cracked." *Fr.* I.
  "Her voice enters the room." *Fr.* II.
  "I wake to the sound of rain." *Fr.* III.
Tunnyng [*or* Tunning] of Elynour [*or* Elinor] Rummyng [*or* Rumming], The, *sels.* John Skelton. AAS; TrGrPo
  "Then Margery [*or* Marjorie] Milkduck." EBEV; OAEL-1; PoE
Tupac Amaru Relegated. Antonio Cisneros, *tr. fr. Spanish by* David Tipton. Per
Tupelo Destruction, The. *Unknown.* AmFP
Turf Carrier on Aranmore. John Hewitt. PoRA
Turf-Stacks. Louis MacNeice. *See* Among These Turf-Stacks.
Turista. Mark Osaki. BrSi
Turkey, A. Hugo Claus, *tr. fr. Dutch by* Theo Hermans. DuIn
Turkey and the Ant, The. John Gay. *Fr.* Fables. PBBP
Turkey in the Straw. *Unknown.* AS, *with music;* FaFP; GBP
Turkey is dancing near the rocks, A. *Unknown, tr. by* Jerome Rothenberg *after* David McAllester. STP
Turkish Bakery, The. *Unknown, tr. fr. Korean by* Peter H. Lee. PBWP
Turkish Carpet, The. Paul Durcan. CIP
Turkish Death Songs. *Unknown, tr. by* Reza Baraheni *and* Zahra-Soltan Shokoohtaezeh. BoWoP
Turkish government allows no law, The. Fulke Greville. FaBoPV
Turkish Legend, A. Thomas Bailey Aldrich. GN
Turkish Love Songs. *Unknown, tr. by* Reza Baraheni *and* Zahra-Soltan Shokoohtaezeh. BoWoP
Turkish Trench Dog, The. Geoffrey Dearmer. Mes
Turn, The. Robert Creeley. LCAP
Turn (a Poem in 4 Parts). Ken Belford. NOBC
Turn again, maiden, twice slain and rotten. Hilaire Kirkland. *Fr.* Observations, III. PeNZ
Turn Again to Life. Mary Lee Hall. BLPL; PoLF

Turn again, turn again, turn once again. Carrousel Tune. Tennessee Williams. NBLV; OBAL
Turn Back, O Man. Clifford Bax. NOCV
Turn Blind. Paul Celan, *tr. fr. German by* Joachim Neugroschel. VWA
Turn from Self. George Macdonald. PWR
Turn from that girl. I Shall Laugh Purely. Robinson Jeffers. LiTA; LiTM; WaP
Turn I my looks unto the skies. Rosader's Sonnet. Thomas Lodge. *Fr.* Rosalynde; or Euphues' Golden Legacy. OBSC
Turn inward on the brain. What the Emanation of Casey Jones Said to the Medium. A. J. M. Smith. MoCV
Turn like a top, spin on your dusty axis. Instead of a Journey. Michael Hamburger. NYBP
Turn me like a waterwheel turning a millstone. After Being in Love, the Next Responsibility. Jalal ed-Din Rumi, *tr. by* John Moyne *and* Coleman Barks. UnAS
Turn Me to My Yellow Leaves. William Stanley Braithwaite. BANP
Turn o'er thy outward man, and judge aright. The Outward Man Accused. Edward Taylor. LiTA
Turn of noontide has begun, The. A Half-Way Pause. Dante Gabriel Rossetti. NOBVV
Turn of the Moon. Robert Graves. TEP
Turn of the Road, The. James Stephens. SO; WSC
Turn of the World, The, *sel.* Sacheverell Sitwell.
  "In the turn of the world." PoPo
Turn on the light, and the water looks more like green. On Drinking. Wakayama Bokusui, *tr. fr. Japanese by* Hiroaki Sato. *Fr.* Forty-four Tanka. FCEI
Turn on Your Side and Bear the Day to Me. George Barker. OxBTC
Turn out more ale, turn up the light. Dum Vivimus Vigilamus. Charles Henry Webb. AA
Turn the page of stone and there. Eeva-Liisa Manner, *tr. fr. Finnish by* Jaakko A. Ahokas. *Fr.* Cambrian, III. PBWP
"Turn to me in the darkness." Titus and Berenice. John Heath-Stubbs. GTBS-P
Turn to right, turn to left. Witches' Spells. Madeleine Edmondson. NTCP
Turn, turn, my wheel! Turn round and round. The Potter's Song. Longfellow. *Fr.* Kéramos. PoEL-5
Turn, turn thy beauteous face away. Beaumont *and* Fletcher. *Fr.* Love's Cure. PoEL-2
Turn, Turn, Unhappy Souls, Return. Henry Alline. AH
Turn under, plow. Plowman's Song. Raymond Knister. CaP
Turn we to survey. Goldsmith. *Fr.* The Travel[l]er; or, A Prospect of Society. OBTV
"Turn, Willie Macintosh." Willie Macintosh. *Unknown.* ESPB, (A *vers.*); OxBoLi
  (Burning of Auchindown.) OxBB
Turn with me from the city's clamorous street. Thomas à Kempis. Richard Rogers Bowker. AA
Turn your face and look. Insha Allah Khan Insha, *tr. by* Ahmed Ali. GoT
Turn your head, look, the light is turning yellow. Villanelle at Sundown. Donald Justice. BLA
Turncoat, The. Imamu Amiri Baraka. NeAP; PoE
Turncoat, The. Priscilla Jane Thompson. CBWP-2
Turner's Camp on the Chippewa. *Unknown.* AmFP
Turners Dish of Lentten Stuffe or A Galymaufery. William Turner. CoMu
Turner's Sunrise. Helen Smith Bevington. EyDe
Turning. Robert Finch. MoCV; OBCV
Turning, The. Philip Levine. VGW
Turning, The. Philip Murray. NePoAm
Turning and turning in the widening gyre. The Second Coming. W. B. Yeats. BIrV; BLPL; CMoP; EaLo; FaBoMo; FaBoPV; FF; GTBS-P; GTBS-P; HAP; HeIP; HoPM; InPK; InPS; LiTB; LiTM; MAT; MoAB; MoBrPo; MoP; NAEL-2; NAWM-2; NIP; NoAM; NOBE; NoP; OAEL-2; OxBTC; PoE; PPP; PrIm; SCV; SeCePo; SoSe; TEP; UnPo; WaP; WeW
Turning and turning, these summer days, to my regret. Teika, *tr. fr. Japanese by* Hiroaki Sato. *Fr.* Eighty-four Tanka. FCEI
Turning Aside from Battles. Sextus Propertius, *tr. fr. Latin by* Ezra Pound. WaaP
Turning Away from Lies. Robert Bly. LCAP
Turning deer flesh over. Blood. Barney Bush. STE
Turning Fifty. Judith Wright. NAs
Turning, following the arrows through. The House of Madam Juju. Kanai Mieko, *tr. by* Christopher Drake. BoWoP
Turning from Shelley's sculptured face aside. On a Grave in Christchurch, Hants. Oscar Fay Adams. AA
Turning Into. Robert Duncan. EAS

Turning it over, considering, like a madman. John Berryman. *Fr.*
Dream Songs. MoP; NoAM
Turning On Daytime TV. Alex Kuo. UL
Turning, returning on world winds that know. Angel Eye of Memory.
John Malcolm Brinnin. PoA
Turning Thirty. Katha Pollitt. InPS; WeW
Turning through a collection. Wes Hardin: From a Photograph.
Raymond Carver. GeTw
Turning to him, who meets me with desire. Bible, *O.T.* *Fr.* The Song
of Solomon, VII: 10–13. PBWP
Turnip Vendor, The. Mother Goose. OxNR
Turns. Tony Harrison. *Fr.* The School of Eloquence. NAEL-2;
NoAM
Turns. Tymoteusz Karpowicz, *tr. fr. Polish by* Czeslaw Milosz. PwPP
Turnstile, The. William Barnes. CH; NOBVV
Turtle. Peter Blue Cloud. HATNAP
Turtle. Robert Lowell. LCAP
Turtle, The. Ogden Nash. FaFP; FiBHP; NoP; OBAL; SoSe; TAP
Turtle, The. *Unknown.* PAH
Turtle and Flamingo, The. James Thomas Fields. *See* Lively young
turtle lived down by the banks, A.
Turtle and the Sparrow, The, *sel.* Matthew Prior.
"Behind an unfrequented glade." PBBP
Turtle Dove, The. Geoffrey Hill. FaBoTw; NePoEA
Turtle-Dove, The. *Unknown.* OxBoLi
Turtle lives 'twixt plated decks, The. The Turtle. Ogden Nash. FaFP;
FiBHP; NoP; OBAL; SoSe; TAP
Turtle on yon withered bough, The. Song of Thyrsis. Philip Freneau.
Fr. Female Frailty. AA; LiTA
Turtle Soup. "Lewis Carroll." *See* Alice's Adventures in Wonderland:
Beautiful Soup, so rich and green.
Turtle thus with plaintive crying, The. John Gay. PBBP
Turtledoves. Jacob Glatstein, *tr. fr. Yiddish by* Benjamin *and* Barbara
Harshav. AYP
Turtledoves don't do it. Observation on a Solitary Tree. Abba Kovner,
tr. by Bernhard Frank. MHeP
Turtle's Belly, The. Ellen Pearce. IHMS
Turtle's Song, The. *Unknown.* BPo
Turvey Top. William Sawyer. NA
Tuscaloosa Sam. "Orpheus C. Kerr." OBAL
Tuscan cypresses. Cypresses. D. H. Lawrence. FaBoPP; NAEL-2
Tuscan Life. Elizabeth Barrett Browning. *Fr.* Aurora Leigh, VII.
FaBoPP
Tuscan, that wanderest through the realms of gloom. Dante.
Longfellow. AA
Tuskegee. Leslie Pinckney Hill. BANP; PoNe
Tusks that clashed in mighty brawls, The. On the Vanity of Earthly
Greatness. Arthur Guiterman. BXAP; HeIP; HoPM; OBCA; TrJP
Tuslag. T. A. Robertson. OxBS
Tusser, they tell me when thou wert alive. Ad Tusserum. *Unknown.*
FaBoUs
Tussock burned to fine gold, and the sheep bore golden fleeces. Evening
Walk in Winter. Mary Ursula Bethell. ATNZ
Tut! Bah! we take as another case. Barry Pain. *Fr.* The Poets at Tea, V.
Par
Tutankhamen. William Dickey. Psk
Tutelage, The. Robert Mowry Bell. AA
Tutivillus, the Devil. *Unknown.* EBEV; MeEL
Tutor not thyself in science: go to masters for perfection. Good Counsel.
Unknown, tr. by James Clarence Mangan. NOIV
Tutor who tooted a flute, A. Carolyn Wells. SoSe
Tutto è Sciolto. James Joyce. OBMV
Tutumantu is like hopscotch, kwani-kwani is like hide-and-seek.
Comprehensive. Carol Ann Duffy. NPo
TV. John Forbes. CBAP
TV Blooper Spotter. Jack Skelley. UL
T.V. (2). Anselm Hollo. UL
Twa Bonny Lads. Burns. OxBSP
Twa Books, The. Allan Ramsay. OxBS
Twa Brothers, The. *Unknown.* CH; EBEV; ESPB, (A *and* B *vers.*);
OxBB
Twa Corbies, The. *Unknown.* AWP; CH; ELP; EnSB; ESPB; FaBoBa;
FaBoCh; GoTS; GTBS; GTBS-P; HAP; InPK; NoP; OBEV; OxBS;
PBBP; PPP; RB; SeCePo; UnPo
Twa Knights, The. *Unknown.* ESPB
Twa Magicians, The. *Unknown.* ESPB; GBP; OAEL-1; OxBB
Twa Sisters, The. *Unknown.* ESPB (B *vers.*); FaBoBa; NoP; OxBS
Twa Sisters [of Binnorie]. *Unknown.* *See* There were twa sisters sat in a
bower [*or* bour *or* bowr.]
Twa Weavers, The. Alexander Rodger. PF

Twain that were foes, while Mary lived, are fled. His Lady's Death.
Pierre de Ronsard, *tr. by* Andrew Lang. AWP
'Twas a balmy summer evening, and a goodly crowd was there. The Face
upon [*or* on] the Floor. Hugh Antoine D'Arcy. BeLS; BLPA;
FaBoBe; FaFP; FPL
'Twas a busy day in the courtroom, and a curious crowd was there. The
Bank Thief. J. R. Farrell. BeLS; BLPA
'Twas a cloudless morn and the sun shone bright. The Cherokee. Mary
Weston Fordham. CBWP-2
'Twas a dangerous cliff, as they freely confessed. A Fence or an
Ambulance. Joseph Malins. BLPA
'Twas a grand display was the prince's ball. Baron Renfrew's Ball.
Charles Graham Halpine. PAH
'Twas a mining town called Golden Gulch. Silver Bells and Golden
Spurs. *Unknown.* CowP
'Twas a new feeling—something more. Did Not. Thomas Moore.
BoLoP; ErPo
(Quantum Est Quod Desit.) EnLoPo
'Twas a night of dreadful horror. The Night of Death. Frances Ellen
Watkins Harper. PWR
'Twas a stylish congregation, that of Theophrastus Brown. Trouble in the
"Amen Corner." Thomas Chalmers Harbaugh. BLPA
'Twas a tough task, believe it, thus to tame. Upon Dr. Davies's British
Grammar. James Howell. OBWVE
'Twas a wonderful brave fight! The Fight at Sumter. *Unknown.* PAH
'Twas after a supper of Norfolk brawn. Turvey Top. William Sawyer.
NA
'Twas after dread Pultowa's day. Mazeppa. Byron. EnRP
'Twas all along the Binder Line. Sensitive Sydney. Wallace Irwin.
FiBHP; ILY
'Twas all on board a ship down in a southern sea. The Golden Vanity.
Unknown. CH; ELP; FaBoCh; OBET; WiR
'Twas an evening in November. *Unknown.* CenHV
'Twas at that sober hour when the light of the day is receding. Southey
Looks out of the Window at Greta Hill. Robert Southey. *Fr.* A
Vision of Judgement. FaBoPP
'Twas at the landing-place that's just below Mount Wyse. Port Admiral.
Frederick Marryat. MOS
'Twas at the Matin Hour. *Unknown.* OHIP
'Twas at the royal feast, for Persia won. Alexander's Feast; or, The
Power of Music [*or* Musique]. Dryden. ACP; FaPoR; FiP; GN;
GTBS; GTBS-P; LiTB; NAEL-1; NOBE; OAEL-1; OBS; SeCV-2;
TrGrPo; WiR
'Twas at the silent, solemn hour. William and Margaret. David Mallet.
NOEC
'Twas August, and the fierce sun overhead. East London. Matthew
Arnold. WGRP
'Twas autumn and 'round me the leaves were descending. The Banks of
Champlain. *Unknown.* AmFP
'Twas battered and scarred, and the auctioneer. The Touch of the
Master's Hand. Myra Brooks Welch. BLPA
'Twas brillig, and the slithy toves. Jabberwocky. "Lewis Carroll." *Fr.*
Through the Looking-Glass, *ch.* 1. AmMo; EBEV; EBVV; FaBoBe;
FaBoCo; FaBoNo; FaBV; FaFP; FaPON; FF; FiBHP; FPL; GoJo;
HeIP; HoPM; InPK; InPS; LiTB; NA; NAEL-2; NBLV; NIP;
NoAM; NOBE; NOBL; NOBVV; NoP; NTCP; OAEL-2; OPOP;
OxBChV; PoRA; PPP; RB; RHPC; TEP; TTTS
'Twas but a single Rose. Upon a Virgin Kissing a Rose. Robert Herrick.
SeCP; SeCV-1
'Twas Captain Church, bescarred and brown. King Philip's Last Stand.
Clinton Scollard. PAH
'Twas Christmas Eve, the month was May. A Tragedy. Tom Masson.
OBAL
'Twas Christmas Eve, the snow lay deep. When the Christ Child Came.
Frederic E. Weatherly. OHIP
'Twas early in 'eighty-two, and I think on March the twentieth day. Tiger
Bay. *Unknown.* OxBSS
'Twas early in the month of May. Barbara Allen. *Unknown.* OBET
'Twas early in the springtime of the year. Early in the Springtime.
Unknown. OBET
'Twas early on a May morning. Lady Isabel. *Unknown.* ESPB
'Twas early one morning a fair maid arose. A Kiss in the Morning Early.
Unknown. GBP
'Twas early one morning by the break of the day. All Jolly Fellows That
Follow the Plough. *Unknown.* OBET
'Twas earlye, earlye in the spring. Earlye, Earlye, in the Spring.
Unknown. AmFP
'Twas Euclid, and the theorem pi. Plane Geometry. Emma Rounds.
ImOP
'Twas eve in sunny Italy. A Tale of Italy. Eloise Bibb. CBWP-4

'Twas evening, though not sun-set, and spring-tide. Tamar's Wrestling.
Walter Savage Landor. *Fr.* Gebir, I. EnRP
(Shepherd and the Nymph, The.) OBNC
'Twas Ever Thus. Henry S. Leigh. FaBoCo; FaBoPa
'Twas Ever Thus. *Unknown.* BXAP
'Twas ever thus from childhood's hour! Disaster. Charles Stuart
Calverley. CenHV; FM; NBLV
'Twas fancy first made Celia fair. Fancy. Jonathan Smedley. OxBSP
'Twas Friday morn: the train drew near. Through Baltimore. Bayard
Taylor. PAH
'Twas going to snow—'twas snowing! Curse his luck! The Drove-Road.
W. W. Gibson. OxBTC
'Twas Goosey Goosey Gander. Goosey Goosey Gander—by Various
Authors (Macaulay's Version). William Percy French. CenHV
'Twas hurry and scurry at Monmouth town. Molly Pitcher. Kate
Brownlee Sherwood. PAH
'Twas in a basement tobble d'hote. Reverie. Don Marquis. FPL; PoLF
'Twas in heaven pronounced, and 'twas muttered in hell. Catherine
Fanshawe. ChTr
("'Twas whispered in Heaven, 'twas muttered in hell.") GN
'Twas in Koolau I met with the rain. The Rain. *Unknown, tr. by* N. B.
Emerson. WTO
'Twas in Rosemary Lane, sirs. Neddy Nibble'm and Biddy Finn.
Unknown. GBP
'Twas in that island summer where. He Loves and He Rides Away.
Sydney Thompson Dobell. OBNC
'Twas in the days of the Revolution. Emily Geiger. *Unknown.* BLPL;
PoLF
'Twas in the middle of the night. Mary's Ghost. Thomas Hood.
FiBHP
'Twas in the month of August, or the middle of July. She Said the Same
to Me. *Unknown.* AS
'Twas in the moon of winter time when all the birds had fled. Jesous
Ahatonhia. Jesse Edgar Middleton. CaP
(The Huron Carol.) OBCP
'Twas in the prime of summer time. The Dream of Eugene Aram [the
Murderer]. Thomas Hood. BeLS; EnRP
'Twas in the reign of George the Third. A New Song Called the Gaspee.
Unknown. PAH
'Twas in the spring of '72. The April Fool. Eugene Field. PWR
'Twas in the town of Jacksboro in the spring [*or* year] of seventy-three.
The Buffalo Skinners. *Unknown.* AmFP; AS, *with music;* GBP
'Twas in the year of 1898, and on the 21st of June. The Albion Battleship
Calamity. William McGonagall. BXAP
'Twas in the year of forty-nine. The Whale. *Unknown.* ChTr
(Greenland Whale, The.) GBP
'Twas Jolly, Jolly Wat. C. W. Stubbs. OHIP
'Twas Juet spoke—the Half Moon's mate. The Death of Colman.
Thomas Frost. PAH
'Twas June on the face of the earth, June with the rose's breath. The Eve
of Bunker Hill. Clinton Scollard. PAH
'Twas just this time, last year, I died. Emily Dickinson. PoE
'Twas late, and the gay company was gone. The Declaration. Nathaniel
Parker Willis. AnAmPo; OBAL
'Twas like a maelstrom, with a notch. Emily Dickinson. CMoP; LiTM;
PoE
(Final Inch, The.) LiTA
'Twas May upon the mountains, and on the airy wing. The Surprise at
Ticonderoga. Mary A. P. Stansbury. PAH
'Twas mercy brought me from my pagan land. On Being Brought from
Africa to America. Phillis Wheatley. FF; GOA; HeIP; NAAL-1;
NOBA; NOEC; TAP; TTY; WPE
'Twas midnight—every mortal eye was closed. The Helmets; a Fragment.
Thomas Penrose. NOEC
'Twas midsummer: cooling breezes all the languid forests fanned. The
Death of Jefferson. Hezekiah Butterworth. PAH
'Twas my pleasure to walk in the river meadows. The Midnight Court.
Brian Merriman, *tr. by* Frank O'Connor. AnIL
'Twas Night. *Unknown.* OBS
'Twas night upon the Darro. The Thanksgiving for America. Hezekiah
Butterworth. PAH
'Twas not as lonesome as it might have been. The Cricket Kept the
House. Edith M. Thomas. OBCA
"'Twas not so in my time," surly Grumio exclaims. Samuel Bishop.
NOEC
'Twas not the brown of chestnut boughs. Gwendoline. Bayard Taylor.
BXAP
'Twas November the fourth, in the year of ninety-one. Sainclaire's
Defeat. *Unknown.* PAH
'Twas of a brisk young sailor, as I have heard it said. Johnny German.
Unknown. AmFP

'Twas of a lovely creature who dwelled by the seaside. Mary in the
Silvery Tide. *Unknown.* OBET
'Twas of a nobleman's daughter. Caroline and Her Young Sailor Bold.
Unknown. AmFP
'Twas of a shepherd's son. Blow Away the Morning Dew. *Unknown.*
OBET
'Twas of a young brickster a-going from his work. The Brickster.
Unknown. OBET
'Twas on a dark and stormy night well southward of the Cape. The
Flying Dutchman. *Unknown.* OxBSS
'Twas on a Holy Thursday, their innocent faces clean. Holy Thursday
(" 'Twas on a Holy Thursday, their innocent faces clean"). Blake.
Fr. Songs of Innocence. CH; EnRP; InPS; NAEL-2; NAWM-2;
NOBE; NOEC; NoP; OAEL-2; OFD; PoE; SCV; TEP; TrCP
'Twas on a lofty vase's side. Ode on [*or* On] the Death of a Favourite [*or*
Favorite] Cat, Drowned in a Tub [*or* Bowl] of Gold Fishes. Thomas
Gray. EBEV; FaBoBe; FM; HoPM; NAEL-1; NBLV; NOBE;
NOBL; NOEC; NoP; OAEL-1; PoE; PoEL-3; PPP; TEP
(Cat and the Fish, The.) WiR
(On a Favorite Cat Drowned in a Tub of Gold Fishes.) BeLS;
FaBoCo; GN; GTBS; GTBS-P; InvP; LiTB; OBEV
(On the Death of a Favorite Cat, Drowned in a Tub of Gold Fishes.)
FPL; InPS; PoLF; PoRA
'Twas on a Monday morning. Charlie, He's My Darling. Burns. CH;
FaBoPV
'Twas on a Monday morning, just at the break of day. Maggie Mac.
Unknown. AmFP
'Twas on a Monday morning, the first I saw my darling. Hanging Out the
Linen Clothes. *Unknown.* AS
'Twas on a night, an evening bright. Proud Lady Margaret. *Unknown.*
ESPB
'Twas on a pleasant mountain. The Battle of King's Mountain.
Unknown. PAH
'Twas on a summer noon, in Stainsford mead. My Ox Duke. John
Dyer. NOEC
'Twas on a summer's day—the sixth of June. Byron. *Fr.* Don Juan, I.
PPP
'Twas on an evening fair I went to take the air. Willie's Fatal Visit.
Unknown. ESPB
'Twas on board the sloop of war *Wasp,* boys. The *Wasp's* Frolic.
Unknown. PAH
'Twas on Lake Erie's broad expanse. John Maynard. Horatio Alger, Jr.
BeLS; BLPA; FaBoBe
'Twas on the eighth of January, just at the dawn of day. The Battle of
New Orleans. *Unknown.* AmFP
'Twas on the field of Antietam where many's the soldier fell. The Battle
of Antietam Creek. *Unknown.* AmFP
'Twas on the glorious day. The Death of General Pike. Laughton
Osborn. PAH
'Twas on The [*or* the] Longstone Lighthouse there dwelt an English maid.
Grace Darling. *Unknown.* OBET; OxBSS
'Twas on the shores that round our coast. The Yarn of the *Nancy Bell.*
W. S. Gilbert. BeLS; BLPA; CenHV; FaBoBe; FaBoCh; FaBoCo;
FaBV; FaFP; HoPM; MOS; MoShBr; NOBL; OnMSP; TrGrPo
'Twas on the twelfth of April. Sumter—a Ballad of 1861. *Unknown.*
PAH
'Twas one October mornin'. Bigerlow. *Unknown.* AS
'Twas one of the charmèd days. The Heart of All Scene. Emerson.
Fr. Woodnotes I ("When the pine tosses its cones"). AA
'Twas out upon mid ocean that the San Jacinto hailed. Death of the
Lincoln Despotism. *Unknown.* PAH
'Twas over hills and over dales. Locks and Bolts. *Unknown.* OBET
'Twas so, I saw thy birth: that drowsy [*or* drowsie] lake. The Shower [*or*
Showre]. Henry Vaughan. BoNaP; ChTr; FaBoPP; LiTB; MePo;
OBS; SeCP
'Twas spring, and dawn returning breathed new-born. Idyll of the Rose.
Ausonius, *tr. by* John Addington Symonds. AWP
'Twas summer, and the spot a cool retreat. A Dream. Elizabeth
Clementine Kinney. AA
'Twas summer, and the sun had mounted high. The Wanderer.
Wordsworth. *Fr.* The Excursion, I. EnRP, *abr.*
(Ruined Cottage, The, *diff. version.*) NoP; OAEL-2
'Twas Sunday morning, quite serene the air. A City Eclogue. "W. J."
NOEC
'Twas sung of old in hut and hall. Birthday Verses Written in a Child's
Album. James Russell Lowell. OxBChV
'Twas sunset's hour, the glorious day. The Exile's Reverie. Mary
Weston Fordham. CBWP-2
'Twas sure a luckless planet. Out of Luck. Abraham ibn Ezra, *tr. by*
Solomon Solis-Cohen. TrJP

'Twas the angel of death that to us downward flew. In Memoriam of E. B. Clark. Lizelia Augusta Jenkins Moorer. CBWP-3

'Twas the angel of Eden, to Adam he said. Dedication Day Poem. Lizelia Augusta Jenkins Moorer. CBWP-3

'Twas the dead of the night. By the pine-knot's red light. New England's Chevy Chase. Edward Everett Hale. PAH

'Twas the dream of a God. Ireland. Dora Sigerson Shorter. OBEV; TIRV

'Twas the end of the nineteenth century. The Throw-Back. Waddie Mitchell. CowP

'Twas the eve before Christmas. "Good night," had been said. Annie and Willie's Prayer. Sophia P. Snow. BeLS; BLPA

'Twas the gray of early morning when the dreadful cry of "Fire! The Milwaukee Fire. *Unknown.* AmFP

'Twas the heart of the murky night, and the lowest ebb of the tide. Wayne at Stony Point. Clinton Scollard. PAH

'Twas the night before Christmas, when all through the house. A Visit from St. Nicholas. Clement Clarke Moore. AA; AiP; AnAmPo; BeLS; BLPA; FaBoBe; FaBV; FaFP; FaPON; FPL; NTCP; OBAL; OBCA; OBCP; OnMSP; OxBChV; PChr; RHPC
(Night before Christmas, The.) OHIP; PWR; WBLP

'Twas the proud Sir Peter Parker came sailing in from the sea. The Boasting of Sir Peter Parker. Clinton Scollard. PAH

'Twas the spring in the air. Danny's Wooing. David McKee Wright. PoAu-1

'Twas the very verge of May. Dewey at Manila. Robert Underwood Johnson. PAH

'Twas the year of the famine in Plymouth of old. Five Kernels of Corn. Hezekiah Butterworth. PAH

'Twas warm—at first—like us. Emily Dickinson. CMoP; LiTA; NAWM-2; QFR; SoSe

'Twas when bright Cynthia with her silver car. A Night-Piece; or, Modern Philosophy. Christopher Smart. NOEC

'Twas when Tacita hushed the noisy world. The Dream. "Brian Bendo." NOEC

'Twas when the friendly shade of night. To Clarissa. Robert, Earl Nugent. NOEC

'Twas when the rain fell steady an' the Ark was pitched an' ready. The Legends of Evil II. Kipling. MoShBr

'Twas When the Seas Were Roaring. John Gay. *Fr.* The What D'Ye-Call-It. HAP

'Twas when the spousal time of May. Coventry Patmore. *Fr.* The Angel in the House, II, vii. GBL

'Twas whispered in Heaven, 'twas muttered in hell. Catherine Fanshawe. *See* "'Twas in heaven pronounced, and 'twas muttered in hell."

'Twas wond'rous, then, a bardling should be found. The Tribulations of an Uneducated Poet in the 1760's. James Woodhouse. *Fr.* The Life and Lucubrations of Crispinus Scriblerus. , NOEC

Tweed and Till. *Unknown.* BoNaP; ChTr; FaBoCh; FaBoPP; GBP; OBEV; OxBSP

Tweed Visited, The. William Lisle Bowles. Son

Tweedle-Dum and Tweedle-Dee. Mother Goose. NA; NOBL; OxNR

"Tweet" pipes the robin as the cat creeps by. The Firetail's Nest. John Clare. EnRP

Twelfth day of Christmas, The. The Twelve Days of Christmas. *Unknown.* OxBoLi

12th Horse Song of Frank Mitchell (Blue), The. Frank Mitchell, *tr. fr. Navajo Indian by* Jerome Rothenberg *and* David P. McAllester. STP

Twelfth Night. Philip Booth. NePoEA

Twelfth Night. Peter Scupham. OBCP

Twelfth Night, *sels.* Shakespeare.
Come Away, Come Away, Death. *Fr.* II, iv. EiL; ELP; GBL; NOBE; NoP
(Clown's Song, The.) CTC
(Come Away, Death.) PoRA
(Dirge: "Come away, come away, death.") OBEV
(Dirge of Love.) GTBS; GTBS-P
(Feste's Song ("Come away, come away, death").) OBSC
(Love's Despair.) TrGrPo
(Song: "Come away, come away, death.") FiP; PoEL-2
Food of Love, The. *Fr.* I, i. TrGrPo
O [*or* Oh] Mistress Mine [Where Are You Roaming?]. *Fr.* II, iii. AWP; CTC; EiL; ELP; FaBV; FaFP; GBL; HAP; HeIP; InPS; LiTB; NAEL-1; NBLV; NOBE; NoP; OAEL-1; OxBoLi; OxBSP; PoRA; TrGrPo
(Carpe Diem.) GTBS; GTBS-P
(Feste's Song ("O mistress mine! where are you roaming?").) BoLoP; OBSC
(Song: "O mistress mine! where are you roaming?.") FiP; GoJo
(Sweet-and-Twenty.) OBEV; PoE
"Once more, Cesario." *Fr.* II, iv. SCV

Patience on a Monument. *Fr.* II, iv. TrGrPo

When That I Was and a Little Tiny Boy. *Fr.* V, i. CH; EBEV; EiL; FaBoCh; HeIP; LiTB; NOBE; NoP; OAEL-1; PoRA
(Feste's Song ("When that I was and a little tiny boy").) NBLV; OBSC; OxBoLi
(Song: "When that I was and a little tiny boy.") FiP; PoEL-2
(Wind and the Rain, The.) WiR

12th Raga: For John Wieners. David Meltzer. *Fr.* Ragas. NeAP

Twelve, The, *sel.* Alexander Blok, *tr. fr. Russian by* Babette Deutsch *and* Avrahm Yarmolinsky.
Black Night./ White snow. AWP

Twelve. Jacob Glatstein, *tr. fr. Yiddish by* Benjamin *and* Barbara Harshav. AYP

Twelve and ugly. Dresses. Kathleen Fraser. NMM

Twelve Articles. Swift. NBLV

Twelve Autumn Lines. Aaron Zeitlin, *tr. fr. Yiddish by* Robert Friend. PeBMYV

Twelve Bells/ Benny's on the ropes. The Memory of Boxer Benny (Kid) Paret. Frank Lima. PoNe

Twelve Days of Christmas, The. *Unknown.* AmFP; FaFP; OxBoLi; OxNR; PChr

Twelve elements in slow orbit, The. Upon Looking at a Book of Astrology. David McFadden. NeAC

Twelve-Elf, The. (Twelve-Elf raises his left hand, The.) Christian Morgenstern, *tr. by* W. D. Snodgrass *and* Lore Segal. WSC

12 Gates to the City. Nikki Giovanni. IHMS; PoBA

Twelve good friends. Peter and John. Elinor Wylie. MoAB; MoAmPo; MoBS

Twelve herds of oxen, no less flockes of sheepe. Homer, *tr. fr. Greek by* George Chapman. *Fr.* Odyssey, XIV. CTC

Twelve Lines about the Burning Bush. Melech Ravitch, *tr. fr. Yiddish by* Ruth Whitman. VWA

Twelve Minutes. J. C. Hall. OBD

Twelve Miscellaneous Poems on the Fang Garden, *sels.* Chang Yü, *tr. fr. Chinese by* Jonathan Chaves. CoBLCP
Butterflies.
Moon Window, The.
Painting ("Slowly I walk the gully path, alone").
Spring Night.
Summer Night at the Pond Pavillion.

Twelve o'clock./ Along the reaches of the street. Rhapsody on a Windy Night. T. S. Eliot. CMoP; HeIP; InPS; PoE

12 o'Clock News. Elizabeth Bishop. OxBC

12 October. Myra Cohn Livingston. NTCP; RHPC

Twelve Oxen, The. *Unknown. See* I Have Twelve Oxen.

Twelve pears hanging high. Mother Goose. OxNR

Twelve snails went walking after night. The Haughty Snail-King. Vachel Lindsay. SO

Twelve-Thousand-Day Honeymoon, The. Anne Sexton. AnAn

Twelve Weapons of Spiritual Battle, The, *sel.* Sir Thomas More.
Peace of a Good Mind, The. FaBoRV

Twelve years old, my father put. Harvest Time. G. A. Watermeyer, *tr. by* Guy Butler, Uys Krige *and* Jack Cope. PeSA

Twentieth Anniversary. Betty Adcock. MT

20th Century, The. Darrell Gray. UL

Twentieth-Century Blues. Kenneth Fearing. CMoP

20th Century Requiem. Patricia M. Saunders. CN

Twentieth Telegram ("Ah my city, my lady"). Abd al-Aziz al-Maqalih, *tr. fr. Arabic by* Lena Jayyusi *and* Christopher Middleton. *Fr.* Telegrams of Tenderness for Sanaa. MAP

Twentieth year is well-nigh past, The. To Mary. William Cowper. EnLoPo; EnRP; FiP; NOEC
(My Mary.) OBEV
(To the Same.) GTBS; GTBS-P

20. Barbara Guest. PoM

Twenty Below. R. A. D. Ford. CaP; NOBC

Twenty brothers of Eynhallow, The. Our Lady of the Waves. George Mackay Brown. NePoEA-2

Twenty-eight Characters Sent to Tung-ts'un. Cheng Hsieh, *tr. fr. Chinese by* Jonathan Chaves. CoBLCP

28 VIII 69. Laura Chester. IHMS

Twenty-Eight Poems Inscribed on T'ien-kuan Mountai, *sels.* Chao Meng-fu, *tr. fr. Chinese by* Jonathan Chaves. CoBLCP
Cutstone Pond.
Dragon Mouth Cliff.
Spirit Pool.
Stone Man Peak.
Thunder God Cliff.

Twenty-eight young men bathe by the shore. Walt Whitman. *Fr.* Song of Myself, XI. HAP; NoP

25th Dance—Saying Things about Making Gardens—22 March 1964.
　Jackson MacLow.　LP
Twenty-fifth Year of His Life, The.　Constantine P. Cavafy, *tr. fr. Greek*
　by Edmund Keeley *and* Philip Sherrard.　PeHV
Twenty-first Day of the Seventh Month.　Yüan Hung-tao, *tr. fr. Chinese*
　by Jonathan Chaves.　CoBLCP
Twenty five/ and she waited.　25.40 P.M. (Past Mourning).　a-dZiko
　Simba.　WS
25 December 1960.　Ingrid Jonker, *tr. fr. Afrikaans by* Jack Cope *and* Uys
　Krige.　PeSA
25.40 P.M. (Past Mourning).　a-dZiko Simba.　WS
25:1:68.　Philip Whalen.　PoM
Twenty-four Hokku, *sels.*　Kito, *tr. fr. Japanese by* Hiroaki Sato.　FCEI
　"An ugly sight—a burn mark on the straw mat."
　"Bright moon: a crab, The."
　"Daybreak: in its madder-red."
　"Escaping a dog, a rooster flaps."
　"Even the soil is withered and saddening."
　"I drink water and my stomach bulges."
　"I see the shadow of a warbler."
　Love.
　"On my stupid face I see white."
　"Out of sadness I eat fish."
　Parting.
　Pitying a Woman Who Has Many Affairs.
　Sitting Quietly at Night.
　"Skylark rises through the dawn, A."
　"Stand of winter trees, A."
　"Stepping on violets."
　"Tumble, fall, crash, then silence, A."
　"Warbler escapes next door, A."
　"Warbler, what are you afraid of?."
　Water Lowers and Stones Show.
　"When evening comes, plovers fly."
　"Winning wrestler leaves, The."
　"Woman who has crossed the river, A."
　"Yawning and praising the moon."
Twenty-four Poems of Living in the Mountains, *sel.*　Zengetsu, *tr. fr.*
　Chinese by Lucien Stryk *and* Takashi Ikemoto.
　"Mind, mind, mind—above the Path."　ZPCJ
Twenty-four Tanka, *sels.*　Sanetomo, *tr. fr. Japanese by* Burton Watson.
　FCEI
　"As evening comes."
　"As the warrior reaches up."
　"Bamboo frond, The."
　"Bitter sight—/ I watch and my tears."
　"Boneset, why are you blooming."
　"By Hakone Road/ I cross over."
　"Fabrics swirled in a thousand."
　"Grown over with straggly saw grass."
　"Gull-haunted,/ the windblown shore of Susaki."
　"I didn't mean/ to recall the past."
　"I open the pine door."
　"If only the world."
　"In the rockbound pool."
　"Is it always so bleak a sight?."
　"Leaves of the small oaks, The."
　"Long-drawn-out autumn, The."
　"Sleet rattles on the leaves."
　"So cold the night."
　"This world—/ call it an image."
　"Though a time come."
　"Too much/ at one time."
　"Waves of the great sea, The."
　"When the wild goose."
　"You erect pagodas."
Twenty-four Years.　Dylan Thomas.　CMoP; MAT; MoAB; NAs; OxBSP
Twenty Golden Years Ago.　James Clarence Mangan.　NOBVV
Twenty Hokku, *sels.*　Kyorai, *tr. fr. Japanese by* Burton Watson.　FCEI
　"Close of day."
　"Coming, coming!'"
　"Cuckoo sings/ at right angles, The."
　"Deep in the family shrine."
　"Distant sailboat never quite, A."
　"Every boatman in."
　"Fall breezes/ time to try out the."
　"Full sail, reefed sail."
　"He doesn't seem."
　"How to tell."
　"In this heat."
　On the Death of His Younger Sister.

Poem of Parting.
"Point of rock."
"Rocky shore/ flocks of plovers."
"So hot the melons."
"That mountain I crossed."
"Too dark to tell the gate."
"Waters of the lake, The."
"What's this?/ wearing a long sword."
Twenty Lines to a Tree.　Judd Teller, *tr. fr. Yiddish by* Grace Schulman.
　PeBMYV
Twenty lost years have stol'n their hours away.　Alone in an Inn at
　Southampton, April the 25th, 1737.　Aaron Hill.　NOEC
Twenty men crossing a bridge.　Metaphors of a Magnifico.　Wallace
　Stevens.　SOTW
Twenty men stand watching the muckers.　Muckers.　Carl Sandburg.
　SaC
29 (A Dream in Two Parts).　Ai.　MAYP
Twenty-nine Hokku, *sels.*　Taigi, *tr. fr. Japanese by* Hiroaki Sato.　FCEI
　"Angry, is he, a wasp drinking water."
　"At daybreak when plovers call."
　"Autumn night: I question."
　"Beautiful sunlight has come."
　"Cold moon—the sound of the bridge."
　"Eyes open, I listen to spring."
　"I feel someone dying of an illness."
　"I lie down, I get up."
　"I peer into quietness."
　"I swept and ended up not sweeping."
　"In the waves rolling in."
　Kyuko and I Stayed at Rittei's.
　"Long night: I wake up, A."
　"Many mosquitoes bloated with blood."
　"Near a fence, young, small grasses."
　"Other end of this long bridge, The."
　"Rat has dropped into the water jar, A."
　"Servant, taking leave, A."
　"Shower: on a raft the pole, A."
　"Sound of casting a net downstream."
　"Sound of the rain, The."
　"Spring night: I frighten a woman, A."
　"Stream's clear: five inches, A."
　"Tree-searing wind: wrinkles of age."
　"Village child with spring grass, A."
　"Warbler: leaves hiding it."
　"Water of a shallow river, The."
　"Way it walks, the snail, The."
　"With a faint scent of river."
29 Poems, *sels.*　Louis Zukofsky.　PoE
　"Blue light is the night harbor-slip."　*Fr.* 27.
　"Not much more than being."　*Fr.* 2.
Twenty nine years of stale cake and flat ale.　The Gorilla at Twenty Nine
　Years.　J. D. Reed.　NeAC
29th Month, The.　Stan Rice.　NPGG
Twenty-odd years in doubt.　Joju, *tr. fr. Chinese by* Lucien Stryk *and*
　Takashi Ikemoto.　ZPCJ
Twenty of My Sons.　Anna Swirszczynska, *tr. fr. Polish by* Magnus Jan
　Krynski *and* Robert A. Maguire.　PwPP
Twenty-one Hokku, *sels.*　Boncho, *tr. fr. Japanese by* Hiroaki Sato.
　FCEI
　"Abandoned boat, An."
　"Ash pail has stopped dripping, The."
　"At an eagle's nest on dead camphor."
　"At this dilapidated hut."
　"Blowing wind's companion, A."
　"Crow wipes its beak on young grass, A."
　"Dark night: a child begins weeping."
　"Elongated line of a river, An."
　"Every bit of water in the paddies."
　"Fording a stream I stop."
　"From the porch, in various ways."
　"I try to call him back."
　"In a shower, black chopped wood."
　"In the heat haze a fox."
　Meeting Etsujin.
　"Not a Bird Singing, the Mountain Is All the More Quiet."
　"Patch of cloud rides the moon tonight, A."
　"Paulownia tree drops dead leaves, A."
　"Razor blade rusted overnight, A."
　"Spring rain isn't even enough, The."
　"Town smells of things, The."

Twenty-one Hokku, *sels.* Kaya Shirao, *tr. fr. Japanese by* Hiroaki Sato. FCEI
"About the time I miss someone."
"Bowman listens to a cuckoo, A."
"Cold moon: a white sheet."
"Floating cloud before my eyes, The."
"For eight or nine yards I watch."
"I put aside a story."
"In a field with scentless winter trees."
"In the dark garden at night."
"In the setting sun even its shadow."
"Just one evening snipe."
"Katydid stops chirping, A."
"Lightning gets to be terrifying."
"Night hailstones fall so hard."
"On a dark night, as long as it's dark."
"Pity the sweetfish after spawning."
"Rafts are moored to cherries."
"Skylark rises, A."
"Sparrows, mating."
"There's even someone combing her hair."
"Tides carry the haze, The."
"Wait a while—this is an evening shower."
Twenty-one Love Poems, *sels.* Adrienne Rich.
"Across a city from you, I'm with you." *Fr.* XVI. GLP; PeHV
"Can it be growing colder when I begin." *Fr.* XIX. GLP; NAAL-2
"Dark lintels, the blue and foreign stones, The." *Fr.* XXI. GLP; NoAM
"Every peak is a crater. This is the law of volcanoes." *Fr.* XI. GLP; NAAL-2; NoAM
"I can see my self years back at Sunion." *Fr.* VIII. GLP
"I come home from you through the early light of spring." *Fr.* IV. BoWoP; GLP
"I wake up in your bed. I know I have been dreaming." *Fr.* II. GLP; NAAL-2; NoAM; UnAS
"If I lay on that beach with you." *Fr.* XV. GLP
"It was your vision of the pilot." *Fr.* XIV. GLP
"No one's fated or doomed to love anyone." *Fr.* XVII. GLP
"Rain on the West Side Highway." *Fr.* XVIII. GLP; NAAL-2
"Rules break like a thermometer, The." *Fr.* XIII. GLP
"Since we're not young, weeks have to do time." *Fr.* III. GLP; UnAS
"Sleeping, turning in turn like planets." *Fr.* XII. GLP; PeHV
"That conversation we were always on the edge." *Fr.* XX. BoWoP; GLP; NoAM
"This apartment full of books could crack open." *Fr.* V. GLP
"What kind of beast would turn its life into words?." *Fr.* VII. GLP
"Whatever happens with us, your body." *Fr. The Floating Poem, Unnumbered.* GLP; NoAM
"Wherever in this city, screens flicker." *Fr.* I. GLP; PeHV
"Your dog, tranquil and innocent, dozes through." *Fr.* X. GLP
"Your silence today is a pond where drowned things live." *Fr.* IX. GLP
"Your small hands, precisely equal to my own." *Fr.* VI. GLP; PoE
Twenty-one Sonnets, *sel.* C. K. Stead.
"Rain, and a flurry of wind shaking the pear's white blossom." *Fr.* II. PeNZ
Twenty-one Years. *Unknown.* AmFP
Twenty Poems in Imitation of Han-shan and Shih-te, *sel.* Wang An-shih, *tr. fr. Chinese by* Burton Watson.
"Once I was a cow, a horse." CoBCP
Twenty-second of August, The. The Cruise of the Fair American. *Unknown.* PAH
Twenty-second of December, The. Bryant. GN
Twenty-seven Bums Give a Prostitute the Once. E. E. Cummings. OBAL
Twenty-seven Hokku, *sels.* Natsume Seibi, *tr. fr. Japanese by* Hiroaki Sato. FCEI
"Butterfly dying right in front, A."
"Deer in the morning look edgy and lost."
"Even gulls appear to feel cold."
"Having eaten fish."
"Hazy moon has detached itself, The."
"I want to die—at times I think."
"Is that the person I once loved."
"Lightning: a man walking."
"Not home! Not home!'"
Old Man's Thought, An.
On the Anniversary of My Father's Death.
"On the violets of the field."
Reading an "Ode to a Widow."
Reading the Analects.

"Sleeping in the grass, laying myself."
"Somehow I can't help looking."
"Spring bird—thinking of what?, A."
"Standing by a plum, a penniless poet."
"Summer night has turned to dawn, The."
Topic for a Painting, A.
"Traveler I saw yesterday, The."
"Under how many layers of fallen leaves."
"Useless acquaintances increase."
Visiting My Wife's Grave.
When Mother Died.
"White peonies about to collapse."
"Wild cat steps over kudzu vines, A."
Twenty-seven Quatrains Discussing Poetry, *sel.* Rai San'yo, *tr. fr. Chinese by* Burton Watson.
"In form most people look to Sung and Yuan models." *Fr.* XXVI. JLIC-2
26th Precinct Station. Louis Simpson. EOEF
Twenty-some years and I've finished my book. Rai San'yo, *tr. fr. Chinese by* Burton Watson. *Fr.* Random Thoughts on the Writing of History, VIII. JLIC-2
Twenty-third Flight. Earle Birney. HeIP; OxBC; SoSe
Twenty-third Street Runs into Heaven. Kenneth Patchen. ErPo
Twenty-three Hokku, *sels.* Onitsura, *tr. fr. Japanese by* Hiroaki Sato. FCEI
At the Opening of Chikubu's Collection of Haikai.
Bright Moon: after an Illness.
Cooling Off in the Evening.
Early Autumn.
"Fir stands sveltely under the moon, A."
"Gargoyle spits out a sparrow to a peach tree, A."
"I poured water in the basin."
"I think the May rains."
"In spring they croak."
"In the mist something's visible."
Late spring.
Leaving Itami in Early February.
Monk Kudo Asked Me, "What's Your Haikai Eye Like?"
Night Grew Late in Kuzuha Village in Hirakata, The.
On My Way Home.
"Profusely in confusion."
Remembering with Feeling.
"Spring day: a sparrow sand-bathing in my garden."
"Spring water's visible here and there, The."
Thirteenth Year of *Genroku* [1700], the Year My Boy Toshiaki Died, The.
"Under flying sweetfish clouds flow in a stream."
"Water bird, looking heavy, floats, A."
"Why are some icicles long, some short?"
Twenty-three Tanka, *sels.* Kyogoku Tamekane, *tr. fr. Japanese by* Burton Watson.
"Bird voices gently calling." FCEI
"Cuckoo,/ repeating his cry, The." FCEI
"Drawn on by moonlight." FCEI
"From peaks in the morning storm." FCEI
"In the path of the late sun." FCEI
"In the snow piled." FCEI
"Late at night." FCEI
"Mountain wind, The." FCEI
On Love. FCEI; LLLT
"On the storm's freezing blast." FCEI
"Plum flowers/ blooming crimson." FCEI
"Rainy night, A." FCEI
"So few rays." FCEI
"Takase Mountain:/ I push along." FCEI
"Though the glow." FCEI
"Traveler's pillow,/ bundled up, undone, A." FCEI
"Warbler's voice, The." FCEI
"Weighed down with dew." FCEI
"Where the bright moon comes up." FCEI
"While day lasted." FCEI
"White dew,/ come from no one knows where, The." FCEI
"Wind/ that for a time blew so wildly, The." FCEI
"Wind that tossed the pines." FCEI
22 Miles. José Angel Gutiérrez. FIA
Twenty-two Quatrains on Receiving the Obituary Notice for my Son, *sel.* T'ang Hsien-Tsu, *tr. fr. Chinese by* Jonathan Chaves.
"My son, you loved telling the story of Prince Nata." CoBLCP
Twenty Views of Wang-ch'uan, *sels.* Wang Wei, *tr. fr. Chinese by* Burton Watson. CoBCP
Bamboo Mile Lodge. *Fr.* 17.

Deer Fence. *Fr.* 5.
Meng-ch'eng Hollow. *Fr.* 1.
Twenty white horses on a red hill. *Unknown.* PrIm
Twenty-Year Marriage. Ai. BoWoP; MAYP; NoAM
Twenty Years After. Evan V. Shute. CaP
Twenty Years Ago. *At.* to A. J. Gault *and also to* Dill Armor Smith. BLPA
Twenty Years Ago. D. H. Lawrence. Mes
Twenty years are gone. Palinode. Oliver St. John Gogarty. OBMV
Twenty Years Hence. Walter Savage Landor. GBL; NAEL-2; NOBVV; TrGrPo; ViBoPo
Twenty years on the road of love. Nizar Qabbani, *tr. fr. Arabic by* Diana Der Hovanessian *and* Lena Jayyusi. *Fr.* Painting with Words. MAP
'Twer May, but ev'ry leaf wer dry. A Wife a-Prais'd. William Barnes. EBVV
'Twere a dree night, a dree night, as the squire's end drew nigh. The Dree Night. *Unknown.* ChTr
'Twere folly if ever/ The Whigs should endeavor. A New Ballad. *Unknown.* APAS
Twere infinit to tell what wondrous things. Astolfo Visits the Moon. Ariosto, *tr. fr. Italian by* Sir John Harington. *Fr.* Orlando Furioso, XXXIV. PFI
'Twere well your judgments but in plays did range. Dryden. *Fr.* The Spanish Friar [*or* Fryar]. OBSV
Twice. M. M. Hutchinson. BoTP
Twice. Christina Rossetti. GBL; NOBE; OBEV; OBNC; TOF; TrCP; ViBoPo
Twice a year. Alma Mater, Forget Me. William Cole. FiBHP
Twice blue and round. Girl of My Generation. Jacob Glatstein. AYP
Twice daily I carried water from the spring. The Water Carrier. John Montague. FaBCIP
Twice happy violets! that first had birth. Violets in Thaumantia's Bosome. Sir Edward Sherburne. OBS
Twice I ended up in a forest. The Woods. Sa'di Yusuf, *tr. by* Sargon Boulus *and* Naomi Shihab Nye. MAP
Twice I have written you that I am unhappy. A Letter to Her Father. Inib-sarri. BoWoP, *tr. by* Willis Barnstone
Twice nineteen years, dear Nancy, on this day. On Our Thirty-ninth Wedding Day. Jonathan Odell. CaP
Twice one are two. Twice. M. M. Hutchinson. BoTP
Twice or thrice had I loved thee. Air[e] and Angels. John Donne. JCP; MeLP; MePo; NAEL-1; OAEL-1; OBS; Prf; SeCP; SeCV-1
Twice recently young girls have/ given me the finger. Finger of Necessity. Coleman Barks. TW
Twice Shy. Seamus Heaney. TwCP
Twice Times Then Is Now. Ibn Hazm Al-Andalusi, *tr. fr. Persian by* Omar Pound. OBVE
Twickham Tweer. Jack Prelutsky. RHPC
Twicknam *or* Twickenham Garden. John Donne. EBEV; EnLoPo; FaBoPP; MeLP; MePo; OBS; OPOP; PoE; PoEL-2; SeCP; TEP
Twig Plummets, A. Hayyim Nahman Bialik, *tr. fr. Hebrew by* Bernhard Frank. MHeP
Twig turned in her hand and the diviner said, The: "Water." The Water-Witch. Martha Eugenie Perry. CaP
Twilight. Robert Frost. AnAmPo
Twilight. Louisa S. Guggenberger. NOBVV
Twilight. Heine, *tr. fr. German by* Louis Untermeyer. AWP
Twilight. D. H. Lawrence. OBMV
Twilight. Longfellow. CH
Twilight. John Masefield. OxBTC
Twilight./ Sad wagons roll in. Wagons. Jacob Glatstein, *tr. by* Benjamin *and* Barbara Harshav. AYP
Twilight at Sea. Amelia B. Welby. AA; AnAmPo
Twilight at the Heights. Joaquin Miller. AA
Twilight. By now the genial sea of dusk. Half Past Four, October. Anna Hajnal, *tr. by* Daniel Hoffman. BoWoP; MHuP
Twilight Calm. Christina Rossetti. BoNaP; OBNC
Twilight cicadas. Masaoka Shiki, *tr. fr. Japanese by* Burton Watson. *Fr.* Thirty-nine Haiku. FCEI
Twilight Comes. Hayden Carruth. AnAn; NNaP
Twilight comes, The; the sun. June Twilight. John Masefield. GoYe
Twilight cuckoo, The. Saigyo, *tr. fr. Japanese by* Burton Watson. *Fr.* Sixty-four Tanka. FCEI
Twilight falls; I soften the dusting feathers, The. Sappho. James Wright. NoAM
Twilight falls on the hill. Vespers. Odell Shepard. TrPWD
Twilight glitters on the fragmented glass. Judeebug's Country. Joe Johnson. PoBA
Twilight had fallen, austere and grey. The Tomtit. Walter de la Mare. FM

Twilight has fallen and the candled gloom. after John Keats. Peter Titheradge. *Fr.* Teatime Variations. FaBoPa
Twilight hours like birds flew by, The. Twilight at Sea. Amelia B. Welby. AA; AnAmPo
Twilight in California. Philip Dow. AmPA
Twilight in Middle March, A. Francis Ledwidge. BIrV
Twilight is sad and cloudy, The. Twilight. Longfellow. CH
Twilight is spacious, near things in it seem far. Miracles. Conrad Aiken. MoAmPo
Twilight it is, and the far woods are dim, and the rooks cry. Twilight. John Masefield. OxBTC
Twilight mist spreads along the damp moss, The. The Drunken Gentleman. Yin O, *tr. by* Lois Fusek. ATF
Twilight Musings. Mary Weston Fordham. CBWP-2
Twilight of Disquietude, The, *sels. Christopher Brennan.* PoAu-1
My Heart Was Wandering in the Sands.
Years That Go to Make Me Man, The.
Twilight of Earth, The. "Æ" AnIL
Twilight of Freedom. Osip Mandelstam, *tr. fr. Russian by* Andrew Glaze. VWA
Twilight on Sumter. Richard Henry Stoddard. PAH
Twilight on Tweed. Andrew Lang. EBVV
Twilight. Red in the west. The Wild Duck. John Masefield. BrPo
Twilight Room. Hagiwara Sakutaro, *tr. fr. Japanese by* Hiroaki Sato. FCEI
Twilight Shadows round Me Fall, The. Ernest Edwin Ryden. AH
Twilight Thoughts in Israel. Melech Ravitch, *tr. fr. Yiddish by* Seymour Levitan. VWA
Twilight Time. Samuel Palmer. *See* Shoreham: Twilight Time.
Twilight turns from amethyst, The. Commonplace. James Joyce. FL
Twilight twiles in the vernal vale, The. In the Gloaming. James C. Bayles. NA
Twilights. James Wright. LCAP; NaP
Twilight's Last Gleaming. Arthur W. Monks. NIP; OFD
Twilit Revelation. Léonie Adams. MoAB; MoAmPo
"'Twill take some getting." "Sir, I think 'twill so." Man and Dog. Edward Thomas. FM
Twin. Phyllis Haring. PeSA
Twin Aces. Keith Wilson. Psk
Twin stars through my purpling pane. Dusk. Angelina Weld Grimké. CDC
Twin streaks twice higher than cumulus. Vapor Trails. Gary Snyder. CAPP; NAAL-2
Twine then the rays. Psycholophon. Gelett Burgess. CenHV; NA
Twined together and, as is customary. Never Such Love. Robert Graves. BoLoP
Twinings Orange Pekoe. Judith Moffett. PoA; SM
Twink Drives Back, in a Bad Mood, from a Party in Massachusetts. George Amabile. NYBP
Twinkle those small stars. *Unknown, tr. by* Arthur Waley. BoS
Twinkle, twinkle/ Little star. Star Struck. Sandra Inskeep-Fox. SoTCo
Twinkle, twinkle, little bat! The Mad Hatter's Song. "Lewis Carroll." *Fr.* Alice's Adventures in Wonderland, *ch.* 7. FaBoNo; NOBL; Par
Twinkle, twinkle, little star. The Star. Jane Taylor. BoTP; FaBoBe; FaFP; FaPON; NTCP; OxBChV; OxNR; Par; PYC; RAR; RHPC
Twinkling Earn, The. John Davidson. *Fr.* Winter in Strathearn. PoSH
Twinkling of an Eye. Benjamin Péret, *tr. fr. French by* Michael Benedikt. POS
Twins, The. Robert Browning. Mes
Twins. Gloria Escoffery. PVCV
Twins. Robert Graves. FaBoEE
Twins, The. Henry Sambrooke Leigh. CenHV; FaPON; RHPC
Twins. William Matthews. MAYP
Twins. "Owen Meredith." ErPo
Twins, The. Karl Shapiro. MoAmPo; TrJP
Twins, The. Judith Wright. PoAu-2
Twirl about, dance about. Dreidel Song. Efraim Rosenzweig. RAR
Twirling your blue skirts, travel[l]ing the sward. Blue Girls. John Crowe Ransom. ChTr; CMoP; GBL; LiTA; MoAB; MoAmPo; NoAM; PrIm; RB; TAP; VGW; WeW
Twirls on the tips of a carnation. The Oriental Ballerina. Rita Dove. NAmP
Twist about, turn about. *Unknown.* OxNR
Twist me a crown of windflowers. A Crown of Windflowers. Christina Rossetti. OxBChV
Twist thou and twine! in light and gloom. Featherstone's Doom. Robert Stephen Hawker. OBNC
Twist Ye, Twine Ye! Even So. Sir Walter Scott. *Fr.* Guy Mannering, *ch.* 4. EnRP
Twisted apple, with rain and magian fire, The. June Morning. Hugh McCrae. PoAu-1

Twister Twisting Twine. John Wallis. *See* When a twister a-twisting will twist him a twist.

Twisting/ swing/ a/ moment of flight. Uneven Parallel Bars. Patricia Gary. ASP

Twisting, circling, the green path slants. Cheng-tao Temple. Tai Piao-yüan, *tr. by* Jonathan Chaves. CoBLCP

Twitching in the cactus. Deathwatch. Michael S. S. Harper. AmPA; PoBA

Twitching, sniffs the liverwurst. Supper. George Keithley. SoTCo

Twittingpan seized my arm, though I'd have gone. The Encounter. Edgell Rickword. OxBTC

'Twixt Carrowbrough Edge and Settlingstones. Old Skinflint. W. W. Gibson. OBMV

'Twixt clouded heights Spain hurls to doom. The *Brooklyn* at Santiago. Wallace Rice. PAH

'Twixt Cup and Lip. Mark Hollis. FiBHP; NBLV

Twixt devil and deep sea, man hacks his caves. Arachne. William Empson. InvP; OBMV

'Twixt East and West a giant shape she grew. Sonnet on the Crimean War. William Forster. CBAP

'Twixt failure and success the point's so fine. Don't Give Up. *Unknown*. FaFP

'Twixt handkerchief and nose. A Rub. John Banister Tabb. OBAL

Twixt nature and Pygmalion there might appear great strife. *Unknown*. OAEL-1

Twixt the Girthhead and Langwoodend. The Lads of Wamphray. *Unknown*. ESPB

Two. Margarita Aliger, *tr. fr. Russian by* Elaine Feinstein. VWA

Two. Robert Canzoneri. HoPM

Two [, The]. Hugo von Hofmannsthal, *tr. fr. German*. AWP, *tr. by* Ludwig Lewisohn; TrJP, *tr. by* Jethro Bithell.

Two. Moishe Kulbak, *tr. fr. Yiddish by* Ruth Whitman. VWA

Two. Winfield Townley Scott. NYBP

Two African Breasts. Nizar Qabbani, *tr. fr. Arabic by* Diana Der Hovanessian *and* Lena Jayyusi. MAP

Two aldermen, three lawyers, five physicians. Of a Zealous Lady. Sir John Harington, *after the Latin of* Martial. FaBoEE

2 a.m./ December, and still no moon. Late Moon. Philip Levine. LCAP

2 a.m.: moonlight. The train has stopped. Track. Tomas Tranströmer, *tr. by* Robert Bly. EAS; RB

Two-an'-Six. Claude McKay. BANP

Two Anchors, The. Richard Henry Stoddard. BeLS

Two and One Are a Problem. Ogden Nash. FiBHP

Two and thirty is the ploughman. Etching. William Ernest Henley. *Fr.* In Hospital, XII. BrPo

Two Angels, The. Whittier. AA

Two angels came through the gate of Heaven. A Song of Two Angels. Laura E. Richards. AA

Two angels from the North. Charm: Burns. *Unknown*. FaBoUs

Two Animals, One Flood. Diane Glancy. STE

Two Appeals to John Harralson, Agent. *Unknown*. OBAL

Two April Mornings, The. Wordsworth. EBEV; EnRP; GTBS; GTBS-P; NAEL-2

Two are left alone, The. It Doesn't Count. István Vas, *tr. by* Edwin Morgan. MHuP

Two Are Together. Geoffrey Grigson. GBL

Two Argosies. Wallace Bruce. AA

Two Armies. Stephen Spender. OBWP; OxBTC; WaP

Two baths in one day! Man and Woman. Don L. Lee. NeAC

Two battles, hundreds of years ago. After the Fifth of June. Yusuf al-Khal, *tr. by* May Jayyusi *and* Naomi Shihab Nye. MAP

Two beers screw my head up. Hustlers. Dennis Cooper. UL

Two bells to pealing through my age. Harald, the Agnostic Ale-loving Old Shepherd Enemy of the Whisky-drinking Ploughmen and Harvesters, Walks over the Sabbath Hill to the Shearing. George Mackay Brown. NePoEA-2

Two Birth Poems, *sels.* Lauris Edmond. ATNZ
    Shift of Emphasis, A. *Fr.* I.
    Zero Population Growth. *Fr.* II.

Two blind mice. Paul Dehn. *Fr.* Rhymes for a Modern Nursery. FiBHP

Two bloated bodies in rotted rags. War. Sulamith Ish-Kishor. GoYe

Two bodies have I. *Unknown*. OxNR

Two books a prayer shawl and one glass eye. Formations. William Freedman. VWA

Two-boots in the forest walks. The Intruder. James Reeves. OnUR; PDV

Two boys uncoached are tossing a poem together. Catch. Robert Francis. ASP; HeIP; InPK

Two boys, whose birth beyond all question springs. Charles Churchill. *Fr.* The Prophecy of Famine. OBSV

Two bronzes, but they were passing bronze before. Two Wrestlers. Robert Francis. TSL

Two Brothers, The. *Unknown*. AmFP

Two brothers devised what at sight. Laurence Perrine. SoTCo

Two Brothers in a Field of Absence. Cynthia MacDonald. NIP

Two brothers we are. *Unknown*. OxNR

Two brown heads with tossing curls. Katie Lee and Willy [*or* Willie] Grey. *At. to* Josie R. Hunt *and to* J. H. Pixley. BeLS; BLPA

Two bubbles found they had rainbows on their curves. Bubbles. Carl Sandburg. TDD

Two Bulls, The. *Unknown, tr. fr. Irish by* Thomas Kinsella. *Fr.* How the Bulls Were Begotten. NOIV

Two Campers in Cloud Country. Sylvia Plath. NYBP

Two campers (King Lear and his clown?). Outward Bound. James Simmons. CIP

Two Captains, The. William Johnson Cory. *See* when George the Third was reigning a hundred years ago.

Two Carols to Our Lady. *Unknown*. ACP

Two caterpillars crawling on a leaf. Immortality. Joseph Jefferson. BLPA

Two Cats, The. Elizabeth Jane Coatsworth. ILY; TDD

Two Cats/ One up a tree. Diamond Cut Diamond. Ewart Milne. FaBoCh; NeIP

Two-Cent Coal. *Unknown*. AmFP

Two Chartist Songs, *sels.* Thomas Cooper. PF
    "Song for the free—the brave and the free, A."
    "Time shall come when wrong shall end, The."

Two Children, The. Emily Brontë. PoEL-5

Two children, dressed in court costume. An Old Picture. Howard Nemerov. OxBSP

Two Chorale-Preludes. Geoffrey Hill. OxBC

Two Christs were at Golgotha. Early Lynching. Carl Sandburg. MoAmPo

Two Chronometers. Kenneth Slessor. *Fr.* Five Visions of Captain Cook. SeCePo

Two circles. The upper circle much smaller. The Crowded Circle. Claude Royet-Journoud, *tr. by* Keith Waldrop. RHTwFP

Two coffees in the Español, the last. Conrad Aiken. *Fr.* Preludes for Memnon; or, Preludes to Attitude. FYAP; LiTA; NoAM

Two Coffins, The. Eugene Field. AnAmPo

Two college sophs of Cambridge growth. Cassinus and Peter. Swift. OAEL-1; PPP

Two Comical Folk. Mother Goose. OxNR

Two Countries. José Martí, *tr. fr. Spanish by* Mona Hinton. TTY

Two cows stand transfixed. Blurry Cow. Chase Twichell. MAYP

Two crows sew themselves onto the lace flag. The Process. Tom Clark. UL

Two Cultures. David Dabydeen. UAS

Two darknesses embraced each other. Bayonets. Jacob Glatstein, *tr. by* Benjamin *and* Barbara Harshav. AYP

Two days ago the sky was. Autumn Rain. Kenneth Rexroth. NU

Two days she miss'd her dove, and then alas! Minnie and Her Dove. Charles Tennyson Turner. FM

Two days there were of colour and of sun. Wartime Report Centre: Solo School. Mabel Ferrett. CN

Two dead divers hauled up in their bell, The. The Divers' Death. Alison Brackenbury. DiPo

Two Decisions. Vernon Watkins. OxBTC

Two Dedications, *sels.* Gwendolyn Brooks.
    Chicago Picasso, The. BPo; EyDe; LiTM
    Wall, The. PoBA
    "South of success and east of gloss and glass are." PoNe

Two Deserts, The. Coventry Patmore. BoNaP

Two Dogs. John Davidson. FM

Two Dogs. Ruth Kim Chun-soo, *tr. fr. Korean by* Koh Chang-soo. ACKP

Two dreams came down to earth one night. The Dreams. Eugene Field. AnAmPo

Two Drinking Songs, *sels.* T'ao Yuan-ming.
    "I built my hut near where people live." *Fr.* 1. NU
    (I Built My Hut.) AWP, *tr. by* Arthur Waley.
    "Such a strong color on the late chrysanthemums." *Fr.* 2. NU

Two Drops. Zbigniew Herbert, *tr. fr. Polish by* Czeslaw Milosz. RB

Two dykes went their separate routes. *Unknown*. PeHV

Two empires by the sea. International Hymn. George Huntington. PoLF

Two Englishmen. Douglas Stewart. CBAP

Two Epigrams, *sels*. James Kenneth Stephen.
  Cynicus to W. Shakspere. CenHV
  Senex to Matt. Prior. CenHV; FiBHP
Two Epigrams, *sels*. Sir William Watson. TrGrPo
  Love.
  Poet, The.
Two evils, monstrous either one apart. Winter Remembered. John
  Crowe Ransom. HAP; MoAB; NOBA; OxBA; PrIm; UnPo; VGW
Two-Faced Too. *Unknown, tr. fr. Welsh by* Glyn Jones. OBWVE
Two Families, The. Joyce L. Brisley. BoTP
Two Fawns That Didn't See the Light This Spring. Gary Snyder. HCAP
Two figures in deep water. Walking to Bellrock. Michael Ondaatje.
  NOBC
Two Figures in Dense Violet Light. Wallace Stevens. MoAB; MoAmPo
Two Figures on Canvas. Gerald William Barrax. MT
Two figures there beneath the dome, walking with similar pace. St.
  Sophia. John Fuller. DiPo
Two Fires, The. Judith Wright. MoBrPo
Two Fish. Katha Pollitt. DiPo
Two Fish by a Willow Embankment. Hsü Wei, *tr. fr. Chinese by*
  Jonathan Chaves. CoBLCP
Two Fishermen. Stanley Moss. CoAP; VWA
  (Fisherman.) DiL
Two fleets have sailed from Spain. The one would seek. The Sailing of
  the Fleet. *Unknown.* PAH
Two forms move among the dead, high sleep. The Owl in the
  Sarcophagus. Wallace Stevens. FaBoMo
Two Foscari, The, *sel*. Byron.
  Swimming. GN
Two Friends. Nikki Giovanni. ILY
Two Friends, The. Charles Godfrey Leland. AA
Two friends at the close of summer. Why She Says No. Ellen Bryant
  Voigt. FaBoWP
Two friends talked of dark politics in light. Night Out. R. A. Simpson.
  PoAu-2
2 f's/ in giraffe, The. The Giraffe. Ron Padgett. *Fr.* Three Animals.
  TTTS
Two full years went by, and in this room. The Woodworm. Erminia Fua
  Fusinato, *tr. by* Muriel Kittel. DMI
Two Fusiliers. Robert Graves. MMA
Two Gardens. Yona Wallach, *tr. fr. Hebrew by* Warren Bargad *and*
  Stanley F. Chyet. IP
Two Garnett brothers who run the Shell station here, The. Sweep.
  Rodney Jones. MT
Two gates unto the road of life there are. The Road of Life. William
  Morris. *Fr.* The Earthly Paradise. OBNC
Two Generations. L. A. G. Strong. OBMV
Two Gentlemen of Verona, The, *sels*. Shakespeare.
  My Thoughts Do Harbour. *Fr.* III, i. CTC
  This Spring of Love. *Fr.* I, iii. ChTr
  "This have I shunned the fire for fear of burning." *Fr.* I, iii. GBL
  Who Is Silvia [*or* Sylvia]? *Fr.* IV, ii. BLPL; EiL; FaBoBe; FaFP;
    GN; LiTB; OAEL-1; TrGrPo
  (Silvia.) OBEV
  (Song to Silvia.) OBSC
Two German officers crossed the Rhine, parlee-voo. Hinky Dinky, Parlee-
  Voo. *Unknown.* AS
Two Gifts. *Unknown, tr. fr. Catalan by* Willis Barnstone. BoWoP
Two girls barefoot walking in the rain. On Growing Old in San
  Francisco. Jack Gilbert. NPGG
Two girls discover. The Secret. Denise Levertov. NaP; NIP
Two girls of twelve or so at a table. Charles Reznikoff. PCP
Two Glasses, The. Ella Wheeler Wilcox. BLPA; BLPL
Two golden parrots perch atop her hand. A Southern Song. Wen T'ing-
  yün, *tr. by* Lois Fusek. ATF
Two Graces, *sels*. *Unknown.*
  "Hurly, hurly, roon the table." FaBoCh
  "Some hae meat that canna eat." FaBoCh
  (Child's Grace, A, *at. to* Burns) FaPON; MoShBr
Two Guitars, *sels*. Gloria A. Maxson. TSM
  Dead, The.
  Living, The.
Two Handfuls of *Waka* for Thelonious Sphere Monk (d. Feb. 1982).
  Walter Lew. BrSi
Two Hands. Anne Sexton. CAPP
Two hands lie still, the hairy and the white. Love for a Hand. Karl
  Shapiro. CoAP; NYBP
Two hands on the Water. Zuhur Dixon, *tr. fr. Arabic by* Patricia Alanah
  Byrne *and* Salma Khadra Jayyusi. MAP
Two hands upon the breast. Now and Afterwards. Dinah Maria Mulock
  Craik. PoLF; WGRP

Two Hangovers. James Wright. LCAP
Two-headed Calf, The. Laura Gilpin. FYAP
Two heads are better than one. Binary. Bob Perelman. LP
Two Hearts Divided. R. Williams Parry, *tr. fr. Welsh by* Joseph P.
  Clancy. OBWVE
Two hearts: two blades of grass I braid together. Weaving Love-Knots 2.
  Hsüeh T'ao, *tr. by* Carolyn Kizer. BoWoP
Two Heavens. Leigh Hunt. GN
Two heavy trestles, and a board. My Table. W. B. Yeats. *Fr.*
  Meditations in Time of Civil War, III. LiTB
Two Heroes. Harriet Monroe. *See* Commemoration Ode: Washington.
Two Hoboes. *Unknown.* WTO
Two Hookers. A. K. Redwing. VoR
Two horses in yellow light. August. Adrienne Rich. CAPP; NNaP;
  PBWP
Two hours, or more, beyond the prime of a blithe April day. The Battle
  of Charleston Harbor. Paul Hamilton Hayne. PAH
Two Houses. Edward Thomas. FaBoCh
Two hummingbirds as evanescent as. Vision. Richard Eberhart. NYBP
Two Hunchbacks. Anna Swirszczynska, *tr. fr. Polish by* Magnus Jan
  Krynski *and* Robert A. Maguire. PwPP
Two hundred men and eighteen killed. James Henry. NOBVV
209 Canal. Richard Howard. TAP
270 The birches are worn out by mirrors. My Final Agonies. Benjamin
  Péret, *tr. by* James Laughlin. POS
225 days under grass. For Jane. Charles Bukowski. HoPM
Two Hundred Unborn Lambs. Alastair Fowler. NPo
Two hundred wagons, rolling out to Oregon. The Oregon Trail. Arthur
  Guiterman. FaPON
Two in August. John Crowe Ransom. AWP; OxBA; PPP
Two in Bed. Abram Bunn Ross. FaPON; NTCP
Two in the afternoon. The restlessness. Down the Nile. Robert Lowell.
  HCAP
Two in the Campagna. Robert Browning. EBEV; EBVV; ELP;
  GTBS-P; NAEL-2; NOBE; NOBVV; NoP; OAEL-2; OBNC; PoE;
  PoEL-5; SeCePo; TOF; TrGrPo
Two in Twilight. Eugenio Montale, *tr. fr. Italian by* William Arrowsmith.
  AnAn
Two infants vis-à-vis. Bleecker Street. Jean Garrigue. TAP
Two Invocations of Death, *sels*. Kathleen Jessie Raine.
  "Death, I repent." *Fr.* I. OxBTC
  (Invocation of Death.) MoAB
  "From a place I came." *Fr.* II. OxBTC
Two Invocations of the Virgin, II. Chaucer. *Fr.* The Canterbury Tales:
  The Prologue of the Prioress's Tale. ACP
Two Japanese Poems, *sels*. Gust Gils. DuIn
  "Fujiyama/ is quite a sight, The." *Fr.* I.
  "Mayor of Fukui, The." *Fr.* II.
Two Jazz Poems. Carl Wendell Hines, Jr.. AmNP
Two Jerusalems rise up. Jerusalem. Ruben Kanalenstein, *tr. by* Yishai
  Tobin. VWA
Two Kids. Saibara, *tr. fr. Japanese by* Hiroaki Sato. FCEI
Two Kitchen Songs. Dame Edith Sitwell. CMoP
Two ladies sit in the spotless driveway. Garage Sale. Karl Shapiro.
  Psk
Two ladies to the summit of my mind. Sonnet: Of Beauty and Duty.
  Dante, *tr. by* Dante Gabriel Rossetti. AWP
Two Landscapes, Grammar. Alain Delahaye, *tr. fr. French by* Anthony
  Barnett. RHTwFP
Two Lean Cats. Myron O'Higgins. PoBA; PoNe
Two leaps the water from its race. A Mill. William Allingham.
  FaBoEE; OxBSP; SeCePo
Two Legends. Ted Hughes. *Fr.* Crow. PoE
Two-Legs. Dan Pagis, *tr. fr. Hebrew by* Bernhard Frank. MHeP
Two legs sat upon three legs. Mother Goose. OxNR
  (Riddle: "Two legs sat upon three legs.") NTCP
Two liddle niggers all dressed in white. Raise a "Rucus" To-Night.
  Unknown. BPo; TAP
Two Limericks after Lear, *sels*. John Updike. SoTCo
  "There was an old poop from Poughkeepsie."
  "Touchy old gent from Cohasset, A."
Two Lines from the Brothers Grimm. Gregory Orr. AmPA
Two Lips. Thomas Hardy. BoLoP
Two little arabs adult and arabesque. Hans Arp, *tr. by* Harriet Watts.
  FaBoNo
Two little beaks went tap! tap! tap! To Let. D. Newey-Johnson. BoTP
Two little birdies, one wintry day. The Birdies' Breakfast. J. M. BoTP
Two Little Blackbirds. *Unknown.* BoTP
Two little clouds, one summer's day. The Rainbow Fairies. *Unknown.*
  BoTP
Two little creatures. Monkeys. Padraic Colum. Mes; OxBTC

Two little dicky-birds. Dicky-Birds. Natalie Joan. BoTP
Two little dicky birds. *Unknown*. OxNR
Two little dogs/ Sat by the fire. *Unknown*. OxNR
Two little elves/ Were lost one night. A Fairy Dream. Dorothy Graddon. BoTP
Two little girls, one fair, one dark. The Lost Children. Randall Jarrell. CoAP; PrIm; TAP
Two Little Kittens. Jane Taylor. BoTP
Two Little Kittens. *Unknown*. OBCA; OxBChV
Two Little Miss Lloyds, The. Elizabeth Turner. OxBChV
Two little ships were sailing by. Upon a Christmas Morning. *Unknown*. AmFP
Two Lives, *sels*. William Ellery Leonard. Son
  Love's Primal Want.
  True Marriage Is True Love.
Two lofty ships of Eng-e-land set sail. The Wild Barbaree. *Unknown*. AmFP
Two Look at Two. Robert Frost. MoAB; MoAmPo; NU
Two Lovers, The. Marie de France, *tr. by* Patricia Terry. BoWoP
Two Loves. Lord Alfred Bruce Douglas. PeHV
Two Loves. Richard Eberhart. CMoP
Two loves had I. Now both are dead. Dead Love. Mary Mathews Adams. AA
"Two loves I have of comfort and despair." Shakespeare. *Fr*. Sonnets, CXLIV. EBEV; InvP; NAEL-1; NIP; OAEL-1; PeHV; PoEL-2; Son
Two Lyrics, *sels*. Lorenzo de' Medici, *tr. fr. Italian by* John Addington Symonds. AWP
  "How can I sing light-souled and fancy-free." *Fr*. II.
  "Into a little close of mine I went." *Fr*. I.
Two Magicians, The. *Unknown*. ChTr; OAEL-1; OxBoLi
Two Magicians, The. *Unknown*. *See* The lady stands in her bower door.
Two Magpies Sat on a Garden Rail. D'Arcy Wentworth Thompson. MoShBr
Two magpies under the cypresses, The. What Birds Were There. William Everson. NoAM
Two Man a Road. *Unknown*. PBCV
Two Masks Unearthed in Bulgaria. William Meredith. EyDe
Two Meetings, The. Eugene Field. PWR
Two Memorial Poems. David Avidan, *tr. fr. Hebrew by* Warren Bargad *and* Stanley F. Chyet. IP
Two men walk along the edge of a country road. Under the Green Ceiling. Stephen Dobyns. NAmP
Two men wrote a lexicon, Liddell and Scott. *Unknown*. CenHV
Two More about a Crow, in the Manner of Zukofsky. *Unknown, tr. fr. Seneca Indian by* Jerome Rothenberg *and* Richard Johnny John. STP
Two Mornings. Lawrence McGaugh. PoBA
Two Mornings and Two Evenings. Elizabeth Bishop. PoA
Two Mountains Men Have Climbed. Pauline Starkweather. GoYe
Two mules stand in front of the brick wall of a warehouse. Mule Team and Poster. Donald Justice. AnAn
Two murders this month. October. Greg Pape. AmPA
Two Musicians, The. Henrietta Cordelia Ray. CBWP-3
Two Mysteries, The. Mary Mapes Dodge. AA; PWR; TrCP; WGRP
Two Neighbours, The. George Campbell Hay. OxBS
Two never-ever-will-be lovers each. Mathematics of Encounter. Isabella Gardner. ErPo
Two Nights, The. Nicki Jackowska. DT
Two nights in Manchester: nothing much to do. Mr. Cooper. Anthony Thwaite. OxBTC
Two nights running I was out there. The Mummies. Maxine W. Kumin. Psk
Two Noble Kinsmen, The, *sels*. John Fletcher *and* Shakespeare.
  Bridal Song, A ("Roses, their sharp spines being gone"). *Fr*. I, i. EIL; NOBE; OBSC
  "Hail Sovereign Queen of secrets, who hast power." *Fr*. V, i. PoEL-2
  Urns and Odours Bring Away! *Fr*. I, v. EIL
    (Dirge of the Three Queens.) OBEV
    (Funeral Song.) ChTr; OBS
2 November 1982. Alan Bold. NPo
Two o'Clock. Katharine Pyle. *Fr*. The Wonder Clock. OBCA
Two of a Kind. Bob Schild. CowP
Two of a Trade. Samuel Willoughby Duffield. AA
Two, of course there are two. Death and Co. Sylvia Plath. CMoP; FF; LCAP; PrIm
Two of Cups, The. Emmett Jarrett. NeAC
Two of the Festivals of Death. João Cabral de Melo Neto, *tr. fr. Portuguese by* W. S. Merwin. ATCBP
Two of Thy children one summer day worked in their garden, Lord. The Garden. Rose Parkwood. WGRP
Two of you went off in a boat, The. *Unknown, tr. by* Arthur Waley. BoS

Two Old Bachelors, The. Edward Lear. BeLS; FiBHP
Two Old Crows. Vachel Lindsay. FaBoNo; OBAL
Two old dancing shoes my grandfather. Genius. Philip Levine. NoAM
Two old friends, dead too early. North Haven. Philip Booth. BLA
Two Old Kings, The. John Byrne Leicester Warren, 3rd Baron De Tabley. OBEV
Two Old Ladies. Siegfried Sassoon. OxBTC
Two Old Lenten Rhymes, *sels*. *Unknown*. ACP
  "Lenten has brought us, as I understand." *Fr*. II.
  "Lenten stuff is come to the town." *Fr*. I.
Two Old Men Look at the Sea. J. R. Hervey. ATNZ
Two old nuns stood in the blizzard. February 4. A. Leyeles, *tr. fr. Yiddish by* Benjamin *and* Barbara Harshav. *Fr*. Fabius Lind's Diary. AYP
Two or Three; a Recipe [*or* Receipt] to Make a Cuckold. Pope. BoLoP; FaBoEE
Two or three lines across; the black ones, down. Crayon House. Muriel Rukeyser. EyDe
Two or three visits, and two or three bows. Two or Three; a Recipe [*or* Receipt] to Make a Cuckold. Pope. BoLoP; FaBoEE
Two Orgasms, *sels*. Nancy Sullivan. NIP
  "At Lascaux they've shut the caves." *Fr*. II.
  "More like the candle going out." *Fr*. I.
Two Paintings by Gustav Klimt. Jorie Graham. SV
Two pairs of hands go round. Korf's Clock. Christian Morgenstern, *tr. by* Geoffrey Grigson. FaBoNo
Two pairs of mallards, tandem. Nearing Winter. Ernest Sandeen. NYBP
Two Parents, The. "Hugh MacDiarmid." FaBoTw; OxBTC
Two Paths. Julia Caroline Ripley Dorr. AA
Two People. Eve Merriam. RHPC
Two People. E. V. Rieu. RHPC
Two people. Fast. John Tagliabue. SD
Two people in a room, speaking harshly. Novella. Adrienne Rich. PPP
Two people live in Rosamund. Two People. E. V. Rieu. RHPC
Two people live side by side. Two. Moishe Kulbak, *tr. by* Ruth Whitman. VWA
Two people meet. The sky turns winter. Glances. William Stafford. SM
Two Performing Elephants. D. H. Lawrence. RB
Two perhaps three. Revelation. Zbigniew Herbert, *tr. by* Czeslaw Milosz. PwPP
Two Pewits. Edward Thomas. CH; FM
Two Pictures. *Unknown*. BeLS; BLPA; FaBoBe
Two Pictures of a Leaf. Marvin Bell. LCAP
Two Pieces for Suetonius. Robert Penn Warren. NOBA
Two pilgrims, broiling in the sun. Beware of Dogmas. Ebenezer Elliott. FaBoEE
Two Poems about President Harding. James Wright. CoAP; MoP
2 Poems for Black Relocation Centers. Etheridge Knight. NNaP
Two Poems on the Catholic Bavarians, *sels*. Edgar Bowers. CRP
  "Fierce and brooding holocaust of faith, The." *Fr*. I.
  "I know a wasted place high in the Alps." *Fr*. 2.
Two Poems Presented to the Gentleman in the Office of Palace Writers Ku Yen-hsien, *sel*. Lu Chi, *tr. fr. Chinese by* Burton Watson.
  "Off at dawn to service in the walled and storied palace." *Fr*. II. CoBCP
Two Poems to the Tune "Chin-tzu ching," *sels*. Ma Chih-yüan, *tr. fr. Chinese by* Jonathan Chaves. CoBLCP
  "At night, in west wind."
  "Catkins flying: floating white snow."
Two Poems to the Tune "Hsiao-t'iao hung," *sels*. Ni Tsan, *tr. fr. Chinese by* Jonathan Chaves. CoBLCP
  "Mist and water of Five Lakes, this body not gone home." *Fr*. II.
  "River of autumn water, pale, cold mist, A." *Fr*. I.
Two Poems to the Tune "Jen-yüeh yüan," *sels*. Ni Tsan, *tr. fr. Chinese by* Jonathan Chaves. CoBLCP
  "It breaks the heart, don't ask."
  "Startled awake, back from a dream."
Two Poems to the Tune "Po pu tuan," *sels*. Ma Chih-yüan, *tr. fr. Chinese by* Jonathan Chaves. CoBLCP
  "Among men of plain clothes."
  Staying in a Mountain Pavilion on a Summer Night.
Two Points of View. Lucian B. Watkins. BANP
Two poles, The. We didn't disagree. Echo ("Two poles. We didn't disagree."). Michael Palmer. IAT
Two policemen laughed, The. Policemen Laughing. Ray Fraser. NeAC
Two Portraits, *sels*. Tanikawa Shuntaro, *tr. fr. Japanese by* Hiroaki Sato. FCEI
  "I see a woman/ I see my wife." *Fr*. D.
  "I see a woman/ it's a woman who was my lover." *Fr*. C.

Two Postures beside a Fire. James Wright. HCAP
Two Prayers, The. Andrew Gillies. BLRP
Two Prayers. Charlotte Perkins Gilman. WGRP
Two purple pigeons circle a London square. The Exiled Heart. Maurice Lindsay. OxBS
Two Pursuits. Christina Rossetti. WPE
Two-quart virgin in my lap, A. The Aged Wino's Counsel to a Young Man on the Brink of Marriage. X. J. Kennedy. FF
Two Quatrains on the "Awash-in-Springtime Garden," sels. Ch'ien Ch'ien-yi, tr. fr. Chinese. WFTU
Lotus Pond. Tr. by Ronald Miao.
Willow Creek. Tr. by Irving Lo.
Two Questions, The. Alice Meynell. WPE
Two Red Roses across the Moon. William Morris. EBVV
Two Refugees. Mordecai Marcus. VWA
Two Rivers. Emerson. AmPP; NOBA; OxBA; PoE; TrGrPo
Two Rivers, The. Unknown. See Says Tweed to Till —.
Two roads diverged in a yellow wood. The Road Not Taken. Robert Frost. AiP; AmPP; ChTr; CMoP; FaBoCh; FaFP; FPL; HAP; HeIP; LiTA; LiTM; MoAB; MoAmPo; MoP; NAAL-2; NIP; NoAM; NoP; OxBA; PoLF; RFM; SoSe; TAP; TwCP
Two Roads, Etc. Dorothy Walters. IHMS
Two rows of foolish faces blent. Bored. Horatio Brown. PeHV
Two Rural Sisters. Charles Cotton. See Resolution in Four Sonnets, of a Poetical Question Put to Me by a Friend, Concerning Four Rural Sisters.
Two Sad. William Cole. RAR
Two sculptors. Four Translations from the English of Robert Hershon. Robert Hershon. NeAC
Two Selves, The. Margaret Avison. MoP
Two separate divided silences. Severed Selves. Dante Gabriel Rossetti. Fr. The House of Life, XL. BoLoP
Two Shadows. Elizabeth Spires. DiPo
Two shall be born, the whole wide world apart. Fate. Susan Marr Spalding. AA; BLPA
Two Shapes. Arthur Gregor. TAP
Two silhouettes. A Story. Yusuf al-Sa'igh, tr. by Diana Der Hovanessian with Salma Khadra Jayyusi. MAP
Two Sisters, The ("There was an old man in the North Countrie"). PrIm
Two Sisters, The ("There was an old woman lived on the seashore"). Unknown. AmFP
Two Sisters, The ("Was two sisters loved one man"). MAT
Two Solitudes. Evelyn Ames. GoYe
Two Songs, sels. C. Day Lewis. HAP; NoAM
"Come, live with me and be my love." Fr. II. BoLoP; NoAM; OBMV
(Song: "Come, live with me and be my love.") NIP; NoP
"I've heard them lilting at loom and belting." HAP; NoAM; OBMV
Two Songs, sels. Adrienne Rich.
"Sex, as they harshly call it." Fr. I. NIP; NOBA; TAP
"That 'old last act'!" Fr. II. NIP; NOBA; TAP
Two Songs about Flowers & Where I Was Walking. Unknown, tr. fr. Seneca Indian by Jerome Rothenberg and Johnny John. STP
Two Songs from a Play. W. B. Yeats.
Fr. The Resurrection, I. CMoP; FaBoTw; HAP; LiTB; NOBE; NoP; OAEL-2; PoE; PPP; PrIm
Fr. The Resurrection, II. CMoP; FaBoTw; HAP; LiTB; NOBE; NoP; OAEL-2; PPP; PrIm
Two Songs of a Fool. W. B. Yeats. CMoP; RB
Two Songs on the Economy of Abundance, sels. James Agee. MoAmPo
Red Sea.
Temperance Note: and Weather Prophecy.
Two Sonnets, sels. John Ashbery. VGW
Dido.
Idiot, The.
Two Sonnets, sels. Charles Hamilton Sorley. MMA; MoBrPo
"Saints have adored the lofty soul of you." Fr. I.
"Such, such is Death: no triumph: no defeat." Fr. II.
Two Sonnets for a Lost Love, sels. Samuel A. DeWitt. GoYe
"If I were less the man, I might have kept." Fr. II.
" 'There is no permanence,' you sagely said." Fr. I.
Two Sonnets on Fame, sels. Keats. EnRP
"Fame, like a wayward girl, will still be coy." Fr. I.
"How fever'd is the man who cannot look." Fr. II.
Two Sons. Laoiseach Mac an Bhaird. NOIV
Two Sons Drowning. Roger Weingarten. NAmP
Two Souls. Marjorie Pickthall. NOBC

Two Spirits, The. James Benjamin Kenyon. AA
Two Spirits [an Allegory], The. Shelley. CH; OAEL-2; Prf; WiR
Two spoons of sherry. The Witch's Work Song. T. H. White. FaBoNo
Two Springs. Li Ch'ing-chao, tr. fr. Chinese by Kenneth Rexroth. BoWoP
Two Stars, The. W. H. Davies. MoBrPo
Two stars there are in one faire firmament. Richard Barnfield. Fr. Sonnets, IV. PeHV
Two statesmen met by moonlight. What the Moon Saw. Vachel Lindsay. FaBoEE; OxBSP
Two steps from my garden rail. Hayyim Nahman Bialik, tr. fr. Hebrew by Maurice Samuel. Fr. Songs of the People, I. AWP
Two Stories. Charles Wright. FYAP
Two Strange Worlds. Francesca Yetunde Pereira. PBA
Two suicides, not in the one season. Waikato Railstop. Kendrick Smithyman. ATNZ
Two Summers in Moravia. Roger McDonald. CBAP
Two Surprises. R. W. McAlpine. PoLF
Two Swans, The. Thomas Hood. CH
Two sweeter babes you nare did see. Unknown. FaBoEE
Two Tales of Clumsy, sel. Gjertrud Schnackenberg.
"When Clumsy harks the gladsome ting-a-lings." Fr. I. NoAM
Two tapsters traded on Thames's side. Ballad of the Two Tapsters. Vernon Watkins. MoBS
Two Temples. Hattie Vose Hall. BLPA
Two that could not have lived their single lives. Two in August. John Crowe Ransom. AWP; OxBA; PPP
Two that through windy nights kept company. The Two Neighbours. George Campbell Hay. OxBS
Two thimblefuls of wine, and slightly later. The Stone-Hitter. Medbh McGuckian. DT
Two Things. Donald C. Babcock. NePoAm
Two things have set the world a-twist. Foxgloves and Snow. Marion Angus. PoSH
Two things I have asked of Thee. Neither Poverty nor Riches. Bible, O.T. Fr. Proverbs, XXX: 7-9. TrJP
"Two things," said Kant, "fill me with breathless awe." The Third Wonder. Edwin Markham. FYAP
Two things there are with Memory will abide. Memories. Thomas Bailey Aldrich. AA
Two things were set. Two Things. Donald C. Babcock. NePoAm
2000. Dave Smith. BLA
Two thousand feet beneath our wheels. Cockpit in the Clouds. Dick Dorrance. FaPON; RHPC
2976. Julia Uceda, tr. fr. Spanish by Willis Barnstone. BoWoP
2001: The Tennyson/ Hardy Poem. Gavin Ewart. FaBoCo
MMDCCXIII½. Lorenzo Thomas. UL
2021: Noon: Idaho. Bruce Hawkins. BWV
Two Tile Beaks. Maria Amalia Fonte Boa, tr. by Willis Barnstone and Nelson Cerqueira. BoWoP
Two Times Two Is Four. H. Leivick, tr. fr. Yiddish by Ruth Whitman. VWA
Two Tramps in Mud Time. Robert Frost. BLPL; CMoP; LiTA; LiTM; MoAB; MoAmPo; MoP; NAAL-2; NoAM; PrIm; TrGrPo
Two Translations from Villon, sel. Villon, tr. by J. M. Synge. Prayer of the Old Woman, Villon's Mother. MoBrPo
Two Travelers on a Summer Evening. Alfred Corn. BLA
Two Trees, The. W. B. Yeats. BrPo; OAEL-2
Two Trinities. Kenneth Mackenzie. CBAP
Two Trunks. Kuan Kuan, tr. fr. Chinese by Dominic Cheung. IFON
Two turbid streams in a confluence of sun's glare. Manhattan Bridge. A. Leyeles, tr. fr. Yiddish by Benjamin and Barbara Harshav. Fr. New York. AYP
Two Variations. Denise Levertov. NaP
2 Variations: All About Love. Philip Whalen. NeAP
Two vases stood on the Shelf of Life. Vases. Nan Terrell Reed. BLPA
Two Vast Enjoyments Commemorated. John Danforth. SCAP
Two Veterans. Walt Whitman. See Last sunbeam, The.
Two Views of a Cadaver Room. Sylvia Plath. CMoP; GoYe
Two Views of Two Ghost Towns. Charles Tomlinson. NoAM
Two virtues ride, by stallion, by nag. The Death of Myth-making. Sylvia Plath. PoA
Two Voices. Edmund Blunden. OBWP
Two voices are there: one is of the deep. James Kenneth Stephen. BXAP; FaBoCo; FaBoPa; FiBHP; NOBL; Par
(Sonnet on Wordsworth, A.) CenHV
Two voices are there; one is of the Sea. Thought [or Thoughts] of a Briton on the Subjugation of Switzerland. Wordsworth. EnRP
(England and Switzerland 1802.) GTBS; GTBS-P
(Sonnet: Thought of a Briton on the Subjugation of Switzerland.) ChER

Two Voices in a Meadow, *sels.* Richard Wilbur. NBLV; UnPo
  Milkweed, A. CRP
  Stone, A. CRP
Two Voyages. Maurice James Craig. NeIP
Two ways I love Thee, selfishly. Rabia, *tr. by* A. J. Arberry.
  TOF
Two webfoot brothers loved a fair. That Gentle Man from Boston Town.
  Joaquin Miller. AnAmPo
Two weeks of rain. Enough. Donald Finkel. BLA
Two Went Up into the Temple to Pray. Richard Crashaw. HAP
Two were silent in a sunless church, The. Her Dilemma. Thomas
  Hardy. BrPo; NOBVV
Two White Horses. *Unknown.* AS
Two White Women in the Sun. Munir Niazi, *tr. fr. Urdu by* Mahmood
  Jamal. PBMUP
Two wild duck of the upland spaces. Duck. John Lyle Donaghy.
  BIrV
Two Wise Generals. Ted Hughes. MoBS
Two Witches, *sel.* Robert Frost. CMoP
  Witch of Coös, The. LiTM; MoAB; NoAM; NOBA
Two Witches, The. Robert Graves. SO
Two Witches. Alexander Resnikoff. RHPC
Two Wives, The. William Dean Howells. AA
Two Women. Naomi Replansky. NMM
Two Women. Tania Van Zyl. PeSA
Two Women. Nathaniel Parker Willis. BeLS
Two Women I Know. Rita Anyiam–St. John. WS
Two women on the lone wet strand. The Watchers. William Stanley
  Braithwaite. PoNe
Two Words. Peter Seaton. LP
Two Words; a Wedding. B. P. Nichol. NOBC
Two words from China: "Ku li"—bitter strength. Ku Li. Robin Hyde.
  PeNZ
Two workmen were carrying a sheet of asbestos. Christo's. Paul
  Muldoon. CIP
Two worlds there are. One you think. Cleaning the Well. Fred
  Chappell. MT
Two Wrestlers. Robert Francis. TSL
Two X. E. E. Cummings. FaBoMo
Two-Year-Old Has Had a Motherless Week, The. Karl Shapiro.
  WeW
Two Years Later. John Wieners. PoM
Two years now since I last came. Arriving at Hangchou. Yüan Mei, *tr.
  by* Jonathan Chaves. CoBLCP
Two years thus spent in gathering knowledge. Tom Brainless as Student
  and Preacher at College. John Trumbull. *Fr.* The Progress of
  Dulness. AmPP
Two years to maturity. A needle injected into the thigh. Thanksgiving
  Dinner during Pelting Season. Mary Moran. GOS
Two years we spent. The Woods. Derek Mahon. NOIV
Two young maids in a beauty fair. *Malay Oral Tradition, tr. by* R. O.
  Winstedt. WTO
Two Young Men, 23 to 24 Years Old. C. P. Cavafy, *tr. fr. Greek by*
  Edmund Keeley *and* Philip Sherrard. PeHV
Twoborn. Rokwaho. STE
'Twould ring the bells of Heaven. The Bells of Heaven. Ralph
  Hodgson. BoTP; BrPo; EaLo; GoJo; LiTM; MoAB; MoBrPo;
  NOBE; OBEV; OxBSP
Tyburn and Westminster. John Heywood. ACP
Tycoon, Poet, Saint. Abdur-Rahman Slade Hopkinson. PBCV
Tyger! Tyger! burning bright. Blake. *See* Tiger! Tiger! burning bright.
Tying her bonnet under her chin. The Love-Knot. Nora Perry.
  AA
Tying Up for the Night at Maple River Bridge. Chang Chi, *tr. fr. Chinese
  by* Burton Watson. CoBCP
Tyl it was noon, they stoden for to se. At the Gate. Chaucer. *Fr.*
  Troilus and Criseyde [*or* Criseide]. SeCePo
Tyndarus attempting too kis a fayre lasse with a long nose. Of Tyndarus,
  That Frumped a Gentlewoman. *Unknown.* BIrV, *tr. by* Richard
  Stanyhurst
Type of the antique Rome! Rich reliquary. The Coliseum. Poe. AmPP;
  NOBA
Typewriter Revolution, The. D. J. Enright. NoP
Typhoon Season, A. Fei Ma, *tr. fr. Chinese by* Dominic Cheung.
  IFON
Tyrannic Love, *sels.* Dryden.
  Ah, How Sweet It Is to Love! *Fr.* IV, i. HoPM
  Epilogue to "Tyrannick Love." SeCV-2
Tyranny of Moths. Gerald Vizenor. VoR
Tyrants were/ people. Pentti Saarikoski, *tr. by* Aili Jarvenpa. SOP
Tyr'd with all these for restfull death I cry. *See* Tired with all these for
  restfull death I cry.

Tyre brought me up, who born in thee had been. Of Himself. Meleager,
  tr. by Richard Garnett. AWP
Tyre of the West, and glorying in the name. England. John Henry,
  Cardinal Newman. ACP
Tyrolean Elephant, The. Hans Arp, *tr. fr. French by* Michael Benedikt.
  POS
Tyson's Corner. Primus St. John. PoBA
Tywater. Richard Wilbur. CMoP; LiTA; LiTM; MoAB
Tzu-yeh Song. Li Po, *tr. fr. Chinese by* Burton Watson. CoBCP
Tzu Yeh Songs, *sels. Unknown, tr. fr. Chinese.*
  "All night I could not sleep." BoWoP, *tr. by* Arthur Waley.
    ("Nights are long and I cannot sleep.") CoBCP, *tr. by* Burton
    Watson.
  "At the time when blossoms." *Tr. by* Arthur Waley. BoWoP
  "Cool breezes—I sleep by the open window." *Tr. by* Burton Watson.
    CoBCP
  "Fragrance comes from the scent I wear, The." *Tr. by* Burton Watson.
    CoBCP
  "Hems gathered up, sash not yet tied." *Tr. by* Burton Watson.
    CoBCP
  "I heard my love was going to Yang-chou." *Tr. by* Arthur Waley.
    BoWoP
  "I will carry my coat and not put on my belt." *Tr. by* Arthur Waley.
    BoWoP
  "In the hottest time, when all is still and windless." *Tr. by* Burton
    Watson. CoBCP
  "Out the southern gate at sundown." *Tr. by* Burton Watson.
    CoBCP
  "When ice on the pond is three feet thick." *Tr. by* Burton Watson.
    CoBCP
Tz'u-yün Poem Written in Response: Tiger Hill, A. Liu Shih, *tr. fr.
  Chinese by* Irving Lo. WFTU

U

U bet u wer. To a Poet I Knew. Jewel C. Latimore. PoBA
U feel that way sometimes. Mixed Sketches. Don L. Lee. BPo;
  TAP
U Name This One. Carolyn M. Rodgers. BlSi; NMM; PoBA
U. S. Coast and Geodetic Survey Ship *Pioneer*, The. Robert Hershon.
  NeAC
U. S. 1946 King's X. Robert Frost. NIP
U. S. Sailor with the Japanese Skull, The. Winfield Townley Scott.
  LiTM; WaP
U-24 Anchors off New Orleans. Turner Cassity. MT
Ubi Sunt Qui ante Nos Fuerunt? *Unknown, tr. fr. Latin into Middle
  English.* NoP
Ubique. Joshua Sylvester. *See* Were I as base as is the lowly plain.
Uccello. Gregory Corso. FF; NeAP; PoM
Uccello on the Heath. Geoffrey Grigson. WaP
Udders dripping. Iida Dakotsu, *tr. by* Geoffrey Bownas *and* Anthony
  Thwaite. PeBJV
Uffia. Harriet R. White. NA
UFO Is Coming, A. Lo Ch'ing, *tr. fr. Chinese by* Dominic Cheung.
  IFON
Ugliest little boy. The Life of Lincoln West. Gwendolyn Brooks. FB;
  NoAM
Ugly Chile. Clarence Williams. TW
Ugly old man, An. No Great Matter. David Lawson. VGW
An ugly sight—a burn mark on the straw mat. Kito, *tr. fr. Japanese by*
  Hiroaki Sato. *Fr.* Twenty-four Hokku. FCEI
Ugly Things. Teresita Fernández, *tr. fr. Spanish by* Margaret Randall.
  AIW
Ugolino. Dante, *tr. fr. Italian by* Seamus Heaney. *Fr.* Divina
  Commedia: Inferno, XXXII-XXXIII. AnAn; FaBoPV; PFI, *sh.
  sel.*
Ugolino took his sons. The Flying Dutchman. Jules Laforgue, *tr. by*
  William Jay Smith. CT
Ugstabuggle, The. Peter Wesley-Smith. AmMo
Uh nebah cross dese courts agen ess uh live un hundred yares. Lizzie and
  Joe in Court. Edward Cordle. PVCV
Uhuru. Mari E. Evans. CNA
Uji River boat piled with brushwood, An. Princess Shikishi, *tr. fr.
  Japanese by* Hiroaki Sato. *Fr.* Seventy-eight Tanka.
  FCEI
Ula Masondo's Dream. William Plomer. MoBS
Ulalume. Poe. AA; AmPP; AnAmPo; AWP; BLPL; LiTA; NOBA;
  OxBA; TAP
  (Ulalume—a Ballad.) NAAL-1

Ulcerated tooth keeps me awake, there is. Letters from a Father. Mona Van Duyn. ER; FYAP; PPR

Ulf in Ireland. Charles De Kay. AA

Ulinda. David Campbell. CBAP

Ulric Dahlgren. Kate Brownlee Sherwood. PAH

Ulster. Kipling. FaBoPV

Ulster Twilight, An. Seamus Heaney. CIP

Ulsterman, An. Lynn Doyle. TIRV

Ultima Ratio Regum. Stephen Spender. CMoP; FaFP; LiTB; LiTM; OAEL-2; OBWP; SeCePo; WaaP; WaP

Ultima Thule. Longfellow. MOS; ViBoPo

Ultimate Antientropy, The. Theodore Weiss. NoAM

Ultimate Distance, The. Fu'ad Rifqa, tr. fr. Arabic by Sargon Boulus and Samuel Hazo. MAP

Ultimate Equality. Ray Durem. PoNe

Ultimate Exile IV. Ralph Nixon Currey. PeSA

Ultimate gesture. Senryu. Robert Frazier. BWV

Ultimate Poem Is Abstract, The. Wallace Stevens. PoA

Ultimate Problems. William Stafford. NU

Ultimate Reality. Ogden Nash. See Limerick: "There was an old man in a trunk."

Ultimatum, The. Ben King. AnAmPo

Ultimatum. Philip Larkin. Fr. Poetry of Departures. FL

Ultra. Alfred Gong, tr. fr. German by Beth Bjorklund. CoAuP

Ulysses. Robert Graves. CMoP; FaBoTw; MoP; NoAM; PrIm

Ulysses, sels. James Joyce.
  Stephen's Vampire Poem. VVA
  Yes. FF

Ulysses. Robert Lowell. NAAL-2

Ulysses. Umberto Saba, tr. fr. Italian by Henry Taylor. PFI

Ulysses. Claude Clayton Smith. TSL

Ulysses. Tennyson. AWP; EBEV; FaPoR; FF; FiP; FPL; HAP; HeIP; HoPM; InPK; InPS; LiTB; MOS; NAEL-2; NAWM-2; NIP; NOBE; NOBVV; NoP; OAEL-2; PoE; PoRA; PPP; PrIm; SCV; SeCePo; SoSe; TEP; TrGrPo; UnPo; WeW

Ulysses Advises Achilles. Shakespeare. Fr. Troilus and Cressida, III, iii. LiTB

Ulysses and His Dog. Homer, tr. fr. Greek by Pope. Fr. Odyssey, XVII. FiP

Ulysses and the Siren. Samuel Daniel. ElL; HAP; NAEL-1; NOBE; NoP; OBEV; OBSC; PoE; PoEL-2; TEP

Ulysses' flying window dodges. Voyage. István Kormos, tr. by Edwin Morgan. MHuP

Ulysses in the Waves. Homer, tr. fr. Greek by George Chapman. Fr. Odyssey, V. OBS

Ulysses Leaves the Nymph Calypso. Homer, tr. fr. Greek by George Chapman. Fr. Odyssey, V. JCP

Ulysses' Library. David Daiches. PoA

Um Hakeem. Salah Niyazi, tr. fr. Arabic by Lena Jayyusi and Charles Doria. MAP

Umber slant lands under the Apennines, The. To the South. Brewster Ghiselin. LiTA

Umber was painting of a lion fierce. Upon Umber: Epigram. Robert Herrick. CaPo

Umbilical. Eve Merriam. RHPC

Umbrella, An/ And a raincoat. Conversation. Buson. NTCP

Umbrella, The. Ann Stanford. NYBP

Umbrella, An. Gertrude Stein. Fr. Tender Buttons. TTTS

Umbrella, the Cane, and the Broom, The. Eliezer Steinbarg, tr. fr. Yiddish by Curt Leviant. VWA

Umbrellas. Barbara Juster Esbensen. RAR

Umpire, The. Milton Bracker. SD

Umpire, The. Walker Gibson. SD

Un-American Investigators. Langston Hughes. BPo

Una fair, my flower of the amber tresses. Una Bhan. At. to Tomas Mac Coisdealbhaigh ("Laider"), tr. fr. Irish by Thomas Kinsella. NOIV

Una fair, my flower of the amber tresses. Una Bhan. At. to Tomas Mac Coisdealbhaigh ("Laider"), tr. by Thomas Kinsella. NOIV

Unable by Long and Hard Travel to Banish Love, Returns Her Friend. George Turberville. OBTV

Unable, Father, Still, to Disavow. Richard Moore. Fr. Word from the Hills, XXXI. Son

Unable to hold on to the dry branches. Ten Lines: Autumn. Hsiang Yang, tr. by Dominic Cheung. IFON

Unable to put thread through a needle. Ozaki Hosai, tr. fr. Japanese by Hiroaki Sato. Fr. One Hundred Haiku in Free Form. FCEI

Unable to settle through the long unending night. Teika, tr. fr. Japanese by Hiroaki Sato. Fr. Eighty-four Tanka. FCEI

Unaccompanied. Harvey Andrews. OBET

Unachieved. Philip Lamantia. BAP

Unalterables. Arthur Gregor. NYBP

Unanswered. Martha Gilbert Dickinson Bianchi. AA

Unanswered Prayers. Ella Wheeler Wilcox. WGRP

Unanswered yet the prayer your lips have pleaded. Pray without Ceasing. Ophelia Guyon Browning. BLPA; BLPL
  (Sometime, Somewhere.) BLRP

Unarmed Combat. Henry Reed. Fr. Lessons of the War. HeIP; LiTB

Unasked For, The. Peter Cooley. NAmP

Unavoidable/ Said Edwards—that and pain, The. The Bracelet. John Peck. AnAn

Unaware I'm growing old. Kaai Chigetsu, tr. fr. Japanese by Hiroaki Sato. Fr. Thirteen Hokku. FCEI

Unaware of coming, going. Eun, tr. by Lucien Stryk and Takashi Ikemoto. ZPCJ

Unaware of my black hair in disorder. Lady Izumi, tr. fr. Japanese by Hiroaki Sato. Fr. Fifty-one Tanka. FCEI

Unaware of the times. Empress Eifuku, tr. by Steven D. Carter. WFTW

Unaware that the ships must wait. Unknown. Fr. Manyo Shu. Ma

Unawares. Emma A. Lent. PoLF

Unbeliever, The. Elizabeth Bishop. LiTA; NAAL-2; NoAM

Unbeliever, An. Anna Hempstead Branch. WGRP

Unbeseechable, The. Frances Cornford. MoBrPo

Unbind Your Angered Tresses, sel. Petronilla Paolini Massimi, tr. fr. Italian by Muriel Kittel.
  Fortune Welcomed Me at Last. DMI

Unblinding, The. Laurence Lieberman. NYBP

Unborn, The. Thomas Hardy. CMoP

Unborn, The. Sarah Stafford. CN

Unborn Child, An. Derek Mahon. FaBCIP

Unborn children are rowing out to the far edge of the sky, The. Cloud River. Charles Wright. GeTw; MT

Unbounded is thy range; with varied style. The Stormy Hebrides. William Collins. Fr. An Ode on the Popular Superstitions of the Highlands of Scotland [Considered as the Subject of Poetry]. NOBE

Unbridled licentiousness with no holds barred. Reading Pornography in Old Age. Howard Nemerov. NoAM

Unbridled Now. Laura Lourene LeGear. GoYe

Unbroken stillnesses: the lake mist. Two Travelers on a Summer Evening. Alfred Corn. BLA

Uncaring, the God of Fire causes the farmers grief. A Song of Bitter Drought. Cha Shen-hsing, tr. by William Schultz. WFTU

Uncertain-aged Miss Thereabouts. Smithereens. Dante Gabriel Rossetti. NOBVV

Uncertain State of a Lover, The. Unknown. EIL

Uncessant minutes, whil'st you move you tell. To His Watch, When He Could Not Sleep. Lord Herbert of Cherbury. JCP; MePo; NOBE; PoEL-2

Unchangeable, The. Shakespeare. See Sonnets: CIX. ("O [or Oh]! Never say that I was false of heart.")

Unchanging as the tsuga-trees. Yakamochi. Fr. Manyo Shu. Ma

Unchanging Jesus. Karl Johann Philipp Spitta, tr. fr. German by R. Massie. BLRP

Unchastity. Hugues C. Pernath, tr. fr. Dutch by James S. Holmes. DuIn

Uncle. Harry Graham. RHPC

Uncle. Philip Levine. NNaP

Uncle Ambrose. James Still. AmFN

Uncle an' Aunt. William Barnes. NOBVV

Uncle Ananias. E. A. Robinson. MoAmPo; NIP

Uncle Avram Pastures the Horses. Moishe Kulbak, tr. fr. Yiddish by Leonard Wolf. Fr. Byelorussia. PeBMYV

Uncle Bull-Boy. June Jordan. PoBA

Uncle Carl: A Home Movie. J. Bernlef, tr. fr. Dutch by Scott Rollins. DuIn

Uncle Dog; the Poet at 9. Robert Sward. CoAP; PrIm; VGW

Uncle Eph's Banjo Song. James Edwin Campbell. BANP

Uncle Fred never gave up. Crying Uncle. Tom Hansen. TSL

Uncle Gabe's White Folks. Thomas Nelson Page. AA

Uncle Harry. W. H. Auden. NOBL; PeHV

Uncle Ike's Holiday. Priscilla Jane Thompson. CBWP-2

Uncle Iv Surveys His Domain from His Rocker. Jonathan Williams. NBLV; OBAL

Uncle Jim. Countee Cullen. BANP; NAAL-2

Uncle Jimmie's Yarn. Priscilla Jane Thompson. CBWP-2

Uncle Mells and the Witches' Tree. Elizabeth Madox Roberts. WSC

Uncle Remus and His Friends, sels. Joel Chandler Harris.
  My Honey, My Love. AA; FaBoBe
  Plough-Hands' Song, The. AA

Uncle Robert. Robert Morgan. GeTw

Uncle Rube on the Race Problem. Clara Ann Thompson. CBWP-2

Uncle Rube to the Young People. Clara Ann Thompson. CBWP-2

Uncle Rube's Defense. Clara Ann Thompson. CBWP-2

Uncle Sam's Soliloquy. George Sands Johnson. PWR

Uncle sent for O. T. told him we have to fight. O. T.'s Blues. Waring Cuney. MAT
Uncle Simon and Uncle Jim. "Artemus Ward." NA
Uncle Time. Dennis Scott. PBCV; UAS
Uncle tries his best, An. Rhapsodies. Cyril Dabydeen. BrSi
Uncle, whose inventive brains. Uncle. Harry Graham. RHPC
Unclean, unclean: my Lord, undone, all vile. Edward Taylor. *Fr.* Preparatory Meditations before My Approach to the Lord's Supper, XXVI. NAAL-1
Unclench Yourself. Marge Piercy. NeAC
Uncle's First Rabbit. Lorna Dee Cervantes. CCP; NoAM
Unconcerned, The. Thomas Flatman. FaBoCh
Unconquerably, men venture on the quest. The Polar Quest. Richard Burton. AA
Unconquer'd captive!—close thine eye. Virginia Capta. Margaret Junkin Preston. PAH
Uncontrollable night, An. Fist Fight. Doug Cockrell. Psk
Uncouth Knight, The. Hugh McCrae. PoAu-1
Uncurtained, my long room floats on. Night Thoughts. Elaine Feinstein. PoPo
Undead, The. Richard Wilbur. CoAP; OxBC
Undefeated. Robert Froman. ILY
Undefined Tenderness, An. Joel Oppenheimer. VGW
Under. George Bowering. NeAC
Under. J. C. Squire. FaBoTw
Under a bent when the night was deep. William Morris. *Fr.* The Earthly Paradise. PChr
Under a dung-cake. D. J. Opperman, *tr. by* Jack Cope. PeSA
Under a Hat Rim. Carl Sandburg. AnAmPo
Under a hedge the other day. Marcabrun, *tr. by* Paul Blackburn. Pro
Under a hill. *Unknown.* OxNR
Under a Lady's Picture. Edmund Waller. EnLoPo
Under a lawne, than skyes more cleare. Upon Roses. Robert Herrick. SeCP
Under a layer of soot and sand—a playground. Future Generations. Margarete Beutler, *tr. by* Susan L. Cocalis *and* Gerlinde Geiger. DMG
Under a low sky. Silence. William Carlos Williams. TDD
Under a ragged loincloth. Year End. Akera Kanko, *tr. by* Burton Watson. FCEI
Under a Reading Lamp. Christine Busta, *tr. fr. German by* Beth Bjorklund. CoAuP
Under a sky studded with asterisks. On the Night in Question. Patricia Goedicke. TAP
Under a splintered mast. A Talisman. Marianne Moore. GoJo; MoAB; MoAmPo
Under a spreading chestnut-tree. The Village Blacksmith. Longfellow. AA; AiP; AnAmPo; BLPL; FaBoBe; FaFP; FaPON; FaPoR; OBAL; OBCA; PWR; WBLP
Under a spreading gooseberry bush the village burglar lies. The Village Blacksmith. *Unknown.* FiBHP
Under a sultry, yellow sky. Mercedes. Elizabeth Stoddard. AA
Under a swaying. El Dorado. Richard Ryan. BIrV
Under a throne I saw a virgin sit. Fulke Greville. FaBoPV
Under a toadstool. The Elf and the Dormouse. Oliver Herford. AA; FaBoBe; FaPON; OnMSP; RHPC
Under a Tree. Basho *and others, tr. fr. Japanese by* Burton Watson. FCEI
Under a tree. Mary Is with Child. *Unknown.* MeEL
Under a tree a frog. Suiko, *tr. by* Sato. FCEI
Under a white coverlet of snow. January. John Heath-Stubbs. OBCP
Under a willow by the road. Teika, *tr. fr. Japanese by* Hiroaki Sato. *Fr.* A Compendium of Good Tanka. FCEI
Under a Wiltshire Apple Tree. Anna Bunston De Bary. CH
Under Attack. Margaret Randall. AIW; ER
Under Ben Bulben ("Swear by what the sages spoke"), *sels.* W. B. Yeats. CMoP; HAP; LiTM; MoP; NAEL-2; NoAM; NoP; OxBTC
"Cast a cold eye." FaBoEE
"Under bare Ben Bulben's head." FaBoRV; WeW
Under broad banners and barbarian. Against the Age. Louis Simpson. NePoEA-2
Under Cancer. John Hollander. CoAP
Under cherries many people have gathered. Cherry. Hagiwara Sakutaro, *tr. by* Hiroaki Sato. FCEI
Under clouds, at the tag end of August. Lighting the Night Sky. Kenneth O. Hanson. FYAP
Under cracking pieces of the moon, eelpout. Spawning in Northern Minnesota. David McElroy. AmPA
Under Creag Mhor. Stewart Conn. PoSH
Under dream interrogation. Dave Calder. BWV

Under enormous and cemented cliffs. The Second Iron Age. Michael Harrington. CaP
Under every cathedral. The Invention of Fire. Andrew Taylor. CBAP
Under 500 kings three kingdoms groan. The Parliament Dissolved at Oxford. *Unknown.* APAS
Under flying sweetfish clouds flow in a stream. Onitsura, *tr. fr. Japanese by* Hiroaki Sato. *Fr.* Twenty-three Hokku. FCEI
Under glass: glass dishes which changed. The Fundamental Project of Technology. Galway Kinnell. BLA; CAPP; SM; SV
Under God's violent unsleeping eye. Difference. T. H. Jones. OBWVE
Under great yellow flags and banners of the ancient cold. The Shadow of Cain. Edith Sitwell. OxBTC
Under her deep plush roof. "Vierge Ouvrante." Miriam Palmer. NMM
Under his careful crown he keeps. King Midas Has Asses' Ears. Donald Finkel. NePoEA-2
Under his helmet, up against his pack. Asleep. Wilfred Owen. MMA
Under his view the wind. The View. Howard Nemerov. NYBP
Under how many layers of fallen leaves. Natsume Seibi, *tr. fr. Japanese by* Hiroaki Sato. *Fr.* Twenty-seven Hokku. FCEI
Under Leafy Bowers. Judah al-Harizi, *tr. fr. Hebrew.* TrJP
Under ledges of snow outthrust from ledges. Seasons. Robert Penn Warren. KS
Under Lenin's portrait. Budapest. Judd Teller, *tr. by* Grace Schulman. PeBMYV
Under light soft as seawater, sounds. The Obscure Pleasure of the Indistinct. Bin Ramke. MAYP
Under mercury light the little pup strives. A sinister shadow. Reveille. John Godfrey. UL
Under Milk Wood, *sel.* Dylan Thomas.
Johnnie Crack and Flossie Snail. FaPON; FiBHP; GoJo; PDV; RHPC
Under my eaves untiring all the spring day. A Natural Grace. C. K. Stead. ATNZ
Under my hood I have a hat. Winter Clothes. Karla Kuskin. RHPC
Under my thoughts may I God-thoughts find. Thoughts of God. *Unknown, tr. by* Douglas Hyde. WTO
Under my window. Letter in Winter. Raymond R. Patterson. PoBA
Under my window-ledge the waters race. Coole Park and Ballylee, 1931. W. B. Yeats. CMoP; GTBS-P; NoAM; NOIV; OBMV; PPP
Under Our Own Wings. Nellie Wong. BrSi
Under pared moons. The Horse. José María Eguren, *tr. by* Cheli Durán. WSC
Under Restless Clouds. Hanny Michaelis, *tr. fr. Dutch by* Marjolijn de Jager. VWA
Under silver wing. Crossing Nation. Allen Ginsberg. AiP
Under Sirius. W. H. Auden. FaBoMo
Under sleepy branches. Moonlight in the Forest. Aaro Hellaakoski, *tr. by* Aili Jarvenpa. SOP
Under Sorrow's Sign. Gofraidh Fionn O'Dalaigh, *tr. fr. Irish by* John Montague. BIrV
Under Stars. Tess Gallagher. GeTw; InPK; MAYP
Under Stone. Elaine Feinstein. VWA
Under the African lintel, Table Mountain. David Wright. *Fr.* South African Broadsheets. PeSA
Under the after-sunset sky. Two Pewits. Edward Thomas. CH; FM
Under the almond tree. In Kensington Gardens. Arthur Symons. EnLoPo
Under the Anheuser Bush. Andrew B. Sterling. OBAL
Under the apple bough. Remembrance. George Parsons Lathrop. AA
Under the Arc de Triomphe: October 17. Marilyn Hacker. PoA
Under the arch of life, where love and death. Soul's Beauty. Dante Gabriel Rossetti. *Fr.* The House of Life, LXXVII. OBEV
Under the azure where the noon sun totters. Antony and Cleopatra. Henri Coulette. NePoEA
Under the Baby Blanket. May Swenson. AnAn
Under the bamboo. T. S. Eliot. *Fr.* Sweeney Agonistes. UnPo
Under the bed. Under Which Heading Does All This Information Go? Mira Teru Kurka. UL
Under the big 500-watted lamps, in the huge sawdusted government inspected slaughter-house. The Slaughter-House. Alfred Hayes. LiTA
Under the Blue. Francis Fisher Browne. AA
Under the Boathouse. David Bottoms. MAYP; MT
Under the Boughs. Gene Baro. BoNaP
Under the bronze crown. A Baroque Wall-Fountain in the Villa Sciarra. Richard Wilbur. AmPP; CAPP; NAAL-2; NePoEA; NoP; NYBP; TwCP
Under the Casuarina. Elizabeth Riddell. PoAu-2
Under the Cliff. Geoffrey Grigson. WaP
Under the concrete benches. Weed Puller. Theodore Roethke. AmPP; HCAP; NAAL-2

Under the cover of night. Cities and Seas. Norman Jordan. PoNe
Under the dark is a star. Sleeping Outdoors. Marchette Chute. RAR
Under the dawn I wake my two-wheel friend. Yevgeny Yevtushenko, tr. fr. Russian by Robin Milner-Gulland and Peter Levi. Fr. On a Bicycle. ILY
Under the Drooping Willow Tree. Unknown. OxBoLi
Under the dusty print of hobnailed boot. Country Press. Rosemary Dobson. FaBoWP
Under the dying sun. The Reaper. Leslie Holdsworth Allen. PoAu-1
Under the Earth. Abraham Sutskever, tr. fr. Yiddish by Ruth Whitman. VWA
Under the Edge of February. Jayne Cortez. BlSi
Under the Eildon Tree, sel. Sydney Goodsir Smith.
   "Here I ligg, Sydney Slugabed Godless Smith." Fr. sec. Elegy V. OxBS
Under the El on Sunday afternoon. Aside. Alan Dugan. PoA
Under the Eyes. Tom Paulin. CIP
Under the financier's. The Jersey Marsh. David Galler. NYBP
Under the fire escape, crouched, one knee in cinders. The Desk. David Bottoms. BLA; MAYP; MT
Under the flowers of green pinks, one illusory corpse sleeps. Pinks and a Blue Cat. Hagiwara Sakutaro, tr. by Hiroaki Sato. FCEI
Under the forest, where the day is dark. The Manzanita. Yvor Winters. VGW
Under the Frontier Post. Wang Chang-ling, tr. fr. Chinese by Rewi Alley. ChTr
Under the great down-curving lilac branches. Lisa. Constance Carrier. SoSe
Under the great hill sloping bare. The King's Missive. Whittier. PAH
Under the Green Ceiling. Stephen Dobyns. NAmP
Under the green hedges, after the snow. Violets. John Moultrie. BoTP
Under the green lamp-light her letter there. Letter of a Mother. Robert Penn Warren. MoAmPo
Under the Greenwood Tree. "Hugh MacDiarmid," after the Cretan. OBVE
Under the Greenwood Tree. Shakespeare. Fr. As You Like It, II, v. AWP; BoNaP; BoTP; CH; EIL; ELP; FaBoBe; FaFP; FaPON; GN; GTBS; GTBS-P; HeIP; HoPM; InPS; LiTB; NAEL-1; NoP; OAEL-1; OBEV; OHIP; TTTS; UnPo; WiR
   (Amiens's Song.) OBSC
   (Song: "Under the greenwood tree.") CTC; FiP
   (Songs of the Greenwood.) TrGrPo
Under the Greenwood Tree. Unknown. GBP
Under the Ground. Rhoda Warner Bacmeister. RAR
Under the Hazy, Blossom-Laden Sky. Okamoto Jun, tr. fr. Japanese by Geoffrey Bownas and Anthony Thwaite. PeBJV
Under the Heaven of Our Holy Ruler. Su Tung-p'o, tr. fr. Chinese by Burton Watson. CoBCP
Under the hemlocks Fancy came. On the Concord River. Henrietta Cordelia Ray. CBWP-3
Under the Hill. Richard Eberhart. PoA
Under the Hill. Daryl Hine. MoCV
Under the hills and veins of water. Last Letter to Pablo. Pat Lowther. NOBC
Under the hive-like dome the stooping haunted readers. The British Museum Reading Room. Louis MacNeice. LiTM; MoAB; MoBrPo; NOBE; SeCePo; WaP
Under the house, between the road the sea-cliff. Grass on the Cliff. Robinson Jeffers. Fr. The Trumpet, V. PoA
Under the ice with its bouldery death's faces. The Bread Hot from the Oven. John Thompson. NOBC
Under the Ladder to Heaven. Elizabeth Fenton. NMM
Under the lamplight that grows feeble. Teika, tr. fr. Japanese by Hiroaki Sato. Fr. Eighty-four Tanka. FCEI
Under the Leaves. Albert Laighton. OHIP
Under the Leaves Green. Unknown. See Who Shall Have My Faire Lady?
Under the Lindens [or Lime Tree]. Walther von der Vogelweide, tr. fr. German. CTC, tr. by Ford Madox Ford
   (Under the Lime Tree.) Tr. by Thomas Lovell Beddoes. ErPo; GBL
   ("Under the lime-tree, on the daisied ground.") OBVE, tr. by Thomas Lovell Beddoes
Under the Locust Blossoms. Frederick Goddard Tuckerman. NOBA
Under the long dark boughs, like jewels red. Cherry Robbers. D. H. Lawrence. MoAB; MoBrPo
Under the longleaf pines. A Quilled Quilt, a Needle Bed. Brad Leithauser. MAYP; SM
Under the lower leaves of hydrangea fireflies cluster. Teika, tr. fr. Japanese by Hiroaki Sato. Fr. Eighty-four Tanka. FCEI
Under the lucent glass. In the Egyptian Museum. Janet Lewis. NYBP; QFR

Under the Maud Moon. Galway Kinnell. CAPP; NNaP
Under the Mirabeau Bridge the Seine/ Flows and [or with] our love[s]. The Mirabeau Bridge. Guillaume Apollinaire. BoLoP, tr. by Quentin Stevenson; OBVE, tr. by W. S. Merwin; RUTwFP, tr. by Richard Wilbur.
Under the Mistletoe. Countee Cullen. PChr
Under the Mountain. Louis MacNeice. FaBCIP
Under the mountain, as when first I knew. Frederick Goddard Tuckerman. Fr. Sonnets, II, xvi. HAP; QFR; TAP
Under the new pond-dam. Looking Before and After. Carter Revard. HATNAP
Under the night shade.. Clickstone. Rokwaho. STE
Under the oak tree, oak tree. Unknown, tr. by Willis Barnstone. BoWoP
Under the Old Elm, sels. James Russell Lowell.
   "Never to see a nation born." Fr. VII. GOA
   New-come Chief, The. Fr. III. PAH
   "That lifted blade transformed our jangling clans." GOA
   Washington. GN; OHIP
Under the orchards, under. Rogation Days. Kenneth Rexroth. NaP
Under the parabola of a ball. How to Kill. Keith Douglas. FaBoMo; NOBE; RB
Under the Pines. Arthur Stanley Bourinot. OBCV
Under the pines. Myoe, tr. fr. Japanese by Burton Watson. Fr. Ten Tanka. FCEI
Under the pines and hemlocks. The Deer. Mary Austin. FaPON
Under the pines I questioned the boy. Looking for a Recluse but Failing to Find Him. Chia Tao, tr. by Burton Watson. CoBCP
Under the pink quilted covers. The Fortress. Anne Sexton. LiTM
Under the plum-blossoms are nightingales. Desolation. Amy Lowell. PoA
Under the pond, among rocks. The Dragonfly. Howard Nemerov. PoA
Under the Pondweed. Unknown, tr. fr. Chinese by Helen Waddell. Fr. Shi King. AWP
Under the Pot. Robert Graves. FaBoEE
Under the quince tree. Bible, O.T. Fr. The Song of Solomon, VIII: 5. PBWP
Under the rain. To Taufiq Sayigh. Riad al-Rayyes, tr. by Abdullah al-Udhari. MPAW
Under the red-and-white striped awning. The Luncheon of the Boating Party. Leon Stokesbury. MT
Under the Red Cross. Chauncey Hickox. AA
Under the rock, in the sand and the gravel run. Charles Wright. Fr. Skins, 6. HCAP
Under the roof and the roof's shadow turns. The Merry-go-round. Rainer Maria Rilke, tr. by C. F. MacIntyre. WeW
"Under the roots of the roses." Mors et Vita. Richard Henry Stoddard. AA
Under the Rose. Unknown. OBET
Under the Ruins of Poland. Itzig Manger, tr. fr. Yiddish by Miriam Waddington. VWA
Under the sagging clotheslines of crepe paper. The Best Slow Dancer. David Wagoner. NoAM
Under the scarlet-licking leaves. My Many-Coated Man. Laurie Lee. NYBP
Under the Scrub Oak, a Red Shoe. Dave Smith. GeTw
Under the September Peach. Robert Wallace. Son
Under the Shade of the Trees. Margaret Junkin Preston. PAH
Under the shadows of a cliff. A Rise. Ernest McGaffey. AA
Under the Shawl. Rose Drachler. VWA
Under the sheet of transparent wool. Penumbra. Pierre Louys, tr. fr. French. Fr. Chansons de Bilitis. PeHV
Under the Sign of Cancer. Carolyne Wright. NAmP
Under the slanting light of the yellow sun of October. The Modern Romans. Charles Frederick Johnson. AA
Under the sloped snow. As Children Together. Carolyne Forché. NAmP; NoAM
Under the slumber and winter of a silent night. In Lord Carpenter's Country. Barry O. Higgs. PeSA
Under the Snow. Robert Collyer. AA
Under the sovereign crests of dead volcanoes. On a Bougainvillaea Vine at the Summer Palace [or in Haiti]. Barbara Howes. MoAmPo; NYBP
Under the Stars. Wallace Rice. AA; OHIP
Under the summer sun, a blue cat. Cat. Kitahara Hakushu, tr. by Hiroaki Sato. FCEI
Under the sun is nothing new? To the Archdeacon. George Farewell. NOEC
Under the surface of flux and of fear there is an underground movement. Louis MacNeice. Fr. The Kingdom. LiTM
Under the Table Manners. Unknown. CRH

Under the tall black sky you look out of your body. Endless. Muriel Rukeyser. NYBP

Under the too white marmoreal Lincoln Memorial. The March 1. Robert Lowell. HCAP; NoP

Under the Trapeze. Ernst David, *tr. fr. German by* Beth Bjorklund. CoAuP

Under the Tread of My Feet. H. Leivick, *tr. fr. Yiddish by* Benjamin *and* Barbara Harshav. AYP

Under the tree with rice-cake flowers. Issa, *tr. by* Hiroaki Sato. FCEI

Under the Umbrella of Blood. William Pitt Root. GeTw

Under the urination of astronauts. Everything Is Wonderful. Jayne Cortez. AIW

Under the viaduct, by the hot canal. Plaque. Bruce Ruddick. CaP

Under the Violets. Oliver Wendell Holmes. *Fr.* The Professor at the Breakfast Table. AA

Under the Violets. Edward Young. AA

Under the Vulture-Tree. David Bottoms. MT

Under the walls of Monterey. Victor Galbraith. Longfellow. PAH

Under the waning moon. Starting at Dawn. Sun Yün-feng, *tr. by* Kenneth Rexroth *and* Ling Chung. PBWP

Under the water tower at the edge of town. To the Evening Star: Central Minnesota. James Wright. NaP

Under the Waterfall. Thomas Hardy. BoLoP; CTC; LiTB; NAEL-2

Under the wide and starry sky. Robert Louis Stevenson. BrPo; DL; EBVV; FaBV; FaPoR; FPL; GoTS; MoBrPo; NBLV; NOBE; NOBVV; OBD; OBEV; OBNC; OHFP; PoLF; PoRA; TrGrPo; WGRP

Under the Willow Shades. Sir William Davenant. BoLoP; ELP

Under the willow the willow. Recruiting Drive. Charles Causley. NePoEA; OxBTC; PrIm

Under the Window: Ouro Preto. Elizabeth Bishop. NYBP

Under the Winter Sky. János Pilinszky, *tr. fr. Hungarian by* Ted Hughes. MHuP

Under the Woods. Edward Thomas. CH

Under the yew-tree's heavy weight. Les Hiboux. Baudelaire, *tr. by* Arthur Symons. AWP

Under these historic skies. From Jerusalem: A First Poem. Gabriel Preil, *tr. by* Robert Friend. VWA

Under this marble, or under this sill. Epitaph on Himself. Pope. FaBoEE

Under this real estate—squared street on street. Asphodel. David Malouf. CBAP

Under this stone/ Lies a Reverend Drone. An Epitaph upon That Profound and Learned Casuist, the Late Ordinary of Newgate. Thomas Brown. OBSV

Under this stone, reader, survey. On Sir John Vanbrugh [Architect]. Abel Evans. FaBoCo; FaBoEE; FiBHP

Under this stone there lieth at rest. An Epitaph of Sir Thomas Gravener [Knight]. Sir Thomas Wyatt. OBSC; SiPS

Under this town's ashes. On Learning That Certain Peat Bogs Contain Perfectly Preserved Bodies. Susan Ludvigson. MAYP

Under thy shadow may I lurk awhile. St. Peter's Shadow. Richard Crashaw. ACP

Under Which Heading Does All This Information Go? Mira Teru Kurka. UL

Under Which Lyre, a Reactionary Tract for the Times. W. H. Auden. MoAB; MoBrPo; NOBL

Under yonder beech-tree single [*or* standing] on the green-sward. Love in the Valley. George Meredith. AWP; EBVV; ErPo, *sel.*, LiTB; NOBE; OAEL-2; OBEV, *abr.*; TrGrPo, *sel.*

Under you shrivels. Ultra. Alfred Gong, *tr. by* Beth Bjorklund. CoAuP

Under your Milky Way. Return of the Goddess Artemis. Robert Graves. PoA

Under Your Voice, among Legends. Phyllis Beauvais. NMM

Underdeveloped Country, An. D. J. Enright. NOBL

Underfoot rotten boards, forest rubble, bones. Remains of an Indian Village. Alfred W. Purdy. NOBC

Undergraduate. Merrill Moore. ErPo

Undergraduates/ By and large shabby. Nakamura Kusadao, *tr. by* Geoffrey Bownas *and* Anthony Thwaite. PeBJV

Underground, The. Guy Boas. CenHV

Underground Gardens, The. Robert Mezey. NaP

Underground grower, blind and a common brown, An. Potato. Richard Wilbur. CAPP; LiTA; MoAB; TrGrPo

Underground joy goes out from me, An. White Haunches. Pierre Jean Jouve, *tr. by* Kenneth Rexroth. RHTwFP

Underground Stream, The. James Dickey. NOBA

Undergrowth's a conveyance of butterflies, The. Hope's Okay. A. R. Ammons. HCAP

Underneath a cypress shade, the Queen of Love sat mourning. *Unknown.* GBL

Underneath an old oak tree. The Raven. Samuel Taylor Coleridge. WiR

Underneath my belt. When I Was Lost. Dorothy Aldis. RHPC

Underneath my lids another eye has opened. From the Prison House. Adrienne Rich. NNaP

Underneath My Window. Sir Philip Sidney. *See* Astrophel and Stella: Who is it that this dark night.

Underneath Pont Mirabeau flows the Seine. Pont Mirabeau. X. J. Kennedy, *from* Guillaume Apollinare. BLA

Underneath the boardwalk, way, way back. The Secret Cavern. Margaret Widdemer. FaPON

Underneath the broad hat is the face of the Ambassador. The Ambassador. Stevie Smith. Mes

Underneath the growing grass. The Bourne. Christina Rossetti. ELP; OBNC

Underneath the water-weeds. The Tadpole. E. E. Gould. BoTP

Underneath this marble stone/ Lie two beauties join'd in one. Epitaph of Pyramus and Thisbe. Abraham Cowley. FaBoEE
(Epitaph: "Underneath this marble stone.") EnLoPo

Underneath this pretty cover. With a Copy of Swift's Works. J. V. Cunningham. QFR

Underneath this sable hearse [*or* herse]. On the Countess Dowager of Pembroke. *At. to* William Browne. AWP; HAP; InvP; JCP; NoP; OAEL-1; PoEL-2; PoRA; ViBoPo; WeW
(Epitaph on the Countess[e] Dowager of Pembroke.) FaBoEE; NOBE; OBEV; OBS
(On the Death of Marie, Countesse of Pembroke.) NIP; OAEL-1

Underneath this wooden cross there lies. Karl Shapiro. *Fr.* Elegy for a Dead Soldier. OFD

Undersea Fever. William Cole. FiBHP

Undersong, The. Emerson. *Fr.* Woodnotes II ("As sunbeams stream through liberal space"). AA

Understand, he is naked in the sea. The Loved One. Joseph Hansen. NYBP

Understand me: I am a mediocre being. Words to My Friend. Renée Vivien, *tr. by* Sandia Belgrade. PeHV

Understanding. Pauline E. Soroka. PoLF

Understanding. Sara Teasdale. AnAmPo

Undertakers' Club, The. *Unknown.* GBP

Undertaker's Horse, The. Kipling. FaBoNo; FM

Undertaking, The. John Donne. MePo; NAEL-1; NOBE

Undertaking, The. Louise Glück. FaBoWP

Undertone. William Bedell Stanford. NeIP

Undertones. George R. Sims. NOBVV

Undertow. Langston Hughes. LiTM

Underwater eyes, an eel's. An Otter. Ted Hughes. CMoP; MoP; NePoEA-2; NoAM

Underwater Lake Michigan Socrates. "Antler." SoTCo

Underwater Pieces. Kendrick Smithyman. ATNZ

Underwear. Lawrence Ferlinghetti. OBAL

Underwood. Howard Moss. NePoEA-2; TwCP

Underworld, The. Margaret Lavington. RAR

Underworld of children becomes the overworld, The. Blue Glass. Fleur Adcock. FaBoWP

Undesirable you may have been, untouchable. September Song. Geoffrey Hill. NAEL-2; NoAM; NoP; OBWP

Undine. Irving Layton. ErPo

Undiscovered Country, The. Thomas Bailey Aldrich. AA

Undo! *Unknown.* NOCV

Undo Your Heart. *Unknown.* MeEL

Undone, undone the lawyers are. The Downfall of Charing Cross. *Unknown.* FaBoCo

Undue significance a starving man attaches. Emily Dickinson. LiTA; LiTM

Undulating, a frog undulates. Hokukon, *tr. by* Hiroaki Sato. FCEI

Undulation, An/ on too many legs. Codes. Diana Chang. BrSi

Unduly elected body of our elders, An. Elegy for Yards, Pounds, and Gallons. David Wagoner. PoA

Undying Thirst. Antipater of Sidon, *tr. fr. Greek by* Robert Bland. AWP

Une Idole du Nord. Francis Stuart. NeIP

Une petite pêche dans un orchard fleurit. The Little Peach. *Unknown.* NA

Unearthing. Betsy Rosenberg. VWA

Uneasy Peace. Edmund Blunden. BrPo

Uneasy Resident. Louis Johnson. ATNZ

Uneasy Rider. Diane Wakoski. NIP

Uneasy Riders. Robert N. Feinstein. SoTCo

Unemployment. William Mills. HoPM

Unemployment in our bones, The. Derry. Seamus Deane. CIP

Unemployment/Monologue. June Jordan. WPOW

Unequal Distribution. Samuel Hoffenstein. TrJP
Unerring Guide, The. Anna Shipton. BLRP
Uneven Parallel Bars. Patricia Gary. ASP
Uneventfully/ and pleasantly I go on putting on weight. Ishikawa Takuboku, *tr. fr. Japanese by* Hiroaki Sato. *Fr.* Forty-seven Tanka in Three Lines. FCEI
Unexpected Pleasure, An. *Unknown.* FaBoCo
Unexpected Visit. Fleur Adcock. ATNZ
Unexpectedly cool, in summer clothes. Teika, *tr. fr. Japanese by* Hiroaki Sato. *Fr.* A Compendium of Good Tanka. FCEI
Unexplainable/ the perpetual attempt. Landscape of a Face. Alfred Gesswein, *tr. by* Beth Bjorklund. CoAuP
Unexplorer, The. Edna St. Vincent Millay. MoShBr; PoA
Unfaded patch, The. *Unknown, tr. by* Burton Watson. FCEI
Unfading, The. "Marie Madelaine", *tr. fr. German by* Ferdinand E. Kappey. PeHV
Unfailing Friend, The. Joseph Scriven. BLRP
Unfailing One, The. Phillips Brooks. BLRP
Unfair to Men. *Unknown, tr. fr. Welsh by* Gwyn Jones. OBWVE
Unfair to Women. *Unknown, tr. fr. Welsh by* Gwyn Jones. OBWVE
Unfaithful Shepherdess. *Unknown.* GTBS; GTBS-P
　(Adieu Love, Untrue Love.) EIL
　(Faithless Shepherdess, The.) OBEV
　(Philon.) OBSC
　(Philon the Shepherd.) NOBE
Unfamiliar Quartet. Stephen Vincent Benét. AnAmPo
Unfathomable sea, and time, and tears, The. To N. V. de G. S. Robert Louis Stevenson. BrPo
Unfathomable Sea! whose waves are years. Time. Shelley. FaBoRV; FPL; MOS; Par; PoLF
Unfinished History, An. Archibald MacLeish. NYBP; VGW
Unfinished Race, The. Norman Cameron. OxBS
Unflinching Dante of a later day. To an Imperilled Traveller. Nathan Haskell Dole. AA
Unflushed Urinals. Donald Justice. AnAn
Unfold, unfold! take in his light. The Revival. Henry Vaughan. NOCV; OBS; PoEL-2; TrGrPo
　(Unfold, Unfold.) ELP
Unforgiven, The. E. A. Robinson. CMoP
Unfortunate admiral! Your poor America. To Columbus. Rubén Darío, *tr. by* Lysander Kemp. TTY
Unfortunate Coincidence. Dorothy Parker. BXAP; FaBoUs; NoP
Unfortunate Male, The. Kalonymos ben Kalonymos, *tr. fr. Hebrew by* J. Chotzner. *Fr.* The Touchstone. TrJP
Unfortunate Miller, The. A. E. Coppard. FaBoTw
Unfortunate Miller; or, The Country Lasses Witty Invention, The. *Unknown.* CoMu; OxBB
Unfortunate Miss Bailey. George Colman, the Younger. FiBHP; GBP
　(Miss Bailey's Ghost.) FaBoBa; OxBoLi
Unfortunate Mole, The. Mary Kennedy. GoYe
Unfortunate Woman, The. Ho Ning, *tr. fr. Chinese by* Lois Fusek. ATF
Unfortunately. Bobbi Katz. RAR
Unfriendly Fortune. John Skelton. MeEL
Unfriendly friendly universe. The Child Dying. Edwin Muir. FaBoTw; GTBS-P; RB
Unfrocked Priest, The. Joseph Campbell. AnIL
Unfulfillment. Frances Louisa Bushnell. AA
Unfurled gull on the tide, and over the skerry, The. December Day, Hoy Sound. George Mackay Brown. OxBS
Unfurls in rain. The Newest Banana Plant Leaf. Ingrid Wendt. NMM
Unfussy lodger, she knows what she wants and gets it. Cat. Michael Hamburger. PoPo
Ungar and Rolfe. Herman Melville. *Fr.* Clarel. OxBA
Ungathered Apples, The. James Wright. ErPo
Ungathered Love. Philip Bourke Marston. OBNC
Ungrateful Garden, The. Carolyn Kizer. CAPP; NePoEA-2
Ungrateful Jenny. Mother Goose. OxNR
Unguarded Gates. Thomas Bailey Aldrich. AA; AnAmPo; PAH
Unhand me nurse! thou saucy quean! Maternal Despotism; or, The Rights of Infants. Richard Graves. NOEC
Unhappie Light. William Drummond of Hawthornden. OBS
Unhappy about some far off things. The Stars Go over the Lonely Ocean. Robinson Jeffers. LiTA; LiTM; WaP
Unhappy Bella. *Unknown.* ErPo
Unhappy Boston. Paul Revere. AiP; PAH
Unhappy childhood, please do not curve. Terms of Surrender. Michael Bachstein. TSM
Unhappy country, what wings you have! Even here. Eagle Valor, Chicken Mind. Robinson Jeffers. LiTA; OxBA; OxBSP; WaP
Unhappy Diary Days. Gerald Vizenor. VoR

Unhappy dreamer, who outwinged in flight. On the Death of a Metaphysician. George Santayana. *Fr.* Sonnets. AnAmPo
Unhappy East (not in that awe). Reply. Sidney Godolphin. OBS
Unhappy Lover, The. Judah Al-Harizi, *tr. fr. Hebrew by* J. Chotzner. TrJP
Unhappy people in a happy world, An. Wallace Stevens. *Fr.* The Auroras of Autumn, X. CMoP
Unhappy Revenge, The, *sels.* Swinburne. FL
　"Thank your engines."
　"What is that death they boast but a frail pageant."
Unhappy Schoolboy, The. *Unknown.* OxBChV
Unhappy summer you. This Summer and Last. Thomas Hardy. OxBTC
Unhappy [*or* Unhappie] Verse, the witness[e] of my unhappy state. Iambicum Trimetrum. Spenser. BoLoP; EBEV; EIL; OBEV; OPoP; PoEL-1
　(Iambica.) OxBoLi
Unharvested. Robert Frost. BoNaP
Unheard of even in the age of mighty gods. Teika, *tr. fr. Japanese by* Hiroaki Sato. *Fr.* A Compendium of Good Tanka. FCEI
Unhistoric Story, The. Allen Curnow. ATNZ
Unholy Missions. Bob Kaufman. CNA; TTY
Unhurried as a snake I saw Time glide. On Time. Richard Hughes. MoBrPo
Unhurt, There Is No Help. Allen Curnow. ATNZ
Unicorn, The. George Darley. *Fr.* Nepenthe. ChTr; OBNC; PoEL-4
Unicorn, The. E. V. Rieu. AmMo
Unicorn, The. Gerrit Komrij, *tr. fr. Dutch by* Jacob Lowland. DuIn
Unicorn, The. Ruth Pitter. MoBrPo
Unicorn, The, *sel.* Rainer Maria Rilke, *tr. fr. German by* Stephen Mitchell.
　"Oh this is the animal that never was." TTTS
Unicorn. William Jay Smith. RHPC; SO
Unicorn, The. Ella Young. FaPON
Unicorn and the Lady, The. Jean Garrigue. NYBP
Unicorn stood, like a king in a dream, The. The Unicorn. E. V. Rieu. AmMo
Unicorn to hand, A. Haste to the Wedding. Alex Comfort. ErPo
Unicorn with the long white horn, The. Unicorn. William Jay Smith. RHPC; SO
Unicornis Tale, The. *Unknown.* *Fr.* The Talis of the Fyve Bestis. OxBLMV
Unicorn's hoofs! The. Dance Song. *Unknown, tr. by* Arthur Waley. Bos; FaBoCh
Unifying Principle, The. A. R. Ammons. CAPP; NOBA
Unillumined Verge, The. Robert Bridges. AA
Uninscribed Monument on One of the Battle-Fields of the Wilderness, An. Herman Melville. AA
Unintelligible Terms. Charles Simic. NoP
Uninterpreted, the days. The Absentee. Denise Levertov. ER
Uninvited, The. Dorothy Livesay. NOBC
Uninvited, The. William D. Mundell. NYBP
Union and Liberty. Oliver Wendell Holmes. OHIP
Union Jack, The. Jeannie Kirby. BoTP
Union Man. Albert Morgan. AmFP
Union Pier Michigan. We called it Shapiro. That Was Then. Isabella Gardner. CAPP
Unique among Girls. *Malay Oral Tradition, tr. by* R. J. Wilkinson *and* R. O. Winstedt. WTO
Unison, A. William Carlos Williams. NOBA
Unitarian Easter. Sandra McPherson. MAYP
Unitas. Edward Gold. ASP
Unite, unite, let us all unite. The Padstow Night Song. *Unknown.* ChTr; GBP
United. Paulus Silentiarius, *tr. fr. Greek by* W. H. D. Rouse. AWP
United Fruit Co, The. Pablo Neruda, *tr. fr. Spanish by* Robert Bly. FaBoPV
United States, The. Goethe, *tr. fr. German by* Robert Bly. AiP
United States and Macedonian, The. *Unknown.* PAH
United States is giving the Suez Canal back to Panama, The. "Some Days," Dorothy Parker Said, "It's Better Than Digging Ditches." Maureen Owen. UL
United States of America We, The. Sam Abrams. UL
United States Prepare for the Permanent Revolution, The. George Hitchcock. EAS
Unity. Jakov de Haan, *tr. fr. Dutch by* David Soetendorp. VWA
Unity of God, The. Panatattu, *tr. fr. Sanskrit.* WGRP
Univac to Univac. Louis B. Salomon. FF
Universal. Ory Bernstein, *tr. fr. Hebrew by* Warren Bargad *and* Stanley F. Chyet. *Fr.* Poems from Mexico. IP
Universal Favorite, The. Carolyn Wells. NBLV

Universal Prayer, The. Pope. BLPA; FaBoBe; FPL; NoP; WGRP
Universe, The. Mary Britton Miller. RHPC
University. Karl Shapiro. LiTA; OxBA
University Curriculum. William Price Turner. OxBS
University Examinations in Egypt. D. J. Enright. OxBTC; TwCP
University Hospital, Boston. Mary Oliver. CAPP
University of Hunger. Martin Carter. PBCV
Unkindness Has Killed Me. *Unknown.* MeEL
Unknown, The. John Davidson. BLPA
Unknown, The. Elmer Osborn Laughlin. BLPA
Unknown, The. Denise Levertov. NAAL-2
Unknown, The. Edward Thomas. GBL
Unknown Bird, The. Edward Thomas. RB
Unknown Child, The. Elizabeth Jennings. PBWP
Unknown Citizen, The. W. H. Auden. FF; HeIP; InPK; LiTA; LiTM;
   MoAB; NBLV; NIP; NOBL; NYBP; OBSV; PoRA; SoSe; UnPo
Unknown City, The. Sir Charles G. D. Roberts. CaP
Unknown Color, The. Countee Cullen. FaPON; OBCA
Unknown Eros, The, *sels.* Coventry Patmore.
   Arbor Vitae. *Fr.* II, iii. OBNC; SeCePo
   Auras of Delight. ACP
   Azalea, The. ELP; GBL
   Departure. *Fr.* I, viii. ACP; NOBE; OBEV; OBNC; SeCePo
   "With all my will, but much against my heart." ACP; BoLoP; EnLoPo;
     GTBS-P; NOBE; OBEV; OBNC; PoEL-5; TrGrPo
   Here, in This Little Bay. BoNaP
   (Magna Est Veritas.) GTBS-P; HAP; NOBE; NOBVV; OBEV;
     OBNC; OxBSP
   (Truth.) TrGrPo
   If I Were Dead. ACP
   Legem Tuam Dilexi. *Fr.* X. PoEL-5
   Saint Valentine's Day. *Fr.* XLIII. OBNC
   To the Body. *Fr.* XL. OAEL-2; PoEL-5
   To the Unknown Eros. NoBVV; PoEL-5
   Toys, The. *Fr.* I, x. ACP; BeLS; EBEV; EBVV; FaFP; OBEV; SoSe;
     TrGrPo; TrPWD
Unknown faces in the street. The Turning. Philip Levine. VGW
Unknown Girl in the Maternity Ward. Anne Sexton. MoP; NAs; NoAM
Unknown God, The. Æ. MoBrPo; WGRP
Unknown God, The. Sir William Watson. WGRP
Unknown in history or in time they stand. Speakers, Columbus Circle.
   Raymond Souster. CaP
Unknown love/ Is as bitter a thing. Lady Otomo no Sakanoe. *Fr.* Manyo
   Shu. AWP; PBWP, *tr. by* Arthur Waley.
   ("Unknown love/ is bitter.") BoWoP; LLLT, *tr. by* Willis Barnstone.
Unknown Man in the Morgue. Merrill Moore. MoAmPo
Unknown Master of Moulins, The. The Cardinal's Dog. John Glassco.
   MoCV
Unknown Shepherd's Complaint, The. Richard Barnfield. EIL
   (Shepherd's Complaint, A.) OBSC
Unknown Shores. D. M. Thomas. BWV
Unknown Smoke. Archie Washburn. NOVW
Unknown Soldier, The. Conrad Aiken. *Fr.* The Soldier, II. WaaP;
   WaP
Unknown Soldier, The. Alun Lewis. MoBrPo
Unknown Soldier, The. Billy Rose. BLPA; FPL; OPP
Unknown Soldiers. Edgar Lee Masters. *Fr.* The New Spoon River.
   NoAM; TAP
Unknown Warrior Speaks, The. Margery Smith. CN
Unknown Wind, The. "Fiona Macleod." BoTP
Unlawful Assembly. D. J. Enright. OxBTC
Unleashed dog walks back and forth, The. The Madman's Wife. Steve
   Orlen. MAYP
Unless. Ella Dietz Glynes. AA
Unless I depart resolved from my dependent coronet. Ten Lines: On
   Seed. Hsiang Yang, *tr. by* Dominic Cheung. IFON
Unless you can dance through a common bar. Mahsati, *tr. fr. Farsi by*
   Deirdre Lashgari. AIW; WPOW
Unless you remind me. Pavlov. Naomi Long Madgett. BPo
Unlike are we, unlike, O princely heart! Elizabeth Barrett Browning. *Fr.*
   Sonnets from the Portuguese, III. OBEV; TrGrPo
Unlike my subject now shall be my song. Earl of Chesterfield. FaBoEE
Unlike the cloud that dwells on Mount Mifune. Prince Yuge. *Fr.* Manyo
   Shu. Ma
Unlike the hawk he has no dream of height. Sea Owl. Dave Smith.
   HCAP
Unloading Rails. *Unknown.* AmFP
Unlovely place/ unlovely association. Numbness. Friederike Mayröcker,
   tr. by Beth Bjorklund. CoAuP
Unlucky Boat. George Mackay Brown. NePoEA-2
Unmanifest Destiny. Richard Hovey. AA; WGRP

Unmarked Ceiling, The. Mary Michaels. DT
Unmarked faces/ fierce with grief. Falls Funeral. John Montague. CIP
"Unmitigated England." Great Central Railway, Sheffield Victoria to
   Banbury. Sir John Betjeman. NYBP
Unmon's barrier pulled down, the old. Daito, *tr. by* Lucien Stryk *and*
   Takashi Ikemoto. ZPCJ
Unmoored, unmanned, unheeded on the deep. The Derelict. Lucius
   Harwood Foote. AA
Unmoved by what the wind does. Sleeping with One Eye Open. Mark
   Strand. CAPP; NYBP; SM
Unmuzzle the broad joke. Catullus, *tr. fr. Latin by* James Michie. *Fr.*
   Hymeneal. PeHV
Unnamed Always. Robert Marteau, *tr. fr. French by* Louis Simpson.
   RHTwFP
Unnamed Lake, The. Frederick George Scott. CaP; NOBC
Unnoted as the setting of a star. Mulford. Whittier. AA
Unnumbered suppliants crowd preferment's gate. Samuel Johnson. *Fr.*
   Vanity of Human Wishes, The: The Tenth Satire of Juvenal Imitated.
   OBSV
Unoccupied Zone, The. Louis Aragon, *tr. fr. French by* Louis MacNeice.
   RHTwFP
Unparalleled Severity. Jules Laforgue, *tr. fr. French by* William Jay
   Smith. CT
Unpardonable Sin, The. Vachel Lindsay. CMoP
Unplait the braided dark. To the Spring Sun. Freda Laughton. NeIP
Unpossessed, The. Adèle Naudé. PeSA
Unposted Birthday Card. Norman MacCaig. NAs
Unpraised Picture, An. Richard Burton. AA
Unpredictable, The. Thomas Blackburn. OPOP
Unpredicted, The. John Heath-Stubbs. BoLoP; OxBC
Unprofitablenes. Henry Vaughan. SeCV-1
Unpurged images of day recede, The. Byzantium. W. B. Yeats.
   CMoP; EBEV; FaBoMo; HAP; InPS; LiTM; MoAB; MoBrPo; MoP;
   NAEL-2; NAWM-2; NIP; NoAM; NOBE; NoP; OAEL-2; OxBTC;
   PoE; PPP; SeCePo; TEP
Unquiet Grave, The. *Unknown.* AmFP; CH; ELP; EnSB; ESPB;
   FaBoBa; GBP; HAP; HeIP; NoP; OAEL-1; OBD; OBET; OxBB;
   PoEL-1; RB; ViBoPo; WeW
Unquiet Ones, The. Stanley Kunitz. CAPP
Unraveled Thought, An. Shlomit Cohen, *tr. fr. Hebrew by* Myra Glazer
   Schotz. VWA
Unreal silence, an. Swallows over the Camp. Uys Krige, *tr. by the*
   author and Jack Cope. PeSA
Unreal Song of the Old, The. James Koller. PoM
Unreal tall as a myth. The Bear on the Delhi Road. Earle Birney.
   HeIP; MoCV; NoAM; NOBC; NoP; NYBP; PrIm
Unreal the Buffalo Is Standing. *Unknown.* GOA
Unrealities, The. Schiller, *tr. fr. German by* James Clarence Mangan.
   AWP
Unrecorded Speech. Anna Adams. BrRo
Unrelenting Flood. William Matthews. GeTw
Unremarkable Year, The. Roy Fuller. OxBC
Unrest. Richard Watson Dixon. OBNC
Unresting, like the people. *Unknown.* *Fr.* Manyo Shu. Ma
Unreturning, The. Wilfred Owen. MoBrPo
Unreturning, The. Clinton Scollard. PAH
Unreturning. Elizabeth Stoddard. AA
Unreturning Native, The. Basil Dowling. ATNZ
Unrhymed, unrhythmical, the chatter goes. At the Party. W. H. Auden.
   OxBSP
Unromantic Awakening, An. Priscilla Jane Thompson. CBWP-2
Unromantic Song. Anthony Brode. FiBHP
Unruly hair, bare feet—busily studying books. Chu Yün-ming, *tr. fr.*
   Chinese by Jonathan Chaves. *Fr.* Improvisations, III. CoBLCP
Unsaid. A. R. Ammons. NOBA
Unsaid Word, An. Adrienne Rich. NMM
Unsatiated Passions. H. Leivick, *tr. fr. Yiddish by* Benjamin *and* Barbara
   Harshav. AYP
Unseasonable/ as bees in April. Vermont: Indian Summer. Philip Booth.
   NePoEA
Unseaworthy Ship, The. J. Smith. OxBSS
Unseemly as a marvellous and astral renegade. Queen Anne's Lace.
   June Jordan. TAP
Unseen. Fanny Crosby. TrPWD
Unseen Deer, An. John Tagliabue. Psk
Unseen Fire. Ralph Nixon Currey. OBWP; OxBTC
Unseen, snow slides from over-laden boughs. Fire-Queen. Ruth
   Fainlight. PoA
Unseen Spirits. Nathaniel Parker Willis. *See* Shadows lay along
   Broadway, The.
Unseen, unknown. The Sylph. Paul Valéry. CT

Unsent Message to My Brother in His Pain. Leon Stokesbury. MAYP
Unsettled again and hearing Russian spoken. Hearing Russian Spoken. Donald Davie. GTBS-P; NePoEA-2
Unsettled Motorcyclist's Vision of His Death, The. Thom Gunn. NePoEA-2; PoA
Unsexed by the cold sea, prone out of it on the beach. Watch Hill. Winfield Townley Scott. ErPo
Unshaken world! Another day of light. Autumn Blitz. Frances Cornford. CN
Unshrinking Faith. W. H. Balhurst. BLRP
Unshunnable is grief; we should not fear. Grief and God. Stephen Phillips. WGRP
Unsolicited Letters to Five Artists. Clive James. FaBoPa
Unsound Condition. Richard Armour. ASP
Unspeakable. Margaret Avison. NOBC
Unspeakable sorrow! Tune: Gazing at the South. Li Yü, tr. by Burton Watson. CoBCP
Unspecifiable/ the inexhaustible novel, The. Anne-Marie Albiach, tr. fr. French by Keith Waldrop. Fr. Enigma, IV. RHTwFP
Unstable dreame, accordyng to the place. The Lover Having Dreamed Enjoying of His Love, Complaineth That the Dreame Is Not either Longer or Truer. Sir Thomas Wyatt. AAS
Unsteady is that cypress boat. Unknown, tr. by Arthur Waley. BoS
Unstill Universe. Lucio Piccolo, tr. fr. Italian by Charles Tomlinson. PFI
Unsullied the white colt. Unknown, tr. by Arthur Waley. BoS
Unsung Heroes, The. Paul Laurence Dunbar. BPo
Unsuspected Fact, An. Edward Cannon. NA
Untidy Dreadful Table. William Sydney Graham. PoPo
Until darkness fell. Evening Snow. Tamekane, tr. by Steven D. Carter. WFTW
Until I lose my soul and lie. Sara Teasdale. TrPWD
Until I Saw the Sea. Lilian Moore. NTCP; RHPC
Until now the earth has been drawn in the shape of a pear. A Grave for New York. "Adunis," tr. by Lena Jayyusi and Alan Brownjohn. MAP
Until recently there was fear. Amir Gilboa, tr. by Warren Bargad and Stanley F. Chyet. IP
Until Tatum passed. Standing on the Corner. Philip Levine. NNaP
Until that sun, which keeps. Trains Made of Stone. Ray A. Young Bear. CDW
Until the desert knows. Emily Dickinson. NOBA
Until They Have Stopped. Sarah E. Wright. PoBA
Until thine hands clasp girdlewise the waist of the Belov'd. Sadi, tr. by R. A. Nicholson. AWP
Until this poem is over, I shall not leave. Windfall. F. R. Scott. CaP
Until today the precious gem's been buried. Ryozan, tr. by Lucien Stryk and Takashi Ikemoto. ZPCJ
Until yesterday I was polite and peaceful. Opinions of the New Student. Regino Pedroso, tr. by Langston Hughes. TTY
Until you wake up to what you really are. Surdas, tr. by John Stratton Hawley and Mark Juergensmeyer. SSI
Until your laughter. Tumult. Charles Enoch Wheeler. PoNe
Untimely alone. Edwin Dickinson's Perspective. William Corbett. PPR
Untimely Thought, An. Thomas Bailey Aldrich. PWR
Untitled. Ellen Bass. PPR
Untitled. Daryl Hine. NoAM
Untitled I. Ishmael Reed. CNA
Untitled Poem. Alan Dugan. CAPP
Untitled Requiem for Tomorrow. Conyus. PoBA
Unto a heavenly course decreed. Star Morals. Friedrich Wilhelm Nietzsche, tr. by Ludwig Lewisohn. AWP
Unto Adam, His Own Scriveyn. Chaucer. See Adam scrivein, if ever it thee bifalle.
Unto God let praise be brought. And It Came to Pass at Midnight. Yannai. TrJP
Unto Jehovah Sing Will I. Henry Ainsworth. AH
Unto my faith as to a spar, I bind. Adrift. Elizabeth Dickinson Dowden. WGRP
Unto my thinking, thou beheld'st all worth. To Dante Alighieri. Guido Cavalcanti, tr. by Dante Gabriel Rossetti. AWP
Unto no body my woman saith she had rather a wife be. Catullus, tr. by Sir Philip Sidney. OBVE
Unto Our God Most High We Sing. John Vance Cheney. AH
Unto the blithe and lordly fellowship [or ffellowship]. Folgore Da San Gimignano, tr. fr. Italian by Dante Gabriel Rossetti. Fr. Sonnets of the Months: Dedication. AWP
Unto the boundless ocean of thy beauty. Samuel Daniel. Fr. To Delia. OBSC
Unto the Breach. Andrea Poliziano, tr. fr. Latin by John Addington Symonds. PeHV

Unto the deep the deep heart goes. The Place of Rest. "Æ." WGRP
Unto the silver night. Revelation. Sir Edmund Gosse. OBEV
Unto the temple of thy beauty. Unknown. OBSC
Unto the Upright Praise, sel. Moses Hayyim Luzzatto, tr. fr. Hebrew by Nina Davis Salaman. "All ye that handle harp and viol." TrJP
Unto this place when as the Elfin Knight. The Hill of the Graces. Spenser. Fr. The Faerie Queene, VI, 10. NOBE
Unto Thy Favor. Robert Tofte. Fr. Laura, I, xxx. Son
Unto you, most froward, this letter I write. A Grotesque Love-Letter. Unknown. MeEL
Untold Want, The. Walt Whitman. MoAmPo
Untouched grandeur in the hinterlands. Life in the Boondocks. A. R. Ammons. HAP
Untrammelled giant of the West. The Parting of the Ways. Joseph B. Gilder. PAH
Untranslatable. Wilhelm Szabo, tr. fr. German by Beth Bjorklund. CoAuP
Untrodden Ways. Agnes Maule Machar. CaP
Untwine those ringlets! Ev'ry dainty clasp. Frangipanni. Unknown. NA
Unusual Shoelaces. X. J. Kennedy. TDD
Unutterable Beauty, The. Geoffrey Anketell Studdert-Kennedy. TrPWD
Unutterable void of Hell is stirred, The. The Lesbian Hell. Aleister Crowley. PeHV
Unuttered Prayer. Josephine D. Henderson Heard. CBWP-4
Unveiling, The. Suzanne Bernhardt. VWA
Unwanted. Edward Field. GLP; Psk
Unwanted, The. Mary Gordon. IHMS
Unwarmed by any sunset light. Whittier. Fr. Snow-bound; a Winter Idyl. AiP
(World Transformed, The.) AA
Unwatch'd [or unwatched], the garden bough shall sway. Tennyson. Fr. In Memoriam A. H. H., CI. ELP; GTBS-P; OBNC; PoEL-5; SCV (Somersby, Lincolnshire; after Leaving the Refectory.) FaBoPP
Unweary'd watch their list'ning leaders keep, Th.' Homer, tr. fr. Greek by Pope. Fr. The Iliad, X. OBVE
Unwed Mother, The, sel. Camille Bélot, tr. fr. French by Beth Archer. Decision, The. DMF
Unwelcome. Mary Elizabeth Coleridge. CH; OBEV; OBNC; WPE
Unwelcome child. The Child Compassion. Margot Ruddock. OBMV
Unwinking frog of malachite, The. Museum-Piece. Audrey Alexandra Brown. CaP
Unworn long gown, meant for dances, The. Disposal. W. D. Snodgrass. CAPP
Unwritten Poems. William Winter. AA
Unwritten Song, The. Ford Madox Ford. BoTP
Unyielding in the pride of his defiance. The Flying Dutchman. E. A. Robinson. MOS
Up. Bill Kushner. GLP; UL
Up/ silvers/ the jet/ plane. Jet. John Travers Moore. RR
Up a ladder weightless as bird legs, thinner. The Fifth Season. Reg Saner. FYAP
Up above the winds. Wind of an Evening Shower. Shotetsu, tr. by Steven D. Carter. WFTW
Up against That Wall Everywhere. Márton Kalász, tr. fr. Hungarian by Jascha Kessler. FOC
Up against the Wall. D. C. Berry. BXAP
Up and Down. James Merrill. GLP
Emerald, The, sel. CAPP
Up and Down. Shakespeare. Fr. A Midsummer Night's Dream, III, ii. CTC
Up and Down. Sándor Weöres, tr. fr. Hungarian by Jascha Kessler. FOC
Up and down, o'er hill and valley. Triumph. L. D. Stearns. BLRP
Up and down the air you float. The Butterfly. Clinton Scollard. RAR
Up and down the beach. The Skin Divers. George Starbuck. NYBP
Up and down the City Road. Pop Goes the Weasel! At. to W. R. Mardale. FaBoNo; OxNR
Up and down without a bridge. Christine Lavant, tr. by Beth Bjorklund. CoAuP
Up, and only up, as the Sun. Upwards. Sándor Weöres, tr. by Jascha Kessler. FOC
Up & Out. Nila NorthSun. STE
Up and up soars the Evening Star, hanging there in the sky. The Evening Star. Aborigine Oral Tradition. Fr. Moon-Bone Song [or Cycle]. WTO
Up and up, the Incense-burner Peak! Having Climbed to the Topmost Peak of the Incense-Burner Mountain. Po Chü-i, tr. by Arthur Waley. SD

Up at a Villa—Down in the City. Robert Browning. FaBoPP; GTBS-P; INPS; NOBE; OBTV; PoRA; PPP

Up at Piccadilly oh! Mother Goose. OxNR

Up at the prow, I wash my mouth, dripping water on my robe. Yang Chi, *tr. fr. Chinese* by Jonathan Chaves. *Fr.* Miscellaneous Impressions of T'an-chou. CoBLCP

Up, black, striped and damasked like the chasuble. The Skunk. Seamus Heaney. FaBCIP; NAEL-2; OxBC; PoE

Up, boy! arise, and saddle quick. The Message. Heine, *tr.* by Kate Freiligrath Kroeker. AWP

Up Early. Kit Robinson. UL

Up, Fairy! quit the chick-weed bower. The Second Quest. Joseph Rodman Drake. *Fr.* The Culprit Fay. AA

Up floats the turf. Watching Tackles in Slow Motion. David Allan Evans. TSL

Up from my belly, up from my back. Chopping Fire-Wood. Robert Pack. NePoEA-2

Up from South Jersey and the low persistent. Toward the Verrazano. Stephen Dunn, *tr.* by Joachim Neugroschel. AnAn

Up from the Bed of the River. James Weldon Johnson. *Fr.* The Creation. EaLo

Up from the bronze, I saw. Roman Fountain. Louise Bogan. NoP; WPOW

Up from the Egg; the Confessions of a Nuthatch Avoider. Ogden Nash. FiBHP; PoRA

Up from the log cabin to the capitol. Edwin Markham. *Fr.* Lincoln, the Man of the People. OFD

Up from the low-roofed dockyard warehouses. Grain Elevator. A. M. Klein. CaP

Up from the meadows rich with corn. Barbara Frietchie. Whittier. AIP; AnAmPo; BeLS; BF; BoTP; CTC; FaBoBe; FaBV; FaFP; FaPON; FaPoR; FPL; GN; NOBA; OBAL; OBCA; PAH; PoLF; TrGrPo; WBLP

Up from the moor came Guldah, with laughter in her eyes. Vampire. Bertrande Harry Snell. VVA

Up from the paddies. Tonna, *tr.* by Steven D. Carter. WFTW

Up from the South at break of day. Sheridan's Ride. Thomas Buchanan Read. AnAmPo; BeLS; FaBoBe; FaBV; FaFP; GN; OHFP; OHIP; PAH; WBLP

Up from the street and the crowds that went. Her Eyes. E. A. Robinson. AnAmPo

Up from the Wheelbarrow. Ogden Nash. FaBoBe

Up, Helsum Hairt. Alexander Scott. OxBS

Up here I can see the/ glimmering lights. At Mexican Springs. Laura Tohe. STE

Up hill and down dale. *Unknown.* OxNR

Up I Arose in Verno Tempore. *Unknown.* GBP

Up in a dirty window in a dark room is a star. The Pilot. Russell Edson. LCAP

Up in the Air. Allan Ramsay. NOEC

Up in the attic, down in the cellar, and under. A Treasure. Reed Whittemore. NePoEA

Up in the carbon, as you play postage. New Jersey. Will Bennett. UL

Up in the hay one evening, darkling. Afanasi Afanasievich Fet, *tr.* by Alan Myers. AAA

Up in the heavenly saloon. Arizona Nature Myth. James Michie. NOBL

Up in the lift go we. *Unknown.* PBBP

Up in the mountains, it's lonesome all the time. The Mountain Whippoorwill. Stephen Vincent Benét. TrGrPo

Up in the North. *Unknown.* OxBoLi

Up in the Pine. Nancy Dingman Watson. RHPC

Up in the sky big ships send out smoke. Clasped Hands. Philippe Soupault, *tr.* by Michael Benedikt. POS

Up into the cherry tree. Foreign Lands. Robert Louis Stevenson. BoTP

Up into the Silence the Green. E. E. Cummings. TTTS

Up Johnie raise in a May morning. Johnie Cock. *Unknown.* ESPB
(Johnie o' Cocklesmuir.) OxBB

Up leaps the lark. Delightful Spring once more. Edmund St. Gascoigne Mackie. *Fr.* Charmides. PeHV

Up-line platform bridges a metal road, The. Ravenglass Railway Station, Cumberland. Norman Nicholson. NYBP

Up on the downs the red-eyed kestrels hover. John Masefield. BrPo
(Up on the Downs.) NOBE

Up on their brooms the witches stream. The Ride-by-Nights. Walter de la Mare. DuDa; FaPON; WSC

Up Rising. Robert Duncan. *Fr.* Passages. NNaP

Up Silver Stairsteps. Jesse Stuart. AmFN

Up street and down street. *Unknown.* OxNR

Up tails all! Down and under! Undersea Fever. William Cole. FiBHP

Up the airy mountain. The Fairies. William Allingham. AnIL; CH; ChTr; FaBoCh; FaBoPP; FaBV; FaPON; Mes; NOBE; NOBVV; OBEV; OnMSP; OxBChV; PDV; RHPC; WSC
(Up the Airy Mountain.) FaFP

Up the ash tree climbs the ivy. Upper Lambourne. Sir John Betjeman. FaBoTw

Up the Country. Henry Lawson. CBAP

Up the crag. Weapons. Anna Wickham. MoBrPo

Up the dark-valleyed river stroke by stroke. The Dawn on the Lievre. Archibald Lampman. CaP

Up the dusty way from Frisco town. Walk, Damn You, Walk! William de Vere. PoLF

Up the hill. Forget Me Not. Austin Clarke. CIP

Up the hill beyond the Mayflower. Generation. Rowena Tiempo Torrevillas. WCI

Up the hillside, down the glen. Texas. Whittier. PAH

Up the Noran Water. Shy Geordie. Helen B. Cruickshank. GoTS; OxBS

Up the reputable walks of old established trees. The Campus on the Hill. W. D. Snodgrass. AiP; LiTM; NIP; NoAM; TAP; TwCP

Up the wooden hill. *Unknown.* OxNR

Up There. W. H. Auden. OxBTC

Up there on the mountain road, the fireworks. Blue Ridge. Ellen Bryant Voigt. AnAn; MAYP; NoAM

Up through a cloudy sky, the sun. The Battle of Bennington. Thomas P. Rodman. PAH

Up through the blue-green furrow. Neptune Rising. Jane Yolen. BWV

"Up, Timothy, up with your staff and away!" The Childless Father. Wordsworth. CH

Up to Date. "Hugh MacDiarmid." FaBoCo

Up to Mount Olivet. William Alabaster. *Fr.* Divine Meditations, VI. Son

Up to the bed by the window, where I be lyin.' Old Shepherd's Prayer. Charlotte Mew. EaLo; MoAB; MoBrPo; OBD; OxBTC; WPE

Up to the top of the haunted turf. Walter de la Mare Tells the Listener about Jack and Jill. Louis Untermeyer. *Fr.* Mother Goose Up-to-Date. MoAmPo

Up to those heights where angels rest. The Perfect Orchestra. Henrietta Cordelia Ray. CBWP-3

Up to thy summit, Lewesdon, to the brow. William Crowe. *Fr.* Lewesdon Hill. NOEC

Up! up! let us a voyage take. The Northern Seas. William Howitt. GN

Up, up, my drowsie soule, where thy new eare. Our Companie in the Next World. John Donne. *Fr.* Of the Progresse of the Soule; the Second Anniversarie. OBS

Up! Up! my friend, and quit your books. The Tables Turned. Wordsworth. EnRP; NAEL-2; OAEL-2; TOF

Up! Up! the time for sleep is past! The Expensive Wife. Judah ibn Sabbatai. *Fr.* The Gift of Judah the Woman-Hater. TrJP

Up, Up! Ye Dames and Lasses Gay. Samuel Taylor Coleridge. BoTP

Up! Up! You brothers, now be strong. Song of the Cape of Good Hope. Christian Schubart, *tr.* by Alfred Baskerville. NU

Up where the world grows cold. A North Pole Story. Menella Bute Smedley. OxBChV

Up with me! up with me into the clouds! Wordsworth. *Fr.* To a Skylark. FPL; TTTS

Up yonder hill, behold how sadly slow. Thomas Parnell. *Fr.* Night Piece on Death. OBD

Up yonder on the mountain. The Shepherd's Lament. Goethe, *tr.* by Bayard Taylor. AWP

An Upbraiding. Thomas Hardy. OPOP

Upcountry. Adrienne Rich. ER

Upended, it crouches on broken limbs. Charles Tomlinson. CMoP

Upgrade, past snow-tangled bramble, past. Sila. Robert Penn Warren. NoP

Uphill [or Up-Hill]. Christina Rossetti. BLPA; CH; EBVV; FaBoBe; FaBoRV; FPL; HAP; InPK; NAEL-2; NOBE; NoP; OAEL-2; OBD; OBEV; OBNC; PoE; PoRA; PPP; TrCP; TrGrPo; WeW; WGRP; WiR; WPE

Upland. A. R. Ammons. NOBA

Upland flocks grew starved and thinned, The. The Lambs of Grasmere, 1860. Christina Rossetti. FM

Upon a Black Twist, Rounding the Arm of the Countess of Carlisle. Robert Herrick. CaPo

Upon a Braid of Hair in a Heart. Henry King. EnLoPo

Upon a Child. Robert Herrick. *See* Here a pretty baby lies.

Upon a Child That Died. Robert Herrick. CaPo; CH; InPK; NoP; OBEV; SeCV-1
(Epitaph Upon a Child that Died.) OBD; OBEV

Upon a Christmas Morning. *Unknown.* AmFP

Upon a cloud among the stars we stood. The Flight. Lloyd Mifflin. AA

Upon a cock-horse to market I'll trot. *Unknown.* OxNR

Upon a dainty hill sometime. Nicholas Breton. PBBP

Upon a dark ball spun in time. Giraffe and Tree. W. J. Turner. CH; GrPl

Upon a dark, light, gloomy, sunshine day. A Messe of Nonsense. *Unknown.* OBS

Upon a darksome night. Saint John of the Cross, *tr. by* E. Allison Peers. ErPo

Upon a day, came sorrow in to me. Sonnet: On the 9th of June 1290. Dante, *tr. by* Dante Gabriel Rossetti. AWP

Upon a Dead Man's Head. John Skelton. HAP; SeCePo
(Gift of a Skull, The.) ACP
(Uppon a Deedmans Hed.) AAS

Upon a Diamond Cut in Form[e] of a Heart. Sent in a New-Yeares [*or* Year's] Gift. Sir Robert Ayton. EiL; OBS

Upon a Dying Lady. W. B. Yeats. LiTB; UnPo

Upon a fibry fern-tree bough. Mid-Noon in January. "Fiona Macleod." *Fr.* Australian Transcripts. FM

Upon a Flie. Robert Herrick. FM

Upon a Fool. John Hoskyns. FaBoEE

Upon a Funeral. Sir John Beaumont. FaBoRV

Upon a Girl of Seven Years Old. Pope. OxBSP

Upon a Great Shower of Snow That Fell on May-Day, 1654. Thomas Washbourne. NOCV

Upon a House Shaken by the Land Agitation. W. B. Yeats. CMoP

Upon A. M. Sir John Suckling. ErPo

Upon a Maid That Died [*or* Dyed] the Day She Was Married [*or* Marryed]. Meleager, *tr. fr. Greek by* Robert Herrick. AWP; CaPo; ChTr; FaBoCh; FaBoEE; OBVE; OxBoLi

Upon a Mole in Celia's Bosom. Thomas Carew. CaPo

Upon a night an aungell bright. Now the Most High Is Born. James Ryman. MeEL

Upon a Notorious Shrew. *Unknown.* FaBoEE

Upon a Passing Bell. Thomas Washbourne. FaBoRV

Upon a Ribband [*or* Ribbon]. Thomas Carew. CaPo; OAEL-1; PoE

Upon a Rich Country Gentleman. *Unknown.* FaBoEE

Upon a Ring of Bells. Bunyan. CH

Upon a Row of Old Books and Shoes in a Pawnbroker's Window. "Furnley Maurice." CBAP

Upon a Sabbath-day it fell. The Eve of Saint Mark. Keats. CH; EnRP

Upon a Second Marriage. James Merrill. *See* Orchards we linger here because.

Upon a simmer Sunday morn. The Holy Fair. Burns. EnRP; OBSV

Upon a Snail. Bunyan. *See* She goes but softly, but she goeth sure.

Upon a Spider Catching a Fly. Edward Taylor. AmPP; NOBA; NoP; OxBA; PoEL-3; SCAP; TAP

Upon a sudden, as I gazing stood. Rachel Speght. *Fr.* A Dream. WPE

Upon a summer Sunday: sweet the sound. The Runaways. Mark Van Doren. PoRA

Upon a summer's time. A Pleasant New Court Song. *Unknown.* CoMu

Upon a time a neighing steed. The Council of Horses. John Gay. GN

Upon a time, before the faery broods. Lamia. Keats. EnRP; NAEL-2; VVA

Upon a tree there mounted guard. The Cock and the Fox. La Fontaine, *tr. by* Elizur Wright. AWP

Upon a tuffet of most soft and verdant moss. Little Miss Muffet. *Unknown.* BXAP; FaBoPa

Upon a Virgin Kissing a Rose. Robert Herrick. SeCP; SeCV-1

Upon a Wasp Chilled [*or* Child] with Cold. Edward Taylor. NAAL-1; NOBA; NOCV; PoEL-3

Upon a white and starched ruff. The Clowns. Jules Laforgue, *tr. by* William Jay Smith. CT

Upon a Young Mother of Many Children. Robert Herrick. CaPo

Upon Absence. Katherine Philips. PBWP

Upon an Ingenious Friend, Over-Vain. Thomas Fitzgerald. OxBSP

Upon an obscure night. The Obscure Night of the Soul. St. John of the Cross, *tr. by* Arthur Symons. AWP; OBMV

Upon an old estate from ancient sires descended. The Portraits. Anna Maria Lenngren, *tr. by* C. W. Stork. WPOW

Upon Apennine Slope. Arthur Hugh Clough. *See* Amours de Voyage: Ah, That I Were Far Away.

Upon Appleton House, to My Lord Fairfax, *sels.* Andrew Marvell. FaBoPV; SeCP; SeCV-1, *sl. abr.*
After Floods on the Wharfe. FaBoPP
"And now to the abyss I pass." OAEL-1
Carrying Their Coracles. ChTr
"From that blest bed the hero came." JCP
Garden of Appleton House, The ("When in the east the morning ray"). NOBE

Hewel, or Woodpecker, The. ChTr
Kingfisher, The. ChTr
"Oh thou, that dear and happy isle." OxBoLi
"See how the flowers, as at parade." TrGrPo
(Garden, A.) OBEV
"When first the eye this forest sees." PBBP

Upon Arriving at Ili, Recalling What I Saw on the Road. Hung Liang-chi, *tr. fr. Chinese by* Irving Lo. WFTU

Upon Batt. Robert Herrick. FaBoEE

Upon Ben Johnson. Edmund Waller. SeCV-1

Upon Ben Jonson. Robert Herrick. CaPo; FaBoEE; NoP; OBS; SeCV-1

Upon Bishop Andrewes His Picture before His Sermons. Richard Crashaw. OBS

Upon Boys Diverting Themselves in the River. Thomas Foxton. OxBChV

Upon Bunce: Epigram. Robert Herrick. CaPo

Upon Christ's Nativity or Christmas. Rowland Watkyns. OBWVE

Upon distant water, rain falls. Waking Up: A Song. Yip Wai-lim, *tr. by* Dominic Cheung. IFON

Upon Dr. Davies's British Grammar. James Howell. OBWVE

Upon Drinking in a Bowl. Earl of Rochester. OBS; OxBoLi; SeCV-2

Upon Fairford Windows. Richard Corbett. EyDe

Upon Ford's Two Tragedies, "Loves Sacrifice" and "The Broken Heart." Richard Crashaw. OBS

Upon Glass: Epigram. Robert Herrick. JCP

Upon Groins: Epigram. Robert Herrick. CaPo

Upon Her Feet. Robert Herrick. CaPo; OxBSP; PoE

Upon her head she weares a crowne of starres. An Angel Describes Truth. Ben Jonson. *Fr.* Hymenaei. OBS

Upon Her Soothing Breast. Emily Brontë. BoWoP

Upon Her Voice. Robert Herrick. CaPo

Upon Himself. Robert Herrick. OxBSP

Upon himself a miracle he wrought. Eugenio Pacelli. Francis Neilson. GoYe

Upon His Departure Hence. Robert Herrick. FaBoRV; QFR

Upon his dull ear fell the stern command. The Black Draftee from Dixie. Carrie Williams Clifford. BISi

Upon his frustrate and unhopeful quest. Fragment from "The Maladjusted: A Tragedy." Morris Bishop. NBLV

Upon His Leaving His Mistress. *See* 'Tis not that I am weary.

Upon His Majesty's Being Made Free of the City. Andrew Marvell. *See* On the Lord Mayor and Court of Aldermen, Presenting the Late King and Duke of York Each with a Copy of Their Freedoms.

Upon His Picture. Thomas Randolph. MePo; NOBE

Upon His Sister-in-Law, Mistress Elizabeth Herrick. Robert Herrick. CaPo

Upon His Spaniell Tracie. Robert Herrick. FM

Upon His Verses. Robert Herrick. NAEL-1

Upon Jack and Jill: Epigram. Robert Herrick. CaPo; NAEL-1

Upon Julia. Ernest Radford. BXAP

Upon Julia Washing Herself in the River. Robert Herrick. CaPo

Upon Julia's Arctics. Bert Leston Taylor. NBLV; OBAL

Upon Julia's Breasts. Robert Herrick. CaPo; NoP

Upon Julia's Clothes. Robert Herrick. AWP; CaPo; ChTr; EBEV; EnLoPo; FaBV; FaFP; FF; FPL; GBL; HAP; HeIP; HoPM; InPS; JCP; LiTB; NAEL-1; NBLV; NIP; NOBE; NoP; OAEL-1; OBEV; OBS; OPOP; OxBSP; PoE; PoEL-3; PPP; SeCP; SeCV-1; TrGrPo; TTTS; WeW
(Whenas in Silks My Julia Goes.) BLPA; GTBS; GTBS-P; TEP

Upon Julia's Clothes. E. V. Knox. BXAP

Upon Julia's Ribband. Robert Herrick. CaPo

Upon Julia's Voice. Robert Herrick. InPK; JCP; NOBE; SeCePo; SeCP; SoSe

Upon Kinde and True Love. Aurelian Townshend. MeLP; MePo; OBS

Upon Lazarus His Teares. Richard Crashaw. SeCV-1

Upon [His] Leaving His Mistress. Earl of Rochester. EnLoPo; GBL; TEP
(Upon Leaving His Mistress.) NBLV; TrGrPo

Upon Leaving the Capital: A Farewell to My Several Friends. K'ang Yu-wei, *tr. fr. Chinese by* Irving Lo. WFTU

Upon Leaving the Parole Board Hearing. Conyus. PoBA

Upon Listening to the Third Brandenburg Concerto. Gerhard Fritsch, *tr. fr. German by* Beth Bjorklund. CoAuP

Upon Looking at a Book of Astrology. David McFadden. NeAC

Upon Love. Robert Herrick. SeCV-1; TrGrPo

Upon Love Fondly Refus'd for Conscience's Sake. Thomas Randolph. OAEL-1

Upon Lulls. Robert Herrick. CaPo

Upon Master Edmund Spenser. Francis Beaumont. FaBoEE

Upon Master Fletcher's Incomparable Playes. Robert Herrick. OBS

Upon Master Walter Montagu's Return from Travel. Thomas Carew. CaPo

Upon Mistress Elizabeth Wheeler under the Name of Amarillis. Robert Herrick. CaPo; PBBP

Upon [Mr.] Ben Jonson: Epigram. Robert Herrick. CaPo

Upon Mrs. Anne Bradstreet Her Poems. John Rogers. SCAP

Upon my bier no garlands lay. Now. Mary Barker Dodge. AA

Upon my darling's beaming eyes. Auf meiner Herzliebsten Äugelein. Heine, tr. by Richard Garnett. AWP

Upon My Lady Carlisle's Walking in Hampton Court Garden. Sir John Suckling. CaPo; NoP

Upon my lap my sovereign sits. Richard Verstegan. CH; EiL; OBEV

Upon My Lord Brohall's Wedding. Sir John Suckling. CaPo

Upon My Lord Chief Justice's Election of My Lady Anne Wentworth for His Mistress. Thomas Carew. CaPo

Upon Nirwána's brink the ráhat stood. The Ráhat. John Jerome Rooney. AA

Upon Nothing. Earl of Rochester. MePo; OBS; OBSV; PoEL-3; TrGrPo

Upon One of the Maids of Honour to Queen Elizabeth. John Hoskyns. FaBoEE

Upon Our Saviour's Tomb Wherein Never Man Was Laid. Richard Crashaw. See To Our Blessed Lord upon the Choice of His Sepulchre.

Upon Pagget. Robert Herrick. CaPo; FaBoCh

Upon Paul's steeple stands a tree. Unknown. OxNR

Upon Phillis Walking in a Morning before Sun-Rising. John Cleveland. MeLP

Upon Prew, His Maid. Robert Herrick. See In this little urn is laid.

Upon Prudence Baldwin Her Sickness. Robert Herrick. JCP; SeCV-1

Upon Prue, His Maid. Robert Herrick. JCP; NAEL-1; NoP; SeCV-1

Upon Re-reading a Poem by Paul Celan. Erich Fried, tr. fr. German by Beth Bjorklund. CoAuP

Upon Reading the Boudoir Poem of Mei-ts'un. Ch'ien Ch'ien-yi, tr. fr. Chinese by Irving Lo. WFTU

Upon Reading the Works of Tu Fu, sel. Sung Hsiang, tr. fr. Chinese by Irving Lo.

"He pledged himself to live with poetry until old age." WFTU

Upon Receipt of a Pound of Coffee in 1863. Mary E. Tucker. CBWP-1

Upon Returning to the Capital in 1923. Cheng Hsiao-hsü, tr. fr. Chinese by Irving Lo. WFTU

Upon Rook: Epigram. Robert Herrick. CaPo

Upon Roses. Robert Herrick. SeCP

Upon St. David's Day. Unknown. FaBoUs

Upon Scobble [Epigram]. Robert Herrick. CaPo; FaBoEE; NoP; TW

Upon Shaving Off One's Beard. John Updike. OxBSP

Upon Showbread: Epigram. Robert Herrick. CaPo

Upon Sir Francis Drake's Return from His Voyage about the World, and the Queen's Meeting Him. Unknown. CoMu; EiL; FaBoCh; OxBSS

Upon Sir John Lawrence's Bringing Water over the Hills. Sir John Suckling. CaPo

Upon Some Alterations in My Mistress, after My Departure into France. Thomas Carew. CaPo

Upon Some Women. Robert Herrick. CaPo

Upon Sybilla. Robert Herrick. CaPo
   (Sibilla.) SeCePo

Upon the Anonymous Author of Legion's Humble Address to the Lords. Thomas Brown. APAS

Upon the Author; by a Known Friend. Benjamin Woodbridge. SCAP

Upon the Author of a Play Called Sodom. John Oldham. TW

Upon the Author of the "Satire against Wit." Sir Charles Sedley. APAS

Upon the Author's First Seven Years' Service. Thomas Tusser. EiL

Upon the Bankruptcy of a Physician. Henricus Selyns. SCAP

Upon the barren man. Pocahontas. George Pope Morris. PAH

Upon the beach are thousands of crabs; they are. Crustaceans. Roy Fuller. NoAM

Upon the Bleeding Crucifix. Richard Crashaw. See On the Bleeding Wounds of Our Crucified Lord.

Upon the Body of Our Blessed Lord, Naked and Bloody. Richard Crashaw. ACP; InvP; SeCP
   (On Our Crucified Lord, Naked and Bloody.) HoPM; OAEL-1; OBS; OxBSP; SeCV-1; TrCP

Upon the Book and Picture of the Seraphical Saint Teresa. Richard Crashaw. See O thou undaunted daughter of desires!

Upon the boughs and tops of trees. Patrick Hannay. Fr. Philomela, the Nightingale. PBBP

Upon the branches of our silence hang our words. The Tree of Silence. Vassar Miller. NePoEA-2

Upon the branches of those trees. Matthew Royden. Fr. An Elegy, or Friend's Passion for His Astrophil [or Astrophel]. PBBP

Upon the Burning of Our House, July 10th, 1666. Anne Bradstreet. See Some Verses upon the Burning of Our House, July 10th, 1666.

Upon the Crucifix. William Alabaster. PoEL-2

Upon the Curtain of Lucasta's Picture It Was Thus Wrought. Richard Lovelace. CaPo

Upon the Death of G. B. John Cotton. SCAP

Upon the Death of His Late Highness the Lord Protector. Andrew Marvell. See I saw him dead, a leaden slumber lyes (or lies).

Upon the Death of His Much Esteemed Friend Mr. Jno Saffin Junr. Grindall Rawson. SCAP

Upon the Death of His Sparrow; an Elegie. Robert Herrick. FM

Upon the Death of Mr. King Drowned in the Irish Seas. John Cleveland. See I like not tears in tune, nor will I prize.

Upon the Death of My Ever Desired Friend Doctor Donne Dean of Pauls. Henry King. SeCP

Upon the Death of Sir Albert Morton's Wife. Sir Henry Wotton. BoLoP; EnLoPo; FaBoEE; NOP; OBD; OBEV; OBS; SeCP; TrGrPo; WeW

Upon the Death of the Earl of Dundee. Dryden. See Oh last and best of Scots! who did'st maintain.

Upon the Death of the Lord Hastings. Dryden. SeCV-2

Upon the Death of the Viscount of Dundee. Dryden. OBS

Upon the Decease of Mrs. Anne Griffin. John Fiske. SCAP

Upon the decks they take beef tea. Passage Steamer. Louis MacNeice. MOS

Upon the deep ocean a schooner is lying. Bird of Passage. Ida Hahn-Hahn, tr. by Susan L. Cocalis. DMG

Upon the Dramatick Poems of Mr. John Fletcher. William Cartwright. OBS

Upon the earth there are so many treasures. Earth Felicities, Heavens Allowances. Richard Steere. SCAP

Upon the Eastern shore of Windermere. On Windermere; Bowness Bay and Belle Isle. Wordsworth. Fr. The Prelude [or, Growth of a Poet's Mind]: Childhood and School-Time. FaBoPP

Upon the ecstatic diving board the diver. Lone Bather. A. M. Klein. HeIP

Upon the eighteenth day of June. Bonny John Seton. Unknown. ESPB

Upon the Ensignes of Christes Crucifyinge. William Alabaster. MePo

Upon the eyes, the lips, the feet. Extreme Unction. Ernest Dowson. ACP; MoBrPo; OAEL-2; OBMV

Upon the fifth day of November. On Mr. Pricke. Unknown. FaBoEE

Upon the gale she stooped her side. The Gallant Ship. Sir Walter Scott. BoTP

Upon the grass. Noontide. Henrietta Cordelia Ray. Fr. Idyl. CBWP-3

Upon the Hill before Centreville. George Henry Boker. PAH

Upon the hill my lover stands. The House o' the Mirror. Helen Adam. MAT; NMM

Upon the hills of Phrygie near a teyle there stands a tree. Ovid, tr. fr. Latin by Arthur Golding. Fr. Metamorphoses: Philemon and Baucis. OBSC, tr. by Arthur Golding.
   (Baucis and Philemon.)

Upon the Holy Sepulchre. Richard Crashaw. FaBoEE

Upon the Horse and His Rider. Bunyan. OxBChV

Upon the Image of Death, sel. Robert Southwell. CH; EiL; NOBE; OBSC

"Before my face the picture hangs." OBD

Upon the Infant Martyrs. Richard Crashaw. NoP; OAEL-1

Upon the King's Return from Flanders. Henry Hall. APAS

Upon the King's Voyage to Chatham to Make Bulwarks against the Dutch. Unknown. APAS

Upon the Lake. Hayim Lenski, tr. fr. Hebrew by Robert Friend. VWA

Upon the lake. The Gramophone. James Reaney. CaP

Upon the Lark and the Fowler. Bunyan. CH; PBBP

Upon the level field behold. Baseball. Frank Dempster Sherman. OBCA

Upon the Lines and Life of the Famous Scenic Poet, Master William Shakespeare. Hugh Holland. OBWVE

Upon the Loss[e] of H[h]is Mistresses. Robert Herrick. CaPo; NAEL-1; PoE; SeCV-1

Upon the man who's buried here. J. E. Thorold Rogers. FaBoEE

Upon the Most Useful Knowledge, Craft or Cunning, Which Is More Wisdom, as 'Tis Less Wit. William Wycherley. SeCV-2

Upon the mountain's edge with light touch resting. A Sunset. Samuel Taylor Coleridge. OxBSP

Upon the Much-to Be Lamented Desease of the Reverend Mr. John Cotton. John Fiske. SCAP

Upon the Nipples of Julia's Breast. Robert Herrick. CaPo; ErPo; NAEL-1

Upon the [or a] Snail. Bunyan. ChTr; OxBSP

Upon the patch of earth that clings. Public Aid for Niagara Falls. Morris Bishop. NBLV

Upon the poop the captain stands. The Shipwreck. E. Harriet Palmer. NA

Upon the Priory Grove, His Usual Retirement. Henry Vaughan. FaBoPP

Upon the Same (Detractor). Robert Herrick. CaPo

Upon the Sand. Ella Wheeler Wilcox. AnAmPo

Upon the Saying That My Verses Were Made by Another. Anne Killigrew. WPE

Upon the slippery tops of humane state. Seneca. *See* Thyestes: Stond [*or* Stand] who so list upon the slipper toppe.

Upon the soft brown pillow of thy shore. Apostrophe to the Parret. E. H. Burrington. FaBoPP

Upon the Springs Issuing out from the Foot of Plimouth Beach. Samuel Sewall. SCAP

Upon the Sudden Restraint of the Earl[e] of Somerset, Then Falling from Favor [*or* Favour]. Sir Henry Wotton. ELP; JCP; MePo; NOBE; NoP; OBS; SeCP

Upon the Swallow. Bunyan. OxBChV

Upon the threshold of the year we stand. The New Year. Homera Homer-Dixon. BLRP

Upon the Tomb of the Most Reverend Mr. John Cotton. Benjamin Woodbridge. SCAP

Upon the topmost branches dies. Doubt. Fernand Gregh, *tr. by* Ludwig Lewisohn. WGRP

Upon the tree of time. A Harvest to Seduce. Melville Cane. NYBP

Upon the Troublesome Time. Robert Herrick. CaPo

Upon the utmost corners of the warld. In Orknay. William Fowler. GoTS; OxBS

Upon the Weathercock. Bunyan. OxBChV

Upon this cake of ice is perched. The Puffin. Robert Williams Wood. RHPC

Upon this leafy bush. The Linnet. Walter de la Mare. LiTB

Upon this marble bust that is not I. To Inez Milholland. Edna St. Vincent Millay. AiP; WPE

Upon this place the great Gustavus died. On Gustavus Adolphus, King of Sweden. Sir Thomas Roe. FaBoEE

Upon this primrose hill. The Primrose, Being at Montgomery Castle, upon the Hill, on Which It Is Situate. John Donne. FaBoPP; GBL

Upon This Rock. Ruthven Todd. PoA

Upon Thought Castara May Die. William Habington. *Fr.* Castara. ACP

Upon Time. Robert Herrick. OBS

Upon Umber: Epigram. Robert Herrick. CaPo

Upon Venus Putting on Mars His Armes. Richard Crashaw. SeCP

Upon Visiting His Lady by Moonlight. "A. W." CTC; OBSC

Upon Wedlock and Death of Children. Edward Taylor. AmPP; NAAL-1; NoP

Upon Your Leaving. Etheridge Knight. NeAC; NNaP

Upon your sunken cheek a hectic stain! Moriturus. "Marie Madelaine", *tr. by* Ferdinand E. Kappey. PeHV

Upone Tabacco. Sir Robert Ayton. OxBS

Upper Broadway. Adrienne Rich. HCAP; InPS

Upper Canadian, The. James Reaney. NOBC

Upper Chamber, An. Frances Bannerman. OBEV

Upper chamber in a darkened house, An. Frederick Goddard Tuckerman. *Fr.* Sonnets, I, x. NOBA; NoP; TAP

Upper Family. Maxwell Bodenheim. OBAL

Upper Garrison Farm: A Ballad a Lament for a Woman Killed by the Soldiery. Shih Jun-chang, *tr. fr. Chinese by* William Shultz. WFTU

Upper Lake, The. Francis Stuart. NeIP

Upper Lambourne. Sir John Betjeman. FaBoTw

Upper Room, An. Daniel Lawrence Kelleher. NeIP

Upper Skies, The. Robert Bridges. BoTP

Upper slopes are busy with the cricket, The. Elegy on the Dust. Thom Gunn. NoAM

Uppon a Deedmans Hed. John Skelton. *See* Your ugly token my mind hath broken.

Uppon the First Sight of New England, June 29, 1638. Thomas Tillam. GOA; SCAP

(Hail, Holy Land.) AH

Upright and shrewd, more woo'd of fame. Henry Charles Beeching. *Fr.* Balliol Rhymes. CenHV

Uprightness. Camouflaged Troop-Ship. Amy Lowell. AiP

Uprising See the Fitful Lark. *Unknown.* NA

Uproar, An/ a spruce-green sky, bound in iron. The Butterfly. Margaret Avison. OBCV

Upshore from the cloud. By a Lake in Minnesota. James Wright. AmFN

Upside-Down World, The. Hamish Hendry. BoTP

Upstairs a young man plays. Inside and Out. Robert Phillips. GeTw

Upstairs Downstairs. Hervey Allen. PoA; PoNe

Upstairs on the third floor. Bottled [New York]. Helene Johnson. BlSi; CDC; PoBA

Upstood upstaffed passing sinuously away over an airy arch. Christophe. Russell Atkins. PoNe

Upstream. Carl Sandburg. MoAB; MoAmPo

Upstream, against the wind, they pull hundreds of feet of rope. Song of the Boat-Pullers. Pien Kung, *tr. by* Jonathan Chaves. CoBLCP

Uptown. Allen Ginsberg. FF; TwCP

("Yellow Budweiser signs over oaken bars.") TW

Uptown on Lenox Avenue. Prime. Langston Hughes. PoBA

Uptown there's not a lot of living matter. Courthouse Square. Herbert Merrill. AmFN

Upturned were cups and spilt. Mohammad Taqi Mir, *tr. by* Ahmed Ali. GoT

Upward through crystal in a kümmel bottle. Dreamscape in Kümmel. Harold Witt. NYBP

Upwards. Sándor Weöres, *tr. fr. Hungarian by* Jascha Kessler. FOC

Ur ol' Hyar lib in ur house on de hill. Ol' Doc' Hyar. James Edwin Campbell. BANP

Urania. Robert Andrews. NOEC

Urania, *sels.* Mary Sidney Wroth, Countess of Montgomery. WPE

Duke's Song, The.

Lindamira's Complaint.

Love Leave to Urge. Son

Morea's Sonnet.

Pamphilia to Amphilanthus.

"Am I thus conquered? have I lost the powers." NAEL-1

"False hope which feeds but to destroy, and spill." NAEL-1

Pamphilia's Sonnet.

Verses of the Talkative Knight, The.

When Night's Black Mantle. Son

Urania, or Spiritual Poems, *sel.* William Drummond of Hawthornden.

Too Long I Followed. Son

Urania takes her morning flight. The Adventurous Muse. Isaac Watts. NOEC

Uranne. Mary Weston Fordham. CBWP-2

Urban Convalescence, An. James Merrill. CoAP; NAAL-2; NOBA

Urban Dream. Victor Hernandez Cruz. NBP

Urban Experience: Part One, The. Lew Blockcolski. VoR

Urban Experience: Part Two, The. Lew Blockcolski. VoR

Urban Guerrilla, An. Allen Curnow. *Fr.* Moro Assassinato, II. PeNZ

Urban Lad, An. David Cram. SoTCo

Urban Ode. Sandra McPherson. MAYP

Urban Pollution. John Armstrong. *Fr.* The Art of Preserving Health. NOEC

Urceus Exit. Austin Dobson. *Fr.* Rose-Leaves. OBEV

Urchin's Dance, The. *At. to* John Lyly *and to* Thomas Ravenscroft. *See* By the moon we sport and play.

Urgency. Sarah E. Wright. PoNe

Urgent the cry of the wild geese, wailing amidst the void. Ditty: Below the Frontier. Shen Te-ch'ien, *tr. by* Marie Chan. WFTU

Urging Her of a Promise. Ben Jonson. *Fr.* A Celebration of Charis in Ten Lyrick Peeces. SeCP

Uriel. Emerson. LiTA; NAAL-1; NOBA; OxBA

Uriel, *sel.* William Force Stead.

"I thought the night without a sound was falling." TrPWD

(How Infinite Are Thy Ways.) OBMV

Uriel to his charge/ Returned on that bright beam. Milton. *Fr.* Paradise Lost, *bk.* IV, *ll.* 589–609.

(Now Came Still Evening On.) FaBoRV

Urizen's Curse upon His Children. Blake. *Fr.* Vala; or The Four Zoas. TW

Urn I: Silent for Twenty-five Years, the Father of My Mother Advises Me, *sel.* Walter Lew.

"Careless/ but not fearless." BrSi

Urn Burial. Ted Hughes. EBEV

Urn for Burial, An. *Unknown, tr. fr. Tamil by* A. K. Ramanujan. PLW

Urns and Odours Bring Away! John Fletcher *and* Shakespeare. *Fr.* The Two Noble Kinsmen, I, v. ElL

(Dirge of the Three Queens.) OBEV

(Funeral Song.) ChTr; OBS

Ursa Major. James Kirkup. ImOP

Ursula. David Ray. VGW

Uru-tu-sendo's Song. *Unknown, tr. fr. Tewa Indian by* H. J. Spinden. WTO

Urumbula Song, The. *Unknown, tr. fr. Aranda by* T. G. H. Strehlow. CBAP

Us. Julius Lester. PoBA

Us. Anne Sexton. CAPP

Us Two. A. A. Milne. OxBChV

Us two wuz boys when we fell out. Our Two Opinions. Eugene Field. AA
Use a decent length of no. 8. The Initiation. Brian Turner. ATNZ
Use all your hidden forces. Do not miss. Attainment. Ella Wheeler Wilcox. WGRP
Use maketh maistry [or mast'ry], this hath been said alway. Of Use. John Heywood. FaBoEE; PBBP
Use of a Wall Mirror, The. Adriaan Morriën, tr. fr. Dutch by James S. Holmes. DuIn
Use of Fiction, The. Naomi Shihab Nye. MAYP
Use, then, my lust for whisky and for thee. The Light of Life. "Hugh MacDiarmid." CMoP
Use three physicians still [or physicians' skill] : first Doctor Quiet. Health Counsel. Sir John Harington. FaBoUs, 2 l.
Use words to describe feelings? 4/13/79. Lewis Warsh. UL
Used jointly: seasons, books, and music. A Kind of Loss. Ingeborg Bachmann, tr. by Beth Bjorklund. CoAuP
Used to lying together. Wakayama Bokusui, tr. fr. Japanese by Hiroaki Sato. Fr. Forty-four Tanka. FCEI
Useful for Avoiding Collisions at Sea. Unknown. FaBoUs
Useless acquaintances increase. Natsume Seibi, tr. fr. Japanese by Hiroaki Sato. Fr. Twenty-seven Hokku. FCEI
Useless Day. Rosario Castellanos, tr. by Maureen Ahern. WPOW
Useless letter, long, yet to be finished, A. Ishikawa Takuboku, tr. fr. Japanese by Hiroaki Sato. Fr. Forty-seven Tanka in Three Lines. FCEI
Useless Machine. André Frénaud, tr. fr. French by Serge Gavronsky. RHTwFP
Uselessness. Ella Wheeler Wilcox. TrPWD
Uses of Adversity, The. Shakespeare. Fr. As You Like It, II, i. LiTB; TrGrPo
Uses of Clouds, The. Gregory O'Brien. ATNZ
Uses of Ocean, The. Sir Owen Seaman. FiBHP
Uses of Poetry. Winfield Townley Scott. PoA
Usk. T. S. Eliot. Fr. Landscapes, III. FaBoCh; NOCV; RB
Usk, The. C. H. Sisson. NOCV
Usual exquisite boredom of patrols, The. Hugh Popham. OxBTC
Usually/ you wake first. Why. Yusuf al-Sa'igh, tr. by Diana Der Hovanessian with Salma Khadra Jayyusi. MAP
Usually a landscape more obviously beautiful. Sheffield East End. Stanley Cook. NPo
Usufruct. Austin Clarke. IPY
Usurpers, The. Edwin Muir. CMoP
Ut, re, mi, fa, sol, la. Unknown. FaBoNo
Utah Iron Horse, The. Unknown. AmFP
Ute Lover, The. Hamlin Garland. AA
Ute Mountain. Charles Tomlinson. RB
Utilitarian View of the Monitor's Fight, A. Herman Melville. AmPP; NAAL-1; UnPo
Utmost grace the Greeks could show, The. Grecian Kindness. Earl of Rochester. OxBSP
Utmost Hour. Yves Bonnefoy, tr. fr. French by Paul Auster. RHTwFP
Utmost island of Europe, loveliest land. Ireland Weeping. William Livingston. GoTS
"Utopia, The." Lee Harwood. EAS
Utopia. Jewel C. Latimore. BPo
Utopia. Wislawa Szymborska, tr. fr. Polish by Czeslaw Milosz. PwPP
Utopia of Lord Mayor Howard, The. Randolph Stow. PoAu-2
Utopia TV Store. Maxine Chernoff. UL
Utter moorland, high, and wide, and flat, An. The Fork of the Road. William Renton. NOBVV
Utter Passion Uttered Utterly, An. John Todhunter. BXAP
Uvavnuk. Unknown, tr. fr. Eskimo by Knud Rasmussen. NU (Song of Joy.) WTO

V

V. Charlotte Calmis, tr. fr. French by Mary Ann Caws. DMF
V. B. Nimble, V. B. Quick ("V. B. Wigglesworth wakes at noon"). John Updike. NYBP
V. Innocentia Veritas Viat Fides Circumdederunt Me Inimici Mei. Sir Thomas Wyatt. AAS
V-Letter. Karl Shapiro. TrJP; WaP (Love Letter.) NYBP
V-Letter to Karl Shapiro in Australia. Selden Rodman. WaP
V. N. and C. I, The. Maggie Pogue Johnson. CBWP-4
Vacancy in the Park. Wallace Stevens. LCAP
Vacant Cage, The. Charles Tennyson Turner. FM
Vacant Lot, The. Gwendolyn Brooks. NAAL-2; NoAM; NOBA

Vacant Lot. Dudley Randall. NoAM
Vacation. William Stafford. AmFN; Psk
Vacation. Nixon Waterman. See It seems to me I'd like to go.
Vacation is over. Leavetaking. Eve Merriam. PDV
Vacation on Earth, A. Thomas M. Disch. BWV
Vacation Time. Frank Hutt. BoTP
Vacation Trip. Donald G. Babcock. NePoAm
Vacation? Well, our children took our love apart. Any Time. William Stafford. LCAP
Vacationer. Walker Gibson. SD
Vacillation. W. B. Yeats. NoAM
Vacillation ("Between extremities."), sel. William Butler Yeats. NoAM "Must we part, Von Hügel, though much alike." OBMV
Vacuous childhood. Salt of Pleasure. Pentti Saaritsa, tr. by Aili Jarvenpa. SOP
Vacuum, The. Howard Nemerov. NePoEA; NIP; RB
Vacuum cleaner held over my head, A. In a Dream. David Ignatow. PoA
Vagabond, The. Robert Louis Stevenson. BrPo
Vagabond, A. James Tate. NoAM
Vagabond House. Don Blanding. BLPA
Vagabond Song, A. Bliss Carman. AnAmPo; FaPON; GN
Vagabondia. Richard Hovey. AnAmPo
Vagabonds. Langston Hughes. SaC
Vagabonds. "Marie Madelaine", tr. fr. German by Ferdinand E. Kappey. PeHV
Vagabonds, The. John Townsend Trowbridge. AA; AnAmPo; BeLS; BLPA
Vague aspirations; enthusiasms. Alma Perdida. Valery Larbaud, tr. by William Jay Smith. CT
Vague Dream, A. Munir Niazi, tr. fr. Urdu by Mahmood Jamal. PBMUP
Vague Lyric by G. M. Max Beerbohm. FaBoEE
Vague sadness, A. Ishikawa Takuboku, tr. fr. Japanese by Hiroaki Sato. Fr. Forty-seven Tanka in Three Lines. FCEI
Vague sea thuds against the marble cliffs, The. Time. Robert Graves. LiTM
Vaguely I hear the purple roar of the torn-down Third Avenue El. You Are Gorgeous and I'm Coming. Frank O'Hara. NeAP; SM
Vaices That Be Gone, The. William Barnes. NOBVV
Vain Advice at the Year's End. James Wright. NYBP
Vain and not to trust. Woman. Irving Layton. ErPo
Vain Britons, boast no longer with proud indignity. War and Washington. Jonathan Mitchell Sewall. PAH
Vain Finding. Walter de la Mare. BrPo
Vain, frail, short liv'd, and miserable Man. A Song of Emptiness to Fill up the Empty Pages Following. Michael Wigglesworth. SCAP
Vain is the chiming of forgotten bells. Poets. Joyce Kilmer. WGRP
Vain is the fleeting wealth. On the Vanity of Man's Life. Unknown. OBSC
Vain World Adieu. Unknown. AmFP
Vainly ("Vainly/the epistles burn"). Nelly Sachs, tr. fr. German by Michael Roloff. NYBP
Vaiont dam is in Val Cellina, The. Official Iconography. Roberto Roversi, tr. by Lawrence R. Smith. NItP
Vala; or The Four Zoas, sels. Blake.
  Enion Replies from the Caverns of the Grave. Fr. The Four Zoas. OBNC
  Enitharmon Revives with Los. Fr. The Four Zoas. OBNC (Enitharmon's Song.) ChTr
  It Is Not So with Me. Fr. The Four Zoas. SeCePo
  Lamentation of Enion, The. Fr. The Four Zoas. OBNC
  Night VIII (The Eternal Man). PoE
  Price of Experience, The. Fr. The Four Zoas. EnRP; Prf (Night II (Enion's Lament).) PoE
  Song of Enitharmon. Fr. The Four Zoas. OAEL-2
  Urizen's Curse upon His Children. Fr. The Four Zoas. TW
  Vala, Night the Ninth Being the Last Judgment. Fr. The Four Zoas. OAEL-2
Vale from Carthage. Peter Viereck. LiTM; MoAmPo
Vale in Dagestan, the noon sun gleaming, A. The Dream. M. Y. Lermontov, tr. by Alan Myers. AAA
Valediction, A: "Before the seas again divide." Walter Adolphe Roberts. PVCV
Valediction, A: "Bid me not go where neither suns nor show'rs." William Cartwright. OBS
Valediction: Forbidding Mourning, A. John Donne. BLPL; FF; HAP; HeIP; HoPM; InPS; JCP; LiTB; MeLP; MePo; NAEL-1; NIP; NOBE; NoP; OAEL-1; OBS; PoE; PoEL-2; PPP; PrIm; SeCP; SeCV-1; SoSe; TEP; UnPo; WeW
Valediction: Forbidding Whining, A. David Shevin. SoTCo

Valediction: "Glory of soundless heaven, wheel of stars." John Hall Wheelock. NePoAm
Valediction, A: "If we must part." Ernest Dowson. BoLoP
Valediction: Of My Name in the Window, A. John Donne. QFR
Valediction of Weeping, A. John Donne. HAP; HeIP; InPS; MeLP; MePo; NAEL-1; NoP; OAEL-1; OBS; PoE; SeCP; WeW
Valediction: "Their verdure dare not show." Louis MacNeice. AnIL; FaBCIP
Valediction Forbidding Mourning, A. Adrienne Rich. NAAL-2; NoAM; NoP
Valediction (Liverpool Docks), A. John Masefield. OBMV
Valediction to My Contemporaries. Horace Gregory. MoAmPo
Valediction to the River Duddon. Wordsworth. See River Duddon, The: I thought of Thee, my partner and my guide.
Valedictory Sonnet to the River Duddon. Wordsworth. See River Duddon, The: I thought of Thee, my partner and my guide.
Valedictory to Standard Oil of Indiana, A. David Wagoner. NYBP
Valentine, A. Matilda Betham-Edwards. PeHV
Valentine, A. Emily Dickinson. FL
Valentine, The. Mary Weston Fordham. CBWP-2
Valentine. Len Gasparini. NeAC
Valentine. Donald Hall. GrPl; LLLT; NTCP; PCP
Valentine. Ernest Hemingway. OBAL; TW
Valentine, A. Laura Richards. AA
Valentine. Shel Silverstein. RHPC
Valentine. Hollis Spurgeon Summers. GoYe
Valentine, A. Priscilla Jane Thompson. CBWP-2
Valentine Browne. Egan O'Rahilly, tr. fr. Irish by Thomas Kinsella. NOIV
Valentine for a Lady, A. Lucilius, tr. fr. Latin by Dudley Fitts. OFD
Valentine for Ben Franklin Who Drives a Truck in California, A. Diane Wakoski. NoAM
Valentine to My Mother, A. Christina Rossetti. OHIP
Valentine to Sherwood Anderson, A. Gertrude Stein. NoAM
Valentine's Day. Charles Kingsley. BoTP
Valentines to My Mother, 1880. Christina Rossetti. OFD
Vales of the Medway, The, sel. A. J. Munby.
    Above the Medway. FaBoPP
Valiant Love. Richard Lovelace. SeCP
Valiant Sailor, The,. Unknown. OxBSS
[Valiant] Seaman's Happy Return [to His Love], The. Unknown. ChTr; GBP
Valley, The. Stanley Moss. NYBP; PCP
Valley and Villa of Horace, The. Arthur Hugh Clough. See Amours de Voyage: Tibur is beautiful, too, and the orchard slopes, and the Anio.
Valley Blood. Barry Sternlieb. SM
Valley Called Moonshine, A. Sam Hunt. ATNZ
Valley floors. A Collage for Richard Davis—Two Short Forms. De Leon Harrison. PoBA
Valley Forge, sel. Maxwell Anderson.
    Lafayette to Washington. OPP
Valley Forge. Thomas Buchanan Read. Fr. The Wagoner of the Alleghanies. PAH
Valley of Men, The. Uri Zvi Greenberg, tr. fr. Hebrew. VWA, tr. by Robert Mezey and Ben Zion Gold
Valley of the Black Pig, The. W. B. Yeats. ChTr
Valley of the Shadow. John Galsworthy. OHIP; TrPWD
Valley of Unrest, The. Poe. AmPP; NAAL-1; PoEL-4
Valley Prince. Mervyn Morris. PBCV
Valley Where I Don't Belong, A. Marge Piercy. IHMS
Valley with a silver-grayish mist, The. A Vision. Hugo von Hofmannsthal, tr. by Charles Wharton Stork. TrJP
Valleys crack and burn, the exhausted plains, The. The Mahratta Ghats. Alun Lewis. OBTV; OBWVE
Valor of Ben Milam, The. Clinton Scollard. PAH
Valse Jeune. Louise Imogen Guiney. AA
Valse Oubliée. John Heath-Stubbs. OxBTC
Valuable. Stevie Smith. OxBTC
Value of Dentistry, The. Solyman Brown. Fr. Dentologia; a Poem on the Diseases of the Teeth and Their Proper Remedies. FaBoUs
Value of pi, The. Unknown. FaBoUs
Vampire. Ray Amorosi. VVA
Vampire, The. Baudelaire, tr. fr. French by Arthur Symons. VVA
Vampire, The. Madison Cawein. VVA
Vampire, The. John DeWitt. VVA
Vampire, The. David Galler. VVA
Vampire, The. Walter H. Kerr. VVA
Vampire, The. Kipling. BLPA; BLPL; NOBVV; VVA
Vampire, The. Gregory Orr. VVA
Vampire, The. Heinrich August Ossenfelder, tr. fr. German by Aloysius Gibson. VVA

Vampire, The. Herbert Edward Palmer. VVA
Vampire. Jean Pedrick. VVA
Vampire, The. Efrén Rebolledo, tr. fr. Spanish by Samuel Beckett. MexPo; VVA
Vampire. Bertrande Harry Snell. VVA
Vampire, The. Arthur Symons. VVA
Vampire Bride, The. Henry Liddell. VVA
Vampire Bride. Felix Stefanile. VVA
Vampire Housewife, The. Ruth Fainlight. VVA
Vampire: 1914, The. Conrad Aiken. VVA
Vampire once was not a bit respectable, The. Enter the Vampire. Clement Wood. VVA
Vampirella. Elaine Equi. UL
Vampires. Lawrence Raab. VVA
Vampire's Aubade. W. D. Snodgrass. VVA
Vampire's Love Song, The. Margaret G. Keyes and Jeanne Youngson. VVA
Vampire's Tryst, The. Wade Wellman. VVA
Vampires Won't Vampire for Me, The. F. Scott Fitzgerald. VVA
Vampyr. Stephen Spera. VVA
Vampyre, The. Vasile Alecsandri, tr. fr. Rumanian by William Beatty-Kingston. VVA
Vampyre, The. James Clerk Maxwell. VVA
Vampyre, The. John Stagg. VVA
Vampyre Legend, A. Kathleen Resch. VVA
Van Amburgh's Menagerie ("Van Amburgh is the man that goes with all the shows"). Unknown. BLPA
Van Dieman's Land. Unknown. CoMu; FaBoBa; OBET; OBTV (A and B vers.)
Van Gogh. David Mitchell. PeNZ
Van Winkle. Hart Crane. Fr. The Bridge: Powhatan's Daughter. AmPP; FaBV; MoAB; MoAmPo
Vancouver Lights. Earle Birney. CaP
Vandals, The. Jenny Mastoraki, tr. fr. Modern Greek by Nikos Germanakos. BoWoP
Vane on Hughley Steeple, The. Hughley Steeple. A. E. Housman. Fr. A Shropshire Lad, LXI. FaBoPP
Vane, young in yeares, but in sage counsell old. To Sir Henry Vane the Younger. Milton. OBS; Son
Vanessa Vanessa. Ewart Milne. BIrV; NeIP
Vanguard of liberty, ye Men of Kent. To the Men of Kent. Wordsworth. OBWP
Vanilla Sugar; or, Verse for a "Hallmark" Greeting Card. Joy Howard. DT
Vanished. Emily Dickinson. AA
Vanished house that for an hour I knew, A. Souvenir. E. A. Robinson. NoAM
Vanishers, The. Whittier. AA; AnAmPo
Vanishing Point. Peter Cooley. AmPA
Vanishing Point, The. Peter Davison. DiPo
Vanishing Points. Sonya Dorman. BWV
Vanishing Valley, The. Ernie Fanning. CowP
Vanitas Vanitatum. John Webster. See All the Flowers of the Spring.
Vanitas Vanitatum. Israel Zangwill. TrJP
Vanity. Robert Graves. GTBS-P
Vanity [or Vanitie]. George Herbert. MePo; NoP; SeCV-1
Vanity. Giuseppe Ungaretti, tr. fr. Italian by Charles Tomlinson. PFI
Vanity. Anna Wickham. FaBoTw
Vanity of All Worldly Things, The. Anne Bradstreet. NoP; SCAP
Vanity of Existence, The. Philip Freneau. AmPP
Vanity of Human Wishes, The: The Tenth Satire of Juvenal Imitated ("Let observation with extensive view."), sels. Samuel Johnson. EBEV; HeIP; LaA; NOEC; NoP; OAEL-1; PoEL-3; PrIm; TEP
    Life's Last Scene. SeCePo
    "On what foundation stands the warrior's pride." OBWP
        (Charles XII of Sweden.) NOBE
    Power of Prayer, The. NOBE
    "Unnumbered suppliants crowd preferment's gate." OBSV
    "When first the college rolls receive his name." OBSV
        (Scholar's Life, The.) NOBE; SeCePo
Vanity of Spirit. Henry Vaughan. TOF
Vanity of the World, The. Siôn Cent, tr. fr. Welsh by Joseph P. Clancy. OBWVE
Vanity of vanities, saith the Preacher, vanity of vanities; all is vanity. Bible, O.T. Fr. Ecclesiastes, I: 2-11. FaBoPV; TrJP, (I: 2-9).
Vanity of vanities, the Preacher saith. The One Certainty. Christina Rossetti. OBNC
Vanity, saith the preacher, vanity! The Bishop Orders His Tomb at Saint Praxed's Church. Robert Browning. AWP; EBVV; FiP; HAP; HeIP; NAEL-2; NAWM-2; NOBVV; NoP; OAEL-2; OBAL; PoE; PPP; PrIm; TEP

Vanity, vanity, all is vanity. Ha! Original Sin. Ogden Nash. FaBoCo; NBLV

Vanquished. Francis Fisher Browne. AA

Vanquished, The. Charles Eglington. PeSA

Vanquished and weary was my soul in me. Sonnet: A Trance of Love. Cino da Pistoia, *tr. by* Dante Gabriel Rossetti. AWP

Vantage Point, The. Robert Frost. OxBA

Vanzetti. Charles Buckmaster. CBAP

Vapor rises from the water's surface at dawn. Chiang Shih, *tr. fr. Chinese by* Irving Lo. *Fr.* Getting Up Early at Lakeside Pavilion. WFTU

Vapor Trail Reflected in the Frog Pond. Galway Kinnell. CAPP; NoP; OBWP; VGW

Vapor Trails. Gary Snyder. CAPP; NAAL-2

Vaporish closeness of this two-month fog, The. 1930's. Robert Lowell. NoP

Vapour and Blue. Wilfred Campbell. CaP

Vaquero. Edward Dorn. NeAP; PoM

Vaquero. Joaquin Miller. AA

Variables of Green. Robert Graves. FaBoEE

Variant, A. A. Leyeles, *tr. fr. Yiddish by* Benjamin *and* Barbara Harshav. AYP

Variation, A. Robert Creeley. DiL

Variation on a Noel. John Ashbery. EOEF

Variation on a Sentence. Louise Bogan. FM; ImOP

Variation on Heraclitus. Louis MacNeice. MoP; NoAM

Variation on Ronsard. T. Sturge Moore. OBMV

Variation on the Gothic Spiral. W. S. Merwin. PoA

Variation on the Word *Sleep*. Margaret Atwood. NIP; NOBC

Variations. Randall Jarrell. VGW

Variations, Calypso and Fugue on a Theme of Ella Wheeler Wilcox. John Ashbery. LCAP

Variations Done for Gerald Van de Wiele. Charles Olson. NeAP; NoAM; NOBA; NoP

Variations for Two Pianos. Donald Justice. NYBP

Variations for Two Voices. Roberta Hill Whiteman. HATNAP; NOVW

Variations of [*or* on] an Air: After Alfred Lord Tennyson. G. K. Chesterton. FaBoPa; NOBL; Par

Variations on a Medieval Theme. Geoffrey Dutton. PoAu-2

Variations on a Still Morning. Thomas Cole. NePoAm

Variations on a Text by Vallejo. Donald Justice. CAPP; NoAM

Variations on a Theme, *sel.* Jacob Glatstein, *tr. fr. Yiddish by* Benjamin *and* Barbara Harshav.
   Steal into the Prayerbook. AYP

Variations on a Theme. John Hay. NePoAm

Variations on a Theme. Mark Vinz. Psk

Variations on a Theme. Anne Wilkinson. MoCV

Variations on a Theme, *sels.* Oscar Williams. LiTA
   Borrower of Salt, The. *Fr.* III.
   On the Death of an Acquaintance. *Fr.* I.
   Spritely Dead, The. *Fr.* II.

Variations on a Theme by George Herbert. Marya Zaturenska. TrPWD

Variations on a theme by morning. Cocoa Morning. Bob Kaufman. AmNP

Variations on a Theme by William Carlos Williams. Kenneth Koch. BXAP; CAPP; FF; NBLV; NIP; NoAM; NoP; PoM

Variations on an Air: After Robert Browning. G. K. Chesterton. BXAP; FaBoPa; NOBL; Par

Variations on an Air: After W. B. Yeats. G. K. Chesterton. BXAP; FaBoPa; NOBL; Par

Variations on an Air: After Walt Whitman. G. K. Chesterton. BXAP; FaBoPa; NOBL; Par

Variations on an Air Composed on Having to Appear in a Pageant as Old King Cole ("Cole, that unwearied prince of Colchester."), *sels.* G. K. Chesterton. FaBoPa; NBLV; NOBL
   (Variations of an Air.) Par
   Old King Cole ("Me clairvoyant"). BXAP
   Old King Cole ("Of an old king in a story"). BXAP
   Old King Cole ("Who smoke-snorts toasts o' My Lady Nicotine"). BXAP

Variations on [*or* of] an Air: After [Algernon Charles] Swinburne. G. K. Chesterton. FaBoPa; NOBL; Par

Variations on Sappho, *sels.* "Michael Field." PeHV
   "Come, Gorgo, put the rug in place."
   "Maids, not to you my mind doth change."

Variations on Southern Themes. Donald Justice. BLA; MT; SV

Variations on the Themes of Little Boys. Sándor Weöres, *tr. fr. Hungarian by* William Jay Smith. MHuP

Variations on the Word *Love*. Margaret Atwood. NoAM

Variations on White, *sel.* Nelo Risi, *tr. fr. Italian by* Lawrence R. Smith.
   "Prisoner/ rendered blind mute, The." NItP

Variations: The Air Is Sweetest That a Thistle Guards. James Merrill. NePoEA

Variegation. Janet Sutherland. DT

Variety. *Yoruba Oral Tradition, tr. by* E. Lasebikan. WTO

Various devices great mechanics gave. Means of Propulsion for Steam-Ships. Thomas Baker. *Fr.* The Steam Engine; or, The Power of the Flame. FaBoUs

Various Ends. Ruthven Todd. SeCePo

Various flowers' bowls and cups. Spring Variation. Miyazawa Kenji, *tr. by* Hiroaki Sato. FCEI

Various Meanings. Jackson MacLow. LP

Various members of the hierarchy move, The. A Morning Letter. Robert Duncan. PoA

Various nostalgias: rock, scissor, and paper. Towards the Vanishing Point. David Lehman. SM

"Various the roads of life; in one." Walter Savage Landor. FaBoEE ("Various the Roads of Life.") EnRP

Various Wakings. Vincent Buckley. PoAu-2

Varitalk. Weare Holbrook. NYBP

Varium et Mutabile. Sir Thomas Wyatt. *See* Is It Possible?

Varuna, The. George Henry Boker. PAH

Varus, whom I chanced to meet. A Fib Detected. Catullus, *tr. by* John Hookham Frere. AWP; OBVE

Vase, The. Gabriela Mistral, *tr. fr. Spanish by* Perry Higman. LPSS

Vase was made of clay, The. Elegy to the Sioux. Norman Dubie. MAYP

Vases. Nan Terrell Reed. BLPA

Vashti. Lascelles Abercrombie. *Fr.* Emblems of Love.
   Woman's Beauty. MoBrPo

Vashti. Frances E. W. Harper. AIW; BlSi

Vashti/ with her one brown. If You Black Get Back. Cheryl Clarke. AIW

Vast and immaculate; no pilgrim bands. The Sea Cathedral. Edwin John Pratt. CaP

Vast bedroom, The. Tracks. John Montague. CIP; FaBCIP

Vast Bodies of Philosophie. To Mr. Hobs. Abraham Cowley. SeCV-1

Vast Light. Richard Eberhart. CMoP

Vast mild melancholy splendid. Canberra in April. J. R. Rowland. PoAu-2

Vast oceanic movements, the flux and reflux of immeasurable. Currents. Emma Lazarus. *Fr.* By the Waters of Babylon. WPE

Vast superstition! Glorious stile of weaknesse! Chorus Quintus: Tartarorum. Fulke Greville. *Fr.* Mustapha. OBS

Vastness. Tennyson. OPOP

Vaticide. Myron O'Higgins. IDB; PoBA

Vaudeville. Lincoln Kirstein. MoP

Vaulting Ambition. Shakespeare. *See* Macbeth:
   If it were done when 'tis done, then 'twere well.

Vaunting Oak. John Crowe Ransom. OxBA; VGW

Vedic Hymns, *sels. Unknown, tr. fr. Sanskrit by* Romesh Dutt.
   Brahma, the World Idea, *Fr.* Rig Veda WGRP
   Indra, the Supreme God, *Fr.* Rig Veda AWP
   Pushan, God of Pasture, *Fr.* Rig Veda AWP

Veery, The. Henry van Dyke. AA

Veery-Thrush, The. Joseph Russell Taylor. AA

Vegas. Charles Bukowski. NoP

Vegetable Air, The. Cathy Song. NoAM

Vegetable Destiny. Nina Cassian, *tr. fr. Rumanian by* Michael Impey *and* Brian Swann. PBWP

Vegetable Garden. Lu Yu, *tr. fr. Chinese by* Burton Watson. CoBCP

Vegetable, I Will Not Be, A. Donna Whitewing. NOVW

Vegetable Loves. Erasmus Darwin. *Fr.* The Botanic Garden: The Loves of the Plants. SeCePo

Vegetables. Eleanor Farjeon. FaPON

Vegetables/ and jewelry, right displayed. For Instance. Robert McAlmon. PoA

Vegetarian in a shabby robe, my spirit's, A. Ryuge, *tr. by* Lucien Stryk *and* Takashi Ikemoto. ZPCJ

Vehicle gives a lurch but seems, The. Foetal Song. Joyce Carol Oates. IHMS; NAs

Veil, The. Denis Johnson. NAmP

Veil not thy mirror, sweet Amine. To Amine. James Clarence Mangan. OBEV

Veil of death hath fallen, The. To a Deceased Friend. Priscilla Jane Thompson. CBWP-2

Veil of haze protects this, A. City Afternoon. John Ashbery. HeIP; InPK

Veil thine eyes, O belovèd, my spouse. The Bridegroom of Cana. Marjorie Pickthall. CaP; TrCP

Veil upon veil. Natura Naturans. Kathleen Jessie Raine. NYBP

Veiled in that light amazing. The Dispraise of Absalom. *Unknown, tr. by Robin Flower.* BIrV

Veiled Land. Kahlil Gibran, *tr. fr. Arabic by* Adnan Haydar *and* Michael Beard. MAP

Veld Eclogue: The Pioneers, A. Roy Campbell. OBSV

Velocity with which they write, The. Movie Actors Scribbling Letters Very Fast in Crucial Scenes. Jean Garrigue. TAP

Velvet Shoes. Elinor Wylie. CH; FaPON; FPL; GoJo; MoAB; MoAmPo; TrGrPo

Velvet Sonneteers, The. Tom MacInnes. CaP

Venders croon their welcoming harangues. Cedar Needles. Chase Twichell. MAYP

Venerable Bee, The. A. M. Klein. TrJP

Venerable Mother Toothache. A Charm against the Toothache. John Heath-Stubbs. NePoEA; TwCP

Veneris Venefica Agrestis. Charles Tomlinson, *after* Lucio Piccolo. OBVE

Venetia. Adah Isaacs Menken. CBWP-1

Venetian Air. Thomas Moore. OxBSP

Venetian Fragment. Alois Hergouth, *tr. fr. German by* Beth Bjorklund. CoAuP

Venetian Night, A. Hugo von Hofmannsthal, *tr. fr. German by* Ludwig Lewisohn. AWP

Vengeance. Mazisi Kunene. WMBCH

Vengeful across the cold November moors. The Pity of the Leaves. E. A. Robinson. AA; AnAmPo; MoAmPo

Veni Coronaberis. Geoffrey Hill. DiPo; NoP

Veni Creator. Bliss Carman. *See* Lord of the grass and hill.

Veni Creator. Alice Meynell. WPE

Veni Creator Spiritus. *At. to* Charlemagne *and to* Hrabanus Maurus, *paraphrased by* Dryden. AWP; FaPoR; SeCV-2; WGRP

Venice. Longfellow. EyDe

Venice. Howard Moss. MoAB

Venice. Arthur Symons. OxBSP

Venice Recalled. Bruce Boyd. NeAP

Venice Revisited. Amy Clampitt. ER

Venom. James Dickey. PoA

'Vention did in Boston meet, The. Convention Song. *Unknown.* PAH

Venus Abandoned. Shakespeare. *Fr.* Venus and Adonis. OBSC

Venus, again thou mov'st a war. To Venus ("Intermissa, Venus"). Horace, *tr. fr. Latin. Fr.* Odes, IV, 1. AWP, *tr. by* Ben Jonson; OBVE, *tr. by* Ben Jonson.
("Again? New tumults in my breast?.") PeHV, *tr. by* Pope.

Venus and Adonis. William Browne. EiL

Venus and Adonis, *sels.* Shakespeare. BeLS
"At this Adonis smiles as in disdain." EBEV
"But, lo! from forth a copse that neighbours by." FM
(Courser, The.) OBSC
(Courser and the Jennet, The.) NOBE
"Fondling," she saith, "since I have hemmed thee here."" OAEL-1
Lo! Here the Gentle Lark. ChTr
Poor Wat. OBSC
"Sweet boy," she says, "this night I'll waste in sorrow."" ErPo

Venus Abandoned. OBSC

Venus and Cupid. Mark Alexander Boyd. *See* Fra Bank to Bank, Fra Wood to Wood I Rin.

Venus and the Rain. Medbh McGuckian. FaBCIP

Venus, by Adonis' side. Venus and Adonis. William Browne. EiL

Venus Fly Trap, The. Readymade. John Perreault. EAS

Venus glows in the east. Work to Do toward Town. Gary Snyder. VGW

Venus has lit her silver lamp. The Lamp in the West. Ella Higginson. AA

Venus of Milo, The. Henrietta Cordelia Ray. CBWP-3

Venus of the Louvre. Emma Lazarus. AA

Venus of the Salty Shell. Denis Devlin. BIrV; NOIV

Venus Poised. Rafael López, *tr. fr. Spanish by* Samuel Beckett. MexPo

Venus Pudica stands, bent. Where her hand is. The Lady at the Castle. John Hollander. NoAM

Venus, take my votive glass. The Lady Who Offers Her Looking-Glass to Venus. Matthew Prior, *after the Greek of* Plato. AWP; FaBoEE; NOEC; OBEV; OxBSP
(Farewell, A: "Venus, take my votive glass.") AWP

Venus Transiens. Amy Lowell. PoA

Ver. Shakespeare. *See* Love's Labour's Lost: When Daisies Pied [and Violets Blue].

Veracruz. Robert Hayden. AmNP

Verandahs. Robert Francis Brissenden. CBAP

Veranius, my dear friend, the friend worth. Catullus, *tr. fr. Latin by* James Michie. PeHV

Verazzano. Hezekiah Butterworth. PAH

Verb "To Think," The. D. J. Enright. OxBC

Verdant branch was swinging here, A. So Long Ago. Morris Jacob Rosenfeld, *tr. by* Elbert Aidline. TrJP

Verdict, The. Norman Cameron. SeCePo

Verdict. Ernst Jandl, *tr. fr. German by* Beth Bjorklund. CoAuP

Vergier. *Unknown, tr. fr. Provençal by* Ezra Pound. GBL

Vergissmeinnicht. Keith Douglas. FaBoMo; GTBS-P; InPS; NAEL-2; NePoEA; NoAM; OBD; OBWP; OxBTC; RB; SoSe

Verification of the Poetic Talents of Young Maidens. Susanna Elisabeth Zeidler, *tr. fr. German by* Susan L. Cocalis *and* Gerlinde Geiger. DMG

Verifying the Dead. James Welch. CDW

Verigin, Moving in Alone. John Newlove. NeAC

Verigin 3. John Newlove. NeAC

Verily/ The sky clears. The Sky Clears. *Unknown, tr. by* Frances Densmore. OBVE

Verily, I am far away from you. From One of My Letters. Moyshe-Leyb Halpern, *tr. by* John Hollander. PeBMYV

Verlaine. E. A. Robinson. NAAL-2

Vermont: Indian Summer. Philip Booth. NePoEA

Vern. Gwendolyn Brooks. ILY

Vernal Equinox. Martin Johnston. CBAP

Vernal Equinox. Ruth Stone. MoAmPo

Verona. James Wright. NNaP

Veronica/ Rose of pale fire. Woven Romance. Lucha Corpi. CCP

Veronica extends her arms, The. Funeral Procession. Oswald de Andrade, *tr. by* Jean R. Longland. ATCBP

Vers de Société. H. D. Traill. Par

Vers Nonsensiques. George Du Maurier. NA

Versailles. Adrienne Rich. NePoEA

Versailles!—Up the chestnut alley. The Pompadour. George Walter Thornbury. BeLS

Verse: "Past ruin'd [or ruined] Ilion Helen lives." Walter Savage Landor. *See* Ianthe: Past Ruined Ilion Helen Lives.

Verse: "What should we know." Oliver St. John Gogarty. AnIL; FaBoCh; OBMV; PoRA

Verse, a breeze 'mid blossoms straying. Youth and Age. Samuel Taylor Coleridge. BLPL; EnRP; FiP; GTBS; GTBS-P; OBEV; OBNC; PoLF

Verse and Fame. John Donne. *Fr.* Anatomy [*or* Anatomie] of the World, An: The First Anniversary. FaBoRV

Verse as of 7 June 1951. Jan Hanlo, *tr. fr. Dutch by* James S. Holmes. DuIn

Verse hath a middle nature; heaven keepes soules. Verse and Fame. John Donne. *Fr.* Anatomy [*or* Anatomie] of the World, An: The First Anniversary. FaBoRV

Verse makes heroic[k] virtue live. To Mr. Henry Lawes, Who Had Then Newly Set a Song of Mine in the Year 1635. Edmund Waller. CTC; SeCP; SeCV-1

Verse may find him who a sermon flies, A. On the Following Work and Its Author. Jonathan Mitchell. SCAP

Verse Written in the Album of Mademoiselle. Pierre Dalcour, *tr. fr. French by* Langston Hughes. PoNe; TTY

Verses: "Poor fellow, what is it to you." Sir Charles Hanbury Williams. OBWVE

Verses about Poland. Adam Zagajewski, *tr. fr. Polish by* Antony Graham. PwPP

Verses Addressed to a Friend, Just Leaving a Favourite Retirement. Samuel Henley. NOEC

Verses against Argula. Argula von Grumbach, *tr. fr. German by* Susan L. Cocalis. *Fr.* An Answer in Verse for Someone Studying in Ingolst. DMG

Verses Composed on the Eve of His Execution. James Graham Marquess of Montrose. *See* Let them bestow on ev'ry airth a limb.

Verses for a First Birthday. George Barker. MoAB; MoBrPo

Verses for Fruitwomen, *sels.* Swift.
Onyons. BIrV; FaBoUs

Verses Found in Thomas Dudley's Pocket after His Death. Thomas Dudley. SCAP

Verses from a Letter. Keats. *See* There Was a Naughty Boy.

Verses from the Shepherd's Hymn. Richard Crashaw. *See* We saw Thee in Thy balmy nest.

Verses Intended to Be Written below a Noble Earl's Picture. Burns. HoPM

Verses Made Sometime Since upon. The Indian Squa. John Josselyn. SCAP

Verses Made the Night before He Died. Michael Drayton. *See* So well I love thee, as without thee I.

Verses Made the Night before He Dyed. Sir Walter Ralegh. *See* Even Such Is Time.

Verses Occasioned by the Sudden Drying Up of St. Patrick's Well, *sel.* Swift.
"Wretched Ierne! with what grief I see." OBSV

Verses of Man's Mortalitie. *At. to* Simon Wastell. *See* Microbiblion: Man's Mortality.

Verses of the Talkative Knight, The. Mary Sidney Wroth, Countess of Montgomery. *Fr.* Urania. WPE

Verses on a Cat. Shelley. FL

Verses on Accepting the World. Joseph Brodsky, *tr. fr. Russian by* Dimitry Pospielovsky *and* Keith Bosley

Verses on Blenheim. Martial, *tr. fr. Latin by* Swift. AWP

Verses on Daniel Good. *Unknown.* CoMu; OxBB

Verses on Sir Joshua Reynolds's Painted Window at New College, Oxford. Thomas Warton the Younger. NOEC; PoEL-3

Verses on the Death of Doctor Swift [D.S.P.D., Occasioned by Reading a Maxim in Rochefoucauld], *sels.* Swift.
"Behold the fatal day arrive!" SCV
"Doctors tender of their fame, The." NOBL
"Here shift the scene, to represent." OBD
"My female friends, whose tender hearts." NOBL; SeCePo
"Perhaps I may allow, the Dean." NOBE
"Suppose me dead; and then suppose." NOBE; NOEC; OxBoLi, *abr.*; PoEL-3; TEP
"Time is not remote when I, The." EBEV; Mes; NOBE; NOBL; NOIV

Verses on the Prospect of Planting Arts and Learning in America. George Berkeley. *See* Muse, disgusted at an age and clime, The.

Verses Said to Be Written on the Union. Swift. APAS

Verses Supposed to Be Written by Alexander Selkirk during His Solitary Abode on the Island of Juan Fernandez. William Cowper. FPL; NOEC; PoEL-3; PoLF

Verses to Be Repeated by an Attorney Leaving His Lodging to Wait upon Judges Riding the Circuits from One County to Another, Least He Forget Some Necessary Thing. John Willis. FaBoUs

Verses to Miss——— J. Wilde. NOEC

Verses to my Heart's-Sister. Henrietta Cordelia Ray. CBWP-3

Verses under a Peacock Portrayed in Her Left Hand. Robert Greene. PBBP

Verses Written at Montauban in France, 1750. Joseph Warton. OBTV

Verses Written at The Hague. Anno 1696. Matthew Prior. OBTV

Verses Written during the War, 1756-1763, *sel. At. to* Thomas Osbert Mordaunt.
Sound, Sound the Clarion. EBEV; FaBoEE; FaPoR; NOBE
(Call, The.) OBEV
(One Crowded Hour.) TrGrPo
(To a Lady on Reading Sherlock "Upon Death.") NOEC

Verses Written in 1872. Robert Louis Stevenson. BLPA; BLPL

Verses Written in a Lady's Sherlock "Upon Death." Earl of Chesterfield. EBEV

Verses Written in the Chiosk at Pera, overlooking Constantinople. Lady Mary Wortley Montagu. OBTV

Verses Written on Sand. Melech Ravitch, *tr. fr. Yiddish by* Seymour Mayne *and* Rivka Augenfeld. VWA

Version. Dennis Scott. PVCV

Versions. Robert Creeley. PPR

Versions. Robert Kelly. *Fr.* The Book of Persephone, 12. PoM

Versions of Love. Roy Fuller. LiTM

Versos de Montalgo. *Unknown, tr. by* Frank J. Dobie. AS

Vertigo is my territory. Eagle. Robin Skelton. NOBC

Vertigos or Contemplation of Something That Is Over. Alejandra Pizarnik, *tr. fr. Spanish by* Yishai Tobin. VWA

Vertue. George Herbert. *See* Sweet day, so cool, so calm, so bright.

Very acme of my woe, The. Little Son. Georgia Douglas Johnson. CDC

Very bitter weeping that ye made, The. Dante, *tr. fr. Italian by* Dante Gabriel Rossetti. *Fr.* Vita Nuova, La, XXV. AWP

Very dark the autumn sky. A Belated Violet. Oliver Herford. AA

Very day the war ended, The. Song of the Tart. Kaneko Mitsuharu, *tr. by* Geoffrey Bownas *and* Anthony Thwaite. PeBJV

Very Early. Karla Kuskin. PDV

Very Fair My Lot. Jacob David Kamzon, *tr. fr. Hebrew by* Sholom J. Kahn. TrJP

Very few can. The Pecan, The Toucan. Robert Williams Wood. NBLV

Very first joy that Mary had, The. The Joys of Mary. *Unknown.* AmFP

Very fownder and begynner of owr fyrst creacyon, The. *Unknown. Fr.* Mankind. OxBLMV

Very friendly, A/ prison. Tripart. Gayl Jones. BlSi

Very grandiloquent goat, A. The Grandiloquent Goat. Carolyn Wells. MoShBr

Very handsome gentleman, A. *Unknown, tr. fr. Chinese by* Arthur Waley. *Fr.* Shih Ching. BoS; BoWoP

Very Heroical Epistle in Answer to Ephelia, A. Earl of Rochester. APAS

Very leafy is that willow tree. *Unknown, tr. by* Arthur Waley. BoS

Very like a Whale. Ogden Nash. BLPL; HAP; InPK; InPS; PoLF; TrGrPo; WeW

Very longest willow branches grow in I-ch'un Park, The. The Willow Branches. Wen T'ing-yün, *tr. by* Lois Fusek. ATF

Very Minor Poet Speaks, A. Isabel Valle. BLPA

Very Nearly. Queenie Scott-Hopper. FaPON

Very Nicest Place, The. *Unknown.* RAR

Very Odd Fish, A. D'Arcy Wentworth Thompson. OxBChV

Very often when you are striving. The Would-be Critic. Mrs. Henry Linden. CBWP-4

Very old are the woods. All That's Past. Walter de la Mare. GoJo; MoAB; NOBE; OAEL-2; OBMV; OxBTC; TrGrPo

Very Old Man. James Henry. NOBVV

Very Old Woman, A. Clayton Eshleman. MAT

Very pitiful lady, very young, A. Dante, *tr. fr. Italian by* Dante Gabriel Rossetti. *Fr.* Vita Nuova, La, XIV. AWP; CTC, *shorter sel.*

Very Pretty Maid of This Town, and the Amorous 'Squire Not One Hundred Miles from the Place, The. *Unknown.* CoMu

Very sharp, the good shares. *Unknown, tr. fr. Chinese by* Arthur Waley. BoS

Very small chickens in tattered feathers. The. A Study in Aesthetics. Robert Peters. BXAP

Very small children in patched clothing, The. The Study in Aesthetics. Ezra Pound. *Unknown.* NoP

Very Softly. Piera Oppezzo, *tr. fr. Italian by* Muriel Kittel. DMI

Very soon the day will darken. Putting My Daughter to Bed. Li Nan, *tr. by* Dominic Cheung. IFON

Very soon the Yankee teachers. Learning to Read. Frances Ellen Watkins Harper. BlSi

Very True, the Linnets Sing. Walter Savage Landor. TrGrPo

"Very, very queer things have been happening to me." Queer Things. James Reeves. WSC

Very well/ but at least let me. Sent to a Woman. Shunzei, *tr. fr. Japanese by* Burton Watson. *Fr.* Thirty Tanka. FCEI

Vesi, the black one, the leaper who sprang. Praises of the King Dingana (Vesi). *Unknown.* PeSA

Vesperal. Ernest Dowson. OBMV

Vespers. W. H. Auden. *Fr.* Horae Canonicae. FaBoMo

Vespers. Thomas Edward Brown. BoTP

Vespers. A. A. Milne. OxBChV

Vespers. S. Weir Mitchell. WGRP

Vespers. Odell Shepard. TrPWD

Vessels. Howard Schwartz. VWA

Vesta. Whittier. TrPWD

Vestal, The. Nathalia Crane. TrJP

Vestal, The. Pope. *Fr.* Eloisa to Abelard. ACP

Vestal Virgin, The. Eloise Bibb. CBWP-4

Vestal Virgin, The, *sel.* John Plummer Derwent Llwyd.
"Night is soft with summer, The; yon faint arch." CaP

Vestige. Jung Han-mo, *tr. fr. Korean by* Koh Chang-soo. ACKP

Vestigia. Bliss Carman. CaP; WGRP

Vestigial. Albert Goldbarth. NAmP

Veteran, The. Edmund Blunden. BrPo

Veteran. Lola Ridge. WPE

Veteran Greeks came home, The. Return, The ("The veteran Greeks came home"). Edwin Muir. CMoP
(Return of the Greeks, The.) NoP; PoE

Veteran of the Great War, A. John Bensko. MAYP

Veteran Sirens. E. A. Robinson. NOBA; QFR; SoSe

Veterans. George Johnston. NOBC

Veterans, The. Donagh MacDonagh. CIP

Veterans Day, 1981. Carole Oles. PPR

Vet's Rehabilitation. Ray Durem. PoBA

Vetus Flamma. Robert Mezey. PoA

Vex no man's secret soul—if that can be. Help. Sadi, *tr. fr. Persian by* Sir Edwin Arnold. *Fr.* The Gulistan. AWP

Vexation of mind. Hi De Buckras Hi! Grace Nichols. AIW

Via, Veritas, et Vita. Alice Meynell. WGRP

Viable. A. R. Ammons. TAP

Viaticum. Ethna MacCarthy. NeIP

Vibrant naive Naabeeho women. Modern on the Surface. Nia Francisco. HATNAP

Vicar, The. George Crabbe. *Fr.* The Borough, Letter III. OBSV
"But let applause be dealt in all we may." OBNC

Vicar, The. Winthrop Mackworth Praed. *Fr.* Every-Day Characters. EnRP; OBEV; OBNC; PoEL-4

Vicar of Bray, The. *Unknown.* FaBoPV; GBP; NOBE; NOBL; OBSV; OxBoLi

Vicar of Wakefield, The, *sels.* Goldsmith.
Elegy on the Death of a Mad Dog, An. *Fr. ch.* 17. BeLS; BLPA; FaBoBe; FaBoCh; FaBoCo; FaFP; FPL; GN; NA; NBLV; NOBE; NOEC; NOIV; OBNV; TEP

When Lovely Woman Stoops to Folly. *Fr. ch.* 24. GTBS; GTBS-P; HAP; HeIP; NoP; PrIm; UnPo
  (Song: "When lovely woman stoops to folly.") AWP; BoLoP; NOBE; NOEC; SeCePo; TrGrPo
  (Stanzas on Woman.) ELP
  (Woman.) FPL; LiTB; OBEV
Vicarious Atonement. Richard Aldington. MoBrPo; WGRP
Vice. Anthony Hecht. OBAL
Vice most obscene and unsavoury, A. *Unknown.* NOBL
Vice now may lift aloft her speckled head. Spoken Extempore on the Death of Mr. Pope. *Unknown.* NOEC
Vice-President of the Universe, The. Don Welch. SoTCo
Vicious winter finally yields, The. William DeWitt Snodgrass. *Fr.* Heart's Needle, X. NePoEA; SM
Vicissitudes of the world, O Olaad, are like the clouds of the seasons, The. To a Dictatorial Sultan. *Somali Oral Tradition, tr. by* B. W. Andrzejewski. WTO
Vickery's Mountain. E. A. Robinson. MoAmPo
Vicksburg. Paul Hamilton Hayne. AA; PAH
Vicomte is wearing a brow of gloom, The. Chez Brébant. Francis Alexander Durivage. AA
Victim, The. Lupenga Mphande. WMBCH
Victim, The. Ellen Bryant Voigt. MAYP
Victim No. 48. Mahmoud Darwish, *tr. fr. Arabic by* Abdullah al-Udhari. MPAW
Victims, The. Sharon Olds. InPS; NIP
Victims of that warrior, The. Mohammad Taqi Mir, *tr. fr. Urdu by* Ahmed Ali. GoT
Victor, The. C. W. Longenecker. PWR
Victor Dog, The. James Merrill. NoAM; NoP
Victor Galbraith. Longfellow. PAH
Victor of Antietam, The. Herman Melville. PAH
Victoria Markets Recollected in Tranquillity, The, *sel.* "Furnley Maurice."
  Winds Are Bleak, Stars Are Bright. PoAu-2
Victorian Grandmother. Margo Lockwood. Psk
Victorian Hangman Tells His Love, A. Bruce Dawe. NoAM
Victorian Idyll, A. David Wagoner. NoAM
Victorian Paraphrase, A. Horace. *See* Odes: I, 38. Simplicity.
Victorian Song. John Chipman Farrar. GoYe
Victories of Love, The, *sels.* Coventry Patmore.
  Lonely Cloud of Care, The. *Fr.* II, viii. FaBoRV
  Music of Forefended Spheres, The. *Fr.* I, ii. FaBoRV
  "Your love lacks joy, your letter says." *Fr.* I, v. GBL
  (Rain That Fell upon the Height, The.) FaBoRV
Victorious beauty, though your eyes. To the Countesse of Salisbury. Aurelian Townshend. MePo; OBS; SeCP
  (Loves Victory.) MeLP
Victorious knights without reproach or fear. To the Returning Brave. Robert Underwood Johnson. PAH
Victorious Men of Earth. James Shirley. *Fr.* Cupid and Death. OBS; TrGrPo
  (Last Conqueror, The.) GTBS; GTBS-P
Victors, The. Denise Levertov. NoP
Victors, The. Anthony McNeill. PBCV
Victory. Eileen Duggan. ATNZ
Victory. Lionel Johnson. NOBVV
Victory, A. R. T. Smith. MOWH
Victory. *Unknown. See* I am a youthful lady, my troubles they are great.
Victory ("Ye that have faith to look with fearless eyes"). *Unknown.* WGRP
Victory Bonfire. Ruth Pitter. CN
Victory comes. The New Victory. Margaret Widdemer. WGRP
Victory comes late. Emily Dickinson. InPK
Victory Dance, A. Alfred Noyes. PoLF
Victory Drive, near Fort Benning, Georgia. Bin Ramke. MT
Victory in Defeat. Edwin Markham. BLPL; PoLF
Victory on the Last Green. Thomas Mathison. *Fr.* The Goff; an Heroi-comical Poem. NOEC
Victory, Victory! Yes, ah, yes, thou republican Zion. Arthur Hugh Clough. *Fr.* Amours de Voyage, Canto II, vi. EBVV
Victory-Wreck, The. Will M. Carleton. PAH
Video Cuisine. Maxine W. Kumin. NoAM
Vield Path, The. William Barnes. NOBVV
Vienna. Peter Porter. OBTV
"Vierge Ouvrante." Miriam Palmer. NMM
Vierzide Chairs, The. William Barnes. NOBVV
Vietnam. Ahmad Faraz, *tr. fr. Urdu by* Mahmood Jamal. PBMUP
Vietnam. Clarence Major. PoBA
Vietnam. Mustafa Zaidi, *tr. fr. Urdu by* Mahmood Jamal. PBMUP
Vietnam #4. Clarence Major. FF; PoBA
Vietnamese Girl in the Madhouse, The. David Fisher. NPGG

Vieux Carré. Walter Adolphe Roberts. PoNe
View. Rae Armantrout. IAT
View. Robin Munro. PoSH
View, The. Howard Nemerov. NYBP
View, A. Beverly Quint. NYBP
View by Color Photography on a Commercial Calendar. William Carlos Williams. LCAP
View from a Cab, The. Henry Taylor. NBLV
View from an Apartment. Michael Palmer. UL
View from an Attic Window, The. Howard Nemerov. CoAP
View from far: beside the gate, The. Returning Home. Yüan Mei, *tr. by* Jonathan Chaves. CoBLCP
View from Here, The. William Stafford. RFM
View from Middle-Earth, A. William Langland. *Fr.* The Vision of Piers Plowman. Mes
View from My Window. Alasdair Maclean. PoSH
View from the dungeon's barred slit is, The/ A tree. Pleasures. Albert Goldbarth. GeTw
View from the Gorge. Ben Belitt. NYBP
View from the Pavilion on a Moonlit Night. Ch'en San-li, *tr. fr. Chinese by* Irving Lo. WFTU
View Mee, Lord. ("View mee, Lord, a work of thine"). Thomas Campion. TrPWD
View of a Pig. Ted Hughes. LiTM; OxBTC; TwCP
View of Christ's Kingdom, A, *sel.* William Williams, *tr. fr. Welsh by* Lewis Saunders *and* Gwyn Jones.
  Marriage in Eden, The. OBWVE
View of Jersey, A. Edward Field. NeAP
View of the Burning, A. James Merrill. NePoEA-2
View of the Capitol from the Library of Congress. Elizabeth Bishop. AmFN
View of the Cathedral, *sels.* Raymond Henri. EyDe
  Chartres.
  Duomo, Milan.
View of the coast of Brazil. Charles Darwin Pays a Visit, December 1971. Michael Ondaatje. HeIP
View of the Present State of Ireland, A. Edmund Blunden. BrPo
View of the Town, A. In an Epistle to a Friend, *sel.* Thomas Gilbert. Against Homosexuality. NOEC
View on Death, A. Roy W. Watson. PWR
View phenomena as void, view phenomena as appearance, such is the ultimate view. Kung Tzu-chen, *tr. fr. Chinese by* Shirleen S. Wong. *Fr.* Miscellaneous Poems of the Year Chi-hai, CCXXVI. WFTU
View to the North. May Swenson. ER
Viewing Nara from a Distance in Wind and Rain. Fujii Chikugai, *tr. fr. Chinese by* Burton Watson. JLIC-2
Viewing the Body. William DeWitt Snodgrass. CAPP
Viewing the cherry-blossom. Issa, *tr. by* Geoffrey Bownas *and* Anthony Thwaite. PeBJV
Viewing the Ocean. Ts'ao Ts'ao, *tr. fr. Chinese by* Burton Watson. CoBCP
Viewing the Plum-Blossoms. Ho Ning, *tr. fr. Chinese by* Lois Fusek. ATF
Viewing the Plum-Blossoms. Sun Kuang-hsien, *tr. fr. Chinese by* Lois Fusek. ATF
Viewing the Sea from the Li-shuo Pavilion. Wang Shih-chen, *tr. fr. Chinese by* Daniel Bryant. WFTU
Viewing the Waterfall at Mount Lu. Li Po, *tr. fr. Chinese by* Burton Watson. CoBCP; TTTS
Viewless thing is the wind, A. Love Is Strong. Richard Burton. AA
Views of an American Writer. Sumio Matsuda. KS
Views of the Favorite Colleges. John Malcolm Brinnin. LiTA; MoAB
Vigil. Marjorie Freeman Campbell. CaP
Vigil. Richard Dehmel, *tr. fr. German by* Ludwig Lewisohn. AWP
Vigil. W. E. Henley. *Fr.* In Hospital, VII. BrPo
Vigil, The. Philippe Jaccottet, *tr. fr. French by* Anthony Rudolf. RHTwFP
Vigil, The. Denise Levertov. NePoEA-2
Vigil, The. Cecília Meireles, *tr. fr. Portuguese by* James Merrill. ATCBP
Vigil, The. Shlomo Reich, *tr. fr. French by* Mira Reich. VWA
Vigil, The. Giuseppe Ungaretti, *tr. fr. Italian by* Charles Tomlinson. PFI
Vigil at Dawn. Gábor Garai, *tr. fr. Hungarian by* Daniel Hoffman. MHuP
Vigil of the Wounded. Phillip Yellowhawk Minthorn. STE
Vigil of Venus, The ("Spring appears, in which the earth, The."), *sels. Unknown, tr. fr. Latin.* AWP, *tr. by* Thomas Stanley; GBL, *tr. by* Allen Tate
  "Goddesse bade the nymphs remove, The." *Tr. by* Thomas Stanley. OBVE
  "Love he to morrow, who lov'd never." *Tr. by* Thomas Stanley. OBVE

Vigil Strange I Kept on the Field One Night. Walt Whitman. MoAmPo; NAAL-1; NOBA; NoP; OBWP; PeHV; PoE; TAP; WaaP
Vigilance. André Breton, tr. fr. French by Michael Benedikt. POS
Vigilantius, or a Servant of the Lord Found Ready. Cotton Mather. SCAP
Vigils ("Lone heart, learning."), sel. Siegfried Sassoon. CMoP
    Down the Glimmering Staircase. PoLF
Vigor, vitality, vim and punch. Pep. Grace G. Bostwick. WBLP
Vigula divina, sorcerers call a rod. Fulke Greville. FaBoPV
Viking Dublin; Trial Pieces. Seamus Heaney. IPY
Viking Terror, The. Unknown, tr. fr. Old Irish by Fred Norris Robinson. AnIL
Vikings, The ("Bitter the storm to-night"). Unknown, tr. fr. Irish. ChTr
Vikings, The ("Bitter the wind tonight"). Unknown, tr. fr. Irish by John Montague. BIrV
Vile Stanhope, demons blush to tell. On Lord Chesterfield and His Son. Unknown. FaBoCo
Villa d'Este Gardens. Siegfried Sassoon. OBTV
Villa Sciarra: Rome. Christine Turner Curtis. GoYe
Village, The, sels. George Crabbe.
    Pauper's Funeral, The. OBNC
    Rural Life. NOBE
    Truth in Poetry. SeCePo
    "Village life, and every care that reigns." EnRP; NAEL-1; NOEC; OAEL-1; PoE
    (Village Life.) PoEL-4
Village, The. Marina Gashe. PBA
Village, The. Goldsmith. See Deserted Village, The: Auburn.
Village. Roland Jooris, tr. fr. Dutch by Theo Hermans. DuIn
Village and Factory. Alexander Ilyich Bezymensky, tr. fr. Russian by Babette Deutsch. TrJP
Village Atheist, The. Edgar Lee Masters. Fr. Spoon River Anthology. EaLo; LiTA
Village before Sunset. Frances Cornford. BoNaP
Village Blacksmith, The. Longfellow. AA; AiP; AnAmPo; BLPL; FaBoBe; FaFP; FaPON; FaPoR; OBAL; OBCA; PWR; WBLP
Village Blacksmith, The. Unknown. FiBHP
Village child with spring grass, A. Taigi, tr. fr. Japanese by Hiroaki Sato. Fr. Twenty-nine Hokku. FCEI
Village Choir, The. Unknown. FaBoPa
Village Cinema, The. Stanislaw Grochowiak, tr. fr. Polish by Czeslaw Milosz. PwPP
Village Coddled in the Valley, The. George Barker. OxBSP
Village-folk told me, saying, The. Unknown. Fr. Manyo Shu. Ma
Village Hairdresser. Anzai Hitoshi, tr. fr. Japanese by Hiroaki Sato. FCEI
Village is a circle, A. Village. Roland Jooris, tr. by Theo Hermans. DuIn
Village is submerged, houses and creatures, The. Ashokan. Dachine Rainer. NePoAm
Village life, and every care that reigns. George Crabbe. Fr. The Village. EnRP; NAEL-1; NOEC; OAEL-1; PoE
    (Village Life.) PoEL-4
Village maid was leaving home, with tears her eyes were wet, A. Heaven Will Protect the Working Girl. Edgar Smith. FaFP
Village Night. Po Chü-i, tr. fr. Chinese by Burton Watson. CoBCP
Village Noon. Mid-Day Bells. Merrill Moore. MoAmPo
Village of Balmaquhapple, The. James Hogg. FaBoCo; FaBoPP
Village of Erith, The. Unknown. See There are men in the village of Erith.
Village of Reason, The. Michael Palmer. NPGG
Village of the Presents, The. James McMichael. AmPA
Village of Tudda, The. Kenneth Patchen. VGW
Village Parson, The. Goldsmith. Fr. The Deserted Village. BeLS; EnRP; FaFP; GoTL; LaA; NOEC; NoP; OAEL-1; PoEL-3; TEP
    (Village Preacher, The.) TIRV
Village Path. Ilse Aichinger, tr. fr. German by Beth Bjorklund. CoAuP
Village Patriarch, The, sels. Ebenezer Elliott. PF
    "Hail, Sabbath! day of mercy, peace, and rest!" Fr. III.
    "Is it the horn that, on this holy day." Fr. IV.
    "Now landed Trader, that, with haughty stare." Fr. V.
Village people/ will be out picking young greens, The. Tameie, tr. by Steven D. Carter. WFTW
Village Preacher, The. Goldsmith. See Deserted Village, The: Village Parson, The.
Village Schoolmaster, The. Goldsmith. Fr. The Deserted Village. BeLS; EnRP; FaFP; GoTL; LaA; NOEC; NoP; OAEL-1; PoEL-3; TEP
Village sleeps, a name unknown, till men, The. Distinction. Mark A. de Wolfe Howe. AA
Village Snowfall. Tamemasa, tr. fr. Japanese by Steven D. Carter. WFTW

Village snuffed asleep. Masaoka Shiki, tr. by Geoffrey Bownas and Anthony Thwaite. PeBJV
Village! thy butcher's son, the steward now. Ebenezer Elliott. Fr. The Splendid Village. OBSV
Village woman makes her five-year-old son, The. Ballad of Selling a Child. Wang Chiu-ssu, tr. by Jonathan Chaves. CoBLCP
Villagers. Iain Crichton Smith. NPo
Villagers all, this frosty tide. Kenneth Grahame. Fr. The Wind in the Willows. PChr
    (Carol: "Villagers all, this frosty tide.") OHIP
    (Christmas Carol: "Villagers all, this frosty tide.") FaPON
Villagers and Death, The. Robert Graves. HeIP; OBD
Villagers who gather round. Spiel of the Three Mountebanks. John Crowe Ransom. MoAmPo; MoAmPo
Villages. Corrado Govoni, tr. fr. Italian by Felix Stefanile. PFI
Villages are going away now, The. Between Evening and Night. Gerhard Fritsch, tr. by Beth Bjorklund. CoAuP
Villages are strewn, The. Villages Démolis. Sir Herbert Read. BrPo
Villain, The. W. H. Davies. MoBrPo; OxBSP; OxBTC; SoSe
Villain shows his indiscretion. Curtain! Paul Laurence Dunbar. CenHV
Villancico. Unknown, tr. fr. Spanish by Thomas Walsh. AWP
Villanelle at Sundown. Donald Justice. BLA
Villanelle: "Every day our bodies separate." Marilyn Hacker. AmPA; SM
Villanelle: "It is the pain, it is the pain, endures." William Empson. CMoP; EnLoPo; MoP; NoAM; OAEL-2; PoE
Villanelle: "It's all a trick, quite easy when you know it." W. W. Skeat. FaBoCo; FiBHP
Villanelle: Man in the Recreation Room, The. Edward Harkness. SM
Villanelle: "O winter wind, lat grievin be." Margaret Winefride Simpson. OxBS
Villanelle of Marguerites. Ernest Dowson. MoBrPo
Villanelle of Sunset. Ernest Dowson. BrPo
Villanelle of the Mystical Cycle. A. Leyeles, tr. fr. Yiddish by Benjamin and Barbara Harshav. AYP
Villanelle of the Poet's Road. Ernest Dowson. OBMV; TrGrPo; UnPo
Villanelle of Washington Square. Walter Adolphe Roberts. PoNe
Villanelle: "Proud inclination of the flesh." Dilys Bennett Laing. ErPo
Villanelle: The Psychological Hour. Ezra Pound. CTC; NAAL-2
Villanelle: "Time can [or will] say nothing but I told you so." W. H. Auden. LiTA; MoAB; MoBrPo
Villanelle: "You cannot rest behind the plate." M. D. Feld. SD
Villeggiatura. Edith Nesbit. NOBVV
Villon's Good-Night. William Ernest Henley. CenHV
Villon's Prayer for His Mother to Say to the Virgin. Villon, tr. fr. French by Robert Lowell. OBD
Villon's Straight Tip to All Cross Coves. W. E. Henley, after Villon. AWP; CenHV; FaBoCo; InvP; NA; SeCePo
Vilna. Moishe Kulbak, tr. fr. Yiddish. PeBMYV, tr. by Nathan Halper; VWA, tr. by Joachim Neugroschel
Vilna Puzzle, A. Sasha Chorny, tr. fr. Russian by Daniel Weissbort. VWA
Vincent Van Gogh. William Jay Smith. EyDe
Vindication. Daniil Kharms, tr. fr. Russian by George Gibian. FaBoNo
Vine, The. Robert Herrick. CaPo; ErPo; NAEL-2; NoP
Vine and the Goat, The. Aesop, tr. fr. Greek by William Ellery Leonard. AWP
Vine I see, and though 'tis time to glean, A. Overripe Fruit. Kasmuneh. TrJP
Vinegrowers dig up. Paul Celan, tr. by Beth Bjorklund. CoAuP
Vines, The. John Gray. NOBVV
Vines tougher than wrists. Forcing House. Theodore Roethke. CAPP
Vineta. Charles Spear. PeNZ
Vineyard, The. W. S. Merwin. NNaP
Vineyard of My Beloved, The. Priscilla Jane Thompson. CBWP-2
Vingtaine, sels. Alice Learned Bunner. AA
    Immutabilis. Fr. II.
    Separation. Fr. I.
Vintage. Robert Hass. AnAn
Vintage to the Dungeon, The. Richard Lovelace. CaPo; SeCV-1
Violence. Robert Lowell. NoAM
Violence on Television. Louis Jenkins. NU
Violent order is disorder, A. Connoisseur of Chaos. Wallace Stevens. LiTM
Violent praise the destructive rites of the hawk, The. The Beaver's Story. Vernon Watkins. NYBP
Violent Space, The. Etheridge Knight. BPo
Violent Storm. Mark Strand. NYBP
Violet. John Hollander. FYAP
Violet, The. Sir Walter Scott. EnRP
Violet, sel. Arthur Symons.
    Declaration. BrPo

Violet Bank, A. Shakespeare. *Fr.* A Midsummer Night's Dream, II, i. FaPON
("I know a place whereon the wild thyme blows.") BoNaP
(Where the Wild Thyme Blows.) TrGrPo
Violet in her greenwood bower, The. The Violet. Sir Walter Scott. EnRP
Violet Star. Philip Lamantia. UL
Violet Twilights. Edith Södergran, *tr. fr. Swedish by* Stina Katchadourian. WPOW
Violet wash is streaked across the clouds, A. Dinosaur Spring. Marilyn Nelson Waniek. ER; MAYP
Violets. Kate Louise. BoTP
Violets. John Moultrie. BoTP
Violets. P. A. Ropes. BoTP
Violets and Roses. *Unknown. See* Sweet Violets.
Violets are in bloom. A Spring Poem. Chikako, *tr. by* Steven D. Carter. WFTW
Violets blue of the eyes divine, The. Die blauen Veilchen der Äugelein. Heine, *tr. by* James Thomson. AWP
Violets, daffodils. Nosegay. Elizabeth Jane Coatsworth. OBCA
Violets for Mother. Lonny Kaneko. BrSi
Violets have withered. Shiba Sonome, *tr. fr. Japanese by* Hiroaki Sato. *Fr.* Fifteen Hokku. FCEI
Violets in Saint Mark's Square. Diego Valeri, *tr. fr. Italian by* I. L. Salomon. PFI
Violets in Thaumantia's Bosome. Sir Edward Sherburne. OBS
Violin Calls, The. Florence Randal Livesay. CaP
Violin Tree, The. Joel Rosenberg. VWA
Violinist, The. Archibald Lampman. CaP
Violinist's shadow vanishes, The. Cadenza. Ted Hughes. CMoP; NYBP
Violins. Eugenio Montale, *tr. fr. Italian by* Jonathan Galassi. *Fr.* Chords, I. PFI
Violin's Complaint, The. William Roscoe Thayer. AA
Violins in Repose. Jorge Plescoff, *tr. fr. Spanish by* Yishai Tobin. VWA
Viper, The. Hilaire Belloc. FaBoNo; NoAM
Viper, The. Ruth Pitter. FaBoTw
Vire will wind in other shadows. Saint-Lô. Samuel Beckett. NOIV
Virgidemiarum, *sels.* Joseph Hall.
"Great is the folly of a feeble brain." *Fr. bk.* I, Satire VII. EBEV
"Sturdy ploughman doth the soldier see, The." *Fr. bk.* IV, Satire VI. OBSV
"Time was, and that was termed the time of Gold." *Fr. bk.* III, Satire I. OBSV
(Olden Days, The.) OBSC
"Who doubts? The laws fell down from heaven's height." OBSV, *fr. bk.* II, Satire III.
Virgil: Georgics, Book IV. Dennis Schmitz. NPGG
Virgil's Farewell to Dante. Dante, *tr. fr. Italian by* Laurence Binyon. *Fr.* Divina Commedia: Purgatorio, XXVII. FaBoTw
Virgil's Tomb. Robert Cameron Rogers. AA
Virgin Country. Roy McFadden. NeIP
Virgin Declares Her Beauties, A. Francesco da Barberini, *tr. fr. Italian by* Dante Gabriel Rossetti. AWP; ErPo
Virgin is thinking of a child, The. Leonardo's Secret. Robert Bly. NNaP
Virgin Martyrs. John Heath-Stubbs. OxBC
Virgin Mary, The. Edgar Bowers. NePoEA; QFR
Virgin Mary, The. *Unknown, tr. fr. Welsh by* Joseph P. Clancy. OBWVE
Virgin mother, daughter of your son. Saint Bernard's Hymn of Praise to the Virgin Mary. Dante, *tr. fr. Italian by* Dana Gioia. *Fr.* Divina Commedia: Paradiso, XXXIII. PFI
Virgin Mother walked barefoot, The. Begotten of the Spleen. Charles Simic. LCAP
(Apocrypha.) AnAn
Virgin of the vestal flame. The Vestal Virgin. Eloise Bibb. CBWP-4
Virgin Pictured in Profile. Rosanna Warren. MAYP
Virgin, sing the Virgin Huntress. To Apollo and Diana ("Dianam tenerae dicite virgines"). Horace, *tr. fr. Latin. Fr.* Odes, I, 21. OBVE, *tr. by* Branwell Brontë.
(Invocation: "Maidens young and virgins tender,".) AWP, *tr. by* Louis Untermeyer.
Virgin Warrior, The. Gwendolyn MacEwen. FaBoWP
Virginal, A. Ezra Pound. CMoP; MoAB; MoAmPo; NAAL-2; NIP; NOBA; OxBA; Son; TAP
Virginia. Hart Crane. *Fr.* The Bridge. NAAL-2
Virginia. T. S. Eliot. *Fr.* Landscapes, II. InPK; RB
Virginia. Elouise Loftin. PoBA

Virginia Capta. Margaret Junkin Preston. PAH
Virginia Lake. James Keir Baxter. PeNZ
Virginia Reel. Charles Wright. AnAn
Virginia Song, The. *Unknown.* PAH
Virginia Woolf, Etc. Cristina Peri Rossi, *tr. fr. Spanish by* Kate Flores. DMH
Virginians of the Valley, The. Francis Orrery Ticknor. AA; PAH
Virginia's Bloody Soil. *Unknown.* AmFP
Virgins, The. Derek Walcott. OxBC; SoSe
Virgins are like the fair flower in its lustre. What Shall I Do to Show How Much I Love Her? John Gay. *Fr.* The Beggar's Opera, I, vii. TEP
Virgins, in vain you labour to prevent. Christopher Marlowe. *Fr.* Tamburlaine the Great. OBD
Virgin's Lullaby, The. *Unknown.* OxBLMV
Virgins promis'd when I died *or* dy'd. An Epitaph upon a Child. Robert Herrick. FaBoEE; SeCV-1
Virgin's Song, The. *Unknown.* NOBE
Virgo Descending. Charles Wright. LCAP
Virile Christ, A. Rex Boundy. WGRP
Virtual Particles. Frank Wilczek. NBLV
Virtue. Nicholas Grimald. OBSC
Virtue. George Herbert. AWP; CH; ELP; HAP; HeIP; InPS; InvP; JCP; NAEL-1; NOBE; NOCV; NoP; OAEL-1; OBD; OBEV; PoE; PoRA; PPP; SoSe; TEP; TrGrPo; WGRP
(Vertue.) FaBoRV; MeLP; MePo; OBS; SeCP; SeCV-1
Virtue. Immanuel di Roma, *tr. fr. Hebrew by* J. Chotzner. *Fr.* Machberoth. TrJP
Virtue. Walter de la Mare. MMA
Virtue conceal'd within our breast. Swift, *after the Latin of* Horace. OBVE
Virtue, dear friends, needs no 'defense.' I, 22. "Virtue, dear friend, needs no 'defence'" ("Integer vitae"). Horace, *tr. fr. Latin. Fr.* Odes. OBVE, *tr. by* Earl of Roscommon.
("Man in righteousness arrayed, The.")
(To Aristius Fuscus.) OBVE, *tr. by* Samuel Johnson.
("To man, my friend, whose conscious heart.")
(To Sally.) AWP, *tr. by* John Quincy Adams.
Virtue dwells rarely in the bright eyed and fair. Virtue. Immanuel di Roma, *tr. fr. Hebrew by* J. Chotzner. *Fr.* Machberoth. TrJP
Virtue may choose the high or low degree. Pope. *Fr.* Epilogue to the Satires [*or* 1738], Dialogue I. OBSV
(Triumph of Vice, The.) NOBE; OBSV
Virtue's branches wither, virtue pines. A Priest's Song. Thomas Dekker. *Fr.* Old Fortunatus. OBSC
(Song: "Virtue's branches wither, virtue pines.") EiL
Virtues of Carnation Milk, The. *Unknown. See* Carnation Milk
("Carnation milk is the best in the land.")
Virtues of Sid Hamet, the Magician's Rod, The. Swift. APAS
Virtues of the cane must now be sung, The. Nathaniel Weekes. *Fr.* Barbados. PBCV
Virtue's way is to heed the canons of heaven. Speaking My Thoughts. Prince Otomo, *tr. by* Burton Watson. JLIC-1
Virtuosa. Mary Ashley Townsend. AA
Virtuous Fox and the Self-righteous Cat, The. John Cunningham. OnMSP
Virtuous Sin, The. Luis Palés Matos, *tr. fr. Spanish by* Perry Higman. LPSS
Virtuous Wife, The. Süsskind von Trimberg, *tr. fr. Middle High German.* TrJP
Virtuous Woman, The. Bible, *O.T. See* Proverbs: Who can find a virtuous woman? for her price is far above rubies.
Virus Poliomyelitis. Mary R. Gaumond. TSM
Viruses, when the lens is right. First Photos of Flu Virus. Harold Witt. SM
Visage becomes armed, The: within. Armed Vision. N. P. van Wyck Louw, *tr. by* Jack Cope *and* Uys Krige. PeSA
Viscous air, wheres' ere she fly, The. The Kingfisher. Andrew Marvell. *Fr.* Upon Appleton House, to My Lord Fairfax. ChTr
Visibility. Maura Stanton. NAmP
Visible Baby, The. Peter Redgrove. NAs
Visible, invisible. A Jellyfish. Marianne Moore. OxBSP; PCP
Visibly here the tide. Wellfleet Harbor. Paul Goodman. CoAP
Vision. Delmira Augustini, *tr. fr. Spanish by* Marti Moody. WPOW
Vision, The. Burns. OxBS
Vision, A. John Clare. ChTr; EBVV; FaBoRV; GTBS-P; NAEL-2; NOBVV; OAEL-2; OBNC; OPOP; PoE; PPP
(I Lost the Love of Heaven.) ELP
Vision. Harry Crosby. EAS
Vision. E. E. Cummings. FL
Vision, The. Daniel Defoe. APAS
Vision. Richard Eberhart. NYBP

Vision, The. Robert Herrick. CaPo; ErPo; JCP; SeCP

Vision. William Dean Howells. AA

Vision. Louis Johnson. PeNZ

Vision, A. Maria Konopnicka, *tr. fr. Polish* by Jerzy Peterkiewicz *and* Burns Singer. WPOW

Vision, A. Lord Herbert of Cherbury. SeCP

Vision, The. Muhammed al-Faituri, *tr. fr. Arabic* by Sargon Boulus *and* Peter Porter. MAP

Vision, The. Egan O'Rahilly, *tr. fr. Irish* by Thomas Kinsella. NOIV
(Reverie, The.) AnIL, *tr.* by Frank O'Connor
(Reverie at Dawn.) FaBoPV, *tr.* by Frank O'Connor

Vision. Francis Reginald. MoCV

Vision. Frank Sidgwick. MMA

Vision, The. William Taylor. NOEC

Vision, The. Kitty Tsui. Fr. Red Rock Canyon, Summer 1977. ER

Vision, A. Henry Vaughan. *See* I saw eternity the other night.

Vision, A. Hugo von Hofmannsthal, *tr. fr. German* by Charles Wharton Stork. TrJP

Vision, A. Sándor Weöres, *tr. fr. Hungarian* by Jascha Kessler. FOC

Vision. Israel Zangwill. TrJP

Vision and breath. Outside White Earth. Gordon Henry. STE

Vision and Prayer. Dylan Thomas. LiTM

Vision as of crowded city streets, A. Shakespeare. Longfellow. AWP

Vision by Sweetwater. John Crowe Ransom. CMoP; FaBoMo; MoAB; NOBA; OxBA; RB

Vision Clear, The. J. M. Westrup. BoTP

Vision from the Small Blue Window. Ernesto Cardenal, *tr. fr. Spanish* by Francisco X. Alarcón. Vol

Vision in long filaments flows. Vision. Francis Reginald. MoCV

Vision of Belshazzar, The. Byron. GN; OnMSP

Vision of Beulah, The ("There is a place where contrarieties are equally true"). Blake. Fr. Milton, II. OAEL-2

Vision of Beulah, The ("Thou hearest the nightingale begin the song of spring"). Blake. *See* Milton: Thou hearest the nightingale begin the song of spring.

Vision of Children, A. Thomas Ashe. EBVV

Vision of Connaught in the Thirteenth Century, A. James Clarence Mangan. AnIL; NOIV

Vision of Delight, The. Ben Jonson. PoEL-2

Vision of Delight Presented at Court in Chistmas, 1617, The. Ben Jonson. SeCV-1

Vision of Eve, The. Henrietta Cordelia Ray. CBWP-3

Vision of Ita, The. Saint Ita. *See* Jesukin.

Vision of Ita, The. *Unknown, tr. fr. Old Irish* by Whitley Stokes. AnIL

Vision of Jesus, The. William Langland. Fr. The Vision of Piers Plowman. ACP

Vision of Judgement, A, *sels*. Robert Southey.
Absolvers, The. EnRP
Southey Looks out of the Window at Greta Hill. FaBoPP

Vision of Judgment, The, *sels*. Byron. EnRP; NAEL-2; OAEL-2; TEP
"At length with jostling, elbowing, and the aid." OBSV
George III. TW
George the Third. FiP
(George III.) TW, *abr*.
"Saint Peter sat by the celestial gate." OBSV; OxBoLi

Vision of Lazarus, The, *sel*. Fenton Johnson.
"Another sate near him, whose harp of gold." BANP

Vision of MacConglinne, The. MacConglinne, *tr. fr. Middle Irish*.
BIrV, *tr.* by John Montague; CH, *tr.* by Kuno Meyer; FaBoNo, *tr.* by Kuno Meyer

Vision of Marsden Hartley, The. John Haines. BLA

Vision of Moonlight, A. Henrietta Cordelia Ray. CBWP-3

Vision of Nature, A. William Langland. *See* Vision of Piers Plowman, The: And I bowed my body and beheld all about.

Vision of Piers Plowman, The, *sels*. William Langland.
Age of Reason, The, *mod*. by Donald Attwater NOCV
"And I bowed my body and beheld all about." CTC
(Vision of Nature, A.) PoEL-1
"As for the birds and the beasts, the men in bygone times." Fr. Passus XII. PBBP
"Birds I beheld building nests in the bushes." Fr. Passus XI. PBBP
Civil Service, The, , *mod*. by Donald Attwater NOCV
Descent into Hell, The. PoEL-1
Entertainment Industry, The, *mod*. by Donald Attwater NOCV
"Envy with heavy heart asked for shrift." Fr. Passus V. NAEL-1
Et Incarnatus Est. NOBE, Passus II (C *text*).
"For trewthe telleth that loue is triacle of hevene." OBEV

(Incarnation, The.) PoEL-1
Glutton [*or* Glutton in the Tavern], The. ACP; PoE
God's Mercy, *mod*. by Donald Attwater NOCV
Good Works, *mod*. by Donald Attwater NOCV
"In a summer [*or* somer] season, when soft[e] was the sun [*or* sunne *or* sonne]."
(Field Full of Folk, The.) PoE
(Field of Folk, The.) PoEL-1
(On Malverne Hilles, the Place of Piers Plowman's Vision.) FaBoPP
(Prologue: "In a summer season, when soft was the sun", *mod*. by J. B. Trapp (B *text*)) EBVV; OAEL-1
Incarnation, The. OBEV; PoEL-1
Palace of Truth, The. ACP
Palmer, The. ACP
Poor, The. PoEL-1
Prologue. FaBoRV
Saint Called "Truth," A, *mod*. by Donald Attwater NOCV
View from Middle-Earth, A, *mod. vers*. by Naomi Lewis Mes
Vision of Jesus, The. ACP
Vision of Nature, A. CTC; PoEL-1
"What for feere of this ferly and of the false Jewes." Fr. Passus XVIII. EBEV
"What this mountain means, and the murky dale." Fr. Passus I (B *text*) *mod*. by J. B. Trapp. OAEL-1
"Wool-chafed and wet-shoed I went forth after." Fr. Passus XVIII. NAEL-1
"Yet I courbed on my knees and cried hire of grace." Fr. Passus II. EBEV

Vision of Sin, The, *sel*. Tennyson. OAEL-2
Song at the Ruin'd Inn. PoEL-5

Vision of Sir Launfal, The, *sels*. James Russell Lowell. OnMSP
Brook in Winter, The. Fr. Prelude to Pt. II. GN
Down swept the chill wind from the mountain peak.
Earth gets its price for what Earth gives us. Fr. Prelude to Pt. I.
"For a cap and bells our lives we pay." Fr. Prelude to Pt. I. AA
(June Weather.) GN
"For Christ's sweet sake, I beg an alms." WGRP, *fr. pt*. II.
"Holy Supper is kept, indeed, The." Fr. pt. II.
Not Only around Our Infancy. Fr. Prelude to Pt. I. FaFP
"Over his keys the musing organist." Fr. Prelude to Pt. I. LiTA
(June "Over his keys the musing organist").) OHFP
Sir Launfal and the Leper. Fr. pt. I. GN
What [*or* And what] Is So Rare as a Day in June?. Fr. Prelude to Pt. I. BLPL; FaBoBe; FaFP; FaPON
(Day in June, A ("And what is so fair as a day in June?").) FaPON
(June ("What is so rare as a day in June?").) FaBV
Winter Morning, A. Fr. II. GN, *fr. pt*. II.

Vision of the Blessed Gabriele, The. Penelope Shuttle. NPo

Vision of the Day of Judgment. Bible, *O.T.* Fr. Isaiah, LXIII, Moulton, Modern Reader's Bible. WGRP

Vision of the Lamentation of Beulah, A. Blake. *See* Milton: Thou hearest the nightingale begin the song of spring.

Vision of the Mermaids, A, *sel*. Gerard Manley Hopkins.
"Rowing, I reach'd a rock—the sea was low." ChTr

Vision of the Sea, A. Shelley. MOS

Vision of the Snow, The. Margaret Junkin Preston. AA

Vision of the World's Instability, A. Richard Verstegan. ElL

Vision of Truth, A. J. C. Squire. NOBL

Vision Song (Cheyenne). Lance Henson. STE

Vision that appeared to me, A [*or* The]. The Vision of MacConglinne. MacConglinne. BIrV, *tr*. by John Montague; CH, *tr*. by Kuno Meyer; FaBoNo, *tr*. by Kuno Meyer

Vision to Electra, The. Robert Herrick. SeCP

Vision upon This Conceit of the Faerie Queene, A. Sir Walter Ralegh. Fr. Commendatory Verses to Edmund Spenser's Fairy Queen. OBSC; Son
("Methought I saw the grave where Laura lay.") NAEL-1
(Of Spenser's Faery Queen.) SiPS

Visionary, The. Emily Brontë. BLPL; LiTB; NOBE; NOBVV; OBNC; PBWP; SCV
(Silent Is the House.) CH; ELP
("Silent is the house—all are laid asleep.") BrRo

Visionary Oklahoma Sunday Beer. James Whitehead. SM

Visions, *sel*. Blake.
"Moment of desire, The! the moment of desire! the virgin." ErPo

Visions, *sel*. William Browne.
Rose, The. CH; OBEV

Visions, *sels*. Joachim Du Bellay, *tr. fr. French* by Spenser.
"I saw the bird that can the sun endure." Fr. VII. Son
"It was the time, when rest, soft sliding downe." Fr. I. AWP; Son

Visions. Kathleen Spivack. AmPA

Visions. William Stafford. NoAM

Visions of beauty, of light, and of love. Dreams of Beauty. Adah Isaacs Menken. CBWP-1

Visions of Mexico While at a Writing Symposium in Port Townsend, Washington. Lorna Dee Cervantes. CCP; ER; FIA
México. NoAM
Washington. NoAM

Visions of the Daughters of Albion, *sel.* Blake. OAEL-2
Take Thy Bliss, O Man. EnRP

Visions of the world beyond these walls recede. Resurrection: Fragments. Felix Mnthali. WMBCH

Visions of the World's Vanity, *sel.* Spenser.
Huge Leviathan, The. ChTr

Visions, The. Petrarch. *Fr.* Sonnets to Laura: To Laura in Life, CLXXXVIII, tr. by C. B. Cayley. AWP

Visions you never saw, The. Grandfather. Lance Henson, *tr. by* Lance Henson. CDW; HATNAP

Visit. A. R. Ammons. CoAP; GrPl; TwCP

Visit, A. Sherwood Anderson. PoA

Visit, The. "Badawi al-Jabal", *tr. fr. Arabic by* Matthew Sorenson *and* John Heath-Stubbs. MAP

Visit. Norman Dubie. *Fr.* The Duchess' Red Shoes, II. AnAn

Visit, The. Emerson. AnAmPo; NOBA

Visit, The. Phillip William George. VoR

Visit, The. Ogden Nash. FiBHP

Visit. James Welch. AmPA

Visit by Water. Floris Clark McLaren. OBCV

Visit from Alphonse, A. Paul Zimmer. OBTV

Visit from St. Nicholas, A. Clement Clarke Moore. AA; AiP; AnAmPo; BeLS; BLPA; FaBoBe; FaBV; FaFP; FaPON; FPL; NTCP; OBAL; OBCA; OBCP; OnMSP; OxBChV; PChr; RHPC
(Night before Christmas, The.) OHIP; PWR; WBLP

Visit from the Sea, A. Robert Louis Stevenson. FM; GN; MOS

Visit Home, A. Joseph Glazer. VWA

Visit of Hope to Sydney Cove, near Botany-Bay. Erasmus Darwin. NOEC; OBTV

Visit of the Gods, The. Schiller, *tr. fr. German by* Samuel Taylor Coleridge. OBVE

Visit to a Hospital. Jean Valentine Chace. GoYe

Visit to Bridge House, A. Richard Weber. BIrV

Visit to Enniskillen, A. Tadhg Dall O'Huiginn. NOIV

Visit to the Art Gallery, A, *sels.* Carlos Baker. EyDe
Chinese Mural, A.
On a Landscape of Sestos.

Visit to the Asylum, A. Edna St. Vincent Millay. SO

Visit to the Author's Paternal Seat, A. Richard Polwhele. *Fr.* The Influence of Local Attachment. NOEC

Visit to the Farm, A. Robert Siegel. GeTw

Visit to the Juvenile Penitentiary. Hermann Gail, tr. fr. German by Beth Bjorklund. CoAuP

Visitant, The. Theodore Roethke. CMoP; PoE; RB; UnPo

Visitant to our dumbly human home. The Great Moth. Robert Gittings. OxBTC

Visitation, The. Elizabeth Jennings. MoBS

Visitation, A. W. D. Snodgrass. SM

Visitation Rights. Heather Wishik. GLP

Visitations. Lawrence Durrell. *Fr.* Eight Aspects of Melissa. MoBrPo

Visitations: VII, *sel.* Louis MacNeice.
And the Lord Was Not in the Whirlwind. EaLo

Visited. Fleur Adcock. PeNZ

Visited by Thieves. Ryokan, *tr. fr. Chinese by* Burton Watson. JLIC-2

Visiting. Tony Beyer. ATNZ

Visiting a Recluse on West Mountain and Not Finding Him In. Ch'iu Wei, *tr. fr. Chinese by* Burton Watson. CoBCP

Visiting Card, A. Gregory O'Brien. ATNZ

Visiting conductor, A. A Simple Story. Gwen Harwood. FaBoWP

Visiting Day. Al Young. NPGG

Visiting Emily Dickinson's Grave with Robert Francis. Robert Bly. LCAP

Visiting Father. Genny Lim. BrSi

Visiting from Britain, I take my ease. The Emigrés. Ted Walker. OBTV

Visiting Grandpa years ago, I. Foreign Soil. Dianne Hai-Jew. BrSi

Visiting Home, *sel.* Edward Field.
"*Yiskidor*, when he dies I won't know the Hebrew words to say." DiL

Visiting home to tell my people. A Long Overdue Thankyou Note to the Girl Who Taught Me Loving. Tom Schmidt. NeAC

Visiting Hour, The. David Wagoner. HoPM

Visiting Ichijo-ji. Ito Jinsai, *tr. fr. Chinese by* Burton Watson. JLIC-2

Visiting Juliet Street. Elizabeth Smither. ATNZ

Visiting Mount Vernon and Paying Homage at George Washingon's Burial Vault. K'ang Yu-wei, *tr. fr. Chinese by* Chang-fang Chen. WFTU

Visiting My Father. Rai San'yo, *tr. fr. Chinese by* Burton Watson. JLIC-2

Visiting My Wife's Grave. Natsume Seibi, *tr. fr. Japanese by* Hiroaki Sato. *Fr.* Twenty-seven Hokku. FCEI

Visiting Rites. Phyllis Janowitz. PPR

Visiting the Graves. Ellen Bryant Voigt. PPR

Visiting the Oracle. Lawrence Raab. AmPA

Visiting the Temple of Accumulated Fragrance. Wang Wei, *tr. fr. Chinese by* Burton Watson. CoBCP

Visiting the Temple of Chang Tzu-fang. Chu Yi-tsun, *tr. fr. Chinese by* Irving Lo. WFTU

Visitor, The. Michael Dennis Browne. OBTV

Visitor, A. "Lewis Carroll." FaBoNo

Visitor, The. W. H. Davies. GBL; OBWVE

Visitor, The. Carolyn Forché. FYAP

Visitor. W. E. Henley. *Fr.* In Hospital, XX. BrPo

Visitor, The. Gregory Orr. MAYP

Visitor, The. Jack Prelutsky. AmMo

Visitor, The. Katharine Pyle. OnUR

Visitor, The. Gibbons Ruark. MT

Visitor. *Unknown.* OxNR

Visitor makes many things of time, The. Tarragona Wine. George McWhirter. UAS

Visitor to Warsaw. Portrait of a Jew Old Country Style. Jerome Rothenberg. NNaP

Visitor Who Never Came, The. Nazik al-Mala'ika, *tr. fr. Arabic by* Matthew Sorenson *and* Christopher Middleton. MAP

Visitors, The. Richard Moore. DiPo

Visitor's Parking. Anne Szumigalski. NOBC

Visits to St. Elizabeths. Elizabeth Bishop. CoAP; VGW

Vistas between the shadowy pines were bright. Starlight Thought. Henrietta Cordelia Ray. *Fr.* A Group of Musings. CBWP-3

Visual Conspiracy. Fyna Dowe. WS

Vita Benefica. Alice Wellington Rollins. AA

Vita Nuova. Stanley Kunitz. VGW

Vita Nuova, La, *sels.* Dante, *tr. fr. Italian by* Dante Gabriel Rossetti.
"All my thoughts always speak to me of Love." *Fr.* VI. AWP
"All ye that pass along Love's trodden way." *Fr.* II. AWP
"At whiles (yea oftentimes) I muse over." *Fr.* IX. AWP
"Beyond the sphere which spreads to widest space." *Fr.* XXIX. AWP; CTC
"Canst thou indeed be he that still would sing." *Fr.* XIII, b. AWP
"Day agone, as I rode sullenly, A." *Fr.* IV. AWP
"Death, always cruel, Pity's foe in chief." *Fr.* III, b. AWP
"Even as the others mock, thou mockest me." *Fr.* VII. AWP
"Eyes that weep for pity of the heart, The." *Fr.* XIX. AWP; WGRP, *sl. diff. vers.*.
"For certain he hath seen all perfectness." *Fr.* XVII. AWP
"Gentle thought there is will often start, A." *Fr.* XXVI. AWP
"I felt a spirit of love begin to stir." *Fr.* XV. AWP
"Ladies that have intelligence in love." *Fr.* X. AWP
"Love and the gentle heart are one same thing." *Fr.* XI. AWP
"Love hath so long possessed me for his own." *Fr.* XVIII. AWP
"Love's pallor and the semblance of deep ruth." *Fr.* XXIV. AWP
"Mine eyes beheld the blessed pity spring." *Fr.* XXIII. AWP
"My lady carries love within her eyes." *Fr.* XII. AWP
"My lady looks so gentle and so pure." *Fr.* XVI. AWP
"Song, 'tis my will that thou do seek out Love." *Fr.* V. AWP
"Stay now with me, and listen to my sighs." *Fr.* XX. AWP
"That lady of all gentle memories." *Fr.* XXII. AWP
"That she hath gone to Heaven suddenly." *Fr.* III. CTC
"Thoughts are broken in my memory, The." *Fr.* VIII. AWP
"To every heart which the sweet pain doth move." *Fr.* I. AWP
"Very bitter weeping that ye made, The." *Fr.* XXV. AWP
"Very pitiful lady, very young, A." *Fr.* XIV. AWP; CTC, *shorter sel.*
"Weep, Lovers, with Love's very self doth weep." *Fr.* III, a. AWP
"Whatever while the thought comes over me." *Fr.* XXI. AWP
"Woe's me! by dint of all these sighs that come." *Fr.* XXVII. AWP
"Ye pilgrim-folk, advancing pensively." *Fr.* XXVIII. AWP; CTC
"You that thus wear a modest countenance." *Fr.* XIII, a. AWP

Vita Sackville West. The Nicolsons. Roberta Simone. SoTCo

Vita with Postscript. Ilse Tielsch, *tr. fr. German by* Beth Bjorklund. CoAuP

Vitae Summa Brevis Spem Nos Vetat Incohare Longam. Ernest Dowson. AWP; BrPo; ChTr; EBVV; FaBoRV; HAP; NOBE; NoP; OBEV; OxBSP; TrGrPo; WGRP

Vitaï Lampada. Sir Henry Newbolt. BLPA; FaPoR; OBWP

Vital Message. Robert Phillips. GeTw
Vital spark of heavenly flame! Pope, *par. fr. the Latin of* Emperor
  Hadrian. BLPL; LiTB
  (Dying Christian to His Soul, The.) AWP; OBEV
Vital Statistics. William Rose Benét. AnAmPo
Vitality. Maria Amalia Fonte Boa, *tr. fr. Portuguese by* Willis Barnstone
  and Nelson Cerqueira. BoWoP
Vitamins and Roughage. Kenneth Rexroth. NoAM
Vitelli rides west toward Fano, the morning sun. The Death of Vitellozzo
  Vitelli. Irving Feldman. TwCP
Vittoria Colonna. Roy Marz. PoA
Vivaldi. Delmore Schwartz. NYBP
Vivamus, Mea Lesbia, atque Amemus. Thomas Campion. *See* My
  Sweetest Lesbia Let Us Live and Love.
Vive Noir! Mari E. Evans. IHMS; PoBA
Vivérols. David Starr Jordan. AA
Vivid, alone, against the wide expanse. Pedro. Phoebe W. Hoffman.
  GoYe
Vivid and heavy, he strolls through dark brick kitchens. The Composer's
  Winter Dream. Norman Dubie. LCAP
Vivid smile of my sweetheart, The. *Unknown. Fr.* Manyo Shu. Ma
Vivien's Song ("But now the wholesome music of the wood"). Tennyson.
  Fr. Idylls of the King: Balin and Balan. OAEL-2
Vixen, The. John Clare. RB
Vixen woman, The. Harold Monro. *Fr.* Natural History. OBMV
Vixi Puellis Nuper Idoneus. Sir Thomas Wyatt. *See* They Flee [*or* Fle]
  from Me That Sometime Did Me Seek [*or* Seke].
Vlamertinghe; Passing the Château, July 1917. Edmund Blunden.
  MMA; OBWP
Vlaminck's Tie, the Persistent Imaginal. Michael Harlow. PeNZ
Vocation. Judith Herzberg, *tr. fr. Dutch by* Manfred Wolf. DuIn;
  WPOW
Vocation. Carol Rumens. DiPo
Vocation. William Stafford. CAPP
Vocation. Rabindranath Tagore. FaPON
Voice, The. Rudolf Bayr, *tr. fr. German by* Beth Biorklund. CoAuP
Voice, A. Yves Bonnefoy, *tr. fr. French by* Paul Auster. RHTwFP
Voice, A. Norman Gale. OHIP
Voice, The. Thomas Hardy. BoLoP; CMoP; EnLoPo; GBL; GTBS-P;
  HAP; InPS; MoP; NAEL-2; NoAM; NoP; OAEL-2; OBNC; PoE;
  PoEL-5
Voice, The. Judith Herzberg, *tr. fr. Dutch by* Shirley Kaufman.
  VWA
Voice. Jung Han-mo, *tr. fr. Korean by* Koh Chang-soo. ACKP
Voice. W. S. Merwin. NNaP
Voice. Ron Padgett. UL
Voice, The. Theodore Roethke. VGW
Voice, A. Tadeusz Rozewicz, *tr. fr. Polish by* Czeslaw Milosz. PwPP
Voice. Harriet Prescott Spofford. AA
Voice. Tamura Ryuichi, *tr. fr. Japanese by* Hiroaki Sato. FCEI
Voice, The. Walter de la Mare. WSC
Voice, The. Edmund Wilson. NYBP
Voice, A, said, "Follow, follow"; and I rose. Two Pursuits. Christina
  Rossetti. WPE
Voice and Address. Michael Palmer. NPGG
Voice at a Seance, A. Anthony Hecht. AnAn
Voice came from the distance, The. Three Voices. Tamura Ryuichi, *tr.
  by* Geoffrey Bownas *and* Anthony Thwaite. PeBJV
Voice from Danang. Thomas Dillon Redshaw. MAT
Voice from heaven was heard on earth, A. St. Andrew's Voyage to
  Mermedonia. *Unknown, tr. fr. Anglo-Saxon by* Charles W. Kennedy.
  Fr. Andreas. AnOE
Voice from the dark called out, A. Making Peace. Denise Levertov.
  ER
Voice from the dark is calling me, A. Divorce. Anna Wickham.
  MoBrPo
Voice from the Invisible World, A. Goethe, *tr. fr. German by* James
  Clarence Mangan. AWP
Voice from the Roses, A. Maxine W. Kumin. NMM
Voice from the Waters, A. Thomas Lovell Beddoes. *See* Death's Jest
  Book: Dirge: "Swallow leaves her nest, The."
Voice from the Well [of Life Speaks to the Maiden], The. George Peele.
  See Old Wives' [*or* Wife's] Tale, The: Gently Dip.
Voice from under the Table, A. Richard Wilbur. AmPP; HAP; NePoEA;
  NOBA
Voice hoarse, the monkey's teeth. Kikaku, *tr. fr. Japanese by* Hiroaki
  Sato. *Fr.* Thirty-three Hokku. FCEI
Voice in Darkness. Richard Dehmel, *tr. fr. German by* Margarete
  Münsterberg. AWP
Voice in the Blood. Barney Bush. STE
Voice in the Crowd. Ted Joans. *See* If you should see a MAN.

Voice in the Dark. A. L. Strauss, *tr. fr. Hebrew by* Robert Friend.
  VWA
Voice in the Garden, A. Selima Hill. FaBoWP
Voice of a Dissipated Woman inside a Tomb. Sor Violante do Céu, *tr. fr.
  Portuguese by* Willis Barnstone. BoWoP
Voice of America, 1961, The. James Liddy. CIP
Voice of Blooming, The. Yip Wai-lim, *tr. fr. Chinese by* Dominic
  Cheung. IFON
Voice of England is a trumpet tone, The. England. George Edgar
  Montgomery. AA
Voice of Experience, The. Goethe, *tr. fr. German by* Walter Kaufman.
  ErPo
Voice of God, The. Katherine R. Barnard. BLRP; WBLP
Voice of God, The. James Stephens. WGRP
Voice of God Is Calling, The. John Haynes Holmes. AH
Voice of King Solomon's nightingale, The. A Snow in Jerusalem.
  Hayim Naggid. VWA, *tr. by* Shlomo Vinner *and* Howard Schwartz
Voice of *mufana*, The. Mamano. José Craveirinha, *tr. by* Chris Searle.
  WMBCH
Voice of my Brothers. Pentti Saaritsa, *tr. fr. Finnish by* Aili Jarvenpa.
  SOP
Voice of my darling, The. Bible, *O.T. See* Song of Solomon, The:
  Hark! My Beloved!
Voice of My White City, The. Abba Kovner, *tr. fr. Hebrew by* Warren
  Bargad *and* Stanley F. Chyet. IP
Voice of Robert Desnos, The. Robert Desnos, *tr. fr. French by* Michael
  Benedikt. POS; RHTwFP, *tr. by* Bill Zavatsky.
Voice of Stone. Fahmida Riaz, *tr. fr. Urdu by* Mahmood Jamal.
  PBMUP
Voice of summer, keen and shrill. To a Cricket. William Cox Bennett.
  BoTP; GN
Voice of the Derwent, The. Wordsworth. FaBoPP
Voice of the Devil, The. Blake. *Fr.* The Marriage of Heaven and Hell.
  NU
Voice of the Dove, The. Joaquin Miller. AA
Voice of the glutton I heard with disdain, The. The Glutton. John
  Oakman. OxBChV
Voice of the Grass, The. Sarah Roberts Boyle. AA
Voice of the last cricket, The. Splinter. Carl Sandburg. FaPON;
  OBCA; SoSe
Voice of the Negro, The. Lizelia Augusta Jenkins Moorer.
  CBWP-3
Voice of the Power of This World, The. Gregory Hall. NU
Voice of the Studio Announcer. Archibald MacLeish. *Fr.* The Fall of
  the City. HoPM
Voice of the Void, The. George Parsons Lathrop. AA
Voice of Webster, The, *sel.* Robert Underwood Johnson.
  Silence was envious of the only voice. AA
Voice on the winds, A. To Morfydd. Lionel Johnson. MoBrPo;
  OAEL-2; OBMV
Voice out of the Sabbaths, A. W. I. Derek Walcott. WeW
Voice peals in this end of night, A. A Thrush before Dawn. Alice
  Meynell. MoBrPo; WPE
Voice said, "Hurl him down!", The. The Lovely Shall Be Choosers.
  Robert Frost. MoAB; MoAmPo; NOBA; OxBA; PoE
Voice Sings, A. Samuel Taylor Coleridge. *Fr.* Remorse. CH
Voice [Speaks] from the Well, A. George Peele. *Fr.* The Old Wives'
  [*or* Wife's] Tale. FaBoCh; NOBE; OBSC; OxBoLi
Voice That Beautifies the Land, The. *Unknown, tr. fr. Navajo Indian by*
  Washington Matthews. AWP
Voice that breathed o'er Eden, The. John Keble. NOCV
Voice went over the waters, The. Cuba to Columbia. Will M. Carleton.
  PAH
Voiceless, The. Oliver Wendell Holmes. *Fr.* The Autocrat of the
  Breakfast Table. AA, *fr.* 12.
Voices. Nora Dauenhauer. HATNAP
Voices. Celia Gilbert. ER
Voices. David Mitchell. UAS
Voices, The. Janine Pommy-Vega. UL
Voices. Walter de la Mare. UnPo
Voices against England in the Night. Stevie Smith. CN
Voices Answering Back: The Vampires. Lawrence Raab. AmPA;
  VVA
Voices at the Window. Sir Philip Sidney. *See* Astrophel and Stella:
  Who is it that this dark night.
Voices from the Other World. James Merrill. TwCP
Voices from Things Growing in a Churchyard. Thomas Hardy. OBD;
  OxBTC
Voices in the Night. Melvin L. Whipple. CowP
Voices Inescapable, The. Ann Stanford. IHMS

Voices lifted high in singing. Music. *Malay Oral Tradition, tr. by* R. O. Winstedt. WTO

Voices moving about in the quiet house. Falling Asleep. Siegfried Sassoon. MoBrPo; OxBTC

Voices of Eden, The. Else Lasker-Schüler, *tr. fr. German by* Robert Alter. OV

Voices of Heroes. Horace Gregory. OFD

Voices of insects at a stag by the fence, The. Princess Shikishi, *tr. fr. Japanese by* Hiroaki Sato. *Fr.* Seventy-eight Tanka. FCEI

Voices of the Rain. Henrietta Cordelia Ray. CBWP-3

Voices That Have Filled My Day. Fay Chiang. BrSi

Voices touch like hesitation. Harmoniums. Kathryn Rantala. BWV

Void, The. Gwendolyn MacEwen. *Fr.* The T. E. Lawrence Poems. NOBC

Void Between, The. John Lancaster Spalding. *Fr.* God and the Soul. AA

Void, damned weed! that hell's dry sweetmeats art. On Tobacco. Thomas Pestel. EIL

Void only. "Ping Hsin", *tr. fr. Chinese by* Kenneth Rexroth *and* Ling Chung. *Fr.* Multitudinous Stars. PBWP

Void that's highly embraceable, The. Jack Kerouac. *Fr.* Mexico City Blues, 225. NeAP

Vois loude in that light to Lucifer seide, A. The Descent into Hell. William Langland. *Fr.* The Vision of Piers Plowman. PoEL-1

Volatile Kerryman, The. Owen Roe O'Sullivan, *tr. fr. Irish by* Sean O'Riada. BIrV

Volcanic Venus. D. H. Lawrence. InPS

Volcano. Ivan Van Sertima. PBCV

Volcano. Derek Walcott. OxBC

Volcano portulaca rain. Loquat. Nishiwaki Junzaburo, *tr. by* Hiroaki Sato. FCEI

Volcanoe Suite, *sel.* "Shake" Keane.
  Soufrière (79). *Fr.* I. PBCV

Volcanoes. Bella Akhmadulina, *tr. fr. Russian by* W. H. Auden. PBWP

Volitions. A. R. Ammons. CAPP

Volleyball Match, The. Bill Pearlman. ASP

Volpone, *sels.* Ben Jonson.
  "Come, my Celia, let us prove." *Fr.* III, vii. EIL; OBVE; TEP
  (Come, My Celia.) FaBV; FF; HeIP; NoP; TrGrPo
  (Song to Celia.) ErPo; JCP; OAEL-1, *with music*; OBS; SeCP; SeCV-1
  Fools, They Are the Only Nation. *Fr.* I, ii. InvP
  (Fools.) EIL
  (Nano's Song.) TrGrPo

Volt. Tristan Tzara, *tr. fr. French by* Lee Harwood. RHTwFP

Voltaire at Ferney. W. H. Auden. LiTA; LiTM; PoA

Volubilis, North Africa. Ralph Nixon Currey. PeSA

Volume, The. Robert Pinsky. AnAn

Volume of Chopin, A. James Picot. PoAu-2

Volumes of books, tea and incense. Wen Cheng-ming, *tr. fr. Chinese by* Jonathan Chaves. *Fr.* Inscribed on a Painting: Cultivating Leisure. CoBLCP

Voluntaries, *sels.* Emerson.
  Duty. *Fr.* III. FaFP; GN
  In an Age of Fops and Toys. *Fr.* III. FPL; LiTA; PoLF

Voluntary Mutilation. Jean Follain, *tr. fr. French by* W. S. Merwin. RHTwFP

Volunteer, The. Herbert Asquith. MMA; OBWP; OxBTC

Volunteer, The. Elbridge Jefferson Cutler. AA

Volunteer, The. *Unknown.* NOEC

Volunteers, The. William Haines Lytle. PAH

Volunteer's Thanksgiving, The. Lucy Larcom. OBCA

Voluptuaries and Others. Margaret Avison. MoCV

Voluspo. *Unknown, tr. fr. Old Norse by* Henry Adams Bellows. *Fr.* The Elder Edda. AWP

Von Tempsky's Dance. Murray Edmond. PeNZ

Voodoo on the Un-Assing of Janis Joplin. Carolyn M. Rodgers. JB

Vor a Gauguin Picture zu Singen. Kurt M. Stein. FiBHP

Voronezh. "Anna Akhmatova", *tr. fr. Russian by* Tom Paulin. FaBoPV

Vorthy cit, von Vitsunday, A. Mr. and Mrs. Vite's Journey. *Unknown.* NOBL

Votaries know. A Poem for Integration. Alvin Saxon. PoBA

Vote, A, *sel.* Abraham Cowley.
  "This only grant me, that my means may lye."
  (Of Myself.) OBS

Votive Song. Edward Coate Pinkney. AA; AnAmPo

Vow, A. Allen Ginsberg. OBWP

Vow, The. Anthony Hecht. InPK; NePoEA; Prf

Vow. Abba Kovner, *tr. fr. Hebrew by* Warren Bargad *and* Stanley F. Chyet. IP

Vow. John Updike. NYBP

Vow-Breaker, The. Henry King. OBS

Vow of Washington, The. Whittier. PAH

Vow to Heavenly Venus, A. Joachim Du Bellay, *tr. fr. French by* Andrew Lang. AWP

Vow to Love Faithfully, Howsoever He Be Rewarded, A. Petrarch. *See* Sonnets to Laura: To Laura in Life.

Vowel Movements. Daryl Hine. PoA

Vowels. Rimbaud, *tr. fr. French by* Kenneth Koch. SOTW; TTTS

Vowels of Another Language, The. Tom Disch. PoA

Vowels plowed into other: opened ground. Seamus Heaney. *Fr.* Glanmore Sonnets, I. NoP

Vows, The. Andrew Marvell. TW

Vox Clero. *Unknown.* APAS

Vox Humana. Thom Gunn. NePoEA-2

Vox Oppressi, to the Lady Phipps. Richard Henchman. SCAP

Vox Populi. Dryden. *Fr.* The Medal [*or* Medall]. NOBE
  "Almighty crowd, thou shorten'st all dispute." OBS

Vox Populi, Vox Dei, *sels. Unknown.* FaBoPV
  "And yet not long ago."
  "I pray you, be not wroth."

Vox Ultima Crucis. John Lydgate. OBEV

"Voy wawm" said the dustman. Hymn to the Sun. Michael Roberts. FaBoCh; OxBTC

Voyage, The. Heine, *tr. fr. German by* John Todhunter. AWP

Voyage. István Kormos, *tr. fr. Hungarian by* Edwin Morgan. MHuP

Voyage, The. Denis Florence MacCarthy. *Fr.* The Voyage of St. Brendan. TIRV

Voyage. Josephine Miles. LiTM

Voyage, The. Edwin Muir. LiTM

Voyage, The. Charles Hubert Sisson. NPo

Voyage. Cesare Vivaldi, *tr. fr. Italian by* Lawrence R. Smith. NItP

Voyage. Stanislaw Wygodski, *tr. fr. Polish by* Isaac Komem. VWA

Voyage of Bran, The, *sels. Unknown, tr. fr. Old Irish by* Kuno Meyer.
  "Branch of the apple-tree from Emain, A." AnIL
  Song of the Woman, The. TIRV
  Worship of Cromm Cruaich, The. TIRV

Voyage of Jimmy Poo, The. James A. Emanuel. AmNP

Voyage of Life, The. Charles Bernstein. UL

Voyage of Life, The. Cynewulf, *tr. fr. Anglo-Saxon by* Charles W. Kennedy. *Fr.* Christ 2. AnOE; MOS

Voyage of Maeldune, The. Tennyson. PoEL-5

Voyage of St. Brendan, The, *sel.* Denis Florence MacCarthy.
  Voyage, The. TIRV

Voyage on the Thames, The. Pope. *See* Rape of the Lock, The: Not with more glories, in th' ethereal plain.

Voyage to the Isle of Love, A, *sel.* Aphra Behn.
  Dream, The. PBWP

Voyage to Tintern Abbey, A, *sel.* Sneyd Davies.
  Crooked bank still winds to something new, The. NOEC

Voyage West. Archibald MacLeish. VGW

Voyager upon life's sea. Paddle Your Own Canoe. Sarah K. Bolton. FaFP

Voyager's Prayer, A. *Unknown, tr. fr. Chippewa Indian.* WGRP, *tr. by* Tanner

Voyages, The. Gregory Orr. BLA

Voyages (I–VI), *sels.* Hart Crane. CMoP; NoAM; NOBA; NoP; TAP
  "Above the fresh ruffles of the surf." *Fr.* I. AmPP; MoP; MOS; NAAL-2; OxBA; PoE; VGW
  "And yet this great wink of eternity." *Fr.* II. AmPP; HAP; LiTM; MoAB; MoAmPo; MOS; OxBA; PoE; PPP; UnPo; VGW
  "Infinite consanguinity it bears." *Fr.* III. OxBA
  "Meticulous, past midnight in clear rime." *Fr.* V. NAAL-2; PoE
  "Where icy and bright dungeons lift." *Fr.* VI. HAP; MoAB; MoAmPo; UnPo

Voyages of Captain Cock, The. William Jay Smith. ErPo

Voyageur. R. E. Rashley. CaP

Voyeur. John Edward Hardy. ErPo

Voyeur's Dream. Barney Bush. HATNAP

Vuillard: "The Mother and Sister of the Artist." W. D. Snodgrass. CoAP

Vulcan contrive me such a cup. Upon Drinking in a Bowl. Earl of Rochester. OBS; OxBoLi; SeCV-2

Vulcan's Song. John Lyly. *Fr.* Sapho and Phao. EBEV; EIL
  (Song in Making of the Arrows.) OBSC

Vulgar Error, A. J. E. Thorold Rogers. FaBoEE

Vulgar of manner, overfed. Owed to New York. Byron Rufus Newton. BLPA; NBLV

Vulnerability. Bartolo Cattafi, *tr. fr. Italian by* Lawrence R. Smith. NItP

Vulnerary, A. Jonathan Williams. PoM

Vulture, The. Samuel Beckett. *Fr.* Echo's Bones. NOAM

Vulture, The. Hilaire Belloc. OxBChV; RHPC

Vulture. Robinson Jeffers. NAAL-2; NoAM; NOBA; NoP

Vulture. Kenneth Rexroth. *Fr.* A Bestiary. NNaP

Vulture and the Husbandman, The. A. C. Hilton. CenHV; FaBoCo

Vulture eats between his meals, The. The Vulture. Hilaire Belloc. OxBChV; RHPC

Vulture! Vulture in Your Mountains. Saul Tchernichowsky, *tr. fr. Hebrew by* Bernhard Frank. MHeP

Vultures, The. David Diop, *tr. fr. French by* Ulli Beier. PBA; TTY

Vultures are being spring-cleaned, The. Building Society Blues. Roger Roughton. EAS

Vultures waft circles. Remnant Ghosts at Dawn. Oliver La Grone. FB

Vusumzi's Song. L. T. Manyase, *tr. fr. Xhosa by* C. M. Mcanyangwa *and* Jack Cope. PeSA

W

W. James Reeves. ChTr; NTCP

W. H. Auden & Mantan Moreland. Al Young. NPGG

W. H. *Eheu!* Samuel Taylor Coleridge. FaBoEE

W. L. M. K. Francis Reginald Scott. NOBC

W. S. Landor. Marianne Moore. OBAL

W. W. Imamu Amiri Baraka. HeIP; NBP; NOBA; PoBA

Waäit till our Sally cooms in, fur thou mun a' sights to tell. The Northern Cobbler. Tennyson. EBEV

Wadasa Nakamoon, Vietnam Memorial. Ray A. Young Bear. HATNAP

Wade/ through black jade. The Fish. Marianne Moore. AmPP; FaBoWP; MoAB; MoAmPo; MoP; MOS; NAAL-2; NoAM; OxBA

Waders and Swimmers. Stanley Plumly. GeTw

Waement the deid. Coronach. Alexander Scott. OxBS

Waes-hael for [the] knight and [the] dame! King Arthur's Waes-hael. Robert Stephen Hawker. OBEV

Wae's me, wae's me. Cauld Lad of Hilton. *Unknown.* OxBoLi

   (Cauld Lad's Song, The.) ChTr

   (Ghost's Song, The.) FaBoCh

   (Song of the Cauld Lad of Hylton.) GBP

   (Wandering Spectre, The.) CH

Wafer; thin and hard and bitter pill I. To His Book. Leon Stokesbury. SM

Wag a leg, wag a leg. *Unknown.* OxNR

Waggon-Maker, The. John Masefield. EBEV

Waggoner, The. *Unknown.* GBP

Wagner. Rupert Brooke. FaBoTw; NOBL

Wagon Full of Thunder. Louis Oliver. HATNAP; STE

"Wagon Wheel Gap is a place I never saw." Localities. Carl Sandburg. AmFN

Wagoner of the Alleghanies, The, *sels.* Thomas Buchanan Read.

   Rising, The. PAH

   Valley Forge. PAH

Wagoner's Lad, The. *Unknown.* AmFP

Wagons. Jacob Glatstein, *tr. fr. Yiddish.* AYP, *tr. by* Benjamin *and* Barbara Harshav; PeBMYV, *tr. by* Chana Bloch.

Wahiawa is still. Leaving. Cathy Song. NoAM

Waif, The. Walter de la Mare. FaBoNo

Waifs. Vivian Virtue. PVCV

Waiheke 1972—Rocky Bay. Christina Beer. PeNZ

Waikato Railstop. Kendrick Smithyman. ATNZ

Waikato-Taniwha-Rau. Vincent O'Sullivan. PeNZ

Waikiki. Rupert Brooke. OBTV

Wail of Archy, The. Don Marquis. *Fr.* Archy and Mehitabel. FiBHP

Wail of Prometheus Bound, The. Aeschylus, *tr. fr. Greek by* Elizabeth Barrett Browning. *Fr.* Prometheus Bound. WGRP

Wail of the Divorced. Mary E. Tucker. CBWP-1

Wail, wail, Ah for Adonis! Lament for Adonis. Bion, *tr. by* John Addington Symonds. AWP

Waile whit ase whalles bon, A. The White Beauty. *Unknown.* MeEL

Wailing, wailing, wailing, the wind over land and sea. Rizpah. Tennyson. PoEL-5

Wailing wind doth not enough despair, The. Awake. Mary Elizabeth Coleridge. OBNC

Wailings of a maiden I recite, The. Wednesday; or, The Dumps. John Gay. *Fr.* The Shepherd's Week. OAEL-1

Waillie, waillie! *Unknown. See* Waly, Waly.

Wain upon the northern steep, The. Astronomy. A. E. Housman. OBWP

Waist thin as the purslane creeper. Peace Poem. Maturai Velacan, *tr. by* A. K. Ramanujan. PLW

Wait. Timothy Steele. PoA

Wait a Little! *Unknown.* NOCV

Wait a while—this is an evening shower. Kaya Shirao, *tr. fr. Japanese by* Hiroaki Sato. *Fr.* Twenty-one Hokku. FCEI

Wait for Me. Robert Creeley. NOBA; PPP

Wait for me. *Unknown, tr. fr. Japanese by* Burton Watson. *Fr.* Kangin Shu. FCEI

Wait for moonlight. Ryokan, *tr. by* Burton Watson. FCEI

Wait for the Wagon. *At. to* R. Bishop Buckley. PAH

Wait for the Wagon. *Unknown.* PAH

Wait here, and I'll be back, though the hours divide. Three Star Final. Conrad Aiken. OxBA

Wait, Kate! You skate at such a rate. To Kate, Skating Better than Her Date. David Daiches. ASP; FiBHP; NYBP; SD

Wait; the great horned owls. Owls. W. D. Snodgrass. Psk

Wait. This seems to be the kind of place. A Roman Temple. Umar Abu Risha, *tr. by* Issa Boullata *and* Thomas G. Ezzy. MAP

Wait till the darkness is deep. Wallada, *tr. fr. Arabic by* James Monroe *and* Deirdre Lashgari. WPOW

Wait till Then. Mark Van Doren. SO

Wait until I too "hang up my carriage." Hsieh Chin, *tr. fr. Chinese by* Jonathan Chaves. *Fr.* Parting from Liu Nan-chou. CoBLCP

Waitekauri Every Time! Edwin Edwards. PeNZ

Waiter, Please. *Unknown. See* Epicure, Dining at Crewe, An.

Waiters. Mary Ann Hoberman. RHPC

Waiting. John Burroughs. AA; AnAmPo; BLPA; FaBoBe; OHFP; WGRP

Waiting. Jane Cooper. TAP

Waiting. Hilary Corke. ErPo

Waiting. Robert Creeley. VGW

Waiting. Jacques Dupin, *tr. fr. French by* Paul Auster. RHTwFP

Waiting. John Freeman. CH

Waiting. W. E. Henley. *Fr.* In Hospital, II. NAEL-2

Waiting. Doris Mühringer, *tr. fr. German by* Beth Bjorklund. CoAuP

Waiting. Robert Pack. GOYP

Waiting, The. Whittier. WGRP

Waiting. Yevgeny Yevtushenko, *tr. fr. Russian by* Robin Milner-Gulland *and* Peter Levi. LLLT; UnAS

Waiting. Herbert Zand, *tr. fr. German by* Beth Bjorklund. CoAuP

Waiting beside the window while you were brushing. Eurydice. Sherod Santos. NAmP

Waiting Both. Thomas Hardy. MoAB; MoBrPo; OxBoLi; TTTS

Waiting Chords, The. Stephen Henry Thayer. AA

Waiting for a Second Time. Tauhindauli. STE

Waiting For Breakfast, While She Brushed Her Hair. Philip Larkin. NoAM

Waiting for Death. Mordecai Gebirtig, *tr. fr. Yiddish by* Joseph Leftwich. TrJP

Waiting for Fidel. John Agard. PBCV

Waiting for Her. Alden Nowlan. NeAC

Waiting for his turn. *Unknown, tr. by* Geoffrey Bownas *and* Anthony Thwaite. PeBJV

Waiting for Icarus. Muriel Rukeyser. NNaP

Waiting for Lilith. Jascha Kessler. VWA

Waiting for Love. Teika, *tr. fr. Japanese by* Steven D. Carter. WFTW

Waiting for Love in Vain. Tonna, *tr. fr. Japanese by* Steven D. Carter. WFTW

Waiting for me. Lady Ishikawa. *Fr.* Manyo Shu. PeBJV

Waiting for Robinson. Roberta Hill Whiteman. HATNAP

Waiting for the Barbarians. C. P. Cavafy, *tr. fr. Greek by* Edmund Keeley *and* Philip Sherrard. VMG

Waiting for the Bus. D. J. Enright. OxBTC

Waiting for the Dawning. *Unknown.* BLRP

Waiting for the Doctor. Colette Inez. IHMS

Waiting for the Emperor Tenji. Princess Nukada, *tr. fr. Japanese.* PBWP, *tr. by* Cid Corman *and* Susumu Kamaike

Waiting for the end, boys, waiting for the end. Just a Smack at Auden. William Empson. FaBoCo; LiTM; MoBrPo; UnPo

Waiting for the Ferry at Inchon. Liu E, *tr. fr. Chinese by* Jonathan Chaves. CoBLCP

Waiting for the gazelles. A Moorish Frigate: 2. Hans Warren, *tr. by* James S. Holmes. DuIn

Waiting for the morning breeze am I. Khwaja Mir Dard, *tr. fr. Urdu by* Ahmed Alli. *Fr.* Tarkib-Bund, II-IV. GoT

Waiting for the Pakeha. Alistair Campbell. ATNZ

Waiting for the Post. Dorothy Auchterlonie. CBAP

Waiting for the Rain. Felix Mnthali. WMBCH

Waiting for the Transformation. Judith Minty. TV

Waiting for the Wind. Donald Finkel. BLA

Waiting for Truth. Susan Griffin. GLP

Waiting for when the sun an hour or less. In Santa Maria del Popolo. Thom Gunn. CMoP; FaBoMo; GTBS-P; NePoEA-2; OxBC; PoE; QFR

Waiting for Winter. George Keithley. NPGG

Waiting for you. Prince Otsu. *Fr.* Manyo Shu. Ma

Waiting for you, I am filled with longing. Princess Nukada. *Fr.* Manyo Shu. FCEI

Waiting for you, I have not entered my bedroom. Princess Shikishi, *tr. fr. Japanese by* Hiroaki Sato. *Fr.* Seventy-eight Tanka. FCEI

Waiting for You to Come By. ' Simon J. Ortiz. CDW

Waiting in Front of the Columnar High School. Karl Shapiro. HAP

Waiting in the place where the cicadas turn the silence. White Light. Linda Gregg. NAmP

Waiting Inside. David Ignatow. CAPP

Waiting is the poem of waiting. On Arrival. Richard Howard. TAP

Waiting like a trap-door spider for a rookie sell-out. Baseball or the name game? Four Poems for *The St. Louis Sporting News.* Jack Spicer. PoM

Waiting on Basho as He Lay Ill. Joso, *tr. fr. Japanese by* Hiroaki Sato. *Fr.* Fifteen Hokku. FCEI

Waiting-Room, The. Robin Fulton. PoA

Waiting Rooms. Howard Nemerov. PoA

Waiting, the Hallways under Her Skin Thick with Dreamchildren. Lyn Lifshin. NeAC

Waiting to Be Fed. Ray A. Young Bear. CDW

Waiting to be served we look from the veranda. From the Other Shore. William Pitt Root. MAYP

Waiting today while planes roar over the seacoast. 1944—On the Invasion Coast. Jack Beeching. WaP

Waitomo. Kendrick Smithyman. ATNZ

Waitress, The/ takes our order. Somewhere Else. Paula Rankin. MAYP

Waitress, with eyes so marvellous black. Salad: After Browning. Mortimer Collins. *Fr.* Salad. Par

Waits, The. John Freeman. BoTP

Wait. that tastes good. already it is on the wing. Rainer Maria Rilke, *tr. fr. German by* Christopher Hawthorne. *Fr.* Sonnets to Orpheus. SOTW

Waka. Dogen, *tr. fr. Japanese by* Lucien Stryk *and* Takashi Ikemoto. ZPCJ

Waka. Sogyo, *tr. fr. Japanese by* Lucien Stryk *and* Takashi Ikemoto. ZPCJ

Waka. *Unknown, tr. fr. Japanese by* Lucien Stryk *and* Takashi Ikemoto. ZPCJ

Waka on Impermanence. Dogen, *tr. fr. Japanese by* Lucien Stryk *and* Takashi Ikemoto. ZPCJ

Waka on Kyosei's Raindrop Sound. Dogen, *tr. fr. Japanese by* Lucien Stryk *and* Takashi Ikemoto. ZPCJ

Waka on Seeing and Hearing Directly. Bunan, *tr. fr. Japanese by* Lucien Stryk *and* Takashi Ikemoto. ZPCJ

Waka on the Correct-Law Eye Treasury. Dogen, *tr. fr. Japanese by* Lucien Stryk *and* Takashi Ikemoto. ZPCJ

Waka on Zen Sitting. Dogen, *tr. fr. Japanese by* Lucien Stryk *and* Takashi Ikemoto. ZPCJ

Wake. Langston Hughes. OBAL

Wake! Omar Khayyám. *See* Rubáiyát of Omar Khayyám of Naishápúr, The: Wake, for the sun, who scattered [*or* scatter'd] into flight.

Wake All the Dead. Sir William Davenant. *Fr.* The Law against Lovers. ELP; FaBoCh; HAP; SeCePo

Wake. And my eyes stun. I Wake, My Friend, I. Faye Kicknosway. IHMS

Wake as you will, but wake in me. To Song. Olga Berggolts, *tr. by* Daniel Weissbort. BoWoP

Wake at the Well, The. *Unknown.* GBP

Wake, child with the flute. Mirabai, *tr. fr. Hindi by* Willis Barnstone *and* Usha Nilsson. BoWoP

Wake Cry. Waring Cuney. BANP

Wake! for the sun has driven in equal flight. The Golfer's Rubaiyat. H. W. Boynton. BXAP

Wake, for the sun, who scattered [*or* scatter'd] into flight. Omar Khayyám, *tr. fr. Persian by* Edward Fitzgerald. *Fr.* The Rubáiyát of Omar Khayyám of Naishápúr. FF; NAEL-2; OBNC; ViBoPo (Wake!) FaPON

Wake, friend, from forth thy lethargy! The drum. An Epistle to a Friend, to Persuade Him to the Wars. Ben Jonson. TEP

Wake, Hercules, awake: but heave up thy black eye. Ben Jonson. *Fr.* Pleasure Reconciled to Virtue. NAEL-1

Wake, Israel, wake! Recall today. The Banner of the Jew. Emma Lazarus. AA; TrJP

Wake me up at five-thirty please. Hotel. Adam Wazyk. VWA, *tr. by* Isaac Komem

Wake not, but hear me, love! Lew Wallace. *Fr.* Ben Hur. AA

Wake Not for the World-heard Thunder. A. E. Housman. CMoP; NoAM

Wake, now my love, awake; for it is time. Spenser. *Fr.* Epithalamion. GBL

Wake of William Orr, The. William Drennan. TIRV

Wake: the silver dusk returning. Reveille. A. E. Housman. *Fr.* A Shropshire Lad, IV. CMoP; FaFP; FPL; LiTB; LiTM; MoAB; MoBrPo; NoP; PoLF; SoSe

Wake the Song of Jubilee. Leonard Bacon. AH

Wake up, dear boy that holds the flute! Mirabai, *tr. fr. Hindi by* Usha Nilsson. WPOW

Wake-up Niggers. Don L. Lee. PoBA

Wake up, wake up, darlin' Cory. Darling Cory. *Unknown.* AmFP

Waked by the Gospel's Powerful Sound. Samson Occom. AH

Wakefield Second Shepherds Play, The. *Unknown. See* Second Shepherds' Play, The.

Wakeful all night I lay and thought of God. Renunciation. Wathen Mark Wilks Call. WGRP

Wakeful for last year's call that I loved. Teika, *tr. fr. Japanese by* Hiroaki Sato. *Fr.* Eighty-four Tanka. FCEI

Wakeful in the Township. Elizabeth Riddell. PoAu-2

Wakeful, vagrant, restless thing. The Power of Fancy. Philip Freneau. AmPP

"Waken from your sleep." The Summons. W. W. Eustace Ross. CaP

Waken, lords and ladies gay. Hunting Song. Sir Walter Scott. *Fr.* The Lay of the Last Minstrel. EnRP; GN; GTBS; GTBS-P; TrGrPo; WiR

Wakening, The. *Unknown. See* On a Time the Amorous Silvy.

Wakepick I. Kristjana Gunnars. NOBC

Wakes that boats make, The. The Ways. Louis Zukofsky. PoE

Waking. Patrick MacDonogh. NeIP

Waking. Hugh Maxton. BIrV; CIP

Waking. Lilian Moore. RHPC

Waking. Katharine Pyle. OBCA

Waking, The. Theodore Roethke. AmPP; CAPP; CoAP; CRP; HAP; HCAP; HeIP; InPK; InPS; LiTM; MoAmPo; MoP; NAAL-2; NIP; NoAM; NOBA; NoP; OPOP; PPP; PrIm; SM; SoSe; TAP; TwCP; WeW

Waking. C. H. Sisson. NPo

Waking Alone. *Unknown.* MeEL

Waking [*or* Walking] alone in a multitude of loves when morning's light. On the Marriage of a Virgin. Dylan Thomas. EnLoPo (Marriage of a Virgin, The.) ErPo

Waking an Angel. Philip Levine. NaP

Waking at Dusk from a Nap. William Matthews. AnAn

Waking at morn, with the accustomed sigh. On the Death of His Son Vincent. Leigh Hunt. NOBVV

Waking at this broad window I discover. The Henri Rousseau Style. Lauris Edmond. ATNZ

Waking Bird Refutes, The. Allen Curnow. ATNZ

Waking, Child, While You Slept. Ethel Anderson. *Fr.* Bucolic Eclogues. PoAu-2; WPE

Waking Early Sunday Morning. Robert Lowell. FaBoMo; HCAP; NOBA; OxBC

Waking from a bad dream, and thrashing out. Dream Time. Anthony Thwaite. DiPo

Waking from a nap. Buson, *tr. fr. Japanese by* Hiroaki Sato. *Fr.* Eighty-seven Hokku. FCEI

Waking from a Nap. Ni Tsan, *tr. fr. Chinese by* Jonathan Chaves. CoBLCP

Waking from a Nap on the Beach. May Swenson. NTCP; PCP; RFM

Waking from Sleep. Robert Bly. CAPP; EAS; NOBA; NoP

Waking from spring dreams. Reading an "Ode to a Widow." Natsume Seibi, *tr. fr. Japanese by* Hiroaki Sato. *Fr.* Twenty-seven Hokku. FCEI

Waking, he found himself in a train, andante. Slow Movement. Louis MacNeice. FaBCIP

Waking ("I strolled across/ An open field"), The. Theodore Roethke. RFM; TTTS

Waking in drifts of whiteness! head to toe. Hospital Breakfast: With Grace After. John Frederick Nims. BLA

Waking in the Blue. Robert Lowell. CoAP; HCAP; MoAmPo; UnPo

Waking in the Dark. Dorothy Livesay. NOBC

Waking in the Dark. Adrienne Rich. FaBoWP

Waking Jed. C. K. Williams. DiL

Waking Jesus sudden riding a scream like a/ train. I Scream You Scream. Don McKay. NOBC

Waking on a Greyhound. Gordon Henry. STE
Waking one morning, he was alarmed to find. He Smelt the Smell of
     Death within the Marrow. Louis Johnson. ATNZ
Waking, the Love Poem Sighs. Jim Hall. GOYP
Waking this morning. This Morning. Muriel Rukeyser. BoWoP; NMM
Waking to the clatter of hot-plate kettle. The Years. John Ennis. CIP
Waking Up. *Unknown.* BoTP
Waking Up: A Song. Yip Wai-lim, *tr. fr. Chinese by* Dominic Cheung.
     IFON
Waking with morning, I note the empty. The Landscape of Love.
     Thomas Cole. NePoAm
Waking's urgency, that sets. Frühling. K. O. Arvidson. *Fr.* The Four
     Last Songs of Richard Strauss at Takahe Creek above the Kaipara, I.
     ATNZ
Wakonda! Talako! deathonic turkey gobbling in the soft-footpatch night!
     Spontaneous Requiem for the American Indian. Gregory Corso.
     MAT; PoM
Walam [*or* Wallum] Olum; or, Red Score, *sels. Unknown, tr. fr.*
     Delaware (Lenape) Indian.
     "After the Seizer there were ten chiefs, and there was much warfare
     south and east." *Tr. by* Daniel G. Brinton. OBVE
     Deluge, The. *Tr. by* C. S. Rafinesque. LiTA
     On the Creation and Ontogony. *Tr. by* C. S. Rafinesque. LiTA
Wald my gude lady luve me best. The Garmont of Gude Ladies. Robert
     Henryson. GoTS
Waldeinsamkeit. Emerson. NOBA; WGRP
Walden, *sel.* Henry David Thoreau.
     Light-winged Smoke, Icarian Bird. *Fr.* ch. 13. NOBA; TAP
     (Smoke.) AA; AWP; HeIP; NoP; OxBA
Walden in July. Donald Junkins. NYBP
Walden Pond/ All those noxious gases rising from it. Jack Spicer. *Fr.*
     Graphemics, 7. VGW
Waldere 1 (". . .heard him gladly"). *Unknown, tr. fr. Anglo-Saxon by*
     Charles W. Kennedy. AnOE
Waldere 2 ("Waldere addressed him, the warrior brave"). *Unknown, tr.*
     by Charles W. Kennedy. AnOE
Waldere addressed him, the warrior brave. *Unknown, tr. by* Charles W.
     Kennedy. AnOE
Wales England wed; so I was bred. An Autobiography. Ernest Rhys.
     OBEV; OBWVE
Wales Visitation. Allen Ginsberg. CAPP; NNaP; NOBA; NYBP; Prf
Wales, which I have never seen. For My Ancestors. Rolfe Humphries.
     PoRA
Walk, A. Ilse Aichinger, *tr. fr. German by* Beth Bjorklund. CoAuP
Walk, The. Conrad Aiken. KS
Walk, The. Celia Gilbert. PPR
Walk, The. Thomas Hardy. CMoP; NAEL-2; PoE; PoEL-5; PrIm
Walk. Frank Horne. BPo
Walk, A. Pierre Jean Jouve, *tr. fr. French by* Keith Bosley. RHTwFP
Walk, A. Hedwig Lachmann, *tr. fr. German by* Jethro Bithell. TrJP
Walk, A. Eeva-Liisa Manner, *tr. fr. Finnish by* Aili Jarvenpa. SOP
Walk. Brian Merriman, *tr. fr. Modern Irish by* Brendan Behan. *Fr.* The
     Midnight Court. BIrV
Walk, The. W. W. Eustace Ross, *tr. fr. Greek.* SD
Walk, A. Gary Snyder. NOBA
Walk, A. Nikolai Alekseevich Zabolotsky, *tr. fr. Russian by* Daniel
     Weissbort. RB
Walk by the Charles, A. Adrienne Rich. NePoEA; NYBP
Walk, Damn You, Walk! William de Vere. PoLF
Walk east. Dawn polishes the sky. Direction. Roberta Hill. CDW
Walk in Early March, A. Paul Mariani. DiL
Walk in Kyoto, A. Earle Birney. GoYe
Walk in March, A. Tim Reynolds. MAT
Walk in Spring, A. K. C. Lart. BoTP
Walk in the half light of rain. Monsoon. Kenneth Slade Alling.
     NePoAm
Walk in the Precepts. Moses Ibn Ezra, *tr. fr. Hebrew by* Solomon Solis-
     Cohen. TrJP
Walk in Würzburg, A. William Plomer. NYBP
Walk in your sleep beyond Yeppoon. Assignation with a Somnambulist.
     John Manifold. CBAP
Walk into the prison, that domed citadel. My Lessons in the Jail.
     Miriam Waddington. MoCV
Walk, Mary, down de Lane. *Unknown.* BoAN-2
Walk on the Moon. N. Scott Momaday. CRP
Walk out into your country. Who Shall Die. James A. Randall, Jr..
     BPo
Walk proud, walk straight, let your thoughts race. Musings. Patty L.
     Harjo. NOVW
"Walk right in, Brother Wilson—how you feelin' today?" The Rain Song.
     Alex Rogers. BANP

Walk Slowly. Adelaide Love. BLPA
Walk this mile in silence. Pastourelle. Donald Jeffrey Hayes.
     AmNP
Walk this way mudra. A glance. Separation of events. Heavy Clouds
     Passing before the Sun. Jean Day. IAT
Walk to the Eastern River Bank, A. Kao Ch'i, *tr. fr. Chinese by* Jonathan
     Chaves. CoBLCP
Walk Together Children. *Unknown.* BPo
Walk with de Mayor of Harlem. David Henderson. PoBA
Walk with the sun. Dream Song. Lewis Alexander. PoBA; PoNe
Walk with thy fellow-creatures: note the hush. Henry Vaughan. WGRP
Walk with Tom Jefferson, A. Philip Levine. BAP
Walken Hwomme at Night. William Barnes. NOBVV
Walker, a large two-hundred-fifty pound blackman. Christmas 1962.
     Paul Mariah. GLP
Walker River Night, The. Adrian C. Louis. STE
Walking. Thomas Traherne. *See* To Walk Abroad.
Walking a flatland and weary. Buson, *tr. fr. Japanese by* Hiroaki Sato.
     Fr. Eighty-seven Hokku. FCEI
Walking a short lane. A Drunkard. Fei Ma, *tr. by* Dominic Cheung.
     IFON
Walking against the Wind. Jon Stallworthy. OxBC
Walking all the day. Song for Ireland. Phil *and* June Colclough.
     OBET
Walking alone in a multitude of love when morning's light. *See* Waking
     alone. . .
Walking along the Hudson. Donald Petersen. CoAP
Walking along the Sea of Galilee. Dovid Knut, *tr. fr. Russian.* VWA,
     tr. by John Glad
Walking among my own this windy morning. The Spring Vacation.
     Derek Mahon. FaBCIP
Walking among sceptre-headed. Walking-Sticks and Paperweights and
     Watermarks. Marianne Moore. PoA
Walking Around. Pablo Neruda, *tr. fr. Spanish by* Robert Bly.
     EAS
Walking around in the park. Toads Revisited. Philip Larkin. CMoP;
     NOBL; SaC
Walking at last by the tame little edge of the sea. Evening before Rain.
     L. A. G. Strong. OxBTC
Walking at Night. Amory Hare. PoLF
Walking at Night. Henry Treece. WaP
Walking at night in a hat fitted with twelve candles. Vincent Van Gogh.
     William Jay Smith. EyDe
Walking at night on asphalt campus. Death News. Allen Ginsberg.
     MoP
Walking becomes unbearable, another year. Antonio Porta, *tr. fr. Italian*
     by Lawrence R. Smith. *Fr.* Human Relations. NItP
Walking by map, I chose unwonted ground. On the Hall at Stowey.
     Charles Tomlinson. CMoP; PoE
Walking docile as you do down the empty street. Abasis. Christopher
     Middleton. *Fr.* Herman Moon's Hourbook. NePoEA-2
Walking down Jalan Thamrin. R. F. Brissenden. CBAP
Walking down to eat my meal. Ozaki Hosai, *tr. fr. Japanese by* Hiroaki
     Sato. *Fr.* One Hundred Haiku in Free Form. FCEI
Walking downhill from Suilven (a fine day, for once). No Accident.
     Norman MacCaig. PoSH
Walking eight hundred. Removal: Last Part. Carroll Arnett. VoR
Walking for the first time. Echo. Leonard Clark. Mes
Walking home at night. Ernst David, *tr. by* Beth Bjorklund. CoAuP
Walking Home at Night. Daniel Weissbort. VWA
Walking, I heard the water dripping, running in the gutter. Partly to My
     Cat. Ellen Bass. NMM
Walking in a Meadowe Greene. *Unknown.* BoLoP; ErPo
Walking in a Swamp. David Wagoner. HAP
Walking in a valley green. The Shepherd's Ode. Robert Greene. *Fr.*
     Tullie's Love. OBSC
Walking in the Country outside T'ai-yüan on a Spring Day. Yang Chi, *tr.*
     fr. Chinese by Jonathan Chaves. CoBLCP
Walking in the 15th Century. Daniel Halpern. NAmP
Walking Late. John Montague. CIP
Walking next day upon the fatal shore. Cyril Tourneur. *Fr.* The
     Atheist's Tragedy. WaaP
Soldier's Death, A. SeCePo
Walking north toward the point, I come on a dead seal. The Dead Seal
     near McClure's Beach. Robert Bly. NNaP; NU
Walking often beside the waves.' Coleridge. R. S. Thomas. TOF
Walking on a child's tender feet. I've Never Come Away, You Know.
     Anna Hajnal, *tr. by* Jascha Kessler. FOC
Walking on Sunday. Richard Murphy. IPY
Walking on the Green Grass. *Unknown.* AmFP
Walking on Water. James Dickey. NePoEA-2

Walking Out. Betty Adcock. MT
Walking out, I flushed some meadowlarks. The Duck Pond at Mini's
	Pasture, a Dozen Years Later. Philip Dow. AmPA; NPGG
Walking out in the late March midnight. Thorn Leaves in March. W. S.
	Merwin. TwCP
Walking out of the "big E." Before the Stuff Comes Down. Gary
	Snyder. HeIP
Walking Outside the City Walls. Pien Kung, tr. fr. Chinese by Jonathan
	Chaves. CoBLCP
Walking Parker Home. Bob Kaufman. PoBA
Walking Past Paul Blackburn's Apt. on 7th St. Diane Wakoski. TAP
Walking Road, The. Richard Hughes. OBMV
Walking Song. William E. Hickson. OxBChV
Walking-Sticks and Paperweights and Watermarks. Marianne Moore.
	PoA
Walking swiftly with a dreadful duchess. Infelice. Stevie Smith.
	FaBoWP
Walking the Beach. Sarah Youngblood. IHMS
Walking the New York Bedrock Alive in the Sea of Information. Gary
	Snyder. BAP
Walking the small oval of Gibbs Pond. I Move to Random Consolations.
	William Heyen. AmPA
Walking the suburbs in the afternoon. Suburban Dreams. Edwin Muir.
	OxBTC
Walking the town as if I owned it all. Severance of Connections, 1946.
	L. E. Sissman. Fr. In and Out. NYBP; TwCP
Walking the Wide Road. Unknown, tr. fr. Chinese by Burton Watson.
	CoBCP
Walking the Wilderness. William Stafford. NaP
Walking this field I remember. The Premonition. Theodore Roethke.
	CAPP
Walking through a Cornfield in the Middle of Winter I Stumble over a
	Cow Pie and Think of the Sixties Press. Barbara Harr.
	BXAP
Walking through a field. Cornfield Myth. Mary Goose. STE
Walking through twisted hollow pathways. Peter Blue Cloud. VoR
Walking to Bellrock. Michael Ondaatje. NOBC
Walking to-day by a cottage I shed tears. Scazons. C. S. Lewis.
	EBEV
Walking to Mou-chou at Dawn. Chu Yi-tsun, tr. fr. Chinese by Chang
	Yin-nan. WFTU
Walking to Sleep. Richard Wilbur. LCAP; NYBP
Walking to the Museum. Bone Thoughts on a Dry Day: Chicago.
	George Starbuck. GoYe; NYBP; TwCP
Walking to the Temple of Precious Light. Wen Cheng-ming, tr. fr.
	Chinese by Jonathan Chaves. CoBLCP
Walking to your place for a love feast. The Same Inside. Anna
	Swirszczynska, tr. by Czeslaw Milosz. PwPP
Walking Tour, The. W. H. Auden. Fr. Paid on Both Sides. CMoP
	(Chorus: "To throw away the key and walk away.") MoBrPo
Walking towards the house, the terraces. Sestina in Time of Winter.
	Patrick Anderson. PoA
Walking up the driftwood beach at day's end. Flood Year. Judith
	Wright. NoAM
Walking West. William Stafford. RB
Walking Westward, sels. C. K. Stead.
	"Art has nothing to do with perfect circles." ATNZ
	Walking Westward. PeNZ
Walking with God. William Cowper. EnRP; NOCV; NOEC; PoEL-3;
	TEP; TOF
	(O [or Oh] for a Closer Walk with God.) FiP
Walking with God. Unknown. BLRP
Walking with Lulu in the Wood. Naomi Lazard. NYBP
Walking with R. B. Evan Jones. PVCV
Walking with the moon. Lamenting Life. Ma Chih-yüan, tr. fr. Chinese
	by Jonathan Chaves. Fr. Three Poems to the Tune "Ssu-k'uai yü", 3.
	CoBLCP
Walking with you. Friend. Gwendolyn Brooks. CNA
Walking with you and another lady. A Dream of Jealousy. Seamus
	Heaney. FaBCIP
Walking with Your Eyes Shut. William Stafford. GOYP
Walking Wounded. Vernon Scannell. OBWP
Walks in a Forest, sel. Thomas Gisborne.
	Spring. PBBP
"Walks in graveyards." Sunday Graveyard. Maura Stanton. NAmP
Walky-talky Jenny. Unknown. AS
Wall, The. Ludvik Askenazy, tr. fr. Czech. VWA
Wall, The. Gwendolyn Brooks. Two Dedications. PoBA
	"South of success and east of gloss and glass are." PoNe
Wall, The. Michel Deguy, tr. fr. French by Clayton Eshleman.
	RHTwFP

Wall, The. David Gascoyne. PoPo
Wall, The. William Hawkins. MoCV
Wall, The. David Jones. PoA
Wall, A./ A blunt wall of human backs, arms, legs. In the Subway. A.
	Leyeles, tr. fr. Yiddish by Benjamin and Barbara Harshav. Fr. New
	York. AYP
Wall, The. Eve Merriam. TrJP
Wall, The. Eugenio Montale, tr. fr. Italian by Maurice English, PFI
Wall, The. Arthur L. Phelps. CaP
Wall, The. Henry Reed. LiTB
Wall, The. Tadeusz Rozewicz, tr. fr. Polish by Czeslaw Milosz. PwPP
Wall, A. Charles Simic. HCAP
Wall, The. Cesare Vivaldi, tr. fr. Italian by Lawrence R. Smith. NItP
Wall, Cave, and Pillar Statements, after Asôka. Alan Dugan. CoAP
Wall continues, The. Before the Actual Cold. Ray A. Young Bear.
	VoR
Wall-Flower, The. Henrik Arnold Thaulov Wergeland, tr. fr. Norwegian
	by Sir Edmund Gosse. AWP
Wall is blackened, The. Encounters. Faiz Ahmad Faiz, tr. by Mahmood
	Jamal. PBMUP
Wall, no! I can't tell whar he lives. Jim Bludso of the Prairie Belle.
	John Milton Hay. AA; AnAmPo; BeLS; FaBoBe; FaFP
Wall of China, The. Padraic Colum. GrPl
Wall of stone against a cloudless sky, A/ a mountain stream by a gate
	gleams bright. An Inscription for a Painting: "A Forest in the Frost."
	Yün Shou-p'ing, tr. by Irving Lo. WFTU
Wall of stone against a cloudless sky, A/ a mountain stream by a trail
	hangs in the void. Early Summer, Jen-tzu Year, in Playful Imitation
	of Ts'ao Yün-hsi. Yün Shou-p'ing, tr. by Irving Lo. WFTU
Wall of Tomorrow, The. Orkhan Muyassar, tr. fr. Arabic by Lena
	Jayyusi and Samuel Hazo. MAP
Wall of Weeping, The, sels. Edmond Fleg, tr. fr. French by Humbert
	Wolfe. TrJP
	End of Sorrow, The.
	Wandering Jew Comes to the Wall, The.
Wall of woodland overlooks me, A. Unknown. Fr. Four Glosses.
	NOIV
Wall Painting by Wu Wei, A. Wang T'ing-hsiang, tr. fr. Chinese by
	Jonathan Chaves. Fr. Miscellaneous Poems on Spirit-Valley Temple.
	CoBLCP
Wall Rev. Jackson MacLow. LP
Wall Shadows. Carl Sandburg. WSC
Wall should be low, as to say, The. The Wall. Arthur L. Phelps.
	CaP
Wall Street. A. Leyeles, tr. fr. Yiddish by Benjamin and Barbara
	Harshav. Fr. New York. AYP
Wallabout Martyrs, The. Walt Whitman. GOA
Wallace, The, sels. Henry the Minstrel.
	Burning of the Barns of Ayr, The. OxBLMV
	Description of Wallace, A. Fr. IX. GoTS
		(Schir William Wallace.) OxBS
	Wallace's Lament for the Graham. Fr. X. GoTS
		(Lament for the Graham.) OxBS
Wallace commaunde a burges for to get. The Burning of the Barns of
	Ayr. Henry the Minstrel. Fr. The Wallace. OxBLMV
Wallace stature of greatness [or gretnes], and of hicht [or hycht]. A
	Description of Wallace. Henry the Minstrel. Fr. The Wallace, IX.
	GoTS
	(Schir William Wallace.) OxBS
Wallace Stevens, what's he done? The Rouse for Stevens. Theodore
	Roethke. OBAL
Wallace's Lament for the Graham. Henry the Minstrel. Fr. The
	Wallace, X. GoTS
	(Lament for the Graham.) OxBS
Walled-in. In the Subway ("Walled-in"). A. Leyeles, tr. fr. Yiddish by
	Benjamin and Barbara Harshav. Fr. New York. AYP
Wallet gone completely empty. Ozaki Hosai, tr. fr. Japanese by Hiroaki
	Sato. Fr. One Hundred Haiku in Free Form. FCEI
Wallflower to a Moonbeam. Louis Untermeyer. BXAP
Walloping Window-Blind, The. Charles Edward Carryl. Fr. Davy and
	the Goblin. NA, fr. ch. 8; NBLV, fr. ch. 8; OBCA, fr. ch. 8.
	(Nautical Ballad, A.) FaPON; OBAL
	("Oh, a capital ship for an ocean trip.") MoShBr
Wallowing in this bloody sty. The Drunken Fisherman. Robert Lowell.
	AmPP; CMoP; LiTA; LiTM; NOBA; OxBA; VGW
Wallpaper, The. Sir Edmund Gosse. Mes
Wallpaper of Mr. R. K., The. Max Jacob, tr. fr. French by Andrei
	Codrescu. RHTwFP
Walls. C. P. Cavafy, tr. fr. Modern Greek by Rae Dalven.
	TrJP

Walls are down to window height, The. At a Ruined Croft. John Manson. PoSH
Walls are made of rain, The. The city's walls. Cant. Imamu Amiri Baraka. NAAL-2
Walls are made of water, pillared by air, The. Ravidas, *tr. by* John Stratton Hawley *and* Mark Juergensmeyer. SSI
Walls are white and the psychiatrists, The. Poetic Institution. Jotie T'Hooft, *tr. by* James S. Holmes. DuIn
Walls divide us from water and from light, The. The City. Charles Brasch. *Fr.* Nineteen Thirty-Nine. ATNZ
Walls Do Not Fall, The, *sels.* Hilda Doolittle ("H. D.").
  "Incident here and there, An." NAAL-2; OBWP
  "Now it appears very clear." NAAL-2
  "O heart, small urn." LLLT
  "Sirius/ what mystery is this?." PBWP
  "We have had too much consecration." NAAL-2
  "We have seen how the most amiable." BoWoP; PBWP
Walls have been shaded for so many years, The. The Soldier Walks under the Trees of the University. Randall Jarrell. OxBA; WaP
Walls. . .iridescent with eyes. The Fifth-Floor Window. Lola Ridge. WPE
Walls of Ice. Janet Campbell Hale. STE
Walls of Jericho, The. Blanche Taylor Dickinson. CDC
Walls of My House, The. Ilse Tielsch, *tr. fr. German by* Beth Bjorklund. CoAuP
Walls of stone, the floor of muddy stone, The. On Broadway. A. Leyeles, *tr. fr. Yiddish by* Benjamin *and* Barbara Harshav. *Fr.* New York. AYP
Walls of the house are paper thin, The. Domestic Quarrel. Sally McInerney. GrPl
Walls of the maelstrom are painted with trees, The. Charles Madge. EAS
Walls of Urbino, The. Paolo Volponi, *tr. fr. Italian by* Lawrence R. Smith. NItP
Walls surrounding them they never saw, The. The Wall. Donald Justice. CRP
Walnut bark, walnut sap. Dogget Gap. *Unknown.* AmFP
Walnut in a walnut shell. Bye Baby Walnut. Norma Farber. TSS
Walnut Tree, The. David McCord. OBCA
Walnutry. Robert Morgan. MT
Walrus, The. Michael Flanders. RHPC
Walrus and the Carpenter, The. "Lewis Carroll." *Fr.* Through the Looking-Glass, *ch.* 4. BeLS; BLPA; FaBoBe; FaBoCo; FaBoNo; FaBV; FaFP; FaPON; FiBHP; FPL; GN; LiTB; NA; NAEL-2; NoAM; NOBL; NOBVV; OxBChV; PoRA; TEP
Walrus Hunting. Aua, *tr. fr. Eskimo.* WTO
Walrus lives on icy floes, The. The Walrus. Michael Flanders. RHPC
Walrus stretches forth a wrinkled hand, The. The Kingsfisher's Boxing Gloves. James Fenton. NoAM
Walsingham[e]. *See* As You [*or* Ye] Came from the Holy Land of Walsingham.
Walsinghame's Song. James Hogg. BXAP
Walt Whitman. Emanuel Carnevali. PoA
Walt Whitman. Edwin Honig. TAP
Walt Whitman. Harrison Smith Morris. AA
Walt Whitman. E. A. Robinson. OxBA
Walt Whitman. Francis Howard Williams. AA
Walt Whitman, a kosmos, of Manhattan the son. Walt Whitman. *Fr.* Song of Myself, XXIV. NoP; SCV
Walt Whitman at Bear Mountain. Louis Simpson. CAPP; LiTM; NePoEA-2; PoCH
Walt Whitman at the Reburial of Poe. Nicholas Christopher. MAYP
Walter de la Mare Tells the Listener about Jack and Jill. Louis Untermeyer. *Fr.* Mother Goose Up-to-Date. MoAmPo
Walter Jenks' Bath. William Meredith. HoPM
Walter Lesly. *Unknown.* ESPB
Walter Rawley of the Middle Temple, in Commendation of the Steele Glasse. Sir Walter Ralegh. *See* In Commendation of George Gascoigne's Steel Glass.
Walter Scott. Gloria A. Maxson. SoTCo
Walthena. Elisabeth Peck. AmFN
Waltz, The, *sel.* Byron.
  Muse of the many-twinkling feet! whose charms. OBSV
Waltz, The. Hilary Corke. NYBP
Waltz, The. Edith Sitwell. *Fr.* Facade. OAEP
Waltz against the Mountains. Thomas Hornsby Ferril. VGW
Waltzer in the House, The. Stanley Kunitz. ErPo; NYBP; RHPC
Waltzing Matilda. Andrew Barton Paterson. CBAP; ChTr; GBP; PoAu-1
Waly, waly! bairns are bonny. A Scottish Proverb. *Unknown.* FaBoUs
Waly, Waly ("O waly, waly, up the bank"). *Unknown.* EnLoPo; EnSB; FaBoBa; GBP; HAP; OBEV; OxBS

(Forsaken Bride, The.) GTBS; GTBS-P
(Jamie Douglas.) ESPB
(Lord Douglas.) OxBB
(O Waly, Waly.) ELP; GoTS; OBS
(Waly, Waly, Love Be Bonny.) PrIm
Waly, Waly ("When cockle shells turn silver bells"). *Unknown.* AmFP
  (Waillie, waillie!) AS
Wan/ Swan. The Bereaved Swan. Stevie Smith. FaBoNo; FaBoTw
Wan, fragile faces of joy! Home-Thoughts from France. Isaac Rosenberg. MMA
Wan leafs shak, atour us like the snaw, The. Farewell to Dostoevski. "Hugh MacDiarmid." *Fr.* A Drunk Man Looks at the Thistle. NAEL-2
Wanaka, mother of Clutha. The Shag. Ellen Duggan. PeNZ
Wander-Lovers, The. Richard Hovey. AA
Wanderer, The. W. H. Auden. CMoP; LiTB; MoP; NoAM; RB; SOTW; WeW
Wanderer, The, *sels.* Christopher John Brennan.
  Come Out, Come Out, Ye Souls That Serve. PoAu-1
  How Old Is My Heart. PoAu-1
  I Cry to You as I Pass Your Windows. PoAu-1
  Land I Came Thro' Last, The. PoAu-1
  O Desolate Eves. PoAu-1
  "When window-lamps had dwindled, then I rose." CBAP
Wanderer, The. John Masefield. BrPo
Wanderer, The, *sel.* Roland Robinson.
  "I reached that waterhole, its mud designed." CBAP
Wanderer, The. *Unknown, tr. fr. Anglo-Saxon by* Charles W. Kennedy. AnOE; NAWM-1; OAEL-1; TEP, *tr. by* Mark Caldwell.
Wanderer, The. Claude Vigée, *tr. fr. French.* VWA, *tr. by* Anthony Rudolf.
Wanderer, The. Wordsworth. *Fr.* The Excursion, I. EnRP, *abr.* (Ruined Cottage, The, *diff. version.*) NoP; OAEL-2
Wanderer, The. "Yehoash," *tr. fr. Yiddish by* Isidore Goldstick. TrJP
Wanderer Recalls the Past, The. Wordsworth. *Fr.* The Excursion, I. OBNC
Wanderers, The. Robert Browning. *Fr.* Paracelsus, IV. OBEV
Wanderers. Charles Stuart Calverley. CenHV
Wanderers. Thomas Curtis Clark. TrPWD
Wanderers, chosen of God. Chosen of God. Stefan Zweig, *tr. fr. German by* Eden *and* Cedar Paul. *Fr.* Jeremiah. TrJP
Wanderer's Litany, A. Arthur Stringer. WGRP
Wanderer's Night-Songs, *sels.* Goethe, *tr. fr. German.*
  "O'er all the hill-tops." *Fr.* II. AWP
  (Second Poem the Night-Walker Wrote, The.) NU, *tr. by* Robert Bly.
  "Over every hill." *Tr. by* Arthur Hugh Clough. OBD
  "Thou that from the heavens art." *Fr.* I. AWP
Wanderer's Song, A. John Masefield. MoAB; MoBrPo
Wanderers, wanderers are we. Emigrant Song. "S. Ansky", *tr. by* Joseph Leftwich. TrJP
Wanderin'. *Unknown.* AS, B *vers.*
Wandering above a sea of glass. Down on My Luck. Arthur Rex Dugard Fairburn. ATNZ; PeNZ
Wandering albatross rides the wind, The. The Celtic Albatross. Alan Bold. NPo
Wandering by the heave of the town park, wondering. On the Closing of Millom Ironworks. Norman Nicholson. FaBoTw
Wandering Chorus. Alquit, B., *tr. fr. Yiddish by* Howard Schwartz. VWA
Wandering, in autumn, the woods of boyhood. Gold Glade. Robert Penn Warren. CRP
Wandering Jack. Emile Jacot. BoTP
Wandering Jew, The. Eloise Bibb. CBWP-4
Wandering Jew, The. E. A. Robinson. QFR
Wandering Jew, The. Benjamin Fondane, *tr. fr. French by* Edouard Roditi. VWA
Wandering Jew, The. Robert Mezey. NePoEA-2; VWA
Wandering Jew Comes to the Wall, The. Edmond Fleg, *tr. fr. French by* Humbert Wolfe. *Fr.* The Wall of Weeping. TrJP
Wandering Jew once met a man, A. The Eternal Jew. Jacob Cohen, *tr. by* I. M. Lask. TrJP
Wandering Jews. Nancy Keesing. VWA
Wandering Knight's Song, The. John Gibson Lockhart. ChTr
Wandering Lunatic Mind, The. Edward Carpenter. WGRP
Wandering Maiden; or, True Love at Length United, The. *Unknown.* CoMu
Wandering Outlaw, The. Byron. *Fr.* Childe Harold's Pilgrimage, III. FiP
Wandering oversea dreamer. Prayer after World War. Carl Sandburg. VGW

Wandering Shepherdess, The. *Unknown.* OBET

Wandering Spectre, The. *Unknown. See* Cauld Lad of Hilton, The *or* The Wandering Spectre.

Wandering through cold streets tangled like old string. Brussels in Winter. W. H. Auden. OBTV; OxBTC

Wandering tribe called the Siouxs, A. Prevalent Poetry. Charles Follen Adams. CenHV

Wandering Ulysses/ While returning to his Mrs. Roberta Simone. SoTCo

Wandering up and down one day. The Cobbler. *Unknown.* BoTP

Wanderings of Oisin, The ("Oisin, tell me the famous story."), sels. W. B. Yeats. BrPo

Old Man Stirs the Fire to a Blaze, An. RB

"We galloped over the glossy sea." SeCePo

Wand'ring in this place as a wilderness. *Unknown.* GBL

Wandsworth Common. David Bromwich. PoA

Waning daylight all round. Instead of an Autobiography. László Kálnoky, *tr. by* Edwin Morgan. MHuP

Waning Moon, The. Shelley. CH; ChER; OxBSP; TrGrPo (Moon, The.) FaBoCh; OBEV

Waning moon looks upward, this grey night, The. Nostalgia. D. H. Lawrence. PoA

Waning of Love, The. "Arthur Lyon Raile." PeHV

Waning Summer. Thomas Nashe. *See* Summer's Last Will and Testament: Fair Summer Droops.

Wanna hear something really funny? A Woman like Me. Eileen Myles. GLP

Wanne mine eyhnen misten. How Death Comes. *Unknown.* MeEL

Want Ad. Bruce Boston. BWV

Want and winter are upon us. *Unknown. Fr.* Toward Winter. NOIV

Want Bone, The. Robert Pinsky. BLA; EOEF

Want of Þ Want of Ö. Anne Szumigalski. FaBoWP

Want of You, The. Ivan Leonard Wright. BLPA; FaBoBe

Want quickens wit: Want's pupils needs must work. The Fishermen. Theocritus, *tr. fr. Greek by* Charles Stuart Calverley. *Fr.* Idylls, XXI. AWP; OBVE

Wanted/ to give away pride. A Defeat. Denise Levertov. PBWP

Wanted. Josiah Gilbert Holland. *See* God, Give Us Men!

Wanted—A Man. Edmund Clarence Stedman. AnAmPo; PAH

Wanted, a Minister's Wife. *Unknown.* BLPA

Wanted—a Witch's Cat. Shelagh McGee. CRH; RHPC

Wanting a Child. Jorie Graham. MAYP

Wanting a Mummy. Sandra McPherson. AmPA; LCAP

Wanting for their young limbs praise. To the Girls of My Graduating Class. Irving Layton. ErPo

Wanting leads to worse than oddity. Where I'll Be Good. Michael Ryan. PPR; SM

Wanting Out. Gavin Ewart. EAS

Wanting things to go on forever. The Extra-Inning Ballgame. Halvard Johnson. TSL

Wanting to Air His Thoughts about and Prove His Respect for Mademoiselle Weichmann's Unusual Talent. H. E. Weichmann, *tr. fr. German by* Susan L. Cocalis. DMG

Wanting to Answer Mr. Darnmann's Undeserved Civility in the Same Rhyme-Scheme. H. E. Weichmann, *tr. fr. German by* Susan L. Cocalis. DMG

Wanting to Die. Anne Sexton. IHMS; MoP; NoAM; TAP

Wanting to say things. My Father's Song. Simon J. Ortiz. HATNAP; MAYP; STE

Wanton, sel. Silabhattarika, *tr. fr. Sanskrit.*

"My husband is the same who took my maidenhead." *Tr. by* Daniel H. H. Ingalls. PBWP

("My husband is the same man who first pierced me.") BoWoP, *tr. by* Willis Barnstone.

Wanton, The, sel. Vidya, *tr. fr. Sanskrit by* Daniel H. H. Ingalls.

"Say, friend, if all is well still with the bowers." PBWP

Wanton Eye. Charles, Duc d' Orléans. OxBLMV

Wanton herd of rakes profest, The. Horace. *Fr.* Odes: I, 25. Ribald Romeos Less and Less Berattle ("Parcius iunctas quatiunt fenestras").

Wanton Seed, The. *Unknown.* OBET

Wanton Trick, The. *Unknown.* CoMu

Wanton troopers riding by, The. The Nymph Complaining for the Death of Her Fawn. Andrew Marvell. CH; FM; GoTL; HeIP; MePo; NAEL-1; OAEL-1; OBS, *abr.;* PoEL-2; SeCP; SeCV-1

Wanton with long delay the gay spring leaping cometh. April, 1885. Robert Bridges. OxBSP; OxBTC

Wants. Philip Larkin. GTBS-P; NoP

Wants of Man, The. John Quincy Adams. OBAL, *abr.;* PoLF

Wants to be admired. The Horse in the Drugstore. Tess Gallagher. AmPA; AnAn

Wantword. Charles Brasch. ATNZ

Wapentake. Longfellow. AA

Wapiti, The. Ogden Nash. MoShBr

War. Guillaume Apollinaire, *tr. fr. French by* Jessie Degen *and* Richard Eberhart. WaaP

War. Sulamith Ish-Kishor. GoYe

War, A. Randall Jarrell. OxBSP

War. Joseph Langland. AiP; FF; NePoEA

War! James Gilchrist Lawson. WBLP

War. Li Po, *tr. fr. Chinese by* Rewi Alley. ChTr

War, The. W. S. Merwin. LCAP

War. Andrei Voznesensky, *tr. fr. Russian by* William Jay Smith *and* Vera Dunham. RB

War. Edgar Wallace. OBWP

War against the Jews, The. Gerald Stern. CAPP

War against the Trees, The. Stanley Kunitz. CAPP; HAP

War and Peace. Barry Goldensohn. NAmP

War and Washington. Jonathan Mitchell Sewall. PAH

War Baby. Pamela Holmes. CN

War-Baby. D. H. Lawrence. NAs

War Bird's Burlesque, A. *Unknown.* AS

War Blinded. Douglas Dunn. DiPo; OBWP

"War-bonnet" we'd say. A Second Molting. Ralph Salisbury. STE

War Bride. Douglas Worth. FF

War canoes were ready. Thirsty Island. Jim Tollerud. VoR

War Casualty in April. Frances Bellerby. CN

War chief danced the old way, The. At the Klamath Berry Festival. William Stafford. InPK

War Comes. Zalman Schneour, *tr. fr. Yiddish by* Joseph Leftwich. TrJP

War Confession. Natan Zach, *tr. fr. Hebrew by* Warren Bargad *and* Stanley F. Chyet. IP

War Down a Monkland. *Unknown.* PBCV

War drum is beating, prepare for the fight, The. "We Conquer or Die." James S. Pierpont. PAH

War God wakened drowsily, The. The Awakened War God. Margaret Widdemer. WGRP

War God's Horse Song, The. *Unknown, tr. fr. Navajo Indian.* LiTA, *tr. by* Dane Coolidge *and* Mary Roberts Coolidge; RB, *tr. by* Louis Watchman; TTTS

War Horse, The. Eavan Boland. BIrV; CIP

War in the Air, The. Howard Nemerov. DiPo

War Is Kind, *sels.* Stephen Crane.

Candid Man, The. *Fr.* IX. MoAmPo

Do Not Weep, Maiden, for War Is Kind. *Fr.* 76. AmPP; FPL; LiTA; NAAL-2; NOBA; OBWP; PoLF

"Fast rode the knight." *Fr.* 83. NAAL-2

Man Said to the Universe, A. *Fr.* XXI. AmPP; FaBoEE; FF; ImOP; LiTM; NAAL-2, *sect.* 96; OBAL; OBSV; PrIm; TAP; WeW

Newspaper Is a Collection of Half-Injustices, A. *Fr.* XII. AmPP; NAAL-2, *sect.* 87.

On the Desert. *Fr.* XI. LiTM

Peaks, The. *Fr.* XVIII. AA; WGRP

Slant of Sun on Dull Brown Walls, A. *Fr.* XIV. LiTM; NAAL-2, *sect.* 89.

There Was a Man with a Tongue of Wood. *Fr.* XVI. LiTA; MoAmPo

Trees in the Garden Rained Flowers, The. *Fr.* XXVI. LiTM; PrIm

War Is Kind, I (title poem). LiTM; TAP; WaaP

Wayfarer, The. *Fr.* XIII. AmPP; LiTA; MoAmPo

War is no longer declared. Every Day. Ingeborg Bachmann. DMG, *tr. by* Kate Flores; PBWP, *tr. by* Michael Hamburger ("War is not declared any more.") BoWoP, *tr. by* Christopher Middleton

War is not declared any more. Ingeborg Bachmann. *See* Every Day.

War Is the Statesman's Game. Shelley. *Fr.* Queen Mab, IV. FF

War Lord in the Early Evening. Patricia K. Page. NoAM

War Memento (Somewhere in France 1915). Roger Hecht. CRP

War of 1793, The. Diodata Saluzzo, *tr. fr. Italian by* Muriel Kittel. DMI

War of the Secret Agents, The, *sels.* Henri Coulette. NePoEA-2

Cinema at the Lighthouse. *Fr.* VI.

Denise: A Letter Never Sent. *Fr.* VIII.

Epilogue: Author to Reader. *Fr.* XII.

Phono, at the Boar's Head. *Fr.* IX.

War of the Worlds, The. Vern Rutsala. Psk

War on the Periphery. George Johnston. NOBC

War Party. Eddy Grant. PBCV

War-path is true and straight, The. Just One Signal. *Unknown.* PAH

War Poet. Roy Fuller. *See* January 1940.

War Poetry. John Philips. *Fr.* Blenheim. NOEC

War Ship of Peace, The. Samuel Lover. PAH

War ships, cold tides. Yün Shou-p'ing, *tr. fr. Chinese by* Jonathan Chaves. *Fr.* Seeing Off Mr. Yang. CoBLCP

War shook the land where Levi dwelt. The Field of Glory. E. A. Robinson. AnAmPo; MoAmPo

War shows what each man's country is to him. Invasion. Ellen Duggan. PeNZ

War Song, A. Bertrans de Born. *See* Well Pleaseth Me the Sweet Time of Easter.

War Song, A. Blake. *See* King Edward the Third: War Song to Englishmen, A.

War Song. John Davidson. OBNC

War Song. *Zulu Oral Tradition, tr. by* D. K. Rycroft. WTO

War Song of Dinas Vawr, The. Thomas Love Peacock. *Fr.* The Misfortunes of Elphin. AWP; EnRP; FaBoCh; FaPoR; HAP; InvP; NAEL-2; NOBE; OAEL-2; OnMSP; PrIm; WaaP; WeW; WiR

War Song of the Saracens. James Elroy Flecker. *Fr.* Hassan, III, iii. FaBV; MoBrPo

War Song to Englishmen, A. Blake. *Fr.* King Edward the Third. CH; OHIP; WaaP

(War Song, A.) OHIP

War Story. Jon Stallworthy. OxBC

War Swaggers. Emanuel Litvinoff. WaP

War that we have carefully for years provoked, The. Black-out. Robinson Jeffers. LiTA; LiTM; WaP

War-Time. William Robert Rodgers. OxBSP

War-Token, The. Longfellow. *Fr.* The Courtship of Miles Standish. PAH

War Tribunal. Elizabeth Daryush. CN

War Walking Near. Ray A. Young Bear. CDW

War Widow. Margaret Hamilton Noël-Paton. CN

Waradgery Tribe, The. Mary Gilmore. PoAu-1

Waratah. Roland Robinson. PoAu-2

Warbler. Anzai Hitoshi, *tr. fr. Japanese by* Sato. FCEI

Warbler escapes next door, A. Kito, *tr. fr. Japanese by* Hiroaki Sato. *Fr.* Twenty-four Hokku. FCEI

Warbler: leaves hiding it. Taigi, *tr. fr. Japanese by* Hiroaki Sato. *Fr.* Twenty-nine Hokku. FCEI

Warbler, what are you afraid of? Kito, *tr. fr. Japanese by* Hiroaki Sato. *Fr.* Twenty-four Hokku. FCEI

Warbler's voice, The. Kyogoku Tamekane, *tr. fr. Japanese by* Burton Watson. *Fr.* Twenty-three Tanka. FCEI

Ward, and still in bonds, one day, A. Regeneration. Henry Vaughan. JCP; MeLP; MePo; NAEL-1; NoP; OBS; PoE

Ward has no heart, they say, but I deny it. On J. W. Ward. Samuel Rogers. FaBoEE

Ward 130 in the passage on the right. 25 December 1960. Ingrid Jonker, *tr. by* Jack Cope *and* Uys Krige. PeSA

Ward Two. Francis Webb. CBAP

Ward X, *sel.* Lola Ridge.

"Salvation Army lass, The." WPE

Wardance. Phillip William George. VoR

Wardance Soup. Phillip William George. VoR

Warden at ocean's gate. Liberty Enlightening the World. Edmund Clarence Stedman. PAH

Warden of the Cinque Ports, The. Longfellow. AA

Warden Said to Me the Other Day, The. Etheridge Knight. FF; MT

Warden with his armed guards stalls, The. No Word. Barry Goldensohn. NAmP

Wardour Street. Humbert Wolfe. OxBTC

Waring. Robert Browning. PoEL-5

Warkin' Mon's Reflections, A. William Baron. PF

Warlike of the Isles, The. *Unknown.* OBTV

Warm. Robert Grenier. IAT

Warm and snug. Hara Sekitei, *tr. by* Geoffrey Bownas *and* Anthony Thwaite. PeBJV

Warm Babies. Keith Preston. FiBHP

Warm green pond is flooded with radiant sunlight, The. Joy at Renewal. Niu Hsi-chi, *tr. by* Lois Fusek. ATF

Warm junk rusts on sunny fields of drained earth. Junk. Berysh Vaynshteyn, *tr. fr. Yiddish by* Benjamin *and* Barbara Harshav. *Fr.* New York Everywhere. AYP

Warm perfumes like a breath from wine and tree. Waikiki. Rupert Brooke. OBTV

Warm rain, sunny wind start to break the chill. Li Ch'ing-chao, *tr. by* Willis Barnstone *and* Sua Chu-chin. BoWoP

Warm shone the sun, the wind as warmly blew. Hay-Time; or, The Constant Lovers. A Pastoral. Josiah Relph. NOEC

Warm stones gather the rainfall. Looking for Buddha. Jaime Jacinto. BrSi

Warm summer sun. Epitaph Placed on His Daughter's Tomb. "Mark Twain." PoLF

Warm sun is failing, The; the bleak wind is wailing. Autumn; a Dirge. Shelley. CH

Warm walnut seats crisscross braces. Powwow remnants. Lew Blockcolski. VoR

Warm, wild, rainy wind, blowing fitfully. May Morning. Celia Thaxter. AA

Warm winds crossed from the eastern coast, The. The Boss's Wife. *Unknown.* CBAP

Warm Winter Day, A. Julian Cooper. BoNaP

Warming a set of new bones. Beating the Drum. Ruth Dallas. *Fr.* Letter to a Chinese Poet. ATNZ

Warming Up for the Real Thing. Lee Rudolph. TW

Warmth. Barton Sutter. GOYP

Warning. John Ciardi. PDV

Warning, The. Adelaide Crapsey. WPE; WSC

Warning, The. Robert Creeley. NeAP; TAP; VGW

Warning. Robert Frost. AnAmPo

Warning. Langston Hughes. BPo

Warning. Jenny Joseph. AIW; FaBoWP; GOYP; OxBTC

Warning. Ursula Krechel, *tr. fr. German by* Susan L. Cocalis. DMG

Warning, A. Alexander Nicolson. PoSH

Warning, A. Coventry Patmore. EnLoPo

Warning, A. Elizabeth Smart. PoPo

Warning. *Unknown.* OxNR; PBBP

Warning and Reply. Emily Brontë. WPE

Warning of dog shit, A. *Unknown, tr. by* Burton Watson. FCEI

Warning of Winter. Mary Ursula Bethell. ATNZ; FaBoWP; PeNZ

Warning to a Guest. John Holloway. NePoEA

Warning to America, A. Philip Freneau. TAP

Warning to Children. Robert Graves. FaBoCh; FaFP; NoP; OAEL-2; SO

Warning to My Love, A. David Wagoner. NePoEA-2

Warning to One. Merrill Moore. MoAmPo; TrGrPo

Warning to Those Who Serve Lords, A. *Unknown.* MeEL

Warning to Travailers Seeking Accomodations at Mr. Devills Inn. Sarah Kemble Knight. SCAP

Warp and Woof. Harry Halbisch. BLRP

Warping bandstand reminds you of the hard rage, The. Return to La Plata, Missouri. Jim Barnes. HATNAP

Warren Phinney. Bernadette Mayer. UL

Warren's Address at Bunker Hill [*or* to the American Soldiers]. John Pierpont. AA; AnAmPo; FaBoBe; GN; GOA; PAH; WBLP

Warrior, A/ I have been. Song of Sitting Bull. *Unknown.* GOA

Warrior Dreams. Ray A. Young Bear. NOVW

Warrior drinks the goat's blood for bravery, A. Weep Not for a Warrior. Mbuyiseni Oswald Mtshali. WMBCH

Warrior is going a journey, The. Incantation. Alistair Paterson. *Fr.* Incantations for Warriors, V. PeNZ

Warrior Nation Trilogy. Lance Henson. NOVW; VoR

Warrior walks, A. Buson, *tr. fr. Japanese by* Hiroaki Sato. *Fr.* Eighty-seven Hokku. FCEI

Warriors. Douglas Dunn. OxBC

Warrior's come home, Th. Ponsonby/Remuera/My Iai. David Mitchell. ATNZ

Warriors go forth, The. Kanamura. *Fr.* Manyo Shu. Ma

Warrior's Lament, The. Sir Owen Seaman. FiBHP

Warriors Prancing, Women Dancing. Niema Rashidd. NBP

Warr'st thou 'gainst Athens? Shakespeare. *Fr.* Timon of Athens, IV, iii. EBEV

Wars, The. Conrad Aiken. *Fr.* The Soldier, I. WaaP

War's End. Dahlia Ravikovich, *tr. fr. Hebrew by* Warren Bargad *and* Stanley F. Chyet. IP

Wars of Santa Fe, The. *Unknown.* AmFP

Wars of the Roses, The. *Unknown.* GBP

Wars we wage, The. Robert Gould Shaw. William Vaughn Moody. *Fr.* An Ode in Time of Hesitation. AA

Wartime Dawn, A. David Gascoyne. LiTM

Wartime Maternity Ward, A. Barbara Catherine Edwards. CN

Wartime Report Centre: Solo School. Mabel Ferrett. CN

Wartime Story, A. Edith Jay Scovell. CN

Warty Bliggens, the Toad. Don Marquis. *Fr.* Archy and Mehitabel. FiBHP

Warum sind denn die Rosen so blass. Heine, *tr. fr. German by* Richard Garnett. AWP

Wary of time O it seizes the soul tonight. Easter Eve. Muriel Rukeyser. VGW

Was a Man. Philip Booth. NePoEA-2; VGW

Was broken./ He bade a warrior abandon his horse. The Battle of Maldon. *Unknown, tr. by* Charles W. Kennedy. AnOE; OAEL-1

Was he a mining on the flat. He Done His Level Best. "Mark Twain." AiP

Was He Married? Stevie Smith. MoP; NoAM

Was he then Adam of the Burning Way? Such Is the Sickness of Many a Good Thing. Robert Duncan. CAPP

Was I born to play? Emperor Go-Shirakawa, *tr. fr. Japanese by* Hiroaki Sato. *Fr.* Ryojin Hisho. FCEI

Was I summoned. Eve's Birth. Kim Chernin. VWA

Was I too glib about eternal things. The Sequel. Theodore Roethke. NYBP

Was I wrong when I thought. Thought on June 26. Mazisi Kunene. WMBCH

Was it a dream. Saigyo, *tr. fr. Japanese by* Burton Watson. *Fr.* Sixty-four Tanka. FCEI

Was it a dream? The Books were men. The Wounded. Louise Louis. GoYe

Was it a dream? We sailed, I thought we sailed. A Dream. Matthew Arnold. GBL; GTBS-P; OBTV; SeCePo

Was it a fragment of rock or of cloud. The Mountain's Side. Shmu'el Shatal, *tr. by* Bernhard Frank. MHeP

"Was it a little baby." A Tonversation with Baby. Morris Bishop. FiBHP

Was it a mirror then across a room. Mirrors. Elizabeth Jennings. NePoEA

Was it a "please urge" or "a police purge" or some combination. The Kiss. John Yau. UL

Was It All Worth While? *Zulu Oral Tradition, tr. by* H. Tracey. WTO

Was it by day or night. The Pathetic Runaway. Philippe Thoby-Marcelin, *tr. by* William Jay Smith. CT

Was it fancy, sweet nurse. Don Marquis. *Fr.* Grotesques. FiBHP

Was It for This. Wordsworth. *Fr.* The Prelude [or, Growth of a Poet's Mind]: Childhood and School-Time. RB

Was it for this I uttered prayers. Grown-up. Edna St. Vincent Millay. NoAM

Was it his face that so unsettled him? Narcissus. Donald Petersen. NePoEA-2

Was it only last night. *Unknown. Fr.* Manyo Shu. FCEI

Was it only the new, old chemical stirrings. Portrait of a Lady. Michael Ryan. NAmP

Was it pleasing to my prince's soul? Princess Tamochi. *Fr.* Manyo Shu. Ma

Was it really you all the time? Dream Sequence, Part 9. Naomi Long Madgett. BPo

Was it that I went to sleep. Komachi, *tr. by* Geoffrey Bownas *and* Anthony Thwaite. PeBJV

Was it the brown eagle feather that. Insight. Mary Goose. STE

"Was it the proud full sail of his great verse." Shakespeare. *Fr.* Sonnets, LXXXVI. InvP; OAEL-1; Son; TEP

Was it there at all. The Bat in the Bedroom. Robert Crum. MOWH

Was it wind off the dumps. Summer Home. Seamus Heaney. FaBCIP; IPY

Was It You? Stewart I. Long. WBLP

Was it you who came to me. Narihira, *tr. by* Geoffrey Bownas *and* Anthony Thwaite. PeBJV

Was never day came on my head. George Turberville. *Fr.* The Lover Abused Renounceth Love. EiL

Was never in Scotland hard nor sene. Christ's Kirk on the Green. *At. to* James V, King of Scotland. OxBS

Was Not the Lost Dauphin. Robert Penn Warren. *Fr.* Audubon, I.

Was She a Witch? Laura E. Richards. PDV

Was that a plover? A Wood Thrush Concealed. Tamemasa, *tr. by* Steven D. Carter. WFTW

Was the arrangement made between the two couples legal? Some Litanies. Michael Benedikt. CoAP; TwCP

Was the love between them. His Lunch Bucket. Doug Cockrell. Psk

Was there ere sic a parish, a parish, a parish. Little Dunkeld. *Unknown.* GBP

Was there ever message sweeter. A Message. Elizabeth Stuart Phelps Ward. PAH

Was there no mute to mourn this crumpled city. Threnody for Berlin—1945. Wrenne Jarman. CN

Was this his face, and these the finding eyes. On a Portrait of Columbus. George Edward Woodberry. AA

Was this the face that launched a thousand ships? Christopher Marlowe. *Fr.* Doctor Faustus, V, i. EBEV; GBL; HeIP; NIP; TrGrPo

   (Face of Helen, The.) FaBV

   (Helen.) BLPL; FaFP; LiTB

   (Helen of Troy.) FF

Was two sisters loved one man. The Two Sisters. *Unknown.* AmFP; MAT; PrIm; TrGrPo

Was very kind. When she regained. The Raper from Passenack. William Carlos Williams. TW

Was you at de hall las' night. Leap Yeah Party, De. Maggie Pogue Johnson. CBWP-4

Wash. Eiléan Ní Chuilleanáin. BIrV; WPOW

Wash-Day. Lilian McCrea. BoTP

Wash Day. Larry Mollin. NeAC

Wash, hands, wash. A Rhyme for Washing Hands. Rodney Bennett. BoTP

Wash it well, and season it hot. To Stew a Rump-Steak. *Unknown.* FaBoUs

Wash man out of the earth, shear off. Wash. Eiléan Ní Chuilleanáin. BIrV; WPOW

Wash the dishes, wipe the dishes. Mother Goose. OxNR

Wash your hands, or else the fire. Another to the Maids. Robert Herrick. OHIP

Washback of the waters, swirl of time. Sea-Ruck. Richard Eberhart. MOS

Washed by the rain, dust and grime are laid. Starting Early from the Ch'u-ch'êng Inn. Po Chü-i, *tr. by* Arthur Waley. OBVE

Washed in the blood of the brave and the blooming. God Save the Flag. Oliver Wendell Holmes. FaFP; OHFP; OPP

Washer-Woman, The. Otto Leland Bohanan. BANP

Washers of the Shroud, The. James Russell Lowell. PAH

Washerwoman, The. Mary Collier. *Fr.* The Woman's Labour; an Epistle to Mr. Stephen Duck. NOEC

Washerwoman, The. Mary Weston Fordham. CBWP-2

Washing. John Drinkwater. FaPON

Washing and Dressing. Ann Taylor. FaBoUs

Washing Day. *Unknown.* CoMu

Washing hanging from the lemon tree, The. The Five-Day Rain. Denise Levertov. NeAP

Washing hangs upon the line, A. Elizabeth Bishop. *Fr.* Songs for a Colored Singer. FaBoWP; RB

Washing Kai in the sauna. The Bath. Gary Snyder. CAPP; DiL; NNaP; TAP

Washing Machine, The. Jeffrey Davies. PCP

Washing My Hair. Tadaomi, *tr. fr. Chinese by* Burton Watson. JLIC-1

Washing the Coins. Douglas Dunn. FaBoPV

Washing the Dishes. Christopher Morley. PoLF

Washing-Up Song, The. Elizabeth Gould. BoTP

Washington. Byron. *Fr.* Ode to Napoleon Buonaparte. OHIP; PAH

Washington. Lorna Dee Cervantes. *Fr.* Visions of Mexico While at a Writing Symposium in Port Townsend, Washington. NoAM

Washington. James Russell Lowell. *Fr.* Under the Old Elm. GN, *fr.* V; OHIP, *fr.* V.

Washington. Geraldine Meyrich. OHIP

Washington. Harriet Monroe. *Fr.* Commemoration Ode. AA; FaBoBe (Two Heroes.) OHIP

Washington. Denis O'Crowley. OHIP

Washington. John A. Prentice. OHIP

Washington. James Jeffrey Roche. PAH

Washington. Nancy Byrd Turner. FaPON; RHPC

Washington. *Unknown. See* Washington, the brave, the wise, the good.

Washington. Mary Wingate. OHIP

Washington and Jefferson made many a joke. Presidents of the United States. *Unknown.* FaBoUs

Washington by the Delaware. Joaquin Miller. AnAmPo

Washington Heights, 1959. Michael C. Blumenthal. HCAP

Washington in Love. John Berryman. LCAP

Washington Monument by Night. Carl Sandburg. CMoP; FaPON; OFD; OHIP

Washington Sequoia, The, *sel.* Milicent Washburn Shinn. Yosemite. AA

Washington, the brave, the wise, the good. Inscription at Mount Vernon. *Unknown.* OHIP

   (Washington.) OFD

Washington's Birthday. Arthur J. Burdick. OHIP

Washington's Monument, February 1885. Walt Whitman. OFD

Washington's Monument. *Unknown.* OHIP; PAH

Washington's Statue. Henry Theodore Tuckerman. AA

Washington's Tomb. Ruth Lawrence. OHIP

Washington's Vow. Whittier. OHIP

Was/Man. Phyllis Gotlieb. BWV

Wasn't it pleasant, O brother mine. Out to Old Aunt Mary's. James Whitcomb Riley. FaFP; OHFP

Wasn't That a Mighty Storm? *Unknown.* AmFP

Wasn't this the site, asked the historian. House and Land. Allen Curnow. ATNZ; PeNZ

Wasn't your mother a woman? Hennamma, *tr. by* Willis Barnstone. BoWoP

Wasp, The. John Davidson. FM
Wasp, The. Daryl Hine. NYBP
Wasp, The. "Fiona Macleod." *Fr.* Transcripts from Nature. BoTP; FaPON; FM
Wasp, The. Joyce Carol Oates. GeTw
Wasp, climbing the window pane. Epigrams, I-IX. Howard Nemerov. OBAL
Wasp Sex Myth (One). Anselm Hollo. PoM
Wasp Sex Myth (Two). Anselm Hollo. PoM
Wasps. Dorothy Aldis. RHPC
Wasp's Frolic, The. Unknown. PAH
Wasps' Nest, The. George MacBeth. OxBTC
Wasps or hornets rattle on the sills. Her Sleep. Jill Hoffman. TV
Wasp's Song, The. "Lewis Carroll." FaBoNo
Wassail Song, The (Here we come a-wassailing). *Unknown.* OHIP
(Here we come a-wassailing.) PChr
Wassail Song ("Wassail! wassail! all round the town"). *Unknown.* OHIP
(Somerset Corol.) OBET
(Wassail Song: "We have been a-walking.") GBP
Wassail Song: "We have been a-walking,." *Unknown. See* Wassail Song ("Wassail! wassail! all round the town").
Wassail the trees, that they may bear. Robert Herrick. *Fr.* Ceremonies for Christmas[se]. PChr
Wassail, Wassail. John Bale. ChTr
Wassail, wassail, all over the town! Gloucestershire Wassail. *Unknown.* OBET
(Thames Head Wassailers' Song.) OBET
Wassail! Wassail! all over the town. Wassailer's Song. Robert Southwell. OHIP
Wassail! wassail! all round [*or* over] the town. Wassail Song ("Wassail! wassail! all round the town"). *Unknown.* OHIP
(Somerset Wassail.) OBET
(Wassail Song: "We have been a-walking.") GBP
Wassail, wassail, out of the milk pail. Wassail, Wassail. John Bale. ChTr
Wassailer's Song. Robert Southwell. OHIP
Wassailing Song. *Unknown.* OBCP
Waste. Harry Graham. FaBoCo
(Aunt Maud.) MoShBr
Waste Land, The ("April is the cruelest month."), sels. T. S. Eliot. AmPP; CMoP; FaBoMo; HAP; LiTA; LiTM; MoAB; MoAmPo; NAWM-2; NoAM; NOBA; NOBE; NoP; OAEL-2; OxBA; OxBTC; TAP; UnPo
Death by Water. *Fr.* IV. OBVE
Game of Chess, A. *Fr.* II. SCV
"When Lil's husband got demobbed, I said." NAs
Waste Land Limericks. Wendy Cope. FaBoWP
Wasted Day, A. Frances Cornford. MoBrPo
Wasted Day, The. Robert Fuller Murray. EBVV
Wasted Land, The. Edward Pygge. FaBoPa
Wasted Sympathy, A. Winifred Howells. AA
Wasted, Weary, Wherefore Stay. Sir Walter Scott. *Fr.* Guy Mannering, ch. 27. EnRP
Wasting in summer. Kawabata Bosha, *tr. by* Geoffrey Bownas *and* Anthony Thwaite. PeBJV
Wasting thistle whitens on my crest, The. The Wild Knight. G. K. Chesterton. WGRP
Wastrel-Woman Poem, The. Brenda Marie Osbey. ER; MT
Wat a joyful news, Miss Mattie. Colonization in Reverse. Louise Bennett. PBCV
Wat a piece of rain, Miss Kate! Wat A Rain. Valerie Bloom. PBCV
Wat A Rain. Valerie Bloom. PBCV
Watch, The. Frances Cornford. HeIP; InPK; MoBrPo; OxBTC; RR
Watch, The. Marge Piercy. GeTw
Watch, The. May Swenson. HAP
Watch/ how high. Just Watch. Myra Cohn Livingston. RAR
Watch Any Day. W. H. Auden. FaBoMo
(Free One, A.) CMoP
Watch, Cima Quattro. Giuseppe Ungaretti, *tr. fr. Italian by* Patrick Creagh. OBD
Watch for the Ice. Brian Turner. UAS
Watch Hill. Winfield Townley Scott. ErPo
Watch how dem touris' like fe look. Fetchin Water. Claude McKay. PBCV
Watch it. That's the body: what goes on. The Body. William Bronk. VGW
Watch long enough, and you will see the leaf. Conrad Aiken. *Fr.* Preludes for Memnon; or, Preludes to Attitude. CMoP; OxBA
Watch me swim! Swimming. Alice Higgins. RAR

Watch, now. Shadow Show. Ruth Dallas. ATNZ
Watch of a Swan, The. Sarah Morgan Bryan Piatt. AA
Watch out for the bus. Mercado. Greg Pape. AmPA
Watch out, my dear. Praxilla, *tr. by* John Dillon. PBWP
Watch people stop by bodies in funeral homes. On the Symbolic Consideration of Hands and the Significance of Death. Miller Williams. InPK
Watch, please, this painted ballet of the fed. Uccello on the Heath. Geoffrey Grigson. WaP
Watch Repair. Charles Simic. NoP
Watch the Lights Fade. Robinson Jeffers. CMoP; NOBA
Watch Them Die. Dennis Trudell. KS
Watch upon my wrist, The. Parable. W. H. Auden. FaBoCo
Watch was up on the topsail-yard a-making fast the sail, The. One of Wally's Yarns. John Masefield. BrPo
Watch well the poor in this late hour. Temperance Note: and Weather Prophecy. James Agee. *Fr.* Two Songs on the Economy of Abundance. MoAmPo
Watch will tell the time of day, A. Mr. Coggs. E. V. Lucas. BoTP
(Mr. Coggs, Watchmaker.) FaPON
"Watch Your Step!" Moyshe-Leyb Halpern, *tr. fr. Yiddish by* Benjamin *and* Barbara Harshav *and* Kathryn Helle. AYP
Watch Your Step—I'm Drenched. Adrian Mitchell. RB
Watch Yourself Go By. Strickland W. Gillilan. BLPA
Watched from the showerblock which I clean. Female Prisoners—Boggo Road. Robin Thurston. UAS
Watcher, The. Sarah Josepha Hale. AA
Watcher, The. John Peck. AmPA
Watcher, The. James Stephens. MoBrPo; OBEV
Watcher, The. Ruth Stone. NYBP
Watcher, The. Clara Ann Thompson. CBWP-2
Watcher, The. Margaret Widdemer. OHIP
Watchers, The. Arlo Bates. AA
Watchers, The. Paul Blackburn. NYBP
Watchers, The. William Stanley Braithwaite. PoNe
Watchers. W. S. Merwin. NaP
Watchers, The. Charles Spear. PeNZ
Watchers and Seekers. Amryl Johnson. WS
Watchful Wakeful. Amir Gilboa, *tr. fr. Hebrew by* Warren Bargad *and* Stanley F. Chyet. IP
Watching. "Fanny Forester." AA
Watching a Child Watching a Witch. Jenny Joseph. *Fr.* Derivations. AIW
Watching a Cloud. Dannie Abse. OxBC; TEP
Watching a Game of Chess: Second Series. Ch'ien Ch'ien-yi, *tr. fr. Chinese by* Irving Lo. WFTU
Watching an Opera: Impressions, *sel.* Chao Yi, *tr. fr. Chinese by* Shirleen S. Wong.
"With sticks and staves on a makeshift stage—all are engrossed in a child's game." WFTU
Watching baseball. Baseball Canto. Lawrence Ferlinghetti. ASP
Watching Fish in the Water. Suemochi, *tr. fr. Chinese by* Burton Watson. JLIC-1
Watching Football on TV. Howard Nemerov. ASP
Watching for Dolphins. David Constantine. OBTV
Watching Gymnasts. Robert Francis. RR
Watching, I have grown lonely. Princess Shikishi, *tr. fr. Japanese by* Hiroaki Sato. *Fr.* Seventy-eight Tanka. FCEI
Watching me approach, Goldilocks asks. I Am Mama Bear. Nedine Davis. TSM
Watching oneself. Poem without a Main Verb. John Wain. NePoEA-2
Watching Salmon Jump. Simon J. Ortiz. CDW
Watching Tackles in Slow Motion. David Allan Evans. TSL
Watching Television. Robert Bly. CoAP
Watching Tennis. John Heath-Stubbs. Son
Watching the beautiful. This Day. Lawrence Raab. BLA; NoP
Watching the competition dancers at the Dakota Wapici. The Ghost Dance: August, 1976. David Jauss. MOWH
Watching the Dance. James Merrill. NIP
Watching the Jets Lose to Buffalo at Shea. May Swenson. ASP
Watching the lightning. Bondage. Hubert Witheford. ATNZ
Watching the Moon with Thoughts of Far Away. Chang Chiu-ling, *tr. fr. Chinese by* Burton Watson. CoBCP
Watching the Native Country from the Border. Lo Fu, *tr. fr. Chinese by* Dominic Cheung. IFON
Watching the Old Man Die. Arthur James Marshall Smith. MoCV
Watching the Sea. Lo Men, *tr. fr. Chinese by* Dominic Cheung. IFON
Watching the shied core. As Bad as a Mile. Philip Larkin. InPK; OxBC; OxBSP
Watching the Sun Rise over Mount Zion. Ruth Whitman. VWA

Watching the Swinging, *sel.* Li K'ai-hsien, *tr. fr. Chinese by* Jonathan Chaves.

"Colorful frames are erected beside the Yellow River, The." CoBLCP

Watching this dawn's mnemonic of old dawning. Sestina in a Cantina. Malcolm Lowry. MoCV

Watching TV, the Elk Bones Up on Metaphysics. John Bensko. MT

Watching War Movies. Lucien Stryk. CAPP

Watching You. Simon J. Ortiz. HATNAP

Watching you in the mirror I wonder. The Mirror. Louise Glück. GeTw; MAYP

Watching You Sleep under Monet's Water Lilies. Gibbons Ruark. SM

Watchmaker God. Robert Lowell. HCAP

Watchmaker's Shop, The. *Unknown.* BoTP

Watchman, The. Charles Kingsley. EBVV

Watchman, The. Abraham Reisen, *tr. fr. Yiddish by* Joseph Leftwich. TrJP

Watchman, watchman on your height. The Watchman. Abraham Reisen, *tr. by* Joseph Leftwich. TrJP

Watchman, What of the Night? Swinburne. WiR

"Watchman, what of the night?" The Watchman. Charles Kingsley. EBVV

Watchman, What of the Night? Bible, *O.T. Fr.* Isaiah, XXI: 11–15. AWP

Water. Hilda Conkling. PDV

Water. John R. Crossland. BoTP

Water. Emerson. AmPP; OxBSP; PoEL-4

Water. Ted Hughes. OxBSP

Water. Edmond Jabès, *tr. fr. French by* Anthony Rudolf. VWA

Water. Philip Larkin. FaBoMo; OxBSP

Water. Lo Fu, *tr. fr. Chinese by* Dominic Cheung. IFON

Water. Robert Lowell. CMoP; HeIP; LCAP; NOBA; NoP; PoE; SM

Water. Leslie Norris. OBWVE

Water, *sel.* Kathleen Jessie Raine.

"There is a stream that flowed before the first beginning." ImOP

Water. Gary Snyder. LCAP

Water. Sa'di Yusuf, *tr. fr. Arabic by* Abdullah al-Udhari. MPAW

Water and marble and that silentness. Venice. Arthur Symons. OxBSP

Water and windmills, greenness, islets green. The Netherlands. Samuel Taylor Coleridge. OBTV

Water and Worship: An Open-Air Service on the Gatineau River. Margaret Avison. HAP

Water astonishing and difficult altogether. Water Raining. Gertrude Stein. *Fr.* Tender Buttons. PBWP

Water at Ayuchi in Oharida, The. *Unknown. Fr.* Manyo Shu. Ma

Water Babies, The, *sels.* Charles Kingsley.

Clear and Cool. GN

(Clear and Cool.) BoNaP; OxBChV

Lost Doll, The. FaPON; MoShBr

(Little Doll, The.) OxBChV

Young and Old. BLPL; EBEV; FaBoBe; FaFP; FaPoR; OxBChV; PoLF

Water Below, The. Fleur Adcock. ATNZ

Water bird, looking heavy, floats, A. Onitsura, *tr. fr. Japanese by* Hiroaki Sato. *Fr.* Twenty-three Hokku. FCEI

Water-Boy. *Unknown.* TrGrPo

Water bridge by the river, the weeds have consumed, The. Weeds. Su Shao-lien, *tr. by* Dominic Cheung. IFON

Water bug is drawing the shadows, The. *Unknown, tr. by* Frances Densmore. OBVE

Water Carrier, The. John Montague. FaBCIP

Water clangs, the crystal flies in shivers, The. The Centaur's Bath. Luis G. Urbina, *tr. by* Samuel Beckett. MexPo

Water closing, The. Together. Maxine W. Kumin. BoWoP; NMM

Water Color. Stephen Mooney. NYBP

Water-Colour of Venice, A. Lawrence Durrell. MoBrPo

Water does not lie heavy and deep, The. Kinneret. Judith Herzberg, *tr. by* Shirley Kaufman. VWA

Water down the rocky wall, The. The Bunyip. Douglas Stewart. AmMo

Water-Drinker, The. Edward Jonson. BXAP

Water fills. Bathing. Sara Boyes. DT

Water, first creature of the gods. Tea Poems. George Mackay Brown. OxBC

Water flooded everywhere. Rebirth. Catriona Stamp. BrRo

Water flushed into paddies. Strolling in a Nearby Village. Tani Rokkoku, *tr. by* Burton Watson. JLIC-2

Water Fowl. Wordsworth. FM

Water fragrant in my hands, I traced it upstream. Princess Shikishi, *tr. fr. Japanese by* Hiroaki Sato. *Fr.* Seventy-eight Tanka. FCEI

Water-Girl. *Gond Oral Tradition, tr. by* V. Elwin *and* S. Hivale. WTO

Water gives, it gets us, The. Late Afternoon on a Good Lake. Dara Wier. MAYP

Water Glass. Jutta Schutting, *tr. fr. German by* Beth Bjorklund. CoAuP

Water has to start, The. Coming Down to It. Malcolm Glass. BXAP

Water hen is hopping, A. May Evening. Eileen Brennan. NeIP

Water Hyacinth. Kitahara Hakushu, *tr. fr. Japanese by* Hiroaki Sato. FCEI

Water I will draw. Ryokan, *tr. by* Geoffrey Bownas *and* Anthony Thwaite. PeBJV

Water in a shallow container. Zuni Derivations. *Unknown, tr. by* Dennis Tedlock. STP

Water in my prison shatters in a prism, The. The Trout. Daryl Hine. CoAP

Water is practical. Mourning Pablo Neruda. Robert Bly. LCAP

Water Is Wide, The. *Unknown.* OBET

Water Island. Howard Moss. CoAP; NePoEA-2; NYBP; Prf

Water Lady, The. Thomas Hood. CH

Water like quartz, with the same kinds of strata, The. Nights Passed on Ward's Island, Toronto Harbour. Doug Fetherling. NeAC

Water-Lilies. Sara Teasdale. MoAmPo

Water-lilies in myriads rocked on the slight undulations. On the Atchafalaya. Longfellow. *Fr.* Evangeline. AA

Water-Lily, The. John Banister Tabb. AA; ACP

Water-Lion is the God verray, The. King Arthur's Dream. *Unknown.* ACP

Water Lowers and Stones Show. Kito, *tr. fr. Japanese by* Hiroaki Sato. *Fr.* Twenty-four Hokku. FCEI

Water Mill, The. Sarah Doudney. BLPA; WGRP

Water mirror. *Unknown, tr. by* Geoffrey Bownas *and* Anthony Thwaite. PeBJV

Water Music. "Hugh MacDiarmid." GoTS

Water Noises. Elizabeth Madox Roberts. BoNaP

Water of a shallow river, The. Taigi, *tr. fr. Japanese by* Hiroaki Sato. *Fr.* Twenty-nine Hokku. FCEI

Water of Contradiction. Shin Dong-jip, *tr. fr. Korean by* Koh Chang-soo. ACKP

Water of Kane, The. *Unknown, tr. fr. Hawaiian by* N. B. Emerson. WTO

Water-Ousel, The. Mary Webb. CH

Water Ouzel. William H. Matchett. CoAP; NePoEA; NYBP

Water Picture. May Swenson. BoNaP

Water plunges to devour us. Travel Song. Hugo von Hofmannsthal, *tr. by* Charles Wharton Stork. TrJP

Water pulls nervously whispering satin across cool roots, cold stones. Interval. Joseph Auslander. FYAP

Water Raining. Gertrude Stein. *Fr.* Tender Buttons. PBWP

Water rushes up. Open Hydrant. Marci Ridlon. RHPC

Water sings along our keel, The. Armistice. Sophie Jewett. AA

Water Song. Steve Crow. HATNAP

Water Song. Solomon ibn Gabirol, *tr. fr. Hebrew by* Israel Abrahams. TrJP

Water spurting out of a pump, The. Ishikawa Takuboku, *tr. fr. Japanese by* Hiroaki Sato. *Fr.* Forty-seven Tanka in Three Lines. FCEI

Water stands high on the place, The. Part of the Question. Ilse Aichinger, *tr. by* Beth Bjorklund. CoAuP

Water still flows. Illegitimate Things. William Carlos Williams. MoAB; MoAmPo; RR

Water strider skates upon the brook, A. Plane Geometer. David McCord. NYBP

Water the ground with his tears. The Light. John Holloway. NePoEA

Water to draw. Ryokan, *tr. by* Burton Watson. FCEI

Water travels a long shot. Water Song. Steve Crow. HATNAP

Water-Truck, The. Patrick Lane. NeAC

Water under the Earth. Robert Bly. NNaP

Water understands, The. Water. Emerson. AmPP; OxBSP; PoEL-4

Water Was Carving Out Tall Grills of Girls, The. Tristan Tzara, *tr. fr. French by* Michael Benedikt. POS

Water, water I desire. The Scare-Fire. Robert Herrick. HAP; NoP

Water water water. And nothing but water. A Flamingo's Dream. Aleksander Wat, *tr. by* Czeslaw Milosz. PwPP

Water Whirligigs. D. J. Opperman, *tr. fr. Afrikaans by* Jack Cope *and* Uys Krige. PeSA

Water Witch, The, *sel.* James Fenimore Cooper.

My Brigantine. *Fr. ch.* 15. AA; MOS

Water-Witch, The. Martha Eugenie Perry. CaP

Water, with lidless stare. Narcissus. Charles Gullans. NePoEA

Water without Sound. Malka Heifetz-Tussman, *tr. fr. Yiddish by* Marcia Falk. OV; PeBMyV; VWA

Waterbird goes up, A. 5 Poems. Robert Gray. CBAP

Waterchew! Gregory Corso. VGW

Waterclock drips heavy. To the Tune "Song of the Plum Blossom at the River Town." Yang Shen, *tr.* by Jonathan Chaves. CoBLCP
Watercolor of Grantchester Meadows. Sylvia Plath. LCAP; NYBP; SM
Watercress & Ice. Chase Twichell. MAYP
Watercress Seller, The. Thomas Miller. OxBChV
Waterfall. Seamus Heaney. HeIP
Waterfall. Pierre Reverdy, *tr. fr. French* by Mark Rudman. RHTwFP
Waterfall [*or* Water-Fall], The. Henry Vaughan. FaBoPP; MeLP; MePo; NAEL-1; NOBE; NOCV; NoP; OBS; OBWVE; PoEL-2; PrIm; SeCV-1; WiR
Waterfall. Anne Welsh. PeSA
Waterfall Song, The. Duane Niatum. NOVW
Waterfalls and Liquor ("Waterfalls sounded.") Kapilar, *tr. fr. Tamil* by A. K. Ramanujan. PLW
Watergaw, The. "Hugh MacDiarmid." GoTS; NAEL-2; NoP
Watering Rhyme, A. P. A. Ropes. BoTP
Watering the Horse. Robert Bly. CAPP; NaP
Waterloo. Byron. *See* Childe Harold's Pilgrimage: There was a sound of revelry by night.
Waterloo, *sel.* Keith Douglas.
  "Napoleon is charging our squares." FL
Waterloo Bridge. Christopher Middleton. *Fr.* Herman Moon's Hourbook. NePoEA-2
Waterloo Station. Rosemary Norman. DT
Watermelons. Charles Simic. OBAL
Waterpot. Grace Nichols. PBCV
Waters above! eternal springs! The Shower. Henry Vaughan. BoNaP; ChTr; OBS
  (Showre, The.) MePo; SeCP
Waters chased him as he fled, The. Emily Dickinson. PoEL-5
Waters deep, the waters dark, The. Casting. Howard Nemerov. OxBSP
Water's Edge. Lillian Morrison. RHPC
Water's flowing. *Unknown, tr.* by Jerome Rothenberg. STP
Waters, Indeed, Are to the Palate, Bitter, The. Hubert Witheford. ATNZ
Waters of earth come and go, The. Here and Now. Philip Levine. PoA; VWA
Waters of Life, The. Humbert Wolfe. MoBrPo
Waters of the lake, The. Kyorai, *tr. fr. Japanese* by Burton Watson. *Fr.* Twenty Hokku. FCEI
Waters of Tyne, The. *Unknown.* GBP
Waters of Waiapu, The. Paraire Henare Tomoana, *tr. fr. Maori* by Margaret Orbell. PeNZ
Waters rippled, gleamed and fell, The. At the Cascade. Henrietta Cordelia Ray. CBWP-3
Waters saw thee, O God, The. Bible, *O.T. Fr.* Psalms: Psalm LXXVII ("I cried unto God with my voice."), 16-19. MOS
Waters we dipped from. Tsurayuki, *tr. fr. Japanese* by Burton Watson. *Fr.* Kokin Shu. FCEI
Watershed, The. W. H. Auden. OAEL-2
Watershed. Margaret Avison. OBCV
Watershed. Robert Penn Warren. PoA
Waterside Village. Yün Shou-p'ing, *tr. fr. Chinese* by Jonathan Chaves. CoBLCP
Waterspout, The. William Hart-Smith. *Fr.* Christopher Columbus. PoAu-2
Waterspout. James Merrill. CAPP
Waterwings. Cathy Song. NoAM
Waterwitch, The. *Unknown.* PoAu-1
Watt happened inn the passed? The Hole Seen. May Swenson. SoTCo
Watteau was slightly silly to equip. L'Embarquement pour Cythère. John Manifold. CBAP
Watteau's Coloration ("Watteau's color: atmospheric May.") Alfred Gesswein, *tr. fr. German* by Beth Bjorklund. CoAuP
Watts. Shirley Kaufman. NMM
Watts. Conrad Kent Rivers. PoBA
Watts. Alvin Saxon. PoBA
Watt's Improvements to the Steam Engine. Thomas Baker. *Fr.* The Steam Engine; or, The Power of the Flame. FaBoUs
Waulking Song: Two. Minnie Bruce Pratt. GLP
Wave, The. Jacques Dupin, *tr. fr. French* by Paul Auster. RHTwFP
Wave, The. Daryl Hine. Prf
Wave, The. David Phillips. NeAC
Wave approaching and the wave returning, The. Sequence. George Barker. PoA
Wave blossoms for my delight, a thousand sheets of snow. Tune: The Fisherman. Li Yü, *tr.* by Burton Watson. CoBCP
Wave of coldness, A. Yosano Akiko, *tr.* by Glenn Hughes *and* Yozan T. Iwasaki. WPOW
Wave swashes. Water's Edge. Lillian Morrison. RHPC

Wave Symphony, The. Arthur Davison Ficke. *Fr.* Four Japanese Paintings. PoA
Wave that is dark piles white and slips to its death, The. Fishing Season. Val Vallis. PoAu-2
Wave, wave your glorious battle-flags, brave soldiers of the North. Gettysburg. Edmund Clarence Stedman. PAH
Wave withdrawing, The. "Dover Beach"—a Note to That Poem. Archibald MacLeish. FF
Wavelets like rippling trees. The Painting, *"Mist and Rain on the Spring River,"* by Hsiao Chao. Tai Piao-yüan, *tr.* by Jonathan Chaves. CoBLCP
Waverley, *sels.* Sir Walter Scott.
  Hie Away, Hie Away. *Fr.* 12. EnRP; MoShBr
  To an Oak Tree. *Fr.* 29. OBNC
Waverley Pen, The. *Unknown.* FaBoUs
Waves. Emerson. *See* Nahant.
Waves are hot, The. Kyotai, *tr. fr. Japanese* by Burton Watson. *Fr.* Sixteen Hokku. FCEI
Waves bluster up the bay and through the throat. A Family Photograph 1939. James Keir Baxter. OxBC
Waves forever move, The. The Sisters. John Banister Tabb. AA
Waves Gleam in the Sunshine, The. Heine, *tr. fr. German* by Emma Lazarus. *Fr.* Songs to Seraphine. TrJP
Waves lingering about the fish-weir stakes, The. Hitomaro. *Fr.* Manyo Shu. Ma
Waves of flapping parrots pierce my head whenever I see you in profile. Twinkling of an Eye. Benjamin Péret, *tr.* by Michael Benedikt. POS
Waves of Pleasure. *"Miraji," tr. fr. Urdu* by Mahmood Jamal. PBMUP
Waves of the great sea, The. Sanetomo, *tr. fr. Japanese* by Burton Watson. *Fr.* Twenty-four Tanka. FCEI
Waves on the ebb. Watanabe Suiha, *tr.* by Geoffrey Bownas *and* Anthony Thwaite. PeBJV
Waves rattling pebbles rocked me asleep. Recitative. Ronald McCuaig. PoAu-2
Waves surge higher still, The. Elegy: Ise Lamenting the Death of Empress Onshi. Lady Ise, *tr.* by Etsuko Terasaki *and* Irma Brandeis. BoWoP
Waves that danced about the rock have gone, The. Grandmother and Child. Ruth Dallas. ATNZ
Waves toss high, The. *Unknown. Fr.* Manyo Shu. Ma
Waves want/ to be wheels. Surf. Lillian Morrison. NTCP
Waves wash off the peach blossoms. To the Tune "Heavenly Immortal" ("Waves wash off the peach blossoms.") Yang Shen, *tr.* by Jonathan Chaves. CoBLCP
Waving a Bough. Boris Pasternak, *tr. fr. Russian* by Babette Deutsch. TrJP
Waving flies off a sick man's shoulders. Buson, *tr. fr. Japanese* by Hiroaki Sato. *Fr.* Eighty-seven Hokku. FCEI
Waving Good-bye to My Father. Michael C. Blumenthal. DiL
Waving of a Hand, The. W. S. Merwin. CAPP; DiL
Wax. Winfield Townley Scott. ErPo
Wax-tree, five-needled pine. Stone. Kusano Shimpei, *tr.* by Geoffrey Bownas *and* Anthony Thwaite. PeBJV
Waxwings. Robert Francis. LCAP; NU
Way, The. Robert Creeley. BoLoP; LiTM; NeAP; PPP
Way/ they lay together, The. Peyanar, *tr. fr. Tamil* by A. K. Ramanujan. *Fr.* Seven Said by the Foster-Mother, 1. PLW
Way. Tristan Tzara, *tr. fr. French.* POS, *tr.* by Michael Benedikt; RHTwFP, *tr.* by Lee Harwood
Way, The. Zoltán Zelk, *tr. fr. Hungarian* by Barbara Howes. MHuP
Way a crow, The. Dust of Snow. Robert Frost. CMoP; MoShBr; OxBA; OxBSP; PDV; PrIm; RHPC; SoSe; TAP; UnPo; WeW
Way a Ghost Dissolves, The. Richard Hugo. NAAL-2; NoAM; NoP; SM
Way a tired Chippewa woman, The. Hush. David St. John. DiL; LCAP; MAYP
"Way back in eighty-two or three." The Dreadful Fate of Naughty Nate. John Kendrick Bangs. OBCA
Way Down, The. Philip Levine. NOBA
Way Down, The, *sel.* Jay Macpherson.
  They Return. NOBC; PoA
Way Down, The. Ernest Sandeen. CRP
Way down in the bottom. Poor Little Johnny. *Unknown.* AmFP
Way down in yonders low valley, in some lonesome place. Pretty Saro. *Unknown.* AmFP
Way down Souf whar de lillies grow. To See Ol' Booker T. Maggie Pogue Johnson. CBWP-4
Way Down South. *Unknown.* Par; RHPC
  (Grasshopper and the Elephant, The.) OnUR

We go out in the stony midnight. Thomas McGrath. *Fr.* Letter to an Imaginary Friend, Part One, VIII, 4. NNaP

We Go Out Together. Kenneth Patchen. MoAmPo

We got away—for just two nights. To Be a Pilgrim. Robert Conquest. OxBC

We Got Everything We Needed Here and Aint It Something. *Unknown, tr. fr. Seneca Indian by* Jerome Rothenberg *and* Richard Johnny John. STP

We got sunlight on the sand. There Is Nothin' like a Dame. Oscar Hammerstein II. OBAL

We got this idea. Our Hands in the Garden. Anne Hébert, *tr. by* A. Poulin, Jr.. BoWoP

We grasp our battle spears: we don our breast-plates of hide. The Battle. Ch'ü Yuan, *tr. by* Arthur Waley. WaaP

We Greet Each Other in the Side. *Unknown.* BXAP

We greet thee now open this festal morn. Greeting. Henrietta Cordelia Ray. CBWP-3

We greet you rarest White Heron of One Flight. A Greeting to Queen Elizabeth, the Rare White Heron of Single Flight. Wiremu Kingi Kerekere, *tr. by* Wiremu Kingi Kerekere. PeNZ

We grew like vines and matured like them. Childhood. David Rokeah, *tr. by* Bernhard Frank. MHeP

We grow to the sound of the wind. Dates. *Unknown, tr. fr. Arabic by* E. Powys Mathers. *Fr.* The Thousand and One Nights. AWP; FaPON

We had a motorbike all through the war. A Motorbike. Ted Hughes. InPS

We had a view once. Ashes. Brian Turner. ATNZ

We had already left him. Ugolino. Dante, *tr. fr. Italian by* Seamus Heaney. *Fr.* Divina Commedia: Inferno, XXXII-XXXIII. AnAn; FaBoPV

We had been in the tall grass for hours. At Midsummer. Norman Dubie. MAYP; NoAM

We had been long in mountain snow. The Greeting of the Roses. Hamlin Garland. AA

We had been school-mates,—she and I. Imogene. Eloise Bibb. CBWP-4

We had expected everything but revolt. Nightmare Number Three. Stephen Vincent Benét. MoAmPo; SaC

We had gathered for the love-feast on the time appointed. Who Is My Neighbor? Josephine D. Henderson Heard. CBWP-4

We had no petnames, no diminutives for you. Mary Gravely Jones. Adrienne Rich. *Fr.* Grandmothers. HCAP; NAAL-2; NoAM

We had red earth once to smear on our cheeks. Arrowy Dreams. Witter Bynner. GOA

We had the selfsame world enlarged for each. "George Eliot." *Fr.* Brother and Sister, IX. GN

We halted in a town the host. A Halt. Zbigniew Herbert, *tr. by* Czeslaw Milosz. PwPP

We hauled trash that summer, the three of us. Garbage. Eric Tretheway. MOWH

We have a bed, and a baby too. The Laborer. Richard Dehmel, *tr. by* Jethro Bithell. AWP

We have a crazy mixed-up school. Mixed-Up School. X. J. Kennedy. TDD

We have a dog named "Here." Birthday. William Stafford. NAs

We have a fiction that we live by: it is the river. Waikato-Taniwha-Rau. Vincent O'Sullivan. PeNZ

We have a mountain at the end of our street. In a Desert Town. Lionel Stevenson. AmFN

We have a pretty witty King. Impromptu on Charles II. John Wilmot, 2nd Earl of Rochester. ChTr; NOBL; OBSV

We have all been in rooms. Adultery. James Dickey. CAPP; MT; TAP

We have all, one time or another, met a famous figure. Back Room Joys. Justin Richardson. FiBHP

We have all seen them circling pastures. Under the Vulture-Tree. David Bottoms. MT

We Have Amazed. Pierre Jean Jouve, *tr. fr. French by* Keith Bosley. RHTwFP

We have an old mother that peevish is grown. The Mother Country. Benjamin Franklin. AiP; PAH

We have ascended to this paradise. The Attic. Henri Coulette. NePoEA-2; PoRA

We have bathed, where none have seen us. Bridal Song to Amala. Thomas Lovell Beddoes. *Fr.* Death's Jest Book, IV, iii. ChER; GBL; OBNC

(Epithalamia.) PoEL-4

(Song: "We have bathed, where none have seen us.") NOBVV

We have been a walking. Wassail Song. *Unknown.* GBP

We Have Been Believers. Margaret Abigail Walker. PoBA; PoNe

We have been helping with the cake. Day before Christmas. Marchette Chute. NTCP

We Have Been Here Before. Morris Bishop. FiBHP; NYBP

We have been on trial for our life for so many years. On the Jewish Day of Judgment in the Year 1942 (5703). Jozef Wittlin. VWA, *tr. by* Isaac Komem

We have been sailing in a certain small fountain. About This Course. David Shapiro. PoA

We have been shown. Six Variations. Denise Levertov. AmPP; LCAP

We have borne good sons to broken men. Miners' Wives. Joe Corrie. OxBS

We have bread and wine. The Last Supper. Yusuf al-khal, *tr. by* Abdullah al-Udhari. MPAW

We have climbed the mountain. Sestina: Here in Katmandu. Donald Justice. SM

(Here in Katmandu.) CoAP; HeIP; RFM

We have come in the winter. Song for a Country Wedding. William Jay Smith. GrPl

We have come to a quiet valley in the hills. Haven. Louis Johnson. *Fr.* Four Poems from the Strontium Age, IV. ATNZ

We have come to the edge of the woods. Jacklight. Louise Erdrich. HATNAP; NOVW; TSL

We have come to the end of a dream. The Cities Have Fallen. Fragano Ledgister. PBCV

We have come to the jungle. Jungle. Phyllis Haring. PeSA

We have come to your shrine to worship. A Plea for Mercy. Kwesi Brew. PBA

We have cried in our despair. When Helen Lived. W. B. Yeats. CMoP

We have done what we wanted. Coming to This. Mark Strand. HCAP

We have done with dogma and divinity. After Trinity. John Meade Falkner. OxBTC

We have faith in old proverbs full surely. Where There's a Will There's a Way. Eliza Cook. BLPA; FaFP

We have for many years been bored. The Pen-guin. The Sword-fish. Robert Williams Wood. NBLV

We have forgotten Paris, and his fate. Helen Grown Old. Janet Lewis. QFR

We have found our peace, and move with a turning globe. Arthur Rex Dugard Fairburn. ATNZ

We have found you out. Arson and Cold Lace. Worth Long. NBP

We have gone out in boats upon the sea at night. Passage over Water. Robert Duncan. NoAM; NOBA

We have grown a tree of knowledge, "Worthy Claflin" is the name. The Tree of Knowledge. Lizelia Augusta Jenkins Moorer. CBWP-3

We have grown too old to complain. Jonah's Canticle. Jean-Paul de Dadelsen, *tr. by* Anselm Hollo. RHTwFP

We have had too much consecration. Hilda Doolittle ("H. D.") *Fr.* The Walls Do Not Fall. NAAL-2

We have heard no nightingales singing. Working Class. Bertram J. Warr. NOBC; OBCV; WaP

We have here, she said, only one sun in the month, and for only a little while. Henri Michaux, *tr. fr. French by* Richard Ellmann. *Fr.* I Am Writing to You from a Far-Off Country, I. RHTwFP

We have kept faith, ye Flanders' dead. In Flanders Now. Edna Jaques. CaP

We Have Lived and Loved Together. Charles Jefferys. BLPA; FaBoBe

We have lived like civilized people. The Silent Piano. Louis Simpson. CAPP

We Have Lost Our Little Hanner. "Max Adeler." FiBHP

We have loved each other in this time twenty years. An Unfinished History. Archibald MacLeish. NYBP; VGW

We have met. To a Butterfly. W. H. Davies. FM

We have met late—it is too late to meet. A Denial. Elizabeth Barrett Browning. GBL; OBNC

We have moving over us, over head and spire. Sunday. Josephine Miles. PoA

We have no heart for the fishing, we have no hand for the oar. The Dykes. Kipling. OBWP

We have no idea what his fantastic head. Archaic Torso of Apollo. Rainer Maria Rilke, *tr. by* Robert Bly. NU

We have no prairies. Bogland. Seamus Heaney. FaBCIP; HeIP; IPY; NoAM; NOIV; NoP

We have no time for bridges. Seagulls. Patricia Hubbell. PDV

We have no visions. Safety Pin. Moshe Dor, *tr. by* Bernhard Frank. MHeP

We have not been happy, my Lord, we have not been too happy. T. S. Eliot. *Fr.* Murder in the Cathedral. OxBTC

We have once more caught. The Bear. Ann Stanford. WSC

We have only known this shadowy world. Asadullah Khan Ghalib, *tr. by* Ahmed Ali. GoT

We have opened the door. The Dead Feast of the Kol-Folk. Whittier. PoEL-4

We have our work. Farewell before Dawn. Nakano Shigeharu, *tr. by* Geoffrey Bownas *and* Anthony Thwaite. PeBJV

We Have Paid Enough Long Since in Our Own Blood. Virgil, *tr. fr. Latin by* Richmond Lattimore. *Fr.* Georgics. WaaP

We have parents who peep through a hole. *Unknown, tr. by* Hiroaki Sato. FCEI

We have plenty of matches in our house. Love Poem. Ron Padgett. UL

We have reached the age. Maturity. Isabelle Vuckovic, *tr. by* Kathleen Weaver. OV

We have reached the end of pastime, for always. End of Play. Robert Graves. EBEV

We have scarcely time to tell thee. Shelly. James McIntyre. FiBHP

We have seen a house in the sleeping town. Death of the Horses by Fire. Tess Gallagher. NAmP

We have seen her/ the world over. Hilda Doolittle ("H. D.") *Fr.* Tribute to the Angels. CRP; VGW

We have seen how the most amiable. Hilda Doolittle ("H. D.") *Fr.* The Walls Do Not Fall. BoWoP; PBWP

We have seen thee, queen of cheese. Queen of Cheese. James McIntyre. FiBHP

We have sent him seeds of the melon's core. Ku Klux. Madison Cawein. AA; PAH

We have shared beauty and have shared grief, too. A Prayer for a Marriage. Mary Carolyn Davies. TrPWD

We have struck the regions wherein we are keel or reef. Zone. Louise Bogan. WPE

We have such plain faces. Joseph Rolnik, *tr. fr. Yiddish by* Irving Feldman. *Fr.* Poets. PeBMYV

We have suffered enough to be wise. Graffiti for a Particle Accelerator. Dexter Masters. KS

We have sweat our share. Stable-Talk. Raymond Knister. CaP

We have tangled together. Growing Together. Joyce Carol Oates. IHMS

We have tested and tasted too much, lover. Advent. Patrick Kavanagh. FaBCIP; TIRV

"We have the mauve or the cerise." Shop Talk. Roy Fuller. OxBC

We have the road here, the gate the key. Moved towards a Future. Laura Chester. NPGG

We have the statue for it—Liberty. Address to the Refugees. John Malcolm Brinnin. GOA

We have these drums. Percussions. Ron Welburn. CNA

We have to bury the urns. Leaving Seoul; 1953. Walter Lew. BrSi

We have tomorrow. Youth. Langston Hughes. AmFN

We have tried words before—always in vain. The Knife. Milton Kaplan. TrJP

We have two ducks. One blue. One black. Quack, Quack! "Dr. Seuss." RAR

We have watched again. Among Hawks. Lance Henson. VoR

We haven't eaten the grape. Letter from Sicily. Emanuel di Pasquale. ILY

We heard the corncrake's call from close at hand. First Corncrake. John Hewitt. NeIP

We heard the thrushes by the shore and sea. In Kerry. John Millington Synge. FaBoPP; GBL; MoBrPo

We hearing them. Shunzei, *tr. fr. Japanese by* Burton Watson. *Fr.* Thirty Tanka. FCEI

We Heart. Laura Chester. NPGG

We, Hermia. Helena and Hermia. Shakespeare. *Fr.* A Midsummer Night's Dream, III, ii. GN

We hesitate along. A Graveyard in Queens. John Montague. IPY

We hold a splendid feast today. *Unknown, tr. fr. Chinese by* Burton Watson. *Fr.* Nineteen Old Poems of the Han, IV. CoBCP

"We hold our flat shields, we wear our jerkins of hide." Hymn to the Fallen. *Unknown, tr. by* Arthur Waley. OBWP

We hold these truths to be self-evident. Decoy. John Ashbery. PoM

We hurry on, nor passing note. Digby Mackworth Dolben. OBNC

We in Antioch were astonished when we heard. On the Outskirts of Antioch. Constantine P. Cavafy, *tr. by* Edmund Keeley *and* Philip Sherrard. VMG

We in our wandering. A Song of the Open Road. *Unknown, tr. by* John Addington Symonds. AWP

We invite him to die. Colobus Monkey. *Unknown, tr. fr. Yoruba by* Ulli Beier. *Fr.* Hunter Poems of the Yoruba. RB

We Irish pride ourselves as patriots. Ireland. John Hewitt. CIP; FaBoPP

We is gathahed hyeah, my brothahs. An Ante-Bellum Sermon. Paul Laurence Dunbar. BPo

We issue from the meat of Pineapple Street. On the Island. L. E. Sissman. NYBP

We jabs him in the ribs for spite. Irish Wake Song. Richard O'Connell. SoTCo

We Just Sit About Quietly. Mihály Ladányi, *tr. fr. Hungarian by* Edwin Morgan. MHuP

We kept him an hour in the/ bottom. A Cocker of Snooks. Phyllis Gotlieb. NOBC

We kissed at the barrier; and passing through. On the Departure Platform. Thomas Hardy. NOBE; OBNC; OxBTC

We knelt on the rocks by the dark green pools. Frances Mayo. CN

We knew it would rain, for all the morn. Before the Rain. Thomas Bailey Aldrich. GN

We knew so much; when her beautiful eyes could lighten. Sagacity. William Rose Benét. MoAmPo

We know/ the winter earth. November Twenty-sixth Nineteen Hundred and Sixty-three. Wendell Berry. LiTM

We know it doesn't rhyme much anymore. What Is Poetry. James Scully. FYAP

We know not what it is, dear, this sleep so deep and still. The Two Mysteries. Mary Mapes Dodge. AA; PWR; TrCP; WGRP

We know nothing. The Death of Guillaume Apollinaire. Tristan Tzara, *tr. by* Lee Harwood. RHTwFP

We ladies sense it is the cuckoo builds no nest. Liberation. Ruth Stone. BoWoP

We Laughed. Rochelle Kraut. UL

We lay in the trenches we'd dug in the ground. The Ballad of Bunker Hill. Edward Everett Hale. PAH

We lay red roses on his grave. Paul Laurence Dunbar. Robert Hayden. NoP

We lay upon the southern slope, and saw. Coruisk. Walter Chalmers Smith. PoSH

We Lay Us Down to Sleep. Louise Chandler Moulton. AA

We lead a boorish existence out here. Bucolic. Simon Rae. NPo

We lean across the kitchen table. Arm Wrestling with My Father. Jack Driscoll. GOYP

We lean together over fuming acid. On the Marriage of Art and Science. Sonya Dorman. BWV

We leaned out of the window. The First Rain. Angelos Sikelianos, *tr. by* Edmund Keeley *and* Philip Sherrard. VMG

We learned that you don't shoot. Statement on Our Higher Education. W. M. Ransom. CDW

We learned to laugh. Although the flying bombs. Coman Leavenworth. *Fr.* Norfolk Memorials, II. LiTA

We leave the farmland for the formless coast. Summer Island. William Logan. MAYP

We leave the well-beloved place. Tennyson. *Fr.* In Memoriam A. H. H., CII. PoEL-5

We leave thy courts to-day. Farewell to Allen University. Josephine D. Henderson Heard. CBWP-4

We left/ The silent forest. Charles Mair. *Fr.* Tecumseh. OBCV

We left our rented farmhouse for three weeks. End of August. Gregory Orr. MAYP

We left the city when the summer day. Indolence. Robert Bridges. BrPo

We left the horses in the draw. A Season of Loss. Jim Barnes. HATNAP

We lie back to back. Curtains. The Suitor. Jane Kenyon. InPK

We lie by towering hollyhocks. August Night, 1953. Elizabeth B. Harrod. NePoEA

We lie in that other darkness, ourselves. Now That My Father Lies Down beside Me. Stanley Plumly. DiL; GeTw

We lie there. Business Partners. Brenda Agard. WS

We lift the curtain of the past to-day. Lincoln. Henrietta Cordelia Ray. CBWP-3

We like March—his shoes are purple. Emily Dickinson. SOTW; TTTS

We, like shades that were first conjured up. And through the Caribbean Sea. Margaret Danner. BPo

We live:—dishonoured, in the shit. So what? it had to be. Iambes VIII. André Marie de Chénier, *tr. by* Tom Paulin. FaBoPV

We Live in a Cage. William J. Harris. PoBA

We Live in a Rickety House. Alexander McLachlan. NOBC; OBCV

We live in fragments. Tight Rope. Imamu Amiri Baraka. CNA

We live in houses of ample weight. Edvard Munch. Charles Wright. HCAP

We live in the oblivion of our metamorphoses. Our Movements. Paul Eluard, *tr. by* Michael Benedikt. POS

We live, while we see the sun. Pedro Calderón de la Barca, *tr. fr. Spanish by* Arthur Symons. *Fr.* Life Is a Dream. AWP

We lived deep in a land of optative moods. From the Canton of Expectation. Seamus Heaney. CIP

We lived in language all our black selves. When the Wine Was Gone. Alvin Aubert. CNA

We lived one and twenty year. Upon a Notorious Shrew. *Unknown*. FaBoEE

We looked over the white sea. Hill Love. James Macmillan. PoSH

We looked the part. Crossing the Border into Canada. Joy Harjo. STE

We looked, we loved, and therewith instantly. Pure Death. Robert Graves. GTBS-P; MoAB

We Lost but Love Gained Nothing. Mahmoud Darwish, *tr. fr. Arabic by* Abdullah al-Udhari. MPAW

We Love Life Whenever We Can. Mahmoud Darwish, *tr. fr. Arabic by* Abdullah al-Udhari. MPAW

We Love the Venerable House. Emerson. AH

We love thee, Ann Maria Smith. The Editor's Wooing. "Orpheus C. Kerr." OBAL

We love with great difficulty. Sing with Your Body. Janice Mirikitani. WPOW

We Love You the Way You Are. David McFadden. NeAC

We loved our nightjar, but she would not stay with us. The Nightjar. Sir Henry Newbolt. Mes

We loved the wild clamor of battle. The Song of the Flags. Silas Weir Mitchell. PAH

We Lying by Seasand. Dylan Thomas. PoA

We made a mistake in this song. *Unknown, tr. by* Jerome Rothenberg *and* Richard Johnny John. STP

We made castles of grass, green halls, enormous stem-lined rooms. The Riders. Ann Stanford. WPE

We make a home so as not to stay at home. Customs. Juan Gelman, *tr. by* Yishai Tobin. VWA

We make both mead and garden gay. Daffodils. P. A. Ropes. BoTP

We make our meek adjustments. Chaplinesque. Hart Crane. CMoP; LiTM; MoP; NAAL-2; NoAM; NOBA; OxBA; VGW

We Manage Most When We Manage Small. Linda Gregg. AmPA; NPGG

We march into the suburbs led by a six-year-old kid. Some of Us Are Exiles from No Land. Diana O Hehir. NPGG

We marched, and saw a company of Canadians. Canadians. Ivor Gurney. FaBoTw

We marched half the day. Nothing Said. Brenda Agard. WS

We married for acceptance; to stall the nagging. My Second Marriage to My First Husband. Alice Fulton. NAmP

We marry our grandfathers. Extensions of Linear Mobility. Jeanine Hathaway. IHMS

We mask our faces. On Halloween. Aileen Fisher. RAR

We may be humble in our ways. Why Should We Sell Our Dreams? Ahmad Faraz, *tr. by* Mahmood Jamal. PBMUP

We May Be Learning How to Tell the Truth. Marilyn Hacker. *Fr.* La Fontaine de Vaucluse, VII. Son

We May Be Lo', We May Be Poor. Thomas Blackah. PF

We may no longer stay on shore. The Greenland Whale Fishery. *Unknown*. OBET

We may not climb the heavenly steeps. Our Master. Whittier. BLRP; WBLP

We may shut our eyes. Joys. James Russell Lowell. BoTP

We may sigh o'er the heavy burdens. The Burdens of All. Frances Ellen Watkins Harper. PWR

We may well wonder at those froward hermits. The Eremites. Robert Graves. LiTB

We Meet in the Lives of Animals. Peter Everwine. NNaP

We meet 'neath the sounding rafter. The Revel. Bartholomew Dowling. BLPA

We meet tonight to pass the point of blame. The Reckoning. Alice R. Friman. KS

We meet upon the Level and we part upon the Square. The Level and the Square. Robert Morris. BLPA

We Men Are of Two Worlds. Mary Elizabeth Colman. CaP

We Met. Mary E. Tucker. CBWP-1

We met, a hundred of us met. The Vision. William Taylor. NOEC

We met for supper in your flat-bottomed boat. Dream Barker. Jean Valentine. PrIm; VGW

We Met on Roads of Laughter. Charles Divine. FaBoBe

We met the British in the dead of winter. Meeting the British. Paul Muldoon. CIP; FaBoPV; NoAM

We might have known it always: music. An die Musik. David Malouf. CBAP

We mind not now the merits of our kind. Marriage and Money. Sir Charles Sedley. *Fr.* The Happy Pair. OBSV

We miss a kinsman more. Emily Dickinson. OxBSP

We more than others have the perfect right. Song of the Moderns. John Gould Fletcher. AWP

We mourn to-day o'er our sister dead. Resting. Josephine D. Henderson Heard. CBWP-4

We move from one. The River. Sam Cornish. PoBA

We move in elephantine row. Express. William Allingham. NOBVV

We Move On to a Country. Mahmoud Darwish, *tr. fr. Arabic by* Lena Jayyusi *and* Christopher Middleton. *Fr.* Poems after Beirut, II. MAP

We move very fast and smoothly. Good Times and No Bread. Reginald Lockett. CNA

We moved like fingers. San Francisco Poem. John Logan. NNaP

We Must Be Free or Die. Wordsworth. *See* It Is Not to Be Thought Of [That the Flood].

We must be nobler for our dead, be sure. The Watchers. Arlo Bates. AA

We must burn up. Vincente Rodríguez Nietzsche, *tr. fr. Spanish by* Julio Marzán. *Fr.* Mural. InW

We Must Free Ourselves Today. Ida Vallerugo, *tr. fr. Italian by* Muriel Kittel. DMI

We must kill our gods before they kill us. Black Trumpeter. Henry Dumas. PoBA

We must leave the handrails and the Ariadne-threads. À l'Ange Avantgardien. Francis Reginald. MoCV

We Must Look at the Harebell. "Hugh MacDiarmid." *Fr.* In Memoriam James Joyce. NAEL-2

We Must Make a Kingdom of It. Gregory Orr. BLA; MAYP

We must not sever, you and I. Brotherhood. "J. J. W." PeHV

We must pass like smoke or live within the spirit's fire. Immortality. "Æ." AWP; OBMV; TIRV; WGRP

We Must Return. Agostinho Neto, *tr. fr. Portuguese by* Marga Holness. WMBCH

We Must Shed our Illusions. Jukka Vieno, *tr. fr. Finnish by* Aili Jarvenpa. SOP

We must sit down. Councils. Marge Piercy. NeAC

We must sleep like air. The Storm. Shauqi Abi Shaqra, *tr. by* Abdullah al-Udhari. MPAW

We must stay away from our fathers. Little Father Poem. Marvin Bell. LCAP

We mustered at midnight, in darkness we formed. Bethel. A. J. H. Duganne. PAH

We named you. Rachel. Linda Pastan. TV

We need him now—his rugged faith that held. Abraham Lincoln, the Master. Thomas Curtis Clark. OHIP

We need no runners here. Booze is law. Harlem, Montana; Just Off the Reservation. James Welch. CDW; HATNAP; NOVW; STE

We, Negroes, will go out with knives. White Moon. H. Leivick, *tr. by* Benjamin *and* Barbara Harshav. AYP

We never half believed the stuff. James Wetherell. E. A. Robinson. MoAmPo

We Never Know. Yusef Komunyakaa. MT

We never know how high we are. Emily Dickinson. AnAmPo

We never know we go. Emily Dickinson. AnAmPo

We never laughed much. Cartwheels. Mary Lonnberg Smith. AIW

We never meet, yet we meet day by day. Thoughts in Separation. Alice Meynell. BoTP

We Never Said Farewell. Mary Elizabeth Coleridge. OxBSP; WPE

We never spent time in the mountains. Interlude. Welton Smith. PoBA

We Object. *Unknown, tr. fr. Maori by* A Armstrong. WTO

We, of the Singing Swords. Jacob Glatstein, *tr. fr. Yiddish by* Benjamin *and* Barbara Harshav. AYP

We offer you, Lord, in our strong, our sensitive hands. Offertory. John F. Deane. TIRV

We often come to the City Park. City Park. Remco Campert, *tr. by* John Scott *and* Graham Martin. DuIn

We only know that in the sultry weather. England and America, 1863. Richard Monckton Milnes. EBVV

We only live between. For Sheridan. Robert Lowell. HCAP

We oughtta take somma these college perfessers. What the Sixties Were Really Like. Sam Abrams. UL

We outgrow love, like other things. Emily Dickinson. NOBA

We owe the ancients something. You have read. Fitz-Greene Halleck. *Fr.* Fanny. OBAL

We Own the Night. Imamu Amiri Baraka. PoBA

We park and stare. A full sky of the stars. The Death of the Sheriff. Robert Lowell. LCAP

(Noli Me Tangere, The.) LCAP

We part/ I go beyond the. *Unknown, tr. fr. Japanese by* Burton Watson. *Fr.* Kokin Shu. FCEI

We pass a stranger. He glances. The Stranger Not Ourselves. William Stafford. NNaP

We passed each other, turned and stopped for half an hour, then went our way. On the Road to the Sea. Charlotte Mew. BrRo; FaBoWP; PeHV

We passed the ice of pain. The Moment. Theodore Roethke. NYBP

We passed their graves. Peace. Langston Hughes. BPo

We photographed everything. The 20th Century. Darrell Gray. UL

We pick/ the bittersweet grapes. Napa, California. Ana Castillo. WPOW

We Pick Ferns, We Pick Ferns. *Unknown, tr. fr. Chinese by* Burton Watson. CoBCP

We planted a garden/ Of all kinds of flowers. Flowers. Harry Behn. FaPON

We pledged our hearts, my love and I. The Exchange. Samuel Taylor Coleridge. FiBHP

We plotted our future, the young city. Here in Netanya. Meir Wieseltier, *tr. by* Warren Bargad *and* Stanley F. Chyet. IP

We plough and sow—we're so very, very low. The Song of the Lower Classes. Ernest Charles Jones. CoMu

We plucked the bracken, plucked the bracken. *Unknown, tr. by* Arthur Waley. BoS

We Poets in Our Youth. Wordsworth. *Fr.* Resolution and Independence. FaBoRV

We poets pride ourselves on what. On Hearing Mrs. Woodhouse Play the Harpsichord. W. H. Davies. BrPo

We Poets Speak. Francis Thompson. *Fr.* Sister Songs. FaBV

We pointed it out to his bed-ridden eyes. Hospital. Geoffrey C. Millard. PeSA

We poor Agawams. Mr. Ward of Anagrams Thus. Nathaniel Ward. SCAP

We Praise Thee, God, for Harvests Earned. John Coleman Adams. AH

We Praise Thee, If One Rescued Soul. Lydia Huntley Sigourney. AH

We praise thee, O God; we acknowledge thee to be the Lord. Te Deum Laudamus. *Unknown.* WGRP

We pray Thee, have mercy on Zion! Prayer for Redemption. *Unknown.* TrJP

We pray to life's source, Mary. The Virgin Mary. *Unknown, tr. by* Joseph P. Clancy. OBWVE

We prayed for miracles: the prairie dry. Epilogue to the Outrider. Dorothy Livesay. CaP

We preside, brothers, over the twilight of freedom. Twilight of Freedom. Osip Mandelstam, *tr. by* Andrew Glaze. VWA

We pulled for you when the wind was against us and the sails were low. Song of the Galley-slaves. Kipling. ChTr; GTBS-P; HAP; PoEL-5

We put more coal on the big red fire. Father's Story. Elizabeth Madox Roberts. FaPON

We put our heads into the window of a car which was passing. Leslie Scalapino. *Fr.* Hmmmm. NPGG

We put out our hands on the window—cold. In Time of Need. William Stafford. UnPo

We put the shoe on him the first time this morning. The First Shoe. Máire Mhac an tSaoi, *tr. by* Brendan O Hehir. OV

We Rainclouds. Marvin Wyche, Jr... AmNP

We raise de wheat. *Unknown.* BPo; TAP

We ran across the meadow scabbed with the cow-dung. Geoffrey Hill. *Fr.* Mercian Hymns, XXII. HAP

We Reached Out Far. Peretz Markish, *tr. fr. Yiddish by* Jacob Sonntag. TrJP

We read and hear about you every day. To the Rulers. Howard Nemerov. OxBC

We read letters of the dead and are like helpless gods. Letters of the Dead. Wislawa Szymborska, *tr. by* Czeslaw Milosz. PwPP

We Read of a People. *Unknown.* AH

We Real Cool. Gwendolyn Brooks. CAPP; FF; HAP; HeIP; HoPM; IDB; InPK; NoP; PoA; PoBA; PoE; PrIm; SM; SoSe; TAP; TTY; WeW

We reconstruct lives in the intensive. Clan Meeting: Births and Nations: A Blood Song. Michael S. Harper. NoAM

We recruits have our commanders to send us off. Tu Fu, *tr. fr. Chinese by* Burton Watson. *Fr.* On the Border, First Series, 4. CoBCP

We remember, we do not forget, O Trail Breakers. Trail Breakers. James Henry Daugherty. AmFN

We remember you/ calling America. Poetry Concert. Michael S. S. Harper. TAP

We retain the flowers in mind as we pass. Lady Izumi, *tr. fr. Japanese by* Hiroaki Sato. *Fr.* Fifty-one Tanka. FCEI

We return again to the steep carving. The Mountain. Musaemura Bonus Zimunya. WMBCH

We ride down the coast hwy through the rain. The Great Santa Barbara Oil Disaster OR. Conyus. AmPA

We rise from the snow where we've. Selective Service. Carolyn Forché. MAYP; NAmP

We road the hiways. The Ballgame. Imamu Amiri Baraka. DiL

We rode at a trot. Grenada. Mikhail Arkadyevich Svetlov, *tr. by* Alexander Kaun. WaaP

We rode the canals. Boxing the Fox. Pearse Hutchinson. CIP

We rode the tawny Texan hills. That Texan Cattle Man. Joaquin Miller. AnAmPo

We run the dangercourse. We Walk the Way of the New World. Don L. Lee. BPo; NeAC; PoBA

We said: there will surely be hawthorn out. Spring Snow and Tui. Mary Ursula Bethell. PeNZ

We sail out of season into an oyster-gray wind. Crossing the Atlantic. Anne Sexton. MOS; NoAM

We sail toward evening's lonely star. Celia Thaxter. AA

We sailed and sailed upon the desert sea. Hope. William Dean Howells. AA; MOS

We sailed in sunshine; but then was black. The Peak. W. W. Gibson. PoSH

We sailed in the Ark. The New Noah. "Adunis," *tr. by* Abdullah al-Udhari. MPAW

We sailed to and fro in Erie's broad lake. Perry's Victory. *Unknown.* PAH

We sat across the table. The Friend. Marge Piercy. CAPP; NMM

We sat at the hut of the fisher. Twilight. Heine, *tr. by* Louis Untermeyer. AWP

We sat before an October fire. The Necessity of Falling. William Mills. MT

We sat in an old, crumbling house. Mah-do-ge Tohee. STE

We sat in the courtyard. Merida, 1969. William Matthews. EOEF

We sat together at one summer's end. Adam's Curse. W. B. Yeats. BIrV; CMoP; NAEL-2; NoAM; NoP; OAEL-2; SOTW; TEP

We sat, two children, warm against the wall. The Gate. Edwin Muir. CMoP; LiTM

We sat within the farm-house old. The Fire of Drift-wood. Longfellow. AmPP; BLPL; NAAL-1; NOBA; NoP; OxBA; TAP

We saw a bloody sunset over Courtland. Remembering Nat Turner. Sterling A. Brown. PoBA; PoNe

We saw a town by the track in Colorado. Holding the Sky. William Stafford. RFM

We saw anchored worlds in a shallow stream. Lying on a Bridge. Van K. Brock. MT; SM

We saw and woo'd each other's eyes. The Reward of Innocent Love. William Habington. *Fr.* Castara. ACP

We saw it all. We saw the souvenir shops, and sitting. Niagara Falls. Alan Dugan. PoA

"We saw reindeer." Rigorists. Marianne Moore. NU

We saw the Brochan spectre from. Poem, 1972. Syd Scroggie. PoSH

We saw the light shine out a-far. The Golden Carol. *Unknown.* OHIP

We saw the swallows gathering in the sky. George Meredith. *Fr.* Modern Love, XLVII. EnLoPo; GTBS-P; Mes; NOBE; NOBVV; OAEL-2; OBNC
(We Saw the Swallows.) ELP

We saw Thee in Thy balmy nest. Shepherd's Hymn, The ("We saw Thee in Thy balmy nest.") Richard Crashaw. *Fr.* In the Holy Nativity of Our Lord God. ACP; TrGrPo, 3 *sts.*
(Verses from the Shepherd's Hymn.) OBEV

We saw truth shining through the shabby compromise. Rededication. Emanuel Litvinoff. WaP

We say he is dead; ah, the word is too somber. Not Dead, but Sleeping. Clara Ann Thompson. CBWP-2

We say that a loon, most graceful and dark. A Woman Gave Me a Red Star to Wear on My Headband. Jimmie Durham. HATNAP

We say the sea is lonely; better say. The Open Sea. William Meredith. CoAP; GrPl; MOS; NePoEA; TAP; UnPo

We Say This Prayer. József Tornai, *tr. fr. Hungarian by* William Jay Smith. MHuP

"We seamen are the bonny boys." A Song of the Seamen and Land Soldiers. *Unknown.* OxBSS

We search the world for truth; we cull. The Book Our Mothers Read. Whittier. *Fr.* Miriam. BLRP

We see each living thing finally die. Louise Labé, *tr. by* Willis Barnstone. BoWoP

We See Jesus. Annie Johnson Flint. BLRP

We see lots of people at the party. The Party. Jerome Sala. UL

We see the dog running. What They Ate What They Wore. Linda Gregg. NAmP

We seek to know, and knowing seek. In Immemoriam. "Cuthbert Bede." NA

We seem to exist in a hazardous time. Evolution. Ben King. AnAmPo

We send you home to a grave on Stone Tower Mountain. Weeping for Ying Yao. Wang Wei, *tr. by* Burton Watson. CoBCP

We sent him to one-with. The Psychonaut Sonnets: Jones. Albert Goldbarth. SM

We set out yesterday upon a winter drive. Alexandre Dumas, *tr. fr. French by* Gerard Manley Hopkins. *Fr.* The Lady of the Pearls. TTY

We Settled by the Lake. F. D. Reeve. NYBP

We shall be called harsh names by men unborn. Contemporary. Hortense Flexner. PoA

"We shall cede with a brotherly embrace." The Rise of Shivaji. Zulfikar Ghose. MoBS

We shall come tomorrow morning, who were not to have her love. Emily Hardcastle, Spinster. John Crowe Ransom. CMoP; OxBSP

We shall do much in the years to come. What Have We Done Today? Nixon Waterman. WBLP

We shall have beds round which light scents are wafted. The Death of Lovers. Baudelaire, *tr. by* Roy Campbell. OBD

We shall have everything we want and there'll be no more dying. Ode to Joy. Frank O'Hara. GLP; NeAP; PPP

We Shall Have Far to Go. James Wreford Watson. CaP

We Shall Know. *Unknown.* PWR

We shall live again. *Unknown, tr. fr. Sioux Indian by* James Mooney. *Fr.* Ghost Dance Songs. STP

We shall not always plant while others reap. From the Dark Tower. Countee Cullen. BANP; BPo; CDC; IDB; LiTM; NAAL-2; PoBA; PoNe; Son

We shall not cease from exploration. T. S. Eliot. *Fr.* Four Quartets: Little Gidding, V. ImOP

We shall not dwell forever in these yellow lands, our pleasance. Anabasis. "St.-John Perse," *tr. by* T. S. Eliot. RHTwFP

We Shall Not Escape Hell. Marina Tsvetayeva, *tr. fr. Russian by* Elaine Feinstein. BoWoP; WPOW

We shall not ever meet them bearded in heaven. On the Death of Friends in Childhood. Donald Justice. InPK; LCAP

We shall not forget anything. Ring Road. Sandra Mangini, *tr. by* Muriel Kittel. DMI

We shall not go up against you. This Be Our Revenge. Saul Tchernichowsky, *tr. by* Shalom Spiegel. TrJP

We Shall Overcome. *Unknown.* AH, *with music;* EaLo

We shall remember him. John Butler Yeats. Jeanne Robert Foster. GoYe

We Shall Say. Miriam Allen DeFord. GoYe

We shan't see Willy any more, Mamie. To a Bull-Dog. J. C. Squire. FM

We shared not one idea in thirty years. A Reformer to His Father. James Simmons. BIrV

We should cultivate our different tastes. Cultivation. Mrs. Henry Linden. CBWP-4

We should have freely known the garden. Mohammad Taqi Mir, *tr. by* Ahmed Ali. GoT

We shut them out, the houses. Time Out. Oliver Jenkins. GoYe

We, sighing, said, "Our Pan is dead." Thoreau's Flute. Louisa May Alcott. AA

We sing our sons who have died red. Song (We Sing). Cosmo Pieterse. WMBCH

We sirens, since we rigged up stereophonic sound. The Sirens. Gordon Challis. PeNZ

We sit around the lamp talking, hating to leave. My Small Daughter. Huang Tsun-hsien, *tr. by* J. D. Schmidt. WFTU

We sit at a sidewalk table. The Firebreathers at the Café Deux Magots. Miller Williams. MT

We sit by the old tent. What Are You Thinking About? James Macmillan. PoSH

We sit, crookbacked, at the bar. At the Telephone Club. Henri Coulette. CoAP

We sit in a *tuk-tuk* with binoculars. This Kampuchea. Jay Parini. BLA

We sit in the basement kitchen, arranging. A Card Game; Kinjiro Sawada. Patricia Y. Ikeda. BrSi

We sit indoors and talk of the cold outside. There Are Roughly Zones. Robert Frost. CMoP; PPP

We sit late, watching the dark slowly unfold. September. Ted Hughes. BoLoP

We sit outside. Death of Dr. King. Sam Cornish. CNA; OFD; PoBA

We Sit Solitary. *Unknown.* TrJP

We sit watching the afternoon summer smell ripely. James Powell on Imagination. Larry Neal. BPo

We six pile in, the engine churning ink. Nigger Song: An Odyssey. Rita Dove. AmPA

We smile at astrological hopes. For the Conjunction of Two Planets. Adrienne Rich. ImOP

We smiled together. Gardens. Neil Curry. NPo

We Soldiers of All Nations Who Lie Killed. James Agee. NIP

We sound like crying bullheads. Voices. Nora Dauenhauer. HATNAP

We sow the fertile seed and then we reap it. Evening Hymn in the Hovels. Francis Lauderdale Adams. OxBS

We spend our morning. The Memory of Elena. Carolyn Forché. ER; MAYP; NoAM

We spent all day fishing and talking. Late at Night During a Visit of Friends. Robert Bly. InPS

We spoke tonight/ of the departure from Egypt. The Departure. Jeremy Robson. VWA

We stand at the edge of the cliff and in the depths beneath us. Molokai. Tomas Tranströmer, *tr. by* Samuel Charters. AnAn

We stand facing each other, our. Stars. Sara Boyes. DT

We stand in line all morning long to see it. The Most Expensive Picture in the World. Howard Nemerov. EyDe

We stand naked behind the line. On the Death of Sylvia Plath. Judith Herzberg. VWA, *tr. by* Shirley Kaufman; WPOW, *tr. by* Manfred Wolf

We stand on the edge of wounds, hugging canned meat. Dream of Rebirth. Roberta Hill Whiteman. CDW

We stand together. Last Journey. John Montague. CIP; FaBCIP

We started early, just as soon. Today Is Saturday. Zilpha Keatley Snyder. ILY

We started off. Exhaustion. Sa'di Yusuf, *tr. by* Abdullah al-Udhari. MPAW

We stayed the night in the pathless gorge. Oh, Lovely Rock. Robinson Jeffers. NU

We step out on the green rectangle. On the Tennis Court at Night. Galway Kinnell. TSL

We still call it mother. The Competitors. Gerald William Barrax. KS

We still have/ To fly. Flight. Hsin Mu, *tr. by* Dominic Cheung. IFON

We still want to say the one true thing. Still. Lisa Zeidner. SM

We still write them. Poems. Vittorio Sereni, *tr. by* Paul Vangelisti. PFI

We stood at the edge of the crowded bar drinking. The Princess. Muhammad al-Asad, *tr. by* Lena Jayyusi *and* Charles Doria. MAP

We stood by a pond that winter day. Neutral Tones. Thomas Hardy. BrPo; CMoP; EBVV; HAP; HeIP; InPK; InPS; MoBrPo; MoP; NAEL-2; NoAM; NOBVV; OAEL-2; PPP; TEP; UnPo

We stood up before day. In the Dordogne. John Peale Bishop. OBWP; VGW

We summoned not the Silent Guest. The Skeleton at the Feast. James Jeffrey Roche. AA

We Survive! Hirsch Glick, *tr. fr. Yiddish by* Ruth Rubin. TrJP

We swing ungirded hips. The Song of the Ungirt Runners. Charles Hamilton Sorley. MoBrPo; OBEV

We take it with us, the cry. Departure. Carolyn Forché. AnAn

We take place in what we believe. Elephant Rock. Primus St. John. PoBA

We take up the halberds of Wu. Those Who Died for Their Country. *Unknown, tr. fr. Chinese by* Burton Watson. *Fr.* Nine Songs. CoBCP

We talk of old men who have forgotten their/ thoughts. Errore. Pier Giorgio Di Cicco. NOBC

We talked and talked. Watching the Native Country from the Border. Lo Fu, *tr. by* Dominic Cheung. IFON

We talked of things but all the time we wanted each other. And What with the Blunders. Kenneth Patchen. NaP

We talked [*or* talk'd] with open heart, and tongue. The Fountain. Wordsworth. EnRP; GTBS; GTBS-P; SeCePo

We Thank Thee. John Oxenham. BLRP

We Thank Thee. *Unknown.* FaPON

We thank Thee for the joy of common things. A Prayer for Thanksgiving. Joseph Auslander. TrPWD

We thank Thee for the morning light. *Unknown.* BLRP

We thank Thee, Heavenly Father. Thanks to Spring. Mary Anderson. BoTP

We Thank Thee, Lord. Calvin W. Laufer. AH

We Thank Thee, Lord. John Oxenham. *Fr.* A Little Te Deum of the Commonplace. WBLP

We thank Thee, Lord, for quiet upland lawns. Grace and Thanksgiving. Elizabeth Gould. BoTP

We thank Thee, Lord, for this our food. *Unknown.* BLRP

We thank Thee, now, O Father. The Most Acceptable Gift. Matthias Claudius, *tr. by* J. M. Campbell. BLRP

We Thank You! L. E. Cox. BoTP

We, that did nothing study but the way. A Renunciation. Henry King. OBEV

We that have done and thought. Spilt Milk. W. B. Yeats. OxBSP

We that were wood. Susan Howe. LP

We that with like hearts love, we lovers twain. A Vow to Heavenly Venus. Joachim Du Bellay, *tr. by* Andrew Lang. AWP

We, the Ancient Ones. Rain Song of the Giant Society. *Unknown, tr. by* Matilda Coxe Stevenson. AnAmPo

We, the boys of Sanpete County, in obedience to the cause. The Boys of Sanpete County. *Unknown.* AmFP

We, the captives of a thousand skies. Farewell to Europe. William Pillen. VWA

We, the rescued. Chorus of the Rescued. Nelly Sachs. VWA, *tr. by* Harry Zohn; WPOW, *tr. by* Ruth Mead *and* Matthew Mead.

We the Revolutionaries; or, This America. Moyshe-Leyb Halpern, *tr. fr. Yiddish by* Benjamin *and* Barbara Harshav. AYP

We, the symmetrians, seek justice here. N. B., Symmetrians. Gene Derwood. LiTA

We, the unborn. Chorus of the Unborn. Nelly Sachs, *tr. by* Ruth Mead *and* Matthew Mead. NYBP

We the White Witches are, that free. Masque of the Virtues against Love. Mary Monck. NOEC

We the Women. Grace Nichols. UAS

We the Wordproletariat. Jacob Glatstein, *tr. fr. Yiddish by* Benjamin *and* Barbara Harshav. AYP

We Think Farewell. Kurt Klinger, *tr. fr. German by* Beth Bjorklund. CoAuP

We think our boat is alone. *Unknown.* Fr. Manyo Shu. PeBJV

We think to create festivals. Antonio Machado, *tr. fr. Spanish by* John Dos Passos. *Fr.* Poems. AWP

We thirst at first—'tis nature's act. Emily Dickinson. NOCV (Thirst.) WGRP

We thought at first, this man is a king for sure. Blue Blood. James Stephens, *after the Irish of* David O'Bruaidar. MoAB; MoBrPo; OBMV

We thought the grass. Photographs: A Vision of Massacre. Michael S. Harper. PoBA

We thought you were a simple peasant. *Unknown, tr. by* Arthur Waley. BoS

We three are on the cedar-shadowed lawn. George Meredith. *Fr.* Modern Love, XXI. NOBVV

We Three Kings. John Henry Hopkins, Jr.. *See* We Three Kings of Orient Are.

We Three Kings of Orient Are. John Henry Hopkins, Jr. AH, *with music;* PChr
(We Three Kings.) OHIP

We too, we too, descending once again. The Too-late Born. Archibald MacLeish. GoJo; MoAB; MoAmPo; OxBA; WaP

We too were created from clay. Vessels. Howard Schwartz. VWA

We took it to the woods, we two. Emerson. Mary Mapes Dodge. AA

We took no notes of contemplated light. To My Friends. Peter Levi. NePoEA-2

We took our work, and went, you see. Recreation. Jane Taylor. OxBoLi

We tore the green tree down. Verifying the Dead. James Welch. CDW

We total it up for. Up & Out. Nila NorthSun. STE

We touched land. Not That Far. May Miller. BlSi

We Travel Like Other People. Mahmoud Darwish, *tr. fr. Arabic. Fr.* Poems after Beirut, III. MAP, *tr. by* Lena Jayyusi *and* Christopher Middleton; MPAW, *tr. by* Abdullah al-Udhari.

We traveled a long journey. Amagoduka at Glencoe Station. Mbuyiseni Oswald Mtshali. WMBCH

We travelers on the road to death. Mohammad Taqi Mir, *tr. by* Ahmed Ali. GoT

We trekked into a far country. Translation. Anne Spencer. BANP

We turn aside from everything. Birthday Wishes to a Minister of the Gospel. Lizelia Augusta Jenkins Moorer. CBWP-3

We turn to look. Kyuko and I Stayed at Rittei's. Taigi, *tr. fr. Japanese by* Hiroaki Sato. *Fr.* Twenty-nine Hokku. FCEI

We Two. Shlomoh Tan'ee, *tr. fr. Hebrew by* Bernhard Frank. MHeP

We two are last in hell: what may we fear. Barley-Break; or, Last in Hell. Robert Herrick. CaPo

We Two Boys Together Clinging. Walt Whitman. PeHV

We two stood simply friend-like side by side. Inapprehensiveness. Robert Browning. NOBVV

We unlock the door. We Are Welcome. Sue Sanders. DT

We used to gather at the high window. When Mahalia Sings. Quandra Prettyman. IDB; PoBA

We used to picnic where the thrift. Trebetherick. Sir John Betjeman. CMoP

We Used to Play. Don Welch. Psk

We used to say "If pigs could fly!" To a Barrage Balloon. May Morton. CN

We used to shadow-box on the shining grass. Dimidium Animae Meae. Charles A. Brady. GoYe

We used to spend the spring together. The Most Beautiful Girl in the World. Lorenz Hart. OBAL

We used to talk a lot. Once rain. Conversations. Ory Bernstein, *tr. by* Bernhard Frank. MHeP

We waged a war within a war. Karl Shapiro. *Fr.* Recapitulations, XI. PoNe

We wait for the moon. Princess Nukada. *Fr.* Manyo Shu. PeBJV

We wait for the moving mountains to break. Sharpshooters. Wu T'e-Liang, *tr. by* Dominic Cheung. IFON

We wait our turn, as still as mice. The Hospital Waiting-Room. W. H. Davies. BrPo

We waited for an omnibus. Walking Song. William E. Hickson. OxBChV

We waited in the desert encircled. Sukkot. Sol Lachman. VWA

We wake and watch the sun make bright. Another Sunday Morning. Derek Mahon. CIP

We wake to hear the storm come down. The Storm. Edward Shanks. BoNaP

We wake; we wake the day. Indian Singing in 20th Century America. Gail Tremblay. HATNAP

We walk across the snow. On Frozen Fields. Galway Kinnell. CAPP

We walk alone on our roots. Prayer for Kafka and Ourselves. Anthony Rudolf. VWA

We walk, as all around walks on creation. In the Shadow of the Valley of Death. Abu al-Qasim al-Shabbi. DL

We Walk the Way of the New World. Don L. Lee. BPo; NeAC; PoBA

We walked a mile from the road and with every step. Daisies. Alden Nowlan. NeAC

We walked along, while bright and red. The Two April Mornings. Wordsworth. EBEV; EnRP; GTBS; GTBS-P; NAEL-2

We Walked among the Whispering Pines. John Henry Boner. AA

We walked that night between the piled houses. The Window. Iain Crichton Smith. NePoEA-2

We wander now who marched before. Old Soldier. Padraic Colum. OBMV

We wandered to the pine forest. Shelley. *Fr.* To Jane: The Recollection. CH

We want to be amused. La Voix du Peuple. Hans Lodeizen, *tr. by* James S. Holmes. DuIn

We want what is real. Song of the Bald Eagle. *Unknown, tr. by* Lewis Henry Morgan. STP

We wanted Li Wing. Lapsus Linguae. Keith Preston. NBLV; OBAL

We watch, fascinated. The Disaster. Bruce Bennet. RR

We watch the heavy-odoured beast. Port of Call: Brazil. Alun Lewis. OBTV

We watch the only eagles in the world. At a Parade. F. T. Prince. WaP

We watched from the house. I Was Sleeping Where the Black Oaks Move. Louise Erdrich. HATNAP

We watched [*or* watch'd] her breathing thro' the night. The Death-Bed. Thomas Hood. EnRP; GTBS; GTBS-P; NOBE; OBD; OBEV; OBNC

We watched our love burn with the lumberyard. The Lumberyard. Ruth Herschberger. LiTA; WPE

We watched the condors winging towards the moon. Condors. Padraic Colum. VWA

We watched thy spirit flickering in the dark. In Memoriam: John Davidson. Ronald Campbell Macfie. GoTS

We Wear the Mask. Paul Laurence Dunbar. AmNP; CDC; FF; IDB; NIP; NoP; PoBA; TTY; UnPo

We weave haunted circles about each other. Afterwards. Fleur Adcock. ATNZ

We welcome these cool auspicious hours. The Sonic Flowerfall of Primes. Andrew Joron. BWV

We went north/ to escape winter. Indian Song: Survival. Leslie Marmon Silko. CDW; VoR

We went off to the wake of the "whelpish youngster." Harvest of the Sea. Máire Mhac an tSaoi. PBWP

We went on a motorcycle on a straight road with people watching us. Areas. Leslie Scalapino. NPGG

We went out, early one morning. Out Fishing. Barbara Howes. ASP; WPE

We went there on the train. Protocols. Randall Jarrell. LCAP; OxBC; VGW

We went there to confer. Detroit Conference of Unity and Art. Nikki Giovanni. HoPM

We went to look for stragglers on a ridge. Mushrooms. Basil Dowling. ATNZ

We were a multitude, until the hunters. Angels. Richard Burns. VWA

We were a people taut for war; the hills. Welsh History. R. S. Thomas. OBWVE

We were a tribe, a family, a people. Scotland 1941. Edwin Muir. OxBS

We were afraid as we built the barricade. Building the Barricade. Anna Swirszczynska, *tr.* by Magnus Jan Krynski and Robert A. Maguire. PwPP

We were agreed on the choice of weapons. Duel among the Roses. Paul Snoek, *tr.* by Alasdair MacKinnon. DuIn

We were all passengers in that motorcade. Channel U.S.A.—Live. Adrien Stoutenburg. AmFN

We were all sitting round the table. Christmas Dinner. Michael Rosen. OBCP

We were all standing outside. Nuptial. Joan Drew Ritchings. SoTCo

We were all under God. God. Boris Slutsky, *tr.* by Dimitry Pospielovsky and Keith Bosley. VWA

We were alone and did your life. To Children. Lawrence McGaugh. PoBA

We were apart; yet, day by day. Isolation: To Marguerite. Matthew Arnold. *Fr.* Switzerland, IV. EBVV; TEP

We were as tough as our glasses. Tyson's Corner. Primus St. John. PoBA

We were born grooms, in stable-straw we sleep still. A Dream of Horses. Ted Hughes. NePoEA-2

We Were Boys Together. George Pope Morris. AA

We were camped just under Hawk's Rest. Dudes. Nick Johnson. CowP

We were camped on the plains at the head of the Cimarron. The Zebra Dun. *Unknown.* CowP

We were challenged by The Dingoes—they're the pride of Squatter's Gap. A Friendly Game of Football. Edward Dyson. CBAP

We were closed, each to each, yet dear. Each to Each. Melville Cane. GoYe

We were crowded in the cabin. Ballad of the Canal. Phoebe Cary. AnAmPo

We were crowded in the cabin. Ballad of the Tempest. James Thomas Fields. AnAmPo; BeLS; BLPL; FaBoBe; PoLF
(Captain's Daughter, The.) FaFP

We were different when we returned to earth. Divers. Charles Ghigna. TSL

We were driving the down express. The Engine Driver's Story. William Wilkins. BeLS

We were forty miles from Albany. The E-ri-e. *Unknown.* AS

We were glad together in gladsome meads. Adam Lindsay Gordon. *Fr.* The Rhyme of Joyous Garde. PoAu-1

We were going to. The Winter Thing. Philip Dacey. NAmP

We were just three. Three. Elizabeth Jane Coatsworth. ILY

We were laying in Surrey Dock one day. Stormy Weather, Boys. *Unknown.* OxBSS

We were nearly. Above the Pool. John Montague. NOIV

We were not even out of sight of land. Sea Monster. W. S. Merwin. WSC

We were not here. Plato was a spider. Spinoza Was a Bee. Jaroslaw Marek Rymkiewicz, *tr.* by Czeslaw Milosz. PwPP

We were not many—we who stood. Monterey. Charles Fenno Hoffman. AA; AnAmPo; FaBoBe; PAH

We were not wrong, believing that it cared. The Empty House. Harold Monro. BrPo

We were ordered to Samoa from the coast of Panama. An International Episode. Caroline Duer. AA; PAH

We were out in Arizona, on the Painted Desert ground. Arizona. *Unknown.* AmFP

We were playing on the green together. "Is It Nothing to You?" May Probyn. OBEV

We were real people. Real People. Merry Harris. GOS

We were smoking some of this knockout weed when. Operation Memory. David Lehman. BAP

We were starving. Resistance in the Ghetto. Jacob Glatstein, *tr.* by Benjamin and Barbara Harshav. AYP

We Were Suntanned Gods. Pentti Saaritsa, *tr. fr. Finnish* by Aili Jarvenpa. SOP

We were sure to interrupt the traveller's siesta. Nausicaa with Some Attendants. Tom Lowenstein. VWA

We were talking about tent revivals. Sects. Jack Gilbert. NPGG

We were talking about the great things. Great Things Have Happened. Alden Nowlan. GOYP

We were the wrecked elect. The Fiction-Makers. Anne Stevenson. DiPo

We were three women, three men. The Sorrow of Kodio. *Unknown, tr.* by Miriam Koshland. PBA

We were together. Yakamochi, *tr.* by Kenneth Rexroth. UnAS

We were together in my time and at your place. In My Time, at Your Place. Yehuda Amichai, *tr.* by Warren Bargad and Stanley F.Chyet. IP

We were twin brothers, tall and hale. A Flight Shot. Maurice Thompson. AA

We were two daughters of one race. The Sisters. Tennyson. InvP

We were two pretty babes, the youngest she. Childhood Fled. Charles Lamb. EnRP

We were very tired, we were very merry. Recuerdo. Edna St. Vincent Millay. AmFN; FaFP; FPL; LiTA; LiTM; NAAL-2; NoAM; OxBA; PoA; TAP

We were waiting at the station. The Parting Kiss. Josephine D. Henderson Heard. CBWP-4

We were walking and talking on the roof of the world. End of the Seers' Convention. Kenneth Fearing. LiTA

We were walls facing walls. Lebanon. Khalil Hawi, *tr.* by Abdullah al-Udhari. MPAW

We were wrong to think. Form. Heather McHugh. GeTw

We were young, we were merry, we were very very wise. Unwelcome. Mary Elizabeth Coleridge. CH; OBEV; OBNC; WPE

We who also linger near the border of insanities. Near the Border of Insanities. Dannie Abse. PoA

We Who Are Left. Nikos Gatsos, *tr. fr. Greek* by Edmund Keeley and Philip Sherrard. *Fr.* Four Songs. VMG

We Who Are Left. George Whalley. CaP

We who are left, how shall we look again. W. W. Gibson. MMA; OxBTC

We who carry the endless seasons. Virginia Cerenio. BrSi

We who devour our unclean dead are now arisen. Letter to Robert. Mary Fabilli. IHMS

We who do not belong in and from. Closedown. Kendrick Smithyman. ATNZ

We who have come all ways into the city. The Trail. Edward Weismiller. WaP

We who must act as handmaidens. A Muse of Water. Carolyn Kizer. NMM

We who play under the pines. The Song of the Rabbits outside the Tavern. Elizabeth Jane Coatsworth. OBCA

We who survived the war and took to wife. Thirtieth Anniversary Report of the Class of '41. Howard Nemerov. HCAP

We Who Were Born. Eiluned Lewis. FaPON

We who with songs beguile your pilgrimage. James Elroy Flecker. *Fr.* The Golden Journey to Samarkand. BrPo; FaPoR; GoJo; OBMV; OxBTC

We will all have to just hang on for awhile. One Coat of Paint. John Ashbery. BAP

We will go no more to Shaemus, at the Nip. Shaemus. Conrad Aiken. OxBA

We will go to the wood, says Robin to Bobbin. *Unknown.* OxNR

"We will kill." After the Killing. Dudley Randall. CNA; SoSe

We Will Live Forever. Yehuda Amichai, *tr. fr. Hebrew* by Warren Bargad and Stanley F.Chyet. IP

We Will Not Fear. David Diamond. AH

We will not find you by going back to London. Robert Lowell: His Death. Alan Williamson. PPR

We will not whisper, we have found the place. Hilaire Belloc. MoBrPo

We will pause. In the mist. For a Certain Night. Tachihara Michizo, *tr.* by Hiroaki Sato. FCEI

We will pull, we will haul, hearty, healthy, and gay. Blow the Man Down. *Unknown.* AmFP

We will remember. R.A.F. Sarah Churchill. CN

We will return to life. Comanche Ghost Dance: An Impression. Lance Henson. VoR

We will strike the new air with our armor-plated heads. Perdition. Aimé Césaire, *tr.* by Clayton Eshleman and Annette Smith. RHTwFP

We will take it seriously as we open our morning paper. Sonnet to Be Written from Prison. Robert Adamson. CBAP

We will watch the Northern Lights. *Unknown.* RFM

We wish to the new child. For C. K. at His Christening. Daniel Lawrence Kelleher. NeIP

We with our Fair pitched among the feathery clover. The Individualist Speaks. Louis MacNeice. OBMV

We woke early. Names in Monterchi: To Rachel. James Wright. AnAn; NNaP

We Women. Klara Müller-Jahnke, *tr. fr. German* by Susan L. Cocalis. DMG

We Women. Edith Södergran, *tr. fr. Swedish* by Samuel Charters. WPOW

We women here all live with tightened throats. Henri Michaux, *tr. fr. French* by Richard Ellmann. *Fr.* I Am Writing to You from a Far-Off Country, VI. RHTwFP

We wonder what the horoscope did show. Shakespeare. Henrietta Cordelia Ray. CBWP-3

We wonder whether the dream of American liberty. Archibald MacLeish. *Fr.* Land of the Free. MoAB

We wondered at the tobacco plants there in France. Tobacco Plant. Ivor Gurney. OBTV

We wondered what our walk should mean. Peace Walk. William Stafford. Psk

We wondered why he always turned aside. Inheritance. Mary Potter Thacher Higginson. AA

We won't pay any attention to this invitation. Konrad Bayer, *tr. by* Beth Bjorklund. CoAuP

We worked in the kitchen. The Function Room. Patrice Phillips. MAT

We would climb the highest dune. With Kit, Age 7, at the Beach. William Stafford. RFM

We Would See Jesus. Anna Bartlett Warner. AH

We wreathed about our darling's head. The Morning-Glory. Maria White Lowell. AA

We zealots, made up of stiff clay. Let Us All Be Unhappy on Sunday. Lord Neaves. FaBoCo

Weak Is the Will of Man, His Judgment Blind. Wordsworth. EnRP

Weak Monk, The. Stevie Smith. BoWoP; FaBoTw

Weak-winged is song. Ode Recited at the Harvard Commemoration. James Russell Lowell. AA; NOBA; OBWP; PAH

Wealth. Emerson. ImOP

Wealth. Sadi, *tr. fr. Persian by* Sir Edwin Arnold. *Fr.* The Gulistan. AWP

Wealth came by water to this farmless island. Delos. Bernard Spencer. NoAM

Wealth covers sin—the poor. Mary Magdalene Kassia, *tr. by* Patrick Diehl. WPOW

Wealth of kings, The. Miser. Gloria A. Maxson. *Fr.* Epitaphs. SoTCo

Wealth; or Song Written for a Beggar. Vali Mohammad Nazir, *tr. fr. Urdu by* Ahmed Ali. GoT

Wealth unto every man, I see. Worldly Wealth. Rowland Watkyns. FaBoEE

Wealthy Cit, grown old in trade, The. The Cit's Country Box. Robert Lloyd. NOEC

Weapon, The. "Hugh MacDiarmid." RB

Weapon shapely, naked, wan. The Broad-Ax. Walt Whitman. *Fr.* Song of the Broad-Ax. MoAmPo

Weapon that comes down as still, A. The Ballot. John Pierpont. AA

Weapon that turns on itself, the fish spears itself. The Boomerang. Adriano Spatola, *tr. by* Lawrence R. Smith. NItP

Weapon that you fought with was a word, The. "He Knoweth Not That the Dead Are Thine." Mary Elizabeth Coleridge. OBNC

Weaponry. Wendy Rose. ER

Weapons. Anna Wickham. MoBrPo

Weapons alone. One Flight Up. Bob Holman. UL

Wear a dress. An Answer to a Man's Question, "What Can I Do about Women's Liberation?" Susan Griffin. GLP

Wear it as a bangle on your arm. Fame. Eleanor Hollister Cantus. GoYe

Wear yourself not out. *Unknown. Fr.* Manyo Shu. Ma

Wearied arm and broken sword. Pocahontas. Thackeray. AmFN; FaPON; GN; OnMSP; OPP; PAH

Wearied arm, and broken sword. Thackeray. *Fr.* Pocahontas. AiP

Wearied, desire invents and seeks refuge. Asadullah Khan Ghalib, *tr. by* Ahmed Ali. GoT

Wearily, still in her dressing gown. Eliza Telefair. Jocelyn Macy Sloan. GoYe

Wearin' o' the Green, The. *Unknown.* NOIV

Weariness. Mary E. Tucker. CBWP-1

Weariness in the Evening of January Thirty-Second. Isam Mahfouz, *tr. fr. Arabic by* Sargon Boulus *and* Samuel Hazo. MAP

Weariness of life that has no will, The. Everyman. Siegfried Sassoon. MoBrPo

Weariness of this dirt and labour, The. Fatigues. Richard Aldington. BrPo

Wearing a flowered nightgown. Shopping in Ferney with Voltaire. Maxine W. Kumin. ER

Wearing a Worn-Out Coat. Chin Nung, *tr. fr. Chinese by* Jonathan Chaves. CoBLCP

Wearing an overcoat in August heat. Bag Woman. Dudley Randall. NoAM

Wearing her yellow rubber slicker. Myrtle. Ted Kooser. GOYP

Wearing of the Green. Aileen Fisher. RHPC

Wearing of [*or* Wearin' o'] the Green, The. *Unknown.* AnIL; AWP; FaFP; FaPoR; GBP; OxBoLi; WTO

Wearing worry about money like a hair shirt. Worry about Money. Kathleen Jessie Raine. FaBoTw

Wearisome Sonnetteer, feeble and querulous. The Soldier's Wife. George Canning *and* John Hookham Frere. Par

Wears dirty clogs. Ozaki Hosai, *tr. fr. Japanese by* Hiroaki Sato. *Fr.* One Hundred Haiku in Free Form. FCEI

Weary already, weary miles to-night. A Match with the Moon. Dante Gabriel Rossetti. NOBVV

Weary at heart with winter yesterday. April. Obadiah Cyrus Auringer. AA

Weary Blues, The. Langston Hughes. FaBV; MoP; NoAM; NOBA; NoP; PoNe

Weary, I open wide the antique pane. Poetry and the Poet. Henry Cuyler Bunner. OBAL

Weary I was, and thought to sit at rest. Elizabeth Melvill, Lady Culross. *Fr.* A Godly Dream. WPE

Weary in Well-doing. Christina Rossetti. SeCePo; TrPWD

Weary is he, and sick of the sorrow of war. The Soldier Is Home. John Shaw Neilson. CBAP

Weary Lot Is Thine, A. Sir Walter Scott. *Fr.* Rokeby, III. CH
(Rover, The.) GTBS; GTBS-P
(Rover's Adieu [*or* Farewell], The.) NOBE; OBEV
(Song: "Weary lot is thine, fair maid, A.") EnLoPo; OBNC

Weary men, what reap ye?—"Golden corn for the stranger." The Famine Year. Lady Wilde. TIRV

Weary of dreams and forays. Don Quixote. Ben-Zion Tomer, *tr. by* Bernhard Frank. MHeP

Weary of erring in this Desert Life. To Our Ladies of Death. James Thomson. GoTS

Weary of myself, and sick of asking. Self-Dependence. Matthew Arnold. WGRP

Weary on ye, sad waves! On an Island. "Ethna Carbery." WPE

Weary one had rest, the sad had joy that day, The. Because We Do Not See. *Unknown.* BLRP

Weary Song to a Slow Sad Tune, A. Li Ch'ing-chao, *tr. fr. Chinese by* Kenneth Rexroth. BoWoP

Weary teacher sat alone, The. The Teacher's Dream. William Henry Venable. BeLS

Weary the cry of the wind is, weary the sea. Sorrow of Mydath. John Masefield. MoBrPo

Weary was when coming on a stream. Aswelay. Norman Henry Pritchard II. PoBA

Weary way-wanderer, languid and sick at heart. The Soldier's Wife. Robert Southey. OxBSP

Weary, weary, desolate. Yuma. Charles Henry Phelps. AA

Weary wind is slumbering on the wing, The. Sunset. Arthur Bayldon. PoAu-1

Weary with life we long for death. Sheikh Ibrahim Zauq, *tr. by* Ahmed Ali. GoT

"Weary with toil, I haste me to my bed." Shakespeare. *Fr.* Sonnets, XXVII. OBSC

Weary, worn, and sorrow-laden. Storm-Beaten. Clara Ann Thompson. CBWP-2

Weary year his race now having run, The. Amoretti, LXII. Spenser. OBSC

Wearyin' for You. Frank Lebby Stanton. AnAmPo

Weasel, The. *Unknown.* ChTr

Weasel, by a person caught, A. The Man and the Weasel. Phaedrus, *tr. by* Christopher Smart. AWP

Weasel (or a stoat), A. The Aesthete Weasel. Christian Morgenstern. FaBoNo, *tr. by* Geoffrey Grigson

Weather. Archibald MacLeish. MoAmPo

Weather. William Meredith. NYBP

Weather. Nishiwaki Junzaburo, *tr. fr. Japanese by* Geoffrey Bownas *and* Anthony Thwaite. PeBJV

Weather. *Unknown.* RHPC

Weather, The. Meir Wieseltier, *tr. fr. Hebrew by* Bernhard Frank. MHeP

Weather came down from Nevis, The. Eagle. Tom Bowker. PoSH

Weather changeable at dusk and dawn, The. Written on the Lake, Returning from the Retreat at Stone Cliff. Hsieh Ling-yün, *tr. by* Burton Watson. CoBCP

Weather Ear. Norman Nicholson. OxBSP

Weather Forecast. Vivian Lamarque, *tr. fr. Italian by* Muriel Kittel. DMI

Weather Forecast. Linda Pastan. AnAn

Weather Forecasters. Eeva Kilpi, *tr. fr. Finnish by* Aili Jarvenpa. SOP

Weather isn't news unless extreme, The. No News at All. Jack Butler. MT

Weather-leech of the topsail shivers, The. Tacking Ship Off Shore. Walter Mitchell. AA; FaBoBe; GN

Weather Newly Cleared. Wang Wei, *tr. fr. Chinese by* Burton Watson. CoBCP

Weather of Olympus, The. Robert Graves. FaBoEE
Weather of Six Mornings, The. Jane Cooper. IHMS; NYBP
Weather or not/ born. Ernst Jandl. *Fr.* Biography. CoAuP
Weather Rhymes. Hamish Brown. PoSH
Weather was fine, The. They took away his teeth. John Berryman. *Fr.* Dream Songs. CAPP
Weather Wisdom [*or* Weather Wise], sels. *Unknown.*
  "Evening red and morning gray." FaBoBe; FaBoUs; OxNR
  "If bees stay at home." OxNR
  "If the oak is out before the ash." OxNR
  "Mackerel sky." FaBoUs; OxNR
  "March winds and April showers." FaBoBe; OxNR
  "Rain before seven." FaBoBe; OxNR
  "Rainbow at night." FaBoBe
  "Red sky at night." OxNR
  "South wind brings wet weather, The." FaBoUs
  "Sunshiny shower, A." FaBoBe
  "When clouds appear like rocks and towers." FaBoUs; OxNR
  "When the clouds are upon the hills." OxNR
  "When the wind is in the east." FaBoUs; OxNR
Weather Words. David McCord. ImOP
Weathercock, The. Rose Fyleman. BoTP
Weathercock. Elizabeth Jennings. NePoEA
Weathercock once again heading south, The. This Morning. Jon Stallworthy. NoP
Weathercock, The: "I puff my breast out, my neck swells." *Unknown, formerly at. to Cynewulf, tr. fr. Anglo-Saxon by Geoffrey Grigson. Fr.* Riddles (Exeter Book). RB
Weathering. Fleur Adcock. DiPo
Weathering Out. Rita Dove. NoAM
Weathering the Depths. Al Lee. AmPA
Weather[s]. Thomas Hardy. BoTP; CH; FaBoCh; FaBV; MoAB; MoBrPo; OBMV; RB; SeCePo
Weather's cleared, The. We're filming at Versailles. Clive James. *Fr.* To Pete Atkin: A Letter from Paris. OBSV
Weave me into a solid rag rug. Rag Rug. Rob Wilborn. SoTCo
Weave no more silks, ye Lyons looms. Our Orders. Julia Ward Howe. AA
Weave the warp, and weave the woof. The Curse upon Edward. Thomas Gray. OBEV
Weaver, The. "Fanny Forester." BLPA
Weaver, The. Giovanni Pascoli, *tr. fr. Italian by* E. J. Scovell. PFI
Weaver, The ("I sat at my loom in silence"). *Unknown.* BLRP
Weaver, The ("I was a bachelor, I lived by myself"). *Unknown.* AS
Weaver, The. William H. Burleigh. BLPA
Weaver and the Factory Maid, The. *Unknown.* OBET
Weaver sat by the side of his loom, A. The Weaver. "Fanny Forester." BLPA
Weavers. Heine. TrJP
Weaving at the Window. Wang Chien, *tr. fr. Chinese by* William H. Nienhauser. SaC
Weaving Love-Knots. Hsüeh T'ao, *tr. by* Carolyn Kizer. BoWoP
Weaving Love-Knots 2. Hsüeh T'ao, *tr. by* Carolyn Kizer. BoWoP
Weaving of the Wing, The. Ralph Hodgson. BrPo
Weaving Song. *Unknown. See* Song of the Ill-Married.
Weaving the Morning. João Cabral de Melo Neto, *tr. fr. Portuguese by* Galway Kinnell. ATCBP
Web, The. Gregory O'Donoghue. BIrV
Web, The. Theodore Weiss. CoAP
Webern. Thomas W. Shapcott. *Fr.* Piano Pieces. CBAP
Webern's Mountain. Fred Chappell. BLA
Webs between the words. Paul Celan, *tr. by* Beth Bjorklund. CoAuP
Webster; an Ode, sel. William Cleaver Wilkinson. At Marshfield. AA
Webster Ross. Naomi Mitchison. PoSH
Webster was much possessed by death. Whispers of Immortality. T. S. Eliot. CMoP; CTC; LiTA; NoAM; NOBA; NoP; OBMV
We'd ever so many kinds of cake. The Pirates' Tea-Party. Dorothy Una Ratcliffe. BoTP
We'd found an old Boche dug-out, and he knew. The Sentry. Wilfred Owen. MMA
We'd gained our first objective hours before. Counter-Attack. Siegfried Sassoon. BrPo; MoBrPo; WaP
We'd have to love the nape of the neck more than the thigh. Conditions. José Luis Vega. InW, *tr. by* Julio Marzán.
We'd rather have the iceberg than the ship. The Imaginary Iceberg. Elizabeth Bishop. FaBoWP; LiTM; MoAB; MoAmPo
Wedded Love. Milton. *See* Paradise Lost: Hail wedded love, mysterious law, true source.

Wedded to a redolence. Honeysuckle Yellow. Pierre Kemp, *tr.* by Fred van Leeuwen. DuIn
Wedding, The. Conrad Aiken. CMoP; TAP
Wedding. Maria Banus, *tr. fr. Rumanian by* Laura Schiff. OV
Wedding. Ewa Lipska, *tr. fr. Polish by* Peter Jay *and* Geri Lipshultz. VWA
Wedding, A. James Tate. NoAM
Wedding and Funeral. *Unknown.* GBP
Wedding-cake face in a paper frill, A. Sylvia Plath. *Fr.* Berck-Plage. OBD
Wedding Coat, The. Harriet Rose. BrRo
Wedding cortège, A. Wedding. Ewa Lipska, *tr. by* Peter Jay *and* Geri Lipshultz. VWA
Wedding Day at Nagasaki. Rodney Hall. CBAP
Wedding Feast, The. Luis de Góngora y Argote, *tr. fr. Spanish by* Edward Meryon Wilson. *Fr.* The First Solitude. OBVE
Wedding Gift, The. Minna Irving. BLPA
Wedding-Hymn. Sidney Lanier. TrPWD
Wedding Morn. D. H. Lawrence. MoAB; MoBrPo
Wedding night/ Graciela bled lightly. Graciela. Gary Soto. NoAM
Wedding Night, The. Anne Sexton. PoA
Wedding of Alcmane and Mya, The. Chapman. *Fr.* Hero and Leander, Fifth Sestiad. OBSC
Wedding of the Clans, The. Aubrey Thomas De Vere. AnIL
Wedding Party. Donald Hall. LCAP
Wedding Reception. Melinda Goodman. GLP
Wedding-Ring. Denise Levertov. CAPP
Wedding Song, A. John White Chadwick. AA
Wedding Song. *Unknown.* OBET
Wedding Song in honor of R. Solomon ben Matir, sel. Moses Ibn Ezra, *tr. fr. Hebrew by* Solomon Solis-Cohen.
  "Rejoice, O youth, in the lovely hind." TrJP
Wedding-Wind. Philip Larkin. MAT
Wedgewood Bowl, A. Frances Beatrice Taylor. CaP
Wedlock; a Satire. Hetty Wright. NOEC
Wednesbury Cocking, The. *Unknown.* EnSB; FaBoBa
Wednesday at North Hatley. Ralph Gustafson. NOBC
Wednesday, February 9th. 9:35 a.m. "And Brief, Good Mother? For I Am In Haste? Whither?" Dezsö Tandori, *tr. by* Daniel Hoffman. MHuP
Wednesday in Holy Week. Christina Rossetti. TrCP
Wednesday, January 1, 1701. Samuel Sewall. *See* Once More, Our God, Vouchsafe to Shine!
Wednesday night, in the zeppelin. Zeppelins. Patrick Conrad, *tr. by* James S. Holmes. DuIn
Wednesday Night Prayer Meeting. Jay Wright. PoBA
Wednesday; or, The Dumps. John Gay. *Fr.* The Shepherd's Week. OAEL-1
Wednesdays at the bone orchard deliveries. Memo. Charles Lynch. PoBA
Wee Davie Daylicht. Robert Tennant. OxBChV
Wee leave Creete Country; and our sayls unwrapped uphoysing. Virgil, *tr. fr. Latin by* Richard Stanyhurst. *Fr.* The Aeneid [*or* Eneados], III. OBVE
Wee little nut lay deep in its nest, A. Among the Nuts. *Unknown.* BoTP
Wee Little Worm, A. James Whitcomb Riley. PDV; RHPC
Wee man o' leather. *Unknown.* ChTr; GBP
Wee, modest, crimson-tippèd flow'r. To a Mountain Daisy. Burns. EnRP; GN; PoLF; WBLP
  (Daisy, The.) BoNaP
Wee nah look no quarrel wi dem. Some Men. Dazzly Anderson. AIW
Wee, sleeket [*or* sleekit], cow'rin' [*or* cowran], tim'rous beastie. To a Mouse on Turning Her Up in Her Nest with the Plough, November, 1785 *or* To a Mouse. Burns. EnRP; FaFP; FF; FM; GoTS; HAP; HeIP; InPS; NAEL-2; NOEC; NoP; OAEL-1; OxBS; PoE; PoLF; PPP; PrIM; TEP; TrGrPo
  (To a Field Mouse.) GTBS; GTBS-P
Wee strippit irritating beastie. To a Midge. Eilidh Nisbet. PoSH
Wee Tammy Tyrie. *Unknown.* OxNR
Wee Wee Man, The. *Unknown.* CH; EBEV; ELP; ESPB; FaBoCh; GBP; OAEL-1, *with music;* OxBB, *with music*
Wee, wee tailor. The Tailor. Thomas Lovell Beddoes. WiR
Wee Willie Gray. Burns. OxBChV
Wee Willie Winkie rins [*or* runs] through the town. William Miller. NOBVV; OxNR
  (Willie Winkie.) FaFP; OxBChV
Weed. Robert Hass. MAYP
Weed Puller. Theodore Roethke. AmPP; HCAP; NAAL-2
Weeds. Ann Stanford. GrPl
Weeds. Su Shao-lien, *tr. fr. Chinese by* Dominic Cheung. IFON

Weeds grow shamelessly/ on my tongue. Self-Portrait. Cecil Bodker, *tr.* by Nadia Christensen. BoWoP

Weedy creek, A. Making a Door. Dennis Schmitz. LCAP

Weedy light through the uncurtained glass, The. Hiatus. Margaret Avison. HAP

Week after week, month after month, in pain. Memorial Poem. Roy Fuller. OxBSP

Week ago I had a fire, A. All in June. W. H. Davies. OxBSP

Week ago to-day, when red-haired Sally, A. Done For. Rose Terry Cooke. AA

Week ago, when I had finished, A. Vikram Seth. *Fr.* The Golden Gate. UAS

Week-end. Harold Monro. SeCePo

Week-End, *sel.* Harold Monro. SeCePo

"Train, The! The twelve o'clock for paradise." *Fr.* I. MoBrPo

Week-End by the Sea. Edgar Lee Masters. MoAmPo

Week-End Indian, The. Anita Endrezze Probst. VoR

Week in August you come home, The. Family Reunion. Maxine W. Kumin. CAPP

Week is dealt out like a hand, The. Hope. Randall Jarrell. MoAB; MoAmPo

Week it, The. The Proposition. Bill Manhire. ATNZ

Week of Che Guevara, hunted, hurt. October and November. Robert Lowell. MAT

Week of Doodle, A. Reed Whittemore. NePoEA

Week on the Concord and Merrimack Rivers, A, *sels.* Henry David Thoreau.

Low-anchored Cloud. ImOP; NoP

(Mist.) AA; AmPP; AWP; OxBA

Woof of the Sun (Ethereal Gauze). TAP

(Haze.) HeIP; NoP

Week one: our expedition slowed. A Scientific Expedition in Siberia, 1913. Kelly Cherry. SM

Week-Seek. Jim Tollerud. VoR

Week to Christmas, A. Louis MacNeice. *Fr.* Autumn Journal. TIRV

Weekend Stroll. Frances Cornford. BoNaP

Weeksville Women. Elouise Loftin. PoBA

Weel, gin ye speir, I'm no inclined. Barry Pain. *Fr.* The Poets at Tea, IX. Par

Weep, ah weep love's losing. Imr el Kais. *Fr.* The Mu'allaqat. AWP

Weep, and weep long, but do not weep for me. To a Troubled Friend. James Wright. Son

Weep balm and myrrh, you sweet Arabian trees. Stanzas from Saint Peter's Complaint. Robert Southwell. *Fr.* Saint Peter's Complaint. ACP

Weep, beloved friends! Gabriello Chiabrera, *tr.* by Wordsworth. *Fr.* Intaglios. AWP

Weep eyes, break heart! Parting. Thomas Middleton. *Fr.* A Chaste Maid in Cheapside. EIL

Weep for me, friends, for now that I am hence. Tears of the World. Mu'tamid, King of Seville, *tr.* by Dulcie L. Smith. AWP

Weep for the dead, for they have lost this light. On Himself. Robert Herrick. FaBoEE

Weep, Israel! your tardy meed outpour. Bar Kochba. Emma Lazarus. TrJP

Weep, Lovers, with Love's very self doth weep. Dante, *tr. fr. Italian by* Dante Gabriel Rossetti. *Fr.* Vita Nuova, La, III, a. AWP

Weep No More. *At.* to John Fletcher. *Fr.* The Queen of Corinth, III, ii. CH; EIL; OBEV

(Mourn No More.) TrGrPo

Weep no more for what is past. What Is Past. Sir William Davenant. TrGrPo

Weep no more, woful shepherds weep no more. Milton. *Fr.* Lycidas. FaBoRV

Weep not,/ You who loved her. Burial of the Young Love. Waring Cuney. BANP

Weep not because this child hath died so young. On the Death of Mistress Mary Prideaux. William Strode. JCP

Weep Not for a Warrior. Mbuyiseni Oswald Mtshali. WMBCH

Weep [*or* Weepe] not, my wanton, smile upon my knee. Sephestia's Song to Her Child[e]. Robert Greene. *Fr.* Menaphon. ELP; PoEL-2; TrGrPo

(Sephestia's Lullaby.) NOBE; OBEV

(Sephestia's Song.) OBSC

(Weep Not My Wanton.) EIL; SeCePo

Weep not, nor backward turn your beams. A Lover, upon an Accident Necessitating His Departure, Consults with Reason. Thomas Carew. CaPo

(Lover Consults with Reason, The.) TrGrPo

Weep not that you no longer feel the tide. Lost Youth. Sir Roger Casement. TIRV

Weep Not To-Day. Robert Bridges. OBMV

Weep not, weep not. Go Down Death. James Weldon Johnson. AmNP; DL; PoBA

Weep o'er the mis'ries of a wretched maid. Dying Prostitute, The; an Elegy. Thomas Holcroft. NOEC

Weep! Weep! Weep! Tumadir al-Khansa for Her Brother. *Unknown, tr. fr. Arabic by* E. Powys Mathers. *Fr.* The Thousand and One Nights. AWP

(For Her Brother.) PBWP

Weep, weep, ye woodmen! wail. Anthony Munday. *Fr.* Death of Robert, Earl of Huntingdon. CH

(Dirge: "Weep, weep, ye woodmen, wail.") CTC; OBSC

(Robin Hood's Funeral.) WiR

(Song: "Weep, weep, ye woodmen, wail.") EIL

Weep [*or* Weepe] with me, all you that read. Epitaph on S. P. [Salomon *or* Salathiel Pavy], a Child of Queen Elizabeth's Chapel. Ben Jonson. EIL; HeIP; HoPM; JCP; MePo; Mes; NAEL-1; NoP; OAEL-1; OBD; OBEV; OBS; PoEL-2; PPP; SeCP; SeCV-1; TrGrPo; UnPo

(On Solomon Pavy, a Child of Queen Elizabeth's Chapel.) NOBE

Weep [*or* Weepe] You No More [Sad Fountains]. *Unknown.* CH; EBEV; EIL; ELP; EnLoPo; GBL; HAP; NoP; OBSC; PoE; PoEL-2; SoSe; TrGrPo

(Sleep Is a Reconciling.) ChTr

Weepe not, my wanton, smile upon my knee. *See* Weep not, my wanton.

Weepe O mine eyes. *Unknown.* PoEL-2

Weeper, The. Richard Crashaw. *See* Saint[e] Mary Magdalene; or, The Weeper.

Weepers Tower in Amsterdam, The. Paul Goodman. VGW

Weepies, The. Paul Muldoon. NoAM

Weeping and Wailing. Gerald Stern. CAPP

Weeping and wakeful all the night I lie. Rhodanthe. Agathias, *tr. by* Andrew Lang. AWP

Weeping as though for a parent, bitter as a dose of herbs. Weeping for My Elder in Poetry Shimada. Michizane, *tr. by* Burton Watson. JLIC-1

Weeping for Hsüeh Tzu-shu. Liu-K'o-chuang, *tr. fr. Chinese by* Burton Watson. CoBCP

Weeping for My Elder in Poetry Shimada. Michizane, *tr. fr. Chinese by* Burton Watson. JLIC-1

Weeping for the Priest Gempin. Emperor Saga, *tr. fr. Chinese by* Burton Watson. JLIC-1

Weeping for Ying Yao. Wang Wei, *tr. fr. Chinese by* Burton Watson. CoBCP

Weeping Melpomene assist my lays. The Fatal Dream; or, The Unhappy Favourite. Emanuel Collins. NOEC

Weeping, murmuring, complaining. Goldsmith. NOIV

Weeping o'er the sacred urn. Ambrose Philips. *Fr.* To the Memory of Lord Halifax. FaBoCo

Weeping rose in her dark night of leaves, The. A Song at Morning. Dame Edith Sitwell. CMoP

Weeping Sinner, Dry Your Tears. Oliver Holden. AH

Weeping, sobbing. Ishikawa Takuboku, *tr. by* Geoffrey Bownas *and* Anthony Thwaite. PeBJV

Weeping sorely as he journeyed. The Canadian Exile. Antoine Gerin-Lajoie, *tr. by* John Boyd. CaP

Weeping tree, A. What Am I? Abo Stoltzenberg, *tr. by* Gabriel Preil *and* Howard Schwartz. VWA

Weeping Willow, The. *Unknown.* AmFP

Weeps out of western country something new. The Birth in a Narrow Room. Gwendolyn Brooks. BlSi; NAs; PoNe

Weevily Wheat. *Unknown.* AmFP; AS, *with music*

'Weh Down Souf. Daniel Webster Davis. BANP

Wei-ch'i Chess. Li K'ai-hsien, *tr. fr. Chinese by* Jonathan Chaves. CoBLCP

Wei Wind, *sel.* Confucius, *tr. fr. Chinese by* Ezra Pound.

Pedlar. CTC; OBVE

Weigh me the fire; or canst thou find. To Finde God. Robert Herrick. WGRP

Weighed down with dew. Kyogoku Tamekane, *tr. fr. Japanese by* Burton Watson. *Fr.* Twenty-three Tanka. FCEI

Weighing the stedfastness and state. Man. Henry Vaughan. MeLP; MePo; NOBE; NOCV; OBEV; OBS; PoEL-2; SeCV-1

Weight distributed. One Down. Richard Armour. SD

Weight of myself, The. The weight of my mother. Things Not of This Union. Linda Gregg. NPGG

Weight of Stones. Philippe Jaccottet, *tr. fr. French by* Paul Auster. RHTwFP

Weight Room, The. Thomas Rabbitt. MAYP

Weightless Now. Giuseppe Ungaretti, *tr. fr. Italian by* Richard Wilbur. PFI

Weir Bridge. Padraic Fallon. CIP

Weir that winds have made in a mountain stream, The. Teika, *tr. fr. Japanese by* Hiroaki Sato. *Fr.* A Compendium of Good Tanka. FCEI

Weird Sister. In Salem. Lucille Clifton. AmPA

Wel/come back, brother. Huey. Etheridge Knight. NNaP

Wel mended tinker! sans dispute. Of John Bunyan's Life. John James. SCAP

Wel, wanton ey, but must ye nedis pley. Wanton Eye. Charles, Duc d' Orléans. OxBLMV

Weland knew fully affliction and woe. Deor's Lament. *Unknown, tr. by* Charles W. Kennedy. AnOE; OAEL-1

Weland, that dauntless man, well learned to bear. Deor. *Unknown, tr. by* Walter Kendrick. TEP

Welcome, The. Abraham Cowley. *Fr.* The Mistress. BoLoP; SeCV-1

Welcome, The. Freda Laughton. NeIP

Welcome! but yet no entrance, till we bless. The Entertainment, or Porch-Verse, at the Marriage of Master Henry Northleigh and the Most Witty Mistress Lettice Yard. Robert Herrick. CaPo

Welcome Christmas! heel and toe. Stocking Song on Christmas Eve. Mary Mapes Dodge. OHIP

Welcome, dear dawn of summer's rising sway. May-Day. Aaron Hill. NOEC

Welcome Eild. *Unknown.* GoTS

Welcome, fayre chylde, what is thy name? Dalyaunce. *Unknown.* CH

Welcome for Etheridge, A. James Cunningham. JB

Welcome freshness over the garden lay, A. Suspended Moment. Mariana B. Davenport. GoYe

Welcome, friend. Newton to Einstein. Jeannette Chappell. GoYe

Welcome, grinned Henry, welcome fifty-one! John Berryman. *Fr.* Dream Songs. TAP

Welcome, happy Easter day! Easter Praise. Rodney Bennett. BoTP

Welcome Home. Josephine D. Henderson Heard. CBWP-4

Welcome home, driving downhill. Lament City. Thomas Lux. AmPA

Welcome home from the exhausting voyage. Sea Legs. Susan Feldman. AmPA

Welcome, kind Death: my long tired spirit bear. Algernon Sidney's Farewell. *Unknown.* APAS

Welcome, little Robin. *Unknown.* BoTP

Welcome, maids of honor. To Violets. Robert Herrick. CaPo; JCP; OBEV; OBS; SeCP; TrGrPo

Welcome me, if you will. For James Dean. Frank O'Hara. NeAP; NNaP

Welcome, most welcome, to our vows and us. To the King, upon His Coming with His Army into the West. Robert Herrick. CaPo

Welcome now, Victoria. Queen Victoria. *Unknown.* CoMu

Welcome O Great Mary. Alice O'Gallacher, *tr. fr. Gaelic by* Douglas Hyde. WTO

Welcome, old friend! These many years. To Age. Walter Savage Landor. EnRP

Welcome! Our Messiah. *Unknown.* MeEL

Welcome, precious stone of the night. Welcome to the Moon. *Unknown.* BoNaP; ChTr

Welcome, Queen Sabbath. Zalman Schneour, *tr. fr. Hebrew by* Harry H. Fein. TrJP

Welcome, red and roundy sun. The Wood-Cutter's Night Song. John Clare. EnRP

Welcome, stranger! glad I greet thee. To Don Juan Baz. Mary E. Tucker. CBWP-1

Welcome, Summer. Chaucer. *See* Parlement of Foules, The: Now Welcom[e], Somer [*or* Summer].

Welcome, Sweet Rest. Michael Wigglesworth. AH

Welcome the lord of light, and lamp of day. Welcome to the Sun. Virgil, *into Middle English by* Gavin Douglas. *Fr.* The Aeneid [*or* Eneados], XII. ACP

Welcome the Wrath. Stanley Kunitz. VGW

Welcome thou of high estate. Welcome O Great Mary. Alice O'Gallacher, *tr. by* Douglas Hyde. WTO

Welcome, thrice welcome to my native place! Mary Gulliver to Captain Lemuel Gulliver. John Gay *and* Alexander Pope. OAEL-1

Welcome to Dr. Benjamin Apthorp Gould, A. Oliver Wendell Holmes. ImOP

Welcome to Freedom's birth-place—and a den! Ode to the Cameleopard. Thomas Hood. FaBoNo

Welcome to Hiroshima. Mary Jo Salter. DiPo

Welcome to Hon. Frederick Douglass. Josephine D. Henderson Heard. CBWP-4

Welcome to Sack, The. Robert Herrick. CaPo; SeCP; SeCV-1

Welcome to Spring. John Lyly. *See* Alexander and Campaspe: Trico's Song.

Welcome to Spring. Irene Thompson. BoTP

Welcome to the Moon. *Unknown, tr. fr. Gaelic.* BoNaP; ChTr

Welcome to the Nations. Oliver Wendell Holmes. PAH

Welcome to the Sun. Virgil, *tr. into Middle English by* Gavin Douglas. *Fr.* The Aeneid [*or* Eneados], XII. ACP

Welcome to this my college, and thought late. To His Kinsman, Master Thomas Herrick, Who Desired to Be in His Book. Robert Herrick. CaPo

Welcome to you, rich Autumn days. Rich Days. W. H. Davies. BoNaP; BoTP

Welcome, wild Northeaster! Ode to the Northeast Wind. Charles Kingsley. FaPoR; GN

Welcome, Ye Hopeful Heirs of Heaven. Phoebe Hinsdale Brown. AH

Welcome Yule. *Unknown.* CH

Welcomed to islands over the long water. Islanders, Inlanders. Michael Mott. PoA

Welcoming Party, A. John Montague. FaBCIP; IPY

Welcoming the Worthy Guest. Mao Wen-hsi, *tr. fr. Chinese by* Lois Fusek. ATF

Weldon Kees in Mexico, 1965. David Wojahn. MAYP

Wele, herying and worshipe be to Christ that dere ous boughte. A Palm-Sunday Hymn. William Herebert. MeEL

Welkin's wind, way unhindered. The Wind. Dafydd ap Gwilym, *tr. by* Joseph P. Clancy. OBWVE

Well, The. T. E. Brown. NOBVV

Well/ we were hauf-roads up Schiehallion. Hauf-Roads up Schiehallion. Donald Campbell. PoSH

Well, The. Manuel de la Parra, *tr. fr. Spanish by* Samuel Beckett. MexPo

Well, The. Luis Palés Matos, *tr. fr. Spanish by* Donald Walsh. InW

Well, The. A. J. Seymour. PVCV

Well-aimed Stare, The. Hugo Margenat, *tr. fr. Spanish by* Julio Marzán. InW

"We'll all be rooned," said Hanrahan. Said Hanrahan. Patrick Joseph Hartigan. PoAu-1

We'll All Go a-Hunting Today. *Unknown.* OBET

Well, all these seamen—sailors and skippers—they. Tristan Corbière, *tr. fr. French by* C. F. MacIntyre. *Fr.* The End. OBD

Well, *alter ego,* Time has trudged. Why Do We Live? Israel Zangwill. TrJP

Well & whatever on whatever in whatever. Plan for Understanding. Reinhard Priessnitz, *tr. by* Beth Bjorklund. CoAuP

Well, as Kavanagh said, we have lived. Singing School. Seamus Heaney. InPS

We'll begin with a box, and the plural is boxes. Why English Is So Hard. *Unknown.* FaBoUs

Well boss did it/ ever strike you. The Hen and the Oriole. Don Marquis. *Fr.* Archy and Mehitabel. FiBHP

Well boss I met. Cheerio My Deario. Don Marquis. *Fr.* Archy and Mehitabel. FaBoCo

Well-bred young girl of Gomorrah, A. *Unknown.* PeHV

Well-buggered boy named Delpasse, A. *Unknown.* PeHV

Well clay it's strange at last we've come to it. The Spark's Farewell to Its Clay. R. A. K. Mason. ATNZ; PeNZ

Well, David said—it was snowing outside and his voice contained many. Paschal Lamb. Robert Hass. NAmP; NPGG

Well, dear Mr. Wright, I must send you a line. To Henry Wright of Mobberley, Esq. on Buying the Picture of Father Malebranche. John Byrom. NOEC

Well, Did You Evah? Cole Porter. OBAL

Well do I know that human life is passing. Yakamochi. *Fr.* Manyo Shu. Ma

Well do I remember how she wept. Osakabe Chikuni. *Fr.* Manyo Shu. Ma

Well dost thou, Love, thy solemn feast to hold. Saint Valentine's Day. Coventry Patmore. *Fr.* The Unknown Eros, XLIII. OBNC

Well Dreams, The, *sel.* John Montague.

"People are different." PoPo

Well fare the nightingale. *Unknown.* PBBP

Well formed is the child, well formed now. The Dawn of Day. Keaulumoku, *tr. fr. Hawaiian by* M. W. Beckwith. *Fr.* Kumulipo, The; a Creation Chant. WTO

Well, Froggie went a-courting and he did ride. Froggie Went a-Courting. *Unknown.* AmFP

Well, gaze thou on the hills, and hedge-side flowers. Steam at Sheffield. Ebenezer Elliott. PF

"Well, General Grant, have you heard the news?" Lee's Parole. Marion Manville. PAH

Well, gentlemen,/ You flag wavers. To Those Who Sing America. Frank Marshall Davis. FB

We'll Go No More a-Roving. Byron. *See* So We'll Go No More a-Roving.

We'll Go to Sea No More. *Unknown.* ChTr; GBP

We'll go to the meadows, where cowslips do grow. The Meadows. Jane *and* Ann Taylor. BoTP

Well, God is/ love. Puerto Rico Song. William Carlos Williams. NYBP

Well hath the powerful hand of majesty. To Sir Thomas Egerton. Samuel Daniel. OBSC

Well, Heaven be thanked my first-love failed. The County Ball. Coventry Patmore. *Fr.* The Angel in the House, II, iii. EBVV

Well! Hello down there. Issa, *tr. by* Harry Behn. ILY; TSS

We'll hoist daddy's vest. Song of the Self-Made Orphans. David Avidan, *tr. by* Warren Bargad *and* Stanley F. Chyet. IP

Well, honest John, how fare you now at home? To John Clare. John Clare. Son

Well, how d'ye do, Private William McBride. No Man's Land. Eric Bogle. OBET

Well, I drink to you, David Campbell, but I drop a curse in the cup. Letter to David Campbell on the Birthday of W. B. Yeats, A, 1965. Alec Derwent Hope. NAs

Well, I have thought on't, and I find. The Retirement. John Norris. OBS

Well, I may now receive, and die: my sin. John Donne. *Fr.* Satires, IV. OBSV

Well I never, did you ever. *Unknown.* FaBoCh

Well I Remember [How You Smiled]. Walter Savage Landor. *Fr.* Ianthe. HAP; OBNC; TrGrPo

   (Ianthe.) HAP; OBNC; TrGrPo

Well, I was at the dresser. Just How It Happened. Priscilla Jane Thompson. CBWP-2

Well, I was camped out on the draw at the head of Cimarron. The Zebra Dun. *Unknown.* AmFP

Well I was travelin' through the country. So Long. Ross Knox. CowP

Well, I went to California in the year of Seventy-six. Root Hog or Die. *Unknown.* AmFP

Well, I would have it so. I should have known. André Marie de Chénier, *tr. fr. French by* Arthur Symons. *Fr.* Elegies, III. AWP

Well, if a King's a lion, at the least. Pope. *Fr.* The First Epistle of the First Book of Horace Imitated. OBSV

Well; if ever I saw such another Man since my Mother bound my Head. Mary the Cook-Maid's Letter to Dr. Sheridan. Swift. OxBoLi

Well! If the Bard was weather-wise, who made. Dejection; an Ode [*or* A Letter to Sara Hutchinson]. Samuel Taylor Coleridge. EnRP; FiP; HeIP; LiTB; NAEL-2; NAWM-2; NOBE; NoP; OAEL-2; OBNC; PoE; PoEL-4; PPP; SeCePo, *st.*1; TOF

Well, if you must know all the facts. "Lewis Carroll." FaBoNo

Well! I'm goin' home. Special Rider Blues. *Unknown.* AmFP

Well, I'm in love with a feller, a feller you have seen. Common Bill. *Unknown.* AmFP; AS, *with music*

Well! in my many walks I've rarely found. The Pettichap's Nest. John Clare. PBBP

Well-intentioned Question, The. Wendy Rose. STE

Well into the distance young leaves of grass undulate. Teika, *tr. fr. Japanese by* Hiroaki Sato. *Fr.* Eighty-four Tanka. FCEI

Well is the hill of Mimoro guarded. *Unknown. Fr.* Manyo Shu. Ma

Well, it was never mine. This Day, under My Hand. David Malouf. CBAP

Well, it's partly the shape of the thing. *Unknown.* SoSe

Well, Jesus died to save me in all of my sin. The Rock Island Line. *Unknown.* AmFP

Well, let's go. Basho, *tr. by* Kenneth Koch *and* Harold Henderson. TTTS

Well look a-here, honey. Depot Blues. *Unknown.* AmFP

Well matched, well matched to mine. Lady Ise, *tr. fr. Japanese by* Burton Watson. *Fr.* Kokin Shu. FCEI

Well may I weene, faire ladies, all this while. Spenser. *Fr.* The Faerie Queene, III, 6. OAEL-1

Well may that kisse be sweet that's giv'n t' a sleek. Sir Richard Fanshawe, *after the Italian of* Giovanni Battista Guarini. *Fr.* Il Pastor Fido. OBVE

Well may they write, that sit in parlours fine. On His Writing Verses. John Hawthorn. NOEC

Well may you question the degree of falsehood. Aviary. Medbh McGuckian. FaBCIP

Well meaning readers! you that come as friends. The Flaming Heart. Richard Crashaw. LiTB; OAEL-1; PoEL-2; SeCePo; SeCV-1; TEP

"We'll meet no more as wont!" she said. Not as Wont. Joseph Skipsey. NOBVV

"Well met, well met, my friend, all on the highway riding." The Husbandman and Serving-Man. *Unknown.* OBET

"Well met, well met, my own true love." The Carpenter's Wife. *Unknown.* OBET; OAEL-1, *with music; diff. vers;* OxBB, *with music.*

   (Demon [*or* Daemon] Lover.) EnSB; HAP; LiTB; MAT; MOS; UnPo; WeW

   (House Carpenter, The.) AmFP;

   (James Harris.) AmFP; ESPB; FaBoBa

   (Well Met, Well Met, My Old True Love.) AmFP

Well Now, the Virgin. Roy Fuller. *Fr.* Mythological Sonnets, VII. Son

We'll o'er the water and o'er the sea. O'er the Water to Charlie. Burns. FaBoCh

Well of Baln, The. Ursula K. Le Guin. BWV

Well of freshness, A. Juxta. Grover Jacoby. GoYe

Well of St. Keyne, The. Robert Southey. BeLS; FaBoBe

Well of the King of Wu, The. Kao Ch'i, *tr. fr. Chinese by* Jonathan Chaves. CoBLCP

Well of Vertew and Flour of Womanheid, The. *Unknown.* OxBS

Well, old spy. Award. Ray Durem. BPo; IDB; PoBA; SoSe; TTY

Well, Paul, when you were nine. Poem for My Son. John Logan. DiL

We'll, placed in Love's triumphant chariot high. William Cavendish, Duke of Newcastle. *Fr.* The Humorous Lovers. OxBSP

We'll play in the snow. Snow. Karla Kuskin. RAR

Well Pleaseth Me the Sweet Time of Easter. Bertrans de Born, *tr. by* Ezra Pound. InvP

   (Song of Battle.) AWP; WaaP

   (War Song, A.) CTC

Well pleasing 'tis to me. Goat's-Leaf. Marie de France, *tr. by* Aline Allard. PBWP

Well Rising, The. William Stafford. NaP; RB

We'll roll, we'll roll the chariot along. Roll the Chariot. *Unknown.* AS

"We'll see who can stick." *Fr.* Anselm Williams *and* Br. Leander Neville. Elizabeth Smither. ATNZ

Well-shadowed landscape, fare ye well! Farewell to Love. Sir John Suckling. CaPo

Well, Sir, 'tis granted, I said D[ryden's] rhimes [*or* rhymes]. An Allusion to Horace; the Tenth Satire of the First Book. John Wilmot, 2nd Earl of Rochester. APAS; OBS

Well, So That Is That ("Well so that is that. Now we must diomantle the tree."). W. H. Auden. *Fr.* For the Time Being; a Christmas Oratorio. LiTA; OAEL-2; OBCP

   (After Christmas.) MoAB; MoBrPo

   (Flight into Egypt, The.) OxBA

Well, some may hate, and some may scorn. Stanzas to———. Emily Brontë. WPE

Well, sometimes it's Heaven, and sometimes it's Hell. Heaven and Hell. Willie Nelson. InPK

Well, son de story of my life. The Favorite Slave's Story. Priscilla Jane Thompson. CBWP-2

Well, son, I'll tell you. Mother to Son. Langston Hughes. AmNP; CDC; NAAL-2; NTCP; OBCA; PoNe; SO; TTY

Well, sorrow is a simple word. The Food-Rioter Banished. William Thom. PF

We'll stock up books. Striking a Pose. Kevin Ireland. ATNZ

Well, Teddy, I have found you. The Lost Teddy Bear. Maggie Pogue Johnson. CBWP-4

Well, that was silly; too near the edge. On Catching a Dog-Daisy in the Mower. Peter Redgrove. NePoEA-2

Well, the day of slavery back again! The Yankees Back. "Mighty Sparrow, The." PBCV

Well the prophets were dancing in the end much. In Sobieski's Shield. Edwin Morgan. BWV

Well the sunset rays are shining. The Wild Mushroom. Gary Snyder. NoP

Well then! I now do plainly see. The Wish. Abraham Cowley. *Fr.* The Mistress. LiTB; NOBE; NoP; OBEV; OBS; SeCV-1; TrGrPo

Well, then, poor G—— lies under ground! Epitaph on G——. Pope. OBD

Well, then, the last day the sharks appeared. The Sharks. Denise Levertov. NeAP

Well then, the promis'd [*or* promised] hour is come at last. To My Dear Friend Mr. Congreve [on His Comedy Called "The Double-Dealer"]. Dryden. EBEV; FiP; OAEL-1; OBS; PoEL-3; SeCV-2

Well then, tomorrow! the wood exalts under the mild. Finally. Vittoria Aganoor Pompili, *tr. by* Brenda Webster. PBWP

Well there is in the west country, A. The Well of St. Keyne. Robert Southey. BeLS; FaBoBe

Well! there you lie already. . .on the board. Before a Corpse. Manuel Acuña, *tr. by* Samuel Beckett. MexPo

Well, they are gone, and here must I remain. Seen from the Quantocks. Samuel Taylor Coleridge. *Fr.* This Lime Tree Bower My Prison. FaBoPP

Well, they are gone, and here must I remain. This Lime-Tree Bower My Prison. Samuel Taylor Coleridge. EnRP; FaBoPP; HeIP; NAEL-2; NIP; PoE; PoEL-4; TOF

Well they'd made up their minds to be everywhere because why not. The Last One. W. S. Merwin. LCAP; NoAM; VGW

Well, they're quite dead, Rambuncto; thoroughly dead. Rambuncto. Margaret Widdemer. BXAP

Well, this bird comes, and under his wing is a crutch. The Bird. Moyshe-Leyb Halpern, *tr. by* John Hollander. PPP

"Well, this is where I go down to the river." Heat. Kenneth Mackenzie. CBAP; PoAu-2

"Well, though it seems." Liddell and Scott; on the Completion of Their Lexicon. Thomas Hardy. OxBoLi

We'll to the woods and gather may. Alons au bois le may cueillir. Charles d'Oréans, *tr. by* W. E. Henley. AWP

We'll to the Woods No More. A. E. Housman. OAEL-2; PoRA

Well-travelled Roadway, The. John Newlove. NeAC

Well: Two Songs, The. *Gond Oral Tradition, tr. by* V. Elwin *and* S. Hivale. WTO

"Well Uncle Ike! This beats me." Uncle Ike's Holiday. Priscilla Jane Thompson. CBWP-2

Well, Wanton Eye. Charles, Duc d' Orléans. HAP

Well Water. Randall Jarrell. InPK; NAAL-2; NOBA; NoP; OxBSP; VGW

Well water. Eight Sandbars on the Takano River. Gary Snyder. NOBA; NoP; VGW

Well—we have reached the precipice at last. On the Masquerades. Christopher Pitt. NOEC

Well, we went down town a-shopping. The Christmas Rush. Clara Ann Thompson. CBWP-2

Well, we will do that rigid thing. Parting with Lucasia; a Song. Katherine Philips. PeHV

Well, well, I know the wise ones talk and talk. Augusta Davies Webster. *Fr.* A Castaway. BrRo

Well, well, 'tis true. Plain Dealing. Alexander Brome. OBS

Well, well, you's cum at las.' People's Literary, De. Maggie Pogue Johnson. CBWP-4

Well, what's in a fire. The Glow. Bill Simpson. CowP

Well, when all is said and done. "Æ." MoBrPo

Well when you can't see the forest. Orange Juice Song. David Phillips. NeAC

Well, wife, I've found the model church! I worshipped there to-day. The Model Church. John H. Yates. PWR

Well-wishing to a Place of Pleasure, A. *Unknown.* GBL

Well, World, you have kept faith with me. He Never Expected Much. Thomas Hardy. NAEL-2; NAs; NoAM; OxBTC; SCV

Well worthy to be magnified are they. The Pilgrim Fathers. Wordsworth. PAH; AiP, *abr.*

Well, yes, I've lived in Texas since the spring of '61. A Spool of Thread. Sophie E. Eastman. PAH

Well, yes, sir, dat am a comical name. Ashcake. Thomas Nelson Page. AA

Well You Caught Me Unprepared. Wendy Rose. GOS

Well you have to remember this place. Living Here. Cilla McQueen. ATNZ

Well, you know the sun is going down. Lowdown Dirty Blues. *Unknown.* AmFP

Welladay, welladay, poor Colin, thou art going to the ground. George Peele. *Fr.* The Arraignment of Paris. ElL

(Shepherd's Dirge, The.) OBSC

"Wellcome, to the Caves of Artá!" Robert Graves. NBLV; NOBL; NYBP

Wellfleet Harbor. Paul Goodman. CoAP

Wellfleet Whale, The. Stanley Kunitz. CAPP; DiPo; NoAM

Wellington. Louis Johnson. ATNZ

Wellington again slaps the face with wind. Return Journey. Paul Henderson. ATNZ

Wells of Jesus Wounds, The. *Unknown.* MeEL

Welsh Ballad, A. Edmwnd Prys, *tr. fr. Welsh by* Gwyn Williams. OBWVE

Welsh History. R. S. Thomas. OBWVE

Welsh Incident. Robert Graves. CMoP; NOBE; OxBTC; WSC

Welsh Landscape. R. S. Thomas. FaBoMo

Welsh Marches, The. A. E. Housman. FaBoTw

Welsh Sea, The. James Elroy Flecker. BrPo

Welshman by the pit whose Sabbath voice, The. Orpheus. E. W. Mandel. *Fr.* Minotaur Poems, VI. OBCV

Welshman in Exile Speaks, The. T. H. Jones. OBWVE

Welshman to Any Tourist, A. Ronald Stuart Thomas. OxBC

Welt. Georgia Douglas Johnson. BANP

Welt ist dumm, die Welt ist blind, Die. Heine, *tr. fr. German by* James Thomson. AWP

Weltschmerz. Frank Yerby. AmNP

Wemen's Wather. T. S. Law. OxBS

Wen the turuf is thi tuur. *Unknown.* SeCePo

We'n you see a man in woe. "Hullo!" Sam Walter Foss. CenHV

Wenberi's Song. Wenberi, *tr. fr. Woiworung by* A. W. Howitt. CBAP

Wendell Phillips. Amos Bronson Alcott. AA

Wendell Phillips, *sel.* John Boyle O'Reilly.

"What shall we mourn? For the prostrate." AA

Wendell Phillips. Henrietta Cordelia Ray. CBWP-3

Wendigo, The. Ogden Nash. AmMo; RHPC

Wendling. Coman Leavenworth. *Fr.* Norfolk Memorials, III. LiTA

Wendy in Winter. Kaye Starbird. RHPC

Wenlock. A. E. Housman. *See* Shropshire Lad, A: Wenlock Edge (" 'Tis time, I think; by Wenlock town").

Wenlock Edge ("On Wenlock Edge the woods's in trouble"). A. E. Housman. *See* On Wenlock Edge.

Wenlock Edge (" 'Tis time, I think; by Wenlock town"). A. E. Housman. *Fr.* A Shropshire Lad, XXXIX. FaBoPP

(Wenlock.) SeCePo

Wensleydale Lad, The. *Unknown.* FaBoPP

Went down to St. Joe's infirmary. Those Gambler's Blues. *Unknown.* AS

Went into a shoestore to buy a pair of shoes. Sale. Josephine Miles. WPE

Went to dinner with her thursday. Pubescence at 39. Vickie Sears. GLP

"Went to NCC for a year." Sheepherder Blues. Luci Tapahonso. STE

Went up a year this evening. Emily Dickinson. HAP; WeW

Went weeping, little bones. But where? I Cry, Love! Love! Theodore Roethke. LCAP

Wenzel knelt to his tied ram. Ram Time. William Heyen. GeTw

We're A' Dry wi' the Drinkin' O't. *Unknown.* ErPo

(We're All Dry.) NOBL, *sl. diff. vers*

("We're all dry with drinking on't.") OxNR, *sl. diff. vers*

"We're all Americans, except the Doc." A Mad Negro Soldier Confined at Munich. Robert Lowell. FaBoMo; OxBC

We're all at home. Having Eaten Breakfast. David Chapman Berry. BXAP

We're All Dry. *Unknown. See* We're A' Dry wi' the Drinkin' O't.

We're all dry with drinking on't. *Unknown. See* We're A' Dry wi' the Drinkin' O't.

Were all our sins so empty of enjoyment. The Muted Screen of Graham Greene. Phyllis McGinley. FaBoEE

We're an Africanpeople. Don L. Lee. *Fr.* African Poems. CNA

Were beth they [that] biforen us weren. Ubi Sunt Qui ante Nos Fuerunt? *Unknown.* NoP

(Contempt of the World.) MeEL

(Ubi Sunt.) PoE

("Were beth they biforen us weren.") PrIm

("Where are the ones who lived before.") HAP

("Where are those that were before us.") NoP; PrIm; WeW

("Where beeth they biforen us weren.") EBEV

("Where beth they, beforen us weren.") MeEL

("Where beth they biforen us weren.") HAP

Were But My Spirit Loosed upon the Air. Louise Chandler Moulton. AA

We're connecting. Poems for the New. Kathleen Fraser. IHMS; NMM

We're crossing the bar of another year. "I Am with Thee." Ernest Bourner Allen. BLRP

We're 'er Majesty's bold troubleshooter; wherever they send us we goes. Bold Troubleshooters. Peter Veale. NOBL

We're flattered they come so close. Animal Song. Heather McHugh. AnAn; MAYP

We're foot—slog—slog—slog—sloggin' over Africa. Boots. Kipling. BLPA; FaPoR; FPL; MoBrPo

We're going to have a party. The Christmas Party. Adeline White. BoTP

We're going to the fair at Holstenwall. Holstenwall. Sidney Keyes. FaBoTw

Were half the power that fills the world with terror. A Message of Peace. Longfellow. *Fr.* The Arsenal at Springfield. WBLP

Were he composer, he would surely write. Portrait of the Boy as Artist. Barbara Howes. MoAmPo

We're hoping to be arrested. Street Demonstration. Margaret Abigail Walker. BPo; CNA
Were I a happy bird. Faith Trembling. "Madeline Bridges." AA
Were I a king, I could command content. A Choice. Edward de Vere, Earl of Oxford. OBSC
  (Doubtful Choice, A.) EiL
  (Epigram: "Were I a king, I could command content.") FaBoEE; OxBSP
Were I as Base as Is the Lowly Plain. *At. to* Joshua Sylvester. Son
  (Love's Omnipresence.) GTBS; GTBS-P
  (Sonnet: "Were I as base as is the lowly plain.") EiL; OBSC
  (Ubique.) OBEV
Were I idiom and. While. Bruce Andrews. LP
Were I in Trouble. Robert Frost. OxBSP
Were I invited to a nectar feast. Sylvia. Samuel Croxall. NOEC
Were I laid on Greenland's coast. John Gay. *Fr.* The Beggar's Opera, I, i. EnLoPo; NAEL-1; OxBoLi; PoEL-3
  (Macheath and Polly.) NOEC
  (Over the Hills and Far Away.) NOBE; PrIm
Were I the palm tree which your love returning. E Questo il Nido in Che la Mia Fenice. A. D. Hope. OxBC
Were I the red-brushed fox, I should go warier. November Fugitive. Henry Morton Robinson. OxBC
Were I to leave no more than a good friend. The Departure; an Elegy. Henry King. SeCP
Were I to take an iron gun. Facts. "Lewis Carroll." FaBoUs
Were I transported to some distant star. A Plain Man's Dream. Frederick Keppel. AA
Were I, who to my cost already am. A Satire [*or* Satyr] against [Reason and] Mankind. John Wilmot, 2d Earl of Rochester. LiTB; NoP; OAEL-1; OBSV
  (Homo Sapiens.) NOBE
  (Satyre against Mankind, A.) OBS; PoEL-3; SeCV-2
  (Satyre against Reason and Mankind, A.) SCV
Were I, who to my cost already am. John Wilmot, 2nd Earl of Rochester. *Fr.* A Satire against [Reason and] Mankind. LiTB; SCV
Were it not for the dresses. Nakatomi Yakamori. *Fr.* Manyo Shu. Ma
Were it undo that is y-do. He Is Far. *Unknown.* OAEL-1
  (Forsaken Maiden's Lament, A.) SeCePo
We're low—we're low—we're very, very low. The Song of the Low. Ernest Charles Jones. NOBVV; PF
We're marching 'round the levee. Marching 'round the Levee. *Unknown.* AmFP
Were My Hart as Some Men's Are. Thomas Campion. AAS
We're not as simple as we seem. Mohammad Taqi Mir, *tr. by* Ahmed Ali. GoT
We're not silent. Lord of Dreams. Abba Kovner, *tr. by* Warren Bargad *and* Stanley F. Chyet. IP
Were Not the Gael Fallen. Peadar O'Mulconry, *tr. fr. Early Modern Irish by* Robin Flower. AnIL
We're OK. Gloria Fuertes, *tr. fr. Spanish by* Philip Levine. WPOW
We're queer folks here. Just Folks. Edgar Albert Guest. FaFP
We're Racing, Racing down the Walk. Phyllis McGinley. RHPC
We're Satisfied. Ilse Tielsch, *tr. fr. German by* Beth Bjorklund. CoAuP
We're standing on a stage. Tableau Mourant. Gerrit Achterberg, *tr. by* James S. Holmes. DuIn
We're striding in your front ranks. Procession. Dovid Hofshteyn, *tr. by* Robert Friend. PeBMYV
We're the D-Day Dodgers, out in Italy. Ballad of the D-Day Dodgers. *Unknown.* WTO
We're the hardrock men. Dynamite Song. *Unknown.* AmFP
Were the Itada bridge to crumble. *Unknown. Fr.* Manyo Shu. Ma
Were the whole world good as you—not an atom better. The Question. *Unknown.* WBLP
Were there no crowns on earth. The Dead President. Edward Rowland Sill. PAH
Were there too many revolving mirrors? Air Circus. Carl Sandburg. AnAmPo
Were these flowers broken off. *Unknown. Fr.* Manyo Shu. Ma
Were we now to fall. The Mechanic. Robert Creeley. NaP
Were-Wolf. Julian Hawthorne. AA
Were you a leper bathed in wounds. Proving. Georgia Douglas Johnson. CDC
Were you an only child? she asks. Southpaw. Lisel Mueller. KS
Were you, as old prints have shown. John Frederick Nims. BLA
Were You There When They Crucified My Lord? *Unknown.* AH, *with music;* BPo
Were yu normal today did yu screw society. Christ I Wudint Know Normal if I Saw It When. Bill Bissett. NOBC

Werena My Heart Licht Wad Dee. Lady Grisel Baillie. OBEV
Werfel dead? Hark. The forest is empty. The Shooting of Werfel. Vernon Watkins. WaP
Werther had a love for Charlotte. The Sorrows of Werther. Thackeray. BLPA; CenHV; FaBoCo; FiBHP; FPL; NA; NBLV; NOBL; NOBVV; OBD
Wes Hardin: From a Photograph. Raymond Carver. GeTw
We's invited down to brudder Browns. Krismas Dinnah. Maggie Pogue Johnson. CBWP-4
Wesley in Heaven. Thomas Edward Brown. OBNC
Wessex Heights. Thomas Hardy. CMoP; EBVV; FaBoPP; OAEL-2; OBNC; PoEL-5
West ascending Lotus Flower Mountain. Poem No. 19 in the Old Manner. Li Po, *tr. by* Burton Watson. CoBCP
West Coast Indian. George Clutesi. HATNAP
West-Country Damosel's Complaint, The. *Unknown.* ESPB
West Creek at Ch'u-chou. Wei Ying-wu, *tr. fr. Chinese by* Burton Watson. CoBCP
West-Easterly Divan, *sels.* Goethe, *tr. fr. German by* John Weiss. PeHV
  Cupbearer Speaks, The. *Fr. bk.* 9.
  "Market square's admiring throngs, The." *Fr. bk.* 9.
West Forties: Morning, Noon, and Night, The. Louis Edward Sissman. CoAP; NYBP
West Indies, The, *sels.* James Montgomery. PBCV
  Inspiration, The. PAH
  Lust of Gold, The. PAH
West Kansas full moon. Directions in Our Blood. Barney Bush. HATNAP
West Lake. Kenneth O. Hanson. CoAP
West London. Matthew Arnold. FF; Son
West of Alice. W. E. Harney. PoAu-1
West of Chicago. John Dimoff. RFM
West of the bridge. Waterside Village. Yün Shou-p'ing, *tr. by* Jonathan Chaves. CoBLCP
West of the Sierras where. The California Phrasebook. Dennis Schmitz. AmPA; NPGG
West of the village, evening rays linger on red leaves. Wu Chen, *tr. fr. Chinese by* Jonathan Chaves. *Fr.* Paintings of Fishermen, I. CoBLCP
West of Your City. William Stafford. LiTM
West of your door, Blue Mountain dreams of melting. Blue Mountain. Roberta Hill. VoR
West Palm Beach Storm, The. *Unknown.* AmFP
West Ridge Is Menthol-Cool, The. D. L. Graham. PoBA
West-running Brook. Robert Frost. BLPL; MoAB; MoAmPo; NOBA; NoP
West Sussex Drinking Song. Hilaire Belloc. MoBrPo
West Virginia Handicrafts. Kathleen Spivack. ER
West Wind, The. John Masefield. FaFP; FPL; LiTB; LiTM; MoAB; MoBrPo
West wind, blow from your prairie nest. The Song My Paddle Sings. E. Pauline Johnson. CaP; FaPON
West wind has come again to the "tower of makeup," The. Cheng Hsieh, *tr. fr. Chinese by* Jonathan Chaves. *Fr.* Yangchou. CoBLCP
West wind slaughters the lingering heat. Once More Following the Rhymes of Pin-lao's Poem "Getting Up After Illness." Huang T'ing-chien, *tr. by* Burton Watson. CoBCP
Wester wind when will thou blow. Western Wind. *Unknown.* BoLoP; CTC; EBEV; EnLoPo; FaBoCh; FF; GBP; HAP; HeIP; InPK; LLLT; MAT; MeEL; NOBE; NoP; OAEL-1; OxBLMV; OxBSP; PPP; PrIM; TEP; UnPo; WeW
  (Absence.) OBSC
  (Lover in Winter Plaineth for the Spring, The.) OBEV
  (Westron Wind[e], When Will Thou Blow.) InvP; MeEL; NAEL-1; NIP; OBTV; PoE; PoEL-1
  ("Westron wynde when wyll thou blow.") GBL
Westering. Douglas V. Kane. GoYe
Western Approaches, The. Howard Nemerov. HCAP; TAP
Western Capital in lawless disorder, The. Wang Ts'an, *tr. fr. Chinese by* Burton Watson. *Fr.* Seven Sorrows, I. CoBCP
Western Civilization. Agostinho Neto, *tr. fr. Portuguese by* Marga Holness. WMBCH
Western Magic. Mary Austin. AmFN
Western Star, *sel.* Stephen Vincent Benét.
  "Americans are always moving on." AmFN
Western sun withdraws the shorten'd day, The. The Autumnal Moon. James Thomson. *Fr.* The Seasons: Autumn. NOBE
  (Autumn ("Western sun withdraws the shorten'd day, The").) NOBE
Western Town. David Wadsworth Cannon, Jr. PoNe

Western Town. Karl Shapiro. NYBP

Western Wagons. Rosemary *and* Stephen Vincent Benét. AiP

Western Waves of Ebbing Day, The. Sir Walter Scott. *Fr.* The Lady of the Lake, I. PoEL-4

Western Wind. *Unknown.* BoLoP; CTC; EBEV; EnLoPo; FaBoCh; FF; GBP; HAP; HeIP; InPK; LLLT; MAT; MeEL; NOBE; NoP; OAEL-1; OxBLMV; OxBSP; PPP; PrIM; TEP; UnPo; WeW

(Absence.) OBSC

(Lover in Winter Plaineth for the Spring, The.) OBEV

(Westron Wind[e], When Will Thou Blow.) InvP; MeEL; NAEL-1; NIP; OBTV; PoE; PoEL-1

("Westron wynde when wyll thou blow.") GBL

Western wind has blown but a few days, The. The Cranes. Po Chü-i, *tr. by* Arthur Waley. OBVE

Westgate-on-Sea. Sir John Betjeman. OxBoLi

Westland Row. Thomas Kinsella. MoP

Westminster Wedding; or, Like unto Like, Quoth the Devil to the Collier, A. *Unknown.* CoMu

Westphalian Song. *Unknown, tr. fr. German by* Samuel Taylor Coleridge. AWP; OBVE

Westron Wind[e], When Will Thou Blow. *Unknown.* See Western Wind.

Westron wynde when wyll thou blow. *Unknown.* See Western Wind.

Westward, hit a low note, for a roarer lost. A Strut for Roethke. John Berryman. NOBA

Westward Ho! Joaquin Miller. AA; AnAmPo; FaBoBe

Westward I watch the low green hills of Wales. Clevedon Church. Andrew Lang. GoTS, *abr*

Westward the field of the cloth of gold. A Visit. Sherwood Anderson. PoA

Westward, the gloom of the remote wilds. Headwaters of the Lung River. Hsü Ts'an, *tr. by* Pao Chia-lin. WFTU

Wet. Yusuf al-Sa'igh, *tr. fr. Arabic by* Diana Der Hovanessian *with* Salma Khadra Jayyusi. MAP

Wet. Lilian Moore. RR

Wet almond-trees, in the rain. Bare Almond-Trees. D. H. Lawrence. FaBoPP; OBTV

Wet Are the Boards. John Ashbery. BLA; NPo

Wet August, A. Thomas Hardy. PPP

Wet Casements. John Ashbery. NAAL-2; PoM

Wet dawn inks are doing their blue dissolve, The. Winter Trees. Sylvia Plath. CAPP; HCAP; LCAP; NMM

Wet Earth. Ramón López Velarde, *tr. fr. Spanish by* Samuel Beckett. MexPo

Wet Evening in April. Patrick Kavanagh. PoPo

Wet gray day, A—rain falling slowly. Morels. William Jay Smith. BoNaP; MAT; NYBP; RFM

Wet Hair: If Now His Mother Should Come. Robert Penn Warren. *Fr.* Penological Study: Southern Exposure, III. NoAM

Wet Morning. Janet Frame. ATNZ

Wet Night, A. Richard Ryan. CIP

Wet paint on the cheeks wings and a sudden wind. Burying Uncle Salomon. David Avidan, *tr. by* Warren Bargad *and* Stanley F. Chyet. IP

Wet Sheet and a Flowing Sea, A. Allan Cunningham. EnRP; GoTS; GTBS; GTBS-P

(Sea-Song, A.) BoTP; FaBoBe; FaPoR; GN

Wet, sickly/ smells of cattle yard silage fill the prairie air. Dream. Elizabeth Cook-Lynn. *Fr.* Journey, I. HATNAP

Wet silence, I. Mad Sweeny. John Montague. FaBCIP

Wet streets are undisturbed by that chronic, The. Sirens in Bad Weather. Sherod Santos. MAYP

Wet streets. It has rained drops big as silver coins. Eighteen. Maria Banus, *tr. by* Willis Barnstone *and* Matei Calinescu. BoWoP; VWA

Wet Summer. May Williams Ward. GoYe

Wet Thursday. Weldon Kees. NaP; NYBP

Wet, wayward fingers of the west wind wave the wheat. Corn Cañon. Patric Stevenson. NeIP

Wet Weather. Patricia Low. VGW

Wet Weather at Cannes. Edward Lear. FaBoNo

Wet-Weather Talk. James Whitcomb Riley. AnAmPo

Wet, wet, wet. Wet. Lilian Moore. RR

Wet wipe out rust dry over oily flame. Sally. Tom Mandel. IAT

Wetness. Paul Eluard, *tr. fr. French by* Michael Benedikt. POS

Wetting his head, he slips in. *Unknown, tr. by* Hiroaki Sato. FCEI

We've all been invited up to Killisnoo. *Unknown, tr. by* James Koller. STP

We've been to the wars together. To Lou Gehrig. John Kieran. SD

We've come intil a gey queer time. Epistle to John Guthrie. Sydney Goodsir Smith. OxBS

We've formed our band and are well manned. The Californian. *Unknown.* AmFP

We've fought with many men acrost the seas. Fuzzy-Wuzzy. Kipling. BrPo; MoBrPo; TrGrPo

We've found this Scott Fitzgerald chap. Effervescence and Evanescence. Keith Preston. OBAL

We've got some. Reservation Girls. Nila NorthSun. GOS

We've hardly parted. Tsurayuki, *tr. fr. Japanese by* Burton Watson. *Fr.* Kokin Shu. FCEI

We've hung David's *La Vierge et Les Saintes*. The Living Room. Gjertrud Schnackenberg. FYAP

We've kept the faith. Our souls' high dreams. To Our Friends. Lucian B. Watkins. BANP

We've lived for forty years, dear wife. The Ideal Husband to His Wife. Sam Walter Foss. AnAmPo

We've made a great mess of love. The Mess of Love. D. H. Lawrence. OAEL-2

We've nothing vast to offer you, no deserts. A Welshman to Any Tourist. Ronald Stuart Thomas. OxBC

We've our business to attend Day's duties. Bending the Bow. Robert Duncan. CAPP

We've put a fine addition on the good old church at home. The Ladies' Aid. *Unknown.* PoLF

We've reached the land of desert sweet. Dakota Land. *Unknown.* AS

We've seen him before. A Charmer Turned Ascetic. Marippittiyar, *tr. by* A. K. Ramanujan. PLW

We've taken our burlap sacks and entered. The Killigrew Wood. Norman Dubie. AmPA

We've taken the dog for his walk. To a Child. S. S. Gardons. NePoEA-2

We've traveled a road. *Unknown. Fr.* Manyo Shu. FCEI

We've traveled long together. Verses to my Heart's-Sister. Henrietta Cordelia Ray. CBWP-3

We've trod the maze of error round. Late Wisdom. George Crabbe. *Fr.* Reflections. OBEV; TrGrPo

Wexford Girl, The ("My tender parents brought me here"). *Unknown.* AmFP

Wha ebah Joe an me duz lib we likes to hab um neat. Lizzie and Joe Catch a Thief. Edward Cordle. PBCV

Wha Fe Call I.' Valerie Bloom. AIW

Wha gangs wi' us owre the hill. Owre the Hill. William Soutar. PoSH

Wha Is Perfyte. Alexander Scott. GoTS

Wha Is That at My Bower-Door? Burns. ErPo; InvP

Wha kens on whatna Bethlehems. The Innumerable Christ. "Hugh MacDiarmid." EaLo; EBEV; NoP; OxBS

Wha lies here? Johnny Dow [*or* Doo]. *Unknown.* FaBoCo; FaBoEE; FiBHP

Wha wadna be in love. Maggie Lauder. *At. to* Francis Sempill. OBS; OxBS

Whack Fol the Diddle. Peadar Kearney. FiBHP

Whaddaya Do for Action in This Place? George Starbuck. NePoEA-2

Whalan of Waitin' a While. James William Gordon. PoAu-1

Whale. William Rose Benét. MoAmPo

Whale. Geoffrey Dearmer. BoTP

Whale, The. John Donne. *Fr.* The Progress[e] of the Soul[e]. ChTr

Whale, The. Herman Melville. *See* Moby Dick: Ribs and Terrors in the Whale, The.

Whale, The. *Unknown, tr. by* Gavin Bone. EBEV

Whale, The. *Unknown.* ChTr

(Greenland Whale, The.) GBP

Whale, The. *Unknown, tr. fr. Anglo-Saxon by* Charles Kennedy. *Fr.* Physiologus. AnOE; MOS

"To explain the nature of fishes in craft of verse." EBEV

Whale, The. *Unknown, tr. fr. Middle English by* Richard Wilbur. *Fr.* The Bestiary. CRP

Whale got my friend, The. One Thousand Feet of Shadow. David Craig. PoSH

Whale, His Bulwark, The. Derek Walcott. OxBC; TTY

Whale, improbable as lust, The. A Tall Tale; or, A Moral Song. Phyllis Webb. OBCV

Whale in the Blue Washing Machine, The. John Haines. AnAn

Whale is the greatest beast in all the ocean waste. The Whale. *Unknown, tr. fr. Middle English by* Richard Wilbur. *Fr.* The Bestiary. CRP

Whale, says Jonah, is the war and its black-outs, The. Jean-Paul de Dadelsen, *tr. by* Anselm Hollo. RHTwFP

Whale Songs. Diane Ackerman. BWV

Whalefeathers. Paul Violi. UL

Whale-hunting we will go, A. The Hunting of Whales. Jacques Prévert, *tr.* by Michael Benedikt. POS

Whales, The. Marguerite Young. WPE

Whales off Wales, The. X. J. Kennedy. OBCA

Whales Weep Not! D. H. Lawrence. CMoP; MOS; NoAM; NU

Whaling for continents coveted deep in the south. The Unhistoric Story. Allen Curnow. ATNZ

Wha'll buy my caller herrin? Caller Herrin.' Lady Nairne. OxBS

Whan bells war rung, an mass was sung. Sweet William's Ghost. *Unknown.* ESPB

(Sweet William and May Margaret.) CH

Whan netilles in winter bere roses rede. Impossible to Trust Women. *Unknown.* MeEL

Whan said was al this miracle, every man. Chaucer. *See* Canterbury Tales, The: Prologue to Sir Thopas.

Whan that Aprill[e] with his shoures [*or* shower] soote. Chaucer. *Fr.* The Canterbury Tales: Prologue. ChTr; CTC, *abr.;* FiP; InPS; NAEL-1; NIP; NoP; OAEL-1; PoE; SCV; TrGrPo

(As soon as April pierces to the root, *mod. vers.* by Theodore Robinson) NAWM-1

(When April with Its Sweet Showers.) PrIm

(When in April the Sweet Showers Fall, *mod. vers.* by Nevill Coghill) TEP

(When the Sweet Showers of April Follow March, *mod. vers.* by Louis Untermeyer) TrGrPo

Whan that Aprille with hise shoures soote. Aprilly. Bert Leston Taylor. OBAL

Whan that the knight had [*or* hadde] thus his tale ytold. Chaucer. *See* Canterbury Tales, The: Miller's Prologue, The.

Whan they unto the paleys were yoemen. Chaucer. *Fr.* Troilus and Criseyde [*or* Criseide], V. PoE

Whane lordes wol leefe theire olde lawes. Prophecia Merlini Doctoris Perfecti. *Unknown.* OxBLMV

Whango Tree, The. *Unknown.* NA

Whanne I this Supplicacioun. The Parting of Venus and Old Age. John Gower. *Fr.* Confessio Amantis, VIII. PoEL-1

Whanne ic se on Rode. I Ought to Weep. *Unknown.* MeEL

"Whar hae ye been a' day, my boy Tammy?" My Boy Tammy. Hector MacNeill. CH

Whare the braid planes in dowy murmurs wave. The Ghaists; a Kirk-yard Eclogue. Robert Fergusson. OxBS

Wharton ("Wharton! the scorn and wonder of our days.") Pope. *Fr.* Epistle to Sir Richard Temple. AWP

What/ has happened. Here. Robert Creeley. NOBA

What? Langston Hughes. NBLV; OBAL

What a beautiful thing to dump everything on the unconscious! The Private Theater. Nelo Risi, *tr.* by Lawrence R. Smith. NItP; PFI

What a calamity! What dreadful loss! Honesty at a Fire. Sir John Collings Squire. FiBHP

What a charming thing's a battle! Isaac Bickerstaffe. *Fr.* The Recruiting Serjeant. NOEC

What a Circus. Alan Dugan. AnAn

What a commanding power. Thomas Washbourne. WGRP

What a commotion there was yesterday around me. On the Butcher Block. Jacob Glatstein, *tr.* by Benjamin *and* Barbara Harshav. AYP

What a cost to be pure! did e'er strike your mind. Refining Fire. Lizelia Augusta Jenkins Moorer. CBWP-3

What a crazy saint I am. I Would Rather Run Back. Sandor Csoori, *tr.* by Alan Dixon. MHuP

What a delight it is. Poems of Solitary Delights. Tachibana Akemi, *tr.* by Geoffrey Bownas *and* Anthony Thwaite. Mes

What a delight it is/ When a guest you cannot stand. Tachibana Akemi, *tr. fr. Japanese* by Geoffrey Bownas *and* Anthony Thwaite. *Fr.* Poems of Solitary Delights. PeBJV

What a delight it is/ When, after a hundred days. Tachibana Akemi, *tr. fr. Japanese* by Geoffrey Bownas *and* Anthony Thwaite. *Fr.* Poems of Solitary Delights. PeBJV

What a delight it is/ when, borrowing. Tachibana Akemi, *tr. fr. Japanese* by Geoffrey Bownas *and* Anthony Thwaite. *Fr.* Poems of Solitary Delights. PeBJV

What a delight it is/ When everyone admits. Tachibana Akemi, *tr. fr. Japanese* by Geoffrey Bownas *and* Anthony Thwaite. *Fr.* Poems of Solitary Delights. PeBJV

What a delight it is/ When I blow away the ash. Tachibana Akemi, *tr. fr. Japanese* by Geoffrey Bownas *and* Anthony Thwaite. *Fr.* Poems of Solitary Delights. PeBJV

What a delight it is/ When I find a good brush. Tachibana Akemi, *tr. fr. Japanese* by Geoffrey Bownas *and* Anthony Thwaite. *Fr.* Poems of Solitary Delights. PeBJV

What a delight it is/ When, of a morning. Tachibana Akemi, *tr. fr. Japanese* by Geoffrey Bownas *and* Anthony Thwaite. *Fr.* Poems of Solitary Delights. PeBJV

What a delight it is/ When on the bamboo matting. Tachibana Akemi, *tr. fr. Japanese* by Geoffrey Bownas *and* Anthony Thwaite. *Fr.* Poems of Solitary Delights. PeBJV

What a delight it is/ When, skimming through the pages. Tachibana Akemi, *tr. fr. Japanese* by Geoffrey Bownas *and* Anthony Thwaite. *Fr.* Poems of Solitary Delights. PeBJV

What a delight it is/ When, spreading paper. Tachibana Akemi, *tr. fr. Japanese* by Geoffrey Bownas *and* Anthony Thwaite. *Fr.* Poems of Solitary Delights. PeBJV

What a fine cow your predecessor was! To a Sacred Cow. *Unknown*, *tr.* by W. E. Mashiel. WGRP

What a fine hunting day, it's as balmy as May. We'll All Go a-Hunting Today. *Unknown.* OBET

What a fine tower the little boy is building with his blocks. Time. Avraham Huss, *tr.* by Mark Elliott Shapiro. VWA

What a Friend We Have in Cheeses! William Cole. OBAL

What a friend we have in Jesus. The Unfailing Friend. Joseph Scriven. BLRP

What a garden, where the tree is. Our Garden. Moyshe-Leyb Halpern, *tr.* by Benjamin *and* Barbara Harshav *and* Kathryn Helle. AYP

What a girl called "the dailiness of life." Well Water. Randall Jarrell. InPK; NAAL-2; NOBA; NoP; OxBSP; VGW

What a grand time was the war! World War II. Langston Hughes. HCAP

What a great battle you and I have fought. The Marriage. Anna Wickham. AIW

What a grudge I am bearing the earth. Petrarch, *tr. fr. Italian. Fr.* Sonnets to Laura: To Laura in Death, XXXIII, *tr.* by J. M. Synge. (Translation from Petrarch, A.) MoBrPo

What a host you are, Mancinus. Martial, *tr.* by Peter Porter. OBVE

What a hot day it is! A Terrestrial Cuckoo. Frank O'Hara. SOTW

What a language to speak! In Hungarian. Gábor Garai, *tr.* by Edwin Morgan. MHuP

What a laugh—the priest is deaf. Spending the Night in a Rundown Temple. Takeuchi Unto, *tr.* by Burton Watson. JLIC-2

What a lovely being is a mother! Mother. Hettye Rayburn Ramsey. PWR

"What a lovely world," said the baby chick. An Easter Chick. Thirza Wakley. BoTP

What a moment of strange dreaming! Mind Flying Afar. Edgar Lee Masters. PoA

What a night! The wind howls, hisses, and but stops. Snowstorm. John Clare. BoNaP; WiR

What a noise they make. Night Bell on the Mountain. Shotetsu, *tr.* by Steven D. Carter. WFTW

What a pox do you mean with your pride and ill-nature. A Solitary Canto to Chloris the Disdainful. John Smith. NOEC

What a Proud Dreamhorse. E. E. Cummings. InvP; VGW

What a quantity of books! A temple with thick walls built of. The Mind Emerges. Pierre Reverdy, *tr.* by William Jay Smith. CT

What a shame—the chaos of the city! Evening View from the Bell Tower at P'ing-ch'ang. T'ang Hsien-Tsu, *tr.* by Jonathan Chaves. CoBLCP

What a thrill. Cut. Sylvia Plath. CAPP; TAP

What a Time! Michael C. Blumenthal. BLA

What a trick. Ragout. William Zaranka. BXAP

"What a waste of a beautiful girl!" Last Letter to the Western Civilization. D. T. Ogilvie. NBP

What a wonderful bird the frog are. The Frog. Carolyn. MoShBr; NBLV; NTCP; RB

What a word and I thought it would be. Alone. Richard Shelton. NYBP

What about each Great Canadian Lake? The Great Lakes of Canada. Gordon Perry. FaBoUs

What about that bad short you saw last week. Black People! Imamu Amiri Baraka. BPo

What about the people who came to my father's office. The Questions. Robert Pinsky. NoAM; NPGG

What about You? Edward Pygge. BXAP; FaBoPa

What ailes Pigmalion? Is it lunacy. Thomas Morton. SCAP

What ails John Winter, that so oft. John Winter. Laurence Binyon. MOS

What! alive and so bold, O Earth? Lines Written on Hearing the News of the Death of Napoleon. Shelley. ChER

What Am I? Abo Stoltzenberg, *tr. fr. Yiddish* by Gabriel Preil *and* Howard Schwartz. VWA

What am I doing here—in this place where. Birds Flying. Alistair Paterson. ATNZ

What am I glad will stay when I have passed. The Things that Will Not Die. Edward Rowland Sill. AnAmPo

What am I in the place of nourishment. A Curse on Uruk. Enheduanna, tr. by Aliki and Willis Barnstone. BoWoP

What Am I, Life? John Masefield. Fr. Sonnets. ImOP

What am I? Nosing here, turning leaves over. Wodwo. Ted Hughes. MoP; NoAM

What am I to do? Ietaka, tr. by Steven D. Carter. WFTW

What am I to do? Prince Munenaga, tr. by Steven D. Carter. WFTW

What am I to do with my sister? Prince Yuhara. Fr. Manyo Shu. AWP

What am I to think? Tameie, tr. by Steven D. Carter. WFTW

What Am I Who Dare. William Habington. TrPWD

What an elusive target. The Fights. Milton Acorn. MoCV; NOBC

What? an English sparrow sing? Did You Ever Hear an English Sparrow Sing? Bertha Johnston. BLPA

What an intolerable deal of history! The Compound Eye. Peter Davison. SM

What! Another Cracked Poet. Samuel Laycock. PF

What are all the hillmen wanting. The Keeper of the Midnight Gate. George Mackay Brown. OxBC

What are days for? Days. Philip Larkin. EBEV; FaBoMo; Mes; OxBC; OxBSP; RB; TOF

What Are Heavy? Christina Rossetti. FaBoRV; OxBChV
(Sea-Sand and Sorrow.) ChTr
("What are heavy? sea-sand and sorrow.") FaBoEE

What are little boys made of, made of? Mother Goose. FaFP; OxNR

What are our light afflictions here. Our Light Afflictions. Unknown. BLRP

"What are ruins to us." At Lindos. Mary Sarton. WPE

"What are the bugles blowin' for?" said Files-on-Parade. Danny Deever. Kipling. BrPo; EBVV; FaBoBa; FaPoR; FPL; GTBS-P; InPS; LiTB; MoBrPo; NAEL-2; NoAM; NOBE; NOBVV; OxBoLi; OxBTC; PoLF; SCV; SeCePo; TEP; TrGrPo; UnPo; WaaP

What are the islands to me. The Islands. Hilda Doolittle ("H. D."). MoAmPo

What are the lays of artful Addison. The Charms of Nature. Joseph Warton. Fr. Enthusiast, The; or, The Lover of Nature. SeCePo

What are the long waves singing so mournfully evermore? Olivia. Edward Pollock. AA

What are the thoughts that are stirring his breast? Under the Shade of the Trees. Margaret Junkin Preston. PAH

What are these women up to? They've gone and strung. The Deodand. Anthony Hecht. DiPo; NoAM

What are they waiting for? Aren't they going to call me? Call Out My Number. Julia de Burgos, tr. by Julio Marzán. InW

What are we first? First, animals; and next. George Meredith. Fr. Modern Love, XXX. GBL; HAP; NoP; PoEL-5

What Are We Playing At? Andrée Chedid, tr. fr. French by Samuel Hazo and Mirene Ghossem. BoWoP

What are we to do with a heaven. Three Songs from the Temple. Don Domanski. NOBC

What are we waiting for, assembled in the forum? Waiting for the Barbarians. Constantine P. Cavafy, tr. by Edmund Keeley and Philip Sherrard. VMG

What Are Years? Marianne Moore. BLPL; CMoP; EaLo; LiTA; MoAB; MoAmPo; MoP; NoAM; NOBA; OxBA; TrGrPo

What are you able to build with your blocks? Block City. Robert Louis Stevenson. EyDe; FaPON; NTCP

What are you carrying, Pilgrims, Pilgrims? Atlantic Charter, A.D. 1620-1942. Francis Brett Young. AmFN

What Are You Doing? Edmund Vance Cooke. PWR

What are you doing? Lizzie, Six. Carol Ann Duffy. NPo

What are you doing here, ghost, among these urns. Father in the Railway Buffet. U. A. Fanthorpe. FaBoWP

What are you doing here in this strange world that goes on and off. Traffic Lights. Lina Kasdaglis, tr. by Edmund and Mary Keeley. BoWoP

What are you doing, my lady, my lady. Unknown. OxNR

What, are you drop't? John Webster. Fr. The White Devil, V, vi. PoEL-2

What are you going to do with us, who have. The Pleaders. Peter Davison. NYBP

What, are you hurt, Sweet? So am I. To a Hurt Child. Grace Denio Litchfield. AA

What are you, Lady?—naught is here. Portrait of a Lady in the Exhibition of the Royal Academy. Winthrop Mackworth Praed. Fr. Every-Day Characters. NOBL; PoEL-4

What are you, then, my love, my friend, my father. The Quarry. Vassar Miller. NePoEA-2; WPE

What are you. . .? they ask, in wonder. Cold Colloquy. Patrick Anderson. Fr. Poem on Canada, V. CaP; NOBC

What Are You Thinking About? James Macmillan. PoSH

What are you waiting for, George, I pray? Tardy George. Unknown. PAH

What art thou, frost? and whence are thy keen stores. Winter ("What art thou, frost? and whence are thy keen stores"). James Thomson. Fr. The Seasons: Winter. OxBS

What art thou, Mignon, child of mystery? Mignon. Henrietta Cordelia Ray. CBWP-3

What asks the Bard? He prays for naught. After Horace. Alfred Denis Godley. NOBL

What authors lose, their booksellers have won. On Authors and Booksellers. Pope. FaBoEE

"What bait do you use," said a Saint to the Devil. The Lure. John Boyle O'Reilly. TIRV

"What be you a-lookin' at, Emily Ann?" The Pear-Tree. Mary Gilmore. PoAu-1

What beast of saliva and suet has moistened my bones. Black Banderillas. Robert Marteau, tr. by Anne Winters. RHTwFP

What beasts and angels practice I ignore. Little Ode. Paul Goodman. PoA

What Became of the Family? Louis Johnson. ATNZ

What Became of Them? Unknown. BoTP; OBCA; OxBChV

What beckoning [or beck'ning] ghost, along the moonlight shade. Elegy to the Memory of an Unfortunate Lady. Pope. FiP; NOBE; NOEC; OAEL-1; OBD; OBEV; TEP

What becomes of the girl who lives always alone? The Sorceress. Eugène Marais, tr. by Jack Cope and Uys Krige. PeSA

What began that bustle in the village. The Birth of Moshesh. David Granmer T. Bereng, tr. by Dan Kunene and Jack Cope. PeSA; TTY

What Belongs to Me. Ilse Tielsch, tr. fr. German by Beth Bjorklund. CoAuP

What big heavy doors! Elizabeth Wyse. Fr. Auschwitz. CN

What binds the atom together. Philip Dow. NPGG

What bird is that, with voice so sweet. A Creole Slave-Song. Maurice Thompson. AA

What bird so sings, yet so does wail. Trico's Song. John Lyly. Fr. Alexander and Campaspe, V, i. EIL; OBSC; PBBP; TrGrPo
(Song: "What bird so sings.") PBBP
(Spring, The.) CH
(Spring's Welcome.) OBEV
(Welcome to Spring.) NOBE

What Birds Were There. William Everson. NoAM

"What bluid's that on thy coat lap." Edward. Unknown. ESPB

What bones? What bones? Stones instead. Georgia. Bin Ramke. MT

What Booker can prognosticate. The King Enjoys His Own Again. Martin Parker. FaBoCh; OBS; OxBoLi

What boots it, thy virtue. Tact. Emerson. AnAmPo

What Bothered Him. David Avidan, tr. fr. Hebrew by Warren Bargad and Stanley F. Chyet. Fr. Samson, Our Hero, 2. IP

What Bright Pushbutton? Samuel Allen. PoNe

What bright soft thing is this? The Tear [or The Teare]. Richard Crashaw. LiTB; SeCP

What bring[s] you, sailor, home from the sea. Luck. W. W. Gibson. MoShBr; OBMV

What brought you to my frozen solitude. Wild Idyll. Manuel José Othón, tr. by Samuel Beckett. MexPo

What bullet killed him? Dead Soldier. Nicolás Guillén, tr. by Langston Hughes. TTY

What business have I here. Autumn Burial; a Meditation. Charles Gullans. QFR

What business, or what hope brings thee to town. To Sextus. Martial, tr. by Sir Charles Sedley. FaBoEE

What calendar do you consult for an explosion of the sun? Sestina to the Common Glass of Beer: I Do Not Drink Beer. Diane Wakoski. SM

What Called Me to the Heights. Lawrence Pilkington. PoSH

What calls itself Crane. Agreeable Monsters. Amy Clampitt. AnAn

What Came to Me. Jane Kenyon. PPR

What can a man do that. Of the Confident Stranger. Clark Coolidge. UL

What can be done? Thoughts of Paradise. Sun Kuang-hsien, tr. by Lois Fusek. ATF

What can be the matter. The Wind. Dorothy Graddon. BOTP; OnUR

What can be wrong. Housewife. Susan Fromberg Schaeffer. IHMS

What can console for a dead world? Believe and Take Heart. John Lancaster Spalding. AA

What can he want. The Panda. Harley Elliott. Fr. Animals That Stand in Dreams. NeAC

What Can I Do? Saibara, *tr. fr. Japanese by* Hiroaki Sato. FCEI
What Can I Do? Horace Logo Traubel. *Fr.* Chants Communal. TrJP
What can I do?—frog dumped. Ransetsu, *tr. by* Hiroaki Sato. FCEI
What can I do, I love you so much! Chu Yün-ming, *tr. fr. Chinese by* Jonathan Chaves. *Fr.* Forest Birds (A Woman Speaks), I. CoBLCP
What can I do in Poetry. The Departure of the Good Daemon. Robert Herrick. FaBoRV
What can I do to drive away. Keats. OAEL-2
What can I do with you. Prince Yuhara. *Fr.* Manyo Shu. Ma
What can I give Him. My Gift. Christina Rossetti. *Fr.* A Christmas Carol, *st.* 5. FaPON; PChr
What can I send you under the earth. Traditional Funeral Songs. *Unknown, tr. by* Willis Barnstone *and* Elene Kolb. BoWoP
What Can I Tell My Bones? Theodore Roethke. AmPP; NOBA
What can it mean? Is it aught to him. God Cares. "Marianne Farningham." BLRP; WBLP
(He Careth.) WBLP
What can lambkins do. A Chill. Christina Rossetti. BoTP
What can melt a traveler's grief? Rhyming a Friend's Poem. Yü Hsüan-chi, *tr. by* Geoffrey Waters. BoWoP
What can the cause be, when the K. have given. An Epigram, to the Household, 1630. Ben Jonson. Son
What, can these dead bones live, whose sap is dried. The New Ezekiel. Emma Lazarus. Son
What can Tommy Onslow [*or* little T. O.] do? On Thomas, Second Earl of Onslow. *Unknown.* FaBoCo
(On Tom Onslow, Earl of Onslow.) FaBoEE
What can you do when you're six five. Lanky Hank Farrow. Harold Witt. ASP
What can you do with a woman under thirty? Green Apples. Dudley Randall. FB
What can you expect. Maryam bint Abi Ya'qub al-Ansari, *tr. by* Elene Margot Kolb. WPOW
What cannot be committed to memory, this can save. Photograph. Quandra Prettyman. PoBA
What can't be cured. *Unknown.* FaFP
What Care I. George Wither. *See* Fair Virtue, the Mistress of Philarete: Shall I Wasting in Despair.
What care I for the leagues o sand. The Mither's Lament. Sydney Goodsir Smith. OxBS
What care I how black I be? *Unknown.* OxNR
What care I if good God be. Egocentric. Stevie Smith. FaBoNo
What care I, so they stand the same. Merops. Emerson. OxBA
"What care I, what cares he." The Cowboy. John Antrobus. AA; FaBoBe; FaPON
What celebration should there be? Holiday ("Festo quid potius die") Horace, *tr. fr. Latin. Fr.* Odes, III, 28. AWP, *tr. by* Louis Untermeyer.
What ceremony can we fit. For a Child Born Dead. Elizabeth Jennings. AIW
What ceremony else? Shakespeare. *Fr.* Hamlet, V, i. EBEV
What chance do I have? No one. Last Song of the Angel of Bad Luck. Philip Levine. KS
What changes take place in the course of a year. The Course of a Year. George Sands Johnson. PWR
What cher? Gud cher; gud cher, gud cher. Cheerful Welcome. *Unknown.* MeEL
What Christ Is to Us. *Unknown.* BLRP
What college kids we've grown up. For Randie. Geof Hewitt. NeAC
What Color Is Lonely. Carolyn M. Rodgers. BPo
What cometh here from west to east a-wending? A Death Song. William Morris. NAEL-2
What, comrade of a night. Life. Alice Brown. AA
What conscience has Venus drunk? Our inebriated beauties. Juvenal, *tr. fr. Latin by* Peter Green. *Fr.* Satires, VI. PeHV
What conscience, say, is it in thee. To Oenone. Robert Herrick. OBEV
What Constitutes a State? Sir William Jones. BLPA
What Could Be. John Gill. NeAC
What could be dafter. John Skelton. Robert Graves. BrPo
What could be done? The house was full of folks! The Inn That Missed Its Chance. Amos Russel Wells. TrCP
What could be nicer than the spring. A Walk in Spring. K. C. Lart. BoTP
What could he know of sky and stars, or heaven's all-hidden life. The Sooth-Sayer. Sadi, *tr. fr. Persian by* Sir Edwin Arnold. *Fr.* The Gulistan. AWP
"What could I make," Socrates might have asked. The Makers. David Galler. NYBP
What could make me more morose. The Ovibos. Robert Beverly Hale. FiBHP

What creature's this with his short hairs. The Character of a Roundhead. *Unknown.* FaBoPV
What crowds by envied power, the wish of all. Sejanus. Juvenal, *tr. fr. Latin by* William Gifford. *Fr.* Satires, X. OBVE
What cruel laws depress the female kind. Elizabeth Tollet. *Fr.* Hypatia. NOEC
What cry was that. Encounter. Geraldine Hammond. IHMS
What cunning can express. White and Red. Edward de Vere, 17th Earl of Oxford. OBSC
(What Cunning Can Express.) EIL
What curses should I choose? Lines on Being Refused a Guggenheim Fellowship. Reed Whittemore. TW
What danger is the pilgrim in. Bunyan. *Fr.* The Pilgrim's Progress. EBEV
What dawn is it? Karl Shapiro. VGW
What day did you come down from that former place. Rejoicing That the Zen Master Pao Has Arrived from Dragon Mountain. Liu Ch'ang-ch'ing, *tr. by* Burton Watson. CoBCP
What day was it she slid. Birth of Venus. Constance Urdang. PoA
What death? John Webster. *Fr.* The Duchess of Malfi, IV, ii. OBD
What death is worse than this. Sir Thomas Wyatt. SiPS
What demented malice, my silly Ravidus. Catullus, *tr. by* Celia *and* Louis Zukofsky. OBVE
What demons moved thee, what malicious fiends. To That Most Senseless Scoundrel, the Author of Legion's Humble Address to the Lords. Thomas Brown. APAS
What desperate nightmare rapts me to this land. Legacy: My South. Dudley Randall. PoBA; PoNe
What did he do except lie. Banneker. Rita Dove. NoAM
What did Hiamovi, the red man, Chief of the Cheyennes have? All One People. Carl Sandburg. AmFN
What did I do on my blooming vacation? The Jokesmith's Vacation. Don Marquis. FiBHP
What Did I Lose? Sun Yü-tang. Mes
What did I say? What did I say? A Monologue. Clark Coolidge. BAP
What did I study in your School of Night? The School Of Night. A. D. Hope. PoA
What did the cuckoo bring? *Unknown, tr. fr. Japanese by* Hiroaki Sato. FCEI
What did the day bring? Letter from a Coward to a Hero. Robert Penn Warren. MoAmPo
What did the Indians call you? To the Avon River above Stratford, Canada. James Reaney. MoCV
What did they feel, those twenty-odd. Temple of the Muses. Beth Bentley. EyDe
What did those girls say when you walked the strip. Words. David Huddle. *Fr.* Tour of Duty. EyDe
What did we say to each other. Simile. N. Scott Momaday. CDW
What did you do for the holiday? Eclogue between the Motherless. Louis MacNeice. FaBCIP
What did you hear? Advent; a Carol. Patric Dickinson. OBCP
What did you see out there, my lad. Face to Face with Reality. John Oxenham. WBLP
What did you think when first. The Triple Mirror. Gloria C. Oden. IHMS
What did you want to welcome. On Love. Tanikawa Shuntaro, *tr. by* Hiroaki Sato. FCEI
What Different Dooms Our Birthdays Bring! Thomas Hood. *Fr.* Miss Kilmansegg and Her Precious Leg. NAs
(Miss Kilmansegg's Birth.) OxBoLi
What dire offense from amorous [*or* am'rous] causes springs. The Rape of the Lock. Pope. HAP; NAEL-1; NOEC; NoP; OAEL-1; OBNV; PoE; PoEL-3; TEP; TrGrPo
What distant thunders rend the skies. On the Death of Captain Nicholas Biddle. Philip Freneau. PAH
What do I care. Pursuit. Hilda Doolittle ("H. D."). WPE
What Do I Care. Jules Supervielle, *tr. fr. French by* William Alwyn. RHTwFP
"What Do I Care." Sara Teasdale. VGW
What do I care for life or death. Otoneribe Chifumi. *Fr.* Manyo Shu. Ma
What Do I Care for Morning. Helene Johnson. CDC
What do I care if my name. *The elder daughter of* Lady Otomo no Sakanoe. *Fr.* Manyo Shu. Ma
What do I remember of my visit to Ravenna? Firstly. Ravenna. Louis MacNeice. OBTV
What do I stare at—not the colt. The White Horse. William Henry Davies. OxBTC
What Do People Do? A. Leyeles, *tr. fr. Yiddish by* Benjamin *and* Barbara Harshav. AYP
What Do the Birds Think? Alfred W. Purdy. MoCV

What do the long years bring us. Retrospection. Henrietta Cordelia Ray. CBWP-3

What do the people say, and what does the government do? Arthur Hugh Clough. *Fr.* Amours de Voyage, Canto II, i. EBVV, i-iv *only;* FaBoPV, i-iv *only.;* OBSV, i-iv *only.*

What Do They Do? Christina Rossetti. *Fr.* Sing-Song. FaPON

What Do They Say. Gary Snyder. NNaP

What do they sing, the last birds. Last Songs. Galway Kinnell. CAPP

What Do We Know, Dear Brothers? Moyshe-Leyb Halpern, *tr. fr. Yiddish by* Benjamin *and* Barbara Harshav. *Fr.* Zarkhi on the Sea Shore. AYP

What do we know of what is behind us? History. Arthur Gregor. TAP

What do we need for love—a midnight fire. Need. Babette Deutsch. PCP

What Do We Plant [When We Plant the Tree]. Henry Abbey. FaPON; OHIP; WBLP

What do we share with the past? Again for Hephaistos, the Last Time. Richard Howard. GLP

What do you call it, bobsled champion. Twentieth-Century Blues. Kenneth Fearing. CMoP

What do you do? Why, everything. Asides. Paul Valéry, *tr. by* William Jay Smith. CT

What do you mean, you "don't like poetry?" Can Zone; or, The Good Food Guide. Rika Lesser. MAYP

"What do you paint, when you paint on a wall?" I Paint What I See. E. B. White. NBLV; NYBP

What Do You Say When a Man Tells You, You Have the Softest Skin. Mary Mackey. FF

What do you seek within, O soul, my brother? Introversion. Evelyn Underhill. WGRP

What do you sell, O ye merchants? In the Bazaars of Hyderabad. Sarojini Naidu. FaPON

What do you take. Bill Manhire. ATNZ; PeNZ

What do you tell me now. Komachi, *tr. fr. Japanese by* Burton Watson. *Fr.* Kokin Shu. FCEI

What do you think I saw to-day. The Fairy Cobbler. A. Neil Lyons. BoTP

What, do you think, is the gypsy bible? The Gypsy Bible. Julian Tuwim, *tr. by* Isaac Komem. VWA

What do you think? Last night I saw. The Dragon. Mary Mullineaux. BoTP

What Do You Want? John Newlove. NOBC

What do you want me to say. Local News. Loretta Merenda, *tr. by* Muriel Kittel. DMI

What does a bird in Cross's air. *Unknown. Fr.* A Collection of Hymns of the Moravian Brethren. NOEC

What does he plant who plants a tree? The Heart of the Tree. H. C. Bunner. OHFP; OHIP

"What does it have to do with me, the crimson banner?" Random Thoughts on the Shinkokinshu: Fujiwara no Teika. Anzai Hitoshi, *tr. by* Hiroaki Sato. FCEI

What Does It Matter? Noah Barker. PWR

What does it mean. Gift. Gerald William Barrax. MT

What does it mean. The Changeling. Marilyn Davis. TSM

What does little birdie say? Tennyson. *Fr.* Sea Dreams. BoTP; OxBChV

What does love look like? The Shape of Death. May Swenson. TAP

What does not change/ is the will to change. The Kingfishers. Charles Olson. CMoP; InPS; NAAL-2; NeAP; NOBA; PoM

What does not fade? The tower that long had stood. Transience. John Armstrong. *Fr.* The Art of Preserving Health. NOEC

What does passion know? Passion. Sue May. DT

"What does reincarnation mean?" Reincarnation. Wallace McRae. CowP

What does she put four whistles beside heated rugs for? Random Generation of English Sentences; or, The Revenge of the Poets. William Jay Smith. OBAL

What Does the Bee Do? Christina Rossetti. *Fr.* Sing-Song. OxBChV

What does the cracker. Self. N. H. Pritchard II. PoBA

What does the farmer in the spring. Spring Work at the Farm. Thirza Wakley. BoTP

What does the forest do Monday through Friday? Clerk's Song II. Norman H. Russell. NOVW

What does the horse give you. Horse. Louise Glück. AnAn; MAYP

What does the jeweller know. Ignorance of the Wise. Iftiqar Arif, *tr. by* Mahmood Jamal. PBMUP

What Does the Little Boy Love?, *sels.* Hsieh Chin, *tr. fr. Chinese by* Jonathan Chaves. CoBLCP

"People say the sun is in heaven." *Fr.* II.

"Sage has the "Six Classics," The." *Fr.* IV.

"What does the little boy dream of?" *Fr.* III.

What does the old man hope from those books like graves. Taghore. Muhammad al-Ghuzzi, *tr. by* May Jayyusi *and* John Heath-Stubbs. MAP

What does the sea want, my clothes, my keys, my face? In Horse Latitudes. Katha Pollitt. PPR

What does the storm say? The Ways and the Peoples. Randall Jarrell. PoA

What Does This Mean? Sir Thomas Wyatt. *See* What meaneth [*or* menethe] this? When I lie [*or* lye] alone.

What domes and pinnacles of mist and fire. Evening in Tyringham Valley. Richard Watson Gilder. AA

What domination of what darkness dies this hour. The City. "Æ" WGRP

What? Dorval, me you applaud. Constance-Marie de Salm-Dyck, *tr. by* Dorothy Backer. DMF

What dost thou here. Moth-Song. Ellen Mackay Hutchinson Cortissoz. AA

What dost thou here, thou shining, sinless thing. A Butterfly in Church. George Marion McClellan. BANP

What! dost thou pray that the outgone tide be rolled back on the strand. A Far Cry to Heaven. Edith Matilda Thomas. AA; WGRP

What doth it serve to see sun's burning face. William Drummond of Hawthornden. EIL

What D'Ye-Call-It, The, *sel.* John Gay.

'Twas When the Seas Were Roaring. HAP

What eagle can behold her sunbright eye. Sir John Davies. *Fr.* The Gulling Sonnets. Son

What ecstasies her bosom fire! To a Lady on Her Passion for Old China. John Gay. FaFP; LiTB

What else can we do. What Are We Playing At? Andrée Chedid, *tr. by* Samuel Hazo *and* Mirene Ghossem. BoWoP

What else could we do, for the doors were guarded. Curfew. Paul Eluard. BoLoP, *tr. by* Quentin Stevenson

What else does a crane spreading its torn wings have. Crane. Maruyama Kaoru, *tr. by* Hiroaki Sato. FCEI

What ever 'tis, whose beauty here below. The Starre. Henry Vaughan. MePo

What Every Boy Knows. Antler. GLP

What face, in the water. William Carlos Williams. VGW

What face she put on it, we will not discuss. Conrad Aiken. *Fr.* Time in the Rock [or, Preludes to Definition], LXXXIV. VGW

What Faire Pompe. Thomas Campion. GBL; PoEL-2; Prf (Love's Pilgrims.) OBSC

"What fairings will ye that I bring?" The Singing Leaves. James Russell Lowell. GN

What fall amounts to is really a cold infusion. The End of Fall. Francis Ponge, *tr. by* Robert Bly. NU

What falls before us like snow. Moth. Lance Henson. VoR

What Family? Yü Chi, *tr. fr. Chinese by* Jonathan Chaves. CoBLCP

What Far Kingdom. Arthur Stanley Bourinot. CaP

What Fifty Said. Robert Frost. NAs

What fills the whisper and. Hadrian's Lane. Ray DiPalma. LP

What Finer Hills? J. K. Annand. PoSH

What flower is my lady like? Of His Lady. *Unknown.* EIL

What flower is this that greets the morn. The Flower of Liberty. Oliver Wendell Holmes. OPP

What For. Garrett Kaoru Hongo. MAYP

What for feere of this ferly and of the false Jewes. William Langland. *Fr.* The Vision of Piers Plowman, Passus XVIII. EBEV

What for Saxon, Frank, and Hun. The Black Hole of Calcutta. Ebenezer Elliott. PF

What fragrant-footed comer. The Little Knight in Green. Katharine Lee Bates. AA

What Frank, Martha and I Know about the Desert. Alice Sadongei. GOS

What Frenzy Has of Late Possess'd the Brain. Samuel Garth. NBLV

What friendship can'st thou boast? what honours claim? Bristol. Richard Savage. FaBoPP

What from the founder Aesop fell. The Purpose of Fable-writing. Phaedrus, *tr. by* Christopher Smart. AWP

What fullness in the life is this which possesses. Eating Lechon, with My Brothers and Sisters. Luis Cabalquinto. BrSi

What fun to keep an ostrich! Bedraggled Ostrich. Takamura Kotaro, *tr. by* Geoffrey Bownas *and* Anthony Thwaite. PeBJV

What fun to work the mountain paddies! *Unknown, tr. by* Hiroaki Sato. FCEI

What gentle Ghost, besprent with April deaw. An Elegie on the Lady Jane Pawlet, Marchion: of Winton. Ben Jonson. SeCP

What gives it power makes it change its mind. The Beautiful Lawn Sprinkler. Howard Nemerov. PCP

What glories would we? Motions of the soul? The Renewal. Theodore Roethke. VGW
What Glorious Vision. *At. to* Thomas Cradock. AH
What God gives, and what we take. A Grace for Children. Robert Herrick. OxBChV
What God Hath [*or Has*] Promised! Annie Johnson Flint. BLRP; WBLP
What God never sees. *Unknown.* OxNR
What gods are these? Bright red, or white and green. The Fox-Hunters. Ebenezer Elliott. TW
What goes on in the pauses. Torture. Margaret Atwood. PoE
What golden gaine made Higginson remove. Reverend Mr, The Higginson. Edward Johnson. SCAP
What good is it to me if long ago. Louise Labé, *tr. by* Willis Barnstone. BoWoP
What Good Poems Are For. Tom Wayman. NoP
What good's world—profit, fame? Living in the Mountains Sen of Kyuho, *tr. by* Lucien Stryk *and* Takashi Ikemoto. ZPCJ
What grandeur makes a man seem venerable? Louise Labé, *tr. by* Willis Barnstone. BoWoP
What Grandma Knew. Edward Field. Psk
What great genius invented the waiting room? Waiting Rooms. Howard Nemerov. PoA
What great yoked brutes with briskets low. Crossing the Plains. Joaquin Miller. AA; AnAmPo; GN
What greater torment ever could have been. Lonely Beauty. Samuel Daniel. *Fr.* The Complaint of Rosamond. CTC; OBSC
What Greece, when learning flourish'd, onle knew. Prologue to the University of Oxford, 1673. Dryden. OBS
What guile [*or* guyle] is this, that those her golden tresses. Amoretti, XXXVII. Spenser. NAEL-1; NoP; OBSC; Son; TrGrPo
What Habacuck once spake, mine eyes. Roger Williams. SCAP
What had become of the young shark? The Birth of a Shark. David Wevill. TwCP
What had become very clear to him. Abraham. Stephen Mitchell. VWA
What had looked like fires. Ryoshun, *tr. by* Steven D. Carter. WFTW
What had November done? The Beautiful Ruined Orchard. Daniel Berrigan. FYAP
What had you been thinking about. The Tennis Court Oath. John Ashbery. NoAM; TAP
What hand trimmed these strident feathers for flight. Night Flight. George Whalley. CaP
What hand, what skill can form the artful piece. Advice to a Painter. *Unknown.* APAS
What Happened? John Wieners. PoM
What Happened Here Before. Gary Snyder. NNaP
What happened? My dear, don't cry. The thing. Lőrinc Szabó, *tr. fr. Hungarian by* Edwin Morgan. *Fr.* Cricket Music. MHuP
What Happened to a Young man in a Place Where He Turned to Water. *Unknown, tr. fr. Apache Indian by* Anselm Hollo. STP
What happened to the iceman after all? The Iceman. Gordon Challis. ATNZ; PeNZ
What Happens. June Jordan. BPo
What happens here happened to my grandfather and my father. Abelardo Sanchez Leon, *tr. by* David Tipton. Per
What Happens in Shakzpeare. Alan Brunton. PeNZ
What happens to a dream deferred. Harlem. Langston Hughes. *Fr.* Lenox Avenue Mural. AIP; AmNP; AmPP; GLP; HCAP; HeIP; HoPM; InPS; NoP; PoNe
(Dream Deferred.) FF; InPk, LiTM; PoBA; PPP; SoSe
(Harlem (A Dream Deferred).) NIP
What happens to the beautiful girls with slender hips and bright round dresses? Hamtramck: The Polish Women. Toi Derricotte. InPS
What happens when the dog sits on a tiger. What Happens. June Jordan. BPo
What Happiness Can Equal Mine. John David. AH
What happiness you gave to me. The Yew-Tree. *Unknown, tr. by* Geoffrey Grigson. ChTr; GBL
What happy, secret fountain. The Dwelling-Place. Henry Vaughan. MeLP; OBS; TrPWD; WGRP
What harm have I done to the stars? Without My Friends the Day Is Dark. Moses ibn Ezra, *tr. by* Solomon Solis-Cohen. TrJP
What Harvest Half So Sweet Is, *sel.* Thomas Campion. "Dove alone expresses, The." PBBP
What has a life must have a death. Poem in the Form of a Coffin-Puller's Song. T'ao Ch'ien, *tr. by* Burton Watson. CoBCP
What has aged you so. Yehuda Amichai. Seymour Mayne. VWA
What has become of our astonishment. The Way We Wonder. Robert Pack. NePoEA

What has been brought to a finish. Disturbing the Sallies Forth. Clark Coolidge. UL
What has bent you. The Pine at Timber-Line. Harriet Monroe. PoA
What has burnt has gone away long since. Polishing the Porcelain Lamp. Park Je-chun, *tr. by* Koh Chang-soo. ACKP
What has happened in the world? Volcanic Venus. D. H. Lawrence. InPS
What has he done to me? I don't know what's become of me. The Painted Madonna Speaks. Berta Lask, *tr. by* Susan L. Cocalis. DMG
What has poor Woman done, that she must be. Aphra Behn. *Fr.* Sir Patient Fancy, Epilogue. WPOW
What has risen in the dark and is? Voice in the Dark. A. L. Strauss, *tr. by* Robert Friend. VWA
What Has This Bugbear Death. Lucretius, *tr. fr. Latin by* Dryden. *Fr.* De Rerum Natura (On the Nature of Things), III. CTC; OBD
What has want to give. Kathleen Jessie Raine. WPE
What, hast thou run thy race? Art going down? Of the Going Down of the Sun. Bunyan. CH
What hath man done that man shall not undo. Mercy Pleads for Mankind. Giles Fletcher the Younger. *Fr.* Christ's Victory and Triumph: Christ's Victory in Heaven, I. JCP
What Hath Man Wrought Exclamation Point. Morris Bishop. NYBP
What have I/ done? All Soul's Day. Paul Celan, *tr. by* Beth Bjorklund. CoAuP
What have I accomplished? Meditation at Seventy. Rudolf Henz, *tr. by* Beth Bjorklund. CoAuP
What have I done for you. England, My England. W. E. Henley. BLPL; MoBrPo; OBEV; PoLF
What have I dreamt of, all this night? Written at Night, after Dreaming That I Had Returned to My Old Home. Li Tz'u-ming, *tr. by* Daniel Bryant. WFTU
"What have I earned for all that work," I said. The People. W. B. Yeats. CMoP
What have I made. The Children. Constance Urdang. CoAP; IHMS
"What, have I thus betrayed my liberty?" Sir Philip Sidney. *Fr.* Astrophel and Stella, XLVII. GBL; NAEL-1; NoP; PoEL-1
(Yoke of Tyranny, The.) TrGrPo
What Have I to Do With. Abraham Reisen, *tr. fr. Yiddish by* Leonard Wolf. PeBMYV
What have I to give? In the Far Years. Wilson Pugsley MacDonald. CaP
What Have We Done Today? Nixon Waterman. WBLP
What have we done? What cruel passion moved thee. Dialogue after Enjoyment. Abraham Cowley. BoLoP
What have we swallowed. Love Gone Cold. Lindsay MacRae. DT
"What have you looked at, Moon." To the Moon. Thomas Hardy. BoNaP; ChTr
What have you more than I, who crave you so? Zora Cross. *Fr.* Love Sonnets, LIV. CBAP
What have you seen on the summits, the peaks that plunge their. Charles Brasch. *Fr.* The Estate, XXIV. PeNZ
"What have you there?" the great Panjandrum said. The Truant. E. J. Pratt. NOBC; NoP; OBCV
What! Hayes acquitted! Armstrong's magazine! True and Joyful News. *Unknown.* APAS
What he lent itself. And the Love of Laughter. Bruce Andrews. LP
What He Said. Allur Nanmullai, *tr. fr. Tamil by* A. K. Ramanujan. PLW
What He Said. Ammuvanar, *tr. fr. Tamil by* A. K. Ramanujan. PLW
What He Said. Catti Natanar, *tr. fr. Tamil by* A. K. Ramanujan. PLW
What He Said. Orerulavanar, *tr. fr. Tamil by* A. K. Ramanujan. PLW
What He Said. Perevin Muruvalar, *tr. fr. Tamil by* A. K. Ramanujan. PLW
What He Said after a Quarrel, Remembering His Wedding Night. Virrurru Muteyinanar, *tr. fr. Tamil by* A. K. Ramanujan. PLW
What He Said ("As the deer begin to hide"). Peyanar, *tr. fr. Tamil by* A. K. Ramanujan. *Fr.* Nine on Happy Reunion, 5. PLW
What He Said ("As wild oxen bellowed"). Peyanar, *tr. fr. Tamil by* A. K. Ramanujan. *Fr.* Nine on Happy Reunion, 3. PLW
What He Said ("Because peacocks moved like you"). Peyanar, *tr. fr. Tamil by* A. K. Ramanujan. *Fr.* Nine on Happy Reunion, 2. PLW
What He Said in the Desert. Otalantaiyar, *tr. fr. Tamil by* A. K. Ramanujan. PLW
What He Said ("In this time of rain and thunder"). Peyanar, *tr. fr. Tamil by* A. K. Ramanujan. *Fr.* Nine on Happy Reunion, 1. PLW
What He Said ("The red earth"). Peyanar, *tr. fr. Tamil by* A. K. Ramanujan. *Fr.* Nine on Happy Reunion, 4. PLW

What He Said to His Charioteer, on His Way Back. Cittalai Cattanar, *tr. fr. Tamil by* A. K. Ramanujan. PLW

What He Said to His Heart, Arguing against Further Ambition and Travel. Ilankiranar, *tr. fr. Tamil by* A. K. Ramanujan. PLW

What He Took. *Unknown.* CoMu

What heart could have thought you? To a Snowflake. Francis Thompson. BoNaP; FaBV; ImOP; MoAB; MoBrPo; SeCePo; TrGrPo

What heartache—ne'er a hill! From the Flats. Sidney Lanier. AnAmPo; NOBA; OxBA

What heave of grapnels will resurrect the fabric. S.S.R., Lost at Sea— *The Times.* Ralph Gustafson. OBCV

What heaven-entreated [*or* heaven-besiegèd heart] is this. To the Noblest and Best of Ladies, the Countess of Denbigh. Richard Crashaw. JCP; MeLP

   (Letter to the Countess of Denbigh.) MePo; SeCP

What heavy-hoofed coursers the wilderness roam. The Fall of Tecumseh. *Unknown*

What Hee Suffered. Ben Jonson. *Fr.* A Celebration of Charis in Ten Lyrick Peeces. SeCP

What helps it if of love I sing. Hadewijch, *tr. by* Frans van Rosevelt. PBWP

What helps it those. For a Musician. George Wither. *Fr.* Hallelujah; or, Britain's Second Remembrancer. OBS

What Her Friend Said. Kapilar, *tr. fr. Tamil by* A. K. Ramanujan. PLW

What Her Friend Said Criticizing Him to Give Her Strength. Kuriyiraiyar, *tr. fr. Tamil by* A. K. Ramanujan. PLW

What Her Friend Said to Her, before the Rains. Kapilar, *tr. fr. Tamil by* A. K. Ramanujan. PLW

What Her Friend Said to Her, within the Lover's Hearing. Paranar, *tr. fr. Tamil by* A. K. Ramanujan. PLW

What Her Friend Said to the Foster Mother. Kapilar, *tr. fr. Tamil by* A. K. Ramanujan. PLW

What Her Girl Friend Asked and What She Replied Regarding His Return. *Unknown, tr. fr. Tamil by* A. K. Ramanujan. PLW

What Her Girl Friend Said ("As the cassias blossom"). Peyanar, *tr. fr. Tamil by* A. K. Ramanujan. *Fr.* Nine on Happy Reunion, 6. PLW

What Her Girl Friend Said before the Elopement. Kutavayir Kirattanar, *tr. fr. Tamil by* A. K. Ramanujan. PLW

What Her Girl Friend Said, Consoling Her when She Was Distressed by the Town's Gossip. Uloccanar, *tr. fr. Tamil by* A. K. Ramanujan. PLW

What Her Girl Friend Said ("Her eyes lined with kohl"). Peyanar, *tr. fr. Tamil by* A. K. Ramanujan. *Fr.* Nine on Happy Reunion, 9. PLW

What Her Girl Friend Said on Her Wedding Day. Ammuvanar, *tr. fr. Tamil by* A. K. Ramanujan. PLW

What Her Girl Friend Said ("Saying to himself"). Peyanar, *tr. fr. Tamil by* A. K. Ramanujan. *Fr.* Nine on Happy Reunion, 8. PLW

What Her Girl Friend Said, Seeing Her Friend Suffer in Silent Dignity over Her Husband's Infidelity. Kayamanar, *tr. fr. Tamil by* A. K. Ramanujan. PLW

What Her Girl Friend Said, the Lover within Earshot, behind a Fence. Uloccanar, *tr. fr. Tamil by* A. K. Ramanujan. PLW

What Her Girl Friend Said to Her. Kovatattan, *tr. fr. Tamil by* A. K. Ramanujan. PLW

What Her Girl Friend Said to Her. Maturai Marutan Ilanakanar, *tr. fr. Tamil by* A. K. Ramanujan. PLW

What Her Girl Friend Said to Her. Palaipatiya Perunkatunko, *tr. fr. Tamil by* A. K. Ramanujan. PLW

What Her Girl Friend Said to Her Lover on His Return. Kakkai Patiniyar Naccellaiyar, *tr. fr. Tamil by* A. K. Ramanujan. PLW

What Her Girl Friend Said to Him. Ammuvanar, *tr. fr. Tamil by* A. K. Ramanujan. PLW

What Her Girl Friend Said to Him. Centan Kannanar, *tr. fr. Tamil by* A. K. Ramanujan. PLW

What Her Girl Friend Said to Him. Kannan, *tr. fr. Tamil by* A. K. Ramanujan. PLW

What Her Girl Friend Said to Him (on Her Behalf) When He Came by Daylight. *Unknown, tr. fr. Tamil by* A. K. Ramanujan. PLW

What Her Girl Friend Said to Him, Trying to Dissuade Him from His Long Journey. *Unknown, tr. fr. Tamil by* A. K. Ramanujan. PLW

What Her Girl Friend Said to Him When He Wanted to Come by Day. Ammuvanar, *tr. fr. Tamil by* A. K. Ramanujan. PLW

What Her Girl Friend Said to the Foster-Mother ("If you think, mother"). Orampokiyar, *tr. fr. Tamil by* A. K. Ramanujan. *Fr.* Five on the Crabs, 4. PLW

What Her Girl Friend Said to the Foster-Mother ("In his fields, mother"). Orampokiyar, *tr. fr. Tamil by* A. K. Ramanujan. *Fr.* Five on the Crabs, 5. PLW

What Her Girl Friend Said when He Sent a Flattering Minstrel on His Behalf. Orampokiyar, *tr. fr. Tamil by* A. K. Ramanujan. PLW

What Her Girl Friend Said, When the Woman Was About to Take Back Her Unfaithful Husband. Orampokiyar, *tr. fr. Tamil by* A. K. Ramanujan. PLW

What Her Girl Friend Said ("Your arms are beautiful again"). Peyanar, *tr. fr. Tamil by* A. K. Ramanujan. *Fr.* Nine on Happy Reunion, 7. PLW

What Her Girlfriends Said to Her. Okkur Macatti, *tr. fr. Tamil by* A. K. Ramanujan. BoWoP

What Her Mother Said. *Unknown, tr. fr. Tamil by* A. K. Ramanujan. PLW

What here you see, in beguiling tints. On Her Portrait. Sister Juana Inés de la Cruz, *tr. by* Kate Flores. DMH

What heroes from the woodland sprung. Seventy-six. Bryant. PAH

What Hiawatha Probably Did. *Unknown.* NBLV

What hideous noyse was that? John Webster. *Fr.* The Duchess of Malfi, IV, ii. PoEL-2

What hills are like the Ochil hills? The Ochil Hills. *Unknown.* PoSH

What His Friend Said, Teasing the Man in Love. Milaipperun Kantan, *tr. fr. Tamil by* A. K. Ramanujan. PLW

What ho! my shepherds, sweet it were. A Sylvan Revel. Edward Cracroft Lefroy, *after the Greek of* Theocritus. *Fr.* Echoes from Theocritus, XXV. AWP

What honey summons these animalcules? Stings. Sylvia Plath. AnAn; NaP

What hope of safety for our realm. On Sympathisers with the American Revolution. Charles Wesley. NOCV

What Horace says is. Eheu Fugaces. "Thomas Ingoldsby." FaBoEE; OxBoLi

What horrid sin condemned the teeming Earth. On Tobacco. Charles Cotton. OBSV

What hosts of women everywhere I see! The Monstrous Regiment. Alice Coats. CN

What hours I spent of precious time. Poetical Economy. Harry Graham. CenHV; FaBoCo; Mes

What How? How now? Hath How such hearing found. On How the Cobler. *Unknown.* SCAP

What hue lies in the slit of anger. Outlines. Audre Lorde. GLP

What humour can be so rare. Sister Juana Inés de la Cruz, *tr. fr. Spanish by* Judith Thurman. *Fr.* A Satirical Romance. PBWP

"What hundred books are best, think you?" I said. John Kendrick Bangs. CenHV

What hurrying human tides, or day or night! Broadway. Walt Whitman. NAAL-1

What I call you. Friederike Mayröcker, *tr. by* Beth Bjorklund. CoAuP

What I Do Is Me. Gerard Manley Hopkins. *See* As Kingfishers Catch Fire [Dragonflies Draw Flame].

What I Expected [Was]. Stephen Spender. MoAB; MoBrPo; NoAM; NOBE

What I fancy, I approve. No Loathsomnesse in Love. Robert Herrick. GBL

What I forgot to mention was the desultory. Postscript to an Elegy. Gibbons Ruark. MT

What I had never imagined: your return. Brief Encounter. Winfield Townley Scott. GOYP

What I "have to do" has nothing to do. Last Words. Richard Howard. *Fr.* Ithaca: The Palace at Four A.M.. DiPo

What I Have to Tell You, Until Next Time. David Avidan, *tr. fr. Hebrew by* Warren Bargad *and* Stanley F. Chyet. IP

What I have written, I cannot unwrite. Ending. Norman Jordan. PoNe

What I heard before the declaration of war. The Day of Pearl Harbor. Takamura Kotaro, *tr. fr. Japanese by* Hiroaki Sato. *Fr.* A Brief History of Imbecility. FCEI

What I hope (when I hope) is that we'll. To the Dead. Frank Bidart. EOEF

What I like about Clive. E. C. Bentley. *Fr.* Clerihews. CenHV; NOBL

   (Lord Clive.) MoShBr

What I like is poems. Ars Poetica: 4. Herman de Coninck, *tr. by* James S. Holmes. DuIn

What I like most is when. Crimes of Passion: The Slasher. Terry Stokes. AmPA

What I Live For. George Linnaeus Banks. BLPA; FaBoBe; WBLP

   (My Aim.) WBLP

   (Why Do I Live?) PWR

What I love best in all the world. Robert Browning. *Fr.* De Gustibus. OBTV

   (Italy of the South.) FaBoPP

What I meant to say to her as she reached. Feed the Mexican Back into Her. Cherríe Moraga. GLP

What I need is lots of money. Take I, 4:11:58. Philip Whalen. NeAP

What I Owe Iowa. Tomislav Longinovic. WCI

What I remember about that day. Eviction. Lucille Clifton. NTCP (1st, The.) InPS

What I remember most was not. Lamplighter: 1914. Stanley Kunitz. BLA

What I saw was just one eye. The Bird at Dawn. Harold Monro. BoTP; MoBrPo

What I shall leave thee none can tell. To His Son [or Sonne], Vincent Corbet[t]. Richard Corbet. FaBoCh; OBS; OxBChV; TrGrPo

What I Tell Him. Simon J. Ortiz. CDW

What I Think of Hiawatha. J. W. Morris. Par

What I thought so unusual about today. The Great Pretenderer. Pat Nolan. UL

What I thought was love. The Liar. Imamu Amiri Baraka. AmPP; NOBA

What I took in my hand. Robert Creeley. NoP; PoA

What I walked down to the highway. Another Sunday Morning. Carter Revard. VoR

What I want from God, feared to be. Breath. Heather McHugh. GeTw

What I wanted. In Weather. Robert Hass. AmPA; GeTw

What I wanted to say to her. Greenwood. Richard Jackson. KS

What I was doing with my white teeth exposed. The Dog. Gerald Stern. BLA

What I will ask, if one free wish comes down. A Boon. William Meredith. NePoEA

What I will say today. Lo Que Digo. Unknown. AS

What If a Day [or a Month or a Year]. Thomas Campion. AAS; EBEV; ElL; PrIm

What If a Much of a Which of a Wind. E. E. Cummings. BLPL; FaFP; LiTA; LiTM; MoAmPo; NAAL-2; NOBA; NoP; OxBA; PoA; PoRA; PPP; SoSe; WaP

What if I bade you leave. Those Images. W. B. Yeats. CMoP

What if I did not mention death to get started. Thin Air. Robert Hass. BAP

What if jealousy is just a bad dream? Miriam Palmer. NMM

What if Orpheus. Orpheus in Greenwich Village. Jack Gilbert. NPGG

What if outside the dying pine trees sing in the clearing gale. Inside the Cave. Geoffrey Grigson. FaBoPP

What if Prince Paris, after taking thought. Judgement of Paris. Robert Graves. KS

What if small birds are peppering the sky. It Is Winter, I Know. Merrill Moore. MoAmPo

What If Some Little Paine the Passage Have. Spenser. Fr. The Faerie Queene, I, 9. CH

What if the body goes the sense. Image-Nation 3. Robin Blaser. PoM

What if the foot, ordain'd the dust to tread. Pope. Fr. An Essay on Man, Epistle I. FaBoPV

What If the Saint Must Die. John Peck. AH

What if the September flowers hurt. Hannah Weiner. LP

What if the soul her real life elsewhere holds. The Soul in the Body. Edith M. Thomas. AA

What if the sun comes out. Boy Remembers in the Field. Raymond Knister. CaP; NOBC

What if the ways be stone. City Songs. Mark Van Doren. NYBP

What if there wasn't a metaphor. Stigmata. Patrick Lane. NOBC

What if these long races go on repeating themselves. Written in Dejection near Rome. Robert Bly. NaP

What if they knew nothing, or what they did. Remove the Predicate. Clark Coolidge. UL

What if this present were the world's last night? John Donne. Fr. Holy Sonnets, XIII. EBEV; HeIP; InPS; JCP; LiTB; MeLP; NAEL-1; NOCV; OBS; PoE; Son; TEP

What I'm saying is. The Bull Rider's Advice. David Allan Evans. TSL

What immense gratitude one feels toward life. Kitchen Range. Umberto Saba, tr. by William Jay Smith. CT; PFI

What in our lives is burnt. August 1914. Isaac Rosenberg. EBEV; NOBE; OBWP; OPOP; OxBTC

What, in the Register of Doom, is writ. Bishop Orders His Tomb in St. Praxed's. Morris Bishop. OBAL

What in the World? Eve Merriam. RHPC

What infants suffer when they breed their teeth. Infant Diseases and Their Treatment. M. Saint-Marthe, tr. fr. French. Fr. Paedotrophiae; or, The Art of Bringing Up Children. FaBoUs

What instinct forces man to journey on. The Poet. Amy Lowell. WGRP

What Interest Have You, World, in Persecuting Me? Sister Juana Inés de la Cruz, tr. fr. Spanish by Kate Flores. DMH

What Invisible Rat. Jean-Joseph Rebéarivelo, tr. fr. French by Alan Ryder. TTY

What! Irving? thrice welcome, warm heart, and fine brain. Irving. James Russell Lowell. Fr. A Fable for Critics. TAP

What Is. E. E. Cummings. MOS

What is/ eternity? Home Alone These Last Hours of the Afternoon, Dusk Now, the Sabbath Setting In, I Sit Back, and These Words Start Welling Up in Me. Stephen Levy. VWA

What is/ a/ voyage. What Is. E. E. Cummings. MOS

"What is a Bongaloo, Daddy?" The Bongaloo. Spike Milligan. AmMo

What is a communist? One who hath yearnings. Ebenezer Elliott. NOBVV

(On Communists.) NBLV; NOBL

(What is a day, what is a year of vain delight and pleasure? Unknown. OBSC

What is a first love worth except to prepare for a second? John Milton Hay. FaBoEE

What is a Jew in solitude? Yom Kippur 1984. Adrienne Rich. ER; GLP; NoAM

What Is a Jewish Poem? Myra Sklarew. CRP; VWA

What is a kiss? Why this, as some approve. A Kiss. Robert Herrick. CaPo

What is a locust? The Locust. Unknown. FaPON, tr. by Frank Cushing; RB, tr. by A. Marre and Willard R. Trask

(Coyote and the Locust, The.) AWP

What is a modern Poet's fate? The Poet's Fate. Thomas Hood. FaBoEE; FiBHP

(To the Reviewers.) TW

("What is a modern poet's fate.") FaBoEE

What is a poet's love? The Poet's Lot. Oliver Wendell Holmes. PoEL-5

What is a shaman? Coyote, Coyote, Please Tell Me. Peter Blue Cloud. STE

What is a sonnet? 'Tis the pearly shell. Richard Watson Gilder. AA

What is a woman that you forsake her. Harp Song of the Dane Women. Kipling. Fr. Puck of Pook's Hill. HAP; OBNC; PoRA; SeCePo

What is a yielded life? The Yielded Life. "W. A. G." BLRP

What is Africa to me. Heritage. Countee Cullen. AmNP; BANP; BPo; FaBV, abr.; HeIP; MoAmPo; NAAL-2; NoAM; NoP; PoBA; TTY

What is all this washing about. Washing. John Drinkwater. FaPON

What is ambition? 'Tis a glorious cheat! Ambition. Nathaniel Parker Willis. OBCA

What is ambition? 'tis unrest, defeat! Ambition. Henrietta Cordelia Ray. CBWP-3

What is an epigram? a dwarfish whole. Samuel Taylor Coleridge. FaBoEE

(What Is an Epigram?) NIP

What is beautiful alters, has undertow. Whole and without Blessing. Linda Gregg. MAYP; NPGG

What Is Black? Mary O'Neill. NTCP

What is black. Gullfish. Tom Weatherly. Fr. Cantos, 4. PoBA

What Is Charm? Louisa Carroll Thomas. BLPA

What is constant. Unknown, tr. fr. Japanese by Burton Watson. Fr. Kokin Shu. FCEI

What is failure? When the maiden. Failure. Henrietta Cordelia Ray. CBWP-3

What is freedom? ask the philosophers. Freedom. Adam Zagajewski, tr. by Antony Graham. PwPP

"What is funny?" you ask, my child. The Anatomy of Humor. Morris Bishop. NBLV

What Is Good? John Boyle O'Reilly. WBLP

What is green in me. Stepping Westward. Denise Levertov. CAPP; NMM; VGW

What Is Happening Now? Hubert Witheford. PeNZ

What is happening to me now that loved faces. Childhood in Jacksonville, Florida. Jane Cooper. TAP

What is he buzzing in my ears? Confessions. Robert Browning. ELP; GTBS-P; NOBE; NOBVV

What is he, this lordling, that cometh from the fight? The Knight Stained from Battle. William Herebert. MeEL

What Is Heaven? Philip James Bailey. PWR

What is hidden in the fruit of summer? Teresa Torres, tr. by James Tipton. OV

What is home without a Bible? Home without a Bible. Charles D. Meigs. WBLP

What is hope? A smiling rainbow. Cui Bono? Thomas Carlyle. WGRP

What is house, and what is home. House and Home. Joseph Beaumont. OBS

What is it/ that is senseless to lament. Tameyo, tr. by Steven D. Carter. WFTW

What Is It? H. E. Wilkinson. BoTP

What is it about homework. Homework. Jane Yolen. RHPC

What is it all language is attempting definitively to say? Once and for All. Louis Aragon, tr. by Michael Benedikt. POS

What is it, inside them and undeniable. The King's Men. William Heyen. PoA

What Is It Makes the Stranger? Robin Hyde. ATNZ

What is it men in women do require? Blake. *Fr.* Several Questions Answered. OAEL-2

(Question Answered [*or* A Question Answered], The.) ErPo; FaBoEE; GBL; NoP

What is it more eyes doth wear. *Unknown.* GBP

What is it now with me. Fear of Death. John Ashbery. FaBoMo; TAP

What is it our mammas bewitches. Written for My Son, and Spoken by Him at His First Putting on Breeches. Mary Barber. NOEC

What is it so transforms the boulevard? Another Spirit Advances. Jules Romains, *tr. by* Joseph T. Shipley. AWP

What is it that stirs the heart and mind. The Hillman Looks Back. Rennie McOwan. PoSH

What is it that troubles you? Liang Ch'i-ch'ao, *tr. fr. Chinese by* Cecile Chu-chin Sun. *Fr.* Thoughts at the End of Spring—A Farewell Poem for Someone Going Home, I. WFTU

"What is it to be dead?" O Life. A Child's Question. Emma Huntington Nason. AA

What is it to grow old? Growing Old. Matthew Arnold. FaFP; FiP; NAEL-2; NOBVV; OAEL-2; PoEL-5

"What is it to me?" *Unknown, tr. by* Geoffrey Bownas *and* Anthony Thwaite. PeBJV

What is it to remember? Bliss Carman. *Fr.* Songs of the Sea-Children, LXVI. OBCV

What is it when a woman sleeps, her head bright. Where You Go When She Sleeps. T. R. Hummer. MAYP; MT

What is it with these people-swallowing streets. All of a Sudden. Teresa de Jesús, *tr. by* Maria A. Proser, Arlene Scully *and* James Scully. WPOW

What is it you remember?—the summer mornings. To Any Member of My Generation. George Barker. WaP

"What is it you're mumbling, old Father my Dad?" By the Exeter River. Donald Hall. MoBS

What Is Left? István Vas, *tr. fr. Hungarian by* Emery George. VWA

What is left in field. An Early Illinois Winter. Alex Kuo. BrSi

What Is Life? Samuel Taylor Coleridge. FiP

What Is Liquid. Margaret Cavendish, Duchess of Newcastle. FaBoUs

What Is Lived. Carmen Valle, *tr. fr. Spanish by* Julio Marzán. InW

What Is Man? Bible, *O.T. See* Psalms: Psalm VIII ("O Lord our Lord, how excellent is thy name. . .").

What Is Man's Body? *Gond Oral Tradition, tr. by* V. Elwin *and* S. Hivale. WTO

What is more beautiful than potatoes in bloom? The Cure. Medbh McGuckian. FaBCIP

What is more gentle than a wind in summer? Sleep and Poetry. Keats. EnRP

What Is Needed. Marcos Rodríguez Frese, *tr. fr. Spanish by* Julio Marzán. InW

What Is Orange? Mary O'Neill. RHPC

What is our innocence. What Are Years? Marianne Moore. BLPL; CMoP; EaLo; LiTA; MoAB; MoAmPo; MoP; NoAM; NOBA; OxBA; TrGrPo

What Is Our Life? A Play of Passion. Sir Walter Ralegh. EBEV; FaBoEE; MePo; OxBSP; SiPS

(All the World's a Stage.) NOBE; OBSC

(On the Life of Man.) NAEL-1

What is—"Paradise." Emily Dickinson. CMoP

What Is Past. Sir William Davenant. TrGrPo

What Is Pink? Christina Rossetti. *Fr.* Sing-Song. GoJo; OnUR; OxBChV; RHPC

What Is Poetry. John Ashbery. LCAP

What Is Poetry. James Scully. FYAP

What is poetry? Is it a mosaic? Amy Lowell. WGRP

What is poetry? Who Knows? Poetry. Eleanor Farjeon. RHPC

What Is Prayer? James Montgomery. BLRP; WGRP

What is reality? Self in 1958. Anne Sexton. HCAP

What Is Red? Mary O'Neill. RHPC

What is so rare as a day in June? Question and Answer. Samuel Hoffenstein. FiBHP

What is song's eternity? Song's Eternity. John Clare. FaBoCh

What Is Terrible. Roy Fuller. WaP

What is that a-billowing there. Firstfruits in 1812. Wallace Rice. PAH

What is that death they boast but a frail pageant. Swinburne. *Fr.* The Unhappy Revenge. FL

What is that growling! Screeching! Barking! Spring Cleaning. Phillip William George. VoR

What is the boy now, who has lost his ball. The Ball Poem. John Berryman. ASP; CoAP; FF; MoAmPo; NoAM; NOBA; NoP

What Is the Case in Point? Abraham Reisen, *tr. fr. Yiddish by* Richard J. Fein. VWA

What is the flower that blooms each year. The Christmas Rose. Cecil Day Lewis. TIRV

What is the head. Some Last Questions. W. S. Merwin. CAPP; HCAP

What is the heart of a girl? The Heart of a Girl Is a Wonderful Thing. *Unknown.* BLPA

What is the horn that the dawn holds. The Horn. James Reaney. OBCV

What is the latest fashion in my city now? My City. Faiz Ahmad Faiz, *tr. by* Mahmood Jamal. PBMUP

What is the life of the rose? Mohammad Taqi Mir, *tr. by* Ahmed Ali. GoT

What is the little one thinking about? Babyhood. Josiah Gilbert Holland. *Fr.* Bitter-sweet. AA

"What is the matter, grandmother dear?" Grandma's Lost Balance. Sydney Dayre. OBCA

What is the matter with Grandpapa? Poor Dear Grandpapa. D'Arcy Wentworth Thompson. NA

What is the meaning of imprisonment. One Year. Ali Sardar J'afri, *tr. by* Mahmood Jamal. PBMUP

What is the meaning of this Ideal. W. J. Turner. *Fr.* The Seven Days of the Sun. OBMV

What is the measure then, the magpie in the field. The Measure. Patrick Lane. NOBC

What is the metre of the dictionary? Dylan Thomas. *Fr.* Altarwise by Owl-Light, IV. CMoP; FaBoMo

What is the minstrel's lot upon the earth? The Minstrel's Lot. John Bolton Rogerson. PF

What is the mirror saying with its O? A Room in the Villa. William Jay Smith. NYBP

What is the misery in one that turns one with gladness. Grace Abounding. A. R. Ammons. HCAP

What is the moral? Who rides may read. The Winners. Kipling. *Fr.* The Story of the Gadsbys. BLPA; FaPoR; FPL; MoBrPo; TrGrPo

(L'Envoi: "What is the moral? Who rides may read.") MoBrPo; TrGrPo

What is the name of King Ringang's daughter? Beauty Rohtraut. Eduard Friedrich Mörike, *tr. by* George Meredith. AWP; OBVE

What is the opposite of a prince? Richard Wilbur. WSC

What is the opposite of riot. Some Opposites. Richard Wilbur. OBCA

What is the opposite of two? The Opposite of Two. Richard Wilbur. ILY; RHPC

"What is the real good?" What Is Good? John Boyle O'Reilly. WBLP

What is the reason. Early Autumn. Joben, *tr. by* Steven D. Carter. WFTW

What is the rhyme for porringer? Mother Goose. OxNR

"What is the song I am singing?" The Founts of Song. "Fiona Macleod." WGRP

What is the subject? It looks like a paragraph. Prose. Bernard Welt. EOEF

"What is the thing your eyes hold loveliest." The Newlyweds. Cloyd Mann Criswell. PoLF

What Is the Use?, *sel.* Erastus Wolcott Ellsworth. AA

"I saw a man, by some accounted wise." AA

What is the use of the rule insane. The Solution. Brian Merriman, *tr. fr. Modern Irish by* Arland Ussher. *Fr.* The Midnight Court. BIrV

What is the voice I hear. To America. Alfred Austin. GN

(Britannia to Columbia.) PAH

What is the word for "death." Flowers for Luis Bunuel. Stuart Z. Perkoff. NeAP

"What is the world, O soldiers?" Napoleon. Walter de la Mare. FaBoCh; FaBoTw; NOBE; RB

What is the world! tell, Worldling (if thou know it). Mundus Qualis. Joshua Sylvester. FaBoEE

What is the Ziz? The Ziz. John Hollander. VWA

What Is There for Us. Arto Melleri, *tr. fr. Finnish by* Aili Jarvenpa. SOP

What is there for us. Song of the Bride. Susan Mernit. VWA

What is there for us two. Fifty-Fifty. Carl Sandburg. ILY

What is there hid in the heart of a rose. Alfred Noyes. CH

What is there in my heart that you should sue. Lachrimae Amantis. Geoffrey Hill. NOCV

What is there left to be said? Arthur Rex Dugard Fairburn. ATNZ; PeNZ

What is there that we can do or say. Ezekiel Mphahlele. WMBCH

What is there they will not do to you? The First Test. Susan Fromberg Schaeffer. IHMS

What is there wanting in the Spring. The Wistful Days. Robert Underwood Johnson. AA

What is this extraordinary crowding. Ague. Sandor Csoori, *tr. by* Edwin Morgan. MHuP

What is this flesh and blood compounded of. Allen Tate. *Fr.* Sonnets of the Blood, I. PoA

"What is this golden bowl, mother." Ballad of the Golden Bowl. Sara Henderson Hay. OnMSP

What is this image in the clouded mirror. Image in a Mirror. Mae Winkler Goodman. GoYe

What Is This Knowledge? Sir John Davies. *Fr.* Nosce Teipsum. FaBoRV
(Knowledge and Reason.) OBSC
(Much Knowledge, Little Reason.) ChTr

What is this life if, full of care. Leisure. W. H. Davies. AWP; BoNaP; BoTP; CH; FaBoBe; FaFP; FaPON; LiTB; LiTM; MoBrPo; MoShBr; NOBE; OBEV; OBMV; PoRA; SeCePo; TrGrPo

What is this life, this active guest. A Solemn Meditation. William Shenstone. NOEC

What is this recompense you'd have from me? From a Woman to a Greedy Lover. Norman Cameron. *Fr.* Three Love Poems, I. FaBoEE

What is this road that separates us. Way. Tristan Tzara. POS, *tr. by* Michael Benedikt; RHTwFP, *tr. by* Lee Harwood

What is this sad legacy. A Dream of Roaming. Sándor Weöres, *tr. by* Jascha Kessler. FOC

What is this sound that wakens me at night? Eeva Kilpi, *tr. by* Aili Jarvenpa. SOP

What is this tempest. W. J. Turner. *Fr.* The Seven Days of the Sun. OBMV

What is this that I can see. Oh! Death. *Unknown.* AmFP

What is this that I have heard? Dawn Has Yet to Ripple In. Melville Cane. MoAmPo

What is this that roareth thus? Motor Bus. Alfred Denis Godley. FaBoCo; NOBL
(On the Motor Bus.) FaBoNo; NBLV

What is this voice I hear. To America. Alfred Austin. GN
(Britannia to Columbia.) PAH

What is this wonderful thing? Brown and everywhere! Looking at a Dry Canadian Thistle Brought In from the Snow. Robert Bly. NNaP

What Is Time? James Marsden. PWR

What Is Truth?, *sel.* James Harold Manning.
"I have been/ Three separate times, in war." CaP

What is under the grass. Under the Ground. Rhoda Warner Bacmeister. RAR

What Is Veal? *Unknown.* FaBoUs

What is weaker than a god? It groans hungry. Rosario Castellanos, *tr. by* Willis Barnstone. BoWoP

What Is Woman? Mrs. Henry Linden. CBWP-4

What is your feeling about the revolutionary spirit. Firebrand. Harry Crosby. EAS

What Is Your Life? Hannu Mäkelä, *tr. fr. Finnish by* Aili Jarvenpa. SOP

"What is your substance, whereof are you made." Shakespeare. *Fr.* Sonnets, LIII. CTC; EBEV; EIL; FaFP; LiTB; OAEL-1; OBEV; OBSC; PeHV

What is't, fine Grand, makes thee my friendship fly. To Fine Grand. Ben Jonson. JCP

What is't, good prying friend, you say? The Alarm. Hildebrand Jacob. NOEC

What Is't to Us? Charles Churchill. *Fr.* Night; an Epistle to Robert Lloyd. SeCePo

What it is to be stone. On Being Stone. Vivienne Finch. TSM

What It Means to Be Naked. Bill Manhire. ATNZ

What it must be like to be an angel. Parents. William Meredith. FYAP

What it showed was always the same. The Night Mirror. John Hollander. NYBP; Prf

What it would look like if really there were only. Allen Curnow. *Fr.* A Small Room with Large Windows, I. PeNZ

What It's Like Living in My Studio Late in Spring, *sel.* Wen Cheng-ming, *tr. fr. Chinese.*
"Quiet courtyard fills with greenery, The." *Tr. by* Jonathan Chaves. CoBLCP

What Jenner Said on Hearing in Elysium That Complaints Had Been Made of His Having a Statue [in Trafalgar Square]. Shirley Brooks. EyDe; FaBoEE

What Johnny Told Me. John Ciardi. ILY

What joy hath yon glad wreath of flowers that is. The Garland and the Girdle. Buonarroti Michelangelo, *tr. by* John Addington Symonds. AWP

What joys attend [*or* joy attends] the fisher's life! The Fisher's Life. *Unknown.* ChTr; GBP

What jungles he swung out of into the imagination. Gorilla Gorilla. Bruce Dawe. NoAM

What, Kaiser dead? The heavy news. Kaiser Dead. Matthew Arnold. FM

What, keep love in perspective?—that old lie. In Perspective. Robert Graves. OxBSP

What Kin' o' Pants Does the Gambler Wear. *Unknown.* AS

What Kind of a Guy Was He? Howard Nemerov. PCP

What kind of beast would turn its life into words? Adrienne Rich. *Fr.* Twenty-one Love Poems, VII. GLP

What Kind of Mistress He Would Have. Robert Herrick. CaPo; TrGrPo

What lack you, sir? What seek you? What will you buy? Thomas Newbery. *Fr.* The Great Merchant, Dives Pragmaticus, Cries His Wares. OxBChV

What large, dark hands are those at the window. Love on the Farm. D. H. Lawrence. CMoP; ErPo; FaBV; FF; MoAB; MoBrPo; NAEL-2; NoAM; TrGrPo

What Larkin bawled to hungry crowds. Inscription for a Headstone. Austin Clarke. BIrV; CIP

What Length of Verse? Sir Philip Sidney. PoE

What lewd, naked and revolting shape is this? Shopping for Meat in Winter. Oscar Williams. LiTA; LiTM

What life can compare with the jolly town-rakes. The Town-Rakes. *At. to* P. A. Motteux. CoMu

What lifts the heron leaning on the air. Snowy Heron. John Ciardi. WeW

What lightning shall light it? What thunder shall tell it? Martin Luther at Potsdam. Barry Pain. NA

What linking of soul to the halcyons of the afternoon! Aegean Melancholy. Odysseus Elytis, *tr. by* Edmund Keeley *and* Philip Sherrard. VMG

What Lips My Lips Have Kissed. Edna St. Vincent Millay. BoLoP; HeIP; HoPM; LiTA; LLLT; MoAB; MoAmPo; NAAL-2; NIP; PrIm; Son

What lithely springs in the corner. The Sound of Matter. J. Bernlef, *tr. by* James S. Holmes. DuIn

What lively lad most pleasured me. A Last Confession. W. B. Yeats. BoLoP; CMoP; ELP; ErPo; HAP; NIP; OAEL-2; WeW

What Love Is. Ella Wheeler Wilcox. PWR

What love is this of thine, that cannot be. Edward Taylor. *Fr.* Preparatory Meditations before My Approach to the Lord's Supper, 1. AmPP; NOCV; PoEL-3; SCAP

What lovely things. The Scribe. Walter de la Mare. CMoP; FaBoCh; OBMV; TrCP; TrPWD

What made the place a landscape of despair. Claus von Stauffenberg. Thom Gunn. OBWP

What made the porter stare so hard? At Devlin's Siding. Barcroft Henry Boake. CBAP

What makes a city great? Huge piles of stone. The City's Crown. William Dudley Foulke. WGRP

What Makes a Happy Life. Martial, *tr. fr. Latin by* Goldwin Smith. AWP

What makes a knave a child of God. Samuel Butler. *Fr.* Hudibras, III, 1. NOBL; OBSV

What Makes a Nation Great? Alexander Blackburn. WBLP

What makes a nation's pillars high. A Nation's Strength. Emerson. OPP

What makes a plenteous harvest. Virgil, *tr. fr. Latin by* Dryden. *Fr.* Georgics, I. AWP

What makes all subjects discontent. Samuel Butler. FaBoEE

What makes me disinclined. Pretences. Ibn Rashiq, *tr. by* A. J. Arberry. TTY

What makes my bed seem hard, seeing it is soft? Captive of Love. Ovid, *tr. fr. Latin by* Christopher Marlowe. *Fr.* Elegies, I, 2. AWP

What makes permeable the ghost? The Ghost. Hilary Corke. NYBP

What makes us rove that starlit corridor. Science Fiction. Kingsley Amis. NePoEA-2; NoAM

What makes you look so black, so glum, so cross? Edward Lear. FaBoNo

What makes your lip so strange? Thomas Middleton. *Fr.* The Changeling, III, iv. PoEL-2

What man dost thou dig it for? Shakespeare. *Fr.* Hamlet, V, i. DL

What man is he that yearneth. Sophocles, *tr. fr. Greek by* A. E. Housman. *Fr.* Oedipus at Colonus. AWP

What man is there so bold that he should say. Liberty. John Hay. AA

What man of ignorance undefiled. Oh Come, Little Children. Phyllis McGinley. FaBV

What? Mars his sword? faire Cytherea say. Upon Venus Putting on Mars His Armes. Richard Crashaw. SeCP

What Matter? *Gond Oral Tradition, tr. by* V. Elwin *and* S. Hivale. WTO

What matter if the sun be lost? Daffodil's Return. Bliss Carman. CaP

What matter makes my spade for tears or mirth. Digging. Edward Thomas. BrPo

What matters all his love for me? A Sailor's Wife. Clara Bernhardt. CaP

What matters here is (can a fish live). The Instinct of Self-Preservation. Nanni Balestrini, tr. by Lawrence R. Smith. NItP

What matters it, O breeze. Mohammad Taqi Mir, tr. by Ahmed Ali. GoT

What mean these dreams, and hideous forms that rise. George the Third's Soliloquy. Philip Freneau. NOBA

What mean these loud aerial cracks I hear? Unknown. Fr. Bedlam; a Poem on His Majesty's Happy Escape from His German Dominions. NOEC

What mean these peals from every tower. The Fall of Richmond. Herman Melville. PAH

What mean these showy and these sounding signs. The Feast of Blood. Joseph Fawcett. Fr. The Art of War. NOEC

What mean these mortall children of mine owne. Chorus Tertius: Of Time; Eternitie. Fulke Greville. Fr. Mustapha. OBS

Eternity's Speech against Time. JCP

What meanes this silence of Harvardine quils. A Supplement. Benjamin Tompson. SCAP

What meanest thou, my fortune. Unknown. EnLoPo

What meaneth [or menethe] this? When I lie [or lye] alone. Sir Thomas Wyatt. GBL; SiPS

(What Does This Mean?) MeEL

What means at this unusual hour the light. Sonnet in the Mail Coach. Henry Taylor. TEP

What means this host of advancing. The Advance of Education. Josephine D. Henderson Heard. CBWP-4

What means this new-born child of planets' motion? Eternity's Speech against Time. Fulke Greville. Fr. Mustapha: Chorus Tertius: Of Time; Eternitie. JCP

What means this stately tablature. To My Noble Kinsman, Thomas Stanley, Esquire, on His Lyric Poems Composed by Master John Gamble. Richard Lovelace. CaPo

What means this vast assemblage here. Dedication Day. Maggie Pogue Johnson. CBWP-4

What means this watery canop' 'bout thy bed. On King Richard the Third, Who Lies Buried under Leicester Bridge. Sir John Suckling. CaPo

What measure fate to him shall mete. Love Serviceable. Coventry Patmore. Fr. The Angel in the House, I, vi. EnLoPo

What Memory Reveals. Susan Wheeler. BAP

What men are they who haunt these fatal glooms. James Thomson ("B. V.") Fr. The City of Dreadful Night, XI. EBVV

What meneth this? When I lye alone. See What meaneth this? When I lie alone.

What Mérida looked like the first time you were there. Things That Happen to You. Alonzo Gonzales Mó, tr. by Allan F. Burns. STP

What miracle is this! I almost blush, I know it. Wanting to Air His Thoughts about and Prove His Respect for Mademoiselle Weichmann's Unusual Talent. H. E. Weichmann, tr. by Susan L. Cocalis. DMG

What miracle is this! what! I should blush, I know it! Wanting to Answer Mr. Darnmann's Undeserved Civility in the Same Rhyme-Scheme. H. E. Weichmann, tr. by Susan L. Cocalis. DMG

What moment in the gradual decay. Pale Fire. Vladimir Nabokov. OBD

What more? Where is the third Calixt. Ballad of the Lords of Old Time. Villon, tr. by Swinburne. AWP

What moved me, was the way your hand. Dorothy Livesay. CaP

What moves that lonely man is not the boom. The Hermit. W. H. Davies. BrPo; MoBrPo

What Mr. Robinson Thinks. James Russell Lowell. Fr. The Biglow Papers: 1st Series, No. III. AA; AmPP; PAH

What My Child Learns of the Sea. Audre Lorde. NBP; PoBA; TV

What my friend? Love this! I who have known. Walking with R. B. Evan Jones. PVCV

What My Lover Said. Homer Greene. AA

What mystery pervades a well! Emily Dickinson. NAAL-1

What name do I have for you? Just Walking Around. John Ashbery. NAAL-2

What nedeth these thretning wordes and wasted wynde? Sir Thomas Wyatt, after the Italian of Serafino. OBVE

What Need Have I for Memory? Georgia Douglas Johnson. CDC

What need you, being come to sense. September 1913. W. B. Yeats. BrPo; CMoP; FaBoPV; GTBS-P; HAP; MoP; NAEL-2; NoAM; PoRA

What Needeth All This Travail. Unknown. EIL

What needs complaints. Comfort to a Youth That Had Lost His Love. Robert Herrick. NOBE; OBEV

What needs my Shakespear[e] for his honoured [or honour'd or honored] bones. On Shakespeare. Milton. InvP; MeLP; MePo; NAEL-1; NoP; PoE; PoRA; SeCePo; TrGrPo

(Epitaph on the Admirable Dramatic Poet, W. Shakespeare, An.) FaBoEE

What new responsibilities are we hatching now. Green Ice. Vivienne Finch. BrRo

What News. Walter Savage Landor. BoLoP

What news for man in a broken house, old trees. Autumn, Thurlby Domain. Charles Brasch. ATNZ

What Night Would It Be? John Ciardi. PDV

What! no more favours? Not a ribbon more. To a Lady That Forbade to Love before Company. Sir John Suckling. CaPo

What No, Perdy. Sir Thomas Wyatt. See "What no, perdy! ye may be sure!"

What no, perdy! ye may be sure! Sir Thomas Wyatt. AAS; OBSC

(No! Indeed.) MeEL

(What No, Perdy.) PoEL-1

What noble courage must their hearts have fired. Oliver Goldsmith, the Younger. Fr. The Rising Village. OBCV

(Lonely Settler, The.) NOBC

What noise of viols is so sweet. Beggars. Francis Davidson. CH

What nothing earthly gives, or can destroy. The Soul's Calm Sunshine. Pope. Fr. An Essay on Man, IV. FaBoRV

What now. Another Poem for Me. Etheridge Knight. NNaP

What now avails to gain a woman's heart. The Mortified Genius. James Graeme. NOEC

What nudity is beautiful as this. Portrait of a Machine. Louis Untermeyer. MoAmPo

What numerous votaries 'neath thy shadowy wing. To the Evening. John Codrington Bampfylde. NOEC

What nymph should I admire or trust. The Question to Lisetta. Matthew Prior. OBEV

What of earls with whom you have supt. The Toad-Eater. Burns. TW

What of her glass without her? The blank gray. Without Her. Dante Gabriel Rossetti. Fr. The House of Life, LIII. GBL; OBNC; PoEL-5; Son

What of it, that the realms of this epoch. The Animal Howl. "M. J.", tr. by A. Glanz-Leyeless. TrJP

What of the faith and fire within us. Men Who March Away. Thomas Hardy. MMA; OBWP

What of the night? Unknown, tr. by Arthur Waley. BoS

What of these verses that I write. Narcissus: To Himself. David Galler. PoA

What of this fabulous country. Canoe-Trip. Douglas Le Pan. CaP; OBCV

"What of vile dust?" the preacher said. The Praise of Dust. G. K. Chesterton. MoBrPo

What offspring other men have got. Upon His Verses. Robert Herrick. NAEL-1

What on earth! I fear and tremble. Darkened in the Soul. Napa. WTO

What Once I Was. Sir Thomas Wyatt. MeEL

What one art thou, thus in torn weed yclad? Virtue. Nicholas Grimald. OBSC

What [or And what] Is So Rare as a Day in June? James Russell Lowell. Fr. The Vision of Sir Launfal, Prelude to Pt. I. BLPL; FaBoBe; FaFP; FaPON

(Day in June, A ("And what is so fair as a day in June?").) FaPON

(June ("What is so rare as a day in June?").) FaBV

What our Dame bids us do. Ben Jonson. Fr. The Masque of Queens. OFD; WSC

What pain and distress. Yakamochi. Fr. Manyo Shu. Ma

What pain, to wake and miss you! Quite Forsaken. D. H. Lawrence. BrPo

What pangs did he merit—so simple, without misdeed ? Death of a Ram. Sedulius Scottus. NOIV

What passing-bells for these who die as cattle? Anthem for Doomed Youth. Wilfred Owen. BrPo; ChTr; CMoP; CMOP; EBEV; FaBoMo; FaBoRV; FaFP; GTBS-P; HAP; HeIP; HoPM; InPK; InPS; LiTM; MoAB; MoBrPo; MoP; NAEL-2; NoAM; NOBE; NoP; OAEL-2; OBEV; OBWP; OxBTC; PoE; PPP; SCV; SeCePo; Son; SoSe; TrGrPo; WaP; WeW

What pen can well report the plight. Another of Seafarers, Describing Evil Fortune. Unknown. OxBSS

What People Say about Paris. Kenneth Koch. BAP

What Piggy-Wig Found. Enid Blyton. BoTP

What place can it be. River Messages. Wei Chuang, tr. by Lois Fusek. ATF

What place have the bells come flying from? Flying Bells. Yüan Mei, tr. by Jonathan Chaves. CoBLCP

What plant is not faded? Unknown, tr. by Arthur Waley. BoS

What pleasure can this gaudy world afford? Consideratus Considerandus. John Saffin. SCAP

What pleasure have great princes. The Quiet Life. *At. to* William Byrd. EIL
  (Herdmen, The.) NOBE; OBSC

What plucky sperm invented Mrs. Gale? A New World Symphony. Kit Wright. NBLV

What poets feel not, when they make. A Caution to Poets. Matthew Arnold. FaBoUs

What poor astronomers are they. *Unknown.* OBSC

What portents, from what distant region, ride. On the Ice Islands Seen Floating in the German Ocean. William Cowper. OAEL-1; PrIm

What Price. Lulu Minerva Schultz. GoYe

What Profit? Immanuel di Roma, *tr. fr. Hebrew by* J. Chotzner. TrJP

What rage is this? what furor [*or* furour] of what kind [*or* kynd]? Sir Thomas Wyatt. AAS; EnLoPo; SiPS

What ran under the rosebush? Could It Have Been a Shadow? Monica Shannon. FaPON; RHPC

What reason first imposed thee, gentle name. The Family Name. Charles Lamb. Son

What remains in the hands. Kamal Sabti, *tr. fr. Arabic by* Lena Jayyusi *and* Naomi Shihab Nye. *Fr.* Jungles. MAP

What remains of summer. The Cold. Lance Henson. CDW

What riches have you that you deem me poor? George Santayana. *Fr.* Sonnets, XXIV. TrGrPo

What Riddle Asked the Sphinx. Archibald MacLeish. HoPM

What Rider Spurs Him from the Darkening East. Edna St. Vincent Millay. TrCP; WPE

What Robin Told. George Cooper. FaPON

What! Roses growing in a meadow. Wild Roses. Mary Effie Lee Newsome. CDC

What! Roses on thy tomb! and was there then. Ave! Nero Imperator. Duffield Osborne. AA

What rots in my heart. Sad Little Round of Life. René Daumal, *tr. by* Kenneth Rexroth. RHTwFP

What Rules the World. William Ross Wallace. OHIP

What rumour'd heavens are these. To the Unknown Eros. Coventry Patmore. *Fr.* The Unknown Eros. PoEL-5

What ruse of vision. The Bear. N. Scott Momaday. CDW; HATNAP; NOVW

What sacrifice so great! A Mother's Love. Josephine D. Henderson Heard. CBWP-4

What Saundra Said about Being Short. Jim Hall. MOWH

What savage beast would willfully consent to ride jammed haunch to haunch. Bus Ride. Lenore Kandel. NMM

What say the Bells of San Blas. The Bells of San Blas. Longfellow. OxBA

What says my brother?/ Death is a fearful thing. On Death. Shakespeare. *Fr.* Measure for Measure, III, i. FiP

What scenes appear where-e'er I turn my view. Eloisa. Pope. *Fr.* Eloisa to Abelard. SeCePo

What Schoolmasters Say. Martin Seymour-Smith. OxBTC

What scope/ is there where. The Rope. Tania Van Zyl. PeSA

What seas did you see. A Conversation. Dylan Thomas. RFM

What seas what shores what grey rocks and what islands. Marina. T. S. Eliot. CMoP; FaBoMo; GTBS-P; HeIP; LiTA; MOS; NAEL-2; NOBE; NOCV; PoE; TOF

What Secret Desires of the Blood. Nelly Sachs, *tr. fr. German by* Keith Bosley. VWA

What seek'st thou at this madman's pace? His Quest. Lewis Frank Tooker. AA

What seems to us for us is true. Perspective. Coventry Patmore. *Fr.* The Angel in the House, II, i. FaBoEE; GBL

What seer is this. Ode on the Twentieth Century. Henrietta Cordelia Ray. CBWP-3

What shakes the eye but the invisible? The Decision. Theodore Roethke. CRP; VGW

What shall avail me. The Border. Edwin Muir. Mes

What shall be said between us here. Félise. Swinburne. BeLS

What shall become of us, O Sun. József Tornai, *tr. by* Jascha Kessler. FOC

What shall he have that killed the deer? Amien's Song. Shakespeare. *Fr.* As You Like It, IV, ii.
  (Song: "What shall he have that kill'd the dear?.") CTC

What shall her silence keep? Madison Cawein. AA

What shall I do. Heaven's Wanderer in Heaven, for Tu Fu. Park Je-chun, *tr. by* Koh Chang-soo. ACKP

What shall I do now? Waiting for Love in Vain. Tonna, *tr. by* Steven D. Carter. WFTW

What shall I do this afternoon? Half Holiday. Olive Enoch. BoTP

What shall I do to be for ever known. The Motto. Abraham Cowley. SeCP

What shall I do to be just? The Cry of the Age. Hamlin Garland. WGRP

What Shall I Do to Show How Much I Love Her? John Gay. *Fr.* The Beggar's Opera, I, vii. TEP

What shall I do with this absurdity. The Tower. W. B. Yeats. CMoP; LiTB; LiTM; NoAM; PoE

What Shall I Give. Gwendolyn Brooks. *Fr.* The Womanhood: The Children of the Poor. BPo, 2 *only*.

What Shall I Give? Edward Thomas. FaBoCh; OxBChV

What Shall I Give My Children? Gwendolyn Brooks. Son

What shall I render to thy Name. In Thankfull Remembrance for My Dear Husband's Safe Arrivall Sept. 3, 1662. Anne Bradstreet. TrPWD

What shall I say, because talk I must? The Yellow Flower. William Carlos Williams. HAP

What shall I say, my Lord? With what begin? Edward Taylor. *Fr.* Preparatory Meditations before My Approach to the Lord's Supper, XXIX. HAP

What shall I say to the people? The People. Thomas Ince. PF

What shall I send my sweet today. A Valentine. Matilda Betham-Edwards. PeHV

What shall I teach in the vivid afternoon. Going to School. Karl Shapiro. TrJP

What shall I tell you? The Beginning of the Day. Lin Huan-ch'ang, *tr. by* Dominic Cheung. IFON

What shall I wish thee? New Year's Wishes. Frances Ridley Havergal. BLRP

What shall I wish thee this New Year? A New Year Wish. *Unknown.* BLRP

What shall I your true-love tell. Messages. Francis Thompson. CH

What Shall it Profit? William Dean Howells. AA

What shall it profit a man. Anastasis. Albert E. S. Smythe. CaP

What shall Presto do for pretty prattle. Swift. Delmore Schwartz. PoA

What! shall that sudden blade. Custer. Edmund Clarence Stedman. PAH

What shall the world do with its children? Romans Angry about the Inner World. Robert Bly. NOBA

What shall we add now? He is dead. "Died. . ." Elizabeth Barrett Browning. NOBWV

What shall we be like when. Seeds. John Oxenham. WGRP

What shall we be, sweet, you and I. These Bones. T. H. Parry-Williams, *tr. by* H. Idris Bell. OBWVE

What shall we do. Songs of the Priestess. Malka Heifetz Tussman, *tr. by* Marcia Falk. VWA

What shall we do for Love these days? Lascelles Abercrombie. *Fr.* Emblems of Love. CH; MoBrPo
  Small Fountains, *sel.* CH

What shall we do for timber? Kilcash. *Unknown, tr. by* Frank O'Connor. BIrV; OBMV

What shall we do now, Mary being dead. Mary Booth. Thomas William Parsons. AA

What shall we do—what shall we think—what shall we say? Conrad Aiken. *Fr.* Preludes for Memnon; or, Preludes to Attitude. FaBoMo

What shall we do with our God-Kissed one. Songs of the Priestess. Malka Heifetz Tussman. VWA

What shall we mourn? For the prostrate. John Boyle O'Reilly. *Fr.* Wendell Phillips. AA

What Shall We Render. *Unknown.* BLRP

What shall we say it is to be forgiven? Forgiveness. Elizabeth Sewell. EaLo

What shall we sing? sings Harry. Themes. Denis Glover. *Fr.* Sings Harry. ATNZ

What she collects is men. The Collector. Raymond Souster. ErPo; OBCV

What She Didn't Say. Ory Bernstein, *tr. fr. Hebrew by* Warren Bargad *and* Stanley F. Chyet. IP

What she made in her body is broken. Poem for J. Wendell Berry. GeTw

What she remembers. Mother of the Groom. Seamus Heaney. OxBSP

What She Said ("And all those horses"). Kapilar, *tr. fr. Tamil by* A. K. Ramanujan. PLW

What She Said ("As the lovely new flowers"). Allur Nanmullai, *tr. fr. Tamil by* A. K. Ramanujan. PLW

What She Said ("Bees, six tiny legs and wings all lovely"). Orampokiyar, *tr. fr. Tamil by* A. K. Ramanujan. *Fr.* Five on the Riverside Cane, 1. PLW

What She Said ("Bigger than earth, certainly"). Tevakulattar, *tr. fr. Tamil by* A. K. Ramanujan. PLW

What She Said ("Bird and Beast"). Nannakaiyar, *tr. fr. Tamil by* A. K. Ramanujan. PLW

What She Said ("Forest animals walk there"). Kapilar, tr. fr. Tamil by A. K. Ramanujan. PLW

What She Said ("Friend, listen"). Ammuvanar, tr. fr. Tamil by A. K. Ramanujan. PLW

What She Said ("Green creepers planted inside the house"). Orampokiyar, tr. fr. Tamil by A. K. Ramanujan. Fr. Five on the Riverside Cane, 5. PLW

What She Said ("He is from those mountains"). Kapilar, tr. fr. Tamil by A. K. Ramanujan. PLW

What She Said Her Lover within Earshot. Kapilar, tr. fr. Tamil by A. K. Ramanujan. PLW

What She Said ("Hovering like the heron"). Orampokiyar, tr. fr. Tamil by A. K. Ramanujan. Fr. Five on the Riverside Cane, 2. PLW

What She Said ("In his fields"). Orampokiyar, tr. fr. Tamil by A. K. Ramanujan. Fr. Five on the Crabs, 3. PLW

What She Said ("In his place, mother,/ field-crabs cut into the pink"). Orampokiyar, tr. fr. Tamil by A. K. Ramanujan. Fr. Five on the Crabs, 2. PLW

What She Said ("In his place, mother,/ mud-spattered spotted crabs"). Orampokiyar, tr. fr. Tamil by A. K. Ramanujan. Fr. Five on the Crabs, 1. PLW

What She Said ("In the full river"). Orampokiyar, tr. fr. Tamil by A. K. Ramanujan. Fr. Five on the Riverside Cane, 3. PLW

What She Said ("Like the high fanning tufts on swift horses"). Orampokiyar, tr. fr. Tamil by A. K. Ramanujan. Fr. Five on the Riverside Cane, 4. PLW

What She Said ("My body"). Ammuvanar, tr. fr. Tamil by A. K. Ramanujan. PLW

What She Said (" 'O your hair,' he said"). Kapilar, tr. fr. Tamil by A. K. Ramanujan. PLW

What She Said ("Only the dim-witted say it's evening"). Milaipperun Kantan, tr. fr. Tamil by A. K. Ramanujan. PLW

What She Said ("Only the thief was there, no one else"). Kapilar, tr. fr. Tamil by A. K. Ramanujan. PLW

What She Said ("Rains, already old, The"). Okkur Macatti, tr. fr. Tamil by A. K. Ramanujan. PBWP

What She Said ("The fishermen who go"). Ammuvanar, tr. fr. Tamil by A. K. Ramanujan. PLW

What She Said, Thinking of Him Crossing the Wilderness Alone. Auvaiyar, tr. fr. Tamil by A. K. Ramanujan. PLW

What She Said to Her Friend ("The colors on the elephant's body"). Kapilar, tr. fr. Tamil by A. K. Ramanujan. PLW

What She Said to Her Friend ("You ask me to forget him"). Kapilar, tr. fr. Tamil by A. K. Ramanujan. PLW

What She Said to Her Girl Friend, after a Tryst at Night (Which Turned Out to Be a Fiasco). Kapilar, tr. fr. Tamil by A. K. Ramanujan. PLW

What She Said to Her Girl Friend, and What Her Girl Friend Said in Reply. Uruttiran, tr. fr. Tamil by A. K. Ramanujan. PLW

What She Said to Her Girl Friend, Her Foster-Mother within Earshot. Kapilar, tr. fr. Tamil by A. K. Ramanujan. PLW

What She Said to Her Girl Friend ("In his country"). Kapilar, tr. fr. Tamil by A. K. Ramanujan. PLW

What She Said to Her Girl Friend ("O you, you wear flowers of gold"). Kapilar, tr. fr. Tamil by A. K. Ramanujan. PLW

What She Said to Her Girl Friend ("On the tall hill"). Paranar, tr. fr. Tamil by A. K. Ramanujan. PLW

What She Said to Her Girl Friend When She Returned from the Hills. Kapilar, tr. fr. Tamil by A. K. Ramanujan. PLW

What She Said to Him, after Meeting His Concubine. Cakalacanar, tr. fr. Tamil by A. K. Ramanujan. PLW

What She Wanted to Be. Ory Bernstein, tr. fr. Hebrew by Warren Bargad and Stanley F. Chyet. IP

What Sheila Tells Him, Softly. Vincent O'Sullivan. ATNZ

What Shines in Winter Burns. T. R. Hummer. MAYP; MT

What Ship Is This? at. to Samuel Hauser. AH

What should be said of him cannot be said. Dante. Buonarroti Michelangelo, tr. by Longfellow. AWP; PFI

What should I care at all from what my name I take. The Trent Again. Michael Drayton. Fr. Polyolbion, Sixth and Twentieth Song. FaBoPP

What should I do? If only I had a hut. Teika, tr. fr. Japanese by Hiroaki Sato. Fr. A Compendium of Good Tanka. FCEI

What should I tell them? Richard Wilbur. Fr. The Mind-Reader. CRP

What should one. The Picture of J. T. in a Prospect of Stone. Charles Tomlinson. PPP

What should I [or shulde] I say[e]. Sir Thomas Wyatt. NoP; PoEL-1; SiPS
    (Farewell: "What should I say.") GBL; Mes; NOBE; OBSC
    (Revocation, A.) OBEV

What should we be without the sexual myth. Men Made out of Words. Wallace Stevens. MoAB; NOBA; OxBSP; TAP; VGW

What should we have taken. Provisions. Margaret Atwood. IHMS

What should we know. Oliver St. John Gogarty. AnIL; FaBoCh; OBMV; PoRA

What shulde I saye. See What should I say.

What sin was mine, sweet, silent boy-god, Sleep. Sleep. Statius, tr. by W. H. Fyfe. AWP

What since August, when the sound. Natural History. Richard Howard. TAP

What siren zooming is sounding our coming. The Exiles. W. H. Auden. OxBTC

What sky! And I remember suddenly. Le Tombeau de Frank O'Hara. Art Lange. UL

What slender youth bedewed with liquid odours. I, 5. "What slender youth bedewed with liquid odours" ("Quis multa gracilis"). Horace, tr. fr. Latin. Fr. Odes. OBVE, tr. by Milton.
    (Another to the Same.) WiR, tr. by William Browne.
    (Fifth Ode of Horace, The.) EBEV, tr. by Milton; EnLoPo, tr. by Milton; PoEL-3, tr. by Milton.
    ("Pyrrha, what slender well-shap'd beau.") OBVE, tr. by Anthony Horneck.
    ("Say what slim youth, with moist perfumes.") OBVE, tr. by Christopher Smart.
    ("Tell me, Pyrrha, what fine youth.") OAEL-1, tr. by William Browne.
    ("Tell me, Pyrrha, what fine youth.")
    (To a Girl.) WiR, tr. by Milton.
    (To Pyrrha.) AWP, tr. by Milton.
    ("To whom now, Pyrrha, art thou kind?.") OBVE, tr. by Abraham Cowley.
    ("What stripling now thee discomposes.") OBVE, tr. by Sir Richard Fanshawe.

What smoldering senses in death's sick delay. The Kiss. Dante Gabriel Rossetti. Fr. The House of Life, VI. Son

What so beyond all madness is the elf. Cupid Far Gone. Richard Lovelace. CaPo; OPOP

What! soar'd the old eagle to die at the sun! The Death of Harrison. Nathaniel Parker Willis. PAH

What soft, cherubic creatures. Emily Dickinson. AmPP; HAP; MoAB; MoAmPo; SoSe; WPE

What solemn sound the ear invades. Mount Vernon. Unknown. AmFP; OFD

What Someone Said When He Was Spanked on the Day before His Birthday. John Ciardi. RHPC

What songs found voice upon those lips. Helen Hunt Jackson. Ina Coolbrith. AA

What sons of so and so. In Order to Say It. Idea Vilariño, tr. by Kate Flores. DMH

What soothes the angry snail? Eine Kleine Snailmusik. May Sarton. NBLV

What sort of a church would our church be. Just like Me. P. W. Sinks. BLRP

What soul hath struck its need of melody. Incompleteness. Henrietta Cordelia Ray. CBWP-3

"What sound awakened me, I wonder." The Deserter. A. E. Housman. OBMV

What sound awoke me? Dragon Skate. Gladys Cardiff. CDW

What sounds are those, Helvellyn, which are heard. The Fair below Helvellyn. Wordsworth. Fr. The Prelude [or, Growth of a Poet's Mind]: Residence in London. FaBoPP

What sounds fetched from far the wind carries tonight. Notes on Life at Home, February, 1942. Valentine Ackland. CN

What sower walked over earth. Sunflower. Rolf Jacobsen, tr. by Robert Bly. NU

What sphinx of cement and aluminum bashed open their skulls. Allen Ginsberg. Fr. Howl, II. NeAP; SOTW, abr.; TAP

What spirit touched the faded lambrequin. The Ilex Tree. Agnes Lee. PoA

What Splendid Rays. Christian Gregor, tr. fr. German. AH

What stands 'tween me and her that I adore? Echo Poem. M. Allan. FiBHP

What starts with f and ends with u-c-k? starts. The World of Expectations. Albert Goldbarth. HCAP

What station we started from. Funeral Trains. Ishihara Yoshiro, tr. by Hiroaki Sato. FCEI

What sticks with me is the pit. Moonwalk. John Engels. MAT

What, Still Alive. Hugh Kingsmill. See What, still alive at twenty-two.

What, still alive at twenty-two. Hugh Kingsmill. FaBoCo; NOBL
    (Poem, after A. E. Housman.) FaBoPa

(What, Still Alive.) BXAP; NBLV

(What, Still Alive at Twenty–Two.) InPK

What strange sound was slithering along the length of the. Despair of the Sun. Robert Desnos, *tr. by* Michael Benedikt. POS

What street is this? Osip Mandelstam, *tr. by* Clarence Brown *and* W. S. Merwin. OBD

What strength! what strife! what rude unrest! Westward Ho! Joaquin Miller. AA; AnAmPo; FaBoBe

What stripling now thee discomposes. Horace. *See* Odes: I, 5. "What slender youth bedewed with liquid odours" ("Quis multa gracilis").

What Sugared Terms. Richard Lynche. *See* Diella: What sugred termes, what all-perswading arte.

What sugred termes, what all-perswading arte. Richard Lynche. *Fr.* Diella, IV. AAS

(What Sugared Terms.) Son

What sweet relief the showers to thirsty plants we see. A True Love. Nicholas Grimald. EIL; OBEV

(Truelove, A.) OBSC

What swords and spears, what daggers bright. Frost. W. H. Davies. BoNaP

What the Birds Said. Whittier. NOBA

What the blind lost when radio. After the Revolution for Jesus the Associate Professor [*or* a Secular Man] Prepares His Final Remarks. Miller Williams. BLA; MT

What the Bullet Sang. Bret Harte. AA; OBEV

What the cats do. The Cats. Weldon Kees. NaP

What the Chairman Told Tom. Basil Bunting. OxBTC

What the Choir Sang about the New Bonnet. M. T. Morrison. BLPA

What the Concubine Said When She Heard the Wife Complain about the Concubine's Wiles. Villakaviralinar, *tr. fr. Tamil by* A. K. Ramanujan. PLW

What the Dead Poets Know. Elizabeth Smither. ATNZ

What the devil are these angels doing perched half-way between. The Angels. Mirko Lauer, *tr. by* David Tipton. Per

What the Devil Said. James Stephens. CMoP

What the Donkey Saw. U. A. Fanthorpe. OBCP

What the Earth Asked Me. James Wright. NYBP

What the Emanation of Casey Jones Said to the Medium. A. J. M. Smith. MoCV

What the eye sees is a dream of sight. To the Hand. W. S. Merwin. EAS

What the Girl Friend Said to the Foster-Mother. Kapilar, *tr. fr. Tamil by* A. K. Ramanujan. PLW

What the Gray Cat Sings. Arthur Guiterman. MoShBr

What the Informant Told to Franz Boas in 1920. *Unknown, tr. fr. Keresan Indian by* Armand Schwerner. STP

What the Light Was Like. Amy Clampitt. FaBoWP

What the Moon Saw. Vachel Lindsay. FaBoEE; OxBSP

What the Motorcycle Said. Mona Van Duyn. NIP

What the Orderly Dog Saw. Ford Madox Ford. CTC

What the Passersby Said to the Lover Eloping with the Girl. Uraiyur Mutukorran, *tr. fr. Tamil by* A. K. Ramanujan. PLW

What the people learn out of lifting and hauling. Carl Sandburg. *Fr.* The People, Yes, *sec.* 32. OBAL

What the Prince of I Dreamt. Henry Cholmondeley-Pennell. NA

What the Red-haired Bo'sun Said. Charles H. Souter. PoAu-1

What the Rooster Does before Mounting. Cyn Zarco. BrSi; UL

What the Servants Said to Him, as He Returned Home. Maturaittamilkkuttan Katuvan Mallanar, *tr. fr. Tamil by* A. K. Ramanujan. PLW

What the seven sages, too. Tabito. *Fr.* Manyo Shu. PeBJV

What the Sixties Were Really Like. Sam Abrams. UL

What the Sonnet Is. Eugene Lee-Hamilton. HoPM; Son

What the Stone Dreams. James B. Hathaway. GOYP

What the Thrush Said. Keats. EBEV

What the Thrush Said. Queenie Scott-Hopper. BoTP

What the Violins Sing in Their Baconfat Bed. Jean Arp, *tr. fr. French by* John Frederick Nims. WeW

What the Weather Does. *Unknown.* BoTP

What the wind harried, the fire worried. Deadfall. Martha Keller. GoYe

What the Winds Bring. Edmund Clarence Stedman. AnAmPo

What the Wing Says. David Swanger. KS

What Then? W. B. Yeats. CMoP

What Then, Dancer? Kay Smith. CaP

What then is poetry. Poetry. Claude Vigée, *tr. by* Anthony Rudolf. VWA

"What then, what if my lips do burn." Ulf in Ireland. Charles De Kay. AA

What There Is. Kenneth Patchen. LLLT

What there is once may not be twice. No Laws. Brian Allwood. WaP

What therefore, what ys thyn entent? An Exchange between the Poet and St. Augustine. Petrarch, *tr. fr. Latin by* W. H. Draper. *Fr.* Secretum, I. OxBLMV

What they are doing is turning. Turn (a Poem in 4 Parts). Ken Belford. NOBC

What They Ate What They Wore. Linda Gregg. NAmP

What They Do to You in Distant Places. Marvin Bell. Psk

What thing/ should I sing. Dove. Norma Farber. PChr

What thing did I love that walks the street. The Contemporary Muse. Edgell Rickword. OBSV

What Thing Is Love. George Peele. *Fr.* The Hunting of Cupid. EIL; ELP; NOBE; SeCePo

(Love.) EIL; ELP; NOBE; OBSC; SeCePo

What thing shall be held up to woman's beauty? Woman's Beauty. Lascelles Abercrombie. *Fr.* Emblems of Love: Vashti. MoBrPo

What things are steadfast? Not the birds. We Manage Most When We Manage Small. Linda Gregg. AmPA; NPGG

What think you of this age now. *Unknown.* APAS

What this mountain means, and the murky dale. William Langland. *Fr.* The Vision of Piers Plowman, Passus I (B *text) mod. by* J. B. Trapp. OAEL-1

What Thomas an Buile Said in a Pub. James Stephens. MoAB; MoBrPo; MoP; PoRA; TrGrPo; WGRP

What thou hast done thou hast done; for the heavenly horses are swift. Irrevocable. Mary Wright Plummer. WGRP

What thou lovest well remains. Ezra Pound. *Fr.* Cantos, LXXXI. CMoP; FaBoTw; MoAB; NOBE; OxBA

What Thou Lovest Well, Remains American. Richard Hugo. NAAL-2; NIP

What though, for showing truth to flatter'd [*or* flattered] state. Sonnet: Written on the Day That Mr. Leigh Hunt Left Prison. Keats. ChER

(Written on the Day That Mr. Leigh Hunt Left Prison.) Son

What though my penne wax faynt. To Maystres Jane Blenner-Haiset. John Skelton. *Fr.* The Garlande [*or* Garlands] of Laurell. AAS

What, though oblivion in her sable shroud. George Keate. *Fr.* Ancient and Modern Rome. OBTV

What Though the Field Be Lost? Milton. *Fr.* Paradise Lost, *bk.* I, *ll.* 105–124. EaLo

What Though the Green Leaf Grow? Maybury Fleming. AA

What thought ye to burn, when ye kindled the pyre. *Unknown, tr. fr. Hebrew. Fr.* Duel with Verses over a Great Man. TrJP

What thoughts I have of you tonight, Walt Whitman. A Supermarket in California. Allen Ginsberg. AmPP; CoAP; HAP; HCAP; HeIP; InPK; InPS; LiTM; NAAL-2; NaP; NeAP; NoAM; NOBA; PoM; PrIm; SOTW; TAP; TwCP; UnPo

What thoughts I have of you tonight, Walt Whitman, for I work late. A Pizza Joint in Cranston. Craig Weeden. BXAP

What throws you out is what drags you in. Overboard. May Swenson. RR

What tidings of reverent gladness are voiced by the bells that ring. On Easter Morning. Eben E. Rexford. BLRP

What time I see you passing by. *Unknown, tr. fr. Italian. Fr.* Popular Songs of Tuscany. AWP, *tr. by* John Addington Symonds

What time I was your one best bet. Horace. *See* Odes: III, 9. Dialogue between Horace and Lydia, A ("Donec gratus eram").

What time soft night had silently begun. Fame and Fortune. Michael Drayton. *Fr.* The Legend of Robert, Duke of Normandy. OBSC

What time the earth takes on the garb of Spring. Incipit Vita Nova. William Morton Payne. AA

What time the gifted lady took. George Sand. Dorothy Parker. FiBHP

What time the Lord drew back the sea. Panama. Amanda T. Jones. PAH

What time the mighty moon was gathering light. Love and Death. Tennyson. OBD

What time the noble Lovewell came. Lovewell's Fight. *Unknown.* PAH

What time the poet hath hymned. Oh, Hollow! Hollow! Hollow! W. S. Gilbert. *Fr.* Patience. FaBoNo

What time the rose of dawn is laid across the lips of night. The Angler's Reveille. Henry Van Dyke. *Fr.* The Toiling of Felix. GN

What time the weary weather-beaten sheep. The Tenth Eclogue. Michael Drayton. *Fr.* The Shepherd's Garland. JCP

What time this world's great workmaster did cast. Beauty. Spenser. *Fr.* An Hymne in Honour of Beautie. OBSC

What tocsin's needed here. Going On Talking. Gyorgy Raba, *tr. by* Jascha Kessler. FOC

What Tomas Said in a Pub. James Stephens. *See* What Thomas an Buile Said in a Pub.

What Tongue Can Her Perfections Tell? Sir Philip Sidney. *Fr.* Arcadia. SiPS

What travellers of matchlesse Venice say. An Elegie Made by Mr. Aurelian Townshend in Remembrance of the Ladie Venetia Digby. Aurelian Townshend. SeCP

What treasure greater than a friend. A Friend. Santob de Carrion. *Fr.* Proverbios Morales. TrJP

What tree would shape itself like this? While Pruning. Dixie Partridge. TSM

What tribute have we failed to pay? After the Guests Departed. Tsfrirah Gar, *tr. by* Bernhard Frank. MHeP

What trifling coil do we poor mortals keep. Human Life. Matthew Prior. FaBoEE

What triumph moves on the billows so blue? Matthew Gregory Lewis. OBTV

What truly is will have no end. For an Amulet. Arthur Rex Dugard Fairburn. ATNZ

What Ulysses Said to Circe on the Beach of Aeaea. Irving Layton. ErPo

What unknown affinity. The Search. Denis Glover. *Fr.* Arawata Bill. ATNZ

What use is prayer. Tameyo, *tr. by* Steven D. Carter. WFTW

What used to be. The Change. Samuel Chimsoro. WMBCH

What vaileth trouth? or by it to take payn? Sir Thomas Wyatt. AAS

What various hindrances we meet. Exhortation to Prayer. William Cowper. NOCV

What Violins Are Singing in Their Beds of Lard. Hans Arp, *tr. fr. French by* Michael Benedikt. POS

What Voice at Moth-Hour. Robert Penn Warren. DiPo; MT; SM

"What voice, what harp, are those we hear." The Minstrel. Goethe, *tr. by* James Clarence Mangan. AWP

What! want to be buggered, and cry when it's done! Epigram: To Papilus. Martial. PeHV

What wants thee, that thou art in this sad taking? London Sad London. *Unknown.* OBS

What Was Ashore, Then. John Berryman. *Fr.* Sonnets, XV. Son

What was he doing, the great god Pan. A Musical Instrument. Elizabeth Barrett Browning. EBVV; FaBoBe; FaPON; NAEL-2; NoP; OAEL-2; OBEV; OnMSP; PoE; WPE

(Great God Pan, The.) WiR

What was he thinking of. *Unknown, tr. by* Burton Watson. FCEI

What was her beauty in our first estate. She. Richard Wilbur. AmPP; NIP

What was his name? I do not know his name. The Nameless Saints. Edward Everett Hale. WGRP

What was I thinking. Summer Night. Emperor Kogon, *tr. by* Steven D. Carter. WFTW

What was is. since 1930. Homecoming. Robert Lowell. CAPP

What was it? The Death of the First Man. Nancy Sullivan. NIP

What was it/ that caught in our throats that day. The Greek Room. James W. Thompson. BPo

What was it called. Custer Lives in Humbolt County. Janet Campbell Hale. STE; VoR

What was it I wonder? The Knife. Richard Tillinghast. MAYP; MT

What was it like? Interview with a Winner. Donald Finkle. ASP

What was it like, that country house? Country Villa. Jean Garrigue. TAP

What was it? What was it? Woman as Market. Muriel Rukeyser. NoAM

What was it you remember—the summer mornings. To Any Member of My Generation. George Barker. LiTM; Son; WaP

What was most striking about them. Concerning the Dead Women: The Munitions Plant Explosion: June, 1918. Elizabeth Libbey. AmPA

What Was My Dream? Joseph O'Connor. AA

What was our trust, we trust not. EMC². Morris Bishop. ImOP

What Was Solomon's Mind? Geoffrey Scott. OBMV

"What was that sound we heard." Why Must You Know? John Wheelwright. VGW

What was the first prophetic word that rang. Peace. Edwin Markham. WBLP

What was the nub of wonder? Was it. Questions of Swimming, 1935. Peter Davison. DiPo

What was the promise that smiled from the maples at evening? Robert Penn Warren. *Fr.* Promises, I. DiL

What Was Your Name in the States? *Unknown.* AS

What watch, what woe, what want, what wrack. The Shipmen. William Hunnis. OBSC

What way does the Wind come? What way does he go? Address to a Child during a Boisterous Winter Evening. Dorothy Wordsworth. OxBChV

(Wind, The.) BoTP

What We Call Living. Heather McHugh. NAmP

What We Can. Ray A. Young Bear. VoR

What we do best is breed. A Christening. Donald Davie. OxBC

What we got, we hardly got in the first place. A Memory. P. Mustapää, *tr. by* Aili Jarvenpa. SOP

What we looked for always remained. The Friendship. Robert Mezey. NaP

What we read and what we argue over. After a Fruitless Argument. Ishikawa Takuboku, *tr. by* Geoffrey Bownas *and* Anthony Thwaite. PeBJV

What We Teach at Claflin. Lizelia Augusta Jenkins Moorer. CBWP-3

What we to-day prize most fondly cherish. Instability. Henrietta Cordelia Ray. CBWP-3

What weight of ancient witness can prevail. Private Judgement Condemned. Dryden. *Fr.* The Hind and the Panther, I. OBS (Confessio Fidei.) NOBE

(Prayer, A: "What weight of ancient witness can prevail.") FiP

What well-heeled knuckle-head, straight from the unisex. An Old Malediction. Anthony Hecht, *after* Horace. NoAM; TW

What Were They Like? Denise Levertov. HeIP; NIP; OBWP; VGW; WPE

What were we playing? Was it prisoner's base? Running. Richard Wilbur. ASP; CoAP

What were you carrying, Pilgrims, Pilgrims? Atlantic Charter: 1942. Francis Brett Young. OPP

What, what, what/ What's the news from Swat? George Thomas Lanigan. AA; FiBHP; NA; NBLV

(Ahkoond of Swat, The.) AnAmPo; CaP

(Threnody on the Ahkoond of Swat, A.) CenHV

What Wild Dawns There Were. Denise Levertov. NOBA

What will become of Hawaii? The Leper. Ka-'ehu, *tr. by* M. K. Pukui *and* A. L. Korn. WTO

What will happen now? What She Said. Maturai Ilampalaciriyan Centan Kuttanar, *tr. by* A. K. Ramanujan. PLW

What will have become. Tamefuji, *tr. by* Steven D. Carter. WFTW

What will it do for him, to have internalized. A Giant Has Swallowed the Earth. Pattiann Rogers. MT

What Will Remain after Me? Mendel Naigreshel, *tr. fr. Yiddish by* Joachim Neugroschel. VWA

What will they give me, when journey's done? Journey's End. Humbert Wolfe. TrJP

What will we do. Poem for Nana. June Jordan. BlSi

What Will We Do for Linen? *Unknown.* GBP; WTO

What will you do. What Then, Dancer? Kay Smith. CaP

What Will You Do, God, When I Die? Rainer Maria Rilke, *tr. fr. German by* Babette Deutsch. EaLo

What will you do with. This Blood. Ali Sardar J'afri, *tr. by* Mahmood Jamal. PBMUP

What will you give to a barefoot lass. A Song of Riches. Katharine Lee Bates. AA

"What will you have for your birthday?" Birthday Gifts. Herbert Asquith. OFD

What will you ride on? Hey! My Pony! Eleanor Farjeon. FaPON

What winter floods, what showers of spring. Emily Brontë. NOBVV

What winter holiday is this? The Man of Peace. Bliss Carman. OHIP

What wisdom have we that by wisdom all. Relativities. Louis Untermeyer. BXAP

What! without feeling? Don't we make pretense. Two Vast Enjoyments Commemorated. John Danforth. SCAP

What Women Are Not. *Unknown.* MeEL

What wonder, Percy, that with jealous rage. To Percy Shelley: On the Degrading Notions of Deity. Leigh Hunt. TW

What wonders now I have to pen, sir. The Female Husband, Who Had Been Married to Another Female for Twenty-one Years. *Unknown.* CoMu

What wondrous life is this I lead! Andrew Marvell. *Fr.* Garden, The ("How vainly men themselves amaze"). BoNaP; CH; ChTr

What Wondrous Love Is This. *At. to* Alex Means. AH, 2 *vers., with music.*

(Wondrous Love.) AmFP

What wondrous pretty things I've seen. Young Master's Account of a Puppet Show. John Marchant. OxBChV

What word have you, interpreters, of men. Of Heaven Considered as a Tomb. Wallace Stevens. PoA; QFR

What Word Spring. Yves Bonnefoy, *tr. fr. French by* Galway Kinnell. RHTwFP

What words are these have fallen from me. Tennyson. *Fr.* In Memoriam A. H. H., XVI. EBEV

What Words Have Passed. Milton. *Fr.* Paradise Lost, *Bk.* IX, *ll.* 1144–1189. TrCP

What work of honour and eternal name. De Guiana, Carmen Epicum. George Chapman. OBSC

What worth to me the seven treasures. Okura. *Fr.* Manyo Shu. Ma (Elegy on the Death of Furuhi.) DL

What would earth do without her blessed boobs. Yes, What? Robert Francis. LCAP

What Would I Do White? June Jordan. NMM

What would I do without this world faceless incurious. Samuel Beckett. NoAM; NOIV

What Would I Give? Christina Rossetti. OPOP; OxBSP

What would it be like. A Sacred Grove. Fran Winant. BrRo

What would it look like if really there were only. A Small Room with Large Windows. Allen Curnow. ATNZ

What would it mean to lose this life. Now It Can Be Told. Philip Levine. VWA

What would our mother say? Distress. Susan Griffin. NPGG

What would this Man? Now upward will he soar. Pope. *Fr.* An Essay on Man, Epistle I. HeIP

What Would You Fight For? D. H. Lawrence. OxBSP

What! would you have the fatal sister lend. For the Dead Gregorians. Ignacio Ramírez, *tr. by* Samuel Beckett. MexPo

What would'st thou have for easement after grief. Comfort of the Fields. Archibald Lampman. CaP

What wourde is that chaungeth not. Sir Thomas Wyatt. AAS

What Yo' Gwine to Do When Yo' Lamp Burn Down? *Unknown.* BPo

"What, you are stepping westward?" Stepping Westward. Wordsworth. CH; EnRP; PoEL-4

What you call me, man? Dopefiends Trip. Hector Angulo. FIA

What you do with time. Mother. Herman de Coninck, *tr. by* James S. Holmes. DuIn

What You Goin' to Do When the Rent Comes 'Round? Andrew B. Sterling. OBAL

What you gwain to do when the meat gives out, my Baby? What Kin' o' Pants Does the Gambler Wear? *Unknown.* AS

What you have heard is true. The Colonel. Carolyn Forché. InPS; OBWP

What You Need. Kathleen Fraser. AmPA

What you see here is a colorful illusion. She Attempts to Refute the Praises That Truth, Which She Calls Passion, Inscribed on a Portrait of the Poet. Sister Juana Inés de la Cruz. BoWoP

"What You See Is Me." Barbara Gibbs. NYBP

What You Should Know to Be a Poet. Gary Snyder. NNaP; PoM

What you think you. The Dream. Robert Creeley. BAP

What you want, is to. Doing Nothing. Dennis Saleh. SoTCo

What Zimmer Would Be. Paul Zimmer. Psk

What'd you get, black boy? Mr. Roosevelt Regrets. Pauli Murray. PoBA

Whate'er Has Been. Sidney Lanier. Son

Whate'er is born of mortal birth. To Tirzah. Blake. *Fr.* Songs of Experience. EnRP; NAEL-2; NOBE; OAEL-2

Whate'er the passion—knowledge, fame, or pelf. Pope. *Fr.* An Essay on Man, Epistle II. TrGrPo
(Human Folly.) FiP

Whate'er thy Countrymen have done. Written in the Beginning of Mezeray's History of France. Matthew Prior. NOBE; PoEL-3

Whate'er we leave to God, God does. Inspiration. Henry David Thoreau. AmPP; AnAmPo; NOBA; OxBA

Whatever brawls disturb the street. Love between Brothers and Sisters. Isaac Watts. FaBoUs

Whatever city or country road. Double Elegy. Michael S. Harper. NoAM

Whatever constitutes. The Act of Love. Robert Creeley. HAP

Whatever good is naturally done. Sonnet: Of Love, in Honor of His Mistress Becchina. Cecco Angiolieri da Siena, *tr. by* Dante Gabriel Rossetti. AWP

Whatever Happened? Philip Larkin. Son

Whatever happens with us, your body. Adrienne Rich. *Fr.* Twenty-one Love Poems, *The Floating Poem, Unnumbered.* GLP; NoAM

Whatever he does, you have to do too. Follow the Leader. Kathleen Fraser. RHPC

Whatever I do, and whatever I say. Aunt Tabitha. Oliver Wendell Holmes. CenHV

Whatever I find if I search will be wrong. The Other. Ruth Fainlight. BrRo

"Whatever is here, it is." Confessions of the Life Artist. Thom Gunn. CMoP

Whatever Is—Is Best. Ella Wheeler Wilcox. BLPA; PWR

Whatever It Is. Jim Simmerman. BLA

Whatever it is, it must have. American Poetry. Louis Simpson. CAPP; MoP; NoAM; NOBA; TAP

Whatever it is, it's a passion. Love in America. Marianne Moore. AiP; GOA

Whatever it is you're missing, whatever. Call Them Back. Chris Petrakos. GOYP

Whatever it was she had so fiercely fought. The Recognition of Eve. Karl Shapiro. *Fr.* Adam and Eve. MoAB

Whatever it was: the grains of the glacier caked in the. Adrienne Rich. *Fr.* Shooting Script, 14. FaBoWP; HCAP

Whatever one toucan can do. Toucannery. Jack Prelutsky. OnUR

Whatever the books may say, or the plausible. December: Of Aphrodite. W. S. Merwin. NePoEA

Whatever they wanted for their sons. Déjà Vu. Shirley Kaufman. LCAP

Whatever we do, whether we light. Dilemma. David Ignatow. VGW

Whatever went wrong, that week, was more than weather. A Hairline Fracture. Amy Clampitt. NoAM

Whatever while the thought comes over me. Dante, *tr. fr. Italian by* Dante Gabriel Rossetti. *Fr.* Vita Nuova, La, XXI. AWP

Whatever You Say Say Nothing. Seamus Heaney. OBWP; OxBC

"Whatever you want is yours." The Lay of the Battle of Tombland. Dunstan Thompson. LiTA

Whatever your eye alights on this morning is yours. Years of Indiscretion. John Ashbery. NOBA

Whatever's lost, it first was won. Elizabeth Barrett Browning. *Fr.* De Profundis. TrPWD

What'll Be the Title? Justin Richardson. FiBHP

What'll the Neighbours Say? Sandra Kerr. AIW

What's a poem? A flat piece of paper. A Poem—Good or Bad—a Thing—with One Attribute—Flat. Melech Ravitch, *tr. by* Ruth Whitman. VWA

What's a toad like? Adman into Toad. Frank Polite. UL

What's an old man like you doing. Golden Age. Mac Hammond. EOEF

What's become of Waring. Waring. Robert Browning. PoEL-5

What's de Use ob Wukin in de Summer Time at All. Maggie Pogue Johnson. CBWP-4

What's filling up the mirror? O, it is not I. The Fat Man in the Mirror. Robert Lowell. PoA

What's going to be the end for both of us—God? Twelve Lines about the Burning Bush. Melech Ravitch, *tr. by* Ruth Whitman. VWA

What's Going to Happen to the Tots? Noel Coward. NBLV

What's Good for the Soul Is Good for Sales. Richard Wilbur. NBLV

What's growing? Will it start. Nothing to Steal. John Ashbery. BLA

What's hallowed ground? Has earth a clod. Hallowed Ground. Thomas Campbell. BLPA

What's Hard. Laurence Lerner. NePoEA-2

What's he that, in yon gilded coach elate. A Remonstrance. John Gerrard. NOEC

What's in a Name? Helen F. More. PAH

What's in a name? What's in a name? Fame. Josephine D. Henderson Heard. CBWP-4

What's in the Cupboard? *Unknown.* CH; ChTr; GBP; OxNR

What's in there? *Unknown.* OxNR

What's life? What's death? Yuzan, *tr. by* Lucien Stryk *and* Takashi Ikemoto. ZPCJ

What's love, when the most is said? When the Most Is Said. "Madeline Bridges." AA

What's Mo' Temptin' to de Palate? Maggie Pogue Johnson. CBWP-4

What's my sweetheart?—A laundress is she. Jeannette. Otto Julius Bierbaum, *tr. by* Jethro Bithell. AWP

What's My Thought Like? Thomas Moore. FaBoEE
(Riddle, A.) FaBoCo

"What's new?"—What's old? what's anything. S. T. Coleridge Dismisses a Caller from Porlock. Gerard Previn Meyer. GoYe

What's Next. Tawfiq Sayigh, *tr. fr. Arabic by* Abdullah al-Udhari. MPAW

What's on this May morning in the hills? Ascension Thursday. Saunders Lewis, *tr. by* Gwyn Morgan. OBWVE

What's sweeter than at the end of a summer's day. Thanksgiving. Kenneth Koch. VGW

What's That? Florence Parry Heide. RHPC

What's that approaching like dust like poverty. Charles Simic. LCAP

What's that cart that nobody sees. Every Day. Norman MacCaig. OBD

What's that red stuff? Blood? Gee. The Last Supper. Stan Rice. NPGG

What's That Smell in the Kitchen? Marge Piercy. NBLV; NIP

"What's that that hirples at my side?" Heriot's Ford. Kipling. PoRA

What's that we see from far? the spring of Day. A Nuptial[l] Song, or Epithalamie [*or* Epithalamy], on Sir Clipseby Crew and His Lady. Robert Herrick. CaPo; JCP; PoEL-3; SeCP; SeCV-1

What's that you're telling me? The Love Charm. *Unknown, tr. by* Jerome Rothenberg. STP

What's the balm. Alan Dugan. CAPP; SM

What's the best thing in the world? The Best. Elizabeth Barrett Browning. OxBSP
(Best Thing in the World, The.) EBVV; NOBVV

What's the brightness of a brow? Evanescence. Harriet Prescott Spofford. AA

What's the good of a wagon. The Gold-tinted Dragon. Karla Kuskin. RAR

What's the good of mourning. Thank You. Geoffrey Grigson. PoPo

What's the greeting for a rajah riding on an elephant? Some Questions to Be Asked of a Rajah, Perhaps by the Associated Press. Preston Newman. FiBHP

"What's the horriblest thing you've seen?" Horrible Things. Roy Fuller. OnUR

What's the Life of a Man? *Unknown.* OBET

What's the matter here? Extinction of Plankton. Ono Tozaburo, *tr. by* Hiroaki Sato. FCEI

What's the news of the day. Mother Goose. OxNR

What's the Plural? *Unknown.* FaBoUs

What's the Railroad to Me? Henry David Thoreau. PoEL-4; TAP (Railroad, The.) FaBV

What's this?/ wearing a long sword. Kyorai, *tr. fr. Japanese by* Burton Watson. *Fr.* Twenty Hokku. FCEI

What's this? A dish for fat lips. The Shape of the Fire. Theodore Roethke. CMoP; LCAP; LiTA; MoAB

What's this dull town to me? Robin Adair. Caroline Keppel. FaBoBe

What's this morn's bright eye to me. Morning Hymn. Joseph Beaumont. TrPWD

What's to be done about the scorching heat after a rain? After Rain. Hsüeh Shao-hui, *tr. by* Irving Lo. WFTU

What's to be done with that ladder. The Ladder. István Vas, *tr. by* Jascha Kessler. FOC

What's up, today, with our lovers? The Lovers Go Fly a Kite. W. D. Snodgrass. NYBP

What's worse than this past century? "Anna Akhmatova," *tr. by* Barbara Einzig. BoWoP

What's wrong with you-zie? Her-zie. Stevie Smith. Mes

What's your name? Pudden Tame. *Unknown.* ChTr; FaBoNo

Whatso men sayn. Men Only Pretend. *Unknown.* MeEL

"Whatsoe'er He bids you—do it!" Leave the Miracle to Him. Thomas H. Allan. BLRP

Whaup o' the Reed, *sel.* Will H. Ogilvie. Blades of Harden, The. GoTS

Whaur are ye gaun. John Hielandman. *Unknown.* GBP

Whaur green abune the banks the links stretch oot. The Planticru. Robert Rendall. OxBS

Whaur yon broken brig hings owre. William Soutar. GoTS; OxBS

Wheat. Gary Gildner. KS

Wheat. Diane Glancy. CRP

Wheat, The. *Unknown, tr. fr. Italian by* Grace Warwick. PFI

Wheat has been quickly harvested, The. Compassion for the Farmers. Li K'ai-hsien, *tr. by* Jonathan Chaves. CoBLCP

Whee hee lo, whee hee. Evening on Howth Head. Eileen Brennan. NeIP

Wheear 'as tha been sin' ah saw thee? Ilkla Moor. *Unknown.* FaBoPP

Wheel, The. Wendell Berry. GeTw

Wheel, The. Aimé Césaire, *tr. fr. French by* Michael Benedikt. POS

Wheel, The. Robert Hayden. BPo

Wheel, The. Edwin Muir. NoAM

Wheel, The. Sully-Prudhomme, *tr. fr. French by* William Dock. ImOP

Wheel, The. W. B. Yeats. GTBS-P

Wheel of Fortune, The. Thom Gunn. OxBC

Wheel of light without beginning. Sunflower. Tuvia Rübner, *tr. by* Bernhard Frank. MHeP

Wheel of the quivering Meat, The. Jack Kerouac. *Fr.* Mexico City Blues, 211. NeAP; PoM

Wheel Revolves, The. Kenneth Rexroth. NoAM

Wheel Turning on the Hub of the Sun. William Pitt Root. MAYP

Wheelbarrow, The. Russell Edson. LCAP

Wheelbarrow. Eleanor Farjeon. FiBHP

Wheelchair Butterfly, The. James Tate. NoAM

Wheeler at Santiago. James Lindsay Gordon. PAH

Wheeler's Brigade at Santiago. Wallace Rice. PAH

Wheels fall innumerably. Yoshioka Minoru, *tr. by* Hiroaki Sato. FCEI

Wheels hurry onward, onward, The. A Cartload of Shoes. Abraham Sutskever, *tr. by* David G. Roskies. VWA

Wheel's inventor, nameless demigod, The. The Wheel. Sully-Prudhomme, *tr. by* William Dock. ImOP

Wheesht, Wheesht. "Hugh MacDiarmid." ErPo; HAP; InPK

Whelp that nipped its mother's dug in turning from her breast, The. The Lion's Cub. Maurice Thompson. AA

When/ Dr./ Edith (Hon. D. Litt. [Leeds], Hon. D. Litt. [Durham]). A Thin Façade for Edith Sitwell. John Malcolm Brinnin. FiBHP; NYBP

When. Dorothy Aldis. RHPC

When. Philip Appleman. BXAP

When/ Water forgets. Fire. Fazil Hüsnü Daglarca. CRP

When/ he wills. Friend. Lilian Moore. ILY

When,/ Halting in front of it, I look. Hitomaro, *tr. fr. Japanese by* Arthur Waley. *Fr.* Shui Shu. AWP

When. Pierre Jean Jouve, *tr. fr. French by* Keith Bosley. RHTwFP

When/ Sir/ Beelzebub. Sir Beelzebub. Dame Edith Sitwell. *Fr.* Façade. BoWoP; FaBoWP; HoPM; MoAB; MoBrPo; OxBTC; PrIm (When Sir Beelzebub.) FaBoMo

When/ my/ grandmother/ died. When My Grandmother Died. Sam Cornish. Psk

When a Beau Goes In. Gavin Ewart. OBWP; OxBTC; WaP

When a brass sun staggers above the sky. Tramp. Richard Hughes. MoBrPo

When a brisk gale against the current blows. John Gay. *Fr.* Rural Sports. FM

When a brown person. Flipochinos. Cyn Zarco. UL

When a casual wind shook it. Absence. Ruth Kim Chun-soo, *tr. by* Koh Chang-soo. ACKP

When a Cat Is Asleep. Karla Kuskin. TDD

When a certain great King, whose initial is G. An Ancient Prophecy. Philip Freneau. PAH

When a clatter came. Sounds of the Day. Norman MacCaig. RB

When a crane cries at the Nine Swamps. *Unknown, tr. by* Arthur Waley. BoS

When a daffadill [*or* daffodil] I see. Divination by a Daffadill [*or* Daffodil]. Robert Herrick. CaPo; OBS; SeCV-1

When a daughter tries suicide. The Risk. Anne Sexton. BoWoP

When a dream is born in you. A Pinch of Salt. Robert Graves. MoBrPo

When a feller hasn't got a cent. Fellowship. *Unknown.* BLPA

When a fellow loves a maiden. La Cucaracha. *Unknown.* AS

When a felon's not engaged in his employment. The Policeman's Lot, A [*or* The]. W. S. Gilbert. *Fr.* The Pirates of Penzance. NOBL; SaC; TrGrPo

When a friend calls to me from the road. A Time to Talk. Robert Frost. ILY

When a gentle wind from the south. *Unknown, tr. fr. Chinese by* Arthur Waley. BoS

When a Girl Looks Down. Kay Smith. CaP; OBCV

When a great tree falls. To Be Answered in Our Next Issue. *Unknown.* RHPC

When a green fox looks. Fox. David Campbell. CBAP

When a helmet becomes God in heaven. Nizar Qabbani, *tr. fr. Arabic by* Diana Der Hovanessian *and* Lena Jayyusi. *Fr.* The Actors, IV. MAP

When a King Asks for a Chieftain's Daughter. Maturai Marutan Ilanakanar, *tr. fr. Tamil by* A. K. Ramanujan. PLW

When a maid is sweet and fair. If a Maid Be Fair. Laura Goodman Salverson. CaP

When a man becomes tired of his life. Song, *Hamlet.* John Poole. BXAP

When a man dies. "Anna Akhmatova," *tr. by* Richard McKane. OBD

When a Man Has Married a Wife. Blake. ErPo; FaBoEE; FF; OAEL-2 (Marriage.) OxBoLi

When a man hath no freedom to fight for at home. Byron. EnRP; FaBoEE; NAEL-2; NBLV; PoLF; TrGrPo (Stanzas: "When a man hath no freedom to fight for at home.") NoP

When a man is in love. Language. Nizar Qabbani, *tr. by* Diana Der Hovanessian *and* Lena Jayyusi. MAP

When a man sleeps, often his dream will break. Hugo von Hofmannsthal, *tr. fr. German by* Michael Hamburger. *Fr.* Death and the Fool. OBD

When a man spends his life on horseback. Cowboy's Favorite. Barney Nelson. CowP

When a Negro comes in question you may watch the Southern press. The Southern Press. Lizelia Augusta Jenkins Moorer. CBWP-3

When a new world is born, the old. Rattle. Peter Blue Cloud. HATNAP

When a person writes. Alfred Kolleritsch, *tr. by* Beth Bjorklund. CoAuP

When a sighing begins. Chansons d'Automne. Paul Verlaine, *tr. by* Arthur Symons. AWP

When a song goes wrong behind. The Damaged Aria. Pamela Stewart. NAmP

When a statue turns its real gaze. After Plotinus. William Stafford. PoA

When a thousand birds. *Unknown, tr. fr. Japanese by* Geoffrey Bownas *and* Anthony Thwaite. *Fr.* Kokin Shu. PeBJV

When a tree falls in a forest. Bedtime Story. Charles Simic. AnAn

When a twister a-twisting will twist him a twist. John Wallis. FaBoNo, 1 *st.;* OxNR, 1 *st.*
  (Twister Twisting Twine.)' ChTr, 3 *sts.*
When a wax candle burns down, ashes are left behind. Cheng Hsieh, *tr. fr. Chinese by* Jonathan Chaves. *Fr.* Mourning for My Son Jun-erh. CoBLCP
When a Woman Blue. *Unknown.* AS
When a woman cannot open her heart. Inscape. Susan Litwack. VWA
When Abraham Lincoln was shoveled into the tombs. Cool Tombs. Carl Sandburg. AmPP; BLPL; CMoP; HAP; HeIP; MoAB; MoAmPo; MoP; NAAL-2; NoAM; NOBA; OPP; OxBSP; PoLF; TAP; TrGrPo
When Adam Day by Day. A. E. Housman. FiBHP
  (Occasional Poem.) NOBL
When Adam delf [*or* dalf] and Eve span. The Pointless Pride of Man. *Unknown.* MeEL
  (Peasant's Song, The.) FaBoPV, *diff. vers.*
When Adam Delved. *Unknown.* SaC
When Adam found his rib was gone. The Lady's-Maid 's Song. John Hollander. ErPo; LiTM; NePoEA; TW; TwCP
When Adam Was First Created. *Unknown.* OBET
When, after holing up for winter, the spring comes. Princess Nukada. *Fr.* Manyo Shu. FCEI
When, after storms that woodlands rue. A Requiem for Soldiers Lost in Ocean Transports. Herman Melville. PoEL-5
When age hath made me what I am not now. Upon His Picture. Thomas Randolph. MePo; NOBE
When alarm bells rang. Where Is the Guard? Ahmad al-Safi al-Najafi, *tr. by* Sharif Elmusa *and* Thomas G. Ezzy. MAP
When Alcuin taught the sons of Charlemagne. The Student's Tale. Longfellow. *Fr.* Tales of a Wayside Inn, *pt.* III. AmPP
When Alexander Pope. Edmund Clerihew Bentley. *Fr.* Clerihews. FiBHP
When Alexander Pope strolled in the city. Mr. Pope. Allen Tate. MoAB; NoAM; NOBA; TwCP; VGW
When Alice called to say. Cardinals in the Ice Age. John Engels. BLA
When all/ My waterfall. Her Time. Theodore Roethke. NAAL-2
When all birds else do of their music fail. Money Makes the Mirth. Robert Herrick. CaPo
When all has passed. Genesis. Lotte Kramer. VWA
When all is done and said, in the end thus shall you find. Of a Contented Mind. Lord Thomas Vaux. EIL
  (Content.) OBSC; QFR
When all is over and you march for home. Spoils. Robert Graves. HAP; Son; WeW
  (Spoils of Love, The.) NYBP
When all is still within these walls. The Man's Prayer. T. A. Daly. TrPWD
When All My Five and Country Senses See. Dylan Thomas. MoAB; MoBrPo; NoAM; PoA; SeCePo; Son
When all my words were said. Enough. Digby Mackworth Dolben. EBVV
When all night long a chap remains. The Contemplative Sentry. W. S. Gilbert. *Fr.* Iolanthe. FiBHP
When all of us wore smaller shoes. Ancient Lights. Austin Clarke. BIrV; CMoP; IPY
When all our hopes are sown on stony ground. A Note of Humility. Arna Bontemps. PoNe
When all the days are hot and long. Swimming. Clinton Scollard. FaPON
When all the other leaves are gone. Buds. Elizabeth Jane Coatsworth. TSS
When all the others were away at Mass. Seamus Heaney. *Fr.* Clearances, III. CIP
When all the witches were haled to the stake and burned. King Duffus. Sylvia Townsend Warner. FaBoWP
When All the World Is Full of Snow. N. M. Bodecker. RHPC
When all the world is young, lad. Young and Old. Charles Kingsley. *Fr.* The Water Babies. BLPL; EBEV; FaBoBe; FaFP; FaPoR; OxBChV; PoLF
  (When All the World Is Young.) BoTP
When All the World's Asleep. Anita E. Posey. RAR
When all this Alt doth pass from age to age. Fulke Greville. *Fr.* Caelica, LXIX. EBEV
"When all this is over," said the swineherd. Swineherd. Eiléan Ni Chuilleanáin. BIrV; CIP; FaBoWP; WPOW
When all was quiet and serene, a storm broke out at the dead. A Riot. Mrs. Henry Linden. CBWP-4
When all within is dark. From Thee to Thee. Solomon ibn Gabirol, *tr. by* Israel Abrahams. EaLo; TrJP
When All's Said and Done. Mihály Ladányi, *tr. fr. Hungarian by* Kenneth McRobbie. MHuP

When Alma Gluck. Conversations from Childhood: the Victrola. Joseph Langland. SM
When Almonds Bloom. Milicent Washburn Shinn. AA
When Alysandyr Our King Was Dede. *Unknown. See* Death of Alexander, The.
When Americans say a man. Language Lesson, 1976. Heather McHugh. MAYP
When an archer is shooting for nothing. The Need to Win. Thomas Merton. ASP
When an elf is as old as a year and a minute. The Seven Ages of Elf-hood. Rachel Lyman Field. RHPC
When and where did you first. Sexual Privacy of Women on Welfare. Pinkie Gordon Lane. BISi
When Angels Came to Zimmer. Paul Zimmer. MOWH
When any mortal (even the most odd). E. E. Cummings. FaBoEE
When April & dew brings primroses here. An Anecdote of Love. John Clare. NOBVV
When April rains make flowers bloom. The Shamrock. Maurice Francis Egan. AA
When April with Its Sweet Showers. Chaucer. *See* Canterbury Tales, The: Prologue.
When are the children all happy and gay? Christmas Times. Maggie Pogue Johnson. CBWP-4
When arms and numbers both have failed. Aguinaldo. Bertrand Shadwell. PAH
When Armstrong, stalwart Anglo-Saxon, put his boot. White Power Poem. Michael Bishop. BWV
When Arthur was homeless and broke. *Unknown.* PeHV
When as I do record. *Unknown.* EBEV
When as if sacrificed the lamb. When. Pierre Jean Jouve, *tr. by* Keith Bosley. RHTwFP
When as man's life, the light of human lust. *See* Whenas man's life, the light of human lust.
When as the chill charocco blows. Thomas Bonham. *See* In Praise of Ale.
When as the nightingales sang Pluto's matins. *See* Whenas the nightingales sang Pluto's matins.
When as the sheriff of Nottingham. Robin Hood and the Golden Arrow. *Unknown.* ESPB
When asked, I used to say. What Zimmer Would Be. Paul Zimmer. Psk
When at break of day at a riverside. Piano and Drums. Gabriel Okara. NIP; PBA; TTY
When at last he was well enough to take the sun. A Leg in a Plaster Cast. Muriel Rukeyser. MoAmPo
When, at our Sovereign's command. Yakamochi. *Fr.* Manyo Shu. Ma
When Aunt Wessie played she. Concert. Robert Morgan. TDD
When Aurelia First I Courted. *Unknown.* OBS
When Autumn bleak and sunburnt do appear. Autumn. Thomas Chatterton. *Fr.* Aella; a Tragycal Enterlude. Mes
When autumn comes we shall meet. *Unknown. Fr.* Manyo Shu. Ma
When autumn is here. *Unknown. Fr.* Manyo Shu. PeBJV
When autumn rains flatten sycamore leaves. Rain. Gary Soto. *Fr.* The Elements of San Joaquin. NoAM
When Autumn smiles, all beauteous in decay. William Somervile. *Fr.* Field Sports. FM
When autumn wounds the bough. Autumnal Spring Song. Vassar Miller. NePoEA
When awful darkness and silence reign. The Dong with a Luminous Nose. Edward Lear. AmMo; CenHV; ChTr; EBVV; FaBoCo; FaBoNo; FaBV; NOBVV; PoEL-5; WiR
When babe hit. Babe & Lou. Franz Douskey. ASP
When baby woke in woolly spread. Where Is My Butterfly Net? David McCord. FiBHP
When Baby's cries grew hard to bear. L'Enfant Glacé. Harry Graham. FaBoCo; NBLV
When Banners Are Waving. *Unknown.* GN
When beauty breaks and falls asunder. Juan's Song. Louise Bogan. NYBP
When beechen buds begin to swell. The Yellow Violet. Bryant. BLPL; NAAL-1; PoLF; TAP
When before those eyes, my life and light. Gaspara Stampa, *tr. by* J. Vitiello. BoWoP
When Bibo thought fit from the world to retreat. Matthew Prior. FaBoEE
When Bill was a lad he was terribly bad. Those Two Boys. Franklin Pierce Adams. FiBHP; TrJP
When birds. Spring Morning. Lin Huan-ch'ang, *tr. by* Dominic Cheung. IFON
When birds break open the sky, a smell of snow. Winter Burn. Roberta Hill. VoR

When Black People Are. A. B. Spellman. BPo; CNA; PoBA
When black snails cross your path. *Unknown*. FaBoUs
When blam! my father's gun began the dash. Birth Report. X. J. Kennedy. *Fr.* Snapshots. NAs
When bold Leander sought his distant fair. On Leander's Swimming over the Hellespont to Hero. Thomas Warton the Younger, *after* Martial. FaBoEE
When bored by the drone of the wedlocked pair. Sacred and Profane Love, or, There's Nothing New Under the Moon Either. Peter De Vries. NBLV
When both hands of the town clock stood at twelve. Village Noon; Mid-Day Bells. Merrill Moore. MoAmPo
When both lights you see ahead. Useful for Avoiding Collisions at Sea. *Unknown*. FaBoUs
When boyhood's fire was in my blood. A Nation Once Again. Thomas Davis. NOIV
When brave Van Rensselaer cross'd the stream. The Battle of Queenstown. William Banker, Jr.. PAH
When breezes are soft and skies are fair. Green River. Bryant. AnAmPo; NOBA; OxBA
When bright Orion glitters in the skies. The Washerwoman. Mary Collier. *Fr.* The Woman's Labour; an Epistle to Mr. Stephen Duck. NOEC
When Britain first, at heaven's command. Rule, Britannia! James Thomson *and* David Mallet. *Fr.* Alfred, A Masque, II, v. FaPoR; GTBS; GTBS-P; NOEC; OBWP; WBLP
(Ode: Rule, Britannia!) NAEL-1
When Britain *really* ruled the waves. The House of Lords. W. S. Gilbert. *Fr.* Iolanthe. NAEL-2; TrGrPo
When Britain, with envy and malice inflamed. Capture of Little York. *Unknown*. PAH
When British troops first landed here. Cornwallis's Surrender. *Unknown*. PAH
When brothers build a city. Malcolm, a Thousandth Poem. Conrad Kent Rivers. CNA
When Brothers Forget. Jill Witherspoon Boyer. CNA
When Bunyan swung his whopping axe. Folk Tune. Richard Wilbur. AmFN
When Burnet perceived that the beautiful dames. An Excellent New Ballad, Called the Brawny Bishop's Complaint. Arthur Mainwaring. APAS
When by thy scorn, O murd'ress[e] [*or* murderess], I am dead. The Apparition. John Donne. EnLoPo; GBL; HeIP; MePo; NAEL-1; NAWM-1; NOBE; NOBL; OAEL-1; OBD; OBEV; OBS; PoE; SCV; SeCP; SeCV-1
When by Zeus relenting the mandate was revoked. Phoebus with Admetus. George Meredith. NOBE; OBEV
When calm is the night, and the stars shine bright. Sleighing Song. John Shaw. AA
When can one be sure. The Spring Moon Concealed. Tamemasa, *tr. by* Steven D. Carter. WFTW
When Carolina's hope grew pale. Sumter's Band. J. W. Simmons. PAH
When cats run home and light is come. The Owl. Tennyson. BoTP; FaBoCh; FaPON; GoJo; MoShBr
(Song—the Owl.) FaPON; GoJo; PBBP
(When Cats Run Home.) CH
When chapman [*or* chapmen] billies leave the street. Tam o' Shanter. Burns. BeLS; EnRP; GoTS; NAEL-2; NoP; OAEL-1; OBNV; OxBS; SeCePo; TrGrPo, *sl. abr.*
When children, blundering on their fathers' guns. Prayer for Light. Stanton A. Coblentz. TrPWD
When Christ was born in Bethlehem. *Unknown, tr. by* Longfellow. OHIP
When Christ was born in Bethlehem. Ballad of the Epiphany. Charles Dalmon. OnMSP
When civil dudgeon first grew high. Samuel Butler. *See* Hudibras: When civil fury first grew high.
When civil fury first grew high. Samuel Butler. *Fr.* Hudibras, I, 1. EBEV; SeCV-2
(Presbyterian Knight.) NOBE
("When civil dudgeon first grew high.") OAEL-1
When clear October suns unfold. Mallee in October. Flexmore Hudson. PoAu-2
When Clenched Teeth Grate. Dovid Hofshteyn, *tr. fr. Yiddish by* Leonard Wolf. PeBMYV
When Cleomira disbelieves. The Force of Love. Samuel Jones. NOEC
When clerks and navvies fondle. Louis MacNeice. *Fr.* Trilogy for X, I. ErPo
(For X.) BoLoP; EnLoPo

When clouds appear like rocks and towers. *Unknown*. *Fr.* Weather Wisdom [*or* Weather Wise]. FaBoUs; OxNR
When clouds inch. The Horizon Is Definitely Speaking. Diana Chang. BrSi
When Clumsy harks the gladsome ting-a-lings. Gjertrud Schnackenberg. *Fr.* Two Tales of Clumsy, I. NoAM
When cockle shells turn silver bells. Waly, Waly. *Unknown*. AmFP (Waillie, waillie!) AS
When, Coelia, must my old day set. To Coelia. Charles Cotton. OBEV
When cold, I huddle up, foetal, cross/ arms. Christmas Eve. A. R. Ammons. NAs
When coldness wraps this suffering clay. The Immortal Mind. Byron. WGRP
When coltsfoot withers and begins to wear. Cuckoos. Andrew Young. ChTr
When consummate the day hangs before you. Three Variations. Boris Pasternak, *tr. by* Babette Deutsch. TrJP
When country hills are soft with snow. Les Chasse-Neige. Ralph A. Lewin. FiBHP
When cowherds begin. Ito Sachio, *tr. by* Geoffrey Bownas *and* Anthony Thwaite. PeBJV
When crazy Frankenstein pulled down the switch. Frankenstein Gets His Man. Frank Carr. AmMo
When cripples throw their crutches into the air. Cripples. Nina Cassian, *tr. by* Herbert Kuhner. VWA
When, cruel fair one, I am slain. The Tombe. Thomas Stanley. OBS
When Daddy Cums from Wuk. Maggie Pogue Johnson. CBWP-4
When daffodils begin to peer. Shakespeare. *Fr.* The Winter's Tale, IV, ii. ChTr; EIL; FaBoBe; FaBoCh; NoP; OxBSP; PrIm
(Autolycus Sings.) NOBE
(Autolycus's Song ("When daffodils begin to peer").) NOBE; OAEL-1; OBSC
(Pedlar's Song, The.) NBLV; OxBoLi
(Song: "When daffodils begin to peer.") FiP; PoEL-2
When Daisies Pied [and Violets Blue]. Shakespeare. *Fr.* Love's Labour's Lost, V, ii. FF; InPK; NAEL-1; NOBE; NoP; PoRA; PrIm ("Now daisies pied, and violets blue.") BoTP
(Song: "When daisies pied and violets blue.") FiP; PBBP; PoEL-2
(Spring.) EIL; HAP; HeIP; NBLV; NIP; OAEL-1; OBEV; PoEL-2; SeCePo; TEP; TrGrPo; UnPo
(Ver.) OBSC
When Daniel Boone goes by, at night. Daniel Boone. Stephen Vincent Benét. AmFN; GOA
When Daphne's lover here first wore the bays. To the River Isca. Henry Vaughan. FaBoPP
When Darby saw the setting sun. Darby and Joan. St. John Honeywood. AA
When darkness comes to city streets. Mister Alley Cat. John McGowan. CRH
When darkness crept and grew. Under the Hill. Richard Eberhart. PoA
When darkness prevail'd and aloud on the air. The Tomb of the Brave. Joseph Hutton. PAH
When darkness settles itself. Winter Solstice. Peter Blue Cloud. *Fr.* Within the Seasons. HATNAP
When day breaks, must I go over the mountain ridge again. Teika, *tr. fr. Japanese by* Hiroaki Sato. *Fr.* A Compendium of Good Tanka. FCEI
When day declining sheds a milder gleam. The Naturalist's Summer-Evening Walk. Gilbert White. NOEC; PBBP
When day is over and the sun hides behind the earth. An Evening with a Black-and-White Feathered Bird. Akhtar-ul-Iman, *tr. by* Mahmood Jamal. PBMUP
When daylight was yet sleeping under the billow. Ill Omens. Thomas Moore. PoEL-4
When de Co'n Pone's Hot. Paul Laurence Dunbar. AnAmPo; BANP
When de Saints Go Ma'chin' Home. Sterling Allen Brown. AmNP
When, dearest, I but think on [*or* of] thee. *At. to* Sir John Suckling *and* to Owen Feltham. MePo
(Song: "When dearest, I but think on [*or* of] thee.") MePo
(When, Dearest, I but Think on [*or* of] Thee.) JCP; OBEV; OBS
When Death Comes. *Unknown*. MeEL
When Death comes near to grimly claim his toll. May God Give Strength. Peter Van Wynen. BLRP
When death, shall part us from these kids. A Dialogue between Thyrsis and Dorinda. Andrew Marvell. SeCP
When Death to Either Shall Come. Robert Bridges. OBEV
When descends on the Atlantic. Seaweed. Longfellow. MOS; OxBA; TAP

When despair for the world grows in me. The Peace of Wild Things. Wendell Berry. GeTw; HeIP; MT; NIP; NU; PCP; VGW
When Dey 'Listed Colored Soldiers. Paul Laurence Dunbar. BPo
When Diamonds, Nibbling in My Ears. W. H. Davies. BrPo
When Did the World Begin. Robert Clairmont. GrPl
When did these gray ones. Duel in the Park. Lisa Grenelle. GoYe
When did you start your tricks. The Mosquito. D. H. Lawrence. RB (Mosquito Knows, The.) FaBoEE; OxBTC
When Dido found Aeneas would not come. A Note on the Latin Gerunds. Richard Porson. FaBoCo; FaBoEE (On the Latin Gerunds.) FaBoUs
When do I see thee most, belovèd one? Lovesight. Dante Gabriel Rossetti. Fr. The House of Life, IV. EBVV; GTBS-P; NAEL-2; OBNC; TrGrPo
When Dobbin and Robin, unharnessed from the plow. The Circus-Postered Barn. Elizabeth J. Coatsworth. MoAmPo
When does it end? When does a new poem. Peter Levi. TOF
When does the soul leave the body? For My Mother. Ellen Bryant Voigt. NIP
When Doris Danced. Richard Eberhart. CMoP; ErPo
When Dorothy and I took tea, we sat upon the floor. Small and Early. Tudor Jenks. AA
When down the crowded aisle my wandering eyes. Eyeing the Eyes of One's Mistress. Ebenezer Jones. NOBVV
When dreaming [or foolish] kings, at odds with swift-paced time. Washington. Harriet Monroe. Fr. Commemoration Ode. AA; FaBoBe (Two Heroes.) OHIP
When dreams like stars collide. Lesson for Dreamers. Paul B. Janeczko. PCP
When Dublin is a mist the quays are lost. Working the Rain Shift at Flanagan's. Gibbons Ruark. MAYP
When Earth slept, like a pig in the sun. Ballad of the Electric Eel. Wayne Brown. PBCV
When Earth's last picture is painted, and the tubes are twisted and dried. Kipling. FaFP; LiTB; OHFP; PWR; WGRP (Envoi, L': "When Earth's last picture is painted, and the tubes are twisted and dried.") LiTB
When Eastern lovers feed the fun'ral fire. Pope. Fr. Three Epitaphs on John Hewet and Sarah Drew, II. NIP
When e'er we enter life's open field. Ambition. Maggie Pogue Johnson. CBWP-4
When Egypt said, "Exterminate." Retribution. Lizelia Augusta Jenkins Moorer. CBWP-3
When England's multitudes observed with frowns. Bungaloid Growth. Colin Ellis. FaBoEE
When Eubolus the Greek learned. Dionysus. Irving Layton. ErPo
When Euclid started out to measure Hades. Hades and Euclid. Harry Martinson, tr. by Robert Bly. BWV
When Eve did with the snake dispute. The Woman's Wish. Matthew Prior. FaBoEE
When Eve first saw the glistering day. Song with Words. James Agee. MoAmPo
When Eve upon the first of men. A Reflection. Thomas Hood. FaBoEE
When even a turning to memory. Against Sadness. Natan Zach, tr. by Warren Bargad and Stanley F. Chyet. IP
When Even Cometh On. Lucy Evangeline Tilley. AA
When evenen sheades o' trees do hide. The Vaices That Be Gone. William Barnes. NOBVV
When evening comes. Yakamochi. Fr. Manyo Shu. AWP, tr. by Arthur Waley; FCEI, tr. by Burton Watson; PeBJV, tr. by Geoffrey Bownas and Anthony Thwaite.
When evening comes, plovers fly. Kito, tr. fr. Japanese by Hiroaki Sato. Fr. Twenty-four Hokku. FCEI
When evening falls, the autumn wind rustles. Teika, tr. fr. Japanese by Hiroaki Sato. Fr. A Compendium of Good Tanka. FCEI
When evening mist. Unknown. Fr. Manyo Shu. FCEI
When every one to pleasing pastime hies. Pamphilia to Amphilanthus. Mary Sidney Wroth, Countess of Montgomery. Fr. Urania. WPE
  "Am I thus conquered? have I lost the powers." NAEL-1
  "False hope which feeds but to destroy, and spill." NAEL-1
When face to face we stand. Paradox. Angelina Weld Grimké. CDC
When faces called flowers float out of the ground. Edward Estlin Cummings. BoNaP; PrIm
When Faction, in league with the treacherous Gaul. The Lords of the Main. Joseph Stansbury. PAH
When fair Columbia was a child. The Daughter's Rebellion. Francis Hopkinson. PAH

When faith and love which parted from thee never. Sonnet: On the Religious Memorie of Mrs. Catherine Thomason My Christian Freind Deceas'd Decem. 1646. Milton. OBS
When faith in God goes, man, the thinker, loses his greatest thought. Have You Lost Faith? Unknown. WBLP
"When far-spent night persuades each mortal eye." Sir Philip Sidney. Fr. Astrophel and Stella, XCIX. OBSC; PoE; Son
When Father Came Home for Lunch. Jim Mitsui. BrSi
When Father Carves the Duck. Ernest Vincent Wright. BLPL; FaBV; FaFP; NTCP; PoLF
When Father goes to town with me to buy my Sunday hat. When Polly Buys a Hat. E. Hill. BoTP
When father takes his spade to dig. The Robin. Laurence Alma-Tadema. BoTP
When fierce Pizarro's legions flew. The Revenge of America. Joseph Warton. OBTV
When First. Edward Thomas. NoAM
When first Apollo got my brain with childe. The Author to His Book. George Alsop. SCAP
When first, descending from the moorlands. An Extempore Effusion [upon the Death of James Hogg]. Wordsworth. EBEV; FaBoRV; FiP; NOBE; NoP; OAEL-2; SCV (Ode: "When first, descending from the moorlands.") NAEL-2
When first, fair mistress, I did see your face. To B. C. Sir John Suckling. CaPo
When first from sea I landed I had a roving mind. The Pride of Kildare. Unknown. OBET
When first I came here I had hope. When First. Edward Thomas. NoAM
When first I came to Louisville, some pleasure for to find. The Lily of the West. Unknown. AmFP
When first I ended, then I first began. Michael Drayton. Fr. Idea's Mirrour, L (also given as LXII in Idea). TrGrPo
When first I landed in Liverpool I went upon the spree. Off to Sea Once More. Unknown. OxBSS
When first I looked into thy glorious eyes. Sarah Helen Whitman. Fr. Sonnets from the Series Relating to Edgar Allan Poe, II. AA
When First I Saw Her. George Edward Woodberry. Fr. Wild Eden, V. AA
When first I saw our banner wave. Astraea at the Capitol. Whittier. PAH
When first I took to cutlass, blunderbuss and gun. The Ballad of O'Bruadir. Frederick Robert Higgins. OBMV
When first I walked here I hobbled. The Seekonk Woods. Galway Kinnell. NoAM
When first I was courtin' sweet Rosie O'Grady. Irish Song (Rosie O'Grady). Noel Coward. NBLV
When first I went a waggoner. The Jolly Waggoner. Unknown. OBET
When first in this country a stranger. The Green Mossy Banks of the Lee. Unknown. OBET
When first mine eyes did view and mark. Sir Thomas Wyatt. SiPS
When first mine infant-ear. Christendom. Thomas Traherne. PoEL-2
When first my lines [or verse] of heav'nly [or heavenly] joy[e]s made mention. Jordan. George Herbert. MePo; NAEL-1; OAEL-1; OBS; OBWVE; PPP; SeCP
When first on board of a man-of-war. The Jolly Sailor's True Description of a Man-of-War. Unknown. OxBSS
When first the busy, clumsy tongue is stilled. Supersensual. Evelyn Underhill. WGRP
When first the college rolls receive his name. Samuel Johnson. Fr. Vanity of Human Wishes, The: The Tenth Satire of Juvenal Imitated. OBSV (Scholar's Life, The.) NOBE; SeCePo
When first the eye this forest sees. Andrew Marvell. Fr. Upon Appleton House, to My Lord Fairfax. PBBP
When first the fiery-mantled sun. Ode to Winter. Thomas Campbell. GTBS; GTBS-P
When first the magick of thine eye. The Vow-Breaker. Henry King. OBS
When first the post arrived at my tent. King Henry to Rosamond. Michael Drayton. Fr. England's Heroical Epistles. OBSC
When first the year, I heard the cuckoo sing. John Gay. Fr. The Shepherd's Week: Thursday; or, The Spell. PBBP
When first thou didst entice to thee my heart. Affliction ("When first thou didst entice to thee my heart"). George Herbert. JCP; LiTB; MeLP; MePo; NAEL-1; NOBE; NoP; OBS; SeCP
When first thou on me, Lord, wrought'st thy sweet print. The Ebb and Flow. Edward Taylor. AmPP; SCAP

When first we hear the shy-come nightingales. Early Nightingale. John Clare. PBBP

When first we met we did not guess. Robert Bridges. BrPo; OxBSP

When first you learn to read a clock. Clock. Harold Monro. BrPo

When first you sang a song to me. Your Songs. Gwendolyn B. Bennett. CDC

When first your glory shone upon my face. Commemoration. Claude McKay. BANP

When fishes flew and forests walked. The Donkey. G. K. Chesterton. ACP; FaBV; FaPoR; FPL; InPK; MoBrPo; OBEV; PoLF; RB; WGRP

When fishes set umbrellas up. Christina Rossetti. Fr. Sing-Song. FM

When fivepence a solid meal cannot supply. The Volunteer. Unknown. NOEC

When flighting time is on, I go. The Birdcatcher. Ralph Hodgson. MoBrPo

When Flora Had Ourfret the Firth. Unknown. NoP
(Four May Poems.) OxBS
(Quhen Flora Had O'erfret the Firth.) OBEV

When fog come creepin' over Beccles. Molly Fitton. BXAP

When for eternal worlds we steer. Vain World Adieu. Unknown. AmFP

When for school o'er Little Field with its brook and wooden brig. John Clare. Fr. Remembrances. SaC

When for the thorns with which I long, too long. The Coronet. Andrew Marvell. MeLP; MePo; NAEL-1; NOCV; NoP; OBS; PoE; SeCV-1; TOF

When forehead full of torments hot and red. Chercheuses de Poux, Les. Rimbaud, tr. fr. French by T. Sturge Moore. Fr. Illuminations. AWP

When formed our band, we are all well manned. California. Unknown. AS

When fortune's blind goddess had shied my abode. Dick Turpin and Black Bess. Unknown. AmFP

When Fortune's shield protects thee, then beware. Fortune's Treachery. Judah Halevi, tr. by Solomon Solis-Cohen. TrJP

"When forty winters shall besiege thy brow." Shakespeare. Fr. Sonnets, II. BLPL; FF; LiTB; OBSC; Son; TEP

When foxes eat the last gold grape. Escape. Elinor Wylie. LiTA; MoAmPo

When Francis preached love to the birds. Saint Francis and the Birds. Seamus Heaney. TIRV

When Francus comes to solace with his whore. In Francum. Sir John Davies. FaBoEE

When Freedom, dressed in bloodstained vest. Ode to Liberty. Thomas Chatterton. Fr. Goddwyn. TrGrPo

When Freedom, fair Freedom, her banner display'd. Truxton's Victory. Unknown. PAH

When Freedom, from her mountain height. The American Flag. Joseph Rodman Drake. AA; AnAmPo; FaBoBe; FaFP; GN; OPP; PAH; WBLP

When frequent rains, and gentle show'rs descend. Nathaniel Weekes. Fr. Barbados. PBCV

When Friday nights are lucky, you. Irving Wexler. Fr. Elegy for My Father. DiL

When Friendship or Love our sympathies move. The Tear. Byron. Par

When from afar these mountain tops I view. The Sonnet of the Mountain. Mellin de Saint-Gelais, tr. by Austin Dobson. AWP

When from dark error's subjugation. Nikolai Alekseyevich Nekrasov, tr. fr. Russian by Juliet Soskice. Fr. A Propos of the Wet Snow. NAWM-2

When from my fumbling hand the tired pen falls. The Scribe's Prayer. Robert W. Service. TrPWD

When from the blossoms of the noiseful day. To My Friend. Francis Thompson. PoA

When from the Calyx-Canopy of Night. Freda Laughton. NeIP

When from the gates of Paradise fair Eve. The Vision of Eve. Henrietta Cordelia Ray. CBWP-3

When from the gloom of earth we see the sky. The Void Between. John Lancaster Spalding. Fr. God and the Soul. AA

When from the hush of this cool wood. The Cell. G. Rostrevor Hamilton. TrPWD

When from the pallid sky the sun descends. Winter ("When from the pallid sky the sun descends"). James Thomson. Fr. The Seasons: Winter. OAEL-1; OxBS

When, from the spring, the stream. Jaufré Rudel, tr. by Paul Blackburn. Pro

When, from the tower whence I derive love's heaven. Sonnet. Unknown. Fr. Zepheria. ElL

When from the Vallais we had turned. Wordsworth. Fr. The Prelude [or, Growth of a Poet's Mind]: Cambridge and the Alps. TOF

When from the vaulted wonder of the sky. Faith's Vista. Henry Abbey. AA

When furrowed fields of shaded brown. The Canadian Rossignol. Edward William Thomson. CaP

When gadding snow makes hill-sides white. Winter. Charles Mair. OBCV

When Gaffer be dead for a month or more. Martin Fagg. BXAP

When gardens shone with flowery pride. On a Little Boy's Endeavouring to Catch a Snake. Thomas Foxton. OxBChV

When Gauguin was visiting Fiji. Victor Gray. NOBL

"When geometric diagrams and digits." "Novalis," tr. by Robert Bly. NU

When George the King would punish folk. How We Became a Nation. Harriet Prescott Spofford. PAH

When George the Third was reigning a hundred years ago. A Ballad for a Boy. William Johnson Cory. FaPoR; OxBChV
(Two Captains, The.) FaPoR

When George's Grandmamma was told. George. Hilaire Belloc. FiBHP

When Georges Seurat. Lila Zeiger. SoTCo

When getting my nose in a book. A Study of Reading Habits. Philip Larkin. InPK; NOBL; PoPo; PPP; SoSe; TW

When God at first made Man. The Pulley. George Herbert. AWP; EaLo; GTBS; GTBS-P; HAP; HeIP; InPK; InPS; LiTB; MePo; Mes; NAEL-1; NOBE; NOCV; NoP; OAEL-1; OBEV; OBS; PPP; PrIm; SeCP; SeCV-1; TEP; TrGrPo
(Gifts of God, The.) GTBS; GTBS-P

When God Descends with Men to Dwell. Hosea Ballou I. AH

When God, disgusted with man. Crow Blacker than Ever. Ted Hughes. TEP

When God First Said. Natan Zach, tr. fr. Hebrew by Peter Everwine and Shula Starkman. VWA

When God gave you to me. Nizar Qabbani, tr. by Lena Jayyusi and W. S. Merwin. MAP

When God had finished Master Messerin. Sonnet: Of the Making of Master Messerin. Rustico di Filippo, tr. by Dante Gabriel Rossetti. AWP; PFI

When God in the Bible makes a promise. Like Sand. Natan Zach, tr. by Warren Bargad and Stanley F. Chyet. IP

When God in the Bible wants to promise. As Sand. Natan Zach. VWA, tr. by Jon Silkin

When God Lets My Body Be. E. E. Cummings. MoAB; MoAmPo; NOBA

When God made this place. Soliloquies. Denis Glover. Fr. Arawata Bill. ATNZ

When God makes a great Man he intends all others to crush him. Arthur Hugh Clough. Fr. Amours de Voyage, Canto II, early variant. OBSV

When God scooped up a handful of dust. They Ask: Is God, Too, Lonely. Carl Sandburg. ILY

When God was learning to draw the human face. Two Masks Unearthed in Bulgaria. William Meredith. EyDe

When God was making the world. The World in Making. Sir Gilbert Parker. CaP

When gods had framed the sweet of women's face. Love and Jealousy. Robert Greene. ElL

When God's holy law is read out. Unity. Jakov de Haan, tr. by David Soetendorp. VWA

When God's parachute failed. Religion Back Home. William Stafford. OBAL

When gold was first discovered at Coloma, near the hill. The National Miner. Unknown. AmFP

When good King Arthur ruled this land. Mother Goose. FaBoNo; NA; OxNR

When good St. David, as old writs record. In Honour of St. David's Day. Unknown. OBWVE

When Goody O'Grumpity baked a cake. Goody O'Grumpity. Carol Ryrie Brink. FaPON

When gooseberries grow on the stem of a daisy. To Mollidusta. James Robinson Planché. NA

When Grandmamma fell off the boat. Indifference. "Harry Graham." NBLV

When Graphicus sat by the baths. Strato. PeHV

When griping grief the heart doth wound. Music's Silver Sound. Shakespeare. Fr. Romeo and Juliet, IV, v. GN

When groping farms are lanterned up. A Country God. Edmund Blunden. MoBrPo

When Gwen heard at last. In Memoriam. W. J. Gruffydd, tr. by R. Gerallt Jones. OBWVE

When, hardly moving, you decorate night's hush. The Waters of Life. Humbert Wolfe. MoBrPo

When harvest is done all thing placed and set. Thomas Tusser. *Fr. A Hundreth Good Poyntes of Husbandry.* FaBoUs

When have I last looked on. Lines Written in Dejection. W. B. Yeats. NAs

When, having carefully put on. Songs Exchanged between Prince Okuninushi and Princess Nunakawa ("When, having carefully put on"). *Unknown, tr. fr. Japanese by* Hiroaki Sato. *Fr.* The Kojiki. FCEI

When, having watched for a long time the trees. Grove and Building. Edgar Bowers. NePoEA

When he bought the old Tompkins place. The Climb Up. Yisroel-Yankev Schwartz, *tr. fr. Yiddish by* Seymour Levitan. *Fr.* Kentucky. PeBMYV

When he breathed his last breath it was he. The Moment of My Father's Death. Sharon Olds. ER

When he brings home a whale. Naughty Boy. Robert Creeley. HeIP; NoAM; NOBA

When he built the Magic Tower. *Unknown, tr. by* Arthur Waley. BoS

When he came home Mother said he looked. My Father's Martial Art. Stephen Shu Ning Liu. BrSi; InPK

When he came out, into the world. Born Tying Knots. Samuel Makidemewabe, *tr. by* Howard Norman. STP

When he comes home at night. Wasp Sex Myth (One). Anselm Hollo. PoM

When he comes home from work. Allegory of Death and Night. Frank Stanford. MT

When he died, far away, no one at the Café. Universal. Ory Bernstein, *tr. fr. Hebrew by* Warren Bargad *and* Stanley F. Chyet. *Fr.* Poems from Mexico. IP

When he first came to see me I forgot that he was dead. Memories of Her Friend Who Died. Ory Bernstein, *tr. by* Warren Bargad *and* Stanley F. Chyet. IP

When he got into bed. Damon and Pythias. Robert Creeley. LCAP

When he heard the owls at midnight. Longfellow. *Fr.* The Song of Hiawatha. FM, *fr.* III.

When He Is Flying. Olivia FitzRoy. CN

When he is ready he is raised and carried. The Glass King. Eavan Boland. CIP

When he kicked the ball under a plum tree. *Unknown, tr. by* Hiroaki Sato. FCEI

When he killed the noble mudjokivis. *See* He killed the noble mudjokivis.

When he left the earth was green. The Starman. Diane Ackerman. BWV

When he left, the waves were flush with the raili ng. Thoughts in the Cold. Li Shang-yin, *tr. by* Burton Watson. CoBCP

When he lies in the night away from her. The Jealous Lovers. Donald Hall. NYBP

When he married her he said. Thalamos. Peter Kane Dufault. ErPo

When he pushed his bush of black hair off his brow. Sicilian Cyclamens. D. H. Lawrence. NoAM

When he recalled the past. Views of an American Writer. Sumio Matsuda. KS

When he returned and opened his eyes and stood there, uncalled for. Honi. Dan Pagis, *tr. by* Warren Bargad *and* Stanley F. Chyet. IP

When he returned from his travels. Profile of the Lover of the Great Bear. Abdul Wahab al-Bayati, *tr. by* Abdullah al-Udhari. MPAW

When he said. What She Said. Nannakaiyar, *tr. by* A. K. Ramanujan. PLW

When he sailed into the harbor. Korinna, *tr. fr. Greek by* Willis Barnstone. BoWoP

When he saw her. *Unknown, tr. by* John Brough. TOF

When He Says So We Dance in All Directions—Wow! *Unknown, tr. fr. Seneca Indian by* Jerome Rothenberg *and* Richard Johnny John. STP

When he showed up on the sidewalk in the old neighborhood. The Yo-Yo King. Syma Cheris Cohn. TSL

When He Spoke to Me of Love. M. A. Mokhomo, *tr. fr. Sotho by* Dan Kunene *and* Jack Cope. PeSA

When he surrendered his eyes to the dream, this lad. A Dream. Muhammad al-Ghuzzi, *tr. by* May Jayyusi *and* John Heath-Stubbs. MAP

When he the nation's heart had won. The Presidents. Lizelia Augusta Jenkins Moorer. CBWP-3

When He Thought Himself Contemned. Thomas Howell. EiL

When he trades in tea—it's right nearby. Song of the Merchant's Wife. Yang Shih-ch'i, *tr. by* Jonathan Chaves. CoBLCP

When He Was barely five. The Boyhood of Christ. Saint Columbanus. NOIV

When he was eight years old he had become. Words and Monsters. Vernon Scannell. OxBC

When he was four years old, he stood at the window during a thunderstorm. A Son with a Future. Charles Reznikoff. *Fr.* Five Groups of Verse. DiL

When he was my age and I was already a boy. The Harp. Bruce Weigl. MAYP

When he was shot he toppled to the ground. Shot Who? Jim Lane! Merrill Moore. MoAmPo

When he was young, he broke horses. The Passion Drinker. Anita Endrezze Probst. VoR

When he went blundering back to God. Of One Self-slain. Charles Hanson Towne. WGRP

When he went down to the square, the pavilions now. Ikhnaton's Night. Agnes Nemes Nagy, *tr. by* Laura Schiff. OV

When he who adores thee has left but the name. Pro Patria Mori. Thomas Moore. GTBS; GTBS-P; HoPM
(When He Who Adores Thee.) HoPM

When he, who, from the scourge of wrong. No Man Knoweth His Sepulchre. Bryant. AnAmPo

When he, who is the unforgiven. The Unforgiven. Edwin Arlington Robinson. CMoP

When He Would Have His Verses Read. Robert Herrick. CaPo; NOBE; OBS; SeCV-1

When heaven's about to withdraw its blessing, signs abound in examination halls. In the City of Wu, I Obtained a Record of Names from the Civil Service Examinations. Kung Tzu-chen, *tr. by* Shirleen S. Wong. WFTU

When Helen first saw wrinkles in her face. Walter Savage Landor. *Fr.* Ianthe. EnLoPo

When Helen Lived. W. B. Yeats. CMoP

When her daughter. *Unknown, tr. by* Geoffrey Bownas *and* Anthony Thwaite. PeBJV

When her need for you dies. In Her Only Way. Robert Graves. OxBSP

When his boat snapped loose. The Long Boat. Stanley Kunitz. BLA

When his bones are as seaweed, when his sweet tongue is parched. The White Rainbow. Starr Nelson. GoYe

When His Excellency Prince Norodom Chantaraingsey. Dead Soldiers. James Fenton. NoAM; OBTV; OBWP

When his hour for death had come. Osceola. Walt Whitman. NAAL-1

When his son-in-law. Shakuhachi. Jim Mitsui. BrSi

When hit come ter de question er de female vote. Brother Baptis' on Woman Suffrage. Rosalie Jonas. BlSi

When holy Patrick full of grace. The White Lake. *Unknown, tr. by* Robin Flower. TIRV

When Howitzers Began. Hayden Carruth. Psk; RR

When I/ see you/ climb the walls. Pressure. Anne Waldman. PoM

When I/ die/ I'm sure. The Rebel. Mari E. Evans. AmNP; CRP; IDB; IHMS; PoBA

When I/ took my. The Watch. May Swenson. HAP

When I a verse shall make. His Prayer to Ben Jonson [*or* Johnson]. Robert Herrick. CaPo; JCP; NAEL-1; NoP; OBS; OxBoLi; OxBSP; SeCV-1; TrGrPo

When I Admire the Greatness. Jacob Steendam, *tr. fr. Dutch.* AH

When I admire the rose. Thomas Lodge. *Fr.* The Life and Death of William Longbeard. OBSC
(Fancy, A.) EIL

When I am alone. The Fisherman's Wife. Amy Lowell. BoWoP

When I am alone, and quite alone. Hide and Seek. A. B. Shiffrin. RAR

When I am alone, no one tells me who I am. A Deficiency. Ute Erb, *tr. by* Susan L. Cocalis. DMG

When I am an old woman I shall wear purple. Warning. Jenny Joseph. AIW; FaBoWP; GOYP; OxBTC

When I Am Dead. Hugh Barrie. PoSH

When I Am Dead. Georgia Douglas Johnson. CDC

When I Am Dead. George MacBeth. OxBTC

When I Am Dead. *Unknown.* OxBoLi

When I Am Dead. James Edward Wilson. PoLF

When I am dead, and Doctors know not why. The Dampe. John Donne. SeCP

When I am dead and over me bright April. I Shall Not Care. Sara Teasdale. MoAmPo; TrGrPo; UnPo

When I am dead and some kind soul. Bahadur Shah Zafar, *tr. by* Ahmed Ali. GoT

When I am dead, even then. Then. Muriel Rukeyser. GLP; LCAP

When I am dead, I hope it may be said. On His Books. Hilaire Belloc. ACP; FaBoCo; FaBoEE; MoBrPo; NBLV; OxBoLi; WeW

When I am dead I want you to dress me. When I Am Dead. *Unknown.* OxBoLi

When I am dead, no pageant train. Dirge of Alaric the Visigoth. Edward Everett. BeLS

When I am dead, withhold, I pray, your blooming legacy. When I Am Dead. Georgia Douglas Johnson. CDC

When I am dead you'll find it hard. He and She. Eugene Fitch Ware. PoLF

When I am four a crippled hospital. Clinics. Michael Bachstein. TSM

When I am gone. Josephine D. Henderson Heard. CBWP-4

"When I am gone." Ute Mountain. Charles Tomlinson. RB

When I am grown to man's estate. Robert Louis Stevenson. CenHV (Looking Forward.) BrPO; NBLV; OxBChV

When I am living in the Midlands. The South Country. Hilaire Belloc. ACP; MoBrPo

When I am lying in the grass. The Underworld. Margaret Lavington. RAR

When I Am Old. Caroline Atherton Briggs Mason. BLPA

When I am old. Young Old Young Old. Jan G. Elburg, tr. by Koos Schuur. DuIn

When I am old. Song: "When I am old." Denis Glover. Fr. Sings Harry, III. PeNZ

When I am old and long turned gray. 2001: The Tennyson/ Hardy Poem. Gavin Ewart. FaBoCo

When I am only fit to go to bed. Resignation. Bliss Carman. AnAmPo

When I am parted from you, my dearest. Unknown. Fr. Manyo Shu. Ma

When I am playing by myself. Water Noises. Elizabeth Madox Roberts. BoNaP

When I am sad and weary. Celia Celia. Adrian Mitchell. FaBoEE

When I am standing on a mountain crest. Love in the Winds. Richard Hovey. AA

When I am the sky. Denise Levertov. PoM

When I am very earnestly digging. Pause. Mary Ursula Bethell. ATNZ; PeNZ

When I Am with You. Ghazi al-Gosaibi, tr. fr. Arabic by Sharif Elmusa and Charles Doria. MAP

When I arsked himb. Fred's Dead Friend. John Powers. SoTCo

When I ask the experts. Immigration Law. Margaret Randall. ER

When I ask what things they fear. Fears of the Eighth Grade. Toi Derricotte. InPS

When I asked for fish in the restaurant facing the Ohio River. Carl Sandburg. Fr. Whiffs of the Ohio River at Cincinnati. PoE

When I asked the very old man. Quotations. George Oppen. NNaP

When I Awake I Am Still with Thee. Harriet Beecher Stowe. See Still, Still, with Thee.

When I awake in the early mist. Very Early. Karla Kuskin. PDV

When I Awoke. Raymond R. Patterson. PoBA

When I awake before the dawn, my head. Ugolino. Dante, tr. fr. Italian by Seamus Heaney. Fr. Divina Commedia: Inferno, XXXIII. PFI

When I awoke this morning. The Blue Animals. Jon Anderson. AmPA; SM

When I awoke with cold. Coffee. James Vincent Cunningham. MoAmPo; PrIm; VGW

When I began my love to sow. Husbandry. William Hammond. JCP

When I beheld the poet blind, yet bold. On Mr. Milton's Paradise Lost. Andrew Marvell. JCP

When I behold Becchina in a rage. Sonnet: Of Becchina in a Rage. Cecco Angiolieri da Siena, tr. by Dante Gabriel Rossetti. AWP

When I behold how black, immortal ink. Silet. Ezra Pound. MoAB; MoAmPo; Son

When I behold the heavens as in their prime. Anne Bradstreet. Fr. Contemplations. PBWP

When I bethinke me on that speech whyleare. Spenser. Fr. The Faerie Queene, VII, 8. OAEL-1

When I bought bubble gum. Why We Bombed Haiphong. Jonathan Holden. MAYP

When I bound up my hair I was reading your poems. The Grave of Li Po. Huang Ching-jen, tr. by Daniel Bryant. WFTU

When I burned our leaves, a wind from the dark. Looking West. William Stafford. NYBP

When I but think upon the great dead days. Piere Vidal Old. Ezra Pound. MoAB

When I Buy Pictures. Marianne Moore. EyDe; OxBA

When I call to you, God. Contact. John F. Deane. TIRV

When I came back, he was gone. My Father's Leaving. Ira Sadoff. AmPA; DiL

When I Came from Colchis. W. S. Merwin. NePoEA; VGW

When I came in that night I found. A Surprise in the Peninsula. Fleur Adcock. ATNZ

When I came into the room I saw. And And. Zoltán Zelk, tr. by Daniel Hoffman. MHuP

When I came last to Ludlow. Friends. A. E. Housman. SeCePo

When I Came to Israel. Bert Meyers. VWA

When I Came to London. Rachael Castelete, tr. fr. Judezmo by Stephen Levy. VWA

When I came to show you my summer cottage. Summer. Josephine Miles. FaBoWP; WPE

When I can hold a stone within my hand. Rumination. Richard Eberhart. LiTA; LiTM

When I can read my title clear. Ninety-fifth. Isaac Watts. AmFP

When I carefully consider the curious habits of dogs. Meditatio. Ezra Pound. FaBoCh; OBAL

When I catch sight of your fair head. Sonnet. Louise Labé, tr. by Joan Keefe and Richard Terdiman. PBWP

When I climb up. Drinking Fountain. Marchette Chute. RAR

When I come down to sleep death's endless night. My City. James Weldon Johnson. BANP; CDC; PoNe

When I come groping back through mists of sleep. Mortal Combat. Countess Alice Fay di Castagnola. GoYe

When I conceived the child with star-green eyes. Sea-Monster. Gertrud Kolmar, tr. by Henry A. Smith. VWA

"When I consider everything that grows." Shakespeare. Fr. Sonnets, XV. AWP; BLPL; NAEL-1; OBSC; Son; TEP; TrGrPo

When I consider how my life is spent. Reminiscent Reflection. Ogden Nash. FaBoCo

When I Consider How My Light Is Spent. Milton. InPK; NAEL-1; PoE (On His Blindness.) AWP; ChTr; FaBV; FiP; FPL; GN; GTBS; HAP; HEiP; LiTB; NOBE; OBEV; PoEL-3; PoLF; PoRA; PrIM; SoSe; TrGrPo; WeW

When I Consider Life. Dryden. Fr. Aureng-Zebe, IV, i. FiP

When I consider Life and its few years. Tears. Lizette Woodworth Reese. AA; AnAmPo; MoAmPo; WGRP

When I consider men of golden talents. So That's Who I Remind Me Of. Ogden Nash. BLPL; PoLF

When I Consider Thy Heavens. Bible, O.T. Fr. Psalms: Psalm VIII ("O Lord our Lord, how excellent is thy name. . ."). FaPON, (3-5); ImOP, (3-8).

When I contemplate o'er me. The Night Serene. Luís de León, tr. by Thomas Walsh. TrJP

When I could not see thee and all thy majesty. Khwaja Mir Dard, tr. by Ahmed Ali. GoT

When I couldn't be always discussed things. Action Would Kill It/A Gamble. Robert Adamson. CBAP

When I crept over the hill, broken with tears. The Comforters. Dora Sigerson Shorter. CH

When I decide I shall assemble you. Identity. Elizabeth Jennings. NePoEA

When I did wake this morn from sleep. Early Morn. W. H. Davies. CH

When I Die. Fenton Johnson. CDC; PoNe

When I Die. Brenda G. Macrow. Fr. All Flesh Is Grass. PoSH

When I died, the circulating library. Seth Compton. Edgar Lee Masters. Fr. Spoon River Anthology. LiTA

"When I do count the clock that tells the time." Shakespeare. Fr. Sonnets, XII. AWP; EIL; InPS; NAEL-1; NoP; OAEL-1; OBSC; Son; TEP

(When I Do Count the Clock.) FaFP

When I do it, I remember how it was with us. Making Love to Myself. James L. White. GLP

When I dragged the rotten log. Kenneth Rexroth. Fr. The Signature of All Things. BoNaP

When I Drink I Become the Joy of Faggots. Dorothy Allison. GLP

When I drive cab. After Anacreon. Lew Welch. Fr. Taxi Suite. NeAP; PoM

When I drive, every bridge is. Together Again. William Stafford. LCAP

When I eat melon. Okura. Fr. Manyo Shu. Ma

When I entered the room and turned on the lights. The Man Hidden behind the Drapes. Pattiann Rogers. MAYP

When I entertained Ruskin. The Vampire. John DeWitt. VVA

When I face north a lost Cree. Returned to Say. William Stafford. NaP

When I faded back to pass. Ties. Dabney Stuart. GrPl

When I fall asleep, and even during sleep. Baudelaire. Delmore Schwartz. TwCP; VGW

When I finished reading a dog story. Dog Story. James Steel Smith. SoTCo

When I first came to live in Japan. The Merchant at Yokohama. Osman Edwards. Fr. Residential Rhymes, I. OBTV

When I first heard about America. Nobody Lives on Arthur Godfrey Boulevard. Gerald Costanzo. MAYP

When I first opened my eyes. Autobiography. Janet Dubé. BrRo

When I first saw a woman after childbirth. Ishtar. Judith Wright. NoAM

When I first saw him he was standing on wet pebbles. Orpheus. Susan Tichy. ER
When I first set foot. Like an Orchid in Deep Muddy Water. Nilene O. A. Foxworth. AIW
When I forth fare beyond this narrow earth. After Death. Charles Francis Richardson. AA
"When I found where we had crashed, in the snow." He Said. Jean Valentine. TAP
When I gaze at the sun. A Moment Please. Samuel Allen. AmNP; IDB; PoBA
When I gaze upon the sky. Reflection from Sea and Sky. Walter Savage Landor. FaBoEE
When I get big. Basketball Star. Karama Fufuka. RHPC
When I Get Time. Thomas L. Masson. BLPA; FPL
When I get to be a composer. Daybreak in Alabama. Langston Hughes. AmFN; CNA
When I get to heaven. Happy Day (or Independence Day). James Cunningham. JB
When I get up in the morning. Getting Up. Lilian McCrea. BoTP
When I go. After Grave Deliberation. Elizabeth Flynn. NBLV
When I go away from you. The Taxi. Amy Lowell. BoWoP; MoAmPo
When I go back to earth. The Answer. Sara Teasdale. PoA
When I go home to the South the river lakes. The Gar. Charles G. Bell. AmFN
When I go into the garden, there she is. There She Is. Linda Gregg. NPGG
When I go musing all alone. The Authors Abstract of Melancholy. Robert Burton. Fr. The Anatomy of Melancholy. OBS
When I, Good Friends, Was Called to the Bar. W. S. Gilbert. Fr. Trial by Jury. NAEL-2
When I Got It Right. Carl Lindner. TSL
When I grow old I hope to be. Growing Old. Rose Henderson. RHPC
When I grow old I will have blond curls. A Child's Mirror. Judith Herzberg, tr. by the author. DuIn
When I had firmly answered "No." The Last Ride Together (from Her Point of View). James Kenneth Stephen. BXAP; CenHV; FaBoCo; Par; UnPo
When I had met my love the twentieth time. Her Merriment. W. H. Davies. EnLoPo
When I had money, money, O! Money. W. H. Davies. OBEV; OBMV
When I Had Need of Him. Samuel Ellsworth Kiser. BLRP
When I had spread it all on linen cloth. The Wife's Tale. Seamus Heaney. CIP; IPY
When I hang up my blue-and-white scarf. Jerusalem. Rose Ausländer, tr. by Ewald Osers. VWA
When I have a house. as I sometime may. Vagabond House. Don Blanding. BLPA
When I have been dead for several years. Poet's Wish. Valery Larbaud, tr. by William Jay Smith. CT; GrPl
When I have Borne in Memory. Wordsworth. EnRP; GTBS; GTBS-P (England, 1802, V.) OBEV
When I have chanted my new poems. K'ang Hai, tr. fr. Chinese by Jonathan Chaves. Fr. Ten Poems on Almond Blossoms. CoBLCP
When I have ended, then I see. Laurence Housman. TrPWD
When I Have Fears [That I May Cease to Be]. Keats. AWP; BLPL; EBEV; EnRP; HAP; HeIP; HoPM; InPS; LiTB; NAEL-2; NIP; NoP; OAEL-2; OBEV; PoE; PoRA; PrIm; Son; TEP; TrGrPo; UnPo (Sonnet: "When I have fears that I may cease to be.") FiP; OBNC
When I have forgotten your lips. The Desolate Lover. Eileen Shanahan. NeIP
When I have grown foolish. Peregrine's Sunday Song. Elinor Wylie. NYBP
When I have heard small talk about great men. Grandeur of Ghosts. Siegfried Sassoon. MoBrPo; OBMV
When I have lost the power to feel the pang. Strangeness of Heart. Siegfried Sassoon. TrJP
"When I have seen by Time's fell hand defaced." Shakespeare. Fr. Sonnets, LXIV. AWP; BLPL; EIL; EnLoPo; FaFP; HAP; HeIP; LiTB; NOBE; NoP; OAEL-1; OBSC; PoE; PoRA; Son (Time and Love, I.) GTBS; GTBS-P
When I have talked for an hour I feel lousy. The Dancers Inherit the Party. Ian Hamilton Finlay. FF
When I Have Time. Unknown. PWR
When I hear deep in the mountains. Teika, tr. fr. Japanese by Hiroaki Sato. Fr. A Compendium of Good Tanka. FCEI
When I hear laughter from a tavern door. Wilfrid Scawen Blunt. Fr. Esther [a Young Man's Tragedy]. OBMV; TrGrPo
When I hear of the beautiful young women divorcing. The Good New Is; the Bad News Is. David Ray. SoTCo

When I hear the old men. A Song of Greatness. Unknown, tr. by Mary Austin. AmFN; FaPON
When I Heard at the Close of the Day. Walt Whitman. AmPP; GBL; NAAL-1; NoAM; OxBA; PoE
When I Heard Dat White Man Say. Zack Gilbert. PoBA
When I heard that thunder, I rose up like a happy animal. Returning to the World. Laura Chester. NPGG
When I Heard the Learn'd Astronomer. Walt Whitman. AmPP; AnAmPo; FF; FPL; HAP; MoAmPo; NAAL-1; NoP; OxBA; SoSe; TAP; TrGrPo; WeW
When I heard the terrible news, that Myris was dead. Myris: Alexandria, A.D. 340. Constantine P. Cavafy, tr. by Edmund Keeley and Philip Sherrard. AnAn; VMG
When I Held You to My Chest, You Fit. Jack Myers. AmPA
When I hit her on the head, it was good. Herbert White. Frank Bidart. AmPA
When I in wild defiance fled. In Tribute. Vernal House. CaP
When I invite the Giraffe to dine. Giraffe. William Jay Smith. ILY
When I lay me down to sleep. Insomnia the Gem of the Ocean. John Updike. NBLV
When I left the room. A Strange City. Sándor Weöres, tr. by Jascha Kessler. FOC
When I lie down to sleep dream the Wishing Well it rings. I Am a Victim of Telephone. Allen Ginsberg. NBLV
When I lie sleepless, longing for Yamato. Empress Otomaro. Fr. Manyo Shu. Ma
When I lie where shades of darkness. Fare Well. Walter de la Mare. GTBS-P; NOBE; OBEV
When I lived down in Devonshire. Autobiographical Fragment. Kingsley Amis. NePoEA-2
When I lived here in the shade of your love. Even the Mirror Dies. Anja Vammelvuo, tr. by Aili Jarvenpa. SOP
When I lived in Naples there was always a beggar at the gate of my palace. The Beggar Woman of Naples. Max Jacob, tr. by John Ashbery. RHTwFP
When I look/ at the wisteria blossoms/ I think of long ago. Masaoka Shiki, tr. fr. Japanese by Burton Watson. Fr. Fifteen Haiku. FCEI
When I look/ at wisteria blossoms/ I want to get out. Masaoka Shiki, tr. fr. Japanese by Burton Watson. Fr. Fifteen Haiku. FCEI
When I look and see. Summer Evening. Emperor Kogon, tr. by Steven D. Carter. WFTW
When I look around in the quiet before dawn. Princess Shikishi, tr. fr. Japanese by Hiroaki Sato. Fr. Seventy-eight Tanka. FCEI
When I look at my elder sister now. The Elder Sister. Sharon Olds. NIP
When I look back upon my life nigh spent. George Macdonald. TrPWD
When I look forth at dawning, pool. Nature's Questioning. Thomas Hardy. TEP
When I look in the mirror. Hysteria. Chu Shu-chen, tr. by Kenneth Rexroth. NaP
When I look into a glass. A Thought. W. H. Davies. MoShBr
When I look into the mountain air. Chiliasm. Richard Eberhart. EaLo
When I look up and gaze. Yakamochi. Fr. Manyo Shu. Ma
When I looked at my poverty. Poverty. Charles Simic. MAT
When I looked at the stubborn dark Buddha. Byzantium Burning. Jack Gilbert. NPGG
When I looked into your eyes. Chinoiseries. Amy Lowell. PoRA
When I love her/ so much. Unknown. Fr. Manyo Shu. Ma
When I loved you, I can't but allow. Thomas Moore. EnLoPo; OxBSP
When I meet the morning beam. The Immortal Part. A. E. Housman. Fr. A Shropshire Lad, XLIII. MoBrPo; UnPo
When I meet the skier she is always. Transit. Adrienne Rich. NoP
When I meet you. Unknown. Fr. Manyo Shu. Ma
When I must come to you, O my God, I pray. A Prayer to Go to Paradise with the Donkeys. Jammes Francis, tr. by Richard Wilbur. EaLo; RB
When I Neared Fifty. Pertti Nieminen, tr. fr. Finnish by Aili Jarvenpa. SOP
When I Now Tell You about the Emperor. Paavo Haavikko, tr. fr. Finnish by Aili Jarvenpa. SOP
When I open the door & let them in. A Desirable Property. Vivienne Joseph. ATNZ
When I opened your letter. A Thought of Marigolds. Janice Farrar. GoYe
When I pass. Four Choctaw Songs. Jim Barnes. STE
When I perceive your blond and graceful head. Louise Labé. BoWoP, tr. by Willis Barnstone (Sonnet: "When I catch sight of your fair head.") PBWP, tr. by Joan Keefe and Richard Terdiman.
When I Peruse the Conquer'd Fame. Walt Whitman. PoEL-5
When I pictured you. Ollie, Answer Me. Stephen Berg. NaP

When I play on my fiddle in Dooney. The Fiddler of Dooney. W. B. Yeats. EBVV; FaBoCh; NBLV

When I, poor Lais, with my crown. Lais to Aphrodite. Edwin Arlington Robinson, *after* Plato. FaBoEE

When I put flowers in an empty flower vase. In June. Ruth Kim Chunsoo, *tr. by* Koh Chang-soo. ACKP

When I put her out, once, by the garbage pail. The Geranium. Theodore Roethke. CoAP; UnPo; WeW

When I put my slate back in the void. André Frénaud, *tr. by* Keith Bosley. RHTwFP

When I put myself out on a saucer. Cannibalism. Diana Chang. WPOW

When I put off the sense in death. The Free Intelligence. Anna Wickham. OBD

When I put on my hat. When I get into my shoes again. Vow. Abba Kovner, *tr. by* Warren Bargad *and* Stanley F. Chyet. IP

When I ran to snatch the wires off our roof. The Powerline Incarnation. Les A. Murray. CBAP

When I reached his place. It Was All Very Tidy. Robert Graves. OxBTC; RB

When I Reached the Post Station at Kaya. Michizane, *tr. fr. Chinese by* Burton Watson. JLIC-1

When I Read Shakespeare. D. H. Lawrence. MoP; NoAM; Son

When I Read the Book. Walt Whitman. NAAL-1

When I Recovered from an Illness, *sels.* Li K'ai-hsien, *tr. fr. Chinese by* Jonathan Chaves. CoBLCP

"All my friends can write them." *Fr.* II.

"While an official, I never wrote lyrics." *Fr.* I.

When I reflect on it now. Yosano Akiko, *tr. fr. Japanese by* Hiroaki Sato. *Fr.* Thirty-nine Tanka. FCEI

When I Reflect on Nature's Cruelty. Stefan Themerson. NPo

When I remember again. John Skelton. *Fr.* Phyllyp Sparowe [*or* Philip Sparrow]. PBBP; SeCePo

(Sparrow's Dirge, The.) FaBoCh; OBSC

When I remember the work camps. Mother. José Montoya, *tr. by* Toni Empringham. FIA

When I return I search for myself. On Going Home. Marjorie L. Agnew. GoYe

When I returned with drinks and nuts, my friend. The Friend of the Fourth Decade. James Merrill. NYBP

When I ride my bicycle. Different Bicycles. Dorothy Walter Baruch. FaPON

When I rolled three 7's. Situation. Langston Hughes. OBAL

When I said "You have grown thin." Meeting after Separation. Marula, *tr. by* Tambimuttu *and* G. V. Vaiyda. BoWoP

When I sailed out of Baltimore. A Child's Pet. W. H. Davies. CH; RB

When I sat beside the river. The Flood. Ann Stanford. MOWH

When I saw that clumsy crow. Night Crow. Theodore Roethke. HoPM; InPK; OxBSP; VGW

When I saw the dark clouds, I wept. The Clouds. Mirabai, *tr. fr. medieval Hindi; English version by* Robert Bly. NU

When I saw the flags fly taut. Winter Race Meeting. Ernest Kroll. SoTCo

When I saw the grapefruit drying, cherries in each center lying. Arrogance Repressed. Sir John Betjeman. FiBHP

When I saw the painter on Kwangbok street. Jung-sup Lee I Saw. Ruth Kim Chun-soo, *tr. by* Koh Chang-soo. ACKP

When I saw the woman's leg on the floor of the subway train. The Leg in the Subway. Oscar Williams. LiTM

When I saw your head bow, I knew I had beaten you. The Last Word. Peter Davison. InPK

When I see a couple of kids. High Windows. Philip Larkin. FaBoMo; NAEL-2; NoAM

When I see a poet's photograph with the name. The Poet's Photograph. Stephen E. Smith. SoTCo

When I see a suckling pig turn. The Animals. Linda Pastan. ER

When I see a woman. *Unknown. Fr.* Manyo Shu. Ma

When I See Another's Pain. Mani Leib, *tr. fr. Yiddish by* Joseph Leftwich. TrJP

When I see birches bend to left and right. Birches. Robert Frost. AmPP; CMoP; FaBV; FPL; HeIP; LiTA; LiTM; MoAB; MoAmPo; MoP; NAAL-2; NIP; NoAM; NoP; OxBA; PoLF; PoRA; RB; TAP; TrGrPo

When I see buildings in a town together. Mr. Frost Goes South to Boston. Firman Houghton. Par

When I see carved so clearly on your face. Two Solitudes. Evelyn Ames. GoYe

When I see him/ gliding gazelle-like. Little Half-Brother, Little Black Star. George Barlow. NAmP

When I see how helplessly the thoughts of many. Without Names. Gerrit Kouwenaar, *tr. by* Koos Schuur. DuIn

When I see how high it is. So Beautiful Is the Tree of Night. Pauline Hanson. TAP

When I See Old Men. Raymond Souster. CaP

When I See on Rood. *Unknown.* OxBSP

When I see peas. Your Eyes and Swiveling Members. Clark Stillman. SoTCo

When I see some kid from Norway. High Wonders. Naomi Marks. BXAP

When I see the earth ornate and lovely. Veronica Gambara, *tr. fr. Italian by* Brenda Webster. PBWP

When I see the evening reds, friend, blusing deep in the west. To Creuzer. Karoline von Günderode, *tr. by* Susan L. Cocalis. DMG

When I see the falling bombs. Conflict. Francis Reginald Scott. CaP

When I see the lark a-moving [*or* stir her wings for joy]. The Lark. Bernart de Ventadorn. CTC, *tr. by* Ezra Pound; Pro, *tr. by* Paul Blackburn

When I see the meadows greening. *Unknown, tr. by* Paul Blackburn. Pro

When I see the moonlight pouring. *Unknown, tr. fr. Japanese by* Burton Watson. *Fr.* Kokin Shu. FCEI

When I see the next century. A Long and Happy Life. Simon Schuchat. UL

When I see you moving in a room with other people. Portrait across a Room. Elizabeth Nannestad. ATNZ

When I see you off to camp, I see you. I See My Girl. Sharon Olds. BLA

When I see your picture in its frame. As If You Had Never Been. Richard Eberhart. EyDe

When I Set Out for Lyonnesse. Thomas Hardy. BrPo; EBVV; InPS; MoBrPo; RB; SeCePo

When I shall be without regret. James Vincent Cunningham. InPK

When I show up. *Unknown, tr. by* Jerome Rothenberg. STP

When I sit by myself at the close of the day. Good Company. *Unknown.* OBET

When I sit up to bread and milk. At Breakfast. Ida M. Mills. BoTP

When I sleep alone, in the Imperial City. Tabito. *Fr.* Manyo Shu. Ma

When I solidly do ponder. Francis Daniel Pastorius. SCAP

When I some antique jar behold. To a Lady. John Gay. OBEV

When I speak now. Volcano. Ivan Van Sertima. PBCV

When I stand in the center of that man's madness. Reflection by a Mailbox. Stanley Kunitz. TrJP; WaP

When I start to compose myself in the morning. In the Morning. Jacob Glatstein, *tr. by* Benjamin *and* Barbara Harshav. AYP

When I started out from home. Mononobe Tatsu. *Fr.* Manyo Shu. Ma

When I stepped homeward to my hill. Home-coming. Léonie Adams. MoAmPo

When I stop to think. Emperor Kogon, *tr. by* Steven D. Carter. WFTW

When I strip./ stop walking/ and drop into sleep. Anne-Marie Kegels, *tr. by* Willis Barnstone. BoWoP

When I survey [*or* survay] the bright. "Nox Nocti Indicat Scientiam." William Habington. *Fr.* Castara, III. ACP; JCP; MeLP; MePo; NOBE; OBEV; OBS

When I Survey the Wondrous Cross. Isaac Watts. AmFP; FaPoR; WGRP

(Crucifixion to the World by the Cross of Christ.) NOCV; NOEC

When I take my girl to the swimming party. The One Girl at the Boys Party. Sharon Olds. InPK; MAYP

When I take the *koto*, sobs break forth. *Unknown. Fr.* Manyo Shu. Ma

When I talk to you folks on other stars. Can You Hear Me, Thinktank Two? Thomas M. Disch. BWV

When I taught you. To a Daughter Leaving Home. Linda Pastan. ER

When I think how far the onion has traveled. The Traveling Onion. Naomi Shihab Nye. MT

When I think of all you've got. A Father's Heart Is Touched. Samuel Hoffenstein. FiBHP

When I think of death. Bop Lyrics. Allen Ginsberg. OBAL

When I Think of Him. *Unknown, tr. fr. Chippewa Indian by* Frances Densmore. OV

When I think of my fear. The Unblinding. Laurence Lieberman. NYBP

When I think of us—Yiddish poets. Yiddish Poets. H. Leivick, *tr. by* Benjamin *and* Barbara Harshav. AYP

When I through all my many poems look. To the Most Virtuous Mistress Pot, Who Many Times Entertained Him. Robert Herrick. CaPo

When I thy singing next shall heare. Againe. Robert Herrick. SeCP

When I traverse the distance. All the Caverns of Light. Ya'akov Beser, *tr. by* Bernhard Frank. MHeP

When I trusted as one trusts in a great ship. *Unknown. Fr.* Manyo Shu. Ma

When I try to skate. Skating. Herbert Asquith. FaPON
When I used to focus on the worries, everybody. Joanne Kyger. UL
When I Vexed You. Robert Browning. *Fr.* Ferishtah's Fancies. OxBSP
When I visited this shrine of truth. The Pavillion-Where-the-Crane-Came. Chao Meng-fu, *tr. by* Jonathan Chaves. CoBLCP
When I wake in the early mist. Very Early. Karla Kuskin. PDV
When I wake up again, when I wake up. The Report. Jon Swan. NYBP
When I walk home through snow or slush. Winter Song. David Daiches. NYBP
When I want some sort of human metronome. Jumper. Tony Harrison. NPo
When I Want to Speak. Rav Abraham Isaac Kook, *tr. fr. Hebrew by* Ben Zion Bokser. VWA
When I want to tell of the laughing throne. Old Flag. W. S. Merwin. AnAn
When I was/ thirteen I. Spring. Ruth Whitman. IHMS
When I was a bachelor bold and young. Bachelor Bold and Young. *Unknown.* AmFP
When I was a bachelor [*or* bach'lor *or* batchelor] I lived all alone [*or* early and young *or* by myself *or* young and gay]. The Foggy, Foggy Dew. *Unknown.* AS; CoMu; ELP; GBP; LiTB; OBET; OxBoLi
When I was a blonde I. First Corinthians at the Crossroads. Bruce Dawe. NoAM
When I was a boy. The Piper's Progress. Francis Sylvester Mahony. FiBHP
When I was a boy, a relative. A Way to Make a Living. James Wright. NNaP
When I was a boy, and saw bright rows of icicles. Conrad Aiken. *Fr.* Improvisations: Light and Snow. BoNaP
When I was a boy desiring the title of man. George. Dudley Randall. BPo; NoAM
When I was a boy I saw the world I was in. Old-Time Childhood in Kentucky. Robert Penn Warren. AiP; BLA
When I was a boy, I used to go to bed. The Remorse for Time. Howard Nemerov. Son
When I was a boy, myself and my girl. Making Love outside Aras an Uachtaráin. Paul Durcan. FaBCIP
When I was a boy, the Milky Way. The Milky Way. Jon Anderson. MAYP
When I was a child. Autobiographia Literaria. Frank O'Hara. CAPP; NNaP; NOBA; TTTS
When I was a child. My People. Margery Himel. IHMS
When I was a child. The Message of the Rain. Norman H. Russell. STE
When I was a child. The Truth about My Sister and Me. Anita Endrezze Probst. CDW
When I was a child. The Witch's Life. Anne Sexton. KS
When I was a child. Why Do You Write about Russia? Louis Simpson. InPS; LCAP
When I was a child and thought as a child, I put. The Wandering Jew. Robert Mezey. NePoEA-2; VWA
When I was a child I knew red miners. Childhood. Margaret Abigail Walker. IHMS; PBWP; PoBA; Son; WPOW
When I was a child I lay in dread. To the Wind. Vicente Riva Palacio, *tr. by* Samuel Beckett. MexPo
When I was a child in the little village. Prologue to "The Boatman in the Moon." Sándor Weöres, *tr. by* Jascha Kessler. FOC
When I was a child of five winters. Poor Wolf Speaks. Poor Wolf. NU
When I Was a Child They Married Me. *Unknown, tr. fr. Spanish by* Kate Flores. DMH
When I was a chile we used to play. Children's Rhymes. Langston Hughes. BPo; InPS
When I was a girl. Two Gifts. *Unknown, tr. by* Willis Barnstone. BoWoP
When I was a girl I saw with the old men. You Call That a Ts'ing; a Letter. Jedediah Barrow. BXAP
When I was a good and quick little girl. *Unknown, tr. by* W. S Merwin. BoWoP
When I was a greenhorn and young. Charles Kingsley. NOBVV
When I was a kid. The External Element. David McFadden. NeAC
When I was a kid and doing my best to. To Be a Top Hand. Georgie Sicking. CowP
When I was a kid in summer. Some One Liked Me when I Was Twelve. Peter Orlovsky. GLP
When I was a lad and so was my dad. *Unknown.* OxNR
When I was a lad I served a term. Sir Josephs's Song. W. S. Gilbert. *Fr.* H. M. S. Pinafore. LiTB
When I was a little boy/ I had but little wit. *Unknown.* OxNR
When I was a little boy/ I lived by myself. *Unknown.* BoTP; OxNR

When I was a little boy/ I washed my mammy's dishes. *Unknown.* OxNR
When I was a little boy/ My mammy kept me in. *Unknown.* OxNR
When I was a little girl,/ About seven years old. Mother Goose. OxNR
When I was a little maid. The Little Maid. Anna Maria Wells. OBCA
When I was a new-born babe. *Unknown.* *Fr.* Manyo Shu. Ma
When I was a servant in Rosemary Lane. The Servant of Rosemary Lane. *Unknown.* OxBSS
When I was a single girl. *See* When I was single.
When I was a single girl, I went dressed very fine. Oh, I Wish I Were Single Again. *Unknown.* AmFP
When I was a teacher. The Teacher. David Fisher. NPGG
When I was a wee thing. The Kirk of the Birds, Beasts and Fishes. *Unknown.* GBP
When I was a windy boy and a bit. Dylan Thomas. ErPo; OPOP; PPP
"When I was a young girl, I used to seek pleasure." One Morning in May; or, The Young Girl Cut Down in Her Prime. *Unknown.* AmFP
When I Was a Young Maid. *Unknown.* AmFP
When I was a young man I carried a pack. The Band Played Waltzing Matilda. Eric Bogle. OBET
When I was a young man I lived rarely. A Poor Man's Work Is Never Done. *Unknown.* OBET
When I was a youngster I sailed with the rest. Liverpool Girls. *Unknown.* OxBSS
When I was about eight, I once stabbed somebody, another kid, a little girl. Blades. C. K. Williams. GeTw
When I was as high as that. A Memory. L. A. G. Strong. FaBoCo; NOBL
"When I was at the party." Betty at the Party. *Unknown.* BOTP; OnUR
When I was born in a world of sin. G. K. Chesterton on His Birth. A. E. Housman. FaBoNo; NBLV
When I was born in the great house on the bank of the sea. Poem of Distant Childhood. Noémia da Sousa. AIW, *tr. by* Kathleen Weaver *and* Allan Francovich
When I was born, my mother and father. Riddle: Cuckoo. *Unknown.* PBBP
When I was born, my mother taped my ears. Youth's Progress. John Updike. FiBHP
When I was born on Amman Hill. The Collier. Vernon Watkins. FaBoTw; OBWVE
When I was born, one of the crooked. Seven-Sided Poem. Carlos Drummond de Andrade, *tr. by* Elizabeth Bishop. ATCBP
When I was bound apprentice, in famous Lincolnshire. The Lincolnshire Poacher. *Unknown.* CH; GBP; OnMSP; OxBoLi; SD (Poacher, The.) WiR
When I was bound for London a lady met me there. The Sheffield Apprentice. *Unknown.* OBET (Sheffield 'Prentice, The.) AmFP
When I was but thirteen or so. Romance. W. J. Turner. CH; GoJo; MoBrPo; NOBE; OBMV; PoRA; TrGrPo
When I Was Christened. David McCord. *Fr.* Perambulator Poems, I-VII, V. OBCA (Perambulator Poem.) OFD
When I was coming down from the country. The Forgotten City. William Carlos Williams. LiTA
When I Was Conceived. Michael Ryan. MAYP; NAmP
When I was down beside the sea. At the Seaside. Robert Louis Stevenson. NTCP; OxBChV
When I Was Dying. William Hathaway. UL
When I was eight I listened to stories of love. Tapestries. Colleen J. McElroy. ER
When I was eighteen years of age. McCaffery. *Unknown.* OBET
When I was eleven and they. Twins. William Matthews. MAYP
When I Was Fair and Young. Elizabeth I, Queen of England. CTC; NIP; NoP; PoRA (Youth and Cupid.) OBSC
When I was fifteen years of age. Phone Number. Jack Collom. UL
When I was five my father kidnapped me. The Gift. Mark Jarman. MOWH
"When I was forced from Stella ever dear." Sir Philip Sidney. *Fr.* Astrophel and Stella, LXXXVII. NAEL-1
When I was forty the stocktaker came. On My Fortieth Birthday. John Tripp. NAs
When I was four my father went to Scotland. The Truth. Randall Jarrell. DiL; OxBC
When I Was Growing Up. David Vogel, *tr. fr. Hebrew by* A. C. Jacobs. VWA

When I was home de/ Sunshine seemed like gold. Po' Boy Blues. Langston Hughes. BANP
When I was Home Last Christmas. Randall Jarrell. MT
When I was in a summer valley. *At.* to Nicholas de Guildford, Middle English. *Fr.* The Owl and the Nightingale. PBBP
When I was in the garden. The Queen Bee. Mary K. Robinson. BoTP
When I was just a little boy. The Ships of Yule. Bliss Carman. CaP
"When I was just as far as I could walk." The Telephone. Robert Frost. SO; SoSe
When I was led again to the Akedah. The Akedah. Matti Megged. VWA, *tr.* by Howard Schwartz
When I was like you I crossed a street. Finding a Lucky Number. Gary Soto. MOWH
When I was little, when. The Poplar's Shadow. May Swenson. NYBP
When I was lonely, I thought of death. The Secret of Poetry. Jon Anderson. MAYP
When I Was Lost. Dorothy Aldis. RHPC
When I was marked for suffering, Love forswore. Cervantes, *tr.* by Sir Edmund Gosse. AWP
When I was on Night Line. Ego. Philip Booth. TwCP
When I was once in Baltimore. Sheep. William Henry Davies. LiTM; MoBrPo; RB
When I was One-and-Twenty. A. E. Housman. *Fr.* A Shropshire Lad, XIII. CMoP; ELP; FaBV; FaFP; FPL; HeIP; InPK; LiTB; LiTM; MoAB; MoBrPo; NAEL-2; NoAM; PoE; PoLF; SoSe; TrGrPo
When I was one and twenty. The Shropshire Lad's Cousin. Samuel Hoffenstein. BXAP
When I was only five years old. The Wallpaper. Sir Edmund William Gosse. Mes
When I was only semen in a gland. James Keir Baxter. *Fr.* Pig Island Letters, VIII. PeNZ
When I was only six years old. When I Was Six. Zora Cross. FaPON
When I was past such thinking. You Came as a Thought. J. Laughlin. GOYP
When I was seven. Growing Up. Harry Behn. PDV; RHPC
When I was seventeen. Just How Crazy Brenda Is. Melinda Goodman. GLP
When I was seventeen, a man in the Dakar Station. Objets d'Art. Cynthia MacDonald. ER; NMM
When I was seventeen I heard. To Critics. Walter Learned. AA
When I was sick and lay a-bed. The Land of Counterpane. Robert Louis Stevenson. BrPo; EBEV; FaBoBe; FaFP; NBLV; NTCP; OxBChV; PWR
When I was single [*or* a single girl]. I Wish I Were [*or* Was] Single Again. *Unknown*. AmFP, *diff. vers.*; AS
When I Was Six. Zora Cross. FaPON
When I Was Small. André Marie de Chénier, *tr. fr. French* by Elizabeth Gerteiny. ErPo
When I was small. Nostalgia. Yu Kuang-chung, *tr.* by Dominic Cheung. IFON
When I was small my mother did my hair. Plaits. Tabitha Tuckett. Mes
When I was the sissy of the block who nobody wanted on their team. The Sleeper. Edward Field. ASP
When I was three years old, my mother passed away. Cheng Hsieh, *tr. fr. Chinese* by Jonathan Chaves. *Fr.* Seven Songs. CoBLCP
When I was told, as Delta children were. Ruby Tells All. Miller Williams. MT
When I was twelve I was kidnapped and sold as a slave. A Psalm of Onan for Harp, Flute and Tambourine. Alden Nowlan. NeAC
When I Was Twenty. Bliss Carman. AnAmPo
When I was very little the lake was blue. Viljo Kajava, *tr.* by Aili Jarvenpa. SOP
When I was very very. Mama Knows. Sharon Scott. JB
When I was very young. Traveling to Town. Duane Big Eagle. AiP
When I was waiting for a haircut at Joe's. Travelling. Denis Johnson. NAmP
When I Was Well into Being Savored. Joanne Kyger. PoM
When I Was Young. Alun Llywelyn-Williams, *tr. fr. Welsh* by Gwyn Williams. OBWVE
When I Was Young. Veijo Meri, *tr. fr. Finnish* by Aili Jarvenpa. SOP
When I was young. *Unknown*, *tr.* by Geoffrey Bownas and Anthony Thwaite. PeBJV
When I was young. Dreams, Yellow Lions. Alistair Campbell. ATNZ
When I Was Young and Foolish. *Unknown*. AS
When I was young and in my prime,/ I thought I never could marry. Devilish Mary. *Unknown*. AmFP
When I was young and in my prime,/ I flourished like a vine. Thyme. *Unknown*. AmFP
When I was young and in my prime, my age twenty-two. The Lightning Flash. *Unknown*. AmFP

When I was young and used to wander. Hubert's Museum. Louis Simpson. OxBC
When I was young and wanted to see the sights. On His Queerness. Christopher Isherwood. OxBTC; PeHV
When I was young I had a care. Soliloquy. Francis Ledwidge. HoPM
When I was young, I had no sense. The Fiddle. Neil Munro. BoTP
When I was young, I said to Sorrow. Sorrow. Aubrey Thomas De Vere. BLPA; WGRP; WiR
When I was young I scribbled, boasting, on my wall. The Summing-up. Stanley Kunitz. OBAL
When I Was Young, I Stopped by a Wine Shop in Chi-men. Yü Chi, *tr. fr. Chinese* by Jonathan Chaves. CoBLCP
When I was young I thought that if death came. When He Is Flying. Olivia FitzRoy. CN
When I was young I us'd to wait on Massa and hand him de plate. The Blue-Tail Fly. *Unknown*. FaFP; GBP
When I was young, I went to school. The One Furrow. R. S. Thomas. HoPM; OxBC
When I was young, it was much simpler. Soliloquy on a Southern Strand. John Montague. FaBCIP
When I was young, just starting at our game. To My Least Favorite Reviewer. Howard Nemerov. TW
When I was young, love, and in full blossom. Love It Is Pleasing. *Unknown*. OBET
When I was young, my ringlets waved. The Wasp's Song. "Lewis Carroll." FaBoNo
When I was young my teachers were the old. What Fifty Said. Robert Frost. NAs
When I was young, not knowing the taste of grief. Tune: Ugly Rogue. Hsin Ch'i-chi, *tr.* by Burton Watson. CoBCP
"When I was young," said Aunt to me. Other Fabrics, Other Mores! Anna Maria Lenngren, *tr.* by Nadia Christensen *and* Marianne Tiblin. AIW; PBWP
When I was young the days were long. The Flying Wheel. Katharine Tynan Hinkson. WGRP
When I was young, with sharper sense. A Summer Commentary. Yvor Winters. LiTM; QFR
When I was younger. William Carlos Williams. AmPP; OxBA
When I watch my two boys, Walter and Robert, at play. I Am as Happy as a Queen on Her Throne. Mrs. Henry Linden. CBWP-4
When I Watch the Living Meet. A. E. Housman. *Fr.* A Shropshire Lad, XII. CMoP; MoBrPo; NOBVV; NoP; TrGrPo
When I watch you. Miss Rosie. Lucille Clifton. AmPA; BlSi; CAPP; CNA; NMM; PoBA; TwCP
When I wear my football jersey to class. Marvin Pickett. Mel Glenn. ASP
When I went/ to Gaza and met. Samson Rends His Clothes. Anadad Eldan, *tr.* by Ruth Nevo. VWA
When I went into my garden, I found. Sister Bertken, *tr.* by Willis Barnstone. BoWoP
When I went into my room, at mid-morning. Man and Bat. D. H. Lawrence. RB
When I Went Off to Prospect. *Unknown*. AmFP
When I went out. A Spike of Green. Barbara Baker. RAR
When I Went Out. Karla Kuskin. NTCP
When I went out to kill myself, I caught. Saint Judas. James Wright. LCAP; NOBA; SM
When I went to bed at night. Through the Porthole. Marjorie Wilson. BoTP
When I Went to the Circus. D. H. Lawrence. CMoP; LiTB; MoP
When I went to visit. Tsurayuki, *tr.* by Geoffrey Bownas and Anthony Thwaite. PeBJV
When I went up the minster tower. At Lincoln. Oscar Fay Adams. AA
When I went up to Clova glen. Change and Immutability. Syd Scroggie. PoSH
When I wer still a bwoy, an' mother's pride. False Friends-like. William Barnes. NOBVV
When I were at home wi' my fayther an' mother, I niver had na fun. The Wensleydale Lad. *Unknown*. FaBoPP
When I wiped you from. Foolishness. Nizar Qabbani, *tr.* by Diana Der Hovanessian *and* Lena Jayyusi. MAP
When I, with the wind against me. Ballad of a Perennially Misunderstood Man. Gust Gils, *tr.* by Manfred Wolf. DuIn
When I woke, the lake-lights were quivering on the wall. Coming Awake. D. H. Lawrence. BrPo
When I woke up this morning I knew there was horror, I. Ice, Ice. Gerald Stern. AnAn
When I woke up this morning, I thought. Salt Peanuts. Riekus Waskowsky. DuIn
When I Would Die. Josephine D. Henderson Heard. CBWP-4
When I Would Image. George Meredith. NOBVV

When ice on the pond is three feet thick. *Unknown, tr. fr. Chinese by* Burton Watson. *Fr.* Tzu Yeh Songs. CoBCP
When icicles by silver eaves. Winter Fairyland in Vermont. Francis P. Osgood. WeW
When Icicles Hang by the Wall. Shakespeare. *Fr.* Love's Labour's Lost, V, ii. AWP; FaPON; FF; GN; GoJo; InPK; InPS; LiTB; NAEL-1; NOBE; PoRA; PrIm
  (Hiems.) FaBoCh; OBSC
  (Merry Note, A.) WiR
  (Song: "When icicles hang by the wall.") FiP; PBBP; PoEL-2
  (Tu-Whit To-Who.) CH
  (Winter.) BoNaP; ChTr; ElL; GTBS; GTBS-P; HAP; HeIP; NIP; OAEL-1; OBEV; SeCePo; TEP; TrGrPo; UnPo; WeW
When ideas, when thought itself. Nizar Qabbani, *tr. fr. Arabic by* Diana Der Hovanessian *and* Lena Jayyusi. *Fr.* The Actors, I. MAP
When idle in a poor Welsh mining valley. Rebel's Progress. Tom Earley. OBWVE
When I'm a little older. My Plan. Marchette Chute. FaPON
When I'm by myself I don't know. But I. Amir Gilboa, *tr. by* Warren Bargad *and* Stanley F. Chyet. IP
When I'm discharged in Liverpool 'n' draws my bit o' pay. Hell's Pavement. John Masefield. BrPo
When I'm driving up Bellefield in spring. For the Margrave of Brandenburg. Ed Ochester. SoTCo
When I'm far out in drink, your musical box. To My Daughter. James Michie. OxBSP
When I'm in bed at night. Noises in the Night. Lilian McCrea. BoTP
When I'm in France, for Frenchmen's sake. The Englishman on the French Stage. Sir Owen Seaman. OBTV
When I'm sealed. The Owl. Sándor Weöres, *tr. by* Jascha Kessler. FOC
When I'm six I'll marry Ibby. Variations on the Themes of Little Boys. Sándor Weöres, *tr. by* William Jay Smith. MHuP
When I'm that far south, the old words. México. Lorna Dee Cervantes. *Fr.* Visions of Mexico While at a Writing Symposium in Port Townsend, Washington. CCP; ER; NoAM
When I'm without you. Nights. Cyn Zarco. UL
When in a dent of the cliff. Slope. Nishiwaki Junzaburo, *tr. by* Hiroaki Sato. FCEI
When in April the Sweet Showers Fall. Chaucer. *See* Canterbury Tales, The: Prologue.
When in Banaras. Lepers Cry. Peter Orlovsky. GLP
When in danger or in doubt. Sound Advice. *Unknown.* FaBoUs; NBLV
"When, in disgrace with fortune and men's eyes." Shakespeare. *Fr.* Sonnets, XXIX. AWP; CTC; EBEV; ElL; FaBoRV; FaBV; GBL; HAP; HeIP; InPK; InPS; InvP; LiTB; NAEL-1; NOBE; NoP; OAEL-1; OBEV; OBSC; OPOP; PeHV; PoEL-2; Son
  (Consolation, A.) GTBS; GTBS-P
When in her face mine eyes I fix. William Alexander, Earl of Stirling. *Fr.* Aurora. ElL
When in My Arms. Pushkin, *tr. fr. Russian by* Babette Deutsch. ErPo
When, in my effervescent youth. Who'd Be a Hero (Fictional)? Morris Bishop. FiBHP; OBAL
When in my walks I meet some ruddy lad. Samuel Ward. AA
When in my youth I travelled. The Migration of the Grey Squirrels. William Howitt. OxBChV
When in nineteen-thirty-seven, Etta Moten, sweetheart. The Convert. Margaret Danner. BPo
When in Rome. Mari E. Evans. AmNP; SoSe
When in some sudden hush of earth. The Retreat. Sir Herbert Read. BrPo
When, in spring, the sun is misted. Mushimaro. *Fr.* Manyo Shu. Ma
"When, in summer." A Poet's Memory Is Counsel. Kallil Attiraiyanar, *tr. by* A. K. Ramanujan. PLW
When in the ardent spells. Echoes. José Peón y Contreras, *tr. by* Samuel Beckett. MexPo
When in the bedded dark of night. Marriage. Donald Hall. NePoEA
"When in the chronicle of wasted time." Shakespeare. *Fr.* Sonnets, CVI. AWP; BLPL; CTC; ElL; EnLoPo; FaBoCh; FaBV; FiP; LiTB; NAEL-1; NOBE; NoP; OBEV; OBSC; PoRA; Son; TEP; TrGrPo
  (To His Love.) GTBS; GTBS-P
When in the cold of a winter evening. On a Winter Evening. Koh Chang-soo, *tr. by the author.* ACKP
When, in the dawn of love and my desire. The Miracle. Allan Dowling. ErPo
When in the east the morning ray. Garden of Appleton House, The ("When in the east the morning ray"). Andrew Marvell. *Fr.* Upon Appleton House, to My Lord Fairfax. NOBE

When in the festival of August heat. Horas Tempestatis Quoque Enumero: The Sundial. John Hollander. NePoEA
When in the First Great Hour. E. M. Thomas. *Fr.* The Inverted Torch. AA
When in the halcyon days of eld, I was a little tyke. Our Biggest Fish. Eugene Field. AnAmPo
When in the mask of night there shone that cut. Landing on the Moon. May Swenson. TAP
When, in the midst of the thriving alien. Declaration of Independence. Michael Brownstein. UL
When in the mirror of a permanent tear. Elegy on Gordon Barber. Gene Derwood. FaFP
  (Elegy: "When in the mirror of a permanent tear.") LiTA; LiTM
When in the silent midnight grove. The Temper of Aristippus. John Gilbert Cooper. *Fr.* Epistles to His Friends in Town. PBBP
When in the sun the hot red acres smoulder. The Zulu Girl. Roy Campbell. OBMV
When in the throes of madness. Mohammad Taqi Mir, *tr. by* Ahmed Ali. GoT
When in the woods flashed forth that sword of fire. The Sword. Mir Babbar Ali Anis, *tr. by* Ahmed Ali. GoT
When in thy glass thou studiest thy face. Afternoon. Wendell Phillips Garrison. *Fr.* Post-Meridian. AA
When Israel against Philistia. David and Goliath. Nathaniel Crouch. OxBChV
When Israel Came Forth out of Egypt. Bible, *O.T. See* Psalms: Psalm CXIV ("When Israel went out of Egypt. . .").
When Israel came out of Egypt. Psalm CXIV: A Fountain from Wilderness Stone. Bible, *O.T.* CRP
When Israel, of the Lord beloved. Rebecca's Hymn. Sir Walter Scott. *Fr.* Ivanhoe, *ch.* 39. EnRP
When Israel out of Egypt Came. A. E. Housman. LiTB
When Israel Was in Egypt's Land. *Unknown. See* Go Down, Moses.
When Israel went out of Egypt. Psalm CXIV ("When Israel went out of Egypt. . ."). Bible, *O.T. Fr.* Psalms.
  (Psalm CXIV: "When Israel came from Egypt's coast", *paraphrased by* Christopher Smart) OBVE
  (When Israel Came Forth out of Egypt. . .) TrJP
When Israel's daughters mourn'd their past offences. Epigram in a Maid of Honour's Prayer-Book. Pope. FaBoEE
When it burns before the harps and freezes behind the easels. Hans Arp, *tr. by* Harriet Watts. FaBoNo
When It Came Time. Aharon Amir, *tr. fr. Hebrew by* Bernhard Frank. MHeP
When it comes to a question of trusting. The Average Man. Margaret E. M. Sangster. WBLP
When it comes to coldness, this is the pinnacle. Flakes of Auspicious Snow Fall Here. Chou Meng-tieh, *tr. by* Dominic Cheung. IFON
When it comes to poets. Yadoyano Meshimori, *tr. by* Sato. FCEI
When it gets towards Christmas. Brief Landing. Sarah Kirsch, *tr. by* Gerda Mayer. OV
When it is all over. Lost Moment. Hoyt W. Fuller. PoBA
When it is finally ours, this freedom, this liberty, this beautiful. Frederick Douglass. Robert Hayden. AmNP; CAPP; CNA; GOA; HCAP; IDB; NIP; PoBA; PoNe; Son; TTY
When It Is Given You to Find a Smile. Enrique Gonzáles Martínez, *tr. fr. Spanish by* Samuel Beckett. MexPo
When it is not yet day. Looking for Mushrooms at Sunrise. W. S. Merwin. NaP; NOBA
When it is only the echo. Echo. Zoltán Zelk, *tr. by* Barbara Howes. MHuP
When it is past—the golden moment—gone! Lost Opportunities. Henrietta Cordelia Ray. CBWP-3
When it snowed hard, cars failed. Bystanders. William Matthews. PPR
When it snows after a train wreck. The Train Wreck. Marcia Southwick. PPR
When it was late/ the Baal Shem Tov. Wonders. Shirley Kaufman. VWA
When it's Easter, someone. Judas. Gerhard Fritsch, *tr. by* Beth Bjorklund. CoAuP
When it's hot. Summer. Frank Asch. NTCP; RHPC
When it's ninety in the shade. Drive a Tractor. *Unknown.* NBLV
When it's of his wife. Senryu, *tr. by* Geoffrey Bownas *and* Anthony Thwaite. PeBJV
When it's time. Listening. Aileen Fisher. NTCP
When I've a saxpence under my thumb. Todlen Butt, and Todlen Ben. *Unknown.* OBS
When Jack had pulled the oar and the boat was gone. Jackie Tar. *Unknown.* OxBSS
When Jack the King's commander. The Fate of John Burgoyne. *Unknown.* PAH

When Jacob from the land of Canaan down. The Exodus from Egypt. Ezekielos of Alexandria, *tr. by* E. H. Gifford. TrJP

When James, our great monarch, so wise and discreet. Upon the King's Voyage to Chatham to Make Bulwarks against the Dutch. *Unknown.* APAS

When Januar' wind war blawing cauld. The Lass That Made the Bed for Me. Burns. InvP

When Jemmy the Second, not Jemmy the First. A New Song Entitled the Warming Pan. *Unknown.* CoMu

When Jesus came to Golgotha they hanged Him on a tree. Indifference. G. A. Studdert-Kennedy. TrCP

When Jesus was a little thing. His Mother in Her Hood of Blue. Lizette Woodworth Reese. OHIP

When Jesus was leaving this sin-accursed land. Whoso Gives Freely, Shall Freely Receive! Josephine D. Henderson Heaven. CBWP-4

When Jill complain[e]s to Jack for want of meat[e]. Upon Jack and Jill: Epigram. Robert Herrick. CaPo; NAEL-1

When John Henry was a little babe [*or* fellow]. John Henry. *Unknown.* AmFP; BPo

When John Henry was about three days old. John Henry. *Unknown.* AmFN

When John Henry was nothin' but a baby. John Henry. *Unknown.* FaBoBe

When Johnny Comes Marching Home. Patrick Sarsfield Gilmore. OPP; PAH

When Johnson sought (as Shakespear says) that bourn. Introduction and Anecdotes. "Peter Pindar." *Fr.* Bozzy and Piozzi. PoEL-3

When Jones's Ale Was New. *Unknown.* AmFP

When Joseph was an old man. The Cherry-Tree Carol. *Unknown.* AmFP

When joy surprises me, I ripen. Quatrains for Joy. Muhammad al-Ghuzzi, *tr. by* May Jayyusi *and* John Heath-Stubbs. MAP

When Judas writes the history of solitude. The Sacrifice. Frank Bidart. GLP; PPR

When Julius Fabricius, Sub-Prefect of the Weald. The Land. Kipling. MoBrPo; OnMSP

When Kavin comes back from the barber. Concerning Kavin. Bliss Carman. AnAmPo

When Klopstock England defied. Blake. OAEL-2

When lads have done with labor. A. E. Housman and a Few Friends. Humbert Wolfe. BXAP; FiBHP; Par

When lads were home from labour. Fancy's Knell. A. E. Housman. FaBoCh; PoRA

When Lalement and de Brébeuf, brave souls. Brébeuf and His Brethren. F. R. Scott. NOBC

When land is gone and money spent. *Unknown.* OxNR

When last I died [*or* When I dyed last], and, dear[e], I die [*or* dye]. The Legacy [*or* Legacie]. John Donne. SeCP; TrGrPo

When last I journeyed down. Tabito. *Fr.* Manyo Shu. Ma

When late I attempted your pity to move. An Expostulation. Isaac Bickerstaffe. FaBoCo; FiBHP; NIP

When late I heard the trembling cello play. The Cello. Richard Watson Gilder. AA

When lately King James, whom our sovereign we call. The Clerical Cabal. *Unknown.* APAS

When Lazarus left his charnel-cave. Tennyson. *Fr.* In Memoriam A. H. H., XXXI. TOF

When learning's triumph o'er her barb'rous [*or* barbarous] foes. Prologue Spoken [by Mr. Garrick] [at the Opening of the Theatre in Drury-Lane, 1747]. Samuel Johnson. EBEV; NAEL-1; NOEC; NoP

When leaves, in evenen winds, do vlee. Jay a-Pass'd. William Barnes. NOBVV

When leaves turn outward to the light. Poet and Lark. "Madeline Bridges." AA

When leaving the primrose, bayberry dunes, seaward. The Constant. A. R. Ammons. HAP; WeW

When leaving with your loving in my veins. Late Light. Barbara Bellow Watson. NYBP

When Lebrun in his felicitous lines. Reply to the Verses of M. Lebrun Entitled "My Last Word on Women Poets." Philippine de Vannoz, *tr. by* Beth Archer. DMF

When Lesbia first I saw so heavenly fair. Lesbia. Congreve. OxBSP

When Letty had scarce pass'd her third glad year. Letty's Globe. Charles Tennyson Turner. NOBVV; OBEV; OnUR

When Levin mowed Mashkin Hill. Mashkin Hill. Louis Simpson. SaC

When liberty is headlong girl. Liberty. Archibald MacLeish. GOA

When Life has borne its harvest from my heart. A Prayer in Late Autumn. Violet Alleyn Storey. TrPWD

When life hath run its largest round. Daniel Webster. Oliver Wendell Holmes. PAH

When like a bud my Julia blows. To Julia under Lock and Key. Sir Owen Seaman. BXAP; FaBoPa

When, like a Running Grave. Dylan Thomas. OAEL-2

When, like all liberal girls and boys. Days Pass: Men Pass. Stephen Vincent Benét. AnAmPo

When like the rising day. Gerald Griffin. *Fr.* Eileen Aroon. OBEV

When lilacs last in the dooryard bloom'd. When Lilacs Last in the Dooryard Bloom'd. Walt Whitman. *Fr.* Memories of President Lincoln. AmPP; AWP; FPL; HAP; LiTA; MoAmPo; NAAL-1; NOBA; NoP; OFD, 24 *ll.*; OxBA; PoEL-5; PoRA; PPP; TAP; TrGrPo

"Come lovely and soothing death." SCV
  (Carol of Death, The.) DL

"In the swamp in secluded recesses." RFM

When Lil's husband got demobbed, I said. T. S. Eliot. *Fr.* The Waste Land. NAs

When Lion sends his roaring forth. The Lion. Mary Howitt. FaPON

When little boys grow [*or* grown] patient at last, weary. Death of Little Boys. Allen Tate. LiTA; MoAB

When little heads weary have gone to their bed. The Plumpuppets. Christopher Morley. FaPON; RHPC

When little John Hardy was four years old. John Hardy. *Unknown.* AmFP; FaBoBa

When little people go abroad, wherever they may roam. To Henrietta, on Her Departure for Calais. Thomas Hood. OBTV; OxBChV

When Liverpool John was just sixteen he went away to sea. Liverpool John. Phil *and* June Colclough. OxBSS

When locked in murd'rous toils of wants and cares. F. I. Tyutchev, *tr. by* Alan Myers. AAA

When London Calls. Victor James Daley. CBAP

When Londons fatal bills were blown abroad. Marlburyes Fate. Benjamin Tompson. SCAP

When lonesome, I always stay in the moist courtyard. Grievance I. Tu Yeh, *tr. by* Dominic Cheung. IFON

When longings/ press too fiercely. Komachi, *tr. fr. Japanese by* Burton Watson. *Fr.* Kokin Shu. FCEI

When longings are too great. Sent to a Woman on a Rainy Day. Shunzei, *tr. fr. Japanese by* Burton Watson. *Fr.* Thirty Tanka. FCEI

When, looking on the present face of things. October 1803. Wordsworth. EnRP

When, loosened from the winter's bonds. Princess Nukada. *Fr.* Manyo Shu. Ma; PBWP

When lordly Saturn in a sable robe. Eurymachus's Fancy. Robert Greene. *Fr.* Francesco's Fortunes. OBSC

When Louis came home to the flat. Meet Me in St. Louis, Louis. Andrew B. Sterling. OBAL

When love/ Had strove. Love. Joseph Beaumont. OBS

When Love Comes Knocking. William Henry Gardner. AA

When love in the faint heart trembles. Song of Eros. George Edward Woodberry. *Fr.* Agathon. AA

When love is a shimmering curtain. On Diverse Deviations. Maya Angelou. BlSi

When love is ripe beyond bearing. What He Said. Perevin Muruvalar, *tr. by* A. K. Ramanujan. PLW

When Love Meets Love. Thomas Edward Brown. UnPo

When love on time and measure makes his ground. False Love. *At. to* John Lilliat. EBEV; OBSC
  (Song: "When love on time and measure makes his ground.") EIL

When Love, our great Immortal. The Rose of Stars. George Edward Woodberry. *Fr.* Wild Eden, IX. AA

When love was structured, so was verse—both fit. The Good Old Days. Barbara Fried. NBLV

When love with unconfinèd wings. To Althea, from Prison. Richard Lovelace. AWP; BLPA; CaPo; FaBoBe; FPL; GBL; GTBS; GTBS-P; HAP; HeIP; InPS; JCP; LiTB; MeLP; MePo; NAEL-1; NOBE; NoP; OBEV; OBS; PoE; PoRA; SeCP; SeCV-1; SoSe; TEP; TrGrPo

When lovely woman, prone to folly. *Unknown.* FaBoPa

"When Lovely Woman Stoops to Folly." Mary Demetriadis. FaBoPa

When Lovely Woman Stoops to Folly. Goldsmith. *Fr.* The Vicar of Wakefield, *ch.* 24. GTBS; GTBS-P; HAP; HeIP; NoP; PrIm; UnPo
  (Song: "When lovely woman stoops to folly.") AWP; BoLoP; NOBE; NOEC; SeCePo; TrGrPo
  (Stanzas on Woman.) ELP
  (Woman.) FPL; LiTB; OBEV

When Lovely Woman ("When lovely woman wants a favor"). Phoebe Cary. FaBoBe

When love's brief dream is done. Remember. Georgia Douglas Johnson. PoNe

When lyart leaves bestrew the yird. Burns. *Fr.* The Jolly Beggars. NOEC

When Magritte died. Homage to René Magritte. George Melly. EAS

When Mahalia Sings. Quandra Prettyman. IDB; PoBA

When maidens are young, and in their spring. Aphra Behn. *Fr.* Emperor of the Moon. FF

When maidens such as Hester die. Hester. Charles Lamb. EnRP; GTBS; GTBS-P; OBEV

When making for the brook, the falconer doth espy. Hawking. Michael Drayton. *Fr.* Polyolbion, Twentieth Song. SD

When Malindy Sings. Paul Laurence Dunbar. PoBA; PoNe

When man first flew beyond the sky. Song in Space. Adrian Mitchell. PoPo

When man has conquered space. Earth's Bondman. Betty Page Dabney. GoYe

When man walketh moon. T. Griffiths. BXAP

When many years we'd been apart. Reminiscence. Wallace Irwin. FiBHP; NOBL

When Mary Goes Walking. Patrick R. Chalmers. BoTP

When Mary thro' the Garden Went. Mary Elizabeth Coleridge. BoTP

When Master Ungo asked. Zuigan, *tr. by* Lucien Stryk *and* Takashi Ikemoto. ZPCJ

When May has come, and all around. The Archer. Clinton Scollard. FaPON

When May is in his prime, then may each heart rejoice. May. Richard Edwards. OBSC

When memory's fabled daughter. Notes for a History of Poetry. David Daiches. PoA

When men a dangerous disease did 'scape. To Doctor Empiric[k]. Ben Jonson. FaBoEE; NoP; SeCP

When men are born in disorderly times. The Ballad of Ch'ao-chou. Huang Tsun-hsien, *tr. by* J. D. Schmidt. WFTU

When men are laid away. Inscription for a Graveyard. Yvor Winters. CRP

When men-folk scoff at us, I have to draw my sword. Letter to Mariana Ziegler. Anna Helena Volckmann, *tr. by* Susan L. Cocalis. DMG

When men shall find thy flower [*or* flow'r], thy glory, pass. Samuel Daniel. *Fr.* To Delia. NAEL-1; NOBE; NoP; OBEV; OBSC; Son; TrGrPo

(Sonnet: "When men shall find thy flower, thy glory, pass.") EiL

When men were all asleep the snow came flying. London Snow. Robert Bridges. BoNaP; BrPo; CH; ChTr; CMoP; EBEV; EBVV; FaBoPP; GTBS-P; LiTB; LiTM; MoAB; MoBrPo; MoP; NoAM; NOBE; NOBVV; OAEL-2; OBNC; OxBTC; PoEL-5; SeCePo; TrGrPo; WiR

When midnight comes a host of dogs and men. Badger. John Clare. EnRP; HAP; LiTB; NoP; NU; OAEL-2; PoE; PoEL-4; PrIm; WeW; WiR

When Mike stuck a knife in Nancy. The Precinct Station. Louis Simpson. EOEF

When mild Favonius breathes, with warbling throat. Hoc Cygno Vinces. Henry Hawkins. ACP

When milder autumn summer's heat succeeds. Pope. *Fr.* Windsor Forest. PBBP

(Field Sports.) SeCePo

When milkweed blows in the pasture. Horse-Chestnut Time. Kaye Starbird. PDV

When Milton sees his "late espoused saint." Confessional Poetry. Tony Harrison. DiPo

When mine eynen misteth. *Unknown.* EBEV

(All too late.) OAEL-1

When Miriam Tazewell heard the tempest bursting. Miriam Tazewell. John Crowe Ransom. TW

When mist rises on the seashore. *Unknown. Fr.* Manyo Shu. Ma

When Mister Mulryan called me into his office. A Deck of Cards. Gail Mazur. PPR

When moiling seems at cease. "According to the Mighty Working." Thomas Hardy. CMoP

When Monday drives the roses through the ground. For Judith. Konrad Bayer, *tr. by* Beth Bjorklund. CoAuP

When 'mongst the youths you lately came. *Unknown, tr. by* Sydney Oswald. PeHV

When Monk laid it down. Two Handfuls of *Waka* for Thelonious Sphere Monk (d. Feb. 1982). Walter Lew. BrSi

When Monmouth the chaste read those impudent lines. An Excellent New Ballad Giving a True Account of the Birth and Conception of a Late Famous Poem Called the Female Nine. Charles Sackville. APAS

When Moonlike ore the Hazure Seas. Thackeray. NA

When Morgan crossed the Murray to Peechelba and doom. Morgan. Edward Harrington. PoAu-1

When morning came. The Brother. Peter Everwine. FYAP; NNaP

When morning has come, all the chief priests and elders of the people. Bible, *N.T. Fr.* St. Matthew, XXVII. NAWM-1

When morning is breaking and darkness has fled. We Are Passing Away. Matilda Caroline Edwards. PWR

When morning's caravan had crossed the night. Morning. Mir Babbar Ali Anis, *tr. by* Ahmed Ali. GoT

When Moses and his people. Just the Same Today. *Unknown.* BLRP; WBLP

When Moses in Horeb struck the rock. On Certain Wits. Howard Nemerov. HCAP; OxBC

When Moses, musing in the desert, found. The Burning Bush. Norman Nicholson. EaLo; SeCePo

When Moses was as old as God. Moses and Joshua. Else Lasker-Schüler, *tr. by* Joachim Neugroschel. VWA

When Mosquitoes Make a Meal. Else Holmelund Minarik. RHPC

When Mother Died. Natsume Seibi, *tr. fr. Japanese by* Hiroaki Sato. *Fr.* Twenty-seven Hokku. FCEI

When mother divorced you, we were glad. She took it and. The Victims. Sharon Olds. InPS; NIP

When Mother Reads Aloud. *Unknown.* FaPON

When mother was small. Fireflies. Li Nan, *tr. by* Dominic Cheung. IFON

When mothers weep and fathers richly proud. The Confirmation. Karl Shapiro. ErPo

When mountain rocks and leafy trees. Nature's Lineaments. Robert Graves. FaBoTw; RB

When mountains are split. Sanetomo, *tr. by* Geoffrey Bownas *and* Anthony Thwaite. PeBJV

When mountains crumble and rivers all run dry. The Line of Beauty. Arthur William Edgar O'Shaughnessy. TIRV

When Mr. Apollinax visited the United States. Mr. Apollinax. T. S. Eliot. PoA

When Mr. Croxford. At the St. Louis Institute of Music. Ronald Wallace. GOYP

When Mrs. Gorm (Aunt Eloise). Opportunity. Harry Graham. FaBoCo

When Mrs. Taflan Gruffyd Lewis left Dai's flat. What about You? Edward Pygge. BXAP; FaBoPa

When music, heav'nly maid, was young. The Passions, an Ode for [*or* to] Music. William Collins. GTBS; GTBS-P

When my Anselm/ drifts away. H. C. Artmann, *tr. by* Beth Bjorklund. CoAuP

When my arms wrap you round I press. He Remembers Forgotten Beauty. W. B. Yeats. CTC; LLLT

(Michael Robartes Remembers Forgotten Beauty.) BrPo

When my Aunt Leratiny now. Make Me Hear You. Reginald Gibbons. MAYP

When my birthday was coming. Little Brother's Secret. Katherine Mansfield. FaPON; NAs

When my blood flows calm as a purling river. Communism. Ella Wheeler Wilcox. AnAmPo

When my brother Tommy. Two in Bed. Abram Bunn Ross. FaPON; NTCP

When My Brothers Come Home. Aires de Almeida Santos, *tr. fr. Portuguese by* Margaret Dickinson. WMBCH

When my devotions could not pierce. Denial. George Herbert. JCP; NAEL-1; NOBE; NoP; OAEL-1

(Deniall.) MePo; PoEL-2; TOF

When My Dog Died. Freya Littledale. NTCP

When my father died. Between Here and Illinois. Ralph Pomeroy. Psk

When my father had been dead a week. White Apples. Donald Hall. TAP

When my flaps peel back, I am seen. Dermis. Anthony McNeill. PBCV

When my gloomy hour comes to me. Alexander McLachlan. *Fr.* Woman. CaP

When My Grandmother Died. Sam Cornish. Psk

When my grandmother left the races with Mr. Hughes. Mr. Hughes. David Campbell. CBAP

When my grandmother was dying. Sorrow. T. R. Hummer. MT

When my grave is broke up again[e]. The Relic. John Donne. EiL; GBL; HAP; HeIP; LiTB; NOBE; NoP; OAEL-1; PoEL-2; PPP

(Relique, The.) MeLP; MePo; OBS; PoEL-2; SeCP; SeCV-1

When my husband. Ten Years and More. Miriam Waddington. NOBC

When my Italian son. In Front of a Poster of Garibaldi. Stanley Moss. DiL

When my life has enough of love, and my spirit enough of mirth. A Wanderer's Litany. Arthur Stringer. WGRP

When my life was thrifty, thrifty. The Shearing. *Unknown, tr. by* Glyn Jones. OBWVE

When my love becomes/ All-powerful. Ono no Komachi, *tr. fr. Japanese by* Geoffrey Bownas *and* Anthony Thwaite. PBWP; PeBJV

"When my love swears [*or* sweares] that she is made of truth." Shakespeare. *Fr.* Sonnets, CXXXVIII. AWP; EBEV; NAEL-1; NoP; OAEL-1; PoEL-2; PPP; SoSe; TEP; TrGrPo

When my mirror clouds up. Emperor Go-Shirakawa, *tr. fr. Japanese by* Hiroaki Sato. *Fr.* Ryojin Hisho. FCEI

When my mother died I was very young. Chimney Sweeper, The. Blake. *Fr.* Songs of Innocence. CH; EnRP; FaBoPV; FF; HeIP; InPK; NAEL-2; NAWM-2; NOEC; OAEL-2; OxBChV; PoE; PPP; SaC; SoSe; TEP

When my mother fell from the cherry tree. My Mother and the Touched Old Woman. Gary Gildner. MOWH; SoTCo

When my mother shall see my brothers. When My Brothers Come Home. Aires de Almeida Santos, *tr. by* Margaret Dickinson. WMBCH

When my older brother. The Rain. Zbigniew Herbert, *tr. by* Czeslaw Milosz. PwPP

When My Sensational Moments Are No More. E. E. Cummings. Son

When My Ship Comes In. Robert J. Burdett. FaFP

When my spring unbound comes o'er us like a flood. In April. Ethelwyn Wetherald. CaP

When my wife brings breakfast. Diary of a Prisoner. Lo Ch'ing, *tr. by* Dominic Cheung. IFON

When my young brother was killed. War. Joseph Langland. AiP; FF; NePoEA

When Narcissus died the pool of his pleasure changed. The Disciple. Oscar Wilde. OAEL-2

When Nature bids us leave to live, 'tis late. To William Roe. Ben Jonson. OAEL-1; OBS; SeCV-1

When Nature dreamt of making bores. Epigram: On Sir Roger Phillimore. *Unknown.* FaBoCo; NBLV

When Nature had made all her birds. The Bobolinks. Christopher Pearse Cranch. AA; GN

When Nature Hath Betrayed the Heart That Loved Her. Sophie Jewett. AA

When Nature heard men thought her old. The Mistress. Sir William Davenant. JCP

"When Nature made her chief work, Stella's eyes." Sir Philip Sidney. *Fr.* Astrophel and Stella, VII. NAEL-1; NIP; Son

When nature once in lustful hot undress. Giantess. Baudelaire, *tr. by* Karl Shapiro. ErPo; OBVE

When nature's God for our offenses died. A Stanza Put on Westminster Hall Gate. *Unknown.* APAS

When Neptune from his billows London spied. Of London Bridge, and the Stupendous Sight, and Structure Thereof. James Howell. ChTr; FaBoPP

When nettles in winter bring forth roses red. Trust in Women. *Unknown.* NA

When news came that your mother'd. Kin. Michael S. Harper. LCAP

When News of Saichi's Death Arrived. Ryokan, *tr. fr. Chinese by* Burton Watson. JLIC-2

When next we met, she bade me turn. Apostasy. Aus of Kuraiza, *tr. by* Hartwig Hirschfeld. TrJP

When night comes down on the children's eyes. At Night in the Wood. Nancy M. Hayes. BoTP

When night comes, even shy stars. Conversing. Lan Ling, *tr. by* Dominic Cheung. IFON

When night comes slippin' up the valley. Greasin' the Miles. Nick Johnson. CowP

When night drifts along the streets of the city. Solitaire. Amy Lowell. MoAmPo

When night fell, when day broke. Tsurayuki, *tr. fr. Japanese by* Burton Watson. *Fr.* Kokin Shu. FCEI

When night first bids the twinkling stars appear. London at Night. John Gay. *Fr.* Trivia; or, The Art of Walking the Streets of London. FaBoPP

When night is come, and all around is still. Safe in His Keeping. Edgar Cooper Mason. BLRP

When night is dark. At Night. Aileen Fisher. RAR

When night plows the meadows of darkness. Lonely Are the Fields of Sleep. Mary Newton Baldwin. GoYe

When night shadows slipped across the plain, I saw a man. A Nation Wrapped in Stone. Roberta Hill. BoWoP; CDW

When night stirred at sea. The Planter's Daughter. Austin Clarke. CIP; OxBTC

When night-time bars me in. Snowdrops. Margiad Evans. OBWVE

When Night's Black Mantle. Mary Sidney Wroth, Countess of Montgomery. *Fr.* Urania. Son

When no one listens. Stranger. Thomas Merton. EaLo

When noon is warm, old Pensioners. Out of Soundings. Padraic Fallon. NeIP

When North first began. Lord North's Recantation. *Unknown.* PAH

When nothing is happening. How Everything Happens. May Swenson. HAP; RFM

When Nothing Remains. Stanislaw Grochowiak, *tr. fr. Polish by* Czeslaw Milosz. PwPP

When nothing whereon to lean remains. The Time to Trust. *Unknown.* BLRP

When Oakwood Burns. Kim Hyun-sung, *tr. fr. Korean by* Koh Chang-soo. ACKP

When Oats Were Reaped. Thomas Hardy. OxBTC

When objects diverge like tree branches. The World of Verna Lisa. Yung Tzu, *tr. by* Dominic Cheung. IFON

When ocean breezes blow the moon. Inscribed on the Painting "Solitary Crane." Yü Chi, *tr. by* Jonathan Chaves. CoBLCP

When ocean-clouds over inland hills. Misgivings. Herman Melville. NAAL-1; NOBA; OxBA

When o'er the hill the eastern star. My Ain Kind Dearie, O. Burns. GoTS

When o'er the wold the heedless lamb. Thomas Holcroft. NOEC

When Ogden his prosaic verse. On Dr. Samuel Ogden. R. P. Arden. FaBoCo

When Ol' Sis' Judy Pray. James Edwin Campbell. BANP

When old cars get retired, they go to Maine. Maine. Philip Booth. AmFN

When old corruption first begun. Blake. *Fr.* An Island in the Moon. RB

(Quid the Cynic's Song.) FaBoNo

When old crones wandered in the woods. Child Naming Flowers. Robert Hass. MAYP; NPGG

When old heads felt to-day. On Hearing a Broadcast of Ceremonies in Connection with Conferring of Cardinals' Hats. Denis Wrafter. NeIP

When Old John Bax drove the mail to Coonabarabran. Old John Bax. Charles Henry Souter. PoAu-1

When old philosophers wrote the world's birth. A Panegyric on the Author of "Absalom and Achitophel." *Unknown.* APAS

When 'Omer Smote 'Is Bloomin' Lyre. Kipling. Par

When on my bed the moonlight falls. Tennyson. *Fr.* In Memoriam A. H. H., LXVII. NoP; SeCePo

When on my day of life the night is falling. At Last. Whittier. TrPWD; WGRP

When on my sick bed I languish. A Thought of Death. Thomas Flatman. OBS

When on my soul in nakedness. The Quiet Pilgrim. Edith M. Thomas. AA

When on my time of living I reflect. My Thirty Years. Juan Fransico Manzano, *tr. by* Oliver Cobarn *and* Ursula Lehrburger. TTY

When on my travels I pine for home. Kurohito. *Fr.* Manyo Shu. Ma

When, on our casual way. The Shakespearean Bear. Arthur Guiterman. CenHV

When on some balmy-breathing night of spring. The Glow-Worm. Charlotte Smith. FM

When on the barn's thatch'd roof is seen. Signs of Christmas. Edwin Lees. OHIP

When, on the bearing mother, death's. Childbirth. Ted Hughes. NAs

When on the high bluff discovering. From the North Saskatchewan. Eli Mandel. NOBC

When once I knew the Lord. Hymn of Sivaite Puritans. *Unknown.* WGRP

When once the scourging prophet, with his cry. The Disused Temple. Norman Cameron. OxBS; OxBTC

When once the sun sinks in the west. Evening Primrose. John Clare. CH; TrGrPo

When one climber fell to his doom, I also fell. The Climbing Rope. Alice V. Stuart. PoSH

When one gathers beans, gathers beans. *Unknown, tr. by* Arthur Waley. BoS

When one looks at it. Tamekane, *tr. by* Steven D. Carter. WFTW

When One Loves Tensely. (Don Marquis). FiBHP; NBLV

When One made love to Zero. Sines. Raymond Queneau, *tr. by* Teo Savory. RHTwFP

When one of the old, little stars doth fall from its place. Sidera Cadentia. Ford Madox Ford. OxBSP

When one of them moved through the center of Selefkia. One of Their Gods. C. P. Cavafy, *tr. by* Edmund Keeley *and* Philip Sherrard. VMG

When one or other rambles. Francis Daniel Pastorius. SCAP

When one's been drunk, the best relief I know. Hangover Cure. Amphis. FaBoUs

When Orion straddled his apex of sky. The White Land. Roberta Hill Whiteman. HATNAP

When Orpheus sent down to the regions below. The Power of Music. Thomas Lisle. NOBL

When other fair ones [*or* ladies] to the shades [*or* groves] go down. Pope. FaBoEE
  (Epigram: "When other Ladies to the Shades go down.") OxBSP; PoEL-3
  (On Certain Ladies.) FaBoCo
When others mustered out in '46, you soldiered. The Sergeant. Don Johnson. MAYP
When others run to windows or out of doors. Part for the Whole. Robert Francis. PoA
When our babe he goeth walking in his garden. Garden and Cradle. Eugene Field. AA
When our brother Fire was having his dog's day. Brother Fire. Louis MacNeice. MoAB; MoP; NoAM; NOBE; WaaP
When our cars touched. Jump Cabling. Linda Pastan. InPK
When our children cried in the shadow of the gallows. Nathan Alterman, *tr. fr. Hebrew by* Simon Halkin. *Fr.* From All Peoples. TrJP
When our dean took a pious young spinster. Victor Gray. NOBL
When Our Earthly Sun Is Setting. Edwin H. Nevin. AH
When our rude and unfashion'd words, that long. To a Lady Who Did Sing Excellently. Herbert of Cherbury. OBS; SeCP
When our tears are dry on the shore. Rediscovery. Kofi Awoonor. TTY
When our two souls stand up erect and strong. Elizabeth Barrett Browning. *Fr.* Sonnets from the Portuguese, XXII. BoWoP; NAEL-2; NOBE; OBEV; TrGrPo; WPE
When Our Voices Broke Off. James Seay. MT
When out at Shellbrook, round by stile and tree. Shellbrook. William Barnes. OBNC
When, over-arched by gorgeous night. The Unknown God. Sir William Watson. WGRP
When over the flowery, sharp pasture's. Flowers by the Sea. William Carlos Williams. CMoP; GoJo; MoAB; MoAmPo; NoAM; RB; TAP
When pails empty the last brightness. O You among Women. F. R. Higgins. BIrV
When Pan Silvester, our neighbor, died. At That Time. Alfred Gong, *tr. by* Beth Bjorklund. CoAuP
When, parched by the thirst of his soul. Manhood. Adela Zamudio, *tr. by* Kate Flores. DMH
When Parnell's Irish in the House. Wilfred Owen's Photographs. Ted Hughes. FaBoPV; OxBC
When passion's trance is overpast. To——— Shelley. EnRP
When pavements were blown up, exposing nerves. Epilogue to a Human Drama. Stephen Spender. CMoP
When pensive on that portraiture I gaze. Sonnet on a Family Picture. Thomas Edwards. NOEC
When people ask me where I come from. Strangers in a Hostile Landscape. Meiling Jin. WS
When people call this beast to mind. The Elephant. Hilaire Belloc. BoTP
When people choose. Life's Will. Abu al-Qasim al-Shabbi, *tr. by* Sargon Boulus *and* Christopher Middleton. MAP
When people come with big muddy feet. Go Throw Them Out. Moyshe-Leyb Halpern, *tr. by* Ruth Whitman. VWA
When people's ill they come to I. On Dr. Isaac Letsome. *Unknown.* FaBoCo
When periwigs came first in wear. The Bald Cavalier. *Unknown.* OxBChV
When Pershing's men go marching into Picardy. Marching Song. Dana Burnet. PAH
When Petula Clark sang "Downtown," I wished I. Meet the Supremes. David Trinidad. UL
When Phoebe formed a wanton smile. William Collins. EnLoPo; OxBSP
When Phoebus had melted the sickles of ice. Robin Hood and the Ranger. *Unknown.* ESPB
When Phoebus in the rainy cloud. Welcome Eild. *Unknown.* GoTS
When Phoebus lifts his head out of the winter's wave. Michael Drayton. *Fr.* Polyolbion, Thirteenth Song. OBS; PBBP
When Piecrust first began to reign. A Fancy. *Unknown.* FaBoNo
When pleasing heat, and fragrant blooms inspire. William Diaper, *after the Greek of* Oppian. *Fr.* Halieutica. BXAP
When poetry walked the live, spring wood. Kingcups. Sacheverell Sitwell. MoBrPo
When poets get quite famous. High Poetic Circles. Gavin Ewart. NPo
When poets print their works, the scribbling crew. To My Ingenious and Worthy Friend William Lowndes, Esq. John Gay. OBSV
When Polly Buys a Hat. E. Hill. BoTP
When Polly lived back in the old deep woods. Stranger. Elizabeth Madox Roberts. MoAmPo
When Poor Mary Came Wandering Home. *Unknown.* AS
When poppies in the garden bleed. The End of Summer. Edna St. Vincent Millay. BoNaP

When President John Quincy. John Quincy Adams. Rosemary *and* Stephen Vincent Benét. OBCA
When primroses are out in Spring. Days Too Short. W. H. Davies. MoBrPo
When Psyche's friend becomes her lover. Friend and Lover. "Madeline Bridges." AA
When quacks with pills political would dope us. Canopus. Bert Leston Taylor. FiBHP; NOBL
When raging [*or* ragyng] love with extreme pain [*or* payne]. Consolation. Earl of Surrey. AAS; EBEV; EnLoPo; NOBE; OBSC; SiPS; TEP
When rain falls gray and unabating. A Different Door. X. J. Kennedy. CRH
When Reason's ray shines over all. On the Triumph of Rationalism. Alfred Ainger. FaBoCo
When Reedisdale and Wise William. Redesdale and Wise William. *Unknown.* ESPB
When Reuben Pantier ran away and threw me. Dora Williams. Edgar Lee Masters. *Fr.* Spoon River Anthology. HAP
When Rilke's writer's block. Just Dessert. Colette Inez. SoTCo
When Rimbaud became a slave-trader. To Rimbaud. Mu'in Besseisso, *tr. by* Abdullah al-Udhari. MPAW
When rising from the bed of death. Joseph Addison. TOF
When rites and melodies begin. The Proof. W. H. Auden. OAEL-2
When ritual was the reason for living. Kekchi Warrior. Marco Antonio Flores, *tr. by* David Volpendesta. Vol
When roaring gloom surged inward and you cried. To His Dead Body. Siegfried Sassoon. NoAM
When Robert Graves got involved. Robert Graves. Gavin Ewart. NoAM
When Robin Hood, and his merry men all. Robin Hood and the Valiant Knight. *Unknown.* ESPB
When Robin Hood and Little John. Robin Hood's Death. *Unknown.* ESPB; FaBoBa; OBET; TrGrPo
When Robin Hood in the green-wood livd. Robin Hood Rescuing Will Stutly. *Unknown.* ESPB
When Robin Hood was about eighteen [*or* twenty] years old. Robin Hood and Little John. *Unknown.* AmFP; ESPB
When Rooks Fly Homeward. Joseph Campbell. TIRV
When rosy plumelets tuft the larch. Tennyson. *Fr.* In Memoriam A. H. H., XCI. OBNC
When Ruth was left half desolate. Ruth; or, The Influences of Nature. Wordsworth. ChER; EnRP; GTBS; GTBS-P; PoEL-4
When ruthful time the South's memorial places. The Stricken South to the North. Paul Hamilton Hayne. PAH
When Saint Mochua knelt to pray. The Little Pets of Saint Mochua. John Irvine. TIRV
When Sam goes back in memory. Sam. Walter de la Mare. FaBV; MoAB; MoBrPo; OnMSP
When Sarah Pierrepont let her spirit rage. Address to the Scholars of New England. John Crowe Ransom. GOA; LiTM
When science starts to be interpretive. Self-Protection. D. H. Lawrence. NoP
When Serpents Bargain for the Right to Squirm. E. E. Cummings. PrIm; SoSe; TwCP
When seven years were come and gane. Sweet William's Ghost. *Unknown.* ESPB
When seyd was al this miracle, every man. Prologue to Sir Thopas. Chaucer. *Fr.* The Canterbury Tales. Par
  ("Whan said was al this miracle, every man.") NAEL-1
When Shakespeare, Jonson, Fletcher ruled the stage. In Defense of Satire. Sir Carr Scroope. APAS
When shall I master this anxiety. August, Graf von Platen. *Fr.* Sonnets to Karl Theodore German, I. PeHV
When shall I see the half-moon sink again. End of Another Home Holiday. D. H. Lawrence. EBEV; FaBoMo
When shall I see the white thorn leaves agen. The Yellowhammer. John Clare. NOBVV
When Shall My Pilgrimage, Jesus My Saviour, Be Ended? *At. to* Andrew Rudman, *tr. fr. Swedish by* Ernest Edwin Ryden. AH
When Shall We All Meet Again? *Unknown.* AH
When shall we be married. *Unknown.* OxNR
When shall we learn, what should be clear as day. W. H. Auden. LiTA
When shawes beene sheene, and shrads [*or* shradds] fyll [*or* full] fayre. Robin Hood and Guy of Gisborne. *Unknown.* ESPB
When She a Maiden Slim. Maurice Hewlett. OHIP
When she asked. Educating the Body. Kevin Ireland. ATNZ
When she asked me to keep an eye on her things. Bewley's Oriental Café, Westmoreland Street. Paul Durcan. CIP
When she came suddenly in. The Door. Robert Graves. LiTB
When she cannot be sure. Woman Alone. Denise Levertov. WPOW
When she carries food to the table and stoops down. Part of Plenty. Bernard Spencer. ErPo; GBL; LiTB; LiTM

When She Comes. O. V. de L. Milosz, *tr. fr. French by* John Peck. RHTwFP

When She Comes Home. James Whitcomb Riley. AA; AnAmPo; BLPL; FaBoBe

When she died, lightning struck in the north. The Devil's Daughter. Lucha Corpi, *tr. fr. Spanish by the author and* Catherine Rodríguez-Nieto. *Fr.* The Marina Poems, III. CCP; OV

When she died no face turned pale, no lips trembled. Elegy for a Woman of No Importance. Nazik al-Mala'ika, *tr. by* Chris Knipp *and* Mohammad Sadiq. OV

When she fed the/ child. The Feeding. Joel Oppenheimer. NeAP

When she gives a "psychic reading." Crepe de Chine. Tennessee Williams. NYBP

When she goes to Hollywood. Helen in Hollywood. Judy Grahn. ER

When she lived near St. Lawrence. William Rossa Cole. *Fr.* A Mini-Samizdat of New River Rhymes. SoTCo

When she opened her eyes the fields were gone into houses. For the Field. Eric Chock. BrSi

When she opens her eye this morning. For the Fourth Birthday of My Daughter. George Barker. NAs

When She Plays upon the Harp or Lute. Moses ibn Ezra, *tr. fr. Hebrew by* Solomon Solis-Cohen. TrJP

When she put her hand on me. The First Time. John Newlove. NeAC

When she rises in the morning. Gloire de Dijon. D. H. Lawrence. BrPo; CMoP; ELP; EnLoPo; ErPo; GBL; NoAM

When she sleeps, her soul, I know. Doubts. Rupert Brooke. CH

When she speaks it is like coming onto a grave. Gray Eyes. Tess Gallagher. NAmP

When she wails. *Unknown, tr. by* Geoffrey Bownas *and* Anthony Thwaite. PeBJV

When she walks through the door, at last. Meeting Up. Vincent O'Sullivan. ATNZ

When she was alive, now a memory. Hitomaro. *Fr.* Manyo Shu. FCEI

When She Was Born. Robert Tofte. *Fr.* Laura, III, vii. Son

When She Was Here, Li Bo. Peter Williams. InPK

When she was in her garden. Ann and the Fairy Song. Walter de la Mare. *Fr.* A Child's Day. FaBV

When she was little. Poem for Aretha. Nikki Giovanni. BPo; PoBA

When she was young and dancing. Jane Austen at the Window. Patricia Beer. FaBoWP

When she who gave you life has departed with pain. Childhood Summers. Helena Anhava, *tr. by* Aili Jarvenpa. SOP

When Sickly Jim Wilson's first wife died. The Courtship. George Ella Lyon. MOWH

When sickness struck me I had thoughts that. Evening. Khalil Mutran, *tr. by* Issa Boullata *and* Thomas G. Ezzy. MAP

When Silence Divests Me. Henry Birnbaum. GoYe

When silver Diane full of beames bright. A Starscape. John Bellenden. ACP

When silver snow decks Susan's clothes. Blind-Man's Buff. Blake. WiR

When, sin-stricken, burdened, and weary. "My Grace Is Sufficient for Thee." *Unknown.* BLRP

When singing songs of scariness. The Worst. Shel Silverstein. WSC

When Sir Beelzebub. Edith Sitwell. *See* Façade: Sir Beelzebub.

When Sir Joshua Reynolds died. Sir Joshua Reynolds. Blake. FaBoCo; FaBoEE; FiBHP; OxBoLi; TW

When Sisyphus was pushing the stone up the mountain. Sisyphus. Josephine Miles. NYBP

When ski-ing in the Engadine. Patience. Harry Graham. FiBHP; MoShBr

When Slavery Seems Sweet. Ed Bullins. NBP

When slaves their liberties require. Phillis's Resolution. William Walsh. OxBSP

When sleeping alone. Hand-Jive. Sandie Castle. UL

When sly Jemmy Twitcher had smugged up his face. The Candidate. Thomas Gray. PPP

When Smoke Stood up from Ludlow. A. E. Housman. *Fr.* A Shropshire Lad, VII. MoBrPo

When snow-balls pack on the horses' hoofs. Sugar Weather. Peter McArthur. CaP

When snow like sheep lay in the fold. In Memory of Jane Fraser [*or* Frazer]. Geoffrey Hill. MoP; NAEL-2; NePoEA; NoAM; OxBTC

When so little of his life remained. Kon Myogun. *Fr.* Manyo Shu. Ma

When soft September brings again. Pont-y-Wern. Arthur Hugh Clough. *Fr.* Ambarvalia. FaBoPP

When Sol did cast no light. The [Valiant] Seaman's Happy Return [to His Love]. *Unknown.* ChTr; GBP

When Sol had loosed his weary teams. Juggy's Christening. *Unknown.* NOEC

When Solomon was reigning in his glory. Solomon and the Bees. John Godfrey Saxe. GN

When some beloved voice that was to you. Substitution. Elizabeth Barrett Browning. WGRP

When some beloveds, 'neath whose eyelids lay. Bereavement. Elizabeth Barrett Browning. WPE

When some boys. Some Boys. Chuck Ortleb. GLP; PeHV

When some brisk youth, the tenant of a stall. Byron. *Fr.* English Bards and Scotch Reviewers. PF

When some great sorrow, like a mighty river. This, Too, Shall [*or* Will] Pass Away. Lanta Wilson Smith. BLPA

When some proud son of man returns to earth. Inscription on the Monument of a Newfoundland Dog. Byron. TEP

When someone asks me who I am. For the Curious. Yisroel Shtern, *tr. by* Robert Friend. PeBMYV

When someone hangs up, having said. The Business Life. David Ignatow. NNaP; TW

When someone talks of the spirit. Human Wisdom. Washington Delgado, *tr. by* David Tipton. Per

When Something Happens. James A. Randall, Jr. BPo

When somewhere life. Beaver Moon—The Suicide of a Friend. Mary Oliver. GOYP

When summer toke in hand the winter to assail. Henry Howard, Earl of Surrey. *See* Love's Rebel.

"When sorrow (using mine own fire's might)." Sir Philip Sidney. *Fr.* Astrophel and Stella, CVIII. AAS; SiPS, (*Sonnets, I–CVIII and 9 Songs*)

When sorrows had begirt me round. For Deliverance from a Fever. Anne Bradstreet. NAAL-1

When souls that have put off their mortal gear. Recognition. John White Chadwick. AA

When Spanky goes. Basketball. Nikki Giovanni. RHPC

When sparrows build churches and steeples high. *Unknown. Fr.* Trust in Women. PBBP

When Spoon River became a ganglion. Marx the Sign Painter. Edgar Lee Masters. *Fr.* The New Spoon River. NoAM; TAP

When sporgles spanned the floreate mead. Uffia. Harriet R. White. NA

When spring arrives, blossoming trees cover the capital. Manifold Little Hills. Ho Ning, *tr. by* Lois Fusek. ATF

When Spring came,/ Leaves grew with a green fresh. *Unknown.* RFM

When spring comes. *Unknown, tr. by* Geoffrey Bownas *and* Anthony Thwaite. PeBJV

When spring comes. For the Children Who Died in a Smallpox Epidemic. Ryokan, *tr. by* Hiroaki Sato. FCEI

When spring comes. Shunzei, *tr. fr. Japanese by* Burton Watson. *Fr.* Thirty Tanka. FCEI

When spring comes, from the paddy dam, small dam. Rice-Planting Song: Aomori Prefecture. *Unknown, tr. by* Hiroaki Sato. FCEI

When spring comes round. *Unknown. Fr.* Manyo Shu. Ma

When stags do rut in the Plym. Alan Gibson. BXAP

When Stars Are Shrouded. "I. T." EIL

When stars pursue their solemn flight. Music in the Night. Harriet Prescott Spofford. AA

When stars ride in on the wings of dusk. Refuge. Lew Sarett. AA

When Statesmen gravely say "We must be realistic." W. H. Auden. FaBoCo

When, staunchly entering port. The Beauty of the Ship. Walt Whitman. MOS

When stealthy age creeps on me unaware. A Litany for Old Age. Una W. Harsen. TrPWD

When storms arise. Paul Laurence Dunbar. TrPWD

When storms blow loud, 't is sweet to watch at ease. Suave Mari Magno. Lucretius, *tr. fr. Latin by* W. H. Mallock. *Fr.* De Rerum Natura (On the Nature of Things). AWP

When stubble-lands were greening, you came among the stooks. The Green Autumn Stubble. *Unknown, tr. by* Patrick Browne. WTO

When suddenly at midnight you hear. The God Abandons Antony. C. P. Cavafy, *tr. by* Edmund Keeley *and* Philip Sherrard. VMG

When Sue Wears Red. Langston Hughes. CNA; TTY

When summer ended. Emplumada. Lorna Dee Cervantes. NoAM

When summer starts to fall. Autumnal Equinox. Edward E. Wilson. MOWH

When summer strikes Tsukiji. The Missionary at Karnizawa. Osman Edwards. *Fr.* Residential Rhymes, II. OBTV

When summer took in hand the winter to assail. Love's Rebel. Henry Howard, Earl of Surrey. OBSC; SiPS

("When sommer toke in hand the winter to assail.") AAS

When summer's in the city. The Ice-Cream Man. Rachel Field. FaPON

When Sun Came to Riverwoman. Leslie Silko. VoR

When Sun Doth Rise. Roger Williams. AH

When sun, light-handed, sows this Indian water. Aubade: Lake Erie. Thomas Merton. NYBP

When sun the earth least shadow spares. The River Lynher. Richard Carew. *Fr.* Survey of Cornwall. FaBoPP

When sunshine met the wave. In the Beginning. Harriet Monroe. AA

When supper time is almost come. Milking Time. Elizabeth Madox Roberts. FaPON; GoJo; OBCA

When surly winter o'er the naked earth. A Winter Night in Manchester. Philip Connell. PF

When Susanna Jones wears red. When Sue Wears Red. Langston Hughes. CNA; TTY

When Susan's work was done, she'd [*or* she would] sit. Old Susan. Walter de la Mare. CMoP; MoBrPo

When swallows lay their eggs in snow. Fool's Song. Thomas Holcroft. NOEC

When swimming and croquet are in full sway, dolor. Dolor. Josephine Miles. FaBoWP

When Sydney and the Bush first met. Sydney and the Bush. Les A. Murray. DiPo

When Tadlow walks the streets the paviours cry. Tadlow. Abel Evans. FaBoCo

When tea with his lovely graduate assistant. Love in the Nuclear Age. Linda Pastan. SoTCo

When tempest winnowed grain from bran. The Victor of Antietam. Herman Melville. PAH

When that day comes, whose evening sayes I'm gone. His Sailing from Julia. Robert Herrick. PoEL-3

When That I Was and a Little Tiny Boy. Shakespeare. *Fr.* Twelfth Night, V, i. CH; EBEV; EiL; FaBoCh; HeIP; LiTB; NOBE; NoP; OAEL-1; PoRA

(Feste's Song ("When that I was and a little tiny boy").) NBLV; OBSC; OxBoLi

(Song: "When that I was and a little tiny boy.") FiP; PoEL-2

(Wind and the Rain, The.) WiR

When that rich Soule which to her heaven is gone. John Donne. *Fr.* Anatomy [*or* Anatomie] of the World, An: The First Anniversary. SeCV-1

(First Anniversary, The.) NAEL-1

When that Seint George hadde sleyne ye draggon. *Unknown.* NA

When that the chill charocco blows. Thomas Bonham. *See* In Praise of Ale.

When that the Eternal deigned to look. Ballade of Illegal Ornaments. Hilaire Belloc. ACP

When that the fields put on their gay attire. To the Redbreast. John Codrington Bampfylde. Son

When the/ sun. August 2. Norman Jordan. PoBA

When the African Arts. At Home in Dakar. Margaret Danner. BlSi; FB

When the agathic capsule factory spews. Bright New Missouri. Steve Sneyd. BWV

When the air is wine and the wind is free. Song of the Queen Bee. E. B. White. NYBP

When the alcoholic passed the crucial point. Point of No Return. Robert Graves. BIrV

When the allegorical man came calling. The Inflatable Globe. Theodore Spencer. LiTA; WaP

When the Angels Are Exhausted. Yona Wallach, *tr. fr. Hebrew by* Leonore Gordon. VWA

When the angry passion gathering in my mother's face I see. The Patter of the Shingle. *Unknown.* BLPA

When the anxious hearts say "Where?" Missing. *Unknown.* WGRP

When the ape. Ay: His Hill. Mutamociyar, *tr. by* A. K. Ramanujan. PLW

When the ash is before the oak. *Unknown.* FaBoUs

When the Ashes. Jaroslav Seifert, *tr. fr. Czech by* Jeffrey Fiskin *and* Erik Vestville. AnAn

When the Assault Was Intended to the City. Milton. GTBS; GTBS-P; NoP; Son

(Sonnet: "Captain or colonel or knight in arms.") OAEL-1

When the Atlantic upsloped itself. Winter Tryst. Mark Van Doren. LiTA

When the autumn winds go wailing. Ungathered Love. Philip Bourke Marston. OBNC

When the autumn's breezes. Mr. Edward Fordham. Mary Weston Fordham. CBWP-2

When the bare branch responds to leaf and light. Spain. Dorothy Livesay. NOBC

When the barn catches fire. The Longing to Be Saved. Maxine W. Kumin. CAPP

When the battle was over. Masses. César Vallejo, *tr. fr. Spanish by* Robert Bly. *Fr.* España, Aparta de me Este Caliz. RB

When the bells justle in the tower. A. E. Housman. NOBVV

When the bird flew from the Columbus hull. Jeremiad. Oscar Williams. LiTA

When the bird saw how innocent they were. Paradise. Steve Orlen. NAmP

When the birds sang. *Unknown, tr. by* Willis Barnstone. BoWoP

When the black. The Hours of a Bridge. W. S. Merwin. LCAP

When the black car came thundering from its pale. Proserpine at Enna. Ronald Bottrall. SeCePo

When the black herds of the rain were grazing. The Lost Heifer. Austin Clarke. BIrV .

When the blackbird, in the new greenery, comes back. Faithful Blackbird. Juan Ramón Jiménez, *tr. by* Perry Higman. LPSS

When the bleak winds of winter. Remember the Poor. Matilda Caroline Edwards. PWR

When the bloated sun stands upon Black Mesa. Black Mesa. Ron Rogers. STE

When the bombs dropped on us at the end of the war. A Chinaman's Chance. Alex Kuo. UL

When the bones are no longer curious. Overture for Bubble-Gum and Flute. Alistair Paterson. ATNZ; PeNZ

When the bones walk out of me. Never. George Reavey. BIrV

When the boy undressed. The Skull. Ian Young. NeAC

When the breath of twilight blows to flame the misty skies. By the Margin of the Great Deep. "Æ." OBEV

When the breeze from the bluebottle's blustering blim. To Marie. *Unknown.* NA

When the bright eyes of the day. Day and Night. James Stephens. BoTP

When the British warrior queen. Boadicea; an Ode. William Cowper. BeLS; FaPoR

When the buds began to burst. The Three Roses. Walter Savage Landor. NAEL-2

When the call comes, be calm. How to Watch Your Brother Die. Michael Lassell. GLP

When the Century Dragged. Robert Penn Warren. MoAmPo

When the Chen and Wei. *Unknown, tr. by* Arthur Waley. BoS

When the cherry-flower blooms. *Unknown. Fr.* Manyo Shu. Ma

When the child's forehead full of red torments. The Lice Seekers. Rimbaud, *tr. fr. French by* Kenneth Koch *and* George Guy. *Fr.* Illuminations. SOTW

When the chilled dough of his flesh went in an oven. Marked with D. Tony Harrison. *Fr.* The School of Eloquence. NAEL-2; NoAM

When the Christ Child Came. Frederic E. Weatherly. OHIP

When the clock strikes five but it's only four. Wrimples. Jack Prelutsky. RHPC

When the clouds are upon the hills. *Unknown. Fr.* Weather Wisdom [*or* Weather Wise]. OxNR

When the clouds' swoln bosoms echo back the shouts of the many and strong. Thomas Hardy. *Fr.* In Tenebris, II. BrPo; CMoP; LiTM; NoAM; OxBTC

When the cold comes. Where? When? Which? Langston Hughes. BPo

When the corpse revived at the funeral. The Piano Player Explains Himself. Allen Grossman. BAP

When the cowboy poets gathered it was nineteen eighty-five. Poets Gathering, 1985. Charles A. Kortes. CowP

When the crop is fair in the olive-yard. The Cocooning. Frédéric Mistral, *tr. fr. Provençal by* Harriet Waters Preston. *Fr.* Mirèio. AWP

When the crowd surrounded those dragged to death. Remembrance. Mieczyslaw Jastrun, *tr. by* Czeslaw Milosz. PwPP

When the crows fly away. My Love. Richard Shelton. GOYP

When the curtain/ rises. A Poem on Theater. Sándor Weöres, *tr. by* Jascha Kessler. FOC

When the curtain of night, 'tween the dark and the light. Whistling Boy. Nixon Waterman. PoLF

When the Curtains of Night Are Pinned Back. *Unknown.* AS; *with music.*

(I'll Remember you, Love, in My Prayers.) BLPA; FaBoBe

When the curtain opens. Front Porch: A Drama Critic Warns of Clichés. Evan Zimroth. ER

When the dark months have run out. Rhyme-Prose on the Snow. Hsieh Hui-lien, *tr. by* Burton Watson. CoBCP

When the dawn comes. *Unknown, tr. fr. Japanese by* Arthur Waley. *Fr.* Kokin Shu. AWP

When the Day. Thomas Sessler, *tr. fr. German by* Herbert Kuhner. VWA

When the day and the night do meete. Cobbe's Prophecies. *Unknown.* NA

When the Day Comes. Manuel Gutiérrez Nájera, *tr. fr. Spanish by* Samuel Beckett. MexPo

When the day darkens. The Unknown Wind. "Fiona Macleod." BoTP

When the day is stormy, and no sun shines through. A Trust-Song. Eben E. Rexford. BLRP

When the days are long in May. Jaufré Rudel, *tr.* by Paul Blackburn. Pro

When the Days Grow Long. Hayyim Nahman Bialik, *tr. fr. Hebrew by* A. C. Jacobs. VWA

When the Days Shall Grow Long. Hayyim Nahman Bialik, *tr. fr. Hebrew* by A. M. Klein. TrJP

When the days were still as deith. The Rowan. Violet Jacob. PoSH

When the dew is on the grass. *Unknown.* OxNR

When the doctor came from Chin-t'an. Weeping for Hsüeh Tzu-shu. Liu-K'o-chuang, *tr.* by Burton Watson. CoBCP

When the dream departs leaving. Salah Fa'iq, *tr.* by Patricia Alanah Byrne *and* Salma Khadra Jayyusi. MAP

When the Drive Goes Down. Douglas Malloch. AmFN

When the droughts hit the backland they make. The Drafted Vulture. João Cabral de Melo Neto, *tr.* by W. S. Merwin. ATCBP

When the Druzes come together. Diaspora Jews. Rachel Boimwall, *tr.* by Gabriel Preil *and* Howard Schwartz. VWA

When the Dumb Speak. Robert Bly. NOBA

When the dying flame of day. Hymn of the Moravian Nuns of Bethlehem. Longfellow. PAH

When the eager squadrons of day are faint and disbanded. The Cult of the Celtic. Anthony C. Deane. BXAP; NOBL

When the earth is turned in spring. The Worm. Ralph Bergengren. FaPON; RHPC

When the east wind blows. Michizane, *tr.* by Geoffrey Bownas *and* Anthony Thwaite. PeBJV

When the echo of the last footstep dies. E. W. Mandel. MoCV; OBCV

When the Emperor had departed from the world of men. The Song of Yüan-yüan. Wu Wei-yeh, *tr.* by John D. Coleman *and* Gloria Shen. WFTU

When the exposed spirit, busy in daytime. Time Exposures. Muriel Rukeyser. PoA

When the Eye of Day Is Shut. A. E. Housman. Mes; NOBVV; OAEL-2

When the fair year. The Jews. Henry Vaughan. OBS

When the Fairies. Edward Dorn. NeAP

When the Faithless One gave me the cold. Hurrah for Trees! László Nagy, *tr.* by Jascha Kessler. FOC

When the far south glittered. Pilgrimage. Austin Clarke. CIP; IPY; TIRV

When the farmer comes to town. The Farmer. *Unknown.* AS

When the feet of the rain tread a dance on the roofs. Gipsy-Night. Richard Hughes. OBWVE

When the fields catch flower. April. Vidame de Chartres, *tr.* by Swinburne. AWP

When the fierce north wind with his airy forces. The Day of Judgement [*or* Judgment]; an Ode. Isaac Watts. HAP; NOBE; NOEC; NoP; OBEV; SeCePo

When the fifth month comes. Lady Ise, *tr.* by Etsuko Terasaki *and* Irma Brandeis. BoWoP

When the first sound of the/ Carabao. Manong Jacinto Santo Tomas. Al Robles. BrSi

When the Five Prominent Poets. Josephine Jacobsen. TAP

When the flaming lute-thronged angelic door is wide. The Travail of Passion. W. B. Yeats. TrCP

When the flesh of summer piecemeal mars the lawn. Sonnet in Autumn. Donald Petersen. NePoEA-2

When the flowers turn to husks. Cells Breathe in the Emptiness. Galway Kinnell. NaP; VGW

When the flush of a newborn sun fell first on Eden's green and gold. The Conundrum of the Workshops. Kipling. MoBrPo

When the Flyin' Scot. Uncle Henry. W. H. Auden. NOBL; PeHV

When the forests have been destroyed their darkness remains. The Asians Dying. W. S. Merwin. CoAP; HCAP; NaP; NOBA; NYBP

When the four quarters shall. Ark Overwhelmed. Jay Macpherson. *Fr.* The Ark. NOBC

When the French fleet lay. Running the Blockade. Nora Perry. PAH

When the Frost Is on the Punkin. James Whitcomb Riley. AnAmPo; BoNaP; FaBoBe; FaBV; FaFP; FPL; OBAL; PoLF

When the full moon rises. Song of Black Cubans. Federico García Lorca, *tr.* by William B. Logan. SOTW

When the game began between them for a jest. Stage Love. Swinburne. PoEL-5

When the gardener has gone this garden. In a Garden. Elizabeth Jennings. NOCV

When the god, needing something, decided to become a swan. Leda. Rainer Maria Rilke, *tr.* by Robert Bly. NU

When the gold fever raged I was doing very well. The Miner's Lament. *Unknown.* AmFP

When the gong sounds ten in the morning/ and I walk to school by our lane. Vocation. Rabindranath Tagore. FaPON

When the Grass Shall Cover Me. Ina Coolbrith. AA

When the grass was closely mown. The Dumb Soldier. Robert Louis Stevenson. OxBChV

When the great golden eagle of the West. Salt Lake City. Hayden Carruth. AmFN

When the Great Gray Ships Come In. Guy Wetmore Carryl. AnAmPo; FaBoBe; PAH

When the great universe hung nebulous. Egoisme à Deux. Louisa S. Guggenberger. NOBVV

When the green grass rose in the spring. On the Bright Side. Carter Revard. NOVW; VoR

When the Green Lies over the Earth. Angelina Weld Grimké. CDC; PoNe

When the green woods laugh with the voice of joy. Laughing Song. Blake. *Fr.* Songs of Innocence. BoTP; NAEL-2 (When the Green Woods Laugh.) CH; EnRP; GoJo; NBLV; OxBChV

When the grey lake-water rushes. The Solitary Woodsman. Sir Charles G. D. Roberts. CaP; OBCV

When the Guests First Take Their Seats. *Unknown, tr. fr. Chinese by* Burton Watson. CoBCP

When the gunner spoke in his sleep the hut was still. The Gunner. Francis Webb. CBAP

When the half-body dies its frightful death. Resurrection of the Right Side. Muriel Rukeyser. LCAP

When the hare and the pig had some pleasure to plan. The Hare and the Pig. L. J. Bridgman. RHPC

When the heart's feeling. Thomas Moore. OxBSP

When the heat of the summer. A Dragonfly. Eleanor Farjeon. FaPON; OnUR; PDV; RHPC

When the heavens with stars are gleaming. For Who? Mary Weston Fordham. CBWP-2

When the herd[s] were watching. William Canton. OHIP (Bethlehem.) BoTP

When the hills are resting calmly. Song of a Silesian Weaver. Louise Aston, *tr.* by Susan L. Cocalis *and* Gerlinde Geiger. DMG

When the hills of spring. "Owari." *Fr.* Manyo Shu. Ma

When the Himalayan peasant meets the he-bear in his pride. The Female of the Species. Kipling. BLPA; FPL

When the horse has been unharnessed and we've flushed the old machine. Cleaning Up. Edward Dyson. PoAu-1

When the Hounds of Spring [Are on Winter's Traces]. Swinburne. *Fr.* Atalanta in Calydon. FaBoBe; HeIP; LiTB; NAEL-2; NoP; PoE; PrIm; TEP; TrGrPo (Chorus: "When the hounds of spring are on winter's traces.") AWP; CTC; EBVV; FaBoBe; GTBS-P; GTBS-P; HAP; HeIP; LiTB; NOBE; NoP; OAEL-2; OBEV; PrIm; TEP; TrGrPo; WeW (Hounds of Spring, The.) FaBV

When the hours of day are numbered. Footsteps of Angels. Longfellow. AnAmPo

When the hunter-star Orion. Retrospection. Sir Arthur Quiller-Couch. CenHV

When the hurricane unfolds. The Hurricane. Luis Palés Matos, *tr.* by Alida Malkus. FaPON

When the inmate stirs, the birds retire discreetly. A Bird-Scene at a Rural Dwelling. Thomas Hardy. FM

When the knight had finished, no one, young or old. Prologue to the Miller's Tale. *Fr.* The Canterbury Tales. NAWM-1

When the Kye Comes Hame. James Hogg. OxBS

When the Lad for Longing Sighs. A. E. Housman. *Fr.* A Shropshire Lad, VI. MoBrPo

When the lake lies still as a mirror. The Travellers. Elizabeth Spires. KS

When the Lamp Is Shattered. Shelley. CH; FiP; NAEL-2; PPP; TEP; TrGrPo (Lines: "When the lamp is shattered.") EnRP; FF; NoP; OBEV; OBNC; PoEL-4

When the landfolk of Galway converse with a stranger. Undertone. William Bedell Stanford. NeIP

When the last bus leaves, moths stream toward lights. Depot in Rapid City. Roberta Hill. BoWoP

When the last Flavius, drunk with fury, tore. Juvenal, *tr. fr. Latin by* William Gifford. *Fr.* Satires, IV. OBVE

When the last H-bomb blast has done its stuff. Brave Old World. Elisabeth Lambert. FaFP

When the last of gloaming's gone. The Shadow. Walter de la Mare. OnUR

When the Last Riders. Natan Zach, *tr. fr. Hebrew by* Peter Everwine *and* Shula Starkman. VWA

When the last sea is sailed, when the last shallow['s] charted. D'Avalos' Prayer. John Masefield. MOS; TrPWD

When the last star breathes like a rose. Sailors. Louis Simpson. NYBP

When the last voyage is ended. Requiem. Joseph Lee. OHIP

When the last weariness. Humbly. Ramón López Velarde, tr. by Samuel Beckett. MexPo

When the leaf spins. Marcabrun, tr. by Paul Blackburn. Pro

When the least whistling wind begins to sing. Her Hair. Sir Robert Chester. Fr. Love's Martyr. ElL

When the leaves in autumn wither. Autumnus. Joshua Sylvester. ElL; OBS; SoSe

When the lessons and tasks are all ended. The Children. Charles Monroe Dickinson. AA

When the Light Falls. Stanley Kunitz. MoAmPo

When the literary man. A Serious Literary Slip. Kevin Ireland. ATNZ

When the little armadillo. Mexican Serenade. Arthur Guiterman. FiBHP

When the little blue-bird. Let's Do It. Cole Porter. OBAL

When the little Grecian cities went a-warring each with each. Little Songs. Marjorie Pickthall. CaP

When the loneliness of the tomb went down into the marketplace. Mona Sa'udi, tr. by Kamal Boullata. WPOW

When the Lord brought back those that returned to Zion. Psalm CXXVI ("When the Lord brought back. . ."). Bible, O.T. Fr. Psalms. (Like unto Them That Dream.) TrJP

When the Lord fashioned man, the Lord his God. The Mother. Catulle Mendès, tr. by W. J. Robertson. TrJP

When the mar. Tomorrow. Henri Michaux, tr. by Armand Schwerner. RHTwFP

When the Martyrs Go to Sleep. Mahmoud Darwish, tr. fr. Arabic by Abdullah al-Udhari. MPAW

When the master lived a king and I a starving hutted slave beneath the lash, and. On Listening to the Spirituals. Lance Jeffers. PoBA

When the master sits at ease. Friend Cato. Anna Wickham. MoBrPo

When the Master was calling the roll. Anseo. Paul Muldoon. CIP; FaBoPV

When the men came. The Wolf Girl Speaks. Nancy Springer. BWV

When the men leave me. Summer in a Small Town. Linda Gregg. MAYP

When the mice awaken. The Vigil. Denise Levertov. NePoEA-2

When the Mint Is in the Liquor. Clarence Ousley. PoLF

When the Mississippi Flowed in Indiana. Vachel Lindsay. CMoP

When the mists have rolled in splendor. We Shall Know. Unknown. PWR

When the mob swerved. Truth and Consequences. Edward Baugh. PBCV

When the monkey in his madness. The Monkey's Glue. Goldwin Goldsmith. NA

When the moon appears. My Mother on an Evening in Late Summer. Mark Strand. FYAP; GeTw

When the moon comes up. The Moon Rises. Federico García Lorca, tr. by William Bryant Logan. SOTW; TTTS

When the moon shines o'er the corn. The Field Mouse. "Fiona Macleod." FaPON; MoShBr

When the moon that shines. Unknown. Fr. Manyo Shu. Ma

When the moon was full they came to the water. Moon Fishing. Lisel Mueller. CoAP

When the moon wraps the earth in silvery light. The Blind Musician. Ali Mahmud Taha, tr. by Issa Boullata and Thomas G. Ezzy. MAP

When the moonlight. Unknown, tr. fr. Japanese by Geoffrey Bownas and Anthony Thwaite. Fr. Kokin Shu. PeBJV

When the moon's splendour shines in naked heaven. To His Friend in Absence. Walafrid Strabo, tr. by Helen Waddell. PeHV

When the morning hymn. The Wonder-Teacher. Cynthia Ozick. VWA

When the morning star bleeds and silver-cry the Pleiades. Dream. Joseph Eliyia, tr. by Rae Dalven. VWA

When the morning warmth enters the window. A Stool with a Broken Leg. Sung Wan, tr. fr. Chinese by William Schultz. Fr. Songs Composed in Prison, III. WFTU

When the morning was waking over the war. Among Those Killed in the Dawn Raid Was a Man Aged a Hundred. Dylan Thomas. Son

When the Most Is Said. "Madeline Bridges." AA

When the mouse died at night. The Mouse. Jean Garrigue. TwCP

When the mouse died, there was a sort of pity. Death of a Whale. John Blight. CBAP; OBD; PoAu-2

When the neat white. Duck. Valerie Worth. NTCP

When the new day dawns. Ietaka, tr. by Steven D. Carter. WFTW

When the Night and Morning Meet. Dora Greenwell. EBVV

When the night begins to fall. Where Are You Now? Mary Britton Miller. RHPC

When the night her visions is weaving. The Harp of David. "Yehoash", tr. by Alter Brody. TrJP

When the night is cloudy. In the Hours of Darkness. James Flexner. FaPON

When the night is still and far. The Highway. William Channing Gannett. WGRP

When the night of butter just emerged from the churn. Nebulous. Benjamin Péret, tr. by Michael Benedikt. POS

When the nightingale to his mate. Alba ("When the nightingale to his mate"). Ezra Pound, after the Provençal of Arnaut Daniel. Fr. Langue d'Oc. OBVE; VGW; WeW

When the Norn Mother saw the whirlwind hour. Lincoln, the Man of the People. Edwin Markham. MoAmPo; OHFP; OHIP; PAH; TrGrPo (Lincoln the Great Commoner.) GN

When the north wind moans thro' the blind creek courses. A Gallop of Fire. Marie E. J. Pitt. PoAu-1

When the nuclear disaster comes. Disaster. Meiling Jin. WS

When the old Cove Creek Dam first was started. The Song of Cove Creek Dam. Unknown. AmFP

When the old flaming prophet climbed the sky. On a Virtuous Young Gentlewoman That Died Suddenly. William Cartwright. HAP

When the old, long-preserved wine stands at the repast. Five Arabic Verses in Praise of Wine. Unknown, tr. by Hartwig Hirschfeld. TrJP

When the old ones die. Karoniaktatie. STE

When the Orient is lit by the great light. Vittoria da Colonna, tr. by Brenda Webster. WPOW

When the other children go. The Invisible Playmate. Margaret Widdemer. FaPON

When the outlook is dark, try the uplook. Try the Uplook. Unknown. BLRP

When the pale moon hides and the wild wind wails. The Wolf. Georgia Roberts Durston. RHPC

When the particular. Latter Day. Rae Armantrout. LP

When the pencil undresses for sleep. The Pencil's Dream. Tymoteusz Karpowicz, tr. by Czeslaw Milosz. PwPP

When the petals of the plum tree. Last Breath. Laura Chester. NPGG

When the Pilgrims. The First Thanksgiving. Jack Prelutsky. NTCP

When the pills don't work any more. Cole Porter's Son. Gerrit Henry. EOEF

When the pistol muzzle oozing blue vapour. That Moment. Ted Hughes. Fr. Crow. FF; PoE

When the place was green with the shaky grass. Where the Lilies Used to Spring. David Gray. OxBS

When the plate was at pawn and the fob at an ebb. The Vows. Andrew Marvell. TW

When the plum-blossoms are gone. Sakiko. Fr. Manyo Shu. Ma

When the pods went pop on the broom, green broom. A Runnable Stag. John Davidson. BrPo; FaPoR; FM; GoTS; HAP; OBEV; OxBTC; PrIm; SD; WiR

When the Present has latched its postern behind my tremulous stay. Afterwards. Thomas Hardy. BoNaP; CH; ChTr; CMoP; EBEV; FaBoRV; GTBS-P; InPS; LiTB; LiTM; MoAB; MoBrPo; NOBE; NoP; OAEL-2; OBNC; PoEL-5; QFR; TOF; TrGrPo

When the priest made his entrance on the altar on the stroke of 10.30. 10.30 AM Mass, June 16, 1985. Paul Durcan. CIP

When the prime mover of my many sighs. To Vittoria Colonna. Michelangelo, tr. by Longfellow. AWP; PFI

When the procession falls to its knees tomorrow. Mortar Salvos. Jaroslav Seifert, tr. by Jeffrey Fiskin and Erik Vestville. AnAn

When the Prophet. Stephen Crane. AnAmPo

When the proud fleet that bears the red-cross flag. Wordsworth. Fr. The Prelude [or, Growth of a Poet's Mind]: Residence in France. FaBoPV

When the proud king rode into the enemy's city. The Proud King. Jacob Glatstein, tr. by Benjamin and Barbara Harshav. AYP

When the proud World does most my world despise. Robert Nichols. Fr. Sonnets to Aurelia. OBMV

"When the Pulitzers showered on some dope." Words for Hart Crane. Robert Lowell. CMoP

When the Queen of Darkness heard his voice. Noch Einmal, an Orpheus. George Bradley. BAP

When the rain drums loud on the leaf. Resemblance. Unknown, tr. by N. B. Emerson. WTO

When the Rain Raineth. Unknown. GBP; RB

When the rains began. The Prophetess. Dorothy Livesay. MoCV

When the reaper's task was ended, and the summer wearing late. The Swan Song of Parson Avery. Whittier. AA

When the returning sun begins to smile. James Dance. Fr. Cricket; an Heroic Poem. NOEC

When the rice paddies slowly dry, and. Frying Fish. Chan Ch'e, tr. by Dominic Cheung. IFON

When the ring gleamed white and your chair hugged the edge of it. Change of Address. Kathleen Fraser. NYBP

When the Ripe Fruit Falls. D. H. Lawrence. CMoP
When the ripe pears droop heavily. The Wasp. "Fiona Macleod." BoTP; FaPON
When the robust and brass-bound man commissioned first for sea. Poseidon's Law. Kipling. MOS
When the roof, the sky. Earthquake. Sándor Weöres, tr. by Jascha Kessler. FOC
When the rooster jumps up on the windowsill. Cuba, 1962. Ai. AmPA
When the rose is brightest. To Giulia Grisi. Nathaniel Parker Willis. AA
When the runner's whistle lights the last miles of darkness. Soldier (T. P.). Randall Jarrell. WaP
When the Sabbath was declining, just at twilight's mystic hour. In Memoriam. Susan Eugenia Bennett. Mary Weston Fordham. CBWP-2
When the Saints Go Marchin' [or Marching] In. Unknown. EaLo
When the scarlet cardinal tells. July. Susan Hartley Swett. GN
When the sea comes in at Horsey Gap. Horsey Gap. Unknown. FaBoPP; GBP
When the sea is as grey as her eyes. Soft White. Lee Harwood. EAS
When the sea is everywhere. North Atlantic. Carl Sandburg. MOS
When the Secretary gave up his office. The Mountain Residence of Secretary Cheng Ching-ssu. Hsü Pen, tr. by Jonathan Chaves. CoBLCP
When the Seed of Thy Word Is Cast. Cotton Mather. AH
When the Septentrion of the First Heaven. Dante, tr. fr. Italian. Fr. Divina Commedia: Purgatorio, XXX-XXXI. NAWM-1, tr. by John Ciardi.
When the shades of night are falling, and the sun goes down. The Dustman. Unknown. BoTP
When the sheen on tall summer grass is pale. The Gazelles. T. Sturge Moore. BrPo; OBMV
When the sheep are in the fauld, and the kye [or cows] at hame. Auld Robin Gray. Lady Anne Lindsay. AIW; BeLS; CH; GoTS; GTBS; GTBS-P; NOEC; OBEV; WPE
When the shoals of plankton. Shooting Whales. Mark Strand. CAPP; LCAP
When the shy, slender thrush. Spring Doggerel. Rhoda Coghill. NeIP
When the sire of Framboisy returned from war his wife reproached him. The Key. Max Jacob, tr. by Ron Padgett. RHTwFP
When the sky. Muskrat. John Engels. AnAn
When the sky starts in a-rainin.' Let Be. Unknown. WBLP
When the snake bit. Snake. Dannie Abse. NoAM
When the snow falls the flakes. The Dance. William Carlos Williams. NAAL-2
When the snow starts melting. The French Mood. Abo Stoltzenberg, tr. by Gabriel Preil and Howard Schwartz. VWA
When the Sorrow of My Heart. Faiz Ahmad Faiz, tr. fr. Urdu by Mahmood Jamal. PBMUP
When the soul sought refuge in the place of rest. Self-Discipline. "Æ" MoBrPo
When the southeastern wall was first put in. The Paintings on My Wall Have Been Damaged by the Weather. T'ang Hsien-Tsu, tr. by Jonathan Chaves. CoBLCP
When the Sovereign Asks. Sirkka Turkka, tr. fr. Finnish by Aili Jarvenpa. SOP
When the Spent Day Begins to Frail. E. E. Cummings. ErPo
When the spent sun throws up its rays on cloud. Acceptance. Robert Frost. CMoP; OxBA
When the spider dropped down from the ceiling. The Grandmother Came Down to Visit Us. Joseph Bruchac. CDW
When the spring comes. Princess Nukada. Fr. Manyo Shu. PeBJV
When the spruce wood ends, I step. The Visitor. Gregory Orr. MAYP
When the stern god. Mythic Fragment. Louise Glück. NoAM
When the storm hit, I was fording the river. My Marriage with Mrs. Johnson. Jack Gilbert. NPGG
When the Storms Come. Lupenga Mphande. WMBCH
"When the Students Resisted, a Minor Clash Ensued." David Knight. MoCV
When the Sultan Goes to Ispahan. Thomas Bailey Aldrich. AA; BeLS; FaBoBe
When the summer fields are mown. Aftermath. Longfellow. NAAL-1; NOBA; TAP
When the sun and the moon. Hymn to Tirumal (Visnu). Kirantaiyar, tr. by A. K. Ramanujan. PLW
When the sun begins to throw. Skimmers. Ted Walker. NYBP
When the sun comes up from the salt sea. Unknown, tr. fr. Anglo-Saxon by Peggy Munsterberg. Fr. The Phoenix. PBBP
When the sun comes up we work. Ground-Thumping Song. Unknown, tr. by Burton Watson. CoBCP
When the sun gets low, in winter. Human Things. Howard Nemerov. BoNaP

When the sun goes down and the world is still. Jock o' Dreams. Rose Fyleman. BoTP
When the sun goes down, it writes. Man Alone. Denise Levertov. CAPP
When the sun has left the hill-top. L. Alma Tadema. Fr. A Blessing for the Blessed. BoTP
When the sun has slipped away. The Skunk. Robert Tristram Coffin. FaPON
When the sun is shining overhead. Shady Woods. E. M. Adams. BoTP
When the sun rises on another day. Charles Angoff. TrPWD
When the sun shines in Iowa, in Poland it's night. Beneath the Apple of Paradise in Iowa. Joanna Salamon, tr. by Christopher Wertz. WCI
When the Sun Shines More Years Than Fear. Janet Frame. ATNZ; PeNZ
When the sun shone hot the girl's arm was detected. Temperature. Gerard Malanga. NYBP
When the sun shouts and people abound. Summer Holiday. Robinson Jeffers. MoAmPo; OxBA
When the Sun Went Down. John Ashbery. NAAL-2
When the sun's perpendicular rays. Beginning of an Undergraduate Poem. Unknown. FaBoCo
When the sun's whiteness closes around us. The Map. Gary Soto. MAYP; NoAM
When the swans turned my sister into a swan. The Black Swan. Randall Jarrell. CAPP; CMoP; PoE
When the Sweet Showers of April Follow March. Chaucer. See Canterbury Tales, The: Prologue.
When the swift-rolling brook, swollen deep. The Storm-Wind. William Barnes. NOBE
When the Sword of Sixty Comes Nigh His Head. Firdausi, tr. fr. Persian by Basil Bunting. NAs; OBVE
When the tall puffy. Couplet. Donald Hall. ASP; TSL
When the tea is brought at five o'clock. Milk for the Cat. Harold Monro. BoTP; FaBoBe; FaFP; MoBrPo; OBMV
When the tender body. An Enchanted Bird. "Zelda", tr. by Bernhard Frank. MHeP
When the tide ebbed in the Ch'in-huai, autumn after spring. Wang Shih-chen, tr. fr. Chinese by Daniel Bryant. Fr. Poems on the Ch'i-huai, XIV. WFTU
When the tide lay under the clouds. The Veil. Denis Johnson. NAmP
When the tide smothers you. On Saying Goodbye to the Lady in Green. Ali Abdallah Khalifa, tr. by Lena Jayyusi and Alistair Elliot. MAP
When the tide was out. A Ship Burning and a Comet All in One Day. Richard Eberhart. NYBP
When the time has arrived. Trala Trala Trala Le-le-la. William Carlos Williams. OFD
When the timeless, daily, tedious affair. The Poet at Seven. Robert Lowell. NaP
When the tiny birds. A Morning Scene. Wu Sheng, tr. by Dominic Cheung. IFON
When the tourists cease from calling, and the heat is. The Minister at Chiuzenji. Osman Edwards. Fr. Residential Rhymes, III. OBTV
When the Tree Bares. Conrad Aiken. MoAmPo
When the troubled sea swells and surrounds. Vittoria da Colonna, tr. by Brenda Webster. PBWP
When the trout rise like compassion. The Stopover. Brian Turner. ATNZ
When the trumpet sounded, it was. The United Fruit Co. Pablo Neruda, tr. by Robert Bly. FaBoPV
When the turf is thy tower. The Grave. Unknown. ChTr
When the two-lane highway was widened. Dreaming America. Joyce Carol Oates. GeTw
When the universe goes up in flame. A Lament for the Willows outside the City Walls. Yün Shou-p'ing, tr. by Jonathan Chaves. CoBLCP
When the Vacation Is Over for Good. Mark Strand. NYBP
When the veil from the eyes is lifted. Si Jeunesse Savait! Edmund Clarence Stedman. AA
When the vengeance wakes, when the battle breaks. Battle Song. Robert Burns Wilson. PAH
When the voices of children are heard on the green/ And whisprings are in the dale. Nurse's Song. Blake. Fr. Songs of Experience. EnRP; FF; NAEL-2
When the voices of children are heard on the green/ And laughing is heard on the hill. Nurse's Song. Blake. Fr. Songs of Innocence. AWP; BLPL; CH; EnRP; FaBoBe; NAEL-2; OxBChV (Play Time.) FaPON
When the war-cry of liberty rang through the land. The Death of Warren. Epes Sargent. PAH
When the War Is Over. W. S. Merwin. OxBSP
When the warl's couped soon' as a peerie. Moonstruck. "Hugh MacDiarmid." NAEL-2

When the warm zummer breeze do blow over the hill. The Shep'erd Bwoy. William Barnes. EBVV

When the water fell. Flooded Mind. Norman MacCaig. OxBC

When the water fowl are found, the falconers hasten. *Unknown. Fr.* The Parlement [*or* Parliament] of the Thre[e] Ages. PBBV

When the water's calm. *Unknown, tr. by* Jerome Rothenberg. STP

When the waves of trouble roll. Show Me Thyself. Margaret Sangster. TrPWD

When the weather is rough, said the anxious child. Contemporary Song. Theodore Spencer. LiTA

When the weather suits you not. Try Smiling. *Unknown.* BLPA; FaFP; PWR; WBLP

When the white feet of the baby beat across the grass. Baby Running Barefoot. D. H. Lawrence. NoP

When the white flame in us is gone. Dust. Rupert Brooke. MoBrPo; OxBTC

When the white fog burns off. The Depths. Denise Levertov. NaP; NU

When the white wave of a glory that is hardly I. Sinfonia Domestica. Jean Starr Untermeyer. MoAmPo

When the wild goose. Sanetomo, *tr. fr. Japanese by* Burton Watson. *Fr.* Twenty-four Tanka. FCEI

"When the Wild Goose Finds Food He Calls His Comrades"—*I Ching.* Jan Kemp. PeNZ

When the Wind. Michel Deguy, *tr. fr. French by* Clayton Eshleman. RHTwFP

When the wind blows. Mibu Tadamine, *tr. by* Geoffrey Bownas *and* Anthony Thwaite. PeBJV

When the wind blows. *Unknown.* OxNR

When the wind blows loud and fearful. The Beggar Boy. Cecil Frances Alexander. OxBChV

When the wind blows, walk not abroad. To the Maids Not to Walk in the Wind. Oliver St. John Gogarty. AnIL; ErPo

When the wind is gentle. Hsü Wei, *tr. fr. Chinese by* Jonathan Chaves. *Fr.* A Kite. CoBLCP

When the wind is in the east. Mother Goose. BOTP; FaBoUs; OxNR

When the wind is in the east. *Unknown. Fr.* Weather Wisdom [*or* Weather Wise]. FaBoUs; OxNR

When the wind is in the thrift. By the Saltings. Ted Walker. NYBP

When the Wind Is Strong. Tanikawa Shuntaro, *tr. fr. Japanese by* Geoffrey Bownas *and* Anthony Thwaite. PeBJV

When the wind patch. Hound's Nest for a Parafen. James Sherry. LP

When the wind works against us in the dark. Storm Fear. Robert Frost. CMoP; OxBA

When the window glass blows in. Alan Dugan. AnAn

When the Wine Was Gone. Alvin Aubert. CNA

When the woods are green again. Midsummer Moon. "E. M. G. R." BoTP

When the words have gone away. Alphabet for Auden. Carol Ann Duffy. NPo

When the words rustle no more. Stillness. James Elroy Flecker. BrPo; CH; GoJo; MoBrPo

When the Work's All Done This Fall. *Unknown.* AS

When the World Ends. Mark Van Doren. GoYe

When the world goes voodoo. Creed. Walter Lowenfels. PoNe

When the World Is Burning. Ebenezer Jones. OBEV; PF

When the world is fast asleep. The Dream-Ship. Eugene Field. AnAmPo

When the world takes over for us. Lear. William Carlos Williams. NAAL-2; NOBA; PoA

When the world turns completely upside down. Wild Peaches. Elinor Wylie. FaBoWP; LiTA; LiTM; NAAL-2; OxBA; WPE

When the world vanishes, I will come back. Some Night Again. William Stafford. GOYP

"When the World Was in Building." Ford Madox Ford. CTC

When the world's folk, one day of freedom. The Labourer. Iolo Goch, *tr. by* Gwyn Williams. OBWVE

When the yellow bird's note was almost stopped. Rejoicing at the Arrival of Chi'en Hsiung. Po Chü-i, *tr. by* Arthur Waley. AWP

When the young Augustus Edward. On the Beach. Charles Stuart Calverley. FiBHP

When Thee (O holy sacrificed Lamb). To the Blessed Sacrament. Henry Constable. ACP

When their last hour shall rise. Ex-Voto. Swinburne. MOS

When their vigilance slipped. One Life. Dinah Butler. AIW

When there are animals about, who else. Talking to Animals. Barbara Howes. GrPl

When there are minds to heal, and you. Girl in a White Coat. John Malcolm Brinnin. SaC

When there are so many we shall have to mourn. In Memory of Sigmund Freud. W. H. Auden. HAP; LiTB; NoAM; OAEL-2; OxBA

When there came days sunk deep in damp your beauty seemed increased. A Lone Woman Asleep. Pierre Jean Jouve, *tr. by* David Gascoyne. RHTwFP

"When There Is Peace." Austin Dobson. PAH

When there was nothing, there was God. Asadullah Khan Ghalib, *tr. by* Ahmed Ali. GoT

When there's hardly a breath of wind to stir. Green Riders. Rachel Lyman Field. TSS

When there's love as unrecognized as a lily. Teika, *tr. fr. Japanese by* Hiroaki Sato. *Fr.* Eighty-four Tanka. FCEI

When these graven lines you see. A Happy Man. Carphyllides, *tr. by* E. A. Robinson. AWP

When these old woods were young. Under the Woods. Edward Thomas. CH

When these small. Beach Stones. Lilian Moore. TSS

When these were past, thus gan the Titaness. Mutability. Spenser. *Fr.* The Faerie Queene, VII, 7 *and* 8. PoEL-1

When they ask your name. Children. Russell Edson. AmPA

When they brought me the newspaper. Josie Bliss, October 1971. Carolyne Wright. NAmP

When they came to that blue harbour. Home. Vincent O'Sullivan. PeNZ

When they confess that they have lost the penial bone. God Bless America. John Fuller. OBSV

When they drink, poor fellows, those planters! *Unknown, tr. by* Sato. FCEI

When they entered through the back door. The Morning They Shot Tony Lopez, Barber and Pusher Who Went Too Far, 1958. Gary Soto. MAYP

When they escaped. Exodus. Harvey Shapiro. VWA

When they found Giotto. Allan M. Laing. FiBHP

When They Grow Old. Nathan Ralph. CaP

When they had pitched their smoked tepees. Indian Dance. Frederick Niven. CaP

When they had won the war. The Inner Part. Louis Simpson. PVCV

When They Have Lost. C. Day Lewis. MoAB; MoBrPo

When they [*or* Quhen thai] him fand, and gude [*or* gud] Wallace him saw. Wallace's Lament for the Graham. Henry the Minstrel. *Fr.* The Wallace, X. GoTS
(Lament for the Graham.) OxBS

When they in throngs a safe retirement seek. William Diaper, *after the Greek of* Oppian. *Fr.* Halieutica. OBVE

When they killed my mother it made me nervous. The State. Randall Jarrell. LiTM

When they light the candles a little propellor. Childish Things. William Stafford. BLA

When they needed a foreign part. Partial Accounts. William Meredith. GLP

When they play like that where everyone is. *Unknown, tr. fr. Tepehua Indian by* Charles Boilès. *Fr.* Tepehua Thought-Songs, III. STP

When they ran over her. Passing Remark. Tawfiq Zayyad, *tr. by* Sharif Elmusa *and* Charles Doria. MAP

When they realize it's no longer evening. Night Robbers. Ishihara Yoshiro, *tr. by* Sato. FCEI

When they said Carrickfergus I could hear. The Singer's House. Seamus Heaney. EBEV

When they said the time to hide was mine. The Rabbit. Elizabeth Madox Roberts. OBCA; RHPC

When they saw off Dai Evan's da. Fforestfawr. Kingsley Amis. *Fr.* The Evans Country. NOBL

When they saw Patroklos dead. The Horses of Achilles. C. P. Cavafy, *tr. by* Edmund Keeley *and* Philip Sherrard. OBD

When they sd to me this. When. Philip Appleman. BXAP

When they shook the box, and poured out its chances. For a Daughter Gone Away. William Stafford. AnAn; SV

When they shot Malcolm Little down. At That Moment. Raymond R. Patterson. PoBA

When they stop poems. Today Is a Day of Great Joy. Victor Hernandez Cruz. TTY

When they took us to the shower I saw. Death Camp. Irena Klepfisz. GLP

When they woke me. Coming Back. Joseph Bruchac. CDW

When They've Finished Shipping Cattle in the Fall. Bruce Kiskaddon. CowP

When Thickly Beat the Storms of Life. Gurdon Robins. AH

When thin-strewn memory I look through. Miss Loo. Walter de la Mare. CMoP; OxBTC

When Things Fall Upwards. István Eörsi, *tr. fr. Hungarian by* Edwin Morgan. MHuP

When things go wrong, as they sometimes will. Don't Quit. *Unknown.* BLPA; FPL

When This Carnival Finally Closes. Jack A. Mapanje. WMBCH

When This Cruel War Is Over. Charles C. Sawyer. AmFP
When this fly lived, she used to play. A Fly That Flew into My
  Mistress's Eye. Thomas Carew. CaPo
When this frothful carnival finally closes, brother. When This Carnival
  Finally Closes. Jack A. Mapanje. WMBCH
When, this incredible thing, the principal of the junior high. Women Who
  Cook. Anita Skeen. GLP
When this is the thing you put on. Armor. James Dickey. CoAP
When This Old Hat Was New. *Unknown.* OBET
When this slow heart was raging. Dogs in the Storm. Michael Waters.
  NAmP
When This Tide Ebbs. Verna Loveday Harden. CaP
When this troubled life is over, hide Thou me. Hide Thou Me.
  Unknown. AmFP
When this yokel comes maundering. The Plot against the Giant. Wallace
  Stevens. CMoP; FF; OxBA
When those renowned noble peers of Greece. Amoretti, XLIV. Spenser.
  PoE
When those we love die. Death in the Home. T. Sturge Moore. BrPo
When thou and I are dead, my dear. Inseparable. Philip Bourke
  Marston. BoLoP
When Thou Did Thinke I Did Not Love. Sir Robert Ayton. OBS
  (When Thou Didst Think I Did Not Love.) EIL
When thou hast spent the ling[e]ring day in pleasure and delight.
  Gascoigne's [*or* Gascoygnes] Good-Night. George Gascoigne.
  AAS; NOCV
When Thou Must Home to Shades of Underground. Thomas Campion,
  after the Latin of Propertius. AWP; EIL; EnLoPo; NoP; OBSC;
  OxBSP; PoEL-2; PoRA
  (To Shades of Underground.) ChTr
When Thou Passest through the Waters. Henry Crowell. BLRP
"When thou passest through the waters." Passing Through. Annie
  Johnson Flint. BLRP
When thou, poor[e] excommunicate. To My Inconstant Mistress [*or*
  Mistris]. Thomas Carew. EnLoPo; MeLP; MePo; NOBE; OBS;
  SeCePo; SeCV-1; TrGrPo
  (Song: To My Inconstant Mistress.) CaPo; GBL; JCP; NoP; SeCP
  (To His Inconstant Mistress.) OBEV
When thou to my true love com'st. Westphalian Song. *Unknown, tr. by*
  Samuel Taylor Coleridge. AWP; OBVE
When through the winding cobbled streets of time. The Noonday April
  Sun. George Love. IDB
When thy beauty appears. Thomas Parnell. OBEV
When thy bright beams, my Lord, so strike mine eye. Edward Taylor.
  Fr. Preparatory Meditations before My Approach to the Lord's
  Supper, XXII. NAAL-1
When Thy Heart with Joy O'erflowing. Theodore Chickering Williams.
  AH
When Thy King Is a Boy, *sel.* Ed Roberson.
  "You black out the sun." PoBA
When time drives you down to the florid savannahs. The Fruits of
  Retirement. James Camp. SoTCo
When time was then. Hunter's Song. Mvula Ya Nangolo. WMBCH
When to assure us on our way. A Rhenish Carol. Robert Finch. NAs
When to Her Lute Corinna [*or* Corrina] Sings. Thomas Campion. AAS;
  NAEL-1; NoP; OAEL-1; OBSC; PoE
When, to my deadly [*or* deadlie] pleasure. Sir Philip Sidney. EnLoPo;
  PoEL-1
When to my lone soft bed at eve returning. Povre Ame Amoureuse.
  Louise Labé, *tr. by* Robert Bridges. AWP
When to My Serene Body. Freda Laughton. NeIP
When to soft sleep we give ourselves away. Sleep. Thomas Bailey
  Aldrich. AA
When to the flowers so beautiful. The Forget-Me-Not. *Unknown.*
  BoTP
When to the music of Byrd or Tallis. King's College Chapel. Charles
  Causley. TOF
"When to the sessions of sweet silent thought." Shakespeare. *Fr.*
  Sonnets, XXX. AWP; CTC; EBEV; EIL; FaBoRV; FaBV; FF; FPL;
  GBL; HAP; InPS; LiTB; NAEL-1; NOBE; NoP; OAEL-1; OBEV;
  OBSC; PoE; PoEL-2; PoLF; PoRA; PPP; PrIM; TEP; TrGrPo
  (Remembrance.) FaFP; GTBS; GTBS-P
When Tom and Elizabeth took the farm. The Magpies. Denis Glover.
  ATNZ; PeNZ
When Tony was found dead in his. Never Be As Fast As I Have Been.
  Robert Hahn. ASP
When torches cast their light. Tsurayuki, *tr. fr. Japanese by* Burton
  Watson. *Fr.* Kokin Shu. FCEI
When Toroi Bandi was alive. Toroi Bandi. *Mongol Oral Tradition, tr.
  by* C. R. Bawden. WTO
When trouble comes your soul to try. The Friend Who Just Stands By.
  Bertye Young William. PoLF

When trout swim down Great Ormond Street. Conrad Aiken. *Fr.*
  Priapus and the Pool, III [IV]. NoAM; NOBA
When tulips bloom in Union Square. An Angler's Wish. Henry Van
  Dyke. AA
When tunes jigged nimbler than the blood. Song from a Country Fair.
  Léonie Adams. GoJo; GrPl
When twilight comes to Prairie Street. The Winning of the TV West.
  John T. Alexander. AmFN; RHPC
When Two Are Parted. Heine, *tr. fr. German by* Louis Untermeyer.
  AWP
When two elephants fight. Some Pieces. Calvin Forbes. MAYP
When two horses run. Horse and Riot. Ishihara Yoshiro, *tr. by* Hiroaki
  Sato. FCEI
When two lovers love each other well. Young Bearwell. *Unknown.*
  ESPB
When two men meet for the first time in all. Law in the Country of the
  Cats. Ted Hughes. TW
When Two Suns Do Appear. Sir Philip Sidney. *Fr.* Arcadia. SiPS
When two who love are parted. When Two Are Parted. Heine, *tr. by*
  Louis Untermeyer. AWP
When Ulysses braved the wine-dark sea. Making the Move. Paul
  Muldoon. NoAM
When under Edward or Henry the English armies. Now as Then. Anne
  Ridler. CN; WaP
When vain desire at last and vain regret. The One Hope. Dante Gabriel
  Rossetti. *Fr.* The House of Life, CI. NAEL-2; OAEL-2
When Venus her Adonis found. The Death of Adonis. Philip Ayres,
  after the Greek of Theocritus. OBVE
When Very was a celibate. Varitalk. Weare Holbrook. NYBP
When Viera was buried we knew it had come to an end. Because One Is
  Always Forgotten. Carolyn Forché. ER; MAYP
When violets were springing. Words. John Hay. AnAmPo
When walking in a tiny rain. Vern. Gwendolyn Brooks. ILY
When Wallaby would come to call on me. The Critic on the Hearth. L.
  E. Sissman. TW
When walnuts grew in stands like oak. Walnutry. Robert Morgan.
  MT
When wand'ring along noisy alleys. Pushkin, *tr. by* Alan Myers. AAA
When war and taxation had fleec'd us right sair. The Twa Weavers.
  Alexander Rodger. PF
When wars and ruined men shall cease. Prayer against Indifference. Joy
  Davidman. TrPWD
When war's red banner trailed along the sky. Robert G. Shaw. Henrietta
  Cordelia Ray. BlSi; CBWP-3; Son
When was it? Ishikawa Takuboku, *tr. fr. Japanese by* Hiroaki Sato. *Fr.*
  Forty-seven Tanka in Three Lines. FCEI
When was it first they called each other mine? Unhurt, There Is No Help.
  Allen Curnow. ATNZ
When was it that the particles became. Wallace Stevens. PoA
When Water Stands Still It's Stone. Gerrit Kouwenaar, *tr. fr. Dutch by*
  Peter Nijmeijer. DuIn
When waves invade the yellowing wheat. Composed While under Arrest.
  Mikhail Yurevich Lermontov, *tr. by* Max Eastman. AWP
When We Are Able. Bernice Zamora. CCP
When we are dead, some Hunting-boy will pass. The Statue. Hilaire
  Belloc. ACP
When we are going toward someone we say. Simple Song. Marge
  Piercy. LLLT
When we are in love, we love the grass. Robert Bly. PCP
When we are like two drunken suns. Yvonne Caroutch. LLLT, *tr. by*
  Carl Hermey
  ("When we are two drunk suns.") BoWoP, *tr. by* Willis Barnstone
  and Elene Kolb
When We Are Men. Stella Mead. BoTP
When we are old and these rejoicing veins. Edna St. Vincent Millay.
  ErPo; VGW
When we are shadows watching over shadows. Two Shadows. Elizabeth
  Spires. DiPo
When we are two drunk suns. Yvonne Caroutch. *See* When we are like
  two drunken suns.
When we as strangers sought. At an Inn. Thomas Hardy. NOBVV
When we behold. Dahlias. Padraic Colum. GoJo
When we came down from the country, we were strangers to the sea.
  Down from the Country. John Blight. CBAP
When we come to that dark house. Dame Edith Sitwell. *Fr.* The
  Sleeping Beauty. OBMV
When we count out our gold at the end of the day. Service. Georgia
  Douglas Johnson. CDC
When we died. Pontianak. Bee Bee Tan. ER
When we fell apart in the Badlands and lay still. In the Badlands. David
  Wagoner. UnPo
When we first rade down Ettrick. Ettrick. Lady John Scott. WPE

When we for age could [or cou'd] neither read nor write. Of the Last Verses in the Book. Edmund Waller. EBEV; FaBoRV; HAP; MePo; NoP; OBS; SeCP; SeCV-1

When we fought the Yankees and annihilation was near. Jubilation T. Cornpone. Johnny Mercer. OBAL

When we go out into the fields of learning. Fields of Learning. Josephine Miles. NoAM

When we have come this long way. Anniversary Poem for the Cheyennes Who Fell at Sand Creek. Lance Henson. VoR

When we have thrown off this old suit. The Question Whither. George Meredith. WGRP

When We Hear the Eye Open. Bob Kaufman. CNA

When we in kind embracements had agre'd [agreed]. *Unknown. Fr.* Zepheria, XXVI. AAS; Son

When we invent a machine to read. Jack Dann. *Fr.* Hospital Songs. BWV

When we know we are on the way out. Only with Radiance. Margit Szécsi, *tr. by* Kenneth McRobbie. MHuP

When we lay where Budmouth Beach is. Budmouth Dears. Thomas Hardy. *Fr.* The Dynasts, *pt.* III, Act II, sc. i. CH

When we learn. It is the Season. Josephine Jacobsen. TAP

When We Let Ourselves Run Down-Hill. H. Leivick, *tr. fr. Yiddish by* Benjamin *and* Barbara Harshav. AYP

When We Looked Back. William Stafford. NYBP

When we loved. Loving. Jane Stembridge. NMM

When we move from this colony. When We Are Able. Bernice Zamora. CCP

When we moved here, pulled. An Oregon Message. William Stafford. CoAP

When we, my love, are gone to dust. A Song of Dust. John Byrne Leicester Warren, 3rd Baron De Tabley. EnLoPo

When we on simple rations sup. Washing the Dishes. Christopher Morley. PoLF

When we parted, it was willow blossom season. One Summer Day, Invited by Mr. Shih Chü-an to Have a Drink. Ch'en Wei-sung, *tr. by* Madeline Chu. WFTU

When we played in the nursery till seven. Hello There. Brian S. Salome. BXAP

When we reach the field. Celebration: Birth of a Colt. Linda Hogan. HATNAP; NOVW

When we rested between marches, I read Aristophanes. The Virgin Warrior. Gwendolyn MacEwen. FaBoWP

When We Return. Daisy Zamora, *tr. fr. Spanish by* Magaly Fernández. VoI

When we returned they asked us questions. More Questions. Ory Bernstein, *tr. by* Warren Bargad *and* Stanley F. Chyet. IP

When we rolled up the three armored vehicles. One Morning We Brought Them Order. Al Lee. FF

When we sailed to the edge of the universe. Cosmology. Phyllis Gotlieb. BWV

When we sat his mother on her tail, he mouthed her teat. Ted Hughes. *Fr.* Sheep. OBD

When we see again the spring blossoming of the world. Guillaume de Poitiers, *tr. by* Paul Blackburn. Pro

When we shuddered and took into ourselves. The Whole Story. William Stafford. NNaP

When we sigh about our trouble. Good Medicine. *Unknown.* PWR

When we slept. Signature. Larry Mollin. NeAC

When we stand on the tops of things. Emily Dickinson. PoE

When we start breaking up in the wet darkness. Consolations of Philosophy. Derek Mahon. BIrV; CIP

When We That Now Ha' Childern Wer Childern. William Barnes. NOBVV

When We Two Parted. Byron. BoLoP; ChER; EnRP; FiP; FPL; GTBS; GTBS-P; HoPM; NAEL-2; NOBE; NoP; OBEV; OBNC; PoLF; TrGrPo

When We Wake. Gary Soto. NAmP

When we were a soft amoeba. Ere You Were Queen of Sheba. Sir Arthur Shipley. FaBoCo

When we were building Skua Light. The Dancing Seal. W. W. Gibson. OnMSP

When we were charming *Backfisch*. Friendship. Katherine Mansfield. PeHV

When we were children, clasping hands. But You, My Darling, Should Have Married the Prince. Kathleen Spivack. AmPA; NMM

When we were children old Nurse used to say. The Quiet House. Charlotte Mew. BrRo; EBEV

When we were farm-boys, years ago. Recollections of "Lalla Rookh." John Townsend Trowbridge. OBAL

When we were girl and boy together. Ballad of Human Life. Thomas Lovell Beddoes. BeLS

When we were idlers with the loitering rills. To a Friend. Hartley Coleridge. PoLF
(Friendship.) OBEV
(Sonnet: To a Friend.) OBNC

When we were little childer we had a quare wee house. Grace for Light. Moira O'Neill. TIRV

When we were married eight years. Tryst. Eve Merriam. NMM

When we were silly sisters seven. Fair Mary of Wallington. *Unknown.* ESPB
(Bonny Earl of Livingston, The.) OxBB

When we were small, folks taught us these precepts. Breaking the Precepts. Yasin Taha Hafiz, *tr. by* Sharif Elmusa *and* Christopher Middleton. MAP

When We Were Very Silly, *sels.* J. B. Morton. FaBoPa
Now We Are Sick.
Someone Asked the Publisher.
Theobald James.

When we would reach the anguish of the dead. Near an Old Prison. Frances Cornford. OBMV

When weariness comes with oblique step. To W.H. Auden at 63. Michael Jackson. UAS

When we're/ Hunting. Dangerous. Dorothy Aldis. RAR

When we're playing tag. No Girls Allowed. Jack Prelutsky. RHPC

When wert thou born, Desire? Of the Birth and Bringing Up of Desire. Edward De Vere, 17th Earl of Oxford. FaBoEE; OBSC

When Wesley died, the Angelic orders. Wesley in Heaven. Thomas Edward Brown. OBNC

When Westwall Downes [or Westwell Downs] I gan to tread. On Westwall Downes [or On Westwell Downs]. William Strode. FaBoPP; JCP; PoEL-2

When what has helped us has helped us enough. The Place of Backs. W. S. Merwin. HoPM

When what hugs stopping earth than silent is. E. E. Cummings. PoA

When whelmed the altar, priest and creed. Sir William Watson. WGRP

When, when, and whenever death closes our eyelids. Ezra Pound. *Fr.* Homage to Sextus Propertius. MoAB; OBMV; PoA

When whispering strains do softly steal. In Commendation of Music. William Strode. ELP; OBEV

When Whistler's Mother's Picture's frame. Don Marquis. *Fr.* To a Lost Sweetheart. FiBHP

When white dew descends on the hundred grasses. Han Yü, *tr. fr. Chinese by* Burton Watson. *Fr.* Autumn Thoughts, 2. CoBCP

When white people speak of being uptight. The Dancer. Al Young. PoBA

When Wild Confusion Wrecks the Air. Mather Byles. AH

When will it break loose. Late Blossoms in the Cold Mountains. Gyoko, *tr. by* Steven D. Carter. WFTW

When will men again. The Leaping Laughers. George Barker. OBMV

When will she come again. White Goddess. Hubert Witheford. ATNZ

When will the bell ring, and end this weariness? Last Lesson of the Afternoon. D. H. Lawrence. NoAM

When Will the Bird Cry Again? René Altmann, *tr. fr. German by* Beth Bjorklund. CoAuP

When will the fountain of my tears be dry? Give Me Leave. "A. W." TrGrPo
(Petition to Have Her Leave to Die.) OBSC

When will you ever, Peace, wild wooddove, shy wings shut. Peace. Gerard Manley Hopkins. ELP; GTBS-P; OxBSP; TrCP

"When will you marry me, William." The West-Country Damosel's Complaint. *Unknown.* ESPB

When will you speak again? George Seferis, *tr. fr. Greek by* Edmund Keeley *and* Philip Sherrard. *Fr.* Three Secret Poems, II: 6. VMG

When willing nymphs and swains unite. The Judgement of Tiresias. Hildebrand Jacob. NOEC

When wilt Thou save the people? God Save the People. Ebenezer Elliott. BLPA; EaLo; WBLP

When Wilt Thou Teach the People? D. H. Lawrence. OBSV

When wind and waves rise upon the river. The Fisherman. Cheng Hsieh, *tr. by* Jan *and* Yvonne Walls. WFTU

When Windsor walles sustain'd my wearied arme. Earl of Surrey. *See* When Windsor walls sustain'd my wearied arme.

When window-lamps had dwindled, then I rose. Christopher John Brennan. *Fr.* The Wanderer. CBAP

When Winds Are Raging. Harriet Beecher Stowe. AH

When winds go organing through the pines. The Wind in the Pines. Madison Cawein. AA

When winds that move not its calm surface sweep. The Ocean. Moschus, *tr. by* Shelley. AWP; MOS; OBVE

When Windsor walls sustain'd my wearied arme. Earl of Surrey. SiPS
("How Each Thing Save the Lover in Spring Reviveth to Pleasure.") Son
("When Windesor walles sustain'd my wearied arme.") AAS

When wine runs low, it is not worth the sparing. Joshua Sylvester, *after the French of* Pierre Mathieu. FaBoEE

When winking stars at dusk peep through. Makes the Little Ones Dizzy. Samuel Hoffenstein. BXAP

When winter is gone and spring comes. *Unknown. Fr.* Manyo Shu. Ma

When winter nights fall like eyelids closing. Montana Remembered from Albuquerque; 1982. Ron Rogers. STE

When winter scourged the meadow and the hill. Ice. Sir Charles G. D. Roberts. BoNaP; OBCV; RHPC

When winter snows upon thy sable hairs. Samuel Daniel. *Fr.* To Delia. CTC; OBSC; Son; TEP

When winter was half over. Another Sarah. Anne Porter. TTTS

When winter's cold tempests and snows are no more. The Blue-Bird. Alexander Wilson. AA

When Winter's royal robes of white. A Parting Hymn. Charlotte Forten. BlSi

When wintry days are dark and drear. The Light'ood Fire. John Henry Boner. AA

When wintry weather's all a-done. The Spring. William Barnes. BoNaP

When wise Minerva still was young. The Origin of Didactic Poetry. James Russell Lowell. PoEL-5

When, with a pain he desires to explain to his servitors, Baby. The Nurses. Kipling. *Fr.* Land and Sea Tales. NoAM

When, with a serious musing, I behold. The Marigold. George Wither. OBS

When with eyes closed as in an opium dream. Parfum Exotique. Baudelaire, *tr. by* Arthur Symons. AWP

When with hot palms, unable to fall asleep. Night. Miyazawa Kenji, *tr. by* Hiroaki Sato. FCEI

When with May the air is sweet. Love, Whose Month Was Ever May. Ulrich von Liechtenstein, *tr. by* Jethro Bithell. AWP

When with much pains this boasted learning's got. Charles Churchill. *Fr.* The Author. OBSV

When with staid mothers' milk and sunshine warmed. Alfred Austin. *Fr.* The Human Tragedy. FaBoCo

When with the first month comes the spring. Ki. *Fr.* Manyo Shu. Ma

When with the virgin morning thou dost rise. Matins, or Morning Prayer. Robert Herrick. CaPo

When, with You Asleep. Juan Ramón Jiménez, *tr. fr. Spanish by* Perry Higman. LPSS

When within my arms I hold you. Aurelia. Robert Nichols. OBMV

When women first Dame Nature wrought. Of Women. Richard Edwards. EIL

When woods are odorous at eve. Wood Carols. Henrietta Cordelia Ray. CBWP-3

When working blackguards come to blows. Ebenezer Elliott. EBEV

When world is water and all is flood, God said. Noah's Ark. Marguerite Young. WPE

When would-be suicides in purpose fail. Thomas Hood. OBD

When ye hunt at the roe, then shall ye see there. Julians Barnes. *Fr.* Book of Hunting. WPE

When Yon Full Moon. W. H. Davies. MoBrPo

When you and I draw close at night and play. Ballade of the Grindstones. Judith Johnson Sherwin. SM

When you and I go down. Midnight Lamentation. Harold Monro. BrPo; OBMV, *abr.*; OxBTC

When you and I have play'd the little hour. Reunited. Sir Gilbert Parker. OBEV

When You and I Must Part. *Unknown.* AmFP

When you and I on the Palos Verdes cliff. Shane O'Neill's Cairn. Robinson Jeffers. NoAM; NOBA

When you and my true lover meet. The Lady's Third Song. W. B. Yeats. *Fr.* The Three Bushes. FaBoTw

"When you are/ ill at ease." Granma's Words. Ted D. Palmanteer. STE

When you are alone. Arithmetic. Aleksander Wat, *tr. by* Czeslaw Milosz. PwPP

When you are away, wherefore should I adorn myself? *Unknown. Fr.* Manyo Shu. Ma

When you are called on to perform a duty. Do Your Best. Mrs. Henry Linden. CBWP-4

When you are caught breathless in an empty station. This Is the Place to Wait. Horace Gregory. *Fr.* The Passion of M'Phail. MoAmPo

When you are discouraged. Try This Once. *Unknown.* WBLP

When you are gone, I lie upon your bed. Suburban Wife's Song. Robert Hutchinson. NYBP

When you are in bed and it's cold outside. Pretending. Bobbi Katz. RAR

When you are in love, we love the grass. Robert Bly. PCP

When You Are Old. W. B. Yeats, *after the French of* Pierre de Ronsard. AWP; BoLoP; CMoP; CTC; EBVV; FaBV; FaFP; FPL; GBL; GoJo; HeIP; InvP; LiTM; MoAB; MoBrPo; MoP; NAEL-2; NAWM-2; NoAM; NOBVV; NoP; OBEV; OxBTC; PCP; PoLF; PrIm; TEP

When you are old and beautiful. At Majority. Adrienne Rich. NePoEA-2

When you are thus gone. Emperor Shomu. *Fr.* Manyo Shu. Ma

When you are traveling. Ijajee's Story. Charlotte DeClue. STE

When you are very old, at evening. Of His Lady's Old Age. Pierre de Ronsard, *tr. by* Andrew Lang. AWP; CTC

When you arrive in our town. Salt and Memory. Zoltán Zelk, *tr. by* Barbara Howes. MHuP

When you awake. The Sleeper. Sydney Clouts. PeSA; VWA

When you bared your china. Party Favour. Daniel David Moses. HATNAP

When you break your heart it changes. End Song. Ruth Krauss. LLLT

When you broke from me. Izumi Shikibu, *tr. fr. Japanese by* Willis Barnstone. BoWoP

When you came and you talked and you read. To William Carlos Williams. Galway Kinnell. NePoAm; NOAM; SM

When you came out of your house. Remembering Althea. William Stafford. NYBP

When you came, you were like red wine and honey. A Decade. Amy Lowell. MoAmPo

When you come, as you soon must, to the streets of our city. Advice to a Prophet. Richard Wilbur. AmPP; CAPP; FYAP; MAT; MoAmPo; NYBP; OBWP; OxBC; PoE; PPP; TwCP

When you come to the end of a perfect day. A Perfect Day. Carrie Jacobs Bond. WBLP

When you come to the other side. The Other. Peter Cooley. MAYP; NAmP

When you consider. Saigyo, *tr. fr. Japanese by* Burton Watson. *Fr.* Sixty-four Tanka. FCEI

When you consider the radiance, that it does not withhold. The City Limits. A. R. Ammons. CAPP; HCAP; MoP; NAAL-2; NoAM; NOBA; NoP

When you dance. Creole Girl. Leslie Morgan Collins. PoNe

When you dance Greek-style. With the Greeks. Naomi Shihab Nye. NAmP

When you destroy a blade of grass. To Iron-Founders and Others. Gordon Bottomley. OBEV; OBMV

When you drive on the freeway, cars follow you. Paranoia. Michael Dennis Browne. AmPA

When you enter. Al Fitnah Muhajir. Nazzam Al Sudan. NBP

When you enter Chin-hua Mountain. Tsung Ch'en, *tr. fr. Chinese by* Jonathan Chaves. *Fr.* Sent to Yü Te-fu upon His Receipt of an Official Commission. CoBLCP

When you feel like saying something. The Most Vital Thing in Life. Grenville Kleiser. SoSe

When you first feel the ground under your feet. Walking in a Swamp. David Wagoner. HAP

When you first rub up against God's own skin. Ars Poetica about Ultimates. Tram Combs. TwCP

When you get down to it, earth. A Physics. Heather McHugh. MAYP

When you get hard knocks and buffets. Keep the Glad Flag Flying. *Unknown.* FaFP

When you get there, do not greet them. Tommorow. Amal Dunqul, *tr. by* Sharif Elmusa *and* Thomas G. Ezzy. MAP

When You Go Away. W. S. Merwin. LCAP

When you go away/ you become everything I believe. The Departure. Frank Steele. GOYP

When you go away the wind clicks around to the north. When You Go Away. W. S. Merwin. LCAP

When you go out at early morn. The Serving Maid. Arthur Munby. NOBVV

When you got up this morning the sun. Wind. Gary Soto. *Fr.* The Elements of San Joaquin. NoAM

When you ground the lenses and the moons swam free. The Emancipators. Randall Jarrell. PoA; WaP

When you had left our pirate fold. A Most Ingenious Paradox. W. S. Gilbert. *Fr.* The Pirates of Penzance. NAs

When you hark to the voice of the knocker. The Quarrelsome Trio. "L. G." WBLP

When you have/ once had. Self Portrait II. Tove Ditlevsen, *tr. by* Ann Freeman. OV

When you have bathed in the river. Submission. *Unknown, tr. by* E. Powys Mathers. ErPo

When you have come, the house is emptied quite. Evening. Mary Matheson. CaP

When You Have Emptied Our Calabashes. Iyamide Hazeley. WS

When You Have Forgotten Sunday: The Love Story. Gwendolyn Brooks. BPo; FF; WPOW

When you have nothing more to say, just drive. The Peninsula. Seamus Heaney. FaBCIP

When you have tidied all things for the night. Solitude. Harold Monro. MoBrPo; TrGrPo

When you have wearied of the valiant spires of this country town. Oxford Canal. James Elroy Flecker. OxBTC

When you kneel below me. Celebration. Leonard Cohen. ErPo

When You Laugh. Ingrid Jonker, *tr. fr. Afrikaans by* Elizabeth Jones. WPOW

When You Leave. Kimiko Hahn. BrSi

When you lie with a woman, at least so girls say. Epigram: To Polycharmus. Martial. PeHV

When you look down from the airplane you see lines. Field and Forest. Randall Jarrell. LCAP; VGW

When you look on my grave. *Unknown.* FaBoEE

When you look upon this ol' Stetson hat. My Ol' Stetson. Owen Barton. CowP

When you lost touch with lovers' bare skin. John Donne. James Simmons. CIP

When you love, or speak of it. Aphra Behn. BoWoP

When you meet a man who is satisfied with one island. One Island. Naomi Shihab Nye. NAmP

When you move away, you see how much depends. Landscape, Dense with Trees. Ellen Bryant Voigt. BLA; MT

When you perceive these stones are wet. Sir William Davenant. ACP

When you plunged. The Otter. Seamus Heaney. FaBCIP; IPY; NoAM

When you press next to me. Negative Space. Michael Waters. NAmP

When you put on the feet be sure. Dr. Potatohead Talks to Mothers. Judith Johnson Sherwin. MoP

When you put up your walls afresh. To You Building the New House. Nelly Sachs, *tr. by* Keith Bosley. VWA

When You Reach the Hilltop the Sky Is on Top of You. Etta Blum. GoYe

When you reach to touch the markings. Indian Rock, Bainbridge Island, Washington. Duane Niatum. CDW

When You Read This Poem. Pinkie Gordon Lane. BlSi

When you scuttled the ship, the shore was still in sight. Meditation of a Mariner. Dorothy Auchterlonie. CBAP

When you see a guy reach for stars in the sky. Guys and Dolls. Frank Loesser. OBAL

When you see a ragged urchin. Boys Make Men. *Unknown.* PWR

When you see me sitting quietly. On Ageing. Maya Angelou. AIW

When You See Millions of the Mouthless Dead. Charles Hamilton Sorley. MMA; OBWP

When you see them. Breath. Mark Strand. HCAP

When you send out invitations, don't ask me. Palladas, *tr. fr. Greek by* Tony Harrison. OBVE

When you shall see me in the toils of Time. She, to Him. Thomas Hardy. OxBTC

When you show me. Colors for Mama. Barbara Mahone. CNA; PoBA

When you smile, the sea becomes fragrant. Wakayama Bokusui, *tr. fr. Japanese by* Hiroaki Sato. *Fr.* Forty-four Tanka. FCEI

When you speak of dauntless deeds. The Deed of Lieutenant Miles. Clinton Scollard. PAH

When you spoke to me——wrapped in your faded, perennial. The Night-Blooming Cereus. Roger Weingarten. NAmP

When you swim in the surf off Seal Rocks, and your family. Family. Josephine Miles. FaBoWP; FYAP; GrPl

When you take off your clothes. In Nakedness. Marnie Pomeroy. ErPo

When You Talk to a Monkey. Rowena Bastin Bennett. RAR

When you the sunburnt pilgrim see. Good Counsel to a Young Maid ("When you the sunburnt pilgrim see"). Thomas Carew. ErPo (Song: Good Counsel to a Young Maid.) CaPo

When you think of it. Teika, *tr. by* Steven D. Carter. WFTW

When you think of the distances. The Distances. W. S. Merwin. NOBA

When you think of the hosts without no. Cautionary Limerick. *Unknown.* FaBoUs; NBLV

When you turn at the road's. Cain the Immortal. Yusuf al-Khal, *tr. by* Sargon Boulus *and* Samuel Hazo. MAP

When you visit the barber. Barbershop. Martin Gardner. RHPC

"When you wait for one to come." *Unknown, tr. by* Geoffrey Bownas *and* Anthony Thwaite. PeBJV

When you wake up, in your fourteenth year. Joe Gillon Hypnotizes His Son. Albert Goldbarth. SM

When You Walk. James Stephens. PDV

When you walk in the country, she further confided to him. Henri Michaux, *tr. fr. French by* Richard Ellmann. *Fr.* I Am Writing to You from a Far-Off Country, II. RHTwFP

When you walked downstairs. In Praise of Beverly. Steve Orlen. MAYP

When you walked here. The Dumbfounding. Margaret Avison. NOBC

When you wardance, sometimes you must. Wardance. Phillip William George. VoR

When you watch for. Feather or Fur. John Becker. FaPON; RHPC

When you well might have wished to live. Fujii Kooyu. *Fr.* Manyo Shu. Ma

When you were. For Angela. Zack Gilbert. PoBA

When you were a girl. Woman. Umberto Saba, *tr. by* Thomas G. Bergin. UnAS

When you were a tadpole and I was a fish. Evolution. Langdon Smith. BeLS; BLPA; FaBoBe; FaFP

When you were drunk you could always whip Joe Louis. My Right Hand Don't Leave Me No More. Carter Revard. HATNAP

When you were here in wonderful Detroit. Goodbye David Tamunoemi West. Margaret Danner. BPo

When you were lying on the white sand. Incident. Fleur Adcock. ATNZ

When you were there, and you, and you. Dining-Room Tea. Rupert Brooke. BrPo; MoBrPo

When you two or three. Battlefield of Dreams. Okamoto Jun, *tr. by* Geoffrey Bownas *and* Anthony Thwaite. PeBJV

When you whom Jules de Goncourt's prose. O Matre Pulchra. Charles Spear. ATNZ

When You Will Walk in the Field. Leah Goldberg, *tr. fr. Hebrew by* Simon Halkin. TrJP

When you with Hogh Dutch Heeren dine. Matthew Prior. OBTV

When you woke [up] among them. After Grief. Stanley Plumly. AmPA; DiL; LCAP

When You Write Again. Ingrid Jonker, *tr. fr. Afrikaans by* Jack Cope *and* William Plomer. PBWP

When you wrote your letter it was April. Response. Mary Ursula Bethell. ATNZ; FaBoWP; PeNZ

When Young Hearts Break. Heine, *tr. fr. German by* Louis Untermeyer. AWP

When young I scribbled, boasting, on my wall. The Summing-up. Stanley Kunitz. OBAL

When Young Ladies Get Married. *Unknown.* AmFP

When Young Melissa Sweeps. Nancy Byrd Turner. FaPON; NTCP

When your boots are full of water and your hat brim's all a-drip. Rain on the Range. S. Omar Barker. CowP

When your boyfriend writes you a letter. Ruth Krauss. RR

When Your Cheap Divorce Is Granted. "Orpheus C. Kerr." OBAL

When your client's hopping mad. The Advertising Agency Song. *Unknown.* FaBoUs; NBLV

When your eyes gaze seaward. Golden Moonrise. William Stanley Braithwaite. PoBA

When your eyes shall be closing, your mouth be opening. *Unknown, tr. by* Douglas Hyde. WTO

When your face/ appeared over my crumpled life. Colors. Yevgeny Yevtushenko, *tr. by* Robin Milner-Gulland *and* Peter Levi. LLLT

When your feet are like lead. Consolatory! St. John Emile Clavering Hankin. CenHV

When your hour was rung at last. Rendez-vous Manqué dans la Rue Racine. J. M. Synge. BIrV

When your lips seek my lips they bring. Isolation. Arthur Symons. OxBSP

When your name is added. Christine Lavant, *tr. by* Beth Bjorklund. CoAuP

When your widow had left the graveside. The Ritual of Memories. Tess Gallagher. GeTw

When you're a duck like me it's impossible. The Duck. Richard Digance. RHPC

When You're Away. Samuel Hoffenstein. FiBHP

When you're away I sleep a lot. The Method. J. D. McClatchy. EOEF

When you're depressed, a toad's distant voice too. Sora, *tr. by* Hiroaki Sato. FCEI

When you're lying awake with a dismal headache. Nightmare. William Schwenck Gilbert. *Fr.* Iolanthe. NOBL; NoP; OxBoli; PoRA (Chancellor's Nightmare, The.) FaBoNo

When You're Not a Poet. Yona Wallach, *tr. fr. Hebrew by* Warren Bargad *and* Stanley F. Chyet. IP

When you're out in smart society. Well, Did You Evah? Cole Porter. OBAL

When you're together with her, and you have a good excuse. Juan Ruiz, Archpriest of Hita, *tr. fr. Spanish by* Hubert Creekmore. *Fr.* The Book of True Love. ErPo

When you're trying to get it. *Unknown, tr. fr. Japanese by* Burton Watson. FCEI

When you're unfilled in ways of worldly entertainment. Tabito. *Fr.* Manyo Shu. FCEI

When Youth and Beauty Meet Together. *Unknown.* EIL
When Youth Had Led. Earl of Surrey. SiPS
When youth was lord of my unchallenged fate. On a Boy's First Reading of "King Henry V." Silas Weir Mitchell. AA
When youthful faith hath fled. John Gibson Lockhart. OBEV
When you've had yourself accoutered. Preparedness. Felicia Lamport. ASP
When you've just been jugged by an upright judge. They Can't Do That. *Unknown.* WTO
Whenas from cups my Julia sups. Teatime Variations: After Robert Herrick. Peter Titheradge. FaBoPa
Whenas galoshed my Julia goes. Upon Julia's Arctics. Bert Leston Taylor. OBAL
Whenas in furs my Julia goes. Upon Julia's Clothes. Edmund George Valpy Knox. BXAP
Whenas in Jeans. Paul Dehn. FiBHP
Whenas in perfume Julia went. Herrick's Julia. Helen Smith Bevington. BXAP
Whenas in silks my Julia goes. Upon Julia's Clothes. Robert Herrick. AWP; CaPo; ChTr; EBEV; EnLoPo; FaBV; FaFP; FF; FPL; GBL; HAP; HeIP; HoPM; InPS; JCP; LiTB; NAEL-1; NBLV; NIP; NOBE; NoP; OAEL-1; OBEV; OBS; OPOP; OxBSP; PoE; PoEL-3; PPP; SeCP; SeCV-1; TrGrPo; TTTS; WeW
(Whenas in Silks My Julia Goes.) BLPA; GTBS; GTBS-P; TEP
Whenas in silks you came and dazzled. Bahadur Shah Zafar, *tr. by* Ahmed Ali. GoT
Whenas [*or* When as] man's life, the light of human[e] lust. Fulke Greville. *Fr.* Caelica, LXXXVII [LXXXVIII]. LiTB; MePo; PoEL-1
(Sonnet: "When as man's life, the light of human lust.") OBS
Whenas—methinks that is a pretty way. They Answer Back. "Francis." FiBHP
(To His Ever-worshipped Will from W. H.) ErPo
Whenas Queen Anne of great renown. A New Ballad. Arthur Mainwaring. APAS
Whenas the chill sirocco blowes. In Praise of Ale. *At. to* Thomas Bonham. OBS
(Pipe and Can II.) OBEV
("When as the chill charocco blows.") OBEV
("When that the chill charocco blows.") FaBoCh
Whenas the mildest month. The Rose. Thomas Howell. EIL; OBSC
Whenas [*or* When as] the Rye [Reach to the Chin]. George Peele. *Fr.* The Old Wives' [*or* Wife's] Tale. ELP; EnLoPo; FaBoCh; GBL; InvP; NoP; SeCePo; TEP
(Song: "When as [*or* whenas] the rye [*or* rie] reach to the chin.") EIL; OBSC; OxBoLi; PoEL-2
(Summer Song, A.) NOBE; OBEV
Whenas to shoot my Julia goes. To Julia in Shooting Togs. Sir Owen Seaman. BXAP
Whence and Whither. Hayyim Nahman Bialik, *tr. fr. Hebrew by* Helena Frank. TrJP
"Whence are you, learning's son?" The End of Clonmacnois. *Unknown, tr. by* Frank O'Connor. CIP
Whence art thou, thirsty wind. O Thirsty Wind. *Unknown, tr. by* N. B. Emerson. WTO
Whence came this man? As if on the wings. Abraham Lincoln. Samuel Valentine Cole. OHIP
Whence come ye, Cherubs? from the moon? The Chanting Cherubs—A Group by Greenough. Richard Henry Dana. AA
Whence come you, all of you so sorrowful? Sonnet: To Certain Ladies; When Beatrice Was Lamenting Her Father's Death. Dante, *tr. by* Dante Gabriel Rossetti. AWP
Whence comes my love? O heart, disclose! A Sonnet Made on Isabella Markham. John Harington. EIL; OBSC
Whence comes this rush of wings afar. Carol of the Birds. *Unknown.* OHIP
Whence comest thou, Gehazi. Gehazi. Kipling. FaBoPV
Whence Had They Come? W. B. Yeats. BoLoP
Whence, hardworn drum. Tambour. István Vas, *tr. by* Jascha Kessler. FOC; VWA
Whence let us go to. "The Nicest Phantasies Are Shared." Brian Coffey. CIP
Whence, O fragrant form of light. The Water-Lily. John Banister Tabb. AA; ACP
Whence should I know who I am? Origins. Barbara Fiedler, *tr. by* Susan L. Cocalis. DMG
Whence the sudden stir that roars through my vitals? Epithalamium for Mary Stuart and the Dauphin of France. George Buchanan. GoTS
Whence this impatience fluttering in my breast! Urania. Robert Andrews. NOEC
Whene'er bitter foe attack thee. Advice to Hotheads. Samuel ben Elhanan Isaac, Archevolti of Padua, *tr. by* A. B. Rhine. TrJP

Whene'er I come where ladies are. Love at Large. Coventry Patmore. *Fr.* The Angel in the House. EBVV, *fr.* I, ii; NOBVV, *fr.* I, ii.
Whene'er I look into your eyes. I Love But Thee. Heine, *tr. by* Louis Untermeyer. AWP
Whene'er I take my walks abroad. Praise for Mercies Spiritual and Temporal. Isaac Watts. NOEC
Whene'er with haggard eyes I view. Rogero's Song. George Canning , George Ellis *and* John Hookham Frere. *Fr.* The Rovers, I. NOEC
(Song by Rogero.) FaBoNo
(Song of One Eleven Years in Prison.) FiBHP
Whenever a butterfly. A Lesson of Silence. Tymoteusz Karpowicz, *tr. by* Czeslaw Milosz. PwPP
Whenever a fellow called Rex. Limerick. *Unknown.* NOBL
Whenever a Little Child Is Born. Agnes Louisa Carter Mason. AA
Whenever a snowflake leaves the sky. Snowflakes. Mary Mapes Dodge. AA
Whenever, Chloe, I begin. Earl of Chesterfield. NOEC
Whenever grief's insistent pressure. The Tear. Prince P. A. Vyazemsky, *tr. by* Alan Myers. AAA
Whenever he observes me purchasing. Sextus the Usurer. Martial, *tr. by* Kirby Flower Smith. AWP
Whenever I dine in a dainty shoppe. Lettuce Pause. Alma Denny. SoTCo
Whenever I go by there nowadays. The Tavern. E. A. Robinson. AnAmPo
Whenever I Go There. W. S. Merwin. NaP
Whenever I pause. The Noise of the Village. *Unknown, tr. by* Frances Densmore. OBVE
"Whenever I plunge my arm, like this." Under the Waterfall. Thomas Hardy. BoLoP; CTC; LiTB; NAEL-2
Whenever I read that poem. Explanation. Hermann Gail, *tr. by* Beth Bjorklund. CoAuP
Whenever I remember. Shamsuddin Mohammad Vali, *tr. by* Ahmed Ali. GoT
Whenever I see. Emperor Meiji, *tr. by* Geoffrey Bownas *and* Anthony Thwaite. PeBJV
Whenever I see him. Waking in the Dark. Dorothy Livesay. NOBC
Whenever I see them ride on high. The Bombers. Sarah Churchill. CN
Whenever I walk to Suffern along the Erie track. The House with Nobody in It. Joyce Kilmer. BLPA; BLPL
Whenever in my daily routine I suddenly look up. Dragon Song. Park Je-chun, *tr. by* Koh Chang-soo. ACKP
Whenever Mr. Edwards spake. The Theology of Jonathan Edwards. Phyllis McGinley. MoAmPo
Whenever Offenbach backed off. Bragatelle. K. F. Lazarus. SoTCo
Whenever Richard Cory went down town. Richard Cory. Edwin Arlington Robinson. AmPP; AnAmPo; CMoP; DL; FaFP; FF; FPL; HAP; InPK; LiTA; LiTM; MoAB; MoAmPo; NAAL-2; NIP; NOBA; NoP; OxBA; PoLF; PoRA; PrIm; SoSe; TAP; TrGrPo
Whenever the dark cloud horses galloped. And Jesus Don't Have Much Use for His Old Suitcase Anymore. Tom Kryss. NeAC
Whenever the moon and stars are set. Windy Nights. Robert Louis Stevenson. BoTP; GoJo; OxBChV; PoRA; RHPC; RR
Whenever the moon went into eclipse he became a man. Was/Man. Phyllis Gotlieb. BWV
Whenever the Snakes Come. Hedva Harkavi, *tr. fr. Hebrew by* Tova Weizman. VWA
Whenever troublous hours I find. Happiness amidst Troubles. Immanuel di Roma, *tr. by* J. Chotzner. TrJP
Whenever war is spoken of. The Great War. Vernon Scannell. OBWP
Whenever we touched, I thought of the Lying-in Hospital. Robert Layzer. NePoEA
Whenever you drink all night you make. Martial, *tr. by* James Michie. FaBoEE
Whenever you see the hearse go by. Be Merry. *Unknown.* RB
Whenne mine eynen misteth. All Too Late. *Unknown.* EBEV; OAEL-1
When/Then. Adrienne Rich. ER
Wher one would be. Sir Edward Dyer. PoEL-1
Where? A. S. J. Tessimond. OBTV
Where? Kenneth Patchen. LiTM
Where. Walter de la Mare. NYBP
Where a Roman judged a foreign people. Notre Dame. Osip Mandelstam, *tr. by* James Greene. OBVE
Where a Roman Villa Stood, above Freiburg. Mary Elizabeth Coleridge. OBNC; OBTV
Where alders spring and a split hollow oak. Before a Journey. Robert Wells. NPo
Where all the winds were tranquil. A Pine-Tree Buoy. Harrison Smith Morris. AA
Where am I now? And what. A Song in Passing. Yvor Winters. CRP; VGW

Where am I, O awesome friend? Yitzhak Lamdan, *tr. fr. Hebrew by* Simon Halkin. *Fr.* For the Sun Declined. TrJP

Where ancient forests round us spread. Hymn for the Dedication of a Church. Andrews Norton. AA

Where angel trumpets hail a brighter sun. My Own Hereafter. Eugene Lee-Hamilton. WGRP

Where are all thy beauties now, all hearts enchaining? Thomas Campion. GBL; OBSC

Where are Elmer, Herman, Bert, Tom and Charley. The Hill. Edgar Lee Masters. *Fr.* Spoon River Anthology. CMoP; FYAP; LiTA; LiTM; NoAM; NOBA; OxBA; TAP

Where are my people? To Egypt. Gloria Davis. NBP

Where are now, in coign or crack. Ballade of England. Louis MacNeice. NYBP

Where are the bay-leaves, Thestylis, and the charms. The Incantations. Theocritus, *tr. fr. Greek by* Charles Stuart Calverley. *Fr.* Idylls. AWP

Where are the braves, the faces like autumn fruit. Indian Reservation: Caughnawaga. Abraham Moses Klein. LiTM; NOBC; NoP; OBCV

Where are the dear domestics, white and black. Familiar Faces, Long Departed. Robert Hillyer. NYBP

Where are the hands and feet. Give Me My Infant Now. Te-whaka-io-roa, *tr. by* John White. NAs; WTO

Where Are the Hebrew Children? *at. to* Peter Cartwright. AH

Where are the heroes of yesteryear? Where, O Where? Milton Bracker. SD

Where are the lumberjacks who came from the woods for Christmas. River Song. Elizabeth Brewster. CaP

Where Are the Men Seized in This Wind of Madness? Alda do Espírito Santo, *tr. fr. Portuguese by* Alan Ryder. TTY; WPOW

Where are the old side-wheelers now. The River Boats. Daniel Whitehead Hicky. AmFN

Where Are the Ones Who Lived Before? *Unknown. See* Ubi Sunt Qui ante Nos Fuerunt?

Where are the passions they essayed. Ballade of Dead Actors. W. E. Henley. EBVV; OBMV

Where are the people as beautiful as poems. The Black Angel. Henri Coulette. CoAP; NYBP

Where are the Quonset huts, fireflies. By the Iowa River. Satoru Sato, *tr. by the author.* WCI

Where are the ribbons I tie my hair with? Ballade of Lost Objects. Phyllis McGinley. CRP; NBLV; PoRA

Where Are the Snows? Leonard Trawick. SoTCo

Where are the tears of shame. Tears of Shame. Ali Sardar J'afri, *tr. by* Mahmood Jamal. PBMUP

Where Are the War Poets? Cecil Day Lewis. FaBoMo; OBWP; OxBSP; OxBTC

Where Are the Waters of Childhood? Mark Strand. HCAP; LCAP; WeW

Where are they all? Some raise their heads. Asadullah Khan Ghalib, *tr. by* Ahmed Ali. GoT

Where are they gone, the old familiar faces? The Old Familiar Faces. Charles Lamb. EnRP; FaBoRV

Where are they now, the softly blooming flowers. Irises. Padraic Colum. BoNaP

Where are those that were before us. *Unknown. See* Were beth they [that] biforen us weren.

Where are we. Bahamas. George Oppen. NYBP

Where are we going? where are we going. Song of Slaves in the Desert. Whittier. OxBA

Where are we to go when this is done? Alfred A. Duckett. AmNP; PoBA; PoNe

Where Are You. Benjamin Péret, *tr. fr. French by* Michael Benedikt. POS

"Where are you coming from, Lomey Carter." Old Christmas Morning. Roy Helton. MoAmPo

Where are you damn'd? Christopher Marlowe. *Fr.* Doctor Faustus, I, iii. OBD

Where are you going. *Unknown.* BoTP

Where are you going? asked Manny the Mayor. Jig Tune: Not for Love. Thomas McGrath. VGW

Where Are You Going, Greatheart? John Oxenham. BLPA

"Where are you going, Master mine?" Whither Away? Mary Elizabeth Coleridge. CH

Where Are You Going, My Pretty Maid. *Unknown.* NBLV

Where are you going, my spiv, my wide boy. Spiv Song. Royston Ellis. PeHV

"Where are you going?" said the knight in the road. The False Knight upon the Road. *Unknown.* AmFP

(False Knight and the Wee Boy, The.) FaBoCh

"Where are you going to, my pretty maid?" Mother Goose. OxNR

"Where are you going to-night, to-night." John Evereldown. E. A. Robinson. AnAmPo; CMoP; OxBA

Where are you going? To Scarborough Fair? Scarborough Fair. *Unknown.* OxBoLi

Where are you going, you little pig? The Little Piggies. Thomas Hood. BoTP

Where Are You My Bright-Eyed Baby? Maureen Ismay. WS

Where Are You Now? Mary Britton Miller. RHPC

Where Are You Now Superman? Brian Patten. FF

Where are your ancient waves, O river. Home-Coming. Albert Ehrenstein, *tr. by* Babette Deutsch *and* Avram Yarmolinsky. TrJP

Where are your heroes, my little black ones. Poem for Black Boys. Nikki Giovanni. BPo

Where are your oranges? The Children's Bells. Eleanor Farjeon. BoTP; CH

Where Art Is a Midwife. Tom Paulin. FaBCIP

Where art thou gone, light-ankled youth? To Youth. Walter Savage Landor. EnRP

"Where art thou, Muse, that thou forget'st so long." Shakespeare. *Fr.* Sonnets, C. OBSC

Where art thou, my beloved son. The Affliction of Margaret. Wordsworth. EnRP; GTBS; GTBS-P; PoEL-4

"Where art thou wandering, little child?" The Little Maid and the Cowslips. John Clare. BoTP

Where Avalanches Wail. *Unknown.* NA

Where Babylon Ends. Nathaniel Tarn. VWA

Where Babylon's high walls erected were. Pyramus and Thisbe. Abraham Cowley. FL

Where Be You Going, You Devon Maid? Keats. ErPo

Where beeth they biforen us weren. *Unknown. See* Were beth they [that] biforen us weren.

Where, behind Keighley, the road. Matthew Arnold. *Fr.* Haworth Churchyard. FaBoPP

Where beneath the Night Did You Get Lost. Eeva Kilpi, *tr. fr. Finnish by* Aili Jarvenpa. SOP

Where beth they beforen us weren. *Unknown. See* Where are those that were before us?

Where beth they biforen us weren. *Unknown. See* Where are those that were before us?

Where broods the Absolute. Quest. Edmund Clarence Stedman. *Fr.* Corda Concordia. AA

Where Cadmus, old Agenor's son, did rest and plant his reign. The Fate of Narcissus. William Warner. *Fr.* Albion's England. OBSC

Where can one live? We inherited sidereal cities. Life on This Star. Christine Busta, *tr. by* Beth Bjorklund. CoAuP

Where can we buy wine? We ask. Mooring Our Boat at Tan-yang Harbor. Kao Ch'i, *tr. by* Jonathan Chaves. CoBLCP

Where can we find in heaven or earth. Adam's Ex. Hannah Fox. SoTCo

Where Cape Delgado strikes the sea. Edwin John Pratt. *Fr.* The Cachalot. CaP; MoCV

Where Children Live. Naomi Shihab Nye. MAYP

Where cider ends there ale begins to reign. The Cambrian Swain. Edward Davies. *Fr.* Chepstow: A Poem. OBWVE

Where clear air blew off the land. York Harbor Morning. George Garrett. MT

Where close the curving mountains drew. Untrodden Ways. Agnes Maule Machar. CaP

Where could I find the words. Arvo Turtiainen, *tr. fr. Finnish by* Aili Jarvenpa. *Fr.* Ballad of Herman's Rose, III. SOP

Where Covent-Garden's famous temple stands. The Dangers of Foot-ball. John Gay. *Fr.* Trivia; or, The Art of Walking the Streets of London. SD

Where Cross the Crowded Ways of Life. Frank Mason North. AH, *with music.*
(City, The.) WGRP

Where Cumbria's mountains in the north arise. James Plumptre. *Fr.* Prologue to "The Lakers; a Comic Opera." NOEC

Where Did He Run To? Mark Van Doren. SO

"Where did I come from, Mother, and why?" Christmas Lullaby for a New-born Child. Yvonne Gregory. AmNP

Where did I see this region before with its bleak earth. Baffling Picture. Lajos Kassák, *tr. by* Edwin Morgan. MHuP

Where did it roll in from, that sea of light. In Two Fields. Waldo Williams, *tr. by* Gwyn Jones. OBWVE

"Where did the blood come from?" On a Line in Sandburg. Ronald Stuart Thomas. NAs

Where did the voice come from? I hunted through the rooms. Bedtime Story for My Son. Peter Redgrove. NePoEA-2

Where did this tiger come from? Ballad of the Ferocious Tiger. Hsü Pen, *tr. by* Jonathan Chaves. CoBLCP

Where did you borrow that last sigh. Sir William Berkeley. *Fr.* The Lost Lady. OxBSP

Where did you come from, baby dear? The Baby. George Macdonald. *Fr.* At the Back of the North Wind, 23. FaPON
(Where Did You Come From.) BLPA; FaFP; OxBChV

Where dips the rocky highland. The Stolen Child. W. B. Yeats. CMoP; NAEL-2; NoP; WSC

Where do insects go at night. When All the World's Asleep. Anita E. Posey. RAR

Where Do School Days End? Josephine D. Henderson Heard. CBWP-4

Where Do the Gipsies Come From? Sir Henry Howarth Bashford. CH

Where do the roots go? The Pit. Theodore Roethke. *Fr.* The Lost Son. NAAL-2

"Where do the stars grow, little Garaine?" Little Garaine. Sir Gilbert Parker. FaPON

Where do these voices stray. The Eccho. Richard Leigh. MePo

Where do we go, my love, who have been led. The Bed. James Merrill. NePoEA

Where do we live? Variations for Two Voices. Roberta Hill Whiteman. HATNAP; NOVW

Where do you go with your fury. Fury's Field. Cecil Bodker, *tr. by* Nadia Christensen. PBWP

Where do you think I've been to-day? The Pigeon's Story. Jeannie Kirby. BoTP

Where do you walk this moment that I fall? Next of Kin. Herbert B. Mallalieu. WaP

Where Does My Sadness Come From? Kao Ch'i, *tr. by* Jonathan Chaves. CoBLCP

Where does Pinafore Palace stand? Lilliput Levee. William Brighty Rands. CenHV

Where does she come from, the wind who comes first. The Ring. Pier Paolo Pasolini, *tr. by* Lawrence R. Smith. NItP

Where does the dragon-ox display its imposing form. Hsü Wei, *tr. fr. Chinese by* Jonathan Chaves. *Fr.* Songs of Yen-ching. CoBLCP

Where does the locus lie. The Gathering. A. R. Ammons. BLA

Where dost [*or* do'st thou careless[e] lie. An Ode to Himself. Ben Jonson. HAP; JCP; LiTB; NOBE; NoP; OBS; PoEL-2; PrIm; QFR; SeCePo; SeCP; SeCV-1

Where Dunwich Used to Be. Swinburne. *Fr.* By the North Sea, VI. FaBoPP

Where dwell the lovely, wild white womenfolk. The White Women. Mary Elizabeth Coleridge. BrRo

Where dwells that wish most ardent of the wise? Edward Young. *Fr.* Night Thoughts. OBD

Where Earth. Philippe Jaccottet, *tr. fr. French by* Paul Auster. RHTwFP

Where-e'er My Flatt'ring Passions Rove. Isaac Watts. NOCV

Where ends our chancel in a vaulted space. The Vicar. George Crabbe. *Fr.* The Borough, Letter III. OBSV

"But let applause be dealt in all we may." OBNC

Where Englands Damon us'd to keep. The Pastoral on the King's Death; Written in 1648. Alexander Brome. OBS

Where every female delights to give her maiden to her husband. Male & Female Loves in Beulah. Blake. *Fr.* Jerusalem, III. OBNC

Where fair Sabrina's wand'ring currents flow. William Somervile. *Fr.* The Bowling-Green. NOEC

Where Fire Burns. Gladys Cardiff. HATNAP

Where five old graves lay circled on a hill. The Graveyard. Jane Cooper. NePoEA-2

Where foam-white openwork. Waterspout. James Merrill. CAPP

Where folds the central lotus. William Yeats in Limbo. Sidney Keyes. MoBrPo

Where from the watch towers. Bay Poem. Lance Henson. VoR

Where go the birds when the rain. Jane Heap. PoA

Where Go the Boats? Robert Louis Stevenson. FaBoBe; FaBoCh; GoJo; Mes; NTCP; OxBChV; PYC

Where goats are slaughtered. Murukan: His Places. Nakkiranar, *tr. by* A. K. Ramanujan. PLW

Where Goblins Dwell. Jack Prelutsky. RHPC

Where had I heard this wind before. Bereft. Robert Frost. LiTM; MoAB; MoAmPo; OxBA; SoSe

Where hae ye been a' the day. *Unknown.* OxNR

Where has he of race divine. Chorus of Satyrs, Driving Their Goats. Euripides, *tr. fr. Greek by* Shelley. *Fr.* Cyclops. AWP

Where has she come from, this lady. Lady of Chaos. Ali Ja far al-Allaq, *tr. by* Sharif Elmusa *and* Thomas G. Ezzy. MAP

Where has tenderness gone, he asked the mirror. Delirium in Vera Cruz. Malcolm Lowry. FaBoTw; OxBTC

Where has the guardian of sleep gone? *Unknown, tr. by* Geoffrey Bownas *and* Anthony Thwaite. PeBJV

Where has ti been, maw canny hinny? Captain Bover. *Unknown.* GBP

Where hast been toiling all day, sweetheart. The Child on the Judgment Seat. Elizabeth Rundle Charles. BLPA

Where hast 'te been, ma' canny hinny? Ma Canny Hinny. *Unknown.* FaBoPP; GBP

Where hast thou floated? in what seas pursued. To the Immortal Memory of the Halibut on Which I Dined This Day, Monday, April 26, 1784. William Cowper. MOS; SeCePo

Where have all the colours gone? The Darkening Garden. *Unknown.* BoTP

Where Have All the Indians Gone? Janet Campbell Hale. STE

Where have these hands been. Musician. Louise Bogan. GoJo; NYBP

Where have they gone. The Saint John. George Frederick Clarke. CaP

Where have they led you, into what disguise. The Kingdom. Jon Swan. NYBP

Where have ye [*or* you] been all the day,/ Billy Boy?" *Unknown.* See Billy Boy.

"Where have you been." Banbury Fair. Edith G. Millard. BoTP

Where have you been? Dialogue. Jeannie Ebner, *tr. by* Beth Bjorklund. CoAuP

"Where have you been all day, Henry my son,/ Where have you been all day, my pretty one?" Green and Yellow. *Unknown.* OBET

"Where have you been all day, Henry my son,/ Where have you been all day, my beloved one?" Henry My Son. *Unknown.* OBET

Where have you been all the day, Billy boy, Billy boy? *Unknown.* OxNR

Where Have You Been Dear? Karla Kuskin. NTCP

Where have you been, South Wind, this May-day morning? South Wind. Siegfried Sassoon. BoTP

Where Have You Gone? Mari E. Evans. BPo; PoNe; TTY

Where Have You Gone, Little Boy. Patty L. Harjo. VoR

Where have you gone to, Yesterday. Yesterday. Hugh Chesterman. BoTP

Where have you soared so still tonight? This Thing Only. Anna Rydstedt-Dannstedt, *tr. by* Joanna Bankier. OV

Where He Hangs His Hat. Deborah Lee. BrSi

Where he really hung, there. One More Time. James Welch. NOVW

Where he rows the dark. The Bear Who Came to Dinner. Adrien Stoutenburg. SO

Where he stood and where. Jew. James A. Randall, Jr.. BPo

Where he stood in boots in water to his calves. The Fishvendor. William Meredith. SaC

Where Helen Comes. John Jerome Rooney. AA

Where Helen Sits. Laura Elizabeth Richards. AA

Where hints of racy sap and gum. Wild Honey. Maurice Thompson. AnAmPo

Where His Lady Keeps His Heart. "A. W." CTC; EIL; OBSC

Where Hudson's Wave. George Pope Morris. AA

Where Hurricane. LeRoy Clarke. PVCV

Where I Am. Marcelino dos Santos, *tr. fr. Portuguese by* Chris Searle. WMBCH

Where I could think of no thoroughfare. Were I in Trouble. Robert Frost. OxBSP

Where I go are flowers blooming. Les Planches-en-Montagnes. Michael Roberts. OBMV

Where I Hang My Hat. Dick Gallup. UL

Where I lived the river. Eclogues. Dennis Schmitz. NPGG

Where I was born, near Stepney Green. Stepney Green. John Singer. WaP

Where icy and bright dungeons lift. Hart Crane. *Fr.* Voyages (I–VI), VI. HAP; MoAB; MoAmPo; UnPo

Where I'll Be Good. Michael Ryan. PPR; SM

Where in blind files. Eavan Boland. CIP

Where in the summer-warm woodlands with the sweet wind. Iphione. Thomas Caulfield Irwin. EnLoPo

Where in what ever-blissfully watered gardens. Rainer Maria Rilke, *tr. fr. German by* James Blair Leishman. *Fr.* Sonnets to Orpheus. OBVE
("Where, in whatever happily watered garden, on what trees.")
SOTW, *tr. by* Christopher Hawthorne.

Where is a written deer running through a written forest? The Joy of Writing. Wislawa Szymborska, *tr. by* Czeslaw Milosz. PwPP

Where is another sweet as my sweet. The Letter. Tennyson. TTTS

Where is every piping lad. Dawn of Day. William Browne. *Fr.* The Shepherd's Pipe. EIL

Where Is He? Mother Goose. OxNR

Where is he, that giddy sprite. Wordsworth. *Fr.* The Kitten and the Falling Leaves. PBBP

Where is he, the wood pecker? The Woodpecker. Ni Tsan, *tr. by* Jonathan Chaves. CoBLCP

Where is it now? Look, there it flies in merry sport. The Swallow's Flight. Louis Levy, *tr.* by Martin S. Alwood *and* Sanford Kaufman. TrJP

Where Is Justice? Eliezer Steinbarg, *tr. fr. Yiddish by* Seth L. Wolitz. VWA

Where is Mount Ararat. Aboard a Ship Leaving Yokohama. Narushima Ryuhoku, *tr.* by Burton Watson. JLIC-2

Where Is My Butterfly Net? David McCord. FiBHP

Where is my Chief, my Master, this bleak night, *mavrone*! O'Hussey's Ode to the Maguire. Eochadh O'Hussey, *tr.* by James Clarence Mangan. NOIV; SeCePo
(Ode to the Maguire.) BIrV

Where is my husband trudging on his journey? *The wife of* Tagima Maro. *Fr.* Manyo Shu. Ma

Where is my ruined life, and where the fame. Hafiz, *tr. fr. Persian by* Gertrude Lowthian Bell. *Fr.* Odes, V. AWP

Where Is My Wandering Boy Tonight? *at.* to Robert Lowry. FaFP

"Where is now Elijah's God?" A Martyr's Death. Menahem ben Jacob. TrJP

Where Is Our Holy Church? Edwin H. Wilson. AH

Where is Paris and Heleyne? Thomas of Hales. *Fr.* A Love-Song. ChTr

Where is poor Jesus gone? Jesus. Francis Lauderdale Adams. OxBS

Where is that sugar, Hammond. Early Evening Quarrel. Langston Hughes. UnPo

Where is the arm I well could trust. Address to My Malay Krees. John Leyden. OBTV

Where is the beautiful song being sung. Hearing a Song from My Boat. Chang Yü, *tr.* by Jonathan Chaves. CoBLCP

Where Is the Black Community? Joyce Carol Thomas. CNA

Where is the first sign of spring?/ Spring comes earliest to a winding pond. Winding Pond. Hung Liang-chi, *tr. fr. Chinese by* Irving Lo. *Fr.* To Dispel the Cold: Two Poems on Spring, II. WFTU

Where is the first sign of spring?/ Spring comes earliest to a small pavilion. Small Pavilion. Hung Liang-chi, *tr. fr. Chinese by* Irving Lo. *Fr.* To Dispel the Cold: Two Poems on Spring, I. WFTU

Where Is the Fruit. Innocent Banda. WMBCH

Where is the gallant race that rose. Thomas Mercer. *Fr.* Arthur's Seat. OxBS

Where is the grave of Sir Arthur O'Kellyn? The Knight's Tomb. Samuel Taylor Coleridge. EnRP; FaBoCh; GN; RB

Where Is the Guard? Ahmad al-Safi al-Najafi, *tr. fr. Arabic by* Sharif Elmusa *and* Thomas G. Ezzy. MAP

Where is the hand to trace. With a Coin from Syracuse. Oliver St. John Gogarty. OBMV

Where is the home for me? The Home of Aphrodite. Euripides, *tr. fr. Greek by* Gilbert Murray. *Fr.* Bacchae. AWP

Where is the Jim Crow section. Merry-go-round. Langston Hughes. PoNe

Where is the man who has been tried and found strong and sound? A Degenerate Age. Solomon Ibn Gabirol, *tr.* by Emma Lazarus. TrJP

Where is the nightingale. Hilda Doolittle "H. D." *Fr.* Songs from Cyprus, II. MoAmPo

Where is the nymph, whose azure eye. Thomas Moore. EnLoPo

Where is the promise of my years. Infelix. Adah Isaacs Menken. CBWP-1

Where is the star of Bethlehem? Christmas 1959 et Cetera. Gerald William Barrax. OFD; PChr

Where is the true man's fatherland? The Fatherland. James Russell Lowell. GN

Where is the woman who unmoored this morning. The Woman. George Keithley. NPGG

Where is the word of Your youth and beauty. To the Young Man Jesus. Annie Charlotte Dalton. CaP

"Where is the world!" cries Young at eighty. Byron. *Fr.* Don Juan, XI. FaBoPV

Where is the world? not about. Merchant Marine. Josephine Miles. TAP; VGW

Where is the world we roved, Ned Bunn? To Ned. Herman Melville. MOS; NAAL-1; NOBA; PoEL-5

Where is this stupendous stranger. The Nativity of Our Lord and Saviour Jesus Christ. Christopher Smart. *Fr.* Hymns and Spiritual Songs, XXXII. EBEV; HAP; NOBE; NOCV; PoEL-3
(Christmas Day, *sts.* 6–9) ChTr; OBCP
(Hymn.) NAs; NOEC

Where it says snow. Errata. Charles Simic. NNaP

Where Knock Is Open Wide. Theodore Roethke. HAP; VGW

Where Late the Sweet Birds Sang. William D. Crago. TSM

Where laurel hedges hide the coal and coke. Crematorium. Sir John Betjeman. PoA

Where Lie All the Slain. Harry Morris. CRP

Where Lies the Land [to Which the Ship Would Go?]. Arthur Hugh Clough. *Fr.* Songs in Absence, VII. FaBoRV; MOS

Where Lies the Land to Which Yon Ship Must Go ? Wordsworth. EnRP; MOS; OBNC; PoEL-4
(Sonnet: Where Lies the Land.) ChER

Where Lies the Truth? Has Man in Wisdom's Creed. Wordsworth. TrCP

Where light is. To a Woman Who Wants Darkness and Time. Gerald Barrax. PoBA

Where, like a pillow on a bed. The Ecstasy. John Donne. BoLoP; FPL; HAP; InPS; JCP; LiTB; NAEL-1; NOBE; NoP; OAEL-1; OBEV; PoE; PrIm; TEP; TOF; TrGrPo
(Ecstacy, The.) SeCePo
(Extasie, The.) EnLoPo; MeLP; MePo; OBS; PoEL-2; SeCP; SeCV-1

Where Liver Eatin' Johnson lies. Old Trail Town, Cody, Wyoming.sie. John Garmon. BoLoP; EnLoPo; FPL; HAP; InPS; JCP; LiTB; MeLP; MePo; NOBE; NoP; OAEL-1; OBEV; PoEL-2; PrIm; SeCePo; SeCP; SeCV-1; TEP; TrGrPo

Where lives the man that never yet did hear. Orchestra; or, A Poem of Dancing. Sir John Davies. OBSC; SiPS

Where long the shadows of the wind had rolled. The Sheaves. E. A. Robinson. AWP; CMoP; FaBV; HAP; MoAB; MoAmPo; MoP; NoAM; NOBA; OxBA; TAP

Where marble stood and fell. Reflection in a Green Arena. Gregory Corso. VGW

Where may the wearied eye repose. Washington. Byron. *Fr.* Ode to Napoleon Buonaparte. OHIP; PAH

Where metalled road invades light thinning air. Sándor Weöres, *tr. fr. Hungarian by* Edwin Morgan. *Fr.* The Lost Parasol. MHuP; OBVE

Where might there be a refuge for me. Tell Me, Tell Me. Marianne Moore. LiTM; NYBP

Where Mountain Lion Lay [or Laid] Down with Deer. Leslie Marmon Silko. STE; VoR; WPOW

Where murdered Mumford lies. Mumford. Ina M. Porter. PAH

Where My Books Go. W. B. Yeats. OBEV

Where my gaze ends. Horizons. Kim Hyun-sung, *tr.* by Koh Chang-soo. ACKP

Where my grandfather is is in the ground. Mi Abuelo. Alberto Ríos. MAYP

Where my grandmother lived. Number Four. Doughtry Long, Jr.. CNA; PoBA; SO

Where my kindred dwell, there I wander. Dawn Boy's Song. *Unknown, tr.* by Washington Matthews. FaBV

Where neither King nor shepheard want comes neare. Homer, *tr. fr. Greek by* George Chapman. *Fr.* Odyssey, IV. CTC

Where Nothing Dwelt but Beasts of Prey. Isaac Watts. AH

Where nothing holds us, where long light. Space Burial. Brian W. Aldiss. BWV

Where now/ are time and space. Wind Gardens. Louis Untermeyer. BXAP

Where Now Are the Hebrew Children? *Unknown.* AH

Where now he roves, by wood or swamp whatever. Proem to "The Kid." Conrad Aiken. *Fr.* The Kid. MoAB

Where now these mingled ruins lie. Stanzas Occasioned by the Ruins of a Country Inn *or* On the Ruins of a Country Inn. Philip Freneau. AnAmPo; OxBA
(On the Ruins of a Country Inn.) AA

Where nowadays the Battery lies. Peter Stuyvesant's New Year's Call. Edmund Clarence Stedman. PAH

Where, O Where? Milton Bracker. SD

Where O Where Is Old Elijah. *Unknown.* AS

Where, Oh Where Are the Hebrew Children? *Unknown.* BLPA

Where, on prairie elevations. Fires. William Heyen. MAYP

Where on the wrinkled stream the willows lean. The Water-Ousel. Mary Webb. CH

Where once my ancestors grubbed for the fern's root. Ancestors. Rowley Habib. PeNZ

Where once the grey scrub's finches cried with thin. The Tank. Roland Robinson. PoAu-2

Where once we danced, where once we sang. An Ancient to Ancients. Thomas Hardy. CMoP; GTBS-P; LiTM; OxBTC

Where once we hunted, white men have built many long-houses. Speech of the Salish Chief. Earle Birney. *Fr.* Damnation of Vancouver. OBCV

Where only flowers fret. Aegean. Louis Simpson. GrPl; NYBP

Where or When. Philip Whalen. PoM

Where others' husbands ride on horseback. *Unknown. Fr.* Manyo Shu. Ma

Where oxen do low and apples do grow. Dialogue, between Crab and Gillian. Thomas D'Urfey. *Fr.* The Bath; or, The Western Lass. NOEC

Where purple cuckoo-clappers quake. Invasion Spring. Ruth Tomalin. CN

Where racial memories, like snakes. Landscape of Violence. Ralph Nixon Currey. PeSA

Where Runs the River. Francis William Bourdillon. WGRP

Where shall Celia fly for shelter. Christopher Smart. EnLoPo

"Where shall I gang, my ain true love?" The Duke of Athole's Nurse. *Unknown*. ESPB

Where shall I have at mine own will. Sir Thomas Wyatt. SiPS

Where shall I hide my head and my face? Breaking. Alexander Allan. PoAu-2

Where shall I lead the flocks to-day? Where the Flocks Shall Be Led. Adah Isaacs Menken. CBWP-1

Where shall I learn to get my peace again? Keats. *Fr.* Lines to Fanny. ChER

Where shall I seek shelter. Kurohito. *Fr.* Manyo Shu. Ma

Where shall the Baby's Dimple Be. Josiah G. Holland. BLPA

Where shall the eyes a darkness find. Huw Menai. *Fr.* Back in the Return. OBWVE

Where shall the lover rest. Sir Walter Scott. *Fr.* Marmion, III. CH, *abr.*; EnRP; GTBS; GTBS-P

Where shall this lust open its mouth? Out of the Inner Shell of a Certain Landscape. Hagiwara Sakutaro, *tr. by* Hiroaki Sato. FCEI

Where shall we find Thee—where art Thou, O God? Search. Margaret Widdemer. TrPWD

Where shall we go? The Hounded Lovers. William Carlos Williams. NYBP; TrGrPo

Where shall we seek for a hero, and where shall we find a story? Crispus Attucks. John Boyle O'Reilly. PAH

Where she lived the close remained the best. The Way a Ghost Dissolves. Richard Hugo. NAAL-2; NoAM; NoP; SM

Where She Was Not Born. Yvonne. CNA

Where should I seat you, where. Márton Kalász, *tr. by* Jascha Kessler. FOC

Where skies are thunderous, by a cypress walk. Some Negatives: X. at the Chateau. James Merrill. NePoEA-2

Where Somnus' temple rises from a ground. Laudanum. *Unknown*. NOEC

Where sunless rivers weep. Dream Land. Christina Rossetti. BrRo

Where swell the songs thou shouldst have sung. A Soldier Poet. Rossiter Johnson. AA

Where Sydney Cove her lucid bosom swells. Visit of Hope to Sydney Cove, near Botany-Bay. Erasmus Darwin. NOEC; OBTV

Where the acorn tumbles down. The Fieldmouse. Cecil Frances Alexander. OxBChV

Where the afternoon sun blears the city. O My Invisible Estate. Bruce Smith. Son

Where the autumn sun shines, on a stone. Ozaki Hosai, *tr. fr. Japanese by* Hiroaki Sato. *Fr.* One Hundred Haiku in Free Form. FCEI

Where the bee sucks, there suck I. Shakespeare. *Fr.* The Tempest, V, i. AWP; BoTP; CH; CTC; EiL; FaBV; HeIP; NAEL-1; NBLV; NoP; OBEV; OxBSP; TTTS

(Ariel's Song: "Where the bee sucks, there suck I.") GN; NOBE; OBSC; PDV

Where the bright moon comes up. Kyogoku Tamekane, *tr. fr. Japanese by* Burton Watson. *Fr.* Twenty-three Tanka. FCEI

Where the buttercups so sweet. The Little Herd-Boy's Song. Robert Buchanan. BoTP

Where the camshaft weeps. Resting Place. Jon Silkin. VWA

Where the Canyon spreads on either hand. Hangman's Tree. Lillian Zellhoefer White. AmFN

Where the castle stood. Masaoka Shiki, *tr. fr. Japanese by* Burton Watson. *Fr.* Thirty-nine Haiku. FCEI

Where the cedar leaf divides the sky. Passage. Hart Crane. CMoP; NOBA; PoE

Where the Cedars. Jacob Glatstein, *tr. fr. Yiddish by* Joseph Leftwich. TrJP

Where the city's ceaseless crowd moves on the livelong day. Sparkles from the Wheel. Walt Whitman. InPS; NAAL-1

Where the Corrib river chops through the Claddagh. The Last Galway Hooker. Richard Murphy. IPY

Where the Dead Men Lie. Barcroft Henry Boake. CBAP; PoAu-1

Where the dews and the rains of heaven have their fountain. The Battle in the Clouds. William Dean Howells. PAH

Where the dropwort springs up lithe and tall. John Lyle Donaghy. NeIP

Where the dusty lane. Daisies. Valerie Worth. PCP

Where the elk stood, stand I, worldly wise. Tall Trees by Still Waters. James Tate. MAYP

Where the Flocks Shall Be Led. Adah Isaacs Menken. CBWP-1

Where the graves were many, we looked for one. In Clonmel Parish Churchyard. Sarah Morgan Bryan Piatt. AA

Where the lazy wall is down. Sierran Vigil. Ewart Milne. NeIP

Where the Light. Marcelin Pleynet, *tr. fr. French by* Harry Mathews. RHTwFP

Where the Lilies Used to Spring. David Gray. OxBS

Where the Lilies Were in Flower. Kumattur Kannanar, *tr. fr. Tamil by* A. K. Ramanujan. PLW

Where the living with effort go. The White Ship. Geoffrey Hill. OxBC

Where the lizard ran to its little prey. The Range in the Desert. Randall Jarrell. NOBA

Where the lone wind on the hilltop. The Empty House. Russell Hoban. WSC

Where the mighty cliffs are frowning. Rajpoot Rebels. Sir Alfred Comyn Lyall. OBTV

Where the mob gathers, swiftly shoot along. John Gay. *Fr.* Trivia; or, The Art of Walking the Streets of London, III. OAEL-1

Where the Moosatockmaguntic. The Ballad of Hiram Hover. Bayard Taylor. AnAmPo; BXAP; FaBoCo; OBAL

Where the orange-branches mingle on the sunny garden-side. The Demon of the Mirror. Bayard Taylor. BeLS

Where the Pelican Builds. Mary Hannay Foott. PoAu-1

Where the Picnic Was. Thomas Hardy. OxBTC

Where the pools are bright and deep. A Boy's Song. James Hogg. BoTP; CH; FaPON; FaPoR; ILY; MoShBr; OBEV; OnUR; OxBChV; WiR

Where the printing-works buttress a church. The Coldness. Jon Silkin. VWA

Where the quiet-colored end of evening smiles. Love among the Ruins. Robert Browning. FaBV; HAP; NAEL-2; NOBE; OAEL-2; OBEV; PoEL-5; PrIm

Where the racing Wairau slows, homesick for its snowshed. Cloudy Bay. Ellen Duggan. PeNZ

Where the Rainbow Ends. Robert Lowell. HCAP; MoAB; MoAmPo; NePoEA; TrGrPo

Where the Rainbow Ends. Richard Rive. PBA; TTY

Where the Red Lion flaring o'er the way. A Description of an Author's Bedchamber. Goldsmith. BIrV

Where the remote Bermudas ride. Bermudas. Andrew Marvell. AWP; CH; ChTr; FaBoCh; GN; JCP; MePo; MOS; NAEL-1; NOBE; NOCV; NoP; OBEV; OBS; OBTV; PAH; PoE; RB; SeCP; SeCV-1

(Song of the Emigrants [in Bermuda].) GTBS; GTBS-P

Where the ripe pears droop heavily. The Wasp. "Fiona Macleod." *Fr.* Transcripts from Nature. FM

Where the river springs: peach blossoms, tree after tree. Evening View from P'eng-lai Pavilion. Chu Yi-tsun, *tr. by* Irving Lo. WFTU

Where the sally tree went pale in every breeze. Field Work. Seamus Heaney. AnAn; FaBCIP

Where the sea gulls sleep or indeed where they fly. The Ballet of the Fifth Year. Delmore Schwartz. MoAB; OxBA; TwCP

Where the short-legged Esquimaux. An Arctic Vision. Bret Harte. PAH

Where the Single Men Go in Summer. Nina Bourne. FiBHP

Where the slanting forest eves. To Nature Seekers. Robert W. Chambers. MoShBr

Where the Slow Fig's Purple Sloth. Robert Penn Warren. NoP

Where the slow river. Leda. Hilda Doolittle ("H. D."). NAAL-2

Where the Song Went Where She Went & What Happened When They Met. *Unknown, tr. fr. Seneca Indian by* Jerome Rothenberg *and* Richard Johnny John. STP

Where the spring mist slowly drifts. *Unknown. Fr.* Manyo Shu. Ma

Where the sturdy ocean breeze. The Ballad of Mr. Cooke. Bret Harte. AnAmPo

Where the summit road twists and turns, I'm soon to lose my way. Chao Chih-hsin, *tr. fr. Chinese by* James M. Hargett. *Fr.* Miscellaneous Poems on Mountain Travel, I. WFTU

Where the sun shines in the street. Fear. Mary Carolyn Davies. WGRP

Where the sun shines so brightly, both daily and nightly. The Poet's Corner. Alexander Wilson. PF

Where the thistle lifts a purple crown. Daisy. Francis Thompson. AWP; BeLS; BrPo; FaBV; MoAB; MoBrPo; OBEV; OBNC

Where the water. Shunzei, *tr. fr. Japanese by* Burton Watson. *Fr.* Thirty Tanka. FCEI

Where the waters gently flow. The Song of the Reed Sparrow. *Unknown*. OxBChV

Where the western zun, unclouded. Zun-zet. William Barnes. PoEL-4

Where the wheel of light is turned. Pole Star for This Year. Archibald MacLeish. OxBA

Where the wife is scouring the frying pan. Land of Little Sticks, 1945. James Tate. MAYP

Where the Wild Thyme Blows. Shakespeare. *See* Midsummer Night's Dream, A: Violet Bank, A.

Where the wild wave, from ocean proudly swelling. Fort Bowyer. Charles L. S. Jones. PAH

Where the wind. Footprints on the Glacier. W. S. Merwin. MoP; NoAM

Where the wind attacks the downs. A Kodak; Tregantle. Horatio Brown. PeHV

Where, then, is Dorothy Parker now? Dig for Her the Narrow Bed. Robert Wallace. SoTCo

Where then shall hope and fear their objects find? An Additional Poem. John Ashbery. FaBoMo

Where then shall Hope and Fear their objects find? The Power of Prayer. Samuel Johnson. *Fr.* Vanity of Human Wishes, The: The Tenth Satire of Juvenal Imitated. NOBE

Where there is personal liking we go. The Hero. Marianne Moore. *Fr.* Part of a Novel, Part of a Poem, Part of a Play. CMoP; NOBA; OxBA; PoA

Where There's a Will There's a Way. Eliza Cook. BLPA; FaFP

Where There's a Will There's a Way. John Godfrey Saxe. AnAmPo

Where they once dug for money. The Old Marlborough Road. Henry David Thoreau. PoEL-4

Where they tamed the wild Libyan. The Parthenon. John Heath-Stubbs. OBTV

Where They Were. *Unknown.* AS

Where this man walks his fences. Relearning the Language of April. Maxine W. Kumin. ER

Where thou dwellest, in what grove. The Birds. Blake. CH

Where, thy true treasure? Gold says, "Not in me,." Edward Young. *Fr.* Night Thoughts, Night VI. OAEL-1

Where Tide. Philip Booth. BLA

Where to escape this steamy heat? Seventh Month, Sixteenth Day. Ryokan, *tr. by* Burton Watson. JLIC-2

Where tom-tom drummed. The Inheritors. Dorothy Livesay. CaP

Where trees deepen. Imitation of Joy. Salvatore Quasimodo, *tr. by* Jack Bevan. PFI

Where, twining subtile fears with hope. Andrew Marvell. *Fr.* An Horatian Ode upon Cromwell's Return from Ireland. OBD

Where Two o'Clock Came From. Kenneth Patchen. SO

Where two or three were flung together, or fifty. The March 2. Robert Lowell. NoP

Where Unimaginably Bright. Oliver Hale. GoYe

Where Venta's Norman castle still appears. On King Arthur's Round Table, at Winchester. Thomas Warton the Younger. Son

Where voices vanish into dream. Elected Silence. Siegfried Sassoon. MoBrPo

Where, vomit-yellow, the lichen crawls. Why You Climbed Up. Robert Penn Warren. BLA

Where was I at the hour of sowing. Questions. Dagmar Hilarova, *tr. by* Ewald Osers. VWA

Where was the boundary between the bitter water. Salmon Cycle. Avner Treinin, *tr. by* Robert Friend. VWA

Where was the monk? Shugen, *tr. by* Hiroaki Sato. FCEI

Where was you last winter, boys. The Horse Trader's Song. *Unknown.* AmFP

Where wast thou when I laid the foundations of the earth? Bible, *O.T.* *Fr.* Job: Then the Lord Answered ("Who is this that darkeneth counsel by words without knowledge?"), XXXVIII: 4–38. ImOP, *abr.*

Where We Are. Judson Mitcham. KS

Where We Could Go. Gary Soto. NAmP

Where we live, the teakettle whistles out. Now. William Stafford. NNaP

Where we made the fire. Where the Picnic Was. Thomas Hardy. OxBTC

Where We Must Look for Help. Robert Bly. NePoEA

Where we went in the boat was a long bay. The Mediterranean. Allen Tate. FaBoMo; GOA; HAP; LiTA; LiTM; MoAB; MoAmPo; MOS; VGW; WeW

Where we were walking in the day's light, seeing. Conrad Aiken. *Fr.* Time in the Rock [or, Preludes to Definition], XXXVII. VGW

Where were the greenhouses going. Big Wind. Theodore Roethke. AmPP; CMoP; GoJo; InvP; NoP; VGW

Where were we going that. The Drive. Janet Reed McFatter. GrPl

Where were we in that afternoon? And where. Anniversary. Richmond Lattimore. NYBP

Where were ye, Birds, that bless His name. John Banister Tabb. *Fr.* The Child. AA

Where were you then? A Story. Margaret Avison. MoCV

Where? When? Which? Langston Hughes. BPo

Where, where are now the great reports. Fuimus Fumus. Joshua Sylvester. FaBoEE

Where, where but here have pride and truth. On Hearing That the Students of Our New University Have Joined the Agitation against Immoral Literature. W. B. Yeats. MoP; NoAM

Where will it find harbor. Kurohito. *Fr.* Manyo Shu. FCEI

Where will that boat find harbour. Kurohito. *Fr.* Manyo Shu. Ma

Where Will You Be? Patricia Parker. GLP

Where will you find this year, Mary. Invitation to Mary. Mairtin O Direain, *tr. by the author.* TIRV

Where will your strange pilgrimage take you next? Saying Good-Bye to Feng the Hermit. Mo Shih-lung, *tr. by* Jonathan Chaves. CoBLCP

Where wit is over-ruled by will. Desire's Government. "A. W." EIL

Where with their magnetic breasts are Susanna and Martha. The Ladies of Bygone Days. Otto Orban, *tr. by* Edwin Morgan. MHuP

Where, without bloodshed, can there be. Long Feud. Louis Untermeyer. MoAmPo

Where yonder ancient willow weeps. Alexander McLachlan. *Fr.* A Backwoods Hero. CaP

Where You Go When She Sleeps. T. R. Hummer. MAYP; MT

Where you going?/ (Getting berries. Think I'll try a little farther.). Getting Berries. *Unknown, tr. by* Franz Boas. STP

Where you going?/ (Going to get firewood.). Getting Firewood. *Unknown, tr. by* Franz Boas. STP

Whereas galoshed my Julia goes. Upon Julia's Arctics. Bert Leston Taylor. NBLV

Whereas, on certain boughs and sprays. The Lawyer's Invocation to Spring. Henry Howard Brownell. PoLF

Whereas the rebels hereabout. Tom Gage's Proclamation. *Unknown.* PAH

Whereat Erewhile I Wept, I Laugh. Robert Greene. *Fr.* Arbasto. EIL

Where'er there's a thistle to feed a linnet. Poets and Linnets. Tom Hood. CenHV

Wherefore Hidest Thou Thy Face, and Holdest Me for Thine Enemie? Francis Quarles. *Fr.* Emblems, III, 7. MePo; OBS

Wherefore, Lucinda, dost aspire. To Miss L. F. on the Occasion of Her Departure for the Continent. Sir John Collings Squire. BXAP

Wherefore peep'st thou, envious day? *Unknown.* GBL

Wherefore should I seek the bud. Bahadur Shah Zafar, *tr. by* Ahmed Ali. GoT

Wherefore these revels that my dull eyes greet? The Royal Mummy to Bohemia. Charles Warren Stoddard. AA

Wherefore this busy labor without rest? Tuskegee. Leslie Pinckney Hill. BANP; PoNe

Wherefore tonight so full of care. Dejection. Robert Bridges. QFR

Wherefore was that cry? Shakespeare. *See* Macbeth: She should have died hereafter.

Wherein Consists the High Estate. Ebenezer Dayton. AH

Wherelings Whenlings. E. E. Cummings. HAP; WeW

Where's Babe Ruth, the King of Swat. The Ballad of Dead Yankees. Donald Petersen. HeIP

Where's Commander All-a-Tanto? Herman Melville. *Fr.* Bridegroom Dick. PoEL-5

Where's he that died o' Wednesday? Falstaff's Song. Edmund Clarence Stedman. AA

Where's Ho Xuan Huong. Saigon Bar Girls, 1975. Yusef Komunyakaa. MT

Where's Peace? I start, some clear–blown night. Mr. Hosea Biglow to the Editor of the Atlantic Monthly. James Russell Lowell. *Fr.* The Biglow Papers: 2d Series, No. X. AA, *abr.*.

("Beaver roars hoarse with meltin' snows.") PoEL-5

Where's the meeting place for. Shir Ma'alot/ A Song of Degrees. Richard Flantz. VWA

Where's the Queen of Sheba? Gone. Walter de la Mare. GoJo

Where's the winning without chocolate. The Chocolate Soldiers. Calvin Forbes. MAT; MAYP

Wheresoe'er I turn mine eyes. God Everywhere. Abraham ibn Ezra, *tr. by* D. E. de L. TrJP

Wheresoe'er I turn my view. Lines on Thomas Warton's Poems *or* Lines in Ridicule of Certain Poems Published in 1777. Samuel Johnson. FaBoCo; FaBoEE

(Lines in Ridicule of Certain Poems Published in 1777.) FaBoCo

Wheresoever ye fare by frith or by fell. Julians Barnes. *Fr.* Book of Hunting. WPE

Whereto should I express. To His Lady. Henry VIII, King of England. CTC; EBEV; OBSC

Whereupon I told/ That once in the stillness of a summer's noon. Books. Wordsworth. *Fr.* The Prelude [or, Growth of a Poet's Mind], V. EnRP; OAEL-2

"He who in his youth." TOF

There Was a Boy ("There was a boy, ye knew him well"). ChER; FaBoCh; FaBoRV; FiP; OBNC; PoE; PoEL-4

(Winander Lake.) FiP

Wherever God erects a house of prayer. Daniel Defoe. *Fr.* The True-born Englishman, I. NOBL; OBSV

Wherever I am, there's always Pooh. Us Two. A. A. Milne. OxBChV

Wherever I go to find. Pigeons. Bert Meyers. EAS

While the blue noon above us arches. Annihilation. Conrad Aiken. GBL; MoAB; MoAmPo

While the Choir Sang. Priscilla Jane Thompson. CBWP-2

While the coarse picture charms his eyes. The Man of Taste. William Parsons. OBTV

While the cobbler mused, there passed his pane. The Great Guest Comes In. Edwin Markham. WBLP

While the Constabulary covered the mob. Summer 1969. Seamus Heaney. CIP

While the Days Are Going By. George Cooper. BLRP; WBLP

While the evening here is approaching the mountain paths. Overnight in the Apartment by the River. Tu Fu. ChTr

While the far farewell music thins and fails. Departure (Southampton Docks: October 1899). Thomas Hardy. Son

While the frozen armies trembled. Autobiographies. Derek Mahon. FaBCIP

While the hum and the hurry. Under a Hat Rim. Carl Sandburg. AnAmPo

While the leaves of the bamboo rustle. *Unknown. Fr.* Manyo Shu. Ma; PeBJV, *tr. by* Geoffrey Bownas *and* Anthony Thwaite.

While the milder Fates consent. A Lyric to Mirth. Robert Herrick. CaPo

While the noon-lustre o'er the land is spread. M. J. Chapman. *Fr.* Barbadoes. PBCV

While the Record Plays. Gyula Illyés, *tr. fr. Hungarian by* William Jay Smith. MHuP

While the south rains, the north. Sled Burial, Dream Ceremony. James Dickey. CAPP

While the Tragedy's afoot. Colophon. Oliver St. John Gogarty. OBMV

While the water-wagon's ringing showers. In the Isle of Dogs. John Davidson. OBNC

While the wind upon the waters still returns. Logbook. Dan Pagis, *tr. by* Warren Bargad *and* Stanley F. Chyet. IP

While the women sliced bread and cold meat. The Thief's Niece. George Keithley. NPGG

While thirteen moons saw smoothly run. Stanzas Subjoined to the Yearly Bill of Mortality of the Parish of All Saints, Northampton; for the Year 1787. William Cowper. NOCV

While this America settles in the mould of its vulgarity, heavily thickening to empire. Shine, Perishing Republic. Robinson Jeffers. CMoP; FF; LiTA; LiTM; MAT; MoAB; MoP; NAAL-2; NoAM; NOBA; NoP; OxBA; PrIm; TAP; UnPo; VGW

While Thracians shal with arrowes war, Iazices with bowe. Ovid, *tr. fr. Latin by* Thomas Underdowne. *Fr.* Invective against Ibis. OBVE

While thus he spake, th' Angelic Squadron bright. Milton. *Fr.* Paradise Lost, *bk.* IV, *ll.* 977–1004. SCV

While thus he thought, a monst'rous wave up-bore. Homer, *tr. fr. Greek by* Pope. *Fr.* Odyssey, V. OBVE

While thus the imprisoned leaves and waking flowers. Spring. Thomas Gisborne. *Fr.* Walks in a Forest. PBBP

While time hustled. James Weigel, Jr.. TSM

While Titian was grinding rose madder. *Unknown.* NOBL

While Trying to Rival Your Hair. Luis de Góngora y Argote, *tr. fr. Spanish by* Perry Higman. LPSS

While upon the journey of life. The Mask. Patty L. Harjo. VoR

While U.S. marshals. Wili Woyi, Shaman, Also Known as Billy Pigeon. Robert J. Conley. STE

While visiting Arundel Castle. Victor Gray. NOBL

While, waiting for you. Princess Nukada. *Fr.* Manyo Shu. Ma

While walking at dusk in a strange city. Pinhas Sadeh, *tr. by* Gabriel Preil *and* Howard Schwartz. VWA

While walking down a crowded. If I Only Was the Fellow. Will S. Adkin. BLPA

While we are at peace. Albatross. Lele-io-Hoku. WTO, *tr. by* S. H. Elbert *and* N. Mahoe

While we bring to dawn the flower and the moon. Teika, *tr. fr. Japanese by* Hiroaki Sato. *Fr.* Eighty-four Tanka. FCEI

While We Lowly Bow before Thee. Daniel C. Colesworthy. AH

While we sail and laugh, joke and fight, comes death. In Memoriam; Ingvald Bjorndal and His Comrade. Malcolm Lowry. OBCV

While We Slept. David Wolff. TrJP

While we unloaded the hay from the truck, building. The Barn. Wendell Berry. EyDe

While we wandered (thus it is I dream!), A. Gray Nights. Ernest Dowson. Son

While we were fearing it, it came. Emily Dickinson. PPP

While we were together. A Painful Love Song. Yehuda Amichai, *tr. by the author.* LLLT

While we were visiting David's grave. Despair. Denise Levertov. NNaP

While we were walking under the top. John Ashbery. EAS

While with a strong and yet a gentle hand. Edmund Waller. *Fr.* A Panegyric[k] to My Lord Protector. JCP; OBS; SeCV-1

While with false pride, and narrow jealousy. On the Use of New and Old Words in Poetry. Anna Seward. Son

While with labour assid'ous due pleasure I mix. Verses Written at The Hague. Anno 1696. Matthew Prior. OBTV

While with my sleeves I sweep the bed. *Unknown. Fr.* Manyo Shu. Ma

While yet the grapes were green, thou didst refuse me. Grapes. *Unknown, tr. by* Alma Strettell. AWP

While yet the Morning Star. The Unicorn. Ella Young. FaPON

While You. Bessy Reyna, *tr. fr. Spanish by* William M. Davis. DMH

While you clambered up ahead. Climbing Gannett. Roberta Hill Whiteman. HATNAP

While you, my friend, from louring wintry plains. William Mickle. *Fr.* Almada Hill: An Epistle from Lisbon. OBTV

While you, my lord, the rural shades admire. A Letter from Italy, to the Right Honourable Charles Lord Halifax. Joseph Addison. NOEC

While you read. The Cat. William Matthews. AmPA

While you that in your sorrow disavow. A Christmas Sonnet. E. A. Robinson. EaLo

While you walk the water's edge. Beach Glass. Amy Clampitt. FaBoWP; NoAM

While you were still asleep. For the Little Girl Who Asked Why the Kitchen Was So Bright. James Ulmer. TDD

While your great-grandmother and her sons. Separate Parties. Dabney Stuart. NYBP

While your widow clatters water into a kettle. Father-in-Law. Derek Mahon. FaBCIP

While you're a white-hot youth, emit the rays. The Star System. Richard Wilbur. NBLV

Whiles someone did chant this lovely lay, The. Spenser. *Fr.* The Faerie Queene, II, 12. OBVE
(Gather the Rose.) EiL
(Song of Bliss.) FF

Whilom in the winter's rage. The Penitent Palmer's Ode. Robert Greene. *Fr.* Francesco's Fortunes. OBSC

Whilom ther was dwellynge in my contree. The Friar's Tale. Chaucer. *Fr.* The Canterbury Tales. PoE

Whil'st Alexis Lay Prest [*or* Press'd]. Dryden. *Fr.* Marriage à la Mode, IV, ii. ErPo; FF; PrIm
(Song: "Whilst Alexis lay pressed.") BoLoP

Whilst Echo cries [*or* eccho cryes], "What shall become of me[e]?" Henry Constable. *Fr.* Diana. AAS; OBSC

Whilst human kind/ Throughout the lands lay miserably crushed. Beyond Religion. Lucretius, *tr. by* William Ellery Leonard. AWP

Whilst I beheld the neck o' th' dove. Patrick Cary. JCP

Whilst in her prime and bloom of years. On a Female Rope-Dancer. *Unknown.* NOEC

Whilst in peaceful quarters lying. The Battle of Monmouth. "R. H." PAH

Whilst in This World I Stay. Philip Pain. AH

Whilst landmen wander, though controlled. *Unknown.* OxBSS

Whilst my soul's eye beheld no light. A Dialogue betwixt God and the Soul. *At. to.* Sir Henry Wotton. MeLP; OBS

Whilst on Septimius' panting breast [*or* brest]. Acme and Septimius. Catullus, *tr. by* Abraham Cowley. AWP
(Ode: Acme and Septimus.) OBVE

Whilst on thy head I lay my hand. A Spell of Invisibility. *At. to.* Christopher Marlowe. ChTr

Whilst our children. Begging A.I.D. David Rubadiri. WMBCH

Whilst some affect the sun, and some the shade. Robert Blair. *See* Grave, The: While some affect the sun, and some the shade.

Whilst the red spittle of the grape-shot sings. Arthur Rimbaud. *See* Eighteen-Seventy: Evil.

Whilst thirst of praise, and vain desire of fame. The Lady's Resolve. Lady Mary Wortley Montagu. BoWoP; OxBSP

Whilst thus my pen strives to eternize thee. Michael Drayton. *Fr.* Idea, XLIV. AAS; OBSC; Son

Whil'st thy weigh'd judgements, Egerton, I heare. To Thomas Lord Chancellor. Ben Jonson. OBS

Whilst walking a crowded city street the other day. Just Try to Be the Fellow That Your Mother Thinks You Are. Will S. Adkin. WBLP

Whilst we sing the doleful knell. Ding Dong. *Unknown. Fr.* Swetnam, the Woman-Hater. EiL

Whilst what I write I do not see. Written in Juice of Lem[m]on. Abraham Cowley. *Fr.* The Mistress. SeCP; SeCV-1

Whilst with his falling wings, the courtly dove. Jealousie Is the Rage of a Man. Finch, Countess of. FM

Whil'st with hot scent, the Popish Tory crew.   A Hue and Cry after Blood and Murder. *Unknown.* APAS
Whilst yet to prove. Farewell to Love. John Donne. OAEL-1
Whim of Time, A. Stephen Spender. MoAB; MoBrPo
Whimper of Awakening Passion. Ebenezer Jones. NOBVV
Whins are blythesome on the knowe, The. A New Spring. Albert D. Mackie. OxBS
Whip, The. Robert Creeley. EOEF; MoP; NaP; NeAP; PoE; PoM
Whip Jamboree. *Unknown.* OxBSS
Whip-poor-will. Donald Hall. BLA
Whiplash. William Matthews. MAYP
Whipped by sorrow now. Miklós Radnóti, *tr. by* Steven Polgar *and* Stephen Berg *and* S. J. Marks. VWA
Whipping, The. Robert Hayden. GrPl; IDB; PoBA; PoE; TW
Whipping Cheare. *Unknown.* FaBoBa
Whippoorwill this/ moonday into. E. E. Cummings. RR
Whipp'will's singin' to de moon. Go Sleep, Ma Honey. Edward D. Barker. AA
Whirl, snow, on the blackbird's chatter. Eager Spring. Gordon Bottomley. MoBrPo
Whirl up, sea. Oread. Hilda Doolittle ("H. D."). AWP; CMoP; GoJo; HeIP; InPS; MoAmPo; MoP; NAAL-2; NoAM; NOBA; OxBA; TAP
Whirl'd off at last, for speech I sought. Coventry Patmore. *Fr.* The Angel in the House, II, xi. GBL
Whirling your deep and gloomy tresses pour. The Vampire. Efrén Rebolledo, *tr. by* Samuel Beckett. MexPo; VVA
Whirlwind Road, The. Edwin Markham. AA
Whirlwind with a vacuum at four a.m. Memorial Days. Ira Sadoff. BLA
Whirring, A. Daisy Aldan. RR
Whiskey on your breath, The. My Papa's Waltz. Theodore Roethke. AnAmPo; CAPP; CMoP; DiL; FF; HAP; HCAP; HeIP; HoPM; InPK; InPS; LCAP; LiTM; MoAB; MoP; NAAL-2; NBLV; NIP; NoAM; NOBA; NoP; PoE; PPP; PrIm; SM; TAP; VGW; WeW
Whisky, frisky,/ Hippity hop. The Squirrel. *Unknown.* FaPON; PDV
Whisky Frisky. *Unknown.* BoTP
Whisky Johnny. *Unknown.* AmFP; AS
Whisper in Agony. Jules Supervielle, *tr. fr. French by* D. J. Enright. OBD
Whisper of yellow globes. Her Lips Are Copper Wire. Jean Toomer. NoAM
Whisper was recorded and rehearsed, The. Black Aggie. Norman Andrew Kirk. TSM
Whisper woke the air, A. Calumny. Frances Sargent Osgood. AA
Whisper Words of Love to Me. Lizelia Augusta Jenkins Moorer. CBWP-3
Whisperer, The. James Stephens. WGRP
Whisperer, The. Mark Van Doren. MoAmPo
Whisperin' Bill. Irving Bacheller. PoLF
Whispering ghosts of the west. *Unknown, tr. by* John White. WTO
Whispering to each handhold, "I'll be back." After Arguing against the Contention That Art Must Come from Discontent. William Stafford. NoAM
Whispering Wind. Catherine Braan Layne. PWR
Whisperings for the Unwashed. William Thom. PF
Whispers. Myra Cohn Livingston. PDV
Whispers. Roberta Hill. CDW
Whispers, for two voices. Sandor Csoori, *tr. fr. Hungarian by* Alan Dixon. MHuP
Whispers of Heavenly Death. Walt Whitman. LiTA
Whispers of Immortality. T. S. Eliot. CMoP; CTC; LiTA; NoAM; NOBA; NoP; OBMV
Whist. Eugene Fitch Ware. PoLF
Whistle, The/ of the bright. Belfast Lough. *Unknown, tr. by* John Montague. BIrV
Whistle, The. Charles Murray. GoTS; OxBS
Whistle Aloud, Too Weedy Wren. Wallace Stevens. *Fr.* Notes toward a Supreme Fiction. LiTA
Whistle, and I'll Come to You, My Lad. Burns. OxBoLi
Whistle Column, The. John Haines. AnAn
Whistle, Daughter, Whistle. *Unknown.* AIW; AmFP; ErPo; OBET; OxNR, *shorter vers*
   ("Mother, I longs to get married.") ErPo
   ("O mother, I longs to get married.") OBET
Whistle o'er the Lave o't. Burns. OxBS
Whistle o'er the Lave o't. *Unknown.* GBP
Whistle shrilled, A; the farm hands left the stack. Jack and Jill. Charles Powell. BXAP
Whistle under the water. Amy Lowell. *Fr.* Flute-Priest Song for Rain. UnS

Whistles like light in leaves, O light. The Heart Flies Up, Erratic as a Kite. Delmore Schwartz. PoA
Whistling. Jack Prelutsky. RAR
Whistling Boy, The. George Crabbe. TrGrPo
Whistling Boy. Nixon Waterman. PoLF
Whistling flew around the corner; it had, The. Peter Rosei, *tr. by* Beth Bjorklund. CoAuP
Whistling like a goat pissing on a tin lid. For an Octogenarian. Brian Turner. UAS
Whistling postman swings along, The. The Postman. *Unknown.* FaPON
Whit Monday. John Hewitt. TIRV
Whit Monday. Louis MacNeice. NYBP; OAEL-2
White. Christopher Buckley. MOWH
White, a shingled path. Icos. Charles Tomlinson. GTBS-P
White an' Blue. William Barnes. GBL; GTBS-P
White and Black, The. N. M. Khaketla
White and black and black and white. Disillusionment. René Daumal, *tr. by* Michael Benedikt. POS
White and blue, an outspread fan. Environs of Vanholt I. Charles Spear. ATNZ; PeNZ
White and curved as a shell she lies. Discoverer. James Michie. DiPo
White and delicate, like white lilies. The Phantom. Salvador Díaz Mirón, *tr. by* Samuel Beckett. MexPo
White and Red. Edward de Vere, Earl of Oxford. OBSC
   (What Cunning Can Express.) EiL
White and red. Still Life. Francis Sullivan. CRP
White and the Black, The. N. M. Khaketla, *tr. fr. Southern Sotho.* OV, *tr. by* Jack Cope *and* Dan Kunene; PeSA, *tr. by* Jack Cope *and* Dan Kunene
White Anemone, The, *sel.* "Owen Meredith."
   "'Tis the white anemone, fashioned so." GN
White Apples. Donald Hall. TAP
White armies. Minnesota Camp Grounds. Gerald Vizenor. STE
White as coal-ash pressed. Queen of Heaven Mausoleum. Dennis Schmitz. LCAP
White as her hand fair Julia threw. The Snow-Ball. Soame Jenyns. OBVE
White as paper a-sail in the air. *Malay Oral Tradition, tr. by* O. Winstedt. WTO
White as snow and snow it isn't. *Unknown.* GBP
White Azaleas. Harriet McEwen Kimball. AA
White beach: a dog barks. Joso, *tr. fr. Japanese by* Hiroaki Sato. *Fr.* Fifteen Hokku. FCEI
White Bears. Veronica Porumbacu, *tr. fr. Rumanian by the author and* Kathleen Weaver. OV
White Beauty, The. *Unknown.* MeEL
White birch blooms, The. Rhythm. Ruth Kim Chun-soo, *tr. by* Koh Chang-soo. ACKP
White Bird, The. Roy McFadden. NeIP
White Bird. Matti Megged, *tr. fr. Hebrew by* Howard Schwartz. VWA
White bird, A. Shira. Howard Schwartz. VWA
White Bird, The. Wilfred Watson. MoCV
White bird cries in a hushed manner, A. Wakayama Bokusui, *tr. fr. Japanese by* Hiroaki Sato. *Fr.* Forty-four Tanka. FCEI
White bird featherless/ Flew from Paradise. *Unknown.* ChTr; GBP; OxNR
White bird floats down through the air, A. *Unknown.* ChTr; GBP
White bird—is it not sad?, A. Wakayama Bokusui, *tr. fr. Japanese by* Hiroaki Sato. *Fr.* Forty-four Tanka. FCEI
White bird of the tempest! O beautiful thing! To a Seagull. Gerald Griffin. TIRV
White Birds, The. W. B. Yeats. UnAS
White Blocks. Hans Arp, *tr. fr. French by* Michael Benedikt. POS
White Blossom, A. D. H. Lawrence. MoBrPo
White blossom, white, white shell; the Nazarene. Music of Colours— White Blossom. Vernon Watkins. LiTM; WaP
White Blossoms. Robert Mezey. NaP; VWA
White buck come in. Anadarko John. Carroll Arnett. VoR
White Butterflies. Swinburne. FaPON; PDV
White butterfly, A. The Graceful Bastion. William Carlos Williams. NYBP
White Canoe, The. Alan Sullivan. CaP
White Captain of my soul, lead on. A Soldier's Prayer. Robert Freeman. TrPWD
White cat, The. Cat Ballerina Assoluta. Emilie Glen. GoYe
White Cat in Moonlight. Douglas Gibson. CRH
White Cat of Trenarren, The. Alfred Leslie Rowse. OxBTC
White cathedral changes into white gloves, The. The White Etc. Hans Arp, *tr. by* Michael Benedikt. POS
White Center. Richard Hugo. NAAL-2; NoP

White chairs in a tall stack against a table. Silverhill. Martin Seymour-Smith. NPo

White chocolate jar full of petals, The. Chez Jane. Frank O'Hara. CoAP; NeAP; NoAM; NOBA; PoA; PoE

White Christmas. W. R. Rodgers. LiTM; MoAB; MoBrPo; SeCePo

White chrysanthemum, A. Miura Chora, *tr. fr. Japanese by* Hiroaki Sato. *Fr.* Sixteen Hokku. FCEI

White chrysanthemums they've set up at Fukiage. Teika, *tr. fr. Japanese by* Hiroaki Sato. *Fr.* A Compendium of Good Tanka. FCEI

White church on the hill, The. A New England Church. Wilson Agnew Barrett. WGRP

"White City, The." Richard Watson Gilder. PAH

White City, The. Claude McKay. BPo; NoAM; TAP; TW

White Cliffs, The, *sels.* Alice Duer Miller.
  English Are Frosty, The. PoLF
  I Have Loved England. BLPL; PoLF

White clock (?) white commu/ nion. White Horse Song. Reinhard Priessnitz, *tr. by* Beth Bjorklund. CoAuP

White cloud passed over the land, The. The Final Painting. Lee Harwood. EAS

White clouds are mindless, they never come to rest, The. Nesting among Clouds. Yang Chi, *tr. by* Jonathan Chaves. CoBLCP

White clouds beyond the sky, The. A Mushroom Gatherer Deep in the Mountains. Hsü Wei, *tr. by* Jonathan Chaves. CoBLCP

White clouds, I cannot see their end. Ch'ang-an. Ho Ching-ming, *tr. by* Jonathan Chaves. CoBLCP

White clouds like a scarf enfold the the mountain's waist. Shen Chou, *tr. by* Jonathan Chaves. CoBLCP

White Clover. Marvin Bell. CAPP

White cock's tail, The. Ploughing on Sunday. Wallace Stevens. FaPON; GoJo; RB; SOTW; TTTS

White columns of towering masonry. Monserrat. William Edwin Collin. CaP

White Conduit House. William Woty. NOEC

White coral bells upon a slender stalk. *Unknown.* PDV

White cormorants shaped like houses stare down at you, The. Party at Hydra. Irving Layton. HeIP

White Crane Hill. Su Tung-p'o, *tr. fr. Chinese by* Burton Watson. CoBCP

White cups white. Turkish Love Songs. *Unknown, tr. by* Reza Baraheni *and* Zahra-Soltan Shokoohtaezeh. BoWoP

White curtains blowing inward. This Song Shows Me Pictures; Morningside Drive, New York City 1950-1960. Richard Oyama. BrSi

White curtains of infinite fatigue. And the Seventh Dream Is the Dream of Isis. David Gascoyne. EAS

White day, black river. The Predicter of Famine. William Carlos Williams. VGW

White delightful swan, The. The Dying Swan. *Unknown.* ChTr

White Devil, The, *sels.* John Webster.
  Call for the Robin Redbreast and the Wren. *Fr.* V, iv. ChTr; EBEV; FaBoCh; HAP; HeIP; NoP; PoEL-2; PoRA; PrIm; RB; SeCePo
  (Cornelia's Song.) OBS; TrGrPo
  (Dirge, A: "Call for the robin-redbreast and the wren.") ElI; LiTB; NOBE; OBEV
  (Land Dirge, A.) CH; GTBS; GTBS-P
  Execration against Whores, An. *Fr.* III, ii. TW
  "What, are you drop't?." *Fr.* V, vi. PoEL-2

White dew,/ come from no one knows where, The. Kyogoku Tamekane, *tr. fr. Japanese by* Burton Watson. *Fr.* Twenty-three Tanka. FCEI

White dew, a dream, this life, an illusion. To a Man I Met Only Briefly. Lady Izumi, *tr. fr. Japanese by* Hiroaki Sato. *Fr.* Fifty-one Tanka. FCEI

White dew: one drop on each prickle. Buson, *tr. fr. Japanese by* Hiroaki Sato. *Fr.* Eighty-seven Hokku. FCEI

White Dou o Truth. The Ineffable Dou. Sydney Goodsir Smith. OxBS

White Dress, The. Roberta Spear. MAYP

White Dress, The. Marya Zaturenska. MoAmPo

White dusk moved ahead of them. Image of City. Lance Henson. VoR

White Dust, The. W. W. Gibson. MoBrPo

White Dwarf. A. R. Ammons. CAPP

White Eagle, The. Nan McDonald. PoAu-2

White Earth. Gerald Vizenor. HATNAP

White Earth Reservation 1980. Gerald Vizenor. STE

White Egret, The. Kenneth Rosen. NAmP

White England, shouldering from the sea. Fair England. Helen Gray Cone. AA

White Etc, The. Hans Arp, *tr. fr. French by* Michael Benedikt. POS

White faces are lit below the high bank, The. Elver Fishers. Ivor Gurney. FaBoPP

White Fields. James Stephens. BoNaP; BoTP; FaPON; MoShBr

White fish clustering in seaweed. Basho, *tr. fr. Japanese by* Burton Watson. *Fr.* Seventy-six Hokku. FCEI

White fish graphically move in the water's color. Raizan, *tr. fr. Japanese by* Hiroaki Sato. *Fr.* Thirteen Hokku. FCEI

White Fisher, The. *Unknown.* ESPB

White Flag, The. John Milton Hay. AnAmPo

White flour, earth-flesh, a cold fleece on the mountain. The Snowfall. Gwerfyl Mechain, *tr. by* Kenneth Hurlstone Jackson. OBWVE

White-flower is twisted into bast, The. *Unknown, tr. by* Arthur Waley. BoS

White fog lifting & falling on mountain-brow. Wales Visitation. Allen Ginsberg. CAPP; NNaP; NYBP; Prf

"White folks is white," says Uncle Jim. Uncle Jim. Countee Cullen. BANP; NAAL-2

White Foolscap/Book of Cordelia, *sel.* Susan Howe.
  "Children of Lir." LP

White founts falling in the courts of the sun. Lepanto. G. K. Chesterton. FaBV; FaPoR; GoTL; MoBrPo; MOS; OBMV; OBNV; RB

White Fox. Elizabeth Alsop Shepard. GoYe

White gem unknown of men, A. *Unknown. Fr.* Manyo Shu. Ma

White Gentian, A. Sam Hunt. ATNZ

White Goat, White Ram. W. S. Merwin. NePoEA

White Goddess, The. Robert Graves. MoBrPo; NAEL-2; OAEL-2; OPOP

"White Goddess"/ to white men, The. Of Utterances. Alma Villanueva. CCP

White Goddess. Hubert Witheford. ATNZ

White-gowned woman making offering, A. Virgin Pictured in Profile. Rosanna Warren. MAYP

White Guardians of the Universe of Sleep. E. E. Cummings. NYBP

White gulls that sit and float. The Echoing Cliff. Andrew Young. PoSH

White gum showing, The. Pine Gum. W. W. E. Ross. OBCV

White hair shrouds both my temples. Blaming Sons. T'ao Ch'ien, *tr. by* Burton Watson. CoBCP

White-haired Lover, *sel.* Karl Shapiro.
  "I swore to stab the sonnet with my pen." PoA

White-haired man, holding a fishing pole, The. Tsung Ch'en, *tr. fr. Chinese by* Jonathan Chaves. *Fr.* Miscellaneous Words on the Lake. CoBLCP

White hands of langourous grace. He Praises His Wife When She Has Left Him. *Unknown, tr. by* Robin Flower. AnIL

White hard rock. Silica Carbonate Rock. Fred Berry. NU

White Hare, The. Lilian Bowes-Lyon. OxBTC

White Haunches. Pierre Jean Jouve, *tr. fr. French by* Kenneth Rexroth. RHTwFP

White Heliotrope. Arthur Symons. BoLoP; EBEV

White hen she cackles, The. *Unknown.* PBBP

White hill-side is prickled with antlers, The. Knole. Charles Hubert Sisson. NOCV

White Horse, The. W. H. Davies. OxBTC

White Horse, The. D. H. Lawrence. SOTW; TTTS

White Horse, The. Tu Fu, *tr. fr. Chinese by* Rewi Alley. ChTr

White Horse of the Father, White Horse of the Son. William Pitt Root. MAYP

White Horse of Westbury, The. Charles Tennyson Turner. EBEV

White Horse Song. Reinhard Priessnitz, *tr. fr. German by* Beth Bjorklund. CoAuP

White Horses. Eleanor Farjeon. PDV

White Horses. Irene F. Pawsey. BoTP

White horses, tails high, rise from the cedar. E Uni Que A The Hi A Tho, Father. Roberta Hill. VoR

White-Hot Blizzard, The. Irina Ratushinskaya, *tr. fr. Russian by* David McDuff. AIW

White-hot midday in the Snake Park, A. In the Snake Park. William Plomer. NYBP; OxBTC

White House, The. Claude McKay. AmNP; AmPP; NIP; PoBA (White Houses.) PoNe

White Houses. Claude McKay. *See* White House, The.

White houses bank the hill. The Rooftop. Thom Gunn. NoP

White hummocks here are rounded to a thigh. Early Summer Sea-Tryst. Frederick Macartney. CBAP

White Hydrangeas. Shotetsu, *tr. fr. Japanese by* Steven D. Carter. WFTW

White in the moon the long road lies. A. E. Housman. *Fr.* A Shropshire Lad, XXXVI. AWP; CMoP; ELP; LiTB

White Iris, A. Pauline B. Barrington. PoLF

White is the sail and lonely. A Sail. Mikhail Yurevich Lermontov, *tr. by* Max Eastman. AWP

White is the thin snow. Night Snow. Emperor Kogon, *tr. by* Steven D. Carter. WFTW

White Island; or, The Place of the Blest [*or* Blessed], The.   Robert Herrick.   ChTr; JCP; NoP; OAEL-1; OBS; TOF; WiR

White Isle of Leuce, The.   Sir Herbert Read.   FaBoTw

White Jade Bitter Melon.   Yu Kuang-chung, *tr. fr. Chinese* by Dominic Cheung.   IFON

White jade trees line the phoenix tower.   The Taoist Nun.   Lu Ch'ien-i, *tr.* by Lois Fusek.   ATF

White January sun on fire through the blinds, A.   Luxury of Sin.   Joyce Carol Oates.   KS

White Knight's Ballad, The.   "Lewis Carroll."   *See* Through the Looking-Glass: I'll tell thee everything I can.

White Knight's Song, The.   "Lewis Carroll."   *See* Through the Looking-Glass: I'll tell thee everything I can.

White Lady has asked me to dance, The.   Fourth Dance Poem.   Gerald W. Barrax.   PoBA

White Lake.   James Applewhite.   MT

White Lake, The.   *Unknown, tr. fr. Irish* by Robin Flower.   TIRV

White lambs leap. Through miles of snow.   The Fire in the Snow.   Vernon Watkins.   LiTM

White Land, The.   Roberta Hill Whiteman.   HATNAP

White Light.   Linda Gregg.   NAmP

White, like a spectre seen when night is old.   The Taj.   H. G. Keene.   OBTV

White Lilac.   John Welch.   NPo

White Lotus Flowers.   Ts'ao Chen-chi, *tr. fr. Chinese* by William H. Nienhauser, Jr..   WFTU

White Magic; an Ode.   William Stanley Braithwaite.   PoNe

White man drew a small circle in the sand, The.   Circles.   Carl Sandburg.   AmFN

White man is, The.   12 Gates to the City.   Nikki Giovanni.   IHMS; PoBA

White man is a tiger at my throat, The.   Tiger.   Claude McKay.   BPo

White Man Pressed the Locks, The.   James C. Kilgore.   InPK

White-maned, wide-throated, the heavy-shouldered children of the wind.   Granite and Cypress.   Robinson Jeffers.   AmPP

White Man's Burden, The.   Kipling.   FaBoPV

White mares lashed to the sulky carriages.   In Ohio.   James Wright.   NNaP

White mares of the moon rush along the sky, The.   Night Clouds.   Amy Lowell.   AnAmPo; MoAmPo

White men's children spread over the earth.   The Riddle.   Georgia Douglas Johnson.   PoBA

White Monster, The.   W. H. Davies.   AmMo; LiTB

White Moon.   H. Leivick, *tr. fr. Yiddish* by Benjamin *and* Barbara Harshav.   AYP

White moon setting and red sun waking.   The Bomber.   Beatrice R. Gibbs.   CN

White moon, The, gleams through scudding/ Clouds.   Sorrow.   Chu Shu-chen, *tr.* by Kenneth Rexroth.   BoWoP

White moons like midnight's in the morning sun.   Autumn Mushrooms.   Kenneth Mackenzie.   CBAP

White moth to the closing vine, The.   The Gipsy Trail.   Kipling.   PoRA

White Motor, The.   André du Bouchet, *tr. fr. French* by Paul Auster.   RHTwFP

White Night.   Kadya Molodowsky, *tr. fr. Yiddish* by Adrienne Rich.   PeBMYV

White Noise.   Andrew Joron.   BWV

White notch as of bone, A.   A Suite of Six Pieces for Siskind.   John Logan.   LCAP

White Notes.   Donald Justice.   LCAP

White nymph wandering in the woods by night, A.   André Marie de Chénier, *tr. fr. French* by Arthur Symons.   *Fr.* Elegies, II.   AWP

White ocean birds that seek the land.   Gulls and Dreams.   Lionel Stevenson.   CaP

White-of-blossoms almond in the rain.   Almond Blossoms.   Eli Netser, *tr.* by Bernhard Frank.   MHeP

White on white, I can never be viewed.   Venus and the Rain.   Medbh McGuckian.   FaBCIP

White, orphaned camel kid, The.   Mongol Oral Tradition, *tr.* by C. R. Bawden.   WTO

White Owl, The.   George Meredith.   *Fr.* Love in a Valley.   ChTr

White Oxen.   Louis Simpson.   NoAM

White Paternoster, The.   *Unknown.*   *See* Matthew, Mark, Luke, and John/ Bless the bed that I lie on.

White Peace, The.   "Fiona Macleod."   FaBoBe

White pearl, sunk under the deep sea, The.   *Unknown. Fr.* Manyo Shu.   Ma

White peonies about to collapse.   Natsume Seibi, *tr. fr. Japanese* by Hiroaki Sato.   *Fr.* Twenty-seven Hokku.   FCEI

White People.   David Henderson.   PoBA

"White phosphorous, white phosphorous."   Overheard over S. E. Asia.   Denise Levertov.   BoWoP

White pine, yellow pine. Southern Pines.   John Peale Bishop.   GOA

White Pines, Felled 1984.   Richard Eberhart.   BLA

White pinnace on lactic waves, The.   Birth by Anesthesia.   George Scarbrough.   GoYe

White Power Poem.   Michael Bishop.   BWV

White Primit Falls.   *Unknown.*   ChTr

White Public Benches.   Hagiwara Sakutaro, *tr. fr. Japanese* by Hiroaki Sato.   FCEI

White Queen.   John Fuller.   NePoEA-2

White Rainbow, The.   Starr Nelson.   GoYe

White Rose, A.   John Boyle O'Reilly.   AA; ACP; OBEV; SoSe

White rose had a sorrow, A.   The Betrayal of the Rose.   Edith M. Thomas.   AA

White Rose: Sophie Scholl 1921-1943, The.   Erika Mumford.   MOWH

White Roses.   John Ashbery.   TAP

White sagebrush desert, The. Noon.   O Pioneers!   John Peale Bishop.   VGW

White sail gleams alone out yonder, A.   The Sail.   Mikhail Yurevich Lermontov, *tr.* by Alan Myers.   AAA

White sail upon the ocean verge.   Arthur.   William Winter.   AA

White sand and cedars; cedars, sand.   Sandy Hook.   George Houghton.   AA

White Season.   Frances Mary Frost.   FaPON

White Serpent.   Nelly Sachs, *tr. fr. German* by Michael Hamburger.   BoWoP

White shape is Loch Fionn, The.   Ascent.   Donald G. Saunders.   PoSH

White Sheep.   W. H. Davies.   BoTP

White sheep, white sheep, on a blue hill.   *Unknown.*   GBP

White sheet on the tail-gate of a truck, A.   Elegy for a Dead Soldier.   Karl Shapiro.   HAP; LiTM; OBWP; OxBA; WaaP; WaP

White Ship, The.   Geoffrey Hill.   OxBC

White Ship, The.   Dante Gabriel Rossetti.   OBNV

White Ships and the Red, The.   Joyce Kilmer.   PAH

White-sided flowers are thrusting up on the hillside.   Hawaii Dantesca.   Charles Wright.   HCAP; LCAP

White Skirt, The.   Stephen Dobyns.   MAYP

White snow fills the lakeside village.   Tsung Ch'en, *tr. fr. Chinese* by Jonathan Chaves.   *Fr.* Miscellaneous Words on the Lake.   CoBLCP

White snow which lies so deep, The.   Yakamochi.   *Fr.* Manyo Shu.   Ma

White, stamen-shadowed petals of wild rose.   Dogrose.   Patric Stevenson.   NeIP

White star! that travellest at old Maggie's pace.   Maggie's Star.   Charles Tennyson Turner.   FM

White stars falling gently.   Winter Joys.   Dorothy Graddon.   BoTP

White Stone Slope.   Yang Shih-ch'i, *tr. fr. Chinese* by Jonathan Chaves.   *Fr.* The Intendant Yao Shan Has Requested Six Poems on Living in the Mountains.   CoBLCP

White sun.   Zebra.   Judith Thurman.   RHPC

White Swan.   A. Leyeles, *tr. fr. Yiddish* by Keith Bosley.   VWA

White swan of cities, slumbering in thy nest.   Venice.   Longfellow.   EyDe

White-tailed Hornet, The.   Robert Frost.   OxBA

White the October air, no snow, easy to breathe.   How to Get There.   Frank O'Hara.   NoP

White though ye be, yet, lies, know.   How Lillies Came White.   Robert Herrick.   CaPo

White-throat flicked into the sunset window, A.   Procession.   Philip Booth.   BLA

White Tiger Battalion, The.   Sahara Morizumi, *tr. fr. Chinese* by Burton Watson.   JLIC-2

White-tin chimneys shimmer in midday under a high sun.   Laundry.   Berysh Vaynshteyn, *tr. fr. Yiddish* by Benjamin *and* Barbara Harshav *and* Kathryn Hellerstein.   *Fr.* Negroes.   AYP

White to the neck he glides and plunges.   Fencing School.   John Streeter Manifold.   CBAP

White Trash.   Jim Hall.   MT

White velvet covers the town.   Jerusalem in the Snow.   Anath Bental, *tr.* by Howard Schwartz.   VWA

White Venus limpid wandering in the sky.   Louise Labé, *tr.* by Aliki *and* Willis Barnstone.   BoWoP

White Violet.   Marian Osborne.   CaP

White violet, The.   Sea Violet.   Hilda Doolittle ("H. D.").   NoP

White waters twist and turn among crumbling embankments.   In the Evening, Walking in the Western Fields.   Chang Yü, *tr.* by Jonathan Chaves.   CoBLCP

White waves springing on my head, in July.   Eye.   Nishiwaki Junzaburo, *tr.* by Geoffrey Bownas *and* Anthony Thwaite.   PeBJV

White Weekend.   Quincy Troupe.   NBP

White wings of commerce sailing far.   In Memory of General Grant.   Henry Abbey.   AA

White winter light, The.   Spoil.   Malka Heifetz Tussman, *tr.* by Marcia Falk.   OV

White Witch, The. James Weldon Johnson. BANP; CDC

White woman have you heard. Montgomery. Sam Cornish. CNA; PoBA; Psk

White Women, The. Mary Elizabeth Coleridge. BrRo

White World. Hilda Doolittle ("H. D."). LLLT

White Zombie. Harrison Fisher. UL

Whitebeard on Videotape. James Merrill. NoP

Whitehall Stairs. Aaron Hill. NOEC

Whiteness. A. Leyeles, *tr. fr. Yiddish by* Benjamin *and* Barbara Harshav. AYP

Whiteness. Yunna Moritz, *tr. fr. Russian by* Elaine Feinstein. VWA

Whiteness of faintly roseate milk. A line. Dayspring. Luis G. Urbina, *tr. by* Samuel Beckett. MexPo

Whitening striations bruise this lake of ice. Lakes. Gabriel Preil, *tr. by* Bernhard Frank. MHeP

Whiter/ than the crust. The Wind Sleepers. Hilda Doolittle ("H. D."). WPE

Whiter than the stones on Stone Mountain. Basho, *tr. fr. Japanese by* Burton Watson. *Fr.* Seventy-six Hokku. FCEI

Whites alone upon the jury in a number of the states. Injustice of the Courts. Lizelia Augusta Jenkins Moorer. CBWP-3

Whitewashed wall is covered with blackberries. As far as the eye can see, The. The Wall. Cesare Vivaldi, *tr. by* Lawrence R. Smith. NItP

Whither. John Vance Cheney. AA

Whither? Wilhelm Müller, *tr. fr. German by* Longfellow. AWP

Whither Away? Mary Elizabeth Coleridge. CH

Whither away, Robin. The Flight of the Birds. Edmund Clarence Stedman. GN

Whither dost thou hide from the magic of my flute-call? The Snake-Charmer. Sarojini Naidu. PBWP

Whither I kneel or stand or sit in prayer. At Communion. Madeleine L'Engle. TrCP

Whither leads this pathway, little one? Whither. John Vance Cheney. AA

Whither, midst falling dew. To a Waterfowl. Bryant. AA; AmPP; AnAmPo; AWP; BLPL; CH; FaBoBe; FaFP; GN; HoPM; LiTA; NAAL-1; NOBA; NoP; OHFP; OxBA; PoEL-4; PoLF; PrIm; PWR; SoSe; TAP; TrGrPo; WBLP; WGRP

Whither, O splendid ship, thy white sails crowding. A Passer-by. Robert Bridges. BrPo; CMoP; LiTB; LiTM; MoAB; MoBrPo; MOS; OAEL-2; OBEV; OBNC; OxBTC; WiR

Whither, O whither didst thou fly. The Eclipse. Henry Vaughan. OxBSP

Whither, O whither wander I forlorn? Oceana and Britannia. John Ayloffe. APAS

Whither, oh! whither wilt thou wing thy way? Flight of the Spirit. Felicia Dorothea Hemans. Son

Whither, say whither shall I fly. The Frozen Zone; or, Julia Disdainful. Robert Herrick. CaPo

Whither shall I go. Unknown, *at. to* John Webster *and* William Rowley. *Fr.* The Thracian Wonder, II, i. GBL

Whither shall I, the fair maiden, flee from Sorrow? Sorrow. *Unknown, tr. by* W. R. S. Ralston. AWP

Whither So Fast? *Unknown.* EIL

Whitley at Three O'Clock. Jeff Worley. GOYP

Whitman. Larry Levis. MAYP

Whitman at a Grain Depot. James Reiss. AnAn

Whitman in Black. Ted Berrigan. UL

Whitman's Ride for Oregon. Hezekiah Butterworth. PAH

Whitsun Weddings, The. Philip Larkin. FaBoMo; HeIP; MoP; NePoEA-2; NoAM; NoP; OxBTC

Whittier. Paul Laurence Dunbar. AnAmPo

Whittier. James Russell Lowell. *Fr.* A Fable for Critics. AmPP; NOBA; OxBA

Whittier. Margaret E. Sangster. AA

Whittingham Fair. *Unknown.* GBP

Whittling. John Pierpont. GN

Who. Moyshe-Leyb Halpern, *tr. fr. Yiddish by* Joseph Leftwich. TrJP

Who? Florence Hoatson. BoTP

Who. Edwin Honig. TAP

Who. Philip Levine. KS

Who/ Are you/ Who is born. Vision and Prayer. Dylan Thomas. LiTM

Who a Mother Is. Roy W. Watson. PWR

Who Am I? Felice Holman. RFM; TSS

Who am I? I am a lady faithful to the ways. Lady of the Ferry Inn. Gwerfyl Mechain. BoWoP, *tr. by* Willis Barnstone

Who am I, my fellow beings? Mohammad Taqi Mir, *tr. by* Ahmed Ali. GoT

Who am I? Who am I? Who could have guessed right. Light—My Word. Moyshe-Leyb Halpern, *tr. by* John Hollander. PeBMYV

Who am I worthless that you spent such pains. A Prayer for the Self. John Berryman. *Fr.* Eleven Addresses to the Lord, VIII. PPP

Who among us would accept. The Final Prospect. Carl L. Stach. KS

Who among you has begun his days. Poet. Ali Ja far al- Allaq, *tr. by* Sharif Elmusa *and* Thomas G. Ezzy. MAP

Who Among You Knows the Essence of Garlic? Garrett Hongo. InPS

Who Are My People? Rosa Zagnoni Marinoni. BLPA

Who are the nobles of the earth. The True Aristocrat. W. Stewart. WBLP

Who are these among you. The Decision. Owen Dodson. PoNe

Who are these from the strange, ineffable places. Arabia. John Meade Falkner. OxBTC

Who are these people at the bridge to meet me? The Bee Meeting. Sylvia Plath. HCAP; InPS; PPP; WPE

Who are these people who have got their grammar and their diction levels. Movement along the Frieze. Caroline Knox. BAP

Who are these? Why sit they here in twilight? Mental Cases. Wilfred Owen. BrPo; CMoP; FaBoMo; MMA; NoAM; WaP

Who are they. The Passengers. David Antin. NYBP

Who are they talking to in the big temple? The Temple. C. H. Sisson. OxBTC

Who are they to be in their skin. The Subway Witnesses. Lorenzo Thomas. PoBA

Who are those marching—such as we are—gnomes? A Short Fairy Tale. Stanislaw Grochowiak, *tr. by* Czeslaw Milosz. PwPP

Who are we here? Intra-Political. Margaret Avison. MoCV

Who are we to love. A Footnote to a Gray Bird's Pause. James Cunningham. JB

"Who are we waiting for?" "Soup burnt?" The Feckless Dinner Party. Walter de la Mare. FaBoTw

Who are ye, spirits, that stand. The Blazing Heart. Alice Williams Brotherton. AA

Who are you. Nizar Qabbani, *tr. by* Lena Jayyusi *and* W. S. Merwin. MAP

Who Are You? "Adunis", *tr. fr. Arabic by* Lena Jayyusi *and* John Heath-Stubbs. MAP

Who are you. To Desi as Joe as Smoky the Lover of 115th Street. Audre Lorde. CNA

Who are you? You and I. Tennessee Williams. GLP

Who are you dusky woman, so ancient hardly human. Ethiopia Saluting the Colors. Walt Whitman. PAH; PoNe

Who are you, listening to me, who are you. Poem for Half White College Students. Imamu Amiri Baraka. BPo; TAP; UnPo

Who Are You, Little I. E. E. Cummings. NYBP

"Who are you, Sea Lady." Santorin. James Elroy Flecker. FaBoTw; GoJo; OBMV

"Who are you that are twisted, brown." Death of a Prominent Business Man. Louis MacNeice. FL

"Who are you that so strangely woke." The Princess of Scotland. Rachel Annand Taylor. GoTS

Who are you there that from your icy tower. The Astronomers of Mont Blanc. Edgar Bowers. PoA; QFR

Who Art Thou, O Great Mountain. Dahlia Ravikovich, *tr. fr. Hebrew by* Warren Bargad *and* Stanley F. Chyet. IP

Who as he rides is weighed down by the burden. Homage. Dezsö Tandori, *tr. by* Daniel Hoffman. MHuP

Who aside from you, King Ram. Tulsidas, *tr. by* John Stratton Hawley *and* Mark Juergensmeyer. SSI

Who Be Kind To. Allen Ginsberg. NNaP

Who beckons the green ivy up. The Miracle. Walter de la Mare. LiTB; UnPo

Who believes/ he is dead? Under Stone. Elaine Feinstein. VWA

Who bends in garden rows. This Poem Is for Nadine. Paul B. Janeczko. GOYP

Who Bids Us Sing? Rhys Carpenter. WGRP

Who borrows all your ready cash. A Friend. Marguerite Power. FaBoCo; FaFP

Who bought a mountain and became a hermit there? Chin Nung, *tr. fr. Chinese by* Jonathan Chaves. *Fr.* I Discuss the Past and Not the Present. CoBLCP

Who but the Lord? Langston Hughes. BPo

Who by Searching Can Find Out God? Eliza Scudder. *See* I cannot find thee! Still on restless pinion.

Who called flowers "mouths"?—these painted lips. Novas. Van K. Brock. MT

"Who called?" I said, and the words. Echo. Walter de la Mare. OBMV

Who calls her two-faced? Faces, she has three. The Three-faced. Robert Graves. FaBoEE

Who calls? Who calls? Who? For a Mocking Voice. Eleanor Farjeon. CH

Who came whirling out of the North. Of the Scythians. Katha Pollitt. DiPo; InPS; SM

Who Can Be Born Black. Mari E. Evans. CNA

Who can bear/ The wail of a young orphan? Rabbi Yussel Luksh of Chelm. Jacob Glatstein, *tr. by* Nathan Halper. TrJP

Who can believe with common sense. Epigram on Fasting. Swift. OBVE

Who can bring back the magic of that story. The Descent of the Child. Susan Langstaff Mitchell. TIRV

Who can divine what the dim future holds. The Sabbath Peal; or, Past, Present, and Future. A Moral Essay. Thomas Nicholson. PF

Who can find a virtuous woman? for her price is far above rubies . Bible, *O.T. Fr.* Proverbs, XXXI: 10-31. SaC
(Good Wife, The.) TrGrPo
(Virtuous Woman, The.) TrJP

Who can forget that ne'er forgotten night. On the Nativity of Our Saviour. Thomas Philipott. JCP

Who can grasp for the first time. New Music. Gwen Harwood. CBAP

Who can live in heart so glad. The Merry Country Lad. Nicholas Breton. *Fr.* The Passionate Shepherd. EIL
(Happy Countryman, The, *shorter sel.*) CH
(Pastoral: "Who can live in heart so glad.") ELP
(Shepherd and Shepherdess.) OBSC

Who can open the door. Overture. Zuhur Dixon, *tr. by* Patricia Alanah Byrne *and* Salma Khadra Jayyusi. MAP

Who can remember back to the first poets. The Makers. Howard Nemerov. DiPo; FYAP

Who can review, without a precious loss. The Passion. Ralph Knevet. JCP

Who can say. Tennyson. FaBoCh

Who Can Say. Alastair Reid. NePoEA

Who can support the anguish of love? Ibn al-Arabi, *tr. by* R. A. Nicholson. AWP

Who Can Tell? *Gond Oral Tradition, tr. by* V. Elwin *and* S. Hivale. WTO

Who can tell a man's real pain. Then Sings My Soul. Paul Mariani. GeTw; MAYP

Who Can Tell When He Is Awake. James Tate. MAYP

Who can tell who was born of what? Doorstep, Lightning, Waif-Dreaming. James Dickey. CAPP

Who can the various city frauds recite. John Gay. *Fr.* Trivia; or, The Art of Walking the Streets of London, III. OAEL-1

Who cannot speak. The Hill, the Frenzy. Alain Delahaye, *tr. by* Anthony Barnett. RHTwFP

Who comes here?/ A grenadier. The Grenadier. *Unknown.* GBP; OxNR

Who comes to-night? We ope the doors in vain. Henry James. Robert Louis Stevenson. OBNC

Who comes to us in our dark. Isaac and Esau. Rose Drachler. VWA

Who could be smaller than this child. The Green Horse. Bin Ramke. MAYP

Who could dispute his choice. The Net and the Sword. Douglas Le Pan. NOBC

Who could have come? The garden is. Asadullah Khan Ghalib, *tr. by* Ahmed Ali. GoT

Who could have thought that men and women could feel. Old Paintings on Italian Walls. Kathleen Raine. NYBP

Who could long for anything but you? Ravidas, *tr. by* John Stratton Hawley *and* Mark Juergensmeyer. SSI

Who could remember cause? The Victim. Ellen Bryant Voigt. MAYP

Who counts himself as nobly born. The Nobly Born. Frances Ellen Watkins Harper. PWR

Who cries that the days of daring are those that are faded far. Deeds of Valor at Santiago. Clinton Scollard. PAH

Who crieth: "Woe"? who: "Alas"? The Drunkard. Bible, *O.T. Fr.* Proverbs, XXIII: 29-35. TrJP

Who dare complain or be ashamed. Celebrations. Austin Clarke. IPY

Who dares to drop the pin destruction of our silence. Can You Change a Shilling? Toni Del Renzio. EAS

Who dat a-knockin' at the door below. What You Goin' to Do When the Rent Comes 'Round? Andrew B. Sterling. OBAL

Who decided what is useful in its beauty. Looking at Quilts. Marge Piercy. SaC

Who died on the wires, and hung there, one of two. The Silent One. Ivor Gurney. MMA; NAEL-2; OBD, *abr.*; OBWP

Who does not love the juniper tree? Juniper. Eileen Duggan. PChr

Who does not love the spring deserves no lovers. Georgian Spring. Roy Campbell. OBSV

Who Does Not Love Wine, Women and Song. J. H. Voss. FaFP

Who Does the Cold Come Early To?, *sels.* Michizane, *tr. fr.* Chinese *by* Burton Watson. JLIC-1

Who does the cold come early to?/ It comes early to the fisherman.

Who does the cold come early to?/ To the old man who lost his wife.

Who does the cold come early to?/ To the peasant fled from another province.

Who does the cold come early to?/ To the relay station house attendant.

Who Done It? Daniel Hoffman. SoTCo

Who doth behold my mistress' face. The Fairest of Her Days. *Unknown.* EIL

Who doth desire that chaste his wife should be. Advice to the Same. Sir Philip Sidney. *Fr.* Arcadia. SiPS

Who doubts? The laws fell down from heaven's height. Joseph Hall. *Fr.* Virgidemiarum. OBSV, *fr. bk.* II, Satire III.

Who doubts the world is a thing of wind and waves. Grieving for the Student Abe. Michizane, *tr. by* Burton Watson. JLIC-1

Who Drags the Fiery Artist Down? Clarence Day. FaBoCo; NBLV

Who dreamed [*or* dream'd] that beauty passes like a dream? The Rose of the World. W. B. Yeats. BrPo; CMoP; MoAB; MoBrPo; NAEL-2

Who drives the horses of the sun. The Happiest Heart. John Vance Cheney. AA; WGRP

Who even dead, yet hath his mind entire! Ezra Pound. *Fr.* Cantos, XLVII. CMoP; PoE; VGW

Who ever had/ Such a whale of a plan? The Wall of China. Padraic Colum. GrPl

Who Ever Loved, That Loved Not at First Sight? Christopher Marlowe. *See* Hero and Leander: It Lies Not in Our Power to Love or Hate.

Who ever saw so fair a sight. Constancy. Samuel Daniel. *Fr.* Hymen's Triumph. OBSC

Who feasts tonight? The Fairies Feast. Charles M. Doughty. CH

Who fed me from her gentle breast. My Mother. Ann Taylor. BLPA; BLPL; OHIP; OxBChV

Who feels a growing hunger for fair eyes. To Liebig. August, Graf von Platen, *tr. by* Reginald Bancroft Cooke. PeHV

Who findeth comfort in the stars and flowers. Thomas Lovell Beddoes. *Fr.* Death's Jest Book. OBNC

Who first reform'd our stage with justest law[e]s. An Elegy on Ben Jonson. John Cleveland. MeLP; OBS

Who folds a leafe downe. *Unknown.* FaBoUs

Who Follows in His Train? Reginald Heber. WGRP

Who forced the Muse to this alliance? On Professor Drennan's Verse. Roy Campbell. GTBS-P

Who gave thee, O Beauty. Ode to Beauty. Emerson. AmPP; PoEL-4

Who goes? On the Bus. Mitsuye Yamada. *Fr.* Camp Notes. WPOW

Who Goes round My Pinfold Wall. *Unknown.* GBP

Who goes there? God knows. I'm nobody. How should I answer? Etosion achthos aroures. Robert Bridges. QFR

Who goes there? hankering, gross, mystical, nude. Walt Whitman. *Fr.* Song of Myself, XX. TrGrPo

Who Goes with Fergus? W. B. Yeats. CMoP; FaBoCh; GoJo; InPK; MoP; NAEL-2; NoAM; NOBE; NOBVV; PoE; PoRA

Who grace, for zenith had, from which no shadowes grow. Fulke Greville. *Fr.* Caelica, LXXXIII. PoEL-1
(Despair.) OBSC

Who half asleep, or waking, does not hear it. The Furnace of Colors. Vernon Watkins. NYBP

Who has a feeling she will come one day. White Queen. John Fuller. NePoEA-2

Who has been drinking our air from the other side? Inuit and Seal. Rosanne Wasserman. BAP

Who has broken the tops of the reeds in the port? *Unknown. Fr.* Manyo Shu. FCEI

Who has but dighted his tricks in a bed. This Is What the Watchbird Sings, Who Perches in the Lovetree. Bruce Boyd. NeAP

Who has ever stopped to think of the divinity of Lamont Cranston? In Memory of Radio. Imamu Amiri Baraka. NAAL-2; NeAP; NoP; PoM

Who Has Known Heights. Mary Brent Whiteside. BLPA

Who has not heard of the dauntless *Varuna?* The Varuna. George Henry Boker. PAH

Who has not heard of the Vale of Cashmere. The Light of the Harem [*or* Haram]. Thomas Moore. *Fr.* Lalla Rookh, The Story of the Sultana Nourmahal. EnRP; TEP

Who has not thought, when scuffing shells. Lower Forms of Life. Mary Winter. GoYe

Who Has Our Redeemer Heard. Stephen Collins Foster. AH

Who has robbed the ocean cave. John Shaw. AA

Who Has Seen the Wind? Christina Rossetti. *Fr.* Sing-Song. FaPON; GoJo; NTCP; PDV; RHPC
(Wind, The.) BLPL; FaBoBe; OxBChV

Who Has Seen the Wind? Christina Georgina Rossetti. BoTP

Who has strangled the tired voice. Appeal. Noémia da Sousa. TTY, *tr. by* Dorothy Guedes *and* Phillippa Rumsey; WPOW, *tr. by* Alan Ryder

Who has you then you pretty wood? Nature Morte. Heidi Pataki, *tr. by* Beth Bjorklund. CoAuP

Who Hath a Book. Wilbur Dick Nesbit. BLPA

Who hath desired the Sea?—the sight of salt water unbounded. The Sea and the Hills. Kipling. FaBV; MOS

Who hath gathered the wind in his fists? The Words of Agur. Bible, *O.T. Fr.* Proverbs, XXX: 4, 15-16, 18-19, 24-28.
Four Things. *Fr. ll.* 24-28.
Too Wonderful. *Fr. ll.* 18-19. TrJP

Who hath given man speech? or what hath set therein. Swinburne. *Fr.* Atalanta in Calydon. OAEL-2

Who hath he[a]rd of such[e] cruelty before? Sir Thomas Wyatt. AAS; SiPS

Who hath his fancy pleasèd. Who Hath His Fancy [*or* Fancie] Pleased. Sir Philip Sidney. EIL; PoEL-1; QFR
(Immortality.) OBSC

Who hath not sent out ships to sea? The Ship That Went Down. Adah Isaacs Menken. CBWP-1

Who have been lonely once. Careless Love. Stanley Kunitz. WaP

Who Here Can Cast His Eyes Abroad. Abiel Holmes. AH

Who, if I cried out, would hear me among the angels? Rainer Maria Rilke, *tr. fr. German by* Stephen Mitchell. *Fr.* Duino Elegies, I. NAWM-2

Who, in the dark, has cast the harbor-chain? Putting to Sea. Louise Bogan. LiTM; PoA

Who, in the garden-pony carrying skeps. Horses. Dorothy Wellesley. OBMV; OxBTC

Who, in the public library, one evening after rain. Public Library. Dannie Abse. OxBC

Who invited him in? What was he doing here. The Dirty Little Accuser. Norman Cameron. OxBS

Who is a mother some one exclaimed? Who a Mother Is. Roy W. Watson. PWR

Who Is at My Window? *Unknown.* TrGrPo

Who is de prutties' gal you say? My Little Lize. James Martinez. PVCV

Who is God. The Questions of Ethne Alba. *Unknown, tr. by* James Carney. TIRV

Who Is It. Benjamin Péret, *tr. fr. French by* Michael Benedikt. POS

Who is it. The Wind. Kazuko Yamada, *tr. by* Miyao Ohara *and* D. J. Enright. OBD

Who is it calling by the darkened river. Voices. Walter de la Mare. UnPo

Who is it rivets broken bands. The Poet's Mission. Ernest Charles Jones. PF

Who is it runs through the many-storied mansion of myth. Dwarf of Disintegration. Oscar Williams. LiTM; PoCH

Who Is It Talks of Ebony? Manmohan Ghose. OBMV

Who is it that this dark night. Sir Philip Sidney. *Fr.* Astrophel and Stella. EIL; NAEL-1; OBSC; PoE; PoEL-1; TEP
(Underneath My Window.) SeCePo
(Voices at the Window.) NOBE; OBEV

Who is like unto thee who teachest knowledge. Hymn of Unity. *Unknown, tr. by* H. M. Adler. TrJP

Who Is My Brother? Pinkie Gordon Lane. BlSi

Who is my father in this world, in this house. The Irish Cliffs of Moher. Wallace Stevens. DiL; LCAP; NOBA; TOF; VGW

Who Is My Neighbor? Josephine D. Henderson Heard. CBWP-4

Who is not a stranger still. Stephany Fuller. BPo

Who is opening his eyes. Baby. Jung Han-mo, *tr. by* Koh Chang-soo. ACKP

Who is she coming, whom all gaze upon. A Rapture Concerning His Lady. Guido Cavalcanti, *tr. by* Dante Gabriel Rossetti. AWP; PFI

Who is she that ascends so high. The Assumption. Sir John Beaumont. ACP

Who is she that comes, makyng turn every man's eye. Sonnet [*or* Sonetto] VII. Guido Cavalcanti, *tr. by* Ezra Pound. CTC; OBVE

Who Is Silvia [*or* Sylvia]? Shakespeare. *Fr.* The Two Gentlemen of Verona, IV, ii. BLPL; EIL; FaBoBe; FaFP; GN; LiTB; OAEL-1; TrGrPo
(Silvia.) OBEV
(Song to Silvia.) OBSC

Who is so proud. The Performing Seal. Rachel Lyman Field. *Fr.* A Circus Garland. OBCA; RHPC

Who is standing behind me I don't know, but I know. A Word to Orphists. Kazimierz Wierzynski, *tr. by* Czeslaw Milosz. PwPP

Who Is Sylvia? Shakespeare. *See* Who Is Silvia?

Who is that. Robe of Flame. Ali Sardar J'afri, *tr. by* Mahmood Jamal. PBMUP

Who Is That a-Walking in the Corn? Fenton Johnson. PoNe

Who is that student pale and importunate. Student. Josephine Miles. NoP

Who is the East? Emily Dickinson. TTTS

Who is the happy warrior? Who is he? Character of the Happy Warrior. Wordsworth. EnRP; FaBoBe; FaFP; LiTB
(The Happy Warrior.) OHFP

Who is the mighty master that can trace. To Haydn. Thomas Holcroft. NOEC

Who is the runner in the skies. The Runner in the Skies. James Oppenheim. TrJP

Who Is the Same, Which at My Window Peepes? Spenser. *Fr.* Epithalamion. NAs

Who is the sleeping giant. Giant's Tomb in Georgian Bay. "Katherine Hale." CaP

Who is this fish, still wearing its wealth. A Wreath to the Fish. Nancy Willard. BLA

Who is this I hear?—Lo, this is I, thine heart. The Dispute of the Heart and Body of François Villon. Villon, *tr. by* Swinburne. AWP; OBVE

Who is this man out walking. Sunday Stroll. Michael Pettit. MAYP

Who is this Moses? who made him, we say. A Soliloquy of One of the Spies Left in the Wilderness. Gerard Manley Hopkins. TrCP

Who is this that comes in splendour, coming from the blazing East? The Airy Christ. Stevie Smith. NOCV

Who is this that cometh from Edom. Vision of the Day of Judgment . Bible, *O.T. Fr.* Isaiah, LXIII, Moulton, Modern Reader's Bible. WGRP

Who is this that darkeneth counsel by words without knowledge? Then the Lord Answered ("Who is this that darkeneth counsel by words without knowledge?"). Bible, *O.T. Fr.* Job, XXXVIII: 2–XXXIX. AWP
Sels.
"Wilt thou hunt the prey for the lion?" *Fr.* XXXVIII: 38–XXXIX. FM
"Where wast thou when I laid the foundations of the earth?." *Fr.* XXXVIII: 4–38. ImOP, *abr.*
"Knowest thou the time when the wild goates of the rocke bring forth?." *Fr.* XXXIX. OBVE
Hast Thou Given the Horse Strength. *Fr.* XXXIX: 19–25. ChTr
(Horse, The.) FaPON, *abr.*; TrGrPo
God Replies, XXXVIII: 2–41
"Then the Lord answered Job out of the whirlwind, and sayd." *Fr.* XXXVIII. AWP; OBVE
"Knowest thou the time when the wild goates of the rocke bring forth." *Fr.* XXXIX. OBVE

Who Is This Who Howls and Mutters? Stevie Smith. OxBC

Who is this whose feet. The Swan's Feet. Edith Jay Scovell. FaBoWP; OxBTC

Who is this ye say is slain? Ellsworth. *Unknown.* PAH

Who is this young corpse. Elegy for the Young Corpse. José Luis Villatoro, *tr. by* Tony Ryan. VoI

Who is to blame that I don't see your tree. In Central Park. Moyshe-Leyb Halpern, *tr. by* Benjamin *and* Barbara Harshav. AYP

Who is, who is the rider there. Who. Moyshe-Leyb Halpern, *tr. by* Joseph Leftwich. TrJP

Who is wise?/ He who learns from everyone. The Good Man. *Unknown, tr. fr. Hebrew. Fr.* The Talmud. TrJP

Who is yonder siren so distressed. An Old Burden. Amado Nervo, *tr. by* Samuel Beckett. MexPo

Who keeps the owl's breath? Whose eyes desire? David St. John. LCAP

Who Kill'd John Keats? Byron. EnRP
(John Keats.) FaBoEE

Who killed Christ?—my favorite subject. Letting in Cold. Marvin Bell. DiL

Who killed Cock [*or* poor] Robin? [*or* Here lies Cock Robin]. Mother Goose. OxNR; PBBP
("Heve hes Cock Robin.") OxBoLi
("Who killed poor Robin?") AmFP

Who Killed Lawless Lean? Stevie Smith. TEP

Who killed poor Robin? Mother Goose. *See* Who killed Cock [*or* poor] Robin? [*or* Here lies Cock Robin].

Who killed the last fighter [*or* commando]? The Dead Witness. Buland al-Haidari. MAP, *tr. by* Patricia Alanah Byrne *and* Salma Khadra Jayyusi; MPAW, *tr. by* Abdullah al-Udhari.

Who knew her. On the Fifth Anniversary of Bluma Sach's Death. Vinnie-Marie D'Ambrosio. IHMS

"Who knocks at my door, so late in the night?" Pilgrims in Mexico. *Unknown.* OBCP

"Who knocks?" "I, who was beautiful." The Ghost. Walter de la Mare. BrPo; CMoP; ELP; EnLoPo; LiTM; MoAB; MoBrPo; NOBE; OAEL-2; OxBTC

Who Knows? A. L. Milner-Brown. PBA; TTY

Who Knows? Nora Perry. AA

Who knows his will? Meditation on a Memoir. J. V. Cunningham. QFR

Who knows how cold, how lonely the west wind? Singde, *tr. by* William Schultz. WFTU

Who Knows if the Moon's. E. E. Cummings. SO

Who knows it not, who loves it not. A Racing Eight. James L. Cuthbertson. PoAu-1

Who knows the thoughts of a child. Who Knows? Nora Perry. AA

Who knows? This Africa so richly blest. Who Knows? A. L. Milner-Brown. PBA; TTY

Who knows this or that? Limits. Emerson. FM; OxBSP; PoEL-4

Who knows through what mysterious tensions these. The Ivory Tower. Robert Hillyer. NYBP

Who knows what days I answer for to-day? The Young Neophyte. Alice Meynell. ACP

Who Knows Where. Detlev von Liliencron, *tr. fr. German by* Ludwig Lewisohn. AWP

Who knows whether the sea heals or corrodes? Plague of Dead Sharks. Alan Dugan. LiTM; NoAM

Who lies here. Saigyo, *tr. fr. Japanese by* Burton Watson. *Fr.* Sixty-four Tanka. FCEI

Who Likes the Rain? Clara Doty Bates. BoTP

Who list the Romane greatnes forth to figure. Joachim Du Bellay, *tr. fr. French by* Spenser. *Fr.* Ruins of Rome. OBVE

Who lit the furnace of the mammoth's heart? The Sun. Francis Thompson. *Fr.* Ode to the Setting Sun. MoAB; MoBrPo

Who lived at the top end of our street. The Retired Colonel. Ted Hughes. NePoEA-2

Who lives here. Saigyo, *tr. fr. Japanese by* Burton Watson. *Fr.* Sixty-four Tanka. FCEI

Who locked me. A Night in the Royal Ontario Museum. Margaret Atwood. PBWP

Who, long before she left her teens. An Old Song Resung. Charles Larcom Graves. CenHV

Who Loves a Garden. Louise Seymour Jones. BLPA

Who lyst his welthe and eas retayne. V. Innocentia Veritas Viat Fides Circumdederunt Me Inimici Mei. Sir Thomas Wyatt. AAS

Who Makes the Journey. Cathy Song. BrSi

Who Maketh the Grass to Grow. Bible, *O.T. Fr.* Psalms: Psalm CXLVII ("Praise ye the Lord"). FaPON, *greatly abr.*.

Who masquerades behind the winds? Moods. Leib Kwitko, *tr. by* Joseph Leftwich. TrJP

Who may this be? Narcissus in Camden. Helen Gray Cone. BXAP

Who might have inhabited the small shoes the small. The Small Shoes (II). Sue Roe. NPo

Who, minter of medallions. Reading a Medal. Terence Tiller. FaBoTw; GTBS-P

Who Misses or Who Wins. Thackeray. SD

Who must be blamed for the young head. The Landscape of the Heart. Geoffrey Grigson. LiTB; WaP

Who nearer Nature's life would truly come. Thoreau. Amos Bronson Alcott. AA

Who needs a raft that can invade the stars? Inscribed on a Painting ("Who needs a raft that can invade the stars?"). Yün Shou-p'ing, *tr. by* Jonathan Chaves. CoBLCP

Who Never Ate with Tears His Bread. Goethe, *tr. fr. German by* Farnsworth Wright. WGRP

Who, now, can speak of gods. The Gods. Dennis Lee. NOBC

Who now dare longer trust thy mother hand? San Francisco. John Vance Cheney. PAH

Who now does follow the foule Blatant Beast. Spenser. *Fr.* The Faerie Queene, VI, 10. OAEL-1

Who now regards Chloris, her tears, and her whining. Advice to the Ladies. William Somervile. FaBoUs

Who, now, seeing Her so. Et in Arcadia Ego. W. H. Auden. CMoP

Who nowadays hears the ancient tune of Ji Peak? Flutist Diviner. Daisen, *tr. by* Lucien Stryk *and* Takashi Ikemoto. ZPCJ

Who often found their way to pleasant meadows. Elegy for Minor Poets. Louis MacNeice. FaBCIP

Who on your breast pillows his head now. The Lost Jewel. Robert Graves. EnLoPo; NYBP

Who or why, or which, or what. The A[h] kond of Swat. Edward Lear. CenHV; FaBoCh; FaBoCo; FaBoNo; FiBHP; NA

Who Ordered That? W. Gregory Stewart. SoTCo

Who owns the land where musket-balls are buried. Richard Murphy. *Fr.* The Battle of Aughrim. IPY

Who owns the moonlit skies, the purple dawn. Owning. Wilmot B. Lane. CaP

Who owns these cattle, Corydon? The Herdsmen. Theocritus, *tr. fr. Greek by* Charles Stuart Calverley. *Fr.* Idylls, IV. AWP

Who owns these scrawny little feet? Death. Examination at the Womb-Door. Ted Hughes. NAEL-2; NAs; OxBC

Who peered from the invisible world. Seven Forbidden Words. Michael Palmer. LP

Who prop, thou ask'st, in these bad days, my mind? To a Friend. Matthew Arnold. NAEL-2; Son

Who puts back into place a fallen bar. The Father's Business. Edwin Markham

Who puts off shift. My Naked Aunt. Archibald MacLeish

Who questions if the punctual sun unbars. William Baylebridge. *Fr.* Love Redeemed, LXXXII. PoAu-1

Who really respects the earthworm. The Earthworm. Harry Edmund Martinson, *tr. by* Robert Bly. RB

Who Reigns? Shelley. *Fr.* Prometheus Unbound. SeCePo, *fr.* II, iv.

Who rides at night, who rides so late? The Invisible King. Goethe, *tr. by* Robert Bly. NU

Who rideth through the driving rain. The King's Son. Thomas Boyd. OBMV

Who rose up like a goddess from the sea. The Museum. William Abrahams. WaP

Who rules the world with iron rod? Tall Hat. Victor Daley. CBAP

Who said, "Peacock Pie"? The Song of the Mad Prince. Walter de la Mare. EBEV; FaBoCh; GoJo; MoP; NoAM; NOBE; OxBChV

Who said the sea's concave. Heishin, *tr. by* Lucien Stryk *and* Takashi Ikemoto. ZPCJ

Who said to the trout. Pisces. R. S. Thomas. OxBC

Who saw the petals. The Secret Song. Margaret Wise Brown. OBCA; PDV; RHPC

Who say we no get beauty for Africa. African Beauty. Taiwo Olaleye-Oruene. AIW

Who say[e]s that fictions onl[e]y and false hair. Jordan. George Herbert. HAP; InPS; JCP; LiTB; MeLP; MePo; NAEL-1; NOCV; NoP; OAEL-1; OBS; PoE; PoEL-2; PPP; SeCP; TEP; TrCP

Who Says. Musa Moris Farhi. VWA

Who Says. Otto Laaber, *tr. fr. German by* Beth Bjorklund. CoAuP

Who says/ the old man/ stayed his hand? Psalm of the Jealous God. Henry Abramovitch. VWA

Who says/ I should wear a skirt. Their Plan. Sista Roots. WS

Who says death is better than sex. Who Says. Musa Moris Farhi. VWA

Who says that death. Who Says. Otto Laaber, *tr. by* Beth Bjorklund. CoAuP

Who says that Giles and Joan at discord be? On Giles and Joan. Ben Jonson. NAEL-1; NOBL; TEP

Who says that in the human world autumn has already gone? Wang Kuo-wei, *tr. by* Irving Lo. WFTU

Who says that in the mountains everything is grand? Huang Tsung-hsi, *tr. fr. Chinese by* Lynn Struve. *Fr.* Songs from Living in the Mountains, II. WFTU

Who says that the river is broad. *Unknown, tr. fr. Chinese by* Arthur Waley. BoS

Who Says the River is Wide? *Unknown, tr. fr. Chinese by* Burton Watson. CoBCP

Who says you have no sheep? *Unknown, tr. fr. Chinese by* Arthur Waley. BoS

Who says you're like one of the dog days? Shall I Compare Thee to a Summer's Day? Howard Moss. InPK

Who seeks perfection in the art. Perfection. Francis Carlin. FaFP

Who seeks the way to win renown. In Praise of Seafaring Men, in Hope of Good Fortune. *Unknown.* OxBSS

Who seeks the way to win renown. In Praise of Seafaring Men, in Hopes of Good Fortune. Sir Richard Grenville. OBTV

Who seeks wisdom in words. Silences. David Mitchell. PeNZ

Who sees him walk the street, can scarce forbear. Marvellous Martin. Charles Harpur. CBAP

Who sees the cross at Christmas? To See the Cross at Christmas. Roger Cooper. TrCP

Who sees you, G, surprises two in one. To Grosphus. Godfrey the Satirist. PeHV

Who serves his country best? The Better Way. "Susan Coolidge." OPP

Who shall console the veiled woman. The Prophecy. Richard Ntiru. UAS

Who Shall Deliver Me? Christina Rossetti. TOF

Who Shall Die. James A. Randall, Jr.. BPo

Who shall doubt, Donne, where [*or* whe'er] I a Poet be[e]. To John Donne. Ben Jonson. JCP; NoP; SeCP; SeCV-1

Who shall have my fair [*or* faire *or* fayre] lady? My Fair Lady. *Unknown.* EnLoPo; PoEL-1

(Under the Leaves Green.) OxBoLi

Who shall I tell of the color rouge? Yosano Akiko, *tr. fr. Japanese by* Hiroaki Sato. *Fr.* Thirty-nine Tanka. FCEI

Who shall invoke when we are gone. Tragic Love. W. J. Turner. OBMV

Who shall speak for the people? Carl Sandburg. *Fr.* The People, Yes, *sec.* 24. OxBA

Who shall tell what did befall. Wealth. Emerson. ImOP

Who shall welcome home. The Hosts. George M. Brady. NeIP

Who Shapes a Balustrade? Conrad Aiken. EyDe

Who Shined Shoes in Times Square. Lance Jeffers. CNA

Who shot the snake? beat it to death on the road? In Memoriam S. L. Akintola. David Knight. MoCV

Who Sleeps by Day and Walks by Night. Henry David Thoreau. PoEL-4

Who smoke-snorts toasts o' My Lady Nicotine. Variations on an Air: After Robert Browning. G. K. Chesterton. FaBoPa; NOBL; Par

   (Old King Cole.) BXAP

Who so late/ at the garden gate. At the Garden Gate. David McCord. FaPON; ILY

Who so valiant to decide? Young Woman at a Window. Mark Van Doren. LiTA

Who sows the seas, or ploughs the easy shore? Woman's Inconstancy. Phineas Fletcher. *Fr.* Sicelides. EIL

Who stands, the crux left of the watershed. The Watershed. W. H. Auden. OAEL-2

Who still believes. Hertha Kräftner, *tr. by* Beth Bjorklund. CoAuP

Who strolls so late, for mugs a bait. French Lisette; a Ballad of Maida Vale. William Plomer. ErPo

"Who stuffed that white owl?" No one spoke in the shop. The Owl-Critic. James Thomas Fields. BLPA; CenHV; OBAL; WBLP

Who stuffed the lark. The Return of the Veil. Salah Niyazi, *tr. by* Abdullah al-Udhari. MPAW

Who take today and jerk it out of joint. Young Africans. Gwendolyn Brooks. NoAM

Who tamed your lawless Tartar blood. To Russia. Cincinnatus Hiner Miller. AA

Who tames the lion now? Lord Alcohol [*or* Song]. Thomas Lovell Beddoes. ViBoPo; WiR

Who telleth a tale of unspeaking death? Shelley. *Fr.* On Death. OBD

Who, then was Cestius. Rome. Thomas Hardy. MoAB

Who Thou art I know not. God the Architect. Harry Hibbard Kemp. WGRP

   (To God, the Architect.) TrPWD

Who thought of the lilac? The Lilac. Humbert Wolfe. FaPON

Who to the North, or South, doth set. Observation. Robert Herrick. FaBoUs

Who tossed those golden coins. Mizumura Kazue. TSS

Who trampled down the ripe raspberry patch? Who Done It? Daniel Hoffman. SoTCo

Who travels by the wearie wandring way. Spenser. *Fr.* The Faerie Queene. OBD

Who travels by the weary wandering way. Despair. Spenser. *Fr.* The Faerie Queene, I, 9. SeCePo

Who understood the storyteller. For Shirley. Denise Panek. GOS

Who used his masterful brush to paint this romantic beauty? T'ang Yin, *tr. fr. Chinese by* Jonathan Chaves. *Fr.* On a Painting of a Woman Shown Half-Length, II. CoBLCP

Who Walks with Beauty. David Morton. BLPA; FaBoBe

Who wants my jellyfish? The Jellyfish. Ogden Nash. FaPON

Who wants to be my lover? St. Valentine. Tu Kuo-ch'ing, *tr. by* Dominic Cheung. IFON

Who was Athena's pet. New Dust. Eleanor Ross Taylor. PPR

Who Was Born Dead. Vicente Aleixandre, *tr. fr. Spanish by* Perry Higman. LPSS

Who was born, not of a virgin but a real woman. Jah Son/ Another Way. Kendel Hippolyte. PVCV

Who Was It Came. Daniel Hoffman. CoAP

Who Was It, Tell Me. Heine, *tr. fr. German by* Richard Garnett. TrJP

   (Sag' Mir Wer Einst die Uhren Erfund.) AWP

Who was it that took away my voice? Silence. Bella Akhmadulina, *tr. by* Daniel Halpern. BoWoP; OV

Who was it who held me on her knee? Mother. Josephine D. Henderson Heard. CBWP-4

Who was responsible for the very first arms deal. Peace. Michael Longley. CIP

Who was this girl. Looking at Pictures to Be Put Away. Gary Snyder. FF; NNaP

Who wd. cope in this Quick. The Web. Gregory O'Donoghue. BIrV

Who weds a sot to get his cot. *Unknown.* FaBoUs

   (Proverbial Advice on Marriage.) NBLV

Who weeps now anywhere in the world. Solemn Hour. Rainer Maria Rilke, *tr. by* C. F. MacIntyre. TrJP

Who Were before Me. John Drinkwater. OBMV

Who were the builders? Question not the silence. Nameless Doon [*or* Dun]. William Larminie. AnIL; BIrV

"Who Wert and Art and Evermore Shalt Be." William Channing Gannett. TrPWD

Who? Who? *Unknown.* CH

Who, who and who? The Dark Lord of Savaiki. Alistair Campbell. PeNZ

"Who—who—the bride will be?" Who? Who? *Unknown.* CH

Who, who will be the next man to entrust his girl to a friend? Ezra Pound. *Fr.* Homage to Sextus Propertius. FaBoMo

"Who will believe my verse in time to come." Shakespeare. *Fr.* Sonnets, XVII. OBSC

Who Will Buy a Poem? Mahon O'Heffernan. *See* I ask, who will buy a poem?

Who Will Endure. W. H. Auden. FaBoPV

   (No Change of Place.) OxBTC

Who Will Give Cover? Anadad Eldan, *tr. fr. Hebrew.* VWA, *tr. by* Ruth Nevo

Who will go drive with Fergus now. Who Goes with Fergus? W. B. Yeats. CMoP; FaBoCh; GoJo; InPK; MoP; NAEL-2; NoAM; NOBE; NOBVV; PoE; PoRA

"Who will in fairest book of Nature know." Sir Philip Sidney. *Fr.* Astrophel and Stella, LXXI. InPS; NAEL-1; NoP; OAEL-1; PoE

Who will last? And what? The wind will stay. 1974. Abraham Sutskever, *tr. fr. Yiddish by* Cynthia Ozick. *Fr.* Poems from a Diary. PeBMYV

Who Will Live in Our Houses When We Die? Michael C. Blumenthal. NoAM

"Who will pay for the milk I gave you?" Let Me Go. *Gond Oral Tradition, tr. by* V. Elwin *and* S. Hivale. WTO

Who will remember, passing through this gate. On Passing the New Menin Gate. Siegfried Sassoon. NAEL-2; NoAM; OBMV; Son

Who will say a word for a country town of a sultry summer night. Not without Beauty. John A. B. McLeish. CaP

Who Will Shoe Your Pretty Little Foot? *Unknown.* AS

Who will show us where. At the Doors. Der Nistor, *tr. by* Joseph Leftwich. TrJP

Who Will Stop His Hand from Giving Warmth. Alejandra Pizarnik, *tr. fr. Spanish by* Alina Rivero. VWA

Who will take away. Spell against Sorrow. Kathleen Jessie Raine. PBWP

Who winds the clumsy flower clock now, I wonder. Heavy Heavy Heavy. John Malcolm Brinnin. NYBP

Who with the soldiers was stanch danger-sharer. The Daughter of the Regiment. Clinton Scollard. PAH

Who with thy leaves shall wipe (at need). To His Book[e]. Robert Herrick. FaBoUs; JCP

Who Wot Nowe That Ys Here. *Unknown.* InPS

Who would/ who could. Now Ain't That Love? Carolyn M. Rodgers. BPo

Who would be/ A mermaid fair. The Mermaid. Tennyson. BoTP, *abr.*; FaPON; GN; WSC

Who would be/ A merman bold. The Merman. Tennyson. BoTP, *abr.*; FaPON; GN; WSC

Who would care to pass his life away. Lotos Eating. Mortimer Collins. NOBVV

Who would ever have thought without this love from you. Dawn. Louis Aragon, *tr. by* Lou Lipsitz *and* Jean Gillou. POS

Who Would Have Said It. Alfredo Giuliani, *tr. fr. Italian by* Lawrence R. Smith. NItP

Who Would Have Thought. Thomas Howell. *Fr.* The Lover Deceived Writes to His Lady. EIL

Who would have thought that a disease of the ordinary world. Hsü Chung-hsing, *tr. fr. Chinese by* Jonathan Chaves. *Fr.* Inquiring about the Health of Li Te-hua. CoBLCP

Who would I show it to. W. S. Merwin. HCAP

Who Would List. *Unknown, tr. fr. French by* Andrew Lang. *Fr.* Aucassin and Nicolette. CTC

Who would live in others' breath? Epitaph: Iohannis Sande. Thomas Bastard. FaBoEE

Who would not be. The Laureate. William Edmonstoune Aytoun. BXAP; Par

Who would suspect, or even know. A Vegetable, I Will Not Be. Donna Whitewing. NOVW

Who would true valour see. Bunyan. *Fr.* The Pilgrim's Progress. EBEV

   (Pilgrim, The.) BoTP; GN

   (Pilgrim Song, The.) CoMu; ELP; NOCV; OBS

   (Pilgrim's Song, The.) WiR

   (To Be a Pilgrim, *sl. diff. vers.*) FaPoR

Who wouldn't want such a bed? Woman Asleep on a Banana Leaf. Katha Pollitt. InPS

Who wrote *Who wrote Icon Basilike? On ["Who Wrote Icon Basilike" by Dr.] Christopher Wordsworth, Master of Trinity.* Benjamin Hall Kennedy. FaBoCo; FaBoEE

Who'd Be a Hero (Fictional)? Morris Bishop. FiBHP; OBAL

Who'd believe me if. The Third Dimension. Denise Levertov. NeAP

Who'd dare read in that. In Praise of the Lowest Line. János Pilinszky, *tr. by* Jascha Kessler. FOC

Who'd ever think that Utah would stir the world so much? Marching to Utah. *Unknown.* AmFP

Who'd have thought it? Shunzei, *tr. fr. Japanese by* Burton Watson. *Fr.* Thirty Tanka. FCEI

Whoe'er he be that to a taste aspires. James Bramston. *Fr.* The Man of Taste.

Whoe'er [*or* Who e'er *or* Who ere] she[e] be[e]. Wishes to His Supposed Mistress[e]. Richard Crashaw. BoLoP; EBEV; MeLP; MePo; OBEV; PoEL-2; SeCP; SeCV-1
(Wishes for the Supposed Mistress[e].) GTBS; GTBS-P

Whoe'er this book, if lost, doth find. *Unknown.* FaBoUs

Whoe'er thou art whose path in summer lies. Mark Akenside. NOEC

Whoever coined the phrase *The Body Politic*? Talking to Myself. W. H. Auden. OBD

Whoever colored the moon tonight didn't stay. A Visit to the Farm. Robert Siegel. GeTw

Whoever [*or* Who ever] comes to shroud me, do not harm[e]. The Funeral[l]. John Donne. AWP; BoLoP; EBEV; EnLoPo; HeIP; MeLP; NAEL-1; NAWM-1; NoP; OAEL-1; OBEV; OBS; PoEL-2; PoRA; SeCP; SeCV-1

Whoever despises the clitoris despises the penis. The Speed of Darkness. Muriel Rukeyser. GLP; LCAP

Whoever [*or* Who ever] guesses, thinks, or dream[e]s he know[e]s. The Curse. John Donne. TW

Whoever has a yod in his name. Bella and the Golem. Rossana Ombres, *tr. by* Edgar Pauk. VWA

Whoever has followed the bag lady. Three Journeys. Edward Hirsch. NAmP

Whoever has heard of St. Gingo. The New Cecilia. Thomas Lovell Beddoes. OAEL-2

Whoever has not choked on a word. Truly. Ingeborg Bachmann, *tr. by* Susan L. Cocalis. DMG

"Whoever hath her wish, thou hast thy Will." Shakespeare. *Fr.* Sonnets, CXXXV. NAEL-1; OAEL-1

Whoever hath washed his hands of living. Courage. Sadi, *tr. fr. Persian by* Sir Edwin Arnold. *Fr.* The Gulistan. AWP

Whoever in this tavern. Mohammad Taqi Mir, *tr. by* Ahmed Ali. GoT

Whoever intends to wage war in the jungle. Tamborillo. Mario Payeras, *tr. by* Barbara Paschke. VoI

Whoever is washed ashore at that place. Legend. Ralph Gustafson. CaP

Whoever is without a home. Hosanna. Heidi Pataki, *tr. by* Beth Bjorklund. CoAuP

Whoever it was who brought the first wood and coal. Banking Coal. Jean Toomer. PoNe

Whoever loves, if he do not propose. Love's Progress. John Donne. *Fr.* Elegies, XVIII. LiTB; OAEL-1

Whoever may by chance or of necessity. Envoi to Poem to the Virgin. Laura Terracina, *tr. by* Muriel Kittel. DMI

Whoever safely went. Mohammad Taqi Mir, *tr. by* Ahmed Ali. GoT

Whoever to finding fault inclines. The Cynic. St. George Tucker. OBAL

Whoever weeps somewhere out in the world. Silent Hour. Rainer Maria Rilke, *tr. by* Jessie Lemont. AWP

Whoever without money is in love. Of Why He Is Unhanged. Cecco Angiolieri da Siena, *tr. by* Dante Gabriel Rossetti. PFI
(Sonnet: Of Why He Is Unhanged.) AWP

Whoever you are, got out into the evening. Initiation. Rainer Maria Rilke, *tr. by* C. F. MacIntyre. TrJP

Whoever You Are Holding Me Now in Hand. Walt Whitman. InvP; NAAL-1; PoEL-1

Whole and without Blessing. Linda Gregg. MAYP; NPGG

Whole Armour of God, The. Charles Wesley. NOCV

Whole church got hot and vivid, The. The Gift of Tongues. Robert Morgan. MT

Whole day long, under the walking sun, The. The Sleeping Giant. Donald Hall. GrPl; NePoEA; NYBP; Psk; TwCP

Whole day's light is not enough, The. Masuhito. *Fr.* Manyo Shu. Ma

Whole Duty of Children. Robert Louis Stevenson. FaBoUs; NBLV; OxBChV

Whole field of poppies billowed, my beloved, The. A Farewell Ballad of Poppies. Eva Brudne. VWA

Whole heap of nickles and a whole heap of dimes, A. Shout, Little Lulu. *Unknown.* AmFP

Whole idea of sanity is intriguing, The. Greedy Seasons. Eileen Myles. UL

Whole landscape drifted away to the north, The. A Window on the North. Robert Arthur Douglas Ford. MoCV

Whole morning I gathered green, The. *Unknown, tr. by* Arthur Waley. BoS

Whole night through, A. Vigil. Giuseppe Ungaretti, *tr. by* Charles Tomlinson. PFI
(Watch, Cima Quattro.) OBD, *tr. by* Patrick Creagh.

Whole process is a lie, The. The Ivy Crown. William Carlos Williams. NAAL-2; NoAM; NoP; PrIm

Whole royal family was living in one room at that time, The. The End of a Dynasty. Zbigniew Herbert, *tr. by* Czeslaw Milosz. FaBoPV; PwPP

Whole Story, The. William Stafford. NNaP

Whole town has come into my room, The. Horizon. Philippe Soupault, *tr. by* Rosmarie Waldrop. POS; RHTwFP

Whole towns shut down. The Late Snow and Lumber Strike of the Summer of Fifty-four. Gary Snyder. NaP

Whole Treasure of All Wordly Bliss, The. Charles, Duc d' Orléans. OxBLMV

Whole tribe dies, A. Duane Big Eagle. STE

Whole universe is full of God, The. Yunus Emre, *tr. by* W. S. Merwin *and* Talat Sait Halman. LLLT

Whole village, The. *Unknown, tr. by* Geoffrey Bownas *and* Anthony Thwaite. PeBJV

Whole villages come. Piarco. Eric Roach. PVCV

Whole weight of history bears down, The. The Awful Mother. Susan Griffin. NPGG

Whole weight of the ocean smashes on rock, The. An Address to the Vacationers at Cape Lookout. William Stafford. NYBP

Whole white world is ours, The. White World. Hilda Doolittle ("H. D."). LLLT

Whole world, The. Cache la Poudre. James Galvin. AnAn

Whole world here, leavened with madness, swells, The. Ben Jonson. *Fr.* An Epistle to a Friend, to Persuade Him to the Wars. JCP

Whole World Now, The. Robert Bridges. *Fr.* The Growth of Love, III. Son

Wholehearted he can't move. The Eye Is More or Less Satisfied with Seeing. Allen Curnow. ATNZ

Wholesome. William Meredith. TAP

Who'll be the lover of that woman on the bench? No Thank You. John Skoyles. NAmP

Who'll buy my laces? I've laces to sell! The Lace Pedlar. Catherine A. Morin. BoTP

Who'll have the crumpled pieces of a heart? Laurana's Song. Richard Hovey. AA; AnAmPo

Who'll Help a Fairy? *Unknown.* BoTP

Who'll marry me? Cold Saturday. Will he leave me? Questions and Answers. Diana O Hehir. NPGG

Who'll walk the fields with us to town? Market Day. Mary Webb. CH

Wholly drunk, I see only. Wakayama Bokusui, *tr. fr. Japanese by* Hiroaki Sato. *Fr.* Forty-four Tanka. FCEI

Whom are you carrying. João Cabral de Melo Neto, *tr. fr. Portuguese by* Elizabeth Bishop. *Fr.* The Death and Life of a Severino, II. ATCBP

Whom first we love, you know, we seldom wed. Changes. Robert Bulwer-Lytton. PoLF

Whom I lay down for dead rises up in blood. In All the Argosy of Your Bright Hair. Dunstan Thompson. WaP

"Whom I shall kiss," I heard a Sunbeam say. Betrayal. John Banister Tabb. ACP

Whom Jesus Loved. John Barford. PeHV

Whom might this shipwrecked man most wish to meet. Odysseus in Phaeacia. Gábor Devecseri, *tr. by* Robert Graves. MHuP

Whom Shall One Teach. Bible, *O.T. Fr.* Isaiah, XXVIII: 9–13. TrJP

Whom the Gods Love. Margaret E. Bruner. PoLF

Whom the Gods Love. Mark Antony De Wolfe Howe. AA

"Whom the Gods Love die young" I used to quote. Whom the Gods Love. Margaret E. Bruner. PoLF

"Whom the Gods Love due young"—if Gods ye be. Whom the Gods Love. Mark Antony De Wolfe Howe. AA

Whom thus answer'd th' Arch Fiend now undisguis'd. Satan's Guile. ("Whom thus answer'd th' Arch Fiend now undisguis'd"). Milton. *Fr.* Paradise Regained, *bk.* I, *ll.* 357-405. LiTB; OBS

Whom when I saw assembled in such wise. Virgil, *tr. fr. Latin, tr. by* the Earl of Surrey. *Fr.* The Aeneid [*or* Eneados], II. PoE

Whon men beth muriest at her mele. All Turns into Yesterday. *Unknown.* MeEL

Whoop! the Doodles have broken loose. "Call All." *Unknown.* PAH

Whoopee-Ti-Yi-Yo. *Unknown.* AS, *with music;* FaPON (Git Along, Little Dogies.) MoShBr

Whoops! *Unknown.* FaFP; NTCP; RHPC

Whore that rides in us abides, The. *Unknown.* SCAP

Who's aware of mutability? Daitetsu, *tr. by* Lucien Stryk *and* Takashi Ikemoto. ZPCJ

Who's been squashing Billy Ray Smith? Billy Ray Smith. Ogden Nash. ASP

Who's In. Elizabeth Fleming. BoTP; RHPC

Who's in the Next Room? Thomas Hardy. PoEL-5; QFR; WSC

Who's killed the leaves? Leaves. Ted Hughes. OxBC

Who's Most Afraid of Death? Thou. E. E. Cummings. CMoP; PoE; VGW

Who's on First? Lloyd Schwartz. PPR

Who's That A-Knocking? Emile Jacot. BoTP

Who's that knocking on the window. Innocent's Song. Charles Causley. GTBS-P; OBCP

Who's that mysterious rider. The Horseman on the Skyline. Henry Lawson. CBAP

Who's that ringing at my door bell? *Unknown.* FaBoCh; OxNR

Who's that ringing at our door-bell? That Little Black Cat. D'Arcy Wentworth Thompson. OxBChV

"Who's that ringing at the front door bell?" *Unknown.* BoTP

"Who's that tickling my back?" said the wall. The Tickle Rhyme. Ian Serraillier. NTCP; OnUR; PYC; RHPC

Who's the Dover-based day tripper. A Trifle for Trafalgar Day. Ted Pauker. NOBL

Who's the most important man this country ever knew? Barney Google. Billy Rose. OBAL

Who's the Pretty Girl Milkin' the Cow? *Unknown.* AS

Who's there? Hamlet. Shakespeare. NAWM-1

Who's Who. W. H. Auden. MoAB; MoBrPo; MoP; NoAM; Son

Whose broken window is a cry of art. Boy Breaking Glass. Gwendolyn Brooks. AiP; MoP; NAAL-2; NoAM; NoP

Whose candles light the tulip tree? Tulip Tree. Sacheverell Sitwell. MoBrPo

Whose cherry tree did young George chop? Mingled Yarns. X. J. Kennedy. OBCA

Whose fault is it that your tree can't be seen. In Central Park. Moyshe-Leyb Halpern, *tr. by* John Hollander. PeBMYV

Whose freedom is by suff'rance, and at will. William Cowper. *Fr.* The Task, V. EnRP

Whose furthest footstep never strayed. Richard Hovey. *Fr.* More Songs from Vagabondia. AA

Whose Hand. *Unknown, tr. fr. Hebrew by* Arthur Davis. TrJP

Whose headless body is this. Beirut. Ahmad Faraz, *tr. by* Mahmood Jamal. PBMUP

"Whose husband this time." *Unknown. Fr.* Manyo Shu. FCEI

Whose is that noble dauntless brow? Verses Intended to Be Written below a Noble Earl's Picture. Burns. HoPM

Whose is the river, Excellency, whose the fish. The Geographers. Karl Shapiro. OxBA

Whose is this horrifying face. Ecce Homo. David Gascoyne. *Fr.* Miserere. LiTM; OBWP

Whose little beast? Donkey. Mark Van Doren. EaLo

Whose little pigs are these, these, these? *Unknown.* OxNR

Whose love is given over-well. Partial Comfort. Dorothy Parker. FaBoCo; OBAL; OBD

"Whose man goes." *Unknown. Fr.* Manyo Shu. PeBJV

Whose minds like horse or ox. The Learned Men. Archibald MacLeish. MoAB

Whose Scene? Ruth Stone. BoWoP

Whose Voice. Barney Bush. STE

Whose Window? Alison Brackenbury. DiPo

Whose woods these are I think I know. Stopping by Woods on a Snowy Evening. Robert Frost. AmPP; BoNaP; CMoP; FaBoCh; FaBV; FaFP; FaPON; FF; FPL; GoJo; GrPl; HAP; HeIP; HoPM; InPK; InPS; LiTA; LiTM; MoAB; MoAmPo; MoP; MoShBr; NAAL-2; NIP; NoAM; NOBA; NoP; NTCP; OBCA; OxBA; PDV; PoE; PoRA; PrIm; PYC; RB; RHPC; SCV; SoSe; TAP; TOF; TTTS

Whoso answers my questions. All or Nothing. Bayard Taylor. BXAP

Whoso Gives Freely, Shall Freely Receive! Josephine D. Henderson Heard. CBWP-4

Whoso in harvest mindeth to reap. To His Child. William Bullokar. OxBChV

Whoso in love would bear the bell. Ballad[e] of Ladies' Love, Number Two. Villon, *tr. by* John Payne. ErPo

Whoso list to hunt, I know where is an hind. Whoso List to Hunt [I Know Where Is an Hind]. Sir Thomas Wyatt. AAS; BoLoP; EBEV; GBL; HAP; InvP; NAEL-1; NoP; OAEL-1; OBVE; PoE; PoEL-1; PrIm (Sonnet: "Whoso list to hunt, I know where is an hind.") SiPS

Whoso maintains that I am humbled now. Epitaph for a Reviewer. Frances Cornford. OBD

Whoso thou art that passest by this place. An Epitaph of Maister Win Drowned in the Sea. George Turberville. FaBoEE

Whoso to marry a minion wife. A Minion Wife. Nicholas Udall. *Fr.* Ralph Roister Doister. EIL

Whoso walks in solitude. Emerson. *Fr.* Woodnotes II ("As sunbeams stream through liberal space"). NOBA

Whoso Would See This Song of Heavenly Choice. John Wilson. AH

"Who've ye got there?" "Only a dying brother." "The Brigade Must Not Know, Sir!" *Unknown.* PAH

Whsst, and away, and over the green. Nothing. Walter de la Mare. WSC

Whummil Bore, The. *Unknown.* CH; ESPB

"Whu's aw thae fflag-poles ffur in Princess Street?" Heard in the Cougate. Robert Garioch. OxBTC

Whut do i keer ef de white-folks do 'buse us! Uncle Rube's Defense. Clara Ann Thompson. CBWP-2

Why. Yusuf al-Sa'igh, *tr. fr. Arabic by* Diana Der Hovanessian *with* Salma Khadra Jayyusi. MAP

Why? Melba Joyce Boyd. BlSi

Why? Richard Augustine Chima. WMBCH

Why? Stephen Crane. *Fr.* The Black Riders, XXV. AA

Why,/ you. Double-barreled Ding-Dong-Bat. Dennis Lee. RHPC

Why? A. Leyeles, *tr. fr. Yiddish by* Benjamin *and* Barbara Harshav. AYP

Why/ do/ you/ sigh. Post-Coitum Tristesse: A Sonnet. Brad Leithauser. EOEF

Why/ Is the sky? Questions at Night. Louis Untermeyer. FaPON

Why. Michael Ryan. PPR

Why? *Unknown, tr. fr. Hebrew. Fr.* The Talmud. TrJP

Why? Walter de la Mare. FiBHP

Why Adam Sinned. Alex Rogers. BANP

Why all the racket, you chattering birds? *Unknown, tr. by* Thomas Meyer. PeHV

Why am I first in thy so sad regard. Twilight. Robert Frost. AnAmPo

Why am I going away from the glass of wine. Who. Philip Levine. KS

Why am I so halfhearted, so doubtful. Ten Thousand Nations. József Tornai, *tr. by* Jascha Kessler. FOC

Why am I tired of this life? To Stay Alive. Paul Snoek, *tr. by* Claire Nicolas White. DuIn

Why and Wherefore set out one day. Metaphysics. Oliver Herford. NA

Why are candles brightly burning. The Christmas Tree. Lizelia Augusta Jenkins Moorer. CBWP-3

Why Are Daddies So Mean? Jane Chambers. GLP

Why are our ancestors. Ancestors. Dudley Randall. BPo; CNA

Why are saints so difficult to recognize. Sainthood. Cristoir O'Flynn. TIRV

Why are some icicles long, some short? Onitsura, *tr. fr. Japanese by* Hiroaki Sato. *Fr.* Twenty-three Hokku. FCEI

Why are the public buildings so high? W. H. Auden. FaBoCo

Why are the things that have no death. Irony. Louis Untermeyer. TrJP

Why are these pipples taking their hets off? E. E. Cummings. FiBHP

Why are those tears? Why droops your head? The Farmer's Wife and the Raven. John Gay. PBBP

Why are we[e] by all creatures waited on? John Donne. *Fr.* Holy Sonnets, XII. JCP; NOCV; OBS; PoE; PoEL-2; TrCP

Why are women so energetic? Energetic Women. D. H. Lawrence. InPS

Why are ye wandering aye 'twixt porch and porch. Arcades Ambo. Charles Stuart Calverley. BXAP

Why are you dragged to be stoned? Why? *Unknown, tr. fr. Hebrew. Fr.* The Talmud. TrJP

Why are you leaving. Song of Farewell. Nellie Wong. BrSi

Why are you waiting? The squirrel in the pine tree. Eugenio Montale, *tr. fr. Italian. Fr.* The Motets, X. Dana Gioia

"Why are your eyes as big as saucers—big as saucers?" Man in the Street. Robert Penn Warren. OBAL

Why Art Thou Silent. Speak! Wordsworth. OBEV

Why art thou silent and invisible. To Nobodaddy. Blake. OAEL-2

Why art thou slow, thou rest of trouble, Death. Death Invoked. Philip Massinger. *Fr.* The Emperor of the East. ACP (Sad Song, A.) OBS

Why be afraid of death, as though your life were breath? Emancipation. Maltbie Davenport Babcock. BLRP; WBLP (Death.) WGRP

Why be so proud of this useless, used-up body? Kabir, *tr. by* John Stratton Hawley *and* Mark Juergensmeyer. SSI

"Why?" Because all I haply can and do. Why I Am a Liberal. Robert Browning. Son

Why blush, dear girl, pray tell me why? On Seeing a Lady's Garter. *Unknown.* ErPo

Why boast we, Glaucus! our extended reign. Homer, *tr. fr. Greek by* Pope. *Fr.* The Iliad, XII. OBVE

Why boastest thou thyself in mischief, O mighty man? Psalm LII ("Why boastest thou thyself in mischief. . ."). Bible, *O.T.* *Fr.* Psalms. (Psalm LII: "Tyrant, why swel'st thou thus", *paraphrased by* the Countess of Pembroke) OBVE

Why Brownlee Left. Paul Muldoon. DiPo

Why, by an ingrained habit, elevate. With the Grain. Donald Davie. NoAM

Why call it dead, wi' life a-vled. All Still. William Barnes. NOBVV

Why call the miser miserable? Byron. *Fr.* Don Juan, XII. UnPo

Why came I so untimely forth. To a Very Young Lady. Edmund Waller. OBS; SeCP; TrGrPo (To a Girl.) WiR (To My Young Lady, Lucy Sidney.) MePo

Why cannot we eat enough for a week. Envying the Pelican. Richard Weber. CIP

Why Can't I Leave You? Ai. AmPA; GeTw

Why cherish thus the senseless thing? That Glove. Mary E. Tucker. CBWP-1

Why, Chloe, thus squander your prime. A Logical Song. *Unknown.* ErPo

Why climb the mountains? I will tell you why. How Small Is Man. John Stuart Blackie. PoSH

Why come ye hither, stranger, your mind what madness fills? Rifleman's Song at Bennington. Joseph Rodman Drake. PAH

Why Come Ye Not to Court, *sel.* John Skelton. "Such a prelate, I trow." OBSV

Why, Damon, with the forward day. The Dying Man in His Garden. George Sewell. GTBS; GTBS-P

Why, Death, what dost thou here. On One Who Died in May. Clarence Chatham Cook. AA

Why did all manly gifts in Webster fail? Emerson. GOA

Why did I laugh tonight? No voice will tell. Keats. TEP

Why did I let things go this far? Stone Song (Zen Rock) the Seer & the Unbeliever. Karoniaktatie. STE

Why did my parents send me to the schools. Nosce Teipsum. Sir John Davies. SiPS, *complete.*

Why did [*or* do] I write? what sin to me unknown. Pope. *Fr.* Epistle from Mr. Pope to Dr. Arbuthnot. ChTr, *short sel.;* EBEV; FiP; TOF

Why did that have to be the only answer? It's true. Abelardo Sanchez Leon, *tr. by* David Tipton. Per

"Why did the children,." Carl Sandburg. *Fr.* The People, Yes, *sec.* 41. OBAL

Why did the sun his beams conceal. The Crucifixion. Mary Weston Fordham. CBWP-2

Why did those people laugh? Memory of Pinks. Kitahara Hakushu, *tr. by* Hiroaki Sato. FCEI

Why did you give me not that night. The Going. Thomas Hardy. EBEV; ELP; LiTB; NOBE; UnPo

Why Did You Go. E. E. Cummings. VGW

Why did you hate to be by yourself. As to Being Alone. James Oppenheim. TrJP

Why did you have to die? Elegy to Li Shuang-tse. Chiang Hsun, *tr. by* Dominic Cheung. IFON

Why did you kiss the girl who cried. What the Earth Asked Me. James Wright. NYBP

Why did you lay there asleep. Fragment from "Clemo Uti—the Water Lilies." Ring Lardner. FiBHP

"Why did you melt your waxen man." Sister Helen. Dante Gabriel Rossetti. BeLS

Why did your spirit. Ark Astonished. Jay Macpherson. *Fr.* The Ark. NOBC

"Why didst thou promise such a beauteous day." Shakespeare. *Fr.* Sonnets, XXXIV. OBSC

"Why do/ You thus devise." Susanna and the Elders. Adelaide Crapsey. WPE

Why do I carry, she said. Road 1940. Sylvia Townsend Warner. CN

Why do I deny manna to another? Sather Gate Illumination. Allen Ginsberg. NeAP

Why Do I Live? George Linnaeus Banks. *See* I live for those who love me.

Why do I post my love letters. Why Don't You Talk to Me? Alistair Campbell. ATNZ; PeNZ

Why do I sleep amid the snows. Roger Williams. Hezekiah Butterworth. PAH

Why do men smile when I speak. Is It Because I Am Black? Joseph Seamon Cotter, Jr. BANP

Why do people sit in darkness as regards the Negro race? The Truth Suppressed. Lizelia Augusta Jenkins Moorer. CBWP-3

Why do poets/ Like to die. More Letters Found near a Suicide. Frank Horne. BANP

Why do the bells for Christmas ring? Christmas Song. *At. to* Eugene Field. BoTP; OHIP

Why do the Graces now desert the Muse? Walter Savage Landor. FaBoEE

Why do the heathen rage. Psalm II ("Why do the heathen rage.") Bible, *O.T.* *Fr.* Psalms. NAAL-1, *paraphrased by* Edward Taylor. (Psalm II: "Why do the Gentiles tumult", *paraphrased by* Milton) OBVE

Why do the lilies goggle their tongues at me. Grotesque. Amy Lowell. BoWoP

Why do the sun rays laugh across the swamp? Huda Na mani, *tr. fr. Arabic by* Lena Jayyusi. *Fr.* To You, I. MAP

Why do we draw the chains tight across thousands of miles? The Suitcases. Abd al-Karim Kassid, *tr. by* Lena Jayyusi *and* Anthony Thwaite. MAP

Why do we fear words? Love Song for Words. Nazik al-Mala'ika, *tr. by* Matthew Sorenson *and* Christopher Middleton. MAP

Why do we grumble because a tree is bent. Variety. *Yoruba Oral Tradition, tr. by* E. Lasebikan. WTO

Why Do We Live? Israel Zangwill. TrJP

Why Do We Love. Sir Benjamin Rudyerd. EiL

Why Do We Mourn Departing Friends? Isaac Watts. AH

Why do we return? Not in the darkened rooms. Roy Fuller. *Fr.* Ghost Voice. OBD

Why do we waste so much time in arguing? Sushi. Paul Muldoon. CIP

Why do [*or* doe] ye weep, sweet babes? To Primroses Filled with Morning Dew. Robert Herrick. OBS; SeCV-1; ViBoPo

Why do you/ still write. Speechless. Erich Fried, *tr. by* Beth Bjorklund. CoAuP

Why do you always dress in gray? Change of Color. Kathinka Zitz-Halein, *tr. by* Susan L. Cocalis *and* Gerlinde Geiger. DMG

Why do you cry out, why do I like to hear you. Sound of Breaking. Conrad Aiken. AWP

Why do you dig like long-clawed scavengers. Verlaine. E. A. Robinson. NAAL-2

Why do you dwell so long in clouds. Song to the Masquers. James Shirley. *Fr.* The Triumph of Peace. OxBSP

Why do you hide, O dryads! when we seek. Chant for Reapers. Wilfrid Thorley. OBEV

Why do you hold the flag so high. Changing of the Guard. Charles G. Ballard. NOVW

Why do you lean beside the window, Will? Schoolroom: 158– James E. Warren, Jr. GoYe

Why do you lie with your legs ungainly huddled. The Dug-out. Siegfried Sassoon. CH; MoBrPo; OHIP; WaaP; WaP

Why do you look so gloomy, Naevolus? Juvenal, *tr. fr. Latin.* *Fr.* Satires, IX. PeHV

Why do you love her? Questions [1]. Donald Hall. FF

Why do you play such dreary music. Radio. Frank O'Hara. PoA

Why do you stand at the window like that? I Say to Myself. Moyshe-Leyb Halpern, *tr. by* Leonard Wolf. PeBMYV

"Why do you stand so silent." Jacob Studies "The Selling of Joseph" with His Sons. Itzig Manger, *after Genesis 37-50, tr. by* Leonard Wolf. PeBMYV

Why do you talk so much. For Robert Frost. Galway Kinnell. NOBA; VGW

Why Do You Want to Suffer Less. David Fisher. NPGG

"Why do you wear your hair like a man?" After Dilettante Concetti. Henry Duff Traill. BXAP; CenHV; FaBoCo; Par

Why do you wrap your wisdom in a multitude of words? I Ask My Teachers. Sister Mary Madeleva. *Fr.* Concerning Death. CRP

Why Do You Write about Russia? Louis Simpson. InPS; LCAP

Why? doan't I pay me car-fare? A Market Basket in the Car. Thomas MacDermot. PVCV

Why doe not all fresh maids appeare. Upon the Death of His Sparrow; an Elegie. Robert Herrick. FM

Why does he keep bruising against me my dead father why still. Sestina with Refrain. Thomas W. Shapcott. CBAP

Why Does It Snow? Laura Elizabeth Richards. OBCA

Why does my husband beat me? Poor Me. *Unknown, tr. by* Richard Beaumont. ErPo

Why does no one say, "Pitiful!" Saigyo, tr. fr. Japanese by Burton Watson. Fr. Sixty-four Tanka. FCEI

Why does the poets abuse us, we that are seamen's poor wives? The Seamen's Wives' Vindication. Unknown. OxBSS

Why does the raven cry aloud and no eye pities her? The Lamentation of Enion. Blake. Fr. Vala; or The Four Zoas, The Four Zoas. OBNC

Why does the sea burn? Why do the hills cry? Zaydee. Philip Levine. CAPP; NNaP; VWA

Why does the sea moan evermore? By the Sea. Christina Rossetti. BoNaP; MOS; NOBVV

Why does the thin grey strand. Sorrow. D. H. Lawrence. CMoP; GTBS-P; OBD; OBMV

Why does the wind so want to be. The Wind. Elizabeth Rendall. BoTP

"Why [or Quhy] does [or dois/ your brand sae [or so] drop wi' blude [or drap wi bluid]." Edward [or Edward, Edward]. Unknown. AmFP; CH; EBEV; ELP; EnRP; ESPB; FaBoBa; FaPoR; GoTS; HAP; HoPM; InPK; InPS; LiTB; Mes; NAEL-1; NOBE; NoP; OBEV; OxBB; OxBS; PoEL-1; PoRA; PrIm; SoSe; TrGrPo; TW; WeW

Why does your name continue. Sa'di Yusuf, tr. fr. Arabic by Sargon Boulus and Naomi Shihab Nye. Fr. Three Dispositions Regarding One Woman, I. MAP

"Why doesn't somebody buy me false ears?" From the Joke Shop. Roy Fuller. OxBC

Why don't I write in the language of air? Mona Sa'udi, tr. by Kamal Boullata. WPOW

Why don't people leave off being lovable. Elemental. D. H. Lawrence. NoP

Why Don't They Go Back to Transylvania? Robert Peters. VVA

Why don't we rock the casket here in the moonlight? The Pale Blue Casket. Oliver Pitcher. PoBA; TTY

Why don't we start all over again. Genesis. Jacob Glatstein, tr. by Cynthia Ozick. PeBMYV

Why Don't You Talk to Me? Alistair Campbell. ATNZ; PeNZ

Why don't you write you never. Dear Reader. Peter Meinke. Psk

Why dost thou hail with songful lips no more. Memnon. Clinton Scollard. AA

Why dost thou haste away? Sir Philip Sidney. Fr. Arcadia. OBSC; SiPS

Why dost thou shade thy lovely face? O why. To His Mistress. Earl of Rochester. OBEV

Why dost Thou shade thy lovely face? Oh why. Francis Quarles. See: Wherefore Hidest Thou Thy Face, and Holdest Me For Thine Enemie?

Why dost thou so explore. Homer, tr. fr. Greek by George Chapman. Fr. The Iliad, VI. OBVE

Why doth heaven bear a sun. Barnabe Barnes. Fr. Parthenophil and Parthenophe. EIL; OBSC

Why Doubt God's Word? Albert Benjamin Simpson. BLRP

Why drink, why touch you now? If it will be. John Hollander. Fr. Sonnets for Roseblush. SM

Why each is striving, from of old. Destiny. Sir Edwin Arnold. NOBVV; OxBSP

Why English Is So Hard. Unknown. FaBoUs

Why fadest thou in death. R. W. Dixon. ChTr

Why Fear to Die? Sir Philip Sidney. Fr. Arcadia. SiPS

Why fearest thou thy outward foe. That Each Thing Is Hurt of Itself. Unknown. EIL

Why Flowers Change Color. Robert Herrick. HAP

Why from the danger did mine eyes not start. Sonnet: Of His Pain from a New Love. Guido Cavalcanti, tr. by Dante Gabriel Rossetti. AWP

Why God Permits Evil: For Answers to This Question of Interest to Many Write Bible Answers Dept. E-7. Miller Williams. MT; SM

Why has our poetry eschewed. Food and Drink. Louis Untermeyer. MoAmPo

Why hast thou breathed, O God, upon my thoughts. The Poet. Angela Morgan. PoPo; TrPWD, abr.; WGRP

Why Hast Thou Forsaken Me? Chad Walsh. Fr. The Psalm of Christ. TrCP

Why hast thou nothing in thy face? Eros. Robert Bridges. CMoP; LiTB; NOBE; PoEL-5; QFR

Why have crowds as magnets drawn. Why We Meet. Lizelia Augusta Jenkins Moorer. CBWP-3

Why have I locked myself inside. John Hollander. EOEF

Why have such scores of lovely, gifted girls. A Slice of Wedding Cake. Robert Graves. BoLoP; NAEL-2; NOBE; OxBTC

Why have these dead birds. Dead Birds. Rutger Kopland, tr. by Ria Leigh-Loohuizen. DuIn

Why have they moved me. O Hada Cibernetica. Carlos German Belli, tr. by Maureen Ahern and David Tipton. Per

Why have ye no reuthe on my child? Mary Suffers with Her Son. Unknown. MeEL

Why have you come to the shining cliffs. The Knight without a Name. Unknown. WiR

Why Have You No Ruth? Unknown. OxBSP

Why have you risen, to stand with naked feet. With the Dawn. Thomas Caulfield Irwin. BIrV; EnLoPo

Why, having won her, do I woo? The Married Lover. Coventry Patmore. Fr. The Angel in the House, II, xii. OBEV; TrGrPo

Why He Was There. E. A. Robinson. CMoP; NOBA

Why here, on this third planet from the sun. Tellus. William Reed Huntington. AA

Why hoard your maidenhead? There'll not be found. Asclepiades, tr. by R. A. Furness. OBD

Why I Am a Liberal. Robert Browning. Son

Why I Am Afraid to Have Children. Bin Ramke. MAYP

Why I Am Not a Painter. Frank O'Hara. CAPP; HCAP; MoP; NeAP; NoAM; NOBA; PoE; PoM

Why I Am Not a Painter. Frank O'Hara. NeAP; NoAM; NOBA; PoM

Why I Can't Write a Poem about Lares. Iván Silén, tr. fr. Spanish by Julio Marzán. InW

Why I Can't Write My Autobiography. Rodger Kamenetz. VWA

Why I Didn't Go to Delphi. James Welch. CDW

Why I Like Movies. Patricia Jones. BlSi

Why I Sing the Blues. B. B. King. MAT

Why I tie about thy wrist. The Bracelet: To Julia. Robert Herrick. OBEV; TrGrPo

Why I Voted the Socialist Ticket. Vachel Lindsay. MoAmPo

Why I Write Not of Love. Ben Jonson. OxBSP

Why, if Becchina's heart were diamond. Sonnet: Of Becchina, the Shoemaker's Daughter. Cecco Angiolieri da Siena, tr. by Dante Gabriel Rossetti. AWP

Why, if this interval of being can be spent serenely. Rainer Maria Rilke, tr. fr. German by Stephen Mitchell. Fr. Duino Elegies, IX. NAWM-2

Why in all the many races of the country where we live. Why Negroes Don't Unite. Lizelia Augusta Jenkins Moorer. CBWP-3

Why is a pump like Viscount Castlereagh? What's My Thought Like? Thomas Moore. FaBoEE

(Riddle, A.) FaBoCo

Why is everything I do in my life like a boomerang? Boomerang. John Perreault. EAS

Why is it. Lover's Meeting. Ray Mathew. CBAP

Why Is It? Lizelia Augusta Jenkins Moorer. CBWP-3

Why is it then that early-spring blue is so deeply distressed? Uri Zvi Greenberg, tr. fr. Yiddish by Robert Friend. Fr. Mephisto. PeBMYV

Why is it, when I am in Rome. On Being a Woman. Dorothy Parker. AnAmPo; FPL; PoLF

"Why is my district death-rate low?" Municipal. Kipling. BrPo; BXAP

"Why is my verse so barren of new pride." Shakespeare. Fr. Sonnets, LXXVI. EBEV; InvP

Why is that graceful female here. The Indian's Bride. Edward Coate Pinkney. AnAmPo

Why is the princess so depressed. Noblesse Oblige. Celeste Turner Wright. Psk

Why is the word pretty so underrated? Pretty. Stevie Smith. NAEL-2; NoAM; NoP; TEP

Why is the world beloved, that fals is and vein. Despise the World. Unknown. MeEL

Why is your forehead deep-furrowed with care? Call Me Not Back from the Echoless Shore. Unknown. BLPA

Why It Was Cold in May. Henrietta Robins Eliot. AA

Why, Jack, how now? I hear strange stories. An Epistle to My Friend J. B. Robert Dodsley. NOEC

Why lament one's fate. Sogi, tr. by Steven D. Carter. WFTW

Why lean over the fire, and who is this. In the Secret House. Christopher Middleton. FaBoMo

Why Linger Yet upon the Strand? Louis FitzGerald Benson. AH

Why listen, even the water is sobbing for something. The Maid's Thought. Robinson Jeffers. ErPo

Why Log Truck Drivers Rise Earlier than Students of Zen. Gary Snyder. NNaP; SOTW

"Why looks my lord so deadly pale?" The Vampyre. John Stagg, tr. by Christopher Middleton, W. E. Aytoun and Theodore. VVA

Why, Lord ("Why Lord, must something in us"). Mark Van Doren. AH, with music; TrPWD

Why lovest thou so this brittle [or brotle] worlde's joy? The Peace of a Good Mind. Sir Thomas More. Fr. The Twelve Weapons of Spiritual Battle. FaBoRV

Why, man, he doth bestride the narrow world. Portrait of Caesar. Shakespeare. Fr. Julius Caesar, I, ii. TrGrPo

Why Mira Can't Go Back to Her Old House. Mirabai, tr. fr. Medieval Hindi; English vers. by by Robert Bly. NU

Why mourns my beauteous friend, bereft? To Urania. Benjamin Colman. SCAP

Why muse wee thus to see the wheeles run cross. The Town Called Providence, Its Fate. Benjamin Tompson. SCAP

Why Must You Know? John Wheelwright. VGW

Why must you play chess with your friends all day? A Poem Expressing My Wife's Response to One I Sent Her. Li K'ai-hsien, *tr. by* Jonathan Chaves. CoBLCP

Why My Hair Is Not Gray. Picirantaiyar, *tr. fr. Tamil by* A. K. Ramanujan. PLW

Why My Mother Made Me. Sharon Olds. ER

Why Negroes Don't Unite. Lizelia Augusta Jenkins Moorer. CBWP-3

Why, no, Sir! If a barren rascal cries. Doctor Major. Lionel Johnson. BrPo

Why Not. Moyshe-Leyb Halpern, *tr. fr. Yiddish by* Benjamin *and* Barbara Harshav *and* Kathryn Helle. AYP

Why not despair of this world. The Radiance of Extinct Stars. Allan Kolski Horvitz. VWA

Why not mark out the land. Hard Questions. Margaret Tsuda. RFM

Why not merely the despaired of. Cascando. Samuel Beckett. NOIV

Why not? The mouths of the ginger blooms slide open. Chinoiserie. Charles Wright. AmPA

Why not view your family's past. Song from the Totem Maker. Duane Niatum. NOVW

Why now so melancholy, Ben? Leviathan; or, A Hymn to Poor Brother Ben. *Unknown.* APAS

Why now tempt me? Why do you do this? OK. Prayer to Aphrodite. Timoshenko Aslanides. UAS

Why now the word "Kalahari." Kalahari. Luis Palés Matos, *tr. by* Rachel Benson. InW

"Why of the sheep do you not learn peace?" An Answer to the Parson. Blake. FaBoEE; NBLV; OxBoLi

Why puts our Grandame Nature on. On the Unusual Cold and Rainie Weather in the Summer, 1648. Robert Heath. OBS

Why quails my heart? God riding with. Saul. Isaac Rosenberg. VWA

Why reclining, interrogating? why myself and all drowsing? To the States. Walt Whitman. CTC; NAAL-1

Why regret to leave. Saigyo, *tr. fr. Japanese by* Burton Watson. *Fr.* Sixty-four Tanka. FCEI

Why rejoice in beauty? What. Reflections. Antoinette Deshoulières, *tr. by* Yvor Winters. PBWP

Why repeat? I heard you the first time. Carl Sandburg. *Fr.* The People, Yes, *sec.* 42. OBAL

Why, Rome was naked once, a bastard smudge. Humble Beginnings. Thomas Lovell Beddoes. NOBVV

Why Rosalie Did It. Jim Wayne Miller. MOWH

Why Run? Norah Smaridge. RHPC

Why say the idiot is not. The Locus. Cid Corman. VGW

Why seraphim like lutanists arranged. Evening without Angels. Wallace Stevens. VGW

Why shall I keep the old name? Blacklisted. Carl Sandburg. SaC

Why She Moved House. Thomas Hardy. FM

Why She Says No. Ellen Bryant Voigt. FaBoWP

Why Should a Foolish Marriage Vow. Dryden. *Fr.* Marriage à la Mode, I, i. HeIP; NAEL-1; NIP
(Song: "Why should a foolish marriage vow.") AWP; SeCV-2

Why should I be awaken by love. James A. Randall, Jr.. BPo

Why Should I Be Jealous. *Unknown, tr. fr. Chippewa Indian by* Frances Densmore. OV

Why Should I Be with a Husband Bound? *Unknown, tr. fr. Spanish by* Kate Flores. DMH

Why should I blame her that she filled my days. No Second Troy. W. B. Yeats. BrPo; CMoP; EnLoPo; GTBS-P; MoP; NAEL-2; NoAM; NOBE; OAEL-2; OxBTC; PoEL-5; PPP; SeCePo; WeW

Why Should I Care for the Men of Thames? Blake. ChTr

Why should I find Him here. Christ in the Clay-Pit. Jack R. Clemo. GTBS-P

Why Should I Grieve? Moses Ibn Ezra, *tr. fr. Hebrew by* Solomon Solis-Cohen. TrJP

Why should I have returned? Noah's Raven. W. S. Merwin. HCAP

Why should I heed their railings? What's a prude? A Marriage Prospect. William Hurrell Mallock. NOBVV

Why should I keep holiday. Compensation. Emerson. AmPP; FPL; LiTA; NOBA; TAP

Why should I let the toad work. Toads. Philip Larkin. CMoP; NePoEA; NoAM; NOBL; OxBTC; PoE; SoSe

Why should I longer long to live. Being Forsaken of His Friend He Complaineth. "E. S." EiL

Why Should I Murmur. Hartley Coleridge. Son

Why should I put my faith in you. Nawab Mirza Khan Dagh, *tr. by* Ahmed Ali. GoT

Why should I resent. A Woman Forsaken in Love. Saigyo, *tr. fr. Japanese by* Burton Watson. *Fr.* Sixty-four Tanka. FCEI

Why should I seek for love or study it? Ribh Considers Christian Love Insufficient. W. B. Yeats. TW

Why should I seek to ease intense desire. To Tommaso de' Cavalieri. Buonarroti Michelangelo, *tr. by* John Addington Symonds. PeHV

Why Should I Sing in Verse. Samuel Daniel. *Fr.* To Delia. Son

Why should I stay? Nor seed nor fruit have I. The Bubble. John Banister Tabb. AA

Why Should I Wander Sadly. Süsskind von Trimberg, *tr. fr. Middle High German.* TrJP

Why should my heart. Saigyo, *tr. fr. Japanese by* Burton Watson. *Fr.* Sixty-four Tanka. FCEI

Why should not we all be merry. *Unknown.* OBS

Why should one care to unpack. Mohammad Taqi Mir, *tr. by* Ahmed Ali. GoT

Why should scribblers discompose. Walter Savage Landor. *See* Why should the scribblers discompose.

Why Should the American Negro Be Proud? Maggie Pogue Johnson. CBWP-4

Why should the scribblers discompose. The Scribblers. Walter Savage Landor. FaBoEE; OBSV
("Why should scribblers discompose.") FaBoEE

Why should this a desert be? Orlando's Rhymes. Shakespeare. *Fr.* As You Like It, III, ii. CTC; OBSC

Why should this flower delay so long. The Last Chrysanthemum. Thomas Hardy. CMoP; LiTB

Why should this Negro insolently stride. August. Elinor Wylie. MoAB; MoAmPo

Why should thy look requite so ill. A Paradox. Earl of Pembroke. EiL

Why Should Vain Mortals Tremble. Niles. AH

Why should we praise them, or revere. Against Seasons. Robert Mezey. NYBP

Why Should We Sell Our Dreams? Ahmad Faraz, *tr. fr. Urdu by* Mahmood Jamal. PBMUP

Why should we waste and weep? Fledglings. Thomas Lake Harris. AA

Why should you believe in magic. Consumed. James Tate. MAT

Why should you [or shouldst thou] swear I am forsworn. The Scrutiny [or Scrutinie]. Richard Lovelace. BoLoP; CaPo; ELP; EnLoPo; GBL; MeLP; MePo; NoP; OBS; SeCP; TrGrPo

Why should you wake, my darling, at this hour. A Fairy Tale. Kenneth Mackenzie. PoAu-2

Why should your fair eyes with such sovereign grace. Michael Drayton. *Fr.* Idea, XLIII. OBSC

Why shouldst thou cease thy plaintive song. To an Obscure Poet Who Lives on My Hearth. Charles Lotin Hildreth. AA

Why, silly Man! so much admirest thou. George Wither. *Fr.* A Collection of Emblemes, Ancient and Moderne. SeCV-1

Why Sit'st Thou by That Ruin'd Hall. Sir Walter Scott, *Fr.* The Antiquary, *ch.* 10. EnRP

Why so drawn, so worn. Vampire's Aubade. W. D. Snodgrass. VVA

Why So Many of Them Die. Susan Wallbank. BrRo

Why So Pale and Wan, Fond Lover? Sir John Suckling. *Fr.* Aglaura, IV, ii. AWP; ELP; FaBV; FPL; HAP; HeIP; HoPM; NOBE; OBEV; OBS; PoE; PoRA; SeCePo; TEP; TrGrPo; UnPo
(Encouragements to a Lover.) FaFP; GTBS; GTBS-P
(Song: "Why so pale and wan, fond lover?.") BoLoP; CaPo; EnLoPo; HeIP; InPS; JCP; MePo; PoEL-3; PrIm; SeCP; SeCV-1

Why so pale and wan, fond lover? Why So Pale and Wan, Fond Lover? Sir John Suckling. NAEL-1; NBLV; NIP; OPOP

Why so valiant to decide? Young Woman at a Window. Mark Van Doren. LiTA

Why, Soldiers, Why? *At. to* James Wolfe. OBET

Why, Some of My Best Friends Are Women. Phyllis McGinley. NMM

Why speak of memory and death. Two Views of Two Ghost Towns. Charles Tomlinson. NoAM

Why speak of the use. Hayden Carruth. VGW

Why stand aghast. He Hath Need of Rest. Josephine D. Henderson Heard. CBWP-4

"Why stand you, gentle mother." Premonition. Laura Goodman Salverson. CaP

Why stay we at home now the season is come? The Greenland Voyage; or, The Whale Fisher's Delight. *Unknown.* OxBSS

Why Stone Does Not Sing by Itself. Anita Endrezze-Danielson. STE

Why talk. I Am Panting. Anna Swirszczynska, *tr. by* Czeslaw Milosz. PwPP

Why That's Bob Hope. William Hathaway. NAmP; SM

Why the blue bruises high up on your thigh. The Farm Woman: 1942. Naomi Mitchison. CH

Why the British Girls Give In So Easily. Nicholas Moore. WaP

Why the Many Words? Gerhard Fritsch, *tr. fr. German by* Beth Bjorklund. CoAuP

Why the Resurrection Was Revealed to Women. Catharina Regina von Greiffenberg, *tr. fr. German by* Michael Hamburger. PBWP

Why the Robin's Breast Was Red. James Ryder Randall. AA

Why the Soup Tastes like the Daily News. Marge Piercy. MAT

Why the unbroken spiral, Virtuoso. Apple Peeler. Robert Francis. LCAP; NePoAm

Why the Wind Comes. Hirini Melbourne. PeNZ

Why They Waged War. John Peale Bishop. NYBP

Why this girl has no fear. Carmen. Victor Hernandez Cruz. PoBA

Why, this is hell. How Many Devils Can Dance on the Point. D. J. Enright. AnAn

Why Thus Longing? Harriet Winslow Sewall. AA

Why Tomas Cam Was Grumpy. James Stephens. CMoP

Why vainly do I hither fly. The Lament of Professor Turbojet. James Laughlin. SoTCo

Why vex thy soul that never nations claim thee? A Citizen of—the World. Donald McDonald. PBCV

Why wait we for the torches' lights? Let Us Drink. Alcaeus, *tr. by* John Hermann Merivale. AWP

Why was a radio sinful? Lord knows. But it was. The Radio under the Bed. Reed Whittemore. NYBP

Why was it that the thunder voice of fate. Robert Gould Shaw. Paul Laurence Dunbar. Son

Why We Always Take Vacations by the Water. Ira Sadoff. BLA

Why We Bombed Haiphong. Jonathan Holden. MAYP

Why We Meet. Lizelia Augusta Jenkins Moorer. CBWP-3

Why We Sometimes Paint by Numbers. Colleen J. McElroy. ER

"Why weep ye by the tide, ladie?" Jock of [*or* o'] Hazeldean. Sir Walter Scott. BeLS; EnRP; GN; GTBS; GTBS-P; NAEL-2; OxBS; TEP (Jock o' Hazeldean.) GTBS; GTBS-P

"Why weep ye by the tide, ladye?" John of Hazelgreen [*or* Haselgreen]. *Unknown.* ESPB

Why were you born when the snow was falling? A Dirge. Christina Rossetti. ChTr; EBVV; NOBVV

Why, who makes much of a miracle? Miracles. Walt Whitman. AnAmPo

Why Why Should I the World Be Minding. Thomas Smith. AiP

Why will Delia thus retire. A Receipt to Cure [*or* for] the Vapours. Lady Mary Wortley Montagu. NOEC; PBWP (Receipt for the Vapours.) PBWP

Why will they never sleep. John Peale Bishop. LiTA; LiTM

Why will they never speak. The Grandfathers [*or* After a Line by John Peale Bishop]. Donald Justice. PoCH

"Why, William, on that old grey [*or* gray] stone." Expostulation and Reply. Wordsworth. EnRP; NAEL-2; OAEL-2

Why without cease do I think of a bold youth. The Haunting. Irving Layton. NeAC

Why Would I Have Survived? Edith Bruck, *tr. fr. Italian by* Anita Barrows. VWA

Why Would I Want. William J. Harris. PoBA

Why would she come to him. Versions. Robert Creeley. PPR

Why Ye Blossome Cometh Before Ye Leafe. Oliver Herford. AA

Why, ye tenants of the lake. On Scaring Some Waterfowl in Loch Turit, a Wild Scene among the Hills of Oughtertyre. Burns. PBBP

Why You Climbed Up. Robert Penn Warren. BLA

Whylom [*or* Whilom] Ther was dwellinge at Oxenford [*or* Oxenforde]. The Miller's [*or* Milleres] Tale. Chaucer. *Fr.* The Canterbury Tales. NAEL-1; OAEL-1; OxBoLi
("Sometime ago there was a rich old codger," *mod. vers. by* Nevill Coghill) TEP
("There used to be a rich old oaf who made," *mod. vers. by* Theodore Morrison) NAWM-1

"Fair was this yonge wyf, and therwithal." EBEV

Whym Chow. "Michael Field." FM

Why'n't you bring me. To Greet a Letter-Carrier. William Carlos Williams. OBAL

Wi da lentenin days ida first o da Voar. Tuslag. T. A. Robertson. OxBS

Wi' patchit brose and ilka pen. Lilt Your Johnnie. *Unknown.* BXAP

Wichita Vortex Sutra, *sel.* Allen Ginsberg. "Face the Nation." NaP

Wicked Hawthorn Tree, The. W. B. Yeats. WSC

Wicked Neighbor, The. Zelda, *tr. fr. Hebrew by* Hannah Hoffman. WPOW

Wicked Who Would Do Me Harm, The. *Unknown, tr. fr. Gaelic by* A. Carmichael. RB

Wickedest Man in Memphis, The. Alex J. Brown. BeLS

Wickedness of Peter Shannon, The. Alden Nowlan. MoCV

Wicker Basket, A. Robert Creeley. CAPP; HAP; MoP; NoAM; NoP; SM

Widdecombe [*or* Widdicombe] Fair. *Unknown.* CH; MoShBr

Wide as this night, old as this night is old and young as it is young. Kenneth Fearing. CMoP

Wide Awake. Myra Cohn Livingston. RAR

Wide awake and dreaming. Of Calico Cats. Kirsty Seymour-Ure. CRH

Wide Empty Landscape with a Death in the Foreground. N. Scott Momaday. CDW

Wide, ho? Ezra Pound, *after the Chinese.* OBVE

Wide is our mouth and. Need Is Our Name. Luci Shaw. TrCP

Wide Land, The. A. R. Ammons. TwCP

Wide Mizzoura, The. *Unknown.* AS

Wide o'er the valley the pennons are fluttering. The Siege of Chapultepec. William Haines Lytle. PAH

Wide open and unguarded stand our gates. Unguarded Gates. Thomas Bailey Aldrich. AA; AnAmPo; PAH

Wide Open Are Thy Loving Hands. Saint Bernard of Clairvaux, *tr. fr. Latin by* Charles P. Krauth. AH, *with music*

Wide sky arching above. Desert Madness. A. Leyeles, *tr. by* Benjamin and Barbara Harshav. AYP

Wide sleeves sway. Dancing. Yang Kuei-fei, *tr. by* Florence Ayscough and Amy Lowell. FaPON

Wide was the land. Patrick Anderson. *Fr.* Poem on Canada: The Coming of the White Man. CaP

Wide, white, wing-boned washboards of twenty, The. Of Oystermen, Workboats. Dave Smith. MAYP

wide wide Yangtze, dragons in deep pools, The. The Merchant's Joy. Lu Yu, *tr. by* Burton Watson. CoBCP

Widely is flung, warning of slaughter. The Song of the Valkyries. *Unknown, tr. by* Lee M. Hollander. WaaP

Widely we are scattered. An Endless Chain. Abraham Reisen, *tr. by* Keith Bosley. VWA

Widgeon. Seamus Heaney. FaBCIP

Widow, The. Susan Ludvigson. MAYP; MT

Widow, The. W. S. Merwin. NYBP; UnPo; VGW

Widow, The. Robert Southey. NOEC

Widow at Windsor, The. Kipling. BrPo; NAEL-2; NoAM; NoP

Widow bird sate mourning for her love, A. Shelley. *Fr.* Charles the First. ELP; GTBS; GTBS-P
(Song, A: "Widow bird sate mourning for her love, A.") NOBE; OBNC; OxBSP; PoEL-4
(Widow Bird, A.) BoTP; CH; FaPON

Widow Brown's Christmas. John Townsend Trowbridge. BeLS

Widow Has Buried Her Second Husband, The. William Dunbar. *Fr.* The Tua Mariit Wemen and the Wedo. OxBLMV

Widow in Wintertime, A. Carolyn Kizer. CAPP; ER

Widow of Drynam, The. Patrick MacDonogh. NeIP

Widow Perez, The. Gary Soto. MAYP

Widow refuses sleep, for sleep pretends, The. Exile. Ellen Bryant Voigt. MAYP

Widow Speaks, The. William Dunbar. *Fr.* The Book of the Two Married Women and the Widow. PoEL-1

Widow That Keeps the Cock Inn, The. *Unknown.* CoMu

Widow under a New Moon. Kevin Clark. KS

Widow, well met; whither go you today? A Contention betwixt a Wife, a Widow, and a Maid. Sir John Davies. OBSC; SiPS

Widowed Heart, The. Albert Pike. AA

Widower, The. Royall Tyler. OBAL

Widower in the Country, The. Les A. Murray. DiPo

Widowhood. Malka Heifetz-Tussman, *tr. fr. Yiddish.* AYP, *tr. by* Kathryn Hellerstein; PeBMYV, *tr. by* Marcia Falk

Widows. Edgar Lee Masters. MoAmPo

Widows be woeful whose husbands be taken, The. A Ballad of the Rising in the North. *Unknown.* ACP

Widow's Curse, The. *Unknown, tr. fr. Irish by* Thomas Kinsella. NOIV

Widow's Hymn, A. George Wither. OBEV

Widow's Lament. *Unknown, tr. fr. Chinese by* Arthur Waley. *Fr.* Shih Ching. BoWoP

Widow's Lament in Springtime, The. William Carlos Williams. CMoP; HAP; LiTM; MoP; NAAL-2; NoAM; NOBA; PoE; TAP

Widow's Old Broom, The. *Unknown.* AmFP

Widow's Plot; or, She Got What Was Coming to Her, The. William Plomer. MoP

Widows' Rice. Okkur Macattanar, *tr. fr. Tamil by* A. K. Ramanujan. PLW

Widow's Walk. Elizabeth Spires. MAYP

Widow's Weeds, A. Walter De la Mare. FaBV

Widow's Yard, The. Isabella Gardner. CAPP

Widsith spoke, his word-hoard unlocked. Widsith, the Minstrel. *Unknown, tr. fr. Anglo-Saxon. Fr.* Widsith. AnOE

Widsith, the Minstrel. *Unknown, tr. fr. Anglo-Saxon.* Fr. Widsith. AnOE

Wie langsam kriechet sie dahin. Heine, *tr. fr. German by* Richard Monckton Milnes. AWP

Wife, The. Robert Creeley. VGW

Wife, The. Anna Peyre Dinnies. AA

Wife, The. Denise Levertov. ErPo

Wife a-Lost, The. William Barnes. BoLoP; EBVV; ELP; EnLoPo; HAP; OBEV

Wife and servant are the same. To the Ladies. Mary Lee, Lady Chudleigh. NOEC; WPE; WPOW

Wife a-Prais'd, A. William Barnes. EBVV

Wife—at daybreak I shall be, A. Emily Dickinson. AmPP

Wife-Hater, The. *Unknown.* CoMu

Wife in London, A. Thomas Hardy. NOBVV; OBWP

"Wife, land of the wave fire.' *Unknown, tr. fr. Icelandic by* George Johnston. *Fr.* The Saga of Gisli. OBVE

Wife of Aed mac Ainmirech, King of Ireland, Laments Her Husband, The. *Unknown, tr. fr. Old Irish by* Myles Dillon. AnIL

Wife of Auchtermuchty, The. *Unknown.* GoTS

Wife of Bath's Prologue, The. Chaucer. *Fr.* The Canterbury Tales. NAEL-1; OAEL-1; OxBoLi, *abr.*.
  (Prologue to the Wife of Bath's Tale, The.) PoEL-1
  "If poor (you say) she drains her husband's purse," *mod. version by* Pope OBSV
  "My fifthe housbonde, god his soule blesse!" FiP

Wife of Bath's Tale, The. Chaucer. *Fr.* The Canterbury Tales. NAEL-1; OAEL-1

Wife of Kohelet. Shlomit Cohen, *tr. fr. Hebrew by* Yishai Tobin. VWA

Wife of Usher's Well, The. *Unknown.* AmFP; AWP; CH; ChTr; EBEV; EnRP; EnSB; ESPB, (A, B, C *and* D *vers.*); FaBoBa; GoTS; LiTB; NAEL-1; NOBE; NoP; OAEL-1, *with music;* OBEV; OnMSP; OxBB, *with music;* OxBS; PoEL-1; PrIm; RB; TrGrPo

Wife of Winter's Tale, The. Michael Dennis Browne. SM

Wife Speaks, The. Mary Stanley. PeNZ

"Wife Takes a Child, The." Ellen Bryant Voigt. SM

Wife Talks to Herself, A. Stephen Berg. NaP

Wife to Husband. Fleur Adcock. ATNZ; PeNZ

Wife was sitting at her reel ae night, A. The Strange Visitor. *Unknown.* ChTr; FaBoCh; GBP

Wife Who Smashed Television Gets Jail. Paul Durcan. CIP

Wife Who Would a Wanton Be, The. *Unknown.* FaBoCo

Wife-Woman, The. Anne Spencer. BANP

Wife won/ and she never, The. *Unknown, tr. by* Burton Watson. FCEI

Wife Wrapt [*or* Wrapped] in Wether's Skin, The. *Unknown.* AmFP; ESPB, F vers.

Wife's Complaint, The. *Unknown, tr. fr. Anglo-Saxon by* Michael Alexander. BoLoP

Wife's Lament, The. *Unknown.* AnOE, *tr. by* Charles W. Kennedy; PBWP, *tr. by* Kemp Malone; PoE, *tr. by* Kemp Malone; WPE
  (Wife's Complaint, The.) BoLoP, *tr. by* Michael Alexander

Wife's Tale, The. Seamus Heaney. CIP; IPY

Wife's Thoughts, The. Hsü Kan, *tr. fr. Chinese by* Burton Watson. CoBCP

Wiggly Giggles. Stacy Jo Crossen *and* Natalie Anne Covell. RHPC

Wigs and Beards. Robert Graves. NOBL

Wil the Merry Weaver, and Charity the Chamber-Maid; or, A Brisk Encounter between a Youngman and His Love. *Unknown.* CoMu

Wilberforce. Josephine D. Henderson Heard. CBWP-4

Wild, The. Wendell Berry. VGW

Wild air, world-mothering air. The Blessed Virgin Compared to the Air We Breathe. Gerard Manley Hopkins. BrPo; NOBVV

Wild and windy was the day. *Unknown, tr. by* Arthur Waley. BoS

Wild as they are, accept them, so were we. Aecclesiae et Reipub. William Strachey. OBTV

Wild Ass. Padraic Colum. MoBrPo

Wild (at Our First) Beasts Uttered Human Words. E. E. Cummings. FaBoMo; NYBP

Wild Barbaree, The. *Unknown.* AmFP

Wild Beasts. Evaleen Stein. RAR

Wild beauty of an eagle, once born to virgin sky, The. The Folding Fan. Grey Cohoe. NOVW

Wild Bees. James Keir Baxter. ATNZ; NoP

Wild Bill Jones. *Unknown.* AmFP

Wild bird singer, sing on. Sand Creek. Charles G. Ballard. UnPo; VoR

Wild bird, whose warble, liquid sweet. Tennyson. *Fr.* In Memoriam A. H. H., LXXXVIII. NoP; PBBP

Wild Boar and the Ram, The. John Gay. *Fr.* Fables. FM; NOEC

Wild Carthage held her, Rome. A Puritan Lady. Lizette Woodworth Reese. MoAmPo

Wild Cat, The. Iain Crichton Smith. CRH

Wild Cat, A. Suad al-Mubarak al-Sabah, *tr. fr. Arabic by* May Jayyusi *and* John Heath-Stubbs. MAP

Wild cat steps over kudzu vines, A. Natsume Seibi, *tr. fr. Japanese by* Hiroaki Sato. *Fr.* Twenty-seven Hokku. FCEI

Wild Cheese, The. James Tate. PPR

Wild Cherry Tree. Edmund Blunden. BrPo

Wild child rolling naked in the snow, The. The Price of Wildness. Judith Moffett. BLA

Wild Colloina Boy, The. *Unknown.* AmFP

Wild Colonial Boy, The. *Unknown.* FaBoBa; PoAu-1

Wild Common, The. D. H. Lawrence. NoAM

Wild Crab. Mary Ellen Solt. BoWoP

Wild Dog Rose, The. John Montague. BIrV; CIP; IPY; PoE

Wild Dreams of Summer What Is Your Grief. George Barker. OxBTC

Wild Duck, The. John Masefield. BrPo

Wild-duck are on the Ching, The. *Unknown, tr. by* Arthur Waley. BoS

Wild duck startles like a sudden thought, The. Autumn Birds. John Clare. PBBP

Wild ducks/ float with the north wind. Sun Children. Leslie Marmon Silko. VoR

Wild Duck's Nest, The. Wordsworth. FM
  (Sonnet: Wild Duck's Nest, The.) ChER

Wild Eden, *sels.* George Edward Woodberry. AA
  Child, The. *Fr.* XXX.
  Divine Awe. *Fr.* XVI.
  Homeward Bound. *Fr.* XXV.
  O, Inexpressible as Sweet. *Fr.* VII.
  O, Struck beneath the Laurel. *Fr.* XXXIII.
  Rose of Stars, The. *Fr.* IX.
  Seaward. *Fr.* XLI.
  Secret, The. *Fr.* VI.
  So Slow to Die. *Fr.* XXXVIII.
  When First I Saw Her. *Fr.* V.

Wild-eyed team with horned and swaying heads, The. The Team. "Furnley Maurice." CBAP

Wild Flower Man, The. Lu Yu, *tr. fr. Chinese by* Kenneth Rexroth. NaP

Wild Flowers. Peter Newell. NA; RHPC

Wild Flower's Song. Blake. BoTP

Wild Garden, The. Pope. *See* Essay on Man, An: Awake, my St. John! leave all meaner things.

Wild Geese. Elinor Chipp. FaPON

Wild Geese, The. James Herbert Morse. AA

Wild geese are flying, The. *Unknown, tr. by* Arthur Waley. BoS

Wild geese departing, The. Saigyo, *tr. fr. Japanese by* Burton Watson. *Fr.* Sixty-four Tanka. FCEI

Wild geese departing, their wings in white clouds, The. Teika, *tr. fr. Japanese by* Hiroaki Sato. *Fr.* A Compendium of Good Tanka. FCEI

Wild geese flying. Watanabe Suiha, *tr. by* Geoffrey Bownas *and* Anthony Thwaite. PeBJV

Wild geese, flying in the night, behold, The. The Wild Geese. James Herbert Morse. AA

Wild geese gone, the cove looks cleared. Issa, *tr. fr. Japanese by* Hiroaki Sato. *Fr.* Forty-four Hokku. FCEI

Wild geese leave no trace in the citadel of water, The. Princess Shikishi, *tr. fr. Japanese by* Hiroaki Sato. *Fr.* Seventy-eight Tanka. FCEI

Wild geese lured by the autumn wind. Teika, *tr. fr. Japanese by* Hiroaki Sato. *Fr.* A Compendium of Good Tanka. FCEI

Wild geese returning, The. Tsumori Kunimoto. PDV

Wild geese, wild geese, ganging to the sea. *Unknown.* PBBP

Wild Goat, The. Claude McKay. CDC

Wild goat on the hill, A. Dilana and Diram. Saleem Barakat, *tr. fr. Arabic by* Lena Jayyusi *and* Naomi Shihab Nye. *Fr.* The Crane. MAP

Wild Goose Lingering on an Inlet. Shinkei, *tr. fr. Japanese by* Steven D. Carter. WFTW

Wild Goose, Wild Goose. Issa, *tr. fr. Japanese by* Kenneth Rexroth. TTTS

Wild Grass. Akhtar-ul-Iman, *tr. fr. Urdu by* Mahmood Jamal. PBMUP

Wild Grass. Wu Sheng, *tr. fr. Chinese by* Dominic Cheung. IFON

Wild has its skills. Lapsed Meadow. Stanley Plumly. AnAn

Wild Honey. Alistair Campbell. ATNZ

Wild Honey. Maurice Thompson. AnAmPo

Wild Honeysuckle, The. Philip Freneau. AA; AmPP; AnAmPo; BLPL; LiTA; NAAL-1; NOBA; OxBA; PoEL-4; PoLF; TAP; TrGrPo

Wild Horse. Elder Olson. GrPl

Wild Horses of Assateague Island, The. John Bensko. MT

Wild Idyll. Manuel José Othón, *tr. fr. Spanish by* Samuel Beckett. MexPo

Wild Iron. Allen Curnow. ATNZ; RB

Wild is its nature, as it were a token. Song of the Palm. Tracy Robinson. AA

Wild Knight, The. G. K. Chesterton. WGRP

Wild man of Ssu-ming Mountain. Li Po, *tr. fr. Chinese by* Burton Watson. *Fr.* Facing Wine with Memories of Lord Ho, 1. CoBCP

Wild Mushroom, The. Gary Snyder. NoP

Wild Mustard River, The. *Unknown.* AmFP

Wild Nature. Charles Newton. *Fr.* Stanzas. NOEC

Wild Negro Bill. *Unknown.* BPo

Wild nights!—wild nights! Emily Dickinson. AmPP; NAAL-1; NIP; NoAM; NOBA; NoP; OxBA; PBWP; TAP; UnAS; WPE

Wild Oats. Philip Larkin. InPS

Wild Oats. Norman MacCaig. OxBTC

Wild Old Wicked Man, The. W. B. Yeats. AnIL; CMoP

Wild orange tree, The. Ietaka, *tr. by* Steven D. Carter. WFTW

Wild patience has taken me this far, A. Integrity. Adrienne Rich. CAPP

Wild Peaches. Elinor Wylie. FaBoWP; LiTA; LiTM; NAAL-2; OxBA; WPE

Wild Peaches ("When the world turns completely upside down."), *sel.* Elinor Wylie. LiTA; LiTM; OxBA; WPE

"Down to the Puritan marrow of my bones." BoWoP (Puritan Sonnet, IV.) FPL; MoAB; MoAmPo; TrGrPo

Wild pigeon of the leaves. Birds. *Unknown, tr. fr. Arabic by* E. Powys Mathers. *Fr.* The Thousand and One Nights. AWP

Wild Pigs. Ted Kooser. SM

Wild Pitches. Philip Dacey. NAmP

Wild Ride, The. Louise Imogen Guiney. AA

Wild Rippling Water, The. *Unknown.* FaBoBa

Wild Rose. William Allingham. GN

Wild Rose of Alloway! my thanks. Burns. Fitz-Greene Halleck. AA

Wild Roses. Mary Effie Lee Newsome. CDC

Wild roved the Indians once. Grand Rapids. Julia A. Moore. OBAL

Wild singing and drunken dancing. Yang Chi, *tr. fr. Chinese by* Jonathan Chaves. *Fr.* Describing My Feelings While Living in the Spring Quarters at Chiang-ning: Four Poems to the Tune "Ching-p'ing-yëh." CoBLCP

Wild Song. Judah Leib Teller, *tr. fr. Yiddish by* Benjamin *and* Barbara Harshav. AYP

Wild strawberries/ fatten. Lilian Moore. ILY

Wild Strawberries. Robert Graves. FaBoCh

Wild Strawberry. Maurice Kenny. HATNAP; NOVW; STE

Wild stream the clouds, and the fresh wind is singing. The Hunt. Harriet Prescott Spofford. AA

Wild Swan: "My attire is noiseless when I tread the earth." *Unknown, formerly at. to* Cynewulf, *tr. fr. Anglo-Saxon. Fr.* Riddles (Exeter Book). AnOE, *tr. by* Charles W. Kennedy.

(Riddle: Mute Swan.) PBBP

Wild Swans. Edna St. Vincent Millay. CMoP; MoAmPo; PBWP; UnPo

Wild Swans at Coole, The. W. B. Yeats. ChTr; CMoP; FaBoPP; FaBoRV; FM; HeIP; InPS; MoAB; MoBrPo; MoP; NAEL-2; NoAM; NoAM; NoP; PBBP; PPP; SoSe; SOTW; TEP; UnPo

Wild, the Free, The. Byron. RHPC

Wild Thyme, The. Blake. *Fr.* Milton, II. WiR

Wild Thyme. Joyce Sambrook. BoTP

Wild was the day; the wintry sea. The Twenty-second of December. Bryant. GN

Wild water and an arching bridge. On the Ninth, outside Feng-yi Gate, I Passed by P'ei-ts'un's Country House. Chu Hsiao-tsang, *tr. by* Li Chi *and* Michael Patrick O'Connor. WFTU

Wild West. Mark Vinz. Psk

Wild white hands snare you with a stray rope. Lynching. Berysh Vaynshteyn, *tr. fr. Yiddish by* Benjamin *and* Barbara Harshav. *Fr.* Negroes. AYP

Wild, wild the storm, and the sea high running. Patrolling Barnegat. Walt Whitman. MOS; NoP

Wild Wind. Li Meng-yang, *tr. fr. Chinese by* Jonathan Chaves. CoBLCP

Wild winds weep, The. Mad Song. Blake. *Fr.* Poetical Sketches. EnRP; NAEL-2; NOEC; OAEL-2; PoE; PoEL-4; PrIm; TEP; TrGrPo

Wildcat sits on the rocks, The. The Wild Cat. Iain Crichton Smith. CRH

Wildcat was walking. *Unknown, tr. by* Jerome Rothenberg. STP

Wildebeest, The. June Daly. FaPON

Wilderness. Ilyas Farhat, *tr. fr. Arabic by* Salma Khadra Jayyusi *and* John Heath-Stubbs. MAP

Wilderness, The, *sel.* Sidney Keyes. LiTB
   "Red rock wilderness, The." OBWP

Wilderness, The. Kathleen Jessie Raine. BoWoP; PoSH; WPE

Wilderness. Martin Seymour-Smith. NPo

Wilderness, The. Maura Stanton. MAYP

Wilderness a secret keeps, The. Ecce in Deserto. Henry Augustin Beers. AA

Wilderness Gothic. Alfred W. Purdy. HeIP; MoCV; NOBC; NoP

Wilderness Is Tamed, The. Elizabeth J. Coatsworth. *See* Axe has cut the forest down, The.

Wilderness Rivers. Elizabeth Jane Coatsworth. AmFN

Wilderness Sacred Wilderness. Philip Lamantia. UL

Wilderness that not always would deliver. Combe Florey. Paul Durcan. FaBCIP

Wilderness, The: but otherwise. Esther K. Comes to America: 1931. Jerome Rothenberg. NNaP

Wilderness Theme. Ian Mudie. PoAu-2

Wildernesse and the solitarie place shall be glad for them, The. Bible, *O.T. Fr.* Isaiah, XXX. OBVE

Wildfire. Judit Tóth, *tr. fr. Hungarian by* Emery George. VWA

Wildflower. Stanley Plumly. AnAn; LCAP; NAmP

Wildflowers. Richard Howard. NoAM

Wildflowers,/ After the burning artillery subsides. The Story of Wildflowers. Yip Wai-lim, *tr. by* Dominic Cheung. IFON

Wilding, The. Philip Booth. NePoEA

Wildly he wandered on. Shelley. *Fr.* Alastor; or, The Spirit of Solitude. TOF

Wildness of haggard flights. Roussan Camille, *tr. by* Seth L. Wolitz. TTY

Wildness sleeps upon the mountain. The Fisher Cat. Richard Eberhart. GrPl

Wildtrack, *sel.* John Wain.
   Lie Easy in Your Secret Cradle. NAs

Wilfred Owen's Photographs. Ted Hughes. FaBoPV; OxBC

Wilful waste brings woeful want. *Unknown.* OxNR

Wilhelm Meister's Apprenticeship, *sel.* Goethe, *tr. fr. German.*
   Mignon. *Fr. bk.* I *ch.* 1, *tr. by* Robert Bly. NU
   ("Knowest thou the land where bloom the lemon trees.") AWP, *tr. by* James Elroy Flecker.

Wilhelm Stekel Gives Up Life. Judah Leib Teller, *tr. fr. Yiddish by* Benjamin *and* Barbara Harshav. *Fr.* Psychoanalysis. AYP

Wili Woyi, Shaman, Also Known as Billy Pigeon. Robert J. Conley. STE

Wilkes Booth came to Washington, an actor great was he. Booth Killed Lincoln. *Unknown.* AmFP; OFD; OPP

Will, The. John Donne. EBEV; LiTB; MePo

Will, The. Moyshe-Leyb Halpern, *tr. fr. Yiddish by* John Hollander. PeBMYV

Will, The. Sipho Sepamla. WMBCH

Will. Ella Wheeler Wilcox. BLPA; FPL

Will days, indeed, yet come in forgiveness and grace. When You Will Walk in the Field. Leah Goldberg, *tr. by* Simon Halkin. TrJP

Will dissolves, the heart becomes excited, The. Soliloquy in an Air-Raid. Roy Fuller. PoA

Will God, always cold, have a temperature? Moral Ode. David Rosenmann-Taub, *tr. by* Charles Guenther. VWA

Will God forever cast us off. Jesse Mercer. AmFP

Will he always love me? Lady Horikawa, *tr. by* Kenneth Rexroth. BoWoP

Will He No Come Back Again? *Unknown.* OBEV

"Will I die?" you ask. And so I enter on. For Andrew. Fleur Adcock. ATNZ

Will I see it again. Teika, *tr. fr. Japanese by* Hiroaki Sato. *Fr.* A Compendium of Good Tanka. FCEI

Will It Be So? Edith M. Thomas. *Fr.* The Inverted Torch. AA

Will it cease, and the snow. Cessation of War. Ellodë Collins. CN

Will it last? he says. The Snowflake Which Is Now and Hence Forever. Archibald MacLeish. NoP

Will lightning strike me if I take. Thoughts of Loved Ones. Margaret Fishback. FiBHP

Will Love again awake. Muse and Poet. Robert Bridges. OBMV

Will night already spread her wings and weave. Night-Thoughts. Solomon Ibn Gabirol, *tr. by* Emma Lazarus. TrJP

Will of a Man Dying in Exile, The. Samih al-Qasim, *tr. fr. Arabic by* Abdullah al-Udhari. MPAW

Will of God be done by us, The. Blessed Be the Holy Will of God. *Unknown, tr. by* Douglas Hyde. TIRV

Will of God we must obey, The. The Death of King Edward VII. *Unknown.* OxBoLi

Will people accept them? Tenzone. Ezra Pound. *Fr.* Contemporania. PoA

Will seeing Concan make a dog a lion? Ritual Not Religious. *Unknown.* WGRP

Will someone/ at the scent of orange blossom. Shunzei, *tr. fr. Japanese by* Burton Watson. *Fr.* Thirty Tanka. FCEI

'Will sprawl, now that the heat of day is best. Caliban upon Setebos; or, Natural Theology in the Island. Robert Browning. AWP; EBEV; NAEL-2; NOBVV; NoP; OAEL-2; WGRP

Will Stewart and John. *Unknown.* ESPB

Will the lady with locker key 43. Will You Come Out Now? Valerie Sinason. BrRo

Will the man who gets clean love his neighbor? Soap (II). Jerome Rothenberg. NNaP

Will the Real Me Please Stand Up? A. L. Hendricks. PVCV

Will the tree bloom again, and the red field. The Unborn. Sarah Stafford. CN

Will the Weaver. *Unknown.* AmFP

Will the wolves lie down with the lambs and feed them? The End of Sorrow. Edmond Fleg, *tr. fr. French by* Humbert Wolfe. *Fr.* The Wall of Weeping. TrJP

Will there be any. Onitsura, *tr. by* Geoffrey Bownas *and* Anthony Thwaite. PeBJV

Will there never come a season. The Pedestrian's Plaint. E. V. Lucas. CenHV

Will there never come a season. To R. K. James Kenneth Stephen. BXAP; CenHV; FaBoCo; FaBoEE; FaBoPa; NBLV; NOBL; Par

Will there really be a morning? Emily Dickinson. OBCA

(Morning.) AA; FaPON

Will They Cry When You're Gone, You Bet. Imamu Amiri Baraka. NAAL-2

Will they fight? They say so. And will the French ? Arthur Hugh Clough. *Fr.* Amours de Voyage, Canto II, iii. FaBoPV

Will they have children? Will they have more children? Neighbors. James Tate. BAP

Will they never fade or pass! The Farmer Remembers the Somme. Vance Palmer. PoAu-1

Will they occur. Brasília. Sylvia Plath. CAPP

Will they stop. Requiem. Kenneth Fearing. CMoP

Will to be tickled wants; has got the itch. *Unknown.* FaBoEE

Will to Change, The. Adrienne Rich. NMM

Will to Live, The. Mekeel McBride. MAYP; NAmP

Will to Win. Francis Reginald Scott. OBCV

Will., Will., Hen. Steph. Hen. Dick, John Hen., Eddy Ned, Edward. The Kings and Queens of England. *Unknown.* FaBoUs

Will wither like grass. Friederike Mayröcker, *tr. by* Beth Bjorklund. CoAuP

Will ye see what wonders love hath wrought. Sir Thomas Wyatt. SiPS

Will ye that I should sing. A Lady of High Degree. *Unknown, tr. by* Andrew Lang. AWP

Will Yer Write It Down for Me? Henry Lawson. CBAP

Will you always catch me unaware. To My Mother at 73. Elizabeth Jennings. NAs

Will You Be as Hard? Douglas Hyde, *tr. fr. Irish by* Lady Gregory. OBMV

Will You Be My Little Wife? Kate Greenaway. MoShBr

Will you buy any tape. Autolycus's Song ("Will you buy any tape"). Shakespeare. *Fr.* The Winter's Tale, IV, iii. OBSC

Will You Come? Edward Thomas. CH; GoJo; GrPl; RR

Will you come a boating, my gay old hag. The Gay Old Hag. *Unknown.* BIrV

Will You Come Out Now? Valerie Sinason. BrRo

Will you come to the bower I have shaded for you? Walter Savage Landor. *Fr.* A Reply to Lines by Thomas Moore. ChTr

Will you come to Turvy Land. Topsy-Turvy Land. Phyllis M. Stone. BoTP

Will you come with me, my Phyllis dear. Wait for the Wagon. *At. to* R. Bishop Buckley. PAH

"Will you gang wi' me, Leezie Lindsay." Leezie Lindsay. *Unknown.* FaBoCh

Will you glimmer on the sea? Moonrise. Hilda Doolittle ("H. D."). PoA

Will you have me? A Popular Romance. Kevin Ireland. ATNZ; PeNZ

Will you hear of a bloody battle. The Downfall of Piracy. *At. to* Benjamin Franklin. PAH

Will you heara tale of Robin Hood. Robin Hood and the Pedlars. *Unknown.* ESPB

Will you leave the hills of Scotland? Highland Mary. Mary Weston Fordham. CBWP-2

Will you lend me your mare to ride but a mile? *Unknown.* OxNR

Will you love me when I'm old. Love. Nilene O. A. Foxworth, *tr. by the author.* AIW

Will You Love Me When I'm Old? *Unknown.* BLPA; BLPL; FaBoBe

Will you never view us without distrust. Marie-Anne Du Boccage, *tr. fr. French by* Dorothy Backer. *Fr.* The Amazons. DMF

Will you sleep forever? Korinna, *tr. by* Willis Barnstone. BoWoP; PBWP, *tr. by* John Dillon

Will you, sometime, who have sought so long, and seek. The Finder Found. Edwin Muir. PoA

Will you take a sprig of hornbeam? Forester's Song. A. E. Coppard. FaPON

"Will you take a walk with me." The Clucking Hen. *Unknown.* BoTP

"Will you walk a little faster?" said a [*or* the] whiting to a [*or* the] snail. "Lewis Carroll." *Fr.* Alice's Adventures in Wonderland, *ch.* 10. NoAM

(Lobster Quadrille, The.) BoTP; FaPON; MoShBr; OxBChV; Par; RR

(Mock Turtle's Song, The.) ChTr; FaBoNo

"Will you walk into my parlor?" said the Spider to the Fly. The Spider and the Fly. Mary Howitt. BeLS; FaFP; FaPON; OHFP; OnUR; OxBChV; Par; PWR; WBLP

Will you wear white, O my dear, O my dear? Jennie Jenkins [*or* Jinnie Jinkins]. *Unknown.* AmFP

Willets, The. May Swenson. WPE

William and Helen. Sir Walter Scott. EnRP

William and Margaret. David Mallet. NOEC

William and Mary,/ George and Anne. *Unknown.* OxNR

William and Mary. *Unknown.* AmFP

William and Phyllis. *Unknown.* OBET

William asked how veal was made. What Is Veal? *Unknown.* FaBoUs

William Blake Sees God. Roy McFadden. NeIP

William Bond. Blake. OxBB

William Brown of Oregon. Joaquin Miller. AnAmPo

William Dewy, Tranter Reuben, Farmer Ledlow late at plough. Friends Beyond. Thomas Hardy. EBVV; FaBoRV; GTBS-P; NOBVV; OBEV

William F. Buckley/ Writes pluckley. Edmund Conti. SoTCo

William Gifford. Walter Savage Landor. FaBoEE; GTBS-P

William Hall. *Unknown.* AmFP

William James (*The Varieties of Religious Experience,* p.84) is to be. Motion Which Disestablishes Organizes Everything. A. R. Ammons. BAP

William Jones. Edgar Lee Masters. *Fr.* Spoon River Anthology. ImOP

William Lisle Bowles. Byron. *Fr.* English Bards and Scotch Reviewers. OBNC

William Lloyd Garrison. Henrietta Cordelia Ray. CBWP-3

William P. Frye, The. Jeanne Robert Foster. PAH

William Street. Kenneth Slessor. CBAP

William Taylor. *Unknown.* OBET; OxBSS, *with music*

William the Bastard. "Lakon." FiBHP

William the Conqueror long did reign. England's Sovereigns in Verse. *Unknown.* BLPA

William the Conqueror, ten sixty-six. *Unknown.* FaBoUs; OxNR

William the Norman conquers England's state. Lines on Succession of the Kings of England. *Unknown.* FaBoUs

William, the wild round plums are falling. The Dressing Stations. Norman Dubie. AmPA

William Wallace. Francis Lauderdale Adams. OxBS

William was a bashful lover. William Taylor. *Unknown.* OBET; OxBSS, *with music*

William Was a Royal Lover. *Unknown.* AmFP

William Wordsworth. Sidney Keyes. OxBTC; SeCePo

William Wordsworth (1770-1850). Gavin Ewart. NoAM

William Yeats in Limbo. Sidney Keyes. MoBrPo

Williams: An Essay. Denise Levertov. InPS

Williams Avenue Zionist Church, The. Russia. William Carlos Williams. VGW

Willie. *Unknown.* AmFP

Willie and Earl Richard's Daughter. *Unknown.* *See* O Willie's large o limb and lith.

Willie and Lady Maisry. *Unknown.* ESPB; ESPB, A *and* B *vers.*

Willie and Lady Margerie [*or* Maisry]. *Unknown.* ESPB; OxBB

Willie and Nellie, one evening sat. Willie's and Nellie's Wish. Julia A. Moore. FiBHP

Willie boy, Willie boy, where are you going? *Unknown.* BoTP

Willie Brew'd [*or* Brewed] a Peck o' Maut. Burns. AWP; EnRP; OxBS

Willie had a purple monkey climbing on a yellow stick. In Memoriam. "Max Adeler." FaBoCo

Willie is fair, an Willë's rair. *Unknown.* *See* Willy's rare. . .

Willie Leonard; or, The Lake of Cold Finn. *Unknown.* AmFP

Willie Macintosh. *Unknown.* ESPB, (A *and* B *vers.*); OxBoLi

Willie Macintosh. *Unknown. See* As I Came in by Fiddich-Side.

Willie o Douglas Dale. *Unknown.* ESPB

Willie o [*or* of] Winsbury. *Unknown.* AmFP; ESPB, A *and* D *vers.*

Willie poisoned Auntie's tea. Willie the Poisoner. *Unknown.* NTCP

Willie saw some dynamite. Little Willie. *Unknown.* FaPON

Willie, take your little drum. Patapan. Bernard de la Monnoye. PChr

Willie the Poisoner. *Unknown.* NTCP

Willie the Weeper. *Unknown.* BeLS; BLPA; OBAL

Willie was a widow's son. Willie and Lady Maisry. *Unknown.* ESPB, (A *and* B *vers.*)

Willie Wastle dwalt on Tweed. Sic a Wife as Willie Had. Burns. GoTS

"Willie, Willie, I'll learn you a wile." Willie's Lyke-Wake. *Unknown.* ESPB

Willie Winkie. William Miller. *See* Wee Willie Winkie rins [*or* runs] through the town.

Willie, with a thirst for gore. Careless Willie. *Unknown.* FaPON

Willie's and Nellie's Wish. Julia A. Moore. FiBHP

Willie's Fatal Visit. *Unknown.* ESPB

Willie's Lady. *Unknown.* ESPB

Willie's Lyke-Wake. *Unknown.* ESPB

Willie's [*or* Willie] has taen him o'er the fame. Willie's Lady. *Unknown.* ESPB

Willing Arawak, The. Ethnocide. Howard Fergus. PBCV

Willingly I'll say. Robert Duncan. *Fr.* Passages.

Willis, The. David Law Proudfit. AA

Willis Beggs. Edgar Lee Masters. *Fr.* The New Spoon River. SaC

Willobie His Avisa, *sel.* Henry Willoby. To Avisa. ElL

Willoughby liked being Willoughby. The Contentment of Willoughby. Frances Alexander. GoYe

Willow. Richard Watson Dixon. *See* Song: "Feathers of the willow, The."

Willow, The. Tu Fu, *tr. fr. Chinese by* Kenneth Rexroth. NaP

Willow Bend and Weep. Herbert Clark Johnson. PoNe

Willow-Boughs, The. Alexander Block. BoTP

Willow Branches. Chang Pi, *tr. fr. Chinese by* Lois Fusek. ATF

Willow Branches, The. Ho Ning, *tr. fr. Chinese by* Lois Fusek. ATF

Willow Branches. Huang-fu Sung, *tr. fr. Chinese by* Lois Fusek. ATF

Willow Branches. Ku Hsiung, *tr. fr. Chinese by* Lois Fusek. ATF

Willow Branches. Niu Chiao, *tr. fr. Chinese by* Lois Fusek. ATF

Willow Branches. Sun Kuang-hsien, *tr. fr. Chinese by* Lois Fusek. ATF

Willow Branches, The. Wen T'ing-yün, *tr. fr. Chinese by* Lois Fusek. ATF

Willow branches are long, The. Song of the Water Clock at Night. Wen T'ing-yün, *tr. by* Lois Fusek. ATF

Willow by the Eastern Gate. *Unknown, tr. fr. Chinese by* Burton Watson. CoBCP

Willow catkins beyond the garden wait for evening tides. Ch'ien Ch'ien-i, *tr. fr. Chinese by* Jonathan Chaves. *Fr.* In Spring of the Year *Ping-shen.* CoBLCP

Willow catkins, white as cotton. Yang Wei-chen, *tr. fr. Chinese by* Jonathan Chaves. Impromptu Inspirations, I. CoBLCP

Willow Creek. Ch'ien Ch'ien-yi, *tr. fr. Chinese by* Irving Lo. *Fr.* Two Quatrains on the "Awash-in-Springtime Garden." WFTU

Willow Flowers. Yüan Mei, *tr. fr. Chinese by* J. P. Seaton. WFTU

Willow flows away, The. Chiyojo, *tr. fr. Japanese by* Hiroaki Sato. *Fr.* Seventeen Hokku. FCEI

Willow in a Gale. Jane Wilson. NPo

Willow leaves dancing. Eveningsong. Ramona Wilson. VoR

Willow-Man, The. Juliana Horatia Ewing. OxBChV

Willow Poem. William Carlos Williams. NAAL-2

Willow shining, The. The Knowledge of Light. Henry Rago. VGW

Willow-tassels grow in tremors of the spring wind. Lines to Do with Youth. Witter Bynner. PoA

Willow tickles awake, A. Issa, *tr. fr. Japanese by* Hiroaki Sato. *Fr.* Forty-four Hokku. FCEI

Willow-Tree, The. Thackeray. CenHV

Willow Tree, The. *Unknown.* OBET

Willow trees screen the tower in darkness. A Southern Song. Chang Pi, *tr. by* Lois Fusek. ATF

Willows, The. Walter Prichard Eaton. FaPON; OHIP

Willows, The. Bret Harte. BXAP

Willows. Joseph Langland. NePoEA

Willows are dancing in the wind, The. Song of the Wine Spring. Ku Hsiung, *tr. by* Lois Fusek. ATF

Willows are taking the old river road, The. Old River Road. Blanche Whiting Keysner. GoYe

Willows are trees of life. They ride. Willows. Joseph Langland. NePoEA

Willows are willows everywhere. Willows in Alma-Ata. Aleksander Wat, *tr. by* Isaac Komem. VWA

Willows by the Water Side, The. *Unknown. See* My little breath, under the willows by the waterside we used to sit.

Willows carried a slow sound, The. Repose of Rivers. Hart Crane. AWP; CMoP; LiTM; MoAB; MoAmPo; NOBA; OxBA; PoE

Willows in Alma-Ata. Aleksander Wat, *tr. fr. Polish by* Isaac Komem. VWA

Willows line the Sui Embankment. Mist on the Willows. Mao Wen-hsi, *tr. by* Lois Fusek. ATF

Willows of Massachusetts, The. Denise Levertov. NAAL-2

Willows weave spring sorrow. To the Tune "Yellow Oriole." Yang Shen, *tr. by* Jonathan Chaves. CoBLCP

Willowware Cup. James Merrill. NoP

Willowwood ("And now love sang: but his was such a song"). Dante Gabriel Rossetti. *Fr.* The House of Life, L. NAEL-2; OAEL-2

Willowwood ("I sat with love upon a woodside well"). Dante Gabriel Rossetti. *Fr.* The House of Life, XLIX. NAEL-2; OAEL-2; PoEL-5

Willowwood ("O ye, all ye that walk in Willowwood"). Dante Gabriel Rossetti. *Fr.* The House of Life, LI. NAEL-2; OAEL-2

Willowwood ("So sang he: and as meeting rose and rose"). Dante Gabriel Rossetti. *Fr.* The House of Life, LII. NAEL-2; OAEL-2

Will's Love, The. Besmilr Brigham. IHMS

Willy boy, Willy boy,/ Where are you going? Mother Goose. OxNR

Willy Drowned in Yarrow. *Unknown.* GTBS; GTBS-P

Willy, enormous Saskatchewan grizzly. Richard Moore. MAT

Willy Lyons. James Wright. HCAP; NNaP; PoE

Willy the Weeper. *Unknown.* AS, *with music;* GBP, *sl. diff. vers.*

Willy, Willy, Harry, Ste. The Kings and Queens of England. *Unknown.* FaBoUs

Willy, Willy Wilkin. Mother Goose. OxNR

Willy's rare, and Willy's fair. Rare Willie Drowned in Yarrow; or, The Water o Gamrie. *Unknown.* ESPB; GoTS (Rare Willy.) OxBB ("Willie is fair, an Willë's rair.") GBP

Wilson and Pilcer and Snack stood before the zoo elephant. Elephants Are Different to Different People. Carl Sandburg. MoAmPo

Wilt Chamberlain. R. R. Knudson. ASP

Wil't please your grace to go along with us? A Quotation from Shakespeare with Slight Improvements. "Lewis Carroll." FaBoNo

Wilt thou forgive that sin where I begun. A Hymn to God the Father. John Donne. AWP; EaLo; EBEV; HAP; InPK; JCP; LiTB; MeLP; MePo; NAEL-1; NOBE; OAEL-1; OBS; PoEL-2; PoRA; SCV; SeCP; SeCV-1; TOF; TrGrPo; TrPWD (For Forgiveness.) WGRP (Hymn: "Wilt Thou forgive that sin where I begun.") NOBE

Wilt thou go with me, sweet maid. An Invite to Eternity. John Clare. NAEL-2; NOBVV; OAEL-2; OBNC

Wilt thou hunt the prey for the lion? Bible, *O.T. Fr.* Job: Then the Lord Answered ("Who is this that darkeneth counsel by words without knowledge?"), XXXVIII: 38–XXXIX. FM

Wilt thou love God, as he thee! then digest. John Donne. *Fr.* Holy Sonnets, XV. JCP; OBS; TrCP

Wilt Thou not visit me? Jones Very. OxBA; TrCP; TrPWD

Wilt Thou Set Thine Eyes upon That Which Is Not? Francis Quarles. *Fr.* Emblems, II, 5. OBS (False World, Thou Liest.) SeCePo

Wilt thou then serve the Philistines with that gift. Milton. *Fr.* Samson Agonistes. EBEV

Wilt thou upon the high and giddy mast. Shakespeare. *Fr.* King Henry IV, Pt. II, III, i. MOS

Wilt was so built. Wilt Chamberlain. R. R. Knudson. ASP

Wiltshire Downs. Andrew Young. GTBS-P; OxBTC

Wily Fox, The. Edward Davies, *tr. fr. Welsh by* Joseph P. Clancy. OBWVE

Win at First and Lose at Last; or, A New Game at Cards. Laurence Price. OxBoLi

Winander Lake. Wordsworth. *See* Prelude [*or*, Growth of a Poet's Mind], The: Books.

Wind. Hamish Brown. PoSH

Wind, The. Padraic Colum. *See* I Saw the Wind Today.

Wind, The. Dafydd ap Gwilym, *tr. fr. Welsh by* Joseph P. Clancy. OBWVE

Wind, The. William Henry Davies. SeCePo

Wind. James Fenton. NAEL-2

Wind, The. Dorothy Graddon. BoTP; OnUR

Wind. Ted Hughes. NAEL-2; SoSe

Wind, The. *Malay Oral Tradition*, *tr. by* R. O. Winstedt. WTO

Wind, The. James Reeves. RHPC

Wind, The. Elizabeth Rendall. BoTP

Wind, The. Christina Rossetti. *See* Sing-Song: Who Has Seen the Wind?
Wind. Gary Soto. *Fr.* The Elements of San Joaquin. NoAM
Wind, The. James Stephens. AnIL; BoNaP; HeIP; InPK; MoP; NoAM
Wind, The. Robert Louis Stevenson. BoTP; GN
Wind, The. *Unknown.* FaBoCh; GBP; OxNR
  (High Wind, The.) ChTr
Wind, The. Dorothy Wordsworth. *See* Address to a Child during a Boisterous Winter Evening.
Wind, The. Kazuko Yamada, *tr. fr. Japanese by* Miyao Ohara *and* D. J. Enright. OBD
Wind/ blows white, the/ bird, The. Cypress. Friederike Mayröcker, *tr. by* Beth Bjorklund. CoAuP
Wind/ flattening its gaunt furious self against. Anne Marriott. *Fr.* The Wind Our Enemy. CaP
Wind/ that for a time blew so wildly, The. Kyogoku Tamekane, *tr. fr. Japanese by* Burton Watson. *Fr.* Twenty-three Tanka. FCEI
Wind, The/ only. Song of the Trees. *Unknown, tr. by* Frances Densmore. OBVE
Wind, a rustle of leaves, The. The Edge of Autumn. Michael Anania. NoAM
Wind above Long River spreads the scent of lotus, leaf after leaf, The. Chu Yi-tsun, *tr. fr. Chinese by* Irving Lo. *Fr.* Mallard Lake Boating Songs, XXXI. WFTU
Wind accounted for all, The. The Scythe. Henry Kanabus. UL
Wind and Glacier Voices. Simon J. Ortiz. HATNAP
Wind and Impulse. Duane Big Eagle. STE
Wind and Mist. Edward Thomas. BrPo
Wind and Rain. Michizane, *tr. fr. Chinese by* Burton Watson. JLIC-1
Wind and rain, chill, chill! *Unknown, tr. by* Arthur Waley. BoS
Wind and Silver. Amy Lowell. BoWoP; HeIP; MoAmPo
Wind and the Bird, The. *Unknown, tr. fr. Bushman by* W. H. I. Bleek. PeSA
Wind and the Leaves, The. George Cooper. *See* Come, Little Leaves.
Wind and the Moon, The. George Macdonald. GoJo; MoShBr; OnMSP
Wind and the Rain, The. Shakespeare. *See* Twelfth Night: When That I Was and a Little Tiny Boy.
Wind and the rain are beating down, The. In My Dreams I Searched for You. *Gond Oral Tradition, tr. by* V. Elwin *and* S. Hivale. WTO
Wind and Wave. Charles Warren Stoddard. AA; AnAmPo
Wind and waves sinking low, The. Yakamochi. *Fr.* Manyo Shu. Ma
Wind and Window Flower. Robert Frost. AnAmPo
Wind at a House in the Paddies, The. Tameshige, *tr. fr. Japanese by* Steven D. Carter. WFTW
Wind at Penistone, The. Donald Davie. LiTM; NePoEA-2
Wind at the Door, The. William Barnes. ELP; GBL; GTBS-P; PoEL-4
Wind: "At times I resort, beyond man's discerning." *Unknown, formerly at. to* Cynewulf, *tr. fr. Anglo-Saxon. Fr.* Riddles (Exeter Book). AnOE
Wind at Your Door, The. Robert David Fitzgerald. PoAu-2
Wind begun to knead the grass, The. Emily Dickinson. NAAL-1
Wind begun to rock the grass, The. Emily Dickinson. HAP; NAAL-1; WeW
  (Thunder-Storm, A.) BoNaP
Wind billowing out the seat of my britches, The. Child on Top of a Greenhouse. Theodore Roethke. LCAP; VGW
Wind, bird, and tree. The Words. David Wagoner. PoA
Wind blew all my wedding-day, The. Wedding-Wind. Philip Larkin. MAT
Wind blew: for you, The. Princess Kagami. *Fr.* Manyo Shu. PeBJV
Wind blew in the reign of Hsuan-t'ung, The. Red Corns. Ya Hsien, *tr. by* Dominic Cheung. IFON
Wind Blew like Water. Alice Sadongei. HATNAP
Wind blew strongly like the voice of fate, The. Christoph. Charles Spear. ATNZ
Wind, blow, and don't blow! *Unknown, tr. fr. Japanese by* Hiroaki Sato. *Fr.* Inutsukuba Shu. FCEI
Wind Blows, The. Donagh MacDonagh. NeIP
Wind blows, and with a little broom, The. Cathleen Sweeping. George Johnston. NOBC
Wind blows east, The—the wind blows west. A Salem Witch. Ednah Proctor Clarke. PAH
Wind blows grey, The. Naito Meisetsu, *tr. by* Geoffrey Bownas *and* Anthony Thwaite. PeBJV
Wind blows hot, The. English and foreign birds. Christmas Eve. Karl Shapiro. NYBP
Wind Blows on the Border, The. Antonio Porta, *tr. fr. Italian by* Lawrence R. Smith. NItP
Wind Blows out of the Gates of the Day, The. W. B. Yeats. *Fr.* The Land of Heart's Desire. RB
  (Fairy Song.) MoBrPo

Wind blows roughly, The. Waiting for Love. Teika, *tr. by* Steven D. Carter. WFTW
Wind blows up the tent like a balloon, The. Crimson Tent. John Dos Passos. PoA
Wind blows wild on Bos'n Hill. Bos'n Hill. John Albee. AA
Wind came up out of the sea, A. Daybreak. Longfellow. BOTP; FPL; PoLF; PWR
Wind can't blow any harder, The. Bottle Creek Blues. Sam Hunt. PeNZ
Wind Carol, The. Lewis Turco. SM
Wind carries the bear's spirit. Vanishing Points. Sonya Dorman. BWV
Wind chases signboards, The. City Highway. Judah Leib Teller, *tr. by* Benjamin *and* Barbara Harshav. AYP
Wind comes from opposite poles, The. The Marriage. Mark Strand. EAS; NoAM
Wind comes from the north, The. Suspense. D. H. Lawrence. MoBrPo
Wind comes rushing from the sea, The. One Night at Victoria Beach. Gabriel Okara. UAS
Wind comes up, clouds depart, the moon just overhead, The. Shu Wei, *tr. fr. Chinese by* Barry L. Gartell. *Fr.* Composed on a Moonlit Night Outing on Ancient West, I. WFTU
"Wind doth blow today, my love, The." The Unquiet Grave. *Unknown.* CH; ELP; ESPB; GBP; HAP; HeIP; NoP; OAEL-1; OBD; OxBB; PoEL-1; RB; ViBoPo; WeW
Wind exultant swept, The. A Mood. Winifred Howells. AA
Wind fills her embroidery loom with willow catkins, The. Springtime Embroidery. Yang Chi, *tr. fr. Chinese by* Jonathan Chaves. *Fr.* Paintings of Ladies Engaged in Four Springtime Occupations. CoBLCP
Wind finds the northwest gap, fall comes. Heart of Autumn. Robert Penn Warren. MT
Wind flapped loose, the wind was still, The. The Woodspurge. Dante Gabriel Rossetti. EBEV; ELP; GTBS-P; HAP; HeIP; NOBE; NoP; OAEL-2; OBEV; OBNC; PoEL-5; PrIm; UnPo; WeW
Wind from off the sea says nothing new, The. The Marrow. Theodore Roethke. NYBP
Wind from the east, oh Lapwing of the day. Hafiz, *tr. fr. Persian by* Gertrude Lowthian Bell. *Fr.* Odes, VII. AWP
Wind from the mountain. Mountain Hut in a Storm. Tamekane, *tr. by* Steven D. Carter. WFTW
Wind from the north: the young spring day. The Song of the Four Winds. Thomas Love Peacock. *Fr.* The Misfortunes of Elphin. WiR
Wind from the south, hook in the mouth. How They Bite. *Unknown.* SD
Wind from the West, A. Lauchlan MacLean Watt. PoSH
Wind gallop up Maiden Lane, The. Last Impression of New York. Mason Jordan Mason. PoNe
Wind Gardens. Louis Untermeyer. BXAP
Wind, hark, The! the wind in the angry woods. Summer Storm. Lionel Johnson. BrPo
Wind has at last got into the clock, The. The Wind, the Clock, the We. Laura Riding. LiTA
Wind has blown that searchlight out, The. Autumn Squall—Lake Erie. Lola Ingres Russo. AmFN
Wind has blown the rain away and blown, A. E. E. Cummings. MoAB; MoAmPo
Wind has changed, and all the signs turned right, The. The Omens. Ann Stanford. WSC
Wind has died, no motion now, The. The Estuary. Arthur Rex Dugard Fairburn. ATNZ
Wind has scattered my city to the sheep, The. Ruins of the City of Hay. Randolph Stow. CBAP; PoAu-2
Wind has such a rainy sound, The. The Sound of the Wind. Christina Rossetti. *Fr.* Sing-Song. OnUR
Wind Has Wings, The. *Unknown, tr. by* Raymond de Coccola *and* Paul King. GrPl
Wind, heavy from the land, irons the surf, The. Offshore Breeze. Milton Acorn. NeAC
Wind hinders your walk. On the Road. Judah Leib Teller, *tr. by* Benjamin *and* Barbara Harshav. AYP
Wind howling through the pines, The. Toshiyori, *tr. by* Geoffrey Bownas *and* Anthony Thwaite. PeBJV
Wind in a Frolic, The. William Howitt. MoShBr; OxBChV
Wind in the Grass, The. Siegfried Emerson. BoTP
Wind in the Grass, The. Mark Van Doren. FaBV
Wind in the Pine. Lew Sarett. TrPWD
Wind in the pines, The. Ishikawa Takuboku, *tr. by* Geoffrey Bownas *and* Anthony Thwaite. PeBJV
Wind in the Pines, The. Madison Cawein. AA
Wind in the Tree, The. F. T. Prince. OxBSP
Wind in the Willows, The, *sels.* Kenneth Grahame.

Ducks' Ditty. BoTP; FaPON; GoJo; MoShBr; NTCP; OxBChV; PDV; RHPC

Song of Mr. Toad, The. FaPON; FiBHP; GoJo; NOBL

"Villagers all, this frosty tide." PChr
  (Carol: "Villagers all, this frosty tide.") OHIP
  (Christmas Carol: "Villagers all, this frosty tide.") FaPON

Wind Increases, The. William Carlos Williams. NAAL-2

Wind is a man and goes out from his hut, The. The Wind and the Bird. *Unknown, tr. by* W. H. I. Bleek. PeSA

Wind Is Blind, The. Alice Meynell. MoBrPo; SeCePo

Wind is blowing harshly on the lake, The. St. Mary's Loch. Geoffrey Faber. PoSH

Wind Is Blowing West, The. Joseph Ceravolo. TTTS

Wind is cold, The. Winter. Princess Shikishi, *tr. by* Hiroaki Sato. PBWP

Wind is crisp and carries, The. Residue. Anthony McNeill. PBCV

Wind is desolate in the fields, The. The Deserted Homestead. Loren C. Eiseley. PoA

Wind is east but the hot weather continues, The. American Letter. Archibald MacLeish. AmPP; OxBA

Wind is fair, The. Arnaut de Mareuil, *tr. by* Paul Blackburn. Pro

Wind is fragrant, the dew is sweet, The. The Taoist Nun. Sun Kuang-hsien, *tr. by* Lois Fusek. ATF

Wind is gentle, The. Ryokan, *tr. by* Geoffrey Bownas *and* Anthony Thwaite. PeBJV

Wind Is Ill, The. John Malcolm Brinnin. LiTA

Wind is making countries, The. Homecoming. Dennis Scott. PBCV

Wind is not nigh. Zone of Death. William Everson. VGW

Wind is not right today, The. Bodega, Goodbye. Edwin Honig. NoAM

Wind is piercing chill, The. Battlefield. Richard Aldington. MMA; OBWP

Wind is rough, The. Landscape: 6. Ono Tozaburo, *tr. by* Sato. FCEI

Wind is ruffling the tawny pelt, A. A Far Cry from Africa. Derek Walcott. HeIP; MoP; NAEL-2; NoAM; PVCV; TTY; UnPo

Wind is rustling, The. Prince Munenaga, *tr. by* Steven D. Carter. WFTW

Wind is shaking this house, The. The Storm House. Elizabeth Jennings. WPE

Wind is thin. *Unknown, tr. fr. Latin by* Willis Barnstone. *Fr.* Cambridge Songs. BoWoP

Wind is wild tonight, The. *Unknown.* NOIV

Wind it blew, and the ship it flew, The. The Earl o' Quarterdeck. George Macdonald. BeLS

Wind it blew from east to west, The. Get Up and Bar the Door. *Unknown.* AmFP

Wind It Blew up the Railroad Track, The. *Unknown.* AS

Wind it wailed, the wind it moaned, The. Alec Yeaton's Son. Thomas Bailey Aldrich. MOS

Wind like an ocean, The. Larry Eigner. PoM

Wind loses its fingers reaching out, The. Ephemeral. Sándor Weöres, *tr. by* Jascha Kessler. FOC

Wind may blow the snow about, The. A Country Boy in Winter. Sarah Orne Jewett. OBCA

Wind meets me at Penistone, The. The Wind at Penistone. Donald Davie. LiTM; NePoEA-2

Wind moves the last line. "101." Alan Davies. IAT

Wind mutters thinly on the sagging wire. Prairie Graveyard. Anne Marriott. CaP; NOBC; OBCV

Wind o' the East dark with rain. The Efficient Wife's Complaint. Confucius, *tr. fr. Chinese by* Ezra Pound. *Fr.* Airs of Pei. CTC

Wind, O you wind who storms my blood. Love of the Scorching Wind. László Nagy, *tr. by* Kenneth McRobbie. MHuP

Wind of an Evening Shower. Shotetsu, *tr. fr. Japanese by* Steven D. Carter. WFTW

Wind of dawning riffles the young furze, The. Drafts for a Quatrain. Edmund Wilson. OBAL

Wind of Hampstead Heath still burns my cheek, The. Breath of Hampstead Heath. Edith M. Thomas. AA

Wind of heaven, the maidens cross the ice. Princess Shikishi, *tr. fr. Japanese by* Hiroaki Sato. *Fr.* Seventy-eight Tanka. FCEI

Wind of Late Summer, The. Pamela Stewart. NAmP

Wind of sage in which the world dreams. Buffalo Marrow on Black. Lance Henson. STE

Wind of the City Streets. To a June Breeze. H. C. Bunner. AA

Wind of the North. The Four Winds. Charles Henry Lüders. AA

Wind of the Prairie. Grace Clementine Howes. GoYe

Wind of the West, that fans with fragrant wing. To the Western Wind. Judah Halevi, *tr. by* Solomon Solis-Cohen. TrJP

Wind on the Corn. Charles Tennyson Turner. EBVV

Wind on the Hills, The. Dora Sigerson Shorter. NOBVV

Wind one morning sprang up from sleep, The. The Wind in a Frolic. William Howitt. MoShBr; OxBChV

Wind Our Enemy, The, *sel.* Anne Marriott.
  "Wind/ flattening its gaunt furious self against." CaP

Wind outside this beach house, The. The Beach House. James Keir Baxter. ATNZ

Wind passes, the mirror of blossoms clouds, A. Teika, *tr. fr. Japanese by* Hiroaki Sato. *Fr.* Eighty-four Tanka. FCEI

Wind picks at the clapboard. Noah in New England. Tom Lowenstein. VWA

Wind picks up and the water grows rough and choppy, The. A Sail on the Lake after Rain. Huang Ching-jen, *tr. by* Daniel Bryant. WFTU

Wind piercing, hill bare, hard to find shelter. *Unknown, tr. fr. Welsh by* Joseph P. Clancy. *Fr.* Winter. OBWVE

Wind roars and the river roars, The. The Sounding Portage. Annie Charlotte Dalton. CaP

Wind rocks the car. Like This Together. Adrienne Rich. VGW

Wind rose cold under our robes, and straw blew loose. The Boy Shepherds' Simile. David Bottoms. MT

Wind runs free across our plains, The. For Adolf Eichmann. Primo Levi. VWA, *tr. by* Ruth Feldman *and* Brian Swann

Wind sang to the cornfields, The. August. Eunice Fallon. BoTP

Wind searching as a sieve of brass. Storm at Sea. *Malay Oral Tradition, tr. by* R. O. Winstedt. WTO

Wind Secrets. Diane Wakoski. AmPA

Wind shakes my window frames. October in the Country: 1983. James Simmons. CIP

Wind shall lull us yet, The. From the Antique. Christina Rossetti. EnLoPo

Wind sighs in the reeds—autumn on the rustic shore, The. T'ang Yin, *tr. fr. Chinese by* Jonathan Chaves. *Fr.* Poems Inscribed on Paintings. CoBLCP

Wind Sleepers, The. Hilda Doolittle ("H. D.") WPE

Wind Song. Carl Sandburg. MoAB; MoAmPo; MoShBr

Wind Sou'west, The. *Unknown.* AmFP

Wind spills plovers, picks them up, The. Chiyojo, *tr. fr. Japanese by* Hiroaki Sato. *Fr.* Seventeen Hokku. FCEI

Wind Sprang Up at Four o'Clock, The. T. S. Eliot. LiTB

Wind sprays pale dirt into my mouth, The. The Elements of San Joaquin. Gary Soto. NPGG

Wind, stirring in the dark foliage, brings, The. God's Harp. Gustav Falke, *tr. by* Ludwig Lewisohn. AWP

Wind stirs the willows, The. Songs of the Ghost Dance. *Unknown.* WSC

Wind stood up, and gave a shout, The. The Wind. James Stephens. AnIL; BoNaP; HeIP; InPK; MoP; NoAM

Wind subsided, The. Note apropos a Light Breeze and an Elderly Couple on a Bench, Together, in the National Park at Ram. Abba Kovner, *tr. by* Bernhard Frank. MHeP

Wind Suffers of Blowing, The. Laura Riding. RB

Wind sways the pines, A. Dirge in Woods. George Meredith. FF; NAEL-2; OBEV; OBNC; OPOP; WiR

Wind-swept Wheat, The. "Madeline Bridges." AA

Wind takes colour from the trees, The. Winds. Hugh McCrae. CBAP

Wind—tapped like a tired man, The. Emily Dickinson. Mes; MoAB; MoAmPo; TOF
  (Wind's Visit, The.) AnAmPo

Wind, That Comes on Suddenly, A. Ory Bernstein, *tr. fr. Hebrew by* Warren Bargad *and* Stanley F. Chyet. IP

Wind that rose, A. Emily Dickinson. RB

Wind That Shakes the Rushes, The. John Clare. PoRA

Wind that speeds the bee and plucks the bee-line. Awake! W. R. Rodgers. LiTM; WaP

Wind that sweeps down Ikaho, The. *Unknown, tr. fr. Japanese. Fr.* Manyo Shu. PeBJV

Wind that tossed the pines. Kyogoku Tamekane, *tr. fr. Japanese by* Burton Watson. *Fr.* Twenty-three Tanka. FCEI

Wind, the Clock, the We, The. Laura Riding. LiTA

Wind Took Up the Northern Things, The. Emily Dickinson. SOTW; TTTS

Wind-tossed catkins fly past a silken blanket of green. Hsiang Hung-tso, *tr. by* Irving Lo. WFTU

Wind turned, The. Volitions. A. R. Ammons. CAPP

Wind voice calls and calls you, The. The Summons. Elizabeth Roberts MacDonald. CaP

Wind wafts his fitful. Waiting for the Wind. Donald Finkel. BLA

Wind wafts palace bells sounding the hour of dawn. Through the Snow to Early Duty at the Office. Michizane, *tr. by* Burton Watson. JLIC-1

Wind was a torrent of darkness among the gusty trees, The. The Highwayman. Alfred Noyes. BeLS; FaBV; FaFP; FaPON, *abr.;* FaPON; FPL; OBNV; OHFP; PoLF

Wind was blowing over the moors, The. Charlotte Brontë. "Susan Coolidge." OBCA

Wind Was There, The. Bravig Imbs. EAS

Wind whines and whines the shingle. On the Beach at Fontana. James Joyce. MoBrPo; OBMV; PoA; RB; SoSe

Wind whistled loud at the window-pane, The. William Brighty Rands. BoTP

Wind-Wolves. William D. Sargent. RHPC

Wind won't come to draw smiles in dream sand, The. Yehuda Amichai, tr. by Warren Bargad and Stanley F.Chyet. IP

Wind would tear a dead man's shroud. Wind. Malay Oral Tradition, tr. by R. O. Winstedt. WTO

Windfall. David Mitchell. ATNZ

Windfall. F. R. Scott. CaP

Windharp. John Montague. CIP; FaBCIP

Windhover, The. Gerard Manley Hopkins. ACP; BrPo; CMoP; EaLo; EBVV; GTBS-P; HAP; InPK; InPS; InvP; LiTB; LiTM; MoAB; MoBrPo; MoP; NAEL-2; NoAM; NOBE; NOBVV; NoP; OAEL-2; OBNC; PBBP; PoE; PoEL-5; PoRA; PPP; PrIm; RB; SCV; TEP; TOF; UnPo; WeW

Windigo. Louise Erdrich. NoAM

Windigo. Paulette Jiles. NOBC

Winding Pond. Hung Liang-chi, tr. fr. Chinese by Irving Lo. Fr. To Dispel the Cold: Two Poems on Spring, II. WFTU

Winding Up. Derek Walcott. NoAM

Winding way the serpent takes, The. Norembega. Whittier. PAH

Winding, winding. The Lost Valley. Gordon J. Gadsby. PoSH

Windlass Song. William Allingham. GN

Windless city built on decaying granite, loose ends. Thomas McGrath. Fr. Letter to an Imaginary Friend, Part Two, II, 2–5. NNaP

Windmill, The. E. V. Lucas. BoTP

Windmill, The. Longfellow. MoShBr

Windmill of Evening, The. Shlomo Reich, tr. fr. French. VWA, tr. by Mira Reich

Windmill on the Cape. William Vincent Sieller. GoYe

Windmill on the riverbank, The. At the Art Exhibit. Manfred Winkler, tr. by Bernhard Frank. MHeP

Window, The. Conrad Aiken. CMoP

Window, The. Robert Creeley. CAPP; NoAM; NOBA; TAP; VGW

Window, The. Stephen Dobyns. MAYP

Window, A. Forugh Farrokhzad, tr. fr. Persian by Deirdre Lashgari. OV

Window, The. Edwin Muir. LiTM

Window. Bruce Smith. DiL

Window, The. Iain Crichton Smith. NePoEA-2

Window and a river. Butterflies, A. Iowa Recollected in Tranquility. Peter Jay. WCI

Window Boxes ("A window box of pansies"). Eleanor Farjeon. FaPON

Window cleaner's life is grand!, A. The Window Cleaner. Elizabeth Fleming. BoTP

Window curtain nodding in the May breeze. Live for It. Ellen Bass. ER

Window-Dreaming with SAS. Haim Guri, tr. fr. Hebrew by Warren Bargad and Stanley F. Chyet. IP

Window Frames the Moon, The. Laureen Mar. BrSi

Window-Glance, The. Heine, tr. fr. German by John Todhunter. AWP

Window insulates me from the street, The. Maternity Gown. David Holbrook. OxBTC

Window into the ground, A. Skara Brae. Michael Longley. FaBCIP

Window is broken, A. The Night Has Twenty-four Hours. Pedro Juan Pietri. InW

Window is wide and lo, beyond its bars, The. Interlude: The Casement. Christopher John Brennan. InW

Window Ledge in the Atom Age. E. B. White. NBLV; OBAL

Window of the Tobacco Shop, The. Constantine P. Cavafy, tr. fr. Greek by Edmund Keeley and Philip Sherrard. PeHV

Window on the North, A. R. A. D. Ford. MoCV

Window pales, and by its paltry light, The. Aubade: Donna Anna to Juan, Still Asleep. Richard Howard. PoA

Window Seat, A. Albert Goldbarth. NAmP

Window Sill, The. Robert Graves. EnLoPo

Window, The; or, The Song of the Wrens, sel. Tennyson. Ay. PBBP

Window was made of ice with bears lumbering across it, The. Bad Dream. Louis MacNeice. FaBCIP; NoAM

Window was open all night long, The. All Night Long. Nina Cassian, tr. by Herbert Kuhner. VWA

Window Washer. Charles Simic. BLA

Windows, The. Constantine P. Cavafy, tr. fr. Greek by Edmund Keeley and Philip Sherrard. VMG

Windows. William Dickey. KS

Windows, The. George Herbert. MeLP; NAEL-1; NOCV; NoP; PoE; SeCP; SeCV-1; TrCP

Windows. Mordechai Husid, tr. fr. Yiddish by Seymour Mayne and Rivka Augenfeld. VWA

Windows. João Cabral de Melo Neto, tr. fr. Portuguese by Jean Valentine. ATCBP

Windows flash, flare up above the square. Evening. A. Leyeles, tr. fr. Yiddish by Benjamin and Barbara Harshav. Fr. New York. AYP

Windows in Providence. Aliki Barnstone. BoWoP

Window's length beyond the Pleiades, A. First Snow on an Airfield. John Ciardi. PoA

Windows of Heaven were open wide, The. A Ballad of the Conemaugh Flood. Hardwick Drummond Rawnsley. PAH

Windows of Sound. Antonin Artaud, tr. fr. French by Michael Benedikt. POS

Windows of the church are bright, The. Christmas Thoughts, by a Modern Thinker. William Hurrell Mallock. NOBVV

Windrush down the timber chutes. Mountain Wind. Barbara Kunz Loots. RHPC

Winds. Hugh McCrae. CBAP

Winds, The. Thomas Tusser. WiR

Winds Are Bleak, Stars Are Bright. "Furnley Maurice." Fr. The Victoria Markets Recollected in Tranquillity. PoAu-2

Winds are dark passages among the stars, The. Turtle. Peter Blue Cloud. HATNAP

Wind's bride seized me, The. In the Open Fields. Hugo Sonnenschein. VWA, tr. by Edouard Roditi

Winds had hushed at last as by command, The. The Sower. Mathilde Blind. WPE

Winds have talked with him confidingly, The. Longfellow. James Whitcomb Riley. AA

Wind's in the heart of me, a fire's in my heels, A. A Wanderer's Song. John Masefield. MoAB; MoBrPo

Wind's Lament, The. John Morris-Jones, tr. fr. Welsh by Anthony Conran. OBWVE

Winds of Africa. Dorothy S. Obi. WPOW

Winds of autumn, The. Basho, tr. by Geoffrey Bownas and Anthony Thwaite. PeBJV

Winds of Change, The. Charles G. Ballard. VoR

Winds of doctrine blow both ways at once, The. Conrad Aiken. Fr. A Letter from Li Po. VGW

Winds of Fate, The. Ella Wheeler Wilcox. AnAmPo; BLPA; FPL; WBLP

Winds of spring, The. Saigyo, tr. by Geoffrey Bownas and Anthony Thwaite. PeBJV

Winds on the stems make them creak like manmade things. Stalin. Robert Lowell. HCAP

Wind's on the wold, The. Inscription for an Old Bed. William Morris. OBEV; WiR

(For the Bed at Kelmscott.) FaBoRV; PoEL-5

(Lines for a Bed at Kelmscott Manor.) CH

Wind's spine is broken, The. Storm Tide on Mejit. Unknown, tr. by Augustin Kramer and Willard Trask. RFM

Winds that drift over the desert. Winds of Africa. Dorothy S. Obi. WPOW

Winds that sweep the southern mountains. Allatoona. Unknown. PAH

Winds they did blow, The. The Squirrel. Unknown. BoTP; OxNR

Winds through [or thro'] the olive trees. Long, Long Ago. Unknown. FaPON; OHIP; PChr; PDV

(Christmas Song, A.) BoTP

Winds tread the autumn's syllables, The. Transmissions. Shin Dong-jip, tr. by Koh Chang-soo. ACKP

Wind's Visit, The. Emily Dickinson. See Wind tapped like a tired man, The.

Winds, whisper gently whilst she sleeps. Laura Sleeping. Charles Cotton. ELP; OBS; ViBoPo

Winds will crack tree trunks. Figure. Judah Leib Teller, tr. by Benjamin and Barbara Harshav. AYP

Winds; words of the wind; rumor of great walls pierced. Hayden Carruth. Fr. The Asylum, II. SM

Wind's Work. T. Sturge Moore. BrPo

Windsor Castle, sel. Earl of Surrey.

Prisoned in Windsor, He Recounteth His Pleasure There Passed. NAEL-1

Windsor Forest, sels. Pope.

"Groves of Eden, vanished now so long, The." OAEL-1

Hunt, The. NIP

"See! from the brake the whirring Pheasant springs." FM; PoEL-3

"Thy forests, Windsor! and thy green retreats." NOEC

"When milder autumn summer's heat succeeds." PBBP

(Field Sports.) SeCePo

Windy Bill. Unknown. CowP

Windy Bishop, The. Wilfred Watson. OBCV
Windy Day, A. Winifred Howard. FaPON
Windy Night, The. Thomas Buchanan Read. GN
Windy night was blowing on Rome, A. The Rider at The Gate. John Masefield. BrPo
Windy Nights. Robert Louis Stevenson. BoTP; GoJo; OxBChV; PoRA; RHPC; RR
Wine. Micah Joseph Lebensohn, *tr. fr. Hebrew.* TrJP, *tr. by* A. M. Klein
Wine and cakes for gentlemen. *Unknown.* OxNR
Wine and Dew. Richard Henry Stoddard. AA
Wine and feasts I followed with the host of officials. Banished from the Palace. Prince Nakao, *tr. by* Burton Watson. JLIC-1
Wine and Grief. Solomon Ibn Gabirol, *tr. fr. Hebrew by* Emma Lazarus. TrJP
Wine and oil gleaming within their heads. Double Ode. Muriel Rukeyser, *tr. by* Edmund Keeley. AnAn; LCAP
Wine and Water. G. K. Chesteron. *Fr.* The Flying Inn. ACP; CenHV; FaBoCo; FiBHP; MoBrPo
Wine and woman and song. Villanelle of the Poet's Road. Ernest Dowson. OBMV; TrGrPo; UnPo
Wine Bowl. Hilda Doolittle ("H. D.") NoP
Wine came in gallon bottles, The. My Early Religious Education. Sally Fisher. SoTCo
Wine comes in at the mouth. A Drinking Song. W. B. Yeats. BoLoP; OAEL-2
Wine, friend, and truth, the proverb says, agree. Theocritus, *tr. fr. Greek by* Thomas Creech. *Fr.* Idylls, XXVI. PeHV
Wine just purchased, The. Enjoying Retirement ("The wine just purchased.") Ma Chih-yüan, *tr. fr. Chinese by* Jonathan Chaves. *Fr.* Three Poems to the Tune "Ssu-k'uai yü", 1. CoBLCP
Wine-maiden. Midnight Dancer. Langston Hughes. FF
Wine Menagerie, The. Hart Crane. NoAM; NOBA; OxBA; VGW
Wine o Living. Matt Marshall. PoSH
Wine of Love is music, The. James Thomson ("B. V.") *Fr.* Sunday up the River, XVIII. OBEV
Wine of the new vintage they brought us. The New Vintage. Douglas Le Pan. OBCV
Wine-Press of Los, The. Blake. *See* Milton: This wine-press is call'd war on earth.
Wine-Songs, sels. Moses Ibn Ezra, *tr. fr. Hebrew by* Solomon Solis-Cohen. TrJP
   Awake, My Soul.
   Bring Me the Cup.
   Drink, Friends.
   Rosy Days Are Numbered, The.
Wine taken with excess. Temperance. *Unknown.* ACP
Wine, the red coals, the flaring gas. At the Cavour. Arthur Symons. NOBVV; OxBSP
Wine upon beer, I counsel thee. *Unknown.* FaBoUs
Wine Vessels: Two Labels. Yang Mu, *tr. fr. Chinese by* Dominic Cheung. IFON
Wineglass, The. E. A. Baratynsky, *tr. fr. Russian by* Alan Myers. AAA
Winemaker's Beat-étude, The. Alfred W. Purdy. MoCV
Wine's inebriety. Asadullah Khan Ghalib, *tr. by* Ahmed Ali. GoT
Wing of Separation, The. Ibn Darraj al-Andalusi, *tr. fr. Arabic by* J. B. Trend. AWP
Wing of the moth were perhaps the sail, The. Asadullah Khan Ghalib, *tr. by* Ahmed Ali. GoT
Wing says, "I am the space behind you", The. What the Wing Says. David Swanger. KS
Wingatui. Bill Manhire. ATNZ
Winged bull trundles to the wired perimeter, The. Cecil Day Lewis. *Fr.* Flight to Italy. OxBTC
Winged Heart, A. Henry Vaughan. *Fr.* Of Life and Death. FaBoRV
Winged horses descend to drink, The. On a Bas-Relief. W. Wesley Trimpi. NePoEA
Winged in Gold. Euros Bowen, *tr. fr. Welsh by the author.* OBWVE
Wingéd lion on top of that column, The. Notes Made in the Piazza San Marco. May Swenson. CoAP
Winged Man. Stephen Vincent Benét. MoAmPo
Winged mimic of the woods! thou motley fool! To the Mocking-bird. Richard Henry Wilde. AA
Winged wonder of motion. The Dragonfly. Theodore Harding Rand. CaP
Winged Worshippers, The. Charles Sprague. AA
Wingfoot Lake. Rita Dove. BLA
Wings. Bible, *O.T. Fr.* Psalms: Psalm LV, 6-7 ("Give ear to my prayer.") FaPON
Wings. Aileen Fisher. RAR
Wings, The. Denise Levertov. CAPP

Wings. Elissa Hamilton Malcohn. BWV
Wings. Maruyama Kaoru, *tr. fr. Japanese by* Geoffrey Bownas *and* Anthony Thwaite. PeBJV
Wings. Judith Wright. CBAP
Wings/ hid by your merciless. Dreamtime I You Dog You. Thulani Davis. ER
Wings and Seeds. Sandra McPherson. GeTw
Wings and Wheels. Nancy Byrd Turner
Wings filmed, the threads of knowledge thicken. The Jam Trap. Charles Tomlinson. MoBrPo
Wings in the Dark. John Gray. NOBVV
Wings like pistols flashing at his sides. The Sparrow Hawk. Russell Hoban. RHPC
Wings of a bird, The. Totem. Nissim Ezekiel. VWA
Wings of a Wild Goose, The. Chrystos. GLP
Wings of the gull flapping in the dark sea sky, The. Song of the Sail. Maruyama Kaoru, *tr. by* Hiroaki Sato. FCEI
Wings of the mayfly. *Unknown, tr. by* Arthur Waley. BoS
Wings of Time are black and white, The. Compensation. Emerson. AmPP; NOBA
Wings outstretched, a horned owl. Signatures. Daniel Hoffman. VGW
Wings stay caught, trapped between the locked shutters, The. There or Elsewhere. Pierre Reverdy, *tr. by* Michael Benedikt. POS
Wingspan. Bartolo Cattafi, *tr. fr. Italian by* Lawrence R. Smith. NItP
Wingtip. Carl Sandburg. PCP
Wingwalking in Oregon. Robert Peterson. NeAC
Winifred Waters. William Brighty Rands. OxBChV
Winifreda. *Unknown.* OBEV
Winked too much and were afraid of snakes. The Monkeys. Marianne Moore. CMoP; LiTA; NOBA; OxBA
Winkte. Maurice Kenny. GLP
Winners, The. Kipling. *Fr.* The Story of the Gadsbys. BLPA; FaPoR; FPL
Winnie Song. Lucille Clifton. ER
Winnie Whiney, all things grieve her. Ten Kinds. Mary Mapes Dodge. RHPC
Winning of Cales, The. Thomas Deloney. CoMu; OBTV; OxBSS
Winning of the TV West, The. John T. Alexander. AmFN; RHPC
Winning wrestler leaves, The. Kito, *tr. fr. Japanese by* Hiroaki Sato. *Fr.* Twenty-four Hokku. FCEI
Wino was eating soup, The. Tornado Soup. A. K. Redwing. VoR
Winslow Crater. Edward Bryant. BWV
Winsome Torment rose from slumber, rubbed his eyes, and went his way. The Hammam Name. James Elroy Flecker. BrPo; PeHV
Wintah Styles, De. Maggie Pogue Johnson. CBWP-4
Winter. Bella Akhmadulina, *tr. fr. Russian by* Barbara Einzig. BoWoP
Winter. Muhammad al-Maghut, *tr. fr. Arabic by* Abdullah al-Udhari. MPAW
Winter. Alexander Barclay. *Fr.* Eclogues, V. OxBLMV
Winter. Enid Blyton. BoTP
Winter. Chang Yü, *tr. fr. Chinese by* Jonathan Chaves. *Fr.* The Four Seasons in the Mountains. CoBLCP
Winter, *sel.* Charles Cotton.
   Winter's Troops. ChTr
Winter. Walter de la Mare. ChTr; OAEL-2; OBMV
Winter. John Lyle Donaghy. BIrV
Winter. Gawin Douglas. SeCePo
Winter. Richard Hughes. OBMV; OBWVE
Winter. W. D. Landor. BoTP
Winter. Mani Leib, *tr. fr. Yiddish by* Keith Bosley. VWA
Winter. Charles Mair. OBCV
Winter. Masayori, *tr. fr. Japanese by* Steven D. Carter. WFTW
Winter. Samuel Menashe. GrPl
Winter. Christina Rossetti. BoTP
Winter. Yankev-Yitskhok Segal, *tr. fr. Yiddish by* Grace Schulman. PeBMYV
Winter. Shakespeare. *See* Love's Labour's Lost: When Icicles Hang by the Wall.
Winter. Shmu'el Shatal, *tr. fr. Hebrew by* Bernhard Frank. MHeP
Winter. Princess Shikishi, *tr. fr. Japanese by* Hiroaki Sato. PBWP
Winter. Spenser. *Fr.* The Faerie Queene, VII, 7. GN
Winter. Ruth Stone. BoWoP
Winter. J. M. Synge. NOIV; OBMV; OxBTC
Winter, *sels.* James Thomson. *Fr.* The Seasons.
   "Fowls of heaven, The." PBBP
   "Keener tempests come, The: and fuming dun." EBEV; EnRP; NoP
Winter ("As thus the snows arise, and foul and fierce"). SeCePo
Winter ("Drooping, the labourer-ox"). FM
Winter ("Now, when the cheerless empire of the sky"). OxBA

Winter ("See, Winter comes, to rule the varied year"). NOEC; TEP
Winter ("What art thou, frost? and whence are thy keen stores"). OxBS
Winter ("When from the pallid sky the sun descends"). OAEL-1; OxBS
Winter Night, A. NOBE
Winter, *sel. Unknown, tr. fr. Welsh by* Joseph P. Clancy.
  "Wind piercing, hill bare, hard to find shelter." OBWVE
Winter. Sheila Wingfield. EnLoPo
Winter and Spring. *Unknown.* BoTP
Winter and Summer. Stephen Spender. MoAB; MoBrPo
Winter and summer, whatever the weather. The Floor and the Ceiling.
  William Jay Smith. GrPl; OBCA
Winter Anemones. Charles Brasch. *Fr.* Night Cries, Wakari Hospital.
  ATNZ; PeNZ
Winter ("As thus the snows arise, and foul and fierce"). James Thomson.
  Fr. The Seasons: Winter. SeCePo
Winter at Night in the Old Hut. Moishe Kulbak, *tr. fr. Yiddish by*
  Leonard Wolf. *Fr.* Byelorussia. PeBMYV
Winter at Tomi. Ovid, *tr. fr. Latin by* F. A. Wright. AWP
Winter Bell. Shotetsu, *tr. fr. Japanese by* Steven D. Carter. WFTW
Winter Birds. Linda Gregg. NAmP
Winter birds, The. Migration. Pinkie Gordon Lane. BlSi
Winter blast. Mukai Kyorai, *tr. by* Geoffrey Bownas *and* Anthony
  Thwaite. PeBJV
Winter Bouquet. Lewis Turco. EOEF
Winter Burn. Roberta Hill. VoR
Winter Climb. Beinn Eunaich. PoSH
Winter Clothes. Karla Kuskin. RHPC
Winter comes, and a crow perches. Kikaku, *tr. fr. Japanese by* Hiroaki
  Sato. *Fr.* Thirty-three Hokku. FCEI
Winter comes I walk alone, The. The Winters Spring. John Clare.
  NOBVV
Winter Coming On. Martin Bell, *after the French of* Jules Laforgue.
  FaBoMo; OBVE; OxBTC
Winter Conversation. Nishiwaki Junzaburo, *tr. fr. Japanese by* Hiroaki
  Sato. FCEI
Winter copse. Kito, *tr. by* Geoffrey Bownas *and* Anthony Thwaite.
  PeBJV
Winter Count of Sean Spotted Wolf. Earle Thompson. STE
Winter Cricket. John Heath-Stubbs. OBCP
Winter Dawn. D. H. Lawrence. BrPo
Winter Day. Susannah Fried, *tr. fr. Czech by* Anthony Rudolf. VWA
Winter Day. Whittier. *See* Snow-bound; a Winter Idyl: Sun that brief
  December day, The.
Winter day, A: frozen on horseback, a shadow. Basho, *tr. fr. Japanese
  by* Burton Watson. *Fr.* Seventy-six Hokku. FCEI
Winter Daybreak above Vence, A. James Wright. InPS; LCAP
Winter Days. Henry Abbey. AA
Winter Days. Gareth Owen. OBCP
Winter days are drawin' nigh, De. Winter is Coming. Waverly Turner
  Carmichael. BANP
Winter Deepening, The. Richard Wilbur. Son
Winter Drive. James McAuley. PoA
Winter ("Drooping, the labourer-ox"). James Thomson. *Fr.* The
  Seasons: Winter. FM
Winter Drought. Michael Ryan. NAmP
Winter: East Anglia. Edmund Blunden. OxBTC
Winter Encounters. Charles Tomlinson. LiTM
Winter Evening. Anzai Hitoshi, *tr. fr. Japanese by* Hiroaki Sato.
  FCEI
Winter Evening. Archibald Lampman. NOBC; OBCV
Winter Evening. Judah Leib Teller, *tr. fr. Yiddish by* Benjamin *and*
  Barbara Harshav. AYP
Winter Evening. Walter de la Mare. FaBoRV
Winter Evening ("Just when our drawing-rooms begin to blaze"). William
  Cowper. *Fr.* The Task. NOEC
Winter Evening Poem. Laura Jensen. LCAP
Winter evening settles down, The. T. S. Eliot. *Fr.* Preludes (I-IV).
  HeIP; LiTA; MoShBr; NoP; OBMV; PPP; SeCePo; SOTW; TwCP;
  UnPo; VGW; WeW
Winter Evening, The ("Hark! 'tis the twanging horn o'er yonder bridge").
  William Cowper. *Fr.* The Task, IV. SeCePo
  (Post-Boy, The.) FiP
Winter Fairyland in Vermont. Francis P. Osgood. WeW
Winter fells. Deathward. John Lyle Donaghy. BIrV
Winter fly, The. *Unknown, tr. by* Geoffrey Bownas *and* Anthony
  Thwaite. PeBJV
Winter for a moment takes the mind; the snow. Conrad Aiken. *Fr.*
  Preludes for Memnon; or, Preludes to Attitude. LiTA; LiTM;
  OxBA
Winter Galaxy. Charles Heavysege. *See* Stars Are Glittering in the
  Frosty Sky, The.

Winter Garden. Donald Britton. EOEF
Winter Garden. David Gascoyne. GTBS-P
Winter goes and weather betters. Marcabrun, *tr. by* Paul Blackburn. Pro
Winter has a pencil. Pencil and Paint. Eleanor Farjeon. PDV
Winter has at last come. Minamoto no Shigeyuki, *tr. fr. Japanese by*
  Arthur Waley. *Fr.* Shui Shu. AWP
Winter Has Come. *Unknown, tr. fr. Old Irish by* Kenneth Jackson.
  AnIL
Winter Has Come. Katri Vala, *tr. fr. Finnish by* Aili Jarvenpa. SOP
Winter has come with scarcity. Winter Has Come. *Unknown, tr. by*
  Kenneth Jackson. AnIL
Winter has wrecked the legend of your wings. To the Ghost of a Kite.
  James Wright. NePoEA
Winter Heavens. George Meredith. NoP
Winter Holding off the Coast of North America. N. Scott Momaday.
  CDW
Winter Homily on the Calton Hill. Douglas Young. OxBS
Winter Hymn—to the Snow, A. Ebenezer Jones. OBNC
Winter in Durnover Field. Thomas Hardy. MoBrPo
Winter in Étienburgh. Stephen Parker. NYBP
Winter in Jerusalem. James Keir Baxter. ATNZ
Winter in Lower Canada. Standish O'Grady. *Fr.* The Emigrant.
  NOBC; OBCV
Winter in Strathearn, *sel.* John Davidson.
  Twinkling Earn, The. PoSH
Winter in the country, Southampton, pale horse. Frank O'Hara. Ted
  Berrigan. UL
Winter in the Fens. John Clare. BoNaP
Winter is cold-hearted. Summer. Christina Rossetti. BoNaP; ELP
Winter is Coming. Waverly Turner Carmichael. BANP
Winter is fallen early. The Children of Stare. Walter de la Mare. BrPo;
  Mes
Winter Is Here. "Katri Vala", *tr. fr. Finnish by* Jaakko A. Ahokas.
  PBWP
Winter is icumen [*or* icummen] in. Ancient Music. Ezra Pound.
  BXAP; FaBoCo; FaBoPa; FF; HeIP; LiTM; NBLV; OBAL; OxBA;
  Par; TW
Winter is passing, and the bells. Spring in the Students' Quarter. Henry
  Murger, *tr. by* Andrew Lang. AWP
Winter Journey. Stanislaw Wygodski, *tr. fr. Polish by* Isaac Komem.
  VWA
Winter Joys. Dorothy Graddon. BoTP
Winter Juniper. Joseph Langland. NePoEA
Winter kept us in the valleys. April, Glengarry. Philip Coxon.
  PoSH
Winter Lakes, The. Wilfred Campbell. BoNaP; NOBC; OBCV
Winter Landscape. John Berryman. LiTA; LiTM; MoAmPo; TwCP
Winter Landscape. Stephen Spender. MoAB; MoBrPo
Winter Landscape with a Girl in Brown Shoes. Sherod Santos. AnAn
Winter Light. Jon Anderson. AnAn
Winter Love, *sel. Hilda Doolittle ("H. D.").*
  "So we were together." FaBoWP
Winter Love. Elizabeth Jennings. BoLoP; NePoEA
Winter Mask. Allen Tate. OxBA; Prf
Winter Memories. Henry David Thoreau. AmPP; AnAmPo; OxBA
Winter Moon. Langston Hughes. RHPC
Winter Moon. Philippe Jaccottet, *tr. fr. French by* Charles Tomlinson.
  RHTwFP
Winter Moon, The. Tagaki Kyozo, *tr. fr. Japanese by* James Kirkup *and*
  Nakamo Michio. LLLT
Winter moon. Myoe, *tr. fr. Japanese by* Burton Watson. *Fr.* Ten
  Tanka. FCEI
Winter Moon. Maria Luisa Spaziani, *tr. fr. Italian by* Lynne Lawner.
  PBWP
Winter Moon. Tameshige, *tr. fr. Japanese by* Steven D. Carter. WFTW
Winter Moon after a Rain, The. Tamesada, *tr. fr. Japanese by* Steven D.
  Carter. WFTW
Winter Morning, A. James Russell Lowell. *Fr.* The Vision of Sir
  Launfal, II. GN, *fr. pt.* II.
Winter Morning. William Jay Smith. BoNaP
Winter Music. Tamura Ryuichi, *tr. fr. Japanese by* Hiroaki Sato. FCEI
Winter must be here, The. What We Can. Ray A. Young Bear. VoR
Winter: My Secret. Christina Rossetti. BrRo; NAEL-2; NOBVV; TEP
Winter my theme confines; whose nitry wind. John Gay. *Fr.* Trivia; or,
  The Art of Walking the Streets of London, II. NOEC
Winter Night, A. William Barnes. ChTr; FaBoRV; NOBE; OBNC
Winter Night. Louis O. Coxe. NYBP
Winter Night. C. Day Lewis. PoA
Winter Night. Arthur Rex Dugard Fairburn. ATNZ
Winter Night. Charles Simic. HCAP
Winter Night, A. Priscilla Jane Thompson. CBWP-2

Winter Night, A. James Thomson. *Fr.* The Seasons: Winter. NOBE

Winter Night. Whittier. *Fr.* Snow-bound; a Winter Idyl. TrGrPo

Winter Night in Manchester, A. Philip Connell. PF

Winter night is cold and drear, The. Across the Delaware. Will M. Carleton. PAH

Winter Night: Mount Royal. A. M. Klein. NoAM

Winter Night, Reading Books. Kan Sazan, *tr. fr.* Chinese by Burton Watson. JLIC-2

Winter-Night Sonnet. A. Leyeles, *tr. fr.* Yiddish by Benjamin *and* Barbara Harshav. AYP

Winter night: the moon, clear beyond a leafless tree, A. Princess Shikishi, *tr. fr.* Japanese by Hiroaki Sato. *Fr.* Seventy-eight Tanka. FCEI

Winter Nightfall. Robert Bridges. MoAB; MoBrPo; OBEV

Winter Nightfall. J. C. Squire. OxBTC

Winter: 1955. Takahashi Mutsuo, *tr. fr.* Japanese by Hiroaki Sato. FCEI

Winter ("Now, when the cheerless empire of the sky"). James Thomson. *Fr.* The Seasons: Winter. OxBA

Winter occasionally changes its mind. Remembering Snow. Sandor Csoori, *tr. by* Jascha Kessler. FOC

Winter Ocean. John Updike. InPK; MOS; SoSe

Winter Offering. D. S. Savage. LiTB

Winter on Black Mingo, *sel.* *Unknown.* "Cold, deserted and silent." FiBHP

Winter owl banked just in time to pass, The. Questioning Faces. Robert Frost. GrPl

Winter owl skirts hemlock tree. Arthur Stanley Bourinot. CaP

Winter Pause: Mt. Liberty, N.H. Martin Robbins. RR

Winter Piece, A. Bryant. AmPP; OxBA

Winter Piece. Guido Gozzano, *tr. fr.* Italian by Charles Tomlinson. PFI

Winter-Piece, A. Ambrose Philips. NOEC; OBTV; SeCePo

Winter-Piece to a Friend Away, A. John Berryman. NOBA

Winter Ploughing. William Everson. NU

Winter Poem, A. Tameie, *tr. fr.* Japanese by Steven D. Carter. WFTW

Winter Pond. Ben Belitt. NYBP

Winter Portrait. Robert Southey. BoNaP

Winter pulls the body inward. In the Van Gogh Room. Traise Yamamoto. BrSi

Winter Race Meeting. Ernest Kroll. SoTCo

Winter rain. Boncho, *tr. by* Geoffrey Bownas *and* Anthony Thwaite. PeBJV

Winter Rain. Christina Rossetti. BoNaP; WiR

Winter Rains: Cataluña. Philip Levine. NaP

Winter Remembered. John Crowe Ransom. HAP; MoAB; NOBA; OxBA; PrIm; UnPo; VGW

Winter Report. Ben Howard. PoA

Winter river: a raft sits, A. Kikaku, *tr. fr.* Japanese by Hiroaki Sato. *Fr.* Thirty-three Hokku. FCEI

Winter Saint. A. R. Ammons. TW

Winter Scene. Marguerite Young. NU; WPE

Winter seagull, A. Kato Shuson. OBD

Winter ("See, Winter comes, to rule the varied year"). James Thomson. *Fr.* The Seasons: Winter. NOEC; TEP

Winter Shore, The. Thomas Wade. OAEL-2

Winter shut in—/ a single fly. Kyotai, *tr. fr.* Japanese by Burton Watson. *Fr.* Sixteen Hokku. FCEI

Winter Sketches. Charles Reznikoff. PoA

Winter-sky began to frown, The. Stella at Wood-Park. Swift. BIrV

Winter Sleep. Edith M. Thomas. AA

Winter snowes, all covered is the grounde, The. Winter. Alexander Barclay. *Fr.* Eclogues, V. OxBLMV

Winter Solstice. Peter Blue Cloud. *Fr.* Within the Seasons. HATNAP

Winter Solstice—for Frank. Asphodel. BrRo

Winter Solstice Poem. Diana Scott. BrRo

Winter Song. Salah Abd al-Sabur, *tr. fr.* Arabic by Lena Jayyusi *and* John Heath-Stubbs. MAP

Winter Song. David Daiches. NYBP

Winter Song. Yankev Fridman, *tr. fr.* Yiddish by Ruth Whitman. PeBMYV

Winter Song. Juan Ramón Jiménez, *tr. fr.* Spanish by H. R. Hays. WSC

Winter Song. George MacDonald. NOBVV

Winter Song. Elizabeth Tollet. NOEC

Winter Stars. Larry Levis. DiL; MAYP; NAmP

Winter sunlight in Assisi, and the birds tilting. Soaping Down for Saint Francis of Assisi: The Canticle of Sister Soap. Gibbons Ruark. MAYP

Winter Sweetness. Langston Hughes. *See* This Little House Is Sugar.

Winter Talent, A. Donald Davie. NePoEA-2; OAEL-2

Winter tells me I shall die alone, The. Winter Song. Salah Abd al-Sabur, *tr. by* Lena Jayyusi *and* John Heath-Stubbs. MAP

Winter ("The wrathful winter, 'proaching on apace"). Thomas Sackville, *fr.* A Mirror [*or* Mirour] for Magistrates. *Fr.* Induction to "A Mirror for Magistrates." AAS; OBSC

Winter Thing, The. Philip Dacey. NAmP

Winter Time. Robert Louis Stevenson. *Fr.* A Child's Garden of Verses. EBVV; ER; MoBrPo; OxBChV

Winter time is bleak, the wind. Caoilte. *Unknown, tr. by* Frank O'Connor. KiLC

Winter Trees. Conrad Diekmann. SD

Winter Trees. Sylvia Plath. CAPP; HCAP; LCAP; NMM

Winter Tryst. Mark Van Doren. LiTA

Winter Tuesday, the city pouring fire, A. Coming Home. Philip Levine. CAPP

Winter Twilight, A. Arlo Bates. AA

Winter Twilight. George Tracy Elliot. AA

Winter Twilight, A. Angelina Weld Grimké. CDC; PoBA; PoNe

Winter Twilight. Lou Lipsitz. GOYP

Winter Twilight, Glowing Black and Gold, The. Delmore Schwartz. NoAM

Winter uses all the blues there are. Blue Winter. Robert Francis. LCAP

Winter Verse for His Sister. William Meredith. NYBP; TAP

Winter Views Serene. George Crabbe. *Fr.* The Borough, Letter IX. OBNC

Winter Visit, A. Dannie Abse. KS; NoAM

Winter [*or* Wynter] Wakeneth All [*or* Al] My Care. *Unknown.* HAP; SeCePo

(Winter Wakens All My Care.) HAP, *mod. English*

Winter Walk at Noon, A, *sel.* William Cowper. *Fr.* The Task, VI. EnRP; TEP

"No noise is here, or none that hinders thought." PBBP

Winter Walking. Alfred Wellington Purdy. NoAM

Winter Warfare. Edgell Rickword. OBWP; OxBTC

Winter ("What art thou, frost? and whence are thy keen stores"). James Thomson. *Fr.* The Seasons: Winter. OxBS

Winter ("When from the pallid sky the sun descends"). James Thomson. *Fr.* The Seasons: Winter. OAEL-1; OxBS

Winter will bar the swimmer soon. Swimming Chenango Lake. Charles Tomlinson. FaBoMo; MoP; NoAM

Winter Will Follow. Richard Watson Dixon. *See* Heaving Roses of the Hedge Are Stirred, The.

Winter will not let go of earth. In Defense of Felons. Robert Mezey. NePoEA

Winter wind: blowing pebbles. Buson, *tr. fr.* Japanese by Hiroaki Sato. *Fr.* Eighty-seven Hokku. FCEI

Winter wind: pebbles in a plowed field. Buson, *tr. fr.* Japanese by Hiroaki Sato. *Fr.* Eighty-seven Hokku. FCEI

Winter wind: the voice of water. Buson, *tr. fr.* Japanese by Hiroaki Sato. *Fr.* Eighty-seven Hokku. FCEI

Winter Winds Cold and Blea. John Clare. GBL; OBNC

Winter winds howled and the great barn creaked. The Barn in Winter. Claire Harris MacIntosh. CaP

Winter Wish, A. Robert Hinckley Messinger. AA

Winter with the Gulf Stream. Gerard Manley Hopkins. CMoP; NoAM

Winter withering. Taigi, *tr. by* Geoffrey Bownas *and* Anthony Thwaite. PeBJV

Winter without Snow, A. J. D. McClatchy. FYAP

Winter Work. Peter Fallon. CIP

Wintered-on windfield: here. Paul Celan, *tr. by* Beth Bjorklund. CoAuP

Wintering. Sylvia Plath. NMM

Winterlong, off La Manche, wind leaning. Gray stones of the gray. Flaubert in Egypt. Robert Penn Warren. NoAM

Winters at home brought wind. Once in a Lifetime, Snow. Les A. Murray. CBAP

Winters close, springs open, no child stirs, The. John Berryman. *Fr.* Homage to Mistress Bradstreet. NAAL-2; NAs

Winter's Cold. W. R. Rodgers. EnLoPo

Winter's coming on, The. Sanctuary. Dorothy Hewett. CBAP

Winter's End. Howard Moss. NePoEA

Winter's Frosty Pangs. Henry Vaughan. *Fr.* To His Retired Friend, an Invitation to Brecknock. FaBoRV

Winter's Glance, The. Tomas Tranströmer, *tr. fr.* Swedish by Samuel Charters. AnAn

Winter's Onset from an Alienated Point of View. Alan Dugan. FF

Winter's Song. *Unknown, tr. fr.* Bohemian. BoTP

Winters Spring, The. John Clare. NOBVV

Winter's Tale, A. Robert Patrick Dana. NYBP

Winter's Tale. Norma Farber. TSS

Winter's Tale, A. D. H. Lawrence. MoAB; MoBrPo

Winter's Tale, The, *sels.* Shakespeare.
  Autolycus as Peddler. *Fr.* IV, iii. OAEL-1
   (Autolycus's Song ("Lawn as white as driven snow")) OBSC
   (Come Buy! Come Buy!) ElL
   (Pedlar, The.) WiR
   (Pedlar's Song, The.) CH
  Autolycus's Song ("Will you buy any tape") *Fr.* IV, iii. OBSC
  "Here's flowers for you." *Fr.* IV, iii. GBL
   (Flowers of Perdita, The.) FiP
   (Some Flowers o' the Spring.) ChTr
  "Jog On, jog on, the footpath way." *Fr.* IV, ii. FaBoCh; GN
   (Autolycus's Song ("Jog on, jog on, the footpath way")) OBSC
   (Merry Heart, A.) ElL; TrGrPo
   (Merry Heart, The.) BoTP
   (Song: "Jog on, jog on, the footpath way.") OxBSP
  "Shepherdess—/ A fair one are you." *Fr.* IV, iv. PoE
  "When daffodils begin to peer." *Fr.* IV, ii. ChTr; ElL; FaBoBe; FaBoCh; NoP; OxBSP; PrIm
   (Autolycus's Song ("When daffodils begin to peer")) NOBE; OAEL-1; OBSC
   (Pedlar's Song, The.) NBLV; OxBoLi
   (Song: "When daffodils begin to peer.") FiP; PoEL-2
Winter's Tale, A. Dylan Thomas. CMoP; LiTB
Winter's Troops. Charles Cotton. *Fr.* Winter. ChTr
Wintertime nighs. Thomas Hardy. *Fr.* In Tenebris, I. NoAM; OAEL-2
Winterward. William Stafford. SM
Wintry. Robert Grenier. IAT
Wintry blast goes wailing by, A. Christmas Night of '62. William Gordon McCabe. AA
Wintry Dawn, *sel.* Meir Wieseltier, *tr. fr. Hebrew by* Warren Bargad *and* Stanley F. Chyet.
  "Blood flows from my brow, The." *Fr.* 12. IP
Wintry haw is burning out of season, The. The Haw Lantern. Seamus Heaney. NoAM
Wintry night, A. The Brewing Stone. Lo Fu, *tr. by* Dominic Cheung. IFON
Wintry rain at Ch'in-yu brings my boat to an evening mooring. Mooring in the Rain at Kao-yu. Wang Shih-chen, *tr. by* Daniel Bryant. WFTU
Winwick, Lancashire. *Unknown.* GBP
Wiped out by the hugeness of the big electric crane. On All Fours. Benjamin Péret, *tr. by* Charles Simic *and* Michael Benedikt. POS; RHTwFP
Wired and wisdomed and ready to roll. Defeat at the Hands of Alien Scholars. Bruce Boston. BWV
Wireless. Rodney Bennett. BoTP
Wirikota Wirikota. For the God of Peyote. *Unknown, tr. by* Jerome Rothenberg. STP
Wisdom. Phyllis Hanson. GoYe
Wisdom. George Sands Johnson. PWR
Wisdom. Hy Sobiloff. VGW
Wisdom. Sara Teasdale. AnAmPo; MoAmPo
Wisdom. W. B. Yeats. TrCP
Wisdom. Frank Yerby. AmNP
Wisdom and spirit of the universe! Wordsworth. *Fr.* The Prelude [or, Growth of a Poet's Mind]: Childhood and School-Time. NOBE
Wisdom found no place where she might dwell. Wisdom's Plight. Bible, Pseudepigrapha. *Fr.* Enoch, XLII: 1–3. TrJP
Wisdom Has Broken My Arms. Anne Hébert, *tr. fr. French by* Kathleen Weaver. OV
Wisdom has nothing to do with age. Wisdom. Hy Sobiloff. VGW
Wisdom hath builded her house. The House of Wisdom. Bible, *O.T. Fr.* Proverbs, IX: 1-6. TrGrPo
Wisdom is better than bread. Nevertheless. Gustav Davidson. GoYe
Wisdom is the finest beauty of a person. *Yoruba Oral Tradition, tr. by* Ulli Beier. WTO
Wisdom of Life, The. "Al-Akhtal al-Saghir," *tr. fr. Arabic by* Issa Boullata *and* Thomas G. Ezzy. MAP
Wisdom of Merlyn, The, *sel.* Wilfrid Scawen Blunt.
  "Wouldst thou be wise, O Man? At the knees of a woman begin." OBMV
Wisdom of the Gazelle. George P. Solomos. GoYe
Wisdom of the World, The. Siegfried Sassoon. MoBrPo
Wisdom, out of Anguish by Denial. Pedigree. Mary Mills. NePoAm
Wisdom's Plight. Bible, Pseudepigrapha. *Fr.* Enoch, XLII: 1–3. TrJP
Wise, The. Countee Cullen. PoNe
Wise Child, The. Edward Lucie-Smith. PBCV
Wise emblem of our politic [*or* politick] world. The Snail. Richard Lovelace. CaPo; OAEL-1
  (Snayl, The.) PoEL-3

Wise fish digs his silver in, The. Night Catch. Heather McHugh. AmPA
Wise guys, The. Kid Stuff. Frank Horne. AmNP; PChr; PoBA; PoNe
Wise king dowered with blessings on his throne, The. The Trophy. Edwin Muir. LiTM
Wise Men, The. Edgar Bowers. NePoEA
Wise Men and Shepherds. Sidney Godolphin. *See* Hymn: "Lord, when the wise men came from far[r]."
Wise Men Ask the Children the Way, The. Heine, *tr. fr. German by* Geoffrey Grigson. OBCP
  (Kings from the East, The.) ChTr
Wise men come here to shit. From a Lavatory Wall. *Unknown.* FaBoEE
Wise Men of Gotham, The. Thomas Love Peacock. *Fr.* Nightmare Abbey, *ch.* 11. BXAP; FaBoNo
  (Men of Gotham, The.) CH
  (Seamen Three.) WiR
  (Three Men of Gotham.) FaBoCh; OBEV
Wise old apple tree in spring, The. Robert Hillyer. BoNaP
Wise Old Owl, A. Edward Hersey Richards. BLPA; FaBoBe; FaFP; OxNR; PYC
Wise Owl. Patricia Goedicke. SM
Wise Rochefoucault a maxim writ. Swift. *Fr.* The life and Genuine Character of Dean Swift. NOBL
Wise to have gone so early to reward. The Wazir Dandan for Prince Sharkan. *Unknown, tr. fr. Arabic by* E. Powys Mathers. *Fr.* The Thousand and One Nights. AWP
Wisely a woman prefers to a lover a man who neglects her. Distichs. John Hay. AnAmPo
Wisely and well was it said of him. Addition to Kipling's "The Dead King (Edward VII), 1910." Max Beerbohm. FaBoEE
Wiser Than the Children of Light. Monk Gibbon. NeIP
"Wisest scholar of the wight most wise, The." Sir Philip Sidney. *Fr.* Astrophel and Stella, XXV. NoP; OAEL-1
Wisga. Lew Blockcolski. VoR
Wish. Ilse Aichinger, *tr. fr. German by* Beth Bjorklund. CoAuP
Wish, The. Abraham Cowley. *Fr.* The Mistress. LiTB; NOBE; NoP; OBEV; OBS; SeCV-1; TrGrPo
Wish, The. Ann Friday. RAR
Wish, A. Hamlin Garland. AA
Wish, A. Elizabeth Gould. BoTP
Wish. Lance Henson. CDW
Wish, A. Jenny Joseph. NPo
Wish, A. Fanny Kemble. WPE
Wish, A. Laurence Lerner. FF; OxBTC
Wish, A. Samuel Rogers. FaPoR; GTBS; GTBS-P; NOBE; OBEV
Wish, The. Thomas Stanley. AWP
Wish, A. J. M. Synge. FaBoEE
Wish. Dorothy Brown Thompson. RAR
Wish for a Young Wife. Theodore Roethke. MoP; NAAL-2; NoAM; NoP; OxBSP; TAP
Wish I was in Tennessee. Tennessee. *Unknown.* AmFP
Wish of Manchin of Liath, The. *Unknown, tr. fr. Irish by* Kenneth Jackson. AnIL
Wish, that of the living whole, The. Tennyson. *Fr.* In Memoriam A. H. H., LV. HAP; NoP; OBNC; TOF
"Wish to Be Believed, The." Mona Van Duyn. PoA
Wish to embroider a twin-budded flower? Ancient Sentiments. Hsüeh Shao-hui, *tr. by* Irving Lo. WFTU
Wishbone, The. Paul Muldoon. CIP
Wished Sunday's come: mirth brightens ev'ry face. White Conduit House. William Woty. NOEC
Wished to have been milk. Story. Dennis Saleh. NeAC
Wishes. Patty L. Harjo. VoR
Wishes. F. Rogers. BoTP
Wishes. *Unknown.* BoTP
Wishes, for Alix. James A. Emanuel. NIP
Wishes for Her. Denis Devlin. CIP; NOIV
Wishes for My Son. Thomas MacDonagh. TIRV
Wishes for the supposed Mistress. Richard Crashaw. *See* Whoe'er she be.
Wishes of an Elderly Man. Sir Walter Alexander Raleigh. CenHV; FaBoCh; FaBoCo; FaBoEE; FiBHP; FPL; NBLV; NOBL
Wishes to His (Supposed) Mistress [*or* Mistresse]. Richard Crashaw. BoLoP; EBEV; MeLP; MePo; OBEV; OBS; PoEL-2; SeCP; SeCV-1
  (Wishes for the supposed Mistress.) GTBS; GTBS-P
Wishful Thinking. Michael C. Blumenthal. HCAP
Wishing. William Allingham. BoTP; FaPON; OHIP; OxBChV
Wishing. John Godfrey Saxe. AnAmPo
Wishing Africa. Marilyn Bowering. NOBC

Wishing Bone Cycle, The, *sel.* Jacob Nibenegenesabe, *tr. fr. Cree Indian* by Howard Norman.
  "One time I wanted two moons." STP
Wishing for roses, I walk through the garden. Summer Garden. "Anna Akhmatova," *tr. by* Stephen Stepanchev. BoWoP
Wishing My Death. *Unknown.* MeEL
Wishing Poem. *Unknown.* NTCP; OxNR
Wishing someone would. Ishikawa Takuboku, *tr. fr. Japanese by* Hiroaki Sato. *Fr.* Forty-seven Tanka in Three Lines. FCEI
Wishmakers' Town, *sels.* William Young. AA
  Bells, The.
  Bridal Pair, The.
  Conscience-Keeper, The.
  Flower-Seller, The.
  Pawns, The.
Wispy clouds drift in the boundless autumn sky. The Drunken Gentleman. Ku Hsiung, *tr. by* Lois Fusek. ATF
Wispy cuttings lie in rows, The. July in Indiana. Robert Fitzgerald. AiP; NYBP
Wisselton, wasselton, who lives here? Wassailing Song. *Unknown.* OBCP
Wisteria in the Rain. Gyoko, *tr. fr. Japanese by* Steven D. Carter. WFTW
Wistful,/ they speak of. The People. Robert Creeley. VGW
Wistful camera caught this four-year-old, The. Self-Portrait. Allen Curnow. ATNZ
Wistful Days, The. Robert Underwood Johnson. AA
Wit, Whither Wilt Thou? *Unknown.* EIL
Wit Wonders. *Unknown.* *See* God and Yet a Man, A?
Witch. Patricia Beer. OxBC
Witch, The. Mary Elizabeth Coleridge. BrRo; WPE
Witch, The. Percy H. Ilott. BoTP
Witch, The, *sels.* Thomas Middleton.
  "Black spirits and white, red spirits and gray." *Fr.* V, i. WSC
  "In a maiden-time professed." OxBSP
Witch, The. Robert Southey. WiR
Witch. Jean Tepperman. AIW; NMM
Witch, The. Katharine Tynan. NOBVV
Witch, The. W. W. Gibson. *Fr.* Skye. PoSH
Witch-Bride, The. William Allingham. NOBVV
Witch Burning. Sylvia Plath. CAPP
Witch Doctor. Robert Hayden. AmNP; MAT; NoAM
Witch-elms that counterchange the floor. Tennyson. *Fr.* In Memoriam A. H. H., LXXXIX. OBNC
Witch flew out on Hallowe'en, The. Oh, Lovely, Lovely, Lovely! *Unknown.* CRH
Witch Going Down to Egypt, A. Raquel Chalfi, *tr. fr. Hebrew.* VWA, *tr. by* Alexandra Meiri *and* Myra Glazer Schotz
Witch in the Glass, The. Sarah Morgan Bryan Piatt. AA
Witch of Atlas, The, *sel.* Shelley.
  "And whilst the outer lake beneath the lash." PBBP
Witch of Coös, The. Robert Frost. *Fr.* Two Witches. InPS; LiTM; MoAB; MoP; NoAM; NOBA; PoE
Witch of East Seventy-second Street, The. Morris Bishop. NYBP
Witch Sycorax Addresses Her Lover, The. Vicki Raymond. UAS
Witch that came (the withered hag), The. Provide, Provide. Robert Frost. AmPP; CMoP; HAP; MoAB; MoP; NAAL-2; NIP; NoAM; NOBA; NoP; OPOP; PoE; PPP; TAP; TwCP; UnPo; WeW
Witch, The! The Witch! Eleanor Farjeon. RHPC
Witchcraft. Nora Naranjo-Morse. GOS
Witchcraft by a Picture. John Donne. EyDe
Witchcraft: New Style. Lascelles Abercrombie. MoBrPo
Witchcraft was hung, in history. Emily Dickinson. WSC
Witchcraft Woman. Nora Naranjo-Morse. GOS
Witches. Ted Hughes. GoYe
Witches, The. *Unknown.* *See* Hey-How for Hallowe'en.
Witches and poets co-embrace like fate. Fatales Poetae. Henry Parrot. FaBoEE
Witches' Ballad, The. William Bell Scott. *See* Witch's Ballad, The.
Witches' Blood. Alma Villanueva. CCP
Witches' Charm, The. Ben Jonson. *Fr.* The Masque of Queens: The Witches' Charms. EIL; FaBoCh
  (Charme.) FM
  (Witches' Sabbath, The.) WSC
Witches' Chasm. Ben Jonson. RB
Witches' Menu. Sonja Nikolay. RHPC
Witches' Ride, The. Karla Kuskin. PDV
Witches' Sabbath, The. Ben Jonson. *See* Masque of Queens, The: Witches' Sabbath, The.
Witches' Song, The. Ben Jonson. CH
Witches' Spells. Madeleine Edmondson. NTCP

Witches' Wood, The. Mary Elizabeth Coleridge. PBWP
Witch's Ballad, The. William Bell Scott. NOBVV; OBEV
  (Witches' Ballad, The.) CH
Witch's Broomstick Spell, The. *Unknown.* ChTr; GBP
Witch's Cat, The. Ian Serraillier. SO; WSC
Witch's Life, The. Anne Sexton. KS
Witch's Spell [*or* Witch's Milking Charm], A. *Unknown.* ChTr; GBP
Witch's Whelp, The. Richard Henry Stoddard. AA
Witch's Work Song, The. T. H. White. FaBoNo
With/Tattered grey fishnet eyes. Just an Old Man. Mary Goose. STE
With a basket, a lovely basket. Emperor Yuryaku. *Fr.* Manyo Shu. FCEI
With a bitter flavor tonight, jealous. Moon. Antonin Artaud, *tr. by* Michael Benedikt. POS
With a bold profile. Something Precise. Bartolo Cattafi, *tr. by* Lawrence R. Smith. NItP
With a Book at Twilight. Jakov Steinberg, *tr. fr. Hebrew by* Mark Elliott Shapiro. VWA
With a China Chamberpot, to the Countess of Hillsborough. Lord Holland. FaBoUs
With a Coin from Syracuse. Oliver St. John Gogarty. OBMV
With a Copy of Swift's Works. James Vincent Cunningham. QFR
With a crossbow, late, in hand ready bent. Of a Daw. John Heywood. PBBP
With a cry of fear. Hidden Bow. Mordecai Temkin, *tr. by* Jeremy Garber. VWA
With a face saying I caught something. Ozaki Hosai, *tr. fr. Japanese by* Hiroaki Sato. *Fr.* One Hundred Haiku in Free Form. FCEI
With a faint scent of river. Taigi, *tr. fr. Japanese by* Hiroaki Sato. *Fr.* Twenty-nine Hokku. FCEI
With a Fool. Malka Heifetz-Tussman, *tr. fr. Yiddish by* Marcia Falk. PeBMYV
With a fork drive Nature out. Marigolds. Robert Graves. BrPo
With a garlande of thornes kene. Christ Complains to Sinners. *Unknown.* MeEL
With a Gift of Rings. Robert Graves. GBL
With a Guitar, to Jane. Shelley. EnRP; OAEL-2
  (To a Lady, with a Guitar.) GTBS; GTBS-P
With a gull's beak I cry. The Bright Hillside. Rhoda Coghill. NeIP
With a half-glance upon the sky. Tennyson. *Fr.* A Character. Mes
With a handful of weeds I weep in the slanting sun. Boudoir Lament. Yü Hsüan-chi, *tr. fr. Japanese by* Geoffrey Waters. BoWoP
With a hint of some coloring. At the Ferry on the Miya River. Shiba Sonome, *tr. fr. Japanese by* Hiroaki Sato. *Fr.* Fifteen Hokku. FCEI
With a hush in their voices. Country Woman Elegy. Margaret Gibson. MT
With a lantern that wouldn't burn. The Draft Horse. Robert Frost. CMoP; HeIP; HoPM; PoE
With a Lifting of the Head. "Hugh MacDiarmid." MoBrPo
With a Little Bit of Luck. Alan Jay Lerner. FaFP
With a long stirrup under fern. Craswall. Roland Mathias. OBWVE
With a movement. The Enclosure. Jules Supervielle, *tr. by* James Kirkup. RHTwFP
With a Nantucket Shell. Charles Henry Webb. AA
With a pale green curly. The Love of Lettuce. Marge Piercy. CAPP
With a pert moustache and a ready candid smile. The Mixer. Louis MacNeice. FaBoTw
With a pleasant/ heaviness. Giraut Riquier, *tr. by* Paul Blackburn. Pro
With a Posthumous Medal. John Malcolm Brinnin. SaC
With a Pressed Flower. James Russell Lowell. AnAmPo
With a pure colour there is little one can do. Morning Glory. Ruth Pitter. FaBoWP
With a Ring. Veronica Porumbacu, *tr. fr. Rumanian by the author and* Kathleen Weaver. OV
With a Rod No Man Alive. Walther von der Vogelweide, *tr. fr. German by* Jethro Bithell. AWP
With a Rose from Conway Castle. Julia Caroline Ripley Dorr. AA
With a sadnes curtained. The Maiden. Rochelle Ratner. PCP
With a Sliver of Marble from Carrara. James Wright. EyDe
With a Spray of Apple Blossoms. Walter Learned. AA
With a sudden gust. Tamekane, *tr. by* Steven D. Carter. WFTW
With a very big yawn. Mr. Beetle. Emily Hover. BoTP
With a wall and a ditch between us, I watched the gate-legged dromedary. The Fruit of the Tree. David Wagoner. NYBP
With a whip as my staff I've come home under autumn's evening sky. Desultory Thoughts on My Old Home. Yu T'ung, *tr. by* Paul W. Kroll. WFTU
With a whirl of thought oppressed. The Day of Judgement. Swift. BlrV; FaBoRV; NOBE; NOEC; OAEL-1; OBSV; PPP
With a yellow lantern. Glow-Worms. P. A. Ropes. BoTP

With a young leaf may I wipe. Basho, *tr. fr. Japanese by* Burton Watson. *Fr.* Seventy-six Hokku. FCEI
With all a woman's virtues but the pox. Pope. *Fr.* The Second Satire of the First Book of Horace. OBSV
With All Deliberate Speed. Don L. Lee. JB
With all its sinful doings, I must say. Italy. Byron. *Fr.* Beppo; a Venetian Story. SeCePo
(Italy versus England.) NOBE
With all my heart, in truth, and passion strong. The Pride of a Jew. Judah Halevi, *tr. by* Israel Cohen. TrJP
With All My Heart, Jehovah, I'll Confess. Henry Ainsworth. AH
With all my will, but much against my heart. Coventry Patmore. *Fr.* The Unknown Eros. ACP; BoLoP; EnLoPo; GTBS-P; NOBE; OBEV; OBNC; PoEL-5; TrGrPo
With all the drifting race of men. Léonie Adams. *Fr.* April Mortality. TrGrPo
With all the heart in my body. Now Jentil Belly Down. *Unknown.* GBP
With all the powres my poor heart hath. The Hymn of Saint Thomas in Adoration of the Blessed Sacrament. Richard Crashaw. OBS
(Hymn in Adoration of the Blessed Sacrament.) MeLP
With all these loads of injuries opprest. Dryden. *Fr.* Absalom and Achitophel, Pt. I. EBEV
With an effort Grant swung the great block. Blocking the Pass. Charles Madge. FaBoMo
With an insane. Learning. Earl Simpson. GrPl
With angry brow and stately tread. The Earthquake of 1886. Josephine D. Henderson Heard. CBWP-4
With Annie gone. For Anne. Leonard Cohen. FF
With B. E. F. June 10. Dear Wife. The Letter. Wilfred Owen. OBD
With banked fire to mark the occasion. Family Evening. Dan Huws. NYBP
With banners and our smiles. Christopher Street Liberation Day, June 28, 1970. Fran Winant. PeHV
With banners furled, the clarions mute. The Night-March. Herman Melville. LiTA
With blackest moss the flower-plots. Mariana. Tennyson. AWP; CH; ChER; InPS; NAEL-2; NOBE; NoP; OAEL-2; OBEV; OBNC; PoE; PoEL-5; TEP; TrGrPo; UnPo; WiR
With blameless carriage I lived here. An Epitaph upon a Sober Matron. Robert Herrick. CaPo
With bland serenity. Issa, *tr. by* Geoffrey Bownas *and* Anthony Thwaite. PeBJV
With bleeding back, from tyrant's lash. The Fugitive. Priscilla Jane Thompson. CBWP-2
With blooms of pampas grass. Saigyo, *tr. fr. Japanese by* Burton Watson. *Fr.* Sixty-four Tanka. FCEI
With burning fervour. The Crystal. George Barker. LiTM; OBMV
With burning horns, two twisted candles under a radiant yellow. Death of an Ox. Abraham Sutskever, *tr. by* Ruth Wisse. PeBMYV
With camel's hair I clothed my skin. Dream. Richard Watson Dixon. EBEV; NOBVV
With candour I confess my love. *Unknown, tr. by* Ezra Pound and Noel Stock. BoWoP
With Child. Genevieve Taggard. AIW; MoAmPo
With Christ and All His Shining Train. Thomas Prince. AH
With cicada's nymphal skin. The Largess. Richard Eberhart. LiTA
With Closed Eyes. Alois Vogel, *tr. fr. German by* Beth Bjorklund. CoAuP
With coat like any mole's, as soft and black. Mole Catcher. Edmund Blunden. OBMV
With collars be they yoked, to prove the arm at length. Wrestlers. Michael Drayton. *Fr.* Polyolbion, First Song. SD
With Corse at Allatoona. Samuel H. M. Byers. PAH
With Cortez in Mexico. Wilfred Campbell. PAH
With courage seek the kingdom of the dead. The Last Journey. Leonidas of Tarentum, *tr. by* Charles Merivale. AWP; OBD
With crayons and pieces of paper, I entered the empty room. The Room. Gregory Orr. GeTw
With crowbars and drag chains. Wrestling Angels. David Bottoms. MAYP
With crumpled leaves flung in his face. October. Zoltán Zelk, *tr. by* Daniel Hoffman. MHuP
With Dad gone, Mom and I worked. Adolescence—III. Rita Dove. NoAM
With dagger drawn I pass through the shop of your lovely toys. Heartfelt Pity. Ben-Zion Tomer, *tr. fr. Hebrew by* Bernhard Frank. *Fr.* Song Sequence. MHeP
With dawn it comes or does not come. The Impossible. Abd al-Wahhab al-Bayyati, *tr. by* Salma Khadra Jayyusi *and* Christopher Middleton. MAP

With death doomed to grapple. Epitaph for William Pitt. Byron. FaBoEE
With deathlace tickling my throat. Death-Lace. David Ray. MAT
With deep affection/ And recollection. The Bells of Shandon. Francis Sylvester Mahony. ACP; CH; ChTr; OBEV
With Deep Repentance for My Wasted Days. Gaspara Stampa, *tr. fr. Italian by* Marya Zaturenska. PFI
With delicate, mad hands, behind his sordid bars. To One in Bedlam. Ernest Dowson. ACP; BrPo; MoBrPo; OBMV; Son
With difficulty the ship was built. The Critics. Theodore Spencer. NYBP
With disheveled head cloths, we sit late on the bench. Summer Night at the Pond Pavillion. Chang Yü, *tr. fr. Chinese by* Jonathan Chaves. *Fr.* Twelve Miscellaneous Poems on the Fang Garden. CoBLCP
With Donne, whose muse on dromedary trots. On Donne's Poetry. Samuel Taylor Coleridge. InvP; NAEL-2; NoP; OAEL-2; SeCePo
With doubt and dismay you are smitten. Opportunity. Berton Braley. WBLP
With drooping sail and pennant. The White Ships and the Red. Joyce Kilmer. PAH
With each step that I take. Asadullah Khan Ghalib, *tr. by* Ahmed Ali. GoT
With earliest spring, while yet in mountain cleughs. James Grahame. *Fr.* The Birds of Scotland. PBBP
With Eastern banners flaunting in the breeze. Marlowe. Arthur Bayldon. PoAu-1
With echoing step the worshippers. Give Me Thy Heart. Adelaide Anne Procter. ACP
With ecstasy I walk. Asadullah Khan Ghalib, *tr. by* Ahmed Ali. GoT
With elbow buried in the downy pillow. Clarimonde. Théophile Gautier, *tr. fr. French by* Lafcadio Hearn. *Fr.* Taches Jaunes, Les. AWP; VVA
With Esther. Wilfrid Scawen Blunt. OBEV; OBMV; OBNC; TrGrPo
With evening the groom and bride in groundfog. There Should Have Been. Sydney Lea. SM
With every blow of the wind. My Soul Hovers over Me. Joshua Tan Pai, *tr. by* Yishai Tobin. VWA
With every movement, the soft particles. The Dusting of the Books. Dorothy Hughes. GoYe
With every note/ of the mountain temple. *Unknown, tr. by* Willis Barnstone. BoWoP
With every rolling stone place me in the breach. Place Me in the Breach. Yehuda Karni, *tr. by* Sholom J. Kahn. TrJP
With every soft gush of my feet. After Picking Rosehips. Harley Elliott. NeAC
With Exultation, As We Can! H. Leivick, *tr. fr. Yiddish by* Benjamin *and* Barbara Harshav. AYP
With Eyes at the Back of Our Heads. Denise Levertov. AmPP
With eyes hand-arched he looks into. Comradery. Madison Cawein. AA
With fair Ceres, Queen of Grain. Praise of Ceres. Thomas Heywood. *Fr.* The Silver Age. EIL
With fairest flowers,/ Whilst summer lasts. Shakespeare. *Fr.* Cymbeline, IV, ii. EBEV; RB
With faith I trust in Christ the Lord. Mrs. Saunder's Experience. *Unknown.* AmFP
With fastidious nails and teeth. The Vampire Housewife. Ruth Fainlight. VVA
With favoring winds, o'er sunlit seas. Ultima Thule. Longfellow. MOS; ViBoPo
With favour and fortune fastidiously blest. The Character of Sir Robert Walpole. Swift. FaBoEE; PoE
With feeling, standing. Bright Moon: after an Illness. Onitsura, *tr. fr. Japanese by* Hiroaki Sato. *Fr.* Twenty-three Hokku. FCEI
With fifteen-ninety or sixteen-sixteen. On an Anniversary. J. M. Synge. FaBoEE; NOIV; OBMV
With fingers weary and worn. The Song of the Shirt. Thomas Hood. EBVV; EnRP; FaPoR; SaC; TEP; WBLP
With flowing tail, and flying mane. The Wild, the Free. Byron. RHPC
With focus sharp as Flemish-painted face. The [or A] Dome of Sunday. Karl Shapiro CMoP; CoAP; LiTM; MoAB; MoAmPo; NoAM; OxBA; WaP
With Fragrant Flowers We Strew the Way. Thomas Watson. *Fr.* The Honourable Entertainment Given to the Queen's Majesty in Progress at Elvetham, 1591. EIL
(Ditty of the Six Virgins, The.) OBSC
With Freedom's Seed. Pushkin, *tr. fr. Russian by* Babette Deutsch. TTY
With frost again the thought is clear and wise. Frost. John Hewitt. NeIP
With Garments Flowing. John Clare. GBL
With gentle step I came at last. Afterward. Mary Matheson. CaP

With gentleness/ his eyes filmed. Monument. Milton Acorn. NeAC
With Giorgio Morandi in Bologna. Wieland Schmied, *tr. fr. German by* Beth Bjorklund. CoAuP
With glass like a bull's eye. Mrs. MacQueen (*or* The Lollie-Shop). Walter de la Mare. BoTP
With God and His Mercy. Carl Olof Rosenius. AH
With God Conversing. Gene Derwood. LiTA; LiTM
With grass for a pillow, on a journey. Hitomaro. *Fr.* Manyo Shu. FCEI
With grief and mourning I sit to spin. The Girl's Lamentation. William Allingham. SeCePo; TIRV
With hairs, which for the wind to play with, hung. On Lydia Distracted. Philip Ayres. EnLoPo; Son
With half a heart I wander here. In the States. Robert Louis Stevenson. AiP; BrPo
With half a hundred sudden loops and coils. The Hurrying Brook. Edmund Blunden. BoNaP
With half the Western world at stake. Sea and Land Victories. *Unknown.* PAH
With hands all reddened and sore. The Washerwoman. Mary Weston Fordham. CBWP-2
With hands and faces nicely washed. Clever Peter and the Ogress. Katharine Pyle. OBCA
With Hands like Leaves. James Still. GrPl
With hands tight clenched through matted hair. The Three Voices. "Lewis Carroll." BXAP
With Happiness Stretch[e]d across the Hills. Blake. EnRP; NAEL-2; NoP
With hateful eyes I wait withdrawal from the world. Self-Derision. Natsume Soseki, *tr. by* Burton Watson. JLIC-2
With Heads Held High. Mark Insingel, *tr. fr. Dutch by* James S. Holmes. DuIn
With Heart and Breast of Brimstone, Flesh of Flax. Michelangelo, *tr. fr. Italian by* Edwin Morgan. PFI
With heart at rest I climbed the citadel's. Baudelaire, *tr. by* Arthur Symons. AWP
With hearts of poor men it is so. The Poor. Emile Verhaeren, *tr. by* Ludwig Lewisohn. AWP
With hearts responsive. John Oxenham. *Fr.* A Little Te Deum of the Commonplace. TrPWD
With hearts revived in conceit, new land and trees they eye. *At.* to Edward Johnson. *Fr.* Good News from New England. GOA
With heavy groans did I approach my friends. Wine and Grief. Solomon Ibn Gabirol, *tr. by* Emma Lazarus. TrJP
With heavy steps the hairy men trudged. Like Chaff. Jacob Glatstein, *tr. by* Benjamin *and* Barbara Harshav *and* Kathryn Helle. AYP
With her basket, her basket. Emperor Yuryaku. *Fr.* Manyo Shu. PeBJV
With her black hair fallen forward. She Who Understands. Alfonsina Storni, *tr. by* Kate Flores. DMH
With her buskins tipped with dew. May's Invocation after a Tardy Spring. Henrietta Cordelia Ray. CBWP-3
With her eyes closed. Sabbath. David Rosenmann-Taub. VWA, *tr. by* Charles Guentheer
With her face to the wall. The Jewish Girls. Berta Lask, *tr. by* Susan L. Cocalis. DMG
With him bound by fear. Tamekane, *tr. by* Steven D. Carter. WFTW
With him ther was his sone, a young Squyer. Chaucer. *Fr.* The Canterbury Tales: Prologue. TrGrPo
("With him there was his son, a youthful Squire," *mod. vers. by* Louis Untermeyer) TrGrPo
With his apology. *Unknown, tr. by* Geoffrey Bownas *and* Anthony Thwaite. PeBJV
With his hat on the table before him. In January, 1962. Ted Kooser. Psk
With his kind[e] mother who partakes thy woe. Temple. John Donne. *Fr.* La Corona. OBS; Son
With his lady your slave must be in love. Yakamochi. *Fr.* Manyo Shu. Ma
With his penis swollen for the girl on the next farm and rigid. Lugete O Veneres. R. A. K. Mason. ATNZ
With his tusk-like fierce moustaches and double-pointed beard. A Bully. *Malay Oral Tradition, tr. by* R. J. Wilkinson. WTO
With his two-fist sword, enscintillant, he cut an apple down. The Uncouth Knight. Hugh McCrae. PoAu-1
With his weapon a shovel. Denis Glover. *Fr.* Arawata Bill. PeNZ
With his work, as with a glove, a man feels the universe. Open and Closed Space. Tomas Tranströmer, *tr. by* Robert Bly. EAS
With honeysuckle, over-sweet, festooned. Arbor Vitae. Coventry Patmore. *Fr.* The Unknown Eros, II, iii. OBNC; SeCePo

With Hopeless Love. Moses Ibn Ezra, *tr. fr. Hebrew by* Solomon Solis-Cohen. TrJP
With horns and [with] hounds, I waken the day. Diana's Hunting-Song. Dryden. *Fr.* The Secular Masque. NOBE; SeCePo
With how! fox, how! With hay! fox, hay! The False Fox. *Unknown.* ChTr; GBP; PBBP
"With how sad steps, O [*or* Oh] Moon, thou climb'st the skies!" Sir Philip Sidney. *Fr.* Astrophel and Stella, XXXI. AWP; BoLoP; CH; ChTr; ElL; EnLoPo; GBL; HAP; HeIP; InPS; InvP; MAT; NAEL-1; NoP; OBSC; PoE; PoEL-1; PoRA; PPP; Son; TEP; TrGrPo; WeW
(His Lady's Cruelty.) OBEV
(Languishing Moon, The.) BoNaP
(To the Sad Moon.) NOBE
With *huarango* branches. Ancient Peru. Antonio Cisneros, *tr. by* Maureen Ahern *and* David Tipton. Per
With hyphens, clip off endings that don't fit. Sonneteering Made Easy. S. B. Botsford. NYBP
With innocent wide penguin eyes, three. Bird-witted. Marianne Moore. CMoP; FM; NAAL-2
With its baby rivers and little towns, each with its abbey or its cathedral. England. Marianne Moore. FaBoWP; LiTA; MoAB; MoAmPo
With its cloud of skirmishers in advance. An Army Corps on the March. Walt Whitman. AiP; InPS; PoLF
With its rat's tooth the clock. The Alarum. Sylvia Townsend Warner. MoBrPo
With its untended garden, its spacious rooms, and its fine. Toto Merumeni. Guido Gozzano, *tr. by* J. G. Nichols. PFI
With joy all relics of the past I hail. Old Ruralities: A Regret. Charles Tennyson Turner. EBVV; Son
With joy Britannia sees her fav'rite goose. To the Marquis of Graham on His Marriage. *Unknown.* OBSV
With Joy erst while, (when knotty doubts arose). Upon the Much-to Be Lamented Desease of the Reverend Mr. John Cotton. John Fiske. SCAP
With Kit, Age 7, at the Beach. William Stafford. RFM
With Lamp in Hand. Agnes Gergely, *tr. fr. Hungarian by* Daniel Hoffman. MHuP
With languages dispersed, men were not able. Four Epigrams on the Naturalization Bill. John Byrom. NOBL
With leaden foot Time creeps along. Absence. Richard Jago. OBEV
With leering looks, bullfac'd, and freckled fair. On Jacob Tonson, His Publisher. Dryden. ChTr; FaBoEE; OBSV
With Life and Death I walked when Love appeared. Hymn to Colour. George Meredith. OBNC
With lifted feet, hands still. Going Down Hill on a Bicycle. Henry Charles Beeching. OBEV
(Bicycling Song.) GN
With lights for eyes, our city turns. Dom Moraes. NePoEA-2
With Lilacs. Charles Henry Crandall. AA
With Lilacs in My Eye. Lucile Coleman. GoYe
With little here to do or see. To the Daisy. Wordsworth. GTBS; GTBS-P
(To the Same Flower.) EnRP
With loitering step and quiet eye. In November. Archibald Lampman. NOBC; OBCV
With Love among the haycocks. Ralph Hodgson. GoJo
With love exceeding a simple love of the things. Melampus. George Meredith. PoEL-5
With love there's never a thought that one might die. Surdas, *tr. by* John Stratton Hawley *and* Mark Juergensmeyer. SSI
With lovers 'twas of old the fashion. To a Young Lady, with Some Lampreys. John Gay. FaBoUs; NOEC
With low thunder, with red bushes smooth. Red Rock Ceremonies. Anita Endrezze Probst. CDW; VoR
With Lullay, Lullay, like a Child. John Skelton. InvP
With marjoram [*or* margerain] gentle. To Mistress Margery Wentworth. John Skelton. *Fr.* The Garlande [*or* Garlands] of Laurell. EBEV; EnLoPo; NOBE; OAEL-1; OBEV; OBSC; TrGrPo
With Me My Lover Makes. Cecil Day Lewis. OBMV
With me while present, may thy lovely eyes. To Miss Lucy F——, with a New Watch. George Lyttelton. FaBoUs
With Mercy for the Greedy. Anne Sexton. CAPP; HCAP; TOF
With merry lark this maiden rose. Old-Time Service. Thomas Churchyard. *Fr.* A Fayned Fancy betweene the Spider and the Gowte. OBSC
With Metaphor. Sarah Wingate Taylor. GoYe
With mighty hand the Holy Lord. The Temptation and Fall of Man. Caedmon, *tr. fr. Anglo-Saxon by* C. W. Kennedy. *Fr.* Genesis. AnOE
With Monmouth cap and cutlass by my side. A Long Prologue to a Short Play. Sir Henry Sheers. APAS

With morning you leave. *Unknown. Fr.* Manyo Shu. FCEI

With much ado you fail to tell. A Critic. Walter Savage Landor. ChTr; FaBoEE

With music strong I come, with my cornets and my drums. Walt Whitman. *Fr.* Song of Myself, XVIII. TrGrPo

With my axe I felled the trees. *Unknown. Fr.* Manyo Shu. Ma

With my breath I cut my way through the six forests. Lalleswari, *tr. by* George Grierson. WPOW

With My Foot in My Mouth. Dennis Lee. ILY

With My God, the Smith. Uri Zvi Greenberg, *tr. fr. Hebrew by* Robert Mezey *and* Ben Zion Gold. VWA

With My Grandfather. Zelda, *tr. fr. Hebrew by* Marcia Falk. VWA

With my looks I am bound to look simple or fast. Magna Est Veritas. Stevie Smith. OxBC

With my luck. My Name in the Star Registry. Michael Bachstein. TSM

With my many illnesses I meet the spring. The First Day of Spring. Pien Kung, *tr. by* Jonathan Chaves. CoBLCP

With my muscles running out into a radio. The Human Use of Human Beings. Sybren Polet, *tr. by* Peter Nijmeijer. DuIn

With Myself. Moyshe-Leyb Halpern, *tr. fr. Yiddish by* Benjamin *and* Barbara Harshav. AYP

With names we summon cosmos out of chaos. The Adam Sign. Muhammad Abd al-Hayy, *tr. fr. Arabic by* Matthew Sorenson *and* Alistair Elliot. *Fr.* Ode of Signs, I. MAP

With nerves all shattered and worn. Song of the Sheet. *Unknown.* BXAP

With nets and kitchen sieves they raid the pond. The Pond. Anthony Thwaite. MAT; NYBP

With night coming on. Tamekane, *tr. by* Steven D. Carter. WFTW

With night full of spring and stars we stand. Young Girls. Raymond Souster. HeIP

With no lover's pledge. Ietaka, *tr. by* Steven D. Carter. WFTW

With no-mind I've enjoyed my stay. Gotsuan, *tr. by* Lucien Stryk *and* Takashi Ikemoto. ZPCJ

With no more fragrance, the *sakaki*, its voice. Teika, *tr. fr. Japanese by* Hiroaki Sato. *Fr.* Eighty-four Tanka. FCEI

With no other identity than the. The Enemy's Testament. Etel Adnan, *tr. by the author.* OV

With noiseless steps good goes its way. The World. Ella Wheeler Wilcox. PWR

With nothing but God's word. The Life-Giving. Brad Leithauser. PPR

With nought to hide or to betray. L'Amitié et l'Amour. John Swanwick Drennan. BIrV

With oaken staff and swinging lantern bright. The Andalusian Sereno. Francis Saltus Saltus. AA

With one consuming roar along the shingle. Felixstowe; or, The Last of Her Order. Sir John Betjeman. OxBC

With one foot on the brick step. Choro, *tr. by* Lucien Stryk *and* Takashi Ikemoto. ZPCJ

With one letter of your many names. Love the Ruins. Malka Heifetz-Tussman, *tr. by* Marcia Falk. VWA

With one stroke I rammed the demon's den. Sogen, *tr. by* Lucien Stryk *and* Takashi Ikemoto. ZPCJ

With one who safeguards Gwynedd. The Stallion. Tudur Aled, *tr. by* Joseph P. Clancy. OBWVE

With only his feeble lantern. Charon's Cosmology. Charles Simic. GeTw; HCAP; NoP

With other women I beheld my love. Ballata: Of His Lady among Other Ladies. Guido Cavalcanti, *tr. by* Dante Gabriel Rossetti. AWP

With paciens thou hast us fed. Farewell! Advent. James Ryman. MeEL

With paste of almonds Syb her hands doth scour[e]. Upon Sybilla. Robert Herrick. CaPo

(Sibilla.) SeCePo

With Paul Engle at Fort Madison, 1978. Thomas McCarthy. WCI

With pinched cheeks hollow and wan. The Outcast. Josephine D. Henderson Heard. CBWP-4

With plucking pizzicato and the prattle of the kettledrum. Narnian Suite. C. S. Lewis. RR

With plum blossoms from the fence visiting my sleeves. Princess Shikishi, *tr. fr. Japanese by* Hiroaki Sato. *Fr.* Seventy-eight Tanka. FCEI

With Poems Already Begun. Rachel Korn, *tr. fr. Yiddish by* Seymour Mayne *and* Rivka Augenfeld. VWA

With poisoned apple, comb, ring, garment. How to Murder Your Best Friend. Diana O Hehir. NPGG

With porcupine locks. The Katzenjammer Kids. James Reaney. MoCV; OBCV

With proud thanksgiving, a mother for her children. For the Fallen. Laurence Binyon. NOBE; OBEV; OBWP; OxBTC

With prune-dark eyes, thick lips, jostling each other. Refugees. Louis MacNeice. LiTB; WaP

With quiet signs of faraway. Wagons. Jacob Glatstein, *tr. by* Chana Bloch. PeBMYV

With reeds and bird-lime from the desert air. On a Fowler. Isidorus, *tr. by* William Cowper. AWP

With restless step of discontent. Balboa. Nora Perry. PAH

With reverence I compose these words. *Unknown. Fr.* Manyo Shu. Ma

With Robert Hughes on Botany Bay. William Rossa Cole. *Fr.* A Mini-Samizdat of New River Rhymes. SoTCo

With rue my heart is laden. Samuel Hoffenstein. *Fr.* The Mimic Muse. NBLV; UnPo

With Rue My Heart Is Laden. A. E. Housman. *Fr.* A Shropshire Lad, LIV. AWP; BLPL; CMoP; FaFP; HAP; HeIP; HoPM; InPK; LiTB; LiTM; MoAB; MoBrPo; NAEL-2; NoAM; NoP; PoE; PrIm; SoSe; TrGrPo; UnPo

"With sacrifice before the rising morn." Laodamia. Wordsworth. EnRP

With sadness I survey our present generation! Meditation. Mikhail Yurevich Lermontov, *tr. by* Alan Myers. AAA

With sails full set, the ship her anchor weighs. Emigravit. Helen Hunt Jackson. AA

With saintly grace and reverent tread. Presentiment. Ambrose Bierce. AA

With sap running early. Valley Blood. Barry Sternlieb. SM

With savoring eyes. Third-World Theme. Angela de Hoyos. ER

With sedative voices we joke and spar. Millie's Date. Dannie Abse. NPo

With Self Dissatisfied. Frederick L. Hosmer. TrPWD

With Serving Still. Sir Thomas Wyatt. EIL; InPK; SiPS

(His Reward.) OBSC

With seven matching calfskin cases for his new suits. Home Leave. Barbara Howes. TwCP

With sharpened pen and wit, one tunes his lays. The Praise of New Netherland. Jacob Steendam. PAH

With Ships the Sea Was Sprinkled Far and Nigh. Wordsworth. EnRP; MOS

With shot and shell, like a loosened hell. The Charge at Santiago. William Hamilton Hayne. PAH

With sick and famisht eyes. Longing. George Herbert. SeCV-1

With six small diamonds for his eyes. The Spider. Robert Peter Tristram Coffin. ImOP

With snort and pant the engine dragged. The Song of the Engine. H. Worsley-Benison. BoTP

With so much suffering. So Much Suffering. Bertalicia Peralta, *tr. by* Robert L. Smith *and* Judith Candullo. DMH

With sober pace an heav'enly Maid walks in. Abraham Cowley. *Fr.* Davideis, III. SeCV-1

With songs and honors sounding loud. Edom. Isaac Watts. AmFP

With spangles gay and candle light. The Christmas Tree. Isabel de Savitzsky. BoTP

With spring manifest on moss-grown. Princess Shikishi, *tr. fr. Japanese by* Hiroaki Sato. *Fr.* Seventy-eight Tanka. FCEI

With steadfast heart and true. "Go Forward." "A. R. G." BLRP

With Stephen in Maine. Stanley Plumly. BLA; NAmP

With sticks and staves on a makeshift stage—all are engrossed in a child's game. Chao Yi, *tr. fr. Chinese by* Shirleen S. Wong. *Fr.* Watching an Opera: Impressions. WFTU

With strollers loitering. A Barren Area. Hagiwara Sakutaro, *tr. by* Hiroaki Sato. FCEI

With such a throb does blood. Joy of Knowledge. Isidor Schneider. TrJP

With such compelling cause to grieve. Tennyson. *Fr.* In Memoriam A. H. H., XXIX. EBVV

With sun on his back and sun on his belly. Pig. Paul Eluard, *tr. by* Kenneth Koch. TTTS

With sweet surprise, as when one finds a flower. On Finding the Truth. Jones Very. TrCP

With sweetest milk and sugar first. The Nymph and Her Fawn. Andrew Marvell. *Fr.* The Nymph Complaining for the Death of Her Faun. FaBoCh

(Girl and Her Fawn, The.) BoTP

With table wines. The Prison's Stream. Shauqi Abi Shaqra, *tr. by* Abdullah al-Udhari. MPAW

With tears thy grief thou dost bemoan. Solomon Ibn Gabirol, *tr. by* Emma Lazarus. TrJP

With Teeth in the Earth. Malka Heifetz Tussman, *tr. fr. Yiddish by* Kathryn Hellerstein. AYP

With teeth of flowers, headdress of dew. I Am Going to Sleep. Alfonsina Storni, *tr. by* Kate Flores. DMH

With Tendrils of Poems. Michael McClure. PoM

With that a thundring noise seem'd shake the skie. The Overthrow of Lucifer. Phineas Fletcher. *Fr.* The Purple Island, XII. OBS

With that crude roof overhead. Crab. François Dodat, *tr. by* Bert *and* Odette Meyers. TSS

With that delight the royal captive's brought. Lady A, The L., My Asylum in a Great Extremity. Richard Lovelace. CaPo

With that he stripped him to the ivory skin. Amorous Neptune. Christopher Marlowe. *Fr.* Hero and Leander, Second Sestiad. NOBE

With that I saw two swans of goodly hue. Spenser. *Fr.* Prothalamion. PBBP

With that low cunning, which in fools supplies. Character of a Critic. Charles Churchill. *Fr.* The Rosciad. NOEC

With the bounteous wine the doughty warrior blesses. Prince Yuhara. *Fr.* Manyo Shu. Ma

With the boys busy. Philomena Andronico. William Carlos Williams. FaBoMo

With the coming of clear days. *Unknown, tr. by* Paul Blackburn. Pro

With the Dawn. Thomas Caulfield Irwin. BIrV; EnLoPo

With the earth and all. Two Landscapes, Grammar. Alain Delahaye, *tr. by* Anthony Barnett. RHTwFP

With the effect as of carving, almost, the hillside. For an Age of Plastics. Plymouth. Donald Davie. NePoEA-2

With the exact length and pace of his father's stride. For a Father. Anthony Cronin. FaBoTw

With the festival hour close at hand. King Killi in Combat. Cattantaiyar, *tr. by* A. K. Ramanujan. PLW

With the fierce rage of winter deep suffused. A Winter Night. James Thomson. *Fr.* The Seasons: Winter. NOBE

With the fine spring weather. Cercamon, *tr. by* Paul Blackburn. Pro

With the first gray light of dawn the remnants. Broken Off by the Music. John Yau. EOEF

With the first rains. The Girl Friend Describes the Bull Fight. Uruttiran, *tr. by* A. K. Ramanujan. PLW

With the flower brocades. Teika, *tr. by* Steven D. Carter. WFTW

With the forks of flowers I eat the meat of morning. Lyric by Nine. *Unknown.* EAS

With the Grain. Donald Davie. NoAM

With the Greeks. Naomi Shihab Nye. NAmP

With the green lamp of the spirit. Into the Glacier. John Haines. CoAP

With the Guerillas. Cecily Pile. CN

With the heavy steps of slow oxen. Slow Oxen. Ilya Rubin, *tr. by* Linda Zisquit. VWA

With the Herring Fishers. "Hugh MacDiarmid." LiTM

With the Holy Poem. H. Leivick, *tr. fr. Yiddish by* Robert Friend. PeBMYV

With the hooves of a doe. Lenox Avenue. Sidney Alexander. PoNe

With the jewels of my anklets. *Unknown. Fr.* Manyo Shu. Ma

With the King's million I struck the proud foe. Song of Victory: the Battle of Port Arthur. Nogi Maresuke, *tr. by* Burton Watson. JLIC-2

With the last whippoorwill call of evening. Birmingham. Margaret Abigail Walker. PoBA

With the Mickey Mouse. The Girl in the Hall. John Stone. MT

With the morning-glories I eat my meal. Basho, *tr. fr. Japanese by* Burton Watson. *Fr.* Seventy-six Hokku. FCEI

With the Most Susceptible Element, the Mind, Already Turned under the Toxic Action. Walter Benton. WaP

With the ninth month when the thunder. *Unknown. Fr.* Manyo Shu. Ma

With the old kindness, the old distinguished grace. Upon a Dying Lady. W. B. Yeats. LiTB; UnPo

With the one and the two and the three. A Beginning and an End. Edouard Roditi. VWA

With the open eyes of their dead fathers. War. Andrei Voznesensky, *tr. by* William Jay Smith *and* Vera Dunham. RB

With the other geese within the goosehouse. January. James Reaney. *Fr.* A Suit of Nettles. OBCV

With the Rain. Amir Gilboa, *tr. fr. Hebrew by* Warren Bargad *and* Stanley F. Chyet. IP

With the Shell of a Hermit Crab. James Wright. NoP; SM

With the ships all in trim. Mariko Omaro. *Fr.* Manyo Shu. Ma

With the shrewd and upright man. Fool and False. *Unknown, tr. fr. Sanskrit by* Arthur Ryder. *Fr.* The Panchatantra. AWP

With the south wind a gentle goddess came. Rain. Nishiwaki Junzaburo, *tr. by* Geoffrey Bownas *and* Anthony Thwaite. PeBJV

With the spring, now. Shune, *tr. by* Geoffrey Bownas *and* Anthony Thwaite. PeBJV

With the stars. For the Coming Year. Peter Everwine. OFD

With the stylish young brood bitch, the old dog showed. Old Dog, New Dog. Sydney Lea. MAYP

With the sun half way down the tall pines. River Water Music. Richard Eberhart. BLA

With the Thin Girl. György Petri, *tr. fr. Hungarian by* William Jay Smith. MHuP

With the thinking of winter. The Cook. Ray A. Young Bear. CDW

With the wasp at the innermost heart of a peach. A Scherzo. Dora Greenwell. NOBVV

With the woodburner cracking hot. The Limestone Cowboy's Luck Runs Out. Greg German. SoTCo

With the years my woes increased. The Paths of Prayer. Edouard Roditi. VWA

With Thee a moment! Then what dreams have play! Desire. "Æ" OBMV; TIRV; TrPWD

With thee conversing, I forget all time. Milton. *Fr.* Paradise Lost, *bk.* IV, *ll.* 639–656. WiR
(Eve Speaks to Adam.) ChTr; GBL
(Eve to Adam.) TrGrPo

With their boxing-glove muzzles. Cattle. Peter Skrzynecki. CBAP

"With their chins high, girls come back from the tennis courts." Czeslaw Milosz, *tr. fr. Polish by the author and* Peter Dale Scott. *Fr.* Throughout Our Lands, VII-VIII. PwPP

With their country bound to the sails and their oars hung on the wind. Amorgos. Nikos Gatsos, *tr. by* Edmund Keeley *and* Philip Sherrard. VMG

With their feet in the earth. Tall Trees. Eileen Mathias. BoTP

With their harsh leaves old rhododendrons fill. The Mountain Cemetery. Edgar Bowers. NePoEA

With their lithe, long, strong legs. Bullfrog. Ted Hughes. NYBP; RFM

With these heaven-assailing spires. New York. "Æ" OBMV

With these missing pieces. A Tribe Searching. Shlomo Reich. VWA, *tr. by* Mira Reich

With this ambiguous earth. Christ in the Universe. Alice Meynell. ACP; MoBrPo; NOBE

With this charm I keep the boy at six. The Magician Suspends the Children. Carole Oles. SoSe

With this overload sweet and tough-hearted like flowers. From the Depths. Friederike Mayröcker, *tr. by* Beth Bjorklund. CoAuP

With this toast the wish is carried. Marriage Toast. William Rossa Cole. SoTCo

With this trusty sword and shield. Heroisms. "Marie." PF

With thise maner yiftes the goddesse Rome the princys herte moevid. Rome Araieth Stilico in Vesture of the Consul. Claudian, *tr. fr. Latin by* Osbern Bokenham. *Fr.* De Consulatu Stilichonis. OxBLMV

With thy rugged, ice-girt shore. Alaska. Mary Weston Fordham. CBWP-2

With thy small stock, why art thou venturing still. To a Weak Gamester in Poetry. Ben Jonson. JCP

With Timbrels. Bible, Apocrypha. *Fr.* Judith. TrJP

With torches I have wandered the dark poppy world. The Double Axe. Anne Hazlewood-Brady. IHMS

With treble vivas and limp hedgerow flags. The Vanquished. Charles Eglington. PeSA

With trembling eyes. Charm. Miklós Radnóti, *tr. by* Steven Polgar, Stephen Berg *and* S. J. Marks. LLLT

With trembling fingers did we weave. Tennyson. *Fr.* In Memoriam A. H. H., XXX. EBVV

With troubled heart and trembling hand I write. In Memory of My Dear Grandchild [Anne Bradstreet]. Anne Bradstreet. BoWoP; NAAL-1; TrCP

With twilight I gather you here. Conjuration. Agnes Gergely. VWA, *tr. by* Emery George

With Two Fair Girls. *Unknown, tr. fr. Greek by* Robert C. MacGregor. ErPo

With two 60's stuck on the scoreboard. Foul Shot. Edwin A. Hoey. RHPC

With two strange fires of equal heat possest. Love and Jealousy. Sir Philip Sidney. *Fr.* Arcadia. SiPS

With two white roses on her breasts. A Brown Girl Dead. Countee Cullen. TAP

With Usura. Ezra Pound. *Fr.* Cantos, XLV. CMoP; LiTM; NAAL-2; NOBA; PoE; TW

With walloping tails, the whales off Wales. The Whales off Wales. X. J. Kennedy. OBCA

With what a gentle sound. September. Henrietta Cordelia Ray. CBWP-3

With what anguish of mind I remember my childhood. The Old Oaken Bucket. *Unknown.* BLPA; FaFP; WBLP

With what attentive courtesy he bent. The Guitarist Tunes Up. Frances Cornford. SoSe

With what attractive charms this goodly frame. Mark Akenside. *Fr.* The Pleasures of Imagination, I. EnRP

With what deep murmurs through time's silent stealth. The Waterfall [*or* Water-Fall]. Henry Vaughan. FaBoPP; MeLP; MePo; NAEL-1; NOBE; NOCV; NoP; OBS; OBWVE; PoEL-2; PrIm; SeCV-1; WiR

With what joy in front. Asadullah Khan Ghalib, *tr. by* Ahmed Ali. GoT

With what, O Codrus! is thy fancy smit? Edward Young. *Fr.* Love of Fame, the Universal Passion, Satire II. OBSV

"With what sharp checks I in myself am shent." Sir Philip Sidney. *Fr.* Astrophel and Stella, XVIII. NAEL-1

With What Stones, What Blood, and What Iron. Odysseus Elytis, *tr. fr. Greek by* Edmund Keeley *and* Philip Sherrard. VMG

With what sword shall I. The Question and the Answer. Muhammad al-Faituri, *tr. by* Sargon Boulus *and* Peter Porter. MAP

With what thou gavest me, O Master. Equipment. Paul Laurence Dunbar. TrPWD

With what voice. Spider. Basho. TTTS

With wild hair, you block out your characters. To Chin Nung. Cheng Hsieh, *tr. by* Jonathan Chaves. CoBLCP

With wild surprise/ Four great eyes. The Christmas Tree in the Nursery. Richard Watson Gilder. OHIP

With wine and words of love and every vow. Seduced Girl. Hedylos, *tr. by* Louis Untermeyer. BoLoP; ErPo

With wings held close and slim neck bent. Swans. Leonora Speyer. FYAP

With woman's form and woman's tricks. Thomas Moore. OxBSP

With words of chastity he adorned my hands. How Crazy Are Those Who Love You So Much. Kishwar Naheed, *tr. by* Mahmood Jamal. PBMUP

With Wordsworth at Rydal. James Thomas Fields. AA

With wrath-flushed cheeks, and eyelids red. Ahmed. James Berry Bensel. AA

With wrinkled hide and great frayed ears. Gunga. Rachel Field. *Fr.* A Circus Garland. OBCA

With yellow pears leans over. Half of Life. Friedrich Hölderlin, *tr. by* James Blair Leishman. ChTr; OBVE

With you a part of me hath passed away. George Santayana. *Fr.* To W. P. TrGrPo

With you first shown to me. William Barnes. EnLoPo

With you for mast and sail and flag. The Narrow Sea. Robert Graves. FaBoEE; FaBoMo; MOS

With you here at Mertu. *Unknown, tr. by* Boris de Rachewiltz; *English version by* Ezra Pound *and* Noel Stock. PBWP

With you, I know, my offering will find grace. Ben Jonson. *Fr.* Epistle to Elizabeth, Countess of Rutland. JCP

With you there are blue seas, safe seas. Note to Isolationists 1940. F. Tennyson Jesse. CN

With your assistance, departed citizens. Certain Dead. John Haines. LCAP

With your fair eyes a charming light I see. Love, the Light-Giver [*or* To Tommaso de' Cavalieri]. Buonarroti Michelangelo, *tr. by* John Addington Symonds. AWP; PeHV

With your other hand support me. Yosano Akiko, *tr. fr. Japanese by* Hiroaki Sato. *Fr.* Thirty-nine Tanka. FCEI

With your wine jars open. Farewell to Pari's Hill. Kapilar, *tr. by* A. K. Ramanujan. PLW

Withal a meager man was Aaron Stark. Aaron Stark. E. A. Robinson. MoAB; MoAmPo; Son

Withdraw thee, soul, from strife. Sleep. Alice Brown. AA

Withdrawal, The. Robert Lowell. NoP

Withdrawn from layers of upper air, ice-blue and clear. Suburb Hilltop. Richard Moore. NYBP

Withdrawn on this warm ledge I lie. Summer Afternoon. Elizabeth B. Harrod. NePoEA

Withered and worn, near a cloud-misted cloister. An Ancient Plum Tree at the K'ai-hsien Buddhist Monastery. Ch'ü Ta-chün, *tr. by* Paul W. Kroll. WFTU

Withered leaves that drift in Russell Square, The. Drilling in Russell Square. Edward Shanks. OBMV

Withered Rose, A. "Yehoash", *tr. fr. Yiddish by* Isidore Goldstick. TrJP

Withered vines, old tree. Autumn Thoughts. Ma Chih-yüan, *tr. fr. Chinese by* Jonathan Chaves. *Fr.* To the Tune "T'ien ching sha." CoBLCP

Withered Willows. Wang Fu-chih, *tr. fr. Chinese by* Irving Lo. WFTU

Withering grass knows not its needs. After the Rain. Edward A. Collier. BLRP

Withering under its bush. Cast Rose. Anna Hajnal, *tr. fr. Hungarian by* Jascha Kessler. *Fr.* Images. FOC

Within a budding grove. Spring: The Lover and the Birds. William Allingham. OBNC

Within a copse, I met a shepherd-maid. Ballata: Concerning a Shepherd-Maid. Guido Cavalcanti, *tr. by* Dante Gabriel Rossetti. AWP

Within a dark and cheerless hut. The Old Saint's Prayer. Priscilla Jane Thompson. CBWP-2

Within a garden all alone. Mary, The Mother of Jesus. Ada Belle Gardner. PWR

Within a gloomy dimble she doth dwell. Mother Maudlin the Witch. Ben Jonson. *Fr.* The Sad Shepherd. ChTr

Within a greenwood sweet of myrtle savour. *Unknown.* GBL

Within a low wall falling away. Jewish Graveyards, Italy. Philip Levine. BLA

Within a native hut, ere stirred the dawn. Nativity. Aquah Laluah. CDC; PBA; TTY

Within a poor man's squalid home I stood. Vision. William Dean Howells. AA

Within a quad of aging brick. John Updike. ASP

Within a thick and spreading hawthorn bush. The Thrush's Nest. John Clare. BoTP; GoJo

Within an Emerald. Salvador Díaz Mirón, *tr. fr. Spanish by* Samuel Beckett. MexPo

Within an open curled Sea of Gold. A Vision. Lord Herbert of Cherbury. SeCP

Within Heaven's circle I had not guessed at this. The Flight into Egypt. Peter Quennell. LiTB; LiTM

Within her gilded cage confined. The Contrast; the Parrot and the Wren. Wordsworth. FM

Within Her Hair. "E. C." *Fr.* Emaricdulfe, VI. EiL; Son

Within his sober realm of leafless trees. The Closing Scene. Thomas Buchanan Read. AA

Within how many metamorphoses. To Primal Matters. Luis de Sandoval y Zapata, *tr. by* Samuel Beckett. MexPo

Within King's College Chapel, Cambridge. Wordsworth. *See* Ecclesiastical Sonnets

Within me are two souls that pity each. Duality. Arthur Sherburne Hardy. AA

Within my bolted infernal gates. Salah Niyazi, *tr. fr. Arabic by* Abdullah al-Udhari. *Fr.* The Thinker. MPAW

Within my casement came one night. The Dawn of Love. Henrietta Cordelia Ray. BlSi; CBWP-3

Within my garden, rides a bird. Emily Dickinson. AmPP

Within my head, aches the perpetual winter. Winter and Summer. Stephen Spender. MoAB; MoBrPo

Within My Heart. Judah al-Harizi, *tr. fr. Hebrew.* TrJP

Within my heart a stab I felt. En las Internas Entrañas. St. Theresa of Avila, *tr. by* Father Benedict Zimmerman. WPOW

Within my heart I long have kept. Blondel. Clarence Urmy. AA

Within my heart when you are here. Muddy Madrigal. Léon-Paul Fargue, *tr. by* William Jay Smith. CT

Within my house of patterned horn. The Tortoise in Eternity. Elinor Wylie. FaPON; ImOP

Within our happy castle there dwelt one. Stanzas Written in My Pocket Copy of Thomson's "Castle of Indolence." Wordsworth. EnRP

Within that porch, across the way. The Cat. W. H. Davies. CRH; NOBE

Within the bounds of heaven and earth. Sanu Chigami. *Fr.* Manyo Shu. Ma

Within the Casket of thy Coelick Breast. An Acrostick on Mrs. Winifret Griffin. John Saffin. SCAP

Within the cave, it is dark. safe. Gimel. Stuart Z. Perkoff. VWA

Within the chukar's call the twilight sun moves westward. On Hearing the Chukar. Yu T'ung, *tr. by* Paul W. Kroll. WFTU

Within the circuit of this plodding life. Winter Memories. Henry David Thoreau. AmPP; AnAmPo; OxBA (Within the Circuit of This Plodding Life.) NOBA

Within the cloister blissful of thy sides. Two Invocations of the Virgin, I. Chaucer. *Fr.* The Canterbury Tales: The Prologue to the Second Nun's Tale. ACP

Within the covert of a shady grove. Love Sleeping. Plato, *tr. by* Thomas Stanley. AWP; FaBoEE

Within the crystal palace, the cassia is in flower. Spring in the Moon Palace. Mao Wen-hsi, *tr. by* Lois Fusek. ATF

Within the curved edge of quarter moon. The Path I Must Travel. Emerson Blackhorse Mitchell. NOVW

Within the dream the thought. Asadullah Khan Ghalib, *tr. by* Ahmed Ali. GoT

Within the Dream You Said. Philip Larkin. InPS

Within the dungeon's noxious gloom. Sonnet: The Cell. John Thelwall. NOEC

Within the flower there lies a seed. Spell of Creation. Kathleen Jessie Raine. FaBoCh; OxBS
Within the gentle heart Love shelters him. Of the Gentle Heart. Guido Guinicelli, *tr. by* Dante Gabriel Rossetti. AWP; CTC; OBVE; PFI
Within the Gorges there is no lack of men. Invitation to Hsiao Ch'u-shih. Po Chü-i, *tr. by* Arthur Waley. OBVE
Within the great grey flapping tent. The Auction Sale. Henry Reed. MoBrPo
Within the great wall's perfect round. The Window. Edwin Muir. LiTM
Within the hard surface of night's bowl. Still Life. Yoshioka Minoru, *tr. by* Hiroaki Sato. FCEI
Within the introspection of my dying. Parable. Robert Pack. NePoEA-2
Within the iron cities. The Garden of God. "Æ" WGRP
Within the letter's rustling fold. Spring Flowers from Ireland. Denis Florence MacCarthy. ACP
Within the night, above the dark. Mary Gilmore. *Fr.* Swans at Night. PoAu-1
Within the oak a throb of pigeon wings. A Twilight in Middle March. Francis Ledwidge. BIrV
Within the pale blue haze above. The Storm. Coventry Patmore. EnLoPo
Within the purple graph of the Hokonuis, the dark. The Foxes. Janet Frame. WPE
Within the sacred fence. Ryoshun, *tr. by* Steven D. Carter. WFTW
Within the sand of what far river lies. Shadows of His Lady. Jacques Tahureau, *tr. by* Andrew Lang. AWP
Within the Seasons, *sels.* Peter Blue Cloud. HATNAP
   Autumn Equinox.
   Spring Equinox.
   Summer Solstice.
   Winter Solstice.
Within the Shelter of Our Walls. Elinor Lennen. AH
Within the sober realm of leafless trees. The Closing Scene. Thomas Buchanan Read. AA; AnAmPo
Within the soul's courts is a temple fair. The Soul's Courts. Henrietta Cordelia Ray. CBWP-3
Within the streams, Pausanias saith. The Last Chance. Andrew Lang. NOBVV; SD
Within the thin. The Madman. S. J. Pretorius, *tr. by* Uys Krige *and* Jack Cope. PeSA
Within the Veil. Margaret E. M. Sangster. BLRP
Within the wires of the post, unloading the cans of garbage. Prisoners. Randall Jarrell. OxBA; WaP
Within the world I was. Khwaja Haider Ali Atish, *tr. by* Ahmed Ali. GoT
Within These Doors Assembled Now. Oliver Holden. AH
Within this [*or* that] ample volume lies. Sir Walter Scott's Tribute. Sir Walter Scott. *Fr.* The Monastery, *ch.* 12. WBLP (Bible, The.) BLRP
Within this black hive to-night. Beehive. Jean Toomer. IDB; PoBA; TTY
Within this lowly grave a Conqueror lies. The Conqueror's Grave. Bryant. AA
Within this mindless vault. J. V. Cunningham. RB; VGW
Within this place. Over Case's Door. John Case. FaBoUs
Within this restless, hurried, modern world. My Voice. Oscar Wilde. BrPo; EBVV
Within this silent palace of the Night. Moonrise. Frank Dempster Sherman. AA
Within this sober frame expect. Upon Appleton House, to My Lord Fairfax. Andrew Marvell. FaBoPV; SeCP; SeCV-1
Within those walls where student zeal. The College Cat. Alfred Denis Godley. CenHV
Within three days we've changed boats twice. Fan Tseng-hsiang, *tr. fr. Chinese by* J. P. Seaton. *Fr.* Random Verses from a Boat, II. WFTU
Within your heart. Hold Fast Your Dreams. Louise Driscoll. BLPA; FaBoBe; FaPON; FPL
Withinner, The. Ursula K. Le Guin. BWV
Without a Beginning nor an End. Sylvia Paskin. DT
Without a door, through the smooth wall. At Night. Rachel Boimwall, *tr. by* Gabriel Preil *and* Howard Schwartz. VWA
Without a pickaxe to my name. Graves. Orkhan Muyassar, *tr. by* Lena Jayyusi *and* Samuel Hazo. MAP
Without a trace it has cleared on this side of the clouds. Princess Shikishi, *tr. fr. Japanese by* Hiroaki Sato. *Fr.* Seventy-eight Tanka. FCEI
Without a winter coat. Raising the Flag. Gerald Vizenor. VoR

Without and Within. James Russell Lowell. AnAmPo
Without Benefit of Declaration. Langston Hughes. AmNP; TTY
Without Benefit of Tape. Dorothy Livesay. NOBC
Without Ceremony. Vassar Miller. MoAmPo; SM
Without Colors. Gerrit Kouwenaar, *tr. fr. Dutch by* Koos Schuur. DuIn
Without dressmakers to connect. Because of Clothes. Laura Riding. LiTA
Without excess (no galaxies). Civilities of Lamplight. Charles Tomlinson. OxBC
Without expectation. Summer Oracle. Audre Lorde. BlSi; PoBA
Without flocks or cattle or the curved horns. A Time of Change. Egan O'Rahilly, *tr. by* Eavan Boland. BIrV; FaBoPV
Without Her. Dante Gabriel Rossetti. *Fr.* The House of Life, LIII. GBL; OBNC; PoEL-5; Son
Without him still this whirling earth. Egotism. Edward Sandford Martin. AA
Without it, nothing exists. The Invention of Zero. Constance Urdang. VWA
Without Jews. Jacob Glatstein, *tr. fr. Yiddish.* AYP, *tr. by* Benjamin *and* Barbara Harshav; PeBMYV, *tr. by* Cynthia Ozick
Without Knowing Why. Sebastian Salazar Bondy, *tr. fr. Spanish by* Ena Hollis *and* David Tipton. Per
Without Me You Won't be Able to See Yourself. Chaim Grade, *tr. fr. Yiddish by* Ruth Whitman. VWA
Without Mercy. László Nagy, *tr. fr. Hungarian by* Tony Connor. MHuP
Without My Friends the Day Is Dark. Moses ibn Ezra, *tr. fr. Hebrew by* Solomon Solis-Cohen. TrJP
Without my having known. The Boy Died in My Alley. Gwendolyn Brooks. NoAM
Without Name. Pauli Murray. AmNP; PoBA; PoNe
Without Names. Gerrit Kouwenaar, *tr. fr. Dutch by* Koos Schuur. DuIn
Without Names. Jeff Tagami. BrSi
Without Offerings. Jacob Glatstein, *tr. fr. Yiddish by* Benjamin *and* Barbara Harshav. AYP
Without so much/ as trying to look. You. Carroll Arnett. VoR
Without Song. Grace Nichols. PBCV
Without support and with Support. Commentary Applied to Spiritual Things. Saint John of the Cross, *tr. by* K. Kavanaugh and O. Rodrigues. TOF
Without Tears for the Roses. Nanni Balestrini, *tr. fr. Italian by* Lawrence R. Smith. NItP
Without that once clear aim, the path of flight. Stephen Spender. CMoP (Without That Once Clear Aim.) Son
Without the hall, and close upon the gate. Gardens of Alcinous, The. Homer, *tr. fr. Greek by* George Chapman. *Fr.* Odyssey, VII. OAEL-1; OBVE
Without the Herdsman. Diotimus, *tr. fr. Greek by* John William Burgon. AWP
Without, the lonely night is sweet with stars. Martyrdom. "Rufus Learsi." TrJP
Without the slightest basis/ for hypochondriasis. How Jack Found That Beans May Go Back on a Chap. Guy Wetmore Carryl. HoPM
Without the Way, there can be no going. The Way; the Truth; the Life. Samuel Judson Porter. BLRP
Without their helmets. Losers. Jonathan Holden. MAYP
Without this/ what is/ worth doing. Land. Carroll Arnett. VoR
Without thought, without remorse, without shame. Walls. C. P. Cavafy, *tr. by* Rae Dalven. TrJP
Without warning their nest. A Call to Action. Ch'iu Chin, *tr. by* Kenneth Rexroth *and* Ling Chung. PBWP
Without you, O Saki, never could I. Mohammad Taqi Mir, *tr. by* Ahmed Ali. GoT
Without your knowledge they are turning your wounds into words. A Latter Purification. Haim Guri, *tr. by* Mark Elliott Shapiro. VWA
Withouten Time is no earthly thinge. Time and Eternity. Stephen Hawes. *Fr.* The Pastime of Pleasure. PoEL-1
Withouten you. Little Elegy. Elinor Wylie. ILY
Witless and dull, I curl up in the hut I love. The Cat in Cold Weather. Rai San'yo, *tr. by* Burton Watson. FCEI; JLIC-2
Witlesse gallant, a young wench that woo'd, A. Michael Drayton. *Fr.* Idea. AAS, *fr.* XXI.
Witness. Jon Anderson. MAYP
Witness. John Montague. CIP
Witness, A. Helga Osswald, *tr. fr. German by* Susan L. Cocalis. DMG
Witness anew, I'm bound to pass on, A. Dan Pagis, *tr. by* Warren Bargad *and* Stanley F. Chyet. IP
Witness Chair, The. Michael Harlow. ATNZ
Witness how it comes to pass. Epitaph in Sirmio. David Morton. PoLF

Witness to Death. Richmond Lattimore. VGW
Witnesses, The. X. J. Kennedy. PChr
Witnesses, The. Longfellow. GOA
Witnesses, The, *sel.* Clive Sansom.
   "It was a night in winter." PChr
Witnesses. W. S. Merwin. LCAP
Wits, The. Sir John Suckling. *See* A session was held the other day.
Wit's End Corner. Antoinette Wilson. BLRP
Wit's perfection, Beauty's wonder. Francis Davison. OBSC
Wit's Pilgrimage, *sel.* John Davies of Hereford.
   Some Blaze the Precious Beauties of Their Loves. Son
Wit's queen (if what the poets sing be true). Upon a Girl of Seven Years
   Old. Pope. OxBSP
Witty as Horatius Flaccus. On Seeing Francis Jeffrey Riding on a
   Donkey. *At. to* Sydney Smith. FaBoEE
Wives, The. Donald Hall. CoAP
Wives in the Sere. Thomas Hardy. BrPo; NOBE; NOBVV
Wives of Mafiosi, The. Erica Jong. AmPA
Wives of Spittal, The. *Unknown.* AS
Wizard of Alderley Edge, The. Peter Coe. OBET
Wizard Oil. *Unknown.* AS
Wizards. Alonzo Gonzales Mó, *tr. fr. Mayan by* Allan F. Burns. STP
Wizard's Funeral, The. Richard Watson Dixon. ELP; NOBVV
Wm. Brazier. Robert Graves. NOBL
Wmffre the Sweep. Rolfe Humphries. EaLo
Wo, his purple an' linen, too. Dives and Laz'us. *Unknown.* TTY
Wo worth the days! The days I spent. A Few Lines to Fill up a Vacant
   Page. John Danforth. SCAP
Wobbly Rock. Lew Welch. PoM
Wodwo. Ted Hughes. MoP; NoAM
Woe for the brave ship *Orient!* The Brave Old Ship, the *Orient.* Robert
   Traill Spence Lowell. AA; FaBoBe
Woe Is Me! VII: 1-6. Bible, *O.T. Fr.* Micah, VII: 1–6. TrJP
Woe is me, my soul says, how bitter is my fate. Rachel Morpurgo, *tr. by*
   Robert Alter. PBWP
Woe to him by this world enticed. A Child in Prison. Gofraidh Fionn
   O'Dalaigh. NOIV
Woe to him who slanders women. Gerald, Earl of Desmond.
   NOIV
Woe to us. The Cry of the Gravediggers. Jacob Glatstein, *tr. by*
   Benjamin *and* Barbara Harshav. AYP
Woe worth thee, woe worth thee, false Scottlande! Earl Bothwell.
   Unknown. ESPB
Woefully Arrayed. *At. to* John Skelton. ChTr
   (Wofully Araide.) MeEL
Woe's me! by dint of all these sighs that come. Dante, *tr. fr. Italian by*
   Dante Gabriel Rossetti. *Fr.* Vita Nuova, La, XXVII. AWP
Wofully Araide. John Skelton. *See* Woefully Arrayed.
Woggly bird sat on the whango tree, The. The Whango Tree. *Unknown.*
   NA
Woken, I lay in the arms of my own warmth and listened. First Things
   First. W. H. Auden. NYBP
Wol ze here a wonder thynge. Riddles Wisely Expounded. *Unknown.*
   ESPB
Wolcum be thu, hevene kyng. Welcome Yule. *Unknown.* CH
Wolf. Peter Blue Cloud. HATNAP; VoR
Wolf, The. Georgia Roberts Durston. RHPC
Wolf, The, *sel.* H. Leivick, *tr. fr. Yiddish by* Benjamin *and* Barbara
   Harshav.
   "And it was on the third day in the morning." AYP
Wolf. Kenneth Rexroth. *Fr.* A Bestiary. NNaP
Wolf, A. *Unknown, tr. fr. Osage Indian.* RHPC
Wolf, The. Unsi al-Haj, *tr. fr. Arabic by* Sargon Boulus *and* Alistair
   Elliot. MAP
Wolf also shall dwell with the lamb, The. Bible, *O.T. Fr.* Isaiah, XI:
   6–9. PDV
   (God's Rule.) FM
   (Peaceable Kingdom.) FaPON
Wolf and the Dog, The. La Fontaine, *tr. fr. French by* Elizur Wright.
   OBVE
Wolf and the Lambs, The. Ivy O. Eastwick. BoTP
Wolf and the Stork, The. La Fontaine, *tr. fr. French by* Marianne Moore.
   FM; OBVE
Wolf "Aunt." Maurice Kenny. HATNAP
Wolf Bezberider. Aba Shtoltsenberg, *tr. fr. Yiddish by* Dennis Silk.
   PeBMYV
Wolf-Boy. David Malouf. CBAP
"Wolf!" cried my cunning heart. The True Encounter. Edna St. Vincent
   Millay. OxBSP
Wolf Cry, The. Lew Sarett. FaPON; RHPC
Wolf Girl Speaks, The. Nancy Springer. BWV
Wolf Hunting near Nashoba. Jim Barnes. STE

Wolf, Khaym-Berl and Zanvl were playing cards. Overtime. Moyshe-
   Leyb Halpern, *tr. by* Benjamin *and* Barbara Harshav *and* Kathryn
   Helle. AYP
Wolf may catch in its own dewlap, The. *Unknown, tr. by* Arthur Waley.
   BoS
Wolf-mouth, enamelled face and golden fret. The Alfred Jewel. Robert
   Wells. NPo
Wolf Said to Francis, The. A. G. Rochelle. Mes
Wolf Strikover in the middle of the room. The Strikover Rabbi. Zishe
   Landau, *tr. by* Irving Feldman. PeBMYV
Wolfe Tone. Austin Clarke. CIP
Wolfhound. Richard Murphy. *Fr.* The Battle of Aughrim. NOIV
Wolfen Creek. James Still. MT
Wolfram's Dirge. Thomas Lovell Beddoes. *See* Death's Jest Book: If
   thou wilt ease thine heart.
Wolf's profile hangs, The. From the Window of the Beverly Wilshire
   Hotel. Michael McClure. EAS
Wolsey, or possibly my John of Gaunt. Santa Claus. Christopher
   Hassall. OxBSP
Wolsey's Farewell to His Greatness. Shakespeare *and probably* John
   Fletcher. *Fr.* King Henry VIII, III, ii. OHFP
   (Cardinal Wolsey's Farewell.) LiTB
   (Farewell to Greatness.) TrGrPo
   (Wolsey.) FaBoRV
Wolves. John Haines. LCAP
Wolves, The. Galway Kinnell. NePoEA-2
Wolves. Louis MacNeice. NoAM; OxBTC
Wolves, The. Allen Tate. LiTA; LiTM; NOBA; OxBA; PoA
Wolves can outeat anyone. The Wolf and the Stork. La Fontaine, *tr. by*
   Marianne Moore. FM; OBVE
Wolves for Company. *Unknown, tr. fr. Irish.* BIrV
Wolves in the Zoo. Howard Nemerov. NoAM
Wolves of evening will be much abroad, The. Runes for an Old Believer.
   Rolfe Humphries. NYBP
Wolves say to the dogs, The. J. Michael Yates. *Fr.* The Great Bear
   Lake Meditations. HoPM
Wolves' voices harmonize. Joso, *tr. fr. Japanese by* Hiroaki Sato. *Fr.*
   Fifteen Hokku. FCEI
Woman. Natalie Clifford Barney, *tr. fr. French by* Barbara Johnson.
   DMF
Woman. Eaton Stannard Barrett. TIRV
Woman. Jane Chambers. IHMS
Woman. "Chrystos." GOS
Woman. Goldsmith. *See* Vicar of Wakefield, The: When Lovely Woman
   Stoops to Folly.
Woman, A. Yasin Taha Hafiz, *tr. fr. Arabic by* Sharif Elmusa *and*
   Christopher Middleton. MAP
Woman! Juana de Ibarbourou, *tr. fr. Spanish by* Kate Flores. DMH
Woman. Randall Jarrell. NOBA
Woman, A. Denis Johnson. MAYP
Woman, The. George Keithley. NPGG
Woman. Irving Layton. ErPo
Woman. Elouise Loftin. PoBA
Woman, *sel.* Alexander McLachlan.
   "When my gloomy hour comes to me." CaP
Woman. Valente Malangatana, *tr. fr. Portuguese by* Dorothy Guedes *and*
   Philippa Rumsey. PBA; TTY
Woman. Milton. *Fr.* Samson Agonistes. OBS
Woman. Magda Portal, *tr. fr. Spanish by* Irene Vegas-Garcia *and*
   Kathleen Weaver. WPOW
Woman. Carl Rakosi. TAP
Woman. Umberto Saba, *tr. fr. Italian by* Thomas G. Bergin. UnAS
Woman, The. R. S. Thomas. OxBC
Woman. *Unknown, tr. fr. Chinese by* H. A. Giles. *Fr.* Shi King.
   AWP
(Wo)man. Alma Villanueva. CCP
Woman, A. Sa'di Yusuf, *tr. fr. Arabic by* Lena Jayyusi *and* Naomi
   Shihab Nye. MAP
Woman/ will you come with me moving. Woman. "Chrystos."
   GOS
Woman, A/ sleeps next to me on the earth. Night in the Forest. Galway
   Kinnell. TAP
Woman, a dog and a walnut tree, A. *Unknown.* FaBoUs
Woman, a pleasing but a short-lived flow'r. An Essay on Woman. Mary
   Leapor. NOEC
Woman Alone. Denise Levertov. WPOW
Woman and Her Dying Warrior, A. Vanparanar, *tr. fr. Tamil by* A. K.
   Ramanujan. PLW
Woman and Nature, *sels.* Susan Griffin. NPGG
   Acoustics.
   Garden, The.
   Silence.

Woman and the Aloe, The. Perseus Adams. PeSA
Woman and Tree. Robert Graves. ErPo
Woman as Market. Muriel Rukeyser. NoAM
Woman Asleep on a Banana Leaf. Katha Pollitt. InPS
Woman at the Piano. Marya Zaturenska. MoAmPo
Woman at the Washington Zoo, The. Randall Jarrell. CAPP; CoAP;
   HAP; HCAP; LiTM; OxBC; TAP; TwCP; UnPo
Woman at the Window. Ernst Jandl, *tr. fr. German* by Beth Bjorklund.
   CoAuP
Woman Back in the Kitchen, The. Nicholas Lloyd Ingraham. PWR
Woman, bathe this head of mine. The Bathing of Oisin's Head.
   Unknown, tr. by Eoin MacNeill. AnIL
Woman Cleaning Lentils, The. Zehrd, *tr. fr. Armenian* by Diana der
   Hovanessian *and* Marzbed Margossian. TSS
Woman coming down the snowy road, A. Grey Woman. Gladys
   Cardiff. CDW
Woman Defending Herself Examines Her Own Character Witness, A.
   Susan Griffin. NPGG
Woman, Don't Be Troublesome. Augustus Young, *tr. fr. Irish.* CIP
Woman fears for man, he goes. Abel's Bride. Denise Levertov.
   FaBoWP; VGW
Woman Forsaken in Love, A. Saigyo, *tr. fr. Japanese* by Burton Watson.
   Fr. Sixty-four Tanka. FCEI
Woman Free, *sel.* Elizabeth Wolstenholme-Elmy.
   "Marriage, which might have been a mateship sweet." BrRo
Woman from the Book of Genesis, A. Dovid Knut, *tr. fr. Russian* by
   John Glad. VWA
Woman full of wile. Growing Old. *Unknown, tr.* by Frank O'Connor.
   ErPo
   (Autumn.) OBMV
Woman, Gallup, N. M. Karen Swenson. NYBP
Woman Gave Me a Red Star to Wear on My Headband, A. Jimmie
   Durham. HATNAP
Woman gave me butter now, A. A Present of Butter. Tadhg Dall
   O'Huiginn. BIrV, *tr.* by the Earl of Longford
Woman, give him alms. For the Poor Blind Man. Francisco A. de
   Icaza, *tr.* by Samuel Beckett. MexPo
Woman grew, with waiting, over-quiet, A. Narrative. Elisabeth Eybers,
   tr. by the author. PeSA
Woman grows hard and skinny, A. Ride the Turtle's Back. Beth Brant.
   ER; STE
Woman Grows Soon Old, A. Larin Paraske, *tr. fr. Finnish* by Jaakko A.
   Ahokas. PBWP
Woman had a dress, The. 1909. Guillaume Apollinaire, *tr.* by Robert
   Bly. POS; RHTwFP
Woman Hanging from the Thirteenth Floor Window, The. Joy Harjo.
   ER; GLP; HATNAP; NOVW
Woman Has a Baby in Her Sleep. Jack Driscoll. SoTCo
Woman has wings all the pilgrim, The. A Painting Entitled Love and the
   Pilgrim. Gregory O'Brien. ATNZ
Woman-Hater, The, *sel.* Francis Beaumont *and* Fletcher.
   Come, sleep. ElL; ELP
Woman, her face between her hands, The. Destiny. Amalia
   Guglielminetti, *tr.* by Muriel Kittel. DMI
Woman I Am, The. Glen Allen. BLPA
Woman I have never seen before, A. Transit. Richard Wilbur. DiPo;
   LCAP
Woman I love carries, A. Body Work. Melinda Goodman. ER
Woman I Mix Men Up, A. Bernadette Mayer. UL
Woman I want, The. No More than Five. Fred Levinson. AmPA
Woman: If you weren't you who would you rather be? Flood. Roger
   McGough. FF
Woman in childbirth, fainting with cruel pain, A. To a Faithless Friend.
   Salaan Arrabey, *tr.* by M. Laurence. WTO
Woman in dark glasses, A. Ozaki Hosai, *tr. fr. Japanese* by Hiroaki
   Sato. *Fr.* One Hundred Haiku in Free Form. FCEI
Woman in her room is standing at the mirror, The. The Importance of
   Mirrors. Helga Sandburg. IHMS
Woman in Love with a Captive King, A. Nakkannaiyar, *tr. fr. Tamil* by
   A. K. Ramanujan. PLW
Woman in My Notebook, The. Lorna Dee Cervantes. WPOW
Woman in Rain. Judah Leib Teller, *tr. fr. Yiddish* by Benjamin *and*
   Barbara Harshav. AYP
Woman in the, The. Marge Piercy. NMM
Woman in the Arts, The. Gerrit Komrij, *tr. fr. Dutch* by Jacob Lowland.
   DuIn
Woman in the garden gathers lilacs, A. A. L. Hendricks. *Fr.* D'Où
   Venons Nous? Que Sommes Nous? Où Allons No. PBCV
Woman in the newspaper, The. Ozaki Hosai, *tr. fr. Japanese* by Hiroaki
   Sato. *Fr.* One Hundred Haiku in Free Form. FCEI
Woman in the shape of a monster, A. Planetarium. Adrienne Rich.
   CAPP; FaBoWP; HCAP; MoP; NAAL-2; NIP; NoAM; NOBA

Woman in the spiked device, The. A Woman's Issue. Margaret Atwood.
   AIW
Woman in whose voice. Nizar Qabbani, *tr.* by Lena Jayyusi *and* W. S.
   Merwin. MAP
Woman inside an enormous sunhat, A. Close-up. Heather McPherson.
   PeNZ
Woman into Man. Susan Wallbank. AIW
Woman Is a Branchy Tree, A. James Stephens. ErPo
Woman Is a Worthy Thing, A. *Unknown.* FaBoCo; GBP
   (Women Are Worthy.) MeEL
Woman is by aptitude. *Unknown, tr. fr. Welsh* by Gwyn Williams. *Fr.*
   Against Women. OBWVE
Woman is kneeling in a stream, A. Her Voice Is the Tidying of a House.
   Gregory O'Brien. ATNZ
Woman is making the tremolo into the wind, A. Tremolo. Joan Shaddox
   Isom. GOS
Woman Is of Man the Best. Lope de Vega, *tr. fr. Spanish* by Perry
   Higman. LPSS
Woman is perfected, The. Edge. Sylvia Plath. FaBoWP; HCAP;
   NAAL-2; PoE; TAP
Woman is planting asters on the south wind side, A. And the Silver Turns
   into Night. Nathan Yonathan. VWA, *tr.* by Richard Flantz
Woman is reading a poem on the street, A. The Hug. Tess Gallagher.
   NAmP
Woman Is Talking to Death, A. Judy Grahn. GLP
Woman knocks on the pearly gates, A. Saint Peter and the Bluestocking.
   Marie von Ebner-Eschenbach, *tr.* by Susan L. Cocalis *and* Gerlinde
   Geiger. DMG
Woman like Me, A. Eileen Myles. GLP
Woman Made of Stars. Earle Thompson. STE
Woman making advances publicly, A. Judith Kazantzis. BrRo
Woman Me. Maya Angelou. BlSi
Woman, Mother of Man. Concha Michel, *tr. fr. Spanish* by Kate Flores.
   Fr. God, Our Lady. DMH
Woman Mourned by Daughters, A. Adrienne Rich. IHMS; TV
Woman Moving with You in Coitus, The. Verena Stefan, *tr. fr. German*
   by Johanna Moore *and* Beth Weckmueller. DMG
Woman much missed, how you call to me, call to me. The Voice.
   Thomas Hardy. BoLoP; CMoP; EnLoPo; GBL; GTBS-P; HAP; InPS;
   MoP; NAEL-2; NoAM; NoP; OAEL-2; OBNC; PoE; PoEL-5
Woman named Tomorrow, The. Four Preludes on Playthings of the
   Wind. Carl Sandburg. CMoP; MoAB; MoAmPo; NOBA
Woman Née Wu, The. Wu Chia-chi, *tr. fr. Chinese* by Jonathan Chaves.
   CoBLCP
Woman of the House, The. Richard Murphy. IPY
Woman of Three Cows, The. *Unknown, tr. fr. Irish* by James Clarence
   Mangan. AnIL; EnRP; NOIV
Woman on a spring night, A. Kikaku, *tr. fr. Japanese* by Hiroaki Sato.
   Fr. Thirty-three Hokku. FCEI
Woman on the other side, The. Kimono. Jorie Graham. MAYP; PPR
Woman one wonderful morning, A. Europa. William Plomer. MoBS
Woman Poem. Nikki Giovanni. BlSi; NMM
Woman Poet, The. Gertrud Kolmar, *tr. fr. German* by Henry A. Smith.
   DMG; VWA
Woman prepared a mouse for her husband's dinner, A. On the Eating of
   Mice. Russell Edson. NAmP; PPR
   (Woman was cooking a mouse for her husband's dinner, A.) SoSe
Woman pulls the cart, The. Inscribed on the Painting "Stabbing a Tiger"
   by Chao Tzu-ang. Yang Shih-ch'i, *tr.* by Jonathan Chaves.
   CoBLCP
Woman Recipe. Vinícius de Moraes, *tr. fr. Portuguese* by Paul
   Blackburn. ATCBP
Woman, rest on my brow your balsam hands. Night of Sine. Léopold
   Sédar-Senghor, *tr.* by Ulli Beier. PBA
Woman sails, man must row. Sail and Oar. Robert Graves. MOS
Woman Seed Player. Roberta Hill Whiteman. HATNAP; STE
Woman '77. Vivienne Joseph. ATNZ
Woman Shopping, A. Denis Glover. ATNZ
Woman singing in the house, The. Another Coast. David Wojahn.
   MAYP
Woman Sings of Her Love. *Somali Oral Tradition, tr.* by B. W.
   Andrzejwski *and* I. M. Lewis. WTO
Woman sits in a corner of sun, A. The Survivor. Katherine Gallagher.
   AIW
Woman sits on her porch. Earle Thompson. HATNAP; STE
Woman Skating. Margaret Atwood. FaBoWP; IHMS
Woman sobs on the toilet, A. Bathroom Walls. Maura Stanton. PPR
Woman steps quietly from my forehead, A. Postcards to Athena.
   Michael Bishop. BWV
Woman, supple frame. Woman. Natalie Clifford Barney, *tr.* by Barbara
   Johnson. DMF

"Woman, take away my tunic." Goll's Parting with His Wife. *Unknown, tr. by* Eoin MacNeill. AnIL
Woman Talk. a-dZiko Simba. WS
Woman Talks to Her Thigh, A. Anna Swirszczynska, *tr. fr. Polish by* Czeslaw Milosz. PwPP
Woman That Had More Babies than That, The. Wallace Stevens. LiTA
Woman: that is to say. Of Women. *Unknown, tr. fr. Arabic by* E. Powys Mathers. *Fr.* The Thousand and One Nights. ErPo
Woman Thing, The. Audre Lorde. BlSi; NMM
Woman! thoughtless, giddy creature. The Declaimer. Henry Baker. NOEC
Woman through the Window. Marcia Falk. VWA
Woman to Child. Judith Wright. PBWP; WPE
Woman to Her Lover, A. Christina Walsh. BrRo
Woman to Man. Ai. NoAM
Woman to Man. Judith Wright. CBAP; PoAu-2; WPE
Woman to man, they lie. In Bloemfontein. Alan Ross. BoLoP
Woman touches her bun, The. Gold. Ferenc Juhász, *tr. by* David Wevill. MHuP
Woman Tung. Wu Chia-chi, *tr. fr. Chinese by* Jonathan Chaves. CoBLCP
Woman Undiscovered. Gertrud Kolmar, *tr. fr. German by* Henry A. Smith. DMG
Woman Waits for Me, A. Walt Whitman. ErPo; NOBA
Woman wants monogamy. General Review of the Sex Situation. Dorothy Parker. NAAL-2
Woman was heavy with child, The. The Flower Vendor. Luis Cabalquinto. BrSi
Woman was old and ragged and gray, The. Somebody's Mother. Mary Dow Brine. BeLS; BLPA; FaFP; WBLP
Woman was sitting, A. Sweet Grass Is around Her. Salli Benedict. GOS
Woman watches her husband rubbing his nose, The. Twenty Below. R. A. D. Ford. CaP; NOBC
Woman weak and woman mortal, through the spirit's open portal. Streets of Baltimore. *Unknown.* BLPA
Woman went into the same resturant every Tuesday night, A. Sandwiches. David Donnell. NoAM
Woman who, as a thirteen-year-old girl, A. Novella. Robert Hass. NAmP
Woman Who Could Read the Minds of Dogs, The. Leslie Scalapino. NPGG
Woman who had been dressed by someone, in the same way that, A. Leslie Scalapino. *Fr.* Hmmmm. NPGG
Woman who has crossed the river, A. Kito, *tr. fr. Japanese by* Hiroaki Sato. *Fr.* Twenty-four Hokku. FCEI
Woman who has grown old, The. The Crows. Louise Bogan. FaBoWP
Woman who is waiting for the evening draws, The. The Window. Stephen Dobyns. MAYP
Woman who lived in Holland, of old, A. Going Too Far. Mildred Howells. OnMSP
Woman Who Loved to Cook, The. Erica Jong. TAP
Woman Who Loved Worms, The. Colette Inez. NMM
Woman Who Loves Old Men, The. Herbert Scott. NAmP
Woman Who Suddenly Entered the Room, A. Mieczyslaw Jastrun, *tr. fr. Polish by* Czeslaw Milosz. PwPP
Woman Who Thought She Was More than a Samba, The. Jessica Hagedorn. BrSi
Woman Who Understands, The. Everard Jack Appleton. PoLF
Woman who writes feels too much, A. The Black Art. Anne Sexton. PoA
Woman whose face/ is a blurred map of roots. To Vera Thompson. John Haines. LCAP
Woman with a burning flame, A. Smothered Fires. Georgia Douglas Johnson. BlSi
Woman with a Past, A. Wilfrid Scawen Blunt. *Fr.* The Love Sonnets of Proteus, XLIX. Son
Woman with broad, rough hands. Woman. Magda Portal, *tr. by* Irene Vegas-Garcia *and* Kathleen Weaver. WPOW
Woman with Flower. Naomi Long Madgett. AmNP; FB
Woman with Gardenia: A Sketch. Pamela White Hadas. BLA
Woman with Girdle. Anne Sexton. ErPo
Woman with no face walked into the light, A. Homage to Hieronymus Bosch. Thomas MacGreevy. BIrV; EAS
Woman with the caught fox. Plea for a Captive. W. S. Merwin. NePoEA-2; NoAM; NYBP
Woman with the crepe paper body, The. A Branch of Nettle Enters through the Window. André Breton, *tr. by* David Antin. POS; RHTwFP
Woman, Woman, let us say these things to each other. Conrad Aiken. NYBP

Woman, women/ 1. An adult female person. The Dictionary Is an *His*torian: A Found Political Poem. Judith McCombs. IHMS
Woman Work. Maya Angelou. SaC
Woman working hard and wisely, A. Mary Magdalene Kassia, *tr. by* Patrick Diehl. WPOW
Woman, you are afraid of the forest. Maria Wine, *tr. by* Nadia Christensen. PBWP
Woman, you'll never credit what. The Shepherd's Tale. James Kirkup, *after the French of* Raoul Ponchon. OBCP
Womanhod, wanton, ye want. John Skelton. AAS
Womanhood, The, *sels.* Gwendolyn Brooks.
    Children of the Poor, The. *Fr.* I. PoA, *complete;* WPE, 1 *and* 2. What Shall I Give. BPo, 2 *only.*
    "One wants a Teller in a time like this." *Fr.* XI. WPE
    Rites for Cousin Vit, The. *Fr.* VI. BPo; HAP; WeW; WPE
Womanisers. John Press. BoLoP; ErPo
Womankind. Gerald Massey. NOBVV
Womanness had formed in a man's hand, A. The Bachelor's Hand. Russell Edson. AnAn
Woman's Answer, A. *At. to* Surrey, Earl of. SiPS
Woman's Answer to "The Vampire," A. Felicia Blake. BLPA
Woman's Beauty. Lascelles Abercrombie. *Fr.* Emblems of Love: Vashti. MoBrPo
Woman's beauty is like a white, A. W. B. Yeats. *Fr.* The Only Jealousy of Emer. MoAB
Woman's Constancy. John Donne. NBLV; NoP; SeCV-1
Woman's Constancy. Sir John Suckling. CaPo
Woman's Dream, The. Frances Horovitz. BrRo
Woman's Execution, A. Edward King. AA
Woman's face is full of wiles, A. Humphrey Gifford. ElL
"Woman's face with nature's own hand painted, A." Shakespeare. *Fr.* Sonnets, XX. ErPo; InvP; NAEL-1; OAEL-1; PeHV
Woman's Inconstancy. Phineas Fletcher. *Fr.* Sicelides. EIL
Woman's Issue, A. Margaret Atwood. AIW
Woman's Labour; an Epistle to Mr. Stephen Duck, The, *sel.* Mary Collier.
    Washerwoman, The. NOEC
Woman's Last Word, A. Robert Browning. BLPA; BLPL; FaBoBe; FaFP; NAEL-2; TrGrPo
Woman's Looks, A. *Unknown.* OBSC; TrGrPo
Woman's Love. *Unknown.* WBLP
Woman's Question, A. Lena Lathrop, *wr. at to* Elizabeth Barrett Browning. BLPA; WBLP
Woman's Reason, A. Gelett Burgess. FaBoNo
Woman's Room in Autumn, A. Yüan Hung-tao, *tr. fr. Chinese by* Jonathan Chaves. CoBLCP
Woman's Shortcomings, A. Elizabeth Barrett Browning. BLPA
Woman's Song, A. Colleen J. McElroy. BlSi
Woman's Song, about Men, A. *Unknown, tr. fr. Eskimo into French by* Paul-Emile Victor; *English vers. by* Armand Schwerner. OV; STP
Woman's Sorrow, A, *sel.* Ho Nansorhon, *tr. fr. Korean by* Peter H. Lee.
    "Yesterday I fancied I was young." PBWP
Woman's Will. John Godfrey Saxe. FaFP
Woman's Wish, The. Matthew Prior. FaBoEE
Woman's worth to the world can never be told. Oh Woman, Blessed Woman! Mrs. Henry Linden. CBWP-4
Womb, The. Apirana Taylor. PeNZ
Womb Song. Susan Fromberg Schaeffer. IHMS
Wombat, The. Ogden Nash. CenHV
Women. Louise Bogan. LiTA; MoAB; MoAmPo; NoAM; TwCP; VGW; WPE
Women. William Cartwright. ErPo
Women. ——Heath. CTC; FaBoCo; OBSC
Women. Adrienne Rich. NMM
Women. Yannis Ritsos, *tr. fr. Greek by* Minos Savvas. AnAn
Women. May Swenson. BoWoP; NMM; Prf
Women. Alice Walker. GOA; WPOW
Women. *Yoruba Oral Tradition, tr. by* Ulli Beier. WTO
Women,/ What fools we are. Two Strange Worlds. Francesca Yetunde Pereira. PBA
Women/ in the district capital went down to work, The. Lombard-Venetian. Luciano Erba, *tr. by* Lawrence R. Smith. NItP
Women and Masks. Gábor Devecseri, *tr. fr. Hungarian by* Robert Graves. MHuP
Women and Men. Hassan Sheikh Mumin, *tr. fr. Somali.* WTO
Women and poets see the truth arrive. Letter to the Front. Muriel Rukeyser. WaP
Women and Roses. Robert Browning. NAEL-2

Women are at their best. Emperor Go-Shirakawa, *tr. fr. Japanese by* Hiroaki Sato. *Fr. Ryojin Hisho.* FCEI

Women are timid, cower and shrink. Betty Zane. Thomas Dunn English. PAH

Women are walking to town, The. The Rainy Season. Linda Hogan. HATNAP

Women Are Worthy. *Unknown. See* Woman Is a Worthy Thing, A.

Women at the Corners Stand, The. Louis Golding. TrJP

Women at the Market. Angela Figueroa-Aymerich, *tr. fr. Spanish by* Hardie St. Martin. PBWP

Women before were strangers. Dispatch Number Nine. Doug Fetherling. NeAC

Women ben full of ragerie. Imitation of Chaucer. Pope. FaBoPa; Par

Women Damned. Baudelaire, *tr. fr. French by* Joanna Richardson. PeHV

Women don't travel in clubcars. George Jonas. NeAC

Women have loved before as I love now. Edna St. Vincent Millay. PoA

Women have no share in the encampments of this world. Women and Men. Hassan Sheikh Mumin. WTO

Women have no wilderness in them. Women. Louise Bogan. LiTA; MoAB; MoAmPo; NoAM; TwCP; VGW; WPE

Women have twisted wings. Feathers. Leo Vroman. DuIn

Women he liked, did shovel-bearded Bob. Bob's Lane. Edward Thomas. PoE

Women, if we held the oxhide shield. Lament for a Warrior. *Unknown, tr. by* Dan Kunene *and* Jack Cope. PeSA

Women in black picked up their violins. The Call. Jules Supervielle, *tr. by* Geoffrey Gardner. NU

Women in every age by nature were. Women's Worth. Modesta dal Pozzo, *tr. by* Muriel Kittel. DMI

Women in Love. Donald Justice. SM

Women in Old Parkas, The. Mary TallMountain. AIW; STE

Women in Vietnam, The. Grace Paley. NMM

Women know how to wait here. Lines for Marking Time. Roberta Hill Whiteman. BoWoP; CDW

Women like mirrors yet who plot with Fate. Don Juan in Winter. Michael Mott. KS

Women Men's Shadows. Ben Jonson. *See* That Women Are but Men's Shadows.

Women much loved, who never had enough. Years. Anna Margolin, *tr. by* Adrienne Rich. OV

Women of All the Ages. Andrée Chédid, *tr. fr. French by* Mary Ann Caws. DMF

Women of Dan Dance with Swords in Their Hands to Mark the Time When They Were Warriors, The. Audre Lorde. ER; NAAL-2; NoAM

Women of My Land. Frankie Armstrong. BrRo

Women of Rubens, The. Wislawa Szymborska, *tr. fr. Polish by* Celina Wieniewska. WPOW

Women of the West, The. G. Essex Evans. PoAu-1

Women of Trachis, *sels.* Sophocles, *tr. fr. Greek by* Ezra Pound.
"Kupris bears trophies away." CTC
"Torn between griefs, which grief shall I lament." OBVE

Women often seem distant. Women. Yannis Ritsos, *tr. by* Minos Savvas. AnAn

Women on the Road to Pine Gap. Wendy Poussard. AIW

Women Open Cautiously. Deborah Lee. BrSi

Women Pleased, *sel.* John Fletcher.
"Oh [*or* O] fair[e] sweet face, oh [*or* O] eyes celestial[1] bright." *Fr.* III, iv. OBS; PoEL-2

Women reminded him of lilies and roses. Thoughts after Ruskin. Elma Mitchell. FaBoWP

Women should be beautiful and fly a lot. Oxygen for a Castle in the Air. Paul Snoek, *tr. by* Peter Nijmeijer. DuIn

Women Songs. Kadya Molodowsky, *tr. fr. Yiddish by* Adrienne Rich. OV

Women spin dreams all hours of the day. Women's Dreams. Shirley Lim. UAS

Women stone breakers. History Makers. George Campbell. PVCV

Women that are loved are more than lovable. The Colours of Love. Denis Devlin. IPY

Women Transport Corps. *Unknown, tr. fr. Chinese by* Kai-yu Hsu. WPOW

Women Who Cook. Anita Skeen. GLP

Women who do not know me, The. The Women Who Hate Me. Dorothy Allison. GLP

Women Who Hate Me, The. Dorothy Allison. GLP

Women who heard. Saying Her Name. Brendan Galvin. KS

Women, whoever wishes to know my lord. Gaspara Stampa, *tr. by* J. Vitiello. BoWoP

Women Wisdom. Larry Mitchell. GLP

Women with hats like the rear ends of pink ducks. To a Waterfowl. Donald Hall. OBAL

Women, women,/ women, women. A Fixture. May Swenson. NYBP

Women's Broadcast. Marie Luise Kaschnitz, *tr. fr. German by* Susan L. Cocalis. DMG

Women's Degrees. Alfred Denis Godley. NOBL

Women's Dreams. Shirley Lim. UAS

Women's Jail, The. Miriam Waddington. NOBC

Women's Locker Room. Marilyn Nelson Waniek. MAYP

Women's Marseillaise, The. F. E. M. Macaulay. BrRo

Women's Songs. *Unknown, tr. fr. Maori by* Margaret Orbell. PeNZ

Women's Songs ("For poor brides who were servant girls"). Kadya Molodovsky, *tr. fr. Yiddish by* Irving Feldman. PeBMYV

Women's Songs ("I will come to him"). Kadya Molodovsky, *tr. fr. Yiddish by* Irving Feldman. PeBMYV

Women's Tug of War at Lough Arrow. Tess Gallagher. ASP; MAYP

Women's Worth. Modesta dal Pozzo, *tr. fr. Italian by* Muriel Kittel. DMI

Won' you ring, old hammer? Hammer, Ring. *Unknown.* AmFP

Wonder. Thomas Traherne. CH; HAP; LiTB; NAEL-1; NoP; PoE; SeCePo; SeCP; SeCV-2; TOF; TrGrPo

Wonder, The/ of the bees. Virgil: Georgics, Book IV. Dennis Schmitz. NPGG

Wonder Castle, The. Gyula Illyés, *tr. fr. Hungarian by* Kenneth McRobbie. MHuP

Wonder Clock, The, *sels.* Katharine Pyle. OBCA
Nine o'Clock.
One o'Clock.
Two o'Clock.

Wonder not if I stay not here. To Master Davenant for Absence. Sir John Suckling. CaPo

Wonder of the world is o'er, The. The Twilight of Earth. "Æ." AnIL

Wonder stranger ne'r was known, A. The Suffolk Miracle. *Unknown.* ESPB

Wonder-Teacher, The. Cynthia Ozick. VWA

Wonder Woman. Genny Lim. BrSi

Wonderful. Julian S. Cutler. PWR

Wonderful bears that walked my room all night. Bears. Adrienne Rich. NePoEA; NYBP

Wonderful bird is the pelican, A. Dixon Lanier Merritt. CenHV

Wonderful breasts, here's a mosquito. Ozaki Hosai, *tr. fr. Japanese by* Hiroaki Sato. *Fr.* One Hundred Haiku in Free Form. FCEI

Wonderful Derby Ram, The. *Unknown. See* As I was going to Derby. . .

Wonderful is the sea. *Unknown. Fr. Manyo Shu.* Ma

Wonderful Mother, A. Pat O'Reilly. BLPA

Wonderful occupation, A,/ Making songs! The Joy of a Singer. Piuvkaq. WTO

Wonderful Old Man, The. *Unknown.* NA

Wonderful "One-Hoss Shay," The. Oliver Wendell Holmes. *See* Autocrat of the Breakfast Table, The: Deacon's Masterpiece, The; or, The Wonderful "One-Hoss Shay."

Wonderful Tangerines, The. John Ash. NPo

Wonderful way is the King's Highway, A. The King's Highway. John Masefield. BLRP

Wonderful weather! The Sea's Last Gift; 1961. Milton Kessler. DiL

Wonderful workings of the world: wonderful, The. Cut the Grass. A. R. Ammons. CAPP; HAP; PPP; TAP; WeW

Wonderful World, The. William Brighty Rands. FaPON
(Child's World, The.) OHIP
(World, The.) BoTP; OxBChV

Wondering, I touched it with my young lips. Yosano Akiko, *tr. fr. Japanese by* Hiroaki Sato. *Fr.* Thirty-nine Tanka. FCEI

Wondering is a typical pastime of the leisure class. The Ex-Poet. Bill Zavatsky. UL

Wonderland. Harry Thurston Peck. AA

Wonders. Shirley Kaufman. VWA

Wonders. Lorenzo Thomas. UL

Wonders, *sel. Unknown.* EiL
(Thule, The Period of Cosmography.) HAP
"Andalusian merchant, that returns, The." FaBoCh

Wonders are many and none is more wonderful that man. Glengormley. Derek Mahon. CIP; FaBCIP

Wondrous is the season. Asadullah Khan Ghalib, *tr. by* Ahmed Ali. GoT

" 'Wondrous life!' cried Marvell at Appleton House." Weldon Kees. CoAP; NaP

Wondrous Love. Alex Means. *See* What Wondrous Love Is This.

Wondrous the gods, more wondrous are the men. A Compliment to the Ladies. Blake. BXAP

Wondrous the Merge. James Richard Broughton. GLP

Wondrous this masonry wasted by Fate! The Ruin. *Unknown, tr. by* Charles W. Kennedy. AnOE; PrIm

Wonga Vine. Judith Wright. PoAu-2

"Won't you look out of your window, Mrs. Gill?" The Mocking Fairy. Walter de la Mare. MoBrPo; MoShBr

Won't you please hasten. Tamesada, *tr. by* Steven D. Carter. WFTW

Woo Not the World. Mu'tamid, King of Seville, *tr. fr. Arabic by* Dulcie L. Smith. AWP

Wood. Thomas Hornsby Ferril. PoRA

Wood Carols. Henrietta Cordelia Ray. CBWP-3

Wood-Cutter's Night Song, The. John Clare. EnRP

Wood Ducks. *Unknown, tr. fr. Japanese by* Sato. FCEI

Wood Floor Dreams. Lance Henson. VoR

Wood green. Grandfather built it. July 4th. Anne Waldman. UL

Wood House over the Wilia, The. Johannes Bobrowski, *tr. fr. German by* Don Bogen. AnAn

Wood is a good place to find, The. Walking with Lulu in the Wood. Naomi Lazard. NYBP

Wood is bare, The: a river-mist is steeping. Robert Bridges. EBVV

Wood is full of shining eyes, The. The Magic Wood. Henry Treece. EAS

Wood Music. Ethel King. GoYe

Wood of Flowers, The. James Stephens. BoTP; PDV

Wood-Pile, The. Robert Frost. AnAmPo; InPK; LiTA; NAAL-2; NoAM; NoP; VGW

Wood shakes in the breeze, The. The Old Tree. Andrew Young. GoJo

Wood So Wild, The. *Unknown. See* I Must Go Walk the Wood So Wild.

Wood Song, A. Ralph Hodgson. GoJo

Wood Song. Sara Teasdale. AnAmPo

Wood-Swallows, The. "Fiona Macleod." *Fr.* Australian Transcripts. FM

Wood, swollen with mushrooms, The. The Circle. Jean Garrigue. LiTA

Wood, the Weed, the Wag, The. Sir Walter Ralegh. *See* Three Things [*or* Thinges] There Be[e] That Prosper All [*or* Up] Apace.

Wood Thrush Concealed, A. Tamemasa, *tr. fr. Japanese by* Steven D. Carter. WFTW

Wood was rather old and dark, The. The Little Boy Lost. Stevie Smith. FaBoTw

Wood Weasel, The. Marianne Moore. CMoP

Woodbines in October. Charlotte Fiske Bates. AA

Woodchuck Who Lives on Top of Mt. Ritter. John Oliver Simon. NeAC

Woodchucks. Maxine W. Kumin. CAPP; HoPM; NIP

Woodchuck's very very fat, The. The Jolly Woodchuck. Marion Edey *and* Dorothy Grider. FaPON; PDV

Woodcutter wakes as mountain moon hangs low, The. The Feelings in Nature ("Woodcutter wakes as mountain moon hangs low. Ma Chih-yüan, *tr. fr. Chinese by* Jonathan Chaves. *Fr.* Four Poems to the Tune "Ch'ing-chiang yin," III. CoBLCP

Woodcutter's Hut. Zotan, *tr. fr. Chinese by* Lucien Stryk *and* Takashi Ikemoto. ZPCJ

Woodcutter's Wife, The. William Rose Benét. AWP

Wooden bridge, gaunt willows. Written on the Night of the Twenty-ninth of the First Month. Yün Shou-p'ing, *tr. by* Jonathan Chaves. CoBLCP

Wooden Chamber, The. Anne Hébert, *tr. fr. French by* Birgit Swenson. WPOW

Wooden Die, A. Zbigniew Herbert, *tr. fr. Polish by* Czeslaw Milosz. PwPP

Wooden gate. Kikaku, *tr. by* Geoffrey Bownas *and* Anthony Thwaite. PeBJV

Wooden hives sealed with a glue of propolis, The. The Apprentice at the Feast. Peter Redgrove. NPo

Wooden Horse then said, The. Jenny Mastoraki, *tr. by* Nikos Germanakos. BoWoP; PBWP

Wooden puppet with tangled, A. Song for My Son. Marilyn Davis. TSM

Wooden shoes resounded and died down. The European Night. Stanislav Vinaver. VWA, *tr. by* Vasa D. Mihailovich

Woodland Mass, The. Dafydd ap Gwilym, *tr. fr. Welsh by* Gwyn Williams. OBWVE

Woodland of silent oak trees, A. Suburb. Buson, *tr. fr. Japanese by* Hiroaki Sato. *Fr.* Eighty-seven Hokku. FCEI

Woodland sprite of the rakish kind, A. A Scandal among the Flowers. Charles S. Taylor. BLPA

Woodland Worship. Ethelwyn Wetherald. CaP

Woodlands, The. William Barnes. BoNaP

Woodlands. Sir Herbert Read. BrPo

Woodlark, The. Gerard Manley Hopkins. RB

Woodlot, The. Amy Clampitt. HCAP

Woodman, Spare That Tree. George Pope Morris. AA; AnAmPo; BLPA; FaBoBe; FaFP; FaPON; FPL; OHIP; PWR; WBLP

Woodnotes I ("When the pine tosses its cones"), *sels.* Emerson. AmPP; NOBA

Heart of All the Scene, The. AA

"In unplowed Maine he sought the lumberers' gang." TAP

Woodnotes II ("As sunbeams stream through liberal space"), *sels.* Emerson. NOBA

"All the forms are fugitive." WGRP

"As the sunbeams stream through liberal space." OHIP

Mighty Heart, The. AA

Undersong, The. AA

Woodpecker, The. Ni Tsan, *tr. fr. Chinese by* Jonathan Chaves. CoBLCP

Woodpecker, The. Elizabeth Madox Roberts. FaPON; OBCA

Woodpecker, The. Joyce Sambrook. BoTP

Woodpecker goes beating a little drum, The. Sleep. Charles Simic. CoAP

Woodpecker in Disguise. Grace Taber Hallock. RAR

Woodpecker pecked out a little round hole, The. The Woodpecker. Elizabeth Madox Roberts. FaPON; OBCA

Woodpecker taps at the apple tree. Woodpecker in Disguise. Grace Taber Hallock. RAR

Woodrow Wilson. Robinson Jeffers. FaBoPV

Woods. Louis MacNeice. FaBCIP

Woods, The. Derek Mahon. NOIV

Woods again holing up for winter, under snow. Teika, *tr. fr. Japanese by* Hiroaki Sato. *Fr.* Eighty-four Tanka. FCEI

Woods are overhead over everywhere, The. James Cunningham. *Fr.* The Narrator's Trance. JB

Woods decay, the woods decay and fall, The. Tithonus. Tennyson. HAP; LiTB; NAEL-2; NAWM-2; NOBE; NOBVV; NoP; OAEL-2; OBNC; PoE; PoEL-5; PPP; TEP

Woods of Arcady are dead, The. The Song of the Happy Shepherd. W. B. Yeats. NoAM

Woods of the horizon, The. Men in the City. Alfonsina Storni. PBWP, *tr. by* Rachel Benson

Woods, the mountain, silent, The. On a Cold Day I Climbed Tiger Hill With Professor Ho. Mo Shih-lung, *tr. by* Jonathan Chaves. CoBLCP

Woodsman passes, The. Leaves Falling on a Bridge. Tamemasa, *tr. by* Steven D. Carter. WFTW

Woodsmen blow their horns, and close the day, The. The Fair in the Woods. Thom Gunn. AnAn

Woodspurge, The. Dante Gabriel Rossetti. EBEV; ELP; GTBS-P; HAP; HeIP; NOBE; NoP; OAEL-2; OBEV; OBNC; PoEL-5; PrIm; UnPo; WeW

Woodstock. Joni Mitchell. NIP

Woodtick. Joy Kogawa. BrSi

Woodtown Manor. John Montague. IPY

Woodworker's Ballad. Herbert Edward Palmer. OBEV

Woodworm, The. Erminia Fua Fusinato, *tr. fr. Italian by* Muriel Kittel. DMI

Woodyards in the Rain. Anne Marriott. CaP

Wooed and Married and A.' Alexander Ross. OxBS

Woof of the Sun (Ethereal Gauze). Henry David Thoreau. *Fr.* A Week on the Concord and Merrimack Rivers. TAP

(Haze.) HeIP; NoP

Wooing Frog, The. James Reeves. SO

Wooing in a Dream. Nicholas Breton. *See* Report Song [in a Dream], A.

Wooing Lady, The. William Jay Smith. NePoEA

Wooing Maid, The. Martin Parker. CoMu

Wooing of Criseide, The, III. Chaucer. *Fr.* Troilus and Criseyde [*or* Criseide]. PoEL-1

Wooing of Etain, The. *Unknown, tr. fr. Irish by* John Montague. BIrV

Wooing Rogue, The. *Unknown.* CoMu

Wooing Song. Giles Fletcher the Younger. *Fr.* Christ's Victory and Triumph: Christ's Victory on Earth, II. ElL; OBEV

Wool-chafed and wet-shoed I went forth after. William Langland. *Fr.* The Vision of Piers Plowman, Passus XVIII. NAEL-1

Wool Trade, The. John Dyer. *Fr.* The Fleece, III. SeCePo

Woolly Words. Robert N. Feinstein. NBLV

Woosel cock so black of hue, The. Bottom's Song. Shakespeare. *Fr.* A Midsummer Night's Dream, III, i. CTC; PBBP

Wops came down to the port, The. The City of Beggars. Alfred Hayes. WaP

Word. Gerrit Achterberg, *tr. fr. Dutch by* James Brockway. DuIn

Word, The. Margaret Avison. MoCV

Word, The. Basil Bunting. PoA

Word, The. Fyna Dowe. WS
Word, The. D. J. Enright. PoPo
Word, The. Gustave Kahn, *tr. fr. French by* Edouard Roditi. VWA
Word, The. Richard Realf. AA; WGRP
Word. Stephen Spender. NYBP
Word/ Meant *arrogant* once, the absolute of pride, The. The Superb Lily.
  Robert Pinsky. AnAn
Word, The. Bible, *N.T. Fr.* St. John, I: 1-5. TrGrPo
Word, The. Neil Weiss. NYBP
Word about Freedom and Identity in Tel Aviv, A. Jon Silkin. VWA
Word and Afterword. Ingeborg Bachmann, *tr. fr. German by* Beth
  Bjorklund. CoAuP
Word bites like a fish, The. Word. Stephen Spender. NYBP
Word by Night. Charles Brasch. ATNZ; PeNZ
Word cemetery, The. Some Words Which, Up until Now, Had Remained
  Mysteriously Forbidding for Me. Paul Eluard, *tr. by* Michael
  Benedikt. POS
Word "dream" is technical and means nothing, The. View from an
  Apartment. Michael Palmer. UL
Word Fitly Spoken, A. Bible, *O.T. Fr.* Proverbs, XXV: 11. FaPON
Word from the Hills, *sels.* Richard Moore.
  It Took TV to Civilize Our Village. *Fr.* XXXIV. Son
  Though the New Teacher Is a Trifle Odd. *Fr.* XXXVII. Son
  Unable, Father, Still, to Disavow. *Fr.* XXXI. Son
Word goes round Repins, The. An Absolutely Ordinary Rainbow. Les
  A. Murray. CBAP
Word has been abroad, The; is back, with a tanned look. Annunciations.
  Geoffrey Hill. NePoEA-2
Word has come from the kitchen. *See* Word's gane to the kitchen.
Word has come to May Margerie. Jellon Grame. *Unknown.* EBEV;
  ESPB, A *vers.;* OxBB
Word has gane thro a' this land. The Bonny Lass of Anglesey.
  Unknown. ESPB
Word I keep near me, The. For Where You Skill. Vincent O'Sullivan.
  ATNZ
Word I Like White Paint Considered, The. James Sherry. LP
Word in Edgeways, A. Charles Tomlinson. NOBL
Word in the bread feeds me, The. Rune. Muriel Rukeyser. SM
Word is a bouncing ball, The. Morphine. Nizar Qabbani, *tr. by*
  Abdullah al-Udhari. MPAW
Word is dead, A. Emily Dickinson. RHPC
Word is out that I have your enemy, The. To Julia de Burgos. Julia de
  Burgos. OV, *tr. by* Maria Arrillaga
Word Made Flesh, The. W. J. Turner. OBMV
Word made flesh is seldom, A. Emily Dickinson. NAAL-1
Word of a snail on the plate of a leaf, The? The Couriers. Sylvia Plath.
  LCAP
"Word" of a Watch-Dog, The. Sandag, *tr. by* C. R. Bawden. WTO
"Word" of a Wolf Encircled by the Hunt, The. Sandag, *tr. fr. Mongolian
  by* C. R. Bawden. WTO
Word of advice about matters and things, A. Written at the White Sulphur
  Springs. Francis Scott Key. OBAL
"Word" of an Antelope Caught in a Trap, The. Sandag, *tr. by* C. R.
  Bawden. WTO
Word of Art. Alan Bernheimer. UL
Word of Encouragement, A. J. R. Pope. FiBHP; FPL; NBLV; NOBL
Word of God, The. Annie Johnson Flint. BLRP
Word of God, Across the Ages. Ferdinand Q. Blanchard. AH
Word of God came unto me, The. In the Garden of the Lord. Helen
  Keller. WGRP
Word of God to Leyden Came, The. Jeremiah Eames Rankin. AA; PAH
Word of Snow. Tony Beyer. *Fr.* Surviving the Journey. ATNZ
Word of the Lord by night, The. Boston Hymn. Emerson. OPP; PAH;
  WGRP
Word of the Lord came unto me, saying, The. Chorus from "The Rock."
  T. S. Eliot. *Fr.* The Rock, III. LiTB
Word of the Lord from Havana, The. Richard Hovey. PAH
Word of Water, The. E. L. Mayo. PoA
Word over all, beautiful as the sky. Reconciliation. Walt Whitman.
  HAP; MoAmPo; NAAL-1; NoP; OBWP; OxBA; OxBSP; TrGrPo;
  WaaP; WeW
Word *Plum*, The. Helen Chasin. NIP
Word Poem (Perhaps Worth Considering). Nikki Giovanni. PoBA
Word "Silk", The. Thomas McCarthy. CIP
Word sticks in the wind's throat, A. Apology. Richard Wilbur. Psk
Word the general's chosen is parsley, The. The Palace. Rita Dove. *Fr.*
  Parsley, II. NoAM
Word to New England, A. William Bradford. SCAP
Word to Orphists, A. Kazimierz Wierzynski, *tr. fr. Polish by* Czeslaw
  Milosz. PwPP
Word to the West End, A. Thomas Ashe. EBVV

Word to the Wise, A. Caroline Duer. AA
Word was brought to the Danish king. The King of Denmark's Ride.
  Caroline E. Norton. BeLS; GN
Word World. Bob Perelman. LP
Wordless, he is whetting a knife. Knife Whetter. Takamura Kotaro, *tr.*
  by Hiroaki Sato. FCEI
Words. Helen Morgan Brooks. PoNe
Words. Robert Finch. PoA
Words. Barbara Guest. BAP
Words. Charles Harpur. PoAu-1
Words, The. Lee Harwood. EAS
Words. John Hay. AnAmPo
Words. David Huddle. *Fr.* Tour of Duty. Son
Words. Philip Levine. VWA
Words. Dan Pagis, *tr. fr. Hebrew by* Warren Bargad *and* Stanley F.
  Chyet. IP
Words. David Phillips. NeAC
Words. Sylvia Plath. HCAP; LCAP; NAAL-2; PoE
Words. W. R. Rodgers. OxBSP
Words. *Unknown.* PoLF
Words, The. David Wagoner. PoA
Words/ across. Persimmons and Plums. Elizabeth Hodges. GrPl
Words and Legacy. Cyril Dabydeen. PBCV
Words and Monsters. Vernon Scannell. OxBC
Words and Music, *sel.* Samuel Beckett.
  "Age is when to a man." BIrV
Words and Truth. Yasin Taha Hafiz, *tr. fr. Arabic by* Sharif Elmusa *and*
  Christopher Middleton. MAP
Words are deeds. The words we hear. Words. Charles Harpur. PoAu-1
Words Are Never Enough. Charles Bruce. CaP; OBCV
Words are sardines packed. Bell Too Heavy to Ring. Tom Kryss.
  NeAC
Words are written/ on the Wailing Wall. Identity. Robert Friend.
  VWA
Words Asleep. Laurie Lee. PoPo
Words can be stuffy, as sticky as glue. Alphabet Stew. Jack Prelutsky.
  RHPC
Words do not grow on the landscape. Jean Malley. PoA
Words don't express your absence. Another Time. Ory Bernstein, *tr. by*
  Bernhard Frank. MHeP
Words dreamed by fire, then erased. The Intense Landscape. Alain
  Delahaye, *tr. by* Paul Auster. RHTwFP
Words for a Resurrection. Leo Kennedy. OBCV
Words for Delmira Agustini. Alfonsina Storni, *tr. fr. Spanish by* Kate
  Flores. DMH
Words for Hart Crane. Robert Lowell. CMoP
Words for the Wind. Theodore Roethke. CoAP; NOBA
Words for You. Hans Andreus, *tr. fr. Dutch by* James S. Holmes. DuIn
Words from a Bottle. Deborah Lee. BrSi
Words from an Old Spanish Carol. *Unknown, tr. fr. Spanish by* Ruth
  Sawyer. PChr
Words from Hell. David Helwig. NOBC
Words from the Goblet of Wisdom. Yüan Mei, *tr. fr. Chinese by*
  Jonathan Chaves. CoBLCP
Words from the Window of a Railway Car. Anatoly Steiger, *tr. fr.*
  Russian by John Glad. VWA
Word's gane to the kitchen. Mary Hamilton. *Unknown.* ESPB, A
  vers.; FaBoBa; NoP
  ("Word has come from the kitchen.") AmFP
Word's gone out, and now they spread the main, The. Daniel Defoe.
  Fr. The Spanish Descent. OBWP
Words have all fled the country, they are not expected back, The.
  Emigration. Anita Barrows. NMM
Words have grown old inside men, The. The Words Will Resurrect.
  Jorge de Lima, *tr. by* John Nist. TTY
Words Heard, by Accident, over the Phone. Sylvia Plath. AnAn
Words in the air, heard. Birthday Visit. P. J. Kavanagh. NPo
Words in the Mourning Time, *sel.* Robert Hayden.
  "For King, for Robert Kennedy." CNA
Words in Time. Archibald MacLeish. PoRA
Words in Works in Russian. Stephen Rodefer. IAT
Words like branches of deadfall. Michael Jackson. *Fr.* Fragments.
  ATNZ
Words Like Freedom. Langston Hughes. *See* There are words like
  Freedom.
Words, like Spiders. P. Wolny. PCP
Words Made of Water. Burns Singer. NePoEA-2
Words May Well Want. Henry Lok. *Fr.* Sundry Christian Passions
  Contained in Two Hundred. Son
Words Most Often Mispronouncd in Poetry. Alex Kuo. UL

Words move, music moves. T. S. Eliot. *Fr.* Four Quartets: Burnt Norton, V. UnS
Words of Agur, The. Bible, *O.T. Fr.* Proverbs, XXX: 4, 15-16, 18-19, 24-28.
  Four Things. *Fr. ll.* 24-28.
  Too Wonderful. *Fr. ll.* 18-19.TrJP
Words of Finn, The. *Unknown, tr. fr. Old Irish.* ChTr
Words of hymns abruptly plod, The. Louise Townsend Nicholl. EaLo
Words of Oblivion and Peace. Gabriel Preil, *tr. fr. Hebrew by* Robert Friend. VWA
Words of our day, The. The Same Side of the Canoe. Alda do Espírito Santo. PBWP, *tr. by* Allan Francovich *and* Kathleen Weaver
Words of Tayko-mol. William Oandasan. *See* Past, The.
Words of the All-Wise, The, *sel. Unknown, tr. fr. Icelandic by* W. H. Auden *and* Paul B. Taylor.
  "Say, dwarf, for it seems to me." OBVE
Words of the Newly Wed Wife. Wang Chien, *tr. fr. Chinese by* Burton Watson. CoBCP
Words Persistently. Gerhard Fritsch, *tr. fr. German by* Beth Bjorklund. CoAuP
Words Read in a Poem in a Dream. Jascha Kessler. FOC
Words say, mispell and mispell your name. Michael Palmer. UL
Words scored upon a bone. Meditation on a Bone. A. D. Hope. NoAM; TW
Words Spoken Alone. Dannie Abse. NYBP
Words Spoken by Pasternak during a Bombing. Bella Akhmadulina, *tr. fr. Russian by* Jean Valentine *and* Olga Carlisle. BoWoP
Words that pass from lip to lip, The. Speech and Silence. Richard Hovey. AnAmPo
Words That Speak of Death. Anadad Eldan, *tr. fr. Hebrew by* Anthony Rudolf *and* Natan Zach. VWA
Words to a Song. Agnes Nemes Nagy, *tr. fr. Hungarian by* Bruce Berlind. BoWoP
Words to My Friend. Renée Vivien, *tr. fr. French by* Sandia Belgrade. PeHV
Words to Remind Me of Grandmother. Andrés Castro Ríos, *tr. by* Julio Marzán. InW
Words were meant. Poet's Protest. Doris Hedges. CaP
Words Wherein Stinging Bees Lurk. Judah Halevi, *tr. fr. Hebrew by* Nina Davis Salaman. TrJP
Words will one day come, The. The Movie Run Backward. Robert Creeley. CAPP
Words Will Resurrect, The. Jorge de Lima, *tr. fr. Portuguese by* John Nist. TTY
Words without Music. Irving Layton. CaP
Words! Words! Jessie Redmond Fauset. CDC
Words would not have come to write to you. Autumn Wind. Ruth Dallas. *Fr.* Letter to a Chinese Poet, VIII. PeNZ
Wordspinning. Olga Kirsch, *tr. fr. Afrikaans by* Jack Cope. PeSA
Wordsworth. William Wilberforce Lord. *Fr.* Ode to England. AA
Wordsworth I love, his books are like the fields. To Wordsworth. John Clare. OAEL-2; Son
Wordsworth Skates on Esthwaite Water. Wordsworth. *Fr.* The Prelude [or, Growth of a Poet's Mind]: Childhood and School-Time. FaBoPP
Wordsworth to the contrary notwithstanding. In Magic Words. Merrill Moore. Son
Wordsworth Unvisited. Hartley Coleridge. *See* He Lived amidst th' Untrodden Ways.
Wordsworth upon Helvellyn! Let the cloud. On a Portrait of Wordsworth by B. R. Haydon. Elizabeth Barrett Browning. HeIP
Wordsworth's Grave. Matthew Arnold. *Fr.* Memorial Verses. FaBoPP
Wordsworth's Grave. Sir William Watson. OBNC
Work. Louis James Block. AA
Work. Andrei Codrescu. EAS
Work, The. Robert Duncan. *Fr.* Dante Études. CAPP
Work. Gyula Illyés, *tr. fr. Hungarian by* William Jay Smith. MHuP
Work. Pierre Jean Jouve, *tr. fr. French by* John Montague. RHTwFP
Work. D. H. Lawrence. OBMV
Work. Pushkin, *tr. fr. Russian by* Babette Deutsch *and* Avrahm Yarmolinsky. AWP
Work. Robert Penn Warren. *Fr.* Boy's Will, Joyful Labor without Pay, and Harvest Home. SaC
Work?/ I don't have to work. Necessity. Langston Hughes. NOBA
Work; a Song of Triumph ("Work!/ Thank God for the might of it"). Angela Morgan. PoLF
Work, for the night is coming. Annie L. Walker. SaC
Work Gangs. Carl Sandburg. SaC
Work is a blessing. Before Breughel the Elder. Aleksander Wat, *tr. by* Czeslaw Milosz. PwPP
Work is a gulf. Oh protect me from that self. Work. Pierre Jean Jouve, *tr. by* John Montague. RHTwFP

Work [*or* Worke] is done, The. Young men and maidens, set. On Himself. Robert Herrick. CaPo; SeCP
Work of Artifice, A. Marge Piercy. IHMS; Psk
Work of Love, The. Margaret E. Sangster. BLRP
Work on the railroad. Roll on the Ground. *Unknown.* AmFP
Work-out, The. Geoffrey Movius. MAT
Work Song. Raymond Mazisi Kunene, *tr. fr. Zulu by* D. K. Rycroft. WTO
Work Song, The. Sipho Sepamla. WMBCH
Work-Songs, *sels. Unknown.* PBCV
  "If me want for go in a Ebo." *Fr.* II.
  "Tink dere is a God in a top." *Fr.* I.
Work-table, litter, books and standing lamp. Night Sweat. Robert Lowell. NAAL-2; TAP; VGW
Work to Do toward Town. Gary Snyder. VGW
Work without Hope. Samuel Taylor Coleridge. BoNaP; EnRP; FiP; NAEL-2; NOBE; NoP; OBEV; SaC; Son; TEP
  (In Springtime.) BoTP, 4 *ll.*
Work—work—work. Thomas Hood. *Fr.* The Song of the Shirt. RR
Workaday Morning. Astrid Tollefsen, *tr. fr. Norwegian by* Nadia Christensen. PBWP
Workbox, The. Thomas Hardy. InPK; NAEL-2; UnPo
Workday. Linda Hogan. HATNAP
Worke is done, The. Robert Herrick. *See* Work is done. . .
Worker, The. Gerald Massey. EBVV
Worker, The. Richard W. Thomas. PoBA; PoNe
Workers earn it. Money. Richard Armour. FaFP; NBLV
Workers of the Sun's Land. Antonio Cisneros, *tr. fr. Spanish by* Maureen Ahern *and* David Tipton. Per
Workhouse Boy, The. *Unknown.* GBP
Working against Time. David Wagoner. MAT
Working and Waiting. Adah Isaacs Menken. CBWP-1
Working Class. Bertram J. Warr. NOBC; OBCV; WaP
Working-Class Woman, A. Louise Colet, *tr. fr. French by* Beth Archer. DMF
Working girl: child-carrying, sensual, The. I See Cleopatra. Nurunnessa Choudhury, *tr. by the author and* Paul Joseph Thompson. AIW
Working Girls. Carl Sandburg. SaC
Working is another way of praying. Song for Dov Shamir. Dannie Abse. VWA
  (Song of a Hebrew.) WTO
Working late. Louis Simpson. DiL; PBCV
Working my way through life's karma. The Year *Chi-wei* (1559), New Year's Day. Wen Cheng-ming, *tr. by* Jonathan Chaves. CoBLCP
Working Party, A. Siegfried Sassoon. CMoP; MMA
Working Song. Buluguru, *tr. fr. Yaoro by* E. A. Worms. CBAP
Working the Rain Shift at Flanagan's. Gibbons Ruark. MAYP
Working with these young kids in the pastel. A School Report. Sam Hunt. ATNZ
Working with Tools. A. R. Ammons. CAPP; NoAM
Working, working. Ishikawa Takuboku, *tr. by* Geoffrey Bownas *and* Anthony Thwaite. PeBJV
Workman plied his clumsy spade, A. Two Surprises. R. W. McAlpine. PoLF
"Workman, what will you make on the bench today?" Carpenter. George Mackay Brown. OxBC
Workman's Home, A. Thomas Ince. PF
Workmen eating lunch. *Unknown, tr. by* Burton Watson. FCEI
Works and Days, *sel.* Hesiod, *tr. fr. Greek by* Thomas Cooke.
  "Next to my counsels an attention pay." FaBoUs
Works of God, The. Moses ibn Ezra, *tr. fr. Hebrew by* Solomon Solis-Cohen. TrJP
World,/ world you are wonderful. A Round Song. Rhyll McMaster. CBAP
World. André Breton, *tr. fr. French by* Michael Benedikt. POS
World, The. Robert Creeley. MoP; NaP; NoP
World, The. William Drummond of Hawthornden. *See* Book, The.
World, The. Frederick William Faber. PWR
World, The. George Herbert. OBS; SeCV-1
World, The. Kathleen Jessie Raine. OxBTC
World, The. William Brighty Rands. *See* Great, wide, beautiful, wonderful world.
World, A. Peter Redgrove. NPo
World, The. Christina Rossetti. BoWoP
World, The. Vern Rutsala. Psk
World, The. Henry Vaughan. AWP; EBEV; FaBV; GoTL; HAP; HeIP; JCP; LiTB; MePo; NAEL-1; NOBE; NOCV; OAEL-1; OBS; PoEL-2; PPP; SeCP; SeCV-1; TEP; TrCP; TrGrPo; WGRP
World, The. Ella Wheeler Wilcox. PWR

World, The. *Wordsworth. See* World is too much with us; late and soon, The.

World, The. Barbara Young. RAR

World a hunting is, The. William Drummond of Hawthornden. OBD (Word a Hunt, A.) NOBE; OBS

World an Illusion, The. *Unknown.* MeEL

World an Old Music Box, The. Hans Lodeizen, *tr. fr. Dutch by* James Brockway. DuIn

World, as fine as a razor-blade, The. The Fan and the Observatory Dome. Shauqi Abi Shaqra, *tr. by* Abdullah al-Udhari. MPAW

World as Meditation, The. Wallace Stevens. HeIP; LCAP; MoAB; NIP; PPP

World Awoke Me, The. Gábor Devecseri, *tr. fr. Hungarian by* Robert Graves. MHuP

World Beautiful, The. Milton. *See* Paradise Lost: Sweet is the breath of morn.

World begins with rough and smooth, The. The School for Objects. Paul Hoover. UL

World below the Brine, The. Walt Whitman. BoNaP; FM; MAT; NoP

World Beyond, A. Nathaniel Ingersoll Bowditch. AA

World can end any time, The. A Reliable Service. Allen Curnow. ATNZ

World Champions. William Jay Smith. ASP

World could fall to pieces any moment now, The. The Thermostatic Man. Gordon Challis. ATNZ

World did say to me, The. The Crazy World. William Gay. PoAu-1

World doesn't crumble apart, The. Watershed. Margaret Avison. OBCV

World feels dusty, The. Emily Dickinson. MoAmPo

World full of sugar and rain, The. A World. Peter Redgrove. NPo

World has held great Heroes, The. The Song of Mr. Toad. Kenneth Grahame. *Fr.* The Wind in the Willows. FaPON; FiBHP; GoJo; NOBL

World Has Many Places Many Ways, The. Norman H. Russell. NOVW

World has room for the manly man, with the spirit of manly cheer, The. The Manly Man. *Unknown.* BLPA; WBLP

World has so many eyes, The. Lady Kasa. *Fr.* Manyo Shu. FCEI

World hath conquered, the wind hath scattered like dust, The. Tara Is Grass. *Unknown, tr. by* Padraic Pearse. AnIL

World Hymn, The. James Gilchrist Lawson. WBLP

World I Am Passing Through, The. Lydia Maria Child. AA

World I did not wish to enter, A. A Necessitarian's Epitaph. Thomas Hardy. FaBoEE

World in gloom and splendour passes by, The. To a Millionaire. Archibald Lampman. NOBC

World in Making, The. Sir Gilbert Parker. CaP

World in turmoil—we came south together, A. The Rebellion Over, I See Off a Friend Who Is Returning North. Ssu-k'ung Shu, *tr. by* Burton Watson. CoBCP

World is, The/ not with us enough. O Taste and See. Denise Levertov. NoP; PBWP; PPP; TAP

World Is a Bundle of Hay, The. Byron. EnRP; FF (Epigram on John Bull.) FaBoCo

World Is a gift again, The. Spring Workman. Alan Creighton. CaP

World Is a Mighty Ogre, The. Fenton Johnson. AmNP

World Is a Musician's Cliff House, The. Rodney Hall. *Fr.* Black Bagatelles. CBAP

World is alive with inspiration to a potter who turns the wheel, The. Chao Yi, *tr. fr. Chinese by* Irving Lo. *Fr.* On Poetry, I. WFTU

World is all orange-round, The. The Walking Road. Richard Hughes. OBMV

World is charged with the grandeur of God, The. God's Grandeur. Gerard Manley Hopkins. AWP; BLPL; BrPo; CMoP; EBVV; FaFP; FF; HAP; InPK; InvP; LiTB; LiTM; MoAB; MoBrPo; MoP; NAEL-2; NIP; NoAM; NOBE; NOBVV; NoP; OAEL-2; OBNC; PoE; PPP; PrIm; Son; SoSe; SOTW; TEP; TrCP; TrGrPo; UnPo; WeW

World is come upon me, I used to keep it a long way off, The. The Deserter. Stevie Smith. FaBoWP

World is complete, The. Complete Thought. Barrett Watten. IAT

World is composed, The. The Grass Is a Reasonable Colour. John Newlove. NeAC

World is dull, the world is blind, The. Die Welt ist dumm, die Welt ist blind. Heine, *tr. by* James Thomson. AWP

World Is Everything That Is the Case, The. Derek Mahon. PPR (Tractatus.) FaBCIP; OxBSP

World Is Full of Beauty, The. Matilda Caroline Edwards. PWR

World is full of colour!, The. Colour. Adeline White. BoTP

World is full of gladness, The. Lemon Pie. Edgar A. Guest. OBAL

World is full of iniquities, The. Ching-wei. Ku Yen-wu, *tr. by* J. P. Seaton. WFTU

World is full of mostly invisible things, The. To David, about His Education. Howard Nemerov. DiL; HCAP

World is full of the effulgence, The. Asadullah Khan Ghalib, *tr. by* Ahmed Ali. GoT

World is full of wistful ones who hoard their souvenirs, The. Ballad of Culinary Frustration. Phyllis McGinley. FiBHP

World is great, The: the birds all fly from me. I Am Lonely. "George Eliot." *Fr.* The Spanish Gypsy. GN

World is heated seven times, The. A Night in June. Duncan Campbell Scott. OBCV

World is in a mess today, The. Song about Whiskers. P. G. Wodehouse. FiBHP

World Is like a Woman of Folly, The. Moses Ibn Ezra, *tr. fr. Hebrew by* Solomon Solis-Cohen. *Fr.* The World's Illusion. TrJP

World Is Mine, The. Florence Earle Coates. AA

World Is Not a Fenced-off Garden, The. Jakov Steinberg, *tr. fr. Hebrew by* Mark Elliott Shapiro. VWA

World Is Not a Pleasant Place to Be, The. Nikki Giovanni. PCP

World is only conjectural, The. Mohammad Taqi Mir, *tr. by* Ahmed Ali. GoT

World Is Really a Sugarplum House in the Forest, The. Aram Boyajian. NeAC

World is Rome, The; Carnuntum, on the Danube. Marcus Antoninus Cui Cognomen Erat Aurelius. Burns Singer. OxBS

World Is Round, The. Veijo Meri, *tr. fr. Finnish by* Aili Jarvenpa. SOP

World is several billion years of age, The. Winter Report. Ben Howard. PoA

World is so full of a number of things, The. Happy Thought. Robert Louis Stevenson. BoTP; FaBoBe; OxBChV; PWR; RAR; RHPC

World is taking off her clothes, The. X. J. Kennedy. SM

World is to me but child's play, The. Asadullah Khan Ghalib, *tr. by* Ahmed Ali. GoT

World Is Too Much with Us, The. Wordsworth. AWP; ChTr; EnRP; FaFP; FaPoR; FiP; FPL; GTBS; GTBS-P; HAP; HeIP; HoPM; InPK; InPS; LiTB; MAT; NAEL-2; NAWM-2; NOBE; NoP; OAEL-2; OBNC; PoE; PoEL-4; PoLF; PoRA; PPP; PrIm; Son; SoSe; TEP; TrGrPo; WeW; WGRP
(Sonnet: The World Is Too Much with Us.) ChER; OHFP
(Sonnet: "This world is too much with us: late and soon.") PWR
(World, The.) OBEV

World is very flat, The. Night Thought of a Tortoise Suffering from Insomnia on a Lawn. E. V. Rieu. FiBHP

World is weaned from this one dead by the thread of a shawl, The. The Spoils of War. Vernon Watkins. WaP

World is what you swim in, or dance, it is simple. The Dolphins. Carol Ann Duffy. NPo

World Is white with cherry-trees, The. June. Wilson Pugsley MacDonald. CaP

World is wise, for the world is old, The. The World. Frederick William Faber. PWR

World Is with Me, The. Thomas Hood. Son

World Is with Me Just Enough, The. Sam Abrams. UL

World is young today, The. Digby Mackworth Dolben. NOBVV; OBNC

World laid low, and the wind blew like a dust, The. *Unknown, tr. by* Thomas Kinsella. NOIV

World, let it be, and good. To the World. Andrea Zanzotto, *tr. by* Lawrence R. Smith. NItP

World Looks On, The. Louis I. Newman. PoNe

World? Moonlit, The. Waka on Impermanence. Dogen, *tr. by* Lucien Stryk *and* Takashi Ikemoto. ZPCJ

World Music. Frances Louisa Bushnell. AA

World, natura, phenomenon. This Too Is Ars Poetica. István Vas, *tr. by* Jascha Kessler. FOC

World of Darkness. Robert Chatain. PoA

World of dew is, The. Issa, *tr. by* Geoffrey Bownas *and* Anthony Thwaite. OBD; PeBJV

World of dew is, yes, The. Issa, *tr. by* Hiroaki Sato. FCEI

World of Expectations, The. Albert Goldbarth. HCAP

World of Fancy. Sami Mahdi, *tr. fr. Arabic by* May Jayyusi. MAP

World of Light, A. Elizabeth Jennings. NePoEA-2

World of Light, The. Henry Vaughan. *See* They Are All Gone into the World of Light.

World of mightie kings and princes I could name, A. Michael Drayton. *Fr.* Polyolbion, Twentieth Song. OBS

World of stars and space being His bauble, The. Receiving Communion. Vassar Miller. NePoEA-2

World of Verna Lisa, The. Yung Tzu, *tr. fr. Chinese by* Dominic Cheung. IFON

World rustles for Esther, The. Lilith Re-Tells Esther's Story. Michelene Wandor. AIW

World-Secret. Hugo von Hofmannsthal, *tr. fr. German by* Charles Wharton Stork. TrJP
World seems smaller, The. That Time in Tangier. Marvin Bell. AnAn
World stretches out, The. Madonna. Ian Wedde. *Fr.* Earthly: Sonnets for Carlos, 1. ATNZ
World, that all contains, is ever moving, The. Fulke Greville. *Fr.* Caelica, VII. NIP
(Change.) OBSC
World, the Devil, and Tom Paine, The. *Unknown.* AH
World Transformed, The. Whittier. *See* Snow-bound; a Winter Idyl: Unwarmed by any sunset light.
World Turned Upside Down, The. *Unknown.* PAH
World turns mild, The; democracy, they say. Tempora Mutantur. James Russell Lowell. HAP
World turns round and leaves the sun, The. Eve in My Legend. Denis Devlin. IPY
World turns softly, The. Water. Hilda Conkling. PDV
World under the sky, The. A Gone. Larry Eigner. NeAP
World uprose as a man to find Him, The. At the End of Things. Arthur Edward Waite. WGRP
World War. Richard Eberhart. WaP
World War. *Unknown.* FaFP
World War II. Edward Field. GLP
World War II. Langston Hughes. HCAP
World War II Premium from Battle Creek, A. John Caddy. TSL
World was everything that was the case?, The. James Merrill. *Fr.* Mirabell: Books of Number, *Bk*. 9. HCAP
World was first a private park, The. The Fisherman. Jay Macpherson. Mes; NOBC
World was made when a man was born, The. Experience. John Boyle O'Reilly. ACP
World Well Lost, The. Edmund Clarence Stedman. AA
World where no nightingale can sing. Stars. Hans Verhagen, *tr. by* Peter Nijmeijer. DuIn
World will burst like an intestine in the sun, The. Passengers. Denis Johnson. MAYP; SM
World Winter. Earle Birney. GrPl
World with all of its thought and action, The. God's Electric Power. Mrs. Henry Linden. CBWP-4
World without End. Charles Brasch. ATNZ
"World without Objects Is a Sensible Emptiness, A. " Richard Wilbur. LiTM; MoAmPo; MoP; NAAL-2; NoAM; NOBA; PoA
World without Peculiarity. Wallace Stevens. HCAP
World world world world/ and the face grave. Enueg II. Samuel Beckett. NoAM
Worldly Vanity. Dryden. *See* Hind and the Panther, The: Conversion.
Worldly Wealth. Rowland Watkyns. FaBoEE
World's a bubble, and the life of man, The. The Life of Man. Francis Bacon. EIL; GTBS; OBSC
(Life.) GTBS-P
World's a Sea, The. Francis Quarles. ChTr
World's a sorry wench, akin, The. The Jester's Plea. Frederick Locker-Lampson. CenHV
World's a stage, The. The trifling entrance fee. Hilaire Belloc. OxBTC
World's a theater, the earth a stage, The. The Author to His Booke. Thomas Heywood. *Fr.* An Apology for Actors. OBS
World's a very happy place, The. The World's Music. "Gabriel Setoun." FaBoBe
World's a weary place, The. All thro' the Year. *Unknown.* BLRP
World's a well strung fidle, mans tongue the quill, The. Nathaniel Ward. SCAP
World's an inn, The; and I her guest. On the World. Francis Quarles. HAP
Worlds are breaking in my head, The. Yves Tanguy. David Gascoyne. EAS
World's Bliss. Alice Notley. UL
World's bright comforter, whose beamsome light, The. God's Virtue. Barnabe Barnes. *Fr.* A Divine Century of Spiritual Sonnets. NOCV; OBSC
(Sonnet: "World's bright comforter, whose beamsome light, The.") EIL
World's Desire, The. William Rose Benét. TrPWD
World's gone forward to its latest fair, The. The Moor. Ralph Hodgson. MoBrPo
World's great age begins anew, The. Shelley. *Fr.* Hellas: Choruses from "Hellas," 4. EnRP; FiP; HeIP; NAEL-2; PoE; TEP
(Chorus from "Hellas.") AWP
(Chorus: "World's great age begins anew, The.") EBEV; HAP; NOBE; NoP; OAEL-2; PoEL-4
(Final Chorus, The.) SeCePo

(Hellas.) ChTr; OBEV
(New World, A.) TrGrPo
World's Greatest Tricycle Rider, The. C. K. Williams. NYBP
World's Illusion, The, *sels.* Moses Ibn Ezra, *tr. fr. Hebrew by* Solomon Solis-Cohen. TrJP
All Ye That Go Astray.
He That Regards the Precious Things of Earth.
In Vain Earth Decks Herself.
Promises of the World, The.
World Is like a Woman of Folly, The.
Ye Anger Earth.
World's Last Unnamed Poem, The. A. K. Redwing. VoR
World's love runs thin, The. To the Tune "The Phoenix Hairpin." T'ang Wan, *tr. by* Kenneth Rexroth *and* Ling Chung. WPOW
World's Music, The. "Gabriel Setoun." FaBoBe
Worlds on worlds are rolling ever. Shelley. *Fr.* Hellas: Choruses from "Hellas." EnRP; NoP; TEP
(Chorus: "Worlds on worlds are rolling ever.") NAEL-2
(Worlds on Worlds.) HeIP
World's so wide I cannot cross it, The. Fond Affection. *Unknown.* AS
World's Wanderers, The. Shelley. TTTS
World's Way, The. Shakespeare. *See* Sonnets, LXVI: "Tired [*or* Tyr'd] with all these, for restful death I cry."
World's Worst Boxer, The. Lucilius, *tr. fr. Greek by* Humbert Wolfe. SD
Worm, The. Willis Barnstone. VWA
Worm, The. Ralph Bergengren. FaPON; RHPC
Worm artist, The. The Earth Worm. Denise Levertov. NOBA
Worm, at long last, must find, The. Seeing the Light. Tsfrirah Gar, *tr. by* Bernhard Frank. MHeP
Worm Either Way. D. H. Lawrence. NoAM
Worm Fed on the Heart of Corinth, A. Isaac Rosenberg. BrPo; OAEL-2
Worm unto his love, The: lo, here's fresh store. The Coffin-Worm. Ruth Pitter. MoBrPo
Wormrunner's Curse. Sonya Dorman. BWV
Worms. A. Leyeles, *tr. fr. Yiddish by* Benjamin *and* Barbara Harshav. AYP
Worms at Heaven's Gate, The. Wallace Stevens. NoAM; OBD
Wormwood. Thomas Kinsella. CIP; FaBCIP
Worn and torn by many fingers. A Family Album. Alter Brody. VWA
Worn-out voice of the clock breaks on the hour, The. Prize for Good Conduct. Kenneth Allott. OBWP
Worried Life Blues. *Unknown.* AmFP
Worried Skipper, The. Wallace Irwin. BLPA
Worry about Money. Kathleen Jessie Raine. FaBoTw
Worschippe ye that loveris bene this May. Spring Song of the Birds. James I, King of Scotland. OBEV
Worsening Situation. John Ashbery. NOBA
Worship, *sel.* William Wilberforce Lord.
"For them, O God, who only worship Thee." AA
Worship. Robert Whitaker. TrPWD
Worship. Whittier. NOCV
Worship of Cromm Cruaich, The. *Unknown, tr. fr. Old Irish by* Kuno Meyer. *Fr.* The Voyage of Bran. TIRV
Worship of virtu is the mede. Carol of St, A George. *Unknown.* MeEL
Worship the Lord, the God of wild cold kind. The Lord in the Wind. James Picot. PoAu-2
Worshiper, The. Vassar Miller. NePoEA-2
Worst, The. Shel Silverstein. WSC
Worst is/ that I don't know, The. Peter Turrini, *tr. by* Beth Bjorklund. CoAuP
Worst side of it all, The. White Roses. John Ashbery. TAP
Worth While. Ella Wheeler Wilcox. BLPA; FPL
Worthless Heart, The. Immanuel di Roma, *tr. fr. Hebrew.* TrJP
Worthy and not worthy of our respect. *Unknown, tr. by* Hiroaki Sato. FCEI
Worthy art Thou,/ O Lord, of praise. Deliverance from a Fit of Fainting. Anne Bradstreet. TAP
Worthy kyng, quhen he has seyn, The. Before Bannockburn. John Barbour. *Fr.* The Bruce. OxBS
Worthy London Prentice, A. The London Prentice. *Unknown.* CoMu
"Wot's in a name?" she sez. An' then she sighs. The Play. C. J. Dennis. *Fr.* The Sentimental Bloke. PoAu-1
Wotton, my little Bere dwells on a hill. Ad Henricum Wottonem. Thomas Bastard. FaBoEE; FaBoPP
Woud ye hear of William Wallace. Gude Wallace. *Unknown.* ESPB
Wou'd you in love succeed, be brisk, be gay. The Advice. Charles Sackville. FaBoUs
Would a circling surface vulture. Mahadevi, *tr. by* A. K. Ramanujan. BoWoP

Would-be bride is here, The. Gladys. Hugo Williams. *Fr.* Calling Your Name in the Zoo. NPo
Would-be Critic, The. Mrs. Henry Linden. CBWP-4
Would Edison get the blues if he blew a fuse? Electricity Is Funny! John Currier. GrPl
Would God that I and my darling. *Unknown, tr. fr. Gaelic by* Frank O'Connor. *Fr.* A Beggarman's Song. WTO
Would God That It Were Holiday! Thomas Deloney. *Fr.* The Gentle Craft. EIL
Would he understand that I wasn't at his grave. Burying. Judith Herzberg, *tr. by the author.* DuIn
Would I again were with you!—O ye dales. That Delightful Time. Mark Akenside. *Fr.* The Pleasures of Imagination. SeCePo
Would I Be Shrived? John D. Swain. BLPA
Would I could cast a sail on the water. The Collarbone of a Hare. W. B. Yeats. OxBTC; RB
Would I had been, beloved. Lady Ishikawa. *Fr.* Manyo Shu. Ma
Would I Might Go Far over Sea. Marie de France, *tr. fr. French by* Arthur O'Shaughnessy. AWP; PoRA
Would I might lie like this, without the pain. In Hospital. James Elroy Flecker. OxBTC
Would I might mend the fabric of my youth. Welt. Georgia Douglas Johnson. BANP
Would I might rouse the Lincoln in you all. Lincoln. Vachel Lindsay. *Fr.* Litany of the Heroes. OHIP
Would I were a king of children. The Child-King. Morris Wintchevsky, *tr. by* Alter Brody. TrJP
Would I were air that thou with heat opprest. Thomas Stanley. FaBoEE
Would I were chang'd into that golden shower. Sir Arthur Gorges. GBL
"Would it had been the man of our wish!" In the Room of the Bride-Elect. Thomas Hardy. *Fr.* Satires of Circumstance, IV. BrPo; InPK
Would It Had Pleased the Lord That I Never Was Born. *Unknown, tr. fr. Italian by* L. R. Lind. PFI
Would it please you if I strung my tears. The Race Question. Naomi Long Madgett. BPo
Would my love were a bracelet. Furu Tamuke. *Fr.* Manyo Shu. Ma
Would she at least want time for combing her hair. Pitying a Woman Who Has Many Affairs. Kito, *tr. fr. Japanese by* Hiroaki Sato. *Fr.* Twenty-four Hokku. FCEI
Would surprise her, his square dark hand, while she. The Hunk. Judson Jerome. SoTCo
Would that I had stayed. Princess Oku. *Fr.* Manyo Shu. Ma
Would that I streamed like water. Like Water down a Slope. Zalman Schneour, *tr. by* Harry H. Fein. TrJP
Would That I Were. Arthur Hugh Clough. TrPWD
Would that the structure brave, the manifold music I build. Abt Vogler. Robert Browning. GoTL; NAEL-2; OAEL-2; TOF; WGRP
Would that they were flowers. Prince Aki. *Fr.* Manyo Shu. Ma
Would the lark sing the sweeter if he knew. An Open Secret. Caroline Atherton Briggs Mason. AA
Would the moon ever tell us to grieve. Teika, *tr. fr. Japanese by* Hiroaki Sato. *Fr.* A Compendium of Good Tanka. FCEI
Would the world know how Godfrey lost his breath? Truth Brought to Light, or Murder Will Out. Stephen College. APAS
Would there were a land. Yakamochi. *Fr.* Manyo Shu. Ma
Would there were other means of consolation. Princess Shikishi, *tr. fr. Japanese by* Hiroaki Sato. *Fr.* Seventy-eight Tanka. FCEI
Would we could coin for thee new words of praise. Washington's Tomb. Ruth Lawrence. OHIP
Would write a letter with/ my scissors mouth. Young Woman's Neo-Aramaic Jewish Persian Blues. Jerome Rothenberg, *after Persian folk poem.* BoWoP
Would you be famous and renowned in story. The Advice. *Unknown.* APAS
Would you be preserved from ruin? The Impartial Inspection. *Unknown.* APAS
Would You Believe It? Remco Campert, *tr. fr. Dutch by* John Scott *and* Graham Martin. DuIn
Would you believe me. A Family. W. S. Merwin. CAPP
Would you believe some-/ one who said he. Dance and Eye Me (Wicked)ly My Breath a Fixed Sphere. Rochelle Owens. NMM
Would you believe, when you this monsieur see. On English Monsieur. Ben Jonson. NBLV; NoP
Would you come back if I said the earth. Nadia Tuéni, *tr. by* Willis Barnstone. BoWoP
Would you Have a Young Virgin? John Gay. *See* Beggar's Opera, The: If the heart of a man is deprest [*or* depressed] with cares.
Would you hear of an old-time [*or* old-fashioned] sea fight. Battle of the *Bonhomme Richard* and the *Serapis.* Walt Whitman. *Fr.* Song of Myself, XXXV-XXXVI. MOS; RB; UnPo

Would you hear of the River-Fight? Henry Howard Brownell. *Fr.* The River-Fight. AA
Would You in Venus' Wars Succeed. *Unknown.* ErPo
Would you like to see a city given over. The City of Golf. Robert Fuller Murray. SD
Would you, mama, believe if I told. In the Golden Land. Moyshe-Leyb Halpern, *tr. by* Benjamin *and* Barbara Harshav *and* Kathryn Helle. AYP
Would you, my friend, in little room express. Martial, *tr. by* Elijah Fenton. OBVE
Would you see the little men. The Little Men. Flora Fearne. BoTP
Would you your son should be a sot or dunce. William Cowper. *Fr.* Tirocinium; or, A Review of Schools. OBSV
Wouldn't it be wonderful to come across in cabaret. Unromantic Song. Anthony Brode. FiBHP
Wouldnt think/t look at m. Panther Man. James A. Emanuel. BPo
Wouldn't this old world be better. I Know Something Good about You. Louis C. Shimon. BLPA
Wouldn't You? John Ciardi. RAR
Wouldn't you like to be a whale. Whale. Geoffrey Dearmer. BoTP
Wouldn't you like to know. Elementary. Jim Tollerud. VoR
Would'st be happy, little child. To Theodora. *Unknown.* OxBChV
Wouldst know the artist? Then go seek. Art. Lilla Cabot Perry. AA
Wouldst know the lark? A Listener's Guide to the Birds. E. B. White. NYBP
Wouldst thou be wise, O Man? At the knees of a woman begin. Wilfrid Scawen Blunt. *Fr.* The Wisdom of Merlyn. OBMV
Wouldst thou hear what man can say. Epitaph on Elizabeth, L. H. Ben Jonson. EIL; ELP; FaBoEE; HAP; HeIP; NAEL-1; NIP; NoP; OBEV; OBS; PoE; SeCP; SeCV-1
Wouldst thou live long? The only means are these. He Lives Long Who Lives Well. Thomas Randolph. WBLP
Wound, The. "Adunis," *tr. fr. Arabic by* Abdullah al-Udhari. MPAW
Wound, The. Louise Glück. NoAM
Wound, The. Thom Gunn. NePoEA
Wound-Dresser, The. Walt Whitman. AmPP; NAAL-1; NOBA; OBWP; PrIm; TAP
Wound in the heart won't redden like a rose, A. Narcissus. Israel Efrat, *tr. by* Bernhard Frank. MHeP
Wound which the dragon had dealt him began, The. Beowulf's Death. *Unknown, tr. fr. Anglo-Saxon by* Charles W. Kennedy. *Fr.* Beowulf. AnOE
Wounded, The. Louise Louis. GoYe
Wounded American Indian. Indians at the Guthrie. Gerald Vizenor. STE
Wounded Bird, The. La Fontaine, *tr. fr. French by* Edward Marsh. OBD
Wounded Breakfast, The. Russell Edson. LCAP
Wounded Cupid, The. Robert Herrick. AWP; OBVE; OFD
Wounded deer leaps highest, A. Emily Dickinson. AWP; TAP
Wounded hare looks out, The. Hare in Winter. Marge Piercy. NeAC
Wounded Hawk, The. Herbert Edward Palmer. FaBoTw
Wounded Man and the Swarm of Flies, The. William Somervile. FM
Wounded Person, The. Walt Whitman. *Fr.* Song of Myself, XXXIII. PoNe
Wounded were coming, The. Black Truth. Brenda Agard. WS
Wounded wilderness of Morris Graves, The. Lawrence Ferlinghetti. *Fr.* A Coney Island of the Mind. NeAP
Wounded with love and piercing deep desire. Unable by Long and Hard Travel to Banish Love, Returns Her Friend. George Turberville. OBTV
Wounds. Michael Longley. FaBCIP; FaBoPV; OBD
Wounds. Judith Minty. GeTw
Woven Romance. Lucha Corpi. CCP
Woyi, The. Lew Blockcolski. VoR
Wraggle Taggle Gipsies, The. *Unknown.* BoTP; CH; FaPON; WiR
Wraith. Edna St. Vincent Millay. WSC
Wraith-Friend, The. George Barker. OBMV
Wrap Me in Blankets of Momentary Winds. Harold Littlebird. VoR
Wrap up in a blanket in cold weather and just read. Things to Do around a Lookout. Gary Snyder. NaP; TAP
Wrapped Hair Bundles. Tauhindauli. STE
Wrapped in a twisted brown stocking, strangled in the rolled. Under the Scrub Oak, a Red Shoe. Dave Smith. GeTw
Wrapped in anger. Landscape. Anne Hébert, *tr. by* Kathleen Weaver. OV
Wrapped up, O Lord, in man's degeneration. Fulke Greville. *Fr.* Caelica, XCVIII [XCIX]. QFR
Wrapt in my careless cloak, as I walk to and fro. Earl of Surrey. SiPS
Wrath of Peleus son, O muse, resound, The. Homer, *tr. fr. Greek by* Dryden. *Fr.* The Iliad, Invocation. OBVE

Wrath to Sadness. Robert Grenier. UL

Wrathful winter, 'proaching on apace, The. Winter ("The wrathful winter, 'proaching on apace"). Thomas Sackville, *fr.* A Mirror [*or* Mirour] for Magistrates. *Fr.* Induction to "A Mirror for Magistrates." AAS; OBSC

Wreath, The. Robert Graves. BoLoP

Wreath, A. George Herbert. JCP; OAEL-1; OxBSP; SeCP

Wreath, A. Gyula Illyés, *tr. fr. Hungarian* by William Jay Smith. MHuP

Wreath for the Suicide Heart, A. Anthony McNeill. PVCV

Wreath of flowers as cold as snow, A. The Birth. Rosemary Dobson. PoAu-2

Wreath that star-crowned Shelley gave, The. After a Lecture on Keats. Oliver Wendell Holmes. AA

Wreath to the Fish, A. Nancy Willard. BLA

Wreathed garland of deserved praise, A. A Wreath. George Herbert. JCP; OAEL-1; OxBSP; SeCP

Wreaths. Geoffrey Hill. PoA

Wreck, The. Walter de la Mare. MOS

Wreck of the *Deutschland*, The ("Thou mastering me."), *sel.* Gerard Manley Hopkins. BrPo; CMoP; FaBoMo; LiTB; LiTM; NoAM; NOBE; OBNC; PoEL-5; TEP

"On Saturday sailed from Bremen." SeCePo

Wreck of the Deutschland, The, *parody*. David Annett. BXAP

Wreck of the *Hesperus*, The. Longfellow. AnAmPo; BeLS; BLPA; FaBoBe; FaFP; FPL; GN; MOS; OBCA; OBNV; PAH; WBLP

Wreck of the *Julie Plante* [*or* The *Julie Plante*], The. William Henry Drummond. BeLS; BeLS; BLPA; BLPA; CaP; FaBoBe; FaPON; NA; OBCV

Wreck of the *Northfleet*, The. *Unknown*. OxBSS

Wreck of the *Rambler*, The. *Unknown*. OxBSS

Wreck of the *Royal Charter*, The. *Unknown*. OxBSS

Wreck of the Royal Palm, The. *Unknown*. AmFP

Wreck of Walsingham, The. *Unknown*. *See* In the wrecks of Walsingham.

Wrecked Boat on the River Shore. Chiang Lu, *tr. fr. Chinese* by Burton Watson. CoBCP

Wrecked castaway. Robinson Crusoe Daniel Defoe. Maurice Sagoff. NBLV

Wrecker Driver Foresees Your Death, The. David Baker. MAYP

Wreckers' Prayer, The. Theodore Goodridge Roberts. OBCV

Wren, The. Issa, *tr. fr. Japanese* by R.H. Blyth. NTCP

Wren, The. *Unknown*. OxBChV

Wren dropped down on my window sill, A. A Little Wren. Priscilla Jane Thompson. CBWP-2

Wren she lies in care's bed, The. *Unknown*. PBBP

Wrestlers. Michael Drayton. *Fr.* Polyolbion, First Song. SD

Wrestling. Kathleen Fraser. RHPC

Wrestling Angels. David Bottoms. MAYP

Wrestling Jacob. Charles Wesley. NOBE; NOCV; NOEC; OBEV; PoEL-5; SeCePo; TOF

Wrestling The Beast. Arnold Adoff. ASP

Wrestling with the Angel. Jacques Prévert, *tr. fr. French* by Michael Benedikt. POS

Wretched Amintor with a flame. The Greater Trial. Countess of Winchilsea. TrGrPo

Wretched Catullus, play the fool no more. To Himself. Catullus, *tr.* by William Ellery Leonard. AWP

Wretched Flavia, on her couch reclined, The. Saturday: The Small-Pox. Lady Mary Wortley Montagu. *Fr.* Six Town Eclogues. NOEC; WPE

Wretched hovel/ of some lowly commoner, The. Evening Faces. Keiun, *tr.* by Steven D. Carter. WFTW

Wretched Ierne! with what grief I see. Swift. *Fr.* Verses Occasioned by the Sudden Drying Up of St. Patrick's Well. OBSV

Wretched Man. John Wilmot, 2nd Earl of Rochester. *Fr.* A Satire against [Reason and] Mankind. SeCePo

Wrights' Biplane, The. Robert Frost. WeW

Wrimples. Jack Prelutsky. RHPC

Wring the Swan's Neck. Enrique Gonzáles Martínez, *tr. fr. Spanish* by Samuel Beckett. MexPo

Wrinkled, but not inured by years. Spring; a Formal Ode. Fyodor Tyuchev, *tr.* by Charles Tomlinson. FaBoRV

Wrinkled, crabbed man they picture thee, A. Winter Portrait. Robert Southey. BoNaP

Wrinkled ostler, grim and thin! Song at the Ruin'd Inn. Tennyson. *Fr.* The Vision of Sin. PoEL-5

Wrinkled, unrelaxing stone. Barbarian Prayer. Sandor Csoori, *tr.* by Edwin Morgan. MHuP

Wrinkling with laughter that made no sound. At a Country Fair. John Holmes. MoShBr

Writ on the Eve of My 32nd Birthday. Gregory Corso. NAs

Write, Do Write. Marilyn Chin. BrSi

Write in a lively style, as fish swim in the water. Li K'ai-hsien, *tr. fr. Chinese* by Jonathan Chaves. *Fr.* Impromptu Poems. CoBLCP

Write it down. Write it. In ordinary ink. Starvation Camp near Jaslo. Wislawa Szymborska, *tr.* by Jan Darowski. WPOW

Write it in gold—a spirit of the sun. Lines Written in a Blank Leaf of the Prometheus Unbound. Thomas Lovell Beddoes. OAEL-2

Write now for the sky. To Himself. Pierre Jean Jouve, *tr.* by Keith Bosley. RHTwFP

Write on my grave when I am dead. Katharine Tynan. WGRP

Write to thine eyes? Why, my poor pen. To Fannie. Mary E. Tucker. CBWP-1

Write! Write! Help! Help! Barnabe Barnes. *Fr.* Parthenophil and Parthenophe, XVIII. Son

Writer, The. Hildebrand Jacob. FaBoCo

Writer, The. Richard Wilbur. CAPP; HCAP; NoAM; OxBC

Writer, attend no schools. The Teacher. Virginia Brady Young. GoYe

Writers, *sel.* Robert Lowell.
Robert Frost. *Fr.* VII. Son

Writing. William Allingham. NOBVV

Writing. Anthony Cronin. PoPo

Writing. Anne French. ATNZ

Writing. Roland Jooris, *tr. fr. Dutch* by Peter Nijmeijer. DuIn

Writing. Andrew Motion. DiPo

Writing. Howard Nemerov. NYBP

Writing a letter he said. Buffalo—Isle of Wight Power Cable. Anselm Hollo. PoM

Writing Again on the Same Theme. Po Chü-i, *tr. fr. Chinese* by Burton Watson. CoBCP

Writing, and Other Avenues. Sue Roe. NPo

Writing in England Now. Philip O'Connor. OxBTC

Writing Letters. Rodney Bennett. BoTP

Writing My Feelings. Yüan Mei, *tr. fr. Chinese* by Jonathan Chaves. CoBLCP

Writing of the Character "Tree", The. Lo Ch'ing, *tr. fr. Chinese* by Dominic Cheung. IFON

Writing on the Wall. Padraic Fallon. NeIP

Writing through a Text by Chris Mann. John Cage. EOEF

Writing while My Father Dies. Linda Pastan. PCP

Writings Recede, The. André Breton, *tr. fr. French* by Michael Benedikt. POS

Written after Swimming from Sestos to Abydos. Byron. MOS; NAEL-2; NBLV; NoP; OBTV

Written after the Revolt. Ogasawara Gokyo, *tr. fr. Chinese* by Burton Watson. JLIC-2

Written Answer, A. Tom Paulin. FaBCIP

Written at [*or* in] an Inn at Henley. William Shenstone. AWP; NOBE; NOEC; OBEV

Written at Cambridge. Charles Lamb. EnRP

Written at Night, after Dreaming That I Had Returned to My Old Home. Li Tz'u-ming, *tr. fr. Chinese* by Daniel Bryant. WFTU

Written at Stonehenge. Thomas Warton the Younger. Son

Written at the End of a Book. Langdon Elwyn Mitchell. AA

Written at the End of Master Ho-ching's Collected Works. Chin Nung, *tr. fr. Chinese* by Jonathan Chaves. CoBLCP

Written at the Graveside. Yüan Mei, *tr. fr. Chinese* by Anthony C. Yu. WFTU

Written at the Po-Shan Monastery. Hsin Ch'i-chi, *tr. fr. Chinese* by Irving Y. Lo. ILY

Written at the White Sulphur Springs. Francis Scott Key. OBAL

Written at the Year's End, While Visiting Chien-ling. Ch'ü Ta-chün, *tr. fr. Chinese* by Paul W. Kroll. WFTU

Written December 1790. Anna Seward. Son

Written for My Neighbor. Shen Yüeh, *tr. fr. Chinese* by Burton Watson. CoBCP

Written for My Own Amusement. Wang An-shih, *tr. fr. Chinese* by Burton Watson. CoBCP

Written for My Son, and Spoken by Him at His First Putting on Breeches. Mary Barber. NOEC

Written for the Pavilion of the Drunken Old Man at Ch'u-chou. Ou-yang Hsiu, *tr. fr. Chinese* by Burton Watson. CoBCP

Written Forty Miles South of a Spreading City. Robert Bly. NNaP

Written granite. Ray DiPalma. *Fr.* Planh, I. IAT

Written in a Blank Leaf of Dugdale's "Monasticon." Thomas Warton the Younger. *See* Deem not devoid of elegance, the sage.

Written in a Carefree Mood. Lu Yu, *tr. fr. Chinese* by Burton Watson. CoBCP

Written in a Cool Breeze. Fan Tseng-hsiang, *tr. fr. Chinese* by J. P. Seaton. WFTU

Written in a Copy of Swift's Poems, for Wayne Burns. James Wright. NOBA
Written in a Lady's Prayer Book. Earl of Rochester. BoLoP
Written in a Public Restaurant, sel. Israel Efrat, tr. fr. Hebrew by Bernhard Frank.
  "Dumpy and obese—a woman." MHeP
Written in an Ovid. Matthew Prior. FaBoEE; FaBoUs
Written in Autumn. Thomas Cole. AiP
Written in Autumn When Spending the Night Near the Grave of His Wife. Shunzei, tr. fr. Japanese by Burton Watson. Fr. Thirty Tanka. FCEI
Written in Blood. Victor Segalen, tr. fr. French by Nathaniel Tarn. RHTwFP
Written in Dejection near Rome. Robert Bly. NaP
Written in Early Spring. Wordsworth. See I heard a thousand blended notes.
Written in Exile. Kathleen Jessie Raine. TrCP; WPE
Written in Her French Psalter. Elizabeth I, Queen of England. PBWP; WPE
Written in Ireland. Mary Alcock. NOEC; OBTV
Written in Jest: On "The Old Man Who Rolled with the Punch." Wu Wei-yeh, tr. fr. Chinese by Irving Lo. WFTU
Written in Juice of Lem[m]on. Abraham Cowley. Fr. The Mistress. SeCP; SeCV-1
Written in London, September, 1802. Wordsworth. FaBoPV; TrGrPo
Written in March. Wordsworth. BoNaP; BoTP; EnRP; FaPON; GoJo; NAEL-2; NTCP; PYC; UnPo
Written in Northampton County Asylum. John Clare. See I am: yet what I am none cares or knows.
Written in Pencil in the Sealed Railway-Car. Dan Pagis, tr. fr. Hebrew by Stephen Mitchell. OBD
Written in Prison. Ch'ien Ch'ien-yi, tr. fr. Chinese by Irving Lo. WFTU
Written in Prison. John Clare. OAEL-2
Written in Response to Wei-yin's Rhymes. Wang Ts'ai-wei, tr. fr. Chinese by Irving Lo. WFTU
Written in the Album of a Child. Wordsworth. See Small service is true service while it lasts.
Written in the Beginning of Mezeray's History of France. Matthew Prior. NOBE; PoEL-3
Written in the Euganean Hills, North Italy. Shelley. See Many a green isle needs must be.
Written in the Mountains. Wang Ts'ai-wei, tr. fr. Chinese by Pao Chia-lin. WFTU
Written in the Office Precincts. Wang T'ing-hsiang, tr. fr. Chinese by Jonathan Chaves. CoBLCP
Written in the Second Month of 1861 when I Left the Temple and Returned to Lay Life. Tomobayashi Mitsuhira, tr. fr. Chinese by Burton Watson. JLIC-2
Written in the Sunset. Hsiung-hung, tr. fr. Chinese by Kenneth Rexroth and Ling Chung. OV
Written in the Visitors' Book at the Birthplace of Robert Burns. George Washington Cable. AA
Written in Unbridled Repugnance near Sioux Falls, Alabama—April 30, 1974. A. K. Redwing. VoR
Written in Very Early Youth. Wordsworth. EnRP
Written on a Boat in Canton, 1882. Wen T'ing-shih, tr. fr. Chinese by Timothy C. Wong. WFTU
Written on a Boat on the Ch'ien-t'ang River. Hung Liang-chi, tr. fr. Chinese by Irving Lo. WFTU
Written on a Fly-Leaf of Theocritus. Maurice Thompson. AA
Written on a Leaf. Unknown, tr. fr. Chinese by Geoffrey Waters. BoWoP
Written on a Looking-Glass. Unknown. FaBoEE
Written on a Painting Entitled "Misty Yangtze and Folded Hills." Su Tung-p'o, tr. fr. Chinese by Burton Watson. CoBCP
Written on a Paper Napkin. Len Gasparini. NeAC
Written on a Summer Night. Kan Sazan, tr. fr. Chinese by Burton Watson. JLIC-2
Written on a Wall at Woodstock. Elizabeth I, Queen of England. PBWP; WPE
Written on a Window. Aaron Hill. OxBSP
Written on an Autumn Day at the Garden of the Official Residence of the Governor of Kansu. T'an Ssu-t'ung, tr. fr. Chinese by Timothy C. Wong. WFTU
Written on an Island off the Breton Coast. Saint Venantius Fortunatus, tr. fr. Latin by Helen Waddell. PeHV
Written on Board a Ship on the Yellow Sea, When a Japanese Friend Asked Me for a Poem. Ch'iu Chin, tr. fr. Chinese by Pao Chia-lin. WFTU
Written on My Way into Exile. Han Yü, tr. fr. Chinese by Burton Watson. CoBCP

Written on New Year's Eve. Rai San'yo, tr. fr. Chinese by Burton Watson. JLIC-2
Written on Parting from Mr. Ying. Ts'ao Chih, tr. fr. Chinese by Burton Watson. CoBCP
Written on Seeing the Flowers, and Remembering My Daughter. Kao Ch'i. DL
Written on the Anniversary of Our Father's Death. Hartley Coleridge. Son
Written on the Day That Mr. Leigh Hunt Left Prison. Keats. See What though, for showing truth to flatter'd state.
Written on the Eve of Execution. Chidiock Tichborne. See My prime of youth is but a frost of cares.
Written on the Lake after a Shower, On the Sixteenth of the Seventh Month. Li E, tr. fr. Chinese by Shirleen S. Wong. WFTU
Written on the Lake, Returning from the Retreat at Stone Cliff. Hsieh Ling-yün, tr. fr. Chinese by Burton Watson. CoBCP
Written on the Night of the Twenty-ninth of the First Month. Yün Shou-p'ing, tr. fr. Chinese by Jonathan Chaves. CoBLCP
Written on the Oi River. Rokunyo, tr. fr. Chinese by Burton Watson. JLIC-2
Written on the Plain of Thebes. J. W. Burgon. OBTV
Written on the Sense of Isolation in Contemporary Ireland. Robert Greacen. NeIP
Written on the Wall at Chang's Hermitage. Tu Fu, tr. fr. Chinese by Kenneth Rexroth. HoPM; NaP
Written on the Wall of Ku Tzu-p'eng's Studio. Cheng Hsiao-hsü, tr. fr. Chinese by Irving Lo. WFTU
Written on the Wall of Pan-shan Temple. Wang An-shih, tr. fr. Chinese by Burton Watson. CoBCP
Written on the Wall of the Flying Cloud Cave in Kweichow. Sung Hsiang, tr. fr. Chinese by Irving Lo. WFTU
Written on the Walls of His Dungeon. Luís De León, tr. fr. Spanish by Thomas Walsh. TrJP
Written on Visiting the Shrine of the Minister of the Right Sugawara no Michizane. Rai San'yo, tr. fr. Chinese by Burton Watson. JLIC-2
Written on Yün-lang's Nuptial Day. Ch'en Wei-sung, tr. fr. Chinese by Madeline Chu. WFTU
Written over a Gate. John Sheffield. NIP
Written the Night Before He Was Beheaded. See My prime of youth is but a frost of cares.
Written the Night before His Execution. Chidiock Tichborne. See My prime of youth is but a frost of cares.
Written under Capricorn, a land. Chris Wallace-Crabbe. PoAu-2
Written upon Coming Again to the Tu-hsü Taoist Temple. Ch'ü Ta-chün, tr. fr. Chinese by Paul W. Kroll. WFTU
Written upon the Top of Ben Nevis. Keats. PoSH
Written When Appointed Commander of the Western Sea Marches. Umakai, tr. fr. Chinese by Burton Watson. JLIC-1
Written When Drunk. Chang Yüeh, tr. fr. Chinese by Burton Watson. CoBCP
Written when He Was Well Over Eighty. Shunzei, tr. fr. Japanese by Burton Watson. Fr. Thirty Tanka. FCEI
Written when the Poet Was Seventy-six. Shunzei, tr. fr. Japanese by Burton Watson. Fr. Thirty Tanka. FCEI
Written While Sick. Wen Cheng-ming, tr. fr. Chinese by Jonathan Chaves. CoBLCP
Written with a Diamond on Her Window at Woodstock. Elizabeth I, Queen of England. PBWP; WPE
Wrong Kind of Love. Ray A. Young Bear. NOVW
Wrong Line, The. Rachael Beck. SoTCo
Wrong Not, Sweete Empress of My Heart. At. to Sir Robert Ayton. Fr. The Silent Lover. OBS
  (Merit of True Passion, The.) LiTB
Wrong Start, The. Marchette Chute. RHPC
Wrong that are, The. Tom. Victor Questel. PBCV
Wronged Lover, The. Sir Philip Sidney. Fr. Arcadia. SiPS
Wrote the clergy: "Our Dear Madame Prynne." A Hawthorne Garland. Richard Harter Fogle. NIP; OBAL
Wry Smile, A. Roy Fuller. WaaP; WaP
Wu Family Thatched Hall. Cheng Hsiao-hsü, tr. fr. Chinese by Irving Lo. WFTU
Wu land mulberry leaves grow green. Sent to My Two Little Children in the East of Lu. Li Po, tr. by Burton Watson. CoBCP
Wu Shan-yang. Yang Chi, tr. fr. Chinese by Jonathan Chaves. Fr. Thinking of My Friends at Kou-jung Subprefecture. CoBLCP
Wu-t'ung tree a hundred feet tall, A. Inscribed on a Painting of a Wu-t'ung Tree by Myself. Tao-chi, tr. by Jonathan Chaves. CoBLCP

Wu Wei grew old and died. Song of the Painting "River and Mountains," by Wu Wei. Ho Ching-ming, *tr. by* Jonathan Chaves. CoBLCP
Wukhand. Paul Keens-Douglas. PBCV
Wulf and Eadwacer. *Unknown, tr. by* Willis Barnstone *and* Elene Kolb. BoWoP
Wulf and Eadwacer. *Unknown.* TrGrPo
Wull ye come in early Spring. Come! William Barnes. CH
Wyatt Resteth Here. Henry Howard, Earl of Surrey. NoP
   (Epitaph on Sir Thomas Wyatt.) NAEL-1
   ("Wyat resteth here, that quicke coulde never rest.") AAS
Wykehamist's Address to Learning, A. P. N. Shuttleworth. FaBoCo
Wyncote, Pennsylvania: A Gloss. Thomas Kinsella. NOIV
Wynken, Blynken, and Nod. Eugene Field. AA; BeLS; BoTP; FaBoBe; FaFP; FaPON; NBLV; NTCP; OBAL; OBCA; OxBChV; PoRA; PYC
   (Dutch Lullaby, A.) AnAmPo; BLPA; FPL
Wynter Wakeneth al My Care. *Unknown. See* Winter Wakeneth All My Care.
Wynyard Sailor. Ray Mathew. CBAP
Wyoming Massacre, The. Uriah Terry. PAH
Wyse men alwaye. A Mery Gest How a Sergeaunt Wolde Lerne to Be A Frere. Sir Thomas More. AAS
Wyth all myn hool herte enter. The Lovers' Mass. *Unknown.* OxBLMV
Wyth that came Ryotte, russhynge all at ones. The Dreamer Meets Riot. John Skelton. *Fr.* The Bowge of Courte. OxBLMV
Wyvern. Charles Connell. AmMo

X

"X." Barrett Watten. LP
X, Oh X. Mark Simpson. GOYP
X-Rated. F. F. Burch. SoTCo
X-Ray. David Ray. NePoEA-2
X-Ray. Leonora Speyer. ImOP
X was asked. Aleksander Wat, *tr. fr. Polish by* Czeslaw Milosz. *Fr.* Notes Written in Obory. PwPP
Xantippe. Amy Levy. BrRo
Xenia. Eugenio Montale, *tr. fr. Italian by* G. Singh. OBD
Xenophanes. Emerson. NOBA
Xenophobia. Rae Armantrout. IAT
Xkoagu, give me your heart. Prayer to the Hunting Star, Canopus. *Unknown, tr. by* W. H. I. Bleek *and* Jack Cope. PeSA
Xmas for the Boys. Gavin Ewart. OBSV
Xochitepec. Malcolm Lowry. *See* Those animals that follow us in dream.
Xylographer started to cross the sea, A. The Zealless Xylographer. Mary Mapes Dodge. AnAmPo; OBAL

Y

Y. M. C. A, The. Mrs. Henry Linden. CBWP-4
Ya know, I got this ranch from my daddy. A Time to Stay, a Time to Go. Baxter Black. CowP
Ya Se Van Los Pastores. Dudley Fitts. FYAP
Yacht, The. Catullus, *tr. fr. Latin by* John Hookham Frere. AWP; OBVE
Yacht for Sale. Archibald MacLeish. ASP
Yachts, The. William Carlos Williams. AmPP; CMoP; HeIP; LiTA; LiTM; MoAB; MoAmPo; MoP; MOS; NoAM; NOBA; NoP; OxBA; PoE; PPP
Yachts on the Nile. Bernard Spencer. NoAM
Yah gee. Robert Grenier. *Fr.* A Sequence/ 28 Separate Poems. IAT
Yahrzeit. Dan Jaffe. VWA
Yahrzeit. Susan Fromberg Schaeffer. VWA
Yai—yai—yai. Musk Oxen. Igjugarjuk. WTO
Yak, The. Hilaire Belloc. FaBV; FaPON; MoBrPo; NA; NBLV; NoAM; NOBL; OxBChV
Yak, The. Jack Prelutsky. RHPC
Yak, The. Virna Sheard. CaP
Yall/ out there. A Chant for Young/Brothas and Sistuhs. Sonia Sanchez. BPo
Yamaha yamaha. Mysterious East. William Cole. OBAL
Yamashiro. Saibara, *tr. fr. Japanese by* Hiroaki Sato. FCEI
Yamato has clusters of mountains. Emperor Jomei. *Fr.* Manyo Shu. FCEI

Yan, tan, tethera, tethera, pethera, pimp. A Lincolnshire Shepherd. *Unknown.* OBET
Yang-Se-Fu. "Yehoash", *tr. fr. Yiddish by* Isidore Goldstick. TrJP
Yangchou, *sel.* Cheng Hsieh, *tr. fr. Chinese by* Jonathan Chaves.
   "West wind has come again to the "tower of makeup," The." CoBLCP
Yangtze River, autumn colors, The. Inscribed on the Painting "River in Autumn." Ni Tsan, *tr. by* Jonathan Chaves. CoBLCP
Yankee boy, before he's sent to school, The. Whittling. John Pierpont. GN
Yankee Doodle. *At.* to Richard Shuckburg *and to* Edward Bangs. AmFP; AnAmPo; ChTr; FaFP; FaPON; GBP; OBAL; OxNR, 4 *ll.*
   (Yankeys' Return from Camp, The.) OPP; OxBoLi; PAH
Yankee Doodle sent to town. The Last Appendix to "Yankee Doodle." *Unknown.* PAH
Yankee Doodle went to war. The Run from Manassas Junction. *Unknown.* PAH
Yankee Doodle's Expedition to Rhode Island. *Unknown.* PAH
Yankee Man-of-War, The. *Unknown.* AA; FaBoBe; OxBSS; PAH
Yankee Privateer, The. Arthur Hale. PAH
Yankee ship and a Yankee crew, A. The *Constitution's* Last Fight. James Jeffrey Roche. PAH
Yankee Thunders. *Unknown.* PAH
Yankees Back, The. "Mighty Sparrow, The." PBCV
Yankee's Return from Camp, The. *Unknown, at.* to Edward Bangs *and also to* Richard Shuckburg. *See* Father and I went down to camp.
Yardbird's Skull. Owen Dodson. AmNP; CNA; IDB; PoBA; VGW
Yardley Oak. William Cowper. LaA; NOEC
Yarn of the *Nancy Bell*, The. W. S. Gilbert. BeLS; BLPA; CenHV; FaBoBe; FaBoCh; FaBoCo; FaBV; FaFP; HoPM; MOS; MoShBr; NOBL; OnMSP; TrGrPo
Yarrow counted eight of them. July the First. Robert Currie. Psk
Yarrow had to learn it but he loved Young Jacob. Brothers. Robert Currie. Psk
Yarrow liked it. In the Music. Robert Currie. TDD
Yarrow Revisited. Wordsworth. EnRP
Yarrow Unvisited. Wordsworth. EnRP; GTBS; GTBS-P; PoRA
Yarrow Visited. Wordsworth. EnRP; GTBS; GTBS-P
Yawning. Eleanor Farjeon. RHPC
Yawning and praising the moon. Kito, *tr. fr. Japanese by* Hiroaki Sato. *Fr.* Twenty-four Hokku. FCEI
Ybba. Elissa Hamilton Malcohn. BWV
Ye Alps audacious, thro' the heavens that rise. The Hasty Pudding. Joel Barlow. AmPP; ANTH , (I); NOBA, (I); OBAL, *abr.*; OxBA, (I); TAP, (I)
Ye Ancient Divine Ones. Arthur Hugh Clough. *Fr.* Amours de Voyage, Canto I, x. OBNC
Ye angells bright, pluck from your wings a quill. Edward Taylor. *Fr.* Preparatory Meditations before My Approach to the Lord's Supper, LX. PoEL-3
Ye Anger Earth. Moses Ibn Ezra, *tr. fr. Hebrew by* Solomon Solis-Cohen. *Fr.* The World's Illusion. TrJP
"Ye are the Duke of Athol's nurse." The Duke of Athole's Nurse. *Unknown.* ESPB
Ye are the temples of the Lord. The Exhortation of a Father to His Children. Robert Smith. OxBChV
Ye ayres and windes, ye elves of hilles. Medea's Incantation. Ovid, *tr. fr. Latin.* *Fr.* Metamorphoses: Magic. OBVE, *tr. by* Arthur Golding.
Ye banks and braes and streams around. Highland Mary. Burns. AWP; EnRP; GTBS; GTBS-P; OBEV; TrGrPo; WBLP
Ye banks and braes o' Bonnie Doon. The Banks of Doon. Burns. BoLoP; GTBS; GTBS-P; NOBE; NOEC; OBEV; PrIm; TrGrPo; WBLP
   (Bonnie Doon.) NoP
   (Ye Banks and Braes [o' Bonnie Doon].) CH; ELP
   (Ye Flowery Banks [o' Bonnie].) AWP; EnRP; NAEL-2; PoEL-4; UnPo
Ye Beauties, Beaux, ye Pleaders at the Bar. *Unknown. Fr.* London Evening Post. FaBoUs
Ye beauties! O how great the sun. On a Bed of Guernsey Lilies. Christopher Smart. NOEC
Ye [*or* Yee] blushing virgins happy are. To Roses in the Bosom[e] of Castara. William Habington. *Fr.* Castara, *Pt.* I. EnLoPo; MeLP; OBEV; SeCP
Ye bold British tars, who out glory are free. The *Dolphin's* Return. *Unknown.* OxBSS
Ye brave bold men of 'Cotia. Robens' Promised Land. George Purdom. WTO
Ye brave Columbian bands! a long farewell! On Disbanding the Army. David Humphreys. PAH

Ye brave sons of Freedom, come join in the chorus. The Times. *Unknown.* PAH

Ye Bruthers Dogg. Jon Anderson. NAmP; NBLV

Ye bubbling springs that gentle music makes. Love's Limit. *Unknown.* TrGrPo

Ye buds of Brutus' land, courageous youths, now play your parts! For Soldiers. Humphrey Gifford. CH; EIL

Ye cats that at midnight spit love at each other. An Appeal to Cats in the Business of Love. Thomas Flatman. EnLoPo; GBL; HAP

Ye Clerke of Ye Wethere. *Unknown.* BXAP

Ye clerks that on your shoulders bear the shield. Preachment for Preachers. Alexander Barclay. *Fr.* The Ship of Fools. ACP

Ye Clouds! that far above me float and pause. France; an Ode. Samuel Taylor Coleridge. EnRP

Ye Columbians so bold, attend while I sing. Hull's Surrender. *Unknown.* PAH

Ye Commons and Peers. Jack Frenchman's Defeat. Congreve. APAS
(Jack Frenchman's Lamentation.) CoMu

Ye coop us up, and tax our bread. Caged Rats. Ebenezer Elliott. EBEV

Ye coopers and hoopers, attend to my ditty. The Cooper o' Dundee. *Unknown.* CoMu

Ye dainty nymphs, that in this blessed brook. Elisa ("Ye dainty nymphs, that in this blessed brook"). Spenser. *Fr.* The Shepheardes [*or* Shepeards *or* Shepherd's] Calender: Aprill. OBSC
(Lay to Eliza, The.) NOBE

Ye distant spires, ye antique towers. Ode on a Distant Prospect of Eton College. Thomas Gray. BLPL; GTBS; GTBS-P; HeIP; LiTB; NAEL-1; NOBE; NOEC; NoP; OAEL-1; PoE; PoEL-3; PrIm

Ye dogg, O'Toole. Ye Bruthers Dogg. Jon Anderson. NAmP; NBLV

Ye elms that wave on Malvern Hill. Malvern Hill. Herman Melville. AmPP; FPL; PAH; TAP

Ye elves of hill, brooks, standing lakes, and groves. Shakespeare. *Fr.* The Tempest, V, i. EBEV; SCV
(Magic.) AWP

Ye famed physicians of this place. A Lamentable Case. Charles Hanbury-Williams. ErPo

Ye flippering soule. An Address to the Soul Occasioned by a Rain. Edward Taylor. NAAL-1; NOBA; OxBA; PoEL-3
(Let by Rain.) NOBA

Ye Flowery Banks [o' Bonnie Doon]. Burns. *See* Ye banks and braes o' Bonnie Doon.

Ye fog that creeps there in the uplands. Invocation for a Storm. *Unknown.* WTO

Ye gallants of Newgate, whose fingers are nice. Newgate's Garland. John Gay. FaBoBa

Ye gentlemen and ladies fair. The Hunters of Kentucky; or, Half Horse and Half Alligator. Samuel Woodworth. AS; PAH

"Ye gie corn to my horse." Clyde's Water. *Unknown.* ESPB

Ye glowing seraphs, that now breathe above. Friendship in Perfection. Andrew Michael Ramsay. NOEC

Ye Goat-herd Gods. Sir Philip Sidney. *Fr.* Arcadia. HAP; NAEL-1; NOBE; NoP; OAEL-1
(Double Sestine.) LiTB; PoEL-1

Ye gods above protect the widow, and with pity look on me. President Parker. *Unknown.* OxBSS

Ye Gods! the raptures of that night! The Enjoyment. *Unknown.* ErPo

"Ye graceful peasant-girls and mountain-maids." Ballata: His Talk with Certain Peasant Girls. Franco Sacchetti, *tr. by* Dante Gabriel Rossetti. AWP

Ye green-rob'd Dryads, oft' at dusky eve. The Enthusiast: or, The Lover of Nature. Joseph Warton. EnRP; NOEC

Ye have been fresh and green. To Meadows. Robert Herrick. AWP; CaPo; CH; JCP; NOBE; OBEV; QFR
(To Meddowes.) OBS; PoEL-3; SeCP; SeCV-1

"Ye have robbed," said he, "ye have slaughtered and made an end." He Fell among Thieves. Sir Henry Newbolt. EBVV; FaPoR; OBEV; OBWP; OnMSP; OxBTC

Ye Heavens, Uplift Your Voice. *Unknown.* OHIP

Ye Highlands [*or* hielands] and ye Lawlands [*or* lowlands]. The Bonny Earl of Murray. *Unknown.* ESPB, (A *vers.*); FaBoBa; OBEV; OxBB, *with music;* OxBS; PrIm
(Bonnie Earl of Moray [*or* Murray], The.) FaBoCh; OBS
(Bonny Earl o' Moray, The.) ELP; GoTS

Ye holy Angels bright. Richard Baxter. *Fr.* A Psalm of Praise. NOCV

Ye humble souls that seek the Lord. Christ's Resurrection and Ascension. Philip Doddridge. NOCV

Ye jolly Yankee gentlemen, who live at home in ease. The C.S.A. Commissioners. *Unknown.* PAH

Ye jovial throng, come join the song. The Battle of Muskingum; or, The Defeat of the Burrites. William Harrison Safford. PAH

Ye know my heart, my lady dear. Sir Thomas Wyatt. SiPS

Ye ladies, walking past me piteous-eyed. Sonnet: To the Same Ladies; With Their Answer. Dante, *tr. by* Dante Gabriel Rossetti. AWP

Ye Laye of Ye Woodpeckore. Henry Augustin Beers. NA

Ye learned sisters which have oftentimes. Spenser. AAS; BoLoP; EIL; InPS; MaSP; NAEL-1; NOBE; NoP; OAEL-1; OBEV; OBSC; PoE; PoEL-1; TEP

Ye lie, friend Pindar! and friend Thales! On a Quaker's Tankard. Walter Savage Landor. FaBoEE

Ye Little Birds That Sit and Sing. *Unknown.* EIL

Ye living lamps, by whose dear light. The Mower to the Glow-Worms [*or* Glowworms]. Andrew Marvell. AWP; ELP; InvP; NAEL-1; NOBE; NoP; OAEL-1; OxBoLi; PPP; TrGrPo
(Mower to the Glo-Worms, The.) EnLoPo; MePo; OBS; PoEL-2; SeCP

Ye lords of creation, men you are called. The Lords of Creation. *Unknown.* PoLF

Ye loyal Britons, I pray draw near. The Battle of Shiloh. *Unknown.* AmFP

Ye maggots, feed on Willie's brains. Burns. FaBoEE

Ye Mariners of England. Thomas Campbell. BLPA; EnRP; FaPoR; GN; GTBS; GTBS-P; NOBE; OBEV; OBWP

Ye mariners of Spain. The Song of the Galley. *Unknown, tr. by* John Gibson Lockhart. AWP

"Ye maun gang to your father, Janet." Fair Janet. *Unknown.* ESPB; OxBB, *with music*

Ye may simper, blush, and smile. To Cherry-Blossomes. Robert Herrick. SeCV-1

Ye members of Parliament all. The Shash. *Unknown.* APAS

Ye merry hearts that love to play. Win at First and Lose at Last; or, A New Game at Cards. Laurence Price. OxBoLi

Ye mitered fathers of the land. The Sentiments. *Unknown.* APAS

Ye Mongers Aye Need Masks for Cheatrie. Sydney Goodsir Smith. OxBS

Ye morning glories, ring in the gale your bells. The New God. James Oppenheim. WGRP

Ye motions of delight, that through the fields. Imagination, How Impaired and Restored. Wordsworth. *Fr.* The Prelude [or, Growth of a Poet's Mind]: Imagination and Taste, How Impaired and Restored, XII *and* XIII. OBNC

Ye mountain valleys, pitifully groan! Lament for Bion. Moschus, *tr. by* George Chapman. AWP

Ye muses, pour the pitying tear. A Great Man. Goldsmith. NA

Ye nymphs and ye swains that trip over the plains. Black Thing. *Unknown.* CoMu

Ye Nymphs forlorn, who pine away in Shades! From a Marriage Broker's Card, 1776. *Unknown.* FaBoUs

Ye nymphs! if e'er your eyes were red. On the Lamented Death of Mrs. Throckmorton's Bullfinch. William Cowper. NOEC; PBBP; PPP

Ye old mule, that thinck your self so fayre. Sir Thomas Wyatt. AAS

Ye Parliament of England. *Unknown.* AmFP; PAH

Ye paultry underlings of state. On the Irish Club. Swift. OBSV

Ye people of Ireland, both country and city. A New Song of Wood's Halfpence. *At. to* Swift. OxBoLi

Ye people that labour the world to measure. Geographers. Alexander Barclay. *Fr.* The Ship of Fools. ACP

Ye people who delight in sin. The Hanging of Sam Archer. *Unknown.* AmFP

Ye pilgrim-folk, advancing pensively. Dante, *tr. fr. Italian by* Dante Gabriel Rossetti. *Fr.* Vita Nuova, La, XXVIII. AWP; CTC

Ye powers above and heavenly poles. On Button the Grave-Maker. *Unknown.* FaBoEE

Ye powers of truth, that bid my soul aspire. On Freedom and Ambition. Goldsmith. *Fr.* The Travel[l]er; or, A Prospect of Society. NOIV

Ye Protestants of Ulster, I pray you join with me. Lisnagade. *Unknown.* WTO

Ye Realms below the Skies. Hosea Ballou II. AH

Ye saints who dwell on Europe's shore. The Handcart Song. *Unknown.* AmFP

Ye saw't floueran in my breist. The Mandrake Hert. Sydney Goodsir Smith. OxBS

Ye say they all have passed away. Indian Names. Lydia Huntley Sigourney. AmFN; FaPON; GOA; OBCA; PAH; PoLF

Ye Scattered Nations. *Unknown, tr. fr. Latin by* Thomas Cradock. AH

Ye seamen who's a mind to go. A New Song on the *Blandford* Privateer. *Unknown.* OxBSS

Ye [or You] should stay longer if we durst. Francis Beaumont. *Fr.* The Masque of the Inner Temple and Gray's Inne, IV. OBS; TrGrPo

Ye silent shades, whose each tree here. To Groves. Robert Herrick. CaPo

Ye Simple Men. John Stuart Blackie. PoSH

Ye sons of Britain in chorus join and sing. Nelson's Death and Victory. *Unknown.* OxBSS

Ye Sons of Columbia. Thomas Green Fessenden. PAH

Ye sons of Columbia, who bravely have fought. Adams and Liberty. Robert Treat Paine. PAH

Ye sons of Columbia, your attention I do crave. Fuller and Warren. *At. to* Moses Whitecotton. AmFP; BeLS

Ye sons of earth prepare the plough. The Sower. William Cowper. SaC

Ye sons of Massachusetts, all who love that honored name. The Sudbury Fight. Wallace Rice. PAH

Ye sons of Sedition, how comes it to pass. On the Snake. *Unknown.* PAH

Ye sons of toil, awake to glory! The Marseillaise. Claude Joseph Rouget de Lisle, *tr. by* Charles H. Kerr. WBLP

Ye Sorrowers. Franz Werfel, *tr. fr. German by* Ludwig Lewisohn. *Fr.* The Eternal Road. TrJP

Ye sorrowing people! who from bondage fly. The Fugitive Slaves. Jones Very. TAP

Ye Swains who roam from fair to fair. Would You in Venus' Wars Succeed. *Unknown.* ErPo

Ye sylvan Muses, loftier strains recite. The Birth of the Squire; an Eclogue. John Gay. NAEL-1; NOEC; PoEL-3

Ye tender-hearted people, I pray you lend an ear. Samuel Allen. *Unknown.* AmFP

Ye that have faith to look with fearless eyes. Victory. *Unknown.* WGRP

Ye that in love delight. On Clarastella Singing. Robert Heath. OBS

Ye that pasen by the weiye. Jesus to Those Who Pass By. *Unknown.* MeEL

Ye, too, marvellous twain, that erect on the Monte Cavallo. Ye Ancient Divine Ones. Arthur Hugh Clough. *Fr.* Amours de Voyage, Canto I, x. OBNC

Ye tourists and travellers, bound to the Rhine. Thomas Hood. OBTV

Ye true lovers bold, come listen unto me. The True Lovers Bold. *Unknown.* AmFP

Ye vig'rous swains! while youth ferments your blood. The Hunt. Pope. *Fr.* Windsor Forest. NIP

Ye walls! sole witnesses of happy sighs. Walter Savage Landor. *Fr.* Ianthe. EnLoPo

Ye Wearie Wayfarer, *sel.* Adam Lindsay Gordon.
Sun and Rain and Dew from Heaven. PoLF

Ye weary, heavy laden souls. The Lonesome Dove. *Unknown.* AmFP

Ye wha are fain to hae your name. Braid Claith. Robert Fergusson. GoTS; NOEC; OxBS

Ye who amid this feverish world would wear. Urban Pollution. John Armstrong. *Fr.* The Art of Preserving Health. NOEC

Ye who have come o'er the sea. Gunnar's Howe above the House at Lithend. William Morris. OBTV

Ye who intelligent the third heaven move. The First Canzone of the Convito. Dante, *tr. by* Shelley. OBVE

Ye who with fortune ever are at strife. James Boswell. OBTV

Ye wild-eyed Muses, sing the Twins of Jove. Hymn to Castor and Pollux. *Unknown, tr. fr. Greek by* Shelley. *Fr.* Homeric Hymns. AWP

Ye worthy patriots go on. An Encomium upon a Parliament. Daniel Defoe. APAS

Ye young debaters over the doctrine. The Village Atheist. Edgar Lee Masters. *Fr.* Spoon River Anthology. EaLo; LiTA

Yea, gold is son of Zeus: no rust. Gold Is the Son of Zeus: Neither Moth nor Worm May Gnaw It. "Michael Field." OBMV

Yea, let me praise my lady whom I love. Sonnet: He Will Praise His Lady. Guido Guinicelli, *tr. by* Dante Gabriel Rossetti. AWP; PFI

Yea, my King. Robert Browning. *Fr.* Saul, XIII-XIX *sl. abr.* WGRP

Yea, the coneys are scared by the thud of hoofs. The Field of Waterloo. Thomas Hardy. *Fr.* The Dynasts. FaBoCh
(Chorus of the Years.) CMoP
("Yes, the coneys are scared by the thud of hoofs.") WaaP

"Yea" to "Yill" for "W". Tina Darragh. LP

Yea, we go down to sea in ships. At Sea. James Whitcomb Riley. MOS

Yeah./ you can really. Rebolushinary X-mas. Carolyn M. Rodgers. JB

Yeah./ they hang you up. To All Brothers. Sonia Sanchez. BPo

Yeah here am I. Two Jazz Poems. Carl Wendell Hines, Jr.. AmNP

Year, The. Coventry Patmore. *See* Crocus, while the days are dark, The.

Year a bird flies against the drum, The. For Now. W. S. Merwin. NaP

Year after year I have watched. Li Ch'ing-chao, *tr. by* Kenneth Rexroth. BoWoP

Year after year in the snow. Tune: Pure Serene Music ("Year after year in the snow"). Li Ch'ing-chao, *tr. by* Burton Watson. CoBCP

Year after year, I've missed the season of flowers. Chang Hui-yen, *tr. fr. Chinese by* Irving Lo. *Fr.* Tune: Joy at Meeting, I. WFTU

Year after year the princess lies asleep. Parabola. A. D. Hope. PoA

Year after year. how many millennia of worldly affairs. The Cave of Gold Essence in Ning-tu. T'ang Hsien-Tsu, *tr. by* Jonathan Chaves. CoBLCP

Year ago how often did I meet, A. Samuel Hoar. Franklin Benjamin Sanborn. AA

Year ago I asked you for your soul, A. The Caged Bird. Arthur Symons. BrPo

Year ago I fell in love with the functional ward, A. The Hospital. Patrick Kavanagh. BIrV; CIP; FaBCIP

Year ago you came, A. Pietà. James McAuley. CBAP; PoAu-2

Year Ahead, The. Horatio Nelson Powers. WBLP

"Year and I are dying out together, The." Lament in Autumn. Harold Stewart. PoAu-2

Year at its turn, The. The Last Day of the Year (New Year's Eve). Annette von Droste-Hülshoff, *tr. by* Willis Barnstone. BoWoP

Year away from the pigpen, and look at him, A. Variation on a Noel. John Ashbery. EOEF

Year *Chi-wei* (1559), New Year's Day, The. Wen Cheng-ming, *tr. fr. Chinese by* Jonathan Chaves. CoBLCP

Year dies fiercely: out of the north the beating storms, The. Year's End. William Everson. MoP; NoAM

Year 1812, The. Donald Davie, *after the Polish of* Adam Mickiewicz. OBVE; OBWP

Year End. Akera Kanko, *tr. fr. Japanese by* Burton Watson. FCEI

Year grows darker, but each day more lamps, The. Autumnal Consummation. Patric Stevenson. NeIP

Year had all the days in charge, The. Why It Was Cold in May. Henrietta Robins Eliot. AA

Year has changed his mantle cold, The. Spring. Charles, Duc d' Orléans, *tr. by* Andrew Lang. AWP; CTC

Year has come to us as though out of hiding, A. Early January. W. S. Merwin. VGW

Year has run thin through the tuning room of my mind, The. A Spring Memorandum. Robert Duncan. PoA

Year *Hsin-hai* (1551), New Year's Eve, The. Wen Cheng-ming, *tr. fr. Chinese by* Jonathan Chaves. CoBLCP

Year *I-mao* (1555), New Year's Eve, The. Wen Cheng-ming, *tr. fr. Chinese by* Jonathan Chaves. CoBLCP

Year is dead, for Death slays even time, The. Year's End. Nathaniel Anketell Benson. CaP

Year is done, the last act of the vaudeville, The. Midnight Show. Karl Shapiro. OxBA

Year is ending, The. Teika, *tr. by* Steven D. Carter. WFTW

Year is gone, beyond recall, The. The Opening Year. *Unknown, tr. by* F. Pott. BLRP

Year is round around me now, The. Green Song. Philip Booth. BoNaP

Year of Jubilee, The. Henry Clay Work. PAH

Year of Our Lord two thousand one hundred and seven, The. John Heath-Stubbs. *Fr.* An Ecclesiastical Chronicle. NOBL

Year of Seeds, The, *sels.* Ebenezer Elliott.
Give Not Our Blankets, Tax-Fed Squire. Son
Ralph Leech Believes. Son
Toy of the Titans. Son

Year of Sorrow, A, *sels.* Aubrey Thomas De Vere.
"Fall, snow, and cease not! Flake by flake." ACP
Spring. OBNC

Year of the Bird. Brian Swann. AmPA

Year of Winter, The. Tauhindauli. STE

Year our neighbors' ancestors' Thor, The. Three Migrations. Ralph Salisbury. STE

Year Outgrows the Spring, The. Ella Wheeler Wilcox. AnAmPo

Year stood at its equinox, The. The Milking-Maid. Christina Rossetti. BeLS

Year was the sixth of Constantine's sway, The. Constantine's Vision of the Cross. Cynewulf, *tr. fr. Anglo-Saxon by* Charles W. Kennedy. *Fr.* Elene. AnOE

Year well remembered! Happy who beheld thee! The Year 1812. Donald Davie, *after the Polish of* Adam Mickiewicz. OBVE; OBWP

Yearly Regret. Kikaku, *tr. fr. Japanese by* Hiroaki Sato. *Fr.* Thirty-three Hokku. FCEI

Yearning, A. Arapera Hineira Blank, *tr. fr. Maori* by Arapera Hineira Blank. PeNZ

Yearning for the moon hazy. Teika, *tr. fr. Japanese* by Hiroaki Sato. *Fr.* Eighty-four Tanka. FCEI

Yearning for the Shore. Saqi Farooqi, *tr. fr. Urdu* by Mahmood Jamal. PBMUP

Years. Jon Anderson. AmPA

Years, The. John Ennis. CIP

Years. Walter Savage Landor. OBEV

Years. Anna Margolin, *tr. fr. Yiddish.* OV, *tr.* by Adrienne Rich; VWA, *tr.* by Ruth Whitman

Years. Alicia Ostriker. ER

Years/ flew by like magpies trailing bright, The. Regine's Rebuke to Kierkegaard. Ruthann Robson. ER

Years ago/ he began dialing your number. The Obscene Caller. Philip Dacey. AmPA

Years ago, as dusk seeped from the blue. The Lost Children. Gregory Orr. GeTw

Years ago, at a private school. An Ever-Fixed Mark. Kingsley Amis. ErPo; MoP; NoAM; PeHV

Years ago feasting on raw whale by the eastern sea. Third Month, Night of the Seventeenth, Written While Drunk. Lu Yu, *tr.* by Burton Watson. CoBCP

Years ago I lost. The Unquiet Ones. Stanley Kunitz. CAPP

Years ago, to the winding banks of this lake in spring. At the Lake— Remembering My Dead Son, Yü. Pien Kung, *tr.* by Jonathan Chaves. CoBLCP

Years ago, when I was young. Juan Chi, *tr. fr. Chinese* by Burton Watson. *Fr.* Singing of Thoughts. CoBCP

Years ago you said. George Seferis, *tr. fr. Greek* by Edmund Keeley *and* Philip Sherrard. *Fr.* Three Secret Poems, I: 4. VMG

Years and months, The. Teika, *tr. fr. Japanese* by Hiroaki Sato. *Fr.* A Compendium of Good Tanka. FCEI

Years and scars later. Jacob. George Garrett. CRP

Years and years I have loved you. Gabriel Gillett. PeHV

Years and years of roses have burst forth here. Oakland Rose Garden. Jacques Roubaud, *tr.* by Neil Baldwin. RHTwFP

Years are but half a score, The. On the Big Horn. Whittier. PAH

Years are flowers and bloom within, The. God's Garden. Richard Burton. WGRP

Years are plucked like feathers, The. Like Feathers. Gabriel Preil, *tr.* by Grace Schulman. PeBMYV

Year's at the Spring, The. Robert Browning. *Fr.* Pippa Passes, sc. 1. BLPA; FaBoBe; FaBV; WGRP
(Pippa's Song.) BLPL; BoTP; FaFP; FaPON; GoJo; LiTB; NTCP; OBEV; OHIP; PDV; TEP; TrCP; UnPo
(Song: "Year's at the Spring, The.") SoSe; TrGrPo

Year's Awakening, The. Thomas Hardy. CMoP; OxBTC

Years, bring little pain, yet they add, The. Joe Ross. *Fr.* Guards of the Heart, I, ii. BAP

Years creep slowly by, Lorena. The. Lorena. H. D. L. Webster. BLPA

Year's End. Nathaniel Anketell Benson. CaP

Year's End. William Everson. MoP; NoAM

Year's End. Ellen Bryant Voigt. NoAM

Year's End. Richard Wilbur. CAPP; CoAP; HeIP; LiTM; NAAL-2; NePoEA; SM

Year's Ending, The. St. J. Page Yako, *tr. fr. Xhosa* by C. M. Mcanyangwa *and* Jack Cope. PeSA

Year's first day, The. Kikaku, *tr. fr. Japanese* by Hiroaki Sato. *Fr.* Thirty-three Hokku. FCEI

Years from You to Me, The. Paul Celan, *tr. fr. German* by Beth Bjorklund. CoAuP

Years go by, and still both moor and mount. Grey Galloway. Thomas S. Cairncross. PoSH

Years have flown since I knew thee first. Richard Watson Gilder. *Fr.* The New Day. AA

Years have gone, The. It is spring. Andrée Rexroth. Kenneth Rexroth. PrIm; VGW

Years have made up my face, The. Toward Myself. Leah Goldberg, *tr.* by Robert Friend. VWA

Years in the blood keep us naked to the bone, The. The Art of Clay. Duane Niatum. HATNAP

Years I've waited for this. Kite-Flying. Kath McKay. DT

Years Later. Laurence Lerner. NAs; PeSA

Years Later. Ruth Stone. BoWoP

Years later the girl died. Linda Pastan. KS

Years, long years ago, I read of a death I envied. Schiehallion. Helen B. Cruickshank. PoSH

Years, many parti-coloured years. Years. Walter Savage Landor. OBEV

Years of Indiscretion. John Ashbery. NOBA

Years of manhood had not tinged, The. Charley du Bignon. Mary E. Tucker. CBWP-1

Years pile up, but there rides with you still, The. As on a Darkling Plain. Henry Taylor. MT

Years ride out from the world like couriers gone to a throne, The. Song of the Riders. Stephen Vincent Benét. *Fr.* John Brown's Body. MoAmPo

Years saw me still Acasto's mansion grace. An Old Cat's Dying Soliloquy. Anna Seward. NOEC

Year's Spinning, A. Elizabeth Barrett Browning. NAEL-2

Years That Go to Make Me Man, The. Christopher Brennan. *Fr.* The Twilight of Disquietude. PoAu-1

Years they come and go, The. Ad Finem. Heine, *tr.* by Elizabeth Barrett Browning. AWP

Years they mistook me for you. Dodo. Henry Carlile. Psk

Years to come. Looking over Poems by Persons of Long Ago. Shunzei, *tr. fr. Japanese* by Burton Watson. *Fr.* Thirty Tanka. FCEI

Years to come (empty boxcars), The. Time. William Stafford. Son

Years, years ago, ere yet my dreams. The Belle of the Ball-Room. Winthrop Mackworth Praed. *Fr.* Every-Day Characters. EnRP; FaBoCo

Yeats could not walk in the disarming field without. The Empty Valley. John Russell Hervey. ATNZ

Yee Shall Not Misse of a Few Lines in Remembrance of Thomas Hooker. Edward Johnson. SCAP

Yeh./ billie. if someone. For Our Lady. Sonia Sanchez. IHMS

Yehuda Amichai. Seymour Mayne. VWA

Yei-ie's Child. Charles C. Long. NOVW

Yelled at/ for praying in his underwear. *Unknown, tr.* by Burton Watson. FCEI

Yellow. Anna Hajnal, *tr. fr. Hungarian* by Jascha Kessler. *Fr.* Images. FOC

Yellow. De Leon Harrison. PoBA

Yellow. Kenton Kilmer. GoYe

Yellow. David McCord. RHPC

Yellow. Charles Wright. AmPA

Yellow-belly, yellow-belly, come and take a swim. *Unknown.* OxBoLi (Yes, by Golly.) SD

Yellow Bird, The. James W. Thompson. PoBA

Yellow Bird Sings, The. Rabindranath Tagore. *Fr.* The Gardener. OBMV

Yellow Bittern, The. Cathal Buidhe Mac Giolla Ghunna, *tr. fr. Irish.* BIrV, *tr.* by Thomas MacDonagh; CIP, *tr.* by Tom MacIntyre; NOIV, *tr.* by Thomas Kinsella.

Yellow blood on the dunes. Before the Pacific. Blanca Varela, *tr.* by Willis Barnstone. BoWoP

Yellow Budweiser signs over oaken bars. Allen Ginsberg. *See* Uptown.

Yellow Butter. Mary Ann Hoberman. RAR

Yellow butterflies. *At.* to Koianimptiwa, *tr.* by Natalie Curtis. AWP; WTO

Yellow canary trilled, A. Jealous Adam. Itzig Manger, *tr.* by Jacob Sonntag. TrJP

Yellow chrysanthemums, The. Sequence for a Young Widow Passing. Deborah Munro. IHMS

Yellow cloud rising up from that fighting. *Aborigine Oral Tradition.* WTO

Yellow clouds, purple ramparts—three thousand *li.* Singde, *tr.* by William Schultz. WFTU

Yellow, dandelion-yellow in the low December. The Cloud-Fish. Rudolf Bayer, *tr.* by Beth Bjorklund. CoAuP

Yellow dusk: messenger fails to appear. *Unknown, tr.* by Arthur Waley. OBVE

Yellow Fairy, The. Charlotte Druitt Cole. BoTP

Yellow Flower, The. William Carlos Williams. HAP

Yellow flower is a yellow well, The. A New Colour in the Colour of Sunlight. Munir Niazi, *tr.* by Mahmood Jamal. PBMUP

Yellow-haired Laddie, The. *Unknown.* GBP

Yellow is for regret, the distal, the second hand. Yellow. Charles Wright. AmPA

Yellow Jessamine. Constance Fenimore Woolson. AA

Yellow leaf, from the darkness, A. Brooding Grief. D. H. Lawrence. CMoP; PoE

Yellow leaves do fly from the trees so high, The. The Lamenting Maid. *Unknown.* OBET

Yellow leaves spiral down through the air. A Record of My Trip to Mount She. Yüan Hung-tao, *tr.* by Jonathan Chaves. CoBLCP

Yellow Light. Garrett Kaoru Hongo. InPS; MAYP

Yellow-lit [*or* Yellow] Budweiser signs over oaken bars. Uptown. Allen Ginsberg. FF; TwCP
("Yellow Budweiser signs over oaken bars.") TW

Yellow northeast afternoon, A. Parameter. Marcos Konder Reis, *tr. by* Mark Strand. ATCBP

Yellow november/comes swaying. Rushing. Ray A. Young Bear. CDW

Yellow paper planes fly. Eagles. Elizabeth Woody. STE

Yellow River. Fei Ma, *tr. fr. Chinese by* Dominic Cheung. IFON

Yellow River winds along, The. Autumn Vista. Li Meng-yang, *tr. by* Jonathan Chaves. CoBLCP

Yellow sand, white reeds. Crossing the Frontier. Li Meng-yang, *tr. by* Jonathan Chaves. CoBLCP

Yellow Season, The. William Carlos Williams. MoAB; MoAmPo

Yellow Sonnets, The, *sel.* C. K. Stead.
  "Spring is a recurring astonishment—like poetry." ATNZ

Yellow sun yellow. The Ballad of Red Fox. Melvin Walker La Follette. NePoEA

Yellow the bracken. Autumn. Florence Hoatson. BoTP

Yellow Violet, The. Bryant. BLPL; NAAL-1; PoLF; TAP

Yellow-White Glow, The. H. Leivick, *tr. fr. Yiddish by* Benjamin *and* Barbara Harshav. AYP

Yellow winds blow in from the north. Seeing Off Commander-In-Chief Li. Li Meng-yang, *tr. by* Jonathan Chaves. CoBLCP

Yellow Woman Speaks. Merle Woo. BrSi

Yellowhammer, The. John Clare. NOBVV

Yellowjacket. Peter Blue Cloud. HATNAP

Yellow's unstitching itself from the sun. Interior with Mme. Vuillard and Son. Kathleen Fraser. NPGG

Yen's sorry. A Magpie Rhyme, Northumberland. *Unknown.* GBP

Yeoman of the Guard, *sels.* W. S. Gilbert.
  Family Fool, The. NBLV
  "Man who would woo a fair maid, A." FaBoUs

Yere yernes ful yerne, and yeldes never like, A. The Passage of a Year. *Unknown, tr. fr. Middle English by* Brian Stone. *Fr.* Sir Gawain and the Green Knight. PoEL-1

Yes. James Joyce. *Fr.* Ulysses. FF

Yes. Brendan Kennelly. CIP

Yes/ come and meet. Very Softly. Piera Oppezzo, *tr. by* Muriel Kittel. DMI

Yes, all the world must sure agree. Against Marriage to His Mistress. William Walsh. FaBoUs

Yes, an angel has summoned me too. The Apparition. Otto Orban, *tr. by* Edwin Morgan. MHuP

Yes as alike as entirely. To My Father. William Sydney Graham. FaBoTw

Yes! Beauty still rebels! Art, I. Alfred Noyes. OBEV

Yes, brother your word had come. Hearing James Brown at the Café des Nattes. Richard A. Long. AmNP

"Yes, But. . ." Theodore Weiss. TAP

Yes, But. James Wright. CAPP

Yes, but all the same. Tameie, *tr. by* Steven D. Carter. WFTW

Yes, by Golly. *Unknown.* *See* Yellow-belly, yellow-belly, come and take a swim.

Yes, contumelious fair, you scorn. The Author Apologizes to a Lady for His Being a Little Man. Christopher Smart. BoLoP

Yes, death is at the bottom of the cup. If. William Dean Howells. AA

Yes, do you remember an inn. Lament for Lost Lodgings. Phyllis McGinley. NYBP

Yes, ducks are valiant things. Frederick William Harvey. *Fr.* Ducks. BoTP

Yes, every poet is a fool. Matthew Prior. FaBoEE
  (Another.) FaBoCo

Yes, faith is a goodly anchor. After the Burial. James Russell Lowell. AA; UnPo

Yes, farewell, farewell forever. Lady Byron's Reply to Lord Byron's "Fare Thee Well." *Unknown.* BLPA

Yes, fickle Cambridge, Perkin's found this true. On the University of Cambridge's Burning the Duke of Monmouth's Picture. George Stepney. APAS

Yes! from mine eyes the tears unbidden start. Distant View of England from the Sea. William Lisle Bowles. EnRP

Yes, from the ingrate heart, the street. The Fugitive. Alice Meynell. NOCV

Yes, he said, darling, yes, of course you tried. The Appointment. L. A. G. Strong. OxBTC

Yes, he was that, or that, as you prefer. T. A. H. Ambrose Bierce. AA

Yes, he's got her now. Blues. John Fuller. NOBL

Yes! hope may with my strong desire keep pace. Michelangelo, *tr. by* Wordsworth. OBVE
  (Love's Justification.) AWP
  (To the Marchesana of Pescara.) CTC
  (Yes! Hope May with My Strong Desire Keep Pace.) PFI

Yes, I Am an African Woman. Nilene O. A. Foxworth. AIW

Yes, I am black! and radiant. Bible, *O.T.* *Fr.* The Song of Solomon, I: 5–6. PBWP

Yes, I believe He loved them, too. The Young Workman. Mary Dillingham Frear. TrCP

Yes, I caught the butterfly. Went crazy for the moment. Amir Gilboa, *tr. by* Warren Bargad *and* Stanley F. Chyet. IP

Yes, I Could Love If I Could Find. *Unknown.* ErPo

Yes, I experienced youth. Wu Sheng, *tr. by* Dominic Cheung. IFON

Yes, I got another Johnny; but he was to Number One. My Other Chinee Cook. Brunton Stephens. PoAu-1

Yes, I have heard the nightingale. Hast Thou Heard the Nightingale? Richard Watson Gilder. AA

Yes! I have seen the ancient oak. Felicia Dorothea Hemans. *Fr.* The Brereton Omen. CTC

Yes, I know what you say. Tempted. Edward Rowland Sill. AA; AnAmPo

Yes, I only got here on my own. On My Own. Philip Levine. FYAP

Yes. I remember Adlestrop. Adlestrop. Edward Thomas. BrPo; CH; FaBoPP; GoJo; HAP; LiTB; NAEL-2; NOBE; OBEV; OxBTC

Yes, I remember that pain precisely. The Blood. Nina Cassian. VWA, *tr. by* Herbert Kuhner; WPOW, *tr. by* Laura Schiff

"Yes, I was only sidesman here when last." Bristol and Clifton. Sir John Betjeman. CMoP

Yes, I will love thee when the sun. W. F. Hawley. OBCV

Yes! I Write Verses. Walter Savage Landor. EnRP

Yes, I'm in love, I feel it now. The "Je Ne Sais Quoi." William Whitehead. SoSe

Yes! in the sea of life enisled. To Marguerite—Continued. Matthew Arnold. *Fr.* Switzerland, V. BoLoP; EBEV; EBVV; ELP; FiP; GTBS-P; MOS; NOBE; NoP; OAEL-2; OBEV; OBNC; PoEL-5; PPP; PrIM; TEP

Yes, in the summer of 1773. Tom Wedgwood Tells. Brian W. Aldiss. NOBL

Yes, injured Woman! rise, assert thy right! The Rights of Woman. Anna Laetitia Barbauld. NOEC

Yes, it is true that the landscape changed a little. Advice. Czeslaw Milosz, *tr. by the author.* PwPP

Yes, It Was the Mountain Echo. Wordsworth. EnRP

Yes, I've sev'ral kivers you can see. Kivers. Ann Cobb. AmFN

Yes, leave it with Him; the lilies all do. Leave It with Him. *Unknown.* BLRP

"Yes, let me go. Yon fields are green." Request of a Dying Child. Lydia Huntley Sigourney. OBCA

Yes! let the rich deride, the proud disdain. Goldsmith. *Fr.* The Deserted Village. OBSV

Yes Miss/ Put up your pretty little mouth for a kiss. Admonition to the Muse. Geoffrey Taylor. FaBoEE

Yes, my darling, when life's shadows. In Memoriam. Alphonse Campbell Fordham. Mary Weston Fordham. CBWP-2

Yes! my Lesbia! let us prove. Catullus, *tr. by* Walter Savage Landor. OBVE

Yes, no, yes, no, yes, no, yes, no, yes, no, yes, no, yes, no, yes. Antonio Porta, *tr. fr. Italian by* Lawrence R. Smith. *Fr.* Zero. NItP

Yes, she is black. Her cheek has no rose tint. Black Girl. Paul-Jean Toulet, *tr. by* William Jay Smith. CT

Yes, so be it, though we already knew. The Sinking of the Mendi. S. E. K. Mqhayi, *tr. by* C. M. Mcanyangwa *and* Jack Cope. PeSA

Yes solid mountain mingle in my brain. Solid Mountain. George Bowering. NeAC

Yes, still I love thee! Time, who sets. Love Unchangeable. Rufus Dawes. AA

Yes, stranger! you well may say so. The Wickedest Man in Memphis. Alex J. Brown. BeLS

Yes. Such were the eyes through which in rage and pain. Aunt Lucrezia. Alistair Campbell. ATNZ

Yes, Tadeusz Rozewicz, I too. In Praise of Old Women. Marya Fiamengo. WPOW

Yes! that fair neck, too beautiful by half. Madame d'Albert's Laugh. Clément Marot, *tr. by* Leigh Hunt. AWP

Yes: that fingery fraction of a rabbit's commodious. Vestigial. Albert Goldbarth. NAmP

Yes, that's how I was. Judgment Day. R. S. Thomas. CRP

Yes, the Agency Can Handle That. Kenneth Fearing. WeW

Yes, the candidate's a dodger. The Dodger. *Unknown.* AmFP; GBP

Yes, the coneys are scared by the thud of hoofs. Thomas Hardy. *See* Dynasts, The: Field of Waterloo, The.

Yes, the Secret Mind Whispers. Al Young. PoBA

"Yes, the Town Clerk will see you." In I went. The Town Clerk's Views. Sir John Betjeman. CMoP

Yes, there is holy pleasure in thine eye! Admonition to a Traveller. Wordsworth. GTBS; GTBS-P

Yes, these are the dog-days, Fortunatus. Under Sirius. W. H. Auden. FaBoMo

Yes, they are alive and can have those colors. A Blessing in Disguise. John Ashbery. PoM

Yes, this family portrait. Family Portrait. Carlos Drummond de Andrade, *tr.* by Elizabeth Bishop. ATCBP

Yes, this is where I stood that day. Ballad of Hector in Hades. Edwin Muir. MoP; NoAM; NOBE

Yes, this is where she lived before she won. Interview. Sara Henderson Hay. OBCA

Yes, thou art gone! and never more. A Reminiscence. Anne Brontë. WPE

Yes: though the brine may from the desert deep. Frederick Goddard Tuckerman. *Fr.* Sonnets, II, iii. HAP

"Yes, 'tis the time," I cried, "impose the chain." On the Benefactions in the Late Frost. Pope. NOEC; OxBSP

Yes to the Earth. Sibilla Aleramo, *tr. fr. Italian* by Muriel Kittel. DMI

Yes, true, children will take advantage of. The Little Girl. Nicholas Moore. ErPo

Yes, we are fighting at last, it appears. Arthur Hugh Clough. *Fr.* Amours de Voyage, Canto II, v. EBVV

Yes, we had gone down to the shore. Songs without Words. John Ashbery. NAAL-2

Yes, we love this land together. Fatherland Song. Björnstjerne Björnson, *tr.* by William Ellery Leonard. AWP

Yes, we were looking at each other. Looking at Each Other. Muriel Rukeyser. GLP; NNaP

Yes, we'll rally round the flag, boys, we'll rally once again. Battle-Cry of Freedom. George Frederick Root. AnAmPo; FaBoBe; PAH

Yes; we'll wed, my little fay. The Conformers. Thomas Hardy. Mes

Yes, What? Robert Francis. LCAP

Yes when the dark withdrew I suffered light. A World of Light. Elizabeth Jennings. NePoEA-2

Yes. Why do we all, seeing of a soldier, bless him? The Soldier. Gerard Manley Hopkins. WaaP

Yes, wonderful are dreams: and I have known. Charles Harpur. *Fr.* The Tower of the Dream. PoAu-1

Yes, write, if you want to, there's nothing like trying. A Familiar Letter to Several Correspondents. Oliver Wendell Holmes. FaBoUs

Yes, yes/ it's time. My Spring Thing. Everett Hoagland. BPo

Yes, yes, dear love! I am dead! Resurgam. Adah Isaacs Menken. CBWP-1

Yes, yes, I grant the sons of earth. The Question. James Beattie. FaBoCo

Yes, yes, my boy, there's no mistake. McIlrath of Malate. John Jerome Rooney. PAH

Yes you have said enough for the time being. The End Is Near the Beginning. David Gascoyne. EAS

Yes, yours, my love, is the right human face. The Confirmation. Edwin Muir. OxBS

Yesterday. Hugh Chesterman. BoTP

Yesterday. W. S. Merwin. DiL; FYAP

Yesterday/ Stark winter crossed the fields with death. Spring in Wartime. Phoebe Hesketh. CN

Yesterday/ God was/ white. The Change. Matabaruka. PVCV

Yesterday/ some people of this town. What She Said to Her Girl Friend. Ammuvanar, *tr.* by A. K. Ramanujan. PLW

Yesterday a Euclid took trees. Bright green. Breaking Green. Michael Ondaatje. NOBC

Yesterday again it was so. Song of Travel on the Chikuma River. Shimazaki Toson, *tr.* by Geoffrey Bownas and Anthony Thwaite. PeBJV

Yesterday all the past. The language of size. Spain 1937. W. H. Auden. FaBoPV; LiTB; NAEL-2; OBWP; WaP (Spain.) WaP

Yesterday, as I went down to the bridge at the river. Hsü Pen, *tr. fr. Chinese* by Jonathan Chaves. *Fr.* Five Things Sought For——In the Manner of Han Wo. CoBLCP

Yesterday, at the Sessions held in Buckingham. A Case at Sessions. Walter Savage Landor. OBSV

Yesterday by the lake bridge, parting hands, returning. The Day after Saying Goodby to Mototada. Rai San'yo, *tr.* by Burton Watson. JLIC-2

Yesterday Down at the Canal. Frank O'Hara. CAPP

Yesterday evening I saw your corpse. Joyce Mansour, *tr.* by Albert Herzing. WPOW

Yesterday feels like a thousand years ago. Yosano Akiko, *tr. fr. Japanese* by Hiroaki Sato. *Fr.* Thirty-nine Tanka. FCEI

Yesterday, I amused myself at the western stream. Song of the West Stream. Mao Wen-hsi, *tr.* by Lois Fusek. ATF

Yesterday I chanced to step. Mohammad Taqi Mir, *tr.* by Ahmed Ali. GoT

Yesterday I dumped on my son the following story. Autobiography. Jacob Glatstein, *tr.* by Benjamin *and* Barbara Harshav. AYP

Yesterday I fancied I was young. Ho Nansorhon, *tr. fr. Korean* by Peter H. Lee. *Fr.* A Woman's Sorrow. PBWP

Yesterday I found one left. The Survivor. R. S. Thomas. FaBoTw

Yesterday I knew no lullaby. Child of Our Time. Eavan Boland. CIP

Yesterday I planted garlic. James Keir Baxter. *Fr.* Jerusalem Sonnets, XVIII. ATNZ; PeNZ

Yesterday I saw my first mirage. At the Cochise Tourist Pavilion. Maura Stanton. NAmP

Yesterday I skipped all day. Tiptoe. Karla Kuskin. PDV

Yesterday I stood on the balcony. Not Often. Ray Fraser. NeAC

Yesterday I wanted to. For Love. Robert Creeley. NOBA

Yesterday I was/ given flowers. Anthology Poem. Petra von Morstein, *tr.* by Rosemarie Waldrop. BoWoP

Yesterday, in a big market, I made seven thousand dollars. Back through the Looking Glass to This Side. John Ciardi. NBLV

Yesterday in drizzling rain. A Tailor Called Sorrow. Betti Alver, *tr.* by Willis Barnstone *and* Felix Oinas. BoWoP

Yesterday in Oxford Street. Rose Fyleman. PDV

Yesterday it was night out. Servitudes. Philippe Soupault, *tr.* by Michael Benedikt. POS

Yesterday it was this way too. Song: Thoughts of a Traveler on the Chikuma River. Shimazaki Toson, *tr.* by Burton Watson. FCEI

Yesterday Mrs. Friar phoned. "Mr. Ciardi." Suburban. John Ciardi. NBLV

Yesterday my gun exploded. The Perils of Obesity. Harry Graham. FiBHP

Yesterday rain fell in torrents. You Could Say. Robert Mezey. NaP

Yesterday, Rebecca Mason. Truth's the Best. Elizabeth Turner. OxBChV

Yesterday, Robin spoke to me. Charlotte DeClue. STE

Yesterday, sitting. Just. Judith Johnson Sherwin. TAP

Yesterday the fields were only gray with scattered snow. A Winter's Tale. D. H. Lawrence. MoAB; MoBrPo

Yesterday the gentle. St. Stephen's Day. Patric Dickinson. OBCP

Yesterday, the laughing blue eyes. Vietnam. Mustafa Zaidi, *tr.* by Mahmood Jamal. PBMUP

Yesterday, the man who calls himself "Our Father." The Prisoner. Ai. ER

Yesterday the twig was brown and bare. Miracle. Liberty Hyde Bailey. OHIP

Yesterday three deer stood at the roadside. Deer at the Roadside. Iain Crichton Smith. *Fr.* Deer on the High Hills—a Meditation. PoSH

Yesterday, we left Dragon River. The Customs Station at Weed Lake. Cha Shen-hsing, *tr.* by William Schultz. WFTU

Yesterday you burnt your olden times. Auto-da-Fe. Kevin Ireland. ATNZ

Yesterday's Illusion *or* Remembering the Thirties. Alun Llywelyn-Williams, *tr. fr. Welsh* by R. Gerallt Jones. OBWVE

Yesterday's Paper. Mabel Watts. RAR

Yestreen I had a pint o' wine. Anna. Burns. TrGrPo

Yestreen I stood on Ben Dorain, and paced its dark-/ grey path. On Ben Dorain. Duncan Ban MacIntyre, *tr. fr. Gaelic* by Robert Buchanan. *Fr.* Last Farewell to the Hills. PoSH

Yet another great truth I record in my verse. The Viper. Hilaire Belloc. FaBoNo; NoAM

Yet Another Poem about a Dying Child. Janet Frame. ATNZ; PeNZ

Yet Another Song. David Rubadiri. WMBCH

Yet but Three? Shakespeare. *Fr.* A Midsummer Night's Dream, III, ii. CTC

Yet Chloe [*or* Cloe] sure was formed without a spot. Pope. *Fr.* Moral Essays: Epistle to a Lady: Of the Characters of Women. ErPo; OBSV (Chloe.) AWP; NOBE

Yet Dish. Gertrude Stein. SOTW

Yet Do I Marvel. Countee Cullen. AmNP; BANP; BPo; CDC; FF; IDB; NAAL-2; NoAM; PoBA; PoNe; Son; TAP; TTY

Yet Each Man Kills the Thing He Loves. Oscar Wilde. *Fr.* The Ballad of Reading Gaol. TEP; TrGrPo

Yet Gentle Will the Griffin Be. Vachel Lindsay. *Fr.* Poems about the Moon, II. PDV

Yet had his sun not risen; from his lips. The Final Struggle. Louis James Block. *Fr.* The New World. PAH

Yet Ha'e I Silence Left. "Hugh MacDiarmid." *Fr.* A Drunk Man Looks at the Thistle. NAEL-2

Yet hard/ The travail is for such as bend their minds. *Unknown, tr. fr. Sanskrit by* Sir Edwin Arnold. *Fr.* The Bhagavad-Gita. TOF

Yet I could think, indeed, the perfect call. Arthur Hugh Clough. *Fr.* Dipsychus, pt. II, sc. v. OBNC

Yet I courbed on my knees and cried hire of grace. William Langland. *Fr.* The Vision of Piers Plowman, Passus II. EBEV

Yet if his majesty, our sovereign [or sovereign] Lord. *Unknown.* FaBoCh; NoP; PoRA
(Coming of the King, The.) TrGrPo
(Guest, The.) EaLo; OBS; TrCP
(Preparations.) NOBE; OBEV
(Royal Guest, A.) CH

Yet in spite/ Of pleasure won, and knowledge not withheld. Summer Vacation. Wordsworth. *Fr.* The Prelude [or, Growth of a Poet's Mind], IV. PoEL-4
"That heartless chase." TOF
Consummate Happiness. OBNC
"Favourite pleasure hath it been with me, A," *Oxford ed.*
Dedicated Spirit, A. SeCePo
"In a throng,/ A festival company." EBEV

Yet it is not all immaculate death. Not All Immaculate. Laura Riding. *Fr.* Three Sermons to the Dead, II. LiTA

Yet London, empress of the northern clime. Dryden. *Fr.* Annus Mirabilis. NAEL-1

Yet, love, mere love, is beautiful indeed. Elizabeth Barrett Browning. *Fr.* Sonnets from the Portuguese, X. CTC

Yet Love will dream and Faith will trust. Life and Love. Whittier. BLRP

Yet much may be performed, to check the force. Bedford Level. John Dyer. *Fr.* The Fleece, II. FaBoPP

Yet, O my friend—pale conjurer, I call. Bring Them Not Back. James Benjamin Kenyon. AA

Yet, O stricken heart, remember, O remember. In Memoriam F. A. S. Robert Louis Stevenson. BrPo

Yet often I think the king of that country. The Gospel of Labor. Henry van Dyke. WBLP; WGRP

Yet on the other side, faine would he start. Giovanni Battista Marino, *tr. fr. Italian by* Richard Crashaw. *Fr.* The Massacre of the Innocents. OBVE

Yet once again do I behold the forms. The Voice of the Derwent. Wordsworth. FaBoPP

Yet once more, O ye laurels, and once more. Lycidas. Milton. AWP; ChTr; EBEV; FiP; GTBS; GTBS-P; HAP; InPK; InPS; JCP; LiTB; Mes; NAEL-1; NIP; NOBE; NoP; OAEL-1; OBEV; OBS; PoE; PoEL-3; PPP; PrIm; TrGrPo; UnPo; WeW; WGRP

Yet one more hour, then comes the night. My Drinking Song. Richard Dehmel, *tr. by* Ludwig Lewisohn. AWP

Yet one smile more, departing, distant sun! November. Bryant. AnAmPo; Son

Yet Ostia boasts of her regeneration. Daniel Defoe. *Fr.* Reformation of Manners. OBSV

Yet, planter, let humanity prevail. Slaves. James Grainger. *Fr.* The Sugar Cane. NOEC

Yet that have hearts vexed with unquiet thought. To Spenser. John Hamilton Reynolds. Son

Yet there is no great problem in the world today. "Hugh MacDiarmid." *Fr.* Lament for the Great Music. OxBTC

Yet there's one scruple with which I am much. Philip Massinger. *Fr.* The Renegado. ACP

Yet to be reconciled with the reality of the dark. Princess Shikishi, *tr. fr. Japanese by* Hiroaki Sato. *Fr.* Seventy-eight Tanka. FCEI

Yet to the wondrous St. Peter's, and yet to the solemn Rotonda. Ah, That I Were Far Away. Arthur Hugh Clough. *Fr.* Amours de Voyage, Canto III *introd..* OBNC
(Upon Apennine Slope.) FaBoPP

Yet, when I muse on what life is, I seem. Continued. Matthew Arnold. Son

Yet wulde I nat the causer fared amisse. Subject to All Pain. *Unknown.* MeEL

Yet, yet a moment, one dim ray of light. Pope. *Fr.* The Dunciad, IV. NAEL-1; OAEL-1; PoEL-3

Yetzer ha Ra. Edward Codish. VWA

Yeux Glauques. Ezra Pound. *Fr.* Hugh Selwyn Mauberley. (Life and Contacts). MoAmPo

Yevtushenko, Voznesensky and I. A Dream. Charles Tomlinson. OxBC

Yew-Tree, The. *Unknown, tr. fr. Welsh by* Geoffrey Grigson. ChTr; GBL

Yew-Tree, The. Vernon Watkins. EaLo; LiTB

Yew Trees. Wordsworth. EnRP; UnPo

Yew trees in ice, The. Friederike Mayröcker, *tr. by* Beth Bjorklund. CoAuP

Yickity-yackity, yickity-yak. The Yak. Jack Prelutsky. RHPC

Yiddish. Judith Herzberg, *tr. fr. Dutch.* DuIn, *tr. by* Manfred Wolf; VWA, *tr. by* Shirley Kaufman

Yiddish. Abraham Sutskever, *tr. fr. Yiddish.* VWA, *tr. by* Seymour Levitan

Yiddish Poet. A. C. Jacobs. VWA

Yiddish poet. Move On, Yiddish Poet. Jacob Glatstein, *tr. by* Ruth Whitman. VWA

Yiddish Poets. H. Leivick, *tr. fr. Yiddish by* Benjamin *and* Barbara Harshav. AYP

Yiddish poets. Yiddishkayt. Jacob Glatstein, *tr. by* Cynthia Ozick. PeBMYV

Yiddish Speaking Socialists of the Lower East Side. Ed Sanders. UL

Yiddishkayt. Jacob Glatstein, *tr. fr. Yiddish by* Cynthia Ozick. PeBMYV

Yield. Ronald Gross. InPK

Yield./ No Parking. Yield. Ronald Gross. InPK

Yield all, my love; but be withal as coy. Upon A. M. Sir John Suckling. ErPo

Yielded Life, The. "W. A. G." BLRP

Yillow, yillow, yillow. Metamorphosis. Wallace Stevens. InPK; VGW

Yip-yap Rattletrap. Clyde Watson. RHPC

Yippee! she is shooting in the harbor! he is jumping. Blocks. Frank O'Hara. EAS; HCAP

Yiskidor, when he dies I won't know the Hebrew words to say. Edward Field. *Fr.* Visiting Home. DiL

Yitskhok Leybush Perets. Moyshe-Leyb Halpern, *tr. fr. Yiddish by* John Hollander. PeBMYV

Yiya wo!/ This land of the Baca. Was It All Worth While? *Zulu Oral Tradition, tr. by* H. Tracey. WTO

Ylen's Song. Richard Hovey. *Fr.* The Birth of Galahad. AA

Yo-Yo King, The. Syma Cheris Cohn. TSL

Yogi, don't go away. Mirabai, *tr. by* Willis Barnstone *and* Usha Nilsson. BoWoP

Yohama, my dear. With Myself. Moyshe-Leyb Halpern, *tr. by* Benjamin *and* Barbara Harshav. AYP

Yohoweyah. When He Says So We Dance in All Directions—Wow! *Unknown, tr. by* Jerome Rothenberg *and* Richard Johnny John. STP

Yoke, The. Kalonymos ben Kalonymos, *tr. fr. Hebrew by* J. Chotzner. *Fr.* The Touchstone. TrJP

Yoke of Tyranny, The. Sir Philip Sidney. *See* Astrophel and Stella: XLVII. "What, have I thus betrayed my liberty?"

Yoke Soft and Dear. John C. Kunze. AH

Yoke uneasy on the ox doth sit, The. Philip Ayres. FaBoEE

Yoko. Thom Gunn. NoAM

Yolp, Yolp, Yolp, Yolp. *Unknown.* EIL

Yom Kippur. Chana Bloch. VWA

Yom Kippur. Eric Chaet. VWA

Yom Kippur. Lucille Day. VWA

Yom Kippur. Linda Pastan. VWA

Yom Kippur. Israel Zangwill. TrJP

Yom Kippur: Fasting. Ruth Whitman. OFD

Yom Kippur 1984. Adrienne Rich. ER; GLP; NoAM

Yomyo Stupa, The. Zotan, *tr. fr. Chinese by* Lucien Stryk *and* Takashi Ikemoto. ZPCJ

Yon clouds that roam the deserts of the air. The Bedouins of the Skies. James Benjamin Kenyon. AA

Yon Far Country. A. E. Housman. *See* Shropshire Lad, A: Into My Heart [an Air That Kills].

Yon is the laddie lo'ed to daunder far. Lintie in a Cage. Alice V. Stuart. OxBS

Yon Island Carrions Desperate of Their Bones. Shakespeare. *Fr.* King Henry V, IV,ii. RB

Yon laddie wi' the gowdan pow. William Soutar. OxBS

Yon spark's a poet, by my troth! The Difference. Tadhg Dall O'Huiginn, *tr. by* Robin Flower. BIrV

Yon white cloud blown. *Unknown. Fr.* Manyo Shu. Ma

Yond cawcrow's way-out. Two More about a Crow, in the Manner of Zukofsky. *Unknown, tr. by* Jerome Rothenberg *and* Richard Johnny John. STP

Yonder. Richard Eberhart. GOA

Yonder. Itamar Ya'oz-kest, *tr. fr. Hebrew by* Bernhard Frank. MHeP

Yonder come Roberta! Tell me how do you know? Midnight Special. *Unknown.* AS

Yonder comes a courteous Knight. The Baffled Knight. *Unknown.* ESPB
(Courteous Knight, The.) OxBB, *with music*
(There Was a Knight [and He Was Young].) CoMu

Yonder comes dat ole Joe Brown. Walky-talky Jenny. *Unknown.* AS

Yonder Comes My Pretty Little Girl. *Unknown.* AS

Yonder comes the dawn. Uru-tu-sendo's Song. *Unknown, tr. by* H. J. Spinden. WTO

Yonder Comes the High Sheriff. *Unknown.* AS

Yonder great shadow—that blot on the passionate glare of the desert. The Dead of the Wilderness. Hayyim Nahman Bialik, *tr. by* Maurice Samuel. AWP

Yonder in the plum-tree. *Unknown. Fr.* Manyo Shu. Ma

Yonder on the plain of Kasuga. *Unknown. Fr.* Manyo Shu. Ma

Yonder See the Morning Blink. A. E. Housman. CMoP; MoShBr; NOBVV

Yonder stands a pretty fair maiden. No, Sir, No. *Unknown.* AmFP

Yonder, that swarm of things insectual. A Sequelula to "The Dynasts,." Max Beerbohm. Par

Yonder they are coming. It Is Mine, This Country Wide. *Unknown.* GOA

Yonder, yonder see the fair rainbow. The Rainbow. *Unknown, tr. by* Natalie Curtis. WTO

Yonder you weep. Jamila. Nazik al-Mala'ika, *tr. by* Kamal Boullata. WPOW

Yond's the Cardinall's window: This fortification. John Webster. *Fr.* The Duchess of Malfi, V, iii. PoEL-2

Yonghy-Bonghy-Bo, The. Edward Lear. *See* Courtship of the Yonghy-Bonghy-Bo, The.

Yonnondio. Walt Whitman. NAAL-1

Yonosa House. R. T. Smith. STE

York Harbor Morning. George Garrett. MT

York Play of the Crucifixion, The. *Unknown.* NAEL-1

Yorktown Centennial Lyric. Paul Hamilton Hayne. PAH

Yorunomado sat in. The Black Hat. Clayton Eshleman. VGW

Yosemite. Milicent Washburn Shinn. *Fr.* The Washington Sequoia. AA

Yoshino. Fujii Chikugai, *tr. fr. Chinese by* Burton Watson. JLIC-2

Yoshino River/ with kerria blossoming. Ietaka, *tr. by* Steven D. Carter. WFTW

Yoshiwara. Hagiwara Sakutaro, *tr. fr. Japanese by* Hiroaki Sato. FCEI

You. Carroll Arnett. VoR

You. Charles Bernstein. LP

You. Barbara Burford. DT

You/ my bell-clapper. Christmas Mass for a Little Atheist Jesus. Claude Maillard, *tr. by* Maxine *and* Judith Kumin. BoWoP

You, sels. Tom Clark. EAS
   "Chords knotted together like insane nouns." *Fr.* IV.
   "Door behind me was you, The." *Fr.* I.
   "Today I get this letter from you and the sun." *Fr.* III.
   "You are bright, tremendous, wow." *Fr.* II.

You. Michel Deguy, *tr. fr. French by* Anthony Rudolf. RHTwFP

You/ Over there/ Beyond the hill. Echo. Mildred Weston. BoNaP

You. D. H. Lawrence. NoAM

You. Kenneth Rexroth. *Fr.* A Bestiary. HoPM

You/ Refuse to see. Out. Riots and Rituals. Richard W. Thomas. PoBA

You/ are the One who put. Stars in Apple Cores. Luci Shaw. TrCP

You/ black man/ made me raw umber. To My Father. Dinah Butler. AIW

You a gentleman and I up from the grime. December 24 and George McBride Is Dead. Richard Hugo. HoPM

You, a man who made me wait but didn't come. Emperor Go-Shirakawa, *tr. fr. Japanese by* Hiroaki Sato. *Fr.* Ryojin Hisho. FCEI ("May the man who gained my trust yet did not come.") PeBJV, *tr. by* Geoffrey Bownas *and* Anthony Thwaite.

You abandon me, woman, because I am very poor. El Abandonado. *Unknown, tr. by* Frank J. Dobie. AS

You accompanied me so far. A Last Address to My Ghosts. Gregory Orr. GeTw

You ain't part Indian. Wake-up Niggers. Don L. Lee. PoBA

You All Are Static; I Alone Am Moving. Peter Viereck. LiTA

You Alone. Suad al-Mubarak al-Sabah, *tr. fr. Arabic by* May Jayyusi *and* John Heath-Stubbs. MAP

You Also, Gaius Valerius Catullus. Archibald MacLeish. NoAM; TAP

You also, our first great. *to* Whistler, American. Ezra Pound. AiP; NAAL-2; PoA

You always know what to expect. The Country House. Louis Simpson. NOBA

You always named it. Horn. Sydney Lea. KS

You always read about it. Cinderella. Anne Sexton. HeIP; InPS; NAAL-2

You and I. Henry Alford. BLPA; FaBoBe

You and I. Tennessee Williams. GLP

You and I/ Have so much love. Married Love. Kuan Tao Sheng, *tr. by* Kenneth Rexroth *and* Ling Chung. UnAS

You and I and Amyas. Desire. William Cornish. OBSC (Latet Anguis.) OBEV

You and I are like an old married couple. Lifesaving. Sandra McPherson. MAYP

You and I are like birds in a forest. Chu Yün-ming, *tr. fr. Chinese by* Jonathan Chaves. *Fr.* Forest Birds (A Woman Speaks), II. CoBLCP

You and I by this lamp with these. Together. Ludwig Lewisohn. TrJP

You and I Saw Hawks Exchanging the Prey. James Wright. NAAL-2; NoAM

You and I—we agitate. Minutes. Denis Johnson. MAYP

You and I will go to Finegall. *Unknown, tr. by* Thomas Kinsella. NOIV

You and It. Mark Strand. NYBP

You and Nell found Aunt Maud. Maud. Mary Swander. MOWH

You, Andrew Marvell. Archibald MacLeish. AWP; CMoP; FaBV; FYAP; HAP; HeIP; HoPM; LiTA; LiTM; MoAB; MoAmPo; MoP; NAAL-2; NoAM; NOBA; NoP; OxBA; PoRA; PPP; PrIm; SoSe; TrGrPo; TwCP; WeW

You approach me carrying a book. Superballs. Tom Clark. EAS

You approach sleep like voices trying to reach. Foam Blanches. Anadad Eldan, *tr. by* Bernhard Frank. MHeP

You are a friend then, as I make it out. Ben Jonson Entertains a Man from Stratford. E. A. Robinson. AmPP; MoAB; MoAmPo

You Are a Jew! Delmore Schwartz. *Fr.* Genesis. TrJP

You are a landscape in the Tale of Terror. For Cora Lightbody, R.N. John Glassco. PoA

You are a murderer. Sleeping Wrestler. Takahashi Mutsuo, *tr. by* Hiroaki Sato. FCEI

You Are a Part of Me. Frank Yerby. AmNP

You are a stool pigeon and. Kenneth Rexroth, *after the Latin of* Martial. NNaP

You are a sunrise. To a Golden-haired Girl in a Louisiana Town. Vachel Lindsay. MoAmPo

You are a traveller to them. Letter from Mama Dot. Frederick D'Aguiar. PVCV

You are a tried and loyal friend. To My Setter, Scout. Frank H. Seldon. BLPA

You are a tulip seen today. A Meditation for His Mistress[e]. Robert Herrick. CaPo; JCP; NOBE; OBEV; OBS; SeCP

You are a victim of life's grief. A. K. Tolstoy, *tr. by* Alan Myers. AAA

You are a woman. Another. Ellen Marie Bissert. PeHV

You are all these people. To a Single Shadow without Pity. Sam Cornish. NBP; PoBA

You Are Alms. James W. Thompson. PoBA

You are already/ asleep. Touch. Thom Gunn. CMoP

You are as gold. Hilda Doolittle ("H. D."). LiTA; LiTM; MoAmPo

You are beautiful. What Ulysses Said to Circe on the Beach of Aeaea. Irving Layton. ErPo

You are beautiful and faded. A Lady. Amy Lowell. AnAmPo; MoAmPo

You are blind like us. Your hurt no man designed. To Germany. Charles Hamilton Sorley. MoBrPo

You Are Born Again and Again. Sirkka Turkka, *tr. fr. Finnish by* Aili Jarvenpa. SOP

You are bright, tremendous, wow. Tom Clark. *Fr.* You, II. EAS

You are carried in a basket. Operation. W. E. Henley. *Fr.* In Hospital, V. BrPo

You are carrying me, full consciousness, god that has desires. Full Consciousness. Juan Ramón Jiménez, *tr. by* Robert Bly. NU

You are clear. Garden. Hilda Doolittle ("H. D."). LiTA; NoAM

You are coming to woo me, but not as of yore. Lips That Touch Liquor. George W. Young. NBLV

You are coming toward us. Aunt Laura Moves toward the Open Grave of Her Father. Joseph De Roche. HeIP

You are coming very slowly, why do you delay. My Cobra Girl. *Gond Oral Tradition, tr. by* V. Elwin *and* S. Hivale. WTO

You are confronted with yourself. Each year. Rembrandt's Late Self-Portraits. Elizabeth Jennings. EyDe

You are dead and your body, beneath a Uruguayan cloak. Words for Delmira Agustini. Alfonsina Storni, *tr. by* Kate Flores. DMH

You are desolate, fort of kings. *Unknown.* NOIV

You are disdainful and magnificent. Sonnet to a Negro in Harlem. Helene Johnson. AmNP; BANP; CDC; NIP

You are drowning. How Metaphor Can Save Your Life. Myra Sklarew. CRP

You are eighty years old today, ma. To Mother. Lessie M. Drown. PWR

You are falling asleep and I sit looking at you. After Dark. Adrienne Rich. LCAP; LiTM; VGW

You are famous in my mind. Before the Big Storm. William Stafford. NaP

You are far away, my father, there in your realm of shadows. My Father. Vicente Aleixandre, *tr.* by Perry Higman. LPSS

You are fortunate, dear friends, that you can tell. Vidya, *tr. fr. Sanskrit* by Daniel Ingalls. WPOW

You are going far away, far away from poor Jeannette. Jeannette and Jeannot. Charles Jefferys. BLPA

You are gone, and I have nothing unhappy to remember. Elegies for Prince Atsumichi ("You are gone, and I have nothing unhappy to remember"). Lady Izumi, *tr. fr. Japanese* by Hiroaki Sato. *Fr.* Fifty-one Tanka. FCEI

You Are Gorgeous and I'm Coming. Frank O'Hara. NeAP; SM

You are here. Minor Things. Heather Ross Miller. MT

You are here now. The Sleeping Fury. Louise Bogan. IHMS; LiTM

You are horizontal. Footpaths Cross in the Rice Field. "Lin Ling." *Unknown, tr.* by Kenneth Rexroth and Ling Chung. PBWP

You are ill and so I lead you away. Alfred W. Purdy. NOBC

You are ill; let me put my slender arm. Yosano Akiko, *tr. fr. Japanese* by Hiroaki Sato. *Fr.* Thirty-nine Tanka. FCEI

You are in love with a country. Where? A. S. J. Tessimond. OBTV

You are just the kind of man. Exorcism of the Straight/Man/Demon. Aaron Shurin. GLP

You are laid low with soil and stones. Word. Gerrit Achterberg, *tr.* by James Brockway. DuIn

You are less than one-half. The Speaker. Charles G. Ballard. VoR

You are like a sun of the tropics. Luxury. Donald Justice. HeIP

You are like a whispering branch. Metaphors. Miklós Radnóti, *tr.* by Steven Polgar and Stephen Berg and S. J. Marks. VWA

You are like those scarves, those white beach waves. *Unknown. Fr.* Manyo Shu. FCEI

You are looking at my ghost. I Am Not the Woman I Am. Diane Glancy. GOS

You are looking now on old Tom Moore. The Days of 'Forty-nine. *Unknown.* PAH

You are lying, O missionary! Raymond Mazisi Kunene, *tr. fr. Zulu* by D. K. Rycroft. WTO

You are made of almost nothing. The Dragonfly. Louise Bogan. HeIP; NIP

You are mistaken: that's not a tiger, black as night, that roars. That's Not a Tiger. Pertti Nieminen, *tr.* by Aili Jarvenpa. SOP

You are my friend. Lorine Niedecker. VGW

You are my friends. You do things. The Game. Harold Bond. TSM

You are, my green island. Neither This nor That. Luis Palés Matos, *tr.* by Julio Marzán. InW

You are my stick, my prop. Houseplant. Felicity Napier. BrRo

You are naked and have no clothes. Your Presence. Mordecai Temkin, *tr.* by Jeremy Garber. VWA

You are no longer here. What I see. Distracted. Pedro Salinas, *tr.* by Perry Higman. LPSS

You are not alone on the mountain. Beinn A' Ghlo. Bill Tulloch. PoSH

You are not beautiful, exactly. To Dorothy. Marvin Bell. CAPP; Psk

You are not here, I cannot touch you, or be still. Gemini Elegy. Margaret Gibson. MAYP

You are not here! the quaint witch Memory sees. To Maria Gisborne in England, from Italy. Shelley. *Fr.* Letter to Maria Gisborne. NOBE

You are not merry, brother. Why not laugh. The Prodigal Son. E. A. Robinson. MoAmPo

You are not nearer God than we. Annunciation. Rainer Maria Rilke, *tr.* by James Blair Leishman. OBVE

You are now/ In London, that great sea. Shelley. *Fr.* Letter to Maria Gisborne. ChER; EBEV

"You Are Old, Father William." Father William. "Lewis Carroll." *Fr.* Alice's Adventures in Wonderland, *ch.* 5. BXAP; FaBoCo; FaBoNo; FaBoPa; FaPON; FiBHP; FPL; GoJo; HoPM; LiTB; NOBL; NOBVV; OxBChV; Par; PDV; PoLF; PoRA; RHPC; TrGrPo; UnPo

"You are old, Father William," the young man cried. The Old Man's Comforts and How He Gained Them. Robert Southey. HoPM; OxBChV; Par; UnPo

"You are old, Father William," the young man said,/ "And your nose has a look of surprise." Father William. *Unknown.* NA

"You are old Munro bagger," the young man said. The Old Munro Bagger. *Unknown.* PoSH

You Are on U.S. 40 Headed West. Vera White. AmFN

You are only one of many. One of Many. Stevie Smith. OxBC

You are over there, Father Malloy. Father Malloy. Edgar Lee Masters. *Fr.* Spoon River Anthology. OxBA

You are perishing like the old men. Already your arms are gone. The Chorus Speaks Her Words as She Dances. Linda Gregg. AnAn; NPGG

You are proof that it can happen. A Tardy Epithalamium for E. and N. Ralph Pomeroy. GLP; PeHV

You are pulling on my riding boot. Fitting. Alastair Fowler. NPo

You are right about it; that wary. Old Tiger. Marianne Moore. AnAn

You are right. In dreams I might well dance. Possession. Marie Ponsot. VGW

You are right. What we call Poetry is the boat. A New Poem. Robert Duncan. NNaP; PoM

You are rumpled like a sweater. Nothing More Will Happen. Marge Piercy. NeAC

You Are Safe. Jacques Roubaud, *tr. fr. French* by Robert Kelly. RHTwFP

You are small and intense. To a Child Running with Outstretched Arms in Canyon de Chelly. N. Scott Momaday. CDW; HATNAP

You are so small, I. Miss Cho Composes in the Cafeteria. James Tate. SM; WeW

You Are So Tender. Berta Freistadt. DT

You are so thick-skinned! A Bull. Ahmad Nadeem Qasmi, *tr.* by Mahmood Jamal. PBMUP

You are so witty, profligate, and thin. Epigram on Voltaire. Edward Young. FaBoCo

You are speaking of Chile. Things That Are Worse than Death. Sharon Olds. MAYP

You are still a child but already your limbs. Sin. János Pilinszky, *tr.* by Ted Hughes. MHuP

You are such a well-rounded sponge. Sediment. David Ignatow. NYBP

You are that frail decision that devised. Hart Crane. AnAn

You Are the Brave. Raymond R. Patterson. NBP; NIP; PoBA

(In Time of Crisis.) IDB

You are the cake of my endeavour, and my jelly-roll forever. The Merry Pieman's Song. John Bennett. ILY

You are the echo when my body calls. The One Who Laughs and Laughs and Laughs. Unsi al-Haj, *tr.* by Sargon Boulus and Alistair Elliot. MAP

You are the first, and You remain the last. Another Testimony. Dan Pagis, *tr.* by Warren Bargad and Stanley F. Chyet. IP

You are the grain. I Think of Housman Who Said the Poem Is a Morbid Secretion, like a Pearl. Judith Kroll. UnPo

You are the lady. The Comet. Paolo Volponi, *tr.* by Lawrence R. Smith. NItP

You Are the Man. Esther Raab, *tr. fr. Hebrew* by Bernhard Frank. MHeP

You are the merry men, dwarfs of soul. The Diakka. Gerald Massey. NOBVV

You are the millions, we are multitude. The Scythians. Aleksandr Aleksandrovich Blok, *tr.* by Babette Deutsch and Avrahm Yarmolinsky. AWP; WaaP

You are the mother of my little ones lost some in the fire. This Way, This Way. Abba Kovner, *tr.* by Bernhard Frank. MHeP

You are the one. To a Dark Moses. Lucille Clifton. CAPP

You are the owner of one complete thought. Voice and Address. Michael Palmer. NPGG

You are the pitying, I the pitiful one. Tulsidas, *tr.* by John Stratton Hawley and Mark Juergensmeyer. SSI

You are the problem I propose. The Metaphysical Amorist. J. V. Cunningham. VGW

You are the town and we are the clock. W. H. Auden. *Fr.* The Dog beneath the Skin. OxBTC

You are tired. The Midnight Tennis Match. Thomas Lux. AmPA; ASP; TSL

You are tired at last this old world. Zone. Guillaume Apollinaire, *tr.* by Roger Shattuck. POS

You are to me my breath, my life. *Unknown. Fr.* Manyo Shu. FCEI

You are traveling to play basketball. Your team's. In Your Young Dream. Richard Hugo. InPK

"You are wise, Mr. Dodgson," the young child said. Lewis Carroll. Eleanor Farjeon. OxBChV

You are with me this evening, all my friends. Evening in the Walls. Jean Wahl, *tr.* by Charles Guenther. VWA

You are writing a gospel. Your Own Version. Paul Gilbert. BLRP

You Arise. Paul Eluard, *tr. fr. French* by Michael Benedikt. POS

You ask a verse, to sing (ah, laughing face!). To a Lady. John James Piatt. AA

You ask for the date. Nizar Qabbani, *tr.* by Diana Der Hovanessian and Lena Jayyusi. MAP

You ask how old am I. Twice Times Then Is Now. Ibn Hazm Al-Andalusi, *tr.* by Omar Pound. OBVE

You Ask Me. Mutabaruka. PVCV

You ask me. To Madame A. V. Pletneff. Karolina Pavlova, *tr.* by Paul Schmidt. PBWP

You ask me for a song, folks. Cousin Jack Song. *At. to* Charley Tregonning. AmFP

You ask me, Fresher, who it is. Ballade of Andrew Lang. Dugald Sutherland MacColl. CenHV

You ask me how Contempt who claims to sleep. J. V. Cunningham. ErPo; NePoAm

You ask me how to pray to someone who is not. On Prayer. Czeslaw Milosz, *tr. by* Robert Hass. AnAn

You ask me to forget him. What She Said to Her Friend ("You ask me to forget him"). Kapilar, *tr. by* A. K. Ramanujan. PLW

You ask me to sing, so I'll sing you a song. The Cranberry Song. Barney Reynolds. AmFP

You Ask Me What It Means. Giovanni Giudici, *tr. fr. Italian by* Lawrence R. Smith. NItP

You ask me *What's love?*—Why, that virtue-fed vapour. Address to Lady———, Who Asked What the Passion of Love Was? Charles Morris. NOEC

You ask what I have found, and far and wide I go. The Curse of Cromwell. W. B. Yeats. BlrV; SeCePo

You ask what place I like the best. The Kinkaiders. *Unknown.* AS

You ask when I will go back home. Ni Tsan, *tr. fr. Chinese by* Jonathan Chaves. *Fr.* Following the Rhymes of Yü-chai's Poems on Autumn. CoBLCP

You ask why gold and velvet bind. On a New Duke. *Unknown.* FaBoEE

You Ask Why Sometimes I Say Stop. Marge Piercy. CAPP; NIP

You asked me for a love poem. Couplets. Natalie Clifford Barney, *tr. by* Barbara Johnson. DMF

You asked me to enter the holy cloister. Banishment from Ur. Enheduanna, *tr. by* W. W. Hallo *and* J. J. A. van Dijk. BoWoP

You asked us to hear the softest vocable of wind. Lines for Roethke Twenty Years after His Death. Duane Niatum. HATNAP

You at God's altar stand, His minister. Written on an Island off the Breton Coast. Saint Venantius Fortunatus, *tr. by* Helen Waddell. PeHV

You bad leetle boy, not moche you care. Leetle Bateese. W. H. Drummond. CaP

You balanced her within a cyclone. Woman Seed Player. Roberta Hill Whiteman. HATNAP; STE

You beat your pate, and fancy wit will come. Pope. FaBoEE (To a Blockhead.) NBLV

You beautious ladies, great and small. The Famous Flower of Serving-Men; or, The Lady Turn'd Serving-Man. *Unknown.* ESPB; OBET; OxBB

You became/ In many acts and quiet observances. My Company. Sir Herbert Read. BrPo; MMA

You Begin. Margaret Atwood. NOBC; NoP

You, being less than either dew or frost. Love Song out of Nothing. Vassar Miller. NePoEA

You bells in the steeple, ring, ring out your changes. Seven Times Two—Romance. Jean Ingelow. *Fr.* Songs of Seven. GN

You beneath rosebud trees in bloom and they. Eleanor——— Hayden Carruth. AnAn

You better sure shall live, not evermore. Horace. *See* Odes: II, 10. "Receive, dear friend, the truths I teach" ("Rectius vives").

You bible-sharps that thump on tubs. Villon's Good-Night. W. E. Henley. CenHV

You bid me to hold my peace. The Poet to the Birds. Alice Meynell. FM

You black-maned, horse-haired, long-faced creature. To the Gentlewoman of Llanarth Hall. Evan Thomas, *tr. by* Gwyn Jones. OBWVE

You black out the sun. Ed Roberson. *Fr.* When Thy King Is a Boy. PoBA

You blame me that I do not write. Letter to a Friend. Jon Stallworthy. NoAM

You Blessed Bowers. *Unknown.* EIL

You blew away, feather-brained for beauty. Ducking: After Maupassant. Dave Smith. AnAn

You bloom/ with a color and fragrance. Tsurayuki, *tr. fr. Japanese by* Burton Watson. *Fr.* Kokin Shu. FCEI

You boast about your ancient line. Family Trees. Douglas Malloch. OHIP

You brave heroic [*or* heroique] minds. To the Virginian Voyage. Michael Drayton. AiP, *sl. abr.*; HAP; NAEL-1; NOBE; OBEV; OBS; PAH; PoEL-2; SeCePo; TEP

You bring the ball down the court. Point Guard. Arnold Adoff. ASP

You bring the Dardevle back fast. The Cedar River. Reginald Gibbons. MAYP

You bring the only changes to this season. For Nicholas, Born in September. Tod Perry. NYBP

You Britons all of courage bold. A Sea Song. *Unknown.* OxBSS

You brought me a little seaweed. Genoa Woman. Dino Campana, *tr. by* Charles Wright. PFI

You build it where you will be heard only by chance. The Cabin North of It All. James McMichael. AmPA

You build your harp frame. The Silence. Tomas Mac Siomoin, *tr. by the author.* TIRV

You built the new Court House, Spoon River. Benjamin Franklin Hazard. Edgar Lee Masters. *Fr.* The New Spoon River. GOA

You burst into the world with smiles wide as April. Sleeping with Foxes. Roberta Hill. CDW

You buy some flowers for your table. Samuel Hoffenstein. *Fr.* Poems in Praise of Practically Nothing. FiBHP; TrJP

You call me love. To the Waitress at the Hickory Pit. Lisa Vice. ER

You Call That a Ts'ing; a Letter. Jedediah Barrow. BXAP

You came already the first summer. In the Year 4 after Father. Aila Meriluoto, *tr. by* Aili Jarvenpa. SOP

You came, and looked and loved the view. Green Sussex. Tennyson. *Fr.* Prologue to General Hamley. FaBoPP

You came. And you did well to come. Sappho, *tr. by* Willis Barnstone. BoWoP

You Came as a Thought. J. Laughlin. GOYP

You came back to us in a dream and we were not here. Come Back. W. S. Merwin. NaP

You came like the dawn. On the Death of a Child. Edward S. Silvera. PoNe

You came to it through wild country, there the sea's voice. The House in the Green Well. John Hall Wheelock. MoAmPo

You came, were seated. Happy and uplifted. To the Muse ("You came, were seated. Happy and uplifted"). Afanasi Afanasievich Fet, *tr. by* Alan Myers. AAA

You Came with Shells. June Jordan. NoAM

You Can. Jutta Schutting, *tr. fr. German by* Beth Bjorklund. CoAuP

You can always fight the foulest grief. The Five Feet. Ed Sanders. UL

You can be a dancing brontosaurus. No Money in Art. Jim Gustafson. UL

"You can be so inconsiderate." Who's on First? Lloyd Schwartz. PPR

You can be walking along the beach. American Landscape with Clouds & a Zoo. Jon Anderson. AnAn; MAYP

You can become a shaman. New Indian Medicine. Emma Lee Warrior. HATNAP

You can call me Herbie Jr. or Ashamah. Unemployment/Monologue. June Jordan. WPOW

You can decorate your office. The Ultimatum. Ben King. AnAmPo

You can feel the muscles and veins rippling in widening and rising circles. Saying Dante Aloud. James Wright. InPK

You can find it only in attics or in ads. The Spinning Wheel. A. M. Klein. CaP

You can go back in a clap of blue metal. Southbound. Betty Adcock. MT

You can have daughters, sons. Inventing a Family. Dennis Saleh. *Fr.* A Guide to Familiar American Incest. NeAC

You Can Have It. Philip Levine. AnAn; CAPP

You can hear the silence of it. David Jones. *Fr.* In Parenthesis. FaBoMo

You can make a tidy leaf-pot out of sarai leaves. Man's Need. *Gond Oral Tradition, tr. by* V. Elwin *and* S. Hivale. WTO

You can never see him. The Figure in the Carpet. James Camp. TW

You can no longer. A Wreath. Gyula Illyés, *tr. by* William Jay Smith. MHuP

You can pull from your head a gray hair. Sacco-Vanzetti. Moyshe-Leyb Halpern, *tr. by* John Hollander. PeBMYV ("You can pull out.") AYP, *tr. by* Benjamin *and* Barbara Harshav ("You can tear a gray hair out of your head.") VWA, *tr. by* David G. Roskies *and* Hillel Schwartz

You can pull out. Moyshe-Leyb Halpern. *See* Sacco-Vanzetti.

You can push. Fourteen Ways of Touching Peter. George MacBeth. CRH

You can see from their faces. Photographs of Pioneer Women. Ruth Dallas. PeNZ

You can sigh o'er the sad-eyed Armenian. An Appeal to My Countrywomen. Frances E. W. Harper. BlSi

You can sing of the maid. The Girl with the Jersey. Ben King. AnAmPo

You can stop me. There's Somethin.' Adam Small. PeSA

You can take a tub with a rub and a scrub in a two-foot tank of tin. Pater's Bathe. Edward Abbott Parry. OxBChV

"You can talk about your sheep dorgs." Daley's Dorg Wattle. W. T. Goodge. PoAu-1

You can talk about your farms and your Chinaman's charms. The Cowboy's Life Is a Very Dreary Life. *Unknown.* AmFP

You can tear a grey hair out of your head. Moyshe-Leyb Halpern. *See* Sacco-Vanzetti.

You cannot cage a field. Lives. Henry Reed. BoNaP; LiTB

You Cannot Do This. Gwendolyn MacEwen. FaBoWP

You cannot dream. Things Lovelier. Humbert Wolfe. TrJP

You cannot find a fossilot. The Fossilot. Jane Yolen. BWV

You cannot from the open window invade. The Crow. Rita Boumi-Pappas, *tr. by* Kimon Friar. PBWP

You Cannot Go Down to the Spring. John Shaw Neilson. CBAP

You cannot hope. The British Journalist. Humbert Wolfe. FaBoEE; FiBHP; OxBTC

You cannot justly of the Court complain. To a Witty Man of Wealth and Quality; Who, after His Dismissal from Court, Said, He Might Justly Complain of It. William Wycherley. SeCV-2

You cannot leave! Cheng Wen-cho, *tr. by* William Schultz. WFTU

You Cannot Leave. Alma Villanueva. CCP

You cannot rest behind the plate. M. D. Feld. SD

You cannot return! Cheng Wen-cho, *tr. by* William Schultz. WFTU

You cannot see mountains and valleys in the clouds. Spyglass Conversations. *Unknown, tr. by* Frances Densmore. STP

You cannot stay! Cheng Wen-cho, *tr. by* William Schultz. WFTU

You can't beat English lawns. Our final hope. Rolling the Lawn. William Empson. MoBrPo

You can't breathe, the hard earth wriggles with worms. Concert at the Station. Osip Mandelstam, *tr. by* Andrew Glaze. VWA

You can't buy baseball bats in Israel. Louisville Feared in Mideast. Steven Bryan Bieler. TSL

You can't count. Don't Count. Ory Bernstein, *tr. by* Warren Bargad *and* Stanley F. Chyet. IP

You can't ever imagine the Virgin Mary having vulvitis or thrush. Sonnet: Supernatural Beings. Gavin Ewart. Son

You Can't Go to the Moon There's No Trains. Joy Howard. DT

"You can't race me," said Johnny the Hare. The Hare and the Tortoise. Ian Serraillier. SO

You can't say it that way any more. And "Ut Pictura Poesis" Is Her Name. John Ashbery. InPS

You can't take three from two, two is less than three. New Maths. Tom Lehrer. FaBoUs

You can't tell me God would have Heaven. A Malemute Dog. Pat O'Cotter. BLPA

You captains and commanders both by land and sea. A Copy of Verses on Jefferys the Seaman. *Unknown.* OxBSS

You captains brave and bold, hear our cries, hear our cries. Captain Kidd. *Unknown.* AmFP

You care naught for the living. Okura. *Fr. Manyo Shu.* Ma

You: caught in the net of the chosen. Patriotic Reflections. Yehuda Amichai, *tr. by* Warren Bargad *and* Stanley F.Chyet. IP

You charm'd me not with that fair face. Dryden. *Fr. An Evening's Love, II, i.* SeCV-2

You claim his poems are garbage. Baldedrash! A Poet Defended. Paul Ramsey. InPK

You, clear of vision, farsighted, penetrating. His Relative Confides in Professor Sigmund Freud. Judd Teller, *tr. by* Grace Schulman. PeBMYV

You come/ in ancestral wisdom. On the Naming Day. Jewel C. Latimore. CNA

You come along. tearing your shirt. yelling about Jesus. To a Contemporary Bunkshooter. Carl Sandburg. WGRP

You come forth/ the color of a stone cliff. To Insure Survival. Simon J. Ortiz. CDW

You come from the line of a Cola king. A Poet's Counsel ("You come from the line of a Cola king"). Kovur Kilar, *tr. by* A. K. Ramanujan. PLW

You come to fetch me from my work tonight. Putting in the Seed. Robert Frost. ErPo; NoAM; OxBA

You complain of your body. A Guide to Perfection. Kevin Ireland. ATNZ

You could be sitting now in a carrel. A Late Aubade. Richard Wilbur. SM; SoSe

You could draw a straight line from the heels. Man Lying on a Wall. Michael Longley. FaBCIP

You could love here, not the lovely goat. The Milltown Union Bar. Richard Hugo. NoAM

You Could Say. Robert Mezey. NaP

You could say I came home to the hooley. Uneasy Resident. Louis Johnson. ATNZ

You could sit there with the stains on your shoes. Robert Frost. *Fr.* Home Burial. OBD

You could smell the river. For E. C. J. Emmett Jarrett. NeAC

You couldn't bear to grow old, but we grow old. John Berryman. *Fr.* Dream Songs. TAP

You couldn't find it in the bird's weight. These Labdanum Hours. Kathleen Fraser. NPGG

You couldn't pack a Broadwood half a mile. The Song of the Banjo. Kipling. FaBoCh; PrIm

You cover my words, my deeds. The Filth of Your Suspicion. Grace Schulman. PeBMYV

You cry, waking from a nightmare. Little Sleep's-Head Sprouting Hair in the Moonlight. Galway Kinnell. InPS; LCAP

You danced a magnetic dance. So Many Feathers. Jayne Cortez. BlSi

You dare not tell me. A Childless Witch. Raquel Chalfi, *tr. by* Alexandra Meiri *and* Myra Glazer Schotz. VWA

You dare to say with perjured lips. Mare Liberum. Henry Van Dyke. PAH

You darling girls of Bagaduce, who live along the shore. The Schooner *Fred Dunbar.* Amos Hanson. AmFP

You day-sun, circling around. Song for Bringing a Child into the World. *Unknown, tr. by* Frances Densmore. OV

You dazzle all eyes by increasing. You Float. Rae Armantrout. IAT

You, dead in '92 and '93. To the French of the Second Empire. Arthur Rimbaud, *tr. fr. French by* Robert Lowell. *Fr.* Eighteen-Seventy. FaBoPV; OBWP

You, dear husband, who have gone forth. Kanamura. *Fr. Manyo Shu.* Ma

You departing geese. Departing Geese. Yoshida no Kenko, *tr. by* Steven D. Carter. WFTW

You did late review my lays. To Christopher North. Tennyson. FaBoEE; FiBHP

You did not come. A Broken Appointment. Thomas Hardy. GBL; NAEL-2; NoAM; NOBVV; NoP

You did not leave this fruited land. Evangeline. Norma E. Smith. CaP

You did not see Him on the mountain of Transfiguration. To the Good Thief. Saunders Lewis, *tr. by* Gwyn Morgan. OBWVE

You did not suck at my mother's breast. Yonathan Ratosh, *tr. by* Howard Schwartz. VWA

You did not walk with me. The Walk. Thomas Hardy. CMoP; NAEL-2; PoE; PoEL-5; PrIm

You did see the forest for the trees, and now in your old age. Generations. István Eörsi, *tr. by* William Jay Smith. MHuP

You didn't have to travel to become an airplane. Communication of His Thirtieth Birthday. Marvin Bell. CoAP

You died nine years ago today. February 11, 1977. Frederick Morgan. DiPo

You dig instant revolution: against. Down Wind against the Highest Peaks. Clarence Major. NBP

You do doo-doo, you do doo-doo. Baby. John Shea. SoTCo

You do look, my son, in a mov'd sort. Prospero. Shakespeare. *Fr.* The Tempest, IV, i. FiP

You do not do, you do not do. Daddy. Sylvia Plath. BoWoP; CAPP; CMoP; CoAP; HCAP; HeIP; InPK; InPS; LiTM; MoP; NAAL-2; NaP; NIP; NMM; NoAM; NOBA; NoP; OPOP; PoE; PrIm; TW; TwCP; UnPo

You do not for a moment imagine. First Ultraviolet Ballad. Cassiano Ricardo, *tr. by* William Jay Smith. CT

You do not know how beautiful you are. Ode to a Beautiful Woman. Carl Clark. JB

You do not know this Byaruhanga: he is short. The Kaleidoscope. David Gill. OBTV

You do not move about, but try. Getting Lost in Nazi Germany. Marvin Bell. VWA

You do not seem to realize that beauty is a liability. Roses Only. Marianne Moore. LiTM

You do not want for words. Wantword. Charles Brasch. ATNZ

You do sunrise as well as anyone. For Ellen after the Publication of Her Stories. James Whitehead. BLA

You do that because I will. In the yard parts of us resemble. Paradise and Lunch. Jean Day. IAT

You, Doctor Martin. Anne Sexton. MoAmPo; NAAL-2

You don't/ know. Confession to Settle a Curse. Rosemarie Waldrop. TW

You don't have to believe this, I'm not asking you to. The Birth of Potchikoo. Louise Erdrich. *Fr.* Old Man Potchikoo. HATNAP

You don't have to give me your seat, lady. Don't, Don't. Huan Fu, *tr. by* Dominic Cheung. IFON

You don't have to tell how you live each day. It's in Your Face. *Unknown.* PoLF

You don't know I pretend my dumb. Plea to Those Who Matter. James Welch. AmPA

You don't know me but you must have seen me reading. A Letter on the Lake. Carl Dennis. BLA

You Don't Know What Love Is. Raymond Carver. BXAP

You don't put salt on anything. The Salt. May Swenson. *Fr.* Poet to Tiger. GLP

You dreamed all night of waking, of turning. A Story You Know. Mark Strand. KS

You dreamed it. From my ground. Ark Parting. Jay Macpherson. *Fr.* The Ark. NOBC

You Drive in a Circle. Ted Hughes. NYBP

You drop a pearl, 'twill keep its hue. *Malay Oral Tradition, tr. by* R. J. Wilkinson *and* R. O. Winstedt. WTO

You earthly Souls that court a wanton flame. La Belle Confidente. Thomas Stanley. JCP; MeLP; MePo; OBS

You empress of the stars, the heavens' worthy crown. Spring-Joy Praising God; Praise of the Sun. Catharina Regina von Greiffenberg, *tr. by* George C. Schoolfield. WPOW

You Englishmen of each degree. The Labouring Man. *Unknown.* OBET

You Enlarge on Near and Distant. Biancamaria Frabotta, *tr. fr. Italian by* Keala Jane Jewell. DMI

You enter a rat's eye. Cytogenetics Lab. Lucille Day. BWV

You enter the areas beyond veiled light. Sleep Watch. Lance Henson. VoR

You enter the garden and do not recognize it. Eden. Lev Mak, *tr. by* Daniel Weissbort. VWA

You entered my life in a casual way. To a Friend. Grace Stricker Dawson. BLPA

You erect pagodas. Sanetomo, *tr. fr. Japanese by* Burton Watson. *Fr.* Twenty-four Tanka. FCEI

You, Farrell O'Reilly, I feared as a boy. Farrell O'Reilly. Oliver St. John Gogarty. OxBTC

You feel a hardcore blankness. Losing It. Alice Fulton. BAP

You feel adequate to the demands of this position? You Will Be Hearing from Us Shortly. U. A. Fanthorpe. AIW

You feeling-hearted Christians all in country or in town. The Mail Boat, *Leinster. Unknown.* OxBSS

You Fight On. *Unknown.* AS

You find one drinking at the creek. Bees Awater. Robert Morgan. WeW

You find them in the darker woods. The Persistence of Nature in Our Lives. Andrew Hudgins. DiPo

You fish for people. Aged Fisherman. Witter Bynner. GoYe

You Fit into Me. Margaret Atwood. InPK; NoAM; NoP; TW

You Float. Rae Armantrout. IAT

You follow foreign ways. Two Sons. Laoiseach Mac an Bhaird. NOIV

You followed rodeo from Calgary to El Paso. For Jeff. Jon Bowerman. CowP

You fondled him. For the Parents of a Dead Child. Ryokan, *tr. by* Burton Watson. FCEI

You fool yourself and live a crazy day. Voice of a Dissipated Woman inside a Tomb. Sor Violante do Céu, *tr. by* Willis Barnstone. BoWoP

You foolish men, who accuse. Arguing That There Are Inconsistencies between Men's Tastes and Their Censure When They Accuse Women. Sister Juana Inés de la Cruz, *tr. by* Muriel Kittel. DMH

You, for whom I have longed standing across the River of Heaven. Okura. *Fr.* Manyo Shu. FCEI

You Frenchmen, don't boast of your fighting. The Tars of the *Blanche. Unknown.* OxBSS

You Gallants all, that love good Wine. A Ballad To the Tune of Bateman. Sir Charles Sedley. CoMu

You gathered incredible strength. To My Father. Blaga Dmitrova, *tr. by* J. Bossolova *and* Guillevic *into French;* Joanna Bake *from French to English.* OV

You gave me roses, love, last night. The Mystery. Lilian Whiting. AA

You gaze at me teasingly through the window. Praxilla, *tr. by* Willis Barnstone. BoWoP

You generals all and champions bold. The Duke of Marlborough. *Unknown.* OBET

You, Genoese Mariner. W. S. Merwin. GOA

You gentlemen of England fair. England's Great Loss by a Storm of Wind. *Unknown.* OxBSS

You gentlemen of England far and near. The Wind Sou'west. *Unknown.* AmFP

You gentlemen of England who live at home at ease. The Bay of Biscay. *Unknown.* AmFP

You get into the tub holding *The Naked Ape.* The Dream. May Swenson. *Fr.* Poet to Tiger. GLP

You girls whose talk is all of pop. Tracy & Co. Hugo Williams. *Fr.* Calling Your Name in the Zoo. NPo

You give your cheeks a rosy stain. Artificial Beauty. Lucianus, *tr. by* William Cowper. AWP

You gnaw at your silence. Requiem For The Sumpul. Mercedes Durand, *tr. by* Tina Alvarez Robles. Vol

You go at night into immensity. Immensity. Mabel Esther Allan. CN

You go somewhere in your sleep. Nocturnal Journey. Ory Bernstein, *tr. by* Warren Bargad *and* Stanley F. Chyet. IP

You go to your church, and I'll go to mine. Your Church and Mine. Phillips H. Lord. BLPA

You gods that have the power. Puerperium. Edmund Waller. JCP

You gods! to fold the charmer in my arms. The Rapture. Henry Baker. NOEC

You good folks of Nottingham I would have you draw near. The Red Wig. *Unknown.* CoMu

You Got to Cross It foh Yohself. *Unknown.* AS

You Gotta Have Your Tips on Fire. Víctor Hernández Cruz. InW

You grow up with music. The Second Violinist's Son. Debora Greger. KS

You Growing. Milton Acorn. NOBC

You guys/ like spring. See You Soon. Tomioka Taeko, *tr. by* Hiroaki Sato. FCEI

You had better tell. *Unknown. Fr.* Manyo Shu. Ma

You had expected more. Now that I leave. The Departure. Robert Pack. NePoEA

You had the legs of a pregnant mare. Love Song. Elio Pagliarani, *tr. by* Lawrence R. Smith. NItP

You Had to Know Her. William Hathaway. NAmP

You had two girls—Baptiste. At the Cedars. Duncan Campbell Scott. CaP; NOBC

You happen to get well. Elegy and Kaddish. David Rosenmann-Taub, *tr. by* Charles Guenther. VWA

You Hated Spain. Ted Hughes. OBTV

You have a taste of tempest on your lips—But where did you wander. Marina of the Rocks. Odysseus Elytis, *tr. by* Edmund Keeley *and* Philip Sherrard. VMG

You have already put too much in my hands. On the Way. Jeannie Ebner, *tr. by* Beth Bjorklund. CoAuP

You have anti-freeze in the car, yes. Christmas Card. Ted Hughes. OBCP

You have been driving for hours. Looking for a Rest Area. Stephen Dunn. AmPA; AnAn

You have been good to me, I give you this. Idolatry. Arna Bontemps. AmNP; PoNe

You have been my love for so many years. René Char, *tr. by* Michael Hamburger. RHTwFP

You have been my treasure, Rose Pilgrim. Elect. Mary Ursula Bethell. PeNZ

You have beheld a smiling Rose [*or* rose]. The Lilly in a Christal. Robert Herrick. NAEL-1; NoP; PoEL-3; SeCePo; SeCP (Lily in a Crystal, The.) NAEL-1; NoP; SeCePo

You have brought pearly beads. Pearly Beads. *Gond Oral Tradition, tr. by* V. Elwin *and* S. Hivale. WTO

You have called at the gate of the True Vehicle. Saying Good-bye to a Singing Girl. Mo Shih-lung, *tr. by* Jonathan Chaves. CoBLCP

You have coats and robes. You Will Die. *Unknown, tr. fr. Chinese by* H. A. Giles. *Fr.* Shi King. AWP

You have come your way, I have come my way. Fronleichnam. D. H. Lawrence. GBL

You have consum'd my language, and my pen. Ovid, *tr. fr. Latin by* Henry Vaughan. *Fr.* De Ponto, Elegy III, 7. OBVE

You have edited a thousand pages of palm-leaf manuscripts. To the Monk Wu-hsia. Mo Shih-lung, *tr. by* Jonathan Chaves. CoBLCP

You have enslaved me with your lovely body. The Apple. Judah Halevi, *tr. by* Robert Mezey. UnAS

You have granted me my full share of days. From the Crag. Mani Leib, *tr. by* David G. Roskies *and* Hillel Schwartz. VWA

You have heaped my hands with rubies. Odysseus' Song to Calypso. Peter Kane Dufault. ErPo

You have heard, I suppose, of the man in the moon. The Coolie Chinee. Septimus Winner. OBAL

You have just come in the door. The Confession. Peter Cooley. AmPA

You have many great sons and daughters, Lord. Song of the Plain. Anna Hajnal, *tr. by* William Jay Smith. MHuP

You have netted this dawn. The Archaeology of Love. Richard Murphy. EnLoPo

You have no heart. Emperor Go-Shirakawa, *tr. fr. Japanese by* Hiroaki Sato. *Fr.* Ryojin Hisho. FCEI ("Oh, my man is so unfeeling.") PeBJV, *tr. by* Geoffrey Bownas *and* Anthony Thwaite.

You have not conquered me—it is the surge. Infidelity. Louis Untermeyer. TrJP

"You have not considered the rose garden." Stavrogin's Return. János Pilinszky, *tr. fr. Hungarian by* Jascha Kessler. *Fr.* Three Poems. FOC

You have not left me usurer's black blood. Lines to My Father. Leslie Daiken. NeIP

You have only to wait, they will find you. Messengers. Louise Glück. AnAn; HCAP

You have put your two hands upon me, and your mouth. Betrothed. Louise Bogan. LLLT

You have red toenails, chestnut. Leda and Her Swan. Olga Broumas. PeHV

You have returned. You have returned, my joy. Edward James. *Fr.* Carmina Amico. PeHV

You have spoken your holy command over the city. Inanna and the City of Uruk. Enheduanna, *tr. by* Aliki *and* Willis Barnstone. BoWoP

You have taken back the promise. Fidelis. Adelaide Anne Procter. BLPA; FaBoBe

You have taken me away from all joy. Christine Lavant, *tr. by* Beth Bjorklund. CoAuP

You Have Taken My Language Away. Heidi Pataki, *tr. fr. German by* Beth Bjorklund. CoAuP

You have the ingredients on hand. Recipe for an Ocean in the Absence of the Sea. Richard Howard. TAP

You Have the Lovers. Leonard Cohen. NOBC

You have to be quick to stamp on your own shadow. The Shadowless Man. Gordon Challis. ATNZ

You have to inhabit poetry. Making Poetry. Anne Stevenson. DiPo

You Have What I Look For. Jaime Sabines, *tr. fr. Spanish by* W. S. Merwin. LLLT

You have withdrawn. Absence. Elizabeth Knies. GOYP

You have your hat and coat on and she says she will be right down. The Evening Out. Ogden Nash. MoAmPo

You have your language too. The Wellfleet Whale. Stanley Kunitz. CAPP; DiPo; NoAM

You have your shadow. Your Shadow. Mark Strand. *Fr.* Elegy for My Father. Prf

You have your water and your grain. My Little Birds. *Unknown, tr. by* Henrietta Siksek-Su'ad. FaPON

You hear my step. To His Children in Darkness. James Dickey. DiL

You Heard Him Say Lonely, Now. Ishihara Yoshiro, *tr. fr. Japanese by* Hiroaki Sato. FCEI

You heartless man. Tameko, *tr. by* Steven D. Carter. WFTW

You held my lotus blossom. To the Tune "Soaring Clouds." Huang O, *tr. by* Kenneth Rexroth *and* Ling Chung. BoWoP; PBWP; WPOW

You Hide ("You hide in the ostrich egg"). Edith Bruck, *tr. fr. Italian by* Ruth Feldman *and* Brian Swann. BoWoP

You hitched a thousand miles. August on Sourdough, a Visit from Dick Brewer. Gary Snyder. SOTW

You hold me now completely in your hands. The Woman Poet. Gertrud Kolmar, *tr. by* Henry A. Smith. DMG; VWA

You hold the bat at eye-level. Sacrifice Bunt. Lucky Jacobs. ASP

You hollow-cheeked son. Baboon 2. *Unknown.* PeSA

You hook it, but it's no fun. Kyosui, *tr. by* Sato. FCEI

You, husband, lying next to/ me. Prowling the Ridge. Judith Minty. GeTw

You husbandmen and ploughmen, of every degree. The Little Farm; or, The Weary Ploughman. *Unknown.* CoMu

You, I. Tom Clark. EAS

You I give no name to/ The mysterious things within you/ are an untrodden bower. Ahmad al-Mushari al-Udwani, *tr. fr. Arabic by* Hilary Kilpatrick *and* Charles Doria. *Fr.* Signs, III. MAP

You I give no name to/ The mysterious things within you/ are fragrance, light and melody. Ahmad al-Mushari al-Udwani, *tr. fr. Arabic by* Hilary Kilpatrick *and* Charles Doria. *Fr.* Signs, IV. MAP

You, I presume, could adroitly and gingerly. How the Women Will Stop War. Aristophanes, *tr. fr. Greek by* B. B. Rogers. *Fr.* Lysistrata. WaaP

You in Anger. James Reeves. OxBTC

You inquire gracefully of a man sick at heart. Separation from the Torah. Solomon Ibn Gabirol, *tr. by* David Goldstein. TOF

You inquire into meaning and truth. Meaning and Truth. Stefan Themerson. NPo

You intimidated me. I was thrown into hell without a trial. Denouement. Ruth Stone. BoWoP

You invaded my country by accident. Ways of Conquest. Denise Levertov. CAPP

You invite me to a war party. War Party. Eddy Grant. PBCV

You (IV). Tom Clark. EAS

You joked, and now are silent; down the years. After Alamein. Prudence Macdonald. CN

You judge a woman. To Some Supposed Brothers. Essex Hemphill. GLP

You judge severely moral values, Fehme. For Women. Louise Aston, *tr. by* Susan L. Cocalis. DMG

You Jump First. Pedro Juan Pietri. InW

You just keep to your tunes. To a Korean Percussion Ensemble. Koh Chang-soo, *tr. by the author.* ACKP

You keep eating and raising a family. A Suite for Marriage. David Ignatow. NNaP

You keep me waiting in a truck. Twenty-Year Marriage. Ai. BoWoP; MAYP; NoAM

You keep our love hidden. Love Story. Adrian Henri. UnAS

You keep silent. On the threshold. The Rain in the Pine Grove. Gabriele D'Annunzio, *tr. by* William Giuliano. PFI

You kin talk about yer anthems. The Ol'Tunes. Paul Laurence Dunbar. AnAmPo

You kiss me like a sister. Pauline de Simiane, *tr. by* Dorothy Backer. DMF

You Kissed Me. Josephine Slocum Hunt. BLPA; FaBoBe; FPL

You knew I was coming for you, little one. Windigo. Louise Erdrich. NoAM

You knew the odds on failure from the start. Archaeology. Katha Pollitt. MAYP

You knew what you did when you laughed. A Soap Bubble: 3. Hans Warren, *tr. by* James S. Holmes. DuIn

You knew,—who knew not Astrophil? On Sir Philip Sidney. Matthew Royden. *Fr.* An Elegy, or Friend's Passion for His Astrophil [*or* Astrophel]. EiL

You know/ I know. Alaskan Drinking Song. Dave Morice. EOEF

You Know. Jean Garrigue. NYBP; UnPo

You know, dear, that this vicious world. Mrs. Myrick's Lecture. Mary E. Tucker. CBWP-1

You know her hustle. Asking for Ruthie. Judy Grahn. ER; NMM

You know how I am at certain times. Letter in the Present and Present Perfect. Daria Menicanti, *tr. by* Muriel Kittel. DMI

You know how I long. Prince Munenaga, *tr. by* Steven D. Carter. WFTW

You know I said to Mark that I'm furious at you. The Quarrel. Diane DiPrima. NMM

You know it's all bullshit. Coda: Revising History. Paul Mariani. MAYP

You know it's April by the falling-off. B Negative. X. J. Kennedy. NePoEA-2

You know, Joe, it's a funny thing. Ultimate Equality. Ray Durem. PoNe

"You know, my friends, with what a brave carouse." The Bride. Ambrose Bierce. AA

You know not how deep was the love your eyes did kindle. Ibn al-Abbar, *tr. by* A. R. Nykl. PeHV

You know nothing of your past. You have dreamed it. L'étrangère. O. V. de L. Milosz, *tr. by* John Peck. RHTwFP

You know, or you don't know, that great Bacon saith. Byron. *Fr.* Don Juan, XIV. NOBL

"You know Orion always comes up sideways." The Star-Splitter. Robert Frost. ImOP

You know, she said, they made you. A Dress of Fire. Dahlia Ravikovich, *tr. by* Chana Bloch. VWA

You know, she said, they sewed you a dress of fire. The Dress. Dahlia Ravikovich, *tr. by* Bernhard Frank. MHeP

You know, sweetheart. A Letter. Rachel Korn, *tr. by* Ruth Whitman. VWA

You know that day at Peach Tree Creek. Logan at Peach Tree Creek. Hamlin Garland. PAH

You know that he is going to die. The Red Dog. Laura Jensen. LCAP

You know that I love you, sweetheart, but every time I come around. *Unknown, tr. by* Kiowa Indian. *Fr.* "49" Songs. STP

You know the answer to the last surmise. Sonnet for My Son. Melanie Gordon Barber. GoYe

You know the day, the month, even the year. Annunciation. Giuseppe Gioacchino Belli, *tr. by* Anthony Burgess. PFI

You know, the feeling that you should have. It's Tough Being American. Mark Irwin. SoTCo

You know the fellow. A Public Nuisance. Reginald Arkell. SD

You know the old woman. The Old Woman. Beatrix Potter. GoJo; NTCP; PDV; RAR

You know the place: then. Sappho, *tr. by* Mary Barnard. PBWP

You know the risks when you work. Risks. Malcolm Glass. SoTCo

You know there goes a tale. The Modern Jonas. *Unknown.* PAH

You know there is not much. To a Friend Concerning Several Ladies. William Carlos Williams. VGW

You know there were others before you. Friends. Mary Goose. STE

You know this art well, but may I venture a thought.   I Saw a Professional Juggler by the Roadside and Presented Him with This Poem.   Kung Tzu-chen, *tr. fr. Chinese* by Shirleen S. Wong.   *Fr.* Miscellaneous Poems of the Year *Chi-hai*, XIX.   WFTU

You know this: I must lose you again and cannot.   Eugenio Montale, *tr. fr. Italian*.   *Fr.* The Motets, I.   Dana Gioia

You know those rose sherbets.   You Know.   Jean Garrigue.   NYBP; UnPo

You know those windless summer evenings, swollen to stasis.   Cigales.   Richard Wilbur.   NePoEA; NOBA

You know w'at for ees school keep out.   Leetla Giorgio Washeenton.   T. A. Daly.   FaPON

You know we French stormed [*or* storm'd] Ratisbon.   Incident of the French Camp.   Robert Browning.   BeLS; FaPoR; GN; OBWP; TrGrPo

You know we must be lonely, you and I.   Souls.   Paul Wertheimer, *tr.* by Jethro Bithell.   TrJP

You know what it is to be born alone.   Baby Tortoise.   D. H. Lawrence.   CMoP

You ladies all that are in fashion.   A New Song called The Curling of the Hair.   *Unknown*.   CoMu

You landsmen and you seamen bold.   The Loss of the *Due Dispatch*.   *Unknown*.   AmFP

You Laughed and Laughed and Laughed.   Gabriel Okara.   PBA

You lay a wreath on murdered Lincoln's bier.   Abraham Lincoln.   Tom Taylor.   PAH

You lay down under a blasting light.   Without Mercy.   László Nagy, *tr.* by Tony Connor.   MHuP

You lay in wait.   Sappho, *tr.* by Willis Barnstone.   BoWoP

You leaned in your wooden chair.   The Gravestone.   Abd al-Karim Kassid, *tr.* by Lena Jayyusi *and* Anthony Thwaite.   MAP

You leaned your body in the doorway.   Talkers in a Dream Doorway.   Judy Grahn.   ER; GLP

You leaped from the white horses.   The Distaff.   Erinna, *tr.* by Marylin Arthur.   WPOW

You learned Lear's *Nonsense Rhymes* by heart, not rote.   A Plea to Boys and Girls.   Robert Graves.   GTBS-P; NAEL-2

You Learned the Stars.   Michael Jackson.   UAS

You leave dead friends in.   Will They Cry When You're Gone, You Bet.   Imamu Amiri Baraka.   NAAL-2

You leave the little temple town.   Between Jejuri and the Railway Station.   Arun Kolatkar.   UAS

You led me to the hills.   To Alan.   Douglas Fraser.   PoSH

You left.   Pearl.   Barbara Brinson Curiel.   ER

You left at morning, my heart at evening in pieces.   Mourning for My Teacher Hokuju.   Buson, *tr.* by Hiroaki Sato.   FCEI

You left, the mist lingered by the hedge.   Lady Izumi, *tr. fr. Japanese* by Hiroaki Sato.   *Fr.* Fifty-one Tanka.   FCEI

You, letters scratched on walls.   Epitaphs.   Abraham Sutskever, *tr.* by Neal Kozodoy.   PeBMYV

You, Letting the Trees Stand as My Betrayer.   Diane Wakoski.   MoP

You lie down in terror of the darkness.   Seek Out Another Heart.   Mikha'il Nu aima, *tr.* by Sargon Boulus *and* Thomas G. Ezzy.   MAP

You lie in my arms.   Apocrypha.   Stanley Moss.   VWA

You lie now in many coffins.   For Malcolm: After Mecca.   Gerald William Barrax.   CNA; PoBA

You lie, snail-like, on your stomach.   Depression.   Wendy Cope.   FaBoWP

You like it under the trees in autumn.   The Motive for Metaphor.   Wallace Stevens.   MoAB; MoAmPo

You like not that French novel? Tell me why.   George Meredith.   *Fr.* Modern Love, XXV.   NOBVV

You like those images of snow that ask emotion.   Snow.   Hubert Witheford.   ATNZ

You like to have contests of size with people.   The Contest Snake.   Cheng Hsieh, *tr.* by Jonathan Chaves.   CoBLCP

You lit a firebrand.   The Floating Candles.   Sydney Lea.   MAYP; SM

You little, eager, peeping thing.   The Awakening.   Angela Morgan.   OHIP

You little know the heart that you advise.   An Answer to a Lady Advising Me to Retirement.   Lady Mary Wortley Montagu.   TEP

You little stars that live in skies.   Fulke Greville.   *Fr.* Caelica, IV.   EIL; NoP

(His Lady's Eyes.)   OBSC

You live here because there's no other place.   So Long Solon.   Jack Myers.   AmPA

You Live There; I Live Here.   Harold Monro.   *Fr.* Strange Meetings.   Mes

You live where the sounds of trucks.   Tapwater.   Laura Jensen.   LCAP

You lived and moved among the best society.   W. H. Auden.   *Fr.* Letter to Lord Byron.   OBSV

You look at me.   A Drop of Dew.   Shmuel Halkin, *tr.* by Jacob Sonntag.   TrJP

You look at me, a hut or cage contains.   Hilda Doolittle ("H. D.").   *Fr.* Sagesse.   NOCV

You look out yellowing leaves of.   Funeral March for a Papagallo.   Michael Malinowitz.   BAP

You Looked the Monster in the Eye.   Hannu Mäkelä, *tr. fr. Finnish by* Aili Jarvenpa.   SOP

You, love, and I.   Counting the Beats.   Robert Graves.   ELP; GBL; GTBS-P; HAP; OxBTC; WeW

You love? That's high as you shall go.   The Attainment.   Coventry Patmore.   *Fr.* The Angel in the House, I, iii.   FaBoEE

You love the roses—so do I. I wish.   Roses.   George Eliot.   BoTP

You love us when we're heroes, home on leave.   Glory of Women.   Siegfried Sassoon.   MMA; NAEL-2; OBWP

You love us yet? Then really, what a One!   Good Friday.   John Frederick Nims.   TW

You loved me for a little.   Midsummer.   Sydney King Russell.   BLPA; FaBoBe

You loved me not at all, but let it go.   Edna St. Vincent Millay.   VGW

You Lovely People.   Virginia Cerenio.   BrSi

You made healing as you wanted us to make bread and poems.   Mendings.   Muriel Rukeyser.   SaC

You Made It Rain.   Ruby C. Saunders.   BlSi

You made me a cup, inscrutable potter.   Destiny.   Angela Figueroa-Aymerich, *tr.* by Kate Flores.   DMH

You madly kiss my lips—I seem to see.   The Pit.   Suad al-Mubarak al-Sabah, *tr.* by May Jayyusi *and* John Heath-Stubbs.   MAP

You make us want to stay alive, Suzanne.   Suzanne.   John Logan.   CAPP

You make yourself new again.   The Marsh.   Beatrice Hawley.   PPR

You males, praised the whole world through.   In Praise of the Male Sex, As Seen by Certain Females.   Christiana Mariana von Ziegler, *tr.* by Susan L. Cocalis *and* Gerlinde Geiger.   DMG

You, man, are the snake in.   Of/To Man.   Alma Villanueva.   CCP

You marched off southward with the fire of twenty.   Danny.   Malcolm Cowley.   PoA

You married men, whom Fate hath assign'd.   The Merry Cuckold.   *Unknown*.   CoMu

You Masks of the Masquerade.   Gustave Kahn, *tr. fr. French by* Jethro Bithell.   TrJP

You, master of delays.   Killing No Murder.   Sylvia Townsend Warner.   MoBrPo

You may be right, divinity.   Francis Sullivan.   CRP

You may brag about your breakfast foods you eat at break of day.   Sausage.   Edgar A. Guest.   OBAL

You may call, you may call.   The Bad Kittens.   Elizabeth J. Coatsworth.   FaPON; OBCA

You may drink to your leman in gold.   Wine and Dew.   Richard Henry Stoddard.   AA

You may get through the world, but 'twill be very slow.   People Will Talk.   Samuel Dodge.   WBLP

You may have troubles manifold.   A Mother's Joy.   Ruth Fortney Maxwell.   PWR

You may lift me up in your arms, lad, and turn my face to the sun.   The Famous Ballad of the Jubilee Cup.   Sir Arthur Quiller-Couch.   NA

You may not believe it, for hardly could I.   The Pumpkin.   Robert Graves.   PDV; RHPC; WSC

You may speak of a grave in a distant land.   A Reverie.   Mary Weston Fordham.   CBWP-2

You may talk about me just as much as you please.   Hold the Wind.   *Unknown*.   GBP; OBD

You may talk o' gin and [*or* an'] beer.   Gunga Din.   Kipling.   BrPo; EBVV; FaFP; FPL; LiTB; MoBrPo; OBTV; OnMSP

You may talk of Columbus's sailing.   "Are Ye Right There, Michael?" (A Lay of the Wild West Clare.)   William Percy French.   WTO

You may tempt the upper classes.   Edgar Smith.   *Fr.* Heaven Will Protect the Working-Girl.   FiBHP

You may write me down in history.   Still I Rise.   Maya Angelou.   BlSi

You mean Josje with the tiny eyes?   Verse as of 7 June 1951.   Jan Hanlo, *tr.* by James S. Holmes.   DuIn

You meaner beauties of the night.   On [*or* To] His Mistress, the Queen of Bohemia.   Sir Henry Wotton.   EIL; ELP; EnLoPo; GBL; HAP; JCP; MeLP; MePo; NoP; OBS; SeCP; TrGrPo

(Elizabeth of Bohemia.)   BoLoP; FaBoCh; GTBS; GTBS-P; NOBE; OBEV

You meet your friend, your face.   Selected Epigrams.   Mary Magdalene Kassia, *tr.* by Patrick Diehl.   PBWP

You men who hold forth.   Reasonings of a Woman Poet.   *Unknown, tr.* by Robert L. Smith *and* Judith Candullo.   DMH

You merchant men of Billingsgate, I wonder how you can thrive. Cordial Advice. *Unknown*. OxBSS

You met me on this lonely hill. Voice of Stone. Fahmida Riaz, *tr. by* Mahmood Jamal. PBMUP

You might ask. Battle Scene. Aricil Kilar, *tr. by* A. K. Ramanujan. PLW

You might at one time, when you were young perhaps. K. O. Arvidson. *Fr.* The Flame Tree. ATNZ

You might call this. Old Men on the Couthouse Lawn, Murray, Kentucky. James Galvin. AnAn

You might come here Sunday on a whim. Degrees of Gray in Philipsburg. Richard Hugo. CAPP; CoAP; NAAL-2; NoAM; NoP

You might suppose it easy. The Boatman. Jay Macpherson. MoCV; OBCV

You, Morningtide Star, now are steady-eyed, over the east. Lying Awake. Thomas Hardy. FaBoRV

You move/ like the sound of pipes. You. Barbara Burford. DT

You Move Forward. Thomas Sessler, *tr. fr. German by* Herbert Kuhner. VWA

You must agree that Rubens was a fool. To English Connoisseurs. Blake. OxBoLi

You must be sad; for though it is to Heaven. To Two Bereaved. Thomas Ashe. NOBVV

You must do as they do at Hoo. Hoo, Suffolk. *Unknown*. GBP

You Must Hand Over. József Tornai, *tr. fr. Hungarian by* William Jay Smith. MHuP

You Must Have Been a Sensational Baby. Harold Norse. GLP

You must have been still sleeping, your wife there. The Sacred Hearth. David Gascoyne. FaBoTw

You must learn how to peel, man. Orange. Barbara Ferland. PVCV

You must leave here. The signs say so. Mene Mene. Ory Bernstein, *tr. by* Warren Bargad *and* Stanley F. Chyet. IP

You must live through the time when everything hurts. The Double Shame. Stephen Spender. LiTB; LiTM

You must move the speckled stone, the dead-tired stone. Stonetalk. Jacques Hamelink, *tr. by* Ria Leigh-Loohuizen. DuIn

You Must Never Bath in an Irish Stew. Spike Milligan. RHPC

You must not wonder, though you think it strange. For That He Looked Not upon Her. George Gascoigne. EIL; NoP

You must remain very much alone. Presences. Zoé Karélli, *tr. by* Kimon Friar. PBWP

You must remember structures beyond cotton plains. If Blood Is Black Then Spirit Neglects My Unborn Son. Conrad Kent Rivers. PoBA

You must show yourself to catch. Lyn Hejinian. IAT

You must stand erect but at your ease, a posture. The Singing Lesson. David Wagoner. NoAM

You mustn't laugh at my tall tower. Yüan Mei, *tr. fr. Chinese by* Anthony C. Yu. *Fr.* Life at the Sui Garden, X. WFTU

You, my branch, my lopped limb! Tree to Flute. Anna Hajnal, *tr. by* Jascha Kessler. FOC; VWA

You, my statue, why do you torment me? The Statue. Orkhan Muyassar, *tr. by* Lena Jayyusi *and* Samuel Hazo. MAP

You need lightning. To the Man Who Sidled Up to Me and Asked: "How Long You In Fer, Buddy?" Etheridge Knight. NeAC

You need not kill the calf for me, a bowl of soup will do. The Prodigal Son. Christine Busta, *tr. by* Beth Bjorklund. CoAuP

You need not see what someone is doing. Sext. W. H. Auden. *Fr.* Horae Canonicae. SaC

You need the untranslatable ice to watch. Appendix to the Anniad. Gwendolyn Brooks. BlSi

"You never attained to Him." "If to attain." Via, Veritas, et Vita. Alice Meynell. WGRP

You Never Can Tell. Ella Wheeler Wilcox. BLPA; BLPL

You never could tell what my deaf Uncle Arthur heard. And Don't Be Deaf to the Singing Beyond. Carter Revard. HATNAP

You never know who has your memory. You Gotta Have Your Tips on Fire. Víctor Hernández Cruz. InW

You never know with a doorbell. Doorbells. Rachel Lyman Field. FaPON

You never left Bologna. With Giorgio Morandi in Bologna. Wieland Schmied, *tr. by* Beth Bjorklund. CoAuP

You never let me have you. Once or Twice. John Skoyles. NAmP

You never married, never took a job—you went completely astray! Written at the End of Master Ho-ching's Collected Works. Chin Nung, *tr. by* Jonathan Chaves. CoBLCP

You never touch. Yosano Akiko, *tr. fr. Japanese by* Geoffrey Bownas *and* Anthony Thwaite. BoWoP; PBWP; PeBJV

You nip at the dried burrs. Stray Dog. Sándor Weöres, *tr. by* Jascha Kessler. FOC

You, no doubt, have heard the story told of Charleston by the sea? The Crum Appointment. Lizelia Augusta Jenkins Moorer. CBWP-3

You noble Diggers all, stand up now, stand up now. The Digger's Song. Gerrard Winstanley. FaBoPV

You Northern Girl. Charles G. Ballard. NOVW

You [*or* You're] not alone when you are still alone. Michael Drayton. *Fr.* Idea, XI. PoEL-2; TrGrPo

You now solicit a few enemy thrusts. D. B. Wyndham Lewis. *Fr.* If So the Man You Are. OBSV

You now, you in the next century, and the next. Poem Touching the Gestapo. William Heyen. GeTw

You nurtured grief until that leap. Waiting for Robinson. Roberta Hill Whiteman. HATNAP

You, O Tsui-Xgoa. Hymn to Tsui-Xgoa. *Unknown*. PeSA

You often went to breathe a timeless air. The Scholar. Frances Cornford. BrRo

You on the Tower. Thomas Hardy. SaC

You, once a belle in Shreveport. Snapshots of a Daughter-in-Law. Adrienne Rich. FaBoWP; HCAP; NAAL-2; NIP; NMM; NoAM; NoP

You only come in the tormenting. Suicide. Robert Lowell. PoE

You Only Know. Mani Leib, *tr. fr. Yiddish by* John Hollander. PeBMYV

You Opened a Door. Marianna Fiore, *tr. fr. Italian by* Muriel Kittel. DMI

You opened up like a plum. We Say This Prayer. József Tornai, *tr. by* William Jay Smith. MHuP

You or I? Ilyas Abu Shabaku, *tr. fr. Arabic by* Adnan Haydar *and* Michael Beard. MAP

You, orphan child. *Unknown, tr. by* Geoffrey Bownas *and* Anthony Thwaite. PeBJV

You ought to see my blue-eyed Sally. Stay All Night, Stay a Little Longer. *Unknown*. AmFP

You over there, young man with the guide book red-bound. Home Sweet Home with Variations. H. C. Bunner. BXAP; CenHV; OBAL

You Owe Them Everything. John Allman. SaC

You passed as through snow; and through snow you passed. A Red and Blue Song. Amir Gilboa, *tr. by* Bernhard Frank. MHeP

You philosophers of the old world. Bengal. "Sahir Ludhianvi," *tr. by* Mahmood Jamal. PBMUP

"You picked a white chrysanthemum and smiled." Yosano Akiko, *tr. fr. Japanese by* Hiroaki Sato. *Fr.* Thirty-nine Tanka. FCEI

You plant like Paul, you water like Apollos. The Rev. Nicholas Noyes to the Rev. Cotton Mather. Nicholas Noyes. SCAP

You play the flute. Longing. *Gond Oral Tradition, tr. by* V. Elwin *and* S. Hivale. WTO

You plummeting shards of the darkness. To the Swallows of Viterbo. Gibbons Ruark. SM

You possess the sturdy elegance of a cannon. For Natalya Correia. Irving Layton. NeAC

You praise the firm restraint with which they write. On Some South African Novelists. Roy Campbell. FaBoCo; FaBoEE; GTBS-P; InPK; MoBrPo; NOBL; OxBTC

You prayer—, you blasphemy, you. Plashes the Fountain. Paul Celan, *tr. by* Michael Hamburger. OBVE

You pried the oval jade. Lapis. Shawn Wong. BrSi

You probably could put their names to them. "As When Emotion Too Far Exceeds Its Cause." Gloria C. Oden. AmNP

You promise heavens free from strife. Mimnermus in Church. William Johnson Cory. NOBE; OBEV

You, proud curve-lipped youth, with brown sensitive face. Through the Long Night. Edward Carpenter. *Fr.* Towards Democracy. PeHV

You, pushed-in window in terribly beautiful countries! Hertha Kräftner, *tr. fr. German by* Beth Bjorklund. *Fr.* Litanies. CoAuP

You put me on Hold. Goodbye Forever. Lillian Morrison. SoTCo

You put your hand on my shoulder. Abdelfatteh. E. A. Lacey. PeHV

You rambling boys of Liverpool I'll have you to beware. The Banks of Newfoundland ("You rambling boys of Liverpool I'll have you to beware"). *Unknown*. OxBSS

You read the New York Times. Alfred Corning Clark. Robert Lowell. RB

You, reading over my shoulder, peering beneath. The Reader over My Shoulder. Robert Graves. NAEL-2

You recline that magnificent pair of buttocks. To Kyris. Strato, *tr. by* Teddy Hogge. PeHV

You recommend that the motive, in Chapter 8, should be changed. Yes, the Agency Can Handle That. Kenneth Fearing. WeW

You refuse to own. Margaret Atwood. NeAC

You reisolate tip. Bruce Andrews. IAT

You remember the big Gaston, for whom everyone predicted a bad end? Monsieur Gaston. A. M. Klein. MoCV

You Remember the Elk. Mirkka Rekola, *tr. fr. Finnish by* Aili Jarvenpa. SOP

You Too? Me Too—Why Not? Soda Pop. Robert Hollander. NIP

You took me to see your friend, a youngish man. Summer Nights. Daniel Halpern. NAmP

You took the world and embraced. Pedro. Luis Omar Salinas. FF

You tossed a blanket from the bed. T. S. Eliot. *Fr.* Preludes (I-IV). HelP; LiTA; NoP; OBMV; PPP; SeCePo; SOTW; TwCP; UnPo; VGW; WeW

You touched my sleeve, and quickly spoke my name. At Swindon. Reginald Brett. PeHV

You tug at words. Modern Kabbalist. Marcia Falk. VWA

You understand it? How they returned from Culloden. Culloden and After. Iain Crichton Smith. OxBS

You Understand the Requirements. Lyn Lifshin. NeAC

You unseen lightning flash, you darkly radiant light. On the Ineffable Inspiration of the Holy Spirit. Catharina Regina von Greiffenberg, *tr. by* Michael Hamburger. PBWP

You use your mind. To Military Progress. Marianne Moore. AnAmPo

You used to ask me once what was wrong. In Memoriam I. Franco Fortini, *tr. by* Ruth Feldman. VWA

You Usually Come in the Morning. György Petri, *tr. fr. Hungarian by* William Jay Smith. MHuP

You vilify me, but I rise above grief. Lament after Her Husband Bishr's Murder. Al-Khirniq, *tr. by* Willis Barnstone. BoWoP

You virgins that did late despair. Piping Peace. James Shirley. *Fr.* The Imposture. ACP; NOBE
(Song: "You virgins that did late despair.") PoEL-2

You, Voyager, with exile-heart that yearns. Speak to the Sun. Dedie Huffman Wilson. GoYe

You waken slowly. In your dream you're straying. William Bell. NePoEA

You walk into a room of voices. Teaching Poetry. Cyn Zarco. BrSi

You walk on. A Door. W. S. Merwin. EAS

You walk on permafrost. Voronezh. "Anna Akhmatova," *tr. by* Tom Paulin. FaBoPV

You want a guarantee. Testament. Nizar Qabbani, *tr. by* Diana Der Hovanessian *and* Lena Jayyusi. MAP

You want clear spectacles: your eyes are dim. The Accusation of the Inward Man. Edward Taylor. LiTA

You want coins? Roman? Greek? Nice vase? Head of god, goddess. Ali Ben Shufti. Anthony Thwaite. OxBTC

You want distraction's collar and necktie. Goddess of Wisdom Whose Substance Is Desire. Anne Waldman. UL

You Want Me White. Alfonsina Storni, *tr. fr. Spanish by* Lynn C. Jacox. LPSS

You want my fingers spread. Iron Eyes. Terence Winch. UL

You want the summer lightning, throw the knives. Ingeborg Bachmann, *tr. fr. German by* Daniel Huws. BoWoP

You want to go back. Margaret Atwood. NeAC

You want to integrate me into your anonymity. Black Narcissus. Gerald William Barrax. PoBA

You want to make some honey? Bee. X. J. Kennedy. OBCA

You wanted the perfect setting. For Anna. Irving Layton. NeAC

You watch—it's clouded. Chora, *tr. by* Geoffrey Bownas *and* Anthony Thwaite. PeBJV

You watched out for him or. Travis, the Kid Was All Heart. Terry Stokes. AmPA

You wear the face. Izumi Shikibu, *tr. by* Willis Barnstone. BoWoP

You wear the morning like your dress. Hilaire Belloc. OBEV

You, weary of the waves rolling into autumn. Teika, *tr. fr. Japanese by* Hiroaki Sato. *Fr.* Eighty-four Tanka. FCEI

You, weeping wide at war, weep with me now. The Coward. Eve Merriam. TrJP

You well-compacted groves, whose light and shade. Sonnet Made upon the Groves near Merlou Castle. Herbert of Cherbury. JCP

You went downstairs. The Hair. May Swenson. *Fr.* Poet to Tiger. GLP

You went to fields madder-red. Princess Nukada. *Fr.* Manyo Shu. PeBJV

You went to the verge, you say, and came back safely. Conrad Aiken. *Fr.* Preludes for Memnon; or, Preludes to Attitude. FaBoMo; LiTA; TwCP

You were/ water to me. Praise Song for My Mother. Grace Nichols. WS

You were a girl of satin and gauze. The Wheel Revolves. Kenneth Rexroth. NoAM

You were a moral dandy, sir. The font. To Max Jacob. Rosanna Warren. DiPo

You were a pretty boy once, Archestratus, and. Philip of Thessalonica, *tr. by* Edith Morgan. PeHV

You were a sophist. Advice. Gwendolyn B. Bennett. BlSi; CDC

You were a tender girl, Sina. Sina. Alistair Campbell. ATNZ

You were amused to find you too could fear. Letter I. William Empson. LiTB

You were born; must die; were loved; must love. Stephen Spender. Son (Sonnet: "You were born; must die; were loved; must love.") MoAB; MoBrPo

You were born on the Esplanade des Invalides. On the Esplanade des Invalides. David Fisher. NPGG

You were brought up. Coming Up and Falling Down. Stephen Vincent. NeAC

You were forgiven. Dialogue of the Night of the Roses. Zuhur Dixon, *tr. by* Patricia Alanah Byrne *and* Salma Khadra Jayyusi. MAP

You Were Humming. Philippe Thoby-Marcelin, *tr. fr. French by* William Jay Smith. CT

You were never told, Mother, how old Illya was drunk. The Czar's Last Christmas Letter: A Barn in the Urals. Norman Dubie. NoAM

You were praised, my books. Salutation the Second. Ezra Pound. NOBA; OxBA

You were separated from me Hori. The Space Invaders Machine. Pita Sharples, *tr. by the author.* PeNZ

You were sitting at your desk and you heard a woman's voice. An Attempt. Adam Wazyk, *tr. by* Czeslaw Milosz. PwPP

You Were Still the Sun's There. Sandor Csoori, *tr. fr. Hungarian by* Jascha Kessler. FOC

You were tall and beautiful. First Love. Mary Dorcey. BrRo

You were the fence standing between our land and the descendants of Ali. Lament for a Dead Lover. Siraad Haad, *tr. by* B. W. Andrzejewski *and* I. M. Lewis. WTO

You were the morning star among the living. Aster ("You were the morning star among the living"). Plato, *tr. by* Peter Jay. PeHV

You Were Wearing. Kenneth Koch. AiP; CoAP; EAS; MoP; NiP; NNaP; NoP

You were with me and it wasn't flying, exactly. A Dream as Reported. Virginia Earle. GoYe

You were writing a long poem, yes. Residue of Song. Marvin Bell. AmPA

You were young—but that was scarcely to your credit. Gerald Gould. *Fr.* Monogamy. OxBTC

You weren't even a. To L. Julianne Perry. PoBA

"You! What d'you mean by this?" I rapped. Inspection. Wilfred Owen. WaP

You white hydrangeas. Teika, *tr. by* Steven D. Carter. WFTW

You "white oneness," I don't want to divide you. Seventh Answer. Erika Mitterer, *tr. by* Beth Bjorklund. CoAuP

You who/ fail. Femina. Daphne Marlatt. NOBC

You who accept the voices of the stars. Tonight. Ada Negri, *tr. by* Brenda Webster. OV

You who are constantly on my mind. Kanamura. *Fr.* Manyo Shu. Ma

You who are earth, and cannot rise. To the World; the Perfection of Love. William Habington. JCP

You who are great both in peace and war. Epistle to the Emperor Napoleon (1810). Constance-Marie de Salm-Dyck, *tr. by* Dorothy Backer. DMF

You who are so beautiful. The Sun Going Down upon Our Wrath. Denise Levertov. AIW

You who are still and white. Slain. T. W. H. Crosland. OBWP

You who ask where I find the courage. A Return to the Tree of Time. Vesna Parun, *tr. by* Vasa D. Mihailovich *and* Ronald Morgan. WPOW

You who can grant, or can refuse, the pow'r. A Sea-Chaplain's Petition to the Lieutenants in the Ward-Room, for the Use of the Quarter-Gallery. "J. T." NOEC

You who descend river by river. Giraffe. *Unknown.* PeSA

You who desired so much—in vain to ask. To Emily Dickinson. Hart Crane. CMoP; NIP; NoAM; NOBA; NoP; Son; TAP

You Who Dog My Footsteps. Leib Kwitko, *tr. fr. Yiddish by* Joseph Leftwich. TrJP

You who dread the cares and labors. The Last Landlord. Elizabeth Akers Allen. AA

You who dump the beer cans in the lake. Malediction. Barry Spacks. TW

You who give sustenance to your creatures, O God. Prayer for Rain. Sheikh Aquib Abdullahi Jama, *tr. by* B. W. Andrzejewski. WTO

You who go out on schedule. Two Variations. Denise Levertov. NaP

You who go through rice paddies in the rain. Traveler. Miyazawa Kenji, *tr. by* Hiroaki Sato. FCEI

You who have from far Cathay. Cathay. Paul-Jean Toulet, *tr. by* William Jay Smith. CT

You who have grown so intimate with stars. To an Aviator. Daniel Whitehead Hicky. RHPC

You who have spoken words in the earth. Reproach to Dead Poets. Archibald MacLeish. NAAL-2

You, who in Cupid's rolls inscribe your name. Ovid, *tr. fr. Latin by* Dryden. *Fr.* The Art of Love. FaBoUs

You, who in sultry weather. A Plea for a Plural. Rudolph Chambers Lehmann. CenHV

You who journey to Shiragi. *Unknown. Fr.* Manyo Shu. PeBJV

You who lead the column marching in step behind you. While Marching Around to Attract Shells. Guillaume Apollinaire, *tr. by* Michael Benedikt. POS

You who like a boulder stand. The Wildebeest. June Daly. FaPON

You who live secure. Shema. Primo Levi, *tr. by* Ruth Feldman *and* Brian Swann. VWA

You who make your escape from the tumult. Hyena. *Unknown.* PeSA

You Who Occupy Our Land. Manuela Margarido, *tr. fr. Portuguese by* Allan Francovich. WPOW

You who snore with your sleeping wife so near. Tristan Corbière, *tr. fr. French by* Christopher Pilling. *Fr.* Litany of Sleep. OBVE

You who softly wane into a shadow. The Unknown Warrior Speaks. Margery Smith. CN

You who were darkness warmed my flesh. Woman to Child. Judith Wright. PBWP; WPE

You who would sorrow even for a token. Reciprocity. Vassar Miller. IHMS; MT; NePoEA

You, Whoever You Are. Walt Whitman. AmFN

You whom I could not save. Czeslaw Milosz, *tr. by the author.* PwPP

You whom the kings saluted; who refused not. To the Unknown Warrior. G. K. Chesterton. MMA

You, whose ancestors in the mighty days. Yanagawa Seigan, *tr. by* Burton Watson. JLIC-2

You will ask how I came to be eavesdropping, in the first place. Confession Overheard in a Subway. Kenneth Fearing. LiTA; LiTM; WaP

You Will Be Hearing from Us Shortly. U. A. Fanthorpe. AIW

You will be obscured by a cloud of postures. Nadar. Richard Howard. AnAn

You will carry this suture. Trauma. Brad Leithauser. InPK

You will come, my bird, Bonita? Juanita. Joaquin Miller. AA

You will come with small words. Chopin Nocturne. Jacob Glatstein, *tr. by* Benjamin *and* Barbara Harshav *and* Kathryn Helle. AYP

You will come, your eyes full of night and of yesterday. Toward Lesbos. Renée Vivien, *tr. by* Sandia Belgrade. PeHV

You Will Die. *Unknown, tr. fr. Chinese by* H. A. Giles. *Fr.* Shi King. AWP

You will do he will do you will do. To My Children. Rosanna Guerrini, *tr. by* Muriel Kittel. DMI

You will find me drinking rum. The Logical Vegetarian. G. K. Chesterton. CenHV

You will have the road gate open, the front door ajar. In Memory of My Mother. Patrick Kavanagh. BIrV

You will know. Story from Bear Country. Leslie Silko. STE

You Will Know When You Get There. Allen Curnow. ATNZ; PeNZ

You will need. Truganinny. Wendy Rose. HATNAP

You will never be alone, you hear so deep. Assurance. William Stafford. CAPP

You will never forget the look on my face. No Need for Nuremberg. Erica Marx. CN

You will not travel. The Ultimate Distance. Fu'ad Rifqa, *tr. by* Sargon Boulus *and* Samuel Hazo. MAP

You will remember that the Twelfth was always dry. The Glorious Twelfth. Robert Greacen. NeIP

You will remember the kisses, real or imagined. Resurrection. Kenneth Fearing. CMoP; PoE

You Will See Far. Väinö Kirstinä, *tr. fr. Finnish by* Aili Jarvenpa. SOP

You will see him any day in Te Kuiti. The Gunfighter. Alistair Campbell. ATNZ

You Will See Your Lord a-Coming. *Unknown.* AH

You wished for a love-letter, Doctor. A Love-letter. Mary E. Tucker. CBWP-1

You with that creeping, twining thing can play. To a Fine Young Woman. William Wycherley. TW

You with yourself. Thanaton Melein. Alfred Gong, *tr. by* Beth Bjorklund. CoAuP

You withdrew. Saw You among Trees. Malka Heifetz Tussman, *tr. by* Kathryn Hellerstein. AYP

You wonder why Drab sells her love for gold? J. V. Cunningham. NePoAm

You work fast in the morning, ladies, as you plant the seedlings. *Unknown, tr. by* Hiroaki Sato. FCEI

You, worldwinged, hoverer. The Hoverer. Margit Szécsi, *tr. by* Jascha Kessler. FOC

You worry me whoever you are. Badman of the Guest Professor. Ishmael Reed. BPo

You Would Have Me Immaculate. Alfonsina Storni, *tr. fr. Spanish by* Kate Flores. DMH

You would have scoffed if we had told you yesterday. To a Child in Death. Charlotte Mew. MoAB; MoBrPo

You would hear, O Lord, woman's lament. Revolt. Adine Brabart Riom, *tr. by* Beth Archer. DMF

You would hoist an old hat on the tines of a fork. A Bat on the Road. Seamus Heaney. PoE

You would not bend. For Kinte. Oliver La Grone. FB

You would not recognize me. The Tourist from Syracuse. Donald Justice. CAPP; NoAM; TwCP

You would not say to children. The Folk Museum. Medbh McGuckian. CIP

You would shrink back/ jump up. July 4, 1984: For Buck. June Jordan. NoAM

You would sleep with the moon. Alternatives. Peter Cooley. AmPA

You would think I'd be a specialist in contemporary. The Put-Down Come On. A. R. Ammons. NoP

You would think the fury of aerial bombardment. The Fury of Aerial Bombardment. Richard Eberhart. CMoP; FaBoMo; FF; FYAP; HeIP; HoPM; InPK; LiTA; LiTM; MoP; NIP; NoAM; NoP; OBWP; PrIm; RB; TAP; TwCP; UnPo; VGW; WaP

You would think with so much going on outside. The Studio. Derek Mahon. FaBCIP

You wouldn't believe all this house has cost me. The Flitting. Medbh McGuckian. FaBCIP

You wound up in the wrong place, Uncle Shaggy. To the Bear. Sándor Rákos, *tr. fr. Hungarian by* Jascha Kessler. *Fr.* Bear Song. FOC

You write of goats, I curl. Another Reading. Nicki Jackowska. DT

You write with ease, to shew your breeding. Clio's Protest. Sheridan. FaBoEE

You wrote a line too much, my sage. Cynicus to W. Shakspere. James Kenneth Stephen. *Fr.* Two Epigrams. CenHV

You wrote a poem. Love Poem. Lindsay MacRae. DT

You X-ari bush. Zebra. *Unknown.* PeSA

You, you are all unloving, loveless, you. The Sea. D. H. Lawrence. BoNaP; MOS

You, you caribou. Magic Words for Hunting Caribou. *Unknown, tr. by* Jerome Rothenberg *and* Johnny John. STP

You. You dwell in this old house. To the Beloved Grown Past Youth. Amin Nakhla, *tr. by* Matthew R. Sorenson. MAP

You. You running across the field. Orpheus and Eurydice. Jean Valentine. FaBoWP; LCAP

You young friskies who to-day. The Next War. Robert Graves. BrPo

You'd have men's hearts up from the dust. Near Perigord. Ezra Pound. FaBoMo; LiTA; LiTM

You'd laugh/ If only you knew. To the Woman in the Office. "Kim." DT

You'd scarce expect one of my age. Tall Oaks from Little Acorns Grow. David Everett. FaFP

(Boy Reciter, The.) BLPA

You'd start at seven, and then you'd bend your back. Washing the Coins. Douglas Dunn. FaBoPV

You'd think I was crazy even if you didn't say it. Letter to the Little Shell. Gretchen Cottrell. GOS

You'd think that at 3:00 A.M. L'Elisir d'Amore. Dallas E. Wiebe. MAT

You'l marvel when I tell ye o. Loudon Hill; or, Drumclog. *Unknown.* ESPB

You'll always be my friend. More Girl Than Boy. Yusef Komunyakaa. PPR

You'll [*or* You'le] ask, perhaps, wherefore I stay. An Excuse of Absence. Thomas Carew. CaPo; SeCP

You'll be my little seven stone missionary! T. S. Eliot. *Fr.* Sweeney Agonistes. UnPo

You'll come to our ball;—since we parted. Our Ball. Winthrop Mackworth Praed. *Fr.* Letters from Teignmouth. EnRP

You'll depart when you feel like it. Nightfall. Robert Desnos, *tr. by* Michael Benedikt. POS

You'll find that I'm the sort. Abner Silver's "Pu-leeze! Mr. Hemingway!" Ring Lardner. OBAL

You'll go on, talking away. Hilda Doolittle ("H. D."). *Fr.* Sigil, IX. AnAn

You'll go to the plaza. Camoes and the Debt. Sophia de Mello Breyner Andresen, *tr. by* Willis Barnstone *and* Nelson Cerqueira. BoWoP

You'll make tea. Just the Two of Us. Tomioka Taeko. FCEI, *tr. by* Hiroaki Sato; WPOW, *tr. by* Harry *and* Lynn Guest *and* Kajima Shozo

You'll Never Know. Ruby Marion Wray. PWR

You'll only make me sad. Mohammad Taqi Mir, *tr. by* Ahmed Ali. GoT

You'll see sometime—half. Memorandum. William Stafford. NYBP

You'll wait a long, long time for anything much. On Looking Up by Chance at the Constellations. Robert Frost. CMoP

Young Acacia, The. Hayyim Nahman Bialik, *tr. fr. Hebrew by* Helena Frank. TrJP

Young Africans. Gwendolyn Brooks. NoAM

Young Allan. *Unknown.* ESPB

Young and Old. Charles Kingsley. *Fr.* The Water Babies. BLPL; EBEV; FaBoBe; FaFP; FaPoR; OxBChV; PoLF

Young and Radiant, He Is Standing. Allen Eastman Cross. AH

Young and tender is this sweet pear-tree. *Unknown, tr. by* Arthur Waley. BoS

Young [*or* Younge] Andrew. *Unknown.* ESPB; OxBB

Young Apollo, golden-haired, A. Youth. Frances Cornford. PCP

Young are quick of speech, The. On Teaching the Young. Yvor Winters. NoAM; NOBA

Young Argonauts. Sheila Wingfield. SD

Young-Autumn. A. Leyeles, *tr. fr. Yiddish by* Benjamin *and* Barbara Harshav. AYP

Young Barnswell. *Unknown.* OBET

Young Bearwell. *Unknown.* OBET

Young bee falls between my window, A. Vincent O'Sullivan. *Fr.* Brother Jonathan, Brother Kafka, 32. ATNZ

Young Beichan. *Unknown.* EnSB; ESPB (A *and* C *vers.*); FaBoBa (Lord Bateman.) AmFP; OBET

Young Beichan and Susie Pye. *Unknown.* OnMSP

Young Ben he was a nice young man. Faithless Sally Brown. Thomas Hood. NOBL; OBNV

(Sally Brown.) FaBoCo

Young Benjie. *Unknown.* ESPB; OxBB, *with music*

Young Birch, A. Robert Frost. BoNaP; LiTA

Young Blondes. Gavin Ewart. ErPo

Young bloods come round less often now, The. Horace. *See* Odes: Ribald Romeos Less and Less Berattle ("Parcius iunctas quatiunt fenestras"), I, 25.

Young bull, The. A Young Chieftain. Auvaiyar, *tr. by* A. K. Ramanujan. PLW

Young Charlottie or, The Frozen Girl. *Unknown.* AmFP; BeLS; BLPA

Young cherry trees, The. April. Linda Pastan. Psk

Young Chess Player, The. Keith Sinclair. ATNZ

Young Chieftain, A. Auvaiyar, *tr. fr. Tamil by* A. K. Ramanujan. PLW

Young Chimera at an orgy left, A. The Chimera. Théophile Gautier, *tr. by* William Jay Smith. CT

Young Colin Clout, a lad of peerless meed. Tuesday; or, the Ditty. John Gay. *Fr.* The Shepherd's Week. NOEC

Young composer, working that summer at an artist's colony, The. A Story about the Body. Robert Hass. GeTw; NPGG

Young Cordwainer, The. Robert Graves. MoBS

Young Corydon [*or* Coridon] and Phyllis [*or* Phillis]. On the Happy Corydon and Phyllis. *At. to* Sir Charles Sedley. BoLoP; CoMu; ErPo

Young David: Birmingham, A. Helen Morgan Brooks. PoNe

Young Dead Soldiers, The. Archibald MacLeish. OFD; WaP

Young Deer/Dust, A. Hemda Roth, *tr. fr. Hebrew by* Myra Glazer Schotz. VWA

Young Democracy, *sel.* Bernard O'Dowd.

"Hark! Young Democracy from sleep." PoAu-1

Young Dove, The. Moses Ibn Ezra, *tr. fr. Hebrew by* Solomon Solis-Cohen. TrJP

Young Earl of Essex's Victory over the Emperor of Germany, The. *Unknown.* ESPB; OBET

Young Edward came to Emily his gold all for to show. Edwin in the Lowlands Low. *Unknown.* AmFP

Young Edwin in the Lowlands Low. *Unknown.* OBET

Young Endymion sleeps Endymion's sleep, The. Keats. Longfellow. Son; TAP

Young engine-driver called Hunt, A. Victor Gray. NOBL

Young eyes leave the volume and stray out, The. History Lesson. Mark Van Doren. NYBP

Young fairy with habits perverse, A. *Unknown.* PeHV

Young Fellers. R. O. Munn. CowP

Young Fenians, The. Padraic Fallon. BIrV

Young fiddlehead ferns, The. Yomono Akara, *tr. by* Burton Watson. FCEI

Young fir-tree grows, A. Soul, Remember This! Eduard Friedrich Mörike. OBD

Young Fir-Wood, A. Dante Gabriel Rossetti. GN

Young fisherboys sing like the endless sea. That's Our Lot. Moyshe-Leyb Halpern, *tr. by* Kathryn Hellerstein. VWA

Young flowers were whispering in melody. Poe. *Fr.* Al Aaaraff. NOBA

Young flute player, The. Flute Player. *Gond Oral Tradition, tr. by* V. Elwin *and* S. Hivale. WTO

Young Frederick the Great was a beaut. *Unknown.* PeHV

Young Gal's Blues. Langston Hughes. NAAL-2

Young Girl. Ricarda Huch, *tr. fr. German by* Janine Canan *and* Deirdre Lashgari. WPOW

Young Girl and the Beach, The. Sophia de Mello Breyner Andresen, *tr. fr. Portuguese by* Alexis Levitin. WPOW

Young girl dancing lifts her face, The. The Dancer. W. J. Turner. OBMV

Young girl moves like an ear of grain, A. The Young Girl and the Beach. Sophia de Mello Breyner Andresen, *tr. by* Alexis Levitin. WPOW

Young girl now comes back from the open fields, The. Saturday Evening in the Village. Giacomo Leopardi, *tr. by* John Heath-Stubbs. PFI

Young girl of thirteen, A. The Cloak. Violet Anderson. CaP

Young girl, only eleven, A. "Mother-in-Law Is Cruel." Cheng Hsieh, *tr. by* Jonathan Chaves. CoBLCP

Young girl stood beside me, The. The Orange Tree. John Shaw Neilson. CBAP; PoAu-1

Young girl took a walk, A. Such Instance. Byron Herbert Reece. KS

Young Girl with a Pitcher Full of Water, A. David Wagoner. NoAM

Young Girls. Raymond Souster. HeIP

Young Glass-Stainer, The. Thomas Hardy. CTC; EyDe; SaC

Young go off, The. Emperor Meiji, *tr. by* Geoffrey Bownas *and* Anthony Thwaite. PeBJV

Young gourds spread and spread, The. *Unknown, tr. by* Arthur Waley. BoS

Young Gray Head, The. Caroline Anne Bowles Southey. BeLS

Young Harvard man, sweet and tender, A. *Unknown.* PeHV

Young, having risen early, had gone, The. The Guardians. Geoffrey Hill. NePoEA-2; NoP

Young Heroes. Gwendolyn Brooks. BPo

Young Highland Girl Studying Poetry, A. Iain Crichton Smith. NePoEA-2

Young Hodge met Mog the miller's maid. Don't Be Foolish Pray. *Unknown.* CoMu

Young homosexuals and hot girls, The. Lone Gentleman. Pablo Neruda, *tr. by* Clayton Eshleman. ErPo

Young Horseman. Lajos Kassák, *tr. fr. Hungarian by* Edwin Morgan. MHuP

Young hound howls, A. Unemployment. William Mills. HoPM

Young Housewife, The. William Carlos Williams. HeIP; NAAL-2; NoP; TAP

Young Hunting (*diff. versions*). *Unknown.* AmFP; ESPB; FaBoBa; OxBB; OxBoLi

Young Hyllus, why refuse today. Epigram: A Riddle. Martial, *tr. by* Brian Hill. PeHV

Young I am, and yet unskill'd. Song for a Girl. Dryden. ELP; ErPo

Young in Fall I said: the birds. Lorine Niedecker. VGW

Young Japanese son was in love with a servant boy, The. Dream Data. Robert Duncan. NeAP

Young Jemmy is a lad. England's Darling; or, Great Britain's Joy and Hope on That Noble Prince James, Duke of Monmouth. *Unknown.* CoMu

Young Jockey he courted sweet Mog the Brunette. Mog the Brunette. *Unknown.* CoMu

Young Johnny sails the sea, young Johnny sails the shore. The Green Bed. *Unknown.* AmFP

Young Johnny the miller he courted of late. The Gray Mare. *Unknown.* AmFP

Young Johnstone ("Young Johnstone and the young Colnel"). *Unknown.* ESPB; OxBB, *with music*

Young Knowledge. Robin Hyde. PeNZ

Young lady, The. Chinese Song. Federico García Lorca, *tr. fr. Spanish by* William Jay Smith. *Fr.* Songs of Childhood. CT

Young Lady Dancing with Soldier. Phyllis Shand Allfrey. CN

Young Lady Named Bright, A. *Unknown, at. to* Arthur Buller. *See* Relativity: There was a young lady called Bright.

Young lady of fair Mytilene, A. *Unknown.* CenHV

Young lady of Lynn, A. *Unknown.* ChTr; RHPC

Young Lady of Norway, A. Edward Lear. *See* There Was a Young Lady of Norway.

Young Lambs. John Clare. TrGrPo

Young Latin-Americans silently follow the burial, The. Notes on the Moving of a Corpse. Mirko Lauer, *tr. by* David Tipton. Per

Young leaves have left Fuji, The. Buson, *tr. fr. Japanese by* Hiroaki Sato. *Fr.* Eighty-seven Hokku. FCEI

Young Lettuce. Rutger Kopland, *tr. fr. Dutch by* Ria Leigh-Loohuizen. DuIn

Young Lincoln. Edwin Markham. OHIP

Young Lochinvar. Sir Walter Scott. *See* Marmion: Lochinvar.

Young Lochinvar. *Unknown.* FiBHP

Young lords o' the north country, The. Lady Maisry ("The young lords o' the north country"). *Unknown.* ESPB; OxBB

Young Love lies sleeping. Dream-Love. Christina Rossetti. CH; HAP; PoEL-5

Young man, alone, on the high bridge over the Tagus, A. The High Bridge above the Tagus River at Toledo. William Carlos Williams. CTC

Young man and an aged man of late, A. On a Young Man and an Old Man. Edward May. OxBSP

Young man and maid, pray lend attention. The Silver Dagger. *Unknown.* AmFP

Young Man and the Young Nun, The. A. D. Mackie. OxBS

Young man came to make you his wife, The. Emperor Go-Shirakawa, *tr. fr. Japanese by* Hiroaki Sato. *Fr.* Ryojin Hisho. FCEI ("Young man came to manhood, The.") PeBJV, *tr. by* Geoffrey Bownas *and* Anthony Thwaite.

Young man came to manhood, The. Emperor Go-Shirakawa. *See* Ryojin Hisho: Young man came to make you his wife, The.

Young man, crouching, ties his shoelaces, A. Myself Departing. Takahashi Mutsuo, *tr. by* Hiroaki Sato. FCEI

Young man, his face dark, A. Apollo. James Wright. LCAP

Young man lately in our Town, A. The Maids Conjuring Book. *Unknown.* CoMu

Young man left his native shores, A. Look Out Below! Charles Robert Thatcher. PoAu-1

Young man of alien beauty. Muireadhach Albanach O Dalaigh. NOIV

Young man of twenty, A. Lost Picture. Ray Fraser. NeAC

Young Man Thinks of Sons, The. R. A. K. Mason. ATNZ; PeNZ

Young Man Who Loved the Girl Who Took Care of Her Aged Father, The. Greg Kuzma. AmPA

Young man, you who stand in the stone-paved plaza of this castle city. Myself in the Disguise of an Ancient Goddess. Takahashi Mutsuo, *tr. by* Hiroaki Sato. FCEI

Young Man's Epigram on Existence, A. Thomas Hardy. BrPo; MoP

Young man's lying in the sky, stretched out, A. Ballad of the Store Clerk. Gerrit Achterberg, *tr. by* James S. Holmes. DuIn

Young Man's Song, A. William Bell. FaBoTw; NePoEA

Young Martins, The. Andrew Young. FM

Young Master's Account of a Puppet Show. John Marchant. OxBChV

Young May Moon, The. Thomas Moore. ELP; EnRP; OBEV

Young Men Come Less Often, The—Isn't It So? Horace, *tr. fr. Latin by* Robert Fitzgerald. ErPo

Young men dancing, and the old. Youthful Age. Thomas Stanley, *after the Greek of* Anacreon. AWP
(Young Men Dancing.) OBVE

Young men give ear to me a while. The Maid's Complaint for Want of a Dil Doul. *Unknown.* CoMu

Young men leave the country for the town, The. The Way to the Sea. Laurence Lerner. NePoEA-2

Young men of the nineteen hundreds, The. My Country. Julio Ortega, *tr. by* Ena Hollis. Per

Young men walking the open streets. Remember Your Lovers. Sidney Keyes. WaP

Young men who banded together, the White Tiger Battalion. The White Tiger Battalion. Sahara Morizumi, *tr. by* Burton Watson. JLIC-2

Young Molly Ban. *Unknown.* FaBoBa

Young moon, take my face up yonder. Re-birth. *Unknown, tr. by* W. H. I. Bleek *and* Jack Cope. PeSA

Young Mrs. Snooks was sick of sex. Nursery Rhyme. Kenneth Burke. OBAL

Young Negro Poet. Calvin C. Hernton. AmNP

Young Neophyte, The. Alice Meynell. ACP

Young niggers/ die old. Dedication to the Final Confrontation. Lloyd M. Corbin, Jr. PoBA

Young Night Thought. Robert Louis Stevenson. PWR

Young Old Young Old. Jan G. Elburg, *tr. fr. Dutch by* Koos Schuur. DuIn

Young Ones, The. Elizabeth Jennings. OxBTC

Young Ones, Flip Side, The. James A. Emanuel. PCP

Young Palmus was a ferryman. Shackley-Hay. *Unknown.* GBP

Young Peggy. *Unknown.* ESPB

Young people all, attention give. Liverpool. *Unknown.* AmFP

Young people, all attention give. Mission. *Unknown.* AmFP

Young People Who Delight in Sin. *Unknown.* AmFP

Young Philander woo'd me long. *Unknown.* ErPo

Young Pilgrim Finds Refuge with the Goatherds, The. Luis de Góngora y Argote, *tr. fr. Spanish by* Edward Meryon Wilson. *Fr.* The First Solitude. OBVE

Young pinoy, A. Pick-up at Chef Rizal Restaurant. Virginia Cerenio. BrSi

Young Poet. Myron O'Higgins. PoBA; PoNe

Young poet Evmenis, The. The First Step. Constantine P. Cavafy, *tr. by* Edmund Keeley *and* Philip Sherrard. Mes

Young Reynard. George Meredith. HoPM

Young Roger came tapping at Dolly's window. Roger and Dolly. Henry Carey. CoMu; NOEC; OxNR, *sl. diff. vers.*

Young Ronald. *Unknown.* ESPB

Young Sailor Cut Down in His Prime, The. *Unknown.* OxBSS

Young Sea. Carl Sandburg. MOS

Young Shepherd Bathing His Feet. Peter Clarke. PBA

Young skull which the wind scrapes, which the sand. On the Relative Merit of Friend and Foe, Being Dead. Donald Thompson. WaP

Young Soul. Amiri Baraka. BPo; CNA

Young squirrel's mother said, "Come out!," The. Squirrel in the Rain. Frances Mary Frost. RAR

Young Stock. Victoria Mary Sackville-West. OxBTC

Young Sycamore. William Carlos Williams. TAP

Young things who frequent picture-palaces, The. Limerick. *Unknown.* NOBL

Young to the end through sympathy with youth. James McCosh. Robert Bridges. AA

Young Training. Lawrence McGaugh. PoBA

Young Traveller Is Presented to the Goddess Dulness, A. Pope. *Fr.* The Dunciad, IV. NOEC

Young trees rise. The Surprised Pen. Gabriel Preil, *tr. by* Grace Schulman. PeBMYV

Young Ukrainians. Aba Shtoltsenberg, *tr. fr. Yiddish by* Dennis Silk. PeBMYV

Young Una, you were a rose in a garden. Tomas Costello, *tr. fr. Gaelic by* Frank O'Connor. *Fr.* A Lament for Una. WTO

Young unmarried man, with a good name, A. Byron. *Fr.* Don Juan. NOBL, XII.

Young viper grows as it sits, The. *Unknown, tr. fr. Zulu by* T. Cope. *Fr.* Shaka, King of the Zulus. WTO

Young Virgins Plucked Suddenly. Berl Pomerantz, *tr. fr. Hebrew by* Harold Schimmel. VWA

Young warbler crying through the Festival of Tombs. Chang Hui-yen, *tr. fr. Chinese by* Michael Duke. *Fr.* Tune: Joy at Meeting, II. WFTU

Young Warrior, A. Ponmutiyar, *tr. fr. Tamil by* A. K. Ramanujan. PLW

Young Warrior, The. Gayle Two Eagles. GOS

Young Washington. Arthur Guiterman. FaPON; OHIP

Young Waters. *Unknown.* ESPB; OxBB, *with music*

Young Wife, A. D. H. Lawrence. BrPo; ELP; MoBrPo

Young Wife, The. Derek Walcott. DiPo

Young will not wear it, The. Kutavayir Kirattanar, *tr. by* A. K. Ramanujan. PLW

Young Willie stands in his stable door. Clyde's Waters. *Unknown.* OxBB

Young Woman. Howard Nemerov. ErPo

Young Woman at a Window. Mark Van Doren. LiTA

Young Woman from Aenos, The. *Unknown.* OBAL

Young Woman of Beare, The. Austin Clarke. MoP; NoAM

Young woman plants seedlings, A. Kikaku, *tr. fr. Japanese by* Hiroaki Sato. *Fr.* Thirty-three Hokku. FCEI

Young woman with, A. Jumping-Jack Flash. Leslie Scalapino. BAP

Young Woman's Neo-Aramaic Jewish Persian Blues. Jerome Rothenberg, *after Persian folk poem.* BoWoP

Young women are obsessed with beauty, The. The Clothes Pit. Douglas Dunn. OxBTC

Young women in their April moodiness. The True Weather for Women. Louis Simpson. NePoAm

Young women, they [*or* they'll] run like hares on the mountain. Hares on the Mountain. *Unknown.* ErPo

Young Wordsworth's London, The. Wordsworth. *Fr.* The Prelude [*or,* Growth of a Poet's Mind]: Residence in London. FaBoPP

Young Workman, The. Mary Dillingham Frear. TrCP

Young Wrestlers. Grace Butcher. ASP

Young Writer Smells a Rat, The. Bonnie Jacobson. SoTCo

Younger Poet, A. Peter Schjeldahl. PoA

Younger sister, The. *Unknown, tr. by* Geoffrey Bownas *and* Anthony Thwaite. PeBJV

Younger Van Eyck, The. E. C. Bentley. FiBHP

Youngest Daughter, The. Cathy Song. MAYP; NoAM

Your absence has gone through me. Separation. W. S. Merwin. HAP; ILY; NoP; PCP

Your Absence Has Not Taught Me. Doug Fetherling. NeAC

Your Air of My Air. Hugo Margenat, *tr. fr. Spanish by* Julio Marzán. InW

Your archival voice. The Music. Everett Hoagland. CNA

Your are/ Getting free. Thoughts for You (When She Came Back from the Mountains). Ranice Henderson Crosby. NMM

Your arms are beautiful again. What Her Girl Friend Said ("Your arms are beautiful again"). Peyanar, tr. fr. Tamil by A. K. Ramanujan. Fr. Nine on Happy Reunion, 7. PLW

Your arms will clasp the gathered grain. The Island. Edwin Muir. OAEL-2

Your art has brought you great respect. Sent to the Painter, Lu Hsiao-feng. Li K'ai-hsien, tr. by Jonathan Chaves. CoBLCP

Your ashes will not stir, even on this high ground. In Carrowdore Churchyard. Derek Mahon. CIP; FaBCIP

Your Attention Please. Peter Porter. OBWP; OxBTC

Your average tourist: Fifty. 2.3. Casual Wear. James Merrill. NIP

Your back is rough all. Margaret Atwood. NeAC

Your baggy lyrics. To a Political Poet. Heine, tr. by Tom Paulin. FaBoPV

Your bards are wearing lotuses. Nettimaiyar, tr. by A. K. Ramanujan. PLW

Your bare white legs. The Beach at Veracruz. George Bowering. NeAC

Your basket, with your pretty basket. Emperor Yuryaku. Fr. Manyo Shu. Ma

Your Beauty and My Reason. Unknown. See Like two proud armies marching in the field.

Your beauty is deep and comforting. African Dancer. Luis Palés Matos, tr. by Perry Higman. LPSS

Your beauty, ripe, and calm. The Philosopher and the Lover: To a Mistress Dying. Sir William Davenant. OBD

Your beauty, ripe and calm, and fresh. Lover and Philosopher. Sir William Davenant. ACP; MePo; NOBE; OBEV; Prf

Your bed's got two wrong sides. Your life's all grouse. Long Distance. Tony Harrison. NAEL-2

Your best friend is gone. Tomorrow. Mark Strand. GOYP

Your Birthday Comes to Tell Me This. E. E. Cummings. NAs

Your Birthday in Wisconsin You Are 140. John Berryman. NAs

Your blond hair and autumn sweater. Janna. King D. Kuka. VoR

Your blood does not flow, not even a little. A Poem for Diane Wakoski. Ray A. Young Bear. CDW

Your blood reappears on my hands. For a Friend. David Steingass. TW

Your body derns. Scunner. "Hugh MacDiarmid." FaBoTw

Your body gleams like copper on the veld. The Fallen Zulu Commander. C. M. Van Den Heever, tr. by Uys Krige and Jack Cope. PeSA

Your body has moved to unstaunchable distance. N. Hugh Seidman. PoA

Your body is a pipeline. Air. Tomaz Salamun, tr. by Aleksandar Nejgebauer. VWA

Your Body Is Stars. Stephen Spender. FaBoTw

Your body might have come from the loins of a prince. Moon of the Earth. Gond Oral Tradition, tr. by V. Elwin and S. Hivale. WTO

Your body to hold, your perfect breasts. Undine. Irving Layton. ErPo

Your Body's Bread. Andras Fodor, tr. fr. Hungarian by Jascha Kessler. FOC

Your bold voice and the light suspended above a trumpet. It Ain't Blues That Blows an Ill Wind. Colleen J. McElroy. ER

Your bottoms are not purple. Horror Comic. Robert Conquest. OxBTC

Your boy's-ambition was to be a Horseman. Stud Groom. John Glassco. OBCV

Your brother brings you home from hunting. One Man Down. Ai. GeTw

Your brother is dead. Dreaming with a Friend. Stephen Berg. NaP

Your Burnt-out Body. Peretz Markish, tr. fr. Yiddish by Keith Bosley. VWA

Your buttonholes for eyes, your solemn face. The Statue. John Fuller. NePoEA-2

Your cage/ (said the caretaker). Peter Henisch, tr. by Beth Bjorklund. CoAuP

Your Catullus is depressed, Cornificus. Catullus. PeHV

Your chance of human birth. Kabir, tr. by John Stratton Hawley and Mark Juergensmeyer. SSI

Your Chase Had a Beast in View. John Peale Bishop. LiTA

Your cheeks flat on the sand. Venus Khoury-Gata, tr. by Willis Barnstone. BoWoP

Your Church and Mine. Phillips H. Lord. BLPA

Your clear eye is the one absolutely beautiful thing. Child. Sylvia Plath. HCAP; PBWP

Your closed eyes bulge like mushrooms. Letter to Kafka. Maura Stanton. AmPA

Your clothes a dark pink heap, a dimming sky. L'Art. Frederick Feirstein. SM

Your clothes of snow and satin and pure blood. The Bed. Karl Shapiro. NYBP

Your comedy I've read, my friend. To a Living Author. Unknown. NBLV

Your correspondent must be kidding when he says. Americana IX. Carl Rakosi. InPS

Your courtiers scorn we country clowns. A Ballad of the Courtier and the Country Clown. Unknown. CoMu

Your cousin tells you it's like fruit juice. Grape Daiquiri. Tina Koyama. BrSi

Your dandelions dotting half. Grass Widows. Robert B. Shaw. CRP

Your death in your own car. Extended Sonnet on the Death of Isaac Danziger. Meir Wieseltier, tr. by Warren Bargad and Stanley F. Chyet. IP

Your death, she said, is covered. The Indian Women Are Listening; to the Nuke Devils. Wendy Rose. GOS

Your doctor, Lord. For Dr. and Mrs. Dresser. Margaret Avison. MoCV

Your Dog Dies. Raymond Carver. GeTw

Your dog, tranquil and innocent, dozes through. Adrienne Rich. Fr. Twenty-one Love Poems, X. GLP

Your door is shut against my tightened face. The White House. Claude McKay. AmNP; AmPP; NIP; PoBA
(White Houses.) PoNe

Your downcast, harlequin, defenceless face. Lynched Negro. Maxwell Bodenheim. PoNe

Your Dress. Moyshe-Leyb Halpern, tr. fr. Yiddish by Benjamin and Barbara Harshav. AYP

Your dressing, dancing, gadding, where's the good in? On Ladies' Accomplishments. Unknown. FaBoUs

Your dusky shadow at the window lingers. Morning and Evening. Antoni Slonimski, tr. by Watson Kirkconnell. TrJP

Your dying was a difficult enterprise. Thom Gunn. GLP

Your ears receive a platter of sound. Walking with Your Eyes Shut. William Stafford. GOYP

Your elephant adolescence in sandlots Brooklyn. 16/53. Marge Piercy. NeAC

Your enemy is not the kind who wears. Poet's Counsel, A ("Your enemy is not the kind who wears"). Kovur Kilar, tr. by A. K. Ramanujan. PLW

Your eyen two will slay me suddenly [or wol slee me sodenly]. Merciles[s] Beauty [or Beaute[e]]. Chaucer. ACP; BoLoP; CTC; EBEV; EnLoPo; HAP; MeEL
(Rondel of Merciless Beauty, A, mod. vers. by Louis Untermeyer.) TrGrPo
(Three Roundels of Love Unreturned.) NoP

Your Eyes. Muhammad al-Ghuzzi, tr. fr. Arabic by May Jayyusi and John Heath-Stubbs. MAP

Your Eyes and Swiveling Members. Clark Stillman. SoTCo

Your eyes are just. Four-Word Lines. May Swenson. GLP; WPE

Your eyes are like a night of rain. Nizar Qabbani, tr. by Lena Jayyusi and W. S. Merwin. MAP

Your eyes are open. Carious Exposure. Gladys Cardiff. CDW

Your eyes are palm groves refreshed by dawn's breath. Rain Song. Badr Shakir al-Sayyab, tr. by Abdullah al-Udhari. MPAW

Your eyes are so deep that leaning down to drink. Elsa's Eyes. Louis Aragon, tr. by William Jay Smith. CT

Your eyes are two palm tree forests in early light. Rain Song. Badr Shakir al-Sayyab, tr. by Lena Jayyusi and Christopher Middleton. MAP

Your eyes glisten, glow, and sparkle. To a Woman Socialist. Abraham Reisen, tr. by Leonard Wolf. PeBMYV

Your Eyes Have Their Silence. Gerald William Barrax. CNA; PoBA

Your Eyes That Gaze. Dov Khomsky, tr. fr. Hebrew by Bernhard Frank. MHeP

"Your eyes that once were never weary of mine." Ephemera. W. B. Yeats. BrPo

Your eyes were ever brown, the colour. On Not Being Your Lover. Medbh McGuckian. FaBCIP

Your eyes, your flowing hair. Auburn. Paul Verlaine, tr. by Lawrence M. Bensky. ErPo

Your face,/so pale now it is blue. David St. John. AmPA

Your face broods from my table, Suicide. John Berryman. Fr. Dream Songs. TAP

Your face did not rot. The Lost Pilot. James Tate. CoAP; DiL; NoAM; NoP; OBWP; TwCP; UnPo

Your face fills the sky. Portrait of a Man. Alan Bernheimer. UL

Your face is the face of all the others. The Face of Love. Ingrid Jonker, tr. by Jack Cope. PeSA

Your face reveals a down so light. Epigram: To Dindymus. Martial, tr. by Brian Hill. PeHV

Your face scrapes my sleep tonight. Letter to Be Disguised as a Gas Bill. Marge Piercy. WPE

Your faith is in what you hold. Chicago. Lola Ridge. PoA

Your father had gangrene. Moenkopi. Arthur Sze. BrSi

Your Father Knoweth. *Unknown. See* Precious thought, my Father knoweth.

"Your father's gone," my bald headmaster said. The Lesson. Edward Lucie-Smith. OxBTC; TwCP

Your fires burnt my forests. The Womb. Apirana Taylor. PeNZ

Your Flag and My Flag. Wilbur Dick Nesbit. FaFP; WBLP

Your foe in war to overrate. Porson on His Majesty's Government. Richard Porson. FaBoCo

Your friends come fondly to your living room. Birthday Card for a Psychiatrist. Mona Van Duyn. IHMS

Your friends shall be the tall wind. For a Child. Fannie Stearns Davis. FaPON

Your friendship oft has made my heart ake. *See* Thy friendship oft has made my heart ache.

Your garden hut stands by the green waters. Yang Chi, *tr. fr. Chinese by* Jonathan Chaves. *Fr.* Living in Master Fang's Garden. CoBLCP

Your gentle, wild rider. Animal Mood. Judah Leib Teller, *tr. by* Benjamin *and* Barbara Harshav. AYP

Your great-grandfather dreamed that his son. Letters to My Daughters, No. 3. Judith Minty. TV

Your great mistake is to disregard the satire. The Mute Phenomena. Derek Mahon. FaBCIP

Your great sin. New Jersey White-tailed Deer. Joyce Carol Oates. GeTw

Your Hair. Ruth Kim Chun-soo, *tr. fr. Korean by* Koh Chang-soo. ACKP

Your hair comes undone when you put it up. Mikata no Sami. *Fr.* Manyo Shu. FCEI

Your hair hovers over the sea with the golden juniper. Your Hair over the Sea. Paul Celan, *tr. by* Joachim Neugroschel. AnAn

Your hair is growing long, Uncle Ambrose. Uncle Ambrose. James Still. AmFN

Your Hair over the Sea. Paul Celan, *tr. fr. German by* Joachim Neugroschel. AnAn

Your hand among them. Poem of Parting. Kyorai, *tr. fr. Japanese by* Burton Watson. *Fr.* Twenty Hokku. FCEI

Your Hand Full of Hours. Paul Celan, *tr. fr. German by* Michael Hamburger. OBVE

Your Hand in Mine. Vicente Aleixandre, *tr. fr. Spanish by* Perry Higman. LPSS

Your handkerchief should be blue. Love Song ("Your handkerchief should be blue"). *Unknown, tr. by* Reza Baraheni *and* Zahra-Soltan Shokoohtaezeh. BoWoP

Your Hands. Angelina Weld Grimké. CDC; PoBA

Your hands lie open in the long fresh grass. Silent Noon. Dante Gabriel Rossetti. *Fr.* The House of Life, XIX. HAP; NAEL-2; NoP; OBNC; PoEL-5; TrGrPo; UnAS

Your hands made a tent o'er mine eyes. Whimper of Awakening Passion. Ebenezer Jones. NOBVV

Your hands, my dear, adorable. The Chilterns. Rupert Brooke. MoBrPo

Your hands, strewn on the sheets, were my dead leaves. To a Sleeping Friend. Jean Cocteau. PeHV

Your hay it is mowed, and your corn is reaped. Harvest Home. Dryden. *Fr.* King Arthur. PrIm
(Song: "Your hay it is mow'd, and your corn is reap'd.") SeCV-2

Your head comes like a ship with full freight. Hunger. Jeannie Ebner, *tr. by* Beth Bjorklund. CoAuP

Your health, Master Willow. Contrive me a bat. Tree Party. Louis MacNeice. FaBCIP; OxBTC

Your heart is a music-box, dearest! Frances Sargent Osgood. AA

Your heavy eyes. Etruscan Statue. Esther Raab, *tr. by* Bernhard Frank. MHeP

Your home is deep in the white clouds. The Mountain Retreat of a Recluse. Chang Yü, *tr. by* Jonathan Chaves. CoBLCP

Your horse stands saddled and ready in the dawn. The Difficulty of Parting. Hsüeh Chao-yün, *tr. by* Lois Fusek. ATF

Your hour approaching, to *Latona* cry,. Labour. M. Saint-Marthe, *tr. fr. French. Fr.* Paedotrophiae; or, The Art of Bringing Up Children. FaBoUs

Your house is near the southern tip of the lake. Hermit Feng's Residence on the Lake. Hsü Pen, *tr. by* Jonathan Chaves. CoBLCP

Your houseplant is a delicate thing. Why So Many of Them Die. Susan Wallbank. BrRo

Your hulk is like some. Cow. Janet Reed McFatter. GrPl

Your husband will be with us at the treat. To His Mistress. Ovid, *tr. fr. Latin by* Dryden. *Fr.* Amores, I, 4. BoLoP; ErPo

Your image is engraved. Nizar Qabbani, *tr. by* Lena Jayyusi *and* W. S. Merwin. MAP

Your immediate worry is over. Melodious Birds. Timothy Holmes. UAS

Your innocence snuffed out. Candle. Jacob Isaac Segal, *tr. by* Seymour Mayne. VWA

Your intestines/ spring up. Pogoing. Cynthia S. Pederson. RR

Your kind of night, David, your kind of night. Night Thoughts. Henri Coulette. FYAP

Your kindness is no kindness now. Kindness. Catherine Davis. NYBP

Your Lad, and My Lad. Randall Parrish. PAH

Your Last Drive. Thomas Hardy. OBNC

Your laughter is like a burst pomegranate. When You Laugh. Ingrid Jonker, *tr. by* Elizabeth Jones. WPOW

Your least and lightest movement may be critical. The Man of Glass. Gordon Challis. ATNZ

Your leaves bound up compact and fair. To an Author. Philip Freneau. AmPP; NOBA; OxBA

Your legend is still green with us, and avid. Prophet Bird. Alfred Corn. BLA

Your legs would be pretty, if you had legs. Portrait of a Nun. Bobi Jones, *tr. by* Joseph P. Clancy. OBWVE

Your letter came.—Glutted the earth and cold. A Winter-Piece to a Friend Away. John Berryman. NOBA

Your light is the basis of creation. Asadullah Khan Ghalib, *tr. by* Ahmed Ali. GoT

Your lips were so laughing. Langston Blues. Dudley Randall. CNA; FB

Your little dog that barked as I came by. To His Wife, for Striking Her Dog. Sir John Harington. OxBSP

Your little hands. Samuel Hoffenstein. *Fr.* Love-songs, at Once Tender and Informative. FiBHP; NBLV; TrJP

Your little house stands in a bamboo grove. Sent in Parting to Yen Kung-su. Shen Chou, *tr. by* Jonathan Chaves. CoBLCP

Your little voice/ Over the wires came leaping. E. E. Cummings. LLLT

Your looks so often cast. Sir Thomas Wyatt. SiPS

Your love is dead, lady, your love is dead. R. S. Thomas. BoLoP; EnLoPo

Your love is like fire, croons the. Peter Rosei, *tr. by* Beth Bjorklund. CoAuP

Your love lacks joy, your letter says. Coventry Patmore. *Fr.* The Victories of Love, I, v. GBL
(Rain That Fell upon the Height, The.) FaBoRV

Your love, love. The Lover to Himself. David Phillips. NeAC

Your love lurks in my veins like a bandit. A Wild Cat. Suad al-Mubarak al-Sabah, *tr. by* May Jayyusi *and* John Heath-Stubbs. MAP

Your love threw me down. Nizar Qabbani, *tr. by* Lena Jayyusi *and* W. S. Merwin. MAP

Your love turned my body into water. Nur, Empress Jahan, *tr. by* Willis Barnstone. BoWoP

Your lynx-eyes, Asia. "Anna Akhmatova," *tr. by* Stanley Kunitz *and* Max Hayward. BoWoP

Your Majesty's reign will never end. Teika, *tr. fr. Japanese by* Hiroaki Sato. *Fr.* A Compendium of Good Tanka. FCEI

Your master dead, your life all out of tune. Epitaph for a Dog. Samuel Twardowski, *tr. by* Jerzy Peterkiewicz *and* Burns Singer. OBD

Your master died from drinking too much. The Taoist Huang Has Died of Alcoholism. Shen Chou, *tr. by* Jonathan Chaves. CoBLCP

Your men of the land, from the king to Jack Ketch. Epistle to a Desponding Sea-Man. Philip Freneau. MOS

Your midnight ambulances, the first knife-saw. Robert Sheridan Lowell. Robert Lowell. *Fr.* Marriage, *st.* 13. NAS

Your midriff sags toward your knees. Woman with Girdle. Anne Sexton. ErPo

Your milk was already poisoned. Childhood. Edith Bruck, *tr. by* Anita Barrows. VWA

Your mind and you are our Sargasso Sea. Portrait d'une Femme. Ezra Pound. CMoP; FF; InPS; MoAB; MoAmPo; MoP; NAAL-2; NoAM; NOBA; NoP; PPP; TAP; TwCP

Your mind lies open like the map of rivers. Five Birds Rise. William Hayward. NYBP

Your Mission. Ellen M. Huntington Gates. BLPA; BLRP

Your mistress, that you follow whores, still taxeth you. A Self Accuser. John Donne. FaBoEE

Your moon face. Leaving. Jenny Vuglar. DT

Your Mother. Sam Cornish. CNA

Your mother poses on black rocks. Black Rocks. Laureen Mar. BrSi

Your Mouth Says, Kiss Me. Charles, Duc d' Orléans. OxBLMV

Your name doesn't appear in the magazines. The Incurable Love. José Luis Quesada, *tr. by* Jack Hirschman. Vol

Your Name in Arezzo. James Wright. SM

"Your name is Achilles Deatheridge?" Achilles Deatheridge. Edgar Lee Masters. AmFN

Your name is the Wheel of Progress—a pleasant name indeed. To the Wheel of Progress. Mrs. Henry Linden. CBWP-4

Your name: the act of worship. Ravidas, tr. by John Stratton Hawley and Mark Juergensmeyer. SSI

Your new blouse, Mercedes. A First-Rate Equation. Luciano Erba, tr. by Lawrence R. Smith. NItP

Your nurse could only speak Italian. Sailing Home from Rapallo. Robert Lowell. HCAP; TAP

Your old hat hurts me, and those black. Dad. Elaine Feinstein. AIW; VWA

Your overtures overjoy me. Let's Not Think about That. Fran Landesman. DT

Your Own Place. Edward Lucie-Smith. PBCV

Your Own Version. Paul Gilbert. BLRP

Your Pain. Armando Guebuza, tr. fr. Portuguese by Margaret Dickinson. WMBCH

Your parents don't like me. Farewell, Sweet Mary. Unknown. AmFP

Your Passing, Fleet Passing. Joseph Eliyia, tr. fr. Modern Greek by Rae Dalven. VWA

Your passion was ever plural, apart. To Thoreau on Rereading Walden. Isabella Gardner. CAPP

Your petals open wet. Lesbian. Paula Jennings. PeHV

Your pinks, your tulips live an hour. To the Gardener at Nuneham. Horace Walpole. FaBoEE

Your Place. John Oxenham. BLRP

Your Presence. David Diop, tr. fr. French by Ulli Beier. PBA

Your Presence. Mordecai Temkin, tr. fr. Hebrew by Jeremy Garber. VWA

Your presence, mother, is the living drama of a race. Black Mother. Viriato da Cruz, tr. by Margaret Dickinson. WMBCH

Your residence on earth, a floating, nothing but adream. Lamenting the Taoist Wei Kung-yüan. Chao Meng-fu, tr. by Jonathan Chaves. CoBLCP

Your Riches Taught Me Poverty. Emily Dickinson. AnAmPo

Your sands are furrowed. What Her Girl Friend Said to Him. Ammuvanar, tr. by A. K. Ramanujan. PLW

Your Shadow. Mark Strand. Fr. Elegy for My Father. Prf

Your shadow I have seen you play with often. The Child and the Shadow. Elizabeth Jennings. NePoEA-2

Your shrunken head was bent. The Murder Trial. Perseus Adams. PeSA

Your silence today is a pond where drowned things live. Adrienne Rich. Fr. Twenty-one Love Poems, IX. GLP

Your sisters all must stay at home. Michizane, tr. fr. Japanese by Burton Watson. Fr. Kokin Shu. FCEI
(To Comfort My Little Son and Daughter.) JLIC-1

Your skin was blue-puddled snow. Early Love. Herbert Scott. MOWH; NAmP

Your sleep is so profound. Aurora. Timothy Steele. DiPo

Your small embattled eyes dispute a face. On Looking in the Looking Glass. Isabella Gardner. CAPP

Your small hands, precisely equal to my own. Adrienne Rich. Fr. Twenty-one Love Poems, VI. GLP; PoE

Your smile/ with the spectacular softness. After the Rain. Paul B. Janeczko. PCP

Your smile, delicate. Woman Me. Maya Angelou. BlSi

Your smiles are not, as other womens be. To the Lady May. Aurelian Townshend. GBL; MePo

Your smiling cheeks, burning clouds. A Poem about Fan the Fourth. Li K'ai-hsien, tr. by Jonathan Chaves. CoBLCP

Your smiling, or the hope, the thought of it. A Simile for Her Smile. Richard Wilbur. HoPM; InPK

Your son is seven years dead. After Labor Day. Sydney Lea. BLA; NAmP

Your son presses against me. The Apple Trees. Louise Glück. HCAP

Your song comes to me in little pieces. Jacob Glatstein, tr. by Benjamin and Barbara Harshav. AYP

Your Songs. Gwendolyn B. Bennett. CDC

Your sore-throat germ may say, "Heh heh." Things on a Microscope Slide. X. J. Kennedy. TSS

Your sorrow overflowed you; I let the stream. Consolation. Gyula Illyés, tr. by Charles Tomlinson. MHuP

Your soul is a sealed garden. Clair de Lune. Paul Verlaine. AWP, tr. by Arthur Symons.

Your Soul Shines. Alice Walker. MT

Your spirit flows out over all the land between. Flow at Full Moon. R. A. K. Mason. ATNZ

Your subjects hope, dread Sire. To the King's Most Excellent Majesty. Phillis Wheatley. TAP

Your sweetness of soul was a mystery to me. Hattie Rice Rich. Adrienne Rich. Fr. Grandmothers. NAAL-2

Your tall French legs, my V for victory. Will to Win. Francis Reginald Scott. OBCV

Your tall, fresh faces stand up in snow. My Students Who Stand in Snow. Michael S. S. Harper. AnAn

Your tears, Niobe. Hayden Carruth. VGW

Your Teeth. Ramón López Velarde, tr. fr. Spanish by Samuel Beckett. MexPo

Your teeth are loose, your head is bald. An Admonition to Myself. Chao Meng-fu, tr. by Jonathan Chaves. CoBLCP

Your thighs are appletrees. Portrait of a Lady. William Carlos Williams. AmPP; CMoP; MoP; NAAL-2; NoAM; NOBA; OxBA

Your thighs your belly. Sea Flower. Mary Dorcey. BrRo
(Sea Change.) AIW

Your thoughts/ dreaming in a softened brain. A Cloud in Trousers. Vladimir Mayakovsky, tr. by Peter Bogdanoff. SOTW

Your threats how vain, Corregidor. A Ballad of Manila Bay. Sir Charles G. D. Roberts. PAH

Your tongue has spent the night. The Dream-Language of Fergus. Medbh McGuckian. CIP

Your Totem Is the Opulent Serpent. Giancarlo Marmori, tr. fr. Italian by Lawrence R. Smith. NItP

"Your touch is abrasive. My blood seethes and smarts." Occasional Verses. Marilyn Hacker. Son

Your turn came, and you chose to take it. Winter Solstice—for Frank. Asphodel. BrRo

Your two great eyes will slay me suddenly. A Rondel of Merciless Beauty. Chaucer, mod. vers. by Louis Untermeyer. TrGrPo

Your ugly token. Upon a Dead Man's Head. John Skelton. HAP; SeCePo
(Gift of a Skull, The.) ACP
(Uppon a Deedmans Hed.) AAS

Your velvet nakedness, in this pitch dark. Flesh from Flesh. Mal'akhi Bet-Aryeh, tr. by Bernhard Frank. MHeP

Your Voice. Michael Burkard. NAmP

Your voice always whacked me right on the funny bone. Burying Blues for Janis. Marge Piercy. GeTw; NeAC

Your voice at times a fist. To a Husband. Maya Angelou. IHMS

Your voice is the color of a robin's breast. A To O. E. Claude McKay. BANP; BPo

Your voice on the telephone. Another Woman. Rosemary Norman. DT

Your voice on the telephone. Donald Hall. FF

Your voice sister. Mississippi Born. Pearl Cleage Lomax. CNA

Your walk sacerdotal and slow, undulant. A Black Girl Goes By. Emile Roumer, tr. by Edna Worthley Underwood. TTY

Your way/ is turning bad. Unknown, tr. by W. S. Merwin. STP

Your weeping gray streets. Seventeenth Telegram ("Your weeping gray streets"). Abd al-Aziz al-Maqalih, tr. fr. Arabic by Lena Jayyusi and Christopher Middleton. Fr. Telegrams of Tenderness for Sanaa. MAP

Your will is done. Its promise, that I fled. Oedipus to the Oracle. W. Wesley Trimpi. NePoEA

Your wistful eyes searched each one as he passed. Stray Dog. Charlotte Mish. PoLF

Your words dropped into my heart like pebbles into a pool. Absence. Claude McKay. CDC

Your words haunt me in the night. Talisman 18. Sharon A. Stern. TSM

"Your words, my friend, right helpful caustics, blame." Sir Philip Sidney. Fr. Astrophel and Stella, XXI. NAEL-1; PoE; TEP

Your World ("Your world is as big as you make it"). Georgia Douglas Johnson. AmNP

Your yellow sails—a shroud. The Burning Ship. Margit Szécsi, tr. by Laura Schiff. MHuP

You're. Sylvia Plath. FaBoTw; FaBoWP; NAs; RB

You're a hillbilly and you come to a place like Detroit. Gracie, 1967. Faye Kicknosway. ER

You're a poet. Unknown. FaFP

You're a traitor convicted, you know very well! Jefferson D. Henry Sylvester Cornwell. PAH

You're an anti-racist person. Anti-Racist Person. Marsha Prescod. AIW

You're backed. I Resigned Myself to Being Here. John Giorno. UL

You're clean shaven in this country. The Vegetable Air. Cathy Song. NoAM

"You're fired, Lane." The Water-Truck. Patrick Lane. NeAC

You're flying back, weighted with half the books. Corona. Marilyn Hacker. BLA

You're fond of details. On Details. Sami Mahdi, *tr. by* May Jayyusi *and* Charles Doria. MAP

You're full, sated with wonder as with bread. You Only Know. Mani Leib, *tr. by* John Hollander. PeBMYV

You're Going to Reap Just What You Sow. *Unknown.* AmFP

You're in my mind. To My Wife. James Forsyth. WaP

You're like a drifting log with iron nails in it. Funeral Song. Hayiaku, *tr. by* James Koller. STP

You're made for my hand. A Hammer. Eugène Guillevic, *tr. by* Denise Levertov. RHTwFP

You're No King. Haim Guri, *tr. fr. Hebrew by* Warren Bargad *and* Stanley F. Chyet. IP

You're not alone when you are still alone. *See* You not alone when you are still alone.

You're not supposed to roast a ghost. The Haunted Oven. X. J. Kennedy. WSC

You're Nothing but a Spanish Colored Kid. Felipe Luciano. PoBA

You're paranoid she says. Home Life. Pat Nolan. UL

You're perfectly right, O Treasure of Knowledge. To the Queen of Sweden, on Her Contempt for Women's Minds. Mlle Certain, *tr. by* Dorothy Backer. DMF

You're right/ I chase after myself. Peter Henisch, *tr. by* Beth Bjorklund. CoAuP

You're right. In the Library. Michael Patrick Hearn. NTCP

You're right I brought a grain. The Sand. May Swenson. *Fr.* Poet to Tiger. GLP

You're right. With feather-light configuration. Butterfly. A. A. Fet, *tr. by* Alan Myers. AAA

You're so brave, you camp-followers of Cain. Once More. István Vas, *tr. by* Jascha Kessler. FOC

You're So Far Away. Iyamide Hazeley. DT

You're so fragile. Silk and Silence. Haim Guri, *tr. by* Warren Bargad *and* Stanley F. Chyet. IP

You're so funny! I'd give you. Kirsten. Ted Berrigan. TTTS

You're so very blue my dear springtime. Seasons Their Asterisks and Their Pawns. Hans Arp, *tr. by* Michael Benedict. POS

You're so well-suited as a lover. Garsenda de Forcalquier, *tr. by* Meg Bogin. WT

You're Sorry, Your Mother Is Crazy, & I'm a Chinese Shiksa. Deborah Lee. BrSi

You're the Top ("At words poetic, I'm so pathetic."), *sel.* Cole Porter. NBLV; OBAL; UnPo

You're the Top. *Unknown.* NBLV

You're there again? Capri as Cloud. Karl Wawra, *tr. by* Beth Bjorklund. CoAuP

You're through—now walking up and down. The Ageing Athlete. Neil Weiss. SD

You're tired of this old world at last. Zone. Guillaume Apollinaire, *tr. by* Ron Padgett. SOTW

You're weary of this ancient world at last. Zone ("You're weary of this ancient world at last"). Guillaume Apollinaire, *tr. by* Louis Simpson. POS

You're wondering if I'm lonely. Adrienne Rich. InPK; PBWP

Youre yen two wol slee me sodeinly. Merciless Beauty. Chaucer. NAEL-1

Yours is the face that the earth turns to me. Kathleen Jessie Raine. LiTB; MoAB; MoBrPo

Yourself. Jones Very. AA; NOBA; OxBA; PoEL-4; Son

Yourself and Myself. *Unknown, tr. fr. Irish by* Thomas Kinsella. NOIV

Youth. Robert Browning. *Fr.* Saul. BOTP

Youth. Virginia Woodward Cloud. AA

Youth. Frances Cornford. PCP

Youth, A. Stephen Crane. *See* Black Riders, The: Youth in Apparel That Glittered, A.

Youth. Bartholomew Griffin. *See* Fidessa, More Chaste than Kind: I have not spent the April of my time.

Youth. "Laurence Hope." WeW

Youth. Langston Hughes. AmFN

Youth. Georgia Douglas Johnson. BANP; PoNe

Youth. Pablo Neruda, *tr. fr. Spanish by* Perry Higman. LPSS

Youth. Barend Toerien, *tr. fr. Afrikaans by the author.* PeSA

Youth. *Unknown.* OBSC

Youth. Robert Wever. *See* Lusty Juventus:
In a herber [*or* a harbour *or* an arbour] green [*or* grene], asleep [*or* aslepe] whereas [*or* where as *or* where] I lay.

Youth. James Wright. DiL; NaP; NoP

Youth and Age. Byron. *See* Stanzas for Music.

Youth and Age. Samuel Taylor Coleridge. BLPL; EnRP; FiP; GTBS; GTBS-P; OBEV; OBNC; PoLF

Youth and Age. Mimnermus, *tr. fr. Greek by* John Addington Symonds. AWP

Youth and Age. Shakespeare. *See* Passionate Pilgrim, The: Crabbed Age and Youth.

Youth and Age. Henry Howard, Earl of Surrey. *See* Laid in My Quiet Bed [in Study as I Were].

Youth and Age. Bible, *O.T. See* Ecclesiastes: Remember Now Thy Creator.

Youth and Age. W. B. Yeats. FaBoEE

Youth and Age on Beaulieu River, Hants. Sir John Betjeman. FaBoTw; TwCP

Youth and Art. Robert Browning. CTC; NAEL-2; NOBVV

Youth and Beauty. Aurelian Townshend. GBL; MePo; SeCP

Youth and Cupid. Elizabeth I, Queen of England. *See* When I Was Fair and Young.

Youth and Love. John Gay. *See* Beggar's Opera, The: Youth's the Season.

Youth and Maturity. Fulke Greville. *See* Caelica: Nurse-life wheat, within his greene huske growing, The.

Youth Dreams, The. Rainer Maria Rilke, *tr. fr. German by* Ludwig Lewisohn. AWP; TrJP

Youth gone, and beauty gone if ever there. Christina Rossetti. *Fr.* Monna Innominata. GBL; OBNC; Son

Youth in Apparel That Glittered, A. Stephen Crane. *Fr.* The Black Riders, XXVII. LiTA; NAAL-2
(Content.) AA
(Youth, A.) MoAmPo

Youth in Arms, *sel.* Harold Monro.
Carrion. *Fr.* IV. MMA

Youth is sweet and well. Triumph of Bacchus and Ariadne. Lorenzo de' Medici, *tr. by* Lorna de' Lucchi. PFI

Youth Mowing, A. D. H. Lawrence. InPK; MoAB; MoBrPo; NoAM; TrGrPo

Youth of a Poet, The. James Beattie. *Fr.* The Minstrel, I. NOEC

Youth of my heart, my beloved one. Love Song to King Shu-Suen. Kubatum, *tr. by* Thorkild Jacobsen. WPOW

Youth of Nature: Wordsworth's Country, The, *sel.* Matthew Arnold. "Raised are the dripping oars." FaBoPP

Youth rambles on life's arid mount. The Progress of Poesy. Matthew Arnold. NOBVV

Youth Sings a Song of Rosebuds. Countee Cullen. BANP; PoLF; PoNe

Youth there was, Elpenor was he nam'd, A. Homer, *tr. fr. Greek by* Pope. *Fr.* Odyssey, X. OBVE

Youth! Thou Wear'st to Manhood Now. Sir Walter Scott. OxBSP

Youth walks up to the white horse, The. The White Horse. D. H. Lawrence. SOTW; TTTS

Youth, with proud heart, pure and strong, A. The After-Glow of Pain. Clara Ann Thompson. CBWP-2

Youth with Red-gold Hair, The. Dame Edith Sitwell. FaBoTw

Youth, you lay out. Violins. Eugenio Montale, *tr. fr. Italian by* Jonathan Galassi. *Fr.* Chords, I. PFI

Youthful Age. Thomas Stanley, *after the Greek of* Anacreon. AWP

Youthful passion seeps through my mind. Tomb. David Semah, *tr. by* Yoffee Berkovitz. VWA

Youthful Picnic Long Ago: Sad Ballad on Box. Robert Penn Warren. BLA

Youths, De. Nefertiti Gayle. WS

Youth's Progress. John Updike. FiBHP

Youth's the Season. John Gay. *Fr.* The Beggar's Opera, II, i. WiR

You've asked me what the lobster is weaving there. Enigmas. Pablo Neruda, *tr. by* Robert Bly. NU

You've Been a Good Old Wagon, but You've Done Broke Down. Ben Harney. OBAL

You've been both exalted and debased. To George Sand. Ida von Reinsberg-Düringsfeld, *tr. by* Susan L. Cocalis *and* Gerlinde Geiger. DMG

You've been holding back. Wild Pitches. Philip Dacey. NAmP

You've got halfway, and found it rather hard. Three Girls on a Buttress. Eilidh Nisbet. PoSH

You've got lots of beer, wine and whiskey. Fill Up Those Glasses, Bartender. Jim Bollers. CowP

You've got nice knees. Gavin Ewart. OxBTC

You've Got to Be Taught. Oscar Hammerstein II. AmFN

You've Got to Learn the White Man's Game. Mbembe Milton Smith. ASP

You've got to speculate. Financial Wisdom. *Unknown.* FaBoUs

You've gotta have heart. Heart. Richard Adler *and* Jerry Ross. *Fr.* Damn Yankees. ASP

You've gotten in through the transom. To a Child Trapped in a Barber Shop. Philip Levine. CAPP; InPK; MoP; NoAM; NOBA; TAP; VGW

"You've grieved enough, my daughter dear." The Ballad of the White Glow. Itzig Manger, *tr. by* Leonard Wolf. PeBMYV

"You've had your operation, Mrs. Brown." The Other Side. Roy Fuller. OxBC

You've heard how a green thumb. My Aunt. Ted Hughes. WSC

You've heard of the Gresford disaster. The Gresford Disaster. *Unknown.* GBP; OBET

You've heard of the Turks and the Greeks. The Battle of Navarino. *Unknown.* CoMu

You've heard that saying brave. Konstantin Nikolayevich Batyushkov, *tr. by* Alan Myers. AAA

You've lived there long, away from the trappings of office. To a Hermit in the Mountains. Hsü Pen, *tr. by* Jonathan Chaves. CoBLCP

You've made a table you say, and are happy. From. Tom Paulin. FaBCIP

You've moved to a house backing the outer wall. Looking for Lu Hung-chien but Failing to Find Him. Chiao-jan, *tr. by* Burton Watson. CoBCP

You've never heard the voice of God? The Voice of God. Katherine R. Barnard. BLRP; WBLP

You've pluck'd [*or* plucked] a curlew, drawn a hen. On an Island. J. M. Synge. BIrV; MoBrPo; OxBSP

You've read of several kinds of cat. The Ad-dressing of Cats. T. S. Eliot. FM

You've seen a pair of youthful lovers die. Dryden. *Fr.* Epilogue to Nathaniel Lee's "Mithridates." OBD

You've seen a strawberry. Nevertheless. Marianne Moore. CMoP; MoAB; NAAL-2; OxBA; SoSe

You've started today on life's journey. Have Courage, My Boy, to Say No! L. M. Hilton. WTO

You've talked to the sun and moon. Charles Wright. *Fr.* Skins, 20. HCAP

You've Told Me, Maro. Martial, *tr. fr. Latin by* F. Lewis. NIP

You've toughed it out pretty well, old Body, done. Remarks of Soul to Body. Robert Penn Warren. NAs

Yowre mouth hit saith me, 'Bas me, bas me.' Your Mouth Says, Kiss Me. Charles, Duc d' Orléans. OxBLMV

Ypres. Laurence Binyon. MMA

Yt fell abowght the Lamasse tyde. The Battle of Otterburn [*or* Oterborne]. *Unknown.* ESPB; OxBS. *See also* It fell about. . .

Yu, yu, cry the deer. *Unknown, tr. by* Arthur Waley. BoS

Yucca clump, The/ is blooming. The Yucca Moth. A. R. Ammons. NOBA

Yugoslav Cemetery. Celeste Turner Wright. WPE

Yuh Lookin Good. Carolyn M. Rodgers. BPo

Yule Days, The. *Unknown.* ChTr; GBP

Yule Log, The. William Hamilton Hayne. AA

Yule Log. Robert Herrick. *See* Come, bring with a noise.

Yule's Come, and Yule's Gane. *Unknown.* GBP

Yuma. Charles Henry Phelps. AA

Yung Wind, *sels.* Confucius, *tr. fr. Chinese by* Ezra Pound. CTC
  Baroness Mu Impeded in Her Wish to Help Famine Victims in Wei.
  Sans Equity and Sans Poise.

Yuola. A. Leyeles, *tr. fr. Yiddish by* Benjamin *and* Barbara Harshav. AYP

Yussouf. James Russell Lowell. BeLS; BLPA; BLPL; BoTP; FaBoBe

Yves Tanguy. Paul Eluard, *tr. fr. French by* Michael Benedikt. POS

Yves Tanguy. David Gascoyne. EAS

Z

Z Is for Zoroaster. Eleanor Farjeon. WSC

Z, Y, X, and W, V. *Unknown.* OxNR

Zack Bumstead uster flosserfize. A Philosopher. Sam Walter Foss. OBAL

Zagonyi. George Henry Boker. PAH

Zalka Peetruza. Ray Garfield Dandridge. BANP; PoBA

Zambra Dance, The. Dryden. *See* Conquest of Granada, The: Song of the Zambra Dance.

Zapata & the Landlord. Alfred B. Spellman. PoBA

Zaph Describes the Haunts of Malzah. Charles Heavysege. *Fr.* Saul. OBCV

Zapolya, *sel.* Samuel Taylor Coleridge.
  Glycine's Song. CH; OBEV
  (Song: "Sunny shaft did I behold, A.") PBBP

Zarian was saying: Florence is youth. A Water-Colour of Venice. Lawrence Durrell. MoBrPo

Zarkhi, His Pipe to the Yard, Cries. Moyshe-Leyb Halpern, *tr. fr. Yiddish by* Benjamin *and* Barbara Harshav. *Fr.* Zarkhi on the Sea Shore. AYP

Zarkhi on the Sea Shore, *sels.* Moyshe-Leyb Halpern, *tr. fr. Yiddish by* Benjamin *and* Barbara Harshav. AYP
  From Zarkhi's Teachings.
  What Do We Know, Dear Brothers?.
  Zarkhi, His Pipe to the Yard, Cries.
  Zarkhi to Himself.

Zarkhi to Himself. Moyshe-Leyb Halpern, *tr. fr. Yiddish by* Benjamin *and* Barbara Harshav. *Fr.* Zarkhi on the Sea Shore. AYP

Zaydee. Philip Levine. CAPP; NNaP; VWA

Zeal and Love. John Henry, Cardinal Newman. TW

Zealless Xylographer, The. Mary Mapes Dodge. AnAmPo; OBAL

Zealot without a Face. Charles Dobzynski, *tr. fr. French by* Anita Barrows. VWA

Zealots of Yearning. David Rokeah, *tr. fr. Hebrew by* I. M. Lask. TrJP

Zealous locksmith died of late, A. On a Puritanicall Lock-Smith. William Camden. FaBoEE

Zealous Puritan, The. *Unknown.* OBS

Zebaoth. Else Lasker-Schüler, *tr. fr. German by* Jethro Bithell. TrJP

Zebra. "Isak Dinesen." GoJo; RFM

Zebra. Judith Thurman. RHPC

Zebra. *Unknown, tr. fr. Hottentot.* PeSA

Zebra Dun, The. *Unknown.* CowP; AmFP, *diff. vers.*

Zebra jumps up and approaches, The. Beaver Skin. Antonio Porta, *tr. by* Lawrence R. Smith. NItP

Zebra Stallion. *Unknown, tr. fr. Hottentot.* PeSA

Zebras, The. Roy Campbell. LiTB; MoBrPo; PrIm

Zechariah, *sels.* Bible, O.T.
  I Return unto Zion. *Fr.* VIII: 3-5. TrJP
  Open Thy Doors, O Lebanon. *Fr.* XI: 1-14. AWP

Zeenty, peenty, heathery, mithery. Counting-out Rhyme. *Unknown.* ChTr; GBP

Zeimbekiko. Robin Magowan. EAS

Zeke. L. A. G. Strong. MoBrPo

Zek'l Weep. *Unknown.* AS

Zelanto, the Fountain of Fame, *sel.* Anthony Munday.
  Love. OBSC

Zella Wheeler! did I evah? The Interrupted Reproof. Priscilla Jane Thompson. CBWP-2

Zen Archer, The. James Kirkup. EaLo

Zen Buddhism and Psychoanalysis/ Psychoanalysis and Zen Buddhism. Jackson MacLow. PoM

Zen priest,/ Meditation finished. *Unknown, tr. by* Geoffrey Bownas *and* Anthony Thwaite. PeBJV

Zepheria, *sels. Unknown.*
  Proud in Thy Love. *Fr.* XIII. Son
  Sonnet. EIL
  "When we in kind embracements had agre'd [agreed]." *Fr.* XXVI. AAS; Son

Zephyr. Eugene Fitch Ware. PoLF

Zeppelin. Andrew Glaze. WeW

Zeppelins. Patrick Conrad, *tr. fr. Dutch by* James S. Holmes. DuIn

Zermatt: To the Matterhorn. Thomas Hardy. OBNC

Zero, *sel.* Antonio Porta, *tr. fr. Italian by* Lawrence R. Smith.
  "Yes, no, yes, no, yes, no, yes, no, yes, no, yes, no, yes, no, yes." NItP

Zero/ zero/ zero/ the museum of modern art. The Story of the Zeros. Victor Hernandez Cruz. PoBA

0[D]G/. Elizabeth Spires. DiPo

Zero hour. Waiting yet again. James Merrill. *Fr.* The Book of Ephraim. HCAP

Zero Life, *sel.* Lamberto Pignotti, *tr. fr. Italian by* Lawrence R. Smith.
  "Place in evidence." NItP

Zero Population Growth. Lauris Edmond. *Fr.* Two Birth Poems, II. ATNZ

Zeroing In. Denise Levertov. ER

Zest of Life, The. Henry van Dyke. *Fr.* The Three Best Things. WBLP

Zeus,/ Brazen-thunder-hurler. The Faun Sees Snow for the First Time. Richard Aldington. MoBrPo

Zeus,—by what name soe'er. Hymn to Zeus. Aeschylus, *tr. fr. Greek by* Gilbert Murray. *Fr.* Agamemnon. WGRP

Zeus lies in Ceres' bosom. Ezra Pound. *Fr.* Cantos, LXXXI. FaBoMo; MoP; NAAL-2; NoAm; NOBA; VGW

Zeus was once overheard to shout at Hera. The Weather of Olympus. Robert Graves. FaBoEE

Zeus, whoever Zeus may be, if he. Aeschylus, *tr. by* Peter Levi. TOF

Zig-zag bee *zzz* and *zzz*-ing, came, A. The Bee. John Fandel. GoYe

Zig-Zag up a Thistle. Rachel McAlpine. ATNZ

Zillebeke Brook. Edmund Blunden. MMA

Zilver-Weed, The. William Barnes. NOBVV

Zimbabwe. F. D. Sinclair. PeSA

Zimmer and His Turtle Sink the House. Paul Zimmer. Psk

Zimmer Drunk and Alone, Dreaming of Old Football Games. Paul Zimmer. MAT

Zimmer to His Students. Paul Zimmer. KS

Zimmer's Head Thudding against the Blackboard. Paul Zimmer. PCP

Zimmer's Street. Paul Zimmer. TDD

Zimmershire Lad, A. Paul Zimmer. SM

Zimri ("In the first rank of These did Zimri stand."). Dryden. *See* Absalom and Achitophel, Pt. I: In the first rank of these did Zimri stand.

Zimri ("Numerous host of dreaming saints succeed."). Dryden. *See* Absalom and Achitophel, Pt. I: Zimri: The Duke of Buckingham ("A numerous host of dreaming saints succeed").

Zimri: ("Some of their chiefs were princes of the land"). Dryden. *See* Absalom and Achitophel, Pt. I: Some of their chiefs were princes of the land.

Zimri: The Duke of Buckingham. Dryden. *Fr.* Absalom and Achitophel, Pt. I. NOBE; OBSV

Zimri: The Duke of Buckingham ("A numerous host of dreaming saints succeed"). Dryden. *Fr.* Absalom and Achitophel, Pt. I. NOBE; OBSV

   (Zimri ("Numerous host of dreaming saints succeed.").) AWP; SeCePo

Zinnias. Valerie Worth. NTCP

Zinnias, ochre, orange, chrome and amber, The. Transition. May Sarton. NePoAm

Zinnias, stout and stiff. Zinnias. Valerie Worth. NTCP

ZINZ. Alma Villanueva. CCP

Zion, or the City of God. John Newton. *See* Glorious Things of Thee Are Spoken.

Zion, wilt thou not ask if peace's wing. Ode to Zion. Judah Halevi, *tr. by* Nina Davis Salaman. TrJP

Zionist Marching Song. Naphtali Herz Imber, *tr. fr. Hebrew by* Israel Zangwill. TrJP

Zion's Sons and Daughters. *Unknown.* AmFP

Zip, zip the valley wind,/ Bring darkness, bringing rain. *Unknown, tr. by* Arthur Waley. BoS

Zip, zip the valley wind!/ Nothing but wind and rain. *Unknown, tr. by* Arthur Waley. BoS

Zippo lighter, A. Off the Back of a Lorry. Tom Paulin. FaBCIP

Zippora Returns to Moses at Rephidim. Rose Drachler. VWA

Ziz, The. John Hollander. VWA

Zizi's Lament. Gregory Corso. NeAP; VGW

Zlochov [*or* Zlotchev, My Home]. Moyshe-Leyb Halpern, *tr. fr. Yiddish by* Benjamin *and* Barbara Harshav. AYP; VWA, *tr. by* Richard J. Fein

Zobo Bird, The. Frank A. Collymore. AmMo; GoJo

Zodiac, The, *sel.* James Dickey.
   "Tenderness, ache on me, and lay your neck." TAP

Zodiac Rhyme, The. *Unknown.* GBP

Zodiac Song, The. John Ruskin. NOBVV

Zoetropes. Bill Manhire. ATNZ; PeNZ

Zohara. Jack Hirschman. VWA

Zola. Edwin Arlington Robinson. OxBA

Zolgotz. *Unknown.* AmFP

Zollicoffer. Henry Lynden Flash. PAH

Zollverein was hardly neutral, The. One recalls. Philatelic Lessons: The German Collection. Lawrence P. Spingarn. NYBP

Zone. Guillaume Apollinaire, *tr. fr. French.* POS, *tr. by* Roger Shattuck; RHTwFP, *tr. by* Samuel Beckett; SOTW, *tr. by* Ron Padgett.

Zone. Louise Bogan. WPE

Zone of Death. William Everson. VGW

Zones of warmth around his heart, The. Sandy Star and Willie Gee. William Stanley Braithwaite. BANP

Zong Belegt Baatar. *Mongol Oral Tradition, tr. by* C. R. Bawden. WTO

Zong, A: "O Jenny, don't sobby! vor I shall be true." William Barnes. BoLoP

Zonnebeke Road, The. Edmund Blunden. MMA; OBWP

Zoo, The. John Logan. LCAP

Zoo, The. Gilbert Sorrentino. NeAP

Zoo, The. Humbert Wolfe. MoShBr

Zoo in the City, The. Sara Van Alstyne Allen. GoYe

Zoo is full of cages and it lies, The. Picture Postcard of a Zoo. Oscar Williams. Son

Zoo Manners. Eileen Mathias. BoTP

Zoo of You, The. Arthur Freeman. ErPo

Zophiël, *sels.* Maria Gowen Brooks. AA
   Palace of the Gnomes.
   Respite, The.

Zoroaster Devoutly Questions Ormazd. Zoroaster. *See* Sacred Book, The.

Zotz! Neil Marcus. TSM

Zounds, gramercy, and rootity-toot! Robin Hood. Phyllis McGinley. *Fr.* Speaking of Television. OBSV

Zounds! how the price went flashing through. Israel Freyer's Bid for Gold. Edmund Clarence Stedman. PAH

Zu fragmentarisch ist Welt und Leben. Heine, *tr. fr. German by* Charles Godfrey Leland. AWP

Zulu Girl, The. Roy Campbell. OBMV

Zum Lazarus, *sel.* Heine, *tr. fr. German by* Alistair Elliot.
   "Heavenly fields of Paradise, The." OBD

Zummer Stream. William Barnes. BoNaP

Zun-zet. William Barnes. PoEL-4

Zuni Derivations. *Unknown, tr. fr. Zuni Indian by* Dennis Tedlock. STP

Zürich, zum Storchen. Paul Celan, *tr. fr. German by* Joachim Neugroschel. VWA

AUTHOR INDEX

Arabic, Chinese, Korean, and old-style Japanese names in the Author Index are alphabetized, following standard practice, in uninverted form. Modern Japanese names, however, are inverted in the Western manner. Pseudonymous names are enclosed in quotation marks.

À Beckett, Gilbert Abbott
  Holiday Task, A.
"A., F. P." *See* Adams, Franklin Pierce
"A. K." *See* "K., A."
"A. R. G." *See* "G., A. R."
"A. W." *See* "W., A."
Aal, Katharyn Machan
  Beets Poem, The.
  Ithaca.
  Leda's Sister and the Geese.
Aaronson, Leonard [*or* Lazarus]
  Homeward Journey, The.
  Pesci Misti.
Abba Arika. *See* Rab
Abbe, George
  Horizon Thong.
  New York City.
  Passer, The.
Abbey, Henry
  Donald.
  Faith's Vista.
  In Memory of General Grant.
  What Do We Plant [When We Plant the Tree].
  Winter Days.
Abbott, Clifton
  Just Keep On.
Abbott, Keith
  Blue Mason Jars.
  French Desire.
  Good News Bad News.
  Persephone.
  To an Old San Francisco Poet.
Abbott, Wenonah Stevens
  Soul's Soliloquy, A.
Abd-al-Haye. *See* "Ludhianvi, Sahir"
Abd al-Hayy, Muhammad
  Adam Sign, The, *sel.*
Abd al-Sabur, Salah
  Expectation: Night and Day.
  Gist of the Story, The.
  People of My Country, The.
  Sun and the Woman, The.
Abe no Hironiwa. *See* Hironiwa
Abeita Louise. *See* "E-Yeh-Shure"
Abelard, Peter
  David's Lament for Jonathan.
  Hymn for the Close of the Week.
Abelardo
  $.
Abercrombie, Lascelles
  All Last Night.
  Epilogue: "What shall we do for Love these days?" *sel.*
  Epitaph: "Sir, you should notice me: I am the Man."
  Fear, The.
  Hope and Despair.
  Hymn to Love, *sel.*
  Mary and the Bramble.
  Seeker, The, *sel.*
  Song: "Balkis was in her marble town," *sel.*
  Stream's Song, The.
  Vashti, *sel.*

  Witchcraft: New Style.
  Woman's Beauty, *sel.*
Abi Shaqra, Shauqi
  Children of a Grieved Mother.
  Fan and the Observatory Dome, The.
  Fresh Air.
  Fugue.
  Hotel, The.
  Miss Lemonada.
  My Arms Became the Month of October.
  Prison's Stream, The.
  Returning to Granny.
  Silver Mouth, The.
  Storm, The.
  Student, The.
Abrahams, Peter
  Lonely Road.
  Me, Colored, *sel.*
Abrahams, William
  In the Henry James Country.
  Museum, The.
  Poem in Time of War.
  Séance.
Abramovitch, Henry
  Psalm of the Jealous God.
Abrams, Sam
  Cakewalkman.
  Not the Arms Race.
  United States of America We, The.
  What the Sixties Were Really Like.
  World Is with Me Just Enough, The.
Abse, Dannie
  Angels.
  Bedtime Story.
  Down the M4.
  Epithalamion: "Singing, today I married my white girl."
  Florida.
  In the Theatre.
  Inscription on the Flyleaf of a Bible.
  Letter to Alex Comfort.
  Millie's Date.
  Mysteries.
  Near the Border of Insanities.
  New Diary, A.
  Not Adlestrop.
  Pathology of Colours.
  Peachstone.
  Poem and Message.
  Public Library.
  Scream, A.
  Snake.
  Song for Dov Shamir.
  Tales of Shatz.
  Tuberculosis.
  Watching a Cloud.
  Winter Visit, A.
  Words Spoken Alone.
Abu Bakr
  Sword, The.
Abu Dharr
  Oranges, The.
Abu Dolama
  Humorous Verse.

Abu Khalid, Fawziyya
  Mother's Inheritance.
  I Love You.
  This Is My Wine.
  You or I?
Abu Zakariya
  Bubbling Wine.
Abulafia, Todros Ben Judah
  From Prison.
Abutsu the Nun
  Against the white beach.
  As you went away.
  If not so my children.
  In the former world.
  Shore wind is cold on my travel clothes, The, *sel.*
  Shower comes up, A.
  Travelers/ are all up and on their way, The.
Acharyaov, Ananda
  My Faith.
  Realization.
Achebe, Chinua
  After a War.
  Beware, Soul Brother.
  Christmas in Biafra (1969).
  Non-Commitment.
Achterberg, Gerrit
  Accountability.
  Ballad of the Store Clerk.
  Bridegroom.
  Grief.
  House.
  Ichthyology.
  Lullaby: "In my memory you flare."
  Ravel's Bolero.
  Skin.
  Sleepwalking.
  Statue.
  Tableau Mourant.
  Word.
Ackerley, J. R.
  After the Blitz, 1941.
Ackerman, Diane
  Driving through Farm Country at Sunset.
  Fatalities.
  Fine, a Private Place, A.
  In the Silks.
  Ode to an Alien.
  Other Night (Comet Kohoutek), The.
  Patrick Ewing Takes a Foul Shot.
  Pumping Iron.
  Soccer at the Meadowlands.
  Space Shuttle.
  Spiders.
  Starman, The.
  Sweep Me through Your Many-Chambered Heart.
  Whale Songs.
Ackermann, Louise
  My Book.
Ackland, Valentine
  Black-Out.
  Notes on Life at Home, February, 1942.
  7 October, 1940.

Ackroyd, Peter
All These.
And the Children.
Day, The.
It Would Be Easy.

Acorn, Milton
Blackfish Poem.
Fights, The.
Ghostly Story.
I'd Like to Mark Myself.
I've Gone and Stained with the Color of
Love.
I've Tasted My Blood.
Knowing I Live in a Dark Age.
Lover That I Hope You Are.
Monument.
Offshore Breeze.
On Saint-Urbain Street.
Poem for a Singer.
Saint-Henri Spring.
You Growing.

Acosta, Teresa Palma
My Mother Pieced Quilts.

Acquah, Kobena Eyi
I want to Go to Keta.

Acton, Ellen M. V.
Exodus from a Renaissance Gallery.

Acuña, Manuel
Before a Corpse.

"Ada"
Lines: "From fair Jamaica's fertile plains."
Lines, Suggested on Reading "An Appeal to
Christian Women of the South."
Oh, when this earthly tenement.Black and
White.
Song for My Little Friends.

Adamo, Ralph
Great Escape, The.
My Answer.

Adams, Anna
Her Dancing Days.
Unrecorded Speech.

Adams, Arthur H.
Australian, The.
Dwellings of Our Dead, The.

Adams, Charles Follen ("Yawcob Strauss")
John Barley-Corn, My Foe.
Misplaced Sympathy.
My Infundibuliform Hat.
Prevalent Poetry.
Repartée.
To Bary Jade.

Adams, E. H.
Action Rhyme.

Adams, E. M.
Haymaking.
Paddling Pool, The.
Sea, The.
Shady Woods.
Snowman, The.

Adams, Elijah
Ashland Tragedy, The.

Adams, Francis Lauderdale
Evening Hymn in the Hovels.
Hagar.
Jesus.
To the Christians.
William Wallace.

Adams, Franklin Pierce ("F.P.A.")
Ballade of Lawn Tennis, A.
Baseball Note.
Baseball's Sad Lexicon.
Composed in the Composing Room.
Double Standard, The.
If.
Lines Where Beauty Lingers.
Rich Man, The.
Song: "Don't Tell Me What You Dreamt Last
Night."
"Such Stuff as Dreams."

Those Two Boys.
To a Lady.
To a Thesaurus.
Tonight.
Translated Way, The.

Adams, H. M.
Johnny's Farm.

Adams, James Barton
Cowboy's Dance Song, The.
Cowboy's Life, The, _at._

Adams, Jean
Dream, or the Type of the Rising Sun, A.

Adams, John Coleman
We Praise Thee, God, for Harvests Earned.

Adams, John G.
Heaven Is Here.

Adams, John Quincy
Lip and the Heart, The.
Send Forth, O God, Thy Light and Truth.
Wants of Man, The.

Adams, John Quincy _after_ Horace
To Sally.

Adams, Léonie
April Mortality.
Bell Tower.
Caryatid.
Counsel to Unreason.
Country Summer.
Death and the Lady.
Early Waking.
Figurehead, The.
Ghostly Tree.
Grapes Making.
Home-coming.
Horn, The.
Kingdom of Heaven.
Lullaby: "Hush, lullay."
Mount, The.
Night-Piece.
River in the Meadows, The.
Song from a Country Fair.
Sundown.
This Measure..
On a Grave in Christchurch, Hants.

Adams, Perseus
Murder Trial, The.
My Grandmother.
Woman and the Aloe, The.

Adams, Sarah Flower
Nearer, My God, to Thee.

Adamson, Robert
Action Would Kill It/A Gamble.
My House.
Ribbon-Fish, The.
Sail Away.
Sonnet to Be Written from Prison.
Things Going out of My Life.

Adcock, Arthur St. John
By Deputy.
Travellers.

Adcock, Betty
Nothing Happened.
Roller Rink.
Southbound.
Twentieth Anniversary.
Walking Out.

Adcock, Fleur
Advice to a Discarded Lover.
Afterwards.
Against Coupling.
Bedroom Window, The.
Before Sleep, _sel._
Below Loughrigg.
Blue Glass.
Composition for Words and Paint.
Crab.
December Morning.
Double-Take.
Drought Breaks, The.
Ex-Queen among the Astronomers, The.
Excavations.

For a Five-Year-Old.
For Andrew.
Foreigner.
Future Work.
Icon.
Illustration to Dante, An.
Incident.
Instead of an Interview.
Kilpeck.
Leaving the Tate.
Message, A.
Mornings After.
Net, The.
Note on Propertius I.5.
Over the Edge.
Poem Ended by a Death.
Surprise in the Peninsula, A.
Unexpected Visit.
Visited.
Water Below, The.
Weathering.
Wife to Husband.

Addison, Joseph
Cato's Soliloquy, _sel._
Immortal glories in my mind revive, _sel._
Letter from Italy, to the Right Honourable
Charles Lord Halifax, A.
Ode: "How are thy servants blest, O Lord!"
Ode: "Spacious firmament on high, The."
Poem to His Grace the Duke of Marlborough,
A, _sel._
Song: "Oh the charming month of May!"
When rising from the bed of death.

Addison, William
Shadows among the Ettrick Hills.

Ade, George
Il Janitoro.
Microbe's Serenade, The.
R-E-M-O-R-S-E.

"Adeler, Max" (Charles Heber Clark)
In Memoriam.
Mr. Slimmer's Funeral Verses for the
Morning Argus .
Sacred to the Memory of Maria (To Say
Nothing of Jane and Martha) Sparks.
We Have Lost Our Little Hanner.

Adler, Mortimer J.
Fearless, The.

Adler, Richard _and_ **Jerry Ross**
Heart, _sel._

Adnan, Etel
Enemy's Testament, The.
Human race is going to the cemetery, The,
sel.

Adoff, Arnold
Chocolate Chocolate.
My Mouth.
Past.
Point Guard.
Wrestling The Beast.

"Adonis." _See_ **"Adunis"**

Adrian, Vonna
By Yon Bonny Banks or Thereabout.
Clerihew: "Jan Vermeer/ liked to paint a
tankard of beer."
Clerihew: "Joseph Mallord Turner/ no slow
learner."

"Adunis," [_or_ **"Adonis"**] **(Ali Ahmad Sa'id)**
Beginning Speech.
Bird, The.
Desert, The.
Fire Tree, The.
Grave for New York, A.
Invasion.
Mihyar, A King!
Minaret, The.
Mirror for Autumn, A.
Mirror for the Twentieth Century, A.
Mirror to Khalida, A.

New Noah, The.
Song, A: "O close of night, I would have you linger."
Who Are You?
Wound, The.

"Æ" (Russell, George William)
Ancient.
By the Margin of the Great Deep.
Cities, The.
City, The.
Continuity.
Dark Rapture.
Desire.
Dust.
Epilogue: "Well, when all is said and done."
Exiles.
Frolic.
Garden of God, The.
Gay, The.
Germinal.
Great Breath, The.
Holy Well, A.
Immortality.
Lonely, The.
Mountain Wind, A.
New York.
On Behalf of Some Irishmen Not Followers of Tradition.
Outcast.
Pain.
Place of Rest, The.
Prayer: "Let us leave our island woods grown dim and blue."
Prisoner, A.
Reconciliation.
Secret, The.
Self-Discipline.
Tragedy.
Truth.
Twilight of Earth, The.
Unknown God, The.

Aengus [or Angus] the Culdee
Prayer for Forgiveness, A.

Aeschylus
Achaians Have Got Troy, upon This Very Day, The, *sel.*
Agamemnon.
Alone of gods death has no love for gifts, *sel.*
Chorus: "Great Fortune is an hungry thing," *sel.*
Eumenides, The.
God of War, Money Changer of Dead Bodies, The, *sel.*
Hymn to Zeus, *sel.*
If I Were to Tell of Our Labours, Our Hard Lodging, *sel.*
Lament for the Two Brothers Slain by Each Other's Hand, *sel.*
Libation Bearers, The.
Salamis, *sel.*
Signal Fire, The, *sel.*
Wail of Prometheus Bound, The, *sel.*
Zeus, whoever Zeus may be, if he.

Aesop (6th century B.C.)
Ass in the Lion's Skin, The ("An ass put on a lion's skin and went").
Mountain in Labor, The.
Shepherd-Boy and the Wolf, The.
Swan and the Goose, The.
Vine and the Goat, The.

Agard, Brenda
Black Truth.
Business Partners.
Nobody.
Nothing Said.

Agard, John
Pan Recipe.
Waiting for Fidel.

Agard, Sandra
House, A.

Agate, James
Eumenides at Home, The.

Agathias
Not Such Your Burden.
Plutarch.
Rhodanthe.

Agee, James
Happy Hen, The.
I loitered weeping with my bride for gladness, *sel.*
In Heavy Mind.
In Memory of My Father.
Permit Me Voyage.
Rapid Transit.
Red Sea, *sel.*
So it begins. Adam is in his earth, *sel.*
Song with Words.
Sonnets, *sels.*
Sunday: Outskirts of Knoxville, Tennessee.
Temperance Note: and Weather Prophecy, *sel.*
Those former loves wherein our lives have run, *sel.*
We Soldiers of All Nations Who Lie Killed.

Agh, István
Dead of My Songs, The.

Agnew, Edith
Let me tell to you the story.
Progress.

Agnew, Joan
Freedom.
Sons of the King.

Agnew, Marjorie L.
On Going Home.

"Agricola"
Daventry Wonder, The.

Agustini, Delmira
Another Breed.
Another Lineage.
Blindness.
Explosion.
From Far Away.
Ineffable, The.

Ai (Florence Anthony)
Abortion.
Almost Grown.
Barquisimeto, Venezuela, October 27, 1561, *sel.*
Buchenwald, 1945, *sel.*
Child Beater.
Cuba, 1962.
Everything: Eloy, Arizona, 1956.
Expectant Father, The.
Guadalajara Hospital.
Hangman.
Hitchhiker, The.
I Have Got to Stop Loving You.
Ice.
Immortality.
Kid, The.
Mexico, 1940.
Mortician's Twelve-year-old Son, The.
One Man Down.
Orinoco, 1561, The, *sel.*
Pentecost.
Peru, 1955, *sel.*
Prisoner, The.
Russia, 1927.
Salome.
She Didn't Even Wave.
Spain, 1929, *sel.*
29 (A Dream in Two Parts).
Twenty-Year Marriage.
Why Can't I Leave You?
Woman to Man.

Ai Shih-te
Human Mind, The.

Aichinger, Ilse
Abroad.
Attempt.
Counted Out.
Game of Cards.
Last Night.
March.

Part of the Question.
Self-Made.
Thirteen Years.
Village Path.
Walk, A.
Wish.

Aidoo, Ama Ata
Cornfields in Accra.

Aig-Imoukhuede, Frank
One Wife for One Man.

Aiken, Conrad
Accomplices, The.
All Lovely Things.
And in the Hanging Gardens.
Annihilation.
At a Concert of Music.
Bend as the Bow Bends, *sel.*
Bend as the bow bends.
Dead Cleopatra lies in a crystal casket, *sel.*
Dear Uncle Stranger.
Doctors' Row.
Farewell Voyaging World!
Green, Green, and Green Again, *sel.*
Habeas Corpus Blues, The.
Hatteras Calling.
Herman Melville.
It is morning, Senlin says, and in the morning, *sel.*
It's time to make love. Douse the glim.
La Belle Morte.
Limerick: "Animula vagula blandula."
Limerick: "On the deck of a ship called the Masm."
Limerick: "There once was a wonderful wizard."
Lovers, The.
Mandrill, The.
Miracles.
Multitudes Turn in Darkness.
Music I heard with you was more than music, *sel.*
Mysticism, but let us have no words, *sel.*
Nameless Ones, The.
Nuit Blanche: North End.
Obituary.
Prelude VII: "Beloved, let us once more praise the rain," *sel.*
Prelude XXI: "First note, simple, The; the second note, distinct," *sel.*
Prelude XLII: "Keep in the heart the journal nature keeps," *sel.*
Prelude LIII: "Nothing to say? Then we'll say nothing," *sel.*
Prelude LVII: "One star fell and another as we walked," *sel.*
Prelude LVI: "Rimbaud and Verlaine, precious pair of poets," *sel.*
Prelude III: "Sleep: and between the closed eyelids of sleep," *sel.*
Prelude XX: "So, in the evening, to the simple cloister," *sel.*
Prelude LII: "Stood, at the closed door," *sel.*
Prelude XXXIII: "Then came I to the shoreless shore of silence," *sel.*
Prelude VI: "This is not you? These phrases are not you?," *sel.*
Prelude XXVIII: "Time has come, the clock says time has come, The," *sel.*
Prelude II: "Two coffees in the Español, the last," *sel.*
Prelude XIX: "Watch long enough, and you will see the leaf," *sel.*
Prelude XXIX: "What shall we do—what shall we think—what shall we say?," *sel.*
Prelude I: "Winter for a moment takes the mind; the snow," *sel.*
Prelude: "Woman, Woman, let us say these things to each other."

Prelude XIV: "You went to the verge, you say, and came back safely," *sel.*
Proem to "The Kid", *sel.*
Puppet Dreams, The, *sel.*
Quarrel, The.
Road, The.
Room, The.
Sea Holly.
Senlin, *sel.*
Shaemus.
Sighed a dear little shipboard divinity.
Snowflake.
This Is the Shape of the Leaf, *sel.*
Three Star Final.
Unknown Soldier, The, *sel.*
Vampire: 1914, The.
Walk, The.
Wars, The, *sel.*
Wedding, The.
What face she put on it, we will not discuss, *sel.*
When I was a boy, and saw bright rows of icicles, *sel.*
When the Tree Bares.
When trout swim down Great Ormond Street, *sel.*
Where we were walking in the day's light, seeing, *sel.*
Who Shapes a Balustrade?
Window, The.
Winds of doctrine blow both ways at once, The, *sel.*

Aiken, Joan
Down Below.
Fable: "Pity the girl with crystal hair."
Fisherman Writes a Letter to the Mermaid, The.
In the Old House.
John's Song.
Night Landscape.

Aikin, John
Picturesque; a Fragment.
Tit for Tat; a Tale.

Aikin, Lucy
Beggar Man, The.
Swallow, The.

Aimeric de Belenoi
No man can utterly fulfill what he has in his heart.

Aimeric de Peguilhan
As much as I've made vers and canso.
At court I'm asked so much I'm sick.

Ainger, Alfred
On the Triumph of Rationalism.

Ainger, Arthur Campbell
God Is Working His Purpose Out.

Ainslie, Douglas
Stirrup Cup, The.

Ainsworth, Henry
Except the Lord, That He for Us Had Been.
Fire in My Meditation Burned.
Give Ear, O Heavens, to That Which I Declare.
How Long, Jehovah?
I Minded God.
I Spread Out unto Thee My Hands.
In the Distress upon Me.
To God Our Strength Shout Joyfully.
Unto Jehovah Sing Will I.
With All My Heart, Jehovah, I'll Confess.

Ainsworth, Ruth
Good Night.

'Aisha bint Ahmad al-Qurtubiyya
I am a lioness.

Aisthorpe, Harry
Looking for a Ship.

Ajukutooq
Song of Sukkaartik, the Assistant Spirit.

Akahito (Yamabe no Akahito)
I passed by the beach.
I wish I were close.
Mists rise over, The.

Akara, Yomo. *See* **Yomo Akara**

Akazome Emon
I, who cut off my sorrows.
In my heart's depth.

Akemi Tachibana. *See* **Tachibana Akemi**

Akenside, Mark
Amoret.
Complaint, The.
Creative Process, The, *sel.*
Farewell to Leyden's lonely bound, *sel.*
For a Statue of Chaucer at Woodstock.
Genius of ancient Greece! whose faithful steps, *sel.*
Hymn to Science.
Inscription for a Grotto, *sel.*
With what attractive charms this goodly frame, *sel.*

Akera Kanko
Autumn Wind.
Year End.

Akerman, John Yonge
Harnet and the Bittle, a Wiltshire Tale, The

Akers, Elizabeth. *See* **Allen, Elizabeth Akers**

Akesson, Sonja
Autobiography.
Ears.
Evening Walk.
Marital Problem, The.

Akhenaton
Hymn to the Sun, The.

Akhmadulina, Bella
At Night.
Autumn.
Bride, The.
Dream, A.
Fifteen Boys, or Perhaps Even More.
Goodbye.
In the Emptied Rest Home.
Names of Georgian Women, The.
Silence.
Sleepwalkers.
Small Aircraft.
Sound of Rain, The.
Volcanoes.
Winter.
Words Spoken by Pasternak during a Bombing.

"Akhmatova, Anna" (Anna Andreyevna Gorenko)
Alone.
Cleopatra.
Epilogue: "There I learned how faces fall apart," *sel.*
Everything Is Plundered.
Grey-eyed King, The.
Hands clenched under my shawl.
He loved three things in life.
How can you look at the Neva.
I Am Not One of Those Who Left the Land.
I taught myself to live simply and wisely.
I wrung my hands under my dark veil.
July 1914.
Land not mine, still, A.
Lot's Wife.
No, not under an alien sky, *sel.*
Pushkin.
Requiem 1935—1940.
Summer Garden.
Tashkent Breaks into Bloom.
There is in human closeness a sacred boundary.
This Cruel Age Has Deflected Me.
Three Things Enchanted Him.
Voronezh.
What's worse than this past century?
When a man dies.
Your lynx-eyes, Asia.

Al-Akhtal al-Saghir (Bishara Abdallah al-Khuri)
In the Arab Maghreb.
Rain Song.

Shadows of Jaikur.
Song in August.

Akhtar-ul-Iman
Evening with a Black-and-White Feathered Bird, An.
My Friend Abul Haul.
Pride of Cities.
Wild Grass.

Akhyaliyya, Laila
Camel.
Laila Boasting.
Lamenting Tauba.

Akiko, Yosano. *See* **Yosano Akiko**

Akimochi, Mononobe. *See* **Mononobe Akimochi**

Akin, Gülten
Ellas and the Statues.

Akjartoq
Old Woman's Song, An.
Remembering.

Alabaster, William
Incarnatio Est Maximum Donum Dei.
Night, the Starless Night of Passion, The, *sel.*
On the Reed of Our Lord's Passion.
Up to Mount Olivet, *sel.*
Upon the Crucifix.
Upon the Ensignes of Christes Crucifyinge.

Al-Adawiyya, Rabi'a (Rabi'a the Mystic)
O my Lord, if I worship you from fear of Hell.
O my Lord, the stars glitter and eyes of men are closed.

Al Ahmad, Muhamml-Andalusi, Ibn Hazm
Twice Times Then Is Now.

Alais, Iselda and Carenza
Lady Carenza of the lovely, gracious body.

Alamanda
If I seek your advice, pretty friend Alamanda.

Alarcón, Juan Ruiz de
Feast by the Manzanares, *sel.*

Al-Asad, Muhammad
Gardens for the Fire and the Rain.
Princess, The.

Alasdair, Alisdair MacMhaighstir. *See* **MacDonald, Alexander**

Alattur Killar
Guide to Patrons, A.

Alba, Nanina
Be Daedalus.
For Malcolm X.

Al-Baraduni, Abd-Allah
From Exile to Exile.
His fame stole his real name, *sel.*

Al-Bayati, [or Abd al-Wahhab al-Bayyati] Abdul Wahab
Apology for a Short Speech, An.
Arab Refugee, The.
Birth of Aisha and Her Death, The.
Elegy for Aisha.
Fugitive, The.
Hamlet.
Impossible, The.
Luzumiyya.
Profile of the Lover of the Great Bear.
To Ernest Hemingway.

Albee, John
Bos'n Hill.
Dandelions.
Landor.
Music and Memory.
Soldier's Grave, A.

Albert, Samuel L.
After a Game of Squash.
Honeymoon.

Albert, Steve
City Lights: I Took That Picture.

Alberti, Rafael
Charlie's Sad Date.
For Aitana.
I went away, *sel.*
Returnings of Love in Vivid Landscapes.

Albiach, Anne-Marie
And the emphasis, *sel.*
Availability/ doesn't mean, *sel.*
For if it's a theme state it, *sel.*
He accepts the circle, speech and so.
Of the unended in the speed of, *sel.*
Unspecifiable/ the inexhaustible novel, The, *sel.*

Albizzi, Niccolò degli
Prolonged Sonnet: When the Troops Were Returning from Milan.
Storm, The.

Al-Buraikan, Mahmoud
Man of the Stone City.
Tale of the Assyrian Statue.

Alcman
Sleep Upon the World.

Alcock, Mary
Chimney-Sweeper's Complaint, The ("A chimney-sweepers' boy am I").
Written in Ireland.

Alcott, Amos Bronson
Bartol.
Channing.
Emerson.
Garrison.
Hawthorne.
Margaret Fuller.
Thoreau.
Wendell Phillips.

Alcott, Louisa May
Little Kingdom I Possess, A.
Our Little Ghost.
Thoreau's Flute.

Alcuin
Lament for the Cuckoo.
Sequence for Saint Michael, A.

Aldan, Daisy
Stones: Avesbury.
Whirring, A.

Aldana, Francesco de
Image of God, The.

Alderson, Brian
Kinder- und Hausmärchen.

Aldington, Richard
After Two Years.
At the British Museum.
Barrage.
Battlefield.
Bombardment.
Epilogue: "Have I spoken too much or not enough of love?"
Evening.
Fatigues.
Faun Sees Snow for the First Time, The.
Her Mouth.
Images.
In the Trenches.
Lesbia.
Loss.
On the March.
Possession.
Prelude: "How could I love you more?"
Reserve.
Ruined House, A.
Soliloquy I.
Soliloquy II.
Three Little Girls.
Vicarious Atonement.

Aldis, Dorothy
Big.
Blum.
Clown, The.
Crunch and Lick.
Dangerous.
Everybody Says.
Hiding.
Little.
My Nose.
Naughty Soap Song.
On a Snowy Day.
Our Silly Little Sister.
Picnic, The.
Setting the Table.
Wasps.
When.
When I Was Lost.

Aldiss, Brian W.
Bridging Hour in Wesciv.
Destruction of the Fifth Planet.
Progression of the Species.
Space Burial.
Thomas Hardy Considers the Newly-Published Special Theory of Relativity.
Tom Wedgwood Tells.

Aldrich, Anne Reeve
April and Dying.
Crowned Poet, A.
Death at Daybreak.
Eternal Justice, The.
Fraternity.
In November.
Little Parable, A.
Love's Change.
Music of Hungary.
Recollection.
Song about Singing, A.

Aldrich, Henry
If all be true that I do think.

Aldrich, James
Death-Bed, A.

Aldrich, Thomas Bailey
Bells at Midnight, The.
By the Potomac.
Circumstance.
Enamoured Architect of Airy Rhyme.
Fannie.
Fredericksburg.
Guilielmus Rex.
Heredity.
Identity.
Lady of Castlenoire.
Maple Leaves.
Marjorie's Almanac.
Masks.
Memories.
Memory.
Ode, on the Unveiling of the Shaw Memorial on Boston Common, May 31st, 1897, An.
On Reading.
Outward Bound.
Palabras Cariñosas.
Petition, A.
Prescience.
Quits.
Reminiscence.
Sargent's Portrait of Edwin Booth at "The Players."
Shadow of the Night, A.
Sleep.
Tennyson.
Thalia.
Tiger-Lilies.
To Hafiz.
Turkish Legend, A.
Undiscovered Country, The.
Unguarded Gates.
When the Sultan Goes to Ispahan.

Aldridge, Richard
Archery Instructor.

Alecsandri, Vasile
Vampyre, The.

Alegría, Claribel
Everything Is Normal in Our Courtyard.
I Thought to Spend My Time.
Loneliness and July Ninth.
On the Beach.
Search.
Small Country.

Aleichem, Sholom
Epitaph: "Here lies a simple Jew."
Sleep, My Child.

Aleixandre, Vicente
Beyond.
Like the Sea, Kisses.
My Father.
Who Was Born Dead.
Your Hand in Mine.

Aleqaajik
Great grief came over me.

Aleramo, Sibilla
I Am So Good.
Night in Prison, A.
Yes to the Earth.

Alexander, Cecil Frances
All Things Bright and Beautiful.
Beggar Boy, The.
Burial of Moses, The.
Evening Song.
Fieldmouse, The.
His Are the Thousand Sparkling Rills.
Once in Royal David's City.
There Is a Green Hill Far Away.

Alexander, Frances
Contentment of Willoughby, The.

Alexander, John T.
Winning of the TV West, The.

Alexander, Joseph Addison
Hidden Line, The.

Alexander, Lewis
Africa.
Dark Brother, The.
Day and Night.
Dream Song.
Enchantment.
Japanese Hokku.
Negro Woman.
Nocturne Varial.
Tanka (I–VIII).
Transformation.

Alexander, Lilla M.
There Is Never a Day So Dreary.

Al-Faituri [*or* Al-Fituri], Muhammad
Closed Door, The.
Dervish, The.
I am a Negro.
Incident.
Knell, The.
Question and the Answer, The.
Scream, A.
Story, The.
Vision, The.

Alfieri, Vittorio
On His Life.
To Dante.
To Fido, His Horse.

Alford, Henry
Harvest Home.
You and I.

Alfred, King of England
Thus queth Alvred:/ "Idelschipe and overprute, that lereth yong wif üvel thewes", *sel.*
Thus queth Alvred:/ "If thu havest seorewe, ne seyethu hit than arewe", *sel.*
Thus queth Alvred:/ "Nevre thu, bi thine lyve, the word of thine wyve", *sel.*
Thus queth Alvred:/ "Ne schaltu nevere thi wif by hire wlyte cheose", *sel.*
Thus queth Alvred:/ "Ne würth thu never so wod ne so wyn-drunke", *sel.*

Alfred, William
Mary Lifted from the Dead.

Alger, Horatio, Jr.
John Maynard.

Al-Ghuzzi, Muhammad
Beggar, The.
Dream, A.
Female.
My Sister.
Pen, The.
Quatrains for Joy.

Taghore.
Your Eyes.
Al-Gosaibi, Ghazi
Octopus.
Silence.
When I Am with You.
Al-Haidari, Buland
Age of the Rubber Seals.
Conversation at the Bend in the Road.
Dead Witness, The.
Dialogue.
Genesis.
Guilty Even if I Were Innocent.
My Apologies.
Postman, The.
Al-Haj, Unsi
Autumn Leaves Are Virgin Mary.
Blue Crest of Fondness.
Days and the Giants, The.
Girl Butterfly Girl.
He Knew Joy on Earth.
Memory.
One Who Laughs and Laughs and Laughs,
The.
Wolf, The.
Al-Harizi, Judah
Heavy-hearted.
Love Song: "Long closed door, oh open it
again, The."
Secret Kept, A.
Song of the Flea.
Song of the Pen, The.
Under Leafy Bowers.
Unhappy Lover, The.
Within My Heart.
Ali, Muhammad
They All Must Fall.
Aliger, Margarita
House in Meudon.
To a Portrait of Lermontov.
Two.
"Al-Jabal, Badawi." *See* **"Badawi al-Jabal"**
Al-Jawahiri, Muhammad Mahdi
Come Down, Darkness.
Lullaby for the Hungry.
Al-Junaid
Now I have known, O Lord.
Alkabez, Solomon Halevi
Come, O Friend, to Greet the Bride.
Al-Kamali, Shafiq
Coda.
Disposition No. 1.
Harvest, The.
Al-Khal, Yusuf
After the Fifth of June.
Cain the Immortal.
Deserted Well, The.
Enough, She Said.
In Death's Field.
Night, The.
On Her Brother.
On Her Brother Sakhr.
Rain to the Tribe.
Sleepless.
Al-Khirniq
Lament after Her Husband Bishr's Murder.
Al-Khuri, Bishara Abdallah. *See* **"Al-Akhtal
al-Saghir"**
Allah, Fareedah. *See* **Saunders, Ruby C.**
Allan, James Alexander
Breaking.
Allan, M.
Echo Poem.
Allan, Mabel Esther
I Saw a Broken Town.
Immensity.
Allan, Thomas H.
Leave the Miracle to Him.
Allen, Alice E.
Life's Common Things.
My Mother's Garden.

Allen, Elizabeth Akers
In a Garret.
Last Landlord, The.
My Dearling.
Rock Me to Sleep, [Mother].
Sea-Birds.
Toad, A.
Allen, Ernest Bourner
"I Am with Thee."
Allen, George Leonard
Portrait.
To Melody.
Allen, Glen
Woman I Am, The.
Allen, Grace Elisabeth
Pinkletinks.
Allen, Grant
Ballade of Evolution, A.
Allen, Heather
Cartographers, The.
Allen, Hervey
Upstairs Downstairs.
Allen, John Alexander
Admiral.
Allen, Jonathan
Sinners, Will You Scorn the Message?
Allen, Leslie Holdsworth
Reaper, The.
Allen, Lillian
Belly Woman's Lament.
I Fight Back.
Allen, Lyman Whitney
Coming of His Feet, The.
Allen, Marie Louise
First Snow.
Five Years Old.
Mitten Song, The.
Allen, Paula Gunn
Beautiful Woman Who Sings, The.
Catching One Clear Thought Alive.
Dear World.
Grandmother.
Kopis'taya.
Lament of my Father.
God of Bethel Heard Her Cries, The.
Allen, Samuel ("Paul Vesey")
Dylan, Who Is Dead.
If the Stars Should Fall.
Love Song: "Arrow rides upon the sky, An."
Moment Please, A.
My Friend.
Nat Turner.
Ski Trail.
Staircase, The.
To Satch (or American Gothic).
What Bright Pushbutton?
Allen, Sara Van Alstyne
Marble Statuette Harpist.
Zoo in the City, The.
Allen, William S.
Erie Canal, The.
Allerton, Ellen Palmer
Beautiful Things.
Allfrey, Phyllis Shand
Child's Return, The.
Cunard Liner 1940.
Love for an Island.
Young Lady Dancing with Soldier.
Alline, Henry
Amazing Sight! The Saviour Stands, *sel.*
Hard Heart of Mine.
Turn, Turn, Unhappy Souls, Return.
Alling, Kenneth Slade
Monsoon.
Onion Skin in Barn.
Allingham, William
Abbot of Inisfalen, The.
An Evening.
At Ballyshannon, Co. Donegal.
Blowing Bubbles.

Dream, A.
Evening, An.
Everything passes and vanishes.
Eviction, The, *sel.*
Express.
Fairies, The.
Four Ducks on a Pond.
Girl's Lamentation, The.
Homeward Bound.
Lion and the Wave, The.
Lord Crashton: The Absentee Landlord, *sel.*
Meadowsweet.
Mill, A.
No funeral gloom, my dears, when I am
gone.
Riding.
Robin Redbreast.
Song: "I walk'd in the lonesome evening."
Spring: The Lover and the Birds.
Swing Song, A.
Up the Airy Mountain.
Wild Rose.
Windlass Song.
Wishing.
Witch-Bride, The.
Writing.
Allison, Dorothy
To the Bone.
When I Drink I Become the Joy of Faggots.
Women Who Hate Me, The.
Allison, Drummond
Brass Horse, The.
Dedication: "Had there been peace there never
had been riven."
King Lot's Envoys.
No Remedy.
Allison, John
Okeechobee.
Reflection: After Visiting Old Friends.
"Allison, Joy" (Mary A. Cragin)
Which Loved Best?
Allison, William Talbot
O Amber Day, amid the Autumn Gloom.
Allison, Young Ewing
Derelict.
Allman, John
You Owe Them Everything.
Allott, Kenneth
Lament for a Cricket Eleven.
Prize for Good Conduct.
Statue, The.
Allston, Washington
America to Great Britain.
On the Late S. T. Coleridge.
Rosalie.
Allur Nanmullai
What He Said.
What She Said.
Allwood, Brian
No Laws.
Al-Maghut, Muhammad
Arab Traveler in a Space Ship, An.
From the Threshold to the Sky.
Noonday Sun and the Shade, The.
Orphan, The.
Postman's Fear, The.
Siege.
Tattoo, The.
Tourist.
Winter.
Al-Mahdi
Preacher, The.
Al-Majdhoub, Muhammad al-Mahdi
Birth (al-Maulid).
Rain, The.
Al-Mala'ika, Nazik
Elegy for a Woman of No Importance.
Jamila.
Lilies for the Prophet.
Love Song for Words.
New Year.

Song for the Moon.
Visitor Who Never Came, The.
Al-Maqalih, Abd al-Aziz
Choice.
Fifteenth Telegram ("Birds that migrated, The"), *sel.*
First Communiqué from One Returning from the Zanj Revolt.
First Telegram ("As I retire, each day, with myself"), *sel.*
Nineteenth Telegram ("Love has changed the face of distances"), *sel.*
Ninth Telegram ("Trains roll over my heart, The"), *sel.*
Second Telegram ("Every evening when night retrieves the substance of our longings"), *sel.*
Seventeenth Telegram ("Your weeping gray streets"), *sel.*
Seventh Telegram ("The day recedes"), *sel.*
Tenth Telegram ("I wish I had a boat"), *sel.*
Thirteenth Telegram ("Faces that stab the eye are familiar, The"), *sel.*
Twentieth Telegram ("Ah my city, my lady"), *sel.*
Alma-Tadema, Laurence
If No One Ever Marries Me.
Robin, The.
Almucs de Castelnau *and* **Iseut de Capio**
Lady Almucs, with your permission.
Al-Najafi, Ahmad al-Safi
Moth, The.
Pleasures of Darkness, The.
Ship of Life, The.
Where Is the Guard?
Alohikea, Alfred
Glory of Hanalei is its heavy rain, The.
Alonso, Ricardo
Tiempo Muerto.
Al-Qasim, Samih
Boring Orbit, The.
Clock on the War, The.
General's Property, The.
Girl from Rafah.
I feel my limbs, *sel.*
Sons of War.
Story of the Unknown Man, The.
Will of a Man Dying in Exile, The.
Al-Qasim al-Shabbi, Abu
In the Shadow of the Valley of Death.
Alquit, B.
Light of the World, The.
Wandering Chorus.
Al-Rahabi, Sayf
Entering the Gardens of Doom.
Al-Rasafi, Maruf
Abyss of Death, The.
Poem to al-Raihani.
Al-Rayyes, Riad
To Taufiq Sayigh.
Al-Sabah, Suad al-Mubarak
Free Harbor.
Mad Woman.
Pit, The.
Wild Cat, A.
You Alone.
"Al-Saghir, Al-Akhtal." *See* **"Al-Akhtal al-Saghir"**
Al-Sayyah, Badr Shakir
Death and the River.
Jaikur and the City.
River and Death, The.
Al-Shabbi, Abu al-Qasim
Cupbearer, take your wine away, *sel.*
Life's Will.
Al-Sharqawi, Ali
I shall knock three times at the door, *sel.*
Alsop, George
Author to His Book, The.
Be just (domestick monarchs) unto them.

Could'st thou (O Earth) live thus obscure, and now.
Heavens bright lamp, shine forth some of thy light.
Lines on a Purple Cap Received as a Present from My Brother.
Poor vaunting earth, gloss'd with uncertain pride.
'Tis said the Gods lower down that chain above.
To My Cosen Mrs. Ellinor Evins.
Trafique Is Earth's Great Atlas.
Alston, Joseph Blynth
"Stack Arms!"
Alta
After Reading Sylvia Plath.
Bitter Herbs.
Euch, are you having your period?
First Pregnancy.
I Don't Have No Bunny Tail on My Behind.
Penus envy, they call it.
Altamirano, Ignacio Manuel
To the Atoyac.
Altamirano, Santiago
Eagle above Us, The.
Al-Tayyib, Abdallah
Breaking of the Glass, The.
Altenburg, Michael
Battle Hymn.
Alterman, Nathan [*or* Natan]
Foundling, The.
Poem about Your Face.
Red Ridinghood.
Saul.
Spinning Girl, The.
Summer Night.
Tammuz.
This Night.
To the Elephants.
Tonight.
When our children cried in the shadow of the gallows, *sel.*
Altmann, René
Impression.
Late Fall.
When Will the Bird Cry Again?
Altrocchi, Julia Cooley
Pigeon-Feeders in Battery Park, The.
Al-Udwani, Ahmad al-Mushari
An Answer.
I asked the grave-digger, "Do you have", *sel.*
Mysterious things within you, The, *sel.*
You I give no name to/ The mysterious things within you/ are fragrance, light and melody, *sel.*
You I give no name to/ The mysterious things within you/ are an untrodden bower, *sel.*
Alurista
Get Stuffed.
In the Barrio.
Must Be the Season of the Witch.
Our Barrio.
Alvarez, Alfred
Cemetery in New Mexico, A.
Dying.
Fortunate Fall, The.
Mourning and Melancholia.
Alvarez, Julia
He: Age Doesn't Matter When You're Both in Love, *sel.*
Mother Asks What I'm Put To, *sel.*
33 Is the Year That Jesus Christ, *sel.*
Alver, Betti
Iron Heaven.
Painter in the Lion Cage, The.
Tailor Called Sorrow, A.
Titans, The.
Al-Wahaybi, Al-Munsif
Camel, The.
Ceremony.
Desert, The.

In the Arab House.
Man Rises from the Cave of Hira', A.
Al-Wugayyan, Khalifa
Elegy: "Newspaper appears in the morning, The."
Letter to a Bedouin Informer.
Alyea, Dorothy
Keepsake from Quinault.
Al-Zahawi, Jamil Sidqi
Both Strangers.
Ama Ata Aidoo, Christine
Prelude: "I am the bird of the wayside."
Amabile, George
Snowfall: Four Variations.
Twink Drives Back, in a Bad Mood, from a Party in Massachusetts.
Amarou
Drunken Rose, The.
Ambapali
Black and glossy as a bee and curled was my hair.
Ambrose, Saint
Hymn: "Framer of the earth and sky."
Ameen, Mark
Monologue of a Dying Beast.
Sonnet No. 21.
Sonnet No. 22.
Amen, Grover
Cot, The.
Amenhotep IV. *See* **Akhenaton**
Amergin
Fish-teeming sea, *sel.*
I am wind on sea, *sel.*
I call the land of Ireland, *sel.*
Mystery, The, at.
Ames, A. S.
Abraham Lincoln.
Ames, Bernice
Country of Water.
Ames, Evelyn
Because I Live.
Two Solitudes.
Amichai [*or* **Amikhai**], **Yehuda**
Advice.
All these stones, all this sadness, all, *sel.*
And in spite of it all I must, *sel.*
And this is how it begins now, my late, *sel.*
Both of Us Together and Each Apart.
Clouds Are the First Fatalities, The.
Clouds have come up from the south, the Nile's, *sel.*
Defoliated Leaves.
Diameter of the Bomb Was Thirty Centimeters, The.
Early in the Morning You Lean.
Elegy: "Wind won't come to draw smiles in dream sand, The."
Evening lies along the horizon and gives blood.
For My Beloved, Combing Her Hair.
For My Birthday.
God Has Mercy on Kindergarten Children.
God Has Pity on Kindergarten Children.
I Am a Leaf.
I Am a Live Man.
I Am Sitting Here.
I have nothing to say about the war, *sel.*
I Think of Oblivion.
In My Time, at Your Place.
In the Old City.
Instructions for the Waitress.
Is all this sorrow? I don't know, *sel.*
Jerusalem, Port City.
Jews in the Land of Israel.
Late in my life I come to you.
Lay Your Head on My Shoulder.
Light on the Tower of David, light on the Church of St. Mary, *sel.*
Like Two Stones at the Bottom of a Slope.
Look, Thoughts and Dreams.
Lovers in Fall.

My Father.
My Father's Memorial Day.
My Mother Once Told Me.
Not like a Cypress.
Now in the Storm.
Of the Three or Four in the Room.
Of Three or Four in a Room.
Old Ice Factory in Petakh Tikva, The.
On the Day of Atonement.
On the Wide Stairs.
Onus of Mercy, The.
Painful Love Song, A.
Patriotic Reflections.
People on This Beach Will Never, The.
Pity; We Were Such a Good Invention, A.
Quick and Bitter.
Shadow of the Old City.
Since Then.
Sodom's Sister City.
Song of Resignation.
Testimonies.
This year I traveled far, *sel.*
Time after time you're placed at the imagined,
    sel.
To Carry on Living.
Tonight I think again.
Town I Was Born In, The.
We Did It.
We Will Live Forever.
Amini, Johari. *See* **Latimore, Jewel C.**
Amir, Aharon
Cock.
Exit from the Garden of Delights.
Nothingness.
Odeon.
Stone.
When It Came Time.
Amiri, Akhtar
My home is the mountain, *sel.*
Amis, Kingsley
Aberdarcy: The Chaucer Road.
Aberdarcy: The Main Square.
After Goliath.
Against Romanticism.
Album-Leaf.
Aldport (Mystery Tour), *sel.*
Alternatives.
Autobiographical Fragment.
Beowulf.
Bookshop Idyll, A.
Brynbwrla, *sel.*
Delivery Guaranteed.
Departure.
Dream of Fair Women, A.
Ever-Fixed Mark, An.
Fforestfawr, *sel.*
Helbatrawss, The.
Langwell, *sel.*
Last War, The.
Masters.
New Approach Needed.
Note on Wyatt, A.
Nothing to Fear.
Ode to Me.
On a Portrait of Mme. Rimsky-Korsakov.
Pendydd, *sel.*
Reborn.
St. Asaph's.
Science Fiction.
Shitty.
Sight Unseen.
Silent Room, The.
Terrible Beauty.
Tribute to the Founder, A.
Amis, Lewis R.
Jehovah, God, Who Dwelt of Old.
Ammer, Sigrid
To My Mothers.
Ammianus
Epitaph of Nearchos.
Ammons, Archie Randolph
Apologia pro Vita Sua.

Arc Inside and Out, The.
Auto Mobile.
Belief.
Bonus.
Breaking Out.
Bridge.
Burnout in the Overshoot.
Cascadilla Falls.
Chasm.
Christmas Eve.
City Limits, The.
Clarity.
Classic.
Cleavage.
Close-up.
Confirmers, The.
Conserving the Magnitude of Uselessness.
Constant, The.
Coon Song.
Corsons Inlet.
Coward.
Cut the Grass.
Dark Song.
Distraction.
Easter Morning.
Eternal City, The.
Extrication.
First Carolina Said-Song.
Gathering, The.
Grace Abounding.
Gravelly Run.
Hardweed Path Going.
Hope's Okay.
I don't know about you,/ but I'm sick of good
    poems, *sel.*
I was pulling Veronica out of the lawn when
    this hornet came, *sel.*
Kind.
Laser.
Life in the Boondocks.
Mechanism.
Mirrorment.
Motion Which Disestablishes Organizes
    Everything.
Motion's Holdings.
Mountain Talk.
My Father Used to Tell of An.
Needs.
Neighbors.
Parting.
Periphery.
Pet Panther.
Play.
Poetics.
Put-Down Come On, The.
Reflective.
Runoff.
Second Carolina Said-Song.
Serpent Country.
Silver.
Singing & Doubling Together.
Sitting Down, Looking Up.
Small Song.
So I Said I Am Ezra.
Spring Coming.
Terminations.
There is a faculty or knack, smallish, in the
    mind that can turn, *sel.*
Transaction.
Treaties.
Triphammer Bridge.
Unifying Principle, The.
Unsaid.
Upland.
Viable.
Visit.
Volitions.
White Dwarf.
Wide Land, The.
Winter Saint.
Yucca Moth, The.

Ammuvanar
Six Said by the Concubines to Him.
What He Said.
What Her Girl Friend Said on Her Wedding
    Day.
What Her Girl Friend Said to Him When He
    Wanted to Come by Day.
What She Said ("Fishermen who go, The").
What She Said ("Friend, listen").
What She Said ("My body").
What She Said to Her Girl Friend.
Amner, John
Motet, A: "Stranger here, as all my fathers
    were, A."
Amon-Re
Hymn of Victory: Thutmose III.
Amorosi, Ray
Vampire.
Amoss, Harry
Pedagogical Principles.
Riding.
Amphis
Hangover Cure.
Anacreon
Picture, The.
Anadad Eldan
Samson Rends His Clothes.
Anania, Michael
Adrift on an oil-drum raft, *sel.*
Among the provisions they carried, *sel.*
Edge of Autumn, The.
Memorial Day.
Which river is this, *sel.*
Andal
Cuckoo, noisy among the Shenbaka flowers.
O people who live in the world.
To Krishna Haunting the Hills.
"Ande" (Angela Milne)
Coconut, The.
Andersen, Astrid Hjertenaes
Before the sun goes down.
Anderson, Alexander ("Surfaceman")
Cuddle Doon.
Heart! But this grand world rolls onward
    through the shadows of the years, *sel.*
Anderson, Bill
Letter from a Black Soldier.
Outbreak.
Anderson, Dazzly
Some Men.
Anderson, Ethel Louisa Mason
Kunai-mai-pa Mo.
Waking, Child, While You Slept, *sel.*
Anderson, Forrest
Beach Homos, The.
Anderson, Jack
Garden of Situations, A.
Invention of New Jersey, The.
Ode to Pornography.
Anderson, Jon
American Landscape with Clouds & a Zoo.
Blue Animals, The.
Cypresses, The.
Each Day Does That.
Face of Dürer, The.
Falling in Love.
Homage to Robert Bresson.
In Autumn.
In Sepia.
John Clare.
Milky Way, The.
Parachutist, The.
Photograph of Myself, The.
Refusals.
Rosebud.
Secret of Poetry, The.
Time Machine, The.
Winter Light.
Witness.
Ye Bruthers Dogg.
Years.

Anderson, Mary
  In the April Rain.
  Praise.
  Thanks to Spring.
Anderson, Mary Désirée
  Black-out, The.
  Harvest.
Anderson, Maxwell
  Lafayette to Washington, sel.
  Parallax.
Anderson, Mildred Leigh
  I Can Be a Tiger.
Anderson, Patrick
  Camp.
  Canoe.
  Capital Square.
  Cold Colloquy, sel.
  Coming of the White Man, The, sel.
  Houses Burning; Quebec.
  Sestina in Time of Winter.
  Sleighride.
Anderson, S. E.
  Junglegrave.
  New Dance, A.
  Sound of Afroamerican History Chapt I, The.
  Sound of Afroamerican History Chapt II, The.
Anderson, Sherwood
  Visit, A.
Anderson, Violet
  Cloak, The.
  Through the Barber Shop Window.
Andeyek
  I know how people get treated when they die.
Andrade, Carlos Drummond de
  Family Portrait.
  In the Middle of the Road.
  Infancy.
  Seven-Sided Poem.
  Travelling in the Family.
Andrade, Costa
  Augusto Ngangula.
  Fourth Poem.
Andrade, Mário de
  Aspiration.
  Improvisation of the Dead Boy.
  Rondeau for You.
Andrade, Oswald de
  Advertisement.
  Epitaph: "I am round, round."
  Funeral Procession.
  National Library.
André, John
  Cow-Chace, The.
Andre, Michael
  My Regrets.
  1,000 Illustrations and a Complete
    Concordance.
Andresen, Sophia de Mello Breyner
  Camoes and the Debt.
  Dead Men, The.
  Dionysius.
  Listen.
  Mirrors, The.
  Small Square, The.
  Sonnet to Eurydice.
  Young Girl and the Beach, The.
Andreus, Hans
  Countryside in France.
  Empty Room Is Still an Empty Room, The.
  Hollow of Light.
  Horror Story.
  I Spoke the Words of the World.
  Mulish.
  Words for You.
Andrew of Wyntoun
  Macbeth.
Andrewes, Francis
  I bear, in sign of love, sel.
Andrews, Albert Charlton
  Our Modest Doughboys.

Andrews, Bruce
  And the Love of Laughter.
  Apart/ meant —licking stick good golly. If,
    sel.
  Cherry red kind of washed-out, sel.
  Equality demands no less; history begins with
    old man crying, sel.
  Funnels In.
  Letters.
  Matter of Fact.
  Silhouette for its Rousseau, A.
  While.
  You reisolate tip.
Andrews, Harvey
  Unaccompanied.
Andrews, John
  To the Detracted, sel.
Andrews, Mary Raymond Shipman
  Call to Arms, A.
Andrews, Robert
  Mercury; on Losing My Pocket Milton at Luss
    near Ben Lomond, and Other Mountains.
  Urania.
Anduza, Clara d'. See **Clara d' Anduza**
Aneirin
  Men went to Catraeth, keen their war-band,
    sel.
  Men went to Gododdin, laughter-loving, sel.
  To Cattraeth's vale in glitt'ring row, sel.
Angel, Ralph
  Shadow Play.
Angell, Barbara
  Street Music.
Angelotti, Mike
  Last Man Killed by Indians in Kimble
    County, Texas, The.
  Still Life.
Angelou, Maya
  Africa.
  Chicken-Licken.
  In Retrospect.
  My Arkansas.
  On Ageing.
  On Diverse Deviations.
  Pickin Em Up and Layin Em Down.
  Sepia Fashion Show.
  Song for the Old Ones.
  Southeast Arkanasia.
  Still I Rise.
  They Went Home.
  Times-Square-Shoeshine-Composition.
  To a Husband.
  Woman Me.
  Woman Work.
"Angelus Silesius" (Johannes Scheffler)
  Cherubic Pilgrim, The.
Angermayer, Frances
  Conversion.
Anghelaki-Rooke, Katerina
  Before they ripen into diffused spirits.
  Black Angel, The.
  Body Is the Victory and the Defeat of
    Dreams, The.
  Diogenes.
  Old man moved into his night, The, sel.
Angiolieri, Cecco, da Siena
  Sonnet: He Argues His Case with Death.
  Sonnet: He Is Past All Help.
  Sonnet: He Rails against Dante, Who Had
    Censured His Homage to Becchina.
  Sonnet: He Will Not Be Too Deeply in Love.
  Sonnet: "I am in love, but am not so in love."
  Sonnet: In Absence from Becchina.
  Sonnet: Of All He Would Do.
  Sonnet: Of Becchina in a Rage.
  Sonnet: Of Becchina, the Shoemaker's
    Daughter.
  Sonnet: Of Love, in Honor of His Mistress
    Becchina.
  Sonnet: Of Love in Men and Devils.
  Sonnet: Of the 20th of June 1291.

  Sonnet: Of Why He Is Unhanged.
  Sonnet: Of Why He Would Be a Scullion.
  Sonnet: To Dante Alighieri (He Writes to
    Dante, Then in Exile at Verona, Defying
    Him as No Better Than Himself).
  Sonnet: To Dante Alighieri on the Last Sonnet
    of the Vita Nuova.
Anglund, Joan Walsh
  Ladybug.
  We Built a Castle near the Rocks.
Angoff, Charles
  Litany: "When the sun rises on another day."
  Little Girl, A.
Angulo, Hector
  Dopefiends Trip.
Angus, Marion
  Foxgloves and Snow.
Angus the Culdee. See **Aengus the Culdee**
Anhava, Helena
  Among the Grieving One Should Speak
    Softly.
  Childhood Summers.
  My Sons Have Grown to Manhood.
Anhava, Tuomas
  I Sleep to the Patter of the Rain.
  May 1964.
  Sky Has Wings, The.
Anis, Mir Babbar Ali
  Morning.
  Sword, The.
  Traveler, The.
Annand, James King
  Arctic Convoy.
  O Aa the Manly Sports.
  On the Croun o Bidean.
  What Finer Hills?
Annett, David
  Wreck of the Deutschland, The, parody.
Ansen, Alan
  Fatness.
  Tennyson.
"Ansky, S." (Solomon Rappoport)
  Emigrant Song.
  Tailor, The.
Anstadt, Henry
  Little Rhyme and a Little Reason, A.
Anstey, Christopher
  Hearken, Lady Betty, hearken, sel.
"Anstey, F." (Thomas Anstey Guthrie)
  Burglar Bill.
  Conscience-Curst! The.
  Limerick: "There was an old man of Bengal."
  Ordinary valour only works, The.
Ant, Howard
  Bucket of Sea-Serpents.
Antar
  Mu'allaqa.
Antella, Simone dall'
  Prolonged Sonnet: In the Last Days of the
    Emperor Henry VII.
Anthony, Edward ("A. C. Gate")
  Advice to Small Children.
  Let Others Share.
Anthony, George
  Autumn Evening.
Anthony, Florence. See **Ai**
Antin, David
  Passengers, The.
  Radical Coherency.
Antipater of Sidon
  Aristeides.
  Erinna.
  Never again, Orpheus.
  Pindar.
  This is Anacreon's grave. Here lie.
  Undying Thirst.
"Antler"
  Underwater Lake Michigan Socrates.
  What Every Boy Knows.
Antokolsky, Pavel Grigoryevich
  Hate!

Antoninus, Brother. *See* **Everson, William**
Antrobus, John
  Cowboy, The.
Anyiam-St. John, Rita
  For Me from You.
  Mama.
Anyiam–St. John, Rita
  I Remember ("I remember/ watching the
    women.").
  I Wondered.
  One Man to Another.
  Two Women I Know.
Anyte [*or*Anytes]
  Alive, this man was Manes, a common slave.
  I am Hermes. I stand in the crossroads by a
    windy.
  I, Hermes, have been set up.
  Lounge in the shade of the luxuriant laurel's.
  Shepherd's Gift, A.
Anzai Hitoshi
  Random Thoughts on the Skinkokinshu:
    Fujiwara no Teika.
Anzaldúa, Gloria
  Interface.
  We Call Them Greasers.
Aphek, Edna
  Sarah.
  Story of Abraham and Hagar, The.
Apolebieji, Odeniyi
  Salute to the Elephant.
Apollinaire, Guillaume
  Always.
  Annie.
  Automne Malade.
  Autumn.
  Calligram, 15 May 1915.
  Carnation, The ("May this carnation announce
    to you").
  Carnation, The ("May this carnation tell
    you").
  Dusk.
  Earth-Ocean.
  Forever.
  Gorgeous Redhead, The.
  Hotel.
  Hunting Horns.
  In this mirror I am enclosed, *sel.*
  It's Raining.
  Kings who have died, *sel.*
  Links.
  Little Car, The.
  Mirabeau Bridge, The.
  Monday Christine Street.
  Musician of Saint-Merry, The.
  My heart like an upside down flame, *sel.*
  1909.
  Phantom of the Clouds.
  Pretty Red-Head, The.
  Rosemonde.
  Saffron.
  Saltimbanques.
  Shadow.
  Sonnet: Zone ("You're weary of this ancient
    world at last").
  There Is.
  War.
  While Marching Around to Attract Shells.
  Zone.
Apollinaris (*or* **Apollinaris Sidonius**)
  Invitation to the Dance.
Appel, Benjamin
  Talker, The.
Appleman, Philip
  Amurrika!
  Fleas.
  Is There a Voice.
  It Is Enough.
  La Misère.
  Maples.
  More.
  My Friend.

So What.
Try.
When.
Appleton, Everard Jack
  Woman Who Understands, The.
Applewhite, James
  Barbecue Service.
  Bordering Manuscript.
  Marriage Portrait.
  My Grandfather's Funeral.
  To Earth.
  White Lake.
Aql, Said
  Dark Beauty.
  Do Not Show Your Love.
  More Beautiful Than Your Eyes.
  My ecstasy is that I have met you, *sel.*
Aragon, Louis
  Beginnings of the Fugitive, The.
  Brothers Lacôte, The.
  C.
  Dawn.
  Definitive Declaration.
  Dirge; for the Barrel-Organ of the New
    Barbarism.
  Drinking Song.
  Elsa's Eyes.
  Homeless.
  I'll Reinvent the Rose for You.
  Lilacs and the Roses, The.
  Once and for All.
  Poem to Shout in the Ruins.
  Pop Tune.
  Safety Lock.
  Special Preference.
  Tapestry of the Great Fear.
  Tercets.
  This is an ancient waltz, *sel.*
  Too Bad for Me.
  Unoccupied Zone, The.
Arakida Moritake. *See* **Moritake**
Arbiter, Petronius
  Encouragement to Exile.
Arbuthnot, John
  Epitaph on Colonel Francis Chartres.
Archer, Kate Rennie
  Lairdless Place, The.
Archestratus
  I write these precepts for immortal Greece,
    sel.
  Recipe: Hare.
**Archevolti, Samuel ben Elhanan Isaac, of
  Padua**
  Advice to Hotheads.
Archias of Byzantium
  Sea Dirge.
Archilochus
  Decks awash,/ Mast-top dipping.
  Like Odysseus under the ram.
  May he lose his way on the cold sea.
  This island, garlanded with wild woods.
Arden, Richard Pepper, Baron Alvanley
  On Dr. Samuel Ogden.
Aretino, Pietro
  Brother Alberto, one hot summer day.
  Brother Astolfo sated appetite.
  Stragglers.
Argentarius, Marcus
  Epigram: "Hetero-sex is best for the man of a
    serious turn of mind."
  Old Story, The.
  Rumoresque Senum Severiorum.
Argüelles, Iván
  Spanish Girls, The.
Aricil Kilar
  Battle Scene.
Arif, Iftiqar
  All the Same.
  Ignorance of the Wise.
  Sad Evenings.

Ariosto, Ludovico
  Alcyna met them at the outer gate, *sel.*
  Angelica and the Ork, *sel.*
  Astolfo Visits the Moon, *sel.*
  Blessed angell not a word replies, The, *sel.*
  Go soule, go sweetest soule for ever blest,
    sel.
  On Poets, *sel.*
Aristaenetus
  Pleasing Constraint, The.
Aristophanes
  Chorus of Birds, *sel.*
  How the Women Will Stop War, *sel.*
  Song of the Clouds, *sel.*
Ariwara no Nahihira. *See* **Narihira**
Ariwara no Yukihira. *See* **Yukihira**
Arkell, Reginald
  Public Nuisance, A.
Arkwright, John S.
  Supreme Sacrifice, The.
"Arkwright, Peleg." *See* **Proudfit, David
  Law**
Armando
  Boxers.
  Ship! the White Ship!, The.
  Trip with Knives.
Armantrout, Rae
  Anti-Short Story.
  Bases.
  Double.
  Extremities.
  Latter Day.
  Necromance.
  Range.
  Single Most.
  Through Walls.
  Tone.
  View.
  Xenophobia.
  You Float.
Armijo, Roberto
  To Patrice Lumumba.
Armitage, Jennifer
  To Our Daughter.
Armknecht, Richard F.
  Crow's Nest.
Armour, Richard
  Hiding Place.
  Money.
  One Down.
  Say Id Isn't So.
  Travelling Companions.
  Unsound Condition.
Armstrong, Frankie
  Collier Lass, The.
  Month of January.
  Out of the Darkness.
  Women of My Land.
Armstrong, J. A.
  Another Reply to "In Flanders Fields."
Armstrong, John
  Advantages of Washing, The, *sel.*
  Advice to Lovers, *sel.*
  Dangers of Sexual Excess, The, *sel.*
  Madness, *sel.*
  Transience, *sel.*
  Urban Pollution, *sel.*
Armstrong, Martin
  Gold.
  On a Little Bird.
  To a Jilt.
Armstrong, Peter
  Butterfly.
Armstrong, Thomas ("Tommy")
  Oakey Street Evictions, The.
  Trimdon Grange Explosion, The.
"Armytage, R." *See* **Watson, Rosamund
  Marriott**
Arnatkoak
  Personal Song.

Arnaut, Daniel
Aura Amara, L.'
Autet e bas.
Arnaut de Mareuil
Lovely to look at.
Wind is fair, The.
Arnett, Carroll
Out in the Woods.
Song of the Breed.
Story of My Life, The.
Arnett, Carroll (Gogisgi)
Anadarko John.
Ayohu Kanogisdi.
Bio-poetic Statement.
Drunk.
Land.
Last May.
Look Back.
Old Man Said, The.
Removal: Last Part.
Rock Painting.
Something for Supper.
You.
Arnold, George
Beer.
Farewell to Summer.
Sweet September.
Arnold, Irene (Mrs. Major Arnold)
Pray!
Thank God for the Country!
Arnold, Lila
Paisley Ceiling, The.
Arnold, Matthew
Below the Surface-Stream.
Buried Life, The.
Calm Soul of All Things! [Make It Mine],
   sel.
Caution to Poets, A.
Children dear, was it yesterday, *sel.*
Continued.
Courage.
Death of Sohrab, The ("He spoke; and Sohrab
   smiled on him, and took"), *sel.*
Desire.
Dover Beach.
Dream, A.
East London.
Epoch ends, the world is still, The, *sel.*
Far far from here, *sel.*
First-born Star, The, *sel.*
Forsaken Merman, The.
Geist's Grave.
Go, for they call you, shepherd, from the hill,
   sel.
Growing Old.
Hayeswater, *sel.*
How changed is here each spot man makes or
   fills!, *sel.*
If Birth Persists, *sel.*
Immortality.
In Utrumque Paratus.
Isolation: To Marguerite, *sel.*
It is so small a thing, *sel.*
Kaiser Dead.
Last Word, The.
Life and Thought, *sel.*
Lines Written in Kensington Gardens.
Longing.
Meeting, *sel.*
Memorial Verses.
Nameless Epitaph, A.
Obermann Once More.
Palladium.
Philomela.
Poor Matthias.
Progress of Poesy, The.
Quiet Work.
Raised are the dripping oars, *sel.*
Requiescat.
Rugby Chapel.
Scenes from Carnac.

Scholar-Gipsy, The.
Second Asgard, The, *sel.*
Self-Dependence.
Shakespeare.
So, on the bloody sand, Sohrab lay dead, *sel.*
Sohrab and Rustum.
Song for Apollo, *sel.*
Song of Callicles, The ("Through the black,
   rushing smoke-burst"), *sel.*
Stanzas from the Grande Chartreuse.
Strayed Reveller, The.
Strayed Reveller to Ulysses, The.
Summer Night, A.
Terrace at Berne, The.
Then Sohrab with is sword smote Rustum's
   helm, *sel.*
Thyrsis.
To a Friend.
To a Republican Friend, 1848.
To Marguerite—Continued, *sel.*
West London.
Where, behind Keighley, the road, *sel.*
Wordsworth's Grave, *sel.*
Arnold, Sir Edwin
After Death in Arabia.
Almond Blossom.
Darien.
Destiny.
He and She.
Musmee, The.
Painted streets alive with hum of noon, The,
   sel.
To a Pair of Egyptian Slippers.
Arnstein, Flora J.
Timers.
Arowa, Omobayode
Dekunle, handsome man, hail!, *sel.*
Arp, Hans
Black Joy.
Black Veins.
Domestic Stones (fragment), The.
Domesticated Stones.
Droplet of Man, A.
Feet of Morning, The.
I Am a Horse.
Infinite Millimeter Manifesto.
Sawdust from the Scales.
Seasons Their Asterisks and Their Pawns.
Two little arabs adult and arabesque.
Tyrolean Elephant, The.
What the Violins Sing in Their Baconfat Bed.
What Violins Are Singing in Their Beds of
   Lard.
When it burns before the harps and freezes
   behind the easels.
White Blocks.
White Etc, The.
Arrabey, Salaan
To a Faithless Friend.
Arriví, Francisco
Sometimes a huge wave of thought, *sel.*
Song for a Day.
This tree/ growing out of me, *sel.*
Arrowsmith, Pat
Christmas Story (1980).
Day I Once Dreamed, The.
Political Activist Living Alone.
Artaud, Antonin
Address to the Dalai Lama.
Bad Dreamer, The.
German Organ.
Invocation to the Mummy.
Love without a Truce.
Moon.
Night Works, The.
Nocturnal Festival.
Organ and Sulphur.
Panes of Sound, The.
Prayer: "O give us skulls of hot coals."
Romance.
Snow.

Trappists.
Tree.
Windows of Sound.
Arthur, Kevyn
Gospel.
I Saw Three Ships.
Arthur, Ruth M.
Snowflakes.
Artmann, H. C.
Every evening a counterfeit minstrel.
Interior.
Mon dieu mon dieu.
My Heart.
Now look here. !
O death you dark master.
Oh, Anselm,/ take/ Schubert.
Salt and bread in our.
When my Anselm/ drifts away.
Arudra
Poeti-c Art ("The poetic cart").
Arundel, Anne Howard, Duchess of. *See*
   Howard, Anne, Duchess of Arundel
Arundel, Philip Howard, 1st Earl of. *See*
   Howard, Philip, 1st Earl of Arundel
Arvey, Verna
All That I Am.
Arvidson, K. O.
Beim Schlafengehen, *sel.*
Fish and Chips on the Merry-Go-Round.
Frühling, *sel.*
Im Abendrot, *sel.*
September, *sel.*
Tall Wind, The.
You might at one time, when you were young
   perhaps, *sel.*
Asada no Yasu. See Yasu
Asatsuna (Oe no Asatsuna)
Most virile of beings-man.
Rhyme-Prose on the Marriage of Man and
   Woman.
Asbaje, Juana de. *See* **Juana Inés de la**
   Cruz, Sister
Asch, Frank
Alley Cat School.
Leaves.
Play.
Sugar Lady, The.
Summer.
Sunflakes.
Sunrise.
Asclepiades
Eumares.
Why hoard your maidenhead? There'll not be
   found.
Ash, John
Epigraphs for Epigones.
Hotel Brown Poems, The.
Memories of Italy (Broken Sestina).
Other Great Composers, The.
Wonderful Tangerines, The.
Ash, Linda
Bellerin' and Bawlin'.
Ash, Sarah Leeds
Changeless Shore.
Ashbery, John
Additional Poem, An.
And "Ut Pictura Poesis" Is Her Name.
Around the Rough and Rugged Rocks the
   Ragged Rascal Rudely Ran.
As One Put Drunk into the Packet-Boat.
As You Came from the Holy Land.
At North Farm.
Bird's-Eye View of the Tool and Die Co.
Blessing in Disguise, A.
Boy, A.
Bungalows, The.
But What Is the Reader to Make of This?
By the Flooded Canal.
Cathedral Is, The.

City Afternoon.
Civilization and Its Discontents.
Crazy Weather.
De Imagine Mundi.
Decoy.
Definition of Blue.
Dido, *sel.*
Down by the Station, Early in the Morning.
Drunken Americans.
Endless Variation.
Everyman's Library.
Farm Implements and Rutabagas in a
    Landscape.
Faust.
Fear of Death.
For John Clare.
Forties Flick.
Friends.
Glazunoviana.
Grand Abacus.
Hard Times.
He.
How Much Longer Will I Be Able to Inhabit
    the Divine Sepulcher.
Ice-Cream Wars, The.
Idiot, The, *sel.*
If the Birds Knew.
Illustration.
Instruction Manual, The.
Introduction: "To be a writer and write
    things."
Just Walking Around.
Knocking Around.
Landscapeople.
Last Month.
Last World, A.
Le Livre Est sur la Table.
Leaving the Atocha Station.
Love Poem, A: "And they have to get it right.
    We just need."
Man of Words, A.
Many Wagons Ago.
Märchenbilder.
Meditations of a Parrot.
Melodic Trains.
Mixed Feelings.
My Erotic Double.
Never Seek to Tell Thy Love.
No Way of Knowing.
Nothing to Steal.
Oh, Nothing.
On Autumn Lake.
One Coat of Paint.
One Thing That Can Save America, The.
Ongoing Story, The.
Our Youth.
Painter, The.
Pantoum.
Paradoxes and Oxymorons.
Picture of Little J.A. in a Prospect of
    Flowers, The.
Poem: "While we were walking under the
    top."
Pyrography.
Rivers and Mountains.
Robin Hood's Barn.
Self-Portrait in a Convex Mirror.
Some Trees.
Songs without Words.
Soonest Mended.
Spring Day.
Statuary.
Street Musicians.
Summer.
Syringa.
Tennis Court Oath, The.
Tenth Symphony.
These Lacustrine Cities.
They Dream Only of America.
Thinnest Shadow, The.
Thoughts of a Young Girl.
To Redouté.

Variation on a Noel.
Variations, Calypso and Fugue on a Theme of
    Ella Wheeler Wilcox.
Wet Are the Boards.
Wet Casements.
What Is Poetry.
When the Sun Went Down.
Whether It Exists.
White Roses.
Worsening Situation.
Years of Indiscretion.
Ashby, Cliff
    Latter Day Psalms.
    Stranger in This Land, A.
Ashby-Sterry, Joseph
    Kindness to Animals.
    Spring's Delights.
Ashe, Thomas
    City Clerk, The.
    Corpse-bearing.
    To Two Bereaved.
    Vision of Children, A.
    Word to the West End, A.
Ashley, Carlos
    Ol' Edgar Martin.
Askenazy, Ludvik
    Wall, The.
Askew, Anne
    Ballad Which Anne Askew Made and Sang
        When She Was in Newgate, The.
Aslan, Odette
    I discover you in bits and pieces.
Aslanides, Timoshenko
    Imitation of Intimations.
    Island of the Sirens, The.
    Prayer to Aphrodite.
Asphodel (Pauline Long)
    Full Moon in Malta.
    On the Pilgrim's Way in Kent, as It Leads to
        the Coldrum Stones.
    Winter Solstice—for Frank.
Asquith, Herbert
    Birthday Gifts.
    Elephant, The.
    Hairy Dog, The.
    Hooded in angry mist, the sun goes down,
        sel.
    Ship Sails Up to Bideford, A.
    Skating.
    Volunteer, The.
Astley, Thea
    Droving Man.
Aston, Louise
    For Women.
    Sacred Ceremony, A.
    Song of a Silesian Weaver.
Astra
    Bloody Pause.
    Daughters.
    Now or Never.
Astrachan, John Mann
    Jenny.
Asturias, Miguel Angel
    Indians Come Down from Mixco, The.
Asukai Masayori. *See* **Masayori**
Asya (Asya Gay)
    Celan.
    Deer, The.
    Grain of Moonlight, A.
    My Strawlike Hair.
    My True Memory.
    Pause a Moment.
At Taliq
    I took leave of my beloved one evening: how
        I wish.
Atherton, John
    Tank Town.
Atimantiyar
    Nowhere, not among the warriors at their
        festival.

Atish, Khwaja Haider Ali
    Bulbul in the garden, The.
    It was the night of love.
    Listen, what a legend.
    Within the world I was.
Atkins, Russell
    At War.
    Christophe.
    "Dangerous Condition": Sign on Inner-City
        House.
    Dark Area.
    Editorial Poem on an Incident of Effects
        Far-reaching.
    Inner-City Lullaby.
    Irritable Song.
    It's Here in The.
    Narrative.
    New Storefront.
    Night and a Distant Church.
    On the Fine Arts Garden, Cleveland.
    Probability and Birds in the Yard.
Attar, Faridu'ddin
    Dervish wept to feel the violence of, A, *sel.*
    Hallaj's corpse was burnt and when the flame,
        sel.
    In India lives a bird that is unique, *sel.*
Attar, Samar
    And you came back, *sel.*
Attika, Mririda n'Ait
    God Hasn't Made Room.
    Like Smoke.
Attwood, A. A.
    Farmyard, The.
Atwell, Roy
    Some Little Bug.
Atwood, Margaret
    Accident Has Occurred, The.
    After the agony in the guest/ bedroom.
    Against Still Life.
    Animals in That Country, The.
    At first I was given centuries.
    At the Tourist Center in Boston.
    Being with you, *sel.*
    Daguerreotype Taken in Old Age.
    Death of a Young Son by Drowning.
    Disembarking at Quebec.
    Dream 2: Brian the Still-Hunter.
    Earth.
    Eden Is a Zoo.
    Elegy for the Giant Tortoises.
    Eventual Proteus.
    Explorers, The.
    Footnote to the Amnesty Report on Torture.
    Game after Supper.
    Habitation.
    I can change my-/ self more easily.
    Interview with a Tourist.
    It Is Dangerous to Read Newspapers.
    Landcrab.
    Lying here, everything in me.
    Marrying the Hangman.
    Men with the heads of eagles, *sel.*
    Night in the Royal Ontario Museum, A.
    Notes towards a Poem That Can Never Be
        Written.
    November.
    Pig Song.
    Postcard.
    Provisions.
    Puppet of the Wolf, The.
    Returning to the room, *sel.*
    Settlers, The.
    Siren Song, *sel.*
    Spelling.
    Summer again, *sel.*
    There Is Only One of Everything.
    They Eat Out.
    This Is a Photograph of Me.
    This year I intended children.
    Torture.

Variation on the Word *Sleep*.
Variations on the Word *Love*.
We are standing facing each other.
Woman Skating.
Woman's Issue, A.
You Begin.
You Fit into Me.
You refuse to own.
You take my hand and.
You want to go back.
Your back is rough all.

Aua
Bear Hunting.
Morning Prayer.
Walrus Hunting.

Aubert, Alvin
Economics.
How It's Done.
Silence.
When the Wine Was Gone.

Aubigné, Théodore Agrippa d'
Portrait of Henri III, A, *sel.*
Portrait of Henri III, A, *sel.*

Auchterlonie, Dorothy
Apopemptic Hymn.
Meditation of a Mariner.
Waiting for the Post.

Audelay, John
Be True to Your Condition in Life.
In His Utter Wretchedness.

Auden, Wystan Hugh
Aesthetic Point of View, The.
After Reading a Child's Guide to Modern Physics.
Always the Following Wind.
Amor Loci.
And the Age Ended, *sel.*
Another Time.
Anthem: "Let us praise our Maker, with true passion extol Him."
As I Walked Out One Evening.
At Last the Secret Is Out.
At the Grave of Henry James.
At the Party.
August for the People.
August 1968.
Autumn 1940.
Ballad of Barnaby, The.
Base Words Are Uttered.
Behold the Manly Mesomorph.
Brussels in Winter.
Canzone: "When shall we learn, what should be clear as day."
Carry Her over the Water.
Chilled by the present, its gloom and its noise, *sel.*
Chorus: "Summer holds, The: upon its glittering lake," *sel.*
Chorus: "You are the town and we are the clock," *sel.*
City, The, *sel.*
City without Walls.
Colonel from Cheltenham stopped everyone, A, *sel.*
Consider This and in Our Time.
Cry went through me like a stab of a knife, A, *sel.*
Dead man, A/ who never caused others to die, *sel.*
Dear, Though the Night Is Gone.
Decoys, The.
Doctors attended behind each chair, *sel.*
Doggerel by a Senior Citizen.
Don Quixote's Credo, *sel.*
Don Quixote's Farewell, *sel.*
Door, The, *sel.*
Earth, receive an honoured guest, *sel.*
Edward Lear.
England, my England—you have been my tutrix, *sel.*
Epitaph for the Unknown Soldier.

Epitaph on a Tyrant.
Et in Arcadia Ego.
Exiles, The.
Fairground.
Fall of Rome, The.
Far from a cultural centre he was used, *sel.*
Far from the Heart of Culture.
Finale, *sel.*
First Things First.
Flight into Egypt, The, *sel.*
For What as Easy.
From gallery-grave and the hunt of a wren-king, *sel.*
From Scars Where Kestrels Hover.
Fugal-Chorus, *sel.*
Gare du Midi.
Get There If You Can and See the Land.
Golden Age, The, *sel.*
Good-bye to the Mezzogiorno.
He is the way, *sel.*
He stayed, and was imprisoned in possession, *sel.*
He turned his field into a meeting-place, *sel.*
He was their servant (some way he was blind), *sel.*
He watched the stars and noted birds in flight, *sel.*
Healthy Spot, A.
Hearing of Harvests Rotting in the Valleys.
Henry Adams.
Here war is harmless like a monument, *sel.*
Herman Melville.
Highway to Glory Song, *sel.*
His care-free swagger was a fine invention, *sel.*
History of Truth, The.
Horatians, The.
I Am Not a Camera.
I Cannot Grow.
I like your muse because she's gay and witty, *sel.*
If on Account of the Political Situation, *sel.*
In corduroy trousers and seedy black coats, *sel.*
In Due Season.
In Memoriam: Ernst Toller.
In Memory of Sigmund Freud.
In Memory of W. B. Yeats.
In Praise of Limestone.
It's No Use Raising a Shout.
James Honeyman.
Jew Wrecked in the German Cell, The.
Journey to Iceland.
Jumbled in the Common Box.
Kingdom of Number is all boundaries, The, *sel.*
Labyrinth, The.
Lakes.
Lauds, *sel.*
Leap before You Look.
Led by the light of an unusual star, *sel.*
Letter, The.
Long time since it seems to-day, A, *sel.*
Lost on a fogbound spit of sand.
Love Feast, The.
Lullaby: "Din of work is subdued, The."
Lullaby: "Lay your sleeping head, my love."
Many Happy Returns.
May with its light behaving.
Miranda, *sel.*
Miss Gee.
More Loving One, The.
Mountains.
Mundus et Infans.
Musée des Beaux Arts.
Night Mail, The.
1929.
Note on Intellectuals.
Now for the spirit of the people. Here, *sel.*
Now the Leaves Are Falling Fast.
Now through Night's Caressing Grip.

O for Doors to Be Open and an Invite with Gilded Edges.
O What Is That Sound [Which So Thrills the Ear]
O Where Are You Going?, *sel.*
Ode: To My Pupils.
Ode to Terminus.
Ode to the Medieval Poets.
On a lorry the centre of a gaping crowd, *sel.*
On Installing an American Kitchen in Lower Austria.
On the Circuit.
On This Island.
Ottava Rima would, I know, be proper, *sel.*
Our Bias.
Our Father, whose creative Will, *sel.*
Our Hunting Fathers.
Our news is seldom good: the heart, *sel.*
Parable.
Petition.
Poem: "He watched with all his organs of concern."
Preface: "Aged catch their breath, The," *sel.*
Prime.
Private faces in public places.
Prologue: "By landscape reminded once of his mother's figure."
Prologue: "O love, the interest itself in thoughtless heaven."
Proof, The.
Runner, The.
Sancho Panza's Dream, *sel.*
Say this city has ten million souls.
September 1, 1939.
Sext, *sel.*
Shield of Achilles, The.
Silly Fool, The.
Since.
Sir Rider Haggard.
So an age ended, and its last deliverer died, *sel.*
So from the years their gifts were showered: each, *sel.*
Soldier Loves His Rifle, The.
Some of our dead are famous, but they would not care, *sel.*
Some thirty inches from my nose.
Song: "Deftly, admiral, cast your fly."
Song: "Fish in the unruffled lakes."
Song for St. Cecilia's Day.
Song: "Make this night loveable."
Song of Dejection, *sel.*
Song of the Barber, The, *sel.*
Song of the Enchanters.
Song of the Knight of the Mirrors, *sel.*
Song of the Master and Boatswain, *sel.*
Song of the Ogres.
Song of the Quest, *sel.*
Spain 1937.
Starling and a Willow-Wren, A.
Stop All the Clocks, Cut Off the Telephone.
Strings' Excitement, The.
Summer Night, A.
T. S. Eliot.
Talking to Myself.
Taller to-day, we remember similar evenings.
Thanksgiving for a Habitat.
That Night When Joy Began.
Their Lonely Betters.
They Wondered Why, *sel.*
They wondered why the fruit had been forbidden, *sel.*
This Lunar Beauty.
Thought of writing came to me today, The, *sel.*
Traction Engine, The.
Truest Poetry Is the Most Feigning; or, Ars Poetica for Hard Times, The.
Uncle Henry.
Under Sirius.

Under Which Lyre, a Reactionary Tract for
  the Times.
Unknown Citizen, The.
Up There.
Vespers, *sel.*
Villanelle: "Time can [*or* will] say nothing
  but I told you so."
Voltaire at Ferney.
Walking Tour, The, *sel.*
Wanderer, The.
Watch Any Day.
Watershed, The.
Well, So That Is That ("Well so that is that.
  Now we must diomantle the tree."), *sel.*
When Statesmen gravely say "We must be
  realistic."
Who Will Endure.
Who's Who.
Why are the public buildings so high?
You lived and moved among the best society,
  sel.

Auerbach, Ephraim
Seismograph.

Augustin, Michael
Kay-You-Enn-Aye Radio, Iowa.

Augustini, Delmira
Vision.

Ault, Norman
Ducks.
Pig's Tail, The.

"Aunt Effie." *See* Browne, Jane Euphemia
"Aunt Mary." *See* Lathbury, Mary
  Artemisia

Auringer, Obadiah Cyrus
April.
Ballad of Oriskany, The.
Flight of the War-Eagle, The.

Aus of Kuraiza
Apostasy.

Auslander, Joseph
Elegy: "Fled is the swiftness of all the
  white-footed ones."
Interval.
Near Dusk.
Prayer for Thanksgiving, A.
Sunrise Trumpets.
Three Things.

Ausländer, Rose
Cézanne.
Evening.
Father.
Harlem at Night.
Hasidic Jew from Sadagora.
In Chagall's Village.
In the Chagall Village.
Jerusalem.
My Nightingale.
Passover.
Phoenix.
Romeo and Juliet in Central Park.
Still Life.
Sunday on Riverside Drive.

Ausonius, Decimus Magnus
Epigram: "Glad youth had come thy sixteenth
  year to crown."
Epigram: "Reincarnating Pythagoras, say."
I am that Dido which thou here do'st see.
Idyll of the Rose.
On the Sicilian strand a hare well wrought.
To His Wife.

Auster, Paul
Covenant.
Hieroglyph.
Scribe.
Song of Degrees.

Austin, Albert Gordon
Chez-Nous.

Austin, Alfred
Is Life Worth Living?
Maiden of the Smile, The.

Thrush, The.
To America.
When with staid mothers' milk and sunshine
  warmed, *sel.*

Austin, Mary
At Carmel.
Beggar Wind, The.
Brown Bear, The.
Deer, The.
Eagle's Song, The.
Feller I Know, A.
Grizzly Bear.
Prairie-Dog Town.
Rathers.
Snow, *sel.*
Western Magic.

Austin Clarke
Last Republicans, The.

Automedon
Epigram: "I dined with Demetrius last night."

Auvaiyar
Chariot Wheel, A.
Earth's Bounty.
Elegy: "If he found a little liquor."
Elegy: "Let day, let night, come no more."
Elegy: "This bright burning pyre."
His Welcome.
Mothers.
Poet to a Dancer, A.
Shall I charge like a bull.
What She Said, Thinking of Him Crossing the
  Wilderness Alone.
You stand and hold the post of my small
  house.
Young Chieftain, A.

Auxier, Sylvia
Breaking Point.

Ava, Frau
I am yours, you are mine.

Avane
Ageing Hunter, The.

Avery, Richard K.
And the Cock Begins to Crow.

Avicolli, Tommi
Rape Poem, The.

Avidan, David
Another Catalogue Item, *sel.*
Burying Uncle Salomon.
Cradle Song: "Come here, little girl, come
  here."
Domination as Another Form of Weakness.
Election Speech for the Presidency of the
  United States of Chinamerica.
End of the Trip, *sel.*
Fire the Babysitter.
First Date, The, *sel.*
For Advanced Seminar Students Only, *sel.*
General Truths, *sel.*
Glimpse of an Open Dream.
Longterm Hatred.
Minor Mythology.
Moment Ago, A.
Moral, The, *sel.*
Not Allowed to Make a Movie in This
  Country, *sel.*
Personal Problems.
Practical Poems.
Prehistory.
Recurring Opportunity.
Sleep, Leopard, Sleep.
Some Futureplans.
Song of the Self-Made Orphans.
Spot Remained on the Wall, The.
Streets at Their Leisure Rise, The.
Three Self-Plagiarisms, *sel.*
Two Memorial Poems.
What Bothered Him, *sel.*
What I Have to Tell You, Until Next Time.

Avison, Margaret
Butterfly, The.
Butterfly Bones; or, Sonnet against Sonnets.

Civility a Bogey.
Dumbfounding, The.
For Dr. and Mrs. Dresser.
Hiatus.
In a Season of Unemployment.
Intra-Political.
Lament, A: "Gizzard and some ruby inner
  parts, A."
Meeting Together of Poles & Latitudes: In
  Prospect.
Nameless One, A.
New Year's Poem.
Party, The.
Perspective.
Rigor Viris.
Snow.
Story, A.
Stray Dog, near Ecully.
Swimmer's Moment, The.
Tennis.
Thaw.
Transit.
Two Selves, The.
Unspeakable.
Voluptuaries and Others.
Water and Worship: An Open-Air Service on
  the Gatineau River.
Watershed.
Word, The.

Avrett, Robert
Renaissance.

Awatere, Arapeta
Lament for Kepa Anaha Ehau.

Awoonor, Kofi (George Williams)
Rediscovery.

Axelrod, David B.
Once in a While a Protest Poem.

Axelrod, Susan
Home, The.

Axionicus
Recipe: Sausage.

Ayala, Ramon Perez de.
She Was a Pretty Little Girl.

Ayer, Ethan
Like a Whisper.

Ayer, Jean
Everyday Things.

Ayer, William Ward
Be Still.

Ayloffe, John
Britannia and Raleigh.
Marvell's Ghost.
Oceana and Britannia.

Ayres, Philip
Cynthia on Horseback.
Describes the Place Where Cynthia Is
  Sporting Herself.
Epigram on Woman, An.
Ever Present.
Invites His Nymph to His Cottage.
Invites Poets and Historians to Write in
  Cynthia's Praise.
Of Lydia Distracted.
On a Fair Beggar.
On Lydia Distracted.
Yoke uneasy on the ox doth sit, The.

Ayres, Philip *after the Greek of* Theocritus
Death of Adonis, The.

Ayres, Philip *after the Spanish of* Quevedo
Fly, The.

Ayton [*or* Aytoun], Sir Robert
I Lov'd Thee Once.
On A Woman's Inconstancy.
To His Forsaken Mistress.
Upon a Diamond Cut in Form[e] of a
  Heart. Sent in a New-Yeares [*or* Year's]
  Gift.
Upone Tabacco.
When Thou Did Thinke I Did Not Love.
Wrong Not, Sweete Empress of My Heart,
  sel.

Aytoun, William Edmonstoune [or Emondstoune]
Execution of Montrose, The.
La Mort d'Arthur.
Laureate, The.
Massacre of the Macpherson, The.
Old Scottish Cavalier, The.
Sonnet to Britain.
Then the Provost he uprose, *sel.*

Aytoun, William Edmonstoune and Sir Theodore Martin
Lay of the Lovelorn, The.

Aytoun, Sir Robert. *See* Ayton, Sir Robert

A'yunini
Killer, The.

Azalais de Porcairages
Now we are come to the cold time.

A'Zmi, Kaifi
Bangladesh.
Stray Prostrations.

Azuma, Konda. *See* Konda Azuma

B

"B., M."
Deportation.

"B., R."
This story's strange, but altogether true.

"B. L. T." *See* Taylor, Bert Leston

"B. V." ("Bysshe Vanolis"). *See* Thomson, James (1834–82)

Ba, Oumar
Drought.

Baba Kuhi of Shiraz
In the market, in the cloister—only God I saw.

Babcock, Donald Campbell
In a Garden.
Neoplatonic Soliloquy.
O God, in Whom the Flow of Days.
Two Things.

Babcock, Donald G.
Vacation Trip.

Babcock, Maltbie Davenport
Be Strong.
Emancipation.
Not to Be Ministered To.
School Days.
This Is My Father's World.

Babcock, William Henry
Bennington.

Baca, Jimmy Santiago
Cloudy Day.
There Are Black.

Bacchylides
Peace on Earth.

Bachar, Eli
Dawn of Jaffa Pigeons, A.
Houses, Past and Present.
Room Poems.

Bacheller, Irving
Whisperin' Bill.

Bachmann, Ingeborg
Curriculum Vitae.
Days in White.
Every Day.
Firstborn Land, The.
Fogland.
Go On, Idea.
Great Freight, The.
Instructed in love, *sel.*
Kind of Loss, A.
My Bird.
Out of the corpse-warm vestibule of heaven steps the sun.
Prague, January 1964.

Psalm: "Be silent with me, as all bells are silent!"
Respite, The.
Theme and Variations.
To the Sun.
Truly.
Word and Afterword.
You want the summer lightning, throw the knives.

Bachstein, Michael
Clinics.
My Name in the Star Registry.
Terms of Surrender.

Backberger, Barbro
I'm Taking Off.

Backus, Bertha Adams
Then Laugh.

Bacmeister, Rhoda Warner
Galoshes.
Icy.
Under the Ground.

Bacon, Francis
Life of Man, The.

Bacon, Leonard
Fly fisherman in Wartime.

Bacon, Leonard (1802–1881)
Hail, Tranquil Hour of Closing Day.
Pilgrim Fathers, The.
Wake the Song of Jubilee.

Bacon, Leonard (1887–1954)
Horatian Variation.
Richard Tolman's Universe.

Bacon, Peggy
Hearth.

"Badawi al-Jabal"
Beauty.
Immortality.
Visit, The.

"Badawi al-Jabal" (Muhammad Sulaiman al-Ahmad)
Dark Mirage.

Baden-Powell, Sir Robert
Man, matron, maiden.

Baez, Joan
Love Song to a Stranger.

Bagg, Robert
Ronald Wyn.
See That One?
Soft Answers.

Baggesen, Jens
Childhood.

"Bagritsky, Eduard" (Eduard Dzyubin)
He Tries out the Concords Gently.
Piece of Black Bread, A.

Baha Ad-din Zuhayr
On a Blind Girl.

Bahadur Shah Zafar (Bahadur Shah II)
As long as I remained asleep.
My life gives out no ray of light.
Suddenly things have changed, my soul.
When I am dead and some kind soul.
When as in silks you came and dazzled.
Wherefore should I seek the bud.

Bahe, Liz Sohappy
And What of Me?
Farewell: "You sang round-dance songs."
Grandmother Sleeps.
Once Again.
Parade, The.
Printed Words.
Ration Card, The.
Talking Designs.

Bai, Mukta
I live where darkness/ is not.

Baildon, Henry Bellyse
Moth, A.

Bailey, Alfred Goldsworthy
Algonkian Burial.
Border River.
Colonial Set.

Miramichi Lightning.
Tâo.

Bailey, Anthony
Green and the Black, The.

Bailey, Liberty Hyde
Miracle.

Bailey, Philip James
What Is Heaven?

Baillie, Joanna
Blackcock, The.
Child to His Sick Grandfather, A.
Disappointment, A.
Horse and His Rider, The.
Mother to Her Waking Infant, A.
Outlaw's Song, The.
Trysting Bush, The.

Baillie, Lady Grisel
Werena My Heart Licht Wad Dee.

Bainbrigge, Philip
Chorus of Scyrian Maidens, *sel.*

Baines, Elizabeth
News of Old Girls.

Bairacli-Levy, Juliette de
Killed in Action.
Threnode for Young Soldiers Killed in Action.

Baird, Joseph L.
Longing for the Birds of Solomon.

Baker, Barbara
Spike of Green, A.

Baker, Carlos
Chinese Mural, A, *sel.*
Men of Sudbury, The.
On a Landscape of Sestos, *sel.*

Baker, David
Caves.
8-Ball at the Twilite.
Ice River.
Running the River Lines.
Wrecker Driver Foresees Your Death, The.

Baker, Donald W.
Formal Application.

Baker, Dorothy
Castles in the Sand.
In the Woods.

Baker, George Augustus
Thoughts on the Commandments.

Baker, Henry
Declaimer, The.
Love.
Rapture, The.

Baker, Howard
Ode to the Sea.

Baker, J. G.
My Trundle Bed.

Baker, Julia Aldrich
Mizpah.

Baker, Karle Wilson ("Charlotte Wilson")
Beauty's Hands Are Cool.
Creeds.
Good Company.
Let Me Grow Lovely.
Ploughman, The.

Baker, Kathleen Leland
Baby Hilary, Sir Edmund, The.
Honey Moon.

Baker, Thomas
Electric Telegraph, The, *sel.*
I dream'd I walk'd in raptures high, *sel.*
Means of Propulsion for Steam-Ships, *sel.*
Watt's Improvements to the Steam Engine, *sel.*

Balaban, John
"Faith and Practice."
Guard at the Binh Thuy Bridge, The.

Balakian, Peter
Father Fisheye.
Homage to Hart Crane.
In the Turkish Ward.
Jersey Bait Shack.

Balbuena, Bernardo de
Immortal Springtime and Its Tokens, *sel.*
Baldenegro, Salomón R., Jr.
Man, I Felt Like Running All Night.
Balderston, Jean
Garbo Stepping In.
Baldwin, A. W. I.
Ten Little Dicky-Birds.
Baldwin, James
Guilt, Desire and Love.
Lover's Question, A.
Baldwin, Mary Newton
Lonely Are the Fields of Sleep.
Baldwin, Michael
Death on a Live Wire.
Baldwin, Thomas
From Whence Doth This Union Arise?
Baldwin, William
Christ, My Beloved.
Christ to His Spouse *or* The Beloved to the
Spouse.
Bale, John
Wassail, Wassail.
Balestrini, Nanni
But We'll Make Another One.
De Cultu Virginis.
Fugitive's Apologue, The.
In This Manner.
Instinct of Self-Preservation, The.
Tape Mark.
Without Tears for the Roses.
Balhurst, W. H.
Unshrinking Faith.
Balkt, H. H. ter
Animal's Crusade, The.
Elegy of the Hogs.
Found, The.
Mill, The.
Ball, Arthur
Above Ben Loyal.
Tall Sky, The.
Ballagas, Emilio
Elegy for María Belén Chacón.
Ballard, Charles G.
Changing of the Guard.
During the Pageant at Medicine Lodge.
Grandma Fire.
Man of Property, The.
Memo.
Navajo Girl of Many Farms.
Now the People Have the Light.
Sand Creek.
Speaker, The.
Spirit Craft, The.
Their Cone-like Cabins.
Time Was the Trail Went Deep.
Winds of Change, The.
You Northern Girl.
Ballard, Colin Robert
Pacific Railway, The.
Ballou, Hosea, I
Dear Lord, Behold Thy Servants.
In God's Eternity.
When God Descends with Men to Dwell.
Ballou, Hosea, II
Ye Realms below the Skies.
Ballou, Silas
Almighty God in Being Was.
While I Am Young.
Balsdon, Dacre
Endurance Test.
Bamberger, Augustus Wright
Each a Part of All.
Bamford, Samuel
Bard's Reformation, The.
Farewell to My Cottage.
Homely Rhymes on Bad Times.
Landowner, The.
Bampfylde, John Codrington
On a Frightful Dream.
On a Wet Summer.

On Hearing That Torture Was Suppressed
throughout the Austrian Dominions.
Sonnet: "As when, to one who long hath
watched, the morn."
To the Evening.
To the Redbreast.
Bancks, John
Description of London, A.
Fragment, A: "In Cloe's chamber, she and I."
Bancroft, Charles
Tadoussac.
Bancroft, James Henry
Brother, Though from Yonder Sky.
Banda, Innocent
Lindedi Singing.
Malawi.
May Bright Mushrooms Grow.
That There Should Be Laughter.
Where Is the Fruit.
Bandeira, Manuel
Anthology.
Brazilian Tragedy.
My Last Poem.
Rondeau of the Little Horses.
Bangs, Carol Jane
Sunday Afternoon.
Touching Each Other's Surfaces.
Bangs, Edward *and also* Richard Shuckburg
Yankee Doodle, at.
Bangs, John Kendrick
"Don't Care" and "Never Mind."
Dreadful Fate of Naughty Nate, The.
Hired Man's Way, The.
If.
Little Elf, The.
May 30, 1893.
My Dog.
On File.
Thanksgiving Day.
To a Withered Rose.
"What hundred books are best, think you?" I
said.
Banim, John
Soggarth Aroon.
Bankei
Alone in mountain fastness.
Banker, William, Jr.
Battle of Queenstown, The.
Banks, George Linnaeus
What I Live For.
Bannerji, Himani
Paki Go Home.
Bannerman, Frances
Upper Chamber, An.
Banning, Lex
Captain Arthur Phillip and the Birds.
Bansui, Tsuchii. *See* Tsuchii Bansui
Bantock, Gavin
Bard.
Dirge: "Body lies under the ground."
Joy.
Banus, Maria
Eighteen.
Gift Hour.
New Notebook, The.
Wedding.
Baraka, Imamu Amiri (Leroi Jones)
After the Ball.
Agony, An. As Now.
Air.
As a Possible Lover.
Audubon, Drafted.
Babylon Revisited.
Balboa, the Entertainer.
Ballad of the Morning Streets.
Ballgame, The.
Beautiful Black Women.
Biography.
Black Art.
Black Bourgeoisie.
Black Dada Nihilismus.

Black People!
Black People: This Is Our Destiny.
Bumi.
Cant.
Cold Term.
Crow Jane.
Das Kapital.
Duncan Spoke of a Process.
Each Morning, *sel.*
End of Man Is His Beauty, The.
Epistrophe.
Evil Nigger Waits for Lightnin.'
For Hettie.
Funeral Poem.
Guerrilla Handbook, A.
I Substitute for the Dead Lecturer.
In Memory of Radio.
In One Battle.
Incident.
Invention of Comics, The.
It's Nation Time.
Ka 'Ba.
Leadbelly Gives an Autograph.
Legacy.
Leroy.
Letter to E. Franklin Frazier.
Liar, The.
Like Rousseau.
Major Bowes' Diary.
New Reality Is Better Than a New Movie!,
A.
New World, The.
Numbers, Letters.
One Night Stand.
Ostriches and Grandmothers!
Poem for Black Hearts, A.
Poem for Half White College Students.
Poem for Speculative Hipsters, A.
Poem Some People Will Have to Understand,
A.
Political Poem.
Politics of Rich Painters, The.
Preface to a Twenty Volume Suicide Note.
Pressures, The.
Red Light.
Return of the Native.
Snake Eyes.
Song Form.
SOS.
Study Peace.
To a Publisher. Cut-out.
Tight Rope.
Turncoat, The.
W. W.
Way Out West.
We Own the Night.
Will They Cry When You're Gone, You Bet.
Young Soul.
Barakat, Saleem
Cows of Heaven, The.
Dilana and Diram, *sel.*
Flamingo, The.
Greyhound, The.
Hoopoe Bird, The.
Squirrel, The.
Baranczak, Stanislaw
Humane Conditions, The.
If Porcelain, Then Only the Kind.
If You Have to Scream, Please Do It Quietly.
Never Really.
Those Men, So Powerful.
Baratynsky, Evgeny Abramovich
All things have their own pace and mode of
motion.
Autumn.
Death.
Desolation.
Disillusion.
Muse, The.
My gift is scant, my voice lacks force behind
it.

Planting a Wood.
Wineglass, The.
Barba, Sharon
Dykes in the Garden.
"Barbara Eve." *See* **Reiss, Barbara Eve**
Barbauld, Anna Laetitia
Life.
Mouse's Petition, The.
Rights of Woman, The.
To Mr. S. T. Coleridge.
Barbeitos, Arlindo
In the Forest of Your Eyes.
Man of Rain, A.
Many years ago.
O Night Flower.
Barber, Frances
Play-acting.
Barber, Mary
On Seeing an Officer's Widow Distracted.
Written for My Son, and Spoken by Him at
His First Putting on Breeches.
Barber, Melanie Gordon
Sonnet for My Son.
Barber, William
Explanation.
Barberini, Francesco da
Sonnet: Of Caution.
Virgin Declares Her Beauties, A.
Barbour, George Hurlbut
Decoration Day.
Barbour, John
Before Bannockburn, *sel.*
Bruce Addresses His Army, *sel.*
Bruce Consults His Men, *sel.*
Freedom [*or* Fredome], *sel.*
Prologue to the Avowis of Alexander, *sel.*
Storys to rede ar delitabill, *sel.*
Barclay, Alexander
Geographers, *sel.*
Of Glotons and Dronkardes, *sel.*
Preachment for Preachers, *sel.*
Star of the Sea, *sel.*
Tudor Rose, The, *sel.*
Winter, *sel.*
Barclay, Edwin
Human Greatness.
Barclay, Robert
Hic liber ad me pertinet.
Bardeen, Charles William
Birds' Ball, The.
Barford, John
Eric.
Serve Her Right.
Sundered.
Toleration.
Whom Jesus Loved.
Barford, Wanda
Conversation with an Angel.
Pool.
Barham, Richard Harris. *See* **"Ingoldsby,**
Thomas"
Baring, Maurice
I Dare Not Pray to Thee.
I. M. H.
Baring-Gould, Sabine
Hymn: "Now the day is over."
Olive Tree, The.
Onward, Christian Soldiers.
Barker, Edna L. S.
Child of the World.
Barker, Edward D.
Go Sleep, Ma Honey.
Barker, George
Allegory of the Adolescent and the Adult.
And now there is nothing left to celebrate,
sel.
At midday they looked up and saw their
death, *sel.*
Channel Crossing.
Crystal, The.
Death of Yeats, The.

Dog, Dog in My Manger.
Elegy V: Separation of Man from God.
Elegy on the Eve.
Epitaph for the Poet.
Evening Star.
For the Fourth Birthday of My Daughter.
From thorax of storms the voices of verbs,
sel.
He Comes Among.
House I Go to in My Dream, The.
I enter and find I stand, *sel.*
I see the young bride move among, *sel.*
I sent a letter to my love, *sel.*
Ikons of the Dead, The.
Images! Venerable as Druidical trees, *sel.*
In Memory of a Friend.
Keelhauled across the star-wrecked death of
God, *sel.*
Leaping Laughers, The.
Meandering abroad in the Lincolnshire
meadows day, *sel.*
Memorial Couplets for the Dying Ego.
Munich Elegy No. 1.
My darkling child the stars have obeyed, *sel.*
My Joy, My Jockey, My Gabriel, *sel.*
News of the World I ("Cold shuttered loveless
star, skulker in clouds").
News of the World III.
News of the World II.
Not in the Poet.
O Golden Fleece ("O golden fleece she is
where she lies tonight"), *sel.*
O Tender under Her Right Breast, *sel.*
Oak and the Olive, The.
Ode against St. Cecilia's Day.
Resolution of Dependence.
Satan Is on Your Tongue, *sel.*
Seagull, spreadeagled, splayed on the wind,
The, *sel.*
Sequence.
Shut the Seven Seas against Us, *sel.*
Sonnet of Fishes.
Sonnet to My Mother.
Sparrow's Feather, A.
Summer Idyll.
Three Dead and the Three Living, The.
To Any Member of My Generation.
Today, the Twenty-sixth of February, *sel.*
Triumphal Ode MCMXXXIX.
Turn on Your Side and Bear the Day to Me.
Verses for a First Birthday.
Village Coddled in the Valley, The.
Wild Dreams of Summer What Is Your Grief.
Wraith-Friend, The.
Barker, Jane
Epitaph on the Secretary to the Muses.
To Her Lover's Complaint.
Barker, Noah
What Does It Matter?
Barker, S. Omar
Bear Ropin' Buckaroo.
Jack Potter's Courtin.'
Rain on the Range.
Barker, Thomas
Baits for Various Fish, *sel.*
How to Catch Trout, *sel.*
Methods of Cooking Trout, *sel.*
Barks, Coleman
Finger of Necessity.
Last Rebirth, The.
So it is, *sel.*
Barksdale, Clement
To My Nephew, J. B.
Barlett, I. J.
Town of Don't-You-Worry, The.
Barlow, George
Little Half-Brother, Little Black Star.
Mellowness and Flight.
Old Man Sweeping.
Stacademia.
Sweet Diane.

Barlow, Joel
Advice to a Raven in Russia [December,
1812]
Along the Banks.
Based on its rock of right your empire lies,
sel.
Eager he look'd. Another train of years, *sel.*
First American Congress, The.
Freedom.
Hasty Pudding, The.
Judge Me, O God.
O God of My Salvation, Hear.
On the Discoveries of Captain Lewis.
Song, A: "Fame let thy trumpet sound."
Barnard, John
Nations That Long in Darkness Walked.
Thrice Blest the Man.
Barnard, Katherine R.
Voice of God, The.
Barnard, Mary
Pleiades, The.
Shoreline.
Barnard, Lady Anne. *See* **Lindsay, Lady**
Anne
As it fell upon a day, *sel.*
Barnefield, Richard. *See* **Barnfield, Richard**
Barnes, Barnabe
Ah, sweet Content! where is thy mylde
abode?, *sel.*
Blast of wind, a momentary breath, A, *sel.*
God's Virtue, *sel.*
Jove for Europa[e]s love took[e] shape of
bull, *sel.*
Mistress, Behold, in This True-Speaking
Glass, *sel.*
No More Lewd Lays, *sel.*
O Powers Celestial, with what sophistry, *sel.*
Ode, An: "Why doth heaven bear a sun," *sel.*
Soft, lovely, rose-like lips, conjoined with
mine, *sel.*
To the Most Beautiful Lady, the Lady Bridget
Manners.
Write! Write! Help! Help!, *sel.*
Barnes, Djuna
Transfiguration.
Barnes, Jane
Hot Dog Poem, The.
How to Dress Like a Femmy Dyke.
How to Dress like a Scary Dyke.
Barnes, Jim
Abukbo, *sel.*
Autobiographical Flashback: Puma and
Pokeweed.
Autobiography, Chapter XLII: Three Days in
Louisville.
Autobiography, Chapter XVII: Floating the
Big Piney.
Autobiography: Last Chapter.
Baii, *sel.*
Bone Yard.
Camping Out on Rainy Mountain.
Captive Stone, The.
Chicago Odyssey, The.
Comcomly's Skull.
Contemporary Native American Poetry.
Ex-Deputy Sheriff Remembers the Eastern
Oklahoma Murderers, An.
Four Choctaw Songs.
Four Things Choctaw.
Halcyon Days.
Heartland.
Isuba, *sel.*
La Plata, Missouri: Clear November Night.
Last Look at La Plata, Missouri.
Lying in a Yuma Saloon.
Nashoba, *sel.*
Paiute Ponies.
Return to La Plata, Missouri.
Season of Loss, A.
Sunday Dreamer's Guide to Yarrow,
Missouri, A.

Sweating It Out on Winding Stair Mountain.
These Damned Trees Crouch.
Tracking Rabbits: Night.
Tracking the Siuslaw Man.
Wolf Hunting near Nashoba.

Barnes, Jo
Clinic Day.

Barnes, Julians
Time of grease beginneth at Midsummer day, *sel.*
When ye hunt at the roe, then shall ye see there, *sel.*
Wheresoever ye fare by frith or by fell, *sel.*

Barnes, Kate
Mare, A.

Barnes, William
All Still.
Bells ov Alderburnham, The.
Be'mi'ster.
Burncombe Hollow.
Childhood.
Clote (Water-Lily, The).
Come!
Day's Work a-Done.
Evenen in the Village.
Evening, and Maidens.
Fall, The.
False Friends-like.
Grammer's Shoes.
Heedless o' My Love.
In the Spring.
Jay a-Pass'd.
Leane, The.
Leaves a-Vallen.
Light or Sheade.
Lost Little Sister, The.
Lwonesomeness.
Mater Dolorosa.
May, *sel.*
May Tree, The.
Melhill Feast.
Mother o' blossoms, and ov all, *sel.*
Musings.
My Love's Guardian Angel.
My Orcha'd in Linden Lea.
Polly Be-en Upzides wi' Tom.
Readen ov a Head-Stwone.
Rustic Childhood.
Rwose in the Dark, The.
Seasons and Times.
Sheep in the Sheade.
Shellbrook.
Shep'erd Bwoy, The.
Shop o' Meat-Weare.
Slow to Come, Quick a-Gone.
Sonnet: "In every dream thy lovely features rise."
Sonnet: Leaves.
Spring, The.
Storm-Wind, The.
Stwonen Steps, The.
Times o' Year.
To Me.
Tokens.
Troubles of the Day.
Turnstile, The.
Uncle an' Aunt.
Vaices That Be Gone, The.
Vield Path, The.
Vierzide Chairs, The.
Walken Hwomme at Night.
When We That Now Ha' Childern Wer Childern.
Which Road?
White an' Blue.
Wife a-Lost, The.
Wife a-Prais'd, A.
Wind at the Door, The.
Winter Night, A.
With you first shown to me.
Woodlands, The.
Zilver-Weed, The.

Zong, A: "O Jenny, don't sobby! vor I shall be true."
Zummer Stream.
Zun-zet.

Barnett, Anthony
Book of Mysteries, The.
Celan.
Cloisters.
Crossing.
Marriage, A.

Barnett, Ratcliffe
For Summer's Here.

Barney, Natalie Clifford
Couplets.
To a Bride-to-Be.
Woman.

Barnfield [or Barnefield], Richard
Ah no; nor I myselfe: though my pure love, *sel.*
As it fell upon a day, *sel.*
But now my Muse toyled with continuall care, *sel.*
Cherry-lipped Adonis, *sel.*
Cherry-lipt Adonis in his snowie shape, *sel.*
Comparison of the Life of Man, A.
Daphnis to Ganymede, *sel.*
Here hold this glove (this milk-white cheveril glove), *sel.*
If thou wilt love me, thou shalt be my boy, *sel.*
Shepherd's Complaint, A.
Sighing, and Sadly Sitting by My Love, *sel.*
Some talk of Ganymede th' Idalian boy, *sel.*
Sometimes I wish that I his pillow were, *sel.*
Sporting at fancie, setting light by love, *sel.*
Sweet corrall lips, where Nature's treasure lies, *sel.*
Sweet Thames I honour thee, not for thou art, *sel.*
Thus was my love, thus was my Ganymed, *sel.*
To His Friend Master R.L., In Praise of Music and Poetry.
Two stars there are in one faire firmament, *sel.*
Unknown Shepherd's Complaint, The.

Barnstone, Aliki
Mating the Goats.
To a Friend's Child.
Windows in Providence.

Barnstone, Willis
Changsha Shoe Factory.
Gas Lamp.
Good Beasts, The.
Grandfather.
Miklos Radnoti.
Paradise.
Worm, The.

Baro, Gene
Cherry.
Ferns, The.
For Hani, Aged Five, That She Be Better Able to Distinguish a Villain.
Horsemen, The.
Judges, Judges.
Ladder, The.
Lament for Better or Worse.
Northern Spring, A.
Northwind.
Street, The.
Travelling Backward.
Under the Boughs.

Baron, Mary
Newborn Neurological Exam.

Baron, William
Warkin' Mon's Reflections, A.

Barr, Isabel Harriss
Madaket Beach.

Barratt, Ken
Burke and Wills.

Barrax, Gerald William
Black Narcissus.
Christmas 1959 et Cetera.
Competitors, The.
Efficiency Apartment.
For Malcolm: After Mecca.
Fourth Dance Poem.
Gift.
I Had a Terror—Since September.
If She Sang.
To a Woman Who Wants Darkness and Time.
Two Figures on Canvas.
Your Eyes Have Their Silence.

Barreno, Maria Isabel, Maria Teresa Horta, and Maria Velho da Costa. See Marias, The Three

Barrett, Carlton. See Cogil, Legon and Carlton Barrett.

Barrett, Eaton Stannard
Woman.

Barrett, Wilson Agnew
New England Church, A.

Barrick, J. R.
No Land like Ours.

Barrie, Hugh
When I Am Dead.

Barrington, Patrick
Air Sentry, The.
I Had a Duck-billed Platypus.
I had a hippopotamus; I loved him as a friend, *sel.*

Barrington, Pauline B.
White Iris, A.

Barrios, Gregorio
Crazy Movie.

Barrios, Miguel de
Epitaph: "Daniel and Abigail."

Barrow, Jedediah
You Call That a Ts'ing; a Letter.

Barrows, Anita
Ancestors, The.
Avenue Y.
Emigration.
Letter to a Friend in an Unknown Place.
Reflections.

Barrows, Marjorie
Bug, The.

Barry, Michael J.
Hymn of Freedom.

Barstow, Henry H.
If Easter Be Not True.

Barth, John
Minstrel's Last Lay, The.

Barth, R. L.
Insert, The.

Barthgate, Dave
Rock Leader.

Bartlett, Elizabeth
After the Storm.
Charlotte, Her Book.
Contre Jour.
999 Call.

Bartole, Genevieve
Canadian Farmer.

Barton, Bernard
Bruce and the Spider.
Land Which No Mortal May Know, The.

Barton, Joan
First News Reel: September 1939.
Mistress, The.

Barton, Joyce
Epitaph on a Soldier.

Barton, Owen
Early Morning Roundup.
My Ol' Stetson.

Baruch, Dorothy Walter
Automobile Mechanics.
Cat.
Different Bicycles.
Funny the Way Different Cars Start.

On a Steamer.
Riding in a Motor Boat.
Riding in an Airplane.
Stop-Go.

Baruch of Worms
Elegy: "Those reckless hosts rush to the wells."

Bashford, Herbert
Song of the Forest Ranger, The.

Bashford, Sir Henry Howarth
Where Do the Gipsies Come From?

Bashir, Al-Tijani Yusuf
Memories of the Village School.
Tormented Mystic.

Basho (Matsuo Basho)
Ah, spring, spring!, *sel.*
Ailing on my travels.
Alive, sea cucumbers frozen in one lump, *sel.*
All That Is Left.
An old pond: a frog jumps in, *sel.*
As if touching a boil a willow bends, *sel.*
At my house small mosquitoes, *sel.*
At night secretly a worm, *sel.*
At Saya-between-the-Hills, *sel.*
At Takadachi in Oshu, *sel.*
Autumn's deep, The—my neighbor, *sel.*
Azaleas arranged, and by them, *sel.*
Beginning of art, The.
Beginning of autumn, The.
Beside the road.
Bright moon: strolling around the pond all night long, *sel.*
By the Roadside in My Birthplace, *sel.*
Chrysanthemum didn't spill a dewdrop, The, *sel.*
Clouds now and then.
Cold Nights, *sel.*
Coming by a mountain path, *sel.*
Composed While Ill, *sel.*
Congratulations on a New House, *sel.*
Cruel: under a helmet, a cricket, *sel.*
Cuckoo—, The/ Its call stretching.
Cuckoo fades away, A, *sel.*
Cuckoo's voice lays itself over the water, A, *sel.*
Daybreak: a white fish, *sel.*
Departing spring: birds cry, *sel.*
Dragonfly—unable to get hold of a grass blade, *sel.*
Enfeebled: I've bitten on the sand in seaweed, *sel.*
First cold rain.
First shower—even a monkey, *sel.*
First snow: luckily I find myself residing in my own hut, *sel.*
Fishermen's faces were seen first, *sel.*
Flash of lightning, A.
Fleas, lice—a horse pisses right by my pillow, *sel.*
Friend sparrow, do not eat, I pray.
Gathering the May rains, *sel.*
Haiku: "Lightning flashes, The!"
Haiku: "Lightning gleam, A."
Hair grown and face pale, *sel.*
Having planted a plantain, *sel.*
How cool it feels.
Hozo Pass, *sel.*
I pluck my gray hair, *sel.*
I usually hate crows, *sel.*
I'd like to be called a traveler, *sel.*
If taken in hand, autumn frost, *sel.*
I'll make a fire tonight, *sel.*
"I'm tired of children!"—to anyone who says that.
In a fisherman's hut crickets mingle, *sel.*
In a rape field sparrows, *sel.*
In Hatchobori, *sel.*
In mists and rains, the day, *sel.*
In morning dew, dirty and cool, *sel.*
In my hut, square light cast, *sel.*
In the middle of a plain, *sel.*

In the old stone pool.
In the old village, no house without a persimmon tree, *sel.*
Iris looks exactly like the one in the water, The, *sel.*
It's spring! nameless mountains, *sel.*
Kite's Feathers, The.
Later, Spending Some Time at Bokusetsu's Hut in Otsu, *sel.*
Lightning: going in the dark side, *sel.*
Lightning in my hand, *sel.*
Lightning in the clouds!
Lonely pond in age-old stillness sleeps, A.
Mistaken for a blind man, *sel.*
Mogami River has poured the hot sun into the sea, The, *sel.*
Month's last day, no moon, The, *sel.*
Moon as your guide, The, *sel.*
Mottoes, *sel.*
Nijiko, *sel.*
O cricket, from your cheery cry.
Old men, white-haired, beside the ancestral graves.
Old pond, An: a frog jumps in.
On a bare branch.
On a withered branch.
On dead branches crows remain, *sel.*
On the Twenty-first of the Seventh Month of the Seventh Year of Genroku, at Bokusetsu's Hut, *sel.*
Only butterflies fly in the field, *sel.*
Pea crab crawls up my leg, A, *sel.*
People's voices: returning by this road as autumn ends, *sel.*
Pines of Karasaki, The, *sel.*
Plum blossoms at their best, *sel.*
Quick-falling dew.
Quietness: piercing the rocks, *sel.*
Rakushisha, *sel.*
Roadside marsh mallow, The, *sel.*
Roadside thistle, eager, The.
Salted breams' gums are cold, *sel.*
Scallions just washed white in this cold, *sel.*
Scudding cloud, A, *sel.*
Sea dark, The.
Sea darkens, and the voices of ducks, The, *sel.*
Sentiment on a Journey, *sel.*
Seven sights were veiled.
Silent and still: then.
Skull exposed in a field in my mind, *sel.*
Soon it will die.
Sound of paddles slapping the waves, *sel.*
Spider.
Spring:/ A hill without a name.
Staying at Horai Temple, *sel.*
Staying Overnight at Akashi, *sel.*
Still baking down.
Stopping by Saigyo's Willow, *sel.*
Summer clothes: I have yet to pick all the lice, *sel.*
Summer grasses.
This road: no one taking it as autumn ends, • *sel.*
This snowy morning, alone,, *sel.*
This white chrysanthemum doesn't have a speck of dust, *sel.*
Though it will die soon.
Through the long day the skylarks, *sel.*
To the sun's path.
Under a Tree.
Well, let's go.
White fish clustering in seaweed, *sel.*
Whiter than the stones on Stone Mountain, *sel.*
Winds of autumn, The.
Winter day, A: frozen on horseback, a shadow, *sel.*
With a young leaf may I wipe, *sel.*
With the morning-glories I eat my meal, *sel.*
You say one word.

Basho *and* **Shita Yaba**
At a Fragrance of Plums.

Bass, Ellen
Celia.
Change.
First Menstruation.
For My Mother.
I am the sorrow in the wheat fields.
In Celebration.
Live for It.
Partly to My Cat.
September 7.
To Praise.
Untitled.

Basse, William
Anglers Song.
As inward love breeds outward talk, *sel.*
Elegy on Shakespeare [*or* On Mr. Wm. Shakespeare]

Bassui
I flung open all six windows on the moon.

Bastard, Thomas
Ad Henricum Wottonem.
De Naevo in Facie Faustinae.
Epitaph: Iohannis Sande.
In Gaetam.
Methinks 'Tis Pretty Sport [to Hear a Child]

Bat-Miriam, Yocheved [*or* **Yokheved]**
Distance Spills Itself.
Just as You See Me, That's How I Am.
Monasteries Lift Gold Domes, The.

Bates, Arlo
America, *sel.*
Cyclamen, The.
In Paradise.
Kitty's Laugh, *sel.*
Kitty's "No.", *sel.*
Like to a Coin.
On the Road to Chorrera.
Watchers, The.
Winter Twilight, A.

Bates, Charlotte Fiske
Character, A.
Clue, The.
Delay.
Living Book, The.
Woodbines in October.

Bates, Clara Doty
At Grandfather's.
Gray Thrums.
Thistle-Down.
Who Likes the Rain?

Bates, David
Speak Gently.

Bates, G. E.
Pentagonia.

Bates, Herbert
Heavens Are Our Riddle, The.
Prairie.

Bates, Katharine Lee
America the Beautiful.
Despised and Rejected.
For Deeper Life.
Kings of the East, The.
Little Knight in Green, The.
Robin's Secret.
Song of Riches, A.
Song of Waking, A.
Thou Knowest.

Bates, Rachel
How Sweet the Night.
Infinite Debt, The.

Bates, Scott
B Is for Baseball.

Bathgate, Dave
For Tony, Dougal, Mick, Bugs, Nick et Al.

Batisti, Silvia
This Rage.

Battcock, Marjorie
Refugee, The.

Batterham, Eric N.
Once.
Batyushkov, Konstantin Nikolayevich
As I was leaving Albion's shore,
    mist-covered.
There is enjoyment in a wilderness of trees.
To My Friends.
You've heard that saying brave.
Baudelaire, Charles
Balcon, Le.
Beauté, La.
Carrion, A.
Correspondences.
Damned Women.
Death of Lovers, The.
Don Juan in Hell.
Élévation.
Epilogue: "With heart at rest I climbed the
    citadel's."
Giantess.
Harmonie du Soir.
Hiboux, Les.
Intimate Associations.
Inward Conversation.
Jewels, The.
Litany to Satan.
Meditation.
Metamorphoses of the Vampire.
Parfum Exotique.
Peace, Be at Peace, O Thou My Heaviness.
Seven Old Men, The.
Spleen LXXVI ("I have more memories than
    if I had lived a thousand years.").
Vampire, The.
Women Damned.
Baugh, Edward
Carpenter's Complaint, The.
Colour-Scheme.
Country Dance.
Truth and Consequences.
Baughan, Blanche Edith
Logs, at the door, by the fence; broadcast
    over the paddock, sel.
Old Place, The.
Toward the dawn, sel.
Baum, Peter
Horror.
Psalms of Love.
Baumel, Judith
Led by the Hebrew School Rabbi.
Bax, Clifford
Turn Back, O Man.
Bax, Vera
Fallen, The.
To Billy, My Son.
To Richard, My Son.
Bax, Sir Arnold. *See* **"O'Byrne, Dermot"**
Baxter, James Keir
Apple Tree, The.
At Akitio.
At Taieri Mouth.
At the Fox Glacier Hotel.
Ballad of Calvary Street.
Ballad of the Stonegut Sugar Works.
Bay, The.
Beach House, The.
Bees that have been hiving above the church
    pond, The, sel.
Buried Stream, The.
Colin, you can tell my words are crippled
    now, sel.
Crossing Cook Straight.
Dark Welcome, The, sel.
Dentist's Window, A.
East Coast Journey.
Election 1960.
Elegy for an Unknown Soldier.
Evidence at the Witch Trials.
Family Photograph 1939, A.
Father Lenin, you understood the moment,
    sel.

First Forgotten, The.
From an old house shaded with macrocarpas,
    sel.
Green Figs at Table.
Haere Ra.
High Country Weather.
Homecoming, The.
Howrah Bridge.
Inflammable Woman, The.
Lament for Barney Flanagan.
Lion Skin, The.
Mandrakes for Supper.
Morgue, The.
My Love Late Walking.
New Zealand.
News from a Pacified Area.
On the Death of Her Body.
Perseus.
Poem in the Matukituki Valley.
Rata blooms explode, the bow-legged tomcat,
    The, sel.
Rope for Harry Fat, A.
Shingle Beach Poem.
Small grey cloudly louse that nests in my
    beard, sel.
Spider crouching on the ledge above the sink,
    The, sel.
Summer 1967.
Three dark buds for the Trinity, sel.
To a Print of Queen Victoria.
To pray for an easy heart is no prayer at all,
    sel.
To wake up with a back sore from the hard
    mattress, sel.
To wish to climb a ladder to the loft, sel.
Virginia Lake.
When I was only semen in a gland, sel.
Wild Bees.
Winter in Jerusalem.
Yesterday I planted garlic, sel.
Baxter, Richard
Ye holy Angels bright, sel.
Bayer, Konrad
For Judith.
Franz was./ was Franz?
We won't pay any attention to this invitation.
Bayer, Rudolf
Cloud-Fish, The.
Late at Night.
Baykov, Hala
Café.
Bayldon, Arthur
Marlowe.
Sunset.
**Baylebridge, William (Charles William
    Blocksidge)**
All that I am to Earth Belongs, sel.
As fire, unfound ere pole approaches pole,
    sel.
Brain, the blood, the busy thews, The, sel.
Choir of spirits on a cloud, A, sel.
God, to get the clay that stayed me, sel.
I worshipped, when my veins were fresh, sel.
Love feeds, like Intellect, his lamp with truth,
    sel.
Quiet moon, immaculate of face, The, sel.
This miracle in me I scan, sel.
Who questions if the punctual sun unbars, sel.
Bayles, James C.
In the Gloaming.
Bayliss, John Clifford
Apocalypse and Resurrection.
Seven Dreams.
Baylor, Byrd
Desert Tortoise.
Bayly, Thomas Haynes
Mistletoe Bough, The.
She Wore a Wreath of Roses.
Bayr, Rudolf
Voice, The.

Beach, Joseph Warren
Dropping Your Aitches.
Horatian Ode.
Beach, Seth Curtis
Mysterious Presence! Source of All.
Thou One in All, Thou All in One.
"Beachcomber." *See* **Morton, John Bingham**
Beadnell, Mary
Hiroshima.
Beardsley, Aubrey
Ballad of a Barber, The.
Three Musicians, The.
**Beatrice [or Beatritz or Beatriz] de Die [or
    Dia]**
Estat ai en greu cossirier.
Fine joy brings me great happiness.
Handsome friend, charming and kind.
I Have Been in Great Distress.
I have been in heavy thought.
I sing a song reluctantly.
I thrive on youth and joy.
I've lately been in great distress.
Lately I've felt a grave concern.
My true love makes me happy.
Of things I'd rather keep in silence I must
    sing.
Beattie, James
Epitaph, An: "Like thee I once have stemm'd
    the sea of life."
Nature and the Poets, sel.
Question, The.
To Mr. Alexander Ross.
Youth of a Poet, The, sel.
Beattie, James Hay
On the Author of the *Treatise of Human
    Nature.*
Beaumont, Francis
Lines on the Tombs in Westminster, at.
Mr. Francis Beaumont's Letter to Ben
    Johnson.
More pleasing were these sweet delights, sel.
Mr. Francis Beaumont's Letter from the
    Country [to Jonson]
On blessed youths, for Jove doth pause, sel.
Peace and silence be the guide, sel.
Shake off your heavy trance!, sel.
True Beauty.
Upon Master Edmund Spenser.
Ye [*or* You] should stay longer if we durst,
    sel.
Beaumont, Francis and John Fletcher
Away, Delights, sel.
Bridal Song ("Cynthia, to thy power"), sel.
Bridal Song ("Hold back thy hours"), sel.
Come, sleep, sel.
Come, You Whose Loves Are Dead, sel.
Jillian of Berry, sel.
Lay a garland on my hearse, sel.
Lovers Rejoice!, sel.
Merrythought's Song, sel.
Mirth, sel.
Month of May, The, sel.
Nose, nose, jolly red nose, sel.
Song: "Turn, turn thy beauteous face away,"
    sel.
Tell Me Dearest, What is Love?, sel.
Beaumont, Joseph
Biothanatos.
Garden, The.
Gentle Check, The.
Gnat, The.
House and Home.
Love.
Morning Hymn.
Beaumont, Sir John
Assumption, The.
Epitaph upon My Dear Brother, Francis
    Beaumont, An.
O Thou Who Art Our Author and Our End.
Of His Dear Son, Gervase, sel.

Of My Dear Son [*or* Deare Sonne], Gervase
  Beaumont.
Of True Liberty.
Richard III's Speech, *sel.*
To His Late Majesty Concerning the True
  Form of English Poetry.
Upon a Funeral.

Beauvais, Phyllis (Phyllis Harris)
Furniture.
Outside.
Under Your Voice, among Legends.

Beauveau, Marquise de Boufflers,
Marie-Françoise-Catherine de
Air: Sentir avec Ardeur.

Beaver, Bruce
Cow Dance.
I shop in the streets of my hometown with/
  my family, *sel.*
I welcome the anonymity of the middle years,
  sel.
Mid-day and a heat haze over all, *sel.*
Sou'wester whips the day awake, The, *sel.*
Three anti-depressants and one diuretic a day,
  sel.
Three images of dying stick in my mind like
  morbid transfers, *sel.*
Today the self-destroying anger, *sel.*

Beccadelli, Antonio. *See* **"Panormitanus"**

Beck, Rachael
Wrong Line, The.

Beck, Victor Emanuel
Sifting.

Becker, Edna
Before the Monkey's Cage.
Beside the Line of Elephants.

Becker, Edwin
Mother's Day.

Becker, John
Feather or Fur.

Beckerman, H. N.
Adjustments.
To: The Access Committee.

Beckett, Samuel
Age is when to a man, *sel.*
Alba.
Cascando.
Dieppe.
Echo's Bones, *sel.*
Enueg I.
Enueg II.
Gnome.
I would like my love to die.
Malacoda.
My way is in the sand flowing.
Ooftish.
Saint-Lô.
Song: "Age is when to a man."
Vulture, The, *sel.*
What would I do without this world faceless
  incurious.
Whoroscope.

Beckford, Slim *and* **Sam Blackwood**
Johnny Tek Away Mi Wife.

Beckford, William
Ode: "To orisons, the midnight bell."

Bécquer, Gustavo Adolfo
Dark-Winged Swallows Will Return, The.
They Closed Her Eyes.

Beddo, Frank
Jeff Buckner.

Beddoes, Thomas Lovell
Alpine Spirit's Song.
Another.
Ballad of Human Life.
Beautiful Night, A, *sel.*
"Bona de Mortuis."
Bridal Song to Amala, *sel.*
Bury Him Deep.
Comet, The.
Crocodile, A, *sel.*
Death Sweet.
Dirge: "Swallow leaves her nest, The", *sel.*

Dirge Written for a Drama.
Dream-Pedlary.
Envoi, L': "Who findeth comfort in the stars
  and flowers," *sel.*
Fair and bright assembly, A: never strode, *sel.*
Fantastic Simile, A.
Humble Beginnings.
Hymn: "And many voices marshalled in one
  hymn."
If thou wilt ease thine heart, *sel.*
Lake, A.
Lines Written in a Blank Leaf of the
  Prometheus Unbound.
Lord Alcohol [*or* Song]
Man's Anxious, but Ineffectual Guard against
  Death.
Mighty Thoughts of an Old World, The, *sel.*
New Cecilia, The.
Old Adam, the Carrion Crow, *sel.*
Old Ghost, The.
Phantom-Wooer, The.
Poor Old Pilgrim Misery, *sel.*
Resurrection Song.
Silenus in Proteus.
Song: "A ho! A ho!/ Love's horn doth blow,"
  sel.
Song: "How many times do I love thee,
  dear?," *sel.*
Song of the Stygian Naiades.
Song: Old Adam, the Carrion Crow.
Song on the Water, *sel.*
Song: "Strew not earth with empty stars," *sel.*
Sonnet: To Tartar, a Terrier Beauty.
Squats on a toad-stool under a tree, *sel.*
Tailor, The.
Threnody.
To Night.
To Sea, *sel.*
To Silence.
We Do Lie beneath the Grass, *sel.*

Bede, The Venerable
Hymn, A: "Hymn of glory let us sing, A."

"Bede, Cuthbert" (Edward Bradley)
Entrance Exams.
In Immemoriam.
Limerick: "There was a queer fellow named
  Woodin."

Beebe, Lucius
Quid Restat.

Beecham, Audrey
Ditty: "If this town should tumble down."
Eichmann.
Song: "There's no more talk and ease."

Beecher, John
I read your testimony and I thought, *sel.*

Beeching, Henry Charles
Going Down Hill on a Bicycle.
Prayers.

Beeching, Jack
1944—On the Invasion Coast.

Beedome, Thomas
Broken Heart, The.
To the Noble Sir Francis Drake.

Beer, Christina
Fox Glove Song.
1974—The Sounds.
Waiheke 1972—Rocky Bay.

Be'er, Hayim
Love Song: "In the light of the moon."
Sequence of Generations, The.
Tabernacle of Peace.

Beer, Morris Abel
Manhattan.

Beer, Patricia
Autobiography.
Birthday Poem from Venice.
Christmas Carols.
Christmas Eve.
Christmas Tree, The.
Creed of Mr. Nicholas Culpeper.
Dilemma.

Fifth Sense, The.
Gallery Shepherds.
In a Country Museum.
In the Cathedral.
Jane Austen at the Window.
Leaping into the Gulf.
Letter, The.
Lion Hunts.
Middle Age.
Postilion Has Been Struck by Lightning, The.
Witch.

Beer-Hofmann, Richard
Evil Man, An!, *sel.*
Jacob's Destiny, *sel.*
Lullaby for Miriam.

Beerbohm, Max
Addition to Kipling's "The Dead King
  (Edward VII), 1910."
Ballade Tragique à Double Refrain.
Brave Rover.
Elegy on Any Lady by George Moore.
Epitaph for G. B. Shaw.
Luncheon, A.
On the Imprint of the First English Edition of
  "The Works of Max Beerbohm."
Police Station Ditties.
Road to Zoagli, The.
Savonarola ("Savonarola looks more grim
  today").
Sequelula to "The Dynasts," A.
Thomas Hardy and A. E. Housman.
Vague Lyric by G. M.

Beerbohm, Max *and* **William Rothenstein**
Eli the Thatcher.

Beers, Ethel Lynn
All Quiet along the Potomac.
Which Shall It Be?

Beers, Henry Augustin
Biftek aux Champignons.
Ecce in Deserto.
On a Miniature.
Posthumous.
Singer of One Song, The.
Ye Laye of Ye Woodpeckore.

Beeton, Douglas Ridley
Autumn.

Beevers, John
Atameros.

Behan, Brendan
Repentance.

Behn, Aphra
Amyntas Led Me to a Grove, *sel.*
And Forgive Us Our Trespasses.
Coquette, The.
Defiance, The.
Dream, The, *sel.*
Love in fantastic triumph sate.
Love's Witness.
Not to sigh and to be tender.
Song: "Ah false Amyntas, can that hour," *sel.*
Song: "All joy to mortals, joy and mirth," *sel.*
Song: "Curse upon that faithless maid, A,"
  sel.
Song: "Oh! Love, that stronger art than
  wine," *sel.*
Song: "When maidens are young, and in their
  spring," *sel.*
Thousand Martyrs I Have Made, A.
What has poor Woman done, that she must
  be, *sel.*
When you love, or speak of it.

Behn, Harry
Christmas Carol, A: "Angel told Mary, An."
Christmas Morning.
Flowers.
Ghosts.
Gnome, The.
Growing Up.
Hallowe'en.
Invitation.

Kite, The.
Mr. Pyme.

Behn, Robin
To Rise, So Suddenly.

Behrend, Alice
Snowflakes.

Beidler, Martha
Mohammed Ibrahim Speaks.

Beirei
All patriarchs are above our understanding.

Beissel, Henry
In the one-two domestic goose one-two
one-two step, *sel.*
Pans at Carnival.

Beissel, Johann Conrad
Sun Now Risen, The.

Beker, Ruth
Don't Show Me.

Belarde, Linda
Precious Bits of Family.

Belev, Georgi
Images from the Midwest.

Belford, Ken
Beside the Road.
Blueline.
Branches Back Into.
Carrier Indians.
Dusk.
For Kelley.
Glove Glue.
Hunchbacked and corrected.
In spots/ it is warm enough.
New Potatoes.
Peanuts.
Stony Brook Tavern.
Stove.
Turn (a Poem in 4 Parts).

Belisarda, Marcia (Sister María de Santa Isabel)
Stanzas Written in Great Haste in Reply to
Some Proposing That Women Are Fickle.

Belitt, Ben
Charwoman.
Karamazov.
Late Dandelions.
Papermill Graveyard.
Sand Painters, The.
View from the Gorge.
Winter Pond.

Belknap, Jeremy
Far from Our Friends.
Thus Spake the Saviour.

Bell, Birdie
I Have Always Found It So.

Bell, Charles G.
Banana.
Baptism.
Blue-Hole, The.
Diretro al Sol.
Flood, The.
From Le Havre.
Gar, The.
Girl Walking.
On a Baltimore Bus.

Bell, Don
Going to the Shawnee Rodeo.

Bell, Henry Glassford
Mary, Queen of Scots.

Bell, J. J.
Boa, The.
Hedgehog, The.
Lights, The.
Shark, The.
Ships, The.

Bell, Julian
Redshanks, The.

Bell, Lindolf
Of This Core I Sample the Bitter Taste.
On Hope.
On Time.

Poem to a Young Man.
Portrait of an Ex-Young Bourgeois.

Bell, Martin
Footnote to Enright's "Apocalypse."
Songs, The.
Winter Coming On.

Bell, Marvin
Acceptance Speech.
Cabin in Minnesota, A.
Communication of His Thirtieth Birthday.
Drawn by Stones, by Earth, by Things That
Have Been in the Fire.
During the War.
Extermination of the Jews, The.
Fresh News from the Past.
Gemwood.
Getting Lost in Nazi Germany.
Here.
Hole in the Sea, The.
Homage to the Runner, *sel.*
Impotence.
Iowa Land.
Israeli Navy, The.
Last Thing I Say, The.
Late Naps.
Letting in Cold.
Little Father Poem.
Long Island.
Music of the Spheres, The.
Mystery of Emily Dickinson, The.
Nest, The.
Obsessive, *sel.*
Origin of Dreams.
Path among the Dunes, A.
Perfection of Dentistry, The.
Quilt, Dutch China Plate.
Residue of Song.
Song for a Little Bit of Breath.
Stars Which See, Stars Which Do Not See.
That Time in Tangier.
These Green-going-to-Yellow.
They.
Things We Dreamt We Died For.
3 Stanzas about a Tree.
Tideline.
To an Adolescent Weeping Willow.
To Dorothy.
Treetops.
Trinket.
True Story, A.
Two Pictures of a Leaf.
What They Do to You in Distant Places.
White Clover.

Bell, Maurice
Alabama, The.

Bell, Robert Mowry
Second Volume, The.
Tutelage, The.

Bell, Walker Meriwether
Jefferson Davis.

Bell, William
Coolin Ridge, The.
Elegy IX: "My dear, observe the rose! though
she desire it."
Elegy X.
Elegy: "Tonight the moon is high, to summon
all."
On a Dying Boy.
On a Ledge.
Sonnet: "You waken slowly. In your dream
you're straying."
To a Lady on Her Marriage.
Young Man's Song, A.

"Bell, Acton."   *See* **Bronte, Anne**

"Bell, Currer."   *See* **Bronte, Charlotte**

"Bell, Ellis."   *See* **Bronte, Emily**

Bellamann, Henry
Charleston Garden, A.

Bellamy, Peter
Sweet Loving Friendship.

Belleau, Remy
April.

Bellenden, John
Starscape, A.

Bellerby, Frances
Bereaved Child's First Night.
Clear Shell, A.
Inconclusive Evening, An.
Invalided Home.
War Casualty in April.

Belli, Carlos German
O Hada Cibernetica.
Segregation.
Tongue-tied.

Belli, Giaconda
Free Country: July 19, 1979.
I rise up, *sel.*
Obligations of the Poet.
Strike.

Belli, Giuseppe Gioacchino
Coffee-House Philosopher, The.
Confessor, The.
Last Judgment, The.
Sonnet: Annunciation.
Sonnet: Good Spiritual Father, The.

Bellman, Carl Michael
Cradle Song: "Lullaby, my little one."

Belloc, Hilaire
A stands for Archibald who told no lies, *sel.*
Almighty God, Whose Justice Like a Sun.
B stands for Bear. When bears are seen, *sel.*
Ballade of Illegal Ornaments.
Ballade to Our Lady of Czestochowa.
Big Baboon, The.
Bison, The.
Camelopard, The.
Chamois, The.
Charles Augustus Fortescue.
Child, Do Not Throw This Book About.
Courtesy.
Discovery.
Dodo, The.
Dreadful Dinotherium he, The, *sel.*
E stands for egg, *sel.*
Early Morning, The.
Elephant, The.
Epitaph on the Favourite Dog of a Politician.
Epitaph on the Politician Himself.
False Heart, The.
Fatigue.
First in his pride the orient sun's display.
Franklin Hyde.
Frog, The.
G.
G stands for Gnu, whose weapons of defence.
Game of Cricket, The.
George.
Godolphin Horne.
Grandmamma's Birthday.
Ha'nacker Mill.
Henry King, Who Chewed Bits of String, and
Was Early Cut Off in Dreadful Agonies.
Heretics All.
Hippopotamus, The.
I am a sundial. Ordinary words.
I am a sundial, turned the wrong way round.
Jim, Who Ran Away from His Nurse, and
Was Eaten by a Lion.
Juliet.
Justice of the Peace, The.
K for the Klondyke, a country of gold, *sel.*
Leader, The.
Lines for a Christmas Card.
Lines to a Don.
Lion, The.
Llama, The.
Lord Abbott.
Lord Finchley.
Lord Heygate.
Lord High-Bo.
Lord Hippo.

Lord Lucky.
Lord Lundy.
Matilda.
Night, The.
On a Dead Hostess.
On a General Election.
On a Politician.
On a Puritan.
On a Sundial.
On His Books.
On Hygiene.
On Jam.
On Lady Poltagrue, a Public Peril.
On Mundane Acquaintances.
On Noman, a Guest.
Python, The.
R the reviewer, reviewing my book, *sel.*
Rebecca, Who Slammed Doors for Fun and
    Perished Miserably.
Rhinoceros, The.
Sarah Byng Who Could Not Read and Was
    Tossed into a Thorny Hedge by a Bull.
Song Called "His Hide Is Covered with Hair,"
    The.
Song of Duke William.
Song: "You wear the morning like your
    dress."
Sonnet: "We will not whisper, we have found
    the place."
South Country, The.
Statesman, The.
Statue, The.
Tarantella.
They Say That in the Unchanging Place, *sel.*
This, the last ornament among the peers.
Tiger, The.
To Dives.
Viper, The.
Vulture, The.
West Sussex Drinking Song.
World's a stage, The. The trifling entrance
    fee.
Yak, The.
Bélot, Camille
Decision, The, *sel.*
Belting, Natalia M.
Dark gray clouds, The.
Put the pine tree in its pot by the doorway.
Some say the sun is a golden earring.
Beman, Nathan S. S.
Jesus, I Come to Thee.
Ben Aaron of Lenczicz, Solomon Ephraim
These Things I Do Remember.
Ben-Amittai, Levi
My Soul in the Palm of Your Hand.
On a Fall Night.
Ben Isaac ben Abun of Mainz, Simeon
All the Hosts of Heaven.
I Come to Supplicate.
Ben Judah, Daniel
Living God, The.
Ben Kalir, Eleazar
O Hark to the Herald.
Palms and Myrtles.
Prayer for Dew.
Prophet Jeremiah and the Personification of
    Israel, The, at.
Terrible Sons, The.
To Him Who Is Feared.
Ben Menahem Hazaken of Le Mans, Elijah
Precepts He Gave His Folk.
Ben Moses of Lucca, Kalonymos
His Sovereignty.
Ben Moses of Lucca, Kalonymos ben
Sovereignty, His.
Ben Shefatiah, Amittai
Hymn of Weeping.
Ben Yeshaq, Yosef Damana
Rusted Chain, The.
Ben-Yitzhak, Avraham
Blessed Are Those Who Sow and Do Not
    Reap.

I Didn't Know My Soul.
Psalm: "There are a very few moments when
    you."
Benally, Nan
Navaho Sings.
Rug of Woven Magic.
"Bendo, Brian"
Dream, The.
Benedict, Salli
Sweet Grass Is around Her.
Benedikt, Michael
Clement Atlee.
Divine Love.
European Shoe, The.
Fate in Incognito.
Fraudulent Days.
Grand Guignols of Love, The.
Some Litanies.
Benét, Laura
Mountain Convent.
Rowers, The.
Benet, Mayster
Alphabet of Aristotle, The.
Benét, Rosemary
Benjamin Franklin 1706-1790.
George Washington.
Hernando De Soto.
John Quincy Adams.
Nancy Hanks.
Peregrine White and Virginia Dare.
Southern Ships and Settlers.
Thomas Jefferson [1743-1826]
Benét, Rosemary and **Stephen Vincent**
Western Wagons.
Benét, Stephen Vincent
American Names.
Americans are always moving on, *sel.*
Ballad of William Sycamore, The.
Battle of Gettysburg, The, *sel.*
Daniel Boone.
Days Pass: Men Pass.
For All Blasphemers.
For City Spring.
Ghosts of a Lunatic Asylum.
He was a farmer, he didn't think much of
    towns, *sel.*
Hemp, The.
Hymn in Columbus Circle.
Innovator, The.
Invocation: "American muse, whose strong
    and diverse heart," *sel.*
Jack Ellyat Heard the Guns, *sel.*
John Brown's Prayer, *sel.*
Litany for Dictatorships.
Love Came By from the Riversmoke, *sel.*
Metropolitan Nightmare.
Mountain Whippoorwill, The.
Negro Spirituals.
Nightmare at Noon.
Nightmare Number Three.
Nightmare, with Angels.
1935.
Nomenclature.
Nonsense Song, A.
Rain after a Vaudeville Show.
Robert E. Lee, *sel.*
Song of the Riders, *sel.*
Three Elements, *sel.*
Unfamiliar Quartet.
Winged Man.
Benét, William Rose
Brazen Tongue.
Eternal Masculine.
Falconer of God, The.
Fancy, The.
Fawn in the Snow, The.
Gate of Horn.
Great Land, The.
Horse Thief, The.
Inscription for a Mirror in a Deserted
    Dwelling.

Jesse James.
Judgment.
Merchants from Cathay.
Night.
On a Dead Poet.
Sagacity.
Stricken Average, The.
Strong Swimmer, The.
Vital Statistics.
Whale.
Woodcutter's Wife, The.
World's Desire, The.
Beney, Zsuzsa
Breaking, The, *sel.*
Color, The, *sel.*
Reflections, *sel.*
Beneyto, Maria
Nocturne in the Women's Prison.
Benford, Lawrence
Beginning of a Long Poem on Why I Burned
    the City, The.
Benjacob, Isaac
Epitaph, An: "Here lies Nachshon, a man of
    great renown."
Benjámin, László
Cave Drawings.
Poem by an Unknown Poet from the
    Mid-Twentieth Century.
Benjamin, Park
Old Sexton, The.
To Arms.
Bennard, George
Old Rugged Cross, The.
Bennet, Bruce
Disaster, The.
Bennett, Alan
Place-Names of China.
Bennett, Anna Elizabeth
Candle Song.
Hush Thee, Princeling.
Bennett, Arnold
Limerick: "There was a young man of
    Montrose."
Love Affair, A.
Bennett, Bruce
Box Step.
Experience, The.
Form, The.
Leader.
Norman; or, The Fungus among Us.
Political Animal, A.
Story of Your Life, The.
Travis Licked Me.
True Story of Snow White, The.
Bennett, Gertrude Ryder
Diary of a Raccoon.
Bennett, Gwendolyn B.
Advice.
Fantasy.
Hatred.
Heritage.
Lines Written at the Grave of Alexander [*or*
    Alexandre] Dumas.
Nocturne: "This cool night is strange."
Quatrains.
Secret.
Song: "I am weaving a song of waters."
Sonnet: "He came in silvern armor, trimmed
    with black."
To a Dark Girl.
To Usward.
Your Songs.
Bennett, Henry Holcomb
Flag Goes By, The.
Bennett, John
God Bless You, Dear, To-Day!
Her Answer.
In a Rose Garden.
Ingenious Little Old Man, The.
Merry Pieman's Song, The.
Sky-Lark's Song, The, *sel.*

Song of the Hunt, The, *sel.*
Tiger Tale, A.
Bennett, Joseph Deericks
Complaint.
Quatrina.
To Eliza, Duchess of Dorset.
Bennett, Lerone, Jr.
And Was Not Improved.
Blues and Bitterness.
Bennett, Louise
Back to Africa.
Colonization in Reverse.
Dutty Tough.
Excitement.
Independance.
Independence Twenty-One.
Bennett, Mary
Cells.
Bennett, Murray
Funeral.
Bennett, Rodney
And Back.
Christmas-Tree Song, A.
Easter Praise.
Fluttering Leaves.
Growing River, The.
Little Brown Seed.
Little Old Lady, The.
Merry Birds.
Mr. Brown.
Mrs. Jenny Wren.
My Dog, Spot.
Pigeons, The.
Postman's Knock.
Robin's Song.
Ten Little Christmas Trees.
Thank You for Friends, A.
There.
Three Little Men in a Boat.
Wireless.
Writing Letters.
Bennett, Rowena Bastin
Airplane, The.
End-of-Summer Poem.
Freight Train, The.
Modern Dragon, A.
Motor Cars.
Smoke Animals.
Thanksgiving Magic.
When You Talk to a Monkey.
Bennett, Will
New Jersey.
Nod.
Poor Movies.
Bennett, William Cox
Invocation to Rain in Summer.
To a Cricket.
Bennis, Mohammad
Belonging to a New Family.
Second Coming, The.
Bensel, James Berry
Ahmed.
Bensho
In T'ang China Longing for Home.
Bensko, John
Elk on Mutability, The.
Elk Uncovers the Heavens, The.
Mail Call.
Mowing the Lawn.
Night-blooming Cactus, The.
Veteran of the Great War, A.
Watching TV, the Elk Bones Up on
  Metaphysics.
Wild Horses of Assateague Island, The.
Bensley, Connie
Charity.
Desires.
Benson, Arthur Christopher
Ant-Heap, The.
Land of Hope and Glory.
Phoenix, The.

Benson, Gerard
Leavings.
Probatioun Officeres Tale, The.
Benson, Louis FitzGerald
O Love That Lights the Eastern Sky.
O Risen Lord upon the Throne.
O Thou Whose Feet Have Climbed Life's
  Hill.
O Thou Whose Gracious Presence Blest.
Why Linger Yet upon the Strand?
Benson, Mary Josephine
Smoking Flax.
Benson, Nathaniel Anketell
Holy Night.
Year's End.
Benson, Robert Hugh
Priest's Lament, The.
Teresian Contemplative, The.
Benson, Stella
Frost.
Now I Have Nothing.
Benson, Steve
Blue Book 42.
Echo.
First and foremost I was trying to realize.
Bent, O. M.
Robin, The.
Bental, Anath
Angel Michael, The.
Jerusalem in the Snow.
Bentley, Beth
Bridges and Tunnels.
Gnomes, The.
Temple of the Muses.
Bentley, Edmund Clerihew
Adam Smith, *sel.*
After dinner Erasmus, *sel.*
Art of Biography, The, *sel.*
Ballade of Liquid Refreshment.
"Dear me!" exclaimed Homer, *sel.*
Dr. Clifford, *sel.*
George the Third, *sel.*
Great Duke of Wellington, The, *sel.*
I am not Mahomet, *sel.*
"I quite realized," said Columbus, *sel.*
If only Mr. Roosevelt, *sel.*
Intrepid Ricardo, The, *sel.*
John Stuart Mill, *sel.*
Liszt, *sel.*
Mr. Bernard Shaw, *sel.*
Mr. Hilaire Belloc, *sel.*
"No," said Charles Peace, *sel.*
"No, sir," said General Sherman, *sel.*
People of Spain think Cervantes, The, *sel.*
Savonarola ("Savonarola/Declined to wear a
  bowler").
Sir Christopher Wren, *sel.*
Sir Humphry Davy, *sel.*
Sir Walter Raleigh, *sel.*
There exists no proof as, *sel.*
What I like about Clive, *sel.*
When Alexander Pope, *sel.*
Younger Van Eyck, The.
Bentley, Nicolas
On Mrs. W——.
Benton, Joel
At Chappaqua.
Grover Cleveland.
Poet, The.
Scarlet Tanager, The.
Benton, Patricia
Desert River.
Benton, Walter
Summary of the Distance between the Bomber
  and the Objective.
With the Most Susceptible Element, the Mind,
  Already Turned under the Toxic Action.
Benveniste, Asa
Alchemical Cupboard, The.
Béranger, Pierre Jean de
King of Yvetot, The.

Berchan
Fort of Rathangan, The, *at.*
Bereng, David Granmer T.
Birth of Moshesh, The.
Berenguer, Amanda
Housework.
Berg, Stephen
Animals, The.
Between Us.
Desnos Reading the Palms of Men on Their
  Way to the Gas Chambers.
Don't Forget.
Dreaming with a Friend.
For My Father.
Glimpse of the Body Shop, A.
Gooseberries.
Holes, The.
Ollie, Answer Me.
People Trying to Love.
Survivor, The, *sel.*
To My Friends.
Wife Talks to Herself, A.
Bergé, Carole
Chiaroscuro.
Berge, H. C. ten
Goldrush.
Greenland Fossil an Icy Poet.
Hartlaub Gull, The.
Song Encountered in the Landscape.
Bergengren, Ralph Wilhelm
Dirigible, The.
Worm, The.
Berger, Bruce
Tallulah at the Schubert.
Berggolts, Olga
Infidelity.
To My Sister.
To Song.
Bergman, Alexander
Chronicler, The.
Letter.
Bergman, David
Blueberry Man.
Bergner, Zekharye Khone. See **Ravitch,**
  Melech
Berkeley, George
On the Prospect of Planting Arts and Learning
  in America.
Berkeley, Sir William
Song: "Where did you borrow that last sigh,"
  sel.
Berkson, Bill
Baby's Awake Now.
Bubbles.
Dream with Fred Astaire.
Familiar Music.
Fixture, A.
Fourth Street, San Rafael.
Ode: "Midnight moonlight mobbed Dante's
  bridge."
Star Motel.
Berlind, Bruce
Cynthia Lodgepole's Bum Rap ("Cynthia
  Lodgepole/ looked over her shoulder").
Berman, Ruth
Computative Oak.
Bernard, Artis
Snowfall.
Bernard, Oliver
That Night.
**Bernard [*or* Bernart] de Ventadour [*or*
  Ventadorn]**
It is worthless to write a line.
Lark, The.
Bernard of Clairvaux, Saint
Jesus, Thou Joy of Loving Hearts.
Wide Open Are Thy Loving Hands.
**Bernard of Cluny [*or* of Morlaix *or* of
  Morlas]**
Jerusalem the Golden, *sel.*

Scarcely believe things shameful to utter which yet I shall speak of, *sel.*

Bernart Arnaut de Moncuc
Now, when the rozier blows.

Bernart de Ventadorn. See **Bernard de Ventadour**

Berners, Dame Juliana
Properties of a Good Greyhound, The.

Bernhardt, Clara
Sailor's Wife, A.

Bernhardt, Suzanne
In a Dream Ship's Hold.
Unveiling, The.

Bernheim, Cathy
Poem of A, The.

Bernheimer, Alan
Amarillo.
Passing Strange.
Portrait of a Man.
Specimen of an Induction to a Poem.
Spinal Guard.
Word of Art.

Berni, Francesco
Deuce, a Roast of Scraggy Quails, a Bit, The.

Bernlef, J.
Art of Being Second, The.
Delight.
Erik Satie.
Sound of Matter, The.
Uncle Carl: A Home Movie.

Bernstein, Charles
For Love Has Such a Spirit That If It Is Portrayed It Dies.
Harbor of Illusion, The.
Kiwi Bird in the Kiwi Tree, The.
Klupzy Girl, The.
Live Acts.
Of Time and the Line.
Part Quake.
St. McC.
Senses of Responsibility.
Sentences My Father Used.
Shreds of Our Webs, The.
Special Pleading.
Stove's Out.
To Which I Never Wanted.
Voyage of Life, The.
You.

Bernstein, Ory [*or* **Ori**]
All This Is My Time.
An Imagined Description of Myself, in Another Scene.
And after a Long While.
And Later by Myself.
Another Time.
At Woods' Edge.
Conversations.
Cuernavaca, *sel.*
Departure.
Dog On the Road.
Don't Count.
Games.
Her Words from the Corner.
In a Park, in Siena, at Twilight.
Mayan Ruins, *sel.*
Memories of Her Friend Who Died.
Mene Mene.
More Questions.
Nocturnal Journey.
Not for You.
Of All the Splendor.
Only from Afar.
Season when Nothing's in Place, A.
Silent Song.
Small War, A, *sel.*
This Is a Poem of Love.
Time to Leave.
Universal, *sel.*
What She Didn't Say.
What She Wanted to Be.
Wind, That Comes on Suddenly, A.

Berridge, Elizabeth
Bombed Church.

Berrigan, Daniel
Beautiful Ruined Orchard, The.
Crucifix, The.
Great God Paused among Men.
On the Birth of Dan Goldman.
Somewhere the Equation Breaks Down.

Berrigan, Ted
Bean Spasms.
Cranston Near the City Line.
Frank O'Hara.
How to Get to Canada.
Kirsten.
Lady.
Last Poem.
Living with Chris.
Love.
My Autobiography.
People of the Future.
People Who Died.
Real Life.
Resolution.
Sonnet: "My dream a drink with Lonnie Johnson."
Stronger than alcohol, more great than song.
Sweeter than sour apples flesh to boys.
Things to Do in New York City.
Things to Do in Providence.
Today's News.
Whitman in Black.

Berrigan, Ted and **Ron Padgett**
Orange Jews.

Berry, David Chapman
Alluding to the One-armed Bandit.
Cosmogony.
Dog.
Faces.
Godiva.
Having Eaten Breakfast.
In Blue.
Leaps over the Aisle of Syllogism.
On Reading Poems to a Senior Class at South High.
Road.
Robert Creeley Also Watches.
Robert Creeley Listens, Too.
Theodore Roethke Foots It.
To the Woodville Depot.
Up against the Wall.

Berry, Francis
Gudveig.

Berry, Fred
Silica Carbonate Rock.

Berry, James
Back to Hometown Kingston.
Distance of a City.
Fantasy of an African Boy.
From Lucy: Holiday Reflections.
Ingrown.
My Father.

Berry, Martyn
Cairngorm, November 1971.

Berry, Wendell
And my love has come to me, *sel.*
Another Sunday morning comes, *sel.*
Barn, The.
Buildings, The.
Earth and Fire.
For the Rebuilding of a House.
Gift of Gravity, The.
Grandmother, The.
Grief.
Healing.
In Rain.
Independence Day.
Lilies, The.
Music, A.
My Great-Grandfather's Slaves.
November Twenty-sixth Nineteen Hundred and Sixty-three.

One thing work gives, *sel.*
Peace of Wild Things, The.
Poem for J.
September 2.
Slip, The.
Snake, The.
To sit and look at light-filled leaves, *sel.*
Wheel, The.
Wild, The.

Berryman, John
Again, his friend's death made the man sit still.
Alcoholic.
American Lights, Seen from Off Abroad.
Apollo 8.
April Fool's Day, or St. Mary Egypt, *sel.*
At Henry's bier let some thing fall out well, *sel.*
Ball Poem, The.
Cage, The.
Canto Amor.
Certainty before Lunch.
Chilled in this Irish pub I wish my loves, *sel.*
Conversation.
Deprived of his enemy, shrugged to a standstill, *sel.*
Desires of Men and Women.
Dispossessed, The.
Elegy for W. C. W., the Lovely Man, An, *sel.*
Father being the loneliest word in the one language, *sel.*
Filling her compact and delicious body, *sel.*
First Night at Sea.
Full moon. Our Narragansett gales subside, *sel.*
Gislebertus' Eve.
Glories of the world struck me, made me aria, once, The, *sel.*
Go, ill-sped book, and whisper to her or.
God bless Henry. He lived like a rat, *sel.*
Governor your husband lived so long, The, *sel.*
Grandfather, sleepless in a room upstairs, *sel.*
Great Citadels whereon the Gold Sun Falls, *sel.*
He lay in the middle of the world, and twitcht, *sel.*
He Resigns.
He stared at ruin. Ruin stared straight back, *sel.*
He yelled at me in Greek, *sel.*
Hello.
Henry hates the world. What the world to Henry, *sel.*
Henry sats in de bar and was odd, *sel.*
Henry's Confession, *sel.*
Henry's mind grew blacker the more he thought, *sel.*
Henry's pelt was put on sundry walls, *sel.*
Henry's Understanding.
His Helplessness, *sel.*
How this woman came by the courage, how she got, *sel.*
Huffy Henry hid the day, *sel.*
I am, outside. Incredible panic rules, *sel.*
I am the little man who smokes and smokes, *sel.*
I can't get him out of my mind, out of my mind, *sel.*
I don't operate often. When I do, *sel.*
I have moved to Dublin to have it out with you, *sel.*
I trundle the bodies, on the iron bars, *sel.*
Ill lay he long, upon this last return, *sel.*
I'm cross with god who has wrecked this generation, *sel.*
Irish have the thickest ankles in the world, The, *sel.*
Keep your eyes open when you kiss: do: when.
King David Dances.

Lauds.
Lay of Ike, The, *sel.*
Let us suppose, valleys and such ago, *sel.*
Life, friends, is boring. We must not say so, *sel.*
Love her he doesn't but the thought he puts, *sel.*
Marble Nor Monuments whereof Then We Spoke, *sel.*
Marker slants, flowerless, day's almost done, The, *sel.*
Master of beauty, craftsman of the snowflake, *sel.*
Minnesota Thanksgiving.
Moon and the Night and the Men, The.
New Year's Eve.
Note to Wang Wei.
Nowhere.
O all your ages at the mercy of my loves, *sel.*
Of Suicide.
Our Sunday morning when dawn-priests were applying.
Parting as Descent.
Peter's not friendly. He gives me sideways looks, *sel.*
Poet's Final Instructions, The.
Prayer for the Self, A, *sel.*
Professor's Song, A.
Sabbath, *sel.*
Scholars at the Orchid Pavilion.
Seedy Henry rose up shy in de world, *sel.*
Sigh as It Ends.
So Long? Stevens, *sel.*
So squeezed, wince you I scream? I love you & hate, *sel.*
Sole watchman of the flying stars, guard me, *sel.*
Some good people, daring and subtle voices, *sel.*
Song of the Tortured Girl, The.
Sonnet 7: "I've found out why, that day, that suicide."
Sonnet: "All we were going strong last night this time."
Sonnet: "Sometimes the night echoes to prideless wailing."
Sonnet: "They may suppose, because I would not cloy your ear."
Soviet Union, The.
Strut for Roethke, A.
Supreme my holdings, greater yet my need, *sel.*
Sympathy, a Welcome, A.
That dark brown rabbit, lightness in his ears, *sel.*
That's enough of that, Mr. Bones. Some lady you make.
There are voices, voices. Light's dying. Birds have quit, *sel.*
There sat down, once, a thing on Henry's heart, *sel.*
This world is gradually becoming a place, *sel.*
Three 'coons come at his garbage. He be cross, *sel.*
Three limbs, three seasons smashed; well, one to go, *sel.*
Thurn, A.
Transit.
Traveller, The.
Turning it over, considering, like a madman, *sel.*
Washington in Love.
Weather was fine, The. They took away his teeth, *sel.*
Welcome, grinned Henry, welcome fifty-one!, *sel.*
What Was Ashore, Then, *sel.*
Whether There Is Sorrow in the Demons.
Winter Landscape.
Winter-Piece to a Friend Away, A.
Winters close, springs open, no child stirs, The, *sel.*

You couldn't bear to grow old, but we grow old, *sel.*
Your Birthday in Wisconsin You Are 140.
Your face broods from my table, Suicide, *sel.*
Bersohn, Robert
Dignity of Labor, The.
Berssenbrugge, Mei-Mei
Chinese Space.
Farolita.
Spring Street Bar.
Bertke, Sister. *See* **Bertken, Sister**
Bertken, Sister (Bertha Jacobs)
Love wears roses' elegance.
When I went into my garden, I found.
Bertram, James
Is It Well-Lighted, Papa?
Bertrans [*or* Bertran *or* Bertrand] de Born
A Perigord pres del muralh.
Count has moved me by sir Arramon Luc d'Esparro, The.
Depressing to dismount the siege-machines.
I have made a sirventes in which no word is missing.
I want to make half-a-sirventes upon two kings.
Lady/ I clear myself toward you.
Rassa, I rise.
Since Oc-e-No has set the fire and drawn blood.
Since Ventadorn and Comborn with Segur on one side.
Spring is a juice, a rejoicing, forcing.
Well Pleaseth Me the Sweet Time of Easter.
Berwick, Thurso
Idleset: "Ill's the airt o the Word the day.")
Besant, Sir Walter
Day Is Coming *parody,* The.
Beser, Ya'akov
All the Caverns of Light.
Child Built a Castle, A.
In the Beginning My Mother Screeched.
It Is the Silence.
Silence Plucks Chords, The.
Snake Skin.
Besseisso, Mu'in
To Rimbaud.
Traffic Lights.
Best, Charles
Sonnet of the Moon, A.
Best, Susie Montgomery
Thanksgiving.
Bet-Aryeh, Mal'akhi
Flesh from Flesh.
Betham-Edwards, Matilda Barbara
Valentine, A.
Bethell, Mary Ursula
Decoration.
Detail.
Elect.
Erica.
Evening Walk in Winter.
Fall.
Hour is dark. The river comes to its end, The, *sel.*
Lever de Rideau.
Long Harbour, The.
Midnight.
9th July, 1932.
October Morning.
Pause.
Response.
Sauntering home from church we lingered, *sel.*
Soothsayer.
Spring Snow and Tui.
That bridge from the city, that was Waimakariri, *sel.*
Time.
Trance.
Warning of Winter.

Bethell, Mary Ursula. *See* **"Hayes, Evelyn"**
Bethune, George Washington
Jesus, Shepherd of Thy Sheep.
O for the Happy Hour.
There Is No Name So Sweet on Earth.
Bethune, John
Spring Song—1834, A.
Bethune, Lebert
Blue Tanganyika.
Bwagamoyo.
Harlem Freeze Frame.
Juju of My Own, A.
To Strike for Night.
Betjeman, Sir John
Advent 1955.
Afternoons/ Brought coconut smell of gorse, *sel.*
Archaeological Picnic, The.
Arrest of Oscar Wilde at the Cadogan Hotel, The.
Arrogance Repressed.
Back Again for the Holidays, *sel.*
Before the Anæsthetic; or, A Real Fright.
Bristol and Clifton.
Christmas.
City, The.
Cottage Hospital, The.
Crematorium.
Dawn.
Death in Leamington.
Diary of a Church Mouse.
East Anglian Bathe.
Executive.
False Security.
Felixstowe; or, The Last of Her Order.
For Patrick, Aetat: LXX.
For the Queen Mother.
Great Central Railway, Sheffield Victoria to Banbury.
Green shutters, shut your shutters! Windyridge, *sel.*
Heart of Thomas Hardy, The.
How to Get On in Society.
Hunter Trials.
Huxley Hall.
Hymn: "Church's Restoration, The."
In a Bath Teashop.
In Memoriam: A. C., R.J.O., K.S.
In Memory of Basil, Marquess of Dufferin and Ava.
In Memory of George Whitby, Architect.
In the Public Gardens.
In Westminster Abbey.
Incident in the Early Life of Ebenezer Jones, Poet, 1828, An.
Inevitable.
Invasion Exercise on the Poultry Farm.
Ireland with Emily.
Last Laugh, The.
Late-flowering Lust.
Licorice Fields at Pontefract, The.
Longfellow's Visit to Venice.
Lord Cozens Hardy.
Matlock Bath.
Meditation on the A30.
Metropolitan Railway, The.
Middlesex.
My dear deaf father, how I loved him then, *sel.*
Myfanwy.
"New King Arrives in His Capital by Air."—Daily Newspaper.
NW5 and N6.
Olympic Girl, The.
On a Portrait of a Deaf Man.
Parliament Hill Fields.
Potpourri from a Surrey Garden.
Remorse.
Seaside Golf.
Senex.
Shropshire Lad, A.
Slough.

Small Towns of Ireland, The.
Subaltern's Love-Song, A.
Sunday Afternoon Service in St. Enodoc
   Church, Cornwall.
Sunday Morning, King's Cambridge.
Town Clerk's Views, The.
Trebetherick.
Tregardock.
Upper Lambourne.
Westgate-on-Sea.
Youth and Age on Beaulieu River, Hants.

Betocchi, Carlo
At noon I watch the sun shine, *sel.*
From the Rooftops.

Bettarini, Mariella
As the Botanist.
But then what do you know about the rights
   of suffocated genitals, *sel.*

Betts, Craven Langstroth
Don Quixote.
Hollyhocks, The.
To the Moonflower.

Beutler, Margarete
Doll, The.
Future Generations.

Bevington, Helen Smith
Herrick's Julia.
It's a debatable land. The winds are variable,
   sel.
Mr. Rockefeller's Hat.
Mrs. Trollope in America.
Nature Study, after Dufy.
Penguins in the Home.
Talk with a Poet.
Turner's Sunrise.

Bewe, ———
I Would I Were Actaeon, at.

Beyer, Evelyn
Jump or Jiggle.

Beyer, Tony
Cut Lilac.
Island Waters.
Rain Games.
Visiting.
Word of Snow, *sel.*

Bezner, Kevin
Kid, The.

Bezymensky, Alexander Ilyich
Village and Factory.

Bhartrihari
In former days we'd both agree.
Peace.
She who is always in my thoughts prefers.
Time.

Bhavabhuti
Deep in love.

**Bialik, Hayyim Nahman [or Khayim
Nakhman or Chaim Nachman]**
After My Death.
Alone.
Beneath Thy Wing.
Between clouds of fire and clouds of blood,
   sel.
City of Slaughter, The.
Come with me to the City of Slaughter, come,
   enter its courtyards, *sel.*
Dance of Despair, The.
Dead of the Wilderness, The.
Death of David, The.
Footsteps of Spring.
Grasshopper's Song, The.
Graveyard, The.
Homecoming.
I Didn't Find Light by Accident.
If Thou Wouldst Know.
Mathmid, The.
Message.
Midnight Prayer.
My Father.
My Song.
Night.

On a hill there blooms a palm, *sel.*
On the Slaughter.
Place Me under Your Wing.
Queen Sabbath.
Sea of Silence Exhales Secrets, The.
Should I Be a Rabbi?
Stars Are Lit, The.
Summer Night.
Sunset.
Take Me under Your Wing.
Talmud Student, The.
Throbs the Night with Mystic Silence.
Twig Plummets, A.
Two steps from my garden rail, *sel.*
When the Days Grow Long.
When the Days Shall Grow Long.
Whence and Whither.
Young Acacia, The.

Bialoszewski, Miron
And Even, Even If They Take Away the
   Stove.
Ballad of Going Down to the Store, A.
Garwolin—a Town for Ever.
My Jacobean Fatigues.
Self-Portrait as Felt.

Bianchi, Martha Gilbert Dickinson
Forgiveness Lane.
Heaven.
Her Music.
Priest's Prayer, A.
Reality.
Separation.
Unanswered.

Bibb, Eloise
An Offering.
Anne Boleyn.
Belshazzer's Feast.
Capt. Smith and Pocahontas.
Catharine of Arragon.
Charmion's Lament.
Class Song of '91.
Destiny.
Early Spring.
Eliza in Uncle Tom's Cabin.
Expulsion of Hagar, The.
Gerarda.
Hermit, The.
Imogene.
In Memoriam Frederick Douglass.
In Memory of Arthur Clement Williams.
Judith.
Leona, dear, twelve months ago.
Lines to Mrs. M. C. Turner.
Lines to the Hon. George L. Knox.
Ode to the Sun.
Sonnet: "O thou who never harbored fear."
Tale of Italy, A.
Tribute.
Vestal Virgin, The.
Wandering Jew, The.

Bibbs, Hart Leroi
Six Sunday.

Bickerstaffe, Isaac
Air: "What a charming thing's a battle!," *sel.*
Expostulation, An.
There was a jolly miller once, *sel.*

Bickersteth, Edward Henry, Bishop of Exeter
O God, the Rock of Ages.
Peace, Perfect Peace.

Bidart, Frank
Another Life.
Confessional.
Ellen West.
Golden State.
Happy Birthday.
Herbert White.
Light, *sel.*
Lineage, *sel.*
Sacrifice, The.
Self-Portrait.
To the Dead.

Bieiris de Romans
Lady Maria, in you merit and distinction.

Bieler, Steven Bryan
Louisville Feared in Mideast.

Bierbaum, Otto Julius
Blacksmith Pain.
Jeannette.
Kindly Vision.
Oft in the Silent Night.

Bierce, Ambrose
Another Way.
Blow, blow, ye spicy breezes, *sel.*
Bride, The.
Creation.
Cur foretells the knell of parting day, The,
   sel.
Death of Grant, The.
Don't steal. Thou'lt never thus compete.
Fiercely the battle raged and, sad to tell, *sel.*
Hail, holy Lead!—of human feuds the great,
   sel.
Megaceph, chosen to serve the State, *sel.*
Montefiore.
Once I seen a human ruin, *sel.*
"One night," a doctor said, "last fall", *sel.*
Presentiment.
Spelling reformer indicted, A, *sel.*
T. A. H.
There's a man with a nose, *sel.*

Big Eagle, Duane
Birthplace.
Elegy: "Whole tribe dies, A."
My Grandfather Was a Quantum Physicist.
Recollection.
Traveling to Town.
Wind and Impulse.

Bigg, J. Stanyan
An Irish Picture.

Biggs, Carrie
Chair That Is Filled, The.

Biggs, Maurice
Spring Offensive, 1941.

Bignold, Thomas Frank
Holiday, The.

Bilal
Muhammedan Call to Prayer.

Bilhana
Black Marigolds.

"Bill o' th' Hoylus End"
Factory Girl, The.

Billings, William
David's Lamentation.
Heavenly Vision.
Let Tyrants Shake Their Iron Rod.

Billington, William
Gerald Massey.
Salford Bridge   That Popular Resort of the
   Great Unwashed.

Bingham, G. Clifton
Love's Old Sweet Song.

Binney, Thomas
Eternal Light!

Binyon, Laurence
Bab-Lock-Hythe.
Beauty.
Belfry, The.
Burning of the Leaves, The.
Fetching the Wounded.
For the Fallen.
House That Was, The.
Hunger.
Invocation to Youth.
John Winter.
Little Dancers, The.
Nothing Is Enough.
Song, A: "For mercy, courage, kindness,
   mirth."
Sower, The.
Statues, The.
This Is England.

Tristram's End.
Ypres.
Bion
Dream of Venus, A.
Lament for Adonis.
Biran, Paddy
Paddy Biran's Song.
Birche, William
Songe betwene the Quenes Majestie and
Englande, A.
Bird, Bessie Calhoun
Proof.
Bird, Dolly
Can I Say.
Bird, Edward
To His Coy Mistress.
Bird, Harold. *See* **Littlebird, Harold**
Birkenhead, Sir John
Four-legg'd Elder; or, A Horrible Relation of
a Dog and an Elder's Maid, The.
Birnbaum, Henry
Room I Once Knew, A.
When Silence Divests Me.
Birney, Earle
Anglo Saxon Street.
Bear on the Delhi Road, The.
Birthday.
Bushed.
Can. Hist.
Can. Lit.
Cartagena de Indias.
Charité Espérance et Foi.
Christchurch, N. Z.
David.
El Greco: Espolio.
For Steve.
From the Hazel Bough.
Gray Woods Exploding, The.
Hot Springs.
Mappemounde.
Monody on a Century.
Museum of Man.
My Love Is Young.
On Going to the Wars.
Poet-Tree.
Road to Nijmegen, The.
Sinalóa.
Slug in Woods.
Small Faculty Stag for the Visiting Poet, A.
Speech of the Salish Chief, *sel.*
There Are Delicacies.
Twenty-third Flight.
Vancouver Lights.
Walk in Kyoto, A.
World Winter.
Birnie, Patrick
Auld Man's Mear's Dead, The.
Bishop, Elizabeth
Armadillo[—Brazil], The.
Arrival at Santos.
At the Fishhouses.
Bight, The.
Brazil, January 1, 1502.
Burglar of Babylon, The.
Cape Breton.
Casabianca.
Cirque d'Hiver.
Cold Spring, A.
Cootchie.
Crusoe in England.
Faustina, or Rock Roses.
Filling Station.
First Death in Nova Scotia.
Fish, The.
Florida.
From Trollope's Journal.
House Guest.
Imaginary Iceberg, The.
In the Waiting Room.
Insomnia.
Jeronimo's House.

Large Bad Picture.
Letter to N. Y.
Little Exercise at 4. A.M.
Man-Moth, The.
Manners [for a Child of 1918]
Manuelzinho.
Map, The.
Miracle for Breakfast, A.
Monument, The.
Moose, The.
North Haven.
One Art.
Over 2000 Illustrations and a Complete
Concordance.
Poem: "About the size of an old-style dollar
bill."
Prodigal, The.
Questions of Travel.
Riverman, The.
Roosters.
Sandpiper.
Seascape.
Sestina: "September rain falls on the house."
Shampoo, The.
Sleeping on the Ceiling.
Some Dreams They Forgot.
Songs for a Colored Singer.
Squatter's Children.
Summer's Dream, A.
12 o'Clock News.
Two Mornings and Two Evenings.
Unbeliever, The.
Under the Window: Ouro Preto.
View of the Capitol from the Library of
Congress.
Visits to St. Elizabeths.
Washing hangs upon the line, A, *sel.*
Bishop, G. E.
Bigger Day, The.
Bishop, John Peale
Always, from My First Boyhood.
Ancestors, The.
Birds of Paradise, The.
Boys, by Girls Held in Their Thighs.
Colloquy with a King-Crab.
Dream, The.
Fiametta.
Hours, The.
Hunchback, The.
Hunger and Thirst.
In the Dordogne.
Interlude, An.
John Donne's Statue.
Metamorphoses of M.
O Pioneers!
Ode: "Why will they never sleep."
Percy Shelley.
Perspectives Are Precipices.
Recollection, A.
Return, The.
Saint Francis.
Sleep Brought Me Vision.
Southern Pines.
Spare Quilt, The.
Speaking of Poetry.
Statue of Shadow, The.
Submarine Bed, The.
This Dim and Ptolemaic Man.
To a Swallow.
Triumph of Doubt, The.
Why They Waged War.
Your Chase Had a Beast in View.
Bishop, Michael
For the Lady of a Physicist.
Postcards to Athena.
White Power Poem.
Bishop, Morris
Ambition.
Anatomy of Humor, The.
Bishop Orders His Tomb in St. Praxed's.
Complete Misanthropist, The.
Dementia Praecox.

Diogenes.
EMC^2.
Englishman with an Atlas; or, America the
Unpronounceable, An.
Epitaph for a Funny Fellow.
Fragment from "The Maladjusted: A
Tragedy."
Gas and Hot Air.
Hog-calling Competition.
How to Treat Elves.
I Hear America Griping.
Immoral Arctic, The.
It Rolls On.
Limerick Is Furtive and Mean, The.
Naughty Preposition, The.
Ozymandias Revisited.
Perforated Spirit, The.
Public Aid for Niagara Falls.
Sales Talk for Annie.
Settling Some Old Football Scores.
Song of the Pop-Bottlers.
Sonnet and Limerick.
There's Money in Mother and Father.
Tonversation with Baby, A.
We Have Been Here Before.
What Hath Man Wrought Exclamation Point.
Who'd Be a Hero (Fictional)?
Witch of East Seventy-second Street, The.
Bishop, Samuel
Epigram: "Need from excess—excess from
folly growing."
Epigram: "'Twas not so in my time," surly
Grumio exclaims."
Bisinger, Gerald
At Lake Lietzen; or, The Search for Identity.
Bissert, Ellen Marie
Another.
Most Beautiful Woman at My Highschool
Reunion, The.
Bisset, James
Next day they rambled round the town, and
swore, *sel.*
Bissett, Bill
Christ I Wudint Know Normal if I Saw It
When.
Dont Worry Yr Hair.
Th Wundrfulness uv th Mountees Our Secret
Police.
Biton, Erez
Beginnings.
Bird's Nest, A.
Buying a Shop on Dizengoff.
Bitton, W. Nelson
Resurgam.
Bixler, William Allen
Beautiful.
Björnson, Björnstjerne
Boy and the Flute, The.
Fatherland Song.
Tree, The.
Bjornvig, Thorkild
Owl, The.
Black, Austin
Soul.
Black, Baxter
Big High and Lonesome, The.
Time to Stay, a Time to Go, A.
Black, Isaac J.
Roll Call: A Land of Old Folk and Children.
Talking to the Townsfolk in Ideal, Georgia.
Black, Jack
Awake!
Black, MacKnight
Rock, Be My Dream.
Blackah, Thomas
We May Be Lo', We May Be Poor.
Blackburn, Alexander
What Makes a Nation Great?

Blackburn, Paul
Assistance, The.
Clickety-Clack.
Continuity, The.
Crossing, The.
Encounter, The.
Hot Afternoons Have Been in West 15th Street.
Invitation Standing.
Night Song for Two Mystics.
Once-over, The.
One-Night Stand: An Approach to the Bridge, The.
Phone Call to Rutherford.
Problem, The.
Proposition, The.
17. IV. 71.
Sirventes.
Slogan, The.
Stone, The.
Tides, The.
Watchers, The.

Blackburn, Thomas
Families.
Felo de Se.
Ganga.
Hospital for Defectives.
Lucky Marriage, The.
Oedipus.
Song for the Infant Judas.
Unpredictable, The.

Blackie, John Stuart
How Small Is Man.
Ye Simple Men.

Blackmore, Richard Doddridge
Dominus Illuminatio Mea.

Blackmore, Sir Richard
Circulation of the Blood, The, *sel.*

Blackmur, Richard Palmer
Before Sentence Is Passed.
Half-Tide Ledge.
Resurrection.
Sonnet: "Three silences made him a single word."

Blackstock, Walter
Old Voyager.

Blackwell, Harriet Gray
Forest.
Hill People.

Blackwood, Algernon
Jack o' the Inkpot.

Blackwood, Sam. *See* **Beckford, Slim** *and* **Sam Blackwood**

Bladen, Peter
Coronation Day at Melrose.

Blaine, Scott
Hockey.

Blair, Robert
Grave, The, *sel.*
Oft in the lone church-yard at night I've seen, *sel.*
Tell us! ye dead! Will none of you in pity, *sel.*
While some affect the sun, and some the shade, *sel.*

Blair, Eric. *See* **Orwell, George**

Blake, Felicia
Woman's Answer to "The Vampire," A.

Blake, Howard
Argent Solipsism.

Blake, James Vila
In Him.

Blake, James W.
Sidewalks of New York, The.

Blake, Mary Elizabeth McGrath
Dawning o' the Year, The.

Blake, Robert
Little Boy Lost, A.

Blake, William
Abstinence Sows Sand All Over, *sel.*

Ah! Sun-Flower ("Ah! Sun-flower, weary of time"), *sel.*
America a Prophecy.
And Did Those Feet in Ancient Time, *sel.*
Angel, The, *sel.*
Angel That Presided o'er My Birth, The, *sel.*
Answer to the Parson, An.
Auguries of Innocence.
Birds, The.
Blind-Man's Buff.
Blossom, The, *sel.*
Book of Thel, The.
But still the thunder of Los peals loud and thus the thunder's cry, *sel.*
Chimney Sweeper ("A little black thing among the snow"), The, *sel.*
Chimney Sweeper, The ("When my mother died I was very young"), *sel.*
Clod and the Pebble, The, *sel.*
Compliment to the Ladies, A.
Cradle Song: "Sleep, sleep, beauty bright."
Cradle Song, A: "Sweet dreams, form a shade," *sel.*
Cromek [*or* On Cromek]
Crystal Cabinet, The.
Divine Image, A ("Cruelty has a human heart"), *sel.*
Divine Image, The ("To mercy, pity, peace, and love"), *sel.*
Door of Death, The, *sel.*
Dream, A, *sel.*
Earth's Answer, *sel.*
Echoing [*or* Ecchoing] Green, The, *sel.*
Empire Is No More, *sel.*
England! awake! awake! awake!, *sel.*
Enion Replies from the Caverns of the Grave, *sel.*
Enitharmon Revives with Los, *sel.*
Epilogue: "Truly my Satan thou art but a dunce," *sel.*
Epitaph, An: "Come knock your heads against this stone."
Eternity ("He who binds [*or* bends] to himself a joy"), *sel.*
Ethinthus, Queen of Waters, *sel.*
Fearing that Albion should turn his back against the Divine Vision, *sel.*
Fields from Islington to Marybone, The, *sel.*
For the Sexes; the Gates of Paradise.
Garden of Love, The, *sel.*
Good English Hospitality, *sel.*
Great Things [Are Done] ("Great things are done when men and mountains meet."), *sel.*
Grown old in love from seven till seven times seven.
He has observed the golden rule, *sel.*
Hear the Voice of the Bard!, *sel.*
Hebrew nation did not write it, The.
Her Whole Life Is an Epigram.
Here lies John Trot, the friend of all mankind.
Holy Thursday ("Is this a holy thing to see"), *sel.*
Holy Thursday (" 'Twas on a Holy Thursday, their innocent faces clean"), *sel.*
Human Abstract, The, *sel.*
I asked a thief to steal me a peach.
I laid me down upon a bank.
I Saw a Chapel All of Gold.
I saw a Monk of Charlemaine, *sel.*
I was buried near this dyke.
Immortal, The, *sel.*
In Deadly Fear, *sel.*
In Obtuse Angle's Study, *sel.*
In seed time learn, in harvest teach, in winter enjoy, *sel.*
Infant Joy, *sel.*
Infant Sorrow, *sel.*
It is easier to forgive an enemy than to forgive a friend, *sel.*
It Is Not So with Me, *sel.*
Jerusalem
Lamb, The, *sel.*

Lamentation of Enion, The, *sel.*
Land of Dreams, The.
Laughing Song, *sel.*
Little Black Boy, The, *sel.*
Little Boy Found, The, *sel.*
Little Boy Lost, A ("Nought loves another as itself"), *sel.*
Little Boy Lost, The ("Father, father, where are you going?"), *sel.*
Little Fly,/ Thy summers play, *sel.*
Little Vagabond, The, *sel.*
London ("I wander through each chartered street"), *sel.*
London ("There souls of men are bought and sold"), *sel.*
Long John Brown and Little Mary Bell.
Louis XVI, *sel.*
Mad Song, *sel.*
Male & Female Loves in Beulah, *sel.*
Memorable Fancy, A ("Angel came to me and said"), *sel.*
Memorable Fancy, A ("As I was walking among the fires of hell."), *sel.*
Mental Traveller, The.
Mock On, Mock On, Voltaire, Rousseau.
Moment of desire, The! the moment of desire! the virgin, *sel.*
Monk, The, *sel.*
Morning.
Mr. Cromek.
Mr. Cromek to Mr. Stothard.
My Pretty Rose Tree, *sel.*
My Spectre around Me Night and Day.
Never Seek to Tell Thy Love.
Night, *sel.*
Night VIII (The Eternal Man), *sel.*
Nurse's Song, *sel.*
O Lapwing!
"O little cloud," the virgin said, "I charge thee tell to me," *sel.*
Old Maid Early, An.
On Another's Sorrow, *sel.*
Orator Prigg.
Piping Down the Valleys Wild, *sel.*
Poems from MSS.
Poison Tree, A, *sel.*
Price of Experience, The, *sel.*
Pride of the peacock is the glory of God, The, *sel.*
Reason and Imagination, *sel.*
Riches.
Rintrah roars & shakes his fires in the burdend air, *sel.*
Robin Redbreast in a cage, A, *sel.*
Schoolboy, The, *sel.*
Secrets of the Earth, The, *sel.*
Shepherd, The, *sel.*
Shuddring the Spectre howls, his howlings terrify the night, *sel.*
Sick Rose, The, *sel.*
Since all the riches of this world.
Sipsop's Song, *sel.*
Sir Joshua Reynolds.
Smile, The.
Soft Snow.
Some people admire the work of a fool.
Song: "Fresh from the dewy hill, the merry year."
Song: "How sweet I roam'd from field to field."
Song: "Memory, hither come."
Song: "My silks and fine array."
Song of Enitharmon, *sel.*
Song of Liberty, A.
Spring, *sel.*
Suction's Anthem, *sel.*
Sword sang on the barren heath, The, *sel.*
Take Thy Bliss, O Man, *sel.*
Thel's Motto, *sel.*
Then Milton rose up from the heaven of Albion ardorous!, *sel.*
They said this mystery shall never cease, *sel.*

This wine-press is call'd war on earth, *sel.*
Thou hearest the nightingale begin the song of
 spring, *sel.*
Tiger [*or* Tyger], The, *sel.*
To Autumn.
To English Connoisseurs.
To Flaxman.
To forgive enemies Hayley does pretend.
To God.
To Hunt.
To Morning.
To My Friend Butts I Write.
To Nobodaddy.
To See a World in a Grain of Sand, *sel.*
To Spring.
To Summer.
To the Christians, *sel.*
To the Evening Star, *sel.*
To the Muses.
To Tirzah, *sel.*
To William Hayley.
To Winter.
Urizen's Curse upon His Children, *sel.*
Vala, Night the Ninth Being the Last
 Judgment, *sel.*
Vision of Beulah, The ("There is a place
 where contrarieties are equally true"), *sel.*
Visions of the Daughters of Albion.
Voice of the Devil, The, *sel.*
War Song to Englishmen, A, *sel.*
What is it men in women do require?, *sel.*
When a Man Has Married a Wife.
When Klopstock England defied.
When old corruption first begun, *sel.*
Why Should I Care for the Men of Thames?
Wild Flower's Song.
Wild Thyme, The, *sel.*
William Bond.
With Happiness Stretch[e]d across the Hills.
Blakely, Henry
 H. Rap Brown.
 Morning Song.
Blaker, Margaret
 Clerihew: "Cecil Beaton,/ Though not
  schooled at Eton."
 Clerihew: "Guillaume Apollinaire/ Didn't
  care."
 Pippa Passes, But I Can't Get Around This
  Truck.
Blamire, Susanna
 From where dark clouds of curling smoke
  arise, *sel.*
Blanchard, Ferdinand Q.
 O Child of Lowly Manger Birth,.
 Word of God, Across the Ages.
Blanchard, Laman
 Ode to the Human Heart.
Bland, James A.
 Carry Me Back to Old Virginny.
Bland, Peter
 Death of a Dog.
 Happy Army, The.
 Kumara God.
 Mother.
 Past the Tin Butterflies and Plaster Gnomes.
 Remembering England.
 So Many Cenotaphs.
Bland, Edith Nesbit. *See* **Nesbit, Edith**
Blandiana, Ana
 Couple, The.
 I Have the Right.
 I need only fall asleep/ to return.
Blanding, Don
 Vagabond House.
Blank, Arapera Hineira
 Yearning, A.
Blankner, Frederika
 Remainder.
Blaser, Robin
 4 Part Geometry Lesson, A.
 Herons.

Image-Nation (the Poesis).
Image-Nation 13 (the Telephone).
Image-Nation 3.
Poem: "And when I pay death's duty."
Poem by the Charles River.
Poem: "For years I've heard."
Suddenly.
Blaustein, Rahel. *See* **Rachel**
Blenkhorn, Ada
 Heavenly Stranger, The.
Blewett, Jean
 At Quebec.
Blight, John
 Becalmed.
 Cormorants.
 Death of a Whale.
 Down from the Country.
 Evolution.
 Gate's Open, The.
 Letter, The.
 Morgan.
 Pearl Perch.
 Tenant at Number 9.
Blind, Mathilde
 After-Glow, The.
 Dead, The.
 Dost thou remember ever, for my sake, *sel.*
 I charge you, O winds of the West, O, *sel.*
 Internal Firesides.
 On a Forsaken Lark's Nest.
 Reapers.
 Sower, The.
"Blind Harry." *See* **Henry the Minstrel**
Blishen, Edward
 Abroad Thoughts.
Bliss, Philip Paul
 Almost Persuaded.
Blitzstein, Marc
 Art for Art's Sake, *sel.*
Blixen, Karen. *See* **"Dinesen, Isak"**
Bloch, Alice
 Six Years.
Bloch, Anne
 Absent Friends, *sel.*
 Dreams.
 On Listening to a Bus Conductor.
 Pied à Terre.
Bloch, Chana
 Death of the Bronx, The.
 Deer in the Bush.
 Goodbye.
 Life, A.
 Noah.
 Paradise.
 Sacrifice, The.
 Yom Kippur.
Bloch, Jean-Richard
 Idea of a Swimmer.
Block, Alexander
 Willow-Boughs, The.
Block, Louis James
 Fate.
 Final Struggle, The, *sel.*
 Garden Where There Is No Winter, The.
 Tuberose.
 Work.
Block, Ron
 Ballade of the Back Road.
Blockcolski, Lew
 After the First Frost.
 Flicker, The.
 Flint Hills, The.
 49 Stomp, The.
 Indian Love Song.
 Langston Hughes.
 My Dream.
 Peyote Vision.
 Playing Pocahontas.
 Powwow remnants.
 Reservation Special.
 Urban Experience: Part One, The.

Urban Experience: Part Two, The.
Wisga.
Woyi, The.
Blocksidge, Charles William. *See*
 Baylebridge, William
Blodgett, E. D.
 Fossil.
 Snails.
Bloede, Gertrude. *See* **"Sterne, Stuart"**
Blok, Aleksandr [*or* **Alexander] Aleksandrovich**
 Black Night./ White snow, *sel.*
 Little Catkins.
 Night, street, a lamp, a chemist's window,
  sel.
 Red Glow in the Sky, A.
 Russia.
 Scythians, The.
Blood, Henry Ames
 Comrades.
 Shakespeare.
Bloom, Valerie
 For Michael.
 Life in Uncle Sam's Backyard.
 Wat A Rain.
 Wha Fe Call I.
Bloomfield, Robert
 Coracle Fishers, The, *sel.*
 Health! I seek thee; dost thou love, *sel.*
 Meandering Wye, *sel.*
 Moonlight. Scattered Clouds, *sel.*
 Summer, *sel.*
Bloomgarden, Solomon. *See* **"Yehoash"**
Blossom, Laurel
 Skate.
 Things to Say When You Quit Smoking.
Blount, Charles
 Dialogue between King William and the Late
  King James on the Banks of the Boyne, A.
Blount, Roy, Jr.
 Against Broccoli.
 For the Record.
 Gryll's State.
 Still Life.
Blue Cloud, Peter
 Autumn Equinox, *sel.*
 Bear: A Totem Dance As Seen by Raven.
 Coyote, Coyote, Please Tell Me.
 Crazy Horse Monument.
 Death Chant.
 Dogwood Blossoms.
 Elderberry Flute Song.
 Hawk Nailed to a Barn Door.
 Oche Iron.
 Old Man's Lazy, The.
 Rattle.
 Spring Equinox, *sel.*
 Summer Solstice, *sel.*
 Sweat Song.
 Sweetgrass.
 To-ta Ti-om.
 Turtle.
 Walking through twisted hollow pathways.
 Winter Solstice, *sel.*
 Wolf.
 Yellowjacket.
Blum, Etta
 When You Reach the Hilltop the Sky Is on
  Top of You.
Blumenthal, Michael C.
 Abandoning Your Car in a Snowstorm:
  Rosslyn, Virginia.
 Back from the Word-Processing Course, I Say
  to My Old Typewriter.
 Dusk: Mallards on the Charles River.
 Elephants Dying, The.
 I Have Lived This Way for Years and Do Not
  Wish to Change.
 In Assisi.
 Inventors.
 Litrajure of Everyday Life, The.

Mushroom Hunting in Late August, Peterborough, N.H.
Squid.
Tip of the Iceberg, The.
Today I Am Envying the Glorious Mexicans.
Washington Heights, 1959.
Waving Good-bye to My Father.
What a Time!
Who Will Live in Our Houses When We Die?
Wishful Thinking.

Blumenthal, Walter Hart
Da Silva Gives the Cue.

Blumenthal-Weiss, Ilse
Jewish Child Prays to Jesus, A.

Blumgarden, Solomon. *See* "**Yehoash**"

Blumstein, Rachel. *See* **Rachel**

Blunden, Edmund
Almswomen.
And mathematics, fresh as May, *sel.*
At the Great Wall of China.
Barn, The.
Bleue Maison.
Cottage at Chigasaki, The.
Country God, A.
Departure.
Eastern Tempest.
Festubert: The Old German Line.
Forefathers.
Giant Puffball, The.
Gods of the Earth Beneath, The.
Hurrying Brook, The.
Idlers, The.
In Festubert.
Late Light.
Les Halles d'Ypres.
Lonely Love.
Midnight Skaters, The.
Mole Catcher.
New Moon, The.
1916 Seen from 1921.
Pike, The.
Poor Man's Pig, The.
Psalm, A: "O God, in whom my deepest being dwells."
Recovery, The.
Report on Experience.
Sheepbells.
Sighing Time, The.
Survival, The.
Thiepval Wood.
Trees on the Calais Road.
Two Voices.
Uneasy Peace.
Veteran, The.
View of the Present State of Ireland, A.
Vlamertinghe; Passing the Château, July 1917.
Wild Cherry Tree.
Winter: East Anglia.
Zillebeke Brook.
Zonnebeke Road, The.

Blunt, Wilfrid Scawen
As to His Choice of Her, *sel.*
Deeds That Might Have Been, The, *sel.*
Depreciating Her Beauty, *sel.*
Falcon, The, *sel.*
Farewell to Juliet, *sel.*
Gibraltar.
He who has once been happy is for aye, *sel.*
Honour Dishonoured.
I Will Not Tell the Secrets, *sel.*
Nocturne, A: "Moon has gone to her rest, The."
Oasis of Sidi Khaled, The.
Old Squire, The.
St. Valentine's Day, *sel.*
Sinner-Saint, The.
Storm in Summer, A.
When I hear laughter from a tavern door, *sel.*
With Esther.

Woman with a Past, A, *sel.*
Wouldst thou be wise, O Man? At the knees of a woman begin, *sel.*

Bly, Robert
After Drinking All Night with a Friend, We Go Out in a Boat at Dawn to See Who Can Write the Best Poem.
After Long Busyness.
After the Industrial Revolution, All Things Happen at Once.
After Working.
Afternoon Sleep.
Asian Peace Offers Rejected without Publication.
At a March against the Vietnam War.
At Mid-Ocean.
August Rain.
Awakening.
Barnfire during Church.
Christmas Eve Service at Midnight at St. Michael's.
Clear Air of October, The.
Come with Me.
Counting Small-boned Bodies.
Dead Seal near McClure's Beach, The.
Depression.
Dream of Suffocation, A.
Driving My Parents Home at Christmas.
Driving through Minnesota during the Hanoi Bombings.
Driving to Town Late to Mail a Letter.
Driving toward the Lac Qui Parle River.
Evolution from the Fish.
Executive's Death, The.
Extra Joyful Chorus for Those Who Have Read This Far, An.
Finding the Father.
Fishing on a Lake at Night.
For My Son, Noah, Ten Years Old.
Great Society, The.
Hatred of Men with Black Hair.
Hearing Men Shout at Night on MacDougal Street.
Hermit, The.
Hockey Poem, The.
Hollow Tree, A.
Hurrying Away from the Earth.
In a Mountain Cabin in Norway.
In a Train.
In Rainy September.
Insect Heads.
Johnson's Cabinet Watched by Ants.
Kneeling Down to Look into a Culvert.
Late at Night During a Visit of Friends.
Laziness and Silence.
Leonardo's Secret.
Long Walk before the Snows Began, A.
Looking at a Dead Wren in My Hand.
Looking at a Dry Canadian Thistle Brought In from the Snow.
Looking at New-fallen Snow from a Train.
Looking at Some Flowers.
Looking into a Face.
Looking into a Tide Pool.
Love Poem: "When we are in love, we love the grass."
Man Whom the Sea Kept Awake, The.
Melancholia.
Missouri Traveller Writes Home: 1830, A.
Mourning Pablo Neruda.
My Father's Wedding.
Night.
November Day at McClure's.
Offering.
Old Boards.
Origin of the Praise of God, The.
Passing an Orchard by Train.
Poem against the Rich.
Poem in Three Parts.
Prayer Service in an English Church.
Puritan on His Honeymoon, The.
Reading in Fall Rain.

Romans Angry about the Inner World.
Shack Poem.
Silence.
Six Winter Privacy Poems.
Sleet Storm on the Merritt Parkway.
Small Bird's Nest Made of White Reed Fiber, A.
Snowbanks North of the House.
Snowfall in the Afternoon.
Solitude Late at Night in the Woods.
Stump, The.
Surprised by Evening.
Teeth Mother Naked at Last, The.
Thinking of "The Autumn Fields."
Those Being Eaten by America.
Three Kinds of Pleasures.
Three Presidents.
Turning Away from Lies.
Visiting Emily Dickinson's Grave with Robert Francis.
Waking from Sleep.
Watching Television.
Water under the Earth.
Watering the Horse.
When the Dumb Speak.
Where We Must Look for Help.
Written Forty Miles South of a Spreading City.
Written in Dejection near Rome.

Blyton, Carey
Manatee, The.

Blyton, Enid
Fairy Music.
Field-Mouse, The.
What Piggy-Wig Found.
Winter.

Boa, Maria Amalia Fonte
Two Tile Beaks.

Boake, Barcroft Henry
Allegory, An.
At Devlin's Siding.
Where the Dead Men Lie.

Boas, Guy
Underground, The.

Bobrowski, Johannes
Memorial for a Fisherman.
Wood House over the Wilia, The.

Bocanegra, Matías de
Song on Beholding an Enlightenment.

Bocanegra, Fernando de Córdova y. *See* **Córdova y Bocanegra, Fernando de**

Boccaccio, Giovanni
Inscription for a Portrait of Dante, *sel.*
Of Fiammetta Singing, *sel.*
Of His Last Sight of Fiammetta, *sel.*
Of Three Girls and of Their Talk, *sel.*
Rape of Mensola, The, *sel.*
Sonnet: To That Fair Kingdom, O My Gentle Lord.
To Dante in Paradise, after Fiammetta's Death, *sel.*
To One Who Had Censured His Public Exposition of Dante, *sel.*

Bock, Frederick
Aubade: The Desert.
Big, Fat Summer—and the Lean and Hard.

Bode, John E.
To the End.

Bodecker, N. M.
Cats and Dogs.
Good-by My Winter Suit.
Island of Yorrick, The.
John.
Miss Bitter.
Mr. 'Gator.
Night Crawler.
Sing Me a Song of Teapots and Trumpets.
When All the World Is Full of Snow.

Bodenheim, Maxwell
Advice to a Forest.
Death.

Lynched Negro.
Negroes.
Poem: "O men, walk on the hills."
Poem to Negro and Whites.
To an Enemy.
Upper Family.
Bodker, Cecil
Calendar.
Fury's Field.
Self-Portrait.
Boethius
Happy he whose eyes have view'd, *sel.*
Happy that first white age! when wee, *sel.*
Happy Too Much, *sel.*
Huc omnes pariter, *sel.*
Hue quam precipiti, *sel.*
O thou whose pow'r o'er moving worlds
    presides, *sel.*
Though countless as the grains of sand, *sel.*
Bogan, Louise
After the Persian.
Alchemist, The.
Animal, Vegetable and Mineral.
Betrothed.
Cassandra.
Come, Break with Time.
Crossed Apple, The.
Crows, The.
Daemon, The.
Decoration.
Didactic Piece.
Dragonfly, The.
Dream, The.
Evening in the Sanitarium.
Exhortation.
Frightened Man, The.
Henceforth, from the Mind.
Hypocrite Swift.
I Saw Eternity.
Juan's Song.
Knowledge.
Last Hill in a Vista.
Late.
M., Singing.
Man Alone.
Medusa.
Meeting, The.
Men Loved Wholly beyond Wisdom.
Musician.
Night.
Old Countryside.
Packet of Letters.
Putting to Sea.
Question in a Field.
Roman Fountain.
Simple Autumnal.
Single Sonnet.
Sleeping Fury, The.
Song for a Lyre.
Song for the Last Act.
Spirit's Song.
Statue and Birds.
To an Artist, to Take Heart.
To Be Sung on the Water.
To My Brother.
Train Tune.
Variation on a Sentence.
Women.
Zone.
Bogart, Elizabeth ("Estelle")
He Came Too Late.
Bogin, George
Abraham.
Attaché Case, The.
Cottontail.
Kiss, The.
Martha Nelson Speaks.
Bogle, Eric
Band Played Waltzing Matilda, The.
No Man's Land.
Now I'm Easy.

Bohanan, Otto Leland
Dawn's Awake, The!
Washer-Woman, The.
Boiardo, Matteo Maria
Sonnet: Poor Drooping Flowers and Pallid
    Violets.
Boimwall, Rachel
At Night.
Diaspora Jews.
Lifelong.
Round.
Boker, George Henry
Awaking of the Poetic Faculty, The.
Ballad of New Orleans, The.
Ballad of Sir John Franklin, A.
Battle of Lookout Mountain, The.
Before Vicksburg.
Black Regiment, The.
Countess Laura.
Crossing at Fredericksburg, The.
Cruise of the *Monitor*, The.
Dirge for a Soldier.
Ferry, The.
God to Thee We Humbly Bow.
Hooker's Across!
Lincoln.
Love Is That Orbit.
On Board the *Cumberland.*
The *Varuna.*
To England.
To My Lady, *sel.*
Upon the Hill before Centreville.
Zagonyi.
Bokusui, Wakayama. *See* **Wakayama**
    Bokusui.
Boland, Eavan
Child of Our Time.
Famine Road, The.
Glass King, The.
Irish Childhood in England: 1951, An.
It's a Woman's World.
Song: "Where in blind files."
War Horse, The.
Bold, Alan
Celtic Albatross, The.
Concerning Cork.
David Hume, Dying, Talks to Boswell.
Malfeasance, The.
Public Wash House, The.
That's Life?
2 November 1982.
Bold, Henry
Song: "Chloris, forbear a while."
Song: "Fire, fire."
Boleyn, Anne
Defiled Is My Name Full Sore, *at.*
Boleyn, George
O Death, Rock Me Asleep, *at.*
Bollers, Jim
Fill Up Those Glasses, Bartender.
Bolles, Matthew
Here, Lord, Retired, I Bow in Prayer.
Bolton, Edmund
Palinode, A.
To Favonius.
Bolton, Frank
Insult before Gift-Giving.
Bolton, Sarah Knowles
His Monument.
Inevitable, The.
Influence.
Now.
Paddle Your Own Canoe.
Bomze, Nahum
City of Light.
Pshytik.
Bonar, Horatius
Be True [*or* Be True Thyself]
Here, O my Lord, I see Thee face to face,
    sel.
Length of Days.

Master's Touch, The.
More of Thee.
My Prayer.
Thy Way, Not Mine.
Boncho (Nozawa Boncho)
Abandoned boat, An, *sel.*
Ash pail has stopped dripping, The, *sel.*
At an eagle's nest on dead camphor, *sel.*
At this dilapidated hut, *sel.*
Blowing wind's companion, A, *sel.*
Brushwood bones.
Cool and fresh.
Crow wipes its beak on young grass, A, *sel.*
Dark night: a child begins weeping, *sel.*
Elongated line of a river, An, *sel.*
Every bit of water in the paddies, *sel.*
Fording a stream I stop, *sel.*
From the porch, in various ways, *sel.*
I try to call him back, *sel.*
In a shower, black chopped wood, *sel.*
In the heat haze a fox, *sel.*
Meeting Etsujin, *sel.*
"Not a Bird Singing, the Mountain Is All the
    More Quiet," *sel.*
Overnight/ My razor rusted.
Patch of cloud rides the moon tonight, A, *sel.*
Paulownia tree drops dead leaves, A, *sel.*
Razor blade rusted overnight, A, *sel.*
Spring rain isn't even enough, The, *sel.*
Town smells of things, The, *sel.*
Winter rain.
Bond, Carrie Jacobs
Perfect Day, A.
Bond, Harold
Dancing on Water.
Detour.
Game, The.
Glove, The.
Bond, Julian
Bishop of Atlanta: Ray Charles, The.
Look at That Gal.
Rotation.
Bondy, Sebastian Salazar
Exiled from the Light.
Interior Patio.
Shades of Origin.
Testament.
Without Knowing Why.
Bone, Edith
On Myself.
Bone, Florence
Prayer for a Little Home, A.
Boner, John Henry
Light'ood Fire, The.
Poe's Cottage at Fordham.
Remembrance.
We Walked among the Whispering Pines.
Bonham, Thomas
In Praise of Ale, at.
Bonnefoy, Yves
Blood, the Note "B."
Imperfections Is the Summit.
Place of the Salamander.
Quiet.
Ravine, The.
Same Voice, Still, The.
Tree, the Lamp, The.
True Name.
Utmost Hour.
Voice, A.
What Word Spring.
Bontemps, Arna
Black Man Talks of Reaping, A.
Blight.
Close Your Eyes!
Day-Breakers *or* Daybreakers , The.
Gethsemane.
God Give to Men ("God give the yellow
    man").
Golgotha Is a Mountain.
Homing.

Idolatry.
Lancelot.
Length of Moon.
Miracles.
Nocturne at Bethesda.
Nocturne of the Wharves.
Note of Humility, A.
Reconnaissance.
Return, The.
Southern Mansion.
To a Young Girl Leaving the Hill Country.
Tree Design, A.

Boodson, Alison
Poem: "He lying spilt like water from a
  bowl."

Booth, Eva Gore. *See* **Gore-Booth, Eva**

Booth, Philip
After the Rebuilding.
Barred Islands.
Countershadow, The.
Crossing.
Day the Tide, The.
Deer Isle.
Ego.
First Lesson.
Green Song.
Hard Country.
Heron.
How to See Deer.
Instruction in the Art.
Jake's Wharf.
Late Spring: Eastport, A.
Maine.
Marin.
Misery of Mechanics, The.
North.
North Haven.
Offshore.
One Man's Wife.
Photographer.
Procession.
Round, The: "Skunk cabbage, bloodroot."
Seeing Auden Off.
Sorting It Out.
Stove.
This Day after Yesterday.
Tower, The.
Twelfth Night.
Vermont: Indian Summer.
Was a Man.
Where Tide.
Wilding, The.

Boothroyd, John Basil
"And Now."
Holy Order.
Please Excuse Typing.
Sanctuary.

Borawski, Walta
Cheers, Cheers for Old Cha Cha Ass
  ("Cheers, cheers for old Patchogue High").
English Was Only a Second Language.
Invisible History.

Borenstein, Emily
Life of the Letters.

Borges, Jorge Luis
Afterglow.
Amorous Anticipation.
Dagger, The ("A dagger rests in a drawer").
Hengest Cyning.
On the Death of Francisco López Merino.
Plainness.

Borgese, G. A.
Easter Sunday, 1945.

Born, Nicholas
Balance Sheet with Incident.

Borregaard, Ebbe
Each Found Himself at the End Of. . .
Some Stories of the Beauty Wapiti.

Borrell, D. E.
Another Death.

Borson, Roo
Flowers.
Gray Glove.
Jacaranda.
Talk.

Borthwick, Jane
Light Shining Out of Darkness.

Boruch, Marianne
Hammer Falls, Is Falling, The.

Bose, Harry
M 13, *sel.*

Bosha, Kawabata. *See* **Kawabata Bosha**

Bosman, Herman Charles
Learning Destiny.
Old I Am.
Seed.

Bossidy, John Collins
Boston.
Boston Toast, A, at.

Boston, Bruce
Defeat at the Hands of Alien Scholars.
FTL Addict Fixes, The.
Human Remains.
If Gravity Were Like Weather.
Mathematician.
Star Drifter Grounded, The.
Want Ad.

Bostwick, Grace G.
Pep.

Boswell, James
Five winter days at Mannheim shall I be.
Here am I, sitting in a German inn.
Ye who with fortune ever are at strife.

Boswell, Margie B.
Texas Ranger, The.

Botrall, Ronald
Icarus.

Botsford, S. B.
Sonneteering Made Easy.

Bottomley, Gordon
Blanid's Song, *sel.*
Dawn.
Eager Spring.
Eagle Song, *sel.*
End of the World, The.
Hymn of Form, A.
Hymn of Touch, A.
"L'Apparition" of Gustave Moreau.
L'Oiseau Bleu.
Louse Crept Out of My Lady's Shift, A.
Maid of Arc, The.
To Iron-Founders and Others.

Bottoms, David
Boy Shepherds' Simile, The.
Copperhead, The.
Desk, The.
Drowned, The.
Ice.
In a U-Haul North of Damascus.
Naval Photograph: 25 October 1942: What the
  Hand May Be Saying.
Sign for My Father, Who Stressed the Bunt.
Smoking in an Open Grave.
Under the Boathouse.
Under the Vulture-Tree.
Wrestling Angels.

Botton, Isaac de
Desire.

Bottrall, Ronald
Darkened Windows.
Mating Answer.
Proserpine at Enna.

Botwood, Edward
Hot Stuff.

Bouchet, André du
Light of the Blade, The.
Postponement.
White Motor, The.

Boulton, Marjorie
Spring Betrayed.

Boulus, Sargon
Lighter.
My Father's Dream.
Poem: "I want to know today."
Siege.

Boumi-Pappas, Rita
Artemis.
Crow, The.
Krinio.

Boundy, Rex
Virile Christ, A.

Boundzekei-Dongala, Emmanuel
Fantasy under the Moon.

Bourdillon, Francis William
Ah, happy who have seen Him, whom the
  world, *sel.*
Night Has a Thousand Eyes, The.
Where Runs the River.

Bourinot, Arthur Stanley
Dark Flows the River.
Fish.
Johnny Appleseed.
Legend of Paul Bunyan, A.
Nicolas Gatineau.
Only Silence.
Paul Bunyan, *sel.*
Snow Anthology.
Sonnets to My Mother.
Tom Thomson.
Under the Pines.
What Far Kingdom.
Winter owl skirts hemlock tree.

Bourke, Sharon
Sopranosound, Memory of John.

Bourne, David
Parachute Descent.

Bourne, Nina
Where the Single Men Go in Summer.

Bourne, Vincent
Cricket, The.
Housekeeper, The.
Jackdaw, The.
Snail, The.

Bouvé, Thomas Tracy
Shannon and the *Chesapeake,* The.

Bovshover, Joseph
To the Laggards.

Bowden, Samuel
Kite, completed thus, is borne along, The,
  sel.

Bowditch, Nathaniel Ingersoll
World Beyond, A.

Bowen, Alice
Circumstance.

**Bowen, Charles Synge Christopher Bowen,
  Baron**
Rain It Raineth, The.

Bowen, Euros
Blackthorn.
Nettles in May.
Winged in Gold.

Bowen, John Eliot
Man Who Rode to Conemaugh, The.

Bowering, George
Beach at Veracruz, The.
Dobbin.
Egg, The.
Envies, The.
Está Muy Caliente.
Grandfather.
Grass, The.
Grass, Grass.
House, The.
I am slowly dying, water evaporating, *sel.*
In the Forest.
Inside the Tulip.
Moon Shadow.
My Atlas Poet.
Smoking Drugs with Strangers.
Solid Mountain.
Under.

Bowering, Marilyn
Russian Asylum.
Seeing Oloalok.
Wishing Africa.

Bowerman, Jon
For Jeff.
Tribute to Freckles and Tornado.

Bowers, Edgar
Adam's Song to Heaven.
Afternoon at the Beach, An.
Aix-La-Chappelle, 1945.
Astronomers of Mont Blanc, The.
Autumn Shade.
Dark Earth and Summer.
Elegy: December, 1970, An.
Fierce and brooding holocaust of faith, The,
   sel.
From William Tyndale to John Frith.
Grove and Building.
I know a wasted place high in the Alps, sel.
Mirror, The.
Mountain Cemetery, The.
Stoic; for Laura von Courten, The.
Virgin Mary, The.
Wise Men, The.

Bowes-Lyon, Lilian
Son, A.
White Hare, The.

Bowie, Walter Russell
God of the Nations.
O Holy City Seen of John.

Bowker, Richard Rogers
Thomas à Kempis.

Bowker, Tom
Eagle.

Bowles, Paul
Extract.

**Bowles, Caroline Anne (Caroline Anne
   Bowles-Southey)**
Young Grey Head, The.

Bowles, William Lisle
An Egyptian Tomb.
At Dover Cliffs.
At Tynemouth Priory, after a Tempestuous
   Voyage.
Distant View of England from the Sea.
Hope.
In Age, sel.
In Youth, sel.
Netley Abbey.
Sonnet: "Evening, as slow thy placid shades
   descend."
Sonnet: "How sweet the tuneful bells'
   responsive peal!"
Time and Grief.
To a Friend.
To the River Itchin, near Winton.
Tweed Visited, The.

Bowman, Louise Hollingsworth
Quiet Hour, The.

Bowman, Louise Morey
Sea Lavender.
She Plans Her Funeral.

Bowndheri, Ilmi
As Camels Who Have Become Thirsty.

Bowring, Sir John
God Is Love.
In the Cross of Christ I Glory.

Boyajian, Aram
American Commencement.
Blok: Let Me Learn the Poem.
Death of the Epileptic Poet Yesenin, The.
George Washington Goes to a Girlie Movie.
Hairs in My Nose, The.
Poetry Is in the Darkness.
World Is Really a Sugarplum House in the
   Forest, The.

Boyars, Arthur
Initial.

Boyd, Bruce
Sanctuary.

This Is What the Watchbird Sings, Who
   Perches in the Lovetree.
Venice Recalled.

Boyd, Mark Alexander
Fra Bank to Bank, Fra Wood to Wood I Rin.

Boyd, Melba Joyce
Beer Drops.
Sunflowers and Saturdays.
Why?

Boyd, Thomas
King's Son, The.

"Boyd, Nancy." See **Millay, Edna St.
   Vincent**

Boyden, Polly Chase
Mud.
Mud ("Mud is very nice to feel").

Boye, Karin
I feel your steps in the hall, sel.
Sword, A.

Boyer, Jill Witherspoon
Detroit City.
Dream Farmer.
King Lives.
When Brothers Forget.

Boyes, Sara
Bathing.
Breaking Days.
Stars.

Boyesen, Hjalmar Hjorth
Thoralf and Synnöv.

Boyle, Kay
Communication to Nancy Cunard, A.
For James Baldwin.
For Marianne Moore's Birthday.
Monody to the Sound of Zithers.
New Emigration, The.
Poets.
Thunderstorm in South Dakota.
To a Seaman Dead on Land.

Boyle, Sarah Roberts
Voice of the Grass, The.

Boyle, Virginia Fraser
Tennessee.

Boynton, H. W.
Golfer's Rubaiyat, The.

Bozhilov, Bozhidar
Poets.

Bracken, Thomas
Not Understood.

Brackenbury, Alison
Divers' Death, The.
Whose Window?

Brackenridge, Hugh Henry and Philip Freneau
Eugenio, sel.
Leander, sel.

Bracker, Milton
P Is for Paleontology.
Umpire, The.
Where, O Where?

Brackett, Anna Callender
Benedicite.
In Hades.

Bradford, Gamaliel
God.

Bradford, William
And Truly It Is a Most Glorious Thing.
Epitaphium Meum.
New England's Growth.
Of Boston in New England.
Word to New England, A.

Bradley, Christine E.
Skippets, the Bad One.

Bradley, George
Noch Einmal, an Orpheus.

Bradley, Mary Emily Neely
Beyond Recall.
Chrysalis, A.
In Death.
Spray of Honeysuckle, A.

Bradley, Edward and **Edith Cooper.** See
   "Field, Michael"

Bradstreet, Anne
As Spring the Winter Doth Succeed.
As Weary Pilgrim, Now at Rest.
Author to Her Book, The.
Before the Birth of One of Her Children.
Contemplations.
Deliverance from a Fit of Fainting.
Flesh and the Spirit, The.
For Deliverance from a Fever.
Four Seasons of the Year, The.
I wist not what to wish, yet sure thought I,
   sel.
In Memory of My Dear Grandchild [Anne
   Bradstreet]
In Memory of My Dear Grandchild Elizabeth
   Bradstreet Who Deceased August, 1665,
   Being a Year and a Half Old.
In Reference to Her Children, 23 June, 1656.
In Thankfull Remembrance for My Dear
   Husband's Safe Arrivall Sept. 3, 1662.
Letter to Her Husband, Absent upon Public
   Employment, A ("as loving hind.").
Letter to Her Husband, Absent upon Public[k]
   Employment, A.
Mariner that on smooth waves doth glide,
   The, sel.
O Thou Most High Who Rulest All.
O Time the fatal wrack of mortal things, sel.
On My Dear Grandchild Simon Bradstreet.
Prologue, The: "To sing of wars, of
   captain[e]s, and of kings."
Shall I then praise the heavens, the trees, the
   earth, sel.
Silent alone, where none or saw, or heard,
   sel.
So he that saileth in this world of pleasure,
   sel.
Some Verses upon the Burning of Our House,
   July 10th, 1666.
To My Dear and Loving Husband.
To the Memory of My Dear and Ever
   Honored Father Thomas Dudley Esq.
Vanity of All Worldly Things, The.
When I behold the heavens as in their prime,
   sel.

Bradstreet, Samuel
Almanack for the Year of Our Lord, 1657,
   An.

Brady, Charles A.
Dimidium Animae Meae.

Brady, Edwin James
Coachman's Yarn, The.
Lost and Given Over.

Brady, George M.
Day, The.
Garden, The.
Generations, The.
Hosts, The.
Land-Fall.
Old Michael.
Settled Men, The.

Brady, June
Far Trek.

Brady, Nicholas and **Nahum Tate.** See **Tate,
   Nahum** and **Nicholas Brady**

Bragdon, Claude
Point, the Line, the Surface and Sphere, The,
   sel.

Bragg, Linda Brown
Our Blackness Did Not Come to Us Whole.
Poem about Beauty, Blackness, Poetry, A.

Brainard, Joe
Nothing to Write Home About.

Brainard, John Gardiner Calkins
Deep, The.
Mr. Merry's Lament for "Long Tom."
On the Death of Commodore Oliver H. Perry.
To Thee, O God, the Shepherd Kings.

Brainard, Mary Gardiner
I know not what will befall me: God hangs a mist o'er my eyes, *sel.*
Not Knowing.

Braine, Sheila
Mr. Scarecrow.

Braithwaite, William Stanley
Del Cascar.
Golden Moonrise.
House of Falling Leaves, The.
In a Grave-Yard.
Ironic: LL.D.
October XXIX, 1795.
Rhapsody.
Rye Bread.
Sandy Star and Willie Gee.
Scintilla.
Sic Vita.
To———.
Turn Me to My Yellow Leaves.
Watchers, The.
White Magic; an Ode.

Braley, Berton
Business Is Business.
Do It Now.
Loyalty.
Opportunity.
Prayer, A: "Lord, let me live like a Regular Man."
Success!
Thinker, The.

Braley, Ephraim
Canada-I-O ("Come all ye jolly lumbermen and listen to my song"), at.

Bramston, James
Huge commentators grace my learned shelves, *sel.*
Time's Changes, *sel.*
Whoe'er he be that to a taste aspires, *sel.*

Branch, Anna Hempstead
Grieve Not, Ladies.
Mathematics or the Gift of Tongues.
Monk in the Kitchen, The.
Song for My Mother, A: Her Hands, *sel.*
Song for My Mother, A: Her Stories, *sel.*
Song for My Mother, A: Her Words, *sel.*
Unbeliever, An.

Branch, M. W
Schmaltztenor!

Brand, Dionne
Give up the bitterness, *sel.*
In the 5 a.m. dusk, *sel.*

Brand, Millen
Lost.

Brandling, Charles
To a Lady, with a Present of a Fan, at.

Brant, Beth
For All My Grandmothers.
Her Name Is Helen.
I write because not to write is a breach of faith, *sel.*
Native Origin.
Ride the Turtle's Back.

Brant, LeRoy V.
Green Plumes of Royal Palms.
Oh, Day of Days.

Brasch, Charles
Always, in these islands, meeting and parting, *sel.*
Ambulando.
Autumn, Thurlby Domain.
Before the light of evening can go out, *sel.*
City, The, *sel.*
Cry Mercy.
Ergo Sum.
Great Sea.
I tramp my streets into recognition, *sel.*
In drab derelict marsh near the madhouse, *sel.*
Letter from Thurlby Domain.
Life Mask.

Man Missing.
No Reparation.
Once more as I gather about me the cloak of the evening, *sel.*
Open the Heart.
Oreti Beach.
Photograph of a Baby.
Physics of Love.
Self to Self.
Shoriken.
Tempora Mutantur, *sel.*
Thistle, briar, thorn, *sel.*
Wantword.
What have you seen on the summits, the peaks that plunge their, *sel.*
Winter Anemones, *sel.*
Word by Night.
World without End.

Brass, Perry
I Think the New Teacher's a Queer.

Brathwaite, Edward
So When the Hammers of the Witnesses of Heaven Are Raised All Together, *sel.*

Brathwaite, Edward Kamau
Harbour.
Horse Weebles.
Schooner.
Starvation and Blues.

Brathwaite, Richard
Nightingale, The, *sel.*
Of Maids' Inconstancy, *sel.*

Braun, Richard Emil
Goose.
Lilies, The.
Seeking an Explanation.

Brautigan, Richard
All Watched Over by Machines of Loving Grace.
Day They Busted the Grateful Dead, The.
Haiku Ambulance.
In a Cafe.
Late Starting Dawn.

Brawley, Benjamin
Chaucer.
My Hero.

Braxton, Jodi
Sometimes I Think of Maryland.

Brazelton, Ethel M. C.
Poor Lil' Brack Sheep.

Breban, Nicolae
Indian Summer.

Brechin, Sandy
Animal House, The.

Brecht, Bertolt
Children's Crusade 1939.
Film of the Comedian Chaplin, A.
First Psalm, The.
God of War, The.
I Need No Gravestone.
Letter to the Actor Charles Laughton concerning the Work on the Play "The Life of Galileo."
Mask of Evil, The.
New House, A.
Of Poor B.B.
Of Swimming in Lakes and Rivers.
On the Suicide of the Refugee W. B.

Brecht, Stefan
Momentariness.

Breck, Mrs. Frank A.
They Two.

Bremser, Ray
Blood.
Let me lay it to you gently, Mr. Gone!, *sel.*

Bremser, Ray. *See* **Leland, Charles Godfrey**

Brennan, Christopher John
Adam to Lilith, *sel.*
Anguish'd Doubt Broods over Eden, The, *sel.*
Because She Would Ask Me Why I Loved Her.

Come Out, Come Out, Ye Souls That Serve, *sel.*
Fire in the heavens, and fire along the hills, *sel.*
How Old Is My Heart, *sel.*
I Cry to You as I Pass Your Windows, *sel.*
I Said, This Misery Must End, *sel.*
I Saw My Life as Whitest Flame, *sel.*
Interlude: The Casement.
Land I Came Thro' Last, The, *sel.*
Let Us Go Down, the Long Dead Night Is Done, *sel.*
Lilith on the Fate of Man, *sel.*
My Heart Was Wandering in the Sands, *sel.*
O Desolate Eves, *sel.*
When window-lamps had dwindled, then I rose, *sel.*
Years That Go to Make Me Man, The, *sel.*

Brennan, D.
Toad Song.

Brennan, Eileen
Evening on Howth Head.
May Evening.
One Kingfisher and One Yellow Rose.

Brennan, Gerald
Mornin's Mornin, The.

Brennan, J. Keirn
Let the Rest of the World Go By.

Brennan, John Michael
Air Is.

Brennan, Joseph Payne
Raccoon on the Road.

Brent, Hally Carrington
I Think I Know No Finer Things than Dogs.

Brenzoni, Caterina Bon
Heart has powerful wings;—take me by the hand, The, *sel.*

Brereton, E. C.
Three Dogs.

Brereton, Jane
On Mr. Nash's Picture at Full Length.

Brereton, John Le Gay
Buffalo Creek.
Cling to Me.

Breton, André
Always for the First Time.
Branch of Nettle Enters through the Window, A.
Curtain Curtain.
Egret.
Free Union.
Freedom of Love.
Go For Broke.
In the Eyes of the Gods.
In the Loverly Half-Light.
Lethal Relief.
Man and Woman Absolutely White, A.
Marquis de Sade, The.
My wife whose hair is a brush fire, *sel.*
No Grounds for Prosecution.
On the Road to San Romano.
Poem-Object.
Postman Cheval.
Spectral Attitudes, The.
Sunflower.
They Tell Me That Over There.
Vigilance.
World.
Writings Recede, The.

Breton, Nicholas
Aglaia, *sel.*
Cradle Song, A: "Come, little babe, come, silly soul."
I would thou wert not fair, or I were wise, *sel.*
Merry Country Lad, The, *sel.*
Odd Conceit, An.
Olden Love-making.
Pastoral, A: "On a hill there grows a flower."
Phillida and Coridon, *sel.*

Phyllis.
Pretty Twinkling Starry Eyes, *sel.*
Rare News.
Report Song [in a Dream], A.
Supplication, A.
To His Muse.
Upon a dainty hill sometime.

Brett, Reginald Baliol, 2d Viscount Esher
At Swindon.

Brew, Kwesi
Ancestral Faces.
Lonely Traveller, The.
Plea for Mercy, A.
Search, The.

Brewer, Ebenezer Cobham
Signs of the Zodiac, The.

Brewster, Elizabeth
Anti-Love Poems.
Death by Drowning.
East Coast—Canada.
Egoist Dead, The.
Eviction.
Great-Aunt Rebecca.
If I Could Walk Out into the Cold Country.
In the Library.
River Song.

Brewster, Martha
Stately Structure of This Earth, The.

Brice, Andrew
Poet's Terror at the Bailiffs of Exeter, The,
sel.

Brick, Norman
Of Snow.

Bricuth, John
Song of the Darkness.

"Bridges, Madeline" (Mary Ainge De Vere)
Breath, A.
Faith Trembling.
Farewell, A: "I put thy hand aside, and turn
away."
Friend and Lover.
God Keep You.
Life's Mirror.
Poet and Lark.
Spinner, The.
When the Most Is Said.
Wind-swept Wheat, The.

Bridges, Robert
April, 1885.
Cliff-Top, The.
Clouds Have Left the Sky, The.
Elegy: "Clear and gentle stream!"
Elegy: Summer-House on the Mound.
Etosion achthos aroures.
First Spring Morning.
Fortunatus Nimium.
Gay Robin Is Seen No More.
I Never Shall Love the Snow Again.
Johannes Milton, Senex.
Low Barometer.
Melancholia.
Poor Poll.
Triolet: "When first we met we did not
guess."
Upper Skies, The.
Winter Nightfall.

Bridges, Robert (1844–1930)
Affliction of Richard, The.
Angel Spirits of Sleep.
Awake, My Heart, to Be Loved.
Cheddar Pinks.
Dejection.
Elegy on a Lady, Whom Grief for the Death
of Her Betrothed Killed.
Elegy: "Wood is bare, The: a river-mist is
steeping."
Eros.
Ethick, *sel.*
Evening Darkens Over, The.
I Have Loved Flowers.
I Heard a Linnet Courting.

I Love All Beauteous Things.
I Will Not Let Thee Go.
Idle Flowers, The.
Idle Life I Lead, The.
Indolence.
London Snow.
Man that sees by chance his picture, made, A,
sel.
Muse and Poet.
My Delight and Thy Delight.
My Lady Pleases Me, *sel.*
Nightingales.
Noel; Christmas Eve, 1913.
November.
O Weary Pilgrims, *sel.*
On a Dead Child.
Passer-by, A.
Pater Filio.
Philosopher to His Mistress, The.
Psalm, The: "While Northward the hot sun
was sinking o'er the trees."
Sky's unresting cloudland, that with varying
play, The, *sel.*
Snow Lies Sprinkled on the Beach, The.
So Sweet Love Seemed.
Spring Goeth All in White.
Storm is over, the land hushes to rest, The.
Thanksgiving Day.
There is a hill beside the silver Thames.
They that in play can do the thing they would,
sel.
Thou Didst Delight My Eyes.
To the United States of America.
Triolet: "All women born are so perverse."
Weep Not To-Day.
When Death to Either Shall Come.
Whole World Now, The, *sel.*

Bridges, Robert (1858–1941)
Gheluvelt.
James McCosh.
Toast to Our Native Land, A.
Unillumined Verge, The.

Bridges-Adams, W.
Fragment from the Elizabethans.

Bridget, Saint.
I Should Like to Have a Great Pool of Ale,
at.

Bridglal, Sindamani
She Lives between Back Home and Home.

Bridgman, L. J.
Hare and the Pig, The.

Briefs, E. Castendyk
Fat Mama at Swenson's.

Brierre, Jean
Harlem.

Briggs, C.
Framework-Knitters Petition, The.

Briggs, Olga Hampel
Brief History.

Brigham, Besmilr
Tell Our Daughters.
Will's Love, The.

Bright, Susan
Contest.

Bright, Verne
Revelation.

Brin, Ruth F.
On Cedar Lake, 1957.

Brinckman, Rosemary
Fish and Bird.

Brine, Mary Dow
Somebody's Mother.

Bringhurst, Robert
Deuteronomy.
Notes to the Reader.
These Poems, She Said ("These poems, these
poems").

Brink, Carol Ryrie
Goody O'Grumpity.

Brinnin, John Malcolm
Address to the Refugees.

American Plan.
Angel Eye of Memory.
Ascension: 1925, The.
At the Airport.
At the Band Concert.
At the Museum.
Cape Ann; a View.
Every Earthly Creature.
Fêtes, Fates.
Girl in a White Coat.
Heavy Heavy Heavy.
Hotel Paradiso e Commerciale.
Letter from an Island.
Letter to Statues.
My Father, My Son.
New England Sampler, A.
Nuns at Eve.
Roethke Plain.
Saul, Afterward, Riding East.
Skin Diving in the Virgins.
Thin Façade for Edith Sitwell, A.
Views of the Favorite Colleges.
Wind Is Ill, The.
With a Posthumous Medal.

Brinson Curiel, Barbara
Pearl.
Recipe for Salt.
Recipe for Sand.

Brisley, Joyce L.
Two Families, The.

Brissenden, Robert Francis
Verandahs.
Walking down Jalan Thamrin.

Bristol, Augusta Cooper
Pyxidanthera, The.

Britton, Donald
Winter Garden.

Bro, Margueritte Harmon
Prayer: "God, listen through my words to the
beating of my heart."

Broaddus, Andrew
Help Thy Servant.

Brock, Edwin
Five Ways to Kill a Man.

Brock, Van K.
Departure.
Lying on a Bridge.
Man in the Rain, The.
Novas.
Sea Birds, The.

Brock-Broido, Lucie
Hitchcock Blue.

Brockman, Zoe Kincaid
Grapevine, The.

Brod, Max
Goldfish on the Writing Desk.

Brode, Anthony
Breakfast with Gerard Manley Hopkins.
Calypsomania.
Obituary.
Unromantic Song.

Brodey, Jim
Little Light.
Noh Play.
To Guillaume Apollinaire.

Brodsky, Joseph
Einem alten Architekten in Rom.
Étude.
Jewish Cemetery near Leningrad, A.
Monument to Pushkin.
Pilgrims.
Soho.
Sonnet: "Month of January has flown Past,
The."
Spring Season of Muddy Roads.
To a Tyrant.
To Urania.
Verses on Accepting the World.

Brody, Alter
 Cry of the Peoples, The.
 Family Album, A.
 Ghetto Twilight.
 Lamentations.
Brome, Alexander
 Love's without Reason.
 Pastoral on the King's Death; Written in
  1648, The.
 Plain Dealing.
 Resolve, The.
 Riddle, The: "No more, no more,/ We are
  already pin'd."
Bromley, Isaac H.
 Passenjare, The.
Bromwich, David
 From the Righteous Man Even the Wild
  Beasts Run Away.
 Wandsworth Common.
Bronk, William
 Aspects of the World like Coral Reefs.
 Body, The.
 Feeling, The.
 March, Upstate.
 Metonymy as an Approach to a Real World.
 Postcard to Send to Sumer, A.
Brontë, Anne ("Acton Bell")
 Arbour, The.
 Captive Dove, The.
 Doubter's Prayer, The.
 If This Be All.
 Lines Composed in a Wood on a Windy Day.
 Memory.
 Prayer, A: "My God (oh, let me call Thee
  mine)."
 Reminiscence, A.
Brontë, Charlotte ("Currer Bell")
 Autumn day its course has run—the Autumn
  evening falls, The.
 Fairies' Farewell, The.
 House was still—the room was still, The.
 I now had only to retrace.
 Nurse believed the sick man slept, The.
 On the Death of Anne Brontë.
Brontë, Emily ("Ellis Bell")
 A.G.A. to A.E.
 Ah! Why, because the Dazzling Sun.
 All Hushed and Still within the House.
 Anticipation.
 Ay—There It Is!
 Come, walk with me.
 Death.
 D.G.C. to J.A.
 Evening Sun, The.
 Fall, Leaves, Fall.
 Had there been falsehood in my breast.
 Harp of Wild and Dream-like Strain.
 He comes with western winds, with evening's
  wandering airs, sel.
 Hope.
 How still, how happy! These [or Those] are
  words.
 I Am the Only Being Whose Doom.
 I die; but when the grave shall press.
 I know not how it falls on me.
 If grief for grief can touch thee.
 I'm Happiest When Most Away.
 In the dungeon-crypts, idly did I stray, sel.
 It will not shine again.
 It's over now; I've known it all.
 Ladybird! Ladybird!
 Last Words.
 Little While, a Little While, A.
 Long neglect has worn away.
 Love and Friendship.
 Mild the mist upon the hill.
 Morning Star, The.
 Night Is Darkening round Me.
 Night Wind, The.
 No Coward Soul [Is Mine]
 O come with me, thus ran the song.

 O dream, where art thou now?
 O for the time when I shall sleep, sel.
 Old Stoic, The.
 Plead for Me.
 Remembrance.
 Shall Earth No More Inspire Thee?
 She dried her tears, and they did smile.
 Song: "Linnet in the rocky dells, The."
 Stanzas: "I'll not weep that thou art going to
  leave me."
 Stanzas: "Often rebuked, yet always back
  returning," at.
 Stanzas to———.
 Still, let my tyrants know, I am not doomed
  to wear, sel.
 Sun Has Set, The.
 Tell me, tell me, smiling child.
 That Wind.
 There Let Thy Bleeding Branch Atone.
 Two Children, The.
 Upon Her Soothing Breast.
 Visionary, The.
 Warning and Reply.
 What winter floods, what showers of spring.
Brooke, Henry
 Air: "Arise, arise, arise!," sel.
 Air: "For often my mammy has told," sel.
Brooke, Rupert
 Busy Heart, The.
 Channel Passage, A.
 Chilterns, The.
 Clouds.
 Colloquial.
 Day That I Have Loved.
 Dead, The ("Blow out, you bugles, over the
  rich dead!"), sel.
 Dead, The ("These hearts were woven of
  human joys and cares").
 Dining-Room Tea.
 Doubts.
 Dust.
 Fish, The.
 Fragment: "I strayed about the deck, an hour,
  to-night."
 Great Lover, The.
 Heaven.
 Hill, The.
 In Freiburg Station.
 Letter to a Live Poet, A.
 Memory, A.
 Menelaus and Helen.
 Mummia.
 Mutability.
 Night Journey, The.
 O Thou/ God of all long desirous roaming,
  sel.
 Old Vicarage, Grantchester, The.
 Peace, sel.
 Safety, sel.
 Second Best.
 Soldier, The, sel.
 Sonnet: "Not with vain tears, when we're
  beyond the sun."
 Sonnet: "Oh! Death will find me, long before
  I tire."
 Sonnet Reversed.
 Success.
 Thoughts on the Shape of the Human Body.
 Tiare Tahiti.
 Wagner.
 Waikiki.
Brooke, Stopford
 Courage.
Brooke, Fulke Greville, 1st Baron. *See*
  Greville, Fulke, 1st Baron Brooke
Brooks, Charles Timothy
 Plea for Flood Ireson, A.
Brooks, Edwin
 Tulips from Their Blood.
Brooks, Francis
 Down the Little Big Horn.

 Intaglios, sel.
 On The Plains.
 Tennessee.
Brooks, Fred Emerson
 Barnyard Melodies.
 Foreigners at the Fair.
Brooks, Gwendolyn
 Anniad, The.
 Appendix to the Anniad.
 Aspect of Love, Alive in the Ice and Fire,
  An.
 Ballad of Rudolph Reed, The.
 Bean Eaters, The.
 Beverly Hills, Chicago.
 Big Bessie Throws Her Son into the Street.
 Birth in a Narrow Room, The.
 Black Wedding Song, A.
 Blackstone Rangers, The.
 Boy Breaking Glass.
 Boy Died in My Alley, The.
 Boys. Black.
 Bronzeville Man with a Belt in the Back.
 Chicago "Defender" Sends a Man to Little
  Rock, The.
 Chicago Picasso, The, sel.
 Children of the Poor, The, sel.
 Egg Boiler, The.
 Empty Woman, The.
 Estimable Mable.
 First Fight. Then Fiddle.
 Five Men against the Theme "My Name Is
  Red Hot. Yo Name Ain Doodley Squat."
 Flags.
 Friend.
 Horses Graze.
 Jessie Mitchell's Mother.
 Keziah.
 Kitchenette Building, sel.
 Last Quatrain of the Ballad of Emmett Till,
  The.
 Life of Lincoln West, The.
 Lovely Love, A.
 Lovers of the Poor, The.
 Malcolm X.
 Martin Luther King, Jr.
 Maxie Allen.
 Medgar Evers.
 Mother, The.
 My Dreams, My Works, Must Wait Till after
  Hell.
 Naomi.
 Narcissa.
 Negro Hero.
 Of De Witt Williams on His Way to Lincoln
  Cemetery.
 Of Robert Frost.
 Old-Marrieds, The.
 Old People Working (Garden, Car).
 Old Tennis Player.
 One wants a Teller in a time like this, sel.
 Otto.
 Paul Robeson.
 Penitent Considers Another Coming of Mary,
  A.
 Pete at the Zoo.
 Piano after War.
 "Pygmies Are Pygmies Still, Though Percht
  on Alps."
 Riot.
 Rites for Cousin Vit, The.
 Robert, Who Is Often a Stranger to Himself.
 Rudolph Is Tired of the City.
 Sadie and Maud.
 Second Sermon on the Warpland, The.
 Sermon on the Warpland, The.
 Song in the Front Yard, A.
 "Still Do I Keep My Look, My Identity. . ."
 Street in Bronzeville: Southeast Corner, A.

Strong Men, Riding Horses.
Sunset of the City, A.
Third Sermon on the Warpland, The.
To Be in Love.
To Don at Salaam.
Vacant Lot, The.
Vern.
Wall, The.
We Real Cool.
What Shall I Give My Children?
When You Have Forgotten Sunday: The Love
   Story.
Young Africans.
Young Heroes.

Brooks, Helen Morgan
Plans.
Words.
Young David: Birmingham, A.

Brooks, Jonathan Henderson
And One Shall Live in Two.
Last Quarter Moon of the Dying Year, The.
Muse in Late November.
My Angel.
Paean.
Resurrection, The.
She Said. . .

Brooks, Maria Gowen ("Maria del
   Occidente")
Farewell to Cuba.
Palace of the Gnomes, sel.
Respite, The, sel.
Song of Egla.

Brooks, Phillips
Christmas Everywhere.
O Little Town of Bethlehem.
Unfailing One, The.

Brooks, Shirley
I paints and paints.
More Luck to Honest Poverty.
New Proverb.
Philosopher and Her Father, The.
Poem by a Perfectly Furious Academician.
"Prize" Poem, A.
To Disraeli.
What Jenner Said on Hearing in Elysium That
   Complaints Had Been Made of His Having
   a Statue [in Trafalgar Square]

Brooks, Walter Rollin
Ants, Although Admirable Are Awfully
   Aggravating.
Ode to Spring.
Ode to the Pig: His Tail.
Thoughts on Talkers.

Broome, William
Rose-Bud, The.

Broomell, Myron Henry
Prayer for the Age.

Brosmer, Mary Pierce
Limited Access.
Mothers: A Meditation.

Brotherton, Alice Williams
Blazing Heart, The.
First Thanksgiving Day, The.
My Enemy.

Brough, Robert Barnabas
Look at this skin—at fourscore years, sel.
My Lord Tomnoddy.

Brougham, Henry Peter, 1st Baron
   Brougham and Vaux
Orator's Epitaph, The.

Broughton, James Richard
Birds of America, The.
Feathers or Lead?
Psalm of St. The Priapus.
Psyche to Cupid: Her Ditty.
Wondrous the Merge.

Broughton, T. Alan
Summer Killer.

Broumas, Olga
Cinderella.
Landscape with Leaves and Figure.

Landscape with Next of Kin.
Leda and Her Swan.
She Loves.

Brown, Abbie Farwell
Fisherman, The.

Brown, Alex J.
Wickedest Man in Memphis, The.

Brown, Alice
Artisan, The.
Candlemas.
Cloistered.
Hora Christi.
Life.
Pagan Prayer.
Revelation, sel.
Seaward Bound.
Sleep.
Trilby.

Brown, Anna Gordon
Gay Goshawk, The, at.

Brown, Audrey Alexandra
Amber Beads.
Goldfish, The.
Museum-Piece.
Night Boat.
Reveillé.

Brown, Beatrice Curtis
Jonathan Bing.

Brown, Catherine Bernard
Prayer for Pentecost, A.

Brown, Charles Walter
If I Should Die To-Night.

Brown, Christy
Good Friday.

Brown, Frank London
Jazz.

Brown, George Mackay
Beachcomber.
Carpenter.
Death of Peter Esson, The.
December Day, Hoy Sound.
Desertion of the Women and Seals, The.
Dream of Winter.
Five Voyages of Arnor, The.
Harald, the Agnostic Ale-loving Old Shepherd
   Enemy of the Whisky-drinking Ploughmen
   and Harvesters, Walks over the Sabbath
   Hill to the Shearing.
Hawk, The.
Keeper of the Midnight Gate, The.
Old Fisherman with Guitar.
Old Women, The.
Our Lady of the Waves.
Roads.
Seven Houses, The.
Shroud.
Stars.
Tea Poems.
Trout Fisher.
Unlucky Boat.

Brown, Hamish
Aye, There's Hills.
Beyond Feith Buidhe.
Footprints.
Harlot, The.
In the Rut.
Pitch Seven.
Ronas Hill.
Weather Rhymes.
Wind.

Brown, Harry
Drill, The.
Incident on a Front Not Far from Castel di
   Sangro.

Brown, Horatio
Bored.
Kodak; Tregantle, A.

Brown, Irene Fowler
Rear Guard, The.

Brown, Isaac Hinton
Honest Deacon, The.
Only a Pin.

Brown, Isabella Maria
Another Day.
Prayer: "I had thought of putting an/ altar."

Brown, Jennifer
Africa and the Caribbean.

Brown, John
Rhapsody, Written at the Lakes in
   Westmorland, A.

Brown, Joseph Brownlee
Thalatta! Thalatta!

Brown, Kate Louise
Five-Fingered Maple, The.
Lady Moon, The.
Pine Music.

Brown, Maimee Lee
Created Clay.

Brown, Margaret Wise
Bumble Bee.
Dear Father/ hear and bless.
Fish with the Deep Smile, The.
Green Stems.
Little Black Bug.
Little Donkey Close Your Eyes ("Little
   donkey on the hill.").
Secret Song, The.

Brown, Palmer
Spangled Pandemonium, The.

Brown, Phoebe Hinsdale
I Love to Steal Awhile Away.
Welcome, Ye Hopeful Heirs of Heaven.

Brown, Rita Mae
Aristophanes' Symposium.
Canto Cantare Cantavi Cantatum.
Dancing the Shout to the True Gospel; or,
   The Song Movement Sisters Don't Want
   Me to Sing.
Disconnection, The.
Fire Island.
New Litany, The.
Sappho's Reply.

Brown, Solyman
Artificial Teeth, sel.
Caries, sel.
Tartar, sel.
Value of Dentistry, The, sel.

Brown, Spencer
In an Old House.

Brown, Sterling Allen
After Winter.
Challenge.
Crispus Attucks McCoy.
Effie.
Foreclosure.
Long Gone.
Maumee Ruth.
Memphis Blues.
Odyssey of Big Boy.
Old Lem.
Old Woman Remembers, An.
Remembering Nat Turner.
Return.
Salutamus.
Sister Lou.
Slim Greer.
Slim in Hell ("Slim Greer went to heaven").
Southern Cop.
Southern Road.
Strange Legacies.
Strong Men.
To a Certain Lady, in Her Garden.
When de Saints Go Ma'chin' Home.

Brown, Stewart
Anthropology: Cricket at Kano.

Brown, T. E.
Bristol Channel, The.
Dartmoor: Sunset at Chagford.

Sermon at Clevedon, A.
Vespers.
Well, The.
Brown, Theron
His Majesty.
Brown, Thomas (Tom)
Colonels here in solemn manner meet, The.
Doctor Fell.
Epitaph upon That Profound and Learned
    Casuist, the Late Ordinary of Newgate, An.
Our fathers took oaths as of old they took
    wives.
Reader, beneath this turf I lie.
Satire upon the French King, A.
To That Most Senseless Scoundrel, the Author
    of Legion's Humble Address to the Lords.
Upon the Anonymous Author of Legion's
    Humble Address to the Lords.
Brown, Thomas Edward
Braddan Vicarage.
Disguises.
High overhead.
I Bended unto Me.
Ibant Obscuræ
My Garden.
O Englishwoman on the Pincian, *sel*.
Preparation.
Salve!
To K. H.
Wesley in Heaven.
When Love Meets Love.
Brown, Wayne
Ballad of the Electric Eel.
Bind, The.
England, Autumn.
Fir Tree.
Mackerel.
Noah.
On the Coast.
Remu.
Brown, William Goldsmith
Mother, Home, Heaven.
Browne, Charles Farrar. *See* **"Ward,**
    Artemus"
Browne, Francis Fisher
Santa Barbara.
Under the Blue.
Vanquished.
Browne, Irving
At Shakespeare's Grave.
Man's Pillow.
My New World.
Browne, Isaac Hawkins
Blest leaf! whose aromatic gales dispense, *sel*.
Boy! bring an ounce of Freeman's best, *sel*.
Fire Side, The; a Pastoral Soliloquy, *sel*.
Thrice happy, who free from ambition and
    pride, *sel*.
Browne, Jane Euphemia ("Aunt Effie")
Great Brown Owl, The.
Pleasant Changes.
Rooks, The.
Browne, Michael Dennis
Delta, The.
Hallowe'en 1971.
Handicapped Children Swimming.
Heaven.
Iowa.
Iowa, June.
King in May, The.
Lamb.
News from the House.
Paranoia.
Paycheck.
Peter.
Power Failure.
Roof of the World, The.
Visitor, The.
Wife of Winter's Tale, The.
Browne, Moses
Shrimp, A! Black thing as widow's crape, *sel*.
Survey of the Amphitheatre, A.

Browne, Sir Thomas
Colloquy with God, A, *sel*.
In yellow meadows I take no delight.
O for a toe, such as the funeral pyre.
Browne, Sir William (1692–1774)
Epigram: "King to Oxford sent a troop of
    horse, The."
Browne, William (1591–1643)
As that Arabian bird (whom all admire), *sel*.
Celadyne's Song, *sel*.
Course of the Tavy, The, *sel*.
Dawn of Day, *sel*.
Devonshire Walk, A, *sel*.
[Epitaph] In Obitum M.S., X° Maij [*or*
    Maii], 1614.
Frolic Mariners of Devon, The, *sel*.
Gentle Nymphs, Be Not Refusing, *sel*.
Glide Soft, Ye Silver Floods, *sel*.
Lo, I the Man, *sel*.
Mounting lark, day's herald, got on wing,
    The, *sel*.
Muses' friend, The (grey-eyed Aurora), yet,
    sel.
Ode, An: "Awake, faire Muse; for I intend."
On the Countess Dowager of Pembroke, at.
Praise of Poets, *sel*.
Rose, The, *sel*.
Shall I Tell You Whom I Love?, *sel*.
Sirens' Song, The, *sel*.
So Sat the Muses, *sel*.
So shuts the marigold her leaves, *sel*.
Song: "Choose now among this fairest
    number."
Song: "For her gait, if she be walking."
Venus and Adonis.
Browne, William (twentieth century)
Harlem Sounds: Hallelujah Corner.
Brownell, Florence Kerr
Coin in the Fist.
Brownell, Henry Howard
Abraham Lincoln.
Battle of Charlestown, The.
Bay Fight, The.
Burial of the Dane, The.
Bury Them.
Eagle of Corinth, The.
Lawyer's Invocation to Spring, The.
Night Quarters.
Old Cove, The.
River Fight, The.
Sphinx, The.
Sumter.
Would you hear of the River-Fight?, *sel*.
Browning, Elizabeth Barrett
And I, I was a good child on the whole, *sel*.
And wilt thou have me fashion into speech,
    sel.
Belovéd, my Belovéd, when I think, *sel*.
Belovéd, thou hast brought me many flowers,
    sel.
Bereavement.
Best, The.
Best Thing in the World, The.
Bianca among the Nightingales.
Books, books, books!, *sel*.
Can it be right to give what I can give?, *sel*.
Child's Thought of God, A.
Convinced by Sorrow, *sel*.
Court Lady, A.
Critics say that epics have died out, The, *sel*.
Cry of the Children, The.
Curse for a Nation, A.
Denial, A.
"Died. . ."
Face of all the world is changed, I think, The,
    sel.
Farewells from Paradise.
First time he kissed me, he but only kissed,
    sel.
First time that the sun rose on thine oath,
    The, *sel*.

Florence, *sel*.
Flush or Faunus.
Go from me. Yet I feel that I shall stand, *sel*.
Grief.
How do I love thee? Let me count the ways,
    sel.
Hymn: "Since without Thee we do no good."
I felt the wind soft from the land of souls, *sel*.
I had a little chamber in the house, *sel*.
I learnt the collects and the catechism, *sel*.
I mused/ Up and down, up and down, the
    terraced streets, *sel*.
I never gave a lock of hair away, *sel*.
I thought once how Theocritus had sung, *sel*.
If I leave all for thee, wilt thou exchange, *sel*.
If thou must love me, let it be for nought, *sel*.
Let the world's sharpness, like a clasping
    knife, *sel*.
Look, The.
Lord Walter's Wife.
Mask, The.
Meaning of the Look, The.
Mediator, The.
Mother and Poet.
Musical Instrument, A.
My Kate.
My letters! all dead paper, mute and white,
    sel.
My poet, thou canst touch on all the notes,
    sel.
Of writing many books there is no end;, *sel*.
Olives and Mountains, *sel*.
On a Portrait of Wordsworth by B. R.
    Haydon.
Out in the fields with God, *at*.
Poet, The.
Reading, *sel*.
Reward of Service.
Romance of the Swan's Nest.
Runaway Slave at Pilgrim's Point, The.
Say over again, and yet once over again, *sel*.
Sleep, The.
Substitution.
Tears.
Then, land!—then, England! oh, the frosty
    cliffs, *sel*.
"There it is!/ You play beside a death-bed like
    a child", *sel*.
They look up with their pale and sunken
    faces, *sel*.
Thou hast thy calling to some palace floor,
    sel.
To George Sand: A Desire.
To George Sand: A Recognition.
To school till five! and then again we fly.
Truth, so far, in my book; the truth which
    draws, *sel*.
Tuscan Life, *sel*.
Unlike are we, unlike, O princely heart!, *sel*.
Whatever's lost, it first was won, *sel*.
When our two souls stand up erect and strong,
    sel.
Woman's Shortcomings, A.
Year's Spinning, A.
Yet, love, mere love, is beautiful indeed, *sel*.
Browning, Frederick G.
Amen.
Browning, Ophelia Guyon
Pray without Ceasing.
Browning, Robert
Abt Vogler.
After.
Among the Rocks, *sel*.
And so I somehow-nohow played, *sel*.
Andrea del Sarto.
Any Wife to Any Husband.
Apparent Failure.
Appearances.
At the midnight in the silence of the
    sleep-time, *sel*.
Awakening of Man, The, *sel*.
Bad Dreams.

Belief and Unbelief, *sel.*
Bishop Blougram's Apology.
Bishop Orders His Tomb at Saint Praxed's
  Church, The.
Boot and Saddle("Boot, saddle, to horse, and
  away!"), *sel.*
By the Fire-Side.
Caliban upon Setebos; or, Natural Theology in
  the Island.
"Childe Roland to the Dark Tower Came."
Cleon ("Cleon the poet from the sprinkled
  isles").
Confessions.
Dîs Aliter Visum; or, Le Byron de Nos Jours.
Earl Mertoun's Song, *sel.*
Earth Breaks Up, *sel.*
Englishman in Italy, The.
Epistle Containing the Strange Medical
  Experience of Karshish, the Arab
  Physician, An.
Evelyn Hope.
Eyes, Calm beside Thee (Lady, Could'st Thou
  Know!).
Face, A.
Fame.
Fever, *sel.*
Flower's Name, The, *sel.*
Fra Lippo Lippi.
Grammarian's Funeral, A.
Grow Old Along with Me, *sel.*
Heretic's Tragedy, The.
Hervé Riel.
Home Thoughts from Abroad.
Home Thoughts, from the Sea.
House.
How It Strikes a Contemporary.
How They Brought the Good News from
  Ghent to Aix.
I shall paint/ God in the midst, *sel.*
Inapprehensiveness.
Incident of the French Camp.
Instans Tyrannus.
Into the street the Piper stept, *sel.*
Italian in England, The.
Johannes Agricola in Meditation.
Karshish, the Arab Physician ("Karshish, the
  picker-up of learning's crumbs").
Laboratory; Ancien Régime, The.
Last Ride Together, The.
Life in a Love.
Likeness, A.
Lost Leader, The.
Lost Mistress, The.
Love.
Love among the Ruins.
Love in a Life.
Madness, *sel.*
Master Hugues of Saxe-Gotha.
May and Death.
Meeting at Night.
Meeting at Night.
Memorabilia.
Misconceptions.
Moth's kiss, first, The!, *sel.*
My God, my God, let me for once look on
  thee, *sel.*
My Last Duchess.
My Star.
Never the Time and the Place.
O God, where do they tend—these struggling
  aims?, *sel.*
O Lyric Love, *sel.*
Oh, the wild joys of living! the leaping from
  rock up to rock, *sel.*
One Word More.
Orpheus and Eurydice.
Parting at Morning.
Patriot, The.
Phases of the Moon, *sel.*
Piano di Sorrento, *sel.*
Pictor Ignotus.
Pied Piper of Hamelin, The.

Popularity.
Porphyria's Lover.
Prologue: "Poet's age is sad, The: for why?,"
  sel.
Prospice.
Rabbi Ben Ezra.
Respectability.
Saul, *sels.*
Serenade at the Villa, A.
Service, *sel.*
Sibrandus Schafnaburgensis, *sel.*
Soliloquy of the Spanish Cloister.
Song, *sel.*
Song: "Heap cassia, sandal-buds and stripes,"
  sel.
Song: "Nay but you, who do not love her."
Song: Wanderers, The.
Summum Bonum.
Thamuris Marching.
Then I tuned my harp—took off the lilies we
  twine round its chords, *sel.*
There's a palace in Florence, the world knows
  well, *sel.*
This was my dream! I saw a forest, *sel.*
Thou wilt remember. Thou art not more dear,
  sel.
Thus the Mayne Glideth, *sel.*
To Edward Fitzgerald.
Toccata of Galuppi's, A.
Tray.
Twins, The.
Two in the Campagna.
Up at a Villa—Down in the City.
Wanderers, The, *sel.*
Waring.
What I love best in all the world, *sel.*
When I Vexed You, *sel.*
Why I Am a Liberal.
Woman's Last Word, A.
Women and Roses.
Yea, my King, *sel.*
Year's at the Spring, The, *sel.*
Youth and Art.

Brownjohn, Alan
Camel.
Cat.
Class Incident from Graves.
Cure.
Elephant.
Of Dancing.
Train, The.

**"Brownjohn, John" (Charles Remington
  Talbot)**
School-Master and the Truants, The.

Brownlie, W. S.
On First Looking into Chapman's Homer.

Brownstein, Michael
Declaration of Independence.
Floating.
For Them.
Triplets.

Bruce, Charles
Attic, The, *sel.*
Back Road Farm.
Biography.
Dreaming Trout, The, *sel.*
Fisherman's Son.
Hayfield, The, *sel.*
Words Are Never Enough.

Bruce, George
My House.
Singers, The.
Sumburgh Heid.

Bruce, John
Pike, The.

Bruce, Michael
Farewell, ye blooming fields! ye cheerful
  plains!, *sel.*

Bruce, Michael *revised by* John Logan
To the Cuckoo.

Bruce, Richard
Cavalier.
Shadow.

Bruce, Wallace
Our Nation Forever.
Parson Allen's Ride.
Two Argosies.

Bruchac, Joseph
Canticle.
City.
Coming Back.
Elegy for Jack Bowman.
For a Winnebago Brave.
From an Inmate Rule Book.
Frozen Hands.
Grandmother Came Down to Visit Us, The.
Hiking.
Not a Thing of Paint or Feathers.
Poem for Jan.
Second Skins—a Peyote Song.
Stone Giant.
There is a stream which rises.
Three Poems for the Indian Steelworkers.

Bruck, Edith
Birth.
Childhood.
Equality, Father!
Go, Then.
Let's Talk, Mother.
Sister Zahava.
Why Would I Have Survived?
You Hide ("You hide in the ostrich egg").

Brucker, H. P
Praise Now Your God.

Brudne, Eva
Farewell Ballad of Poppies, A.
Memento Vivendi.

Bruner, Margaret E.
Epitaph for a Cat.
Whom the Gods Love.

Bruno, Giordano
Philosophic Flight, The.

Bruns, John Dickson
Foe at the Gates, The.

Brunton, Alan
Her voice is like some angel picking at the
  door.
I say hello to the sunshine.
Oh me/ is that the ambulance chasing out of
  town?
What Happens in Shakzpeare.

Brutus, Dennis
Beauty of My Land Peers Warily, The.
Blood River Day.
Letter No. 18.
On the Island.
Somehow We Survive.
Sounds Begin Again, The.

Bryan, Elizabeth Mabel
Father of the Man.

Bryan, Sharon
Big Sheep Knocks You About.
Corner Lot.
Hollandaise.
Lunch with Girl Scouts.

Bryant, Edward
Winslow Crater.

Bryant, Frederick, Jr.
Cathexis.
Languages We Are, The.
Patience of a People.

Bryant, John Frederick
On a Piece of Unwrought Pipeclay.

Bryant, William Cullen
African Chief, The.
Antiquity of Freedom, The.
As Shadows Cast by Cloud and Sun.
Battle-Field, The.
Centennial Hymn.

Conqueror's Grave, The.
Death of Lincoln, The.
Death of Slavery, The.
Death of the Flowers, The.
Dedication: "Thou, whose unmeasured temple stands."
Earth's Children Cleave to Earth.
Evening Wind, The.
Father, thy hand/ Hath reared, *sel.*
Flood of Years, The.
Forest Hymn, A.
Green Mountain Boys, The.
Green River.
Hunter of the Prairies, The.
Hymn of the Sea, A.
In Memory of John Lothrop Motley.
Indian at the Burial-Place of His Fathers, An.
Inscription for the Entrance to a Wood.
June.
March.
May Sun Sheds an Amber Light, The.
Meditation on Rhode Island Coal, A.
Mighty One, before Whose Face.
Monument Mountain.
Mother's Hymn, The.
My Autumn Walk.
No Man Knoweth His Sepulchre.
November.
O thou great Movement of the Universe, *sel.*
O Thou Whose Own Vast Temple Stands.
Oh [*or* O] Fairest of the Rural Maids.
Oh Mother of a Mighty Race.
Other Sheep I Have, Which Are Not of This Fold.
Our Country's Call.
Past, The.
Planting of the Apple-Tree, The.
Poet, The.
Prairies, The.
Presentiment, A.
Robert of Lincoln.
Scene on the Banks of the Hudson, A.
Seventy-six.
Song of Marion's Men.
Summer Wind.
Thanatopsis.
Tides, The.
To a Waterfowl.
To Cole, the Painter, Departing for Europe.
To the Fringed Gentian.
Twenty-second of December, The.
Winter Piece, A.
Yellow Violet, The.

Brydges, Sir Samuel Egerton
Lines Written Immediately after Parting from a Lady.
On Dreams, October 15, 1782.
To Miss M———, Written by Moonlight, July 18, 1782.

Bryher, Winifred
Blue Sleep.
Thessalian.

Bryll, Ernest
Ballad of the Bayonet, A.
Leviathan.
Nike.

Bryusov, Valery Yakovlevich
Radiant Ranks of Seraphim.

Buber, Martin
Fiddler, The.
I Consider the Tree.

Buchan, John, "1st Baron Tweedsmuir"
Leap in the Smoke, *sel.*

Buchanan, Dugald
Day of Judgment, The.
Omnia Vanitas.

Buchanan, George
Epithalamium for Mary Stuart and the Dauphin of France.
Of the Sad Lot of the Humanists in Paris.

Buchanan, Robert
Little Herd-Boy's Song, The.

Little Milliner, The.
Starling, The.

Buchanan, Robert Williams
Blind Linnet, The.

Buck, Byron
Song from a Two-Desk Office.

Buck, Chief John
Memorial Ode.

Buck, Richard Henry
Kentucky Babe.

Buckham, James
Child of To-Day, A.
Heart's Proof, The.

Buckham, John Wright
Hills of God, Break Forth in Singing.
O God, above the Drifting Years.

Buckingham, George Villiers, 2nd Duke of
Prayer: "Lord God of the oak and the elm."

Buckingham and Normanby, Duke of. *See* **Sheffield, John, Duke of Buckingham and Normanby.**

Buckley, Christopher
White.

Buckley, R. Bishop
Wait for the Wagon, at.

Buckley, Vincent
Good Friday and the Present Crucifixion.
Late Tutorial.
No New Thing.
Parents.
Return of a Popular Statesman.
Various Wakings.

Buckmaster, Charles
Vanzetti.

Buckner, Samuel O.
Do It Right.

Buddingh', Cees
Ars Poetica.
Historical Materialism.
Monkey, The.
Music Makers, The.
Ode to the Yorkshire Dales.
Petit Salon des Indépendants.
Physics.
Shopping.
Sometimes, in the Evening.
Step by Step.
Sufficient unto the Day.

Budy, Andrea Hollander
Pigs.

Buist, A. A.
Hills of God, The.

Bukowski, Charles
For Jane.
Loser, The.
Short Order.
Style.
Sun Wields Mercy, The.
Tragedy of Leaves, The.
Trash Men, The.
Vegas.

Bulcke, Karl
There Is an Old City.

Bulfinch, Stephen Greenleaf
Hail to the Sabbath Day.

Bulkeley, Peter, the Younger
Like to the Grass That's Green Today.

Bull, Arthur J.
Eve.

Buller, Arthur
Limerick: "There was a young lady named [*or* called] Bright," at.
There was a young lady called Bright, *sel.*

Bullett, Gerald
Footnote to Tennyson.

Bulley, Anne
Leave Poem.

Bullins, Ed
When Slavery Seems Sweet.

Bullokar, William
To His Child.

Buluguru
Working Song.

Bulwer-Lytton, Robert
Changes.

Bulwer-Lytton, Edward Robert, 1st Earl of Lytton. *See* **"Meredith, Owen"**

Bumstead, Eudora S.
Summer Lullaby, A.

Bunan
To One Who Hankers after Buddhahood.
To One Who Reveres Buddhism.
Waka on Seeing and Hearing Directly.

Bunch, David R.
Of Time and Us.
On Passing by Those Icy Stones (and Yes, Columbia!).

Bungay, George W.
Creeds of the Bells.

Bunge, Patricia
Clerihew: "Scarlett O'Hara/ in time came to care a."

Bunin, Ivan
Flax.

Bunki, Ozaki. *See* **Ozaki Bunki.**

Bunner, Alice Learned
Immutabilis, *sel.*
Separation, *sel.*

Bunner, Henry Cuyler
Appeal to Harold, The.
Behold the Deeds!
Chaperon, The.
Deaf.
Feminine.
Heart of the Tree, The.
"Home, Sweet Home," with Variations ("As sea-foam blown of the winds, as blossom of brine that is drifted"), *par.*
"Home, Sweet Home," with Variations ("Brown o' San Juan"), *par.*
"Home, Sweet Home," with Variations ("Mid pleasures and palaces though we may roam"), *par.*
J. B.
Les Morts Vont Vite.
Old Flag, The.
On Reading a Poet's First Book.
One, Two, Three.
Pitcher of Mignonette, A.
Poetry and the Poet.
Shake, Mulleary, and Go-ethe.
To a June Breeze.
Way to Arcady, The.

Bunrin
Right next to a mud turtle a frog.

Bunsoku
His tail fell off, but the frog.

Bunting, Basil
Brag, sweet tenor bull, *sel.*
Chomei at Toyama.
Coda, *sel.*
Complaint of the Morpethshire Farmer, The.
Fearfull Symmetry.
Fishermen.
Gin the Goodwife Stint.
Grass caught in willow tells the flood's height, *sel.*
Light lifts from the water, *sel.*
On the Fly-Leaf of Pound's Cantos.
Orotava Road, The.
To Violet [with Prewar Poems]
What the Chairman Told Tom.
Word, The.

Bunya Yasuhide. *See* **Yasuhide.**
Bunyan, John
He that is down needs fear no fall, *sel.*
My Little Bird.
Neither Hook nor Line.
Of the Boy and Butterfly.
Of the Cuckoo.
Of the Going Down of the Sun.
Time and Eternity.
Upon a Ring of Bells.
Upon the Horse and His Rider.
Upon the Lark and the Fowler.
Upon the [*or* a] Snail.
Upon the Swallow.
Upon the Weathercock.
What danger is the pilgrim in, *sel.*
Who would true valour see, *sel.*
Buonarroti. *See* **Michelangelo Buonarroti.**
Burbank, Elevena
I Danced to the Rumble of the Drum.
Burbidge, Thomas
She Bewitched Me.
Burch, F. F.
X-Rated.
Burden, Jean
Poem before Departure.
Burdett, Robert J.
When My Ship Comes In.
Burdette, Robert Jones
Limerick: "There was a young man of Cohoes."
Orphan Born.
Russian and Turk.
"Soldier, Rest!"
Burdick, Arthur J.
Washington's Birthday.
Burford, Barbara
Manumission.
Reflections.
Scheherazade.
September Blue.
You.
Burford, William
Christmas Tree, A.
On the Apparition of Oneself.
Burge, Maureen
Diet, The.
Disillusion.
Burgess, Anthony
Lines: Inspired by the Controversy on the Value or Otherwise of Old English Studies.
Burgess, Gelett
Abstemia.
Abstrosophy.
Ah, Yes, I Wrote the "Purple Cow."
Felicia Ropps.
I seen a dunce of a poet once, a-writin' a little book, *sel.*
Invisible Bridge, The.
Lazy Roof, The.
Limerick: "I wish that my room had a floor."
Limerick: "I'd rather have habits than clothes."
Low Trick, A.
My Feet.
Nonsense Quatrains: "I sent my Collie to the wash."
On Digital Extremities.
On Drawing-Room Amenities.
Psycholophon.
Purple Cow, The.
Radical Creed, A.
Sunset, The.
Table Manners.
Trapping fairies in West Virginia.
Woman's Reason, A.
Burgess, George
Harvest Dawn Is Near, The.
While o'er the Deep Thy Servants Sail.
Burgess, Joseph
Ten Heawrs a Day.

Burghley, William Cecil, Lord
To Mistress Anne Cecil, upon Making Her a New Year's Gift, January 1, 1567-8.
Burgon, John William
Pedra.
Written on the Plain of Thebes.
Burgos, Juan Sáez
That Poem.
Burgos, Julia de
Call Out My Number.
Pentachromatic.
Poem to My Death.
Poem with the Final Tune.
Río Grande de Loíza.
To Julia de Burgos.
Burgoyne, Arthur G.
"Everybody Works but Father" as W. S. Gilbert Would Have Written It.
Burgunder, Rose
Boy's Place, A.
Joyful.
Buri, Monique
Train to Hell, The.
Burkard, Michael
Feeling from the Sea, A.
Star for a Glass.
Story of Marie, The.
Strangely Insane.
Time When the Day Ended.
Your Voice.
Burke, James
Missionary Hymm.
Burke, Kenneth
Civil Defense.
Frigate Jones, the Pussyfooter ("Frigate Jones was very slow and fat").
Know Thyself.
Nursery Rhyme.
Burket, Gail Brook
From Countless Hearts.
So Touch Our Hearts with Loveliness.
Burkholder, Clarence M.
Easter Beatitudes.
Burleigh, William Henry
Abide Not in the Realm of Dreams.
Lead Us, O Father, in the Paths of Peace.
Weaver, The.
Burnand, Sir Francis Cowley
Oh, My Geraldine.
Tubby or not tubby—there's the rub.
Burnat-Provins, Marguerite
Fruits you give me are more savory than others, The.
Sylvius, your hands near my mouth are heady flowers.
You told me: "I am not worthy of you."
Burnet, Dana
Marching Song.
Road to Vagabondia, The.
Burns, Diane
Big Fun.
DOA in Dulse.
Gadoshkibos.
Our People.
Sure You Can Ask Me a Personal Question.
Burns, Jim
End Bit, The.
Burns, Michael
Drunken Satyr from Newton County Tells How He Met Daphne, A.
Burns, Richard
Angels.
Mandelstam.
Burns, Robert
Address to the Deil.
Address to the Unco Guid, or the Rigidly Righteous.
Ae Fond Kiss.
Anna.
As I Came O'er Cairney Mount.
Auld Lang Syne.

Banks o'Doon, The.
Birks of Aberfeldy, The.
Bonnie Lesley.
Book-Worms, The.
Ca' the Yowes.
Charlie, He's My Darling.
Child's Grace, A.
Chloe.
Comin' thro' the Rye.
Cotter's Saturday Night, The.
Dead Player, The.
Death and Doctor Hornbook.
Drinking Song, *sel.*
Duncan Gray ("Duncan Gray cam here to woo").
Epistle to a Young Friend.
Epistle to John Lapraik an Old Scottish Bard.
Epitaph on a Schoolmaster.
Epitaph on James Grieve, Laird of Boghead.
Epitaph on John Dove.
Exciseman, The.
Farewell, The: It Was A' for Our Rightfu' King.
For A' That and A' That .
Flow Gently, Sweet Afton.
Gie the Lass her Fairin.'
Godly Girzie.
Grace after Dinner.
Grace at Kirkudbright.
Green Grow the Rashes, O.
Guid-Mornin to Your Majesty!, *sel.*
Head pure, sinless quite of brain or soul, A.
Here cursing swearing Burton lies.
Highland Harry Back Again, at.
Highland Mary.
Holy Fair, The.
Holy Willie's Prayer.
How Can I Keep My Maidenhead.
How daur ye ca' me "Howlet-face."
Hunting Song.
I am a bard of no regard, *sel.*
I Once Was a Maid, *sel.*
Inventory, in Answer to the Usual Mandate Sent by a Surveyor of the Taxes, Requiring a Return of the Number of Horses, Servants, Carriages, etc., Kept, The.
John Anderson, My Jo.
John Barleycorn.
Jolly Beggars, The.
Justice to Scotland, *at.*
Kirk's Alarm, The.
Lass That Made the Bed for Me, The.
Lo worms enjoy the seat of bliss.
Lord Galloway.
Lovely Lass o' Inverness, The.
Man's Inhumanity to Man.
Mary Morison.
Morality, thou deadly bane, *sel.*
Mother's Lament for the Death of Her Son, A.
Mourn, ye wee songsters o' the wood, *sel.*
Muirland Meg.
My Ain Kind Dearie, O.
My Heart's in the Highlands.
My Luve's like a Red, Red Rose.
My Nannie's Awa'.
Nine Inch Will Please a Lady.
No more of your titled acquaintances boast.
O Mally's Meek, Mally's Sweet.
O Were My Love Yon Lilac Fair.
O [*or* Oh], Wert Thou in the Cauld Blast.
O'er the Water to Charlie.
Of A' the Airts [the Wind Can Blaw]
Oh, My Love Is Like a Red, Red Rose.
On a Dog of Lord Eglinton's.
On a Noisy Polemic.
On a Wag in Mauchline.
On Elphinston's Translation of Martial.
On Lord Galloway.
On Mr. Pitt's Hair-Powder Tax.

On Scaring Some Waterfowl in Loch Turit, a
    Wild Scene among the Hills of Oughtertyre.
On the Birth of a Posthumous Child, Born in
    Peculiar Circumstances of Family Distress.
Open the Door to Me, Oh!
Parson's Looks, The.
Patriarch, The.
Poet's Grace, A.
Poet's Welcome to His Love-begotten
    Daughter, A.
Poor Mailie's Elegy.
Prayer in the Prospect of Death, A.
Prayer under the Pressure of Violent Anguish.
Rantin' Dog, the Daddie o't, The.
Rantin, Rovin Robin.
Red, Red Rose, A.
Rigs o' Barley, The.
Scots Wha Hae [wi' Wallace Bled]
See the smoking bowl before us, sel.
Sic a Wife as Willie Had.
Silver Tassie, The.
Simmer's a Pleasant Time.
So vile was poor Wat, such a miscreant slave.
Sober laverock, warbling wild, The, sel.
Song: "Again rejoicing Nature sees."
Song: My luve is like a red, red rose.
Song: "O once I loved a bonnie lass."
Sonnet upon Sonnets, A.
Such a Parcel of Rogues in a Nation.
Supper Is Na Ready.
Tam Glen.
Tam o' Shanter.
Tam Samson's Elegy.
Thou Ling'ring Star.
To a Louse [on Seeing One on a Lady's
    Bonnet at Church]
To a Mountain Daisy.
To a Mouse on Turning Her Up in Her Nest
    with the Plough, November, 1785 or To a
    Mouse.
To an Artist.
To James Smith.
To Terraughty, on His Birth-Day.
To William Simpson, Ochiltree.
Toad-Eater, The.
Tommie Makes My Tail Toddle.
Tree of Liberty, The.
Twa Bonny Lads.
Verses Intended to Be Written below a Noble
    Earl's Picture.
Vision, The.
Wee Willie Gray.
Wha Is That at My Bower-Door?
When lyart leaves bestrow the yird, sel.
Whistle, and I'll Come to You, My Lad.
Whistle o'er the Lave o't.
Willie Brew'd a Peck o' Maut.
Ye maggots, feed on Willie's brains.

Burnshaw, Stanley
    Bread.
    End of the Flower World (A.D. 2300).
    House in St. Petersburg.
    Isaac.
    Strange.
    Talmudist.
Burr, Amelia Josephine
    Pershing at the Tomb of Lafayette.
Burr, Gray
    Sailing, Sailing.
Burrell, Sophia
    Epigram on Two Ladies.
Burrington, E. H.
    Apostrophe to the Parret.
Burroughs, Alethea S.
    Savannah.
Burroughs, John
    Song of the Toad, The.
    Waiting.
Burroughs, Margaret Goss
    Black Pride.
    Everybody but Me.

Only in This Way.
To Soulfolk.
"Burroughs, Ellen." See **Jewett, Sophie.**
Burroway, Janet
    Scientist, The.
Burrowes, Elizabeth
    O God, Send Men.
Bursk, Christopher
    First Aid at 4 A.M.
Burstein, Abraham
    Love of Hell, The.
Burt, Bates G.
    O God of Youth.
Burt, Della
    Little Girl's Dream World, A.
    On the Death of Lisa Lyman.
    Spirit Flowers.
Burt, J. F. A.
    Southward Bound.
Burt, Struthers
    My People Came to This Country.
Burton, Henry
    Jesus Himself.
    Pass It On.
Burton, John
    Holy Bible, Book Divine.
Burton, Richard
    Black Sheep.
    Extras.
    First Song, The.
    Forefather, The.
    God's Garden.
    Idols.
    In Sleep.
    Love Is Strong.
    Old Santa Fe Trail, The.
    On a Ferry Boat.
    Polar Quest, The.
    Song of the Unsuccessful, The.
    Unpraised Picture, An.
Burton, Robert
    Authors Abstract of Melancholy, The, sel.
Busch, Wilhelm
    Bird is tangled in a tree, A.
Bush, Barney
    Another Old Song.
    Autumn Warrior.
    Blood.
    Directions in Our Blood.
    Her Voice.
    It Is Finished.
    Leaving Oklahoma Again.
    Memory Sire, The.
    Taking a Captive/ 1984.
    Voice in the Blood.
    Voyeur's Dream.
    Whose Voice.
Bushnell, Frances Louisa
    In the Dark.
    Unfulfillment.
    World Music.
Buson (Taniguchi Buson)
    As the tides flow, in the rain, sel.
    At Kaya in Tamba, sel.
    Bandit chief composes a tanka, The, sel.
    Barrier guard's brazier, The, sel.
    Burnt in the fireplace, sel.
    Butterfly settles on the neckplate, A, sel.
    Camellia drops and spills, A, sel.
    Chipped away, the moon disappears, sel.
    Chopping with an ax, sel.
    Coming out of the dark of the short night, sel.
    Coming out of the privy, sel.
    Conversation.
    Coolness: separating from a bell.
    Dead of winter: crows are black, sel.
    Deep in a windless/ wood.
    Departing spring: a boat with brushwood, sel.
    Departing spring: I've lost the eyeglasses, sel.
    Departing spring: on the carriage, sel.
    Distant from warblers all day, sel.

Each time a wave rolls in, sel.
Even the floating weeds sink, sel.
Evening downpour: clutching grass blades,
    sel.
Evening wind: the water strikes, sel.
Flowing in the spring rain, sel.
Flying kite, in the spot in the sky, A, sel.
Footfall of someone I wait for, The, sel.
For white plum blossoms, sel.
From the acorns on a round tray, sel.
Fuji alone.
Gleaners walk toward where the sunlight is,
    The, sel.
Huge gate and its heavy doors, A, sel.
I buy scallions and go home through leafless
    trees, sel.
I look around: humans like green stalks, sel.
I mistook a warbler for a sparrow, sel.
In a water pail, nodding at each other, sel.
In an old pond a frog, sel.
In an old pond a sandal lies sunken, sel.
In the autumn dusk a woman, sel.
In the candlelight in my hand, sel.
In the pear orchard someone stands, sel.
Into the darkness of an old well, sel.
Leaving my gate, I too am someone, sel.
Lightning spills a noise, sel.
Lonely—still, I've forgotten, sel.
Looking at a passing cloud, sel.
Love in many forms, sel.
May rain: in front of a wide river.
May rain: in front of a wide river, sel.
May rain: paddy by paddy, sel.
May rain: the muddy water thrusts, sel.
Moon about to set, The, sel.
Moon after rain—who's that!
Moon at heaven's center, sel.
Morning glories: a single flower, sel.
Mosquito-buzz.
Mosquito whirs each time, A, sel.
Mountains are low, The, sel.
Mountains darkened, The, sel.
Mountains, darkening, have robbed, sel.
Mourning for My Teacher Hokuju.
Not yet dark, but stars glitter, sel.
Old Man's Thoughts, An ("Lonelier still than
    last year"), sel.
On the one-ton temple bell.
On the temple bell.
Path ending, a fragrance, The, sel.
Peony in a wide garden, sel.
Piercing Chill I Feel, The.
Rape flowers: the moon in the east, sel.
Roof repairman steps on dead leaves, The,
    sel.
Running out of the nets.
Scampering over saucers.
Settled on a temple bell and asleep, sel.
Short night: on a hairy caterpillar, sel.
Shower silently wets the roots, A, sel.
Sitting at an edge, sel.
Sparks from a stonemason, sel.
Spring at dusk, sel.
Spring rain:/ A man lives here.
Spring rain:/ In our sedan.
Spring rain:/ Soaking on the roof.
Spring rain:/ Telling a tale as they go.
Spring rain: small clams, sel.
Spring rain: telling stories, sel.
Spring sea sloshes, The, sel.
Spring water flows through the mountainless
    land, sel.
Spring water flows, wetting violets, sel.
Stonemason cools his chisels, The, sel.
Suburb ("A woodland of silent oak trees"),
    sel.
Suburb ("Cold moon: amidst dead trees"), sel.
Suburb ("Heat haze: a bug I don't know"),
    sel.
Sudden shower.
Summer mountains: across the span of Kyoto,
    sel.

Swimming, a frog looks as if, *sel.*
That the autumn has come, *sel.*
Though divorced, she steps, *sel.*
Waking from a nap, *sel.*
Walking a flatland and weary, *sel.*
Warrior walks, A, *sel.*
Waving flies off a sick man's shoulders, *sel.*
White dew: one drop on each prickle, *sel.*
Winter wind: blowing pebbles, *sel.*
Winter wind: pebbles in a plowed field, *sel.*
Winter wind: the voice of water, *sel.*
Young leaves have left Fuji, The, *sel.*

Buson *and* **Kito**
Peony Fallen.

Bussan, Murakami. *See* **Murakami Bussan.**

Busse, Carl
In the Night of the Full Moon.
Quiet Kingdom, The.

Busta, Christine
An Olive Tree in Corfu.
Anatolia.
Angel with the Sun Dial (Cathedral at Chartres), The.
Experiences.
Life,/ preserved in amber.
Life on This Star.
Prodigal Son, The.
Raymondsville.
Recorded in time/ coming to be.
Salt Gardens.
Scars, touchable.
Under a Reading Lamp.

Bustamante, Cecilia
Birth.
Civil Marriage.
Facts.
Notes.
Resonances.

Butcher, Grace
Hurdler.
Motorcycle Racer Thinks of Quitting.
Young Wrestlers.

Butler, Dinah
Do You Fancy Me?
One Life.
To My Father.

Butler, Guy
Cape Coloured Batman.
Common Dawn.
Giotto's Campanile.
Myths.
Surveyor.

Butler, Jack
Afterglow.
No News at All.
One Reason for Stars.
Preserves.
Subplot.

Butler, Lynne
Man in the Dream Is Death, The.

Butler, Samuel (1612–80)
Argument, The, *sel.*
Ass will with his long ears fray, An.
Authority is a disease, and cure.
Convert's but a fly, that turns about, A.
Description of Holland.
Devil was more generous than Adam, The.
Egyptians say, the sun has twice, The, *sel.*
Far greater numbers have been lost by hopes.
For his religion it was fit, *sel.*
For what mad lover ever died, *sel.*
Godly Casuistry ("The sun had long since in the lap"), *sel.*
Great philosopher did choke, A.
Greatest saints and sinners have been made, The.
How silly were those sages heretofore, *sel.*
Hudibras the Sectarian ("Besides he was a shrewd Philosopher"), *sel.*
Hypocrisy will serve as well.
In mathematic[k]s he is greater, *sel.*

Independent Squire ("A squire he had whose name was Ralph"), *sel.*
Law, The.
Lovers, like wrestlers, when they do not lay, *sel.*
Married man comes nearest to the dead, A.
Metaphysical Sectarian, The ("He was in logick a great critic"), *sel.*
O God! O Montreal!
On William Prynne.
Portrait of Sidrophel, *sel.*
Presbyterian Church Government ("Synods are whelps of the Inquisition"), *sel.*
Question then, to state it first, The, *sel.*
Quoth he, My faith as adamantine, *sel.*
Quoth he, to bid me not to love, *sel.*
Sidrophel, the Rosicrucian Conjurer ("This said, he turned about his steed"), *sel.*
Some were for setting up a king, *sel.*
There is a tall long-sided dame, *sel.*
This place (quoth she) they say's enchanted, *sel.*
What makes a knave a child of God, *sel.*
What makes all subjects discontent.
When civil fury first grew high, *sel.*

Butler, Samuel (1835–1902)
O God! O Montreal!
Prayer, A: "Searcher of souls, you who in heaven abide."
Righteous Man, The.

Butler, William Allen
Incognita of Raphael.
Nothing to Wear.

Butterfield, Frances Westgate
Time Out.

Butterworth, Hezekiah
Bird with a Broken Wing, The.
Church of the Revolution, The.
Death of Jefferson, The.
First Voyage of John Cabot, The.
Five Kernels of Corn.
Fountain of Youth, The.
Garfield's Ride at Chickamauga.
Legend of Waukulla, The.
Ortiz.
Roger Williams.
Thanksgiving for America, The.
Thanksgiving in Boston Harbor, The.
Verazzano.
Whitman's Ride for Oregon.

"Buttle, Myra" (Victor William Williams Saunders Purcell)
Sunday is the dullest day, treating, *sel.*

Butts, Antony
Massenet/ Never wrote a Mass in A.

Butts, Mary Frances
Christmas Trees, The.
In Galilee.
Million Little Diamonds, A.

Buzea, Constanta
I'm Not Here/ Never Was.

Byatt, Howard
Death.

Bye, Reed
Spring.

Byer, Kathryn Stripling
All Hallows Eve.

Byers, Samuel H. M.
Sherman's March to the Sea.
With Corse at Allatoona.

Byles, Mather
Great God, How Frail a Thing Is Man.
Great God, Thy Works.
To Thee the Tuneful Anthem Soars.
When Wild Confusion Wrecks the Air.

Bynner, Witter ("Emanuel Morgan")
Aged Fisherman.
Arrowy Dreams.
Autumn Walk, An.
Defeat.
Driftwood.

Ecce Homo.
Grieve Not for Beauty ("Grieve not for the invisible, transported brow").
I Need No Sky.
Lines to Do with Youth.
New God, The, *sel.*
Pittsburgh.
Poet, The.
Prayer: "Let us not look upon."
Republic to Republic.
Sandpiper, The.
To a President.

Byrd, William
Quiet Life, The, *at.*

Byrom, John
Careless Content.
Dear Martin Folkes, dear scholar, brother, friend, *sel.*
Epigram on the Feuds between Handel and Bononcini.
Four Epigrams on the Naturalization Bill.
Hymn for Christmas Day, A.
Hymn on the Omnipresence, An.
Jacobite Toast.
My Dog Tray.
My Spirit Longeth for Thee.
On Clergymen Preaching Politics.
On the Origin of Evil.
On Two Monopolists.
To Henry Wright of Mobberley, Esq. on Buying the Picture of Father Malebranche.
Tom the Porter.

Byron, Abel
On a Carrier Who Died of Drunkenness.

Byron, George Gordon Noel Byron, 6th Baron
Alas, the country! how shall tongue or pen, *sel.*
All Is Vanity, Saith the Preacher.
And Angling, Too, *sel.*
And Thou Art Dead.
Answer to — — —'s Professions of Affection.
As Sisyphus against the infernal steep, *sel.*
At length with jostling, elbowing, and the aid, *sel.*
At Thirty Years, *sel.*
Behold! in various throngs the scribbling crew, *sel.*
Beppo; a Venetian Story.
Bright Be the Place of Thy Soul!
But thou, false infidel! shall writhe, *sel.*
Childe Harold's Farewell to England, *sel.*
Cornelian, The.
Darkness.
Death of Haidée, The, *sel.*
Dedication: "Bob Southey! You're a poet— poet-laureate," *sel.*
Dedication: To Ianthe, *sel.*
Destruction of Sennacherib, The.
Donna Julia, *sel.*
Dream, The.
Dying Gladiator, The, *sel.*
Elegy: "O [*or* Oh] snatch'd away in beauty's bloom!"
England! with all thy faults I love thee still, *sel.*
Epilogue: "There's something in a stupid ass."
Epistle to Augusta.
Epistle to Mr. Murray.
Epitaph for Castlereagh, An.
Epitaph for William Pitt.
Epitaph to a Dog.
Evening, *sel.*
Fame, *sel.*
Fare Thee Well.
Farewell! If Ever Fondest Prayer.
Farewell to Malta.
Fourth day came, but not a breath of air, The, *sel.*
Fragment: "I would to heaven that I were so much clay," *sel.*

George the Third, *sel.*
Growing old, *sel.*
Gulbeyaz, *sel.*
Haidée, *sel.*
Haidée and Don Juan, *sel.*
Hail, Muse! et caetera.—We left Juan
     sleeping, *sel.*
He that has sail'd upon the dark blue sea, *sel.*
I know that what our neighbours call
     longueurs, sel.
I stood in Venice on the Bridge of Sighs, *sel.*
I want a hero: an uncommon want, *sel.*
I wonder if his appetite was good?, *sel.*
Illustrious Holland! hard would be his lot, *sel.*
Immortal Mind, The.
In her first passion woman loves her lover,
     sel.
In him inexplicably mixed appeared, *sel.*
In Nottingham county there lives at Swan
     Green.
In the great world—which, being interpreted,
     sel.
Inscription on the Monument of a
     Newfoundland Dog.
Is thy face like thy mother's, my fair child!,
     sel.
Isles of Greece, The, *sel.*
Isolation of Genius, The.
It Is the Hush of Night, *sel.*
Italy, *sel.*
Juan embark'd—the ship got under way, *sel.*
Juan in England, *sel.*
Juan knew several languages—as well, *sel.*
Kind of change came in my fate, A, *sel.*
Lachin y Gair.
Lady Adeline Amundeville, *sel.*
Lake Leman woos me with its crystal face,
     sel.
"Let there be light!" said God, and there was
     light!, *sel.*
Lines on Hearing That Lady Byron Was Ill.
Lines Written beneath a Picture.
Lisbon Packet, The.
Love and Death.
Maid of Athens [Ere We Part]
Manfred.
Mazeppa.
Milton's the prince of poets—so we say, *sel.*
Muse of the many-twinkling feet! whose
     charms, *sel.*
My Days of Love Are Over, *sel.*
Newstead Abbey.
Nurse's Dole in the Medea, The.
O love! O glory! what are you who fly, *sel.*
Ocean, *sel.*
Ode to the Framers of the Frame Bill, An.
Oh love! no habitant of earth thou art, *sel.*
Oh, thou! in Hellas deemed of heavenly birth,
     sel.
Oh Wellington! (Or "Villainton," for Fame),
     sel.
Oh ye! who teach the ingenuous youth of
     nations, *sel.*
Old Lambro pass'd unseen a private gate, *sel.*
On Jordan's Bank.
On My Thirty-third Birthday.
On, on the vessel flies, the land is gone, *sel.*
On the Bust of Helen by Canova.
On This Day I Complete My Thirty-sixth
     Year.
Over the stones still rattling, up Pall Mall,
     sel.
Poet and the World, The, *sel.*
Poetical Commandments, *sel.*
Prisoner of Chillon, The.
Prometheus.
Remember Thee! Remember Thee!
Romantic to Burlesque, *sel.*
Rome by Metella's Tomb, *sel.*
Sagest of women, even of widows, she, *sel.*
Saint Peter sat by the celestial gate, *sel.*
She Walks in Beauty.

Shore looked wild, without a trace of man,
     The, *sel.*
Sketch from Private Life, A.
So We'll Go No More a-Roving.
Sonnet on Chillon, *sel.*
Sonnet to Lake Leman.
Stanzas for Music.
Stanzas to a Lady, with the Poems of
     Camoëns.
Stanzas to Augusta.
Stanzas to the Po.
Stanzas Written on the Road between Florence
     and Pisa.
Stars are forth, the moon above the tops, The,
     sel.
Stop! for thy tread is on an empire's dust!,
     sel.
Sunset over the Ægean.
Swimming, *sel.*
The Tear.
There was a sound of revelry by night, *sel.*
They Say That Hope Is Happiness.
They were alone once more; for them to be,
     sel.
This day of all our days has done.
Though somewhat large, exuberant, and
     truculent, *sel.*
'Tis thus with people in an open boat, *sel.*
To Eddleston, *sel.*
To Mr. Murray.
To My Son.
To our theme.—The man who has stood on
     the Acropolis, *sel.*
To Thomas Moore.
'Twas on a summer's day—the sixth of June,
     sel.
Vision of Belshazzar, The.
Vision of Judgment, The.
Wandering Outlaw, The, *sel.*
Washington, *sel.*
When a man hath no freedom to fight for at
     home.
When some brisk youth, the tenant of a stall,
     sel.
When We Two Parted.
"Where is the world!" cries Young at eighty,
     sel.
Who Kill'd John Keats?
Why call the miser miserable?, *sel.*
Wild, the Free, The.
William Lisle Bowles, *sel.*
World Is a Bundle of Hay, The.
Written after Swimming from Sestos to
     Abydos.
You know, or you don't know, that great
     Bacon saith, *sel.*
Young unmarried man, with a good name, A,
     sel.

Byron, Henry James
Adage, An: "Gardener's rule applies to youth
     and age, The."
Rural Simplicity.

Byron, William
So the struck eagle, stretch'd upon the plain.

C

"C., E."
Emaricdulfe.
My Heart Is like a Ship, *sel.*
Within Her Hair, *sel.*

"C., J."
Frailty of Beauty, The, *sel.*

C———, Mme De
Letter to Madame la Marquise de S[imiane],
     on Sending Her Tobacco.

"C. A. L. T."   *See* T. C. A. L.
"C. A. W."   *See* "W. C. A."
"C. B. B."   *See* "B., C. B."
"C. G. H."   *See* "H., C. G."
"C. N. S."   *See* "S., C. N."
"C. T."   *See* "T., C."
"C. W. T."   *See* "T., C. W."
Cabalquinto, Luis
     Big One, The.
     Blue Tropic.
     Eating Lechon, with My Brothers and Sisters.
     Flower Vendor, The.
     Hometown.
Cabell, James Branch
     Story of the Flowery Kingdom.
Cable, George Washington
     New Arrival, The.
     Written in the Visitors' Book at the Birthplace
       of Robert Burns.
Cabral de Melo Neto, Joaõ.   *See* **Melo Neto,**
     Joaõ Cabral de
Caddy, John
     Passage Rite.
     World War II Premium from Battle Creek, A.
Cadenet
     Once I was lovely, had renown.
Cadnum, Michael
     Dislike for Flowers, A.
Caedmon
     Approach of Pharaoh, The, *sel.*
     Caedmon's Hymn.
     Hymn: "Now we must praise
       heaven-kingdom's Guardian."
     Noah's Flood, *sel.*
     Son of Lamech let a black raven, The, *sel.*
     Temptation and Fall of Man, The, *sel.*
Cage, John
     Writing through a Text by Chris Mann.
Cairncross, Thomas S.
     Grey Galloway.
Cakalacanar
     What She Said to Him, after Meeting His
       Concubine.
Calder, Dave
     At Kirk Yetholm.
     On Passing by Those Icy Stones (and Yes,
       Columbia!).
     Under dream interrogation.
Calderón de la Barca, Pedro
     Dream Called Life, The.
     Thou Art of All Created Things.
     We live, while we see the sun, *sel.*
Calhoun, John
     Peter Amberley.
Call, Frank Oliver
     Blue Homespun.
     Old Habitant, An.
Call, Wathen Mark Wilks
     Renunciation.
     Summer Days.
Callimachus
     Art thou the grave of Charidas? If for
       Arimmas' son, *sel.*
     Crethis.
     His Son.
     Saon of Acanthus.
     Sopolis.
     To Archinus.
Callinus
     Call to Action, A.
Calmis, Charlotte
     Am I Not the Lacemaker of Shadow.
     V.
Calverley, Charles Stuart
     And, if you asked of him to say, *sel.*
     Arcades Ambo.
     Ballad: "Auld wife sat at her ivied door,
       The."
     Beer.
     But hark! a sound is stealing on my ear, *sel.*
     Cat, The, *sel.*

Changed.
Cock and the Bull, The.
Companions.
Contentment.
Disaster.
Dover to Munich.
First Love.
"Forever."
Hic Vir, Hic Est.
In the Gloaming.
Lines on Hearing the Organ.
Love.
Lovers, and a Reflection.
Morning.
Motherhood.
Ode to Tobacco.
On the Beach.
Palace, The.
Peace.
Proverbial Philosophy: Of Reading.
Sad Memories.
Schoolmaster Abroad with His Son, The.
Striking.
Wanderers.
Calvert, George Henry
Bunker Hill.
Calvin, John
Salutation to Jesus Christ.
Cambridge, Ada
Faith.
Oh, to be there to-night!, *sel.*
Cambridge, Richard Owen
Fakir, The.
Camden, William
On a Puritanicall Lock-Smith.
Camerino, Aldo
Calm.
Fear.
For a Voice That Is Singing.
Mother.
Night.
Recluse.
Cameron, George Frederick
Ah Me! the Mighty Love.
Future, The.
In After Days.
Standing on Tiptoe.
Cameron, Norman
Compassionate Fool, The.
Dirty Little Accuser, The.
Disused Temple, The.
Firm of Happiness, Limited, The.
For the Fly-Leaf of a School-Book.
Forgive Me, Sire.
From a Woman to a Greedy Lover, *sel.*
Green, Green Is El Aghir.
Hook for Leviathan, A.
In the Queen's Room, *sel.*
She and I.
Shepherdess, *sel.*
Thespians at Thermopylae, The.
Unfinished Race, The.
Verdict, The.
Camille, Roussan
Nocturne: "Wildness of haggard flights."
Camões [or Camoens], Luis de
Babylon and Sion (Goa and Lisbon).
Dear gentle soul, who went so soon away.
Now through the ocean in great haste they flunder, *sel.*
On Revisiting Cintra after the Death of Catarina.
On the Death of Catarina de Attayda.
Shores are crown'd with people, The, *sel.*
Sonnet: "Leave me, all sweet refrains my lip hath made."
Sonnet: "Time and the mortal will stand never fast."
Camp, James
Bruckner.
Claritas.

Female Dancer.
Figure in the Carpet, The.
Fruits of Retirement, The.
Campana, Dino
Chimera, The.
Genoa Woman.
In a moment/ The roses have faded, *sel.*
Sonnet: Autumn Garden.
Campanella, Tomasso
People, The.
Campbell, Alice B.
Sally and Manda.
Campbell, Alistair
Against Te Rauparaha, *sel.*
Akaotu.
At a Fishing Settlement.
Aunt Lucrezia.
Bitter Harvest.
Blue Rain.
Daisy Pinks.
Dark Lord of Savaiki, The.
Dreams, Yellow Lions.
Gathering Mushrooms.
Gunfighter, The.
Hut near Desolated Pines.
Laid-out Body, The, *sel.*
Looking at Kapiti.
Mahuta.
Memo to Mr. Auden, 29/8/66.
My Mother.
Now He Is Dead, *sel.*
Purple Chaos.
Return, The.
Sina.
Stranger from Rakahanga, A.
Waiting for the Pakeha.
Why Don't You Talk to Me?
Wild Honey.
Campbell, Archibald Y.
Murie Sing.
Campbell, Calder
Ossian's Serenade.
Campbell, David
Ariel.
Australian Dream, The.
End of Exploring, The.
Fox.
Harry Pearce.
Men in Green.
Mr. Hughes.
Night Sowing.
On Frosty Days.
Pallid Cuckoo.
Speak with the Sun.
Ulinda.
Campbell, Donald
Hauf-Roads up Schiehallion.
Campbell, George
History Makers.
Holy.
In the Slums.
Campbell, James Edwin
Compensation.
De Cunjah Man.
Negro Serenade.
Ol' Doc' Hyar.
Uncle Eph's Banjo Song.
When Ol' Sis' Judy Pray.
Campbell, Joseph
Every Shuiler Is Christ.
Herb-Leech, The.
I Am the Gilly of Christ.
I Am the Mountainy Singer.
I Will Go with My Father a-Ploughing.
O Glorious Childbearer.
When Rooks Fly Homeward.
Campbell, Joseph (Seosamh MacCathmhaoil)
Ad Limina.
Antiquary, The.
As I Came Over the Grey, Grey Hills.
Blind Man at the Fair, The.

Dancer, The.
Darkness.
Gombeen, The.
Harvest Song.
Ideal and Reality.
Old Age Pensioner, The.
Old Woman, The.
Unfrocked Priest, The.
Campbell, Marion
Levavi Oculos.
Campbell, Marjorie Freeman
Only the Heart.
Vigil.
Campbell, Meg
Journeys.
Maui.
Campbell, Roy
Attend my fable if your ears be clean, *sel.*
Autumn.
Ballad of Don Juan Tenorio and the Statue of the Comendador.
Buffel's Kop.
Choosing a Mast.
Driving Cattle to Casas Buenas.
Fishing Boats in Martigues.
Georgian Spring.
Good Resolution, A.
Hail, mediocrity, beneath whose spell, *sel.*
Heartbreak Camp.
Here, where relumed by changing seasons, burn, *sel.*
Horses on the Camargue.
Luis de Camões.
Mass at Dawn.
Maternal Earth stirs redly from beneath, *sel.*
Next him Jack Squire through his own tear-drops sploshes, *sel.*
On Professor Drennan's Verse.
On Some South African Novelists.
On the Same.
Palm, The.
Rounding the Cape.
Secret Muse, The.
Serf, The.
Sisters, The.
Theology of Bongwi, the Baboon, The.
To the Sun, *sel.*
Toledo.
Tristan da Cunha.
Veld Eclogue: The Pioneers, A.
Zebras, The.
Zulu Girl, The.
Campbell, Thomas
At summer eve, when Heaven's ethereal bow, *sel.*
Battle of the Baltic.
Dead Eagle, The.
Epistle, from Algiers, to Horace Smith.
Freedom and Love.
Hallowed Ground.
Hohenlinden.
Jilted Nymph, The.
Last Man, The.
Lines on Leaving a Scene in Bavaria.
Lochiel's Warning ("Lochiel, Lochiel! beware of the day").
Lord Ullin's Daughter.
Maid of Neidpath, The.
Napoleon and the British Sailor.
Ode to Winter.
Parrot, The.
River of Life, The.
Soldier's Dream, The.
The Irish Harper and His Dog.
To the Evening Star.
Ye Mariners of England.
Campbell, Wilfred
Bereavement of the Fields.
Vapour and Blue.
Campbell, Wilfred (William Wilfred Campbell)
Hills and the Sea, The.

How One Winter Came in the Lake Region.
Indian Summer.
Morning on the Shore.
Winter Lakes, The.
With Cortez in Mexico.

Campert, Remco
City Park.
Hurrah, Hurrah.
Imagine.
Letters.
1975.
Poetry Is an Act.
President in His Country Residence, A.
Sparrows.
This Happened Everywhere.
Tuft by Tuft.
Would You Believe It?

Campion, Thomas
And Would You See My Mistress' Face? *at.*
Are you what your faire lookes expresse?
Author of light, revive my dying spright.
Awake, Awake!
Be thou then my beauty named.
Beauty, Since You So Much Desire.
Blame not my cheeks, though pale with love they be.
Breake now my heart and dye! Oh no, she may relent.
Come, Cheerful Day!
Come, You Pretty False-eyed Wanton.
Content.
Dance, The, *at.*
Dove alone expresses, The, *sel.*
Elegye, An: "Constant to none, but ever false to me."
Fain Would I Wed.
First Love.
Follow, follow.
Follow Thy Fair Sun [Unhappy Shadow]
Follow Your Saint [Follow with Accents Sweet]
Give beauty all her right.
Harden now thy tyred hart with more then flinty rage.
Hark, All You Ladies.
Heart's Music, *at.*
Hours of Sleepy Night, The, *sel.*
Hymn[e] in Praise [*or* Prayse] of Neptune, A.
I Care Not for These Ladies.
I must complain, yet doe enjoy my love.
It Fell on a Summer's Day.
Jack and Joan they think no ill.
Kind Are Her Answers.
Kisses, *at.*
Lamentation, A.
Love Me or Not.
Man of Life Upright, The.
Mistress, Since You So Much Desire.
My Life's Delight.
My Sweetest Lesbia [Let Us Live and Love]
Never Weather-beaten Sail[e]
Now Winter Nights Enlarge.
Raving warre, begot.
Rose-cheeked [*or* cheekt] Laura, Come.
Roses, *sel.*
Secret Love or Two I Must Confess[e], A.
Seek the Lord.
Shall I come, if I swim? wide are the waves, you see.
Shall I Come, Sweet Love, to Thee?
Shall I then hope when faith is fled?
Sleep, Angry Beauty.
So Quick, So Hot, So Mad is Thy Fond Sute.
Stars Dance, The, *sel.*
There Is a Garden in Her Face.
There Is None, O None but You.
Think'st Thou to Seduce Me Then.
Thou Art Not Fair.
Though you are young and I am old.
Though your strangenesse frets my hart.

Thrice Toss [*or* Tosse] These Oaken Ashes in the Air [*or* Ayre]
Thus I Resolve.
To Music Bent Is My Retired Mind.
View Mee, Lord.
Were My Hart as Some Men's Are.
What Faire Pompe.
What If a Day [or a Month or a Year]
When Thou Must Home to Shades of Underground.
When to Her Lute Corinna [*or* Corrina] Sings.
Where are all thy beauties now, all hearts enchaining?
Whether Men Do Laugh or Weep, *at.*

Canales, Tirso
City of San Salvador.
Nocturne for Freedom.

Canan, Janine
Dear Body.

Candiani, Livia
Death of Poetry, The.

Cane, Melville
Dawn Has Yet to Ripple In.
Each to Each.
Harvest to Seduce, A.
Hymn to Night.
Presence of Snow.
Rural Dumpheap.
Snow toward Evening.
Tree in December.

Canfield, Harry Clifford
Entrapped inside a submarine, *sel.*

Cannan, May Wedderburn
Rouen.

Canning, George
Ballynahinch.
Cat and the Bird, The.
Elderly Gentleman, The.
Ipecacuanha.
Mark the dark rook, on pendent branches hung, *sel.*
Political Despatch, A.

Canning, George *and* John Hookham Frere
Friend of Humanity and the Knife Grinder, The.
From mental mists to purge a nation's eyes, *sel.*
Inscription: "For one long term, or e'er her trial came."
Soldiers' Friend, The.
Soldier's Wife, The.

Canning, George , George Ellis *and* John Hookham Frere
Rogero's Song, *sel.*

Cannon, David Wadsworth, Jr.
Freedom in Mah Soul.
Western Town.

Cannon, Edward
Unsuspected Fact, An.

Cannon, Hughie
Bill Bailey, Won't You Please Come Home.

Canton, William
Carol: "When the herd[s] were watching."
Child's Prayer, A.
Day-Dreams.

Cantus, Eleanor Hollister
Fame.

Canzoneri, Robert
Two.

Capern, Edward
My Latest Publication.

Capetanakis, Demetrios
Abel.
Isles of Greece, The.

Caprani, Menotti Vincent
Prizefighter's Prayer, The.

Caragher, Mary E.
Tree Tag.

"Carbery, Ethna" (Anna Johnson MacManus)
King of Ireland's Cairn, The.
Love-Talker, The.
Mea Culpa.
On an Island.

Carden, Ramona
Moccasins of an Old Man, The.
Tumbleweed.

Cardenal, Ernesto
Ecology.
Vision from the Small Blue Window.

Cardenal, Peire
Clerks pretend to be shepherds, and under, The.
Kites and vultures cannot smell out carrion.
Our neighbors are so courteous, worthy and human!
Truth and right are my bases.

Cárdenas, Reyes
Lowriders #2 ("Lowriders/ cruising the barrio").

Cardiff, Gladys
Candelaria and the Sea Turtle.
Carious Exposure.
Combing.
Dragon Skate.
For His Ring and Watch on the Night Stand.
Grey Woman.
Hunting the Dugong.
Leaves like Fish.
Long Person.
Making Lists.
Owl and Rooster.
Swimmer.
Tlanusi' Yi, the Leech Place.
To Frighten a Storm.
Tsa'lagi Council Tree.
Where Fire Burns.

Cardozo, Joaquim
Cemetery of Childhood.
Elegy for Maria Alves.

Carducci, Giosuè
Leave-Taking.
Petrarch.
Primo Vere.
Snow-Storm, A.
Snowfall.

Carenza *and* **Iselda**
Tenson.

Carew, Jan
Cliffs at Manzanilla, The.
Faces and Skulls.
Our Home.

Carew, Richard
River Lynher, The, *sel.*

Carew, Thomas
Another [Epitaph on the Lady Mary Villiers]
Ask Me No More Where Jove Bestows.
Beautifull Mistress, A.
Boldness[e] in Love.
Celia Bleeding, to the Surgeon.
Deposition from Love, A.
Elegy upon the Death of the Dean of St. Paul's, Dr. John Donne, An.
Epitaph on Maria Wentworth.
Epitaph on the Lady Mary Villiers, An.
Eternity of Love Protested.
Excuse of Absence, An.
Fly That Flew into My Mistress's Eye, A.
For a Picture Where a Queen Laments over the Tomb of a Slain Knight.
Good Counsel [*or* Counsell] to a Young Maid.
Good Counsel to a Young Maid ("When you the sunburnt pilgrim see").
Hymeneal Song on the Nuptials of the Lady Anne Wentworth and the Lord Lovelace, An.
Hymeneall Dialogue, An.
Ingrateful [l] Beauty Threatened.
Lady's Prayer to Cupid, A.

Looking-Glass, A.
Lover, upon an Accident Necessitating His
Departure, Consults with Reason, A.
Love's Force.
Maria Wentworth.
New Year's Sacrifice: To Lucinda, A.
On His Mistress Looking in a Glass.
On Sight of a Gentlewoman's Face in the
Water.
On the Death of Donne, sel.
On the Marriage of T. K. and C. C., the
Morning Stormy.
Pastorall Dialogue, A.
Persuasions to Enjoy.
Rapture, A.
Second Rapture, The.
Secrecy [or Secresie] Protested.
Song: Murdring Beautie.
Song: The Willing Prisoner to His Mistress.
Song: To Her Againe, She Burning in a
Feaver.
Song: To One That Desired To Know My
Mistris.
Spring, The.
Tinder, The.
To A. L.: Perswasions to Love.
To a Lady That Desired I Would Love Her.
To Ben Jonson [or Johnson]
To Her in Absence; a Ship.
To My Cousin (C.R.) Marrying My Lady
(A.).
To my Friend G.N., from Wrest.
To My Inconstant Mistress [or Mistris]
To My Mistress Sitting by a River's Side; an
Eddy.
To My Mistresse in Absence.
To My Mistris, I Burning in Love.
To My Worthy Friend Master George Sands [
or Sandys], on His Translation of the
Psalms.
To Saxham.
To T. H., a Lady Resembling My Mistress.
To the King, at His Entrance into Saxham: By
Master John Crofts.
To the New Year.
To the Reader of Master William Davenant's
Play, The Wits.
Upon a Mole in Celia's Bosom.
Upon a Ribband.
Upon Master Walter Montagu's Return from
Travel.
Upon My Lord Chief Justice's Election of My
Lady Anne Wentworth for His Mistress.
Upon Some Alterations in My Mistress, after
My Departure into France.

Carey, Henry
Drinking-Song, A.
God Save the King, at.
Happy Myrtillo.
Huntsman's Rouse, The.
Lilliputian Ode on Their Majesties'
Accession, A.
Namby-Pamby; or, A Panegyric on the New
Versification.
Roger and Dolly.
Sally in Our Alley.
Sally Sweetbread.

Carey, Lady Elizabeth
Fairest action of our human life, The, sel.
'Tis not enough for one that is a wife, sel.

Carey [or Cary], Patrick
And now a fig for the lower house.

Carleton, Sara King
Late October.

Carleton, Will M.
Across the Delaware.
Country Doctor, The.
Cuba to Columbia.
Doctor's Story, The.
Little Black-eyed Rebel, The.
New Church Organ, The.

Out of the Old House, Nancy.
Over the Hill to the Poor-House.
Prize of the *Margaretta*, The.
Victory-Wreck, The.

Carlile, Henry
Dodo.
Fish Story.
Havana Blues.
Listening to Beethoven on the Oregon Coast.
Spider Reeves.

**Carlin, Francis (James Francis Carlin
MacDonnell)**
Perfection.
Plea for Hope.

Carlyle, Thomas
Cui Bono?
Morning.
To-Day.
Today.

Carman, Bliss
Concerning Kavin.
Daffodil's Return.
Daisies, The.
Daphne.
Earth's Lyric.
Eavesdropper, The.
First Julep, The.
Grave-Tree, The.
Gravedigger, The.
Hack and Hew.
Hem and Haw.
Heretic, The.
I Loved Thee, Atthis, in the Long Ago.
I see the golden hunter go, sel.
In a Copy of Browning.
Joys of the Road, The.
Lord of My Heart's Elation.
Lord of the Far Horizons.
Low Tide on Grand Pré.
Man of Peace, The.
More Ancient Mariner, A.
Morning in the Hills.
Mr. Moon.
Nancibel.
Northern Vigil, A.
Old Grey Wall, The.
Overlord.
Resignation.
Rover's Song, A.
Ships of Yule, The.
Spring Song.
Threnody for a Poet.
Trees.
Vagabond Song, A.
Vestigia.
What is it to remember?, sel.
When I Was Twenty.

Carmer, Carl
Antique Shop.

Carmi, T.
Author's Apology, The.
Condition, The.
Examination of Conscience before Going to
Sleep.

Carmichael, Amy
Last Defile, The.

Carmichael, Waverly Turner
Keep Me, Jesus, Keep Me ("Keep me 'neath
Thy mighty wing").
Winter is Coming.

"Carnelian." *See* Coslett, Coslett

Carnevali, Emanuel
Queer Things.
Walt Whitman.

Carney, Julia A. Fletcher
Little Things, at.

Carolan [or O'Carolan], Turlough
Mabel Kelly.
Peggy Browne.

Carolyn
Frog, The.

Caroutch, Yvonne
Child of silence and shadow.
I come to you with the vertigoes of the
source.
Limb of forests rises up, The.
Night opens like an almond.
When we are like two drunken suns.

Carpenter, Amelia Walstien Jolls
Old Flemish Lace.
Recollection.
Ride to Cherokee, The.

Carpenter, Edward
Among the Ferns.
Have Faith.
Love of men for each other, The—so tender,
heroic, constant, sel.
Love's Vision.
Over the Great City.
Songs of the Birds, The.
Stupid Old Body, The.
Through the Long Night, sel.
Wandering Lunatic Mind, The.

Carpenter, Henry Bernard
Reed, The.

Carpenter, Margaret Haley
September Afternoon.

Carpenter, Maurice
To S. T. C. on His 179th Birthday, October
12th, 1951.

Carpenter, Rhys
Master Singers, The.
Who Bids Us Sing?

Carpenter, William
Autumn.
Fire.
Keeper, The.

Carphyllides
Happy Man, A.

Carr, Alan J.
Old Man.

Carr, Frank
Frankenstein Gets His Man.

Carr, John
Memories of Childhood, sel.
Sonnet upon a Swedish Cottage.

Carrier, Constance
At Tripolis.
Black Water and Bright Air.
Commencement.
Fugue.
Lisa.
Pro Patria.
Transformation Scene.

Carrillo, Francisco
All Souls Day.
Composition 1.
I Love My Country.
Procession.
Provincia.
Tannery, The.

Carrington, N. T.
Is she not beautiful? reposing there, sel.

Carroll, Jim
Distances, The.

"Carroll, Lewis" (Charles Lutwidge Dodgson)
Alice's Recitation, sel.
Atalanta in Camden-Town.
Baker's Tale, The, sel.
Beautiful Soup, so rich and green, sel.
Brother and Sister.
Disillusioned.
Evidence Read at the Trial of the Knave of
Hearts, sel.
Facts.
Father William, sel.
Fragment of a Song.
Fury Said to a Mouse, sel.
Hiawatha's Photographing.
His sister named Lucy O'Finner.
How doth the little crocodile, sel.
Hunting of the Snark, The.

I'll tell thee everything I can, *sel.*
In winter, when the fields are white, *sel.*
Jabberwocky, *sel.*
King-Fisher Song, The, *sel.*
Little Birds ("Little birds are playing"), *sel.*
Mad Gardener's Song, The, *sel.*
Mad Hatter's Song, The, *sel.*
Manlet, The.
My dismal sister! Couldst thou know, *sel.*
My Fairy.
Palace of humbug, The.
Pig-Tale, A, *sel.*
Poeta Fit, Non Nascitur.
Quotation from Shakespeare with Slight
  Improvements, A.
Rules and Regulations.
Sea Dirge, A.
She's All My Fancy Painted Him.
Song of Love, A.
Speak roughly to your little boy, *sel.*
Tèma con Variazióni.
There Was a Young Lady of Station.
There was once a young man of Oporta.
Three Badgers, The.
Three Voices, The.
To the Looking-Glass world it was Alice that
  said, *sel.*
Visitor, A.
Walrus and the Carpenter, The, *sel.*
Wasp's Song, The.
"Will you walk a little faster?" said a [*or* the]
  whiting to a [*or* the] snail, *sel.*

Carroll, Paul
  Father.

Carruth, Hayden
  Ah, you beast of love.
  Bouquet in Dog Time.
  Contra Mortem.
  Cows at Night, The.
  Eleanor — — —
  Emergency Haying.
  Fear and Anger in the Mindless Universe.
  Hard Journey, A. Yes.
  Insomniac Sleeps Well for Once and, The.
  Johnny Spain's White Heifer.
  Language As Inevitable Metaphor. Idea As
    Inevitable Figment.
  Late Sonnet.
  Little Fire in the Woods, The.
  Loneliness.
  Mending the Adobe.
  My Father's Face.
  New Orleans.
  No Matter What, after All, and That Beautiful
    Word So.
  On a Certain Engagement South of Seoul.
  Once more by the brook the alder leaves.
  Our Tense and Wintry Minds.
  Post-Impressionist Susurration for the First of
    November, 1983, A.
  Rimrock, Where It Is.
  Salt Lake City.
  Smallish Son, The.
  So be it. I am.
  Sonnet: "Cry, crow."
  Summer's Early End at Hudson Bay.
  "Sure," Said Benny Goodman.
  This Decoration.
  Twilight Comes.
  When Howitzers Began.
  Wherever shadow falls wherever the
    drowning, *sel.*
  Why speak of the use.
  Winds; words of the wind; rumor of great
    walls pierced, *sel.*
  Your tears, Niobe.

Carruth, William Herbert
  Dreamer of Dreams.
  Each in His Own Tongue.

Carryl, Charles Edward
  My Recollectest Thoughts, *sel.*
  Plaint of the Camel, The, *sel.*

Robinson Crusoe, *sel.*
Sleepy Giant, The.
Song in the Dell, The.
Walloping Window-Blind, The, *sel.*

Carryl, Guy Wetmore
  Ballad, A: "As I was walkin' the jungle
    round, a-killin' of tigers an' time."
  Domineering Eagle and the Inventive Bratling,
    The.
  Embarrassing Episode of Little Miss Muffet,
    The.
  How a Girl Was Too Reckless of Grammar
    [by Far]
  How Jack Found That Beans May Go Back
    on a Chap.
  Little Red Riding Hood.
  Singular Sangfroid of Baby Bunting, The.
  Sycophantic Fox and the Gullible Raven, The.
  When the Great Gray Ships Come In.

Carsley, Sara E.
  Little Boats of Britain, The.
  Portrait of a Very Old Man.

Carson, Ciaran
  Belfast Confetti.
  Campaign.
  Car Cemetery, The.
  Dresden.
  Insular Celts, The.
  It Used to Be.

Carson, Mary Newland
  My "Patch of Blue."

Carson, Robert
  Old Sailor Looking at a Container Ship.

Carter, Aline Badger
  Give Our Conscience Light.

Carter, D.
  Mrs. Indiarubber Duck.

Carter, Hodding
  In the Jury Room.
  Slave Story.

Carter, Jared
  At the Sign-Painter's.
  Errata Slip.
  Madhouse, The.
  Purpose of Poetry, The.
  Shriving, The.

Carter, Martin
  As New and as Old.
  Bent.
  For a Man Who Walked Sideways.
  Great Dark, The.
  I come from the nigger yard of yesterday, *sel.*
  Our Number.
  There Is No Riot.
  University of Hunger.

Carter, Sydney
  First of My Lovers, The.
  Lord of the Dance.

Cartwright, Kent
  Scoring.

Cartwright, Peter
  Our Bondage It Shall End, *at.*
  Where Are the Hebrew Children? *at.*

Cartwright, William
  Dead Sparrow, The.
  Falsehood.
  New-Years-Gift to Brian Lord Bishop of
    Sarum, A.
  No Platonic Love.
  On a Virtuous Young Gentlewoman That Died
    Suddenly.
  On the Queen's Return from the Low
    Countries.
  Saint Francis and Saint Benedight, *sel.*
  Song of Dalliance, A.
  To Chloe, Who Wished Herself Young
    Enough for Me.
  Upon the Dramatick Poems of Mr. John
    Fletcher.

Valediction, A: "Bid me not go where neither
  suns nor show'rs."
Women.

Carver, Mabel MacDonald
  Codicil.

Carver, Raymond
  Bobber.
  Catch, The.
  Elk Camp.
  Forever.
  Looking for Work.
  Marriage.
  My Boat.
  Photograph of My Father in His
    Twenty-second Year.
  Prosser.
  Wes Hardin: From a Photograph.
  You Don't Know What Love Is.
  Your Dog Dies.

Cary, Alice
  Among the Beautiful Pictures.
  Balder's Wife.
  Gray Swan, The.
  Her Mother.
  Kemp Owyne.
  My Creed.
  Nobility.
  November.
  Order for a Picture, An.
  To Mother Fairie.

Cary, Patrick
  Whilst I beheld the neck o' th' dove.

Cary, Phoebe
  Ballad of the Canal.
  Day Is Done, The.
  Jacob.
  Keep a Stiff Upper Lip.
  Leak in the Dike, The.
  Legend of the Northland, A.
  Nearer Home.
  Our Heroes.
  Peace.
  Psalm of Marriage.
  Ready.
  Samuel Brown.
  Suppose.
  Thaddeus Stevens.
  When Lovely Woman ("When lovely woman
    wants a favor").

Cary, Thomas
  On His Mistresse Going to Sea.

Cary, Patrick. *See* **Carey, Patrick**

Caryll, John
  Hypocrite, The.
  Naboth's Vineyard.

Casal, Lourdes
  I Live in Cuba.

Cascorbi, H. F.
  Clerihew: "Frederick the Great/ Accepted
    quite late."

Case, Elizabeth York
  There Is No Unbelief.

Case, John
  From One of Case's Pill-Boxes.
  Over Case's Door.
  To Saffold's Customers, *at.*

Casement, Sir Roger
  Forest Thoughts.
  Fragment: "He is an inharmonious note."
  Lost Youth.

Casey, Michael
  Iliad.

Casey, Peter
  Merry Jovial Beggar, The.

Cassian, Nina
  All Night Long.
  Blood.
  Cripples.
  Hills picking up the/ moonlight like.
  Kiwi Bird, The.
  Knowledge.

Lady of Miracles.
Like Gulliver.
Man, A.
Ordeal.
Self-Portrait.
Thanks.
Vegetable Destiny.

Cassity, Turner
Calvin in the Casino.
Chronology.
Flying Friendly Skies.
Gardens of Proserpine, The.
Links.
Professionals.
Technique on the Firing Line.
U-24 Anchors off New Orleans.

Castelete, Rachael
When I Came to London.

Castellanos, Rosario
Daily Round of the Spinster.
Foreign Woman.
Great fish's eyes never shut, The.
Meditation at the Threshold.
O cloud that wants to be the sky's arrow.
Silence Concerning an Ancient Stone.
Speaking of Gabriel.
Useless Day.
What is weaker than a god? It groans hungry.

Castelloza
Friend, if you had shown consideration.
God knows I should have had my fill of song.
You stayed a long time, friend.

Casterline, Helen Annis
God Cares.

Castile, Juan II of
Cancion: "O love, I never, never thought."

Castillejo, Cristobal de
Some Day, Some Day.

Castillo, Ana
Napa, California.

Castillo, Otto René
October.
Prayer for the Soul of My Country.

Castle, Sandie
Blake Mistake, The.
Hand-Jive.
Mother's Day.

Casto, Robert Clayton
Salt Pork, The.

Castorrivas, Ricardo
Bitter Sonnet to a Cup of Coffee.
Consecration of the Corn Tortilla.

Castro, Juana
Maria Enchained.

Castro, Michael
Grandfathers.
Percolating Highway.

Castro, Rosalía de
Crickets and locusts, cicadas.
Feeling Her End Would Come with Summer's End.
From the Cadenced Roar of the Waves.
How placidly shine/ The river, the spring, and the sun.
Justice of Men! I Look for You.
Lieder.
Long May.
Now all that sound of laughter, sound of singing.
Plants don't talk, people say.
They say that plants don't talk, nor do.
This One Goes and That One Goes.
Today Black Hair.

Cater, Catherine
Here and Now.

Cather, Willa
Dedicatory: "Somewhere, sometime, in an April twilight."
Grandmither, Think Not I Forget.
Spanish Johnny.

Cato, Nancy
Independence.

Catri, Franca Maria
Sister Mother.

Catri, Liana
Spiral Staircase, The.

Cattafi, Bartolo
Anthracite.
Black Thread.
Darkness.
On the Sixth Floor.
Something Precise.
Tabula Rasa.
Vulnerability.
Wingspan.

Cattantaiyar
King Killi in Combat.

Catti Natanar
What He Said.

Catton, Bruce
Names from the War.

Catullus, Caius [or Gaius] Valerius
Acme and Septimius.
Attis.
Come and let us live my deare.
Death of Lesbia's Bird, The.
Each moment of the long-liv'd day.
Egnatius has fine teeth, and those.
Fabullus I will treat you handsomely.
Fib Detected, A.
Flavius, If Your Girl Friend.
Gellius, what reason can you give why those ruddy lips of yours.
Hymn to Diana.
I entrust my all to you, Aurelius.
I have something for you to laugh at, Cato.
I love and hate. Ah! never ask why so!
If I could go on kissing your honeyed eyes.
I'll have you by the short and curly hair.
Invitation to an Invitation, An.
Juventius, could you not find in this great crowd of men.
Juventius, my honey, while you played.
Lesbia.
Lesbia Forever on Me Rails.
Lesbia loads me night and day with her curses.
Love and Death.
Miss her, Catullus? don't be so inept to rail.
My Lesbia let us love and live.
My mistress sayes she'll marry none but me.
Odi et Amo.
Of all our bath-house thieves the cleverest one.
On the Burial of His Brother.
Phyllis Corydon clutched to him.
Sappho.
Sirmio.
Sirmio, thou dearest dear of strands.
That me alone you lov'd, you once did say.
That no fair woman will, wonder not why.
This racer of the watry plain.
Thou saidst that I alone thy heart cou'd move.
To Himself.
To Naso.
To Varus.
True or False.
Unmuzzle the broad joke, *sel*.
Unto no body my woman saith she had rather a wife be.
Veranius, my dear friend, the friend worth.
What demented malice, my silly Ravidus.
Yacht, The.
Yes! my Lesbia! let us prove.
Your Catullus is depressed, Cornificus.

"Caudwell, Christopher" (Christopher St. John Sprigg)
Classic Encounter.
Progress of Poetry, The.

Causley, Charles
Angel's Song.

Animals' Carol, The.
Armistice Day.
At Candlemas.
At Kfar Kana.
At the British War Cemetery, Bayeux.
Autobiography.
Ballad for Katharine of Aragon, A.
Ballad of the Bread Man.
Betjeman, 1984.
Bible Story.
By St. Thomas Water.
Chief Petty Officer.
Colonel Fazackerley.
Cowboy Song.
Death of a Poet.
Death of an Aircraft.
Envoi: "I am the Prince."
For an Ex-Far East Prisoner of War.
H.M.S. Glory at Sydney.
I Am the Great Sun.
I Saw a Jolly Hunter.
Infant Song.
Innocent's Song.
King's College Chapel.
Legend.
Loss of an Oil Tanker.
Mary's Song.
Night before a Journey.
Nursery Rhyme of Innocence and Experience.
On Seeing a Poet of the First World War on the Station at Abbeville.
On the Thirteenth Day of Christmas.
Ou Phrontis.
Recruiting Drive.
Riley.
Sailor's Carol.
Song of Samuel Sweet, The.
Ten Types of Hospital Visitor.
Timothy Winters.

Cavafy, Constantine P.
Afternoon Sun, The.
Alexander Jannai.
Alexandrian Kings.
As Much as You Can.
Body, Remember. .
Che Fece. Il Gran Rifiuto.
City, The.
Dareios.
Days of 1896.
Exiles.
First Step, The.
Footsteps, The.
For Ammonis, Who Died at 29, in 610.
From the School of the Renowned Philosopher.
God Abandons Antony, The.
Half an Hour.
He Asked about the Quality.
Hidden Things.
Horses of Achilles, The.
Ides of March, The.
In a Large Greek Colony, 200 B.C.
In a Township of Asia Minor.
In Despair.
In Sparta.
In the Evening.
In the Tavernas.
In the Year 200 B.C.
Interruption.
Ionic.
Ithaka.
Kaisarion.
Longings.
Lovely White Flowers.
Mirror in the Front Hall, The.
Myris: Alexandria, A.D. 340.
Next Table, The.
On Board Ship.
On the Outskirts of Antioch.
On the Street.

One of the Jews.
One of Their Gods.
Philhellene.
Prince from Western Libya, A.
Return.
Satrapy, The.
Since Nine O'Clock.
Their Beginning.
Theodotos.
Thermopylae.
To Have Taken the Trouble.
To Remain.
Trojans.
Twenty-fifth Year of His Life, The.
Two Young Men, 23 to 24 Years Old.
Waiting for the Barbarians.
Walls.
Window of the Tobacco Shop, The.
Windows, The.
Cavalcanti, Guido
Ballata II: Last Song: from Exile.
Ballata: Concerning a Shepherd-Maid.
Ballata: He Reveals, in a Dialogue, His
  Increasing Love for Mandetta.
Ballata II: "Fair women I saw passing where
  she passed."
Ballata: In Exile at Sarzana.
Ballata: Of a Continual Death in Love.
Ballata: Of His Lady among Other Ladies.
Ballata V: "Light do I see within my Lady's
  eyes."
Canzone: A Lady Asks Me.
Canzone: Donna Mi Priegha.
Sonetto XXXV: To Guido Orlando.
Sonnet [or Sonetto] VII.
Sonnet: A Rapture Concerning His Lady.
Sonnet: He Compares All Things with His
  Lady, and Finds Them Wanting.
Sonnet: He Speaks of a Third Love of His.
Sonnet IV: "If I should pray this lady
  pitiless."
Sonnet: Of an Ill-Favored Lady.
Sonnet: Of His Pain from a New Love.
Sonnet: Of the Eyes of a Certain Mandetta.
Sonnet: On the Detection of a False Friend.
Sonnet: To a Friend Who Does Not Pity His
  Love.
Sonnet: To His Lady Joan, of Florence.
Sonnet: You Have in You the Flowers and the
  Green Grass.
To Dante.
To Dante Alighieri: He Mistrusts the Love of
  Lapo Gianni.
To Dante Alighieri: He Reports, in a Feigned
  Vision, the Successful Issue of Lapo
  Gianni's Love.
Cavalli, Patrizia
How Many Temptations I Pass Through.
I Have No Seed to Scatter through the World.
Cavendish, William
Love's Matrimony.
Cavendish, Margaret Duchess of Newcastle.
  See **Newcastle, Margaret Cavendish,**
  Duchess of
Cavendish, William, Duke of Newcastle. *See*
  Newcastle, William Cavendish, Duke of
Cavin, Susan
Christmas with the Holy Family.
Look Away child.
Cawein, Madison
Attainment.
Comradery.
Creek-Road, The.
Death.
Dirge: "What shall her silence keep?"
Flight.
Ku Klux.
"Mene, Mene, Tekel, Upharsin."
Mosby at Hamilton.
Opportunity.
Proem: "There is no rhyme that is half so
  sweet."

Rain-Crow, The.
Soul, The.
To a Wind-Flower.
Vampire, The.
Wind in the Pines, The.
Cawthorn, James
Time was, an Englishman would join, *sel.*
Cayley, George John
Epitaph, An: "Lovely young lady I mourn in
  my rhymes, A."
Cecco, Angiolieri da Siena. *See* **Angiolieri,**
  Cecco, da Siena
Cedering, Siv. *See* **Fox, Siv Cedering**
"Ceiriog." *See* **Hughes, John Ceiriog**
Celan, Paul
All Soul's Day.
Also raised/ from the noises.
And power and pain.
Ash-Glory.
Brand.
Broken-down taboos, The.
By Day.
Cello Entry.
Corona.
Death Fugue.
Etched Away From.
Eyes:/ shining with rain that poured down.
Flower.
He who tears his heart out of his breast at
  night reaches for the rose.
Here.
Hut Window.
Ice, Eden.
In Egypt.
In Prague.
Into the Rivers.
Irish.
Jugs, The.
Just Think.
Leap-Centuries.
Memory of France.
No more sand art, no sand book, no masters.
Notepad-pain.
Nothingness, for the, The.
Over Three Nipple-Stones.
Pale-voiced, flayed.
Plashes the Fountain.
Psalm: "No one kneads us again out of earth
  and clay."
Soul-blind, behind the ashes.
Speck of Sand, A.
Standing, in the shadow.
Summer Report.
Tenebrae.
Thread suns/ above the gray-black [or
  grey-black] wasteland [or wilderness]
To speak with the blind alleys.
Turn Blind.
Vinegrowers dig up.
Webs between the words.
Wintered-on windfield: here.
Years from You to Me, The.
Your Hair over the Sea.
Your Hand Full of Hours.
Zürich, zum Storchen.
Cendrars, Blaise
At the Five Corners.
Clearings.
Head, The.
Homage to Guillaume Apollinaire.
In the World's Heart.
Me Too Boogie.
On the Way to Dakar.
Orion.
Sputterings.
Stop Press.
Cennick, John
Be Present at Our Table, Lord, *at.*
Children of the Heavenly King.
Centamputan, Maturai Eruttalan
What She Said.

Centan Kannanar
What Her Girl Friend Said to Him.
Ceraman Kanaikkal Irumporai
King's Last Words, A.
Ceravolo, Joseph
Wind Is Blowing West, The.
Cercamon
Seeing love end.
True love/ warms my heart.
With the fine spring weather.
Cerenio, Virginia
Manong Benny.
Pick-up at Chef Rizal Restaurant.
Pinay.
We who carry the endless seasons.
You Lovely People.
Cernuda, Luis
Birds in the Night.
Some Bodies Are like Flowers.
Certain, Mlle
To the Queen of Sweden, on Her Contempt
  for Women's Minds.
Cervantes
Sonnet: "When I was marked for suffering,
  Love forswore."
Cervantes, Lorna Dee
Beneath the Shadow of the Freeway.
Cannery Town in August.
Como lo Siento.
Emplumada.
Freeway 280.
In January.
México, *sel.*
Poem for the Young White Man Who Asked
  Me How I, an Intelligent, Well-read
  Person, Could Believe in the War between
  Races.
Shells.
Starfish.
Uncle's First Rabbit.
Visions of Mexico While at a Writing
  Symposium in Port Townsend, Washington.
Washington, *sel.*
Woman in My Notebook, The.
Césaire, Aimé
Beyond.
Demons.
Have No Mercy.
I shall not regard my swelled head as a sign
  of real glory, *sel.*
Inclination.
Judgment of the Light.
Millibars of Storm.
Moment of Calm.
Offering to the Storm.
Perdition.
Prophecy.
Rains.
Samba.
Sentence.
Serpent Sun.
Since Akkad Since Elam Since Sumer.
Swamp Nocturne.
Thunder's Son, The.
To Scream.
Tornado, The.
Wheel, The.
Céu, Sor Violante do
Voice of a Dissipated Woman inside a Tomb.
Ceyti Valluvan Peruncattan
What She Said.
Cha Shen-hsing
After a Rain.
Chrysanthemum pistils daily yellow, *sel.*
Cricket chirrups near my bed, A, *sel.*
Customs Station at Weed Lake, The.
Song of Bitter Drought, A.
Song of Crows Gleaning the Grain, A.
Chace, Jean Valentine
Visit to a Hospital.

Chadwick, John White
Abiding Love, The.
Full Cycle.
His Mother's Joy.
Hymn: "Eternal Ruler of the ceaseless round."
Hymn: "Father, we come not as of old."
Making of Man, The.
Mugford's Victory.
O Love, That Dost with Goodness Crown.
Recognition.
Rise of Man, The.
Starlight.
Wedding Song, A.
Chaet, Eric
Letter Catches Up with Me, A.
Yom Kippur.
Chaikin, Miriam
I Hate Harry.
Light Another Candle.
Ms. Whatchamacallit Thingamajig.
One-Upmanship.
Chaim Guri. *See* **Guri, Haim**
Chalfi, Abraham [*or* **Avraham Khalfi**]
Certain Man, A.
Digger for Gold, The.
Flowers Pink with Ebony.
Golden-Green Dawn, A.
In the Night Birds Fell.
My Father.
One Who Is Missing, The.
Suburb.
Tonight the Moon Fell.
Chalfi, Raquel
Childless Witch, A.
Like a Field Waiting.
Witch Going Down to Egypt, A.
Chalkhill, John
Coridon's Song.
Rhotus on Arcadia, *sel.*
Challis, Gordon
Asbestos-suited Man in Hell, The.
Iceman, The.
Inflammable Man, The.
Man of Glass, The.
Oracle, The.
Postman, The.
Shadowless Man, The.
Sirens, The.
Thermostatic Man, The.
Thin Partition.
Chalmers, Patrick Reginald
Cuckoo, The.
Hay Harvest.
My Woodcock.
Puk-Wudjies.
When Mary Goes Walking.
Chamberlain, Brenda
Dead Ponies.
Give No White Flower.
Islandman.
Lament: "My man is a bone ringèd with weed."
Second Woman's Lament.
Song: "Bone-aged is my white horse."
Song: "Heron is harsh with despair."
Chamberlain, Richard
To the Much Honoured R. F. Esq.
Chambers, Jane
Why Are Daddies So Mean?
Woman.
Chambers, Nancy
It's Eleven O'Clock.
Chambers, Robert William
"Grey Horse Troop," The.
To Nature Seekers.
Chamisso, Adelbert von
Tragic Story, A.
Chan Ch'e
Broken Bowl, A.
Frying Fish.
Mirror, The.

Old Liu's Dawn.
She Is Not Mute.
Chan Fang-sheng
Sailing Homeward.
Chandler, Christine
Tree in the Garden, The.
Chandler, Len
I Would Be a Painter Most of All.
Chandler, Ellen Louise. *See* **Moulton, Louise Chandler**
Chang, Diana
Artists East and West.
Cannibalism.
Codes.
Horizon Is Definitely Speaking, The.
Once and Future.
Second Nature.
Chang Chi
Tying Up for the Night at Maple River Bridge.
Chang Chiu-ling
Watching the Moon with Thoughts of Far Away.
Chang Heng
Bones of Chuang Tzu, The.
Dead man answered me, The, *sel.*
Chang Hsian-hua
Brooch, The.
Chang Hui-yen
Boating on Feng Stream on the Double Fifth.
Royal air comes from the east: hundreds of hard battles, A.
Spring breeze is a loafer, The, *sel.*
Year after year, I've missed the season of flowers, *sel.*
Young warbler crying through the Festival of Tombs, *sel.*
Chang Pi
Flowers Fill the Palace.
Immortal at the River.
Mountain Hawthorns.
River Messages.
Sand of Silk-Washing Stream.
Song of the Butterflies.
Song of the River City.
Song of the Wine Spring.
Southern Song, A.
Spirit of the Yellow River.
Taoist Nun, The.
Thoughts of the Yüeh Beauty.
Willow Branches.
Chang Ts'o
Confused.
Double Jade Ring Grievance.
Drinking Tea.
Empty Promises.
Legend of Tea, The.
Reliance.
Tears of Pearl, The.
To the Hosts: A Reply.
Chang Wen-t'ao
My script soars up, flies away, but I'm too drunk to know.
Poem on Returning Home, A.
Poem without a self is fit only to be excised, A, *sel.*
Pure is the sandalwood incense—a good place to live, *sel.*
This floating life—a grain of millet on a boundless sea!, *sel.*
To condone rotten rubbish is to deny the miraculous, *sel.*
Chang Yü
Artemisia Tiger, The, *sel.*
Autumn, *sel.*
Brewing Tea at Moon Pond, *sel.*
Butterflies, *sel.*
Cliff of the Ancient Tomb, The, *sel.*
Hearing a Song from My Boat.
His pole and paddle have been with him a long time, *sel.*

Hundred-Fold Cord, The, *sel.*
I close the book in my hands, *sel.*
In a Boat on the Cha River.
In a Book-Box I Found the Lost Manuscript of a Poem.
In the Evening, Walking in the Western Fields.
Lamenting for Kao Ch'ing-ch'iu, Chi-ti.
Looking at Chrysanthemums, *sel.*
Merchant's Joy, The.
Moon Window, The, *sel.*
Mountain Retreat of a Recluse, The.
Painting ("A jade cave, ten thousand flowering peach trees of immortality").
Painting ("Slowly I walk the gully path, alone"), *sel.*
Pavilion for Listening to Fragrance, The.
Quatrain: "At this remote village, I have no neighbors."
Reading the Poetry Collection of Lü Fang-ch'ing.
Retreat of Liu Kuo-pao, The.
Retreat of Sun Ching-hsiang, The.
Song of the Old Oak.
Spring, *sel.*
Spring Night, *sel.*
Staying Overnight at T'ien-ning Ch'an Temple.
Summer, *sel.*
Summer Night at the Pond Pavillion, *sel.*
To the Innkeeper at Five Rivers, Sun Pen.
Winter, *sel.*
Chang Yüeh
Written When Drunk.
Chanler, Isaac
Awake My Soul, Betimes Awake.
Thrice Welcome First and Best of Days.
Channing, William Ellery
Barren Moors, The.
Edith.
Hymn of the Earth.
Lady, there is a hope that all men have, *sel.*
Prayer, A: "To Thy continual Presence, in me wrought."
Tears in Spring.
Chao Chih-hsin
Evening clouds suddenly scatter and peaks come into view, *sel.*
Fireflies.
Mid-Autumn Night, A.
On Poetry.
Presented to a Mountain Dweller.
Where the summit road twists and turns, I'm soon to lose my way, *sel.*
Ch'ao Li-houa
Thank You for Your Letter.
Chao Li-hua
Farewell: "My boat goes west, yours east."
Chao Luan-luan
Slender Fingers ("Slender, delicate, soft jade").
Chao Meng-fu
An Admonition to Myself.
Cutstone Pond, *sel.*
Dragon Mouth Cliff, *sel.*
Eulogy of the Sagely Virtue of His Imperial Majesty Emperor Shih-tsu, A.
Fisherman's Lyric.
In the Ancient Manner.
Inscribed on a Landscape by Mi Yüan-hui.
Inscribed on a Wall Painting of Assembled Immortals.
Inscribed on Sun An-chih's "Painting of Pines and Catalpas."
Inscribed on the Painting, "Spring Dawn at Peach Blossom Spring," by Scholar Shang Te-fu.
Lamenting the Taoist Wei Kung-yüan.
Living in Retirement at Te-ch'ing.
Pavillion-Where-the-Crane-Came, The.
Poem of Prefectural Judge Yang T'ien-jui.

Song of an Autumn Night.
Spirit Pool, *sel.*
Stone Man Peak, *sel.*
Thunder God Cliff, *sel.*
To a Pyrotechnist.

Chao Yi
Best of poetry comes from the destitute, but my pocket is not yet empty, The, *sel.*
Mocking Myself.
Poems of Li Po and Tu Fu, passed along by myriad voices, The, *sel.*
Red Cliff, The.
Responding to a Poem on T'ai-po Pavilion at Colored Stone.
Sleepless at the Fifth Watch.
With sticks and staves on a makeshift stage—all are engrossed in a child's game, *sel.*
World is alive with inspiration to a potter who turns the wheel, The, *sel.*

Chao Ying-tou
Decrees of God, The.

Chapin, Christina
On a Bomb Heard through a Violin Concerto.

Chapin, Edwin Hubbell
Hark! Hark! with Harps of Gold.
O Thou, Who Didst Ordain the Word.

Chapin, Katherine Garrison
On a Sea-Grape Leaf.
Plain-Chant for America.
Portrait in Winter.

Chaplin, Kathleen M.
Merry Little Men.

Chapman, Arthur
Out Where the West Begins ("Out where the hand-clasp's a little stronger").

Chapman, George (1559?–1634)
And, now gives Time, her states description, *sel.*
Bridal Song, *sel.*
But Dwell in Darkness, *sel.*
Corinna Bathes, *sel.*
De Guiana, Carmen Epicum.
Descend, Fair Sun!, *sel.*
Epithalamion Teratos, *sel.*
Hymne to Our Saviour on the Crosse, A.
Hymnus in Noctem, *sel.*
Ile sooth his plots: and strow my hate with smiles, *sel.*
Leander to the envious light, *sel.*
Learning, *sel.*
Love Flows Not from My Liver, *sel.*
Muses That Sing Love's Sensual Empery, *sel.*
New light gives new directions, fortunes new, *sel.*
Night, *sel.*
Now all the peacefull regents of the night, *sel.*
Now from Leander's place she rose, and found, *sel.*
Now shall we see, that nature hath no end, *sel.*
Poet Questions Peace, The, *sel.*
Poetry and Learning, *sel.*
Praise of Homer.
Repentance, *sel.*
Rich Mine of Knowledge.
Shadow of Night, The.
Shine Out, Fair Sun, with All Your Heat, *sel.*
Tragedy of Charles Duke of Byron, The.
Wedding of Alcmane and Mya, The, *sel.*

Chapman, Jean
Territory.

Chapman, John Alexander
Gipsy Queen.

Chapman, John Jay
Lines on the Death of Bismarck.
Song: "Old Farmer Oats and his son Ned."

Chapman, M. J.
African Dirge.
Still sparkles here the glory of the west, *sel.*
While the noon-lustre o'er the land is spread, *sel.*

Chappell, Fred
Cleaning the Well.
Earthsleep.
First time I met your Pa he took my slip off, *sel.*
Forever Mountain.
Guess Who.
Lost Carnival, The.
Message.
My Father Washes His Hands.
My Grandfather's Church Goes Up.
My Grandmother Washes Her Feet.
My Grandmother Washes Her Vessels.
My Mother Shoots the Breeze.
Narcissus and Echo.
Northwest Airlines.
Remodeling the Hermit's Cabin.
Rimbaud Fire Letter to Jim Applewhite.
Second Wind.
Skin Flick.
Webern's Mountain.

Chappell, Jeannette
Newton to Einstein.

Char, René
Assembled Whole, The.
Convergence of the Many.
Every Life.
Faction du Muet.
Festival of the Hunter and the Trees.
Fighters.
Hermetic Workmen.
Lightning Victory.
Lords of Maussane, The.
Room in Space.
Septentrion.
To———: "You have been my love for so many years."
To Friend-Tree of Counted Days.
To the Health of the Serpent.
Torn Mountain.

Charlemagne
Veni Creator Spiritus, *at.*

Charles I, King of England
On a Quiet Conscience.

Charles, Dorthi
Concrete Cat.

Charles, Elizabeth Rundle
Child on the Judgment Seat, The.

Charles, Faustin
Fireflies.
Sugar Cane.

Charles, Mary Grant
Flood.

Charles, Robert E.
Roundabout Turn, A.

Charles d'Orléans. *See* **Orleáns, Charles, Duc d'**

Charmoy, Cozette de
From Delphi.

Chartier, Alain
I turn you out of doors.
Lady Resists the Lover's Pleas, The, *sel.*

Chartres, Vidame de
April.

Chasin, Helen
City Pigeons.
Falling Out.
Looking Out.
Mythics.
Photograph at the Cloisters: April 1972.
Poetess Ko Ogimi, The.
Recovery Room: Lying-in, The.
Telemann to A.C.
Word *Plum*, The.

Chatain, Robert
World of Darkness.

Chatt, George
At Elsdon.

Chatterjee, Debjani
I Was That Woman.

Chatterton, Thomas
Autumn, *sel.*
Bristowe Tragedie: or, The Dethe of Syr Charles Bawdin.
Budding floweret blushes at the light [*Boddynge flourettes bloshes atte the lyghte*], *sel.*
Copernican System, The.
Excelente Balade of Charitie, An.
If Wishing for the Mystic Joys of Love.
Last Verses.
Mynstrelles Songe: "Angelles bee wrogte to bee of neidher kynde", *sel.*
Oh! sing unto my roundelay [*or* O! Synge untoe mie roundelaie], *sel.*
Ode to Liberty, *sel.*
Ode to Miss Hoyland.
Resignation.
Sentiment.
Sly Dick.

Chaucer, Geoffrey
And as for me, though that I konne [*or* can] but [*or* my wit be] lyte, *sel.*
At the Gate, *sel.*
Balade de Bon Conseill.
Clerk's Tale, The, *sel.*
Complaint [*or* Compleint *or* Compleinte] of Chaucer to His Empty Purse, The.
Complaint of Troilus, The, *sel.*
Cook's Tale, The, *sel.*
Courtly Scene and a Sudden Storm, A, *sel.*
Dream, The, *sel.*
Epilogue of the Man of Law's Tale, The, *sel.*
Fair was this yonge wyf, and therwithal, *sel.*
Franklin's Prologue, The, *sel.*
Franklin's Tale, The, *sel.*
Friar's Prologue, The, *sel.*
Friar's Tale, The, *sel.*
Gentilesse.
Go, Little Book ("Go, litel book, go litel myn tragedy"), *sel.*
Hyd, Absalon, thy gilte tresses clear, *sel.*
If no love is, O God, what fele I so, *sel.*
Introduction to the Franklin's Prologue, The, *sel.*
Introduction to the Man of Law's Prologue, *sel.*
Introduction to the Pardoner's Prologue, The, *sel.*
Knight's Tale, The, *sel.*
Lak of Stedfastnesse.
Letter of Dydo to Eneas, The.
Love Unfeigned, *sel.*
Manciple's Tale, The, *sel.*
Merciless Beauty.
Miller's Prologue, The, *sel.*
Miller's [*or* Milleres] Tale, The, *sel.*
Months, The.
Now Welcom[e], Somer [*or* Summer], *sel.*
Nun's Priest's Prologue, The, *sel.*
Nun's Priest's Tale, The, *sel.*
Pardoner's Prologue, The, *sel.*
Pardoner's Tale, The, *sel.*
Parson's Prologue, The, *sel.*
Prioress's Tale, The, *sel.*
Prologue, *sel.*
Prologue of the Prioress's Tale, The, *sel.*
Prologue to Sir Thopas, *sel.*
Prologue to the Man of Law's Tale, *sel.*
Prologue to the Miller's Tale, *sel.*
Prologue to the Second Nun's Tale, The, *sel.*
Rondel of Merciless Beauty, A.
Sir Thopas, *sel.*
Sorrow of Troilus, The, *sel.*
Swich fyn hath, lo, this Troilus for love!, *sel.*
There mighte men the royal eagle find, *sel.*
This Fresshe Flour, *sel.*
This Troilus [*or* Troylus], with blisse [*or* Blysse] of that supprysed [*or* surprised], *sel.*
To Adam, His Scribe.

To Rosamond.
Whan they unto the paleys were yoemen, *sel.*
Wife of Bath's Prologue, The, *sel.*
Wife of Bath's Tale, The, *sel.*
Wooing of Criseide, The, III, *sel.*

Chaudhari, Kirti
Inertia.

Chaundler, Christine
Child's Christmas Carol, A.

Chawner, George F.
Prayer, A: "Those who love Thee may they find."

Chear, Abraham
To My Youngest Kinsman, R. L.

Chedid, Andrée
Future and the Ancestor, The.
What Are We Playing At?
Women of All the Ages.

Cheever, George Barrell
Blest Be the Wondrous Grace.
Thy Loving Kindness, Lord, I Sing.

Cheke, Henry
Of Perfect Friendship.

Ch'en Ch'ien-wu. *See* **Huan Fu**

Ch'en Lin, Susan
Song: "I watered my horse at the Long Wall caves."

Ch'en Pao-shen
Inscription for My Evergreen Pavilion.
On the Twenty-Second Night of the Seventh Month, Facing the Moon at Listening-to-the-Water Studio.
Quatrain: "Dare I dislike the green pond for the reflection of my unkempt hair?"
Quatrain: "Three peaks beyond my pavilion show no human feelings, The."

Ch'en San-li
Night at My Lodge, A.
On the Night of the Fourteenth of the Eleventh Month Setting Out for Nanchang by Boat on a Moonlit Night.
Prospect of the Wilds.
Strolling in the Moonlight.
View from the Pavilion on a Moonlit Night.

Ch'en Shih-tao
Cold Night.

Ch'en Tao
Song of Lung-hsi.

Ch'en Tzu-ang
Song on Climbing Yu-chou Gate Tower.

Ch'en Wei-sung
Hungry Crow, The.
Listlessness.
One Summer Day, Invited by Mr. Shih Chü-an to Have a Drink.
Song of the Boat Trackers, The.
Written on Yün-lang's Nuptial Day.

Cheney, Ednah Dow
Larger Prayer, The.

Cheney, Elizabeth
Overheard in an Orchard.

Cheney, John Vance
Every One to His Own Way.
Happiest Heart, The.
Lincoln.
Man with the Hoe; a Reply, The.
San Francisco.
Skilful Listener, The.
Strong, The.
Unto Our God Most High We Sing.
Whither.

Cheng Chen
Born to cling to this human road, *sel.*
Butterflies and dragonflies come in succession, *sel.*
Dim, dim the light from the small window, *sel.*
Discussion of Poetry to Demonstrate to the Students the Coming of a New Age, A.
Evening Prospect.
I read books beside Ox Tail River, *sel.*

Lament for Those Who Hanged Themselves, A.
On Hearing That on the Sixteenth Day of the Tenth Month the Magistrate of Li-po, Chiang Hsiao-yün, *tzu* Chia-ku, of Shao-hsing/ Attacked the Rebels.
On Hearing That the Market outside the East Gate of the City Has Been Burned Down.
Sad, sad is the bird in a cage, *sel.*
Tall willows canopy the thrashing ground with their shade, *sel.*

Cheng Ch'ou-yu
Abode of the Roaming Immortals.
Gateway Arch.
Ladder-Climbing and Grocery.
Rain Says, The.

Cheng Hsiao-hsü
Night of the Full Moon.
Random Poem, A.
Returning to Nanking.
Upon Returning to the Capital in 1923.
Written on the Wall of Ku Tzu-p'eng's Studio.
Wu Family Thatched Hall.

Cheng Hsieh
At the dawn of your life, you ate gruel, *sel.*
Collecting Antiques.
Contest Snake, The.
Fisherman, The.
Flight from Famine: A Ballad.
Girl from Ch'ang-kan, The.
Kings and Emperors.
Martyred Widow Liu of Hai-ling: A Ballad.
Master Cheng is thirty—and doesn't have a job!, *sel.*
Monk, The.
"Mother-in-Law Is Cruel."
On a Painting of a Knight-Errant.
Poem for My Wet Nurse, A.
Poor Scholar.
Powerful Officials.
Song of Surfing on the Bore.
Tavernkeeper, The.
To Chin Nung.
Twenty-eight Characters Sent to Tung-ts'un.
West wind has come again to the "tower of makeup," The, *sel.*
When a wax candle burns down, ashes are left behind, *sel.*
When I was three years old, my mother passed away, *sel.*

Cheng Min
Drought, The.
Student.

Cheng Wen-cho
Fellow Wanderers Gather for the Night in Late Autumn.
Tune: Willow Branch.
You cannot leave!
You cannot return!
You cannot stay!

Cheng Wen-tao
Leaving Knee-prints in the Warm Earth.
Possibilities of Snow.

Chénier, André Marie de
Every Man has his sorrows; yet each still, *sel.*
Iambes VIII.
Well, I would have it so. I should have known, *sel.*
When I Was Small.
White nymph wandering in the woods by night, A, *sel.*

Cherbury, Edward Herbert, 1st Baron. *See* **Herbert of Cherbury**

Chernin, Kim
Eve's Birth.

Chernoff, Maxine
Breasts.
How Lies Grow.
Name, A.

Phantom Pain.
Utopia TV Store.

Cherry, Kelly
Letter to a Censor.
Love.
Scientific Expedition in Siberia, 1913, A.

Cherwinski, Joseph
Manhattan Menagerie.

Chester, Anson G.
Tapestry Weavers, The.

Chester, Laura
Bees inside Me.
Go Round.
In a Motion.
Last Breath.
Moved towards a Future.
On the Wallowy.
Returning to the World.
Simply.
Trellis.
28 VIII 69.
We Heart.

Chester, Sir Robert
Ditty: "O holy Love, religious saint!," *sel.*
Her Hair, *sel.*

Chesterfield, Philip Dormer Stanhope, 4th Earl of
Advice to a Lady in Autumn.
On Miss Eleanor Ambrose, a Celebrated Beauty in Dublin.
On Mr. Nash's Present of His Own Picture at Full Length.
Song: "Whenever, Chloe, I begin."
To Miss Eleanor Ambrose on the Occasion of Her Wearing an Orange Lily at a Ball in Dublin Castle on July the 12th.
Unlike my subject now shall be my song.
Verses Written in a Lady's Sherlock "Upon Death."

Chesterman, Hugh
Outside.
Rhyme Sheet of Other Lands, A.
Sir Nicketty Nox.
Yesterday.

Chesterton, Frances
How Far Is It to Bethlehem?

Chesterton, Gilbert Keith
After W. B. Yeats.
Antichrist, or the Reunion of Christendom; an Ode.
Ballad of Abbreviations, A.
Ballade d'une Grande Dame.
Ballade of Suicide, A.
Before the gods that made the gods, *sel.*
By the Babe Unborn.
Christmas Carol, A: "Christ child lay on Mary's lap, The."
Citizenship; Form 8889512, Sub-Section Q.
Dedication, A: "He was, through boyhood's storm and shower."
Donkey, The.
Ecclesiastes.
Elegy in a Country Churchyard.
For a War Memorial.
For the Crèche, *sel.*
Geography, *sel.*
Glencoe.
Gold Leaves.
History, *sel.*
Holy of Holies, The.
Home at Last.
House of Christmas, The.
Hymn *or* Prayer, A.
Lepanto.
Logical Vegetarian, The.
Old King Cole ("Me clairvoyant"), *sel.*
Old King Cole ("Of an old king in a story"), *sel.*
Old King Cole ("Who smoke-snorts toasts o' My Lady Nicotine"), *sel.*
Old Song, The.

On the Dangers Attending Altruism on the
    High Seas.
Oneness of the Philosopher with Nature, The.
Praise of Dust, The.
Prayer in Darkness, A.
Rolling English Road, The.
Secret People, The.
Skeleton, The.
Song against Grocers, The.
Song of Quoodle, The.
Sonnet: "High on the wall that holds
    Jerusalem."
Sword of Surprise, The.
To the Unknown Warrior.
Variations of [*or* on] an Air: After Alfred
    Lord Tennyson.
Variations on an Air: After Robert Browning.
Variations on an Air: After W. B. Yeats.
Variations on an Air: After Walt Whitman.
Variations on an Air Composed on Having to
    Appear in a Pageant as Old King Cole.
Variations on [*or* of] an Air: After [Algernon
    Charles] Swinburne.
Wild Knight, The.
Wine and Water, *sel.*

Chettle, Henry
Aeliana's Ditty, *sel.*

Chevremont, Evaristo Ribera
Boy and the Lantern, The.

Ch'i, Kao
Written on Seeing the Flowers, and
    Remembering My Daughter.

Chia Tao
Last Night of the Third Moon, The.
Looking for a Recluse but Failing to Find
    Him.

Chia Yi
Rhyme-Prose on the Owl.

Chiabrera, Gabriello
Epitaphs, VII.
Epitaphs, IX.

Chiang, Fay
Letter to Peter, A.
Snow.
Voices That Have Filled My Day.

Chiang Ch'un-lin
Crystal curtains rolled-up have cleared the
    dense mist.
Descriptive Piece for April, 1853, A.
Moon on the Night of the Third of the Month,
    The.
On 19 December 1853, the Rebels Are
    Approaching the Capital.

Chiang Hsun
Chinatown.
Climbing the Mountain.
Elegy to Li Shuang-tse.
Song of Greece, The.

Chiang Lu
Wrecked Boat on the River Shore.

Chiang Shih
Crossing Several Mountain Ridges on My
    Way to P'u-ch'eng from Chiang-shan after
    a Snowfall.
Morning light floods my room overlooking the
    lake, *sel.*
Night at an Inn: Written in the Style of Meng
    Chiao.
Vapor rises from the water's surface at dawn,
    sel.

Chiang Shih-ch'üan
An Evening Prospect: City Lights.
Expelling Witches.
Sixteen Songs of the Capital: Chicken Feather
    Shop.
Toasting the Moon at Ten-Thousand-Year
    Bridge.

Chiao-jan
Looking for Lu Hung-chien but Failing to
    Find Him.

Ch'iao Lin
Face of Christ, The.
Falling Leaves.
Pay the Bill.

Chicken, Edward
At last the beef appears in sight, *sel.*

Ch'ien Ch'ien-i [*or* Ch'ien-yi]
Clusters of cold-weather blossoms, *sel.*
Desolate poems of chaotic times—could I
    bear, *sel.*
Drinking Wine: Second Series.
In hermit's robe, clean and simple, *sel.*
Lotus Pond, *sel.*
Miscellaneous Poems Written While in Jail.
Narcissus and chrysanthemum, *sel.*
No Flowers.
Pavilions of dance, terraces of song, *sel.*
Poem on Drinking Wine with the
    Degree-Holder Ku.
Poem Written during a Dream.
Upon Reading the Boudoir Poem of
    Mei-ts'un.
Watching a Game of Chess: Second Series.
Willow catkins beyond the garden wait for
    evening tides, *sel.*
Willow Creek, *sel.*
Written in Prison.

Ch'ien Wen-ti, Emperor
Lo-yang.

Chigetsu. *See* Kaai Chigetsu

Chikako
He made no promise.
"I long for you."
I sit idly here.
In dawn's first light.
In front of my eyes.
In the valley shade.
It was long ago.
Not even the moon.
Outside my window.
Someone passes on.
Spring Poem, A.

Chikamatsu Monzaemon
To this world, farewell, *sel.*

Chikugai, Fujii. *See* Fujii Chikugai

Child, Lydia Maria
Apple-Seed John.
Thanksgiving Day.
World I Am Passing Through, The.

Child, Philip
Basilisk, The.
Dancing Partners.
Descent for the Lost.
Lyric: "I touched a shining mote of sand."
Macrocosm.
Oak.

Childress, W. Lomax
Beautiful World, The.

Childress, William
Korea Bound, 1952.
Metamorphosis of Aunt Jemima, The.

Chima, Richard Augustine
Chronique Scandaleuse.
In This Shanty Shebeen without You.
Why?

Chimako, Tada
Mirror.

Chimedza, Polycarp
Factory Hands, The.
Raid on the Market.

Chimombo, Steve
Four Ways of Dying.

Chimsoro, Samuel
Change, The.
Curfew Breakers, The.
I Love.
Laborer, The.
To Come Back Home.

Chin, Marilyn
Chinaman's Chance, A.

Grandmother Poems.
Landlord's Wife, The.
We Are a Young Nation, Uncle.
Write, Do Write.

Chin Ch'ang-hsü
Spring Grievance.

Chin-doba
Mountain slopes crawl with lumberjacks, The.

Chin Ho
Ballad of the Girl from Lan-ling.
Strolling in Simplicity Garden for the First
    Time.

Chin Jen-Jui
Capriciousness.
Don't Ask.
Last Word: For My Son Yung.
Tiniest of Lives, The.

Chin Nung
An Inkstone Inscription for the Blind Scholar
    Ho Yung-kuang.
Evening Scene at Twin Forests.
I get so drunk, I could be called the Earl of
    Dissipation!, *sel.*
I remember when he took me on a trip to this
    place, *sel.*
In the silences between peals of the bell, *sel.*
Inscribed on the Wall of a Rice Cake Shop.
Mooring in the Rain at Sung-ling.
Three lines of "clerk script" calligraphy, *sel.*
Traveler, I've been through a thousand
    changes, A, *sel.*
Wearing a Worn-Out Coat.
Who bought a mountain and became a hermit
    there?, *sel.*
Written at the End of Master Ho-ching's
    Collected Works.

Ching An
Elegy for Myself.
Inscribed on a Painting "Fishing in the Snow
    on a Wintry River."
Mountain Dwelling.
Thoughts on Climbing the Swept-Leaves
    Pavilion on the Third Day before the
    Double-Ninth Festival.

Ching-chao, Li
Tune: Endless Union.
Tune: The Butterfly Woos the Blossoms.
Two Springs.

Chipasula, Frank Mkalawile
Hanging, A.
Love Poem for My Country, A.
Those Makheta Nights.

Chipp, Elinor
Wild Geese.

Chiri
Arms spread, a frog floats.

Chittendon, Larry
Cowboy's Christmas Ball, The.

Ch'iu Chin
Call to Action, A.
Random Feelings: Written in Japan.
Song of the Precious Knife, A.
Song: Promoting Women's Rights, A.
To the Tune "The River Is Red."
Tune: Full River Red.
Written on Board a Ship on the Yellow Sea,
    When a Japanese Friend Asked Me for a
    Poem.

Ch'iu Wei
Visiting a Recluse on West Mountain and Not
    Finding Him In.

Chivers, Thomas Holley
As an egg, when broken, never, *sel.*
Lily Adair.
Moon of Mobile, The.

Chiyo
After a long winter, giving/ each other
    nothing.
Don't dress for it.
Hardly spring, with ice.
Once my parents were older.

Chiyojo
At the Ferry in Kuwana, *sel.*
Butterfly: now in front, *sel.*
Butterfly: what's it dreaming of, *sel.*
By its own wind, a small butterfly, *sel.*
Clear water has no front or back, *sel.*
Dandelion: from time to time, *sel.*
From time to time, a butterfly, *sel.*
Green willow's quiet, A, *sel.*
I forget my lips are rouged, *sel.*
I go on, and the clear water meets me again, *sel.*
I raise my hands, and the clear water, *sel.*
Mistaking birds for leaves, *sel.*
Only over the river, darkness flows: fireflies, *sel.*
To tangle or untangle a willow, *sel.*
Touching the line from a fishing pole, *sel.*
Willow flows away, The, *sel.*
Wind spills plovers, picks them up, The, *sel.*

Chock, Eric
For the Field.
Mango Tree, The.
Papio.
Pulling Weeds.
Termites.

Chokei
All's harmony, yet everything is separate.
Rolling the bamboo blind, I.

Chokyusei
Frogs croak in moonlight.

Cholmondeley-Pennell, Henry
Bloated Biggaboon, The.
I've Lost My———
Night Mail North, The.
What the Prince of I Dreamt.

Chora (Miura Chora)
Peering at the stars.
You watch—it's clouded.

Chorley, Henry Fothergill
Brave Old Oak, The.

Chorley, Josiah
All things created, Moses writes, *sel.*

Chorny, Sasha
Vilna Puzzle, A.

Choro
With one foot on the brick step.

Chosa, Martha
Drums.

Chosetsu
Light everywhere, I live in all.

Chosha
Every thing, every place is real.
Nansen said: It's everywhere.

Chou Meng-tieh
Flakes of Auspicious Snow Fall Here.
Impressions at the Vulture Peak.
Thirteen White Chrysanthemums.

Chou Pang-yen
Tune: Palace of Night Revels.

Choudhury, Nurunnessa
Blue Specks.
Death of a Dove.
I See Cleopatra.
Sun Witness, The.

Christensen, Inger
Men's Voices.

Christian, Marcus B.
Craftsman, The.
Dialect Quatrain.
McDonogh Day in New Orleans.

Christopher, Nicholas
Driver in Italy, The.
John Garfield.
Miranda in Reno.
Track, The.
Walt Whitman at the Reburial of Poe.

"Chrystos"
Dance a Ghost.
I'm Making You Up.

Wings of a Wild Goose, The.
Woman ("Woman/ will you come with me moving").

Chu Hsi
Boats Are Afloat, The.

Chu Hsiao-tsang
New Year's Eve in the Year *Keng-tzu.*
On the Ninth, outside Feng-yi Gate, I Passed by P'ei-ts'un's Country House.
Solitary bird crashing into the waves wings off in joy, A.

Ch'u Kuang-hsi
Farmer's Thoughts, A.
Streets of Ch'ang-an, The.

Chu Shu-chen
Hysteria.
Morning.
Old Anguish, The.
Sorrow.
Stormy Night in Autumn.

Ch'ü Ta-chün
Ancient Plum Tree at the K'ai-hsien Buddhist Monastery, An.
Fishing Jetty.
Inscribed on T'ai-po Shrine, at Colored Stone Jetty.
Lament the falling leaves:/ The falling leaves, let them fall in spring, *sel.*
Lament the falling leaves:/ The falling leaves sever the date of return, *sel.*
Snow.
Written at the Year's End, While Visiting Chien-ling.
Written upon Coming Again to the Tu-hsü Taoist Temple.

Chu Yi-tsun
Brown Oxen Knoll, *sel.*
Chia Mountain Monastery, *sel.*
Climbing Ch'ing-shuo Tower at Yün-chung.
Crossing Ta-yü Mountain Ridge.
Evening View from P'eng-lai Pavilion.
Pine Pavilion Hill, *sel.*
Sandbar egrets, sleeping, nestle close to my boat, *sel.*
Self-Portrait: Inscribed upon My Own Collection of Lyrics, A.
Sent to My Beloved Far Away.
Southern Pavilion, *sel.*
Visiting the Temple of Chang Tzu-fang.
Walking to Mou-chou at Dawn.
Wind above Long River spreads the scent of lotus, leaf after leaf, The, *sel.*

Chu Yuan
Battle, The.
Great Summons, The.

Chu Yün-ming
As I Looked at a Lake, My Thoughts Turned to a Certain Friend.
Bamboo bed, rattan pillow, A, *sel.*
Clouds are swept into the sunset—a sky beyond the sky, *sel.*
Drinking.
Fan from Korea, A.
For Several Years I Have Wanted to Grow a Garden.
Landscape Painted on a Fan, A.
Late Spring—Traveling through the Mountains.
Little Landscape, A.
Making Fun of the Well at the Inn below the Mountain.
No robe, no sleeves, my hair uncombed, *sel.*
Old man Chih-shan has a head of white hair, *sel.*
Painting of the Butterfly Dream by the Master Artist Li Tsai, A.
Remembering My Late Wife.
Rumble of thunder brings evening rain, The, *sel.*
Shrine of General Pien, The.
Too Lazy to Write Poetry.

Unruly hair, bare feet—busily studying books, *sel.*
What can I do, I love you so much!, *sel.*
You and I are like birds in a forest, *sel.*

Chuang Tzu
Joy of Fishes, The.
P'eng That Was a K'un, The, *at.*

Chuang Yü
Gossamer threads trail endlessly in the courtyard.
I was somewhere in a dream just a while ago.
Slanting sun across the city wall clings to green trees, The.

Chubb, Ralph
At the time of puberty I had obsessions, *sel.*
Liveliest effigy of the human race, *sel.*
Song of My Soul.

Chubb, Thomas Caldecot
Praise of New England.

Chudleigh, Mary Lee, Lady
Offering: Part One, The.
Resolve, The.
To the Ladies.

Chugan Engetsu
Atami.
Spring Snow.

Chuilleanáin, Eileán Ní. *See* **Ní Chuilleanáin, Eileán.**

Chung-ch'ang T'ung
Speaking My Mind.

Chung-ju, Wang
Complaint of a Young Girl.

Church, Richard
Alchemist, The.
Be Frugal.
On Hearing the First Cuckoo.

Churchill, Charles
Character of a Critic, *sel.*
Dedication, The: "Health to great Gloucester—from a man unknown."
European Crimes, *sel.*
First (entitled to the place), The, *sel.*
Go where we will, at ev'ry time and place, *sel.*
Gods! with what pride I see the titled slave, *sel.*
Is a son born into this world of woe?, *sel.*
Nut, a World, a Squirrel, and a King, A, *sel.*
Oft have I heard thee mourn the wretched lot, *sel.*
On His Own Poetry, *sel.*
Pains of Education, The, *sel.*
Poet as King of Gotham, The, *sel.*
Pomposo (insolent and loud), *sel.*
Spectators only on this bustling stage, *sel.*
Two boys, whose birth beyond all question springs, *sel.*
What Is't to Us?, *sel.*
When with much pains this boasted learning's got, *sel.*

Churchill, Sarah
Bombers, The.
R.A.F.

Churchyard, Thomas
Farewell to a Fondling, A.
Old-Time Service, *sel.*

Chusin, Zekkai. *See* **Zekkai Chusin**

Chute, Marchette
Crayons.
Day before Christmas.
Drinking Fountain.
Going to Bed.
My Dog.
My Plan.
My Teddy Bear.
Showers.
Sleeping Outdoors.
Snowflakes.
Spring Rain.
Wrong Start, The.

Chuya, Nakahara. *See* **Nakahara Chuya**
Ciardi, John
About the Teeth of Sharks.
At My Father's Grave.
Back through the Looking Glass to This Side.
Ballad of the Icondic.
Birthday.
Camptown.
Captain Spud and His First Mate, Spade.
Cat Heard the Cat-Bird, The.
Censorship.
Dawn of the Space Age.
Death's the Classic Look.
Elegy Just in Case.
Elegy: "My father was born with a spade in his hand and traded it."
Evil Eye, The.
Exit Line.
Faces.
First Snow on an Airfield.
For My Twenty-fifth Birthday in Nineteen Forty-one.
Gift, The.
Goodmorning with Light.
Goodnight.
Home Revisited: Midnight.
Homecoming—Massachusetts.
I Wish I Could Meet the Man That Knows.
I Wouldn't.
It Is for the Waking Man to Tell His Dreams.
Journal.
Light-House Keeper's White-Mouse, The.
Love Letter from Mars.
Magus, A.
Man from the Woods, The.
Man in the Onion Bed, The.
Man Who Sang the Sillies, The.
Most Like an Arch This Marriage.
Mummy Slept Late and Daddy Fixed Breakfast.
My Cat Mrs. Lick-a-Chin.
My Father's Watch.
Myra Song, The ("Myra, Myra, sing-song").
Mystic River.
Ode for the Burial of a Citizen.
On a Photo of Sgt. Ciardi a Year Later.
On Being Much Better Than Most and Yet Not Quite Good Enough.
On Evolution.
On Learning to Adjust to Things.
Pinwheel's Song, The.
Plea.
Read This with Gestures.
Reason for the Pelican, The.
River Is a Piece of Sky, The.
Snowy Heron.
Some Cook.
Some Sound Advice from Singapore.
Someone's Face.
Sometimes Running.
Song: "Bells of Sunday rang us down, The."
Stranger in the Pumpkin, The.
Suburban.
That Summer's Shore.
To a Reviewer Who Admired My Book.
To Judith Asleep.
Warning.
What Johnny Told Me.
What Night Would It Be?
What Someone Said When He Was Spanked on the Day before His Birthday.
Wouldn't You?
Cibber, Colley
Blind Boy, The.
Cino da Pistoia
Canzone: His Lament for Selvaggia.
Madrigal: To His Lady Selvaggia Vergiolesi; Likening His Love to a Search for Gold.
Sonnet: A Trance of Love.
Sonnet: All That's to Others Pleasing, I Dislike.
Sonnet: Death Is Not without but within Him.

Sonnet: Of the Grave of Selvaggia, on the Monte della Sambuca.
Sonnet: To Love, In Great Bitterness.
To Dante Alighieri: He Conceives of Some Compensation in Death.
To Dante Alighieri: He Interprets Dante's Dream.
Cisneros, Antonio
Ancient Peru.
Between the Quay of San Nicolas and the Sea.
Chronicle of Lima.
Dead Conquerors, The.
Description of a Plaza, a Monument and Allegories in Bronze.
I'm Getting Out and Going Some 30 Kilometers towards the Coast.
In 62 the Starving Seabirds Reached the Center of Lima.
Karl Marx Died 1883 Aged 65.
Loneliness 2.
Pachacamac.
Paracas.
Prayers of a Repentant Gentleman.
Question of Time.
Sonnet in Which I Say My Son Is a Long Way Off and Has Been for More Than a Year, A.
Tarma.
Three Testimonies of Ayacucho.
Tupac Amaru Relegated.
Workers of the Sun's Land.
Citèkù Ndaaya
Ndaaya, I, am so poor, *sel.*
Citino, David
Sister Mary Appassionata Lectures the Journalism Class.
Cittalai Cattanar
What He Said to His Charioteer, on His Way Back.
Ciullo d'Alcamo
Dialogue: Lover and Lady.
Clairmont, Robert
When Did the World Begin.
Clampitt, Amy
Agreeable Monsters.
Beach Glass.
Burial in Cypress Hills.
Cormorant in His Element, The.
Cure at Porlock, A.
Dancers Exercising.
George Eliot Country.
Gooseberry Fool ("The gooseberry's no doubt an oddity").
Hairline Fracture, A.
Kingfisher, The.
Portola Valley.
Procession at Candlemas, A.
Time.
Venice Revisited.
What the Light Was Like.
Woodlot, The.
Clancy, Joseph P.
Boxer.
Clanvowe, Sir Thomas
But as I lay this other night waking, *sel.*
Clapp, Ross B.
Mother's Love.
Clara d'Anduza
Lauzengiers and the deceitful spies, The.
Clare, John
Anecdote of Love, An.
Autumn.
Autumn Birds.
Autumn Robin, The.
Autumn ("Summer is gone and all the merry noise").
Autumn ("The thistledown's flying. ").
Autumn Wind, The.
Badger.

Badger ("Badger grunting on his woodland track, The"), *sel.*
Beanfield, The.
Birds' Lament.
Birds' Nests.
Bonny Lassie O!
Cat runs races with her tail, The, *sel.*
Clock-a-Clay.
Come Hither.
Come Hither, My Dear One.
Crows in Spring.
Death.
December.
Deluge.
Dying Child, The.
Early Nightingale.
Emmonsail's Heath in Winter.
Eternity of Nature, The.
Evening.
Evening Primrose.
Fallen Elm, The.
Farewell: "Farewell to the bushy clump close to the river."
February, *sel.*
Field Path.
Firetail's Nest, The.
Firewood.
First Love.
Flitting, The.
Flood, The.
Fragment: "Cataract, whirling to the precipice, The."
Fragment: "Language has not the power to speak what love indites."
Fragment: "Love's memories haunt my footsteps still."
Frightened Ploughman, The.
Gipsies ("The gipsies seek wide sheltering wood again").
Gipsies ("The snow falls deep").
Grasshoppers.
Happy Bird, The.
Hares at Play.
Hen's Nest.
Hesperus.
Hymn to the Creator.
I Am.
I Feel I Am.
Invitation to Eternity.
Invite to Eternity, An.
I've Had Many an Aching Pain.
Landrail, The.
Lark's Nest, The.
Lines Written on a Very Boisterous Day in May, 1844.
Little Maid and the Cowslips, The.
Little Trotty Wagtail.
London versus Epping Forest, *sel.*
Lord, Hear My Prayer.
Love, Meet Me in the Green Glen.
Love's Emblem.
Love's Pains.
Maid o' the West, The.
Martin cat long shaged of courage good, The.
Milking Shed, The.
Mother's Lullaby, The.
Mouse's Nest.
My Early Home.
Nightingale, The.
No single hour can stand for naught.
Noon.
Northamptonshire Fens, *sel.*
Now is Past.
Old Year, The.
Or, trying simple charms and spells, *sel.*
Pastoral Poesy.
Peasant Poet, The.
Peggy Said Good Morning.
Pettichap's Nest, The.
Ploughboy, The.
Poets Love Nature.
Ragwort, The.

Remember Dear Mary.
Robin, The.
Sand Martin, The.
Schoolboys in Winter.
Sea Boy on the Giddy Mast, A.
Secret, The.
Secret Love.
She Tied Up Her Few Things.
Shepherd Boy, The.
Signs of Winter.
Silent Love.
Snowstorm.
Solitude.
Song: "I peeled bits of straw and I got switches too."
Song: "I went my Sunday mornings round."
Song: "I wish I was where I would be."
Song: "I would not feign a single sigh."
Song: "Mist rauk is hanging, The."
Song: "Soft falls the sweet evening."
Song's Eternity.
Spring Morning, A.
Stanzas: "Black absence hides upon the past."
Stanzas from "Child Harold", sel.
Stanzas: "Passing of a dream, The."
Summer.
Summer Evening.
Summer Images.
Sunrise in Summer.
There is a charm in solitude that cheers.
Thrush's Nest, The.
Thunder mutters louder & more loud, The.
To an Infant Daughter.
To John Clare.
To Mary: I Sleep with Thee, and Wake with Thee.
To Mary: It Is the Evening Hour.
To Miss B.
To the Snipe.
To Wordsworth.
Vision, A.
Vixen, The.
When for school o'er Little Field with its brook and wooden brig, sel.
Wind That Shakes the Rushes, The.
Winter in the Fens.
Winter Winds Cold and Blea.
Winters Spring, The.
With Garments Flowing.
Wood-Cutter's Night Song, The.
Written in Prison.
Yellowhammer, The.
Young Lambs.

Clark, Carl
Allegory in Black.
Conundrum.
No More.
Ode to a Beautiful Woman.
Second Coming, The.
Thoughts from a Bottle.

Clark, Charles Badger, Jr. (Badger Clark)
Cowboy's Prayer, A.
Pioneers.

Clark, G. Orr
Night Is a Big Black Cat, The.

Clark, J.
Maxims in Rhyme for the Young.

Clark, John Pepper
Agbor Dancer.

Clark, Kevin
Widow under a New Moon.

Clark, Leonard
Echo.
House. For Sale.
November the Fifth.
Parakeet.

Clark, Leslie Savage
In the Time of Trouble.

Clark, Lewis Gaylord
Flamingo, The.

Clark, Lois
Flashback.
Fly Past Alderney.
Picture from the Blitz.

Clark, Martha Haskell
Red Geraniums.

Clark, Robert
Generations.

Clark, Thomas Curtis
Abraham Lincoln, the Master.
Bugle Song of Peace.
Common Blessings.
He Shall Speak Peace.
Keep Love in Your Life.
Poet's Call, The.
Search, The.
Trust the Great Artist.
Wanderers.

Clark, Tom
Alpha November Golf Sierra Tango.
Arc.
Chords knotted together like insane nouns, sel.
Climbing.
Daily News.
Dispersion and Convergence.
Door behind me was you, The, sel.
Final Farewell.
Greeks, The.
Last Baseball Samurai, The.
Lines Composed at Hope Ranch.
Process, The.
Rec Room in Paradise.
Sonnet: "Orgasm completely, The."
Superballs.
Today I get this letter from you and the sun, sel.
You (III).
You are bright, tremendous, wow, sel.
You, I.
You (IV).

Clark, Badger. *See* **Clark, Charles Badger, Jr.**

Clark, Charles Heber. *See* **"Adeler, Max"**

Clarke, Aidan
Journey, The.

Clarke, Andrew Stuart Currie
Prayer for a Happy New Year, A.

Clarke, Austin
Anacreontic.
Ancient Lights.
Burial of An Irish President.
Celebrations.
Cypress Grove.
Early Unfinished Sketch.
Envy of Poor Lovers, The.
Fair at Windgap, The.
Forget Me Not.
Her Voice Could Not Be Softer.
Inscription for a Headstone.
Intercessors.
Irish-American Dignitary.
Japanese Print.
Jest, The.
Jewels, The.
Loss of Strength, The.
Lost Heifer, The.
Lucky Coin, The.
Marriage.
Martha Blake.
Martha Blake at Fifty-one.
Maurice was in an Exhibition Hall, sel.
Men were looking up, sel.
Miss Marnell.
My mother wept loudly, sel.
Night and Morning.
One night he heard heart-breaking sound, sel.
Past the house where he was got, sel.
Penal Law.
Pilgrimage.
Pill, The.

Planter's Daughter, The.
Rememorised, Maurice Devane, sel.
Respectable People.
Scholar, The.
Sermon on Swift, A.
Straight-jacketing sprang to every lock, sel.
Straying Student, The.
Strong Wind, A.
Subjection of Women, The.
Summer was sauntering by, sel.
Tall, handsome, tweeded Dr. Leeper, sel.
Tenebrae.
They are the spit of virtue now, sel.
Three Poems about Children.
Usufruct.
Wolfe Tone.
Young Woman of Beare, The.

Clarke, Cheryl
If You Black Get Back.
Of Althea and Flaxie.
Older American, The.
Palm Leaf of Mary Magdalene.

Clarke, Ednah Proctor
Mocking-Bird, The.
Salem Witch, A.

Clarke, F. W.
Rhyme of the Rain Machine, The.

Clarke, George Frederick
Saint John, The.

Clarke, George Herbert
Fog-Horn.
Halt and Parley.
Over Salève.
Santa Maria del Fiore.

Clarke, Gillian
Baby-Sitting.
Seamstress at St. Léon, sel.

Clarke, James Freeman
Brother, Hast Thou Wandered Far.
Dear Friend, Whose Presence in the House.

Clarke, John Cooper
Evidently Chicken Town.

Clarke, John Henrik
Determination.
Sing Me a New Song.

Clarke, Joseph I. C.
Fighting Race, The.
Pro Libra Mea.

Clarke, LeRoy
Where Hurricane.

Clarke, Macdonald
In the Graveyard.

Clarke, Pauline
My Name Is.

Clarke, Peter
In Air.
Play Song.
Young Shepherd Bathing His Feet.

Clarke, Willis Gaylord
Remembrance, A.

Claudian (Claudius Claudianus)
Epitaph: "Fate to beauty still must give."
Lonely Isle, The.
Old Man of Verona, The.
Rome Araieth Stilico in Vesture of the Consul, sel.

Claudius, Matthias
Most Acceptable Gift, The.

Claus, Hugo
Ambush.
Behind Bars.
Family.
In Flanders Fields.
Isis and the Animals: I.
Marsyas.
Mother, The.
Pigeon, A.
Tollund Man, The.
Turkey, A.

Clausen, Jan
After Touch.

Claytor, Gertrude
Grant at Appomattox.
Cleanthes
God Leads the Way.
Hymn to Zeus.
Cleary, Michael
After Reading *The Great American Marble Book* and Reflecting on Life's Lessons Learned at An Early.
Fingers, Fists, Gabriel's Wings.
Cleaveland, Elizabeth H. Jocelyn
No Sects in Heaven.
Cleaver, Thomas
Day is o'er! yet pleasure, commerce, gain, The, *sel.*
Cleavland, Benjamin
O Could I Find from Day to Day.
Cleghorn, Sarah Norcliffe
Comrade Jesus.
Golf Links, The.
Cleland, William
Hallo My Fancy.
Clémens, Éric
Epilogue: "There is, for me, now, in my life."
Clemens, Samuel Langhorne. *See* **"Twain, Mark"**
Clement of Alexandria
Earliest Christian Hymn.
Clementelli, Elena
Cerveteri road, *sel.*
From gorge to gorge, *sel.*
Net rests on the water's surface, The, *sel.*
Clements, John R.
God's Trails Lead Home.
Clemmons, Carole Gregory
Ghetto Lovesong—Migration.
I'm Just a Stranger Here, Heaven Is My Home.
Love from My Father.
Spring.
Clemo, Jack R.
Burnt Bush, The.
Charlotte Nicholls.
Christ in the Clay-Pit.
Growing in Grace.
Mould of Castile.
Neither Shadow of Turning.
On the Death of Karl Barth.
Clephane, Elizabeth C.
There Were Ninety and Nine.
Clerbout, Marguerite
Matinal.
Spring in the Woods.
Clerk, Sir John, of Penicuik
Fane Wald I Luve, *at.*
Miller, The.
Clerke, William
So, So.
Cleveland, John
And why so coffined in this vile disguise, *sel.*
Antiplatonick, The.
Come keen iambicks with your badger's feet, *sel.*
Elegy on Ben Jonson, An.
Epitaph on the Earl of Strafford.
Lord! what a goodly thing is want of shirts, *sel.*
Nature herself doth Scotchmen beasts confess, *sel.*
On the Memory of Mr. Edward King, Drowned in the Irish Seas.
To the State of Love; or, The Senses' Festival.
Upon Phillis Walking in a Morning before Sun-Rising.
Cleveland, Philip Jerome
I Yield Thee Praise.
Cliff, Michelle
I-Tie-All-My-People-Together.
Land of Look Beyond, The.

Clifford, Carrie Williams
Black Draftee from Dixie, The.
Clifford, Ethel
Harp of Sorrow, The.
Clifford, John
Anvil—God's Word, The.
Clifton, Lucille
Admonitions.
Africa.
Album.
April.
At Last We Killed the Roaches.
Breaklight.
Carver, The.
Come Home from the Movies.
Confession.
Cutting Greens.
Daddy.
Driving through New England.
Everett Anderson's Friend.
Eviction.
Explanations.
For de Lawd.
For the Lame.
For the Mute.
Forgiving My Father.
Friends Come.
God Send Easter.
God's Mood.
Good Times.
Holy Night.
Homage to My Hips.
I Once Knew a Man.
I went to the valley.
If I Stand in My Window.
If Something Should Happen.
In Populated.
In Salem.
In the Inner City.
Incandescence.
Jackie Robinson.
Light That Came, The.
Listen Children.
Lost Baby Poem, The.
Love Rejected.
Malcolm.
Miss Rosie.
Mother, I Am.
My Mama Moved among the Days.
Perhaps.
Poem: "Atlantic is a sea of bones."
Raising of Lazarus, The.
Roots.
She Understands Me.
Speaking of Loss.
Still.
Testament.
There Is a Girl Inside.
Thirty eighth year, The.
Those Boys That Ran Together.
To a Dark Moses.
To Bobby Seale.
To Joan.
To the Unborn and Waiting Children.
Way It Was, The.
Winnie Song.
Clinton, Michelle T.
Anti Apart Hate Art.
Close, Eunice
Here We Come A-Haying.
Way to Fairyland, The.
Close, John
And have we lost another friend?, *sel.*
Clother, Cal
Soaring.
Cloud, Maurice B.
Jazz Vamp.
Cloud, Peter Blue
Composition.
Cloud, Virginia Woodward
Ballad of Sweet P, The.

Care.
Mother's Song, The.
Old Street, An.
Youth.
Clough, Arthur Hugh
Ah, That I Were Far Away, *sel.*
Ah, you have much to learn, we can't know all things at twenty, *sel.*
As at return of tide the total weight of ocean, *sel.*
As I Sat at the Café, *sel.*
As I sat at the café, I said to myself, *sel.*
Columbus.
Come along, 'tis the time, ten or more minutes past, *sel.*
Come Home, Come Home!
Darkness.
Dear Eustatio, I write that you may write me an answer, *sel.*
Dulce it is, and *decorum*, no doubt, for the country to fall, *sel.*
Duty.
Epi-strauss-ium.
Farewell, politics, utterly! What can I do? I can not, *sel.*
Have you the Giesbach seen? a fall, *sel.*
Here Have I Been These One and Twenty Years.
Hope Evermore and Believe.
I dreamed a dream: I dreamt that I espied.
I Dreamt a Dream, *sel.*
Is it illusion? or does there a spirit from perfecter ages, *sel.*
Juxtaposition, *sel.*
Latest Decalogue, The.
Natura Naturans.
Nodding and beckoning across, observed of Attaché and Guardsman, *sel.*
O Thou Whose Image.
Only think, dearest Louisa, what fearful scenes we have witnessed!, *sel.*
Pont-y-Wern, *sel.*
Put forth thy leaf, thou lofty plane.
Qua Cursum Ventus.
Qui Laborat, Orat.
Reply to Dipsychus.
Rome disappoints me still; but I shrink and adapt myself to it, *sel.*
Rome ("Rome disappoints me much"), *sel.*
Say Not the Struggle Nought Availeth.
Sic Itur.
So, I have seen a man killed!, *sel.*
There are two different kinds, I believe, of human attraction, *sel.*
There is a stream, I name not its name, *sel.*
"There is no God," the wicked saith, *sel.*
This is the letter of Hobbes the kilted and corpulent hero, *sel.*
Thoughts of Home.
Tibur is beautiful, too, and the orchard slopes, and the Anio, *sel.*
To spend uncounted years of pain.
Victory, Victory! Yes, ah, yes, thou republican Zion, *sel.*
What do the people say, and what does the government do?, *sel.*
When God makes a great Man he intends all others to crush him, *sel.*
Where Lies the Land [to Which the Ship Would Go?], *sel.*
Will they fight? They say so. And will the French ?, *sel.*
Would That I Were.
Ye Ancient Divine Ones, *sel.*
Yes, we are fighting at last, it appears, *sel.*
Yet I could think, indeed, the perfect call, *sel.*
"Clout, Colin." *See* **Spenser, Edmund**
Clouts, Sydney
Animal Kingdom.
Dawn Hippo.
Earth, Sky.
Firebowl.

Grave's Cherub, The.
Of Thomas Traherne and the Pebble Outside.
Poetry Is Death Cast Out.
Portrait of Prince Henry, The.
Prince Henry the Navigator.
Sea and the Eagle, The.
Sleeper, The.
Clutesi, George
Beast in Man, The.
Ko-Ishin-Mit Goes Fishing.
Song of the Yellow Cedar Face, A.
West Coast Indian.
Coan, Titus Munson
Crystal, The.
Dream of Flowers, A.
Nihil Humani Alienum.
Coates, Carol
Choral Symphony Conductor.
Circle, The.
Country Reverie.
Light.
Coates, Florence Earle
Be Thou My Guide.
Buffalo.
By the Conemaugh.
Hero, A.
His Face.
India.
Perdita.
Pilgrim Song.
Requiem for a Young Soldier.
Seeker in the Night, A.
Suppliant.
Survival.
Tennyson.
Thanksgiving.
To-Morrow.
World Is Mine, The.
Coates, Grace Stone
Prairie Birth.
Coats, Adelbert Sumpter
Common Lot, The.
Pentecost.
Coats, Alice
Monstrous Regiment, The.
Sky-Conscious.
Coatsworth, Elizabeth Jane
All on a Christmas Morning.
Bad Kittens, The.
Barn, The.
Buds.
Circus-Postered Barn, The.
Columbus and the Mermaids.
Conquest.
Country Barnyard.
Daniel Webster's Horses.
Lady Comes to an Inn, A.
March.
Mountain Brook.
Mouse, The.
Navajo, The.
No Shop Does the Bird Use.
Nosegay.
Old Mare, The.
On a Night of Snow.
Pleiades, The.
Rhyme: "I like to see a thunder storm."
Roosters.
Song of the Camels.
Song of the Rabbits outside the Tavern, The.
Storm, The.
Straws.
Sunday.
This Is the Hay That No Man Planted.
Three.
Toad, The.
Two Cats, The.
Violets, daffodils. Nosegay.
Wilderness Rivers.
Cobb, Alice S.
Angela Davis.
Searching, The.

Cobb, Ann
Kivers.
Cobb, Charlie
"Containing Communism."
For Sammy Younge.
Nation.
To Vietnam.
Coblentz, Catherine Cate
Housewife, The.
Our History.
Coblentz, Stanton Arthur
Prayer for Light.
"Cockatoo Jack"
Numerella Shore, The.
Cockrell, Doug
Field Work.
Fist Fight.
His Lunch Bucket.
Cocteau, Jean
To a Sleeping Friend.
Codish, Edward
Juggle of Myrtle Twigs, A.
Yetzer ha Ra.
Codrescu, Andrei
Against Meaning.
Au Bout du Temps.
De Rerum Natura.
En Passant.
Grammar, A.
Imagination of Necessity, The.
Inner Source, The.
Petite Histoire of Red Fascism, A.
Poetry Paper.
Threat, The.
Work.
Coe, Peter
Wizard of Alderley Edge, The.
Coffey, Brian
Awakening like return to Earth from Moon,
   sel.
Blooms such as wither at finger-touch, *sel.*
Cold.
Headrock.
Nightfall, Midwinter, Missouri, *sel.*
"The Nicest Phantasies Are Shared."
Coffin, Robert Peter Tristram
Christening-Day Wishes for My God-Child.
Covered Bridge.
Graveyard.
Skunk, The.
Spider, The.
Square-toed Princes.
Starfish, The.
Coghill, Mary
Knowing.
Coghill, Rhoda
Bright Hillside, The.
In Wicklow.
Poem: "Is to love, this—to nurse a name."
Runaway.
Spring Doggerel.
Cogil, Legon and Carlton Barrett
Dem Belly Full.
Cohan, George M.
Life's a Funny Proposition after All.
Cohen, Arleen
Chinese Checkers.
Cohen, Jacob
Eternal Jew, The.
Harp of David, The.
Surely My Soul. .
Cohen, Leonard
All There Is to Know about Adolph
   Eichmann.
As the Mist Leaves No Scar.
Ballad: "My lady was found mutilated."
Bus, The.
Celebration.
Elegy: "Do not look for him."
For Anne.
Genius, The.

Heirloom.
I Have Not Lingered in European
   Monasteries.
Killers That Run, The.
Kite Is a Victim, A.
Music Crept by Us, The.
Out of the Land of Heaven.
Prayer for Messiah.
Story of Isaac.
Suzanne Takes You Down.
You Have the Lovers.
Cohen, Marc
Mecox Road.
Silhouette.
Cohen, Robert David
Bones of Incontention, The.
Day on Kind Continent.
Storm, The.
Street of Named Houses, The.
Cohen, Shlomit
Same Dream, The.
Unraveled Thought, An.
Wife of Kohelet.
Cohn, Syma Cheris
Yo-Yo King, The.
Cohoe, Grey
Folding Fan, The.
Coignard, Gabrielle de
Prayer: "Fear of death disturbs me constantly,
   The."
Cokayne, Sir Aston
Epitaph on a Great Sleeper.
Funeral Elegy on the Death of His Very Good
   Friend, Mr. Michael Drayton.
Colclough, Phil
Blood on the Sails.
Liverpool John.
Colclough, Phil and June Colclough
Song for Ireland.
Cole, Barry
Men Are Coming Back! The.
Cole, Charlotte Druitt
Christmas Eve.
Clothes-Line, The.
Dormouse, The.
Green Lady, The.
Pimpernel.
Pudding Charms.
Sun and Moon.
Three Mice.
Yellow Fairy, The.
Cole, Eugene Roger
Oh, You Wholly Rectangular.
Cole, George Douglas Howard
And you'll say a nation totters, *sel.*
Cole, Harriet
End of the Way, The.
Cole, Henri
Prince Enters the Forest, The.
Cole, Henry
Thy Best.
Cole, Joanna
Driving to the Beach.
Happy New Year, Anyway.
Hippopotamus.
Cole, Samuel Valentine
Abraham Lincoln.
Hammer and Anvil.
Satisfied.
Trees, The.
Cole, Thomas
Landscape of Love, The.
Memories of a Dorset Childhood in the
   1730's, *sel.*
Spider.
Time allowed for sleep at length elapsed, The,
   sel.
Tray, The.
Variations on a Still Morning.
Written in Autumn.

Cole, William
Alma Mater, Forget Me.
Back Yard, July Night.
Banananananananana.
Did You?
Just Dropped In.
Marriage Couplet.
Mutual Problem.
Mysterious East.
Oh, Noa, Noa!
Poor Kid.
Sneaky Bill.
Time Piece.
Two Sad.
Undersea Fever.
What a Friend We Have in Cheeses!
Cole, William Rossa
Anna Livia Plurabelle, *sel.*
Dirty Work on the Appellation Trail.
Marriage Toast.
On Ireland's Roaringwater Bay, *sel.*
On the beach near Port St. Joe, *sel.*
Sailing on Lac d'Annecy, *sel.*
When she lived near St. Lawrence, *sel.*
With Robert Hughes on Botany Bay, *sel.*
Coleman, Emily Holmes
Liberator, The.
Coleman, Helena
As Day Begins to Wane.
More Lovely Grows the Earth.
Coleman, Herbert T. J.
Cockle-Shell and Sandal-Shoon.
Poet Confides, The.
Coleman, Lucile
With Lilacs in My Eye.
Coleman, Marion
Monte Cassino 1945.
Coleman, Victor
Day Twenty-three.
How the Death of a City Is Never More than
  the Sum of the Deaths of Those Who
  Inhabit Its Spaces.
Coleman, Wanda
Essay on Language.
Coleridge, Hartley
Death-Bed Reflections of Michel-Angelo.
Dedicatory Sonnet to S. T. Colerige.
Early Death.
Full Well I Know.
Hast Thou Not Seen an Aged Rifted Tower.
He Lived amidst th' Untrodden Ways.
How Long I Sailed.
Lines———: "I have been cherish'd and
  forgiven."
Long Time a Child.
"Multum Dilexit."
November, *sel.*
Poietes Apoietes.
Song: She Is Not Fair to Outward View.
There Lived among the Untrodden Ways.
Think upon Death.
To a Cat.
To a Deaf and Dumb Little Girl.
To a Friend.
To Wordsworth.
Why Should I Murmur.
Written on the Anniversary of Our Father's
  Death.
Coleridge, Mary Elizabeth
After Reading Certain Books.
After St. Augustine.
An Insincere Wish Addressed to a Beggar.
At a Friends' Meeting.
Awake.
Bid me remember, O my gracious Lord, *sel.*
Blue and White.
Chillingham.
Clever Woman, A.
Dedication, A: "Life of my learning, fire of
  all my Art."
Depart from Me.

Deserted House, The.
Egypt's Might Is Tumbled Down.
From My Window.
Gifts.
Gone.
"He Knoweth Not That the Dead Are Thine."
I Saw a Stable.
In Dispraise of the Moon.
Jealousy.
L'Oiseau Bleu.
Lord of the Winds.
Marriage.
"My True Love Hath My Heart and I Have
  His."
Nurse's Lament, The.
Other Side of a Mirror, The.
Our Lady.
Punctilio.
Street Lanterns.
Three Helpers in Battle.
Train, The.
Unwelcome.
We Never Said Farewell.
When Mary thro' the Garden Went.
Where a Roman Villa Stood, above Freiburg.
White Women, The.
Whither Away?
Witch, The.
Witches' Wood, The.
Coleridge, Samuel Taylor
All Seasons Shall Be Sweet.
And haply, bason'd in some unsunn'd cleft,
  sel.
Answer to a Child's Question.
Apologia Pro Vita Sua.
Ballad of the Dark Ladie, The.
Christabel.
Christabel and Geraldine, *sel.*
Cologne.
Composed on a Journey Homeward; the
  Author Having Received Intelligence of the
  Birth of a Son.
Constancy to an Ideal Object.
Dejection; an Ode [*or* A Letter to Sara
  Hutchinson]
Delinquent Travellers, The.
Dirge: Metrical Feet.
Eolian [*or* Aeolian] Harp, The.
Epitaph on Himself.
Epitaph: "Stop, Christian passer-by!—Stop,
  child of God."
" 'Even so' (the exulting Maiden said)," *sel.*
Exchange, The.
Fears in Solitude.
For what is Freedom, but the unfettered use,
  sel.
For when it dawn'd—they dropp'd their arms,
  sel.
Fragment: "Spruce and limber
  yellow-hammer, The."
France; an Ode.
Frost at Midnight.
Fruit Plucker, The.
Glycine's Song, *sel.*
Good Great Man, The.
He Prayeth Best, *sel.*
Human Life; on the Denial of Immortality.
Hymn before Sunrise, in the Vale of
  Chamouni.
If I Had but Two Little Wings.
In the Touch of This Bosom There Worketh a
  Spell, *sel.*
Knight's Tomb, The.
Koskiusko.
Kubla Khan; or, A Vision in a Dream.
LaFayette.
Lewti.
Life.
Limbo.
Lines Written in the Album at Elbingerode, in
  the Hartz Forest.
Looking Down on Nether Stowey, *sel.*

Love.
Lovely was the death, *sel.*
Love's Apparition and Evanishment.
Mathematical Problem, A.
Modern Critics.
My Baptismal Birthday.
Ne Plus Ultra.
Netherlands, The.
Nightingale, The.
Nightingales, *sel.*
No cloud, no relique of the sunken day, *sel.*
O My Mother Isle!, *sel.*
Ode to the Departing Year.
On a Bad Singer.
On a Discovery Made Too Late.
On a Lord.
On a Ruined House in a Romantic Country.
On an Infant Which Died before Baptism.
On Donne's Poem "To a Flea."
On Donne's Poetry.
On Imitation.
On My Joyful Departure from the City of
  Cologne.
On the green sheep-track, up the healthy hill,
  sel.
Or wren or linnet.
Pains of Sleep, The.
Pantisocracy.
Pensive at Eve, *sel.*
Phantom or Fact.
Raven, The.
Recollections of Love.
Reflections on Having Left a Place of
  Retirement.
Religious Musings.
Rime of the Ancient Mariner, The.
Scars Remaining, The, *sel.*
Sea-ward, white gleaming through the busy
  scud.
Seen from the Quantocks, *sel.*
Self-Knowledge.
Silent Icicles, The, *sel.*
So gentle Ellen now no more, *sel.*
Sonnet to a Friend Who Asked, How I Felt
  When the Nurse First Presented My Infant
  to Me.
Sonnet: To the River Otter.
Sunset, A.
Swans Sing before They Die.
There is one Mind, one omnipresent, *sel.*
This Lime-Tree Bower My Prison.
Time, Real and Imaginary.
To a Young Ass.
To Nature.
To Simplicity, *sel.*
To the Reverend W. L. Bowles.
To William Wordsworth.
Truth I pursued, as Fancy sketch'd the way.
Up, Up! Ye Dames and Lasses Gay.
Voice Sings, A, *sel.*
W. H. *Eheu!*
What is an epigram? a dwarfish whole.
What Is Life?
Work without Hope: Lines Composed 21st
  February 1827
Youth and Age.

Coleridge, Sara
Garden Year, The.
O sleep, my babe, hear not the rippling wave,
  sel.
Trees.

Coles, Don
Natalya Nikolayevna Goncharov.
Photograph in a Stockholm Newspaper for
  March 13, 1910.

Colesworthy, Daniel C.
Be Never Discouraged.
While We Lowly Bow before Thee.

Colet, Louise
Working-Class Woman, A.

Coletti, Ed
Mourning a Lost Poem.

College, Stephen
Raree Show, A.
Truth Brought to Light, or Murder Will Out.

Collier, Edward A.
After the Rain.

Collier, John
Pluralist and Old Soldier, The.

Collier, Mary
Washerwoman, The, *sel.*

Collier, Thomas Stephens
Cleopatra Dying.
Compensation.
Disappointment.
Infallibility.
Power.
Time.

Collin, William Edwin
Monserrat.
Sancho.

Collins, Anne
Song: "My straying thoughts, reduced stay."

Collins, Billy
High Stick.

Collins, Ellodë
Cessation of War.

Collins, Emanuel
Fatal Dream; or, The Unhappy Favourite,
The.

Collins, Helen Johnson
To an Avenue Sport.

Collins, John
Chapter of Kings, The.
Tomorrow.

Collins, Leslie Morgan
Creole Girl.
Stevedore.

Collins, Martha
Story We Know, The.

Collins, Merle
How Times Have Changed!
Images.
No Dialects Please.
Same But Different.
Shipmates.

Collins, Mortimer
If.
Lotos Eating.
Positivists, The.
Salad: After Browning.
Salad: After Swinburne.
Salad—After Tennyson.
To F. C.

Collins, Ruth
Song of a Factory Worker, The.

Collins, W. F.
Lincoln Statue, The.

Collins, William
Fidele, A.
How Sleep the Brave.
Ode Occasioned by the Death of Mr.
Thomson.
Ode on the Poetical Character.
Ode on the Popular Superstitions of the
Highlands of Scotland, An.
Ode to Evening.
Ode to Fear.
Ode to Simplicity.
Passions, an Ode for [or to] Music, The.
Persian Eclogue the Second.
Sonnet: "When Phoebe formed a wanton
smile."
Stormy Hebrides, The, *sel.*

Collinson, Laurence
Sea and the Tiger, The.

Collom, Jack
Phone Number.
Sidonie.

Collop, John
Leper Cleansed, The.
To the Soul.

Collyer, Robert
Under the Snow.

Collymore, Frank A.
Ballad of an Old Woman.
Monkeys.
Triptych.
Zobo Bird, The.

Colman, Benjamin
Another to Urania.
God of My Life!
Poem on Elijahs Translation, A.
Quarrel with Fortune, A.
To Philomela.
To Urania.

Colman, George, the Younger
Cold blows the blast—the night's obscure,
sel.
On Sir Nathaniel Wraxall the Historian.
Unfortunate Miss Bailey.

Colman, Mary Elizabeth
We Men Are of Two Worlds.

Colombo, John Robert
How They Made the Golem.
Ideal Angels.

Colonna, Giuseppina Turrisi
To My Mother.

Colonna, Vittoria, Marchesa di Pescara
As a hungry fledgling, who sees and hears.
As When Some Hungry Fledgling Hears and
Sees.
Between Hard Rocks and Savage Winds I
Try.
I live on this depraved and lonely cliff.
I Write Only to Relieve My Inner Grief.
Like a hungry fledgeling that watches and
hears.
O what transparent waves, what a tranquil
sea.
When the Orient is lit by the great light.
When the troubled sea swells and surrounds.

Colony, Horatio
Ghost Pet.

Colton, Arthur Willis
Harps Hung Up in Babylon.
Song with a Discord, A.

Colum, Padraic
After Speaking of One Dead a Long Time.
Belfast: High Street.
Book of Kells, The.
Condors.
Cradle Song, A.
Dahlias.
Drover, A.
Fuchsia Hedges in Connacht.
Garland Sunday.
I Saw the Wind Today.
Interior.
Irises.
Knitters, The.
Monkeys.
No Child.
Old Soldier.
Old Woman of the Roads, An.
Peach Tree with Fruit.
Plower, The.
Poor Scholar of the 'Forties, A.
Poplar Tree.
River-Mates.
She Moved through the Fair.
Toy-Maker, The.
Tulips.
Wall of China, The.
Wild Ass.

Columba, Saint. *See* **Columcille, Saint**

Columbanus, Saint
Boat Song, A.
Boyhood of Christ, The.

Columcille [or Columba], Saint
Clamour of the wind making music.
Farewell to Ireland, *at.*
If I owned all of Alba.
Invocation, An: "My claw is tired of
scribing!"
Lon's away,/ Cill Garad is sad today, *sel.*
Mary mild, good maiden.
O Son of God, it would be sweet.
On some island I long to be.
Prayer to the Virgin.
St. Columcille the Scribe, *at.*
Three places most loved I have left.

Colvin, Norma Thomas
Cowboy-Boot Sale.
On Forgetting to Cry.

Combs, Tram
Ars Poetica about Ultimates.
Aware Aware.
Just after Noon with Fierce Shears.

Cometas
Country Gods.

Comfort, Alex
After Shakespeare.
After You, Madam.
Atoll in the Mind, The.
Epitaph: "One whom I knew, a student and a
poet."
Fear of the Earth.
Haste to the Wedding.
Hoc Est Corpus.
Letter to an American Visitor.
Love Poem: "There is a white mare that my
love keeps," *sel.*
Lovers, The.
Notes for My Son, *sel.*
Song for the Heroes.
Sublimation.

Compiuta Donzella
In the Season When the World's in Leaf and
Flower.
This World I'd Wish to Leave and God to
Serve.
To leave the world and serve God.

Compton, S. R.
Imagination of the Retina, The.
Photomicrograph: Last Centimeter of the
Human Airway.

Comyn, Michael
Oisin in the Land of Youth.

Concanen, Matthew
Heaps on Heaps, *sel.*

Conder, Josiah
Bread of Heaven, on Thee We Feed.
Day by Day the Manna Fell.

Cone, Helen Gray ("Coroebus Green")
Arraignment.
Contrast, The.
Fair England.
Last Cup of Canary, The.
Narcissus in Camden.
Spring Beauties, The.
Thisbe.

Confucius
Alba, *sel.*
Aliter, *sel.*
Baroness Mu Impeded in Her Wish to Help
Famine Victims in Wei, *sel.*
Be kind, good sir, and I'll lift my sark, *sel.*
"Chkk! chkk!" hopper-grass, *sel.*
Efficient Wife's Complaint, The, *sel.*
Fraternitas, *sel.*
Hep-Cat Chung, 'ware my town, *sel.*
In chariot like an hibiscus flower at his side,
sel.
In the South be drooping trees, *sel.*
Marsh bank, lotus rank, *sel.*

Pedlar, *sel.*
Sans Equity and sans Poise, *sel.*
So he won't talk to me when we meet?, *sel.*
Three stars, five stars rise over the hill, *sel.*
Congdon, Kirby
Daredevil.
Congreve, William
Doris.
Epilogue: "After our Epilogue this crowd
dismisses," *sel.*
False Though She Be.
Hue and Cry after Fair Amoret, A.
Jack Frenchman's Defeat.
Lesbia.
Pious Selinda [*or* Celinda]
Prologue: "Of those few fools, who with ill
stars are cursed," *sel.*
Soldier and a Sailor, A, *sel.*
Song: "See, see, she wakes, Sabina wakes!"
Coninck, Herman de
Ars Poetica: 4.
Briton, A.
Every Day Here Is like This.
Frédérique, or How I Became a Historian.
Mother.
Rhinoceros, The.
Conkling, Hilda
Dandelion.
Fairies.
I Am.
Little Papoose.
Little Snail.
Water.
Conley, Robert J.
Hills of *Tsa la gi* , The.
Ned Christie.
Rattlesnake Band, The.
Tom Starr.
Wili Woyi, Shaman, Also Known as Billy
Pigeon.
Conn, Stewart
Marriage on a Mountain Ridge.
Under Creag Mhor.
Connell, Charles
Wyvern.
Connell, Hugh
Dream, A.
Erris Coast, 1943.
Mountain Tree, The.
Connell, Philip
Winter Night in Manchester, A.
Connor, Tony
Apologue.
Elegy for Alfred Hubbard.
Lancashire Winter.
Last of the Poet's Car.
Conolly, John
Fiddler's Green.
Conolly, John *and* Bill Meek
Grimsby Lads, The.
Conover, Carl
Nude Reclining at Word Processor, in Pastel.
Conquest, Robert
Agents, The.
Appalachian Convalescence.
Excerpt from a Report to the Galactic
Council.
Generalities.
Guided Missiles Experimental Range.
Horror Comic.
Lake Success.
Man and Woman.
Semantic.
747 (London-Chicago).
To Be a Pilgrim.
Conrad, Patrick
Back Seat Dodge '38, The.
Illegal Operation, The.
Roxy's.
Zeppelins.

Constable, Henry
Dear to my soul! then leave me not forsaken!,
sel.
Diaphenia, *at.*
Fair sun, if you would have me praise your
light, *sel.*
Grace full of grace, though in these verses
here, *sel.*
Hope, like the hyaena [*or* hyena], coming to
be old, *sel.*
If ever Sorrow spoke from soul that loves,
sel.
Love's Franciscan.
Miracle of the world, I never will deny, *sel.*
My tears are true, though others be divine,
sel.
Needs must I leave and yet needs must I love,
sel.
Not that thy hand is soft, is sweet, is white,
sel.
Of the Nativity of the Lady Rich's Daughter.
On the Death of Sir Philip Sidney.
Ready to seek out death in my disgrace, *sel.*
Resolved to Love, *sel.*
Sonnet: "If ever Sorrow spoke from soul that
loves," *sel.*
Sonnet: "My lady's presence makes the roses
red."
Sonnet: "My lady's presence makes the roses
red," *sel.*
Sun, his journey ending in the west, The, *sel.*
To God the Son.
To His Flocks, *at.*
To live in hell, and heaven to behold, *sel.*
To Our Blessed Lady.
To Saint Margaret.
To Saint Mary Magdalen ("Blessed Offendour:
who thyself haist try'd").
To Saint Mary Magdalen ("Sweet Saint, thou
better canst declare to me").
To St. Peter and St. Paul.
To the Blessed Sacrament.
Whilst Echo cries [*or* eccho cryes], "What
shall become of me[e]?", *sel.*
You secret vales, you solitary fields, *sel.*
Constantine, David
Watching for Dolphins.
Conti, Edmund
Clerihew: "Orson Welles/ Suffered from
eating spells."
Clerihew: "Said Henry VIII/ Accepting his
fate."
Clerihew: "William F. Buckley/ Writes
pluckley."
Contreras, José Peón y. *See* **Peón y
Contreras, José.**
Converse, Florence
Rune of Riches, A.
Conway, Hugh
Falkland at Newbury, 1643.
Conway, Jack
Clothes Make the Man.
Conway, Katherine Eleanor
Heaviest Cross of All, The.
Saturninus.
Conyus
Great Santa Barbara Oil Disaster OR, The.
He's Doing Natural Life.
San Francisco County Jail Cell B-6.
Six Ten Sixty-nine.
Untitled Requiem for Tomorrow.
Upon Leaving the Parole Board Hearing.
Coogler, J. Gordon
Alas! Carolina!
Alas! for the South.
Byron.
In Memorial.
Mustacheless Bard, A.

Poor South! Her books get fewer and fewer.
Pretty Girl, A.
Cook, Clarence Chatham
On One Who Died in May.
Cook, Edmund Vance
Are You You?
Cook, Mrs. M. A. W
In Some Way or Other the Lord Will Provide.
Indian Hunter, The.
Many a lip is gaping for drink, *sel.*
Mouse and the Cake, The.
My Old Straw Hat.
Old Arm-Chair, The.
Sailor's Grave, The, *at.*
Try Again.
Where There's a Will There's a Way.
Cook, Mike
Bootie Black and the Seven Giants.
Cook, Russell Sturgis
Just as Thou Art.
Cook, Stanley
Blind Upholsterer, The.
Calder Valley: At the Top of the Ainleys.
Christmas Tree.
Firth Park Road: 9:30 A.M.
Sheffield East End.
Survivor, The.
Cook, Warren F.
Revelation.
Cooke, Edmund Vance
Born without a Chance.
Fin de Siècle.
How Did You Die?
Moo-Cow-Moo, The.
"Off Manilly."
Pass.
Perfect Gift, The.
Plug.
Rags.
What Are You Doing?
You Too.
Cooke, John Esten
Band in the Pines, The.
Cooke, Philip Pendleton
Florence Vane.
Cooke, Rose Terry
Arachne.
Bluebeard's Closet.
Death of Goody Nurse, The.
Done For.
In Vain.
Lise.
Segovia and Madrid.
Snow-filled Nest, The.
Cook-Lynn, Elizabeth
Dream, *sel.*
Grandfather at the Indian Health Clinic.
Memory, *sel.*
My Grandmother's Burial Ground.
Sacristans, *sel.*
Coolbrith, Ina
Fruitionless.
Helen Hunt Jackson.
Mariposa Lily, The.
When the Grass Shall Cover Me.
Cooley, Julia. *See* **Altrocchi, Julia Cooley**
Cooley, Peter
Alternatives.
Ararat.
Confession, The.
For Alissa.
Frog Hunting.
Last Gift, The.
Naked Poetry.
Other, The.
Sparrows, The.
Such Comfort as the Night Can Bring to Us.
To a Wasp Caught in the Storm Sash at the
Advent of the Winter Solstice.
Unasked For, The.
Vanishing Point.

Coolidge, Clark
Album—A Runthru.
Back Always.
Blocks, The.
Codex.
Death of Floyd Collins, The.
Dial around forth enough means that there
   since, *sel.*
Disturbing the Sallies Forth.
Fed Drapes.
I Drove Through This Old World This
   Afternoon.
Manlius to Coeymans.
Monologue, A.
Mud of the bulk of the back yard, The.
Of the Confident Stranger.
Remove the Predicate.
Risen Matters.
Rome Once Alone.
Thin Places.
To Mind.
"Coolidge, Susan" (Sarah Chauncey Woolsey)
Better Way, The.
Bind-Weed.
Calvary and Easter.
Charlotte Brontë.
Child's Thought of Harvest, A."
Edenhall.
Gulf Stream.
Helen.
Measles in the Ark.
Time to Go.
Cooper, Charles
Dreams.
Rubin.
Cooper, Dennis
Being Aware.
Hustlers.
My Past.
Cooper, George
Baby-Land.
Come, Little Leaves.
October's Party.
Only One Mother.
What Robin Told.
While the Days Are Going By.
Cooper, James Fenimore (1789–1851)
My Brigantine, *sel.*
Cooper, James Fenimore (1892–1918)
To a Friend.
Cooper, Jane
Childhood in Jacksonville, Florida.
Circle, a Square, a Triangle and a Ripple of
   Water, A.
Conversation by the Body's Light.
Dispossessions.
El Sueño de la Razón.
Faithful, The.
For a Very Old Man, on the Death of His
   Wife.
Graveyard, The.
In the House of the Dying.
In the Last Few Moments Came the Old
   German Cleaning Woman.
Jittoku, Buddhist Mystic—15th Century.
Knowledge That Comes through Experience,
   The.
Morning on the St. John's.
My Young Mother.
Obligations.
Poem with Capital Letters, A.
Praise.
Rent.
Rock Climbing.
Waiting.
Weather of Six Mornings, The.
Cooper, John Gilbert
Temper of Aristippus, The, *sel.*
Cooper, Julian
Warm Winter Day, A.

Cooper, Karen
Native Woman—1982, A.
Cooper, Leonard
Rhyming Prophecy for a New Year.
Cooper, Roger
To See the Cross at Christmas.
Cooper, Thomas
Methought, on this aspiring form I gazed, *sel.*
Song for the free—the brave and the free, A,
   sel.
Time shall come when wrong shall end, The,
   sel.
Cooper, Edith Katherine Bradley. *See*
   "Field, Michael"
Cooperman, Hasye
Mists Are Rising Now, The.
Cope, Jack
Flying Fish, The.
If You Come Back.
Rock Painting.
Sappho.
Sons.
Cope, Wendy
Budgie Finds His Voice.
Depression.
English Weather.
Mr. Strugnell.
Policeman's Lot, A.
Waste Land Limericks.
Copeland, Benjamin
Christ's Life Our Code.
Our Fathers' God.
Copenhaver, Laura S.
Heralds of Christ.
Coppard, Alfred Edgar
Apostate, The.
Epitaph: "Like silver dew are the tears of
   love."
Forester's Song.
Mendacity.
Unfortunate Miller, The.
Corbet, Richard
Distracted Puritan, The.
Great Tom.
Like to the Thundering Tone.
Little lute, when I am gone.
Non Sequitor, A.
On Mr. Francis Beaumont (Then Newly
   Dead).
To His Son [*or* Sonne], Vincent Corbet[t]
Corbett, E. R.
Inventor's Wife, The.
Corbett, Elizabeth T.
Misspelled Tail, A.
Tail of the See, A.
Three Wise Couples, The.
Three Wise Old Women.
Corbett, Richard
Certain True Woords Spoken Concerning One
   Benet Corbett after Her Death.
Upon Fairford Windows.
Corbett, William
Edwin Dickinson's Perspective.
My Uncle.
Corbière, Tristan (Edouard Joachim
   Corbière)
Epitaph: "Or many things adulterate."
To My Mouse-colored Mare.
To the Eternal Feminine.
Well, all these seamen—sailors and
   skippers—they, *sel.*
You who snore with your sleeping wife so
   near, *sel.*
Corbin, Alice (Alice Corbin Henderson)
Echoes of Childhood.
Harvest, The.
Listening.
Corbin, Lloyd M., Jr. (Djangatolum)
Ali.
Dedication to the Final Confrontation.

Corder, W.
Murder of Maria Marten, The.
Cordle, Edward
Lizzie and Joe Catch a Thief.
Lizzie and Joe in Court.
Lizzie Discourses on the Small-Pox.
Córdova y Bocanegra, Fernando de
Song to the Most Holy Name of Jesus.
Coren, Alan
By the Klondike River.
Corey, Stephen
Bread.
Corgo, Emanuel
Against Negritude.
"Corinna"
Sehnsucht; or, What You Will.
Corinna (fl. c.500? B.C.). *See* **Korinna**
Corke, Hilary
Any Man to His Secretary.
Calm Winter Sleep.
Chair, Dog, and Clock.
Choice, The.
Destroying Angel.
Ghost, The.
November Poppies.
Poem at Equinox.
Storm of Love, A.
Waiting.
Waltz, The.
Cormack, Barbara Villy
Reprieve.
Corman, Cid
Call it a louse—I'm.
Container, The.
Deceased.
Desk, The.
Detail, The.
I have come far to have found nothing, *sel.*
La Selva.
Locus, The.
Old Men, The.
There are things to be said. No doubt.
Three Tiny Songs.
Tortoise, The.
Cormican, P. J.
True Son of God, Eternal Light.
Corn, Alfred
Darkening Hotel Room.
Deception.
Documentary on Brazil, The.
Fire: The People, *sel.*
Grass.
Infinity Effect at the Hôtel Soubise.
Moving: New York—New Haven Line.
Naskeag.
New Year.
Older Men.
Prophet Bird.
Remembering Mykenai.
Two Travelers on a Summer Evening.
Cornelius, Maxwell N.
Some Time We'll Understand.
Cornelius, Peter
Christmas Tree, The.
Cornell, Annette Patton
Sailor's Woman.
Cornford, Adam
Our Sorcerers.
Cornford, Frances (Darwin)
All Souls' Night.
At Night.
Autumn Blitz.
Autumn Morning at Cambridge.
Casualties.
Childhood.
Coast, The: Norfolk.
Country Bedroom, The.
Daybreak.
Epitaph for a Reviewer.
For M.S. Singing *Fruhlingsglaube* in 1945.
From a Letter to America on a Visit to
   Sussex: Spring 1942.

Glimpse, A.
Guitarist Tunes Up, The.
Herd, The.
Hills, The.
In the Backs.
Inscription for a Wayside Spring.
London Despair.
Near an Old Prison.
Night Song.
Parting in Wartime.
Recollection, A.
Scholar, The.
She Warns Him.
Soldiers on the Platform.
Spring Morning.
Summer Beach.
To a Fat Lady Seen from the Train.
Unbeseechable, The.
Village before Sunset.
Wasted Day, A.
Watch, The.
Weekend Stroll.
Youth.

Cornford, John
Full Moon at Tierz; before the Storming of
    Huesca.
Huesca.
Letter from Aragon, A.

Cornish, Sam
April 68.
Black Man, A.
Death of Dr. King.
Dory Miller.
Frederick Douglass.
Home.
Hometown.
Lenox Christmas Eve 68.
Montgomery.
One Eyed Black Man in Nebraska.
Panther.
Ray Charles.
River, The.
Sam's World ("Sam's mother has").
Sooner or Later.
To a Single Shadow without Pity.
When My Grandmother Died.
Your Mother.

Cornish, William
Desire.
Pleasure It Is.

"Cornwall, Barry" (Bryan Waller Proctor)
"Blood Horse, The."
Fate of the Oak, The.
For a Fountain.
Hunter's Song, The.
Sea, The.

Cornwall, Ursula
Sowing Seeds.

Cornwallis, Kinahan
Battle of Murfreesboro, The.

Cornwell, Henry Sylvester
Jefferson D.

Coronel Urtecho, José
Past Will Not Return, The.

Corpi, Lucha
Blind Woman, The.
Crystal Bridge, The.
Dark Romance.
Devil's Daughter, The.
Marina Mother.
Marina Virgin.
Nocturnal Sunscape.
Passion without a Name.
Secret Society of Failures.
She (Marina Distant).
Sunscape.
Woven Romance.

Corretjer, Juan Antonio
Convoy, The.
In Jail.

Corrie, Joe
Image o' God, The.
Miners' Wives.

Corrington, John William
For a Woodscolt Miscarried.
On the Flesh of Christ.
Second Coming, The.

Corrothers, James David
At the Closed Gate of Justice.
Dream and the Song.
In the Matter of Two Men.
Indignation Dinner, An.
Negro Singer, The.
Paul Laurence Dunbar.
Road to the Bow, The.

Corsellis, Timothy
Engine Failure.
Repression.
They Have Taken It from Me.
Thrush, The.
To Stephen Spender.

Corso, Gregory
Birthplace Revisited.
Body Fished from the Seine.
But I Do Not Need Kindness.
Dialogue—2 Dollmakers.
Difference of Zoos, A.
Dream of a Baseball Star.
Dreamed Realization, A.
From Another Room.
Hello.
I Held a Shelley Manuscript.
I Met This Guy Who Died.
In the Fleeting Hand of Time.
Marriage.
New York City—1935.
Notes after Blacking Out.
Paranoia in Crete.
Paris.
Poets Hitchhiking on the Highway.
Reflection in a Green Arena.
Requiem for "Bird" Parker.
Seed Journey.
Spontaneous Requiem for the American
    Indian.
Uccello.
Waterchew!
Writ on the Eve of My 32nd Birthday.
Zizi's Lament.

Cortez, Jayne
Acceptance Speech.
Big Fine Woman from Ruleville.
Everything Is Wonderful.
For Real.
Grinding Vibrato.
I Am New York City.
In the Morning.
Initiation.
Lead.
Orange Chiffon.
Orisha.
Phraseology.
So Long.
So Many Feathers.
Tell Me.
Under the Edge of February.

Cortínez, Carlos
Poetry Reading in the Iowa City Railroad
    Station.

Cortissoz, Ellen Mackay Hutchinson
April Fantasie.
Bride's Toilette, The.
Cry from the Shore, A.
Harvest.
Her Picture.
Moth-Song.
On Kingston Bridge.
Pamela in Town.
Praise-God Barebones.
Quaker Ladies.
Sea-Way.
So Wags the World.

Corvo, Baron. *See* **Rolfe, Frederick William**

Corwin, Norman
Man unto His Fellow Man, *sel.*

Cory, David
Miss You.

Cory, William Johnson
Ballad for a Boy, A.
Bride's Song, The.
Dirge, A: "Naiad, hid beneath the bank."
Eton Boating Song.
Heraclitus.
Hersilia.
Mimnermus in Church.
Poor French Sailor's Scottish Sweetheart, A.
Separation, A.

Coslett, Coslett
Pole Star, The.

Costanzo, Gerald
In the Blood.
Introduction of the Shopping Cart.
Jeanne Dixon's America.
Meeting, The.
Nobody Lives on Arthur Godfrey Boulevard.
Seeing My Name in TV Guide.

Costello, Tomas
Young Una, you were a rose in a garden, *sel.*

Cothi, Lewis Glyn
Lament for Siôn y Glyn.

Cotrell, Gretchen
Letter to the Little Shell.

Cottam, Samuel Elsworth
To G. R.

Cotter, Joseph Seamon, Jr.
And What Shall You Say?
April Day, An.
Band of Gideon, The.
Deserter, The.
Is It Because I Am Black?
Prayer, A: "As I lie in bed."
Rain Music.
Sonnet to Negro Soldiers.
Supplication.

Cotter, Joseph Seamon, Sr.
Tragedy of Pete, The.
Way-Side Well, The.

Cottle, Joseph
Industrial Evils, *sel.*

Cotton, Charles
Alice Is Tall and Upright as a Pine, *sel.*
Epitaph on M. H., An.
Evening.
Laura Sleeping.
Litany, The: "From a ruler that's a curse."
Madrigal.
Marg'ret of Humbler Stature by the Head, *sel.*
Martha Is Not So Tall, *sel.*
Mary Is Black, *sel.*
New Year, The.
On My Pretty Marten.
On Tobacco.
Retirement, The, *sel.*
Song of Sack, A, *at.*
Song: "See, how like twilight slumber falls."
Tempest, The.
To Coelia.
Winter's Troops, *sel.*

Cotton, John (1584–1652)
In Saram.
Pumpkins.
Thankful Acknowledgment of God's
    Providence, A.
To My Reverend Dear Brother, M. Samuel
    Stone.

Cotton, John (*fl.* 1676)
Bacon's Epitaph, Made by His Man, at.
Upon the Death of G. B.

Cotton, John
Old Movies.

Cotton, Nathaniel
Bee, the Ant, and the Sparrow, The.
Contentment.

Early Thoughts of Marriage.
To a Child Five Years Old.

Coulette, Henri
Antony and Cleopatra.
At the Telephone Club.
Attic, The.
Black Angel, The.
Blue-eyed Precinct Worker, The.
Cinema at the Lighthouse, *sel.*
Correspondence.
Denise: A Letter Never Sent, *sel.*
Emeritus, n.
Epilogue: Author to Reader, *sel.*
Family Goldschmitt, The.
Intaglio.
Junk Shop, The.
Night Thoughts.
Phono, at the Boar's Head, *sel.*
Postscript.
Sickness of Friends, The.

Coulter, John
Morning Bus.

Counselman, Mary Elizabeth
Gift with the Wrappings Off.

Coursen, H. R.
Suburban.

Court, Wesli
Academic Curse; an Epitaph.
Sirvente of the Linden Tree.

Cousens, Mildred
American Vineyard.

Coutts, Francis Burdett Money-. *See* **Crossen, Stacy Jo** *and* **Natalie Anne Covell.**

Coward, Noel
A. Stands for Absolutely Anything, *sel.*
Any Part of Piggy.
Bar on the Piccola Marina, A.
Boy Actor, The.
Convalescence.
He Never Did That to Me.
Irish Song (Rosie O'Grady).
I've Been to a Marvelous Party.
Mad Dogs and Englishmen.
Stately Homes of England, The.
There Are Bad Times Just around the Corner.
To Noël Coward.
What's Going to Happen to the Tots?

Cowdery, Mae V.
I Sit and Wait for Beauty.

Cowen, Joseph R.
Recessional for the Class of 1959 of a School for Delinquent Negro Girls.

Cowley, Abraham
Against Hope, *sel.*
Age.
Beauty.
Change, The, *sel.*
Chronicle; a Ballad, The.
Clad All in White, *sel.*
Country-Mouse, The.
Coy Nature (which remain'd, though aged grown), *sel.*
Creation, The, *sel.*
Crown me with roses whilest I live, *sel.*
David and Jonathan, *sel.*
Destinie.
Dialogue after Enjoyment.
Drinking.
Epicure, The ("Fill the bowl with rosie wine").
Epitaph of Pyramus and Thisbe.
Extasie, The.
Grasshopper, The.
Great Diocletian, *sel.*
Honour.
Hymn: To Light.
Innocent Ill, The.
It was a dismal and a fearful night, *sel.*
Love.
Motto, The.

Ode: Of Wit.
Ode upon Doctor Harvey.
Of Solitude.
On the Death of Mr. Crashaw.
On the Death of Mr. William Hervey [*or* Harvey]
Philosophy, the great and only heir, *sel.*
Platonic[k] Love, *sel.*
Power of Numbers, The, *sel.*
Prophet, The.
Pyramus and Thisbe.
Sleep.
Solitude and Reason, in the Village, *sel.*
Spring, The, *sel.*
Supplication, A, *sel.*
Swallow, The.
Thief, The, *sel.*
This only grant me, that my means may lye, *sel.*
Thraldome, The, *sel.*
To Mr. Hobs.
To Sir William Davenant, Upon His Two First Books of Gondibert.
To the Royal Society.
Welcome, The, *sel.*
Wish, The, *sel.*
With sober pace an heav'enly Maid walks in, *sel.*
Written in Juice of Lem[m]on, *sel.*

Cowley, Malcolm
Danny.
Hill above the Mine, The.
Nocturnal Landscape.
Piney Woods.
Stone Horse Shoals.
Streets of Air, The, *sel.*
Tumbling Mustard.

Cowper, William
Beau's Reply.
Boadicea; an Ode.
Capability Brown.
Castaway, The.
Come evening once again, season of peace, *sel.*
Comparison, A.
Ease, *sel.*
England, *sel.*
Epigram on the Refusal of the University of Oxford to Subscribe to His Translation of Homer.
Epistle to Robert Lloyd, Esq., An.
Epitaph on a Free but Tame Redbreast.
Epitaph on a Hare.
Epitaph on Fop.
Exhortation to Prayer.
Faithful Friend, The.
Father, who designs his babe a priest, The, *sel.*
Fragment: "Pity, Religion has so seldom found."
From school to Cam or Isis, and thence home, *sel.*
Garden, The, *sel.*
God Made the Country, *sel.*
Groans of nature in this nether world, The, *sel.*
Hatred and Vengeance, My Eternal Portion, *sel.*
How to Grow Cucumbers, *sel.*
I praise the Frenchman, his remark was shrewd, *sel.*
Jehovah Our Righteousness.
John Gilpin.
Joy and Peace in Believing.
Light Shining out of Darkness.
Lines Written during a Period of Insanity.
Lines Written upon a Window-Shutter at Weston.
London Suburbs, *sel.*
Lord it is my chief complaint, *sel.*
Lord of all, himself through all diffused, The, *sel.*

Lord Will Happiness Divine, The.
Love Constraining to Obedience.
Man on the dubious waves of error toss'd, *sel.*
My Soul Thirsts for God.
Night was winter in his roughest mood, The, *sel.*
Nightingale and the Glowworm, The.
Oh that those lips had language! Life has pass'd, *sel.*
Old-Testament Gospel.
On a Certain Occasion for the Year 1790.
On a Goldfinch Starved to Death in His Cage.
On a Similar Occasion for the Year 1792.
On a Spaniel Called Beau Killing a Young Bird.
On His Portrait.
On Observing Some Names of Little Note Recorded in the "Biographia Britannica."
On the Ice Islands Seen Floating in the German Ocean.
On the Lamented Death of Mrs. Throckmorton's Bullfinch.
On the Loss of the *Royal George*.
On the Receipt of My Mother's Picture out of Norfolk.
Playthings.
Poetic Pains, *sel.*
Poplar Field, The.
Praise for the Fountain Opened.
Prudent Simplicity.
Retired Cat, The.
Retirement.
Self-Acquaintance.
Shrubbery, The.
Sofa, The, *sel.*
Sower, The.
Stanzas Subjoined to the Yearly Bill of Mortality of the Parish of All Saints, Northampton; for the Year 1787.
Sweet Meat Has Sour Sauce; or, The Slave-Trader in the Dumps.
Thou knowest my praise of nature most sincere, *sel.*
Though clasp'd and cradled in his nurse's arms, *sel.*
Time-Piece, The, *sel.*
Tis morning; and the sun with ruddy orb, *sel.*
To a Young Lady.
To Mary.
To Mary Unwin [*or* Sonnet to Mrs. Unwin]
To Mr. Newton on His Return from Ramsgate.
To the Immortal Memory of the Halibut on Which I Dined This Day, Monday, April 26, 1784.
To the Swallow.
To William Hayley, Esq.: In Reply to His Solicitation to Write with Him in a Literary Work.
To William Wilberforce, Esq.
To you, then, tenants of life's middle state, *sel.*
Verses Supposed to Be Written by Alexander Selkirk during His Solitary Abode on the Island of Juan Fernandez.
Walking with God.
Whose freedom is by suff'rance, and at will, *sel.*
Winter Evening ("Just when our drawing-rooms begin to blaze"), *sel.*
Winter Evening, The ("Hark! 'tis the twanging horn o'er yonder bridge"), *sel.*
Winter Walk at Noon, A, *sel.*
Would you your son should be a sot or dunce, *sel.*
Yardley Oak.

Cox, Eleanor Rogers
Return, The.

Cox, Elizabeth
Mask.

Cox, Kenyon
Octopussycat, The.
Cox, L. E.
We Thank You!
Cox, Leo
Bell of Ste. Anne Des Monts, The.
Cornfield.
Easter Thought.
Cox, Palmer
Brownies' Celebration, The.
Lazy Pussy, The.
Mouse's Lullaby, The.
Cox, Samuel K.
Lord, Thou Hast Promised.
Coxe, Arthur Cleveland
America.
Father, Who Mak'st Thy Suff'ring Sons.
Iona.
Present Age, The.
Saviour, Sprinkle Many Nations.
Coxe, Louis O.
Dead Marine.
From the Window Down.
Lake, The.
Nightsong.
Pin-up Girl.
Red Right Returning.
Squaring the Circle.
Winter Night.
Coxon, Philip
April, Glengarry.
Crabbe, George
Ancient Virgin, An, *sel.*
Burials, *sel.*
Caroline, The, *sel.*
East Anglian Fen, *sel.*
Frank Courtship, The, *sel.*
Frenzy, *sel.*
Inebriety.
Late Wisdom.
Lo! now with red rent cloak and bonnet black,
    sel.
Marriage Ring, A.
Marriages, *sel.*
Meeting.
My Birthday.
Now is it pleasant in the summer-eve, *sel.*
Pauper's Funeral, The, *sel.*
Peace, peace, my friend; these subjects fly,
    sel.
Peter Grimes, *sel.*
Rural Life, *sel.*
Sad Lover, The, *sel.*
Sailing upon the River, *sel.*
Schools, *sel.*
Slum Dwelling, A, *sel.*
Something one day occurr'd about a bill, *sel.*
Spring to Winter, *sel.*
Suffolk Shore, The, *sel.*
Then those ill-favour'd Ones, whom none,
    sel.
Truth in Poetry, *sel.*
Vicar, The, *sel.*
Village life, and every care that reigns, *sel.*
Whistling Boy, The.
Winter Views Serene, *sel.*
Craddle, W.
Egoism.
Cradock, Thomas
What Glorious Vision, at.
Cragin, Mary A. *See* **"Allison, Joy"**
Crago, William D.
Where Late the Sweet Birds Sang.
Craig, Alexander
Hillside.
Sonnet: "Go you, O winds that blow from
    north to south."
To His Pandora, from England.
Craig, Christine
Chain, The.

For D. S.
Poem for a Marriage.
Craig, David
One Thousand Feet of Shadow.
One Way Down.
Craig, John
O Hear My Prayer, Lord.
O Lord, That Art My God and King.
Craig, Maurice James
Ballad to a Traditional Refrain.
Fable: "Tale is every time the same, The."
From Burton the Anatomist.
Love Poem.
Poem: "High on a ridge of tiles."
Two Voyages.
Craik, Dinah Maria Mulock
Autumn's Processional.
Douglas, Douglas, Tender and True.
Down the wintry mountain, *sel.*
Friendship.
God Rest You [*or* ye] Merry, Gentlemen.
Green Things Growing.
Now and Afterwards.
Cram, David
An Urban Lad.
Boomerang.
Cricket Match.
Cranch, Christopher Pearse
After the Centennial.
Bear and the Squirrels, The.
Bobolinks, The.
Hours, The.
Old Cat's Confessions, An.
Pines and the Sea, The.
So Far, So Near.
Thought.
Crandall, Charles Henry
Human Plan, The.
Stella.
Three Trees.
With Lilacs.
Crane, Hart
Above the fresh ruffles of the surf, *sel.*
Air Plant, The.
All this—and the housekeeper.
And yet this great wink of eternity, *sel.*
At Melville's Tomb.
Atlantis, *sel.*
Ave Maria, *sel.*
Black Tambourine.
Broken Tower, The.
Cape Hatteras, *sel.*
Capped arbiter of beauty in this street, *sel.*
Carrier Letter.
Chaplinesque.
Cutty Sark, *sel.*
Did one look at what one saw.
Dust now is the old-fashioned house.
Emblems of Conduct.
Enrich My Resignation.
For the Marriage of Faustus and Helen.
Heart, The
Her eyes had the blue of desperate days.
Hurricane, The.
I have that sure enclitic to my act.
I rob my breast to reach those altitudes.
Imperator Victus.
In Shadow.
Infinite consanguinity it bears, *sel.*
Island Quarry.
Key West.
Legend.
March.
Meticulous, past midnight in clear rime, *sel.*
My Grandmother's Love Letters.
Name for All, A.
North Labrador.
O Carib Isle!
Passage.
Phantom Bark, The.
Powhatan's Daughter, *sel.*

Praise for an Urn.
Quaker Hill, *sel.*
Recitative.
Reliquary.
Repose of Rivers.
Royal Palm.
Sad Indian, The.
Southern Cross, *sel.*
There are the local orchard boughs.
They were there falling.
Three Songs, *sel.*
To Brooklyn Bridge, *sel.*
To Conquer Variety.
To Emily Dickinson.
To Shakespeare.
Tunnel, The, *sel.*
Virginia, *sel.*
Where icy and bright dungeons lift, *sel.*
Wine Menagerie, The.
You are that frail decision that devised.
Crane, Nathalia
Janitor's Boy, The.
Vestal, The.
Crane, Stephen
Ancestry, *sel.*
Behold, from the land of the farther suns, *sel.*
Behold, the Grave of a Wicked Man, *sel.*
Black riders came from the sea, *sel.*
Blades of Grass, The, *sel.*
Book of Wisdom, The, *sel.*
Candid Man, The, *sel.*
Do Not Weep, Maiden, for War Is Kind, *sel.*
Fast rode the knight, *sel.*
God fashioned the ship of the world carefully,
    sel.
God in Wrath, A, *sel.*
God lay dead in heaven, *sel.*
I saw a man pursuing the horizon, *sel.*
I Stood upon a High Place, *sel.*
I walked in a desert, *sel.*
In a Lonely Place.
In the Desert, *sel.*
"It Was Wrong to Do This" Said the Angel,
    sel.
Learned Man, A, *sel.*
Man Adrift on a Slim Spar, A.
Man feared that he might find an assassin, A,
    sel.
Man Said to the Universe, A, *sel.*
Man Saw a Ball of Gold in the Sky, A, *sel.*
Many red devils ran from my heart, *sel.*
Many Workmen, *sel.*
Newspaper Is a Collection of Half-Injustices,
    A, *sel.*
Ocean said to me once, The, *sel.*
On the Desert, *sel.*
Once There Came a Man.
Peaks, The, *sel.*
Scaped, *sel.*
Should the wide world roll away, *sel.*
Slant of Sun on Dull Brown Walls, A, *sel.*
Tell me not in joyous numbers.
There is a grey thing that lives in the
    tree-tops.
There Was a Crimson Clash of War.
There Was a Man with a Tongue of Wood,
    sel.
There Was One I Met upon the Road.
Think as I Think, *sel.*
Trees in the Garden Rained Flowers, The, *sel.*
War Is Kind, I, *sel.*
Wayfarer, The, *sel.*
When the Prophet.
Why?, *sel.*
Youth in Apparel That Glittered, A, *sel.*
Crane, Walter
Crocus, The.
Crapsey, Adelaide
Amaze.
For Lucas Cranach's Eve.
Guarded Wound, The.
Night Winds.

November Night.
Roma Aeterna.
Snow.
Susanna and the Elders.
To Man Who Goes Seeking Immortality.
Triad.
Warning , The.
Crase, Douglas
Dog Star Sale.
Heron Weather.
If I could raise rivers, I'd raise them, *sel.*
Once the Sole Province.
Summer.
Crashaw, Richard
And He Answered Them Nothing.
And now where're he strayes, *sel.*
Apology for the Foregoing Hymn, An.
Charitas Nimia; or, The Dear[e] Bargain.
Christ Crucified.
Dear soul be strong!, *sel.*
Death's Lecture at the Funeral of a Young
 Gentleman.
Epitaph upon Husband and Wife Who Died
 and Were Buried Together, An.
Epitaph upon Mr. Ashton, a Conformable
 Citizen, An.
Epithalamium: "Come, virgin tapers of pure
 wax."
Flaming Heart, The.
For Hope.
Hymn of Saint Thomas in Adoration of the
 Blessed Sacrament, The.
Hymn to the Name and Honour of the
 Admirable Saint[e] Teresa, A.
I Am the Door.
In the Glorious Epiphanie of Our Lord God.
In the Holy Nativity of Our Lord God.
Jesu, no more! It is full tide, *sel.*
Live here, great heart; and love and dy and
 kill, *sel.*
Love, thou are absolute sole lord, *sel.*
Love's Horoscope.
Luke XI: Blessed Be the Paps Which Thou
 Hast Sucked.
Music[k]'s Duel[l]
New Year's Day.
O Heart! the equal poise of love's both parts,
 sel.
O thou undaunted daughter of desires!, *sel.*
On Dives.
On Marriage.
On Mr. G. Herberts Booke Intituled the
 Temple of Sacred Poems, Sent to a
 Gentlewoman.
On Our Crucified Lord, Naked and Bloody.
On the Baptized Ethiopian (*or* Aethiopian).
On the Blessed Virgin's Bashfulness.
On the Glorious Assumption of Our Blessed
 Lady.
On the Miracle of Loaves.
On the Miracle of Multiplied Loaves.
On the Wounds of Our Crucified Lord.
Out of the Italian; a Song.
Quaerit Jesum Suum Maria.
Qui Perdiderit Animam Suam.
Saint Mary Magdalene; or, The Weeper.
St. Peter's Shadow.
Samson to His Delilah.
Shepherd's Hymn, The ("We saw Thee in
 Thy balmy nest"), *sel.*
Song, A: "Lord, when the sense of Thy sweet
 grace."
Tear, The.
Temperance or the Cheap Physitian upon the
 Translation of Lessius.
Thou art love's victim; and must die, *sel.*
To a Young Gentle-Woman, Councel
 Concerning Her Choice.
To Our Blessed Lord upon the Choice of His
 Sepulchre.
To Our Lord, upon the Water Made Wine.
To the Infant Martyrs.

To the Name above Every Name, the Name
 of Jesus, a Hymn.
To the Noblest and Best of Ladies, the
 Countess of Denbigh.
Two Went Up into the Temple to Pray.
Upon Bishop Andrewes His Picture before His
 Sermons.
Upon Ford's Two Tragedies, "Loves
 Sacrifice" and "The Broken Heart."
Upon Lazarus His Teares.
Upon the Body of Our Blessed Lord, Naked
 and Bloody.
Upon the Holy Sepulchre.
Upon the Infant Martyrs.
Upon Venus Putting on Mars His Armes.
Wishes to His Supposed Mistress[e]
Craveirinha, José
Black Cry.
Mamana Saquina.
Mamano.
Mamparra M'gaiza.
Ode to a Lost Cargo in a Ship Called *Save.*
Poem of the Future Citizen.
Song of the Negro on the Ferry.
Crawford, Dan
Jesus and I.
Crawford, Francis Marion
New National Hymn.
Crawford, Isabella Valancy
Axe of the Pioneer, The.
Battle, A.
Bite deep and wide, O Axe, the tree, *sel.*
Camp of Souls, The.
City Tree, The.
Dark Stag, The.
Laughter.
Love's Land.
Said the Canoe.
Song of the Arrow, The, *sel.*
South Wind laid his moccasins aside, The,
 sel.
Crawford, Louisa Macartney
Kathleen Mavourneen, at.
Crawford, Robert
My Iambic Pentameter Lines.
Crawford, Vesta Pierce
Pioneer Woman.
Creekmore, Hubert
Concert at Sea.
Dividends.
Music in the Rec Hut.
Pocket Guide for Service Men.
Creeley, Robert
Act of Love, The.
After Lorca.
Age.
Air: "Cat bird singing."
Air: "Love of a woman, The."
All That Is Lovely in Men.
America.
And.
Anger.
Awakening, The.
Ballad of the Despairing Husband.
Business, The.
Car, The.
City, The.
Counterpoint, A.
Crisis, The.
Crow, The.
Damon and Pythias.
Death of Venus, The.
Door, The.
Dream, The.
Faces, The.
Fancy.
Figures, The.
Fire, The.
First Rain.

Flower, The.
For Love.
For My Mother: Genevieve Jules Creeley.
For No Clear Reason.
For the New Year.
Form of Women, A.
Gift, The.
Gift of Great Value, A.
Here.
Heroes.
Hill, The.
I Keep to Myself Such Measures.
I Know a Man.
If You.
Immoral Proposition, The.
Innocence, The.
Invoice, The.
Joy.
Just Friends.
Kind of Act Of, The.
Kore.
Language, The.
Love Comes Quietly.
Man, The.
Marriage, A.
Mechanic, The.
Memory, The.
Moment.
Moon, The.
Mother's Voice.
Movie Run Backward, The.
Naughty Boy.
Oh No.
On Vacation.
Operation, The.
Outside.
People, The.
Pool, The.
Prayer to Hermes.
Quick-Step.
Rain, The.
Reason, A.
Rescue, The.
Rhythm, The.
Self-Portrait.
She Went to Stay.
Sight, A.
Something.
Somewhere.
Song: "Those rivers run from that land."
Song: "What I took in my hand."
Statue, The.
Three Ladies, The.
Time.
Token, A.
Turn, The.
Variation, A.
Versions.
Wait for Me.
Waiting.
Warning, The.
Way, The.
Whip, The.
Wicker Basket, A.
Wife, The.
Window, The.
World, The.
Creelman, Josephine Rice
My Mother.
Creighton, Alan
Pastoral: "Farmhouse skyline, draped with
 trees, The."
Return of a Reaper.
Spring Workman.
Crew, Louie
Gay Psalm from Fort Valley, A.
"Crichton, John"
Bed of Campanula, A.
Crinagoras
Epitaph on an Infant.
Criswell, Cloyd Mann
Newlyweds, The.

Crites, Lucile
Folks and Me.
"Critics, The"
Grey October.
Croasdell, Ann
Muffin Man, The.
Crocker, Henry
Evangelize!
Crocker, T. F. Dillon
To shave, or not to shave? that is the
question.
Croffut, William Augustus
Living Memory, A.
Croft, Roy
Love, at.
Croly, George
Death and Resurrection.
Death of Leonidas, The.
Cronin, Anthony
Apology.
Baudelaire in Brussels.
For a Father.
Man Who Went Absent from the Native
Literature, The.
Middle Years, The.
On the bog road the blackthorn flowers, the
turf-stacks, *sel.*
Writing.
Crooker, Barbara
Deliverance.
Skating after School.
Cros, Charles
Smoked Herring, The.
Crosby, Ernest
Choir Practice.
"Rebels."
Search, The.
Soul of the World, The.
Crosby, Fanny (Frances Jane Crosby)
Best of All, The.
Blessed Assurance.
Jesus, Keep Me Near the Cross.
Keep Thou My Way, O Lord.
Unseen.
Crosby, Harry
Firebrand.
Telephone Directory.
Vision.
Crosby, Ranice Henderson
Poem about a Seashell.
Thoughts for You (When She Came Back
from the Mountains).
Crosland, T. W. H.
Slain.
Cross, Allen Eastman
Gray Hills Taught Me Patience, The.
Though Fatherland Be Vast.
Young and Radiant, He Is Standing.
Cross, Zora
In me there is a vast and lonely place, *sel.*
O brother in the restless rest of God!, *sel.*
What have you more than I, who crave you
so?, *sel.*
When I Was Six.
Cross, Marian Evans Lewes. See **"Eliot,
George"**
Crossen, Stacy Jo and **Natalie Anne Covell**
Wiggly Giggles.
Crossland, John R.
Water.
Crossley-Holland, Kevin
Postcards from Kodai.
Crossman, Samuel
My Song Is Love Unknown.
Crosson, John
Cripple in Sight.
Croswell, William
Clouds, The.
Lord! Lead the Way the Saviour Went.

Crouch, Nathaniel
David and Goliath.
Tower of Babel, The.
Crouch, Stanley
After the Rain.
Albert Ayler: Eulogy for a Decomposed
Saxophone Player.
Blackie Thinks of His Brothers.
Chops Are Flyin.
No New Music.
Riding across John Lee's Finger.
Crow, Steve
El Alamein.
Louisiana.
Revival.
They say a man dies, *sel.*
Water Song.
Crowe, William
Up to thy summit, Lewesdon, to the brow,
sel.
Crowell, Charmaine
Fat Blues.
Crowell, Grace Noll
Because of Thy Great Bounty.
Poet Prays, The.
Quiet Things.
Crowell, Henry
When Thou Passest through the Waters.
Crowley, Aleister
Lesbian Hell, The.
Crowne, John
Kind Lovers, Love On.
Song: "Kind lovers, love on," *sel.*
"Crowquill Alfred." See **Forrester, Alfred
A.**
Croxall, Samuel
Sylvia.
Cruceius, Annibal
Fair Ursly, in a merry mood.
Cruickshank, Alfred
Convict Song, The.
God or Mammon.
Let Us Be Frank.
Cruickshank, Helen B.
Caenlochan.
Comfort in Puirtith.
Schiehallion.
Shy Geordie.
Cruikshank, N. K.
Enemy Action.
Snowy Morning, 1940.
Crum, Lady Erskine
"Good Night," Says the Owl.
Crum, Robert
Bat in the Bedroom, The.
Child Explains Dying, A.
Crummy, Biddy
Poem to Be Said on Hearing the Birds Sing,
A.
Cruz, Victor Hernandez
African Things.
Anonymous.
Carmen.
Confusion.
Electric Cop, The.
Energy.
Going Uptown to Visit Miriam.
Listening to the Music of Arsenio Rodríguez
Is Moving Closer to Knowledge.
Physics of Ochun, The.
Sonsito.
Spirits.
Story of the Zeros, The.
Today Is a Day of Great Joy.
Urban Dream.
Cruz, Viriato da
Black Mother.
Crystal, Catherine Nomura
Embroidery.
Csanádi, Imre
Confession of Faith.

Holiday-Afternoon Rhapsody.
Silent Prayer of Peasants.
Small Craftsman.
Csoóri, Sandor
Afternoon of Grand Old Men.
Ague.
Barbarian Prayer.
E. K.'s Will.
Golden Pheasants Flying.
I Would Rather Run Back.
Maybe Elegies.
Print of Your Hand, The.
Remembering Snow.
Stranger, A.
Summer Haloed.
Sunday before Christmas, The.
Whispers, for two voices.
You Were Still the Sun's There.
Csukás, István
Macadam Road Remembers, The.
Cuevish, Lucario
Before They Made Things Be Alive They
Spoke.
Cullen, Cornelius C.
Battle of Somerset.
Cullen, Countee
Black Magdalens.
Black Majesty.
Brown Boy to Brown Girl.
Brown Girl Dead, A.
For a Lady I Know, *sel.*
For a Mouthy Woman.
For a Poet.
For a Virgin Lady.
For Amy Lowell.
For John Keats, Apostle of Beauty, *sel.*
For My Grandmother, *sel.*
For Paul Laurence Dunbar, *sel.*
From the Dark Tower.
Fruit of the Flower.
Heritage.
I Have a Rendezvous with Life.
Incident.
Judas Iscariot.
Lines to Our Elders.
Litany of the Dark People, The.
Mary, Mother of Christ.
Only the Polished Skeleton.
Protest.
Saturday's Child.
Scottsboro, Too, Is Worth Its Song.
Simon the Cyrenian Speaks.
Tableau.
That Bright Chimeric Beast.
Timid Lover.
To Certain Critics.
To John Keats, Poet, at Springtime.
To Lovers of Earth: Fair Warning.
Uncle Jim.
Under the Mistletoe.
Unknown Color, The.
Wise, The.
Yet Do I Marvel.
Youth Sings a Song of Rosebuds.
Cumbie, Richard
New Jersey Turnpike.
Cumbo, Kattie M.
Black Sister.
Ceremony.
Domestics.
I'm a Dreamer.
Morning after. Love, The.
Nocturnal Sounds.
Cummings, David
Emily's Haunted Housman.
From the Brothers Grimm to Sister Sexton to
Mother Goose; One Transmogrification.
Sweeney, Old and Phthisic, among the
Hippopotami.
Cummings, Edward Estlin
All Ignorance Toboggans into Know.

All in Green Went My Love Riding.
All Nearness Pauses, While a Star Can Grow.
All Which Isn't Singing Is Mere Talking.
Always before Your Voice My Soul.
Annie Died the Other Day.
Anyone Lived in a Pretty How Town.
As Freedom Is a Breakfastfood.
As Is the Sea Marvelous.
As Joe Gould says in.
Being to Timelessness as It's to Time.
Buffalo Bill's.
Buy Me an Ounce and I'll Sell You a Pound.
Cambridge Ladies Who Live in Furnished
  Souls, The, *sel.*
Come, Gaze with Me upon This Dome.
Darling! Because My Blood Can Sing.
Faithfully Tinying at Twilight Voice.
First of All My Dreams, The.
For prodigal read generous.
Four III.
Gee I Like to Think of Dead.
Goodby Betty, Don't Remember Me.
Great, A.
Greedy the People, The.
He as O, A.
Her Careful Distinct Sex Whose Sharp Lips
  Comb.
Hist Whist.
Hours Rise Up, The.
How many moments must (amazing each).
I.
I Am So Glad and Very.
I carry your heart with me (I carry it in).
I Like My Body.
I Like My Body When It Is With Your Body,
  sel.
I Sing of Olaf Glad and Big.
I Thank You God for Most This Amazing.
I Was Sitting in McSorley's.
I Will Be.
If Everything Happens That Can't Be Done.
If I Have Made, My Lady, Intricate.
If I Should Sleep with a Lady Called Death.
If in Beginning Twilight.
If There Are Any Heavens [My Mother Will
  (All by Herself) Have]
If (touched by love's own secret) we, like
  homing.
If You Can't Eat You Got To.
(Im)C-A-T(mo).
IN) all those who got.
In Heavenly Realms of Hellas Dwelt.
In just-/ spring when the world is mud, *sel.*
It Is at Moments after I Have Dreamed.
It Is So Long Since My Heart Has Been with
  Yours.
It May Not Always Be So, *sel.*
It Really Must Be Nice.
It Was a Goodly Co.
Item.
It's Over a (See Just).
Jimmie's got a goil.
L(a.
La Guerre.
Ladies and Gentlemen This Little Girl.
Life Is More True.
Listen.
Little joe gould has lost his teeth and doesn't
  know where.
Little tree, *sel.*
Love is a place.
Maggie and Milly and Molly and May.
Man Who Had Fallen among Thieves, A.
May I Feel Said He.
May My Heart Always.
Me Up at Does.
Mr. U Will Not Be Missed.
My Father Moved through Dooms of Love.
My Love.
My specialty is living said.
My Sweet Old Etcetera.
My Uncle Daniel.

Next to of Course God America I.
Nine Birds.
No Man, if Men Are Gods.
No Time Ago.
Nobody Loses All the Time.
Notice the Convulsed Orange Inch of Moon.
Now Comes the Good Rain Farmers Pray for
  (and).
Now Does Our World Descend.
O By the By.
O Sweet Spontaneous.
Off a pane)the.
Old Age Sticks.
One X.
Out of Midsummer's Blazing Most Not Night.
Paris; This April Sunset Completely Utters.
Pity This Busy Monster, Manunkind.
Plato told/ him:he couldn't, *sel.*
Plato Told Him.
Poem, or Beauty Hurts Mr. Vinal.
Politician, A.
Ponder, Darling, These Busted Statues.
Pretty a Day, A.
Purer than Purest Pure.
Q:dwo.
?
R-P-O-P-H-E-S-S-A-G-R.
Raise the Shade.
"Right Here the Other Night Something."
Salesman Is an It That Stinks Excuse, A.
Season 'Tis, My Lovely Lambs, The.
She Being Brand.
Silence.
Since Feeling Is First.
(Sitting in a tree-).
Slightly before the middle of Congressman
  Pudd.
Somewhere I have never travelled, gladly
  beyond.
Song: "Thy fingers make early flowers of all
  things."
Sonnet: "Wind has blown the rain away and
  blown, A."
Space Being (Don't Forget to Remember)
  Curved.
Spring is like a perhaps hand.
Spring omnipotent goddess thou dost, *sel.*
Sunset.
Than (By Yon Sunset's Wintry Glow).
Thanksgiving (1956).
This Is the Garden.
This Little Bride and Groom Are.
Twenty-seven Bums Give a Prostitute the
  Once.
Two X.
Up into the Silence the Green.
Vision.
Way to Hump a Cow Is Not, The.
What a Proud Dreamhorse.
What If a Much of a Which of a Wind.
What Is.
When any mortal (even the most odd).
When faces called flowers float out of the
  ground.
When God Lets My Body Be.
When My Sensational Moments Are No
  More.
When Serpents Bargain for the Right to
  Squirm.
When the Spent Day Begins to Frail.
When what hugs stopping earth than silent is.
Wherelings Whenlings.
Whippoorwill this/ moonday into.
White Guardians of the Universe of Sleep.
Who Are You, Little I.
Who Knows if the Moon's.
Who's Most Afraid of Death? Thou.
Why Did You Go.
Wild (at Our First) Beasts Uttered Human
  Words.
You Shall above All Things Be Glad and
  Young.

Your Birthday Comes to Tell Me This.
Your little voice/ Over the wires came
  leaping.

Cummins, Evelyn Atwater
I Know Not Where the Road Will Lead.

Cumpian, Carlos
Cuento.

Cuney, Waring
Burial of the Young Love.
Conception.
Crucifixion.
Death Bed, The.
Dust.
Finis.
I Think I See Him There.
My Lord, What a Morning.
No Images.
O. T.'s Blues.
Radical, The.
Threnody: "Only quiet death."
Triviality, A.
Troubled Jesus.
True Love.
Wake Cry.

Cunningham, Allan
Gone Were but the Winter Cold.
Hame, Hame, Hame.
John Grumlie.
Wet Sheet and a Flowing Sea, A.

Cunningham, J. M.
Epigraph from *The Judge Is Fury.*

Cunningham, James (Olumo)
And birds came crying, *sel.*
City Rises, The.
Covenant, The.
Footnote to a Gray Bird's Pause, A.
For Cal.
From a Brother Dreaming in the Rye.
Happy Day (or Independence Day).
High-cool/2.
Incidental Pieces to a Walk.
Lee-ers of Hew.
Leg-acy of a Blue Capricorn.
Plea to My Sister, A.
Portrait of Rudy, A.
Rapping Along with Ronda Davis.
St. Julien's Eve.
Slow Riff for Billy.
Solitary Visions of a Kaufmanoid.
Song thumbed down a cruiser for a ride, A,
  sel.
Street in Kaufman-ville, A.
Tambourine.
There were blood spots on the skirt, *sel.*
Welcome for Etheridge, A.
While Cecil Snores: Mom Drinks Cold Milk.
Woods are overhead over everywhere, The,
  sel.

Cunningham, James Vincent
Aged Lover Discourses in the Flat Style, The.
Agnosco Veteris Vestigia Flammae.
All in Due Time.
And Now You're Ready Who While She Was
  Here, *sel.*
Ars Amoris.
Bride loved old words, and found her pleasure
  marred, *sel.*
Choice.
Coffee.
Dear Child Whom I Begot.
Envoi: "Hear me, whom I betrayed."
Epigram: "After some years Bohemian came
  to this."
Epigram: "And what is love?
  Misunderstanding, pain."
Epigram: "Dark thoughts are my companions.
  I have wined."

Epigram: "Dear, if unsocial privacies obsess me."
Epigram: "Here lies my wife. Eternal peace."
Epigram: "Homer was poor. His scholars live at ease."
Epigram: "How we desire desire! Joy of surcease."
Epigram: "I had gone broke, and got set to come back."
Epigram: "I who by day am function of the light."
Epigram: "If wisdom, as it seems it is."
Epigram: "In whose will is our peace? Thou happiness."
Epigram: "Life flows to death as rivers to the sea."
Epigram: "This is my curse, Pompous, I pray."
Epigram: "Time heals not: it extends a sorrow's scope."
Epigram: "Within this mindless vault."
Epigram: "You ask me how Contempt who claims to sleep."
Epigram: "You wonder why Drab sells her love for gold?"
Epitaph for Someone or Other, *sel.*
Epitaph: "When I shall be without regret."
For My Contemporaries.
Friend, on This Scaffold Thomas More Lies Dead.
Hang up your weaponed wit.
Here lies New Critic who would fox us, *sel.*
History of Ideas.
I had gone broke, and got set to come back, *sel.*
I Married in My Youth a Wife.
I married in my youth a wife, *sel.*
In Innocence.
Interview with Doctor Drink.
Lady, of anonymous flesh and face.
Lector Aere Perennior.
Lip was a man who used his head.
Meditation on a Memoir.
Meditation on Statistical Method.
Metaphysical Amorist, The.
Miramar Beach, *sel.*
Montana Fifty Years Ago.
Montana Pastoral.
Moral Poem, A.
Neaera when I'm there is adamant.
On a cold night I came through the cold rain.
On the Calculus.
Periphrastic Insult, Not a Banal, A.
Phoenix, The.
Pope from penance purgatorial, The.
Rome.
Sonnet on a Still Night.
This *Humanist* Whom No Beliefs Constrained.
To a Friend, on Her Examination for the Doctorate in English.
To the Reader.
To Whom It May Concern.
With a Copy of Swift's Works.
Cunningham, John
  Epigram: "Member of the modern great, A."
  Morning.
  On a Certain Alderman.
  Sent to Miss Bell H——, with a Pair of Buckles.
  Virtuous Fox and the Self-righteous Cat, The.
Cunningham, Julia
  Hymn to Joy.
  Little Bird.
  Trapped Mouse.
Cunninghame-Graham, Robert. *See* **Graham, Robert**
Curnow, Allen
  An Urban Guerrilla, *sel.*
  Balanced Bait in Handy Pellet Form, A.
  Canst Thou Draw Out Leviathan with an Hook.
  Dead Lamb, A.

Eden Gate.
Elegy on My Father.
Eye Is More or Less Satisfied with Seeing, The.
Family Matter, A, *sel.*
He Cracked a Word.
House and Land.
In the interim, how the children should be educated, *sel.*
Incorrigible Music, An.
Jack-in-the-Boat.
Keep in a Cool Place.
Kingfisher's naked arc alight, A, *sel.*
Landfall in Unknown Seas.
Lone Kauri Road ("First time I looked seaward, westward"), *sel.*
Lone Kauri Road ("Too many splashes, too many gashes"), *sel.*
Old Provincial Council Buildings, Christchurch, The.
Oldest of us burst into tears and cried, The, *sel.*
Out of Sleep.
Polynesia.
Reliable Service, A.
Sailing or Drowning.
Self-Portrait.
Seven ageing pine tree hide, *sel.*
Skeleton of the Great Moa in the Canterbury Museum, Christchurch, The.
Small Room with Large Windows, A.
Spectacular Blossom.
Time.
To Forget Self and All.
Tomb of an Ancestor.
Touch of the Hand, A.
Unhistoric Story, The.
Unhurt, There Is No Help.
Waking Bird Refutes, The.
What it would look like if really there were only, *sel.*
Wild Iron.
You Will Know When You Get There.
Curran, John Philpot
  Deserter's Lamentation , The.
Currey, R. N.
  Unseen Fire.
Currey, Ralph Nixon
  Children Waking: Indian Hill Station.
  Cock-Crow.
  Halo.
  In Memoriam: Roy Campbell.
  Jersey Cattle.
  Landscape of Violence.
  Marrakech.
  Remembering Snow.
  Song: "There is no joy in water apart from the sun."
  Ultimate Exile IV.
  Unseen Fire.
  Volubilis, North Africa.
Currie, Robert
  Brothers.
  In the Music.
  July the First.
  Schoolbus Comes before the Sun, The.
Currie, Mary Montgomerie Currie, Baroness. *See* **"Fane, Violet"**
Currier, John
  Electricity Is Funny!
Curry, Neil
  Gardens.
  John Clare and the Acts of Enclosure.
  Maidenhair Tree, The.
  Memorial to the Vicars of Urswick.
Curtis, Christine Turner
  Villa Sciarra: Rome.
Curtis, George William
  Ebb and Flow.
Curtis, Simon
  Satie, at the End of Term.

Curtright, Wesley
  Close of Day, The.
  Heart of the Woods.
Curzon, Colin
  Not Tonight, Josephine.
Cusack, Cyril
  Cross Talk.
  Summer Reflection.
Cushing, William O.
  We Are Watching, We Are Waiting.
Cushman, Ralph Spaulding
  His Presence Came Like Sunrise.
Cussons, Sheila
  1945.
Cussrooee, Biddy
  My Grief on the Sea, at.
Cust, Henry
  Non Nobis.
Cuthbertson, David Cunninghame
  Picture, A.
Cuthbertson, James Lister
  Racing Eight, A.
Cutler, Elbridge Jefferson
  Volunteer, The.
Cutler, Julian S.
  Through the Year.
  Wonderful.
Cutler, William
  One Talent, The.
Cutting, Sewall Sylvester
  God of the World, Thy Glories Shine.
  Gracious Saviour, We Adore Thee.
"Cynddelw." *See* **Ellis, Robert**
Cynddelw Brydydd Mawr
  In Praise of Owain Gwynedd.
  Petition for Reconciliation.
  Poem on His Death-Bed.
Cynewulf
  Anchor: "Oft I must strive with wind and wave.", *sel.*
  Book Moth: "A moth ate a word. To me it seemed.", *sel.*
  Constantine's Vision of the Cross, *sel.*
  Cuckoo: "In former days my father and mother.", *sel.*
  Death of Saint Guthlac, *sel.*
  Dream of the Rood, A, at.
  Fish in River: "My house is not quiet, I am not loud.", *sel.*
  Helena Embarks for Palestine, *sel.*
  Honey-Mead: "I am valued by men, fetched from afar.", *sel.*
  Horn: "Time was when I was weapon and warrior.", *sel.*
  I have great need that the Saint grant help, *sel.*
  Now I pray the man who may love this lay, *sel.*
  Plow: "My beak is bent downward, I burrow below.", *sel.*
  Shield: "Lonely wanderer, wounded with iron, A.", *sel.*
  Swan, The: "Clothes make no sound when I tread ground.", *sel.*
  Voyage of Life, The, *sel.*
  Weathercock, The: "I puff my breast out, my neck swells.", *sel.*
  Wild Swan: "My attire is noiseless when I tread the earth.", *sel.*
  Wind: "At times I resort, beyond man's discerning.", *sel.*

Czaykowski, Bogdan
Prayer, A: "Throw me into a cloud o lord."
Revolt in Verse, A.

D

"D., J."
Essay on the Fleet Riding in the Downes, An.
"D., H." *See* **Doolittle, Hilda ("H. D.")**
Dabir, Ali
Hot is the sun, so hot the birds complain.
Dabney, Betty Page
Earth's Bondman.
Dabydeen, Cyril
Fat Men, The.
Folklore.
Fruit of the Earth.
Lives.
Posterity.
Rehearsal.
Rhapsodies.
Words and Legacy.
Dabydeen, David
Men and Women.
Slave Song.
Two Cultures.
Dacey, Philip
Amputee Soldier, The.
Birthday, The.
Crime.
Form Rejection Letter.
Jack, Afterwards.
Jill, Afterwards.
Mystery Baseball.
No, The.
Obscene Caller, The.
Pac-Man.
Prisms.
Rondel: "Beautiful snow falls on a bed, A."
Skating.
Wild Pitches.
Winter Thing, The.
Dadelsen, Jean-Paul de
Great Book, The.
Jonah's Canticle.
Poplars and Aspens.
Psalm: "Whale, says Jonah, is the war and its
black-outs, The."
Dadié, Bernard
Dry Your Tears, Africa!
I Give You Thanks My God.
Dafydd ab Edmwnd
Girl's Hair, A.
Dafydd ap Gwilym
Cywdd to Morvydd, The.
Girls of Llanbadarn, The.
In Morfudd's Arms.
Rain, The.
Rattle Bag, The.
Seagull, The.
Wind, The.
Woodland Mass, The.
Dafydd Bach ap Madog Wladaidd
Christmas Revel, A.
Dafydd Benfras
From Exile.
Dafydd Nanmor
Ode to Rhys ap Maredudd of Tywyn.
Dagh, Nawab Mirza Khan
I lose my head, but not your madness from
my brain.
It seems the breeze has quarreled with.
My life is a story for the world to hear.
Permanence in the sea of life, The.
They call it love; but it's the lover's distress.
Why should I put my faith in you.

Daglarca, Fazil Hüsnü
Fire.
Hollow Echo.
Thought.
D'Aguiar, Frederick
Letter from Mama Dot.
On Duty.
Dahbur, Ahmad
Death of the Shoemaker, The.
In Memory of Izziddin al-Qalaq.
Dahl, Roald
Aunt Sponge and Aunt Spiker.
Dahlberg, Edward
Kansas City West Bottoms.
Daibai
I'm at one with this, this only.
Daiches, David
Notes for a History of Poetry.
To Kate, Skating Better than Her Date.
Ulysses' Library.
Winter Song.
Daigaku, Horiguchi. *See* **Horiguchi Daigaku**
Daiken, Leslie
June Song of a Man Who Looks Two Ways.
Lines to My Father.
Nostalgie d'Automne.
Dailey, Joel
Everyone in the World.
Good Night.
Joie de Vivre.
Known.
Meanwhile.
Revving Up la Rêve.
Dainty, Evelyn
Birds on the School Windowsill, The.
Daio
I tongue-lashed wind and rain.
Mind and object scrapped.
No longer aware of mind and object.
Daisen
Flutist Diviner.
Daitetsu
Who's aware of mutability?
Daito
Unmon's barrier pulled down, the old.
Daive, Jean
Brain-Cry.
Dakin, Laurence
All night I raced the moon, *sel.*
How gently sings my soul and whets its
wings, *sel.*
How sweetly sings this stream, *sel.*
Song: "Peasant sun went crushing grapes,
The," *sel.*
Dakotsu, Iida. *See* **Iida Dakotsu**
Dalcour, Pierre
Verse Written in the Album of Mademoiselle.
Dale, Peter
Few ever came to help you speak or sell, *sel.*
Rite, The.
Daley, Frank
Piano, The.
Daley, Victor James
Ascetic, The.
Dreams.
Faith.
In a Wine Cellar.
Lachesis.
Narcissus and Some Tadpoles.
Suns, planets, stars, in glorious array, *sel.*
Tall Hat.
Tamerlane.
When London Calls.
Dali, Salvador
Art of Picasso, The.
Dallas, Mary Kyle
He'd Nothing but His Violin.
Dallas, Ruth
Among Old Houses.
Autumn Wind, *sel.*
Beating the Drum, *sel.*

Boy, The.
Clouds on the Sea, *sel.*
Deserted Beach.
Girl with Pitcher.
Grandmother and Child.
In the Giant's Castle.
Milking before Dawn.
Photographs of Pioneer Women.
Shadow Show.
Striped Shell, A.
Tea-shop, A.
Telemachus with a Transistor.
Dallas, Sir George
If you my dear mother, had e'er been at sea,
sel.
Miss Emily Brittle Sails for India, *sel.*
Dallman, Elaine
From the Dust.
Dalmon, Charles
Ballad of the Epiphany.
Early Morning Meadow Song.
Sussex Legend, A.
Dalton, Annie Charlotte
For an Eskimo.
Neighing North, The.
Robin's Egg, The.
Sounding Portage, The.
To the Young Man Jesus.
Dalton, Henry
Emigrant Ship, The.
Dalton, John
Agape the sooty collier stands, *sel.*
Dalton, Roque
Act.
Jubilant Poem.
Poem of Love.
Toward a Better Love.
Dalven, Rae
My Father.
Daly, John Jay
Toast to the Flag, A.
Daly, June
Wildebeest, The.
Daly, Thomas Augustin
Boy from Rome, Da.
Leetla Giorgio Washeenton.
Man's Prayer, The.
Mia Carlotta.
Pennsylvania Places.
Sanctum, The.
Dalziel, Kathleen
He Could Have Found His Way.
Da Maiano, Dante
To Dante Alighieri: He Interprets Dante
Alighieri's Dream.
Damas, Léon
Put Down.
They Came This Evening.
Damascene, Saint John. *See* **John of
Damascus, Saint**
D'Ambrosio, Vinnie-Marie
Grace of Cynthia's Maidenhood, The.
Moon as Medusa.
On the Fifth Anniversary of Bluma Sach's
Death.
Dana, Mary Stanley Bunce
O Sing to Me of Heaven.
Dana, Richard Henry
Chanting Cherubs—A Group by Greenough,
The.
Immortality.
Little Beach-Bird, The.
Moss Supplicateth for the Poet, The.
Murder of a Spanish Lady by a Pirate.
Pleasure-Boat, The.
Soul, The.
Dana, Robert Patrick
Winter's Tale, A.
Dance, James
When the returning sun begins to smile, *sel.*

Dandridge, Danske Bedinger
Dead Moon, The.
On the Eve of War.
Spirit of the Fall, The.

Dandridge, Ray Garfield
Drum Majah, De.
'Ittle Touzle Head.
Sprin' Fevah.
Time to Die.
Zalka Peetruza.

D'Anduza, Clara. *See* **Clara d'Anduza**

Danforth, John
Few Lines to Fill up a Vacant Page, A.
Mercies of the Year, The.
On My Lord Bacon.
Poem upon the Triumphant Translation of
  Mrs. Anne Eliot, A.
Profit and Loss: An Elegy upon the Decease
  of Mrs. Mary Gerrish.
Two Vast Enjoyments Commemorated.

Danforth, Samuel (1626–74)
Almanac Verse.
Awake yee westerne nymphs, arise and sing.

Danforth, Samuel, Jr. (1666–1727)
Ad Librum.
Elegy in Memory of the Worshipful Major
  Thomas Leonard Esq, An.

Dangel, Leo
Gathering Strength.
New Lady Barber at Ralph's Barber Shop,
  The.

Daniel, Arnaut
Bel m'es quan lo vens m'alena.
Mot eran dous miei cossir.
On this gay and slender tune.

Daniel, George
One Desiring Me to Read, But Slept It Out,
  Wakening.
Robin, The.

Daniel, H. J. (1818–89)
My Epitaph.

Daniel, Hal J., III
Light Bulbs and Bananas.

Daniel, Robert T.
Time Will Surely Come, The.

Daniel, Samuel
And yet I cannot reprehend the flight, *sel.*
Are They Shadows [That We See]?
Beauty, sweet Love, is like the morning dew,
  sel.
But love whilst that thou mayst be loved
  again, *sel.*
Care-charmer sleep[e], son[ne] of the sable
  night, *sel.*
Chorus: "How dost thou wear and weary out
  thy days," *sel.*
Chorus: "Then thus we have beheld," *sel.*
Constancy, *sel.*
Description of Beauty, A.
Early Love, *sel.*
English Poetry, *sel.*
Enjoy Thy April Now, *sel.*
Eyes Hide My Love, *sel.*
Fair is my love, and cruel as she's fair, *sel.*
Had Sorrow Ever Fitter Place, *sel.*
Henry's Lament, *sel.*
I must not grieve my love, whose eyes would
  read, *sel.*
I once may see when yeares shall wreck my
  wrong, *sel.*
If it so hap, this of-spring of my care, *sel.*
If this be love, to draw [*or* drawe] a weary
  [*or* wearie] breath, *sel.*
It was upon the twilight of that day, *sel.*
Let others sing of knights and paladins [*or*
  palladines], *sel.*
Lonely Beauty, *sel.*
Look, Delia, how we esteem the half-blown
  rose, *sel.*
Love Is a Sickness, *sel.*
My cares draw on mine everlasting night, *sel.*

My spotless love hovers, with purest wings,
  sel.
None other fame mine unambitious muse, *sel.*
O Blessed Letters, *sel.*
O fearfull, frowning nemesis, *sel.*
Ode: "Now each creature joys the other."
Poet and Critic, *sel.*
Rosamond's Appeal, *sel.*
Star of my mishap imposed this pain, The,
  sel.
These plaintive verse, the posts [*or* postes] of
  my desire, *sel.*
Thou canst not die whilst any zeal abound,
  sel.
Time, cruel time, come and subdue that brow,
  sel.
To Delia.
To Sir Thomas Egerton.
To the Lady Lucy, Countess of Bedford.
To the Lady Margaret, Countess of
  Cumberland.
To the Reader.
Ulysses and the Siren.
Unto the boundless ocean of thy beauty, *sel.*
When men shall find thy flower [*or* flow'r],
  thy glory, pass, *sel.*
When winter snows upon thy sable hairs, *sel.*
Why Should I Sing in Verse, *sel.*

Daniells, Roy
Buffalo.
Journey.
Noah.
So They Went Deeper into the Forest.
Summer Days.

Daniels, Jim
Blubber Lips.
Bookkeepers Talk Baseball, The.
Detroit Hymns, Christmas Eve.
Farewell to Winnipeg.

Dann, Jack
Ceremony.
Stone Stars.
When we invent a machine to read, *sel.*

Danner, Margaret
And through the Caribbean Sea.
At Home in Dakar.
Best Loved of Africa.
Convert, The.
Dance of the Abakweta.
Elevator Man Adheres to Form, The.
Garnishing the Aviary, *sel.*
Goodbye David Tamunoemi West.
Grandson Is a Hoticeberg, A.
Painted Lady, The.
Rhetoric of Langston Hughes, The.
Sadie's Playhouse.
Slave and the Iron Lace, The.
This Is an African Worm.

D'Annunzio, Gabriele
Crescent Moon.
Rain in the Pine Grove, The.

Dante Alighieri
All my thoughts always speak to me of Love,
  sel.
All ye that pass along Love's trodden way,
  sel.
At whiles (yea oftentimes) I muse over, *sel.*
Ballata: He Will Gaze upon Beatrice.
Beyond the sphere which spreads to widest
  space, *sel.*
Canst thou indeed be he that still would sing,
  sel.
Canzone: He Beseeches Death for the Life of
  Beatrice.
Day agone, as I rode sullenly, A, *sel.*
Death, always cruel, Pity's foe in chief, *sel.*
Even as the others mock, thou mockest me,
  sel.
Eyes that weep for pity of the heart, The, *sel.*
First Canzone of the Convito, The.
For certain he hath seen all perfectness, *sel.*

Gentle thought there is will often start, A, *sel.*
I felt a spirit of love begin to stir, *sel.*
Inferno, *sel.*
Ladies that have intelligence in love, *sel.*
Love and the gentle heart are one same thing,
  sel.
Love hath so long possessed me for his own,
  sel.
Love's pallor and the semblance of deep ruth,
  sel.
Mine eyes beheld the blessed pity spring, *sel.*
My lady carries love within her eyes, *sel.*
My lady looks so gentle and so pure, *sel.*
Paradiso, *sel.*
Purgatorio, *sel.*
Sestina I: Of the Lady Pietra degli Scrovigni.
Song, 'tis my will that thou do seek out Love,
  sel.
Sonnet: Comes Often to My Memory.
Sonnet: "Guido, I wish that you and Lapo and
  I."
Sonnet: Of Beatrice de' Portinari, on All
  Saints' Day.
Sonnet: Of Beauty and Duty.
Sonnet: On the 9th of June 1290.
Sonnet: To Brunetto Latini.
Sonnet: To Certain Ladies; When Beatrice
  Was Lamenting Her Father's Death.
Sonnet: To Guido Cavalcanti.
Sonnet: To the Lady Pietra degli Scrovigni.
Sonnet: To the Same Ladies; With Their
  Answer.
Stay now with me, and listen to my sighs,
  sel.
That lady of all gentle memories, *sel.*
That she hath gone to Heaven suddenly, *sel.*
Thoughts are broken in my memory, The, *sel.*
To every heart which the sweet pain doth
  move, *sel.*
Very bitter weeping that ye made, The, *sel.*
Very pitiful lady, very young, A, *sel.*
Weep, Lovers, with Love's very self doth
  weep, *sel.*
Whatever while the thought comes over me,
  sel.
Woe's me! by dint of all these sighs that
  come, *sel.*
Ye pilgrim-folk, advancing pensively, *sel.*
You that thus wear a modest countenance, *sel.*

Dante da Maiano. *See* **Maiano, Dante da**

Da Ponte, Lorenzo
"Giovinette, Che Fate All'Amore" *sel.*
To an Artful Theatre Manager, *sel.*

D'Aquino, Rinaldo
Lament for the Sailing of the Crusade.

D'Arcy, Hugh Antoine
Face upon [*or* on] the Floor, The.

Dard, Khwaja Mir
Blame was all.
Loved ones' irresistible ways, The.
Mukhammas.
Rubai Enlarged.
Rubai: "In vain, in vain, my love, to the river
  bank you go."
So long as life remains.
They say the rose garden.
Waiting for the morning breeze am I, *sel.*
When I could not see thee and all thy
  majesty.
Whether school or mosque or tavern.

Dargan, Olive Tilford
Rescue.

Darío, Rubén (Félix Rubén García Sarmiento)
Alleluya.
Flesh, Celestial Flesh of Woman!
It Was a Gentle Air.
Three Kings, The.
To Columbus.

Darley, George
Dove's Loneliness, The.
Elfin Pedlar, The.

Enchanted Spring, The.
Fallen Star, The.
Hundred-gated Thebes, *sel.*
In Dreamy Swoon, *sel.*
It Is Not Beauty I Demand.
Lilian's Song.
Mermaidens' Vesper-Hymn, The, *sel.*
O Blest Unfabled Incense Tree, *sel.*
O'er the Wild Gannet's Bath, *sel.*
Onward to Far Ida, *sel.*
Sea-Ritual, The, *sel.*
Solitary wayfarer!, *sel.*
Song: "Sweet in her green cell the flower of
    beauty slumbers."
Speckle-black Toad and freckle-green Frog,
    sel.
Syren Songs, *sel.*
To Mie Tirante.
To Poets.
Unicorn, The, *sel.*

Darnley, Henry Stuart, Lord
Gife Langour.
To the Queen.

Darr, Ann
About Motion Pictures.
Love Is.

Darragh, Tina
"Bounded" to "Bower" for "E."
Ludicrous Stick.
"Oilfish" to "Old Chap" for "C."
"Oran" to "Ordain" for "J."
Raymond Chandler's Sentence.
"Yea" to "Yill" for "W."

Darring, Walter
Surprised by Me.

Darwin, Erasmus
Action of Electricity, The, *sel.*
Action of Invisible Ink, The, *sel.*
Economy of Vegetation, The, *sel.*
"How few," the Muse in plaintive accents
    cries, *sel.*
Loves of the Plants, The, *sel.*
Protection of Plants, The, *sel.*
Reproduction of Life, *sel.*
Visit of Hope to Sydney Cove, near
    Botany-Bay.

Darwish, Mahmoud
Apple for the sea, marble narcissus flower,
    An, *sel.*
Bread.
Brief Reflections on an Ancient and Beautiful
    City on the Coast of the Mediterranean Sea.
Earth Poem.
Earth Scrapes Us, *sel.*
Flute Cried, The.
Horses Neighing at the Foot of the Mountain.
Passport, The.
Psalm 3: "Day my poems, The."
Sky for the Sea, A.
Victim No. 48.
We do not need to be reminded, *sel.*
We Lost but Love Gained Nothing.
We Love Life Whenever We Can.
We Move On to a Country, *sel.*
We Travel like Other People.
When the Martyrs Go to Sleep.

Daryush, Elizabeth
Anger Lay by Me All Night Long.
Autumn, Dark Wanderer.
Eyes That Queenly Sit.
Farewell for a While.
Fresh Spring.
Frustration.
How on Solemn Fields of Space.
Look, The.
November.
O Strong to Bless.
Still-Life.
Subalterns.
Throw Away the Flowers.
War Tribunal.

Das, Kamala
House-Builders, The.
Introduction, An: "I don't know politics but I
    know the names."

Da Todi, Jacopone.   *See* **Jacopone da Todi**

Dauenhauer, Nora
Kelp.
Skiing on Russian Christmas.
Voices.

Daugherty, James Henry
Trail Breakers.

Daugherty, Michael
Buzzard.

Daumal, René
Artifice Afire.
Consolatrice.
Deceptions.
Disillusionment.
Fires at Will.
Flesh of Terror.
Icily.
It Comes from Deep Caverns.
Land of Metamorphoses, The.
Monster-Mender, The.
One Word Will Do.
Phantom Skin, The.
Return to an Evil Domain.
Revolution in Summertime.
Sad Little Round of Life.
Skin of Light, The.
Sorcery.

Davenant [*or* D'Avenant], Sir William
By what bold passion am I rudely led, *sel.*
Christmas Reply to the Phylosopher, The.
Endimion Porter and Olivia.
Epitaph: "When you perceive these stones are
    wet."
For the Lady Olivia Porter; a Present upon a
    New Year's Day.
Lark Now Leaves His Water [*or* Wat'ry]
    Nest.
Life and Death, *sel.*
Lover and Philosopher.
Mistress, The.
My lodging it is on the cold ground, *sel.*
O Thou That Sleep'st like Pig in Straw.
Of all the Lombards, by their Trophies
    knowne, *sel.*
Philosopher and the Lover: To a Mistress
    Dying, The.
Praise and Prayer, *sel.*
Soldier Going to the Field, The.
To the Queene, Entertain'd at Night by the
    Countesse of Anglesey.
Under the Willow Shades.
Wake All the Dead, *sel.*
What Is Past.

Davenport, Mariana B.
Suspended Moment.

Davey, Frank
She'd Say.

David, Ernst
After Going Astray in the Underbrush.
Haiku: "As if the first time."
Haiku: "Off the beaten track."
Haiku: "Prevailing west wind."
Haiku: "Solitary crow/ upward over the
    summit."
Haiku: "Strewn out in the smog."
Haiku: "Walking home at night."
Listen to the voice at its root.
Under the Trapeze.

David, John
What Happiness Can Equal Mine.

David ap Gwilym.   *See* **Dafydd ap Gwilym**

David ben Meshullam
Be Not Silent.

Davide, Adèle
I Know Things.
My Youngest Daughter Getting Up in the
    Morning.

Davidman, Joy
Prayer against Indifference.

Davidson, Francis
Beggars.

Davidson, Gustav
Ambushed by Angels.
Nevertheless.

Davidson, John
Ballad of a Nun, A.
Ballad of Heaven, A.
Ballad of Hell, A.
Christmas Eve.
Cinque Port, A.
Dedication to the Generation Knocking at the
    Door.
Eclogue: Queen Elizabeth's Day.
Holiday at Hampton Court.
Imagination, *sel.*
In a Music-Hall.
In Romney Marsh.
In the Isle of Dogs.
Labourer's Wife, A, *sel.*
Last Journey, The, *sel.*
London.
Northern Suburb, A.
Price, The.
Runnable Stag, A.
Song: "Boat is chafing at our long delay,
    The."
Song: "Closes and courts and lanes."
Song of a Train.
Summer.
Thirty Bob a Week.
Twinkling Earn, The, *sel.*
Two Dogs.
Unknown, The.
War Song.
Wasp, The.

Davidson, Michael
Brahms.
Summer Letters.

Davidson, Peter
My Lady the Lake.
Peeper, The.

Davie, Donald
Across the Bay.
At Knaresborough.
Autumn Imagined.
Barnsley and District.
But this, so feminine?
Christening, A.
Compline, *sel.*
Devil on Ice.
Evangelist, The.
For an Age of Plastics. Plymouth.
Fountain, The.
G. M. B.
Garden Party, The.
Gardens No Emblems.
Hearing Russian Spoken.
Heigh-ho on a Winter Afternoon.
Homage to William Cowper.
In California.
Life Encompassed.
Life of Service, The.
Meeting of Cultures, A.
Mushroom Gatherers, The.
On Bertrand Russell's "Portraits from
    Memory."
Orpheus.
Ox-Bow.
Prime, *sel.*
Priory of St. Saviour, Glendalough, The.
Prose for Des Esseintes.
Remembering the 'Thirties.
Rousseau in His Day.
Thanks to Industrial Essex.
Time Passing, Beloved ("Time passing, and
    the memories of love").
To a Teacher of French.
Wind at Penistone, The.

Winter Talent, A.
With the Grain.
Year 1812, The.
Davieau, Robert Stiles
Arizona Village.
Davies, Alan
If the devices fail pens, *sel.*
"101."
Shared Sentences.
Davies, Edward
Cambrian Swain, The, *sel.*
Tintern Abbey, *sel.*
Wily Fox, The.
Davies, Gareth Alban
Dance, The.
Davies, Gloria Evans
Banquet.
Her Name like the Hours.
Davies, Hugh Sykes
Music in an Empty House.
Poem: "In the stump of the old tree, where
the heart has rotted out."
Poem: "It doesn't look like a finger it looks
like a feather of broken glass."
Davies, Idris
Consider Famous Men, Dai Bach.
Do You Remember 1926?
High Summer on the Mountains.
Lay Preacher Ponders, The.
Mrs. Evans Fach, You Want Butter Again.
Davies, J. Kitchener
Today,/ there came a breeze thin as the needle
of a syringe, *sel.*
Davies, Jeffrey
Washing Machine, The.
Davies, Sir John
Affliction, *sel.*
As when the bright cerulean firmament, *sel.*
Contention between Four Maids Concerning
That Which Addeth Most Perfection to That
Sex.
Contention betwixt a Wife, a Widow, and a
Maid, A.
Dance of Love, The, *sel.*
Dancing Sea, The, *sel.*
Dauncing (bright Lady) then began to bee,
sel.
Dedication II: "Strongest and the noblest
argument, The," *sel.*
Dedications, I: To His Very Friend, Master
Richard Martin, *sel.*
Dedications [of Orchestra], I: To His Very
Friend, Master Richard Martin.
Dedications [of Orchestra], II: To the Prince.
Hardness of her heart and truth of mine, The,
sel.
If you would know the love which I you bear,
sel.
In Francum.
In Fuscum.
In Librum.
In What Manner the Soule Is United to the
Body, *sel.*
Into the middle temple of my heart, *sel.*
Lover, under burthen of his mistress' love,
The, *sel.*
Man, *sel.*
Mariner's Song, The.
Mine eye, mine ear, my will, my wit, my
heart, *sel.*
Muse Reviving, The.
My case is this, *sel.*
Nosce Teipsum.
Of Astraea, *sel.*
Oft did I hear our eyes the passage were, *sel.*
On a Pair of Garters.
On the Deputy of Ireland's Child.
Once did my Philomel reflect on me, *sel.*
Or from what spring doth your opinion rise,
sel.

Orchestra; or, A Poem of Dancing.
Sacred muse that first made love divine, The,
sel.
Sickness, intending my love to betray, *sel.*
Sole heir of virtue, and of beauty both, *sel.*
To His Good Friend, Sir Anthony Cooke, *sel.*
To His Lady.
To His Very Friend, Master Richard Martin,
sel.
To love, My Lord, I do knight's service owe,
sel.
To Queen Elizabeth, *sel.*
To the Nightingale, *sel.*
To the Prince, *sel.*
To the Rose, *sel.*
To the Spring, *sel.*
What eagle can behold her sunbright eye, *sel.*
What Is This Knowledge?
Davies, John, of Hereford
Against Gaudy-Bragging-Undoughty Daccus.
Against Proud Poor Phryna.
Although We Do Not All the Good We Love,
sel.
Author Loving These Homely Meats, The,
sel.
Of Kate's Baldness.
Remembrance of My Friend Mr. Thomas
Morley, A.
Some Blaze the Precious Beauties of Their
Loves, *sel.*
Sonnet: "It is as true as strange, else trial
feigns."
Sonnet: "So shoots a star as doth my mistress
glide."
Davies, Mary Carolyn
Be Different to Trees.
Day before April, The.
Easter.
Feet.
Fishing Pole, The ("A fishing pole's a curious
thing").
If I Had Known.
Man's Woman, A.
Prayer for a Marriage, A.
Prayer for a Sleeping Child, A.
Prayer for Every Day, A.
Tree Birthdays.
Davies, Russell
Book Review.
Dear Father Christmas.
Davies, Samuel
Eternal Spirit, Source of Light.
Lord, I Am Thine.
While o'er Our Guilty Land, O Lord.
Davies, Sneyd
Crooked bank still winds to something new,
The, *sel.*
Scene after Hunting at Swallowfield in
Berkshire, A.
Davies, T. Glynne
Caernarfon, 2 July 1969.
Old Man in a Moon Loft.
Sentences While Remembering Hiraethog.
Davies, Walter (Gwalter Mechain)
Nightfall.
Davies, William Henry
All in June.
Ambition.
Battle, The.
Best Friend, The.
Bird of Paradise, The.
Black Cloud, The.
Bright Day, A.
Cat, The.
Chase, The.
Child and the Mariner, The.
Child's Pet, A.
Christ, the Man.
D is for Dog.
Days That Have Been.
Days Too Short.

Dog, The.
Dumb World, The.
Early Morn.
Elements, The.
Example, The.
Eyes.
Facts.
Flirt, The.
Flying Blossoms.
Frost.
Ghost, The.
Great Time, A.
Greeting, A.
Heap of Rags, The.
Her Merriment.
Hermit, The.
Hospital Waiting-Room, The.
Hour of Magic, The.
I Am the Poet Davies, William.
Inquest, The.
Jenny Wren.
Joy and Pleasure.
Kingfisher, The.
Lamorna Cove.
Last Years, The.
Leaves.
Leisure.
Loyalty.
Maiden and Her Hair, A.
Mind's Liberty, The.
Money.
Moon, The.
Moon and a Cloud, The.
Muse, The.
My Garden.
Oh, Sweet Content.
On Hearing Mrs. Woodhouse Play the
Harpsichord.
One Poet Visits Another.
One Token.
Power of Silence, The.
Rain, The.
Rainbow, The.
Rat, The.
Rich Days.
School's Out.
Sea, The.
Sheep.
Sluggard, The.
Songs of Joy.
Sweet Stay-at-Home.
Thought, A.
To a Butterfly.
To a Lady Friend.
Truly Great.
Truth, The.
Two Stars, The.
Villain, The.
Visitor, The.
When Diamonds, Nibbling in My Ears.
When Yon Full Moon.
White Horse, The.
White Monster, The.
White Sheep.
Wind, The.
Davis, Abijah
Blest Is the Man Whose Tender Breast.
Davis, Catherine
After a Time.
Insights.
Kindness.
Nausea.
Davis, Daniel Webster
Hog Meat.
'Weh Down Souf.
Davis, Dick
Chebutykin.
Childhood of a Spy.
Ibn Battuta.
Davis, Fannie Stearns
For a Child.

Davis, Florence Boyce
This and That.
Three Wise Monkeys, The.
Davis, Frank Marshall
Arthur Ridgewood, M.D.
Dancing Gal.
Flowers of Darkness.
Four Glimpses of Night.
Giles Johnson, Ph.D.
I Sing No New Songs.
"Onward Christian Soldiers!"
Robert Whitmore.
Snapshots of the Cotton South.
To Those Who Sing America.
Davis, Gloria
To Egypt.
Davis, Glover
Burial, The.
Lost Moments.
Davis, H. L.
Stalks of Wild Hay.
Davis, Helen Bayley
Jack Frost.
Davis, Jack
Day Flight.
Davis, John
Sun, The.
Davis, Marilyn
Changeling, The.
Song for My Son.
Davis, Nedine
I Am Mama Bear.
Davis, Norma L.
Daydreamers.
Davis, Ossie
To a Brown Girl.
Davis, Ozora Stearns
At Length There Dawns the Glorious Day.
Davis, Robert A.
Dust Bowl.
Davis, Robert H.
At the Door of the Native Studies Director.
Black Buoy.
Raven is Two-Faced.
Raven Tells Stories.
Davis, Ronda
Invitation (To the Night and All Other Things
Dark).
Parasitosis.
Personality Sketch: Bill, A.
Poems about Playmates.
Spacin.
Davis, Thadious M.
Asante Sana, Te Te.
Double Take at Relais de L'Espadon.
"Honeysuckle Was the Saddest Odor of All, I
Think."
It's All the Same.
Remembering Fannie Lou Hamer.
Davis, Thomas
Nation Once Again, A.
This Native Land.
Davis, Thomas Osborne
Girl I Left behind Me, The.
Lament for the Death of Eoghan Ruadh
O'Neill.
Davis, Thulani
Dreamtime I You Dog You.
Moviestar.
Davison, Edward
In This Dark House.
Nocturne: "Be thou at peace this night."
Novice, The.
Owl, The.
Sonnet: "She is so young, and never never
before."
Davison, Francis
Epitaph: "Lovely boy, thou art not dead."
Epitaph: "Thou alive on earth, sweet boy."
Epitaph: "Wit's perfection, Beauty's wonder."
Her Commendation.

His Farewell to His Unkind and Unconstant
Mistress.
I Muse Not.
Madrigal: "Sound of thy sweet name, my
dearest treasure, The."
My Only Star.
Song: "Lady, you are with beauties so
enriched."
To Cupid.
Davison, Peter
Artemis.
Bed Time.
Compound Eye, The.
Cost of Pretending, The.
Housing Starts.
Last Word, The.
Lunch at the Coq d'Or.
Magpie.
Money Cry, The.
Motley.
Pleaders, The.
Poem in the Park, The.
Questions of Swimming, 1935.
Star Watcher, The.
Vanishing Point, The.
Davison, Walter
At Her Fair Hands.
To His Lady, Who Had Vowed Virginity.
Dawe, Bruce
Abandonment of Autos.
Americanized.
City: Midnight, The.
Dogs in the Morning Light.
Drifters.
First Corinthians at the Crossroads.
Gorilla Gorilla.
Happiness Is the Art of Being Broken.
Homecoming.
Not-so-good Earth, The.
Only the Beards Are Different.
Perpetuum Immobile.
Victorian Hangman Tells His Love, A.
Dawes, Rufus
Love Unchangeable.
Dawson, Daniel Lewis
Seeker in the Marshes, The.
Dawson, Grace Stricker
To a Friend.
Dawson, James
Labourer's Song, A.
Dawson, William James
Inspirations.
Day, Clarence
Egg, The.
Man Is but a Castaway.
Might and Right.
Who Drags the Fiery Artist Down?
Day, Dorothea
My Captain.
Day, James William
Rowan County Crew, The.
Day, Jean
Gas.
Heavy Clouds Passing before the Sun.
Paradise and Lunch.
Day, John
Ditty, A, sel.
Day, Lucille
Cytogenetics Lab.
Labor.
Neural Folds.
Yom Kippur.
Day, Richard Edwin
England.
To Shakespeare.
Day, William
Mount Vernon, the Home of Washington.
Day Lewis, Cecil
Album, The.
Almost Human.
As One Who Wanders into Old Workings.

Bombers.
Can the Mole Take.
Chiefly to Mind Appears.
Christmas Eve.
Christmas Rose, The.
Come, live with me and be my love, sel.
Come Up, Methuselah.
Committee, The.
Conflict, The.
Consider These, for We Have Condemned
Them.
Dead, The.
Departure in the Dark.
Desire is a witch.
Do Not Expect Again a Phoenix Hour.
Emily Brontë.
Failure, A.
Few Things Can More Inflame.
For us, born into a still, sel.
Great Magicians, The.
Happy View, A.
It Is Becoming Now to Declare My
Allegiance.
I've heard them lilting at loom and belting,
sel.
"Let Us Now Praise Famous Men."
Maple and Sumach.
Meeting, A.
My Mother's Sister.
Nabara, sel.
Nearing Again the Legendary Isle, sel.
Newsreel.
Now I have come to reason.
Now She Is like the White Tree-Rose, sel.
Offertorium, sel.
On Not Saying Everything.
On the Sea Wall.
Reconciliation.
Rest from Loving and Be Living.
Sheepdog Trials in Hyde Park.
Son and Father.
Stand-to, The.
Sun Came Out in April, The.
Symbols of Gross Experience, sel.
Tempt Me No More, sel.
Third Enemy Speaks, sel.
This Man Was Strong.
Though Bodies Are Apart, sel.
To travel like a bird, lightly to view, sel.
Tourists, The.
When They Have Lost.
Where Are the War Poets?
Winged bull trundles to the wired perimeter,
The, sel.
Winter Night.
With Me My Lover Makes.
You That Love England.
Dayre, Sydney
Grandma's Lost Balance.
Lesson for Mamma, A.
Morning Compliments.
Dayton, Ebenezer
Wherein Consists the High Estate.
Dayton, Irene
Ear Is Not Deaf.
De———, Mlle
Fair Sex Avenged by—, The.
Thalia, you will remember that recently I
made, sel.
Deagon, Ann
Certified Copy.
Man and Wife Is One Flesh.
Deamer, Dulcie
Artemis.
Dean, Elma
Old Men's Ward.
Deane, Anthony C.
Cult of the Celtic, The.
Here Is the Tale.
Jack and Jill—as Kipling Might Have Written
It.

Mary, Mary.
Ode, An: "I sing a song of sixpence, and of rye."
Rustic Song, A.

Deane, John F.
Contact.
Offertory.

Deane, Seamus (Osip Mandelstam)
Burial, A.
Derry.
History Lessons.
Northern Ireland: Two Comments.
Return.
Scholar I.
Scholar II.
Schooling, A.

Dearmer, Geoffrey
Turkish Trench Dog, The.
Whale.

De Bary, Anna Bunston
Snowdrop.
Under a Wiltshire Apple Tree.

De Boully, Monny
Beyond Memory.

De Brun, Padraig
Calvary.
In Memoriam.
Is It Not You, Lord!

De Burgos, Julia
Nothing.
Poem of the Intimate Agony.

Dec, Frederick
Bulldozers.
Class of 19——.

De Carrion, Santob [or Shem-Tob]
Friend, A, sel.
Resignation.
Self-Defense.

De Casseres, Benjamin
Moth-Terror.

DeClue, Charlotte
Ijajee's Story.
In Memory of the Moon (A Killing).
Morning Song.
Place-of-Many-Swans.
To the Spirit of Monahsetah.
Yesterday, Robin spoke to me.

Ded, Lal
Impermanence.

Dederick, Robert
Karoo Town.
Robben Island.

Deems, Charles F.
I Shall Not Want: In Deserts Wild.

Defoe, Daniel
Breed's described, The: Now, Satire, if you can, sel.
Encomium upon a Parliament, An.
In northern climes where furious tempests blow, sel.
In their religion they are so unev'n, sel.
Labouring poor, in spite of double pay, The, sel.
London, sel.
Search all the Christian climes from pole to pole, sel.
Spanish Descent, The.
Then let us boast of ancestors no more, sel.
To sin's a vice in nature, and we find, sel.
True-born Englishman, The.
Vision, The.
Wherever God erects a house of prayer, sel.
Word's gone out, and now they spread the main, The, sel.
Yet Ostia boasts of her regeneration, sel.

DeFoe, Mark
13 Ways of Eradicating Blackbirds.

DeFord, Miriam Allen
We Shall Say.

De Forest, John William
National Hymn, A, sel.

De France, Marie
Nightingale, The.
Song from Chartivel.
Two Lovers, The.

DeFrees, Madeline
Letter to an Absent Son.
New England Interlude.
Pendant Watch.

De Guildford, Nicholas
When I was in a summer valley, sel.

Deguy, Michel
Alluvium.
Eyes, The.
It's between Ourselves.
O Great Apposition.
Wall, The.
When the Wind.
You.

Dehmel, Richard
Before the Storm.
Harvest Song.
Laborer, The.
My Drinking Song.
Silent Town, The.
To———?
Trysting, A.
Vigil.
Voice in Darkness.

Dehn, Paul
Alternative Endings to an Unwritten Ballad.
Armistice.
At the Dark Hour.
Game of Consequences, A.
Hey diddle diddle/ The physicists fiddle, sel.
In a cavern, in a canyon, sel.
Jack and Jill went up the hill/ To fetch some heavy water, sel.
Jenny kiss'd me when we met, sel.
Lament for a Sailor.
Little Miss Muffet/ Crouched on a tuffet, sel.
Nuclear wind, when wilt thou blow, sel.
St. Aubin d'Aubigne.
Two blind mice, sel.
Whenas in Jeans.

Dei-Anang, Michael
My Africa.

DeJong, David Cornel
On the Twenty-fifth of July.

De Kay, Charles
Arcana Sylvarum.
Draft Riot, The.
Ulf in Ireland.

Dekker, Thomas
Art thou poor, yet hast thou golden slumbers?, sel.
Beauty, Arise!, sel.
Drinking Song, sel.
Fortune and Virtue, sel.
Golden Slumbers, sel.
Haymakers, Rakers, sel.
O, the Month of May, sel.
Pleasant Comedy of Patient Grisselle, The.
Priest's Song, A, sel.
Troynovant, sel.

Delafield, Harriet L.
No Escape.

Delahaye, Alain
Because in Destroying He Creates.
Broad Meadow.
Hill, the Frenzy, The.
Intense Landscape, The.
Logic.
Two Landscapes, Grammar.

De la Mare, Walter
Afraid.
Alas, Alack!
All but Blind.
All That's Past.
Alone.
Ann and the Fairy Song, sel.
Antiques.

Archery.
Arrogance.
At Ease.
At the Keyhole.
Autumn.
Away.
Ballad of Christmas, A.
Bandog, The.
Barber's, The.
Bards, The.
Berries.
Bindweed, The.
Birthnight; to F, The.
Bishop Winterbourne.
Bones.
Breughel's Winter.
Bunches of Grapes.
Buttons.
Children of Stare, The.
Comb, The.
Corner Stone, The.
Corporal Pym.
Crazed.
Cupboard, The.
Dark Château, The.
De Profundis.
Double Dutch.
Drugged.
Dunce, The.
Dust to Dust.
Echo.
Empty House, The.
Epitaph, An: "Here lies a most beautiful lady."
Eyes.
Faint Music.
False Dawn.
False Gods.
Fare Well.
Feckless Dinner Party, The.
Five Eyes.
Fly, The.
Full Moon.
Funeral, The.
Galliass, The.
Ghost, The.
Gone.
Good-bye.
Green.
Hare, A.
Hawthorn Hath a Deathly Smell, The.
Here All We See.
Hi!
Holly, The.
Horseman, The.
Huntsmen, The.
Immanent.
In the Dock.
In the Local Museum.
Iron.
It Might Be a Lump of Amber.
J. J.
Jim Jay.
John Mouldy.
Keys of Morning, The.
Last Chapter, The.
Last Coachload, The.
Linnet, The.
Listeners, The.
Little Bird, The.
Lucy.
Many a Mickle.
March Hares.
Marionettes, The.
Martha.
Me.
Mermaids, The.
Mima.
Miracle, The.

Miss Loo.
Miss Pheasant.
Miss T.
Mistletoe.
Mocking Fairy, The.
Moonlight.
Moonshine.
Moth, The.
Motley.
Mountains, The.
Mrs. MacQueen (or The Lollie-Shop).
Napoleon.
Ned Vaughan.
Never More, Sailor.
Nicholas Nye.
Nod.
Nostalgia.
Nothing.
Old Men, The.
Old Shellover.
Old Summerhouse, The.
Old Susan.
Owl, The.
Peace.
Peak and Puke.
Pooh!
Portrait, A.
Quiet Enemy, The.
Railway Junction, The.
Reserved.
Revenant, The.
Ride-by-Nights, The.
Robin, A.
Sam.
Santa Claus.
Scarecrow, The.
Scholars.
Scribe, The.
Shadow, The.
She Said.
Ship of Rio, The.
Shubble, The.
Silver.
Silver Penny, The.
Sleeper, The.
Slim Cunning Hands.
Snow.
Snowflake, The.
Solitude.
Someone [or Some One]
Somewhere.
Song of Finis, The.
Song of the Mad Prince, The.
Song of the Shadows, The.
"Sooeep!"
Spotted Flycatcher, The.
Still Life.
Stranger, The.
Summer Evening.
Sunk Lyonesse.
Supper.
Susannah Prout.
Tartary.
Tat for Tit.
Theologians.
There Blooms No Bud in May.
Things.
Thomas Hardy.
Thomas Logge.
Three Cherry Trees, The.
Three Sisters.
Thunder.
Tired Tim.
Titmouse.
To a Candle.
Tom's Angel.
Tomtit, The.
Trees.
Truants, The.
Vain Finding.
Virtue.
Voice, The.

Voices.
Waif, The.
Where.
Why?
Widow's Weeds, A.
Winter.
Winter Evening.
Winter is fallen early, sel.
Wreck, The.
De la Monnoye, Bernard
Patapan.
Deland, Margaret
Christmas Silence, The.
Clover, The.
Doubt.
Love and Death.
Love's Wisdom.
Sent with a Rose to a Young Lady.
While Shepherds Watched Their Flocks by
Night.
Delany, Clarissa Scott
Interim.
Joy.
Mask, The.
Solace.
Delany, W. W. *See* **"Lee, Andy"**
Delarue-Mardrus, Lucie
If You Come.
Injustice.
Refusal.
De La Tierra, Tatiana
De Ambiente.
De Ledrede, Richard
Festival of the Nativity, The.
De León, Luís
Life of the Blessed, The.
Love Song: "That haughty tyranny of thine."
Night Serene, The.
Written on the Walls of His Dungeon.
De León, Nephtalí
In the Plaza We Walk.
Delétang-Tardif, Yanette
Song: "I want my dance."
Delgado, Washington
Foreign Land.
Globetrotter.
Good Manners.
History of Peru.
Human Wisdom.
Imperfect Times.
Life Explains and Death Spies Out.
Monologue of the Inhabitant.
Plurality of Worlds.
Pure Thoughts.
De Lisle, Leconte. *See* **Leconte de Lisle,
Charles Marie**
Delius, Anthony
Brief Farewell.
Deaf-and-Dumb School.
Distance.
Footnote.
Gamblers, The.
Intuition.
Lady Anne Bathing.
Shadow.
Thinker, The.
Della Casa, Giovanni
To Sleep.
Delle Colonne, Guido
Canzone: To Love and to His Lady.
Del Medigo, Joseph Solomon
Epigram: "If men be judged wise."
Del Monte, Crescenzo
One Thing to Take, Another to Keep.
Roman Roman, A.
Those Zionists.
Deloney, Thomas
Joyful [or Joyfull] New Ballad, A.
Princely Ditty in Praise of the English Rose,
A.

Winning of Cales, The.
Would God That It Were Holiday!
De Long, Juanita
My Hereafter.
Delp, Mike
Fishing the Dream.
Del Renzio, Toni
Can You Change a Shilling?
Del Valle, Adriano
Cradle Song of the Elephants.
Demarest, Mary Lee
My Ain Countree.
Demetriadis, Mary
"When Lovely Woman Stoops to Folly."
Demetrio, Herrera S.
Training.
De Mille, James
Lines to Miss Florence Huntingdon
De Morgan, Augustus
Great Fleas.
Dempster, Roland Tombekai
Africa's Plea.
Is This Africa.
Demus, Klaus
Morning Stillness.
Oh brother, sister—man.
Summer Report.
DenBoer, James
Charming the Moon.
Denby, Edwin
Dishonor.
Denham, Sir John
Cooper's Hill.
Elegie upon the Death of the Lord Hastings,
An.
Had Cowley ne'er spoke, Killigrew ne'er
writ.
Here have I seen the king, when great affairs,
sel.
Here should my wonder dwell, and here my
praise, sel.
My eye descending from the Hill, surveys,
sel.
On Mr. Abraham Cowley, His Death and
Burial amongst the Ancient Poets.
Preface to The Progress of Learning.
There Faunus and Sylvanus keep their courts,
sel.
Denis, Philippe
Already.
Earth.
Moored.
On the Butterfly's.
Star, A.
To Live.
Denney, Reuel
Fixer of Midnight.
Laboratory Midnight, The.
Tennis in San Juan.
Dennis, C. J.
Martyred Democrat, The.
Play, The, sel.
Triantiwontigongolope, The.
Dennis, Carl
Dream of Fair Women, The.
Letter on the Lake, A.
List, The.
Looking at a Photograph on My Forty-Fourth
Birthday.
Pen Pal.
Denny, Alma
Birds of 9th Ave, The.
Lettuce Pause.
Thought While Dressing to Meet the "Girls."
Dennys, John
Angler's Song, The, sel.
Dent, Tom
Blue Light, The.
Mississippi Mornings.
Denwood, Jonathan
Bleeberrying.

De Regnier, Henri
Night.
De Regniers, Beatrice Schenk
I Looked in the Mirror.
Keep a Poem in Your Pocket.
Night Comes.
Der Hovanessian, Diana
Poultry.
Derleth, August
Planetary Arc-Light, The.
Der Nistor
At the Doors.
De Roche, Joseph
Aunt Laura Moves toward the Open Grave of
Her Father.
Blond.
Derricke, John
No table there is spread, *sel.*
Derricotte, Toi
Fears of the Eighth Grade.
Good Old Dog, The.
Hamtramck: The Polish Women.
Mirror Poems, The.
On Stopping Late in the Afternoon for
Steamed Dumplings.
Derwood, Gene
After Reading St. John the Divine.
Bird, Bird.
Elegy on Gordon Barber.
In the Proscenium.
Innocent, The.
N. B., Symmetrians.
Rides.
Spring Air.
With God Conversing.
Derzhavin, Gavril Romanovich
O, Thou Eternal One!
De Savitzsky, Isabel
Christmas Tree, The.
Desbordes-Valmore, Marceline
Roses of Sa'adi, The.
Deshoulières, Antoinette
Reflections.
**Desmond, Gerald Fitzgerald, 4th Earl of
(Gearold Iarla Mac Gearailt)**
Against Blame of Woman.
Woe to him who slanders women.
Desnos, Robert
Arbitrary Destiny.
At the World's Last Outpost.
Cuckoo.
Cuckoo-Clock.
Despair of the Sun.
Ebony Life.
Epitaph: "I lived in those times. For a
thousand years."
For a Daylight Dream.
Great Days of the Poet, The.
Half Way.
I Have Dreamed of You So Much.
Idée Fixe.
Identity of Imagery.
If You Only Knew.
I've Dreamed of You So Much.
Lying Down.
Midway.
Nightfall.
No, Love Is Not Dead.
One Day When It Was Night Out.
Remarks from the Rocks.
Rose of Marble and the Rose of Iron, The.
Spaces inside Sleep, The.
Suicided by Night.
Voice of Robert Desnos, The.
Desnoues, Lucienne
First Things.
Desportes, Philippe
Conquest *or* His Lady's Might.
Desprez, Frank
Lasca.

Des Roches, Catherine
Agnodicia, or Ignorance Banished from the
Presence of Women.
To My Distaff.
Des Roches, Madeleine
First Ode.
Reply to Her Daughter, IV.
**De Tabley, John Byrne Leicester Warren, 3d
Baron**
Anticipation.
Chorus: "Sweet are the ways of death to
weary feet," *sel.*
Churchyard on the Sands, The.
Circe.
Knight in the Wood, The.
Lines to a Lady-Bird.
Nuptial Song.
Philoctetes.
Pilgrim Cranes, The.
Power of Interval, The.
Song of Dust, A.
Sonnet: "Record is nothing, and the hero
great."
Study of a Spider, The.
Two Old Kings, The.
Dett, Robert Nathaniel
Rubinstein Staccato Etude, The.
Deutsch, Babette
Barges on the Hudson.
Destruction of Letters.
Earliness at the Cape.
Fireworks.
Homage to the Philosopher.
Late Reflections.
Memory.
Morning Workout.
Need.
New York—December, 1931.
No Moon, No Star.
Paradigm.
Pig Is Never Blamed, A.
Poem, The: "Painter of Dante's awful
ferry-ride, The."
Scene with Figure.
Small Colored Boy in the Subway.
Stranger than the Worst.
Tak for Sidst.
Devaney, James
Evening Gleam, The.
Mortality.
Song of the Captured Woman.
De Veaux, Alexis
Sisters, The.
Devecseri, Gábor
Bath in Pylos, The.
His Life.
Odysseus in Phaeacia.
Women and Masks.
World Awoke Me, The.
De Vere, Sir Aubrey
Children Band, The.
Reality.
Right Use of Prayer, The.
De Vere, Aubrey Thomas
Autumnal Ode.
Correggio's Cupolas at Parma.
Dominica Pentecostes.
Fall, snow, and cease not! Flake by flake, *sel.*
Feast of the Most Holy Trinity.
In Ruin Reconciled.
Little Black Rose, The.
Poet to a Painter, A.
Sacraments of Nature, The.
Serenade: "Softly, O midnight Hours!"
Sorrow.
Spring, *sel.*
Sun God, The.
Wedding of the Clans, The.
De Vere, Edward, 17th Earl of Oxford
Choice, A.
If Women Could Be Fair.

Of the Birth and Bringing Up of Desire.
Pains and Gains.
White and Red.
De Vere, William
Walk, Damn You, Walk!
De Viau, Theophile
Sleep.
Devlin, Denis
Ank'hor Vat.
Anteroom: Geneva.
Ascension.
Colours of Love, The.
Daphne Stillorgan.
Encounter.
Eve in My Legend.
Evenings ever more willing lapse into my
world's evening, *sel.*
Farewell and Good.
From Government Buildings.
Jansenist Journey.
Lancet, The.
Little Elegy.
Lough Derg.
Memoirs of a Turcoman Diplomat.
Passion of Christ, The.
Renewal by Her Element.
Spires, firm on their monster feet rose light
and thin, The, *sel.*
Venus of the Salty Shell.
Wishes for Her.
Devlin, John Dacres
November Primrose, The.
De Vries, Peter
Bacchanal.
Christmas Family Reunion.
Loveliest of Pies.
Mirror.
Psychiatrist.
Sacred and Profane Love, or, There's Nothing
New Under the Moon Either.
Theme and Variation.
To His Importunate Mistress.
To My Friends.
Dewar, A. W.
Life and the Weaver.
Dewdney, Christopher
Out of Control; the Quarry.
This Is of Two Worlds.
Dewey, George Washington
Blind Louise.
DeWitt, John
Vampire, The.
DeWitt, Samuel A.
If I were less the man, I might have kept, *sel.*
"There is no permanence," you sagely said,
sel.
Two Sonnets for a Lost Love, II.
Dhomhnaill, Nuala Ni
As for the Quince.
Feeding a Child.
Labasheedy (the Silken Bed).
Móir Hatching.
Parthenogenesis.
Race, The.
Shannon Estuary Welcoming the Fish, The.
Dhu 'L-nun
I die, and yet not dies in me.
Dia, Contess Beatritz de. See Beatrice de Die
Diamond, David
We Will Not Fear.
Diamond, Lucy
Eskimo Baby, An.
Greenland Winter, A.
Kayak Song, A.
Diaper, William
Eclogue: "Lycon begin—begin the mournful
tale," *sel.*
Had mournful Ovid been to Brent condemned,
sel.
Happy are you, whom Quantock overlooks,
sel.

Lamprey, glowing with uncommon fires, The,
  sel.
Shelly crawlers each returning year, The, sel.
Strange the formation of the eely race, sel.
When pleasing heat, and fragrant blooms
  inspire, sel.
When they in throngs a safe retirement seek,
  sel.

Díaz Mirón, Salvador
Corpse, The.
Example, The.
Grief.
Nox.
Phantom, The.
To an Araucaria.
Within an Emerald.

Dibdin, Charles
Anchorsmiths, The.
Captain Wattle and Miss Roe.
Jolly Young Waterman, The.
Lady's Diary, The.
Poor Jack.
Poor Tom.
Popular Functionary, A.

Dibdin, Thomas
Child That Has a Cold, A.

Di Castagnola, Countess Alice Fay
Mortal Combat.

Di Cicco, Pier Giorgio
Errore.
Flying Deeper into the Century.
Head Is a Paltry Matter, The.
Male Rage Poem.

Dickenga, I. E.
Building.

Dickens, Charles
Cannibals' Grace before Meat, The.
Fine Old English Gentleman; New Version,
  The.
Ivy Green, The, sel.

Dickenson, John
Tityrus to His Fair Phyllis, sel.

Dickey, James
Adultery.
After the Night Hunt.
Armor.
At Darien Bridge.
Bee, The.
Birth, A.
Birthday Dream, The.
Bread.
Breath.
Buckdancer's Choice.
Bums, on Waking.
By Canoe through the Fir Forest.
Call, The.
Celebration, The.
Cherrylog Road.
Coming Back to America.
Common Grave, The.
Deborah as Scion.
Deer among Cattle.
Dog Sleeping on My Feet, A.
Doorstep, Lightning, Waif-Dreaming.
Driver, The.
Dusk of Horses, The.
Faces Seen Once.
Falling.
False Youth: Autumn: Clothes of the Age.
Fence Wire.
Fiend, The.
Firebombing, The.
Flash, The.
For the Death of Vince Lombardi.
For the Nightly Ascent of the Hunter Orion
  over a Forest Clearing.
Gamecock.
Goodbye to Serpents.
Heaven of Animals, The.
Hedge Life.
Hospital Window, The.

Hunting Civil War Relics at Nimblewill
  Creek.
Ice Skin, The.
In the Marble Quarry.
In the Mountain Tent.
In the Pocket.
In the Pocket.
In the Tree House at Night.
Inside the River.
Island, The.
Landfall, The.
Leap, The.
Lifeguard, The.
Madness.
Magus, The.
Movement of Fish, The.
On the Hill below the Lighthouse.
Performance, The.
Power and Light.
Pursuit from Under.
Reincarnation (I) ("Still, passed through the
  spokes of an old wheel").
Shark's Parlor, The.
Sheep Child, The.
Slave Quarters.
Sled Burial, Dream Ceremony.
So long, sel.
Tenderness, ache on me, and lay your neck,
  sel.
To His Children in Darkness.
Trees and Cattle.
Underground Stream, The.
Venom.
Walking on Water.

Dickey, R. P.
Browsing in Roget's Thesaurus.

Dickey, William
Anniversary, The.
Canonical Hours.
Fish Upstairs, The.
Happiness.
Hootali Ajignat.
Poet's Farewell to His Teeth, The.
Resolving Doubts.
Teaching Swift to Young Ladies.
Things Kept.
Three Songs.
Tutankhamen.
Windows.

Dickinson, Blanche Taylor
Four Walls.
Poem: "Ah, I know what happiness is!"
Revelation.
That Hill.
To an Icicle.
Walls of Jericho, The.

Dickinson, Charles Monroe
Children, The.

Dickinson, Emily
Afraid! Of whom am I afraid?
After a hundred years.
After great pain, a formal feeling comes.
Ah, necromancy sweet!
Ah, Teneriffe!
Alter! When the hills do.
Altered look about the hills, An.
Although I put away his life.
Ample make this bed.
And with what body do they come?
Apparently with no surprise.
Arcturus is his other name.
As imperceptibly as grief.
At half past three, a single bird.
Auctioneer of parting, The.
Autum: "Wind—tapped like a tired man,
  The."
Bat is dun, with wrinkled wings, The.
Beauty—be not caused—it is.
Beauty is not caused—it is.
Because I could not stop for death.
Because you are going.

Bee, The.
Bee his burnished carriage, A.
Bee! I'm expecting you!
Bees are black, with gilt surcingles.
Before I got my eye put out.
Behind me—dips eternity.
Besides the autumn poets sing.
Bible is an antique volume, The.
Bird came down the walk, A.
Birthday of but a single pang.
Bloom is result. To Meet a flower.
Bone that has no marrow, The.
Brain, within its groove, The.
Bring me the sunset in a cup.
Bustle in a house, The.
Cause: "Brain is wider than the sky, The."
Clock stopped, A.
Color—caste—denomination.
Color of the grave is green, The.
Come slowly, Eden.
Could mortal lip divine.
Crickets sang, The.
Crumbling is not an instant's act.
Death is a dialogue between.
Delayed till she had ceased to know.
Did our best moment last.
Did the harebell loose her girdle.
Difference between despair, The.
Distance that the dead have gone, The.
Drama's vitallest expression is the common
  day.
Drop fell on the apple tree, A.
Drowning is not so pitiful.
Drunkard cannot meet a cork, A.
Dying tiger—moaned for drink, A.
Elysium is as far as to.
Essential oils—are wrung.
Eternity.
Faded boy in sallow clothes, A.
Faith is a fine invention.
Faith—is the pierless bridge.
Fame is a fickle food.
Farthest thunder that I heard, The.
Finding is the first act.
First day's night had come, The.
Floss won't save you from an abyss.
For each ecstatic instant.
Four trees upon a solitary acre.
Frigid and sweet her parting face.
Further in summer than the birds.
Fuzzy fellow without feet, A.
Gentian weaves her fringes, The.
Glass was the street.
Go not too near a house of rose.
God is a distant, stately lover.
God is indeed a jealous God.
God made a little gentian.
Going—to—her!
Great streets of silence led away.
Have you got a brook in your little heart.
He ate and drank the precious words.
He fumbles at your soul.
He preached upon "Breadth" till it argued him
  narrow.
He scanned it, staggered, dropped the loop.
He showed me hights I never saw.
Heart asks pleasure—first, The.
Heart, we will forget him!
Heaven is what I cannot reach.
"Heavenly Father," take to thee.
Her breast is fit for pearls.
Her face was in a bed of hair.
Her sweet weight on my heart a night.
His mansion in the pool.
Hope is the thing with feathers.
How happy is the little stone.
How many times these low feet staggered.
How noteless men, and Pleiads, stand.
How soft a caterpillar steps.
How the old mountains drip with sunset.
How the waters closed above him.
I am afraid to own a body.

I am alive—I guess.
I asked no other thing.
I can wade grief.
I cannot live with you.
I could bring you jewels—had I a mind to.
I died for beauty—but was scarce.
I dreaded that first robin, so.
I dwell in possibility.
I felt a cleavage or cleaving in my mind.
I felt a funeral, in my brain.
I found the phrase or words to every thought.
I gave myself to him.
I got so I could take his name.
I had been hungry, all the years.
I had no time to hate, because.
I had not minded walls.
I have never seen volcanoes.
I have not told my garden yet.
I heard a fly buzz—when I died.
I know some lonely houses off the road.
I know that He exists.
I like a look of agony.
I like to see it lap the miles.
I measure every grief I meet.
I never hear the word "escape."
I never lost as much but twice.
I never saw a moor.
I read my sentence steadily.
I reason, earth is short.
I Reckon—When I Count at All.
I saw no way—the heavens were stitched.
I shall know why—when time is over.
I should have been too glad, I see.
I started early, took my dog.
I stepped from plank to plank.
I taste a liquor never brewed.
I think that the root of the wind is water.
I went to heaven.
I would not paint—a picture.
I years had been from home.
If I can stop one heart from breaking.
If I should die.
If I shouldn't be alive.
If recollecting were forgetting.
If you were coming in the Fall.
I'll tell you how the sun rose.
I'm ceded—I've stopped being theirs.
I'm nobody! Who are you?
I'm wife; I've finished that.
Immortal is an ample word.
In winter in my room.
It dropped so low—in my regard.
It is an honorable thought.
It sifts from leaden sieves.
It sounded as if the streets were running.
It struck me every day.
It troubled me as once I was.
It was not death, for I stood up.
It's such a little thing to weep.
I've seen a dying eye.
Just lost, when I was saved!
Lad of Athens, faithful be.
Lady red upon the hill, A.
Lamp burns sure, within, The.
Last night that she lived, The.
Lest any doubt that we are glad that they were born today.
Light exists in spring, A.
Lightly stepped a yellow star.
Lightning is a yellow fork, The.
Like rain it sounded till it curved.
Little East of Jordan, A.
Little Madness in the spring, A.
Love can do all but raise the dead.
Love is that later thing than death.
Martyr poets, The—did not tell.
Mine—by the right of the white election!
Mine enemy is growing old.
Moon, The.
Moon upon her fluent route, The.
Morns are meeker than they were, The.
Mountain sat upon the plain, The.

Mountains grow unnoticed, The.
Much madness is divinest sense.
Murmur of a bee, The.
Musicians Wrestle Everywhere.
My cocoon tightens—Colors tease.
My country need not change her gown.
My friend must be a bird.
My life closed twice before its close.
My life had stood—a loaded gun.
My period had come for prayer.
My portion is defeat—today.
My triumph lasted till the drums.
Name—of it—is "Autumn," The.
Narrow fellow in the grass, A.
Nature—sometimes sears a sapling.
No rack can torture me.
Not Any Higher Stands the Grave.
Not with a club the heart is broken.
Now I knew I lost her.
Of all the souls that stand create.
Of course I prayed.
Of God we ask one favor.
Of nearness to her sundered things.
Oh sumptuous moment.
One blessing had I, than the rest.
One dignity delays for all.
Only ghost I ever saw, The.
Only news I know, The.
Our journey had advanced.
Our little kinsmen after rain.
Our lives are Swiss.
Our share of night to bear.
Ourselves we do inter with sweet derision.
Ourselves were wed one summer—dear.
Pain—has an element of blank.
Papa above!
Pass to thy rendezvous of light.
Past is such a curious creature, The.
Pedigree of honey, The.
Perception of an object costs.
Pink, small and punctual.
Poets Light But Lamps, The.
Precious to me—she still shall be.
Presentiment—is that long shadow—on the lawn.
Publication—is the auction.
Purple Clover.
Read, sweet, how others strove.
Rearrange a wife's affection?
Remorse is memory awake.
Reportless subjects, to the quick.
Resurgam.
Return, The.
Robin is the one, The.
Route of evanescence, A.
Safe in their alabaster chambers.
Satisfaction—is the agent.
Savior! I've no one else to tell.
Science, Also the savants say.
She dealt her pretty words like blades.
She lay as if at play.
She sweeps with many-colored brooms.
Show is not the show, The.
Sky is low, the clouds are mean, The.
So proud she told.
Softened by time's consummate plush.
Some keep the Sabbath going to church.
Some things that fly there be.
Sorrow.
Soul selects her own society, The.
Spider holds a silver ball, The.
Spider sewed at night, A.
Spring is the period.
Stars are old, that stood for me, The.
Stimulus beyond the Grave, The.
Success is counted sweetest.
Superfluous Were the Sun.
Surgeons must be very careful.
Tell all the truth but tell it slant.
That it will never come again.
That love is all there is.
That such have died enables us.

There are two Mays.
There came a day at summer's full.
There came a wind like a bugle.
There is a flower that bees prefer.
There is a languor of the life.
There is a morn by men unseen.
There is a pain—so utter.
There is no frigate like a book.
There is no silence in the earth—so silent.
There's a certain slant of light.
There's been a death in the opposite house.
These are the days when birds come back.
They dropped like flakes, they dropped like stars.
They shut me up in prose.
This consciousness that is aware.
This dirty little heart.
This is my letter to the world.
This quiet dust was gentlemen and ladies.
This was a poet—It is that.
This world is not conclusion.
Those—dying then.
Though the great waters sleep.
Thought beneath so slight a film, The.
Thought went up my mind today, A.
Through the strait pass of suffering.
Tie the strings to my life, my Lord.
Tint I cannot take is best, The.
'Tis not that dying hurts us so.
'Tis so appalling—it exhilarates.
'Tis so much joy! 'tis so much joy!
Title divine—is mine!
To fight aloud is very brave.
To flee from memory.
To hear an oriole sing.
To know just how He suffered would be dear.
To learn the transport by the pain.
To make a prairie it takes a clover and one bee.
To see her is a picture.
Too happy time dissolves itself.
Truth is as old as God.
'Twas just this time, last year, I died.
'Twas like a maelstrom, with a notch.
'Twas warm—at first—like us.
Undue significance a starving man attaches.
Until the desert knows.
Valentine, A.
Vanished.
Victory comes late.
Waters chased him as he fled, The.
Way I read a letter's—this, The.
We do not play on graves.
We dream—it is good we are dreaming.
We like March—his shoes are purple.
We miss a kinsman more.
We never know how high we are.
We never know we go.
We outgrow love, like other things.
We thirst at first—'tis nature's act.
Went up a year this evening.
What is—"Paradise."
What mystery pervades a well!
What soft, cherubic creatures.
When we stand on the tops of things.
While we were fearing it, it came.
Who is the East?
Wife—at daybreak I shall be, A.
Wild nights!—wild nights!
Will there really be a morning?
Wind begun to knead the grass, The.
Wind begun to rock the grass, The.
Wind that rose, A.
Wind Took Up the Northern Things, The.
Wind's Visit, The.
Witchcraft was hung, in history.
Within my garden, rides a bird.
Word is dead, A.
Word made flesh is seldom, A.
World feels dusty, The.
Wounded deer leaps highest, A.
Your Riches Taught Me Poverty.

Dickinson, Goldsworthy Lowes
I never asked for more than thou hast given.
Dickinson, Patric
Advent; a Carol.
St. Stephen's Day.
Dickinson, Peter
By-Election Idyll.
Di Costanzo, Angelo
Sonnet: The Death of Virgil.
Die [*or* Dia], Countess Beatrice de. *See*
Beatrice de Die
Diego Padró, José I. de
Epistolary Briefs to Proclus.
Friend Proclus, the world isn't a fantasy, *sel.*
Diekmann, Conrad
Winter Trees.
Dienstag, Alan
Three Women.
Diespecker, Dick
All these are your essence, you are their flesh
and their force, *sel.*
Dietmar von Aist
Bird Was Singing, A.
Parting at Morning.
Di Filippo, Rustico
Sonnet: Of the Making of Master Messerin.
Digance, Richard
Ants at the Olympics, The.
Duck, The.
Digby, John
Grieve Not, Dear Love.
One Night Away from Day.
Sooner or Later.
Digby, Sir Kenelm
On His Late Espoused Saint.
Dillard, Richard H. W.
Meditation for a Pickle Suite.
Mullins Farm, The.
Diller, John Irving
Lullaby Town.
Dillon, George
Hard Lovers, The.
Kind Inn, A.
Remember, Though the Telescope Extend.
Di Michele, Mary
Moon and the Salt Flats, The.
Dimmette, Celia
Apology of the Young Scientists.
Dimoff, John
West of Chicago.
Dimond, William
Mariner's Dream, The.
Di Montecanti, Guerzo
Sonnet: He Is Out of Heart with His Time.
Di Montorio, Antonio
El Ropero.
"Dinesen, Isak" (Karen Blixen)
Zebra.
Dinnies, Anna Peyre
Wife, The.
Diop, Birago
Breaths.
Diop, David
Africa.
He Who Has Lost All.
Suffer, Poor Negro!
Those Who Lost Everything.
Vultures, The.
Your Presence.
Diotimus
Without the Herdsman.
DiPalma, Ray
Anecdote That Went with It, The.
Bed, The.
Ceremony/ the triumph, *sel.*
Exile.
Geo.
Hadrian's Lane.
New world/ artful as monkeys, A, *sel.*
One deep in the dark, *sel.*
Poem: "Face to face and in the face."

Ripe Tack.
Table, The.
Written granite, *sel.*
DiPasquale, Emanuel
Incantation to Get Rid of a Sometime Friend.
Letter from Sicily.
Rain.
Di Piero, W. S.
Fat Tuesday.
Four Brothers.
Lines to a Friend in Trouble.
Second Horn.
Dipoko, Mbella Sonne
Autobiography.
DiPrima, Diane
Day lay like a pearl on her lap, The, *sel.*
Goodbye Nkrumah.
In Memory of My First Chapatis.
Jungle, The.
Loba Recovers the Memory of a Mare, The,
sel.
Moon Mattress.
O lost moon sisters, *sel.*
Practice of Magical Evocation, The.
Quarrel, The.
Revolutionary Letter #19.
Ruses: A Coyote Tale, The, *sel.*
Di Roma, Immanuel
Happiness amidst Troubles.
Love.
My Sweet Gazelle!
Paradise.
What Profit?
Worthless Heart, The.
Disch, Tom
Cow of Our Time, A.
Donna Anna Writes to Her Sister.
Duelling Platitudes.
Economy, Convenience, Good Taste.
Homage to the Carracci.
In Memoriam.
Vowels of Another Language, The.
Disch, Thomas M.
Can You Hear Me, Thinktank Two?
Cosmology and Us.
In the Picture.
La, La, La!
On Science Fiction.
Outer Space Haiku.
Rapist's Villanelle, The.
Vacation on Earth, A.
Dismond, Binga
At Early Morn.
Status Quo.
Ditlevsen, Tove
He would/ in the case of a divorce, *sel.*
It is not easy, *sel.*
Morning.
Old Folk, The.
Self Portrait I.
Self Portrait II.
Self Portrait IV.
Divine, Charles
We Met on Roads of Laughter.
Dix, William Chatterton
As with Gladness Men of Old.
Dixon, Henry
Description of a Good Boy, The.
Dixon, Richard Watson
All who have loved, be sure of this from me,
sel.
By the Sea.
Dawning.
Dream.
Heaving Roses of the Hedge Are Stirred, The.
Judgment of the May, The.
Ode: The Spirit Wooed.
Song: "Feathers of the willow, The."
Song: "Why fadest thou in death."

Unrest.
Wizard's Funeral, The.
Dixon, Sarah
Lines Occasioned by the Burning of Some
Letters.
Dixon, Zuhur
Dialogue of the Night of the Roses.
Overture.
Season of Beginning and End.
Two Hands on the Water.
DiZazzo, Raymond
On the Speed of Sight.
Djabali, Leila
For My Torturer, Lieutenant D— —.
Djangatolum. *See* **Corbin, Lloyd M., Jr.**
Djanikian, Gregory
How I Learned English.
Djellaladin Pasha, Mahmud
Song: "If you love God, take your mirror
between your hands and look."
Djurberaui
All You Others, Eat.
Dmitrova, Blaga
To My Father.
Doane, George Washington
Bishop Doane on His Dog.
Evening Contemplation.
Fling Out the Banner!
Life Sculpture.
Once More, O Lord.
Robin Redbreast.
Thou Art the Way.
Doane, William Croswell
Ancient of Days.
Modern Baby, The.
Preacher's Mistake, The.
"Doane, Jerry." *See* **Morse, Katharine**
Duncan
Dobbs, Kildare
Exequy: To Peter Allt.
Dobell, Sydney Thompson
Ballad of Keith of Ravelston, The, *sel.*
Chanted Calendar, A, *sel.*
Desolate.
He Loves and He Rides Away.
"How's My Boy?"
Nuptial Eve, A.
Orphan's Song, The.
Perhaps.
Dobson, A. M.
Bidean Nam Bian.
Dobson, Austin (Henry Austin Dobson)
All passes. Art alone, *sel.*
Ballad of Heroes, A.
Ballad to Queen Elizabeth, A.
Child-Musician, The.
City Flower, A.
Clean Hands.
Dora versus Rose.
Fame and Friendship.
Garden Song, A.
In After Days.
Incognita.
Ladies of St. James's, The.
Rose-Leaves.
Urceus Exit, *sel.*
"When There Is Peace."
Dobson, John
Robin; a Pastoral Elegy.
Dobson, Rosemary
Across the Straits.
Being Called For.
Birth, The.
Bystander, The.
Child with a Cockatoo.
Country Press.
Detail from an Annunciation by Crivelli.
Fever, The.
In a Café.

Methuselah, *sel.*
Raising of the Dead, The.
Three Fates, The.
Dobyns, Stephen
Black Dog, Red Dog.
Bleeder.
Cemetery Nights.
Counterparts.
Delicate, Plummeting Bodies, The.
Dream.
Face in the Ceiling, The.
Farmyard at Chassy.
Getting Up.
Girl in White.
Gun, The.
How to Like It.
Japanese Girl with Red Table.
Seeing Off a Friend.
Spider Web.
Triangular Field, The.
Under the Green Ceiling.
White Skirt, The.
Window, The.
Dobzynski, Charles
Fable Merchant, The.
Memory Air.
Never Again, The.
Zealot without a Face.
"Doc Long." *See* Long, Doughtry, Jr.
Dock, Christopher
O Children, Would You Cherish?
Dodat, François
Crab.
Glowworm.
Ladybug.
Dodd, Leonard
Compel Them to Come In.
Dodd, Wayne
Of Sitting Bear, *sel.*
Sometimes Music Rises.
Doddridge, Philip
Awake, My Soul!
Christ's Resurrection and Ascension.
Meditations on the Sepulchre in the Garden.
O God of Bethel.
Dodge, Mary Barker
Now.
Dodge, Mary Mapes
Emerson.
Letters at School, The.
Mayor of Scuttleton, The.
Minuet, The.
Once before, this self-same air.
Poor Crow!
Shadow Evidence.
Snowflakes.
Stars, The.
Stocking Song on Christmas Eve.
Ten Kinds.
That's What We'd Do.
Two Mysteries, The.
Zealless Xylographer, The.
Dodge, Samuel
People Will Talk.
Dodgson, Charles Lutwidge. *See* "Carroll, Lewis"
Dodsley, Robert
An Epistle to My Friend J. B.
Method of Preserving Hay from Being
  Mow-Burnt, or Taking Fire, A, *sel.*
Song: "Man's a poor deluded bubble."
Dodson, Owen
Ballad of Badmen.
Confession Stone, The.
Counterpoint.
Decision, The.
Drunken Lover.
Epitaph for a Negro Woman.
For Edwin R. Embree.
Hymn Written after Jeremiah Preached to Me
  in a Dream.

I Break the Sky.
Job's Ancient Lament.
Mary Passed This Morning.
Morning Duke Ellington Praised the Lord and
  Six Little Black Davids Tapped Danced
  Unto, The.
Rag Doll and Summer Birds.
Sailors on Leave.
Sickle Pears.
Six o'Clock.
Sleep late with your dream, *sel.*
Sorrow Is the Only Faithful One.
Yardbird's Skull.
Dogen
Firm on the seven Buddhas' cushion.
Four and fifty years.
Waka.
Waka on Impermanence.
Waka on Kyosei's Raindrop Sound.
Waka on the Correct-Law Eye Treasury.
Waka on Zen Sitting.
Döhl, Reinhold
Pattern Poem with an Elusive Intruder.
Doji
In Early Spring, While at the Temple at
  Bamboo Ravine Mountain.
Dolben, Digby Mackworth
Enough.
He Would Have His Lady Sing.
Homo Factus Est.
Requests.
Sea Song, A.
Song, A: "World is young today, The."
Strange, All-absorbing Love.
We hurry on, nor passing note.
Dole, Nathan Haskell
Russia.
Russian Fantasy, A.
To an Imperilled Traveller.
Dollard, James B.
Fairy Harpers, The.
Döltz, Emma
Give Us the Right to Vote!
Piece Worker, The.
Domanski, Don
Deadsong.
Three Songs from the Temple.
Domett, Alfred
Christmas Hymn, A.
It was a wondrous realm beguiled, *sel.*
Domin, Hilde
Birthdays.
Catalogue.
Cologne.
Dreamwater.
Dominick, Peter
Origami for Two.
Domino, Ruth
Sparrow in the Dust, A.
Donaghy, John Lyle
Deathward.
Duck.
Ebb.
Fossil, The.
Glenarm.
Grave, The.
Heron, The.
Portrait.
Seeing.
Where the dropwort springs up lithe and tall.
Winter.
Donahue, Jack
Brave Donahue
Donald, C. M.
Eye for an Eye, An.
I Expect You Think This Huge Dark Coat.
Donald, Christine
Good Old Body.
Poor Old Fat Woman.
Thin women woo each other, The.

Donaldson, Islay Murray
Skye Summer ("Skye rasps the mind").
Donatus, St.
Land Called Scotia, The.
Donne, John
Air[e] and Angels.
Anatomy of the World; the First Anniversary,
  An.
Anniversary [*or* Anniversarie], The.
Annunciation, *sel.*
Antiquary.
Apparition, The.
As due by many titles I resign[e], *sel.*
Ascension [*or* Ascention], *sel.*
At the round earths imagined corners, blow,
  sel.
Autumnal[l], The, *sel.*
Bait[e], The.
Batter my heart, three person'd God; for you,
  sel.
Blossom [*or* Blossome], The.
Break[e] of Day.
Broken Heart, The.
Burnt Ship, A.
Calme, The.
Canonization, The.
Change, *sel.*
Comparison, The.
Computation, The.
Contemplation of Our State in Our Deathbed,
  sel.
Crucifying.
Curse, The.
Dampe, The.
Dark Churches, *sel.*
Death be not proud, though some have called
  thee, *sel.*
Dissolution, The.
Doth Not a Tenarif, or Higher Hill, *sel.*
Dream[e], The.
Ecstasy, The.
Elegy on Mistress Boulstred.
Epithalamion Made at Lincolnes Inne.
Expiration, The.
Farewell to Love.
Father, The, *sel.*
Father, part of his double interest, *sel.*
Fever, A.
First Anniversary, The, *sel.*
Flea, The.
Funeral[l], The.
God grant thee thine own wish, and grant thee
  mine.
Going to Bed, *sel.*
Good Friday [*or* Goodfriday], 1613. Riding
  Westward.
Good-Morrow, The.
Hail, Bishop Valentine, whose day this is,
  sel.
His Parting from Her, *sel.*
His Picture, *sel.*
Holy Ghost, The, *sel.*
Hymn to God the Father [*or* For Forgiveness
  or To Christ], A.
Hymn[e] to Christ, at the Author's Last Going
  into Germany, A.
Hymn[e] to God My God, In my Sickness[e].
I am a little world made cunningly, *sel.*
If faithful soules be alike glorifi'd, *sel.*
If poisonous [*or* poysonous] mineral[l]s, and
  if that tree, *sel.*
Indifferent, The.
It quicknd next a toyful Ape, and so, *sel.*
Jealousy, *sel.*
Jet Ring Sent, A.
Kind pity [*or* kinde pitty] chokes my
  spleen[e]; brave scorn forbids, *sel.*
La Corona.
Lame Beggar, A.
Lecture upon the Shadow, A.
Legacy [*or* Legacie], The.
Lovers' Infiniteness [e]

Love's Alchemy [or Alchemie]
Love's Deity [or Deitie]
Love's Growth.
Love's Progress, sel.
Message, The.
Nativity [or Nativitie], sel.
Nature's lay idiot, I taught thee to love, sel.
Nocturnal[l] upon Saint Lucy's [or S. Lucies] Day, Being the Shortest Day, A.
O might those sighes and teares returne againe, sel.
Of the Progres of the Soule; the Second Anniversary.
Oh my black[e] soule! now thou art summoned, sel.
Oh, to vex me, contraries [or contraryes] meet in one, sel.
On His Mistress [or Mistris], sel.
Our Companie in the Next World, sel.
Perfume, The, sel.
Phryne.
Poor soul, in this thy flesh what dost thou know?
Primrose, Being at Montgomery Castle, upon the Hill, on Which It Is Situate, The.
Prohibition, The.
Relic, The.
Resurrection.
Seek True Religion!
Seek true religion, O where? Mirreus, sel.
Self Accuser, A.
She, she is dead; she's dead: when thou knowest this, sel.
Show me dear[e] Christ, thy spouse, so bright and clear, sel.
Since she whom I lov'd hath paid [or payd] her last debt, sel.
Sir: though (I thank God for it) I do hate, sel.
Son, The, sel.
Song: "Go and catch a falling star."
Song: "Sweetest love, I do not go[e]"
Spit in my face you Jew[e]s, and pierce my side, sel.
Storm at Sea, A, sel.
Sun [or Sunne] Rising, The.
Temple.
This is my play's [or playes] last scene, here heavens appoint, sel.
Thou hast made me, and shall thy work[e] decay?
Thou shalt not laugh in this leaf, Muse, nor they, sel.
To Mr. George Herbert.
To Mr. I. L.
To Mr. Rowland Woodward.
To Mr. Tilman after He Had Taken Orders.
To Sir Edward Herbert at Julyers.
To Sir H. W. at His Going Ambassador to Venice.
To the Countesse of Bedford ("Honour is so sublime perfection").
To the Countesse of Bedford, on New-Yeares Day.
Triple Fool, The.
Twicknam Garden.
Undertaking, The.
Valediction: Forbidding Mourning, A.
Valediction: Of My Name in the Window, A.
Valediction: Of Weeping, A.
Verse and Fame, sel.
Well, I may now receive, and die: my sin, sel.
Whale, The, sel.
What if this present were the world's last night?, sel.
When that rich Soule which to her heaven is gone, sel.
Why are we[e] by all creatures waited on?
Will, The.
Wilt thou love God, as he thee! then digest, sel.

Witchcraft by a Picture.
Woman's Constancy.
Donnell, David
Canadian Prairies View of Literature, The.
Lakes.
Potatoes.
Sandwiches.
Stepfathers.
Donnelly, Charles
Flowering Bars, The.
Last Poem.
Tolerance of Crows, The.
Donnelly, Dorothy
Blue Flag.
Girandole.
Donnelly, Susan
That Time, That Country.
Donnelly, Tom
Myself When Young.
Dooley, Ebon
Easter Bunny Blues or All I Want for Xmas Is the Loop, The.
Prophet's Warning or Shoot to Kill, The.
Query.
Doolittle, Hilda ("H. D.")
Acon.
Adonis.
Ah (you say), this is Holy Wisdom, sel.
Alas, my brothers, sel.
Another shout from the wharves, sel.
Are these ashes in my hand, sel.
Are we unfathomable night, sel.
At Baia.
At Ithaca.
Birds in Snow.
Blue-geese, white-geese, you may say, sel.
But it won't be that way, sel.
Centaur Song.
Circe.
Epigram: "Golden one is gone from the banquets, The."
Erige Cor Tuum ad Me in Caelum.
Eurydice.
Evadne.
Evening.
Every hour, every moment, sel.
Flute Song.
Fragment 113: "Not honey/ not the plunder of the bee."
Fragment Sixty-eight: "I envy you your chance of death."
Fragment Thirty-six: "I know not what to do."
Garden.
Gather for festival, sel.
Heat, sel.
Helen.
Helmsman, The.
Hermes of the Ways.
Holy Satyr.
I could say, sel.
"I love you," sel.
I made god upon god, sel.
If you take the moon in your hands, sel.
I'm not here, sel.
In Time of Gold.
Incident here and there, An, sel.
Invisible, indivisible Spirit, sel.
Islands, The.
It is no madness to say, sel.
Lais.
Leda.
Let me be, sel.
Lethe.
Moon in Your Hands, The.
Moonrise.
Mysteries Remain, The.
Never more will the wind, sel.
Not in our time, O Lord, sel.
Now it appears very clear, sel.
Now let the cycle sweep us here and there, sel.
O heart, small urn, sel.

Orchard.
Oread.
Pear Tree.
Pool, The.
Pursuit.
Sea Gods.
Sea Rose.
Sea Violet.
Sigil.
Sirius/ what mystery is this?
So if you love me, sel.
So we were together, sel.
Socratic.
Song: "You are as gold."
Stars wheel in purple, yours is not so rare, sel.
There is no signpost to say, sel.
This is no rune nor riddle, sel.
Time breaks the barrier, sel.
Time has an end, they say, sel.
We have had too much consecration, sel.
We have seen her/ the world over, sel.
We have seen how the most amiable, sel.
Where is the nightingale, sel.
White World.
Wind Sleepers, The.
Wine Bowl.
You look at me, a hut or cage contains, sel.
You'll go on, talking away, sel.
Doom, Alixa
Snorkeling in the Caribbean.
Dor, Moshe [or Mosheh]
Among the Pine Trees.
At a Loss.
Dwelling, The.
Nightingales Are Not Singing.
Safety Pin.
Small Bones Ache.
There's a Certain Difference in the Air.
Dorcey, Mary
Daughter.
First Love.
Return.
Sea Flower.
Trying On for Size.
Doreski, William
Thanksgiving, Growing Older.
Dorgan, John Aylmer
Beautiful, The.
Dead Solomon, The.
Doria, Prinzivalle
Canzone: Of His Love, with the Figure of a Sudden Storm.
Dorman, Sonya
Corruption of Metals.
Elegy for Bella, Sarah, Rosie, and All the Others.
Lullaby, a Farewell, A.
N.Y. to L.A. by Jet Plane.
On the Marriage of Art and Science.
Vanishing Points.
Wormrunner's Curse.
Dorn, Alfred
Accidents.
Ballade of Bones.
Challengers.
Dorn, Edward
Air of June Sings, The.
Are They Dancing.
Biggest Killing, The.
Comforted by Limestone, sel.
For the New Union Dead in Alabama.
From Gloucester Out.
Hide of My Mother, The.
Idle Visitation, An, sel.
La Máquina a Houston.
Los Mineros.
Morning to Remember, A; or, E Pluribus Unum.
Rick of Green Wood, The.
Song, The: "So light no one noticed."
Thesis.

Vaquero.
When the Fairies.
Dorney, Elizabeth
Chemistry of Character, The.
Dornin, Christopher L.
In a Building Named for a Governor.
Dorr, Henry R.
Comrades.
Dorr, Julia Caroline Ripley
Fallow Field, The.
Legend of the Organ-Builder, The.
No More the Thunder of Cannon.
Not Mine.
O Earth! Art Thou Not Weary?
Two Paths.
With a Rose from Conway Castle.
Dorrance, Dick
Cockpit in the Clouds.
Dorset, Catherine Ann
Peacock "At Home," The.
Dorset, Charles Sackville, 6th Earl of. *See*
Sackville, Charles, 6th Earl of Dorset
Dorset, Thomas Sackville, 1st Earl of. *See*
Sackville, Thomas, 1st Earl of Dorset
Dos Passos, John
Crimson Tent.
Doten, Elizabeth
In a Hundred Years, at.
Doten, Elizabeth (Lizzie)
God of the Granite and the Rose!
Doty, Mark
Gardenias.
Late Conversation.
Latin Dances.
Double-face
If there is someone above.
Doudney, Sarah
Christian's "Good-Night," The.
Sweet Surprises.
Water Mill, The.
Doughtry Long
Poem No. 21.
Doughty, C. M.
Bladyn's Song of Cloten, *sel.*
Gauls Sacrifice, The, *sel.*
Hymn to the Sun, *sel.*
Roman Officer Writes, A, *sel.*
Doughty, Charles Montague
Fairies Feast, The.
Douglas, Lord Alfred Bruce
Dead Poet, The.
Green River, The.
Hen, The.
Impression de Nuit; London.
Prayer, A: "Often the western wind has sung
to me."
Shark, The.
To Olive.
To———, with an Ivory Hand-Glass.
Two Loves.
Douglas, Gawin [or Gavin]
As bryght Phebus, scheyn soverane
hevynnys e, *sel.*
Calliope's Nymph Brings the Poet to the
Palace to Honour, *sel.*
Difficulties of Translation, The, *sel.*
Hart's Castle, *sel.*
Nightmare, *sel.*
Towart the evyn, amyd the symmyris heit,
sel.
Winter.
Douglas, Keith
Aristocrats.
Behaviour of Fish in an Egyptian Tea Garden.
Cairo Jag.
Deceased, The.
Desert Flowers.
Gallantry.
How to Kill.
Knife, The.
Landscape with Figures.
Marvel, The.

Napoleon is charging our squares, *sel.*
On a Return from Egypt.
Oxford.
Russians.
Simplify Me When I'm Dead.
Snakeskin and Stone.
Soissons.
Song: "Do I venture away too far."
.303.
Vergissmeinnicht.
**"Douglas, Marian" (Annie Douglas Green
Robinson)**
Ant-Hills.
One Saturday.
Snow-Man, The.
Douglas, William
Annie Laurie.
Douglass, Frederick
Just God! and these are they, *sel.*
Parody, A.
Douglass, Suzanne
No Holes Marred.
Douskey, Franz
Babe & Lou.
Dove, Rita
Adolescence—I.
Adolescence—II.
Adolescence—III.
After Reading *Mickey in the Night Kitchen* for
the Third Time before Bed.
Banneker.
Beauty and the Beast.
Canary.
Cane Fields, The, *sel.*
Champagne.
Dusting.
Event, The.
Fish in the Stone, The.
Geometry.
Grape Sherbet.
Great Palaces of Versailles, The.
Hill of Beans, A.
House Slave, The.
Nigger Song: An Odyssey.
Ö.
Oriental Ballerina, The.
Palace, The, *sel.*
Parsley.
Planning the Perfect Evening.
Pomade.
Receiving the Stigmata.
Secret Garden, The.
Taking In Wash.
"Teach Us to Number Our Days."
This Life.
Weathering Out.
Wingfoot Lake.
Dow, Philip
Air.
Bottom's Dream.
Doe.
Dried Fruit.
Drunk Last Night with Friends, I Go to Work
Anyway.
Duck Pond at Mini's Pasture, a Dozen Years
Later, The.
Elegy: "And if our lives spill."
Ghazal.
Goodbye "Hello."
It Comes during Sleep.
Letter.
Life, The.
Mother.
My son & I, between *Fu-Sang* and/ Cathay,
sel.
Skunk, The.
Snow Geese in the Wind.
Song: "What binds the atom together."
Suite for Celery and Blind Date.
Twilight in California.
Dowden, Edward
Burdens.

Communion.
I found Thee in my heart, O Lord, *sel.*
In the Cathedral Close.
Seeking God.
Dowden, Elizabeth Dickinson
Adrift.
Dowe, Fyna
Bubble Burs, De.
Visual Conspiracy.
Word, The.
Dower, E.
New River Head, a Fragment, The.
Dowland, John
Come Away, Come, Sweet Love.
Flow Not So Fast.
Dowling, Allan
I Sought with Eager Hand.
Joy of Love, The.
Miracle, The.
Dowling, Bartholomew
Revel, The.
Dowling, Basil
Autumn Scene.
Halfwit.
Mushrooms.
Scything.
Through a Glass, Darkly.
Trapped Hare, The.
Unreturning Native, The.
Downie, Freda
Elsdon.
Great-Grandfather.
Her Garden.
Miss Grant.
Starlight.
Dowson, Ernest Christopher
Autumnal.
Breton Afternoon.
Carthusians.
De Amore.
Dead Child, The.
Dregs.
Epigram: "Because I am idolatrous and have
besought."
Exchanges.
Exile.
Extreme Unction.
Flos Lunae.
Garden of Shadow, The.
Gray Nights.
Impenitentia Ultima.
Last Word, A.
Lord over life and all the ways of breath, *sel.*
Non Sum Qualis Eram Bonae sub Regno
Cynarae [or Cynara]
O Mors! Quam Amara Est Memoria Tua
Homini Pacem Habenti in Substantiis Suis.
Spleen.
Terre Promise.
To One in Bedlam.
Valediction, A: "If we must part."
Vesperal.
Villanelle of Marguerites.
Villanelle of Sunset.
Villanelle of the Poet's Road.
Vitae Summa Brevis Spem Nos Vetat
Incohare Longam.
Doyle, Sir Francis Hastings
Private of the Buffs; or, The British Soldier in
China.
Doyle, Kirby
Strange.
Doyle, Lynn
Ulsterman, An.
Doyu
Fifty-six years, above Buddhas, Patriarchs.
Drachler, Rose
As I Am My Father's.
Dark Scent of Prayer, The.

Isaac and Esau.
Letters of the Book, The.
Under the Shawl.
Zippora Returns to Moses at Rephidim.

Drake, Barbara
Photograph, The.

Drake, Francis
To the Memory of the Learned and Reverend,
   Mr. Jonathan Mitchell.

Drake, Joseph Rodman
American Flag, The.
An Elfin Knight.
Assembling of the Fays, The, *sel.*
Bronx.
Culprit Fay, The.
Elfin Song, *sel.*
Fairy Dawn, *sel.*
Fairy in Armor, A, *sel.*
Fay's Crime, The, *sel.*
Fay's Departure, The, *sel.*
Fay's Sentence, The, *sel.*
If the spray-bead gem be won, *sel.*
Rifleman's Song at Bennington.
Second Quest, The, *sel.*
Throne of the Lily-King, The, *sel.*
To the Defenders of New Orleans.

Drake, Joseph Rodman and **Fitz-Greene**
  Halleck. *See* Halleck, Fitz-Greene and
  Joseph Rodman Drake

Drake, Leah Bodine
Precarious Ground.

Dransfield, Michael
Bum's Rush.
Epiderm.
In the forest, in unexplored, *sel.*
Loft.
Pas de Deux for Lovers.
Portrait of the Artist as an Old Man.
Rainpoem.
Sky ceases. There is only, *sel.*
That Which We Call a Rose.

Draper, George
Rink Keeper's Sestina.

Drayson, Phyllis
Blackbird, The.
Hide and Seek.

Drayton, Michael
Agincourt.
And as our God the beasts had given in
  charge, *sel.*
And every bird shew'd in his proper kind, *sel.*
And, now that every thing may in the proper
  place, *sel.*
As love and I, late harbour'd in one inn.
As other men, so I myself do muse, *sel.*
Away yee barb'rous woods; how ever yee be
  plac't, *sel.*
Baron's war, The, *sel.*
Black pitchy night, companion of my woe,
  sel.
Calling to my mind [*or* minde] since first my
  love begun, *sel.*
Cassamen and Dowsabell, *sel.*
Charnwood Forest, *sel.*
Christopher Marlowe, *sel.*
Clear [*or* Cleere] had the day been [*or* bin]
  from the dawn [*or* dawne], *sel.*
Crier, The.
Deare [*or* Dear], why should you command
  [*or* commaund] me to my rest, *sel.*
Description of Elizium, The, *sel.*
Duck, and Mallard first, the falconers only
  sport, The, *sel.*
Dwindling Forest of Arden, The, *sel.*
Earl of Surrey to Geraldine, The.
Earle Douglasse for this day doth with the
  Percies stand, The, *sel.*
Eclogue: "Late 'twas in June, the fleece when
  fully grown," *sel.*
Endymion's Convoy, *sel.*

Eternall and all-working God, which wast,
  sel.
Evil [*or* Evill] spirit, your beauty, haunts me
  still, An, *sel.*
Fame and Fortune, *sel.*
Fen-Men of Lincolnshire's Holland, The, *sel.*
Fools Gaze at Painted Courts, *sel.*
Forest so much fallen from what she was
  before, The, *sel.*
Glorious sun went blushing to his bed, The,
  sel.
Hawking, *sel.*
His Remedie for Love, *sel.*
How many paltry, foolish, painted things, *sel.*
I hear some say, this man is not in love, *sel.*
If chaste and pure devotion of my youth, *sel.*
If he, from heaven that filched the living fire,
  sel.
Into these loves, who but for passion looks,
  sel.
It was not long e're he perceiv'd the skies,
  sel.
King Henry to Rosamond, *sel.*
Like an Adventurous Seafarer Am I, *sel.*
Lincolnshire's Holland Speaks of Her
  Waterfowl, *sel.*
Methinks I See Some Crooked Mimic Jeer,
  sel.
My fair, look from those turrets of thine eyes,
  sel.
My heart, imprisoned in a hopeless isle, *sel.*
My various fleets for fowl, O who is he can
  tell, *sel.*
Nothing but no and I, and I and no, *sel.*
Ode: To the Virginian Voyage.
Ode Written in the Peak[e], An.
Of all the beasts which we for our veneriall
  name, *sel.*
Phoebe on Latmus, *sel.*
Pigwiggen.
Pigwiggin Arms Himself, *sel.*
Queen's Chariot, The, *sel.*
Read here (sweet maid) the story of my woe,
  sel.
Roundelay, A: "Tell me, thou skilful
  shepherd's swain," *sel.*
Rowland's Rhyme, *sel.*
Sacrifice to Apollo, The.
Second Nimphall, The, *sel.*
Severn, The, *sel.*
Shepheard's Daffodil, The, *sel.*
Since there's [*or* ther's] no help[e], come let
  us kiss[e] and part, *sel.*
Skeltoniad, A.
So well I love thee, as without thee I.
Song to Beta: "O thou fair silver Thames,"
  sel.
Stay, speedy time; behold, before thou pass,
  sel.
Stay, Thames, to heare my Song, thou great
  and famous Flood, *sel.*
Stonehenge, *sel.*
Tenth Eclogue, The, *sel.*
Tenth Nimphall, The, *sel.*
There's nothing grieves me, but that age
  should haste, *sel.*
This Edward in the Aprill of his age, *sel.*
This Palace Standeth in the Air, *sel.*
To Cupid.
To Himselfe and the Harpe.
To His Valentine.
To My Most Dearly-loved Friend, Henry
  Reynolds, Esquire, of Poets and Poesy.
To nothing fitter can I thee compare, *sel.*
To the New Yeere.
To these, the gentle South, with kisses smooth
  and soft, *sel.*
Trent, The, *sel.*
Trent Again, The, *sel.*
Truce, gentle love, a parley now I crave, *sel.*
When first I ended, then I first began, *sel.*

When Phoebus lifts his head out of the
  winter's wave, *sel.*
Whilst thus my pen strives to eternize thee,
  sel.
Why should your fair eyes with such
  sovereign grace, *sel.*
Witlesse gallant, a young wench that woo'd,
  A, *sel.*
World of mightie kings and princes I could
  name, A, *sel.*
Wrestlers, *sel.*
You [*or* You're] not alone when you are still
  alone, *sel.*

Drennan, John Swanwick [*or* Swanick]
Epigram: "Golden casket I designed, A."
Epigram: "Love signed the contract blithe and
  leal."
L'Amitié et l'Amour.
On the Telescopic Moon.

Drennan, William
Wake of William Orr, The.

Dresbach, Glenn Ward
Cave, The.
Last Corn Shock, The.

Drewry, Carleton
Evensong.

"Drinan, Adam." *See* Maclead, Joseph
  Gordon

Drinkwater, John
Bird's Nest, The.
Birthright.
Bobby Blue.
Deer.
I Want to Know.
Invocation: "As pools beneath stone arches
  take."
Moonlit Apples.
Morning Thanksgiving.
Petition.
Prayer, A: "Lord, not for light in darkness do
  we pray."
Reciprocity.
Snail.
Sun, The.
Sunrise on Rydal Water.
Town Window, A.
Washing.
Who Were before Me.

Driscoll, Jack
Arm Wrestling with My Father.
Boxing towards My Birth.
Touch Football.
Woman Has a Baby in Her Sleep.

Driscoll, Louise
Epitaph: "Here lies the flesh that tried."
God's Pity.
Grace for Gardens.
Hold Fast Your Dreams.
Marigolds.
My garden is a pleasant place.

Driver, C. J.
Birthdays.
In Solitary Confinement, Sea Point Police
  Cells.
To Jann, in Her Absence.

Dromey, John H.
Perspective.

Dromgoole, Will Allen
Building the Bridge.
Old Ladies.

Dropkin, Celia
Adam.
Circus Dancer, The.
Like Snow on the Alps.
Poem: "You sowed in me, not a child."

Droste-Hülshoff, Annette von
Ailing Eagle, The.
In the Grass.
Last Day of the Year (New Year's Eve), The.
On the Tower.

Drown, Lessie M.
To-Day.
To Mother.

Drummond, William, of Hawthornden (1585–1649)
Angels, The, *sel.*
Book, The.
Change Should Breed Change.
Doth then the world go thus, doth all thus move?
For the Magdalene.
Hymne of the Ascension, An.
Iöas' Epitaph.
Ivory, Coral, Gold, The.
Kiss, A.
Kisses Desired.
Madrigal: "Beauty [*or* Beautie], and the life, The."
Madrigal: "Like the Idalian Queen [e]"
Madrigal: "Poor turtle, thou bemoans."
Madrigal: "This world a hunting is."
Madrigal: "Unhappie Light."
Of Phyllis.
On Mary Magdalene.
On the Margin Wrought.
Phoebus, Arise.
Regrat.
Saint John Baptist.
Sanquhar, whom this earth could scarce contain.
Sleep, Silence' Child.
Song: "It Autumnne was, and on our hemispheare."
Sonnet: "Alexis, here she stayed; among these pines."
Sonnet: "As in a duskie and tempestuous night."
Sonnet: Content and Resolute.
Sonnet: Death's Last Will.
Sonnet: "How that vast heaven intitled First is rolled."
Sonnet: "I know that all beneath the moon decays."
Sonnet: "In minds pure glasse when I my selfe behold."
Sonnet: "Lamp of heaven's crystal hall that brings the hours."
Sonnet: "My lute, be as thou wast [*or* wert] when thou didst grow."
Sonnet: "Sweet soul, which in the April of thy years."
Sonnet: "That learned Graecian (who did so excell)."
Sonnet: "What doth it serve to see sun's burning face."
Spring Bereaved.
Spring Bereaved 2.
Statue of Medusa, The.
Stolen Pleasure.
Tell Me No More.
Thrice Happy He.
Thy Sun Posts Westward.
To a Nightingale.
To Chloris.
To Sir William Alexander.
Too Long I Followed, *sel.*
Trojan Horse, The.
World a hunting is, The.

Drummond, William Henry (1854–1907)
Johnnie Courteau.
Leetle Bateese.
Log Jam, The.
Madeleine Verchères.
Wreck of the *Julie Plante* [*or* The *Julie Plante*], The.

Drummond de Andrade, Carlos
Don't Kill Yourself.
Looking for Poetry.
Table, The.

Dryden, John
Achitophel: The Earl of Shaftsbury, *sel.*

After the Pangs of a Desperate Lover, *sel.*
Ah, Fading Joy
Ah, How Sweet It Is to Love!
Alexander's Feast; or, The Power of Music [*or* Musique]
All, All of a Piece Throughout, *sel.*
All human[e] things are subject to decay, *sel.*
And welcom now (Great Monarch) to your own, *sel.*
Ave atque Vale, *sel.*
But gratious [*or* gracious] God, how well dost thou provide, *sel.*
But if there be a power too just and strong, *sel.*
By viewing Nature, Natures hand-maid, Art, *sel.*
Can Life Be a Blessing, *sel.*
Catholic Church, The, *sel.*
Character of a Good Parson, The.
Charm, A.
Church of England, The, *sel.*
Cleopatra and Antony, *sel.*
Conversion, *sel.*
Cymon and Iphigenia.
Dame, said the Panther, times are mended well, *sel.*
Damon and Celimena, *sel.*
Death the Consequence of the Fall, *sel.*
Diana's Hunting-Song, *sel.*
Dim, as the borrow'd beams of moon and stars, *sel.*
Epilogue Spoken by Mrs. Boutell.
Epilogue: "They who have best succeeded on the stage," *sel.*
Epilogue to "Tyrannick Love."
Epitaph on His Wife.
Farewell, Ungrateful Traitor, *sel.*
Fife and Drum, *sel.*
Fire of London, The, *sel.*
Fourth Day's Battle, The, *sel.*
Great Fire, The, *sel.*
Harvest Home, *sel.*
Heroique Stanzas, Consecrated to the Glorious Memory of His Most Serene and Renowned Highnesse, Oliver, Late Lord Protector of This Common-Wealth.
Human Happiness, *sel.*
In pious times ere [*or* e'r] priestcraft did begin, *sel.*
In the first rank of these did Zimri stand, *sel.*
Incantation to Oedipus, *sel.*
King James II, *sel.*
Lines Printed under the Engraved Portrait of Milton [in Tonson's Folio of the "Paradise Lost"]
Love, *sel.*
MacFlecknoe.
Malcontents, The, *sel.*
Mark how the lark and linnet sing, *sel.*
Midnight.
Militia, The, *sel.*
Milk white Hind, immortal and unchang'd, A, *sel.*
Momus' Song to Mars, *sel.*
New London, The, *sel.*
No, No, Poor Suffering Heart, *sel.*
No porter guards the passage of your door, *sel.*
Now van to van the foremost squadrons meet, *sel.*
Now with a general peace the world was blest, *sel.*
Oak, *sel.*
Of these the false Achitophel was first, *sel.*
On Jacob Tonson, His Publisher.
One evening, while the cooler shade she sought, *sel.*
Parts of the Whole Are We; but God the Whole, *sel.*
Popish Plot, The, *sel.*

Portly prince, and goodly to the sight, A, *sel.*
Power of Love, The, *sel.*
Predestination and Free Will, *sel.*
Presbyterians, The, *sel.*
Priestcraft and Private Judgement, *sel.*
Private Judgement Condemned, *sel.*
Prologue: "As needy gallants in the scriv'ners' hands," *sel.*
Prologue: "He who writ this, not without pains and thought," *sel.*
Prologue: "Our author by experience finds it true," *sel.*
Prologue: "See my lov'd Britons, see your Shakespeare rise," *sel.*
Prologue to "Love Triumphant," *sel.*
Prologue to "Secret-Love; or, The Maiden-Queen."
Prologue to "The Tempest."
Prologue to the University of Oxford, 1673.
Religio Laici.
Scriptures, The, *sel.*
Sea Battle, The, *sel.*
Secular Masque, The.
Some by their friends, more by themselves thought wise, *sel.*
Some of their chiefs were princes of the land, *sel.*
Song, A: "Calm was the even, and clear [*or* cleer] was the sky," *sel.*
Song: "Fair Iris I love, and hourly I die," *sel.*
Song, A: "Fair, sweet and young, receive a prize."
Song for a Girl
Song for St. Cecilia's Day, 1687.
Song from the Italian, A, *sel.*
Song: "I feed a flame within, which so torments me," *sel.*
Song of the Zambra Dance, *sel.*
Song of Venus, *sel.*
Song: "Sylvia the fair, in the bloom of fifteen."
Song to a Fair Young Lady, Going Out of the Town in the Spring.
Song, A: "You charm'd me not with that fair face," *sel.*
Sound the trumpet, beat the drum, *sel.*
Swell'd with our late successes on the foe, *sel.*
Thus man by his own strength to Heaven would soar, *sel.*
Time seems not now beneath his years to stoop, *sel.*
To My Dear Friend Mr. Congreve [on His Comedy Called "The Double-Dealer"].
To My Friend, Dr. Charleton, on His Learned and Useful Works; and More Particularly This of Stone-Heng, by Him Restored to the True Founders.
To My Honour'd Kinsman, John Driden, of Chesterton.
To the Memory of Mr. Oldham.
To the Pious Memory of the Accomplished [*or* Accomplisht] Young Lady, Mrs. Anne Killigrew [Excellent in the Two Sister-Arts of Poesie and Painting].
To this the Panther, with a scornful smile, *sel.*
Tradition, *sel.*
'Twere well your judgments but in plays did range, *sel.*
Upon the Death of the Lord Hastings.
Upon the Death of the Viscount of Dundee.
Vox Populi, *sel.*
When I Consider Life, *sel.*
Whil'st Alexis Lay Prest [*or* Press'd], *sel.*
Why Should a Foolish Marriage Vow, *sel.*
With all these loads of injuries opprest, *sel.*
Yet London, empress of the northern clime, *sel.*
You've seen a pair of youthful lovers die, *sel.*
Zimri: The Duke of Buckingham ("A numerous host of dreaming saints succeed"), *sel.*

Dryden, John *and* **Nahum Tate**
Doeg, though without knowing how or why, *sel.*
Next These, a troop of busy [*or* buisy] spirits press, *sel.*
Og [and Doeg], *sel.*
Thomas Shadwell the Poet, *sel.*
To make quick way I'll leap o'er heavy blocks, *sel.*
Dryden, Myrtle May
Just Forget.
Dubé, Janet
Autobiography.
Happily Ever After, from the Story of the Same Name.
No One's Land.
Penelope.
Reflections.
So to Tell the Truth.
Du Bellay, Joachim
He that has seen a great oak dry and dead, *sel.*
Hereux Qui, comme Ulysse, A Fait un Beau Voyage, *sel.*
Hope ye, my verses, that posterity, *sel.*
Hymn to the Winds.
I saw the bird that can the sun endure, *sel.*
I Saw the Bird That Dares Behold the Sun.
It Was the Time.
It was the time, when rest, soft sliding downe, *sel.*
Rome.
Sonnet to Heavenly Beauty, A.
Thou stranger, which for Rome in Rome here seekest, *sel.*
Thou that at Rome astonished doth behold, *sel.*
To His Friend in Elysium.
Vow to Heavenly Venus, A.
Who list the Romane greatnes forth to figure, *sel.*
Dubie, Norman
At Midsummer.
Balalaika.
Circus Ringmaster's Apology to God, The.
Coleridge Crossing the Plain of Jars; 1833.
Comes Winter, the Sea Hunting.
Composer's Winter Dream, The.
Czar's Last Christmas Letter: A Barn in the Urals, The.
Dream.
Dressing Stations, The.
Duchess after the Burial, The, *sel.*
Einstein's Exile in an Old Dutch Winter.
Elegy for Wright & Hugo.
Elegy to the Sioux.
Elizabeth's War with the Christmas Bear.
Everlastings, The.
February; the Boy Breughel.
Fox Who Watched for the Midnight Sun, The.
Funeral, The.
Ganges, The.
Grandfather's Last Letter, A.
Hours, The.
Huts at Esquimaux, The.
In the Dead of the Night.
Killigrew Wood, The.
Lamentations.
Lord Myth.
New England, Springtime.
Norway.
Obscure, The.
Parish.
Pastoral: "It all happened so fast. Fenya was in the straight chair."
Sacrifice of a Virgin in the Mayan Ball Court.
Sketchbook Ashes of Jehoshaphat, The.
Swann had gone to the estate that afternoon to tell his, *sel.*
Swann has visited the Duc and Duchess de Guermantes, *sel.*
There Is a Dream Dreaming Us.

To Michael.
Visit, *sel.*
Du Boccage, Marie-Anne
Will you never view us without distrust, *sel.*
Dubois, Gaston
Caught.
Insanity.
DuBois, William Edward Burghardt
Litany of [*or* at] Atlanta, A.
Song of the Smoke, The.
Duché, Jacob
Chilled by the Blasts of Adverse Fate.
Great Lord of All, Whose Work of Love.
Duck, Stephen
On Mites; to a Lady.
Soon as the harvest hath laid bare the plains, *sel.*
Duckett, Alfred A.
Portrait Philippines.
Sonnet: "Where are we to go when this is done?"
Dudek, Louis
Air by Sammartini, An.
Avant Garde, *sel.*
Coming Suddenly to the Sea.
Commotion of these waves, however strong, cannot disturb, The, *sel.*
Dead, The.
Fishing Village, *sel.*
García Lorca.
I Have Seen the Robins Fall.
Marine Aquarium, The, *sel.*
Mountains, The.
Narrative.
News, *sel.*
Ocean, The, *sel.*
Pomegranate, The.
Sea retains such images, The, *sel.*
Store-House, A.
Street in April, A.
Dudley, Thomas
Verses Found in Thomas Dudley's Pocket after His Death.
Dudley, William E.
City, Lord, Where Thy Dear Life, The.
Duer, Caroline
International Episode, An.
Portrait, A.
Word to the Wise, A.
Duerden, Richard
Dance with Banderillas.
Moon Is to Blood.
Musica No. 3.
Dufault, Peter Kane
Black Jess.
First Night, A.
In an Old Orchard.
Letter for Allhallows, A.
Notes on a Girl.
Odysseus' Song to Calypso.
On Aesthetics, More or Less.
Owl.
Possibilities.
Thalamos.
Tour de Force.
Duffield, George, Jr.
Stand Up! Stand Up for Jesus.
Duffield, Samuel Willoughby
Two of a Trade.
Duffy, Carol Ann
Alphabet for Auden.
Comprehensive.
Dear Norman.
Dolphins, The.
Lizzie, Six.
Duffy, Maureen
Evesong.
Sonnet: "Afterwards there are dogends in."
Dufresnoy, Adelaïde-Gillette
Deliverance of Argos, The.

Dugan, Alan
Actual Vision of Morning's Extrusion.
Against a Sickness: To the Female Double Principle God.
American against Solitude.
Aside.
Coat of Arms.
Decimation before Phraata, The.
Elegy for a Puritan Conscience.
Elegy: "I know but will not tell."
Fabrication of Ancestors.
For an Obligate Parasite.
For Masturbation.
From Heraclitus.
From Rome, for More Public Fountains in New York City.
Funeral Oration for a Mouse.
Glad at the Cold (1955).
How We Heard the Name.
Internal Migration: On Being on Tour.
Last Statement for a Last Oracle.
Let Heroes Account to Love.
Love Song: I and Thou.
Memorial Service for the Invasion Beach Where the Vacation in the Flesh Is Over.
Memories of Verdun.
Mirror Perilous, The.
Mock Translation from the Greek.
Monarchs, the butterflies, are commanded, The.
Niagara Falls.
On a Seven-Day Diary.
On Alexander and Aristotle, on a Black-on-Red Greek Plate.
On Being a Householder.
On Don Juan del Norte, Not Don Juan Tenorio del Sur.
On Finding the Tree of Life.
On Hurricane Jackson.
On Leaving Town.
On Trees.
Plague of Dead Sharks.
Poem: "Person who can do, The."
Poem: "What's the balm."
Prayer: "God, I need a job because I need money."
Prison Song.
"Space Is Not Merely a Background for Events, But Possesses an Autonomous Structure." A. Einstein.
Stutterer.
Thesis, Antithesis, and Nostalgia.
To a Red-headed Do-good Waitress.
Tribute to Kafka for Someone Taken.
Untitled Poem.
Wall, Cave, and Pillar Statements, after Asôka.
What a Circus.
When the window glass blows in.
Winter's Onset from an Alienated Point of View.

Dugan, Mrs. D. H.
Christ Is Risen!

Dugan, Michael
Gumble.

Duganne, A. J. H.
Bethel.

Duggan, Eileen
Ballad of the Bushman.
Booty.
Bushfeller, The.
Cloudy Bay.
Have No Fear!
Invasion.
Juniper.
Pilgrimage.

Prophecy.
Rosa Luxembourg.
Shag, The.
Tides Run up the Wairau, The.
Truth.
Victory.
Du Guillet, Pernette
Chanson.
Epigram: "As the body denies the means to look."
Maiden's Lament, A, *sel.*
Duke, Richard
After the fiercest pangs of hot desire.
Epithalamium upon the Marriage of Captain William Bedloe, An.
Panegyric upon Oates, A.
Duke, William
Hail Our Incarnate God!
"Dum-Dum." *See* **Kendall, John Kaye**
Dumas, Alexandre
We set out yesterday upon a winter drive, *sel.*
Dumas, Edmund
Our School Now Closes Out.
Dumas, Henry
America.
Black Star Line.
Black Trumpeter.
Buffalo.
Knock on Wood.
Du Maurier, George
Legend of Camelot, A.
Little Work, A, *sel.*
Lost Illusion, A.
Music.
Vers Nonsensiques.
Dunann, Louella
Hot Line.
Dunbar, Jennie
A-Hunting.
Dunbar, Paul Laurence
Accountability.
After the Quarrel.
Ante-Bellum Sermon, An.
Banjo Song, A.
Compensation.
Conscience and Remorse.
Curtain!
Dawn.
Death Song, A.
Debt, The.
Deserted Plantation, The.
Dilettante, The: A Modern Type.
Douglass.
Equipment.
Ere Sleep Comes Down to Soothe the Weary Eyes.
Frederick Douglass.
Get Somebody Else.
Harriet Beecher Stowe.
Haunted Oak, The.
Howdy, Honey, Howdy!
Hymn: After Reading "Lead, Kindly Light."
Hymn: "When storms arise."
In the Morning.
Lawyers' Ways, The.
Life.
Little Black Sheep, The.
Little Brown Baby.
Lover's Lane.
Master-Player, The.
Misapprehension.
My Sort o' Man.
Negro Love Song, A.
Old Apple-Tree, The.
Old Cabin, The.
Ol'Tunes, The.
Paradox, The.
Party, The.
Philosophy.
Place Where the Rainbow Ends, The.
Poet, The.

Prayer, A: "O Lord, the hard-won miles."
Robert Gould Shaw.
Ships That Pass in the Night.
Signs of the Times.
Soliloquy of a Turkey.
Song, A: "Thou art the soul of a summer's day."
Spiritual, A.
Sympathy.
To a Captious Critic.
Unsung Heroes, The.
We Wear the Mask.
When de Co'n Pone's Hot.
When Dey 'Listed Colored Soldiers.
When Malindy Sings.
Whittier.
Dunbar, Robert
Angelica has gain'd the dell, *sel.*
Summit gain'd how glorious the reward, The, *sel.*
Dunbar, William
Amendis to the Telyouris and Sowtaris for the Turnament Maid on Thame, The.
Ballad of Kynd Kittok, The.
Ballad of Our Lady.
Bot of ane bowrd in to bed I sall yow breif yit, *sel.*
Dance of the Sevin Deidly Synnis, The.
Done Is a Battle.
Empryce of prys, imperatrice, *sel.*
Fenyeit Freir of Tungland, The.
Golden Targe, The.
In Winter.
Lament for the Makaris.
Man of Valour to His Fair Lady, The.
Meditatioun in Wyntir.
Petition of the Gray Horse, Auld Dunbar, The.
Poet's Dream, The, *sel.*
Quod Dunbar to Kennedy.
Remonstrance to the King.
Testament of Mr. Andro Kennedy, The.
To a Lady[e].
To Aberdein.
To the City of London [*or* In Honour of the City of London].
To the Merchantis of Edinburgh.
Tretis of the Tua Mariit Wemen and the Wedo, The.
Widow Has Buried Her Second Husband, The, *sel.*
Widow Speaks, The, *sel.*
Dunbar-Nelson, Alice
Music.
Duncan, Mary Lundie
Jesus Tender Shepherd.
Duncan, Rea Lubar
Juncture.
Duncan, Robert
African Elegy, An.
After a Passage in Baudelaire.
At the Loom, *sel.*
Ballad of Mrs. Noah, The.
Bending the Bow.
Childhood's Retreat.
Correspondences.
Dance, The.
Dream Data.
Envoy: "Good Night, at last," *sel.*
Eyesight II.
Fire, The, *sel.*
Food for Fire, Food for Thought.
Fountain of forms! Life springs of unique being!, *sel.*
Fourth Song the Night Nurse Sang.
Homage and Lament for Ezra Pound in Captivity.
I know a little language of my cat, tho Dante says, *sel.*
Ingmar Bergman's "Seventh Seal."
Interlude, An.

Little Language, A.
Lover, The.
Morning Letter, A.
My Mother Would Be a Falconress.
New Poem, A.
Night Scenes.
Often I Am Permitted to Return to a Meadow.
Owl Is an Only Bird of Poetry, An.
Part-Sequence for Change, A.
Passage over Water.
Persephone.
Poem Beginning with a Line by Pindar, A.
Poetry, a Natural Thing.
Question, The.
Returning to Roots of First Feeling.
Roots and Branches.
Shelley's "Arethusa" Set to New Measures.
Something is taking place, *sel.*
Song of the Borderguard, The.
Spring Memorandum, A.
Strains of Sight.
Such Is the Sickness of Many a Good Thing.
Temple of the Animals, The.
This Place Rumord to Have Been Sodom.
Torso: Passages 18, The.
Tribal Memories, *sel.*
Turning Into.
Up Rising, *sel.*
Willingly I'll say, *sel.*
Work, The, *sel.*
Dunkin, William
Hibernia's Helicon is dry, *sel.*
Dunn, Douglas
After the War.
Clothes Pit, The.
Dream of Judgement, A.
Elegy for the Lost Parish.
Emblems.
Estuarial Republic, The.
Glasgow Schoolboys, Running Backwards.
Green Breeks.
House Next Door, The.
Musical Orchard, The.
On Roofs of Terry Street.
Patricians, The.
Remembering Lunch.
Removal from Terry Street, A.
Supreme Death.
War Blinded.
Warriors.
Washing the Coins.
Dunn, Gwen
Journey Back to Christmas.
Dunn, Max
I Danced before I Had Two Feet.
Dunn, Stephen
At the Smithville Methodist Church.
Basketball: A Retrospective.
Because We Are Not Taken Seriously.
Birthday Gift, A.
Choosing to Think of It.
Completion.
Day and Night Handball.
Enough Time.
Looking for a Rest Area.
On Hearing the Airlines Will Use a Psychological Profile to Catch Potential Skyjackers.
Poem for People Who Are Understandably Too Busy to Read Poetry.
Sacred, The.
Tangier.
Toward the Verrazano.
Dunn, Stephen P.
Prayer of the Young Stoic.
Dunn, Susan L.
They Are All Too Kind.
Today, Again, the Jagged Black Line.
Tonight I Stood Looking.
Dunnam, Ouida Smith
Prayer of a Beginning Teacher.

Dunqul, Amal
City a Wrecked Ship, The.
Corner.
Scaffold, The.
Tommorow.
Trains.
Dupin, Jacques
Gripped by the Dread.
Mineral Kingdom.
My Body.
Only Beating, The.
Opened.
Thirst.
Waiting.
Wave, The.
Dupree, Edgar
Light of Faith, The.
Dupuy, J.
Michael Met a Duck.
Durack, Mary
Red Jack.
Durand, Mercedes
Requiem For The Sumpul.
They Fell on the Stairway.
Durand, Oswald
Black Man's Son, The.
Durbin, Harriet Whitney
Little Dutch Garden, A.
Durcan, Paul
Bewley's Oriental Café, Westmoreland Street.
Combe Florey.
General Vallencey's Waltz.
Going Home to Mayo, Winter, 1949.
In Memory of Those Murdered in the Dublin Massacre.
Ireland 1977.
Ireland 1972.
Kilfenora Teaboy, The.
Letter to Ben, 1972.
Making Love outside Aras an Uachtaráin.
Micheál Mac Liammóir.
Nessa.
November 1967.
Sally.
10.30 AM Mass, June 16, 1985.
They Say the Butterfly Is the Hardest Stroke.
Turkish Carpet, The.
Wife Who Smashed Television Gets Jail.
Durell, Ann
Cornish Magic.
Durem, Ray
Award.
Basic.
Friends.
I Know I'm Not Sufficiently Obscure.
Problem in Social Geometry—the Inverted Square!
Ultimate Equality.
Vet's Rehabilitation.
D'Urfey, Thomas
Born with the Vices.
Bright Was the Morning.
Chloe Divine.
Dialogue, between Crab and Gillian, sel.
I'll Sail upon the Dog-Star, sel.
Shepherd Kept Sheep on a Hill So High, A.
Du Toit, J.D. See "Totius"
Durgnat, Raymond
Scrap Iron.
Durham, Jimmie
Columbus Day.
Justiniano Lamé Has Been Killed.
Middle.
Woman Gave Me a Red Star to Wear on My Headband, A.
Durivage, Francis Alexander
Chez Brébant.
Durrell, Lawrence
Adepts, The, sel.
At Epidaurus.
Ballad of the Good Lord Nelson, A.

Ballad of the Oedipus Complex.
Coptic Poem ("A Coptic deputation, going to Ethiopia").
Cradle Song: "Curled like a hoop in sleep."
Epitaph: "Stavro's dead. A truant vine."
Green Coconuts: Rio.
In Arcadia.
In Crisis.
Keepsake.
Lesbos.
Levant.
My uncle sleeps in the image of death, sel.
Mythology.
Nemea.
On First Looking into Loeb's Horace.
On Seeming to Presume.
Owed to America.
Paphos.
Poggio.
Salamis.
Sarajevo.
Seferis.
Stoic.
Swans.
This Unimportant Morning.
Visitations, sel.
Water-Colour of Venice, A.
Durston, Georgia Roberts
Wolf, The.
Duryee, Mary Ballard
Homestead—Winter Morning.
Dutcher, Roger
Antaeus (The Prodigious Builders).
Dutton, G. J. F.
February Thaw.
Hut.
Magma.
Of Only a Single Poem.
Dutton, Geoffrey
January.
Stranded Whales, The.
Time of Waiting.
Variations on a Medieval Theme.
Duyn, Mona Van
Gardener to His God, The.
Dwight, Timothy
As Down a Lone Valley.
Assault on the Fortress, The.
Columbia.
Here stood Hypocrisy, in sober brown, sel.
I Love Thy Kingdom, Lord.
Shall Man, O God of Light.
Sing to the Lord Most High.
To the Federal Convention.
Dybek, Stuart
Clothespins.
Dyer, John
Ah gentle shepherd, thine the lot to tend, sel.
Bedford Level, sel.
English Fog, The, sel.
Ever charming, ever new, sel.
Grongar Hill, sel.
Happy Workhouse and the Good Effects of Industry, The, sel.
How to Shear Sheep, sel.
My Ox Duke.
O may I with myself agree, sel.
To Clio, from Rome.
Wool Trade, The, sel.
Dyer, Lady Catherine
Epitaph on the Monument of Sir William Dyer at Colmworth, 1641, sel.
Dyer, Sir Edward
Corydon to His Phyllis.
Cynthia.
Lowest Trees Have Tops, the Ant her Gall, The.
My Mind [or Minde or Mynde] to Me a Kingdom [or Kyngdome] Is.
Wher one would be.

Dylan, Bob
Dear Mister Congressman.
Dyment, Clifford
As a boy with a richness of needs I wandered.
Fox.
Sanctuary.
Dyson, Edward
Cleaning Up.
Friendly Game of Football, A.
Old Whim Horse, The.
Dzyubin, Edward. See "Bagritsky, Edward"

E

"E." See Fullerton, Mary Elizabeth
"E. H. K." See "K., E.H."
"E. M. G. R." See "R., E. M. G."
"E. O. G." See "G., E.O."
"E-Yeh-Shure" (Louise Abeita)
Beauty.
"Eagle, Solomon." See Squire, Sir John Collings
Earle, Virginia
Dream as Reported, A.
Earley, Tom
Rebel's Progress.
Eason, Amanda
Matauwhi Bay V.
Some Things.
"Eastaway Edward." See Thomas, Edward
Eastburn, James Wallis
O Holy, Holy, Holy, Lord.
Easter, Marguerite Elizabeth
My Laddie's Hounds.
Eastman, Barrett
How We Burned the Philadelphia.
Joy Enough.
Richard Somers.
Eastman, Charles Gamage
Dirge: "Softly!/ She is lying/ With her lips apart."
Eastman, Elaine Goodale
Ashes of Roses.
Baby.
Countrywoman of Mine, A.
Eastman, Gordon
Buckskin Flats.
Eastman, Max
Animal.
At the Aquarium.
Hymn to God in Time of Stress, A.
Invocation: "Truth, be more precious to me than the eyes."
Rainy Song.
Eastman, Sophie E.
Spool of Thread, A.
Eastwick, Ivy O.
At Sunset.
Cherry Tree.
Dark Danny.
Feather for My Cap, A.
Larch Wood Secrets.
Lucy Lavender.
Miller, Miller.
Morning.
Pretty Maid Marion.
Puppy Chased the Sunbeam, The.
Scarf, The.
Singing in the Spring.
Snow in Spring.
Ten to One.
Thanksgiving.
Trouble at the Farm.
Wolf and the Lambs, The.
Eaton, Anthony
Dove Apologizes to His God for Being Caught by a Cat, The.

Eaton, Arthur Wentworth Hamilton
Egyptian Lotus, The.
Phantom Light of the Baie des Chaleurs, The.
Pray for the Dead.
Eaton, Burnham
Technique.
Eaton, Charles Edward
Biography of a Still LIfe.
Lynx, The.
Peony for Apollo, A.
Eaton, Evelyn Sibyl Mary
Gardener, The.
Eaton, Walter Prichard
Willows, The.
Eberhart, Richard
Angels, The.
As If You Had Never Been.
At Lake Geneva.
Attic, The ("The attic and the cedar closet—
    nostalgia!"), sel.
Cancer Cells, The.
Chiliasm.
Dam Neck, Virginia.
Dead Skunk.
Father and Son.
Fisher Cat, The.
Flux.
For a Lamb.
Fury of Aerial Bombardment, The.
Go to the Shine That's on a Tree.
Groundhog, The.
Half-bent Man.
Hard Structure of the World, The.
Hardy Perennial.
Horse Chestnut Tree, The.
I walked over the grave of Henry James.
I Went to See Irving Babbitt.
If I Could Only Live at the Pitch That Is near
    Madness.
Imagining How It Would Be to Be Dead.
In a Hard Intellectual Light.
Inability to Depict an Eagle.
La Crosse at Ninety Miles an Hour.
Largess, The.
Man Is God's Nature.
Marrakech.
Matin Pandemoniums, The.
Meditation, A.
Mystical Beast in the Shadows, The.
New England Bachelor, A.
New Hampshire, February.
On a Squirrel Crossing the Road in Autumn,
    in New England.
On Shooting Particles beyond the World.
Plain Song Talk.
Preacher Sought to Find Out Acceptable
    Words, The.
Rainscapes, Hydrangeas, Roses, and Singing
    Birds.
Reading Room, The New York Public
    Library.
River Water Music.
Roc, The.
Rumination.
Sea Burial from the Cruiser "Reve."
Sea-Hawk.
Sea-Ruck.
Seals, Terns, Time.
Ship Burning and a Comet All in One Day,
    A.
Soul Longs to Return Whence It Came, The.
Spider, The.
Spring Mountain Climb.
To Auden on His Fiftieth.
Two Loves.
Under the Hill.
Vast Light.
Vision.
When Doris Danced.
White Pines, Felled 1984.
World War.
Yonder.

Ebner, Jeannie
Dialogue.
Hunger.
Moment after the Rain.
On the Way.
Ebner-Eschenbach, Marie von
Saint Peter and the Bluestocking.
Ebright, Frederick
Memorial to the Great Big Beautiful
    Self-sacrificing Advertisers.
Echeruo, Michael
Melting Pot.
Eddy, Gary
Desire.
Eddy, Mary Baker
O'er Waiting Harp-Strings of the Mind.
Shepherd, Show Me How to Go.
Eddy, Zachary
Floods Swell around Me, Angry, Appalling.
Jesus, Enthroned and Glorified.
Edelman, Elaine
How Beautiful You Are: 3.
Edelman, Katherine
Irish Grandmother.
Edelstein, Hyman
Indian Night Tableau.
Last Mathematician.
Palimpsest.
Eden, Helen Parry
Four-Paws.
Edey, Marion and Dorothy Grider
Ant Village, The.
Jolly Woodchuck, The.
Edgar, Marriott
Lion and Albert, The.
Edgar, Mary S.
Prayer-Poem, A.
Edman, Irwin
La Donna È Perpetuum Mobile.
Peace.
Prayer for All Poets at This Time.
Edmond, Lauris
All Possession Is Theft.
August, Ohakune.
Before a Funeral.
Difficult Adjustment, A.
Femme Agée.
Ghost Moth, The.
Ghosts II.
Going to Moscow.
Greek Antiquities: First Floor.
Henri Rousseau Style, The.
Latter Day Lysistrata.
Morning in Christchurch.
Names, The.
Noh Plays, The.
Ohakune Fires.
Shift of Emphasis, A, sel.
Study of Geography, or History, The.
Sums, The.
Third Person, The.
To an Old Rebel.
Tristesse d'animal.
Zero Population Growth, sel.
Edmond, Murray
Cell Lay Inside Her Body, The, sel.
House, sel.
My Return to Czechoslovakia.
Shack.
Sprig of Karo, A.
Von Tempsky's Dance.
Edmonds, Paul
Little Tommy Tiddler.
Edmondson, Madeleine
Witches' Spells.
Edmondstoune Aytoun. See **Aytoun, William
    Edmonstoune**
Edmunds, William H.
To Be or Not to Be.
Edson, C. L.
Ravin's of Piute Poet Poe.

Edson, Russell
Automobile, The.
Bachelor's Hand, The.
Childhood of an Equestrian, The.
Children.
Cottage in the Wood, A.
Counting Sheep.
Death of an Angel, The.
Fall, The.
Good Son Jim.
Having to Love Something Else, The.
Hourglass, The.
In All the Days of My Childhood.
In the Forest.
Journey through the Moonlight, A.
Long Picnic, The.
Love Affair, The.
Manure Book, The.
Melting, The.
Mouse Dinners, The.
Old Man's Son, An.
On the Eating of Mice.
Out of Whack.
Performance at Hog Theater, A.
Philosophers, The.
Pilot, The.
Rat's Legs, The.
Rat's Tight Schedule, The.
Retirement of the Elephant, The.
Sculptor, The.
Thickening, The.
Tunnel, The.
Wheelbarrow, The.
Wounded Breakfast, The.
Edwards, Amelia Blandford
Give Me Three Grains of Corn, Mother.
Edwards, Barbara Catherine
Bomb Incident.
Wartime Maternity Ward, A.
Edwards, Edwin
Waitekauri Every Time!
Edwards, Harry
How to Change the U.S.A.
Edwards, Jeannette Slocomb
Hester MacDonagh.
Edwards, Matilda Caroline
Church Walking with the World, The.
Do As You Would Be Done By.
Home.
I Love the Night.
Remember the Poor.
There's a Silvery Lining to Every Cloud.
Time to Die, The.
To a Loved One of Other Days.
We Are Passing Away.
World Is Full of Beauty, The.
Edwards, Osman
Merchant at Yokohama, The, sel.
Minister at Chiuzenji, The, sel.
Missionary at Karnizawa, The, sel.
Professor in Nirvana, The, sel.
Edwards, Richard
Amantium Irae Amoris Redintegratio.
May.
Of Women.
Edwards, Solomon
Dream.
Edwards, Thomas
On the Edition of Mr. Pope's Works with a
    Commentary and Notes.
Sonnet on a Family Picture.
To Shakespeare.
To the Author of Clarissa.
To the Editor of Mr. Pope's Works.
Tongue-Doughty Pedant.
Edwards, Matilda Barbara Betham. See
    Betham-Edwards, Matilda Barbara
Eedes, Richard
No Love, to Love of Man and Wife.
Efrat, Israel
Bird of My Being, The.

Certain Days.
Dumpy and obese—a woman, *sel.*
Heart Will Have Its Way, The.
Interstice in the Deep.
Marine Biology.
Narcissus.
Seashell.
Egan, Maurice Francis
He Made Us Free.
Maurice de Guérin.
Old Violin, The.
Shamrock, The.
Egar, J. H.
Sing, Sing for Christmas.
Egerton, Helen Merrill
Sandpipers.
Egerton, J. A.
Tell Him So.
Egerton, Sarah Fyge
Emulation, The.
Eggleton, David
Painting Mount Taranaki.
These Rumours of Hexagonal Rooms in Gone
   Bee City.
Eglington, Charles
Arrival and Departure.
Buffalo.
Lourenço Marques.
Lowveld, The.
Vanquished, The.
Eguren, José María
Horse, The.
Ehrenburg, Ilya Grigoryevich
Our Children's Children Will Marvel.
Sons of Our Sons, The.
Tree, The.
Trumpet, The.
Ehrenstein, Albert
Ares.
Home-Coming.
Homer.
Suffering.
Ehrlich, Gretel
Cutting Wood on Shell Creek.
Orchard, The.
Sheeprancher Named John, A.
Way of Speaking, A.
Ehrmann, Max
Prayer, A: "Let me do my work each day."
Eibel, Deborah
Freethinkers.
Hagar to Ishmael.
Kabbalist, The.
Eichenrand, Lazer
From Life.
Mute City, The.
Prologue: "In your words."
Eifuku, Empress
Autumn Dusk.
Blossoms at Evening.
Dawn Blossoms.
Deep into the night.
Even the night wind.
Evening shower, An.
Evening sunlight, The.
For just a moment.
If even now/ in the midst of rejection.
In just the same way.
In the whole wide world.
It is the breezes.
Love Poem, A: "He made no promise."
Love Poem, A: "Night has fallen, The."
My heart is moved.
On evenings like this.
River plovers, The.
Scattering blossoms.
Unaware of the times.
We dressed each other.
Eigner, Larry
All Intents.
B.

Bare trees, The/ alternate.
Closed System, The.
Dark swimmers, The.
Do It Yrself.
Don't go.
Elysee.
Environs.
Fete, A.
Flake diamond of/ the sea.
Fleche.
From the sustaining air.
Gone, A.
I have felt it as they've said.
Keep Me Still, for I Do Not Want to Dream.
Letter for Duncan.
Noise Grimaced.
Open.
Passages.
Remember Sabbath Days.
That the neighborhood might be covered.
Wind like an ocean, The.
Eiseley, Loren C.
Beware, My Successor.
Deserted Homestead, The.
Ejo
I'm but a festering lump.
Ejong, Yityangu
Love Song: "Tiny children."
Ela, David H.
Chosen Three, on Mountain Height, The.
Elam, William C.
Mecklenburg Declaration, The.
Elburg, Jan G.
Axes Rust, The.
Knowledge of What Is.
Satie.
Sometimes Believing.
Young Old Young Old.
Eldan, Anadad
At Your Naked Back.
Between the White Stone Canyons.
Candle of Brief Times, The.
Foam Blanches.
Who Will Give Cover?
Words That Speak of Death.
Elder, Anne
Carried Away.
Farmer Goes Beserk.
One Foot in the Door.
School Cadets.
Eldridge, Paul
To a Courtesan a Thousand Years Dead.
Eldridge, Richard Burdick
Soul Remembers, The.
Eleazar
Thy Faithful Sons.
"Elfed." See **Lewis, Howell Elvet**
Elgin, Suzette Haden
McLuhan Transposed.
**"Eliot, George" (Mary Ann Evans Lewes
   Cross)**
Brother and Sister.
But sudden came the barge's pitch-black
   prow, *sel.*
Choir Invisible, The.
I Am Lonely, *sel.*
I Cannot Choose but Think upon the Time,
   sel.
Long hears have left their writing on my
   brow, *sel.*
O may I join the choir invisible, *sel.*
Our brown canal was endless to my thought,
   sel.
Our mother bade us keep the trodden ways,
   sel.
Plaça Santiago, The, *sel.*
Quit now the town, and with a journeying
   dream, *sel.*
Roses
School Parted Us, *sel.*

Those long days measured by my little feet,
   sel.
Tide of Faith, The, *sel.*
We had the selfsame world enlarged for each,
   sel.
Eliot, Henrietta Robins
Why It Was Cold in May.
Eliot, Thomas Stearns
Ad-dressing of Cats, The.
Although I do not hope to turn again, *sel.*
Animula.
Ash-Wednesday.
At the first turning of the second stair, *sel.*
Aunt Helen.
Boston Evening Transcript , The.
Burnt Norton, *sel.*
Cape Ann, *sel.*
Cat Morgan Introduces Himself.
Chorus from "The Rock," *sel.*
Chorus: "We do not wish anything to
   happen," *sel.*
Chorus: "We have not been happy, my Lord,
   we have not been too happy," *sel.*
Cousin Nancy.
Cultivation of Christmas Trees, The.
Death by Water, *sel.*
Dedication to My Wife, A.
Dry Salvages, The, *sel.*
Eagle soars in the summit of heaven, The,
   sel.
East Coker, *sel.*
Eyes That Last I Saw in Tears.
Forgive Us, O Lord, *sel.*
Fragment of an Agon.
Game of Chess, A, *sel.*
Gerontion.
Growltiger's Last Stand.
Gus: The Theatre Cat.
Hippopotamus, The.
His soul stretched tight across the skies, *sel.*
Hollow Men, The.
Journey of the Magi.
La Figlia Che Piange.
Lines for an Old Man.
Lines for Cuscuscaraway and Mirza Murad
   Ali Beg.
Lines to Ralph Hodgson, Esqre.
Little Gidding, *sel.*
Love Song of J. Alfred Prufrock, The.
Lyric, A: "If time and space, as sages say."
Macavity: The Mystery Cat.
Marina.
Morning at the Window.
Morning comes to consciousness, The, *sel.*
Mr. Apollinax.
Naming of Cats, The.
New Hampshire, *sel.*
O Light Invisible, we praise Thee!, *sel.*
Portrait of a Lady.
Preludes, II.
Rannoch, by Glencoe, *sel.*
Rhapsody on a Windy Night.
Rum Tum Tugger, The.
Skimbleshanks: The Railway Cat.
Song for Simeon, A.
Song of the Jellicles, The.
Sweeney among the Nightingales.
Sweeney Erect.
Triumphal March, *sel.*
Under the bamboo, *sel.*
Usk, *sel.*
Virginia, *sel.*
Waste Land, The.
When Lil's husband got demobbed, I said,
   sel.
Whispers of Immortality.
Wind Sprang Up at Four o'Clock, The.
Winter evening settles down, The, *sel.*
You tossed a blanket from the bed, *sel.*
You'll be my little seven stone missionary!,
   sel.

Eliyia, Joseph
Dream.
Epilogue: "I too was a little child once."
Rebecca.
Slender Maid.
Your Passing, Fleet Passing.
Elizabeth I, Queen of England
Doubt of Future Foes, The.
On Fortune.
On Monsieur's Departure.
When I Was Fair and Young.
Written in Her French Psalter.
Written on a Wall at Woodstock.
Written with a Diamond on Her Window at
Woodstock.
Elizabeth of York, Queen
My heart is set upon a lusty pin.
Eller, David
To a God Unknown.
Ellerton, John (1826-1893)
Day Thou Gavest, Lord, Is Ended, The.
God of the Living, The.
Ellerton, John Lodge
Now the Laborer's Task Is O'er.
Elliot, George Tracy
Winter Twilight.
Elliot, Harley
On a Country Road.
Elliot, Henry Rutherford
Laugh It Off.
Elliot, Jane
Flowers of the Forest, The.
Elliot, Jean
Exercise in a Meadow.
Elliott, Ebenezer
Beware of Dogmas.
Black Hole of Calcutta, The.
Caged Rats.
Drone v. Worker.
Epigram: "Prepare to meet the King of
Terrors," cried."
Epigram: "What is a communist? One who
hath yearnings."
Four Dears, The.
Fox-Hunters, The.
Give Not Our Blankets, Tax-Fed Squire, sel.
God Save the People.
Hail, Sabbath! day of mercy, peace, and rest!,
sel.
Here lies the man who stripp'd Sin bare.
How Different!
In These Days.
Is it the horn that, on this holy day, sel.
John.
Now landed Trader, that, with haughty stare,
sel.
On a Rose in December.
Paddy, I have but stol'n your living.
People's Sabbath Prayer, The.
Plaint.
Poet vs. Parson.
Press, The.
Ralph Leech Believes, sel.
Song: "Child, is thy father dead?"
Song: "Donought would have everything."
Song: "When working blackguards come to
blows."
Steam at Sheffield.
Toy of the Titans, sel.
Village! thy butcher's son, the steward now,
sel.
Elliott, F. Ann
Pictures.
Snow, The.
Elliott, George P.
Her Dwarf.
Elliott, Harley
After Picking Rosehips.
Blessed and Resting Uncle.
Brothers Together in Winter.
Crazy Horse Returns to South Dakota.

Natural Order of Things, The.
Panda, The, sel.
Planting, The.
Thinking Twice in the Laundromat.
Ellis, Alice Thomas
To Joshua.
Ellis, Colin
Adder's Epigrams.
Bungaloid Growth.
Epitaph, An: "He worshipped at the altar of
Romance."
International Conference.
Modern World, The.
New Vicar of Bray, The.
Old Ladies, The.
On a Gentleman Marrying His Cook.
Ellis, Edwin John
At Golgotha I stood alone, sel.
Ellis, John
Sarah Hazard's Love Letter.
Ellis, Robert
Hour of Sleep, The.
Ellis, Royston
All my sex life, I had been drifting, sel.
It was an international rage, sel.
Spiv Song.
Ellis, Vivian Locke
At Common Dawn.
Ellsworth, Erastus Wolcott
I saw a man, by some accounted wise, sel.
Mayflower, The.
Ellwanger, William De Lancey
To Jessie's Dancing Feet.
"Elmo"
Our Ernest.
Elton, Charles
Luriana, Lurilee.
Elton Hill
Theme Brown Girl.
Eluard, Paul
Ageless.
Confections.
Curfew.
Deaf and Blind, The.
Earth Is as Blue as an Orange, The.
Ecstasy.
End to Everything, The.
Feathers.
For Pablo Picasso.
From Outside.
From the Depth of the Abyss.
Hen.
Hunted.
In honour of the dumb the blind the deaf, sel.
Invention, The.
Lady Love.
Liberty.
Max Ernst.
Medusas.
On my school notebooks, sel.
One Moment's Mirror.
Out of Sight in the Direction of My Body.
Painted Words.
Paw.
Pig.
"Poetry Ought to Have a Practical Purpose."
Some Words Which, Up until Now, Had
Remained Mysteriously Forbidding for Me.
To Live Here.
To Ride.
We Are.
Wetness.
You Arise.
Yves Tanguy.
Elwood, Thomas
Prayer, A: "O that mine eyes might closed
be."
Elytis, Odysseus
Adolescence of Day.
Aegean Melancholy.

Age of Blue Memory, The.
All Day Long We Walked in the Fields.
Anniversary.
Autopsy, The.
Beauty and the Illiterate.
Body of Summer.
Burnished Day, Conch of the Voice.
Drinking the Sun of Corinth.
For those men night was a more bitter day,
sel.
Form of Boeotia.
He was a fine young man. The first day he
was born, sel.
Helen.
I Lived the Beloved Name.
I No Longer Know the Night.
In the distance crystal bells ring out, sel.
Laconic.
Mad Pomegranate Tree, The.
Marina of the Rocks.
Now that his fatherland has darkened on
earth, sel.
Now with a still wind in his quiet hair, sel.
Sleep of the Brave, The.
Sun, bronze voice, and holy etesian wind, sel.
There where the sun first dwelt, sel.
This Wind That Loiters.
With What Stones, What Blood, and What
Iron.
Ema Saiko
To Inscribe on My Portrait.
Emanuel, James A.
Black Muslim Boy in a Hospital.
Church Burning: Mississippi.
Emmett Till.
For "Mr. Dudley," a Black Spy.
Get Up, Blues.
Negritude.
Negro, The.
Nightmare.
Old Black Men Say.
Panther Man.
Son.
Treehouse, The.
Voyage of Jimmy Poo, The.
Wishes, for Alix.
Young Ones, Flip Side, The.
Emanuel, Lynn
Berlin Interior with Jews, 1939.
Frying Trout While Drunk.
Of Your Father's Indiscretions and the Train
to California.
Sleeping, The.
Technology of Inspiration, The.
You Tell Me.
Embury, Emma Catherine
Love Unsought.
Pilgrim, The.
Emerson, G. R.
Dream of the Artisan, The.
Emerson, Ralph Waldo
All the forms are fugitive, sel.
Alphonso of Castile.
Apology, The.
April and May, sel.
As the sunbeams stream through liberal space,
sel.
Atom from Atom, sel.
Bacchus.
Beyond Winter.
Blight.
Bohemian Hymn, The.
Boston Hymn.
Brahma.
Character.
Chickadee, The.
Compensation.
Concord Hymn.
Days.
Duty, sel.
Each and All.

Earth, The.
Eros.
Experience.
Fable: Mountain and the Squirrel, The.
Fame.
Flower Chorus.
Forbearance.
Forerunners.
Gardener, *sel.*
Give All to Love.
Good-bye.
Grace.
Guy.
Hamatreya
Hand that rounded Peter's dome, The, *sel.*
Heart of All the Scene, The, *sel.*
Humble-Bee, The.
In an Age of Fops and Toys, *sel.*
In unplowed Maine he sought the lumberers'
    gang, *sel.*
Informing Spirit, The.
Letter, A.
Letters.
Limits.
Merlin.
Merops.
Mighty Heart, The, *sel.*
Miracle, The.
Mithridates.
Music.
Nahant.
Nation's Strength, A.
Nature.
Nemesis.
Ode Inscribed to W. H. Channing.
Ode: "O tenderly the haughty day."
Ode to Beauty.
Orator, *sel.*
Parks and Ponds.
Past, The.
Poet, *sel.*
Problem, The.
Prudence.
Quatrain: Poet.
Rhodora [On Being Asked Whence Is the
    Flower], The.
Saadi.
Sea-Shore.
Snow-Storm, The.
Solution.
Song of Seyd Nimetollah of Kuhistan.
Sphinx, The.
Spring Prayer.
Tact.
Terminus.
Test, The.
Thine Eyes Still Shined.
Thought.
Threnody: "South-wind brings, The."
Two Rivers.
Undersong, The, *sel.*
Uriel.
Visit, The.
Waldeinsamkeit.
Water.
We Love the Venerable House.
Wealth.
Whoso walks in solitude, *sel.*
Why did all manly gifts in Webster fail?
Xenophanes.
Emerson, Siegfried
Wind in the Grass, The.
Emeruwa, Leatrice W.
Personals.
Emery, Frances D.
Long-billed Gannets.
Emmett, Daniel Decatur
Dixie.
Empson, William
Arachne.
Aubade: "Hours before dawn we were woken
    by the quake."

Bacchus
Camping Out.
China.
Courage Means Running.
Dissatisfaction with Metaphysics.
Earth Has Shrunk in the Wash.
God who fled down with a standard yard,
    The, *sel.*
Herm whose length measured degrees of heat,
    The, *sel.*
Homage to the British Museum.
I said I wouldn't fly again, *sel.*
Ignorance of Death.
Invitation to Juno.
Just a Smack at Auden.
Legal Fiction.
Let It Go.
Letter I.
Letter IV.
Missing Dates.
Note on Local Flora.
Reflection from Rochester.
Rolling the Lawn.
Scales, The.
Sea Voyage.
Sonnet: "Not wrongly moved by this
    dismaying scene."
Success.
Teasers, The.
This Last Pain.
To an Old Lady.
Villanelle: "It is the pain, it is the pain,
    endures."
Emre, Yunus
Whole universe is full of God, The.
Endrezze, Anita. *See* **Endrezze-Danielson,
    Anita**
Endrezze-Danielson, Anita
Birdwatching at Fan Lake.
Blue Horses; West Winds.
Canto Llano.
Dream Feast (Three Poems), The.
Girl Who Loved the Sky, The.
Hansel, Gretel and Ruby Redlips.
Language of Fossils, The.
Learning the Spells; a Diptych.
Manifest Destiny.
Meditating on Star Light While Traveling
    Highway.
Night Mare.
November Harvest.
October Morning Walk.
Red Rock Ceremonies.
Return of the Wolves.
Reviewing Past Lives while Leaf-Burning.
Shaman//Bear.
Song-Maker.
Sunset at Twin Lake.
There Are Three Bones in the Human Ear.
Why Stone Does Not Sing by Itself.
Engels, John
Cardinals in the Ice Age.
Goldfinch.
Harbor, The.
Homer Mitchell Place, The.
Moonwalk.
Muskrat.
Orchard.
Revisit.
Sestina for My Dead in the First Snow.
Terribilis Est Locus Iste.
Engetsu, Chugan. *See* **Chugan Engetsu**
Engle, John D., Jr.
Reminder.
Engle, Paul
American Child.
Ending, The.
Heartland.
In a Bar near Shibuya Station, Tokyo.
Lord of Each Soul.
Moving In.

New World, The.
Together.
English, Maurice
Form Was the World.
English, Thomas Dunn
Arnold at Stillwater.
Assunpink and Princeton.
Battle of Monmouth, The.
Battle of New Orleans, The.
Battle of the Cowpens, The.
Battle of the King's Mill.
Ben Bolt.
Betty Zane.
Burning of Jamestown, The.
Charge by the Ford, The.
Fall of Maubila, The.
Old Mill, The.
Sack of Deerfield, The.
English, William
Cashel of Munster, *at.*
Enheduanna
Antiphonal Hymn in Praise of Inanna.
Appeal to the Moongod Nanna-Suen to Throw
    Out Lugalanne.
Banishment from Ur.
Condemning the Moongod Nanna.
Crimes of Lugalanne.
Curse on Uruk, A.
Final Prayer.
Inanna and An.
Inanna and Ebih.
Inanna and Enlil.
Inanna and Ishkur.
Inanna and the Anunna.
Inanna and the City of Uruk.
Inanna and the Divine Essences.
O lady of all truths bright light going forth,
    sel.
Restoration of Enheduanna to Her Former
    Station, The.
Enkei
Monk from Etsu Returning to a Hermitage.
On Seeing Lute Priest Off.
Ennis, John
Drink of Spring, A.
Meeting at a Salesyard.
Years, The.
Ennius, Quintus
Like a Shower of Rain, *sel.*
Enoch, Olive
Bluebells.
Half Holiday.
Laughter.
Enomoto Kikaku. *See* **Kikaku**
Enright, Dennis Joseph
After Brecht.
Anecdote from William IV Street.
Apocalypse.
Buy One Now.
Deir El Bahari: Temple of Hatshepsut.
Development.
Dreaming in the Shanghai Restaurant.
Guest.
History of World Languages.
How Many Devils Can Dance on the Point.
In Cemeteries.
Laughing Hyena, by Hokusai, The.
Midstream.
Monuments of Hiroshima, The.
Names.
No Offence.
Noodle-Vendor's Flute, The.
Of Growing Old.
Poet Wondering What He Is Up To.
R-and-R Centre: An Incident from the
    Vietnam War.
Royalties.
Since Then.
Typewriter Revolution, The.
Underdeveloped Country, An.
University Examinations in Egypt.

Unlawful Assembly.
Verb "To Think," The.
Waiting for the Bus.
Word, The.

Enriqueta, María
Thoughts of a Little Girl.

Ensing, Riemke
Already 5 drownings 32, *sel.*
Northern Building Society Office Showing
 Police Headquarters, Auckland.

Enslin, Theodore
Fire Poem, The.

Enzensberger, Hans Magnus
Karl Heinrich Marx.

Eörsi, István
Generations.
When Things Fall Upwards.

"Ephelia" (Joan Philips)
Maidenhead.
To Phylocles, Inviting Him to Friendship.

Epstein, Daniel Mark
At the Millinery Shop.
Barrel Organ, The, *sel.*
Cash Only, No Refund, No Return.
Follies, The.
Mannequins.
Miami.
Old Times.

Equena
Before he died.

Equi, Elaine
Condo Girl.
For Hollis Sigler.
Girl Friday.
Hi-Fashion Girl.
Think Small.
Vampirella.

Erb, Ute
Deficiency, A.
Socialism, I Say.

Erba, Luciano
First-Rate Equation, A.
Incompatibility.
La Grande Jeanne.
Land and Sea.
Lombard-Venetian.
Tabula Rasa?

Erdrich, Louise
Birth of Potchikoo, The, *sel.*
Butcher's Wife, The.
Captivity.
Death of Potchikoo, The, *sel.*
Family Reunion.
Francine's Room.
How Potchikoo Got Old, *sel.*
I Was Sleeping Where the Black Oaks Move.
Indian Boarding School: The Runaways.
Jacklight.
King of Owls, The.
Lady in the Pink Mustang, The.
Love Medicine, A.
Night Sky.
Potchikoo Marries, *sel.*
Strange People, The.
That Pull from the Left.
Windigo.

Erickson, C. L.
Light in the Window, The.

Erinna
Baucis.
Distaff, The.

Eristi-Aya
Letter to Her Mother, A.

Ernst, John F.
O Jesus Christ, True Light of God *with music.*

Erskine, John
Kings and Stars.
Shepherd Speaks, The.

Erskine, Thomas, 1st Baron
On Scott's Poem "The Field of Waterloo."
On Tom Moore's Translation of Anacreon.

Erskine, Thomas Erskine, 1st Baron
James Alan Park/ Came naked stark.

Erumai Veliyanar
Horse Did Not Come Back, The.

Esbensen, Barbara Juster
Snow Print Two: Hieroglyphics.
Umbrellas.

Escoffery, Gloria
After the Fall.
Farewell to a Jovial Friend.
No Man's Land.
Twins.

Esher, Reginald Baliol Brett, 2d Viscount.
 See **Brett, Reginald Baliol, 2d Viscount
 Esher**

Eshleman, Clayton
Black Hat, The.
Very Old Woman, A.

Espaillat, Rhina P.
From the Rain Down.

Espina-Villafan, Eduardo
Iowa City under the Sky of the Mayflower.

Espírito Santo, Alda do
Far from the Beach.
Same Side of the Canoe, The.
Where Are the Men Seized in This Wind of
 Madness?

Espy, Willard R.
Can We Make It Next Weekend Instead?
Did She Say "Hmp—mp" instead of "Mp—
 hmp"?
Gemini Jones.
Graduation of Pasta, A.
Singular Singulars, Peculiar Plurals.

Espy, William R.
Inelegant Proposal, An.

Essex, Edwin
Loneliness.

Essex, Robert Devereux, 2d Earl of
Change Thy Mind since She Doth Change.
Happy Were He.

Esson, Thomas Louis Buvelot
Shearer's Wife, The.

"Estelle." *See* **Bogart, Elizabeth**

E'tesami, Parvin
To His Father on Praising the Honest Life of
 the Peasant.

Etherege, Sir George
Chloris, 'Tis Not in Your Power.
Ephelia to Bajazet.
Letter to the Earl of Middleton, A.
Song: "Ladies, though to your conquering
 eyes," *sel.*
To a Lady Asking Him How Long He Would
 Love Her.

Etherege, Sir George
Rivals, *at.*

Etsudo
Dried Bones under the Pine.

Etsuzan
Day the Emperor treated me, The.
Light dies in the eyes, hearing.

Etter, Dave
Chicken.
Old Dubuque.
Romp.
Snow Country.

Eubulus
Benefits and Abuse of Alcohol, The.

Eun
Disciplined by wind and snow.
Unaware of coming, going.

Eunaich, Beinn
Winter Climb.

Euripides
Aftermath, The, *sel.*
Breed of Athletes, The.
Chorus: "And Pergamos,/ City of the
 Phrygians," *sel.*
Chorus of Satyrs, Driving Their Goats, *sel.*
Chorus: The Kings of Troy, *sel.*

Earth and Sky.
Home of Aphrodite, The, *sel.*
Love Song: "One with eyes the fairest," *sel.*
Medea.
No More, O My Spirit, *sel.*
O for the Wings of a Dove, *sel.*
Strength of Fate, The, *sel.*
There Are No Gods, *sel.*

Euwer, Anthony
As a Beauty I Am Not a Star, *sel.*
True Facts of the Case, The.

Evald, Johannes
King Christian.

Evans, Abbie Huston
Fundament Is Shifted, The.
On the Curve-Edge.
Return to Life.
Sun-up in March.

Evans, Abel
Author's Epitaph, Written by Himself, An.
Keep the commandments, Trapp, and go no
 further.
On Sir John Vanbrugh [Architect]
Tadlow.

Evans, David Allan
Bull Rider's Advice, The.
Bullfrogs.
Bus Depot Reunion.
Neighbors.
Pole Vaulter.
Retired Farmer.
Sound of Rain, The.
Story of Lava, The.
Watching Tackles in Slow Motion.

Evans, Evan ("Ieuan Fardd")
Hall of Ifor Hael, The.

Evans, George Essex
Women of the West, The.

Evans, H. A. C.
If Not.

Evans, Humphrey
And Again.

Evans, Margiad
Rain.
Resurrection.
Snowdrops.

Evans, Mari E.
And the Old Women Gathered.
Black Jam for Dr. Negro.
Daufuskie.
Emancipation of George-Hector (a Colored
 Turtle), The.
How Will You Call Me, Brother.
I Am a Black Woman.
If There Be Sorrow.
Into Blackness Softly.
Langston.
Marrow of My Bone.
Rebel, The.
Spectrum.
Status Symbol.
To Mother and Steve.
Uhuru.
Vive Noir!
When in Rome.
Where Have You Gone?
Who Can Be Born Black.

Evans, Nathaniel
To Thee, Then, Let All Beings Bend.

Evans, Ruth
Roman in Libya, A.

Evans, Sebastian
Fifteen Days of Judgment, The.
Seven Fiddlers, The.

Evans, Mary Ann [Marian] *See* **"Eliot,
 George"**

Everard, Harrison
Holloe Menn, The.

Everett, David
Tall Oaks from Little Acorns Grow.

Everett, Edward
Dirge of Alaric the Visigoth.

Everhard, Jim
Curing Homosexuality.

Everson, Ronald G.
Cold-Weather Love.
Injured Maple.
Laprairie Hunger Strike.
Letter from Underground.
Loaves, The.
Old Snapshot.
One-Night Expensive Hotel.
Pauper Woodland.
Stranded in My Ontario.

Everson, William (Brother Antoninus)
Advent.
Canticle to the Waterbirds, A.
Daughter of earth and child of the wave be
appeased, *sel.*
First Winter Storm.
Flight in the Desert, The.
In All These Acts.
Kingfisher Flat.
Making of the Cross, The.
Man-Fate, The.
March.
Narrows of Birth, The.
Poet Is Dead, The.
Presence, The.
Raid, The.
Runoff.
Song the Body Dreamed in the Spirit's Mad
Behest, The.
South Coast, The.
Stranger, The.
What Birds Were There.
Winter Ploughing
Year's End.
Zone of Death.

Everts, Lillian
Playmates.

Everwine, Peter
Brother, The.
Burden of Decision, The.
Clearing, The.
Distance.
Drinking Cold Water.
For the Coming Year.
Going.
In the End.
Learning to Speak.
Marsh, New Year's Day, The.
Night.
Perhaps It's as You Say.
Routes.
Someone Knocks.
We Meet in the Lives of Animals.

"Evoe." *See* **Knox, Edmund George Valpy**

Evtushenko, Evgeny. *See* **Yevtushenko,
Yevgeny**

Ewart, Gavin
An Old Husband Suspects Adultery.
Anthem: "Our bones will all be built into the
runway."
Bofors A. A. Gun, The.
Christmas Message, A.
Cigarette for the Bambino.
Country Matters.
Deceptive Grin of the Gravel Porters, The.
Dell, The.
Dying Animals, The.
Ella Mi Fu Rapita!
Ending.
Exeter Riddle, An.
Fiction: A Message.
"For Whom the Bell Tolls."
14-Year-Old Convalescent Cat in the Winter,
A.
From V. C. (a Gentleman of Verona).

High Poetic Circles.
Hymn to Proust.
John Betjeman's Brighton.
Larkin Automatic Car Wash, The.
Laureate's Complaint, The.
Lifelines.
Lines: "Other day I was loving a sweet little
fruitpie-and-cream, The."
Love Song: "You've got nice knees."
Lovesleep, The.
Miss Twye.
New Poet Arrives, A.
Officers' Mess.
On First Looking into Michael Grant's *Cities
of Vesuvius.*
On the Tercentenary of Milton's Death.
Pastoral: "Dominic Francis Xavier
Brotherton-Chancery."
Prayer: "Lord I am not entirely selfish."
Psychoanalysis.
Robert Graves.
Sadomasochistic Satisfactions of Seafood,
The.
Short Time.
Sonnet: Dolce Stil Novo.
Sonnet: Equality of the Sexes.
Sonnet: "Point where beauty and intelligence
meet, The."
Sonnet: Supernatural Beings.
Tennysonian Reflections at Barnes Bridge.
They Flee from Me That Sometime Did Me
Seek.
2001: The Tennyson/ Hardy Poem.
Wanting Out.
When a Beau Goes In.
William Wordsworth (1770-1850).
Xmas for the Boys.
Young Blondes.

Ewer, W. N.
Chosen People, The.

Ewing, Annemarie
Sleep, Madame, Sleep.

Ewing, Juliana Horatia
Bluebells.
Burial of the Linnet, The.
Dolls' Wash, The.
For Good Luck.
Friend in the Garden, A.
Garden Lore.
Willow-Man, The.

Exler, Samuel
Cats, The.

Eybers, Elisabeth
Hagar.
Narrative.
Röntgen Photograph.
Sleep-Walking Child.
Snail.

Ezekiel, Nissim
How My Father Died.
Lamentation.
Totem.

Ezekielos of Alexandria
Exodus from Egypt, The.

Ezobi, Joseph
Barren Soul, A, *sel.*

Ezra, Abraham Ibn
My Stars.

F

"F. B. P."
O Mother Dear, Jerusalem.
"F. L. H." *See* **"H., F. L."**
"F. P. A." *See* **Adams, Franklin Pierce**
Faber, Frederick William
All-embracing, The.

Dog, The.
Eternal Years, The.
Expectation, The, *sel.*
God Our Father.
Mundus Morosus.
My God, How Wonderful Thou Art, *sel.*
O Paradise! O Paradise!
Our Lady in the Middle Ages.
Right Is Right.
Right Must Win, The.
There's a Wideness.
World, The.

Faber, Geoffrey
St. Mary's Loch.

Faber, Norma
Hatch, The.

Fabiani, Marta
Poetess, The.

Fabilli, Mary
Letter to Robert.

Fabio, Sarah Webster
All Day We've Longed for Night.
Back into the Garden.
Black Man's Feast.
Chromo.
Evil Is No Black Thing.
To Turn from Love.

Facknitz, Mark A.R.
Topography.

Facos, James
Sonnet: Fable.

Fadiman, Clifton
Jacobean.
Theological.

Fagg, Martin
Burialle of the Dede.
Elegy on Thomas Hood.
When Gaffer be dead for a month or more.

Faidit, Gaucelm
Gaucelm, three plays of love.
Knight once lay beside and with, A.

Fainlight, Harry
Bride, A.

Fainlight, Ruth
Another Full Moon.
Fire-Queen.
God's Language.
Hebrew Sibyl, The.
Lilith.
Other, The.
Sibyl of the Waters.
Sleep-Learning.
Vampire Housewife, The.

Fa'iq, Salah
Poem: "As I traveled from the city."
Poem: "I know/ how fascinated we are with
clarity."
Poem: "If I speak always of the dead."
Poem: "Nothing is more cruel than to see."
Poem: "When the dream departs leaving."

"Fair, C. A."
Chinese Poems: Arthur Waley.

Fairbridge, Wolfe Seymour
Consecration of the House.

Fairburn, Arthur Rex Dugard
Back Street, *sel.*
Beggar to Burgher.
Cave, The.
Conversation in the Bush, *sel.*
Diogenes.
Down on My Luck.
Elements.
Epithalamium: "We have found our peace,
and move with a turning globe."
Estuary, The.
Farewell, A: "What is there left to be said?"
For an Amulet.
Full Fathom Five.
I'm Older than You, Please Listen.
Imperial, *sel.*
Naked Girl Swimming, A.

Possessor, The, *sel.*
Rhyme of the Dead Self.
Solitude.
Tapu.
Terms of Appointment.
Winter Night.

Fairchild, B. H.
Shooting.

Faiz, Faiz Ahmad
Crosses.
Do Not Ask of Me, My Love.
Encounters.
Freedom's Dawn.
I Search Again for a Word Today.
Last Night Your Lost Memory.
Loneliness.
My City.
My Guests.
Nowhere, No Trace Can I Discover.
Poetry's Theme.
Prayer: "Come let us also raise our hands to pray."
Scene.
Smell of Blood, The.
That Day Is Not So Far, My Love.
They Were the Lucky Ones.
To Those Palestinians Martyred in Foreign Lands.
When the Sorrow of My Heart.

Falckner, Justus
Rise, Ye Children.

Falconer, E. J.
Cradle Song at Bethlehem.
Doves.
Elephant, The.
Little Finger Game, A.
Marketing.

Falconer, Raymond
No Voice of Man.

Falconer, William
As the proud horse with costly trappings gay, *sel.*
But now Athenian mountains they descry, *sel.*
Four hours the sun his high meridian throne, *sel.*
Midshipman, The.
Shortening Sail, *sel.*

Faleti, Adebayo
Independence.

Falk, Marcia
Modern Kabbalist.
Shulamit in Her Dreams.
Woman through the Window.

Falke, Gustav
God's Harp.
Strand-Thistle.

Falkner, John Meade
After Trinity.
Arabia.
Christmas Day; the Family Sitting.
Epilogue: "Painted autumn overwhelms, The."

Fallis, Edwina
September.

Fallon, Eunice
August.

Fallon, Padraic
Assumption.
Dardanelles 1916.
Elegy for a Countryman.
For Paddy Mac.
Head, The.
Hedge Schoolmaster, A.
Kiltartan Legend.
Lady Day.
Lakshmi.
Long John.
Mater Dei.
Odysseus.
Out of Soundings.
Painting of My Father.
Pot Shot.

Weir Bridge.
Writing on the Wall.
Young Fenians, The.

Fallon, Peter
My Care.
Spring Song.
Winter Work.

"Falstaff, Jake" (Herman Fetzer)
Beautiful Sunday.

Fan Tseng-hsiang
Before dawn passing Chiang-k'ou town, *sel.*
My good wife was born in the Capital, *sel.*
Within three days we've changed boats twice, *sel.*
Written in a Cool Breeze.

Fandel, John
Bee, The.
Indians.

Fane, Mildmay, Earl of Westmorland. *See* Westmorland, Mildmay Fane, 2d Earl of

Fanning, Ernie
One Red Rose.
Vanishing Valley, The.

Fanshawe, Catherine Maria
Fragment in Imitation of Wordsworth.
Riddle, A: "'Twas in heaven pronounced, and 'twas muttered in hell."

Fanshawe, Sir Richard
Fair Golden Age! When milk was th' onely food, *sel.*
Fall, The, *sel.*
Hope, *sel.*
How I forsook/ Elias and Pisa after, and betook, *sel.*
Learn women all from this housewifery, *sel.*
Ode on His Majesty's Proclamation, *sel.*
Of Beauty, *sel.*
Our beauty is to us that which to men, *sel.*
Rose, A, *sel.*
Well may that kisse be sweet that's giv'n t' a sleek, *sel.*

Fanthorpe, U. A.
At the Ferry.
BC:AD.
Father in the Railway Buffet.
Growing Up.
Not My Best Side.
Reindeer Report.
Resuscitation Team.
What the Donkey Saw.
You Will Be Hearing from Us Shortly.

Faraz, Ahmad
Beirut.
Crucifixion of the Word.
Demon.
Don't Think.
Mercenaries.
Preface: "It's an old story."
Prophecy of the Winds.
Vietnam.
Why Should We Sell Our Dreams?

Farber, Norma
Beyond the Tapestries.
Bow Down, Mountain.
Bye Baby Walnut.
Dove.
Hog at the Manger.
How They Brought the Good News by Sea.
Jubilate Herbis.
Ladybug's Christmas.
Oh the Toe-Test!
Spider.
Sun after Rain.
Winter's Tale.

"Fardd, Ieuan." *See* **Evans, Evan**

Farewell, George
Adieu to My Landlady, An.
Crunking crane heard high amongst the clouds, The, *sel.*
Molly Moor.
Privy-Love for My Landlady.

Quaerè.
There's Life in a Mussel; a Meditation.
To the Archdeacon.

Fargue, Léon-Paul
Boulevard, The.
Fragrance of Night, A.
In a Quarter.
In Yellow Towns.
Muddy Madrigal.
Nocturne: "long arm embossed with gold slides from the tree tops, A."
On the Body.
Tumult.

Farhat, Ilyas
My Burned Suit.
Quatrain: "I saw that thieves had burgled as they do."
Quatrain: "I've learnt to laugh now at adversity."
Quatrain: "Just life and death make up our worldly state."
Quatrain: "My foolish heart keeps beckoning to me."
Quatrain: "O gold, a deep contempt for you I own."
Quatrain: "Seekers of peace, enough hypocrisy!"
Quatrain: "Time promises, should I in that confide?"
Salma.
Wilderness.

Farhi, Musa Moris
God and Nature.
Paths to God.
Smile at Me.
Thirst.
Who Says.

Faricy, Austin
Through Warmth and Light of Summer Skies.

Farjeon, Eleanor
Bedtime.
Blackfriars.
Bliss.
Blow the Stars Home.
C Is for Charms.
Cat.
Cats.
Children's Bells, The.
Children's Carol, The.
Down! Down!
Dragonfly, A.
Elizabeth Cried.
Fairies.
Flower-Seller, The ("The flower-seller's fat").
For a Mocking Voice.
For Snow.
Geography.
Hallowe'en.
Hey! My Pony!
Holly and Mistletoe.
In the Week When Christmas Comes.
Jenny White and Johnny Black.
Keeping Christmas.
Kingfisher.
Kitten, A.
Lewis Carroll.
Light the Lamps Up, Lamplighter!
Moon-Come-Out.
Mrs. Malone.
Mrs. Peck-Pigeon.
Night Will Never Stay, The.
Pencil and Paint.
Poetry.
Quarrel, The.
School-Bell.
Sisters.
Tailor.
There Are Big Waves.
There Isn't Time.
Vegetables.
Wheelbarrow.

White Horses.
Window Boxes ("A window box of pansies").
Witch, The! The Witch!
Yawning.
Z Is for Zoroaster.

Farley, Henry
Bounty of Our Age, The.

Farmer, Philip José
Pterodactyl, The.

Farnham, Jessie
Garland for a Storyteller.

"Farningham, Marianne" (Mary Ann Hearn)
God Cares.
Last Hymn, The.

Farnsworth, Robert
Sketch.

Farooqi, Saqi
Alchemy.
Dog Poem, A.
Morning Sounds.
Sher Imdad Ali's Tadpole.
Spider.
Yearning for the Shore.

Farrar, Janice
Thought of Marigolds, A.

Farrar, John Chipman
Brest Left Behind.
Comparison, A.
Parenthood.
Roller Skates.
Time Is Today, The.
Victorian Song.

Farrell, J. R.
Bank Thief, The.

Farren, Robert
Lineage.
Stable Straw.
While now I lay me down to sleep, *sel.*

Farren, Robert (Roibéard O'Faracháin)
Cool Gold Wines of Paradise, The.
Immolation.

Farrokhzad, Forugh
Born Again.
I Feel Sorry for the Garden.
I'm Sad.
In the land of dwarfs.
Mechanical Doll.
O Realm Bejewelled.
On Earth.
Once More.
Someone like No One Else.
Window, A.

Fatchen, Max
So Big!

Fauset, Jessie Redmond
Christmas Eve in France.
Dead Fires.
Enigma.
Fragment: "Breath of life imbued those few dim days, The."
La Vie C'est la Vie.
Noblesse Oblige.
Oblivion.
Oriflamme.
Rencontre.
Return, The.
Touché.
Words! Words!

Faverey, Hans
Chrysanthemums, Rowers ("The chrysanthemums// that stand in the vase on the table").
First the Message Kills.
Staring at an Empty Space.

Fawcett, Brian
Hand, The.

Fawcett, Edgar
Fireflies.

Fawcett, Joseph
Feast of Blood, The, *sel.*

Fawkes, Francis
Elegy on the Death of Dobbin, the Butterwoman's Horse, An.

Fazio degli Uberti
Of England, and of Its Marvels.

Fearing, Kenneth
American Rhapsody.
Any Man's Advice to His Son.
C Stands for Civilization.
Confession Overheard in a Subway.
Cultural Notes.
Dirge: "1-2-3 was the number he played but today the number came 3-2-1."
Elegy in a Theatrical Warehouse.
End of the Seers' Convention.
Evening Song.
Green Light.
Love, 20 Cents the First Quarter Mile.
Lullaby: "Wide as this night, old as this night is old and young as it is young."
Memo.
Minnie and Mrs. Hoyne.
No Credit.
Obituary.
Operative No. 174 Resigns.
Pact.
Pay-off.
People vs. the People, The.
Portrait.
Readings, Forecasts, Personal Guidance.
Requiem.
Resurrection.
Tomorrow.
Twentieth-Century Blues.
Yes, the Agency Can Handle That.

Fearne, Flora
Little Men, The.

Fefer, Itsik
Dead Gentile women in greatcoats.
I've Never Been Lost.
So what if I've been circumcised.

Fei Ma
Drunkard, A.
Night Flute.
One Thousand and One Arabian Nights.
Television.
Typhoon Season, A.
Yellow River.

Fein, Cheri
Obscene Caller, The.

Feinman, Alvin
November Sunday Morning.

Feinstein, Elaine
Against Winter.
Calliope in the Labour Ward.
Coastline.
Dad.
June.
Lais.
Magic Apple Tree, The.
Marriage.
Medium, The.
Night Thoughts.
Patience.
Quiet War in Leicester, A.
Survivors.
Under Stone.

Feinstein, Martin
Burning Bush.

Feinstein, Robert N.
Heaven Can't Wait.
Uneasy Riders.
Woolly Words.

Feiritear, Piaras
Lay your weapons down, young lady.

Feirstein, Frederick
L'Art.

Feld, M. D.
Villanelle: "You cannot rest behind the plate."

Feldman, Irving
Curse, A.
Death of Vitellozzo Vitelli, The.
Double, The.
Gymnasts, The.
Little Lullaby.
My Olson Elegy.
Old Men, The.
Pripet Marshes, The.
Scene of a Summer Morning.

Feldman, Ruth
Lilith.

Feldman, Susan
How the Invalids Make Love.
Intruder.
Lamentations of an Au Pair Girl.
Sea Legs.

Fell, Alison
Significant Fevers.

Felltham, Owen
On the Duke of Buckingham, Slain by Felton, the 23rd August, 1628.

Fenollosa, Ernest Francisco
Golden Age, The.

Fenton, Elizabeth
Masks.
Under the Ladder to Heaven.

Fenton, James
Dead Soldiers.
German Requiem, A.
God, A Poem.
Kingsfisher's Boxing Gloves, The.
Pitt-Rivers Museum, Oxford, The.
This Octopus Exploits Women.
Wind.

Fenton, James and John Fuller
Poem against Catholics.

Ferebe, George
Houseless Downs, The, *sel.*

Fergus, Howard
Ethnocide.
Forecast.
Lament for Maurice Bishop.

Ferguson, James
Auld Daddy Darkness.

Ferguson, Roy
Island of Rhum, The.

Ferguson, Sir Samuel
Abdication of Fergus Mac Roy, The.
Aideen's Grave.
At the Polo-Ground.
Burial of King Cormac, The.
Fairy Thorn, The.
Lament for the Death of Thomas Davis.

Fergusson, Robert
Braid Claith.
Daft Days, The.
Epigram on a Lawyer's Desiring One of the Tribe to Look with Respect to a Gibbet.
Ghaists; a Kirk-yard Eclogue, The.
Hallow-Fair.
My Winsome Dear, *sel.*
Rising of the Session, The.
Sow of Feeling, The.

Ferland, Barbara
Ave Maria.
Expect No Turbulence.
Orange.

Ferlinghetti, Lawrence
Away above a harborful, *sel.*
Baseball Canto.
Christ Climbed Down.
Constantly risking absurdity, *sel.*
Crazy/ to be alive in such a strange.
Dada would have liked a day like this, *sel.*
Dog.
Don't Let That Horse.
Frightened/ by the sound of my own voice, *sel.*
Funny Fantasies Are Never So Real as Oldstyle, *sel.*

He.
I Am Waiting.
I am waiting for my case to come up, *sel.*
In Golden Gate Park That Day, *sel.*
In Goya's Greatest Scenes We Seem to See.
Lost Parents.
Monet's Lilies Shuddering.
One Thousand Fearful Words for Fidel
   Castro.
Pennycandystore beyond the El, The, *sel.*
People Getting Divorced.
Phoenix at Fifty, A.
Photo of Emily, The.
Poet's yes obscenely seeing, The, *sel.*
Pound at Spoleto.
Retired Ballerinas, Central Park West.
Sarolla's women in their picture hats, *sel.*
Sea and Ourselves at Cape Ann, The.
Sometime during eternity, *sel.*
Terrible/ a horse at night.
This life is not a circus where, *sel.*
True Confessional.
Underwear.
Wounded wilderness of Morris Graves, The,
   sel.

Fernández, Abraham
If You Happy Would Be.

Fernández, Teresita
Every Day that I Love You.
Ugly Things.

Fernández Moreno, Baldomero
Castillian Mother Speaks, The.

Ferne, Doris
Light as a leaping faun!
Sounding.

Ferrarelli, Rina
Joan Benoit.

Ferré, Rosario
Envoi: "To my mother, and to my mother's
   monument."
I Hear You've Let Go.

Ferrett, Mabel
John Douglas White.
Wartime Report Centre: Solo School.

Ferril, Thomas Hornsby
Always Begin Where You Are.
House in Denver.
Morning Star.
Swallows.
Train Butcher, The.
Waltz against the Mountains.
Wood.

Ferriter, Pierce
He Charges Her to Lay Aside Her Weapons.
Lay Your Arms Aside.

Ferry, David
At the Bus Stop: Eurydice.
Beach at Evening, The.
Cythera.
Ellery Street.
Rereading Old Writing.

Fertig, Nelle
I Have Come to the Conclusion.

Fessenden, Thomas Green
Ye Sons of Columbia.

Fet [or Foeth], Afanasi Afanasievich
Breathing seems much easier at nighttime.
Butterfly.
By the Fireside.
Morning Song.
My dear, mere words have no power.
Never.
Old Park, The.
Stars glowed red in leaf-still weather, The.
To the Muse ("Is it for long you deign to visit
   my seclusion").
To the Muse ("You came, were seated. Happy
   and uplifted").
Up in the hay one evening, darkling.

Fetherling, Doug
Bathing with Father.

Dialogues 4 1 Voice Only.
Diseases of the Moon.
Dispatch Number Nine.
Dispatch Number Sixteen.
Dispatch Number Sixty.
Elijah Speaking.
Explorers as Seen by the Natives.
Genius Loci of the Morning.
Nights Passed on Ward's Island, Toronto
   Harbour.
Sex Play in Four Acts.
Shacked Up at the Ritz.
She Employed the Familiar "Tu" Form.
Your Absence Has Not Taught Me.

Fetzer, Herman. *See* **"Falstaff, Jake."**

Fewster, Ernest
Cliff Rose, The.
Pearly Everlasting, The.

Fiacc, Padraic
Boy and the Geese, The.
Deranged.
Gloss.
Goodbye to Brigid / An Agnus Dei.
Haemorrhage.
Introit.
Poet, The.
Stolen Fifer, The.

Fiamengo, Marya
In Praise of Old Women.

Fiawoo, F. K.
Soliloquy on Death.

Fichman, Jacob [or Jakov]
Abishag.
Eve.
In the Old City.

Ficke, Arthur Davison
Father.
Perspective of Co-ordination.
Wave Symphony, The, *sel.*

Fiedler, Barbara
Origins.

Fiedler, Leslie A.
Dumb Dick.
No Ghost Is True.

Field, Edward
Bride of Frankenstein, The.
Curse of the Cat Woman.
Event, An.
Floor Is Dirty, The.
Frankenstein.
Mae West.
My Polish Grandma.
Sleeper, The.
Snowfish, The.
Sonja Henie Sonnet.
Tulips and Addresses.
Unwanted.
View of Jersey, A.
What Grandma Knew.
World War II.
Yiskidor, when he dies I won't know the
   Hebrew words to say, *sel.*

Field, Eugene
Angel's Visit, The.
April Fool, The.
Bachelor Hall.
Bethlehem Town.
Bibliomaniac's Prayer, The.
Boy, The.
Christmas Eve.
Christmas Song, at.
Clink of the Ice, The.
Dibdin's Ghost.
Dinkey-Bird, The.
Dream-Ship, The.
Dreams, The.
Duel, The.
Garden and Cradle.
In the Firelight.
Japanese Lullaby.
Jest 'fore Christmas.

Johnny's Team.
Little Boy Blue.
Little Peach, The.
Lyttel Boy, The.
Mr. Billings of Louisville.
Night Wind, The.
Nightfall in Dordrecht.
Norse Lullaby.
Our Biggest Fish.
Our Two Opinions.
Piazza Tragedy, A.
Rock-a-by Lady, The.
Sioux, The.
Sugar-Plum Tree, The.
Three Kings, The.
To a Soubrette.
Truth about Horace, The.
Two Coffins, The.
Two Meetings, The.
Wynken, Blynken, and Nod.

"Field, Michael" (Katharine Bradley *and*
   Edith Cooper)
After Mass.
And on My Eyes Dark Sleep by
   Night.
Aridity.
Bury Her at Even.
Come, Gorgo, put the rug in place, *sel.*
Cyclamens.
Descent from the Cross.
Dying Viper, A.
Gold Is the Son of Zeus: Neither Moth nor
   Worm May Gnaw It.
If They Honoured Me, Giving Me Their
   Gifts.
Macrinus against Trees.
Maids, not to you my mind doth change, *sel.*
Noon.
Sweeter Far than the Harp, More Gold than
   Gold.
To the Lord Love.
Tragic Mary Queen of Scots, The.
Whym Chow.

Field, Nathaniel
Rise, Lady Mistress, Rise!, *sel.*

Field, Rachel Lyman
Animal Store, The.
At the Theater.
Barefoot Days.
City Lights.
Dancing Bear, The.
Doorbells.
Elfin Town.
Epilogue: "Nothing now to mark the spot,"
   sel.
Equestrienne, *sel.*
Green Riders.
Gunga, *sel.*
Gypsies.
Ice-Cream Man, The.
I'd Like to Be a Lighthouse.
If Once You Have Slept on an
   Island.
Little Rose Tree, The.
Manhattan Lullaby.
My Inside-Self.
Parade, *sel.*
Performing Seal, The, *sel.*
Picnic Day.
Playhouse Key, The.
Pointed People, The.
Roads.
Seven Ages of Elf-hood, The.
Skyscrapers.
Some People.
Something Told the Wild Geese.
Song for a Blue Roadster.

Summer Morning, A.
Taxis.
Field, Thomas
Common Sense.
Fielding, Henry
Hunting Song, *sel.*
Fields, Annie
Cedar Mountain.
Little Guinever.
On Waking from a Dreamless Sleep.
Return, The.
"Song to the Gods, Is Sweetest Sacrifice."
Theocritus.
Fields, James Thomas
Alarmed Skipper, The.
Ballad of the Tempest.
Jupiter and Ten.
On a Watchman Asleep at Midnight.
Owl-Critic, The.
Song of the Turtle and the Flamingo, The.
With Wordsworth at Rydal.
Fields, Julia
Aardvark.
Alabama.
Birmingham, *sel.*
Black Students.
Harlem in January.
High on the Hog.
I play the Masonic Funeral March, *sel.*
Moths, *sel.*
No Time for Poetry.
Poem for Heroes, A.
Fieldson, Jr., Eugene
Colorado Sand Storm, A.
Figueroa, John
At Home the Green Remains.
Birth Is.
Portrait of a Woman (and a Man).
Figueroa, R. Olivares
Sower, The.
Figueroa-Aymerich, Angela
Destiny.
Market Women.
Mothers.
Women at the Market.
Filicaia, Vincenzo da
Italy.
Finch, Anne, Countess of Winchilsea. *See*
Winchilsea, Anne Finch, Countess of
Finch, Anne (b. 1908)
Essay on Marriage.
O, love, in your sweet name enough, *sel.*
Finch, Francis Miles
Blue and the Gray, The.
Nathan Hale.
Finch, Robert
Alone.
Aria Senza da Capo.
Collective Portrait, The.
Crib, The.
Egg-and-Dart.
Last Visit.
Lost Tribe, The.
Mountain, The.
Network, The.
Peacock and Nightingale.
Rhenish Carol, A.
Room.
Silverthorn Bush.
Statue, The.
Time's Bright Sand.
Train Window.
Turning.
Words.
Finch, Vivienne
Earthquake Somewhere Else, An.
Green Ice.
Inertia.
Journey, The.
On Being Stone.

Finkel, Donald
Cain's Song.
Clothing's New Emperor, The.
Cross-eyed Lover, The.
Crumbs.
Enough.
Esthetic of Imitation, An.
Feeding the Fire.
Finders Keepers.
Flagpole Sitter, The.
Genealogy.
Gesture.
Give Way.
Hands.
How Things Fall.
Hunting Song.
Imbecile, The.
Joyful Noise, A.
Juan Belmonte, Torero.
King Midas Has Asses' Ears.
Lame Angel.
Letter to My Daughter at the End of Her
  Second Year.
Lilith.
Metaphysic of Snow.
Oracle.
Sirens, The.
Solo for Bent Spoon.
Spring Song.
Target Practice.
Time Out.
Waiting for the Wind.
Finkelstein, Caroline
My Father's Store.
Finkle, Donald
Interview with a Winner.
Finlay, Ian Hamilton
Classical warfare, *sel.*
Dancers Inherit the Party, The.
Finley, John
Birthday Prayer, A.
Finnigan, Joan
Stoop on the log-house is brown with sweet
  rain-rot, The, *sel.*
Finnin, Olive Mary
Farm near Norman's Lane, The.
Fiore, Marianna
You Opened a Door.
Firdausi (Abul Kasim Mansor)
Alas for Youth.
Dream of Dakiki, The.
When the Sword of Sixty Comes Nigh His
  Head.
Firer, Susan
Miss Summerfest.
Night Game in Menomonie Park, A.
Firestone, Laya
Crow, Straight Flier, but Dark.
For Gabriel.
Listen to the Bird.
Thoughts for My Grandmother.
Firsoff, Axel
Spirit of the Cairngorms, The.
Fischer, Helen Field
Mystic Borderland, The.
Fischer, Joseph C.
Kind of Thanks, A, *sel.*
Fischer, Otakar
From the Depths.
Fishback, Margaret
Complacent Cliff-Dweller, The.
In Extremis.
Sentimental Lines to a Young Man Who
  Favors Pink Wallpaper While I Personally
  Lean to the Blue.
Sitting Pretty.
Thoughts of Loved Ones.
Fisher, Aileen
At Night.
Birthday Cake.
But I Wonder.

Cat in the Snow.
Christmas Tree.
Houses.
I Like It When It's Mizzly.
June.
Light the Festive Candles.
Listening.
Little Talk.
Merry Christmas.
Mouse Dinner.
On Halloween.
On Mother's Day.
Open House.
Pussy Willows.
Raccoons.
Raindrops.
Seed, The.
Snail's Pace.
Wearing of the Green.
Wings.
Fisher, Archie
Final Trawl, The.
Fisher, David
Analyst.
Birds of Arles, The.
Child's Christmas without Jean Cocteau, A.
Death of Rimbaud.
Emergency Room, The.
Harvest Poem.
Junkie with a Flute in the Rain, A.
Keepsake Corporation, The.
Lost.
Mutilated Soldier, The.
Mycenae.
Old Man, The.
On the Esplanade des Invalides.
Pastor Speaks Out, The.
Rehearsal.
Retarded Class at F. A. O. Schwarz's
  Celebrates Christmas, The.
Teacher, The.
Vietnamese Girl in the Madhouse, The.
Why Do You Want to Suffer Less.
Fisher, Ed
Talk of the Town, The.
Fisher, Harrison
Controls, The.
White Zombie.
Fisher, K.
Story of the Corn.
Fisher, Mahlon Leonard
In Cool, Green Haunts.
Fisher, Robert
Minotaur.
Monster Alphabet.
Phoenix, The.
Fisher, Roy
As He Came near Death.
Entertainment of War, The.
Fisher, Salih Michael
Assumption about the Harlem Brown Baby.
Fisher, Sally
My Early Religious Education.
Fisher, I.H. *See* "**Hume, Isobel**"
Fishman, Rachel
Even If.
In the Beginning.
Fiske, John
Upon the Decease of Mrs. Anne Griffin.
Upon the Much-to Be Lamented Desease of
  the Reverend Mr. John Cotton.
Fitch, Eleazar Thompson
By Vows of Love Together Bound *with
  music.*
Lord, at This Closing Hour.
Fitch, Robert
High Brow.
Fitger, Arthur
Evening Prayer.

Fitton, Molly
When fog come creepin' over Beccles.
Fitts, Dudley
Southwest Passage.
Ya Se Van Los Pastores.
Fitz-Geffry [or Fitzgeffrey], Charles
Bee, The, *sel.*
Take Frankincense, O God, *sel.*
Fitzgerald, Edward
Old Song.
Fitzgerald, F. Scott (Francis Scott Key Fitzgerald)
Football.
Obit on Parnassus.
There'd be an orchestra, *sel.*
Vampires Won't Vampire for Me, The.
Fitzgerald, Gerald, 4th Earl of Desmond. *See* Desmond, Gerald Fitzgerald, 4th Earl of
Fitzgerald, Pierce (Piaras Mac Gearailt)
Answer to Thomas Barry, An.
Fitzgerald, Robert
Cobb Would Have Caught It.
Entreaty.
Errantry.
History.
Imprisoned, The.
Jesu, Joy of Man's Desiring.
July in Indiana.
Metaphysical.
Metaphysician.
Midsummer.
Miraculously, through prayer to Saint Anthony, *sel.*
Mise en Scène.
Patrum Propositum.
Queens, The.
Shore of Life, The.
Song for September.
Souls Lake.
Fitzgerald, Robert David
Back from the Paved Way.
Bog and Candle.
Edge.
Face of the Waters, The.
Favour.
Macquarie Place.
1918-1941.
Rain in my ears: impatiently there raps, *sel.*
Wind at Your Door, The.
Fitzgerald, Thomas
Upon an Ingenious Friend, Over-Vain.
Fitzgerald, Zelda Sayre
I Do Love My Charlie So.
Over the Top with Pershing.
Fitzherbert, Sir Anthony
Memorial Verses for Travellers, *sel.*
Fitzpatrick, Kevin
Sneaking in the State Fair.
FitzRoy, Olivia
Fleet Fighter.
Toast.
When He Is Flying.
Fitzsimon, Henry
Swearing.
Flaccus
Epigram: "Just as he is growing a beard."
Flagg, James Montgomery *and* **Julian Street.**
See **Street, Julian** *and* **James Montgomery Flagg**
Flaischlen, Cäsar
Most Quietly at Times.
Flanders, Jane
Other Lives of the Romantics.
Flanders, Michael
First and Second Law.
Hummingbird, The.
Walrus, The.
Flanner, Hildegarde
Hawk Is a Woman.
Hearing a sound that may be thy return, *sel.*
Let Us Believe.

Memo.
Prayer for This Day.
Swift Love, Sweet Motor.
Thee sets a bell to swinging in my soul, *sel.*
This Day.
Flantz, Richard
Shir Ma'alot/ A Song of Degrees.
Flanzbaum, Hilene
Schools and Schoolmasters.
Flash, Henry Lynden
Gallant Fifty-one, The.
Stonewall Jackson.
Zollicoffer.
Flatman, Thomas
Appeal to Cats in the Business of Love, An.
Death.
Defiance, The.
Nudus Redibo.
On Marriage.
Sad Day, The.
Thought of Death, A.
Unconcerned, The.
Flavell, Thomas
County of Mayo, The, *at.*
Flax, Hjalmar
Art.
Littoral.
Flecker, James Elroy
And how beguile you? Death has no repose, *sel.*
Ballad of Hampstead Heath, The.
Ballad of the Londoner.
Brumana.
Epilogue: "Away, for we are ready to a man!," *sel.*
Epithalamion: "Smile then, children, hand in hand."
From Grenoble.
Gates of Damascus.
Hammam Name, The.
Hassan's Serenade, *sel.*
In Hospital.
Inscription for Arthur Rackham's Rip Van Winkle.
No Coward's Song.
Old Ships, The.
Oxford Canal.
Painter's Mistress, The.
Parrot, The.
Prayer: "Let me not know how sins and sorrows glide."
Prologue: "We who with songs beguile your pilgrimage," *sel.*
Queen's Song, The.
Rioupéroux.
Saadabad.
Santorin.
Ship, an Isle, a Sickle Moon, A.
Stillness.
Tenebris Interlucentem.
To a Poet a Thousand Years Hence.
Town without a Market, The.
War Song of the Saracens, *sel.*
Welsh Sea, The.
Flecknoe, Richard
Invocation of Silence.
Noble Love.
On the Death of Our Lord.
Fleg, Edmond
Dead Cities Speak to the Living Cities, The.
End of Sorrow, The, *sel.*
Wandering Jew Comes to the Wall, The, *sel.*
Fleming, Elizabeth
Balloon Seller, The.
Fires.
Hedgehog and His Coat, The.
Hurdy-Gurdy Man, The.
If I Were a Pig.
In the Mirror.
Lavender Bush, The.
Old Mrs. Jarvis.

Patchwork Quilt, The.
Secret, The.
Toadstools.
Who's In.
Window Cleaner, The.
Fleming, Marjory
Melancholy Lay, A.
On Jessy Watson's Elopement.
Sonnet on a Monkey, A.
Fleming, Maybury
To Demeter.
To Sleep.
What Though the Green Leaf Grow?
Fletcher, Bob
Love Dirge to the Whitehouse, A.
Fletcher, Curley W.
Cowboy's Prayer, The.
Flyin' Outlaw, The.
High-loping Cowboy, The.
Strawberry Roan, The.
Fletcher, Giles, the Elder
Are Those Two Stars, *sel.*
First Did I Fear, *sel.*
I wish sometimes, although a worthlesse thing, *sel.*
In time [*or* tyme] the strong and stately [*or* statelie] turrets fall, *sel.*
Like [*or* Lyke] Memnons rock, touched [*or* rocke toucht] with the rising sun[ne], *sel.*
Sad, All Alone, Not Long I Musing Sat, *sel.*
Fletcher, Giles, the Younger
Christ's Triumph after Death, IV, *sel.*
Christ's Victory in Heaven, I, *sel.*
Christ's Victory on Earth, II, *sel.*
Fletcher, John
Arm, Arm, Arm, Arm!, *sel.*
Beauty clear and fair, *sel.*
Bloody Brother, The.
Care-charming Sleep [Thou Easer of All Woes], *sel.*
Come Hither, You That Love.
Come, Shepherds, Come!, *sel.*
Dead Host's Welcome, The, *sel.*
God Lyaeus, Ever Young, *sel.*
God of Sheep, The, *sel.*
Hear, Ye Ladies [That Despise], *sel.*
Let the bells ring, and let the boys sing, *sel.*
Love's Emblems.
Melancholy, *sel.*
Merciless love, whom nature hath denied, *sel.*
Now the Lusty Spring [Is Here], *sel.*
O divine star of heaven, *sel.*
Orpheus I am, come from the deeps below, *sel.*
Priest's Chant, The, *sel.*
River God, The ("I am this fountain's god"), *sel.*
River-God's Song, The ("Do not fear to put thy feet"), *sel.*
Satyr's Farewell, The, *sel.*
Satyr's Song, *sel.*
Sing his praises that doth keep, *sel.*
Song in the Wood, *sel.*
Song: "Oh [*or* O] fair[e] sweet face, oh [*or* O] eyes celestial[l] bright," *sel.*
Weep No More, *sel.*
Fletcher, John *and* **William Shakespeare**
Bridal Song, A ("Roses, their sharp spines being gone"), *sel.*
Hail Sovereign Queen of secrets, who hast power, *sel.*
Urns and Odours Bring Away!, *sel.*
Fletcher, John *and* **William Rowley**
Now having leisure, and a happy wind, *sel.*
Fletcher, John Gould
Before Olympus.
Down the Mississippi.
Elegy on a Nordic White Protestant.
Flickering of incessant rain, *sel.*
Green Symphony.
Last Judgment.
Lincoln.

London Nightfall.
Monadnock, The.
Morning is clean and blue and the wind blows up the clouds, The, *sel.*
O seeded grass, you army of little men, *sel.*
Over the roof-tops race the shadows of clouds, *sel.*
Rebel, A.
Skaters, The.
Song of the Moderns.
There was a darkness in this man, *sel.*
Trees, like great jade elephants, The, *sel.*

Fletcher, Louisa
Land of Beginning Again, The.

Fletcher, Phineas
All-seeing Intellect, The, *sel.*
Cambridge and the Cam, *sel.*
Desiderium, *sel.*
Fisher-lad, A (no higher dares he look), *sel.*
Hymn: "Drop, drop, slow tears."
Lines Written at Cambridge, to W. R., Esquire, *sel.*
Me, Lord? Canst thou mispend.
Of Men, nay Beasts: worse, Monsters: worst of all, *sel.*
Overthrow of Lucifer, The, *sel.*
Sin, Despair, and Lucifer, *sel.*
Song: "Fond men! whose wretched care the life soon ending," *sel.*
Woman's Inconstancy, *sel.*

Fletcher, Robert H.
Drinking Song, *sel.*
Take, Oh, Take Those Lips Away, *sel.*

Flexner, Hortense
Contemporary.

Flexner, James
In the Hours of Darkness.

Flint, Annie Johnson
At the Place of the Sea.
Blessings That Remain, The.
"Daily with You."
Everlasting Love, The.
He Giveth More.
His Will Be Done.
Hitherto and Henceforth.
In Him.
Old Year and the New, The.
Our Father's Hand.
Passing Through.
Pray—Give—Go.
This Moment.
Thou Remainest.
We See Jesus.
What God Hath [*or* Has] Promised!
Word of God, The.

Flint, Francis Stewart
Eau-Forte.
Prayer: "As I walk through the streets."

Flint, James
In Pleasant Lands Have Fallen the Lines.

Flint, Roland
August from My Desk.

Flood, John
To His Coy Mistress.

Flook, Maria
Discreet.

Flores, Manuel M.
Eve.

Flores, Marco Antonio
Kekchi Warrior.

Florio, John
Of Books.

Flower, Robin
Troy.

Flynn, Desirée (Sheila Desirée Savory Rodd)
Collector, The.
From the Rain Forest.

Flynn, Elizabeth
After Grave Deliberation.

Fodor, Andras
Field Hospital, 1945.
Your Body's Bread.

Foeth, Afanasi Afanasievich. *See* **Fet, Afanasi Afanasievich**

Fogel, Ephim G.
Shipment to Maidanek.

Fogle, Richard Harter
Hawthorne Garland, A.

Folcachiero de' Folcachieri
Canzone: He Speaks of His Condition through Love.

Foley, James William
Drop a Pebble in the Water.
Song of Summer Days.

Folger, Peleg
Praise Ye the Lord. O Celebrate His Fame.

Folgore da San Gemignano. *See* **San Geminiano, Folgore da**

Folk, Pat
Empty Holds a Question.
Senile.

Follain, Jean
Child's Blackness.
Dog with Schoolboys.
Egg, The.
End of a Century.
Eve.
Evening Suit, The.
Evenings of Ink.
Landscape of a Child on His Way to the Place of the Regents.
Life.
October Thoughts.
Voluntary Mutilation.

Follen, Eliza Lee (Cabot)
Good Moolly Cow, The.
Lord, Deliver, Thou Canst Save.
Oh! Look at the Moon.
Three Little Kittens, The, *at.*

Fondane, Benjamin
By the Waters of Babylon.
Hertza.
Lullaby for an Emigrant.
Plain Song.
Wandering Jew, The.

Fonte Boa, Maria Amalia
Vitality.

Foot, Edward Edwin
Long live our dear and noble Queen, *sel.*

Foote, Lucius Harwood
Derelict, The.
Don Juan.
El Vaquero.
On the Heights.
Poetry.

Foote, Samuel
Great Panjandrum Himself, The.

Foott, Mary Hannay
Where the Pelican Builds.

Forbes, Calvin
Chocolate Soldiers, The.
Gabriel's Blues.
Lullaby for Ann-Lucian.
M. A. P.
Other Side of This World, The.
Reading Walt Whitman.
Some Pieces.

Forbes, John
Four Heads & How to Do Them.
TV.

Forché, Carolyn
As Children Together.
Because One Is Always Forgotten.
Burning the Tomato Worms.
City Walk-up, Winter 1969.
Colonel, The.
Departure.
Dulcimer Maker.
Endurance.
For the Stranger.

Kalaloch.
Memory of Elena, The.
On Returning to Detroit.
Photograph of My Room.
Reunion.
Selective Service.
Taking Off My Clothes.
Visitor, The.

Ford, Charles Henri
Bad Habit, The.
January wraps up the wound of his arm.
Overturned Lake, The.
Plaint.
Somebody's Gone.
There's No Place to Sleep in This Bed, Tanguy.

Ford, Ford Madox (*originally* **Ford Madox Hueffer**)
Old Houses of Flanders, The.
On Heaven.
Sanctuary, The.
Sidera Cadentia.
Unwritten Song, The.
What the Orderly Dog Saw.
"When the World Was in Building."

Ford, Gena
Legacy.
Lines for a Hard Time.
Nude on the Bathroom Wall, The.

Ford, John
Beasts onely capable of sense, enjoy, *sel.*
Can You Paint a Thought?, *sel.*
Dawn, *sel.*
If thou canst wake with me, forget to eate, *sel.*
Minutes are numbered by the fall of sands, *sel.*
Oh [*or* O], no more, no more, too late, *sel.*
Song, A: "Glories, pleasures, pomps, delights, and ease," *sel.*
There is a place,/ List, daughter! in a black and hollow vault, *sel.*

Ford, Mary A.
Hundred Years from Now, A.

Ford, Robert
Bonniest Bairn in a' the Warl', The.

Ford, Robert Arthur Douglas
Back to Dublin.
Earthquake.
Lynx.
Revenge of the Hunted.
Sakhara.
Twenty Below.
Window on the North, A.

Ford, Thomas
There Is a Lady Sweet and Kind, *at.*

Fordham, Mary Weston
Alaska.
Atlanta Exposition Ode.
Bells of St. Michael.
"By the Rivers of Babylon."
Cherokee, The.
Chicago Exposition Ode.
Christ Child, The.
Coming Woman, The.
Creation.
Crucifixion, The.
Death of a Grandparent. Mrs. Jennette Bonneau.
Dedicated to the Right Rev'd D. A. Payne.
Dying Girl, The.
Exile's Reverie, The.
For Who?
Grafted Bud, The.
Highland Mary.
In Memoriam. Alphonse Campbell Fordham.

In Memoriam. Susan Eugenia Bennett.
June.
Lines To———: "O come to me in my
  dreams love!"
Lines to Florence.
Lines to Mrs. Isabel Peace.
Magnolia.
Maiden and River.
Marriage.
Mother's Recall.
Mr. Edward Fordham.
Mrs. E. Cohrs Brown.
Mrs. Louise B. Weston.
Mrs. Mary Furman Weston Byrd.
Mrs. Rebecca Weston.
Nativity, The.
Nestle-down Cottage.
October.
Ode to Peace.
On Parting with a Friend.
Passing of the Old Year.
Past, The.
Pen, The.
Queenie.
Rally Song.
Requiem, A.
Rev. Samuel Weston.
Reverie, A.
Saxon Legend of Language, The.
Serenade: "Sleep, love sleep."
Shipwreck.
Snow Storm, The.
Snowdrop, The.
Song to Erin.
Sonnet to My First Born.
Stars and Stripes.
Sunset.
To a Loved One.
To an Infant.
To My Mother.
To Rev. Thaddeus Saltus.
To the Eagle.
To the Mock-Bird.
Tribute to a Lost Steamer.
Tribute to Capt. F. W. Dawson.
Twilight Musings.
Uranne.
Valentine, The.
Washerwoman, The.

Foresman, Rebecca
If.

"Forester, Fanny" (Emily Chubbuck Judson)
Lowly Bard, The.
My Bird.
Watching.
Weaver, The.

Forgaill, Dallán
Poem in Praise of Colum Cille, A, at.

Forman, Nicole
Labour of the Brain, Ballad of the Body.

Forrest, Frederick
St. Anthony and His Pig; a Cantata.

Forrest, William
Marigold, The.
New Ballade of the Marigolde, A.

Forrester, Alfred A. ("Alfred Crowquill")
To My Nose.

Forster, Frederick J.
Lobsters and the Fiddler Crab, The ("The
  lobsters came ashore one night").

Forster, William
In New South Wales, as I plainly see, *sel.*
Love Has Eyes.
Poor of London, The.
Sonnet on the Crimean War.

Forsyth, James
Artillery Shoot.
Soldier's Dove.
To My Wife.

Forsyth, Sarah
My Christmas; Mum's Christmas.

Fort, Paul
Ballade: "Pretty maid she died, she died, in
  love-bed as she lay, The."
Pan and the Cherries.
Sailor and the Shark, The.

Forten, Charlotte
Parting Hymn, A.
Poem: "In the earnest path of duty."
To W. L. G. on Reading His "Chosen Queen."

Fortini, Franco
Bitter Winter.
Communism.
Deportation Order.
English Cemetery, The.
For Our Soldiers Who Fell in Russia.
Guests, The.
Gutter, The.
In Memoriam I.
In Memoriam II.
In Santa Croce.
Letter.
Present, The.
To Friends.

Fortney, Steven
Playing Solitaire.

Fortunatus. *See* **Venantius Fortunatus,**
  Saint.

Foscolo, Ugo
My Father's Death.
Self-Portrait.

Fosdick, Harry Emerson
O God, in Restless Living.
Prince of Peace His Banner Spreads, The.

Foss, Sam Walter
Bring me men to match my mountains, *sel.*
Calf-Path, The.
Higher Catechism, The.
House by the Side of the Road, The.
"Hullo!"
Husband and Heathen.
Ideal Husband to His Wife, The.
Man from the Crowd, The.
Philosopher, A.
Town of Hay, The.

Foster, Jeanne Robert
John Butler Yeats.
William P. Frye, The.

Foster, Stephen Collins
Camptown Races, The.
Jeanie with the Light Brown Hair.
Massa's in de Cold Cold Ground.
My Old Kentucky Home, [Good Night]
Oh! [*or* O] Susanna.
Old Black Joe.
Old Folks at Home, The.
Who Has Our Redeemer Heard.

Foulke, William Dudley
City's Crown, The.
Land of my heart,/ What future is before
  thee?, *sel.*
Life's Evening.

Foulkes, William H.
Take Thou Our Minds, Dear Lord.

Fourtouni, Eleni
Eurynome.

Fowler, Alastair
Fitting.
Happy.
Love's Promises.
Nature Morte.
Our Love Is Made, Your Heavy Head.
That Fabulous Nebula.
Two Hundred Unborn Lambs.

Fowler, Andrew
Awake, My Soul! In Grateful Songs.
O Gracious Jesus, Blessed Lord!

Fowler, Hazel J.
Prayer: "Take from the earth its tragic hunger,
  Lord."

Fowler, Laurence
Gather Ye Rosebuds.

Fowler, Russell T.
In Blanco County.

Fowler, William
If When I Die.
In Orknay.
Ship-broken Men Whom Stormy Seas Sore
  Toss.

Fowles, John
Amor Vacui.
Barbarians.
It Is a Lie.

Fox, Gail
For Anne, Who Doesn't Know.
It Is Her Cousin's Death.
Portrait.
She Lay Wrapped.

Fox, Hannah
Adam's Ex.

Fox, Janet
Institutions.
Quotella.

Fox, Lucia
Dream of the Forgotten Lover.

Fox, Robert
It's My Fault.

Fox, Ruth
Another Kind of Burning.

Fox, Siv Cedering
In the Morning.
Nightmares.
Poem for My Mother.

Fox, Henry, 1st Baron Holland. *See*
  Holland, Henry Fox, 1st Baron

"Foxton, E." (Sarah Hammond Palfrey)
Pilgrim, The.

Foxton, Thomas
On a Little Boy's Endeavouring to Catch a
  Snake.
Upon Boys Diverting Themselves in the
  River.

Foxworth, Nilene O. A.
Be Still Heart.
Like an Orchid in Deep Muddy Water.
Love.
Sho Nuff.
Yes, I Am an African Woman.

Frabotta, Biancamaria
Heloise.
You Enlarge on Near and Distant.

Fraire, Isabel
If night takes the form of a whale and.

Frame, Janet
At Evans Street.
Christmas and Death.
Clown, The.
Flowering Cherry, The.
Foxes, The.
Letter.
Place, The.
Rain on the Roof.
Telephonist.
Wet Morning.
When the Sun Shines More Years Than Fear.
Yet Another Poem about a Dying Child.

France, Marie de
Lay of the Honeysuckle, The.

France, Ruth. *See* **"Henderson, Paul."**

Frances, Emmanuel ben David
Price of Begging, The.

Frances, Immanuel
Epitaph on a Dwarf.

Frances, Jacob ben David
Song of Hate.

Francescato, Martha Paley
Parody.

Francesco da Barberino. *See* **Barberino,**
  Francesco da

"Francis"
They Answer Back.

Francis, Colin
Tony O!

Francis, Jammes
Prayer to Go to Paradise with the Donkeys,
A.
Francis, Marilyn
Neighbors.
Francis, Robert
Apple Peeler.
Base Stealer, The.
Blue Jay [or Bluejay]
Blue Winter.
Boy Riding Forward Backward.
Buzz Plane, The.
By Night.
Catch.
Cats.
Cold.
Come Out into the Sun.
Curse, The.
Cypresses.
December.
Eagle Plain.
Everyman/ Preacher or lecher, saint or sot,
sel.
Exclusive Blue.
Fair and Unfair.
Fall.
High Diver.
His Running My Running.
History.
Hogwash.
Hound, The.
Juniper.
Like Ghosts of Eagles.
Mr. Eliot's Day.
"Paper Men to Air Hopes and Fears."
Part for the Whole.
Pitcher.
Sailboat, Your Secret.
Salt.
Seagulls.
Sheep.
Silent Poem.
Skier.
Squash in Blossom.
Swimmer.
That Dark Other Mountain.
Three Darks Come Down Together.
Two Wrestlers.
Watching Gymnasts.
Waxwings.
Yes, What?
Francis of Assisi, Saint
Cantica: Our Lord Christ.
Canticle of Created Things.
Canticle of the Sun.
Cantico del Sole.
Praise of Created Things.
Prayer of St. Francis of Assisi for Peace.
Francis Xavier, Saint
Hymn: "My God, I love thee, not because."
Francisco, Edward
Lilith's Child.
Francisco, Nia
Awéé.
Kayenta Times Yet Dreaming On.
Men Tell and Talk.
Modern on the Surface.
Morning and Myself.
One Who Is Within, The.
Roots of Blue Bells.
Story Tellers Summer, 1980.
To a Man Who is Rob Southland.
Francisco Arriví
Song for a Transformation.
Francisco, Slinger. *See* **"Mighty Sparrow,
The."**
Franco, Veronica
Naked and Alone and Unwary You Caught
Me.
No more words! To the field, to arms.

Frank, Florence Kiper
Jew to Jesus, The.
Jewish Conscript, The.
Now in the Bloom.
Frank, John Frederick
One No. 7.
Frankau, Gilbert
Gun Teams.
Frankel, Doris
Song of the Truck.
Frankenberg, Lloyd
Autumn Song on Perry Street.
Existentialism.
Hide in the Heart.
Sea, The.
Franklin, Benjamin
Downfall of Piracy, The, *at*.
Jack and Roger, *at*.
Mother Country, The.
Franklin, Michael
Scarecrow, The.
Franklin, William (Bob Grove)
"Gotta' Smoke?"
Franzen, John
O God of Stars and Distant Space.
Fraser, Alexander Louis
By Cobequid Bay.
Fraser, Barclay
Mountain Days.
Fraser, C. Lovat
Robin's Song, The.
Fraser, Douglas
Far in the West.
Freedom of the Hills.
Growing Old.
Lost Leader, The.
Mountain Vigil.
On Looking at an Old Climbing Photograph.
Quiet Glen, The.
Spell o' the Hills, The.
To Alan.
Fraser, George Sutherland
Bought Embrace, A.
Christmas Letter Home.
Lean Street.
Letter to Anne Ridler.
Nilotic Elegy.
Rostov.
S. S. *City of Benares*.
Traveller Has Regrets, The.
Fraser, George Sutherland (G. S. Fraser)
Time, The.
Fraser, Hermia Harris
Copper Song, The.
Rousing Canoe Song, The.
Song of Welcome.
Fraser, Kath
Song (October 1969).
Fraser, Kathleen
Broom Balancing.
Casa de Pollos.
Change of Address.
Dresses.
Flowers.
Follow the Leader.
How Tuesday Began.
Interior with Mme. Vuillard and Son.
Joan Brown, about Her Painting.
Know, The.
La Reproduction Interdite// Not to Be
Reproduced.
Les Jours Gigantesques/The Titanic Days.
Lily, Lois & Flaubert; the Site of Loss.
Locations.
Medusa's Hair Was Snakes. Was Thought,
Split Inward.
1930.
Nuts and Bolts Poem for Mr. Mac Adams, Sr.
Poem in Which My Legs Are Accepted.
Poem Wondering If I'm Pregnant.
Poems for the New.

These Labdanum Hours.
What You Need.
Wrestling.
Fraser, Olive
Benighted to the Foothills of the Cairngorms.
Fraser, Ray
Cry of an Aged One, The.
Ecole St. Luc.
Flora.
Grotto, The.
In an Empty Window.
Lost Picture.
Not Often.
On Learning to Play the Guitar.
Policemen Laughing.
Souster.
Frayn, Michael
Life of T. S. Eliot.
Frazier, Robert
Flash Sleep.
Loren Eiseley's Time Passages.
Senryu.
Frear, Mary Dillingham
Young Workman, The.
Free, Spencer Michael
Human Touch, The.
Freedman, Martha H.
Clerihew: "Dorothy Parker/ Knew the darker."
Clerihew: "Henry James/ Only liked dames."
Freedman, William
Benediction.
Formations.
Freeman, Anne Hobson
I'll Tell You What a Flapper Is.
Freeman, Arthur
Cell of Himself, The.
Conversation Piece.
Naples Again.
Zoo of You, The.
Freeman, Carol [or Carole]
Christmas Morning I.
Do Not Think.
I Saw Them Lynch.
Freeman, Enoch W.
Hither We Come, Our Dearest Lord.
Freeman, James
Lord of the Worlds Below!
Freeman, John
Armistice Day.
Asylum.
Crowns, The.
Hounds, The.
It Was the Lovely Moon.
Stone Trees.
To End Her Fear.
Tree, The.
Waiting.
Waits, The.
Freeman, Mary Eleanor Wilkins
Blue-eyed Mary.
Marm Grayson's Guests.
Ostrich is a Silly Bird, The.
Pretty Ambition, A.
Freeman, Robert
Braving the Wilds All Unexplored *with music*.
Soldier's Prayer, A.
Freeth, John
Botany Bay.
Bunker's Hill, or the Soldier's Lamentation.
Colliers' March, The.
Cottager's Complaint, on the Intended Bill for
Enclosing Sutton-Coldfield, The.
New Navigation, The.
Frei, Frederike
Stroke Units.
Freistadt, Berta
Don't Call Me Pedant.
Get Your Body off My Mind.
I Dreamt You Went.
You Are So Tender.
You Take Off Your Jumper.

Freke, John
  History of Insipids, The.
Frémont, John Charles
  On Recrossing the Rocky Mountains after
    Many Years.
Frénaud, André
  Epitaph: "When I put my slate back in the
    void."
  Hatefully Poetry My Love.
  House for Sale.
  I Have Never Forgotten You.
  There Is No Paradise.
  To Drink to Friends.
  Useless Machine.
French, Anne
  Evening in November, An.
  Simultaneous Equations.
  Summer Storm, A.
  Writing.
French, William Percy
  "Are Ye Right There, Michael?" (A Lay of
    the Wild West Clare.).
  Fighting McGuire.
  Goosey Goosey Gander—by Various Authors
    (Kipling's Version).
  Goosey Goosey Gander—by Various Authors
    (Longfellow's Version).
  Goosey Goosey Gander—by Various Authors
    (Macaulay's Version).
  Goosey Goosey Gander—By Various Authors
    (Swineburne's Version).
Freneau, Philip
  Adventures of Simon Swaugum, a Village
    Merchant, The.
  American Soldier, The.
  Ancient Prophecy, An.
  Barney's Invitation.
  Battle of Lake Champlain, The.
  Battle of Stonington on the Seaboard of
    Connecticut, The.
  Bonhomme Richard and *Serapis*, The.
  By Babel's Streams *with music.*
  By some sad means, when reason holds no
    sway, *sel.*
  Captain Jones' Invitation.
  Columbus in Chains.
  Columbus to Ferdinand.
  Death's Epitaph, *sel.*
  Emancipation from British Dependence.
  Epistle to a Desponding Sea-Man.
  Epitaph: "Here—for they could not help but
    die," *sel.*
  George the Third's Soliloquy.
  Hospital Prison Ship, The, *sel.*
  Hurricane, The.
  Indian Burying Ground, The.
  Indian Convert, The.
  Indian Student; or, Force of Nature, The.
  Literary Importation.
  Occasioned by General Washington's Arrival
    in Philadelphia, on His Way to His
    Residence in Virginia.
  Ode: "God save the Rights of Man!"
  On a Honey Bee *or* To a Honey Bee.
  On a Travelling Speculator.
  On Mr. Paine's Rights of Man.
  On Observing a Large Red-Streak Apple.
  On the British Invasion.
  On the British King's Speech.
  On the Capture of the *Guerrière.*
  On the Death of Benjamin Franklin.
  On the Death of Captain Nicholas Biddle.
  On the Departure of the British from
    Charleston.
  On the Emigration to America [and Peopling
    the Western Country]
  On the Religion of Nature.
  On the Uniformity and Perfection of Nature.
  Parting Glass, The.
  Plato to Theon.
  Power of Fancy, The.

Prophecy of King Tammany, The.
Royal Adventurer, The.
Scurrilous Scribe, The.
Sick of thy northern glooms, come, shepherd,
  seek, *sel.*
Sir Henry Clinton's Invitation to the
  Refugees.
Song: "O'er the waste of waters cruising."
Song of Thyrsis, *sel.*
Stanzas Occasioned by the Ruins of a Country
  Inn *or* On the Ruins of a Country Inn.
Stanzas: "Princes and kings decay and die."
To a Caty-did.
To a New England Poet.
To a Noisy Politician.
To an Author.
To Sir Toby.
To the Memory of the Brave Americans.
Tobacco.
Trembling I write my dream, and recollect,
  sel.
Vanity of Existence, The.
Warning to America, A.
Wild Honeysuckle, The.
Frere, John Hookham
  Boy and the Parrot, The.
  Fable, A: "Dingy donkey, formal and
    unchanged, A."
  Fable of the Piece of Glass and the Piece of
    Ice, The.
  Stay your rude steps, or e'er your feet invade,
    sel.
  To a Lady, with a Present of a Walking-Stick.
Frere, John Hookham *and* **George Canning.**
  See **Canning, George** *and* **John Hookham**
  Frere
Frere, John Hookham, George Canning, *and*
  George Ellis. *See* **Canning, George,**
  George Ellis, *and* **John Hookham Frere**
Frese, Marcos Rodríguez
  Leit.
Frezza, Luciana
  Requiem for Sylvia Plath.
Friday, Ann
  Wish, The.
Fridman, Yankev
  Batlonim.
  God No Longer Speaks.
  Poetry.
  Winter Song.
Fried, Barbara
  Good Old Days, The.
Fried, Elliot
  Man Who Owned Cars, The.
Fried, Erich
  Description of a Landscape.
  Deserted Room.
  Goal Consciousness.
  Revenue.
  Rural.
  Speechless.
  Upon Re-reading a Poem by Paul Celan.
Fried, Rivka
  Sabbath.
Fried, Susannah
  Scraps.
  To My Father.
  Winter Day.
Friedlaender, Violet Helen
  Planting Trees.
Friedman, S. L.
  On Seeing a Construction of a Sheet Metal
    Man.
Friedmann, Pavel
  Butterfly, The.
Friend, Robert
  Identity.
  Letter to P.
  Practice of Absence, The.
Friman, Alice R.
  Reckoning, The.

Frink, A. L.
  Rose Still Grows beyond the Wall, The.
Frisch, Anthony
  Convict, The.
  Joan of Arc to the Tribunal.
Frischmuth, Barbara
  My Chinese Summer.
Fritsch, Gerhard
  Afternoon.
  August Night.
  Between Evening and Night.
  Fear.
  I Thought Myself to be Guest.
  Judas.
  Look in the Landscape.
  Poppy.
  Saint Maria Maggiore.
  Sunflowers in October.
  Upon Listening to the Third Brandenburg
    Concerto.
  Why the Many Words?
  Words Persistently.
Fritsch, H. S.
  How Old Are You?
Froissart, Jean
  Rondel: "Love, love, what wilt thou with this
    heart of mine?"
Froman, Robert
  Undefeated.
Frost, Frances Mary
  Apple Song.
  Christmas in the Wood.
  Father.
  Little Whistler, The.
  Maple Feast.
  Night Heron.
  Night of Wind.
  Night Plane.
  Nocturne: "Over New England now, the
    snow."
  Sandpiper, The.
  Squirrel in the Rain.
  White Season.
Frost, Lesley
  Rock 'n' Roll.
Frost, Richard
  Mephisto's Flea Song.
  Sen-Sen.
  Standing Broad Jump, The.
Frost, Robert
  Acceptance.
  Acquainted with the Night.
  After Apple-picking.
  Aim Was Song, The.
  America Is Hard to See.
  Armful, The.
  At Woodward's Gardens.
  August.
  Away!
  Axe-Helve, The.
  Bear, The.
  Bearer of Evil Tidings, The.
  Bereft.
  Beyond Words.
  Birches.
  Birthplace, The.
  Black Cottage, The.
  Blue-Butterfly Day.
  Bonfire, The.
  Boundless Moment, A.
  Brook in the City, A.
  Brown's Descent; or, The Willy-Nilly Slide.
  But God's Own Descent, *sel.*
  Canis Major, *sel.*
  Choose Something like a Star.
  Code, The.
  Come In.
  Considerable Speck, A.
  Cow in Apple Time, The.
  Death of the Hired Man, The.
  Demiurge's Laugh, The.

Departmental.
Desert Places.
Design.
Directive.
Draft Horse, The.
Drumlin Woodchuck, A.
Dust of Snow.
Egg and the Machine, The.
Empty Threat, An.
Fear, The.
Fire and Ice.
Fireflies in the Garden.
Flower-Boat, The.
For Allan, Who Wanted to See How I Wrote
    a Poem.
For Once, Then, Something.
For Travelers Going Sidereal.
Forgive, O Lord, My Little Jokes on Thee.
Fountain, a Bottle, a Donkey's Ears and Some
    Books, A.
From a Milkweed Pod.
From Plane to Plane.
Gathering Leaves.
Ghost House.
Gift Outright, The.
Good-by and Keep Cold.
Good Hours.
Happiness Makes Up in Height for What It
    Lacks in Length.
Hardship of Accounting, The.
Hill Wife, The.
Hillside Thaw, A.
Home Burial.
House Fear, sel.
Hyla Brook.
I Shall Say What Inordinate Love Is.
Immigrants.
Importer, An.
Impulse, The, sel.
In Dives' Dive.
In Hardwood Groves.
In Neglect.
In Winter in the Woods Alone.
Innate Helium.
Investment, The.
John L. Sullivan Enters Heaven.
Kitchen Chimney, The.
La Noche Triste.
Last Word of a Bluebird, The.
Leaf-Treader, A.
Leaves Compared with Flowers.
Lesson for Today, The.
Line-Gang, The.
Lockless Door, The.
Lone Striker, A.
Loneliness, sel.
Lost in Heaven.
Love and a Question.
Lovely Shall Be Choosers, The.
Meeting and Passing.
Mending Wall.
Middleness of the Road, The.
Minor Bird, A.
Mood Apart, A.
Most of It, The.
Mountain, The.
Mowing.
My November Guest.
Need of Being Versed in Country Things,
    The.
Neither Out Far nor In Deep.
Never Again Would Birds' Song Be the
    Same.
Not All There.
Not to Keep.
Nothing Gold Can Stay.
Objection to Being Stepped On, The.
October.
Old Man's Winter Night, An.
On a Tree Fallen across the Road.
On Looking Up by Chance at the
    Constellations.

On the Heart's Beginning to Cloud the Mind.
Once by the Pacific.
Onset, The.
"Out, Out."
Oven Bird, The.
Pan with Us.
Parting. To———.
Pasture, The.
Patch of Old Snow, A.
Peaceful Shepherd, The, sel.
Peck of Gold, A.
Plowmen.
Prayer in Spring, A.
Pride of Ancestry.
Provide, Provide.
Putting in the Seed.
Questioning Faces.
Rabbit Hunter, The.
Range-finding.
Reluctance.
Road Not Taken, The.
Rose Family, The.
Runaway, The.
Sand Dunes.
Secret Sits, The.
Semi-Revolution, A.
Servant to Servants, A.
Silken Tent, The.
Soldier, A.
Sound of Trees, The.
Span of Life, The.
Spring Pools.
Star-Splitter, The.
Stopping by Woods on a Snowy Evening.
Storm Fear.
Strong Are Saying Nothing, The.
Subverted Flower, The.
Telephone, The.
There Are Roughly Zones.
Time to Talk, A.
To a Young Wretch.
To Earthward.
To the Thawing Wind.
Tree at My Window.
Trespass.
Tuft of Flowers, The.
Twilight.
Two Look at Two.
Two Tramps in Mud Time.
U. S. 1946 King's X.
Unharvested.
Vantage Point, The.
Warning.
Were I in Trouble.
West-running Brook.
What Fifty Said.
White-tailed Hornet, The.
Wind and Window Flower.
Wood-Pile, The.
Wrights' Biplane, The.
You could sit there with the stains on your
    shoes, sel.
Young Birch, A.

Frost, Thomas
Death of Colman, The.
Guns in the Grass, The.

Frothingham, Nathaniel Langdon
Crossed Swords, The.
O God Whose Presence Glows in All.

Frothingham, Octavius Brooks
Thou Lord of Hosts, Whose Guiding Hand.

Frug, Simeon Grigoryevich
Sail Peacefully Home.
Talmud, The.

Fry, Christopher
In our fields, fallow and burdened, in grass
    and furrow, sel.

Frym, Gloria
Season Ticket.
Training for the Apocalypse.

Fu Hsien
Ruinous Rains.

Fu Hsüan
Gentle Wind, A.

Fuboku
Looking like a guide to the Joined Bridge.

Fuertes, Gloria
Autobiography.
Birds Nest in My Arms, The.
Climbing.
Human Geography.
I Make Poems, Gentlemen!
I Write Poems.
Interior Landscape.
It's Useless.
I've Never Got Anything.
I've Slept.
Love Which Frees.
Not Allowed to Write.
Now.
To Have a Child These Days.
We're OK.

Fuest, Milan
Moses' Account.

Fufuka, Karama
Basketball Star.
Lil' Bro.'

Fujii Chikugai
Traveling down the Yodo River on a Winter
    Night.
Viewing Nara from a Distance in Wind and
    Rain.
Yoshino.

Fujita Koshiro
In the Army.

Fujiwara no Fuyutsugu. *See* **Fuyutsugu**
Fujiwara no Ietaka. *See* **Ietaka**
Fujiwara no Mototoshi. *See* **Mototoshi**
Fujiwara no Sanesada. *See* **Sanesada**
Fujiwara no Shunzei. *See* **Shunzei**
Fujiwara no Tadamichi. *See* **Tadamichi**
Fujiwara no Tameie. *See* **Tameie**
Fujiwara no Tameuji. *See* **Tameuji**
Fujiwara no Teika. *See* **Teika**
Fujiwara no Umakai. *See* **Umakai**
Fujiwara no Yoshitsune. *See* **Yoshitsune**

Fukao Sumako
Bright House.

Fuller, Hoyt W.
Lost Moment.
Seravezza.

Fuller, Jean Overton
Not Marching Away to Be Killed.

Fuller, John
Band Music.
Blues.
De Sade.
God Bless America.
In a Railway Compartment.
Morvin.
St. Sophia.
Snapshot.
Sonata.
Statue, The.
White Queen.

Fuller, Margaret
Jesus a Child His Course Begun.

Fuller, Margaret Witter
Dryad Song.

Fuller, Roy
Autobiography of a Lungworm.
Be a Monster.
Bringing Up Babies.
Christmas Day.
Consolations of Art.
Crustaceans.
Day, The.
Death.
During a Bombardmant by V-Weapons.
Edmond Halley.
Family Cat, The.
Faust's Servant.

From the Joke Shop.
Green Hills of Africa, The.
Hedge-Sparrows and House-Sparrows.
Hittites, The.
Horrible Things.
How startling to find the portraits of the gods,
  sel.
Image, The.
January 1940.
Last Sheet.
Meetings and Absences.
Memorial Poem.
Metamorphoses.
Middle of a War, The.
Nino, the Wonder Dog.
October 1942.
Of Kings and Dukes.
Other Side, The.
Outside the Supermarket.
Perturbations of Uranus, The.
Reading in the Night.
Sadness, Glass, Theory.
Schizophrenics, The.
Shop Talk.
Singing, 1977.
Soliloquy in an Air-Raid.
Sonnet: "Crumbled rock of London is dripping
  under, The."
Spring 1943.
Spring 1942.
Suns in a skein, the uncut stones of night, *sel.*
There Actually Stood, *sel.*
Those of Pure Origin.
Translation.
Tribes, The.
Unremarkable Year, The.
Versions of Love.
Well Now, the Virgin, *sel.*
What Is Terrible.
Why do we return? Not in the darkened
  rooms, *sel.*
Wry Smile, A.
Fuller, Stephany
In the Silence.
Let Me Be Held When the Longing Comes.
My Love When This Is Past.
That We Head Towards.
Who is not a stranger still.
Fullerton, Mary Elizabeth ("E.")
Communal.
Cubes.
Emus.
Flesh.
Inspiration.
Lichen.
Lion.
Lovers.
Man's Sliding Mood, A.
Martyr.
Stupidity.
Fulton, Alice
Dance Script with Electric Ballerina.
Days through Starch and Bluing.
Everyone Knows the World Is Ending.
From Our Mary to Me.
Losing It.
My Second Marriage to My First Husband.
News of the Occluded Cyclone.
Terrestrial Magnetism.
Traveling Light.
Fulton, Robin
More than People, *sel.*
Stopping by Shadows.
Waiting-Room, The.
Fumi Saito
Palm of the hand, The,/ is not aware of
  dying.
Funge, Robert
Pulitzer Prize Winning Refrigerator, The.
Funk, Wilfred John
Rest in Peace.

Furness, Richard
To the Memory of Ebenezer Elliott the
  Corn-Law Rhymer.
Furness, William Henry
Evening Hymn.
In the Morning I Will Pray.
Light of Stars.
Furse, Margaret Cecilia
Lamp Flower, The.
Fushimi, Emperor
Birds at a Mountain Home.
Buffeted and blown.
Come to me tonight.
Cooled down at last.
Echoing high/ in the tips of the pines.
Evening windstorm, An.
From the broad sea plain.
Has dawn come so soon?
In a hidden bay.
In morning's first light.
In the hazy night.
In the midst of love.
Is the hour that late?
Late into the night.
My gaze comes to rest.
Pure with starlight.
So many nights.
Those tender feelings.
Fusinato, Erminia Fua
Woodworm, The.
Füst, Milán
If My Bones Must Be Handed Over.
Old Age.
Fuyuji, Tanaka. *See* **Tanaka Fuyuji**
Fuyutsugu (Fujiwara no Fuyutsugu)
Hearing Flutes along the Road in the Autumn
  Night.
Fyleman, Rose
Balloon Man, The.
Birthday Child, The.
Child Next Door, The ("The child next door
  has a wreath on her hat").
Christmas Wish, A.
Conversation.
December.
Donkey, The.
Fairies.
Fairies Have Never a Penny to Spend, The.
Fairy Flute, The.
Fairy Went a-Marketing, A.
Frog, The.
Goblin, The.
Good Morning.
I Don't Like Beetles.
Jock o' Dreams.
Mary Middling.
Mice.
Mrs. Brown.
Pretty Lady.
Primrose Hill.
Singing-Time.
Spring, The.
Temper.
Weathercock, The.
Yesterday in Oxford Street.

G

"G., A. R."
"Go Forward."
"G., E. O."
My Church ("My church has but one
  temple").
"G., G."
To W. J. M.
"G., L."
Quarrelsome Trio, The.

"G., W. A."
Yielded Life, The.
"G. S. O." *See* **"O., G. S."**
Gabbard, G. N.
News from the Basement Laundromat.
Gabriel, Charles H.
My Evening Prayer.
Gadbury, John
Ballad upon the Popish Plot, A.
Gadsby, Gordon J.
Lost Valley, The.
Gail, Hermann
Description of an American Billionaire.
Explanation.
Sunday Morning in the Park.
Visit to the Juvenile Penitentiary.
Galai, Benyamin [*or* Benjamin]
Days of Sarah, The.
From the North Pole.
Of the Travelers That Won't Come Again.
To My Generation.
Galassi, Jonathan
Our Wives.
Gale, Norman
Bobby's First Poem.
Child of Loneliness.
Country Faith, The.
Fairy Book, The.
Prayer, A: "Tend me my birds, and bring
  again."
Question, The.
Voice, The.
Gale, Vi
Shore Birds.
Gale, Zona
Credo.
Gal'ed, Zerubavel
Chickory.
Galef, David
Loosely from the Latin.
Gallagher, Joseph
John J. Curtis.
Gallagher, Katherine
Distances.
Survivor, The.
Gallagher, Tess
Bird-Window-Flying.
Black Money.
Black Silk.
Breasts.
Candle, Lamp & Firefly.
Complicity.
Crêpes Flambeau.
Death of the Horses by Fire.
Each Bird Walking.
Gray Eyes.
Horse in the Drugstore, The.
Hug, The.
Instructions to the Double.
Into the Known.
Kidnaper.
Meeting, The.
Ritual of Memories, The.
Shirts, The.
Skylights.
Some Painful Butterflies Pass Through.
Stepping Outside.
Tableau Vivant.
Under Stars.
Women's Tug of War at Lough Arrow.
Gallagher, William Davis
Autumn in the West.
Cardinal Bird, The.
Mothers of the West, The.
Gallaudet, Thomas H.
Jesus, in Sickness and in Pain.
Galler, David
Jersey Marsh, The.
Makers, The.
Narcissus: To Himself.
Vampire, The.

Galloway, George
To the Memory of Gavin Wilson (Boot, Leg and Arm Maker).

Gallup, Dick
Backing into the Fan Mail (Unreceived).
40 Acres and a Mule.
On the Meatwheel.
Relaxation.
Where I Hang My Hat.

Galsworthy, John
Limerick: "Angry young husband called Bicket, An."
Peace in the World.
Prayer for Gentleness to All Creatures.
So Might It Be.
Valley of the Shadow.

Galt, John
Canadian Boat Song, *at.*

Galván, Ignacio Rodríguez
Space is azure and the mountains bathe, *sel.*

Galván, Kyra
Ideological Contradictions in Washing a Dish.

Gálvez, Javier
This Morning.

Galvin, Brendan
Old Map of Barnstable County.
Saying Her Name.

Galvin, James
Cache la Poudre.
Last Man's Club, The.
Man's Vocation Is Nobody's Business, A.
Old Men on the Couthouse Lawn, Murray, Kentucky.

Gambara, Veronica
Since I, by My Good Fortune, Return to Look On.
When I see the earth ornate and lovely.

Gambold, John
Mystery of Life, The.

Gammons, Susan E.
Just One Day.

Gannett, William Channing
From Heart to Heart.
He Hides within the Lily.
Highway, The.
"Who Wert and Art and Evermore Shalt Be."

Ganse, Hervey Doddridge
Lord, I Know Thy Grace Is nigh Me.

Gar, Tsfrirah
After the Guests Departed.
First Rain.
Grown Old and Full of Years.
In the House at Midnight.
Only Statues Don't Shy Away.
Salt Statues.
Seeing the Light.
Spot on the Sun, A.
Tin Toys.

Garai, Gábor
Calcutta.
In Hungarian.
Man Is Beaten Up, A.
Vigil at Dawn.

Garbovsky, Gleb
After the War.

Garbutt, Vin
Mr. Gunman.

García Laviana, Gasper
For the Land Barons.
Meditation on the Lake.

García Lorca, Federico
Ballad of Luna, Luna.
Casida of the Rose.
Chinese Song, *sel.*
Dawn.
Evening.
Faithless Wife, The.
Farewell.
Ghazel of Unforseen Love.
Guitar.
Half Moon.

Lament for Ignacio Sánchez Mejías.
Landscape, *sel.*
Little Mute Boy, The.
Little Song of Seville, *sel.*
Little Viennese Waltz.
Madrigal de Verano.
Moon Rises, The.
Mr. Lizard is Crying.
Narcissus./ Your fragrance.
New York.
Ode to Walt Whitman.
Serenade.
Silly Song.
Six Strings, The.
Sleepwalkers' Ballad.
Snail.
Song Longs to Be Light.
Song of Black Cubans.
Song Sung, A, *sel.*

Garcia Villa, José. *See* **Villa, José Garcia**

Garcilaso de la Vega, Baldomero
Oh Sweet Souvenirs.

Gardner, Ada Belle
Mary, The Mother of Jesus.

Gardner, Alan
On Walking Back to the Bus.

Gardner, Carl
Dead Man Dragged from the Sea, The.
Reflections.

Gardner, Edmund
Sonnet Written in Tintern Abbey, Monmouthshire.

Gardner, Fred
Take Who Takes You.

Gardner, Gail
Dude Wrangler, The.
Sierry Petes, The.

Gardner, Isabella
At a Summer Hotel.
Cock-a-Hoop.
Gimboling.
In the Museum.
Letter from Slough Pond.
Lines to a Seagreen Lover.
Masked Shrew, The.
Mathematics of Encounter.
Milkman, The.
Nightmare.
On Looking in the Looking Glass.
Part of the Darkness.
Summers Ago.
That "Craning of the Neck."
That Was Then.
To Thoreau on Rereading Walden.
Widow's Yard, The.

Gardner, John
Lizard, The.

Gardner, Martin
Barbershop.
Soap.

Gardner, William Henry
When Love Comes Knocking.

Gardons, S. S.
Mother, The.
To a Child.

Garey, Terry A.
Full House.
Partial View of a Supernova.

Garioch, Robert (Robert Sutherland)
At Robert Fergusson's Grave, October 1962.
Campidoglio.
Elegy: "They are lang deid, folk that I used to ken."
Embro to the Ploy.
Heard in the Cougate.
I Was Fair Beat.
Judgment Day.
On Seein an Aik-Tree Sprent Wi Galls.
Sanct Christopher II ("Sanct Christopher's a muckle sanct and strang").
Sisyphus.

Garland, Hamlin
Cry of the Age, The.
Dakota Wheat-Field, A.
Do You Fear the Wind?
Gift of Water, The.
Goin' Back T'morrer.
Gold-Seekers, The.
Greeting of the Roses, The.
Horses Chawin' Hay.
In the Grass.
Logan at Peach Tree Creek.
Massasauga.
Meadow Lark, The.
My Prairies.
Pioneers.
Prairie Fires.
Sport.
Tribute of Grasses, A.
Ute Lover, The.
Wish, A.

Garlick, Phyllis L.
Fairy Feet.
Fairy Shoemaker, The.
Lullaby: "Lullaby, lullaby."

Garmon, John
Old Trail Town, Cody, Wyoming.

Garnett, Richard
Fading-Leaf and Fallen-Leaf.

Garrett, George
Bubbles.
Buzzard.
Giant Killer.
Jacob.
Luck's Shining Child.
Magi, The.
Revival.
Romantic.
Saints.
Tiresias.
York Harbor Morning.

Garrick, David
Epitaph on Laurence Sterne.
Friend Col and I, both full of whim.
Heart of Oak.
On a Certain Lord Giving Some Thousand Pounds for a House.
On Oliver Goldsmith.
On Sir John Hill, M. D., Playwright.

Garrigue, Jean
Amsterdam.
Amsterdam Letter.
Apologia.
Bleecker Street.
Catch What You Can.
Circle, The.
Cortege for Colette.
Country Villa.
Dialog.
Epitaph for My Cat.
False Country of the Zoo.
Forest.
From Venice Was That Afternoon.
Mouse, The.
Movie Actors Scribbling Letters Very Fast in Crucial Scenes.
Now Snow Descends.
Of History More Like Myth.
Old Haven.
Primer of Plato.
Remember That Country.
Shore.
Song for "Buvez les Vins du Postillion"— Advt.
Stranger, The.
Unicorn and the Lady, The.
You Know.

Garrison, Theodosia Pickering
Closed Door, The.
Ilicet.
Memorial Day.
Poplars, The.

Prayer, A: "Let me work and be glad."
Shade.
Shepherd Who Stayed, The.
Stains.
Torch, The.

Garrison, Wendell Phillips
Afternoon, *sel.*
Evening, *sel.*

Garrison, William Lloyd
Freedom for the Mind.
Liberty for All.

Garrison, Winfred Ernest
Thy Sea So Great ("Thy sea, O God, so great").

Garrod, Heathcote William
Thou should'st be living at this hour.

Garsenda de Forcalquier
You're so well-suited as a lover.

Garstin, Crosbie
Nocturne: "Red flame flowers bloom and die, The."

Garth, Sir Samuel
How impotent a deity am I!
Oft has this planet rolled around the sun.
This wight all mercenary projects tries.
What Frenzy Has of Late Possess'd the Brain.

Garthwaite, Wymond
Peter and Wendy.

Garvey, Marcus
Centenary's Day.
Keep Cool.

Garvin, Amelia Beers Warnock. *See* **"Hale, Katherine"**

Gary, Patricia
Uneven Parallel Bars.

Gascoigne, George
All were to little for the merchauntes hande.
All Were Too Little.
And Every Year a World.
And every yeare a worlde my will did deeme.
And if I did, what then?
Arraignment of a Lover, The.
Before Mine Eye.
Before mine eye to feede my greedy will.
Conference among ourselves we called, A.
Constancy of a Lover, The.
Councell Given to Master Bartholmew Withipoll.
Divorce of a Lover, The ("Divorce me nowe good death").
Farewell with a Mischeife.
Fie, Pleasure, Fie!
For That He Looked Not upon Her.
For why? the gaines doth seldome quitte the charge.
For Why the Gains.
Gascoigne's Good-Morrow.
Gascoigne's [*or* Gascoygnes] Good-Night.
Gascoigne's Woodmanship.
Green Knight's Farewell to Fancy, The.
I Could Not though I Would.
In haste poste haste, when first my wandring minde.
Inscription in a Garden.
Looks of a Lover Enamoured, The.
Lullaby [*or* Lullabie] of a Lover, The.
No haste but good, where wisdome makes the waye.
Of All the Birds That I Do Know.
Sonet Written in Prayse of the Browne Beautie, A.
Steele Glas, The.
Straunge Passion of a Lover, A.
To Prink Me Up.
To prinke me up and make me higher plaste.

Gascoyne, David
And the Seventh Dream Is the Dream of Isis.
Cage, The.
Cubical Domes, The.
Ecce Homo.

Elegy: "Friend, whose unnatural early death."
End Is Near the Beginning, The.
Eve.
Ex Nihilo.
Landscape.
Mood.
On the Grand Canal.
Orpheus in the Underworld.
Patmos.
Sacred Hearth, The.
Salvador Dali.
"The Truth Is Blind."
Tough Generation, A.
"Truth Is Blind, The."
Wall, The.
Wartime Dawn, A.
Winter Garden.
Yves Tanguy.

Gashe, Marina
Village, The.

Gasparini, Len
Accident, The.
Greasy Spoon Blues.
Kafka's Other Metamorphosis.
Niagara Falls Nocturne.
Valentine.
Written on a Paper Napkin.

Gasztold, Carmen Bernos de
Noah's Prayer.
Prayer of the Cat, The.
Prayer of the Donkey, The.
Prayer of the Goldfish, The.
Prayer of the Little Ducks, The.
Prayer of the Mouse, The.
Prayer of the Old Horse, The.

"Gate, A.C." *See* **Anthony, Edward**

Gates, Beatrix
Deadly Weapon.

Gates, Ellen M. Huntington
Home of the Soul.
Sleep Sweet.
Your Mission.

Gatsos, Nikos
Amorgos.
Black Sun, The.
Death and the Knight (1513).
Evening at Colonos.
Myrtle Tree, The.
We Who Are Left.

Gatty, Sir Alfred Scott
Three Little Pigs, The.

Gault, A. J.
Twenty Years Ago, *at.*

Gaumond, Mary R.
Rose, The.
Virus Poliomyelitis.

Gautier, Théophile
Art.
Chimera, The.
Clarimonde.
Posthumous Coquetry.

Gavaudan
This vers I make.

Gawsworth, John
Skye.

Gaxe
I wonder what eagle did to him.

Gay, John
About in London.
Air.
Air: "Fox may steal your hens, sir, A."
Air: "O ruddier than the cherry!"
Air: "Since laws were made for ev'ry degree."
Ballad: "Of all the girls that e'er were seen."
Birth of the Squire; an Eclogue, The.
Butterfly and the Snail, The.
Council of Horses, The.
Damon and Cupid.
Dangers of Foot-ball, The.

Epistle to the Right Honourable William Pulteney, Esq.
Experienced men, inured to city ways.
Farmer's Wife and the Raven, The.
Fly-fishing.
Great Frost, The.
Highwaymen, The.
I rage, I melt, I burn.
If the heart of a man is deprest [*or* depressed] with cares.
I'm like a skiff on the ocean tost.
Let due civilities be strictly paid.
Lion and the Cub, The.
London at Night.
Love in Her Eyes.
Modes of the Court, The.
Molly Mog; or, The Fair Maid of the Inn.
Mr. Pope's Welcome from Greece.
My Own Epitaph.
New Song of New Similies , A.
Newgate's Garland.
Nor less the spaniel, skillful to betray.
O Polly, you might have toy'd and kist.
Ode for the New Year, An, *at.*
Painter Who Pleased Nobody and Everybody, The.
Poet and the Rose, The.
Receipt for Stewing Veal, A, *at.*
She who hath felt a real pain.
Song: "Before the barn-door crowing."
Song: "Can love be controlled by advice?"
Song: "If any wench Venus's girdle wear."
Song: "Thus when the swallow, seeking prey."
Song: "Were I laid on Greenland's coast."
Sweet William's Farewell to Black-eyed Susan.
Think of dress in every light.
Three children sliding on the ice, *at.*
Thursday; or, The Spell.
To a Lady.
To a Lady on Her Passion for Old China.
To a Young Lady, with Some Lampreys.
To My Ingenious and Worthy Friend William Lowndes, Esq.
Tuesday; or, the Ditty.
Turkey and the Ant, The.
Turtle thus with plaintive crying, The.
'Twas When the Seas Were Roaring.
Wednesday; or, The Dumps.
What Shall I Do to Show How Much I Love Her?
When a brisk gale against the current blows.
Where the mob gathers, swiftly shoot along.
Who can the various city frauds recite.
Wild Boar and the Ram, The.
Winter my theme confines; whose nitry wind.
Youth's the Season.

Gay, John and Alexander Pope
Mary Gulliver to Captain Lemuel Gulliver.

Gay, William
Crazy World, The.

Gay, Zhenya
In the Summer We Eat.

Gay, Asya. *See* **Asya**

Gayle, Nefertiti
Black Woman Out Dere.
Youths, De.

Gebirtig, Mordecai
Waiting for Death.

Geddes, Alexander
Epistle to the President of the Scottish Society of Antiquaries: On Being Chosen a Correspondent Member.
Satire.

Geddes, Gary
Inheritors, The.
Mess Sergeant.
Transubstantiation.

Geilt, Suibne
Starry frost descends, The, *at.*

Geisel, Theodor Seuss. *See* "Seuss, Dr."
Gellert, Leon
  Anzac Cove.
  Before Action.
  House-Mates.
  In the Trench.
  Jester in the Trench, The.
  These Men.
Gelman, Juan
  Customs.
  Knife, The.
  Stranger, The.
Gen of Kohoin
  At ninety-nine, snowy side-locks.
Genet, Jean
  Murderers of the wall wrap themselves in
    sunrise, The, *sel.*
Gensei
  Autumn, a Visit to the Byodo-in Temple.
  Hut: Thinking of a Friend.
Geoghegan, J. B.
  Down in a Coal Mine.
Georgakas, Dan
  Acrobat from Xanadu disdained all nets, The.
George, Marguerite
  Prisoner.
George, Phil
  Ask the Mountains.
  Night Blessing.
  Old Man, the Sweat Lodge.
George, Phillip William
  America's Wounded Knee.
  Battle Won Is Lost.
  Favorite Grandson Braid.
  First Grade.
  Moon of Huckleberries.
  Morning Vigil.
  Name Giveaway.
  Prelude to Memorial Song: 100 Years Later.
  Spokane Falls.
  Spring Cleaning.
  Spruce.
  Sunflower Moccasins.
  Visit, The.
  Wardance.
  Wardance Soup.
George, Stefan
  Invocation and Prelude.
  Lord of the Isle, The.
  Lyre Player, The.
  No way too long—no path too steep, *sel.*
  Prelude XXIII: "We are those same
    children. . . "
  Rapture.
  Stanzas Concerning Love.
  To a Young Leader of the First World War.
Geppa
  Crossing Lake Biwa.
Gerard, Edwin ("Trooper Gerardy")
  Lofty Lane.
Gerber, Dan
  In the Winter Dark.
Gerez, Jozef Habib
  Call from the Afterworld.
  We Are Acrobats.
  We Fooled Ourselves.
Gergely, Agnes
  Birth of a Country.
  Conjuration.
  Crazed Man in Concentration Camp.
  Desert.
  Sign on My Door Jamb.
  With Lamp in Hand.
Gerhardt, Paul
  Courage.
Gerin-Lajoie, Antoine
  Canadian Exile, The.
German, Greg
  Limestone Cowboy's Luck Runs Out, The.
German, Norman
  New World in the Morning.

Gerondi, Abraham
  Hymn for the Eve of the New Year.
Gerrard, John
  Remonstrance, A.
Gershon, Karen
  Home.
  Jew's Calendar, A.
Gershwin, Ira
  Blah, Blah, Blah.
  It Ain't Necessarily So.
Gerstl, Elfriede
  Cornbush, the name Cornbush.
  Höbinger.
Gerstler, Amy
  Direct Address.
Gessho
  On Hearing that the Port of Shimoda Has
    Been Opened to the Foreigners.
Gesswein, Alfred
  Days Count Again, The.
  Landscape of a Face.
  Possible Landscape.
  Sometimes/ only in the reflection of.
  Watteau's Coloration ("Watteau's color:
    atmospheric May.").
Getsudo
  Perfect way out, The.
Getsuo
  Sea touches sky, and now, moon down.
Gezelle, Guido
  To the Sun from a Flower.
Ghalib, Asadullah Khan
  Again I remember.
  Age has passed away since love, An.
  All that I had in the world.
  Ambition is busy with many and many.
  As ink is spilt on paper.
  Be not deceived by life, O Asad.
  Beauty shall be freed.
  Burnt has been the heart.
  End of life's journey, The.
  Full moon is the mirror, The.
  Full of warning is the solution.
  Garden close from end, The.
  Gone is the pain of absence.
  Having committed the heart to love.
  Heart has learnt, The.
  Heart, I thought, The.
  Heavens revolve both night and day, The.
  How could one struggle for freedom.
  How the wanton hunter tamed.
  Hundred beauties are present, A.
  I am the lip parched with thirst.
  I can no longer plead for love.
  I keep the heart engaged, the heart.
  I wish to go away and live.
  If at my death you do not believe.
  If the loved one had not made.
  I'm neither sound.
  In life I had a fear of death.
  In so far as we are filled.
  In the absence of the great wine-drinkers the
    world.
  Intelligence unconcerned.
  It is not easy to achieve a thing.
  It is the selfsame thing.
  It's merely idleness to believe.
  Joy of every drop, The.
  Last night I was grieved for love's lovelorn
    face and hair.
  Life's leisure is a mirror of the hundred hues.
  Lightning heat of heart's anguish filled the
    cloud, The.
  Listen, you who have just arrived.
  Mad of mind, The.
  Men with the fire of deep desire.
  Moon is lovely when it's full, The.
  My breast is rent asunder.
  My foolish heart what is ailing thee?
  My heart is a temple of fire.
  My life is the great expanse.

  My mad despair is the enemy.
  My sorrow makes you sad, alas.
  Nature of creation itself, The.
  Open are the arms of the rose.
  Pain did not wish to be indebted.
  Plaint has no melody.
  Print of love could not, The.
  Ray of light becomes the track, The.
  Right in the morning appear the signs of the
    close of day.
  Scent of the rose, the heart's lament, The.
  Shamed have I been.
  Sigh needs an age to have effect; who would,
    The.
  Spring has come again, The.
  Steed of life is galloping fast, The.
  Talk was of that lovely one, The.
  There is no hope or light.
  There is no place for me in any heart.
  This garden of Paradise.
  We have only known this shadowy world.
  Wearied, desire invents and seeks refuge.
  When there was nothing, there was God.
  Where are they all? Some raise their heads.
  Whether I wept or not.
  Who could have come? The garden is.
  Wine's inebriety.
  Wing of the moth was perhaps the sail, The.
  With each step that I take.
  With ecstasy I walk.
  With what joy in front.
  Within the dream the thought.
  Wondrous is the season.
  World is full of the effulgence, The.
  World is to me but child's play, The.
  Your light is the basis of creation.
Ghalib, Mirza
  Ghazal XII.
Ghigna, Charles
  Divers.
  Father of the Bride.
  Fighter Learns of Hands, A.
  Prefontaine.
Ghiselin, Brewster
  Catch, The.
  Credo.
  Headland.
  Rattler, Alert.
  To the South.
Ghose, Manmohan
  Who Is It Talks of Ebony?
Ghose, Zulfikar
  Rise of Shivaji, The.
Gibbon, Monk
  Forebears.
  French Peasants.
  Poetry of Gerard Manley Hopkins, The.
  Prayer of the Arab Physician, The.
  Shawls, The.
  Song: "Singer within the little streets."
  Wiser Than the Children of Light.
Gibbons, James Sloan
  Three Hundred Thousand More.
Gibbons, Orlando
  Silver Swan, The, *at.*
Gibbons, Reginald
  Breath.
  Cedar River, The.
  Eating.
  Hoppy.
  "Luckies."
  Make Me Hear You.
  Ruined Motel, The.
Gibbs, Barbara
  "What You See Is Me."
Gibbs, Beatrice R.
  Bomber, The.

Gibbs, Jessie Wiseman
If We Believed in God.
Gibbs, Margaret E.
On the Banisters.
Song of the Bath, The.
Gibford, Dick
Cowboy's Toast.
Last Buckaroo, The.
Old Cowman, The.
Gibran, Kahlil
Earth.
Fame.
Of Love, *sel.*
Then Almitra spoke, saying, We would ask
    now of Death, *sel.*
Veiled Land.
Gibson, Alan
When stags do rut in the Plym.
Gibson, Barbara
After the Quarrel.
Gibson, Douglas
January.
White Cat in Moonlight.
Gibson, George Herbert ("Ironbark")
Ballad of Queensland (Sam Holt), A.
My Mate Bill.
Gibson, Margaret
Burning the Root.
Catechism Elegy.
Country Woman Elegy.
Gemini Elegy.
Invisible Work.
Long Walks in the Afternoon.
October Elegy.
Onion, The.
To Speak of Chile.
Gibson, Morgan
Beyond the Presidency.
Gibson, Walker
Advice to Travelers.
Athletes.
Blues for an Old Blue.
Essay on Lunch.
In Memory of the Circus Ship *Euzkera.*
Killer Too, The.
Mountains, The.
Soliloquy in a Motel.
Umpire, The.
Vacationer.
Gibson, Wilfrid Wilson
All Being Well.
Breakfast.
Dancers, The.
Dancing Seal, The.
Drove-Road, The.
Eagles and Isles.
Flannan Isle.
Henry Turnbull.
Ice, The.
Inspiration.
Lament: "We who are left, how shall we look
    again."
Long Tom.
Luck.
Mark Anderson.
Messages, The.
Michael's Song.
Old Skinflint.
Parrot, The.
Parrots, The.
Peak, The.
Prelude: "As one, at midnight, wakened by
    the call."
Question, The.
Sight.
Stone, The.
White Dust, The.
Witch, The, *sel.*
Gibson, William
Circe.

Gidlow, Elsa
For the Goddess Too Well Known.
Invocation to Sappho.
Gifford, Fannie Stearns Davis. *See* **Davis,**
Fannie Stearns
Gifford, Humphrey [or Humfrey]
For Soldiers.
Song: "Woman's face is full of wiles, A."
Gilbert, Celia
Lot's Wife.
Private Life, A.
Voices.
Walk, The.
Gilbert, Christopher
Blue, *sel.*
Charge.
Now.
Saturday Morning at the Laundry.
Touching.
Gilbert, Jack
Abnormal Is Not Courage, The.
All the Way from There to Here.
Bird Sings to Establish Frontiers, A.
Burning and Fathering; Accounts of My
    Country.
Byzantium Burning.
Don Giovanni on His Way to Hell II ("How
    could they think women a creation?").
Fashionable Heart, The.
Lives of Famous Men, The.
Lord Sits with Me Out in Front, The.
More than Fifty.
Movies, The.
My Marriage with Mrs. Johnson.
New York, Summer.
On Growing Old in San Francisco.
Orpheus in Greenwich Village.
Perspective He Would Mutter Going to Bed.
Pewter.
Playing House.
Prospero Dreams of Arnaud Daniel Inventing
    Love in the Twelfth Century.
Prospero on the Mountain Gathering Wood.
Prospero without His Magic.
Revolution, The.
Sects.
Susanna and the Elders.
Translation into the Original.
Gilbert, James Stanley
Beyond the Chagres.
Gilbert, Paul
Your Own Version.
Gilbert, R. V.
Great Victory, The.
Gilbert, Ruth
Green Hammock, White Magnolia Tree.
Jacob, *sel.*
Gilbert, Sandra M.
Elegy: "Pages of history open, The."
Fog Dream, The.
Sonnet: The Ladies' Home Journal.
Gilbert, Sir William Schwenck
Anglicized Utopia.
Arac's Song.
Bishop of Rum-ti-Foo, The.
Bunthorne's Song [The Aesthete].
Captain Reece.
Contemplative Sentry, The.
Darned Mounseer, The.
Disagreeable Man, The.
Duke of Plaza-Toro, The.
Englishman, The.
Etiquette.
Fable of the Magnet and the Churn, The.
Family Fool, The.
Ferdinando and Elvira, or the Gentle Pieman.
General John.
Gentle Alice Brown.
Grand Inquisitor's Song, The.
House of Lords, The.

I Am the Very Model [*or* Pattern] of a
    Modern Major-General.
If You're Anxious for to Shine in the High
    Aesthetic Line.
King of Canoodle-Dum, The.
Ko-Ko's Song ("As someday it may happen
    that a victim must be found").
Ko-Ko's Winning Song.
Man who would woo a fair maid, A.
Mikado's Song, The.
Most Ingenious Paradox, A.
Nightmare.
Oh, Hollow! Hollow! Hollow!
Oh! my name is John Wellington Wells.
Policeman's Lot, A [*or* The].
Rival Curates, The.
Sing for the Garish Eye.
Sir Joseph's Song.
Story of Prince Agib, The.
There Lived a King.
There Was an Old Man of St. Bees.
To Sit in Solemn Silence.
To the Terrestrial Globe.
When I, Good Friends, Was Called to the
    Bar.
Yarn of the *Nancy Bell,* The.
Gilbert, Thomas
Against Homosexuality.
Gilbert, Virginia
Finding You.
Gilbert, Zack
For Angela.
For Stephen Dixon.
In Spite of All This Much Needed Thunder.
My Own Hallelujahs.
"O. D."
When I Heard Dat White Man Say.
"Gilbertulus." *See* **Howe, Mark Antony De**
Wolfe
Gilboa, Amir
After a Thousand Years.
Against the Wind.
Ancient Song.
Back and forth. As in a swing. When there's.
Birth.
City defenseless by day one sees desolation,
    A.
Death in Spring, A.
Ends of Things, The.
Gazelle I send you to the wolves not in the
    wood they're.
Havdala.
I Don't Want to See Black But.
I guess it will come suddenly. And every.
I looked outside. Pools of water.
I Love This Sunlight Cold.
I pray from the heart a prayerbook.
I Pray from the Heart a Psalter.
I press pen to paper like a pistol to the
    temple.
I Put the Tip of the Pen to the Paper.
I wanted to write the lips of sleepers.
I Went Out into That Welcome Cold.
I'll grab hold of a butt of dream.
In a night hour this is how the things are
    written. And now night.
In the Dark.
Isaac.
I've Come to the Simplest Words.
Joshua's Face.
Kingdom of Silence.
Me—I Am but One.
Morning-Selah.
Moses.
My Brother Was Silent.
My city mine. No more can I.
My left hand's like after a vow. It hurts. I'm
    trying to dream again.
My Soul Wanders About.
Of late from time to time there's risen.

Our Dreams.
Rain Falls and Floods.
Red and Blue Song, A.
Riders' Horses, The ("The riders' spears touched heaven").
Samson.
Saul.
Seeds of Lead.
That very day I saw that is we saw.
They'll all get up. I know I see them.
This isn't what I want to write I.
This whole land belongs to me sleeping and awake I see.
Times stir in me uncalendrically, chaotically.
To come free to a city under siege.
To run a night's distance, distances by night, nothing's easier than traveling distances.
Until recently there was fear.
Watchful Wakeful.
When I'm by myself I don't know. But I.
With the Rain.
Yes, I caught the butterfly. Went crazy for the moment.

Gilchrist, Alan
Assynt.

Gilchrist, Marie Emilie
Apples in New Hampshire.

Gilder, Jeanette Leonard
My Creed.

Gilder, Joseph B.
Parting of the Ways, The.

Gilder, Richard Watson
After-Song.
Ah, Be Not False.
At the President's Grave.
Birds of Bethlehem, The.
Call Me Not Dead.
Celestial Passion, The.
Cello, The.
Charleston.
Child, A.
Christ of Judea, look thou in my heart!, sel.
Christmas Tree in the Nursery, The.
Comfort of the Trees, The.
Doubter, The.
Evening in Tyringham Valley.
Failure and Success.
Hast Thou Heard the Nightingale?
Heroic Age, The.
How to the Singer Comes the Song?
Hymn: "God of the strong, God of the weak."
I Count My Time by Times That I Meet Thee.
Invisible, The.
Land That We Love.
Memorial Day.
Midsummer Song, A.
Noel.
Ode: "I am the spirit of the morning sea."
On the Life-Mask of Abraham Lincoln.
Prelude: "Night was dark, though sometimes a faint star, The," sel.
Sherman.
Song: "Not from the whole wide world I chose thee," sel.
Song of a Heathen, The.
Song: "Years have flown since I knew thee first," sel.
Sonnet, The: "What is a sonnet? 'Tis the pearly shell."
To Thee, Eternal Soul, Be Praise.
"White City, The."

Gildner, Gary
Dear wife and bosom friend I hat seen hart, sel.
Digging for Indians.
First Practice.
House on Buder Street, The.
In My Meanest Daydream.
Letter to a Substitute Teacher.
Life of the Wolf, The.

Meeting My Best Friend from the Eighth Grade.
Meeting the Reincarnation Analyst.
My Father after Work.
My Mother and the Touched Old Woman.
Nails.
Poems.
Runner, The.
Wheat.

Gilead, Zerubavel
Absalom.
Flying Letters.

Gilfillan, Caroline
Lesbian Play on T.V.

Gilkey, James G.
O God, in Whose Great Purpose.
Outside the Holy City.

Gill, David
Kaleidoscope, The.

Gill, John
As a Child Seeing a Cardinal.
Before the Thaw.
First Hymn.
"I Don't Hear Any Melody Breathing I Hear."
Late Spring: A Heaving, a Turning.
Poem: "Something broke the dream."
What Could Be.

Gill, Julia
Christ and the Little Ones.

Gillett, Gabriel
Years and years I have loved you.

Gillies, Andrew
Two Prayers, The.

Gillies, Valerie
Clouds and Clay.

Gillilan, Strickland W.
Finnigin to Flannigan.
Just stand aside, and watch yourself go by, sel.
Need of Loving.
On the Antiquity of Microbes.
Other Fellow's Job, The.
Reading Mother, The.
Watch Yourself Go By.

Gillom, Arthur L.
I Want You.

Gilman, Caroline
Anna Playing in a Graveyard.
Boat, The.
Dead Sister, The.

Gilman, Charlotte Perkins Stetson
Beds of Fleur-de-Lys, The.
Child Labor.
Common Inference, A.
Conservative, A.
Give Way!
Living God, The.
Resolve.
Similar Cases.
To Labor.
Two Prayers.

Gilman, Samuel
O God, Accept the Sacred Hour with music.

Gilmore, Joseph Henry
He Leadeth Me.

Gilmore, Mary
Baying Hounds, The.
Eve-Song.
Fourteen Men.
Heritage.
Myall in Prison, The.
Nationality.
Never Admit the Pain.
Nurse No Long Grief.
Old Botany Bay.
Pear-Tree, The.
Shepherd, The.
Song of the Woman-Drawer, The.
Sudden autumn winds, like hounds, The, sel.
Tenancy, The.

Waradgery Tribe, The.
Within the night, above the dark, sel.

Gilmore, Patrick Sarsfield ("Louis Lambert")
When Johnny Comes Marching Home.

Gilpin, Laura
Two-headed Calf, The.

Gils, Gust
Ballad of a Perennially Misunderstood Man.
Fairy Tale.
Fine Divine Marquis, The.
Fujiyama/ is quite a sight, The, sel.
How Fine N'est-ce Pas.
Mayor of Fukui, The, sel.
Swallowing of the Earth, The.

Gingell, Dave
In Memoriam.
Older Now.

"Ginger." *See* **Irwin, Wallace**

Ginsberg, Allen
America.
American Change.
Back on Times Square, Dreaming of Times Square.
Bayonne Turnpike to Tuscarora.
Bop Lyrics.
Cafe in Warsaw.
Chances "R."
Crossing Nation.
Death News.
Death to Van Gogh's Ear!
Don't Grow Old.
Dream Record: June 8, 1955.
Face the Nation, sel.
Father Death Blues, sel.
Fourth Floor, Dawn, Up All Night Writing Letters.
Friday the Thirteenth.
Homework.
Howl.
Hymmnn.
I Am a Victim of Telephone.
I saw the best minds of my generation destroyed by madness, sel.
Ignu.
In Back of the Real.
In the Baggage Room at Greyhound.
Kaddish.
Kral Majales.
Last Night in Calcutta.
Lion for Real, The.
Love Poem on Theme by Whitman.
Malest Cornifici Tuo Catullo.
Maybe Love.
Memory Gardens.
Message.
Mugging.
My Alba.
My Sad Self.
Ode to Failure.
On Burroughs' Work.
On Neal's Ashes.
Please Master.
Poem Rocket.
Prophecy, A.
Psalm III: "To God: to illuminate all men. Beginning with Skid Road."
Sather Gate Illumination.
S.F. Southward, sel.
Shrouded Stranger, The.
Song: Fie My Fum.
Sunflower Sutra.
Supermarket in California, A.
Sweet Levinsky.
This Form of Life Needs Sex.
Thus Crosslegged on Round Pillow Sat in Space.
To Aunt Rose.
Tonite I walked out of my red apartment door on East tenth street's dusk, sel.
Uptown.
Vow, A.

Wales Visitation.
What sphinx of cement and aluminum bashed open their skulls, *sel.*
Who Be Kind To.
Ginsberg, Louis
Biography of an Agnostic.
Clocks.
Hounds of the Soul, The.
Hymn to Evil.
Morning in Spring.
Prices.
Roots.
Song: "I know that any weed can tell."
Soon at Last My Sighs and Moans.
Gioia, Dana
California Hills in August.
Lives of the Great Composers.
Next Poem, The.
Sunday News, The.
Sunday Night in Santa Rosa.
Giorno, John
I Resigned Myself to Being Here.
Giovanni, Nikki
Adulthood.
Basketball.
Beautiful Black Men.
Certain Peace, A.
Concerning One Responsible Negro with Too Much Power.
Covers.
Dance Poem.
Detroit Conference of Unity and Art.
Dreams.
Ego Tripping.
For Saundra.
Funeral of Martin Luther King, Jr., The.
Kidnap Poem.
Knoxville, Tennessee.
Master Charge Blues.
Mothers.
Mother's Habits.
My Poem.
Nikki-Rosa [*or* Nikki-Roasa]
One ounce of truth benefits.
Poem for Aretha.
Poem for Black Boys.
Poem for Unwed Mothers.
Poem of Angela Yvonne Davis.
Poetry.
Reason I Like Chocolate, The.
Revolutionary Dreams.
Robin's Poem, A.
Scrapbooks.
Seduction.
They Clapped.
True Import of Present Dialogue, Black vs, The Negro.
12 Gates to the City.
Two Friends.
Woman Poem.
Word Poem (Perhaps Worth Considering).
World Is Not a Pleasant Place to Be, The.
Gippius, Zinaida Nikolayevna
She.
Giroux, Roger
And Perhaps.
Center, The.
Far.
It Was.
Lost Beauty.
Naked/ Come shivering.
Once More.
Queen of Going.
Surface.
This Memory.
Touched.
Gisborne, Thomas
Spring, *sel.*
Giten
I've swallowed the Eastern Ocean's iron ball.
Gittings, Robert
Great Moth, The.

Giudici, Giovanni
Is It Right to Move to the Country?
Roman Epigram.
You Ask Me What It Means.
Giuliani, Alfredo
Animal Song.
Days Clinging to the City, The.
Friday, You Look Blue.
Letter from the Mountain Sanitarium.
Old Man, The.
Predilections.
Resurrection after the Rain.
Who Would Have Said It.
Giun
Abusing Scripture, cursing Zen.
Giusti, Giuseppe
Latest in Guillotines, The.
Snail, The.
Gizan
Coming and going, life and death.
Gjuzel, Bogomil
Flood at the International Writing Program.
Gladden, Washington
O Lord of Life.
O Master, Let Me Walk with Thee.
Glading, Jan
Arthritis.
Gladwin, Herman
Dear Miss.
Glaenzer, Richard Butler
Ballad of Redhead's Day, A.
Glancy, Diane
At the Pauwels.
I Am Not the Woman I Am.
Johnna at the Windmill.
Looking for My Old Indian Grandmother in the Summer Heat of 1980.
Lunar Eclipse.
Mary Ackerman, 1938.
Rahab.
There Won't Be Another.
Two Animals, One Flood.
Wheat.
Glanz [*or* Glantz]-Leyeles, A. *See* **Leyeles, A.**
Glasgow, Alex
Escalator, The.
Hands.
Little Tommy Yesterday.
Glass, Malcolm
Boy; or, Son of Rip-off, The.
Coming Down to It.
Risks.
Glassco, John
Brummell at Calais.
Burden of Junk, The.
Cardinal's Dog, The.
Day, The.
Deserted Buildings under Shefford Mountain.
Entailed Farm, The.
For Cora Lightbody, R.N.
One Last Word.
Quebec Farmhouse.
Rural Mail, The.
Stud Groom.
Glatstein [*or* Glatsteyn], Jacob
1919.
Abishag.
Arteriosclerosis.
Autobiography.
Autumn.
Back to the Ghetto.
Ballad: "Shoot, comrades."
Baron Tells of His Last Experience, The.
Bayonets.
Beginning.
Boy and a Roll, A, *sel.*
Bratslaver to His Scribe, The.
Bratzlav Rabbi to His Scribe, The.
Chopin Nocturne.
Clock and Mommie, *sel.*

Cry of the Gravediggers, The.
Death-Charade.
Dissolution.
Dostoevsky.
Evening Bread ("Fresh bread on the table").
Evening Jews.
Few Lines, A.
From Our Yoke.
Gaggie.
Genesis.
Girl of My Generation.
Good Night, World.
Hear and Be Stunned.
Here I Have Never Been.
How Much Christian.
Hunger Fell upon Us, A.
I Am Coming to You.
I Shall Remember.
I Shall Transport Myself.
I'll Find My Self-Belief.
In a Ghetto.
In the Middle of the Road.
In the Morning.
Jewish Kingdoms.
Let Us.
Like Chaff.
Like Weary Trees.
Loyal Sins.
Memorial Poem.
Move On, Yiddish Poet.
Mozart.
My Children's-Children's Past.
My Grandchild-Generation.
My Wander-Brother.
Nakhman of Bratslav to His Scribe.
Night, Be Mood to Me, *sel.*
1919.
Oh, let me through to the joy of the Yiddish word, *sel.*
Old Age.
On My Two-Hundredth Birthday.
On the Butcher Block.
Our Jewish Quarter.
Our Teacher Moses.
Poet Lives, The.
Prayer: "Inmost sense, The."
Property.
Proud King, The.
Rabbi Yussel Luksh of Chelm.
Resistance in the Ghetto.
Sabbath.
Sheeny Mike.
Small Night-Music.
Song, A: "Your song comes to me in little pieces."
Soon.
Steal into the Prayerbook, *sel.*
Sunday Shtetl.
To a Friend Who Wouldn't Bother to Strain His Noodleboard because Even So It Is Hard to Go Hunting When Your Rifle Is Blunt and Love Is Soft as an Old Blanket.
Trust me from here to there, *sel.*
Turtledoves.
Twelve.
Wagons.
We, of the Singing Swords.
We the Wordproletariat.
Where the Cedars.
Without Jews.
Without Offerings.
Yiddishkayt.
Glatsteyn, Jacob. *See* **Glatstein, Jacob**
Glaukos
Epigram: "Time was when once upon a time, such toys."
Glaze, Andrew
Outlanders, The.
Zeppelin.
Glazer, Joseph
Visit Home, A.

Gleason, Madeline
Once and Upon.
Gleason, Marian
Near Myth.
Glen, Duncan
Ane to Anither.
Stanes.
Glen, Emilie
Cat Ballerina Assoluta.
Glenn, Mel
Crystal Rowe.
Greg Hoffman.
Marvin Pickett.
Glick, Hirsch
We Survive!
Glider, Richard Watson
Of One Who neither Sees nor Hears.
Glik, Hirsh. *See* **Glick, Hirsch**
Gloag, John
Board Meets, The.
Glover, Denis
All of These.
Brightness.
Camp Site.
Casual Man, The.
Holiday Piece.
Home Thoughts.
Magpies, The.
Old Jason, the Argonaut, The.
Once the Days.
Prayer: "Mother of God, in this brazen sun."
Printers.
River Crossing, The.
Scene, The.
Search, The.
Soliloquies.
Song: "If everywhere in the street".
Song: "These songs will not stand".
Song: "When I am old".
Themes.
Thistledown.
To the Coast.
With his weapon a shovel.
Woman Shopping, A.
Glover, Guy
Lucifer, The.
Glover, R. W.
It Isn't the Town, It's You.
Glover, Richard
Admiral Hosier's Ghost.
Glück, Louise
All Hallows.
Apple Trees, The.
Aubade: "Today above the gull's call."
Bridal Piece.
Brooding Likeness.
Cottonmouth Country.
Dedication to Hunger.
Descending Figure.
Deviation, The, *sel.*
Drowned Children, The.
Elms.
Eros, *sel.*
For Jane Myers.
For My Mother.
From the Suburbs, *sel.*
Garden, The.
Gift, The.
Grandmother, *sel.*
Gratitude.
Gretel in Darkness.
Happiness.
Horse.
Hyacinth.
Jeanne d'Arc.
Labor Day.
Lamentations.
Magi, The.
Messengers.
Mirror, The.
Mock Orange.

Mountain, The.
My Neighbor in the Mirror.
Mythic Fragment.
Night Song.
Palais des Arts.
Phenomenal Survivals of Death in Nantucket.
Poem: "In the early evening, as now, a man is
bending."
Racer's Widow, The.
Sacred Objects, *sel.*
School Children, The.
Undertaking, The.
Wound, The.
Glynes, Ella Dietz
Unless.
Go-Komatsu, Emperor
Is it not time now.
Go-Shirakawa, Emperor
Bamboo grass in front of the Oji Shrine, The,
sel.
Brocade and rush hat you loved, The, *sel.*
Dance, dance, snail!, *sel.*
Even if I had to sleep alone, *sel.*
Even the moon, *sel.*
Head-lice make merry on my head, *sel.*
It's raining, but you say, "Go away!", *sel.*
Let's make love. The night has turned, *sel.*
Listen, waves, tell of this, beach, *sel.*
Looking at you, my beauty, *sel.*
Lord Buddha is present everywhere, *sel.*
Lying awake quietly at daybreak, *sel.*
Much, much in love, you see her by chance,
sel.
My daughter must be past ten by now, *sel.*
My son must be twenty by now, *sel.*
Potter at Mimaki in Kusuha, The, *sel.*
Stay, stay, dragonfly!, *sel.*
Things a prostitute likes, *sel.*
Things a sage likes, *sel.*
Things a terrifying exorcist likes, *sel.*
Things exceedingly swift, *sel.*
Things hilariously bent, *sel.*
Things lately fashionable in the capital, *sel.*
Things that dance well, exquisitely, *sel.*
Things that pierce the heart, *sel.*
Was I born to play?, *sel.*
When my mirror clouds up, *sel.*
Women are at their best, *sel.*
You, a man who made me wait but didn't
come, *sel.*
You have no heart, *sel.*
Young man came to make you his wife, The,
sel.
Godai Chitsu
Lifting hands, I climb the south star.
Godeschalk
Sequaire.
Godfrey, John
Errant.
Reveille.
Godfrey the Satirist
To Grosphus.
Godley, Alfred Denis
After Horace.
College Cat, The.
Eureka!
Football and Rowing—an Eclogue.
Lines on a Mysterious Occurrence.
Motor Bus.
On the Motor Bus.
Switzerland.
Women's Degrees.
Godley, Elizabeth
Ragged Robin.
Godolphin, Sidney
Constancye.
Hymn: "Lord, when the wise men came from
far[r]"
Reply.
Song: "Noe more unto my thoughts appeare."

Song: "Or love me less [*or* mee lesse], or
love me more."
Song: "'Tis affection but dissembled."
Sonnet: "Madam, "tis true, your beauties
move."
To the Tune of, In Fayth I Cannot Keepe My
Father's Sheepe.
Godric, Saint
Cry to Mary, A.
Godsey, Edwin S.
I Hope I Don't Have You Next Semester,
But.
Godwin, A.
Song for My Lady.
Goedicke, Patricia
After the Second Operation.
Circus Song.
Daily the Ocean between Us.
In the Ocean.
On the Night in Question.
Serious Merriment of Women, The.
Wise Owl.
Goethe, Johann Wolfgang von
Bride of Corinth, The.
Chanting sun, as ever, rivals, The, *sel.*
Christ Is Arisen, *sel.*
Cupbearer Speaks, The.
Erl-King, The.
Holy Longing, The.
Invisible King, The.
Irish Lamentation, An.
King of Thule, The.
Lay of the Captive Count, The.
Limits of the sphere of dream, The, *sel.*
Lose This Day Loitering, *sel.*
Market square's admiring throngs, The, *sel.*
Mignon.
Minstrel, The.
O'er all the hill-tops, *sel.*
Permanence in Change.
Poet to the Sleeping Saki, The.
Prologue in Heaven [*or* The Chorus of the
Archangels], *sel.*
Prometheus.
Rose, The.
Second Poem the Night-Walker Wrote, The.
Shepherd's Lament, The.
Soldier's Song, *sel.*
Stop playing with your melancholy, *sel.*
Symbolum.
Thou that from the heavens art, *sel.*
Thought Eternal, The.
To a Golden Heart, Worn round His Neck.
To the Parted One.
True Rest.
United States, The.
Voice from the Invisible World, A.
Voice of Experience, The.
Wanderer's Night-Song.
Who Never Ate with Tears His Bread.
Goffstein, M. B.
On This Day.
Gogan, Cothrai
Mountain Drive.
Prayer of a Pagan Woman.
Gogarty, Oliver St. John
After Galen.
Airman's Breastplate, The.
Anachronism.
Colophon.
Conquest, The.
Crab Tree, The.
Death May Be Very Gentle.
Dedication: "Tall unpopular men."
Exorcism.
Farrell O'Reilly.
Hay Hotel, The.
Image-Maker, The.
Leda and the Swan.
Marcus Curtius.
Non Dolet.

On the Use of Jayshus.
Palinode.
Per Iter Tenebricosum.
Plum Tree by the House, The.
Portrait with Background.
Ringsend.
To a Boon Companion.
To Death.
To Petronius Arbiter.
To the Liffey with the Swans.
To the Maids Not to Walk in the Wind.
To W. B. Yeats Who Says That His Castle of
    Ballylee Is His Monument.
Verse: "What should we know."
With a Coin from Syracuse.

Gogisgi. *See* **Arnett, Carroll**

Gokei
Flint spark? Lightning? All too late.

Gokyo, Ogasawara. *See* **Ogasawara Gokyo**

Gold, Artie
I Don't Have the Energy.
Life.

Gold, Edward
Unitas.

Gold, Jiri
In the Cellars.
Inhabited Emptiness, An.

Goldbarth, Albert
Accountings, The.
All-Nite Donuts.
"And Now Farley Is Going to Sing *While I
    Drink a Glass of Water!* ."
Before.
Dime Call.
Distances.
Family Grove.
Film, A.
Form and Function of the Novel, The.
History of Civilization, A.
History of Photography, A.
Joe Gillon Hypnotizes His Son.
Numbering at Bethlehem, The.
Pleasures.
Psychonaut Sonnets: Jones, The.
Recipe.
Saucer Station: Monday-Friday.
Starbirth.
Theory of Wind, A.
Tip, The.
Vestigial.
Window Seat, A.
World of Expectations, The.

Goldberg, Leah
Answer.
Blade of Grass Sings to the River, The.
Elul in Galilee.
From My Mother's House.
God Once Commanded Us, A.
Heat Spell in Venice.
Heavenly Jerusalem, of the Earth.
Illuminations.
Khamsin of Nisan.
Last Brightness.
My mother's mother died, *sel.*
My room is so small, *sel.*
Observation of a Bee.
Of Myself.
On Myself.
On the Hazards of Smoking.
Open Window in Florence.
Our Backs Are to the Cypress.
Outside the cats are wailing, *sel.*
Toward Myself.
Tree Celebrates the River, The.
When You Will Walk in the Field.

Goldberg, Israel. *See* **"Learsi, Rufus"**

Goldemberg, Isaac
Bar Mitzvah.
Jews in Hell, The.

Goldensohn, Barry
Dream as Calculation, The.

Garrotted Man, The.
Love And Work: Apple Picking.
No Word.
War and Peace.

Goldensohn, Lorrie
Changing the Tire.
Letter for a Daughter.
Plains of Heaven, The.
Real Estate.
Terms.
Trees, and What They Raise, The.

Golding, Louis
"I."
Is It Because of Some Dear Grace.
Jack.
Judaeus Errans.
O Bird, So Lovely.
Ploughman at the Plough.
Quarries in Syracuse.
Second Seeing.
Women at the Corners Stand, The.

Goldman, Michael
Crack, The.

Goldowsky, Barbara
Playing the Game.

Goldsmith, Frederica
Capes.

Goldsmith, Goldwin
Monkey's Glue, The.

Goldsmith, Oliver
Auburn.
Britain, *sel.*
David Garrick.
Description of an Author's Bedchamber, A.
Double Transformation, The.
Elegy on That Glory of Her Sex, Mrs. Mary
    Blaize, An.
Elegy on the Death of a Mad Dog, An.
Even now the devastation is begun.
First, Best Country, The.
Great Man, A.
Here lies our good Edmund, whose genius
    was such.
Ill fares the land, to hastening ills a prey.
Lud! what a group the motley scene discloses!
O luxury! Thou curst by Heaven's decree.
O Memory, Thou Fond Deceiver.
On Freedom and Ambition.
Parson Gray.
Poem, A: "Of old, when Scarron his
    companions invited."
Remote, unfriended, melancholy, slow.
Retaliation.
Sir Joshua Reynolds.
Song: "Let school-masters puzzle their brain."
Sonnet, A: "Weeping, murmuring,
    complaining."
Sweet Auburn! parent of the blissful hour.
Sweet smiling village, loveliest of the lawn.
Translation of a South American Ode.
Turn we to survey.
Village Parson, The.
Village Preacher, The.
Village Schoolmaster, The.
When Lovely Woman Stoops to Folly.
Yes! let the rich deride, the proud disdain.

Goldsmith, Oliver, the Younger
How sweet it is, at first approach of morn.
Not fifty summers yet have passed thy clime.
What noble courage must their hearts have
    fired.
While now the Rising Village claims a name.

Goldsworthy, Peter
Act Six.
Arson.
Ecclesiastes.
Shoeshine for Louis Armstrong, A.

Golffing, Francis C.
Higher Empiricism, The.

Goll, Claire
Prayer: "In the bright bay of your morning, O
    God."
She-Fox, The.

Goll, Iwan [*or* Yvan]
Clandestine Work.
John Landless Leads the Caravan.
Lilith.
Neïla.
Pear-Tree, The.
Raziel.
Song for a Jewess.

Gombrowicz, Witold
Game/ Suppose it's just a game, A.
Oh, the insanities I took part in!

Gomei
On a summer hill a doe appears.

Gomez, Antonio Enriquez
Elegy: "I die for Your holy word without
    regret."

Gomez, Jewelle
My Chakabuku Mama.

Gomez de Avellaneda, Gertrudis
On Leaving.
On Leaving Cuba, Her Native Land.

Gonçalves Dias, Antônio
There are palm trees in my homeland, *sel.*

Gong, Alfred
At That Time.
Boedromion.
Echo.
Failure.
Limbo.
Robinson.
Somnia.
Studium Generale.
Thanaton Melein.
Ultra.

Góngora, Carlos de Sigüenza y. *See*
    Sigüenza y Góngora, Carlos de

Góngora y Argote, Luis de
River Compared to an Oratorical Sentence,
    The.
Rosemary Spray, The.
Sweet Mouth, The.
Wedding Feast, The.
While Trying to Rival Your Hair.
Young Pilgrim Finds Refuge with the
    Goatherds, The.

Góngoray, Luis de
Let Me Go Warm.

Gonsalves, Ricardo
And.

Gonzales, Alonzo
Chipmunk can't drag it along.
Chipmunk was standing.

Gonzales, Rebecca
South Texas Summer Rain.

Gonzáles de Eslava, Fernán
To the Nativity.

Gonzáles Martínez, Enrique
Condemned, The.
House with Two Doors.
Last Journey.
Pain.
Romance of the Living Corpse.
When It Is Given You to Find a Smile.
Wring the Swan's Neck.

González León, Francisco
Hours.

Gonzalo Rose, Juan
Confidence, A.

Goodale, Dora Read
Flight of the Heart, The.
Judgment, The.
Soul of Man, The.

Goodbrand, D. S.
Kola Run, The.

Goode, Kate Tucker
Failure.

Goodge, W. T.
Daley's Dorg Wattle.

Goodison, Lorna
For Don Drummond.
"Mine, O Thou Lord of Life, Send My Roots
Rain."
Mulatta as Penelope, The.

Goodman, Mae Winkler
Image in a Mirror.

Goodman, Melinda
Body Work.
I Am Married to Myself.
Just How Crazy Brenda Is.
Wedding Reception.

Goodman, Mitchell
Coming and Going.
Man and Wife.

Goodman, Paul
April 1962.
Classical Quatrain, A.
Don Larsen's Perfect Game.
"Dreams Are the Royal Road to the
Unconscious."
Engingines, The.
Good Riddance to Bad Rubbish O at Last.
I planned to have a border of lavender.
Kent State, May 4, 1970.
Lines: "His cock is big and red when I am
there."
Little Ode.
Little Prayer, A.
Long Lines: Youth and Age.
Lordly Hudson, The.
March, 1941.
Pagan Rites, sel.
Saint Harmony my patroness.
Sonnet 21.
Sprayed with strong poison.
Stanzas: "I thought I woke: the midnight sun."
Surfers at Santa Cruz.
The *Weepers Tower* in Amsterdam.
Wellfleet Harbor.

Goodman, Ryah Tumarkin
Silence Spoke with Your Voice.

Goodrich, Samuel Griswold ("Peter Parley")
Higglety, Pigglety, Pop!
Lake Superior.

Goodwill, E. S.
Here is a beetle as black as my hat.

Goodwin, Edward B.
Aeneas built, in days of yore, sel.
Growth of Heptarchy we trace, The, sel.
Principal British Writers.

Googe, Barnabe
Coming Homeward out of Spain.
Of Money.
Once Musing as I Sat.
Out of Sight, Out of Mind.
Refusal, A.
To Alexander Neville.

Goose, Mary
Cornfield Myth.
Friends.
Insight.
Just an Old Man.
Last Night in Sisseton, S. D.

**Gorbanyevskaya [or Gorbanevskaya], Natalya
Yevgenevna**
And there is nothing at all—neither fear.
Cricket sings on Twelfth-night, The.
"Don't touch me!" I scream at passers-by.
Here, as in a painting, yellow noon burns [or
noon burns yellow]
In my own twentieth century.
In the bird scream and whistle.
Love, love! What nonsense it is.
Not because of you, not because of me, just
that.
This world/ is amazingly flat.
To I. Lavrentevaya.

Gordon, A. C.
Kree.
Roses of Memory.

Gordon, Adam Lindsay
Dedication, A: "They are rhymes rudely
strung with intent less."
How We Beat the Favourite.
Rest, and be thankful! On the verge, sel.
Sick Stockrider, The.
Sun and Rain and Dew from Heaven, sel.
We were glad together in gladsome meads,
sel.

Gordon, Charles F.
Long Night Home, The.

Gordon, Don
Laocoon.

Gordon, J.
To Amy.

Gordon, James Lindsay
Wheeler at Santiago.

Gordon, James William ("Jim Grahame")
Whalan of Waitin' a While.

Gordon, Judah Leib
Simhat Torah.

Gordon, Mary
Unwanted, The.

Gore-Booth, Eva
Crucifixion.
Heretic's Pilgrimage, A.

Gorenko, Anna Andreyevna. *See*
"Akhmatova, Anna"

Gorey, Edward
Babe, with a cry brief and dismal, The.
From the bathing machine came a din.
Lady who signs herself "Vexed," The.
Limerick: "There was a young woman named
Plunnery."
Lord Cray.
Some Harvard men, stalwart and hairy.

Gorges, Sir Arthur
Henceforth I will not set my love.
Her face her tongue her wit, at.
She that holds me under the laws of love.
Would I were chang'd into that golden
shower.

Görgey, Gábor
Anatomy of a Supper.
I'm fine, thanks, sel.
Interview.
Some Notes on the Wind.

Goring, J. H.
Home.

Gormley, Queen of Ireland
I have loved thirty by three, sel.

Gorton, Samuel
Serpent with a voyce, so slie and fine, The.

Gosse, Sir Edmund William
Lying in the Grass.
On Yes Tor.
Revelation.
Wallpaper, The.

Gotlieb, Phyllis
Cocker of Snooks, A.
Cosmology.
Death's Head.
Haiku and ½.
Late Gothic.
Morning Prayers of the Hasid, Rabbi Levi
Yitzhok, The.
This One's on Me.
Three-handed Fugue.
Was/Man.

Gotoba, Emperor
Faintly the spring, it seems.
Though the nightingale sings.

Gotsuan
With no-mind I've enjoyed my stay.

Gottfried von Strassburg
Tristan und Isolt.

Gottheil, Gustav
Come, O Sabbath Day.

Gottlieb, Ann
Lady Luck.

Gottlieb, Frantisek
Between Life and Death.
Just a While.

Gottlieb, Lynn
Eve's Song in the Garden.

Gottlieb, Michael
Focke-Wulfs.

Gould, E. E.
Tadpole, The.

Gould, Elizabeth
Grace and Thanksgiving.
Midsummer Night.
Mincemeat.
Mistress Comfort.
My New Rabbit.
Red in Autumn.
Shining Things.
Slumber in Spring.
Such a Blustery Day!
Washing-Up Song, The.
Wish, A.

Gould, Gerald
Child's Song.
Happy Tree, The.
This is the horror that, night after night.
You were young—but that was scarcely to
your credit, sel.

Gould, Hannah Flagg
Day of God! Thou Blessed Day.
Dying Child's Request, The.
Frost, The.
Name in the Sand, A.
Spider, The.

Gould, Janice
Caves, The.
Dispossessed.
Oregon Story, An.

Gould, Mona
This Was My Brother.

Goulder, Dave
January Man.
Long and Lonely Winter, The.

Gouri, Haim. *See* **Guri, Haim**

Gourmont, Remy de
Hair.

Govan, Donald D.
Recollection.

Govoni, Corrado
Little Trumpet, The.
Villages.

Gowar, Mick
Christmas Thank You's.

Gower, John
Jason and Medea, sel.
Parting of Venus and Old Age, The, sel.

Gozan, Kikuchi. *See* **Kikuchi Gozan**

Gozzano, Guido
Difference, The.
Last Betrayal, The.
Most Beautiful, The.
Toto Merumeni.
Winter Piece.

Graddon, Dorothy
Fairy Dream, A.
North Wind, The.
Travelling.
Wind, The.
Winter Joys.

Grade, Chaim
Miracle, The.
Refugees.
Sodom.
To Life I Said Yes.
Without Me You Won't be Able to See
Yourself.

Graeme, James
Mortified Genius, The.

Grafflin, Margaret Johnston
To My Son.

Grafton, Richard
Months of the Year, The.
Graham, A. M.
Aconite, The.
Graham, Al
Casey's Daughter at the Bat.
Graham, D. L.
Soul.
Tony Get the Boys.
West Ridge Is Menthol-Cool, The.
Graham, David
Landscape of Domestic Life.
Graham, Harry ("Col. D. Streamer")
Aunt Eliza.
Auntie, did you feel no pain.
Bath, The.
Bob was bathing in the Bay.
Cockney of the North, The.
Father, chancing to chastise.
Gourmand, The.
Grandpapa.
Impetuous Samuel.
Indifference.
L'Enfant Glacé.
Lord Gorbals.
Misfortunes Never Come Singly.
Mr. Jones.
My First Love.
O'er the rugged mountain's brow.
Opportunity.
Patience.
Perils of Obesity, The.
Philip, foozling with his cheek.
Poetical Economy.
Some Ruthless Rhymes, VII.
Stern parent, The.
Tender-heartedness.
There's been an accident.
Uncle.
Waste.
Graham, James, Marquess of Montrose
Epistle on King Charles I.
His Metrical Vow.
My dear and only Love, I pray, sel.
On Himself, upon Hearing What Was His
    Sentence.
Graham, Jorie
Age of Reason, The.
Artichoke for Montesquieu, An.
At Luca Signorelli's Resurrection of the
    Body.
At the Long Island Jewish Geriatric Home.
Drawing Wildflowers.
Erosion.
Evening Prayer.
Geese, The.
Haying.
History.
How Morning Glories Could Bloom at Dusk.
In What Manner the Body Is United with the
    Soule.
Jackpot.
Kimono.
Love.
Masaccio's Expulsion.
Mind.
My Garden, My Daylight.
Netting.
On Difficulty.
Over and Over Stitch.
Prayer: "Fabric I must keep mended. Rend."
Ravel and Unravel.
Reading Plato.
Sacrament of Gravity, The.
Salmon.
San Sepolcro.
San Xavier Du Bac/ for Jon.
Self Portrait as Both Parties.
Sundial.
Two Paintings by Gustav Klimt.

Wanting a Child.
Way Things Work, The.
Graham, Rachel
New Hampshire Farm Woman.
**Graham, Robert (Robert
    Cunninghame-Graham)**
If Doughty Deeds ("If daughty deeds my lady
    pleases.").
Graham, Rudy Bee
Memorandum.
Graham, Virginia
Disillusionment.
It's All Very Well Now.
1939 Somewhere in England.
Graham, William Sydney
Almost I, yes, I hear, sel.
Baldy Bane.
Beast in the Space, The.
Children of Greenock, The.
Constructed Space, The.
Hill of Intrusion, The.
I Leave This at Your Ear.
Johann Joachim Quantz's Five Lessons.
Language Ah Now You Have Me.
Letter V.
Letter VI.
Letter II.
Listen. Put on Morning.
Many without Elegy.
Note to the Difficult One, A.
Now in the third voice, sel.
Thermal Stair, The.
To My Father.
Untidy Dreadful Table.
Graham, Joyce Anstruther Maxtone. See
    "Struther, Jan"
Grahame, James
With earliest spring, while yet in mountain
    cleughs, sel.
Grahame, Kenneth
Ducks' Ditty, sel.
Song of Mr. Toad, The, sel.
Villagers all, this frosty tide, sel.
"Grahame, Jim." See **Gordon, James
    William**
Grahn, Judy
Asking for Ruthie.
Carol, in the Park, Chewing on Straws, sel.
Ella, in a Square Apron, along Highway 80,
    sel.
Frigga with Hela.
Funeral Plainsong from a Younger Woman to
    an Older Woman, A.
Helen in Hollywood.
History of Lesbianism, A.
In the place where, sel.
Meanings in the Pattern, The.
My name is Judith meaning, sel.
Talkers in a Dream Doorway.
They Say She Is Veiled.
Woman Is Talking to Death, A.
Grainger, James
Compost, sel.
How to Exterminate Rats, sel.
On festal days; or when their work is done,
    sel.
Slaves, sel.
Then earthquakes, nature's agonizing pangs,
    sel.
Grainger, Muriel
Love among the Ruins of London.
Granade, John A.
Come All Ye Mourning Pilgrims.
Sweet Rivers of Redeeming Love.
Grandsen, K. W.
Interview, An.
Grano, Paul
"New Shirt, A!" Why?
Grant, Eddy
War Party.

Grant, James Russell
Africa.
Grant, Lillian
Lines Written in a Mausoleum.
Grant, Richard E.
Broken Heart, Broken Machine.
Grant, Sir Robert
Majesty and Mercy of God, The.
Granville, George, Baron Lansdowne
Cloe.
Impatient with Desire.
Love.
To Cloe.
Grave, John
If Thou Wilt Hear.
Graves, A. P.
Haymaking.
Graves, Charles Larcom
Horace, Book V, Ode III.
Old Song Resung, An.
Graves, John Woodcock
John Peel.
Graves, Richard
Maternal Despotism; or, The Rights of
    Infants.
Graves, Robert
Advice to Colonel Valentine.
Allansford Pursuit, The.
Allie ("Allie, call the birds in").
Ambrosia of Dionysus and Semele, The.
At First Sight.
Beach, The.
Beauty in Trouble.
Bedpost, The.
Birth of a Great Man.
Blue-Fly, The.
Broken Girth, The.
Call It a Good Marriage.
Carol of Patience.
Cat Goddesses.
Certain Mercies.
Change.
Clearing, The.
Climate of Thought, The.
Confess, Marpessa.
Conversation Piece.
Cool Web, The.
Corner Knot, The.
Corporal Stare.
Counting the Beats.
Cry Faugh!
Damocles.
Dead Cow Farm.
Death Room, The.
Defeat of the Rebels.
Devil's Advice to Story-Tellers, The.
Door, The.
Down, Wanton, Down!
Dr. Newman with the crooked pince-nez, sel.
1805.
End of Play.
English Wood, An.
Epitaph on an Unfortunate Artist.
Eremites, The.
Escape.
Eugenist, The.
Face in the Mirror, The.
Fallen Tower of Siloam, The.
Finland.
Flying Crooked.
For the Rain It Raineth Every Day.
Forced Music, A.
Foreboding, The.
Frog and the Golden Ball, The.
From the Embassy.
Frosty Night, A.
Full Moon.
Gift of Sight.
Glutton, The.
Grotesques.
Hag-ridden.

Hedges Freaked with Snow.
Henry and Mary.
Hero, The.
Hide and Seek.
Homage to Texas.
I sat in my chamber yesternight.
I Will Write.
I Wonder What It Feels Like to Be Drowned?
I'd Love to Be a Fairy's Child.
In Her Only Way.
In Her Praise.
In Perspective.
In Procession.
In the Beginning Was a Word.
In the Wilderness.
In Time.
Intercession in Late October.
Interruption.
It Was All Very Tidy.
It's a Queer Time.
Jealous Man, A.
John Skelton.
Judgement of Paris.
Lament for Pasiphae.
Last Post, The.
Laureate, The.
Legion, The.
Legs, The.
Lollocks.
Lost Acres.
Lost Jewel, The.
Lost Love.
Lost World, A.
Love Story, A.
Love without Hope.
Lovers in Winter.
Marigolds.
Mid-Winter Waking.
My Name and I.
Naked and the Nude, The.
Narrow Sea, The.
Nature's Lineaments.
Neglectful Edward.
Never Such Love.
Next War, The.
Ogres and Pygmies.
Oleaster, The.
On Dwelling.
On Portents.
Penthesileia.
Persian Version, The.
Philatelist Royal.
Pier-Glass, The.
Pinch of Salt, A.
Plea to Boys and Girls, A.
Poets' Corner.
Point of No Return.
Portrait, The.
Primrose Bed, The.
Pumpkin, The.
Pure Death.
Pure Death.
Queen Mother to New Queen.
Quiet Glades of Eden, The.
Read Me, Please!
Reader over My Shoulder, The.
Recalling War.
Reproach to Julia.
Return of the Goddess Artemis.
Richard Roe and John Doe ("Richard Roe
  wished himself Solomon.").
Rocky Acres.
Sail and Oar.
Saint.
Sea Horse, The.
Sergeant-Major Money.
Sharp Ridge, The.
She Is No Liar.
She Tells Her Love while Half Asleep.
Sick Love.
Sir John addressed the Snake-god in his
  temple, *sel.*

Six Badgers, The.
Slice of Wedding Cake, A.
Song: How Can I Care?
Song: One Hard Look.
Spoils.
Star-Talk.
Straw, The.
Succubus, The.
Surgical Ward: Men.
Survivor, The.
Symptoms of Love.
Theseus and Ariadne.
Thieves, The.
Three-faced, The.
Tilth.
Time.
To Bring the Dead to Life.
To Calliope.
To Juan at the Winter Solstice.
To Lucia at Birth.
To Walk on Hills.
To Whom Else?
Travel[l]er's Curse after Misdirection, The.
Troll's Nosegay, The.
Trudge, Body.
Turn of the Moon.
Twins.
Two Fusiliers.
Two Witches, The.
Ulysses.
Under the Pot.
Vanity.
Variables of Green.
Villagers and Death, The.
Warning to Children.
Weather of Olympus, The.
"Wellcome, to the Caves of Artá!"
Welsh Incident.
White Goddess, The.
Wigs and Beards.
Wild Strawberries.
Window Sill, The.
With a Gift of Rings.
Wm. Brazier.
Woman and Tree.
Wreath, The.
Young Cordwainer, The.
Gray, Darrell
Foreplay of the Alphabet.
Moving.
Ode to Food.
20th Century, The.
Gray, David
Cross of Gold, The.
Divided.
Golden Wedding, The.
My Epitaph.
On Lebanon.
Sonnet I: "If it must be; if it must be, O
  God!," *sel.*
Where the Lilies Used to Spring.
Gray, John
Barber, The.
Battledore.
Flying Fish, The.
Gazelles and Unicorn, *sel.*
Les Demoiselles de Sauve.
Lord, If Thou Art Not Present.
Mishka.
Night Nurse Goes Her Round, The.
Odiham.
Of the birds that fly in the farthest sea, *sel.*
On the South Coast of Cornwall.
Poem: "Geranium, houseleek, laid in oblong
  beds."
Poem: Spleen.
They say, in other days.
Tobias and the Angel.
Vines, The.
Wings in the Dark.
Gray, Patrick Worth
Necessity Is the Mother of the "Bullet."

Gray, Robert
5 Poems.
Gray, Sir Alexander
Scotland.
Sir Halewyn.
Gray, Stephen
Girl with Doves.
Girl with Long Dark Hair.
Gray, Thomas
Bard a Pindaric Ode, The.
Boast of heraldry, the pomp of pow'r, The,
  sel.
Candidate, The.
Curse upon Edward, The.
Death of Hoel, The.
Elegy Written in a Country Churchyard.
Epitaph: "Here rests his head upon the lap of
  earth," *sel.*
Epitaph on Dr. Keene.
Epitaph on Dr. Keene's Wife.
Fatal Sisters, The.
Fragment: "There pipes the wood-lark, and
  the song thrush there."
Hymn to Adversity.
Lines Spoken by the Ghost of John Dennis at
  the Devil Tavern.
Now the golden morn aloft, *sel.*
Ode on a Distant Prospect of Eton College.
Ode on [*or* On] the Death of a Favourite [*or*
  Favorite] Cat, Drowned in a Tub [*or*
  Bowl] of Gold Fishes.
Ode on the Pleasure Arising from Vicissitude.
Ode on the Spring.
On Dr. Keene, Bishop of Chester.
On Lord Holland's Seat near Margate, Kent.
Pindaric Ode, A, *sel.*
Progress of Poesy, The.
Satire upon the Heads.
Sonnet on the Death of Mr. Richard West.
Stanzas to Mr. Bentley.
Tophet.
Triumphs of Owen, The.
Gray, Victor
Ballad, A: "All the World's a Stage."
Limerick: "Charlotte Brontë said, "Wow,
  sister! *What* a man!"
Limerick: "Old East End worker called Jock,
  An."
Limerick: "One morning old Wilfrid Scawen
  Blunt."
Limerick: "Taxi-cab whore out at Iver, A."
Limerick: "There was a young fellow called
  Crouch."
Limerick: "When Gauguin was visiting Fiji."
Limerick: "When our dean took a pious young
  spinster."
Limerick: "While visiting Arundel Castle."
Limerick: "Young engine-driver called Hunt,
  A."
Gray, William B.
She Is More to Be Pitied than Censured.
Grayson, Caroline
After.
Grazia, Emilio de
Pasttime.
Greacen, Robert
Bird, The.
Curse.
Far Country, The.
Glorious Twelfth, The.
Michael Walked in the Wood.
Written on the Sense of Isolation in
  Contemporary Ireland.
Greeff, Adele
Sonnet XI: "Is God invisible? This very
  room."
Green, Brenda Heloise
New England Is New England Is New
  England.
Green, David H.
Down East Drama.

Green, F. Pratt
Old Couple, The.
Green, H. M.
Cicada, The.
Green, Jane
Songs of Divorce.
Green, Joseph
Permit Us, Lord, to Consecrate.
Green, Judith
Bush-Fiddle, The.
Green, Matthew
But now more serious let me grow, *sel.*
First know, my friend, I do not mean, *sel.*
In Praise of Water-Gruel, *sel.*
On Barclay's Apology for the Quakers.
Sparrow and Diamond, The.
Green, Melissa
More than novelty crooked its finger—silent, austere.
Green, Roger Lancelyn
On First Looking into the Dark Future.
"Green, Coroebus." See Cone, Helen Gray
Greenaway, Kate
Boat Sails Away, The.
Five Little Sisters Walking in a Row.
Happy Child, A.
In go-cart so tiny.
Little Jumping Girls, The.
Little Wind.
On the Bridge.
Ring-a-Ring.
Will You Be My Little Wife?
Greenberg, Barbara L.
Faithful Wife, The.
Greenberg, Samuel
Blank Book Letter, The.
Conduct.
Essentials.
Glass Bubbles, The.
I Cannot Believe That I Am of Wind.
Immortality.
Killing.
Soul's Kiss.
Spirituality.
To Dear Daniel.
Greenberg, Uri Zvi [or Tsvi]
Cutting Off, The.
Forest's black and dense, The; it grows out of the flatlands, *sel.*
Great Sad One, The.
Hour, The.
How It Is.
Jerusalem the Dismembered, *sel.*
King Shabtai Tsvi.
Like a Woman.
On the Pole.
Song at the Skirts of Heaven.
There Is a Box.
Valley of Men, The.
Why is it then that early-spring blue is so deeply distressed?, *sel.*
With My God, the Smith.
Greene, Albert Gorton
Baron's Last Banquet, The.
Old Grimes.
Greene, Ashton
Lagoon, The.
Parade, The.
Greene, Homer
What My Lover Said.
Greene, Richard L.
Song to Imogen [in Basic English]
Greene, Robert
Ah Were She Pitiful.
Barmenissa's Song.
Coridon and Phillis.
Description of Sir Geoffrey Chaucer, The.
Doralicia's Song.
Doron's Description of Samela.
Doron's Jigge.
Eurymachus's Fancy.

Fair Is My Love.
Fie, Fie on Blind Fancy!
Hexametra Alexis in Laudem Rosamundi.
Infida's Song.
Love and Jealousy.
Maesia's Song.
Mars and Venus.
Menaphon's Ditty.
Menaphon's Song.
Of His Mistress.
Palinode, A.
Palmer's Ode, The.
Penitent Palmer's Ode, The.
Philomela's Second Ode.
Sephestia's Song to Her Child[e].
Shepherd's Ode, The.
Shepherd's Wife's Song, The.
Sitting by a river['s] side.
Song: "Sweet are the thoughts that savour of content."
Verses under a Peacock Portrayed in Her Left Hand.
Whereat Erewhile I Wept, I Laugh.
Greene, Sarah Pratt McLean
De Dheepfol.'
Lamp, The.
Sheepfol', De.
Greenfield, Eloise
Moochie ("Moochie likes to keep on playing").
Greenfield, Freddie
Oh God Forbid.
Greenfield, Marjorie H.
Things I Like.
Greenwald, Ted
And, Hinges.
Complete Balancing Weather Meets.
Experience a table of.
Lapstrake.
Lies.
Privets Come into Season at High Tide.
Greenwell, Bill
King Ethelred the Unready.
Greenwell, Dora
Picture, A.
Saturday Review, The.
Scherzo, A.
Sun-Flower, The.
When the Night and Morning Meet.
Greenwood, Dr. ———
Epitaph—on the Wife of Dr. Greenwood.
"Greenwood, Grace" (Sarah Jane Clarke Lippincott)
Illumination for Victories in Mexico.
Greger, Debora
Armorer's Daughter, The.
Light Passages, The.
Man on the Bed, The.
Of.
Patches of Sky.
Second Violinist's Son, The.
Snow White and Rose Red.
Gregg, Linda
Alma to Her Sister.
As When the Blowfish Perishing.
At the Gate in the Middle of My Life.
Beckett Kit, The.
Being with Men.
Children among the Hills.
Choosing the Devil.
Chorus Speaks Her Words as She Dances, The.
Color of Many Deer Running, The.
Coming Back.
Copperhead, The.
Death Looks Down.
Euridice Saved.
Eurydice.
Girl I Call Alma, The.
Gnostics on Trial.
Gods Must Not Know Us, The.

Goethe's Death Mask.
Growing Up.
How the Joy of It Was Used Up Long Ago.
Lilith.
Marriage and Midsummer's Night.
Not Saying Much.
Not Wanting Myself.
River Again and Again, The.
Sigismundo.
Small Lizard, The.
Summer in a Small Town.
Sun Moon Kelp Flower or Goat.
There She Is.
Things Not of This Union.
Trying to Believe.
We Manage Most When We Manage Small.
What They Ate What They Wore.
White Light.
Whole and without Blessing.
Winter Birds.
Gregh, Fernand
Doubt.
Gregor, Arthur
Enough.
History.
Irreconcilables.
Late Last Night.
Likeness, The.
Lyric: "Embodiment of what, The."
Poem: "So many pigeons at Columbus."
Spirit-like before Light.
Spirits, Dancing.
Two Shapes.
Unalterables.
Gregor, Christian
What Splendid Rays.
Gregory, Carole C.
Freedom Song for the Black Woman, A.
Greater Friendship Baptist Church, The.
Love Letter.
Revelation.
Gregory, Horace
And of Columbus.
Ask no return for love that's given, *sel.*
Death and Empedocles 444 B.C.
Elegy and Flame.
For You, My Son.
Foreigner Comes to Earth on Boston Common, A.
Longface Mahoney Discusses Heaven.
On a Celtic Mask by Henry Moore.
Poems for My Daughter.
Postman's Bell Is Answered Everywhere, The.
Rehearsal, The.
They Found Him Sitting in a Chair.
They Were All like Geniuses.
This Is the Place to Wait.
To the Last Wedding Guest.
Valediction to My Contemporaries.
Voices of Heroes.
Gregory, Leona
Silence, an Eloquent Applause.
Gregory, Yvonne
Christmas Lullaby for a New-born Child.
Gregory the Great, Saint
Behold, the Shade of Night Is Now Receding.
Morning Hymn.
Greiffenberg, Catharina Regina von
Anti-Cupid.
On the Ineffable Inspiration of the Holy Spirit.
Spring-Joy Praising God; Praise of the Sun.
Greig, Andrew
Marry the Lass?
On Falling.
Greig, Desmond A.
On a Scooter.
To a Flea in a Glass of Water.
Gréki, Anna
Before Your Waking.
Future is for tomorrow, The.

Grenelle, Lisa
Duel in the Park.

Grenfell, Joyce
Joyce: By Herself and Her Friends.
March Day, 1941.

Grenfell, Julian
Into Battle.

Grenier, Robert
Crossing Ontario.
For Windows.
Long walk, A.
Of life days like.
Prewar Late October Sea Breeze.
Snow/ blue/ eyes.
Snow covers the slopes, covers the slopes.
Spring.
Sticky Fingers.
Striped Canvas.
Warm.
Wintry.
Wrath to Sadness.
Yah gee.

Grenville, R. H.
Pawnshop Window.

Grenville, Sir Richard
In Praise of Seafaring Men, in Hopes of Good
  Fortune.

Grenville, George, Baron Lansdowne. *See*
  Granville, George, Baron Lansdowne

Grépon, Marguerite
Story in Poetic Form: The Androgyne.

Gresham, Walter S.
Crowded Ways of Life.

Greville, Frances (Fanny Macartney)
I ask no kind return of love.
Prayer for Indifference, A.

Greville, Fulke, 1st Baron Brooke
Absence, the noble truce.
All my senses, like beacon's flame.
Away with these self-loving lads.
Caelica, I overnight was finely used.
Caelica, XCIV.
Caelica, when I did see you every day.
Chiefe use then in man of that he knowes,
  The.
Chorus Primus: Wise Counsellors.
Chorus Quintus: Tartarorum.
Chorus Sacerdotum.
Chorus Tertius: Of Time; Eternitie.
Cupid, thou naughty boy, when thou wert
  loathed.
Down in the depth of mine iniquity.
Earth with thunder torn[e], with fire blasted,
  The.
Epitaph on Sir Philip Sidney, *at.*
Eternall Truth, almighty, infinite.
Faction, that ever dwells.
Farewell, sweet boy; complain not of my
  truth.
Fie [*or* Fye], foolish Earth, think[e] you the
  heaven wants glory.
Golden age was when the world was young,
  The.
I, with whose colors [*or* colours] Myra
  dressed [*or* dress'd] her head.
In night, when colors [*or* colours] all to
  black[e] are cast.
In the time when herbs and flowers.
In the window of a grange.
In those years when our sense, desire and wit.
Love is the peace, whereto all thoughts do[e]
  strive.
Love, the delight of all well-thinking minds.
Man, dream[e] no more of curious mysteries.
Manicheans did no idols make, The.
Men, that delight to multiply desire.
More than most fair, full of that heavenly fire.
Nurse-life wheat, within his greene huske
  growing, The.

O false and treacherous Probability.
Sion lies [*or* Syon lyes] waste, and thy
  Jerusalem.
Three things there be in man's opinion
  dear[e].
Turkish government allows no law, The.
Under a throne I saw a virgin sit.
Vigula divina , sorcerers call a rod.
When all this All doth pass from age to age.
Whenas [*or* When as] man's life, the light of
  human[e] lust.
Who grace, for zenith had, from which no
  shadowes grow.
World, That All Contains, Is Ever Moving,
  The.
World, that all contains, is ever moving, The.
Wrapped up, O Lord, in man's degeneration.
You little stars that live in skies.
You that seek what life is in death.

Grew, Gwendolyn
Burning the Letters.

Grey of Fallodon, Pamela Grey, Viscountess
Echo.

Grier, Eldon
I Am Almost Asleep.
Kissing Natalia.
More Than Most People.
Mountain Town—Mexico.
My Winter Past.
On the Subject of Waves.
Sensible Is the Label.

Grierson, Constantia
To Miss Laetitia Van Lewen.

Grieve, Christopher Murray. *See*
  "MacDiarmid, Hugh"

Griffin, Bartholomew
Care-Charmer Sleep.
Faire Is My Love.
Fly [*or* Flye] to her heart; hover about her
  heart.
I have not spent the April of my time.
My ladies haire is threeds of beaten gold.

Griffin, Caroline
Elizabeth.
If My Life Could Be Simple.
Strong Thighs astride My Chest.

Griffin, Gerald
I Love My Love in the Morning.
O Brazil, the Isle of the Blest.
Song: "Place in thy memory, dearest, A."
To a Seagull.
To the Blessed Virgin Mary.
When like the rising day.

Griffin, "Sin-Killer"
Man of Calvary, The.
Roman soldiers come riding in full speed.

Griffin, Susan
Acoustics.
An Answer to a Man's Question, "What Can I
  Do about Women's Liberation?"
Awful Mother, The.
Bad Mother, The.
Chance Meeting.
Chile.
Distress.
Dogs.
Field.
Garden, The, *sel.*
I Like to Think of Harriet Tubman.
I Wake Thinking of Myself as a Man.
Letter to the Revolution.
Love Should Grow Up like a Wild Iris in the
  Fields.
My Child.
Perfect Mother, The.
Perversity.
Pot of Tea.
Prayer for Continuation.
Prologue: "He says that woman speaks with
  nature."

Silence.
Sitting.
Song My.
Song of the Woman with Her Parts Coming
  Out, The.
Teeth.
Three Poems for Women.
Three Shades of Light on the Windowsill.
Tissue.
Trying to Say, #15.
Waiting for Truth.
Woman Defending Herself Examines Her
  Own Character Witness, A.

Griffith, Llewelyn Wyn
From his own solitude to the world
  unheeding.
Silver Jubilee.

Griffiths, Ann
Lo, between the Myrtles Standing.

Griffiths, I. T.
On First Looking into Chapman's Homer.

Griffiths, Monique
Girl Talk.
Nothing to Say.

Griffiths, T.
La Belle Dame sans Merci.
When man walketh moon.

Grigson, Geoffrey
Above the High.
Administrator, An.
And Forgetful of Europe.
Before a Fall.
Bibliotheca Bodleiana.
Burials.
By the Road.
Crematorium, The.
Critics and Poets.
Discoveries of Bones and Stones.
End of the Affair.
Four, The.
Glen Lough.
Hardy's Plymouth.
His Swans.
Inside the Cave.
June in Wiltshire.
Landscape of the Heart, The.
May Trees in a Storm.
Meeting by the Gjulika Meadow.
On a Birth.
On a Lover of Books.
On the Eve of a Birthday.
On the Relinquishment of a Title.
Professionals, The.
Sandy Burial, A.
Thank You.
To Wystan Auden.
Tresco.
Two Are Together.
Uccello on the Heath.
Under the Cliff.

Grilikhes, Alexandra
Runner, The.
Statue, The.

Grimald, Nicholas
Garden, The.
True Love, A.
Virtue.

Grimes, Willard M.
Piazza di Spagna.

Grimké, Angelina Weld
At April.
Black Finger, The.
Dusk.
Eyes of My Regret, The.
For the Candle Light.
Grass Fingers.
Greenness.
Hushed by the Hands of Sleep.
I Weep.
Mona Lisa, A.
Paradox.

Puppet Player, The.
Surrender.
Tenebris.
To Clarissa Scott Delany.
To Keep the Memory of Charlotte Forten
   Grimké.
Ways o' Men, The.
When the Green Lies over the Earth.
Winter Twilight, A.
Your Hands.

Grindal, Edmund
Give Peace in These Our Days, O Lord.

Griswold, Alexander V.
Holy Father, Great Creator.

Grochowiak, Stanislaw
Breasts of the Queen Are Turned out of
   Wood, The.
Clean Men.
Painting.
Short Fairy Tale, A.
To a Lady.
Village Cinema, The.
When Nothing Remains.

Groesbeck, Amy
Momist.

Gross, Ronald
Yield.

Grossman, Allen
Department, The.
Lilith.
Piano Player Explains Himself, The.
Thrush Relinquished, The.

Grossman, Andrew J.
Sometime the Cow Kick Your Head.

Grossman, Martin
Bread of Our Affliction, The.
Into the Book.

Grossman, Reuben
Therefore, We Thank Thee, God.

Grove, C. L.
5th Stanza For Dr. Johnson, Donald Hall,
   Louis Phillips, and X. J. Kennedy, A.

Grove, Matthew
In Praise of His Lady, sel.

Grove, Bob. See **Franklin, William**

Gruber, Abraham L.
My Neighbor's Roses.

Gruber, Johann A.
Love That's Pure, Itself Disdaining.

Grudin, Louis
Dust on Spring Street.

Gruffudd ab yr Ynad Coch
Lament for Llywelyn ap Gruffudd.

Gruffydd, Owen
Old, old/ To live on, wretched to behold, sel.

Gruffydd, W. J.
Gwladys Rhys.
In Memoriam.
This Poor Man.

Grumbach, Argula von
Argula's Answer.
Verses against Argula.

Grundtvig, Nicolai Frederik Severin
I Know a Flower So Fair and Fine.

Grünewald, Alfred
Lamp Now Flickers, The.

Grynberg, Henryk
Anti-Nostalgia.
Dead Sea, The.
Listening to Confucius.
Poplars.

Guadamuz, Carlos José
Flower, A.

Guan
Eighty years, a day's journey.

Guarini, Giovanni Battista
Claim to Love.
Fair Eyes, Ye Mortal Stars Below.
Golden Age, The, sel.
Spring.
Thus saith my Chloris bright.

Guchu
Not seeing that a "Zen man" is no Zen man.

Gudo
Right's fine, wrong's fine.

Guebuza, Armando
If You Ask Me Who I Am.
Your Pain.

Guérin, Charles
Partings.

Guernsey, Bruce
Louis B. Russell.

Guerrini, Rosanna
To My Children.

Guest, Barbara
Direction.
Green Revolutions.
Luminous, The.
Parachutes, My Love, Could Carry Us
   Higher.
Parade's End.
Piazzas.
Poem: "Disturbing to have a person."
Red Lilies.
River Road Studio.
Santa Fe Trail.
Sunday Evening.
20.
Words.

Guest, Edgar Albert
Becoming a Dad.
Friend's Greeting, A.
Grace at Evening.
Home.
It Couldn't Be Done.
Just Folks.
Lemon Pie.
Lesson from Golf, A.
Lord, Make a Regular Man out of Me.
Myself.
Out Fishin.'
Sausage.
Stick to It.
Things that Make a Soldier Great, The.

Guevara, Miguel de
Sonnet: "I am not moved to love thee, my
   Lord God."

Guevara, Pablo
An Attack, 1940.
Babylon, O Babylon.
Bourgeois Are Beasts, The.
Guita Bruner.
Heaven and Hell.
I remember, sel.
My Father.

Guggenberger, Louisa S.
Afternoon.
"Am I to Lose You?"
Egoisme à Deux.
Love and Language.
Twilight.

Guglielminetti, Amalia
Destiny.
My Voice.

Guidacci, Margherita
All Saints' Day; November sky, sel.
At Night.
Many Times November Has Come Back.

Guiducci, Armanda
Equality.
Man.
Song of the Hammer.

Guilhem de Cabestanh
Sweet softness with which love serves me
   often, The.

Guillaume de Lorris and **Jean de Meun**
Garden of Amour, The, sel.
Short space my feet had traversed ere, sel.
There is no place in paradise, sel.

Guillaume de Poitiers
Behold, the Meads.
Count William's Escapade.

I shall make a new song now.
I shall make a vers about/ nothing.
I would like it if people knew this song.
I'll make a vers while I'm asleep here.
I'm going to make a vers boys,. good
   enough?
In the new season.
I've heard the talk.
Luckily, I take great joy of love.
So much bad food and worse liquor, friends.
Song seizes me, but my own vers gives me
   dolor.
When we see again the spring blossoming of
   the world.

Guillelma de Rosers
Dame Guillelma, several knights travelling by
   dark.

Guillén, Jorge
Faithful Lovers, The.
Summit of Delight.

Guillén, Nicolás
Bars.
Dead Soldier.
Go Get Some Bread.
Guadalupe, W.I.
Proposition.
Sightseers in a Courtyard.

Guillet, Pernette de
Non Que Je Veuille Ôter la Liberté.

Guillevic, Eugène
Be Fair.
Cabinet, A.
Eternity.
Face.
Flame, The.
Hammer, A.
Let Me Get Up Early.
Sea, The.
Spain.

Guiney, Louise Imogen
Deo Optimo Maximo.
Footnote to a Famous Lyric, A.
In Leinster.
John Brown; a Paradox.
Martyr's Memorial.
Ode for a Master Mariner Ashore.
Of Joan's Youth.
On First Entering Westminster Abbey.
Outdoor Litany, An.
Pax Paganica.
Sanctuary.
Valse Jeune.
Wild Ride, The.

Guinicelli [or Guinizelle], Guido
Canzone: Of the Gentle Heart.
He Perceives His Rashness in Love, but Has
   No Choice.
Sonnet: He Will Praise His Lady.
Sonnet: Of Moderation and Tolerance.

Guiterman, Arthur
Ain't Nature Commonplace!
Alibi.
Ancient History.
Anthologistics.
Bears.
Blessing on Little Boys.
Brief Essay on Man.
Call to the Colors, The.
Chums.
Consolation.
Daniel Boone.
Eight Oars and a Coxswain ("Eight oars
   compel").
Everything in Its Place.
Haarlem Heights.
Habits of the Hippopotamus.
Harvest Home.
He Leads Us Still.
Heredity.
House Blessing.
In Praise of Llamas.

In the Hospital.
Lament for the Alamo.
Legend of the First Cam-u-el, The.
Local Note.
Mavrone.
Mexican Serenade.
Ode to the Hayden Planetarium.
Of Certain Irish Fairies.
Of Tact.
Offer, An.
On the Vanity of Earthly Greatness.
Oregon Trail, The.
Polliwog, The.
Quivíra.
Routine.
Rush of the *Oregon, The.*
School Days in New Amsterdam.
Scribe's Prayer, The.
Sea-Chill.
Shakespearean Bear, The.
Song of Hate for Eels.
Storming of Stony Point, The.
Strictly Germ-proof.
What the Gray Cat Sings.
Young Washington.

Gulick, Alida Carey
On Waking.

Gullans, Charles
Autumn; an Ode.
Autumn Burial; a Meditation.
First Love.
Narcissus.
Poema Morale.
Satyr.
To a Friend.

Gullar, Ferreira
August 1964.
Clouds' Work.
Man Seated.
Pears, The.
Subversive.
Things of the Earth.

Gullette, David
Angling.

Gumilev, Nikolai Stepanovich
How Could We, Beforehand, Live in Quiet.
Listen:/ There roams, far away, by the waters
    of Clead, *sel.*

Gummere, Francis Barton
John Bright.

Günderode, Karoline von
Dream Kiss, The.
To Creuzer.

Gundersheimer, Karen
Happy Winter, Steamy Tub.

Gunn, Louise D.
Conversation with Rain.

Gunn, Thom
Allegory of the Wolf Boy, The.
Annihilation of Nothing, The.
Apartment Cats.
As Expected.
Autobiography.
Autumn Chapter in a Novel.
Baby Song.
Back to Life.
Before the Carnival.
Black Jackets.
Breakfast.
Byrnies, The.
Carnal Knowledge.
Cherry Tree, The.
Claus von Stauffenberg.
Confessions of the Life Artist.
Considering the Snail.
Corridor, The.
Courage, a Tale.
Das Liebesleben.
Discovery of the Pacific, The.
Donahue's Sister.
Elegy on the Dust.

Encolpius, *sel.*
Expression.
Fair in the Woods, The.
Faustus Triumphant.
Fever.
For Signs.
From the Highest Camp.
From the Wave.
Hampstead; the Horse Chestnut Trees.
High Fidelity.
Hitching into Frisco, *sel.*
Idea of Trust, The.
In Santa Maria del Popolo.
In the Tank.
Incident on a Journey.
Innocence.
Iron Landscapes (and the Statue of Liberty).
Jesus and His Mother.
Lament: "Your dying was a difficult
    enterprise."
Lights among Redwood.
Loot.
Map of the City, A.
Merlin in the Cave: He Speculates without a
    Book.
Messengers, The.
Mirror for Poets, A.
Modes of Pleasure.
Moly.
My Sad Captains.
Nature of an Action, The.
No Speech from the Scaffold.
On the Move.
Rooftop, The.
St. Martin and the Beggar.
Serving man, A. Curled my hair, *sel.*
Street Song.
Tamer and Hawk.
To Yvor Winters, 1955.
Touch.
Trucker, A.
Unsettled Motorcyclist's Vision of His Death,
    The.
Vox Humana.
Wheel of Fortune, The.
Wound, The.
Yoko.

Gunnars, Kristjana
Changeling VIII.
Wakepick I.

Gurevitch, Zali
Not Going with It.
Short Eulogy.

Guri [*or* Gouri], Haim [*or* Khayim *or* Chaim]
Age Is Ended, An.
Album.
Anath.
And of all that was theirs only the letters were
    left.
And on My Return.
And This Happened.
At the Train Station.
But We Shall Bloom.
Dance.
Flame and wood and blackened stones like
    these.
His Mother.
Holiday's End.
I Fancy That I'm Standing Guard.
I live now in an ancient book.
I pray you, forgive me in the stillness of your
    shoes swollen on these sands.
If.
I'll be an amulet, I'll be good news.
In the Amorite City.
Isaac.
It seems to me I'm watching over walls.
Jericho.
Latter Purification, A.
Mistake.
My Samsons.
Nine Men out of a Minyan.

Northern Romance.
Odysseus.
Of the Azazmeh Too.
Pictures of Jews.
Piraeus.
Piyyut for Rosh Hashana.
Piyyut for the New Year.
Prayer: "Thy blessing on the boys—for time
    has come."
Rain.
Silk and Silence.
There Once Was a Dove.
Thorns.
Window-Dreaming with SAS.
You're No King.

Gurney, Dorothy Frances
Lord God Planted a Garden, The.

Gurney, Ivor
After War.
Ballad of the Three Spectres.
Bohemians, The.
Canadians.
Dawns I Have Seen.
December 30th.
Elver Fishers.
Epitaph on a Young Child.
Escape, The.
High Hills, The.
It Is Near Toussaints'.
Larches.
Love Song, The: "Out of the blackthorn
    hedges."
Moments.
On the Night.
Possessions.
Rainy Midnight.
Requiem: "Pour out your light, O stars."
Silent One, The.
Song: "Only the wanderer."
Strange Hells.
To His Love.
Tobacco Plant.
Towards Lillers.
Who died on the wires, and hung there, one
    of two, *sel.*

Gurney, Lawrence
Nevada.

Gusai
Highly Renowned.

Gustafson, Jim
Ambitious.
Dance, The.
Idea of Detroit, The.
Idea of San Francisco, The.
Nervous Miracles.
No Money in Art.

Gustafson, Ralph
Armorial.
At the Ocean's Verge.
Columbus Reaches Juana, 1492.
Dedication: "They shall not die in vain," we
    said.
Fish, The.
In the Yukon.
Legend.
Meaning, The.
Mothy Monologue.
My Love Eats an Apple.
On the Road to Vicenza.
On the *Struma* Massacre.
S.S.R., Lost at Sea— *The Times.*
Swans of Vadstena, The.
Transfigured Night.
Wednesday at North Hatley.

Guthrie, Charles E.
God's Will.

Guthrie, James
Last Song.

Guthrie, Ramon
Homage to Paul Delvaux.
Magi, The.

Noël Tragique.
Today Is Friday.

Guthrie, Woody
Jesus Christ ("Jesus Christ was a man that
    travelled through the land").
Pastures of Plenty.
Plane Wreck at Los Gatos (Deportee).
This Land Is Your Land.

Guthrie, Thomas Anstey. *See* "Anstey, F."

Gutiérrez, José Angel
22 Miles.

Gutiérrez Nájera, Manuel
Dead Waters.
Non Omnis Moriar.
To Be.
To remember. To forgive. To have loved,
    sel.
When the Day Comes.

Guttenbrunner, Michael
Dead Poet in the Mountains.
Guardian Angel, The.
Landing, The.
Metamorphosis.
Occupation.
Reflection.
Return.
Snake Star, The.
Test, The.

Gutteridge, Bernard
Burma Hills.
Man into a Churchyard.
Namkwin Pul.
Patrol; Buonamary.

Guxnawu
Song for the Richest Woman in Wrangell.

Guyon, Jeanne Marie Bouvier de la Motte
Adoration.
Little Bird I Am, A.

Gwala, Mafika Pascal
From the Outside.
Promise!
Shebeen Queen, The.
Sunset.

"Gwallter Mechain." *See* **Davies, Walter**

"Gwenallt." *See* **Jones, David Gwenallt**

Gwerfyl Mechain
Hostess of the Ferry Inn, The.
Snowfall, The.

Gwynn, R. S.
Among Philistines.
1916.
Snow White and the Seven Deadly Sins.

Gwynn, Stephen Lucius
On One Dying in a Convent.

Gyodai (Kato Gyodai)
Autumn hills.
I light the lamp.
Mournful wind.
Snow melting!

Gyoko
Coming, I don't enter at the gate.
Even as it falls.
Late Blossoms in the Cold Mountains.
Mist.
Moon, The.
Moon from a Boat, The.
Moonlight remains, The.
Pellucid moon, The.
Summer Grasses in the Fields at Dusk.
Travel.
Wisteria in the Rain.

Gyokuchu
Life—not coming.

Gyozan
I've reached my seventy-seventh year.

H

"H., C. G."
Power of Innocence, The.
H., Domna
Rosin, tell me from the heart.
"H., F. L."
Father Knows, The.
"H., R."
Battle of Monmouth, The.
"H—, Captain"
Imitation of Martial, Book II Ep, An 105.
"H., H." *See* **Jackson, Helen Hunt**
Ha-Nagid, Samuel
I Look Up to the Sky.
Proverbs.
Haad, Siraad
Lament for a Dead Lover.
Haan, Jakov de
All Is God's.
God's Gifts.
Hanukah.
Sabbath.
Unity.
Haavikko, Paavo
I Look Outside.
Recorders of Life.
When I Now Tell You about the Emperor.
Habergham, Mrs. Fleetwood
Seeds of Love, The, at.
Habib, Rowley (Nga Pitiroirangi)
Ancestors.
Moment of Truth.
Habib Gerez, Jozef. *See* **Gerez, Jozef Habib**
Habington, William
Against Them Who Lay Unchastity to the Sex
    of Women, *sel.*
Castara, *sels.*
Compliment, The.
Fine Young Folly, *sel.*
"Nox Nocti Indicat Scientiam", *sel.*
Quoniam Ego in Flagella Paratus Sum.
Reward of Innocent Love, The, *sel.*
To a Wanton.
To Castara, upon Beautie, *sel.*
To Roses in the Bosom[e] of Castara, *sel.*
To the Right Honourable the Countesse of C.
To the World; the Perfection of Love.
Upon Thought Castara May Die.
What Am I Who Dare.
Hacker, Marilyn
After the Revolution.
Almost Aubade.
April Interval I.
Aube Provençale.
Azure Striation Swirls beyond the Stones, *sel.*
Before the War.
Canzone: "Consider the three functions of the
    tongue."
Canzone: "No better lost than any other
    woman."
Conclusion: "Did you love well what very
    soon you left?," *sel.*
Corona.
Eight Days in April.
Elektra on Third Avenue.
Feeling and Form.
Fifteen to Eighteen.
Hang-Glider's Daughter, The.
Imaginary Translation.
La Fontaine de Vaucluse.
Letter from the Alpes-Maritimes.
Lines Declining a Transatlantic Dinner
    Invitation.

Mythology.
1974.
Occasional Verses.
Presentation Piece.
Rondeau after a Transatlantic Telephone Call.
Runaways Café II.
Sonnet Ending with a Film Subtitle.
Three Sonnets for Iva.
Under the Arc de Triomphe: October 17.
Villanelle: "Every day our bodies separate."
We May Be Learning How to Tell the Truth,
    sel.
Hacker, Mary
Achtung! Achtung!
Hadas, Pamela White
Case of Ample Ora: Sweetness and Light,
    The.
Poem Not about a Zebra, A.
Queen Charming.
Woman with Gardenia: A Sketch.
Hadas, Rachel
Codex Minor.
Nourishment.
Haddad, Qasim
All of Them.
Book of the defeated man, *sel.*
Children, The.
Interrogation.
Like the White.
Hadden, Maude Miner
Creative Force.
Hadewijch
Ah yes, when love allows.
All Things Confine.
Had I been mindful of my high descent.
Love has seven names.
What helps it if of love I sing.
Hadley, Drummond
Gathering Cattle in the Deertracks Pasture.
Hadrian, Emperor (Publius Aelius Hadrianus)
Adriani Morientis ad Animam Suam.
Ah! gentle, fleeting, wav'ring sprite, *sel.*
Animula Vagula, Blandula.
Emperor Hadrian to His Soul, The.
Hadrian's Address to His Soul When Dying.
Hafiz
Comrades, the morning breaks, the sun is up,
    sel.
Days of spring are here, The! the eglantine,
    sel.
Grievous folly shames my sixtieth year, A,
    sel.
I cease not from desire till my desire, *sel.*
I have borne the anguish of love, which ask
    me not to describe, *sel.*
I said to heaven that glowed above, *sel.*
Jewel of the secret treasury, The, *sel.*
Lady that hast my heart within thy hand, *sel.*
Lips of the one I love are my perpetual
    pleasure, The.
Love's hidden pearl is shining yet.
Mortal never won to view thee.
Oft have I said, I say it once more, *sel.*
Persian Song of Hafiz, A.
Rose is not the rose unless thou see, The, *sel.*
Saki, for God's love, come and fill my glass,
    sel.
Where is my ruined life, and where the fame,
    sel.
Wind from the east, oh Lapwing of the day,
    sel.
Hafiz, Solomon
My soul is the veil of his love.
Hafiz, Yasin Taha
Breaking the Precepts.
Gazelle, The.
Woman, A.
Words and Truth.
Hafsa bint al-Hajj
Shall I come there, or you here?

Hagarty, Sir John H.
Funeral of Napoleon I.
Hagedorn, Hermann
Mother in the House, The.
Prayer during Battle.
Troop of the Guard, A.
Hagedorn, Jessica Tarahata
Chiqui and Terra Nova.
Listen.
Ming the Merciless.
Motown// Smokey Robinson.
Song for My Father.
Song of Bullets, The.
Woman Who Thought She Was More than a
Samba, The.
Hagenau, Reinmar von
Childish Game, A.
Hagiwara Sakutaro
Army, The.
Bamboo.
Barren Area, A.
Cherry.
Corpse of a Cat, The.
Hand Is a Cake, The.
Impression of Early Summer, An.
In the Horse Carriage.
Lover of Love.
Night Train.
On a Trip.
Out of the Inner Shell of a Certain Landscape.
Pinks and a Blue Cat.
Sick Face at the Base of the Earth.
Sickly Face at the Bottom of the Ground.
Spring Night.
Sunny Spring.
Twilight Room.
White Public Benches.
Yoshiwara.
Hahn, Kimiko
Dance Instructions for a Young Girl.
Daughter.
Girl Combs Her Hair, A.
When You Leave.
Hahn, Robert
Never Be As Fast As I Have Been.
Hahn-Hahn, Ida
Bird of Passage.
My Language.
Rosane.
Hai-Jew, Dianne
Days Ago.
Foreign Soil.
Thirst of the Dragon.
This Night.
Haicead, Padraigin
On Hearing It Has Been Ordered in the
Chapterhouse of Ireland That the Friars
Make No More Songs or.
"Haida Charlie"
How is it all gonna turn out.
Haines, Gladys M.
In War.
Haines, John
Ancestor of the Hunting Heart.
Awakening.
Certain Dead.
Cloud Factory, The.
Dream of the Lynx.
End of the Street, The.
Flight, The.
From the Workshop of Brancusi and
Giancometti.
Ghost Hunter, The.
Homage to David Smith.
If the Owl Calls Again.
Into the Glacier.
Lake in the Sky, The.
Men against the Sky.
Middle Ages, The.
Paul Klee.
Poem like a Grenade, A.

Ryder.
Snowbound City, The.
To Turn Back.
To Vera Thompson.
Vision of Marsden Hartley, The.
Whale in the Blue Washing Machine, The.
Whistle Column, The.
Wolves.
Hairston, William [Will]
Alabama Bus.
Hajnal, Anna
Cast Rose, *sel.*
Dead Girl.
Fear.
Felled Plane Tree, The.
Half Past Four, October.
I've Never Come Away, You Know.
May It Not Run Down.
Rains.
Separate Time.
Song of the Plain.
That's All?
Tree to Flute.
Yellow, *sel.*
Hakuin
On Wisdom.
Senryu.
Hakushi, Kitahara. *See* **Kitahara Hakushu**
Hakutei
Awakened under stick and *kwatz.*
Hakyo, Ishida. *See* **Ishida Hakyo**
Halas, František
Again.
Halbisch, Harry
Warp and Woof.
Haldane, John Burdon Sanderson
Cancer's a Funny Thing.
Haldeman, Joe W.
Saul's Death: Two Sestinas.
Hale, Arthur
Manila Bay.
Yankee Privateer, The.
Hale, Edward Everett
Adrian Block's Song.
Alma Mater's Roll.
Anne Hutchinson's Exile.
Ballad of Bunker Hill, The.
Columbus.
From Potomac to Merrimac.
Lamentable Ballad of the Bloody Brook, The.
Look Up *or* Lend a Hand.
Marching Song of Stark's Men, The.
Nameless Saints, The.
New England's Chevy Chase.
Omnipresence.
Put It Through.
Hale, Janet Campbell
Aaron Nicholas, Almost Ten.
Backyard Swing.
Cinque.
Custer Lives in Humbolt County.
Desmet, Idaho, March 1969.
On Death and Love.
Salad La Raza.
Scene from a Dream.
Six Feet Under.
Tribal Cemetery.
Walls of Ice.
Where Have All the Indians Gone?
"Hale, Katherine" (Amelia Beers Warnock
Garvin)
Eternal Moment.
Giant's Tomb in Georgian Bay.
Lost Garden.
Portrait of a Cree.
Hale, Oliver
Where Unimaginably Bright.
Hale, Robert Beverly
Big Nasturtiums, The.
Denise.
Ovibos, The.

Hale, Sarah Josepha Buell
Alice Ray.
Mary's Lamb [*or* Mary and Her Lamb]
Mole and the Eagle, The.
Our Father in Heaven.
Watcher, The.
Halevi, Judah
Apple, The.
Awake, My Fair.
Dove, The.
Earth in Spring, The.
Fortune's Treachery.
God, Whom Shall I Compare to Thee?
Grey Hair, The.
He Cometh.
Heal Me, My God.
Hymn for Atonement Day.
Immortal Israel.
Israel's Duration.
Jerusalem.
Letter to His Friend Isaac, A.
Longing.
Longing for Jerusalem.
Lord, Where Shall I Find Thee?
Love Song A: "Let my sweet song be pleasing
unto Thee."
Love Song: "See'st thou o'er my shoulders
falling."
Marriage Song.
Meditation on Communion with God.
Mirror, The.
My Heart Is in the East.
My Sweetheart's Dainty Lips.
Ode to Zion.
On Parting with Moses ibn Ezra.
Ophra.
Parting.
Pride of a Jew, The.
Sabbath, My Love.
Song of Loneliness.
Time-Servers.
To the Western Wind.
To Zion.
Words Wherein Stinging Bees Lurk.
"Haliburton Hugh." *See* **Robertson, James**
Logie
Halkin, Shimon
Do Not Accompany Me.
Halkin, Shmuel
Ah, When Will Dawn Begin to Break?
Drop of Dew, A.
Of Things Past.
Russia.
Hall, Amanda Benjamin
Great Farewells, The.
It Seems That God Bestowed Somehow.
Hall, Carolyn
Fireflies.
Hall, Charles Sprague *and at.* **Thomas**
Brigham Bishop
John Brown's Prayer, *at.*
Hall, Donald
Abroad Thoughts from Home.
Airstrip in Essex, 1960, An.
Alligator Bride, The.
Apples.
Black Faced Sheep, The.
Body Politic, The.
Brain Cells, The.
Breasts.
By the Exeter River.
Calvinist's Caribbean, The.
Child, The.
Christ Church Meadows, Oxford.
Christmas Eve in Whitneyville, 1955.
Clown, The.
Couplet.
Crew-cuts.
Detroit.
Digging.
Farm, The.

For an Early Retirement.
Foundation of American Industry, The.
Funeral, The.
Granite and Grass.
Henyard Round, The.
In the Old House.
Je Suis une Table.
Jealous Lovers, The.
Kicking the Leaves.
Long River, The.
Man in the Dead Machine, The.
Maple Syrup.
Marriage.
Merle Bascom's .22.
Mr. Wakeville on Interstate 90.
Munch's Scream.
My Son, My Executioner.
Names of Horses.
New Hampshire.
O Cheese.
Old Pilot, The.
On a Horse Carved in Wood.
Ox Cart Man.
Philander.
Poet at Twenty, A.
Professor Gratt.
Prophecy.
Proverbs.
Questions [1] ("Why do you love her").
Questions [2] ("How is it now").
Reclining Figure.
Second Stanza for Dr. Johnson, A.
Self-Portrait, as a Bear.
Sestina: "Hang it all, Ezra Pound, there is
　only the one sestina!"
Shudder, The.
Sister on the Tracks, A.
Six Poets in Search of a Lawyer.
Sleeping Giant, The.
Snow, The.
Sudden Things.
Swan.
T. R.
Three Movements, The.
To a Waterfowl.
Town of Hill, The.
Toy Bone, The.
Valentine.
Wedding Party.
Whip-poor-will.
White Apples.
Wives, The.
Your voice on the telephone.

Hall, Elaine
　Spider Dream.
　Spider, World-Spinner.
Hall, Gertrude
　Angels.
　Dust, The.
　Mrs. Golightly.
　My Old Counselor.
Hall, Gregory
　Voice of the Power of This World, The.
Hall, Hattie Vose
　Two Temples.
Hall, Henry
　Ballad on the Times, A.
　On Sir John Fenwick.
　Upon the King's Return from Flanders.
Hall, J. C.
　Twelve Minutes.
Hall, James Baker
　Stafford in Kansas.
Hall, James Norman
　Eat and Walk.
Hall, Janet Campbell
　On a Catholic Childhood.
Hall, Jim
　In the Spring.
　Laughing Backwards.
　Maybe Dats Your Pwoblem Too.

Preposterous.
Waking, the Love Poem Sighs.
What Saundra Said about Being Short.
White Trash.
Hall, John
　Epicurean Ode, An.
　On an Hour[e]-Glass[e]
　Pastoral[l] Hymn[e], A.
　Song: "Distil not poison in mine ears."
Hall, John (1627–56)
　Call, The.
Hall, Joseph
　Great is the folly of a feeble brain, *sel.*
　Sturdy ploughman doth the soldier see, The,
　　sel.
　Time was, and that was termed the time of
　　Gold, *sel.*
　Who doubts? The laws fell down from
　　heaven's height, *sel.*
Hall, Kay DeBard
　Deer in Aspens.
Hall, Mary Lee
　Turn Again to Life.
Hall, Radclyffe
　As a lamp of fine crystal, wonderfully
　　wrought, *sel.*
Hall, Rodney
　After a Sultry Morning, *sel.*
　Eyewitness.
　Lips and Nose, *sel.*
　Mrs. Macintosh.
　My Coffin Is a Deckchair, *sel.*
　October, *sel.*
　Some Magnetism in the Sea, *sel.*
　Text for These Distracted Times, A.
　They're Dying Just the Same in Station
　　Homesteads, *sel.*
　Wedding Day at Nagasaki.
　World Is a Musician's Cliff House, The, *sel.*
Hall, Sharlot M.
　Arizona.
Hall, William
　Auctioneer's Handbill, An.
Hall, Agnes Maxwell. *See* **Maxwell-Hall,
　Agnes.**
Hall-Evans, Jo Ann
　Cape Coast Castle Revisted.
　Seduction.
Hallack, Cecily
　Divine Office of the Kitchen, The.
Hallaman, E. G.
　Exploding Poem, The.
Halleck, Fitz-Greene
　Alnwick Castle.
　At midnight, in his guarded tent, *sel.*
　Burns.
　Fanny was younger once than she is now, *sel.*
　Field of the Grounded Arms, The.
　Marco Bozzaris.
　On the Death of Joseph Rodman Drake.
　Red Jacket.
　Song: "There's a barrel of porter at Tammany
　　Hall."
　We owe the ancients something. You have
　　read, *sel.*
**Halleck, Fitz-Greene and Joseph Rodman
　Drake**
　Man Who Frets at Worldly Strife, The, *sel.*
　National Paintings, The, *sel.*
　Ode to Fortune, *sel.*
Halley, Anne
　Against Dark's Harm.
　Autograph Book/ Prophecy.
　Housewife's Letter: To Mary.
　O Doctor Dear My Love.
　Pride of Ladies, A.
　Rumors of the Turning Wheel.
Halliday, Caroline
　Connection.

Halliday, Mark
　Blue Spruce.
　Functional Poem.
Hallock, Grace Taber
　Woodpecker in Disguise.
Halloran, Laurence Hynes
　Animal Magnetism; the Pseudo-Philosopher
　　Baffled.
Halperin, Mark
　John Clare.
Halpern, Daniel
　Arriving.
　Dance, The.
　Dutch April.
　Epithalamium: "In the streets the crowds go
　　about their business."
　Ethnic Life, The.
　Fish.
　Gossip, The.
　How to Eat Alone.
　Landing, The.
　Nude.
　Portoncini dei Morti.
　Return, Starting Out.
　Señor Excellent.
　Snapshot of Hue.
　Street Fire.
　Summer Nights.
　Summer, 1970.
　Summer Rentals, The.
　To a Friend Shot on a Mexican Bus.
　Walking in the 15th Century.
Halpern, Leivick. *See* **Leivick, H.**
Halpern, Moyshe-Leyb
　Aby Kirly, the War Hero.
　Bird, The.
　Bird Mertsyfint, The.
　Considering the Bleakness.
　End of the Book, The.
　From My Royzele's Diary.
　From One of My Letters.
　From Zarkhi's Teachings, *sel.*
　Oh, Ghingeli [*or* Gingilee], my bleeding
　　heart.
　Go Throw Them Out.
　He Who Calls Himself Leader.
　How Long Will I Stand.
　I and You.
　I Say to Myself.
　I Shall Never Go On Bragging.
　I Walk Along.
　In a "Speakeasy"—the Flower Girl.
　In Central Park.
　In the Golden Land.
　Isaac Leybush Peretz.
　Just Because.
　Kol-Nidre.
　Light—My Word.
　Make for Him a Revolution, If You Can!
　Married.
　Memento Mori.
　My Crying-Out-Loud.
　My Only Son.
　My Portrait.
　My Restlessness Is of a Wolf.
　Night in Manhattan.
　O, Shmuel My Brother!
　Old Leader Complains, The.
　Our Garden.
　Overtime.
　Restless as a Wolf.
　Sacco-Vanzetti.
　Salute.
　Shalamouses.
　So Far, So-So.
　So It Shall Be.
　Story of the World, The.
　Street Drummer, The.
　Tale of the Fly, The.
　That's Our Lot.
　There Wasn't.

This I Said to My Only Son at Play—and to
  Nobody Else.
"Watch Your Step!"
We the Revolutionaries; or, This America.
What Do We Know, Dear Brothers?, *sel.*
Who.
Why Not.
Will, The.
With Myself.
Yitskhok Leybush Perets.
Your Dress.
Zarkhi, His Pipe to the Yard, Cries, *sel.*
Zarkhi to Himself, *sel.*
Zlochov [*or* Zlotchev, My Home].

Halpine, Charles Graham
Baron Renfrew's Ball.
Lecompton's Black Brigade.
Mr. Johnson's Policy of Reconstruction.
Sambo's Right to Be Kilt.
Song of Sherman's Army, The.

Halsall, Martyn
Return to Ararat.

Ham, Marion Franklin
As Tranquil Streams.
O Thou Whose Gracious Presence Shone.
Prayer, A: "I pray not for the joy that
  knows."
Touch Thou Mine Eyes.

Hambleton, Ronald
Comrades as We Rest Within.
Sockeye Salmon.
That Strain Again.

Hamburger, Michael
At Staufen.
Blind Man.
Cat.
Death of an Old Man, The.
Dostoievsky's Daughters.
Dual Site, The.
Epitaph for a Horseman.
In October.
Instead of a Journey.
Man of the World.
Mathematics of Love.
Memory.
Poet's Progress, A.
Search, The.
Song about Great Men, A.
Squares.
Townsman on his yielding bed, The, *sel.*

Hame'iri, Avigdor
Silence.
That Very Night.

Hamelink, Jacques
Ammonite, The.
For the Shadow.
Pyrenees, The.
Stonetalk.

Hamill, Gerry
It was far in the night and the bairnies grat.
Song of the GPO, A.
To His Coy Mistress.

Hamill, Janet
Carravagio.

Hamilton, Anna Elizabeth
Hem of His Garment, The.

Hamilton, Bobb
Poem to a Nigger Cop.

Hamilton, Cicely
March of the Women, The.

Hamilton, Elizabeth
My Ain Fireside.

**Hamilton, George Rostrevor ("George
  Rostrevor")**
Cell, The.
Don's Holiday.
Exchange.
Exile.
No Occupation.
Old Ox.

On a Distant Prospect of an Absconding
  Bookmaker.
On a Statue of Sir Arthur Sullivan.
Schoolmaster.
To the Greek Anthologists.

Hamilton, Harold
School of Sorrow, The.

Hamilton, Horace
Before Dawn.

Hamilton, Janet
Rhymes for the Times.

Hamilton, John
Cold Blows the Wind.

Hamilton, Marion Ethel
Bird at Night.

Hamilton, Robert Browning
Along the Road.

Hammarskjöld, Dag
Lord—Thine the Day.

Hammerstein, Oscar II
Kansas City.
Money Isn't Everything!
There Is Nothin' like a Dame.
You've Got to Be Taught.

Hammon, Jupiter
Evening Thought, An.
O come you pious youth! adore, *sel.*

Hammond, Geraldine
Encounter.

Hammond, Mac
Golden Age.
In Memory of V. R. Lang.

Hammond, William
Husbandry.
Man's Life.
Mutual Love.
Rose, The.
To Her Questioning His Estate.

Hammond, "Doc" *and* **Judy Scott.** *See* **Scott,
  Judy** *and* **"Doc" Hammond**

Hampl, Patricia
August's dense astronomy fits itself, all stars,
  sel.
Blue Bottle.
Hand, Eye.
Leading to your Hands.

Han-shan
My father and mother left me a good living.

Han Yü
Girl of Mt. Hua, The.
Leaves fall turning turning to the ground, *sel.*
My ceramic lake in dawn, water settled clear,
  sel.
Old men are like little boys, *sel.*
Pond shine and sky glow, blue matching blue,
  sel.
This morning I can't seem to get out of bed,
  sel.
When white dew descends on the hundred
  grasses, *sel.*
Written on My Way into Exile.

Hanafi, Amiq (Abdul Aziz Hanafi)
Apology.
Habit.
In the Valley of Death.
Poem (3.11.66).
Poems Are Cheap.
Thinking in the Dark.

Hanaford, Phoebe A.
Cast Thy Bread upon the Waters.

Hanazono, Emperor
As day fades away.
Beneath a clear sky.
Cutting past the front.
Down from the branches.
I arise and see.
In every household.
Love in the Night.
Mist clears away, The.
Nothing is left now.
On the Road at Dusk.

So far from springlike.
Sparrows twitter, The.
Tatsuta River/ carries its red autumn
  leaves.

Hanbury-Williams, Charles
Lamentable Case, A.

Hand, Jack
Death Stairs/Life House.
Pain.
Pain Is My Brother.

Handke, Peter
Austrian Poem 1979/80.
Course of a Day in a Summer Garden, The.
Farewell in the Basilica.
Métro Balard-Charenton.
Occasional Poem.

Handley, Helen
Deer Hunt, Salt Lake Valley.

Hands, Rina
Chatterton.

Handy, William Christopher
St. Louis Blues.

Hanes, Leigh
Old Fence Post.

Hanim, Leylâ
Let's get going.

Hanim, Nigâr
Tell Me Again.

Hankin, St. John Emile Clavering
Consolatory!
De Gustibus.
Editor's Tragedy, The.
Elegy on the Late King of Patagonia, An.
Soul-Severance.

Hanlo, Jan
One Morning.
Roof, The.
To Archangel.
Verse as of 7 June 1951.

Hann, Isaac
After Reading the Life of Mrs. Catherine
  Stubbs in Isaac Ambrose's "War with the
  Devils."

Hannay, Patrick
Upon the boughs and tops of trees, *sel.*

Hannigan, Des
Ben Alder 1963-1977.

Hannigan, Paul
Fiesta.

Hanscombe, Gillian Eve
From her grave, *sel.*
Men made myths, *sel.*
Mrs. Snatcher Thatcher, *sel.*

Hanscombe, Gillian Eve *and* **Suniti Namjoshi**
All the Words.
Christ How My Circumspect Heart.
I Moved in My House.
Measure.

Hansen, Chadwick
Creator of Infinities.

Hansen, Joseph
Dakota: Five Times Six.
Loved One, The.

Hansen, Tom
Crying Uncle.

Hanson, Amos
Schooner *Fred Dunbar* , The.
Trip to the Grand Banks, A.

Hanson, Joseph Mills
November 1918.

Hanson, Kenneth O.
Before the Storm.
Lighting the Night Sky.
Take It from Me.
West Lake.

Hanson, Pauline
And I Am Old to Know.
From Creature to Ghost.
So Beautiful Is the Tree of Night.

Hanson, Phyllis
Wisdom.

Hanzlik, Josef
Clap Your Hands for Herod.
Hara Sekitei
Haiku: "Autumn storm dying, The."
Haiku: "Feeling lonely."
Haiku: "On scattered hailstones."
Haiku: "Stepping on a tendril."
Haiku: "Warm and snug."
Hara Tamiki
Glittering Fragments.
In the fire, a telegraph pole.
Harada, Gail N.
First Winter.
New Year.
Painted Passages.
Pomegranate.
Harasymowicz, Jerzy
Green Lowland of Pianos, A.
Leda and the Swan.
Sister.
Thistle, The.
Harata Tangikuku
Invalid's Song.
Harbaugh, Henry
Aloe Plant, The.
Jesus, I Live to Thee.
Harbaugh, Thomas Chalmers
Trouble in the "Amen Corner."
Harbord, A. M.
At Euston.
Harburg, E. Y. ("Yip" Harburg)
Brother, Can You Spare a Dime?
Hard, Walter
Medical Aid.
Harden, Verna Loveday
Post Mortem.
When This Tide Ebbs.
Hardenberg, Friedrich von. *See* "Novalis"
Hardie, Doris
Song for Susannah: A Lullaby.
Harding, George
Reply to a Creditor.
Harding, Mike
Christmas 1914.
Hardison, O. B., Jr.
Marina.
Small Talk in a Garden.
Stella Maris.
Hardt, Ernst
Specter, The.
Hardy, Arthur Sherburne
Duality.
Immortality.
Iter Supremum.
Hardy, Elizabeth Clark
Some Time at Eve.
Hardy, Elizabeth Stanton
Echo.
Hardy, Jane L.
Lincoln.
Hardy, John Edward
Voyeur.
Hardy, Thomas
"According to the Mighty Working."
After a Journey.
After Jena, *sel.*
After the Fair, *sel.*
After the Visit.
Afterwards.
Agnosto Theo (To an Unknown God).
Ah, Are You Digging on My Grave?
Albuera, *sel.*
An Upbraiding.
Ancient to Ancients, An.
"And There Was a Great Calm."
Anniversary, An.
Architectural Masks.
At a Pause in a Country Dance.
At a Watering Place.
At an Inn.
At Castle Boterel.

At Tea, *sel.*
At the Altar-Rail, *sel.*
At the Draper's.
August Midnight, An.
Backward Spring, A.
Bags of Meat.
Ballad-Singer, The, *sel.*
Beeny Cliff.
Before Life and After.
Bereft.
Beyond the Last Lamp Near Tooting
   Common.
Bird-Scene at a Rural Dwelling, A.
Birds at Winter Nightfall.
Blinded Bird, The.
Boatman's Song, The, *sel.*
Broken Appointment, A.
Budmouth Dears, *sel.*
By Her Aunt's Grave, *sel.*
Cardinal Bembo's Epitaph on Raphael.
Channel Firing.
Children and Sir Nameless, The.
Christmas Ghost-Story, A.
Christmas: 1924.
Church Romance, A.
Colonel's Soliloquy, The.
Comet at Yell'ham, The.
Commonplace Day, A.
Compassion.
Conformers, The.
Contretemps, The.
Convergence of the Twain (Lines on the Loss
   of the *Titanic*, The).
Country Wedding (A Fiddler's Story), The.
Curtains Now Are Drawn, The.
Dark-eyed Gentleman, The.
Darkling Thrush, The.
Dead and the Living One, The.
Dead "Wessex" the Dog to the Household.
Departure (Southampton Docks: October
   1899).
Domicilium.
Drizzling Easter Morning, A.
Drummer Hodge.
During Wind and Rain.
Embarcation.
Enemy's Portrait, The.
Epitaph for George Moore.
Epitaph: "I never cared for Life: Life cared
   for me."
Epitaph on a Pessimist.
Eve of Waterloo, The, *sel.*
Exeunt Omnes.
Faded Face, The.
Faintheart in a Railway Train.
Fallow Deer at the Lonely House, The.
Field of Talavera, The, *sel.*
Field of Waterloo, The, *sel.*
First or Last.
First Sight of Her and After.
Five Students, The.
For Life I Had Never Cared Greatly.
Former Beauties, *sel.*
Friends Beyond.
Garden Seat, The.
God's Funeral.
Going, The.
Going and Staying.
Great Things.
Green Slates.
Hap.
Harbour Bridge, The.
Haunter, The.
He Abjures Love.
He Never Expected Much.
He Resolves to Say No More.
Her Dilemma.
Her Second Husband Hears Her Story.
Heredity.
His Immortality.
Horses Aboard.
House of Hospitalities, The.

How Great My Grief.
I Am the One.
I Found Her Out There.
I Look into My Glass.
I Looked Up from My Writing.
I Need Not Go.
I Said to Love.
I Say I'll Seek Her.
If It's Ever Spring Again.
If You Had Known.
Impercipient, The.
In a Cathedral City.
In a Museum.
In a Wood.
In Childbed.
In Church, *sel.*
In Front of the Landscape.
In the Cemetery.
In the Evening.
In the Moonlight.
In the Nuptial Chamber, *sel.*
In the Old Theatre, Fiesole.
In the Restaurant, *sel.*
In the Room of the Bride-Elect, *sel.*
In the Servants' Quarters.
In the Study, *sel.*
In Time of "The Breaking of Nations."
Jezreel.
Lacking Sense, The.
Last Chrysanthemum, The.
Last Words to a Dumb Friend.
Lausanne.
Let Me Enjoy [(Minor Key)]
Levelled Churchyard, The.
Liddell and Scott; on the Completion of Their
   Lexicon.
Lines: To a Movement in Mozart's E-Flat
   Symphony.
Lodging-House Fuchsias, The.
Long Plighted.
Looking at a Picture on an Anniversary.
Lying Awake.
Man He Killed, The.
Marble-streeted Town, The.
Men Who March Away.
Midnight on the Great Western.
Moments of Vision.
Mound, The.
Mute Opinion.
My Spirit Will Not Haunt the Mound.
Nature's Questioning.
Near Lanivet, 1872.
Necessitarian's Epitaph, A.
Nettles, The.
Neutral Tones.
New Year's Eve.
Newcomer's Wife, The.
Night of the Dance, The.
Night of Trafalgar, The, *sel.*
No Buyers; a Street Scene.
Old Furniture.
On an Invitation to the United States.
On Sturminster Foot-Bridge.
On the Death-Bed, *sel.*
On the Departure Platform.
On the Portrait of a Woman about to Be
   Hanged.
Once at Swanage.
One We Knew.
Outside the Window, *sel.*
Over the Coffin, *sel.*
Overlooking the River Stour.
Oxen, The.
Peace-Offering, The.
Phantom Horsewoman, The.
Pink Frock, The.
Pity of It, The.
Placid Man's Epitaph, A.
Poet, A.
Popular Personage at Home, A.
Practical Woman, A.
Proud Songsters.

Puzzled Game Birds, The.
Refusal, A.
Reminder, The.
Respectable Burgher, The.
Roman Road, The.
Rome.
Rome: Building a New Street in the Ancient
     Quarter.
Ruined Maid, The.
Satires of Circumstance.
Schreckhorn, The.
Self-Unseeing, The.
Selfsame Song, The.
Shadow on the Stone, The.
She Hears the Storm.
She, to Him.
Sheep Fair, A.
Shelley's Skylark.
Shut Out That Moon.
Snow in the Suburbs.
Souls of the Slain, The.
Statue of Liberty, The.
Stranger's Song, The.
Subalterns, The.
Sunshade, The.
Tess's Lament.
There have been times when I well might
     have passed and the ending have come, sel.
This love puts all humanity from me, sel.
This Summer and Last.
Thoughts of Phena [at News of Her Death]
Thunderstorm in Town, A.
To an Unborn Pauper Child.
To C. F. H. on Her Christening-Day.
To Lizbie Browne.
To Meet, or Otherwise.
To the Moon.
Trampwoman's Tragedy, A.
Transformations.
Tree and the Lady, The.
Two Lips.
Unborn, The.
Under the Waterfall.
Voice, The.
Voices from Things Growing in a
     Churchyard.
Waiting Both.
Walk, The.
Weather[s]
Wessex Heights.
Wet August, A.
When I Set Out for Lyonnesse.
When Oats Were Reaped.
When the clouds' swoln bosoms echo back
     the shouts of the many and strong, sel.
Where the Picnic Was.
Who's in the Next Room?
Why She Moved House.
Wife in London, A.
Winter in Durnover Field.
Wintertime nighs, sel.
Wives in the Sere.
Workbox, The.
Year's Awakening, The.
You on the Tower.
Young Glass-Stainer, The.
Young Man's Epigram on Existence, A.
Your Last Drive.
Zermatt: To the Matterhorn.
Hare, Amory
Walking at Night.
Hare, Maurice Evan
There once was a man [or There was a
     young man] who said, "Damn!"
Haresnape, Geoffrey
African Tramp, The.
Harford, Lesbia
Beauty and Terror.
Day's End.
Experience.
He Had Served Eighty Masters.

Revolution.
This Way Only.
Hargreaves, Kay
Patent No. 1.
Haring, Phyllis
Earth Asks and Receives Rain, The.
Foetus.
Forbidden, The.
Jungle.
Overture to Strangers.
Twin.
Harington, Henry
Abbey Church at Bath, The.
Harington, John (fl. 1550)
Elegy Wrote in the Tower, 1554.
I See My Plaint, at.
Sonnet Made on Isabella Markham, A.
Harington [or Harrington], Sir John
     (1561–1612)
Against an Old Lecher.
Author, of His Own Fortune, The.
Author to His Wife, of a Woman's
     Eloquence, The.
Fair, Rich, and Young.
Health Counsel.
Of a Zealous Lady.
Of an Heroical Answer of a Great Roman
     Lady to Her Husband.
Of Treason.
To His Wife, for Striking Her Dog.
To My Lady Rogers, the Authors Wives
     Mother, How Doctor Sherwood
     Commended Her House in Bathe.
Harington, Lucy, Countess of Bedford
Elegy: "Death be not proud, thy hand gave
     not this blow."
Haritsu
Deep in the bamboo grove.
Harjo, Joy
Anchorage.
"Are You Still There."
Bleed Through.
Crossing the Border into Canada.
Eagle Poem.
For Alva Benson, and for Those Who Have
     Learned to Speak.
From the Salt Lake City Airport—82.
I Give You Back.
Mercy.
New Orleans.
Nine Below.
Remember.
Resurrection.
She Had Some Horses.
Transformations.
Woman Hanging from the Thirteenth Floor
     Window, The.
Harjo, Patty L. ("Ya-Ka-Nes")
Death.
Mask, The.
Musings.
Taos Winter.
To an Indian Poet.
Where Have You Gone, Little Boy.
Wishes.
Harkavi, Hedva
It Was Gentle.
Talk to Me, Talk to Me.
Whenever the Snakes Come.
Harkness, Edward
Villanelle: Man in the Recreation Room, The.
Harlow, Michael
Anima Has a Predilection, The, sel.
Composition in Glass, for.
Final Arrangement, The.
Paschal Transfiguration.
Vlaminck's Tie, the Persistent Imaginal.
Witness Chair, The.
Harmon, William
Bureaucratic Limerick ("The Bureau of Labor
     Statistics").

Dawn Horse, A.
Mother-land'scape (Letters).
Harmsen van Beek, Fritzi
Good Morning? Heavenly Madam Ping.
Introduction to a Prayer.
Harnden, Ruth
If I Were Bigger Than Anyone.
Harney, Ben
Mister Johnson.
You've Been a Good Old Wagon, but You've
     Done Broke Down.
Harney, W. E.
West of Alice.
Harney, William Wallace
Adonais.
Stab, The.
Harp, Jerry
Idea of Mick Jagger at a Concert, The.
Harper, Frances Ellen Watkins
Appeal to My Countrywomen, An.
Burdens of All, The.
Bury Me in a Free Land.
Crocuses, The.
Deliverance.
Double Standard, A.
Go Work in My Vineyard.
God Bless Our Native Land.
Grain of Sand, A.
He "Had Not Where to Lay His Head."
Learning to Read.
Let the Light Enter.
Mission of the Flowers, The.
Night of Death, The.
Nobly Born, The.
Nothing and Something.
Present Age, The.
Pure in Heart Shall See God, The.
Refiner's Gold, The.
Renewal of Strength.
Save the Boys.
She's Free!
Slave Auction, The.
Songs for the People.
Sparrow's Fall, The.
Thank God for Little Children.
Then and Now.
Vashti.
Harper, Michael S.
American History.
Barricades.
"Bird Lives": Charles Parker in St. Louis.
Black Study.
Blue Ruth: America.
Borning Room, The.
Br'er Sterling and the Rocker.
Buck.
Cannon Arrested.
Chief.
Clan Meeting: Births and Nations: A Blood
     Song.
Come Back Blues.
Dance of the Elephants, The.
Dark Way Home: Survivors, The.
Dear John, Dear Coltrane.
Deathwatch.
Debridement.
Double Elegy.
Effendi.
Elvin's Blues.
For Bud.
Grandfather.
Healing Song.
Here Where Coltrane Is.
Homage to the New World.
Jazz Station.
John Gibson's Bat.
Kin.
Landfill.
Last Affair: Bessie's Blues Song.

Lecturing on the Theme of Motherhood.
Love Medley: Patrice Cuchulain.
Makin' Jump Shots.
Martin's Blues.
Mother Speaks: The Algiers Motel Incident,
　Detroit, A.
My Students Who Stand in Snow.
New Season.
Newletter from My Mother.
Nightmare Begins Responsibility.
Photographs: A Vision of Massacre.
Poetry Concert.
Reuben, Reuben.
Sandra: At the Beaver Trap.
Song: I Want a Witness.
Tongue-tied in Black and White.
We Assume: On the Death of Our Son,
　Reuben Masai Harper.

Harpur, Charles
Bush Justice.
But hark! What hubbub now is this that
　comes, sel.
Dead city walls may pen us in, but still, sel.
I verse a settler's tale of olden times, sel.
Love Sonnets, VIII.
Marvellous Martin.
Midsummer Noon in the Australian Forest, A.
Settler in the olden times went forth, A, sel.
Words.
Yes, wonderful are dreams: and I have
　known, sel.

Harr, Barbara
Walking through a Cornfield in the Middle of
　Winter I Stumble over a Cow Pie and
　Think of the Sixties Press.

"Harriet Annie"
Death of Gaudentis.

Harrigan, Edward
My Dad's Dinner Pail.

Harriman, Dorothy
Cat on the Porch at Dusk.

Harrington, Edward
Bushrangers, The.
Morgan.
My Old Black Billy.

Harrington, Michael
Gazeteer of Newfoundland.
Second Iron Age, The.

Harrington, Sir John. See **Harington, Sir
John**

Harris, Benjamin
Account of the Cruelty of the Papists, An.
God save the King, that King that sav'd the
　land.
Of the French Kings Nativity.

Harris, Claire
Framed.
Policeman Cleared in Jaywalking Case.

Harris, Jana
Roan Hunter, The.

Harris, Joel Chandler
My Honey, My Love, sel.
Plough-Hands' Song, The, sel.

Harris, Marguerite
My Sun-killed Tree.

Harris, Max
Martin Buber in the Pub.
Tantanoola Tiger, The.

Harris, Merry
Green Corn Festival.
Real People.

Harris, Norman
Fable: "There is an inevitability."

Harris, Phyllis. See **Beauvais, Phyllis**

Harris, Sydney Justin
I Come to Bury Caesar.

Harris, Thomas Lake
Fledglings.
Sea-Sleep.

Harris, William J.
For Bill Hawkins, a Black Militant.

Give Me Five.
Grandfather Poem, A.
Practical Concerns.
Rib Sandwich.
They Live in Parallel Worlds.
We Live in a Cage.
Why Would I Want.

Harris, Wilson
Charcoal.
Laocoön.

Harrison, De Leon
Collage for Richard Davis—Two Short
　Forms, A.
Room, The.
Seed of Nimrod, The.
Some Days/ Out Walking Above.
Yellow.

Harrison, Florence
Faerie Fair, The.
Summer Day, A.

Harrison, Gregory
Distracted the Mother Said to Her Boy.

Harrison, James
Dusk.
Helen.
Leda's Version.
Penelope.

Harrison, Jim
After the Anonymous Swedish.
Ghazals, sels.
Locations.
Poem: "Form is the woods: the beast."
Returning at Night.
She/ pulls the sheet of this dance, sel.
Sketch for a Job Application Blank.
Sound.
Suite to Fathers.

Harrison, Sam
After the Show.
Chez Madame.
Journey.
Meeting.
Poem: "This room is very old and very wise."
Rain.

Harrison, Susan Frances ("Seranus")
Chateau Papineau.

Harrison, Tony
Book Ends.
Brazil, sel.
Call of Nature, The.
Changing at York.
Confessional Poetry.
Durham.
Hands, The.
Heredity.
History Classes, sel.
Jumper.
Lines to My Grandfathers, sel.
Long Distance.
Marked with D.
Me Tarzan, sel.
National Trust.
On Not Being Milton.
Pain-Killers.
Prague Spring.
Queen's English, The.
Self Justification, sel.
Still.
Timer, sel.
Turns.

Harrison, William
In Praise of Laudanum.

Harrod, Elizabeth B.
August Night, 1953.
Calvinist Autumnal.
Sonnet against the Too-Facile Mystic.
Summer Afternoon.

Harryman, Carla
Beginning to End.
For She.

Harsen, Una W.
Litany for Old Age, A.
Prayer before Meat.

Hart, Elizabeth Anna
Mother Tabbyskins.
Sweeping the Skies.

Hart, Kevin
Departure, The.

Hart, Lorenz
Blue Room, The.
Lady Is a Tramp, The.
Manhattan.
Most Beautiful Girl in the World, The.
Mountain Greenery.

Harte, Bret (Francis Bret Harte)
Aged Stranger, The.
Arctic Vision, An.
At the Hacienda.
Ballad of Mr. Cooke, The.
Ballad of the Emeu, The.
Caldwell of Springfield.
Chicago.
Chiquita.
Colenso Rhymes for Orthodox Children.
Coyote.
Crotalus.
Dickens in Camp.
Dow's Flat.
Further Language from Truthful James.
Greyport Legend, A.
Grizzly.
Her Letter.
His Answer to "Her Letter."
How Are You, Sanitary?
Jessie ("Jessie is both young and fair").
"Jim."
John Burns of Gettysburg.
Madroño.
Mrs. Judge Jenkins (Being the Only Genuine
　Sequel to "Maud Muller").
Personified Sentimental, The.
Plain Language from Truthful James ("Which
　I wish to remark").
Ramon.
Reveille, The.
Sanitary Message, A.
Schemmelfennig.
Second Review of the Grand Army, A.
Society upon the Stanislaus, The.
Swiss Air.
Tale of a Pony, The.
What the Bullet Sang.
Willows, The.

Harte, Walter
Enchanted Region; or, Mistaken Pleasures,
　The.

Harteis, Richard
Grace of Animals, The.
Star Trek III.

Hartford, John
Poor Old Prurient Interest Blues, The.

Hartigan, Anne
Advent.
Brazen Image.
No Easy Harbour.
St. Bridget's Cross.
Salt.

Hartigan, Patrick Joseph ("John O'Brien")
Said Hanrahan.
Tangmalangaloo.

Hartman, Charles O.
Double Mock Sonnet.
Inflation.
Little Song, A.

Hartmann von Aue
None Is Happy.

Hartnett, Michael
All That Is Left.
All the Death-Room Needs.
All the Same, It Would Make You Laugh.
Death of an Irishwoman.

Domestic Scene.
Enamoured of the Miniscule.
For My Grandmother, Bridget [*or* Bridgid]
   Halpin.
Gaelic is the conscience of our leaders, *sel.*
Half afraid to break a promise, *sel.*
I Have Heard Them Knock.
Lament for Tadhg Cronin's Children.
Pity the Man Who English Lacks.
Possibility That Has Been Overlooked Is the
   Future, The.
Retreat of Ita Cagney, The.
Small Farm, A.
Sonnet: "I saw magic on a green country
   road."
Hart-Smith, William
Cipangu, *sel.*
Comes Fog and Mist, *sel.*
Departure, *sel.*
Space, *sel.*
Waterspout, The, *sel.*
Hartsough, Lewis
Come, Friends and Neighbors, Come.
Let Me Go Where Saints Are Going.
Haruo, Sato. *See* **Sato Haruo**
Harvey, Anthony
Old Man at the Window, The.
Harvey, Frederick William
Ducks.
November.
Prisoners.
Sleepers, The.
Yes, ducks are valiant things, *sel.*
Harwood, Gwen
At the Sea's Edge.
Carnal Knowledge.
Father and Child.
Hospital Evening.
In the Bistro.
In the Park.
Last Meeting.
Lion's Bride, The.
New Music.
Night Thoughts: Baby & Demon.
Panther and Peacock.
Prize-giving.
Second Life of Lazarus, The.
Simple Story, A.
Suburban Sonnet.
Harwood, Lee
Final Painting, The.
Rain Journal: London: June 65.
Soft White.
"Utopia, The."
Words, The.
Hasan, Mir Ghulam
From Mathnavi Sehrul Bayaan.
"Hashimura Togo." *See* **Irwin, Wallace**
Haskell, Jefferson
My Latest Sun Is Sinking Fast.
Hass, Robert
After the Gentle Poet Kobayashi Issa.
Against Botticelli.
Apple Trees at Olema, The.
Calm.
Child Naming Flowers.
Churchyard.
Fall.
Feast, The.
Harbor at Seattle, The.
In Weather.
January.
Late Spring.
Maps.
Measure.
Meditation at Lagunitas.
Monticello.
Museum.
Novella.
Old Dominion.
Origin of Cities, The.

Palo Alto; the Marshes.
Paschal Lamb.
Return of Robinson Jeffers, The.
Rusia en 1931.
San Pedro Road.
Santa Lucia II.
Song: "Afternoon cooking in the fall sun."
Songs to Survive the Summer.
Spring Drawing II.
Story about the Body, A.
Tall Windows.
Thin Air.
Vintage.
Weed.
Hassall, Christopher Vernon
Santa Claus.
Hassan, Mahammed Abdille
Denunciation, A.
To a Friend Going on a Journey.
Haste, Gwendolen
Montana Wives.
Tomorrow Is a Birthday.
Hastings, Fanny de Groot
Late Comer.
Hastings, Thomas
Exhortation.
Hail to the Brightness of Zion's Glad
   Morning.
In Sorrow.
Jesus, Merciful and Mild!
Now Be the Gospel Banner.
Now from Labor and from Care.
Hatfield, Edwin Francis
Hallelujah! Praise the Lord.
Hathaway, James B.
What the Stone Dreams.
Hathaway, Jeanine
Extensions of Linear Mobility.
Name of God Is, The.
Reflections on a Womb Which Is Called
   "Vacant."
Hathaway, William
American Poet—"But Since It Came to
   Good. ", The.
Dear Wordsworth.
Iceball, The.
My Words.
Still Life.
This Tree.
When I Was Dying.
Why That's Bob Hope.
You Had to Know Her.
Hatshepsut
Now my heart turns to and fro, *sel.*
Hatton, Joseph
Christmas Bills.
Hatun, Mihri
At one glance/ I loved you.
Hauroa, Matangi
Lament: "I lie in darkness, as the dead shades
   gather."
Hauser, Samuel
What Ship Is This? at.
Havelin, Jim Lavella
Enos Slaughter.
Havens, Mrs.
Ask, and Ye Shall Receive.
Havergal, Frances Ridley
Afterwards.
Another Year Is Dawning.
At the Portal.
For Every Day, *sel.*
God Is Faithful.
Happy Christmas, A.
Life-Mosaic.
Lord, speak to me, that I may speak.
New Year Wish, A.
New Year's Wishes.
Reality.
Take My Life and Let It Be.
Thou Art Coming!

"Havesp, Dewi." *See* **Roberts, David**
Haweis, Hugh Reginald
Homeland, The.
Hawes, Stephen
Dame Music, *sel.*
Epitaph of Graunde [*or* La Graunde]
   Amoure, The, *sel.*
Pair of Wings, A.
Seven Deadly Sins, The, *sel.*
Time and Eternity, *sel.*
True Knight [*or* True Knighthood], The, *sel.*
Hawi, Khalil
Bridge, The.
Flute and Wind in the Hermit's Cell.
Lebanon.
Magi in Europe, The.
Hawker, Robert Stephen
Aishah Schechinah.
Aunt Mary.
Butterfly, The.
Cornish Emigrant's Song, The.
Croon on Hennacliff, A.
Death Song.
Featherstone's Doom.
King Arthur's Waes-hael.
Land is lonely now, The: Anathema, *sel.*
Legend of the Hive, A.
Mystic Magi , The.
Poor Man and His Parish Church, The.
Song of the Western Men, The.
Hawkins, Bruce
Great Annelid Worm, A.
2021: Noon: Idaho.
Hawkins, Henry
Bee, The.
Hoc Cygno Vinces.
Hawkins, Hunt
Prejohn, The.
Hawkins, Maureen
Inheritance, The.
Miracle, The.
Hawkins, Walter Everette
Death of Justice, The.
Spade Is Just a Spade, A.
Hawkins, William
New Light, A.
Spring Rain.
To a Worm Which the Author Accidentally
   Trode Upon.
Wall, The.
Hawkshawe, Ann
Little Raindrops, *at.*
Moonlight, The.
Muffin-Man's Bell, The.
Old Kitchen Clock, The.
Hawley, Beatrice
Marsh, The.
Hawley, W. F.
Love Song, A: "Yes, I will love thee when
   the sun."
Hawling, Francis
Author Consults a Critic and Sells His
   Manuscript, The, *sel.*
Hawthorn, John
Deathbed, A, *sel.*
On His Writing Verses.
"Hawthorne Alice." *See* **Winner, Septimus**
Hawthorne, Hildegarde
Song, A: "Sing me a sweet, low song of
   night."
Hawthorne, Julian
Were-Wolf.
Hawthorne, Nathaniel
Star of Calvary, The.
Hay, Clarence Leonard
Down and Out.

"Hay, Elijah." *See* **Seiffert, Marjorie Allen**
Hay, George Campbell
Flooer o the Gean.
Song: "Day will rise and the sun from
   eastward."
Sonnet: "Beckie, my luve!—What is't, ye
   twa-faced tod?"
Two Neighbours, The.
Hay, John (b. 1915)
And Grow.
Defend Us, Lord, from Every Ill.
Railway Station.
Variations on a Theme.
Hay, John Milton (1838–1905)
Advance Guard, The.
Christine.
Distichs.
Enchanted Shirt, The.
Good Luck and Bad.
Jim Bludso of the Prairie Belle.
Liberty.
Light of Love, The.
Little Breeches.
Miles Keogh's Horse.
Not in Dumb Resignation.
Pledge at Spunky Point, The.
Religion and Doctrine.
Silver Leaf, The.
Stirrup-Cup, The.
Surrender of Spain, The.
What is a first love worth except to prepare
   for a second?
White Flag, The.
Words.
Hay, Sara Henderson
Ballad of the Golden Bowl.
"Bottle Should Be Plainly Labeled 'Poison.' "
Christmas, the Year One, A.D.
Daily Manna, The.
For a Dead Kitten.
Interview.
Prayer in April.
Hayakawa, Samuel Ichiye
To One Elect.
Hayden, Robert Earl
Aunt Jemima of the Ocean Waves.
Bahá'u'lláh in the Garden of Ridwan.
Ballad of Nat Turner, The.
Ballad of Remembrance, A.
Ballad of Sue Ellen Westerfield, The.
Bone-Flower Elegy.
Crispus Attucks.
Diver, The.
Double Feature.
El-Hajj Malik El-Shabazz.
For a Young Artist.
For King, for Robert Kennedy, *sel.*
Frederick Douglass.
From the Corpse Woodpiles, from the Ashes.
Full Moon.
Homage to the Empress of the Blues.
In the Mourning Time.
Incense of the Lucky Virgin.
Letter from Phillis Wheatley, A.
Locus.
Middle Passage.
Monet's "Waterlilies."
Mourning Poem for the Queen of Sunday.
"Mystery Boy' Looks for Kin in Nashville."
Night-blooming Cereus, The.
Night, Death, Mississippi.
O Daedalus, Fly Away Home.
On Lookout Mountain.
Paul Laurence Dunbar.
Peacock Room, The.
Perseus.
Plague of Starlings, A.
Plowdens, Finns, *sel.*
Prisoners, The.
Richard Hunt's Arachne.
Road in Kentucky, A.

Runagate Runagate.
Sojourner Truth, *sel.*
Soledad.
Sphinx.
Stars.
Sub Specie Aeternitatis.
"Summertime and the Living."
Tattooed Man, The.
Those Winter Sundays.
To the Virginian Voyage.
Tour 5.
Veracruz.
Wheel, The.
Whipping, The.
Witch Doctor.
Hayes, Alfred
Angel, The.
City of Beggars, The.
Death of the Craneman, The.
Epistle to the Gentiles.
Joe Hill.
Nice Part of Town, A.
Slaughter-House, The.
Hayes, Donald Jeffrey
After All.
Alien.
Appoggiatura.
Auf Wiedersehen.
Benediction.
Confession.
Haven.
Inscription: "He wrote upon his heart."
Night.
Nocturne: "Softly blow lightly."
Pastourelle.
Poet.
Prescience.
Threnody: "Let happy throats be mute."
"Hayes, Evelyn" (Mary Ursula Bethell)
Garden-Lion.
Hayes, J. Milton
Green Eye of the Yellow God, The.
Hayes, John Russell
Old-fashioned Garden, The.
Hayes, Nancy M.
At Night in the Wood.
Shiny Little House, The.
Hayford, Gladys May Casely (Aquah Laluah)
Baby Cobina.
Rainy Season Love Song.
Serving Girl, The.
Shadow of Darkness.
Hayford, James
Mason's Trick.
Haygarth, William
Genius of Greece! thou livest, though thy
   domes, *sel.*
Mournful is the remembrance which awakes,
   sel.
Hayiaku
Funeral Song.
Hayley, William
To Mr. William Long, On His Recovery from
   a Dangerous Illness, 1785.
To Mrs. Smith, Occasioned by the First of
   Her Sonnets.
Hayman, Jane
Murdered Girl Is Found on a Bridge, The.
Hayman, Robert
Mad Answer of a Madman, A.
Of the Great and Famous. Sir Francis Drake,
   and of My Little-Little Selfe.
Pleasant Life in Newfoundland, The.
To My Very Loving and Discreet Friend,
   Master Peter Miller of Bristol.
Hayne, Paul Hamilton
Aspects of the Pines.
Battle of Charleston Harbor, The.
Between the Sunken Sun and the New Moon.
Beyond the Potomac.
Butler's Proclamation.

Charleston.
In Harbor.
Little while (my life is almost set!), A.
Love Scorns Degrees, *sel.*
Macdonald's Raid.
Mocking Bird, The.
Pre-Existence.
Rose and the Thorn, The.
South Carolina to the States of the North.
Storm in the Distance, A.
Stricken South to the North, The.
True Heaven, The.
Vicksburg.
Yorktown Centennial Lyric.
Hayne, William Hamilton
Autumn Breeze, An.
Charge at Santiago, The.
Cyclone at Sea, A.
Exiles.
Moonlight Song of the Mocking-Bird.
Night Mists.
Sleep and His Brother Death.
Southern Snow-Bird, The.
To a Cherokee Rose.
Yule Log, The.
Haynes, Albert E., Jr.
Law, The.
Haynes, Carol
Any Wife or Husband.
Hays, Hoffman Reynolds
Case, The.
For One Who Died Young.
January.
Manhattan.
Sacred Children, The.
Hays, Will S.
O'Grady's Goat.
Hayward, William
Five Birds Rise.
Hazard, Caroline
Great Swamp Fight, The.
Hazeley, Iyamide
Beloved.
When You Have Emptied Our Calabashes.
You're So Far Away.
Hazlewood-Brady, Anne
Closer First to Earth.
Double Axe, The.
Hazo, Samuel
After the Hurricane.
Between You and Me.
Challenge.
Skycoast.
To a Blind Student Who Taught Me to See.
"H.D." *See* **Doolittle, Hilda**
Healy, Ian
Advice from a Nightwatchman, *sel.*
Air Shaft, *sel.*
Heaney, Seamus
Alphabets.
At a Potato Digging.
Barn, The.
Bat on the Road, A.
Birthplace, The.
Black water. White waves. Furrows
   snowcapped, *sel.*
Blackberry-picking.
Bog Queen.
Bogland.
Cana Revisited.
Casualty.
Changes.
Constable Calls, A.
Cool that came off sheets just off the line,
   The, *sel.*
Death of a Naturalist.
Digging.
Diviner, The.
Docker.
Dream of Jealousy, A.
Drink of Water, A.

Heap

Exposure.
Field Work.
Follower.
Forge, The.
From the Canton of Expectation.
Gifts of Rain.
Girls Bathing, Galway 1965.
Given Note, The.
Guttural Muse, The.
Harvest Bow, The.
Haw Lantern, The.
Hazel Stick for Catherine Ann, A.
I dreamt we slept in a moss in Donegal, *sel.*
I had come to the edge of the water, *sel.*
I perched for rest, and imagined, *sel.*
I stirred wet sand and gathered myself, *sel.*
In Memoriam Francis Ledwidge.
In the last minutes he said more to her, *sel.*
Kinship.
Kite for Michael and Christopher, A.
Like a convalescent, I took the hand.
Limbo.
Mid-Term Break.
Mossbawn Sunlight, *sel.*
Mother.
Mother of the Groom.
"My brain dried like spread turf, my
  stomach", *sel.*
Near Anahorish.
New Song, A.
Night Drive.
North.
October Thought.
Other Side, The.
Otter, The.
Outlaw, The.
Peacock's Feather, A.
Peninsula, The.
Personal Helicon.
Plantation, The.
Play Way, The.
Poor Women in a City Church.
Postcard from North Antrim, A.
Punishment.
Rain comes down through the alders, *sel.*
Requiem for the Croppies.
Rite of Spring.
Road ahead, The, *sel.*
Saint Francis and the Birds.
Scaffolding.
Seed Cutters, The, *sel.*
Shooting Script, A.
Singer's House, The.
Singing School.
Skunk, The.
Sloe Gin.
Song: "Rowan like a lip-sticked girl, A."
Strand at Lough Beg, The.
Summer 1969.
Summer Home.
Sweeney kept going until he reached the
  church at/ Swim-two-birds, *sel.*
Thatcher.
This evening the cuckoo and the corncrake,
  sel.
Thunderlight on the split logs: big raindrops,
  sel.
Tollund Man, The.
Traditions.
Twice Shy.
Ulster Twilight, An.
Viking Dublin; Trial Pieces.
Vowels plowed into other: opened ground,
  sel.
Waterfall.
Whatever You Say Say Nothing.
When all the others were away at Mass, *sel.*
Widgeon.
Wife's Tale, The.

Heap, Jane
Where go the birds when the rain.

Heard, Josephine D. Henderson
Admiration.
Advance of Education, The.
Assurance.
Bereft.
Birth of Jesus, The.
Birth of Time, The.
Bishop James A. Shorter.
Black Sampson, The.
City by the Sea, The.
Day after Conference, The.
December.
Deception.
Decoration Day.
Do You Think?
Doxology.
Earthquake of 1886, The.
Easter Morn.
Epitaph, An: "When I am gone."
Eternity.
Fame.
Farewell to Allen University.
Forgetfulness!
General Robert Smalls.
Happy Heart, A.
He Comes Not To-night.
He Hath Need of Rest.
Heart-Hungry.
Hope.
Hope Thou in God.
I Love Thee.
I Will Look Up.
In Memory of James M. Rathel.
Judge Not.
Love Letters.
Matin Hymn.
Message to a Loved One Dead, A.
Morn.
Mother.
Mother's Love, A.
Music.
My Canary.
My Grace Is Sufficient.
My Husband's Birthday.
My Mocking Bird.
National Cemetery, Beaufort, South Carolina,
  The.
New Organ, The.
Night.
On Genessarett.
Out in the Desert.
Outcast, The.
Parting, The.
Parting Kiss, The.
Quarrel, The.
Quarto Centennial, The.
Question, The.
Resting.
Retrospect.
Rev. Andrew Brown, over the Hill to Rest.
Rt. Rev. Richard Allen.
Sabbath Bells.
Slumbering Passion.
Solace.
Sunshine after Cloud.
Tennyson's Poems.
They Are Coming?
Thine Own.
Thou Lovest Me.
To Clements' Ferry.
To Whittier.
To Youth.
Truth.
Unuttered Prayer.
Welcome Home.
Welcome to Hon. Frederick Douglass.
When I Would Die.
Where Do School Days End?
Who Is My Neighbor?
Whoso Gives Freely, Shall Freely Receive!
Wilberforce.

Hearn, Michael Patrick
In the Library.
Rhinos Purple, Hippos Green.

Hearn, Mary Ann. *See* **"Farningham,
  Marianne"**

Heath, ——
Women.

Heath, Ella
Poetry.

Heath, Robert
On Clarastella Singing.
On Clarastella walking in Her Garden.
On the Unusual Cold and Rainie Weather in
  the Summer, 1648.
Seeing Her Dancing.
Song in a Siege.
To Clarastella on St. Valentines Day
  Morning.

Heath-Stubbs, John
Age of Bronze awoke now in brutality, The,
  sel.
Beggar's Serenade.
Carol for Advent.
Charm against the Toothache, A.
Churchyard of St. Mary Magdalene, Old
  Milton.
Crow in Bayswater, A.
Dark Planet, The.
Death of Digenes Akritas, The.
December: Prayer to St. Nicholas.
Epitaph: "Mr. Heath-Stubbs as you must
  understand."
February.
Gifts, The.
History of the Flood, The.
It was the virgin Zennora, who dwelt, *sel.*
January.
Lady's Complaint, The.
Mozart.
Not Being Oedipus.
Old King, The.
Parthenon, The.
Poet of Bray, The.
Preliminary Poem.
Send for Lord Timothy.
Titus and Berenice.
To a Poet a Thousand Years Hence.
Unpredicted, The.
Valse Oubliée.
Virgin Martyrs.
Watching Tennis.
Winter Cricket.
Year of Our Lord two thousand one hundred
  and seven, The, *sel.*

Heaton, John Langdon
Sea Irony.

Heavysege, Charles
How Great unto the Living Seem the Dead!
Malzah's Song, *sel.*
Night.
Oh! think how hard it is to die when young!,
  sel.
Stars Are Glittering in the Frosty Sky, The.
To hunt and to be hunted make existence, *sel.*
Zaph Describes the Haunts of Malzah, *sel.*

Heber, Reginald
An Evening Walk in Bengal.
Brightest and Best of the Sons of the
  Morning.
By Cool Siloam's Shady Rill.
From Greenland's Icy Mountains.
Holy, Holy, Holy.
Providence.
Sympathy.
Who Follows in His Train?

Hébert, Annabelle
Dream about Sunsets.

Hébert, Anne
Alchemy of Day, The.
Bread Is Born.
Crown of Happiness.

Eve.
Great Fountains, The.
Landscape.
Life in the Castle.
Night.
Offended, The.
Our Hands in the Garden.
Skinny Girl, The.
Someone Could Certainly Be Found.
Spring over the City.
Tomb of the Kings, The.
Wisdom Has Broken My Arms.
Wooden Chamber, The.

Hecht, Anthony
Adam.
Alceste in the Wilderness.
Application for a Grant.
Avarice.
Behold the Lilies of the Field.
Birdwatchers of America.
Book of Yolek, The.
Clair de Lune.
Cost, The.
Deodand, The.
Double Sonnet.
Dover Bitch, The.
End of the Weekend, The.
Feast of Stephen, The.
Firmness.
From the Grove Press.
Ghost in the Martini, The.
Gift of Song, The.
Going the Rounds; a Sort of Love Poem.
Hill, A.
Improvisations on Aesop.
"It Out-Herods Herod. Pray You, Avoid It."
Japan.
Jason.
La Condition Botanique.
Letter, A.
Lizards and Snakes.
Lot of Night Music, A.
Meditation.
"More Light! More Light!"
Murmur.
Old Malediction, An.
Origin of Centaurs, The.
Paradise Lost, Book V: An Epitome.
Pig.
Samuel Sewall.
Sestina d'Inverno.
Still Life.
Tarantula or the Dance of Death.
Third Avenue in Sunlight.
Transparent Man, The.
Vice.
Voice at a Seance, A.
Vow, The.

Hecht, Roger
War Memento (Somewhere in France 1915).

Hedge, Frederic Henry
Sovereign and Transforming Grace.

Hedges, Doris
Onwardness.
Poet's Protest.
Prayer: "O God of goodness, forwardness, and fulness."

Hedylos
Seduced Girl.

Heffernan, Michael
Colloquy of Silences, A.
Daffodils.
Naked War.
Putting On My Shoes I Hear the Floor Cry Out beneath Me.
Sunday Service.
Table, The.

Heffernan, William
Kathaleen Ny-Houlahan.

Heginbothom, Ottiwell
Great God, let all my tuneful pow'rs.

Heguri, Lady
Thousand years, you said, A.

Heide, Florence Parry
Rocks.
What's That?

Heifetz-Tussman, Malka
At the Well.
Desert Wind.
Earthquake.
Faker.
Her Oak.
I say.
Keep Me.
Last Apple.
Love the Ruins.
Mount Gilboa.
Out and In Again.
Slavery.
Songs of the Priestess.
Sweet Father.
Thou Shalt Not.
Thunder My Brother.
Water without Sound.
Widowhood.
With a Fool.

Heikel, Karin Alice. *See* **"Vala, Katri"**

Heimler, Eugene
After an Eclipse of the Sun.
Psalm: "Oh Lord, I have been staring into a mirror."

Heine, Heinrich
Ad Finem.
And When I Lamented, *sel.*
Anniversary.
Anno 1829.
Auf meiner Herzliebsten Äugelein.
Azra, The.
Best Religion, The, *sel.*
By the Waters of Babylon, *sel.*
Coffin, The.
Dear Maiden.
Dearest Friend, Thou Art in Love, *sel.*
Der Mond ist aufgegangen.
Die blauen Veilchen der Äugelein.
Die Lotusblume ängstigt.
Die Rose, die Lilie, die Taube, die Sonne.
Die Welt ist dumm, die Welt ist blind.
Du bist wie eine Blume, *sel.*
Ein Fichtenbaum steht einsam.
Enfant perdu.
Epilogue: "Like the stalks of wheat in the fields," *sel.*
Es fällt ein Stern herunter.
Es Stehen Unbeweglich.
Evening Twilight, *sel.*
Farewell: "Linden blossomed, the nightingale sang, The."
Fresco-Sonnets to Christian Sethe.
Heavenly fields of Paradise, The, *sel.*
I, a Most Wretched Atlas, *sel.*
I Love But Thee.
I Met by Chance.
I Wept as I Lay Dreaming.
Ich Weiss Nicht Was Soll es Bedeuten.
If, Jerusalem, I Ever Should Forget Thee.
I'm Black and Blue.
Im Traum sah ich ein Männchen klein und putzig.
It's Going Out.
Kings from the East, The.
Lassie, What Mair Wad You Hae?
Lorelei.
Loreley, The.
Love's Résumé.
Mädchen mit dem rothen Mündchen.
Maiden Lies in Her Chamber, A.
Mein Herz, Mein Herz Ist Traurig.
Mein Liebchen, wir sassen zusammen.
Message, The.
Mir träumte von einem Königskind.
Mir träumte wieder der alte Traum.

Morning After, The.
Mortal, Sneer Not at the Devil, *sel.*
Mutilated choir boys, The, *sel.*
My child, we were two children.
My Songs Are Poisoned ("My songs, they say, are poisoned").
New Jewish Hospital at Hamburg, The.
Night by the Sea, A, *sel.*
Oh Lovely Fishermaiden.
Princess Sabbath.
Proem: "Out of my own great woe."
Sag', wo ist dein schönes Liebchen.
Sea Hath Its Pearls, The.
Shadow-Love, *sel.*
Shepherd Boy, The.
Solomon.
Song: "There stands a lonely pine-tree."
Sonnet to My Mother, A.
Storm, The.
Tell me where thy lovely love is, *sel.*
Tell me where thy lovely love is, *sel.*
This delightful young man, *sel.*
This mad carnival of loving, *sel.*
Thou Hast Diamonds, *sel.*
Three Holy Kings from Morgenland.
To a Political Poet.
To Edom.
To My Mother.
Twilight.
Voyage, The.
Warum sind denn die Rosen so blass.
Waves Gleam in the Sunshine, The, *sel.*
We Cared for Each Other.
Weavers.
When Two Are Parted.
When Young Hearts Break.
Who Was It, Tell Me.
Wie langsam kriechet sie dahin.
Window-Glance, The.
Wise Men Ask the Children the Way, The.
Zu fragmentarisch ist Welt und Leben.

Heinrich von Rugge
He That Loves a Rosy Cheek.

Heishin
Who said the sea's concave.

Hejinian, Lyn
Agreement swerves.
"Angels, it seems, don't always know."
Determinism.
Erosion of rocks blooms, The. The world.
Guard, 8, The.
Ideas move and move the thinker.
If There's Nothing out the Windows Look at Books.
Imagine observing ones fear.
Inanimate are rocks, desks, bubble, The.
Like Plump Birds along the Shore.
Nostalgia is the elixir drained.
Pandemonium hews/ no clouds.
Rain on the macadam quaver ticks.
Sun is just appearing, The.
Tidal throughway from a distance, The.
We are parting with description.
You must show yourself to catch.

Hekigoto, Kawahigashi. *See* **Kawahigashi Hekigoto**

Helburn, Theresa
Mother.

Helen Gray Cone
Ride to the Lady, The.

Hellaakoski, Aaro
Hawk.
Moonlight in the Forest.

Heller, Binem
Pesach Has Come to the Ghetto Again.

Helmer, Charles D.
Battle of Oriskany, The.

Helmore, Thomas
Christmas Carol: "Christ was born on Christmas day."

Helton, Roy
　Lonesome Water.
　Old Christmas Morning.
Helwig, David
　Considerations.
　Dead Weasel, A.
　Drunken Poem.
　For Edward Hicks.
　Words from Hell.
Hemans, Felicia Dorothea
　Agony in the Garden, The.
　Casabianca.
　Child's First Grief, The.
　Corinne at the Capitol.
　Dirge: "Calm on the bosom of thy God," *sel.*
　Flight of the Spirit.
　Graves of a Household, The.
　Homes of England, The.
　Hour of Death, The.
　Hymn for Christmas.
　Landing of the Pilgrim Fathers [in New
　　England], The.
　Prayer, A: "Father in Heaven! from whom the
　　simplest flower."
　Sabbath Sonnet.
　To the Poet Wordsworth.
　Yes! I have seen the ancient oak, *sel.*
Hemingway, Ernest
　Champs d'Honneur.
　Chapter Heading.
　Dedicated to F. W.
　Earnest Liberal's Lament, The.
　Neo-Thomist Poem.
　Valentine.
Hemminger, Graham Lee
　Tobacco ("Tobacco is a dirty weed.").
Hemp, Christine E.
　To Build a Poem.
Hemphill, Essex
　Cordon Negro.
　Family Jewels.
　Isn't It Funny?
　To Some Supposed Brothers.
Hemphrey, Malcolm
　Lanes in Summer.
Hempseed, Isabell
　Rufty and Tufty.
Hemschemeyer, Judith
　Dirty-billed Freeze Footy, The.
　First Love.
　Gift.
　I Remember the Room Was Filled with Light.
　Painters, The.
　Petals of the Tulips, The.
　Settlers, The.
　Survivors, The.
　This Love.
Hemsley, Stuart
　S.P.C.A. Sermon.
Henchman, Richard
　In Consort to Wednesday, Jan. 1st. 1701.
　Vox Oppressi, to the Lady Phipps.
Henderson, Alice C. *See* **Corbin, Alice**
Henderson, Daniel
　Road to France, The.
Henderson, David
　Do Nothing till You Hear from Me.
　Documentary on Airplane Glue, A.
　Downtown-Boy Uptown.
　Keep on Pushing.
　Louisiana Weekly #4, The.
　Psychedelic Firemen.
　Sketches of Harlem.
　They Are Killing All the Young Men.
　Walk with de Mayor of Harlem.
　White People.
Henderson, E. H.
　March Wind, The.
Henderson, Hamish
　First Elegy for the Dead in Cyrenaica.
　Flyting o' Life and Daith, The.

Henderson, Nyle A.
　"Bueno," Which in Spanish Means Good.
　How Many Cows?
"Henderson, Paul." (Ruth France)
　Elegy: "Morning after death on the bar was
　　calm."
　I Think of Those.
　Object Lesson.
　Return Journey.
　Shag Rock.
Henderson, Peggy
　Serpent Muses, The.
Henderson, Rose
　Growing Old.
Hendricks, A. L.
　Boundary.
　Hot Summer Sunday.
　I touch jig-saw fragments, *sel.*
　Looking out toward the stars, *sel.*
　Migrant, The.
　Will the Real Me Please Stand Up?
　Woman in the garden gathers lilacs, A, *sel.*
Hendrie, K. G. P.
　Beckon Me, Ye Cuillins.
Hendry, Hamish
　Silver Bells.
　Silver Road, The.
　Upside-Down World, The.
Hendry, J. F.
　Constant North, The.
Henisch, Peter
　Everything is/ in order folks.
　In protest/ against government policies.
　Your cage/ (said the caretaker).
　You're right/ I chase after myself.
Henjo, Bishop
　Blow wind of heaven.
Henley, Samuel
　Verses Addressed to a Friend, Just Leaving a
　　Favourite Retirement.
Henley, William Ernest
　After, *sel.*
　All in a Garden Green.
　Anterotics, *sel.*
　Apparition, *sel.*
　Ave, Caesar, *sel.*
　Ballade Made in the Hot Weather.
　Ballade of Dead Actors.
　Before, *sel.*
　Bowl of Roses, A.
　Casualty, *sel.*
　"Chief, The", *sel.*
　Children: Private Ward, *sel.*
　Clinical, *sel.*
　Culture in the Slums.
　Discharged, *sel.*
　England, My England.
　Enter Patient, *sel.*
　Envoy: "Do you remember/ That afternoon."
　Etching, *sel.*
　From a Window in Princes Street.
　Gulls in an äery morrice.
　Home *or* Falmouth.
　House-Surgeon, *sel.*
　In the Dials.
　Interior, *sel.*
　Interlude: "O, the fun, the fun and frolic",
　　sel.
　Lady-Probationer, *sel.*
　Largo e mesto, *sel.*
　Madam Life's a Piece in Bloom.
　Music ("Down the quiet eve"), *sel.*
　Nocturn: "At the barren heart of midnight",
　　sel.
　Operation, *sel.*
　Out of Tune.
　Pastoral: "It's the Spring", *sel.*
　Romance, *sel.*
　Rondel: "Beside the idle summer sea."
　Scherzando, *sel.*
　Scrubber, *sel.*

　Since Those We Love and Those We Hate.
　Staff-Nurse: New Style, *sel.*
　Staff-Nurse: Old Style, *sel.*
　Street Scene.
　Suicide, *sel.*
　To Robert Louis Stevenson.
　Vigil, *sel.*
　Villon's Good-Night.
　Villon's Straight Tip to All Cross Coves.
　Visitor.
　Waiting, *sel.*
Henn, Mary Ann
　Chimera.
Hennamma
　Wasn't your mother a woman?
Hennell, Thomas
　Mermaiden, A.
　Queen Anne's Musicians.
　Shepherd and Shepherdess.
Henniker-Heaton, Peter J.
　Post Early for Space.
Henri, Adrian
　Love Story.
　Mrs. Albion You've Got a Lovely Daughter.
Henri, Raymond
　At the Woodpile.
　Chartres, *sel.*
　Duomo, Milan, *sel.*
　Roebling, his life and mind reprieved enough,
　　sel.
Henry, Gerrit
　Cole Porter's Son.
　Confessions of Gerrit, The.
Henry, Gordon
　Freeze Tag.
　Leaving Smoke's.
　Outside White Earth.
　Pine Point, You Are.
　Waking on a Greyhound.
Henry, James
　Another and another and another.
　My Stearine Candles.
　Old Man.
　Once on a time a thousand different men.
　Out of the Frying Pan into the Fire.
　Pain.
　Two hundred men and eighteen killed.
　Very Old Man.
"Henry, O." (William Sidney Porter)
　Options.
Henry VIII, King of England
　Love Ever Green.
　Pastime *or* Good Company.
　To His Lady.
Henry the Minstrel ("Blind Harry")
　Burning of the Barns of Ayr, The, *sel.*
　Description of Wallace, A, *sel.*
　Wallace's Lament for the Graham, *sel.*
Henryson, Robert
　Assembly of the Gods, The, *sel.*
　Cresseid's Complaint against Fortune, *sel.*
　Cressida's Leprosy, *sel.*
　Garment of Good Ladies, The.
　I mend the fyre and beikit me about, *sel.*
　Preiching of the Swallow, The.
　Robin [*or* Robene] and Makyne.
　Taill of the Foxe, That Begylit the Wolf, in
　　the Schadow of the Mone, The.
　Taill of the Wolf and the Wedder, The.
　Tale of the Upland Mouse and the Burgess
　　Mouse, The.
　Testament of Cresseid, The.
　To Our Lady.

Henson, Lance
Among Hawks.
Anniversary Poem for the Cheyennes Who
   Fell at Sand Creek.
At Chadwicks Bar and Grill.
Bay Poem.
Between Rivers and Seas.
Buffalo Blood.
Buffalo Marrow on Black.
Cold, The.
Comanche Ghost Dance: An Impression.
Coyote Fragments.
Curtain.
Dawn in January.
Day Song.
Eight Poems for August.
Epitaph: Snake River.
Flock.
Grandfather.
I Am Singing the Cold Rain.
Image of City.
Last Words, 1968.
Moon at Three A.M.
Moth.
Near Twelve Mile Point.
North.
Old Man Told Me.
Old Story.
Other.
Our Smoke Has Gone Four Ways.
Poem for Carroll, Descendant of Chiefs.
Poem near Midway Truck Stop.
Rain.
Scattered Leaves.
Sitting Alone in Tulsa Three A.M.
Sleep Watch.
Solitary.
Splitting Wood Near Morris, Oklahoma on
   Robbie and Lesa McMurtry's Farm.
Sundown at Darlington 1878.
Travels with the Band-Aid Army.
Vision Song (Cheyenne).
Warrior Nation Trilogy.
We Are a People.
Wish.
Wood Floor Dreams.

Henson, Pauline
On the Edge of the Copper Pit.

Henz, Rudolf
Meditation at Seventy.
Once Again.

Henze, Helen Rowe
Etruscan Warrior's Head.

Hepburn, Thomas Nicoll. *See* **"Setoun,**
   Gabriel"

Heppenstall, Rayner
Actaeon.
Fleur de Lys.
Tammuz.

Heraud, Javier
Guerrilla's Goodbye, A.
Guerrilla's Word, A.
I want two geraniums, *sel.*
New Journey, A.
Summer.

Herbert, E.
Balloon Man, The.

Herbert, Edward. *See* **Herbert of Cherbury,**
   Edward Herbert, 1st Baron

Herbert, George
Aaron.
Affliction ("Broken in pieces all asunder").
Affliction ("When first thou didst entice to
   thee my heart").
Altar, The.
Ana(Mary-Army)gram.
Answer, The.
Artillerie.
Avarice.
Bag, The.
Be Useful.

Bitter-sweet.
Bunch of Grapes, The.
Christmas.
Church-Floor [*or* Floore], The.
Church Lock and Key.
Church Monuments.
Church-Music[k]
Clasping of Hands.
Collar, The.
Come away, *sel.*
Confession.
Death.
Decay.
Denial.
Dialogue, A.
Discipline.
Dooms-Day.
Easter ("I got me flowers to straw Thy Way").
Easter ("I got me flowers to strew thy way.").
Easter ("Rise, heart, thy Lord is risen. Sing
   his praise").
Easter Wings.
Elixir, The.
Employment ("He that is weary, let him
   sit.").
Employment ("If as a flowre doth spread and
   die.").
Flower, The.
Forerunners, The.
Frailty.
Grace.
Heaven.
Holy Baptisme.
Hope.
Jesu.
Jews, The.
Jordan.
Judgement.
Life.
Longing.
Love.
Love ("Immortal heat, O let thy greater
   flame"), *sel.*
Love ("Immortal love, authour of this great
   frame").
Love-Joy.
Love Unknown.
Man.
Mattens.
Miserie.
Mortification.
Odour, The.
Our Life Is Hid with Christ in God.
Paradise.
Parodie, A: "Souls joy, when thou art gone."
Peace.
Pearl, The.
Pilgrimage, The.
Prayer: "Prayer the church's banquet, Angel's
   age," *sel.*
Pulley, The.
Quidditie, The.
Quip, The.
Redemption.
Rose, The.
Sacrifice, The.
Sighs and Grones.
Sin.
Son, The, *sel.*
Sonne, The.
Sonnet: "My God, where is that ancient heat
   towards Thee."
Sonnet: "Sure, Lord, there is enough in Thee
   to dry."
Submission.
Sunday.
Superliminare.
Temper, The.
Time.
To All Angels and Saints.
Trinity Sunday.
True Hymn, A.

Vanity [*or* Vanitie]
Virtue.
Windows, The.
World, The.
Wreath, A.

Herbert, Henry William
Come Back.

Herbert, Mary Sidney, Countess of
   Pembroke. *See* **Pembroke, Mary Sidney**
   Herbert, Countess of

Herbert, Moss
Gentle Park, A.

Herbert, Sir Alan Patrick
At the Theater.
Beaucourt Revisited.
Centipede, The.
Chameleon, The.
Cupid's Darts.
Farmer, The.
Hattage.
"He Didn't Oughter."
I Can't Think What He Sees in Her.
I Like Them Fluffy.
Inst., Ult., and Prox.
I've Got the Giggles Today.
Less Nonsense.
Lines for a Worthy Person Who Has Drifted
   by Accident into a Chelsea Revel.
Mullion.
Racing-Man, The.
Saturday Night.
Stop, Science—Stop!
To a Junior Waiter.
Triangular Legs.

Herbert, William, Earl of Pembroke. *See*
   Pembroke, William Herbert, Earl of

Herbert, Zbigniew
Apollo and Marsyas.
At the Gate of the Valley.
Beethoven.
Devil, A.
Elegy of Fortinbras.
Emperor's Dream, The.
End of a Dynasty, The.
Envoy of Mr. Cogito, The.
Fathers of a Star, The.
From Mythology.
Halt, A.
Jonah.
Mr. Cogito—The Return.
Murderers of Kings, The.
Naked Town, A.
Our Fear.
Pan Cogito's Thoughts on Hell.
Pebble, The.
Power of Taste, The.
Rain, The.
Report from Paradise.
Report from the Besieged City.
Return of the Proconsul, The.
Revelation.
Study of the Object.
Tongue, The.
Two Drops.
Wooden Die, A.

Herbert of Cherbury, Edward Herbert, 1st
   Baron
Description, A.
Ditty in Imitation of the Spanish ["Entre
   Tanto Que L'Avril"], A.
Echo to a Rock.
Elegy over a Tomb.
Epitaph. Caecil. Boulstr.
In a Glass-Window for Inconstancy.
Inconstancy's the Greatest of Sins.
Kissing.
Loves End.
Madrigal: "Dear, when I did from you
   remove."

Madrigal: "How should I love my best?"
Ode upon a Question Moved, Whether Love Should Continue for Ever, An?
Ode, upon a Question Moved, Whether Love Should Continue Forever? An.
Parted Souls.
Platonick Love.
Sinner's Lament, A.
Sonnet: "Innumerable Beauties, thou white haire."
Sonnet Made upon the Groves near Merlou Castle.
Sonnet of Black Beauty.
Tears, Flow No More.
Thought, The.
To a Lady Who Did Sing Excellently.
To Her Eyes.
To His Mistress for Her True Picture.
To His Watch, When He Could Not Sleep.
Vision, A.

Herbertson, Agnes Grozier
Lament for a Cornish Soldier.
Little Betty Blue.

Herbin, John Frederic
Diver, The.
Haying.

Herder, Johann Gottfried von
Esthonian Bridal Song.
Sir Olaf.

Herea, Te Heuheu
Mourning-Song for Rangiaho, A.

Herebert, William
Devout Man Prays to His Relations, The.
Knight Stained from Battle, The.
Palm-Sunday Hymn, A.

Heredia, José-Maria de
Flute; a Pastoral, The.
Laborer, The.

Herford, Oliver
Belated Violet, A.
Bunny Romance, A.
Cat, The.
Chimpanzee, The.
Cow, The, sel.
Crocodile, The.
Dog, The.
Elf and the Dormouse, The.
Eve.
Fall of J. W. Beane, The.
Hen, The.
Hippopotamus, The.
I Heard a Bird Sing.
Japanesque.
Last Violet, The.
Metaphysics.
Missing Link, The.
Mon-Goos, The, sel.
Music of the Future, The.
Musical Lion, The.
Penguin, A.
Platypus, The.
Proem: "If this little world to-nigh," sel.
Silver Question, The.
Smile of the Goat, The.
Smile of the Walrus, The.
Snail's Dream, The.
Some Geese, sel.
Stairs.
Why Ye Blossome Cometh Before Ye Leafe.

Hergouth, Alois
Fall, The.
Farewell: "It will be hard."
Interim Balance.
Venetian Fragment.

"Hermes, Paul." See Thayer, William Roscoe

Hernández, Miguel
Song: "House is a cote for doves, The."
Songhous, The: Love Was Rising between Us.

Hernández Cruz, Víctor
You Gotta Have Your Tips on Fire.

Hernton, Calvin C.
D Blues.
Distant Drum, The.
Elements of Grammar.
Fall Down.
Jitterbugging in the Streets.
Madhouse.
Young Negro Poet.

Herrick, Robert
Againe.
All Things Decay and Die.
Amber Bead, The.
Ambition.
Anacreontic.
Another to the Maids.
Apparition of His Mistress[e] Calling Him to Elizium [or Elysium], The.
Apron of Flowers, The.
Argument of His Book, The.
Bad Season Makes the Poet Sad, The.
Barley-Break; or, Last in Hell.
Beggar to Mab, the Fairy [or Fairie] Queen, The.
Bell-Man, The.
Bellman, The.
Body, The.
Bracelet: To Julia, The.
Bubble; a Song, The.
Canticle to Apollo, A.
Captived Bee; or, The Little Filcher, The.
Ceremonies for Candlemas[se] Eve.
Ceremonies for Christmas.
Ceremony upon Candlemas Eve.
Changes to Corinna, The.
Charm, A.
Charm me asleep, and melt me so, sel.
Charme, or an Allay for Love, A.
Charmes.
Cheat of Cupid; or The Ungentle Guest.
Cherry-ripe.
Chop-Cherry.
Christmas Eve—Another Ceremony.
Clothes Do but Cheat and Cozen Us.
Cock-Crow.
Comfort to a Youth That Had Lost His Love.
Coming of Good Luck, The.
Conjuration, to Electra, A.
Corinna's Going a-Maying.
Country Life: To His Brother, Master Thomas Herrick, A.
Crosses.
Cruel Maid, The.
Crutches.
Curse, The; a Song.
Darling of the world is come, The, sel.
Dean-bourn, a Rude River in Devon, by Which Sometimes He Lived ("Dean-bourn, farewell; I never look to see").
Definition of Beauty, The.
Delight in Disorder.
Departure of the Good Daemon, The.
Dew Sat on Julia's Hair.
Dirge upon the Death of the Right Valiant Lord, Bernard Stuart, A.
Discontents in Devon.
Distrust.
Divination by a Daffadill [or Daffodil]
Dreams.
End of His Work, The.
Entertainment, or Porch-Verse, at the Marriage of Master Henry Northleigh and the Most Witty Mistress Lettice Yard, The.
Epitaph on the Tomb of Sir Edward Giles and His Wife.
Epitaph upon a Child, An.
Epitaph upon a Sober Matron, An.
Epitaph upon a Virgin, An.
Epithalamy to Sir Thomas Southwell and His Lady, An.
Eternity.

Eye, The.
Fair Days; or, Dawns Deceitful.
Fairies, The.
Fairy Temple; or, Oberon's Chapel, The.
Fame.
Fame Makes Us Forward.
Farewell Frost; or, Welcome the Spring.
Four Sweet Months, The.
Four Things Make Us Happy Here.
Frolic, A.
Frozen Zone; or, Julia Disdainful, The.
Funeral Rites of the Rose, The.
God to Be First Served.
Good Christians.
Good Men Afflicted Most.
Good-Night, or Blessing, The.
Grace for a Child.
Grace for Children, A.
Hag, The ("The hag is astride").
Here a pretty baby lies.
His Age, Dedicated to His Peculiar Friend, Master John Wickes, under the Name of Posthumus.
His Cavalier.
His Charge to Julia at His Death.
His Content in the Country.
His Desire.
His Ejaculation to God.
His Farewell to Sack.
His Grange, or Private Wealth.
His Hope or Sheet-Anchor.
His Lachrimae or Mirth, Turn'd to Mourning.
His Litany to the Holy Spirit.
His Own Epitaph.
His Poetry [or Poetrie] His Pillar.
His Prayer for Absolution.
His Prayer to Ben Jonson [or Johnson].
His Request to Julia.
His Return to London.
His Sailing from Julia.
His Saviour's Words, Going to the Cross.
His Tears to Thamesis.
His Winding-Sheet.
Hock-Cart, or Harvest Home, The.
Hour-Glass, The.
How Lillies Came White.
How Marigolds Came Yellow.
How Roses Came Red.
How Violets Came Blue.
Hymn to Bacchus, A.
I Call and I Call ("I call, I call. Who do ye call?").
Impossibilities to His Friend.
In the Dark None Dainty.
Invitation, The.
Julia's Petticoat.
Julius Caesar.
Kiss, A.
Kisses Loathesome.
Lilly in a Christal, The.
Littles, sel.
Long and Lazy.
Love Me Little, Love Me Long.
Love What It Is.
Lovers How They Come and Part.
Lyric[k] for Legacies.
Lyric to Mirth, A.
Mad Maid's Song, The.
Man's Dying-Place Uncertain.
Matins, or Morning Prayer.
Meddow Verse; or, Aniversary to Mistris Bridget Lowman, The.
Meditation for His Mistress[e], A.
Mercy and Love.
Mirth.
Moderation.
Money Gets the Mastery.
Money Makes the Mirth.
Mount of the Muses, The.
Music.
Neutrality Loathesome.

New-Year's Gift Sent to Sir Simeon Steward, A.

New-Yeeres Gift, or Circumcisions Song, Sung to the King in the Presence at White Hall, The.

Night-Piece, to Julia, The.

No Coming to God without Christ.

No Difference in the Dark.

No Loathsomnesse in Love.

No Lock against Lechery.

Not Every Day Fit for Verse.

Not to Love.

Nothing New.

Nuptial[l] Song, or Epithalamie [or Epithalamy], on Sir Clipseby Crew and His Lady, A.

Oberon's Feast.

Oberon's Palace.

Observation.

Ode for Ben Jonson, An.

Ode on the Birth of Our Saviour, An.

Ode to Master Endymion Porter, upon His Brother's Death, An.

Old Wives Prayer, The.

On Himself.

Orpheus.

Panegyric to Sir Lewis Pemberton, A.

Parcae; or, Three Dainty Destinies: The Armillet, The.

Parcae, The, or Three Dainty Destinies: The Armillet.

Parting Verse, the Feast There Ended, The.

Perfume, The.

Peter-Penny, The.

Pillar of Fame, The.

Plaudite, or End of Life, The.

Poet Loves a Mistress, but Not to Marry, The.

Poetry Perpetuates the Poet.

Power and Peace.

Power in the People, The.

Prayers Must Have Poise.

Primrose, The, at.

Scare-Fire, The.

Science in God.

Shoe-tying, The.

Silken Snake, The.

Sins Loathed, and Yet Loved.

So Look the Mornings.

Spell, The.

Star-Song; a Carol to the King; Sung at White-Hall, The.

Steam in Sacrifice.

Supreme Fortune Falls Soonest.

Temple, The.

Temptation.

Ternarie of Littles, upon a Pipkin of Jellie [or Jelly] Sent to a Lady, A.

Thanksgiving.

Thanksgiving to God for His House, A.

This Cross-Tree Here.

Tips Tongueless.

'Tis Hard to Find God.

Tithe: To The Bride, The.

To a Bed of Tulips.

To a Gentlewoman Objecting to Him His Grey Hairs.

To Anthea.

To Anthea Lying in Bed.

To Anthea, Who May Command Him Anything.

To Blossoms.

To Cherry-Blossomes.

To Critics.

To Crown It.

To Daffodils [or Daffadills]

To Daisies, Not to Shut So Soon[e]

To Dianeme.

To Dianeme ("Dear, though to part it be a hell").

To Electra.

To Finde God.

To Fortune.

To God.

To Groves.

To His Book[e]

To his book's end this last line he'd have placed.

To His Conscience.

To His Dying Brother, Master William Herrick.

To His Ever-loving God.

To His Friend, on the Untunable.

To His Honoured and Most Ingenious Friend, Master Charles Cotton.

To His Kinsman, Master Thomas Herrick, Who Desired to Be in His Book.

To His Kinswoman, Mistress Penelope Wheeler.

To His Lovely Mistresses.

To His Maid Prew.

To His Mistress.

To His Mistress Objecting to Him neither Toying or Talking.

To His Mistresses.

To His Saviour, a Child; a Present, by a Child.

To His Tomb-Maker.

To Julia.

To Julia, the Flaminica Dialis, or Queen-Priest.

To Keep a True Lent.

To Larr.

To Laurels.

To Live Merrily, and to Trust to Good Verses.

To Marygolds.

To Master Henry Lawes, the Excellent Composer, of His Lyrics.

To Meadows.

To Mistress Katherine Bradshaw, the Lovely, That Crowned Him with Laurel.

To Music.

To Music: A Song.

To Music, to Becalm a Sweet-sick Youth.

To Music [or Musique], to Becalm [e] His Fever.

To My Ill Reader.

To Oenone.

To Perilla.

To Phyllis, to Love and Live with Him.

To Primroses Filled with Morning Dew.

To Robin Redbreast.

To Sycamores.

To the Generous Reader.

To the King, upon His Coming with His Army into the West.

To the Most Fair and Lovely Mistress Anne Soame, Now Lady Abdie [or Abdy].

To the Most Learned, Wise, and Arch-Antiquary, M. John Selden.

To the Most Virtuous Mistress Pot, Who Many Times Entertained Him.

To the Reverend Shade of His Religious Father.

To the Rose; a Song.

To the Sour[e] Reader.

To the Virgins, to Make Much of Time.

To the Water Nymphs, Drinking at the Fountain.

To the Western Wind.

To the Willow-Tree.

To the Yew and Cypress to Grace His Funeral.

To Violets.

To Virgins.

To Vulcan.

To Women, to Hide Their Teeth, if They Be Rotten or Rusty.

Transfiguration, The.

Upon a Black Twist, Rounding the Arm of the Countess of Carlisle.

Upon a Child That Died.

Upon a Flie.

Upon a Maid.

Upon a Maid That Died the Day She Was Married.

Upon a Virgin Kissing a Rose.

Upon a Young Mother of Many Children.

Upon Batt.

Upon Ben Jonson.

Upon Bunce: Epigram.

Upon Glass: Epigram.

Upon Groins: Epigram.

Upon Her Feet.

Upon Her Voice.

Upon Himself.

Upon His Departure Hence.

Upon His Sister-in-Law, Mistress Elizabeth Herrick.

Upon His Spaniell Tracie.

Upon His Verses.

Upon Jack and Jill: Epigram.

Upon Julia Washing Herself in the River.

Upon Julia's Breasts.

Upon Julia's Clothes.

Upon Julia's Ribband.

Upon Julia's Voice.

Upon Love.

Upon Love, by Way of Question and Answer.

Upon Lulls.

Upon Master Fletcher's Incomparable Playes.

Upon Mistress Elizabeth Wheeler under the Name of Amarillis.

Upon Mr. Ben Jonson: Epigram.

Upon Pagget.

Upon Prudence Baldwin Her Sickness.

Upon Prue, His Maid.

Upon Rook: Epigram.

Upon Roses.

Upon Scobble [Epigram]

Upon Showbread: Epigram.

Upon Some Women.

Upon Sybilla.

Upon the Death of His Sparrow; an Elegie.

Upon the Loss [e] of His Mistresses.

Upon the Nipples of Julia's Breast.

Upon the Same (Detractor).

Upon the Troublesome Time.

Upon Time.

Upon Umber: Epigram.

Vine, The.

Vision, The.

Vision to Electra , The.

Wassail the trees, that they may bear, sel.

Welcome to Sack, The.

What Kind of Mistress He Would Have.

When He Would Have His Verses Read.

White Island; or, The Place of the Blest [or Blessed], The.

Why Flowers Change Color.

Wounded Cupid, The.

Herschberger, Ruth

Coup d'Etat.

Huron, The.

In Panelled Rooms.

Lumberyard, The.

Song: "Sergei's a flower."

Herschell, William M.

Kid Has Gone to the Colors, The.

Hershenson, Miriam

Husbands and Wives.

Love Poem—1940.

Hershon, Robert

Boy Who Smells like Cocoa, A.

Cooper & Bailey Great London Circus, The.

Four Translations from the English of Robert Hershon.

How to Walk in a Crowd.

Ireland Lake.

Kelly.

Spitting on Ira Rosenblatt.

Swimming Lesson, The.
U. S. Coast and Geodetic Survey Ship
  Pioneer, The.
Hervey, Christopher
Confusion.
Hervey, John Russell
Children among the Tombstones.
Empty Valley, The.
Man on a Raft.
Somnambulist.
Two Old Men Look at the Sea.
Herzberg, Judith
After a Photo.
Bear in Bed.
Burying.
Child's Mirror, A.
Commentaries on the Song of Songs.
Dishwasher, The.
Kinneret.
Kitten.
Magic.
Nearer.
On the Death of Sylvia Plath.
Reunion.
Sneakers.
Tree Surgeon.
Vocation.
Voice, The.
Yiddish.
Herzing, Albert
Small Boy, Dreaming, A.
Hesiod
Next to my counsels an attention pay, *sel.*
Hesketh, Phoebe
Dipper, The.
Post-War Christmas.
Spring in Wartime.
Hesse, Hermann
Night.
Sometimes.
Spring Song.
Hessey, Vera
Frog and the Bird, The.
Hester, M. L.
Lightning Rod Salesman, The.
Hetherington, George
Palm House, Botanic Gardens.
Sonnet: "Now keep that long revolver at your
  side."
Sonnet: "Since I keep only what I give away."
Hewett, Dorothy
Moon-Man.
Sanctuary.
This Version of Love.
Hewison, R. J. P.
Genius.
Hewitt, Geof
Behind That Wall My Roommate Fucks His
  Girl.
Conversion.
Emergency at 8.
Explanation.
For Bill.
For Randie.
Rip-off #1: Hippie Capitalism.
Hewitt, John
Because I Paced My Thought.
Calling on Peadar O'Donnell at Dungloe.
First Corncrake.
From a Museum Man's Album.
Frontier, The.
Frost.
Glens, The.
Ireland.
Irishman in Coventry, An.
Leaf.
Little Lough, The.
Lyric: "Let but a thrush begin."
Once Alien Here.
Poem in May.
Ram's Horn, The.

Rome Sunday June 1960.
St. Stephen's Day.
Scar, The.
Swathe Uncut, The.
Turf Carrier on Aranmore.
Whit Monday.
Hewlett, Maurice
When She a Maiden Slim.
Hey, Phil
Old Clothes.
Sweetheart.
True Ballad of the Great Race to Gilmore
  City, The.
Heyen, William
Arrows.
Auction.
Berries, The.
Birds and Roses Are Birds and Roses.
Children, The.
Dark, The.
Dark in the Reich of the Blond.
Dog Sacrifice at Lake Ronkonkoma.
Driving at Dawn.
Elm's Home, The.
Existential.
Fires.
I Move to Random Consolations.
King's Men, The.
Mantle.
Mill, The.
Mother and Son.
Plague Sermon.
Poem Touching the Gestapo.
Ram Time.
Riddle: "From Belsen a crate of gold teeth."
Snapper, The.
Spirit of Wrath, The.
This Night.
Trail beside the River Platte, The.
Heyrick, Thomas
On a Sunbeam.
On an Indian Tomineois, the Least of Birds.
On the Crocodile.
On the Death of a Monkey.
Heyward, DuBose
Equinox, The.
Porgy, Maria, and Bess.
Heywood, Jasper
Look or You Leap.
Heywood, John
All a green willow, willow, willow.
Cardinal Fisher.
Cock and the Hen, The.
English Schoolboy, The, *sel.*
"Gloria Patri," The.
If Love, for Love of Long Time Had.
Of a Daw.
Of Birds and Birders.
Of Use.
On Botching.
Palmer, The, *sel.*
Praise of His Lady, A, *at.*
Tyburn and Westminster.
Heywood, Thomas
Author to His Booke, The, *sel.*
Epitaph, An: "I was, I am not; smiled, that
  since did weep."
Good Morrow, *sel.*
Hymn to Diana, *sel.*
I sought thee round about, O thou my God!,
  sel.
Jupiter and Ganimede.
Pack, Clouds, Away.
Passing Bell, The, *sel.*
Praise of Ceres, *sel.*
She That Denies Me [I Would Have], *sel.*
Hezutsu Tosaku
Affluence—define it as.
Dawn Cherries.
Hickey, Agnes MacCarthy
Old Essex Door.

Hickey, Margarita
Of Property Naught.
Truly Wise Man, The.
Hickock, Eliza M.
Prayer: "I know not by what methods rare."
Hickox, Chauncey
Under the Red Cross.
Hicks, Berryman
Time Is Swiftly Rolling On, The.
Hickson, William E.
Walking Song.
Hicky, Daniel Whitehead
Georgia Towns.
Nocturne: Georgia Coast.
Okefenokee Swamp.
River Boats, The.
To an Aviator.
Hidalgo, José
Autumn, Again Grass.
Hiebert, Paul Gerhardt
Farmer and the Farmer's Wife, The.
Hien Luong
Songs That Cannot Be Silenced.
Hiers, Lois Smith
On Laying Up Treasure.
Higgins, Alice
Swimming.
Higgins, Brian
Analogy.
Baedeker for Metaphysicians.
Corrupt Man in the French Pub, The.
Genesis.
Higgins, Frederick Robert
Ballad of O'Bruadir, The.
Chinese Winter.
Father and Son.
Little Clan, The.
O You among Women.
Old Air, An.
Old Jockey, The.
Padraic O'Conaire—Gaelic Storyteller.
Song for the Clatter-Bones.
Tennis in the City.
Higginson, Ella
Beggars.
Four-Leaf Clover.
Grand Ronde Valley, The.
Lamp in the West, The.
Moonrise in the Rockies.
Higginson, Mary Potter Thacher
Changelings.
Ghost-Flowers.
In the Dark.
Inheritance.
Higginson, Thomas Wentworth
Decoration.
Ode to a Butterfly.
Past Is Dark with Sin and Shame, The.
Since Cleopatra Died.
Snowing of the Pines, The.
Such Stuff as Dreams Are Made Of.
Things I Miss, The.
To Duty.
To Thine Eternal Arms, O God.
Higgons, Bevil
Mourners, The.
Higgs, Barry O.
Deaf.
In Lord Carpenter's Country.
Night Shore.
Parson's Pleasure.
Reversion.
Higham, Charles
Barnacle Geese.
Highet, Gilbert
Homage to Ezra Pound.
Higo, Aig
Hidesong.
Hijazi, Ahmad Abd al-Muti
Elegies, or the Stations of the Other Time.
Lonely Woman's Room, The.

Rendezvous in the Cave.
Secrets.
Hikmet, Nazim
Things I Didn't Know I Loved.
Hilarova, Dagmar
Questions.
Hilberry, Conrad
Instruction.
Hildegard von Bingen
Like the honeycomb dropping honey.
O crimson blood.
Hildreth, Charles Lotin
At the Mermaid Inn.
Implora Pace.
To an Obscure Poet Who Lives on My
Hearth.
Hill, Aaron
Alone in an Inn at Southampton, April the
25th, 1737.
Lord's Prayer in Verse, The.
May-Day.
Modesty.
Whitehall Stairs.
Written on a Window.
Hill, Benjamin Dionysius
To St. Mary Magdalen.
Hill, E.
When Polly Buys a Hat.
Hill, Geoffrey
And it seemed, while we waited, he began to
walk, *sel.*
Annunciations.
Asmodai.
At Pavia, a visitation of some sorrow.
Boethius' dungeon, *sel.*
Brooding on the eightieth letter of *Fors
Clavigera* , *sel.*
Christmas Trees.
Clash of salutation. As keels thrust into
shingle, *sel.*
Coins handsome as Nero's; of good substance
and weight, *sel.*
Dead Bride, The.
Dear lords of life, stump-toothed, with ragged
breath, *sel.*
Dismissing reports and men, he put pressure
on the wax, *sel.*
Distant Fury of Battle, The.
Doctor Faustus.
"Domaine Public."
Eia, with handbells, jews' harps, risible, *sel.*
Gasholders, russet among fields, *sel.*
Genesis.
Gideon at the Well.
God's Little Mountain.
Guardians, The.
He adored the desk, its brown-oak inlaid with
ebony, *sel.*
I was invested in mother-earth, the crypt of
roots, *sel.*
Idylls of the King, *sel.*
Imaginative Life, The.
In Memory of Jane Fraser [*or* Frazer]
In Piam Memoriam.
King of the perennial holly-groves, the riven
sandstone, *sel.*
Lachrimae Amantis.
Lachrimae Verae, *sel.*
Laurel Axe, The, *sel.*
Mad are predators, The. Too often lately they
harbor, *sel.*
Masque of Blackness, The, *sel.*
Merlin.
My little son, when you could command
marvels, *sel.*
Not as we are but as we must appear, *sel.*
Not strangeness, but strange likeness, *sel.*
Of Commerce and Society.
On the morning of the crowning we chorused
our remission from school, *sel.*
Orpheus and Eurydice.

Ovid in the Third Reich.
Pastoral, A: "Mobile, immaculate and
austere."
Pentecost Castle, The.
Pet-name, a common name. Best-selling
brand, curt, A, *sel.*
Picture of a Nativity.
Pre-Raphaelite Notebook, A.
Princes of Mercia were badger and raven,
The, *sel.*
Processes of generation; deeds of settlement,
sel.
Quaint Mazes, *sel.*
Re-Birth of Venus, The.
Requiem for the Plantagenet Kings.
September Song.
Short History of British India, A.
So much for the elves' wergild, the true
governance, *sel.*
Song from Armenia, A.
Strange church smelled a bit "high," of
censers, The, *sel.*
Their spades grafted through the
variably-resistant, *sel.*
To the (Supposed) Patron.
Trim the lamp; polish the lens; draw, one by
one, rare coins, *sel.*
Turtle Dove, The.
Two Chorale-Preludes.
Veni Coronaberis.
We ran across the meadow scabbed with the
cow-dung, *sel.*
White Ship, The.
Wreaths.
Hill, George
Song of the Elfin Steersman.
Hill, Hyacinthe
Old Emily.
Rebels from Fairy Tales.
Hill, Joe
Preacher and the Slave, The, at.
Hill, Leslie Pinckney
Christmas at Melrose.
So Quietly.
Summer Magic.
Teacher, The.
Tuskegee.
Hill, Quentin
Time Poem.
Hill, Roberta
Beginning the Year at Rosebud, S.D.
Blue Mountain.
Depot in Rapid City.
Direction.
E Uni Que A The Hi A Tho, Father.
Falling Moon.
In the Madison Zoo.
Leap in the Dark.
Midnight on Front Street.
Nation Wrapped in Stone, A.
Night along the Mackinac Bridge.
Seal at Stinson Beach.
Sleeping with Foxes.
Song for Healing.
Star Quilt.
Steps.
Swamp.
Winter Burn.
Hill, Roberta. *See* **Whiteman, Roberta Hill**
Hill, Selima
Below Hekla.
Voice in the Garden, A.
Hille, Peter
Beauty.
Maiden, The.
Hillert, Margaret
About Feet.
Blowing Bubbles.
Hide-and-Seek Shadow.
Just Me.
My Teddy Bear.

Hillhouse, Augustus Lucas
Trembling before Thine Awful Throne.
Hillhouse, James Abraham
Demon-Lover, The, *sel.*
Hillila, Bernhard
Shore Thing.
Hillman, Brenda
Ophelia.
Hillyer, Robert Silliman
As One Who Bears beneath His Neighbor's
Roof.
Assassination, The.
Bats, The.
Book of the Dead, *sel.*
Eppur Si Muove?
Eternal Return, The.
Familiar Faces, Long Departed.
Hills turn hugely in their sleep, The, *sel.*
Ivory Tower, The.
Letter to Robert Frost, A.
Lullaby: "Long canoe, The."
Moo!
Nocturne.
Other World, The.
Over Bright Summer Seas.
Pastoral: "So soft in the hemlock wood."
Pastoral, A: "Wise old apple tree in spring,
The."
Relic, The.
Thought in Time, A.
Hilton, Arthur Clement
Ding Dong.
Heathen Pass-ee, The.
Limerick: "There was a young critic of
King's."
Limerick: "There was a young genius of
Queens"
Limerick: "There was a young gourmand of
John's."
Limerick: "There was an old fellow of
Trinity" *at.*
Octopus.
Vulture and the Husbandman, The.
Hilton, David
I Try to Turn In My Jock.
Melmac Year, The.
Hilton, John
Madrigal: "My mistress frowns when she
should play."
Hilton, L. M.
Have Courage, My Boy, to Say No!
Hime, Iwa no, Empress. *See* **Iwa no Hime**
Himel, Margery
My People.
Himmell, Sophie
In the Month of Green Fire.
Hind bint Utba
Fury against the Moslems at Uhud.
Tambourine song for Soldiers Going into
Battle.
Hind bint Uthatha
To a Hero Dead at al-Safra.
Hindley, Charles
Mother Shipton's Prophecies, at.
Hine, Daryl
Bewilderment at the Entrance of the Fat Boy
into Eden, A.
Doppelganger, The.
Fabulary Satire IV.
In Praise of Music in Time of Pestilence.
Lady Sara Bunbury Sacrificing to the Graces,
by Reynolds.
Once when I was coming from art class they
surprised me, *sel.*
Plain Fare.
Point Grey.
Si Monumentum Requiris.
Survivors, The.
Trompe L'Œil.
Trout, The.
Under the Hill.

Untitled.
Vowel Movements.
Wasp, The.
Wave, The.
Hiner, Cincinnatus. *See* Miller, Joaquin
Hines, Carl Wendell, Jr.
Two Jazz Poems.
Hines, Debra
If Our Dogs Outlived Us.
Hinkson, Katharine Tynan. *See* Tynan,
Katharine
Hinostroza, Rodolfo
Night, The.
Othello's Report.
To a Dead Childhood.
Hippius, Zinaida
Grey Frock, A.
L'Imprévisibilité.
Hippolyte, Kendel
Jah Son/ Another Way.
Hironiwa (Abe no Hironiwa)
Autumn Day at the Home of Prince Nagaya.
Hirsch, Edward
At Kresge's Diner in Stonefalls, Arkansas.
Commuters.
Dawn Walk.
Dino Campana and the Bear.
Execution.
Fast Break.
For the Sleepwalkers.
I Need Help.
In the Middle of August.
Indian Summer.
Poor Angels.
Three Journeys.
Hirsch, Mannie
Cry for a Disused Synagogue in Booysens.
Hirsch, Thomas L.
History of Golf—Sort Of, A.
Hirschman, Jack
NHR.
Zohara.
Hirshbein, Peretz
Captive.
I Shall Weep.
Stars Fade.
Hirst, Henry Beck
Fringilla Melodia, The.
Funeral of Time, The.
Hitchcock, George
Figures in a Ruined Ballroom.
May All Earth Be Clothed in Light.
One Whose Reproach I Cannot Evade, The.
Song of Expectancy.
Three Found Poems.
Three Portraits.
United States Prepare for the Permanent
Revolution, The.
Hitomaro (Kakinomoto no Hitomaro)
Bay of Tsunu, The.
This morning I will not.
Hitoshi, Anzai
Hitomaro.
Village Hairdresser.
Warbler.
Winter Evening.
Hittan of Tayyi
His Children, *sel.*
Hix, H. Edgar
Calling.
Ho Ching-ming
Alone I Stand.
Ballad of the Government Granary Clerk.
Ballad of Yi River.
Bamboo Branch Song.
Ch'ang-an.
Ch'en-hsi County.
Fish in a Painting.
Night of the Fourteenth.
Presented to Wang Wen-hsi.
Rainy Night.

Seeing Off Han Ju-Ch'ing.
Song of the Painting "River and Mountains,"
by Wu Wei.
Ho Nansorhon
Yesterday I fancied I was young, *sel.*
Ho Ning
Beautiful Spring Scene, The.
Deva-like Barbarian.
Fisherman, The.
Gathering the Mulberry.
Heaven's Immortal.
Immortal at the River.
Manifold Little Hills.
Mountain Flowers.
Song of Ho Man-tzu.
Unfortunate Woman, The.
Viewing the Plum-Blossoms.
Willow Branches, The.
Ho Shao-chi
Contrary Wind, A.
I Love Mountains.
Mountain Rain.
Samantabhadra Facing Westward.
Ho Sun
At Parting.
Ho Xuan Huong
Buddhist Priest, A.
Jackfruit, The.
Hoagland, Everett
Anti-Semanticist, The.
It's a Terrible Thing!
Love Child—a Black Aesthetic.
Music, The.
My Spring Thing.
Night Interpreted.
Hoare, Florence
Pedlar Jim.
Hoare, Prince
Arethusa, The.
Hoatson, Florence
Autumn.
Bird Bath, The.
Who?
Hoban, Russell
Boy with a Hammer.
Crow, The.
Empty House, The.
Friendly Cinnamon Bun, The.
Homework.
Jigsaw Puzzle.
Skilly Oogan.
Small, Smaller.
Soft-boiled Egg.
Sparrow Hawk, The.
Stupid Old Myself.
Tin Frog, The.
Hobbs, Valine
One Day When We Went Walking.
Hoben, Sandra
Burns.
Hoberman, Mary Ann
Ants.
Birthdays.
Changing.
Clickbeetle.
Cockroach, *sel.*
Combinations, *sel.*
Fish.
Folk Who Live in Backward Town, The.
Jumping Bean.
Meg's Egg.
Neighbors.
Night.
Oak Leaf Plate.
Praying Mantis.
Waiters.
Yellow Butter.
Hobsbaum, Philip
Credential, A.
Last Memo.

Lesson in Love, A.
Timon Speaks to a Dog.
Hobson, Geary
Barbara's Land Revisited—August 1978.
For My Brother and Sister Southwestern
Indian Poets.
Going to the Water.
Lonnie Kramer.
Tiger People.
Hobson, Katherine Thayer
Duality.
Hoccleve [*or* Occleve], Thomas
A Description of His Ugly Lady, a.
Balade and Roundel to Master Somer.
Cupid Defends Women, *sel.*
Description of His Ugly Lady, A.
Hoccleve Remembers His Madness, *sel.*
Lament for Chaucer.
O maister deere and fader reverent!, *sel.*
Prologue: "Musing upon the restless
bisinesse," *sel.*
To Chaucer, *sel.*
Hochman, Sandra
Couple, The.
Eyes of Flesh, The.
Goldfish Wife, The.
Postscript.
Thoughts about My Daughter before Sleep.
Hocquard, Emmanuel
Anno Aetatis XXXV.
Of a Sea-Born Aphrodite.
Three Moral Tales.
Hoddis, Jakov van
Tohub.
Hodes, Aubrey
Jew Walks in Westminster Abbey, A.
Hodgdon, Florence B.
How Can I Smile?
Hodge, Arthur J.
Five Were Foolish.
Hodges, Elizabeth
Persimmons and Plums.
Hodgson, Ralph
After.
Babylon.
Bells of Heaven, The.
Birdcatcher, The.
Bull, The.
Dust thou art, but dust carefully, *sel.*
Eve.
Ghoul Care.
Gipsy Girl, The.
Great Auk's Ghost, The.
Hammers, The.
House across the Way, The.
Hymn to Moloch.
I Love a Hill.
Late, Last Rook, The.
Moor, The.
Movement, she explained, would bring poetry
to the rich, The, *sel.*
Mystery, The.
Reason Has Moons.
Silver Wedding.
Song of Honor [*or* Honour], The.
Song, A: "With Love among the haycocks."
Stupidity Street.
Time.
Time, You Old Gypsy Man.
Weaving of the Wing, The.
Wood Song, A.
Hodgson, William Noel
Before Action.
Hoey, Edwin A.
Foul Shot.
Hoey, George
Asleep at the Switch.
Hofer, Jim
Matching Green Ribbon.
Hoffenstein, Samuel
Babies Haven't Any Hair.

Bird, The.
Birdie McReynolds.
Breathes there a man with hide so tough.
Come, live with me and be my love, *sel.*
Dry.
Early bird may catch the worm, The, *sel.*
Father's Heart Is Touched, A.
I Burned My Candle at Both Ends.
I'd rather listen to a flute.
If you love me, as I love you.
Invocation: "Come, lovely Muse, desert for me."
Love-Songs, at Once Tender and Informative.
Lullaby: "Sleep, my little baby, sleep."
Makes the Little Ones Dizzy.
Miss Millay Says Something Too.
Mr. Vachel Lindsay Discovers Radio.
Mr. Walter de la Mare Makes the Little Ones Dizzy.
Nothing from a straight line swerves, *sel.*
Of all the birds that sing and fly, *sel.*
Only the wholesomest foods you eat, *sel.*
Poem Intended to Incite the Utmost Depression, A.
Question and Answer.
Sheep.
Shropshire Lad's Cousin, The.
Unequal Distribution.
When You're Away.
With Rue My Heart Is Laden.
You buy some flowers for your table, *sel.*
Your Little Hands.

Hoffman, Balthasar
Be Glorified Eternally.

Hoffman, Charles Fenno
Mint Julep, The.
Monterey.
Sparkling and Bright.

Hoffman, Daniel Gerard
Armada of Thirty Whales, An.
As I Was Going to Saint Ives.
Ballad of No Proper Man.
Center of Attention, The.
City of Satisfactions, The.
È, the Feasting Florentines.
Exploration.
Finish, The.
First Flight.
In the Days of Rin-Tin-Tin.
Inviolable.
Lines Written near Linton, on Exmoor.
Outwit Song, The.
Saturday.
Seals in Penobscot Bay, The.
Signatures.
Three Jovial Gentlemen.
Who Done It?
Who Was It Came.

Hoffman, Heinrich
Story of the Wild Huntsman, The.

Hoffman, Jill
Her Sleep.

Hoffman, Phoebe W.
Pedro.

Hoffman, William M.
Screw Spring.

Hoffmann, Heinrich
Story of Augustus, Who Would Not Have Any Soup, The.
Story of Fidgety Philip, The.
Story of Johnny Head-in-Air, The.

Hofmann, Michael
Ancient Evenings.
Means of Production, The.

Hofmannsthal, Hugo von
Ballad of the Outer Life.
Many Indeed Must Perish in the Keel.
Ship's Cook, a Captive Sings, The.
Stanzas on Mutability.
Two, The.

Venetian Night, A.
When a man sleeps, often his dream will break, *sel.*
World-Secret.

Hofshteyn [*or* Hofstein], Dovid
City.
In Winter's Dusk, *sel.*
My Thread.
Procession.
When Clenched Teeth Grate.

Hofuku Seikatsu
Don't tell me how difficult the Way.

Hogan, Linda
Black Hills Survival Gathering, 1980.
Blessing.
Celebration: Birth of a Colt.
Cities behind Glass.
Eclipse II.
Gamble.
Man in the Moon.
New Apartment, Minneapolis, The.
Other Side, The.
Rainy Season, The.
Saint Coyote.
Seeing through the Sun.
Song for My Name.
To Light.
Truth Is, The.
Workday.

Hogan, Michael
Spring.

Hogan, Wayne
Seriousness on the Rise.

Hogg, James
Flying Tailor, The.
Kilmeny, *sel.*
Skylark, The.

Hogg, James ("The Ettrick Shepherd")
Boy's Song, A.
Isabelle.
James Rigg.
Lock the Door, Lariston.
McLean's Welcome.
Village of Balmaquhapple, The.
Walsinghame's Song.
When the Kye Comes Hame.

Hogg, Robert
Little Falls.

Hoggra, Robert
Poem: "In its going down, the moon."

Hoju
Evening shadow: frogs call out.

Hokukon
Undulating, a frog undulates.

Holbrook, David
Coming Home from Abroad.
Day in France, A.
Delivering Children.
Drought.
Fingers in the Door.
Living? Our Supervisors Will Do That for Us!
Maternity Gown.
Poor Old Horse.

Holbrook, Weare
Varitalk.

Holcroft, Thomas
Dying Prostitute, The; an Elegy.
Fool's Song.
Gaffer Gray.
On Shakespeare and Voltaire.
Seasons, The.
Song: "When o'er the wold the heedless lamb."
To Haydn.

Holden, Jonathan
Alone.
American Boyhood, An.
Cutting Beetle-Blighted Ponderosa Pine.
Dancing School.
Driving through Coal Country in Pennsylvania.

First Kiss.
Full Moon, Rising.
Liberace.
Losers.
Poem for Ed "Whitey" Ford, A.
Seventeen.
Swimming Pool, The.
Why We Bombed Haiphong.

Holden, Molly
Giant Decorative Dahlias.
Hare.
Photograph of Haymaker, 1890.
Seaman, 1941.

Holden, Oliver
How Sweet Is the Language of Love.
Weeping Sinner, Dry Your Tears.
Within These Doors Assembled Now.

Holden, Stephen
In Praise of Antonioni.

Holder, C. S.
King's Wood, The.

Hölderlin, Friedrich
All the fruit is ripe, plunged in fire, cooked.
Half of Life.
Oh friend, we arrived too late, *sel.*
Ripe, Being Plunged into Fire.
Sanctimonious Poets, The.
To the Fates.

Holland, Henry Fox, 1st Baron
With a China Chamberpot, to the Countess of Hillsborough.

Holland, Hugh
Epitaph on Prince Henry.
Shakespeare Dead.
Upon the Lines and Life of the Famous Scenic Poet, Master William Shakespeare.

Holland, Josiah Gilbert
Babyhood, *sel.*
Christmas Carol, A: "There's a song in the air!"
Daniel Gray.
God, Give Us Men!
Gradatim.
Hymn: "For Summer's bloom and Autumn's blight," *sel.*
Lullaby: "Rockaby, lullaby, bees in the clover!," *sel.*
Song of Doubt, A.
Song of Faith, A.
To My Dog "Blanco."
Where Shall the Baby's Dimple Be.

Holland, Norah M.
Little Dog-Angel, A.
Sea Song.

Holland, Sir Richard
Roye Robert the Bruss the rayke he avowit, The, *sel.*

Hollander, Gad
Argument against Metaphor.
Axioms.
Fugato (Coda).
In Memoriam Paul Celan.

Hollander, John
Adam's Task.
An Old Story Is Retold.
Appearance and Reality.
Back to Town.
Breadth. Circle. Desert. Monarch. Month. Wisdom.
Curse, The.
Danish Wit.
Disagreements.
Fear of Trembling, The.
Flears, The.
Great Bear, The.
Hall of Ocean Life.
Heliogabalus.
Historical Reflections.
Horas Tempestatis Quoque Enumero: The Sundial.
Jefferson Valley.

Lady at the Castle, The.
Lady's-Maid 's Song, The.
Last Words.
Lion Named Passion, A.
Monuments.
Movie-Going.
Night Mirror, The.
Ninth of July, The.
No Foundation.
Non Sum Qualis Eram in Bona Urbe Nordica
    Illa.
Old Guitar, The.
Paysage Moralisé.
Refrains.
Russian Soul II, The.
Skeleton Key.
Slepynge Long in Greet Quiete Is Eek a Greet
    Norice to Leccherie.
Some Walks with You.
State of Nature, A.
Sunday Evenings.
Swan and Shadow.
Tales Told of the Fathers.
There was an end to hearts and rhymes.
To the Lady Portrayed by Margaret Dumont.
Under Cancer.
Violet.
Why drink, why touch you now? If it will be,
    sel.
Why have I locked myself inside.
Ziz, The.

Hollander, Robert
You Too? Me Too—Why Not? Soda Pop.

Holley, Horace
Hill, The.

Hollis, Mark
Careless Talk.
'Twixt Cup and Lip.

Hollo, Anselm
Amazing Grace.
Anthropology.
Aubade: "Night's ride's over."
Behaviorally.
Big Dog.
Buffalo—Isle of Wight Power Cable.
Discovery of LSD a True Story, The.
If.
Language, The.
Le Jazz Hot.
Lecture.
Manifest Destiny.
No Complaints.
Rain.
T.V. (1).
Terrorist Smiles, The.
That Old Sauna High.
Troll Chanting, sel.
T.V. (2).
Wasp Sex Myth (One).
Wasp Sex Myth (Two).

Holloway, John
Elegy for an Estrangement.
Journey through the Night.
Light, The.
Warning to a Guest.

Holloway, John Wesley
Black Mammies.
Calling the Doctor.
Corn Song, The.
Miss Melerlee.

Holloway, Lucy Ariel Williams
Northboun.'
Origin of the Skagit Indians, The.

"Holm, Saxe." See **Jackson, Helen Hunt**

Holman, Bob
One Flight Up.

Holman, Felice
City Dump, The.
Clock, The.
Friend.
Halloween Witches.

I Can Fly.
Leave Me Alone.
Loneliness.
My Toe.
Sulk.
They're Calling.
Who Am I?

Holman, Jesse L.
Lord, in Thy Presence Here.

Holman, M. Carl
And on This Shore.
Letter across Doubt and Distance.
Mr. Z.
Notes for a Movie Script.
Picnic: the Liberated.
Song: "Dressed up in my melancholy."

Holmes, Abiel
To Thee, O God.
Who Here Can Cast His Eyes Abroad.

Holmes, John
At a Country Fair.
Carry Me Back.
Evening Meal in the Twentieth Century.
Herself.
Map of My Country, A.
Misery.
Peace Is the Mind's Old Wilderness.
Poetry Defined.
Portrait: My Wife.
Rhyme of Rain.
Somerset Dam for Supper, The.
Thrifty Elephant, The.

Holmes, John Haynes
God of the Nations, Near and Far.
Hymn: "Great Spirit of the speeding spheres."
Hymn: "Thou God of all, whose presence
    dwells."
O'er Continent and Ocean.
Voice of God Is Calling, The.

Holmes, Oliver Wendell
Additional Verses to Hail Columbia.
Aestivation [an Unpublished Poem, by My
    Late Latin Tutor], sel.
After a Lecture on Keats.
After the Fire.
Angel of Peace, Thou Hast Wandered Too
    Long.
Angel-Thief, The.
As on the gauzy wings of fancy flying, sel.
Aunt Tabitha.
Ballad of the Boston Tea-Party, A.
Ballad of the Oysterman, The.
Bill and Joe.
Boys, The.
Brother Jonathan's Lament for Sister Caroline.
Cacoëthes Scribendi.
Chambered Nautilus, The, sel.
Contentment.
Daily Trials.
Daniel Webster.
Deacon's Masterpiece, The; or, The
    Wonderful "One-Hoss Shay", sel.
Dorchester Giant, The.
Dorothy Q.
Epilogue to the Breakfast-Table Series, sel.
Familiar Letter to Several Correspondents, A.
Farewell to Agassiz, A.
Flower of Liberty, The.
God Save the Flag.
Grandmother's Story of Bunker-Hill Battle.
Height of the Ridiculous, The.
It chanced to be our washing day, sel.
La Grisette.
Last Leaf, The.
Lexington.
Limerick [or An Eggstravagance or Henry
    Ward Beecher], at.
Living Temple, The, sel.
Look out! Look out, boys! Clear the track!,
    sel.
Lord of All Being, Throned Afar, sel.

My Aunt.
O Love Divine, That Stooped to Share, sel.
Ode for a Social Meeting.
Old Ironsides.
Old Man Dreams, The.
On Lending a Punch-Bowl.
On the Death of President Garfield.
Our Father! While Our Hearts Unlearn.
Parody on "A Psalm of Life", A, at.
Poem, A: "Father of all! in Death's relentless
    claim."
Poem for the Meeting of the American
    Medical Association, A.
Poet's Lot, The.
Reflections of a Proud Pedestrian.
Sea Dialogue, A.
Sherman's in Savannah.
Strong Heroic Line, The.
Sun and Shadow.
To an Insect.
Under the Violets, sel.
Union and Liberty.
Voiceless, The, sel.
Welcome to Dr. Benjamin Apthorp Gould, A.
Welcome to the Nations.

Holmes, Pamela
Missing, Presumed Killed.
Parting in April.
War Baby.

Holmes, R. Ernest
Black Lady in an Afro Hairdo Cheers for
    Cassius.

Holmes, Ruth
No Thoroughfare.

Holmes, Timothy
Melodious Birds.
Snow Fell.

Holmes, W. F.
Old Brown Horse, The.

Holmes, W. K.
Dream Ship, The.
Old Mountaineer, The.
On the Heights.

Holmes, Georgiana Klingle. See "**Klingle,
    George**"

Holstein, Michael
Charley's Green Guide.

Hölty, Ludwig Heinrich Christoph
Harvest Song.

Holtz, Barry
Isaac.

Holub, Miroslav
Bullfight.
Fairy Tale.
Five Minutes after the Air Raid.
Fly, The.
Great and Strong.
History Lesson, A.
How to Paint a Perfect Christmas.
Swans in Flight.

Holyday, Barten
Bogs, purgatory, wolves and ease, by fame.
Clay, sand, and rock, seem of a diff'rent
    birth.
Pride cannot see itself by mid-day light.
Song: "O harmless feast," sel.

Holz, Arno
Buddha.
Leave-Taking, A.
On a mountain of sugar-candy, sel.
Phantasus.
Roses Red.

Hölzer, Max
And the cunning of the poem, that it
    consumes the world.
He Let the House Be.
I accompanied the Castilian.
In the "Trocadero."
Mysterious Geometry.
Sète.
Summer's Cold, The.

"Home, Cecil." *See* **Webster, Augusta**

Homer
Achilles Shows Himself in the Battle by the Ships, *sel.*
Achilles to Lycaon, *sel.*
Achilles with wild fury in his heart, *sel.*
Ajax the swift swerv'd never from the side, *sel.*
All grave old men, and souldiers they had bene, but for age, *sel.*
And as in winter time when Jove his cold-sharpe javelines throwes, *sel.*
And as when with the West-wind's flawes the sea thrusts up her waves, *sel.*
And now Eurynome had bath'd the king, *sel.*
And now his well-known bow the master bore, *sel.*
And now man-slaughtering Pallas took in hand, *sel.*
And now the Queene of women had intent, *sel.*
And now was Paris come/ From his high towres, *sel.*
And when they came together in one place, *sel.*
Andromache's Lamentation, *sel.*
As when an architect some palace wall, *sel.*
As when devouring flames some forest seize, *sel.*
As when of frequent bees, *sel.*
As when the winds, ascending by degrees, *sel.*
Ascend my shoulders, firmly keep thy seat, *sel.*
At her departure his disdain return'd, *sel.*
At this th' impatient hero sowrly smil'd, *sel.*
Big with great purposes and proud, they sat, *sel.*
But ere sterne conflict mixt both strengths, faire Paris stept before, *sel.*
But now, no longer deaf to honour's call, *sel.*
Cave we found, but vacant all within, The, *sel.*
Close to the gates a spacious garden lies, *sel.*
Death of Hector, The, *sel.*
Embodied close, the lab'ring Grecian train, *sel.*
Fierce they drove on, impatient to destroy, *sel.*
For my part, I'le not meddle with the cause, *sel.*
Frail as the leaves that quiver on the sprays, *sel.*
From her bed's high and odoriferous roome, *sel.*
Gardens of Alcinous, The ("Close to the gates a spacious garden lies"), *sel.*
Gardens of Alcinous, The ("Without the hall, and close upon the gate"), *sel.*
Ghost of Patroclus, The, *sel.*
God who mounts the winged winds, The, *sel.*
He ended, nor the Argicide refus'd, *sel.*
He spake, to whom I, answ'ring, thus replied, *sel.*
Hektor to Andromache, *sel.*
Helen's Lamentation, *sel.*
His hand came out of the east, *sel.*
Hornets occasionally build their nests near roads, *sel.*
Just then, forgetful of the strict command, *sel.*
Like leaves on trees the race of man is found, *sel.*
Meanwhile the troops beneath Patroclus' care, *sel.*
Mighty wave rush'd o'er him as he spoke, A, *sel.*
Nausicaa.
New Coasts and Poseidon's Son, *sel.*
Nor lingered Paris in the lofty house, *sel.*
Nor long the trench or lofty walls oppose, *sel.*
Now front to front the hostile armies stand, *sel.*

Now gently winding up the fair ascent, *sel.*
Now side by side, with like unweary'd care, *sel.*
Now to dispose of the dead, the care remains, *sel.*
Now toils the Heroe; trees on trees o'erthrown, *sel.*
Now when the solemn rites of pray'r were past, *sel.*
Now, when twelve days complete had run their race, *sel.*
Nymph turnd home, The. He fell to felling downe, *sel.*
Oileus by his brother's side stood close, *sel.*
Parting of Hector and Andromache, The, *sel.*
Patroclus' Body Saved, *sel.*
Priam and Achilles, *sel.*
Sacrifice, The, *sel.*
Sarpedon to Glaukos, *sel.*
Sarpedon's Speech, *sel.*
Scylla and Charybdis, *sel.*
She thus; when I had great desire to prove, *sel.*
So saying, light-foot Iris passed away, *sel.*
Son of Enops, Thestor next he smote, The, *sel.*
Their ardour kindless all the Grecian pow'rs, *sel.*
Their ground they stil made good, *sel.*
Then he form'd th' immense and solid shield, *sel.*
Then rising in his rage above the shores, *sel.*
Then tooke they seate, and forth our passage strooke, *sel.*
There grew two olives, closest of the grove, *sel.*
There sate the seniors of the Trojan Race, *sel.*
This said, he reacht to take his sonne, *sel.*
This spoke, a huge wave tooke him by the head, *sel.*
Thus at the panting dove a falcon flies, *sel.*
Thus charg'd he; nor Argicides denied, *sel.*
Thus to Glaucus spake/ Divine Sarpedon, *sel.*
Trembling the spectres glide, and plaintive vent, *sel.*
Trojans Outside the Walls, The, *sel.*
Troops exulting sate in order round, The, *sel.*
Twelve herds of oxen, no less flockes of sheepe, *sel.*
Ulysses and His Dog, *sel.*
Ulysses in the Waves, *sel.*
Ulysses Leaves the Nymph Calypso, *sel.*
Unweary'd watch their list'ning leaders keep, Th', *sel.*
Where neither King nor shepheard want comes neare, *sel.*
While thus he thought, a monst'rous wave up-bore, *sel.*
Why boast we, Glaucus! our extended reign, *sel.*
Why dost thou so explore, *sel.*
Without the hall, and close upon the gate, *sel.*
Wrath of Peleus son, O muse, resound, The, *sel.*
Youth there was, Elpenor was he nam'd, A, *sel.*

Homer-Dixon, Homera
New Year, The.

Honei
Fisherman.

Honestus
Requirements ("Not too old, and not too young").

Honeywood, St. John
Darby and Joan.
Radical Song of 1786, A.

Hongo, Garrett Kaoru
Hiking Up Hieizan with Alam Lau/Buddha's Birthday 1974.
Hongo Store 29 Miles Volcano Hilo, Hawaii, The.

Off from Swing Shift.
Something Whispered in the *Shakuhachi*.
What For.
Who Among You Knows the Essence of Garlic?
Yellow Light.

Honig, Edwin
Being Somebody.
Bodega, Goodbye.
1925, *sel.*
November through a Giant Copper Beech.
Now, My Usefullness Over.
Tête-à-Tête.
Through You.
Walt Whitman.
Who.

Hood, E. P
God, Who Hath Made the Daisies.

Hood, Thomas
Address to Mr. Cross, of Exeter 'Change, on the Death of the Elephant.
Athol Brose.
Autumn.
Bed-time.
Born in wealth and wealthily nursed, *sel.*
Bridge of Sighs, The.
Carelesse Nurse Mayd, The.
Centipede along the threshold crept, The, *sel.*
Death-Bed, The.
Death of Leander, The, *sel.*
Domestic Asides; or, Truth in Parentheses.
Dream Fairy, The.
Dream of Eugene Aram [the Murderer], The.
Dust to Dust.
Epigram: "When would-be suicides in purpose fail."
Fair Ines.
Fairy's Reply to Saturn, The, *sel.*
Faithless Nelly Gray.
Faithless Sally Brown.
Farewell, Life.
Friendly Address, A.
Gold.
Green Dryad's Plea, The, *sel.*
Haunted House, The, *sel.*
Her Accident, *sel.*
Her Christening, *sel.*
Her Death, *sel.*
Her Education, *sel.*
Her Precious Leg, *sel.*
I Remember.
I Remember, I Remember.
Irish Schoolmaster, The.
It Was Not in the Winter.
Lay of the Labourer, The.
Little Piggies, The.
Mary's Ghost.
Melodies of Time, The, *sel.*
No!
Nocturnal Sketch, A.
O, very gloomy is the House of Woe, *sel.*
Ode on a Distant Prospect of Clapham Academy.
Ode to the Cameleopard.
On a Royal Demise.
On the Death of the Giraffe.
Our Village—by a Villager.
Parental Ode to My Son, Aged Three Years and Five Months, A.
Poet's Fate, The.
Poor dear dead have been laid out in vain, The.
Quadrupedremian Song, A.
Reflection, A.
Ruth.
Sailor's Apology for Bow-Legs, A.
Sally Simpkin's Lament.
Scylla's Lament, *sel.*
Sea of Death, The.
Serenade, A, *sel.*
Shakespeare: The Fairies' Advocate, *sel.*
She Is Far from the Land.

Silence.
Song of the Shirt, The.
Sonnet: "It is not death, that sometime in a sigh."
Sonnet to Vauxhall.
Stars Are with the Voyager, The.
Sun Was Slumbering in the West, The.
Tim Turpin.
To———: "I gaze upon a city."
To Henrietta, on Her Departure for Calais.
To Minerva.
Two Swans, The.
Water Lady, The.
What Different Dooms Our Birthdays Bring!, sel.
Work—work—work, sel.
World Is with Me, The.
Ye tourists and travellers, bound to the Rhine.

Hood, Tom
Catch, A.
Muddled Metaphors.
Ravings.

Hood, Tom (Thomas Hood, Jr.)
All in the Downs.
Confounded Nonsense.
How Singular.
Little tigers are at rest, The.
Poets and Linnets.
Sunset in the Sea.

Hook, Theodore
Cautionary Verses to Youth of Both Sexes.

Hooper, Edward L.
I Know, You'd Rather Be Dead.
Way Downtown, The.

Hooper, Ellen S.
Duty.

Hooper, Lucy H.
Three Loves.

Hooper, Peter
Pencilled by the Rain.

Hooton, Earnest Albert
Ode to a Dental Hygienist.

Hoover, Paul
Long History of the Short Poem.
Ode to the Protestant Poets.
Poems We Can Understand.
School for Objects, The.
Trumpet Voluntary.

Hope, Alec Derwent
Advice to Young Ladies.
As Well as They Can ("As well as it can, the hooked fish while it dies"), at.
Australia.
Bed, The.
Beware of Ruins.
Brides, The.
Chorale: "Often had I found her fair."
Circe.
Death of the Bird, The.
Double Looking Glass, The.
E Questo il Nido in Che la Mia Fenice?
Elegy, The: "Madam, no more! The time has come to eat."
Epistle, An: "First, last and always dearest, closest, best."
Female Principle, The.
Gateway, The.
Hay Fever.
House of God, The.
Imperial Adam.
Letter to David Campbell on the Birthday of W. A. B. Yeats, 1965.
Lingam and the Yoni, The.
Martyrdom of St. Theresa, The.
Meditation on a Bone.
Moschus Moschiferus.
Now Muse assist me, aptly to describe, sel.
Observation Car.
On an Engraving by Casserius.
On Shakespeare Critics, sel.
Parabola.

Paradise Saved.
Prometheus Unbound.
Pyramis; or, The House of Ascent.
School Of Night, The.
Tiger.

Hope, Allan. *See* **Mutabaruka**

Hope, Francis
Peeping Tom.

Hope, James Barron
John Smith's Approach to Jamestown.

Hope, Laurence
Kashmiri Song.

"Hope, Laurence" (Adela Florence Cory Nicolson)
For This Is Wisdom, sel.
Youth.

Hope, T.
Death Again.

Hopegood, Peter
Dithyramb in Retrospect.
Protagonist, The.

Hopes, David Brendon
Lament for Turlough O'Carolan.

Hopkins, Gerard Manley
Alchemist in the City, The.
Andromeda.
As Kingfishers Catch Fire [Dragonflies Draw Flame]
Barnfloor and Winepress.
Binsey Poplars (Felled 1879).
Blessed Virgin Compared to the Air We Breathe, The.
Bugler's First Communion, The.
By Magdalen Bridge, Oxford.
Caged Skylark, The.
Candle Indoors, The.
Carrion Comfort.
"Child Is Father to the Man, The."
Christmas Carol: Moonless Darkness Stands Between.
Cuckoo, The.
Duns Scotus's Oxford.
Easter Communion.
Felix Randal.
Fragment: "Mark you how the peacock's eye."
God's Grandeur.
Habit of Perfection, The.
Harry Ploughman.
Heaven-Haven.
Henry Purcell.
How Looks the Night?
Hurrahing in Harvest.
In Honour of St. Alphonsus Rodriguez.
I wake and feel the fell of dark, not day
In the Valley of the Elwy.
Inversnaid.
It was a hard thing to undo this knot.
Lantern out of Doors, The.
Leaden Echo and the Golden Echo, The.
Moonrise.
Mrs. Hopley, on Seeing Her Children Say Goodnight to Their Father.
My own heart let me more have pity on.
No, they are come; their horn is lifted up, sel.
No Worst, There Is None.
Not of All My Eyes See.
O Deus, Ego Amo Te.
Of virtures I most warmly bless.
On St. Winefred.
On Saturday sailed from Bremen, sel.
Oxford Bells.
Peace.
Pied Beauty.
Rainbow, The.
Rosa Mystica.
Rowing, I reach'd a rock—the sea was low, sel.
Sea and the Skylark, The.
She Schools the Flighty Pupils of Her Eyes.
Soldier, The.

Soliloquy of One of the Spies Left in the Wilderness, A.
Sonnet: "Patience, hard thing! the hard thing but to pray."
Spelt from Sibyl's Leaves.
Spring.
Spring and Death.
Spring and Fall.
Starlight Night, The.
Summer Malison, The.
That Nature Is a Heraclitean Fire and of the Comfort of the Resurrection.
Thou Art Indeed Just, Lord, If I Contend.
To His Watch.
To Oxford.
To R. B.
To Seem the Stranger Lies My Lot.
Tom's Garland: Upon the Unemployed.
Windhover, The.
Winter with the Gulf Stream.
Woodlark, The.

Hopkins, John (1520–70)
Thou, Lord, Hast Been Our Sure Defense.

Hopkins, John Henry, Jr. (1820–1891)
Alleluia! Christ Is Risen Today.
God of Our Fathers, Bless This Our Land.
We Three Kings of Orient Are.

Hopkins, Josiah
O Turn Ye, O Turn Ye.

Hopkins, Lee Bennett
Girls Can, Too!

Hopkins, Tim
Do Not Go Gentle ("Do not go gentle into Death's esteemed vale").

Hopkinson, Abdur-Rahman Slade
December 1974: a Lament.
Madwoman of Papine, The.
Tycoon, Poet, Saint.

Hopkinson, Francis
American Independence.
Arise and See the Glorious Sun.
At Length the Busy Day Is Done.
Battle of the Kegs, The.
Daughter's Rebellion, The.
New Roof, The.
On the Late Successful Expedition against Louisbourg.

Hopkinson, Joseph
Hail, Columbia.

Hoppe, Anna
Precious Child, So Sweetly Sleeping.

Hopper, Edward
Jesus Saviour, Pilot Me.
They Pray the Best Who Pray and Watch.

Hopper, Nora
King of Ireland's Son, The.

Horace
Ad Leuconoen, sel.
Ad Xanthiam Phoceum ("Ne sit ancillae"), sel.
Albi, Ne Doreas, sel.
As woods whose change appeares, sel.
"Behold yon mountain's hoary height." ("Vides ut alta"), sel.
By the Flat Cup ("Quid dedicatum"), sel.
Counterblast against Garlic, A, sel.
Country Life, sel.
"Dear Molly, why so oft in tears?" ("Quid sles, asterie"), sel.
"Descended of an ancient line" ("Tyrrhena regum progenies"), sel.
Dialogue between Horace and Lydia, A ("Donec gratus eram"), sel.
Extremum Tanain, sel.
"Gold or iv'ry's not intended" ("Non ebur neque aureum"), sel.
Good bailiff of my farm, that snug domain.
Holiday ("Festo quid potius die"), sel.
If, O Maecenas, versed in lore antique.
Immortality of Verse, The, sel.

"Let the youth hardened by a sharp soldier's life" ("Angustam amice"), *sel.*
"Lydia, in Heavens Name" ("Lydia, dic, per omnes"), *sel.*
"O Ligurinus" ("O crudelis adhuc"), *sel.*
Ode: "Hold! pale death, at the poor man's shack and the pasha's palace", *sel.*
Pine Tree for Diana, The ("Montium custos memorumque"), *sel.*
"Pompeius, best of all my comrades, you and I" ("O saepe mecum"), *sel.*
Praise of Pindar, The ("Pindarum quisquis studet aemulari"), *sel.*
"Receive, dear friend, the truths I teach" ("Rectius vives"), *sel.*
Revenge ("Audivere, Lyce"), *sel.*
Ribald Romeos Less and Less Berattle ("Parcius iunctas quatiunt fenestras"), *sel.*
"Seek not, Leuconöe, to know how long you're going to live yet" ("Tu ne qualsieris"), *sel.*
Ship of State, The ("O navis, referent"), *sel.*
Should some ill painter, in a wild design, *sel.*
Simplicity, *sel.*
"The snow dissolv'd no more is seen" ("Diffugere nives"), *sel.*
This Monument Will Outlast ("Exegi monumentum aere perennius," *sel.*
To an Ambitious Friend ("Quid bellicosus"), *sel.*
To Apollo and Diana ("Dianam tenerae dicite virgines"), *sel.*
To Chloe ("Vitas hinnuleo"), *sel.*
To Fuscus Arustus, *sel.*
To Phidyle ("Caelo supinas si tuleris"), *sel.*
To the Fountain[s] of Bandusia ("O fons Bandusiae"), *sel.*
To the Ship on Which Virgil Sailed to Athens ("Sic te diva potens Cyri"), *sel.*
To Venus ("Intermissa, Venus"), *sel.*
"Tread back—and back, the lewd and lay!" ("Odi profanum vulgus"), *sel.*
"Virtue, dear friend, needs no 'defence'" ("Integer vitae"), *sel.*
"What slender youth bedewed with liquid odours" ("Quis multa gracilis"), *sel.*
Young Men Come Less Often, The—Isn't It So?

Horan, Robert
By Hallucination Visited.
Farewell to Narcissus.
Horder, John
Sick Image of My Father Fades, The.
Horgan, Paul
Now Evening Puts Amen to Day.
Horiguchi Daigaku
Hammock.
Landscape.
Memories.
Horikawa, Lady
How long will it last?
Will he always love me?
Horn, Edward Newman
Darling, If You Only Knew.
Horne, Frank
Immortality.
Kid Stuff.
Mamma!
More Letters Found near a Suicide.
Nigger.
On Seeing Two Brown Boys in a Catholic Church.
Patience.
Resurrection.
Symphony.
To a Persistent Phantom.
To "Chick", *sel.*
To James, *sel.*
To Mother, *sel.*
To You, *sel.*
Toast.
Walk.

Horne, Richard Henry [*or* Hengist]
Pelters of Pyramids.
Plough, The.
Horner, Joyce
Public Holiday: Paris.
Horovitz, Frances
Messenger, The.
Moon.
Woman's Dream, The.
Horovitz, Michael
For Leon Bismarck Beiderbecke (1903-1931).
Horsburgh, Wilma
Train to Glasgow, The.
Horta, Maria Teresa
Saved.
Secret.
Swimming Pool.
Horta, Maria Teresa *and* Maria Isabel Barreno *and* Maria Velho da Costa. *See* **Marias, The Three**
Horton, George
Night in Lesbos, A.
Horton, George Moses
New Fashions.
On Liberty and Slavery.
Snaps for Dinner, Snaps for Breakfast, and Snaps for Supper.
Horvitz, Allan Kolski
King Saul.
Radiance of Extinct Stars, The.
Hosack, William
Blazing noon, fierce, unrelenting noon!, The, *sel.*
But hark! The sharp beat of the Afric drum, *sel.*
Hosai (Osaki Hosai)
Haiku: "After scolding my wife," *sel.*
Haiku: "Already dawn, before the Buddha's altar," *sel.*
Haiku: "Althea nodding all day, it has darkened," *sel.*
Haiku: "An early morning road, a dog," *sel.*
Haiku: "Ants stopped coming," *sel.*
Haiku: "Big pine's darkening, The," *sel.*
Haiku: "Biting hard pears, arguing," *sel.*
Haiku: "Blowing the evening sun," *sel.*
Haiku: "Carrying fresh water with both hands," *sel.*
Haiku: "Carved into Buddha's form," *sel.*
Haiku: "Children are shouting," *sel.*
Haiku: "Chrysanthemums have all withered," *sel.*
Haiku: "Cigarette is dead, The," *sel.*
Haiku: "Clipped the nails, the fingers," *sel.*
Haiku: "Crow wordlessly flew away, A," *sel.*
Haiku: "Daybreak, big waves, the clear sky," *sel.*
Haiku: "Driving huge bulls up the hill," *sel.*
Haiku: "Emptying the boat, they all climbed up," *sel.*
Haiku: "Farewell said, cover lowered," *sel.*
Haiku: "Festival, letting a baby sleep, A," *sel.*
Haiku: "For a hollow mind," *sel.*
Haiku: "For laughing, front teeth," *sel.*
Haiku: "From the pipe pointing the way for me," *sel.*
Haiku: "Frost-packed morning," *sel.*
Haiku: "Getting time off from the Buddha," *sel.*
Haiku: "Gun, glinting, deep snow, A," *sel.*
Haiku: "Handkerchief still lying there, A," *sel.*
Haiku: "Having washed the gravestone," *sel.*
Haiku: "He moves his quiet shadow," *sel.*
Haiku: "Heart that seeks something, The," *sel.*
Haiku: "Here's a dying invalid," *sel.*
Haiku: "Holding a child's hand intently," *sel.*
Haiku: "Houses are crowding the town," *sel.*
Haiku: "I cough and am still alone," *sel.*
Haiku: "I go around to the back of the grave," *sel.*
Haiku: "I have no vessel, I receive," *sel.*
Haiku: "I hold a dog, my skin," *sel.*
Haiku: "I know the footsteps of the sparrow," *sel.*
Haiku: "I leave the paper doors open," *sel.*
Haiku: "I look at the evening sky," *sel.*
Haiku: "I look back at the shore," *sel.*
Haiku: "I release a turtle," *sel.*
Haiku: "I rescue a needle from the ashes," *sel.*
Haiku: "I slip a boiled egg out of its shell," *sel.*
Haiku: "I walk over a moistened bridge," *sel.*
Haiku: "I'm looking for a single flea, midnight," *sel.*
Haiku: "I'm thinking of sweeping," *sel.*
Haiku: "In a pond of silence a turtle," *sel.*
Haiku: "In a sharp wind trying to part," *sel.*
Haiku: "In the darkness of the well," *sel.*
Haiku: "In the great wind, in the sky," *sel.*
Haiku: "In the mountain sunset the graveyard," *sel.*
Haiku: "In the sun, counting the money," *sel.*
Haiku: "It came as a stray dog and still is," *sel.*
Haiku: "It's been raining for days," *sel.*
Haiku: "It's wet around the well," *sel.*
Haiku: "Just the ants at the bottom of the burning sky," *sel.*
Haiku: "Late moon, shut out of the town, A," *sel.*
Haiku: "Late night wheat flour spilled," *sel.*
Haiku: "Leaving only the noise of dead leaves," *sel.*
Haiku: "Lord Buddha's yellow flowers, The," *sel.*
Haiku: "Moonlight night I return," *sel.*
Haiku: "Morning-glories' white continues to bloom," *sel.*
Haiku: "Mountain water, trickly," *sel.*
Haiku: "On a warm roof, working," *sel.*
Haiku: "On the straw roof grass grows," *sel.*
Haiku: "One or two, immersed in darkness," *sel.*
Haiku: "Pine cone, as it is, A," *sel.*
Haiku: "Pomegranate opened its mouth, A," *sel.*
Haiku: "Praying mantis drops with a thud, A," *sel.*
Haiku: "Ran and caught up, in the wind," *sel.*
Haiku: "Rejecting a slanderous mind," *sel.*
Haiku: "Right under the big sky," *sel.*
Haiku: "Sea becomes light, a window is open, The," *sel.*
Haiku: "Single set of footsteps coming, A," *sel.*
Haiku: "Small rural newspaper, The," *sel.*
Haiku: "Snake, killed, A," *sel.*
Haiku: "Snap, the thong broke," *sel.*
Haiku: "Snow fades into the river, The," *sel.*
Haiku: "Snow has cleared, The," *sel.*
Haiku: "Snowy sky turns into a single crow, The," *sel.*
Haiku: "Sound of the florist's scissors, The," *sel.*
Haiku: "Sparrows all at once are gone, The," *sel.*
Haiku: "Splashing hot water over my navel," *sel.*
Haiku: "Supper eaten, still blessed," *sel.*
Haiku: "Their many children each reading," *sel.*
Haiku: "There it was, my face," *sel.*
Haiku: "These are the mornings and evenings," *sel.*
Haiku: "Thinking about something," *sel.*
Haiku: "To one of the ears," *sel.*
Haiku: "Unable to put thread through a needle," *sel.*
Haiku: "Walking down to eat my meal," *sel.*

Haiku: "Wallet gone completely empty," *sel.*
Haiku: "We drained the pond," *sel.*
Haiku: "Wears dirty clogs," *sel.*
Haiku: "Where the autumn sun shines, on a stone," *sel.*
Haiku: "With a face saying I caught something," *sel.*
Haiku: "Woman in dark glasses, A," *sel.*
Haiku: "Woman in the newspaper, The," *sel.*
Haiku: "Wonderful breasts, here's a mosquito," *sel.*

Hosking, Arthur Nicholas
Land of the Free.

Hoskins, Katherine
Baucis and Philemon.
Bee and the Petunia, The.
Byfield Rabbit, The.
Côte d'Azur.
Not Lotte.

Hoskyns, John
Absense.
Bellows Maker of Oxford, The.
Epitaph on Sir Walter Pye.
Epitaph on the Fart in the Parliament House.
Here lies the man that madly slain.
His Own Epitaph, When He Was Sick.
Of the Loss of Time.
On a Contentious Companion.
On a Whore.
On One That Lived Ingloriously.
To His Little Son Benedict from the Tower of London.
To His Son Bennet.
Upon a Fool.
Upon One of the Maids of Honour to Queen Elizabeth.

Hosmer, Frederick Lucian
From Age to Age They Gather.
Hear, Hear, O Ye Nations.
My Dead.
O Beautiful, My Country.
O Day of Light and Gladness.
Through Unknown Paths.
Through Willing Heart and Helping Hand.
Thy Kingdom Come, O Lord.
Thy Kingdom Come ("Thy kingdom come— on bended knee").
With Self Dissatisfied.

Hosmer, William Henry Cuyler
Song of Texas.

Hoss, E. Embree
O God, Great Father, Lord, and King.

Hotei
Maitreya! Maitreya!

Hough, Graham
Age of Innocence.

Hough, Lindy
Portrait of the Father.

Houghton, Firman
Mr. Frost Goes South to Boston.
She Sees Another Door Opening.

Houghton, George Washington Wright
Handsel Ring, The.
Legend of Walbach Tower, The.
Manor Lord, The.
Sandy Hook.

Houghton, Richard Monckton Milnes, 1st Baron. *See* **Milnes, Richard Monckton, 1st Baron Houghton**

House, Vernal
In Tribute.

Housman, Alfred Edward
Along the Field as We Came By, *sel.*
Amelia Mixed the Mustard.
As I Gird on for Fighting.
As into the Garden Elizabeth Ran.
Astronomy.
Be still, my soul, be still; the arms you bear are brittle, *sel.*
Because I Liked You Better.
Bredon Hill, *sel.*

Carpenter's Son, The, *sel.*
Could Man Be Drunk for Ever, *sel.*
Crossing Alone the Nighted Ferry.
Day of Battle, The, *sel.*
Deserter, The.
Easter Hymn.
Eight o'Clock.
Elephant, or the Force of Habit, The.
1887, *sel.*
Fairies Break Their Dance, The.
Fancy's Knell.
Far In a Western Brookland, *sel.*
Farewell to Barn and Stack and Tree, *sel.*
For My Funeral.
Fragment of a Greek Tragedy.
Friends.
From Far, from Eve and Morning, *sel.*
G. K. Chesterton on His Birth.
Good Creatures, Do You Love Your Lives.
Grenadier.
Half-way, for One Commandment Broken.
Hallelujah!
He Would Not Stay for Me; and Who can Wonder?
Hell Gate.
Her Strong Enchantments Failing.
Here dead lie we because we did not choose.
Ho, Everyone That Thirsteth.
Hughley Steeple, *sel.*
I Did Not Lose My Heart in Summer's Even.
I Hoed and Trenched and Weeded, *sel.*
I Knew a Cappadocian.
I Promise Nothing.
I to My Perils.
Immortal Part, The, *sel.*
In my own shire, if I was sad, *sel.*
In valleys green and still.
Infant Innocence.
Inhuman Henry.
Into My Heart [an Air That Kills], *sel.*
Is My Team Ploughing [*or* Plowing], *sel.*
Isle of Portland, The, *sel.*
It nods and curtseys and recovers, *sel.*
Jar of Nations, The.
Lads in Their Hundreds, The, *sel.*
Lancer.
Laws of God, the Laws of Man, The.
Lent Lily, The, *sel.*
Look Not in My Eyes, for Fear, *sel.*
Loveliest of Trees [the Cherry Now], *sel.*
March.
Mill-stream, now that noises cease, The.
New Mistress, The, *sel.*
Night Is Freezing Fast, The.
Now Dreary Dawns the Eastern Light.
Now hollow fires burn out to black, *sel.*
O Billows Bounding Far.
O Have You Caught the Tiger?
Oh, See How Thick the Goldcup Flowers, *sel.*
Oh, When I Was in Love with You, *sel.*
Oh Who Is That Young Sinner with the Handcuffs on His Wrists?
Olive, The.
On Moonlit Heath and Lonesome Bank, *sel.*
On the idle hill of summer, *sel.*
On Wenlock Edge [the Wood's in Trouble], *sel.*
Oracles, The.
Others, I am not the first, *sel.*
Parta Quies.
Rain, it streams on stone and hillock, The.
Rainy Pleiads Wester, The.
Recruit, The.
Reveille, *sel.*
Shades of Night, The.
Shot? So Quick, So Clean an Ending?, *sel.*
Sigh that heaves the grasses, The.
Soldier from the Wars Returning.
Some can gaze and not be sick.
Stars Have Not Dealt Me, The.
Stars, I Have Seen Them Fall.
Street Sounds to the Soldiers' Tread, The.

Tell Me Not Here [It Needs Not Saying]
Terence, This Is Stupid Stuff, *sel.*
They Say My Verse Is Sad: No Wonder.
Think no more, lad; laugh, be jolly.
'Tis spring; come out to ramble, *sel.*
To an Athlete Dying Young, *sel.*
To Stand Up Straight.
To Think That Two and Two Are Four.
Wake Not for the World-heard Thunder.
We'll to the Woods No More.
Welsh Marches, The.
Wenlock Edge (" 'Tis time, I think; by Wenlock town"), *sel.*
When Adam Day by Day.
When I was One-and-Twenty, *sel.*
When I Watch the Living Meet, *sel.*
When Israel out of Egypt Came.
When Smoke Stood up from Ludlow, *sel.*
When the bells justle in the tower.
When the Eye of Day Is Shut.
When the Lad for Longing Sighs, *sel.*
White in the moon the long road lies, *sel.*
With Rue My Heart Is Laden, *sel.*
Yonder See the Morning Blink.

Housman, Laurence
Continuing City, The.
Dear love, when with a two-fold mind, *sel.*
Dedication: "When I have ended, then I see."
Gardener, The.
Spikenard.

Houston, Libby
Post-War.

Houston, Peyton
Canzone: "Love, which is least sure and most dared, the pure, keen," *sel.*
Doll, The, *sel.*
The/ Quick Gold, Slant Blue, Sharp Scarlet, *sel.*
Time's Mirror, *sel.*

Hovell-Thurlow, Edward, 2d Baron Thurlow
May.

Hover, Emily
Mr. Beetle.

Hovey, Richard
Barney McGee.
Battle of Manila, The.
Call of the Bugles, The.
Dartmouth Winter-Song.
Distillation.
Eleazar Wheelock.
Envoy: "Whose furthest footstep never strayed," *sel.*
Evening on the Potomac.
Here falls no light of sun nor stars, *sel.*
Immanence.
In a Silence.
Isabel.
Kavin Again.
Laurana's Song.
Love in the Winds.
Premonition.
Sea Gypsy, The.
Secrets.
Speech and Silence.
Three of a Kind.
Transcendence.
Unmanifest Destiny.
Vagabondia.
Wander-Lovers, The.
Word of the Lord from Havana, The.
Ylen's Song, *sel.*

Howard, Anne, Duchess of Arundel
Elegy on the Death of Her Husband.

Howard, Ben
Diver, The.
Lynx.
Winter Report.

Howard, Dorothy S.
Birkett's Eagle.

Howard, Frances Minturn
Heron in Swamp.
Narcissus in a Cocktail Glass.
Prophecy in Flame.
Sampler from Haworth.
Howard, Henry. *See* **Surrey, Henry Howard, Earl of**
Howard, Joy
Casablanca Time Again.
Vanilla Sugar; or, Verse for a "Hallmark" Greeting Card.
You Can't Go to the Moon There's No Trains.
Howard, Leonard
Humours of the King's Bench Prison, a Ballad, The.
Howard, Philip, 1st Earl of Arundel
Hymn: "O Christ, the glorious Crown."
Howard, Richard
Again for Hephaistos, the Last Time.
At the Monument to Pierre Louÿs.
Aubade: Donna Anna to Juan, Still Asleep.
Author of *Christine*, The.
Bonnard; a Novel.
Comedy of Art: Henri de Toulouse Lautrec, The.
Crepuscular.
Far Cry after a Close Call, A.
Foreigner Remembered by a Local Man, The.
Giovanni da Fiesole on the Sublime; or, Fra Angelico's "Last Judgment."
Howard's Way.
Landed: A Valentine.
Last Words, *sel.*
Nadar.
Natural History.
On Arrival.
Oystering.
Personal Values.
Queer's Song, *sel.*
Recipe for an Ocean in the Absence of the Sea.
Richard, may I ask a question? What is an episteme?, *sel.*
Richard, what will it be like when you ask the questions?, *sel.*
Saturday Morning.
Secular Games.
Stitching in Time: Dorothy Ruddick.
209 Canal.
Wildflowers.
Howard, Sir Robert *and* **John Dryden**
Poor mortals that are clogged with earth below, *sel.*
Howard, Winifred
Windy Day, A.
Howard-Jones, Stuart
Hibernia.
Howarth, B. L.
Brown paper worn next to the skin.
Howarth, Ellen Clementine
'Tis But a Little Faded Flower.
Howe, Fanny
Alsace-Lorraine.
Nursery, The.
Onlie X.
Poem for Potential.
Howe, George
Sun-Witch to the Sun, The.
Howe, Joseph
In ev'ry thought, in ev'ry wish I own, *sel.*
Song of the Micmac, The.
Howe, Julia Ward
Battle Hymn of the [American] Republic, The.
Decoration Day.
J. A. G.
Our Country.
Our Orders.
Pardon.

Parricide.
Robert E. Lee.
Howe, Mark Antony De Wolfe ("Gilbertulus")
Distinction.
Travellers, The.
Whom the Gods Love.
Howe, Solomon
Our Kind Creator.
Howe, Susan
Age of earth and us all chattering.
Children of Lir, *sel.*
Come in light variable and with calm.
Do not come down the ladder.
Dream of wandering in woods with.
Earliest before sunrise.
He plodded away through drifts of ice.
Right or ruth, *sel.*
Running rings.
Say that a ballad, *sel.*
Torn away from number weight, *sel.*
We that were wood.
Howe, William Walsham
Funeral Hymn.
Howell, Anthony
Age of the Street, The.
Belmore.
Nudes.
Out Together.
Ramble.
Squirrel, The.
Howell, Elizabeth Lloyd
Milton's Prayer for [*or* of] Patience.
Howell, James
An Elegy upon His Tomb in Herndon-Hill Church, Erected by His Wife, Who Speaks.
Of London Bridge, and the Stupendous Sight, and Structure Thereof.
Upon Dr. Davies's British Grammar.
Howell, Thomas
Of Misery.
Rose, The.
When He Thought Himself Contemned.
Who Would Have Thought, *sel.*
Howells, Mildred
Going Too Far.
Howells, William Dean
Battle in the Clouds, The.
Change.
Earliest Spring.
From Generation to Generation.
Heredity.
Hope.
If.
In August.
Judgment Day.
Prayer, A: "Lord, for the erring thought," *sel.*
Thanksgiving, A.
Two Wives, The.
Vision.
What Shall it Profit?
Howells, Winifred
Forthfaring.
Mood, A.
Past.
Poet and the Child, The.
Wasted Sympathy, A.
Howes, Barbara
At Mrs. Alefounder's.
Chimera.
City Afternoon.
Conversation, A.
Danaë.
Death of a Vermont Farm Woman.
Early Supper.
Flight.
Home Leave.
Indian Summer.
Landscape, Deer Season.
Letter from the Caribbean, A.
Looking Up at Leaves.

Mistral.
Monkey Difference.
On a Bougainvillaea Vine at the Summer Palace [*or* in Haiti].
On Galveston Beach.
Out Fishing.
Portrait of an Artist.
Portrait of the Boy as Artist.
Returning to Store Bay.
Rune for C., A.
Sea School.
Talking to Animals.
Howes, Grace Clementine
Wind of the Prairie.
Howitt, Mary
Buttercups and Daisies.
Fairies of the Caldon-Low, The.
Lion, The.
Monkey, The.
Old Christmas.
Sale of the Pet Lamb, The.
Sea-Gull, The.
September.
Spider and the Fly, The.
Spring Song, A.
Squirrel, The.
Howitt, William
Migration of the Grey Squirrels, The.
Northern Seas, The.
Wind in a Frolic, The.
Howland, Edward
Condemned, The.
Hoyem, Andrew
Circumambulation of Mt. Tamalpais.
Hoyers, Anna Owena
For the Christian Reader.
Hoyland, Michael
Flute-Players.
Hoyos, Angela de
For Marsha.
Rosario, en la Cima.
Third-World Theme.
Hoyt, Helen
Memory.
Hoyt, Ralph
Old.
Hroswitha
In Praise of Virginity.
Hroswitha von Gandersheim
I bring you a goat, *sel.*
Hsi-chün
Lament of Hsi-chün.
Hsi K'ang
Sent to the Hsiu-ts'ai on His Entry into the Army.
Hsiang Hung-tso
In Imitation of Sun Kuang-hsien's Style.
Sent to Wu Tzu-lü Who Wished to See My Recent Lyrics.
Wind-tossed catkins fly past a silken blanket of green.
Hsiang Ssu
Ailing Japanese Monk, The.
Hsiang Yang
Floral Invasions.
Grampaw's Smoking Pipe.
Sailing in the Rain.
Soil and Flower.
Ten Lines: Autumn.
Ten Lines: On Seed.
Hsiao Yen
Spring Song of Tzu-yeh, A.
Hsieh Chin
Government wine of Peking is sweeter than honey, The, *sel.*
I still remember Conch-Shell Slope, west of the River Tzu, *sel.*
Inscribed on a Painting of Dragons by Ch'en So-weng.
People say the sun is in heaven, *sel.*
Playful Poem on a Chicken Egg, A.

Poem on a Little Pine, A.
Sage has the "Six Classics", The, *sel.*
Sandal Mountain.
Song of Cursive Calligraphy.
To Hsiao Shih-ying.
To the Fortuneteller Hsüeh T'ieh-yai.
Wait until I too "hang up my carriage", *sel.*
"What does the little boy dream of?", *sel.*
"What does the little boy love?", *sel.*

Hsieh Hui-lien
Fulling Cloth for Clothes.
Rhyme-Prose on the Snow.

Hsieh Ling-yün
How fetching! Somebody's husband, *sel.*
How fetching! somebody's wife, *sel.*
Replying to a Poem from My Cousin
    Hui-lien.
Written on the Lake, Returning from the
    Retreat at Stone Cliff.

Hsieh Shang
Song of the Thoroughfare.

Hsieh T'iao
In a Provincial Capital Sick in Bed.

Hsieh Wang-ying. *See* **"Ping Hsin"**

Hsin Ch'i-chi
Tune: Ugly Rogue.
Written at the Po-Shan Monastery.

Hsin Mu
Flight.
Meadow upon the Mercy of Heaven, The.
Second Winery, The.

Hsiung-hung
Written in the Sunset.

Hsü Chün-ch'ien
Beginning of Spring—A Stroll with My Wife.
Sitting Up with My Wife on New Year's Eve.

Hsü Chung-hsing
Cane of Ch'iung Bamboo, The.
How brave the peasant who lives beside the
    lake, *sel.*
I shake my robe—and mists disperse, leaving
    clear autumn sky, *sel.*
This metal is engraved with Shang-style
    markings, *sel.*
Traveling by Boat at Shun-ch'ang.
Trees are ancient, thick with patterns of moss,
    The, *sel.*
Who would have thought that a disease of the
    ordinary world, *sel.*

Hsü Kan
Wife's Thoughts, The.

Hsü Pen
Ballad of the Ferocious Tiger.
Ballad of the Merchant.
By nature I love to dress my hair, *sel.*
Deserted Estate at South Garden, The.
Following the Rhymes of Kao Chi-ti's Poem
    "We Had Planned to Travel to Cloud Cliff."
Hermit, The.
Hermit Feng's Residence on the Lake.
Hermit Li's Herb Garden Retreat at
    T'ung-ch'uan.
I love the p'i-p'a's music in my heart, *sel.*
In Harmony with Kao "The Second" Ch'i's
    Poem "On Hearing a P'i-p'a Played Next
    Door."
Mountain of green trees and orioles
    everywhere!
Mountain Residence of Secretary Cheng
    Ching-ssu, The.
Poem on Buddha's Begging Bowl, A.
Saying Goodbye to a Monk from Japan.
Time after time, afraid of the chilly spring
    weather, *sel.*
To a Hermit in the Mountains.
To the Filial Son, Ts'ui.
Tomb of the Singing Girl Ch'iung-i, The.
Yesterday, as I went down to the bridge at the
    river, *sel.*

Hsü Ts'an
Boudoir Feeling.

Headwaters of the Lung River.
Moon over the Mountain Pass.
Rain on the Night of the Full Moon.

Hsü Wei
Buddhist Monk Cut and Burned His Own
    Flesh to Make the Rains Stop, A.
Fifth day of the fifth month, *sel.*
From Chekiang I Went to Hsin-an.
I Once Did a Bamboo Painting for Somebody.
I Tried to Exchange Two Painting for Some
    Grain But Failed.
In one place, flying clubs, *sel.*
In the northwestern pond there is a dragon-ox,
    sel.
Inscribed on a Painting.
Mushroom Gatherer Deep in the Mountains,
    A.
On the Road through the Wu-i Mountains.
Painting of People Strolling through a Pine
    Forest, A.
Puppets which perform before the curtains,
    The, *sel.*
Returning from the Seventy-Two Mountains.
Rock among Bamboo, *sel.*
To Hsü Shih-t'ing.
Two Fish by a Willow Embankment.
When the wind is gentle, *sel.*
Where does the dragon-ox display its
    imposing form, *sel.*

Hsüan-chi, Yü
Elegy for the Wife of a Friend.
For Hidden Mist Pavilion.
For Kuo Hsiang.
Letting My Feelings Out.
Rhyming with a Friend.
Selling Ruined Peonies.
Spring Thoughts Sent to Tzu-an.
Telling My Feelings.
To Tzu-an.

Hsüan-yeh
Gift for an Old Official.
Hunting in the Ordos, the Pheasants and
    Hares Were Many.
Lines in Praise of a Self-Chiming Clock.

Hsüeh Chao-yün
Delight in the High-Flying Orioles.
Difficulty of Parting, The.
Drunken Gentleman, The.
Joy of Meeting, The.
Manifold Little Hills.
Paying Homage at the Golden Gate.
Sand of the Silk-Washing Stream.
Taoist Nun, The.

Hsüeh Shao-hui
After Rain.
Ancient Sentiments.
Emperor Wen.
For My Husband Who Sent Me Several
    Rubbings of Ancient Egyptian Stone
    Tablets.
In Honor of My Husband's Fiftieth Birthday.

Hsüeh T'ao
Spring-gazing Song.
Weaving Love-Knots.
Weaving Love-Knots 2.

Huan Fu [*or* Ch'en Ch'ien-au]
Don't, Don't.
Lotus.

Huang Ching-jen
Caged Tiger: A Ballad, A.
Dawn Snow.
Grave of Li Po, The.
Note to My Friends, While Slightly Ill, A.
Sail on the Lake after Rain, A.

Huang E
Pearl-teardrops roll and gather.

Huang-fu Jan
Spring Thoughts.

Huang-fu Sung
Dreaming of the South.

Gathering Lotus.
Heaven's Immortal.
Picking Fresh Flowers.
Ripples Sifting Sand.
Willow Branches.

Huang O [*or* Ho]
Farewell to a Southern Melody, A.
To the Tune "A Floating Cloud Crosses
    Enchanted Mountain."
To the Tune "Red Embroidered Shoes."
To the Tune "Soaring Clouds."
To the Tune "The Fall of a Little Wild
    Goose."

Huang T'ing-chien
Once More Following the Rhymes of
    Pin-lao's Poem "Getting Up After Illness."
Song of the Clear River.
To Go with Shih K'o's Painting of an Old
    Man Tasting Vinegar.

Huang Tsun-hsien
Ballad of Ch'ao-chou, The.
Ballad of the Great London Fog.
My Small Daughter.
Song of the Exile.

Huang Tsung-hsi
Cold-night Moon—In the Manner of Meng
    Tung-yeh.
Encountering Fire Again in the Fifth Month.
Encountering Fire in Early Spring, 1662.
For fifty years I followed an "overturned
    cart."
Hearing the Cuckoo on the Nineteenth Day of
    the Third Month.
I've come again to Yen Bend and built a hut
    of thatch, *sel.*
Rising Early with My Son Chih to Leave
    Tung-ming Ch'an Monastery.
Who says that in the mountains everything is
    grand?

Hubbard, P. M.
Subjectivity at Sestos.
To Cynthia, Not to Let Him Read the Ladies'
    Magazines.

Hubbell, Patricia
Abandoned House, The.
Autumn.
Black Snake, The.
Christmas Present, The.
Concrete Mixers.
Conjugation.
Fairies, The.
Message from a Mouse, Ascending in a
    Rocket.
Night.
Our Washing Machine.
Prayer for Reptiles.
Seagulls.
Shadows.

Huch, Ricarda
Arrival in Hell.
Death Seed.
Music stirs me, for you.
Young Girl.

Huckel, Oliver
O Mind of God, Broad as the Sky.

Huddle, David
Janie Swecker and Me and Gone with the
    Wind.
My Brother, Beautiful Shinault, That Goat.
My Brother Flies Over Low.
My Grandaddy Mostly with His Knife.
Nerves, *sel.*
Shooting Crows.
Stopping by Home.
Words, *sel.*

Hudgins, Andrew
Around the Campfire.
At the Piano.
Burial Detail.
Persistence of Nature in Our Lives, The.
Postcards of the Hanging: 1869.

Hudson, Deatt
Some Tips on Watching Birds.
Hudson, Flexmore
Mallee in October.
Hueffer, Ford Madox. *See* **Ford, Ford Madox**
Huff, Barbara A.
Afternoon with Grandmother.
Library, The.
Huff, Robert
Although I Remember the Sound.
Course, The.
Getting Drunk with Daughter.
Rainbow.
Smoker, The.
Traditional Red.
Huggins, Horatio Nelson
But mark you well the words I say, *sel.*
Introduction: "Clear transparent sea with light,
The," *sel.*
Hughes, Dorothy
Age of Sheen, The.
Dusting of the Books, The.
Hughes, James D.
My Son.
Hughes, John Ceiriog ("Ceiriog")
Epilogue to Alun Mabon.
Mountain Stream, The.
Hughes, Langston
Advice.
African Dance.
Alabama Earth.
American Heartbreak.
Angola Question Mark.
April Rain Song.
As I Grew Older.
Backlash Blues, The.
Bad Morning.
Ballad of the Landlord.
Be-Bop Boys.
Beale Street.
Birmingham Sunday.
Birth.
Bound No'th Blues.
Brass Spittoons.
Cafe: 3 A.M.
Carol of the Brown King.
Catch.
Children's Rhymes.
Christ in Alabama.
City.
Cross.
Cultural Exchange.
Cycle.
Daybreak in Alabama.
Death in Yorkville.
Dinner Guest: Me.
Down and Out.
Dream Boogie.
Dream Variation [*or* Variations].
Dreams.
Drum.
Dust Bowl.
Early Evening Quarrel.
Ennui.
Esthete in Harlem.
Fantasy in Purple.
50—50.
Fire.
Florida Road Workers.
Frederick Douglass: 1817-1895.
Freedom.
Go Slow.
Hard Daddy.
Harlem ("Here on the edge of hell").
Harlem Sweeties.
Harlem ("What happens to a dream
deferred"), *sel.*
Havana Dreams.
Heaven, Heaven, Heaven Is the Place.
High to Low.

Homesick Blues.
Hope.
House in Taos, A.
I Dream a World.
I Thought It Was Tangiers I Wanted.
I, Too.
I, Too, Sing America.
Impasse.
Island.
Jazz Band in a Parisian Cabaret.
Jazzonia.
Juke Box Love Song.
Junior Addict.
Justice.
Ku Klux.
Let America Be America Again.
Letter.
Life Is Fine.
Lincoln Monument: Washington.
Little Lyric (of Great Importance).
Long Trip.
Lord Has a Child, The.
Lumumba's Grave.
Madam and the Minister.
Madam's Past History.
Mama and Daughter.
Me and the Mule.
Merry-go-round.
Mexican Market Woman.
Midnight Dancer.
Militant.
Misery is when your.
Miss Blues'es Child.
Moonlight Night: Carmel.
Morning After.
Mother to Son.
Motto.
Mulatto.
Necessity.
Negro Servant.
Negro Speaks of Rivers, The.
Night Funeral in Harlem.
October 16: The Raid.
Old Walt.
Oppression.
Peace.
Pennsylvania Station.
Personal.
Po' Boy Blues.
Poem: "I loved my friend."
Poem: "Night is beautiful, The."
Prayer: "I ask you this."
Preference.
Prime.
Question and Answer.
Refugee in America.
Sailor.
Same in Blues, *sel.*
Saturday Night.
Share-Croppers.
Shepherd's Song at Christmas.
Situation.
Slave.
Snail.
Song for a Dark Girl.
Song for a Suicide.
Special Bulletin.
Stars.
Still Here.
Stony Lonesome.
Subway Rush Hour.
Suicide's Note.
Sun Song.
Sylvester's Dying Bed.
Theme for English B.
Third Degree.
This Little House Is Sugar.
Today.
Trip: San Francisco.
Troubled Woman.
Trumpet Player.
Un-American Investigators.

Undertow.
Vagabonds.
Wake.
Warning.
Weary Blues, The.
What?
When Sue Wears Red.
Where? When? Which?
Who but the Lord?
Winter Moon.
Without Benefit of Declaration.
World War II.
Young Gal's Blues.
Youth.
Hughes, Richard
Burial of the Spirit of a Young Poet.
Felo de Se.
Gipsy-Night.
Glaucopis.
Image, The.
Invocation to the Muse.
Lover's Reply to Good Advice.
Old Cat Care.
On Time.
Ruin, The.
Sermon, The.
Tramp.
Walking Road, The.
Winter.
Hughes, Rupert
Martyrs of the *Maine,* The.
Hughes, Ted
After Lorca.
Bear, The.
Bess My Badger.
Birth of Rainbow.
Bridestones.
Bull Moses, The.
Bullfrog.
Buzz in the Window, *sel.*
Cadenza.
Cat and Mouse.
Childbirth.
Childish Prank, A.
Christmas Card.
Cleopatra to the Asp.
Cockcrow.
Crag Jack's Apostasy.
Crow Blacker than Ever.
Crow's First Lesson.
Dawn's Rose, *sel.*
Deaf School.
Dove, A.
Dream of Horses, A.
Esther's Tomcat.
Examination at the Womb-Door.
Famous Poet.
Fern.
Full Moon and Little Frieda.
Hawk Roosting.
Heptonstall Old Church.
Her Husband.
His Legs Ran About.
Horses, The.
Howling of Wolves, The.
Jaguar, The.
Kreutzer Sonata.
Lake, The.
Law in the Country of the Cats.
Leaves.
Littleblood, *sel.*
Lupercalia.
March Calf, A.
Minstrel's Song.
Moon-Witches.
Motorbike, A.
My Aunt.
My Brother Bert.
My Sister Jane.
Nessie.
New Year's [*or* Year] Song.
November.

Now I know I never shall, *sel.*
Old Age Gets Up.
Orf.
Otter, An.
Pause for Breath, A.
Pennines in April.
Pets.
Pibroch.
Pike.
Prometheus on his crag/ began to admire the vulture, *sel.*
Ravens.
Relic.
Retired Colonel, The.
Reveille.
Revenge Fable.
River.
River in March, The.
Roarers in a Ring.
Roe Deer.
Roger the Dog.
Salmon Eggs.
Second Glance at a Jaguar.
Secretary.
September.
Seven Sorrows, The.
Singing on the Moon.
Six Young Men.
Skylarks.
Snowdrop.
Song: "O lady, when the tipped cup of the moon blessed you."
Song of a Rat.
Stations.
Stealing Trout.
Still-Life.
Teaching a Dumb Calf.
That Moment, *sel.*
Theology.
Thistles.
Thought-Fox, The.
Thrushes.
Trees.
Two Legends, *sel.*
Two Wise Generals.
Urn Burial.
View of a Pig.
Water.
When we sat his mother on her tail, he mouthed her teat, *sel.*
Wilfred Owen's Photographs.
Wind.
Witches.
Wodwo.
You Drive in a Circle.
You Hated Spain.

Hughes, Thomas
Dolgelley Hotel, The.

Hugo, Richard
Church on Comiaken Hill, The.
Death in the Aquarium.
Death of the Kapowsin Tavern.
December 24 and George McBride Is Dead.
Degrees of Gray in Philipsburg.
Distances.
Druid Stones at Kensaleyre.
Drums in Scotland.
1805 Gratiot.
Farmer, Dying.
Ferniehirst Castle.
Freaks at Spurgin Road Field, The.
G. I. Graves in Tuscany.
Graves at Elkhorn.
Here, but Unable to Answer.
Hilltop, The.
House on 15th S.W., The.
In Your Bad Dream.
In Your Young Dream.
Lady in Kicking Horse Reservoir, The.
Last Days.
Last Words to James Wright.
Letter to Bell from Missoula.

Letter to Levertov from Butte.
Letter to Logan from Milltown.
Letter to Mantsch from Havre.
Letter to Reed from Lolo.
Letter to Scanlon from Whitehall.
Letter to Wagoner from Port Townsend.
Letter to Welch from Browning.
Map of Montana in Italy, A.
Maratea Porto: Saying Goodbye to the Vitolos.
Milltown Union Bar, The.
Missoula Softball Tournament.
Montana Ranch Abandoned.
Napoli Again.
Night with Cindy at Heitman's, A.
Note to R. H. from Strongsville.
Open Country.
Places and Ways to Live.
Plans for Altering the River.
Salt Water Story.
Skykomish River Running.
To Women.
Way a Ghost Dissolves, The.
What Thou Lovest Well, Remains American.
White Center.

Hugo, Victor
After Six Thousand Years.
Age Is Great and Strong, The.
Be like the Bird.
Genesis of Butterflies, The.
Good Night.
Grave and the Rose, The.
Heard on the Mountain, *sel.*
Is it children we are killing now? My God, *sel.*
More Strong Than Time.
Poet's Simple Faith, The.
Poor Children, The.
Russia 1812.
Sunset, A, *sel.*

Hull, George
To the Memory of William Billington.
Toiler's Wife, The.

Hulme, Keri
He Hola.

Hulme, Thomas Ernest
Above the Dock.
Autumn.
Conversion.
Embankment [*or* Fantasia of a Fallen Gentleman], The.
Image.

Hume, Alexander
Midsummer Day in France, *sel.*
Of Gods Omnipotencie.
Of the Day Estivall.
Summer's Day, A.

Hume, Tobias
Fain Would I Change That Note, at.

Hummer, T. R.
Any Time, What May Hit You.
Beating, The.
Cruelty.
Empty Backstreet in a Small Southern Town.
Inner Ear.
Love Poem: The Dispossessed.
Rural Carrier Stops to Kill a Nine-Foot Cottonmouth, The.
Second Story, The.
Sorrow.
Sun, The.
What Shines in Winter Burns.
Where You Go When She Sleeps.

Humphrey, Paul
Seasoning.

Humphreys, David
Genius of Culture! thou, whose chaster taste, *sel.*
On Disbanding the Army.

Humphreys, Emyr
An Apple Tree and a Pig.
From Father to Son.

Humphries, Rolfe
Aria.
Around Thanksgiving.
Dafydd ap Gwilym Resents the Winter.
For My Ancestors.
Frisbee.
Offering of the Heart Tapestry from Arras, XV Century, The.
Polo Grounds.
Runes for an Old Believer.
Seasons, The.
Summer Landscape; or, The Dragon's Teeth, The.
Wmffre the Sweep.

Hung Liang-chi
Ballad of a Springtime River: Presented to Wang the Elder, A.
Chatting about the Past with Huang the Elder.
On the Road to An-hsi.
Small Pavilion, *sel.*
Upon Arriving at Ili, Recalling What I Saw on the Road.
Winding Pond, *sel.*
Written on a Boat on the Ch'ien-t'ang River.

Hung Sheng
Fire of the Fireflies, The.
Old Sophora Tree, An.
On Rising at Dawn and Seeing the Mountains.
Passing the Night at the Monastery of Eternal Peace.
Thatched Cottage, The.

Hunnis, William
Nosegay Always Sweet, for Lovers to Send for Tokens of Love at New Year's Tide, or for Fairings, A.
Shipmen, The.

Hunt, Josephine Slocum
You Kissed Me.

Hunt, Josie R.
Katie Lee and Willy Grey, at.

Hunt, Leigh
Abou Ben Adhem.
Captain Sword.
Christmas.
Fish Answers, A, *sel.*
Glove and the Lions, The.
Jaffar.
Jenny Kiss'd [*or* Kissed] Me.
Nile, The.
Noble range it was, of many a rood, A, *sel.*
On Receiving a Crown of Ivy from the Same.
On Seeing a Pigeon Make Love.
On the Death of His Son Vincent.
Royal Line, The.
Song of the Grass, The.
There are the fair-limbed nymphs o' the woods, *sel.*
To a Fish.
To Hampstead.
To John Keats.
To Percy Shelley: On the Degrading Notions of Deity.
To the Grasshopper and the Cricket.
To the Spirit Great and Good.
Two Heavens.

Hunt, Sam
At Castor Bay.
Birth of a Son.
Bottle Creek Blues.
Just like That.
Maintrunk Country Roadsong.
My Father Scything.
My Father Today.
Porirua Friday Night.
Requiem.
School Policy on Stickmen.
School Report, A.
Stabat Mater.
Sunday Evening.
Valley Called Moonshine, A.
White Gentian, A.

Hunter, William
"Go Bring Me," Said the Dying Fair.
Joyfully, Joyfully Onward I Move.
Hunter-Duvar, John
First halt. They heard within a sugar patch,
sel.
Here, then, we stand, on the Canadian shore,
sel.
La Belle Sauvage, sel.
Huntington, George
International Hymn.
Huntington, William Reed
Authority.
Tellus.
Huong, Ho Xuan
Carved on an Areca Nut.
Hurdis, James
But most of all subdued, or fearful least, sel.
Hurvits, Ya'ir
For My Love Rising Early.
On a Clear Night.
Sorrow My Love.
Husain (or Hussein), Rashid
Jerusalem and the Hour.
Lessons in Parsing.
Husid, Mordechai
Cry of Generations, The.
On the Way.
Windows.
Huss, Avraham
Classical Idyll, A.
Green Refrain, A.
Nocturnal Thoughts.
Time.
Hussein, Rashid. See Husain, Rashid
Hussey, Norah E.
I Spy.
My Garden.
Toad the Tailor.
Hutchinson, Abby
Kind Words Can Never Die.
Hutchinson, Barney
Cold Logic.
Hutchinson, M. M.
Dancing on the Shore.
Harvest.
Making Tens.
My New Umbrella.
Ten Little Indian Boys.
Thames, The.
Tug-of-War, A.
Twice.
Hutchinson, Pearse
Boxing the Fox.
Gaeltacht.
Malaga.
Manifest Destiny.
Hutchinson, Robert
Suburban Wife's Song.
Hutchinson, Ellen Mackay. See Cortissoz,
Ellen Mackay Hutchinson
Hutchison, A. G.
A'Chuilionn.
Hutt, Frank
Vacation Time.
Hutton, Joseph
Tomb of the Brave, The.
Hutton, Laurence
Doves of Venice, The.
Hutton, Virgil
Dusk over the lake.
Moving shadows, The.
Huws, Daniel
Family Evening.
Goodbye to Regal.
Huxley, Aldous
First Philosopher's Song.
Jonah.
September.
Hwang Chin-i
Blue hill is my desire, The.

I cut in two/ A long November night.
Mountains are steadfast but the mountain
streams.
Hyde, Abby Bradley
And Canst Thou, Sinner, Slight.
Dear Saviour, If These Lambs Should Stray.
Hyde, Douglas
Cold, Sharp Lamentation.
He Meditates on the Life of a Rich Man.
Will You Be as Hard?
Hyde, Michael
To 'ave a garden in fettle.
Hyde, Robin
Adolicus; that's a creeper rug, its small, sel.
Bronze Rider, Wellington, The.
Close under here, I watched two lovers once,
sel.
Cool and certain, their oars will be lifted in
dusk, sel.
Hares on their forms at dusk were not so still,
sel.
Ku Li.
Last Ones, The.
None of it true; for Christ's sake, spill the
ink, sel.
Old nursery chair; its legs, cut down, are
broken, sel.
What Is It Makes the Stranger?
Young Knowledge.
"Hyde, Robin" (Iris Gulver Wilkinson)
Deserted Village, The.
Pihsien Road.
Hyde, William deWitt
Creation's Lord, We Give Thee Thanks.
Hymes, Lucia
Ears Hear.
Hymes, Lucia Lucia and James L. Hymes, Jr.
Oodles of Noodles.
Tombstone.
Hywel ab Owain Gwynedd
Exultation.
Poet's Loves, The.

I

I Nagashiro
On a Winter Day Drinking Wine at a Friend's
House in the Country.
"I. T." See "T., I."
Ibarbourou, Juana de
Assignation, The.
Caress, The.
Dawn.
Life-Hook.
Rebel.
Strong Bond, The.
Time.
Woman!
Ibbetson, Julius Caeser
O mortal man, that lives by bread, at.
Ibn Abithur, Joseph
Sanctification.
Ibn Adiya, Al-Samau'al
Now listen to boasting which leaves the heart
dazed, sel.
Oh, Would That I Knew.
Oh, Ye Censurers.
Ibn al-Abbar
You know not how deep was the love your
eyes did kindle.
Ibn al-Arabi
Ode: "They journeyed,/ When the darkness of
night."
Ode: "Who can support the anguish of love?"
Ibn Chasdai, Abraham
Advice to Bores.
Elusive Maid, The.

Meek and the Proud, The.
Poor Scholar, The.
Ibn Darraj al-Andalusi
Wing of Separation, The.
Ibn Ezra, Abraham
Ages of Man, The, at.
Far Sweeter than Honey.
Freedom.
God Everywhere.
God Supreme.
Law, The.
Living God, The.
Out of Luck.
Song of Chess, The.
Ibn Ezra, Moses
All Ye That Go Astray, sel.
Awake, My Soul, sel.
Beautiful Is the Loved One.
Beauty of the Stars, The.
Bring Me the Cup, sel.
Drink, Friends, sel.
Dying Wife to Her Husband, A.
Elegy: "In pain she bore the son who her
embrace."
Elegy: "My thoughts impelled me to the
resting-place."
End of Man Is Death, The.
Garden of Song, The.
God That Doest Wondrously.
He That Regards the Precious Things of
Earth, sel.
Hot Flame of My Grief, The.
I Went Out into the Garden.
In Vain Earth Decks Herself, sel.
Joy of Life, sel.
Man Is a Weaver.
Men Are Children of This World.
My Love is Like a Myrtle.
On My Sorrowful Life.
Promises of the World, The, sel.
Rejoice, O youth, in the lovely hind, sel.
Rosy Days Are Numbered, The, sel.
Sources of My Being, The.
Splendor of Thine Eyes, The.
Strange Love.
Those Beauteous Maids.
To a Plagiarist.
Walk in the Precepts.
When She Plays upon the Harp or Lute.
Why Should I Grieve?
With Hopeless Love.
Without My Friends the Day Is Dark.
Works of God, The.
World Is like a Woman of Folly, The, sel.
Ye Anger Earth, sel.
Young Dove, The.
Ibn Gabirol, Solomon
Almighty! What Is Man?
Before I Was Born.
Defiance.
Degenerate Age, A.
From Thee to Thee.
His Illness.
In Praise of Wisdom.
In the Morning I Look for You.
Invitation.
Meditations.
Morning Song.
My God, sel.
Night.
Night-Thoughts.
O Soul, with Storms Beset.
Separation from the Torah.
Song of the Wind and the Rain.
Stanzas: "With tears thy grief thou dost
bemoan."
Water Song.
Wine and Grief.
Ibn Rashiq
Pretences.
Ibn Sabbatai, Judah
Expensive Wife, The, sel.

Ibn Tibbon, Judah
Father's Testament, A.
Ibn Zaydun
Cordova.
Ibnu 'L-Farid
Let passion's swelling tide my senses drown!
Ibnu 'L-arabi
My heart is capable of every form.
Oh, her beauty—the tender maid! Its
    brilliance gives light.
Ibrahim, Hafiz
Describing a Suit.
Ibsen, Henrik
Brand Speaks, *sel.*
In the Orchard.
Icaza, Francisco A. de
For the Poor Blind Man.
Golden.
Responding Voice.
Wayfaring.
Ichijo Kaneyoshi. *See* **Kaneyoshi**
"Idas." *See* **Wayland, John Elton**
Iddings, Kathleen
Skating in Pleasant Hill, Ohio.
Idley, Peter
Covetousness.
Sources of Good Counsel.
Ietaka (Fujiwara no Ietaka)
Ah, the Sea of Grebes!
All things have an end.
And what now, wood thrush.
As day nears its end.
Autumn.
Bay at Shiga, The.
Bring your first song.
Cries of crickets, The.
Gazing at the sky.
I awoke from sleep.
I look out today.
In my native home.
In the broad dawn sky.
In the evening light.
Lowermost leaves, The.
My ruminations/ are still far from exhausted.
Old Scent of the Plum Tree.
Only yesterday/ I had thought I must visit.
Spring Dawn.
Those cherry blossoms.
To those who await.
What am I to do?
When the new day dawns.
Wild orange tree, The.
With no lover's pledge.
Yoshino River/ with kerria blossoming.
"Ieuan Fardd." *See* **Evans, Evan**
Igjugarjuk
Musk Oxen.
Ignacio, Bruce
Lost.
Ignatow, David
1905.
Against the Evidence.
Allegory, An.
And the Same Words.
Bagel, The.
Boxing Match, The.
Brightness as a Poignant Light.
Business Life, The.
City, The.
Communion.
Dialogue, A.
Dilemma.
Dream.
Dream, The.
Each Day.
Elegy: "I must wait for a stranger to knock on
    my door."
Europe and America.
Father and Son.
First Coffin Poem.
Fly, The.

For One Moment.
Gardeners.
Get the Gasworks.
He got his friends to agree to shoot him
    standing against a stone wall, *sel.*
He Puts Me to Rest.
Heart, The.
I am proud of your soft, brown eyes, *sel.*
In a Dream.
In the spaces between the stars still water
    dances, *sel.*
Journey, The.
Kaddish.
Last Night.
Lying quietly on the bed, *sel.*
My infinite child, hold me to sleep, *sel.*
My Place.
News Report.
Night at an Airport.
No Theory.
Notes for a Lecture.
Park.
Professional, The.
Promenade.
Question, The.
Requiem, A: "My father listening to opera,
    that's me."
Rescue the Dead.
Sediment.
Self-employed.
Signal, The.
Simultaneously.
Six Movements on a Theme.
Sky Is Blue, The.
Suite for Marriage, A.
Sunday at the State Hospital.
There were no hidden motives to his life.
Waiting Inside.
Ihaka, Kingi M.
Te Atairangikaahu.
Iida Dakotsu
Haiku: "Above her sash."
Haiku: "Dragging across."
Haiku: "In the winter lamp."
Haiku: "Iron autumn."
Haiku: "Udders dripping."
Ikeda, Patricia Y.
Card Game; Kinjiro Sawada, A.
Recovery.
Translations.
Ikhnaton. *See* **Akhenaton**
Ikinilik
Song of the Trout Fisher, The.
Ikku, Jippensha. *See* **Jippensha Ikku**
Ikkyu
South of Mount Sumeru.
Ikkyu Sojun
Ten years in the brothels—hard to wear out
    desire.
Iku, Takenaka. *See* **Takenaka Iku**
Ikuzanchu
I was born with a divine jewel.
Ilam Peruvaluti
This World Lives Because.
Ilankiranar
What He Said to His Heart, Arguing against
    Further Ambition and Travel.
Illyés, Gyula
Aboard the Santa Maria.
Afterward.
Approaching Silence, The.
At the Turning Point of Life.
Brazilian Rain Forest.
Cannibal Future.
Complaint on Solipsism.
Consolation.
Early Darkness.
Grass Snake and Fish.
How Soon.
In Dante's Whirlwind.
It Is Five Years Now.

Logbook of a Lost Caravan.
Maker, The.
My Old Man's Dawdling.
On an Infant.
Record, A.
Ruler.
Tilting Sail.
While the Record Plays.
Wonder Castle, The.
Work.
Wreath, A.
Ilott, Percy H.
Witch, The.
Imagawa Ryoshun. *See* **Ryoshun**
Image, Selwyn
Meditation for Christmas, A.
Iman, Yusef
Love Your Enemy.
"I, Mary"
Christmas.
Imber, Naphtali Herz
Hatikvah—a Song of Hope.
Zionist Marching Song.
Imbs, Bravig
Sleep.
Wind Was There, The.
Immanuel di Roma
Elegy: "Floods of tears well from my deepest
    heart, The."
Oh, Let Thy Teachings, *sel.*
On the Wall.
Virtue, *sel.*
Inada, Lawson Fusao
From Our Album.
Plucking Out a Rhythm.
Since When As Ever More.
Inber, Vera
Leningrad: 1943, *sel.*
Ince, Thomas
People, The.
Workman's Home, A.
Inez, Colette
Apothegms and Counsels.
Better to Spit on the Whip than Stutter Your
    Love like a Worm.
Just Dessert.
Mercedes, Her Aloneness.
Waiting for the Doctor.
Woman Who Loved Worms, The.
Ingalls, Jeremy
My Head on My Shoulders.
Ingalls, John James
Opportunity.
Tribute to Grass.
Ingamells, Rex
Golden Bird, The.
Ship from Thames.
There are rock-rooted ranges to dominate, *sel.*
They made impudent inspection of our coast,
    sel.
Inge, Charles Cuthbert
Limerick: "Certain young gourmet of
    Crediton, A."
On Monsieur Coué.
Inge, William Ralph
Limerick: "There was a good Canon of
    Durham."
Limerick: "There was an old man of
    Khartoum," *at.*
Ingelow, Jean
About the Fairies.
Child and Boatman, *sel.*
Dappled sky, a world of meadows, A, *sel.*
Echo and the Ferry.
For Exmoor.
High Tide on the Coast of Lincolnshire
    (1571), The.
Long White Seam, The.
Longing for Home.
Maternity, *sel.*
Noble Tuck-Man, The.

One Morning, Oh, So Early!
Seven Times One—Exultation, *sel.*
Seven Times Three—Love, *sel.*
Seven Times Two—Romance, *sel.*
Sorrow Humanize Our Race.
Ingemann, Bernard Severin
Pilgrim's Song.
Ingen
My sacred sword's invisible.
Ingham, John Hall
Genesis.
George Washington.
Summer Sanctuary, A.
"Ingoldsby, Thomas" (Richard Harris Barham)
Confession, The.
Cynotaph, The, *sel.*
Eheu Fugaces.
Jackdaw of Rheims, The, *sel.*
Lines Left at Mr. Theodore Hook's House in June, 1834.
Ingraham, Nicholas Lloyd
She Would Have Roses.
Woman Back in the Kitchen, The.
Inib-sarri
Letter to Her Father, A.
Inman, P.
Colloam.
Debris clud.
Silos all by a stillness, *sel.*
Inman, Will
Dark brother touches me, The, *sel.*
Innes, Guy
It's Three No Trumps.
"Innsley, Owen" (Lucy White Jennison)
Bondage.
Burden of Love, The.
Dream of Death, A.
Insana, Jolanda
Because I Did Not Want to Ask.
Insha, Insha Allah Khan
Alas, the days of youth fly past.
Away, away, O breeze of the spring.
Billows in love's stormy sea, The.
My heart is constant and of him.
No news whatever came of those.
O Saki, hold my hand awhile.
Turn your face and look.
Insingel, Mark
Descartes.
Gardens, Betrayed, The.
With Heads Held High.
Inskeep-Fox, Sandra
Star Struck.
Iolo Goch
Labourer, The.
Ipcar, Dahlov
Fishes' Evening Song.
Ireland, Kevin
An Open Door.
Auto-da-Fe.
Caroline beside the Sundial.
Deposition.
Educating the Body.
Founder of the Nation, A.
Guide to Perfection, A.
Hidden Message, A.
Literary Exile, The.
Literary Man Observes a Window to the Sky, The.
Literary Tag, A.
My First Forty Years.
Parade: Liberation Day.
Popular Romance, A.
Serious Literary Slip, A.
Striking a Pose.
Ireland, W. H.
To starve, or not to starve? that is the question.
Iremonger, Valentin
Dog, The.

Evening in Summer.
Going Down the Mountain.
Hector.
Icarus.
In New Ross.
In This River.
Invocation: "Ten bloody years with this quill lying."
These Apple Trees.
This Houre Her Vigill.
Toy Horse, The.
Irish, Jeff
Boy Thirteen, A.
"Ironbark." *See* **Gibson, George Herbert**
"Ironquill." *See* **Ware, Eugene Fitch**
Irvin, Eric
Christmas 1942.
Irvin, Margaret
Chanticleer.
Irvine, John
Invocation to Saint Bride.
Little Pets of Saint Mochua, The.
Saint Colm-Cille and the Cairn of Farewell.
Saint Fiacre.
Irving, Minna
Betsy's Battle Flag.
Lincoln Leads.
Wedding Gift, The.
Irving, Washington
Certain Young Lady, A.
Irwin, Mark
Cheese.
It's Tough Being American.
Irwin, Thomas Caulfield
Iphione.
It was a dim October day, *sel.*
With the Dawn.
Irwin, Wallace ("Ginger"; "Hashimura Togo")
Aunt Nerissa's Muffin.
Constant Cannibal Maiden, The.
Fate of the Cabbage Rose, The.
Powerful Eyes o' Jeremy Tait, The.
Reminiscence.
Sea Serpant, The.
Sensitive Sydney.
Worried Skipper, The.
Isaac ben Samuel of Dampière
His Hand Shall Cover Us.
Isaacs, Jorge
Nima, The.
Isaacson, Jose
Pre-Positions.
Isabella (b. c.1180)
Elais Cairel, I want to know.
Isan
Seventy-seven long years.
Isanos, Magda
Apricot Tree.
Ise, Lady
Because we suspected/ the pillow would say "I know."
Correspondence:/ when I have sad thoughts.
Elegy: Ise Lamenting the Death of Empress Onshi.
Even in my dreams/ I must no longer meet you.
Flower of waves, A.
Forsaking the mists.
Hanging from the branches of a green/ willow tree.
If I consider/ My body like the fields.
If it is you, there/ in the light boat on the pond.
Like a ravaged sea/ this bed.
Near a Waterfall at Ryumon.
News of the palace.
Not even in dreams/ Can I meet him anymore.
On Seeing the Field Being Singed.
Seeing the Plum Blossoms by the River.
Seeing the Returning Geese.

They are rebuilding/ the old bridge, the Nagara.
When the fifth month comes.
Ise Tayu
Clear water of the imperial pond, The.
Farmer's clothes are soaked through and never dried, The.
Iselda. *See* **Alais, Iselda** *and* **Carenza**
Ish-Kishor, Sulamith
War.
Ishak, Abu. *See* **Hill, E.**
Isherwood, Christopher
Common Cormorant [or Shag], The.
On His Queerness.
Ishida Hakyo
Haiku: "Dead fly husk."
Haiku: "Sick-room window."
Haiku: "Sparrows scurrying."
Ishigaki Rin
Clams.
Cocoon.
Festival of the Blind.
Island.
Landscape.
Pan, the Pot, the Burning Fire I Have in Front of Me, The.
Roof.
Tseutsuki Pass.
Ishihara Yoshiro
Commerce in the Caucasus.
Fog and Town.
Funeral Trains.
Horse and Riot.
Last Enemy, The.
Night Robbers.
Night's Invitation.
Sancho Panza's Homecoming.
Song of the Ringing in the Ear.
You Heard Him Say Lonely, Now.
Ishikawa Takuboku
Act like a wizard, *sel.*
After a Fruitless Argument.
All I'd wanted was to get on a train, *sel.*
As if my thoughts were secretly listened to, *sel.*
By accident I broke a rice bowl, *sel.*
By the eastern sea, *sel.*
Calling out the station name as if singing, *sel.*
Carrying mother on my back.
Chin buried in the collar of my overcoat, *sel.*
Come to think of it, *sel.*
Coming in front of a mirror store, *sel.*
Cover myself with the quilt, *sel.*
Day when I yearn for home, A.
Die for a thing like that?, *sel.*
Even while pillowing her lap, *sel.*
Everyone's/ heading in the same direction, *sel.*
For fun I carried mother on my back, *sel.*
For thinking somehow tomorrow will bring something good, *sel.*
Heart felt/ as if being sucked into a very dark hole, *sel.*
I believe in the coming of a new tomorrow, I say, *sel.*
I get anxious to die, at times, *sel.*
I got out and for about five blocks, *sel.*
I look at my dirty hands, *sel.*
I push the door and step out, *sel.*
I said those words casually, *sel.*
I scolded my child, *sel.*
I write in the sand.
In a single night.
In the crowd at the station.
In the snow.
It rains,/ and the people of my house look depressed, *sel.*
Let down, I stood in the hall, *sel.*
Like a weak-minded scout, *sel.*
Little man I always see on the streetcar, The, *sel.*

Name known, but no relations or kin in this place, *sel.*
No better than the ordinary in talent, *sel.*
Nurse's hand taking my pulse, The, *sel.*
Old letters!/ I was on such familiar terms, *sel.*
On the far river bank.
On the sand of a sandhill, *sel.*
On the way, a whim, I changed my mind, *sel.*
Parted, I came away and years have passed, *sel.*
Rather than Cry.
Sadness of the lifeless sand, *sel.*
Somehow,/ I feel there are more people than I expect, *sel.*
Taking off my gloves, my hands stop, *sel.*
That creepy feeling you have, *sel.*
That kiss from the past, *sel.*
They might have hurled stones.
Those days I didn't even notice, *sel.*
Though I close my eyes, *sel.*
Through the train window.
Today, my friends seemed.
Uneventfully/ and pleasantly I go on putting on weight, *sel.*
Useless letter, long, yet to be finished, A, *sel.*
Vague sadness, A, *sel.*
Water spurting out of a pump, The, *sel.*
Weeping, sobbing.
When was it?, *sel.*
Wind in the pines, The.
Wishing someone would, *sel.*
Working, working.

Isidorus
On a Fowler.

Ismay, Maureen
Frailty Is Not My Name.
My Grandmother.
Picture of a Woman.
Surviving.
Where Are You My Bright-Eyed Baby?

Isom, Joan Shaddox
Tremolo.

Isonokami no Yakatsugu. *See* **Yakatsugu**

Issa (Kobayashi Issa)
Among the fleeing silverfish, *sel.*
Another round of farting, *sel.*
Asked, "How old?" a child shows its palm.
Awakened by a horse's fart, I see a firefly in the air, *sel.*
Awakened by someone gnashing his teeth, *sel.*
Beautiful, seen through holes.
Beautiful—the sky, *sel.*
Big cat teases a butterfly, A, *sel.*
Blossom drops, and that, A, *sel.*
Brat, tied up, The.
Buddha's Birthday: April 8, 1819, *sel.*
Buddha's Death Day: February 15, 1815, *sel.*
Butterfly comes and takes a butterfly, A, *sel.*
By a clump of grass, *sel.*
Child jumps out of a willow, A.
Child says, "Nammu, Nammu", A.
Cold night: I keep a vigil, *sel.*
Counting the fleabites while suckling her baby.
Crawl, laugh.
Departing wild geese, *sel.*
Door-latch rusted, A, *sel.*
Dragonflies' resting place, *sel.*
Emerging from the nose.
Falling leaves, making no sound, *sel.*
Far-off mountain peaks.
Firefly: a frog opens his mouth a bit, *sel.*
For a fresh start, *sel.*
For fleas, also, the night.
Frog keeps still, A, *sel.*
Frog looks at me, A, *sel.*
Frogs play hide-and-seek, *sel.*
From a brat's sleeve, *sel.*
Garden: a butterfly, The.
Get me that bright moon!

Great sky splendidly darkens, The, *sel.*
He ties him to a breezy tree.
How our child carries them piggyback.
Huge firefly, undulating, A, *sel.*
I know, I know it, *sel.*
I let the sparrows play, *sel.*
In Celebration of a Child's Future.
In the autumn wind a beggar, *sel.*
I've survived, I've survived, *sel.*
Just one mosquito raises a fuss, *sel.*
Kitten twirls around, A, *sel.*
Laconic crow flies by, A, *sel.*
Lending a branch of his antlers, *sel.*
Lying on the ground, I pick young herbs, *sel.*
Melting snow.
Midnight shower—that crying.
Mosquito larva plays alone, A, *sel.*
Mountain mist: a horse-dung cleaner, *sel.*
Must be a good day, *sel.*
My home, where all I touch.
On a potato leaf, by a dewdrop, a snail, *sel.*
On the heavily loaded bull's head, *sel.*
Once upon a time.
One person.
Only one guy and.
Our child, our treasure.
Parent deer hurries back at the wind, A.
Pissing and trembling, *sel.*
Radish-picker, The.
Red sky in the morning.
Seeking in my hut.
Shrike call takes a persimmon thief, A, *sel.*
Slowly, slowly, climb.
Snow gone, the village fills up, *sel.*
Snowy day: the temple hall's, *sel.*
Someone, somewhere—there's.
Sparrow goes in and out of jail, A, *sel.*
Sparrows' friendship breaks up, *sel.*
Spring rain:/ The uneaten ducks.
Stop! don't swat the fly.
Thin little frog.
This is mine, this is mine.
Three ha'pence worth.
Through a long night, *sel.*
Trying to hide her nestlings, a skylark cries.
Under the tree with rice-cake flowers.
Viewing the cherry-blossom.
Well! Hello down there.
Wild geese gone, the cove looks cleared, *sel.*
Wild Goose, Wild Goose.
Willow tickles awake, A, *sel.*
With bland serenity.
World of dew, A.
World of dew is, The.
World of dew is, yes, The.
Wren, The.

Issaia, Nana
Dream.
Sacrifice.

Issan
I've stalked the world.
I've walked the world over.

Ita, Saint
Jesukin, *at.*

Ito Jinsai
Visiting Ichijo-ji.

Ito Sachio
Beyond the back door.
I have forsaken.
No high mountains.
Standing there.
When cowherds begin.

Ito Togai
Impressions of the Countryside.

Ivanov, Vyacheslav Ivanovich
Holy Rose, The.

Ives, George
Message, A.
Once.

Iwa no Hime, Empress
Longing for the Emperor.

Iwaszkiewicz, Jarosław
Quentin Matsys.

Izumi, Lady (Lady Izumi Shikibu)
After the Death of Her Daughter in Child-birth.
As the rains of spring.
Aware that your body cannot follow, *sel.*
Breaking off rock azaleas, *sel.*
Dew that formed remains, The, *sel.*
Don't tell people how it was, *sel.*
Down the mountain into the path of darkness, *sel.*
Elegies for Her Daughter, Ko-Shikibu ("That she may know I love her and miss her"), *sel.*
Elegies for Prince Atsumichi ("Because I do not know where you are"), *sel.*
Elegies for Prince Atsumichi ("Clearly he would notice: in my eyes"), *sel.*
Elegies for Prince Atsumichi ("Dead people come to visit tonight"), *sel.*
Elegies for Prince Atsumichi ("Discard myself—just the thought is bitter"), *sel.*
Elegies for Prince Atsumichi ("I miss your voice as you talked to me"), *sel.*
Elegies for Prince Atsumichi ("I wish I could see you like this snow"), *sel.*
Elegies for Prince Atsumichi ("It would console me to see you"), *sel.*
Elegies for Prince Atsumichi ("No dreams through the night"), *sel.*
Elegies for Prince Atsumichi ("One body, but heart shattered into a thousand pieces"), *sel.*
Elegies for Prince Atsumichi ("Though my heart isn't a summer field"), *sel.*
Elegies for Prince Atsumichi ("You are gone, and I have nothing unhappy to remember"), *sel.*
Even my pillow, not knowing, won't talk, *sel.*
From darkness/ I go onto the road/ of darkness.
From Prince Atsumichi ("I tell myself not to doubt you"), *sel.*
From Prince Atsumichi ("If I speak of love you'll think I am like everyone else"), *sel.*
From that first night.
Harbor plovers calling to their friends, *sel.*
Having waited for this one for this, *sel.*
Here in this world/ I won't live.
I go out of darkness/ Onto a road of darkness.
I left my hills.
I wish you would come.
I look around: because charcoal firing warms the air, *sel.*
I want to see and be seen by you, *sel.*
If I should forget you because of this unhappiness, *sel.*
If you have no time.
If you love me.
If you'd left me unhappy and hadn't come, *sel.*
In Reply ("Don't keep your heart from resenting me"), *sel.*
In Reply ("I don't think you are like everyone else"), *sel.*
In the dusk the path.
It is the time of rain and snow.
Less troublesome than unforgettable, *sel.*
Looking at My Grandchildren, *sel.*
Lost in thought—even the firefly from the marsh, *sel.*
Loving you, my heart may shatter, *sel.*
Moon above the clouds doesn't look like the moon, The, *sel.*
Never could I think/ Our love a worldly commonplace.
No soothing time for someone who thinks of blossoms, *sel.*
No wonder you're grieved this morning, *sel.*
On nights when hail/ falls noisily.
On spring fields there was only snow, *sel.*
On this winter night.

Orange leaves are gone.
Plum fragrance startles me again and again,
  sel.
Recklessly/I cast myself away.
Since that night/ I cannot know myself.
Someone else/ looked at the sky.
There's no color called love in this world, *sel.*
To a Man I Met Only Briefly, *sel.*
To a Man Who Left Me Early in My Life,
  sel.
To a Man Who Said, "You've forgotten me",
  sel.
To a Sage in Harima, *sel.*
To Someone, when I Was Distressed, *sel.*
Today again, quietly and leisurely I make my
  ablutions, *sel.*
Tonight, as hail falls on bamboo leaves, *sel.*
Unaware of my black hair in disorder, *sel.*
We retain the flowers in mind as we pass, *sel.*
When you broke from me.
Which is worse, to love someone far away,
  sel.
Which is worse, to miss someone dead, *sel.*
Which should I think shouldn't exist in this
  world, *sel.*
You left, the mist lingered by the hedge, *sel.*
You told me it was/ because of me.
You rose with eastern clouds and left, *sel.*
You wear the face.

J

"J., L."
  Day at the Farm, A.
"J., M."
  Animal Howl, The.
  Funeral, The.
  Song of a Jewish Boy.
"J., W."
  City Eclogue.
"J. C." *See* **"C., J."**
"J. D." *See* **"D., J."**
"J. H. S." *See* **"S., J. H."**
"J. J. W." *See* **"W., J. J."**
"J. T." *See* **"T., J."**
Jabès, Edmond
  Book Rises Out of the Fire, The.
  Circular Cry, A.
  Condemned, The.
  Pulverized Screen, The.
  Song: "By the wayside," *sel.*
  Song of the Last Jewish Child.
  Song of the Trees of the Black Forest.
  Song: "On the side of the road."
  Water.
Jabra, Jabra Ibrahim
  After Golgotha.
Jaccottet, Philippe
  Black Cascade.
  Dawn.
  Flowers.
  I Walk.
  Perfect.
  Sowing of Tears, A.
  Vigil, The.
  Weight of Stones.
  Where Earth.
  Winter Moon.
Jacinto, Antonio
  Letter from a Contract Worker.
  Monangamba.
  People Went to War, The.
  Punishment for a Wayward Train.
Jacinto, Jaime
  Beads, The.
  Fire Breather, Mexico City, The.

Looking for Buddha.
Reflections on the Death of a Parrot.
Jackett, Will
  Extraordinary Will.
Jackowska, Nicki
  Another Reading.
  Family Outing—a Celebration.
  Insect Kitchen, The.
  Making a Season.
  Meeting, The.
  Sisters, The.
  Two Nights, The.
Jackson, Ada
  Blessed Event.
  I Have a Roof.
Jackson, Angela
  Blackmen: Who Make Morning.
Jackson, Byron. *See* **Jackson, Kathryn** *and*
  Byron Jackson
Jackson, David
  Grandmother Jackson.
Jackson, Fleda Brown
  Jogging Injury, A.
Jackson, Helen Hunt ("H. H."; "Saxe Holm")
  Coronation.
  Doubt.
  Down to Sleep.
  Emigravit.
  Grab-Bag.
  Habeas Corpus.
  Last Prayer, A.
  Morn.
  October's Bright Blue Weather.
  Poppies in the Wheat.
  September [Days Are Here]
  Song of Clover, A.
  That Things Are No Worse, Sire.
Jackson, Kathryn
  Noonday Sun.
Jackson, Kathryn *and* **Byron Jackson**
  Open Range.
Jackson, Laura Riding. *See* **Riding, Laura**
Jackson, Leroy F.
  Beela by the Sea.
  Fun.
  Grandpa Dropped His Glasses.
  How a Puppy Grows.
  I've Got a New Book from My Grandfather
  Hyde.
Jackson, Mae
  Blues Today, The.
  For Some Poets.
  I Remember ("I remember/ January,/ 1968").
  January 3, 1970.
  Reincarnation.
Jackson, Michael
  Art Market: Leopoldville.
  Fille de Joie: Congo.
  Initiation at Firawa.
  Macrocarpas.
  Marriage, A.
  Mask-Maker.
  Moths, The.
  Red Flag, The.
  Return from Luluabourg.
  River Man.
  Seven Mysteries.
  Shape-Shifter.
  Socrates' Death.
  To W.H. Auden at 63.
  Words like branches of deadfall, *sel.*
  You Learned the Stars.
Jackson, Richard
  Greenwood.
Jacob, Hildebrand
  Alarm, The.
  Here Delia's buried at fourscore.
  Judgement of Tiresias, The.
  Swain, give o'er your fond pretension.
  To Cloe.

To Geron.
Writer, The.
Jacob, Max
  Beggar Woman of Naples, The.
  Bibliophile, The.
  Centaur.
  Declamatory Poem.
  In the Hill Country.
  Key, The.
  Literary Manners I.
  Literary Manners II.
  Literature and Poetry.
  Little Poem.
  Miracles Real Miracles.
  My Life.
  Poem: "Hail falls on the ocean, the night
  falls"
  Rue Ravignan, The.
  To Modigliani to Prove to Him That I Am a
  Poet.
  Wallpaper of Mr. R. K., The.
Jacob, Violet
  Gean Trees, The.
  Last o' the Tinkler, The.
  Pride.
  Rowan, The.
  Tam i' the Kirk.
Jacobs, A. C.
  Isaac.
  Painting.
  Poem for My Grandfather.
  Yiddish Poet.
Jacobs, Alex. *See* **Karoniaktatie**
Jacobs, Bertha. *See* **Bertken, Sister.**
Jacobs, Catherine Haydon
  Secret.
Jacobs, Elijah L.
  High Wheat Country.
  Saturday in the County Seat.
Jacobs, Frank
  Bat, The.
Jacobs, Henry Eyster
  Lord Jesus Christ, We Humbly Pray.
Jacobs, Henry S.
  How Goodly Is Thy House.
Jacobs, Leland B.
  Queenie ("Queenie's strong and Queenie's
  tall").
  Taste of Purple.
  That May Morning.
Jacobs, Lucky
  Sacrifice Bunt.
Jacobsen, Josephine
  Animals, The.
  Destinations.
  For Any Member of the Security Police.
  It Is the Season.
  Matadors, The.
  Murmurers, The.
  Rainy Night at the Writers' Colony.
  Reindeer and Engine.
  Sea Fog, The.
  Shade-Seller, The.
  Thief, The.
  When the Five Prominent Poets.
Jacobsen, Rolf
  Country Roads.
  Road's End.
  Sunflower.
Jacobson, Bonnie
  Ah, Miss Barton, *sel.*
  Earl and Lady Chatham, The, *sel.*
  Head Table Wives.
  Sitting Around Waiting for Your Cat to Die.
  Young Writer Smells a Rat, The.
Jacobson, Ethel
  Atomic Courtesy.

Jacoby, Grover
Juxta.

Jacopo da Lentino
Canzonetta: He Will Neither Boast nor
Lament to His Lady.
Canzonetta: Of His Lady, and of His Making
Her Likeness.
Sonnet: Of His Lady in Heaven.
Sonnet: Of His Lady's Face.

Jacopone da Todi
Nativity Song.
Praise of Diseases.
Stabat Mater, at.

Jacot, Emile
Jack Tar.
Wandering Jack.
Who's That A-Knocking?

Jafar, Hasab al-Shaikh
Descent of Abu Nuwas.

Jaffe, Dan
Owl in the Rabbi's Barn, The.
Yahrzeit.

Jago, Richard
Absence.
Goldfinches, The.
Hamlet's Soliloquy Imitated.
Iron Industry in Birmingham, The, sel.

Jahan, Nur, Empress
Moon of Id came, The.
Your love turned my body into water.

Jahin, Salah
Quatrains.

Jakuan
Listening to the Lute.

Jakuren
Drops of pattering rain, The.
Now spring's over, I know not.
One cannot ask loneliness.

Jakushitsu
Mugo's life cry: "Don't be."

Jakusho
Death Bed Poem.

Jalal ed-Din Rumi. See **Rumi, Jalal ed-Din**

Jalib, Habib
My Daughter.

Jallais, Denise
Lullaby for My Dead Child.

Jama, Sheikh Aquib Abdullahi
Prayer for Rain.

James
Graffiti.

James, Alice Archer Sewall
Butterfly, The.
Processionals.
Sinfonia Eroica.

James, Clive
Blood has soaked the bone which hides the
stone, The, sel.
Unsolicited Letters to Five Artists.
Weather's cleared, The. We're filming at
Versailles, sel.

James, Diana
Munition Workers, The.

James, Edward
He had a many-coloured glance like flowers,
sel.
You have returned. You have returned, my
joy, sel.

James, John
Of John Bunyan's Life.
On the Decease of the Religious and
Honourable Jno Haynes Esqr.

James, John and Robert Wedderburn
Balulalow.

James, Nicholas
May poverty, without offence, approach, sel.

James, Thomas
Hunting for Blueberries.
Letter to a Mute.
Letters to a Stranger.

Mummy of a Lady Named Jemutesonekh XXI
Dynasty.
Reasons.
Snakebite.

James I, King of England
Admonition to Montgomerie.
Epitaph on Sir Philip Sidney, An.
Sonnet: "Azured [or Azur'd] vault, the
crystal circles bright, The.
Sonnet on Sir William Alexander's Harsh
Verses after the English Fashion, A.

James I, King of Scotland
Good Counsel.
He Sees His Beloved, sel.
Kingis Quair, The., abr.
Now was there maid fast by the towris wall,
sel.
Spring Song of the Birds.

James V, King of Scotland
Christ's Kirk on the Green, at.
Jolly Beggar, The. at.

Jami, Nuru'ddin Abdu 'R-Rahman
Even from earthly love thy face avert not.

Jamison, Roscoe Conkling
Negro Soldiers, The.

Jammes, Francis
Amsterdam.
Child Reads an Almanac, The ("The child
reads on; her basket of eggs stands by").
Little Donkey, The.
Love.
Prayer to Go to Paradise with the Asses.

Jana Bai
She was my staff and I am blind.

Jandl, Ernst
Death/ Coming, sel.
Dilection.
Figure of Speech.
Forenoons.
Four Attempts at Definition.
Jupiter uninhabited.
Lifeboat/ drown, sel.
Lying, with You.
On Rainy Shadows.
On the Life of Trees.
Perfection.
Pockets.
Travelogue.
Verdict.
Weather or not/ born, sel.
Woman at the Window.

Jandl, Hermann
Bad Mirror.
Happiness.
It.
Jogger from Schönbrunn, The.
Reading, The.
Successful Attempt.

Janeczko, Paul B.
After the Rain.
Lesson for Dreamers.
Teresa's Red Adidas.
This Poem Is for Nadine.

Janik, Phyllis
In the Field.
Story of Good, The.

Janitschek, Marie
Modern Woman, A.

Janosco, Beatrice
Garden Hose, The.

Janowitz, Phyllis
Although I Am Taking Courses in the
Language.
Change.
Fat Lena's Recipe for Crocodile Soup.
Visiting Rites.

Janvier, Francis DeHaes
God Save Our President.

Janvier, Thomas A.
Santiago.

Janvier, Margaret Thomson. See
"Vandegrift, Margaret"

Jaques, Edna
In Flanders Now.

Jaques, Florence Page
Dragonfly.
There Once Was a Puffin.

Jarman, Mark
By-Blows.
Cavafy in Redondo.
Clues to Displaced Persons.
Desire of Water, The.
Gift, The.
In Hell.
Le Touquet.
Supremes, The.
To the Reader.

Jarman, Wrenne
It Happened Before.
Neutral, The.
Plastic Airman.
Threnody for Berlin—1945.

Jarrell, Randall
Aging.
Augsburg Adoration, The.
Author to the Reader, The.
Bats.
Bird of Night, The.
Black Swan, The.
Blind Sheep, The.
Burning the Letters.
Camp in the Prussian Forest, A.
Chipmunk, The.
Chipmunk's Day , The.
Cinderella.
Come to the Stone.
Country Life, A.
Death of the Ball Turret Gunner, The.
Eighth Air Force.
Elementary Scene, The.
Emancipators, The.
Field and Forest.
Front, A.
Game at Salzburg, A.
Girl in a Library, A.
Gunner.
Hope.
House in the Wood, The.
Hunt in the Black Forest, A.
In Galleries.
In Montecito.
In Nature There Is neither Right nor Left nor
Wrong.
Islands, The.
Jamestown.
Jerome.
Jews at Haifa.
Kirilov on a Skyscraper.
Knight, Death, and the Devil, The.
Lonely Man, The.
Losses.
Lost Children, The.
Lullaby, A: "For wars his life and half a
world away."
Märchen, The.
Mockingbird, The.
Nestus Gurley.
Next Day.
90 North.
Officer's Prison Camp Seen from a Troop
Train, An.
Old and the New Masters, The.
Orient Express, The.
Owl's Bedtime Story, The.
Pilots, Man Your Planes.
Player Piano, The.
Prisoners.
Protocols.
Range in the Desert, The.
Refugees, The.
Say Goodbye to Big Daddy.

Second Air Force.
Seele im Raum.
Sick Child, A.
Sick Nought, The.
Sleeping Beauty; Variation of the Prince, The.
Snow-Leopard, The.
Soldier (T. P.).
Soldier Walks under the Trees of the
     University, The.
Soul, A.
State, The.
Thinking of the Lost World.
To the New World.
Truth, The.
Variations.
War, A.
Ways and the Peoples, The.
Well Water.
When I was Home Last Christmas.
Woman at the Washington Zoo, The.
Jarrett, Emmett
Dear Mother.
For E. C. J.
"Hamlet."
Human Relations.
Song: "Help me now."
Trip, The.
Two of Cups, The.
Jastrun, Mieczyslaw
Beyond Time.
Jews, The.
Man.
Remembrance.
Woman Who Suddenly Entered the Room, A.
Jaszi, Jean
Home.
Jaufré Rudel
When, from the spring, the stream.
When the days are long in May.
Jausbert de Puycibot
Because I had reproached him where he
     failed.
Jauss, David
Ghost Dance: August, 1976, The.
Oliver Johnson Comes Back to Bed the
     Morning after the Ice Storm and Tells His
     Wife Why.
On Certain Mornings Everything Is Sensual.
Javitz, Alexander
Old Men, The.
Jay, Peter
Iowa Recollected in Tranquility.
Jayadeva
Hymn to Vishnu, *sel.*
Sandal and garment of yellow and lotus
     garlands upon his body of blue, *sel.*
Jayyusi, Salma Khadra
April Woman.
On Visiting the M. D. Anderson.
Scrapping Limits.
Ship of Love, The.
Jean Valentine
He Said.
Jeffers, Lance
Black Soul of the Land.
Breath in My Nostrils.
Grief Streams Down My Chest.
How High the Moon.
Love Pictures You as Black and Long-faced.
My Blackness Is the Beauty of This Land.
Nina Simone.
On Listening to the Spirituals.
Trellie.
Who Shined Shoes in Times Square.
Jeffers, Robinson
Age in Prospect.
Animals.
Answer, The.
Ante Mortem.
Antrim.
Apology for Bad Dreams.

Artist, An.
Ascent to the Sierras.
Ave Caesar.
Beaks of Eagles, The.
Beauty of Things, The.
Birds.
Birds and Fishes.
Birth-Dues.
Black-out.
Bloody Sire, The.
Boats in a Fog.
But I Am Growing Old and Indolent.
Calm and Full the Ocean.
Carmel Point.
Cassandra.
Clouds of Evening.
Compensation.
Continent's End.
Credo.
Crumbs or the Loaf.
Deer Lay Down Their Bones, The.
Divinely Superfluous Beauty.
Eagle Valor, Chicken Mind.
Evening Ebb.
Eye, The.
Fawn's Foster-Mother.
Fire on the Hills.
Fourth Act.
Gale in April.
Granite and Cypress.
Grass on the Cliff, *sel.*
Gray Weather.
Hands.
Haunted Country.
Hurt Hawks.
I Shall Laugh Purely.
Inquisitors, The.
Iona; the Graves of the Kings.
Joy.
Life from the Lifeless.
Love the Wild Swan.
Maid's Thought, The.
May-June, 1940.
New Mexican Mountain.
Night.
Noon.
Nova.
November Surf.
Oh, Lovely Rock.
Original Sin.
Pelicans.
Phenomena.
Place for No Story, The.
Post Mortem.
Prescription of Painful Ends.
Promise of Peace.
Purse-Seine, The.
Rearmament.
Return.
Roan Stallion.
Rock and Hawk.
Salmon-fishing.
Science.
Self-Criticism in February.
Shane O'Neill's Cairn.
Shine, Perishing Republic.
Shine, Republic.
Shiva.
Signpost.
Stars Go over the Lonely Ocean, The.
Still the Mind Smiles.
Summer Holiday.
To His Father.
To the Stone-Cutters.
Vulture.
Watch the Lights Fade.
Woodrow Wilson.
Jefferson, Joseph
Immortality.
Jefferys, Charles
Jeannette and Jeannot.

Jeannot's Answer.
We Have Lived and Loved Together.
Jeffrey, Francis, Lord Jeffrey
Epitaph: "Here lies the body of Richard
     Hind."
Like to a baker's oven is the grave.
On Peter Robinson.
Jeffrey, William
Carlyle on Burns, *sel.*
Glen Rosa.
Stones.
Jeffries, Christie
Lone Huntsman.
Jeffries, Charles.   *See* **Jefferys, Charles**
Jeitteles, Alois
To My Distant Beloved.
Jeitteles, Benedict
Epitaph for a Judge.
Jékely, Zoltán
Elegy of a Bronze Age Man, The.
Jekyll, Joseph
See, one physician, like a sculler, plies.
Jemmat, Catherine
Rural Lass, The.
Jenkins, Christina
Sunday Morning.
Jenkins, Louis
Library.
Violence on Television.
Jenkins, Oliver
Merry-go-round.
Time Out.
Jenks, Orville
Dying Mine Brakeman, The.
Jenks, Tudor
Accommodating Lion, An.
Hard to Bear.
On the Road.
Small and Early.
Spirit of the.
Jenner, Edward
Sent to a Patient, with the Present of a Couple
     of Ducks.
Signs of Rain.
Jennett, Sean
Cycle.
Island, The.
Mahoney.
Merchandise.
My Subtle and Proclamant Song.
Old Joyce.
Omphalos: The Well.
Jennings, Elizabeth
Afterthought.
Ago.
Animals' Arrival, The.
Answers.
Beyond Possession.
Birthday in Hospital, A.
Child and the Shadow, The.
Climbers, The.
Communication.
Counterpart, The.
Delay.
Disguises.
Escape and Return.
Father to Son.
Fear of Death, The.
For a Child Born Dead.
Fountain.
Fragment for the Dark.
Ghosts.
Harvest and Consecration.
I Feel.
I wish, God, for some end I do not will, *sel.*
Identity.
Idler, The ("Idler holds that rose as always
     rose, An.").
In a Garden.
In the Night.
Interrogator, The.

Meditation on the Nativity.
Men Fishing in the Arno.
Mirrors.
Not in the Guide-Books.
Old Man.
One Flesh.
Parting, The.
Rembrandt's Late Self-Portraits.
Room, The.
Song at the Beginning of Autumn.
Song for a Birth or a Death.
Song for a Departure.
Storm, The.
Storm House, The.
Teresa of Avila.
Thinking of Love.
To a Friend with a Religious Vocation.
To My Mother at 73.
Unknown Child, The.
Visitation, The.
Way of Looking, A.
Weathercock.
Winter Love.
World of Light, A.
Young Ones, The.

Jennings, Humphrey
Prose Poem.

Jennings, Leslie Nelson
Belden Hollow.

Jennings, Paula
Lesbian.

Jennison, Lucy White. *See* **"Innsley, Owen"**

Jensen, Laura
After I Have Voted.
Age, An.
Ajax Samples, The.
As the Window Darkens.
Candles Draw Well after All, The.
Cloud Parade, The.
House Is an Enigma.
Household.
In the Hospital.
Indian.
Kite.
Probably the Farmer.
Red Dog, The.
Retired Lion by the Clothesline in the Cold Attic.
Sleep in the Heat.
Talking to the Mule.
Tapwater.
Winter Evening Poem.

Jenyns, Soame
Dare I in such momentous points advise, *sel.*
Doctor Johnson.
For love no time has she, or inclination, *sel.*
In days, my Lord, when mother Time, *sel.*
Just broke from school, pert, impudent, and raw, *sel.*
Modern Fine Gentleman, The.
Modern Fine Lady, The.
Now haste, my Muse, pursue thy destin'd way, *sel.*
Snow-Ball, The.
Temple of Venus, The.

Jephcott, Sydney
Thredbo River.

Jerome, Judson
Child's Game.
Deer Hunt.
Eve: Night Thoughts.
Hunk, The.
Private Feast, A.

"Jerry, Bongo" (Robin Small)
Mabrak.

Jesse, F. Tennyson
Note to Isolationists 1940.

Jesús, Teresa de
All of a Sudden.
They go by, go by, love, the days and the hours.

Jewett, Ellen A.
Sermon in a Stocking.

Jewett, John H.
Those Rebel Flags.

Jewett, Sarah Orne
Country Boy in Winter, A.

Jewett, Sophie ("Ellen Burroughs")
Armistice.
If Spirits Walk.
In the Dark.
Least of Carols, The.
Smiling Demon of Notre Dame, A.
Song: "Thy face I have seen as one seeth."
When Nature Hath Betrayed the Heart That Loved Her.

Jewsbury, Maria Jane
Partings.
To a Young Brother.

Jigmed, Chimedin
For the Cultural Campaign.
There is drink fermented, *sel.*

Jiles, Paulette
Paper Matches.
Time to Myself.
Tin Woodsman, The.
Windigo.

Jiménez, Juan Ramón
Faithful Blackbird.
Full Consciousness.
Galente Garden: II.
Lamb Was Bleating Softly, The.
She Came, at First, Pure.
When, with You Asleep.
Winter Song.

Jin, Meiling
Disaster.
No More Fighting.
On Hurt.
Secret Woman.
Strangers in a Hostile Landscape.

Jinsai, Ito. *See* **Ito Jinsai**

Jippensha Ikku
Deathbed Verse.

Jisso
Fifty-four years I've entered.

Jito, Empress
Spring is passing and.

Jitrik, Noe
Addio a la Mamma.

Jittei
Life and death? Shoving a cart.

Joachim, Paulin
Burial.

Joad, C. E. M.
Materialism.

Joan, Natalie
Dicky-Birds.
Kind Mousie, The.

Joans, Ted
Its Curtains.
Lester Young.
Love Tight.
Miles' Delight ("Miles Davis").
Protective Grigri, The.
Scenery.
.38, The.
Truth, The.

Joben
Cherries are blooming.
Cold Reeds around the Inlet.
Crimson Leaves.
Did it perhaps.
Early Autumn.
If not for the bamboos.

Jodorowsky, Raquel
Here We Are.
I Do Not Relate.
Man Is an Animal That Laughs.
Secret.

Johannes Secundus (Jan Nicolai Everaerts)
Not alwayes give a melting kiss, *sel.*

Johansson, Majken
Proportion Poetry.

"John"
Ode to the Last Pot of Marmalade.

John, Gwen
Child's Winter Evening, A.

John Damascene, St. *See* **John of Damascus, Saint**

John of Damascus, Saint
Day of Resurrection, The.

John of the Cross, Saint
Commentary Applied to Spiritual Things.
Dark Night, The.
I live without inhabiting/ Myself, *sel.*
More Stanzas Applied to Spiritual Things.
O Flame of Living Love.
Obscure Night of the Soul, The.
Song of the Soul That Knows God by Faith.
Song of the Soul that Rejoices in Knowing God through Faith.
Stanzas Concerning an Ecstasy Experienced in High Contemplation.
Stanzas of the Soul that Suffers with Longing to See God.
Upon a darksome night.

Johnson, Alicia Loy
Black Lotus.

Johnson, Amryl
Blue Flame, The.
Circle of Thorns.
Dying in the Street.
Like Dogs.
Watchers and Seekers.

Johnson, Burges
Anxious Farmer, The.
Soap, the Oppressor.

Johnson, Charles Bertram
Little Cabin, A.
Negro Poets.

Johnson, Charles Frederick
Modern Romans, The.
Then and Now.

Johnson, Denis
Boarding, The.
In Palo Alto.
Minutes.
Movie within a Movie.
Passengers.
Rockefeller Collection of Primitive Art, The.
Sway.
Travelling.
Veil, The.
Woman, A.

Johnson, Don Allen ("Mustafa")
Above the Falls at Waimea.
Brainwashing Dramatized.
Fountain, The.
For Wilma.
I Traveled with Them.
Night Dive.
Sergeant, The.
Thy Garden.
Tick Picking in the Quetico.

Johnson, Dorothy Vena
Epitaph for a Bigot.
Green Valley.

Johnson, Edward
Among These Troopes of Christs Souldiers, Came. Mr. Roger Harlackenden.
Good News from New-England.
Mr. Eliot Pastor of the Church of Christ at Roxbury.
Mr. Thomas Shepeard.
Oh King of Saints, how great's thy work, say we.
Onely the Reverend Grave and Godly Mr. Buckly Remaines.
Reverend Mr, The Higginson.
With hearts revived in conceit, new land and trees they eye, *sel.*
Yee Shall Not Misse of a Few Lines in Remembrance of Thomas Hooker.

Johnson, Emily Pauline ("Tekahionwake")
Cattle Thief, The.
Corn Husker, The.
Marshlands.
Ojistoh.
Shadow River.
Song My Paddle Sings, The.
Trail to Lillooet, The.
Johnson, Esther ("Stella")
To Dr. Swift on His Birthday, 30th November
  1721.
Johnson, Fenton
Another sate near him, whose harp of gold,
  sel.
Aunt Jane Allen.
Banjo Player, The.
Children of the Sun.
Counting.
Daily Grind, The.
Lonely Mother, The.
Marathon Runner, The.
Negro Peddler's Song, A.
New Day, The.
Old Repair Man, The.
Puck Goes to Court.
Rulers: Philadelphia.
Scarlet Woman, The.
Tired.
When I Die.
Who Is That a-Walking in the Corn?
World Is a Mighty Ogre, The.
Johnson, Fred
Arabesque.
Coda.
Fire, Hair, Meat and Bone.
Noises.
Johnson, George Sands
Beyond the Beaten Way.
By the Pasture Bars.
Christmas Rhyme, A.
Course of a Year, The.
Deacon Brown's Conclusion.
I Am Growing Old.
If We Try.
Old Rustic Mill, The.
Uncle Sam's Soliloquy.
Wisdom.
Johnson, Georgia Douglas
Common Dust.
Conquest.
Credo.
Dreams of the Dreamer, The.
Escape.
Heart of a Woman, The.
Hope.
I Closed My Shutters Fast Last Night.
I Want to Die While You Love Me.
Interracial.
Lethe.
Little Son.
Lovelight.
My Little Dreams.
Old Black Men.
Poet Speaks, The.
Prejudice.
Proving.
Recessional.
Remember.
Riddle, The.
Service.
Smothered Fires.
Suppliant, The.
Trifle.
Welt.
What Need Have I for Memory?
When I Am Dead.
Your World ("Your world is as big as you
  make it").
Youth.
Johnson, Halvard
Americans Playing Slow-Pitch Softball at an
  Airbase near Kunsan, South Korea.

Extra-Inning Ballgame, The.
Spiel.
Johnson, Helen Armstead
Affirmation.
Philodendron.
Johnson, Helene
Bottled [New York]
Fulfillment.
Invocation: "Let me be buried in the rain."
Magalu.
Poem: "Little brown boy."
Remember Not.
Road, The.
Sonnet to a Negro in Harlem.
Summer Matures.
Trees at Night.
What Do I Care for Morning.
Johnson, Herbert Clark
Boy's Need, A.
Crossing a Creek.
On Calvary's Lonely Hill.
Willow Bend and Weep.
Johnson, Hilda
Ballade of Expansion.
Johnson, James Weldon
Brothers.
Creation, The.
Envoy: "If homely virtues draw from me a
  tune."
Fifty Years.
From the German of Uhland.
Glory of the Day Was in Her Face, The.
Go Down Death.
Lift Every Voice and Sing.
Listen, Lord—[a Prayer]
Mother Night.
My City.
O Black and Unknown Bards.
Sence You Went Away.
Up from the Bed of the River, *sel.*
White Witch, The.
Johnson, Joe
Anna.
If I Ride This Train.
Judeebug's Country.
Samurai and Hustlers.
True Love.
Johnson, Josephine
Supplication.
Johnson, Judith Emlyn
Argument One: The Lady Shews How She Is
  Foresaken for a Piece of Wood.
Johnson, Linton Kwesi
Bass Culture.
Great Insohreckshan, Di.
Reggae fi Dada.
Johnson, Lionel Pigot
Age of a Dream, The.
Ah! fair face gone from sight, *sel.*
Beyond.
By the Statue of King Charles at Charing
  Cross.
Church of a Dream, The.
Dark Angel, The.
Darkness, The.
Dead.
Doctor Major.
Laleham: Matthew Arnold's Grave.
Lambeth Lyric.
London Town.
Mystic and Cavalier.
Oxford.
Oxford Nights.
Precept of Silence, The.
Roman Stage, The.
Saint Columba.
Sancta Silvarum.
Stranger, A.
Summer Storm.
Te Martyrum Candidatus.
To a Traveler.

To Morfydd.
Troopship, The.
Victory.
Johnson, Louis
At Large in the Eighties.
Before the Day of Wrath, *sel.*
Birthday, The.
Bread and a Pension.
Coming and Going.
Death of the Bosun's Mate.
Elephant.
Haven, *sel.*
He Smelt the Smell of Death within the
  Marrow.
Here Together Met.
Magpie and Pines.
Marrows.
Matter of Urgency.
Mouse, The.
New Guinea Time.
New Worlds for Old.
Perfect Symbol, The.
Seventies, The.
Spring, *sel.*
Tahiti.
Uneasy Resident.
Vision.
Wellington.
What Became of the Family?
Johnson, Maggie Pogue
Ambition.
As We Sow We Shall Reap.
Christmas Times.
Dat Mule ob Brudder Wright's.
De Day befo' Thanksgibin.'
Dedicated to Dr. W. H. Sheppard.
Dedication Day.
Dream, A.
I Wish I Was a Grown Up Man.
James Hugo Johnston.
Krismas Dinnah.
Leap Yeah Party, De.
Lost Teddy Bear, The.
Meal Time.
Men Folks ob Today, De.
Negro Has a Chance, The.
Old Maid's Soliloquy.
People's Literary, De.
Poet of Our Race.
Sister Johnson's Speech.
Sometimes.
Story of Lovers Leap, The.
Strawberry, The.
Superstitions.
Thoughts.
To Professor Byrd Prillerman.
To See Ol' Booker T.
V. N. and C. I, The.
What's de Use ob Wukin in de Summer Time
  at All.
What's Mo' Temptin' to de Palate?
When Daddy Cums from Wuk.
Why Should the American Negro Be Proud?
Wintah Styles, De.
Johnson, Margaret
Day Dreams, or Ten Years Old.
Johnson, Nick
Dudes.
Greasin' the Miles.
Johnson, Norman M.
Hob the Elf.
Johnson, Pauline. *See* **Johnson, Emily**
  Pauline.
Johnson, Pyke, Jr.
Picnic at the Beach.
Report after a Walk along the Avenue.
Toucan, The.
Johnson, Robert
Love in Vain.
Johnson, Robert Underwood
As a Bell in a Chime.

Blossom of the Soul, The.
Browning at Asolo.
Dewey at Manila. In Tesla's Laboratory.
Silence was envious of the only voice, *sel.*
To the Returning Brave.
Wistful Days, The.

Johnson, Roger
To His Mistress, Dead and Darkly Return'd.

Johnson, Ronald
But are these landscapes to be imagined, *sel.*
I, too, have plucked a stalk of grass, *sel.*
Let us tunnel, *sel.*
Letters to Walt Whitman, II.
Slant sheen/ wrinkled silver, *sel.*

Johnson, Rossiter
Evelyn.
Soldier Poet, A.

Johnson, Samuel (1709–84)
Anacreon's Dove.
Ballad: "I put my hat upon my head."
By numbers here from shame or censure free, *sel.*
City of God.
Comets and Princes.
Epitaph on William Hogarth.
Epitaph upon the Celebrated Claudy Phillips, Musician, Who Died Very Poor, An.
Hermit Hoar.
Life's Last Scene, *sel.*
Lines on Thomas Warton's Poems *or* Lines in Ridicule of Certain Poems Published in 1777.
London.
On a Daffodil, the First Flower the Author Had Seen That Year.
On the Death of Mr. [*or* Dr.] Robert Levet, a Practiser in Physic.
On what foundation stands the warrior's pride, *sel.*
Power of Prayer, The, *sel.*
Prepare for death, if here at night you roam, *sel.*
Prologue Spoken [by Mr. Garrick] [at the Opening of the Theatre in Drury-Lane, 1747]
Prologue to Hugh Kelly's "A Word to the Wise."
Short Song of Congratulation [*or* To a Young Heir], A.
To Mrs. Thrale [on Her Thirty-fifth Birthday]
Translation of Lines by Benserade.
To robbers furious, and to lovers tame.
Unnumbered suppliants crowd preferment's gate, *sel.*
When first the college rolls receive his name, *sel.*

Johnson, Samuel (1822–82)
Father, in Thy Mysterious Presence Kneeling.
I Bless Thee, Lord, for Sorrows Sent.
Life of Ages, Richly Poured.

Johnson, Siddie Joe
Midnight in Bonnie's Stall.

Johnson, Victoria Saffelle
Dedication: "Holy Jesus, Thou art born."

Johnson, William Martin
On Snow-Flakes Melting on His Lady's Breast.

Johnston, Bertha
Did You Ever Hear an English Sparrow Sing?

Johnston, George
Bliss.
Bulge, The.
Cathleen Sweeping.
Indoors.
Music on the Water.
Noctambule.
O Earth, Turn!
Veterans.
War on the Periphery.

Johnston, Martin
Airport.

Directions for Dreamfishing.
Quantum.
Vernal Equinox.

Johnston, Sir Charles
Air Travel in Arabia.

Joho
Fathomed at last!

Joju
Twenty-odd years in doubt.

Jokushi
Carrying his wife on his back a frog.

Jonas, George
Eight Lines for a Script Girl.
Exit Lines.
For the Record.
Four Stanzas Written in Anxiety.
Glass Eaters, The.
Let me put it this way.
Once More.
Peace.
Portrait: The Freedom Fighter.
Single naked wire at ground level, A, *sel.*
Sleep only with strangers.
Temporal.
We all have/ A bench in the park to reach.
Women don't travel in clubcars.

Jonas, Gerald
In Passing.
Night Thought.

Jonas, Rosalie
Ballade des Belles Milatraisses.
Brother Baptis' on Woman Suffrage.

Jonas, Samuel Alroy
Lines on the Back of a Confederate Note.

Jonas, Steve
Poem: "It's a dull poem."

Jones, Amanda Theodosia
Panama.

Jones, Bobi
Portrait of a Nun.
Portrait of a Pregnant Woman.
Portrait of an Engine Driver.
Spring at Nant Dywelan.

Jones, Charles L. S.
Fort Bowyer.
Hero of Bridgewater, The.

Jones, Cullen
Now That the Flowers.

Jones, D. G.
River; North of Guelph, The.

Jones, David
A, a, a, Domine Deus.
And the place of their waiting a long burrow, *sel.*
And to Private Ball it came, *sel.*
Angle-Land, *sel.*
But sweet sister death has gone debauched today and stalks, *sel.*
But why is Father Larkin talking to the dead?, *sel.*
Did he meet Lud at the Fleet Gate? did count the top, *sel.*
Five Unmistakable Marks, The, *sel.*
King Pellam's Launde, *sel.*
Ship's master:/ before him, in the waist and before it, *sel.*
Tawny-black sky-scurries, *sel.*
Wall, The.
You can hear the silence of it, *sel.*

Jones, David Gwenallt ("Gwenallt")
Cymru.
Earth, The.
Old Woman, An.
Rhydcymerau.

Jones, Douglas G.
Beautiful Creatures Brief as These.
For Spring.
From Sex, This Sea.
I Thought There Were Limits.
On a Picture of Your House.
Perishing Bird, The.

Soliloquy to Absent Friends.
These Trees Are No Forest of Mourners.

Jones, Ebenezer
Development of Idiotcy, A.
Eyeing the Eyes of One's Mistress.
High Summer.
When the World Is Burning.
Whimper of Awakening Passion.
Winter Hymn—to the Snow, A.

Jones, Edward Smyth
Song of Thanks, A.

Jones, Elijah
How Big Was Alexander?

Jones, Ellis
Eaves.

Jones, Ernest Charles
Chartist Chorus, A.
Leawood Hall.
Poet's Mission, The.
Song of the Low, The.
Song of the Lower Classes, The.

Jones, Evan
Genesis.
Lament of the Banana Man, The.
Noah's Song.
November 1956.
Song of the Banana Man, The.
Walking with R. B.

Jones, G. W.
Portrait of the Pornographer.

Jones, Gayl
Many Die Here.
3-31-70, *sel.*
Satori.
Tripart.

Jones, Glyn
Again.
Esyllt.
Profile of Rose.

Jones, Gwilym R.
Psalm to the Creatures.

Jones, Gwyn
Blue Day Journey, The.

Jones, H. Bedford
How Do You Do?

Jones, Howard
Fall To.

Jones, John
To Lydia, with a Coloured Egg, on Easter Monday.

Jones, John P.
Silver Jack.

Jones, Joshua Henry
To a Skull.

Jones, Lawrence M.
I Am the Flag.

Jones, LeRoi. *See* **Baraka, Imamu Amiri**

Jones, Louise Seymour
Who Loves a Garden.

Jones, M. Keel
Election Reflection.

Jones, Mary Hoxie
Four Deer, The.

Jones, Patricia
I Done Got So Thirsty That My Mouth Waters at the Thought of Rain.
Why I Like Movies.

Jones, Rae Desmond
Age.

Jones, Rodney
First Birth, The.
For the Eating of Swine.
Mosquito, The.
Remembering Fire.
Sweep.
Thoreau.

Jones, Samuel
Force of Love, The.

Ploughman, in Imitation of Milton, The.
Poverty, in Imitation of Milton.

Jones, T. Gwynn
Argoed.

Jones, T. H.
Difference.
Welshman in Exile Speaks, The.

Jones, Thomas
This is Thomas Jones's book.

Jones, Thomas S., Jr.
As in a Rose-Jar.
Path of the Stars, The.

Jones, Thomas Samuel, Jr.
Daphne.

Jones, Sir William
Epigram: "On parent knees, a naked new-born child."
What Constitutes a State?

Jong, Erica
Alcestis on the Poetry Circuit.
Becoming a Nun.
Buddha in the Womb, The.
Climbing You.
How You Get Born.
In Praise of Clothes.
In Sylvia Plath Country.
Jubilate Canis.
Man under the Bed, The.
Mother.
Seventeen Warnings in Search of a Feminist Poem.
Wives of Mafiosi, The.
Woman Who Loved to Cook, The.

Jonker, Ingrid
Begin Summer.
Child Who Was Shot Dead by Soldiers at Nyanga, The.
Dark Stream.
Dog.
Don't Sleep.
Face of Love, The.
I Am with Those.
I Don't Want Any More Visitors.
I Drift in the Wind.
Journey round the World.
Ladybird.
Lost City.
Pregnant Woman.
This Journey.
Time of Waiting in Amsterdam.
25 December 1960.
When You Laugh.
When You Write Again.

Jonson, Ben
All Your Fortunes We Can Tell Ye, *sel.*
Angel Describes Truth, An, *sel.*
Another Ladyes Exception Present at the Hearing, *sel.*
Begging Another, on Colour of Mending the Former, *sel.*
Ben. Johnsons Sociable Rules for the Apollo.
Buz, Quoth the Blue Fly, *sel.*
Chorus: "Spring all the Graces of the age," *sel.*
Clayming a Second Kisse by Desert, *sel.*
Come, my Celia, let us prove, *sel.*
Come on, sir. Now, you set your foot on shore, *sel.*
Dream[e], The.
Elegie, An: "Let me be what I am, as Virgil cold."
Elegie on the Lady Jane Pawlet, Marchion: of Winton, An.
Elegy, An: "Though beauty be the mark of praise."
Epigram, to the Household, 1630, An.
Epistle Answering to One That Asked to be Sealed of the Tribe of Ben, An.
Epistle to a Friend, to Persuade Him to the Wars, An.

Epitaph on Elizabeth, L. H.
Epitaph on Master Philip Gray, An.
Epitaph on Master Vincent Corbett, An.
Epitaph on S. P. [Salomon *or* Salathiel Pavy], a Child of Queen Elizabeth's Chapel.
Epode.
Execration upon Vulcan, An.
Faery Beam upon You, The, *sel.*
Fit of Rime against Rime, A.
Fools, They Are the Only Nation, *sel.*
Glove, The.
Glove, The, *sel.*
Have you seen but a bright lily grow, *sel.*
Her Man Described by Her Owne Dictamen, *sel.*
Her Triumph.
Here She Was Wont to Go, *sel.*
His Discourse with Cupid, *sel.*
His Excuse for Loving, *sel.*
Hour Glass, The ("Consider this small dust, here in the glass").
Hourglass [*or* The Houre-Glasse], The ("Do but consider this small dust").
How did she leave the world? with what contempt?, *sel.*
How He Saw Her, *sel.*
Hymn [*or* Hymne] on the Nativity [*or* Nativitie] of My Saviour, A.
Hymn to Comus, *sel.*
Hymn to Diana, *sel.*
Hymn to God the Father, A.
I, therefore, will begin. Soul of the age!, *sel.*
I will have all my beds blown up, not stuft, *sel.*
In the Person of Woman Kind.
Inviting a Friend to Supper.
It Is Not Growing Like a Tree, *sel.*
It Was a Beauty That I Saw, *sel.*
Lincolnshire; from the Wolds to the Fens, *sel.*
Mab the Mistress-Fairy, *sel.*
Masque of Christmas, The.
Mother Maudlin the Witch, *sel.*
My Picture Left in Scotland.
New yeares, expect new gifts: Sister, your Harpe.
New-Yeares-Gift Sung to King Charles, 1635, A.
Noble Balm, The.
Nymph's Secret, A.
O sacred poesie, thou spirit of artes, *sel.*
Ode to Himself, An.
Ode to Himsel[f]e ("Come leave the loathed stage").
Ode to Sir William Sydney, on His Birth-Day.
On Court-Worme.
On Don Surly.
On English Monsieur.
On Giles and Joan.
On Gut.
On Lieutenant Shift.
On Lucy Countesse of Bedford.
On Margaret Ratcliffe.
On My First Daughter.
On My First Son [*or* Sonne]
On Playwright.
On Poet-Ape.
On Something, That Walks [*or* Walkes] Somewhere.
On Spies.
Pans Anniversarie.
Praises of a Country Life, The.
Queen and Huntress.
Return of Astraea, The.
Slow, Slow, Fresh Fount, *sel.*
Song: "An eye of looking back were well," *sel.*
Song: "Come on, come on! and where you go," *sel.*

Song: "Great friend and servant of the good," *sel.*
Song: "If I freely may discover," *sel.*
Song: "It follows now you are to prove," *sel.*
Song: "O more, and more! this was so well," *sel.*
Song, A: "Oh do[e] not wanton with those eyes."
Song: "Ope, aged Atlas, open then thy lap," *sel.*
Song: "Still to be neat, still to be dressed," *sel.*
Song: "To the old, long life and treasure," *sel.*
Song: "Wake, Hercules, awake: but heave up thy black eye," *sel.*
Still to Be Neat [Still to Be Drest (*or* Dressed)], *sel.*
Sweet Swan of Avon! what a sight it were, *sel.*
There is no bountie to be shew'd to such, *sel.*
Though I Am Young and Cannot Tell, *sel.*
Thy copp's, too, nam'd of Gamage, thou hast there, *sel.*
To a Weak Gamester in Poetry.
To Celia.
To Celia ("Drink to me only with thine eyes").
To Doctor Empiric[k]
To Edward Allen (Alleyne).
To Elizabeth, Countess of Rutland.
To Fine Grand.
To Fine Lady Would-Be.
To Fool, or Knave.
To Francis Beaumont.
To Heaven.
To John Donne.
To Lucy, Countesse of Bedford, with Mr. Donnes Satyres.
To Mary Lady Wroth.
To My Book.
To Penshurst.
To Pertinax Cob.
To Sir Henrie Savile upon His Translation of Tacitus.
To Sir Henry Cary.
To Sir Robert Wroth.
To the Immortal Memory and Friendship of That Noble Pair, Sir Lucius Cary and Sir Henry Morison.
To the Memory of My Beloved Master [*or* the Author, Mr.] William Shakespeare and What He Hath Left Us.
To the Reader.
To the World; a Farewell for a Gentlewoman, Virtuous and Noble.
To Thomas Lord Chancellor.
To William Camden.
To William Earle of Pembroke.
To William Roe.
Triumph of Charis, The, *sel.*
Urging Her of a Promise, *sel.*
Vision of Delight, The.
Vision of Delight Presented at Court in Chistmas, 1617, The.
What Hee Suffered, *sel.*
What our Dame bids us do, *sel.*
Whole world here, leavened with madness, swells, The, *sel.*
Why I Write Not of Love.
Witches' Charms, The, *sel.*
Witches' Chasm.
Witches' Song, The.
With you, I know, my offering will find grace, *sel.*

Jonson, Edward
Water-Drinker, The.

Jooris, Roland
Cuckoo.
Density.
Minimal.
Somewhat Minimal.

Village.
Writing.
Jordan, A. C.
You Tell Me to Sit Quiet.
Jordan, Barbara Leslie
Desert Shipwreck.
Jordan, Charlotte Brewster
To Borglum's Seated Statue of Abraham
Lincoln.
Jordan, David Starr
Men Told Me, Lord!
Vivérols.
Jordan, John
Lolek.
Jordan, June
All the World Moved.
Cameo No. II.
Clock on Hancock Street.
DeLiza Spend the Day in the City ("DeLiza
drive the car to fetch, Alexis").
For My Mother.
Getting Down to Get Over.
If You Saw a Negro Lady.
In Memoriam: Martin Luther King, Jr.
July 4, 1984: For Buck.
My Sadness Sits around Me.
New Pietà: For the Mothers and Children of
Detroit, The.
Nobody Riding the Roads Today.
Notes on the Peanut.
Okay "Negroes."
Onesided Dialog.
Poem about My Rights.
Poem for My Family: Hazel Griffin and Victor
Hernandez Cruz.
Poem for Nana.
Poem from the Empire State.
Poem to My Sister, Ethel Ennis, Who Sang
"The Star-spangled Banner" at the Second
Inauguration of Richard Milhous Nixon.
Queen Anne's Lace.
Reception, The.
Second Poem from Nicaragua Libre: War
Zone.
Snow, The.
Sunflower Sonnet Number One.
Sunflower Sonnet Number Two.
Uncle Bull-Boy.
Unemployment/Monologue.
What Happens.
What Would I Do White?
You Came with Shells.
Jordan, Margot
Hidden Reason.
Silence Is Nearer to Truth.
Jordan, Norman
August 2.
Black Warrior.
Cities and Seas.
Ending.
Feeding the Lions.
July 31.
Jordan, Raimon
I see the clear weather darken.
Jordan, Thomas
Careless Gallant, The.
Pyms Anarchy, at.
Jordana, Elena
Tango.
Joron, Andrew
Agency.
Asleep in the Arms of Mother Night.
Hunter: 20,000 A.D, The.
Sonic Flowerfall of Primes, The.
White Noise.
Joron, Andrew and Robert Frazier
Aging of Clones, The.
Joseph, Jenny
Back to Base.
Ballad of Rodborough Common, The.
Dog body and cat mind, The.

Letter, A.
Lost Continent, The.
One That Got Away.
Rose in the Afternoon.
Warning.
Watching a Child Watching a Witch, *sel.*
Wish, A.
Joseph, Lawrence
That's All.
Joseph, M. K.
Distilled Water.
Epilogue to a Poetry Reading.
Girl, Boy, Flower, Bicycle.
Granada the Last City, *sel.*
Mercury Bay Eclogue.
Nurse's Song.
Off Cape Leeuwen.
Joseph, Vivienne
By Return Mail.
Desirable Property, A.
Sex Films.
Woman '77.
Joseph of the Studium, Saint
Finished Course, The.
Joso (Naito Joso)
Below the boulder where I sit, *sel.*
Blackening the offing, *sel.*
Both fields and mountains, *sel.*
Bottom of loneliness, The, *sel.*
Colder than the snow, *sel.*
Dragonfly catches a fly, A, *sel.*
From my sleeve a katydid, *sel.*
I run into fireflies, *sel.*
Ill in Bed, *sel.*
Its sloughed-off shell.
I've just come up.
"I've seen it all."
Just seen the bottom of the water, *sel.*
On the boulder at the bottom, *sel.*
That duck, bobbing up.
Thinking I'm after them, *sel.*
Waiting on Basho as He Lay Ill, *sel.*
White beach: a dog barks, *sel.*
Wolves' voices harmonize, *sel.*
Josselyn, John
And the bitter storm augments; the wild winds
wage.
Description of a New England Spring.
Verses Made Sometime Since upon. the
Indian Squa.
Jouve, Pierre Jean
After the Flood.
For White Skin.
Gravida.
Lone Woman Asleep, A.
To Himself.
Walk, A.
We Have Amazed.
When.
White Haunches.
Work.
Joyce, James
Alone.
Ballad of Persse O'Reilly, The, *sel.*
Commonplace.
Ecce Puer.
Flood.
Flower Given to My Daughter, A.
Gas from a Burner.
Goldenhair.
Holy Office, The.
Memory of the Players in a Mirror at
Midnight, A.
Nightpiece.
On the Beach at Fontana.
Ondt and the Gracehoper, The, *sel.*
Right Heart in the Wrong Place, The.
Sleep now, O sleep now.
Stephen's Vampire Poem, *sel.*
There was a kind lady called Gregory.
Thou leanest to the shell of night.

Though I Thy Mithridates Were.
Tilly.
Tutto è Sciolto.
Yes, *sel.*
Jozef Wittlin
Hymn about a Spoonful of Soup, A.
József, Attila
Seventh, The.
Juan Chi
Beautiful trees make paths beneath
themselves, *sel.*
In North Ward they do many strange dances,
sel.
Long ago, at fourteen or fifteen, *sel.*
This summer's burning heat, *sel.*
Tung-ling melons—men say that long ago,
sel.
Years ago, when I was young, *sel.*
Juan de la Cruz, San. *See* **John of the
Cross, Saint**
Juan Ramón Jiménez
Oceans.
Juana Inés de la Cruz, Sister (*originally*
Juana de Asbaje)
Amorous of Laura's Loveliness.
Arguing That There Are Inconsistencies
between Men's Tastes and Their Censure
When They Accuse Women.
But Venus first, *sel.*
Carol to Catherine.
Christmas Hymn.
Crimson Lute That Comest in the Dawn.
Critics: in your sight, *sel.*
Describes Rationally the Irrational Effects of
Love.
Diuturnal Infirmity of Hope.
Divine Rose, That in a Pleasant Garden.
Green Enravishment of Human Life.
I can't hold you and I can't leave you.
Ignorant men, who disclaim, *sel.*
In Which She Satisfies a Fear with the
Rhetoric of Tears.
On Her Portrait.
She Attempts to Refute the Praises That
Truth, Which She Calls Passion, Inscribed
on a Portrait of the Poet.
She Proves the Inconsistency of the Desires
and Criticism of Men Who Accuse Women
of What They Themselves Cause.
Sonnet: Verses Expressing the Feelings of a
Lover.
Stay, shade of my shy treasure! Oh, remain.
Stop, Shadow of My Elusive Beloved.
Tarry, Shadow of My Scornful Treasure.
This coloured counterfeit that thou beholdest.
This evening, my love, even as I spoke
vainly.
This Evening When I Spake with Thee,
Beloved.
What humour can be so rare, *sel.*
What Interest Have You, World, in
Persecuting Me?
"Judah"
Fragrant Thy Memories.
Judit Tóth
Southeast Ramparts of the Seine, The.
Judson, Adoniram
Come Holy Spirit, Dove Divine.
Our Father, God.
Judson, Sarah
Proclaim the Lofty Praise.
Judson, Emily Chubbuck. *See* **"Forester,
Fanny."**
Juhász, Ferenc
Birth of the Foal.
Boy Changed into a Stag Cries Out at the
Gate of Secrets, The.
Crown of Hatred and Love.
Gold.
Power of the Flowers.
Silver.

Juhasz, Suzanne
Dancer from the Dance, The.
Saying Goodbye.
Jukichi, Yagi. *See* **Yagi Jukichi**
Julian, V. M.
Mr. Squirrel.
Jumper, Will C.
California Quail in January.
Jun, Okamoto. *See* **Okamoto Jun**
Jung Han-mo
Baby.
Baby's Room.
Bird.
In the Field.
Remnant.
Song of Sungbuk.
Today.
Vestige.
Voice.
Junkins, Donald
Walden in July.
Junna, Emperor
At a Farewell Party for Fujiwara no Yoshino.
Junzaburo, Nishiwaki
Afterword.
Autumn.
Broadax.
Ceylon.
Decorations.
Far down the Koshu Road.
Rain.
Travelogue.
Way to the Lighthouse, The.
Junzaburo, Nishiwaki. *See* **Nishiwaki Junzaburo**
Jusammi Chikako. *See* **Chikako**
Justema, William
Song: "This is the song of those who live alone."
Justice, Donald
About My Poems.
American Scenes (1904).
Anonymous Drawing.
Another Song.
Assassination, The.
Beyond the Hunting Woods.
Birthday Candle, A.
Bus Stop.
But That Is Another Story.
Childhood.
Children Walking Home from School through Good Neighborhood.
Complaint of the Grandparents.
Counting the Mad.
Crossing Kansas by Train.
Dancer's Life, A.
Dreams of Water.
Elegy Is Preparing Itself, An.
Elsewheres.
First Death.
Furies, The.
Grandfathers [*or* After a Line by John Peale Bishop], The.
Hard, but you can polish it, *sel.*
Heart.
Houses.
In Bertram's Garden.
In Memory of the Unknown Poet, Robert Boardman Vaughn.
In the Attic.
Incident in a Rose Garden.
Landscape with Little Figures.
Lethargy.
Love's Stratagems.
Luxury.
Man Closing Up, The.
Memo from the Desk of X.
Men at Forty.
Missing Person, The.
Mule Team and Poster.
Nostalgia and Complaint of the Grandparents.

Nostalgia of the Lakefronts.
October.
Ode to a Dressmaker's Dummy.
On a Painting by Patient B of the Independence State Hospital for the Insane.
On the Death of Friends in Childhood.
Poem: "This poem is not addressed to you."
Poem to Be Read at 3 A.M.
Presences.
Psalm and Lament.
Sestina: Here in Katmandu.
Sestina: "I woke by first light in a wood."
Snowfall, The.
Sonatina in Yellow.
Sonnet: The Poet at Seven.
Sonnet to My Father.
Sonnet: Wall, The.
Southern Gothic.
Stone.
Summer Anniversaries, The.
Tales from a Family Album.
Thin Man, The.
Thinking about the Past.
To Waken a Small Person.
Tourist from Syracuse, The.
Tremayne.
Unflushed Urinals.
Variations for Two Pianos.
Variations on a Text by Vallejo.
Variations on Southern Themes.
Villanelle at Sundown.
White Notes.
Women in Love.
Justus, May
Good Neighbors.
Jessica Jane ("Jessica Jane is the kind of cook").
Rain Has Silver Sandals, The.
Strawberry Jam.
Juvenal
But of all the plagues, the greatest is untold, *sel.*
Celestial Wisdom, *sel.*
Faggots in Ancient Rome, *sel.*
Give store of days, good Jove, give length of years, *sel.*
Hannibal ("Produce the urn that Hannibal contains"), *sel.*
Hannibal ("Put Hannibal i' th' scale"), *sel.*
Hannibal ("Throw Hannibal on the scales, how many pounds"), *sel.*
Hear what Claudius suffered: When his wife knew he was asleep, *sel.*
In Saturn's reign, at Nature's early birth, *sel.*
"Life! length of life!' for this, with earnest cries, *sel.*
Return we to the dangers of the night, *sel.*
Sejanus ("How many men are killed by power, by power"), *sel.*
Sejanus ("Some ask for envy'd pow'r; which publick hate"), *sel.*
Sejanus ("What crowds by envied power, the wish of all"), *sel.*
What conscience has Venus drunk? Our inebriated beauties, *sel.*
When the last Flavius, drunk with fury, tore, *sel.*
Why do you look so gloomy, Naevolus?, *sel.*
Jylhä, Yrjö
Holy Night.
Meeting in the Forest, A.
More.

K

"K., A."
La Donna È Mobile.

"K."
How Firm a Foundation.
"K., E. H."
City Church, The.
Ka-'ehu
Leper, The.
Kaai Chigetsu
Cricket chirps in a scarecrow's sleeve, A, *sel.*
Despite myself I become so childish, *sel.*
Each morning a wren comes, *sel.*
Fifteenth of the Eighth Month, The, *sel.*
I know and I don't know what I am, *sel.*
I sleep alone; throughout the night, *sel.*
In a wide garden peonies open amply, *sel.*
In autumn a dove looks as if loneliness, *sel.*
Loving My Grandchild, *sel.*
Lying Awake Endlessly in Old Age, *sel.*
On the Anniversary of Basho's Death I Visited His Grave in Kiso, *sel.*
Today's moon—if there were another, *sel.*
Unaware I'm growing old, *sel.*
Kaberry, C. J.
Indian Elephant, The.
Kabir
Clay Jug, The.
Go naked if you want.
God is the jewel.
Hey brother, why do you want me to talk?
Hey Qazi.
If caste was what the Creator had in mind.
I'm dead—/ dead of bad company.
Kabir:/ Even worthless bushes.
Kabir:/ My mind was soothed.
Kabir:/ The hut was made of sticks.
Kabir:/ The instrument is still.
Kabir is done with stretching thread and weaving.
Lean doe, The.
Pundit, how can you be so dumb?
Pundit, so well-read, go ask God.
Pundits have taken, The.
Radiance, The.
Scorched by the forest fire.
Sense of separation, The.
Simple Purification, The.
So I'm born a weaver.
Songs of Kabir.
Tell me, Ram: what will happen to me?
That master weaver, whose skills.
That thief has gone thieving, careening around the world.
They burn:/ The bones like tinder.
True Master, The.
Why be so proud of this useless, used-up body?
Your chance of human birth.
Kaccipettu Nannakaiyar
My lover capable of terrible lies.
Kadhani, Mudereri
Rekayi Tangwena.
Kaffka, Margit
Father.
Kaga no Chiyo
Haiku: "Autumn's bright moon."
Haiku: "Dew of the rouge-flower, The."
Haiku: "Spring rain."
Kagank
It's only whiskey that makes you pity me.
Kageyama, Yuri
Day in a Long Hot Summer, A.
Disco Chinatown.
Love Poem: "I like/ the feel of your pulsating fibers."
My Mother Takes a Bath.
Strings/Himo.
Kahanovitch, Pinhas. *See* **"Der Nistor"**
Kahclamet, Philip
Crier, The.
Kahn, Gustave
Homage.
Paris by Night.

Pilgrim from the East, The.
Song: "O lovely April, rich and bright."
Temple, The.
Word, The.
You Masks of the Masquerade.

Kahn, Hannah
Signature.
To Be Black, to Be Lost.

Kaiama
Song: "Misty and dim, a bush in the wilds of Kapa'a."

Kailas, Uuno
Guilty Man.
House, The.
In a Small Country.
My Son.

Kaiseki
Dream Palace, The.
Restless mind, all night, A.

Kajava, Viljo
Father Is Leaving.
I Am a Guitar.
Love Is Not Cleansed by Fire.
Sky went before me wherever I went, The.
Torn widow's veil, *sel.*
When I was very little the lake was blue.

Kakayek
Song on the Way to Jail.

Kakinomoto No Hitomaro. *See* **Hitomaro**

Kakkai Patiniyar Naccellaiyar
King's Double Nature, A.
Mothers.
What Her Girl Friend Said to Her Lover on His Return.

Kakua
Fisting, shouting like a petty merchant.
Forgetting mind, its complications.
How can I tell what I've seen?
I've crossed the sea after truth.
Satori seekers make me sick!

Kalász, Márton
Age of Snow, The.
Ghost Psalms.
Hymn: "Where should I seat you, where."
Impromptu.
Legacy.
Maiden.
Nearly Nameless.
Time's No Grammar.
Up against That Wall Everywhere.

Kaléko, Mascha
Interview with myself.
Love in the City.
Mannequins.

Kalidasa
Seasons, The.

Kalikoff, Beth
Bad Sport.

Kallil Attiraiyanar
Poet's Memory Is Counsel, A.

Kallman, Chester
Dead Center.
Romance, A.

Kalmar, Bert *and* **Harry Ruby**
"America, I Love You."

Kálnoky, László
De Profundis.
Despair.
Glass Hat, The.
Instead of an Autobiography.
Quarry, The.

Kalola
Fathomless Is My Love.

Kalonymos ben Judah
Although Tormented.

Kalonymos ben Kalonymos
Hypocrite, The, *sel.*
Unfortunate Male, The, *sel.*
Yoke, The, *sel.*

Kambara Yumei
Oyster Shell.

Kamenetz, Rodger
Pilpul.
Scraps.
Why I Can't Write My Autobiography.

Kametani Seiken
Airing Books.

Kaminsky, Marc
Erev Shabbos.

Kamzon, Jacob David
Very Fair My Lot.

Kan Sazan
For My Younger Brother Shinkei on the Seventeenth Anniversary of His Death.
On the Road to Takaya.
Rainy Season.
Summer Day.
Winter Night, Reading Books.
Written on a Summer Night.

Kanabus, Henry
Access, The.
Accordance.
Scythe, The.

Kanalenstein, Ruben
Jerusalem.

Kandel, Lenore
Blues for Sister Sally.
Bus Ride.

Kane, Douglas V.
Westering.

Kaneko, Lonny
Coming Home from Camp.
Family Album.
Secret, The.
Violets for Mother.

Kaneko Mitsuharu
Ascension.
Opposition.
Sharks.
Song of the Tart.

Kanemasa (Minamoto no Kanemasa)
How many nights have you wakened.

Kanemori (Taira no Kanemori)
I would conceal it, yet.

Kaneyoshi (Ichijo Kaneyoshi)
Blossoms at Their Height.
Cherry Blossoms at Shiga, The.
Each time they break.
End of the Third Lunar Month, The.
Garden Moss under Snow.
Out in the paddies.

Kang, Baljit
Midnight.

K'ang Hai
Dreaming of Master Chung-lu.
Listening to the Rain.
Sitting by Myself.
When I have chanted my new poems, *sel.*

K'ang Yu-wei
Discussing Poetry with Shu-yüan.
In Lieu of a Preface to *The Great Commonwealth Book.*
Seeing Spring Off.
Upon Leaving the Capital: A Farewell to My Several Friends.
Visiting Mount Vernon and Paying Homage at George Washington's Burial Vault.

Kangan
These eighty-four years.

Kanié, Anoma
All That You Have Given Me, Africa.

Kanik, Orban Veli
Being Sad.
People.

Kaniyan Punkunran
Every Town a Home Town.

Kanko, Akera. *See* **Akera Kanko**

Kannan
What Her Girl Friend Said to Him.

Kao Ch'i
Along the River, Seeing the Home of Absconded Farmers.
Ballad of the Deserted Mansion.
Ballad of the Neighborhood Shaman.
Going Out to the Country on a Boat Trip.
In the Mountains, Parting from Master Ning.
Lying at Leisure during Rain.
Mooring Our Boat at Tan-yang Harbor.
Moss below the Stairs.
Nodding Off.
Passing by the Battlefield at Feng-k'ou.
Returning to Lotus Village.
Seeing Flowers I Remember My Late Daughter, Shu.
Seeking out Hermit Hu.
Silkworm Song of Torchlit Fields.
Song of the Duck Hunters.
Song of the Man of Green Hill, The.
Spring Day—Remembering Living on the River, A.
Walk to the Eastern River Bank, A.
Well of the King of Wu, The.
Where Does My Sadness Come From?

Kaoru, Maruyama. *See* **Maruyama Kaoru**

Kapilar
Farewell to Pari's Hill.
His Hill.
Kari Sober.
Memory of the Hill, A.
Pari! Pari! they cry.
Pari's Green Land, Remembered.
Pari's Hill Is Partial to Dancers.
Then and Now.
True Protocol of Poets, The.
Waterfalls and Liquor.
What Her Friend Said to Her, before the Rains.
What Her Friend Said to the Foster-Mother (Who Is Guarding Her Carefully).
What She Said ("And all those horses").
What She Said ("Forest animals walk there").
What She Said ("He is from those mountains").
What She Said (" 'O your hair,' he said").
What She Said ("Only the thief was there, no one else").
What She Said to Her Friend ("Colors on the elephant's body").
What She Said to Her Friend ("You ask me to forget him").
What She Said to Her Girl Friend ("In his country").
What She Said to Her Girl Friend ("O you, you wear flowers of gold").
What She Said to Her Girl Friend, after a Tryst at Night (Which Turned Out to Be a Fiasco).
What She Said to Her Girl Friend, Her Foster-Mother within Earshot.
What She Said to Her Girl Friend When She Returned from the Hills.
What She Said to Her Lover within Earshot.
What the Girl Friend Said to the Foster-Mother.

Kaplan, Allan
Marvelous.

Kaplan, Milton
Circus, The.
Knife, The.

Kappiyarrukkappiyanar
Harvest of War.

Karélli, Zoé
Presences.

Karibo, Minji
Superstition.

Kariuki, Joseph E.
New Life.

Karni, Yehuda
Chambers of Jerusalem.
Four of Them, The.
Place Me in the Breach.

Károlyi, Amy
Coffee-stained, knife-cut tablecloth, *sel.*
Jewel towers relay to jewel towers, *sel.*
Like a cloud haunted by the moon, *sel.*
Karoniaktatie (Alex Jacobs)
Dead Heroes.
Elegy: "When the old ones die."
Face, The.
Stone Song (Zen Rock) the Seer & the
    Unbeliever.
Karpowicz, Tymoteusz
Lesson of Silence, A.
Love.
Pencil's Dream, The.
Turns.
Karsch, Anna Louisa
My Young Days Were Oppressed with Cares.
Kasa, Lady
I dreamed I held/ A sword against my flesh.
I love and fear him.
To love somebody/ Who doesn't love you.
To love someone/ Who does not return that
    love.
Kaschnitz, Marie Luise
Cat, The.
Girl thinks if I can only manage, The, *sel.*
Humility.
Only the Eyes.
Resurrection.
Women's Broadcast.
Kasdaglis, Lina
Traffic Lights.
Kasenduaxtc
Throw him into the river.
Kashiku
Among floating weeds, frogs.
Kasmuneh
Overripe Fruit.
Timid Gazelle, The.
Kassák, Lajos
Baffling Picture.
Craftsmen.
I Am with You.
Like This.
No. 42.
No. 96.
No. 65.
No. 12.
Snapshot.
Young Horseman.
Kassia, Mary Magdalene
Epigram: "Poverty? wealth? seek neither."
Epigram: "Wealth covers sin—the poor."
Epigram: "Woman working hard and wisely,
    A."
Lord, this woman who fell into many sins.
Selected Epigrams.
Sticheron for Matins, Wednesday of Holy
    Week.
Kassid, Abd al-Karim
Gravestone, The.
Suitcases, The.
Tales about My Father.
Kästner, Erich
Moral Taxi Ride, The.
Ragoût Fin de Siècle (with Reference to
    Certain Cafés).
Kataiyan Kannanar
In Praise of a Cremation Ground.
Katav, Shalom
Pleading Voices.
Katda
My wife went away, left me.
Katene-Horvath, Hera
In Days Gone By.
Kato Gyodai. *See* **Gyodai**
Kato Kyotai. *See* **Kyotai**
Kato Shuson
Haiku: "Autumn wind—/ I open out."
Haiku: "Sad and forlorn: the shrike."
Haiku: "Sticking out my head from."

Katrovas, Richard
Bloomfield, Inc.
Blues' Body.
Elegy for My Mother.
Mystic Pig, The.
Our Island.
Star Boys.
Katuvan Ilaveyinanar
Tirumal.
Katz, Bobbi
Cat Kisses.
Patience.
Pretending.
Runaway, The.
Samuel.
Spring Is.
Things to Do If You Are a Subway.
Unfortunately.
Katzin, Olga. *See* **"Sagittarius"**
Kaufman, Bob
African Dream.
Afterwards, They Shall Dance.
Battle Report.
Benediction.
Blues Note.
Cincophrenicpoet.
Cocoa Morning.
Falling.
Forget Me Not.
I Have Folded My Sorrows.
I, Too, Know What I Am Not.
Mingus.
Patriotic Ode on the Fourteenth Anniversary
    of the Persecution of Charlie Chaplin.
To My Son Parker, Asleep in the Next Room.
Unholy Missions.
Walking Parker Home.
When We Hear the Eye Open.
Kaufman, Shirley
Always She Moves from Me.
Apples.
Beetle on the Shasta Daylight.
Déjà Vu.
Her Going.
His Wife.
I see bodies in the morning kneel.
Leah.
Looking at Henry Moore's Elephant Skull
    Etchings in Jerusalem during the War.
Looking for Maimonides: Tiberias.
Loving.
Mothers, Daughters.
Mountain, The.
Nechama.
New Graveyard: Jerusalem.
Next Year, in Jerusalem.
Room.
Starting Over.
There are caverns/ under our feet.
Watts.
We are going down a long slide.
Wonders.
Kavanagh, P. J.
Beside the Bed.
Birthday.
Birthday Visit.
First Light.
Moving.
Praying.
Temperance Billiards Rooms, The.
Kavanagh, Patrick
Advent.
Ante-natal Dream.
April, and no one able to calculate, *sel.*
Art McCooey.
Bluebells for Love.
Canal Bank Walk.
Candida ("Candida is one today").
Christmas Childhood, A.
Clay is the word and clay is the flesh, *sel.*
Come Dance with Kitty Stobling.

Dear Folks.
Epic.
Father Mat.
Gold Watch.
Great Hunger, The.
He gave himself another year, *sel.*
Health and wealth and love he too dreamed of
    in May, *sel.*
Hospital, The.
I Had a Future.
I May Reap.
If Ever You Go to Dublin Town.
In a meadow/ Beside the chapel three boys
    were playing football, *sel.*
In Memory of My Mother.
Inniskeen Road: July Evening.
Innocence.
Intimate Parnassus.
Is.
Kerr's Ass.
Leave Them Alone.
Lecture Hall.
Lines Written on a Seat on the Grand Canal,
    Dublin.
Long Garden, The.
Maguire is not afraid of death, the Church
    will light him a candle, *sel.*
Memory of Brother Michael.
Memory of my Father.
My father played the melodion, *sel.*
October.
On an apple-ripe September morning, *sel.*
On Looking into E. V. Rieu's Homer.
One, The.
Peace.
Pegasus.
Ploughman.
Poor Paddy Maguire, a fourteen-hour day, *sel.*
Prelude: "Give us another poem, he said."
Pursuit of an Ideal.
Question to Life.
Road to Hate, The.
Sanctity.
Self-slaved, The.
Shancoduff.
Spraying the Potatoes.
Stony Grey Soil.
Temptation in Harvest.
Tinker's Wife.
To Hell with Commonsense.
To the Man after the Harrow.
Wet Evening in April.
Kavarpentu
Mothers.
Kawabata Bosha
Haiku: "Bright moonlight."
Haiku: "Hearing the thunder-clap."
Haiku: "Nothing there but."
Haiku: "On the snow."
Haiku: "Pillow hard as stone!"
Haiku: "Wasting in summer."
Kawahigashi Hekigoto
Haiku: "Cold spring day."
Haiku: "*No* by torchlight, The."
Kawai Chigetsu-ni
Grasshoppers/ Chirping in the sleeves.
"Kay"
Christmas Verse, A.
Kay, Ellen
Pathedy of Manners.
Kay, Ellen de Young
Cante Hondo.
Magnanimous, The.
Tiresias' Lament.
To a Blue Hippopotamus.
Kay, Jackie
Diary of Days for Adjoa.
Peony.
Kaya Shirao
About the time I miss someone, *sel.*
Bowman listens to a cuckoo, A, *sel.*

Cold moon: a white sheet, *sel*.
Floating cloud before my eyes, The, *sel*.
For eight or nine yards I watch, *sel*.
I put aside a story, *sel*.
In a field with scentless winter trees, *sel*.
In the dark garden at night, *sel*.
In the setting sun even its shadow, *sel*.
Just one evening snipe, *sel*.
Katydid stops chirping, A, *sel*.
Lightning gets to be terrifying, *sel*.
Night hailstones fall so hard, *sel*.
On a dark night, as long as it's dark, *sel*.
Pity the sweetfish after spawning, *sel*.
Rafts are moored to cherries, *sel*.
Skylark rises, A, *sel*.
Sparrows, mating, *sel*.
There's even someone combing her hair, *sel*.
Tides carry the haze, The, *sel*.
Wait a while—this is an evening shower, *sel*.

Kayamanar
What Her Girl Friend Said, Seeing Her Friend
   Suffer in Silent Dignity over Her Husband's
   Infidelity.

Kazan'in Nagachika. *See* **Nagachika**
"Kazanova, Kid." *See* **Stack, Philip**
Kazantzis, Judith
Arachne.
At the National Gallery.
For My Daughter.
Frightened Flier Goes North, The.
In Memory, 1978.
No War.
Static.
We Can Try Again Another Day.
Woman making advances publicly, A.

Kazuko Yamada
Wind, The.

Keach, Benjamin
How Glorious Are the Morning Stars.

Keams, Geraldine
Canyon Day Woman Blues.

Keane, Ellsworth McGranaham ("Shake")
Coming Back.
Soufrière (79), *sel*.

Kearney, Peadar
Whack Fol the Diddle.

Kearns, Lionel
Environment.
Foreign Aid.
Stuntman.

Keary, E.
Old Age.

Keate, George
Midst the fair range of buildings which,
   new-reared, *sel*.
What, though oblivion in her sable shroud,
   sel.

Keating, Geoffrey (Seathrum Ceitinn)
At the news from Fal's high plain I cannot
   sleep.
Keen Thyself, Poor Wight.
Mourn for Yourself.
O lady full of guile.

Keating, Norma
Never, Never Can Nothingness Come.

Keats, John
After Dark Vapours.
Ah! dearest love, sweet home of all my fears,
   sel.
And can I ever bid these joys farewell?, *sel*.
Banquet, The, *sel*.
Bright Star, Would I Were Steadfast as Thou
   Art!
Bruised Titans, The, *sel*.
Could all this be forgotten? Yes, a schism,
   sel.
Daisy's Song.
Darkling I listen; and for many a time, *sel*.
Day Is Gone, The.
Deep in the shady sadness of a vale, *sel*.
Dream, A, *sel*.

Epistle to John Hamilton Reynolds.
Eve of St. Agnes, The.
Eve of Saint Mark, The.
Fairy Song.
Fame, like a wayward girl, will still be coy,
   sel.
Fanatics have their dreams, wherewith they
   weave, *sel*.
Fancy.
Fragment of an Ode to Maia Written on May
   Day, 1818.
Great Spirits Now on Earth.
How fever'd is the man who cannot look, *sel*.
How Many Bards Gild the Lapses of Time!
Human Seasons, The.
Hymn to Pan, *sel*.
Hyperion.
Hyperion and Saturn, *sel*.
Imitation of Spenser.
In a Drear-nighted December.
Isabella; or, The Pot of Basil.
La Belle Dame sans Merci.
Lamia.
Life Again, *sel*.
Magic Casements, *sel*.
Meg Merrilies [*or* Merrilees]
Minnows, *sel*.
Modern Love.
Muse of native land! loftiest Muse!, *sel*.
O for ten years, that I may overwhelm, *sel*.
O Moon! the oldest shades 'mong oldest trees,
   sel.
O sovereign power of love! O grief! O balm!,
   sel.
O that our dreamings all, of sleep or wake,
   sel.
Ode: "Bards of passion and of mirth."
Ode on a Grecian Urn.
Ode on Indolence.
Ode on Melancholy.
Ode to a Nightingale.
Ode to Psyche.
Oft have you seen a swan superbly frowning,
   sel.
On a Dream.
On First Looking into Chapman's Homer.
On Oxford.
On Seeing the Elgin Marbles.
On Sitting Down to Read "King Lear" Once
   Again.
On the Grasshopper and [the] Cricket.
On the Sea.
On the Sonnet.
Portrait, A.
Realm of Fancy, The, *sel*.
Recollection of the Stone Circle near
   Keswick, A, *sel*.
Robin Hood.
Sharing Eve's Apple.
Sleep and Poetry.
Sleeping Youth, A, *sel*.
Solitude.
Sometimes goldfinches one by one will drop,
   sel.
Song: "I had a dove, and the sweet dove
   died", *sel*.
Song of Spring.
Song of the Indian Maid ("O Sorrow,/ Why
   dost borrow"), *sel*.
Song of the Indian Maid, The ("Beneath my
   palm-trees, by the riverside"), *sel*.
Sonnet: Keen, Fitful Gusts.
Sonnet: On a Picture of Leander.
Sonnet: To a Young Lady Who Sent Me a
   Laurel Crown.
Sonnet: To One Who Has Been Long in City
   Pent.
Sonnet: Written at the End of "The Floure and
   the Lefe."
Sonnet: Written on the Day That Mr. Leigh
   Hunt Left Prison.
Stop and consider! life is but a day, *sel*.

Sweet Peas, *sel*.
There Was a Naughty Boy.
Thing of beauty is a joy forever, A, *sel*.
This Living Hand, Now Warm and Capable.
'Tis the witching hour of night.
To———: "What can I do to drive away."
To a Cat.
To Ailsa Rock.
To Autumn.
To Charles Cowden Clarke.
To Fanny.
To Homer.
To Leigh Hunt, Esq.
To My Brother George.
To My Brothers.
To Sleep.
Towards the altar sober-paced I went, *sel*.
Two Sonnets on Fame, II.
What the Thrush Said.
When I Have Fears [That I May Cease to Be]
Where Be You Going, You Devon Maid?
Where shall I learn to get my peace again?,
   sel.
Why did I laugh tonight? No voice will tell.
Written upon the Top of Ben Nevis.

Keaulumoku
Birth of Sea and Land Life, *sel*.
Crawlers, The, *sel*.
Dawn of Day, The, *sel*.
Dog Child, The, *sel*.

Keble, John
Balaam.
Epitalamium: "Voice that breathed o'er Eden,
   The."
Evening.
Fill High the Bowl.
New every morning.
November, *sel*.
Purity of Heart.

Keegan, John
Irish Reaper's Harvest Hymn.

Keeler, Greg
American Falls.
Duct Tape Psalm.

Keeling, Mildred
God's World.

Keene, H. G.
Taj, The.

Keens-Douglas, Paul
Tell Me Again.
Wukhand.

Kees, Weldon
1926.
Aspects of Robinson.
Back.
Beach in August, The.
Cats, The.
Colloquy.
Coming of the Plague, The.
Contours of Fixation, The.
Conversation in the Drawing Room, The.
Crack is moving down the wall, The, *sel*.
Crime Club.
Early Winter.
For My Daughter.
Guide to the Symphony.
Heat in the Room, The.
Henry James at Newport.
Homage to Arthur Waley.
January.
La Vita Nuova.
Patient Is Rallying, The.
Problems of a Journalist.
Relating to Robinson.
River Song.
Robinson.
Robinson at Home.
Round: "Wondrous life!" cried Marvell at
   Appleton House."
Saratoga Ending.
Small Prayer.

Smiles of the Bathers, The.
Wet Thursday.
Keeshig-Tobias, Lenore
Act Respecting Indians, An.
Mother with Child.
Keesing, Nancy
Bread.
Revelation.
Reverie of a Mum.
Wandering Jews.
Kefala, Antigone
Saturday Night.
Kegels, Anne-Marie
I write to make you suffer.
Nocturnal Heart.
When I strip,/ stop walking/ and drop into
    sleep.
Keijo Shurin
Torn Windows, No Paper.
Keisen
Any moment now I'll knock my master down.
First illusion, The.
Keiter, Anne
Past Love.
Keith, Joseph Joel
In the First House.
Keithley, George
Black Hawk in Hiding.
Buster Keaton & the Cops.
Child, The.
Morning Star Man.
Old Graves fell asleep, *sel.*
On Clark Street in Chicago.
Song for New Orleans, A.
Supper.
Thief's Niece, The.
To Bring Spring.
Waiting for Winter.
Woman, The.
Keiun
At this late date.
Early Autumn.
Even in my dreams.
Evening Faces.
From my little hut.
Grasses and trees, When.
Hawking.
Mountain Haze.
Keizan
I've plowed and sown my field.
Kelleher, Daniel Lawrence
For C. K. at His Christening.
Its Name Is Known.
Mother.
Upper Room, An.
Keller, Helen
In the Garden of the Lord.
Keller, Martha
Andrew Jackson.
Deadfall.
Mountain Meadows.
Kelley, Reeve Spencer
Back Again from Yucca Flats.
Rain in the Southwest.
Sound of Morning in New Mexico, The.
Kelly, Blanche Mary
Mirror, The.
Omniscience.
Kelly, Dennis
Chicken.
Kelly, John W.
Slide, Kelly, Slide.
Kelly, Robert
Dance, The, *sel.*
Earth is a woman who imagines us. She
    sings, *sel.*
Fourth Ode to Persephone, *sel.*
Glade, The, *sel.*
Hercules Musarum.
Last Light.
Persephone is the woman buried, *sel.*

Poem for Easter.
Second Ode to Persephone, *sel.*
Sound, The.
Third Ode to Persephone, *sel.*
Versions, *sel.*
Kelly, Roy
Death, Don't Be Boring.
Ode to a Nightingale.
Kelly, Walt
Boston Charlie.
How Low Is the Lowing Herd.
Kelpius, Johannes
I Love My Jesus Quite Alone, *at.*
Kelso, Ian
Busy Old Fool.
Kemble, Frances Anne (Fanny)
Faith.
Lament of a Mocking-Bird.
To Shakespeare
Wish, A.
Kemp, Harry Hibbard
God the Architect.
He Did Not Know.
Hummingbird, The.
Prayer: "I kneel not now to pray that Thou."
Seaman's Confession of Faith, A.
Kemp, Jan
Atalanta.
Cinderella.
If You're My Friend for Life.
In Golden Smock, Walking.
Letter to the Immigration Officer.
Poem: "Puriri moth's wing, A."
"When the Wild Goose Finds Food He Calls
    His Comrades"— *I Ching.*
Kemp, Pierre
Gamble on Red.
Honeysuckle Yellow.
Karma.
Life Sentence.
Ken, Thomas
Evening Hymn, An.
Glory to Thee, My God, This Night.
Morning Hymn.
Kendall, Henry Clarence
Bell-Birds.
Beyond Kerguelen.
Christmas Creek.
Jim the Splitter.
Last of His Tribe, The.
Mooni.
Orara.
September in Australia.
Kendall, John Kaye ("Dum-Dum")
Cat That Followed His Nose, The.
My Last Illusion.
Kendall, Laura E.
Evening Prayer, An.
Kendall, May
Lay of the Trilobite, The.
Seraph and the Snob, The.
Taking Long Views.
Kendrick, Deborah
For Mama.
Me and Hercule Poirot.
Question of Art, A.
Kendrick, John F.
Christians at War.
Kenji, Miyazawa. *See* **Miyazawa Kenji**
Kenko (Yoshida no Kenko)
Cold in the Grass.
Geese Departing at Early Dusk.
I awake from sleep.
I have made a pledge.
If one is not used.
In the capital.
Just where do you find.
Live here for awhile.
Off the beach at dusk.
Person I meet, A.
Plovers on the Coast.

Secret Affair Comes to Its End, A.
There is no place.
Kennedy, Benjamin Hall
Memorial Lines on the Gender of Latin
    Substantives.
On ["Who Wrote Icon Basilike" by Dr.]
    Christopher Wordsworth, Master of Trinity.
Roman Calendar, The.
Kennedy, Edwin O.
Prayer for Charity, A.
Kennedy, Geoffrey Anketell Studdert-. *See*
    Studdert-Kennedy, Geoffrey Anketell
Kennedy, Gerta
Chesapeake.
Kennedy, James
Chased from my calling to this hackneyed
    trade, *sel.*
Kennedy, Leo
Epithalamium: "This body of my mother,
    pierced by me."
Rite of Spring.
Words for a Resurrection.
Kennedy, Mary
Indolent Gardener, The.
Unfortunate Mole, The.
Kennedy, Sara Beaumont
Prayer Rug, The.
Kennedy, Walter
Honour with Age.
Kennedy, X. J.
Abominable Baseball Bat, The.
Abyss.
Aged Wino's Counsel to a Young Man on the
    Brink of Marriage, The.
Agnes Snaggletooth.
Airport in the Grass.
Ambition.
Ars Poetica.
Artificer.
At a Low Mass for Two Hot-Rodders.
At Mount Rushmore I looked up into one, *sel.*
At the Body Club.
B Negative.
Bee.
Birth Report, *sel.*
Brats.
Cat Who Aspired to Higher Things, The.
Certain Sandpiper, A.
Cross Ties.
Different Door, A.
Down in Dallas.
Driving Cross-Country.
Epitaph for a Postal Clerk.
Evening Tide.
Faces from a Bestiary.
Father and Mother.
First Confession.
Fresh Brats.
From Emily Dickinson in Southern California.
Golgotha.
Great-great Grandma, Don't Sleep in Your
    Treehouse Tonight.
Hangover Mass.
Haunted Oven, The.
Help!
Hickenthrift and Hickenloop.
In a Prominent Bar in Secaucus [One Day]
In the Motel.
Japanese Beetles.
Keep a Hand on Your Dream.
Last Child.
Last Lines.
Last Lines on a Wrestler.
Lighting a Fire.
Little Elegy.
Loose Woman.
Mingled Yarns.
Mixed-Up School.
Mother's Nerves.
My Dragon.
Nothing in Heaven Functions as It Ought.

Nude Descending a Staircase.
On a Child Who Lived One Minute.
One Winter Night in August.
Pont Mirabeau.
Paperclips.
People.
Rondel: "World is taking off her clothes, The."
Solitary Confinement.
Terse Elegy for J.V. Cunningham.
Things on a Microscope Slide.
To an Angry God.
To Dorothy on Her Exclusion from the *Guinness Book of World Records*.
Unusual Shoelaces.
Whales off Wales, The.
Witnesses, The.

Kennelly, Brendan
Horse's Head, The.
My Dark Fathers.
Pilgrim, The.
Proof.
Thatcher, The.
Yes.

Kenner, Peggy Susberry
Black Taffy.
Comments.
Image in the Mirror.
No Bargains Today.

Kenney, Richard
In Retrospect, *sel.*
La Brea.
Light.
One might as well conceive this story in the cirrose, *sel.*
Perfect Disc of the Moon, The.

Kenny, Maurice
Corn-Planter.
December.
First Rule.
Going Home.
Legacy.
O Wendy, Arthur.
Reverberation.
Strawberrying.
Sweetgrass.
They Tell Me I Am Lost.
Wild Strawberry.
Winkte.
Wolf "Aunt."

Kensai, Yaguchi. *See* **Yaguchi Kensai**

Kent, Rolly
Old Wife, The.

Kenyon, James Benjamin
Bedouins of the Skies, The.
Bring Them Not Back.
Challenge, A.
Come Slowly, Paradise.
Death and Night.
Tacita.
Two Spirits, The.

Kenyon, Jane
Camp Evergreen.
November Calf.
Suitor, The.
What Came to Me.

Kenyon, John
Champagne Rosée.

Keppel, David
Trouble.

Keppel, Frederick
Plain Man's Dream, A.

Keppel, Lady Caroline
Robin Adair.

Ker, L.
Death of the Gods; an Ode Written in Imitation of Pindar, The.

Ker, W. P.
Song of Degrees, A.
Theme and Variations.
There Is Snowdrift on the Mountain.

Kerekere, Wiremu Kingi
Greeting to Queen Elizabeth, the Rare White Heron of Single Flight, A.

Kernahan, Coulson
I ran for a catch.

Kerner, Justinus
Home-Sickness.

Kerouac, Jack
Chorus: "Big Engines, The," *sel.*
Chorus: "Essence of Existence, The," *sel.*
Chorus: "Glenn Miller and I were heroes," *sel.*
Chorus: "Got up and dressed up," *sel.*
Chorus: "In the ocean there's a very sad turtle," *sel.*
Chorus: "Love's multitudinous boneyard," *sel.*
Chorus: "Nobody knows the other side," *sel.*
Chorus: "Old Man Mose," *sel.*
Chorus: "Only awake to Universal Mind," *sel.*
Chorus: "Praised be man, he is existing in milk," *sel.*
Chorus: "Saints, I give myself up to thee," *sel.*
Chorus: "Void that's highly embraceable, The," *sel.*
Chorus: "Wheel of the quivering Meat, The," *sel.*
How to Meditate.
My Gang.
Pull My Daisy.
Sea Shroud, The.

Kerr, Alexander
Mary and Her Dead Canary.

Kerr, Hugh Thomson
Thy Will Be Done.

"Kerr, Orpheus C." (Robert Henry Newell)
American Traveller, The.
Columbia's Agony.
Dear Father, Look Up.
Editor's Wooing, The.
Neutral British Gentleman, The.
O, Be Not Too Hasty, My Dearest.
Rejected "National Hymns, The."
Tuscaloosa Sam.
When Your Cheap Divorce Is Granted.

Kerr, Sandra
What'll the Neighbours Say?

Kerr, Walter H.
She Walks in Ugly.
Vampire.

Kerr, Watson
Ancient Thought, The.

Keso
Drop by drop, seventy-seven winters.

Keso Shogaku
For twenty years I've sought the other.

Kessler, Jascha
Waiting for Lilith.
Words Read in a Poem in a Dream.

Kessler, Milton
Sea's Last Gift; 1961, The.

Ketchum, Annie Chambers
Bonnie Blue Flag, The.

Ketchum, Arthur
Spirit of the Birch, The.

Kethe, William
Old Hundredth.
Such as in God the Lord Do Trust.
Thy Mercies, Lord, to Heaven Reach.

Kettle, Thomas Michael
Lady of Life, The.
To My Daughter Betty.

Kevorkian, Karen
Softball Dreams.

Key, Francis Scott
Hymn: "Lord, with glowing heart I'd praise thee."
Star-spangled Banner, The.
To My Cousin Mary, for Mending My Tobacco Pouch.
Written at the White Sulphur Springs.

Keyes, Margaret G. *and* **Jeanne Youngson**
Vampire's Love Song, The.

Keyes, Scott
Interference.

Keyes, Sidney
Death and the Plowman.
Early Spring.
Elegy: "April again, and it is a year again."
Gardener, The.
Grail, The.
Greenwich Observatory.
Holstenwall.
Moon is a poor woman, The, *sel.*
Neutrality.
Plowman.
Red rock wilderness, The, *sel.*
Remember Your Lovers.
Rome Remember.
Time Will Not Grant.
Timoshenko.
Wilderness, The.
William Wordsworth.
William Yeats in Limbo.

Keysner, Blanche Whiting
Old River Road.

Kgositsile, Keorapetse
For Eusi, Ayi Kwei and Gwen Brooks.
Ivory Masks in Orbit.
My Name Is Afrika.
New Age.
Origins.
Requiem for My Mother.
Spirits Unchained.

Khaketla, B. Makalo
Lesotho.

Khaketla, N. M.
White and [the] Black, The.

Khalifa, Ali Abdallah
Clover Flower, The.
On Saying Goodbye to the Lady in Green.

Khansa
Tears.

Kharik, Izi
August.
Here I bend my young head and am still.
Pass On, You Lonely Grandfathers.

Kharms, Daniil
Connection, The.
Sonnet, A: "Amazing thing happened to me, An."
Vindication.

Khayyám, Omar
Ah, with the grape my fading life provide, *sel.*
Awake! for morning in the bowl of night, *sel.*
Book of verses underneath the bough, A, *sel.*
Come, fill the cup, and in the fire of spring, *sel.*
Iram indeed is gone with all his rose, *sel.*
Myself when young did eagerly frequent, *sel.*
O Thou, who man of baser earth didst make, *sel.*
Rubáiyát of Omar Khayyám, The.
They say the lion and the lizard keep, *sel.*
Think, in this batter'd caravanserai, *sel.*
Wake, for the sun, who scattered [*or* scatter'd] into flight, *sel.*

Khazak, Yekhi'el
All Night Long Burned the Bridges.

Kherdian, David
That Day.

Khomsky, Dov
Cloudless Morning, A.
Distance from Me to You, The.
Even on the Loveliest of Nights.
Moon Dips in the Puddle's Flow, The.
Paper Flowers.

Sunbeams Diagonally.
Your Eyes That Gaze.
Khouri, Khalil
Ants and the Sun.
Cripple, The.
Khoury-Gata, Venus
Autumn made colors burn, The.
Backed up against time.
My father has big skin like a soldier's cape.
Poem: "Our walls were thick."
Your cheeks flat on the sand.
Ki no Suemochi. *See* **Suemochi**
Ki no Tsurayuki. *See* **Tsurayuki**
Kibkarjuk
Song of the Rejected Woman.
Kicknosway, Faye
After Hilary, Age 5.
Cigarette Poem, The.
Crystal.
Gracie.
Gracie, 1967.
Horse, The.
I am the woman of sweaty language, the belly, *sel.*
I Wake, My Friend, I.
In Mysterious Ways.
Lament: "And what shall I be today, what."
Mr. Muscle-On.
Old Man.
Rapunzel.
There Is No.
"Kid Kazanova." *See* **Stack, Philip**
Kidman, Fiona
Guy Fawkes '58.
Train Song.
Kido
Hearing the Snow.
Kie Tapu
Song by a Woman Accused of Adultery.
Kieran, John
There's This That I Like about Hockey, My Lad.
To Lou Gehrig.
Kifu
Pitifully baby frogs.
Kii, Lady
I know the reputation/ of the idle ways.
Kiju
Frog has legs, The.
Kikaku (Takarai [*or* Enomoto] Kikaku)
Against the morning glories, *sel.*
Amused at My Own Figure while Traveling, *sel.*
An evening shower, *sel.*
At a grass hut I eat smartweed, *sel.*
Autumn sky has detached itself, The, *sel.*
Baby sparrows.
Began drinking sake at fifteen, *sel.*
Bosho's Old Hut, *sel.*
Breaking a branch off my cherry tree.
Bright moon: on the straw mat, *sel.*
Darkening mountains are distant, *sel.*
Even on the bridge, *sel.*
Even swallows seem to have no time, *sel.*
Evening dusk: flying in the middle, *sel.*
Evening shower has washed, The, *sel.*
Harvest moon:/ On the bamboo mat.
Haziness is the blackness of pines, *sel.*
He goes, his horse as his shield, *sel.*
Here and there frogs croak.
In an evening shower ducks walk around, *sel.*
In the sleet too, the heron, *sel.*
In the tree-searing wind, *sel.*
Lightning: again the sky's morning glow, *sel.*
Lightning: in the east yesterday, *sel.*
On charcoal dust, *sel.*
On New Year's dawn.
Shoes going over rocks have fins, *sel.*
Shrike calls when I kiss my infant's cheek, A.
Slashed in a dream, *sel.*
Sleeping butterfly, *sel.*

Swallow has erased a rainbow, A, *sel.*
Think it's your snow, *sel.*
Voice hoarse, the monkey's teeth, *sel.*
Winter comes, and a crow perches, *sel.*
Winter river: a raft sits, A, *sel.*
Woman on a spring night, A, *sel.*
Wooden gate.
Yearly Regret, *sel.*
Year's first day, The, *sel.*
Young woman plants seedlings, A, *sel.*
Kikuchi Gozan
Abandoned Garden.
Kilgore, James C.
White Man Pressed the Locks, The.
Killian, Kevin
Pasolini.
Killigrew, Anne
Farewel to Worldly Joyes, A ("Farewel to unsubstantial joyes").
On Death.
Upon the Saying That My Verses Were Made by Another.
Killigrew, Henry
Song: "While Morpheus thus doth gently lay."
Kilmer, Joyce
Easter.
House with Nobody in It, The.
Mid-Ocean in War-Time.
Poets.
Roofs.
Rouge Bouquet.
Trees.
White Ships and the Red, The.
Kilmer, Kenton
Yellow.
Kilner, Dorothy
Henry's Secret.
Kilpi, Eeva
And Dreams Paled.
Even nature gives you no choice.
Fifth Day, The.
He Stepped inside my Door.
Midsummer's Rose, A.
One Morning the Earth Stirred.
Thistle.
Tomorrow I Will Heat the Sauna.
Weather Forecasters.
What is this sound that wakens me at night?
Where behind the Night Did You Get Lost.
"Kim"
To the Woman in the Office.
Kim Chun-soo
Absence.
After the Leaves Fall.
At Gesthemane.
Bare Tree and Poetry.
Death.
Flower.
In June.
Insect Eyes.
It was raining in winter, *sel.*
Jung-sup Lee I Saw.
Just a Little Wind.
Lilac Blossoms.
Little Boy, A.
Mrs. West of West Village ("Mrs. West's hands are younger than her age").
Painter Jung-sup Lee.
Prelude for a Flower.
Rhythm.
Snow That Falls on Chagall's Village.
Stepping-stone.
Tears.
Two Dogs.
Your Hair.
Kim Chun-soo, Ruth
Sketch of Flower.
Kim Hyun-sung
Absolute Faith.
Absolute Solitude.
Ash.

Autumn's Fragrance.
Autumn's Poem.
End of Solitude.
Horizons.
My Mind is Dry Boughs.
Night Fog, The.
When Oakwood Burns.
Kimball, Hannah Parker
Beyond.
Soul and Sense.
Kimball, Harriet McEwen
All's Well.
Guest, The.
White Azaleas.
Kimball, Jacob
Thy Praise, O God, in Zion Waits.
Kimpu
This moonlit evening.
King, Anna M.
Faith and Sight.
King, B. B.
Why I Sing the Blues.
King, Ben (Benjamin Franklin King)
Appearances.
Cow Slips Away, The.
Cultured Girl Again, The.
Evolution.
Flowers' Ball, The.
Girl with the Jersey, The.
Hair-Tonic Bottle, The.
If I Should Die.
Mermaid, The.
Owl and the Crow, The.
Pessimist, The.
Sum of Life, The.
Sunrise.
That Cat.
Tramp, The.
Ultimatum, The.
King, Dorothy
Billy Boy.
Gipsy Man.
Jenny and Johnny.
King, E. L. M.
Cobwebs.
King, Edith
Duck, The.
Evening Song.
Hedgehog, The.
Pebbles.
Rabbit, The.
To the Bat.
King, Edward
Tsigane's Canzonet, The.
Woman's Execution, A.
King, Eleanor Hamilton
Garden of the Holy Souls, The, *sel.*
King, Ethel
Wood Music.
King, Francis
Séance.
King, Henry, Bishop of Chichester
Anniverse; an Elegy, The.
Contemplation upon Flowers, A.
Departure; an Elegy, The.
Exequy, The.
My Midnight Meditation.
Renunciation, A.
Sic Vita, *at.*
Since lovers' joys then leave so sick a taste, *sel.*
Sleep on, my love, in thy cold bed, *sel.*
Sonnet: Double Rock, The.
Sonnet: "Go, thou that vainly dost mine eyes invite."
Sonnet: "Tell me[e] no more how fair[e] she[e] is."
Surrender, The.
Thou from th' enthroned martyrs blood-stain'd line, *sel.*
To My Dead Friend Ben: Johnson.

Upon a Braid of Hair in a Heart.
Upon the Death of My Ever Desired Friend
    Doctor Donne Dean of Pauls.
Vow-Breaker, The.

King, Jenny
I Enter by the Darkened Door.

King, Jill
Grief Plucked Me Out of Sleep.

King, Stoddard
Breakfast Song in Time of Diet.
Crime at Its Best.
Difference, The.
Étude Géographique.
Hearth and Home.
Idyll.
Trombone Solo.

King, William
Beggar Woman, The.
Far from the parlour have your kitchen plac'd,
    sel.
How fleet is air! how many things have
    breath, *sel.*
Mountown! Thou Sweet Retreat, *sel.*
Sometimes the frugal matron seems in haste,
    sel.

Kingsley, Charles
Airly Beacon.
Ballad: "It was Earl Haldan's daughter."
Clear and Cool, *sel.*
Easter Week.
Farewell, A: "My fairest child, I have no song
    to give you."
Farewell, To C. E. G, A.
Instruction sore long time I bore.
Invitation, The.
Last Buccaneer, The.
Lost Doll, The, *sel.*
Myth, A.
Ode to the Northeast Wind.
Sands of Dee, The, *sel.*
Song: "When I was a greenhorn and young."
Three Fishers, The.
Valentine's Day.
Watchman, The.
When All the World Is Young.
Young and Old, *sel.*

Kingsley, Henry
At Glastonbury.

Kingsmill, Hugh
'Tis summer time on Bredon.
What, still alive at twenty–two.

Kingston, Jeremy
Distances.

Kinnell, Galway
After Making Love We Hear Footsteps.
Angel, The.
Another Night in the Ruins.
Bear, The.
Behind the Power Station on 14th, the held
    breath, *sel.*
Black bear sits alone, A, *sel.*
Blackberry Eating.
Braemar.
Burning.
Cells Breathe in the Emptiness.
Children set fires in ashbarrels, *sel.*
Correspondence School Instructor Says
    Goodbye to His Poetry Students, The.
Crying.
Daybreak.
Dead Shall Be Raised Incorruptible, The.
December Day in Honolulu.
Driftwood from a Ship.
Duck-chasing.
Fergus Falling.
First Song.
First Sun Day of the year. Tonight, *sel.*
Fishmarket closed, the fishes gone into flesh,
    The, *sel.*
Flower Herding on Mount Monadnock.
For Robert Frost.

For the Lost Generation.
Fossils, The.
Freedom, New Hampshire.
Fundamental Project of Technology, The.
Getting the Mail.
Hen Flower, The.
Homecoming of Emma Lazarus, The.
How Many Nights.
In a Parlor Containing a Table.
In Fields of Summer.
In sunlight on the Avenue, *sel.*
In the pushcart market, on Sunday, *sel.*
In the Twentieth Century of My Trespass on
    Earth, *sel.*
La Bagarède.
Last Songs.
Lastness.
Little Sleep's-Head Sprouting Hair in the
    Moonlight.
Man Splitting Wood in the Daybreak, The.
Middle of the Way.
Night in the Forest.
On Frozen Fields.
On Hardscrabble Mountain.
On the Oregon Coast.
On the Tennis Court at Night.
Path among the Stones, The.
Pcheek pcheek pcheek pcheek pcheek, *sel.*
Poem, The: "On this hill crossed."
Poems of Night.
Porcupine, The.
Promise was broken too freely, The, *sel.*
Reply to the Provinces.
Ruins under the Stars.
Saint Francis and the Sow.
Seekonk Woods, The.
Sometimes I see them, *sel.*
Spindrift.
Spring Oak.
Supper after the Last, The.
To Christ Our Lord.
To William Carlos Williams.
Under the Maud Moon.
Vapor Trail Reflected in the Frog Pond.
Wolves, The.

Kinney, Elizabeth Clementine
Blind Psalmist, The.
Dream, A.
Quakeress Bride, The.
To the Boy.

Kino Sadamaru
Though this body, I know.

Kinoshita Yuji
Late Summer.

Kinsella, Thomas
Ancestor.
Another September.
At the Crossroads.
Baggot Street Deserta.
Ballydavid Pier.
C. G. Jung's "First Years."
Carol: "Garden and gardener He made."
Character, indistinct, entered, A, *sel.*
Chrysalides.
Clarence Mangan.
Country Walk, A.
Cover Her Face.
Crab Orchard Sanctuary, Late October.
Death Bed.
Dispossessed, The.
Downstream.
Finistére.
First Light.
Folk Wisdom.
Hand of Solo, A.
Hen Woman.
His Father's Hands.
I must lie down with them all soon and sleep,
    sel.
In the Ringwood.
Inside, it is bare but dimly alive, *sel.*
It is hard to beat a good meal, *sel.*

Je T'Adore.
Landscape and Figure.
Laundress, The.
Leaf-eater.
Love.
Mask of Love.
Midsummer.
Mirror in February.
Model School, Inchicore.
Nightwalker.
Point, greatly enlarged, The, *sel.*
Ritual of Departure.
Sacrifice.
Scylla and Charybdis.
Secret Garden, The.
Song: "Engine screams and Murphy, isolate,
    The."
Spark of Laurel.
Tao and Unfitness at Inistiogue on the River
    Nore.
Tear.
Thinking of Mr. D.
Touching the River.
Westland Row.
Wormwood.
Wyncote, Pennsylvania: A Gloss.

Kipling, Francis Hastings
Buddha at Kamakura.

Kipling, Rudyard
Appeal, The.
Arithmetic on the Frontier.
Astrologer's Song, An.
Ballad of East and West, The.
Ballad of Fisher's Boardinghouse, The.
Batteries Out of Ammunition, *sel.*
Beginner, The.
Big Steamers.
Boots.
Bridegroom, The, *sel.*
Bridge-Guard in the Karroo.
By the Hoof of the Wild Goat, *sel.*
Chant-Pagan.
Cities and Thrones and Powers, *sel.*
Code of Morals, A.
Cold Iron.
Common Form, *sel.*
Conundrum of the Workshops, The.
Coward, The, *sel.*
Dane-Geld.
Danny Deever.
Dead Statesman, A.
Dead Statesman, A, *sel.*
Dedication, A: "My new-cut ashlar takes the
    light."
Delilah.
Derelict, The.
Dove of Dacca, The.
Drifter off Tarentum, A, *sel.*
Dykes, The.
'Eathen, The.
Eddi's Service.
Equality of Sacrifice, *sel.*
Evarra and His Gods.
Female of the Species, The.
Flight of the Bucket, The.
For All We Have and Are.
For to Admire.
Ford o' Kabul River.
Fuzzy-Wuzzy.
Galley-Slave, The.
Gehazi.
Gentlemen-Rankers.
Gethsemane.
Gipsy Trail, The.
Gods of the Copybook Headings, The.
Gunga Din.
Harp Song of the Dane Women, *sel.*
Heriot's Ford.
Hump, The, *sel.*
Hyaenas [*or* Hyenas], The.
I am the cat that walks by himself.
If.

In Springtime.
In the Neolithic Age.
Jobson's Amen.
La Nuit Blanche.
Ladies, The.
Land, The.
Land of Our Birth.
Last Chantey, The.
Last Lap, The.
Law of the Jungle, The.
Legends of Evil I, The.
L'Envoi: "There's a whisper down the field where the year has shot her yield."
L'Envoi: "When Earth's last picture is painted, and the tubes are twisted and dried."
Lie, The.
Liner She's a Lady, The.
Look, You Have Cast Out Love!, sel.
Looking Glass, The.
McAndrew's Hymn.
Mandalay.
Mary Gloster , The.
Mesopotamia.
Morning Song in the Jungle.
Mother o' Mine.
Municipal.
My Rival.
Nativity, A.
Nurses, The, sel.
Old Men, The.
Pagett, M. P.
Philadelphia.
Pict Song, A, sel.
Pink Dominoes.
Poseidon's Law.
Post That Fitted, The.
Power of the Dog, The.
Prodigal Son, The, sel.
Puck's Song, sel.
Rebirth.
Recessional.
Refined Man, The, sel.
Return, The.
Return of the Children, The.
Rhyme of the Three Captains, The.
Runes on Weland's Sword, The.
St. Helena Lullaby, A.
Sea and the Hills, The.
Seal Lullaby, sel.
Sergeant's Weddin', The.
Service Man, The.
Sestina of the Tramp-Royal.
Shillin' a Day.
Sing-Song of Old Man Kangaroo, The.
Skating.
Smuggler's Song, A, sel.
"Soldier an' Sailor Too."
Son, A, sel.
Song of the Banjo, The.
Song of the Galley-slaves.
Song to Mithras, A, sel.
Sons of Martha, The.
Storm Cone, The.
Story of Uriah, The.
Supplication of the Black Aberdeen.
There Is a Tide, sel.
There was a young boy [or man] of Quebec, at.
Tomlinson.
Tommy.
Ulster.
Undertaker's Horse, The.
Vampire, The.
Way Through the Woods, The.
We and They, sel.
When 'Omer Smote 'Is Bloomin' Lyre.
White Man's Burden, The.
Widow at Windsor, The.
Winners, The, sel.
Kipling, Sir Alfred
Stellenbosch.

Kirantaiyar
Hymn to Tirumal (Visnu).
Kirby, David
Nocturne: "Toughs walk by in groups explosive."
Kirby, Jeannie
Aeroplane, The.
Child's Morning Prayer, A.
I Wonder.
Pigeon's Story, The.
Proud Little Spruce Fir.
Timid Bunnies.
Union Jack, The.
Kircher, Pamela
Intimate Earth, The.
Kirk, Norman Andrew
Black Aggie.
Crip.
Tingle, The.
Kirkconnell, Watson
Ah, Flood of Life on which I am a wave, sel.
Crow and the Nighthawk, The.
Kirkland, Hilaire
Arranged on the opposite porch is a male, sel.
Atropos, sel.
Clotho, sel.
Daily the neighbour's dog is withdrawn to the park, sel.
Lachesis, sel.
Turn again, maiden, twice slain and rotten, sel.
Kirkup, James
Baby's Drinking Song.
Correct Compassion, A.
Earth Tremor in Lugano.
Gay Boys.
Giving and Taking.
Japanese Fan.
Lonely Scarecrow, The.
Love of Older Men, The.
Nature of Love, The.
Old Gramophone Records.
Shepherd's Tale, The.
Sumo Wrestlers.
To My Children Unknown, Produced by Artificial Insemination.
Ursa Major.
Zen Archer, The.
Kirsch, Olga
Blockhouse.
Wordspinning.
Kirsch, Sarah
Before the Sun Rises.
Brief Landing.
Dandelions for Chains ("Dandelions meet me wherever I am").
Sad Day in Berlin.
Kirschenbaum, Blossom S.
Portrait of the Consort to Louis XIV.
Realpolitik.
Kirstein, Lincoln
Fall In.
Foresight.
Rank.
Vaudeville.
Kirstinä, Väinö
Fierce Old Trees.
Propaganda Art.
This Rocky Land.
You Will See Far.
Kiser, Samuel Ellsworth
Fighter, The.
When I Had Need of Him.
Kishun Ryuki
At Shoraku-ji in Omi, First Poem of the Year.
First Poem of the Year.
Kiskaddon, Bruce
Cowboy's Dream, The.
Old Night Hawk, The.

That Little Blue Roan.
When They've Finished Shipping Cattle in the Fall.
Kiss, Anna
Cosmic Tapestry.
Miniatures.
Kiss, Jozsef
New Ahasuerus, The.
Kitahara Hakushu
Cat.
Caterpillar.
First Love.
Larch Trees.
Larches.
Memory.
Memory of Pinks.
Okaru and Kampei.
One-sided Love.
Rain on Castle Island.
Terror.
Time Passes.
Water Hyacinth.
Kitchell, Marilyn
Three.
Kitchen, Judith
Perennials.
"Kitchener, Lord"
Miss Tourist.
Kito (Takei Kito)
Bright moon: a crab, The, sel.
Daybreak: in its madder-red, sel.
Escaping a dog, a rooster flaps, sel.
Even the soil is withered and saddening, sel.
I drink water and my stomach bulges, sel.
I see the shadow of a warbler, sel.
Love, sel.
On my stupid face I see white, sel.
Out of sadness I eat fish, sel.
Parting, sel.
Pitying a Woman Who Has Many Affairs, sel.
Sitting Quietly at Night, sel.
Skylark rises through the dawn, A, sel.
Stand of winter trees, A, sel.
Stepping on violets, sel.
Tumble, fall, crash, then silence, A, sel.
Ugly sight—a burn mark on the straw mat, An, sel.
Warbler escapes next door, A, sel.
Warbler, what are you afraid of?, sel.
Water Lowers and Stones Show, sel.
When evening comes, plovers fly, sel.
Winning wrestler leaves, The, sel.
Winter copse.
Woman who has crossed the river, A, sel.
Yawning and praising the moon, sel.
See also Buson and Kito
Kitsujo
Lodging in the puddle from the straw coat.
Kittaararter
Take Your Accusation Back!
Kittner, Alfred
Blue Owl Song.
Old Jewish Cemetery in Worms.
Kivkarjuk
I am but a little woman.
Kiwus, Karin
All Splendor on Earth.
Hommes à Femme.
Lesson on the Facts of Life.
Make-off.
Kiyo
For eighty years I've talked of east and west.
Kiyoko Tsuda
To be a mistress.
Kiyowara Fukuyabu
River-Fog.
Shui Shu.
Kizer, Carolyn
Amusing Our Daughters.
Blessing, The.
Columns and Caryatids.

Copulating Gods, The.
Exodus.
For Jan, in Bar Maria.
From Sappho to myself, consider the fate of women, *sel.*
Great Blue Heron, The.
Hera, Hung from the Sky.
Hiding Our Love.
Horseback.
I take as my theme, "The Independent Woman", *sel.*
I will speak about women of letters, for I'm in the racket, *sel.*
Intruder, The.
Lines to Accompany Flowers for Eve.
Lovemusic.
Muse of Water, A.
One to Nothing.
Semele Recycled.
Singing Aloud.
Skein, The.
Summer near the River.
Thrall.
Through a Glass Eye, Lightly.
To a Visiting Poet in a College Dormitory.
Ungrateful Garden, The.
Widow in Wintertime, A.

Klappert, Peter
Ellie Mae Leaves in a Hurry.
For the Poet Who Said Poets Are Struck by Lightning Only Two or Three Times.
Invention of the Telephone, The.
Lord's Chameleons, The.
Poem for L. C.

Klauber, Edgar
On Buying a Dog.

Klein, Abraham Moses
And in That Drowning Instant.
Autobiographical.
Baal Shem Tov.
Ballad of the Days of the Messiah.
Bestiary.
Biography.
Break-up, The.
Design for Mediæval Tapestry.
For the Sisters of the Hôtel Dieu.
Grain Elevator.
Haggadah.
Heirloom.
In re Solomon Warshawer.
Indian Reservation: Caughnawaga.
Lone Bather.
Monsieur Gaston.
Montreal.
Political Meeting.
Portrait of the Poet as Landscape.
Psalm VI: Upon the Heavenly Scarp, *sel.*
Quebec Liquor Commission Store.
Rabbi Yom-Tob of Mayence Petitions His God.
Rev Owl.
Rocking Chair, The.
Spinning Wheel, The.
Still Small Voice, The.
Sugaring, The.
Venerable Bee, The.
Winter Night: Mount Royal.

Kleinzahler, August
Soda Water with a Boyhood Friend.

Kleiser, Grenville
Challenge, The.
Most Vital Thing in Life, The.
My Daily Prayer.

Klepfisz, Irena
Death Camp.
Dedication: "These words are dedicated to those who died," *sel.*
Few Words in the Mother Tongue, A.
From the Monkey House and Other Cages: Monkey II.
Royal Pearl.

Klinger, Kurt
Beginning.
Cats, The.
Cinema.
Crazy Lady, The.
Mattina.
Miracle in Milan.
Never.
We Think Farewell.

"Klingle, George" (Georgiana Klingle Holmes)
As Thy Days So Shall Thy Strength Be.
He Will Give Them Back.

Kloefkorn, William
Taking the Milk to Grandmother.

Knapp, Shepherd
Lord God of Hosts.
Not Only Where God's Free Winds Blow.

Knevet, Ralph
Passion, The.

Knibbs, Henry Herbert
Boomer Johnson.
Out There Somewhere.

Knies, Elizabeth
Absence.

Knight, David
Chief of the West, Darkling, The.
In Memoriam S. L. Akintola.
Palms, The.
"When the Students Resisted, a Minor Clash Ensued."

Knight, Etheridge
Another Poem for Me.
Apology for Apostasy?
As You Leave Me.
Bones of My Father, The.
Cell Song.
Feeling Fucked Up.
For Black Poets Who Think of Suicide.
For Dan Berrigan.
For Freckle-faced Gerald.
Haiku: "Eastern guard tower."
Hard Rock Returns to Prison from the Hospital for the Criminal Insane.
He Sees Through Stone.
Huey.
I Sing of Shine.
Idea of Ancestry, The.
It Was a Funky Deal.
My Life, the Quality of Which.
On the Birth of a Black/Baby/Boy.
On Watching Politicians Perform at Martin Luther King's Funeral.
Poem to Galway Kinnell, A.
Portrait of Malcolm X.
Sun Came, The.
To Dinah Washington.
To the Man Who Sidled Up to Me and Asked: "How Long You In Fer, Buddy?"
2 Poems for Black Relocation Centers.
Upon Your Leaving.
Violent Space, The.
Warden Said to Me the Other Day, The.

Knight, Henry Coggswell
Lunar Stanzas.

Knight, John
Father to the Man.

Knight, Sarah Kemble
Pleasant Delusion of a Sumpteous Citty.
Resentments Composed because of the Clamor of Town Topers Outside My Apartment.
Thoughts on Pausing at a Cottage near the Paukataug River.
Thoughts on the Sight of the Moon.
Warning to Travailers Seeking Accomodations at Mr. Devills Inn.

Knister, Raymond
Boy Remembers in the Field.
Change.
February's Forgotten Mitts.

Feed.
Hawk, The.
Nell.
Nell, *sel.*
Plowman, The.
Plowman's Song.
Stable-Talk.

Knoepfle, John
She says how/ is it when you, *sel.*

Knott, William ("Saint Geraud")
Breeze Nomadly Coupling Summer Sounds (Precision Insects Chomping).
Death.
(End) of Summer (1966).
Goodbye.
Hair Poem.
Poem: "After your death."
Poem: "At your light side trees shy."
(Poem) (Chicago) (The Were-Age).
Poem: "Only response, The."
Poem: "Our eyes unlash slowly one."
Sleep.
Song: "She was lyin face down in her face."
Stillborn (Domesticity # three), The.

Knowles, Frederic Lawrence
L'Envoi: "O love triumphant over guilt and sin."
Nature: The Artist.
Out of the Depths.
Pasture, A.
To Jesus of Nazareth.

Knowles, James D.
O God, though Countless Worlds of Light.

Knowles, Suzanne
Fox Dancing.
Tails and Heads.

Knox, Caroline
Movement along the Frieze.
Reggae Blue Sweater.

Knox, Edmund George Valpy ("Evoe")
Inspiration.
Last Bus, The.
Limerick: "There was a young curate of Hants."
To the God of Love.
Tryst, The.
Upon Julia's Clothes.

Knox, J. Mason
Co-operation.

Knox, Ronald Arbuthnott
Absolute and Abitofhell.
Anglican curate in want, An.
Idealism.
Limerick: "Evangelical vicar in want, An."

Knox, Ross
Dying Times, The.
Easy Chairs and Saddle Sores.
So Long.

Knox, William
Oh! Why Should the Spirit of Mortal Be Proud?

Knudson, R. R.
Wilt Chamberlain.

Knut, Dovid
Haifa.
Rosh Pina.
Safed.
Walking along the Sea of Galilee.
Woman from the Book of Genesis, A.

Kocan, Peter
Bill.
Hospital Kangaroos, The.
Sleepers, The.

Koch, Christopher
Half-heard.

Koch, James
Fitness Center Chant, A.

Koch, James H.
To a Young Lady Swinging Upside Down on a Birch Limb over a Winter-swollen Creek.

Koch, Kenneth
Down at the Docks.
Fresh Air.
Geography.
I certainly have lost something, *sel.*
Locks.
Lunch.
Mending Sump.
Permanently.
Poem for My Twentieth Birthday.
Poem of the Forty-eight States, A.
Poem: "Thing, The/ To do/ Is organize."
Railway Stationery, The.
Schoolyard in April.
Sleeping with Women.
Stones of Time, The, *sel.*
Thank You.
Thanksgiving.
To Marina.
To win the love of women one should first
   discover, *sel.*
Variations on a Theme by William Carlos
   Williams.
What People Say about Paris.
You Were Wearing.
Koehn, Adam
Divorce.
Koenig, Alma Johanna
Intimations.
Koertge, Ron
Jockey, A.
Koethe, John
Mission Bay.
Mistral.
Substitute for Time, The.
Kogawa, Joy
Ancestors' Graves in Kurakawa.
Dream after Touring the Tokyo Tokei.
Hiroshima Exit.
On Meeting the Clergy of the Holy Catholic
   Church in Osaka.
Woodtick.
Kogetsu
Numskull for eighty-five years!, A.
Kogon, Emperor
As the night grows late.
Autumn Poem, An.
Burning sun and clouds.
Crow in the night, A.
Dream.
Even the frog's voices.
Evening sun shines, The.
From a clump of grass.
Hung low with clouds.
Last weak rays, The.
Love Poem, A: "That widowed crow."
Moon at evening, The.
Night Snow.
Plain of Heaven, The.
Shapes of swallows.
Summer Evening.
Summer Night.
When I stop to think.
Koh Chang-soo
Agnes.
Aspiring Poet.
At the Art Gallery.
Between August and November.
By the River.
By the Sea on a Winter Day.
Christmas.
Face.
In a Remote Korean Village.
Jane's Village.
Landscape.
Memory of a Rose.
Mirror Fantasy.
Ocean Liner.
On a Snowy Night.
On a Winter Evening.
Sketch of Hands.

Snow Fall.
To a Korean Percussion Ensemble.
Koho
Death sitting, death standing.
Koianimptiwa
Yellow butterflies, at.
Kokan Shiren
Autumn Day Stroll in the Country.
Earthquake.
For seventy-four years.
On Something Observed.
Kokuin
I'm twenty-seven years.
Kokuo
Difficult road, The.
Kolatkar, Arun
Between Jejuri and the Railway Station.
Heart of Ruin.
Station Master, The.
Kollan Alici
What She Said.
Koller, James
I Have Cut an Eagle.
O Dirty Bird Yr Gizzard's Too Big & Full of
   Sand.
Some Magic.
Unreal Song of the Old, The.
Kolleritsch, Alfred
House is closed, The.
I don't trust my impressions.
It is increasingly less difficult to get up.
It wants to reveal itself as progress.
Night in which one re-reads the sentences,
   The.
"These poems were anticipations."
This time we have not returned from a trip.
Thus pressed to the edge.
When a person writes.
Kolmar, Gertrud
Jewish Woman, The.
Out of the Darkness.
Paris.
Sea-Monster.
Woman Poet, The.
Woman Undiscovered.
Komachi (Ono no Komachi)
Color of the flowers, The/ has faded.
Doesn't he realize/ that I am not/ like the
   swaying kelp.
How helpless my heart!
If it were real/ Perhaps I'd understand it.
Lustre of the flowers, The.
Ninekeen Tanka, *sels.*
Was it that I went to sleep.
When my love becomes.
Komey, Ellis Ayitey
Oblivion.
Komparu Zenchiku
Teika, a No Play, *at.*
Komrij, Gerrit
Afternoon, An.
Comreigh Critter, The.
Dragons, The.
Fertile.
Homecoming, The.
On Your Back.
Unicorn, The.
Woman in the Arts, The.
Komunyakaa, Yusef
April Fools' Day.
Copacetic Mingus.
Facing It.
Ia Drang Valley.
More Girl Than Boy.
Saigon Bar Girls, 1975.
Somewhere near Phu Bai.
Starlight Scope Myopia.
We Never Know.
Konda Azuma
Fire.
Mediterranean Woman.

Konek, Carol
Daring.
Konishi Raizan. *See* **Raizan**
Konopnicka, Maria
Vision, A.
Koo Siu-sun
Song of Moon and Snow.
Kook, Rav Abraham Isaac
First One Drew Me, The.
Radiant Is the World Soul.
When I Want to Speak.
Ko'oku
At human footfalls a frog.
Koopman, Harry Lyman
Icarus.
John Brown.
Revealed.
Satirist, The.
Sea and Shore.
Kooser, Ted
Anniversary.
At Midnight.
Beer Bottle.
Camera.
Central.
Child's Grave Marker, A.
First Snow.
Flying at Night.
For a Friend.
Genuine Poem, Found on a Blackboard in a
   Bowling Alley in Story City, Iowa.
In January, 1962.
In Tennessee.
In the Basement of the Goodwill Store.
Just Now.
Myrtle.
Wild Pigs.
Kopelke, Kendra
Eager Street.
Kopland, Rutger
Among the Flowers.
Blackbird.
Conversation.
Dead Birds.
G ("G, I wrote a poem about your face").
Johnson Brothers Ltd.
No Generation.
Tarzan Once More.
Young Lettuce.
Kopp, Karl
Incident.
Koran, Yanagawa. *See* **Yanagawa Koran**
Korelitz, Jean Hanff
Properties of Breath, The.
Korin
Narrow path: frog, A.
Korinna
Although I was her pupil,/ even I reproach
   Myrtis.
I blame Myrtis.
I disapprove even of eloquent/ Myrtis.
I Korinna am here to sing the courage.
Kithairon sang of cunning Kronos.
Terpsichore looks kindly on me.
To the white-mantled maidens.
When he sailed into the harbor.
Will you sleep forever?
Kormos, István
After Us.
Deep Sea.
I Am Being Dragged by Red Dolphins.
Lament of Orpheus, The.
Voyage.
Korn, Rachel
From Here to There.
I'm Soaked Through with You.
Keep Hidden from Me ("Keep from me all
   that I might comprehend!").
Letter, A.

Longing.
My Body.
New Dress, A.
Put Your Word to My Lips.
Sometimes I Want to Go Up.
Thirty-one Camels, The.
Too Late.
With Poems Already Begun.

Korn, Rokhl
Crazi Levi.
I Stand in the Midday.
Last Night I Felt a Poem on My Lips.
On the Other Side of the Poem.

Korran
What She Said to Her Girl Friend.

Körte, Sister Mary Norbert
Ghost Poem Five.

Kortes, Charles A.
Poets Gathering, 1985.

Korzhavin, Naum
Children of Auschwitz.

Kosai
Frog climbs up a willow, A.

Koseisoku
Arms stretching from the precipice, finally.

Koshiro, Fujito. *See* **Fujito Koshiro**

Kosovic, Ante
Ah Dalmatia, if only I could send word of
your dear sons.

Kostelanetz, Richard
Concentric.
Disintegration.

Kotaro, Takamura. *See* **Takamura Kotaro**

Kouwenaar, Gerrit
Elba.
Found Subjects.
4 Variations On.
Hand Etc.
Landscape Left Behind.
Like an Object.
Place: Somewhere.
When Water Stands Still It's Stone.
Without Colors.
Without Names.

Kovatattan
What Her Girl Friend Said to Her.

Kovner, Abba
Between mountains coils a city. Wind.
Dimmed Observation.
Dinosaurs.
Front Page.
Hour's Late, The.
How Many Poems Were Lost.
I Don't Know if Mount Zion.
Lookout on a Rock on the Heights of Mount
Hermon.
Lord of Dreams.
My Sister.
Near.
Note apropos a Light Breeze and an Elderly
Couple on a Bench, Together, in the
National Park at Ram.
Note apropos the Neighbor's Garden.
Observation at Dawn.
Observation on a Small Harbor outside the
Military Zone.
Observation on a Solitary Tree.
Of All My Loves.
On My Words.
Poem: Alte Zachen.
Scientists Are Mistaken, The.
Sun-Watchers.
Tashlich.
This Way, This Way.
To the Things That Are Immortal.
Voice of My White City, The.
Vow.
While at Prayer.

Kovur Kilar
Poet's Counsel ("You come from the line of a
Cola king"), A.
Poet's Counsel, A ("Your enemy is not the
kind who wears").

Kowit, Steve
Dracula.
Hate Mail.
It Was Your Song.
Lullaby.
Renewal.
Swell Idea, A.

Koyama, Tina
Definitions of the Word *Gout.*
Grape Daiquiri.
Next.
Ojisan after the Stroke; Three Notes to
Himself.

Kozan, Yabu. *See* **Yabu Kozan**

Kozer, José
Cleaning Day.
My Father, Who's Still Alive.
Store in Havana, The.

Koziol, Urszula
Alarum.

Kräftner, Hertha
I idolize you with litanies, *sel.*
If One Had a Blue Vase and a Clock in an
Old Wooden Cabinet.
Who still believes.
You, pushed-in window in terribly beautiful
countries!, *sel.*
You stony angel over the pain, *sel.*

Kramer, Aaron
Portrait by Alice Neel.

Kramer, Edgar Daniel
Sequence.

Kramer, Lotte
Cissie.
Genesis.
Scrolls.

Krapf, Norbert
Basketball Season Begins.

Kraus, Karl
Express Train.
On the Threshold.

Krauss, Ruth
Duet.
End Song.
Song.
Song: "I'd much rather sit there in the sun."
Song: "Reading about the Wisconsin Weeping
Willow."
Song: "When your boyfriend writes you a
letter."

Kraut, Rochelle
My Makeup.
No Regret.
Sheep.
We Laughed.

Krechel, Ursula
All of the Easiness Gone.
Hymn to the Women of the Middle Class.
To Mainz!
Warning.

Kredenser, Gail
Brontosaurus.
Polar Bear.

Kreps, Gretchen
Leopard.

Kreymborg, Alfred
To W. C. W. M. D.

Kriebel, Casper
Now Sleep My Little Child So Dear.

Krige, Uys
Distant View.
Encounter.
Farm Gate.
Soldier, The.
Swallows over the Camp.

Kriloff, Ivan Andreevich
Peasant and the Sheep, The.

Krinagoras, Robert
From the Greek Anthology.

Krishnamurti, M.
Spirit's Odyssey, The.

Krmpotic, Vesna
December Forest, A.

Kroetsch, Robert
Stone Hammer Poem.

Kroll, Ernest
California Zephyr, The.
Winter Race Meeting.

Kroll, Judith
Dick and Jane.
I Think of Housman Who Said the Poem Is a
Morbid Secretion, like a Pearl.
Not Thinking of America.
Sestina: "Is this the object."

Kroll, Steven
McIntosh Apple.

Kruger, Fania
Passover Eve.

Kryss, Tom
And Jesus Don't Have Much Use for His Old
Suitcase Anymore.
Ballad of an Empty Table.
Bell Too Heavy to Ring.
Breaking Ground in Me.
Nothing Strange.
Suicide, A.
This Wind.

Kshetrayya
Dancing-Girl's Song.

Ku Hsiung
Beautiful Lady Yü, The.
Drunken Gentleman, The.
Echoing Heaven's Everlastingness.
Hatred of Distant Places.
Immortal at the River.
Lotus Leaf Cup.
Offering Deep Affection.
River Messages.
Sand of Silk-Washing Stream.
Song of Kan-chou.
Song of the Fisherman.
Song of the Jade Tower in Spring.
Song of the Water Clock at Night.
Song of the Wine Spring.
Speaking of Love.
Tune: Telling of Innermost Feelings ("Long
nights when he neglects me—where's he
gone?").
Willow Branches.

Ku T'ai-ch'ing
In a Dream, I Visited a Place Called the
Monastery of Heavenly Music.
Sitting in Meditation: A Random Thought.
Sitting Up at Night.

Ku Yen-wu
Ching-wei.
Eight Feet.
Mocking Myself.
Po-hsia.

Kuan Kuan
Autobiography of a Sloppy Sluggard.
Two Trunks.

Kuan Tao Sheng
Married Love.

K'uang Chou-yi
Coolness creeping through the willows, rain
upon the flowers.
I Awake Crying on My Birthday.
One sound after another.
Thoughts upon Hearing a Singer.

Kuapakaa
Ocean Is like a Wreath, The.

Kubatum
Love Song to King Shu-Suen.

Kudaka, Geraldine
Birthright.

Death Is a Second Cousin Dining with Us
  Tonight.
Giving Up Butterflies.
Okinawa Kanashii Monogatari.
On Writing Asian-American Poetry.

Kuder, Blanche Bane
Blue Bowl, The.

Kuijper, Jan
Annemarie Fischer: Portrait of Robbert.
Bullrush Basket.
Starchart.

Kuka, King D.
"A Taste of Honey."
Evening.
February Morning.
Gallery of My Heart.
Jackie.
Janna.
My Friend the Wind.
My Song.
Tiny baby, you're ugly.

Kulbak, Moishe
Ball, A.
Grandfather Dying, *sel.*
Grandpa and the Uncles, *sel.*
I Just Walk Around, Around, Around.
In the attic, at night, a poor man sits, *sel.*
In the Tavern.
Nastasya, *sel.*
Spring.
Summer.
Ten Commandments.
Two.
Uncle Avram Pastures the Horses, *sel.*
Vilna.
Winter at Night in the Old Hut, *sel.*

Kumattur Kannanar
Where the Lilies Were in Flower.

Kumin, Maxine W.
Accidentally.
After Love.
Apostrophe to a Dead Friend.
Appointment, The.
At a Private Showing in 1982.
At the End of the Affair.
Changing the Children.
Envelope, The.
Excrement Poem, The.
Family Man, A.
Family Reunion.
For My Son on the Highways of His Mind.
400-Meter Freestyle.
Fräulein Reads Instructive Rhymes.
Grace of Geldings in Ripe Pastures, The.
Grandchild.
Halfway.
Hermit Has a Visitor, The.
Hermit Picks Berries, The.
Hermit Wakes to Bird Sounds, The.
How It Is.
How to Survive Nuclear War.
In the Absence of Bliss.
In the Pea Patch.
In the Root Cellar.
January 25th.
Longing to Be Saved, The.
Making the Jam without You.
Masochist, The.
May 10th.
Microscope, The.
Morning Swim.
Mummies, The.
Orb.
Our Ground Time Here Will Be Brief.
Presence, The.
Prothalamion.
Relearning the Language of April.
Remembering You.
Retrieval System, The.
Riding in the Rain.

Seeing the Bones.
Shelling Jacobs Cattle Beans.
Shopping in Ferney with Voltaire.
Sneeze.
Sound of Night, The.
Spending the Night.
Spree.
Stones.
To Swim, to Believe.
Together.
Video Cuisine.
Voice from the Roses, A.
Woodchucks.

Kunaikyo
Bringing flowers with it.
By the light or dark.

Kunene, Mazisi
Political Prisoner, The.
Thought on June 26.
To Africa.
Vengeance.

Kunene, Raymond Mazisi
Work Song.
You are lying, O missionary!

Kung Tzu-chen
By chance I composed "Ascending the
  Clouds," by chance I grew tired of flying,
  sel.
I Saw a Professional Juggler by the Roadside
  and Presented Him with This Poem, *sel.*
In the City of Wu, I Obtained a Record of
  Names from the Civil Service
  Examinations.
Tending a bare hill takes no small talent, *sel.*
There is a tall tower by the river.
This trip shall take me through hills to the
  north and east, *sel.*
View phenomena as void, view phenomena as
  appearance, such is the ultimate view, *sel.*

Kunimoto, Tsumori
Wild geese returning, The.

Kunitz, Stanley Jasspon
Abduction, The.
After the Last Dynasty.
An Old Cracked Tune.
Approach to Thebes, The.
Artist, The.
Benediction.
Careless Love.
Choice of Weapons, A.
Daughters of the Horseleech, The.
End of Summer.
Father and Son.
First Love.
For the Word Is Flesh.
Foreign Affairs.
Goose Pond.
He.
Hemorrhage, The.
I Dreamed That I Was Old.
Illumination, The.
Indian Summer at Land's End.
Intimations of Mortality.
Knot, The.
Lamplighter: 1914.
Last Picnic.
Long Boat, The.
Portrait, The.
Prophecy on Lethe.
Quinnapoxet.
Reflection by a Mailbox.
River Road.
Robin Redbreast.
Science of the Night, The.
She Wept, She Railed.
Single Vision.
Snakes of September, The.
Summing-up, The.
Testing-Tree, The.
Thief, The.

Three Floors.
Unquiet Ones, The.
Vita Nuova.
Waltzer in the House, The.
War against the Trees, The.
Welcome the Wrath.
Wellfleet Whale, The.
When the Light Falls.

Kunjufu, Johari M.
Promise, The.
Return.

Kunjufu, Johari M. *See* **Latimore, Jewel C.**

Kuntsch, Margaretha Susanna von
To a Good Friend Who Would Prove the
  Fickleness of Women with the Example of
  Queen Anne.

Kunze, John C.
Yoke Soft and Dear.

Kuo, Alex
Chinaman's Chance, A.
Did You Not See.
Early Illinois Winter, An.
Loss.
On a Clear Day I Can See Forever.
Sheltering the Same Needs.
There Is Something I Want to Say.
Turning On Daytime TV.
Words Most Often Mispronounced in Poetry.

Kuo P'o
Poem on the Wandering Immortal.

Kuramakal Ilaveyini
Tiger, The.

Kuriyiraiyar
What Her Friend Said Criticizing Him to Give
  Her Strength.

Kurka, Mira Teru
Crocodiles.
Fruit and Government.
Under Which Heading Does All This
  Information Go?

Kuroda, Saburoh
Afternoon 3.

Kurohito (Tami no Kurohito). *See* **Tami no
  Kurohito**

Kuroyanagi Shoha. *See* **Shoha**

Kusadao, Nakamura. *See* **Nakamura
  Kusadao**

Kusano Shimpei
Mount Fuji, Opus 5.
Stone.

Kushner, Aleksander
To Boris Pasternak.

Kushner, Bill
I Am.
My Sisters.
Up.

Kushniroff, Aaron
Die My Shriek.

Kuskin, Karla
Balloon, The.
Bug Sat in a Silver Flower, A.
Catherine.
Full of the Moon.
Giraffes Don't Huff.
Gold-tinted Dragon, The.
If you could be small, *sel.*
Lewis Has a Trumpet.
Me.
Meal, The.
Middle of the Night, The.
Miss M. F. H. E. I. I. Jones.
Moon/ Have you met my mother?
Question, The.
Rose on My Cake, The.
Rules.
Snow.
Spring.
Tiptoe.
Very Early.
When a Cat Is Asleep.

When I Went Out.
Where Have You Been Dear?
Winter Clothes.
Witches' Ride, The.

Kutavayir Kirattanar
Elegy: "Young will not wear it, The."
What Her Girl Friend Said before the
Elopement.

Kuzma, Greg
Dump, The.
Great Poems, The.
Hose and Iron.
In Love with the Bears.
Journal of the Storm.
Monster, The.
Pelican, The.
Poetry.
Sometimes.
Young Man Who Loved the Girl Who Took
Care of Her Aged Father, The.

Kvitko, Leyb
Day and Night.
Esau ("Esau,// Hairy Esau [or Shaggy]").
Inscrutable Cat.
Russian Death.

Kwitko, Leib
Moods.
My Fiddle.
You Who Dog My Footsteps.

Kyd, Thomas
Of Fortune, sel.

Kyei, Kojo Gyinaye
African in Louisiana.
Talking Drums, The.

Kyger, Joanne
And with March a Decade in Bolinas.
August 18.
Destruction.
Don't Hope to Gain by What Has Preceded.
I Have No Strength for Mine.
My Father Died This Spring.
Not Yet.
Of All Things for You to Go Away Mad.
Pigs for Circe in May, The.
September.
When I used to focus on the worries,
everybody.
When I Was Well into Being Savored.

Kynaston, Sir Francis
To Cynthia, on Concealment of Her Beauty.
To Cynthia on Her Being an Incendiary.
To Cynthia. On Her Changing.
To Cynthia, on Her Embraces.

Kyochu
One question, and master thunders.

Kyogoku Tamekane. See Tamekane
Kyogoku Tameko. See Tameko
Kyogoku Tamenori. See Tamenori

Kyohaku
Frog crawls out and rubs his back, A.

Kyohei, Rai. See Rai Kyohei

Kyorai (Mukai Kyorai)
Close of day, sel.
"Coming, coming!", sel.
Cuckoo sings/ at right angles, The, sel.
Deep in the family shrine, sel.
Distant sailboat never quite, A, sel.
Every boatman in, sel.
Fall breezes/ time to try out the, sel.
Full sail, reefed sail, sel.
He doesn't seem, sel.
How to tell, sel.
I called to the wind.
In this heat, sel.
On the Death of His Younger Sister, sel.
One paddy ceases croaking for a while.
Poem of Parting, sel.
Point of rock, sel.
Rocky shore/ flocks of plovers, sel.
So hot the melons, sel.
That mountain I crossed, sel.

Too dark to tell the gate, sel.
Waters of the lake, The, sel.
What's this?/ wearing a long sword, sel.

Kyoroku (Morikawa Kyoroku)
Autumn so soon.
Long, long ago now.

Kyoshi, Takahama. See Takahama Kyoshi

Kyosui
You hook it, but it's no fun.

Kyotai (Kato Kyotai)
Cold night/ pasania nuts rolling down, sel.
Column of mosquitoes, A, sel.
Day ending/ and again it starts, sel.
Daybreak/ whales trumpet, sel.
Falling leaves/ fall and pile up, sel.
Leaves falling/ on top of the smoke, sel.
Melting snow/ among deep mountains clouded
over, sel.
Nights when the muddy river, sel.
Observing as I go along, sel.
On her way, the little nun, sel.
Quivering/ in the heat waves, sel.
Start of winter, sel.
Sun has set, The, sel.
Waves are hot, The, sel.
Winter shut in—/ a single fly, sel.

Kyozo, Tagaki
Winter Moon, The.

L

"L., C. G."
Master, The.

L. J. See J., L.

La Coste, Marie
Somebody's Darling.

La Farge, Christopher
Prayer for Living and Dying.

La Farge, Peter
Ballad of Ira Hayes.

La Follette, Melvin Walker
Ballad of Red Fox, The.
Blue Horse, The.
Didactic Sonnet.
Hunt.
I Knew a Boy with Hair like Gold.
Love for a Hare.
Spring Landscape.
Summerhouse.

La Fontaine, Jean de
Aesop's Fable of the Frogs.
Cock and the Fox, The.
Crow and the Fox, The.
Death and the Woodman.
Donkey and the Lapdog, The.
Eagle and the Beetle, The.
Fox and the Crow, The.
Fox and the Grapes, The.
Hag and the Slavies, The.
Love and Folly.
Man and His Image, The.
Rat and the Elephant, The.
Saddled Ass, The.
Wolf and the Dog, The.
Wolf and the Stork, The.
Wounded Bird, The.

La Grone, Oliver
Africland.
For Kinte.
Remnant Ghosts at Dawn.
This Hour.

La Parra, Manuel de
Well, The.

La Vigne, Anne de
Ladies to Mademoiselle de Scudéry: Ode,
The.
Reply to the Shade of Descartes.

Laaber, Otto
Collected Time.
From the Milky Way.
Inventory.
Positive.
September Heath.
These Days.
Who Says.

Labé, Louise
Elegy XXIII: "How does it help me if, with
flawless art."
Povre Ame Amoureuse.
Sonnet XVI: "After an age when thunderbolts
and hail."
Sonnet XIX: "After having slain very many
beasts."
Sonnet XIV: "Although I cry and though my
eyes still shed."
Sonnet: "As long as I continue weeping."
Sonnet IX: "As soon as I lie down in my soft
bed."
Sonnet VI: "Coming of that limpid star is
twice, The."
Sonnet XXIV: "Don't blame me, ladies, if
I've loved. No sneers."
Sonnet IV: "From that first flash when awful
Love took flame."
Sonnet XVII: "I flee the city, temples, and
each place."
Sonnet VIII: "I live, I die, I burn myself and
drown."
Sonnet XX: "I was foretold that on a certain
day."
Sonnet XIII: "If I could linger on his lovely
chest."
Sonnet XVIII: "Kiss me again, re-kiss and
kiss me whole."
Sonnet XII: "Lute, companion of my
calamity."
Sonnet I: "Not Ulysses, no, nor any other
man."
Sonnet XXII: "O blazing Sun, how happy you
are there."
Sonnet XI: "O eyes clear with beauty, O
tender gaze."
Sonnet II: "O handsome chestnut eyes,
evasive gaze."
Sonnet III: "O interminable desires, O futile
hope."
Sonnet: "Seer foretold that I would love one
day, A."
Sonnet XV: "To honor the return of sparkling
sun."
Sonnet VII: "We see each living thing finally
die."
Sonnet XXIII: "What good is it to me if long
ago."
Sonnet XXI: "What grandeur makes a man
seem venerable?"
Sonnet X: "When I perceive your blond and
graceful head."
Sonnet V: "White Venus limpid wandering in
the sky."

LaBombard, Joan
By the Beautiful Ohio.
Dreamers and Flyers.
Marbles.
Sibyl, The.
To My Daughter Riding in the Circus Parade.

Labriola, Gina
Orgy (That Is, Vegetable Market, at Sarno).

Labrunie, Gerard. See Nerval, Gerard de

Lacaussade, Auguste
My lips from this day forgot how to smile,
sel.

Lacey, E. A.
Abdelfatteh.
Guest.
Mesón Brujo.
Ramon.

Lacey, Florence
Promise.
Lachman, Sol
Sukkot.
Lachmann, Hedwig
Home-Sickness.
Walk, A.
Ladányi, Mihály
About the Hero.
Business, *sel.*
Entrance, *sel.*
For Example.
For the Record.
Inventory.
Lenin.
No Denying.
Phalanstery, *sel.*
Quietude.
Three Drawings.
We Just Sit About Quietly.
When All's Said and Done.
Lady of the Arbour
And at the last I cast my mine eye aside, *sel.*
Lady of the Assembly
Palace of Pleasant Regard, The, *sel.*
Laederach, Monique
And so I speak/ in place of that primordial cry, *sel.*
(Leaving the island, she believes, to go to the child.), *sel.*
Laforgue, Jules
Another Complaint of Lord Pierrot.
Apotheosis.
Cigarette, The.
Clair de Lune.
Clowns, The.
Coming of Winter, The.
Complaint of the King of Thule.
Complaint of the Moon in the Provinces.
Complaint of the Oblivion of the Dead.
Five-Minute Water Color.
Flying Dutchman, The.
For the Book of Love.
Foreword.
Funeral March for the Death of the Earth.
Gentlemen.
Impossible, The.
Lady.
Legend.
Moon Solo.
Mystery of the Three Horns, The.
Sunday Piece.
Unparalleled Severity.
LaGrone, Oliver
Africland.
Lahpu
Butterfly Maidens.
"Laidir." *See* **Mac Coisdealbhaigh, Tomas**
Laight, Frederick E.
Drought.
Laighton, Albert
Under the Leaves.
Laing, Alexander Kinnan
Original Sin.
Laing, Allan M.
Family Life.
Jack the Ripper.
Samuel Pepys.
When they found Giotto.
Laing, Dilys Bennett
Eros Out of the Sea.
Farm Hands, The.
Lines on the Sea.
Villanelle: "Proud inclination of the flesh."
Laing, Ronald David
Jill.
Laing, V. R.
Suicide, The.
Laird, Christopher
Sea at Evening, The.

Laird, Ursula
Cats Crept Up on Me Slowly.
Partly Because.
"Lakon"
William the Bastard.
Lal Ded
I drag a boat over the ocean.
Lalleswari
Good repute is water carried in a sieve.
I set forth hopeful—cotton-blossom Lal.
With my breath I cut my way through the six forests.
Laluah, Aquah
Nativity.
Laluah, Aquah. *See* **Hayford, Gladys May Casely**
Lamantia, Philip
Hermetic Bird.
Irrational.
Man Is in Pain.
Morning Light Song.
She Speaks the Morning's Filigree.
Still Poem 9.
Surrealism in the Middle Ages.
Terror Conduction.
Unachieved.
Violet Star.
Wilderness Sacred Wilderness.
Lamar, Mirabeau Buonaparte
Daughter of Mendoza, The.
Lamarque, Vivian
Weather Forecast.
Lamarre, Hazel Washington
Time and Tide.
Lamartine, Alphonse Marie Louis de
Cedars of Lebanon, The.
Lamb, Charles
Anger.
As When a Child.
Childhood Fled.
Choosing a Name.
Cleanliness.
Envy.
Family Name, The.
Farewell to Tobacco, A.
Feigned Courage.
Free Thoughts on Several Eminent Composers.
Going into Breeches.
Going or Gone.
Hester.
Hypochondriacus.
Io! Paean! Io! sing, *sel.*
Methinks How Dainty Sweet It Were.
Nonsense Verses.
Old Familiar Faces, The.
On an Infant Dying as Soon as Born.
To John Lamb, Esq.: Of the South-Sea House.
Triumph of the Whale.
We Were Two Pretty Babes.
Written at Cambridge.
Lamb, Charles and Mary Lamb
Boy and the Snake, The.
Lamb, Mary
Parental Recollections.
Lambert, Elisabeth
Brave Old World.
"Lambert, Louis." *See* **Gilmore, Patrick Sarsfield**
Lambert, Mary Eliza Tucker. *See* **Tucker, Mary E.**
Lamblin, Barbara
Medals and Money: A Re-evaluation.
Lamdan, Yitzhak
On an autumn night, lying restless, far from her broken homeland, *sel.*
Where am I, O awesome friend?, *sel.*
LaMers, Joyce
Observation by a Formerly Rose-Lipt Maiden.
River Nile, The.

Lamont, Colin
Rothiemurchus.
Lampman, Archibald
After the Shower.
Among the Millet.
City of the End of Things, The.
Comfort of the Fields.
Dawn on the Lievre, The.
Heat.
In November.
January Morning, A.
Largest Life, The.
Midnight.
Morning on the Lièvre.
Prayer, A: "O Earth, O dewy mother, breathe on us."
Solitude.
Sunset at Les Éboulements, A.
Temagami.
Thunderstorm, A.
To a Millionaire.
Truth, The.
Violinist, The.
Winter Evening.
Lamport, Felicia
Buck Up.
Clobber the Lobber.
Eggomania.
Mother, Mother, Are You All There?
Poll Star.
Preparedness.
Lan Ling
Approaching.
Car, A.
Conversing.
Listening to Red Maples on an Empty Mountain.
Lancaster, Osbert
Eireann, *sel.*
English, *sel.*
French, *sel.*
Italian, *sel.*
Manhattan, *sel.*
Lancaster, Sarah
Come on, my fellow pilgrims, come, *at.*
Lance Henson
Crazy Horse: The Last Morning.
Landau, Zishe
Epilogue: "Because the papers meanly ignore me."
I Have a Big Favour to Ask You, Brothers.
In the Tavern.
Little Pig, The.
Of Course I Know.
Parts.
Strikover Rabbi, The.
Strikover Rabbi's Wife, The.
This Evening.
Tuesday.
Landesman, Fran
I Quite Like Men.
Let's Not Think about That.
Landeweer, Elizabeth
Dakota Badlands.
Landles, William
Border Forecast, A.
On Ellson Fell.
Landor, W. D.
Winter.
Landor, Walter Savage
Above all gifts we most should prize.
Absence, *sel.*
Age.
Alas! 'Tis Very Sad to Hear.
Alciphron and Leucippe.
Art thou afraid the adorer's prayer.
Before a Saint's Picture.
Behold, O Aspasia! I Send You Verses, *sel.*
Bourbons.
Called Proud.
Case at Sessions, A.

Corinna, from Athens, to Tanagra, *sel.*
Corinna, to Tanagra, from Athens.
Critic, A.
Dead Marten, The.
Death of Artemidora, The, *sel.*
Death of the Day.
Death Stands above Me.
Dirce, *sel.*
Distribution of Honours for Literature.
Do You Remember Me?, *sel.*
Dragon-Fly, The.
Duke of York's Statue, The.
Dull Is My Verse.
Epigrams must be curt, nor seem.
Exhausted now her sighs, and dry her tears.
Fiesolan Idyl, A.
Florence.
For an Epitaph at Fiesole.
Foreign Ruler, A.
From you, Ianthe, little troubles pass, *sel.*
Garden at Heidelberg.
Georges, The.
God Scatters Beauty.
Graceful Acacia.
Had We Two Met.
Hamadryad, The, *sel.*
Have I, this moment, led thee from the beach.
Heart's Abysses, The.
Hearts-Ease.
Here lies Landor.
How often, when life's summer day.
How to Read Me.
I Know Not Whether I Am Proud.
I Strove with None, *sel.*
Ianthe! you resolve [*or* are called] to cross
  the sea!, *sel.*
Idle Words.
Interlude.
Iphigeneia and Agamemnon, *sel.*
Ireland Never Was Contented.
Is it no dream that I am he.
Izaac Walton, Cotton, and William Oldways.
La Promessa Sposa.
Lately Our Poets.
Love and Age.
Loves who many years held all my mind,
  The.
Maid's Lament, The, *sel.*
Malvolio.
Memory.
Mild is the parting year, and sweet, *sel.*
Mimnermus Incert.
Mother, I Cannot Mind My Wheel.
My hopes retire; my wishes as before, *sel.*
Neither in idleness consume thy days.
No charm can stay, no medicine can assuage.
No, thou hast never griev'd but I griev'd too.
O fond, but fickle and untrue.
O friends! who have accompanied thus far.
O Friendship! Friendship! the shell of
  Aphrodite.
Observing a Vulgar Name on the Plinth of an
  Ancient Statue.
On a Quaker's Tankard.
On Catullus.
On Himself.
On Man.
On Music.
On Seeing a Hair of Lucretia Borgia.
On the Death of M. D'Ossoli and His Wife,
  Margaret Fuller.
On the Heights.
On the Hellenics, *sel.*
On the smooth brow and clustering hair.
Our youth was happy: why repine.
Past Ruined Ilion Helen Lives.
Pigmies and Cranes.
Plays.
Poem: "I cannot tell, not I, why she."
Poet! I like not mealy fruit; give me.
Progress of Evening.

Proud word you never spoke, but you will
  speak, *sel.*
Quarrelsome Bishop, A.
Reflection from Sea and Sky.
Remain, Ah Not in Youth Alone.
Retired this hour from wondering crowds.
Rose Aylmer.
Scentless laurel a broad leaf displays, The.
Scribblers, The.
Sensible Girl's Reply to Moore's, A.
Silent, you say, I'm grown of late.
So Then, I Feel Not Deeply!
Some of Wordsworth.
Tamar's Wrestling, *sel.*
Ten thousand flakes about my window blow.
Ternissa! You Are Fled, *sel.*
There Are Sweet Flowers.
There are two miseries in human life.
There falls with every wedding chime, *sel.*
Thou hast not rais'd, Ianthe, such desire, *sel.*
Three Roses, The.
To a Lady Lately Married.
To a Spaniel.
To Age.
To My Child Carlino.
To My Ninth Decade I Have Tottered On.
To One Who Quotes and Detracts.
To Our House-Dog Captain.
To Poets.
To Robert Browning.
To Wordsworth.
To Youth.
Twenty Years Hence.
Various the roads of life; in one.
Very True, the Linnets Sing.
Well I Remember [How You Smiled], *sel.*
What News.
When Helen first saw wrinkles in her face,
  sel.
Why do the Graces now desert the Muse?
Will you come to the bower I have shaded for
  you?, *sel.*
William Gifford.
Ye walls! sole witnesses of happy sighs, *sel.*
Years.
Yes: I Write Verses.
You see the worst of love, but not the best.
You Smiled, You Spoke, and I Believed.

Landy, Francis
Lament for Azazel.
Midrash on Hamlet.
Princess Who Fled to the Castle, The.
Selichos.

Lane, Franklin K.
I Am What You Make Me ("I am whatever
  you make me, nothing more").

Lane, Patrick
At the Edge of the Jungle.
Beware the Months of Fire.
Elephants.
Gray Silk Twisting.
If.
Love.
Loving She Stood Apart.
Measure, The.
Mountain Oysters.
Passing into Storm.
Sleep on the Fraser.
Stigmata.
Surcease.
Treaty-Trip from Shulus Reservation.
Water-Truck, The.

Lane, Pinkie Gordon
Migration.
Nocturne: "Listening for the sound."
On Being Head of the English Department.
Sexual Privacy of Women on Welfare.
When You Read This Poem.
Who Is My Brother?

Lane, Wilmot B.
Owning.

Lang, Andrew
Brahma.
But now the dentist cannot die.
Clevedon Church.
I'd Leave.
Jubilee before Revolution.
Last Chance, The.
Limerick: "There was a young lady of
  Limerick."
Limerick: "There was an auld birkie ca'ed
  Milton."
New Shakespeare, A.
Odyssey, The.
Psalm of Life, A.
Scythe Song.
Tired of Towns.
Twilight on Tweed.

Lang, Andrew *and* **Edward Burnett Tylor**
Double Ballade of Primitive Man.

Lang, Elizabeth
Honey Bear.

Lange, Art
Confirmation.
History.
Le Tombeau de Frank O'Hara.
Poem: "Some who are uncertain compel me."

Langer, Jiri Mordecai
On the Margins of a Poem.
Riddle of Night.

Langfield, Angela
Living with You.

Langfield, June Mercer
Full fathom five thy father lies.

Langhorne, John
Country Justice, The.
Does nature bear a tyrant's breast?, *sel.*
Gypsies, *sel.*
Poor, The, *sel.*

Langland, Joseph
Aria for Flute and Oboe.
Conversations from Childhood: the Victrola.
Crane.
Ecclesiastes.
Hunters in the Snow: Brueghel.
Pruners: Conca di Marini ("Pruners have come
  again among the vineyards").
Sacrifice of a Red Squirrel.
Sea-Change: For Harold, A.
War.
Willows.
Winter Juniper.

Langland, William
Age of Reason, The, *sel.*
And I bowed my body and beheld all about,
  sel.
As for the birds and the beasts, the men in
  bygone times, *sel.*
Birds I beheld building nests in the bushes,
  sel.
Civil Service, The, *sel.*
Descent into Hell, The, *sel.*
Entertainment Industry, The, *sel.*
Envy with heavy heart asked for shrift, *sel.*
Et Incarnatus Est, *sel.*
For trewthe telleth that loue is triacle of
  hevene, *sel.*
Glutton [*or* Glutton in the Tavern], The, *sel.*
God's Mercy, *sel.*
Good Works, *sel.*
Grace for Theology.
In a summer [*or* somer] season, when soft[e]
  was the sun [*or* sunne *or* sonne], *sel.*
Incarnation, The, *sel.*
Palace of Truth, The, *sel.*
Palmer, The, *sel.*
Poor, The, *sel.*
Rectors and parish priests complained to the
  bishop, *sel.*
Saint Called "Truth," A, *sel.*
View from Middle-Earth, A, *sel.*
Vision of Jesus, The, *sel.*

Vision of Nature, A, *sel.*
What for feere of this ferly and of the false Jewes, *sel.*
What this mountain means, and the murky dale, *sel.*
Wool-chafed and wet-shoed I went forth after, *sel.*
Yet I courbed on my knees and cried hire of grace, *sel.*

Langley, Eve
Native Born.

Langton, Stephen
Hymn to the Holy Spirit.

Langworthy, Yolande
Drifting Sands and a Caravan.

Lanier, Emilia
Eves Apologie.

Lanier, H. Glenn
O Christ of Bethlehem.

Lanier, Sidney
Ballad of Trees and the Master, A.
Betrayal, *sel.*
But Thee, but Thee, O sovereign Seer of time, *sel.*
Centennial Meditation of Columbia, The.
Dear Land of All My Love, *sel.*
Dying Words of Stonewall Jackson, The.
Evening Song.
From the Flats.
Harlequin of Dreams, The.
Hound, The, *sel.*
Land of the Wilful Gospel, *sel.*
Laus Mariae.
Lexington, *sel.*
Marsh Song—at Sunset.
Marshes of Glynn, The.
Mocking Bird, The.
My Springs.
Night and Day.
Opposition.
Raven Days, The.
Resurrection.
Revenge of Hamish, The.
Ship of Earth, The.
Song of the Chattahooche.
Song of the Chattahoochee.
Stirrup-Cup, The.
Story of Vinland, The, *sel.*
Struggle.
Sunrise, *sel.*
Symphony, The.
Tampa Robins.
Thar's More in the Man than Thar Is in the Land.
Triumph, The, *sel.*
Wedding-Hymn.
Whate'er Has Been.

Lanigan, George Thomas
Dirge of the Moolla of Kotal.
Threnody, A: "What, what, what/ What's the news from Swat?"

Lankford, Frances Stoakley
Required Course.

Lanusse, Armand
Epigram: "Do you not wish to renounce the Devil?"

Lanyon, Carla Lanyon
Crusade in Europe.

Lao Tzu
Tao Te Ching.

LaPage, Geoffrey
Mr. Giraffe.

LaPena, Frank. *See* **Tauhindauli**

Lapidus, Jacqueline
Coming Out.

Lara, Countess (Eva Cattermole Mancini)
In the Evening.

Larbaud, Valery
Alma Perdida.

And you, Italy, one day I knelt, *sel.*
At the end of a little sloping street, I recognize, *sel.*
Death of Atahuallpa, The.
Eterna Voluttà, L.'
Gift of Oneself, The.
Images.
In Colombo or Nagasaki I examine the Baedekers, *sel.*
Mask, The.
Midnight at sea like so many other midnights at sea, *sel.*
Music after Reading.
My Muse.
November Morning Near Abingdon.
Ode: "Lend me thy great noise, thy powerful, gentle gait."
Old Station of Cahors, The.
Poet's Wish.
Prologue: "Borborygms! Borborygms!"
Scheveningen, Off Season.
Thalassa.

Larcom, Lucy
Brown Thrush, The.
Dumpy Ducky.
For the rosebud's break of beauty, *sel.*
Giles Corey.
Hannah Binding Shoes.
Hymn Written for the Two Hundredth Anniversary of the Old South Church, Beverly, Massachusetts.
In the Tree-Top.
Mistress Hale of Beverly.
Mountains.
Nature's Easter Music.
Nineteenth of April, The.
Plant a Tree.
Sinking of the *Merrimac, The.*
Spring Whistles.
Strip of Blue, A.
Thanksgiving, A.
Tolling.
Trees, The.
Volunteer's Thanksgiving, The.

Lardner, Ring
Abner Silver's "Pu-leeze! Mr. Hemingway!"
Fragment from "Clemo Uti—the Water Lilies."
Hail to Thee, Blithe Owl.
Hardly a Man Is Now Alive.
Parodies of Cole Porter's "Night and Day."
Quiescent, a Person Sits Heart and Soul.

Larkin, Joan
Clifton.
Rape.
Rhyme of My Inheritance.

Larkin, Mary Ann
House of Broughton Street, The.
Riding on a Streetcar with My Father.

Larkin, Philip
Age.
Ambulances.
Annus Mirabilis.
Arrivals, Departures.
Arundel Tomb, An.
As Bad as a Mile.
At Grass.
Aubade: "I work all day, and get half drunk at night."
Born Yesterday.
Card-Players, The.
Church Going.
Coming.
Cut Grass.
Days.
Deceptions.
Dedicated, The.
Dry-Point.
Dublinesque.
Explosion, The.
Faith Healing.

Fiction and the Reading Public.
First Sight.
Forget What Did.
Going.
Going, Going.
Heads in the Women's Ward.
Here.
High Windows.
Homage to a Government.
Home Is So Sad.
I Remember, I Remember.
If, My Darling.
Lines on a Young Lady's Photograph Album.
Love Songs in Age.
Maiden Name.
Mr. Bleaney.
Myxomatosis.
Naturally the Foundation Will Bear Your Expenses.
Next, Please.
Night-Music.
MCMXIV.
No Road.
North Ship, The.
Nothing to Be Said.
Places, Loved Ones.
Poetry of Departures.
Posterity.
Sad Steps.
Self's the Man.
Send No Money.
Seventy Feet Down, *sel.*
So through that unripe day you bore your head.
Spring.
Study of Reading Habits, A.
Sunny Prestatyn.
Take One Home for the Kiddies.
Talking in Bed.
This Be the Verse.
To the Sea.
Toads.
Toads Revisited.
Trees, The.
Ultimatum.
Waiting For Breakfast, While She Brushed Her Hair.
Wants.
Water.
Wedding-Wind.
Whatever Happened?
Whitsun Weddings, The.
Wild Oats.
Within the Dream You Said.

Larminie, William
Nameless Doon [*or* Dun]

Larner, Sam
Smacksman, The.

Larremore, Wilbur
Blossom Time.
Madam Hickory.

Larsen, Carl
Plot to Assassinate the Chase Manhattan Bank, The.

Lart, K. C.
Walk in Spring, A.

Lask, Berta
Jewish Girls, The.
Painted Madonna Speaks, The.
Self-Judgment.

Lasker-Schüler, Else
Abel.
Abraham and Isaac.
Always in the Parting Year.
End of the World.
Hagar and Ishmael.
Homesick.
I Have a Blue Piano.
I Know That I Must Die Soon.
Jacob.
Jacob and Esau.

Jacob ("Jacob: a bull among his herd").
Lord, Listen.
Love Song, A: "Come to me in the night—we shall sleep closely together [*or* Let us sleep entwined]"
Love-Song: "Out of one golden breath."
Love's Flight.
Moses and Joshua.
My Love-Song.
My People.
Pharaoh and Joseph ("Pharaoh rejects his blossoming wives").
Reconciliation.
Rock Crumbles, The.
Saul.
Shulamite, The.
Voices of Eden, The.
Zebaoth.

Lassell, Michael
Dino, *sel.*
Going Rate, The, *sel.*
How to Find Love in an Instant, *sel.*
How to Watch Your Brother Die.
Stud, *sel.*

Lathbury, Mary Artemisia ("Aunt Mary")
Break Thou the Bread of Life.
Day Is Dying in the West, at.
Easter Song.
Song of Hope.

Lathrop, Adele
Because He Lives.

Lathrop, George Parsons
Child's Wish Granted, The.
Feather's Weight, A.
Flown Soul, The.
Keenan's Charge.
Marthy Virginia's Hand.
Remembrance.
South-Wind.
Sunshine of Thine Eyes, The.
Voice of the Void, The.

Lathrop, Lena
Woman's Question, A.

Lathrop, Rose Hawthorne
Clock's Song, The.
Dorothy.
Give Me Not Tears: Despair.
Give Me Not Tears: Joy.
Song before Grief, A.

Lathrop, Walter
Here Is a Toast That I Want to Drink.

Latimer, Bette Darcie
For William Edward Burghardt Du Bois on His Eightieth Birthday.

Latimore, Jewel C.
Positives.
Saint Malcolm.
Utopia.

Latimore, Jewel C. (Johari Amini; Johari M. Kunjufu)
Before/ and After.
Brother.
Ceremony.
Childhood.
On the Naming Day.
Signals.
Sun Heals, A.
To a Poet I Knew.

Lattimore, Richmond
Anniversary.
Bathtubs.
December Fragments.
Dislike of Tasks.
Failure.
Father, The.
Game Resumed.
Krankenhaus of Leutkirch, The.
Max Schmitt in a Single Scull.
Monastery on Athos.
North Philadelphia, Trenton, and New York.

Remorse.
Report from a Planet.
Reports of Midsummer Girls.
Rise and Shine.
Shadowgraphs, The.
Siding near Chillicothe, A.
Tudor Portrait.
Witness to Death.

Lau, Alan Chong
Crossing Portsmouth Bridge.
Day of the Parade.
Father Takes to the Road and Lets His Hair Down.
Letters from Kazuko (Kyoto, Japan—Summer 1980).
Living in the World.

Laube, Clifford James
At the Battery Sea-Wall.

Lauer, Mirko
Amphibians, The.
Angels, The.
Classics Revisited, The.
Cruel Photograph without Light at Daybreak.
Finger-print.
Leit-Motif: Oh Great City of Lima.
Lynx.
1916.
Notes on the Moving of a Corpse.
Patios of Ithaca.
Tanks.
To the Memory of a Pre-Incaic Wiseman.

Laufer, Calvin W.
We Thank Thee, Lord.

Laughlin, Elmer Osborn
Unknown, The.

Laughlin, J.
You Came as a Thought.

Laughlin, James
Lament of Professor Turbojet, The.
Letter to Hitler, A.
Martha Graham.
Mountain Afterglow, The.
Step on His Head.
Summons, The.
Swarming Bees, The.

Laughton, Freda
At the Party.
Bull, The.
Evacuees, The.
To the Spring Sun.
Welcome, The.
When from the Calyx-Canopy of Night.
When to My Serene Body.

Lauren, Joseph
Butterfly and the Caterpillar, The.

Laurence, Elsie
Alone.

Lauterbach, Ann
Psyche's Dream.

Lavant, Christine
Buy Us a Little Grain.
Do Not Ask.
For you I have exchanged the lights.
I asked the headless snake.
In the empty center of the cyclone.
None of the easy remedies has proved effective.
Similar people don't hear one another.
Slyly, the sadness trickles down.
Through these glassy afternoons.
Up and down without a bridge.
When your name is added.
You have taken me away from all joy.

Lavater, Louis
Faithless.
Mopoke.

Lavelle, Thomas.　*See* **Flavell, Thomas**

Lavington, Margaret
Underworld, The.

Lavoie, Steven
Cloud Spots.

In Mutual Time.
Make Way.

Law, T. S.
Wemen's Wather.

Lawless, Emily
After Aughrim.

Lawner, Lynne
In Your Arrogance.
Possession.
Rino's Song.

Lawrence, David Herbert
All Souls.
All Souls' Day.
Almond Blossom.
American Eagle, The.
Andraitx—Pomegranate Flowers.
Argonauts, The.
Autumn Rain.
Aware.
Baby Tortoise.
Baby Running Barefoot.
Ballad of Another Ophelia.
Bare Almond-Trees.
Bat.
Bavarian Gentians.
Bei Hennef.
Birthday.
Blue Jay, The.
Bombardment.
Bride, The.
Britannia's Baby.
Brooding Grief.
Butterfly.
Cherry Robbers.
Collier's Wife, The.
Coming Awake.
Cypresses.
Delicate Mother Kangaroo.
Desire Is Dead.
Doe at Evening, A.
Don Juan.
Don'ts.
Dreams Old and Nascent.
Elemental.
Elephant Is Slow to Mate, The.
End of Another Home Holiday.
Energetic Women.
Enkindled Spring, The.
Fate and the Younger Generation.
Figs.
Flowers and Men ("Flowers achieve their own floweriness and its's a miracle").
Food of the North.
Fronleichnam.
Gazelle Calf, The.
Giorno dei Morti.
Gloire de Dijon.
Glory.
Gods! The Gods!, The.
Green.
"Gross, Coarse, Hideous" (Police Description of My Pictures).
He drank enough, *sel.*
Hibiscus and Salvia Flowers.
History.
How Beastly the Bourgeois Is.
Humming-Bird.
Hymn to Priapus.
I Am like a Rose.
In Trouble and Shame.
Intimates.
It's No Good!
Kangaroo.
Kisses in the Train.
Last Lesson of the Afternoon.
Lightning.
Little Fish.
Living, A.
Lizard.
Lord Tennyson and Lord Melchett.
Love on the Farm.
Lui et Elle.

Man and Bat.
Man of Tyre, The.
Maximus.
Medlars and Sorb-Apples.
Mess of Love, The.
Middle of the World.
Moonrise.
Morning Work.
Mosquito, The.
Mountain Lion.
My Way Is Not Thy Way.
New Heaven and Earth.
New Moon.
New Year's Eve.
Nostalgia.
Nothing to Save.
O! Start a Revolution.
On the Balcony *or* Illicit.
Passing Visit to Helen.
Pax.
Peace.
Peacock.
People.
Piano.
Proper Pride.
Quite Forsaken.
Red Geranium and Godly Mignonette.
Release.
River Roses.
Roses on the Breakfast Table.
Sea, The.
Sea-Weed.
Self-Pity.
Self-Protection.
Shadows.
Ship of Death.
Sicilian Cyclamens.
Snake.
Snap-Dragon.
Song of a Man Who Has Come Through.
Sorrow.
Spray.
Spring Morning.
Stand Up!
Suburbs on a Hazy Day.
Sunday Afternoon in Italy.
Suspense.
Swan.
They Say the Sea Is Loveless.
Things Men Have Made.
To Women, as Far as I'm Concerned.
Tommies in the Train.
Tortoise Family Connections.
Tortoise Gallantry.
Tortoise-Shell.
Tortoise Shout.
Towards the sun, towards the south-west, *sel.*
Trees in the Garden.
Twenty Years Ago.
Twilight.
Two Performing Elephants.
Volcanic Venus.
War-Baby.
We Are Transmitters.
Wedding Morn.
Whales Weep Not!
What Would You Fight For?
When I Read Shakespeare.
When I Went to the Circus.
When the Ripe Fruit Falls.
When Wilt Thou Teach the People?
Whether or Not.
White Blossom, A.
White Horse, The.
Wild Common, The.
Willy Wet-Leg.
Winter Dawn.
Winter's Tale, A.
Work.
Worm Either Way.
You.

Young Wife, A.
Youth Mowing, A.
Lawrence, J. B.
I Believe.
Lawrence, Margery
Garden in the Sky.
Lawrence, Ruth
Washington's Tomb.
Lawrence, Thomas Edward
To S. A.
Lawson, David
No Great Matter.
Lawson, Henry
Andy's Gone with Cattle.
Ballad of the Drover.
Faces in the Street.
Horseman on the Skyline, The.
Ned's Delicate Way.
Ripperty! Kye! Ahoo!
Sliprails and the Spur, The.
Talbragar.
Teams, The.
Up the Country.
Will Yer Write It Down for Me?
Lawson, James Gilchrist
All Nature Has a Voice to Tell.
O Lord, I Come Pleading.
War!
World Hymn, The.
Lawson, Sylvia
Trader's Return.
Lawson, Will
Bill the Whaler.
Lawton, William Cranston
My Fatherland.
Song, Youth, and Sorrow.
Lay, Norma
Sea Sonnet.
Layamon
Passing of Arthur, The, *sel.*
Laycock, Samuel
Bowton's Yard.
Homely Advice to the Unemployed.
Shurat Weaver's Song, The.
What! Another Cracked Poet.
Layne, Catherine Braan
Whispering Wind.
Layton, Irving
Aran Islands.
Bacchanal.
Berry Picking.
Birth of Tragedy, The.
Boys in October.
Bull Calf, The.
Butterfly on Rock.
Cain.
Cold Green Element, The.
Day Aviva Came to Paris, The.
Dionysus.
Fertile Muck, The.
For Anna.
For Mao Tse-tung; a Meditation on Flies and
    Kings.
For Musia's Grandchildren.
For My Brother Jesus.
For Natalya Correia.
From Colony to Nation.
Golfers.
Gothic Landscape.
Grand Finale.
Haunting, The.
Improved Binoculars, The.
Jewish Main Street.
Letter to a Librarian.
Nausicäa.
Newsboy.
Ohms.
Osip Mandelshtam.
Party at Hydra.
Tall Man Executes a Jig, A.
To the Girls of My Graduating Class.

Undine.
What Ulysses Said to Circe on the Beach of
    Aeaea.
Woman.
Words without Music.
Layzer, Robert
Elegy: "Whenever we touched, I thought of
    the Lying-in Hospital."
Insult, The.
Lawn Roller, The.
Saint's Parade.
Sleeping Beauty, The.
Lazard, Naomi
In Answer to Your Query.
Walking with Lulu in the Wood.
Lazarus, A. L.
Questions & Answers.
Lazarus, Emma
Banner of the Jew, The.
Bar Kochba.
Cranes of Ibycus, The.
Crowing of the Red Cock, The.
Currents, *sel.*
Exodus (August 3, 1492), The, *sel.*
1492.
Gifts.
Kindle the Taper.
Lines on Carmen Sylva.
Mater Amabilis.
New Colossus, The.
New Ezekiel, The.
On the Proposal to Erect a Monument in
    England to Lord Byron.
Venus of the Louvre.
Lazarus, K. F.
Bragatelle.
Lea, Fanny Heaslip
Dead Faith, The.
Lea, John
Silver House, The.
Lea, Margery
Bomb Story (Manchester, 1942).
Lea, Sydney
After Labor Day.
Bernie's Quick-Shave (1968).
Coon Hunt, Sixth Month (1955).
Fall.
Floating Candles, The.
Horn.
Issues of the Fall.
Natural Shame, A.
Night Trip across the Chesapeake and After.
Old Dog, New Dog.
Return: Intensive Care, The.
Sereno.
Telescope.
There Should Have Been.
To the Summer Sweethearts.
Train Out, The.
Leaf, Ebba M.
Dear Mother.
Her Son.
Leaf, Walter
Better Way, The.
Leale, B. C.
Rat, The.
Renderings and Sunderings of Cobbett's
    "Rural Rides."
Leapor, Mary
Epistle to a Lady, An.
Essay on Woman, An.
Mira's Will.
Lear, Edward
After Tennyson.
A[h] kond of Swat, The.
Alphabet.
Alphabet, An.
Animal Alphabet, An.
Calico Pie.
Children of the Owl and the Pussy-Cat, The.
Cold Are the Crabs.

Courtship of the Yonghy-Bonghy-Bo, The.
Cummerbund, The.
Dingle Bank.
Dong with a Luminous Nose, The.
Duck and the Kangaroo, The.
Eclogue: "What makes you look so black, so glum, so cross?"
How Pleasant to Know Mr. Lear.
Incidents in the Life of My Uncle Arly.
Jumblies, The.
Letter to Evelyn Baring, A.
Limerick: "There was a young lady of Corsica."
Limerick: "There was a young lady of Hull."
Limerick: "There was a young lady of Russia."
Limerick: "There was a young person of Crete."
Limerick: "There was a young person of Smyrna."
Limerick: "There was an old man in a boat."
Limerick: "There was an old man in a pew."
Limerick: "There was an old man in a tree."
Limerick: "There was an old man of Cape Horn."
Limerick: "There was an old man of Dunblane."
Limerick: "There was an old man of Dundee."
Limerick: "There was an old man of El Hums."
Limerick: "There was an old man of Girgenti."
Limerick: "There was an old man of Hong Kong."
Limerick: "There was an old man of Ibreem."
Limerick: "There was an old man of Kamschatka."
Limerick: "There was an old man of Leghorn."
Limerick: "There was an old man of Madras."
Limerick: "There was an old man of Spithead."
Limerick: "There was an old man of the coast."
Limerick: "There was an old man of the Dargle."
Limerick: "There was an old man of the Dee."
Limerick: "There was an old man of Thermopylae."
Limerick: "There was an old man of Three Bridges."
Limerick: "There was an old man of Vesuvius."
Limerick: "There was an old man of Whitehaven."
Limerick: "There was an old man on the Border."
Limerick: "There was an old man who said: 'How.'"
Limerick: "There was an old man who said, 'Hush!'"
Limerick: "There was an old man who supposed."
Limerick: "There was an old man whose despair."
Limerick: "There was an old man with a gong."
Limerick: "There was an old man with a ribbon."
Limerick: "There was an old person of Anerley."
Limerick: "There was an old person of Bar."
Limerick: "There was an old person of Brussels."
Limerick: "There was an old person of Crowle."
Limerick: "There was an old person of Dean."
Limerick: "There was an old person of Diss."
Limerick: "There was an old person of Dover."

Limerick: "There was an old person of Grange."
Limerick: "There was an old person of Gretna."
Limerick: "There was an old person of Harrow."
Limerick: "There was an old person of Hove."
Limerick: "There was an old person of Lear."
Limerick: "There was an old person of Philae."
Limerick: "There was an old person of Skye."
Limerick: "There was an old person of Twickenham."
Limerick: "There was an old person of Ware."
Limerick: "There was an old person of Wick."
Limerick: "There was an old person of Woking."
Limerick: "There was an old person whose habits."
Limerick: "There was once a man with a beard."
Menu.
Mr. and Mrs. Discobbolos.
Mr. and Mrs. Spikky Sparrow.
Mrs. Jaypher.
Mrs. Jaypher on Lemons.
New Vestments, The.
Nutcrackers and the Sugar-Tongs, The.
Owl and the Pussy-Cat, The.
Pelican Chorus, The.
Pobble Who Has No Toes, The.
Quangle Wangle's Hat, The.
Says I to Myself.
Scraps of Lear.
She sits upon her Bulbul.
Teapots and Quails.
There was a young lady of Norway.
There was a young lady of Portugal.
There was a young lady of Ryde/ Whose shoe-strings were seldom untied.
There was a young lady of Sweden.
There was a young lady whose bonnet.
There was a young lady whose eyes.
There Was a Young Lady Whose Nose.
There was an old lady of Chertsey.
There was an old man in a Barge.
There was an Old Man of Dumbree.
There was an old man of Peru/ Who never knew what he should do.
There was an old man of Peru/ Who watched his wife making a stew.
There was an old man of the East.
There was an old man of the West.
There was an old man of West Dumpet.
There was an old man on some rocks.
There was an old man who screamed out.
There was an old man with a beard.
There was an old party of lyme, at.
There was an old person of Basing.
There was an old person of Blythe.
There was an old person of Bow.
There was an old person of Burton.
There was an old person of Cassel.
There was an old person of Dutton.
There was an old person of Prague.
There was an old person of Rhodes.
Two Old Bachelors, The.
Wet Weather at Cannes.

Lear, Edward *and* **Cosmo Monkhouse**
Limerick: "There once was an old man of Lyme," *at.*

Learmont, John
Poor crawlin' bodies, sair neglectit, *sel.*

Learned, Walter
In Explanation.
Last Reservation, The.
On the Fly-Leaf of Manon Lescaut.
To Critics.
With a Spray of Apple Blossoms.

"Learsi, Rufus" (Israel Goldberg)
Martyrdom.

Leavenworth, Coman
North Pickenham, *sel.*
We learned to laugh. Although the flying bombs, *sel.*
Wendling, *sel.*

Leax, John
Fire Burns Low, The.
Her Seventeenth Winter.
Incarnation Poem.
That Day.

Lebensboim, Razel. *See* **Margolin, Anna**

Lebensohn, Micah Joseph
Wine.

LeBrasseur, Margot
Song for Healing, A.

Lechlitner, Ruth
Kansas Boy.

Lecky, William E. H.
Of an Old Song.

LeClaire, Gordon
Love.
Miser.
Old Seawoman.

Leconte de Lisle, Charles Marie
Hialmar Speaks to the Raven.

LeCron, Helen Cowles
Little Charlie Chipmunk.

Ledgister, Fragano
Cities Have Fallen, The.
On Parade.

Ledoux, Louis V.
Slumber Song.

Ledward, Patricia
Air-Raid Causalties: Ashridge Hospital.
Evening in Camp.

Ledwidge, Francis
Fear, A.
God, whose kindly hand doth sow, *sel.*
God's Remembrance.
Herons, The.
June.
Lament for the Poets: 1916.
Lament for Thomas MacDonagh.
My Mother.
Soliloquy.
Twilight in Middle March, A.

Lee, Agnes
Ilex Tree, The.
Motherhood.
Sweeper, The.

Lee, Alfred M. ("Al")
Among Sharks.
Beside My Grandmother.
Far Side of Introspection, The.
Karl Marx.
Lie, The.
One Morning We Brought Them Order.
Poem for the Year Twenty Twenty.
Weathering the Depths.

"Lee, Andy" (W. W. Delaney)
Crazy Song to the Air of "Dixie."

Lee, Arthur
Prophecy, A.

Lee, B. J.
Eight Witches.

Lee, Deborah
Taking Care of It.
Where He Hangs His Hat.
Women Open Cautiously.
Words from a Bottle.
You're Sorry, Your Mother Is Crazy, & I'm a Chinese Shiksa.

Lee, Dennis
Alligator Pie.
Double-barreled Ding-Dong-Bat.
Dreadful Doings of Jelly Belly, The.
Freddy.
Gods, The.
Good Night, Good Night.
Jenny the Juvenile Juggler.
Last Cry of the Damp Fly, The.

Muddy Puddle, The.
Often I sit in the sun and brooding over the
   city, always, *sel.*
Question, The.
Silverly.
Skyscraper.
Three Tickles.
Tony Baloney ("Tony Baloney is fibbing
   again").
With My Foot in My Mouth.

Lee, Don L. (Haki R. Madhubuti)
Afterword: For Gwen Brooks, An.
Assassination.
Awareness.
Back Again, Home.
Big Momma.
Black Sketches.
But He Was Cool; or, He Even Stopped for
   Green Lights.
Change Is Not Always Progress.
Change-up.
Communication in Whi-te.
Education.
Judy-One.
Man and Woman.
Man Thinking about Woman.
Mixed Sketches.
Mwilu/ or Poem for the Living.
Nigerian Unity/ or Little Niggers Killing Little
   Niggers.
One Sided Shoot-out.
Poem for a Poet, A.
Poem to Complement Other Poems, A.
Positives for Sterling Plumpp.
Primitive, The.
Re-act for Action ("Re-act to Animals").
Self-Hatred of Don L. Lee, The.
Stereo.
To Be Quicker.
Wake-up Niggers.
We Walk the Way of the New World.
We're an Africanpeople, *sel.*
With All Deliberate Speed.

Lee, John Robert
Kite.
Return.
Third World Snapshots.

Lee, Joseph
Requiem: "When the last voyage is ended."

Lee, Laurie
Boy in Ice.
Christmas Landscape.
Day of These Days.
Edge of Day, The.
Field of Autumn.
Home from Abroad.
Invasion Summer.
Long Summer.
Milkmaid.
Moment of War, A.
My Many-Coated Man.
Sunken Evening [in Trafalgar Square]
Words Asleep.

Lee, Nathaniel
Nathaniel Lee to Sir Roger L'Estrange.

Lee, Rena
Old Story, An.

Lee-Hamilton, Eugene
Among the Firs.
Idle Charon.
Luther to a Bluebottle Fly, *sel.*
My Own Hereafter.
Noon's Dream-Song.
Snail's Derby, A.
Sunken Gold.
To My Tortoise Chronos.
What the Sonnet Is.

Lees, Edwin
Signs of Christmas.

Le Fanu, Joseph Sheridan
Hymn: "Hush! oh ye billows," *sel.*

Lefcowitz, Barbara F.
At the Western Wall.
Driftwood Dybbuk.
Emily Dickinson's Sestina for Molly Bloom.
Mirrors of Jerusalem, The.

Lefroy, Edward Cracroft
Cleonicos, *sel.*
Epitaph of Eusthenes, The, *sel.*
Flute of Daphnis, The, *sel.*
Grave of Hipponax, The, *sel.*
Monument of Cleita, The, *sel.*
Sacred Grove, A, *sel.*
Sylvan Revel, A, *sel.*
Thyrsis, *sel.*

Leftwich, Joseph
Tailor, The.

Le Gallienne, Richard
After the War.
Ballad of London, A.
Beatus Vir.
Easter Hymn, An.
May Is Building Her House.
Melton Mowbray Pork Pie, A.
Prayer, A: "Out of the deeps I cry to thee, O
   God!"
Second Crucifixion, The.
Song: "She's somewhere in the sunlight
   strong."

Legaré, James Matthew
Ahab Mohammed.
Amy.
To a Lily.

LeGear, Laura Lourene
Unbridled Now.

Leger, Alexis Saint-Leger. *See* **"Perse,
St.-John"**

Le Guin, Ursula K.
Morden Lecture, 1978.
Song of the Dragon's Daughter, The.
To Siva, the Unmaker.
Well of Baln, The.
Withinner, The.

Lehman, David
Amnesia.
For David Shapiro.
Operation Memory.
Towards the Vanishing Point.

Lehmann, Geoffrey
Auntie Bridge and Uncle Pat, *sel.*
I Was Born at a Place of Pines, *sel.*
Last Campaign, The.
Music Is Unevennesses, *sel.*
My Father's a Still Day, *sel.*
Pigs, The.
Saving the Harvest.
Some of Our Koorawatha Saints, *sel.*
Song for Past Midnight.
There Are Some Lusty Voices Singing, *sel.*

Lehmann, John
Ballad of Banners (1944), The.
Coming into Your Room.
This Excellent Machine.

Lehmann, Rudolph Chambers
Plea for a Plural, A.

Lehrer, Tom
Alma.
Elements, The.
New Maths.

Leib, Mani
Christmas.
Door and Window Bolted Fast.
From the Crag.
Hush.
Hush, Hush.
I Am.
In Little Hands.
Indian Summer.
Inscribed on a Tombstone.
Odors.
Plum, A.
Psalmodist.

Pyre of My Indian Summer, The.
Strangers.
Sun Is Good, The.
They.
They.
Through the Eye of the Needle.
To the Gentile Poet.
When I See Another's Pain.
Winter.
You Only Know.

Leifer, Jay
Six-forty-two Farm Commune Struggle Poem.

Leigh, Amy E.
If I But Knew.

Leigh, Henry Sambrooke
Cossimbazar.
Only Seven.
Rhymes (?).
Saragossa.
'Twas Ever Thus.
Twins, The.

Leigh, Richard
Eccho, The.
Thus Lovely Sleep.

Leigh-Fermor, Patrick
Greek Archipelagoes.

Leigh, Frederick *and* **Frederick Murray.**
See **Murray, Frederick** *and* **Frederick Leigh**

Leighton, Louise
Earthly Illusion.

Leighton, Robert
Bunch of Larks, The.

Leino, Eino
Äijö's Song.
Drifter's Song.
Goodness.
I.
Nocturne: "Song of a blackbird in my ears."

Leipoldt, C. Louis
Banded Cobra, The.
On My Old Ramkiekie.

Leiser, Joseph
Kol Nidra.

Leithauser, Brad
Angel.
Between Leaps.
Expanded Want Ad, An.
Ghost of a Ghost, The.
Life-Giving, The.
Post-Coitum Tristesse: A Sonnet.
Quilled Quilt, a Needle Bed, A.
Tigers of Nanzen-ji, The.
Trauma.

Leivick (*or* Leyvik), H. (Leivick Halpern)
Again a Neighbor Died, *sel.*
And it was on the third day in the morning,
   sel.
Bull-Fights.
Clouds behind the forest come close to the
   tops of the trees, *sel.*
Do not wake the sick birds, *sel.*
First Grass.
Holiday, *sel.*
Holy Song of the Holy Grocer, The.
How Did He Get Here?
I Hear a Voice.
In Fire.
In Snow.
Kabbalists in Safed.
Mima'amakim.
Night Is Dark, The.
On the Roads of Siberia.
Open up, Gate, *sel.*
Over the Sleeping Eyes.
Sacrifice.
Sanatorium.
Somewhere Far Away.
Song of the Yellow Patch, *sel.*
Stubborn Back—And Nothing More, A.
Sturdy in Me, The, *sel.*
Through the Whole Long Night.

To America.
Towering life of the towering city, The, *sel.*
Two Times Two Is Four.
Under the Tread of My Feet.
Unsatiated Passions.
When We Let Ourselves Run Down-Hill.
White Moon.
With Exultation, As We Can!
With the Holy Poem.
Yellow-White Glow, The.
Yiddish Poets.

Leland, Charles Godfrey ("Hans Breitman")
Ballad by Hans Breitmann.
Dere's a liddle fact in hishdory vitch few hafe onnershtand, *sel.*
El Capitan-General.
Hans Breitmann's Party [*or* Barty]
Out and Fight.
Two Friends, The.

Leland, John
Day Is Past and Gone, The.
Now Behold the Saviour Pleading.

Lele-io-Hoku
Albatross.

Lemos, Gouveia de
Song of Agony.

L'Engle, Madeleine
At Communion.
O Simplicitas, *sel.*

Lengyel, Cornel
Fool Song.

Lenhart, Gary
Around the World.
Old Girl, The.
Satellites.

Lennen, Elinor
Prayer for a Play House.
Within the Shelter of Our Walls.

Lenngren, Anna Maria
Other Fabrics, Other Mores!
Portraits, The.

Lennon, Florence Becker
Little White Schoolhouse Blues.

Lennon, John
Fat Budgie, The.

Lennon, John *and* **Paul McCartney**
Eleanor Rigby.
For No One.

Lenowitz, Harris
Fringes, The.
Panegyric.

Lenski, Hayim
Language of Ancients.
Purity.
Upon the Lake.

Lenski, Lois
People.
Sing a Song of People.

Lent, Emma A.
Memorial Day.
Unawares.

Lentino, Jacopo da.　*See* **Jacopo da Lentino**

Lento, Takako Uchino
Glass.

Leon, Abelardo Sanchez
Poem 1: "What happens here happened to my grandfather and my father."
Poem 2: "Why did that have to be the only answer? It's true."
Poem 3: "You thought that I could help you out?"

León, Luis de
To Retirement.

Leonard, Priscilla
Happiness.

Leonard, William Ellery
Love's Primal Want, *sel.*
True Marriage Is True Love, *sel.*

Leone da Modena.　*See* **Modena, Leone da**

Leong, George
Sometimes Love Poem, A.
This Is Our Music.

Leonidas of Alexandria
Menodotis.

Leonidas of Tarentum
Cleitagoras.
Fisherman, The.
Last Journey, The.
Philocles.
Remember Eubolus, who lived and died sober?
Spinning Woman, The.
Tomb of Crethon, The.

Leopardi, Giacomo
Infinite, The.
Infinito, L'.
Last Song of Sappho, The.
Saturday Night in the Village.
Sè Stesso, A.
Setting of the Moon, The.
Sonnet: Saturday Evening in the Village.
To Himself.
To Italy.
To the Moon.

Le Pan, Douglas
Canoe-Trip.
Country without a Mythology, A.
Coureurs de Bois.
Incident, An.
Lion, Leopard, Lady.
Net and the Sword, The.
New Vintage, The.
Nimbus.
One of the Regiment.

Lermontov, Mikhail Yurevich
Boredom, the sadness, and no one to take by the hand, The.
Composed While under Arrest.
Dagger.
Dream, The.
Farewell to Russia's unwashed features.
Gratitude.
I walk out alone into the darkness.
Meditation.
Mountain, The.
Native Land.
No, I'm not Byron, it's my role.
On the sightless seas of ether, *sel.*
Prayer: "At life's most testing moment, when."
Prophet, The.
Reed, The.
Sail, A.
Testament.
Thought, A.

Lerner, Alan Jay
With a Little Bit of Luck.

Lerner, Laurence David
All Day and All October.
14 July 1956.
In a Shoreham Garden.
Meditation upon the Toothache, A.
Poet at Fifty, The.
Raspberries.
St Enda.
Way to the Sea, The.
What's Hard.
Wish, A.
Years Later.

Leslie, Cy
On Riots.

Leslie, Kenneth
From Soil Somehow the Poet's Word.
Halibut Cove Harvest.
My Love Is Sleeping.
Silver herring throbbed thick in my seine, The, *sel.*

Leslie, Sir Shane
Forest Song.

Leone da Modena.
Holy Cross.
Priest or Poet.
Saint Patrick.

Lesoro, E. A. S.
Muscovy Drake, The.

Lesser, Rika
Can Zone; or, The Good Food Guide.
Canopic Jar.
Degli Sposi.
La Banditaccia, 1979.
News & the Weather, The.
Translation.

Lessing, Gotthold Ephraim
Three Kingdoms of Nature, The.

Lester, Julius
It cannot be/ reasoned with, *sel.*
On the Birth of My Son, Malcolm Coltrane.
One needs a lyric poet in this, *sel.*
Us.

Lestey, George
Lament of the Sodomites, *sel.*

L'Estrange, Sir Roger
Loyalty Confin'd.

LeSueur, Meridel
I Light Your Streets.
Rites of Ancient Ripening.
Shelter Him in Milk and Meadow.

Letts, W. M.
Pensioners.

Letts, Winifred M.
Boys.
Elfin People Fill the Tubes, The.
Harbour, The.
Irish Skies.
Spires of Oxford, The.
Spring, the Travelling Man.
To Scott.

Leurgans, Lois
Olympic Event.

Leuty, Helen
Apple Harvest.
Night, The.
Poplars.

Levenson, Christopher
Prophecy, A.

Leveridge, Lilian
Cry from the Canadian Hills, A.
First Robin, The.

Levertin, Oscar
At the Jewish Cemetery in Prague.
Solomon and Morolph, Their Last Encounter.

Levertov, Denise
Abel's Bride.
About Marriage.
Absence, The.
Absentee, The.
Ache of Marriage, The.
Adam's Complaint.
Advent 1966.
Altars in the Street, The.
At the Edge.
Bedtime.
Beyond the End.
Brass Tacks.
Breathing, The.
By Rail through the Earthly Paradise, Perhaps Bedfordshire.
Caedmon.
Cancion: "When I am the sky."
Cat as Cat, The.
Charge, The.
Claritas.
Closed World, The.
Come into Animal Presence.
Common Ground, A.
Continuum.
Credo, *sel.*
Day Begins, A.
Dead Butterfly, The.
Defeat, A.
Depths, The.

Despair.
Dog of Art, The.
Dragonfly-Mother, The.
Earliest Spring.
Earth Psalm.
Earth Worm, The.
"Else a Great Prince in Prison Lies."
Embroidery, An.
Epilogue: "I thought I had found a swan."
Everything flows, *sel.*
Everything That Acts Is Actual.
February Evening in New York.
Five-Day Rain, The.
From the Roof.
Gathered at the River.
Goddess, The.
Goethe's Blues.
Good Dream, The.
Goodbye to Tolerance.
Gulf, The.
Hands, The.
Hypocrite Women.
Illustration—a Footnote, The.
Illustrious Ancestors.
In Mind.
Intrusion.
Invocation: "Silent, about-to-be-parted-from
    house."
Jacob's Ladder, The.
Last Night's Dream.
Leaving Forever.
Life at War.
Like Loving Chekhov.
Living.
Losing Track.
Mad Song.
Making Peace.
Malice of Innocence, The.
Man Alone.
Map of the Western Part of the County of
    Essex in England, A.
Matins.
Merritt Parkway.
Mockingbird of Mockingbirds, The.
Movement.
Mutes, The.
Novices, The.
O Taste and See.
Obsessions.
Offender, The.
Old Adam, The.
Old People Dozing.
Olga Poems.
Our Bodies.
Overheard.
Overheard over S. E. Asia.
Overland to the Islands.
Partial Resemblance.
Passage.
Pilots, The.
Pleasures.
Poem Unwritten, The.
Presence, The.
Prisoners.
Psalm Concerning the Castle.
Psalm Praising the Hair of Man's Body, A.
Quarry Pool, The.
Rainwalkers, The.
Recognition, The.
Relearning the Alphabet.
Resolve, The.
Scenes from the Life of the Peppertrees.
Secret, The.
Seeing for a Moment.
Seems Like We Must Be Somewhere Else.
Sharks, The.
Shlup, shlup, the dog, *sel.*
Six Variations.
Solitude, A.
Song for Ishtar.
Springtime, The.
Stepping Westward.

Sun Going Down upon Our Wrath, The.
Sunday Afternoon.
Supermarket in Guadalajara, Mexico, A.
Tenebrae.
Terror.
Third Dimension, The.
Time Past, A.
To the Reader.
To the Snake.
Triple Feature.
Two Variations.
Unknown, The.
Victors, The.
Vigil, The.
Way Through, The.
Ways of Conquest.
Wedding-Ring.
What Were They Like?
What Wild Dawns There Were.
Wife, The.
Williams: An Essay.
Willows of Massachusetts, The.
Wings, The.
With Eyes at the Back of Our Heads.
Woman Alone.
Zeroing In.

Levi, Adele
    Death of Friends, The.

Levi, David
    Thou, Zion, old and suffering, *sel.*

Levi, Peter
    City built in darkness and cold air, A, *sel.*
    Greenhouse in October, The.
    He Met Her at the Green Horse.
    I imagine where God has never been.
    In a Corner of Eden.
    In stone settlements when the moon is stone.
    L'Aurore Grelottante.
    Ship-Building Emperors Commanded.
    Smoke when the sun fell and when it rose,
       sel.
    To My Friends.
    Tree of roses. The water crashed headlong.
    When does it end? When does a new poem.

Levi, Primo
    For Adolf Eichmann.
    Lilith.
    Shema.

Levi ben Amittai
    Kibbutz Sabbath.

Levi Yitzhok
    Kaddish.

Levi Yitzhok (Isaac of Berditshev)
    Invocation: "Good morning to you, Lord of
       the world!"

Levien, Michael
    In the Falling Deer's Mouth.

Levin, Gabriel
    Adam's Death.
    Étude for Voice and Hand.
    Ishmael.

Levine, Al
    Bottle, The.

Levine, Molly Myerowitz
    Safed and I.

Levine, Norman
    Crabbing.

Levine, Philip
    Above It All.
    After.
    Animals Are Passing from Our Lives.
    At Bessemer.
    At the Fillmore.
    Autumn.
    Baby Villon.
    Blasting from Heaven.
    Businessman of Alicante, The.
    Cemetery at Academy, California, The.
    Children's Crusade, The.
    Clouds.
    Coming Home.

Commanding Elephants.
Cutting Edge, The.
Distant Winter, The.
Drunkard, The.
Face, The.
For Fran.
Gangrene.
Genius.
Harvest.
He Faces the Second Winter, *sel.*
Heaven.
Helmet, The.
Here and Now.
Horse, The.
House, The.
How Much Earth.
In the New Sun.
Jewish Graveyards, Italy.
Keep Talking.
Last Song of the Angel of Bad Luck.
Late Moon.
Let Me Begin Again.
Life Ahead, The.
Look.
Lost Angel, The.
Mad Day in March.
Midget, The.
Milkweed.
Montjuich.
My Son and I.
Negatives, The.
Night Thoughts over a Sick Child.
1933.
Now It Can Be Told.
On a Drawing by Flavio.
On My Own.
On the Edge.
Paraguay.
Poem Circling Hamtramck, Michigan All
    Night in Search of You, The.
Red Dust.
Reply, The.
Salami.
Salts and Oils.
Second Angel, The.
7 Years from Somewhere.
Silent in America.
Something Has Fallen.
Standing on the Corner.
Starlight.
Sunday Afternoon.
Sweet Will.
Then.
They Feed They Lion.
To a Child Trapped in a Barber Shop.
To My God in His Sickness.
Turning, The.
Uncle.
Waking an Angel.
Walk with Tom Jefferson, A.
Way Down, The.
Who.
Winter Rains: Cataluña.
Words.
You Can Have It.
Zaydee.

Levine, Steve
    Gothic Gesture, A.
    Pure Notations.
    Tiny Catullus.

Levinson, Fred
    No More than Five.
    Poem against Rats, A.
    Poem: "Country, The/ was back in the hands
       of the patriots."
    Sharks in Shallow Water.
    Translation From, A.

Levis, Larry
    Adolescence.

Bat Angels.
Blue Stones.
Family Romance.
Fish.
For Zbigniew Herbert, Summer, 1971, Los Angeles.
García Lorca: A Photograph of the Granada Cemetery, 1966.
Irish Music.
Linnets.
Lost Fan, Hotel Californian, Fresno, 1923.
Ownership of the Night, The.
Picking Grapes in an Abandoned Vineyard ("Picking grapes alone in the late autumn sun").
Poem You Asked For, The.
Poet at Seventeen, The.
Quilt, The.
Sensationalism.
To a Wall of Flame in a Steel Mill, Syracuse, New York, 1969.
Whitman.
Winter Stars.

Levitt, W. T.
Ski Song of the U.S. Army's Tenth Mountain Division.

Levy, Amy
Birch-Tree at Loschwitz, The.
Epitaph: "This is the end of him, here he lies."
On the Threshold.
Xantippe.

Levy, Deborah
Flesh.
Frolic.
Nine Reasons Why.
On the State of Englishness (A Fairy Tale).

Levy, Louis
Swallow's Flight, The.

Levy, Newman
Ballad of Sir Brian and the Three Wishes, The.
Belle of the Balkans, The.
Carmen.
Midsummer Jingle.
Rigoletto.
Tannhauser.
Thaïs.

Levy, Stephen
Freely, from a Song Sung by Jewish Women of Yemen.
Friday Night after Bathing.
Home Alone These Last Hours of the Afternoon, Dusk Now, the Sabbath Setting In, I Sit Back, and These Words Start Welling Up in Me.
Judezmo Writer in Turkey Angry, A.

Lew, Walter
Careless/ but not fearless, sel.
Fan.
Leaving Seoul; 1953.
Two Handfuls of Waka for Thelonious Sphere Monk (d. Feb. 1982).

Lewin, Ralph A.
Les Chasse-Neige.

Lewis, Alonzo
Death Song.

Lewis, Alun
All Day It Has Rained.
Dawn on the East Coast.
Goodbye.
In Hospital: Poona, I.
Jungle, The.
Mahratta Ghats, The.
Peasants, The.
Port of Call: Brazil.
Postscript for Gweno.
Song: "First month of his absence, The."
To a Comrade in Arms.
To Edward Thomas.

Troopship in the Tropics.
Unknown Soldier, The.

Lewis, Angelo
America Bleeds.
Clear.

Lewis, Cecil Day. See **Day Lewis, Cecil**

Lewis, Claudia
Frightening.
How Strange It Is.

Lewis, Clive Staples
Apologist's Evening Prayer, The.
Awake, My Lute!
Evensong.
Evolutionary Hymn.
Late Passenger, The.
Love's as Warm as Tears.
Naked Seed, The.
Narnian Suite.
Nativity, The.
On a Vulgar Error.
Pilgrim's Problem.
Prayer: "Master, they say that when I seem."
Save yourself. Run and leave me. I must go back, sel.
Scazons.
Sonnet: "Bible says Sennacherib's campaign was spoiled, The."

Lewis, Dominic Bevan Wyndham ("Timothy Shy")
Am I too dangerous, that no man can let, sel.
Envoi: "I warmed both hands before the fire of Life."
Having a Wonderful Time.
I'm no He-man you know, I'm not a He, sel.
Jig for Sackbuts.
Sapphics.
Shot at Random, A.
You now solicit a few enemy thrusts, sel.

Lewis, Eiluned
Children's Party, The.
We Who Were Born.

Lewis, Gardner E.
How to Tell Juan Don from Another.
Poem, Neither Hilláryous Norgay.

Lewis, Howell Elvet [or Elfed]
Life's Morning.

Lewis, J. Patrick
Feline Fine.
Lonely Monday.

Lewis, Janet
April Hill, The.
At Carmel Highlands.
Country Burial.
For Elizabeth Madox Roberts.
Fossil, 1975.
Girl Help.
Helen Grown Old.
In the Egyptian Museum.
Lines with a Gift of Herbs.
Love Poem: "Instinctively, unwittingly."
Lullaby: "Lullee, lullay."
Remembered Morning.

Lewis, Matthew Gregory
What triumph moves on the billows so blue?

Lewis, Naomi
Counsel.
Creatures of Early Morning.

Lewis, Percy Wyndham
I would set all things whatsoever front to back, sel.
Song of the Militant Romance, The.

Lewis, Saunders
Ascension Thursday.
Deluge 1939, The.
Mary Magdalene.
Pine, The.
To the Good Thief.

Lewisohn, Ludwig
Heinrich Heine.
Together.

Leybourne, George
Man on the Flying Trapeze, The, at.

Leyden, John
Address to My Malay Krees.
Christmas in Penang.
Lay of the Ettercap, The.

Leyeles, A. (Aaron Glanz-Leyeles)
An Encounter.
Autumn.
Bolted Room.
Castles.
Cold Night.
Desert Madness.
Disorder.
Evening, sel.
Fabius Lind Is Riding the Wind.
Fabius Lind to Comrade Death.
Fabius Lind to Fabius Lind.
Fabius Lind's Days.
Fatal Longing.
February 15, sel.
February 4, sel.
February 1, sel.
February 7, sel.
February 17, sel.
February 10, sel.
February 23, sel.
Foreign Fencers.
God of Israel, The.
Gray Light, The.
Herod.
I Came from Ethiopia.
Immobile.
In the Subway ("Rush hour"), sel.
In the Subway ("Wall, A"), sel.
In the Subway ("Walled-in"), sel.
Isaiah and Homer.
Islandish.
It Will Pour.
January 30, sel.
January 28, sel.
Late Hour.
Madison Square.
Madonna in the Subway, The.
Manhattan Bridge, sel.
Moscow Night, End of December 1934.
My Poems.
New York.
Night, sel.
November.
On a Sixth Floor.
On Broadway, sel.
On the Hudson.
On the Way Back.
Poem, The: "In the beginning was the tune."
Red Beard, A.
Rondeau of My Life's Walk.
Sabbath Hours.
Shlomo Molkho Sings on the Eve of His Burning.
Storms and Towers.
Symmetry.
Tao.
That's It.
Variant, A.
Villanelle of the Mystical Cycle.
Wall Street, sel.
What Do People Do?
White Swan.
Whiteness.
Why?
Winter-Night Sonnet.
Worms.
Young-Autumn.
Yuola.

Leyvik, H. See **Leivik, H.**

L'Heureux, John
Discovering God Is Waking One Morning.

Liagarang
Snails.

Liang Ch'i-ch'ao
After the Rain.

Night of the First Full Moon.
Random Thoughts on Autumn.
Scarlet Red Tree, The.
Trying to stay the departing spring is of no
  avail, *sel.*
What is it that troubles you?, *sel.*

Libbey, Elizabeth
Before the Mountain.
Concerning the Dead Women: The Munitions
  Plant Explosion: June, 1918.
Gesture, The.
Marceline, to Her Husband.
To Her Dead Mate: Montana, 1966.

Libera, Sharon Mayer
How You Were Born.
Mother.
Patty, 1949–1961.

Li Chien
Bent Willows.
Dying Lamp, The.
Modern Poem in Response to "Wild Geese on
  the Lake" by Shen Yüeh, A.
My Little Garden.
Strolling under the Moon.

Li Ch'ing-chao
After kicking on the swing.
Clear Bright.
How many evenings in the arbor by the river.
I let the incense grow cold.
Last night thin rain, gusty wind.
Light mist, then dense fog.
Melting in thin mist and heavy clouds.
Poem to the Tune of "Tsui hua yin."
Poem to the Tune of "Yi chian mei."
Rattan bed, paper netting. I wake from
  morning sleep.
Red lotus incense fades on/ the jewelled
  curtain.
Sky links cloud waves, links dawn fog.
To The Tune "Eternal Happiness."
Tune: As in a Dream ("Always I recall the
  river arbor at twilight").
Tune: Crimson Lips Adorned.
Tune: Magnolia Blossom.
Tune: Pure Serene Music ("Year after year in
  the snow").
Tune: Song of Picking Mulberry ("Evening
  comes with an onslaught of wind and
  rain.").
Tune: Telling of Innermost Feelings ("Night
  comes and, drowsy with drink, I'm slow to
  shed my ornaments.").
Warm rain, sunny wind start to break the
  chill.
Weary Song to a Slow Sad Tune, A.
Year after year I have watched.

Lichtenstein, Alfred
Journey to the Insane Asylum, The.
Repose.

Li Chü
Harvesting Wheat for the Public Share.

Liddell, Henry
Vampire Bride, The.

Liddy, James
History.
Paean to Eve's Apple.
Strand Hotel, Rosslare, The.
Voice of America, 1961, The.

Li E
Cowherd's Song: In Imitation of Chang Chi,
  A.
Leaving Southern Screen Hill at Dawn and
  Crossing the Lake.
Passing Seven-Mile Rapids on a Moonlit
  Night.
Passing through South Lake Again.
South Lake in the Rain.
Spending the Night at Monk Ch'ao Yün's
  Retreat on Mount Lung-men.
Written on the Lake after a Shower, On the
  Sixteenth of the Seventh Month.

Lieber, Francis
Ship Canal from the Atlantic to the Pacific,
  The.

Lieberman, Elias
Classroom in October.
Heart Specialist.
I Am an American.
Notation in Haste.
Sholom Aleichem.

Lieberman, Laurence
Coral Reef, The.
Lamb and Bear; Jet Landing.
Unblinding, The.

Liechtenstein, Ulrich von
Love, Whose Month Was Ever May.

Liessin, Abraham
Spring Nocturne.

Lifshin, Lyn
Afterward.
Beryl.
Even There.
Family 8.
For a Friend.
In Spite of His Dangling Pronoun.
My Mother and the Bed.
No More Apologizing the No More Little
  Laughing Blues, The.
Not Quite Spring.
On the New Road.
Plymouth Women.
Pulling Out.
38 Main Street.
Thirty Miles West of Chicago.
To Poem.
Waiting, the Hallways under Her Skin Thick
  with Dreamchildren.
Way Sun Keeps Falling Away from Every
  Window, The.
You Understand the Requirements.

Lighthall, William Douw
Caughnawaga Beadwork Seller, The.

Lightman, Alan P.
First Rainfall.

Li Ho
At Ch'ang-ku, Reading: To Show to My Man
  Pa.
My Man Pa Replies.
Northland in Cold, The.
Song of the Sacred Strings.
Stars rest cold by shoals of cloud, *sel.*

Li Hsün
Beautiful Lady Yü, The.
Deva-like Barbarian, The.
Gazing After the Distant Traveler.
Immortal at the River.
River Messages.
Sand of Silk-Washing Stream.
Song of the Fisherman.
Song of the Southern Country.
Song of the West Stream.
Song of the Wine-Spring.
Stretch of Cloud over Mount Wu, A.
Taoist Nun, The.

Li K'ai-hsien
All morning long I correct my books, *sel.*
All my friends can write them, *sel.*
Beside the river—waterbirds, in the river—
  fish, *sel.*
Colorful frames are erected beside the Yellow
  River, The, *sel.*
Commiserating with the Poor.
Compassion for the Farmers.
Crack soldiers get no sleep, The, *sel.*
Crossing the ridge, the woodcutter loses his
  way, *sel.*
Drunk, Climbing to the Peak of Iron Tomb on
  Wei Mountain.
Earthquake covered Shansi and Shensi, The,
  sel.
Flying sand darkens the air, the moon is a
  dull yellow, *sel.*

Gazing at Ch'ang-po Mountain.
In my house is my book collection, filled with
  book-worms, *sel.*
In the Second Month of Summer, Taking My
  Family to the Villages East of the City.
I've decided to study agriculture, *sel.*
I've followed the billowing dust as a traveler
  too long, *sel.*
Jade trees from the rear courtyard of the
  empire of Ch'en, *sel.*
Meeting Trappers on the Road in Heavy
  Snow.
Men plow, and know everything about "late"
  and "early", The, *sel.*
Night of the First Full Moon, The.
Night of the Seventeenth, The.
Not a day goes by without someone
  borrowing books from me, *sel.*
On My Birthday—Sick.
On the Cold Food Festival, Entertaining at the
  Southern Estate.
Parable, A.
Poem about Fan the Fourth, A.
Poem Expressing My Wife's Response to One
  I Sent Her, A.
Prosperous Villager, The.
Record of a Past Affair, A.
Recording a Weird Happening.
Sent to the Master Physician, "Almond
  Orchard" Shih.
Sent to the Painter, Lu Hsiao-feng.
Sitting by the riverside with a torn net, *sel.*
Staying Overnight on the Banks of
  Embroidered River.
Thanking Doctor Jen.
To drink, no fine wines, to eat, no fish, *sel.*
Trip to a Mountain Village, A.
Wei-ch'i Chess.
While an official, I never wrote lyrics, *sel.*
Write in a lively style, as fish swim in the
  water, *sel.*

Liliencron, Detlev, Freiherr von
After the Hunt.
Autumn.
Death in the Corn.
Who Knows Where.

Lili'u-o-ka-lani, Princess
Puna's Fragrant Glades.

Lillard, Charles
Bushed.
Lobo.

Lilliard, R. W.
America's Answer.

Lilliat, John
False Love, at.

Lillington, Kenneth
Ballade to My Psychoanalyst.

Lily, John. *See* **Lyly, John**

Lim, Genny
Departure.
Sweet 'n Sour.
Visiting Father.
Wonder Woman.

Lim, Shirley
Modern Secrets.
Monsoon History.
Women's Dreams.

Lima, Frank
Memory of Boxer Benny (Kid) Paret, The.

Lima, Jorge de
Enormous Hand, The.
Papa John.
Words Will Resurrect, The.

Li Meng-yang
An Oriole at Dawn.
Autumn Vista.
Crossing the Frontier.
Mooring at Hsai-k'ou at Night.
Seeing Off Commander-In-Chief Li.
Song of Lin Liang's Painting "Two Horned
  Falcons."

Spring Vista from the Tower of Illuminated
  Distance.
Wild Wind.

Li Nan
Breeze, The.
Dog, The.
Dream, The.
Fifteenth Evening of the First Lunar Month,
  The.
Fireflies.
Letter from Home, A.
Papa and Mama.
Putting My Daughter to Bed.
Rooster, The.
Telephone, The.

Lin Huan-ch'ang
Beginning of the Day, The.
Doorway, The.
Spring Morning.

Lincoln, Abraham
Memory.

Lincoln, Mary W.
Kings of France.

Lindbergh, Anne Morrow
Even.

Linden, Eddie
Sunday in Cambridge, A.

Linden, Mrs. Henry
All We Ask Is Justice.
As Women of Our Race.
Bird Song, The.
Brave Man and Brave Woman.
Church Bells, The.
Count Your Blessings.
Cultivation.
Do Your Best.
Encouragement.
Fall Is Here, The.
For the Good of the Pythian Order.
God's Electric Power.
Golden Jubilee of Wilberforce.
Gossip.
Household of Ruth, The.
I Am as Happy as a Queen on Her Throne.
Last Day of the Year; or, New Year's Eve,
  The.
Let Us Strive to Do Something.
Life's Golden Sunset.
Lonely World.
Man Is What He Wills to Be.
Marriage Vow.
May.
Missionary, The.
New Year's Morning; or, the First Day of the
  Year.
October Is Here.
Oh Woman, Blessed Woman!
Orphan Girl, An.
Our Club Work.
Our Noble Booker T. Washington.
Parting Lovers, The.
Paul Laurence Dunbar.
Pay Your Debts.
Prospect of the Future, The.
Riot, A.
Scraps of Time.
Silent Night, The.
Sun of Our Existence, The.
Tell Her So.
This Country's Needs ("This country needs
  more noble men").
To the Conference.
To the Queen of the British Government.
To the Wheel of Progress.
Wayward Son, The.
What Is Woman?
Would-be Critic, The.
Y. M. C. A, The.

Lindh, Stewart
Settler.

Lindner, Carl
First Love.
When I Got It Right.

Lindon, J. A.
My Garden.

Lindsay, Forbes
Ball and the Club, The.

Lindsay, Jack
Budding Spring.

**Lindsay, Lady Anne (Lady Anne Lindsay
  Barnard)**
Auld Robin Gray.

Lindsay, Maurice
Exiled Heart, The.
Highland Shooting Lodge.
Hurlygush.
In the Cheviots.

Lindsay, Sir David
After the Flood, *sel.*
Complaint of the Common Weill of Scotland,
  sel.
Have I nocht made ane honest shift, *sel.*
My patent pardouns ye may see, *sel.*
Of the Realme of Scotland, *sel.*
So Young Ane King.
Squire Meldrum at Carrickfergus, *sel.*

Lindsay, T.
Theological Limerick.

Lindsay, Vachel
Abraham Lincoln Walks at Midnight.
An Explanation of the Grasshopper.
Apple-Barrel of Johnny Appleseed, The.
At Mass.
Bryan, Bryan, Bryan, Bryan.
Chinese Nightingale, The.
Congo, The.
Daniel.
Dove of New Snow, The.
Eagle That Is Forgotten, The.
Euclid, *sel.*
Factory Windows Are Always Broken.
Flower-fed Buffaloes, The.
General William Booth Enters into Heaven.
Ghosts of the Buffaloes, The.
Haughty Snail-King, The.
Horrid Voice of Science, The.
I Heard Immanuel Singing.
I Went Down into the Desert to Meet Elijah.
Indian Summer Day on the Prairie, An.
John Brown.
Johnny Appleseed.
King of Yellow Butterflies, The.
Leaden-eyed, The.
Lincoln, *sel.*
Little Turtle, The.
Moon's the North Wind's Cooky, The.
My Fathers Came from Kentucky.
Mysterious Cat, The.
Nancy Hanks, Mother of Abraham Lincoln.
Net to Snare the Moonlight, A.
On the Building of Springfield.
Potatoes' Dance, The.
Rain.
Sea Serpent Chantey, The.
Simon Legree—a Negro Sermon, *sel.*
Sorceress, The!
Spider and the Ghost of the Fly, The.
To a Golden-haired Girl in a Louisiana Town.
Traveler, The.
Two Old Crows.
Unpardonable Sin, The.
What the Moon Saw.
When the Mississippi Flowed in Indiana.
Why I Voted the Socialist Ticket.
Yet Gentle Will the Griffin Be, *sel.*

Lindsey, Jim
Blank Verse for a Fat Demanding Wife.

Lindsey, William
En Garde, Messieurs.
Hundred-Yard Dash, The.

Link, Carolyn Wilson
Elements.

Link, Gordden
Artist and Ape.

Link, Lenore M.
Holding Hands.

Linton, William James
Epicurean.
Gathering of the People, The.
Life and Adventure of Bob Thin, The, *sel.*
Song: "Leaves are still; not a breath is heard,
  The."
Spring and Autumn.

Lipkin, Jean
Apocalypse.
Credo.
Father.
Pre Domina.

Li Po
At Su Terrace Viewing the Past.
At Yellow Crane Tower Taking Leave of
  Meng Hao-jan.
Autumn Cove.
Bring the Wine!
Clearing at Dawn.
Drinking Alone in the Moonlight.
Exile's Letter.
Girls on the Yueh River.
In Reply When Lesser Officials of Chung-tu
  Brought a Pot of Wine and Two Fish to My
  Inn as Gifts.
In the Mountains on a Summer Day.
In Yüeh Viewing the Past.
Jewel Stairs' Grievance, The ("The jewelled
  steps are already quite white with dew").
Lament of the Frontier Guard.
Long War, The.
Moon at the Fortified Pass, The.
Night with a Friend, A.
Oath of Friendship.
One set on the highway to sing.
Poem by the Bridge at Ten-shin.
Poem No. 19 in the Old Manner.
Presented to Wang Lun.
River Merchant's Wife; a Letter, The.
Seafarers tell of the Eastern Isle of Bliss, The,
  sel.
Seeing a Friend Off.
Sent to My Two Little Children in the East of
  Lu.
Separation on the River Kiang.
Song of a Dream Visit to T'ien-mu.
Spring Night in Lo-Yang—Hearing a Flute.
Still Night Thoughts.
Summer Day in the Mountains.
Taking Leave of a Friend.
Thinking of East Mountain.
To Tan Ch'iu.
Tzu-yeh Song.
Viewing the Waterfall at Mount Lu.
War.
Wild man of Ssu-ming Mountain, *sel.*

Lippincott, Sara Jane Clarke. *See*
  "Greenwood, Grace"

Lippmann, Julie Mathilde
Love and Life.
Pines, The.
Stone Walls.

Lipshitz, Fay
Aleph Bet, The.
Encounter in Jerusalem.
Judean Summer.

Lipsitz, Lou
Bedtime Story.
Prospect Beach.
Thaw in the City.
Winter Twilight.

Lipska, Ewa
Cock, The.
Flood, The.

If God Exists.
Wedding.
Lipton, James
Misericordia!
Lisboa, Henriqueta
Minor Elegy.
Li Shang-yin
At eight stealing a mirror glance.
Last night's planets and stars, last night's
   wind.
Poem for My Little Boy.
Spring Rain.
Thoughts in the Cold.
Li Shen
Pitying the Farmer.
Lisle, Thomas
Letter from Smyrna to His Sisters at
   Crux-Easton, 1733.
Power of Music, The.
Lisle, Rouget de. *See* **Rouget de Lisle,**
Claude Joseph
List, Amedie Eva
Mon that wist for raine, The.
Lister, Richard Percival
At the Ship.
Bone China.
Gemlike Flame, The.
Human Races, The.
Lament of an Idle Demon.
Revolutionaries, The.
Tale of Jorkyns and Gertie; or, Vice
   Rewarded, The.
Time Passes.
Litchfield, Grace Denio
My Letter.
My Other Me.
To a Hurt Child.
Lithgow, William
Painted whore, the mask of deadly sin, A.
Still this, still that I would! all I surmise.
Little, Jack
Poème de Terre; or, Love Song to a Potato.
Little, Katharine Day
Hazlitt Sups.
Littlebird, Harold (Harold Bird)
Alone Is the Hunter.
Circle Begins, A.
Coming Home in March.
Could I Say I Touched You.
Death in the Woods.
For Drum Hadley.
For the Girls 'cause They Know.
For Tom Numkena, Hopi/Spokane.
Gaa-a-Muna, a Mountain Flower.
Hummingbird.
Hunter's Morning.
I tell him how it used to be in Paguate, *sel.*
If You Can Hear My Hooves.
In a Double Rainbow.
Mother/ Deer/ Lady.
Oh but It Was Good.
Old Moke.
Pennsylvania Winter Indian 1974.
Wrap Me in Blankets of Momentary Winds.
Littledale, Freya
When My Dog Died.
Littlefield, Hazel
Not for Its Own Sake.
Littlefield, Milton S.
Come, O Lord, Like Morning Sunlight.
O Son of Man, Thou Madest Known.
Littleton, Edward
Spider, The.
Littlewort, Dorothy
Prayer of a Teacher.
Li Tung
For the Monk San-tsang on His Return to the
   Western Regions.
Li Tung-yang
Following the Rhymes of Yang T'ing-ho's
   Poem "On the Road Back."

Inscribed on the Painting "Meaning of a Poem
   by Wang Wei."
Long Handscroll of Bamboo by Wang
   Meng-tuan, The.
Song of the Painting "Catching Fish."
To Yung-erh.
Trip to Yüeh-lu Temple, A.
Litvinoff, Emanuel
All Ruin Is the Same.
Garrison Town.
If I Forget Thee.
Rededication.
To T. S. Eliot.
War Swaggers.
Litwack, Susan
Creation of the Child.
Havdolah.
Inscape.
Tonight Everyone in the World Is Dreaming
   the Same Dream.
Li Tz'u-ming
On a Rainy Evening: Written in Playful
   Imitation of Yi-shan's "Untitled Poems."
While on an Evening Stroll Outside the Gates,
   I Stood Alone Looking Out on the Water.
Written at Night, after Dreaming That I Had
   Returned to My Old Home.
Liu, Stephen Shu Ning
Adultery at a Las Vegas Bookstore.
I Lie on the Chilled Stones of the Great Wall.
My Father's Martial Art.
On Pali Lookout.
Pair of Fireflies, A.
Liu Ch'ang-ch'ing
Rejoicing That the Zen Master Pao Has
   Arrived from Dragon Mountain.
Liu Ch'e
Song of the Autumn Wind.
Emperor Wu of the Han.
Liu Cheng
Poem without a Category.
Liu E
Academics? Politics? I've nothing to do with
   them!, *sel.*
Beautiful women—we've vowed to be lovers!,
   sel.
Boiling Falls.
Cotton blankets left in the cold, *sel.*
House of Red Leaves, The.
I Remember.
Last year, with jade hands, you offered cups
   of tea, *sel.*
My thoughts flow in streams around this
   tower, *sel.*
New Year's Eve.
"Next year you must come again", *sel.*
On the Night of the Sixteenth of the Eighth
   Month.
On the Road to Pyongyang—An
   Improvisation.
Pleasures of Shinbashi.
Poem on Falling Leaves.
Teahouse at Hoshioka, A.
Waiting for the Ferry at Inchon.
Liu-K'o-chuang
Beggar in patched robe stands in my doorway,
   A, *sel.*
Leaving the City.
Weeping for Hsüeh Tzu-shu.
Liu K'o-hsiang
1970s.
Small Is Beautiful.
Stray Bird's Homeland, A.
Liu Ling-hsien
Inscribed on a Plantain Leaf to Show to a
   Certain Person.
Liu Shih
Poem in Response.
Poem on a Sleeping Butterfly.
Sending a Letter.
Tz'u-yün Poem Written in Response: Tiger
   Hill, A.

Liu Tsung-yüan
Poem to Send to Friends in the Capital, A.
River Snow.
Liu Yü-hsi
Bamboo Branch Song.
To the Tune "Glittering Sword Hilts."
Livesay, Dorothy
Children's Letters, The.
Contact.
Epilogue to the Outrider.
Fantasia.
Green Rain.
Improvisation on an Old Theme.
Inheritors, The.
Interval with Fire.
Lament: "What moved me, was the way your
   hand."
Leader, The.
On Looking into Henry Moore.
Prophetess, The.
Serenade for Strings.
Signature.
Spain.
Uninvited, The.
Waking in the Dark.
Without Benefit of Tape.
Livesay, Florence Randal
Tim, the Fairy.
Violin Calls, The.
Livingston, Edna
Question, A.
Livingston, Myra Cohn
Car Wash.
Conversation with Washington.
Driving.
Father.
German Shepherd.
Grunion.
Halloween.
History.
Jacaranda.
Just Watch.
Lazy Witch.
Lonesome.
Martin Luther King.
Math Class.
Mill Valley.
Mr. Pratt ("Mr. Pratt has never left").
Mrs. Spider.
Night, The.
October Magic.
Tape, The.
Time for Building, A.
12 October.
We Could Be Friends.
Whispers.
Wide Awake.
Livingston, William
Ireland Weeping.
Message to the Bard.
Livingstone, Dinah
Desire.
In Perfect Time.
Night Prayers.
Praise.
Livingstone, Douglas
Evasion, An.
One Time.
Peace Delegate.
Sunstrike.
To a Dead Elephant.
Li Yü
Tune: Crows Crying at Night.
Tune: Deva-like Barbarian ("Blossoms bright,
   the moon dark, shadowed in thin mist").
Tune: Gazing at the South.
Tune: Pure Serene Music ("Since we parted,
   spring half over").
Tune: Ripples Sifting Sand.
Tune: Song of Tzu-yeh.
Tune: The Fisherman.

Llawdden
No Place Like Home.
Lloréns Torres, Luis
Love without Love.
Maceo.
Lloyd, Cecil Francis
March Winds.
Truth.
Lloyd, Donald J.
Bridal Couch.
Lloyd, Evan
Helen like the Rose, *sel.*
Religion and the Lower Classes, *sel.*
Sons of War sometimes are known, The, *sel.*
Lloyd, Robert
Cit's Country Box, The.
Mark yon round parson, fat and sleek, *sel.*
Public Schools, *sel.*
Sent to a Lady, with a Seal.
True Genius, *sel.*
Lloyd, Roseann
Hunting for Grouse.
Song of the Fisherman's Lover.
Lluellyn, Martin
Cock-throwing.
Llwyd, Huw
Fox's Counsel, The.
Llwyd, John Plummer Derwent
Night is soft with summer, The; yon faint arch, *sel.*
Llywarch the Aged
Hearth of Urien, The.
"Llywelyn"
Birds.
Llywelyn ab y Moel
Battle of Waun Gaseg, The.
Llywelyn Goch ap Meurig Hen
Lament for Lleucu Llwyd.
Llywelyn-Williams, Alun
In Berlin, August 1945: Lehrte Bahnhof.
Pont y Caniedydd.
When I Was Young.
Yesterday's Illusion *or* Remembering the Thirties.
Lobel, Arnold
There was a light pig from Montclair.
There Was a Small Pig Who Wept Tears.
Lo Chih-ch'eng
Candle Has Slept in Its Own Flame, A.
Lo Ch'ing
Diary of a Prisoner.
Landscape in a Pot.
Lone Swordsman, The.
Six Ways of Eating Watermelons.
Story of Bitter Tea, The.
Sword of Li Ling, The.
UFO Is Coming, A.
Writing of the Character "Tree", The.
Locke, Lawrence
Animal Pictures.
Leaving Mendota, 1956.
River.
Locker, Malka
Clocks.
Drunken Streets.
Locker-Lampson, Frederick
Jester's Plea, The.
Old Buffer, An.
On an Old Muff.
Our Photograph[s]
Terrible Infant, A.
Lockett, Reginald
Good Times and No Bread.
Lockhart, John Gibson
Lines: "When youthful faith hath fled."
Wandering Knight's Song, The.
Locklin, Gerald
Since You Seem Intent.
Lockman, John
Penitent Nun, The.

Lockwood, Margo
December Eclipse.
Health.
Oxford Street Museum.
Victorian Grandmother.
Lockyer, Milton
Dark Mountains.
Lodeizen, Hans
Dishonorable Seaman's Grave.
Empty Mailman Drowns in the Country Road, An.
Evening at the Merrills.
He Was the Best of All.
Jim I Would Like to Know.
La Voix du Peuple.
World an Old Music Box, The.
Lodge, Edith
Song of the Hill.
Lodge, Thomas
Devoide of reason, thrale to foolish ire, *sel.*
Earth, Late Choked with Showers, The, *sel.*
Fancy, A, *sel.*
For Pity, Pretty Eyes, Surcease.
Her Rambling, *sel.*
I Hope and Fear, *sel.*
I would in rich and golden coloured raine, *sel.*
Love Guards [*or* Guides] the Roses of Thy Lips, *sel.*
Love's Witchery.
Montanus' Sonnet, *sel.*
My Mistress, *sel.*
No Stars Her Eyes, *sel.*
O Pleasing Thoughts, *sel.*
Ode, An: "Now I find thy looks were feigned," *sel.*
Old Damon's Pastoral.
Phillis ("My Phillis hath the morning sun"), *sel.*
Pluck the Fruit and Taste the Pleasure, *sel.*
Rosader's Sonnet, *sel.*
Rosalind's [*or* Rosalynd's] Madrigal[l], *sel.*
Rosaline, *sel.*
Rose, The, *sel.*
Sonnet: "O shady vales, O fair enriched meads," *sel.*
Truth's Complaint over England.
Lodge, Thomas and Robert Greene
Beauty, Alas, Where Wast Thou Born, *at.*
Loesser, Frank
Guys and Dolls.
Loewenthal, Tali
Hebrew Script.
Loewinsohn, Ron
Against the Silences to Come.
Insomniac Poem.
Mrs. Loewinsohn &c.
My Sons.
Pastoral: "Death./ The death of a million."
Stillness of the Poem, The.
Thing Made Real, The.
Loftin, Elouise
Pigeon.
Virginia.
Weeksville Women.
Woman.
Lofting, Hugh
Mister Beers.
Picnic.
Lo Fu
After Dawn.
Beyond Logic.
Brewing Stone, The.
Crab-Legged Flower, The.
Early Snow.
Having Followed the Sound of Rain into the Mountain but Found No Rain.
Peeling Pears at Midnight.
Song of the Cricket.
To Mr. Hsiao Ch'ien.
Watching the Native Country from the Border.
Water.

Logan, John
Avocado.
For My Daughter.
Happening on Aegina.
He told the crowd "The devils", *sel.*
Lines for a Young Wanderer in Mexico.
Lines to His Son on Reaching Adolescence.
On the Death of Keats.
Pass, The.
Saint, who overlaps, *sel.*
Suzanne.
Topcliffe's horses shake, *sel.*
Trip to Four or Five Towns, A.
Logan, John (1748–88)
Braes of Yarrow, The.
Logan, John (b. 1923)
Believe It.
Century Piece for Poor Heine, A.
Coming of Age.
Concert Scene.
Experiment That Failed, The.
First Prelude. Dream in Ohio; the Father, *sel.*
Love Poem: "Last night you would not come."
Monument and the Shrine, The.
Nude Kneeling in Sand.
Picnic, The.
Poem for My Son.
Rescue, The.
San Francisco Poem.
Saturday Afternoon at the Movies.
Second Prelude. Reality in Albuquerque: The Son, *sel.*
Shore Scene.
Spring of the Thief.
Suite of Six Pieces for Siskind, A.
Three Moves.
To a Young Poet Who Fled.
Trip to Four or Five Towns, A.
Zoo, The.
Logan, John Daniel
Heliodore.
Logan, William
Debora Sleeping.
Green Island.
Moorhen.
New York.
Summer Island.
Sutcliffe and Whitby.
Tatiana Kalatschova.
Logau, Friedrich von
Retribution.
Logue, Christopher
Aardvark, The.
Coma.
Epitaph: "I am old."
Footnote.
Foreword to New Numbers.
Friday. Wet Dusk.
Last Night in London Airport.
Lit. Crit.
Melissima's Waltz.
To My Now Distant But Once Much Loved Friend, Mr. Michael White.
Loines, Russell Hillard
On a Magazine Sonnet.
Lok, Henry
It Is Not, Lord, the Sound of Many Words, *sel.*
Words May Well Want, *sel.*
Lom, Iain (John MacDonald)
Day of Inverlochy, The.
To Mackinnon of Strath.
Lomax, Pearl Cleage
Glimpse.
Jesus Drum.
Mississippi Born.
Poem: "You said./ don't write me/ a love poem."
Lombarda
I'd like to be a Lombard for Lombarda.

Lo Men
Tree and the Bird: A Duet, The.
Watching the Sea.
London, Sara
Rare Rhythms.
Long, Charles C.
Yei-ie's Child.
Long, Doughtry, Jr.
Negro Dreams.
Long, Doughtry, Jr. ("Doc Long")
Ginger Bread Mama.
Number Four.
One Time Henry Dreamed the Number.
Long, Elizabeth-Ellen
Mountain Medicine.
Rain Clouds.
Long, Pauline. *See* **Asphodel**
Long, Peter
Remember Thy Creator Now.
Long, Richard A.
Hearing James Brown at the Café des Nattes.
Juan de Pareja: Painted by Velazquez.
Long, Richard Hoopell
Poet and Peasant.
Skylark's Nest, The.
Long, Robert
Burning Out.
Chelsea.
Debts.
First Day of Spring.
Somewhere on the Coast of Maine.
Long, Stewart I.
Was It You?
Long, Worth
Arson and Cold Lace.
Longbottom, Audrey
Resolution.
Longchamps, Joanne de
Blind, I Speak to the Cigarette.
Longenecker, C. W.
Victor, The.
Longfellow, Henry Wadsworth
Aftermath.
Arrow and the Song, The.
Arsenal at Springfield, The.
Ballad of the French Fleet, A.
Battle of Lovell's Pond, The.
Beleaguered City, The.
Belisarius.
Bells of Lynn, The.
Bells of San Blas, The.
Birds of Killingworth, The (The Poet's Tale),
  sel.
Birds of Passage.
Builders, The.
Charlemagne.
Chaucer.
Children's Hour, The.
Christmas Bells.
Christmas Carols.
Courtship of Miles Standish, The.
Cross of Snow, The.
Cumberland, The.
Curfew.
Dante.
Day Is Done, The.
Daybreak.
Death of Minnehaha, The, *sel.*
Decoration Day.
Divina Commedia (*poems introductory to*
  Longfellow's *tr. of the* Divine Comedy,
  I-VI.
Do you ne'er think what wondrous beings
  these?, *sel.*
Drowned Mariner, The.
Dutch Picture, A.
Embarkation, The, *sel.*
Endymion.
Evangeline.
Evangeline in Acadie, *sel.*
Excelsior.

Expedition to Wessagusset, The, *sel.*
Fate of the Prophets, The, *sel.*
Fiftieth Birthday of Agassiz, The.
Finding of Gabriel, The, *sel.*
Fire of Drift-wood, The.
Footsteps of Angels.
From his pouch he took his colors, *sel.*
From his wanderings far to eastward, *sel.*
From My Arm-Chair.
Galley of Count Arnaldos, The.
Giotto's Tower.
Give me of your bark, O Birch-tree!, *sel.*
Golden Mile-Stone, The.
Harvest Moon, The.
Haunted Houses.
Hawthorne.
Hiawatha's Brothers, *sel.*
Hiawatha's Childhood, *sel.*
Hiawatha's Wooing, *sel.*
Home Song.
Hymn of the Moravian Nuns of Bethlehem.
Hymn to the Night.
In the Churchyard at Cambridge.
Introduction: "Should you ask me, whence
  these stories," *sel.*
It Is Not Always May.
It Is Too Late, *sel.*
Jericho's Blind Beggar.
Jewish Cemetery at Newport, The.
Jugurtha.
Keats.
Killed at the Ford.
King Robert of Sicily (The Sicilian's Tale),
  sel.
Lakes of the Atchafalaya, The, *sel.*
Let War's Tempest Cease.
Life, *sel.*
Little Hiawatha, The, *sel.*
Little Moon, The.
Message of Peace, A, *sel.*
Mezzo Cammin.
Milton.
Monk of Casal-Maggiore, The (The Sicilian's
  Tale), *sel.*
My Books.
My Lost Youth.
Nature.
New Household, A, *sel.*
Nuremberg.
O Ship of State.
Ode to the Inhabitants of Pennsylvania.
Old Bridge at Florence, The.
Old Clock on the Stairs, The.
On the Atchafalaya, *sel.*
Paul Revere's Ride.
Poet and His Songs, The.
Potter's Song, The, *sel.*
President Garfield.
Proclamation, The, *sel.*
Prologue: "Delusions of the days that once
  have been," *sel.*
Prologue: "To-night we strive to read, as we
  may best," *sel.*
Psalm of Life, A.
Rain in Summer.
Rainy Day, The.
Revenge of Rain-in-the-Face, The.
Seaweed.
Serenade: "Stars of the summer night!," *sel.*
Shakespeare.
Ships That Pass in the Night (The
  Theologian's Tale), *sel.*
Sir Humphrey Gilbert.
Skeleton in Armor, The.
Slave Singing at Midnight, The.
Slave's Dream, The.
Snow-Flakes.
Song of the Bird, The.
Sound of the Sea, The.
Student's Tale, The, *sel.*
Sunset.
Tell Me Not in Mournful Numbers, *sel.*

Then the Master, *sel.*
This is the forest primeval. The murmuring
  pines and the hemlocks, *sel.*
Thou, too, sail on, O Ship of State!, *sel.*
Three Kings, The.
Tide Rises, the Tide Falls, The.
To the Driving Cloud.
Trial, The, *sel.*
Twilight.
Ultima Thule.
Venice.
Victor Galbraith.
Village Blacksmith, The.
Wapentake.
War-Token, The, *sel.*
Warden of the Cinque Ports, The.
When he heard the owls at midnight, *sel.*
Windmill, The.
Witnesses, The.
Wreck of the *Hesperus,* The.
Longfellow, Samuel
Again as Evening's Shadow Falls.
Christian Life, The.
Church Universal, The.
Holy Spirit, Truth Divine.
O Life That Maketh All Things New.
'Tis Winter Now.
Longinovic, Tomislav
What I Owe Iowa.
Longley, Michael
Amish Rug, An.
Caravan.
Desert Warfare.
Detour.
Emily Dickinson.
Epithalamion: "These are the small hours
  when."
Fleance.
In Memoriam.
Kindertotenlieder.
Leaving Inishmore.
Letter to Derek Mahon.
Letter to Seamus Heaney.
Letter to Three Irish Poets, A.
Linen Industry, The.
Linen Workers, The.
Lodger, The.
Man Lying on a Wall.
No Continuing City.
Peace.
Persephone.
Second Sight.
Skara Brae.
Swans Mating.
Third Light, The.
Wounds.
Longstaff, W. D.
Take Time to Be Holy.
Lonzano, Menahem ben Judah
Gentleman, The.
Looke, John
Famous Sea-Fight, A.
Loomis, Charles Battell
Classic Ode, A.
Jack and Jill.
O-U-G-H.
Timon of Archimedes.
Loots, Barbara Kunz
Mountain Wind.
Lope de Vega Carpio, Félix
At Dawn the Virgin Is Born.
Little Carol of the Virgin, A.
Song of the Virgin Mother, A.
To-Morrow.
Woman Is of Man the Best.
Lopez, Alonzo
Celebration.
Direction.

I Am Crying from Thirst.
Lavender Kitten, The.

López, Rafael
Venus Poised.

Lopez-Penha, Abraham Z.
Dusk.

López Velarde, Ramón
Ants.
Humbly.
I Honour You in Dread.
In the Wet Shadows.
Malefic Return, The.
My Cousin Agueda [or Agatha]
My Heart Atones.
Now, as Never.
Tear, The.
Wet Earth.
Your Teeth.

Lorca, Federico Garciá. *See* **Garciá Lorca, Federico**

Lord, Everett W.
Legend of the Admen, The.

Lord, May Carleton
Old Man with a Mowing Machine.

Lord, Phillips H.
Your Church and Mine.

Lord, William Wilberforce
Brook, The.
For them, O God, who only worship Thee, *sel.*
Keats, *sel.*
On the Defeat of Henry Clay [or of a Great Man]
To Rosina Pico.
Wordsworth, *sel.*

Lorde, Audre
And What About the Children.
Beams.
Between Ourselves.
Birthday Memorial to Seventh Street, A.
Chain.
Coal.
Coniagui Women.
Dahomey.
Eulogy for Alvin Frost.
Father Son and Holy Ghost.
Father, the Year Is Fallen.
For Each of You.
From the House of Yemanjá.
Hanging Fire.
Harriet.
If You Come Softly.
Love Poem: "Speak earth and bless me with what is richest."
Memorial I.
Movement Song.
Naturally.
Now That I Am Forever with Child.
On a Night of the Full Moon.
One Year to Life on the Grand Central Shuttle.
Outlines.
Oya.
Poem for a Poet, A.
Political Relations.
Power.
Question of Climate, A.
Recreation.
Rite of Passage.
Rock Thrown into the Water Does Not Fear the Cold, A.
Sisters in Arms.
Suffer the Children.
Summer Oracle.
This Urn Contains Earth from German Concentration Camps.
To Desi as Joe as Smoky the Lover of 115th Street.
To My Daughter the Junkie on a Train.
Trip on the Staten Island Ferry, A.

What My Child Learns of the Sea.
Woman Thing, The.
Women of Dan Dance with Swords in Their Hands to Mark the Time When They Were Warriors, The.

Lorentz, Pare
Black spruce and Norway pine, *sel.*
Down the Yellowstone, the Milk, the White and Cheyenne, *sel.*

Loring, Frederick Wadsworth
In the Old Churchyard at Fredericksburg.

"Lothrop, Amy." *See* **Warner, Anna Bartlett**

Lothrop, Harriett Mulford
Little Brown Seed, The.

Lott, Henry F.
Sonnet: "Dream not, poor poet, that th' ephemeral breath."
Sonnet: "If 'twere not for the dignity inborn."
Sonnet: My Friend's Library.
Sonnet: "O! how my poet's-spirit doth it vex."

Louis, Adrian C.
Captivity Narrative, September 1981.
Elegy for the Forgotten Oldsmobile.
Hemingway Syndrome, The.
Indian Education.
Walker River Night, The.

Louis, Louise
Wounded, The.

Lourie, Dick
Dream about Junior High School in America, The.
Getting a Poem in the Rain.
Gift, The.
Pearl Harbor Day 1970.
September 30.
Sharks.
Stumbling.
Telegram.
Thinking of You.

Louw, N. P. van Wyk
Armed Vision.
At Dawn the Light Will Come.
Ballad of the Drinker in His Pub.
From the Ballad of Evil.
Gods Are Mighty, The.
Little Chisel, The.
Oh the Inconstant.

Louÿs, Pierre
Agonizing Memory, The, *sel.*
Breasts of Mnasidice, The, *sel.*
Complaisant Friend, The, *sel.*
Love, *sel.*
Meeting, The, *sel.*
Penumbra, *sel.*

Love, Adelaide
Poet's Prayer.
Walk Slowly.

Love, George
Noonday April Sun, The.

Lovejoy, George Newell
Easter Carol.

Lovelace, Richard
A la Bourbon.
Advice to My Best Brother, Colonel Francis Lovelace.
Anniversary on the Hymeneals of My Noble Kinsman, Thomas Stanley, Esquire, An.
Another ("As I beheld a winters evening air").
Another ("The centaur, siren I forgo").
Ant, The.
Apostasy of One and But One Lady, The.
Black Patch on Lucasta's Face, A.
Calling Lucasta from Her Retirement.
Cupid Far Gone.
Dual, The.
Elinda's [or Ellinda's] Glove.
Falcon, The.
Fly about a Glass of Burnt Claret, A.
Fly Caught in a Cobweb, A.
Fool much bit by fleas put out the light, A.

Grasshopper, The.
Gratiana Dancing [or Dauncing] and Singing.
In Allusion to the French Song.
La Bella Bona Roba.
Lady A. L., My Asylum in a Great Extremity, The.
Lady with a Falcon on Her Fist, A.
Loose Saraband, A.
Love Enthroned.
Love Made in the First Age: To Chloris.
Lucasta Laughing.
Lucasta's Fan, with a Looking-Glass in It.
Lucasta's World.
Mock Charon, A.
Mock Song, A.
Night.
Orpheus to Beasts.
Orpheus to Woods.
Painture.
Scrutiny [or Scrutinie], The.
Snail, The.
Song: "In mine own monument I lie."
To a Lady That Desired Me I Would Bear My Part with Her in a Song.
To Althea, from Prison.
To Amarantha, That She Would Dishevel Her Hair.
To Dr. F. B. on His Book of Chess.
To Fletcher Reviv'd.
To Lucasta.
To Lucasta, from Prison.
To Lucasta, Going to the Wars [or Warres]
To Lucasta: Her Reserved Looks.
To Lucasta, [on] Going beyond the Seas.
To Lucasta: The Rose.
To My Noble Kinsman, Thomas Stanley, Esquire, on His Lyric Poems Composed by Master John Gamble.
To My Truly Valiant, Learned Friend, Who in His Book Resolved the Art Gladiatory into the Mathematics.
To My Worthy Friend Master Peter Lely.
Upon the Curtain of Lucasta's Picture It Was Thus Wrought.
Valiant Love.
Vintage to the Dungeon, The.

Loveman, Robert
April Rain.
Hobson and His Men (Hobson went toward death and hell).

Lover, Samuel
Quaker's Meeting, The.
St. Kevin, at.
War Ship of Peace, The.

Loving, Pierre
Black Horse Rider, The.

Low, Patricia
First Day of the Hunting Moon, The.
Wet Weather.

Low, Samuel
To a Segar.

Lowbury, Edward
In the Old Jewish Cemetery, Prague, 1970.
Monster, The.
Roc, The.
Swan.
Tree of Knowledge.

Lowe, C. M.
Hay-Time.

Lowe, Robert, Viscount Sherbrooke
Songs of the Squatters.

Lowell, Amy
Camouflaged Troop-Ship.
Carrefour.
Chacago.
Chinoiseries.
Cyclists, The.
Decade, A.
Desolation.
Epitaph on a Young Poet Who Died before Having Achieved Success.

Fisherman's Wife, The.
Fragment: "What is poetry? Is it a mosaic."
Free Fantasia on Japanese Themes.
Fringed Gentians.
From One Who Stays.
Gift, A.
Grotesque.
I dug a grave under an oak-tree, *sel.*
Katydids.
Lady, A.
Lilacs.
Madonna of the Evening Flowers.
Meeting-House Hill.
Night Clouds.
Nostalgia.
Painted Ceiling, The.
Patterns.
Poet, The.
Proportion.
Sea Shell.
Seeing You Stand Once More before My
    Eyes, *sel.*
Solitaire.
Sprig of Rosemary, A.
Taxi, The.
Texas.
Thorn Piece.
To a Friend.
To John Keats.
Venus Transiens.
Whistle under the water, *sel.*
Wind and Silver.

Lowell, James Russell
After the Burial.
Auspex.
Autograph, An.
Birthday Verses Written in a Child's Album.
Boss, The.
Brook in Winter, The, *sel.*
Bryant, *sel.*
Cooper, *sel.*
Count me o'er earth's chosen heroes—they
    were souls that stood alone, *sel.*
Courtin', The.
Day in June, A ("And what is so rare as a day
    in June?"), *sel.*
Dear common flower, that grow'st beside the
    way, *sel.*
Down swept the chill wind from the mountain
    peak, *sel.*
Earth gets its price for what Earth gives us,
    sel.
Fatherland, The.
1st Series, No. V, *sel.*
1st Series, No. I, *sel.*
1st Series, No. VII, *sel.*
1st Series, No. III, *sel.*
1st Series, No. II, *sel.*
First Snowfall [*or* Snow-Fall], The.
Fitz Adam's Story.
Flawless His Heart.
For a cap and bells our lives we pay, *sel.*
"For Christ's sweet sake, I beg an alms," *sel.*
Forgetfulness.
Fountain, The.
God Is Not Dumb, *sel.*
Hawthorne, *sel.*
Hear now this fairy legend of old Greece, *sel.*
Hebe.
His Throne Is with the Outcast.
Hob Gobbling's Song.
Holmes, *sel.*
Holy Supper is kept, indeed, The, *sel.*
I with uncovered head, *sel.*
In a Copy of Omar Khayyám.
In an Album.
In the Twilight.
International Copyright.
Irving, *sel.*
Joys.
Longing.
Lowell, *sel.*

Misconception, A.
My Love.
Never to see a nation born, *sel.*
New-come Chief, The, *sel.*
Not Only around Our Infancy, *sel.*
Ode Recited at the Harvard Commemoration.
On Board the '76.
Once to Every Man and Nation, *sel.*
Oriental Apologue, An.
Origin of Didactic Poetry, The.
Our Martyr-Chief.
Over his keys the musing organist, *sel.*
Palinode.
Poe and Longfellow, *sel.*
2d Series, Introduction, *sel.*
2d Series, No. IV, *sel.*
2d Series, No. VI, *sel.*
2d Series, No. X, *sel.*
2d Series, No. II, *sel.*
She Came and Went.
Singing Leaves, The.
Sir Launfal and the Leper, *sel.*
Sixty-eighth Birthday.
Slaves, *sel.*
Snow had begun in the gloaming, The, *sel.*
Stanzas on Freedom.
Street, The.
Tempora Mutantur.
That lifted blade transformed our jangling
    clans, *sel.*
There are truths you Americans need to be
    told, *sel.*
There comes Emerson first, whose rich words,
    every one, *sel.*
'Tis Sorrow Builds the Shining Ladder Up.
To His Countrymen, *sel.*
To the Dandelion.
To the Spirit of Keats.
Washers of the Shroud, The.
Washington, *sel.*
What [*or* And what] Is So Rare as a Day in
    June?, *sel.*
Whittier, *sel.*
Winter Morning, A, *sel.*
With a Pressed Flower.
Without and Within.
Yussouf.

Lowell, Maria White
An Opium Fantasy.
Morning-Glory, The.
Song: "O Bird, thou dartest to the sun."

Lowell, Robert (1917–1977)
After the Convention.
After the Surprising Conversions.
Alfred Corning Clark.
At the Altar, *sel.*
As a Plane Tree by the Water.
At the Indian Killer's Grave.
Between the Porch and the Altar.
Beyond the Alps.
Black Spring.
Bomber, The ("Bomber climb out on the
    roof").
Central Park.
Children of Light.
Child's Song.
Christ./ May I die at night.
Christmas Eve under Hooker's Statue.
Coastguard House, The.
Colloquy in Black Rock.
Commander Lowell.
Dead in Europe, The.
Death and the Bridge.
Death from Cancer, *sel.*
Death of the Sheriff, The.
Difficulties, the impossibilities, The, *sel.*
Dolphin.
Down the Nile.
Drunken Fisherman, The.
End of a Year.
Epilogue: "Those blessed structures, plot and
    rhyme."

Exile's Return, The.
Eye and Tooth.
Ezra Pound.
Fall 1961.
Falling Asleep over the Aeneid.
Fat Man in the Mirror, The.
Father.
Fishnet.
For George Santayana.
For John Berryman.
For Sheridan.
For the Union Dead.
Ford Madox Ford.
George III.
Ghost, The.
Grandparents.
Harriet.
Her Dead Brother.
History.
Holy Innocents, The.
Home after Three Months Away.
Homecoming.
Identification in Belfast (I.R.A. Bombing).
In Memory of Arthur Winslow.
In the Cage.
In the Ward.
It Did.
July in Washington.
Lady Ralegh's Lament.
Last Things, Black Pines at 4 a.m.
Lesson, The.
Mad Negro Soldier Confined at Munich, A.
Magnolia's Shadow, The.
Man and Wife.
March 1, The.
March 2, The.
Mary Winslow.
Memories of West Street and Lepke.
Mouth of the Hudson, The.
Mr. Edwards and the Spider.
My Last Afternoon with Uncle Devereux
    Winslow.
Near the Ocean.
Neo-Classical Urn, The.
New Year's Day.
News from Mount Amiata.
Night Sweat.
1930's.
Ninth Month, *sel.*
North Sea Undertaker's Complaint, The.
Notice.
Obit.
October and November.
Old Flame, The.
On the Eve of the Feast of the Immaculate
    Conception: 1942.
Opposite House, The.
Overhanging Cloud, *sel.*
Public Garden, The.
Poet at Seven, The.
Quaker Graveyard in Nantucket, The.
Reading Myself.
Robert Frost.
Robert Sheridan Lowell, *sel.*
Robespierre and Mozart as Stage.
Sailing Home from Rapallo.
Saint-Just 1767-93 ("Saint-Just: his name
    seems stolen from the Missal").
Salem.
September.
Shako, The.
Sheridan.
Shifting Colors.
Skunk Hour.
Soft Wood.
South of Boston, south of Washington, *sel.*
Sparrow Hills.
Stalin.
Suicide.
Sylvia.
This Golden Summer.
Those before Us.

Three Poems for Kaddish.
"To Speak of Woe That Is in Marriage."
T. S. Eliot.
Turtle.
Ulysses.
Violence.
Waking Early Sunday Morning.
Waking in the Blue.
Watchmaker God.
Water.
Where the Rainbow Ends.
Withdrawal, The.
Words for Hart Crane.

Lowell, Robert Traill Spence (1816–91)
After-Comers, The.
Brave Old Ship, the *Orient,* The.

Lowenfels, Walter
Creed.

Lowenstein, Tom
Horizon without Landscape.
Nausicaa with Some Attendants.
Noah in New England.

Lowery, Mike
Nam.
Smell of Old Newspapers Is Always Stronger
    after Sleeping in the Sun, The.
Stroke.

Lowman, Bill
Great Wanagan Creek Flood, The.

Lowry, H. D.
Spring Will Come, The.

Lowry, Malcolm
After Publication of Under the Volcano.
Cain Shall Not Slay Abel Today on Our Good
    Ground.
Christ Walks in This Infernal District Too.
Delirium in Vera Cruz.
Drunkards, The.
Epitaph: "Malcolm Lowry."
For *Under the Volcano.*
He Liked the Dead.
In Memoriam; Ingvald Bjorndal and His
    Comrade.
Lighthouse Invites the Storm, The.
Lupus in Fabula.
Salmon Drowns Eagle.
Sestina in a Cantina.

Lowry, Robert
Where Is My Wandering Boy Tonight? *at.*

Lowther, Pat
Last Letter to Pablo.
Stone Diary, A.

Loy, Mina
Apology of Genius.
Der Blinde Junge.
Love Songs.
Lunar Baedeker.

Lu Chi
Off at dawn to service in the walled and
    storied palace, *sel.*

Lu Ch'ien-i
Beautiful Lady Yü, The.
Immortal at the River.
Taoist Nun, The.
Thoughts of the Yüeh Beauty.

Lu Yu
After Getting Drunk, I Scribble Songs and
    Poems.
Autumn Thoughts.
Blue Rapids.
Border Mountain Moon.
Feeling Sorry for Myself.
Harp Song.
Herd Boy, The.
I Had Occasion to Tell a Visitor about an Old
    Trip I Took.
Idle Thoughts.
In a Boat on a Summer Evening.
It's late, the children come home from school,
    sel.
Long Sigh.

Merchant's Joy, The.
My Village Home.
Sending Tzu-lung Off to a Post in Chi-chou.
Sitting Outdoors.
Sitting Up at Night.
Snug—the robe sewn from coarse cotton, *sel.*
Stone on the Hilltop, The.
Third Month, Night of the Seventeenth,
    Written While Drunk.
To Show My Sons.
Trip to Mountain West Village, A.
Tune: Phoenix Hairpin.
Vegetable Garden.
Wild Flower Man, The.
Written in a Carefree Mood.

Lu Yün
For Ku Yen-hsien, A Poem for Him to Give
    to His Wife.

Lubke, Bernice W.
All-sufficient Christ, The.

Lucan (Marcus Annaeus Lucanus)
Coracle, The.
Just and fit actions Ptolemy (he saith), *sel.*
O wastfull riot, never well content, *sel.*
Portents, The, *sel.*
Thee Pompey thy past deeds by turns infest,
    sel.

Lucas, Alice
Prayer before Sleep.

Lucas, Daniel Bedinger
In the Land Where We Were Dreaming.

Lucas, Edward Verrall
Mr. Coggs.
O England, Country of My Heart's Desire.
Pedestrian's Plaint, The.
Windmill, The.

Lucas, Russell
Bishop's hand on a widow's breast, A.

Lucas, St. John
Curate Thinks You Have No Soul, The.

Lucas, Duchess of Newcastle, Margaret
Hunting of the Hare, The.

"Lucebert" (L. J. Swaanswijk)
Breyten Breytenbach May Look at the Moon.
Death of the Lord of the Flies.
Great Wall, The.
I Try in Poetic Fashion.
Indigo Eater, The.
9000 Jackals Swimming to Boston.
School of Poetry.
Slowly I Begin to Play the Game.
Tired Lovers They Are Machines, The.

Lucian
Bewail not much, my parents! me, the prey.

Luciano, Felipe
You're Nothing but a Spanish Colored Kid.

Lucianus
Artificial Beauty.

Lucie-Smith, Edward
At the Roman Baths, Bath.
Fault, The.
Hymn Tunes, The.
Imperialists in Retirement.
Lesson, The.
Meeting Myself.
My own head. Seen in mirrors. Cleanly axed,
    sel.
On Looking at Stubb's Anatomy of the Horse.
Parrot, The.
Poet in Winter.
Rabbit Cry.
Wise Child, The.
Your Own Place.

Lucilius
Boxer's Face, The.
Eutychides is dead, and what is worse.
Lean Gaius, who was thinner than a straw.
On an Old Woman.
Sluggard, The.
Treasure.

Valentine for a Lady, A.
World's Worst Boxer, The.

Lucretius (Titus Lucretius Carus)
Address to Venus, *sel.*
Against the Fear of Death, *sel.*
Beyond Religion.
Child is like a sailor cast up by the sea, The,
    sel.
Concerning the Nature of Love, *sel.*
Delight of humane kind, and gods above, *sel.*
No Single Thing Abides, *sel.*
Now since the members of the world we
    view, *sel.*
Suave Mari Magno, *sel.*
What Has This Bugbear Death, *sel.*

Lucy, Sean
Friday Evening.
Longshore Intellectual.
Senior Members.
Supervising Examinations.
These Six.

Lüders, Charles Henry
Four Winds, The.
Haunts of the Halcyon, The.
Heart of Oak.
Mountebanks, The.
Old Thought, An.

"Ludhianvi, Sahir"
Bengal.
Foreign Agents.

"Ludhianvi, Sahir" (Abel-al-Haye)
Before Suicide.
Market Place.

Ludlow, Fitz Hugh
Socrates Snooks.
Too Late.

Ludlum, William
Business Man's Prayer, A.
Radio Religion, The.

Ludvigson, Susan Bartels
Child's Dream, The.
I Arrive in a Small Boat, Alone.
Jeanne d'Arc.
Lesson.
Man Arrested in Hacking Death Tells Police
    He Mistook Mother-in-Law for Raccoon.
On Learning That Certain Peat Bogs Contain
    Perfectly Preserved Bodies.
Punishment, The.
Some Notes on Courage.
Widow, The.

Lui Chi
Poet Thinks, A.

Luis Palés Matos
Elegy for the Duke of Marmalade.
Kalahari.

Lum, Wing Tek
At a Chinaman's Grave.
Chinatown Games.
My Mother Really Knew.
Poet Imagines His Grandfather's Thoughts on
    the Day He Died, The.
To the Old Masters.
Translations.

Lummis, Charles Fletcher
John Charles Frémont.
Poe-'em of Passion, A.

Lumumba, Patrice Emery
Dawn in the Heart of Africa.

Lunde, David
Monster, The.
Singularity in Cygnus XI Viewed with Pity
    for HDE 226868, The.

Lunt, George
Requiem: "Breathe, trumpets, breathe."

Luria, Isaac
Sabbath of Rest, A.

Lushington, Franklin
No More Words.

Luswat
Shaman Song.

Luther, Martin
All Hail, Thou Noble Guest.
Ane Sang of the Birth of Christ, with the Tune of Baw Lula Low.
Away in a Manger, *at.*
Ein feste Burg ist unser Gott.
From Heaven High I Come to You, *at.*
Mighty Fortress Is Our God, A.

Luttinger, Abigail
My Mother Was Always Dressed.

Luttrell, Henry
O death, thy certainty is such.
On a Man Run Over by an Omnibus.

Lutz, Gertrude May
Prisoner of War.

Lux, Thomas
All the Slaves.
Barn Fire.
Elegy for Frank Stanford.
Empty Pitchforks.
Farmers.
Flying Noises.
Graveyard by the Sea.
History and Abstraction.
Hunting, The.
If You See This Man.
It's the Little Towns I Like.
Lament City.
Man Asleep in a Child's Bed.
Man Asleep in the Desert.
Midnight Tennis Match, The.
Milkman and His Son, The.
My Grandmother's Funeral.
Night above the Town.
Pedestrian.
Solo Native.
There Were Some Summers.
This Is a Poem for the Fathers and for Michael Ryan.

Luzi, Mario
Animas, Las.
Ivory.
Night Washes over the Mind.

Luzzatto, Isaac
Death, Thou Hast Seized Me.

Luzzatto, Moses Hayyim, of Padua
Chorus: "All ye that handle harp and viol," *sel.*

Lyall, Sir Alfred Comyn
Meditations of a Hindu Prince.
Night in the Red Sea, A.
Rajpoot Rebels.
Studies at Delhi, 1876.

Lydgate, John
Against Women's Fashions.
Balade Simple.
Boy Serving at Table, The.
Duplicity of Women, The.
Henry before Agincourt: October 25, 1415.
Lament: "Farewell Mercy, farewell thy piteous grace," *sel.*
Letter of Compleynt of Canace, The, *sel.*
Lover's New Year's Gift, A.
On the Departing of Thomas Chaucer.
Then I heard a voice celestial, *sel.*
To the Virgin.
Transient as a Rose.
Vox Ultima Crucis.

Lyle, K. Curtis
Lacrimas or There Is a Need to Scream.
Sometimes I Go to Camarillo and Sit in the Lounge.
Songs for the Cisco Kid; or, Singing for the Face.
Songs for the Cisco Kid: or, Singing: Song #2.
Terra Cotta.

Lyly, John
Cupid and my Campaspe played, *sel.*
Cupid's Indictment, *sel.*
Daphne, *sel.*
Fairy Song, A, *sel.*
O Cupid! Monarch over Kings, *sel.*
Oh, For a Bowl of Fat Canary.
Pan's Syrinx, *sel.*
Sapho's Song, *sel.*
Song: "It is all one in Venus' wanton school."
Song of Apollo, *sel.*
Syrinx.
Trico's Song, *sel.*
Vulcan's Song, *sel.*

Lyly, John and Thomas Ravenscroft
By the Moon ("By the moon we sport and play"), *sel.*
Elves' Dance, The, *sel.*

Lynch, Annette
Bridgework.
Gratitude.

Lynch, Charles
If We Cannot Live as People.
Memo.
Shade.

Lynch, Janice M.
Friend asks why I swim, A, *sel.*
Sixty-four Capries for a Long-Distance Summer, *much abr.*

Lynch, Thomas Toke
Lift Up Your Heads, Rejoice!
Thousand Years Have Come, A.

Lynche, Richard
But thou my deere sweet-sounding lute be still, *sel.*
Love's Despair, *sel.*
Soon as the Azure-colored Gates, *sel.*
What sugred termes, what all-perswading arte, *sel.*

Lynd, Sylvia
Migrants.
Searchlights, The.

Lynde, Benjamin
Lines Descriptive of Thomson's Island.

Lyndsay, Sir David
Ane Supplicatioun in Contemptioun of Syde Taillis.

Lyon, George Ella
Courtship, The.
My Grandfather in Search of Moonshine.
Progress.
Testimony, A.

Lyon, Lilian Bowes. See Bowes-Lyon, Lilian

Lyon, P. H. B.
Envoi: "Earth puts her colours by."

Lyon, Roger H.
Keep On Praying.

Lyons, A. Neil
Fairy Cobbler, The.

Lysaght, Sidney Royse
Deserted Home, A.

Lyte, Henry Francis
Abide with Me.

Lytle, William Haines
Antony to Cleopatra.
Siege of Chapultepec, The.
Volunteers, The.

Lyttelton, George
To Miss Lucy F——, with a New Watch.

Lytton, Edward Robert Bulwer-Lytton, 1st Earl of. See "Meredith, Owen"

M

"M."
On the Frequent Review of the Troops.

"M. B." See "B., M."

"M. J." See "J., M."

Maas, Willard
Letter to R.

Mabuza, Lindiwe
Summer 1970.

MacAdams, Lewis
Moguls and Monks.
Raw Honey.

Macainsh, Noel
Kangaroo by Nightfall ("Kangaroo by the roadside, The").

McAlmon, Robert
For Instance.
Frost in the Corn, The.

McAlpine, R. W.
Two Surprises.

McAlpine, Rachel
Bird-Woman.
Surprise Surprise.
Te Kaha.
Zig-Zag up a Thistle.

Mac An Bhaird, Geoffrey Mac Briain
Morning Prayer.

Mac an Bhaird, Laoiseach
Civil Irish and Wild Irish.
Fond greeting, hillock there, A.
Two Sons.

MacAndrew, Rachel
Pony, The.
Robin Hood.

Macarthur, Bessie J. B.
Nocht o' Mortal Sicht.

MacArthur, Gloria
Phineas Pratt.

McArthur, Mary
Song of Granny Smith.

McArthur, Peter
Earthborn.
Sugar Weather.

Macartney, Frederick Thomas Bennett
Desert Claypan.
Early Summer Sea-Tryst.
No Less than Prisoners.

Macaulay, F. E. M.
Women's Marseillaise, The.

Macaulay, Thomas Babington Macaulay, 1st Baron
Armada, The.
Country Clergyman's Trip to Cambridge, The.
Horatius, *sel.*
Horatius at the Bridge, *sel.*
Ivry.
Jacobite's Epitaph, A.
Night sank upon the dusky beach, and on the purple sea, *sel.*
Radical War Song, A.

McAuley, James Philip
Art of Poetry, An.
At Bungendore.
Because.
Canticle.
Convalescence.
Dear John, whoever now takes pen to write, *sel.*
In the Huon Valley.
Jesus.
Late Winter.
Merry-go-round.
New Guinea.
Pietà.
Winter Drive.

MacBeth, George
Basket of Walnuts, A.
Bedtime Story.
Compasses, The.
Drawer, The.
Five-Minute Orlando Macbeth, The.
Fourteen Ways of Touching Peter.
I needed somewhere with a flirt of grace, *sel.*
Killing, The.
Land-Mine, The.
Little Brown Celery, The.
Miner's Helmet, The.
Orlando Commercial, The.

Political Orlando, The.
Red Herring, The.
Remembering Mincemeat.
Return, The.
Scissor-Man.
Snowdrops.
Star, A.
Wasps' Nest, The.
When I Am Dead.

McBride, Arthur
I once knew a fellow named Arthur McBride.

McBride, Mekeel
Aubade: "She wakes long before he does. A fierce shock."
Blessing, A.
Going Under of the Evening Land, The.
Lessons.
Once upon a Time.
Over the Phone.
Red Letters.
Transmigration.
Will to Live, The.

McBurney, William B. ("Carroll Malone")
Croppy Boy, The.

McCabe, Angela
Back.
Blind Adolphus.
Bloom Street.
From Lois in London.
Inside History.

McCabe, Victoria
For Starters.

McCabe, William Gordon
Christmas Night of '62.
Dreaming in the Trenches.

MacCaig, Norman
Aspects.
Aunt Julia.
Beach Talk.
Betweens.
By Achmelvich Bridge.
By the Graveyard, Luskentyre.
Celtic Cross.
Close-ups of Summer.
Cock before Dawn.
Dark Centre.
Drowned, The.
Ego.
Every Day.
Family.
Feeding Ducks.
Fetching Cows.
Flooded Mind.
Golden Calf.
Gone Are the Days.
High Up on Suilven.
In My Mind.
Incident.
Interruption to a Journey.
Man Walking through Clachtoll, A.
Memory.
Milne's Bar.
Moment Musical in Assynt.
Moorings.
Movements.
No Accident.
Nude in a Fountain.
Old Maps and New.
On the North Side of Suilven.
One of the Many Days.
Orgy.
Over and Over Again.
Poem: "There is a wailing baby under every stone."
Praise of a Collie.
Ringed Plover by a Water's Edge.
Sheep Dipping.
Sleet.
Sonnet: Sounds of the Day.
Space Fiction.
Spate in Winter Midnight.

Stars and Planets.
Summer Farm.
Too Bright a Day.
Truth in Two Halves, A.
Unposted Birthday Card.
Wild Oats.

McCall, James Edward
New Negro, The.

McCanless, Allen
Cowboy's Soliloquy, The.

McCann, Richard
Fat Boy's Dream, The.

McCarroll, James
Grey Linnet, The.

McCarthy, Denis Aloysius
Land Where Hate Should Die, The.

MacCarthy, Denis Florence
Dead Tribune, The.
Paschal Fire, The.
Pillar Towers of Ireland, The.
Spring Flowers from Ireland.
Voyage, The, *sel.*

MacCarthy, Ethna
Ghosts.
Insomnia.
Viaticum.

McCarthy, Eugene
Kilroy.
Tamarack.

McCarthy, Harry
Bonnie Blue Flag.

McCarthy, Joseph Huntly
If I Were King.

McCarthy, Thomas
Feeding Ground.
In the Luxembourg Gardens.
Poet of the Mountains, The.
Question Time.
State Funeral.
With Paul Engle at Fort Madison, 1978.
Word "Silk", The.

McCartney, Mabel E.
Refuge.

MacCathmhaoil, Seosamh. *See* **Campbell, Joseph**

McClatchy, J. D.
At a Reading.
Method, The.
Pleasure of Ruins, The.
Winter without Snow, A.

McClaurin, Irma
I, Woman.
Mask, The.
To a Green Era.

McClellan, George Marion
Butterfly in Church, A.
Dogwood Blossoms.
Feet of Judas, The.
Hills of Sewanee, The.

McCloskey, Mark
Rude, The.
Too Dark.

McClure, Michael
Aelf-Scin, The.
Breech, The.
Canticle.
Clear—the senses bright—sitting in the black chair—Rocker, *sel.*
Flowers of Politics, II, The.
Flowers of Politics, I, The.
For Artaud.
From the Window of the Beverly Wilshire Hotel.
Gesture the gesture the gesture the gesture, The, *sel.*
List, The.
Mad Sonnet 1.
May Morn.
Moiré.
Ode for Soft Voice.
Rant Block.

Rug, The.
With Tendrils of Poems.

Mac Coisdealbthaigh, Tomas ("Laidir")
Una Bhan, *at.*

MacColl, Dugald Sutherland
Ballade of Andrew Lang.

MacColl, Ewan
Dove, The.
First Time Ever I Saw Your Face, The.
Freeborn Man.
Shoals of Herring, The.

McCombs, Judith
Dictionary Is an *His* torian: A Found Political Poem, The.

Mac Con Brettan, Bláthmac
I call you with honest words, *sel.*

MacConglinne
Vision of MacConglinne, The.

Mac Con Midhe, Giolla Brighde
Defence of Poetry, A.

McCord, David
Afreet
Ascot Waistcoat.
At the Garden Gate.
Axolotl, The.
Baccalaureate.
Blessed Lord, What It Is to Be Young.
Books Fall Open.
Cities and Science.
Cocoon.
Come Christmas.
Conversation.
Crew Cut.
Crickets.
Crows.
Crows, The.
Epitaph on a Waiter.
Euterpe; a Symmetric, *sel.*
Every Time I Climb a Tree.
Father and I in the Woods.
Fisherman, The.
Gloss.
Glowworm.
Go Fly a Saucer.
Gone.
Grasshopper, The.
Hex on the Mexican X, A.
History of Education.
I've seen one flying saucer. Only when, *sel.*
Kite.
Lacquer Liquor Locker, The.
Mantis.
Mr. Bidery's Spidery Garden.
Mr. Macklin's Jack O'Lantern ("Mr. Macklin takes his knife").
My stocking's where, *sel.*
Notes on a Track Meet.
Perambulator Poem, V.
Pickety fence, The.
Plane Geometer.
Progress.
Rainbow, The.
Second Half.
Singular Indeed.
Snowman.
Song of the Train.
That broken star, *sel.*
This Is My Rock.
Tiggady Rue.
To a Certain Most Certainly Certain Critic.
To Walk in Warm Rain.
Walnut Tree, The.
Weather Words.
When I Was Christened, *sel.*
Where Is My Butterfly Net?
Yellow.

McCoy, T. J.
Alkali Pete Hits Town.

McCrae, George Gordon
Day had fled, the moon arose, The, *sel.*

McCrae, Hugh Raymond
Ambuscade.
Camden Magpie.
Colombine.
Enigma.
Evening.
I Blow My Pipes.
Joan of Arc.
June Morning.
Mad Marjory.
Mouse, The.
Muse-haunted.
Song of the Rain.
Uncouth Knight, The.
Winds.

McCrae, John
Anxious Dead, The.
In Flanders Fields.

MacCraig, Norman
Above Inverkirkaig.

McCray, Chirlane
I Used to Think.

McCrea, Lilian
Boots and Shoes.
Getting Up.
My Toys.
Noises in the Night.
Pussy-Cat and Puppy-Dog.
Rain.
Wash-Day.

McCreery, John Luckey
There Is No Death.

McCuaig, Ronald
Au Tombeau de Mon Père.
L'Après Midi d'une Fille aux Cheveux de
Lin.
Music in the Air.
Recitative.

Mac Cuarta, Seamas Dall
Houses of Corr an Chait are cold, The.

McCully, Laura E.
Canoe Song at Twilight.

McDaniel, Judith
For My Mother's Mother.

MacDermot, Thomas
Cuba.
Dark foreboding haunts me lest I die, A, sel.
Market Basket in the Car, A.

**"MacDiarmid, Hugh" (Christopher Murray
Grieve)**
Another Epitaph on an Army of Mercenaries.
Antenora.
At My Father's Grave.
Bagpipe Music.
Bonnie Broukit Bairn, The.
Bracken Hills in Autumn.
British Leftish Poetry, 1930-40.
By Wauchopeside.
Cattle Show.
Cloudburst and Soaring Moon.
Cophetua.
Crowdieknowe.
Crystals like Blood.
Dae what ye wull ye canna parry, sel.
De Profundis.
Dead Liebknecht, The.
Deep-Sea Fishing.
Eemis-Stane, The.
Empty Vessel.
Facing the Chair.
Farewell to Dostoevski, sel.
Fleggit Bride, The.
Glen of Silence, The.
Great Wheel, The.
Harry Semen.
I heard Christ sing.
In the Children's Hospital.
In the Fall, sel.
In the Pantry.
Innumerable Christ, The.
It was Landor who first said, sel.

Let the only consistency, sel.
Light of Life, The.
Love.
Moonlight among the Pines.
Moonstruck.
Octopus, The.
Old Wife in High Spirits.
On the Ocean Floor.
On the Oxford Book of Victorian Verse.
One of the Principal Causes of War.
Parley of Beasts.
Parrot Cry, The.
Perfect.
Prayer for a Second Flood.
Reflections in a Slum.
Robber, The.
Royal Stag, The.
Sauchs in the Reuch Heuch Hauch, The.
Scotland Small?
Scunner.
Second Hymn to Lenin.
Sic Transit Gloria Scotia.
Skeleton of the Future, The.
Spanish War, The.
Storm-Cock's Song, The.
To a Sea Eagle.
Two Parents, The.
Under the Greenwood Tree.
Up to Date.
Water Music.
Watergaw, The.
We Must Look at the Harebell, sel.
Weapon, The.
Wheesht, Wheesht.
With a Lifting of the Head.
With the Herring Fishers.
Yet Ha'e I Silence Left, sel.
Yet there is no great problem in the world
today, sel.

MacDonagh, Donagh
Ballade which Villon Made.
Childhood.
Dublin Made Me.
Galway.
Going to Mass Last Sunday.
Hungry Grass, The.
Just an Old Sweet Song.
Love's Language.
Of what a quality is courage made, sel.
Prothalamium.
Revel, A.
Veterans, The.
Wind Blows, The.

MacDonagh, Thomas
John-John.
Lifting of the Cloud, The.
Man Upright, The.
Song: "Love is cruel, Love is sweet."
Wishes for My Son.

Macdonald, Agnes Foley
Eternal.

**MacDonald, Alexander (Alasdair
MacMhaighstir Alasdair)**
Birlinn Chlann-Raghnaill.

Macdonald, Andrew
Lover's Leap; a Tale, The.

Macdonald, Cynthia
By the Sea.
Celebrating the Freak.
Instruction from Bly.
Lady Pitcher, The.
Late Mother, The.
Objets d'Art.
Two Brothers in a Field of Absence.

McDonald, Donald
Breakfast in Bed (Influenza in War-time).
Citizen of—the World, A.
Song of Those Who Died, A.

MacDonald, Elizabeth Roberts
Summons, The.

Macdonald, George
Baby, The, sel.

Baby-Sermon, A.
Be With Me, Lord, sel.
Better Things.
Carpenter, The.
Christmas Prayer, A.
Come Down.
Earl o' Quarterdeck, The.
Here lie I, Martin Elginbrodde, at.
Hurt of Love, The.
Lost and Found.
Mammon Marriage.
No End of No-Story.
O God, whose daylight leadeth down, sel.
Obedience.
Prayer, A: "When I look back upon my life
nigh spent."
Professor Noctutus.
Shall the Dead Praise Thee?
Sheep and the Goat, The.
Shortest and Sweetest of Songs, The.
Sir Lark and King Sun; a Parable, sel.
Sweet Peril.
That Holy Thing, sel.
That Thou Art Nowhere to Be Found, sel.
This Day Be with Me, sel.
To My God.
Turn from Self.
Where Did You Come From?
Wind and the Moon, The.
Winter Song.

MacDonald, Goodridge
Elegy, Montreal Morgue.
Sailor, The.

MacDonald, James Edward Hervey
Gallows and Cross.
Hanging, The.
Kitchen Window.

MacDonald, John. See **Lom, Iain**

Macdonald, Mary
Alligator, The.

McDonald, Nan
Hatters, The.
White Eagle, The.

Macdonald, Prudence
After Alamein.
Spring 1940.

McDonald, Roger
Bachelor Farmer.
Components.
Flights.
Hollow Thesaurus, The.
Two Summers in Moravia.

McDonald, S. P.
Casey—Twenty Years Later.

MacDonald, Susan
Children, The.

McDonald, Walter
First Solo.
Hauling over Wolf Creek Pass in Winter.
Never in My Life.
Starting a Pasture.

MacDonald, Wilson Pugsley
Exit.
In a Wood Clearing.
In the Far Years.
John Graydon.
June.
Moonlight on Lake Sydenham.
Song of the Ski, The.
Toll-Gate Man, The.

MacDonnell, James Francis Carlin. See
Carlin, Francis

MacDonogh, Patrick
Alone and Godless, stopped by the sudden
edge, sel.
Be Still as You Are Beautiful.
Dodona's Oaks Were Still.
Flowering Currant.
No Mean City.
Now the Holy Lamp of Love.
River, The.

She Walked Unaware.
Snare, The.
Song: "She spoke to me gently with words of sweet meaning."
This Morning I Wakened among Loud Cries of Seagulls.
Waking.
Widow of Drynam, The.
McDougal, Violet
Sea Wolf, The.
McDougall, Joseph Easton
New House, The.
Mace, Frances Laughton
Alcyone.
Only Waiting.
Succession, The.
McElroy, Colleen J.
Caledonia.
Defining It for Vanessa.
It Ain't Blues That Blows an Ill Wind.
Looking for a Country under Its Original Name.
Ruth.
Tapestries.
Why We Sometimes Paint by Numbers.
Woman's Song, A.
McElroy, David
Before Breakup on the Chena outside Fairbanks.
Dragging in Winter.
Making It Simple December 8, 1969.
Nocturn at the Institute.
Ode to a Dead Dodge.
Report from the Correspondent They Fired.
Spawning in Northern Minnesota.
MacEwen, Gwendolyn
Arcanum One.
Breakfast for Barbarians, A.
Caravan, The.
Dark Pines under Water.
Discovery, The.
Manzini; Escape Artist.
Sea Things.
There Is No Place to Hide, sel.
Thing is Violent, The.
Virgin Warrior, The.
Void, The, sel.
You Cannot Do This.
MacEwen, Pearl Forbes
Kite, The.
My Little Dog.
McFadden, David
Art's Variety.
Day of the Pancreas, The.
External Element, The.
Fiddlehead, The.
Form of Passion, A.
House Plants.
It's a Different Story When You're Going into the Wind.
Kicking from Centre Field.
Lennox Island.
Pop.
Upon Looking at a Book of Astrology.
We Love You the Way You Are.
McFadden, Roy
Address to an Absolute.
Aged Writer, An.
Elegy: "Out on the roads of sky the moon stands poised."
Epithalamium: "So you are married, girl. It makes me sad."
March.
Mihailovich.
Virgin Country.
White Bird, The.
William Blake Sees God.
McFarlane, Basil
Arawak Prologue.
McFarlane, J.E. Clare
On National Vanity.

McFatter, Janet Reed
Cow.
Drive, The.
Go Home.
Indian Camp.
Moving.
Sinkholes.
MacFayden, H. R.
Lone Wild Fowl, The.
McFee, Michael
Passing the Corporate Forest.
McFerren, Martha
Mountain Soprano.
Macfie, Ronald Campbell
In Memoriam: John Davidson.
Macfield, David
Black Is Black.
MacGabhrain, Aodh. See MacGowran, Hugh
McGaffey, Ernest
As the Day Breaks.
Geronimo.
I Fear No Power a Woman Wields.
Little Big Horn.
Mark.
Rise, A.
McGaffin, Audrey
Avalon.
McGahey, Jeanne
Oregon Winter.
McGarvey, Margaret
D-Dawn.
McGaugh, Lawrence
To Children.
Two Mornings.
Young Training.
McGavin, Joan
Torn-Word.
McGavin, Stewart
Kythans.
MacGearilt, Pieras. See Fitzgerald, Pierce
McGee, Clyde
Gratitude.
McGee, Shelagh
Wanted—a Witch's Cat.
McGee, Thomas D'Arcy
Jacques Cartier.
MacGill-Eain, Somhairle. See MacLean, Sorley
Macgillivray, Pittendrigh
Return, The.
McGinley, Phyllis
About Children.
Adversary, The.
Ballad of Culinary Frustration.
Ballade of Lost Objects.
Ballroom Dancing Class.
B's the Bus, sel.
Conversation in Avila.
Daniel at Breakfast.
Day after Sunday, The.
Daylight Saving Time.
Demagogue, The.
Evening Musicale.
F is the fighting Firetruck, sel.
5:32, The, sel.
Garland of Precepts, A.
Giveaway, The.
Good Humor Man, The.
How to Start a War.
Independent, The.
Journey toward Evening.
J's the jumping Jay-walker, sel.
Lament for Lost Lodgings.
Last Year's Discussion: The Nobel Russian.
Muted Screen of Graham Greene, The.
My Six Toothbrushes.
New Order, The.
Notes for a Southern Road Map.
Occupation: Housewife, sel.
Ode to the End of Summer.
Office Party.

Oh Come, Little Children.
Old Beauty, The.
On the Farther Wall, Marc Chagall, sel.
Public Journal.
Publisher's Party.
Reflections at Dawn.
Reflections Outside of a Gymnasium.
Robin Hood, sel.
Spanish Lions, The.
Squeeze Play, sel.
Temptations of Saint Anthony, The.
Theology of Jonathan Edwards, The.
Thunderer, The.
Trinity Place.
Triolet against Sisters.
We're Racing, Racing down the Walk.
Why, Some of My Best Friends Are Women.
Mac Giolla Ghunna, Cathal Buidhe
Yellow Bittern, The.
McGonagall, William
Alas! England now mourns for her poet that's gone, sel.
Albion Battleship Calamity, The.
Hen It Is a Noble Beast, The.
Jottings of New York.
McGouch, Roger
Tide and Time.
McGough, Robert
Fight of the Year, The.
McGough, Roger
Flood.
Goodbat Nightman.
Gruesome.
If Life's a Lousy Picture, Why Not Leave before the End.
Mother the Wardrobe Is Full of Infantrymen.
My Cat and I.
Newly Pressed Suit, The.
P.C. Plod versus the Dale St. Dog Strangler.
Survivor.
McGowan, John
Mister Alley Cat.
MacGowran, Hugh (Aodh MacGabhrain)
Description of are Irish Feast, The.
O'Rourke's Feast.
Macgoye, Marjorie Oludhe
For Miriam.
McGrath, Thomas
Against the False Magicians.
And I hear the pad of feet to the union hall, sel.
Begun before Easter. / Sign of the Fish, sel.
Coal Fire in Winter, A.
Death for the Dark Stranger.
End of the World, The.
Evening—another evening—and the lights flare, sel.
Jig Tune: Not for Love.
Letter for Marian, A.
Long Way outside Yellowstone, A.
Ode for the American Dead in Korea.
Remembering That Island.
Repeated Journey, The.
Song: "Lovers in ladies' magazines."
We go out in the stony midnight, sel.
Windless city built on decaying granite, loose ends, sel.
MacGreevy, Thomas
Aodh Ruadh O'Domhnaill.
De Civitate Hominum.
Homage to Hieronymus Bosch.
Homage to Jack Yeats.
Homage to Marcel Proust.
Nocturne of the Self-evident Presence.
Recessional.
McGreevy, Thomas. See MacGreevy, Thomas
MacGregor, Malcolm
Rannoch Moor.
McGuckian, Medbh
Aphrodisiac, The.

Aviary.
Champagne.
Coleridge.
Cure, The.
Death of a Ceiling.
Dream-Language of Fergus, The.
Felicia's Café.
Flitting, The.
Flower Master, The.
Folk Museum, The.
Gateposts.
Girls in the Plural.
Hard Summer, The.
June.
Mast Year, The.
Moon Pond, The.
Mr. McGregor's Garden.
On Not Being Your Lover.
Power-Cut.
Seed-Picture, The.
Slips.
Smoke.
Sofa, The.
Standing, The.
Stone-Hitter, The.
To My Grandmother.
Tobacco Hole.
Tulips.
Venus and the Rain.

Machado, Antonio
Figures in the fields against the sky!, *sel.*
Frail sound of a tunic trailing, A, *sel.*
Lament of the Virtues and Verses on Account
of the Death of Don Guido.
Let the rich man fill his belly, *sel.*
Love and the Mountains.
My father was a sailor, *sel.*
Naked is the earth, *sel.*
Poems.
Rebirth.
Spanish Folk Songs.
Train, The.
We think to create festivals, *sel.*

Machado de Assis, Joaquim Maria
Blue Fly.

Machar, Agnes Maule
Untrodden Ways.

Machel, Josina
This Is the Time.

Machel, Samora M.
Josina, You Are Not Dead.

Machiavelli, Niccolò
Opportunity.
Song: "He who offends a woman."

Ma Chih-yüan
Among men of plain clothes, *sel.*
At night, in west wind, *sel.*
Autumn Thoughts, *sel.*
Catkins flying: floating white snow, *sel.*
Dew on roses, *sel.*
Enjoying Retirement ("Beside green water"),
sel.
Enjoying Retirement ("The wine just
purchased"), *sel.*
Evening Bell from Misty Temple, *sel.*
Feelings in Nature ("Bamboo fishing coat,
purple official gown"), *sel.*
Feelings in Nature ("In the western village the
day grows long"), *sel.*
Feelings in Nature ("Woodcutter wakes as
mountain moon hangs low, The"), *sel.*
Lamenting Life, *sel.*
Returning Sails at a Distant Shore, *sel.*
Staying in a Mountain Pavilion on a Summer
Night, *sel.*
To the Tune "Shui hsien-tzu."

"Machreth." *See* **Rees, John Machreth**

McHugh, Heather
Animal Song.
Breath.
Brightness.

Capital.
Corps d'Esprit.
Double Agent.
Down, Down, and Down.
Fence, The.
Form.
Ghost, The.
Gig at Big Al's.
Having Read Books.
I Knew I'd Sing.
Impressionist.
Language Lesson, 1976.
Lines: "Some are waiting, some can't wait."
Meantime.
Memento Vitae.
Message at Sunset for Bishop Berkeley.
Night Catch.
Note Delivered by a Female Impersonator.
Oven Loves the TV Set, The.
Physics, A.
Squeal.
Touble With In, The.
What We Call Living.

McHugh, Vincent
Crawl Blues.
Deposition by John Wilmot, A.
I am very fond of the little ribs of women,
sel.
Suite from Catullus.

McInerney, Sally
Domestic Quarrel.

MacInnes, Tom
Ballade of Faith.
Chinatown Chant.
Modernists, The.
Tiger of Desire, The.
To Walt Whitman.
Velvet Sonneteers, The.

McInnis, Edgar
Fire Burial.

MacInnis, Joseph
Barracuda.

MacIntosh, Claire Harris
Barn in Winter, The.
Spirit of the *Bluenose, The.*

McIntosh, Peter. *See* **Tosh, Peter**

McIntosh, Sandy
Lost, One Soul.

MacIntyre, Duncan Ban
Last Leave of the Hills.
On Ben Dorain, *sel.*
Praise of Ben Dorain, The.

McIntyre, James
On the High Cost of Dairy Products.
Queen of Cheese.
Shelly.

MacIntyre, Tom
Drumlin Prayer.
On Sweet Killen Hill.

Mack, Alexander
I Am the Lord.

Mack, L. V.
Biafra.
Death Songs.

MacKay, Charles
Little and Great.
Louise on the Door-Step.
Mowers: An Anticipation of the Cholera,
1848, The.
Poor Man's Sunday Walk, The.
Ship, The.
Three Preachers, The.
Tubal Cain.

McKay, Claude
Absence.
Africa.
After the Winter.
America.
Baptism.
Barrier, The.
Commemoration.

Desolate.
Enslaved.
Exhortation: Summer, 1919.
Fetchin Water.
Flame-Heart.
Harlem Dancer, The.
Harlem Shadows.
I Know My Soul.
If We Must Die.
In Bondage.
Lynching, The.
My House.
Negro's Tragedy, The.
North and South.
Outcast.
Pagan Isms, The.
St. Isaac's Church, Petrograd.
Song of the Moon, A.
Spring in New Hampshire.
Subway Wind.
Tiger.
Tired Worker, The.
To O. E. A.
To the White Fiends.
Tropics in New York, The.
Truth.
Two-an'-Six.
White City, The.
White House, The.
Wild Goat, The.

McKay, Don
Barbed Wire Fence Meditates upon the
Goldfinch, A.
I Scream You Scream.
March Snow.

MacKay, Isabel Ecclestone
Fires of Driftwood.
Helen—Old.

McKay, James Thompson
Cenotaph of Lincoln.

McKay, Kath
Differences.
Kite-Flying.

**MacKay, Louis Alexander ("John
Smalacombe")**
Admonition for Spring.
Battle Hymn of the Spanish Rebellion.
I Wish My Tongue Were a Quiver, *sel.*
Nunc Scio, Quid Sit Amor.

MacKay Brown, George
Poet, The.

MacKaye, Percy
After Tempest.
God of us who kill our kind!, *sel.*
Prayer of the Peoples, A.

McKee, Gladys
Spring Cellar.

MacKellar, Dorothea
Dusk in the Domain.
Fancy Dress.
My Country.

McKellar, John Alexander Ross
Love in a Cottage, *sel.*

Mackellar, Thomas
At the door of Mercy Sighing.

McKelway, St. Clair
Boogie-woogie Ballads.

McKenty, Bob
Andujar in the Pique of His Career.
General Custer.
Mona Leo.

Mackenzie, Kenneth
Autumn Mushrooms.
Caesura.
Earth Buried.
Fairy Tale, A.
God! How I Long for You.
Heat.
Hospital—Retrospections, The.
Legerdemain.
Old Inmate, An.

Pat Young.
Table-Birds.
Two Trinities.
Mackey, Mary
Cleopatra.
Desire.
First Position, *sel.*
Grande Jetée.
Second Position, *sel.*
What Do You Say When a Man Tells You,
  You Have the Softest Skin.
Mackey, Nate
New and Old Gospel.
Mackey, Nathaniel
Degree Four.
MacKie, Alastair
Passin Ben Dorain, *sel.*
Mackie, Albert D.
Molecatcher.
New Spring, A.
Young Man and the Young Nun, The.
Mackie, Edmund St. Gascoigne
Up leaps the lark. Delightful Spring once
  more, *sel.*
McKiernan, Ethna
Catch.
McKim, Elizabeth
Creaming.
I Have Always Been.
To Stay Alive.
McKinney, Laurence
Oboe.
McKinnon, Barry
Bushed.
North, The.
MacKinstry, Elizabeth
Man Who Hid His Own Front Door, The.
Mackintosh, Newton
Fin de Siècle.
Limerick: "Cleopatra, who thought they
  maligned her."
Lucy Lake.
McKuen, Rod
Thoughts on Capital Punishment.
McLachlan, Alexander
And art thou come to this at last, *sel.*
Arrival, The, *sel.*
Hail, Thou great mysterious Being!, *sel.*
Song: "Old England is eaten by Knaves," *sel.*
We Live in a Rickety House.
When my gloomy hour comes to me, *sel.*
Where yonder ancient willow weeps, *sel.*
Maclagan, Sir Douglas
Battle of Glentilt (1847), The.
McLaren, Floris Clark
Frozen Fire.
No More the Slow Stream.
Visit by Water.
McLaughlin, Joe-Anne
Great-Aunt Francesca.
McLaughlin, Kathy
Suicide Pond.
Maclaurin, John, Lord Dreghorn
Elegy: "Nor Hammond's love nor Shenstone's
  was sincere."
MacLead, Joseph Gordon ("Adam Drinan")
Below the dancing larches freckled, *sel.*
Fire the heather, *sel.*
Our pastures are bitten and bare, *sel.*
Maclean, Alasdair
Death of a Hind.
Envoy: "On Meall nan Con, the Peak of the
  Dogs."
View from My Window.
MacLean, Sorley (Somhairle MacGill-Eain)
Kinloch Ainort.
McIntyre and Ross.
Sgurr Nan Gillean, *sel.*
MacLeish, Archibald
Aeterna Poetae Memoria.
America is West and the wind blowing, *sel.*

America was always promises, *sel.*
American Letter.
Ars Poetica.
Brave New World.
Burying Ground by the Ties, *sel.*
Calypso's Island.
Corporate Entity.
Critical Observations.
Curse God and Die, You Said to Me, *sel.*
Discovery of This Time.
"Dover Beach"—a Note to That Poem.
Dr. Sigmund Freud Discovers the Sea Shell.
Eleven.
Empire Builders.
End of the World, The.
Epistle to Be Left in the Earth.
Epistle to the Rapalloan.
Ezry.
Final Chorus, *sel.*
Grazing Locomotives.
He lies upon his bed, *sel.*
Hypocrite Auteur.
Immortal Autumn.
Invocation to the Social Muse.
L'An Trentiesme de Mon Eage.
Land of the Free.
Landscape as a Nude, *sel.*
Learned Men, The.
Liberty.
Lines for an Interment.
Memorial Rain.
Men.
Mother Goose's Garland.
My Naked Aunt.
National Security.
"Not Marble nor the Gilded Monuments."
Panic ("Slowly the thing comes"), *sel.*
Poet Speaks from the Visitors' Gallery, A.
Pole Star for This Year.
Prologue: "And the way goes on in the worn
  earth," *sel.*
Prologue: "These alternate nights and days,
  these seasons."
Psyche with the Candle.
Rape of the Swan, The.
Reconciliation, The.
Reproach to Dead Poets.
Seafarer.
Signature for Tempo.
Snowflake Which Is Now and Hence Forever,
  The.
Space-time, our scientists tell us, is
  impervious, *sel.*
Speech to a Crowd.
Speech to Those Who Say Comrade.
Survivor.
Thunderhead.
Too-late Born, The.
Tourist Death.
Unfinished History, An.
Voice of the Studio Announcer, *sel.*
Voyage West.
We wonder whether the dream of American
  liberty, *sel.*
Weather.
What Riddle Asked the Sphinx.
Words in Time.
Yacht for Sale.
You Also, Gaius Valerius Catullus.
You, Andrew Marvell.
Young Dead Soldiers, The.
McLeish, John A. B.
Not without Beauty.
MacLellan, Robert
Sang: "There's a reid lowe in yer cheek."
McLellan, Isaac, Jr.
New England's Dead!
McLeod, Doug
Kitty.
"Macleod, Fiona" (William Sharp)
Bell-Bird, The, *sel.*

Bells of Youth, The.
Deep peace, pure white of the moon to you,
  sel.
Dream Fantasy.
Eagle, The, *sel.*
Field Mouse, The.
Fireflies, *sel.*
Founts of Song, The.
Madonna Natura.
Mid-Noon in January, *sel.*
Moon-Child, The.
Mystic's Prayer, The.
Redeemer, The.
Rookery at Sunrise, The, *sel.*
Unknown Wind, The.
Wasp, The, *sel.*
White Peace, The.
Wood-Swallows, The, *sel.*
**McLeod, Irene Rutherford (Mrs. Aubrey de
  Sélincourt)**
Beyond the murk that swallows me, *sel.*
Lone Dog.
Prayer, A.
MacLeod, Mairi
Complaint about Exile, A.
Macleod, Norman
Creed, A.
Trust in God, *sel.*
MacLow, Jackson
Giant Otters.
Measures.
Recommend.
2nd Light Poem: For Diane Wakoski.
Trope Market.
25th Dance—Saying Things about Making
  Gardens—22 March 1964.
Various Meanings.
Wall Rev.
Zen Buddhism and Psychoanalysis/
  Psychoanalysis and Zen Buddhism.
McMahon, M. J.
Nonpareil's Grave, The.
MacManus, Anna Johnston. See "Carbery,
  Ethna"
McManus, Cornelius
John Barleycorn's Diary: An Uncoloured
  Picture.
MacManus, Seumas
In Dark Hour.
MacMarcuis, Aindrias
This Night Sees Ireland [*or* Eire] Desolate.
McMaster, Guy Humphreys
Carmen Bellicosum.
McMaster, Rhyll
Profiles of My Father.
Round Song, A.
Tanks.
McMichael, James
Apple Fell in the Night and a Wagon
  Stopped, An.
Cabin North of It All, The.
From the McMichael's.
Great Garret, or 100 Wheels, The.
Inland Lighthouse, The.
Lutra, the Fisher.
Terce.
Village of the Presents, The.
Macmillan, James
Hill Love.
Nightmare on Rhum.
To This Hill Again.
What Are You Thinking About?
McMillan, Peter
Anchors Weighed.
MacMuireadach, Niall Mor
Soraidh Slan Don Oidhche Areir.
Macnab, Roy
El Alamein Revisited.
Majuba Hill.
River, The.

Road to Bologna, The.
Seven of the Clock.
MacNamee, Giolla Brighde
Childless.
MacNeice, Louis
Alcohol.
Among These Turf-Stacks.
And I remember Spain, *sel.*
And love hung still as crystal over the bed, *sel.*
And the Lord Was Not in the Whirlwind, *sel.*
Apple Blossom.
August.
Autobiography.
Bad Dream.
Bagpipe Music.
Ballade of England.
Bar-Room Matins.
Birmingham.
Blasphemies, The.
Brandy Glass, The.
British Museum Reading Room, The.
Brother Fire.
Carrickfergus.
Cats, *sel.*
Charon.
Christina.
Christmas Shopping.
Circe.
Coda.
Conferences, adjournments, ultimatums, *sel.*
Conversation.
Corncrakes, *sel.*
Cradle Song: "Clock's untiring fingers wind the wool of darkness, The."
Creditor, The.
Cushendun, *sel.*
Dandelions, *sel.*
Day of Renewal.
Death of a Prominent Business Man.
Didymus.
Dublin.
Ear, The.
Eclogue between the Motherless.
Eclogue for Christmas, An.
Elegy for Minor Poets.
Entered in the Minutes.
Entirely.
Epitaph for Liberal Poets.
Fanfare for the Makers, A.
Figure of Eight.
Flight of the Heart.
Gardener, The, *sel.*
Grey Ones, The.
Hold-up.
Homage to Wren.
House on a Cliff.
Il Piccolo Rifiuto.
In Lieu.
Individualist Speaks, The.
Introduction, The: "They were introduced in a grave glade."
Invocation: "Dolphin plunge, fountain play."
Jehu.
June Thunder.
Leaving Barra.
Left-Behind, The, *sel.*
Les Sylphides.
Letter to Graham and Anna.
Libertine, The.
London Rain.
Mahabalipuram.
Meeting Point.
Mixer, The.
Morning Sun.
Museums.
National Gallery, The.
Nature Morte.
Night Club.
Nightmare leaves fatigue, *sel.*
Nuts in May.
Old Story, The.

Once-in-Passing, The, *sel.*
Passage Steamer.
Perdita.
Perseus.
Poussin.
Prayer before Birth.
Prayer in Mid-Passage.
Precursors.
Prognosis.
Ravenna.
Reflections.
Refugees.
River in Spate.
Sea, The, *sel.*
Sense of Smell, The.
Shelley and jazz and lieder and love and hymn-tunes, *sel.*
Sligo and Mayo.
Slow Movement.
Snow.
Soap Suds.
Solitary Travel.
Spring Voices.
Springboard, The.
Star-Gazer.
Streets of Laredo, The.
Suicide, The.
Sunday Morning.
Sunlight on the Garden, The.
Take this old man with the soldierly straight back, *sel.*
Tam Cari Capitis.
Taxis, The.
Thalassa.
This Is the Life.
To work. To my own office, my own job, *sel.*
Train to Dublin.
Tree Party.
Truisms, The.
Under the Mountain.
Under the surface of flux and of fear there is an underground movement, *sel.*
Valediction: "Their verdure dare not show."
Variation on Heraclitus.
Week to Christmas, A, *sel.*
When clerks and navvies fondle, *sel.*
Whit Monday.
Wolves.
Woods.
McNeill, Anthony
Dermis.
Don.
Residue.
Saint Ras.
Victors, The.
Wreath for the Suicide Heart, A.
MacNeill, Hector
My Boy Tammy.
Macoubrie, John
Boethius at Cavalzero.
McOwan, Rennie
Highland Loves.
Hillman Looks Back, The.
Hooded Crow, The.
Mountaineering Bus.
Things of the North, The.
McPherson, Heather
Close-up.
Have You Heard of Artemisia?
Theology and a Patchwork Absolute.
Macpherson, James ("Ossian")
Carthon; a Poem.
I sit by the mossy fountain; on the top of the hill of winds, *sel.*
Macpherson, Jay
Ark Anatomical, *sel.*
Ark Apprehensive, *sel.*
Ark Artefact, *sel.*
Ark Articulate, *sel.*
Ark Astonished, *sel.*
Ark Overwhelmed, *sel.*

Ark Parting, *sel.*
Ark to Noah, *sel.*
Beauty of Job's Daughters, The.
Boatman, The.
Eurynome.
Eve in Reflection.
Fisherman, The.
Go Take the World.
Hail Wedded Love!
Ill Wind, The.
Innocents, The.
Leviathan.
Lost Soul, A.
Marriage of Earth and Heaven, The.
Martyrs, The.
Sun and Moon.
They Return, *sel.*
Third Eye, The.
McPherson, Sandra
Alleys.
Butchery.
Centerfold Reflected in a Jet Window.
Children.
Coconut for Katerina, A.
Collapsars.
Compound Eye, The.
Conception.
Elegies for the Hot Season.
Firefly, The.
For Elizabeth Bishop.
Games.
Gnawing the Breast.
Helen Todd: My Birthname.
His Body.
If the Cardinals Were like Us.
7,22,66.
Lament, with Flesh and Blood.
Letter with a Black Border.
Lifesaving.
Marlow and Nancy.
Michael.
Morning Glory Pool.
Museum of the Second Creation, The.
1943.
On Being Told "You Have Stars in Your Eyes."
Open Casket.
Page.
Peter Rabbit.
Pisces Child.
Poem Begun in the Haro Strait When I Was 28 and Finished When I Was 38.
Poppies.
Pornography, Nebraska.
Pregnancy.
Red Seeds Opening in the Shade.
Resigning from a Job in a Defense Industry.
Seaweeds.
Sentience.
Sisters.
To an Alcoholic.
Triolet: "She was in love with the same danger."
Unitarian Easter.
Urban Ode.
Wanting a Mummy.
Wings and Seeds.
McQueen, Cilla
Living Here.
Matinal.
Studio Poem.
To Ben, at the Lake.
MacRae, Lindsay
Dear John.
Immaculate Conception, The.
Love Gone Cold.
Love Poem.
True Life Romance.
McRae, Wallace
Lease Hound, The.
Reincarnation.

Macrow, Brenda G.
At the Shelter-Stone.
Climb in Torridon.
In Praise of Ben Avon.
When I Die, *sel.*
Mac Siomoin, Tomas
Silence, The.
McTair, Roger
Guerrillas.
Politics Kaiso.
McTell, Ralph
First and Last Man.
McTurk, Michael
Deh 'Pon Um Again.
Query.
Macuilxochitl
Battle Song.
MacWard, Owen Roe
Dark Rosaleen, *at.*
McWhirter, George
Madame.
Surreal Appetite.
Tarragona Wine.
Macy, Arthur
Peppery Man, The.
Rollicking Mastodon, The.
Madden, F. A. V.
I put my hat upon my head.
Maddow, Ben
City, The.
Maddox, Everette
1941.
Breakfast.
Great Man's Death: An Anecdote, The.
"Madelaine, Marie" (Baroness von Puttkamer)
Crucifixion.
End Is Now, The.
Foiled Sleep.
Moriturus.
Unfading, The.
Vagabonds.
Madeleva, Sister Mary
Ballade on Eschatology.
Candlemas Day.
Dumb Oxen, *sel.*
From an Afternoon Caller.
I Ask My Teachers, *sel.*
O/ Holy/ Wood.
Madge, Charles
At War.
Birds of Tin, The.
Blocking the Pass.
Fortune.
Loss.
Lusty Juventus.
Monument, A.
On One Condition.
Poem: "Character of a landscape stands always in a mysterious relation, The."
Poem: "Walls of the maelstrom are painted with trees, The."
Solar Creation.
Times, The.
Madgett, Naomi Long (Naomi Long Witherspoon)
Alabama Centennial.
Black Woman.
Deacon Morgan.
Dream Sequence, Part 9.
Exits and Entrances.
Her Story.
Midway.
Mortality.
New Day.
Nomen.
Offspring.
Pavlov.
Quest.
Race Question, The.
Refugee.

Simple.
Star Journey.
Woman with Flower.
Madhubuti, Haki R.   *See* **Lee, Don L.**
Madison, Dolly
La Fayette.
Maeterlinck, Maurice
Last Words, The.
Song: "Three little maidens they have slain."
Magaret, Helene
Lord, I have not time to pray, *sel.*
Magarrell, Elaine
Joy of Cooking, The.
Magee, John Gillespie, Jr.
High Flight.
Magee, Michael
It Is the Stars That Govern Us.
Magee, Thomas D'Arcy
Celtic Cross, The.
Celts, The.
Magee, William Kirkpatrick.   *See* **"Eglinton, John"**
Mager, Don
Beloved,/ What does it take to put a house in order?, *sel.*
Magid, Margo
Night Watch.
Magil, A. B.
They Are Ours.
Maginn, William
Rime of the Auncient Waggonere, The.
Magogo, Princess
Teasing Song.
Magowan, Robin
Days of 1956.
Paros.
Susan.
Zeimbekiko.
Mahadevi (Mahadeviyakka)
Like/ treasure hidden in the ground.
Like a silkworm weaving.
Like an elephant.
O brothers, why do you talk.
Other men are thorn.
People,/ male and female.
Riding the blue sapphire mountains.
Till you've earned.
Would a circling surface vulture.
Mahaka, Solomon
Building Bridges.
If I Leave Here Alive.
In the Zoo.
Mahapatra, Jayanta
Rain of Rites, A.
Snow in Iowa City.
Mahdi, Sami
Beirut.
Inheritance, The.
Mistake, The.
Morning.
On Details.
World of Fancy.
Mahfouz, Isam
Weariness in the Evening of January Thirty-Second.
Mahlmann, Siegfried August
Allah ("Allah gives light in darkness").
Mahon, Derek
Afterlives.
An Unborn Child.
Another Sunday Morning.
Autobiographies.
Banished Gods, The.
Consolations of Philosophy.
Courtyards in Delft.
Dark Country, A.
Derry Morning.
Disused Shed in Co. Wexford, A.
Ecclesiastes.
Father-in-Law.
Garage in Co. Cork, A.

Girls in Their Seasons.
Glengormley.
Grandfather.
Homage to Malcolm Lowry.
I Am Raftery ("I am Raftery, hesitant and confused").
In Carrowdore Churchyard.
Last of the Fire Kings, The.
Lighthouse in Maine, A.
Lives.
Matthew V. 29-30.
Mute Phenomena, The.
My Wicked Uncle.
Nostalgias.
Poem Beginning with a Line by Cavafy.
Poets of the Nineties, The.
Snow Party, The.
Spring Vacation, The.
Studio, The.
Table Talk.
Woods, The.
World Is Everything That Is the Case, The.
Mahone, Barbara
Colors for Mama.
Poem for Positive Thinkers, A.
Sugarfields.
Mahony, Francis Sylvester ("Father Prout")
Attractions of a Fashionable Irish Watering-Place, The.
Bells of Shandon, The.
Piper's Progress, The.
Mahsati
Better to live as a rogue and a bum.
Gone are the games we played all night.
Good-looking, I'll never stoop for you.
I knew like a song your vows weren't strong.
Unless you can dance through a common bar.
"Mai, Trebor."   *See* **Williams, Robert**
Maiano, Dante da
Sonnet: He Craves Interpreting of a Dream of His.
Maiden, Jennifer
Climbing.
Dew.
Slides.
Mailer, Norman
Devils.
Eternities.
Maillard, Claude
Christmas Mass for a Little Atheist Jesus.
Mainwaring, Arthur
Excellent New Ballad, Called the Brawny Bishop's Complaint, An.
Excellent New Song Called "Mat's Peace, An."
New Ballad, A.
Queen's Speech, The.
Tarquin and Tullia.
Mainwaring, M. G.
Gothic columns of petrified motion.
Mair, Alexander
Hesiod, 1908.
Mair, Charles
How dreamy-dark it is!, *sel.*
I love you better than I love my race, *sel.*
Song: "Hear me, ye smokeless skies and grass-green earth," *sel.*
Tell me more of those unrivalled wastes, *sel.*
There was a time on this fair continent, *sel.*
We are not wholly blest who use the earth, *sel.*
We left/ The silent forest, *sel.*
Winter.
Maisel, Carolyn
Dream of Women, A.
Girl in the Willow Tree, The.
Letter from a Friend, A.
Maitland, Sir Richard
Aganis the Thievis of Liddisdale.
Solace in Age.

Major, Clarence
Blind Old Woman.
Celebrated Return.
Design, The.
Down Wind against the Highest Peaks.
Dressed to Kill.
Inside Diameter.
Swallow the Lake.
Vietnam.
Vietnam #4.
Major, Joseph
Poem for Thel—the Very Tops of Trees.
Majorino, Giancarlo
Anniversary.
Doubly Employed.
Industrial Landscape.
Myopia.
Rip.
Mak, Lev
Eden.
Flood, The.
Prayer: "From your high bridge wave &
wail."
Makai, Emil
Comet, The.
Mäkelä, Hannu
Garden.
Into Snowy Night.
What Is your Life?
You Looked the Monster in the Eye.
Makere
Lament for Taramoana.
Makhfi (Zibu'n-Nisa)
Beauty of the Friend it was that taught me,
The.
Makidemewabe, Samuel
Born Tying Knots.
Saw the Cloud Lynx.
Tree Old Woman.
Maksimovic, Desanka
For All Mary Magdalenes.
Malam, Charles
Steam Shovel.
Malancioiu, Ileana
Bear's Blood.
Malanga, Gerard
Temperature.
Malangatana, Valente Goenha
To the Anxious Mother.
Woman.
Malcohn, Elissa Hamilton
Wings.
Ybba.
Maleska, Eugene T.
Assembly: Harlem School.
Countee Cullen.
To a Negro Boy Graduating.
Malfaiera, Anna
I Can No Longer Laugh with Real Joy.
Malik de Coteau, Delano Abdul
Motto Vision 1971.
Oui Papa.
Malikongwa, Albert G. T. K.
Protest from a Bushman (Masarwa), A.
Malinowitz, Michael
Funeral March for a Papagallo.
Glose.
Malins, Joseph
Fence or an Ambulance, A.
Mallalieu, Herbert B.
Cozzo Grillo.
Empedocles on Etna.
Epilogue: "Phoenix on the hot sirocco's
breath."
Look for Me on England.
New Year's Eve.
Next of Kin.
Platform Goodbye.
To Naples.
Mallarmé, Stéphane
Album Leaf.

Anguish.
Glazier, The.
L'Après-Midi d'un Faune.
Proud of my music, let me often make, *sel*.
Sea-Wind.
Sigh.
Mallet, David
William and Margaret.
Mallet, David *and* **James Thomson.** *See*
Thomson, James *and* **David Mallet**
"Malley, Ern" (James McAuley *and* **Harold**
Stewart)
Dürer; Innsbruck, 1495.
Malley, Jean
Words do not grow on the landscape.
Malloch, Douglas
Ain't It [*or* It's] Fine Today.
Be the Best of Whatever You Are.
Family Trees.
When the Drive Goes Down.
Mallock, William Hurrell
Brussels and Oxford.
Christmas Thoughts, by a Modern Thinker.
Marriage Prospect, A.
Softly the Evening.
Malone, Walter
October in Tennessee.
Opportunity.
"Malone, Carroll." *See* **McBurney, William**
B.
Malouf, David
Asphodel.
At My Grandmother's.
die Musik, An.
Early Discoveries.
Snow.
This Day, under My Hand.
Wolf-Boy.
Mamaro, Hasetsukabe. *See* **Hasetsukabe**
Mamaro
Man, Gill
Mist.
Manchán, Saint
Manchán's Prayer.
Mandel, Eli W.
Envoi: "My country is not a country."
Fire Place, The.
Four Songs from the Book of Samuel.
From the North Saskatchewan.
Houdini.
It has been hours in these rooms, *sel*.
Madwomen of the Plaza de Mayo, The.
My father was always out in the garage, *sel*.
On the Death of Ho Chi Minh.
On the 25th Anniversary of the Liberation of
Auschwitz.
Orpheus, *sel*.
Song: "When the echo of the last footstep
dies."
Mandel, Tom
All These Examples.
Hungry and Waiting.
Sally.
Mandela, Zindzi
Drink from My Empty Cup.
Echo of Mandela.
I Saw as a Child.
Lock the Place in Your Heart.
My Country.
There's an Unknown River in Soweto.
Mandelstam, Osip Emilyevich
Age, The.
Ariosto.
Arteries Juicy with Blood, *sel*.
Batyushkov.
Bitter Bread.
Concert at the Station.
Feodosia.
I Was Washing Outside in the Darkness.
Leningrad.
Like a Young Levite.

Mounds of Human Heads Are Wandering into
the Distance.
Not yet dead, not yet alone.
Notre Dame.
On a board of raspberry and pure gold.
Phaedra.
Reed, A.
Stalin Epigram, The.
Stanzas: "I don't want to pay down the last
penny of my soul."
Take from my palms, to soothe your heart.
This Night.
Twilight of Freedom.
What street is this?
Mander, John
As It Was.
Mandeville, Bernard
On Honour.
Mangan, James Clarence
Gone in the Wind.
Hymn for Pentecost.
Nameless One, The.
Rest Only in the Grave.
St. Patrick's Hymn before Tara.
Siberia.
Song from the Coptic, A.
Time of the Barmecides, The.
To Amine.
To My Native Land.
To Sultan Murad II.
Twenty Golden Years Ago.
Vision of Connaught in the Thirteenth
Century, A.
Manger, Itzig
Abishag Writes a Letter Home.
Abraham and Sarah.
Adam and Eve.
Alone.
Autumn.
Ballad of the White Glow, The.
Crucified and the Verminous Man, The.
Dark Hand, A.
Dying Thief.
Eve and the Apple Tree.
Evening.
Fairy Tales.
For Years I Wallowed.
Hagar Leaves Abraham's House.
I Am the Autumn.
In the Train.
Jacob Studies "The Selling of Joseph" with
His Sons.
Jealous Adam.
"Lovers of Israel" at the Belzhets Death
Camp, The.
Mother Sarah's Lullaby ("Mother Sarah rocks
the cradle").
November.
On the Road There Stands a Tree.
Patriarch Jacob Meets Rachel, The.
Rachel Goes to the Well for Water ("Rachel
stands by the mirror and plaits").
Saint Besht.
Strange Guest, The.
There Is a Tree That Stands.
Under the Ruins of Poland.
Manger, Itsik. *See* **Manger, Itzig**
Mangini, Sandra
Ring Road.
Mangoaela, Z. D.
Boast of Masopha.
Manhire, Bill
Children.

Manifold (continued)
Cinema, The.
Contemplation of the Heavens.
Death in the Family, A.
Distance between Bodies, The.
Elaboration, The.
How to Take Off Your Clothes at the Picnic.
In the Tent, Elche.
It Is Nearly Summer.
Kiss, The.
Last Sonnet.
Late Victorian Girl, The.
Old Man's Example, The.
On Originality.
Pavilion.
Pickpocket, The.
Prayer, The: "What do you take."
Proposition, The.
Red Horse.
Scottish Bride', A.
Selenologist, The.
She Says.
Song about the Moon, A.
Song, The: "My body as an act of derision."
Trees, The.
What It Means to Be Naked.
Wingatui.
Zoetropes.

Manifold, John Streeter
Assignation with a Somnambulist.
Bunyip and the Whistling Kettle, The.
Camouflage.
Defensive Position.
Deserter, The.
Fencing School.
Fife Tune.
Garcia Lorca Murdered in Granada.
Griesly Wife, The.
"Heureux Qui comme Ulysse."
L'Embarquement pour Cythère.
Listening to a Broadcast.
Makhno's Philosophers.
Making Contact.
Night Piece.
Ration Party.
Sirens, The.
Tomb of Lt. John Learmonth, A.I.F., The.

Manner, Eeva-Liisa
And So the Oracles, sel.
Apathy, sel.
Assimilation.
Bach.
From My Life I Make a Poem.
Here.
If they wanted freedom, sel.
Into the Silence of the Forest.
Last Year in Capricorn.
Lunar Games, The.
Skin like burnt glass or/ prepared leather,
   The.
Speculation.
To move over shifting borders, sel.
Turn the page of stone and there, sel.
Walk, A.

Mannin, Ethel
Song of the Bomber.

Manning, James Harold
I have been/ Three separate times, in war, sel.

Manning, Robert. See **Mannyng, Robert**

Manning-Sanders, Ruth
Come Wary One.
Old City, The.

**Mannyng [or Manning], Robert (Robert De
   Brunne)**
Bishop's Harp, The.
Dancers of Colbek, The, sel.
Praise of Women.
Round Table, The.

Mansei (Sami Mansei)

Mansel, William Lort
Sun's Perpendicular Rays, The.

Mansfield, Katherine
Friendship.
Little Brother's Secret.
Man with the Wooden Leg, The.
Sanary.
To L. H. B.
To Stanislaw Wyspianski.

Mansfield, Margery Swett
Blessing Mrs. Larkin.

Mansfield, Richard
Eagle's Song, The.

Manson, John
At a Ruined Croft.

Mansour, Joyce
Drowned at the Bottom of a Boring Dream.
Embrace the Blade.
Last night I saw your corpse.
North Express.
Seated on her bed legs spread open.
Sun in Capricorn, The.
Yesterday evening I saw your corpse.

Mansour, Khairi
Day.
I see trees breaking off their branches, sel.

Manville, Marion
Lee's Parole.
Surrender of New Orleans, The.

Manyase, L. T.
Mother Crab and Her Family, The.
Vusumzi's Song.

Manzano, Juan Fransico
My Thirty Years.

Mao Hsi-chen
Deva-like Barbarian.
Flowers in the Rear Garden, The.
Immortal at the River.
Magnolia Flower, The.
Manifold Little Hills.
Pacifying the Western Barbarians.
Pure Serene Music.
Sand of Silk-Washing Stream.
Song of Ho Man-tzu.
Song of the Water Clock at Night.
Song of the Wine Spring.
Southern Song, A.
Taoist Nun, The.

Mao Tse-tung
Chinese Ballad.
Midstream.

Mao Wen-hsi
Barbarian Chieftain, The.
Beautiful Lady Yü, The.
Deep Love, A.
Delight in the High-Flying Orioles.
Drunk among the Flowers.
Echoing Heaven's Everlastingness.
Feeling Regret at the Silk Window.
Immortal at the River.
In Praise of Merit.
Joy at Renewal.
Mist on the Willows.
Roaming in Kan-chou.
Sand of the Silk-Washing Stream.
Song of Ho Man-tzu.
Song of the Water Clock at Night.
Song of the West Stream.
Song of the Wine Spring.
Speaking of Love.
Spring in the Moon Palace.
Stretch of Cloud over Mount Wu, A.
Tune: Drunk among the Flowers.
Welcoming the Worthy Guest.

Mapanje, Jack A.
Before Chilembwe Tree.
Marching Litany to Our Martyrs, A.
New Platform Dances, The.
On His Royal Blindness Paramount Chief
   Kwangala.
When This Carnival Finally Closes.

Mapes, Edith L.
Oh, If They Only Knew!

Mar, Laureen
At Wonder Donut.
Black Rocks.
Immigration Act of 1924, The.
My Mother, Who Came from China, Where
   She Never Saw Snow.
Window Frames the Moon, The.

Mar, Yekhi'el
Anglers, The.
One Tiny Bird.
That Street of Mine.

Maraini, Dacia
Canine Mother.
Poems by Women.

Marais, Eugène
Dance of the Rain, The.
Heart-of-the-Daybreak.
Sorceress, The.

Maran, René
Human Soul.

Marcabrun
Against winter which advances.
At the Fountain.
At the point of separating out.
God sends us from I don't know where.
I'll tell you/ in my own way.
In April around Easter the streams grow clear.
No doubt at all.
Now hear this!
Since my courage is clarified.
Starling didn't loaf around, The.
Starling, take wing and go.
Under a hedge the other day.
When the leaf spins.
Winter goes and weather betters.

Marcela de Carpio de San Felix, Sister
Amor Mysticus.

March, Caeia
Ms World.

March, Susana
To a Man.

Marchant, John
Little Miss and Her Parrot.
Young Master's Account of a Puppet Show.

Marckant, John
O Lord, Turn Not Away Thy Face, at.

Marcus, Adrianne
Physicist's Purpose, The.
Science/Fiction.
Thermodynamics.

Marcus, Mordecai
Two Refugees.

Marcus, Morton
Angel of Death Is Always with Me, The.
Dance, The.
Look Closely.
Swan Song.
Tongue.
Tuba.

Marcus, Neil
Zotz!

Marcus Argentarius. See **Argentarius,
   Marcus**

Mardale, W. R.
Pop Goes the Weasel! at.

Maresuke, Nogi
Song of victories: Battle of Point Arthur

Margarido, Manuela
You Who Occupy Our Land.

Margenat, Hugo
Living Poetry.
Well-aimed Stare, The.
Your Air of My Air.

Margetson, George Reginald
Fledgling Bard and the Poetry Society, The.

Margolin, Anna
Dear Monsters.
Entr'acte.
Epitaph: "Say that she couldn't forgive."
Girls in Crotona Park.
Once I Was Young.

Slender Ships.
Years.

Margolin, Anna (Razel Lebensboim)
Ancient Murderess Night.
Homecoming.
Mother Earth.
My Kin Talk.
Years.

Margolis, Gary
First Green Heron.

Margolis, Silvia
Never Ask Me Why.

Marguerite de Navarre
Autant En Emporte le Vent.

Mariá de Santa Isabel, Sister.　*See* **Belisarda, Marcia**

Maria de Ventadorn.　*See* **Marie de Ventadour**

Mariah, Paul
Christmas 1962.
Quarry/Rock.

Mariani, Paul
Coda: Revising History.
Girl Who Learned to Sing in Crow, The.
Golden Oldie.
Goodnight Irene.
Lesson, The.
Lines I Told Myself I Wouldn't Write.
Matadero, Riley and Company.
News That Stays News.
North/South.
Ring, The.
Sarcophagus.
Then Sings My Soul.
Walk in Early March, A.

Marias, Eugène
Desert Lark, The.

Marias, The Three (Maria Isabella Barreno *and* **Maria Teresa Horta** *and* **Maria Velho da Costa)**
Conversation between the Chevalier de Chamilly and Mariana Alcoforado in the Manner of a Song of Regret.
Saddle and Cell.

"Marie"
Fellow Workers.
Heroisms.
Labour.

Marie de France
Goat's-Leaf.
Hath any loved you well, down there, *sel.*
Honeysuckle (Chevrefoil).
Would I Might Go Far over Sea.

Marie de Ventadour
Dialogue.
Gui d'Ussel, because of you I'm quite distraught.

Marikawa Kyoroku.　*See* **Kyoroku**

Marinetti, Filippo Tommaso
Futurist Aviator Speaks to His Father, Vulcan, The.

Marini, Giambattista.　*See* **Marino, Giovanni Battista**

Marino, Giovanni Battista
Beautiful Slave, The.
Fading Beauty.
Lips and Eyes.
Madrigal: "Love now no fire hath left him."
Sospetto d'Herode, *sel.*
Yet on the other side, faine would he start, *sel.*

Marinoni, Rosa Zagnoni
Who Are My People?

Marippittiyar [*or* Marpittiyar]
Charmer Turned Ascetic, A.
Hunter Once, Now an Ascetic, A.

Mark, Diane Mei Lin
And the Old Folks Said.
Kula.　a Homecoming.
Liberation.

Rice and Rose Bowl Blues.
Susie Wong Doesn't Live Here.

Mark, Rickman
Snow in Town.

"Mark Twain."　*See* **"Twain, Mark"**

Markham, E. A.
An Old Thought for a New Couple.
Don't Talk to Me about Bread.
Grandfather's Sermon and Michael Smith.
Late Return.
Rewrite.

Markham, Edwin
Avengers, The.
Creed, A.
Father's Business, The.
Forgotten Man, The.
Great Guest Comes In, The.
Guard of the Sepulcher, A.
How the Great Guest Came.
Joy of the Morning.
Last Furrow, The.
Lincoln, the Man of the People.
Look into the Gulf, A.
Man with the Hoe, The.
My Comrade.
O Christ of Olivet, you hushed the wars, *sel.*
Outwitted.
Peace.
Poet, The.
Poetry.
Prayer, A: "Teach me, Father, how to go."
Preparedness.
Revelation.
Right Kind of People, The.
Shine on Me, Secret Splendor.
Song to a Tree.
Task That Is Given to You, The.
There Is a High Place.
Third Wonder, The.
Up from the log cabin to the capitol, *sel.*
Victory in Defeat.
Whirlwind Road, The.
Young Lincoln.

Markham, Gervase
Fragment, A: "I walked [*or* walk'd] along a stream for pureness rare."

Markish, Perets
After you, the killed of the Ukraine, *sel.*
Cattle carry on their horns.
Day's not enough for my idle meandering, The.
Galilee.
Hey, women, spotted with typhus and riddled with rakes of fingers.
I recall: beside some rivulet, lonely shepherds arrange their fires.
It's good, it's good not to shield the heart this way.
Marketplace sleeps, its booths like skulls, The.
My homeless one, will you ever fly again?, *sel.*
No! Heavenly tallow, don't lick my gummy beards, *sel.*
On the mute walls of empty shops.
Out of frayed sackcloth—breasts of filthy cataracts.
Rinsed fences dry themselves in the wind, The.
Shards.

Markish, Peretz
In the Last Flicker of the Sinking Sun.
We Reached Out Far.
Your Burnt-out Body.

Markman, Stephanie
They lived out in a women's house, *sel.*

Marks, Naomi
Come Live with Me.
High Wonders.

Marks, S. J.
How.

Marlatt, Daphne
Femina.
Imagine: A Town, *sel.*

Marlatt, Earl Bowman
Spirit of Life, in This New Dawn.
Through the Dark the Dreamers Came.

Marley, Bob
Trenchtown Rock.

Marlowe, Christopher
Ah, fair Zenocrate, divine Zenocrate, *sel.*
Ah, Faustus,/ Now hast thou but one bare hour [*or* hower] to live, *sel.*
Amorous Leander, beautiful and young, *sel.*
Amorous Neptune, *sel.*
And now the sun that through the horizon peeps, *sel.*
And Ride in Triumph through Persepolis, *sel.*
Beauty, *sel.*
Bloody Conquests of Mighty Tamburlaine, The, *sel.*
By this, Leander, being near the land, *sel.*
Her veil was artificial flowers and leaves, *sel.*
Hero and Leander.
Hero Feels the Shaft of Love, The.
I Have an Orchard, *sel.*
If All the Pens That Ever Poets Held, *sel.*
It Lies Not in Our Power to Love or Hate, *sel.*
Love at First Sight, *sel.*
Mine Argosy from Alexandria, *sel.*
Nature That Framed Us of Four Elements, *sel.*
Now Clear the Triple Region of the Air, *sel.*
On Hellespont, guilty of true love's blood, *sel.*
Overreacher, The, *sel.*
Passionate Shepherd to His Love, The.
So on she goes, and in her idle flight, *sel.*
Spell of Invisibility, A, *at.*
To Entertain Divine Zenocrate, *sel.*
Virgins, in vain you labour to prevent, *sel.*
Was this the face that launched a thousand ships?, *sel.*
Where are you damn'd?, *sel.*

Marmori, Giancarlo
He Was Always Nursing Some Human Wound of His.
I Know Nothing of the Sleep Which Tames You.
Still Your Footprint Delicate as an Animal's.
Your Totem Is the Opulent Serpent.

Maro, Tagima.　*See* **Tagima Maro**

Marot, Clément
Friar Lubin.
Love-Lesson, A.
Madame d'Albert's Laugh.
Posy Ring, The.

Marpittiyar.　*See* **Maripittiyar**

Marquis, Don (Donald Robert Marquis)
Archy at the Zoo.
Archy, the Cockroach, Speaks, *sel.*
Archy Confesses, *sel.*
Ballade of the Under Side, *sel.*
Certain Maxims of Archy.
Cheerio My Deario, *sel.*
God-Maker, Man, The.
Hen and the Oriole, The, *sel.*
Honey Bee, The.
I oft stand in the snow at dawn, *sel.*
I once heard the survivors, *sel.*
In the Bayou.
Jokesmith's Vacation, The.
Noah an' Jonah an' Cap'n John Smith.
Old Trouper, The, *sel.*
Only Thy Dust.
Reverie.
Song of Mehitabel, The, *sel.*
Time time said old King Tut.
Tom-Cat, The.
Wail of Archy, The, *sel.*
Warty Bliggens, the Toad, *sel.*
Was it fancy, sweet nurse, *sel.*

When One Loves Tensely.
When Whistler's Mother's Picture's frame, *sel.*

Marr, Barbara
Prayer: "Lord, make me sensitive to the sight."

Marriot, John
On John Donne's Book of Poems.

Marriott, Anne
As You Come In.
Beaver Pond.
Prairie Graveyard.
Sandstone.
Wind/ flattening its gaunt furious self against, *sel.*
Woodyards in the Rain.

Marryat, Frederick
Captain Stood on the Carronade, The, *sel.*
Port Admiral.

Mars, Ann (Annalita Marsigli)
Shadow.

Marsden, James
What Is Time?

Marsh, Corinna
Before the Bath.

Marsh, Daniel L.
Greatest Person in the Universe, The.

Marsh, E. L.
Magic Piper, The.

Marshak, Samuel
Little House in Lithuania, The.

Marshall, Archibald
Limerick: "There was a young man of Devizes," *at.*

Marshall, Austin John
Dancing at Whitsun.

Marshall, Edward
Leave the Word Alone.

Marshall, Jack
Glimmers.
Hitchhiker.

Marshall, Lenore G.
Invented a Person.

Marshall, Matt
Wine o Living.

Marshall, Peter
Prayer for America.

Marshall, Tom
Interior Monologue 666.
Politics.
Summer.

Marshall, William E.
But see this happy village festival, *sel.*
To a Mayflower.

Marson, Una
Brown Baby Blues.
Gettin de Spirit.
Kinky Hair Blues.
Politeness.
Repose.
To Wed or Not to Wed.

Marston, John
I cannot sleepe, my eyes ill neighbouring lids, *sel.*
O gracious gods, take compassion, *sel.*
Song: "Delicious beauty that doth lie."
Song: "O Love, how strangely sweet."
To Detraction I Present My Poesie, *sel.*
To Everlasting Oblivion, *sel.*

Marston, Philip Bourke
After.
Inseparable.
Not Thou but I.
Old Churchyard of Bonchurch, The.
Speechless [upon the Marriage of Two Deaf and Dumb Persons]
Too Late.
Ungathered Love.

Marteau, Robert
Black Banderillas.
Down There.

Metamorphosis of Lovers, The.
Stele.
Unnamed Always.

Martí, José
I am a sincere man, *sel.*
I grow a white rose, *sel.*
Two Countries.

Martial (Marcus Valerius Martialis)
Advantages of Learning, The.
Believe me, sir, I'd like to spend whole days.
Bought Locks.
Country Pleasures.
Critics.
Dasius, chucker-out/ at the Turkish Baths.
De Coenatione Micae.
Either get out of my house or conform to my tastes, woman.
Epigram: A Riddle.
Epigram: "Charm of my life, my dearest care."
Epigram: Go, Happy Rose.
Epigram: "Me Polytimus vexes and provokes."
Epigram: "Milo's from home; and, Milo being gone."
Epigram: "My better half, why turn a peevish scold."
Epigram: On a Slanderer.
Epigram: On Bassa.
Epigram: On Hedylus.
Epigram: The Likeness.
Epigram: To Charinus, a Catamite.
Epigram: To Dindymus.
Epigram: To Labienus.
Epigram: To Lygdus.
Epigram: To Papilus.
Epigram: To Philaenis.
Epigram: To Phoebus.
Epigram: To Polycharmus.
Epitaph for Erotion.
Erotion.
For Erotion's Grave.
Garland of roses, whether you come.
Happy Life.
Hinted Wish, A.
Laid with papyrus to catch fire.
Lentinus! thou dost nought but fume, and fret.
Near Neighbors.
Near the Vipsanian columns where the aqueduct.
On the Death of a Young and Favorite Slave.
Post-Obits and the Poets.
Prithee die and set me free.
Procrastination.
Roman Presents.
Roman Thank-You Letter, A.
Sextus the Usurer.
Temperament.
Things that make the happier life, are these, The.
To Cloe.
To His Book[e]
To Julius.
To Sextus.
Verses on Blenheim.
What a host you are, Mancinus.
What Makes a Happy Life.
Whenever you drink all night you make.
Would you, my friend, in little room express.
You Serve the Best Wines Always, My Dear Sir.
You've Told Me, Maro.

Martin, Angus
Bait-Gathering.
Grandfather.
I Laughed When the Painter, Caroline.

Martin, C. D.
God's Goodness.

Martin, Charles
Leaving Buffalo.

Sharks at the New York Aquarium.
Signs.

Martin, David
Gordon Childe.
I Am a Jew.

Martin, Edward Sandford
Egotism.
Girl of Pompeii, A.
Little Brother of the Rich, A.

Martin, Egbert
National Anthem.
Trade.

Martin, Herbert
Antigone I.
Antigone VI.
Lines: "Singularly and in pairs the decade has been ripped by bullets."
Negro Soldier's Viet Nam Diary, A.

Martin, I. L.
At the Tennis Club.
Dark Eyes at Forest Hills.

Martin, John
God's Dark.
Toad and the Rabbit, The.

Martin, Mairin
All of a Piece.

Martin, Michael C.
Electric Storm.
Guard.

Martin, Philip
In March.

Martin, Sarah Catherine
Old Mother Hubbard.

Martin, Sir Theodore
I met a cracksman coming down the Strand, *sel.*

Martin, William
Apple Orchard in the Spring, An.

Martin, Sir Theodore and William Edmonstoune Aytoun. *See* **Aytoun, William Edmonstoune and Sir Theodore Martin.**

Martinez, David W.
New Way, Old Way.
This Is Today.

Martinez, James
Dis Time No Stan' Like befo' Time.
My Little Lize.

Martinez, Maurice
Suburbia.

Martínez, Walter
Oil Painting.

Martínez de Navarrete, José Manuel
Morning.

Martínez Rivas, Carlos
Port Morazán.

Martinson, Harry Edmund
Cable Ship, The.
Cotton.
Dusk in the Country.
Earthworm, The.
Hades and Euclid.
On the Congo.
Sea Wind, The.

Martos, Marco
Our House.
Politics.
Quijote.
Sometimes I visit the city, *sel.*

Marty, Sid
In the Dome Car of the "Canadian."

Marula
Meeting after Separation.

Marutanilanakanar
Hunchback and the Dwarf, The.

Maruyama Kaoru
Anchor.
Crane.
Dusk.
Estuany.
Fragments.

Funeral Song.
Gun Base.
Gun Emplacement.
Sad Parting.
Song of the Gull.
Song of the Lamp.
Song of the Sail.
Sorrow of Parting.
Wings.

Marvell, Andrew
After Floods on the Wharfe, *sel.*
After two sittings, now our Lady State, *sel.*
Ametas and Thestylis Making Hay-Ropes.
And now to the abyss I pass, *sel.*
Bermudas.
Carrying Their Coracles, *sel.*
Character of Holland, The.
Clorinda and Damon.
Coronet, The.
Damon the Mower.
Definition of Love, The.
Dialogue between the Resolved Soul and
  Created Pleasure, A.
Dialogue between the Soul and [the] Body, A.
Dialogue between Thyrsis and Dorinda, A.
Dutch in the Medway, The, *sel.*
Epitaph, An: "Enough; and leave the rest to
  fame."
Execution of King Charles, The.
Eyes and Tears.
Fair Singer, The.
From that blest bed the hero came, *sel.*
Gallery, The.
Garden, The.
Garden of Appleton House, The ("When in
  the east the morning ray"), *sel.*
Girl and Her Fawn, The.
Hewel, or Woodpecker, The, *sel.*
Holland, that scarce deserves the name of
  land, *sel.*
Horatian Ode upon Cromwell's Return from
  Ireland, An.
I saw him dead, a leaden slumber lyes [*or*
  lies], *sel.*
King Charles on [*or* upon] the Scaffold, *sel.*
Kingfisher, The, *sel.*
Last Instructions to a Painter, The.
Match, The.
Mourning.
Mower against Gardens, The.
Mower to the Glow-Worms [*or* Glowworms],
  The.
Mower's Song, The.
Nymph and Her Fawn, The, *sel.*
Nymph Complaining for the Death of Her
  Fawn, The.
Oh thou, that dear and happy isle, *sel.*
On a Drop of Dew.
On Mr. Milton's Paradise Lost.
On the Lord Mayor and Court of Aldermen,
  Presenting the Late King and Duke of York
  Each with a Copy of Their Freedoms.
Paint Castlemaine in colours that will hold,
  sel.
Paint last the King, and a dead shade of night,
  sel.
Picture of Little T. C. in a Prospect of
  Flowers, The.
Second Advice to a Painter, The.
See how the flowers, as at parade, *sel.*
Third Advice to a Painter, The.
To His Coy Mistress.
Upon Appleton House, to My Lord Fairfax.
Vows, The.
What wondrous life is this I lead!, *sel.*
When first the eye this forest sees, *sel.*
Where, twining subtile fears with hope, *sel.*

Marvin, Jean H.
Circle Sleeper.

Marx, Anne
Lacemaker (Vermeer, The).

Marx, Erica
No Need for Nuremberg.
To One Put to Death in a Gas Chamber.
Mary Queen of Scots
Prayer before Execution.
Maryam bint Abi Ya'qub al-Ansari
What can you expect.
Marz, Roy
Vittoria Colonna.
Marzán, Julio
Epitaph.
Epitaph: "Hours before my death."
Friday Evening.
Graduation Day, 1965.
Masahongva
Corn-blossom maidens.
Now from the east.
Masanés, Josefa
That I be a writer? Absolutely not!, *sel.*
Masaoka Shiki
Country road/ boys whacking at a snake.
Crimson berry, A.
Haiku: "Above the treetops," *sel.*
Haiku: After I'm Dead, *sel.*
Haiku: "Again and again."
Haiku: "Airing books," *sel.*
Haiku: "Always someone resting there," *sel.*
Haiku: "As the bat flies."
Haiku: "Before the/ red blossoms," *sel.*
Haiku: "Clog with a broken thong," *sel.*
Haiku: "Country road—/ boys whacking at a
  snake," *sel.*
Haiku: "Cricket singing, A," *sel.*
Haiku: "Crickets/ in the corner of the garden."
Haiku: "Daily routine," *sel.*
Haiku: "Dead squid, A," *sel.*
Haiku: "Fall rains/ scum collecting on," *sel.*
Haiku: "Fluttering, fluttering," *sel.*
Haiku: "For eating persimmons, too," *sel.*
Haiku: "Forsythia blossoms gone," *sel.*
Haiku: "From the firefly," *sel.*
Haiku: "Getting lazy," *sel.*
Haiku: "He washes his horse."
Haiku: "Home alone/ my mother off
  cherry-viewing," *sel.*
Haiku: "I checked/ three thousand haiku," *sel.*
Haiku: "I don't know when," *sel.*
Haiku: "I pulled on a creeper," *sel.*
Haiku: "I think I'll die," *sel.*
Haiku: "I want to sleep."
Haiku: "I, who/ plant the pit," *sel.*
Haiku: "I, who/ listen to a man," *sel.*
Haiku: "I, who/ hear the drums," *sel.*
Haiku: "I, who/ think so often of," *sel.*
Haiku: "If I were to paint," *sel.*
Haiku: "If you stick the stems," *sel.*
Haiku: In a Strong Wind at the Suma
  Seashore, *sel.*
Haiku: In the Hospital at the Suma Seashore.
Haiku: "Last year in spring," *sel.*
Haiku: "Lonely sound—/ simmering in the
  firepit," *sel.*
Haiku: "Long night/ when the waterfall," *sel.*
Haiku: "Looking through."
Haiku: "Morning fog/ one man's got a fire
  going," *sel.*
Haiku: "Peeling pears/ sweet juice drips," *sel.*
Haiku: "People going home," *sel.*
Haiku: "Purple so deep, A," *sel.*
Haiku: "Sketching from life," *sel.*
Haiku: "Sky blazing/ as I go down the gravel
  path," *sel.*
Haiku: "Snake falls, A."
Haiku: "Snake-gourd in bloom."
Haiku: "So few the cicadas."
Haiku: "Soon to die."
Haiku: "Sprays of wisteria, The/ arranged in
  the vase/ are so short," *sel.*
Haiku: "Sprays of wisteria/ arranged in a
  vase—/ the blossoms hang down," *sel.*
Haiku: "Sprays of wisteria/ arranged in a
  vase—/ one cluster," *sel.*

Haiku: "Stray cat, A," *sel.*
Haiku: "Summer grass/ way in the distance,"
  sel.
Haiku: "Summer storm/ all the sheets of blank
  paper," *sel.*
Haiku: "These wisterias," *sel.*
Haiku: "They've cut down the willow," *sel.*
Haiku: "This year/ I took sick with the
  peonies," *sel.*
Haiku: "Twilight cicadas," *sel.*
Haiku: "When I look/ at wisteria blossoms/ I
  want to get out," *sel.*
Haiku: "When I look/ at the wisteria
  blossoms/ I think of long ago," *sel.*
Haiku: "Where the castle stood," *sel.*
Haiku: Written when Sick in Bed.
I thought to make.
Poor Man's Hut.
Village snuffed asleep.
Masayori (Asukai Masayori)
Insects near a Hut in the Fields.
Now I realize/ it is my sovereign's light.
So cold is this spring.
Sunlight Shining of Red Leaves.
Trees of the same age.
Winter.
Maschler, Fay
Little Bits of Soft-boiled Egg.
Masefield, John
All through the windless night the clipper
  rolled, *sel.*
C. L. M.
Captain Stratton's Fancy.
Cargoes.
Choice, The.
Consecration, A.
Creed, A.
Crowd, The.
D'Avalos' Prayer.
Dawn.
Dead Knight, The.
Epilogue, An: "I have seen flowers come in
  stony places."
Flesh, I Have Knocked at Many a Dusty
  Door, *sel.*
Fox knew well, that before they tore him,
  The, *sel.*
Hell's Pavement.
How Many Ways ("How many ways, how
  many times"), *sel.*
I could not sleep for thinking of the sky, *sel.*
I never see the red rose crown the year, *sel.*
I opened the window wide and leaned, *sel.*
If I could get within this changing I, *sel.*
Is there a great green commonwealth of
  Thought, *sel.*
June Twilight.
King's Highway, The.
Laugh and Be Merry.
Lemmings, The.
Lollingdon Downs.
Man is a sacred city built of marvelous earth,
  sel.
Meet was at "The Cock and Pye," The, *sel.*
Midnight.
Night is on the downland, on the lonely
  moorland, *sel.*
O little self, within whose smallness lies, *sel.*
Ock Gurney and old Pete were there, *sel.*
Old Song Re-sung, An.
On Eastnor Knoll.
On Growing Old.
One of Wally's Yarns.
Other bright days of action have seemed
  great, *sel.*
Partidges.
Passing Strange, The.
Port of Holy Peter.
Port of Many Ships.
Posted.
Rider at The Gate, The.
Roadways.

Rose of the World, The.
Rounding the Horn, *sel.*
Sea Change.
Sea Fever.
Seekers, The.
Sonnet: "Here in the self is all that men can know," *sel.*
Sonnet: "There, on the darkened deathbed, dies the brain."
Sonnets, ("Long, long ago"), *sels.*
Sorrow of Mydath.
Spanish Waters.
Tewkesbury Road.
There is no God, as I was taught in youth.
Tomorrow.
Trade Winds.
Truth.
Twilight.
Up on the downs the red-eyed kestrels hover.
Valediction (Liverpool Docks), A.
Waggon-Maker, The.
Wanderer, The.
Wanderer's Song, A.
West Wind, The.
What Am I, Life?, *sel.*
Wild Duck, The.

Masini, Donna
Cherry Ice.
Hands.
Rubber.

Mason, Agnes Louisa Carter
Whenever a Little Child Is Born.

Mason, Caroline Atherton Briggs
Open Secret, An.
President Lincoln's Grave.
Reconciliation.
When I Am Old.

Mason, Edgar Cooper
Safe in His Keeping.
Satisfied.

Mason, Guy
Adventure.
Independence.

Mason, John
Red Fred exhumed the orangepeels.

Mason, Madeline
Janus.

Mason, Mary Augusta
My Little Neighbor.
Scarlet Tanager, The.

Mason, Mason Jordan
Big Man.
In War.
Last Impression of New York.
Pen Hy Cane ("Pen Hyrogliphic Cane").
Pico della Mirandola.
Things of the Spirit.

Mason, Ronald
Self-Congratulatory Ode on Mr. Auden's Election to the Professorship of Poetry at Oxford.

Mason, Ronald Allison Kells
Be Swift O Sun.
Body of John.
Ecce Homunculus.
Flow at Full Moon.
Footnote to John II: 4.
If the Drink.
Judas Iscariot.
Latter-day Geography Lesson.
Lugete O Veneres.
Nails and a Cross.
Oils and Ointments.
Old Memories of Earth.
On the Swag.
Our Love Was a Grim Citadel.
Prelude: "This short straight sword."
Song of Allegiance.
Sonnet of Brotherhood.
Spark's Farewell to Its Clay, The.
Young Man Thinks of Sons, The.

Mason, Walt
Football.

Mason, William
How to Build a Ha-ha, *sel.*
Thomas Gray's View of Nature, *sel.*

Massey, Gerald
All's Right with the World.
As proper mode of quenching legal lust.
Awakening of the People, The.
Desolate.
Diakka, The.
His Banner over Me.
Hundred years ago this morn, A, *sel.*
O, Lay Thy Hand in Mine, Dear!
Womankind.
Worker, The.

Massimi, Petronilla Paolini
Fortune Welcomed Me at Last, *sel.*
To Female Duties Clorinda Scorned.

Massinger, Philip
Death Invoked, *sel.*
Look on this maid of honour, now, *sel.*
Men May Talk of Country-Christmasses.
Yet there's one scruple with which I am much, *sel.*

Masso
Crossing the Sento River.
Frogs Croaking.

Masson, Tom (Thomas Lansing Masson)
Enough.
He Took Her.
My Poker Girl.
Tragedy, A.
When I Get Time.

Masters, Carol
Fly Ball.

Masters, Dexter
Graffiti for a Particle Accelerator.

Masters, Edgar Lee
Aaron Hatfield, *sel.*
Achilles Deatheridge.
Amanda Barker, *sel.*
Anne Rutledge, *sel.*
Arlo Will, *sel.*
Benjamin Franklin Hazard, *sel.*
"Butch" Weldy, *sel.*
Carl Hamblin, *sel.*
Cassius Hueffer, *sel.*
Chase Henry.
Circuit Judge, The, *sel.*
Cooney Potter, *sel.*
Daisy Fraser, *sel.*
Davis Matlock, *sel.*
Dora Williams, *sel.*
Editor Whedon.
Edmund Pollard, *sel.*
Elliott Hawkins, *sel.*
Elsa Wertman, *sel.*
English Thornton, *sel.*
Father Malloy, *sel.*
Franklin James, *sel.*
Hamilton Greene, *sel.*
Henry C. Calhoun, *sel.*
Herman Altman, *sel.*
Hill, The, *sel.*
In Memory of Bryan Lathrop.
Jacob Godbey, *sel.*
Jonathan Houghton, *sel.*
Jonathan Swift Somers, *sel.*
Judge Somers, *sel.*
Keats to Fanny Brawne.
Knowlt Hoheimer, *sel.*
Lost Orchard, The.
Lucinda Matlock, *sel.*
Marx the Sign Painter, *sel.*
Meredith Phyfe, *sel.*
Mind Flying Afar.
My Dog Ponto.
Ollie McGee.
Petit, the Poet, *sel.*
Rutherford McDowell, *sel.*

Scholfield Huxley, *sel.*
Seth Compton, *sel.*
Silence.
Spooniad, The.
Supplication.
Thing Is Sex, Ben, The, *sel.*
This America is an ancient land, *sel.*
Unknown Soldiers, *sel.*
Village Atheist, The, *sel.*
Week-End by the Sea.
Widows.
William Jones, *sel.*
Willis Beggs, *sel.*

Masters, Marcia Lee
At My Mother's Bedside.
Country Ways, *sel.*

Mastin, Florence Ripley
Return to Spring.

Mastoraki, Jenny
Bridal bed, The. Above it.
Crusaders knew the Holy Places, The.
Death of a Warrior, The.
Prometheus.
Then they paraded Pompey's urn.
Vandals, The.
Wooden Horse then said, The.

Matabaruka
Change, The.

Mataira, Katerina Te Hei Koko
Restoring the Ancestral House.

Matar, Muhammad Afifi
Recital.

Matchett, William H.
Head Couples.
Old Inn on the Eastern Shore.
Packing a Photograph from Firenze.
Water Ouzel.

Mather, Cotton
Epitaph: "Dummer the shepherd sacrific'd."
Eternal God, How They're Increased.
Go then, my dove, but now no longer mine.
I Lift My Eyes Up to the Hills.
My Heart, How Very Hard It's Grown.
O Glorious Christ of God; I live.
Vigilantius, or a Servant of the Lord Found Ready.
When the Seed of Thy Word Is Cast.

Mather, Joseph
File-Hewer's Lamentation, The.
God Save Great Thomas Paine.

Matheson, George
Christian Freedom.
O Love That Wilt Not Let Me Go.

Matheson, Mary
Afterward.
Evening.

Matheus, John Frederick
Requiem: "She wears, my beloved, a rose upon her head."

Mathew, Ray
At a Time.
Good Thing, A.
Love and Marriage.
Lover's Meeting.
'Morning, Morning.
Wynyard Sailor.

Mathews, Aidan Carl
At the Wailing Wall.
Descartes at Daybreak.
Library, The.
Minding Ruth.
Severances.

Mathews, Albert
To an Autumn Leaf.

Mathews, Cornelius
Poet, The.

Mathews, Esther
Song: "I can't be talkin' of love, dear."

Mathews, Harry
Condition of Desire.
Histoire.

Mathias, Eileen
All in Red.
Go Out.
In the Wood.
Just Jumbo.
Little Things.
My Hut.
Sea Fairies.
Tall Trees.
Zoo Manners.
Mathias, Roland
Craswall.
Departure in Middle Age.
God Is.
Mathis, Cleopatra
Aerial View of Louisiana.
Elegy for the Other.
For Maria.
Getting Out.
Mimosa.
Traveler, The.
Mathison, Thomas
Victory on the Last Green, *sel.*
Matimatirattanar. *See* **Mocikiranar**
Matos, Luis Palés
Doorway to Time in Three Voices.
Hurricane, The.
Neither This nor That.
Well, The.
Matraini, Chiara
Liberty.
Matsuda, Sumio
Views of an American Writer.
Matsumoto Takashi
Haiku: "Cicadas shrieking."
Haiku: "Her summer *kimono.*"
Haiku: "In the brothel."
Haiku: "On an onion tuft."
Matsunaga Teitoku. *See* **Teitoku**
Matsuo Basho. *See* **Basho**
Mattam, Donald
In a Town Garden.
Table Talk.
Mattera, Don
At Least.
Of Reason and Discovery.
Protea.
Matthews, Alice Clear
Of the Mathematician.
Matthews, Brander
American Girl, An.
Matthews, Harley
Return of the Native, The.
Matthews, Jack
People in These Houses, The.
Matthews, Marc
Guyana not Ghana.
Matthews, William
Accompanist, The.
Airline Breakfast, An.
Bring the War Home.
Bystanders.
Cat, The.
Charming.
Clearwater Beach, Florida.
Directions.
Elegy for Bob Marley, An.
Flood.
Hello, Hello.
Hummer, The.
In Memory of the Utah Stars.
Introduction: "I have a few remarks," he
　smiled."
Living among the Dead.
Loyal.
Lucky and Unlucky.
Lust.
Merida, 1969.
Nabokov's Death.
Oh Yes.

On the Porch at the Frost Place, Franconia,
　NH.
Photo of the Author with a Favorite Pig.
Praise.
Prolific.
Psychopathology of Everyday Life, The.
Search Party, The.
Spring Snow.
Taking the Train Home.
Twins.
Unrelenting Flood.
Waking at Dusk from a Nap.
Whiplash.
Mattison, Alice
Cool Day in July.
Hunter Radiation Center: Halloween.
Maturai Ilampalaciriyan Centan Kuttanar
What She Said.
Maturai Marutan Ilanakanar
What Her Girl Friend Said to Her.
When a King Asks for a Chieftain's Daughter.
Maturai Velacan
Peace Poem.
Maturaipputan Ilanakanar
Mothers.
Maturaittamilkkuttan Katuvan Mallanar
What the Servants Said to Him, as He
　Returned Home.
Matveyeva, Novella
Eggplants Have Pins and Needles, The.
Maud
Finger Play.
Maughan, Henry Neville
Song: "There was a Knight of Bethlehem,"
　sel.
Maura, Sister
Blessing of St. Francis, The.
Creation of Light, The.
Deirdre's Song at Sunrise.
Each Day.
"Maurice, Furnley" (Frank Wilmot)
Agricultural Show, Flemington, Victoria, The.
On a Grey-haired Old Lady Knitting at an
　Orchestral Concert.
Supremer Sacrifice, The.
Team, The.
Upon a Row of Old Books and Shoes in a
　Pawnbroker's Window.
Winds Are Bleak, Stars Are Bright, *sel.*
Maurice, Thomas
How cursed that country, how severe its
　doom, *sel.*
Mavimbela
My money! O, my money!
Maxson, Gloria A.
Baker, *sel.*
Dead, The, *sel.*
Enid Field: In Memoriam.
Golfer, *sel.*
Living, The, *sel.*
Miser, *sel.*
Walter Scott.
Maxton, Hugh
At the Protestant Museum.
Cernunnos.
Waking.
Maxtone Graham, Joyce Anstruther. *See*
　"Struther, Jan"
Maxwell, James Clerk
Rigid Body Sings.
Vampyre, The.
Maxwell, Ruth Fortney
Mother's Joy, A.
Maxwell-Hall, Agnes
Jamaica Market.
May, Derwent
"A Midsummer Night's Dream" in Regent's
　Park.
Child in the 80's, A.
May, Edward
Five Things White.

On a Young Man and an Old Man.
To a Covetous Churl.
To Barba.
To Her Love.
You tender virgins, fairer than the snow with
　which you play.
May, John
Six Things for Christmas.
May, Julia Harris
Day by Day.
May, Sue
Haircut.
Passion.
Photograph.
Mayakovsky, Vladimir Vladimirovich
Cloud in Trousers, A.
Last Statement.
Our March.
Maybin, Patrick
April 1940.
Ballykinlar: May 1940.
Fallen Tree, The.
Monks at Ards, The.
Thoughts from Abroad.
Mayer, Bernadette
Booze Turns Men into Women.
Complete Introductory Lectures on Poetry,
　The.
Essay.
Eve of Easter.
Holding the Thought of Love.
It Was Miss Scarlet with the Candlestick in
　the Billiard Room.
Laundry and School Epigrams.
Sonnet: Kamikaze.
Tragic Condition of the Statue of Liberty,
　The.
Warren Phinney.
Woman I Mix Men Up, A.
Mayer, Gerda
Chopin's Minute Waltz.
Old Wife Speaks, The.
Small Park in East Germany: 1969.
There'll Be No Better.
Mayer, Hansjörg
Oil.
Mayhall, Jane
City Sparrow.
For the Market.
Human Animal, The.
Marshes, The.
Maynard, Don
Athlete.
Maynard, Theodore
Faith's Difficulty.
Mayne, Jasper
Scorne then their censure, who gave out thy
　wit, *sel.*
Time.
Mayne, John
Logan Braes.
Mayne, Seymour
Abraham Sutskever.
Afternoon's Angel.
Before Passover.
In the First Cave.
Locusts of Silence.
Roots.
Yehuda Amichai.
Mayo, Edward Leslie
Diver, The.
El Greco.
Word of Water, The.
Mayo, Frances
Lament: "We knelt on the rocks by the dark
　green pools."
Mayröcker, Friederike
After Reading the Poetry of Yannis Ritsos.
Crouched in the chirping.
Cypress.
From the Depths.

Maze
Marble the stone-cool the, The.
Model 3/ Melpomene.
Numbness.
Oceanic World.
Ostia Will Receive You.
Patron of Flawless Serpent Beauty.
Something like coasts clover-colored.
Sometimes in some chance.
Squadron-blue the hemp-yellow drink of triumph, The.
What I call you.
Wherever you go.
Will wither like grass.
Yew trees in ice, The.

Maze, Mack
If you see my mother, partner, tell her pray for me.

Mazur, Gail
Baseball.
Deck of Cards, A.
Listening to Baseball in the Car.

M'Baye, Annette
Silhouette.

"McK., S. C."
Quiet from Fear of Evil.

Meacham, Harry M.
To a Young Poet.

Mead, Edward P.
Steam King, The.

Mead, Margaret
Misericordia.

Mead, Stella
Last Gate, The.
When We Are Men.

Means, Alex
What Wondrous Love Is This, *at*.

Mearns, Hughes
Lady with Technique, The, *sel*.
Little Man Who Wasn't There, The.
Perfect Reactionary, The.

Mechain, Gwerfyl
In the Snowfall.
Lady of the Ferry Inn.

Mechain, Gwallter. *See* **Davies, Walter**

Mechtel, Angelika
Children They, The.
Cooking the Rice.

Mechthild of Magdeburg
About This Book.

Mechthild von Magdeburg
Ah dearest Love, for how long, *sel*.
Love Flows from God.
On the Divine Power of Courtly Love.

Medici, Lorenzo de'
How can I sing light-souled and fancy-free.
Into a little close of mine I went.
Leave, Cytherea, Your Enchanted Isle.
Triumph of Bacchus and Ariadne.

Medicine, Bea
Ina, 1979.

Medicine-Tail
He was there/ Old Man Coyote.

Meehan, John James
Race of the *Oregon, The.*

Meek, Bill. *See* **Conolly, John** *and* **Bill Meek.**

Meeks, Brian
Coup-clock Clicks, The.
Las' Rights.

Megged, Matti
Akedah, The.
Phoenix, The.
White Bird.

Mehri
Coming Across.

Mei Yao-ch'en
Aboard a Boat at Night, Drinking with My Wife.
An Offering for the Cat.
At Night, Hearing Someone Singing in the House Next Door.
Back from Green Dragon.

Dappled Horse, The.
Friend Advises Me to Stop Drinking, A.
Lunar Eclipse.
Marrying Again.
My Neighbor to the South, the Office Clerk Hsiao, Came in the Evening to Say Good-bye.
On the Death of a New Born Child.
Out and Back on the Fifteenth Night of the First Month.
Sad Remembrance.
Sharing Lodging with Hsieh Shih-hou.
Shih-hou Pointed Out to Me That from Ancient Times There Had Never Been a Poem on the Subject of Li.

Meidhre, Brian MacGiolla. *See* **Merriman, Brian**

Meigs, Charles D.
Home without a Bible.
Others.

Meigs, Mildred Plew (Mildred Plew Merryman)
Pirate Don Durk of Dowdee, The.
Shepherd Left Behind, The.
Silver Ships.

Meiji, Emperor
"For ever and ever."
In my garden.
In newspapers, all see.
Whenever I see.
Young go off, The.

Meilyr Brydydd
Poem on His Death-Bed.

Meinke, Peter
Advice to My Son.
Atomic Pantoum.
Dear Reader.
Elegy for a Diver.
Everything We Do.
50 on 50.
Heart's Location, The.
Last Mountain Lion on Maple Crest Mountain, The.
Student, The.
To a Daughter with Artistic Talent.

Meïr of Rothenburg
Burning of the Law, The.

Meireles, Cecília
Ballad of the Ten Casino Dancers.
Dead Horse, The.
Pyrargyrite Metal, 9.
Roosters Will Crow, The.
Second Rose Motif.
Song: "I placed my dream in a boat."
Vigil.

Meisetsu, Naito. *See* **Naito Meisetsu**

Meissner, William
Death of the Trackstar.
Kicker's Last Steps, The.
Reunion: Swimming, The.

Meister, Shirley Vogler
Prevaricator, The.

Mejía Sánchez, Ernesto
Death of Somoza, The.

Melbourne, Hirini
Tamaki of a Hundred Lovers.
Why the Wind Comes.

Meleager
Busy with love, the bumble bee.
Epigram: "And now I, Meleager, am among them."
Epigram: "As honey in wine/ wine, honey."
Epigram: "At 12 o'clock in the afternoon."
Epigram: "Boys of Tyre are beautiful, The."
Epigram: "Breath of my life, The—no less."
Epigram: "Diodorus is nice, isn't he, Philocles?"
Epigram: "Drink, unhappy lover, drink."
Epigram: "I was thirsty."
Epigram: "It is true that I held Thero fair."

Epigram: "Listen, you know the pains of love."
Epigram: "Lo! Beauty flashed forth sweetly; from his eyes."
Epigram: "Love brought me quietly in the dreaming night."
Epigram: "One boy alone in all the world for me."
Garland for Heliodora, A.
I'll Twine White Violets.
In the Spring.
Little Love-God, The.
Lost Desire.
Love at the Door.
Love's night and a lamp.
O Gentle Ships.
Of Himself.
Of His Death.
Spring.
Upon a Maid That Died [*or* Dyed] the Day She Was Married [*or* Marryed]

Melinescu, Gabriela
Birth.
Time of Fish Dying.

Mellen, Grenville
Lonely Bugle Grieves, The, *sel*.

Melleri, Arto
Love's Rocky Forest.
Proportions.
What Is There for Us.

Mello Breyner Andresen, Sophia de. *See* **Andresen, Sophia de Mello Breyner**

Melly, George
Belle de Jour.
Homage to René Magritte.

Melnick, David
Men in Aïda, they appeal, eh? A day, O Achilles!
Seta/ colecc.
Thoeisu.

Melo, David Abenatar
Thanksgiving.

Melo Neto, João Cabral de
All the heaven and earth, *sel*.
Canefield and the Sea, The.
Cemetery in Pernambuco ("Nobody lies in this earth").
Cemetery in Pernambuco ("This is a marine cemetery").
Clouds, The.
Daily Space.
Drafted Vulture, The.
Education by Stone.
Emptiness of Man, The.
End of the World, The.
Engineer, The.
Imitation of Water.
Knife All Blade, A.
Man from Up-Country Talking, The.
My name is Severino, *sel*.
Poem: "My eyes have telescopes."
Sea and the Canefield, The.
Two of the Festivals of Death.
Weaving the Morning.
Whom are you carrying, *sel*.
Windows.

Meltzer, David
Eyes, the Blood, The.
15th Raga: For Bela Lugosi, *sel*.
Prayerwheel: 2.
Revelations.
Tell Them I'm Struggling to Sing with Angels.
12th Raga: For John Wieners, *sel*.

Melvill, Elizabeth, Lady Culross
I looked down and saw a pit most black, *sel*.
Into that pit when I did enter in, *sel*.
Then up I rose, and made no more delay, *sel*.
This pit is Hell where through thou now must go, *sel*.
Weary I was, and thought to sit at rest, *sel*.

1713   AUTHOR INDEX   Meredith

Melville, Herman
Aeolian Harp, The.
After the Pleasure Party.
Apparition, The.
Art.
At the Cannon's Mouth.
Attic Landscape, The.
Ball's Bluff.
Bench of Boors, The.
Berg, The.
Billy in the Darbies, *sel.*
Blue-Bird, The.
Buddha.
College Colonel, The.
Commemorative of a Naval Victory.
Conflict of Convictions, The.
Crossing the Tropics.
Dirge for McPherson, A.
Eagle of the Blue, The.
Enthusiast, The.
Enviable Isles, The.
Envoi, L': "My towers at last! These rovings
    end."
Epilogue: "If Luther's day expand to Darwin's
    year," *sel.*
Fall of Richmond, The.
"Formerly a Slave."
Fragments of a Lost Gnostic Poem of the
    Twelfth Century.
Greek Architecture.
Healed of My Hurt.
House-Top, The.
In a Garret.
In the Pauper's Turnip-Field.
In the Prison Pen.
Inscription for Marye's Heights,
    Fredericksburg.
Lone Founts.
Lover and the Syringa-Bush, The.
Maldive Shark, The.
Malvern Hill.
March into Virginia, The.
Martyr, The.
Meditation, A.
Memorial: On the Slain at Chickamauga.
Misgivings.
Monody.
My Jacket Old.
New Ancient of Days, The.
Night-March, The.
Of Rama.
Of Rome, *sel.*
Old Age in His Ailing.
Old Counsel.
On Mammon, *sel.*
Pontoosuce.
Portent, The.
Prelusive, *sel.*
Ravaged Villa, The.
Requiem for Soldiers Lost in Ocean
    Transports, A.
Ribs and Terrors in the Whale, The, *sel.*
Running the Batteries.
Sheridan at Cedar Creek.
Shiloh; a Requiem.
Sodom, *sel.*
Southern Cross.
Surrender at Appomattox, The.
Temeraire, The.
The *Cumberland.*
To Ned.
Tuft of Kelp, The.
Ungar and Rolfe, *sel.*
Uninscribed Monument on One of the
    Battle-Fields of the Wilderness, An.
Utilitarian View of the *Monitor's* Fight, A.
Victor of Antietam, The.
Where's Commander All-a-Tanto?, *sel.*

Menahem ben Jacob
Harvesting of the Roses, The.
Martyr's Death, A.

Menahem ben Makhir of Ratisbon
How Sweet Thy Precious Gift of Rest.
Menai, Huw
Where shall the eyes a darkness find, *sel.*
Menashe, Samuel
Pot Poured Out, A.
Sheep Meadow.
Winter.
Mendelssohn, Asher
Cordoba.
Mendelssohn, Moses
Self-Portrait.
Mendès, Catulle
I Go by Road.
Mother, The.
Mendes, Moses
Ass, The, *sel.*
On the Death of a Lady's Owl.
Philanderer, The, *sel.*
Mendes, Murilo
Horses.
Map.
Mendes Zapata, Santiago
Story of the Eaters, A.
Menebroker, Ann
To the Man I Live With.
Meneses, Vidaluz
Cachikel Woman.
Meng Chiao
On Failing the Examination.
Menicanti, Daria
Letter in the Present and Present Perfect.
Menken, Adah Isaacs
Adelina Patti.
Answer Me.
Aspiration.
Autograph on the Soul, The.
Battle of the Stars.
Dreams of Beauty.
Drifts That Bar My Door.
Dying.
Fragment, A: "Cold chain of life presseth
    heavily on me tonight, The."
Genius.
Hear, O Israel!
Hemlock in the Furrows.
In Vain.
Infelix.
Into the Depths.
Judith.
Karazah to Karl.
Memory, A.
Miserimus.
My Heritage.
Myself.
One Year Ago.
Pro Patria.
Release, The.
Resurgam.
Sale of Souls.
Saved.
Ship That Went Down, The.
Venetia.
Where the Flocks Shall Be Led.
Working and Waiting.
Menzies, G. K.
Poaching *in Excelsis.*
Mercantini, Luigi
Garibaldi Hymn, The.
Mercer, Jesse
Will God forever cast us off.
Mercer, Johnny
Glow-Worm, The.
I'm an Old Cowhand.
Jubilation T. Cornpone.
Mercer, Margaret
Exhortation to Prayer.
Mercer, Thomas
Where is the gallant race that rose, *sel.*
Merchant, Jane
Flight Plan.

Meredith, George
Along the garden terrace, under which, *sel.*
Am I failing? For no longer can I cast, *sel.*
At dinner, she is hostess, I am host., *sel.*
Ballad of Past Meridian, A.
But where began the change; and what's my
    crime?, *sel.*
By this he knew she wept with waking eyes,
    sel.
Dirge in Woods.
"Dream is the thought in the ghost, The", *sel.*
He felt the wild beast in him betweenwhiles,
    sel.
He found her by the ocean's moaning verge,
    sel.
Here Jack and Tom are paired with Moll and
    Meg, *sel.*
Hymn to Colour.
I am to follow her. There is much grace, *sel.*
'I play for seasons, not eternities!', *sel.*
I think she sleeps: it must be sleep, when low,
    sel.
In fellowship Religion has its founts, *sel.*
In our old shipwrecked days there was an
    hour, *sel.*
Islet the Dachs.
It chanced his lips did meet her forehead cool,
    sel.
It is no vulgar nature I have wived, *sel.*
It is the season of the sweet wild rose, *sel.*
Juggling Jerry.
Lark Ascending, The.
Love in the Valley.
Lucifer in Starlight.
Madam would speak with me. So, now it
    comes, *sel.*
Mark where the pressing wind shoots
    javelin-like, *sel.*
Melampus.
Message from her set his brain aflame, A, *sel.*
My lady unto Madam makes her bow, *sel.*
Not solely that the future she destroys, *sel.*
Ode to the Spirit of Earth in Autumn.
Orchard and the Heath, The.
Out in the yellow meadows, where the bee,
    sel.
Phoebus with Admetus.
Pictures of the Rhine.
Question Whither, The.
Sense and Spirit.
She issues radiant from her dressing-room,
    sel.
Should Thy Love Die.
Sweet o' the Year, The.
Their sense is with their senses all mixed in,
    sel.
This golden head has wit in it. I live, *sel.*
This Was the Woman, *sel.*
Thrush in February, The.
Thus piteously Love closed what he begat,
    sel.
'Tis Christmas weather, and a country house,
    sel.
Under yonder beech-tree single on the
    greensward, *sel.*
We saw the swallows gathering in the sky,
    sel.
We three are on the cedar-shadowed lawn,
    sel.
What are we first? First, animals; and next,
    sel.
When I Would Image.
White Owl, The, *sel.*
Winter Heavens.
You like not that French novel? Tell me why,
    sel.
Young Reynard.
**"Meredith, Owen" (Edward Robert
    Bulwer-Lytton, 1st Earl of Lytton)**
Aux Italiens.
Going Back Again.
Last Wish, The.

Lord! if in love, though fainting oft, I have
tended thy gracious Vine, *sel.*
One Thing.
Tears, *sel.*
'Tis the white anemone, fashioned so, *sel.*
Twins.

Meredith, Ralph
Here and There.

Meredith, William
Accidents of Birth.
Bachelor.
Battle Problem.
Boon, A.
Chinese Banyan, The.
Country Stars.
Couple Overheard, The.
Crossing Over.
Do Not Embrace Your Mind's New Negro
Friend.
Dying Away.
Earth Walk.
Effort at Speech.
Fishvendor, The.
For Guillaume Apollinaire.
Hazard's Optimism.
His Plans for Old Age.
Homage to Paul Mellon, I. M. Pei, Their
Gallery, and Washington City.
Iambic Feet Considered as Honorable Scars.
Illiterate, The.
Korean Woman Seated by a Wall, A.
Last Things.
Love Letter from an Impossible Land.
Old Field Mowed, An.
On Falling Asleep by Firelight.
Open Sea, The.
Parents.
Partial Accounts.
Perhaps the Best Time.
Picture of a Castle.
Poem about Morning.
Rainy Season, The.
Rhode Island.
Starlight.
Thoughts on One's Head.
To the Thoughtful Reader.
Transport.
Tree Marriage.
Two Masks Unearthed in Bulgaria.
Walter Jenks' Bath.
Weather.
Wholesome.
Winter Verse for His Sister.

Meredith, William Tuckey
Farragut.

Meredyth, Mr.
To Miss— — —on the Death of Her Goldfish.

Merenda, Loretta
Local News.

Meri, Veijo
Bucharest.
Rhythm.
When I Was Young.
World Is Round, The.

Meriluoto, Aila
I Look at Your Land.
In the Year 4 after Father.
On the Shore.
Still.
Stone God, The.

Merivale, Herman Charles
Darwinity.

Merkel, Andrew
Ann stood and watched the combers race to
shore, *sel.*

Mernit, Susan
Scholar's Wife, The.
Song of the Bride.

Merriam, Eve
Alligator on the Escalator.
Bam, Bam, Bam.

Blue Alert.
Catch a Little Rhyme.
City Traffic.
Coward, The.
Fertile Valley of the Nile, The.
Finding a Poem.
Five Little Monsters.
Grandmother, Rocking.
It Fell in the City.
Kitty Cornered.
Leavetaking.
Misnomer.
One, Two, Three—Gough!
Onomatopoeia.
Rainbow Writing.
Restricted.
Rodomontade in the Menagerie.
Secret Talk.
Sing a Song of Subways.
Some Uses for Poetry.
Summer Rain.
Toaster Time.
Tryst.
Two People.
Umbilical.
Wall, The.
What in the World?
Which Washington?

Merrill, Boynton, Jr.
Fossil, The.
Mite, The.
Mule, The.

Merrill, Herbert
Courthouse Square.

Merrill, James
About the Phoenix.
After Greece.
Angel.
Backdrop: The dining room at Stonington, *sel.*
Bed, The.
Between Us.
Birthday.
Black Mesa, The.
Book of Ephraim, The, *sel.*
Broken Bowl, The.
Broken Home, The.
Casual Wear.
Charles on Fire.
Chimes for Yahya.
Cloud Country.
Current, The.
Days of 1941 and '44.
Days of 1964.
Dedication, A: "Hans, there are moments
when the whole mind."
Emerald, The, *sel.*
Empty perfection, as I take you in, *sel.*
Farewell Performance.
Foliage of Vision.
For a Second Marriage [*or* Upon a Second
Marriage]
Friend of the Fourth Decade, The.
Furnished Room, The.
Geode, the troll's melon, *sel.*
Getting Through.
Grand Canyon, The.
Green Eye, The.
Hotel de l'Univers et Portugal.
Ideas.
It starts in the small hours. An interlude, *sel.*
Kite Poem.
Laboratory Poem.
Last Words.
Life like the periodical not yet, *sel.*
Look Askance, A.
Losing the Marbles.
Lost in Translation.
Mad Scene, The.
Manos Karastefanís.
Matinees.
Mirabell's Books of Number, *sel.*

Mirror.
Octopus, The.
Page from the Koran.
Parnassians, The.
Parrot Fish, The.
Pier: Under Pisces, The.
Preface to the Memoirs, A.
Renewal, A.
Samos, *sel.*
Scenes of Childhood.
Seventh Round, The.
16. ix. 65.
Snapshot of Adam.
Some Negatives: X. at the Chateau.
Swimming by Night.
Syrinx.
Thistledown.
Thousand and Second Night, The.
Timepiece, A.
Tomorrows.
Transfigured Bird.
Up and Down.
Urban Convalescence, An.
Variations: The Air Is Sweetest That a Thistle
Guards.
Victor Dog, The.
View of the Burning, A.
Voices from the Other World.
Watching the Dance.
Waterspout.
Whitebeard on Videotape.
Willowware Cup.
World was everything that was the case?,
The, *sel.*
Zero hour. Waiting yet again, *sel.*

Merrill, William Pierson
Call to the Strong, The.
Not Alone for Mighty Empire.
Rise Up, O Men of God.

Merriman, Brian
Country's Crisis, The, *sel.*
Husband's Lament, The, *sel.*
Irish Marriage Night, An, *sel.*
Lament of the Unmarried Girl, The, *sel.*
Maiden's Plight, The, *sel.*
Midnight Court, The.
Now God Stand Up for Bastards, *sel.*
Old Man's Tale, The, *sel.*
Solution, The, *sel.*
Walk, *sel.*

Merritt, Dixon Lanier
Limerick: "Wonderful bird is the pelican, A."

Merry, Robert
Sir Roland; a Fragment.

**Merryman, Mildred Plew. See Meigs,
Mildred Plew**

Mersar
Allace! So Sobir Is the Micht.

Merton, Thomas
Aubade: Lake Erie.
Cana.
Dark Morning, The.
Elegy for the Monastery Barn.
In the Year 1945 an Original Child Was Born,
sel.
Lent in a Year of War.
Need to Win, The.
Reader, The.
Responsory, 1948, A.
St. Malachy.
Stranger.
There Has to Be a Jail for Ladies.

Merwin, W. S.
Air.
Animula.
Another Year Come.
Asians Dying, The.
Avoiding News by the River.
Ballad of John Cable and Three Gentlemen.
Ballade of Sayings.
Bathers, The.

Beggars and Kings.
Birds Waking.
Black Jewel, The.
Blind Girl.
Bones, The.
Broken, The.
Burning Mountain.
Burning the Cat.
Burnt Child, The.
Caesar.
Chaff, The.
Colloquy at Peniel.
Come Back.
Daybreak.
December among the Vanished.
Departure's Girl-Friend.
Diggers, The.
Distances, The.
Do Not Die.
Door, A.
Drunk in the Furnace, The.
Dusk in Winter.
Early January.
Elegy: "Who would I show it to."
Evening.
Falcons, The.
Family, A.
Fate.
February.
Fields, The.
Finding a Teacher.
Fly.
Footprints on the Glacier.
For a Coming Extinction.
For Now.
Glass.
Gods, The.
Hearing.
Highway, The.
Home for Thanksgiving.
Hours of a Bridge, The.
In the Winter of My Thirty-eighth Year.
Indigestion of the Vampire, The.
Initiate, The.
It Is March ("It is March and black dust falls
   out of the books").
Judgment of Paris, The.
Late Spring.
Lemuel's Blessing.
Letter.
Leviathan.
Looking for Mushrooms at Sunrise.
Low Fields and Light.
Mariners' Carol.
Master, The.
Moths, The.
Native, The.
Noah's Raven.
Odysseus.
Old Flag.
Old Room, The.
Owl, The.
Piper, The.
Place of Backs, The.
"Portland" Going Out, The.
Resolution.
River of Bees, The.
River Sound Remembered.
Room, The.
Sapphire, The.
Separation.
Sire.
Small Woman on Swallow Street.
Snowfall.
Some Last Questions.
Song of Man Chipping an Arrowhead.
Spring.
Stairs.
Sunset after Rain.
Surf-casting.
Tergvinder's Stone.
Thorn Leaves in March.

To My Brother Hanson.
Trail into Kansas, The.
Variation on the Gothic Spiral.
Vineyard, The.
Voice.
War, The.
Watchers.
When I Came from Colchis.
When the War Is Over.
When You Go Away.
Whenever I Go There.
Widow, The.
Yesterday.
You, Genoese Mariner.
Merwin, William Stanley
Approaches, The.
Black Plateau, The.
Bread.
Carol of the Three Kings.
Dead Hand.
December Night.
December: Of Aphrodite.
Divinities.
Door, A.
Exercise.
For the Anniversary of My Death.
Grandfather in the Old Men's Home.
Grandmother and Grandson.
Grandmother Watching at Her Window.
Herds, The.
Last One, The.
Mountain, The.
Old Boast, The.
Peasant.
Plea for a Captive.
Sea Monster.
Song of Three Smiles.
Students of Justice, The.
Things.
To the Hand.
Waving of a Hand, The.
Way to the River, The.
We Continue.
White Goat, White Ram.
Witnesses.
Mesens, E. L. T.
Arid Husband, The.
Meshimori, Yadoyano. *See* **Yadoyano
   Meshimori**
Messinger, Robert Hinckley
Winter Wish, A.
Metastasio, Pietro
Age of Gold.
Metz, Jerred
Angels in the House.
Divination.
Her True Body.
Speak like Rain.
Metz, Roberta
Exactly.
Mew, Charlotte
À Quoi Bon Dire.
Absence.
Again.
Beside the Bed.
Cenotaph, The.
Changeling, The.
Domus Caedet Arborem.
Fame.
Farmer's Bride, The.
Here Lies a Prisoner.
I Have Been through the Gates.
I So Liked Spring.
In Nunhead Cemetery.
In the Fields.
Le Sacré-Coeur.
Not for That City.
Old Shepherd's Prayer.
On the Asylum Road.
On the Road to the Sea.
Quiet House, The.

Rambling Sailor, The.
Rooms.
Saturday Market.
Saturday Market ("In Saturday Market, there's
   eggs a-plenty"), *sel.*
Sea Love.
Smile, Death.
Song: "Love, love today, my dear."
To a Child in Death.
Trees Are Down, The.
Meyer, Conny Hannes
Beast That Rode the Unicorn, The.
Of the Beloved Caravan.
Meyer, Gerard Previn
S. T. Coleridge Dismisses a Caller from
   Porlock.
Meyers, Bert
Dark Birds, The.
Daybreak.
Funeral.
Garlic, The.
Pigeons.
Stars Climb Girders of Light.
Suburban Dusk.
When I Came to Israel.
Meyette, Terri
Celebration 1982.
Trading Post—Winslow, Arizona.
Meynell, Alice (Mrs. Wilfrid Meynell)
After a Parting.
At Night.
Chimes.
Christ in the Universe.
Cradle-Song at Twilight.
Easter Night.
Father of Women, A.
Fugitive, The.
General Communion, A.
"I Am the Way."
In Portugal, 1912.
In Sleep.
Lady Poverty, The.
Launch, The.
Letter from a Girl to Her Own Old Age, A.
Maternity.
November Blue.
October Redbreast, The.
Poet to the Birds, The.
Rainy Summer, The.
Renouncement.
Roaring Frost, The.
Shepherdess, The.
Singers to Come.
Song of Derivations, A.
Song of the Night at Daybreak.
Summer in England, 1914.
Thoughts in Separation.
Threshing Machine, The.
Thrush before Dawn, A.
To a Daisy.
To the Body.
Two Questions, The.
Veni Creator.
Via, Veritas, et Vita.
Wind Is Blind, The.
Young Neophyte, The.
Meynell, Viola
Frozen Ocean, The.
Meynell, Wilfrid
Folded Flock, The.
Meyrich, Geraldine
Washington.
Mezey, Robert
After Hours.
Against Seasons.
April Fourth.
Back.
Bedtime Story, A.
Being a Giant.
Confession, A.
Couplets, XX.

Evening, An.
Friendship, The.
How Much Longer?
I Am Here.
In Defense of Felons.
In the Environs of the Funeral Home.
In the Soul Hour.
In your watercolor, Nely Silvínová, sel.
Lovemaker, The.
My Mother.
New Year's Eve in Solitude.
Night on Clinton.
No Country You Remember.
One Summer.
Reaching the Horizon.
Salesman, The.
Simpler Thing, a Chair, A.
Street Scene.
There.
To Her.
Touch It.
Underground Gardens, The.
Vetus Flamma.
Wandering Jew, The.
White Blossoms.
You Could Say.

Mhac an tSaoi, Máire
First Shoe, The.
Harvest of the Sea.

Mhone, Guy C. Z.
Chisizas I, The.
Lament to My Mother, A.

Mibu Tadamine
Since that parting.
When the wind blows.

Miccolis, Leila
I wanted to see you,/ thighs showing.
Till Death Do Us Part.

Michael of Kildare, Friar
Swet Jesus.

Michaelis, Hanny
Alarm's Callous Racket, The.
Body, The.
Brilliantly Speculating.
Involuntarily.
Irredeemably Buried.
Listening.
Somewhere in the House.
Three Flights Up.
Under Restless Clouds.
We Carry Eggshells.

Michaels, Mary
Unmarked Ceiling, The.

Michal, M. L.
From Skye, Early Autumn.

Michaux, Henri
Dawn is grey here, she went on to tell him. It
   was not always like this, The, sel.
Education regarding chills is not well handled
   in this country, The, sel.
I add one further word to you, a question
   rather, sel.
I am writing to you from the end of the
   world, sel.
Intervention.
My Occupations.
Repose in Calamity.
She writes to him again, sel.
There are constantly, she told him further,
   lions in the village, sel.
Tomorrow.
We have here, she said, only one sun in the
   month, and for only a little while, sel.
We women here all live with tightened
   throats, sel.
When you walk in the country, she further
   confided to him, sel.

Michel, Concha
Woman, Mother of Man, sel.

Michelangelo Buonarroti
Celestial Love.

Dante.
Doom of Beauty, The.
Eternal Lord! Eased of a Cumbrous Load.
For Inspiration.
From thy fair face I learn, O my loved lord.
Garland and the Girdle, The.
Haven and Last Refuge of My Pain, The.
I know not if from uncreated spheres, sel.
In me is death, in you my life.
Joy May Kill.
Love, the Light-Giver [or To Tommaso de'
   Cavalieri]
"Night" in the Medici Chapel.
On the Brink of Death.
Prayer for Purification, A.
Ravished by all that to the eyes is fair, sel.
Thou knowest, love, I know that thou dost
   know.
To Giovanni da Pistoia on the Painting of the
   Sistine Chapel, 1509.
To Luigi del Riccio, after the Death of
   Cecchino Bracci.
To Pope Julius II.
To Tommaso de' Cavalieri.
To Vittoria Colonna.
Transfiguration of Beauty, The.
With Heart and Breast of Brimstone, Flesh of
   Flax.
Yes! hope may with my strong desire keep
   pace.

Michell, David
Voices.

Michelson, Max
Bird, The.
Hymn to Night, A.

Michie, James
Arizona Nature Myth.
Closing Time.
Discoverer.
Dooley Is a Traitor.
Ghost of an Education, The.
Nine Times.
Three Dreams.
To My Daughter.

Michizane
Autumn Night.
Dreaming of Amaro.
Grieving for the Student Abe.
I Give up Trying to Learn to Play the Lute.
I Stopped along the Road to Look at the Old
   House of Lord Minamoto.
Lamp Goes Out, The.
New Years Day at the Official Lodge.
Ninth Month, Tenth Day.
On a Snowy Night Thinking of the Bamboos
   at Home.
On Lo-tien's Poem on the Three Friends of
   the Northern Window.
On Not Going Out the Gate.
On the Road I Met a White-Haired Old Man.
On Vacation: a Poem to Record My
   Thoughts.
Planting Chrysanthemums.
Plum Blossoms.
Rainy Night.
Reading a Letter from Home.
Sitting in a Circle, Speaking Our Thoughts.
Spider, The.
Sudden Inspiration on a Summer Day.
Surprised by Winter.
Through the Snow to Early Duty at the Office.
To Comfort My Little Son and Daughter.
Weeping for My Elder in Poetry Shimada.
When I Reached the Post Station at Kaya.
When the east wind blows.
Who does the cold come early to?/ It comes
   early to the fisherman, sel.
Who does the cold come early to?/ To the old
   man who lost his wife, sel.

Who does the cold come early to?/ To the
   peasant fled from another province, sel.
Who does the cold come early to?/ To the
   relay station house attendant, sel.
Wind and Rain.

Michizo, Tachihara. See **Tachihara Michizo**

Mickle, William
Sonnet on Passing the Bridge of Alcantra,
   near Lisbon.
While you, my friend, from louring wintry
   plains, sel.

Mickle, William Julius
Cumnor Hall.
Sailor's Wife, The.

Middleton, Christopher
Abasis, sel.
Alba after Six Years.
Ant Sun, The, sel.
Edward Lear in February.
Forenoon, The, sel.
In Some Seer's Cloud Car.
In the Secret House.
Male Torso.
News from Norwood.
Ode on Contemplating Clapham Junction, sel.
Oystercatchers.
Pointed Boots, sel.
Thinking of Hölderlin.
Thousand Things, The.
Waterloo Bridge, sel.

Middleton, Jesse Edgar
Jesous Ahatonhia.

Middleton, Richard
Carol of the Poor Children, The.
On a Dead Child.

Middleton, Thomas
Black spirits and white, red spirits and gray,
   sel.
Here we are, if you have any more, sel.
Midnight, sel.
Noises in the Night.
Parting, sel.
Song: "In a maiden-time professed," sel.
Song: "Love for such a cherry lip," sel.
True Love Ditty, A, sel.
What makes your lip so strange?, sel.

Middleton, Thomas and William Rowley
Song: "Trip it Gipsies, Trip it Fine," sel.

Midlane, Albert
There's a Friend for little children, sel.

Midnight Sun
Canada's Natural Resource.

Mieko, Kanai
House of Madam Juju, The.

Mifflin, Lloyd
Battle-Field, The.
Doors, The.
Fiat Lux.
Flight, The.
Half-Mast.
Milton.
Sesostris.
Ship, The.
Sovereigns, The.
Theseus and Ariadne.
To a Maple Seed.
To the Milkweed.

"Mighty Chalkdust, The"
Brain Drain.

"Mighty Sparrow, The" (Slinger Francisco)
Get to Hell Outa Here.
Yankees Back, The.

Miguel de Guevara
Raise Me Up, Lord.
Sonnet: Time and Account.
Sonnet: To Crucify the Son.

Miki Rofu
After the Kiss.
Home.

Mikisaburo, Rai. *See* **Rai Mikisaburo**
Milaipperun Kantan
What His Friend Said, Teasing the Man in Love.
What She Said ("Only the dim-witted say it's evening").
Milbauer, Joseph
Interior.
Milburn, Ken
Motive for Mercy.
Miles, George Henry
Said the Rose.
Miles, Josephine
Album.
As Difference Blends into Identity.
Belief.
Bibliographer.
Bounty.
Campaign, The.
Care.
Civilian.
Conception.
Day the Winds, The.
Doctor Who Sits at the Bedside of a Rat, The.
Dolor.
Dream.
Entrepreneur chicken shed his tail feathers, surplus, The.
Family.
Fields of Learning.
Find.
Forecast.
Government Injunction.
Gypsy.
Housewife.
I've been going around everywhere without any skin.
Made Shine.
Memorial Day.
Merchant Marine.
Midweek.
Monkey.
Moving In.
None.
Oedipus.
Officers.
On Inhabiting an Orange.
Preliminary to Classroom Lecture.
Purchase of a Blue, Green, or Orange Ode.
Reason.
Ride.
Sale.
Savages, The.
Sisyphus.
So Graven.
Student.
Summer.
Sunday.
Tally.
Voyage.
Miles, Judy
Seasons Greetings, Love and Revolution.
Miles, Susan (Ursula Roberts)
He Sports by Himself.
Microcosmos.
Millard, Edith G.
Banbury Fair.
Millard, Geoffrey C.
Hospital.
Millay, Edna St. Vincent ("Nancy Boyd")
Above These Cares.
Afternoon on a Hill.
All I could see from where I stood, *sel.*
Ashes of Life.
Ballad of the Harp-Weaver, The.
Bean-Stalk, The.
Cameo, The.
Childhood Is the Kingdom Where Nobody Dies.
City Trees.
Conscientious Objector.

Counting-out Rhyme.
Departure.
Dirge without Music.
Ebb.
Elegy before Death.
Elegy: "Let them bury your big eyes," *sel.*
End of Summer, The.
Euclid Alone Has Looked on Beauty Bare.
Even in the moment of our earliest kiss.
Exiled.
Feast.
First Fig.
From a Very Little Sphinx.
God's World.
Grown-up.
Hearing your words, and not a word among them.
I, Being Born a Woman and Distressed.
I Do But Ask That You Be Always Fair.
I Dreamed I Moved among the Elysian Fields.
I read with varying degrees, *sel.*
I Shall Forget You Presently, My Dear.
I Shall Go Back.
I Think I Should Have Loved You Presently.
I Too beneath Your Moon, Almighty Sex.
I Will Put Chaos into Fourteen Lines.
In the evening I would sit, *sel.*
In the Grave No Flower.
Justice Denied in Massachusetts.
Lament: "Listen, children:/ Your father is dead."
Look, Edwin!
Love Is Not All, *sel.*
Love is not all; it is not meat nor drink.
Loving You Less than Life, a Little Less.
Men Working.
Moriturus.
My most distinguished guest and learnèd friend.
Never May the Fruit Be Plucked.
Night is my sister, and how deep in love.
Not in a silver casket cool with pearls.
O God, I Cried, No Dark Disguise.
Oh, oh, you will be sorry for that word!
Oh, Sleep Forever in the Latmian Cave.
On Hearing a Symphony of Beethoven.
On the Wide Heath.
Passer Mortuus Est.
Pear Tree, The.
Penitent, The.
Philosopher, The.
Poet and His Book, The.
Portrait by a Neighbor.
Ragged Island.
Recuerdo.
Renascence.
Return, The.
See where Capella with her golden kids, *sel.*
Since of no creature living the last breath.
Snow Storm, The.
Song of a Second April.
Sonnet: And You as Well Must Die, Beloved Dust.
Sonnet: Oh, Think Not I Am Faithful to a Vow!
Sonnet to Gath.
Sonnet XXVIII: "When we are old and these rejoicing veins."
Sonnet XXIX: Pity Me Not [Because the Light of Day]
Sonnet: "Women have loved before as I love now."
Spring.
Strawberry Shrub, The.
Think not, nor for a moment let your mind.
This Beast That Rends Me.
Those Hours When Happy Hours Were My Estate.
Thursday.
Time Does Not Bring Relief.
To a Calvinist in Bali.
To a Young Poet.

To Inez Milholland.
To Jesus on His Birthday.
Travel.
True Encounter, The.
Unexplorer, The.
Visit to the Asylum, A.
What Lips My Lips Have Kissed.
What Rider Spurs Him from the Darkening East.
Wild Swans.
Wraith.
You loved me not at all, but let it go.
Miller, Adam David
Crack in the Wall Holds Flowers.
Hungry Black Child, The.
Miller, Alice Duer
English Are Frosty, The, *sel.*
I Have Loved England, *sel.*
Song: "Light of spring, The."
Sonnet, A: "Dear, if you love me, hold me most your friend."
Miller, Chris
Blue Flag, The.
Miller, Cincinnatus Heiner (Hiner). *See* **Miller, Joaquin**
Miller, E. S.
To My Lady.
Miller, Heather Ross
Girl, Prince, Lizard.
Minor Things.
Miller, Hiner. *See* **Miller, Joaquin**
Miller, J. Corson
Epicedium.
Miller, Jane
Stagger of the Wind That I Think Is Your Turning, The.
Time; or, How the Line about Chagall's Lovers Disappears.
Miller, Jeffrey
Day Glo Question of Identity, The.
Death.
Jeremy.
Sexy Food Stamps.
Truth Made Breakfast, The.
Miller, Jim Wayne
Closing the House.
For Richard Chase.
Hanging Burley.
Hungry Dead, The.
Kinsman, A.
Living with Children.
Rechargeable Dry Cell Poem.
Spring Storm.
Squirrel Stand.
Why Rosalie Did It.
Miller, Joaquin (Cincinnatus Heine Miller)
Alaska.
At the Grave of Walker.
Bravest Battle, The.
By the Pacific Ocean.
Columbus.
Crossing the Plains.
Cuba Libre.
Dead in the Sierras.
Defense of the Alamo, The.
Fortunate Isles, The.
In Men Whom Men Condemn as Ill, *sel.*
Juanita.
Mothers of Men, The.
Peter Cooper.
Rejoice.
Resurge San Francisco.
San Francisco
That Gentle Man from Boston Town.
That Texan Cattle Man.
To Russia.
Twilight at the Heights.
Vaquero.
Voice of the Dove, The.
Washington by the Delaware.

Westward Ho!
William Brown of Oregon.
Miller, Madeleine Sweeny
How Far to Bethlehem?
Miller, Mary Britton
Cat.
Foal.
Shore.
They've All Gone South.
Universe, The.
Where Are You Now?
Miller, May
Gift from Kenya.
Not That Far.
Miller, Peter
Capture of Edwin Alonzo Boyd, The.
Prevention of Stacy Miller, The.
Miller, Ruth
Birds.
Cover my eyes with your palm, *sel.*
Dropped leaf, The, *sel.*
It Is Better to Be Together.
Long Since Last.
Penguin on the Beach.
Plankton.
Sterkfontein.
To eat pain like bread is a condition, *sel.*
Miller, Thomas
Evening.
See yonder smoke, before it curls to heaven, *sel.*
Watercress Seller, The.
Miller, Vassar
Adam's Footprint.
Apology.
At a Child's Baptism.
Autumnal Spring Song.
Beat Poem by an Academic Poet.
Beside a Deathbed.
Bird in the Hand, A.
Bout with Burning.
Ceremony.
Christmas Mourning.
Defense Rests.
Dramatic Monologue in the Speaker's Own Voice.
Epithalamium: "Crept side by side beyond the thresh."
Final Hunger, The.
Fulfillment.
Judas.
Lesson in Detachment, A.
Lord, hush this ego as one stops a bell, *sel.*
Love Song out of Nothing.
On Approaching My Birthday.
Paradox.
Quarry, The.
Receiving Communion.
Reciprocity.
Slump.
Spastic Child.
Spinster's Lullaby.
Subterfuge.
Though He Slay Me.
Tree of Silence, The.
Trimming the Sails.
Without Ceremony.
Worshiper, The.
Miller, William
Wee Willie Winkie rins [Hiner]
Millett, William
I Am Ham Melanite.
Milligan, Spike
Baby Sardine, A.
Bongaloo, The.
Cat Will Rhyme with Hat.
Christmas 1970.
Gofongo, The.
Hipporhinostricow.
Look at All Those Monkeys.
My Sister Laura.

On the Ning Nang Nong.
Tell Me Little Woodworm.
Thousand Hairy Savages, A.
You Must Never Bath in an Irish Stew.
Millikin, Richard Alfred
Groves of Blarney, The.
Mills, Ida M.
At Breakfast.
In Days Gone By.
Mills, Mary
Pedigree.
Postscript.
Mills, William
Motel.
Necessity of Falling, The.
Pity.
Rituals along the Arkansas.
Unemployment.
Mills, William G.
Arise, O Glorious Zion.
Millward, Pamela
Just as the Small Waves Came Where No Waves Were.
Milne, Alan Alexander
At the Zoo.
Ballad of Private Chadd, The.
Buckingham Palace.
Disobedience.
Forgiven.
Four Friends, The.
Halfway Down.
Hoppity.
If I Were King.
King's Breakfast, The.
Lines Written by a Bear of Very Little Brain.
Miss James.
Missing.
More It Snows, The.
Old Sailor, The.
Puppy and I.
Teddy Bear.
Three Foxes, The.
Us Two.
Vespers.
Milne, Ewart
Deirdre and the Poets.
Diamond Cut Diamond.
Dublin Bay.
Hills of Pomeroy, The.
In a Valley of this Restless Mind.
Martyred Earth, The.
Sierran Vigil.
Vanessa Vanessa.
Milne, J. C.
Dolomites.
Faur Wid I Dee?
Feels.
Lairig, The.
Patriot, The.
Milne, Angela. *See* **"Ande"**
Milner, B. E.
Christmas Night.
Milner-Brown, A. L.
Who Knows?
Milnes, Richard Monckton, 1st Baron Houghton
Columbus and the Mayflower.
Corfou, *sel.*
England and America, 1863.
Good Night and Good Morning.
Lady Moon.
Men of Old, The.
Our Mother Tongue.
Sir Walter Scott at the Tomb of the Stuarts in St. Peter's.
Tranquil above the rapids, rocks, and shoals, *sel.*
Milns, William
Federal Constitution, The.
Milosz, Czeslaw
Advice.

Ars Poetica?
Between her and me there was a table, *sel.*
Bobo, a nasty boy, was changed into a fly, *sel.*
Cabeza, if anyone knew all about civilization, it was you, *sel.*
Consciousness ("Consciousness enclosed in itself every separate birch").
Dedication: "You whom I could not save."
Elegy for N. N.
Esse.
Fall, The.
I liked him as he did not look for an ideal object, *sel.*
If I had to tell what the world is for me, *sel.*
Into the Tree.
Magic Mountain, A.
On the Other Side.
Paulina, her room behind the servants' quarters, *sel.*
Poet at Seventy.
Poor Christian Looks at the Ghetto, A.
Proof.
Song on the End of the World, A.
Stanzas: On Prayer.
They are so persistent, that give them a few stones, *sel.*
To Raja Rao.
"With their chins high, girls come back from the tennis courts," *sel.*
Milosz, O. V. de L.
H.
King Don Luis.
L'étrangère.
Strophes.
When She Comes.
Milton, John
Adam the goodliest man of men since born, *sel.*
All Is Best, *sel.*
And God created the great whales, and each, *sel.*
And God said, let the waters generate, *sel.*
Another side, umbrageous grots and caves, *sel.*
As when a Scout/ through dark and desert wayes with peril gone, *sel.*
At a Solemn Music [k]
At thy nativity a glorious quire, *sel.*
Ay me! whilst thee the shores and sounding seas, *sel.*
Be it so, for I submit; his doom is fair, *sel.*
Beneath him with new wonder now he views, *sel.*
Birds their quire apply; airs, vernal airs, The, *sel.*
Blest pair of Sirens, pledges of Heaven's joy, *sel.*
Blindness of Samson, The, *sel.*
Brandish't sword of God before them blaz'd, The, *sel.*
But he his wonted pride, *sel.*
But peaceful was the night, *sel.*
But see here comes thy reverend Sire, *sel.*
Chastity, *sel.*
Come, come, no time for lamentation now, *sel.*
Comus.
Comus's Praise of Nature, *sel.*
Delilah, *sel.*
Descend from Heav'n Urania, by that name, *sel.*
Descended, Adam to the bower where Eve, *sel.*
Dungeon horrible, on all sides round, A, *sel.*
Earth was form'd, but in the womb as yet, The, *sel.*
Echo, *sel.*
Egypt, divided by the river Nile, *sel.*
Epitaph on the Marchioness of Winchester, An.

Father, Thy word is past, man shall find grace, *sel.*
Feast and noon grew high, and Sacrifice, The, *sel.*
Fiend/ Saw undelighted all delight, all kind, The, *sel.*
For now too nigh/ The archangel stood, and from the other hill, *sel.*
Forsake me not thus, Adam, witness Heav'n, *sel.*
Hail holy light, ofspring [*or* offspring] of Heav'n first born, *sel.*
Hail native language, that by sinews weak, *sel.*
Hail wedded love, mysterious law, true source, *sel.*
Half yet remains unsung, but narrower bound, *sel.*
Haste thee, nymph, and bring with thee, *sel.*
He ceased; and Satan stayed not to reply, *sel.*
He ended, and they both descend the hill, *sel.*
He ended; and thus Adam last replied, *sel.*
He scarce had ceas't when the superior Fiend, *sel.*
He stood and call'd/ His legions, angel forms, who lay intranced, *sel.*
Hell ("At once with him they rose"), *sel.*
Her long with ardent look his eye pursu'd, *sel.*
Heroic Vengeance, *sel.*
High on a throne of royal state, which far, *sel.*
His pride/ Had cast him out from Heaven, with all his host, *sel.*
How shall I behold the face, *sel.*
How Soon Hath Time [the Subtle Thief of Youth]
How to th' ascent of that steep savage hill, *sel.*
Hymn on the Morning of Christ's Nativity [*or* On the Morning of Christ's Nativity], *sel.*
If thou beest he; but O how fall'n! how chang'd, *sel.*
Il Penseroso.
In bower and field he sought, where any tuft, *sel.*
Into thir inmost bower, *sel.*
Is this the region, this the soil, the clime, *sel.*
It was the hour of night, when thus the Son, *sel.*
Lady That in the Prime.
L'Allegro.
Last Came, and Last Did Go, *sel.*
Let me obtain forgiveness of thee, Samson, *sel.*
Let Us with a Gladsome Mind.
Look once more ere we leave this specular Mount, *sel.*
Love thou saist, *sel.*
Lycidas.
Magi, The, *sel.*
"Me miserable! which way shall I fly", *sel.*
Meanwhile the adversary of God and man, *sel.*
Meanwhile the tepid caves and fens and shores, *sel.*
Messiah, The ("So they in Heav'n their odes and vigils tun'd"), *sel.*
My author and disposer, what thou biddest, *sel.*
Next came one/ Who mourn'd in earnest, *sel.*
No more of talk where God or Angel Guest, *sel.*
No sooner had th' Almighty ceas't, but all, *sel.*
Now came still evening on, and twilight gray, *sel.*
Now had th' Almighty Father from above, *sel.*
Now Morn her rosy steps in the eastern clime, *sel.*

Nymphs and Shepherds, *sel.*
O favorable spirit, propitious guest, *sel.*
O for that warning voice, which he who saw, *sel.*
O hell! what do mine eyes with grief behold!, *sel.*
O thou in heaven and earth the only place, *sel.*
O thou that with surpassing glory crown'd, *sel.*
O'er [*or* O're] the smooth enameled green, *sel.*
Of man's first disobedience, and the fruit, *sel.*
Oh [*or* O], how comely it is, and how reviving, *sel.*
Oh, why did God,/ Creator wise, *sel.*
On His Deceased Wife.
On Shakespeare.
On the Detraction Which Followed upon My Writing Certain Treatises.
On the Detraction Which Followed upon My Writing Certain Treatises.
On the Late Massacre *or* Massacher in Piedmont *or* Piemont.
On the Lord Gen. Fairfax at the Siege of Colchester.
On the New Forcers of Conscience Under the Long Parliment.
On the Oxford Carrier.
On the University Carrier (Who Sickn'd in the Time of His Vacancy).
On Time.
Parthians, The ("He look't and saw what numbers numberless"), *sel.*
Pensive here I sat, *sel.*
Psalm LXXXIV.
Rivers Arise; a Fragment.
Rome ("The City which thou seest no other deem"), *sel.*
Sabrina, *sel.*
Sabrina Fair, *sel.*
Samson before the Prison in Gaza, *sel.*
Satan's Guile ("Whom thus answer'd th' Arch Fiend now undisguis'd"), *sel.*
She, as a veil down to the slender waist, *sel.*
So passed they naked on, nor shunned the sight, *sel.*
So Satan spake, and him Beëlzebub, *sel.*
So spake our Mother Eve, and Adam heard, *sel.*
So spake th' archangel Michael; then paused, *sel.*
So spake the enemy of mankind, enclosed, *sel.*
So spake the godlike power, and thus our sire, *sel.*
So stretched out huge in length the Arch-Fiend lay, *sel.*
So to the sylvan lodge, *sel.*
Song on [*or* of] May Morning.
Sonnet: On the Religious Memorie of Mrs. Catherine Thomason My Christian Freind Deceas'd Decem. 1646.
Sonnet: To Mr. Lawrence.
Standing on Earth ("Standing on Earth, not rapt above the Pole"), *sel.*
Star That Bids the Shepherd Fold, The, *sel.*
Stygian council thus dissolved; and forth, The, *sel.*
Sweet bird that shunn'st the noise of folly, *sel.*
Sweet is the breath of Morn, her rising sweet, *sel.*
Table Richly Spread, A, *sel.*
Temperance and Virginity, *sel.*
Th' other way Satan went down, *sel.*
Then both ourselves and seed at once to free, *sel.*
There Leviathan/ Hugest of living creatures, on the deep, *sel.*
There stood a hill not far whose grisly top, *sel.*

There the companions of his fall, o'erwhelmed, *sel.*
Therefore let pass, as they are transitory, *sel.*
These are thy glorious works, Parent of good, *sel.*
They ended parle, and both addressed for fight, *sel.*
This having learnt, thou hast attaind the summe, *sel.*
This, this is he; softly a while, *sel.*
Thus Adam himself lamented loud, *sel.*
Thus began/ Outrage from lifeless things; but Discord first, *sel.*
Thus Belial with words clothed in reason's garb, *sel.*
Thus saying, from her husband's hand her hand, *sel.*
Thus saying, from her side the fatal key, *sel.*
Thus talking hand in hand alone they pass'd, *sel.*
Thus they in Heav'n, above the starry sphear, *sel.*
To Cyriack Skinner ("Cyriack, whose grandsire").
To Mr. Cyriack Skinner upon His Blindness.
To Mr. H. Lawes on His Airs.
To Sir Henry Vane the Younger.
To the Lady Margaret Ley.
To the Lord General Cromwell.
To the ocean now I fly, *sel.*
To whom thus also th' angel last replied, *sel.*
To whom thus Michael. Justly thou abhorr'st, *sel.*
To whom thus Michael. Those whom last thou saw'st, *sel.*
Transcendence of God, The, *sel.*
True and False Glory ("To whom our Saviour calmly thus reply'd"), *sel.*
Uriel to his charge/ Returned on that bright beam, *sel.*
Ways of God to Men, The, *sel.*
Weep no more, woful shepherds weep no more, *sel.*
What Though the Field Be Lost?, *sel.*
What Words Have Passed, *sel.*
When I Consider How My Light Is Spent.
When the Assault Was Intended to the City.
While thus he spake, th' Angelic Squadron bright, *sel.*
Wilt thou then serve the Philistines with that gift, *sel.*
With thee conversing, I forget all time, *sel.*
Woman, *sel.*

Mimnermus
Youth and Age.
Minamoto no Kanemasa. *See* **Kanemasa**
Minamoto no Muneyuki. *See* **Muneyuki**
Minamoto no Sanetomo. *See* **Sanetomo**
Minamoto no Shigeyuki. *See* **Shigeyuki**
Minamoto no Shitago. *See* **Shitago**
Minamoto no Toshiyori. *See* **Toshiyori**
Minar, Scott
Luminare.
Minarik, Else Holmelund
Little Seeds.
When Mosquitoes Make a Meal.
Minck, Peter
Pain Paint.
Minor, James
Gid dy/ up gid/ dy up.
Minoru, Yoshioka. *See* **Yoshioka Minoru**
Minot, Laurence
Burgesses of Calais, The.
"Minsky, Nicolai Maksimovich" (Nicolai Maksimovich Vilenkin)
Immortality.
Minthorn, Phillip Yellowhawk
Daybreak.
Earth Cycle Dream, The.
From Which War.

This Earth.
Vigil of the Wounded.
Minty, Judith
Burning against the Wind.
End of Summer, The.
Legacy, The.
Letters to My Daughters, No. 3.
Look to the Back of the Hand.
Making Music.
Orchids.
Prowling the Ridge.
Waiting for the Transformation.
Wounds.
Mir, Mohammad Taqi
As a mirror on which has set.
Ask me not of the heart's.
At every step there was.
At times the rose, at times the hue.
Be not deceived by the surge.
Beggar I came and cried my say, A.
Between the two main destinations.
Borrowed is all glory.
Caressing one another noise.
Clanking of the chain is now, The.
Come into the garden.
Commodity of the heart, The.
Crowd of love's torments, A.
Cup's rotation has, The.
Did I not tell you, avoid the path.
Entire garden of the world, The.
Ever since the heart was created.
For days the thought of parting.
From door to door in the land of love.
Heart has like a mirror, The.
Heart was always the enemy, The.
Heart was filled to flowing, The.
Her drunken eye led to the ruin.
His ways are strange: sometimes.
How much had happened on the earth.
I chanced to see one day.
I could not save the heart.
I did see the moth go up.
I grieve in my frenzy for the heart.
I never knew happiness.
If ever sad and lonely Mir.
If one has the eye this world.
If pure is the heart why should it not.
If you have yourself come to God.
If you like to visit the garden, go.
In endless caravans had men.
In every street and bylane.
In one breath you have consumed.
Instead of oil love feeds.
It is no longer one whose noise.
It matters not, O breeze.
It was but until yesterday.
It was in search of they you lost.
It's all dust like the quicksand.
It's only the dawn of love, the way winds up
    the hill.
I've known the indifference.
Kingdom of the heart, The.
Last night I heard a strange.
Last night within my dream.
Locked up within the prison I.
Look at the bulbul and the rose.
Lost in dream I slept.
Love is pain and cure.
Love's secret had remained concealed.
May it be you or I.
Moments of happiness, The.
My eyes are dry of tears.
My heart could never win your heart.
My heart is filled to overflowing.
My heart's afflictions and its pain.
My precious life was spent.
My tale remained, alas, untold within my
    heart.
Neither does the heart remain.
None knows since when the sea.
Nonexistent are men.
Nowhere did I ever meet.

O keeper of the tavern.
Object of creation, The.
Object of our search, The.
Of the flaming rose, The.
On whose assurance shall I pass.
One day I walked into the shop of those who
    blow the glass.
Our life is like a bubble.
Put each step here.
Remained I all my life.
Right from the evening it burns.
Serenely I walked along my own.
Since I've assumed this form of life.
Sorrow of parting, unfulfilled, The.
Spring of life is only a wink, The.
Strange appears the garden.
Swirling in circles I see.
That leaven of my soul is like.
This is the time when fresh, green leaves.
This world is not, as you may think.
Thousand words lie under the dust, A.
Upturned were cups and spilt.
Victims of that warrior, The.
We are travelers along the road.
We could not laugh or open out.
We should have freely known the garden.
We travelers on the road to death.
We're not as simple as we seem.
What is the life of the rose?
What matters it, O breeze.
When in the throes of madness.
Who am I, my fellow beings?
Whoever in this tavern.
Whoever safely went.
Why should one care to unpack.
Without you, O Saki, never could I.
World is only conjectural, The.
Yesterday I chanced to step.
You'll only make me sad.
Mira Bai. *See* **Mirabai**
Mirabai (*or* **Mira Bai**)
At the Holi festival of color.
Bhil woman tasted them, plum after plum,
    The.
Clouds, The.
Friend, don't be angry.
Friend, how can I meet my lord?
Go to where my loved one lives.
Hari helps his people.
Hari, look at me a while.
Hey love bird, crying cuckoo.
I can't break with the Dark One.
I don't sleep. All night.
I have talked to you, talked.
I saw the dark clouds burst.
I'm colored with the color of dusk, oh *rana*.
Keep me as your servant, O Girdhar.
Let me see you.
Let us go to a realm beyond going.
Life without Hari is no life, friend.
Mira is dancing with bells tied on her ankles.
Murali sounds on the banks of the Jumna.
My eyes are thirsty.
My love is in my house.
O King, I know you gave me poison.
Oh, the yogi—/ my friend, that clever one.
Rana, I know you gave me poison.
Rana, why do you treat me as your enemy?
Sister, I had a dream that I wed.
Today your Hari is coming.
Wake, child with the flute.
Wake up, dear boy that holds the flute!
Why Mira Can't Go Back to Her Old House.
Yogi, don't go away.
"Miraji"
Progress.
Waves of Pleasure.
Miranda, Gary
Horse Chestnut.
Love Poem: "Kind of slant—the way a ball
    will glance, A."
Magician, The.

Mirikitani, Janice
Breaking Silence.
Breaking Tradition.
Sing with Your Body.
Miroń, Salvador Diáz. *See* **Diáz Miroń,**
    Salvador
Mish, Charlotte
Stray Dog.
Mistral, Frédéric
Cocooning, The, *sel.*
Leaf-picking, The.
Mares of the Camargue, The, *sel.*
Mistral, Gabriela (**Lucila Godoy Alcayaga**)
Alien, The.
Ballad: "He went with another."
Bread.
Death Sonnet I.
Drops of Gall.
Dusk.
Emigré Jewess.
Everything Is Round.
Little Girl That Lost a Finger, The.
Midnight.
Rocking My Child.
Silent Love.
Sister.
Sleep Close to Me.
Slow Rain.
Stranger.
To Drink.
To Noel.
Vase, The.
Mitcalfe, Barry
Lamentation on Ninety-Mile Beach.
Mitcham, Judson
Where We Are.
Mitchell
Net of Moon, The.
Mitchell, Adrian
Accountant in His Bath, The ("The accountant
    dried his imperfect back").
Another Prince Is Born.
Autobahnmotorwayautoroute.
Beatrix Is Three.
Beggar, The.
Calypso's Song to Ulyssess.
Celia Celia.
Fifteen Million Plastic Bags.
Giving Potatoes.
Norman Morrison.
Private Transport.
Quite Apart from the Holy Ghost.
Remember Suez?
Riddle: "Their tongues are knives, their forks
    are hands and feet."
Song in Space.
To Whom It May Concern.
Watch Your Step—I'm Drenched.
Mitchell, Archie
Hills of the Middle Distance.
Mitchell, Cynthia
Frog and a Flea, A.
Mitchell, Cyprus R.
Soul of Jesus Is Restless, The.
Mitchell, David
At Pakiri Beach.
My Lai/ Remuera/ Ponsonby.
Ponsonby/Remuera/My lai.
Silences.
Van Gogh.
Windfall.
Mitchell, Elma
Good Old Days.
Thoughts after Ruskin.
Mitchell, Emerson Blackhorse
Four Directions, The.
Miracle Hill.
New Direction, The.
Path I Must Travel, The.

Mitchell, Frank
13th Horse Song of Frank Mitchell (White), The.
12th Horse Song of Frank Mitchell (Blue), The.
Mitchell, James
Gay Epiphany.
Mitchell, John
Reply to "In Flanders Fields."
Mitchell, John Hanlon
City Song, A.
Farm Wife.
Mitchell, Jonathan
On the Following Work and Its Author.
Mitchell, Joni
Woodstock.
Mitchell, Langdon Elwyn
Carol: "Mary, the mother, sits on the hill."
Fear.
Purpose, sel.
Sweets That Die.
Technique, sel.
To One Being Old.
Wayside Virgin, The.
Written at the End of a Book.
Mitchell, Larry
Faggots and their friends now live in Ramrod, The.
Men love papers, The. They love to sign them, file them and.
Men spread disease among the faggots, one of the things they, The.
Sons and Fathers.
Women Wisdom.
Mitchell, Lorna
Hermaphrodite's Song, The.
Mitchell, Lucy Sprague
Back and Forth.
House of the Mouse, The.
Mitchell, Matthew
Printing Jenny ("Printing Bibles is Jenny's daily chore").
Mitchell, Noah
Those Not Confused Are Prisoners of War.
Mitchell, Silas Weir
Decanter of Madeira, Aged 86, to George Bancroft, Aged 86, A.
Herndon.
How the *Cumberland* Went Down.
Idleness.
Kearsarge.
Lincoln.
Of One Who Seemed to Have Failed.
On a Boy's First Reading of "King Henry V."
Quaker Graveyard, The.
Song of the Flags, The.
To a Magnolia Flower in the Garden of the Armenian Convent at Venice.
Vespers.
Mitchell, Stephen
Abraham.
Adam in Love.
Jacob and the Angel.
Mitchell, Susan
Blackbirds.
Boone.
Bread.
From the Journals of the Frog Prince.
Once, Driving West of Billings, Montana.
Story, A.
Mitchell, Susan Langstaff
Descent of the Child, The.
Immortality.
Mitchell, Waddie
Book, The.
Throw-Back, The.
Mitchell, Walter
Tacking Ship Off Shore.
Mitchison, Naomi
1943.

Boar of Badenoch and the Sow of Atholl, The.
Buachaille Etive Mor and Buachaille Etive Beag.
Farm Woman: 1942, The.
Webster Ross.
Mitsuharu, Kaneko. *See* **Kaneko Mitsuharu**
Mitsuhashi Takajo
Hair ornament of the sun, The.
Mitsui, Jim
Graffiti in a University Restroom: "Killing People Is Easier than Writing Poetry."
Letter to Tina Koyama from Elliot Bay Park.
Mexico City, 150 Pesos to the Dollar.
Shakuhachi.
When Father Came Home for Lunch.
Mitsune
At the great sky.
Blowing wind, The.
End of my journey, The.
I must grope as I pick.
Mitsuye Yamada
In the Outhouse, sel.
On the Bus, sel.
Mitterer, Erika
Departure.
Dialogue.
Lord, The.
Portrait of an Old Man.
Seventh Answer.
Third Letter.
Miu Hsi
Poem in the Form of a Coffin-Puller's Song ("In life I stroll the capital city.").
Miura Chora
As the evening shower clears, sel.
Brightness: not even a wind blowing, sel.
Brushing aside the clouds, sel.
Delightful at night, quiet during the day, sel.
Even the day with cherries, sel.
Glancing near the hands cutting, sel.
I broil shrimp and play with my illness, sel.
I first see the spring light, sel.
I think of flowers and birds, sel.
I turn to look: everything behind me, sel.
Insect spills its notes, An, sel.
It's dark around the earth mortar, sel.
Moon in the cold, The, sel.
Mountain temple: no one comes, A, sel.
Out of the grass in a storm, sel.
Seeing the stars through a willow, sel.
White chrysanthemum, A, sel.
Miura Chora. *See* **Chora**
Miyazawa Kenji
Bamboo and Oak.
Breeze Comes Filling the Valley, The.
Landscape Inspector, The.
Last Farewell, The.
Night.
November Third.
Okhotsk Elegy.
Prefectural Engineer's Statement Regarding Clouds, The.
Rest.
Snow on Saddle Mountain, The.
Spring and Asura.
Spring Variation.
Traveler.
Miyoshi Tatsuji
Lake.
On the Grass.
Thunder Moth.
Mizer, Ray
To a Loudmouth Pontificator.
Mizuhara Shuoshi
Haiku: "Everywhere, everywhere."
Haiku: "Gathering water-oats."
Haiku: "Pear blossoms."
Haiku: "Reed-warbler, The."
Haiku: "Stars above the peaks."

Mizumura, Kazue
Gently, gently, the wind blows.
Who tossed those golden coins.
Mkalimoto, Ernie
Energy for a New Thang.
Mnthali, Felix
Antonina.
Beauty of Dawn, The.
Resurrection: Fragments.
Riddles of Change, The.
Waiting for the Rain.
Mó, Alonzo Gonzales
Conversations in Mayan.
How Just One Poor Man Lives.
Things That Happen to You.
Wizards.
Mo Shih-lung
Drinking Wine.
Flower Shadows.
Friend Comes to Visit on a Summer Night, A.
Gathering Lotus with Singing Girls.
I Waited for Chuang Hsüan-yüan.
I Went to Gold Mountain to Visit a Ch'an Master.
Meditation Rock, The.
On a Cold Day I Climbed Tiger Hill With Professor Ho.
Saying Good-bye to a Singing Girl.
Saying Good-Bye to Feng the Hermit.
Staying Overnight at Blue Cloud Temple.
To the Monk Wu-hsia.
Mocikiranar
Not Rice, Not Water.
Modena, Leone da
Epitaph: "Implacable angel, The/ Has shot his dart."
Modisane, Bloke
Black Blues.
Blue Black.
Lonely.
Moffatt, Gertrude MacGregor
All Night I Heard.
Moffett, Judith
Diehard.
Hear Now the Fable of the Missing Link.
Mezzo Cammin.
Now or Never.
Price of Wildness, The.
Twinings Orange Pekoe.
Moffitt, John
To Look at Any Thing.
Mohodahi
On the holy day of your going out to war.
Mohr, Joseph
Silent Night! Holy Night!
Moise, Penina *and* **Edward N. Calisch**
God Supreme! To Thee We Pray.
Mokhomo, M. A.
When He Spoke to Me of Love.
Mokichi, Saito. *See* **Saito Mokichi**
Mokuchin Juro
I've remained in Mokuchin thirty years.
Mokurai
In India, Deeply Moved.
Molesworth, Charles
Horned Lizard.
Molière
Tartuffe.
To Monsieur de la Mothe le Vayer.
Moll, Ernest G.
Eagles over the Lambing Paddock.
Gnarled Riverina Gum-Tree, A.
Mollin, Larry
As the World Turns.
Bunky Boy Bunky Boy Who's My Little Bunky Boy.
My Elbow Ancestry.
Signature.
Tubes.
Wash Day.

Molodovsky, Kadya
And Yet.
God of Mercy.
In Life's Stable.
Invitation.
Night Visitors.
Song of the Sabbath.
Stool at the Head of My Bed, A.
White Night.
Women's Songs ("For poor brides who were
  servant girls").
Women's Songs ("I will come to him").

Momaday, N. Scott
Angle of Geese.
Bear, The.
Before an Old Painting of the Crucifixion.
Burning, The.
But Then and There the Sun Bore Down.
Buteo Regalis.
Carriers of the Dream Wheel.
Colors of Night, The.
Comparatives.
Delight Song of Tsoai-Talee, The.
Eagle-Feather Fan, The.
Earth and I Gave You Turquoise.
Fear of Bo-talee, The.
Forms of the Earth at Abiquiu.
Four Notions of Love and Marriage.
Gourd Dancer, The.
North Dakota, North Light.
Pit Viper.
Plainview: 3.
Rainy Mountain Cemetery.
Simile.
Story of a Well-made Shield, The.
To a Child Running with Outstretched Arms
  in Canyon de Chelly.
Trees and Evening Sky.
Walk on the Moon.
Wide Empty Landscape with a Death in the
  Foreground.
Winter Holding off the Coast of North
  America.

Mombert, Alfred
Along the Strand.
Chimera, The.
Idyl: "And my young sweetheart sat at board
  with me."
Sleeping They Bear Me.

Momin, Momin Khan
Elegy on the Death of His Mistress Hoor
  Tal'at.
My heart no longer is.
Nothing on her has any effect.
O Doomsday come, shake up the world.
Spring rain falling on my bed, The.
There was a bond between you and me.
There was a young man who was famed
  among.
Whichever way my loved one's eyes.

Mommu, Emperor
Singing of the Moon.

Monat, Donald
Rhymed Mnemonic of the Forty Counties of
  England.

Monck, Mary
Masque of the Virtues against Love.
On a Romantic Lady.

Monette, Paul
Bathing the Aged.
Degas.
Into the Dark.

Money-Coutts, Francis Burdett
On A Wife.

Monkhouse, Cosmo
Any Soul to Any Body.
Limerick: "There once was a girl of New
  York."
Limerick: "There once was a person of
  Benin."
There Was a Young Lady of Niger, at.

Monks, Arthur W.
Twilight's Last Gleaming.

Monod, Theodore
None of Self and All of Thee.

Monro, Harold
Bird at Dawn, The.
Birth, *sel.*
Bitter Sanctuary.
Carrion, *sel.*
Cat's Meat.
Children of Love.
City-Storm.
Clock.
Dog.
Empty House, The.
Every Thing.
Flower Is Looking, A, *sel.*
Foundered Tram, The.
Fresh Air, The.
God, *sel.*
Goldfish.
Hearthstone.
Hurrier, The.
If Suddenly a Clod of Earth, *sel.*
Living.
London Interior.
Man Carrying Bale.
Midnight Lamentation.
Milk for the Cat.
Nightingale near the House, The.
Officers' Mess (1916).
One Blackbird.
Overheard on a Saltmarsh.
Real Property.
Rebellious Vine, The.
Silent Pool, The.
Solitude.
Street Fight.
Terrible Door, The.
This Our Life.
Thistledown.
Train, The! The twelve o'clock for paradise,
  sel.
Vixen woman, The, *sel.*
Week-end.
When you and I go down, *sel.*
You Live There; I Live Here, *sel.*

Monroe, Harriet
Democracy, *sel.*
Farewell, A: "Good-bye!—no [*or* nay] do not
  grieve that it is over."
Fortunate One, The.
In High Places.
In the Beginning.
Lincoln, *sel.*
Nancy Hanks.
Pine at Timber-Line, The.
Washington, *sel.*

Monsell, John Samuel Bewley
Light of the World.

Montagu, Charles
Story of the Pot and the Kettle, The.

Montagu, Lady Mary Wortley
Answer to a Lady Advising Me to Retirement,
  An.
Be plain in dress and sober in your diet.
Epistle from Mrs. Yonge to Her Husband.
Epitaph: "Here lies John Hughes and Sarah
  Drew."
Farewell to Bath.
Lady's Resolve, The.
Lover; a Ballad, The.
On the Death of Mrs. Bowes.
Receipt to Cure [*or* for] the Vapours, A.
Saturday: The Small-Pox, *sel.*
Such soft ideas all my pains beguile.
Verses Written in the Chiosk at Pera,
  overlooking Constantinople.

Montague, John
Above the Pool.
All Legendary Obstacles.

Answer, The.
Bright Day, A.
Cage, The.
Clear the Way.
Coming Events.
Country Fiddler, The.
Courtyard in Winter.
Dowager.
Drink of Milk, A.
Edge.
11 rue Daguerre.
Falls Funeral.
Flowering Absence, A.
Grafted Tongue, A.
Graveyard in Queens, A.
Herbert Street Revisited.
Hero's Portion.
Lament for the O'Neills.
Last Journey.
Leaping Fire, The.
Like Dolmens Round My Childhood, the Old
  People.
Lost Tradition, A.
Mad Sweeny.
Mother Cat.
Old lady, I now celebrate, *sel.*
Penal Rock: Altamuskin.
People are different, *sel.*
Point, The.
Process.
Return.
Rifled honeycomb, The, *sel.*
Road's End, The, *sel.*
Same Gesture, The.
Silver Flask, The.
Soliloquy on a Southern Strand.
Special Delivery.
Summer Storm.
Sunset, *sel.*
That Room.
Tim.
Tracks.
Trout, The.
Walking Late.
Water Carrier, The.
Welcoming Party, A.
Wild Dog Rose, The.
Windharp.
Witness.
Woodtown Manor.

Montale, Eugenio
Dora Markus.
Gondola that glides, The, *sel.*
Hitler Spring.
I run my hand across your forehead, *sel.*
In the Park.
Inhuman, The.
La Belle Dame Sans Merci.
Little Testament.
Oboe, *sel.*
Reed that sheds its, The, *sel.*
Sunflower, The.
Two in Twilight.
Violins, *sel.*
Wall, The.
Why are you waiting? The squirrel in the pine
  tree, *sel.*
Xenia.
You know this: I must lose you again and
  cannot, *sel.*

Montanhagol, Guillem de
On all sides I see valor pull up short.

Montaudon, the Monk of
By good luck a few days back.
I ascended to heaven again last week.
I like gayety and horsing around.
I was in paradise the other day.
Since Peter of Auvergne once sang.
So you'll know it—what annoys me most, and
  right.

Montemayor, Jorge de
Song: "Shepherd, who can pass such wrong,"
   sel.
Montgomerie, Alexander
About ane bank, where birdis on bewis, *sel.*
Away Vane World.
Cherry and the Slae, The.
Description of Tyme, A.
Night Is Near [*or* Neir] Gone, The.
Royal Palace of the Highest Heaven, The.
Solsequium, The.
To Henry Constable and Henry Keir.
To His Maistres [*or* Mistress]
To R. Hudson.
Montgomerie, William
Author Unknown.
Elegy for William Soutar.
Epitaph: "My brother is skull and skeleton
   now."
Glasgow Street.
Is there no vision in a lovely place?, *sel.*
Stags.
Montgomery, George Edgar
At Night.
Dead Soldier, A.
England.
To a Child.
Montgomery, James
Inspiration, The, *sel.*
Lust of Gold, The, *sel.*
Nativity.
There is a flower, a little flower, *sel.*
There Is a Land.
West Indies, The.
What Is Prayer?
Montgomery, John
America Greets an Alien.
Montgomery, Lucy Maud
Off to the Fishing Ground.
Montgomery, Marion
Second Year, The.
Montgomery, Niall
Eyewash.
Montgomery, U. M.
Grey Brother.
Montgomery, Leslie Alexander. *See* **"Doyle,
   Lynn"**
**Montgomery, Mary Sidney Wroth, Countess
   of.** *See* **Wroth, Mary Sidney, Countess
   of Montgomery**
Montoya, José
Louie.
Mother.
**Montrose, James Graham, 5th Earl and 1st
   Marquess of.** *See* **Graham, James,
   Marquess of Montrose**
Montross, Percy
Oh, My Darling Clementine, *at.*
Monzaemon, Chikamatsu. *See* **Chikamatsu
   Monzaemon**
Moodie, Susanna-Strickland
Canadian Herd-Boy, The.
Indian Summer.
Moody, Minnie Hite
Say This of Horses.
Moody, William Vaughn
Departure, The.
Faded Pictures.
Gloucester Moors.
Harmonics.
I Stood within the Heart of God, *sel.*
Menagerie, The.
No Hint of Stain, *sel.*
Ode in Time of Hesitation, An.
On a Soldier Fallen in the Philippines.
On the River.
Robert Gould Shaw, *sel.*
This earth is not the steadfast place, *sel.*
Mooney, Stephen
Water Color.
Moor, George
Eternale Footeman's Tale, The.

Moore, Charles Leonard
Disenchantment.
Or Ever the Earth Was.
Soul unto Soul Glooms Darling.
Then Shall We See.
Thou Livest, O Soul!
To England.
Moore, Clement Clarke
Lord of Life, All Praise Excelling.
Visit from St. Nicholas, A.
Moore, Edward
Goose, affected, empty, vain, A, *sel.*
To the Right Hon. Henry Pelham.
Moore, George
Sonnet: "Idly she yawned, and threw her
   heavy hair."
Moore, Honor
First Time: 1950.
Ladies and Gentlemen, my mother is, *sel.*
Memoir.
Moore, Janice Townley
At the National Air and Space Museum.
Moore, John Travers
Going Up.
Jet.
Tree Frog, The.
Moore, Julia A.
And now, kind friends, what I have wrote.
Ashtabula Disaster, The.
"Departed Friend, A."
Grand Rapids.
Little Libbie.
"Lord Byron was an Englishman", *sel.*
Sketch of Lord Byron's Life.
Willie's and Nellie's Wish.
Moore, Lilian
Animals Sick of the Plague, The.
Ants Live Here.
Beach Stones.
Bedtime Story.
Chestnuts Are Falling, The.
Cloud Shadow.
Dragon Smoke.
Foghorns ("The foghorns moaned").
Friend.
Ground Hog Day.
Hey, Bug!
Letter to a Friend.
Listen!
Something Is There.
Sunset.
Until I Saw the Sea.
Waking.
Wet.
Wild strawberries/ fatten.
Moore, Marianne
Animals Sick of the Plague, The.
Arctic Ox, The.
Armour's Undermining Modesty.
Arthur Mitchell.
At Rest in the Blast.
Baseball and Writing.
Bird-witted.
Black Earth.
Buffalo, The.
Carriage from Sweden, A.
Charity Overcoming Envy.
Critics and Connoisseurs.
Dream.
Egyptian Pulled Glass Bottle in the Shape of a
   Fish, An.
England.
Enough.
Face, A.
Fish, The.
Four Quartz Crystal Clocks.
Frigate Pelican, The.
Glory.
Granite and Steel.
Grave, A.
He "Digesteth Harde Yron."

Hero, The, *sel.*
His Shield.
Hometown Piece for Messrs. Alston and
   Reese.
I May, I Might, I Must.
Icosasphere, The.
In Distrust of Merits.
In the Public Garden.
Jellyfish, A.
Keeping Their World Large.
Labors of Hercules, The.
Leonardo Da Vinci's.
Love in America.
Marriage.
Mind, Intractable Thing, The.
Mind Is an Enchanting Thing, The.
Monkeys, The.
Nevertheless.
New York.
Nine Nectarines and Other Porcelain.
No Swan So Fine.
O to Be a Dragon.
Old Amusement Park.
Old Tiger.
Pangolin, The.
Paper Nautilus, The.
Past Is the Present, The.
Peter.
Pigeons.
Poetry.
Rigorists.
Roman had an, A/ artist, a freedman, *sel.*
Roses Only.
Saint Nicholas.
St. Valentine.
See in the Midst of Fair Leaves.
Silence.
Snakes, Mongooses, Snake-Charmers and the
   Like.
Spenser's Ireland.
Staff of Aesculapius, The.
Steeple-Jack, The.
Student, The.
Talisman, A.
Tell Me, Tell Me.
That Harp You Play So Well.
Then the Ermine.
To a Chameleon.
To a Snail.
To a Steam Roller.
To Military Progress.
Tom Fool at Jamaica.
W. S. Landor.
Walking-Sticks and Paperweights and
   Watermarks.
What Are Years?
When I Buy Pictures.
Wood Weasel, The.
Moore, Merrill
And to the Young Men.
Book of How, The.
Domestic: Climax.
How She Resolved to Act.
In Magic Words.
It Is Winter, I Know.
Noise That Time Makes, The.
Old Men and Old Women Going Home on the
   Street Car.
Pandora and the Moon.
Shot Who? Jim Lane!
Transfusion.
Undergraduate.
Unknown Man in the Morgue.
Village Noon; Mid-Day Bells.
Warning to One.
Moore, Nicholas
Fivesucked the features of my girl by glory.
Fred Apollus at Fava's.
Incidents in Playfair House.
Island and the Cattle, The.
Little Girl, The.
Love.

Patient, The.
Song: "Little onion lay by the fireplace, A."
Why the British Girls Give In So Easily.

Moore, Richard
Aubade: "Leave me, dawn! I'm in wretched fettle."
Blimps and Nightingales.
Busby, Whose Verse No Piercing Beams, No Rays.
Friends.
It Took TV to Civilize Our Village, *sel.*
Spring.
Suburb Hilltop.
Though the New Teacher Is a Trifle Odd, *sel.*
Unable, Father, Still, to Disavow, *sel.*
Visitors, The.
Willy, enormous Saskatchewan grizzly.

Moore, Rosalie
Catalogue.
Cats sleep fat and walk thin, *sel.*

Moore, Thomas
After dreaming some hours of the land of Cockaigne, *sel.*
Argument, An.
And is there then no earthly place, *sel.*
At length, my Lord, I have the bliss, *sel.*
At the Mid Hour of Night.
Believe Me, If All Those Endearing Young Charms.
Cherries; a Parable, The.
Come, Ye Disconsolate.
Copy of an Intercepted Despatch from His Excellency Don Strepitoso Diabolo.
Dear Harp of My Country.
Did Not.
Duke Is the Lad to Frighten a Lass, The.
Echo.
Epitaph on Robert Southey.
Epitaph on Tuft-Hunter.
Fly to the desert, fly with me, *sel.*
Fragment of a Character.
Fum and Hum, the Two Birds of Royalty.
Garden Song, A.
Glory of God in Creation *or* Thou Art, O God, The.
Go Where Glory Waits Thee.
Golden Hour, The, *sel.*
Hark! the Vesper Hymn Is Stealing.
Harp That Once through Tara's Halls, The.
How Oft Has the Banshee Cried.
I pray you, let us roam no more, *sel.*
I Saw from the Beach.
I Wish I Was by That Dim Lake.
Ill Omens.
Irish Antiquities.
Irish Peasant to His Mistress, The.
Joke Versified, A.
Journey Onwards, The.
Kiss, The.
Lake of the Dismal Swamp, The.
Let Erin Remember the Days of Old.
Light of the Harem [*or* Haram], The, *sel.*
Long, Long Be My Heart with Such Memories Filled.
Love's Young Dream.
Lying.
Meeting of the Waters, The.
Minstrel Boy, The.
Nay, tempt me not to love again, *sel.*
Nonsense.
Of All the Men.
Oft, in the Stilly Night.
Oh! blame not the bard, if he fly to the bowers.
Oh, Breathe Not His Name!
Oh, Come to Me When Daylight Sets.
Oh, Thou! Who Dry'st the Mourner's Tear.
Oh! where's the slave so lowly.
On a Squinting Poetess.
Pastoral Ballad by John Bull, A.
Peri's Lament for Hinda, The, *sel.*
Petition of the Orangemen of Ireland, The.

Pro Patria Mori.
Scene from a Play, Acted at Oxford, Called "Matriculation."
She Is Far from the Land.
Song of Fionnuala, The.
Song of the Evil Spirit of the Woods.
Song: "When the heart's feeling."
Song: "Where is the nymph, whose azure eye."
Sweet Innisfallen.
Take Back the Virgin Page.
Temple to Friendship, A.
Thee, Thee, Only Thee.
They May Rail at This Life.
This Life Is All Chequer'd with Pleasures and Woes.
Thou Art, O God.
Thy Heaven.
Time I've Lost in Wooing, The.
'Tis the Last Rose of Summer.
To———: "When I loved you, I can't but allow."
To Ladies' Eyes.
To Miss———: "With woman's form and woman's tricks."
To My Mother.
To Sir Hudson Lowe.
Tory Pledges.
Venetian Air.
What's My Thought Like?
Young May Moon, The.

Moore, Thomas Sturge
Beautiful Meals.
Before Rereading Shakespeare's Sonnets.
Daughter of Admetus, A.
Death in the Home.
Duet, A.
Dying Swan, The.
Event, The.
From Titian's "Bacchanal" in the Prado at Madrid.
Gazelles, The.
Kindness.
Lubber Breeze.
On Harting Down.
Response to Rimbaud's Later Manner.
Sent from Egypt with a Fair Robe of Tissue to a Sicilian Vinedresser.
Shells.
Silence.
Summer Lightning.
To Silence.
Variation on Ronsard.
Wind's Work.

Moore, Tom Inglis
Comrade in Arms.
Star Drill.

Moore, William H. A.
Dusk Song.
It Was Not Fate.

Moorer, Lizelia Augusta Jenkins
Accompanying a Gift ("From thy patient, who while here").
Accompanying a Gift ("One whose love will never end").
Africa.
Benefits of Sorrow.
Bible, The.
Birthday Wishes to a Husband.
Birthday Wishes to a Minister of the Gospel.
Birthday Wishes to a Physician.
Christmas Eve.
Christmas Tree, The.
Circle, The.
Claflin's Alumni.
Crum Appointment, The.
Dedication Day Poem.
Dialogue, A.
Door of Hope, The.
Duty, or Truth at Work.
Easter; or, Spring-Time.
Emancipation Day.

Eutawville Lynching, The.
Hallowe'en.
Immortality.
In Memoriam of E. B. Clark.
Injustice of the Courts.
Jim Crow Cars.
Legal Mouse, A.
Lela's Charms.
Lines to a Graduate.
Loyalty to the Flag.
Lynching.
Misunderstood.
Mountain Tops.
Must Be Freed.
Negro Ballot, The.
Negro Heroines.
Negro Schools, The.
Notable Dinner, A.
Peonage System, The.
Pharaohs of Today, The.
Prejudice.
Presidents, The.
Price of Disrespect, The.
Refining Fire.
Retribution.
Russia's Resentment.
Social Glass, The.
Social Life, The.
Song of the Angels.
Southern Press, The.
Southern Pulpit, The.
Southern Work of Dr. and Mrs. L. M. Dunton.
Sympathy.
Thanksgiving.
Tree of Knowledge, The.
Truth Suppressed, The.
Voice of the Negro, The.
What We Teach at Claflin.
Whisper Words of Love to Me.
Why Is It?
Why Negroes Don't Unite.
Why We Meet.

Moraes, Dom
Final Word, The.
Girl.
Lullaby: "With lights for eyes, our city turns."
Queen.
Santa Claus.
Song: "Gross sun squats above, The."

Moraes, Vinícius de
Christmas Poem.
Pear, The.
Song: "Never take her away."
Sonnet of Intimacy.
Sonnet on Fidelity.
Sonnet on Separation.
Woman Recipe.

Moraff, Barbara
Let us suppose the mind.

Moraga, Cherríe
Feed the Mexican Back into Her.
For You, Mamá.

Morales Santos, Francisco
Great Figure, The.

Moran, Mary
Barbara.
I Picked Up Your Cast Away Hide.
Thanksgiving Dinner during Pelting Season.

Moran, Michael ("Zozimus")
Pharao's Daughter.

Mordaunt, Charles, Earl of Peterborough
I Said to My Heart.

Mordaunt, Thomas Osbert
Sound, Sound the Clarion, *sel.*

Mordecai ben Isaac
Fair Thou Art.
Rock of My Salvation.

Mordecai, Pamela
For Eyes to Bless You.

Shooting the Horses.
Tell Me.

Morden, Phyllis B.
Godmother.

More, Hannah
Riddle, A: "I'm a strange contradiction; I'm new, and I'm old."
Riot; or, Half a Loaf Is Better than No Bread, The.
Solitude, *sel.*

More, Helen F.
What's in a Name?

More, Henry
Argument of Democritus Platonissans, or the Infinitie of Worlds, The.
Hymne in Honour of Those Two Despised Virtues, Charitie and Humilitie, An.

More, Sir Thomas (Saint Thomas More)
Consider Well.
I Am Called Childhood.
Lewis, the Lost Lover.
Mery Gest How a Sergeaunt Wolde Lerne to Be A Frere, A.
Pageant Verses.
Peace of a Good Mind, The, *sel.*
Rueful Lamentation on the Death of Queen Elizabeth, A.
To Fortune.

Moreh, Shmuel
Melody.
Return, The.
Tree of Hatred, The.

Morejón, Nancy
Black Woman.
Central Park *Some People (3 P.M.).*
I Love My Master.
Mother.
Reason for Poetry, The.
Richard Brought His Flute.
To a Boy.

Moreland, John Richard
Birch Trees.
Faith.

Moreland, Wayne
Sunday Morning.

Moreton, J. B.
Ballad: "Altho' a slave me is born and bred."

Morgan, Albert
Union Man.

Morgan, Angela
Awakening, The.
Choice.
God Prays.
God, the Artist.
Poet, The.
Reality.
Thanksgiving.
Today.
Why hast thou breathed, O God, upon my thoughts, *sel.*
Work; a Song of Triumph ("Work!/ Thank God for the might of it").

Morgan, Edwin
Canedolia.
Computer's First Christmas Card, The.
In Sobieski's Shield.
In the Snack-Bar.
Instamatic.
Instamatic The Moon February 1973.
Poet, The
Second Life, The.
Siesta of a Hungarian Snake.
Spacepoem 3: Off Course.
Strawberries.
To Hugh MacDiarmid.

Morgan, Elizabeth
Caravati's Junkyard.

"Morgan, Emanuel." *See* **Bynner, Witter**

Morgan, Frederick
Christmas Tree, The.
February 11, 1977.

I Saw My Darling.
1904.
Song: "In Ireland, in Ireland."

Morgan, James Appleton
Malum Opus.

Morgan, Jean
Misogynist, The.

Morgan, Robert
Bees Awater.
Bricking the Church.
Buffalo Trace.
Cedar.
Chant Royal.
Concert.
Cow Pissing.
Death Crown.
Elevation.
Face.
Finding an Old Newspaper in the Woods.
Gift of Tongues, The.
Grandma's Bureau.
Hay Scuttle.
Hollow, The.
Horace Kephart.
Lightning Bug.
Mountain Bride.
Passenger Pigeons.
Pumpkin.
Secret Pleasures.
Uncle Robert.
Walnutry.

Morgan, Robin
And blessed be the women who get you through, *sel.*
Invisible Woman, The.
Lesbian Poem.
On the Watergate Women.

Morgan, Sydney, Lady Morgan
Kate Kearney.

Morgan-Browne, L. E.
Purple, White and Green, The.

"Morganwg, Tolo." *See* **Williams, Edward**

Morgenstern, Christian
Aesthete Weasel, The.
Delayed Action.
Fish's Nightsong.
Funnels, The.
Ghost.
Hen, The.
Klabauterwife's Letter.
Knee, The.
Knee on Its Own, The.
Korf's Clock.
Korf's Enchantment.
Midnightmouse, The.
Moonsheep, The.
On the Planet of Flies.
Philosophy Is Born.
Picket Fence, The.
Rabbi, The.
Salmon, The.
Twelve-Elf raises his left hand, The.

Morgridge, Harriet S.
Jack and Jill, *sel.*
Simple Simon.

Morhange, Pierre
Jew.
Lullaby in Auschwitz.

Morice, Dave
Alaskan Drinking Song.

Mörike, [*or* Möricke] Eduard Friedrich
Beauty Rohtraut.
Prayer: "Lord, as thou wilt, bestow."
Soul, Remember This!

Morin, Catherine A.
High June.
Lace Pedlar, The.

Morin, Maud
Bachelors' Buttons.
Shower and Sunshine.

Moritake (Arakida Moritake)
As the morning glory.
Fallen flower I see.
Haiku: "Fallen flowers rise."
Haiku: "Falling flower, The."
Pine Resin.
Summer night.

Moritz, Yunna
In Memory of Francois Rabelais.
Snow-Girl.
Whiteness.

Morley
"Pussy, Pussy Baudrons."

Morley, Christopher
Animal Crackers.
At the Dog Show.
Dial Call.
Elegy Written in a Country Coal-Bin.
Forever Ambrosia.
Gospel of Mr. Pepys, The.
In Honour of Taffy Topaz.
Old Swimmer, The.
Pennsylvania Deutsch.
Plumpuppets, The.
Public Beach (Long Island Sound).
Scuttle, scuttle little roach, *sel.*
Secret Laughter.
Six Weeks Old.
Song for a Little House.
To a Post-Office Inkwell.
Trees, The.
Washing the Dishes.

Morley, David J.
Climbing Zero Gully.

Moroe, Tachibana. *See* **Tachibana Moroe**

Moronelli da Fiorenza, Pier
Canzonetta: A Bitter Song to His Lady.

Morpurgo, Rachel
Song: "Ah, vale of woe, of gloom and darkness moulded."
Sonnet: "My soul surcharged with grief now loud complains."
Woe is me, my soul says, how bitter is my fate.

Morpurgo, Rahel. *See* **Morpurgo, Rachel**

Morra, Isabella di
Since You Have Clipped the Wings of Fine Desire.

Morriën, Adriaan
Gastronomy.
My Parent's House.
Shipwreck.
Use of a Wall Mirror, The.

Morris, Betty
Strath of Kildonan, The.

Morris, Charles
Address to Lady———, Who Asked What the Passion of Love Was?
Country and Town.

Morris, George Hornell
Sailor's Prayer, A.

Morris, George Pope
Jeannie Marsh.
Main-Truck; or, A Leap for Life, The, at.
My Mother's Bible.
Near the Lake.
Pocahontas.
Retort, The.
We Were Boys Together.
Where Hudson's Wave.
Woodman, Spare That Tree.

Morris, Harrison Smith
Destiny.
Fickle Hope.
Lonely-Bird, The.
Mohammed and Seid.
Pine-Tree Buoy, A.
Walt Whitman.

Morris, Harry
Because Thou Did'st Give.
Girod Street Cemetery: New Orleans.
Maine Lake at Night.
Where Lie All the Slain.
Morris, Herbert
Road, The.
Spanish Blue.
This Alice.
Morris, Ida Goldsmith
Give to the Living.
Morris, J. W.
Collusion between a Alegaiter and a
Water-Snaik.
What I Think of Hiawatha.
Morris, Jenny
Sane, Plain, and Tedious to Know.
Terracotta Flower Pot, The.
Morris, John N.
Mirror, The.
Thanksgiving.
Morris, Lewis
Poem of the Frost and Snow.
Morris, Mervyn
Early Rebels, The.
Family Pictures.
For Consciousness.
House-Slave, The.
One, Two.
Peace-Time.
To an Expatriate Friend.
Valley Prince.
Morris, Robert
Level and the Square, The.
Morris, Sir Lewis
Beginnings of Faith, The.
I praise Thee not, with impious pride, *sel.*
'Tis nigh two thousand years, *sel.*
Morris, Thomas
Sapphics: At the Mohawk-Castle, Canada.
Morris, Thomas Lake
California.
Morris, William
Another for the Briar Rose.
Apology, An, *sel.*
Brooding of Sigurd, The, *sel.*
Christ keep the Hollow Land, *sel.*
Day Is Coming, The.
Death Song, A.
Defense of Guenevere, The.
Earthly Paradise, The.
End of May, The.
Fair Is the World.
For the Briar Rose.
From Far Away.
Garden by the Sea, A, *sel.*
Gunnar's Howe above the House at Lithend.
Haystack in the Floods, The.
Iceland First Seen.
Inscription for an Old Bed.
Love is enough: though the World be
a-waning, *sel.*
Masters, in This Hall.
Message of the March Wind, The.
Midways of a walled garden, *sel.*
Near Avalon.
October, *sel.*
Outlanders, The, *sel.*
Pomona.
Prologue: The Wanderers, *sel.*
Riding Together.
Road of Life, The, *sel.*
Shameful Death.
Sigurd Rideth to the Glittering Heath, *sel.*
Song of Jehane du Castel Beau, The, *sel.*
Summer Dawn.
Tapestry Trees.
Two Red Roses across the Moon.
Under a bent when the night was deep, *sel.*
Morris-Jones, John
North Star, The.

Old Age.
Wind's Lament, The.
Morrison, Lillian
Air Traveler.
Burning Bright.
Goodbye Forever.
If my legs cannot move.
Just for One Day.
Knockout, The.
Let's Go, Mets.
Lobster Cove Shindig.
Nine Triads.
On the Sidelines.
Ratio.
Sailing, Sailing.
Sidewalk Racer; or, On the Skateboard, The.
Surf.
Too Slow.
Water's Edge.
Morrison, M. T.
What the Choir Sang about the New Bonnet.
Morrison, Mary
Nobody Knows but Mother.
Morse, Carl
Dream of the Artfairy.
Fairy Straighttalk.
Scenes of Childhood.
Morse, James Herbert
Brook Song.
His Statement of the Case.
Silence.
Wayside, The.
Wild Geese, The.
Morse, Samuel French
Song in the Cold Season.
Morstein, Petra von
For one who says he feels.
In the Case of Lobsters.
Justice.
Thing Poem.
Mortensen, Vern
Range Cow in Winter.
Morton, David
Beyond Wars.
Dead, The.
Epitaph in Sirmio.
Touring.
Who Walks with Beauty.
Morton, John Bingham ("Beachcomber")
Another Canto.
Dancing Cabman, The.
Epitaph: "Glassblower lies here at rest, A."
Epitaph: "Tread softly; bid a solemn music
sound."
Health and Fitness.
Let poets praise the softer winds of spring.
Now We Are Sick, *sel.*
Someone Asked the Publisher, *sel.*
Song of the Ballet.
Theobald James, *sel.*
Morton, May
To a Barrage Balloon.
Morton, Sarah Wentworth
To Aaron Burr, under Trial for High Treason.
Morton, Thomas
Carmen Elegiacum.
Epitaph: "Time that bringes all things to
light."
New Canaans Genius; Epilogus.
New English Canaan; Prologue.
Poem, The: "I sing th' adventures of mine
worthy wights."
Poem, The: "Rise Oedipus, and if thou canst
unfould."
Poem, The: "What ailes Pigmalion? Is it
lunacy."
Song, The: "Drinke and be merry, merry,
merry boyes."

Morus, Huw
In Praise of a Girl.
Moryson, Fynes
To thee, dear Henry Morison.
Moschus
Cupid Turned Plowman.
Lament for Bion.
Ocean, The.
Pan loved his neighbour Echo—but that child.
Moses, Daniel David
Corn, The.
Party Favour.
Report on Her Remains.
Some Grand River Blues.
Moses, William Robert
American History.
Angina Pectoris.
Big Dam.
Boy at Target Practice; a Contemplation.
Old Theme.
Spurt of Literary Criticism, A.
Moskowitz, Cheryl
At Times.
Mosley, Jr, Joseph M.
Black Church on Sunday.
Moss, Howard
Arsenic.
At the Algonquin.
Balcony with Birds, A.
Burning Love Letters.
Cats and Dogs.
Crossing the Park.
Dead Leaf, A.
Elegy for My Father.
Elizabethan Tragedy; a Footnote.
Finding Them Lost.
Front Street.
Game of Chance, A.
Gift to Be Simple, The.
Great Spaces.
Hand, The.
Heaven.
Horror Movie.
It.
King Midas.
King's Speech, The, *sel.*
Lesson from Van Gogh, A.
Lie, The.
Local Places.
Long Island Springs.
Meeting, The.
Morning Glory.
Movies for the Home.
Piano Practice.
Problem in Morals, A.
Pruned Tree, The.
Rain.
Roof Garden, The.
Shall I Compare Thee to a Summer's Day?
Stars.
Still Pond, No More Moving.
Storm Warning.
Summer Gone, A.
To the Islands.
Tourists.
Traction: November 22, 1963.
Tragedy.
Underwood.
Venice.
Water Island.
Winter's End.
Moss, Stanley
Apocrypha.
Branch, The.
Centaur Song.
Central Park West.
God Poem.
Hangman's Love Song, The.
In Front of a Poster of Garibaldi.
Prayer: "Give me a death like Buddha's. Let
me fall."

Sailing from the United States.
Scroll.
Squall.
Two Fishermen.
Valley, The.
Moss, Thomas
Beggar, The.
Mossman, Bina
I'm going to California.
Motaung, Bonisile Joshua
Garden Boy, The.
Mother Goose
A was an apple pie, B bit it, C cut it.
As I was going along, long, long.
As I was going o'er London Bridge.
As I was going to St. Ives.
As I was going to sell my eggs.
As I was going up Pippen Hill.
As little Jenny Wren/ Was sitting by the shed.
As round as an apple, as deep as a cup.
As soft as silk, as white as milk.
As Tommy Snooks and Bessy Brooks.
At the siege of Belle Isle.
Awake, arise,/ Pull out your eyes.
Baa, baa, black sheep, have you any wool?
Baby, baby, naughty baby.
Barber, barber, shave a pig.
Bat, bat, come under my hat.
Bell horses, bell horses, what time of day?
Bessy Bell and Mary Gray.
Betty Blue.
Betty Pringle's Pig.
Black I am and much admired.
Black within, and red without.
Bless you, bless you, burnie-bee [or bonnie-bee]
Blind man, blind man.
Blow the fire, blacksmith.
Blow, wind, blow! and go, mill, go!
Bob Robin.
Bobby Shaftoe's gone to sea.
Bonny Cravet, The.
Bow-wow, says the dog.
Bow, wow, wow,/ Whose dog art thou?
Boys and girls come out to play.
Buttons, a farthing a pair.
By the Fire.
Bye, baby bunting.
Carrion crow sat upon an oak, The.
Catch.
Christmas comes but once a year.
Cobbler, cobbler, mend my shoe.
Cock a doodle doo!/ My dame has lost her shoe.
Cock crows in the morn, The.
Cock doth crow, The/ To let you know.
Cock doth crow, the wind doth blow, The.
Come, butter, come.
Come dance a jig.
Come, let's to bed.
Come when you're called.
Cross Patch/ Draw the latch.
Curly Locks! Curly Locks! wilt thou be mine?
Curr dhoo, curr dhoo.
Cushy cow, bonny, let down thy milk.
Daffy-down-dilly is new come to town [or Daffadowndilly has come up to town]
Dame Trot and her cat.
Dance a baby diddy.
Dance, Thumbkin, dance.
Dance to your [or thee] daddy.
Dickery, dickery, dare.
Diddle, diddle, dumpling, my son John.
Diddlety, diddlety, dumpty.
Dillar, a dollar, A,/ A ten o'clock scholar.
Ding, dong, bell,/ Pussy's in the well.
Dingty diddlety.
Doctor Foster went to Gloucester [or Glo'ster]
Dove says, Coo, coo, The.
Duck and a drake, A.
Elizabeth, Elspeth, Betsy, and Bess.

Every lady in this land.
Farmer went trotting on [or upon] his grey mare, A.
Flour of England, fruit of Spain.
For every evil under the sun.
For want of a nail.
Formed long ago, yet made today.
Four and twenty tailors.
Georgie Porgie, pudding and pie.
Girl in the lane, The.
God made the bees.
Goosey, goosey, gander, where shall I wander?
Great A, little a.
Hark, hark, the dogs do bark.
Hart he loves the high wood, The.
Hector Protector was dressed all in green.
Here am I, little jumping Joan.
Here sits the Lord Mayor.
Here's Sulky Sue.
Hey diddle diddle/ And hey diddle dan!
Hey [or Sing hey], diddle, diddle,/ The cat and the fiddle.
Hey diddle dinkety, poppety, pet.
Hey, my kitten, my kitten.
Hick-a-more, Hack-a-more.
Hickory, dickory, dock.
Hie, hie, says Anthony.
Higgledy, piggledy, my black hen.
Higher than a house,/ Higher than a tree.
Hot cross buns! Hot-cross buns!/ One a penny, two a penny.
Hot Pease Man, The.
House That Jack Built, The.
How many days has my baby to play?
How many miles to Babylon [or Barley-Bridge]?
Humpty Dumpty sat on a wall.
Hush-a-bye, baby, on the tree-top.
I had a little hobby horse, it was well shod.
I had a little moppet.
I had a little nut-tree, nothing would it bear.
I had a little pony.
I have a little sister, they call her Peep-Peep.
I love sixpence, jolly little sixpence.
I saw a ship a-sailing.
I saw three ships come sailing by.
I won't be my father's Jack.
I would, if I could.
If all the seas were one sea.
If all the world were apple-pie.
If I had [or I'd] as much money as I could spend.
If wishes were horses.
I'll tell you a story/ About Jack a Nory.
In marble walls [or halls] as white as milk.
Intery, mintery, cutery corn.
Is John Smith within?
Jack and Jill went up the hill.
Jack be nimble.
Jack Sprat could eat no fat.
Jacky, come give me thy fiddle.
Jerry Hall.
John Cook had a little grey mare.
Johnny shall have a new bonnet.
King of France, the king of France, The/ with forty thousand men.
Ladybird, Ladybird fly away home.
Leg over leg.
Lion and the unicorn, The.
Little Bo-Peep has lost her sheep.
Little Boy Blue, come blow up your horn.
Little cock sparrow sat on a green tree, A.
Little Girl.
Little Jack Horner.
Little King Pippin.
Little maid, pretty maid,/ Whither goest thou?
Little Miss Muffet/ Sat on a tuffet.
Little Nancy [or Nanny] Etticoat.
Little Polly Flinders.
Little Tommy Tittlemouse/ Lived in a little house.

Long legs, crooked thighs.
Long-tailed pig, A.
Lucy Locket lost her pocket.
Man in the wilderness asked [of] me [or said to me], The [or A]
March, march, head erect.
Margery Mutton-pie.
Mary, Mary [or Mistress Mary], quite contrary.
Master and Man.
Monday's child is fair of face.
My father he died, but I can't tell you how.
My little old man and I fell out.
My maid Mary,/ She minds the dairy.
Niddle Noddle.
North wind doth blow, The.
Nose, nose, jolly red nose.
Old King Cole was a merry old soul.
Old Mother Goose.
Old Mother Goose/ When she wanted to wander.
Old Mother Twitchett had [or has] but one eye.
Old woman, old woman,/ Shall we go a-shearing?
On Saturday night shall be my care.
Once I saw a little bird.
One misty, moisty morning.
One, two,/ Buckle my shoe.
One, two, three, four,/ Mary at the cottage door.
One, two, three, four, five/Once I caught a fish alive.
Pat-a-cake, pat-a-cake, baker's man.
Pease porridge [or pudding] hot.
Peter, Peter, pumpkin eater.
Peter Piper picked a peck of pickled peppers.
Peter White will ne'er go right.
Pit, pat, well-a-day.
Polly put the kettle on.
Poor old Robinson Crusoe!
Pretty John Watts.
Pussy Cat, Pussy Cat, where have you been?
Pussycat.
Queen of Hearts, The.
Rain, rain, go away.
Rain, rain, go to Spain.
Riddle, a riddle, A/ As I suppose.
Riddle me, riddle me ree.
Ride a cock-horse [or a-cock horse] to Banbury Cross,/ To see a fine lady upon a white horse.
Ride away, ride away/ Johnny shall ride.
Ring-a-ring o' roses, A.
Robert Barnes, fellow fine.
Robert Rowley rolled a round roll round.
Robin-a-bobin.
Robin and Richard.
Robin Hood, Robin Hood,/ Is in the mickle wood.
Rock-a-bye, baby, thy cradle is green.
Roses are red.
Rub a dub dub,/ Three men in a tub.
See-saw, Margery Daw,/ Jack[y] shall have a new master.
See-saw, Margery Daw,/ The old hen flew over the malt house.
See-saw, sacradown.
See, see, what shall I see?
Shoe the colt, shoe the colt.
Simple Simon met a pieman.
Sing a song of sixpence.
Sing, sing,/ What shall I sing?
Six little mice sat down to spin.
Smiling girls, rosy boys.
Solomon Grundy.
Sow came in with the saddle, The.
Speak when you're spoken to,/ Come for one call.
Taffy was a Welshman, Taffy was a thief.
There was a crooked man, and he went [or walked] a crooked mile.

There was a little boy and a little girl.
There was a little girl.
There was a little man,/ And he had a little gun.
There was a little man,/ and he wooed a little maid.
There was a man and he had nought.
There was a man of our town.
There was a piper had a cow.
There was an old man in a velvet coat.
There was an old woman/ Lived under a hill/ She put a mouse in a bag.
There was an old woman, and what do you think?
There was an old [*or* little woman], as I've heard tell.
There was an old woman called Nothing-at-all.
There was an old woman in Surrey.
There was an old woman sat spinning.
There was an old woman tossed up in a basket [*or* blanket]
There was an old woman who lived in a shoe.
There were two birds sat on a stone.
They that wash on Monday.
Thirty days hath September.
Thirty white horses upon a red hill.
This is the way the ladies ride.
This little pig went to market.
Three blind mice, see how they run!
Three crooked cripples went through Cripplegate.
Three wise men of Gotham.
To make your candles last for aye.
To market, to market/ To buy a plum bun.
Tom, Tom, the piper's son.
Tommy Tucker.
Trip upon trenchers, and dance upon dishes.
Turnip Vendor, The.
Tweedle-Dum and Tweedle-Dee.
Twelve pears hanging high.
Two Comical Folk.
Two legs sat upon three legs.
Ungrateful Jenny.
Up at Piccadilly oh!
Wash the dishes, wipe the dishes.
What are little boys made of, made of?
What is the rhyme for porringer?
What's the news of the day.
When good King Arthur ruled this land.
When I was a little girl,/ About seven years old.
When the wind is in the east.
"Where are you going to, my pretty maid?"
Where Is He?
Who killed Cock [*or* poor] Robin? [*or* Here lies Cock Robin]
Willy boy, Willy boy,/ Where are you going?
Willy, Willy Wilkin.

Motherwell, William
Cavalier's Song, The.
Sing On, Blithe Bird.

Motion, Andrew
These Days.
Writing.

Moto, Mauro
Clock, The.

Moto Mokuami
Sweat dripping down.

Mototoshi
At the end of autumn.

Mott, Michael
Don Juan in Winter.
Islanders, Inlanders.

Motteux, Peter Anthony
Town-Rakes, The, at.

Motteux, Pierre Antoine. *See* **Motteux, Peter Anthony**

Moulton, Louise Chandler (Ellen Louise Chandler)
At End.

Hic Jacet.
Last Good-by, The.
Laura Sleeping.
Laus Veneris.
Louisa May Alcott.
Love's Resurrection Day.
Painted Fan, A.
Shadow Dance, The.
To-Night.
We Lay Us Down to Sleep.
Were But My Spirit Loosed upon the Air.

Moultrie, John
Forget Thee?
Violets.

Mounsey, Messenger
Here lie my old bones: my vexation now ends.

Mountain, George J.
Indian's Grave, The.

Mousley, James P.
Prayer: "God of light and blossom."

Movius, Geoffrey
Work-out, The.

Mowrer, Paul Scott
Mozart's Grave.

Moyles, Lois
Report from California.
Tale Told by a Head, A.
Thomas in the Fields.

Mozeen, Thomas
Bedlamite, The.
Kilruddery Hunt, The.

Mphahlele, Ezekiel
Exile in Nigeria.
Homeward Bound.
Poem, A: "What is there that we can do or say."
Somewhere.

Mphande, Lupenga
Dwarf of the Hill Caves, The.
Song of a Prison Guard.
Victim, The.
When the Storms Come.

Mqhayi, S. E. K.
Black Army, The.
Sinking of the Mendi, The.

Mririda n'Ait Attik
Azouou.
Mririda.

Msham, Mwana Kupona
Daughter, take this amulet, *sel.*

Mtshali, Mbuyiseni Oswald
Amagoduka at Glencoe Station.
Birth of Shaka, The.
Nightfall in Soweto.
Raging Generation, The.
Shepherd and His Flock, The.
Weep Not for a Warrior.

Mu Hua
Rhyme-Prose on the Sea.

Muchemwa, Kizito Z.
Circular Roads.
My Friends, This Storm.
Redeemer.
Tourists.

Mudie, Ian
They'll Tell You about Me.
Wilderness Theme.

Mueller, Lisel
Alive Together.
Blind Leading the Blind, The.
Historical Museum, Manitoulin Island.
Lonesome Dream, The.
Merce Cunningham and the Birds.
Milkweed Pods in Winter.
Monet Refuses the Operation.
Moon Fishing.
Palindrome.
Reading the Brothers Grimm to Jenny.
Southpaw.

Mueller, Marnie
Strategy for a Marathon.

Muhlenberg, William Augustus
Fulfillment.
Heaven's Magnificence.
I Would Not Live Alway.
Like Noah's Weary Dove.
Saviour, Who Thy Flock Art Feeding.

Mühringer, Doris
Dalmatian Ballad.
Do Not Lock Your House.
I Have a House.
Les Enfants du Paradis.
Lost Goldfish in a Dream.
On the Death of Paul Celan (A Vindication).
Owl/ you/ my frightful friend.
To Sing in the Darkness.
To Stay.
Waiting.

Muir, Edwin
Absent, The.
Animals, The.
Annunciation, The.
Antichrist.
Ballad of Hector in Hades.
Ballad of the Flood.
Birthday, A.
Border, The.
Brothers, The.
Castle, The.
Child Dying, The.
Childhood.
Cloud, The.
Combat, The.
Confirmation, The.
Escape, The.
Face, The.
Fathers, The.
Finder Found, The.
For Ann Scott-Moncrieff.
Gate, The.
Good Man in Hell, The.
Good Town, The.
Great House, The.
Grove, The.
Horses.
Human Fold, The.
In Love for Long.
Interrogation, The.
Island, The.
Labyrinth, The.
Love's Remorse.
Mary Stuart.
Merlin.
Myth, The.
Mythical Journey, The.
Oedipus.
Old Gods, The.
One Foot in Eden.
Reading in War Time.
Refugees, The.
Return, The ("The doors flapped open in Ulysses' house").
Return, The ("The veteran Greeks came home").
Rider Victory, The.
Road, The.
Robert the Bruce.
Salem, Massachusetts.
Scotland 1941.
Scotland's Winter.
Suburban Dreams.
Then.
Three Mirrors, The.
Too Much.
Town Betrayed, The.
Transfiguration, The.
Trophy, The.
Troy.
Usurpers, The.
Voyage, The.

Wayside Station, The.
Wheel, The.
Window, The.
Muir, Henry D.
Soldier's Grave, The.
Muir, John
From garden to garden, ridge to ridge.
Muju
For eight-seven years.
Mukai Kyorai
My native town.
Which is tail? Which head?
Winter blast.
Mukai Kyorai. *See* **Kyorai**
Mukta Bai
Although he has no form.
Muldoon, Paul
Anseo.
Big House, The.
Brock.
Christo's.
Clonfeacle.
Cuba.
Dancers at the Moy.
Field Hospital, The.
Gathering Mushrooms.
Glad Eye, The.
Hedgehog.
Lass of Aughrim, The.
Making the Move.
Meeting the British.
Mirror, The.
Right Arm, The.
Sightseers, The.
Sushi.
Weepies, The.
Why Brownlee Left.
Wishbone, The.
Müller, Wilhelm
Whither?
Müller-Jahnke, Klara
We Women.
Mullineaux, Mary
Dragon, The.
Mulock, D. M.
Blackbird, The.
Mumford, Erika
White Rose: Sophie Scholl 1921-1943, The.
Mumford, Lewis
Consolation in War.
Munby, A. J.
Above the Medway, *sel.*
Munby, Arthur
One Way of Looking at It.
Post Mortem.
Serving Maid, The.
Munday, Anthony
Beauty Sat Bathing by a Spring, *sel.*
I Serve a Mistress, *sel.*
Love, *sel.*
Weep, weep, ye woodmen! wail, *sel.*
Mundell, William D.
Uninvited, The.
Mundorf, Frank
Letter from a State Hospital.
Remembering Lincoln.
Munenaga, Prince
Above Ohara/ the fallen snow has piled up.
At this year's end too.
Fallen away now.
I send these along.
If I left this place.
In times yet to come.
Pain is greater now, The.
Take pity on me!
Tell just this one thing.
What am I to do?
Wind is rustling, The.
You know how I long.
Muneyuki
In my mountain hamlet.

Mungoshi, Charles
If You Don't Stay Bitter for Too Long.
Important Matters.
Munkittrick, Richard Kendall
At the Shrine.
Bulb, A.
Ghosts.
Molasses River.
Old King Cabbage.
Redingote and the Vamoose, The.
Song of the Owl, The.
To Miguel de Cervantes Saavadra.
Munn, R. O.
Young Fellers.
Munro, Deborah
Sequence for a Young Widow Passing.
Song of the Strange Young Duckling.
Munro, Neil
Fiddle, The.
Nettles.
Munro, Robin
Apprentices.
Hills.
Shetland, Hill Dawn.
View.
Munso, Felix
On the Job.
Munson, C. C.
Dead Past, A, at.
Mura, David
Hibakusha's Letter (1955), The.
Lan Nguyen; the Uniform of Death, 1971.
Natives, The.
Nisei Picnic, A.
Relocation.
Murakami Bussan
Long Ago.
Murano Shiro
Beggar.
Black Song.
Flesh, The.
Pole Vault.
Present Winter.
Murasaki Shikibu
Lady Murasaki says, *sel.*
Troubled waters, The/ are frozen fast, *sel.*
Murchison, Lee
In the Beginning Was the.
Sprinters, The.
Murger, Henry
Old Loves.
Spring in the Students' Quarter.
Murguía, Alejandro
O California.
Small Towns.
Murillo, Rosario
Christmas Carol: "I walk today, the pain of
childbirth in each step."
I'm Going to Plant a Heart on the Earth.
Song of Wandering Times.
Murphy, Beatrice M.
Letter, The.
Murphy, Joseph Colin
Skydivers, The.
Murphy, R. D.
Back Lane.
Murphy, Richard
Archaeology of Love, The.
Beehive Cell.
Care.
Casement's Funeral, *sel.*
Coppersmith.
Deep red bogs divided, *sel.*
Epitaph on a Fir-Tree.
Girl at the Seaside.
Green Martyrs, *sel.*
High Island.
Last Galway Hooker, The.
Little Hunger.
Moonshine.
Nest in a Wall, A.

Nocturne: "Blade of a knife, The."
Orange March, *sel.*
Pat Cloherty's Version of *The Maisie*.
Philosopher and the Birds, The.
Planter, *sel.*
Poet on the Island, The.
Rapparees, *sel.*
Reading Lesson, The.
Sailing to an Island.
Seals at High Island.
Stormpetrel.
Walking on Sunday.
Who owns the land where musket-balls are
buried, *sel.*
Wolfhound, *sel.*
Woman of the House, The.
Murray, Anne B.
Drumochter.
Then and Now.
Murray, Bertram
I Caught a Fish ("I caught a little fish one
day").
Murray, Charles
Bennachie.
In Lythe Strathdon.
Whistle, The.
Murray, G. E.
California Dead.
On the Upside.
Shopping for Midnight.
Sketch for a Morning in Muncie, Indiana.
Murray, John
Hark! 'Tis the Saviour of Mankind.
Murray, Frederick and Frederick Leigh
Charlie Piecan.
Murray, Les A.
Absolutely Ordinary Rainbow, An.
Bagman O'Reilly's Curse.
Names of the Humble, The.
Once in a Lifetime, Snow.
Portrait of the Autist as a New World Driver.
Powerline Incarnation, The.
Sydney and the Bush.
Widower in the Country, The.
Murray, Millie
No Say.
Murray, Patrick J.
God's Little Angel.
Murray, Paul
Rain.
Murray, Pauli
Dark Testament.
Death of a Friend.
For Mack C. Parker.
Harlem Riot, 1943.
Inquietude.
Mr. Roosevelt Regrets.
Ruth.
Song: "Because I know deep in my own
heart."
Without Name.
Murray, Philip
Little Litany to St. Francis, A.
Turning, The.
Murray, Raymond
Carmelite.
Murray, Robert Fuller
Andrew M'Crie.
City of Golf, The.
End of April, The.
Man from Inversnaid, The.
Wasted Day, The.
Murray, Rona
Lizard, The.
Murray, Sir David
Sonnet: "Ponder thy cares, and sum them all
in one," *sel.*
Murry, Ann
Familiar Epistle, A.
Murton, Jessie Wilmore
Song of the Builders.

Mus, David
Conserves, *sel.*
Musgrave, Susan
Burial of the Dog.
I Am Not a Conspiracy Everything Is Not
Paranoid.
Judas Goat, The.
Returning to the Town Where We Used to
Live.
Salad Days.
Muske, Carol
Child with Six Fingers.
Found.
Hyena.
Immunity.
Real Estate.
Rice.
Swansong.
Musset, Alfred de
Juana.
Souvenir.
"Mustafa." *See* **Johnson, Don Allen**
Mustapää, P.
Folk Melody.
Lachesis Net.
Memory, A.
Song, A: "I wrote a song shining as glass."
Mutabaruka (Allan Hope)
Free Up de Lan, White Man.
Revolutionary Poets.
You Ask Me.
Mu'tamid, King of Seville
Tears of the World.
Woo Not the World.
Mutamociyar
Ay: A Gift of Elephants.
Ay: His Hill.
Muth, Carol Sue
Love.
Mutran, Khalil
Boycott.
Evening.
Mutsuo, Takahashi. *See* **Takahashi Mutsuo**
Muuse, 'Abdillaahi
Elder's Reproof to his Wife, An.
Muyassar, Orkhan
Graves.
Lost.
Race.
Statue, The.
Transformations.
Wall of Tomorrow, The.
Mycall, John
Our States, O Lord.
Myers, F. W. H.
Inner Light, The, *sel.*
Myers, Frederic William Henry
Inner Light, The.
Prayer, A: "O for one minute hark what we
are saying!"
Myers, Jack
Apprentice Painter, The.
As Long as You're Happy.
Coming to the Surface.
Day of Atonement.
Diaspora, The.
Do You Know What I Mean?
Manner of Speaking, A.
Minyan, The.
Mirror for the Barnyard.
Natural Ice Cream.
So Long Solon.
When I Held You to My Chest, You Fit.
Myles, Eileen
Dawn.
Greedy Seasons.
Medium Poem.
My Cheap Lifestyle.
On the Death of Robert Lowell.
Poetry Reading.

Public Television.
Woman like Me, A.
Myles, Glenn
Percy/ 68.
Mylonas, Eva
Holidays.
Myoe
Because fog engulfs, *sel.*
Bright bright!/ bright bright bright!, *sel.*
Floating cloud, A, *sel.*
How they sting!, *sel.*
Night deepening, *sel.*
Set now,/ and I too will go below, *sel.*
Shining moon, A, *sel.*
Under the pines, *sel.*
While I, with no guide, *sel.*
Winter moon, *sel.*
Myogun, Kon. *See* **Kon Myogun**
Myotan
Great poisoned drum, The.

N

Na mani, Huda
Blind man asked me, A, *sel.*
Love Poem: "In your quest or request God is
remote."
Why do the sun rays laugh across the
swamp?, *sel.*
You sever a hand, *sel.*
Nabbes, Thomas
Love Sets Order in the Elements, *sel.*
Nabokov, Vladimir
Ballad of Longwood Glen, The.
Evening of Russian Poetry, An.
Lines Written in Oregon.
Literary Dinner, A.
Ode to a Model.
On Discovering a Butterfly.
Pale Fire.
Rain.
Room, The.
Nabors, Claudia
How Dumb Is He?
Nachman, Chaim. *See* **Bialik, Hayyim**
Nahman
Nadaud, Gustave
Carcassonne.
Nadir, Moishe (Yitzhok Reis)
Adjectives.
Nadson, Semion Yakovlevich
Brother, The.
Nagachika
Beneath the new green.
My mind on the form.
O distant cuckoo.
Shall I retire now.
Thinking of the past.
Nagase Kiyoko
Mother.
Naggid, Hayim
After the War.
Like a Pearl.
My Mother.
Snow in Jerusalem, A.
Nagy, Agnes Nemes
Between.
Bird.
Comparison, A.
Consciousness.
Defend It.
I Carried Statues.
Ikhnaton's Night.
Shapelessness, The.
Snow.
Statues.

Storm.
Words to a Song.
Nagy, László
Bells Are Calling for Me, The.
Bliss of Sunday, The.
Break-up, The.
Coalmen, The.
Cognition, Language, Poetry.
Fair in Frosty May.
Ferryman, The.
Frosts Are Coming.
Headboard to Headboards, A.
Here Is No Southern Island.
Hurrah for Trees!
Little Jesus of the Barren, The.
Love of the Scorching Wind.
Peacock Woman, The.
Prayer to the White Lady.
Squared by Walls.
Without Mercy.
Naheed, Kishwar
Agreement.
How Crazy Are Those Who Love You So
Much.
I Am Not That Woman.
Listen to Me.
Nahman of Bratzlav, Rabbi
Annul Wars.
Heart of the World, The.
Nahum
Spring Song.
Naidu [or Nayadu], Sarojini
Cradle Song: "From groves of spice."
In the Bazaars of Hyderabad.
Snake-Charmer, The.
Naigreshel, Mendel
Nation.
What Will Remain after Me?
Nairne, Carolina Oliphant, Baroness
Caller Herrin.'
Laird o'Cockpen, The.
Land o' the Leal, The.
N'Ait Attik, Mririda
Abandoned, The.
Second Wife, The.
Sister.
Naito Joso. *See* **Joso**
Naito Meisetsu
Haiku: "Clods of earth."
Haiku: "Early winter."
Haiku: "Hill field: under the moon."
Haiku: "Wind blows grey, The."
Najara, Israel
God of the World.
Loved of My Soul.
Naji, Ibrahim
Farewell: "Leave me, my love, it's time to
part."
Oblivion.
Najmájer, Marie von
Sappho.
Nakahara Chuya
Cold Night.
Leaves of the Fig-Tree.
Marunouchi Building, The.
Nakajima Soin
Before Gion Shrine, determined to drive away
poverty, *sel.*
No more light from second-story lamps, *sel.*
Nakamura Kusadao
Haiku: "Already winter."
Haiku: "Family reunion."
Haiku: "Father at last, A."
Haiku: "Gentle as my dead friend's hand."
Haiku: "Undergraduates/ By and large
shabby."
Nakano Shigeharu
Imperial Hotel, The.
Song: "Don't sing of crimson flowers or
wings of the dragonfly."

Song: Farewell before Dawn.
Tokyo Imperial University Students.
Nakao, Prince
Banished from the Palace.
Nakasuk
Great Farter, The.
Gull, it is said, The.
Invocation: "Land earth-root."
Magic Words to Feel Better.
Nakhla, Amin
Black Song.
To the Beloved Grown Past Youth.
Nakkannaiyar
Woman in Love with a Captive King, A.
Nakkiranar
Murukan: His Places.
Murukan, the Red One.
Nalungiaq
Heaven and Hell.
Nam Jo, Kim
My Baby Has No Name Yet.
Namani, Huda
Both Earth and Heaven.
Namjoshi, Suniti
Cythera.
From the Travels of Gulliver.
Look, Medusa!
Nanak
Beyond number/ are the fools, who simply
cannot see.
By order/ shapes take shape.
Discipline is the workshop.
From listening,/ a depth, a well of virtues.
From listening/ Siddhas, Pirs, Gods, Naths.
From listening,/ Siva, Brahma, Indra.
From listening,/ truth, fulfillment, knowledge.
Guru is the stepping stone, The.
If the true guru is gracious.
If you ponder it,/ no obstacle blocks your
path.
If you ponder it,/ there is mindfulness,
wisdom of mind.
If you ponder it,/ you find the door of
deliverance.
In the realm of action the sound is pure force.
In the realm of wisdom, wisdom reigns.
Nights, seasons, dates, times.
Omkar/ True name.
Realm of truth: there dwells the Formless
One, The.
That was the religion of the realm of religion.
Way one ponders it, The.
Nance, Berta Hart
Moonlight.
Nangaku Gentai
This year turning sixty-four, elements.
Nangolo, Mvula Ya
Contrast.
Flower, A.
Guerrilla Promise.
Hunter's Song.
Nannakaiyar
What She Said.
Nannestad, Elizabeth
My Mother's Mother, Dearly Beloved.
Portrait across a Room.
Portrait of a Lady.
Queen of the River.
Nansen
How long the stars.
Naone, Dana
Girl with the Green Skirt.
I make all the poetic pauses.
Long Distance.
Presence, The.
Sleep.
Napa
Darkened in the Soul.
Napier, Felicity
Houseplant.

Napier, George
To a Lady, with a Compass.
Naranjo-Morse, Nora
Oklahoma Rt. 66.
Witchcraft.
Witchcraft Woman.
Nardi, Rafaela Chacón
Mountain Girl.
Narihira (Ariwara no Narihira)
Can it be that the moon has changed?
Dream of the night, The.
If you are true to your name.
In the blackness.
In the capital is the one I love, like.
It was not that I could not see her.
Like a passion-plant pattern.
Seeing such blooming beauty.
Shallow our union.
Tossing in my bed.
Was it you who came to me.
Narushima Ryuhoku
Aboard a Ship Leaving Yokohama.
Niagara Falls.
Pronouncement on Returning Home.
Saigon.
Nash, Dorothy
Road Moves On, The, *sel.*
Nash, Ogden
Adventures of Isabel.
Among the Anthropophagi.
Anatomy of Happiness, The.
Ant, The.
Arthur.
Bankers Are Just like Anybody Else, except
Richer.
Between Birthdays.
Billy Ray Smith.
Birthday on the Beach.
Boy Who Laughed at Santa Claus, The.
Calling Spring VII-MMMC.
Camel, The.
Canary, The.
Carol for Children, A.
Cat, The.
Celery.
Centipede, The.
Chipmunk, The.
Columbus.
Come On in, the Senility Is Fine.
Cow, The.
Decline and Fall of a Roman Umpire.
Do You Plan to Speak Bantu?
Duck, The.
Eel, The.
Evening Out, The.
Exit, Pursued by a Bear.
Family Court.
Firefly, The.
First Families Move Over!
Fish, The.
Fly, The.
Genealogical Reflection.
Germ, The.
Golly, How Truth Will Out.
Goodbye Now, or, Pardon My Gauntlet.
Grackle, The ("Grackle's voice is less than
mellow.").
Ha! Original Sin.
Hippopotamus, The.
Hunter, The.
I Can't Have a Martini, Dear, but You Take
One.
I Never Even Suggested It.
I pray the Lord my soul to take, *sel.*
Ill Met by Zenith.
Introduction to Dogs, An.
Introspective Reflection.
Invocation: "Senator Smoot (Republican,
Ut.)."
Jellyfish, The.
Kind of an Ode to Duty.

Kindly Unhitch That Star, Buddy.
Kitten, The.
Limerick: "There was an old man in a trunk."
Lines to a World-famous Poet Who Failed to
Complete a World-famous Poem; or, Come
Clean, Mr. Guest!
Lines to Be Embroidered on a Bib; or, The
Child Is Father of the Man, but Not for
Quite a While.
Lion, The.
Little girl marched around her Christmas tree,
A, *sel.*
Man Can Complain, Can't He?, A.
Max Schling, Max Schling, Lend Me Your
Green Thumb.
Morning Prayer.
Mr. Artesian's Conscientiousness.
Notes for the Chart in 306.
Octopus, The.
Old Men.
One-l lama, the.
Panther, The.
Peekaboo, I Almost See You.
People upstairs, The.
Perfect Husband, The.
Phoenix, The.
Pig, The.
Pizza, The.
Portrait of the Artist as a Prematurely Old
Man.
Poultries, The.
Private Dining Room, The.
Purist, The.
Reflection on Babies.
Reflection on Ingenuity.
Reflections on Ice-breaking.
Reminiscent Reflection.
Requiem: "There was a young belle of old
Natchez."
Rhinoceros, The.
Sea-Gull, The.
Seven Spiritual Ages of Mrs. Marmaduke
Moore, The.
Shrew, The.
So That's Who I Remind Me Of.
Song of the Open Road.
Song to be Sung by the Father of Infant
Female Children.
Spring Comes to Murray Hill.
Squirrel, The.
Swallow, The.
Sweet Dreams.
Tableau at Twilight.
Taboo to Boot.
Tale of Custard the Dragon, The.
Termite, The.
That Reminds Me.
They Don't Speak English in Paris.
To a Small Boy Standing on My Shoes While
I Am Wearing Them.
Turtle, The.
Two and One Are a Problem.
Up from the Egg; the Confessions of a
Nuthatch Avoider.
Up from the Wheelbarrow.
Very like a Whale.
Visit, The.
Wapiti, The.
Wendigo, The.
Wombat, The.
Nashe [or Nash], Thomas
Adieu, Farewell, Earth's Bliss[e], *sel.*
A-Maying, a-Playing.
Autumn, *sel.*
Fair Summer Droops, *sel.*
Harvest, *sel.*
Spring, the Sweet Spring, *sel.*
Summer's Farewell, *sel.*
Summer's Last Will and Testament.
Nasir, Amjad
Bent Branches.

Exile.
Loneliness.
Nason, Emma Huntington
Child's Question, A.
Natalya Gorbanyevskaya
In my own twentieth century.
Nathan, Leonard
Carrying On.
Emeritus, The.
Fall, The.
Jane Seagrim's Party.
Just Looking, Thank You.
Nathan, Leonard E.
Diver, The.
Nathan, Robert
Christian, Be Up.
Mountaineer, The.
Now Blue October.
Sonnet: "Because my grief seems quiet and
  apart."
These Are the Chosen People.
Natsume Seibi
Butterfly dying right in front, A, *sel.*
Deer in the morning look edgy and lost, *sel.*
Even gulls appear to feel cold, *sel.*
Having eaten fish, *sel.*
Hazy moon has detached itself, The, *sel.*
"I want to die"—at times I think, *sel.*
Is that the person I once loved, *sel.*
Lightning: a man walking, *sel.*
"Not home! Not home!", *sel.*
Old Man's Thought, An, *sel.*
On the Anniversary of My Father's Death,
  sel.
On the violets of the field, *sel.*
Reading an "Ode to a Widow", *sel.*
Reading the Analects, *sel.*
Sleeping in the grass, laying myself, *sel.*
Somehow I can't help looking, *sel.*
Spring bird—thinking of what?, A, *sel.*
Standing by a plum, a penniless poet, *sel.*
Summer night has turned to dawn, The, *sel.*
Topic for a Painting, A, *sel.*
Traveler I saw yesterday, The, *sel.*
Under how many layers of fallen leaves, *sel.*
Useless acquaintants increase, *sel.*
Visiting My Wife's Grave, *sel.*
When Mother Died, *sel.*
White peonies about to collapse, *sel.*
Wild cat steps over kudzu vines, A, *sel.*
Natsume Soseki
I have no mind to bow to the Buddha, peer
  into the heart.
I spat up streams of crimson blood.
Not a Christian, not a Buddhist, not a
  Confucian either.
Once I was a poor man's son.
Once I was the master of a city.
Self-Derision.
True path is shadowy and still, far away and
  hard to find, The.
Naudé, Adèle
Africa.
From a Venetian Sequence.
Idiot, The.
Portrait.
Unpossessed, The.
Nauen, Elinor
History of the Human Body// Winfield's
  Infield Hit// The Lassitude of the Infinite,
  The.
If I Ever Grow Old: Grim and Gleeful
  Resolutions.
Maine.
3 More Things.
Navarre, Marguerite de
Smell of death is so powerful, The.
Nayadu, Sarojini. *See* **Naidu, Sarojini**
Naydus, Leyb
Intimate Melodies.

Naylor, James Ball
King David and King Solomon.
Nazir, Vali Mohammad
Gipsy, The.
How full of joy were the days of youth.
Man.
Moonlight.
We are like tears of grief.
Wealth; or Song Written for a Beggar.
Neal, John
Men of the North.
Music of the Night.
Neal, Larry
Harlem Gallery: From the Inside.
James Powell on Imagination.
Malcolm X—an Autobiography.
Orishas.
Neale, John Mason
Hymn for Easter Morn.
Oh, Give Us Back the Days of Old.'
Neaves, Lord
Let Us All Be Unhappy on Sunday.
Neef-Uthoff, Maria
Names.
Negri, Ada
Challenge.
Make Way!
Tonight.
Neidhart von Reuental
On the Mountain.
Neidus, Leib
I Love the Woods.
I Often Want to Let My Lines Go.
In an Alien Place.
Neihardt, John G.
Easter, 1923.
Envoi: "Oh, seek me not within a tomb."
One more rendezvous, *sel.*
Prayer for Pain.
Neilson, Francis
Eugenio Pacelli.
Neilson, John Shaw
Beauty Imposes.
Break of Day.
Cool, Cool, Country, The.
Crane Is My Neighbor, The.
Flowers in the Ward.
In the Street.
Love's Coming.
May.
Orange Tree, The.
Poor Can Feed the Birds, The.
Soldier Is Home, The.
Song Be Delicate.
Strawberries in November.
Sundowner, The.
Take Down the Fiddle, Karl!
'Tis the White Plum Tree.
To a Blue Flower.
To a School-Girl.
You Cannot Go Down to the Spring.
Nekrasov, Nikolai Alekseyevich
Capitals Are Rocked, The.
Do you know of just one habitation, *sel.*
Farewell.
No storm, but the forest is drumming, *sel.*
When from dark error's subjugation, *sel.*
Nelms, Sheryl L.
Cumulus Clouds.
Into Fish.
Outhouse Blues.
Real Talent.
Nelson, Alice Dunbar Moore
I Sit and Sew.
Snow in October.
Sonnet: "I had no thought of violets of late."
Nelson, Barney
Cowboy's Favorite.
Nelson, David
My Days are Gliding Swiftly By.

Nelson, Eric
Everywhere Pregnant Women Appear.
Nelson, Howard
Cows near the Graveyard, The.
Nelson, Paula
House, The.
Nelson, Sharon
Pedlar.
Nelson, Starr
White Rainbow, The.
Nelson, Willie
Heaven and Hell.
Nemerov, Howard
Angel and Stone.
At a Country Hotel.
Author to His Body on Their Fifteenth
  Birthday, 29.ii.80, The.
Backward Look, The.
Beautiful Lawn Sprinkler, The.
Because You Asked about the Line between
  Prose and Poetry.
Blue Swallows, The.
Book of Kells, The.
Boom!
Brainstorm.
Brief Journey West, The.
Cabinet of Seeds Displayed, A.
Carol: "Now is the world withdrawn all."
Casting.
Companions, The.
Death of God, The.
Dial Tone, The.
Dialogue.
Dragonfly, The.
Dying Garden, The.
Easter.
Elegy for a Nature Poet.
Epigrams, I-IX.
Eve.
Extract from Memoirs.
Fable of the War, A.
Fugue.
Ginkgoes in Fall.
Glass Dialectic.
"Good-bye," said the river, "I'm going
  downstream."
Goose Fish, The.
Grace to Be Said at the Supermarket.
Guide to the Ruins.
Gyroscope.
Historical Judas, The.
History of a Literary Movement.
Holding the Mirror Up to Nature.
Human Things.
I Only Am Escaped Alone to Tell Thee.
Icehouse in Summer, The.
Insomnia I.
Learning by Doing.
Life Cycle of Common Man.
Lives of Gulls and Children, The.
Lot Later.
Make Love Not War.
Makers, The.
Manners.
Mapmaker on His Art, The.
Marriage of Heaven and Earth, The.
May Day Dancing, The.
Metamorphoses.
Money.
More Joy in Heaven.
Most Expensive Picture in the World, The.
Mousemeal.
Mud Turtle, The.
Murder of William Remington, The.
Mystery Story.
Negro Cemetery Next to a White One, A.
Old Picture, An.
On Being Asked for a Peace Poem.
On Certain Wits.
Ozymandias II.
Phoenix, The.

Picture, A.
Primer of the Daily Round, A.
Reading Pornography in Old Age.
Redeployment.
Reflexions on the Seizure of the Suez, and on a Proposal to Line the Banks of That Canal with Bill.
Remorse for Time, The.
Salt Garden, The.
Sanctuary, The.
Santa Claus.
Scales of the Eyes, The.
September, the First Day of School.
Sestina on Her Portrait.
Sigmund Freud.
Small Moon.
Snowflakes.
Sparrow in the Zoo, The.
Speculation.
Spell before Winter, A.
Statues in the Public Gardens, The.
Storm Windows.
Style.
Sunday at the End of Summer.
Sweeper of Ways, The.
Tapestry, The.
Thirtieth Anniversary Report of the Class of '41.
Three Towns, The.
To D— —, Dead by Her Own Hand.
To David, about His Education.
To My Least Favorite Reviewer.
To the Rulers.
Town Dump, The.
Translation.
Trees.
Truth.
Vacuum, The.
View, The.
View from an Attic Window, The.
Waiting Rooms.
War in the Air, The.
Watching Football on TV.
Way of Life, A.
Western Approaches, The.
What Kind of a Guy Was He?
Wolves in the Zoo.
Writing.
Young Woman.

Nemjoshi, Suniti. *See* **Hanscombe, Gillian**

Nerber, John
Castaway.

Neruda, Pablo (Neftalí Ricardo Reyes Basualto)
Almería.
Battle of the Jarama, The.
Drunk as drunk on turpentine.
Enigmas.
Fickle One, The.
Fleas interest me so much.
Full Woman, Carnal Apple.
Ghost of the Cargo Boat, The.
Great Rain of the South, The.
Gross innocent, *sel.*
International Brigade Arrives at Madrid, The.
Lone Gentleman.
Materia Nupcial.
Nothing but Death.
Ode to Her Aroma.
Ode to Salt.
Ode to the Watermelon.
Our Child.
Rain (Rapa Nui), The.
To the Foot from Its Child.
Tonight I can write the saddest line.
United Fruit Co, The.
Walking Around.
Youth.

Nerval, Gérard de (Gérard Labrunie)
Delfica.
Golden Lines.
Old Tune, An.

Nervo, Amado
And Thou, Expectant.
Entreaty to the Cloud.
Evocation.
Old Burden, An.

Nesbit, Edith (Edith Nesbit Bland)
Among His Books.
Baby Seed Song.
Child's Song in Spring.
Claim, The.
Gray Folk, The.
Love's Guerdons.
Mr. Ody met a body.
Song: "Oh, baby, baby, baby dear."
Things That Matter, The.
Villeggiature.

Nesbit, Wilbur Dick
All to Myself.
Friend of Two, A.
Hymn of Thanksgiving, A.
Let Us Smile.
Who Hath a Book.
Your Flag and My Flag.

Nesmith, James Ernest
Statue of Lorenzo de' Medici, The.

Netherclift, Beryl
London Trees.

Neto, Agostinho
Farewell at the Hour of Parting.
Friend Mussunda.
Kinaxixi.
Marketwoman, The.
We Must Return.
Western Civilization.

Neto, Joaõ Cabral de Melo. *See* **Melo Neto, Joaõ**

Netser, Eli
Almond Blossoms.
Looking at a Chagall Painting.
More, The.
My Best Clothes.
Night Walk.
Star-Sown.
These Colors This Tune.
This Fugitive Beauty.

Nettimaiyar
Your bards are wearing lotuses.

Netumpalliyattan
What She Said about Her Unfaithful, Estranged Husband.

Neugroschel, Joachim
Doves.
Eve's Advice to the Children of Israel.

Nevin, Alice
God's Will.

Nevin, Edwin H.
Happy, Saviour, Would I Be.
When Our Earthly Sun Is Setting.

Newbery, Thomas
What lack you, sir? What seek you? What will you buy?, *sel.*

Newbolt, Sir Henry
Admirals All.
Cities Drowned.
Clifton Chapel.
Commemoration.
Craven.
Drake's Drum.
Final Mystery, The.
From Generation to Generation.
He Fell among Thieves.
Master and Man.
Messmates.
Moonset.
Nightjar, The.
Rilloby-Rill.
Song: "Flowers that in thy garden rise, The."
To a River in the South.
Toy Band, The.
Vitaï Lampada.

Newcastle, Margaret Cavendish, Duchess of
Death is the cook of nature, and we find, *sel.*
Love, how thou'rt tired out with rhyme!
Mirth and Melancholy.
My Cabinets Are Oyster-Shells, *sel.*
O do not grieve, Dear Heart, nor shed a tear.
Of the Theme of Love.
Soul and Body.
Soul's Garment, The.
What Is Liquid.

Newcastle, William Cavendish, Duke of
Love Play.
Love's Epitaph.
Song: "We'll, placed in Love's triumphant chariot high," *sel.*

Newell, J. R.
Christmas Carol: "From the starry heav'ns descending."

Newell, Peter
Educated Love Bird, The.
Her Dairy.
Her Polka Dots.
Timid Hortense.
Wild Flowers.

Newell, Robert Henry
Picciola.

Newell, Robert Henry. *See* **"Kerr, Orpheus C."**

Newey-Johnson, D.
To Let.

Newlove, John
America.
Double-headed Snake, The.
First Time, The.
Grass Is a Reasonable Colour, The.
Pride, The.
Samuel Hearne in Wintertime.
Succubi.
Verigin, Moving in Alone.
Verigin 3.
Well-travelled Roadway, The.
What Do You Want?

Newman, John Henry, Cardinal
Chorus of Angels, *sel.*
England.
Good Samaritan, The.
Jesu, Maria—I am near to death, *sel.*
Judaism.
Refrigerium.
Sensitiveness.
Thanksgiving, A.
Zeal and Love.

Newman, Joseph S.
Hero and Leander.

Newman, Lance
Clean.

Newman, Louis I.
World Looks On, The.

Newman, Michael
Negative Passage.

Newman, Preston
Some Questions to Be Asked of a Rajah, Perhaps by the Associated Press.

Newsome, Mary Effie Lee
Arctic Tern in a Museum.
Baker's Boy, The.
Little Birches.
Morning Light.
Pansy.
Quilt, The.
Quoits.
Sky Pictures.
Wild Roses.

Newton, Byron Rufus
Owed to New York.

Newton, Charles
Wild Nature, *sel.*

Newton, John
Glorious Things of Thee Are Spoken.
Jesus! my Shepherd, Husband, Friend, *sel.*

Newton, Mary Leslie
Queen Anne's Lace.
Nga Pitiroirangi. *See* **Habib, Rowley**
Ngani, A. Z.
Praises of King George VI.
Ngata, Apirana
Cream Song, The.
Ngatho, Stella
Footpath.
Ngawai, Tuini
Great King.
News, The.
Niarchus [or Niarchos]
Requirements.
Niatum, Duane
After the Death of an Elder Klallam.
Apology.
Art of Clay, The.
Ascending Red Cedar Moon.
Chief Leschi of the Nisqually.
Crow's Way.
Digging Out the Roots.
Drawings of the Song Animals.
Elegy for Chief Sealth.
First Spring.
Homage to Chagall.
Indian Rock, Bainbridge Island, Washington.
Lines for Roethke Twenty Years after His
    Death.
Maggie.
No One Remembers Abandoning the Village
    of White Fir.
Novelty Shop, The.
Old Woman Awaiting the Greyhound Bus.
On Hearing the Marsh Bird's Water Cry.
On Leaving Baltimore.
On Visiting My Son, Port Angeles,
    Washington.
Owl in the Rearview Mirror, The.
Pieces.
Raven.
Reality of Autumn, The.
Slow Dancer That No One Hears but You.
Snowy Owl near Ocean Shores ("Snowy owl,
    storm cast from the arctic tundra").
Song from the Maker of Totems.
Song from the Totem Maker.
Street Kid.
To Your Question.
Traveler, The.
Tribute to Chief Joseph, A.
Waterfall Song, The.
Niazi, Munir
Half-Open Window at Midnight, A.
Let Us Leave Something Unsaid.
New Colour in the Colour of Sunlight, A.
Night at a Port, A.
Rain, Wind and a New City.
Song of the Wind.
Two White Women in the Sun.
Vague Dream, A.
Niazi, Salah. *See* **Niyazi, Salah**
Nibenegenesabe, Jacob
One time I wanted two moons, *sel.*
Ni-buttsu
One who rises, rises of himself.
Nicander
Recipe: Gourds.
Niccolai, Giulia
From Outside Comes the Adequate Cause.
GN Is Happy.
Nichol, B. P.
Gorg, a Detective Story.
Two Words; a Wedding.
Nicholas, Michael
Today: The Idea Market.
Nicholl, Louise Townsend
Architect.
Ark of the Covenant.
Cigar Smoke, Sunday, after Dinner.
Creation.

Cruse, The.
Different Speech, A.
Hymn: "Words of hymns abruptly plod, The."
Physical Geography.
Shape of the Heart, The.
Nichols, Grace
Ala.
Epilogue: "I have crossed an ocean."
Eulogy.
Even Tho.
Hi De Buckras Hi!
I Will Enter.
In My Name.
Invitation.
My Black Triangle.
Old Magic.
Praise Song for My Mother.
Skin-Teeth.
Waterpot.
We the Women.
Without Song.
Nichols, Jeannette
My Father Toured the South.
Nichols, Kevin
Feast of Stephen, The.
Nichols, Robert
Aurelia.
Battery Moving Up to a New Position from
    Rest Camp: Dawn.
Before I woke I knew her gone, *sel.*
Burial in Flanders, The.
But piteous things we are—when I am gone,
    sel.
By the Wood.
Casualty.
Come, let us sigh a requiem over love, *sel.*
Day's March, The.
Don Juan's Address to the Sunset.
Full Heart, The.
Harlot's Catch.
Moon behind High Tranquil Leaves, The.
Our Dead.
Secret Garden, The.
Sprig of Lime, The.
Talking of Ezra Pound and long-dead pantos,
    sel.
Thanksgiving.
Though to your life apparent stain attach, *sel.*
To D'Annunzio: Lines from the Sea.
When the proud World does most my world
    despise, *sel.*
Nicholson, John
Genius and Intemperance.
On a Calm Summer's Night.
Nicholson, John Gambril
I love him wisely if I love him well, *sel.*
Nicholson, L.
Bubbles.
Nicholson, Norman
Blackberry, The.
Burning Bush, The.
Caedmon.
Carol for the Last Christmas Eve.
Carol: "Mary laid her Child among."
Cleator Moor.
Cowper's Tame Hare.
For All Sorts and Conditions.
For the Bicentenary of Isaac Watts.
Glacier.
Michaelmas.
Motion of the Earth, The.
On the Closing of Millom Ironworks.
Ravenglass Railway Station, Cumberland.
Rockferns.
Safe Side, The.
Shepherds' Carol.
Song at Night.
To a Child before Birth.
Weather Ear.
Nicholson, Thomas
Sabbath Peal; or, Past, Present, and Future. A
    Moral Essay, The.

Ni Chonaill, Eibhlín Dhubh. *See* **O'Connell,**
    Eibhlin Dubh
Ní Chuilleanáin, Eiléan
At alarming bell daybreak, before, *sel.*
Dead Fly.
Letter to Pearse Hutchinson.
Old Roads.
Swineherd.
Wash.
Nicias
Fountain at the Tomb, The.
Nicochares
Hangover Cure.
Nicoïdski, Clarisse
Breaking Off from Waiting.
Eyes.
Mouth.
Open Earth.
Remembering.
Nicol, Abioseh
African Easter.
Meaning of Africa, The.
Nicoll, Robert
Mossy Stane, The.
We Are Lowly.
Nicolson, Adela Florence Cory. *See* **"Hope,**
    Laurence"
Nicolson, Alexander
Warning, A.
Nicophon
Beware of Figs.
Niedecker, Lorine
As praiseworthy/ the power of breathing.
For best work.
Lake Superior.
My mother saw the green tree toad.
Old man who seined.
Smile/ to see the lake.
You are my friend.
Young in Fall I said: the birds.
Nieminen, Pertti
I Drink the Wine of Your Dreams.
My Sister.
That's Not a Tiger.
They Were Pure Gold.
When I Neared Fifty.
Nietzche, Vincente Rodríguez
Poem H.
We must burn up, *sel.*
Nietzsche, Friedrich Wilhelm
Solitary, The.
Star Morals.
Nightingale, Madeleine
Apple Rhyme, The.
Caravan, The.
Scissor-Man, The.
Nigot
You surprise me, crow.
Nihoniho, Tuta
Government!
Nijo Tamesada. *See* **Tamesada**
Nijo Tameshige. *See* **Tameshige**
Nijo Tameyo. *See* **Tameyo**
Nijo Yoshimoto. *See* **Yoshimoto**
Nikitin, Ivan Savvich
Night in a Village, A.
Nikolay, Sonja
Witches' Menu.
Niles
Why Should Vain Mortals Tremble.
Niles, John Jacob
In All the Magic of Christmas-Tide.
Nilsen, Solveig
Fishing.
Nims, Bonnie
How to Get There.
Nims, John Frederick
Agamemnon before Troy.
Clock without Hands.
Conclusion: "If what began (look far and
    wide) will end."

Contemplation.
Elegy for a Bad Poet, Taken from Us Not
    Long Since.
Elegy: "Were you, as old prints have shown."
Eminent Critic.
Good Friday.
Gravity.
Hospital Breakfast: With Grace After.
Love and Death.
Love Poem: "My clumsiest dear, whose hands
    shipwreck vases."
Occasions of Grace at a Poetry Performance.
Parting: 1940.
Tide Turning.

Nisbet, Eilidh
Three Girls on a Buttress.
To a Midge.

Nishiwaki Junzaburo
Cup's Primitivism.
Eye.
For Memories.
In an Abandoned Garden.
January.
Loquat.
Modern Fable, The.
Pheasant.
Rain.
Sad.
Shepherd in Capri.
Slope.
Weather.
Winter Conversation.

Nishiyama Soin
I'm a Flower, *abr.*

Ni Tsan
Following the Rhymes of the Six Poems
    "Thinking of the Past at Ku-Su."
Inscribed on a Painting.
Inscribed on a Painting by Myself.
Inscribed on the Painting "River in Autumn."
It breaks the heart, don't ask, *sel.*
Lamenting Noble Scholar Chu.
Man in Hangchou Spread Word That I Had
    Died, A.
Mist and water of Five Lakes, this body not
    gone home, *sel.*
On the Fifteenth Day of the Ninth Month of
    the Year *Kuei-mao* of the *Chih-cheng*
    Period.
On the Twentieth Day.
Painting "Solitary Fisherman by a Spring
    River,," The.
River of autumn water, pale, cold mist, A,
    sel.
Startled awake, back from a dream, *sel.*
To the Retired Scholar Chang.
Waking from a Nap.
Woodpecker, The.
You ask when I will go back home, *sel.*

Nitschmann, Anna
This Flock So Small.

Niu Chiao
Deep Gratitude.
Deva-like Barbarian.
Dreaming of the South.
Echoing Heaven's Everlastingness.
Pacifying the Western Barbarians.
Song of the Jade Tower in Spring.
Song of the River City.
Song of the Water Clock at Night.
Song of the West Stream.
Song of the Wine Spring.
Sorrow on Gazing at the River.
Taoist Nun, The.
Willow Branches.

Niu Hsi-chi
Immortal at the River.
Joy at Renewal.
Mountain Hawthorns.
Paying Homage at the Golden Gate.
Song of the Wine Spring.

Niven, Frederick
Indian Dance.

Niyazi [or Niazi], Salah
Hameed.
Return of the Veil, The.
Third World.
Um Hakeem.
Within my bolted infernal gates, *sel.*

No Ch'ŏn-myŭng
Cricket.
Deer.

Noailles, Anna de
Image.
Poem on Azure.

Nobile, Maria Guacci
Suffering.

Noble, Fay Lewis
Prayer for Song.

Noel, Henry
Beauty Extoll'd, at.

Noel, Thomas
Old Winter.

Noël-Paton, Margaret Hamilton
War Widow.

"Nogar, Rui"
Poem of the Conscripted Warrior.

Nogi Maresuke
Song of Victory: the Battle of Port Authur.

Noguchi, Yone
Poet, The.

Noguere, Suzanne
Pervigilium Veneris.

Noho-mai-te-Rangi
Lullaby: "O my son, born on a winter's
    morn."
Song for Te Hauapu.

Noin
I left the capital.

Nolan, Edward
Oxford Is a Stage.

Nolan, Pat
Doubt.
Exercise ("Get loaded").
Exercise ("Just as I stood up").
Great Pretenderer, The.
Home Life.
Senryu.
Stone Age.
Tea for Two.

Noll, Bink
Divorce.
Moving between Beloit and Monroe.

Nomberg, David
Russian Cradle Song, A.

Nooteboom, Cees
Fear Makes the Spectator.
Fuji.
Sleeping Gods, The.
Thousand Nights and Days, A.
Titicaca.

Norman, Rosemary
Another Woman.
Cabbage.
My Son and I.
Waterloo Station.

Norris, Alfred
Humble Heart, A.
Prayer for Faith, A.

Norris, John
Hymn to Darkness.
Retirement, The.

Norris, John W.
Give Peace, O God, the Nations Cry.

Norris, Kathleen
Evaporation Poems.
Her Application to Elysium.
Memorandum/ The Accountant's Notebook.
Running through Sleep.
Stomach.

Norris, Leslie
Ballad of Billy Rose, The.

Buying a Puppy.
Camels, the Kings' Camel, The.
Elegy for Lyn James.
In Black Chasms.
Merlin and the Snake's Egg.
Mice in the Hay.
Quiet-eyed Cattle, The.
Shepherd's Dog, The.
Stable Cat, The.
Water.

Norse, Harold
Behind the Glass Wall.
Breathing the Strong Smell.
Colosseum.
I'm Not a Man.
We Bumped Off Your Friend the Poet.
You Must Have Been a Sensational Baby.

Norskog, Howard
Grey's River Roundup.

North, Dudley
Air: "So full of courtly reverence."

North, E.
Out of Doors.

North, Frank Mason
Where Cross the Crowded Ways of Life.

NorthSun, Nila
Falling Down to Bed.
49, The.
Future Generation.
Red Road, The.
Reservation Girls.
Stories from the Res.
Sweat, The.
Up & Out.

Nortje, Arthur
All Hungers Pass Away.
Brief Thunder at Sharpeville.
Letter from Pretoria Central Prison.
Midnight.
Soliloquy: South Africa.

Norton, Andrews
Hymn for the Dedication of a Church.
My God, I Thank Thee.

Norton, Caroline Elizabeth
Arab to His Favorite Steed, The.
Bingen on the Rhine.
I Do Not Love Thee.
King of Denmark's Ride, The.
Not Lost, but Gone Before.

Norton, John
Funeral Elogy, upon . . . Mrs. Anne
    Bradstreet, A.

Norvig, Gerda
Desert March.
Joining, The.
Tree of Life Is Also a Tree of Fire, The.

Norwood, Eille
Limerick: "Pretty young actress, a stammerer,
    A."

Norwood, Robert
But, this I found, *sel.*

Norworth, Jack
Take Me Out to the Ball Game.

Noshiwaki Junzaburo
Sorrow.

Notley, Alice
After Tsang Chih.
Backyard.
Flowers of the Foothills and Mountain
    Valleys.
I the People.
In Ancient December.
Night Sits in This Chair, The.
Poem: "Clitoris is a kind of brain, A."
Poem: "I believe the yellow flowers think with
    me."
World's Bliss.

Nottage, May Hastings
My Father's Voice in Prayer.

Novak, Helga
Letter to Medea.

Report on the Situation.
Spring in Westend.
"Novalis" (Friedrich von Hardenberg)
Aphorism.
Second Hymn to the Night, The, *sel.*
"When geometric diagrams and digits."
Nowak, Ernst
I let a stranger.
Sooner or later they will go in.
That knife/ has stabbed me in the eye a long
    time.
Nowak, Tadeusz
I Leave Myself.
Nowell, M. H.
Of Disdainful Daphne.
Nowlan, Alden
Aunt Jane.
Beginning.
Daisies.
For Jean Vincent d'Abbadie, Baron
    St.-Castin.
God Sour the Milk of the Knacking Wench.
Great Things Have Happened.
Grove Beyond the Barley, The.
Gypsies.
He Runs into an Old Acquaintance.
He Sits Down on the Floor of a School for the
    Retarded.
In the Operating Room.
Kyran's Christening.
Loneliness of the Long Distance Runner, The.
Party at Bannon Brook.
Porch.
Psalm of Onan for Harp, Flute and
    Tambourine, A.
Semi-Private Room.
Stoney Ridge Dance Hall.
Suppose This Moment Some Stupendous
    Question.
Therese.
Waiting for Her.
Wickedness of Peter Shannon, The.
Noyce, Wilfred
Breathless.
Noyes, Alfred
Art, I.
Art, II.
Barrel-Organ, The.
Betsy Jane's Sixth Birthday.
Daddy Fell into the Pond.
Epilogue: "Carol, every violet has," *sel.*
Forty Singing Seamen.
Highwayman, The.
New Duckling, The.
River of Stars, The.
Sea-Distances.
Sherwood.
Song: "What is there hid in the heart of a
    rose."
Song of Sherwood, A.
Spring, and the Blind Children.
Sunlight and Sea.
Victory Dance, A.
Noyes, Nicholas
Consolatory Poem Dedicated unto Mr. Cotton
    Mather, A.
Prefatory Poem, on. *Magnalia Christi
    Americana.*
Præfatory Poem to the Little Book, Entituled,
    Christianus per Ignem, A.
Rev. Nicholas Noyes to the Rev. Cotton
    Mather, The.
To My Worthy Friend, Mr. James Bayley.
Noyle, Ken
Sea, The.
Nozawa Boncho. *See* **Boncho.**
Ntiru, Richard
Prophecy, The.
Nu aima, Mikha'il
Seek Out Another Heart.
To a Worm.

Nugent, Robert, Earl Nugent
Epigram: "I loved thee beautiful and kind."
Epigram: "My heart still hovering round about
    you."
Epigram: "Since first you knew my am'rous
    smart."
To Clarissa.
Nukada, Princess
Waiting for the Emperor Tenji.
When, loosened from winter's bonds.
Nunan, Thomas
Dreamer, The.
Nunes, Cassiano
Episode.
Nurton, C.
My Doggie.
Nutter, Medora Addison
Mountain Creed.
Nutter, Medora Addison. *See* **Addison,
    Medora C.**
Nuur, Faarah
Limits of Submission, The.
Our Country Is Divided.
Nweke, Chuba
Moon Song.
Nye, Naomi Shihab
Catalogue Army.
Flying Cat, The.
Garden of Abu Mahmoud, The.
Going for Peaches, Fredericksburg, Texas.
Hello.
House in the Heart, The.
Hugging the Jukebox.
Making a Fist.
Mother of Nothing.
New Year.
One Island.
Sure.
Traveling Onion, The.
Trying to Name What Doesn't Change.
Use of Fiction, The.
Where Children Live.
With the Greeks.

O

"O., G. S."
Engine Driver, The.
Oakes, Urian
Away loose-reined careers of poetry!, *sel.*
Elegie upon that Reverend. Mr. Thomas
    Shepard, An.
To the Reader.
Oakes-Smith, Elizabeth. *See* **Smith,
    Elizabeth Oakes**
Oakley, Ebenezer S.
Thoughts That Move the Heart of Man, The.
Oakman, John
Glutton, The.
Oandasan, William
Acoma.
Grandmothers Land.
Past, The.
Round Valley Reflections.
Song of Ancient Ways, The.
Oates, Joyce Carol
Acceleration near the Point of Impact.
Baby.
Back Country.
Child-Bride, The.
Dreaming America.
Foetal Song.
Growing Together.
How Delicately.
Lines for Those to Whom Tragedy Is Denied.
Luxury of Sin.
New Jersey White-tailed Deer.

Night.
Stone Orchard, The.
Suicide, The.
Wasp, The.
Obi, Dorothy S.
Winds of Africa.
Obregón, Roberto
Fears, The.
That Sleepless Flame.
O'Brien, Edward J.
Her Fairness, Wedded to a Star.
O'Brien, Fitz-James
Ghost, The.
Kane.
Legend of the Easter Eggs, The.
Second Mate, The.
O'Brien, Gregory
Comfort for the Sick Child.
Fable, The, *sel.*
Her Voice Is the Tidying of a House.
Light, The, *sel.*
Painting Entitled Love and the Pilgrim, A.
Riverbed for Damien.
Uses of Clouds, The.
Visiting Card, A.
O'Brien, Katharine
In Winter.
Opening Letter to Manufacturers of Bathroom
    Wallp aper.
Spring Song.
O'Brien, Thomas
Always Battling.
International Brigade Dead.
Terror.
"O'Brien, John." *See* **Hartigan, Patrick
    Joseph**
O Brolchain, Mael Isu
I give Thee thanks, my King.
My sins in their completeness.
To an Elderly Virgin.
O'Bruadair, David [*or* Daibhi]
Adoramus Te, Christe.
Change, The.
Eire.
For the Family of Cuchonnacht O Dalaigh.
New Style, The.
O it's best to be a total boor.
O'Bruadair.
O'Byrne, Cathal
Donegal Hush Song, A.
O Canainn, Tomas
Nuala's Fiddle.
O'Carolan, Turlough. *See* **Carolan,
    Turlough**
Occleve, Thomas. *See* **Hoccleve, Thomas**
Occom, Samson
Waked by the Gospel's Powerful Sound.
Ochester, Ed
For the Margrave of Brandenburg.
Gift, The.
In the Library.
110 Year Old House.
Poem for Dr. Spock.
O'Coileain, Sean
Lament for Timoleague.
**O'Connell, Eibhlin Dubh (Eibhlin Dubh
    NiChonaill)**
Lament for Art [*or* Arthur] O'Leary, The.
My Steadfast Love, *sel.*
O'Connell, Richard
Arthur Hugh Clough, *sel.*
Irish Wake Song.
Sir John Suckling, *sel.*
O'Connor, Frank (Michael O'Donovan)
Angry Poet, The.
Hope.
O'Connor, J. F.
Accent Schmaccent.
O'Connor, Joseph
General's Death, The.
What Was My Dream?

O'Connor, Michael
Reveille.
O'Connor, Patrick
Exiles.
Lights of Dublin, The.
My Prayer.
O'Connor, Philip
Fag-End.
Poems (I-XI).
Raspberry in the Pudding, The.
Writing in England Now.
O'Cotter, Pat
Malemute Dog, A.
O'Crowley, Denis
Washington.
O'Dala, Donnchadh Mor
At Saint Patrick's Purgatory.
O'Dalaigh, Gofraidh Fionn
Child in Prison, A.
Under Sorrow's Sign.
O Dalaigh, Lochlann Og
In Praise of Three Young Men.
O'Dalaigh, Muireadach Albanach
Invocation, An: "Last night my soul
  departed."
Mighty Mary, hear me.
On the Death of His Wife.
On the Gift of a Knife.
Young man of alien beauty.
Odell, Jonathan
On Our Thirty-ninth Wedding Day.
Oden, Gloria C.
"As When Emotion Too Far Exceeds Its
  Cause."
Carousel, The.
Man White, Brown Girl and All That Jazz.
Map, The.
Private Letter to Brazil, A.
Review from Staten Island.
Riven Quarry, The.
This Child Is the Mother.
Triple Mirror, The.
Way It Is, The.
O Direain, Mairtin
Homage to John Millington Synge.
Invitation to Mary.
Trees on a Frosty Night.
O Domhnaill, Maghnas
Famished end to my tale this night, A.
Heart made full of thought, A.
Love, I think, is a disease.
O'Donnell, Charles L.
Process.
Resolution.
Security.
O'Donnell, George Marion
Semmes in the Garden.
O'Donoghue, Gregory
Web, The.
O'Donovan, Michael. *See* O'Connor, Frank
O'Dowd, Bernard
As many, Mother, are your moods and forms,
  sel.
Australia.
Cow, The.
Door of existence, beacon of our haze, *sel.*
Hark! Young Democracy from sleep, *sel.*
To other eyes and ears you are a great, *sel.*
Oe no Asatsuno. *See* Asatsuna
Oehlenschläger, Adam
There Is a Charming Land.
Oemaru (Otomo Oemaru)
Fall on, frost!
Oengus Céile Dé
Time is ripe and I repent, The.
Oerke, Andrew
Sun, The.
Offen, Yehudah
Air Drips from Rock.
Inwards.

O'Flynn, Cristoir
God?
Sainthood.
Og MacWard, Fearghal
All Ireland's now one vessel's company, *sel.*
O'Gallagher, Alice
Welcome O Great Mary.
Ogarev, Nikolay Platonovich
Road, The.
Ogasawara Gokyo
Written after the Revolt.
Ogburn, Charlton
Nature in Couplets.
O'Gillan, Angus
Dead at Clonmacnois [*or* Clonmacnoise],
  The.
Ogilvie, D. T.
Last Letter to the Western Civilization.
Ogilvie, Will H.
Blades of Harden, The, *sel.*
Death of Ben Hall, The.
From the Gulf.
How the Fire Queen Crossed the Swamp.
If I Were Old.
Kingship of the Hills, The.
O'Gnive [*or* O Gnimh], Fearflatha
After the Flight of the Earls.
Downfall of the Gael, The.
Passing of the Poets, The.
O'Gorman, Ned
Kiss, The.
O'Grady, Desmond
Day concludes burning, The, *sel.*
Dying Gaul, The.
Finn's Wishes.
If I Went Away.
My darling, my love, *sel.*
Page from a Diary.
Poet in Old Age Fishing at Evening, The.
Professor Kelleher and the Charles River.
O'Grady, Standish
And first Morency, far famed water, you, *sel.*
Old Nick in Sorel, *sel.*
Winter in Lower Canada, *sel.*
Ogunsiji, Bunmi
Pretty Girls Just Are.
O'Halloran, Elspeth MacDuffie. *See*
  "Elspeth"
O'Hara, Frank
Abortion, An.
Answer to Voznesensky and Evtushenko.
Aubade: "Million stars are dreaming out, A."
Autobiographia Literaria.
Ave Maria.
Blocks.
Blocks.
Chez Jane.
Day Lady Died, The.
Easter.
For James Dean.
Having a Coke with You.
Homosexuality.
Hôtel Transylvanie.
How to Get There.
Hunter, The.
I Don't Remember Anything of Then, *sel.*
Image of Leda, An.
In Favor of One's Time.
In Memory of My Feelings.
John Button Birthday.
Les Luths.
Meditations in an Emergency.
Music.
Ode: "Idea of justice may be precious, An."
Ode: Salute to the French Negro Poets.
Ode: Salute to the French Negro Poets.
Ode to Joy.
Ode to Michael Goldberg's Birth and Other
  Births.
On Rachmaninoff's Birthday.
Poem: "All the mirrors in the world."

Poem: "At night Chinamen jump."
Poem: "Eager note on my door said "Call
  me," The."
Poem: "Hate is only one of many responses."
Poem: "I watched an armory combing its
  bronze bricks."
Poem: "I will always love you."
Poem: "Khrushchev is coming on the right
  day!"
Poem: "Lana Turner has collapsed!"
Poem: "O sole mio, hot diggety, nix "I wather
  think I can."
Poem: "There I could never be a boy."
Poetry.
Princess Elizabeth of Bohemia, as Perdita.
Radio.
Rhapsody.
Shine, "O world!" don't weary the gulping
  Pole, *sel.*
Sleeping on the Wing.
Song: "Did you see me walking by the Buick
  Repairs?"
Step Away from Them, A.
Steps.
Terrestrial Cuckoo, A.
To Hell with It.
To John Ashbery.
To My Dead Father.
To the Film Industry in Crisis.
To the Harbormaster.
To the Poem.
Today.
True Account of Talking to the Sun at Fire
  Island, A.
Why I Am Not a Painter.
Yesterday Down at the Canal.
You Are Gorgeous and I'm Coming.
O'Hara, Theodore
Bivouac of the Dead, The.
O'Hare, Felix
Shoofly, The.
**O'Heffernan, Mahon (Mathghamhain O
  Hifearnain)**
I ask, who will buy a poem?
My Son, Forsake Your Art.
O Hehir, Diana
Alone by the Road's Edge.
Anima.
Courtship.
House.
How to Murder Your Best Friend.
Infant.
Learning to Type.
Old Lady under the Freeway, The.
Payments.
Plan to Live My Life Again, A.
Power to Change Geography, The.
Private Rooms.
Questions and Answers.
Retarded Children Find a World Built Just for
  Them, The.
Shore.
Some of Us Are Exiles from No Land.
Summoned.
Tarantula.
Terminal Vision.
They Grow Up Too Fast, She Said.
O Heigeartaigh, Padraig
My sorrow, Donncha, my thousand-cherished.
"O. Henry." *See* **"Henry, O."**
O Heoghusa, Eochaidh. *See* O'Hussey,
  Eochaidh.
O Hifearnain, Mathghamhain. *See*
  O'Heffernan, Mahon
O'Higgins, Brian
Mountain Altar, The.
O'Higgins, Myron
Blues for Bessie.
Sunset Horn.
Two Lean Cats.

Vaticide.
Young Poet.

O'Huiginn, Tadhg Dall
Difference, The.
Present of Butter, A.
Satire on the O'Haras, A.
Second Vision, The.
Visit to Enniskillen, A.

O'Huiginn, Tadhg Og
Lament for Fearghal Ruadh.
On the Breaking-up of a School.

O'Hussey [or O Heoghusa], Eochaidh [or Eochy]
Change in Style, A.
Hugh Maguire.
Mag Uidhir's Winter Campaign.
O'Hussey's Ode to the Maguire.

Ojenke. *See* **Saxon, Alvin**

O'John, Calvin
Dancing Teepees.
You Smiled.

Okamoto Jun
Battlefield of Dreams.
Under the Hazy, Blossom-Laden Sky.

O'Kane, T. C.
My Mother's Prayer.

Okara, Gabriel
Call of the River Nun, The.
Dispensing Morning Balm.
Mystic Drum, The.
Once upon a Time.
One Night at Victoria Beach.
Piano and Drums.
Snowflakes Sail Gently Down, The.
To Adhiambo.
You Laughed and Laughed and Laughed.

O'Keefe, John
Air: "Flaxen-headed cow-boy, as simple as may be, A."
Amo, Amas.
I Want a Tenant; a Satire.

O'Keeffe, Adelaide
Beasts and Birds.
Kite, The.
Rather Too Good, Little Peggy!
To George Pulling Buds.

O'Keeffe, John. *See* **O'Keefe, John**

Okigbo, Christopher
Death lay in ambush, *sel.*
Lament of the Flutes.

Okita, Dwight
Art of Holding On, The.
Crossing with the Light.
In Response to Executive Order 9066: All Americans of Japanese Descent Must Report to Relocation Centers.
Parachute.

Okkur Macattanar
Widows' Rice.

Okkur Macatti
What Her Girlfriends Said to Her.
What She Said ("Rains, already old, The").

Okopenko, Andreas
Brooding Afternoon in July, *sel.*
Edith.
End of a Summer Sunday, *sel.*
First Sunshine.
Hannelore will thus be my wife, *sel.*
July Morning, *sel.*
Prose behind the Insanity.

Oku, Princess
How will you cross the autumn mountain alone?

Okubo Shibutsu
Sudden Shower.

Okura (Yamanoue [or Yamanoe] no Okura)
Elegy on the Death of Furuhi, An.

Olaleye-Oruene, Taiwo
African Beauty.

"Old Shoju." *See* **Shoju-rojin**

Older, Julia
RDA (Recommended Daily Addictions).

Oldham, John
Careless Good Fellow, The.
Cup, The.
If you for orders, and a gown design, *sel.*
Of all the creatures, in the world, that be, *sel.*
On Butler who can think without rage, *sel.*
Prologue: "For who can longer hold? when every Press," *sel.*
Quiet Soul, A.
Satyr III: "When shaven Crown, and hallow'd Girdle's Power", *sel.*
Upon the Author of a Play Called *Sodom.*

Olds, Peter
E Flat.
My Mother Spinning.
Psycho.
Thoughts of Jack Kerouac—& Other Things.

Olds, Sharon
Armor.
Cambridge Elegy.
Death of Marilyn Monroe, The.
Elder Sister, The.
End, The.
First Love.
Fish Story.
I Cannot Forget the Woman in the Mirror.
I See My Girl.
Leningrad Cemetary, Winter of 1941.
Moment of My Father's Death, The.
Month of June: 13½, The.
My Mother's College.
One Girl at the Boys Party, The.
Race Riot, Tulsa, 1921.
Rite of Passage.
Sex without Love.
Sign of Saturn, The.
Things That Are Worse than Death.
Tricks.
Victims, The.
Why My Mother Made Me.

Oldys, William
On a Fly Drinking out of [or from] His Cup.
On Himself.

O'Leary, Eileen
Lament for Art O'Leary, The.

Oles, Carole
Between Talcy and Mer.
Magician Suspends the Children, The.
Manifesto for the Faint-Hearted, A.
Preparing for Weather.
They Set Out in Fog.
To a Daughter at Fourteen Forsaking the Violin.
Veterans Day, 1981.

Oliphant, Carolina. *See* **Nairne, Carolina Oliphant, Baroness**

Olitski, Leib
My Song to the Jewish People.

Oliver, Louis (Little Coon)
Horned Snake, The.
Indian Macho.
Sharpbreasted Snake, The.

Oliver, Louis (LittleCoon)
Empty Kettle.
Materialized into an Owl.
Wagon Full of Thunder.
Wagon Full of Thunder.

Oliver, Mary
At Loxahatchie.
Aunt Leaf.
Beaver Moon—The Suicide of a Friend.
Black Walnut Tree, The.
Diviners, The.
Fish, The.
Grandmothers, The.
In Blackwater Woods.
Kitten, The.
Music Lessons.

Mussels.
Old Whorehouse, An.
Poem for My Father's Ghost.
Rain in Ohio.
Skunk Cabbage.
Sleeping in the Forest.
Storm.
Strawberry Moon.
Swimming Lesson, The.
Tasting the Wild Grapes.
Through Ruddy Orchards.
Truro Bear, The.
University Hospital, Boston.

Oliver, Robert S.
Toad, The.

Oliver, W. H.
Augury.
Counter-Revolution.
In the Fields of My Father's Youth.
Parihaka.
Silent Revolution.

Oliver, William
I'll Have a Collier for My Sweetheart.

Olney, D. A.
Just Like This.

Olson, Charles
Across Space and Time.
As the Dead Prey upon Us.
Celestial Evening, October 1967, *sel.*
Cole's Island, *sel.*
Colored pictures, *sel.*
Death of Europe, The.
Distances, The.
I, Maximus of Gloucester, to You ("By ear, she sd"), *sel.*
I, Maximus of Gloucester, to You ("Off-shore, by islands hidden in the blood"), *sel.*
In Cold Hell, in Thicket.
Kingfishers, The.
La Chute.
La Préface.
Later Note on Letter 15, A, *sel.*
Librarian, The.
Lordly and Isolate Satyrs, The.
Maximus Poems, *sels.*
Merce of Egypt.
Moon Is the Number 18, The.
Moonset, Gloucester, December 1, 1957, 1:58 A.M.
Newly Discovered "Homeric" Hymn, A.
Praises, The.
Ring Of, The.
Songs of Maximus, *sel.*
Variations Done for Gerald Van de Wiele.

Olson, Elder
Childe Roland, etc.
Ice-Skaters.
In Defense of Superficiality.
Knight, with Umbrella.
Reflections on Mirrors.
Wild Horse.

Olson, Ernst W.
God of Peace, in Peace Preserve Us.

Olson, Kirby
Summer in Academia (Sumerian Academia).

Olson, Ted
Hawk's Way.
Things That Endure.

Olumo. *See* **Cunningham, James**

O'Malley, D. J.
Tenderfoot, The.

Omar b. Abi Rabi'a
Damsel, The.

Ombres, Rossana
Bella and the Golem.
Flower Ensnarer of Psalms.
Nocturne: "Today now at this moment the world flies against me."

Ome, Taniha. *See* **Taniha Ome**

O'Meallain, Fear Dorcha
Exodus to Connacht.

O'Meally, Bob
Make Music with Your Life.

O'Mulconry, Peadar
Were Not the Gael Fallen.

Onakatoni Yoshinobu. *See* **Yoshinobu**

Ondaatje, Michael
Biography.
Birth of Sound.
Breaking Green.
Burning Hills.
Charles Darwin Pays a Visit, December 1971.
Cinnamon Peeler, The.
Dog in San Francisco, A.
Elizabeth.
Gold and Black.
House Divided, A.
Inner Tube.
King Kong Meets Wallace Stevens.
Letters & Other Words.
Notes for the Legend of Salad Woman.
Strange Case, The.
To a Sad Daughter.
Walking to Bellrock.

Onderdonk, Henry Ustic
On Zion and on Lebanon.
Spirit in Our Hearts, The.
Though I Should Seek.

Oneil, Henrietta
Ode to the Poppy.

O'Neill, Eugene
It's Great When You Get In.

O'Neill, Mary
Feelings about Words.
Mark's Fingers.
Miss Norma Jean Pugh.
Sound of Water.
What Is Black?
What Is Orange?
What Is Red?

O'Neill, Mary Devenport
Dead in Wars and in Revolutions.
Galway.
Old Waterford Woman, An.
Scene-Shifter Death.

"O'Neill, Moira" (Nesta Higginson Skrine)
Corrymeela.
Grace for Light.
Her Sister.

Onitsura (Uejima Onitsura)
At the Opening of Chikubu's Collection of
    Haikai, *sel.*
Bright Moon: after an Illness, *sel.*
Come, come, I say.
Cooling Off in the Evening, *sel.*
Daybreak/ On the corn shoots.
Early Autumn, *sel.*
Fir stands sveltely under the moon, A, *sel.*
Gargoyle spits out a sparrow to a peach tree,
    A, *sel.*
Green cornfield.
Human parent chases a crow away, A, *sel.*
I poured water in the basin, *sel.*
I think the May rains, *sel.*
In spring they croak, *sel.*
In the mist something's visible, *sel.*
It's summer; then.
Late spring, *sel.*
Leaving Itami in Early February, *sel.*
Monk Kudo Asked Me, "What's Your Haikai
    Eye Like?', *sel.*
Night Grew Late in Kuzuha Village in
    Hirakata, The, *sel.*
On My Way Home, *sel.*
Profusely in confusion, *sel.*
Remembering with Feeling, *sel.*
Spring day: a sparrow sand-bathing in my
    garden, *sel.*
Spring water's visible here and there, The,
    sel.
They bloom and then.

Thirteenth Year of *Genroku* [1700], the Year
    My Boy Toshiaki Died, The, *sel.*
Trout leaping.
Under flying sweetfish clouds flow in a
    stream, *sel.*
Water bird, looking heavy, floats, A, *sel.*
Why are some icicles long, some short?, *sel.*
Will there be any.

Ono no Komachi. *See* **Komachi**

Ono Takamura
Masked by the snowflakes.

Ono Tozaburo
Dislike of Nature.
Extinction of Plankton.
In the Eyes of a Screech Owl.
Landscape: 6.
Landscape: 7.
One Plant for Man-made Oil.
Sparrow Bathing.
Sparrow Flock.
Stealing.
Today's Ferns.

Onuora, Oku (Orlando Wong)
Last Night.
Pressure Drop.
Reflection in Red.

Opoku, Andrew Amankwa
River Afram.

Oppen, George
Bahamas.
Birthplace; New Rochelle.
Book of Job and a Draft of a Poem to Praise
    the Paths of the Living, The.
Building of the Skyscraper, The.
Forms of Love, The.
From Virgil, *sel.*
Gesture, The, *sel.*
If It All Went Up in Smoke.
It Is Difficult Now to Speak of Poetry.
It Is Difficult Now to Speak of Poetry, *sel.*
Of Being Numerous #24, *sel.*
Population.
Psalm: "In the small beauty of the forest."
Quotations.
Sara in Her Father's Arms.
Some San Francisco Poems.

Oppenheim, James
Action.
As to Being Alone.
Death.
Future, The.
Handful of Dust, A.
Hebrews.
New God, The.
Runner in the Skies, The.
Slave, The.

Oppenheimer, Joel
Bath, The.
Blue Funk.
Bus Trip, The.
Father Poem.
Feeding, The.
For Hoyt Wilhelm.
Innocent Breasts, The.
Leave It to Me Blues.
Love Bit, The.
Mare Nostrum.
Mother Poem.
Undefined Tenderness, An.

Opperman, D. J.
Christmas Carol: "Three outas from the bleak
    Karoo."
Fable of the Speckled Cow.
Fable: "Under a dung-cake."
Water Whirligigs.

Oppezzo, Piera
Great Fear, The.
Very Softly.

**O'Rahilly [*or* O'Reilly], Egan [*or* Aogan O
    Rathaille]**
Brightest of the Bright, The.

Brightness most bright I beheld on the way,
    forlorn.
Drenching night drags on: no sleep or snore,
    The.
Geraldine's Daughter, The.
Grey Eye Weeping, A.
Inis Fal.
Lament for Banba, at.
More Power.
No help I'll call till I'm put in the narrow
    coffin.
Reverie, The.
Sleepless Night, A.
Time of Change, A.
Valentine Browne.
Vision, The.

Orampokiyar
What Her Girl Friend Said to the
    Foster-Mother ("If you think, mother'), *sel.*
What Her Girl Friend Said to the
    Foster-Mother ("In his fields', mother'), *sel.*
What Her Girl Friend Said when He Sent a
    Flattering Minstrel on His Behalf.
What Her Girl Friend Said, When the Woman
    Was About to Take Back Her Unfaithful
    Husband.
What She Said ("Bees, six tiny legs and
    wings all lovely'), *sel.*
What She Said ("Green creepers planted
    inside the house'), *sel.*
What She Said ("Hovering like the heron'),
    sel.
What She Said ("In his fields'), *sel.*
What She Said ("In his place, mother,/
    field-crabs cut into the pink'), *sel.*
What She Said ("In his place, mother,/
    mud-spattered spotted crabs'), *sel.*
What She Said ("In the full river'), *sel.*
What She Said ("Like the high fanning tufts
    on swift horses'), *sel.*

O Rathaille, Aogan. *See* **O'Rahilly, Egan**

Oravecz, Imre
By Then You'd Dressed.
9:00 A.M.

Orban, Otto
Apparition, The.
Certain Years.
Computer.
Concert.
Face of Creation, The.
Gaiety and Good Heart.
Hymn: "Some sort of fire leaped out of the
    dirty and poor and merciless city."
Ladies of Bygone Days, The.
Ray.
Report on the Poem.
Requiem: "He tossed a life preserver to the
    young castaway in '55."
Summer on the Lake, A.
To Be Poor.

O'Reilly, Dowell
Sea-Grief.

O'Reilly, John Boyle
Art Master, An.
At Best.
At Fredericksburg.
Boston.
Builder's Lesson, A.
Chicago.
Crispus Attucks.
Cry of the Dreamer, The.
Disappointment.
Experience.
Forever.
Infinite, The.
Lure, The.
Mayflower.
Midnight—September 19, 1881.
Ride of Collins Graves, The.
Savage, A.
Song: "Love was true to me."

O'Reilly (cont.)

What Is Good?
What shall we mourn? For the prostrate, *sel.*
White Rose, A.

O'Reilly, Pat
Wonderful Mother, A.

O'Reilly, Egan. *See* **O'Rahilly, Egan**

Orente, Rose J.
Master City, The.

Orerulavanar
Relations.
What He Said.

"Orestes"
Sonnet to Opium; Celebrating Its Virtues, A.

"Orinda." *See* **Philips, Katherine**

O'Riordan, Conor [*or* Conal]
Hymn to the Virgin Mary.

O Riordain, Sean
Claustrophobia.
Death.
Freedom.
Ice Cold.
Moths, The.
My Mother's Burying.

Orléans, Charles, Duc d'
Alons au bois le may cueillir.
Alas, Death.
Come, Death—My Lady Is Dead, *at.*
Dieu Qu'il la Fait.
Go, Sad Complaint.
In the Forest of Noyous Heaviness.
Mistress without Compare, A. *at.*
My Ghostly Father, I me confess.
Oft in My Thought.
Rondel: "Strengthen, my Love, this castle of my heart."
Smiling Mouth and Laughing Eyen Grey, The.
Spring.
Wanton Eye.
Well, Wanton Eye.
Whole Treasure of All Wordly Bliss, The.
Your Mouth Says, Kiss Me.

Orleans, Ilo
Frog on the Log, The.
Poor Shadow.

Orlen, Steve (Stephen Orlen)
Acts of Grace.
Acts without Consequence.
Aga Khan, The.
All That We Try to Do.
Bagatelles.
Big Friend of the Stones.
Biplane, The.
Boy Hiding in a Closet.
Drunken Man, The.
House, A.
In Praise of Beverly.
Life Drawing.
Life Study.
Madman's Wife, The.
Paradise.
Permission to Speak.

Orlovitz, Gil
If I could rise and see my father young, *sel.*
Night comes. Day runs for its life into my eyes, *sel.*

Orlovsky, Peter
Lepers Cry.
Second Poem.
Some One Liked Me when I Was Twelve.

Ormond, John
Ancient Monuments.
At His Father's Grave.
Lament for a Leg.
To a Nun.

Ormsby, Frank
At the Jaffé Memorial Fountain, Botanic Gardens.
Interim.
Ornaments.

School Hockey Team in Amsterdam, The.
Some of us stayed forever, under the lough, *sel.*
Spot the Ball.
Survivors.

Orozco, Olga
Sphinxes Inclined to Be.

Orpingalik
In a Time of Sickness.
My Breath.

Orr, Bob
Here.
Parable.

Orr, Christine
Road, The.

Orr, Ed
Shopping in Chicago.

Orr, Gregory
Abandoned, Overgrown Cemetery in the Pasture near Our House, An.
Adolescence.
After a Death.
Concerning the Stone.
Doll, The.
Driving Home after a Funeral.
End of August.
Gathering the Bones Together.
Haitian Suite.
Last Address to My Ghosts, A.
Like Any Other Man.
Lost Children, The.
Love Poem: "Black biplane crashes into [*or* through] the window, The."
Morning Song.
On the Lawn at Ira's.
Poem: "This life like no other."
Project, The.
Room, The.
Shelf Is a Ledge, A.
Silence.
Song of the Invisible Corpse in the Field.
Spring Floods.
"Transients Welcome."
Two Lines from the Brothers Grimm.
Vampire, The.
Visitor, The.
Voyages, The.
We Must Make a Kingdom of It.

Orred, Meta
In the Gloaming.

Orrery, Robert Boyle, 1st Earl of
On Christmas Day.

Ortega, Julio
Avenida Abancay.
Catastrophe (Chimbote), The.
Cecilia.
End of Autumn.
Fishermen.
Memory of Dust and Light.
My Country.
October.
Report for Isolda.
Sound of Water.

Ortiz, Simon J.
At the Salvation Army, *sel.*
Bend in the River.
Bony.
Creation, According to Coyote, The.
Dry Root in a Wash.
Forming Child Poems.
Four Bird Songs.
Hunger in New York City.
Indian Guys at the Bar.
Juanita, Wife of Manuelito.
My Father's Song.
New Story, A.
Pretty Woman, A.
Relocation.
Returned from California.
San Diego Poem, A.
Serenity in Stones, The.

Smoking My Prayers.
Spreading Wings on Wind.
Story of How a Wall Stands, A.
Survival This Way.
Telling about Coyote.
Ten O'Clock News.
This Preparation.
To Insure Survival.
Waiting for You to Come By.
Watching Salmon Jump.
Watching You.
What I Tell Him.
Wind and Glacier Voices.

Ortleb, Chuck
Metaphor as Illness.
Militerotics.
On Finding Out that the One You Slept with the Night Before Was Murdered the Next Day.
Some Boys.

Ortmayer, Constance
Dawn.

Orwell, George (Eric Blair)
As One Non-Combatant to Another.
Dressed man and a naked man, A.
Italian soldier shook my hand, The.
Lesser Evil, The.

Osadebay, Dennis C.
African Trader's Complaint, The.

Osaki, Mark
Amnesiac.
Contentment.
For Avi Killed in Lebanon.
Icon.
Turista.

Osaki Hosai. *See* **Hosai**

Osbey, Brenda Marie
Bone Step-Women, The.
"In These Houses of Swift Easy Women."
Portrait.
Wastrel-Woman Poem, The.

Osborn, Laughton
Death of General Pike, The.

Osborn, Margot
Always the Melting Moon Comes.

Osborn, Mary
Every Day.

Osborn, Mary I.
My Playmate.
Swing, The.

Osborn, Selleck
Modest Wit, A.

Osborne, Duffield
Ave! Nero Imperator.

Osborne, Edith D.
Path of the Padres, The.

Osborne, Louis Shreve
Riding Down from Bangor.

Osborne, Marian
Trinity, The.
White Violet.

Osgood, Frances Sargent
Calumny.
Celeste Dancing.
On a Dead Poet.
On Sivori's Violin.
Song: "Your heart is a music-box, dearest!"
To Sleep.

Osgood, Francis P.
Winter Fairyland in Vermont.

Osgood, Kate Putnam
Driving Home the Cows.

O'Shaughnessy, Arthur William Edgar
Fair Maid and the Sun, The.
Line of Beauty, The.
Ode.
Silences.
Song: "I made another garden, yea."
Song: "I went to her who loveth me no more."

O'Sheel, Shaemas
They Went Forth to Battle but They Always Fell.
Oshikochi Mitsune. *See* Mitsune
Oshima Ryota. *See* Ryota
Ossenfelder, Heinrich August
Vampire, The.
Osswald, Helga
Witness, A.
Ostenso, Martha
Return, The.
Ostriker, Alicia
April One.
Everywoman Her Own Theology.
Meeting the Dead.
Years.
O Suilleabhain, Eoghan Kua. *See* O'Sullivan, Owen Roe
O Suilleabhain, Tadhg Gaelach. *See* O'Sullivan, Teig Gallach
O'Sullivan, Daniel James
Glaucous-Gull's Death, The.
January.
Lament for Seán.
Moschatel.
Nightfall in Inishtrahull.
O'Sullivan, Owen Roe [*or* Eoghan Rua O Suilleabhain]
His Request.
Magic Mist, A.
Seamus, light-hearted and loving friend of my breast, *sel.*
Volatile Kerryman, The.
"O'Sullivan, Seumas" (James Starkey)
In North Great George's Street.
Lamplighter, The.
Piper, A [*or* The]
Starling Lake, The.
Trains, The.
O'Sullivan, Teig Gaelach [*or* Tadhg Gaelach O Suilleabhain]
Poem to the Heart of Jesus, A.
O'Sullivan, Vincent
Butcher and Co.
Children, The.
Clown, and All the Sea behind Him.
Dogknotting in Quezaltenango.
Don't Knock the Rawleigh's Man.
Elegy for a Schoolmate.
Elegy: "Today, because I am not dead."
Fault/line.
Figure who stands on the beach, A, *sel.*
For Where You Skill.
Home.
I Have Taken a Thrush.
Last things/ the turning leaves slip in the wind, *sel.*
Liberal, *sel.*
Look Sheila Seeing You've Asked Me.
Magpie vicious or mute on his frozen tree, The, *sel.*
Medusa.
Meeting Up.
On the day my father died a flame-tree, *sel.*
Rat at the Foot of the Cross.
Sententiae.
Still Shines When You Think of It.
TELEX FOR JIX RE SUNDAY.
Them.
There is a day when elaborate weathers ease down, *sel.*
To be in a place for spring and not have lived its winter, *sel.*
Waikato-Taniwha-Rau.
What Sheila Tells Him, Softly.
Which Wing the Angel Chooses.
Young bee falls between my window, A, *sel.*
Osundare, Niyi
Dawncall.
Harvestcall.
Raindrum.

Otalantaiyar
Six on the Desert Ways.
What He Said in the Desert.
Othón, Manuel José
Elegy: "Along the tangled path and in the red."
Steppe in the Nazas Country, A.
Wild Idyll.
Otomo, Prince
Speaking My Thoughts.
Otomo no Sakanoe, Lady
My brother has on/ a thin robe.
My heart, thinking/ "How beautiful he is."
Sent from the Capital to Her Elder Daughter.
Otomo No Yakamochi. *See* Yakamochi
Otomo Oemaru. *See* Oemaru
Otsu, Prince
Approaching Death.
Otsuji
Into a forest.
Otto, Harold
Cows and Logs.
Otto, Heinrich
Lord, Dear God! to Thy Attending.
Otto-Peters, Louise
Confession.
For All.
Otway, Thomas
Enchantment, The.
Ou-ty, Emperor. *See* Wu Ti, Emperor
Ou-yang Chiung
Offering Congratulations to the Enlightened Reign.
Offering Deep Affection.
Sand of Silk-Washing Stream.
Song in Three Characters, A.
Song of the River City.
Song of the Southern Country.
Spring in the Phoenix Tower.
Ou-yang Hsiu
Calligraphy Practice.
Cicada, The.
Distant Mountains.
Green Jade Plum Trees in Spring.
Tune: Song of Picking Mulberry ("Ten years ago I was a visitor at the wine jar").
Tune: Treading on Grass.
Written for the Pavilion of the Drunken Old Man at Ch'u-chou.
Ousley, Clarence
When the Mint Is in the Liquor.
Ouston, Hugh
Climber Surveys His Mountain, The.
Outram, George
On Hearing a Lady Praise a Certain Rev. Doctor's Eyes.
Strictures on the Economy of Nature.
Overstreet, Bonaro W.
First Day of Teaching.
Ovid (Publius Ovidius Naso)
Acteon, *sel.*
And from the Citie Tegea there came the Paragone, *sel.*
And here I wish my soul died with my breath, *sel.*
And on this day, which poets unto thee, *sel.*
Attend, ye nymphs, by wedlock unconfin'd, *sel.*
Captive of Love, *sel.*
Complaisant Swain, The, *sel.*
Constant Penelope sends to thee, careless Ulysses, *sel.*
Corinna, Having Tried, with Her Own Hand, *sel.*
Corinnae Concubitus, I, 5, *sel.*
Cypassis, that a thousand ways trimm'st hair, *sel.*
Daedalus, *sel.*
Daphne and Apollo, *sel.*
Death of Eurydice and Orpheus' Journey to Hell, The, *sel.*

Either she was foule, or her attire was bad, *sel.*
Floods, by nature enemies to land, The, *sel.*
Graecinus (well I wot) thou told'st me once, *sel.*
I ask but right: let her that caught me late, *sel.*
I Ovid poet of my wantonnesse, *sel.*
I pray thee Nymph Penaeis stay, I chase not as a fo, *sel.*
In the Shire of Phestos hard by Cnossus dwelt of yore, *sel.*
King Midas, *sel.*
Kiss, if you can: Resistance if she make, *sel.*
Lente, Lente, *sel.*
Look, he is superfluous—for of what use was it to be born?, *sel.*
Magic, *sel.*
Meleager, *sel.*
More whyght thou art than primrose leaf my Lady Galatee, *sel.*
My intention is to tell of bodies changed, *sel.*
Near the Cymmerians, in his dark abode, *sel.*
Neare Enna walles there standes a Lake Pergusa is the name, *sel.*
Northern breath, that freezes floods, he binds, The, *sel.*
Not Pallas, not ev'n Spleen it self could blame, *sel.*
Now have I brought a woork to end which neither Joves fierce [*or* feerce] wrath, *sel.*
Now in this while gan Daedalus a wearinesse to take, *sel.*
Now ore the sea from her old love comes she, *sel.*
Now whyle Hippomenes/ Debates theis things, *sel.*
Of the Pythagorean Philosophy, *sel.*
Philemon and Baucis, *sel.*
Phoenix Self-born, The, *sel.*
Pygmalion seeing these to spend their times, *sel.*
Pygmalion's Statue Comes to Life, *sel.*
Seeing as the father saw the rosy morn, *sel.*
Seeing thou art faire, I barre not thy false playing, *sel.*
Shall I complain or not? Or shall I mask, *sel.*
Stones (a miracle to mortal view), The, *sel.*
Then sprang up first the golden age, which of itself maintained, *sel.*
Then thus the sire of gods, with look serene, *sel.*
There was a man here, Samian born, but he, *sel.*
To His Mistress, *sel.*
To Paris that was once her owne though now it be not so, *sel.*
To thee obeyeth all the East as far as Ganges goes, *sel.*
To Verse Let Kings Give Place, *sel.*
While Thracians shal with arrowes war, Iaziges with bowe, *sel.*
Winter at Tomi.
You have consum'd my language, and my pen, *sel.*
You, who in Cupid's rolls inscribe your name, *sel.*
Owen, Gareth
Winter Days.
Owen, Goronwy
Elegy for His Daughter Ellen.
Invitation, The.
Owen, Guy
Epitaph for a Beatnik Poet.
Epitaph for a Meat-Packer.
Owen, J. Elgar
Maturity.
Owen, John L.
City Singers, The.
Owen, Maureen
African Sunday.

For Emily (Dickinson).
Heart that's been broken, A.
Narcolepsy.
Novembers or Straight Life.
"Some Days," Dorothy Parker Said, "It's
    Better Than Digging Ditches."
Three Mile Island.

Owen, Wilfred
Antaeus; a Fragment.
Anthem for Doomed Youth.
Apologia pro Poemate Meo.
Arms and the Boy.
Asleep.
Chances, The.
Conscious.
Disabled.
Dulce et Decorum Est.
End, The.
Exposure.
Fragment: "I saw his round mouth's crimson
    deepen as it fell."
From My Diary, July 1914.
Futility.
Greater Love.
Hospital Barge at Cérisy.
Insensibility.
Inspection.
Le Christianisme.
Letter, The.
Mental Cases.
Miners.
Next War, The.
Parable of the Old Man and the Young, The.
Roads Also, The.
Send-off, The.
Sentry, The.
Shadwell Stair.
Show, The.
Sonnet: "Three colours have I known the
    Deep to wear."
Sonnet to My Friend, with an Identity Disc.
Spring Offensive.
Strange Meeting.
Terre, A.
To a Child.
Unreturning, The.

Owens, Rochelle
Dance and Eye Me (Wicked)ly My Breath a
    Fixed Sphere.
Power of Love He Wants Shih (Everything),
    The.

Owl Woman (Juana Manwell)
Songs for the Four Parts of the Night.

Oxenham, John (William Arthur Dunkerley)
All One in Christ.
Credo.
Everymaid.
Face to Face with Reality.
God's Sunshine.
Live Christ.
Love.
Love's Prerogative.
Per Ardua ad Astra.
Prayer, A: "Through every minute of this
    day."
Prince of Life, The.
Sacrament of Sleep, The.
Seeds.
So Little and So Much.
Some Blesseds.
To Whom Shall the World Henceforth
    Belong?
Thanksgiving.
Ways, The.
We Thank Thee.
We Thank Thee, Lord, *sel.*
Where Are You Going, Greatheart?
With hearts responsive, *sel.*
Your Place.

Oxford, Earl of. *See* **De Vere, Edward, 17th
    Earl of Oxford**
Oyama, Richard
Day after Trinity, The.
Dreams in Progress.
Obon by the Hudson.
This Song Shows Me Pictures; Morningside
    Drive, New York City 1950-1960.
Ozaki Bunki
Night Thoughts.
Ozerov, Lev
Babi Yar.
Ozick, Cynthia
Riddle, A: "I walk on two legs."
Wonder-Teacher, The.

P

Pace, Charles Nelson
Cross, The.
Pacernick [or Pacernik], Gary
I Want to Write a Jewish Poem.
Pacheco, José Emilio
Mosquitoes.
Pack, Richardson
Epistle from a Half-Pay Officer in the Country
    to His Friend in London, An.
Pack, Robert
Adam on His Way Home.
Bird in Search of a Cage, A.
Boat, The.
Chopping Fire-Wood.
Clayfeld's Anniversary Song.
Clayfeld's Daughter Reveals Her Plans.
Clayfeld's Glove.
Clayfeld's Twin.
Cleaning the Fish.
Departing Words to a Son.
Departure, The.
Descending.
Don't Sit under the Apple Tree with Anyone
    Else but Me.
Everything Is Possible.
Faithful Lover, The.
Ghost Story.
Idyl in Idleness, An.
In a Field.
On the Seventh Anniversary of the Death of
    My Father.
Pack Rat, The.
Parable.
Poem for You.
Raking Leaves.
Resurrection.
Secrets.
Trying to Separate.
Waiting.
Way We Wonder, The.
Packard, Frederick
Balearic Idyll.
Padeshah Khatun
Sovereign Queen.
Padgett, Ron
After the Broken Arm.
Butterfly, The, *sel.*
Chocolate Milk.
December.
Electric Eel, The, *sel.*
Giraffe, The, *sel.*
High Heels.
Louisiana Perch.
Love Poem.
Ode to Bohemians.
Strawberries in Mexico.
Voice.
Pagan, Isobel
Ca' the Yowes to the Knowes.

Pagaza, Joaquín Arcadio
Chest of Perote, The.
Crag, The.
Page, G. K.
Kaleidoscope.
Page, Geoff
Country Nun.
Page, Patricia K.
Adolescence.
After Rain.
Arras.
Brazilian Fazenda.
Cullen ("Cullen renounced his cradle at
    fifteen").
Deaf-Mute in the Pear Tree.
Element.
Evening Dance of the Grey Flies.
Images of Angels.
Landlady, The.
Man with One Small Hand.
Permanent Tourists, The.
Photos of a Salt Mine.
Puppets.
Schizophrenic.
Snowman, The.
Stenographers, The.
Stories of Snow.
Suffering.
Summer Resort.
T-Bar.
War Lord in the Early Evening.
Page, Thomas Nelson
Ashcake.
Dragon of the Seas, The.
Uncle Gabe's White Folks.
Pagis, Dan
Acrobatics.
Another Testimony.
Ararat.
Armchairs.
Autobiography.
Balloons.
Biped.
Brothers.
Decline of an Empire.
Draft of a Reparations Agreement.
Elephant, The.
Epilogue to Robinson Crusoe.
Final Exam.
Fossils.
Grand Duke of New York, The.
Honi.
Houses.
I Was Before I Was.
Impromptu Heart.
Instructions for Crossing the Border.
Journey, The.
Last Ones, The.
Letter, A.
Limits of Physics, The.
Logbook.
Moment at the Louvre, A.
Needless Return.
November '73.
Outside the Line.
Pages of an Album.
Photo at the Bridge.
Plans.
Point of Origin.
Scrawled in Pencil in a Sealed Railway Car.
Siege.
Souvenir, The.
Testimony.
Tower, The.
Tropical Greenhouse.
Two-Legs.
Witness anew, I'm bound to pass on, A.
Words.
Written in Pencil in the Sealed Railway-Car.
Pagliarani, Elio
Humbly I Confess That I Am Mortal.

It's Already Autumn.
Love Song.
Narcissus Pseudonarcissus.
Poème Antipoème.
Subjects and Arguments for an Act of
   Desperation.
Pagnucci, Gianfranco
Death of an Elephant, The.
Pai, Joshua Tan
My Soul Hovers over Me.
Trees Once Walked and Stood.
"Pai Ta-shun." *See* **Peterson, Frederick**
"Pai Wei"
Madrid.
Pain, Barry
As the sin that was sweet in the sinning, *sel.*
Come, little cottage girl, you seem, *sel.*
Cosy fire is bright and gay, The, *sel.*
Here's a mellow cup of tea, golden tea!, *sel.*
I think that I am drawing to an end, *sel.*
Macaulay at Tea, *sel.*
Martin Luther at Potsdam.
Oh! Weary Mother, *sel.*
One cup for my self-hood, *sel.*
Poets at Tea, III, The.
Ride a Cock Horse.
Tut! Bah! we take as another case, *sel.*
Weel, gin ye speir, I'm no inclined, *sel.*
Pain, Philip
Meditation 8.
Meditation 9 ("Man's life is like a rose that in
   Spring"), *sel.*
Meditation 62.
Meditation 10.
Meditation 29 ("How mutable is every thing
   that here"), *sel.*
Meditations for August 1, 1666.
Meditations for July 19, 1666.
Meditations for July 25, 1666.
Porch, The.
Whilst in This World I Stay.
Paine, Albert Bigelow
Cooky-Nut Trees, The.
Dancing Bear, The.
Hills of Rest, The.
In Louisiana.
Little Child, The.
Mis' Smith.
Paine, Robert Treat
Adams and Liberty.
Paine, Thomas
Liberty Tree.
Palacio, Vicente Riva
To the Wind.
Palagyi, Louis
Aimless.
Palaipatiya Perunkatunko
What Her Girl Friend Said to Her.
What She Said.
Palazzeschi, Aldo
So Let Me Have My Fun.
Palea
Piano at Evening.
Palen, Jennie M.
Early Dutch.
Palés Matos, Luis
African Dancer.
Virtuous Sin, The.
Paley, Grace
One day when I was a child, long ago.
Women in Vietnam, The.
Paley Francescato, Martha
Semen.
Palfrey, Sarah Hammond. *See* **"Foxton, E."**
Palgrave, Francis Turner
City of God, The.
Creçy.
Eutopia.
Linnet in November, The.
Trafalgar.

Palladas
Grammar commences with a 5-line curse.
Loving the rituals that keep men close.
Naked I Came.
Poor devil that I am, being so attacked.
Racing, reckoning fingers flick.
This Life a Theater.
When you send out invitations, don't ask me.
Pallades. *See* **Palladas**
Pallottini, Renata
Message.
Palmanteer, Ted D.
Granma's Words.
Pass It On Grandson.
Palmer, Alice Freeman
Communion Hymn, A.
On a Gloomy Easter.
Palmer, E. Harriet
Parterre, The.
Shipwreck, The.
Palmer, Herbert Edward
Aunt Zillah Speaks.
Ishmael.
Rock Pilgrim.
Vampire, The.
Woodworker's Ballad.
Wounded Hawk, The.
Palmer, John F.
Band Played On, The.
Palmer, John Williamson
Fight at [the] San Jacinto, The.
Maryland Battalion, The.
Ned Braddock.
Reid at Fayal.
Stonewall Jackson's Way.
Theodosia Burr: The Wrecker's Story.
Palmer, Michael
Barely anything to say, everything said. But
   you break.
Book of the Yellow Castle.
Changes around the Bay.
Classical Style, The.
Comet, The.
Dearest Reader.
Desire was a quotation from someone.
Documentation.
Echo ("Two poles. We didn't disagree.").
Echo ("Which in a dry season might").
Echo ("Which resound. Re-sounds. Where
   first would").
Facades for Norma Cole.
From C.
I have answers to all of your questions.
Lens.
Library Is Burning, The.
Notes for Echo Lake 5.
On the Way to Language.
Seven Forbidden Words.
She says, you are the negative.
Song of the Round Man.
Symmetrical Poem.
Theory of the Flower, The.
View from an Apartment.
Village of Reason, The.
Voice and Address.
Words say, mispell and mispell your name.
Palmer, Miriam
Raccoon Poem.
"Vierge Ouvrante."
What if jealousy is just a bad dream?
Palmer, Nettie
Mother, The.
Palmer, Ray
Jesus, These Eyes Have Never Seen.
Lord, My Weak Thought in Vain Would
   Climb.
My Faith Looks Up to Thee.
Palmer, Samuel
Shoreham: Twilight Time.
Palmer, T. H.
Try, Try Again, *at.*

Palmer, Vance
Farmer Remembers the Somme, The.
Palmer, Winthrop
Arlington Cemetery Looking toward the
   Capitol.
Palquera, Shem-Tob ben Joseph
Adapt Thyself.
Mouth and the Ears, The.
Paman, Clement
On Christmas Day to My Heart.
Pan, Lady (Pan Chieh-yü)
Present from the Emperor's New Concubine,
   A.
Song of Regret.
Panatattu
True Knowledge.
Unity of God, The.
Pan Chao
Needle and Thread.
Panek, Denise
Evelyn Searching.
For Shirley.
Pankey, Eric
Tending the Garden.
"Panormitanus" (Antonio Beccadelli)
Epitaph on Pegasus, a Limping Gay.
This Quintus, Corydon, for whom you lust.
Pantiyan Arivutai Nampi
Children.
"Pantycelyn." *See* **Williams, William
   ("Pantycelyn")**
P'an Yüeh
Lamenting the Dead.
Rhyme-Prose on the Idle Life.
Thinking of My Wife.
Pao Chao
Imitating the Old Poems.
In Imitation of "The King of Huai-nan."
Rhyme-Prose on the Desolate City.
Paoli, Betty
To a Man of the World.
Pape, Greg
Boquillas.
Endless Nights of Rain.
Flower Farm, The.
For Rosa Yen, Who Lived Here.
In the City of Bogotá.
La Llorona.
Mercado.
My Happiness.
October.
Porpoise, The.
Put Your Mother on the Ceiling.
Sharks, Caloosahatchee River.
Pappas, Theresa
Playing Time.
Paramore, Edward E., Jr.
Ballad of Yukon Jake, The.
Paranar
What Her Friend Said to Her, within the
   Lover's Hearing.
What She Said.
What She Said to Her Girl Friend ("On the
   tall hill").
Paraone, Tiwai
Chant to Io.
Paraske, Larin
My Little Love Lies on the Ground.
Sad Is the Seagull.
Woman Grows Soon Old, A.
Paredes, Rigoberto
Memorial.
Salon Chronicle.
Pari
That Month.
Parini, Jay
Amores (after Ovid).
Function of Winter, The.
Missionary Visits Our Church in Scranton,
   The.
Skater in Blue.

Skiing Home at Dusk.
Snake Hill.
Suburban Swamp.
This Kampuchea.
To His Dear Friend, Bones.

Park, Frances
Sad Song about Greenwich Village, A.

Park Je-chun
Captain Michael.
Chuangtzu Poem No. 6.
Dong Jin.
Dragon Song.
Famous Archer, The.
Festival in Fishing Village No. 25.
Festival in Fishing Village No. 19.
Festival in Fishing Village No. 3.
Futile Rhetoric No. 1.
Gosan.
Heaven's Wanderer in Heaven, for Tu Fu.
Lady Suro.
Moon Bright.
Offering Wine.
Parrot.
Polishing the Porcelain Lamp.
Recent Status.
That Heaven.

Park, Roswell
Jesus Spreads His Banner o'er Us.

Parke, Walter
His Mother-in-Law.
Limerick: "There was a princess of Bengal,"
    at.
Limerick: "There was a young man who was
    bitten," *at.*
Limerick: "There was an old stupid who
    wrote," *at.*

Parker, Dorothy
Bohemia.
Certain Lady, A.
Comment.
De Profundis.
Experience.
Flaw in Paganism, The.
General Review of the Sex Situation.
George Sand.
Godmother.
Indian Summer.
Inventory.
Little Old Lady in Lavender Silk, The.
News Item, *sel.*
Observation, *sel.*
On Being a Woman.
One Perfect Rose.
Partial Comfort.
Pictures in the Smoke.
Résumé.
Sanctuary.
Social Note.
Tombstones in the Starlight: The
    Fisherwoman.
Unfortunate Coincidence.

Parker, Edgar
Contrary Waiter, The.

Parker, Edwin Pond
Master, No Offering.

Parker, Henry Adams
Apple Blossoms.

Parker, Martin
Description of a Strange (and Miraculous)
    Fish, A.
Keep a Good Tongue in Your Head.
King Enjoys His Own Again, The.
Maunding Soldier, The; or, The Fruits of
    Warre Is Beggery.
Saylors for My Money.
Wooing Maid, The.

Parker, Patricia
From the Cavities of Bones.
I Followed a Path.
My Brother.
Prologue from "Legacy."

There Is a Woman in This Town.
Where Will You Be?

Parker, Sir Gilbert
Little Garaine.
Reunited.
World in Making, The.

Parker, Stephen
Winter in Étienburgh.

Parker, Theodore
Higher Good, The.
Jesus.
Way, the Truth, and the Life, The.

Parkes, Francis Ernest Kobina
Apocalypse.
Blind Steersmen.
Three Phases of Africa.

Parkwood, Rose
Garden, The.

"Parley, Peter." *See* **Goodrich, Samuel
    Griswold**

Parnell, Thomas
Elegy, to an Old Beauty, An.
Hymn to Contentment, A.
Night-Piece on Death, A.
Song: "When thy beauty appears."
Up yonder hill, behold how sadly slow, *sel.*

Parone, Edward
Morning Track, The.

Parra, Nicanor
Forgetfulness.
I Move the Meeting Be Adjourned, *sel.*
Teachers, The.

Parra, Violeta
Goddamn the Empty Sky.

Parrish, Elsie
Some Things That Easter Brings.

Parrish, Essie
Essie Parrish in New York.

Parrish, John
Democratic Barber; or, Country Gentleman's
    Surprise, The.

Parrish, Randall
Your Lad, and My Lad.

Parrot, Henry
Fatales Poetae.
In Obitum Promi.
On a Poet.

Parrott, E. O.
Ode on a Grecian Urn.
Round about the cauldron go!

Parry, David Fisher
Miniver Cheevy, Jr.

Parry, Edward Abbott
I Would Like You for a Comrade.
Jam Fish, The.
Pater's Bathe.

Parry, Joseph
New Friends and Old Friends.

Parry, R. Williams
Branwen's Starling.
Fox, The.
Miraculous Dawn.
Old Boatman of Death's River, The.
On a Soldier Killed in the Great War.
Two Hearts Divided.

Parry, Robert
Except I Love, *sel.*
Song: "Fond affection, hence, and leave me!,"
    sel.

Parry-Williams, T. H.
Christmas Carol, A: "Close to a quarter of a
    century since then."
Llyn y Gadair.
These Bones.

Parsons, Clere
Different.
Introduction: "I bespeak words."

Parsons, Thomas William
Andrew.
Dirge for One Who Fell in Battle [*or* Dirge]
Her Epitaph.

Into the Noiseless Country.
Like as the Lark.
Mary Booth.
Obituary.
On a Bust of Dante.
Paradisi Gloria.
To a Lady.
To a Young Girl Dying.

Parsons, William
Epigram on the Play-House at Amsterdam.
Man of Taste, The.
Ode to the Lake of Geneva.
On Descending the River Po.
To a Friend in Love during the Riots.

Parthasarathy, Rajagopal
Exile: 2, *sel.*

Partridge, Dixie
Angles.
At Nuclear Medicine.
While Pruning.

Partridge, William Ordway
Nathan Hale.

Parun, Vesna
Mother of Man.
Return to the Tree of Time, A.

Pascal, Paul
Tact.

Pascoli, Giovanni
November.
Weaver, The.

Paskin, Sylvia
Bi-Lingual.
Demon-Lover.
Without a Beginning nor an End.

Pasolini, Pier Paolo
Day of My Death, The.
February.
Gramsci's Ashes.
Only loving, only knowing, *sel.*
Prayer to My Mother.
Ring, The.
Sea Promenade, A.
Sun, the Sun, The.
Tears of the Excavator, The.
To a Pope.

Passerat, Jean
Love in May.
Song: "Shephard loveth thow me vell?"

Pastan, Linda
After Reading Nelly Sachs.
Animals, The.
April.
Aspects of Eve.
At the Jewish Museum.
Aubade: "In the early morning."
David.
Death of a Parent, The.
Dido's Farewell.
Elsewhere.
Epilogue: "Years later the girl died."
Ethics.
Family Scene: Mid-Twentieth Century.
Grammar Lesson.
I Think Table.
In the Old Guerilla War.
Jump Cabling.
Last Words.
Love in the Nuclear Age.
Marks.
Notes for an Elegy: for John Gardner.
Overture.
Pears.
Printer, The.
Prologue: "Nothing has happened yet."
Rachel.
September.
Shadows.
Suffocation.
Symposium: Apples, A.
To a Daughter Leaving Home.
To the Field Goal Kicker in a Slump.

Weather Forecast.
Writing while My Father Dies.
Yom Kippur.

Pasternak, Boris Leonidovich
Definition of the Soul.
Fresh Paint.
Hamlet in Russia, A Soliloquy.
Hops.
In the Breeze.
May It Be.
Poem: "So they begin. With two years gone."
Three Variations.
Waving a Bough.

Pastor, Ned
Career Women Who Marry Today.
Double Occupancy—Sahara Style.
No Regrets.

Pastorius, Francis Daniel
As often as some where before my feet.
Delight in books from evening.
Epigram: "At ten a clock, when I the fire
   rake."
Extract the quint-essence.
Great God, Preserver of All Things.
I have a pretty little flow'r.
If Any Be Pleased to Walk into My Poor
   Garden.
If thou wouldest roses scent.
Learn, lads and lasses, of my garden.
Most weeds, whilst young.
On His Garden Book.
Though My Thoughts.
Thy garden, orchard, fields.
To God alone, the only donour.
When I solidly do ponder.
When one or other rambles.

Pataki, Heidi
Hosanna.
Nature Morte.
On the Journey to Your Heart.
You Have Taken My Language Away.

Patchen, Kenneth
All the Roary Night.
And What with the Blunders.
Animal I wanted, The.
As We Are So Wonderfully Done with Each
   Other.
At the New Year.
Because Going Nowhere Takes a Long Time.
Because He Liked to Be at Home.
Because in This Sorrowing Statue of Flesh.
Because Sometimes You Can't Always Be So.
Because They Were Very Poor That Winter.
Behold, One of Several Little Christs.
Biography of Southern Rain.
But there is no black jaw which cannot be
   broken by our word, sel.
Character of Love Seen as a Search for the
   Lost, The.
Constant Bridegrooms, The.
Deer and the Snake, The.
Do the Dead Know What Time It Is?
Elegy for the Silent Voices and the Joiners of
   Everything.
Empty Dwelling Places.
Everlasting Contenders, The.
Fog.
From My High Love.
Gautama in the Deer Park at Benares.
Geography of Music.
I/ want you/ to listen, sel.
I Have Lighted the Candles, Mary.
I'd Want Her Eyes to Fill with Wonder.
In Judgment of the Leaf.
In Memory of Kathleen.
In Order To.
In the footsteps of the walking air.
Known Soldier, The.
Like a Mourningless Child.
Lions of fire, The.
Little hill climbs up to the village and puts its
   green hands, The, sel.

Magical Mouse, The.
Midnight Special.
Moon, Sun, Sleep, Birds, Live.
Naked Land, The.
Nice Day for a Lynching.
O All Down within the Pretty Meadow.
O my love/ The pretty towns.
O Now the Drenched Land Wakes.
O terrible is the highest thing.
Orange Bears, The.
Origin of Baseball, The.
Pastoral: "Dove walks with sticky feet, The."
Reason for Skylarks, The.
Saturday Night in the Parthenon.
Snow Is Deep on the Ground, The.
Street Corner College.
Temple, A.
Trueblue Gentleman, A.
Twenty-third Street Runs into Heaven.
Village of Tudda, The.
We Go Out Together.
What There Is.
Where?
Where Two o'Clock Came From.

Pater, Walter
Mona Lisa.

Paterson, A. B.
Bush Christening, A.
Man from Ironbark, The.

Paterson, Alistair
Birds Flying.
Complaint, sel.
Incantation, sel.
Overture for Bubble-Gum and Flute.
They do it with knives, sel.

Paterson, Andrea
Because I Could Not Dump.

Paterson, Andrew Barton
Bushman's Song, A.
Clancy of the Overflow.
Man from Snowy River, The.
Road to Hogan's Gap, The.
Travelling Post Office, The.
Waltzing Matilda.

Paterson, Evangeline
Female War Criminal.
History Teacher in the Warsaw Ghetto Rising.
Poem for Putzi Hanfstaengel.

Patey, Tom
Last of the Grand Old Masters, The.
Macinnes's Mountain Patrol.

Patmore, Coventry Kersey Dighton
Across the sky the daylight crept, sel.
Arbor Vitae, sel.
Attainment, The, sel.
Auras of Delight, sel.
Azalea, The, sel.
Barren Shore, The.
Cathedral Close, The, sel.
County Ball, The, sel.
Departure, sel.
Devonshire Scenes, sel.
Farewell, A: "With all my will, but much
   against my heart," sel.
Flesh-Fly and the Bee, The.
From the small life that loves with tooth and
   nail.
Here, in This Little Bay, sel.
How fair a flower is sown.
I vow'd unvarying faith; and she, sel.
If I Were Dead, sel.
In Love, at Stonehenge, sel.
King William's Dispatch to Queen Augusta.
Kiss, The, sel.
Legem Tuam Dilexi, sel.
London Fete, A.
Lonely Cloud of Care, The, sel.
Love at Large, sel.
Love Serviceable, sel.
Married Lover, The, sel.
Music of Forefended Spheres, The, sel.

Night and Sleep.
Perspective, sel.
Rainbow, The, sel.
Revelation, The, sel.
Rosy Bosom'd Hours, The.
Round the Year.
Sahara, sel.
Saint Valentine's Day, sel.
Save by the Old Road none attain the new.
Science, the agile ape, may well.
Spirit's Epochs, The, sel.
Storm, The.
To the Body, sel.
To the Unknown Eros, sel.
Toys, The, sel.
Tribute, The, sel.
'Twas when the spousal time of May, sel.
Two Deserts, The.
Warning, A.
Whirl'd off at last, for speech I sought, sel.
Your love lacks joy, your letter says, sel.

Paton, Alan
I Have Approached.
Prison House, The.

Patrick, Bishop of Dublin
Invocation, An: "Almighty God, who fillest
   the recesses of the heavens."

Patrick, Johnstone G.
Closing Prayer.
Grace.
Prayer for Peace.

Patrick, Luther
Sleepin' at the Foot o' the Bed.

Patrick, St.
Deer's Cry, The, at.
St. Patrick's Breastplate, at.

Patten, Brian
After Frost.
Beast, The.
Ode on Celestial Music.
Party Piece.
Portrait of a Young Girl Raped at a Suburban
   Party.
Small Dragon, A.
Through All Your Abstract Reasoning.
Where Are You Now Superman?

Patterson, Charles
Listen.

Patterson, Lindsay
At Long Last.

Patterson, Raymond R.
At That Moment.
Birmingham 1963.
Black All Day.
I've Got a Home in That Rock.
Letter in Winter.
Night-Piece.
When I Awoke.
You Are the Brave.

Pattison, William
Ad Coelum.

Patton, Charlie
34 Blues.

Pauker, Ted
Garland for a Propagandist.
Grouchy Good Night to the Academic Year,
   A.
Limeraiku.
Trifle for Trafalgar Day, A.

Paul, Dorothy
Captive Ships at Manila, The.

Paul, Louis
Cynical Portraits.

"Paul, John." *See* **Webb, Charles Henry**

Paul the Silentiary. *See* **Paulus Silentiarius**

Paulding, James Kirke
Ode to Jamestown.
Old Man's Carousal, The.

Paulin, Tom
Anastasia McLaughlin.
And Where Do You Stand on the National
  Question.
Arthur.
Ballywaire.
Black Bread.
Book of Juniper, The.
Cadaver Politic.
Descendancy.
Desertmartin.
From.
Hyperboreans, The.
Impossible Pictures, The.
Inishkeel Parish Church.
Manichean Geography I.
Newness.
Of Difference Does It Make.
Off the Back of a Lorry.
Other Voice, The.
Personal Column.
Politik.
Rum Cove, a Stout Cove, A.
Settlers.
Song for February.
States.
Still Century.
Surveillances.
Thinking of Iceland.
Under the Eyes.
Where Art Is a Midwife.
Written Answer, A.

Paulinaoq
Dead Man's Song, Dreamed by One Who Is
  Alive.

Paulinus of Nola
To Ausonius.

Paulos
Epigram: "Kissing Hippomenes, I crave."

Paulus Silentarius
In Peterborough Churchyard.
No Matter.
Tantalos.
United.

Pavese, Cesare
Death Will Come and Will Have Your Eyes.
Goat God, The.
Morning Star.
South Seas.

Pavlova, Karolina
To Madame A. V. Pletneff.

Pawsey, Irene F.
Bramble Jam.
Browny Bee.
Browny Hen, The.
Egg for Easter, An.
Eggs for Breakfast.
Found in the Woods.
Greedy Little Pig, The.
Haytime.
June.
Thief, The.
White Horses.

Payack, Peter
Assembling the Model.
Microcosmos.
Migration of Darkness, The.
Motorcycle Evolution.
Spinning Yarns, Relatively Speaking.

Payeras, Mario
Tamborillo.

Payn, James
I Never Had a Piece of Toast.

Payne, John Howard
Home, Sweet Home.

Payne, Nina
Bubble Gum.
Chocolate Cake.
Tag Along.

Payne, William Morton
"Ej Blot til Lyst."
Incipit Vita Nova.
Lohengrin.
Tannhäuser.

Paz, Octavio
Beyond Love.
Landscape.
Street, The.
Touch.

Peabody, Josephine Preston
Hymn: "Dear Lord, Whose serving-maiden."
Song of a Shepherd Boy at Bethlehem.
To a Dog.

Peabody, William Bourne Oliver
Lament of Anastasius.

Peach, Arthur Wallace
Mosaic Worker, The.

Peacham, Henry
Nuptial Hymn, *sel.*

Peacock, Molly
Just About Asleep Together.
Lull, The.
Now Look What Happened.
Old Roadside Resorts.
She Lays ("She lays each beautifully mooned
  finger").
So, When I Swim to the Shore.

Peacock, Thomas
Andonis, My Daughter.
Earth Song.
For the Children.
In Respect of the Elderly.
Six Eagles.

Peacock, Thomas Love
Border Ballad, A.
Chorus: "If I drink water while this doth last."
Fear.
For the Slender Beech and the Sapling Oak.
Friar, The.
Grave of Love, The.
In His Last Binn Sir Peter Lies.
Letter from School, A.
Love and Age.
Margaret Love Peacock [for Her Tombstone,
  1826]
New Order of Chivalry, A.
Newark Abbey.
Priest and the Mulberry-Tree, The.
Rich and Poor; or, Saint and Sinner.
Song by Mr. Cypress.
Song of the Four Winds, The.
Sun-Dial, The.
War Song of Dinas Vawr, The.
Wise Men of Gotham, The.

Peake, Mervyn Laurence
My Uncle Paul of Pimlico.
Sensitive, Seldom and Sad.

Pearce, Ellen
Orange Tree, The.
Turtle's Belly, The.

Pearl, Robert
Mourning Song.

Pearlman, Bill
Volleyball Match, The.

Pearse, Mark Guy
Don't Trouble Trouble.
Facing the New Year.

Pearse, Padraic
Fool, The.
I Am Ireland.
Ideal.
Mother, The.
Prayer to Mother Mary.
Renunciation.

Peck, Elisabeth
Between the Walls of the Valley.
Walthena.

Peck, Harry Thurston
Heliotrope.

Other One, The.
Wonderland.

Peck, John
Bracelet, The.
Cider and Vesalius.
Colophon for Lan-t'ing Hsiu-hsi.
Here Is a Song.
In Front of a Japanese Photograph.
October Cycle.
Ringers, The.
Rowing Early.
Spring Festival on the River, The.
Watcher, The.
What If the Saint Must Die.

Peck, Samuel Minturn
Autumn's Mirth.
Captain's Feather, The.
Kiss in the Rain, A.
My Little Girl.
Sassafras.
Southern Girl, A.

Pederson, Cynthia S.
Pogoing.

Pedrick, Jean
Vampire.

Pedro III, King of Aragon
Peire Salvatge, it's the flowers.

Pedroso, Regino
Opinions of the New Student.

Peele, George
And Who Has Seen a Fair Alluring Face.
Bethsabe's Song, *sel.*
Dirge: "Welladay, welladay, poor Colin, thou
  art going to the ground," *sel.*
Fair and Fair, *sel.*
Fair Maiden, *sel.*
Farewell to Sir John Norris and Sir Francis
  Drake, A.
Gently Dip, *sel.*
Harvester's Song, *sel.*
His Golden Locks Time Hath to Silver
  Turned, *sel.*
O Gentle Love, *sel.*
Oenone's Complaint, *sel.*
Song: "Lo! here we come a-reaping,
  a-reaping," *sel.*
Song of Coridon and Melampus, *sel.*
Spell, A, *sel.*
Voice [Speaks] from the Well, A, *sel.*
What Thing Is Love, *sel.*
Whenas [*or* When as] the Rye [Reach to the
  Chin], *sel.*

Péguy, Charles
Happy Are Those Who Have Died.

Peire d'Alvernhe
My tune is of troubadours who sing variously.

Pellew, George
Death.
On a Cast from an Antique.

Peloubet, Maurice E.
Eternal Kinship, The.

Pembroke, Mary Sidney Herbert, Countess of
If Ever Hapless Woman Had a Cause.
Of Death, *sel.*
Psalm LXXIV: "O God, why hast thou cast us
  off for ever?"
Psalm CXXXIX.
Psalm CXLVII: "Praise ye the Lord."

Pembroke, William Herbert, Earl of
Disdain Me Still.
Paradox, A.
Song: "Soules joy, now I am gone," *at.*

Pendleton, Denise
Ice-Fishing.

Penfold, Merimeri
Land Laws, The.
Tamaki of a Hundred Lovers.

P'eng Sun-yü
As the tenth month comes to a river district,
  sel.

From withered trees we gather the silkworm
   floss, *sel.*
Mounted on a mule, to ford the shallow
   stream, *sel.*
Musing beneath a Pine.
On the Road to Tang Lake.
Summer Solstice.
Traveler's Night, A.

Penkethman, John
   Schoolmaster's Precepts, A.
   Some Boys.

Penna, Sandro
   As You Pass High Upon.
   I Loved Everything in the World.
   Train Will Be at Least an Hour Late, The.

Pennant, Edmund
   Delete? Yes/No?
   Lost Explorer.

Pennecuik, Alexander
   Below fair Peebles, on the river's side, *sel.*

Pennell, Henry Cholmondeley. *See*
   Cholmondeley-Pennell, Henry

Penny, Rob
   And We Conquered.
   Be Cool, Baby.
   I Remember How She Sang.
   Real People Loves One Another, The.

Penny, W. E.
   Town of Nogood, The.

Penrose, Roland
   They breathe with the night, *sel.*

Penrose, Thomas
   Helmets; a Fragment, The.

Peón y Contreras, José
   Echoes.

Peralta, Bertalicia
   Only Woman, The.
   So Much Suffering.

Percival, James Gates
   Apostrophe to the Island of Cuba.
   Coral Grove, The.
   Elegiac.
   May.
   New England.
   To Senaca Lake.

Percy, William
   Judged by my goddess' doom to endless pain,
   sel.
   Relent, my dear yet unkind Coelia, *sel.*
   Sonnet: "It shall be said [*or* sayd] I died [*or*
   dy'de] for Coelia," *sel.*

Percy, William Alexander
   Epilogue: "Giver of bliss and pain, of song
   and prayer."
   Farmers.
   Hymn to the Sun.
   Page's Road Song, A.
   They Cast Their Nets in Galilee.

Pereira, Francesca Yetunde
   Burden, The.
   Mother Dark.
   Paradox, The.
   Two Strange Worlds.

Perelman, Bob
   Binary.
   Book Years.
   God.
   History.
   My One Voice.
   Oceanography.
   Pastoral: "One person each, out."
   Politics.
   Primer.
   Seduced by Analogy.
   Streets.
   Word World.

Péret, Benjamin
   And on the Very First Day.
   Clubs Are Trump.
   Hello.
   It Keeps Going On.

Just Now.
Little Song of the Maimed.
Louis XVI Goes to the Guillotine.
Making Feet and Hands.
My Final Agonies.
Nebulous.
North Wind.
On All Fours.
Round of the Sidewalks.
Sleepless Nights.
Someone's Knocking.
Song in Time of Drought.
Staircase with a Hundred Steps, The.
Thousand Times, A.
To Be Continued.
To Pass the Time.
Twinkling of an Eye.
Where Are You.
Who Is It.

Perets, Yitskhok Leybush. *See* **Peretz, Isaac**
   Leibush

Peretz, Isaac Leibush
   All through the Stranger's Wood.
   Believe Not.
   Eternal Sabbath.
   Hope and Faith.
   In the Silent Night.
   Little People.
   Monish.
   Three Seamstresses, The.

Peretz, Yitzchok Leibush. *See* **Peretz, Isaac**
   Leibush

Perevin Muruvalar
   Elegy: "He has held."
   What He Said.

Peri Rossi, Cristina
   Virginia Woolf, Etc.

Perkins, Emily Swan
   Thou Art, O God, the God of Might.

Perkins, Louis Saunders
   Genius.

Perkins, Lucy Alice
   "Laborers Together with God."

Perkins, Silas H.
   Common Road, The.

Perkoff, Stuart Z.
   Aleph.
   Feasts of Death, Feasts of Love.
   Flowers for Luis Bunuel.
   Gimel.
   Hai.
   Recluses, The.

Perlberg, Mark
   Hiroshige.

Pernath, Hugues C.
   Answer Is, The.
   In the Loveless Landscape of my Solitude.
   Since Dew the Day.
   This is a request, a realization, *sel.*
   Unchastity.

Pernette du Guillet. *See* **Du Guillet,**
   Pernette

Perreault, John
   Boomerang.
   Metaphysical Paintings, The.
   Readymade.
   Shoe.

Perrine, Laurence
   Janus.
   Limerick: "Professional dancer, Miss
   Fairleigh, A."
   Limerick: "Roared her father, severest of
   men."
   Limerick: "Two brothers devised what at
   sight."
   Riddle: "Limrick's writtn to plas, A."

Perronet, Edward
   All Hail the Power of Jesus' Name.

Perry, Georgette
   Neutrinos.

Perry, Gordon
   Aids for Latin.
   Great Lakes of Canada, The.

Perry, Julianne
   No Dawns.
   To L.

Perry, Lilla Cabot
   Art.
   As It Was, *sel.*
   As She Feared It Would Be, *sel.*
   Life and Death.

Perry, Martha Eugenie
   Lonely Shell, The.
   Mainspring, The.
   Water-Witch, The.

Perry, Nora
   Balboa.
   Coming of Spring, The.
   Cressid.
   Love-Knot, The.
   Riding Down.
   Running the Blockade.
   Who Knows?

Perry, Ronald
   Prologue for a Bestiary.
   Shellpicker, The.
   Still-Life.

Perry, Thomas
   Antarctic Muse, The.

Perry, Tod
   For Nicholas, Born in September.

"Perse, St.-John" (Alexis Saint-Léger Léger)
   Anabasis.
   Birds, birds held by long affinity close to
   man's frontiers, *sel.*
   I, only accountant, from the height of this
   corner room surrounded by an, *sel.*
   Poem for Valery Larbaud.
   Such is the way of the world, *sel.*
   Syntax of lightning! O pure speech of exile!
   Far is that other shore where, *sel.*

Persius (Aulus Persius Flaccus)
   Prologue to the First Satire.

Peruncittiranar
   Bard's Family, A.

Perunkunrur Kilar
   Parade, A.

Pesado, José Joaquín
   Huntress, The.

Peseroff, Joyce
   Hardness Scale, The.
   Long March, The.

Pestel, Thomas
   On Tobacco.
   Song: "Silly boy, there is no cause."

Pestell, Thomas. *See* **Pestel, Thomas**

"Peter" (Robert Louis)
   Bus, The.
   Out of the Dark Wood.
   Poetry.
   Saint Wears a Halo, The.
   Speed Track, The.

Peters, Edmund W.
   Bicycalamity.

Peters, Lenrie
   After They Put Down Their Overalls.

Peters, Robert
   Arrival, New York Harbor.
   Blessing a Bride and Groom; a Wedding
   Night Poem.
   Blood stains the feather, *sel.*
   Buying a Record.
   Crazy Bill to the Bishop.
   Darkling Chicken, The.
   Feathered Friends.
   Final Soliloquy on a Randy Rooster (in a Key
   of Yellow).
   I, Lessimus, of Salt Lake City.
   Meeting Mick Jagger.

Melon-Slaughterer; or, A Sick Man's Praise
for a Well Woman.
Reflecting on the Aging-Process.
Study in Aesthetics, A.
Why Don't They Go Back to Transylvania?
Peters, Phillis Wheatley. *See* **Wheatley,**
Phillis
Petersen, Donald
Ballad of Dead Yankees, The.
Narcissus.
Sonnet in Autumn.
True to a Dream.
Walking along the Hudson.
Peterson, Arthur
Kelpius's Hymn.
Peterson, Eileen Blacker
Now and Then.
Peterson, Frederick ("Pai Ta-shun")
Solitude.
Peterson, Henry
Death of Lyon, The.
O gallant brothers of the generous South, *sel.*
Ode for Decoration Day.
Rinaldo.
Peterson, Peter
On First Looking into Chapman's Homer II.
Peterson, Robert
At Veronica's.
For the Minority.
Groom's Lament, The.
Hands folded like napkins in my lap.
Highway Patrol Stops Me, Going Too Slow.
In the 2 A.M. Club, a working man's bar.
Swim in Ohuira Bay, A.
To Myself, Late, in a Myrtle Grove.
Wingwalking in Oregon.
Peterson, Ruth Delong
Midwest Town.
Petoskey, Barbara J.
Into the Wind.
Petrakos, Chris
Call Them Back.
Petrarch (Francesco Petrarea)
Bicause I have the still kept fro lyes and
blame.
Ever myn happe is slack and slo in commyng.
Exchange between the Poet and St.
Augustine, An, *sel.*
How Oft Have I My Dere and Cruell Foo.
How the Lover Perisheth in His Delight, As
the Fly in the Fire, *sel.*
In Wintry Midnight, o'er a Stormy Main.
Madrigal 121: "Now Love, see how this lady,
young and fair."
Madrigal: "Diana, naked in the shadowy
pool."
My Galley.
Songs, *sel.*
Sonnet: When She Walks by Here.
To Laura in Death, *sel.*
To Laura in Life, *sel.*
Translation from Petrarch.
Triumphs.
Petri, György
Song: "I long for nothing more."
With the Thin Girl.
You Usually Come in the Morning.
Petrie, Paul
Church of San Antonio de la Florida, The.
Dream, The.
Enigma Variations, The.
Murderer, The.
Not Seeing Is Believing.
Old Pro's Lament, The.
Phases of Darkness, The.
Petröczi, Kata Szidónia
Swift Floods.
Petronius Arbiter (Calus Petronius Arbiter)
Doing, a Filthy Pleasure Is, and Short.
Good God, What a Night That Was.

Malady of Love Is Nerves, The.
We Are Such Stuff as Dreams.
Petrosky, Anthony
Jurgis Petrakas, the Workers' Angel,
Organizes the First Miner's Strike in
Exeter, Pennsylvania.
Petrova, Olga
To a Child Who Inquires.
Pett, Stephen
Trench.
Pettingell, Phoebe
Ode on Zero.
Pettit, Michael
A Cappella.
Celestial.
Day in My Union Suit, A.
Driving Lesson.
Fire and Ice.
Herdsman.
Sunday Stroll.
Pewhairangi, Kumeroa Ngoingoi
Do Not Turn Away.
I Sit Here.
Peyanar
Embracing the young mother from behind,
sel.
Embracing this woman, *sel.*
Evening in the yard, *sel.*
His heart swells, *sel.*
Like the red flame, *sel.*
Minstrels sing the jasmine songs, *sel.*
Way/ they lay together, The, *sel.*
What He Said ("As the deer begin to hide"),
sel.
What He Said ("As wild oxen bellowed"), *sel.*
What He Said ("Because peacocks moved like
you"), *sel.*
What He Said ("In this time of rain and
thunder"), *sel.*
What He Said ("The red earth"), *sel.*
What Her Girl Friend Said ("As the cassias
blossom"), *sel.*
What Her Girl Friend Said ("Her eyes lined
with kohl"), *sel.*
What Her Girl Friend Said ("Saying to
himself"), *sel.*
What Her Girl Friend Said ("Your arms are
beautiful again"), *sel.*
Peynetsa, Andrew
Boy and the Deer, The.
Pfeiffer, Emily Jane
Song of Winter, A.
Pfingston, Roger
Of Stories Fathers Tell.
Phaedrus
Aesop at Play.
Dog in the River, The.
Man and the Weasel, The.
Purpose of Fable-writing, The.
Phair, George E.
Old-fashioned Pitcher, The.
Phelps, Arthur Leonard
Wall, The.
Phelps, Charles Henry
Henry Ward Beecher.
Rare Moments.
Yuma.
Phelps, Sylvanus D.
Saviour, Thy Dying Love.
Phelps, Elizabeth Stuart. *See* **Ward,**
Elizabeth Stuart Phelps
Philemon
Recipe: Onions.
Philip, Marlene
Oliver Twist.
Salmon Courage.
Philip of Thessalonica
Epigram: "You were a pretty boy once,
Archestratus, and."

Philipott, Thomas
On the Death of a Prince; a Meditation.
On the Nativity of Our Saviour.
Philipps, Stephen
Poet's Prayer, The.
Philipps, Thomas
I Love a Flower, *at.*
Peace of the Roses, The.
Philips, Ambrose
Happy Swain, The.
To Miss Charlotte Pulteney in Her Mother's
Arms [*or* To Charlotte Pulteney]
Weeping o'er the sacred urn, *sel.*
Winter-Piece, A.
Philips, David
If you hear rustling in the straw.
Philips, John
How to Catch Wasps, *sel.*
Pruning, *sel.*
War Poetry, *sel.*
Philips, Katherine ("Orinda")
Against Love.
Answer to Another Persuading a Lady to
Marriage, An.
Friendship's Mystery; to My Dearest Lucasia.
Lucasia, Rosania and Orinda Parting at a
Fountain, July 1663.
Orinda to Lucasia.
Orinda to Lucasia Parting, October, 1661, at
London.
Parting with Lucasia; a Song.
Sea-Voyage from Tenby to Bristol, A.
Song: "'Tis true our life is but a long
dis-ease."
To Mr. Henry Lawes.
To My Excellent Lucasia, on Our Friendship.
To My Lucasia, in Defence of Declared
Friendship.
Upon Absence.
Philips, Joan. *See* **"Ephelia"**
Phillimore, John Swinnerton
In a Meadow.
Phillip, John
Lullaby: "Lullaby baby, lullaby baby."
Phillipps, Thomas. *See* **Philipps, Thomas**
Phillips, Alice Golembiewski
Rapture Is Coming, The.
Phillips, David
Fighting Her.
Lover to Himself, The.
Notes on a Long Evening.
Old Storm.
Orange Juice Song.
Things of Late.
Wave, The.
Words.
Phillips, Frank Lamont
Daybreak.
Genealogy.
Maryuma.
No Smiles.
Phillips, Harriet C.
We Bring No Glittering Treasures.
Phillips, J. A.
Factory Girl, The.
Phillips, John
Happy the man, who, void of cares and strife,
sel.
Splendid Shilling, The.
Thus while my joyless hours I lingring spend,
sel.
Phillips, Louis
Clerihew: "Charles J. Correll/ Sang in no
chorale."
On National Data Banks.
Phillips, Marie Tello
Sorrow.
Phillips, Patrice
Function Room, The.
Phillips, Robert
Decks.

Inside and Out.
Married Man, The.
Miss Crustacean.
Persistence of Memory, the Failure of Poetry,
   The.
Pool & the Cow, The.
Running on Empty.
Six Haiku for Graham V. Phillips Who First
   Said the First One.
Vital Message.

Phillips, Stephen
Apparition, The.
Grief and God.

Phillips, Susan Kelly
Rose of Eden, The.

Phillpotts, Eden
Badgers, The.
Houses, The.
Man's Days.
Miniature.

Philpot, William
Maritae Suae.

Phylip, Siôn
Seagull, The.

Phylip, William
Farewell to Hendre Fechan.

P'i Jih-hsiu
Impromptu on a Hangover.

Piatt, John James
Child in the Street, The.
Dear President, The.
Farther.
Guerdon, The.
Ireland.
Leaves at My Window.
Lost Genius, The.
Mower in Ohio, The.
Purpose.
Rose and Root.
To a Lady.
To Abraham Lincoln.
Torch-Light in Autumn.

Piatt, Sarah Morgan Bryan
After Wings.
Call on Sir Walter Raleigh, A.
Envoy: "Sweet World, if you will hear me
   now."
In Clonmel Parish Churchyard.
Irish Wild-flower, An.
My Babes in the Wood.
Term of Death, The.
Tradition of Conquest.
Transfigured.
Watch of a Swan, The.
Witch in the Glass, The.

Picano, Felice
Gilded Boys, The.
Heart Has Its Reasons, The.

Picasso, Pablo
Poem: "Hasten on your childhood to the hour
   when white."
Poem: "In secret/ be quiet say nothing."
Poem: "In the corner a violet jug the bells the
   folds of paper."

Piccolo, Lucio
Landscape, sel.
Unstill Universe.

Picirantaiyar
Why My Hair Is Not Gray.

Pickard, Tom
Rape.

Pickering (or Pikerying), John
Haltersick's Song, sel.

Pickthall, Edith
Evacuee.

Pickthall, Marjorie Lowry Christie
Bega.
Bridegroom of Cana, The.
Child's Song of Christmas, A.
Ebb Tide.
Immortal, The.

Little Songs.
Mother in Egypt, A.
Père Lalement.
Quiet.
Resurgam.
Swallow Song.
Two Souls.

Picot, James
Lord in the Wind, The.
Volume of Chopin, A.

Piddington, R. A.
Tudor Aspersions.

Pien Kung
Apricot trees form a grove, sel.
At the Lake—Remembering My Dead Son,
   Yü.
Done playing the lute, but still full of feeling,
   sel.
First Day of Spring, The.
Inscribed on an Album Leaf Painted by Dr.
   Lin.
Morning sun climbs the eastern peak, The,
   sel.
New Year's Day—Following the Rhymes of
   Inspector Luan-chiang.
On Hearing That San-p'ing's Newly Brewed
   Chrysanthemum Wine Is Ready to Drink.
On the Sixteenth Day I Visit the Temple
   Again.
Paintings of Various Subjects by Fang
   Jih-sheng.
Song of the Boat-Pullers.
Song of the Transport Workers.
Song of the Woodcutter of the Sea.
This year of famine, old and young suffer
   many strange diseases, sel.
Walking Outside the City Walls.

Pierce, Edith Lovejoy
In the Wilderness.
Let Me Not Die.
O Christ, Thou Art within Me Like a Sea.
Prayer: "Bear with me, Master, when I turn
   from Thee."
Prayer for the Useless Days.
Supplication.

Piercy, Marge
Answer to All Problems, The.
Apron Strings.
Attack of the Squash People.
Barbie Doll.
Burying Blues for Janis.
Cast Off, The.
Cats like Angels.
Common Living Dirt, The.
Councils.
Crabs.
Crows.
Cyclist, The.
Development, The.
Digging In.
For the Young Who Want To.
Friend, The.
Gracious Goodness.
Hare in Winter.
Hello Up There.
Hummingbird.
I Awoke with the Room Cold.
Joy Road and Livernois.
Kneeling Here, I Feel Good.
Last Scene in the First Act.
Learning Experience.
Let Us Gather at the River.
Letter to Be Disguised as a Gas Bill.
Looking at Quilts.
Love of Lettuce, The.
Market Economy, The.
Meaningful Exchange, The.
Moon Is Always Female, The.
Morning Athletes.
My Mother's Body.
My Mother's Novel.

Night Letter.
Noon of the Sunbather.
Nothing More Will Happen.
Peaceable Kingdom, The.
Postcard from the Garden.
Quiet Fog, The.
September Afternoon at Four O'Clock.
Simple Song.
16/53.
Skyscrapers of the Financial District Dance
   with Gasman, The.
Someplace Else.
Something to Look Forward To.
Song of the Fucked Duck.
Spring Offensive of the Snail, The.
Story Wet as Tears, A.
To Be of Use.
To Have without Holding.
Total Influence or Outcome of the Matter: The
   Sun, The.
Unclench Yourself.
Valley Where I Don't Belong, A.
Watch, The.
We Become New.
What's That Smell in the Kitchen?
Why the Soup Tastes like the Daily News.
Woman in the, The.
Work of Artifice, A.
You Ask Why Sometimes I Say Stop.

Pierpont, James S.
Jingle Bells.
"We Conquer or Die."

Pierpont, John
Ballot, The.
Exile at Rest, The.
Fourth of July, The.
Fugitive Slave's Apostrophe to the North Star,
   The.
Kidnapping of Sims, The.
My Child.
On Laying the Corner-Stone of the Bunker
   Hill Monument.
Pilgrim Fathers, The.
Warren's Address at Bunker Hill [or to the
   American Soldiers]
Whittling.

Pierre Morhange
Salomon.

Pieterse, Cosmo
Guerrilla.
Song (We Sing).
To White South Africa.

Pietri, Pedro Juan
Night Has Twenty-four Hours, The.
Silent Movies.
You Jump First.

Pignotti, Lamberto
Here you get alarmed at the confusion, sel.
Place in evidence, sel.
Poetry and Politics.

Pike, Albert
Buena Vista.
Dixie.
To the Mocking-Bird.
Widowed Heart, The.

Pike, Cecily E.
Jack Frost.

Pikeryng, John.   *See* **Pickering, John**

Pile, Cecily
All Clear.
With the Guerillas.

Pilinszky, János
All That Is Needed.
Apocrypha.
As I Was.
Bow down. (Prostrates himself.), sel.
Cattle Brand.
Celebration of the Nadir.
Desert of Love, The.
Every Breath.
Exhortation.

Fable: "Once upon a time/ there was a lonely wolf."
Harbach 1944.
I Shall Be Watching.
In Praise of the Lowest Line.
Meditation, A.
Meetings.
Metronome.
Passion of Ravensbrück.
Postscript.
Rest Is Grace, The.
Sin.
Stavrogin's Farewell, *sel.*
Stavrogin's Return, *sel.*
Under the Winter Sky.

Pilkington, Laetitia
Song: "Lying is an occupation."

Pilkington, Lawrence
What Called Me to the Heights.

Pillen, William
Farewell to Europe.
Night Poem in an Abandoned Music Room.
O, Beautiful They Move.
Ode on a Decision to Settle for Less.
Poem for Anton Schmidt, A.
Poem: "To be sad in the morning."

Pillin, William. *See* **Pillen, William**

Pilling, Christopher
Adoration of the Magi, The.

Pinar, Florencia del
Another Song of the Same Woman, to Some
    Partridges, Sent to Her Alive.
On Some Partridges Sent to Her Alive.
So Wily Are the Ways of Love.

Pincas, Israel
Mediterranean.

Pindar
I Bless This Man, *sel.*
Life after Death.
Ode on Theoxenos.

"Pindar, Peter" (John Wolcot)
Apple Dumplings and a King, The.
Epigram: "Midas, they say, possessed the art
    of old."
Introduction and Anecdotes, *sel.*
George III and the Sailor, *sel.*
George III Visits Whitbread's Brewery, *sel.*
Ode to a Country Hoyden.
Ode: "That I have often been in love, deep
    love."
On a Stone Thrown at a Very Great Man, But
    Which Missed Him.
Royal Tour, The.
Sons of Saint Crispin, 'tis in vain!, *sel.*
Susan, the constant slave to mop and broom,
    sel.
To a Fly, Taken out of a Bowl of Punch.

"Ping Hsin" (Hsieh Wang-ying)
Builder of Continents, The, *sel.*
Falling Star, The, *sel.*
Fishing boats have returned, The!, *sel.*
In shaping the snow into blossoms, *sel.*
O, Lord/If in life eternal, *sel.*
Orphan beat of my heart, The.
Receiving Buddha.
Sprays of frost flowers form.
Three Poems.
Void only, *sel.*

Pinkerton, H. A.
Error Pursued.

Pinkerton, Helen
Indecision.

Pinkney, Dorothy Cowles
Dame Liberty Reports from Travel.

Pinkney, Edward Coate [or Coote]
Health, A.
Indian's Bride, The.
Memory.

Serenade, A: "Look out upon the stars, my
    love."
Song: "We break the glass, whose sacred
    wine."
Votive Song.

Pinsker, Sanford
Response of Telemachus, The.

Pinsky, Robert
Beach Women, The.
Changes, The.
December Blues.
Dionysus as Psychiatrist, *sel.*
Discretions of Alcibiades.
Doctor Frolic.
Dying.
Faeryland.
Figured Wheel, The.
Hearts, The.
History of My Heart.
Icicles.
Invocation, *sel.*
Late Child, *sel.*
Living, The.
Local Politics.
Mad, The, *sel.*
Memorial.
New Saddhus, The.
Peroration, Concerning Genius, *sel.*
Poem about People.
Proposition, *sel.*
Prostate Operation, *sel.*
Questions, The.
Ralegh's Prizes.
Senior Poet, *sel.*
Serpent Knowledge, *sel.*
Some Terms, *sel.*
Song of Reasons.
Sonnet: "Afternoon sun on her back."
Street, The.
Superb Lily, The.
Their Patients, *sel.*
Their Philistinism Considered, *sel.*
Their Seriousness, with Further Comparisons,
    sel.
Their Speech, Compared with Wisdom and
    Poetry, *sel.*
Volume, The.
Want Bone, The.

Pinto, Vivian de Sola
At Piccadilly Circus.

Piper, Edwin Ford
Church, The.

Piper, Linda
Missionaries in the Jungle.
Sweet Ethel.

Piron, Alexis
Here lies Piron—a man of no position.
My Epitaph.

Pisan, Christine de
Adam, David, Samson, Solomon, *sel.*
Alone am I, and alone I wish to be.
Ballad: "A Hundred ballads I have written."
Ballade: "Lone am I, and would be."
Christine to Her Son.
Fountain of tears, river of grief.
From Darts of Love That Do Such Dole, *sel.*
Here Are Told the Misfortunes of Women,
    sel.
I am a widow, robed in black, alone.
I'll always dress in black and rave.
Marriage is a lovely thing.
Phoebus, the goddess variant and changeable,
    sel.

Pise, Constantine
Let the Deep Organ Swell.

Pistoia, Cino da. *See* **Cino da Pistoia**

Pitcher, Oliver
Pale Blue Casket, The.
Raison d'Etre.
Salute.

Pitchford, Kenneth
Lobotomy.
104 Boulevard Saint-Germain.
Pickup in Tony's Hashhouse, *sel.*
Queen, The.
Surgery.

Pitt, Christopher
On the Masquerades.

Pitt, Marie Elizabeth Josephine
Gallop of Fire, A.

Pitt, William
Sailor's Consolation, The, *at.*

Pitter, Ruth
Bat, The.
But for Lust.
Coffin-Worm, The.
Dun-Colour [*or* Dun-Color]
Eternal Image, The.
For Sleep, or Death.
Hen under Bay-Tree.
Lost Tribe, The.
Military Harpist, The.
Morning Glory.
Old Woman Speaks of the Moon, An.
Sparrow's Skull, The.
Stockdove, The.
Swan Bathing, The.
Task, The.
Time's Fool.
To a Lady, in a Wartime Queue.
Unicorn, The.
Victory Bonfire.
Viper, The.

Pittis, William
Battle Royal between Dr. Sherlock, Dr.
    South, and Dr. Burnet, The.

Piuvkaq
It Is Hard to Catch Trout.
Joy of a Singer, The.
Mocking Song against Qaqortingneq.

Pixner, Stef
Day in the Life. . ., A.
Near Death.

Pizarnik, Alejandra
Apart from Oneself.
Dawn.
Mask and the Poem, The.
Privilege.
Tree of Diana, The.
Vertigos or Contemplation of Something That
    Is Over.
Who Will Stop His Hand from Giving
    Warmth.

"Placido"
Farewell to My Mother.
Prayer to God.

Plaice, Stephen
Farewell, My Latin Master.
Ghosts of the Victorians, The.
Melancholia.

Planché, James Robinson
Ching a Ring.
Literary Squabble, A.
Love, You've Been a Villain.
Sea-Serpent, The.
To Mollidusta.

Plantier, Thérèse
Doors.
Men Po Men with Glasses.
Overdue Balance Sheet.

Plarr, Victor
Epitaphium Citharistriae.
Of Change of Opinions.
Shadows.

Platen, August, Graf von
To Liebig.

**Platen, August, Graf von (Karl August Georg
Maximilian, Graf von
Platen-Hallermünde)**
How shall I still mankind's good will retrieve,
    sel.

To Bülow.
To Rotenham.
To Schmidlein.
When shall I master this anxiety, *sel.*

Plath, Sylvia
All the Dead Dears.
Amnesiac.
Among the Narcissi.
Applicant, The.
Ariel.
Arrival of the Bee Box, The.
Babysitters, The.
Balloons.
Barren Woman.
Bee Meeting, The.
Beekeeper's Daughter, The.
Black Rook in Rainy Weather.
Blackberrying.
Blue Moles.
Brasília.
Candles.
Child.
Colossus, The.
Couriers, The.
Crossing the Water.
Cut.
Daddy.
Death and Co.
Death of Myth-making, The.
Disquieting Muses, The.
Edge.
Elm.
Event.
Fever 103°.
Flute Notes from a Reedy Pond.
Frog Autumn.
Full Fathom Five.
Ghost's Leavetaking, The.
Goring, The.
Gulliver.
Hanging Man, The.
Hardcastle Crags.
I see her in my sleep, my red, terrible girl, *sel.*
Kindness.
Lady Lazarus.
Last Words.
Life, A.
Love Letter.
Manor Garden, The.
Mary's Song.
Medallion.
Memoirs of a Spinach-Picker.
Metamorphosis.
Metaphors.
Mirror.
Moon and the Yew Tree, The.
Morning Song.
Most beds are beds, *sel.*
Munich Mannequins, The.
Mushrooms.
Mussel Hunter at Rock Harbor.
Mystic.
New Year on Dartmoor.
Nick and the Candlestick.
Night Dances, The.
Paralytic.
Parliament Hill Fields.
Pheasant.
Point Shirley.
Poppies in July.
Poppies in October.
Sheep in Fog.
Sleep in the Mojave Desert.
Snakecharmer.
Spinster.
Stars over the Dordogne.
Stings.
Stones, The.
Suicide off Egg Rock.
These are the beds, *sel.*
Three Women.

To Ariadne.
Tulips.
Two Campers in Cloud Country.
Two Views of a Cadaver Room.
Watercolor of Grantchester Meadows.
Wedding-cake face in a paper frill, A, *sel.*
Winter Trees.
Wintering.
Witch Burning.
Words.
Words Heard, by Accident, over the Phone.
You're.

Plato
Apple, The, *at.*
Aster.
Epigram: "All I said was—Alexis is gorgeous."
Epigram: "For Hekabé and the women of Ilion."
Farewell: "Far from the deep roar of the Aegean main."
Kissing Helena.
Love Sleeping.
Lover to His Lady, The, *at.*
On a Seal.
On Alexis.
On Archaeanassa.
Once you shone among the living as the morning star.
Pan Piping.
To Stella.

Plato, Ann
Natives of America, The.
Reflections, Written on Visiting the Grave of a Venerated Friend.
To the First of August.

Platt, Anna M.
Crocuses.

Playford, John
Jovial Marriner; or, The Sea-Man's Renown, The.

Plenty-hawk
If all of me is still there.

Plescoff, Jorge
Ladder Has No Steps, The.
Ourobouros.
Tongues of Fire.
Violins in Repose.

Pleynet, Marcelin
Black.
It's Always.
New Republic, The.
Of Coal.
These Mornings.
Where the Light.

Plimpton, Florus B.
Fort Duquesne.

Plomer, William
Atheling Grange; or, The Apotheosis of Lotte Nussbaum.
Away she flies and he follows, *sel.*
Bamboo.
Blind Samson.
Devil-Dancers, The.
Europa.
Father and Son: 1939.
French Lisette; a Ballad of Maida Vale.
Ganymede.
Headline History.
In the Snake Park.
Levantine, A.
Mews Flat Mona.
Playboy of the Demi-World: 1938, The.
Prisoner, The.
Scorpion, The.
September Evening, 1938.
Seven Rainy Months.
Ula Masondo's Dream.

Walk in Würzburg, A.
Widow's Plot; or, She Got What Was Coming to Her, The.

Plumly, Stanley
After Grief.
After Rilke.
After Whistler.
Against Starlings.
American Ash.
Another November.
Blossom.
Cows.
Early Meadow-Rue.
End of the Indian Poems, The.
For Esther.
Fungo.
Giraffe.
Ground Birds in Open Country.
Heron.
Iron Lung, The.
Karate.
Lapsed Meadow.
Linoleum: Breaking Down.
My Mother's Feet.
Now That My Father Lies Down beside Me.
Out-of-the-Body Travel.
Peppergrass.
Posthumous Keats.
Tree Ferns.
Waders and Swimmers.
Wildflower.
With Stephen in Maine.

Plummer, Mary Wright
Irrevocable.

Plumpp, Sterling
Beyond the Nigger ("Beyond the outstretched hands").
For Mattie and Eternity.
Half Black, Half Blacker.
I Told Jesus.
Living Truth, The.

Plumptre, Annabella
To thee, whose cautious step and specious air, *sel.*

Plumptre, James
Where Cumbria's mountains in the north arise, *sel.*

Plunkett, Joseph Mary
I Saw the Sun at Midnight, Rising Red.
I See His Blood upon the Rose.
Saint Augustine.
Sic Transit.
Spark, The.
Stars Sang in God's Garden, The.

Plutzik, Hyam
And in the 51st Year of That Century, While My Brother Cried in the Trench, While My Enemy Glared from the Cave.
Begetting of Cain, The.
Dream about Our Master, William Shakespeare, The.
I Am Disquieted When I See Many Hills.
Jim Desterland.
King of Ai, The.
Mythos of Samuel Huntsman, The.
Of Objects Considered as Fortresses in a Baleful Place.
On the Photograph of a Man I Never Saw.

Pluvkag. *See* **Piuvkaq**

Po Chü-i
Aboard a Boat, Reading Yüan Chen's Poems.
After Eating.
Cranes, The.
Don't go climbing up to the blue clouds, *sel.*
Don't go hide in the deep mountains, *sel.*
Don't go into the realm of red dust, *sel.*
Don't go off and be a farmer, *sel.*
Drunk, Facing Crimson Leaves.
Eating Bamboo-Shoots.
Feelings Wakened by a Mirror.

Poe

Going Alone to Spend a Night at the
    Hsien-Yu Temple.
Half in the Family, Half Out.
Having Climbed to the Topmost Peak of the
    Incense-Burner Mountain.
Idle Droning.
Invitation to Hsiao Ch'u-shih.
Last Poem.
Lazy Man's Song.
Liao-ling.
Light Furs, Fat Horses.
Lodging with the Old Man of the Stream.
Losing a Slave-Girl.
Madly Singing in the Mountains.
New Thatched Hall, A.
Night Snow.
Old Charcoal Seller, An.
On Being Sixty.
People of Tao-chou, The.
Pine Sounds.
Planting Flowers on the Eastern Embankment.
Pouring Out My Feelings after Parting from
    Yüan Chen.
Question Addressed to Liu Shih-chiu, A.
Quiet House in Ch'ang-lo Ward, A.
Red Cuckatoo, The.
Rejoicing at the Arrival of Chi'en Hsiung.
Remembering Golden Bells.
Sentimental Poem.
Song of the Lute.
Spring River.
Starting Early from the Ch'u–ch'eng Inn
Temple, The.
Temple of Bequeathed Love, The.
To Li Chien.
Traveler's Moon, The.
Village Night.
Writing Again on the Same Theme.

Poe, Edgar Allan

Al Aaraaf.
Annabel Lee.
Bells, The.
City in the Sea or The Doomed City, The.
Coliseum, The.
Conqueror Worm, The.
Dream-Land.
Dream within a Dream, A.
Dreams.
Eldorado.
Enigma, An.
Eulalie.
Fairyland.
For Annie.
From Childhood's Hour.
Happiest Day, the Happiest Hour, The.
Haunted Palace, The.
I stand amid the roar, sel.
Israfel.
Lake, The.
Lenore.
Raven, The.
Romance.
Sleeper, The.
Song From "All Aaraaf."
Song: "Young flowers were whispering in
    melody," sel.
Sonnet—Silence.
Sonnet to Science.
To Helen.
To My Mother.
To One in Paradise.
To Science.
Ulalume.
Valley of Unrest, The.

Polet, Sybren

Alienation & Alliteration.
Celebration.
Human Use of Human Beings, The.
Re-education.
Shadow.
Tomorrow's Ideas.

Polite, Frank

Adman into Toad.
Empty at the Heart of Things.
Imitations Based on the American.
Japanese Consulate, The.
Mine.

Polito, Robert

First Love.
Spring Training.

Poliziano, Angelo (Politian)

Dance Song.
He who knows not what thing is Paradise, sel.
I found myself one day all, all alone, sel.
I went a roaming, maidens, one bright day,
    sel.
Three Ballate, I.
Unto the Breach.

Poliziano, Andrea. See **Poliziano, Angelo**

Pollak, Felix

Another transparent skin has grown, sel.
First the light cracked, sel.
Her voice enters the room, sel.
I dream of the finger of the statue, sel.
I look out of my window at night, sel.
I may pass through once more next month,
    sel.
I wake to the sound of rain, sel.
Incident.
Reality.

Pollet, Sylvester

Elegy for John Wilborg.

Pollitt, Katha

Archaeology.
Ballet Blanc.
Composition in Black and White.
Discussion of the Vicissitudes of History
    under a Pine Tree, A.
In Horse Latitudes.
In Memory.
Night Blooming Flowers.
Of the Scythians.
Seal Rock.
Turning Thirty.
Two Fish.
Woman Asleep on a Banana Leaf.

Pollock, Edward

Olivia.

Pollock, John Hackett. See **"An Pilibín"**

Polonsky, Yakov Petrovich

Cosmic Fabric, The.

Polwhele, Richard

Visit to the Author's Paternal Seat, A, sel.

Pomerantz, Berl

End of Summer.
Young Virgins Plucked Suddenly.

Pomerantz, Charlotte

Door Number Four.
Moon Boat.
Tamarindo Puppy, The.

Pomerantz, Marsha

Adam and Eve at the Garden Gate.
How to Reach the Moon.

Pomeroy, Marnie

In Nakedness.

Pomeroy, Ralph

Between Here and Illinois.
High Wind at the Battery.
Leather Bar, The.
Snow.
Tardy Epithalamium for E. and N., A.
To Janet.

Pomfret, John

Choice, The.

Pomfret, Richard

July Wakes.

Pommy-Vega, Janine

Rites of the Eastern Star.
Voices, The.

Pompili, Vittoria Aganoor

Fear.

Finally.
Sappho's Last Song.

Ponciano, Angelo de

Empties Coming Back.

Ponge, Francis

Delights of the Door, The.
End of Fall, The.
Fauna and Flora.
Horse, The.
Oyster, The ("The oyster, about as large as a
    medium-sized stone").
Pleasures of the Door, The.
Trees Lose Parts of Themselves Inside a
    Circle of Fog.

Ponika, Kohine Whakarua

Call Together.
Song of Yearning, A.

Ponmutiyar

Mother's List of Duties, A.
Young Warrior, A.

Pons de Capdueill

Anyone who swallows foolishly.

Ponsot, Marie

Communion of Saints: The Poor Bastard
    under the Bridge.
Mustipara: Gravida 5.
Possession.
Subject.
To the Age's Insanities.

Ponting, Herbert George

Sleeping-bag, The.

Poole, John

Song, Hamlet.

Poole, Tom

I wonder why.

Popa, Vasco

Ashes, sel.
Before Play, sel.
He, sel.
Hide-and-Seek, sel.
Nail, The, sel.
Pig.
Rose Thieves, The, sel.
Seed, The, sel.

Pope, Alexander

All are but parts of one stupendous whole,
    sel.
Alley; an Imitation of Spenser, The.
Apologia pro Vita Sua, sel.
Ask you what provocation I have had?, sel.
Atticus ("How did they fume, and stamp, and
    roar, and chafe"), sel.
Atticus ("Peace to all such! but were there one
    whose fires"), sel.
Awake, my St. John! leave all meaner things,
    sel.
Bard whom pilf'red pastorals reknown, The,
    sel.
Behold the child, by Nature's kindly law, sel.
Bliss of man, The (could pride that blessing
    find), sel.
Bounce to Fop; an Heroick Epistle from a
    Dog at Twickenham to a Dog at Court.
Bred up at home, full early I begun, sel.
Bufo, sel.
But grant I may relapse, for want of grace,
    sel.
But most by numbers judge a poet's song, sel.
Carnations and Butterflies, sel.
Challenge, The.
Cibber! write all thy verses upon glasses.
Close by those meads, for ever crowned with
    flow'rs, sel.
Descend, Ye Nine, sel.
Duke of Buckingham, The, sel.
Elegy to the Memory of an Unfortunate Lady.
Eloisa, sel.
Eloïsa to Abelard.
Epigram Engraved on the Collar of a Dog
    Given [or Which I Gave] to His Royal
    Highness.
Epigram in a Maid of Honour's Prayer-Book.

Epigram on One Who Made Long Epitaphs.
Epigram: "Sir, I admit your general [or gen'ral] rule."
Epigram: "You beat your pate, and fancy wit will come."
Epistle from Mr. Pope, to Dr. Arbuthnot, An.
Epistle to a Lady: Of the Characters of Women, sel.
Epistle to Miss [or Miss Teresa] Blount, on Her Leaving the Town after the Coronation.
Epitaph, at.
Epitaph for One Who Would Not Be Buried in Westminster Abbey.
Epitaph on G——
Epitaph on Himself.
Epitaph on James Moore Smythe.
Epitaph on the Stanton-Harcourt Lovers.
Essay on Criticism, An.
Faith, sel.
Far as creation's ample range extends, sel.
First follow Nature, and your judgment frame, sel.
First Satire of the Second Book of Horace, The.
Groves of Eden, vanished now so long, The, sel.
Happy Life of a Country Parson, The.
Here lie two poor lovers, who had the mishap, sel.
Honor and shame from no condition rise, sel.
Hope humbly then; with trembling pinions soar, sel.
Hunt, The, sel.
Ideals of Satire, The, sel.
Imitation of Chaucer.
In wit, as nature, what affects our hearts, sel.
Inscriptio.
Know then thyself, presume not God to scan, sel.
Let Sporus tremble—"What? That thing of silk", sel.
Life's Poor Play, sel.
Lines by a Person of Quality, at.
Lines on Bounce.
Lines on Swift's Ancestors.
Lines Written in Windsor Forest.
Little learning is a dangerous thing, A, sel.
Lo, the poor Indian! whose untutor'd mind, sel.
Look round our world; behold the chain of love, sel.
Lord Coningsby's Epitaph.
Mighty mother, and her son who brings, The, sel.
Most souls, 'tis true, but peep out once an age, sel.
Nature and Nature's laws lay hid in Night.
Next bidding all draw near on bended knees, sel.
Nor think, in nature's state they blindly trod, sel.
Not with more glories, in th' ethereal plain, sel.
Ode on [or to] Solitude.
Of all the causes which conspire to blind, sel.
Of little use the man you may suppose, sel.
On a Certain Lady at Court.
On a Lady Who P-ssed at the Tragedy of Cato.
On Authors and Booksellers.
On Dennis.
On Dullness.
On her white breast a sparkling cross she wore, sel.
On J. M. S. Gent.
On Poets.
On Queen Caroline's Deathbed.
On the Benefactions in the Late Frost.
On the Candidates for the Laurel.
On the Erection of Shakespeare's Statue in Westminster Abbey.
Paraphrase on Thomas à Kempis, A.

Placed on this isthmus of a middle state, sel.
Playing Cards, The, sel.
Pleasure of Hope, The, sel.
Prayer of St. Francis Xavier.
Question of Libel, A, sel.
Quoth Cibber to Pope, tho' in verse you foreclose.
Rape of the Lock, The.
Rise, Crowned with Light Imperial Salem Rise, sel.
See! from the brake the whirring Pheasant springs, sel.
Some are bewildered in the maze of schools, sel.
Some beauties yet no precepts can declare, sel.
Some ne'er advance a judgment of their own, sel.
Soul's Calm Sunshine, The, sel.
Spare then the person, and expose the vice, sel.
Speak, Gracious Lord, oh speak; thy Servant hears, sel.
Such shameless bards we have; and yet 'tis true, sel.
Sylvan Delights, sel.
Think not by rigorous judgment seized, sel.
Thy forests, Windsor! and thy green retreats, sel.
Timon's Villa, sel.
'Tis hard to say, if greater want of skill, sel.
To Mr. C., St. James's Place, London, October 22nd.
To Mr. Gay, Who Wrote Him a Congratulatory Letter on the Finishing His House.
To Mrs. M. B. on Her Birthday.
To Richard Boyle, Earl of Burlington: Of the Uses of Riches, sel.
Toilet, The, sel.
Tom Southerne's Birth-Day Dinner at LD. Orrery's.
Triumph of Dullness [or Dulness], The, sel.
True ease in writing comes from art, not chance, sel.
Two or Three; a Recipe [or Receipt] to Make a Cuckold.
Universal Prayer, The.
Upon a Girl of Seven Years Old.
Vestal, The, sel.
Virtue may choose the high or low degree, sel.
Vital spark of heavenly flame!
Well, if a King's a lion, at the least, sel.
Wharton ("Wharton! the scorn and wonder of our days"), sel.
What beck'ning ghost, along the moonlight shade, sel.
What dire offence from am'rous causes springs, sel.
What if the foot, ordain'd the dust to tread, sel.
What would this Man? Now upward will he soar, sel.
Whate'er the passion—knowledge, fame, or pelf, sel.
When Eastern lovers feed the fun'ral fire, sel.
When milder autumn summer's heat succeeds, sel.
When other fair ones [or ladies] to the shades [or groves] go down.
Why did [or do] I write? what sin to me unknown, sel.
With all a woman's virtues but the pox, sel.
Yet, yet a moment, one dim ray of light, sel.
Young Traveller Is Presented to the Goddess Dulness, A, sel.

Pope, Alexander and Thomas Parnell
On Riding to See Dean Swift in the Mist of the Morning.
Pope, J. R.
Word of Encouragement, A.

Pope, Walter
Old Man's Wish, The.
Popham, Hugh
Usual exquisite boredom of patrols, The.
Popham, Ivor
Child, The.
Poquelin, Jean Baptist. See **Molière**
Porson, Richard
Bathos, The.
Here lies a Doctor of Divinity.
Mutual Congratulations of the Poets Anna Seward and Hayley, The.
Note on the Latin Gerunds, A.
On a German Tour.
Porson on German Scholarship.
Porson on His Majesty's Government.
Porson's Visit to the Continent.
To Dr. Kipling.
Porta, Antonio
Beaver Skin.
Dialogue with Herz.
Europa Rides a Black Bull.
Nomad's Utopia.
To Open.
Walking becomes unbearable, another year, sel.
Wind Blows on the Border, The.
Yes, no, yes, no, yes, no, yes, no, yes, no, yes, no, yes, no, yes, sel.
Portal, Magda
Film Vermouth: Six o'Clock Show.
Shores of anguish.
Woman.
Porter, Adrian
Perfect Child, The.
Porter, Anne
Another Sarah.
Porter, Bruce
Limerick: "H was an indigent Hen."
Porter, Cole
Anything Goes.
Brush Up Your Shakespeare.
Bull-Dog!
If a custom-tailored vet, sel.
Let's Do It.
My Heart Belongs to Daddy.
Well, Did You Evah?
You're the Top.
Porter, Fairfield
Island in the Evening, The.
Porter, Hal
Lalique.
Sheep.
Porter, Ina M.
Mumford.
Porter, Jenny Lind
In the Beginning.
Porter, Kenneth Wiggins
Street Scene—1946.
Porter, Mrs. David
Thou Has Wounded the Spirit That Loved Thee.
Porter, Peter
Cats of Campagnatico, The.
Christenings.
Consumer's Report, A.
Cost of Seriousness, The.
Death of a Comic Opera Composer, sel.
Evolution.
Exequy, An.
Gertrude Stein at Snails Bay.
Happening at Sordid Creek.
It is time to recompose the face, sel.
King of the Cats is Dead, The.
London is full of chickens, on electric spits, sel.
Metamorphosis.
Mort aux Chats.
May, 1945.

Non Piangere, Liù.
On This Day I Complete My Fortieth Year.
Phar Lap in the Melbourne Museum.
Queer Assayers of the Frontier, The, *sel.*
Retrieval System.
Sydney Cove, 1788.
Vienna.
Your Attention Please.

Porter, Samuel Judson
Way; the Truth; the Life, The.

Porter, William Sidney. *See* "Henry, O."

Porumbacu, Veronica
Of Autumn.
White Bears.
With a Ring.

Poseidippus
Doricha.

Posey, Anita E.
When All the World's Asleep.

Posner, David
Birds, The.
Campus, The.
On a Recent Protest against Social Conditions.

Post, Jonathan V.
Neurophysiologist, The.

Poster, Carol
Robert Bly Finds Something in New Jersey.
Synthesizing Several Abstruse Concepts with
an Experience.

Potamkin, Harry Alan
Cargoes of the Radanites.

Poteat, Edwin McNeill
Eternal God Whose Searching Eye Doth Scan.
Grace at Evening.
Prayer at Dawn.
Prayer for Contentment.

Potter, Beatrix
Old Woman, The.

Potts, Paul
For My Father.
Muse to an Unknown Poet, The.
Note.

Poulin, A., Jr.
I Woke Up. Revenge.

Poulsson, Emilie
First Christmas, The.
Pigs, The.
While Stars of Christmas Shine.

Pound, Ezra
Age demanded an image, The, *sel.*
Alas, eheu, one question that sorely vexes,
sel.
Alba, *sel.*
Alchemist, The.
Ancient Music.
Ancient Wisdom, Rather Cosmic.
And the days are not full enough.
And then went down to the ship, *sel.*
And Thus in Nineveh.
April.
Ballad for Gloom.
Ballad of the Goodly Fere.
Ballatetta.
Bathtub [*or* Bath Tub], The.
Beautiful Toilet, The.
Beneath the sagging roof, *sel.*
Brennhaum, *sel.*
Cantico del Sole.
Cino.
Coda.
Come, my songs, let me express our baser
passions, *sel.*
Coming of War; Actaeon, The.
Commission.
Dance Figure.
De Aegypto.
Doria.
Ed ascoltando al leggier mormorio, *sel.*
Eleanor (she spoiled in a British climate), *sel.*

Elegy VII, *sel.*
Encounter, The.
Envoi (1919), *sel.*
Epilogue: "O chansons foregoing."
Fan-Piece, for Her Imperial Lord.
Faun, The.
Fine fish to net.
For an officer/ in the old Capital, fox fur.
For deep deer-copse beneath Mount Han.
For E. McC.
For three years, out of key with his time, *sel.*
Four more days until vacation.
Fragmenti.
"From the colour the nature," *sel.*
Full be the year, abundant be the grain.
Further Instructions.
Garden, The.
Garret, The.
Girl, A.
Greek Epigram.
Hang it all, Robert Browning, *sel.*
Has he tempered the viol's wood, *sel.*
I dreamt that I was God Himself.
I sat on the Dogana's steps, *sel.*
If you'd have me go on loving you, *sel.*
Immorality, An.
In a Station of the Metro.
Ité.
Know then:/ Toward summer when the sun is
in Hyades.
Kung walked/ by the dynastic temple, *sel.*
Lake Isle, The.
L'Art, 1910.
Liu Ch'e.
Meditatio.
Monumentum Aere, Etc.
Mr. Housman's Message.
Mr. Nixon, *sel.*
Near Perigord.
Now if ever it is time to cleanse Helicon, *sel.*
O Atthis.
O helpless few in my country, *sel.*
Oh to be in England now that Winston's out,
sel.
Ortus.
Pact, A.
Phyllidula.
Piccadilly.
Pick a fern, pick a fern, ferns are high.
Piere Vidal Old.
Pine boat a-shift.
Portrait d'une Femme.
Provincia Deserta.
Reflection and Advice.
Return, The.
Said Jim X. . ., *sel.*
Salutation.
Salutation the Second.
Scientists are in terror, The, *sel.*
Serenely in the crystal jet, *sel.*
Sestina: Altaforte.
Shades of Callimachus, Coan ghosts of
Philetas, *sel.*
Siena Mi Fe'; Disfecemi Maremma, *sel.*
Silet.
So that the vines burst from my fingers, *sel.*
Song: "Love thou thy dream."
Song of the Bowmen of Shu.
Study in Aesthetics, The.
South-Folk in Cold Country.
Tame Cat.
Tea-rose tea-gown, etc., The, *sel.*
Tea Shop, The.
Temperaments, The.
Tenzone, *sel.*
Then a partridge-shaped cloud over dust
storm, *sel.*
There died a myriad, *sel.*
These fought in any case, *sel.*
'Tis of my country that I would endite, *sel.*
To Kalon.
Toujours la Politesse.

To Whistler, American.
Translator to Translated.
Tree, The.
Ts'ai Chi'h.
Tudor indeed is gone and every rose, *sel.*
Villanelle: The Psychological Hour.
Virginal, A.
What thou lovest well remains, *sel.*
When, when, and whenever death closes our
eyelids, *sel.*
Who even dead, yet hath his mind entire!, *sel.*
Who, who will be the next man to entrust his
girl to a friend?, *sel.*
Wide, ho?
With Usura, *sel.*
Yeux Glauques, *sel.*
Zeus lies in Ceres' bosom, *sel.*

Pound, Ezra *and* **Noel Stock**
Swallow sings "Dawn," The.
There are flowers of Zait in the garden.
With candour I confess my love.

Poussard, Wendy
Greenham Women.
Women on the Road to Pine Gap.

Powell, Anthony
Caledonia.

Powell, Charles
Jack and Jill.

Powell, Marcy S.
Long Island.
Precedented.

Power, John
Thy Name We Bless and Magnify.

Power, Marguerite (Countess of Blessington)
Friend, A.

Power, Prunella
End of Term.
First Day at Boarding School.

Powers, Horatio Nelson
Year Ahead, The.

Powers, John
Fred's Dead Friend.

Powers, Star
Harvest Time.

Powys, John Cowper
Aye! What a thing is the passing of Cronos,
the angular-minded, *sel.*
In a Hotel Writing-Room.

Pozzi, Antonia
Awakening.
Canzonetta.
Closing Door, The.
Landing.
Premonition.
To Trust.

Pozzo, Modesta dal
Women's Worth.

Praed, Winthrop Mackworth
Arrivals at a Watering-Place.
Belle of the Ball-Room, The, *sel.*
Charade.
County Member, The, *sel.*
Epitaph on the Late King of the Sandwich
Isles.
Fairy Song.
Goodnight to the Season!
I think the thing you call Renown, *sel.*
Letter of Advice, A.
Our Ball, *sel.*
Portrait of a Lady in the Exhibition of the
Royal Academy, *sel.*
Royal Education.
Song of Impossibilities, A.
Song: "Pints and the pistols, the pike-staves
and pottles, The," *at.*
Stanzas: On Seeing the Speaker Asleep in His
Chair.
Talented Man, The.
Time's Song.
To Helen.
Vicar, The, *sel.*

Prager, Marie-Francoise
I Think about the Dead Woman in a Poem.
I'll act out a weird dream.
Pratt, Agnes
Death Takes Only a Minute.
Empathy.
Pratt, Anna Maria
Early News.
Mortifying Mistake, A.
Pratt, Charles W.
Hoity-Toity Oyster, The, *sel.*
Pratt, Edwin John
Burial at Sea, *sel.*
Come Not the Seasons Here.
Erosion.
Final Moments, The, *sel.*
From Stone to Steel ("From stone to bronze, from bronze to steel").
Gathering, The, *sel.*
Ground-Swell, The.
Ice-Floes, The.
Invisible Trumpets Blowing, *sel.*
Martyrdom of Brébeuf and Lalemant, 16 March 1649, The, *sel.*
Precambrian [*or* Pre-Cambrian] Shield, The, *sel.*
Prize Cat, The.
Ritual, The.
Sea Cathedral, The.
Shark, The.
Silences.
There is a language in a naval log, *sel.*
Thousand years now had his breed, A, *sel.*
Truant, The.
Where Cape Delgado strikes the sea, *sel.*
Pratt, Lenore
Midwinter Thaw.
Old Boat, The.
Pratt, Minnie Bruce
Child Taken from the Mother, The.
Waulking Song: Two.
Praxilla
Adonis, Dying.
Lovely girl, you look at me through the window.
Most beautiful of things I leave is sunlight.
Watch out, my dear.
You gaze at me teasingly through the window.
Pray, Benjamin Sturgis
Motorcycle.
Preil, Gabriel
Arriving.
Autumn Music.
Beyond the Imaginary Garden.
Biographical Note.
Eternal Now.
Fishermen.
From Jerusalem: A First Poem.
Giving Up on the Shore.
Lakes.
Late Manuscript at the Schocken Institute, A.
Lecture, A.
Lesson in Translation, A.
Letter Out of the Gray.
Like David.
Like Feathers.
Memory of Another Climate.
Parting.
Rains on the Island.
Record, The.
Shining Thing.
Sober.
Summing Up, A.
Surprised Pen, The.
Words of Oblivion and Peace.
Prelutsky, Jack
Alphabet Stew.
Bogeyman, The.
Children, Children Everywhere.
City, Oh, City!

Cow, The.
Creature in the Classroom, The.
Darkling Elves, The.
Dogs and Cats and Bears and Bats.
Don't Ever Seize a Weasel by the Tail.
First Thanksgiving, The.
Four Seasons, The.
Ghoul, The.
Harvey Always Wins.
Herbert Glerbett.
Hippopotamus, The.
Home! You're Where It's Warm Inside.
House Mouse, The.
I'm Hungry!
It's Halloween.
Land of Potpourri, The.
Lion, The.
Long Gone.
Me I Am!
Mistletoe, The.
Nature Is.
No Girls Allowed.
Nonsense!
Pancake Collector, The.
Pumberly Pott's Unpredictable Niece.
Skeleton Parade.
Some People I Know.
Somersaults.
Sometimes.
Toucannery.
Troll, The.
Twickham Tweer.
Visitor, The.
Ways of Living Things, The.
Where Goblins Dwell.
Whistling.
Wrimples.
Yak, The.
Prentice, George Denison
Memories.
New England.
Prentice, John A.
Washington.
Prentiss, Elizabeth Payson
Kitty.
More Love to Thee, O Christ.
Prescod, Marsha
Anti-Racist Person.
Prescot, Kenrick
Balsham Bells.
Press, John
African Christmas.
Farewell: "Smell of death was in the air, The."
Womanisers.
Preston, James
Sunfish Races.
Preston, Keith
Complete Cynic, The.
Effervescence and Evanescence.
Lapsus Linguae.
Parental Critic, The.
Probably.
Warm Babies.
Preston, Margaret Junkin
Acceptation.
Dirge for Ashby.
First Proclamation of Miles Standish, The.
First Thanksgiving Day.
Grave in Hollywood Cemetery, Richmond, A.
Hero of the Commune, The.
Last Meeting of Pocahontas and the Great Captain, The.
Mystery of Cro-a-tàn, The.
Ready.
Under the Shade of the Trees.
Virginia Capta.
Vision of the Snow, The.
Pretorius, S. J.
Madman, The.

Prettyman, Quandra
Mood, The.
Photograph.
Still Life: Lady with Birds.
When Mahalia Sings.
Prévert, Jacques
Alicante.
And the Fete Continues.
Attempt at a Description of a Supper of Various Heads in Paris, France.
Barbara.
Bird-Catcher's Song.
Broken Mirror, The.
Dunce, The.
Eclipse, The.
Familial.
Free Quarters.
Garden, The.
Glory.
Hunting of Whales, The.
I Saw Several of Them.
Immense and Red.
In Vain.
Last Supper, The.
Message, The.
Pall-Bearers.
Pater Noster.
To Paint the Portrait of a Bird.
Wrestling with the Angel.
Prewett, Frank
I Shall Take You in Rough Weather.
If I Love You.
Pack, The.
Plea for Peace.
Red-Man, The.
Price, Jonathan
Considered Reply to a Child, A.
Price, Laurence
Honour of Bristol, The, *at.*
Local Motions.
Seaman's Compass, The.
Win at First and Lose at Last; or, A New Game at Cards.
Price, Nancy
Harbor.
One-Night Fair.
Take a Gun.
Price, Victor
Highland Region.
Prideaux, Tom
Skip-Scoop-Anellie.
Priessnitz, Reinhard
Innery.
Plan for Understanding.
Privilegium Minus.
Snowsong.
Trip.
Tropic Circle.
White Horse Song.
Primrose, Lady Diana
Fourth Pearl: Temperance, The, *sel.*
Prince, Frank Templeton
At a Parade.
Babiaantje, The.
Old Age of Michelangelo, The.
Question, The.
Soldiers Bathing.
To a Friend on His Marriage.
Token, The.
Wind in the Tree, The.
Prince, John Critchley
Blest hour of peace, of poetry, and love!, *sel.*
Death of the Factory Child, The.
To Poesy.
Prince, Thomas
Give Ear, O God, to My Loud Cry.
O Lord, Bow Down Thine Ear.
With Christ and All His Shining Train.
Pringle, Thomas
Desolate Valley, The.

Hottentot, The.
Lion-Hunt, The.
Prior, Matthew
Adriani Morientis ad Animam Suam.
Advice to the Painter.
Against Modesty in Love.
Another True Maid.
Answer to Cloe [or Chloe] Jealous.
Behind an unfrequented glade, sel.
Chameleon, The.
Chaste Florimel.
Democritus and Heraclitus.
Divine Blacksmith, The.
Dutch Proverb, A.
Earning a Dinner.
English Ballad, on the Taking of Namur by
the King of Great Britain, 1695, An.
Epigram: "Thy nags (the leanest things
alive)."
Epigram: "To John I ow'd great obligation."
Epigram: "Tom's sickness did his morals
mend."
Epigram: "When Bibo thought fit from the
world to retreat."
Epigram: "Yes, every poet is a fool."
Epitaph, An: "Interred [or Interr'd] beneath
this marble stone."
Epitaph: "Meek Francis lies here, friend,
without stop or stay."
Epitaph on True, Her Majesty's Dog, An.
Fable, A: "In Aesop's tales an honest wretch
we find."
Fatal Love.
Fix thy corporeal, and internal eye, sel.
For My Own Monument.
Great Bacchus: From the Greek.
Human Life.
In Britain's isles, as Heylyn notes, sel.
In Imitation of Anacreon.
Insatiable Priest, The.
Jinny the Just.
Lady Who Offers Her Looking-Glass to
Venus, The.
Les Estreines.
Letter to the Honourable Lady Miss Margaret
Cavendish Holles-Harley, A.
Lover's Anger, A.
Nonpareil.
Ode, An: "The Merchant, to secure his
treasure."
On Exodus 3: 14: "I am that I am."
On Himself.
On My Birthday, July 21.
Paraphrase from the French, A.
Pass we the ills, which each man feels or
dreads, sel.
Phillis's or Phyllis's Age.
Question to Lisetta, The.
Quid Sit Futurum Cras Fuge Quaerere.
Reasonable Affliction, A.
Remedy Worse than the Disease, The.
Simile, A.
To a Child of Quality [Five Years Old, the
Author Supposed Forty]
To a Lady: She Refusing to Continue a
Dispute with Me, and Leaving Me in the
Argument.
To a Young Gentlemen in Love; a Tale.
Town Mouse and the Country Mouse, The.
True Maid, A.
Verses Written at The Hague. Anno 1696.
When you with Hogh Dutch Heeren dine.
Woman's Wish, The.
Written in an Ovid.
Written in the Beginning of Mezeray's History
of France.
Pritam, Amrita
Annunciation, The.
Breadwinner, The.
Daily Wages.
Pritchard, Norman Henry, II
Aswelay.

Gyre's Galax.
Metagnomy.
Self.
Probst, Anita Endrezze
Eclipse.
Exodus.
In the Flight of the Blue Heron: To
Montezuma.
Notes from an Analyst's Couch.
Passion Drinker, The.
Raven/Moon.
Red Rock Ceremonies.
Stripper, The.
Truth about My Sister and Me, The.
Week-End Indian, The.
Probst, Anita Endrezze. See
Endrezze-Danielson, Anita
Probyn, May
Christmas Carol: "Lacking samite and sable."
"Is It Nothing to You?"
Procter, Adelaide Anne
Cleansing Fires.
Envy.
Fidelis.
Give Me Thy Heart.
Lost Chord, A.
One by One.
Per Pacem ad Lucem.
Present, The.
Thankfulness.
Procter, Ida
One, The.
Procter, Bryan Waller. See "Cornwall,
Barry"
Proctor, Edna Dean
Brooklyn Bridge, The.
Captive's Hymn, The.
Columbia's Emblem.
Columbus Dying.
Heaven, O Lord, I Cannot Lose.
John Brown.
Lost War-Sloop, The.
Respice Finem.
Sa-cá-ga-we-a.
Song of the Ancient People, The.
Proctor, Thomas
Proper Sonnet, How Time Consumeth All
Earthly Things, A, at.
Prokosch, Frederic
Conspirators, The.
Fable: "O the vines were golden, the birds
were loud."
Festival, The.
Gothic Dusk, The.
Propertius, Sextus
Ah Woe Is Me, sel.
Hylas, sel.
Revenge to Come, sel.
Turning Aside from Battles.
Prospere, Susan
Passion.
Sub Rosa.
Proudfit, David Law ("Peleg Arkwright")
Willis, The.
"Prout, Father." See **Mahony, Francis
Sylvester**
Prowse, William Jeffery
City of Prague, The.
Prudhomme, Sully-. See **Sully-Prudhomme**
Prys, Edmwnd
Welsh Ballad, A.
Prys, Thomas
Poem to Show the Trouble That Befell Him
When He Was at Sea, A.
Prys-Jones, A. G.
Day Which Endures Not, A.
St. Govan.
Przybos, Julian
Mother.
On the Shore.

Pudney, John
After Bombardment.
For Johnny.
Map Reference T994724.
Missing.
On Seeing My Birthplace from a Jet Aircraft.
Stiles.
To You Who Wait.
Pugliesi, Giacomino
Canzone: Of His Dead Lady.
Canzonetta: Of His Lady in Absence.
Pulci, Luigi
Morgante and the Boars.
Prophecy, sel.
Pullen, Elisabeth Jones Cavazza
Alicia's Bonnet.
Derelict.
Her Shadow.
Love and Poverty.
Sea-Weed, The.
Pullen, Eugene Henry
"Now I Lay Me Down to Sleep."
Now I wake and see the light.
Pulsifer, Susan Nichols
Sounding Fog, The.
Punkanuttiraiyar
Mothers.
Purcell, Victor William Williams Saunders.
See "Buttle, Myra"
Purdom, George
Robens' Promised Land.
Purdy, Alfred Wellington (Al Purdy)
Alive or Not.
Cariboo Horses, The.
Country North of Belleville, The.
Dead Poet, The.
Dead Seal.
Evergreen Cemetery.
Lament for the Dorsets.
Landscape.
Love at Roblin Lake.
Madwoman on the Train, The.
Night Song for a Woman.
Poem: "You are ill and so I lead you away."
Remains of an Indian Village.
Spinning.
Trees at the Arctic Circle.
What Do the Birds Think?
Wilderness Gothic.
Winemaker's Beat-étude, The.
Winter Walking.
Purevich, Edith
Artifact.
Purohit, Swami
I Know That I Am a Great Sinner.
Miracle Indeed, A.
Shall I Do This.
Pushkin, Aleksandr Sergeyevich
Arion.
Autumn.
Elegy: "Extinguished are my years of carefree
laughter."
Elegy: "I visit once again."
For God's sake, let me not go mad.
Georgian hills above lie shrouded in the night,
The.
I Loved You Once.
It's time, my dear, it's time! The heart
demands its quittance.
K***.
Message to Siberia.
No, Never Think.
Phantoms of the Steppe.
Prophet, The.
Sweet boy, gentle boy.
To a Poet.
To Chaadaev.
To Vyazemsky.
When in My Arms.
When wand'ring along noisy alleys.

With Freedom's Seed.
Work.

Putnam, Howard Phelps (Phelps Putnam)
Ballad of a Strange Thing.
Hasbrouck and the Rose.
Romeo and Juliet.

Puttenham, George
Cruel You Be.

Puttkamer, Baroness von. *See* "**Madelaine, Marie**"

Pye, Henry James
Air Balloon, The, *sel.*

Pygge, Edward
Crow Resting.
Notes for a Revised Sonnet.
Notes for a Sonnet.
Occam's Razor Starts in Massachusetts.
Revised Notes for a Sonnet.
Shantih shantih shantih.
Wasted Land, The.
What about You?

Pyke, B. K.
Blacksmith.

Pyle, Katharine
August.
Circus Parade, The.
Clever Peter and the Ogress.
Nine o'Clock, *sel.*
One o'Clock, *sel.*
Toys Talk of the World, The.
Two o'Clock, *sel.*
Visitor, The.
Waking.

Pyrlaeus, Johann C.
Jesu, Come on Board.

Q

"**Q.**" *See* **Quiller-Couch, Sir Arthur Thomas**

Qabbani, Nizar
Between us.
Child Scribbles, The.
Cup and Rose.
Day I met you I tore up, The.
Disrobe, my love.
Equation.
Foolishness.
Footnotes to the Book of the Setback.
God how is it that we surrender.
I am afraid to.
I Am the Train of Sadness.
I Conquer the World with Words.
I knew when I said.
If an audience could be arranged, *sel.*
June war is over, The, *sel.*
Language.
Morphine.
Ruler and the Sparrow, The.
Stage is burned, The, *sel.*
Testament.
There is nothing I can do.
Twenty years on the road of love, *sel.*
Two African Breasts.
When a helmet becomes God in heaven, *sel.*
When God gave you to me.
When ideas, when thought itself, *sel.*
Who are you.
Woman in whose voice.
You ask for the date.
You asked for the date.
Your eyes are like a night of rain.
Your image is engraved.
Your love threw me down.

Qaqatcguk
I keep dreaming I'm dead.

Qarshe, Cabdullaahi
Colonialism ("The colonialist governments").

Qasmi, Ahmad Nadeem
Bull, A.
Civilized.
Firing.

Qorratu'l-Ayn
Cupbearer, O victorious Falcon, come!, *sel.*

Quarles, Francis
Are all such off'rings, as are crusht, and bruis'd.
Authour's Dreame, The, *sel.*
Be Sad, My Heart.
Epigram: "My soul, sit thou a patient looker-on."
Epigram: "My soul, thy love is dear: 'twas thought a good," *sel.*
Forbear, fond taper: what thou seek'st, is fire, *sel.*
Forme of Prayer, A.
Good-Night, A.
Great All in All, that art my rest, my home, *sel.*
Hos Ego Versiculos, *sel.*
Like to the Arctic Needle, *sel.*
My Beloved Is Mine, and I Am His; He Feedeth among the Lillies, *sel.*
My soul, what's lighter than a feather? Wind.
On Change of Weathers.
On Judas Iscariot.
On the Infancy of Our Saviour.
On the Needle of a Sundial.
On the Plough-Man.
On the World.
On Those That Deserve It.
On Zacheus [*or* Zacchaeus]
Our God and soldiers we alike adore.
Wherefore Hidest Thou Thy Face, and Holdest Me for Thine Enemie?, *sel.*
Wilt Thou Set Thine Eyes upon That Which Is Not?, *sel.*
World's a Sea, The.

Quasimodo, Salvatore
Agrigentum Road, The.
And Then Suddenly It's Dark.
Dead, The.
Imitation of Joy.
In This City.
Letter to My Mother.
Milan August 1943.
Snow.

Queneau, Raymond
Conch.
Human Species, The.
If You Imagine.
Poor Fellow.
Seyes, The.
Sines.
Toward a Poetic Art.

Quennell, Peter
Divers, The.
Flight into Egypt, The.
Hero Entombed I.
Music met Leviathan returning, A, *sel.*
Procne.

Queremel, Angel Miguel
Manifesto of the Soldier Who Went Back to War.

Quesada, José Luis
Incurable Love, The.

Questel, Victor
This Island Mopsy.
Tom.

Quevedo, Francisco de
Constant Love Even beyond Death.
Defining Love.

Quevedo y Villegas, Francisco de
Sonnet: Death Warnings.

Quick, Richard
Reagan, The.

Quickenden, Beatrice
Hail, Oh Hail to the King.

Quigless, Helen G.
Concert.

Quijada Urías, Alfonso
Before Death.
Chronicle.

Quiller-Couch, Sir Arthur Thomas ("Q")
De Tea Fabula.
Doom Ferry.
Famous Ballad of the Jubilee Cup, The.
Lady Jane.
Letter, A.
Lion is the [*or* a] beast to fight, The.
New Ballad of Sir Patrick Spens, The.
Planted Heel, The.
Retrospection.

Quillet, Claude
Best Time for Conception, The, *sel.*
How to Conceive Boys, *sel.*
Process of Conception, The, *sel.*

Quinlan, Vess
Spring.

Quinn, Roderic
Camp within the West, The.
Fisher, The.

Quiñónez, Delia
March, Vigilant Fire.

Quint, Beverly
View, A.

Quirino, Giovanni
Sonnet: To Dante Alighieri (He Commends the Work of Dante's Life).

Quirk, Cathleen
Another Night on the Porch Swing.
No Dead Ends.

R

"**R., E. M. G.**"
Midsummer Moon.

"**R. B.**" *See* "**B., R.**"

"**R. C.**" *See* "**C., R.**"

"**R. L. B.**" *See* "**B., R. L.**"

Raab, Esther
Etruscan Statue.
Folk Tune.
Like a Bird Dead in the Stream.
My Arms Are Raised towards You.
Self Portrait.
Serenade for Two Poplars, A.
Today I Am Modest as a Beast.
You Are the Man.

Raab, Lawrence
Assassin's Fatal Error, The.
Attack of the Crab Monsters.
Desire and Revenge.
Familiar Landscapes.
Pastoral: "Today in Peru, this first day of summer."
Room, The.
This Day.
Vampires.
Visiting the Oracle.
Voices Answering Back: The Vampires.

Rab (Abba Arika)
Kingdom of God, The.

Raba, Gyorgy
Conversation.
Epos.
Going On Talking.
Greeks Are Blinding Polyphemus, The.
Himalaya Days.
Message.
My Faces.
Night Meeting.
Preface to Dying.
Study: A Hand.

Rabbitt, Thomas
Casino Beach.
Coon Hunt.
County Roads.
Dancing Sunshine Lounge, The.
Gargoyle.
Old Sipsey Valley Road, The.
Rape.
Weight Room, The.
Rabéarivelo, [or Rebéarivelo]
Here She Stands.
What Invisible Rat.
Rabelais, François
Inscription above the Entrance to the Abbey
of Theleme, sel.
Shrovetide's Countenance.
Rabia
Two ways I love Thee, selfishly.
Rabi'a al-Adawiyya (Rab'a the Mystic)
My Lord/ if I worship Thee from fear of Hell.
Stars are shining/ the eyes of men are closed.
Rabi'a bint Isma'il of Syria
Sufi Quatrain.
Rabi'a of Balkh
My wish for you/ that God should make your
love.
Rabi'a the Mystic. See **Rabi'a al-Adawiyya**
Rabinovitch, Sacha
Bookworm, The.
Lipogram.
Raboff, Paul
Jars.
Reb Hanina.
Rabon, Yisroel
Cat Merchant, The.
Funeral, A.
Mendacious Song.
**Rachel [or Rahel] (Rahel Blumstein or Rahel
Blaustein)**
Barren.
Dawn.
His Wife.
Jonathan.
Kinnereth.
My Dead.
My White Book of Poems.
Perhaps.
Rachel.
Revolt.
To My Country.
Racine, Jean
God whose goodness filleth every clime, The,
sel.
Phaedra.
Radcliffe, Alexander
As Concerning Man.
Radcliffe, Anne
Night.
Sonnet: "Now the bat circles on the breeze of
eve."
Stanzas: "How smooth that lake expands its
ample breast!"
Radford, Dollie (Mrs. Ernest Radford)
Soliloquy of a Maiden Aunt.
Radford, Ernest
Upon Julia.
Radiguet, Raymond
To a Nude Walking.
Radnóti, Miklós
Charm.
Forced March.
Fragment: "I lived on this earth in an age."
Hesitating Ode.
I Hid You.
In Your Arms.
Letter to My Wife.
Metaphors.
Picture Postcards.
Root.
Seventh Eclogue.
Song: "Whipped by sorrow now."

Rae, Hugh C.
Mountain Creed.
Rae, Simon
Bucolic.
Cataloguing, The.
Draining the Ornamental Lake.
Gentle Ghosts.
Raffel, Burton
On Watching the Construction of a
Skyscraper.
Raftery, Anthony [or Antoine Raifteiri]
County Mayo.
I Am Raftery [or Raferty]
I am Raifteiri, the poet, full of courage and
love.
Lass from Bally-na-Lee, The.
Raftery, Gerald
Apartment House.
Rago, Henry
Coming of Dusk upon a Village in Haiti, The.
Green Afternoon, The.
Knowledge of Light, The.
Monster, The.
Summer Countries, The.
Rahel. See **Rachel**
Rai Kyohei
Daikon Song.
Rai Mikisaburo
Crossing Hakone Pass.
In Prison.
Rai San'yo
Cat in Cold Weather, The.
Coming Home.
Day after Saying Goodby to Mototada, The.
Delighted that Jippo Has Come to See Me in
My Illness.
Dutch Ship.
Eastern hills—dense and lush, sel.
Escorting My Mother Home.
Farewell Talk with Saiko by a Rainy
Window.
Fist like the mountain fern half unfurled, sel.
Grieving for Tatsuzo: Today Spring Ended.
Hearing of the Earthquake in Kyoto.
I Accompanied My Mother on a Visit to the
Itsukushima Shrine.
I Accompanied My Uncle Shumpo on an
Outing to Lake Biwa.
I intend her palanquin a hundred miles, sel.
I chastise the bones of an old villain of a
thousand years ago, sel.
I Heard of Master Kan's Illness but Couldn't
Get There in Time.
I put away my book, chin in hand, alone, sel.
In form most people look to Sung and Yuan
models, sel.
Inscribed on Landscapes I Painted Myself.
Isuzu River.
Mongols Are Coming, The.
Mourning for My Younger Sister.
New House.
New Year's Day.
No fields, no house, one poor scholar, sel.
On flowered paths, squeaks of flying squirrels,
sel.
On the road I meet descendants of the Korean
prisoners, sel.
Out the gate I meet a friend, sel.
Parting Talk with Seigan, A.
Reading Books ("Eastern hills—dense and
lush").
Reading Books ("This morning, splendid
breeze and sunlight").
Returning Home.
Setting Out from Hiroshima, Saying Goodby
to My Father.
So stupid of me to hope you'll take to books,
sel.
Ten thousand heaps of fragrant snow fallen in
the dust, sel.

This morning, splendid breeze and sunlight,
sel.
Twenty-some years and I've finished my
book, sel.
Visiting My Father.
Written on New Year's Eve.
Written on Visiting the Shrine of the Minister
of the Right Sugawara no Michizane.
Raifteiri, Antoine. See **Raftery, Anthony**
**"Raile, Arthur Lyon" (Edward Perry
Warren)**
Waning of Love, The.
"Raimar, Freimund." See **Ruckert,
Friedrich**
Raimbaut de Vaqueiras
High waves that come riding across the sea.
Kalenda Maya.
So often, lady, I have asked you.
Raine, Craig
An Attempt at Jealousy.
Birth, sel.
City Gent.
Dandelions.
In Modern Dress.
Martian Sends a Postcard Home, A.
Nature Study.
Onion, Memory, The.
Plain View.
Raine, Kathleen Jessie
Afternoon Sunlight Plays.
Air.
Ancient Speech, The, sel.
By the River Eden.
Daisies of Florence.
Death, I repent, sel.
Easter Poem.
Envoi: "Take of me what is not my own."
Envoi: "What has want to give."
Eudaimon.
From a place I came, sel.
Human Form Divine, The.
I Used to Watch You, Sleeping, sel.
Images.
In Time.
Instrument, The.
Isis Wanderer.
Lachesis.
Last Things.
Love Poem: "Yours is the face that the earth
turns to me."
Message from Home.
Natura Naturans.
Old Paintings on Italian Walls.
Oreads.
Puer Aeternus.
Pythoness, The.
Question and Answer.
Rose.
Scala Coeli.
Shells.
Spell against Sorrow.
Spell of Creation.
Statues.
Still Pool, The.
Summit, The, sel.
There is a stream that flowed before the first
beginning, sel.
There is stone in me that knows stone, sel.
To My Mountain.
"Tu Non Se' in Terra, Si Come Tu Credi."
Wilderness, The.
World, The.
Worry about Money.
Written in Exile.
Rainer, Dachine
Ashokan.
Rainsford, Christina
Shadbush.
Raizan (Konishi Raizan)
Blossoms bloom, I don't wanna die, but this
illness, sel.

Both have whiskers—I mean, the cat's wife, too, *sel.*
Girls planting paddy.
Green, green, the young herbs are green in the snowy field, *sel.*
How many autumns? unable to soothe myself, *sel.*
I hug myself and again it's hard to breathe, *sel.*
I pluck, I pluck and throw away spring grasses, *sel.*
I turn to look: cold in the evening dusk, mountain cherries, *sel.*
Mosquitoes came in, and while the two, *sel.*
Spring breeze.
Spring dream—that I don't go mad is what I resent, A, *sel.*
Spring rain falls, unknown to the cow's eyes, *sel.*
Spring rain: I put my foot out of the footwarmer, *sel.*
Spring wind: over the river bank comes a bull's voice, *sel.*
White fish graphically move in the water's color, *sel.*

Rako
Say "flower," say it again.

Rákos, Sándor
Creature.
Interrogation.
Pheasant.
Three Dostoievskian Masks.
To the Animal Lover, *sel.*
To the Bear, *sel.*
To the Hunter, *sel.*

Rakosi, Carl
Americana IX.
Florida.
In a Warm Bath.
Lamentation, A.
Meditation.
Medium IV, The: Sights.
Memoirs, The.
Woman.

Ralegh, Sir Walter
Advice, The.
Another of the Same.
But true love is a durable fire, *sel.*
Conceit Begotten by the Eyes.
Diana.
Epitaph on Sir Philip Sidney, *at.*
Epitaph on the Earl of Leicester.
Even Such Is Time.
Excuse, The.
Farewell to False Love, A.
Farewell to the Court.
His Petition to Queen Anne of Denmark (1618).
If Cynthia Be a Queen.
In Commendation of George Gascoigne's Steel Glass.
Lie, The.
My Body in the Walls Captived.
My thoughts are winged with hopes, *at.*
My Woe Must Ever Last.
Nature, That Washed [*or* Washt] Her Hands in Milk[e]
Nymph's Reply to the Shepherd, The.
Ocean's Love to Cynthia, The.
On Dulcina, *at.*
On the Cards and Dice.
On the Snuff of a Candle.
Passionate Man's Pilgrimage, The.
Poem Entreating of Sorrow, A.
Poem Put into My Lady Laiton's Pocket, A.
Silent Lover, The, *sel.*
Sonnet: "Like to an hermit poor, in place obscure," *at.*
Sun [*or* Sunne] may set and rise, The.
Sweet Unsure.
Three Things [*or* Thinges] There Be[e] That Prosper All [*or* Up] Apace.

To His Mistress.
To the Translator of Lucan's Pharsalia (1614).
Vision upon This Conceit of the Fairy Queen, A, *sel.*
What Is Our Life? A Play of Passion.
Wrong Not, Sweet[e] Empress of My Heart.

Raleigh, Sir Walter Alexander (1861–1922)
Wishes of an Elderly Man.

Ralph, Nathan
When They Grow Old.

"Ramal Walter." *See* **De la Mare, Walter.**

Ramanujan, A. K.
Hindoo: He Doesn't Hurt a Fly or a Spider Either, The.
Last of the Princes, The.
Small-scale Reflections on a Great House.
Some Indian Uses of History on a Rainy Day.

Ramírez, Ignacio
For the Dead Gregorians.

Ramírez, Lil Milagro
Awakening.

Ramke, Bin
Another Small Town in Georgia.
Eclipse.
Georgia.
Green Horse, The.
Jacob.
Magician, The.
Martyrdom: A Love Poem.
Nostalgia.
Obscure Pleasure of the Indistinct, The.
Sadness and Still Life.
Syllogism.
Victory Drive, near Fort Benning, Georgia.
Why I Am Afraid to Have Children.

Ramsay, Allan
Carle He Came o'er the Croft, The.
Caterpillar and the Ant, The.
Epigram: "Lasses, like nuts at bottom brown."
Lass with a Lump of Land.
My Peggy [Is a Young Thing], *sel.*
Ode to Mr. F—[*or* Mr. Forbes]
Poet's Wish; an Ode, The.
Polwart on the Green.
Twa Books, The.
Up in the Air.

Ramsay, Allen Beville
No teacher I of boys or smaller fry.

Ramsay, Andrew Michael
Friendship in Perfection.

Ramsbottom, Joseph
Coaxin'.
Preawd Tum's Prayer.
Sorrowin'.

Ramsey, Hettye Rayburn
Home and Mother.
Mother.

Ramsey, Jarold
Hand-Shadows.
Ontogeny.
Tally Stick, The.

Ramsey, Paul
Angels, The.
Consolations, *sel.*
Exiles, The, *sel.*
Hours, The.
Images for the Gospel of Christ.
Modern Theologian, A, *sel.*
On Words and Concepts and Things.
Poet Defended, A.

Ranaivo, Flavien
Love Song: "Do not love me, my friend."
Song of a Common Lover.

Ranasinghe, Anne
Auschwitz from Colombo.
Holocaust 1944.

Ranchiku
Morning fodder: a frog.

Rand, Theodore Harding
Dragonfly, The.

June.
Loon, The.

Randall, Belle
City Hall.
Mabel Woo, *sel.*
Playing at Cards.

Randall, Dudley
Abu.
After the Killing.
Analysands.
Ancestors.
Bag Woman.
Ballad of Birmingham.
Black Poet, White Critic.
Blackberry Sweet.
Booker T. and W. E. B.
Different Image, A.
George.
Green Apples.
Hail, Dionysos.
Idiot, The.
Intellectuals, The.
Langston Blues.
Legacy: My South.
Melting Pot, The.
Memorial Wreath.
Old Witherington.
On Getting a Natural.
Pacific Epitaphs.
Perspectives.
Poet Is Not a Jukebox, A.
Primitives.
Profile on the Pillow, The.
Rite, The.
Roses and Revolutions.
Southern Road, The.
Souvenirs.
To the Mercy Killers.
Vacant Lot.

Randall, James A., Jr.
Don't Ask Me Who I Am.
Execution.
Jew.
When Something Happens.
Who Shall Die.
Why should I be eaten by love.

Randall, James Ryder
John Pelham.
My Maryland.
Why the Robin's Breast Was Red.

Randall, Julia
For a Homecoming.
Miracles.
Rockland.
To William Wordsworth from Virginia.

Randall, Margaret
Ever Notice How It Is with Women?
Immigration Law.
Talk to Me.
Under Attack.

Randall-Mills, Elizabeth
Crossing the County Line.

Randolph, Anson Davies Fitz
Master's Invitation, The.

Randolph, Innes
Rebel, The.

Randolph, Thomas
Come from Thy Palace, *sel.*
Devout Lover, A.
Elegie, An: "Love, give me leave to serve thee, and be wise."
From Witty Men and Mad.
Gratulatory to Mr. Ben Johnson for His Adopting of Him to Be His Son, A.
He Lives Long Who Lives Well.
Milkmaid's Epithalamium, The.

Ode to Mr. [*or* Master] Anthony Stafford to
  Hasten Him into the Country, An.
On a Maid [*or* Maide] of Honour Seen by a
  Scholar in Somerset Garden.
Parley with His Empty Purse, A.
Phyllis.
Poetry and Philosophy, *sel.*
Song, A: "Music, thou queen of souls, get up
  and string."
This definition poetry doth fit.
Upon His Picture.
Upon Love Fondly Refus'd for Conscience's
  Sake.
Rands, William Brighty ("Matthew Browne")
Cat of Cats, The.
Dream of a Boy Who Lived at Nine Elms,
  The.
Dream of a Girl Who Lived at Sevenoaks,
  The.
Drummer-Boy and the Shepherdess, The
  ("Drummer-boy, drummer-boy, where is
  your drum?").
Fishing Song, A.
Gipsy Jane.
Godfrey Gordon Gustavus Gore.
Lilliput Levee.
Lullaby: "Wind whistled loud at the
  window-pane, The."
Pedlar's Caravan, The.
Shooting Song, A.
Stalky Jack.
Thought, The.
Topsy-turvy World.
Winifred Waters.
Wonderful World, The.
Rangiaho
Song of Despair.
Rankin, Jeremiah Eames
Fairest of Freedom's Daughters.
God Be with You till We Meet Again.
Laboring and Heavy Laden.
Word of God to Leyden Came, The.
Rankin, Paula
Being Refused Local Credit.
For My Mother, Feeling Useless.
Hot Bath in an Old Hotel.
Middle Age.
Somewhere Else.
Rankins, William
By this time long-gowned Lumen walked
  abroad, *sel.*
Ranko (Takakuwa Ranko)
Plum Trees.
Rain of a winter storm.
Ranran
Shifty-eyed, the frog.
Ransetsu (Hattori Ransetsu)
Harvest moon.
New Year's Day/ Dawns clear, and sparrows.
Painting pines.
What can I do?—frog dumped.
Ransford, R. W.
She Found Me Roots.
Ransom, John Crowe
Address to the Scholars of New England.
Agitato ma Non Troppo.
Amphibious Crocodile.
Antique Harvesters.
Armageddon.
Bells for John Whiteside's Daughter.
Blackberry Winter.
Blue Girls.
Captain Carpenter.
Conrad in Twilight ("Conrad, Conrad, aren't
  you old").
Dead Boy.
Dog.
Emily Hardcastle, Spinster.
Equilibrists, The.
First Travels of Max.
Good Ships.

Her Eyes.
Here Lies a Lady.
Inland City.
Janet Waking.
Judith of Bethulia.
Lady Lost.
Little Boy Blue.
Man without Sense of Direction.
Miriam Tazewell.
Miss Euphemia.
Morning.
Old Man Pondered.
Old Mansion.
Our Two Worthies.
Painted Head.
Painting: A Head.
Parting at Dawn.
Parting, without a Sequel.
Persistent Explorer.
Philomela.
Piazza Piece.
Prelude to an Evening.
Somewhere Is Such a Kingdom.
Spectral Lovers.
Spiel of the Three Mountebanks.
Survey of Literature.
Swimmer, The.
Tall Girl, The.
Two in August.
Vaunting Oak.
Vision by Sweetwater.
Winter Remembered.
Ransom, W. M.
Catechism, 1958.
Critter.
Grandpa's .45.
Indian Summer: Montana, 1956.
Message from Ohanapecosh Glacier.
On the Morning of the Third Night above
  Nisqually.
Statement on Our Higher Education.
Ransome, Basil
Travellers Turning Over Borders.
Rantala, Kathryn
Gran Mal.
Harmoniums.
Noah at Sea.
Slipping in Orbit.
Toast for the Original Survivors.
Raphael, Lennox
Infants of Summer.
Mike 65.
Rappoport, Solomon. *See* "Ansky, S."
Rarawa Kerehoma
Sentinel's Song, A.
Rascas, Bernard
Love of God, The.
Rashed, N. M.
Afraid of Life?
Dance.
Dust Is Upon Us, The.
Eyes of Dark Sorrow, The.
Hand of Music, The.
In the Silence of Endless Night.
My Insect Soul.
Pledge.
Revenge.
Speak.
Rashidd, Amir
Eclipse.
Rashidd, Niema
Warriors Prancing, Women Dancing.
Rashley, R. E.
Caterpillar.
Portrait of an Indian.
Voyageur.
Ratcliffe, Dorothy Una
February.
Pirates' Tea-Party, The.
Ratner, Rochelle
Davening.

Maiden, The.
Poor Shammes of Berditchev, The.
Ratosh, Yonathan [*or* Yonatan]
Lament: "You did not suck at my mother's
  breast."
Million, A.
Ratti, John
Division.
Ratushinskaya, Irina
I Will Live and Survive.
To My Unknown Friend.
White-Hot Blizzard, The.
Raven, John
Assailant.
Inconvenience, An.
Roach, The.
Ravenel, Beatrice
Alligator, The.
Ravenscroft, Thomas
Hawking for the Partridge.
Madrigal: "My mistress is as fair as fine."
Ravidas
Day it comes, it goes, The.
Family that has a true follower of the Lord,
  A.
House is large, its kitchen vast, The.
It's just a clay puppet, but how it can dance!
I've never known how to tan or sew.
Mother, she asks, with what can I worship?
Oh well born of Benares, I too am born well
  known.
Peddler,/ the first watch of night.
Peddler,/ the fourth watch of night.
Peddler,/ the second watch of night.
Peddler,/ the third watch of night.
Regal realm with the sorrowless name, The.
This bodily world is a difficult road—hilly,
  overgrown.
Walls are made of water, pillared by air, The.
Who could long for anything but you?
Your name: the act of worship.
**Ravikovich [*or* Ravikovitch], Dahlia [*or*
  Daliah]**
Blue West, The.
Clockwork Doll.
Dear Mickey.
Dress, The.
Dress of Fire, A.
Everlasting Forests, The.
Hills of Salt.
How Hong Kong Was Destroyed.
Human Qualities.
King over Israel.
Like Rachel.
Man of Mystery.
Marionette.
On the Road at Night There Stands the Man.
Personal Opinion, A.
Poem of Explanations.
Portrait.
Pride.
Private View, A.
Requiem after Seventeen Years.
Sinking Rising.
Surely You Remember.
Time Caught in a Net.
Tirzah and the Wide World.
War's End.
Who Art Thou, O Great Mountain.
Ravitch, Melech (Zekharye Khone Bergner)
Conscience.
Excommunication, The.
Horses.
Let Us Learn.
Poem—Good or Bad—a Thing—with One
  Attribute—Flat, A.
Tropic Nightmare in Singapore.
Twelve Lines about the Burning Bush.
Twilight Thoughts in Israel.
Verses Written on Sand.

Rawlinson, Gloria
Hare in the Snow, The.
Islands Where I Was Born, The.
Merry-go-round.
Simple Matter, A.
Rawnsley, Hardwick Drummond
Ballad of the Conemaugh Flood, A.
Raworth, Tom
Collapsible.
Empty Pain-Killer Bottles, The.
Hot Day at the Races.
My Face Is My Own, I Thought.
Rawson, Grindall
To the Learned and Reverend Mr. Cotton
   Mather, on His Excellent Magnalia.
Upon the Death of His Much Esteemed Friend
   Mr. Jno Saffin Junr.
Ray, David
At the Washing of My Son.
Card-Players, The.
Death-Lace.
Entrepreneur, The.
Genitori.
Good New Is; the Bad News Is, The.
Greens.
Love Letter.
On a Fifteenth-Century Flemish Angel.
On the Poet's Leer.
Problems of a Writing Teacher, The.
Throwing the Racetrack Cats at Saratoga.
Ursula.
X-Ray.
Ray, Henrietta Cordelia
After the Storm.
Afterglow, The.
Ambition.
Among the Berkshire Hills.
An Idyl of Spring.
Anita and Giovanni.
Antigone and Oedipus.
April.
Aspiration.
At Christmas-Tide.
At Nature's Shrine.
At Sunset.
At the Cascade.
August.
Awakening.
Beethoven.
Boat Song.
Broken Heart.
Charity.
Charles Sumner.
Chateaux en Espagne.
Cloud Fantasy.
Cloud Song.
Coming of Spring, The.
Compensation.
Cuckoo Song.
Dante.
Dawn of Love, The.
Dawn's Carol.
December.
Dream of Elfland, A.
Dream within a Song, A.
Easter Carol.
Echo Reverie.
Echo's Complaint.
Emerson.
Enchanted Shell, The.
Evening Prayer.
Fading Skiff, The.
Failure.
Fancy and Imagination.
February.
Fisherman's Story, The.
Fragment, A: "Our fancies are but joys all
   unexprest."
Full Vision.
God's Ways, Not Our Ways.
Greeting.

Hermit and the Soul, The.
Hidden Essence.
Hour's Glory, The.
Hymn to the Thousand Islands.
Ideal, An.
Idyl: Sunrise.
Idyl: Sunset.
In Memoriam Frederick Douglass.
In Memoriam Paul Laurence Dunbar.
Incompleteness.
Instability.
Invocation to the Muse.
January.
July.
June.
Life.
Life's Boundary.
Limitations.
Lincoln.
Lines Written on a Farewell View of the
   Franconia Mountains at Twilight.
Listening Nydia.
Little Fay's Thanksgiving.
Longfellow.
Lost Opportunities.
Love's Vista.
Maid of Ehrenthal, The.
March.
May.
May's Invocation after a Tardy Spring.
Messengers, The.
Midnight, sel.
Mignon.
Mildred's Doves.
Milton.
Mist Maiden, The.
Musidora's Vision.
My Easter Dove.
My Spirit's Complement.
Nature's Minor Chords.
Nature's Uplifting.
Niobe.
Noonday Thought, sel.
Noontide, sel.
November.
O Restless Heart, Be Still!
Ocean Musing, An.
October.
Ode on the Twentieth Century.
On a Nook Called Fairyland.
On the Concord River.
On the Picture of a Child.
On the rapids of the St. Lawrence.
Our Task.
Pastoral: "Annette came through the
   meadows."
Perfect Orchestra, The.
Picture, A.
Poet's Ideal, The.
Poet's Ministrants, The.
Prayer: "O Christ, who in Gethsemane."
Quebec.
Quest of the Ideal, The.
Questioning.
Raphael.
Recompensed?
Repose.
Retrospection.
Reunited.
Reverie.
Rhyme of the Antique Forest.
Robert G. Shaw.
Sculptor's Vision, The.
Sea Cadences.
Self-Mastery.
September.
Shadow and Sunrise.
Shakespeare.
Siren Bird, The.
Sky Picture.
Snow Song.
Song: "O sweet, sad, singing river."

Soul Incense.
Soul's Courts, The.
Star Song.
Starlight Thought, sel.
Sunrise, sel.
Sunrise Thought, sel.
Sunset, sel.
Sunset Picture.
Sunset Thought, sel.
Thought at Walden, A.
Thought of Lake Ontario, A.
Tireles Sculptor, The.
To Laura.
To My Father.
To My Mother.
Toussaint L'Ouverture.
Triple Bension, The.
Two Musicians, The.
Venus of Milo, The.
Verses to my Heart's-Sister.
Vision of Eve, The.
Vision of Moonlight, A.
Voices of the Rain.
Wendell Phillips.
William Lloyd Garrison.
Wood Carols.
Ray, Maude Louise
My Task.
Raymond, Grace (Annie Raymond Grace
   Stillman)
Birth.
Raymond, Monica
Limerick: "There was a young lady of Spain."
Raymond, Vicki
Holiday Girls.
Witch Sycorax Addresses Her Lover, The.
Read, Sir Herbert
Beata l'Alma.
Champ de Manœuvres.
Childhood.
Cranach.
Crucifix, The.
End of a War, The.
Equation.
Execution of Cornelius Vane, The.
Falcon and the Dove, The.
Garden Party.
Happy Warrior, The.
My Company.
1945.
Northern Legion, A.
Phoenix, bird of terrible pride, sel.
Refugees, The.
Retreat, The.
Seven Sleepers, The.
Sic et Non.
Sorrow of Unicume, The.
Summer Rain.
To a Conscript of 1940.
Villages Démolis.
White Isle of Leuce, The.
Woodlands.
Read, Sylvia
For the War-Children.
Owl.
Read, Thomas Buchanan
Angler, The.
Attack, The.
Blennerhassett's Island, sel.
Brave at Home, The.
Closing Scene, The.
Drifting.
Eagle and Vulture, The.
Lines to a Blind Girl.
Rising, The, sel.
Sheridan's Ride.
Valley Forge, sel.
Windy Night, The.
Read, Vail
This New Day.
Realf, Richard
Defence of Lawrence, The.

Indirection.
Old Man's Idyl, An.
Word, The.
Reaney, James
Baby, The, *sel.*
Branwell's Sestina, *sel.*
Chough, The.
Gramophone, The.
Granny Crack.
Horn, The.
January, *sel.*
Katzenjammer Kids, The.
Le Tombeau de Pierre Falcon.
Lost Child, The.
November, *sel.*
Oracular Portcullis, The.
Plum Tree, The.
Red Heart, The.
School Globe, The.
To the Avon River above Stratford, Canada.
Upper Canadian, The.
Reavey, George
Bridge of Heraclitus, The.
Dismissing Progress and Its Progenitors.
How many fires.
Never.
Rebeárivelo, Jean-Joseph. *See* **Rabeárivelo,**
Jean-Joseph
Rebelo, Jorge
Poem: "Come, brother, and tell me your life."
Rebolledo, Efrén
Vampire, The.
Rechter, Judith
Fay Wray to the King.
Reck, Michael
Once More O Ye Etc.
Reckord, Margaret
Ama Credo.
Journey, The.
Miss Geeta.
Red Cloud, Fred
Machu Picchu, Peru.
Tale of Last Stands, A.
Redfern, Roger A.
Night Expedition from Ben Alder Cottage.
Redgrove, Peter
Apprentice at the Feast, The.
Bedtime Story for My Son.
Christiana.
Corposant.
Curiosity-Shop, The.
Design.
Dog Prospectus.
Eggs, The.
For No Good Reason.
Ghostly Father, The.
I Stroll.
Idea of Entropy at Maenporth Beach, The.
Intimate Supper.
Light Hotel.
Man and His Wife, A.
Million, The.
Minerals of Cornwall, Stones of Cornwall.
Not Machines.
On Catching a Dog-Daisy in the Mower.
Red Indian Corpse.
Required of You This Night.
Secretary, The.
Serious Readers.
Shearing Grass.
Some Love.
Story from Russian Author.
Visible Baby, The.
World, A.
Redi, Francesco
Bacchus on Beverages, *sel.*
Bacchus's Opinion of Wine, and Other
    Beverages, *sel.*
Creation of My Lady, The.
Redmond, Eugene B.
Definition of Nature.

Gods in Vietnam.
Love Necessitates.
Redpath, Beatrice
But I Shall Weep.
Star, The.
Redshaw, Thomas Dillon
Voice from Danang.
Redwing, A. K.
Agent of Love.
Blue Jeaned Rock Queen in Search of
    Happiness on a Blind Thursday at 1/3
    Speed and Crying, A.
Chrome Babies Eating Chocolate Snowmen in
    the Moonlight.
Cosmic Eye.
Hoofer, The.
Lost Mohican Visits Hell's Kitchen, A.
Sitting Bull's Will versus the Sioux Treaty of
    1868 and Monty Hall.
Tornado Soup.
Two Hookers.
World's Last Unnamed Poem, The.
Written in Unbridled Repugnance near Sioux
    Falls, Alabama—April 30, 1974.
Reece, Byron Herbert
Such Instance.
Reece, Duane
No Imposter.
Reed, Edward Bliss
Poplars.
Reed, Henry
Auction Sale, The.
Chard Whitlow.
Judging Distances, *sel.*
Lives.
Naming of Parts, *sel.*
Sailor's Harbor.
Unarmed Combat, *sel.*
Wall, The.
Reed, Ishmael
Al Capone in Alaska.
Badman of the Guest Professor.
Beware: Do Not Read This Poem.
Black Power Poem.
Dialog outside the Lakeside Grocery.
Feral Pioneers, The.
Gangster's Death, The.
I Am a Cowboy in the Boat of Ra.
Instructions to a Princess.
Katskills Kiss Romance Goodbye, The.
Rain Rain on the Splintered Girl.
Reactionary Poet, The.
Sermonette.
Skirt Dance.
Sky Diving.
Untitled I.
Reed, J. D.
Cripples.
Gorilla at Twenty Nine Years, The.
Lost Silvertip.
Out from Lobster Cove.
Reports Come In, The.
Reed, Langford
Limerick: "Consider the lowering Lynx."
Reed, Nan Terrell
Life.
Vases.
Reedy, Arnold
Lament for Apirana Ngata.
Rees, John Machreth ("Machreth")
Merioneth.
Reese, Lizette Woodworth
Anne.
At Cockcrow.
Christmas Folk-Song, A.
Daffodils.
Flower of Mullein, A.
Good Joan, The.
His Mother in Her Hood of Blue.
Holiday, A.
Immortality.

In Harbor.
In Time of Grief.
Keats.
Little Song of Life, A.
Lydia.
Lydia Is Gone This Many a Year.
Ownership.
Prayer of an Unbeliever.
Puritan Lady, A.
Reserve.
Spicewood.
Spring Ecstasy.
Street Scene, A.
Taps.
Tears.
Telling the Bees.
Thomas à Kempis.
To a Town Poet.
Trust.
Reese, S. Carolyn
Letter from a Wife.
Reeve, F. D.
Alcoholic.
Falls, The.
Hope.
Plaque in the Reading Room for My
    Classmates Killed in Korea, The.
We Settled by the Lake.
Reeve, Paul Eaton
Succumbing.
Reeves, James
Beech Leaves.
Black Pebble, The.
Bogus-Boo, The.
Catullus to Lesbia.
Ceremonial Band, The.
Cows.
Doctor Emmanuel ("Doctor Emmanuel
    Harrison-Hyde").
Double Autumn, The.
Doze, The.
Fireworks.
Giant Thunder.
Horn, The.
If Pigs Could Fly.
Intruder, The.
Little Brother, The.
Little Fan.
Mr. Kartoffel.
Mr. Tom Narrow.
Nonny, The ("Nonny-bird, I love particularly,
    The").
Old Crabbed Men.
Old Mole.
Old Wife and the Ghost, The.
Queer Things.
Run a Little.
Seeds.
Snail, The.
Snitterjipe, The.
Stocking and Shirt.
Stone Gentleman, The.
Things to Come.
Three Singing Birds, The.
Toadstool Wood, The.
W.
Wind, The.
Wooing Frog, The.
You in Anger.
Reeves, Trish
Silver Coin, The.
Reeves, William Pember
Passing of the Forest, The.
Regan, J. M.
Partial Luetic History of an Individual at Risk.
Regelson, Abraham
Moses on Mount Nebo.
Reginald, Francis
À l'Ange Avantgardien.
Cloth of Gold.

Lass in Wonderland, A.
Vision.
Regnier, Henri de
Je ne veux de personne aupres de ma tristesse.
Reich, Asher
Poems from Iowa City.
Reich, Chamutal
And the rain came. And the water came, *sel.*
At twilight amidst the currents of water, *sel.*
Other days on another continent, *sel.*
Reich, Max Isaac
One Thing Needful, The.
Reich, Shlomo
Golem, The.
Tribe Searching, A.
Vigil, The.
Windmill of Evening, The.
Reid, Alastair
Calenture.
Casa d'Amunt.
Curiosity.
Daedalus.
Figures on the Frieze, The.
Game of Glass, A.
Geneva.
Ghosts.
Ghosts' Stories.
Glass Town, The.
In Memory of My Uncle Timothy.
Lesson in Handwriting, A.
Me to You.
Outlook Uncertain.
Pigeons.
Small Sad Song.
Tale the Hermit Told, The.
To Lighten My House.
Who Can Say.
Reid, Christopher
Gardeners, The.
Letter to Myself.
Reid, Tina
Dry Rock Number.
He May Be a Photograph of Himself.
Reid of Stobo, John
In Peblis town sum tyme, as I heard tell, *sel.*
Reidy, Mykie Silz
Hunting Season.
Night Runner's Prayer.
Reingold, Paula
And This Is Love.
Reinmar von Hagenau
As on the Heather.
Reinmar von Zweter
I Came a-Riding.
Reinsberg-Düringsfeld, Ida von
To George Sand.
Reis, Marcos Konder
Map.
Parameter.
Reis, Yitzhok. *See* **Nadir, Moishe**
Reisen, Abraham
Burn Out Burn Quick.
Children's Games.
Endless Chain, An.
Family of Eight, The.
Future Generations.
Girls from Home.
Healing.
Household of Eight.
Kinds of Luck.
Last Street, The.
Newcomers.
Prayer, A: "Teach me, teach me how."
So!
To a Woman Socialist.
Watchman, The.
What Have I to Do With.
What Is the Case in Point?
Reiss, Barbara Eve ("Barbara Eve")
My Daughter's Ring.
Scenario.

Reiss, James
Breathers, The.
Candystore in Washington Heights, A.
Green Tree, The.
Habla Usted Español?
On Hot Days.
Slight Confusion, A.
Whitman at a Grain Depot.
Reizei Tamehide. *See* **Tamehide**
Reizei Tamemasa. *See* **Tamemasa**
Reizei Tamesuke. *See* **Tamesuke**
Rekola, Mirkka
Among Dark Trees.
In This Wind.
You Remember the Elk.
Relph, Josiah
Hay-Time; or, The Constant Lovers. A
Pastoral.
Rendall, Elizabeth
Wind, The.
Rendall, Robert
Angle of Vision.
Planticru, The.
Shore Tullye.
Rendon, Marcie
This Woman That I Am Becoming.
Renton, William
After Nightfall.
Crescent Moon.
Foal, The.
Fork of the Road, The.
Moon and Candle-light.
Shadow of Himself, The.
Replansky, Naomi
Housing Shortage.
I Met My Solitude.
In the Sea of Tears.
Two Women.
Resch, Kathleen
Revenant.
Vampyre Legend, A.
Resnikoff, Alexander
Bad and Good.
Josephine.
Two Witches.
Revard, Carter
Advice from Euterpe.
And Don't Be Deaf to the Singing Beyond.
Another Sunday Morning.
"But Still in Israel's Paths They Shine."
Coming of Age in the County Jail.
Coyote, The.
Discovery of the New World.
Driving in Oklahoma.
ESP.
Getting Across.
Home Movies.
In Kansas.
January 15 as a National Holiday.
Looking Before and After.
My Right Hand Don't Leave Me No More.
North of Santa Monica.
Not Just Yet.
On the Bright Side.
Support Your Local Police Dog.
Revell, Donald
Belfast.
In Lombardy.
St. Lucy's Day.
Reverdy, Pierre
At the End of the Street of Stars.
Bell-Toll.
Central Heating.
Clear Winter.
Colors of the Windows, The.
Departure.
Endless Journeys.
Flower Market.
Flower-Market Quay.
For the Moment.
Forever There.

Heartbreak.
Inn.
Invasion, The.
Live Flesh.
Love Again.
Memory.
Mind Emerges, The.
One More Explanation for the Mystery.
Perspective.
Saltimbanques.
Show for the Eyes.
Spirit Escapes, The.
Struggles of Words, The.
That Memory.
There or Elsewhere.
Time of the Sea.
Waterfall.
Revere, Paul
Unhappy Boston.
Rexford, Eben Eugene
On Easter Morning.
Silver Threads among the Gold.
Trust-Song, A.
Rexroth, Kenneth
Andrée Rexroth.
Autumn Rain.
Bad Old Days, The.
Bestiary, A.
Dawn in a tree of birds, A.
Deer, *sel.*
Dialogue of Watching, A.
Fact.
Fifty.
Fish Peddler and Cobbler.
For a Masseuse and Prostitute.
Fox, *sel.*
Further Advantages of Learning.
Heart of Herakles, The, *sel.*
Here is Klito's little shack.
Herring, *sel.*
Horse, *sel.*
I have sworn ten thousand times.
I Lais, once an arrow.
I used to tell you, "Frances, we grow old."
Kings River Canyon.
Letter to William Carlos Williams, A.
Lion, *sel.*
Living Pearl, A.
Lute Music.
Lysidike dedicates.
Marichi.
Marthe Away (She Is Away).
Mother Goose Rhyme.
Naked out of the dark we came.
Observations in a Cornish Teashop.
On the Eve of the Plebiscite.
Only Years.
Our Canoe Idles in the Idling Current.
Proust's Madeleine.
Quietly.
Raccoon, *sel.*
Rogation Days.
Signature of All Things, The.
Snow Storm.
Song for a Dancer.
Strength through Joy.
Time Is the Mercy of Eternity.
Vitamins and Roughage.
Vulture, *sel.*
Wheel Revolves, The.
When I dragged the rotten log, *sel.*
Wolf, *sel.*
You are a stool pigeon and.
Reyes, Alfonso
Menace of the Flower, The.
Monterrey Sun.
River of Oblivion.
Scarcely.
Tarahumara Herbs ("Tarahumara Indians have
come down, The").
To-and-Fro of Saint Theresa.

Reyes, Margarita Baldenegro
Old Man Who Is Gone Now, The.
Reyes Basualto, Neftali Ricardo. *See*
Neruda, Pablo
Reyna, Bessy
While You.
Reynolds, Barney
Cranberry Song, The.
Reynolds, Elizabeth Gardner
Little Black Dog, The.
Reynolds, John
Mysteries Revealed after Death, *sel.*
Nosegay, A.
Reynolds, John Hamilton
Gallantly within the Ring.
Peter Bell.
To Keats: On Reading His Sonnet Written in
Chaucer.
To Spenser.
Reynolds, Tim
To a Bad Heart.
Walk in March, A.
Reznikoff, Charles
About an Excavation.
After I Had Worked All Day, *sel.*
Autobiography: Hollywood, *sel.*
Body Is like Roots Stretching, The.
He was afraid to go through their grocery
store, *sel.*
Hebrew of Your Poets, Zion, The.
I Will Go into the Ghetto.
I Will Write Songs against You.
Jacob.
Lament of the Jewish Women for Tammuz.
Lamps Are Burning, The.
Let other people come as streams.
Letter, The.
Luzzato.
New Year's.
Out of the Strong, Sweetness.
Raisins and Nuts.
Son with a Future, A, *sel.*
Te Deum.
These Days the Papers in the Street.
This is the autumn and our harvest, *sel.*
Two girls of twelve or so at a table.
Winter Sketches.
Rhianus
Epigram: "Most inexplicable the wiles of boys
I deem."
Rhinow, Arthur B.
And Yet.
Rhodes, Hugh
Rising in the Morning.
Rhodes, Margaret G.
Best of All, The.
Carol Singers, The.
Rhodes, R.
Prize-winning Limerick, A.
Rhys, Ernest
Autobiography, An.
Rhys, Jean
Obeah Night.
Rhys, Keidrych
Letter to My Wife.
Tragic Guilt.
Riaz, Fahmida
Between You and Me.
Doll.
Inhibition.
Mohajir.
She Is a Woman Impure.
Truth.
Voice of Stone.
Ribback, Alan
Ar(chibald')s Poetica.
Ribemont-Dessaignes, Georges
Sliding Trombone.
Ricardo, Cassiano
First Ultraviolet Ballad.

Nightfall.
Song of the Wild Dove, The.
Rice, Albert
Black Madonna, The.
Rice, Cale Young
Litany for Latter-Day Mystics, A.
Mystic, The.
Rice, Grantland
Alumnus Football.
Babe Didrikson.
Rice, Harvey
Cuba.
Rice, Stan
America the Beautiful.
Bicycle, The.
Cry-Bird Journey, The.
Dogchain Gang, The.
Flesh.
History: Madness.
Incanto.
Last Supper, The.
Metaphysical Shock while Watching a TV
Cartoon.
Poem Following Discussion of Brain.
Round Trip.
Singing Death.
Skyjacker, The.
Some Lamb.
29th Month, The.
Rice, Wallace
Battle-Song of the *Oregon.*
Blood Is Thicker than Water.
Brooklyn at Santiago, The.
Defeat and Victory.
Destroyer of Destroyers, The.
Dewey and His Men.
End, The.
First American Sailors, The.
Firstfruits in 1812.
Immortal Flowers.
Jackson at New Orleans.
Minute-Men of Northboro', The.
Spain's Last Armada.
Sudbury Fight, The.
The *Armstrong* at Fayal.
Under the Stars.
Wheeler's Brigade at Santiago.
Rich, Adrienne
Abnegation.
Across a city from you, I'm with you, *sel.*
After Dark.
Afterwake, The.
At a Bach Concert.
At Majority.
Attention.
August.
Aunt Jennifer's Tigers.
Autumn Sequence.
Bears.
Blood-Sister.
Burning of Paper instead of Children, The.
Can it be growing colder when I begin, *sel.*
Celebration in the Plaza, The.
Charleston in the 1860s.
Clock in the Square, A.
Coast to Coast.
Dark lintels, the blue and foreign stones, The,
sel.
Demon Lover, The.
Dialogue.
Diving into the Wreck.
Double Monologue.
Epilogue for a Masque of Purcell.
Every peak is a crater. This is the law of
volcanoes, *sel.*
Face to Face.
5:30 A.M.
Focus.
For the Conjunction of Two Planets.
For the Dead.
For the Record.

From a Survivor.
From an Old House in America.
From the Prison House.
Gabriel.
Granddaughter, *sel.*
Grandmothers.
Hattie Rice Rich, *sel.*
Heart of cold. Bones of cold. Scalp of cold,
sel.
"I Am in Danger—Sir."
I came out of the hospital like a woman, *sel.*
I can see my self years back at Sunion, *sel.*
I come home from you through the early light
of spring, *sel.*
I Dream I'm the Death of Orpheus.
I wake up in your bed. I know I have been
dreaming, *sel.*
If I lay on that beach with you, *sel.*
In a bald skull sits our friend in a helmet, *sel.*
Insomniacs, The.
Insusceptibles, The.
Integrity.
It was your vision of the pilot, *sel.*
Like This Together.
Living in Sin.
Living in the Cave.
Love in the Museum.
Lucifer in the Train.
Mare's skeleton in the clearing: another sign
of life, The, *sel.*
Mary Gravely Jones, *sel.*
Meditations for a Savage Child.
Merced.
Middle-aged, The.
Mirror in Which Two Are Seen as One, The.
Mourning Picture.
Necessities of Life.
New Year's Eve in Troy.
Newsreel, *sel.*
Nightbreak.
Ninth Symphony of Beethoven Understood at
Last as a Sexual Message, The.
No one's fated or doomed to love anyone, *sel.*
Novella.
November 1968.
Of simple choice they are the villagers; their
clothes come, *sel.*
Old blanket. The crumbs of rubbed wool
turning up, The, *sel.*
Orient Wheat.
Origins and History of Consciousness.
Orion.
Paula Becker to Clara Westhoff.
Peeling Onions.
Phenomenology of anger, The.
Planetarium.
Power.
Primary Ground, A.
Prospective Immigrants Please Note.
Rain on the West Side Highway, *sel.*
Raven, The.
Re-forming the Crystal.
Revivalist in Boston, A.
Roofwalker, The.
Rules break like a thermometer, The, *sel.*
Sex, as they harshly call it, *sel.*
Since we're not young, weeks have to do
time, *sel.*
Sisters.
Sleeping, turning in turn like planets, *sel.*
Snapshots of a Daughter-in-Law.
Song: "You're wondering if I'm lonely."
Splittings.
Springboard, The.
Storm Warnings.
Stranger, The.
Survivors, The.
That conversation we were always on the
edge, *sel.*
That "old last act"!, *sel.*
They come to you with their descriptions of
your soul, *sel.*

This apartment full of books could crack
   open, *sel.*
Tobacco fields lie fallow the migrant pickers,
   The, *sel.*
Tourist and the Town, The.
Toward the Solstice.
Transit.
Translations.
Trees, The.
Trying to Talk with a Man.
Tryst in Brobdingnag, A.
Two Songs, I.
Unsaid Word, An.
Upcountry.
Upper Broadway.
Valediction Forbidding Mourning, A.
Versailles.
Waking in the Dark.
Walk by the Charles, A.
We are driven to odd attempts; once it would
   not have occurred, *sel.*
What kind of beast would turn its life into
   words?, *sel.*
Whatever happens with us, your body, *sel.*
Whatever it was: the grains of the glacier
   caked in us, *sel.*
When/Then.
Wherever in this city, screens flicker, *sel.*
Will to Change, The.
Woman Mourned by Daughters, A.
Women.
Yom Kippur 1984.
Your dog, tranquil and innocent, dozes
   through, *sel.*
Your silence today is a pond where drowned
   things live, *sel.*
Your small hands, precisely equal to my own,
   sel.

Rich, Hiram
   Morgan Stanwood.
Rich, Mark
   Amassing Knowledge.
Rich, Richard
   Newes from Virginia.
Rich, Vera
   Lion Gate.
Richard of Caistre
   Hymn to Jesus, A.
Richards, Edward Hersey
   Wise Old Owl, A.
Richards, George
   Almighty Spake, and Gabriel Sped, Th'.
   Long as the Darkening Cloud Abode.
Richards, Ivor Armstrong
   End of a Course.
   Nothing at All.
   Trinity Brethren Attend.
Richards, Laura Elizabeth
   Alibazan.
   Antonio.
   At Easter Time.
   Cave-Boy, The.
   Eletelephony.
   Giraffe and the Woman, The.
   Kindness to Animals.
   King of the Hobbledygoblins, The.
   Little John Bottlejohn.
   Mermaidens, The.
   Molly Pitcher.
   Monkeys and the Crocodile, The.
   Mouse, The.
   Mrs. Snipkin and Mrs. Wobblechin.
   My Uncle Jehoshaphat.
   Owl and the Eel and the Warming-Pan, The.
   Punkydoodle and Jollapin.
   Snail and the Mouse, The.
   Song of Two Angels, A.
   Valentine, A.
   Was She a Witch?
   Where Helen Sits.
   Why Does It Snow?

Richards, Michael
   After Christmas.
Richardson, Charles Francis
   After Death.
   Conjecture, A.
   Prayer: "If, when I kneel to pray."
Richardson, Dorothy M.
   Message.
Richardson, George
   England! my persecuted isle, *sel.*
Richardson, Jonathan
   On My Late Dear Wife.
   Self-Consciousness Makes All Changes
      Happy; Ode.
Richardson, Justin
   Back Room Joys.
   La Carte.
   Oocuck, The.
   Rhyme for Remembering How Many Nights
      There Are in the Month.
   Rhyme for Remembering the Date of Easter.
   What'll Be the Title?
Richardson, Thomas
   Take Heed of Gazing Overmuch, *sel.*
Richman, Elliot
   On the Tomb of Kalamachius, the Jogger.
Richman, Norma Hope
   Daughter's House, A.
Richstone, May
   Constructive Criticism.
Richter, C. F.
   My Soul before Thee Prostrate Lies.
Richter, Franz
   Course of Life.
   Memorial in Aachen.
   Night Flight.
Rickert, Wendy G.
   Somedays now/ I can squash a cockroach.
Rickword, Edgell
   Cascade, The.
   Complaint after Psycho-Analysis.
   Contemporary Muse, The.
   Cosmogony.
   Encounter, The.
   Handmaid of Religion, The.
   Winter Warfare.
Riddell, Elizabeth
   Children March, The.
   Soldier in the Park, The.
   Suburban Song.
   Under the Casuarina.
   Wakeful in the Township.
Ridge, Lola
   Bees, The.
   Chicago.
   Edge, The.
   Electrocution.
   Fifth-Floor Window, The.
   Réveille.
   Saint's Bridge.
   Salvation Army lass, The, *sel.*
   Song, The: "That day, in the slipping of
      torsos and straining flanks."
   Spring.
   Veteran.
Ridhiana
   Tricked Again.
Riding, Laura (Laura Riding Jackson)
   All the Way Back, *sel.*
   Around the Corner, *sel.*
   Auspice of Jewels.
   Because of Clothes.
   Children, *sel.*
   Dear Possible.
   Flowering Urn, The.
   For-ever Morning.
   Forgiven Past, The.
   Head Itself.
   In Laddery Street Herself, *sel.*
   Into Laddery Street, *sel.*
   Map of Places, The.

Nor Is It Written, *sel.*
Not All Immaculate, *sel.*
Respect for the Dead.
Sad Boy, The.
Way of the Air, The, *sel.*
Wind Suffers of Blowing, The.
Wind, the Clock, the We, The.
Ridings, Elijah
   Hail! muse of my Lancastria fair, *sel.*
   My Uncle Tum.
   Simple Minstrelsy.
Ridland, John
   Another Easter.
   Assassination Poems.
   Light Year, The.
Ridler, Anne
   At Parting.
   Backgrounds to Italian Paintings: Fifteenth
      Century.
   Bathing Song.
   Before Sleep.
   Choosing a Name.
   Christmas and Common Birth.
   For a Child Expected.
   Lumber of Spring.
   Night passed and the fog froze, *sel.*
   Nothing Is Lost.
   Now as Then.
   Now Phillipa Is Gone.
   O Love, Answer.
   On a Picture by Michele Da Verona, of Arion
      as a Boy Riding upon a Dolphin.
   River God's Song.
   Stone Angel.
Ridlon, Marci
   City, City.
   Fernando ("Fernando has a basketball").
   Hamsters.
   Johnny.
   My Brother.
   Open Hydrant.
   That Was Summer.
Riedemann, Myra von
   Horses.
   Last Will of the Drunk.
   There Are Places.
Rieu, Emile Victor
   Flattered Flying Fish, The.
   Green Train, The.
   Hippopotamus's Birthday, The.
   Lesser Lynx, The.
   Lost Cat, The.
   Meditations of a Tortoise Dozing under a
      Rosetree Near a Beehive at Noon While a
      Dog Scampers About and a Cuckoo Calls
      from a Distant Wood.
   Night Thought of a Tortoise Suffering from
      Insomnia on a Lawn.
   Paint Box, The.
   Sir Smasham Uppe.
   Tony the Turtle ("Tony was a turtle").
   Two People.
   Unicorn, The.
Rifqa, Fu'ad
   Elegy for Hölderlin, An.
   Fortune Teller, The.
   Mirrors.
   Setting Off.
   Straw Mat.
   Threshold, The.
   Ultimate Distance, The.
Rigby, Carlos
   If I Were May.
Rigsbee, David
   Crickets.
Rijunkyoku
   Iron will's demanded of.
Rika
   Straw-coat vendor saw the frog last year, The.
Riley, C. L.
   There Are Gods.

Riley, James Whitcomb
At Sea.
Away.
Back to Griggsby's Station.
Barefoot Boy, A.
Bereaved.
Billy Could Ride.
Boy's Mother, A.
Clover, The.
Craqueodoom.
Days Gone By, The.
Diners in the Kitchen, The.
Dwainie, sel.
Extremes.
Good-by er Howdy-do.
Honey Dripping from the Comb.
Hoss, The.
Ike Walton's Prayer.
Just Be Glad.
Knee-deep in June.
Life-Lesson, A.
Lincoln.
Little Orphant Annie.
Longfellow.
Love's Prayer.
Lugubrious Whing-Whang, The.
Man by the Name of Bolus, A.
Man in the Moon, The.
My Fiddle.
My Philosofy.
Name of Old Glory, The.
Nine Little Goblins, The.
Old Man and Jim, The.
Old Sweetheart of Mine, An.
Old Swimmin'-Hole, The.
Old Times Were the Best, The.
On a Dead Babe.
On a Splendid Match.
On the Death of Little Mahala Ashcraft.
Out of the Hitherwhere.
Out to Old Aunt Mary's.
Raggedy Man, The.
Rain.
Rose in October, A.
Sea-Song from the Shore, A.
Shrilling locust slowly sheathes, The, sel.
Song, A: "There is ever a song somewhere,
    my dear."
Summer's Day, A.
Tale of the Airly Days, A.
Thoughts on a Pore Joke.
Town and Country.
Way the Baby Slept, The.
Way the Baby Woke, The.
Wee Little Worm, A.
Wet-Weather Talk.
When She Comes Home.
When the Frost Is on the Punkin.
Riley, Tom
Charitable Stranger, The.
Professional Individual.
Rilke, Rainer Maria
Abishag.
Annunciation.
Archaic Torso of Apollo.
Autumn.
Autumn Day.
Childhood.
Christ's Descent into Hell.
Closing Piece.
Death of the Beloved, The.
For, Lord, the Crowded Cities Be.
From a Childhood.
Full, ripe apple, a pear and banana, sel.
I live my life in growing orbits.
Initiation.
Joseph's Suspicion.
Kings of the world are growing old, The.
Lament: "Oh, everything is far."
Last Evening.
Last Supper, The.
Leda.

Look up, you men. Men there at the fire, sel.
Man Watching, The.
Merry-go-round, The.
Mirrors, no one yet has really described, sel.
Moving Ahead.
O Lord, grant each his own, his own death
    indeed, sel.
Oh this is the animal that never was, sel.
Palm of the Hand.
Panther, The.
Pieta.
Praise.
Prayer of the Maidens to Mary.
Presaging.
Put out my eyes, and I can see you still.
Rose, Oh Pure Contradiction.
Sappho to Eranna.
Silent Hour.
Solemn Hour.
Solitary, The.
Solitude.
Song of Love, The.
Spring has come again. The earth, sel.
This is the creature there has never been, sel.
Tree ascending there. O pure transcension, A,
    sel.
Wait. that tastes good. already it is on the
    wing, sel.
We Are All Workmen.
What Will You Do, God, When I Die?
Where in what ever-blissfully watered
    gardens, sel.
Who, if I cried out, would hear me among the
    angels?, sel.
Why, if this interval of being can be spent
    serenely, sel.
Youth Dreams, The.
Rimbaud, Arthur
After the Flood, sel.
Chercheuses de Poux, Les, sel.
Dawn, sel.
Evil.
Hunger.
Lice Seekers, The, sel.
My mouth is often joined against his mouth.
Napoleon after Sedan.
Ophelia.
Poets Seven Years Old.
Poster of Our Dazzling Victory at
    Saarbrücken, A.
Royalty.
Sensation.
Sleeper in the Valley, The.
Song of the Highest Tower.
Sonnet: "Dead men of 'ninety-two, also of
    'ninety-three."
Strolling Player, The.
To the French of the Second Empire.
Tortured Heart, The.
Vowels.
Rimbaud, Arthur and Paul Verlaine
Sonnet: To the Asshole.
Rimon, I. Z.
I Am a King.
Rimos of Majorca, Moses
Elegy (for Himself).
Rin, Ishigaki. See **Ishigaki Rin**
Ringelnatz, Joachim
Ambition.
Rioff, Suzanne Berger
Cycles, Cycles.
Seduction, The.
Riom, Adine Brabart
Revolt.
Ríos, Alberto
At Kino Viejo, Mexico.
Combing My Hair in the Hall.
Dream of Husbands, A.
I Held His Name.
I Would Visit Him in the Corner.

In the Woman Arms of the Ground.
Incident at Imuris.
Island of the Three Marias.
Juan Rulfo Moved Away.
Lost on September Trail, 1967.
Madre Sofía.
Man She Called Honey, and Married, The.
Man Then Suddenly Stops Moving, A.
Man Who Became Old, The.
Mi Abuelo.
Morning.
Nani.
Purpose of Altar Boys, The.
Saints, and Their Care.
Sleeping on Fists.
Ríos, Andrés Castro
For Nothing.
Words to Remind Me of Grandmother.
Ripley, Sherman
Raggedy Dog, The.
Riquier, Giraut
With a pleasant/ heaviness.
Risi, Nelo
Apple Trees Apple Trees Apple Trees.
Loud voices are needed, sel.
Maneuvers.
Other Side, The.
Prisoner/ rendered blind mute, The, sel.
Private Theater, The.
Tautology.
To deny what we know, sel.
Trinità dei Monti.
Risley, Richard Vorhees
Dewey in Manila Bay.
Ritangen
For thirty-eight years totally unaware.
Ritchie, Elisavietta
International Ski-Flying Championship,
    Obersdorf.
I've Never Written a Baseball Poem.
On Weathering Gales.
Ritchings, Joan Drew
April Fool.
Attic Dance.
Nuptial.
Ritsos, Yannis
Augmentation of the Unknown.
Disfigurement.
Marpessa's Choice.
Our Land.
Penelope's Despair.
Philomela.
Women.
Rittenhouse, Jessie Belle
My Wage.
Ritter, Margaret Tod
Faith, I Wish I Were a Leprechaun.
Rive, Richard
Where the Rainbow Ends.
Rivera, Etnairis
I pull out of the depths of the earth.
Rivera, Marina
Man of O, The.
Rivera, Tomás
My Son Doesn't See a Thing.
Rivera-Avilés, Sotero
Good Memory.
Rainy Morning.
Rivers, Conrad Kent
Death of a Negro Poet, The.
For All Things Black and Beautiful.
Four Sheets to the Wind and a One-Way
    Ticket to France.
If Blood Is Black Then Spirit Neglects My
    Unborn Son.
In Defense of Black Poets.
Malcolm, a Thousandth Poem.
Mourning Letter from Paris, A.
On Passing Two Negroes on a Dark Country
    Road Somewhere in Georgia.

On the Death of William Edward Burghardt
  Du Bois by African Moonlight and
  Forgotten Shores.
Prelude: "Night and the hood."
Still Voice of Harlem, The.
To Richard Wright.
Train Runs Late to Harlem, The.
Watts.

Rives, Amélie
  Before the Rain.
  Mood, A.
  Sonnet, A: "Take all of me, I am thine own,
    heart, soul."

Rixson, Denis
  Glen Pean.
  Ice Has Spoken, The.

Roach, Eric
  At Guaracara Park.
  Love Overgrows a Rock.
  Piarco.

Robbins, Howard Chandler
  And Have the Bright Immensities.
  Put Forth, O God, Thy Spirit's Might.
  Sabbath Day Was By, The.
  Saviour, Whose Love Is Like the Sun.
  Spirit from Whom Our Lives Proceed.

Robbins, Martin
  Cantor's Dream before the High Holy Days,
    A.
  On Seeing a Torn Out Coin Telephone.
  Spring Is a Looping-free Time.
  Winter Pause: Mt. Liberty, N.H.

Roberson, Ed
  Blue Horses.
  Eclipse.
  18,000 Feet.
  If the Black Frog Will Not Ring.
  Mayday.
  Othello Jones Dresses for Dinner.
  Poll.
  Seventh Son.
  You black out the sun, *sel.*

Robert II, King of France
  Strength, Love, Light.

Robert de Brunne. *See* **Mannyng, Robert**

Roberts, Aldwin. *See* **"Kitchener, Lord"**

Roberts, Cecil
  Prayer for a Pilot.

Roberts, Daniel C.
  God of Our Fathers, Whose Almighty Hand.

Roberts, David ("Dewi Havhesp")
  Beloved, The.

Roberts, Dick (Richard Edwin Roberts)
  Duty to Death, LD.

Roberts, Dorothy
  Cold.
  Dazzle.
  Goose Girl, The.
  Sisters.

Roberts, Elizabeth Madox
  Big Brother.
  Butterbean Tent, The.
  Christmas Morning.
  Circus, The.
  Cold Fear.
  Cornfield, The.
  Father's Story.
  Firefly.
  Hens, The.
  In the Night.
  Milking Time.
  Mr. Wells.
  Mumps.
  Orpheus.
  People, The.
  Rabbit, The.
  Sky, The.
  Strange Tree.
  Stranger.
  Uncle Mells and the Witches' Tree.

Water Noises.
Woodpecker, The.

Roberts, G. D.
  Old Morgan.

Roberts, George
  Lament: "My old red Schwinn had a carrier
    over the back fender."
  Scrut Gets Marty Crowe for Social Studies.
  While Dissecting Frogs in Biology Class Scrut
    Discovers the Intricacies of the Scooped
    Neckline in His Lab Partner's Dress.

Roberts, Lloyd
  Deep Dark River.
  Fruit Rancher, The.
  One Morning When the Rain-Birds Call.

Roberts, Mary M.
  Little Pudding.

Roberts, Michael
  "Already," Said My Host.
  H. M. S. *Hero.*
  Hymn to the Sun.
  In Our Time.
  In the Flowering Season.
  Les Planches-en-Montagnes.
  Midnight.
  St. Gervais.
  St. Ursanne.

Roberts, Michele
  After My Grandmother's Death.
  Madwoman at Rodmell.
  Magnificat.
  Out of Chaos Out of Order Out.
  Sibyl's Song, The.

Roberts, Richard Edwin. *See* **Roberts, Dick**

Roberts, Sir Charles G. D.
  Afoot.
  Autochthon.
  Ballad of Manila Bay, A.
  Brook in February, The.
  Brooklyn Bridge.
  Herring Weir, The, *sel.*
  Ice.
  Iceberg, The.
  In Apia Bay.
  In the Wide Awe and Wisdom of the Night.
  Kinship.
  Mowing, The.
  O Earth, Sufficing All Our Needs.
  O Solitary of the Austere Sky.
  Pea-Fields, The, *sel.*
  Potato Harvest, The.
  Salt Flats, The.
  Skater, The.
  Solitary Woodsman, The.
  Sower, The.
  Tantramar Revisited, The.
  Unknown City, The.

Roberts, Theodore Goodridge
  Blue Heron, The.
  Fiddler's Green.
  Lost Shipmate, The.
  Maid, The.
  Wreckers' Prayer, The.

Roberts, Walter Adolphe
  Maroon Girl, The.
  On a Monument to Martí.
  Peacocks.
  San Francisco.
  Valediction, A: "Before the seas again
    divide."
  Vieux Carré.
  Villanelle of Washington Square.

Roberts, William H.
  I Will Believe.

Roberts, Ursula. *See* **Miles, Susan**

Robertson, Clyde
  Mistress of the Matchless Mine.

Robertson, Edith Anne
  Deean Tractorman, Clear, The.
  Deean Tractorman, Deleerit, The.

Robertson, Harry
  Deep Sea Tug.

Robertson, James Logie
  Discovery of America, The.
  Schule Laddie's Lament on the Lateness o'
    the Season, A.

Robertson, T. A.
  Tuslag.

Robertson, Winifred
  Perfect Garden, The.

Robey, George
  Limerick: "Eccentric old person of Slough,
    An."

Robins, Gurdon
  There Is a Land Mine Eye Hath Seen.
  When Thickly Beat the Storms of Life.

Robinson, Agnes Mary Frances
  An Orchard at Avignon.
  Aubade Triste.
  Celia's Home-coming.
  Neurasthenia.
  Pallor.

Robinson, Annie Douglas Green. *See*
  "Douglas, Marian"
  Good Thanksgiving, A.

Robinson, Charles
  Had I but strength enough, and time.

Robinson, Corinne Roosevelt
  Lincoln.
  Path that Leads to Nowhere, The.

Robinson, Edwin Arlington
  Aaron Stark.
  As It Looked Then.
  Ballade by the Fire.
  Ballade of Dead Friends.
  Ben Jonson Entertains a Man from Stratford.
  Bewick Finzer.
  Boston.
  Calvary.
  Calverly's.
  Cassandra.
  Charles Carville's Eyes.
  Children of the Night, The.
  Christmas Sonnet, A.
  Clavering.
  Clerks, The.
  Cliff Klingenhagen.
  Companion, The.
  Corridor, The.
  Credo.
  Dark Hills, The.
  Eros Turannos.
  Eutychides.
  Exit.
  Field of Glory, The.
  Firelight.
  Flammonde.
  Flying Dutchman, The.
  For a Dead Lady.
  George Crabbe.
  Gift of God, The.
  Her Eyes.
  Hillcrest.
  House on the Hill, The.
  How Annandale Went Out.
  I doubt if ten men in all Tilbury Town, *sel.*
  Inscription by the Sea, An.
  Isaac and Archibald.
  James Wetherell.
  John Evereldown.
  John Gorham.
  Karma.
  Klondike, The.
  Lais to Aphrodite.
  L'Envoi: "Now in a thought, now in a
    shadowed word."
  Llewellyn and the Tree.
  Lost Anchors.
  Luke Havergal.
  Man against the Sky, The.
  Many Are Called.

Master, The.
Mighty Runner, A.
Mill, The.
Miniver Cheevy.
Mr. Flood's Party.
New England.
New Tenants, The.
Old Story, An.
Pasa Thalassa Thalassa.
Pity of the Leaves, The.
Prodigal Son, The.
Raven, The.
Reuben Bright.
Reunion.
Richard Cory.
Sheaves, The.
Sonnet: Oh for a Poet—for a Beacon Bright.
Souvenir.
Story of the Ashes and the Flame, The.
Supremacy.
Tact.
Tavern, The.
Too Much Coffee.
Toussaint L'Ouverture.
Uncle Ananias.
Unforgiven, The.
Verlaine.
Veteran Sirens.
Vickery's Mountain.
Walt Whitman.
Why He Was There.
Zola.
Robinson, Elsie
Beauty as a Shield.
Robinson, Grant P.
I Fights Mit Sigel!
Robinson, Harriet H.
"Oh! isn't it a pity, such a pretty girl as I."
Robinson, Henry Morton
November Fugitive.
Second Wisdom.
Robinson, Kenneth Allan
Lines to Dr. Ditmars.
Robinson, Kit
Archangel.
In the American Tree.
In the Orpheum Building.
It's A.
On the Corner.
Separateness of the Fingers in Trance, The.
7 Days in Another Town.
Severance.
Tribute to Nervous.
Up Early.
Robinson, Leonard Wallace
Sicilian Airs.
Robinson, Lucy Catlin
Ballade of Islands, A.
Fire i' the Flint, The.
"Hic Me, Pater Optime, Fessam Deseris."
Robinson, Mary K.
Brown Frog, The.
Dandelion Puff, The.
Queen Bee, The.
Robinson, Roland
I am at Deep Well where the spirit-trees, sel.
I reached that waterhole, its mud designed, sel.
Lyre-Bird, The.
Rock-Lily.
Tank, The.
Waratah.
Robinson, Selma
Bus Ride, sel.
Gentle Name.
Robinson, Tom
Little Lady Wren.
Rabbit.
Swallow Tails.
Robinson, Tracy
Song of the Palm.

Robinson, Wey
Horse & Rider.
Robles, Al
Boyang the Wandering Recluse.
Manong Federico Delos Reyes and His Golden Banjo.
Manong Jacinto Santo Tomas.
Mountain-Toilet Thief, A.
Sushi-Okashi and Green Tea with Mitsu Yashima.
Robson, Jeremy
Departure, The.
Robson, Ruthann
Consort, The.
Regine's Rebuke to Kierkegaard.
Roche, Denis
Eros Possessed.
Roche, James Jeffrey
"Albemarle" Cushing.
Andromeda.
Fight of the *Armstrong* Privateer, The.
Flag, The.
Gettysburg.
Gospel of Peace, The.
Jack Creamer.
Men of the Alamo, The.
My Comrade.
Panama.
Reuben James.
Sailor's Yarn, A.
Skeleton at the Feast, The.
The *Constitution's* Last Fight.
The *Kearsarge*.
Washington.
Roche, Paul
Brick, The.
Courage for the Pusillanimous.
Rochelle, A. G.
Wolf Said to Francis, The.
Rochester, John Wilmot, 2nd Earl of
Against Constancy.
Allusion to Horace; the Tenth Satire of the First Book, An.
Bully, The, *at.*
Chaste Arabian Bird, The.
Commons' Petition to Charles II, The.
Constancy.
Description of Maidenhead, A.
Dialogue between Strephon and Daphne, A.
Disabled Debauchee, The.
Epistolary Essay from M. G. to O. B. upon Their Mutual Poems, An.
Epitaph on Charles II.
Fall, The.
Grecian Kindness.
Imperfect Enjoyment, The.
Impromptu on Charles II.
King's Epitaph, The.
Letter from Artemisia in the Town to Chloe in the Country, A.
Love a woman! y'are an ass.
Love and Life.
Lovely Lass to a Friar Came, A, *at.*
Lycias.
Mistress; a Song, The.
On Poet Ninny.
On the Supposed Author of a Late Poem "In Defense of Satire."
Poet, whoe'er thou art, God damn thee.
Restless he rolls about from whore to whore, *sel.*
Rodomontade on His Cruel Mistress, A.
Satire [*or* Satyr] against [Reason and] Mankind, A.
Song, A: "Absent from thee, I languish still."
Song, A: "As Chloris [*or* Cloris] full of harmless thoughts."
Song: "I promised Sylvia to be true."
Song: "Leave this gaudy gilded stage."
Song, A: "My dear mistress has a heart."
Song of a Young Lady to Her Ancient Lover, A.

Song to Cloris, A.
Spoken Extempore.
Tired with the noisome follies of the age, *sel.*
To Chuse a Friend, but Never Marry, *at.*
To His Mistress.
To Love and Nature all their rights restore, *sel.*
To My More Than Meritorious Wife.
Tunbridge Wells.
Upon Drinking in a Bowl.
Upon [His] Leaving His Mistress.
Upon Nothing.
Very Heroical Epistle in Answer to Ephelia, A.
Were I, who to my cost already am, *sel.*
Wretched Man, *sel.*
Written in a Lady's Prayer Book.
Rock, Madeleine Caron
He Is the Lonely Greatness.
Rockwell, Levi
From a Connecticut Newspaper.
Rodefer, Stephen
Codex.
Pretext.
Words in Works in Russian.
Rodenko, Paul
February Sun.
He.
Robot Poetry.
Roderick, John M.
Passage.
Rodger, Alexander
Bundle of Truths—A Parody, A.
Twa Weavers, The.
Rodgers, Carolyn M.
And While We Are Waiting.
Breakthrough.
Common Poem, A.
For H. W. Fuller.
For Muh' Dear.
For Sapphires.
How I Got Ovah.
"In This House, There Shall Be No Idols."
Jazz.
Jesus Was Crucified or: It Must Be Deep.
Look at My Face, a Collage.
Masquerade.
Me, in Kulu Se and Karma.
Missing Beat.
Newark, for Now (68).
Now Ain't That Love?
One.
Phoenix.
Poem for Some Black Women.
Poem/ Ditty-Bop.
Proclamation/ From Sleep, Arise.
Rebolushinary X-mas.
Remember Times for Sandy.
Setting/ Slow Drag.
Some Me of Beauty.
Somebody Call.
Testimony.
U Name This One.
Voodoo on the Un-Assing of Janis Joplin.
We Dance Like Ella Riffs.
What Color Is Lonely.
Yuh Lookin Good.
Rodgers, William Robert
Airman, The.
Apollo and Daphne.
Awake!
Beagles.
Carol: "Deep in the fading leaves of night."
Christ Walking on the Water.
Directions to a Rebel.
Field Day.
Irish Lake, An.
Lent.
Life's Circumnavigators.
Lovers, The.
Neither Here nor There.

Net, The.
Paired Lives.
Party, The.
Raider, The.
Scapegoat.
Sing, Brothers, Sing!
Snow.
Spring.
Stormy Day.
Summer Holidays.
Summer Journey.
War-Time.
White Christmas.
Winter's Cold.
Words.

Roditi, Edouard
Aurora Borealis.
Beginning and an End, A.
Habakkuk.
Hand.
Kashrut.
Night Prayer of Glückel of Hameln, The.
Paths of Prayer, The.
Seance.
Shekhina and the Kiddushim.

Rodman, Frances
Spring Cricket.

Rodman, Selden
Daphne.
Harpers Ferry.
Man, Not His Arms.
Norris Dam.
On a Picture by Pippin, Called "The Den."
Time of Day.
V-Letter to Karl Shapiro in Australia.

Rodman, Thomas P.
Battle of Bennington, The.

Rodohin
Meeting Master Oryu taught me this.

Rodríguez, Aleida
Explorations/ Bronchitis: The Rosario Beach House.

Rodriguez, Judith
At the Nature-Strip.
Eskimo Occasion.
Handloom, The.
How Come the Truck-Loads?
Rebeca in a Mirror.

Rodriguez, Magdalena de
June 10.

Rodríguez Frese, Marcos
Beginning.
What Is Needed.

Rodríguez Nietzche, Vicente
As Yet.

Roe, Sir Thomas
On Gustavus Adolphus, King of Sweden.

Roe, Sue
Mid-Winter.
No Taker for the Small Shoes.
Small Shoes (II), The.
To See the Minstrels.
Writing, and Other Avenues.

Roethke, Theodore
Academic.
All Morning.
Bat, The.
Beast, The.
Big Wind.
Bound.
Bring the Day!
Ceiling, The.
Chair, The.
Child on Top of a Greenhouse.
Coming of the Cold, The.
Cow, The.
Cuttings ("Sticks-in-a-drowse droop over sugary loam").
Cuttings ("This urge, wrestle, resurrection of dry sticks").

Decision, The.
Dinky.
Dolor.
Donkey, The.
Dream, The.
Elegy for Jane.
Epidermal Macabre.
Far Field, The.
Field of Light, A.
First Meditation, *sel.*
Flight, The, *sel.*
For an Amorous Lady.
Forcing House.
Four for Sir John Davies.
Frau Bauman, Frau Schmidt, and Frau Schwartze.
Geranium, The.
Gibber, The, *sel.*
Give Way, Ye Gates.
Heard in a Violent Ward.
Her Longing.
Her Time.
Heron, The.
Hippo, The.
I Cry, Love! Love!
I Knew a Woman [Lovely in Her Bones]
I'm Here, *sel.*
In a Dark Time.
In Evening Air.
Infirmity.
It Was Beginning Winter, *sel.*
Journey to the Interior.
Kitty-Cat Bird, The.
Lady and the Bear, The.
Light Breather, A.
Light Listened.
Lizard, The.
Long Live the Weeds.
Long Waters, The.
Lost Son, The.
Marrow, The.
Meadow Mouse, The.
Meditation at Oyster River.
Mid-Country Blow.
Minimal, The.
Mips and Ma the Mooly Moo, *sel.*
Mistake, The, *sel.*
Moment, The.
Moss-gathering.
My Papa's Waltz.
Night Crow.
Night Journey.
North American Sequence.
Old Florist.
Open House.
Orchids.
Otto.
Pike, The.
Pipling, *sel.*
Pit, The, *sel.*
Praise to the End!
Prayer before Study.
Prayer: "If I must of my senses lose."
Premonition, The.
Reckoning, The.
Renewal, The.
Reply, The.
Return, The, *sel.*
Root Cellar.
Rose, The.
Rouse for Stevens, The.
Running Lightly over Spongy Ground.
Saginaw Song, The.
Second Shadow.
Sensualists, The.
Sequel, The.
Serpent, The.
Shape of the Fire, The.
She.
Sloth, The.

Small, The.
Snake.
Song for the Squeeze-Box.
Swan, The.
They Sing.
Thing, The.
Visitant, The.
Voice, The.
Waking, The.
Waking ("I strolled across/ An open field"), The.
Weed Puller.
What Can I Tell My Bones?
Where Knock Is Open Wide.
Wish for a Young Wife.
Words for the Wind.

Rofu, Miki. *See* **Miki Rofu**

Rogers, Alex
Rain Song, The.
Why Adam Sinned.

Rogers, F.
Wishes.

Rogers, George
As Gentle Dews Distill.

Rogers, John
Upon Mrs. Anne Bradstreet Her Poems.

Rogers, Pattiann
Achieving Perspective.
Concepts and Their Bodies (The Boy in the Field Alone).
Creation of the Inaudible, The.
Discovering Your Subject.
Finding the Tattooed Lady in the Garden.
First Notes from One Born and Living in an Abandoned Barn.
For Stephen Drawing Birds.
Giant Has Swallowed the Earth, A.
Inside God's Eye.
Justification of the Horned Lizard.
Love Song.
Man Hidden behind the Drapes, The.
Pieces of Heaven, The.
Possible Salvation of Continuous Motion, The.
Suppose Your Father Was a Redbird.
Trinity.

Rogers, Robert Cameron
Dancing Faun, The.
Doubt.
Health at the Ford, A.
Rosary, The.
Shadow Rose, The.
Sleeping Priestess of Aphrodite, A.
Virgil's Tomb.

Rogers, Ron
Bear Dance.
Black Mesa.
Death of Old Joe Yazzie, The.
Elf Night.
Kindergarten.
Montana Remembered from Albuquerque; 1982.
Taking Off.

Rogers, Samuel
Another and the Same, *sel.*
Byron Recollected at Bologna, *sel.*
Captivity.
Epitaph on a Robin Redbreast, An.
Ginevra.
Great St. Bernard, The.
Interview near Florence, An, *sel.*
Man's Going Hence, *sel.*
Naples.
On J. W. Ward.
Sleeping Beauty, The.
Wish, A.

Rogers, Thomas
Spirit of Night, The.

Rogers, J. E. Thorold. *See* **Thorold Rogers, J. E.**
Rogerson, John Bolton
Manchester.
Minstrel's Lot, The.
Rogoff, Jay
Teaching My Students Prosody.
Rohan, Anne de
On a Lady Named Beloved.
Rokeah [or Rokeakh], David
Beginning.
Childhood.
Every City.
Fleeting Too, The.
I Am like a Book.
Spring of Cities, The.
Then.
Zealots of Yearning.
Rokkoku, Tani. *See* **Tani Rokkoku**
Rokunyo
Early Autumn Evening.
Early Summer, Paying a Second Visit to the
Kankantei of the Kansho-in in the Toei.
Frosty Dawn.
Morning-Glories.
Written on the Oi River.
Rokwaho
Amber the sky.
Clickstone.
Owl.
Prelude: "Lake loon paddles, A."
Twoborn.
Roland, Patrick
Spring Burning.
Roland-Holst, Henriëtte
Concerning the Awakening of My Soul.
I Looked for a Sounding-Board.
Mother of Fishermen.
Small Paths.
Throughout the day we are able to ban the
voices.
Rolfe, Edwin
Elegy for Our Dead.
No Man Knows War.
Song (2): "Keep the dream alive and growing
always."
Rolfe, Frederick William (Baron Corvo)
Ballade of Boys Bathing.
Rolland, John
In haist ga hy thee to sum hoill, *sel.*
Rolle of Hampole, Richard
Ghostly Gladness.
Love Is Life.
Love is Life, *sel.*
Song of Love for Jesus, A.
Rolleston, Thomas William Hazen
Grave of Rury, The.
Rollins, Alice Wellington
Death of Azron, The.
Many Things Thou Hast Given Me, Dear
Heart.
Vita Benefica.
Rolls, Eric
Little Sticks.
Sheaf-Tosser.
Rolnik, Joseph
At God's Command.
First Cigarette, The.
Home from Praying.
I'm Not Rich.
In Disguise.
Neighbors, *sel.*
Net, The.
Thank God.
We have such plain faces, *sel.*
Romaine, Harry
Ad Coelum.
Romains, Jules
Another Spirit Advances.
Church, The.

Romanelli, Samuele
From Battle Clamour.
Love.
Romanes, George John
Sloth, The.
Romano, Liboria E.
Lyric Barber.
Romano de Sant'Anna, Affonso
Of Time and River.
Romieu, Marie de
Brief Discourse: That Woman's Excellence
Surpasses Man's.
Romilu, Myrtle
If to Die.
Rónay, György
Teaching Staff Disbanded, The.
Ronksley, William
To Cheer Our Minds.
Ronsard, Pierre de
And Lightly, like the Flowers.
Corinna in Vendome.
Deadly Kisses.
Fragment of a Sonnet.
His Lady's Death.
His Lady's Tomb.
Of His Lady's Old Age.
On His Lady's Waking.
Paradox of Time, The.
Revenge, The.
Rose, The.
Roses.
To His Young Mistress.
To the Moon.
Rooney, John Jerome
Beam of Light, A.
Homing, The.
Joined the Blues.
McIlrath of Malate.
Men behind the Guns, The.
Ráhat, The.
Where Helen Comes.
Root, Edward Merrill
Prayer for Dreadful Morning.
Root, George Frederick
Battle Cry of Freedom, The.
Root, William Pitt
Answering Dance.
Circle of Struggle.
Exchanging Glances.
Fleshflower.
From the Other Shore.
Kraa.
Natural History of Unicorns and Dragons My
Daughter and I Have Known, A.
Nightswim.
Sea-Grape Tree and the Miraculous.
Sometimes Heaven Is a Mean Machine.
Song of Returnings.
Under the Umbrella of Blood.
Wheel Turning on the Hub of the Sun.
White Horse of the Father, White Horse of
the Son.
Roots, Sista (Ras Tina)
Dictionary Black.
Great Escape, The.
Guess Who!
She.
Their Plan.
Ropes, P. A.
Before Spring.
Bluebells.
Daffodils.
Disappointed Shrimper, The.
Dust.
Glow-Worms.
I Will Keep Christmas.
If.
In February.
Poppies.

Violets.
Watering Rhyme, A.
Rorie, David
Pawky Duke, The.
Ros, Villeam. *See* **Ross, William**
Roscoe, William
Butterfly's Ball, The.
Hard was thy fate in all the scenes of life.
Roscommon, Wentworth Dillon, 4th Earl of
Each poet with a different talent writes, *sel.*
Rose, Billy
Barney Google.
Does the Spearmint Lose Its Flavor on the
Bedpost Overnight?
Unknown Soldier, The.
Rose, Greta Leora
Spring Is at Work with Beginnings of Things.
Rose, Harriet
Mellisandra.
Succubus, The.
Wedding Coat, The.
Rose, Juan Gonzalo
Beak of the Dove, The.
Faith, Hope and Charity.
From the Liturgy.
Nata Natal.
Rose, Margaret
Autumn Song.
Butterfly, The.
Little Bird's Song, A.
Little Fir Tree, The.
Magic Whistle, The.
November.
Rose, Sir George
Forensic Jocularities.
Rose, Wendy
Alaskan Fragments June 1981—Summer
Solstice.
America.
Caged Wings: First Impressions from the Boat
Alcatraz Island/ Indian Land, 1970.
Calling the Scientists Home.
Celebration for My Mother.
Coming of Age in "The Movement."
Comment on Ethnopoetics and Literacy.
Comparison of Hands One Day Late Summer
El Sobrante.
Day They Cleaned Up the Border El
Salvador, February, 1981, The.
Epitaph.
For My People.
For Steph.
For Walter Lowenfels.
Grunion.
How I Came to Be a Graduate Student.
I Expected My Skin and My Blood to Ripen.
If I Am Too Brown or Too White for You.
Indian Women Are Listening; to the Nuke
Devils, The.
Julia.
Leaving Port Authority for the St. Regis
Rezz.
Loo-wit.
Oh Father.
Oh My People I Remember.
Poem to a Redskin.
Robert.
Saint Patrick's Day, 1973.
Sarah: Cherokee Doctor.
Self Dirge.
Sideshow: Julia the Lion Woman.
Six Nations Museum Onchiota, New York—
January.
They Sometimes Call Me.
Throat Song: The Whirling Earth.
To an Imaginary Father.
To the Vision-Seekers: Remember This.
Truganinny.
Weaponry.
Well-intentioned Question, The.
Well You Caught Me Unprepared.

Ryozan
Until today the precious gem's been buried.
Ryuge
One room, one bed—enough.
Vegetarian in a shabby robe, my spirit's, A.
Ryuhoku, Narushima. *See* **Narushima Ryuhoku**
Ryuichi, Tamura. *See* **Tamura Ryuichi**
Ryuki, Kishun. *See* **Kishun Ryuki**
Ryuko
Escaping the world, I became a priest.
Ryushu Shutaku
Sweeping Leaves.
Ryusui
Hidden in water plants, a frog.
Ryuwan, Tate. *See* **Tate Ryuwan**
Ryvel
Pilgrimage to Testour, The.

S

"S., A. W."
Life That Counts, The.
"S., E."
Being Forsaken of His Friend He Complaineth.
"S., J. H."
New Year's Wish, A.
Saadi. *See* **Sadi**
Saadi, Rose
Factory Rainbow, A.
Saarikoski, Pentti
Good Society, A.
History of the Revolution.
I Live in Helsinki.
Long Journey, A.
On two tables I spread out old legends.
Parliament Had Been Dissolved.
Sun Sets, Sun Rises, The.
Tyrants were/ people.
Saaritsa, Pentti
Salt of Pleasure.
Voice of my Brothers.
We Were Suntanned Gods.
Saba, Umberto
After a Long Time in the Provinces, I Returned to My Old School in My Late Years.
Boy and the Shrike, The.
Fruits and Vegetables.
Goat, The.
Kitchen Range.
One Night.
Sleepless on a Summer Night.
Three Streets.
Ulysses.
Woman.
Sabin, Edwin L.
Easter.
Sabina, María
Ah, Jesu Kri, *sel.*
Shaman.
Sabines, Jaime
You Have What I Look For.
Saboly, Nicolas
Boots and Saddles.
Bring a Torch, Jeanette, Isabella.
Shepherd Boys, The.
Sabti, Kamal
What remains in the hands, *sel.*
Sacchetti, Franco
Ballata: His Talk with Certain Peasant Girls.
Catch: On a Wet Day.
Sachio, Ito. *See* **Ito Sachio**
Sachs, Nelly
Above the rocking heads of the mothers.
Awakening—/ Voices of birds.

Burning Sand of Sinai.
But Look.
But Perhaps.
Chorus of the Rescued.
Chorus of the Unborn.
Hasidim Dance.
In flight in escape.
In the blue distance.
Landscape of Screams.
Last one, The/ to die here.
Line Like.
O Night of the Crying Children.
O the Chimneys.
Oblivion! Skin.
One Chord.
To You Building the New House.
Vainly ("Vainly/ the epistles burn").
What Secret Desires of the Blood.
White Serpent.
Sackville, Charles, 6th Earl of Dorset
À Madame, Madame B, Beauté Sexagenaire.
Advice, The.
Excellent New Ballad Giving a True Account of the Birth and Conception of a Late Famous Poem Called the Female Nine, An.
On Mr. Edward Howard, upon His British Princes.
On the Countess of Dorchester.
On the Young Statesmen.
Phillis for Shame Let Us Improve.
Song: "Dorinda's sparkling wit, and eyes."
Song: "Methinks the poor town has been troubled too long."
Song Written at Sea in the First Dutch War (1665), the Night before an Engagement.
To Mr. Bays.
Sackville, Thomas, 1st Earl of Dorset
Midnight ("Midnight was come, when every vital thing"), *sel.*
Mirror for Magistrates, A.
Shield of War, The, *sel.*
Thomas Sackevyll in Commendation of the Worke to the Reader.
Troy, *sel.*
Winter ("The wrathful winter, 'proaching on apace"), *sel.*
Sackville-West, Victoria Mary
Bull, The.
Craftsmen.
Full Moon.
Greater Cats, The.
On the Lake.
Persia.
Sometimes When Night.
Spring, *sel.*
Young Stock.
Sadamaru, Kino. *See* **Kino Sadamaru**
Sadeh, Pinhas [*or* Pinkhas]
Angel, The.
Elegy: "While walking at dusk in a strange city."
In the Forest.
In the Garden of the Turkish Consulate.
Raya Brenner.
Sadi (Musli [*or* Muslih]-Ud-Din)
Alas!
Courage.
Dancer, The, *sel.*
Friendship.
Gift of Speech, The.
Great Physician, The, *sel.*
He Hath No Parallel.
Help.
Hyacinths to Feed Thy Soul.
Love's Last Resource.
Mesnevi.
Ode: "Until thine hands clasp girdlewise the waist of the Belov'd."
On the Deception of Appearances.
Sooth-Sayer.
Take the Crust.
Wealth.

Sadoff, Ira
Concise History of the World, A.
Fifties, The.
Memorial Days.
Mood Indigo.
My Father's Leaving.
Nazis.
Poem after Apollinaire.
Why We Always Take Vacations by the Water.
Sadongei, Alice
After Seeing Paintings in a Small Book by T. C. Cannon (1946-1978).
Don't Forget.
For Carlos Charles Bucillio.
Poems Come to Me in the Night.
What Frank, Martha and I Know about the Desert.
Wind Blew like Water.
Sáez Burgos, Juan
This Afternoon.
Saffarzadeh, Tahereh
Birthplace.
Saffin, John
Acrostick on Mrs. Elizabeth Hull, An.
Acrostick on Mrs. Winifret Griffin, An.
Brief Elegie on My Dear Son John, A.
Consideratus Considerandus.
Elegie on the Deploreable Departure of the Honered and Truely Religious Chieftain John Hull, An.
Lamentation on My Dear Son Simon, A.
One Presenting a Rare Book to Madame Hull.
Satyretericall Charracter of a Proud Upstart , A.
Sweetly (my Dearest) I left thee asleep.
To His Excellency Joseph Dudley.
Saffold, Thomas
Saffold's Cures, *at.*
Safford, William Harrison
Battle of Muskingum; or, The Defeat of the Burrites, The.
Safiya bint Musafir
At the Badr Trench.
Saga, Emperor
Spring Dawn by the River.
Weeping for the Priest Gempin.
Sagami, Lady
In the gathering dew.
Sage, Betty
Humming Birds.
"Sagittarius" (Olga Katzin)
Nerves.
Sagoff, Maurice
Clerihew: "John Henry, Cardinal Newman."
Clerihew: "Oscar Wilde/ Married and fathered a child."
Preface Shrinklit: Elements of Style.
Robinson Crusoe Daniel Defoe.
Sahara Morizumi
White Tiger Battalion, The.
Sahl, Hans
Greeting from a Distance.
Memo.
Saibara
Cock Crows, The.
Deep in the Mountain.
House.
My Wife and I.
Powerless Frog.
Summer Spinning.
Two Kids.
What Can I Do?
Yamashiro.
Said, Hameed
Daily Delights.
Dying at the Edge of Death.
Emanations.

Sa'id, 'Ali Ahmad. *See* **"Adunis"**
Saigan, Yanagawa. *See* **Yanagawa Saigan**
Saigyo (Saigyo Hoshi)
Across the face of the field.
After Entering Religious Life.
Although I do not know, *at.*
As banked clouds.
As I look at the moon.
At the roadside.
Butterflies darting.
Cherry petals/ like the tears.
Clear waters unchanged.
Crickets—/ as the cold of the night.
Cry of the crickets, The.
Cuckoo—/ I've yet to hear him.
Deep snow that, The.
Did I ever think.
Did I hear you ask.
Does the moon say "Grieve!".
Drawing his/ sparrow-hunting bow.
Even a person free of passion.
Every single thing.
Float-rigged strands, The.
Garden that recalls the past, A.
Gazing at them.
How lonely, the light of the moon.
I cannot accept.
I know/ how you must feel!
Ice wedged fast.
If only there were.
In a channel.
In a hailstorm.
In a mountain village.
In Akishino/ is it raining.
In my boat that goes.
In some far-off.
In the little weeds.
In the shade of a remote mountain.
In willow shade.
Is it a shower of rain?
Leaves have fallen.
Let me die in spring.
Let me take a good look.
Let us seek the past.
Like those boats which are returning.
Little boat with no treadboard.
Man who has grown distant, A.
Man without feelings, A.
Mingling my prayer.
Moon-viewings in the capital.
Mount Arachi so steep.
Neglectful, we've yet.
Now I understand.
Observing Children.
On Mount Yoshino.
On the Impermanence of Life.
On the road with not a soul.
One lone pine tree.
Pearls plucked,/ the oyster shells.
Perilous Love Affair, A.
Shut in by spring showers.
Side by side.
Since I am convinced.
Since I no longer think.
Startled/ By a single scream.
Startled by the sound.
Those ships which left.
To the dead.
Today again/ I'll go to the hill.
Trailing on the wind.
Twilight cuckoo.
Was it a dream.
When you consider.
Who lies here.
Who lives here.
Why does no one say, "Pitiful!".
Why regret to leave.
Why should my heart.
Wild geese departing, The.
Winds of spring, The.
With blooms of pampas grass.
Woman Forsaken in Love, A.

Saijo Yaso
Crow's Letter, The.
Saiko, Ema. *See* **Ema Saiko**
Sail, Lawrence
Christmas Night.
Sainctonge, Louise Geneviève de
Drinking Song.
Letter to Madame la Marquise de C———.
Sainsbury, Ian
I put my hat upon my head.
Loveliest of Counties, Shropshire Now.
Saint, Assotto
Triple Trouble.
Saint-Gelais, Mellin de
Sonnet of the Mountain, The.
"Saint Geraud." *See* **Knott, William**
St. Germain, Mark
Cannon Park.
St. John, Bruce
Bajan Litany.
Subtlety.
St. John, David
Acadian Lane.
Avenues, The.
Blue Waves.
Day of the Sentry, The.
Dolls.
Elegy: "Who keeps the owl's breath? Whose eyes desire?"
For Lerida.
Guitar.
Hotel Sierra.
Hush.
Iris.
Orange Piano, The.
Poem: "Your face,/so pale now it is blue."
Providence.
Shore, The.
Slow Dance.
33.
St. John, Peter
Descent on Middlesex, The.
St. John, Primus
Benign Neglect/ Mississippi, 1970.
Elephant Rock.
Lynching and Burning.
Morning Star, The.
Tyson's Corner.
St. Leger, Warham
False Gallop of Analogies, A.
To My Hairdresser.
Saint-Marthe, M.
Choosing a Wet-Nurse, *sel.*
Cravings during Pregnancy, *sel.*
Infant Diseases and Their Treatment, *sel.*
Labour, *sel.*
St. Martin, Laura
As I look out from the desk window.
Ocean is a strange, The.
Saito, Fumi. *See* **Fumi Saito**
Saito Mokichi
Close to death.
Crimson tomato.
Faded vine flowers.
Light pink, The.
Mother Dies.
On the mountain.
Sakanoe [Sakanone], Lady Otomo of [*or no*]
Sakanoe, Lady. *See* **Otomo no Sakanoe, Lady**
Sakuma Shozan
Song of History: Peter the Great.
Sakutaro, Hagiwara. *See* **Hagiwara Sakutaro**
Sala, Jerome
At the Treatment Center.
"Ballad of Helmut Franze, The."
Mother's Day.
Party, The.

Salamon, Joanna
Beneath the Apple of Paradise in Iowa.
Thank You, America.
Salamun, Tomaz
Air.
Eclipse.
Saldaña, Diego de
Eyes So Tristful.
Saleh, Dennis
Bed, The.
Doing Nothing.
Furniture of the Poem, The.
Inventing a Family, *sel.*
Nesting.
Return, The.
Story.
Thumb, The.
Salih, Saniyya
Exile.
Goodbye, Zenobia.
Salinas, Luis Omar
I Go Dreaming Roads in My Youth.
Pedro.
Salinas, Pedro
Distracted.
Fear.
I Wonder, Love.
Now I love you/ as the sea loves its water, *sel.*
Salisbury, Ralph
"Among the Savages."
By Now.
Second Molting, A.
This Is My Death-Dream.
Three Migrations.
Salkeld, Blanaid
Evasion.
Leave Us Religion.
Men Walked To and Fro.
Now Is Farewell.
Optimism.
Templeogue.
Terenure.
Salkey, Andrew
Clearsightedness.
Drifting.
Dry River Bed.
Postcard from Mexico, 16.x.1973.
Remember Haiti, Cuba, Vietnam.
Song for England, A.
Soufrière.
Salm-Dyck, Constance-Marie de
Epistle to the Emperor Napoleon (1810).
Letter to Women.
To M———: "What? Dorval, me you applaud."
Salom, Philip
Bushfire.
Cattle Sale.
Salome, Brian S.
Hello There.
Salomon, I. L.
Song for the Greenwood Fawn.
Salomon, Louis B.
Univac to Univac.
Salsbury, Nate
Apex.
Salter, Mary Jo
England.
Refrain.
Welcome to Hiroshima.
Saltillo, José de
Rio Bravo—a Mexican Lament.
Saltman, Benjamin
Fathers, The.
Journey with Hands and Arms, The.
Saltus, Francis Saltus
Andalusian Sereno, The.
Bayadere, The.
Ideal, The.

Pastel.
Sphinx Speaks, The.
Salusbury, Sir John
Buen Matina.
Saluzzo, Diodata
War of 1793, The.
Salverson, Laura Goodman
If a Maid Be Fair.
Premonition.
Salz, Helen
Late.
Samain, Albert
Pannyra of the Golden Heel.
Sambrook, Joyce
Wild Thyme.
Woodpecker, The.
Samik
Hunger.
Sammis, J. H.
All Needs Met.
Sampley, Arthur M.
Defender, The.
Sampter, Jessie E.
Kadia the Young Mother Speaks.
Promised Land, The.
Summer Sabbath.
Sampu (Sugiyama Sampu)
Cherries, cuckoo.
Glint of hoe.
Mountain spring: near the black sleeve, A.
San Garde, Evelina
Giant's Cake, A.
San Geminiano [or Gimignano], Folgore Da
April, *sel.*
August, *sel.*
December, *sel.*
Dedication: "Unto the blithe and lordly
    fellowship," *sel.*
February, *sel.*
January, *sel.*
July, *sel.*
June, *sel.*
March, *sel.*
May, *sel.*
November, *sel.*
October, *sel.*
On Knighthood.
September, *sel.*
Sonnet: Of Virtue.
Sonnets of the Months: Conclusion.
Sonnets of the Months: Dedication.
Sonnets of the Months: November.
Sonnets of the Months: October.
Sonnets of the Months: September.
Sana'ullah, Mohammad. *See* **"Miraji"**
Sanborn, Franklin Benjamin
Ariana.
Samuel Hoar.
Sánchez, Magaly
Almost Love.
Sánchez, Ricardo
I Remember.
Sanchez, Sonia
Answer to Yo/ Question.
Black Magic.
Chant for Young/ Brothas and Sistuhs, A.
Definition for Blk/ Children.
Don't Wanna Be.
For Our Lady.
Homecoming.
Hospital/ Poem.
Kwa Mama Zetu Waliotuzaa.
Listenen to Big Black at S. F. State.
Memorial.
Nigger.
Now Poem. For Us.
Poem at Thirty.
Poem for Etheridge.
Poem for My Father, A.
Poem: "Look at me 8th."

Poem Written after Reading Wright's
    "American Hunger."
Present.
Right On: White America.
Small Comment.
Summary.
Summer Words of [*or* for] a Sistuh [*or*
    Sister] Addict.
To All Brothers.
To All Sisters.
Sanchez Leon, Abelardo
Poem 4: "Irresponsible citizen."
Sandag
"Word" of a Watch-Dog, The.
"Word" of a Wolf Encircled by the Hunt,
    The.
"Word" of an Antelope Caught in a Trap,
    The.
Sandburg, Carl
A. E. F.
Air Circus.
Alice Corbin Is Gone.
All One People.
Aprons of Silence.
Arithmetic ("Arithmetic is where numbers fly
    like pigeons in and out of your head").
At a Window.
Auctioneer.
Baby Toes.
Balloon Faces.
Bar of steel—it is only, A, *sel.*
Bee Song.
Being Born Is Important.
Blacklisted.
Blue Island Intersection.
Bones.
Broadway.
Broken-Face Gargoyles.
Broken Sky.
Bronzes.
Bubbles.
Buffalo Dusk.
Bundles.
Caboose Thoughts.
Chicago.
Chicago Boy Baby.
Child of the Romans.
Circles.
Clinton South of Polk.
Cool Tombs.
Crapshooters.
Daybreak.
Death Snips Proud Men.
Early Copper.
Early Lynching.
Elephants Are Different to Different People.
Englishman in the old days, An, *sel.*
Falltime.
Fence, A.
Fifty-Fifty.
Fire-Logs.
Fish Crier.
Flash Crimson.
Fog.
For You.
Four Preludes on Playthings of the Wind.
Fourth of July Night.
From the four corners of the earth, *sel.*
Gargoyle.
Gone.
Grass.
Grassroots.
Halsted Street Car.
Happiness.
Harbor, The.
Hazardous Occupations.
Hits and Runs.
Horses and Men in the Rain.
I Am the People, the Mob.
Ice Handler.
Improved Farm Land.
In Tall Grass.

Jazz Fantasia.
Laughing Child.
Lawyers Know Too Much, The.
Limited.
Lines Written for Gene Kelly to Dance To.
Little Candle.
Little Girl, Be Careful What You Say.
Localities.
Look at Six Eggs, *sel.*
Losers.
Lost.
Love in Labrador.
Mammy Hums.
Man in the street is fed, The.
Manufactured Gods.
Milk-white Moon, Put the Cows to Sleep.
Mist Forms.
Moist Moon People.
Mr. Attila.
Muckers.
Mysterious Biography.
New Farm Tractor.
Nocturne in a Deserted Brickyard.
North Atlantic.
Now it's Uncle Sam sitting on top of the
    world, *sel.*
Old Deep Sing-Song.
Old Timers.
On a Flimmering Floom You Shall Ride.
One Modern Poet.
Ossawatomie.
People, Yes, The.
People Who Must.
People will live on, The, *sel.*
Population Drifts.
Prairie Waters by Night.
Prayer after World War.
Prayers of Steel.
Precious Moments.
Primer Lesson.
Psalm of Those Who Go Forth before
    Daylight.
Rat Riddles.
River Roads.
Sandhill People.
Sea Hold, The.
Sea-Wash.
Shovel Man, The.
Sins of Kalamazoo, The.
Slippery.
Smoke of the fields in spring is one, *sel.*
Soup.
Southern Pacific.
Splinter.
Spring Grass.
Street Window.
Summer Stars.
Sunset from Omaha Hotel Window.
Sunsets.
Ten Definitions of Poetry.
They All Want to Play Hamlet.
They Ask: Is God, Too, Lonely.
They have yarns, *sel.*
Three Spring Notations on Bipeds.
Threes.
To a Contemporary Bunkshooter.
Under a Hat Rim.
Upstream.
Wall Shadows.
Washington Monument by Night.
What the people learn out of lifting and
    hauling, *sel.*
When I asked for fish in the restaurant facing
    the Ohio River, *sel.*
Who shall speak for the people?, *sel.*
"Why did the children," *sel.*
Why repeat? I heard you the first time, *sel.*
Wind Song.
Wingtip.
Work Gangs.

Working Girls.
Young Sea.
Sandburg, Helga
Importance of Mirrors, The.
Sandeen, Ernest
Nearing Winter.
Plaint of Flowers, A.
Poète Manqué.
They Are Wicked.
Way Down, The.
Sanders, Donald T.
Poem for Shane on Her Brother's Birthday.
Sanders, Edward (Ed)
Five Feet, The.
Fugs, The.
Holy Was Demeter Walking th' Corn Furrow.
Pindar's Revenge.
Yiddish Speaking Socialists of the Lower East
Side.
Sanders, Mark
Death of the Vaudevillian, The.
Sanders, Sue
We Are Welcome.
Sandford, James
Of Love.
Sandoval y Zapata, Luis de
Sonnet: Beauty on a Western Balcony.
Sonnet: Grievous Peril of a Gallant in Moth
Metaphor.
Sonnet: To Primal Matters.
Sonnet: To the Admirable Transubstantiation
of the Roses into the Marvellous Image of
Our Lady of Guadalupe.
Sonnet: White Lily.
To a Dead Actress.
Sands, Robert Charles
Green Isle of Lovers, The.
Sandstrom, Flora
Stately Lady, The.
Sandy, Stephen
Ballad of Mary Baldwin, The.
Declension.
Et Quid Amabo Nisi Quod Aenigma Est.
Hunter's Moon.
Sandys, Edwin
In Pilgrim Life Our Rest.
Sandys, George
Bounty of Jehovah Praise, The.
Judah in Exile Wanders.
O Blest Estate, Blest from Above.
Psalm XXIII: "Lord my shepherd, me His
sheep, The," sel.
Psalm CIV: Deo Opt. Max, sel.
Psalme CXXXVII: "As on Euphrates shady
banks we lay," sel.
Saner, Reg
Fifth Season, The.
Orchestra.
Sanesada (Fujiwara no Sanesada)
Cuckoo called, The.
Sanetaka (Sanjonishi Sanetaka)
Moon on a Spring Dawn.
My thoughts on the past.
Sanetomo (Minamoto no Sanetomo)
As evening comes.
As the warrior reaches up.
Bamboo frond, The.
Bitter sight—/ I watch and my tears.
Boneset, why are you blooming.
Breakers of the ocean, The.
By Hakone Road/ I cross over.
Fabrics swirled in a thousand.
Grown over with straggly saw grass.
Gull-haunted,/ the windblown shore of Susaki.
I didn't mean/ to recall the past.
I open the pine door.
If only the world.
In the rockbound pool.
Is it always so bleak a sight?.
Leaves of the small oaks, The.
Long-drawn-out autumn, The.

Sleet rattles on the leaves.
So cold the night.
That it might be so always.
This world—/ call it an image.
Though a time come.
Too much/ at one time.
Waves of the great sea, The.
When mountains are split.
When the wild goose.
You erect pagodas.
Sanford, Christy Sheffield
Dreams of Snakes, Chocolate and Men.
Romance of Citrus, The.
Romance of Imprinting, The.
Scattered Fog.
Traveling through Ports That Begin with "M."
Sangster, Charles
Evening.
Meadow-Field, The, sel.
Our life is like a forest, where the sun, sel.
Rapid, The.
Red Men, The.
Thousand Islands, The, sel.
Sangster, Margaret Elizabeth (b. 1894)
Mother's Prayer, A.
Security.
Work of Love, The.
**Sangster, Margaret Elizabeth Munson
(1898–1912)**
At Sunset.
Average Man, The.
Awakening.
Our Own.
Show Me Thyself.
Song for Our Flag, A.
Thanksgiving.
They Never Quite Leave Us.
Whittier.
Within the Veil.
Sanguineti, Edoardo
Barbed wire awaits you, the wasp, the viper,
the bright, The, sel.
Compound earths in structural compositions
are Palus Putredinis, sel.
Grab this mercury, this cold gum, this honey,
this sphere, sel.
Sanjonishi Sanetaka. See **Sanetaka**
**Sannazaro, Jacopo (Actius Sincerus
Sannazarius)**
Like to these unmesurable montayns.
Sanpu
May rains!
Sanso
Arrival/ departure: what difference?
Sansom, Clive
Dustman, The.
Innkeeper's Wife, The.
It was a night in winter, sel.
Ladybird.
Milkman, The.
Postman, The.
Snowflakes.
Sant' Angelo, Bartolomeo di
Sonnet: He Jests Concerning His Poverty.
Sant'Ana, Gloria de
African Day.
Santayana, George
A perfect love is nourished by despair, A, sel.
After Grey Vigils, sel.
Among the Myriad Voices of the Spring.
As in the Midst of Battle There Is Room.
Cape Cod.
Deem not, because you see me in the press,
sel.
Dreamt I Today the Dream of Yesternight.
Have I the Heart to Wander.
I Sought on Earth a Garden of Delight.
I Would I Might Forget That I Am I.
Mightier Storms than This.
Minuet on Reaching the Age of Fifty, A.

O Martyred Spirit.
O world, thou choosest not the better part!,
sel.
On the Death of a Metaphysician.
Perfect Love Is Nourished by Despair, A.
Sonnets, sels.
Sorrow.
Sweet Are the Days.
There May Be Chaos Still.
'Tis Love That Moveth the Celestial Spheres.
What riches have you that you deem me
poor?, sel.
With you a part of me hath passed away, sel.
Santen
Beside a dewless, noonday mugwort.
Santob de Carrion
Jewish Poet Counsels a King, A, sel.
Santos, Aires de Almeida
When My Brothers Come Home.
Santos, Arnaldo
Season of Blood.
Santos, Marcelino dos
Dream of the Black Mother.
Here We Were Born.
Where I Am.
Santos, Sherod
Betrayal.
Breakdown, The.
Death.
Enormous Aquarium, The.
Eurydice.
Evening Light along the Sound, The.
Evening Refrain.
First Child, Born Out of Breach in Mid-May,
sel.
Goodbye.
I Bent to Touch a Damp Cloth to Your
Mouth, sel.
Late November.
Madame Orchidée.
Married Love.
Sirens in Bad Weather.
Terra Incognita.
Winter Landscape with a Girl in Brown
Shoes.
Sanuki, Lady
Sleeve of my dress, The.
Sanyo, Rai. See **Rai Sanyo**
Sappho
About the cool water.
Achtung.
All the while, believe me, I prayed.
Alone.
Already old age is wrinkling my.
Andromache's Wedding.
Andromeda/ forgot.
Be kind to me.
Come, holy tortoise shell.
Come out of Crete/ and find me here.
Come to me from Crete to this holy temple.
Don't ask me what to wear.
Dust of Timas, The.
Farewell to Anactoria.
Forever Dead.
Full Moon.
Glow and beauty of the stars, The.
He is more than a hero.
Here are fine gifts, children.
Hermes came to me in a dream. I said.
Hesperos, you bring home all the bright dawn
disperses.
Honestly I wish I were dead!
I could not hope/ to touch the sky.
I have had not one word from her.
I have no embroidered headband.
I hear that Andromeda.
If my nipples were to drip milk.
Immortal Aphrodite, on your patterned throne.
In gold sandals.
It was you, Atthis, who said.
It would be wrong for us. It is not right.

Leave Krete and come to this holy temple.
Leaving Crete, come visit again our temple.
Like a mountain whirlwind.
Like a sweet apple reddening on the high.
Like the very gods in my sight is he.
Love.
Love—bittersweet, irrepressible.
Lucky bridegroom.
Marriage of Hector and Andromache, The.
Moon Has Set, The.
Mother darling, I cannot work the loom.
My Atthis, although our dear Anaktoria.
My mother always said.
My muse, what ails this ardour?
Now in my/ heart I/ see clearly.
O dream from the blackness.
O Gongyla, my darling rose.
Ode to Anactoria.
Ode to Aphrodite.
On your dazzling throne, Aphrodite.
One Girl.
Peer of the gods is that man, who.
People do gossip.
Round about Me.
"Sappho, if you do not come out."
Seizure.
Some say cavalry and others claim.
Some there are who say that the fairest thing
   seen.
Someone, I tell you,/ will remember us.
Thank you, my dear.
That labor/ a face to remember in wonder.
Then I said to the elegant ladies.
There's a man I really believe's in heaven.
To me he seems like a god.
You came. And you did well to come.
You know the place: then.
You lay in wait.

Sardar J'afri, Ali
Final Night, The.
One Year.
Robe of Flame.
Tears of Shame.
This Blood.

Sarett, Lew
Four Little Foxes.
God Is at the Anvil.
Let Me Flower as I Will.
Let Me Go Down to Dust.
Refuge.
Sheepherder, The.
Wind in the Pine.
Wolf Cry, The.

Sargent, Elizabeth Nancy
Break, The.
Child.
Paradise.
Sailor at Midnight, A.

Sargent, Epes
Death of Warren, The.
Heart's Summer, The.
Life on the Ocean Wave, A.

Sargent, John Osborne
Horace.

Sargent, N. B.
Building for Eternity.

Sargent, Nettie M.
Hymn of Trust, A.

Sargent, William D.
Wind-Wolves.

Sarmèd the Yahud
Quatrain: "Sarmèd, whom they intoxicated
   from the cup of love."
Quatrain: "This existence has, without the
   azure sphere, no reality."

"Sarnicol." See **Thomas, Thomas Jacob**

Saroyan, Aram
Crickets.

Sarson, H. M.
I Must Away.

Lovely Things.
Road to Town, The.

Sarton, May
After the palaces, sel.
At Lindos.
Boulder Dam.
Conversation in Black and White.
Der Abschied.
Dutch Interior.
Eine Kleine Snailmusik.
Fruit of Loneliness.
In Time like Air.
Lady and the Unicorn, The.
Monticello.
Muse as Medusa, The.
My Sisters, O My Sisters.
On a Winter Night.
Prayer before Work.
Sacred Order, The.
Santos: New Mexico.
Snow Light, The.
There was your voice, astonishment.
Transition.

Sassoon, Siegfried
Absolution.
Aftermath.
Ancient History.
At Daybreak.
At the Grave of Henry Vaughan.
Attack.
Base Details.
Before Day.
"Blighters."
Brevities.
Case for the Miners, The.
Child's Prayer, A.
Concert Party.
Conclusion: "Image dance of change, An."
Counter-Attack.
Daybreak in a Garden.
Dead Musicians.
Death-Bed, The.
December Stillness.
Does It Matter?
Down the Glimmering Staircase, sel.
Dreamers.
Dug-out, The.
Elected Silence.
Everyman.
Everyone Sang.
Extra Inch, The.
Falling Asleep.
Fancy Dress.
Fathers, The.
General, The.
Glory of Women.
Grandeur of Ghosts.
Haunted.
Hero, The.
Imperfect Lover, The.
In Barracks.
In Me, Past, Present, Future Meet.
"In the Pink."
Invocation: "Come down from heaven to meet
   me when my breath."
Kiss, The.
Lamentations.
Limitations.
Middle Ages.
Morning Glory.
Musical Critic Anticipates Eternity, A.
Mystic as Soldier, A.
Need, The.
On Passing the New Menin Gate.
One-legged Man, The.
One Who Watches.
Phoenix, The.
Picture-Show.
Power and the Glory, The.
Prayer from 1936, A.
Prehistoric Burials.
Presences Perfected.

Rear-Guard, The.
Redeemer, The.
Repression of War Experience.
South Wind.
Sporting Acquaintances.
Stand-to: Good Friday Morning.
Strangeness of Heart.
Suicide in [the] Trenches.
"They."
To a Very Wise Man.
To His Dead Body.
Together.
Troops, The.
Two Old Ladies.
Vigils.
Villa d'Este Gardens.
Wisdom of the World, The.
Working Party, A.

Sato Harua
Song of the Pike.

Sato, Satoru
By the Iowa River.

Satz, Mario
Coconut.
Fish.
Lemon.

Saucedo, María
About Women's Liberation.

Sauda, Mirza Mohammad Rafi
Beggars have no one, The.
How can your playful ways, my love.
I well remember, Sauda.
Incongruity of the Age, Satire on a Miser's
   Horse.
Life of spring is no more than, The.
Like summer's first rain drops are the candle's
   waxen tears.
Rubai: "How long, how long within this
   world will you remain."
To what unfriendly lands.

Sa'udi, Mona
How do I enter the silence of stones.
When the loneliness of the tomb went down
   into the marketplace.
Why don't I write in the language of air?

Saul, George Brandon
Spring Song.

Saunders, Donald G.
Ascent.
On Foinaven.

Saunders, Lesley
Mothers of Sons.

Saunders, Patricia M.
One of Our Aircraft Failed to Return.
20th Century Requiem.

Saunders, R. Crombie
Empty Glen, The.
Ressaif My Saul.

Saunders, Ruby C. (Fareedah Allah)
Cinderella.
Funky Football.
Generation Gap, The.
Hush Honey.
Lawd, Dese Colored Chillum.
You Made It Rain.

Saunders, Thomas
End of Steel.
Horizontal World.

Savage, Derek S.
Fall of Leaves.
Separation.
Winter Offering.

Savage, Frances Higginson
Duck in Central Park.

Savage, Minot Judson
Decorating the Soldiers' Graves.
Life's Common Duties.
My Birth.

Savage, Philip Henry
Infinity.
Morning.

Silkweed.
Solitude.
Savage, Richard
Bristol.
First, let me view what noxious nonsense
reigns, *sel.*
In gayer hours, when high my fancy ran, *sel.*
Now in the patron's mansion see the wight,
sel.
Savile, Jeremy
Health unto His Majesty, A.
Sawyer, C. P
I Used to Love My Garden.
Sawyer, Charles Carroll
When This Cruel War Is Over.
Sawyer, Paul
Garage Sales.
Sawyer, Ruth
Feast o' Saint Stephen, The.
Sawyer, William
Turvey Top.
Saxe, John Godfrey
Blind Men and the Elephant, The.
Comic Miseries.
Early Rising.
Echo.
Expected Ship, The.
Game of Life, The.
Head and the Heart, The.
How Cyrus Laid the Cable.
My Familiar.
News, The.
Pyramus and Thisbe.
Rhyme of the Rail[s]
Solomon and the Bees.
Sonnet to a Clam.
Where There's a Will There's a Way.
Wishing.
Woman's Will.
Saxe, Susan
Questionnaire.
Saxon, Alvin (Ojenke)
Black Power.
Poem for Integration, A.
Watts.
Saxton, Andrew Bice
First Step, The.
Sayers, A. M.
It Always Seems.
Prithee, let no raindrop fall.
Sayers, Dorothy Leigh
Choice of the Cross, The, *sel.*
Sayigh, Mai
Lament: "Those we love die like birds."
Sayigh, Tawfiq
Out of the Depths I Cry unto You, O Death!
Phantom.
What's Next.
Sayigh, Taufiq. *See* **Sayigh, Tawfiq**
Sayles, James M.
Star of the Evening.
Sayres, Cortlandt W.
Bankrupt.
Sazan, Kan. *See* **Kan Sazan**
Scalapino, Leslie
Areas.
As Rimbaud said, I thought today sitting in
the library.
Epilogue: Anemone.
Haven't I said that part of having intercourse
"Having her under me," the man said, "in
bed, and remembering."
How can I help myself, as one woman said to
me about wanting.
How was I to know that the woman, seated
next to me on the bus.
Jumping-Jack Flash.
Seeing the Scenery.
So I decided watching an old woman like her,
who could rise so easily.
That They Were at the Beach.

We put our heads into the window of a car
which was passing.
Woman Who Could Read the Minds of Dogs,
The.
Woman who had been dressed by someone, in
the same way that, A.
Scannell, Vernon
Act of Love.
Any Complaints?
Apple Poem.
Autumn.
Cat.
Dead Dog.
Discriminator, The.
Felo de Se.
Five Domestic Interiors.
Great War, The.
Incendiary.
Jailbird.
Jealous Wife, The.
Lady and the Gypsy, The.
Men Who Wear My Clothes, The.
Moods of Rain.
Moth, The.
Old Books, The.
Poetry Reading.
Six Reasons for Drinking.
Spot-Check at Fifty.
Walking Wounded.
Words and Monsters.
Scantlebury, Elizabeth E.
Hymn of Dedication.
Scarborough, George L.
To the Men Who Lose.
Scarbrough, George
Birth by Anesthesia.
Scarfe, Francis
Grotto, The.
Kitchen Poem.
Merry Window, The.
Ode in Honour.
Scarron, Paul
Philosophiae Consolationis.
Schacht, Marshall
Not to Forget Miss Dickinson.
Schaechter-Gottesman, Beyle
Meditation.
Schaefer, Sister M.
Cherubim.
Rejoice, Let Alleluias Ring.
Schaeffer, Susan Fromberg
First Test, The.
Housewife.
Truth.
Womb Song.
Yahrzeit.
Schaukal, Richard
Images.
Scheele, Roy
Dancer.
Gap in the Cedar, The.
Keeping the Horses.
Nothing but Net.
Scheffauer, Ethel Talbot
Reply from the Akond of Swat, A.
Scheinert, David
Drunken Stones of Prague, The.
Stone and the Blade of Grass in the Warsaw
Ghetto, The.
Scherzo, I. O.
Threnody: "Truth is a golden sunset far
away."
Scheuer, Marjorie Somers
Fox, The.
Schevill, James
Freud: Dying London, He Recalls the Smoke
of His Cigar Beginning to Sing.
Green Frog at Roadstead, Wisconsin.
Huck Finn at Ninety, Dying in a Chicago
Boarding House Room.

London Pavement Artist.
Screamer Discusses Methods of Screaming,
A.
Schierbeek, Bert
Death, Said Remco.
I Fasten Down the Day.
Ishi.
Look a Man Goes to Kansas.
Sun: Day, The.
Thu Sun: Night.
Schierloh, Samuel
Bucko-Mate.
Schild, Bob
Kid Solos, The.
Two of a Kind.
Schiller, Johann Christoph Friedrich von
Columbus.
Lament: "Even beauty must die! That which
subdues both gods and mortals."
Maid of Orleans, The.
Steer, Bold Mariner, On!
Thekla's Song, *sel.*
To My Friends.
Unrealities, The.
Visit of the Gods, The.
Schimmel, Harold
Ancestors.
Schippers, K.
Bianca's First Steps in the Arts.
Brickbat for Krazy Kat, A.
Grains of Sand on a Radio.
How a Guitar Can Lie on a Chair.
Jigsaw Puzzles.
Schjeldahl, Peter
Younger Poet, A.
Schlichter, Norman C.
Sledding Song, A.
Schlipf, Benjamin
Contentment.
Schloerb, Rolland W.
O Thou Eternal Source of Life.
Thou Light of Ages.
Schloss, David
Poem, The: "I had never heard of the
whiteness."
Schmeltz, Susan Alton
Paper Dragons.
Schmid, Constance M.
Synekdechestai.
Schmidt, Lorenza
Heading for Eugene.
Schmidt, Tom
Black and White.
Butcherboy.
Butter.
Civilization.
Creeper, The.
Drowning in Spain.
In the Garden.
Long Overdue Thankyou Note to the Girl
Who Taught Me Loving, A.
Seven Mexican Children.
Schmied, Wieland
Francis Bacon Paints Velázquez's Pope.
In Memory of Reinhold Koehler.
Mark Tobey's Legacy.
Max Ernst's Walk.
Meeting with Giorgio de Chirico.
Opinions about the Painter de Chirico.
Remembrances of Guernica.
Things of René Magritte, The.
Thinking of Constantin Brancusi.
With Giorgio Morandi in Bologna.
Schmitz, Dennis
Arbeit Macht Frei.
California Phrasebook, The.
Chalk Angel, The.
Chicago: Near West-Side Renewal.
Coma.
Dressing Game.
Eclogues.

Gill Boy.
Goodwill, Inc.
If I Could Meet God.
Instructions for Fishing the Eel.
Kindergarten.
Letter to Ron Silliman on the Back of a Map
  of the Solar System, A.
Making a Door.
Making Chicago.
Man Who Buys Hides, The.
Mile Hill.
Mole, The.
Name of Our Country, The.
Navel.
News.
Picture of Okinawa, A.
Planting Trout in the Chicago River.
Poke-Pole Fishing.
Queen of Heaven Mausoleum.
Skinning-the-Cat.
Star & Garter Theater.
String.
Virgil: Georgics, Book IV.

Schmolck, Benjamin
Consecration.

Schmuller, Aaron
Legend of His Lyre.

Schnackenberg, Gjertrud
Darwin in 1881.
Holding a Raccoon's Jaw.
How Did It Seem to Sylvia?
Living Room, The.
Paper Cities.
Paperweight, The.
Signs.
Supernatural Love.
When Clumsy harks the gladsome
  ting-a-lings, sel.

Schneider, Bart
Basket Catch.

Schneider, Isidor
Insects.
Joy of Knowledge.

Schneider, Myra
Drawing a Banana.

Schneour, Zalman
Besieged.
Cherries.
Forsaken.
Last Words of Don Henriquez, The.
Like Water down a Slope.
Road, The.
War Comes.
Welcome, Queen Sabbath.

Schneurson, Zelda. *See* **"Zelda"**

Schoeck, R. J.
Homage.

Scholem, Gershom
Trial, The.

Scholten, Martin
Soliloquy by the Shore.

Schomberg, Ralph
Ay or Nay?, sel.
Courtier's a Riddle, A, sel.
Like Birds of a Feather, sel.

Schonborg, Virginia
Crowds.
Stickball.

Schönwiese, Ernst
Bird that fell out of the nest, A.
Everything is only an image.
Forget everything you have seen.
If they really lived.
Secret Ballgame.

Schott, Penelope Scambly
Rock of This Odd Coincidence, The.

Schotz, Myra Glazer
First Love Poem, The.
Santa Caterina.
Thespian in Jerusalem.

Schreiber, Dale A.
Cool Mule.
Great Vocabulary.

Schreiber, Ron
An Alarming New Development.
House Is Old, The.

Schroeder, Margot
I'm Doing Fine.
I'm Thinking of You.

Schroeder, Peter
All Human Things.

Schubart, Christian
Song of the Cape of Good Hope.

Schuchat, Simon
Anti-Memoirs.
Long and Happy Life, A.

Schull, Joseph
Pirates' Fight, The, sel.

Schulman, Grace
Birds on a Blighted Tree.
Burial of a Fisherman in Hydra.
Filth of Your Suspicion, The.
Messenger, The.

Schultz, Lulu Minerva
What Price.

Schultz, Philip
Balance.
For My Father.
Hemingway House in Key West, The.
Like Wings.
Mrs. Applebaum's Sunday Dance Class.
My Guardian Angel Stein.

Schulz, Lillian
Fuzzy Wuzzy, Creepy Crawly.

Schulze, Axel
Airmail Letter.

Schutting, Jutta
Blundering.
Clouds.
Dove-Late Afternoon, A.
Doves.
First Vacation Day, A.
I Dedicate to You.
Interpretations.
Kinsey Report.
Poems.
Trees.
Water Glass.
You Can.

Schuyler, James
Buried at Springs.
"Can I Tempt You to a Pond Walk?"
Crocus Night.
Crystal Lithium, The.
"Elizabethans Called It Dying, The."
February.
Freely Espousing.
Growing Dark.
Head, A.
I Think.
Let's All Hear It for Mildred Bailey!
Poem: "This beauty that I see."
Salute.
Self-Pity Is a Kind of Lying, Too.
Sleep.
Song: "I'm about to go shopping."
Stun.
Sunday.
Tom.

Schuyler, Montgomery
Carlyle and Emerson.

Schuyler-Lighthall, William Douw
Battle of La Prairie, The.

Schwartz, Delmore
Abraham.
All Clowns Are Masked, sel.
All of us always turning away for solace.
Aria.
Ballet of the Fifth Year, The.
Baudelaire.
Beautiful American Word, Sure, The.

Calmly We Walk through This April Day.
Dark and Falling Summer, The.
Deceptive Present, the Phoenix Year, The.
Do They Whisper behind My Back?
Dog Named Ego, the Snowflakes as Kisses,
  A.
Dogs Are Shakespearean, Children Are
  Strangers.
During December's Death.
Exercise in Preparation for a Pindaric Ode to
  Carl Hubbell.
Father and Son.
For the One Who Would Take Man's Life in
  His Hands.
Heart Flies Up, Erratic as a Kite, The.
Heavy bear who goes with me, The, sel.
I Am a Book I neither Wrote nor Read.
I Am Cherry Alive.
I Did Not Know the Truth of Growing Trees.
In the Naked Bed, in Plato's Cave.
Jacob.
Let Us Consider Where the Great Men Are,
  sel.
Little Morning Music, A.
Look, in the Labyrinth of Memory.
Mind Is an Ancient and Famous Capital, The
  ("The mind is a city like London").
Passionate Shepherd to His Love, The.
Poem: "Old man in the crystal morning after
  snow."
Prothalamion.
Sarah.
Self Unsatisfied Runs Everywhere, The.
Sequel, The.
Socrates' Ghost Must Haunt Me Now.
Sonnet on Famous and Familiar Sonnets and
  Experiences.
Swift.
Time's Dedication.
Tired and Unhappy, You Think of Houses.
Today Is Armistice, a Holiday.
Vivaldi.
Winter Twilight, Glowing Black and Gold,
  The.
You Are a Jew!, sel.

Schwartz, Howard
Abraham in Egypt.
Adam's Dream.
Blessing of the Firstborn.
Eve, The.
Gathering the Sparks.
Iscah.
New Year for Trees, The.
Our Angels.
Prayers, The.
Psalm: "Father/ You are the trunk."
Shira.
Song, A: "Song, A/ That seemed so brief at
  first."
These Two.
Vessels.

Schwartz, Lloyd
Recital, The.
Tom Joanides.
Who's on First?

Schwartz, Yisroel-Yankev
Climb Up, The, sel.
In the End-of-Summer Light.

Schwob, Marcel
Actions.
Moments.
Things Dead.

Scollard, Clinton
Ad Patriam.
Archer, The.
As I Came Down from Lebanon.
At the Tomb of Washington.
Ballad of Paco Town, The.
Battle of Plattsburg Bay, The.

Be Ye in Love with April-Tide.
Bell, A.
Boasting of Sir Peter Parker, The.
Butterfly, The.
Daughter of the Regiment, The.
Deed of Lieutenant Miles, The.
Deeds of Valor at Santiago.
Eve of Bunker Hill, The.
First Thanksgiving, The.
First Three, The.
Khamsin.
King Philip's Last Stand.
Man! A.
Memnon.
Men of the *Maine*, The.
Men of the *Merrimac*, The.
Montgomery at Quebec.
On a Bust of Lincoln.
Prayer, A: "Each day I walk with wonder."
Private Blair of the Regulars.
Riding with Kilpatrick.
Saint Leger.
Sidney Godolphin.
Song for Memorial Day.
Swimming.
Unreturning, The.
Valor of Ben Milam, The.
Wayne at Stony Point.

Scoloker, Anthony
Her Praises.

Scotellaro, Rocco
Country Night.
Economics Lesson.
Full Moon, The.
Portrait's All Feet, The.
Rustlers, The.
They Walk on Cat's Paws.
Threshing, The.
To the Carter's Daughter.
To the Wagoner's Daughter.

Scott, Alexander (1520?–1590?)
Bequest of His Heart, A.
Coronach.
Lament of the Master of Erskine.
Letter to Robert Fergusson.
My Heart Is High Above, *at.*
Of May.
Quha Is Perfyte.
Rondel of Luve [*or* Love], A.
To Luve Unluvit.
Up, Helsum Hairt.
Wha Is Perfyte.

Scott, Alexander (b. 1920)
Calvinist Sang.
Problems.

Scott, Clement
Oh Promise Me.

Scott, Dennis
Compleat Anglers, The.
Epitaph: "They hanged him on a clement
   morning, swung."
Exile.
For the Last Time, Fire.
Grampa.
Homecoming.
Mouth.
Uncle Time.
Version.

Scott, Diana
Lucy Taking Birth.
Prayer for the Little Daughter between Death
   and Burial.
Winter Solstice Poem.

Scott, Duncan Campbell
At Gull Lake; August, 1810.
At the Cedars.
Bells.
Ecstasy.
En Route.
Fallen, The.
Forsaken, The.

Half-Breed Girl, The.
In the Selkirks.
Night and the Pines.
Night Hymns on Lake Nipigon.
Night in June, A.
Off Rivière du Loup.
On the Way to the Mission.
Prairie Water Colour, A.
Rapids at Night.
Song, A: "In the air there are no coral-/ Reefs
   or ambergris."

Scott, Elizabeth
Now Let Our Hearts Their Glory Wake.
See How the Rising Sun.

Scott, Francis Reginald
Bangkok.
Bonne Entente.
Brébeuf and His Brethren.
Canadian Authors Meet, The.
Conflict.
Full Valleys.
Lakeshore.
Laurentian Shield.
Night Club.
Recovery.
Saturday Sundae.
W. L. M. K.
Will to Win.
Windfall.

Scott, Frederick George
Dawn.
Easter Island.
In the Woods.
Requiescant.
Sting of Death, The.
Unnamed Lake, The.

Scott, Geoffrey
All Our Joy Is Enough.
Frutta di Mare.
Hector, the captain bronzed, from simple
   fight, *sel.*
What Was Solomon's Mind?

Scott, Herbert
Achilles' Heel.
Early Love.
Fathers of Desire.
Man Who Would Be a Mother, The.
Woman Who Loves Old Men, The.

Scott, John
How to Fertilize Soil, *sel.*

Scott, Johnie
Speech, or dark cities screaming, *sel.*

Scott, Lady John
Ettrick.

Scott, Peter Dale
Argenteuil County.
Loon's Egg, The.

Scott, Robert Balgarnie Young
O Day of God, Draw Nigh.

Scott, Sharon
Between Me and Anyone Who Can
   Understand.
Come On Home.
Discovering.
Fisk is/ a/ negroid/ institution.
For Both of Us at Fisk.
Just Taking Note.
Little More about the Brothers and Sisters, A.
Mama Knows.
Oh—Yeah!
Okay.
On My Stand.
Our Lives.
Sharon Will Be No/ Where on Nobody's
   Best-selling List.
Sometimes/ the poems.

Scott, Sir Walter
Alice Brand.
Allen-a-Dale.
And What though Winter Will Pinch Severe
Annot Lyle's Song.

Battle, The ("But as they left the dark'ning
   heath").
Battle, The ("By this, though deep the
   evening fell").
Battle, The ("Not for advanc'd was morning
   day").
Bonny [*or* Bonnie] Dundee.
Border Ballad.
Breathes There the [*or* a] Man [with Soul So
   Dead].
Brignall Banks.
Chase, The.
Christmas in England ("Heap on more
   wood!—the wind is chill") Time.
Coronach.
Datur Hora Quieti.
Dreary Change, The.
Edinburgh from the Pentland Hills.
Ettrick Forest in November.
Eve of Saint John, The.
Farewell, Thou Minstrel Harp.
Father's Notes of Woe.
Fire, The.
Football Song.
Friday.
Gallant Ship, The.
Gathering, The.
Gin by Pailfuls.
Hail to the Chief Who in Triumph
   Advances.
Hellvellyn.
Herring loves the merry moonlight,
   The.
Hie Away, Hie Away.
Hour with Thee, An.
Hunting Song.
Hymn to the Virgin.
It's up Glenbarchan's braes I gaed.
Jock of [*or* o'] Hazeldean.
Lochinvar.
Lucy Ashton's Song.
Lullaby of an Infant Chief.
MacGregor's Gathering.
Maid of Neidpath, The.
Man the Enemy of Man.
Marmion and Douglas.
Melrose Abbey.
Minstrel Responds to Flattery, The.
Nativity Chant, The.
Nelson, Pitt, Fox.
Now, yield thee, or by Him who made.
On Having Piles.
Pibroch of Donuil Dhu.
Pride of Youth, The.
Proud Maisie.
Rebecca's Hymn.
Red Harlaw.
Rosabelle.
Saint Cloud.
St. Swithin's Chair.
Serenade.
Sir Walter Scott's Tribute.
Soldier Rest! [Thy Warfare O'er].
Song of Albert Graeme.
Song of the Mermaids and Mermen.
Song of the Reim-Kennar, The.
Speak not of niceness, when there's chance of
   wreck.
Tis Merry in Greenwood.
To a Lock of Hair.
To an Oak Tree.
To-Day I Leave Mrs. Brown's Lodgings.
Toils Are Pitched, The.
Twist Ye, Twine Ye! Even So.
Violet, The.
Wasted, Weary, Wherefore Stay.
Weary Lot Is Thine, A.
Western Waves of Ebbing Day, The.
Where shall the lover rest.
Why Sit'st Thou by That Ruin'd Hall.
William and Helen.
Youth! Thou Wear'st to Manhood Now.

Scott, Tom
Real Muse, The.
Scott, William Bell
Death.
Music.
Rhyme of the Sun-Dial, A.
Robin, The.
Witch's Ballad, The.
Scott, Winfield Townley
Annual Legend.
Brief Encounter.
First Reader, The.
Five for the Grace of Man.
Grant Wood's American Landscape.
Ivory Bed, The.
Landscape as Metal and Flowers.
Let us record/ The evenings when we were
   innocents of twenty, *sel.*
May 1506 (Christopher Columbus Speaking).
Mr. Whittier.
Mrs. Severin.
O Lyric Love.
Sonnet XV: "This is the way we say it in our
   time."
Sonnet XIII.
Swedish Angel.
Two.
U. S. Sailor with the Japanese Skull, The.
Uses of Poetry.
Watch Hill.
Wax.
Scott-Hopper, Queenie
Amy Elizabeth Ermyntrude Annie.
My Party.
Very Nearly.
What the Thrush Says.
Scott, John (1730–1783). *See* **Scott of
   Amwell, John**
Scott of Amwell, John
Ode: "I hate that drum's discordant sound."
Scottus, Sedulius
Apologia pro Vita Sua.
Easter Sunday.
Scovell, Edith Jay
After Midsummer.
Alone.
Betrothal, A.
Boy Fishing, The.
Days Drawing In.
Days fail: night broods over afternoon, The,
   sel.
In a Wood.
Love's Immaturity.
Swan's Feet, The.
Wartime Story, A.
"Scrace, Richard" (Mrs. J. B. Williamson)
At the Place of the Roman Baths.
Gipsies, The.
Scriven, Joseph
Unfailing Friend, The.
Scriven, R. C.
Marrog, The.
Scroggie, Syd
And Happy Am I.
Ante Mortem.
At Last.
Change and Immutability.
Drunken Dee, The.
Loch Ossian.
Long Ago.
Poem, 1972.
Space and Time.
Scroope, Sir Carr
Author's Reply, The.
In Defense of Satire.
Scudder, Eliza
Quest, The.
Thou Grace Divine, Encircling All.
Thou Long Disowned, Reviled, Oppressed.
To a Young Child.

Scudder, Vida
Thy Kingdom, Lord, We Long For.
Scully, James
Crew Practice on Lake Bled, in Jugoslavia.
Fantasy of Little Waters, A.
Glass Blower, The.
Grandson, The.
Late Spring, A.
Midsummer.
What Is Poetry.
Scupham, Peter
To His Coy Mistress.
Twelfth Night.
Seager, Francis
Prayer to Be Said When Thou Goest to Bed,
   A.
Seager, Millicent
Birds' Nests.
Seager, Ralph W.
Taste of Prayer, The.
Seagrave, Artis
Let All Created Things.
Seale, Doris
His Half-Breed Wife.
Seaman, E. William
Higgledy-piggledy/ Ludwig van Beethoven.
Seaman, Sir Owen
Ballad of a Bun, A.
Birthday Ode to Mr. Alfred Austin, A.
Bulbul, The ("The bulbul hummeth like a
   book").
England Expects?
Englishman on the French Stage, The.
Ode to Spring in the Metropolis, An.
Of Baiting the Lion.
Of the Stalking of the Stag.
Penalties of Baldness, The.
Plea for Trigamy, A.
Rhyme of the Kipperling, The.
Schoolmaster Abroad, The.
Sitting Bard, The.
Song of Renunciation, A.
Time's Revenges.
To a Boy-Poet of the Decadence.
To Julia in Shooting Togs.
To Julia under Lock and Key.
Uses of Ocean, The.
Warrior's Lament, The.
Searing, Laura Redden
Disarmed.
Sears, Edmund Hamilton
Calm, on the Listening Ear of Night.
It Came upon the Midnight Clear.
Sears, Vickie
Pow Wow.
Pubescence at 39.
Seaton, Peter
Antonville.
Two Words.
Seaver, Edwin
To My People.
Seaver, George
Communion Hymn.
Seay, James
Clouds over Islands.
It All Comes Together Outside the Restroom
   in Hogansville.
When Our Voices Broke Off.
Secundus, Johannes. *See* **Johannes Secundus**
Sédar-Senghor, Léopold
Night of Sine.
Paris in the Snow.
Songs for a Three-String Guitar.
To New York.
Sedgwick, Henry Dwight
Leo to His Mistress.
Sedley, Sir Charles
Advice to the Old Beaux.
Ah Cloris! That I Now Could Sit, *sel.*
Ballad To the Tune of Bateman, A.
Child and Maiden, *sel.*

Get You Gone.
Indifference, The.
Marriage and Money, *sel.*
Not, Celia, that I juster am.
On a Cock at Rochester.
On Fruition.
On the Happy Corydon and Phyllis, at.
Out of French.
Song: "Hears not my Phillis how the birds."
Song: "Love still has something of the sea."
Song: "Phillis is my only joy."
Song: "Phillis, let's shun the common fate."
Song: "Smooth was the water, calm the air."
To Cloris.
To Nysus.
To Scilla.
To Sergius.
Upon the Author of the "Satire against Wit."
Sedulius Scottus
Death of a Ram.
Heavens, ocean, and all earth, rejoice!, *sel.*
Nunc Viridant Segetes.
Request for Meat and Drink.
Seeger, Alan
I Have a Rendezvous with Death.
Ode in Memory of the American Volunteers
   Fallen for France.
Seferis, George
And if the soul, *sel.*
Angel/ three years we waited intently for him,
   The, *sel.*
Anges Sont Blancs, Les.
Epiphany, 1937.
Euripides the Athenian.
Flame is healed by flame, *sel.*
Harbor is old, I can't wait any longer, The.
   sel.
Helen.
I woke with this marble head in my hands,
   sel.
In the Manner of G. S.
Interlude of Joy.
King of Asini, The.
Last Day, The.
Last Stop.
Memory I.
Memory II.
Narration.
Now/ with the lead melted for divination, *sel.*
Old Man on the River Bank, An.
On the track, on the track again, on the track,
   sel.
Our country is closed in, all mountains, *sel.*
Our Sun.
Sleep wrapped you in green leaves like a tree,
   sel.
So very much having passed before our eyes,
   sel.
Stratis Thalassinos among the Agapanthi.
Summer Solstice.
We didn't know them, *sel.*
When will you speak again?, *sel.*
Years ago you said, *sel.*
Segal, Jacob Isaac
Candle.
Rest.
Segal, Yankev-Yitskhok
At My Wedding.
In Me.
Korets Landscape.
Psalms.
Winter.
Segalen, Victor
Bad Craftsmen.
Hidden Name.
I Am Told.
Mongol Libation.
To That Person.
To the Ten Thousand Years.
Written in Blood.

Segall, Pearl Bloch
Pie Are Square.
Segooa, Demetrius
Praises of the Train.
Seibi Natsume. *See* **Natsume Seibi**
Seidel, Frederick
Dimpled Cloud, A.
Seidman, Hugh
Drop the Wires.
Great Nebula in Andromeda, The.
He imagines her, *sel.*
He knows he must explain this, *sel.*
Making of Color, The.
Modes of Vallejo Street, San Diego, Los
Angeles, 9, The.
Modes of Vallejo Street, San Diego, Los
Angeles, 3, The.
N.
Science as Art.
Tale of Genji.
Seifert, Jaroslav
Burning Ship.
Mortar Salvos.
When the Ashes.
Seiffert, Marjorie Allen ("Elijah Hay")
Cubist Portrait.
Seigan
To a Monk Departing for Mid Stream.
Seigensai
This grasped, all's dust.
Seiken Kametani
There I was, hunched over office desk.
Seiken, Terakado. *See* **Terakado Seiken**
Seiko
Eighty-eight, my head's pure white.
Seisen
Kwatz too weak, stick too short.
Seitz, Don C.
Night at Gettysburg.
Sekirin
Master Suian's Birthplace.
Sekitei, Hara. *See* **Hara Sekitei**
Seldon, Frank H.
To My Setter, Scout.
Seligman, Ulma
Truth Has Perished.
Selkirk, J. B.
Border Burn, A, *sel.*
Sellar, Walter Carruthers *and* **Robert Julian**
Yeatman. *See* **Yeatman, Robert Julian**
and **Walter Carruthers Sellar**
Sellers, Bettie M.
If Justice Moved.
In the Counselor's Waiting Room.
Seltzer, George R.
Come, All Ye People.
Selyns, Henricus
Epitaph for Peter Stuyvesant.
O Christmas Night.
Of Scolding Wives and the Third Day Ague.
On Maids and Cats.
On Mercenary and Unjust Bailiffs.
Reasons for and against Marrying Widows.
Upon the Bankruptcy of a Physician.
Semah, David
Prostration.
Tomb.
Sempill, Francis
Blythsome Bridal, The, *at.*
Maggie Lauder, *at.*
Sempill, Robert
Life and Death of [Habbie Simson] the Piper
of Kilbarchan, The.
Sen of Kyuho
Living in the Mountains ("It's not easy to live
in the mountains").
Living in the Mountains ("What good's
world—profit, fame?").
Sendak, Maurice
January.
October.

Seneca
After death nothing is, and nothing, death,
sel.
End of Being, The.
Her chaunging lookes no colour longe can
holde, *sel.*
Let oken club now strike, and poast of might,
sel.
Let other mount aloft, let other sore, *sel.*
O yee, whome lorde of lande and waters
wyde, *sel.*
Stond [*or* Stand] who so list upon the slipper
toppe, *sel.*
That Orpheus Calliops sonne who stayde the
running brooke, *sel.*
Senesh, Hannah
Blessed Match, The.
One—Two—Three.
Senghor, Léopold Sédar
Black Woman.
Elephant of Moissel, hear my pious prayer,
sel.
I Want to Say Your Name.
On the Appeal from the Race of Sheba: II.
Prayer for Peace: II.
We Delighted, My Friend.
Senior, Olive
Ancestral Poem.
Epitaph: "Last year the child died."
Senka
Innocently a frog squats.
Senryu
When it's of his wife.
Sensai
From the start there's no.
Sensetsu
At daybreak frogs begin.
Sepamla, Sipho
Home.
Pimville Station.
Soweto.
Tell Me News.
Will, The.
Work Song, The.
"Seranus." *See* **Harrison, Susan Frances**
Sereni, Vittorio
Poems.
Terrace, The.
Sergeant, Howard
Inundation, The.
Man Meeting Himself.
Soft Landings.
Seroke, Jaki
Era.
Serote, Mongane Wally
City Johannesburg.
Heat and Sweat.
Hell, Well, Heaven.
Ofay-Watcher Looks Back.
Poem in Black and White, A.
Serraillier, Ian
After Ever Happily.
Death of the Cat.
Falling Asleep.
Hare and the Tortoise, The.
Hen and the Carp, The.
Mouse in the Wainscot, The.
Old Sussex Road, The.
Suppose you met a witch. There's one I
know, *sel.*
Tickle Rhyme, The.
Witch's Cat, The.
Service, Robert W.
Call of the Wild, The.
Cremation of Sam McGee, The.
Inspiration.
Law of the Yukon, The.
Men That Don't Fit In, The.
My Madonna.
Scribe's Prayer, The.

Shooting of Dan McGrew, The.
Spell of the Yukon, The.
Sessler, Thomas
Burnt Debris.
When the Day.
You Move Forward.
Sesson Yubai
In heaven and earth, no ground to plant my
single staff.
Setcho
Fisherman.
Seth, Vikram
Humble Administrator's Garden, The.
Week ago, when I had finished, A, *sel.*
"Setoun, Gabriel" (Thomas Nicoll Hepburn)
Jack Frost.
Romance.
World's Music, The.
Settle, Elkanah
Medal Reversed, The.
"Seuss, Dr." (Theodore Seuss Geisel)
If We Didn't Have Birthdays.
Quack, Quack!
Too Many Daves.
Severy, Bruce
Deserted Farms Poem.
First and Last.
Opening Day.
Poems.
Struggle for the Roads.
Sewall, Frank
Roll Out, O Song.
Sewall, Harriet Winslow
Why Thus Longing?
Sewall, Jonathan Mitchell
On Independence.
War and Washington.
Sewall, Samuel
Once More, Our God, Vouchsafe to Shine!
This Morning Tom Child, the Painter, Died.
To Be Engraven on a Dial.
To the Rev'd Mr. Jno. Sparhawk on the Birth
of his Son.
Upon the Springs Issuing out from the Foot of
Plimouth Beach.
Seward, Anna
Elegy Written at the Sea-Side, and Addressed
to Miss Honoria Sneyd.
Favourite Cat's Dying Soliloquy, A.
In scenes paternal, not beheld through years,
sel.
Now with a vestal lustre glows the Vale, *sel.*
Old Cat's Dying Soliloquy, An.
On Catania and Syracuse Swallowed Up by an
Earthquake, from the Italian of Filicaja.
On the Use of New and Old Words in Poetry.
Sonnet: "Ingratitude, how deadly is the
smart."
Sonnet: To the Departing Spirit of an
Alienated Friend.
While neighbouring cities waste the fleeting
hours, *sel.*
Written December 1790.
Sewell, Elizabeth
Epiphany: For the Artist.
Forgiveness.
Job.
Sewell, George
Dying Man in His Garden, The.
Sexton, Anne
Abortion, The.
All My Pretty Ones.
Black Art, The.
Child Bearers, The.
Cinderella.
Consorting with Angels.
Crossing the Atlantic.
Death King, The.
Division of Parts, The.
End, Middle, Beginning.

Farmer's Wife, The.
Flee on Your Donkey.
For God While Sleeping.
For My Lover, Returning to His Wife.
Fortress, The.
Funnel.
Fury of Cocks, The.
Fury of Flowers and Worms, The.
Fury of Hating Eyes, The.
Hansel and Gretel.
Her Kind.
Hornet.
Housewife.
In Celebration of My Uterus.
In the Beach House.
In the Deep Museum.
January 1st.
Kind Sir: These Woods ("Kind Sir: This is an old game").
Lament: "Someone is dead."
Letter Written on a Ferry while Crossing Long Island Sound.
Little Girl, My Stringbean, My Lovely Woman.
Lobster.
Locked Doors.
Man and Wife.
Menstruation at Forty.
Moon Song, Woman Song.
Moss of His Skin, The.
Nude Swim, The.
Pain for a Daughter.
Ringing the Bells.
Risk, The.
Road Back, The.
Rowing.
Self in 1958.
Snow.
Snow White and the Seven Dwarfs.
Some Foreign Letters.
Starry Night, The.
Sun, The.
Sylvia's Death.
That Day.
Three Green Windows.
To a Friend Whose Work Has Come to Triumph.
To Like, to Love.
Truth the Dead Know, The.
Twelve-Thousand-Day Honeymoon, The.
Two Hands.
Unknown Girl in the Maternity Ward.
Us.
"Wanting to Die.
Wedding Night, The.
Witch's Life, The.
With Mercy for the Greedy.
Woman with Girdle.
You, Doctor Martin.
Seymour, A. J.
And so the day beginning, sel.
Drums/ Then again drums.
First of August.
He dreamed not that the ocean would bear ships, sel.
Slaves/ Humming in the twilight by the shanty door.
Well, The.
Seymour-Smith, Martin
Appetite of Quiet Enchantment.
Après un Rêve.
Chrysanthemums.
He Came to Visit Me.
In My Eye.
Internal Saboteur, The.
Rachmaninov.
Silverhill.
To My Daughters.
What Schoolmasters Say.
Wilderness.
Seymour-Ure, Kirsty
Of Calico Cats.

Shackleford, Theodore Henry
Big Bell in Zion, The.
Shadwell, Bertrand
Aguinaldo.
Cervera.
Shadwell, Thomas
Medal of John Bays; a Satire against Folly and Knavery, The.
Shahid (Roosevelt Williamson)
Letters Come to Prison.
Shakely, Lauren
Definition.
Shakespeare, William
All That Glisters Is Not Gold, sel.
All the World's a Stage, sel.
All tongues speak of him, and the bleared sights, sel.
Ambition, sel.
Amien's Song, sel.
And Will He Not Come Again, sel.
Angels and ministers of grace defend us!, sel.
Antony's Oration [over Caesar's Body], sel.
As we paced along/ Upon the giddy footing of the hatches, sel.
Asleep, My Love?, sel.
At My Nativity, sel.
At this Adonis smiles as in disdain, sel.
Autolycus as Peddler, sel.
Autolycus's Song ("Will you buy any tape"), sel.
Any [or Aye], but to die, and go we know not where, sel.
Barge she sat in, like a burnish'd throne, The, sel.
Be Absolute for Death, sel.
Be Not Afeard: The Isle Is Full of Noises, sel.
Beauty, sel.
Beauty Is a Witch, sel.
Blow, Blow, Thou Winter Wind, sel.
Blow, Winds, sel.
Bottom's Song, sel.
Brave New World, sel.
But, lo! from forth a copse that neighbours by, sel.
Cares of Majesty, The, sel.
Claudio's Lament: "Pardon, goddess of the night."
Cleopatra's Lament, sel.
Come Away, Come Away, Death, sel.
Come, Philomele, that sing'st of ravishment, sel.
Come unto these yellow sands, sel.
Commonwealth of the Bees, The, sel.
Cowards die many times before their deaths, sel.
Crabbed Age and Youth, sel.
Cranmer's Prophecy of Queen Elizabeth, sel.
Death of Antony, sel.
Death of Cleopatra, sel.
Death of Lear, sel.
Death of Othello, sel.
Did Not the Heavenly Rhetoric of Thine Eye, sel.
Dover, the Samphire Cliff, sel.
Dream of Wrecks, A, sel.
Drinking Song, A, sel.
Epilogue: "If we shadows have offended," sel.
Epilogue: "Now my charms are all o'erthrown," sel.
Epilogue: "Thus far, with rough and all-unable pen," sel.
Epitaph: "Done to death by slanderous tongues," sel.
Eros, thou yet behold'st me?
Even or odd, of all days in the year, sel.
Fair Is My Love, sel.
Farewell content, sel.
Fear No More the Heat o' the Sun, sel.
Fire Seven Times Tried This, The, sel.
Flower of This Purple Dye, sel.
"Fondling," she saith, "since I have hemmed thee here."

Food of Love, The, sel.
For here lies Juliet, and her beauty makes, sel.
Frost on the Flower, sel.
Full Fathom Five, sel.
Full fathom [or fadom] five thy father lies, sel.
Gallop apace, you fiery-footed steeds, sel.
Give me your pardon, sir. I have done you wrong, sel.
Good Name, A, sel.
Good sir, whose powers are these?
Grief fills the room up of my absent child, sel.
Hamlet.
Hang out our banners on the outward walls, sel.
Hark! Hark! the Lark, sel.
He Jests at Scars [That Never Felt a Wound], sel.
He that will give good words to thee, will flatter, sel.
He wakes; speak to him, sel.
Heavens themselves, the planets and this center, The, sel.
Helena and Hermia, sel.
Henry V before Agincourt, sel.
Her father loved me; oft invited me, sel.
Here's flowers for you, sel.
How all occasions do inform against me, sel.
How now, spirit! whither wander you?
How Should I Your True Love Know, sel.
How Sweet the Moonlight Sleeps, sel.
Howl, howl, howl! O! you are men of stones, sel.
I am dead, Horatio. Wretched queen, adieu!
I am thy father's spirit, sel.
I have done the deed—Didst thou not hear a noise?
I Have Lived Long Enough, sel.
I saw him beat the surges under him, sel.
If by your art, my dearest father, you have, sel.
If I profane with my unworthiest hand, sel.
If it were done when 'tis done, then 'twere well, sel.
If she be made of white and red, sel.
It faded on the crowing of the cock, sel.
It is the cause, it is the cause, my soul, sel.
It Was a Lording's Daughter, sel.
It Was a Lover and His Lass, sel.
Jog On, jog on, the footpath way, sel.
John of Gaunt's Dying Speech, sel.
King Henry the Fourth, Pt. I.
King Is Dead, A, sel.
Lear and Cordelia, sel.
Lear's Curse on Goneril, sel.
Let Me Play the Fool, sel.
Let the bird of lowdest lay, sel.
Let's Talk of Graves, sel.
Lo! Here the Gentle Lark, sel.
Love-in-Idleness, sel.
Lover's eyes will gaze an eagle blind, A, sel.
Lunatic, the Lover, and the Poet, The, sel.
Master, the swabber, the boatswain and I, The, sel.
Methought That I Had Broken from the Tower, sel.
Midnight, sel.
Mis-shapen Time, copesmate of ugly Night, sel.
Miserable change now at my end, The, sel.
Moon shines bright, The. In such a night as this, sel.
Motley's the Only Wear, sel.
Music's Silver Sound, sel.
My desolation does begin to make, sel.
My liege, I did deny no prisoners, sel.
My Thoughts Do Harbour, sel.
Now Entertain Conjecture of a Time, sel.
Now is the winter of our discontent, sel.
Now sways it this way, like a mighty sea, sel.

Now the Hungry Lion Roars, *sel.*
Now, Until the Break of Day, *sel.*
O for a Muse of fire, that would ascend, *sel.*
O! Full of Scorpions, *sel.*
O my love, my wife!, *sel.*
O [*or* Oh] Mistress Mine [Where Are You Roaming?]
O, that this too too solid flesh would melt, *sel.*
O [*or* Oh], then, I see Queen Mab hath been with you, *sel.*
On a Day—Alack the Day, *sel.*
On Death, *sel.*
Once more, Cesario, *sel.*
Once more unto the breach, dear friends, once more, *sel.*
Opportunity, *sel.*
Orlando's Rhymes, *sel.*
Orpheus with His Lute [Made Trees], *sel.*
Our Revels Now Are Ended, *sel.*
Over Hill, over Dale, *sel.*
Patience on a Monument, *sel.*
Phoenix and the Turtle, The.
Please you, draw near.—Louder the music there!
Polonius' Advice to Laertes, *sel.*
Poor Wat, *sel.*
Portrait of Brutus, *sel.*
Portrait of Caesar, *sel.*
Portrait of Cressida, *sel.*
Portrait of Helen, *sel.*
Power of Music, The, *sel.*
Prospero, *sel.*
Quality of Mercy [Is Not Strain'd], The, *sel.*
Rape of Lucrece, The.
Rugged Pyrrhus, he whose sable arm, The, *sel.*
Sense of death is most in apprehension, The, *sel.*
She should have died hereafter, *sel.*
Shepherdess—/ A fair one are you, *sel.*
Sigh No More, Ladies [Sigh No More], *sel.*
So Sweet a Kiss, *sel.*
Some say that ever 'gainst that season comes, *sel.*
Song: "Hark, hark!/ Bow-wow./ The watch-dogs bark," *sel.*
Song: "If the scorn of your bright eyne," *sel.*
Sonnet: "Against my love shall be, as I am now."
Sonnet: "Ah wherefore with infection should he live."
Sonnet: "Alas, 'tis true I have gone here and there."
Sonnet: "As an unperfect actor on the stage."
Sonnet: "Being your slave, what should I do but tend."
Sonnet: "Beshrew that heart that makes my heart to groan."
Sonnet: "Betwixt mine eye and heart a league is took."
Sonnet: "But be contented: when that fell arrest."
Sonnet: "Devouring Time, blunt thou the lion's paws [lyons pawes]."
Sonnet: "Expense of spirit in a waste of shame, The."
Sonnet: "Farewell! Thou art too dear for my possessing."
Sonnet: "Forward violet thus did I chide, The."
Sonnet: "From fairest creatures we desire increase."
Sonnet: "From you have I been absent in the spring."
Sonnet: "Full many a glorious morning have I seen[e]."
Sonnet: "How can I then return in happy plight."
Sonnet: "How like a winter hath my absence been."

Sonnet: "How oft, when thou, my musiuc, music play'st."
Sonnet: "How sweet and lovely dost thou make the shame."
Sonnet: "If the dull substance of my flesh were thought."
Sonnet: "If thou survive my well-contented day."
Sonnet: "In faith I do not love thee with mine eyes."
Sonnet: "Is it thy wil, thy Image should keepe open."
Sonnet: "Let me confess that we two must be twain."
Sonnet: "Let me not to the marriage of true minds."
Sonnet: "Let those who are in favour with their stars."
Sonnet: "Like as the waves make towards the pebbled shore."
Sonnet: "Look in thy glass, and tell the face thou viewest."
Sonnet: "Love is too young to know what conscience is."
Sonnet: "Mine eye and heart are at a mortal war."
Sonnet: "Mine eye hath play'd the painter, and hath steel'd."
Sonnet: "Music[k] to hear[e], why hear'st thou music[k] sadly?"
Sonnet: "My glass shall not persuade me I am old."
Sonnet: "My love is as a fever longing still."
Sonnet: "My love is strengthen'd, though more weak in seeming."
Sonnet: "My mistress' eyes are nothing like the sun."
Sonnet: "My tongue-tied muse in manners holds her still."
Sonnet: "No longer mourn for me when I am dead."
Sonnet: "No more be grieved at that which thou hast done."
Sonnet: "No, Time, thou shalt not boast that I do change!"
Sonnet: "Not from the stars do I my judgement pluck."
Sonnet: "Not marble, nor the gilded monuments."
Sonnet: "Not mine own fears nor the prophetic soul."
Sonnet: "O how much more doth beauty beauteous seem."
Sonnet: "O me! what eyes hath love put in my head."
Sonnet: "O! Never say that I was false of heart."
Sonnet: "O thou, my lovely boy, who in thy power."
Sonnet: "Or I shall live your epitaph to make."
Sonnet: "Poor[e] soul[e], the centre of my sinful[l] earth."
Sonnet: "Shall I compare thee to a summer's day?"
Sonnet: "Sin of self-love possesseth all mine eye."
Sonnet: "Since brass, nor stone, nor earth, nor boundless sea."
Sonnet: "So am I as the rich, whose blessed key."
Sonnet: "So are you to my thoughts as food to life."
Sonnet: "So is it not with me as with that muse."
Sonnet: "So now I have confessed that he is thine."
Sonnet: "So shall I live, supposing thou art true."
Sonnet: "Sweet love, renew thy force, be it not said."

Sonnet: "Take all my loves, my Love, yea, take them all."
Sonnet: "That thou hast her, it is not all my grief."
Sonnet: "That time of year thou may'st in me behold."
Sonnet: "That you were once unkind befriends me now."
Sonnet: "Then hate me when thou wilt; if ever, now."
Sonnet: "They that have power to hurt, and will do none."
Sonnet: "Thine eyes I love, and they, as pitying me."
Sonnet: "Those hours, that with gentle work did frame."
Sonnet: "Those lips that love's own hand did make."
Sonnet: "Those petty wrongs that liberty commits."
Sonnet: "Thou blind fool, Love, what dost thou to mine eyes."
Sonnet: "Thus is this cheek the map of days outworn."
Sonnet: "Thy bosom is endeared with all hearts."
Sonnet: "Thy glass will show thee how thy beauties wear."
Sonnet: "Tired with all these, for restful death I cry."
Sonnet: " 'Tis better to be vile than vile esteemed."
Sonnet: "To me, fair friend, you never can be old."
Sonnet: "Two loves I have of comfort and despair."
Sonnet: "Was it the proud full sail of his great verse."
Sonnet: "Weary with toil, I haste me to my bed."
Sonnet: "What is your substance, whereof are you made."
Sonnet: "When forty winters shall besiege thy brow."
Sonnet: "When I consider everything that grows."
Sonnet: "When I do count the clock that tells the time."
Sonnet: "When I have seen by Time's fell hand defaced."
Sonnet: "When in the chronicle of wasted time."
Sonnet: "When my love swears, that she is made of truth."
Sonnet: "When, in disgrace with fortune and men's eyes."
Sonnet: "When to the sessions of sweet silent thought."
Sonnet: "Where art thou, Muse, that thou forget'st so long."
Sonnet: "Who will believe my verse in time to come."
Sonnet: "Whoever hath her wish, thou hast thy Will."
Sonnet: "Why didst thou promise such a beauteous day."
Sonnet: "Why is my verse so barren of new pride."
Sonnet: "Woman's face with nature's own hand painted, A."
Sonnet: "O! that you were yourself! but, love, you are."
Sunrise on the Sea, *sel.*
Suppose that you have seen, *sel.*
"Sweet boy," she says, "this night I'll waste in sorrow."
Sweet Rose, Fair Flower, *sel.*
Take, O Take Those Lips Away, *sel.*
Take Physic, Pomp, *sel.*
Tell Me Where Is Fancy [*or* Fancie] Bred, *sel.*

Terrible childbed hast thou had, my dear, A,
sel.
There is a willow grows aslant a brook, *sel.*
This England, *sel.*
This is the foul fiend Flibbertigibbet: he
begins at, *sel.*
This Spring of Love, *sel.*
This Royal Infant, *sel.*
Thou God of This Great Vast, Rebuke These
Surges, *sel.*
Thrice the Brinded Cat Hath Mewed, *sel.*
Through the Forest Have I Gone, *sel.*
Through the House, *sel.*
Thus have I shunned the fire for fear of
burning, *sel.*
Thus with imagin'd wing our swift scene flies,
sel.
Time's Glory, *sel.*
Timon Curses Athens and Mankind, *sel.*
Timon's Epitaph, *sel.*
To be, or not to be, that is the question, *sel.*
To Gild Refinèd Gold, *sel.*
Tomorrow Is Saint Valentine's Day, *sel.*
Tongues of Dying Men, The, *sel.*
Troy Depicted, *sel.*
Ulysses Advises Achilles, *sel.*
Under the Greenwood Tree, *sel.*
Up and Down, *sel.*
Uses of Adversity, The, *sel.*
Venus Abandoned, *sel.*
Venus and Adonis.
Violet Bank, A, *sel.*
Warr'st thou 'gainst Athens?, *sel.*
We few, we happy few, we band of brothers,
sel.
What ceremony else?, *sel.*
What man dost thou dig it for?, *sel.*
When daffodils begin to peer, *sel.*
When Daisies Pied [and Violets Blue], *sel.*
When Icicles Hang by the Wall, *sel.*
When That I Was and a Little Tiny Boy, *sel.*
Where the bee sucks, there suck I, *sel.*
Who Is Silvia [or Sylvia]?, *sel.*
Wilt thou upon the high and giddy mast, *sel.*
With fairest flowers,/ Whilst summer lasts,
sel.
Wolsey, *sel.*
Wolsey's Farewell to His Greatness, *sel.*
Ye elves of hill, brooks, standing lakes, and
groves, *sel.*
Yet but Three?
Yon Island Carrions Desperate of Their
Bones, *sel.*
You Spotted Snakes [with Double Tongue],
sel.

Shalom, Shin
All's Not That Simple.
Evenings, When Sparks.
Marvel Down.
Splendor.

Shanahan, Eileen
Desolate Lover, The.
Epiphany.
Kilkenny Boy, The.
Shankill.

Shange, Ntozake
At 4:30 AM/ she rose, *sel.*
Dark Phrases, *sel.*
Frank Albert and Viola Benzena Owens.
Nappy Edges (A Cross Country Sojourn).
No More Love Poems #1, *sel.*
Somebody almost walked off wid alla my
stuff.

Shanks, Edward
Boats at Night.
Drilling in Russell Square.
Going In to Dinner.
High Germany.
Sleeping Heroes.
Storm, The.
To the Unknown Light.

Shanley, Kate
Returning.

Shanly, Charles Dawson
Civil War.

Shannon, Monica
Could It Have Been a Shadow?
Country Trucks.
How to Tell Goblins from Elves.
Only My Opinion.
Our Hired Man (And His Daughter, Too).
Tree Toad, The ("The tree Toad is a creature
neat").

Shannon, Sheila
On a Child Asleep in a Tube Shelter.

Shao Yung
Arriving in Lo-yang Again.
Song of Delight.
Song on Being Too Lazy to Get Up.
Thoughts on T'ien-chin Bridge.

Shapcott, Thomas William
Autumn.
Bicycle Rider, The.
Finches, The.
Flying Fox.
Litanies of Julia Pastrana (1832-1860), The.
Near the School for Handicapped Children.
Schoenberg Op. 11, *sel.*
Sestina with Refrain.
Three Kings Came.
Webern, *sel.*

Shapiro, Alan
Familiar Story.

Shapiro, Arnold L.
I Speak, I Say, I Talk.

Shapiro, David
About This Course.
Canticle.
Empathy for David Winfield.
From Malay.
Memory of the Present.
Sonnet: "Ice over time."

Shapiro, Harvey
Exodus.
Feast of the Ram's Horn.
For the Yiddish Singers in the Lakewood
Hotels of My Childhood.
Happiness of 6 A.M.
Heart, The.
Like a Beach.
Lines for the Ancient Scribes.
Mountain, Fire, Thornbush.
Musical Shuttle.
National Cold Storage Company.
Provincetown, Mass.
Riding Westward.
Saul's Progress.
Six Hundred Thousand Letters, The.

Shapiro, Karl
All Tropic Places Smell of Mold.
Alphabet, The.
Americans Are Afraid of Lizards.
Aubade: "What dawn is it?"
Auto Wreck.
Bathers, The.
Bed, The.
Boy-Man.
Buick.
Calder, A.
California Winter.
Christmas Eve.
Confirmation, The.
Conscientious Objector, The.
Construction.
Cut Flower, A.
D. C.
Dirty Word, The.
Dome of Sunday, The [or A]
Drug Store.
Elegy for a Dead Soldier.
Elegy for Two Banjos.

Epitaph: "Underneath this wooden cross there
lies," *sel.*
Exile, *sel.*
First Time, The.
Fly, The.
Garage Sale.
Geographers, The.
Girls Working in Banks.
Going to School.
Haircut.
Hollywood.
Hospital.
I sing the simplest flower, *sel.*
I swore to stab the sonnet with my pen, *sel.*
In India.
Intellectual, The.
Jew.
Jew at Christmas Eve, The.
Leg, The.
Love for a Hand.
Lower the Standard: That's My Motto.
Man on Wheels.
Manhole Covers.
Midnight Show.
Moving In.
Murder of Moses, The.
My Father's Funeral.
My Grandmother.
Necropolis.
Nigger.
Nostalgia.
October 1.
151st Psalm, The.
Party in Winter.
Phenomenon, The.
Piano.
Piano Tuner's Wife, The.
Poet.
Poets of Hell, The.
Progress of Faust, The.
Puritan, The.
Quintana Lay in the Shallow Grave of Coral.
Recognition of Eve, The, *sel.*
Scyros.
Sickness of Adam, The, *sel.*
Southerner, The.
Sunday: New Guinea.
This land grows the oldest living things, *sel.*
Travelogue for Exiles.
Troop Train.
Twins, The.
Two-Year-Old Has Had a Motherless Week,
The.
University.
V-Letter.
Waiting in Front of the Columnar High
School.
We waged a war within a war, *sel.*
Western Town.

Shapiro, Mark Elliott
Dying under a Fall of Stars.

Sharfman, Bern
Raw Cowardice.

Shargel, Zvi
I Will Go Away.
Let Us Laugh.
Pictures on the Wall.

Sharman, Lyon (Abbie Mary Lyon Sharman)
Old Man Pot.

Sharp, William. *See* "Macleod, Fiona"

Sharpe, R. L.
Bag of Tools, A.

Sharpe, Richard Scrafton
Country Mouse and the City Mouse, The.
Dame Wiggins of Lee and Her Seven
Wonderful Cats.

Sharples, Pita
Haka: The Blossoming.
Space Invaders Machine, The.

Sharpless, Stanley J.
Betjeman at the Post Office.

Better a day in Oxbridge.
"Go to the Ant."
Hamlet.
In Praise of Cocoa, Cupid's Nightcap.
King Canute.
Low Church.
Paradise Lost.
Summonee's Tale, The.
To His Coy Mistress.

Shatal, Shmu'el
Between You and Me.
Mountain's Side, The.
Winter.

Shaul, Anwar
Mother.
Prayers to Liberty.
To a Cactus Seller.

Shauqi, Ahmad
Andalusian Exile, An.
Bois de Boulogne.
Thoughts on Schoolchildren.

Shaw, Charles
Dissembler.

Shaw, David T.
Columbia, the Gem of the Ocean.

Shaw, John
Sleighing Song.
Song: "Who has robbed the ocean cave."

Shaw, Knowles
Handwriting on the Wall, The.

Shaw, Luci
Craftsman.
For They Shall See God.
Getting Inside the Miracle.
Groundhog, The.
Man Cannot Name Himself.
Need Is Our Name.
Stars in Apple Cores.
To a Christmas Two-Year-Old.

Shaw, Neufville
Drowned Sailor.

Shaw, Richard
Cat's Menu.

Shaw, Robert B.
Gargoyle.
Grass Widows.

Shaw, Winifred
Fine Clay.

Shea, John
Baby.
Notre Dame Victory March, The.

Shea, Robin Gathany
Caught behind Words.
Don't Smile.

Sheard, Virna
Yak, The.

Shebelski, R. C.
Out of Sight.

Sheedy, Jack
Hunting.

Sheers, Sir Henry
Long Prologue to a Short Play, A.

Sheffield, John, Duke of Buckingham and Normanby
Essay upon Satire, An, *at.*
Nine, The.
On Mr. Hobbs, and His Writings.
On One Who Died Discovering Her Kindness.
On Writing for the Stage, *sel.*
Reconcilement, The.
Written over a Gate.

Shegonee, Loyal
Loneliness.

Sheikh Mumin, Hassan
Women and Men.

Sheldon, Gilbert
St. Anthony's Township.

Shelley, Percy Bysshe
Alastor; or, The Spirit of Solitude.
Among the guests who often stayed, *sel.*
And whilst the outer lake beneath the lash, *sel.*
Arethusa.
As an eagle grasped, *sel.*
As I lay asleep in Italy, *sel.*
At Pompeii, *sel.*
Autumn; a Dirge.
Aziola, The.
Beatrice's Last Words, *sel.*
Canst thou imagine where those spirits live, *sel.*
Cenci, The.
Cenci's Curse upon His Daughter, The, *sel.*
Child of Twelve, A, *sel.*
Choruses from "Hellas," *sel.*
Cloud, The.
Daybreak.
Devil now knew his proper cue, The, *sel.*
Dirge, A: "Rough wind, that moanest loud."
Dirge for the Year.
Eagle so caught in some bursting cloud, An, *sel.*
England in 1819.
Epipsychidion.
Ever as We Sailed, *sel.*
Feelings of a Republican on the Fall of Bonaparte.
Fragment: Rain.
From the Arabic; an Imitation.
Go Thou to Rome, *sel.*
Hate-Song, A.
He is made one with Nature, *sel.*
Heigho! the lark and the owl!
Hell is a city much like London, *sel.*
Hymn of Apollo.
Hymn of Pan.
Hymn to Intellectual Beauty.
I could not choose but gaze; a fascination, *sel.*
I rode one evening with Count Maddalo, *sel.*
I wandering went/ Among the haunts and dwellings of mankind, *sel.*
Indian Serenade, The.
Invitation, The.
Invocation: "Earth, ocean, air, belovèd brotherhood!"
Islands and the mountains in the day, The, *sel.*
Julian and Maddalo.
Lament, A.
Let us become the overhanging day, *sel.*
Life of Life, *sel.*
Lifting the thunder of their acclamation, *sel.*
Lines: "Cold earth slept below, The."
Lines to a Reviewer.
Lines Written among the Euganean Hills.
Lines Written in the Bay of Lerici.
Lines Written on Hearing the News of the Death of Napoleon.
Loud deep calls me home even now to feed it, The, *sel.*
Love's Philosophy.
Magic Car Moved On, The, *sel.*
Mask [*or* Masque] of Anarchy, The.
'Mid the mountains Euganean, *sel.*
Monarch of Gods and Dæmons, and all Spirits, *sel.*
Mont Blanc.
Music.
Music, When Soft Voices Die.
Mutability.
O Thou Immortal Deity.
Ode to the West Wind.
On a Painted Woman.
On a poet's lips I slept, *sel.*
On Fanny Godwin.
On Keats.
One remains, the many change and pass, The, *sel.*
Our boat is asleep on Serchio's stream, *sel.*
Over the utmost hill at length I sped, *sel.*
Ozymandias [*or* Ozymandias of Egypt *or* Sonnet: Ozymandias]
Peace, peace! he is not dead, he doth not sleep, *sel.*
Political Greatness.
Prometheus Unbound.
Question, The.
Question, The ("I dream'd that, as I wander'd by the way").
Rarely, Rarely, Comest Thou.
Semichorus II: "There the voluptuous nightingales," *sel.*
She is still, she is cold, *sel.*
Should he upon an evening ramble fare, *sel.*
Similes for Two Political Characters of 1819.
Song: "Men of England," A.
Song to the Men of England.
Sonnet: "Lift not the painted veil which those who live."
Soon as the sound had ceased whose thunder filled, *sel.*
Sphere, which is as many thousand spheres, A, *sel.*
Spouse! Sister! Angel! Pilot of the Fate, *sel.*
Stanzas—April, 1814.
Stanzas to Edward Williams.
Stanzas Written in Dejection [December 1818] near Naples.
Summer and Winter.
There was a poet whose untimely tomb, *sel.*
Thou, Earth, calm empire of a happy soul, *sel.*
Thou knowest that toads and snakes and loathly worms, *sel.*
Thy wisdom speaks in me, and bids me dare, *sel.*
Time.
To — — —: "I fear thy kisses, gentle maiden."
To— — —: "One word is too often profaned."
To a Skylark.
To Constantia Singing.
To Jane: The Recollection.
To Maria Gisborne in England, from Italy, *sel.*
To Mary.
To Night.
To the Moon.
To William Shelley.
To Wordsworth.
Tribute to America.
Triumph of Life, The.
True Love in this differs from gold and clay, *sel.*
Two Spirits [an Allegory], The.
Verses on a Cat.
Vision of the Sea, A.
Waning Moon, The.
War Is the Statesman's Game, *sel.*
We wandered to the pine forest, *sel.*
When the Lamp Is Shattered.
Whether the sensitive plant, or that, *sel.*
Who Reigns?
Who telleth a tale of unspeaking death?
Widow bird sate mourning for her love, A, *sel.*
Wildly he wandered on, *sel.*
With a Guitar, to Jane.
World's Wanderers, The.
You are now/ In London, that great sea, *sel.*

Shelton, Richard
Alone.
Certain Choices.
Connais-Tu le Pays?
My Love.
On Lake Pend Oreille.
Prophets, The.
Requiem for Sonora.
Soldiers Returning, The.

Shelton, Thomas Russell
Patches.

Shembe, Isaiah
Come In.

Dance Hymn.
I Am the Beginning.
Let Zulu Be Heard.
Springtime of the earth has come, The.
Shen Chou
Bamboo Villa, The.
Consoling Wu Te-cheng on the Death of His
  Son.
Drinking at Night with Yen Kung-mou.
Lady Picking Flowers, A.
Moon in a Winecup, The.
On the Fifteenth Day of the Seventh Month I
  Came Home Late from the City.
Painting of Peach Blossom Spring, A.
Paying a Sick-call to Yao Ts'un-tao in the
  Rain.
Sent in Parting to Yen Kung-su.
South of the Bridge, *sel*.
Taoist Huang Has Died of Alcoholism, The.
Temple of the Ocean of Awakening.
To the Tune "Bamboo at West Lake."
To the Tune "Nan-hsiang-tz."
White clouds like a scarf enfold the the
  mountain's waist.
Shen Ch'üan
Therefore We Preserve Life.
Shen Te-ch'ien
Ditty: Below the Frontier.
Mooring My Boat at Pan-ch'a.
Song on a Pine on Yellow Mountain.
Shen Yüeh
I think of when she comes, *sel*.
I think of when she sits, *sel*.
I think of when she sleeps, *sel*.
Out Early One Morning, I Met an Old
  Acquaintance.
Written for My Neighbor.
Shenhar, Aliza
Akedah, The.
Drunkenness of Pain, The.
Expectation.
Resurrection of the Dead.
Sea-Games.
Song of the Closing Service.
Trembling.
Shenstone, William
Elegy XI: "Ah me, my friend! it will not, will
  not last!"
Hint from Voiture.
Lines Written on a Window at The Leasowes.
My banks they are furnished with bees, *sel*.
O Sweet Anne Page.
On the Clerk of a Country Parish.
School-Mistress, The.
Shepherd's Home, The.
Solemn Meditation, A.
Song: The Landscape.
Written at [*or* in] an Inn at Henley.
Shepard, Elizabeth Alsop
White Fox.
Shepard, Odell
Hidden Weaver, The.
In the Dawn.
Vespers.
Shepherd, Sir Fleetwood
Epitaph on the Duke of Grafton.
Shepherd, Hope
Trains.
Shepherd, Nan
Hill Burns, The.
Sgoran Dhu.
Shepherd, Nathaniel Graham
Roll-Call.
Shepherd, Thomas
Alas, my God, that we should be, *sel*.
Shepherd, W. G.
Englishry.
Piss Artist, The.
Suburban Garden a Nature Reserve.
Shepherd, William
Ode on Lord Macartney's Embassy to China.

Sherburne, Sir Edward
And She Washed His Feet with Her Tear[e]s,
  and Wiped Them with the Hairs of Her
  Head.
Christus Mattaeum et Discipulos Alloquitur.
Conscience.
Dream, The.
Violets in Thaumantia's Bosome.
Sheridan, Helen Selina
Charming Woman, The.
Sheridan, John D.
Joe's No Saint.
Priestin' of Father John, The.
To the New Ordained.
Sheridan, Michael
From the Illinois Shore.
Homecoming.
In America.
Michael.
Shooting the Loop.
Sheridan, Richard Brinsley
Air: "I ne'er could any lustre see," *sel*.
Clio's Protest.
Drinking Song, *sel*.
Geranium, The.
On Lady Anne Hamilton.
Song: "Give Isaac the nymph who no beauty
  can boast," *sel*.
Sherlock, Philip
Beauty Too of Twisted Trees, A.
Dinner Party 1940.
Jamaican Fisherman.
Pocomania.
Sherman, Francis
Builder, The.
House of Colour, The.
In Memorabilia Mortis.
Let Us Rise Up and Live.
Sherman, Frank Dempster
At Midnight.
Baseball.
Blossoms.
Golden Rod, The.
Hollyhock, A.
Library, The.
Moonrise.
On a Greek Vase.
On Some Buttercups.
Quatrain, A: "Hark at the lips of this pink
  whorl of shell."
Rose's Cup, The.
Shadows, The.
To a Rose.
Sherman, Joseph
Sarai.
Sherman, Kenneth
My Father Kept His Cats Well Fed.
Sherry, James
About.
Disinterment.
Drawing.
Drawing on Kreisler.
Hound's Nest for a Parafen.
No Chance Operations.
Nothing.
She'll Be Comin' 'Round.
Symbiosis.
Word I Like White Paint Considered, The.
Sherry, Ruth Forbes
Promises.
Sherwin, Judith Johnson
Ballade of the Grindstones.
Dr. Potatohead Talks to Mothers.
Gentle Heart, A: Two.
Goddess.
Just.
Light Woman's Song, The.
Rhyme for the Child as a Wet Dog.
Spoilers and the Spoils, The.
Sherwin, Richard
Jacob's Winning.

Sherwood, Grace Buchanan
After Laughter.
Sherwood, Kate Brownlee
Albert Sidney Johnston.
Molly Pitcher.
Thomas at Chickamauga.
Ulric Dahlgren.
Sherwood, Margaret
In Memoriam—Leo: A Yellow Cat.
Sherwood, Robert E.
Old Hokum Buncombe, The.
Shevin, David
Dawn.
From "Growl."
"Hope" is the Thing with Whiskers.
On the Late Mass of Curs in Piedmont.
Shechem.
Valediction: Forbidding Whining, A.
Shiba Sonome
After a wind a firefly, *sel*.
At the Ferry on the Miya River, *sel*.
Busy, the winter clouds, *sel*.
Child I carry on my back, The, *sel*.
Each time they roll in, *sel*.
Evening dusk: crowned with fans, *sel*.
Heat's so intense I dry my towel, The, *sel*.
Ice has vanished—don't be left behind, *sel*.
Leaves of trees rend, The, *sel*.
Not content, the violets have dyed, *sel*.
Robin's call has stumbled on a rock, A, *sel*.
Rouge vendors come, *sel*.
So cool: brow laid on the green straw mat,
  sel.
Spilled from a tree-searing wind, *sel*.
Violets have withered, *sel*.
Shibutsu, Okubo. See Okubo Shibutsu
Shido
For their son who wears his first *hakama*.
Shiffert, Edith Marcombe
Manners.
Monkeys on Mt. Hiei.
Shadow of a Branch, The.
Shiffrin, A. B.
Hide and Seek.
Shigeharu, Nakano. See Nakano Shigeharu
Shigeji, Tsuboi. See Tsuboi Shigeji
Shigeyuki (Minamoto no Shigeyuki)
Making no sound.
Shih Jun-chang
Ballad of Hu-hsi, A.
Ballad of One Hundred Fathoms, A.
Drums and horns rouse the river town, *sel*.
Falling Teeth.
On the battlefield, the spring wind is harsh,
  sel.
Random Song on Approaching a River, A.
Upper Garrison Farm: A Ballad a Lament for
  a Woman Killed by the Soldiery.
Shih Shan-chi
Fording.
Shihab, Naomi. See Nye, Naomi Shihab
Shiki
For a companion.
Shiki, Masaoka. See Masaoka Shiki
Shikibu, Lady Izumi. See Izumi, Lady
Shikibu, Murasaki
Someone passes.
Shikishi, Princess
Allured outside by someone's plum branches
  in bloom, *sel*.
"And still," I say, and wait, *sel*.
As I gaze, the moon dims, *sel*.
As I grow used to the mattress of moss, *sel*.
As I look, there's no place for my thoughts to
  go, *sel*.
As I looked, winter came, *sel*.
As I sleep somewhere near a mountain away
  from home, *sel*.
As winter comes, the sound from the valley
  stream stops, *sel*.
Autumn.

Autumn night grows late, The, *sel.*
Away from home, in Fushimi village, *sel.*
Away from home: over the dewdrops fragile on my pillow, *sel.*
Be a guide—this is a boat rowing in the traceless waves, *sel.*
Blossoms have fallen, The.
Brocades left at the treetops ceased to be, The, *sel.*
Calls of a clapper rail far into the night, *sel.*
Clear-toned cicadas have exhausted their voices, The, *sel.*
Clouds of May rain have closed into one, The, *sel.*
Counting the dewdrops that vie in falling off, *sel.*
Days accumulate; the more snow falls, *sel.*
Deep in the mountains, the pine door isn't aware of spring, *sel.*
Deep in the mountains, through the pine door closed, *sel.*
Did the cuckoo pity me in the sky, *sel.*
Does he not know how, *sel.*
Dream broken by the sound of a mallet, *sel.*
Evening mists in the depths of my heart, *sel.*
Every day, throwing my heart down into the valley, *sel.*
Faintly as a fisherman's bonfire way in the offing, *sel.*
First day starts, The "All's changed," *sel.*
For a moment we lay in the village of Fushimi, *sel.*
Forgetting, I grieve this evening, *sel.*
Frost that will not fall from the grebe's wings, *sel.*
How could I possibly have lived until today, *sel.*
I look far to the end of the haze, *sel.*
"I'm much in love, but look at me," *sel.*
In spring too, what first stands out is Mount Otowa, *sel.*
In the cold winds, leaves are cleared from the trees, *sel.*
In the garden where no one comes, *sel.*
I've grown used to the pine door unclosed, *sel.*
Layers of eightfold kerria roses in such a glow, *sel.*
Leaves of bamboo near my window stirring with the wind, *sel.*
Moonlight is and is not as of old, The, *sel.*
Night deepens, the sound of water trickling, The, *sel.*
No one to lose his way among the heaped up leaves, *sel.*
Not even for a moment have we joined, *sel.*
Not knowing the dream without beginning has been a dream, *sel.*
O my soul, my string of gems.
October: as a storm sweeps down Mount Mimuro, *sel.*
On the evening when, alone, I leave my village, *sel.*
Only intermittent beads of water, *sel.*
Opening on plum twigs in the unfaded snow, *sel.*
Oppressing all, sunken in autumn sorrows, *sel.*
Over the shingled roof the shower has passed, *sel.*
Passing the cedar grove at Osaka Barrier, *sel.*
Piercing to the marrow: beyond a garden fire, *sel.*
Rim of a foot-wearying mountain hazy at dawn, The, *sel.*
Shallow of me: I have grieved over this uncertain life, *sel.*
Short night, A—outside the window bamboo rustles, *sel.*
Since a wind over the rushes told me that autumn came, *sel.*

Sleeping, wanting to have the past that does not return, *sel.*
Spring.
String of beads, if you must break, break, *sel.*
Summer nights—little time to see the crescent moon decline, *sel.*
Things I have seen, the future I have yet to see, *sel.*
Though the shining sun is clearly of the summer sky, *sel.*
Through the autumn night, quiet and dark, *sel.*
Tumultuous winter sky all day, *sel.*
Uji River boat piled with brushwood, An, *sel.*
Voices of insects and a stag by the fence, The, *sel.*
Waiting for you, I have not entered my bedroom, *sel.*
Watching, I have grown lonely, *sel.*
Water fragrant in my hands, I traced it upstream, *sel.*
When I look around in the quiet before dawn, *sel.*
Which peak do these blossoms come from?
Wild geese leave no trace in the citadel of water, The, *sel.*
Wind of heaven, the maidens cross the ice, *sel.*
Winter.
Winter night: the moon, clear beyond a leafless tree, A, *sel.*
With plum blossoms from the fence visiting my sleeves, *sel.*
With spring manifest on moss-grown, *sel.*
Without a trace it has cleared on this side of the clouds, *sel.*
Would there were other means of consolation, *sel.*
Yet to be reconciled with the reality of the dark, *sel.*
Shillito, Edward
Prayer for a Preacher, A.
Shimada no Tadaomi. *See* **Tadaomi**
Shimazaki Toson
Birdless Country.
By the Old Castle at Komoro.
Coconut.
Coconut, The.
Song for the Burial of My Mother.
Song of Travel on the Chikuma River.
Shimon, Louis C.
I Know Something Good about You.
Shimpei, Kusano. *See* **Kusano Shimpei**
Shin Dong-jip
And You Woods.
Bush Clover.
Dizziness.
Face, The.
First Ice, The.
Life.
Meditation.
Peasant and Ox.
Sea.
Snow.
Someone Burning Firewood.
Sorrow.
Sparrow.
Suburbs on Spring Day.
Transmissions.
Water of Contradiction.
Shinkashi, Takahashi. *See* **Takahashi Shinkichi**
Shinkei
Now only the moon.
Plum Blossoms Late at Night.
Those who lift the sword.
Wild Goose Lingering on an Inlet.
Shinn, Milicent Washburn
Song and Science.
When Almonds Bloom.
Yosemite, *sel.*

Shinsho
Does one really have to fret.
Shipley, Sir Arthur
Ere You Were Queen of Sheba.
Shipman, Thomas
Resolute Courtier, The.
Shippen, William
Character of a Certain Whig, The.
Pasquin to the Queen's Statue at St. Paul's.
Shipton, Anna
Unerring Guide, The.
Shiraishi Kazuko
Phallus Root.
Shirao, Kaya. *See* **Kaya Shirao**
Shiren, Kokan. *See* **Kokan Shiren**
Shirley, James
Bard, The.
Bard's Chant, *sel.*
Cupids Call.
Fie on Love.
Garden, The.
Glories of Our Blood and State, The, *sel.*
Heigh-ho, what shall a shepheard doe, *sel.*
O Fly My Soul, *sel.*
On the Duke of Buckingham.
Passing Bell, The.
Piping Peace, *sel.*
Song to the Masquers, *sel.*
To His Mistris Confined.
Victorious Men of Earth, *sel.*
Shiro, Murano. *See* **Murano Shiro**
Shita Yaba. *See* **Basho and Shita Yaba**
Shitago (Minamoto no Shitago)
I have an ox but its tail is missing.
Shlonsky, Avraham
Citizen's Dissertation on His Neighborhood, A.
Dress Me, Dear Mother.
Grape-gathering.
New Genesis, A.
Pledge.
Prayer: "Forgive me, you whom they cast in a name."
Stars on Shabbat, The.
Shne'ur, Zalman
Snow Song.
Shockley, Martin Staples
Crossedroads.
Shoda
On a young rush blade a frog.
Shoha (Kuroyanagi Shoha)
Deep in the temple.
Heavy cart rumbles, A.
Shohaku (Botange Shohaku)
Fireflies.
On a Journey.
Three Poets at Yuyama.
Shoju-rojin
One look at plum blossoms.
Shokusanjin
Haiku monkey's, The.
Shonen
Mount Sumeru mallet firmly gripped, The.
Shore, Jane
Astronomer's Journal, An.
Haiti: Skin Diving.
Other Woman, The.
Russian Doll, The.
Shoreham, William of
Song to Mary, A, *at.*
Short, Clarice
Old One and the Wind, The.
Short, John
Carol: "There was a boy bedded in bracken."
Shorter, Dora Sigerson
Comforters, The.
Ireland.
Sixteen Dead Men.
Wind on the Hills, The.
Shoten
Leaving, where to go? Staying, where?

Shotetsu
Autumn Evening.
Autumn sunlight, The.
Bird.
Cool beneath the Summer Moon.
Distant Love.
Dream.
Early Autumn.
Evening Bell.
Falling Leaves before the Wind.
Hawking.
Heron Standing in a River, A.
House in the Fields.
I speak to him.
Lament, A: "I have grown old."
Leaves Making a Sound as They Fall.
Love in Spring.
Man Walking through the Snow, A.
Monkey.
Night Bell on the Mountain.
Paddy House.
Plum Scent through a Window closed against the Snow.
Red Leaves on a Buried Tree.
Snow on the Mountain at Dusk.
Spring Moon in Lingering Cold.
Summer Wisteria.
Traveling past a Market Town.
White Hydrangeas.
Wind of an Evening Shower.
Winter Bell.
Shove, Fredegond
Farmer, The.
Showell, Jr., Samuel
To the Borrower of This Book.
Shozan, Sakuma. *See* **Sakuma Shozan**
Shtern, Yisroel
Adage Concerning a Man and an Old Book, An.
For the Curious.
Men Who Hunger.
Shteynbarg, Eliezer
Clever River, The.
Lion and the Mouse, The.
Pig and the Nightingale, The.
Shtoltsenberg, Aba
Bolsheviks.
Boring Days.
Dream Canaan.
Galician Winter.
Wolf Bezberider.
Young Ukrainians.
Shu-chen, Chu
Alone.
Lost.
Plum Blossoms.
Shu Wei
And so, wine and meat markets are proscribed, *sel.*
I Hate Mosquitoes.
I neither trim the sail nor tend the mast, *sel.*
My, my! My, oh my!, *sel.*
Price of rice this year is so dear, The, *sel.*
Wind comes up, clouds depart, the moon just overhead, The, *sel.*
Shuckburg, Richard
Yankee Doodle, *at.*
Shuford, Gene
Harvest.
Shugen
Where was the monk?
Shulman, David
Diary of the Sailors of the North, A.
Shulman, Max
Honest Abe Lincoln.
Shumaker, Peggy
Ladybugs.
Shune
With the spring, now.
Shuntaro, Tanikawa
Beginning of Love.

I see a woman/ it's a woman who was my lover, *sel.*
I see a woman/ I see my wife, *sel.*
Night.
On Love.
On Obscenity.
Reason For Your Suffering.
Shuntaro, Tanikawa. *See* **Tanikawa Shuntaro**
Shunzei
As evening comes, *sel.*
Congratulations, *sel.*
Cuckoo, what are you, *sel.*
Dawn, *sel.*
Even at midnight.
Glowing moon, The, *sel.*
Has it flown away.
In my grass hut, *sel.*
In this world, *sel.*
Journey is a short one, The, *sel.*
Kibune River—/ the rocky waves of its rapids, *sel.*
Looking over Poems by Persons of Long Ago, *sel.*
Mountain stream, The, *sel.*
Oh, this world of ours.
Old though I am, *sel.*
On the Fushimi hills, *sel.*
One-Sided Love, *sel.*
Sailing close to shore, *sel.*
Sent to a Woman, *sel.*
Sent to a Woman on a Rainy Day, *sel.*
Showers wet/ the orange blossoms, *sel.*
Spring night, *sel.*
This world/ no road that takes us out of it, *sel.*
We hearing them, *sel.*
When spring comes, *sel.*
Where the water, *sel.*
While I gaze far off, *sel.*
Who'd have thought it?, *sel.*
Will someone/ at the scent of orange blossom, *sel.*
Written in Autumn When Spending the Night Near the Grave of His Wife, *sel.*
Written when He Was Well Over Eighty, *sel.*
Written when the Poet Was Seventy-six, *sel.*
Shuoshi, Mizuhara. *See* **Mizuhara Shuoshi**
Shuraikh
Distich.
Shurin, Aaron
Exorcism of the Straight/Man/Demon.
Shurin, Keijo. *See* **Keijo Shurin**
Shurtleff, Ernest W.
Lead On, O King Eternal.
Shuson, Kato
Winter seagull, A.
Shuson, Kato. *See* **Kato Shuson**
Shute, Evan V.
Luck.
Poor Fool.
Twenty Years After.
Shuttle, Penelope
Early Pregnancy.
Expectant Mother.
Flower-Press, The.
Gone Is the Sleepgiver.
Hide and Seek.
Locale.
Maritimes.
Mother and Child.
Outdoor Anniversary with Maria.
Vision of the Blessed Gabriele, The.
Shuttleworth, P. N.
Wykehamist's Address to Learning, A.
Shuzan
Silvery world, golden body.
"Shy, Timothy." *See* **Lewis, Dominic Evan Wyndham**
Sica, Gabriella
Oath.

Sickels, David Banks
Reincarnation.
Sicking, Georgie
Old Tuff.
To Be a Top Hand.
Siddal, Elizabeth
Dead Love.
Silent Wood, A.
Sidgwick, Frank
Cheerful Chilterns, The.
Christmas Legend, A.
Vision.
Sidney, James A.
Irish Schoolmaster, The.
Sidney, Sir Philip
Absence.
Advice to the Same, *sel.*
Astrophel and Stella, III.
Complaint of Love, *sel.*
Country Song, A, *sel.*
Cupid, *sel.*
Echo, *sel.*
Eighth Song: "In a grove most rich of shade," *sel.*
Eleventh Song: "Who is it that this dark night," *sel.*
Epithalamium: "Let mother Earth now deck herself in flowers," *sel.*
Farewell, A: "Oft have I mused, but now at length I find," *sel.*
First Song: "Doubt you to whom my Muse these notes intendeth," *sel.*
Fortune, Nature, Love.
Fourth Song: "Only joy, now here you are," *sel.*
Geron and Histor, *sel.*
Get Hence Foule Griefe, *sel.*
Graven Thoughts, *sel.*
He That Loves.
His Being Was in Her Alone.
In Vain, Mine Eyes, *sel.*
In wonted walkes.
Lady My Treasure.
Like as the Dove.
Like Those Sick Folks.
Love and Jealousy, *sel.*
Love and Reason, *sel.*
Love Me, O Love.
Madrigal: "Why dost thou haste away?" *sel.*
My Sheep Are Thoughts, *sel.*
My True Love Hath My Heart [and I Have His], *sel.*
Night, *sel.*
"Oft with true sighs, oft with uncallèd tears," *sel.*
Old Age, *sel.*
Ring Out Your Bells.
Rural Poesy, *sel.*
Sapphics, *sel.*
Shepherd Song, *sel.*
Shepherd's Tale, A, *sel.*
Since So Mine Eyes, *sel.*
Sixth Song: "O you that hear this voice," *sel.*
Sleep, *sel.*
Sleep, Baby Mine, Desire.
Solitariness, *sel.*
Song: "No, no, no, no, I cannot hate my foe."
Song: "O fair! O sweet! when I do look on thee."
Song: Who Hath His Fancy [*or* Fancie] Pleased.
Sonnet: "Ah bed! the field where joy's peace some do see."
Sonnet: "Alas, have I not pain enough, my friend."
Sonnet: "Because I breathe not love to every one."
Sonnet: "Come sleep! O sleep, the certain knot of peace."
Sonnet: "Dear, why make you more of a dog than me?"

Sonnet: "Desire, though thou my old companion art."
Sonnet: "Envious wits, what hath been mine offense."
Sonnet: "Fie, school of patience, fie, your lesson is."
Sonnet: "Fly, fly, my friends, I have my death wound; fly."
Sonnet: "Good brother Philip, I have borne you long."
Sonnet: "Having this day my horse, my hand, my lance."
Sonnet: "Highway, since you my chief Parnassus be."
Sonnet: "I might—unhappy word—oh me, I might."
Sonnet: "I never drank of Aganippe well."
Sonnet: "I on my horse, and Love on me, doth try."
Sonnet: "In highest way of heaven the Sun did ride."
Sonnet: "In martial sports I had my cunning tried."
Sonnet: "In nature apt to like when I did see."
Sonnet: "In truth, O Love, with what a boyish kind."
Sonnet: "It is most true that eyes are formed to serve."
Sonnet: Leave Me, O Love.
Sonnet: "Let dainty wits cry on the Sisters nine."
Sonnet: "Love, by sure proof I may call thee unkind."
Sonnet: "Love still a boy and oft a wanton is."
Sonnet: "Loving in truth, and fain in verse my love to show."
Sonnet: "My mouth doth water, and my breast doth swell."
Sonnet: "No more, my dear, no more these counsels try."
Sonnet: "Now that of absence the most irksome night."
Sonnet: "Not at the first sight, nor with a dribbed shot."
Sonnet: "Nymph of the garden where all beauties be."
Sonnet: "O grammar-rules, O now your virtues show."
Sonnet: "O joy too high for my low style to show!"
Sonnet: "O kiss, which dost those ruddy gems impart."
Sonnet: "O tears, no tears, but rain from beauty's skies."
Sonnet: "Queen Virtue's court, which some call Stella's face."
Sonnet: "Reason, in faith thou art well served, that still."
Sonnet: "Some lovers speak, when they their muses entertain."
Sonnet: "Soul's joy, bend not those morning stars from me."
Sonnet: "Stella oft sees the very face of woe."
Sonnet: "Stella! since thou so right a princess art."
Sonnet: "Stella, think not that I by verse seek fame."
Sonnet: "Stella, while now by honor's [or honor's] cruel might."
Sonnet: "Stella, the only planet of my light."
Sonnet: "Strife is grown between Virtue and Love, A."
Sonnet: "Thou blind man's mark, thou fool's self-chosen snare."
Sonnet: "Though dusty wits dare scorn astrology."
Sonnet: "What, have I thus betrayed my liberty?"
Sonnet: "When I was forced from Stella ever dear."

Sonnet: "When Nature made her chief work, Stella's eyes."
Sonnet: "When far-spent night persuades each mortal eye."
Sonnet: "When sorrow (using mine own fire's might)."
Sonnet: "Whether the Turkish new-moon minded be."
Sonnet: "Who will in fairest book of Nature know."
Sonnet: "Wisest scholar of the wight most wise, The."
Sonnet: "With how sad steps, O [or Oh] Moon, thou climb'st the skies!"
Sonnet: "With what sharp checks I in myself am shent."
Sonnet: "You that do search for every purling spring."
Sonnet: "You that with allegory's curious frame."
Sonnet: "Your words, my friend, right helpful caustics, blame."
Stonehenge, sel.
Sweeter Saint I Serve, A, sel.
Tale for Husbands, A, sel.
Third Song: "If Orpheus voyce had force to breathe such musickes love," sel.
What Length of Verse?
What Tongue Can Her Perfections Tell?, sel.
When, to my deadly [or deadlie] pleasure.
When Two Suns Do Appear, sel.
Why Fear to Die?, sel.
Wronged Lover, The, sel.
Ye Goat-herd Gods, sel.

Siebert, Diane
Train Song.

Siegel, Danny
Binni the Meshuggener.
Crippler, The.
Snow in the City.

Siegel, Eli
All the Smoke.
Fare Thee Well.

Siegel, June
Apologia Pro Vita.

Siegel, Robert
Air Field.
Christmas Eve.
Ego.
Mr. Brunt.
Revenant, The.
Rinsed with Gold, Endless, Walking the Fields.
Visit to the Farm, A.

Siegrist, Mary
League of Nations, The.

Sieller, William Vincent
Windmill on the Cape.

Sierra, Justo
Bucolic Funeral.

Sigerson, George
My Own Cáilin Donn.

Sigourney, Lydia Huntley
Advertisement of a Lost Day.
Blessed Comforter Divine.
California.
Columbus.
God Save the Plough.
God Save the Plough.
Indian Names.
Indian's Welcome to the Pilgrim Fathers, The.
Laborers of Christ! Arise.
Onward, Onward, Men of Heaven.
Request of a Dying Child.
Return of Napoleon from St. Helena, The.
We Praise Thee, If One Rescued Soul.

Sigüenza y Góngora, Carlos de
Invocation and Proposition, sel.

Sikelianos, Angelos
Agraphon.
Because I Deeply Praised.

Caique.
Daedalus.
First Rain, The.
Letter IV.
Mother of Dante, The.
On Acrocorinth.
Pan.
Rehearsing for Death.
Sacred Way, The.
Sparta.
Suicide of Atzesivano Disciple of Buddha, The.
Thalero.

Sikelianos, Angelos
Doric.

Silabhattarika
He who stole my virginity/ is the same man.
My husband is the same who took my maidenhead, sel.

Silberschlag, Eisig
Abraham.
Proust on Noah.

Silén, Iván
To Teresa.
Why I Can't Write a Poem about Lares.

Silentarius, Paulus. See **Paulus Silentarius**

Silesius, Angelus. See "**Angelus Silesius**"

Silk, Dennis
Guide to Jerusalem.
Matronita.

Silkin, Jon
Chisel Grows Heavy, The.
Coldness, The.
Death of a Bird.
Death of a Son.
Death to Us, A.
First It Was Singing.
Furnished Lives.
It Says.
Jerusalem.
Respectabilities.
Resting Place.
Return, The.
Space in the Air, A.
Word about Freedom and Identity in Tel Aviv, A.

Silko, Leslie Marmon
Alaskan Mountain Poem #1.
Deer Song.
Four Mountain Wolves.
Hawk and Snake.
Horses at Valley Store.
How to Write a Poem about the Sky.
In Cold Storm Light.
Indian Song: Survival.
Invention of White People, The.
It Was a Long Time Before.
Long Time Ago.
Love Poem: "Rain smell comes with the wind."
Poem for Ben Barney.
Poem for Myself and Mei: Abortion.
Prayer to the Pacific.
Preparations.
Slim Man Canyon.
Story from Bear Country.
Sun Children.
Time We Climbed Snake Mountain, The.
Toe'osh; a Laguna Coyote Story.
When Sun Came to Riverwoman.
Where Mountain Lion Lay [or Laid] Down with Deer.

Sill, Edward Rowland
Baker's Duzzen uv Wize Sawz, A.
Before Sunrise in Winter.
Coup de Grace, The.
Crickets in the Fields, The.
Dead President, The.
Deserter, The.
Eve's Daughter.
Fool's Prayer, The.

For the Gifts of the Spirit.
Force.
Life.
Lost Love.
Lover's Song, The.
Opportunity.
Philosopher, The.
Prayer for Peace, A.
Prayer, A: "O God, our Father, if we had but
　truth!"
Space.
Tempted.
Things that Will Not Die, The.
'Tis not by guilt the onward sweep, *sel.*
To a Maid Demure.

Sillè, Nicasius de
God Set Us Here.

Sillitoe, Alan
Picture of Loot.

Silvera, Edward S.
Forgotten Dreams.
Jungle Taste.
On the Death of a Child.
South Street.

Silverman, Maxine
Hair.

Silvers, Frances
Frankie Silvers.

Silverstein, Shel (Shelley)
Beware, My Child.
Clarence ("Clarence Lee from Tennessee").
Dirtiest Man in the World, The.
Fancy Dive.
Fourth, The.
Friendship.
Hug o' War.
Jimmy Jet and His TV Set.
Lazy People, The.
Little Boy and the Old Man, The.
Longmobile.
Magical Eraser.
One Inch Tall.
Pie Problem.
Sarah Cynthia Sylvia Stout Would Not Take
　the Garbage Out.
Slithergadee, The.
Smart.
Thumbs.
Valentine.
Worst, The.

Simba, a-dZiko
25.40 P.M. (Past Mourning).
Woman Talk.

Simcox, George Augustus
Love's Votary.

Simiane, Pauline de
Madrigal: "You kiss me like a sister."

Simic, Charles
Against Whatever It Is That's Encroaching.
Ancient Autumn.
Animal Acts.
Animals, The.
Apocrypha.
Baby Pictures of Famous Dictators.
Ballad: "What's that approaching like dust
　like poverty."
Bedtime Story.
Begotten of the Spleen.
Bestiary for the Fingers of My Right Hand.
Bird, The.
Breasts.
Brooms.
Butcher Shop.
Charon's Cosmology.
Classic Ballroom Dances.
Cold, The.
Crows.
Dimly Outlined by a Police Artist.
Elementary Cosmogony.
Empire of Dreams.
Errata.

Euclid Avenue.
Evening.
Fear.
Fork.
Garden of Earthly Delights, The.
George Simic.
Great Infirmities.
Harsh Climate.
Healer, The.
Hearing Steps.
Hunger.
Lesson, The.
Midpoint.
My Shoes.
Nothing.
October Arriving.
Old Couple.
Old Mountain Road.
On Pretext.
Partial Explanation, The.
Pastoral: "I came to a field."
Poem: "Every morning I forget how it is."
Poem without a Title.
Poverty.
Prodigy.
Progress Report.
Psalm: "Old ones to the side."
Return to a Place Lit by a Glass of Milk.
St. Thomas Aquinas.
Severe Figures.
Shirt.
Sleep.
Soup, The.
Spoon, The.
Stone.
Story, The.
Strictly Bucolic.
Strictly for Posterity.
Tapestry.
Theory, A.
Unintelligible Terms.
Wall, A.
Watch Repair.
Watermelons.
Window Washer.
Winter Night.

Simmerman, Jim
Almost Dancing.
Child's Grave, Hale County, Alabama.
Hide-and-Go-Seek.
Whatever It Is.

Simmias of Thebes
To Prote.

Simmons, Gerald L., Jr.
Take Tools Our Strength.

Simmons, Herbert A.
Ascendancy.

Simmons, James
Art and Reality.
Birthday Poem, A.
Claudy.
Experience.
Fear Test: Integrity of Heroes.
Goodbye, Sally.
John Donne.
Letter to a Jealous Friend.
October in the Country: 1983.
Outward Bound.
Playing with Fire.
Reformer to His Father, A.

Simmons, James Wright
Sumter's Band.

Simmons, Judy Dothard
Alabama.
Generations.
It's Comforting.
Survivor.

Simms, William Gilmore
Battle of Eutaw, The.
Decay of a People, The.
Glory and Enduring Fame.

Lost Pleiad, The.
Night Storm.
Song in March.
Swamp Fox, The.
Triumph, The.

Simoko, Patu
Africa Is Made of Clay.
Corruption.
Did We Laugh or Did We Cry?

Simon, István
Rhapsody on Time.

Simon, John Oliver
Cities are washed into time, The.
Dont Tell Bad Dreams Says Tita's Mother.
For Alan Blanchard.
Hanged Man, The.
Headlands, 2365.
Living in the Boneyard.
Tryptych for Jan Bockelson, A.
Woodchuck Who Lives on Top of Mt. Ritter.

Simon, Paul
Richard Cory.

Simone, Nina
Four Women.

Simone, Roberta
Clerihew: The Nicolsons.
Clerihew: "Wandering Ulysses/ While
　returning to his Mrs."

Simonides
At Thermopylae.
On the Lacedaemonian Dead at Plataea.
On the Spartan Dead at Thermopylae.
On Two Brothers.
Someone is glad that I, Theodorus, am dead.
Stranger, when you come to/ Lakedaimon.
Thermopylae.
Thermopylae Ode, The.

Simpson, Albert Benjamin
Why Doubt God's Word?

Simpson, Bill
Glow, The.
Like It or Not.

Simpson, Earl
Learning.

Simpson, Louis
Aegean.
After Midnight.
Against the Age.
American Dreams.
American Poetry.
Arm in Arm.
As a Man Walks.
As Birds Are Fitted to the Boughs.
Battle, The.
Before the Poetry Reading.
Bird, The.
Boarder, The.
Carentan O Carentan.
Chocolates.
Climate of Paradise, The.
Columbus.
Constant Lover, The.
Country House, The.
Custom of the World, The.
Doubting.
Dream of Governors, A.
Dvonya.
Early in the Morning.
Friend of the Family, A.
Heroes, The.
Hot Night on Water Street.
Hubert's Museum.
I Dreamed That in a City Dark as Paris.
In the Suburbs.
Isidor.
It Was the Last of the Parades.
Jamaica.
John the Baptist.
Laurel Tree, The.
Legend of Success, The Salesman's Story,
　The.
Luminous Night.

Man Who Married Magdalene, The.
Mashkin Hill.
Memories of a Lost War.
Middleaged Man, The.
Music in Venice.
My Father in the Night Commanding No.
New Lines for Cuscuscaraway and Mirza
  Murad Ali Beg.
Night in Odessa, A.
On the Lawn at the Villa.
Outward.
Photographer, The.
Physical Universe.
Port Jefferson.
Precinct Station, The.
Quiet Desperation.
Redwoods, The.
Rough Winds Do Shake.
Sacred Objects.
Sailors.
Silent Piano, The.
Simplicity.
Son of the Romanovs, A.
Song: "Let's sing a song together once."
Squeal.
Stumpfoot on 42nd Street.
Summer Storm.
Sway.
Tailor's Wedding, The.
Things.
To the Western World.
Tonight the Famous Psychiatrist.
True Weather for Women, The.
26th Precinct Station.
Walt Whitman at Bear Mountain.
White Oxen.
Why Do You Write about Russia?

Simpson, Lucy Jane
Sheep's Skull.

Simpson, Margaret Winefride
Villanelle: "O winter wind, lat grievin be."

Simpson, Mark
X, Oh X.

Simpson, Ronald Albert
Antarctica.
Diver.
Lake.
Night Out.

Sims, George R.
Christmas Day in the Workhouse.
Garden Song, A.
'Ostler Joe.
Undertones.

Sinason, Valerie
Ghostly Love.
In the Beginning.
Jealousy.
Love Poem: "My love the sun sets."
Nuclear Unit.
Renaming, The.
Will You Come Out Now?

Sinclair, Donald
Path of the Old Spells, The.

Sinclair, F. D.
Zimbabwe.

Sinclair, John
Breakthrough.

Sinclair, Keith
Bomb Is Made, The.
Memorial to a Missionary.
Parakeet, The.
Sonnet from Below the Age Gap.
Young Chess Player, The.

Sinclair, May
Field Ambulance in Retreat.

Singde
After the leaves have quivered and fallen, *sel.*
Even the crows have gone, *sel.*
Heading for cloud-mantled mountains, I press
  on to the other side.
Heart turned to ashes, *sel.*

North wind blowing through the barren
  willows, The, *sel.*
North wind blows, scattering the third-watch
  snow, The.
Sent to Liang-fen.
Song of the Wild Crane: Presented to a
  Friend, A.
Stopping Overnight at Black Dragon River.
Tune: Cuckoo Sky.
Tune: Remembering the South.
Who knows how cold, how lonely the west
  wind?
Yellow clouds, purple ramparts—three
  thousand *li.*

Singer, Burns (James Burns Singer)
Birdsong.
Christ comes to mind and comes across the
  mind, *sel.*
Epilogue: "That death might not be casual."
I promise you by the harsh funeral, *sel.*
Marcus Antoninus Cui Cognomen Erat
  Aurelius.
Nothing.
Old man dozed, The. The hospital quietened,
  sel.
Peterhead in May.
Still and All.
Those flaming Christians with their hygienic
  rose, *sel.*
To see the petrel cropping in the farmyard,
  sel.
Words Made of Water.

Singer, John
Stepney Green.

Singleton, John
Ah me! How differently th'untutor'd slave,
  sel.
But lo! The reaking surface of the vale, *sel.*

Sinks, P. W.
Just like Me.

Siôn Cent
Vanity of the World, The.

Sipe, Muriel
Good Morning.

Siraj, Mir Sirajuddin
Come, hear the tale of love's romance.
Now in the garden Spring's the saki.

Sissman, Louis Edward
Brick plant like a school. The winter set, The,
  sel.
Cockaigne: A Dream.
Critic on the Hearth, The.
Day in the City, A.
December 27, 1966.
Disappearance in West Cedar Street, A.
Dying: An Introduction.
Elegy: E. W.
Henley, July 4: 1914-1964.
In and Out [Severence of Connections, 1946]
My father casts a stone whose ripples ride,
  sel.
New York Woman, The.
On the Island.
Safety at Forty; or, An Abecedarian Takes a
  Walk.
Severance of Connections, 1946, *sel.*
Sweeney to Mrs. Porter in the Spring.
Talking Union: 1964.
West Forties: Morning, Noon, and Night,
  The.
Whether the rivals for a wife and mother can,
  sel.

Sisson, Charles Hubert
A and B.
Adam and Eve.
At First.
Beware of age, *sel.*
Black Rocks.
Cato.
Cotignac Again ("Cotignac is full of spies").
Cranmer.
Easter.

Family Fortunes.
God Bless Karl Marx.
Hare, The.
Human Relations.
Knole.
Letter to John Donne, A.
Looking at Old Note-Books.
Marcus Aurelius.
Money.
Nature of Man, The.
Over the Wall: Berlin, May 1975.
Queen of Lydia, The.
Temple, The.
Usk, The.
Voyage, The.
Waking.

Sitwell, Dame Edith
Ass-Face.
Aubade: "Jane, Jane,/ Tall as a crane."
Bat, The.
Bells of Grey Crystal.
Colonel Fantock.
Country Dance.
Dark Song.
Dirge for the New Sunrise, *sel.*
Drum; the Narrative of the Demon of
  Tedworth, The.
Elegy for Dylan Thomas.
Evening.
Façade.
Gardener Janus Catches a Naiad.
Hambone and the Heart, The.
Heart and Mind.
Hornpipe, *sel.*
How Many Heavens.
In the great gardens, after bright spring rain,
  sel.
Interlude.
King of China's Daughter, The.
Lament of Edward Blastock, The.
Lullaby: "Though the world has slipped and
  gone."
Madam Mouse Trots.
Most Lovely Shade ("Most lovely dark, my
  Æthiopia born").
Neptune—Polka.
Old Woman Laments in Spring-Time, An.
One fantee wave, *sel.*
Panope.
Poet Laments the Coming of Old Age, The.
Scotch Rhapsody.
Shadow of Cain, The.
Sir Beelzebub.
Solo for Ear-Trumpet.
Song at Morning, A.
Song: "Now that Fate is dead and gone."
Spinning Song.
Still Falls the Rain.
Street Song.
Swans, The.
Switchback.
Tears.
Trio for Two Cats and a Trombone.
Two Kitchen Songs.
When we come to that dark house, *sel.*
Youth with Red-gold Hair, The.

Sitwell, Sacheverell
Agamemnon's Tomb.
Fountains ("This night is pure and clear as
  thrice refinèd silver").
In the turn of the world, *sel.*
Kingcups.
One by one, as harvesters, all heavy laden,
  sel.
"Psittachus Eois Imitatrix Ales ab Indis."
Red-Gold Rain, The.
Rio Grande, The.
River God, The.
Tulip Tree.

Sitwell, Sir Osbert
Elegy for Mr. Goodbeare.
English Beach Memory: Mr. Thuddock.

Fountains ("Proud fountains, wave your plumes").
How Shall We Rise to Greet the Dawn?
Maxixe.
Mrs. Busk.
Next War, The.
On the Coast of Coromandel.
Therefore Is the Name of It Called Babel.
Sivan, Arye
Children's Song.
Forty Years Peace.
In Jerusalem Are Women.
To Xanadu, Which Is Beth Shaul.
Sizemore, George
Drill Man Blues.
Skeat, Walter William
Clerk Ther Was of Cauntebrigge Also, A.
Villanelle: "It's all a trick, quite easy when you know it."
Skeen, Anita
Instructions.
Letter to My Mother.
Modern Poetry.
Sailing in Crosslight.
Women Who Cook.
Skelley, Jack
To Marie Osmond.
TV Blooper Spotter.
Skelton, John
And if ye stand in doubt, *sel.*
Auncient Acquaintance, Madam, The.
Ballade of the Scottyshe Kynge, A.
Bowge of Courte, The.
Colin Clout.
Commendations of Mistress Jane Scrope, The, *sel.*
Doctors that learned be, *sel.*
Dreamer Meets Riot, The, *sel.*
Funeral of Philip Sparrow, The, *sel.*
Gup, Scot!
Knowledge, Acquaintance.
Mannerly Margery Mylk and Ale.
My name is Parrot, a byrd of paradise, *sel.*
O Cat of Carlishkind, *sel.*
O ye wretched Scots, *sel.*
Phyllyp Sparowe.
Pla ce bo! Who is there, who?, *sel.*
Prayer to the Father of [*or* in] Heaven, A.
Prelates, The, *sel.*
Skelton Laureate, Defender, against Lusty Garnesche, Well-beseen Christopher, Challenger.
Such a prelate, I trow, *sel.*
Then Margery [*or* Marjorie] Milkduck, *sel.*
Though Ye Suppose.
To Maystres Jane Blenner-Haiset, *sel.*
To Mistress [*or* Maystres] Isabell Pennell, *sel.*
To Mistress Margaret Hussey.
To Mistress Margaret Tilney, *sel.*
To Mistress Margery Wentworth, *sel.*
Tunnyng [*or* Tunning] of Elynour [*or* Elinour] Rummyng [*or* Rumming], The.
Unfriendly Fortune.
Upon a Dead Man's Head.
When I remember again, *sel.*
With Lullay, Lullay, like a Child.
Woefully Arrayed, *at.*
Womanhod, wanton, ye want.
Skelton, Robin
Ballad of a Mine, A.
Eagle.
Lakeside Incident.
Skinner, Constance Lindsay
Bear's Song, The, *sel.*
Love Song, *sel.*
Song for Fine Weather, *sel.*
Song of Cradle-making.
Song of the Full Catch.
Skinner, John
Tullochgorum.

Skinner, Knute
Brockton Murder; a Page out of William James, The.
Cold Irish Earth, The.
Imagine Grass.
Introduction to a Pub in Limerick.
Location.
Skinner, Thomas
Suttee, The.
Skipsey, Joseph
A Golden Lot.
Brooklet, The.
Get Up!
Hey Robin.
Minstrel, The.
Mother Wept.
Not as Wont.
Stars Are Twinkling, The.
Skirrow, Desmond
Ode on a Grecian Urn Summarized.
Skirving, Adam
Johnnie Cope.
Sklarew, Myra
Benediction.
Goodbye, The.
Holocaust.
How Metaphor Can Save Your Life.
Instructions for Elijah.
Instructions for the Messiah.
Ninth of Av.
Speech Warts.
Teaching the Children.
What Is a Jewish Poem?
Skloot, Floyd
Hook.
I Am Getting a Mountain View.
My Daughter Considers Her Body.
Skoyles, John
Burlesque.
Evidence.
If You Have an Enemy.
Knockout.
No Thank You.
Once or Twice.
Skrine, Nesta Higginson. *See* **"O'Neill, Moira"**
Skrzynecki, Peter
Cattle.
Feliks Skrzynecki.
Skythinos
Epigram: "Great woe, fire & war come on me."
Sladen, Douglas Brook Wheelton
Summer Christmas in Australia, A.
Slater, Eleanor
Petition.
Sight and Insight.
Slavitt, David R.
Another Letter to Lord Byron.
Broads.
Dead Bird.
Eczema.
Griefs of Women, The.
In Memory of W. H. Auden.
In the Seraglio.
Intermission Greetings at the Paris Opera—1898.
That Everything Moves Its Bowels.
Sleigh, Tom
Elk at Black Fork Canyon.
Hope.
Slemp, John Calvin
O Christ, Who Died.
Slessor, Kenneth
Beach Burial.
Bushranger, A.
Country Towns.
Dutch Seacoast, *sel.*
Five Bells.
Flowers turned to stone! Not all the botany, *sel.*

King of Cuckooz, The, *sel.*
Leaning against the golden undertow, *sel.*
Mermaids, *sel.*
North Country.
Polarities.
Post-Roads, *sel.*
South Country.
Two Chronometers, *sel.*
William Street.
Sloan, Errol B.
And Yet.
Sloan, Jocelyn Macy
Eliza Telefair.
Sloman, Joel
In a Remote Cloister Bordering the Empyrean.
Tree, The.
Slonimski, Antoni
All.
Conrad.
Conversation with a Countryman.
Defence of the Moon.
Elegy: "No more, no more Jewish townships in Poland."
Hamletism.
He Is My Countryman.
Jerusalem.
London Spring.
Morning and Evening.
Remembrance.
To the Germans.
Slutsky, Boris
Burnt.
Dreams of Auschwitz.
God.
How They Killed My Grandmother.
Sly, Muriel
Chimpanzee, The/ Is a most embarrassing animal to see.
Slyman, Ernest
Chinese Restaurant.
Lightning Bugs.
Scoop.
"Smalacombe John." *See* **MacKay, Louis Alexander**
Small, Adam
There's Somethin.'
Small, Robin. *See* **"Jerry, Bongo"**
Smaridge, Norah
Footnote.
Toothsome.
Why Run?
Smart, Christopher
All the Scenes of Nature Quicken.
Ascension of Our Lord Jesus Christ, *sel.*
Author Apologizes to a Lady for His Being a Little Man, The.
Beauteous, Yea Beauteous More than These, *sel.*
But, O immortals! What had I to plead, *sel.*
Elegance, *sel.*
Epiphany, *sel.*
For I bless the Prince of Peace and pray that all the guns may be nail'd up, *sel.*
For I Will Consider My Cat Jeoffry [*or* Jeoffrey], *sel.*
For Saturday, *sel.*
For the air is purified by prayer which is made aloud, *sel.*
For the doubling of flowers is the improvement of the gardners talent, *sel.*
For the spiritual musick is as follows, *sel.*
Glorious the sun in mid career, *sel.*
Gratitude, *sel.*
Hops along the Medway, *sel.*
How to Cure Hops and Prepare Them for Sale, *sel.*
Instruments, The.
Let Elizur[e] rejoice with the Partridge, *sel.*
Let Ephah rejoice with Buprestis, the Lord endue us with temperance and humanity, *sel.*

Let Shobi rejoice with the Kastrel—blessed be
the name Jesus, *sel.*
Long-Suffering of God, *sel.*
Loveliness, *sel.*
Madam if you please.
Man of Prayer, The, *sel.*
Mirth, *sel.*
Moderation, *sel.*
Morning Hymn, A.
Morning-Piece; or, An Hymn for the
Hay-Makers, A.
Mutual Subjection, *sel.*
Nativity of Our Lord and Saviour Jesus
Christ, The, *sel.*
Night-Piece; or, Modern Philosophy, A.
O David, highest in the list, *sel.*
O thou, that sitst upon a throne, *sel.*
On a Bed of Guernsey Lilies.
On My Wife's Birth-Day.
Praise.
Pray Remember the Poor.
Psalm CXLVII: "Praise ye the Lord."
Rejoice in God, *sel.*
St. Philip and St. James, *sel.*
Song to David, A.
Song: "Where shall Celia fly for shelter."
Stars of the superior class, *sel.*
Strong is the lion—like a coal, *sel.*
Sublime—invention ever young, *sel.*
Taste, *sel.*
Tell them, I AM, Jehovah said, *sel.*
To the Rev. Mr. Powell.
Smart, Elizabeth
Warning, A.
Smedley, Jonathan
Fancy.
Smedley, Menella Bute
North Pole Story, A.
Smeeton, John P.
Jack Frost in the Garden.
Smiley, Joseph Bert
St. Peter at the Gate.
Smith, Alexander
Barbara.
Smith, Ann
Desire makes you.
Smith, Arabella Eugenia
If I Should Die Tonight.
Smith, Arthur James Marshall
Archer, The.
Ballade un Peu Banale.
Brigadier.
Common Man, The.
Dead, The.
Fountain, The.
Good Friday.
Like an Old Proud King in a Parable.
Lonely Land, The.
My Death.
News of the Phoenix.
Ode: On the Death of William Butler Yeats.
Plot against Proteus, The.
Political Intelligence.
Prothalamium.
Resurrection of Arp.
To Henry Vaughan.
Watching the Old Man Die.
What the Emanation of Casey Jones Said to
the Medium.
Smith, Barbara
Lines.
Smith, Bessie
Empty Bed Blues.
Smith, Bruce
Address, *sel.*
Laundry.
O My Invisible Estate.
Window.
Smith, Caroline Sprague
Tarry with Me, O My Saviour.

Smith, Charlotte
Captive Escaped in the Wilds of America
Addressed to the Honorable Mrs. O'Neill,
The.
Glow-Worm, The.
I once was happy, when, while yet a child,
sel.
Invitation to the Bee.
Sonnet Written in the Church-Yard at
Middleton, in Sussex.
Swift fleet the billowy clouds along the sky,
sel.
Thirty-eight.
To Sleep.
To Spring.
To the Moon.
Smith, Claude Clayton
Ulysses.
Smith, Dave
Ancestor, The.
Antipastoral Memory of One Summer, An.
At Frost's Grave.
Bats.
Blues for Benny Kid Paret.
Caravati's Salvage: Richmond, Virginia.
Chopping Wood.
Cleaning a Fish.
Collector of the Sun, The.
Cooking Eggs.
Cumberland Station.
Desks.
Dome Poem.
Drag Race.
Ducking: After Maupassant.
Elk Ghosts: A Birth Memory.
Hawktree.
Hole, Where Once in Passion We Swam.
In the House of the Judge.
Leafless Trees, Chickahominy Swamp.
Looking for the Melungeon.
Mending Crab Pots.
Night Fishing for Blues.
Of Oystermen, Workboats.
Old Whore Speaks to a Young Poet, The.
On a Field Trip at Fredericksburg.
Perspective and Limits of Snapshots, The.
Photographic Plate, Partly Spidered, Hampton
Roads, Virginia, with Model T Ford
Mid-Channel.
Pink Slip at Tool & Dye.
Pinto Mare, A.
Pornography Box, The.
Purpose of the Chesapeake & Ohio Canal,
The.
Rain Forest.
Reading the Books Our Children Have
Written.
Roundhouse Voices, The.
Roundhouse Voices, The.
Sailing the Back River.
Sea Owl.
Smithfield Ham.
Snapshot of a Crab-Picker among Barrels
Spilling Over, Apparently at the End of Her
Shift.
Snow Owl.
2000.
Under the Scrub Oak, a Red Shoe.
Smith, David
Mean Rufus Throw-Down.
Smith, Dexter
Our National Banner.
Smith, Don Ian
Old Horse.
Smith, Edgar
Heaven Will Protect the Working Girl.
You may tempt the upper classes, *sel.*
Smith, Elizabeth Oakes
Her ways were gentle while a babe, *sel.*
Smith, Eunice
Dear Brethren, Are Your Harps in Tune?
Dear Happy Souls.

Smith, Florence
Song: "How pleasant it is that always."
Smith, Francis J.
First Prelude.
Smith, George
Country Lovers; or, Isaac and Marget Going
to Town, on a Summer's Morning, The.
Smith, Gwen A.
Off We Go to Market.
Smith, Harry Bache
Armorer's Song, The.
My Angeline.
Song of the Turnkey, The.
Smith, Horace [or Horatio]
Bit of Colour, A.
Evening; an Elegy.
Gouty Merchant and the Stranger, The.
On a Stupendous Leg of Granite, Discovered
Standing by Itself in the Deserts of Egypt,
with the Inscription Inserted Below.
Tale of Drury Lane, A.
Smith, Horace and James Smith
Baby's Debut, The.
Macbeth.
Theatre, The.
Smith, Iain Crichton
Aberdeen University 1945-49: I, *sel.*
Culloden and After.
Deer at the Roadside, *sel.*
End of the Season on a Stormy Day—Oban.
For Angus MacLeod.
For My Mother.
In Those Days.
John Knox.
Nose, The.
Not in Heaven.
Old Woman.
Poor Relations, The.
Reflection.
Schoolgirl on Speech-Day in the Open Air.
Story, The.
Villagers.
Wild Cat, The.
Window, The.
Young Highland Girl Studying Poetry, A.
Smith, J.
Unseaworthy Ship, The.
Smith, J. Moyr
Four and Twenty Merulae.
She Lost Her Sheep.
Smith, James
On the American Rivers.
Smith, James and Sir George Rose
Conversation in Craven Street, Strand.
Smith, James Steel
Dog Story.
Smith, Janet M.
Corries.
Smith, Jesse
Saturday Night in Woody.
Smith, Jessie Welborn
Sew a Pocket.
Smith, John
First, Goodbye.
Smith, John (1580-1631)
In the Due Honor of the Author Master
Robert Norton.
John Smith of His Friend Master John Taylor.
Sea Marke, The.
Smith, John (1662-1717)
Solitary Canto to Chloris the Disdainful, A.
Smith, Jordan
For Dulcimer and Doubled Voice.
Smith, Kay
Annunciation.
Eye of Humility, The.
Heaven which art in Heaven Our Father in
Heaven, *sel.*
What Then, Dancer?
When a Girl Looks Down.

Smith, Ken
Possessions.
Train.
Smith, Langdon
Evolution.
Smith, Lanta Wilson
This, Too, Shall [or Will] Pass Away.
Smith, Laurence
Christmas Tree.
Smith, LeRoy, Jr.
Spring Song.
Smith, Lewis Worthington
News from Yorktown.
Smith, Lucy
Face of Poverty.
Smith, Margery
For Freda.
Unknown Warrior Speaks, The.
Smith, Margoret
Cataract.
Smith, Marion Couthouy
King of the Belgians.
Star, The.
Smith, Mary Brainerd
Poor for Our Sakes.
Smith, Mary Carter
Clubwoman.
Jungle.
Smith, Mary Lonnberg
Cartwheels.
Smith, May Riley
Departure.
God's Plans.
If We Knew.
My Life Is a Bowl.
My Uninvited Guest.
Scatter Seeds of Kindness.
Sometime.
Smith, Mbembe Milton
You've Got to Learn the White Man's Game.
Smith, Michael
Black Bud.
Fall.
From the Chinese.
I an I Alone; or Goliath.
Mitching.
Smith, Norma E.
Evangeline.
Smith, R. T.
Beneath the Mound.
Long Joke, The.
Red Anger.
Victory, A.
Yonosa House.
Smith, Ray
Apple, The.
Smith, Ray Riley
In Prison.
Smith, Robert (d. 1555)
Exhortation of a Father to His Children, The.
Smith, Roger
Lochan.
Smith, Samuel Francis
America.
As Flows the Rapid River.
Down to the Sacred Wave.
Morning Light Is Breaking, The.
Softly Fades the Twilight Ray.
Tree-planting.
Smith, Samuel J.
Arise, My Soul! With Rapture Rise!
Smith, Stephen E.
Poet's Photograph, The.
Smith, Stevie
Admire Cranmer!
After-Thought, The.
Airy Christ, The.
Ambassador, The.
Anger's Freeing Power.
Away, Melancholy.
Be Off!

Bereaved Swan, The.
Bog-Face.
Bye Baby Bother.
Celtic Fringe, The.
Celts, The.
Childe Rolandine.
Cold as no love, and wild with all negation.
Correspondence between Mr. Harrison in
    Newcastle and Mr. Sholto Peach Harrison
    in Hull.
Dear Female Heart.
Death Sentence, The.
Deserter, The.
Distractions and the Human Crowd.
Drugs Made Pauline Vague.
Edmonton, thy cemetery.
Egocentric.
Everything Is Swimming.
Exeat.
Fafnir and the Knights.
Frog Prince, The.
From the Coptic.
Galloping Cat, The.
Goodnight.
"Great Unaffected Vampires and the Moon."
He Told His Life Story to Mrs Courtly.
Heavenly City, The.
Her-zie.
Here Lies.
Hop hop, thump thump, *sel.*
House of Mercy, A.
I Love.
I Remember.
I Rode with My Darling.
In My Dreams.
Infelice.
Is It Wise?
Jungle Husband, The.
Lads of the Village, The.
Lady "Rogue" Singleton.
Lament of a Slug-a-Bed's Wife.
Little Boy Lost, The.
Longing for Death because of Feebleness.
Lord Barrenstock.
Love Me!
Magna Est Veritas.
Major Macroo.
Man Is a Spirit.
Mother, among the Dustbins.
Mr. Over.
Murderer, The.
My Cats.
My Hat.
New Age, The.
No Categories!
Not Waving but Drowning.
Occasional Yarrow, The.
One of Many.
Our Bog is Dood.
Parklands, The.
Persian, The.
Pretty.
Private Means Is Dead.
Reversionary.
River God, The.
Satin-clad.
Scorpion.
Singing Cat, The.
Small Lady, The.
Some Are Born.
Sunt Leones.
Tenuous and Precarious.
This Englishwoman is so refined.
Thoughts about the Person from Porlock.
To Carry the Child.
To School!
To the Tune of the Coventry Carol.
Valuable.
Voices against England in the Night.
Was He Married?
Weak Monk, The.

Who Is This Who Howls and Mutters?
Who Killed Lawless Lean?
Smith, Sydney
On Seeing Francis Jeffrey Riding on a
    Donkey, at.
Smith, Sydney Goodsir
Bishop Blomfield's First Charge to His
    Clergy, at.
But ae braithless note, *sel.*
Can I Forget? ("Can I forget the sickle
    mune.").
Cokkils.
Deevil's Waltz, The.
Epistle to John Guthrie.
Here I ligg, Sydney Slugabed Godless Smith,
    sel.
Ineffable Dou, The.
Leander Stormbound.
Mandrake Hert, The.
Mither's Lament, The.
Salad, A.
Under the Eildon Tree.
Ye Mongers Aye Need Masks for Cheatrie.
Smith, Thomas
Why Why Should I the World Be Minding.
Smith, Vivian
At an Exhibition of Historical Paintings,
    Hobart.
Bedlam Hills.
Fishermen, Drowned beyond the West Coast.
Last Summer, The.
Reflections.
Summer Band Concert.
Smith, Walter Chalmers
Coruisk.
Glenaradale.
Smith, Welton
Beast Section, The.
Folding and Unfolding, A.
Interlude.
Malcolm.
Nigga Section, The.
Strategies.
Smith, William
Feed, silly sheep, *sel.*
Some in their harts their mistris colours bears,
    sel.
Sonnet: "My Love, I cannot thy rare beauties
    place," *sel.*
To the Most Excellent and Learned Shepherd,
    Colin Clout, *sel.*
Smith, William Jay
Abruptly All the Palm Trees.
American Primitive.
Autumn.
Bachelor's-Buttons.
Butterfly.
Closing of the Rodeo, The.
Coati-Mundi.
Convoy.
Crocodile.
Cupidon.
Dachshunds ("The dachshund leads a quiet
    life").
Dog.
Elegy: "I stood between two mirrors when
    you died."
Floor and the Ceiling, The.
Giraffe.
Green Place, A.
Hotel Continental.
Independence Day.
Jittery Jim.
Journey to the Interior.
Laughing Time.
Lion.
Love.
Lovebirds.
Lovers, The.
Massacre of the Innocents, The.
Moon.

Morels.
Morning at Arnheim.
Mr. Smith.
Neo-Classical Poem.
Nightwood.
Owl, The.
Park in Milan, The.
Pavane for the Nursery, A.
Persian Miniature.
Plain Talk.
Quail in Autumn.
Queen of the Nile, The.
Random Generation of English Sentences; or,
    The Revenge of the Poets.
Rear Vision.
Room in the Villa, A.
Seal.
Song for a Country Wedding.
Tempest, The.
3 for 25.
Toaster, The.
Today I Have Touched the Earth.
Unicorn.
Vincent Van Gogh.
Voyages of Captain Cock, The.
Winter Morning.
Wooing Lady, The.
World Champions.

Smith-Bowers, Cathy
Fat Lady Travels, The.

Smith, Sidney Goodsir. *See* **Smith, Sydney**
    Goodsir

Smither, Elizabeth
Beak, The.
Best Cowboy Movie, The.
Casanova's Ankle ("Casanova was turned by
    an ankle").
City Girl in the Country.
Finger to Finger.
Fr. Anselm Williams and Br. Leander
    Neville.
Graves as Exercises.
Man Watching His Wife in a Play.
Something Has Swept over Him.
Temptations of St. Antony by His
    Housekeeper.
Terrapin, The.
Visiting Juliet Street.
What the Dead Poets Know.

Smithon, Sebald
Mother in the Snow-Storm, The.

Smithyman, Kendrick
After.
Anzac Ceremony.
Blackleg.
Building Programme.
Circus at the Barber's Shop.
Closedown.
Colville 1964.
Die Bauernhochzeit.
High in the afternoon the dove, *sel.*
Hint for the Incomplete Angler.
Idyll: "Adam and Eve, without serpent."
In Our Manner of Speaking.
Inheritance.
Last Moriori, The.
Night-Piece.
Note on the Social Arts, A.
Parable of Two Talents.
Simple Ode.
Te Rangi Hiroa/ Buck.
Thing Remembered, A.
To Be Absent without Leave.
Tomarata.
Underwater Pieces.
Waikato Railstop.
Waitomo.

Smollet, Tobias
To Leven Water.
Tears of Scotland, The.

Smukler, Linda
Shower, The.

Smyth, Florida Watts
Eternal Contour.
Green Mountain Boy.

Smyth, Paul
Spring that I was six I found in the woods,
    The, *sel.*

Smyth, John. *See* **Smith, John (1662–1717)**

Smythe, Albert Ernest Stafford
Anastasis.

Smythe, Daniel
Driftwood.
From My Thought.

Snapp, Thomas
Actor, The.

Snell, Bertrande Harry
Vampire.

Sneyd, Steve
Asteroid Lil.
Astronaut's Widow.
Bright New Missouri.
Lure, The.

Snodgrass, William DeWitt
After Experience Taught Me.
Albert Speer.
April Inventory.
Campus on the Hill, The.
Child of My Winter Born, *sel.*
Disposal.
Dr. Joseph Goebbels, *sel.*
Easter has come around, *sel.*
Eva Braun, *sel.*
Flat One, A.
Friend, A.
He fed them generously who were his flocks.
Heart's Needle.
Here in the scuffled dust, *sel.*
I thumped on you the best I could, *sel.*
Lady, A.
Late April and you are three; today, *sel.*
Leaving the Motel.
Lobsters in the Window.
Lovers Go Fly a Kite, The.
Lying Awake.
Magic Flute, The.
Marsh, The.
Mementos, I: "Sorting out letters and piles of
    my old."
Mementos, II ("I found them there today.").
Men's Room in the College Chapel, The.
Monet: "Les Nymphéas."
Mother, The.
Mutability.
No one can tell you why, *sel.*
No Use.
Old Apple Trees.
Operation, The.
Owls.
Powwow.
Setting Out.
Song: "Sweet beast, I have gone prowling."
Teen-Ager, A.
Ten Days Leave.
Valediction, A.
Vampire's Aubade.
Vicious winter finally yields, The, *sel.*
Viewing the Body.
Visitation, A.
Vuillard: "The Mother and Sister of the
    Artist."

Snoek, Paul
Ballad of a General.
Duel among the Roses.
End of the Ice Age.
Oxygen for a Castle in the Air.
Panic on the Oil Rig.
Rustic Landscape.
Say It with Vegetables.
Swedish Organs.
To Stay Alive.

Snow, Eliza R.
Think Not When You Gather to Zion.

Snow, Karen
Gifts.

Snow, Laura A. Barter
God Is in Every Tomorrow.

Snow, Sophia P.
Annie and Willie's Prayer.

Snyder, Gary
Above Pate Valley.
After weeks of watching the roof leak.
After weeks of watching the roof leak, *sel.*
After Work.
All the Spirit Powers Went to Their Dancing
    Place.
As for Poets.
August on Sourdough, a Visit from Dick
    Brewer.
August Was Foggy.
Autumn Morning in Shokoku-ji, An, *sel.*
Axe Handles.
Bath, The.
Bedrock.
Before the Stuff Comes Down.
Burning, *sel.*
Burning the Small Dead.
By Frazier Creek Falls.
Dead by the Side of the Road, The.
December.
December at Yase, *sel.*
Eight Sandbars on the Takano River.
Elwha River, The.
Fire in the Hole.
For a Far-out Friend.
For John Chappell.
For Nothing.
For the Children.
For the West.
Four Poems for Robin.
Foxtail Pine.
Front Lines.
Geese Gone Beyond.
Getting in the Wood.
Grand Entry, The.
Hay for the Horses.
Hitch Haiku.
Hop, Skip, and Jump.
How Do You Shape an Axe Handle?
Hunting, *sel.*
I Went into the Maverick Bar.
It.
Journeys.
Kyoto: March.
Late Snow and Lumber Strike of the Summer
    of Fifty-four, The.
LMFBR.
Logging, *sel.*
Long Hair.
Looking at Pictures to Be Put Away.
Manichaeans, The.
Meeting the Mountains.
Mid-August at Sourdough Mountain Lookout.
Milton by Firelight.
Mother Earth; Her Whales.
Nature Green Shit.
Nooksack Valley.
Oil.
Old Dutch Woman, The.
Old Woman Nature.
Out West.
Pine Tree Tops.
Piute Creek.
Praise for Sick Women.
Prayer for the Great Family.
Riprap.
Seventy-five feet hoed rows equals, *sel.*
Siwashing It Out Once in Siuslaw Forest, *sel.*
Sixth-Month Song in the Foothills.
Some Good Things to Be Said for the Iron
    Age.
Song of the Taste.
Soy Sauce.
Spring Night in Shokoku-ji, A, *sel.*
There is another world above this one, *sel.*

They Didn't Hire Him, *sel.*
Things to Do around a Lookout.
Things to Do around Kyoto.
This Tokyo.
Through the Smoke Hole.
To Hell with Your Fertility Cult.
Trail Crew Camp at Bear Valley.
Truth Like the Belly of a Woman Turning, The.
Two Fawns That Didn't See the Light This Spring.
Vapor Trails.
Walking the New York Bedrock Alive in the Sea of Information.
Water.
What Do They Say.
What Happened Here Before.
What You Should Know to Be a Poet.
Why Log Truck Drivers Rise Earlier than Students of Zen.
Wild Mushroom, The.
Work to Do toward Town.

Snyder, Richard
Aging Poet, on a Reading Trip to Dayton, Visits the Air Force Museum and Discovers There a Plane He Once Flew, The.
Blue Sparks in Dark Closets.
Chicago, Summer Past.
Mongoloid Child Handling Shells on the Beach, A.
O I Have Dined on This Delicious Day.
Small Elegy, A.

Snyder, Zilpha Keatley
Silent Hill.
To Dark Eyes Dreaming.
Today Is Saturday.

Sobiloff, Hy
Child's Sight, The.
Wisdom.

Socolow, Liz
Laughing Angel: Reims, The.
Taint.

Södergran, Edith
Decision, A.
Hope.
I saw a tree that was greater than all the others.
Love.
Pain.
Violet Twilights.
We Women.

Sodo
Frogs in rain—as their croaks rise.

Sogen
In all of earth and heaven.
With one stroke I rammed the demon's den.

Sogi
Can't you see it there.
Fallen Leaves in a Valley.
Why lament one's fate.

Sogyo
Waka.

Soha
Frog has lifted a fallen blossom, A.

Soin, Nakajima. *See* **Nakajima Soin**
Soin, Nishiyama. *See* **Nishiyama Soin**
Sojun, Ikkyu. *See* **Ikkyu Sojun**
Sokan (Yamazaki Sokon)
Folding its hands.
If it rains.

Sologub, Fyodor
Amphora, The.
Austere the Music of My Songs.

Sologuren, Javier
Nazca Pottery.
Poem: "At the edge of the window that limits space."
Snow.

Solomon, Marvin
Cages.

Solomos, George P.
Wisdom of the Gazelle.

Solon
Boys and Sport.

Solt, Mary Ellen
Forsythia.
Marriage.
Moonshot Sonnet.
Rain Down.
Wild Crab.

Somervile, William
Advice to the Ladies.
Hare-hunting, *sel.*
Hudibras and Milton Reconciled.
When Autumn smiles, all beauteous in decay, *sel.*
Where fair Sabrina's wand'ring currents flow, *sel.*
Wounded Man and the Swarm of Flies, The.

Somerville, William. *See* **Somervile, William**
Somlyó, György
And June. ?
Marginalia.
Mimesis.
Tale about a Flower.
Tale about a/an.
Tale of the Double Helix.
Today.

Sondheim, Stephen
Gee, Officer Krupke.

Soné
Blessed.

Sone Yoshitada. *See* **Yoshitada**
Song, Cathy
Beauty and Sadness.
Blue Lantern.
Day You Are Born, The.
Girl Powdering Her Neck.
Heaven.
Leaving.
Losing Track.
Lost Sister.
Lucky.
Picture Bride.
Vegetable Air, The.
Waterwings.
Who Makes the Journey.
Youngest Daughter, The.

Soniat, Katherine
Something Left to Say.

Sonnenschein, Hugo
In the Ghetto.
In the Open Fields.

Sonome, Shiba. *See* **Shiba Sonome**
Soodley, F. W.
I love this boy, not for his beauty only.

Sophocles
Antigone.
Chorus: "Fair Salamis, the billow's roar," *sel.*
Chorus: "Oh, may my constant feet not fail," *sel.*
Chorus: "What man is he that yearneth," *sel.*
Colonus' Praise, *sel.*
Endure what life God gives and ask no longer span, *sel.*
Kupris bears trophies away, *sel.*
Thebes of the Seven Gates, *sel.*
Torn between griefs, which grief shall I lament, *sel.*

Sora
When you're depressed, a toad's distant voice too.

Sordello
Simply, it is a man who has died.

Sorell, Walter
All That Matters.

Sorley, Charles Hamilton
All the Hills and Vales Along.
Barbury Camp.
Expectans Expectavi.
In Memoriam S.C.W., V.C.

Rooks.
Saints have adored the lofty soul of you, *sel.*
Seekers, The.
So, there, when sunset made the downs look new, *sel.*
Song of the Ungirt Runners, The.
Such, such is Death: no triumph: no defeat, *sel.*
To Germany.
When You See Millions of the Mouthless Dead.

Soroka, Pauline E.
Understanding.

Sorrells, Helen
Child in a Blue Linen Dress.
From a Correct Address in a Suburb of a Major City.
Mountain Corral.
To a Child Born in Time of Small War.
Town I Left.

Sorrentino, Gilbert
Classic Case, A.
Handbook of Versification.
Zoo, The.

Sosa, Rafael
Guatemalan *Huipil.*

Sosa, Roberto
Freehand Sketch.
Other Death, The.
Poor, The.

Soseki, Natsume. *See* **Natsume Soseki**
Sotades
Banquet, A.

Sotheby, William
Netley Abbey; Midnight.

Soto, Gary
After Tonight.
At the Cantina.
Behind Grandma's House.
Between Words.
Black Hair.
Brown like Us.
Chiapas.
Cruel Boys.
Drought, The.
Elements of San Joaquin, The.
Evening of Ants, The.
Finding a Lucky Number.
Firstborn, The.
Getting Serious.
Graciela.
Heaven.
How Things Work.
In the Madness of Love.
Jungle Café, The.
Kearney Park.
Making Money: Drought Year in Minkler, California.
Map, The.
Mission Tire Factory, 1969.
Morning They Shot Tony Lopez, Barber and Pusher Who Went Too Far, 1958, The.
Oranges.
Plum's Heart, The.
Point, The.
Rain, *sel.*
Saturday under the Sky.
Stars.
Street, The.
Summer.
Tale of Sunlight, The.
When We Wake.
Where We Could Go.
Widow Perez, The.
Wind, *sel.*

Soule, Jean Conder
Surpise.

Soupault, Philippe
Clasped Hands.
Comrade.
Georgia.
Gold Medal.
Horizon.
Life-Saving Medal.
Poet's Counsel, The.
River.
Route.
Say It with Music.
Servitudes.
Sport Items.
Sporting Goods.
Sunday.
Swimmer, The.

Sousa, John Philip
Feast of the Monkeys, The.
Have You Seen the Lady?

Sousa, Noémia da
Appeal.
If You Want to Know Me.
Magaiça.
Our Voice.
Poem of Distant Childhood.
Poem of João, The.

Souster, Raymond
Bed without a Woman, A.
Choosing Coffins.
Collector, The.
Falling of the Snow, The.
Flight of the Roller Coaster.
Hunter, The.
Ladybug.
Lagoons, Hanlan's Point.
Man Who Finds That His Son Has Become a
    Thief, The.
May 15th.
Need of an Angel.
Not Wholly Lost.
On the Rouge.
Reality.
Search.
Six-Quart Basket, The.
Speakers, Columbus Circle.
Summer Afternoon.
Sunday Night Walk.
This Poem Will Never Be Finished.
Ties.
When I See Old Men.
Young Girls.

Soutar, William
Among High Hills.
Auld House, The.
Auld Sang.
Gowk, The.
Hint o' Snow, A.
Makar, The.
On the Hill.
Owre the Hill.
Permanence of the Young Men, The.
Riddle, A: "Yon laddie wi' the gowdan pow."
Room, The.
Scotland.
Song: "Whaur yon broken brig hings owre."
Supper.
Tryst [or Trysting Place], The.
Whigmaleerie, A.

Souter, Charles Henry
After Johnson's Dance.
Irish Lords.
Old John Bax.
What the Red-haired Bo'sun Said.

Southey, Caroline Anne Bowles
Young Gray Head, The.

Southey, Robert
Absolvers, The, sel.
Battle of Blenheim, The.
Bower of Peace, The, sel.
Cataract of Lodore, The.
Dancing Bear, The.

Ebb Tide, The.
Epitaph: "Time and the World, whose
    magnitude and weight."
Filbert, The.
From its sources which well, sel.
Go, Valentine.
God's Judgment on a Wicked Bishop.
High in the Air Exposed.
Hold Your Mad Hands.
Holly Tree, The.
Inchcape Rock, The.
Kehama's Curse, sel.
Lord! Who Art Merciful as Well as Just.
Love Indestructible, sel.
March to Moscow, The.
My days among the dead are past.
Night.
Night of darkness and of storms!, A, sel.
O God! Have Mercy, in This Dreadful Hour.
Ode to a Pig while His Nose Was Being
    Bored.
Old Man's Comforts and How He Gained
    Them, The.
On a Picture by J. M. Wright, Esq.
On the Death of a Favourite Old Spaniel.
Recollections of a Day's Journey in Spain.
She Comes Majestic with Her Swelling Sails.
Soldier's Wife, The.
Southey Looks out of the Window at Greta
    Hill, sel.
Thalaba and the Banquet, sel.
Thalaba and the Magic Thread.
To a Goose [or Gosse]
To a Spider.
Two Poems concerning the Slave trade.
Well of St. Keyne, The.
Widow, The.
Winter Portrait.
Witch, The.

Southey, Robert and Samuel Taylor Coleridge
Devil's Thoughts, The.

Southwell, Robert
At Fotheringay.
Before my face the picture hangs, sel.
Burning Babe, The.
Content and Rich.
Ensamples of Our Savior.
Lewd Love Is Loss.
Look Home.
Loss in Delay.
Love's Servile Lot.
Marie Magdalens Complaint at Christs Death.
Martyrdom of Mary, Queen of Scots, The.
New Heaven, New War [re]
New Prince, New Pomp.
Of the Blessed Sacrament of the Altar.
Seek Flowers of Heaven.
Stanzas from Saint Peter's Complaint, sel.
Times Go by Turns.
Upon the Image of Death.
Wassailer's Song.

Southwick, Marcia
Burial, Green, A.
Dusk.
Finches.
Marsh, The.
Owning a Dead Man.
Solo.
Train Wreck, The.

Souza, Eunice De
Remember Medusa?

Soyinka, Wole
Abiku.
Telephone Conversation.

Spacks, Barry
Counting the Losses.
Emblem of Two Foxes, An.
Finding a Yiddish Paper on the Riverside
    Line.
Freshmen.
Malediction.

Muse, The.
Nursing Home.
October.

Spalding, John Lancaster
At the Ninth Hour, sel.
Believe and Take Heart.
Et Mori Lucrum, sel.
Forepledged.
Nature and the Child, sel.
Silence.
Starry Host, The, sel.
Void Between, The, sel.

Spalding, Susan Marr
Fate.
Sea's Spell, The.
Song's Worth, A.

Spargur, Jill
Tragedy.

Spark, Muriel
Canaan.
Faith and Works.
She Wolf, The.

Sparshott, Francis
Entanglement.
Improperia.
Naming of the Beasts, The.
Paysage Choisi.
Reply to the Committed Intellectual.
Three Seasons.

Spatola, Adriano
Boomerang, The.
Sterility in Metamorphosis.

Spaziani, Maria Luisa
Journey in the Orient.
Pagan Prayer.
To Retreat into Myself, to Accept.
Winter Moon.

Spear, Charles
Animae Superstiti.
At a Danse Macabre.
Balthasar.
Christoph.
Disinherited, The.
1894 in London.
Environs of Vanholt I.
Environs of Vanholt II.
Escape.
From a Book of Hours.
God Save the Stock.
Joachim of Flora.
Karl ("All day he stood at Weeping Cross").
Karl ("Outside among the talking criss-cross
    reeds").
Memoriter.
News from Paris.
O Matre Pulchra.
Prisoner, The.
Promised Land.
Remark.
Scott-Moncrieff's Beowulf.
Vineta.
Watchers, The.

Spear, Roberta
Anniversary, The.
August//Fresno 1973.
Bat, The.
Boundaries.
Bringing Flowers.
Sale of Smoke, A.
White Dress, The.

Spears, Dorothea
Begetting.

Spears, Heather
My Love behind Walls.

Spears, Woodridge
Restoration.

Speght, Rachel
I sought, I found, she asked me what I would,
    sel.
My grief, quoth I, is called Ignorance, sel.

Quoth she, I wish I could prescribe your help, *sel.*
Upon a sudden, as I gazing stood, *sel.*

Spelius, Carol D.
Swimmer's Chant, The.

Spellman, Alfred B.
For My Unborn and Wretched Children.
I Looked and Saw History Caught.
In Orangeburg My Brothers Did.
John Coltrane—an Impartial Review.
Tomorrow the Heroes.
When Black People Are.
Zapata & the Landlord.

Spence, Lewis
Prows o' Reekie, The.

Spence, Michael
Bengal Tiger, The.

Spence, Skip
Motorcycle Irene.

Spencer, Anne
Before the Feast of Shushan.
Creed.
Dunbar.
For Jim, Easter Eve.
I Have a Friend.
Innocence.
Lady, Lady.
Letter to My Sister.
Life-long, Poor Browning.
Lines to a Nasturtium.
Neighbors.
Questing.
Substitution.
Translation.

Spencer, Bernard
Behaviour of Money.
Blue Arm.
Boat Poem.
Castanets.
Cold Night, A.
Delos.
Egyptian Dancer at Shubra.
Empire Clock, The.
Letters.
Olive Trees.
On the "Sievering" Tram.
Part of Plenty.
Regent's Park Terrace.
Rendezvous, The.
Sarcophagi.
Spring Wind, A.
Thousand Killed, A.
Yachts on the Nile.

Spencer, James Harvey
For You.

Spencer, Theodore
Californians, The.
Circle, A.
Circus; or One View of It, The.
Contemporary Song.
Critics, The.
Entropy.
Epitaph: "She was a high-class bitch and a dandy."
Inflatable Globe, The.
Invocation: "Empty my heart, Lord, of daily vices."
Return.

Spencer, Thomas E.
How McDougal Topped the Score.

Spencer, William Robert
Beth Gêlert.

Spender, Stephen
Acts passed beyond the boundary of mere wishing.
After They Have Tired of the Brilliance of Cities.
Auden at Milwaukee.
Auden's Funeral.
Auf dem Wasser zu Singen.
Awaking.

Barn, The.
Beethoven's Death Mask.
Central Heating System.
Daybreak.
Double Shame, The.
Drowned, The.
Elementary School Classroom in a Slum, An.
Empty House, The.
Epilogue: "Time is a thing."
Epilogue to a Human Drama.
Express, The.
Farewell in a Dream.
From All These Events.
Funeral, The.
How strangely this sun reminds me of my love!
"I" Can Never Be a Great Man, An.
I Think Continually of Those Who Were Truly Great.
Ice.
In Railway Halls.
Judas Iscariot.
Landscape near an Aerodrome, The.
Late Stravinsky Listening to Late Beethoven.
Lost.
Madam, your face half-hidden by your hair.
Marginal Field, The.
Marston.
Mask.
Missing My Daughter.
Moving through the silent crowd.
New Year.
Not Palaces [an Era's Crown]
O Night O Trembling Night.
One More New Botched Beginning.
Polar Exploration.
Port Bou.
Prisoners, The.
Pylons, The.
Rolled over on Europe: the sharp dew frozen to stars.
Room above the Square, The.
Seascape.
Shapes of Death, The.
Skull Changed to Glass, A.
Song: "Stranger, you who hide my love."
Statistics.
Stopwatch and an Ordnance Map, A.
Thoughts during an Air Raid.
To Poets and Airmen.
To T. A. R. H.
Two Armies.
Ultima Ratio Regum.
What I Expected [Was]
Whim of Time, A.
Winter and Summer.
Winter Landscape.
Without that once clear aim, the path of flight.
Word.
You were born; must die; were loved; must love.
Your Body Is Stars.

Spenser, Edmund ("Colin Clout")
Address to Venus, *sel.*
Amoretti, *sels.*
And is there care in heaven? and is there love, *sel.*
Aprill, *sel.*
Artegall and Radigund, *sel.*
As pilot well expert in perilous wave, *sel.*
At length nigh to the sea they drew, *sel.*
August, *sel.*
Autumn, *sel.*
Ay me, how many perils doe unfold, *sel.*
Balme, *sel.*
Beauty, *sel.*
Behold, O Man, *sel.*
Bower of Bliss, The, *sel.*
Britomart at Isis' Church, *sel.*
But whoso may, thrice happy man him hold, *sel.*

Calm was the day, and through the trembling air, *sel.*
Cave of Despair, The, *sel.*
Colin Clout at Court, *sel.*
Cymochles and Phaedria, *sel.*
Dame Nature, *sel.*
Dance of the Graces, The, *sel.*
Despair, *sel.*
Dragon, The, *sel.*
Elegy, An: "She fell away in her first ages spring," *sel.*
Envy, *sel.*
Epithalamion: "Ye learned sisters which have oftentimes."
Faire knight (quoth he) Hierusalem that is, *sel.*
"Faire sir," quoth she, "be not displeasd at all," *sel.*
February, *sel.*
Fight of the Red Cross Knight and the Heathen Sansjoy, The, *sel.*
Garden of Adonis, The, *sel.*
Garden of Proserpina, The, *sel.*
Gentle knight was pricking on the plaine, A, *sel.*
Happy Isle, *sel.*
Hard is the doubt, and difficult to deeme, *sel.*
He there now does enjoy eternal rest, *sel.*
Her Heards Be Thousand Fishes, *sel.*
Hill of the Graces, The, *sel.*
House of Ate, The, *sel.*
House of Richesse, The, *sel.*
Huge Leviathan, The, *sel.*
Iambicum Trimetrum.
In such luxurious plentie of all pleasure, *sel.*
It fortuned (as faire it then befell), *sel.*
January Eclogue, *sel.*
Kinds of Trees to Plant, *sel.*
Lament for Daphnaida.
Legend of Britomartis, or of Chastitie, The, *sel.*
Legend of the Knight of the Red Cross, or of Holiness, The, *sel.*
Like as the tide that comes from th' Ocean main, *sel.*
Mask of Cupid, The, *sel.*
Mask of Mutability, The, *sel.*
May, *sel.*
Mermaids, The, *sel.*
Mutability.
Nature's Reply to Mutability, *sel.*
Nought is on earth more sacred or divine, *sel.*
November, *sel.*
Now al is done; bring home the bride againe, *sel.*
Now, at the time that was before agreed, *sel.*
Now strike your sailes, ye jolly mariners, *sel.*
O what an endelesse worke have I in hand, *sel.*
October, *sel.*
Of loves perfection perfectly to speake, *sel.*
Pastoral, A: "From thence into the open fields he fled," *sel.*
Prayer to Venus, *sel.*
Prince Arthur, *sel.*
Prothalamion.
Redoubted knights, and honorable Dames, *sel.*
Right well I wrote, most mighty soveraine, *sel.*
Rivers Come to the Hall of Proteus for the Marriage of the Thames and the Medway, The, *sel.*
Rugged forhead that with grave foresight, The, *sel.*
Scudamor in the Temple of Venus, *sel.*
Sea Monsters, *sel.*
So forth she comes, and to her coche does clyme, *sel.*
So oft as I with state of present time, *sel.*
Sonnet: "After long storms and tempests sad assay."

Sonnet: "Coming [or Comming] to kiss [or kisse] her lips [or lyps], (such grace I found)."

Sonnet: "Doubt which ye misdeeme, fayre love, is vaine, The."

Sonnet: "Fair bosom! fraught with virtue's richest treasure."

Sonnet: "Fair [or Fayre] is my love, when her fair [or fayre] golden heares."

Sonnet: "Fair proud, now tell me, why should fair be proud."

Sonnet: "Fair ye be sure, but cruel and unkind."

Sonnet: "Fresh Spring, the herald of love's mighty king."

Sonnet: "Glorious image of the Maker's beauty, The."

Sonnet: "Happy ye leaves whenas those lily [or lilly] hands."

Sonnet: "How long shall this like dying life endure."

Sonnet: "I joy to see how, in your drawen work."

Sonnet: "In That proud port, which her so goodly graceth."

Sonnet: "Joy of my life, full oft for loving you."

Sonnet: "Lacking my Love, I go from place to place."

Sonnet: "Let not one sparke of filthy lustfull fyre."

Sonnet: "Like [or Lyke] a huntsman after weary chase [or chace]."

Sonnet: "Like as a ship, that through the ocean wyde."

Sonnet: "Like as the culver on the bared bough."

Sonnet: "Mark when she smiles with amiable cheer."

Sonnet: "Men call you fair [or fayre], and you do[e] credit it,"

Sonnet: "Merry cuckoo, messenger of spring, The."

Sonnet: "More than most fair [or fayre], full of the living fire [or fyre]."

Sonnet: "Most glorious Lord of Life [or Lyfe]! that on this day."

Sonnet: "Most happy letters framed by skilfull trade."

Sonnet: "My Love is like to ice, and I to fire."

Sonnet: "Of this world's theatre in which we stay."

Sonnet: "Oft when my spirit doth spread her bolder wings."

Sonnet: "One day as I unwarily did gaze."

Sonnet: "One day I wrote her name upon the strand."

Sonnet: "Rudely thou wrongst my dear heart's desire."

Sonnet: "So as they travelled, the drouping night."

Sonnet: "So oft as I her beauty do behold."

Sonnet: "Sweet is the rose, but grows upon a brere."

Sonnet: "This holy season, fit to fast and pray."

Sonnet: "Trust not the treason of those smiling looks."

Sonnet: "Unrighteous Lord of love, what law is this."

Sonnet: "Was it a dream, or did I see it plain?"

Sonnet: "Weary year his race now having run, The."

Sonnet: "What guile [or guyle] is this, that those her golden tresses."

Sonnet: "When those renowned noble peers of Greece."

Sonnet: "Ye tradeful merchants that, with weary toil."

"Soverayne beauty which I doo admire, The", sel.

Such skill, matcht with such courage as he had, sel.

Sudden upriseth from her stately palace, sel.

Summer, sel.

Temple of Venus, The, sel.

Then said that royall Pere in sober wise, sel.

Thence forward by that painfull way they pas, sel.

There the most daintie Paradise on ground, sel.

They sate to meat, and Satyrane his chaunce, sel.

Tho when as chearelesse night ycovered had, sel.

Thus being entered, they behold around, sel.

Wake, now my love, awake; for it is time, sel.

Well may I weene, faire ladies, all this while, sel.

What If Some Little Paine the Passage Have, sel.

When I bethinke me on that speech whyleare, sel.

Whiles someone did chant this lovely lay, The, sel.

Who Is the Same, Which at My Window Peepes?, sel.

Who now does follow the foule Blatant Beast, sel.

Who travels by the wearie wandring way, sel.

Winter, sel.

With that I saw two swans of goodly hue, sel.

Spera, Stephen
Vampyr.

"Speranza." *See* **Wilde, Lady Jane Francesca**

Speyer, Leonora
A B C's in Green.
Measure Me, Sky.
Swans.
X-Ray.

Spicer, J. L.
Communion.

Spicer, Jack
Among the coffee cups and soup toureens walked Beauty.
Book of Gawain, The, sel.
Book of Music, A.
Central Park West.
Five Words for Joe Dunn on His 22nd Birthday.
Four Poems for *The St. Louis Sporting News*.
"Graphemics," 1.
"Graphemics," 10.
Imaginary Elegies, I-IV.
Like a scared rabbit running over and, sel.
Love is not mocked whatever use, sel.
Walden Pond/ All those noxious gases rising from it, sel.

Spilka, Arnold
Don't Tell Me That I Talk Too Much!
Flowers are a Silly Bunch.
I Saw a Little Girl I Hate.
I'm Not Really Lazy.
Puzzle.
Slippery Sam.

Spingarn, Lawrence P.
Museum Piece.
Philatelic Lessons: The German Collection.

Spire, André
Abishag.
Ancient Law, The.
Dust.
Hear, O Israel!
It Was Not You.
Lonely.
Now You're Content.
Nudities.
Poetics.
Pogroms.
Spring.

Spires, Elizabeth
Courtesan with Fan.
Skins.
Tequila.
Travellers, The.
Two Shadows.
Widow's Walk.
0°.

Spitta, Karl Johann Philipp
O Blessèd House, That Cheerfully Receiveth.
Unchanging Jesus.

Spivack, Kathleen
But You, My Darling, Should Have Married the Prince.
Child's Visit to the Biology Lab, A.
Daughterly.
Dido: Swarming.
Drifting.
Dust.
Judgment, The.
Love u.s.a.
March 1st.
Meeting, The.
Moments-of-Past-Happiness Quilt, The.
Mythmaking.
Private Pain in Time of Trouble.
Servant of Others, The.
Visions.
West Virginia Handicrafts.

Spofford, Harriet Prescott
Can't.
Evanescence.
Every Day Thanksgiving Day.
Fossil Raindrops, The.
How We Became a Nation.
Hunt, The.
Music in the Night.
Phantoms All.
Pines, The.
Sigh, A.
Snowdrop, A.
Voice.

Spooner, Lawrence
On Giving Up Smoking, sel.

Sprague, Charles
Brothers, The.
Fiction, sel.
Indians.
News, The, sel.
Winged Worshippers, The.

Spratt, Thomas
On His Mistress Drown'd.

Sprigg, Christopher St. John. *See* **"Caudwell, Christopher"**

Spring-Rice, Cecil Arthur
Day.
God of all power and might, sel.
I Vow to Thee, My Country.

Springer, Nancy
Wolf Girl Speaks, The.

Springer, Sherma
Ms Understood.

Sprod, G. N.
Request Number.

Sprouse, Sarah Elizabeth
Little Song of Work, A.

Squier, Charles
No Se Van Los Pastores.

Squire, Sir John Collings ("Solomon Eagle")
Ballade of the Poetic Life.
Birds, trees and flow'rs they bring to me, sel.
Celtic Lyric, The.
Dog's Death, A.
Everlasting Mercy, The.
Honesty at a Fire.
I left thee with a courage high, sel.
If Gray Had Had to Write His Elegy in the Cemetery of Spoon River Instead of in That of Stoke Poges.
If Pope Had Written "Break, Break, Break."
Interior.

It did not last; the Devil howling Ho.
March, The.
Now the declining fulgent orb of day, *sel.*
Numerous Celts.
O let your strong imagination turn, *sel.*
Passing of Arthur, The.
She Dwelt among the Untrodden Ways.
Ship, The.
So lay the youth with Mary in his arms, *sel.*
Sonnet: "There was an Indian, who had known no change."
Stockyard, The.
To a Bull-Dog.
To Miss L. F. on the Occasion of Her Departure for the Continent.
Under.
Vision of Truth, A.
Winter Nightfall.

Ssu-k'ung Shu
In Illness, Dismissing My Singing Girl.
Rebellion Over, I See Off a Friend Who Is Returning North, The.

Stach, Carl L.
Final Prospect, The.

Stack, Philip ("Kid Kazanova")
Admonition.

Staff, Leopold
Bridge, The.
Foundations.
Three Towns.

Stafford, Sarah
Unborn, The.

Stafford, Wendell Phillips
Invocation: "O Thou whose equal purpose runs."

Stafford, William
Accountability.
Across Kansas.
Address to the Vacationers at Cape Lookout, An.
Adults Only.
After Arguing against the Contention That Art Must Come from Discontent.
After Plotinus.
Among Strangers.
Animal That Drank Up Sound, The.
Answerers.
Any Time.
Assurance.
At Cove on the Crooked River ("At cove at our camp in the open canyon").
At the Bomb Testing Site.
At the Edge of Town.
At the Klamath Berry Festival.
At the Playground.
At the Un-National Monument along the Canadian Border.
Baby Ten Months Old Looks at the Public Domain, A.
Before the Big Storm.
Behind the Falls.
Bess.
Bifocal.
Birthday.
Bring the North.
Broken Home.
Burning a Book.
Ceremony.
Certain Bend, A.
Chickens the Weasel Killed.
Childish Things.
Christianite.
Coming to Know.
Concealment: Ishi, the Last Wild Indian, The.
Day You Are Reading This, The.
Early Ones, The.
Earth Dweller.
Epitaph Ending in And, The.
Escape, The.
Fall Journey.
Family Turn, A.

Farm on the Great Plains, The.
Father's voice.
Fish Counter at Bonneville, The.
For a Daughter Gone Away.
For the Grave of Daniel Boone.
Found in a Storm.
Friend Who Never Came.
Glances.
Holding the Sky.
Humanities Lecture.
In a Museum in the Capital.
In Dear Detail, by Ideal Light.
In Fur.
In the Deep Channel.
In the Oregon Country.
In Time of Need.
Indian Cave Jerry Ramsey Found, The.
Introduction to Some Poems, An.
Lake Chelan.
Late at Night.
Late, Passing Prairie Farm.
Letter from Oregon.
Lifting Illegal Nets by Flashlight.
Listening.
Long Distance.
Looking West.
Maybe Alone on My Bike.
Memorandum.
Moles.
Moment, The.
Monday.
Montana Eclogue.
Monuments for a Friendly Girl at a Tenth Grade Party.
My Father; October 1942.
Notice What This Poem Is Not Doing.
Now.
Observation Car and Cigar.
Ode to Garlic.
One Home.
Oregon Message, An.
Peace Walk.
People of the South Wind.
Pilgrims.
Priest Lake.
Quiet Town.
Religion Back Home.
Remembering Althea.
Report from a Far Place.
Report from K9 Operator Rover on the Motel at Grand Island.
Report to Crazy Horse.
Requiem: "Mother is gone. Bird songs wouldn't let her breathe."
Rescued Year, The.
Returned to Say.
Right Now.
Rover.
Sayings from the Northern Ice.
School Days.
Shepherd.
Some Night Again.
Sound from the Earth, A.
Stared Story, A.
Stick in the Forest, The.
Stories from Kansas.
Story, A.
Story That Could Be True, A.
Stranger Not Ourselves, The.
Strangers.
Strokes.
Survey, A.
Swerve, The.
Temporary Facts.
These Days.
These Leaves.
Things That Happen.
Things That Happen Where There Aren't Any People.
Tides.
Time.
Together Again.

Tornado.
Tourist Country.
Traveling through the Dark.
Trip, The.
Trusting Each Other.
Ultimate Problems.
Vacation.
View from Here, The.
Visions.
Vocation.
Walking the Wilderness.
Walking West.
Walking with Your Eyes Shut.
Well Rising, The.
West of Your City.
When We Looked Back.
Whole Story, The.
Winterward.
With Kit, Age 7, at the Beach.

Stagg, John
Vampyre, The.

Stagnelius, Erik Johann
Memory.

Stalker, Philip A.
Talk.

Stallworthy, Jon
Again.
Almond Tree, The.
At Half Past Three in the Afternoon.
Beginning of the End, The.
Letter to a Friend.
Miss Lavender.
Mother Tongue.
Poem about Poems about Vietnam, A.
Pour Commencer.
Question of Form and Content, A.
Sindhi Woman.
Source, The.
This Morning.
Walking against the Wind.
War Story.

Stamp, Catriona
Rebirth.

Stampa, Gaspara
At dawn of the day the Creator.
By Now I Am So Tired of Waiting.
Deeply repentant of my sinful ways.
Holy angels, in envy I cast no sigh.
Hunger.
I am now so weary with waiting.
If I could believe that death.
Often I compare my lord to heaven.
Often when alone I liken my lord/ to the cosmos.
Oh Count, Where Has Gone.
Stars have given me a hard fate, The.
When before those eyes, my life and light.
With Deep Repentance for My Wasted Days.
Women, whoever wishes to know my lord.

Standish, Celia
New Year's Days.

Stanfield, Leontine
Little Cat Angel, The.

Stanford, Ann
Bear, The.
Beating, The.
Flood, The.
Genia, The.
Night of Souls.
Omens, The.
Riders, The.
Umbrella, The.
Voices Inescapable, The.
Weeds.

Stanford, Anne
Brother Symmes conversed with her on the ship, *sel.*

Stanford, Derek
In Memoriam M. Tambimuttu.
Janus Season.

Stanford, Frank
Allegory of Death and Night.
Between Love and Death.
Intruder, The.
Inventory.
Island Funeral.
Place on a Grave.
Stanford, William Bedell
Angelus-Time near Dublin.
Before Salamis.
To a Greek Ship in the Port of Dublin.
Undertone.
Stanhope, Philip Dormer. *See* **Chesterfield,**
Philip Dormer Stanhope, 4th Earl of
Stanley, Mary
Put Off Constricting Day.
Sestina: "Body of my love is a familiar
country, The."
Wife Speaks, The.
Stanley, Thomas
All Things Drink.
Beauty.
Combat, The.
Divorce, The.
Exequies, The.
Expectation.
Grasshopper, The.
La Belle Confidente.
Magnet, The.
Old I Am.
On a Violet in Her Breast.
Relapse, The.
Repulse, The.
Roses.
Song: "Fool, take up thy shaft again."
Self-Deceaver, The.
Spring.
Swallow, The.
Time Recover'd.
To One That Pleaded Her Own Want of
Merit.
Tombe, The.
Wish, The.
Would I were air that thou with heat opprest.
Youthful Age.
Stansbury, Joseph
Lords of the Main, The.
New Song, A.
To Cordelia
Stansbury, Mary Anna Phinney
How He Saved St. Michael's.
Surprise at Ticonderoga, The.
Stanton, Frank Lebby
Good Lawd Know My Name, De.
Graveyard Rabbit, The.
Keep a-Goin.'
Little Way, A.
Mocking-Bird, The.
Old Hymns, The.
One Country.
Plantation Ditty, A.
Sweetes' Li'l' Feller.
"Tollable Well!"
Wearyin' for You.
Stanton, Henry T.
Moneyless Men, The.
Stanton, Maura
All-Night Waitress, The.
At the Cochise Tourist Pavilion.
At the Landing.
Atlantis.
Bathroom Walls.
Biography.
Childhood.
Cuckoo Clock, The.
Extracts: From the Journal of Elisa Lynch.
Good People.
Judith Recalls Holofernes.
Letter to Kafka.
Little Ode for X.
Palinode.
Shoplifters.

Sunday Graveyard.
Visibility.
Wilderness, The.
Stanyhurst, Richard
Prayer to the Holy Trinity, A.
Stapylton, Sir Robert
Bard's Song, The.
Starbird, Kate
Mother.
Starbird, Kaye
Cockroaches.
Don't Ever Cross a Crocodile.
Eat-It-All Elaine.
Flying.
Horse-Chestnut Time.
Measles.
Wendy in Winter.
Starbuck, George
Amazing Gracious Living on I-93.
Aspects of Spring in Greater Boston, *sel.*
Bone Thoughts on a Dry Day: Chicago.
Chip.
Cold Fire.
Communication to the City Fathers of Boston.
Double Semi-Sestina.
Hardearned Overturned Caribbean Basin
Stomp.
High Renaissance.
Last Straw.
Margaret Are You Drug.
Monarch of the Sea.
New Republic Is Infuriated at the News
Coverage, The.
New Strain.
Of Late.
On First Looking in on Blodgett's *Keats's*
"Chapman's Homer."
Out in the Cold.
Pit Viper.
Poems from a First Year in Boston.
Purple Goatee.
S. L. A. B. S. for George Herbert.
Said.
Skin Divers, The.
Songs for the Old New Jersey Shelling the
Shouf.
Sonnet with a Different Letter at the End of
Every Line.
Spell against Spelling, The.
Spin Control.
Starry Night, The.
Technologies.
Things Keep Dawning on President Joshua.
To His Chi Mistress.
Translations from the English.
Whaddaya Do for Action in This Place?
Starbuck, Victor
Seekers, The.
Starck, Mary
Reign of Peace, The.
Starkey, James. *See* **"O'Sullivan, Seumas"**
Starkweather, Pauline
Two Mountains Men Have Climbed.
Starr, Hattie
Little Alabama Coon.
Statius (Publius Papinius Statius)
Sleep.
Too harsh the man who setting bounds to
grief, *sel.*
Stauffer, Donald A.
Bulldozer, The.
Lemmings, The.
Time Zones for Forty-four.
Staughton, William
Tell Us, Ye Servants of the Lord.
Stead, Christian Karlson
Air New Zealand, *sel.*
All Night It Bullied You, *sel.*
All over the plain of the world lovers are
being hurt, *sel.*
April Notebook.
Art has nothing to do with perfect circles, *sel.*

Carpe Diem.
Dulcinea walks, *sel.*
End of scene Catullus, *sel.*
Fucking, I feel at one with the world, *sel.*
He said God who gave the wound would give
the cure, *sel.*
Is there another poetry than the poetry of
celebration?, *sel.*
Natural Grace, A.
Odysseus under wet snapping sheets, *sel.*
Pictures in a Gallery Undersea.
Quesada on the dunes hurls himself at the
elements, *sel.*
Rain, and a flurry of wind shaking the pear's
white blossom, *sel.*
Spring is a recurring astonishment—like
poetry, *sel.*
That the balls of the lover are not larger than
the balls of the priest, *sel.*
This May Be Your Captain Speaking.
Walking westward/ you have it all before you,
sel.
Stead, William Force
I Closed My Eyes To-Day and Saw.
I thought the night without a sound was
falling, *sel.*
Stearns, L. D.
Triumph.
Stebbins, Mary Elizabeth DeWitt
Harold the Valiant.
Sunflower to the Sun, The.
Stedman, Edmund Clarence
Aaron Burr's Wooing.
Abraham Lincoln.
Ballad of Lager Bier, The.
Cuba.
Custer.
Discoverer, The.
Falstaff's Song.
Flight of the Birds, The.
Gettysburg.
Going a-Nutting.
Hand of Lincoln, The.
Helen Keller.
How Old Brown Took Harper's Ferry.
Hymn of [*or* to] the West.
Invocation: "Thou, whose endearing hand
once laid in sooth."
Israel Freyer's Bid for Gold.
Kearny at Seven Pines.
Liberty Enlightening the World.
Morgan.
Mors Benefica.
Mother's Picture, A.
On a Great Man Whose Mind Is Clouding.
Pan in Wall Street.
Peter Stuyvesant's New Year's Call.
Prelude: "I saw the constellated matin choir."
Quest, *sel.*
Salem.
Si Jeunesse Savait!
Song from a Drama.
Sumter.
Thou, who dost feel Life's vessel strand, *sel.*
Treason's Last Device.
Wanted—A Man.
What the Winds Bring.
World Well Lost, The.
Steegmuller, Francis
Le Hibou et la Poussiquette.
Steel, M.
Little Lucy Lester.
Steele, Anne
O How Sweet Are Thy Words!
Steele, Frank
Close to Home.
Country Greeting.
Departure, The.
Greener Grass.
Markers.
Markings.
Moving.

Steele, Paul Curry
Clerihew: "Mata Hari/ Was later sorry."
Steele, Sir Richard
Trim's Song: The Fair Kitchen-Maid, *sel.*
Steele, Timothy
Aurora.
Devotional Sonnet, A.
Epitaph: "Here lies Sir Tact, a diplomatic
fellow."
One Morning.
Rural Colloquy with a Painter.
Sapphics against Anger.
Sheets, The.
Timothy.
Wait.
Steendam, Jacob
Complaint of New Amsterdam, The.
Oh, Sing to God.
Praise of New Netherland, The.
When I Admire the Greatness.
Steere, Richard
Earth Felicities, Heavens Allowances.
Monumental Memorial of Marine Mercy, A.
On a Sea-Storm nigh the Coast.
Poem upon the Caelestial Embassy, A.
Steese, Edward
Tenth Reunion.
Stefan, Verena
Woman Moving with You in Coitus, The.
Stefanile, Felix
Vampire Bride.
Steiger, Anatoly
Ancient Custom, An.
Words from the Window of a Railway Car.
Stein, Evaleen
Baby's Baking.
Budding-Time Too Brief.
Flood-Time on the Marshes.
In Mexico.
In Youth.
Wild Beasts.
Stein, Gertrude
Blue Coat, A, *sel.*
Cézanne.
Colored Hats, *sel.*
Dog, A, *sel.*
Full well I know that she is there, *sel.*
George Hugnet.
How do you like what you have, *sel.*
How I wish I were able to say what I think,
sel.
I Am Rose.
I love my love with a v, *sel.*
Ladies' Voices.
More, *sel.*
New Cup and Saucer, A, *sel.*
Nothing Elegant, *sel.*
Petticoat, A, *sel.*
Piano, A, *sel.*
Pigeons on the grass alas, *sel.*
Red Roses, *sel.*
Roast Potatoes.
Sacred.
Sound, A, *sel.*
Stanzas in Meditation.
Susie Asado.
Umbrella, An, *sel.*
Valentine to Sherwood Anderson, A.
Water Raining, *sel.*
Yet Dish.
Stein, Kurt M.
Morning Song.
Vor a Gauguin Picture zu Singen.
Stein, Rose M.
Lines to Mother.
Steinbarg, Eliezer
Bayonet and the Needle, The.
Horse and the Whip, The.
"Shatnes" or Uncleanliness.
Terrible Thought, A.

Umbrella, the Cane, and the Broom, The.
Where Is Justice?
Steinberg, Jakov
Donkey Will Carry You, A.
Heart, The.
With a Book at Twilight.
World Is Not a Fenced-off Garden, The.
Steinberg, Jacob. *See* **Steinberg, Jakov**
Steinbergh, Judith W.
Secret Place, A.
Steingart, Moishe
Generations.
Last Fire, The.
Steingass, David
For a Friend.
Steingesser, Martin
Skibomber, The.
Steinman, D. B.
Blueprint.
"Stella." *See* **Johnson, Esther**
Stembridge, Jane
City.
Loving.
Mrs. Hamer.
Stencl, A. N.
Ezekiel.
Stennett, Samuel
Promised Land, The.
Stepanchev, Stephen
Inner Brother.
Japanese.
No Furlough.
Strength to War.
Stephanou, Lydia
"Case of Assault, A."
Stephen, Alexander Maitland
Bring Torches.
Capilano ("Capilano, in the canyon").
Stephen, James Kenneth
After the Golden Wedding.
Cynicus to W. Shakspere, *sel.*
Drinking Song.
Grievance, A.
Heaven and Hell.
In the Backs.
Last Ride Together (from Her Point of View),
The.
Old School List, The.
On a Parisian Boulevard.
On a Rhine Steamer [*or* England and
America, I]
Remonstrance, A.
Senex to Matt. Prior, *sel.*
She's not a faultless woman; no!, *sel.*
Sincere Flattery of R. B.
Sincere Flattery of W. W. (Americanus).
Sonnet, A: "Two voices are there: one is of
the deep."
Splinter, The.
Thought, A.
To R. K.
Stephens, Alan
Prologue: Moments in a Glade.
Stephens, Brunton
Dominion of Australia, The.
My Other Chinee Cook.
Stephens, James
Blue Blood.
Cage, The.
Canal Bank, The.
Centaurs, The.
Check.
Christmas at Freelands.
College of Surgeons, The.
Crest Jewel, The.
Daisies, The.
Danny Murphy.
Dark Wings.
Day and Night.
Devil's Bag, The.
Donnybrook.
Evening.

Fifteen Acres, The.
Goat Paths, The.
Good and Bad.
Hate.
In the Night.
In the Orchard.
In the Poppy Field.
In Waste Places.
Lake, The.
Little Things.
Main-Deep, The.
Night, The.
Odell.
Outcast, The.
Red-haired Man's Wife, The.
Secret, The.
Seumas Beg.
Shell, The.
Snare, The.
Sweet Apple.
To the Four Courts, Please.
Turn of the Road, The.
Voice of God, The.
Watcher, The.
What the Devil Said.
When You Walk.
Whisperer, The.
White Fields.
Why Tomas Cam Was Grumpy.
Wind, The.
Woman Is a Branchy Tree, A.
Wood of Flowers, The.
Stephens, Michael
Good Ship, The.
Mom's Homecooked Trees.
Stephenson, John
If angels sung a Savior's birth, at.
Stephenson, Shelby
Rose and a Baby Ruth, A.
Stepney, George
On the University of Cambridge's Burning the
Duke of Monmouth's Picture.
Sterling, Andrew B.
Meet Me in St. Louis, Louis.
On a Sunday Afternoon.
Under the Anheuser Bush.
What You Goin' to Do When the Rent Comes
'Round?
Sterling, George
Omnia Exeunt in Mysterium.
Sterling, John
Alfred the Harper.
Louis XV.
Stern, Gerald
At Bickford's.
Baja.
Cemetery of Orange Trees in Crete, The.
Dancing, The.
Days of 1978.
Dog, The.
Fritz.
Ground Hog Lock.
Hidden Justice.
I Remember Galileo.
I Sometimes Think of the Lamb.
Ice, Ice.
In Carpenter's Woods.
Lord, Forgive a Spirit.
My Swallows.
Pick and Poke.
Power of Maples, The.
Romance.
Sensitive Knife, The.
Shirt Poem, The.
Song: "There's nothing in this gardenous
world more delightful."
This Was a Wonderful Night.
War against the Jews, The.
Weeping and Wailing.
Stern, Noah
Grave at Cassino.
His Mother's Love.

Stern, Sharon A.
Bitter Herbs.
Kol Nidre.
Reawakening.
Talisman 18.
Sternberg, Jacob
Little Birds.
Sternburg, Janet
My Mother's Breakfront.
"Sterne, Stuart" (Gertrude Bloede)
My Father's Child.
Night after Night.
Soul, Wherefore Fret Thee?
Sternhold, Thomas
I Lift My Heart to Thee.
Lord Descended from Above, The.
My Shepherd Is the Living Lord.
Sternlieb, Barry
Valley Blood.
Sterry, Joseph Ashby. *See* **Ashby-Sterry, Joseph**
Stetler, Charles B.
Man of Action, A.
Stetson, Charlotte Perkins. *See* **Gilman, Charlotte Perkins Stetson**
Stevens, Alex
In Scorching Time.
Stevens, George Alexander
Bartleme Fair.
Pastoral, A: "By the side of a green stagnate pool."
Repentance.
Simple Pastoral, A.
Stevens, George W.
Organist, The.
Stevens, Wallace
And for what, except for you, do I feel love?, *sel.*
Anecdote of the Jar.
Anecdote of the Prince of Peacocks.
Angel Surrounded by Paysans.
Annual Gaiety.
Arrival at the Waldorf.
Asides on the Oboe.
Auroras of Autumn, The.
Autumn.
Autumn Refrain.
Bantams in Pine-Woods.
Begin, ephebe, by perceiving the idea, *sel.*
Beginning, The.
Bethou me, said sparrow, to the crackled blade, *sel.*
Bouquet of Belle Scavoir.
Brave Man, The.
Candle, a Saint, The.
Comedian as the Letter C, The.
Connoisseur of Chaos.
Continual Conversation with a Silent Man.
Contrary Theses (I).
Course of a Particular, The.
Crude Foyer.
Cuisine Bourgeoise.
Curtains in the House of the Metaphysician, The.
Dance of the Macabre Mice.
Death of a Soldier, The.
Depression before Spring.
Disillusionment of Ten o'Clock.
Domination of Black.
Dry Loaf.
Earthy Anecdote.
Emperor of Ice-Cream, The.
Esthétique du Mal.
Evening without Angels.
Extract from Addresses to the Academy of Fine Ideas, An.
Farewell to an idea. A cabin stands, *sel.*
Farewell to an idea. The mother's face, *sel.*
Farewell to Florida.
Final Soliloquy of the Interior Paramour.
First idea was not our own, The. Adam, *sel.*

Flyer's Fall.
Gallant Château.
Girl in a Nightgown.
Glass of Water, The.
Great Statue of the General Du Puy, The, *sel.*
Gubbinal.
He was at Naples writing letters home, *sel.*
Hibiscus on the Sleeping Shores.
High poetry and low.
High-toned Old Christian Woman, A.
Holiday in Reality.
Homunculus et la Belle Étoile.
House Was Quiet and the World Was Calm, The.
How red the rose that is the soldier's wound, *sel.*
I cannot bring a world quite round, *sel.*
I feel an apparition.
Idea of Order at Key West, The.
Idiom of the Hero.
In the Carolinas.
Indigo Glass in the Grass, The.
Irish Cliffs of Moher, The.
Is there an imagination that sits enthroned, *sel.*
It feels good as it is without the giant, *sel.*
It is a theatre floating through the clouds, *sel.*
Large Red Man Reading.
Less and Less Human, O Savage Spirit.
Life is a bitter aspic. We are not, *sel.*
Life Is Motion.
Major abstraction is the idea of man, The, *sel.*
Man on the Dump, The.
Man with the Blue Guitar, The.
Martial Cadenza.
Men Made out of Words.
Metamorphosis.
Metaphor as Degeneration.
Metaphors of a Magnifico.
Motive for Metaphor, The.
Mrs. Alfred Uruguay.
No Possum, No Sop, No Taters.
Not Ideas about the Thing but the Thing Itself.
Nuances of a Theme by Williams.
Of Heaven Considered as a Tomb.
Of Mere Being.
Of Modern Poetry.
Of the Manner of Addressing Clouds.
Old Lutheran Bells at Home, The.
On an Old Horn.
On the Manner of Addressing Clouds.
On the Road Home.
Ordinary Women, The.
Our Stars Come from Ireland.
Owl in the Sarcophagus, The.
Paltry Nude Starts on a Spring Voyage, The.
Parochial Theme.
Peter Quince at the Clavier.
Plain Sense of Things, The.
Planet on the Table, The.
Pleasures of Merely Circulating, The.
Plot against the Giant, The.
Ploughing on Sunday.
Poem That Took the Place of a Mountain, The.
Poems of Our Climate, The.
Poetry Is a Destructive Force.
Polo Ponies Practicing.
Postcard from the Volcano, A.
Prejudice against the Past, The.
President Ordains the Bee to Be, The, *sel.*
Primitive like an Orb, A.
Prologues to What Is Possible.
Puella Parvula.
Quiet Normal Life, A.
Rabbit as King of the Ghosts, A.
Reality Is an Activity of the Most August Imagination.
Repetitions of a Young Captain.
River of Rivers in Connecticut, The.
Room on a Garden, A.

Sad Strains of a Gay Waltz.
Sea Surface Full of Clouds.
Sense of the Sleight-of-Hand Man, The.
Snow Man, The.
So-and-So Reclining on Her Couch.
Soldier, There Is a War between the Mind, *sel.*
Song of Fixed Accord.
Souls of Women at Night, The.
Statue against a Clear Sky, *sel.*
Study of Two Pears.
Sun, in clownish yellow, but not a clown, The, *sel.*
Sunday Morning.
Table Talk.
Tattoo.
Tea at the Palaz of Hoon.
These locusts by day, these crickets by night.
Thirteen Ways of Looking at a Blackbird.
This is where the serpent lives, the bodiless, *sel.*
This Solitude of Cataracts.
To an Old Philosopher in Rome.
To the One of Fictive Music.
Tom-tom, c'est moi. The blue guitar, *sel.*
Tune beyond us as we are, A, *sel.*
Two Figures in Dense Violet Light.
Ultimate Poem Is Abstract, The.
Unhappy people in a happy world, An, *sel.*
Vacancy in the Park.
When was it that the particles became.
Whistle Aloud, Too Weedy Wren, *sel.*
Woman That Had More Babies than That, The.
World as Meditation, The.
World without Peculiarity.
Worms at Heaven's Gate, The.
Stevenson, Anne
Attitudes and Beliefs.
By the Boat House, Oxford.
Demolition, The.
Fiction-Makers, The.
From an Asylum; Kathy Chattle to Her Mother, Ruth Arbeiter.
Giving Rabbit to My Cat Bonnie.
Hands.
Himalayan Balsam.
Making Poetry.
Naming the Flowers.
Price, The.
Shale.
Sous-Entendu.
Suburb, The.
Suicide.
This.
Stevenson, Burton Egbert
Henry Hudson's Quest.
Peace Message, The.
Stevenson, Candace Thurber
Public Library.
Signatures.
Stevenson, James
Gallant Fighting "Joe," The.
Stevenson, Lionel
Gulls and Dreams.
In a Desert Town.
Summer Interlude.
Stevenson, Patric
Anglo-Eire Vignette.
Autumnal Consummation.
Corn Cañon.
Dogrose.
Stevenson, Robert Louis
Alcaics; to H. F. B.
Armies in the Fire.
As with heaped bees at hiving time.
At the Seaside.
Bed in Summer.
Block City.
Blows the Wind Today.
Bright is the ring of words.

Brilliant kernel of the night, The, *sel.*
Browning.
Careful Angler, The.
Celestial Surgeon, The.
Child's Thought, A.
Christmas at Sea.
Christmas Prayer, A.
Cow, The.
Ditty: "Cock shall crow, The."
Dumb Soldier, The.
Escape at Bedtime.
Evensong.
Fair Isle at Sea—thy lovely name.
Far-Farers, The.
Farewell to the Farm.
Flowers, The.
Foreign Children.
Foreign Lands.
Fragment: "Thou strainest through the
    mountain fern."
From a Railway Carriage.
Good and Bad Children.
Good Boy, A.
Good Play, A.
Happy Thought.
Henry James.
Home No More Home to Me.
House Beautiful, The.
I Am a Hunchback.
I saw red evening through the rain.
If This Were Faith.
Ille Terrarum.
In autumn when the woods are red.
In Memoriam F. A. S.
In the Highlands.
In the States.
It's an owercome sooth for age an' youth.
Lamplighter, The.
Land of Counterpane, The.
Land of Nod, The.
Land of Story-Books, The.
Last night we had a thunderstorm in style.
Last Sight, The.
Man Sails the Deep a While.
Marching Song.
Mile an' a Bittock, A.
Moon, The.
Morning drum-call on my eager ear, The.
My Bed Is a Boat ("My bed is like a little
    boat").
My house, I say. But hark to the sunny
    doves.
My Shadow.
Nest Eggs.
Not I.
O dull, cold northern sky.
On the great streams the ships may go, *sel.*
Pirate Ditty, *sel.*
Pirate Story.
Portrait, A.
Prayer: "I ask good things that I detest."
Rain.
Requiem: "Under the wide and starry sky."
Romance.
Say not of me that weakly I declined.
Sick Child, The.
Since Thou Hast Given Me This Good Hope,
    O God.
Sing me a song of a lad that is gone.
Skerryvore.
So live, so love, so use that fragile hour.
Song of the Road, A.
Spaewife, The.
Stormy Nights.
Summer Sun.
Sun's Travels, The.
Swallows travel to and fro.
Swing, The.
System.
Ticonderoga; a Legend of the West
    Highlands.
Time to Rise.

To an Island Princess.
To Be Honest, to Be Kind, *sel.*
To K[atharine de M]attos.
To Mrs. Will H. Low.
To N. V. de G. S.
To S. R. Crockett, *sel.*
To the Muse.
Travel.
Tropic Rain.
Vagabond, The.
Verses Written in 1872.
Visit from the Sea, A.
When I am grown to man's estate.
Where Go the Boats?
Whole Duty of Children.
Wind, The.
Windy Nights.
Winter Time.
Young Night Thought.
Stevenson, William
    Back and Side Go Bare, Go Bare, *sel.*
Stevenson, William Frederick
    Life and Impellance.
    Planet of Descendance, A.
Steward, Joseph
    God from His Throne with Piercing Eye.
    My Soul Would Fain Indulge a Hope.
Steward of Baldynnis, John
    To His Darrest Freind.
Stewart, Anna Bird
    Baby Talk.
Stewart, Carole
    Angry Children.
    Don't Call Me Mama.
    I Love You It's True.
    Jerry Perm Poem.
Stewart, Douglas
    At the Entrance.
    Brindabella.
    Bunyip, The.
    Dosser in Springtime, The.
    Garden of Ships, The.
    Glencoe.
    Mahony's Mountain.
    Nesting Time.
    Oh the corrugated-iron town, *sel.*
    Rock Carving.
    Silkworms, The.
    Snow-Gum, The.
    Two Englishmen.
Stewart, George Craig
    As I Went Down to David's Town.
Stewart, Gervase
    I Burn for England with a Living Flame.
    Landscape Lies within My Head, The.
    Poem: "I take four devils with me when I
    ride."
    Red Cross Nurses.
Stewart, Harold
    Lament in Autumn.
    Leaf-Makers, The.
Stewart, Jane G.
    June.
Stewart, Pamela
    Damaged Aria, The.
    Jack Yazzie's Girl.
    Postcard.
    Punk Pantoum.
    Spring.
    Wind of Late Summer, The.
Stewart, Phillips
    Hope.
Stewart, Susan
    Consecration.
    Evening of Montale's Death, The.
    Man Dancing with a Baby.
    Secret Ceremony: The Sailboat.
Stewart, W.
    True Aristocrat, The.
Stewart, W. Gregory
    Who Ordered That?

Stewart, William
    Thir Lenterne Dayis Ar Luvely Lang, *at.*
Stewart, Harold James Philip McAuley. See
    "Malley, Ern"
Stewart of Baldynneis, John. See Steward of
    Baldynnis, John
Stickney, Helen Frith
    Habitué.
Stickney, Trumbull
    At Sainte-Marguerite.
    Be Still. The Hanging Gardens Were a
    Dream.
    Dramatic Fragment.
    Fidelity.
    He Said: "If in His Image I Was Made."
    In the Past.
    Leave Him Now Quiet.
    Live Blindly.
    Mnemosyne.
    Mount Lykaion, *sel.*
    Near Helikon.
    Now in the Palace Gardens, *sel.*
    On Some Shells Found Inland.
    Six o'Clock.
    Soul of Time, The.
Stidger, William Leroy
    I Saw God Wash the World.
Stigall, John
    Dying.
Still, James
    Ballad: "They were a man's words, a ballad
    of an old time."
    Clabe Mott.
    Dance on Pushback.
    On Double Creek.
    Rain on the Cumberlands.
    Spring.
    Trees in the Road, The.
    Uncle Ambrose.
    With Hands like Leaves.
    Wolfpen Creek.
Stillman, Clark
    David and Delilah.
    Grotto, The.
    Life.
    Your Eyes and Swiveling Members.
Stillman, Michael
    In Memoriam John Coltrane.
Stillman, Annie Raymond. See "Raymond,
    Grace"
Stilwell, Joseph W.
    Lyric to Spring.
Stimson, Louis
    Back in the States.
    Fine Day for Straw Hats, A.
    Working late.
Stirling, William Alexander, Earl of
    Aurora.
    I Envy Not Endymion, *sel.*
    I Hope, I Fear, *sel.*
    Madrigal: "When in her face mine eyes I fix,"
    sel.
    O happy Tithon! if thou know'st thy harp, *sel.*
    Oh, If Thou Knew'st How Thou Thyself Dost
    Harm, *sel.*
    Sonnet: "Cleare moving cristall, pure as the
    Sunne beames," *sel.*
    Sonnet: "Ile give thee leave my love, in
    beauties field," *sel.*
    Sonnet: "Let others of the world's decaying
    tell," *sel.*
Stirling, Zan
    I put my hat upon my head.
Stites, Edgar P.
    I've Reached the Land of Corn and Wine.
Stockard, Henry Jerome
    As Some Mysterious Wanderer of the Skies.
    Mocking-Bird, The.
    Over Their Graves.
Stocking, Jay Thomas
    O Master-Workman of the Race.

Stockton, John H.
Come, Every Soul.
Stockwell, Jeffrey
Parallel Bars.
Stodart-Walker, Archibald
Counsel to Girls, *sel.*
Early Bacon, *sel.*
I had a duck and the young duck died.
Inflictis, *sel.*
Stoddard, Charles Warren
Albatross.
Cocoa-Tree, The.
Royal Mummy to Bohemia, The.
Stigmata.
Wind and Wave.
Stoddard, Elizabeth
In the Still, Star-lit Night.
Last Days.
Mercedes.
November.
On the Campagna.
Poet's Secret, The.
Summer Night, A.
Unreturning.
Stoddard, Lavinia
Soul's Defiance, The.
Stoddard, Richard Henry
Abdication of Noman, The.
Abraham Lincoln.
Adsum.
Arab Song.
Birds.
Catch, A.
Colonel Ellsworth.
Divan, The.
Dying Lover, The.
Falcon, The.
Flight of the Arrow, The.
Gazelle, A.
Jar, The.
Little Drummer, The.
Lover, The.
Men of the North and West.
Mors et Vita.
Sea, The.
Shadow, The.
Sky, The.
Songs.
There Are Gains for All Our Losses.
Twilight on Sumter.
Two Anchors, The.
Wine and Dew.
Witch's Whelp, The.
Stoddart, Thomas Tod
Angler's Invitation, The.
Her, a Statue.
Mirthful Lunacy, *sel.*
Stokes, Francis G.
Blue Moonshine.
Stokes, Terry
All Morning.
Crimes of Passion: The Phone Caller.
Crimes of Passion: The Slasher.
Man All Grown Up Is Supposed To, A.
Travis, the Kid Was All Heart.
Stokes, Will
Bugs.
Stokesbury, Leon
Adventures in Bronze.
Day Begins at Governor's Square Mall.
East Texas.
Funny Joke, A.
Lover Remembereth Such as He Sometimes
    Enjoyed and Showeth How He Would Like
    to Enjoy Her Again, The.
Luncheon of the Boating Party, The.
To His Book.
To Laura Phelan: 1880-1906.
Unsent Message to My Brother in His Pain.
Stoloff, Carolyn
Built Bridge, Footnotes, A.
Dinosaurs.

Stoltzenberg, Abo
French Mood, The.
In Vistas of Stone.
What Am I?
Stone, Arlene
Germination.
Stone, Gillian
Midwinter Warm.
Stone, John
After Love.
Coming around the Horn.
Coming Home.
Death.
Early Sunday Morning.
Girl in the Hall, The.
Stone, P. M.
Mr. Pennycomequick.
Stone, Phyllis M.
Topsy-Turvy Land.
Stone, Ruth
Advice.
Burned Bridge, The.
Codicil.
Dark Conclusions.
Denouement.
Green Apples.
Hunger.
I Have Three Daughters.
In an Iridescent Time.
In the Interstices.
Latest Hotel Guest Walks over Particles That
    Revolve in Seven Other Dimensions
    Controlling Latti, The.
Liberation.
Magnet, The.
My Son.
On the Mountain.
Private Pantomime.
Repetition of Words and Weather.
Room.
Salt.
Snow.
Talking Fish, The.
Vernal Equinox.
Watcher, The.
Whose Scene?
Winter.
Years Later.
Stone, Samuel John
Church's One Foundation, The.
Stone, Walter
Compelled to Love.
Couple.
Nature.
On the Welsh Marches.
Stopple, Libby
Calvary.
Storer, Thomas
Rivers.
Storey, Violet Alleyn
Prayer after Illness, A.
Prayer for a Very New Angel.
Prayer for the New Year, A.
Prayer in Affliction.
Prayer in Late Autumn, A.
Stork, Charles Wharton
Bronze Statuette of Kwan-yin, A.
God, You Have Been Too Good to Me.
Troubadour of God, The.
Storm, Jannick
Thanksgiving Day.
Storni, Alfonsina
Aching.
Ancestral Weight.
Dog and Sea.
Epitaph for My Tomb.
Forgetting.
I Am Going to Sleep (Suicide Poem).
It Could Be.
It May Be.

Lighthouse in the Night.
Little Man.
Men in the City.
My Sister.
Pain.
She Who Understands.
Sierra.
Small Man.
They've Come.
Words for Delmira Agustini.
You Want Me White.
You Would Have Me Immaculate.
Story, Robert
My Own Hills.
Story, William Wetmore
Cleopatra.
English Language, The.
Io Victis!
Praxiteles and Phryne.
Stott, John G.
Scottish Mountaineering Club Song, The.
Stoutenburg, Adrien
Ants and Others.
Avalanche.
Bear Who Came to Dinner, The.
Brobdingnag.
Channel U.S.A.—Live.
Cicada.
Jack Rabbit.
Night Train.
Rain.
Traveller's Guide to Antarctica.
Stow, Randolph
Dust.
Jungle, The, *sel.*
Ruins of the City of Hay.
Singing Bones, The.
Sleepers, The, *sel.*
Strange Fruit.
Utopia of Lord Mayor Howard, The.
Stowe, Harriet Beecher
Abide in Me, O Lord, and I in Thee.
Other World, The.
Still, Still, with Thee.
When Winds Are Raging.
Strabo, Walafrid
To His Friend in Absence.
Strabo, Walafrid. *See* **Walafrid Strabo**
Strachan, Ian
Silent Walls, The.
Silver in the Wind.
Strachey, William
Aecclesiae et Reipub.
Strand, Mark
Always.
Babies, The.
Black Maps.
Breath.
Coming of Light, The.
Coming to This.
Continental College of Beauty, The.
Courtship.
Dance, The.
Dead, The.
Dress, The.
Eating Poetry.
Elegy for My Father.
Empty Body, The, *sel.*
For Her.
Franz.
From a Litany.
Garden, The.
In Celebration.
Kite, The.
Last Bus, The.
Late Hour, The.
Letter.
Mailman, The.
Man in Black, The.
Man in the Mirror, The.

Man in the Tree, The.
Map, The.
Marriage, The.
Moontan.
Morning, A.
My Life.
My Mother on an Evening in Late Summer.
New Year, The, *sel.*
Nights in Hackett's Cove.
Old People on the Nursing Home Porch.
One Song, The.
Poem after Leopardi.
Poor North.
Prediction, The.
Remains, The.
Ruins.
She.
Shooting Whales.
Sleep, The.
Sleeping with One Eye Open.
Story, The.
Story You Know, A.
"The Dreadful Has Already Happened."
Tomorrow.
Tunnel, The.
Violent Storm.
When the Vacation Is Over for Good.
Where Are the Waters of Childhood?
You and It.
Your Shadow, *sel.*

Strato (Straton)
Epigram: "All through the night my eyes have streamed with rain."
Epigram: "At even, when the hour drew nigh at which we say farewell."
Epigram: "Boys' cocks, Diodore."
Epigram: "But yesterday, when from the bath he stept."
Epigram: "Even if I try not to ogle a boy in the street."
Epigram: "Gathering the bloom of all the fairest boys that be."
Epigram: "How shall I know if my love lose his youth."
Epigram: "I am provoked."
Epigram: "I delight in the prime of a boy of twelve."
Epigram: "I like them pale, fair or honey-skinned."
Epigram: "Like when the burning sun doth rise."
Epigram: "Long hair, endless curls trained by the devoted."
Epigram: "Now art thou fair, Diodorus."
Epigram: "Passing the flower-stalls there did I perceive."
Epigram: "Perchance some coming after."
Epigram: "Stolen kisses, wary eyes."
Epigram: "There was this gym-teacher."
Epigram: "Those snooty boys in all their purple drag!"
Epigram: "Thy eyes are sparks, Lycines, god-like made."
Epigram: "When Graphicus sat by the baths."
To Kyris.

Straton. *See* **Strato**
Straus, Austin
Announcer, The.
Juggler, The.

Strauss, A. L.
In Discreet Splendor.
Lament for the European Exile.
On the Path.
Voice in the Dark.

Strauss, Avner
Hollow Flute, The.
Portrait of a Widow.

"Strauss Yawcob." *See* **Adams, Charles Follen**
"Streamer Col. D." *See* **Graham, Harry**
Strebeck, George
Joyful Sound It Is, A.

Street, Alfred Billings
Loon, The.
Settler, The.
Street, Julian and James Montgomery Flagg
To Be Continued.
Street, T.
Tim tryeth truth convicting all that strive.
Streeter, Sebastian
King Shall Reign in Righteousness, A.
Lo, What Enraptured Songs of Praise.
Stringer, Arthur
Morning in the North-west.
Sappho's Tomb.
Sod-Breaker, The.
There Is Strength in the Soil.
Wanderer's Litany, A.
Stringer, R. E. C.
Sartorial Solecism.
Strobel, Marion
Captive.
Pastoral: "This is a place of ease."
Stroblas, Laurie
How to Sign.
Strode, William
Devonshire Song, A, at.
In Commendation of Music.
My love and I for kisses play'd.
Nightingale, The.
On Chloris Walking in the Snow in the Snow.
On the Death of Mistress Mary Prideaux.
On Westwall Downes [*or* On Westwall Downs]
Strong, George
Epiphany, The.
Modern Hiawatha, The, *sel.*
Strong, Julia Hurd
Huckster's Horse, The.
Son and Surf.
Strong, L. A. G.
Brewer's Man, The.
Evening before Rain.
Mad Woman of Punnet's Town, The.
Memory, A.
Old Dan'l.
Rufus Prays.
Zeke.
Strong, Leonard Alfred George
Appointment, The.
Coroner's Jury.
Door, The.
Knowledgeable Child, The.
Lowery Cot.
March Evening.
Old Man at the Crossing, The.
Old Woman, Outside the Abbey Theater, An.
Two Generations.
Strong, Nathan
Almighty Sovereign of the Skies!
Summer Harvest Spreads the Fields, The.
Swell the Anthem, Raise the Song.
Strong, Phillips Burrows
Tongue, The.
Strongin, Lynn
Emily Dickinson Postage Stamp.
Miniatures IV.
Sayre.
Sensuous Latin poet, now I will go off with a thermos, A, *sel.*
Stroud, Joseph
Above Machu Picchu, 129 Baker Street, San Francisco.
As for Me, I Delight in the Everyday Way.
Below Mount T'ui K'oy, Home of the Gods, Todos Santos Cuchumatán, Guatemalan Highlands.
City.
Documentary.
Dragon.
Exile.
Gold Country, The; Hotel Leger, Mokelumne Hill, Revisited, The.

Grandfather.
Lament: "Because the moon became my mother."
Machupuchare. What the Mountain Said. Shaking the Dead Bones, Christmas Eve, 1974.
Memory.
Monte Albán.
Naming.
Poem on the Suicide of My Teacher.
Poem to Han-shan.
Poem to My Father.
Proportions.
Room above the White Rose, The.
Sibyl.
Signature III ("Tsangyang Gyatso was twelve years old").
Signature II.
To Christopher Smart.
"Struther, Jan" (Joyce Anstruther Maxtone Graham)
Traveling America.
Stryk, Lucien
Awakening.
Cannery, The.
Cherries.
Dawn.
Exterminator.
Farmer.
Juggler.
Letter to Jean-Paul Baudot, at Christmas.
Savants.
Summer.
To a Japanese Poet.
Watching War Movies.
Stryker, Melancthon Woolsey
Almighty Lord, with One Accord.
God of Our Fathers.
Stuart, Alice V.
Climbing Rope, The.
Lintie in a Cage.
Stuart, Dabney
Ballad of the Frozen Field, The.
Discovering My Daughter.
Exchange.
Fall Practice.
Mining in Killdeer Alley.
Rescue.
River, The.
Separate Parties.
Soup Jar, The.
Ties.
Stuart, Francis
Coogan's Wood.
Ireland.
Southern Summer.
Une Idole du Nord.
Upper Lake, The.
Stuart, Jesse
By Sandy Waters.
Heart-summoned.
I Sing America Now!
My land is fair for any eyes to see.
Our Heritage.
Speaks the Whispering Grass.
Up Silver Stairsteps.
Stuart, Muriel
In the Orchard.
Seed Shop, The.
Stuart, Ruth McEnery
Endless Song, The.
Stubbs, Charles William
Conscience.
'Twas Jolly, Jolly Wat.
Stubbs, Jane
Sim Ines.
Stubbs, John Heath-. *See* **Heath-Stubbs, John**
Stubbs, Marcia
In a Mirror.

Stubbs, William
Hymn on Froude and Kingsley, A.
Studdert-Kennedy, Geoffrey Anketell
("Woodbine Willie")
Great Wager, The.
Indifference.
Kiss of God, The.
Patience.
Roses in December.
Unutterable Beauty, The.
Studer, Constance E.
Reflections.
Suspension.
Stull, Richard
Romance.
Sturm, Frank Pearce
Still-Heart.
Su Shao-lien
Blackbird, The.
Frost on the Ground.
Little Girl's Show, A.
Mountain Barrier.
Weeds.
Su Tung-p'o
Abandoned earthworks nobody tends, sel.
Beginning to Autumn: A Poem to Send to
Tzu-yu.
Black Muzzle.
Children.
Days of Rain; the Rivers Have Overflowed.
Following the Rhymes of Chiang Hui-shu.
I planted rice before Spring Festival, sel.
I Travel Day and Night.
Lament of the Farm Wife of Wu.
Little stream used to cross my land, A, sel.
Long Ago I Lived in the Country.
Lotus Viewing.
Mid-Autumn Moon.
Moon, Flowers, Man.
New Year's Blizzard, The.
New Year's Eve.
On the Birth of His Son.
On the Road to Hsin-ch'eng.
Presented to Liu Ching-wen.
Rhyming with Tzu-yu's "Treading the Green."
Spring Night.
Terrace in the Snow, The.
To a Traveler.
Tune: Immortal at the River.
Tune: Partridge Sky.
Tune: Prelude to Water Music.
Tune: Sand of Silk-washing Stream ("Flutter
flutter on clothes and cap, jujube flowers
fall").
Tune: Sand of Silk-washing Stream ("Layer
on layer of hemp leaves, jute leaves
shining").
Tune: Sand of Silk-washing Stream ("Soft
grasses, a plain of sedge fresh with
passing").
Tune: Sand of Silk-washing Stream ("Throw
on rouge and powder, watch the governor
pass!").
Tune: Song of River City.
Under the Heaven of Our Holy Ruler.
White Crane Hill.
Written on a Painting Entitled "Misty Yangtze
and Folded Hills."
Suárez, Clementina
Combat.
Suárez Quemain, Jaime
Collective Shot, A.
Dictators, The.
Suasnavar, Constantino
I Have Lost My Shoes.
Sublett, Dyan
Simple Rituals.
Succorsa, Janice Appleby
My Garden.
Suckling, Henry Hughes
Song: "I prithee send me back my heart," at.

Suckling, Sir John
Against Absence.
Against Fruition.
Barley-Break , A.
Bride, The, sel.
Candle, A.
Deformed Mistress, The.
Farewell to Love.
Love's Offence.
Loves World.
Loving and Beloved.
Lutea Allison.
Metamorphosis, The.
Miracle, The.
My dearest Rival, least our Love.
On King Richard the Third, Who Lies Buried
under Leicester Bridge.
On New-Year's Day 1640, to the King.
Out upon it! I have loved.
Pedlar of Small-Wares, A ("A pedlar I am,
that take great care").
Proffered Love Rejected.
Session[s] of the Poets, A ("A session was
held the other day").
Sir Toby Matthews.
Soldier, A.
Song: "No, no, fair heretic[k], it needs must
be," sel.
Song to a Lute, A.
Song: "When, dearest, I but think on [or of]
thee," at.
Song: Why So Pale and Wan, Fond Lover?
Sonnet: "Do'st see how unregarded now."
Sonnet: "Of thee (kind boy) I ask no red and
white."
Sonnet: "Oh! [or O!] for some honest lover's
ghost."
That None Beguiled Be.
'Tis Now, Since I Sat[e] Down Before.
To a Lady That Forbade to Love before
Company.
To B. C.
To Master Davenant for Absence.
Upon A. M.
Upon My Lady Carlisle's Walking in
Hampton Court Garden.
Upon My Lord Brohall's Wedding.
Upon Sir John Lawrence's Bringing Water
over the Hills.
Why So Pale and Wan, Fond Lover?, sel.
Woman's Constancy.
Sudan, Nazzam Al
Al Fitnah Muhajir.
Suemochi (Kino Suemochi)
Watching Fish in the Water.
Sugawara no Michizane.   See **Michizane**
Sugiyama Sampu.   See **Sampu**
Suhl, Yuri
And the Earth Rebelled.
Suibne Geilt
Bellower with the antlers.
I am in great misery tonight.
I am Suibne the wanderer.
My fixed abode is Glen Bolcain.
Rich tuft of ivy, A.
Sweet voice of the Garb.
Though my wanderings are many.
Suiko
Under a tree a frog.
Suiyu
Hopping frog—is a cat chasing you.
Sukenick, Lynn
Parting; a Game.
Suknaski, Andrew
Chinese Camp, Kamloops (circa 1883).
Snake, The.
Sukunamaro, Kose.   See **Kose Sukunamaro**
Sullam, Sarah Copia
My Inmost Hope.

Sullivan, Alan
Suppliant.
White Canoe, The.
Sullivan, Aloysius Michael
Measurement.
Monument.
Psalm to the Holy Spirit.
Sullivan, Charles
Nights along the River.
Sullivan, Francis
Prayer: "You may be right, divinity."
Still Life.
Sullivan, Jonny Kyoko
Sagimusume: The White Heron Maiden.
Sullivan, Nancy
At Lascaux they've shut the caves, sel.
Death of the First Man, The.
Eclipses.
His Necessary Darkness.
More like the candle going out, sel.
Telling It.
To My Body.
Sully-Prudhomme, René François Armand
Naked World, The.
Struggle, The.
Wheel, The.
Sulpicia
At last love has come. I would be more
ashamed.
Darling, I won't be your hot love.
Do you have a sweet thought, Cerinthus.
Drat my hateful birthday.
Have you heard? The troubles.
I'm grateful, really grateful.
It's nice that though you are casual about me.
Let your longing for me, my love.
My hated birthday is here, and I must go.
Sulter, Maud
Babe.
Dance, The.
Full Circle.
Once.
Sumako, Fukao.   See **Fukao Sumako**
Sumangala, the mother of
Free woman, A. At last free!
Summers, Hal
My Old Cat.
Summers, Hollis Spurgeon
Concerning Unnatural Nature: An Inverted
Form.
Family Reunion.
Lost Pictures, The.
Valentine.
Summers, Thomas O.
Morning Bright, with Rosy Light, The.
Sumrall, Amber Coverdale
Mirage.
Owl Woman.
Question of Energy, A.
Questions.
Sun Kuang-hsien
Beautiful Lady Yü, The.
Deva-like Barbarian.
Eight-Beat Barbarian Tune.
Flowers in the Rear Garden, The.
Immortal at the River.
Jade Butterflies.
Mountain Hawthorns.
Pacifying the Western Barbarians.
Paying Homage at the Golden Gate.
Pure Serene Music.
River Messages.
Sand of Silk-Washing Stream.
Song of a Dandy.
Song of Ho Man-tzu.
Song of the Bamboo Branches.
Song of the Fisherman.
Song of the Water Clock at Night.
Song of the Wine Spring.
Spirit of the Yellow River.
Taoist Nun, The.

Thoughts of Paradise.
Thoughts of the Yüeh Beauty.
Toast to the Traveler, A.
Viewing the Plum-Blossoms.
Willow Branches.

Sun-Ra
Nothing Is.
Plane: Earth, The.
Primary Lesson: The Second Class Citizens.

Sun Yü-tang
What Did I Lose?

Sun Yün-feng
On the Road through Chang-te.
Trail up Wu Gorge, The.

Sund, Robert
Bunch Grass #37.

Sung Chang-kyung
Conversation with Mr. Yao, A.
It Rains on Friday.

Sung Hsiang
Did every one of the three hundred poets have
  a teacher?, *sel.*
Emulate Han, emulate Tu, emulate the
  bearded Su, *sel.*
First Rain: Sent to Magistrate Mo-ch'ing.
He pledged himself to live with poetry until
  old age, *sel.*
True, one must read ten thousand volumes
  until threadbare, *sel.*
Written on the Wall of the Flying Cloud Cave
  in Kweichow.

Sung Wan
Ballad of the Righteous Tiger, A.
Earthen *K'ang*, An, *sel.*
Earthen Stove, An, *sel.*
Miscellany on the Garden of Autumn Clouds:
  Peach-Blossom Pond, A.
On Hearing a Cricket in the Boat.
Piece of Rush Matting, A, *sel.*
Random Poem on the Lake.
Song of a Fisherman, A.
Stool with a Broken Leg, A, *sel.*

Supervielle, Jules
Call, The.
Deep Sea.
Enclosure, The.
Entangled.
Flame Point.
Homage to Life.
I Dream You.
Pot Of Earth, A.
Rain and the Tyrants.
What Do I Care.
Whisper in Agony.

Surdas
Away! Go back to where you spent the night!
Black storm clouds have risen in the sky.
Ever since your name has entered Hari's ear.
Far off and furtive, Gopal's in the butter.
Gopal has slipped in and stolen my heart,
  friend.
Hari has fashioned an offering of lights.
Having seen Hari's face, our eyes are opened
  wide.
I, only I, am best at being worst, Lord.
If you drink the milk of the black cow,
  Gopal.
Life has stumbled, stumbled, unraveled.
Look, my friend, look at Hari's nimble eyes.
Lord of Braj, the memory of my passion
  remains.
Madhav, even those who haven't a shred of
  worth.
Madhav, please, control that cow.
Now I am blind; I've shunned Hari's name.
Radha is lost to the onslaught of love.
She's found him, she has, but Radha
  disbelieves.
Those Mathura people, they're rife with vice.
Thoughts of him stalk me even in my dreams.

Until you wake up to what you really are.
With love there's never a thought that one
  might die.

"Surfaceman." *See* **Anderson, Alexander**

Surrey, Earl of
Brittle beauty [*or* beautie], that nature made
  so frail[e].
Complaint by Night of a Lover not Beloved,
  The.
Consolation.
Death of Wyatt, The.
Epitaph on Thomas Clere.
Exhortation to Learn of Others' Trouble.
From Tuscan came my lady's worthy race.
Golden gift that nature did thee give, The.
Golden Mean, The.
I never saw you madam, lay [*or* sawe my
  Ladye] laye apart.
If care do cause men cry, why do not I
  complain.
If he that erst the form so lively drew.
In Cipres springes [*or* Cyprus springs]
  (wheras [*or* whereas] dame Venus dwelt).
In winter's just return, when Boreas gan his
  reign.
Lady Again Complains, The.
Oh loathsome place! where I.
Prisoned in Windsor, He Recounteth His
  Pleasure There Passed, *sel.*
Since fortune's wrath envieth the wealth.
So cruel [*or* cruell *or* crewell] prison how
  could betide [*or* howe coulde betyde], alas.
Such[e] wayward[e] ways [*or* wais] hath
  love, that most[e] part[e] in discord[e].
Too dearly had I bought my green and
  youthful years.
When Windsor walls sustain'd my wearied
  arm.
When Youth Had Led.

Surrey, Henry Howard, Earl of
Although I had a check.
As oft as I behold and see.
Bonum Est Mihi Quod Humiliasti Me.
Complaint of the Absence of Her Lover Being
  upon the Sea.
Give [*or* Geve] Place, Ye Lovers.
In Praise of Wyatt's Psalms.
In the rude age when seyence was not so rife.
Laid in My Quiet Bed [in Study as I Were].
Love's Rebel.
Of a Lady That Refused to Dance with Him.
Portrait of Henry VIII, The.
Restless Heart, The.
Restless State of a Lover, The.
Satire on London, A.
Soote Season, The.
Though I regarded not.
Woman's Answer, A, *at.*
Wrapt in my careless cloak, as I walk to and
  fro.
Wyatt Resteth Here.

Sutheim, Susan
For Witches.

Sutherland, Janet
Cat Got Your Tongue?
Leaning Over.
To the Spider in the Crevice behind the Toilet
  Door.
Touching Heartsease.
Variegation.

Sutherland, Robert. *See* **Garioch, Robert**

Sutoku, Emperor
Blossom to the roots, The.
Swift rapids, The.

Sutskever [*or* Sutzkever], Abraham
Banks of a River, The.
Cartload of Shoes, A.
Death of an Ox.
Deer at the Red Sea.
Epitaphs.
Firemen.

Frozen Jews.
Here I Am.
How?
In the Hamlet.
In the Sack of the Wind.
Landscape.
Lead Plates at the Rom Press, The.
Like Groping Fingers.
1980, *sel.*
1981, *sel.*
1975, *sel.*
1974, *sel.*
1976, *sel.*
On My Wandering Flute.
Poetry.
Secret Town, The.
Song for a Dance.
Song of Praise for an Ox.
Songs to a Lady Moonwalker.
To My Child.
Toys.
Under the Earth.
Yiddish.

Sutter, Barton
Curse against the Owner, A.
Shoe Shop.
Swedish Lesson.
Warmth.

Sutton, David
Not to Be Born.
Taxonomical Note.

Sutton, Henry Septimus
Inward Light, The.

Sutu, S. D. R
Night.
Thaba Bosio.

Sutzkever, Abraham. *See* **Sutskever,
  Abraham**

Svetlov, Mikhail Arkadyevich
Grenada.

Swain, Charles
Home Is Where There Is One to Love Us.
Thin are, oh Mind!—the colours which
  delight, *sel.*

Swain, John D.
Would I Be Shrived?

Swain, Leonard
My Soul, Weigh Not Thy Life.

Swallow, Debra
Keep a Dime.

Swan, Jon
Father Father Son and Son.
In Her Song She Is Alone.
Kingdom, The.
March Weather.
Nebraska.
Report, The.
Their Party, Our House.

Swander, Mary
Maud.
Novena.

Swanger, David
What the Wing Says.

Swann, Brian
Desert in the Sea.
Paradigms of Fire.
Quiet.
Year of the Bird.

Swann, Thomas Burnett
Japanese Birthday Wish, A.

Sward, Robert
American Heritage.
Concert.
Movies, Left to Right.
Uncle Dog; the Poet at 9.

Swart, Edward Vincent
Casey Jones.
Tired of Eating Kisses.

Swarth, Hélène
Candles.
Ecstasy.

Swartz, Roberta Teale
Prayer by Moonlight.

Swenson, Karen
Come with Me into Winter's Disheveled
Grass.
Quarrel, The.
Woman, Gallup, N. M.

Swenson, May
Above the Arno.
All That Time.
Almanac.
Analysis of Baseball.
Beginning to Squall.
Bronco Busting, Event #1.
Café Tableau.
Cardinal Ideograms.
Cat and the Weather.
Centaur, The.
Choosing Craft.
Cloud-Mobile, The.
Death Invited.
Dream, The, *sel.*
Dummy, 51, to Go to Museum. Ventriloquist
Dead at 75.
Evolution.
Feel like a Bird.
Fire Island.
First Walk on the Moon.
Fixture, A.
Flying Home from Utah.
Four-Word Lines.
Frontispiece.
Garden at St. John's, The.
Green Red Brown and White.
Hair, The, *sel.*
Hearing the Wind at Night.
Hole Seen, The.
How Everything Happens.
How to Be Old.
In a Museum Cabinet.
James Bond Movie, The.
July 4th.
Key to Everything, The.
Landing on the Moon.
Lion.
Living Tenderly.
Morning at Point Dume.
Motherhood.
Naked in Borneo.
News from the Cabin.
Night Practice.
Notes Made in the Piazza San Marco.
O'Keeffe Retrospective.
On Addy Road.
On Its Way.
Out of the Sea, Early.
Over the Field.
Overboard.
Painting the Gate.
Pair, A.
Poplar's Shadow, The.
Promontory Moment, The.
Question.
Rain at Wildwood.
Salt, The, *sel.*
Sand, The, *sel.*
Shape of Death, The.
Snow by Morning.
Some Small Shells from the Windward
Islands.
Southbound on the Freeway.
To the Statue.
Under the Baby Blanket.
View to the North.
Waking from a Nap on the Beach.
Watch, The.
Watching the Jets Lose to Buffalo at Shea.
Water Picture.

Willets, The.
Women.

Swett, Herbert B.
Gathering, The.

Swett, Susan Hartley
July.

Swift, Egan
Ireland.
Prometheus.

Swift, Hildegarde Hoyt
I Came to the New World Empty-handed.
My Name Was Legion.

Swift, Joan
Line-up, The.
Oxygen.

Swift, Jonathan
A E I O U.
All human race would fain be wits, *sel.*
Apples, *sel.*
As I strole the city, oft I, *sel.*
Baucis and Philemon; Imitated from the
Eighth Book of Ovid.
Beautiful Young Nymph Going to Bed, A.
Behold the fatal day arrive!, *sel.*
Cassinus and Peter.
Character of Sir Robert Walpole, The.
Clever Tom Clinch Going to Be Hanged.
Daphne.
Day of Judgement, The.
Day will come, when't shall be said, The, *sel.*
Description of a City Shower, A.
Description of the Morning, A.
Dick, a Maggot.
Doctors tender of their fame, The, *sel.*
Epigram: "As Thomas was cudgell'd [*or*
cudgel'd] one day by his wife."
Epigram on Fasting.
Epigram on Scolding.
Excellent New Song, Being the Intended
Speech of a Famous Orator against Peace,
An.
Excellent New Song on a Seditious Pamphlet,
An.
Excellent New Song upon His Grace Our
Good Lord Archbishop of Dublin, An.
Fable of Midas, The.
Fool, to put up four crosses at your door.
Gentle Echo on Woman, A.
Here shift the scene, to represent, *sel.*
Herrings, *sel.*
Hobbes clearly proves that every creature, *sel.*
Holyhead, Sept. 25th, 1727.
In Sickness Written Soon after the Author's
Coming to Live in Ireland, upon the
Queen's Death, October 1714.
Lady's Dressing Room, The.
Mary the Cook-Maid's Letter to Dr. Sheridan.
Mollis Abuti.
My female friends, whose tender hearts, *sel.*
New Song of Wood's Halfpence, A, *at.*
On a Curate's Complaint of Hard Day.
On Burning a Dull Poem.
On Dreams.
On His Own Deafness.
On Poetry; a Rhapsody.
On the Astrologer and Almanac Maker, John
Partridge.
On the Collar of Mrs. Dingley's Lap-Dog.
On the Irish Club.
On the Vowels—a Riddle.
Onyons, *sel.*
Oysters.
Perhaps I may allow, the Dean, *sel.*
Phyllis; or, The Progress of Love.
Place of the Damn'd, The.
Power of Time, The.
Progress of Poetry, The.
Roam not from pole to pole, but enter here,
sel.
Satirical Elegy on the Death of a Late Famous
General, A.

Stella at Wood-Park.
Stella's Birthday; March 13, 1726/27.
Stella's Birth-day, 1718/19.
Stella's Birthday, 1725.
Stella's Birthday, 1721 ("All travelers at first
incline").
Suppose me dead; and then suppose, *sel.*
Time is not remote when I, The, *sel.*
To Form a Just and Finish'd Piece, *sel.*
To the Earl of Oxford, Late Lord Treasurer.
To Stella.
To Their Excellencies the Lords Justices of
Ireland, the Humble Petition of Frances
Harris, Who Must Starve, and Die a Maid
if It Miscarries.
True and Faithful Inventory of the Goods
Belonging to Dr. Swift, Vicar of Laracor,
A; upon Lending His House to the Bishop
of Meath, till His Palace Was Rebuilt.
Twelve Articles.
Verses on the Death of Dr. Swift, D.S.P.D.,
Occasioned by Reading a Maxim in
Rochefoucauld.
Verses Said to Be Written on the Union.
Virtue conceal'd within our breast.
Virtues of Sid Hamet, the Magician's Rod,
The.
Wise Rochefoucault a maxim writ, *sel.*
Wretched Ierne! with what grief I see, *sel.*

Swinburne, Algernon Charles
After Death.
August.
Ave atque Vale.
Baby's feet, like sea-shells pink, A, *sel.*
Ballad of Dead Men's Bay, The.
Ballad of François Villon, A.
Before Parting.
Before the Beginning of Years, *sel.*
Ben Jonson, *sel.*
Child's Laughter, A.
Chorus: "Who hath given man speech? or
what hath set therein," *sel.*
Christopher Marlowe.
Cleopatra.
Come into the orchard, Anne.
Dialogue, A.
Duriesdyke.
Erotion.
Evening by the Sea.
Evening on the Broads.
Ex-Voto.
Faustine.
Félise.
Forsaken Garden, A.
From too much love of living, *sel.*
Garden of Proserpine, The.
Glad, but not flush'd with gladness, *sel.*
Hendecasyllabics.
Here, where the world is quiet, *sel.*
Hermaphroditus.
Hertha.
Hesperia.
Higher Pantheism in a Nutshell, The, *sel.*
Hope and Fear.
Hymn to Proserpine.
I Will Go Back to the Great Sweet Mother,
sel.
Ilicet.
In Memory of Walter Savage Landor.
In the Orchard.
Interpreters, The.
Itylus.
John Jones, *sel.*
John Webster.
Lake of Gaube, The.
Land that is lonelier than ruin, A, *sel.*
Leave-taking, A.
Leper, The.
Love and Sleep.
Love at Sea.
Maiden, and mistress of the months and stars,
sel.

Match, A.
Nephelidia, *sel.*
On Arthur Hugh Clough.
On the Russian Persecution of the Jews.
Poeta Loquitur.
Proserpine, *sel.*
Rondel: "Kissing her hair, I sat against her feet."
Sapphics.
Sark, *sel.*
Shakespeare.
Song: "Love laid his sleepless head."
Sonnet for a Picture, *sel.*
Stage Love.
Suffolk, *sel.*
Sundew, The.
Super Flumina Babylonis.
Swimming, *sel.*
Thank your engines, *sel.*
Thou whose birth on earth, *sel.*
Watchman, What of the Night?
What is that death they boast but a frail pageant, *sel.*
When the Hounds of Spring [Are on Winter's Traces], *sel.*
Where Dunwich Used to Be, *sel.*
White Butterflies.

Swingler, Randall
Letter VIII.
Letter I.
They Live.

Swirszczynska [or Swir], Anna
Building the Barricade.
He Steals Furs.
I Am Panting.
I Knocked My Head against the Wall.
It Smashes Barricades.
I've Been Waiting These Thirty Years.
Kill Me.
Old Woman, The.
Same Inside, The.
Second Madrigal, The.
She Does Not Remember.
Song of Plenitude.
Twenty of My Sons.
Two Hunchbacks.
Woman Talks to Her Thigh, A.

Sykes, Velma West
Diptych.

Sylvester, Janet
Arrowhead Christian Center and No-Smoking Luncheonette.
Hard Strain in a Delicate Place.
Late Show, The.
That Mulberry Wine.

Sylvester, Joshua
Autumnus.
Beware Fair Maide, at.
Fifth Day of the First Week, The, *sel.*
Fuimus Fumus.
Go, Silly Worm.
I hate these phrases: Of power absolute.
Mundus Qualis.
Omnia Somnia.
Rome, Conqueror, Conquered.
Seventh Day of the First Week, The, *sel.*
Sonnet: "They say that shadow[e]s of deceased ghosts."
Sweet mouth, that send'st a musky-rosed breath.
Were I as Base as Is the Lowly Plain, *at.*
When wine runs low, it is not worth the sparing.

Syme, James
Labour Song.

Symmens, Robert
Dam, Glen Garry, The.

Symonds, John Addington
Camera Obscura, The.
Invocation, An: "To God, the everlasting, who abides."

Midnight at Baiae; a Dream Fragment of Imperial Rome.
O God, unknown, invisible, secure, *sel.*
On a Picture by Poussin Representing Shepherds in Arcadia.
Rebuke Me Not.
That night, when storms were spent and tranquil heaven, *sel.*
To Night, the Mother of Sleep and Death.

Symons, Arthur
Absinthe-Drinker, The.
After Sunset, *sel.*
At Carbis Bay.
At Dawn.
At Dieppe: Grey and Green.
At the Cavour.
At Toledo.
Barrel-Organ, The.
By the Pool at the Third Rosses, *sel.*
Caged Bird, The.
Dance of the Daughters of Herodias, The.
Declaration, *sel.*
Dreams.
During Music.
Emmy ("Emmy's exquisite youth and her virginal air").
Episode of a Night of May, *sel.*
Gardener, The.
Grey and Green, *sel.*
Grey Wolf, The.
In Bohemia.
In Ireland: By the Pool at the Third Rosses.
In Kensington Gardens.
In the Bay, *sel.*
In Winter.
Isolation.
Laus Virginitatis.
Maquillage.
Nerves.
Night and Wind.
Nun, The.
On an Air of Rameau.
Palm Sunday: Naples.
Paris.
Pastel: Masks and Faces.
Prodigal Son, The.
Prologue to "London Nights."
Rain on the Down, *sel.*
Return, The, *sel.*
Spain.
Temptation of Saint Anthony, The.
Tune, A.
Vampire, The.
Venice.
White Heliotrope.

Symons, Julian
And the World's Face.
For My Wife.
For the Depressed.
Gladstone.
Hart Crane.
Hospital Observation.
Mr. Symons at Richmond, Mr. Pope at Twickenham.
Pub.
Reflections in Bed.
Second Man, The.
Sunday, July 14th; a Fine Day at the Baths.

Synge, John Millington
Beg-Innish.
Curse, The.
Dread.
Epitaph after Reading Ronsard's Lines from Rabelais.
I curse my bearing, childhood, youth.
I read about the Blaskets and Dunquin.
In Glencullen.
In Kerry.
In May.
Is It a Month.
I've Thirty Months.
On a Birthday.

On an Anniversary.
On an Island.
Passing of the Shee, The.
Prelude: "Still south I went and west and south again."
Queens.
Question, A.
Rendez-vous Manqué dans la Rue Racine.
To the Oaks of Glencree.
Winter.
Wish, A.

Syquia, Luis
New Manong, The.
Pan-Asian Holiday Tour.

Szabó, Lörinc
All for Nothing.
Dreams of the One, The.
Farewell: "What happened? My dear, don't cry. The thing," *sel.*
Prisons.

Szabo, Wilhelm
Don't Trust Anyone over Thirty.
During the Day He Held a Low-level Position.
Resignation.
See, It Begins to Come Down.
Threshing Machine.
Untranslatable.

Sze, Arthur
Black Lightning.
Chance, The.
Cloud Chamber, The.
Dazzled.
Magnetized.
Moenkopi.
Network, The.

Szécsi, Margit
Angel with Horn.
Burning Ship, The.
Death of Moses, The.
Hoverer, The.
Love's Fool.
Man.
Only with Radiance.

Szelki, Karl
Chestnut vendor, The.

Szumigalski, Anne
Angels.
In the Heat of the Morning.
Midwife's Story; Two, A.
Visitor's Parking.
Want of Þ want of Ð.

Szymborska, Wislawa
Autonomy.
Every Case.
Great Number, A.
I Am Too Near.
Joy of Writing, The.
Laughter.
Letters of the Dead.
Starvation Camp near Jaslo.
Utopia.
Women of Rubens, The.

T

"T., I."
When Stars Are Shrouded.

"T., J."
Sea-Chaplain's Petition to the Lieutenants in the Ward-Room, for the Use of the Quarter-Gallery, A.

"T., B. L." *See* **Taylor, Bert Leston**

Ta' Abbata Sharra
Ever Watchful.

Tabb, John Banister
Anonymous.
At Bethlehem, *sel.*

Becalmed.
Betrayal.
Bicycles! Tricycles!
Bubble, The.
Child's Prayer, A.
Christ and the Pagan.
Close Quarters.
Clover.
Communion.
Departed, The.
Druid, The.
Evolution.
Faith.
Fame.
Father Damien.
Foot Soldiers.
Indian Summer.
Insomnia.
Inspiration.
Missing.
Reaper, The.
Rub, A.
Sisters, The.
Tax-Gatherer, The.
To his Mother, sel.
To Shelley.
To the Christ.
Tryst, The.
Water-Lily, The.
Where were ye, Birds, that bless His name, sel.

Tabermann, Tommy
Possessive Love.
Seas Are My Eyes, Birches My Voice.

Tablada, José Juan
Alternating Nocturne.
Dawn in the Cockloft.
Haiku of a Day.
Haiku of the Flowerpot.
Idol in the Porch, The.
Parrot, The.

Tachibana Akemi
Deafening noise!, sel.
Happiness Is When, sel.
Ingots of silver, sel.
Poems of Solitary Delights.
Scenes in a Silver Mine, sel.
Sending up billows, sel.
Servant ("The gourd of wine"), The, sel.
Soaked in sluices, sel.
Stark naked, sel.
Stepping through the sleet, sel.
What a delight it is/ When, skimming through the pages, sel.
What a delight it is/ When, spreading paper, sel.
What a delight it is/ when, borrowing, sel.
What a delight it is/ When I blow away the ash, sel.
What a delight it is/ When everyone admits, sel.
What a delight it is/ When a guest you cannot stand, sel.
What a delight it is/ When, after a hundred days, sel.
What a delight it is/ When, of a morning, sel.
What a delight it is/ When on the bamboo matting, sel.
What a delight it is/ When I find a good brush, sel.

Tachihara Michizo
Afterthoughts.
For a Certain Night.
For a Lost Night.
For a Memory.
In Mourning for the Summer.
Night Song of a Traveller.
Rainbow and You.
Soon Autumn.

Tadamichi (Fujiwara no Tadamichi)
Puppeteers, The.

Tadamine, Mibu. *See* Mibu Tadamine
Tadanori (Taira Tadanori)
Capital at Shiga, The.
Overtaken by the dark.
Tadaomi (Shimada no Tadaomi)
Washing My Hair.
Tadema, L. Alma
Bed-Time.
Playgrounds.
Snowdrops.
When the sun has left the hill-top, sel.
Taeko, Tomioka. *See* Tomioka Taeko
Taft, Margo
I have been my arm.
Tagami, Jeff
Foreman's Wife, The.
Horn Blow, The.
Now It Is Broccoli.
Stonehouse.
Without Names.
Taggard, Genevieve
American Farm, 1934.
Dilemma of the Elm.
Doomsday Morning.
Enamel Girl, The.
Geraniums, The.
In the Tail of the Scorpion.
Little Girl with Bands on Her Teeth, The.
Millions of Strawberries.
Poem to Explain Everything about a Certain Day in Vermont, A.
Solar Myth.
Song for Unbound Hair.
Squirrel near Library.
To the Veterans of the Abraham Lincoln Brigade.
Train: Abstraction.
Try Topic.
With Child.
Tagliabue, John
Bare Arms of Trees, The.
Fast.
I Sought All Over the World.
Maine Vastly Covered with Much Snow.
Pinta, the Nina and the Santa Maria, The.
Unseen Deer, An.
Tagore, Rabindranath
Autumn.
Day after Day, sel.
Deliverance is not for me in renunciation, sel.
Echo always mocks the sound, The, sel.
Fairyland.
Have you not heard his silent steps?, sel.
He it is, the innermost one, who awakens my being with his deep hidden touches, sel.
Here is thy footstool and there rest thy feet, sel.
Home, The.
I Have Got My Leave, sel.
I know not from what distant time thou art ever coming nearer to meet me., sel.
If It Is Not My Portion, sel.
In the Dusky Path of a Dream, sel.
Journey Nears the Road-End, The.
Leave this chanting and singing and telling of beads, sel.
My Song.
On the Slope of the Desolate River, sel.
Paper Boats.
Thou Art the Sky, sel.
Vocation.
Yellow Bird Sings, The, sel.
Taha, Ali Mahmud
Blind Musician, The.
Egyptian Serenade.
Tahureau, Jacques
Moonlight.
Shadows of His Lady.
Tai Piao-yüan
As My Way Passed through T'ung-ch'uan.
Cheng-tao Temple.

In the Year *Chi-hai*.
Painting, *"Mist and Rain on the Spring River,"* by Hsiao Chao, The.
Painting of One Hundred Wild Geese, A.
Returning to Yin-ch'eng Early in the Year *Ting-ch'ou*.
South of the house, north of the house, sel.
Supervisor, Han Chün-mei, Has Shown Me Five Poems He Has Written, The.
T'ai-shang
In Reply to Questions.
Taigi (Tan Taigi)
Angry, is he, a wasp drinking water, sel.
As I picked it up.
At daybreak when plovers call, sel.
Autumn night: I question, sel.
Beautiful sunlight has come, sel.
Bridge broken, The.
Chilling moon, A.
Cold moon—the sound of the bridge, sel.
Eyes open, I listen to spring, sel.
I feel someone dying of an illness, sel.
I lie down, I get up, sel.
I peer into quietness, sel.
I swept and ended up not sweeping, sel.
In the waves rolling in, sel.
"It's the east wind blowing."
Kyuko and I Stayed at Rittei's, sel.
Long night: I wake up, A, sel.
Many mosquitoes bloated with blood, sel.
Near a fence, young, small grasses, sel.
On the dust-heap
Other end of this long bridge, The, sel.
Rat has dropped into the water jar, A, sel.
Servant, taking leave, A, sel.
Shower: on a raft the pole, A, sel.
Sound of casting a net downstream, sel.
Sound of the rain, The, sel.
Spring night: I frighten a woman, A, sel.
Stream's clear: five inches, The, sel.
Tree-searing wind: wrinkles of age, sel.
Village child with spring grass, A, sel.
Warbler: leaves hiding it, sel.
Water of a shallow river, The, sel.
Way it walks, the snail, The, sel.
Winter withering.
With a faint scent of river, sel.
Taiko
Straw sandals worn through, soles blistered.
Taikyoku Zosu
Improvised while Living in the Outskirts of the Capital.
Taira no Kanemari. *See* Kanemari
Taira Tadanori. *See* Tadanori
Tait, William J.
Gallow Hill.
Takahama Kyoshi
Haiku: "Against the broad sky."
Haiku: "Autumn wind:/ Everything I see."
Haiku: "First butterfly."
Haiku: "In the old man's eyes."
Haiku: "Like dust swirling."
Haiku: "On far hills."
Haiku: "On the stolen."
Haiku: "Shuttlecock:/ Smooth as oil."
Haiku: "Sky is high, The."
Haiku: "Snake fled, The."
Takahashi Mutsuo
Dream of Barcelona.
Forecome and Come.
Myself Departing.
Myself in an Anatomical Chart of Sexual Intercourse.
Myself in the Disguise of an Ancient Goddess.
Myself of the Onan Legend.
Myself with a Glory Hole.
Sleeping Wrestler.
We Do Not Know the Name of the King.
Winter: 1955.

Takahashi Shinkichi
Beach Rainbow.
Birth.
Fish.
Snail ("The snail crawls over blackness").
Sparrow in Winter.
Takai Kito. *See* **Kito**
Takakuwa Ranko. *See* **Ranko**
Takamura Kotaro
Artless Talk.
Bedraggled Ostrich.
Chieko Mounting on the Wind.
Comic Verse.
Cooperative Council, *sel.*
Day of Pearl Harbor, The, *sel.*
In Adoration of Love.
Sculpting in the Imperial Presence, *sel.*
Shoan Temple.
Spouting Whale.
Takamura, Ono. *See* **Ono Takamura**
Takarai Kikaku. *See* **Kikaku**
Takashi, Matsumoto. *See* **Matsumoto Takashi**
Takechi no Kurohito. *See* **Kurohito**
Takenaka Iku
Stars.
Story.
Thinking Stone.
Tourist Japan.
Takeuchi Unto
Spending the Night in a Rundown Temple.
Takuboku, Ishikawa. *See* **Ishikawa Takuboku**
Talbot, Charles Remington. *See* **"Brownjohn, John"**
Taliesin
Battle of Argoed Llwyfain, The.
Death Song for Owain ab Urien.
Song to the Wind, A.
Tall, Grace Cornell
Needle, The.
Tallet, José Zacarías
Rumba.
TallMountain, Mary
Good Grease.
Indian Blood.
Matmiya.
Peeling Pippins.
There Is No Word for Goodbye.
Ts'eekkaayah.
Women in Old Parkas, The.
Tamefuji
What will have become.
Tamehide (Reizei Tamehide)
As the mist clears away.
Blooming everywhere.
First one notices.
I may well once more.
I thought it was mist.
In the gloom of dusk.
Lightning.
Tameie (Fujiwara no Tameie)
Always in the past.
Cuckoo calls out, A.
Dangling sacred cords.
Even the dead leaves.
Footprints are gone, The.
Globeflowers on a Riverbank.
I had lost myself.
In dawn's early glow.
Isuzu River—/ like a mirror left behind.
On my way back home.
To Akashi's strand/ I came in hope of finding.
Village people/ will be out picking young greens, The.
What am I to think?
Winter Poem, A.
Yes, but all the same.
Tamekane (Kyogoku Tamekane)
As the night wears on.
At Takase Mountain.

Bird voices gently calling, *sel.*
Blocked by thick branches.
Cuckoo,/ repeating his cry, The, *sel.*
Distant View of the Sea, A.
Drawn on by moonlight, *sel.*
Easy River, they call it.
Even the bird calls.
Evening Snow.
From peaks in the morning storm, *sel.*
From today forward.
He passes the inn.
How many times.
In the path of the late sun, *sel.*
In the snow piled up.
Late at night, *sel.*
Moon in the garden.
Mountain Hut in a Storm.
Mountain wind, The, *sel.*
My mind is made up.
On an evening/ aglow with the crimson.
On Love, *sel.*
On the storm's freezing blast, *sel.*
Out in the garden.
Over empty limbs.
Plum flowers/ blooming crimson, *sel.*
Rainy night, A, *sel.*
Round and round time turns.
Scent of plum flowers, The.
So few rays, *sel.*
So much more forlorn.
Starting, then stopping.
Sun is almost down, The.
Takase Mountain:/ I push along, *sel.*
Those bitter feelings.
Though the glow, *sel.*
Traveler's pillow,/ bundled up, undone, A, *sel.*
Warbler's voice, The, *sel.*
Weighed down with dew, *sel.*
When one looks at it.
Where the bright moon comes up, *sel.*
While day lasted, *sel.*
White dew,/ come from no one knows where, The, *sel.*
Wind/ that for a time blew so wildly, The, *sel.*
Wind that tossed the pines, *sel.*
With a sudden gust.
With him bound by fear.
With night coming on.
Tameko (Kyogoku Tameko)
Clouds from the peak.
Even at its longest.
Even my own heart.
Following the wind.
"I can't come tonight."
In the pines, a storm.
In their seasons.
Kept Indoors on a Winter Evening.
Love Poem, A: "In sad revery."
Mankind and man's world.
On the fine new robes.
Out on Kara Cape.
Pines along the Coast.
Sheets of rain, The.
Showers are falling.
So worn out with worry.
To the sound of the wind.
You heartless man.
Tamemasa (Reizei Tamemasa)
Deep loneliness/ was something I was used to.
Fireflies over a Marsh.
Irises in a Marsh.
Lark along the Road, A.
Leaves Falling on a Bridge.
Love Expresses with Candle as a Metaphor.
Night at the End of the Year.
Snipe in the Marshes, A.
Sprigs of Blossoms.
Spring Moon Concealed, The.
Spring Sea.
Summer Moon.

Taking the Cool in the Shade of the Trees.
Taking the Cool to Forget Summer.
Village Snowfall.
Wood Thrush Concealed, A.
Tamenori (Kyogoku Tamenori)
Above in the clear.
As autumn wears on.
Enough—so be it!
In the dusky light.
Over heavy dew.
Tamesada (Nijo Tamesada)
Love Likened to Clouds.
Moon, The, *sel.*
Passing Miscanthus on the Road.
Sao Princess/ borrows a new robe of haze, The.
Smoke rising, The.
Spring having passed.
Winter Moon after a Rain, The.
Won't you please hasten.
Tameshige (Nijo Tameshige)
Autumn Evening.
Cold Reeds around an Inlet.
He must be heading.
If our love too.
Leaves Falling at Dusk.
Red Leaves.
Snow is all gone, The.
Wind at a House in the Paddies, The.
Winter Moon.
Tamesuke (Reizei Tamesuke)
Born into the world.
How can it be.
I wish I could tell.
In this mountain village.
Mountain winds, The.
Showers go on, The.
Sun must be setting, The.
Tameuji (Fujiwara no Tameuji)
At Sasanami/ the pines are just as they were.
Dew and the frost, The.
Did it not signal.
If anyone asks.
"Not a leaf shall stay."
On a spring night.
Sao Princess/ has donned her new robe of haze, The.
Since the moon resides.
Tameyo (Nijo Tameyo)
Because this village.
Cooler than the wind.
Cormorant boats, The.
If I could have my way.
In the mountain stream.
Not even waiting.
Now even the sound.
O moon at dawn.
That just one of you.
What is it/ that is senseless to lament.
What use is prayer.
Tami No Kurohito
Sitting Alone in the Mountains.
Tamiki, Hara. *See* **Hara Tamiki**
Tam'si, Tchicaya U
Here is the stream again under the rainbow, *sel.*
Tamura Ryuichi
Autumn.
Emperor, The.
Etching.
Four Thousand Days and Nights.
Golden Fantasy.
Image, The.
October Poem.
Premonition.
Study in Terror, A.
Sunken Temple.
Three Voices.
Voice.
Winter Music.

Tan, Bee Bee
Curfew.
Pontianak.

Tanaka, Ronald P.
Big Trimmer, The.
Snacks.

Tanaka Fuyuji
Autumn Night.
Blue Night Road.
Lakeside Hotel.

Tandori, Dezsö
"And Brief, Good Mother? For I Am In
Haste? Whither?"
Details.
Homage.
Sadness of the Bare Copula.

Tan'ee, Shlomoh
End of Summer.
End Song.
We Two.

Tanfield, Lady
Here shadowe lie.

T'ang Hsien-Tsu
Autumn River.
Cave of Gold Essence in Ning-tu, The.
Descending the Ridge of Flying Clouds.
Evening View from the Bell Tower at
P'ing-ch'ang.
Hsiu-chou.
Inspector Hsü Claims He Has Found the
Secret of Youth.
My son, you loved telling the story of Prince
Nata, sel.
On the Day of Washing the Buddha in the
Year Ting-wei.
Paintings on My Wall Have Been Damaged
by the Weather, The.
Spending the Night on the River.

T'ang Wan
To the Tune "The Phoenix Hairpin."

T'ang Yin
Among red leaves and green mountains, white
clouds fly, sel.
Fog of night envelops the flowering trees,
The, sel.
Galloping around, north and south, sel.
Inscribed on a Painting ("At the country inn,
thousands of peach trees").
Inscribed on a Painting of a Fisherman.
Inscribed on a Painting of Bamboo.
Inscribed on a Painting ("On the mountain,
old trees, still green in autumn").
Inscribed on a Painting ("Thatched hut among
the pines, door open near a cliff").
Inscribed on a Painting ("The places I go,
leaning on my bramble cane").
Mountain pavilion is silent—few people visit
me here, The, sel.
Nature has endowed her with complete charm,
sel.
On the Butterflies.
Pines and cedars, a hundred feet of green,
clinging to the earth, sel.
Scene at Heaven Gate, The.
Song of Peach Blossom Retreat.
Ten days of wind and rain, depressing
darkness!, sel.
Who used his masterful brush to paint this
romantic beauty?, sel.
Wind sighs in the reeds—autumn on the rustic
shore, The, sel.

Tangikuku, Hine
Song of Sickness, A.

Tani Rokkoku
Strolling in a Nearby Village.

Tanikawa Shuntaro
Family.
Growing Up.
Isolation of Two Milliard Light Years, The.
Kiss ("I close my eyes, the world recedes").

Kiss ("She came home, smelling of another
man").
Nero.
Sounds.
That Act.
When the Wind Is Strong.

Tannahill, Robert
Midges Dance aboon the Burn, The.
O! Are Ye Sleepin [or Sleeping], Maggie?

Tan Pai, Joshua
Life of Hard Times, The.

T'an Ssu-t'ung
Fen-chou.
Mooring at Night.
Parting Chant.
Tao-wu Mountain.
T'ung Pass.
Written on an Autumn Day at the Garden of
the Official Residence of the Governor of
Kansu.

Tan Taigi. See **Taigi**

Tan Ying
Drinking the Wind.

Tao-chi
Bend after bend, the long embankment.
Flower-Rain Terrace, The.
Inscribed on a Painting.
Inscribed on a Painting of a Wu-t'ung Tree by
Myself.
Inscribed on "Drunk in the Autumn Woods."
Inscribed on My Ink Landscape Painting.
Inscribed on My Large Landscape Hanging
Scroll "Listening to a Waterfall."
Inscribed on My Little Painting of Plum
Blossom and Bamboo.
Inscribed on the Wall at the Temple of the
Auspicious Talisman.
Mood comes on—I want to cross Hsi-ling,
The.
Riding a Boat on Wu-ling Stream.
Searching for Herb Brazier and Cinnabar
Well.
Trip to Hua-yang Mountain, A.
Trip to the Village of the River of White
Sand, A.

T'ao Ch'ien [or T'ao Yuan-ming]
Blaming Sons.
Fall chrysanthemums have beautiful colors,
sel.
I built my hut in a place where people live,
sel.
I built my hut near where people live, sel.
Imitating the Old Poems.
In the Year with the Cyclical Sign Mou-shen.
Long I Have Loved to Stroll.
Long time ago, A.
Matching a Poem by Secretary Kuo.
Motionless Clouds.
Moving House ("A long time I've wanted to
live in the southern village").
Moving House ("In spring and fall there are
many days").
On Being Assigned as Military Adviser to the
Garrison Army.
Once more Fields and Gardens.
Poem in the Form of a Coffin-Puller's Song
("A plain of wild grasses, broad and
tangled").
Poem in the Form of a Coffin-Puller's Song
("In the old days I had no wine to drink").
Poem in the Form of a Coffin-Puller's Song
("What has a life must have a death").
Poem without a Category ("Sun and moon
refuse to slow their pace").
Poem without a Category ("The brave man
has ambitions wide as the four seas").
Prosperity and decline have no fixed dwelling,
sel.
Reading The Classic of Hills and Seas.
Returning to My Home in the Country ("I
planted beans at the foot of the southern
mountain").

Returning to My Home in the Country ("In
youth I couldn't sing to the common tune").
Returning to My Home in the Country ("Out
here in the fields, few social affairs").
Returning to My Home in the Country ("So
long since I've enjoyed the hills and
ponds").
Shadow Replies to Substance, sel.
Shady, Shady.
Spirit Expounds, sel.
Stopping Wine.
Substance Addresses Shadow, sel.
Such a strong color on the late
chrysanthemums, sel.
Way's been lost for a thousand years, The,
sel.

Tao Tschung Yu, Lyall
Richer now the body's juices.

T'ao Yuan-ming. See **T'ao Ch'ien**

Tapahonso, Luci
Belly of the Land, The.
Breeze Swept Through, A.
Dust Will Settle, The.
Hills Brothers Coffee.
It Was a Special Treat.
Sheepherder Blues.
Trees along the River, The.

Tappan, William Bingham
Hour of Peaceful Rest, The.
Ransomed Spirit to Her Home, The.

Tapscott, Stephen
Hank.

Taranci, Cahit Sitki
One of the Dead Speaks.

Tarn, Nathaniel
Where Babylon Ends.

Tarrant, Susan Navarre
Kate and I.

Tasso, Torquato
Cats of Santa Anna, The.
Joyous birds, hid under greenwood shade,
The, sel.
Love.
O lovely age of gold!, sel.
Pluto's Council, sel.
Prayer Brings Rain, A, sel.
Silent the Forests.
Sweet Armida tooke this charge on hand,
The, sel.
To His Mistress in Absence.

Tastu, Amable
Guardian Angel, The.

Tate, Allen
Aeneas at Washington.
Ah, Christ, sel.
Citizen myself, or personal friend, sel.
Cross, The.
Death of Little Boys.
Emblems.
Eye, The.
Fire I praise was once perduring flame, The,
sel.
Gay citizen, myself, and thoughtful friend,
sel.
Horatian Epode to the Duchess of Malfi.
Idiot.
Jubilo.
Mediterranean, The.
More Sonnets at Christmas, I.
Mother and Son.
Mr. Pope.
Near to me as my flesh, my flesh and blood,
sel.
Not power nor the storied hand of God, sel.
Ode: "Once more the country calls."
Ode to the Confederate Dead.
Paradigm, The.
Pauper, A.
Seasons of the Soul.
Shadow and Shade.

Sonnets at Christmas, II.
Swimmers, The.
This Is the Day, *sel.*
This is the day His hour of life draws near, *sel.*
Times have changed, there is not left to us, The, *sel.*
To the Lacedemonians.
Traveller, The.
What is this flesh and blood compounded of, *sel.*
Winter Mask.

Tate, James
Blue Booby, The.
Book of Lies, The.
Chaste Stranger, The.
Coda.
Conjuring Roethke.
Constant Defender.
Consumed.
Dear Reader.
Distant Orgasm, The.
Horseshoe, The.
If It Would All Please Hurry.
Intimidations of an Autobiography.
Jelka Revisited.
Land of Little Sticks, 1945.
Lost Pilot, The.
Love Making.
Miss Cho Composes in the Cafeteria.
Motorcyclists, The.
My Great Great etc. Uncle Patrick Henry.
Mystic Moment.
Neighbors.
On to the Source.
Pet Deer, The.
Poem for the Sandman.
Poem to Some of my Recent Poems.
Powder of Sympathy, The.
President Slumming, The.
Professor Waking, The.
Riven Doggeries.
Shadowboxing.
Sloops in the Bay.
Soup of Venus, The.
Spring Was Begging to Be Born.
Stray Animals.
Summer Nights.
Tall Trees by Still Waters.
Vagabond, A.
Wedding, A.
Wheelchair Butterfly, The.
Who Can Tell When He Is Awake.
Wild Cheese, The.

Tate, Nahum
As Pants the Hart.
Choice, The.
Lord, Have Mercy.
Now if thou hast one dram of grace.
Old England.
Prologue: "If yet there be a few that take delight," *sel.*
While Shepherds Watched [Their Flocks by Night]

Tate, Nahum and Nicholas Brady
Lord, Who's the Happy Man.

Tate Ryuwan
Playing Bowl-and-Bead.

Tatersal, Robert
Bricklayer's Labours, The.

Tatnall, Frances Dorr
Art Thou the Same.

Tatsuji, Miyoshi. *See* **Miyoshi Tatsuji**

Tauhindauli
I Am Stone of Many Colors.
Waiting for a Second Time.
Wrapped Hair Bundles.
Year of Winter, The.

Tauhindauli (Frank LaPena)
There was a time when the stars fell like rain.
Waiting for a Second Time.

Tawney, Cyril
Diesel and Shale.
Grey Funnel Line, The.
On a Monday Morning.
Reunion.
Sally Free and Easy.

Taylor, Allan
Ballad for the Unknown Soldier.
Still He Sings.
Time.

Taylor, Andrew
Developing a Wife.
Invention of Fire, The.
Nature.

Taylor, Ann
Baby, The.
Baby's Dance, The, *at.*
Cow, The.
Meddlesome Matty.
My Mother.
Notorious Glutton, The.
Pin, The.
Sheep, The.
Washing and Dressing.

Taylor, Ann and Jane Taylor
Cow and the Ass, The.
Little Fish That Would Not Do as It Was Bid, The.

Taylor, Apirana
Sad Joke on a Marae.
Taiaha Haka Poem.
Womb, The.

Taylor, Bayard
A Night with a Wolf.
Ah, moment not to be purchased, *sel.*
All or Nothing.
America, *sel.*
Angelo Orders His Dinner.
Ariel in the Cloven Pine.
Ballad of Hiram Hover, The.
Bedouin Song.
Camerados.
Cantelope, The.
Cimabuella.
Demon of the Mirror, The.
Fight of Paso del Mar, The.
God, to whom we look up blindly, *sel.*
Gwendoline.
Lincoln at Gettysburg, *sel.*
National Ode, The.
Nauvoo.
Ode on [*or* to] a Jar of Pickles.
Palabras Grandiosas.
Promissory Note, The.
Quaker Widow, The.
Sir Eggnogg.
Song: "Daughter of Egypt, veil thine eyes!"
Song of the Camp, The.
Through Baltimore.
To M. T.

Taylor, Benjamin Franklin
Isle of the Long Ago, The.

Taylor, Bert Leston ("B.L.T.")
Aprilly.
Canopus.
Dinosaur, The.
Doxology.
Hence These Rimes.
Passionate Professor, The.
Those Flapjacks of Brown's.
Upon Julia's Arctics.

Taylor, Caleb J.
O Jesus, My Savior, I Know Thou Art Mine.

Taylor, Charles S.
Scandal among the Flowers, A.

Taylor, Edward
Accusation of the Inward Man, The.
Address to the Soul Occasioned by a Rain, An.
Am I thy gold? Or purse, Lord, for thy wealth, *sel.*
Angels Sung a Carol, The.
Apples of gold, in silver pictures shrined, *sel.*
Deity of Love Incorporate, A, *sel.*
Ebb and Flow, The.
Elegy upon the Death of That Holy Man of God Mr, An John Allen.
Fig for Thee, Oh! Death, A.
Frowardness of the Elect in the Work of Conversion, The.
Glory of and Grace in the Church Set Out, The, *sel.*
God's Selecting Love in the Decree, *sel.*
Huswifery.
Joy of Church Fellowship Rightly Attended, The, *sel.*
Leaf gold, Lord of thy golden wedge o'erlaid, *sel.*
Like to the marigold, I blushing close, *sel.*
Lord, art thou at the table head above, *sel.*
Methinks I spy Almighty holding in, *sel.*
My Blessed Lord, how doth thy Beautious Spouse, *sel.*
My gracious Lord, I would thee glory doe, *sel.*
My Lord, my life, can envy ever bee, *sel.*
My shattred phancy stole away from mee, *sel.*
My sin! my sin, my God, these cursed dregs, *sel.*
Oh! Golden Rose! Oh. Glittering Lilly White, *sel.*
Oh! Good, good, good, my Lord. What more love yet, *sel.*
Oh leaden heeld. Lord, give, forgive I pray, *sel.*
Oh, that I always breath'd in such an air, *sel.*
Oh that I was the Bird of Paradise!, *sel.*
Oh! what a thing is man? Lord, who am I?, *sel.*
Our Insufficiency to Praise God Suitably for His Mercy.
Outward Man Accused, The.
Peace, peace, my hony [*or* honey], do not cry, *sel.*
Preface, The: "Infinity, when all things it beheld," *sel.*
Prologue: "Lord, can a crumb of dust the earth outweigh," *sel.*
Should I with silver tooles delve through the hill, *sel.*
Soul's Groan to Christ for Succo[u]r, The, *sel.*
Still I complain; I am complaining still, *sel.*
Stupendious love! all saints astonishment, *sel.*
Thou Art the Tree of Life.
Thy grace, dear Lord's my golden wrack I find, *sel.*
Thy human frame, my glorious Lord, I spy, *sel.*
Unclean, unclean: my Lord, undone, all vile, *sel.*
Upon a Spider Catching a Fly.
Upon a Wasp Chilled [*or* Child] with Cold.
Upon Wedlock and Death of Children.
What love is this of thine, that cannot be, *sel.*
What shall I say, my Lord? With what begin?, *sel.*
When thy bright beams, my Lord, so strike mine eye, *sel.*
Ye angells bright, pluck from your wings a quill, *sel.*

Taylor, Eleanor Ross
In the Churchyard.
New Dust.
Painted Bridge, The.

Taylor, Eric Clough
Catmint.

Taylor, Frances Beatrice
Husbandman, The.
Wedgewood Bowl, A.
Taylor, Geoffrey
Admonition to the Muse.
Bluebell.
Boat-Haven, Co. Mayo.
Cruel, Clever Cat.
English Liberal.
Epitaph: "Nor practising virtue nor committing crime."
From an Irish-Latin Macaronic.
Gentlemen.
Song: "Rousing to rein his pad's head back."
Taylor, George Lansing
Dare to Do Right.
Taylor, Henry
Artichoke.
As on a Darkling Plain.
At the Swings.
Breakings.
Campaign Promise.
Country Curate, The.
Depressed by the Death of the Horse That He Bought from Robert Bly.
Flying Change, The.
Getting at the Root of the Matter.
In Orbit.
J. V. Cunningham Gets Hung Up on a Dirty, of All Things, Joke.
Landscape with Tractor.
Miss Creighton.
Riding a One-eyed Horse.
Riding Lesson.
Robert Bly Says Something Too.
Shapes, Vanishings.
Sonnet in the Mail Coach.
Speech.
Taking to the Woods.
To Hear My Head Roar.
View from a Cab, The.
Way It Sometimes Is, The.
Taylor, James Bayard
To G. H. B.
Taylor, Jane
Disappointment, The.
Field Daisy, The.
Gleaner, The.
Greedy Richard.
I Like Little Pussy.
Meadows, The.
Pigs, The.
Recreation.
Star, The.
Two Little Kittens.
Taylor, Jeffreys
Lion and the Mouse, The.
Taylor, Jeremy
My Soul Doth Pant towards Thee.
Penitent, The.
Taylor, John
I come from Bohem, yet no news I bring, sel.
Prague is a famous, ancient, kingly seat, sel.
Sonnet: "Sweet semi-circled Cynthia played at maw," sel.
Trumpet of Liberty, The.
Taylor, Joseph Russell
Breath on the Oat.
Flute, The.
Veery-Thrush, The.
Taylor, Lucy
Leac A'Chlarsair.
Taylor, Rachel Annand
Ecstasy.
Princess of Scotland, The.
Taylor, Rod
Dakota: October, 1822, Hunkpapa Warrior.
Taylor, Sarah Wingate
With Metaphor.
Taylor, Sir Henry
Elena's Song, sel.

Taylor, Tom
Abraham Lincoln.
Taylor, William
Vision, The.
Tchaikovsky, Peter Ilich
Legend, A, at.
Tchernichowsky, Saul [or Sha'ul Chernikhovsky]
Before the Statue of Apollo.
Dance of Saul with the Prophets, The.
Death of Tammuz, The.
Grave in Ukraine, A.
I Believe.
Man Is Nothing But.
Saul's Song of Love.
This Be Our Revenge.
To Ashtaroth and Bel.
Vulture! Vulture in Your Mountains.
Te Aomuhurangi Te Maaka
Go Down, O Sun, Out from the Motu River.
Haka: Hinemotu.
Te Apakura, Irihapeti Rangi
Reply to a Marriage Proposal.
Te Heuheu Tukino
Lament for Te Heuheu Herea.
Te Kooti Rikirangi
Song of Instruction, A.
Te Puea Herangi
Remain, Rata.
Te-whaka-io-roa
Give Me My Infant Now.
Te Whetu
Sound of My Sneezing Nose, The.
Teasdale, Sara
Answer, The.
Appraisal.
April.
August Night.
Barter.
Calm Morning at Sea.
Crystal Gazer, The.
Epitaph: "Serene descent, as a red leaf's descending."
Falling Star, The.
February Twilight.
Full Moon; Santa Barbara.
Grace before Sleep.
"I Am Not Yours."
I Shall Not Care.
Immortal.
Inn of Earth, The.
Long Hill, The.
Mastery.
May Day.
Moonlight.
Morning Song.
Night.
Night Song at Amalfi.
On the South Downs.
Prayer, A: "Until I lose my soul and lie."
September Midnight.
Solitary, The.
Song: "Let it be forgotten, as a flower is forgotten."
Song Making.
Spring in War-Time.
Spring Night.
Stars.
There Will Come Soft Rains.
Understanding.
Water-Lilies.
"What Do I Care."
Wisdom.
Wood Song.
Tegnér, Esaias
Frithiof's Farewell, sel.
Frithiof's Homestead, sel.
Teika (Fujiwara no Taika)
About people, no, I don't know how they feel, sel.
Above a clear, penetrating wind, sel.

Above crimson leaves.
Above the wind the starlight is clear, sel.
After his tryst.
Against the cherries on the hazy hilltop, sel.
As a warbler flits from one plum twig to another, sel.
As far as one can see.
As far as the eye can see.
As far away as distant China, sel.
As I lay awake.
As I look around, I see a weir of waves, sel.
As I look out, there are neither blossoms nor crimson leaves, sel.
As I look, the moon has moved West, sel.
As I pick young herbs for you, sel.
As I searched for cherry blossoms, sel.
As it begins to dawn, I almost take for daybreak, sel.
As soon as it blows, autumn grass and trees wither, sel.
As winds blow over white dewdrops, sel.
At the rising, climbing, southern limit there are clouds, sel.
Autumn gone, the past distant in the great sky, sel.
Autumn has come.
Autumn has come; crimson leaves have fallen, sel.
Autumn wind is and is not as of old, The, sel.
"Autumn's come"—"The year's half gone", sel.
Away from the direction of falling blossoms, sel.
Because limits are set, sel.
Because my home village is close to Mount Yoshino, sel.
Bitter—that I should not have decayed, sel.
Black of my hair, The, sel.
Blossoming plum.
Blossoms of plum.
Building a Sano boat-bridge, sel.
Bush clovers must have shed their flowers, sel.
Carried overhead and wished upon, sel.
Cherries bloom on distant hills, sel.
Cherry blossoms must have opened, sel.
Cicada voices rising continually, far away, sel.
Cloud, a reminder of my lover, The, sel.
Coming to an end and leaving the moon as a keepsake, sel.
Could it be I wait.
Crimson leaves flow in Tatsuta River, sel.
Dew at the tip of a leaf, sel.
Dew on my sleeves, The, sel.
Dew, scatter if you will, sel.
Didn't we make a vow, sel.
Do not let it be known, sel.
Dozing, thoughts interminable in paths of dream, sel.
Drawn by the memory of your face I turn to look, sel.
Dream broken by the sound of a mallet, sel.
Even her heart again a stranger's, sel.
Even in a remote place eightfold heaps, sel.
Evening voices of cicadas, The, sel.
Everyone else has changed to a flowery robe, sel.
Fading, desolate: at the autumn coloring, sel.
Faintly, in the dawn moonlight, sel.
Familiar sound/ of a dog's rough bark, The.
Floating bridge of dreams this spring night, The, sel.
Flower's color has passed, The, sel.
For the jewel-like dew.
For the one I await the path must have ended, sel.
From now on may it go on falling, sel.
From the outer gate.
From tomorrow, who will visit, sel.
Frost has touched the bamboo grass, sel.

Great sky hazy with scents of plum blossoms, The, *sel.*
Had I expected this?, *sel.*
He does not come, but I wait, *sel.*
He for whom I wait.
Here again, another useless sign of the floating world, *sel.*
Hint at the hilltop of the moon, A, *sel.*
How can I forget?—spring hazes lost, *sel.*
How many autumns have I passed, *sel.*
I do not complain.
I had never guessed.
I lifted her hair strand by strand, *sel.*
I remember, I burn brushwood, *sel.*
I shall not forget.
I suffer enough, now it would all be the same, *sel.*
I want only to forget.
I will return and look on Matsushima once again, *sel.*
Ice on my laid-out sleeve still frozen, The, *sel.*
If by chance someone asks, *sel.*
If I can't twist my thread with yours, *sel.*
If I must, I'll have to pick them haphazardly, *sel.*
If only I had my phantom to send to you, *sel.*
If you do not come, must I sleep alone, *sel.*
In a patch of sky.
In a winter-seared forest, *sel.*
In Akishino is it raining on the villages, *sel.*
In May rain, the smoke from the seaweed, *sel.*
In May rains the water, the waves, *sel.*
In my birthplace, the garden and the hedges, *sel.*
In the autumn paddies, the roof mats for the makeshift, *sel.*
In the evening my thoughts go toward the end of the clouds, *sel.*
In the past too, hearts have separated from hearts, *sel.*
In Yatano Field the reeds have turned color, *sel.*
Is it because autumn dew has collected, *sel.*
Its dark green—what if it should be unable to resist, *sel.*
Its rope broken.
It's the start of spring, they say, *sel.*
Izumi River: like the bubbles on a pole, *sel.*
Just because you said, "I'll come right away", *sel.*
Lamplight in the window at slow dawn, A, *sel.*
Light of the moon that crosses the Plain of Heaven, The, *sel.*
Like a mountain stream whose rapids are blocked, *sel.*
Like some ailing leaf, *sel.*
Like the foam on the ever-flowing Thinking River, *sel.*
Like the white dewdrop that forms at the leaf-tip, *sel.*
Like tinkling gems, neither dewdrops nor tears stay, *sel.*
Like trees buried in the shallows of Natori River, *sel.*
Lodging in a hut where the Naniwa men burn reeds, *sel.*
Loneliness has no special color, *sel.*
Loneliness is more intense with frost than with snow, *sel.*
Long as the foot-wearying mountain, *sel.*
Look, this must be love that fills the sky!, *sel.*
Looking at it, just thinking about it, *sel.*
Looking at the moon, I feel sad, *sel.*
Love Poem, A: "Year is ending, The."
Lovely rock buried under the seaweed, A, *sel.*
Lush emerald the summer color becomes, *sel.*
Missives, fleeting, my lover's only trace, *sel.*
Mists above the crimson leaves, *sel.*
More melancholy than the bright moon, *sel.*

My love affair is like the clumps of bush clover, *sel.*
My thought grows like rock azaleas, *sel.*
My thoughts, useless dreams in midair, *sel.*
Neglectful, I have not died of love, *sel.*
Negligently the day opens before I have time to sleep, *sel.*
No shade for halting the horse to shake my sleeves, *sel.*
No shelter in sight.
Not a soul is left.
Not a trace is left.
Not like an ordinary cloud, *sel.*
Not many days have passed, *sel.*
Now, today, I'll lose myself, *sel.*
Off at Tatsuta/ white clouds are piling up.
On a spring day when boundless light, *sel.*
On his way home, he may be watching this, *sel.*
On Matsuo Beach/ I wait in the pines at dusk.
On Mount Moru where both white dew, *sel.*
On my way home at dusk, *sel.*
On the sea god's plain the waves and the sky merge, *sel.*
On this Spring night.
On this trip I couldn't come with offerings, *sel.*
One who's unkind is like you, The, *sel.*
Only one or two nights since winter came, *sel.*
Orange flowers scatter in a village, *sel.*
Parting from you, I go to Inaba, *sel.*
People of the hundred-acre palace, The, *sel.*
Pining for one who does not come.
Pity, how the dew must spill from grass leaves, *sel.*
Plain of Heaven, think of it, The, *sel.*
Plum blossoms are hard to make out, *sel.*
Princess Tatsuta's headband loosened, *sel.*
Raindrops drip down, The.
Rampant rank reed, to repress it I try, *sel.*
Regarding my infants as friends from old days, *sel.*
Relished as cooler than usual tonight, *sel.*
Retaining the colors of snow and moon, *sel.*
Rippling, a wind from the Bay of Grebes, *sel.*
Rising sun casts the same light, The, *sel.*
Scent of the plum blossoms, The, *sel.*
Seasonless waves/ of the Izumi River, The.
Since our parting when the moon at dawn looked unfriendly, *sel.*
Since the mountain cherries began to bloom, *sel.*
Since the sparse bush clover began to flower, *sel.*
Snow falling in quantities and the valley deep, The, *sel.*
So far apart our meetings, *sel.*
So light the sleeves of this cicada-wing robe, *sel.*
Somehow my heart settles on the hill's rim, *sel.*
Sound of pine winds and their color are one, The, *sel.*
Spring passed, and summer it seems has come, *sel.*
Stalling ox, shuffling, swirls up dust, A, *sel.*
Straw mattress: the Bridge Princess of Uji, *sel.*
Suddenly darkening, the sky beyond my eaves, *sel.*
Suma fisherman/ may know the ring of the sea breeze, A.
Take it as a pledge: a dewdrop on a lotus leaf, *sel.*
Tears of wild geese crying, The, *sel.*
They become fragrant, and the Spring ends, *sel.*
Thinking of the past I wake, *sel.*
This spring night.
Those early-rice paddies by the hill, *sel.*
Those long black tresses, *sel.*

Though false rumors pop up as at a fair, *sel.*
Though the space may be short, *sel.*
Through a rift in evening rainclouds, *sel.*
Throughout the land, blossoms are in their prime, *sel.*
To have grown old.
To my hut overgrown with burdocks, *sel.*
Tomorrow I'll come again to this wild path, *sel.*
Too momentary/ to be called evanescent.
Too restless to sleep.
Too tired to move fast.
Travel Poem, A.
Traveler's sleeves fluttered by an autumn wind, A, *sel.*
Troubled throughout the year, *sel.*
Turning and turning, these summer days, to my regret, *sel.*
Unable to settle through the long unending night, *sel.*
Under a willow by the road, *sel.*
Under the lamplight that grows feeble, *sel.*
Under the lower leaves of hydrangea fireflies cluster, *sel.*
Unexpectedly cool, in summer clothes, *sel.*
Unheard of even in the age of mighty gods, *sel.*
Waiting for Love.
Wakeful for last year's call that I loved, *sel.*
Weir that winds have made in a mountain stream, The, *sel.*
Well into the distance young leaves of grass undulate, *sel.*
What should I do? If only I had a hut, *sel.*
When day breaks, must I go over the mountain ridge again, *sel.*
When evening falls, the autumn wind rustles, *sel.*
When I hear deep in the mountains, *sel.*
When there's love as unrecognized as a lily, *sel.*
When you think of it.
While we bring to dawn the flower and the moon, *sel.*
White chrysanthemums they've set up at Fukiage, *sel.*
Wild geese departing, their wings in white clouds, The, *sel.*
Wild geese lured by the autumn wind, *sel.*
Will I see it again, *sel.*
Wind passes, the mirror of blossoms clouds, A, *sel.*
With no more fragrance, the *sakaki* , its voice, *sel.*
With the flower brocades.
Woods again holing up for winter, under snow, *sel.*
Would the moon ever tell us to grieve, *sel.*
Yearning for the moon hazy, *sel.*
Years and months, The, *sel.*
You, weary of the waves rolling into autumn, *sel.*
You white hydrangeas.
Your Majesty's reign will never end, *sel.*

Teishitsu (Yasuhara Teishitsu)
Oh! oh! is all I can say.

Teitoku (Matsunaga Teitoku)
Ah, he stood up, stood up by himself this year!
Both my child.
Dumplings before cherries.

"Tekahionwake." *See* **Johnson, Emily Pauline**

Telemaque, Harold Milton
Adina.

Telesilla
O Artemis and your virgin girls.

Telfer, James
Goblin's Song, The.

Teller, Judah Leib
Animal Mood.

City Highway.
Deportation.
Desire.
Etude.
Evening Motif.
Figure.
Flood, *sel.*
In a Minor Key.
Jud' Süss Oppenheimer on His First Visit with Professor Sigmund Freud, *sel.*
Jud' Süss Tells about Them and about Himself, *sel.*
Knight Sings, The.
Landscape.
Late Evening.
Letter to Sigmund Freud, *sel.*
Lines to a Tree.
Meditation at Stuyvesant Church.
Midnight, *sel.*
Minor Key.
New York in a Jewish Mood.
New York Landscapes.
98 Fahrenheit.
October.
On the Road.
Pantheism: 1968.
Passport, *sel.*
Perhaps it is God.
Poem: "Today I am like a."
Rock.
Ruins.
Sharp Hour.
Sigmund Freud at the Age of Eighty-Two, *sel.*
Switzerland 1938-1965.
Three, *sel.*
To a Christian Woman.
To the Divine Neighbor.
Wild Song.
Wilhelm Stekel Gives Up Life, *sel.*
Winter Evening.
Woman in Rain.

Teller, Judd
Budapest.
His Relative Confides in Professor Sigmund Freud.
Jews of Brisk, The.
Minor.
Three Jewish Boys Write to an Ancient Chinese Poet.
Twenty Lines to a Tree.

Tellez, Fanor
Miss Babian Tending a Bar on the Atlantic Coast ("Miss Babian, in this coast bar").

Tem, Steve Rasnic
ESP.
Lighting the Colony.
Syrup.

Temkin, Mordecai
Foul Water.
Hidden Bow.
Seal of Fire.
Your Presence.

Ten Berge, H. C. *See* **Berge, H. C. ten**
Ten-i
One-two-three-four-five-six-seven.
Tennant, Robert
Wee Davie Daylicht.
Tenneimyo
Hands released, I twirl the letter-board.
Tennyson, Alfred Tennyson, 1st Baron
Again at Christmas did we weave, *sel.*
Ah, what shall I be at fifty, *sel.*
Ancient Pistol, peacock Payne.
Ancient Sage, The.
And answer made King Arthur, breathing hard, *sel.*
And, star and system rolling past, *sel.*
As sometimes in a dead man's face, *sel.*
As thro' the Land at Eve, *sel.*
As When a Man, *sel.*

Ask Me No More [the Moon May Draw the Sea], *sel.*
At Farringford, *sel.*
At Flores in the Azores Sir Richard Grenville lay, *sel.*
Ay, *sel.*
Balin and Balan, *sel.*
Be Near Me, *sel.*
Beggar Maid, The.
Birds in the high Hall-garden, *sel.*
Blackbird, The.
Black Bull of Aldgate.
"Blame not thyself too much," I said, "nor blame", *sel.*
Break, Break, Break.
Brook, The.
Buonaparte.
"But now farewell. I am going a long way", *sel.*
By night we linger'd [*or* lingered] on the lawn, *sel.*
Calm Is the Morn, *sel.*
Captain, The.
Catch not my breath, O clamorous heart, *sel.*
Chains, my good lord: in your raised brows I read, *sel.*
Charge of the Light Brigade, The.
City Child, The.
Come Down, O Maid, *sel.*
Come into the garden, Maud, *sel.*
Come Not When I Am Dead.
Coming of Arthur, The, *sel.*
Contemplate all this work of Time, *sel.*
Cradle Song: "What does little birdie say."
Crossing the Bar.
Daisy, The.
Danube to the Severn gave, The, *sel.*
Dark house, by which once more I stand, *sel.*
Dash back that ocean with a pier, *sel.*
Dawn, The.
Dead, long dead, *sel.*
Dedication, A: "Dear, near and true—no truer Time himself."
Deep Dark Night, The, *sel.*
Defence of Lucknow, The.
Do we indeed desire the dead, *sel.*
Doors, where my heart was used to beat, *sel.*
Duet, *sel.*
Dying Swan, The.
Eagle, The.
England and America in 1782.
Enoch Arden.
Epic, The.
Fair ship, that from the Italian shore, *sel.*
Farewell, A: "Flow down, cold rivulet, to the sea."
Fatima.
Flower in the Crannied Wall.
For I Dipped [*or* Dipt] into the Future, *sel.*
"Frater Ave atque Vale."
From Sorrow Sorrow Yet Is Born.
Geraint and Enid, *sel.*
Go not, happy day, *sel.*
Godiva.
Green Sussex, *sel.*
Hendecasyllabics.
Hesperides, The.
Higher Pantheism, The.
Holy Grail, The, *sel.*
Home They Brought Her Warrior Dead, *sel.*
I cannot see the features right, *sel.*
I climb the hill: from end to end, *sel.*
I dreamed there would be spring no more, *sel.*
I envy not in any moods, *sel.*
I hate the dreadful hollow behind the little wood, *sel.*
I have led her home, my love, my only friend, *sel.*
I hear the noise about thy keel, *sel.*

I Held It Truth, *sel.*
I past [*or* passed] beside the reverend walls, *sel.*
I ran upon life unknowing, without or science or art.
I sometimes hold it half a sin, *sel.*
I Stood on a Tower in the Wet.
I trust I have not wasted breath, *sel.*
I wage not any feud with death, *sel.*
I was walking a mile, *sel.*
In my youth the growls.
If I Were Loved, as I Desire to Be.
If sleep and death be truly one, *sel.*
In Memoriam A. H. H., XCVI.
In the Garden at Swainston.
In the Spring, *sel.*
In the Valley of Cauteretz.
June Bracken and Heather.
Kraken, The.
Lady Clare.
Lady of Shalott, The.
Lancelot and Elaine, *sel.*
Last Tournament, The, *sel.*
Leolin and Edith, *sel.*
Letter, The.
Lincolnshire Shores ("A still salt pool locked in with bars of sand"), *sel.*
Lines: "Here often, when a child, I lay reclined."
Locksley Hall.
Lotos-Eaters, The.
Love and Death.
Love is and was my lord and king, *sel.*
Lucretius.
Make me feel the wild pulsation that I felt before the strife, *sel.*
Mariana.
Marriage Morning.
Memory.
Merlin and the Gleam.
Merlin and Vivien, *sel.*
Mermaid, The.
Merman, The.
Miller's Daughter, The.
Minnie and Winnie.
Morte d'Arthur.
My life has crept so long on a broken wing, *sel.*
My own dim life should teach me this, *sel.*
Northern Cobbler, The.
Northern Farmer.
Not only with no sense of shame.
November in the Isle of Wight, *sel.*
Now fades the last long streak of snow, *sel.*
Now Sleeps the Crimson Petal, *sel.*
O let the solid ground, *sel.*
O living will that shalt endure, *sel.*
O sorrow, cruel fellowship, *sel.*
O [*or* Oh] that 'twere possible, *sel.*
Oak, The.
Of One Dead, *sel.*
Oh yet We Trust, *sel.*
Old warder of these buried bones, *sel.*
Old yew, which graspest at the stones, *sel.*
Olivia, *sel.*
On that last night before we went, *sel.*
On the Jubilee of Queen Victoria.
One seem'd all dark and red—a tract of sand, *sel.*
One writes, that "other friends remain", *sel.*
Owl, The.
Over the Dark World Flies the Wind.
Pallid Thunderstricken Sigh for Gain, The.
Passing of Arthur, The, *sel.*
Path by which we twain did go, The, *sel.*
Peace; come away: the song of woe, *sel.*
Pelleas and Ettarre, *sel.*
Poet's Song, The.
Popular.
Prayer: "More things are wrought by prayer," *sel.*

Prologue: "Over! the sweet summer closes,"
  sel.
Revenge, The.
Ring Out, Wild Bells, *sel.*
Risest thou thus, dim dawn, again, *sel.*
Rizpah.
Sad Hesper o'er the buried sun, *sel.*
Sadness.
Sailor Boy, The.
St. Agnes' Eve.
St. Simeon Stylites.
See what a lovely shell, *sel.*
She came to the village church, *sel.*
Sir Gawain Encounters Sir Priamus, *sel.*
Sisters, The.
Sleeping House, The, *sel.*
So all day long the noise of battle rolled, *sel.*
"So careful of the type?" but no, *sel.*
Somebody.
Somebody Being a Nobody.
Song at the Ruin'd Inn, *sel.*
Song: "Spirit haunts the year's last hours, A."
Song: "Who can say."
Sonnet: "She took the dappled partridge
  flecked [*or* fleckt] with blood."
Spirit haunts the year's last hours, A, *sel.*
Splendor Falls [on Castle Walls], The, *sel.*
Strong Son of God, *sel.*
Sweet after showers, ambrosial air, *sel.*
Sweet and Low [Sweet and Low], *sel.*
Tears of the widower, when he sees, *sel.*
Tears, Idle Tears [I Know Not What They
  Mean], *sel.*
That which we dare invoke to bless, *sel.*
Then loudly cried the bold Sir Bedivere, *sel.*
There Is None like Her, *sel.*
There Is Sweet Music Here, *sel.*
There Rolls the Deep, *sel.*
This world was once a fluid haze of light, *sel.*
Thou comest, much wept for: such a breeze,
  sel.
Throstle, The.
Thy voice is heard through rolling drums, *sel.*
Thy voice is on the rolling air, *sel.*
Till now the doubtful dusk reveal'd, *sel.*
Time draws near the birth of Christ, The, *sel.*
'Tis well, 'tis something; we may stand, *sel.*
Tithonus.
To Christopher North.
To E. Fitzgerald.
To E.L., on His Travels in Greece.
To the Rev. F. D. Maurice.
To-night the Winds Begin, *sel.*
To Virgil [*or* Vergil]
Ulysses.
Unwatch'd [*or* unwatched], the garden bough
  shall sway, *sel.*
Vastness.
Vision of Sin, The.
Voyage of Maeldune, The.
We leave the well-beloved place, *sel.*
What words are these have fallen from me,
  sel.
When Lazarus left his charnel-cave, *sel.*
When on my bed the moonlight falls, *sel.*
When rosy plumelets tuft the larch, *sel.*
Wild bird, whose warble, liquid sweet, *sel.*
Wish, that of the living whole, The, *sel.*
Witch-elms that counterchange the floor, *sel.*
With a half-glance upon the sky, *sel.*
With such compelling cause to grieve, *sel.*
With trembling fingers did we weave, *sel.*
You say, but with no touch of scorn, *sel.*
Tennyson, Frederick
  Glory of Nature, The.
  Holy Tide, The.
  Old Age.
  Skylark, The.
Tennyson, Charles. *See* **Turner, Charles**
  Tennyson
Tennyson-Turner, Charles
  Old Stephen.

Tentije, Hans
  Barges, Rivers.
  Icarian Is the Sea.
Tepperman, Jean
  Going through Changes.
  Witch.
Ter Balkt, H. H. *See* **Balkt, H. H. ter**
Teresa, Saint, of Avila. *See* **Theresa, Saint,
  of Avila**
Terracina, Laura
  Envoi to Poem to the Virgin.
  To the Most Excellent Lady Veronica
    Gambara, *sel.*
Terrazas, Francisco de
  Sonnet: "I dreamed that I was thrown from a
    crag."
Terrell, Myra Burnham
  Theodosia Burr.
Terry, Ellen
  No Funeral Gloom.
Terry, Lucy
  Bar's Fight, August 28, 1746.
Terry, Uriah
  Wyoming Massacre, The.
Tessimond, Arthur Seymour John
  Daydream.
  Jamaican Bus Ride.
  Postscript to a Pettiness.
  Where?
Tettsu
  One thousand and one tumbles.
  Saddled as everyone with karma.
Tevakulattar
  What She Said ("Bigger than earth,
    certainly").
Thackeray, Mary
  Peg of Limavaddy.
Thackeray, William Makepeace
  At the Zoo.
  Ballad of Bouillabaisse, The.
  Damages, Two Hundred Pounds.
  Due of the Dead, The.
  End of the Play, The, *sel.*
  Foreign Literature.
  George I—Star of Brunswick, *sel.*
  George II, *sel.*
  George III, *sel.*
  George IV, *sel.*
  King of Brentford's Testament *abr, The.*
  Little Billee.
  Pocahontas.
  Sorrows of Werther, The.
  Speculators, The.
  This Bouillabaisse a noble dish is, *sel.*
  Wearied arm, and broken sword, *sel.*
  When Moonlike ore the Hazure Seas.
  Who Misses or Who Wins.
  Willow-Tree, The.
Tharp, H. M.
  Finger Folk.
Thatcher, Charles Robert
  Look Out Below!
Thatcher, Thomas
  Love Letter to Elizabeth Thatcher, A.
Thaxter, Celia (Laighton) ("Laighton")
  August.
  Cruise of the *Mystery* , The.
  Favorite Flower, The.
  Flowers for the Brave.
  Jack Frost.
  Little Gustava.
  May Morning.
  Nikolina.
  On Easter Day.
  Sandpiper, The.
  Schumann's Sonata in A Minor.
  Seaward.
  Song: "We sail toward evening's lonely star."
Thayer, Ernest Lawrence
  Casey at the Bat.

Thayer, Louis E.
  Hang to Your Grit!
Thayer, Mary Dixon
  Prayer, A: "God, is it sinful if I feel."
Thayer, Stephen Henry
  Europa.
  Poet of Earth.
  Waiting Chords, The.
Thayer, William Roscoe ("Paul Hermes")
  Last Hunt, The.
  Man in Nature.
  Violin's Complaint, The.
"The Jewish Sibyl"
  There Is a City, *sel.*
Thelwall, John
  Day of my double birth, if such the year, *sel.*
  Sonnet: The Cell.
Themerson, Stefan
  Amateur Thinks, An.
  England, Table, Hamlet, and I.
  King of Sweden, The.
  Meaning and Truth.
  When I Reflect on Nature's Cruelty.
Theocritus
  Amorous shepherd lov'd a charming boy, An,
    sel.
  And so an easier life our Cyclops drew, *sel.*
  Countryman's Wooing, A.
  Death of Daphnis, The, *sel.*
  Enchantment, The, *sel.*
  Epitaph of Cleonicus.
  Epitaph of Hipponax.
  Eunica skornde me, when her I would have
    sweetly kist, *sel.*
  Fishermen, The, *sel.*
  Harvest-Home, *sel.*
  Herdsmen, The, *sel.*
  Incantations, The, *sel.*
  Ortho's Epitaph.
  Shepheard Paris bore the Spartan bride, The,
    sel.
  Wine, friend, and truth, the proverb says,
    agree, *sel.*
Theognis
  Enjoyment.
  Hope.
  Poverty.
  To Kuvos.
Theresa [*or* Teresa], Saint, of Avila
  En las Internas Entrañas.
  I Die because I Do Not Die.
  I gave myself to Love Divine.
  If, Lord, Thy Love for Me Is Strong.
  Let Mine Eyes See Thee.
  Life Above, the Life on High, The.
  Lines Written in Her Breviary.
  Poem: "Nothing move thee."
  Shepherd, Shepherd, Hark.
  Soul, thou must seek thyself in Me.
  To-Day a Shepherd.
Thesen, Sharon
  Kirk Lonegren's Home Movie Taking Place
    Just North of Prince George, with Sound.
  Loose Woman Poem.
  Mean Drunk Poem.
Thewlis, John
  Song of a Happy Rising, The.
Thibaudeau, Colleen
  Brown Family, The.
  Green Family, The.
  Poem: "I do not want only."
Thiele, Colin
  Bert Schultz.
  Tom Farley.
Thoby-Marcelin, Philippe
  Little Stream, A.
  Night of My Return, The.
  Noble Servant, The.
  Pathetic Runaway, The.
  Song: "Living or dead, the one I love."
  You Were Humming.

Thom, William
Blind Boy's Pranks, The.
Food-Rioter Banished, The.
Whisperings for the Unwashed.

Thomas, Cheryl
I have friends.

Thomas, D. M.
Elegy for an Android.
Head-Rape, The.
Puberty Tree, The.
Unknown Shores.

Thomas, Donald
Tangier: Hotel Rif.

Thomas, Dylan
After the Funeral.
Among Those Killed in the Dawn Raid Was a
   Man Aged a Hundred.
And Death Shall Have No Dominion.
Before I Knocked and Flesh Let Enter.
Ceremony after a Fire Raid.
Conversation, A.
Conversation of Prayer, The.
Countryman's Return, The.
Do Not Go Gentle into That Good Night.
Ears in the Turrets Hear.
Especially When the October Wind.
Fern Hill.
First there was the lamb on knocking knees,
   sel.
Force That through the Green Fuse Drives the
   Flower, The.
Ghost Story.
Hand That Signed the Paper Felled a City,
   The.
Holy Spring.
Hunchback in the Park, The.
I, in My Intricate Image.
I See the Boys of Summer.
If I Were Tickled by the Rub of Love.
In a shuttered room I roast.
In Country Sleep.
In My Craft or Sullen Art.
In the White Giant's Thigh.
It is the sinners' dust-tongued bell claps me to
   churches.
January 1939.
Johnnie Crack and Flossie Snail, *sel.*
Lament: "When I was a windy boy and a bit."
Light Breaks Where No Sun Shines.
Marriage of a Virgin, The.
Not from This Anger.
Now stamp the Lord's Prayer on a grain of
   rice, *sel.*
O make me a mask and a well to shut from
   your spies.
On No Work of Words.
On the Marriage of a Virgin.
Out of a War of Wits.
Over Sir John's Hill.
Poem in October.
Poem on His Birthday.
Process in the Weather of the Heart, A.
Refusal to Mourn the Death, by Fire, of a
   Child in London, A.
Song of the Mischievous Dog, The.
Spire cranes, The. Its statue is an aviary.
There Was a Saviour.
This Bread I Break Was Once the Oat.
Tombstone told when she died, The.
Vision and Prayer.
We Lying by Seasand.
What is the metre of the dictionary?, *sel.*
When All My Five and Country Senses See.
When, like a Running Grave.
Winter's Tale, A.

Thomas, Edith Matilda
Babushka.
Betrayal of the Rose, The.
Breath of Hampstead Heath.
Christopher of the Shenandoah, A.

Cricket Kept the House, The.
Far Cry to Heaven, A.
Fir-Tree, The.
Frost.
If Still They Live, *sel.*
Insomnia.
Little Boy's Vain Regret, A.
Mother England.
Mother Who Died Too, The.
Mrs. Kriss Kringle.
Ponce de Leon.
Quiet Pilgrim, The.
Reply of Socrates, The.
Soul in the Body, The.
Talking in Their Sleep.
Tears of the Poplars, The.
Tell Me, *sel.*
Thefts of the Morning.
To Imagination.
To Spain—a Last Word.
When in the First Great Hour, *sel.*
Will It Be So?, *sel.*
Winter Sleep.

Thomas, Edward ("Edward Eastaway")
Adlestrop.
And You, Helen.
As the Team's Head-Brass.
Aspens.
Barn, The.
Birds' Nests.
Bob's Lane.
Bright Clouds.
Brook, The.
By the Ford.
Cat, A.
Celandine.
Chalk-Pit, The.
Cherry Trees, The.
Clouds That Are So Light, The.
Cock-Crow.
Combe, The.
Cuckoo, The.
Dark Forest, The.
Digging.
February Afternoon.
Fifty Faggots.
Gallows, The.
Glory, The.
Good-Night.
Green Roads, The.
Gypsy, The.
Haymaking.
Head and Bottle.
Health.
If I Should Ever by Chance.
In Memoriam (Easter, 1915).
It Rains ("It rains, and nothing stirs within the
   fence").
Liberty.
Lights Out.
Like the Touch of Rain.
Long Small Room, The.
Man and Dog.
March the 3rd.
Melancholy.
Mill-Pond, The.
New House, The.
No One So Much as You.
October.
Old Man.
Out in the Dark.
Owl, The.
Parting.
Penny Whistle, The.
Private, A.
Rain.
Sheiling, The.
Snow.
Some Eyes Condemn.
Sun Used to Shine, The.
Swedes.

Tale, A.
Tall Nettles.
Tears.
Thaw.
There Was a Time.
There's Nothing like the Sun.
Trumpet, The.
Two Houses.
Two Pewits.
Under the Woods.
Unknown, The.
Unknown Bird, The.
What Shall I Give?
When First.
Will You Come?
Wind and Mist.

Thomas, Evan
To the Gentlewoman of Llanarth Hall.

Thomas, Evelyn
Covering All Bases.

Thomas, F. Richard
After Sin, Penitence.

Thomas, Frederick William
Song: "'Tis said that absence conquers love!"

Thomas, Gilbert
Cup of Happiness, The.
Invocation: "There is no balm on earth."

Thomas, Gwyn
Horses.
Little Death.
Microscope.

Thomas, J. H.
If the maiden coughs immediately after.

Thomas, Joyce Carol
Church Poem.
I Know a Lady.
MJQ, The.
Poem for Otis Redding.
Where Is the Black Community?

Thomas, Lorenzo
Canzone: "Strained daybreak breaks in past
   the blinds."
Faith.
Guilt.
Historiography.
Leopard, The.
Onion Bucket.
Otis.
Shake Hands with Your Bets, Friend.
Subway Witnesses, The.
MMDCCXIII½.
Wonders.

Thomas, Louisa Carroll
What Is Charm?

Thomas, R. S.
Alpine.
Ancients of the World, The.
Blackbird Singing, A.
Coleridge.
Day in Autumn, A.
Hand, The.
Here.
Hill Farmer Speaks, The.
In a Country Church.
Ire.
Judgment Day.
Moor, The.
On the Farm.
Peasant, A.
Person from Porlock, A.
Petition.
Poetry for Supper.
Porch, The.
Son, The.
They.
Welsh History.
Welsh Landscape.

Thomas, Richard W.
Amen.
Just Making It.
Life after Death.

Martyrdom.
Riots and Rituals.
To the New Annex to the Detroit County Jail.
Worker, The.

Thomas, Ronald Stuart
After Jericho.
Aside.
At It.
Country Clergy, The.
Farm Child.
Lore.
Madrigal: "Your love is dead, lady, your love is dead."
On a Line in Sandburg.
One Furrow, The.
Over.
Pisces.
Postscript.
Selah.
Self-Portrait.
Survivor, The.
Welshman to Any Tourist, A.
Woman, The.

Thomas, Rosemary
Between Two Worlds.
East River.

Thomas, Rudy
One to Grieve, The.

Thomas, Thomas Jacob ("Sarnicol")
Dic Siôn Dayfydd.

Thomas Aquinas, Saint
Hymn: "Sing, my tongue, the Saviour's glory."

Thomas More, Saint. *See* **More, Sir Thomas**

Thomas of Celano
Day of Judgment, The.
Dies Irae.

Thomas of Erceldoune
Tristrem and the Hunters, *sel.*

Thomas of Hales
Where is Paris and Heleyne?, *sel.*

Thompson, A. R.
Looking Down a Hill.

Thompson, Alexander R.
Wayfarers in the Wilderness.

Thompson, Benjamin
Seaconk Plain Engagement.

Thompson, Clara Ann
After-Glow of Pain, The.
An Autumn Day.
An Opening Service.
Angel's Message, The.
Autumn Leaves.
Christmas Rush, The.
Church Bells.
Doubt.
Drift-Wood.
Dying Year, The.
Easter Bonnet, The.
Easter Light, The.
Empty Tomb, The.
His Answer.
Hope.
Hope Deferred.
If Thou Shouldst Return.
I'll Follow Thee.
Johnny's Pet Superstition.
Lullaby, A: "Hush ye, hush ye! honey, darlin.'"
Memorial Day.
Mrs. Johnson Objects.
Not Dead, but Sleeping.
Oh List to My Song!
Old and the New, The.
Out of the Deep.
Parted.
She Sent Him Away.
Skeptic, The.
Storm-Beaten.
Submission.

To My Dead Brother.
Uncle Rube on the Race Problem.
Uncle Rube to the Young People.
Uncle Rube's Defense.
Watcher, The.

Thompson, D'Arcy Wentworth
Crazy Arithmetic.
Funny Old Man and His Wife, The, at.
Poor Dear Grandpapa.
That Little Black Cat.
Two Magpies Sat on a Garden Rail.
Very Odd Fish, A.

Thompson, Donald
On the Relative Merit of Friend and Foe, Being Dead.

Thompson, Dorothy Brown
Autosonic Door.
Continental Crossing.
Good Will to Men—Christmas Greetings in Six Languages.
I Like Housecleaning.
Maps.
Our House.
Pony Express, The.
This Is Halloween.
Wish.

Thompson, Dunstan
Articles of War.
In All the Argosy of Your Bright Hair.
Largo.
Lay of the Battle of Tombland, The.
Moment of the Rose, The.
Ovid on the Dacian Coast.
This Loneliness for You Is like the Wound.

Thompson, Earle
Corral, The.
Juniper Moon Pulls at My Bones, The.
Love Song: "She is a reed swaying in blue."
Mythology.
No Deposit.
Song: "Woman sits on her porch."
Winter Count of Sean Spotted Wolf.
Woman Made of Stars.

Thompson, Edward
I never yet arraigned the will of heaven, *sel.*
Indian Maid, The; Demararie, Oct. 27, 1781.
I've served my country nine and twenty years, *sel.*
To Emma, Extempore; Hyaena, off Gambia, June 4, 1779.

Thompson, Francis
Ad Amicam.
All Flesh.
All's Vast.
Any Saint.
Arab Love-Song, An.
At Lord's.
But lo! at length the day is lingered out, *sel.*
Contemplation.
Counsel of Moderation, A.
Daisy.
End of It, The.
Envoy: "Go, songs, for ended is our brief, sweet play."
Epilogue: "Heaven, which man's generations draws," *sel.*
Ex Ore Infantium.
Fallen Yew, A.
Heart you hold too small and local thing, The, *sel.*
Heaven and Hell.
Hound of Heaven, The.
Kingdom of God, The.
Lillium Regis.
Messages.
Mistress of Vision, The.
Nature one hour appears a thing unsexed, *sel.*
Now of that vision I, bereaven, *sel.*
Now that the red glare of thy fall is blown, *sel.*
O nothing in this corporal earth of man, *sel.*

Poppy, The.
Sun, The, *sel.*
To a Snowflake.
To My Friend.
To Olivia.
We Poets Speak, *sel.*

Thompson, Irene
Caravans.
Country Child, The.
Feet.
Holiday Train, The.
Penny Wish, A.
Rainy Nights.
Secret Places.
Swinging.
Town Child, The.
Welcome to Spring.

Thompson, James W.
Constant Labor, A.
Greek Room, The.
Plight, The.
Spawn of Slums, The.
Yellow Bird, The.
You Are Alms.

Thompson, John
Adventurers, The.
Bread Hot from the Oven, The.
Homecoming.
Letter to a Friend.
Now You Have Burned.
Onion, The.

Thompson, John, Jr.
Love for Patsy, A.

Thompson, John Randolph
Lee to the Rear.
Obsequies of Stuart.

Thompson, John Reuben
Ashby.
Burial of Latané, The.
Music in Camp.
On to Richmond.

Thompson, Larry
Black Is Best.

Thompson, Leslie
There Are So Many Ways of Going Places.

Thompson, Maurice
Ballad of Chickamauga, The.
Creole Slave-Song, A.
Early Bluebird, An.
Flight Shot, A.
Lion's Cub, The.
Prophecy, A, *sel.*
Wild Honey.
Written on a Fly-Leaf of Theocritus.

Thompson, Priscilla Jane
Address to Ethiopia.
Adieu, Adieu, Forever.
Adown the Heights of Ages.
After the Quarrel.
Afternoon Gossip, An.
Alberta.
Athelstane.
Autumn ("List to the sad wind, drearily moaning").
Autumn ("The sun shines bright, but sadly").
Christmas Ghost, A.
Common Occurrence, A.
Consumptive, The.
David and Goliath.
Death and Resurrection.
Domestic Storm, A.
Emancipation.
Evelyn.
Examination, The.
Favorite Slave's Story, The.
Freedom at McNealy's.
Fugitive, The.
Glimpses of Infancy.
Happy Pair, A.
Home Greeting, A.
Husband's Return, The.

Hymn, A: "Lord, within thy fold I be."
In the Valley.
Inner Realm, The.
Insulted.
Interrupted Reproof, The.
Just How It Happened.
Kindly Deed, A.
King's Favorites, The.
Knight of My Maiden Love.
Lines on a Dead Girl.
Lines to an Old School-House.
Lines to Emma.
Little Wren, A.
Muse's Favor, The.
My Father's Story.
Oh, Whence Comes the Gladness?
Old Freedman, The.
Old Saint's Prayer, The.
Old Year, The.
Prayer, A: "Oh, Lord! I lift my heart."
Precious Pearl, The.
Raphael.
Snail's Lesson, The.
Snow-Flakes, The.
Soft Black Eyes.
Song of the Moon.
Song, The: "Oh, foully slighted Ethiope
    maid!"
Southern Scene, A.
They Are the Same.
Thwarted.
To a Deceased Friend.
To a Little Colored Boy.
To the New Year.
Tribute to the Bride and Groom, A.
Turncoat, The.
Uncle Ike's Holiday.
Uncle Jimmie's Yarn.
Unromantic Awakening, An.
Valentine, A.
Vineyard of My Beloved, The.
While the Choir Sang.
Winter Night, A.
Thompson, Samuel
April.
To a Hedgehog.
Thompson, Vance
Linen Bands.
Symbols.
Thompson, Will Henry
High Tide at Gettysburg, The.
Thompson, Jr, John
Birthday Poem, November 4th.
Thomson, Edward William
Canadian Rossignol, The.
Thomson, James (1700–48)
All–intellectual eye, our solar round, *sel.*
Autumn, *sel.*
For ever, Fortune, wilt thou prove.
Hymn on Solitude.
Hymn on the Seasons, A, *sel.*
In lowly dale, fast by a river's side, *sel.*
Ode: Rule, Britannia.
On the Death of a Particular Friend, *sel.*
Sometimes the pencil, in cool airy halls, *sel.*
Song: "One day the god of fond desire."
Spring, *sel.*
Summer, *sel.*
Winter, *sel.*
**Thomson, James (1700–1748) and David
    Mallet**
Rule, Britannia!, *sel.*
**Thomson, James (1834–82; "B. V." or
    "Bysshe Vanolis")**
Although lamps burn along the silent streets,
    sel.
Anear the centre of that northern crest, *sel.*
As I came through the desert thus it was, *sel.*
City is of Night, The; perchance of Death,
    sel.
City of Dreadful Night, The.

Gifts, *sel.*
He stood alone within the spacious square,
    sel.
I wandered in a suburb of the north, *sel.*
In a Christian Churchyard.
In the Room.
In the Train.
Large glooms were gathered in the mighty
    fane, *sel.*
Mighty river flowing dark and deep, The, *sel.*
Mr. MacCall at Cleveland Hall.
Once in a Saintly Passion.
Proem: "Lo, thus, as prostrate, "In the dust I
    write." *sel.*
Singing is sweet; but be sure of this, *sel.*
Song: "My love is the flaming sword."
To Our Ladies of Death.
What men are they who haunt these fatal
    glooms, *sel.*
Wine of Love is music, The, *sel.*
Thomson, Mary A.
O King of Saints, We Give Thee Praise and
    Glory.
O Sion, Haste, Thy Mission High Fulfilling.
T'Hooft, Jotie
Kicking the Habit.
Lenny Bruce Fixes.
Love and Misery.
Poetic Institution.
Starships.
Thoreau, Henry David
Among the Worst of Men That Ever Lived.
At Midnight's Hour I Raised My Head.
Between the Traveller and the Setting Sun.
Each More Melodious Note I Hear.
Epitaph on an Engraver.
Epitaph on the World.
Fisher's Boy, The.
For Though the Eaves [*or* Caves] Were
    Rabbeted [*or* Rabbited]
Forever in My Dream and in My Morning
    Thought.
Great Friend.
Great God, I Ask Thee for No Meaner Pelf.
I Am a Parcel of Vain Strivings Tied.
I Am the Little Irish Boy.
I Was Born upon Thy Bank, River.
I Was Made Erect and Lone.
If with light head erect I sing, *sel.*
I'm Thankful That My Life Doth Not
    Deceive.
Indeed Indeed, I Cannot Tell.
Inspiration.
Inward Morning, The.
Lately, Alas, I Knew a Gentle Boy.
Light-winged Smoke, Icarian Bird, *sel.*
Love Equals Swift and Slow.
Low-anchored Cloud, *sel.*
Men Say They Know Many Things.
Mist.
Moon Now Rises to Her Absolute Rule, The.
Nature.
Old Marlborough Road, The.
On the Sun Coming Out in the Afternoon.
Our Country.
Pray to What Earth Does This Sweet Cold
    Belong.
River Swelleth More and More, The.
Tall Ambrosia.
They Made Me Erect and Lone.
This is my Carnac, whose unmeasured dome.
Though All the Fates Should Prove Unkind.
To a Marsh Hawk in Spring.
To the Maiden in the East.
To the Mountains.
What's the Railroad to Me?
Who Sleeps by Day and Walks by Night.
Winter Memories.
Woof of the Sun (Ethereal Gauze), *sel.*
Thorley, Wilfrid
Buttercups.
Chant for Reapers.

Fan, the Filly.
Song for a Ball-Game.
Thornbury, George Walter
Cavalier's Escape, The.
Jester's Sermon, The.
La Tricoteuse.
Pompadour, The.
Three Troopers, The.
Thorne, Cyril Morton
To My Unborn Son.
Thornley, Wilfred
Of a Spider.
Thorold Rogers, J. E.
Here X. lies dead, but God's forgiving.
On a Distinguished Politician.
On the Historians Freeman and Stubbs.
Suggestion Made by the Posters of the *Globe*,
    A.
Upon the man who's buried here.
Vulgar Error, A.
Thorpe, Rose Hartwick
Curfew Must Not Ring Tonight.
Thorson, Marie
Closed Doors.
Thrale, Hester Lynch
Three Warnings, The.
Thrilling, Isobel
Lover.
Thumboo, Edwin
Autumn, Iowa City.
Thurber, James
Morals, *sel.*
Thurlow, Edward, 2nd Baron. *See*
    **Hovell-Thurlow, Edward, 2nd Baron
    Thurlow.**
Thurman, Judith
Lumps.
Rags.
Zebra.
Thurston, Robin
Female Prisoners—Boggo Road.
Thwaite, Anthony
Ali Ben Shufti.
Arabic Script.
At Birth.
At Dunwich.
By the Sluice.
Child Crying.
Dream Time.
Looking On.
Mr. Cooper.
Pond, The.
Rites for a Demagogue.
Simple Poem.
Sunday Afternoons.
Switzerland.
Thwaites, Michael
Thermopylae.
Thynne, Francis
Ingratitude.
Tibble, Anne
Trials of a Tourist.
Tibors
Sweet handsome friend, I can tell you truly.
Tibullus, Albius
And you, whate'er your Fav'rite does,
    approve, *sel.*
Dicamus Bona Verba.
Far from the tender tribe of boys remove, *sel.*
Pastoral Elegy, A.
Tichborne [*or* Tichbourne], Chidiock
Tichborne's Elegy.
Written the Night Before He Was Beheaded.
Tichy, Susan
Cry That Kills the Senses: Meditation after a
    Nightmare, The.
Hours, The.
Identity Card.

In an Arab Town.
Irrigation.
Orpheus.
Tickell, Thomas
To the Earl of Warwick, on the Death of Mr.
   Addison.
Ticknor, Francis Orrery [or Orray]
Albert Sidney Johnston.
Battle Ballad, A.
Little Giffen.
"Our Left."
Song for the Asking, A.
Virginians of the Valley, The.
Tieck, Johann Ludwig
Autumn Song.
Tielsch, Ilse
Final reply/ to a first conversation.
Not Provable.
Vita with Postcript.
Walls of My House, The.
We're Satisfied.
What Belongs to Me.
Tiemer-Wille, Gertrude
Repast.
Tiempo, César (Israel Zierlin)
Harangue on the Death of Hayyim Nahman
   Bialik.
I Tell of Another Young Death.
Jewish Cemetery, The.
Tietjens, Eunice
Fun with Fishing.
Great Man, The.
Pioneer Woman—in the North Country, The.
Psalm to My Beloved.
Tilden, Stephen
Braddock's Fate, with an Incitement to
   Revenge.
British Lyon Roused, The.
O Heaven Indulge.
Song of Braddock's Men, The.
Tillam, Thomas
Uppon the First Sight of New England, June
   29, 1638.
Tiller, Terence
Egyptian Dancer.
Reading a Medal.
Street Performers, 1851.
Tillett, Wilbur Fisk
Incarnate Love.
My Father Knows.
Tilley, Lucy Evangeline
When Even Cometh On.
Tillinghast, Richard
Envoi: "Go little book, par avion."
Firstness.
Fossils, Metal, and the Blue Limit.
Hearing of the End of the War.
Knife, The.
Our Flag Was Still There.
Return.
Savannah, Sleepless.
September: Last Day at the Beach.
Shooting Ducks in South Louisiana.
Summer Rain.
Things Past.
Tilney, Charles
Cobbler's Song, The, *sel.*
Tilton, Theodore
Coeur de Lion to Berengaria.
Even This Shall Pass Away.
Flight from the Convent, The.
God Save the Nation.
Great Bell Roland, The.
Sir Marmaduke's Musings.
Timrod, Henry
Carolina.
Charleston.
Cotton Boll, The.
Cry to Arms, A.

Ethnogenesis.
Faint Falls the Gentle Voice.
Ode: "Sleep sweetly in your humble graves."
Quatorzain.
Sonnet: Most Men Know Love But as a Part
   of Life.
Tina, Ras. *See* **Roots, Sista**
Ting, Walasse
Pepsi Generation.
Tió, Elsa
I am furious with myself.
Tiplady, Thomas
Grace, A.
Tippett, James Sterling
Building a Skyscraper.
Ducks in the Rain.
Familiar Friends.
Freight Boats.
Old Log House.
Sunning.
Trains.
Trucks.
Tugs.
Tipputtolar
Red is the battlefield.
Titheradge, Peter
After A. E. Housman, *sel.*
After a Thirties Poet, *sel.*
After Algernon Charles Swinburne, *sel.*
After John Keats, *sel.*
After Robert Herrick, *sel.*
After W. B. Yeats, *sel.*
After Walter de la Mare, *sel.*
New Improved Sonnet XVIII.
Teatime Variations: After A. E. Housman.
Teatime Variations: After Algernon Charles
   Swinburne.
Teatime Variations: After Robert Herrick.
Titherington, Richard Handfield
Faithful unto Death.
To no Tsuneyori. *See* **Tsuneyori**
Todd, Alice
If.
Postman, The.
Todd, Barbara Euphan
Stray, The.
Todd, Gail
To My Four-Year-Old Daughter.
Todd, Ruthven
Joan Miró.
Mantelpiece of Shells, A.
Paul Klee.
Poem.
Upon This Rock.
Various Ends.
Todhunter, John
Aghadoe.
Utter Passion Uttered Utterly, An.
Toerien, Barend
Absent Daughter.
Campi Flegrei.
Firmament Displays on High, The.
Quatrain: "My bloodstream chokes on gall and
   spleen."
Youth.
Tofte, Robert
Love's Labour Lost, *sel.*
Rich damask roses in fair cheeks do bide, *sel.*
Unto Thy Favor, *sel.*
When She Was Born, *sel.*
Togai, Ito. *See* **Ito Togai**
Tohe, Laura
At Mexican Springs.
Cat or Stomp.
Female Rain.
Male Rain.
Shooting, The.
To Shimá Sání.
Tohee, Mah-do-ge
Agnes.

Indian America.
We sat in an old, crumbling house.
Toin
Glittering sky: thirty blows of the staff!
Tokken
Seventy-six years.
Tokugaku
Original face is the reality of realities.
Tolkien, John Ronald Reuel
Cat.
Dragon's Hoard, The.
Far over the misty mountains cold, *sel.*
Goblin Feet.
Mewlips, The.
Old Walking Song, The.
Oliphaunt.
Roads Go Ever On and On.
Shadow-Bride.
Stone Troll, The.
Tollefsen, Astrid
Toulouse Lautrec.
Workaday Morning.
Toller, Ernst
Book I Held Grew Cold, The.
Corpses in the Wood.
O Heavy Step of Slow Monotony.
O Master Masons.
O My Swallows!
One Who Struggles, The.
To the Mothers.
Tollerud, Jim
Bird of Power.
Buzz.
Earth.
Elementary.
Eye of God.
Rainier.
Sunrise.
Thirsty Island.
Week-Seek.
Tollet, Elizabeth
What cruel laws depress the female kind, *sel.*
Winter Song.
Tolson, Melvin Beaunearus
African China.
Birth of John Henry, The, *sel.*
Dark Symphony.
Lamda.
Legend of Versailles, A.
On the Founding of Liberia, *sel.*
PSI.
Satchmo.
Sea-Turtle and the Shark, The, *sel.*
Tolstoy, A. K.
As wave after wave of the turbulent sea.
Lord, when arming me for living, The.
O land of mine where I was bred.
Should you love—be it a furnace.
You are a victim of life's grief.
Tomalin, Ruth
Invasion Spring.
Tomei
Sixty-nine years.
Tomer, Ben-Zion
Copy, *sel.*
Don Quixote.
Heartfelt Pity, *sel.*
Phantoms.
Tomioka Taeko
Age.
Between.
Just the Two of Us.
Let Me Tell You about Myself.
Life Story.
Please Say Something.
See You Soon.
There's Nothing to Do in New York.
Tomkis, Thomas
Gordion Knot, The, *sel.*
Tomkiw, Lydia
Six of Ox Is.

Tomlinson, Charles
Against Portraits.
At Barstow.
At Delft.
Cavern, The.
Chances of Rhyme, The.
Charlotte Corday.
Chestnut Avenue at Alton House, The.
Civilities of Lamplight.
Crane, The.
Death in the Desert, A.
Death of Will, The.
Descartes and the Stove.
Distinctions.
Door, The.
Dream, A.
Farewell to Van Gogh.
Fiascherino.
Hand at Callow Hill Farm, The.
How Still the Hawk.
Icos.
In Arden.
In Defense of Metaphysics.
Jam Trap, The.
Las Trampas U.S.A.
Le Musée Imaginaire.
MacDuff.
Mackinnon's Boat.
Meditation on John Constable, A.
More Foreign Cities.
Mr. Brodsky.
Observation of Facts.
Ode to Arnold Schoenberg.
On a Pig's Head.
Oxen: Ploughing at Fiesole.
Paring the Apple.
Picture of J. T. in a Prospect of Stone, The.
Poem: "Upended, it crouches on broken limbs."
Return to Hinton.
Rhymes.
Ruin, The.
Shaft, The.
Snow Signs.
Swimming Chenango Lake.
Through Binoculars.
Tramontana at Lerici.
Two Views of Two Ghost Towns.
Ute Mountain.
Winter Encounters.
Word in Edgeways, A.
Tomlinson, Charles *after* Lucio Piccolo
Veneris Venefica Agrestis.
Tomoana, Paraire Henare
Full Tide.
Waters of Waiapu, The.
Tomobayashi Mitsuhira
Written in the Second Month of 1861 when I Left the Temple and Returned to Lay Life.
Tompson, Benjamin
Chelmsfords Fate.
Edmund Davie 1682; Annagram.
Marlburyes Fate.
New-Englands Crisis.
On a Fortification at Boston Begun by Women.
Seaconk or Rehoboths Fate.
Supplement, A.
To My Honoured Patron Humphery Davie.
Town Called Providence, Its Fate, The.
"Tomson, Graham R." *See* **Watson, Rosamund Marriott**
Tonan
Sound of rain dripping, The.
Tonks, Rosemary
Farewell to Kurdistan.
Story of a Hotel Room.
Tonna
As swift as the moon.
At my mountain home.
Even the showers/ fall, then stop.

Fields, the mountains, The.
Gone on before me.
Has it grown so late?
If only the world.
In my mountain home.
In the thick grasses.
In this world of ours.
Lark, A.
Mountain wind blows, The.
Old man now, An.
Since all things must end.
Up from the paddies.
Waiting for Love in Vain.
Tontaiman Ilantiraiyan
Great Wagon, The.
Tooker, Lewis Frank
His Quest.
Last Fight, The.
Sleep.
Toomer, Jean
Banking Coal.
Beehive.
Brown River, Smile, *sel.*
Cotton Song.
Evening Song.
Face.
Georgia Dusk.
Harvest Song.
Her Lips Are Copper Wire.
Lost Dancer, The.
November Cotton Flower.
Portrait in Georgia.
Reapers.
Seventh Street.
Song of the Son.
Toosey, Catherine Brewster
Colour Symphony.
Toplady, Augustus Montague
Living and Dying Prayer for the Holiest Believer in the World, A.
Lord, it is not Life to live, *sel.*
Rock of Ages.
Torai
Spring rain: a child's hands.
Torberg, Friedrich
Amalek.
Seder, 1944.
Torlino
Therefore I Must Tell the Truth.
Tornai, József
Ars Poetica.
Mr. T. S. Eliot Cooking Pasta.
Names of the Idols, The.
Psalm: "What shall become of us, O Sun."
Solar Eclipse.
Ten Thousand Nations.
To Die for Something.
We Say This Prayer.
You Must Hand Over.
Torrence, Ridgely
Adam's Dying.
Adam's Song of the Visible World.
Bird and the Tree, The.
Son, The.
Torres, Teresa
Poem: "What is hidden in the fruit of summer?"
Torrevillas, Rowena Tiempo
Generation.
Tosaku, Hezutsu. *See* **Hezutsu Tosaku**
Tosh [or McIntosh], Peter
African.
Toshiyori (Minamato no Toshiyori)
Wind howling through the pines, The.
Toson, Shimazaki
Song: Thoughts of a Traveler on the Chikuma River.
Toson, Shimazaki. *See* **Shimazaki Toson**
Tosu
Forget everything—everything!

Totaku
Out from the moat, a frog.
Tóth, Éva
Creation of the World, The.
Tóth, Judit
Dead Embryos.
Notes on Saint Maurice.
Remembering.
To the Newborn.
Wildfire.
"Totius"
Forgive and Forget.
Toulet, Paul-Jean
Black Girl.
Cathay.
Flight.
Touma, Khalil
Song of Job, A.
Touré, Askia Muhammad
Floodtide.
JuJu.
Tauhid.
Tourneur, Cyril
Epitaph on a Soldier, *sel.*
Madame, his grace will not be absent long, *sel.*
Soldier's Death, A, *sel.*
Thou sallow picture of my poison'd love, *sel.*
Walking next day upon the fatal shore, *sel.*
Toussaint L'Ouverture, Isaac
Farewell: "Shores of my native land."
Towne, Anthony
Dead of Winter.
Towne, Charles Hanson
Around the Corner ("Around the corner I have a friend").
At Nightfall.
City Roofs.
Easter Canticle, An.
Of One Self-slain.
Prayer for the Old Courage, A.
Silence.
Song at Easter, A.
Townsend, Aurelian. *See* **Townshend, Aurelian**
Townsend, Charles
On the Lake Poets.
Townsend, Emily
Fish.
Townsend, F. H.
To the Cuckoo.
Townsend, George Alfred
Army Correspondent's Last Ride.
Fire Guest, The.
In Rama.
Townsend, Mary Ashley ("Xariffa")
At Set of Sun.
Creed.
Dead Singer, The.
Down the Bayou.
Embryo.
Georgia Volunteer, A.
Her Horoscope.
Reserve.
Virtuosa.
Townshend [or Townsend], Aurelian
Dialogue betwixt Time and a Pilgrime [*or* Pilgrim], A.
Elegie Made by Mr. Aurelian Townshend in Remembrance of the Ladie Venetia Digby, An.
Let not thy beauty make thee proud.
Paradox, A.
Pure Simple Love.
Though Regions Far [*or* Farr] Divided.
To the Countesse of Salisbury.
To the Lady May.
Upon Kinde and True Love.
Youth and Beauty.
Toxaoci
I don't know why you tell me I'm drunk.

Toyo
Frog emerges with its child on its back, A.
Tozaburo, Ono. *See* **Ono Tozaburo**
Track, Soge
Indian Love Letter.
Tracy, Neil
I Doubt a Lovely Thing Is Dead.
Traherne, Thomas
All music, sauces, feasts, delights and
  pleasures, *sel.*
Amendment.
Childhood.
Christendom.
Christian Ethics.
Consummation.
Contentment, *sel.*
Eden.
Hosanna.
Love.
My Spirit.
News, *sel.*
O Lord, I wonder at thy lov, *sel.*
On Christmas-Day.
On Leaping over the Moon.
Poverty.
Preparative, The.
Rapture, The.
Right Apprehension.
Salutation, The.
Serious and a Curious Night-Meditation, A.
Shadows in the Water.
Solitude.
Thanksgiving for the Body.
Thanksgivings for the Beauty of His
  Providence.
To the Same Purpos[e]
To Walk Abroad.
Wonder.
Traill, Henry Duff
After Dilettante Concetti.
Drawing-Room Ballad, A.
Put case I circumvent and kill him: good, *sel.*
Vers de Société.
Trainin, Avner
Ancient Song.
Cat in the Dovecot.
Sunbeams.
Trakl, Georg
At Night.
En Route.
Sleep.
Tranströmer, Tomas
Allegro.
Breathing Space July.
Gallery, The.
Gogol.
Man Awakened by a Song above His Roof,
  The.
Molokai.
Morning Bird Songs.
Open and Closed Space.
Schubertiana.
Solitude.
Track.
Winter's Glance, The.
Tranter, John
Chicago "Manuel of Style" is really neat,
  The, *sel.*
Death Circus, The.
Giving up women is worse than animal
  laxatives, *sel.*
Great Artist Reconsiders the Homeric Simile,
  The.
It's bad luck with a coughing baby, *sel.*
Mark.
Spy bears his bald intent like a maniac, The,
  sel.
Sweat is a style of the body, *sel.*
They burn the radio and listen to the blues,
  sel.

Trapp, Joseph
Epigram: "King George, observing with
  judicious eyes."
Trask, Katrina (Kate Nichols Trask)
Aidenn.
At Last.
Love.
Sorrow.
Traubel, Horace Logo
Epicedium.
How Are You, Dear World, This Morning?
I Served in a Great Cause.
If All the Voices of Men.
What Can I Do?, *sel.*
Trawick, Leonard
At the Flying School.
Suthun Accent.
Where Are the Snows?
Traxler, Patricia
Contest of Nerves, The.
Treasone, Grace
Life.
Treece, Henry
Ballad: "Oh, come my joy, my soldier boy."
Birdwatcher.
Conquerors.
Crimson Cherry Tree, The.
Dyke-Builder, The.
Heart's Wild Geese, The.
Horror.
In the Beginning Was the Bird.
In the Third Year of War.
Magic Wood, The.
Prayer in Time of War.
That Summer.
Walking at Night.
Tregear, Edward
Te Whetu Plains.
Tregonning, Charley
Cousin Jack Song, at.
Treinin, Avner
Cage, The.
Deserted Shrine.
Salmon Cycle.
Tremayne, Sydney
Discomfort in High Places.
Moses.
Tremblay, Gail
Indian Singing in 20th Century America.
Medicine Bearer.
Night Gives Old Woman the Word.
Reflections on a Visit to the Burke Museum,
  University of Washington, Seattle.
To Grandmother on Her Going.
Trench, Herbert
Charge, A.
I Heard a Soldier.
I Seek Thee in the Heart Alone.
Jean Richepin's Song.
She Comes Not When Noon Is on the Roses.
Trench, Richard Chenevix
Gibralter.
If There Had Anywhere Appeared.
Kingdom of God, The.
Legend of Alhambra, A.
Prayer: "Lord, what a change within us one
  short hour."
Sonnet: "Open wound which has been healed
  anew, An."
Tretheway, Eric
Garbage.
Trías, Arturo
Act of Faith.
Ars Poetica.
This Shirt.
Triem, Eve
Gardens Are All My Heart.
Trifonov, Gennady
For three swift days.
Trimpi, W. Wesley
Lines for a Wedding Gift.

Oedipus to the Oracle.
On a Bas-Relief.
To Giotto.
Trinidad, David
Meet the Supremes.
Monday, Monday.
Tripp, John
On My Fortieth Birthday.
Tropp, Stephen
My Wife Is My Shirt.
Trott, Norman L.
No Time for God.
Trott, Perient
Negro Spiritual.
Trotter, Bernard Freeman
Poplars, The.
"Troubadour."
Law of Averages, The.
Troubetzkoy, Ulrich
Out of the Wilderness.
Troupe, Quincy
Dirge: "It is the endless dance of the dead."
For Malcolm Who Walks in the Eyes of Our
  Children.
In Texas Grass.
Old People Speak of Death, The.
Poem for Friends.
Sense of Coolness, A.
South African Bloodstone.
Transformation.
White Weekend.
Trowbridge, John Townsend
Charcoalman, The.
Columbus at the Convent.
Darius Green and His Flying-Machine.
Evening at [*or* on] the Farm.
Farmer John.
Filling an Order.
Midsummer.
Midwinter.
Recollections of "Lalla Rookh."
Vagabonds, The.
Widow Brown's Christmas.
Trowbridge, William
Kong Hits the Road with Dan-Dee Carnivals,
  Inc.
Suppose.
Truax, Hawley
Half.
Morning, Noon, And.
Trudell, Dennis
Green Tomatoes.
Hotel in Paris.
Jump Shooter, The.
Watch Them Die.
Trumbull, Annie Eliot
To O. S. C.
Trumbull, John
Amorous Temper, An, *sel.*
At once with resolution held, *sel.*
Dick Hairbrain Learns the Social Graces, *sel.*
Harriet Simper Has Her Day, *sel.*
Prospect of the Future Glory of America.
Rise then, ere ruin swift surprize, *sel.*
Tom Brainless as Student and Preacher at
  College, *sel.*
Truth, Sojourner
Ain't I a Woman?
Ts'ai Yen
I have no desire to live, but I am afraid of
  death, *sel.*
I never believed that in my broken life, *sel.*
I was born in a time of peace, *sel.*
Seventeenth stanza, The. My heart aches, my
  tears fall, *sel.*
Sun sets, The. The wind moans, *sel.*
Tatar chief forced me to become his wife, A,
  sel.
Tsakak
I'm gonna die & won't see you all any more.

Tsaloumas, Dimitris
They brought him one morning, *sel.*
Ts'ao Chen-chi
Inscribed on a Painting.
Lat Spring.
On a Historical Topic.
White Lotus Flowers.
Ts'ao Chih
Forsaken Wife, The.
Presented to Piao, the Prince of Pai-ma.
Rhyme-Prose on the Goddess of the Lo.
Written on Parting from Mr. Ying.
Ts'ao P'i
Lotus Lake.
Emperor Wien of the Mei.
Ts'ao Sung
Protest in the Sixth Year of Ch'ien Fu, A.
Ts'ao Ts'ao
Viewing the Ocean.
Ts'ao Ts'ao, Susan
Song on Enduring the Cold.
Tso Ssu
Scholar in the Narrow Street, The.
Tso Yen-nien
Call to Arms.
Tsuboi Shigeji
Autumn in Gaol.
Butterfly.
English—ugh!
Silent, But.
Star and Dead Leaves.
Tsuchii Bansui
Moon over the Ruined Castle.
Tsuchiya Kyutai
Atomic Bomb.
Tsuda, Margaret
Hard Questions.
Tsui, Kitty
Chinatown Talking Story.
Chinese Banquet, A.
Don't Call Me Sir Call Me Strong.
It's in the Name.
Vision, The, *sel.*
Ts'ui Hao
Songs of Ch'ang-kan.
Tsuneyori
In a mountain stream.
Tsung Ch'en
Drinking at the Cave Mouth.
Glittering, glittering, fireflies in the grass, *sel.*
Night of rain on the autumn river, A, *sel.*
On Hearing That the Sea-Barbarians Are
about to Attack Hu-chou.
On the spring river, you depart, *sel.*
Rebels' cavalry are everywhere, The, *sel.*
Scorching sun, enough to parch the Yangtze!,
A, *sel.*
Side by side, we ride out of the city, *sel.*
Snowstorm: At a Gathering at Chang Chu-fu's
House.
Snowy Mountains.
Song of Meeting.
Song of Selling Flowers.
When you enter Chin-hua Mountain, *sel.*
White-haired man, holding a fishing pole,
The, *sel.*
White snow fills the lakeside village, *sel.*
Tsurayuki
As if it were a relic.
I crossed the spring mountains.
Now, I cannot tell.
Summer night/ I close my eyes.
We drink with palms cupped.
When I went to visit.
Tsvetayeva, Marina
And now the riverbank. For the last time, *sel.*
And now the riverbank. I cling, *sel.*
André Chénier.
Ars.
Attempt at Jealousy, An.

Black as the centre of an eye, the centre, a
blackness, *sel.*
Blatant as factory buildings, *sel.*
Blow muffled through years of, The, *sel.*
I catch the movement of his lips, *sel.*
I didn't want this, not, *sel.*
I know the truth——give up all other truths!
I'd like to live with you.
Last bridge I won't, *sel.*
Our last bridge, *sel.*
Past factory workshops, empty, *sel.*
Rain. A heavy mane, *sel.*
Single post, a point of rusting, A, *sel.*
To lose it all at once, *sel.*
We Shall Not Escape Hell.
Tu Fu
Chüeh-chü.
Dreaming of Li Po.
Emperor, The.
Excursion, The.
Guest Arrives, A.
I have a sister, little sister, living in Chung-li,
sel.
I have brothers, younger brothers in a place
far away, *sel.*
If you draw a bow, draw a strong one, *sel.*
Jade Flower Palace.
Little Rain, The.
Long hoe, long hoe, handle of white wood,
sel.
Lovely Lady.
Man with No Family to Take Leave of, The.
Moon Festival.
Moonlight Night.
Night in the House by the River.
Night Thoughts while Travelling.
On the River.
On the Spur of the Moment.
Overnight in the Apartment by the River.
Passing Chao-ling Again.
Presented to Wei Pa, Gentleman in
Retirement.
Restless Night.
Road to Pengya, The.
Song of P'eng-ya.
Song of the Beautiful Ladies.
Spring Prospect.
They Say You're Staying in a Mountain
Temple.
To the south there is a dragon living in a
mountain pool, *sel.*
Traveler, a traveler, Tzu-mei his name, A,
sel.
Traveler at Night Writes His Thoughts, A.
We recruits have our commanders to send us
off, *sel.*
White Horse, The.
Willow, The.
Written on the Wall at Chang's Hermitage.
Tu Hsün-ho
Traveler's Thoughts.
Tu-kehu
Oh, how my love/ With a whirling power.
Tu-kehu *and* **Wetea**
O beautiful calm.
Tu Kuo-ch'ing
Dogs.
Isle and the Lake, No. 5, The.
Rats.
St. Valentine.
Tu Mu
Sent in Parting.
Tu Yeh
Chrysanthemum and the Sword, The.
Glove and Love.
Grievance I.
In Memory of My Forever-Gone Nineteenth
Year.
Spring Worm I.
Spring Worm II.
Telephone Booth in the Rain.

Tucker, F. Bland
All Praise to Thee.
Our Father, by Whose Name.
Tucker, Mary Eliza
Adieu.
All Alone.
Apple Dumplings.
Arria to Poetus.
Autumn Thoughts.
Beautiful, The.
Beautiful Sea, The.
Blight of Love, The.
Burial of a Fairy Queen.
Charley du Bignon.
Child Life.
Christmas Eve, South, 1865.
Christmas, South, 1866.
Crazed.
Crushed Flower, The.
"Did You Call Me, Father?"
Disappointment.
Drink On.
Drunkard's Wife, The.
Evanishings.
Family Portraits.
Father's Love, The.
First Grey Hair, The.
Found—Who Lost?
Gone.
Heart's Ease.
Hope.
Hugging the Shore.
Humming-Bird, The.
I Am Fashion's Toy.
I am Weary, Mother.
I Smile, but Oh! My Heart Is Breaking.
"I Was a Stranger and Ye Took Me In."
Kindness.
Kiss, A.
Knitting.
Life.
Life for a Life.
Lift Me Higher.
Light in Darkness.
Lines on the Death of the Rev. S. K.
Talmage.
Lines to an Old Dress.
Little Bell.
Loew's Bridge, a Broadway Idyl.
Love-letter, A.
Mail Has Come, The.
Mine.
Mistletoe.
Mother's Lament, The.
Mrs. Myrick's Lecture.
My Mother's Voice.
Mysteries of Life.
No Letter.
Old Crib, The.
Only a Blush.
Opium-Eater, The.
Revenge.
Signal Gun, The.
Silvery Fountain.
Soldier Boy's Dream, The.
Speak to Her Tenderly.
Spring.
That Glove.
To Annie.
To Don Juan Baz.
To Fannie.
To Father.
To Mary.
To One Who Sleepeth.
Tryst, The.
Upon Receipt of a Pound of Coffee in 1863.
Wail of the Divorced.
We Met.
Weariness.
Tucker, St. George
Cynic, The.
Days of My Youth.

Discontented Student, The.
Judge with the Sore Rump, The.
Once at a merry wedding feast, *sel*.

Tuckerman, Frederick Goddard
And change with hurried hand has swept these
   scenes, *sel*.
And faces, forms and phantoms, numbered
   not, *sel*.
And me my winter's task is drawing over, *sel*.
But we are set to strive to make our mark,
   sel.
Cricket, The.
Gertrude and Gulielma, sister-twins, *sel*.
Hast thou seen reversed the prophet's miracle,
   sel.
Here, where the red man swept the leaves
   away, *sel*.
How Oft in Schoolboy Days.
Not the round natural world, not the deep
   mind, *sel*.
November.
O hard endeavor, to blend in with these, *sel*.
Put off thy bark from shore, though near the
   night, *sel*.
Roll on, sad world! Not Mercury or Mars,
   sel.
Sometimes I walk where the deep water dips,
   sel.
Still pressing through these weeping solitudes,
   sel.
Thin little leaves of wood fern, ribbed and
   toothed, *sel*.
Under the Locust Blossoms.
Under the mountain, as when first I knew,
   sel.
Upper chamber in a darkened house, An, *sel*.
Yes: though the brine may from the desert
   deep, *sel*.

Tuckerman, Henry Theodore
Washington's Statue.

Tuckett, Tabitha
Plaits.

Tudur Aled
Stallion, The.

Tuéni, Nadia
More distant than the dead sea.
Nothing but a man.
Of course/ the sun is angry.
This evening.
Would you come back if I said the earth.

Tullar, Grant Colfax
As Thy Days.

Tulloch, Bill
Beinn A' Ghlo.
NN 616410.

Tulsidas
Blind, mean-minded, A.
Fire of my stomach has forced me, The.
Flame offered to Ram, The.
I was born in a beggar family.
It is said in the ancient writings.
It's as if you thought your body.
Madhav, you'll find none duller than I.
Name of King Ram: think of it with love,
   The.
Oh Siva, great giver.
River of the gods, the act of recalling you.
Say Ram, say Ram, say Ram.
This darkest of ages has destroyed.
To those who look to Hanuman.
"Tomorrow, a body of youth."
Who aside from you, King Ram.
You are the pitying, I the pitiful one.

Tupper, Helen Isabella
Give Thanks *or* Thanks for Everything.

Tupper, Kathryn Munro
Fallen Leaves.

Tupper, Martin Farquhar
How beautiful their feet, *sel*.
Simoom, The.

Tuqan, Fadwa
Face Lost in the Wilderness.
From the Diary of——, *sel*.
I Found It.
In the Aging City.
In the Flux.
My mother's phantom hovers here, *sel*.
To Christ.

Tuqan, Ibrahim
Martyr, The.
Perplexity.

Tuquan, Fadwa
After Twenty Years.

Turberville, George
Epitaph of Maister Win Drowned in the Sea,
   An.
Lover to the Thames of London, to Favour [
   or Favor] His Lady Passing Thereon, The.
Of Drunkenness.
Of One That Had a Great Nose.
That He Findeth Others as Fair, but Not So
   Faithful as His Friend.
To an Old Gentlewoman That Painted Her
   Face.
To His Friend, Promising That Though Her
   Beauty Fade, Yet His Love Shall Last.
To His Ring, Given to His Lady, Wherein
   Was Graven This Verse, "My Heart Is
   Yours."
To Parker.
To Spencer.
Unable by Long and Hard Travel to Banish
   Love, Returns Her Friend.
Was never day came on my head, *sel*.

Turbyfill, Mark
Benediction.

Turco, Lewis
Depot, The.
Ordinary Evening in Cleveland, An.
Rick De Travaille, *sel*.
Simon Judson, *sel*.
Wind Carol, The.
Winter Bouquet.

Turei, Mohi
Ruaumoko—the Earthquake God.

Turkka, Sirkka
I See Trees Falling.
Poems of Pain.
Tenderness Closed like a Flower.
Thus the Trees Change Places.
When the Sovereign Asks.
You Are Born Again and Again.

Turner, Alberta
Choosing a Death.
Learning to Count.

Turner, Brian
Ashes.
Coming Home.
Country Hotel.
Drive on the Peninsula, A.
For an Octogenarian.
Hawk.
Initiation, The.
Late Winter Snow.
Listening to the Mountain.
Nichita Stanescu.
Responses to Montale.
Stopover, The.
Tree-Felling, Upper Junction Road.
Trout.
Watch for the Ice.

Turner, Charles Tennyson
Artist on Penmaenmawr, The.
Bee-Wisp, The.
Brilliant Day, A.
Buoy-Bell, The.
Cader Idris at Sunset.
Calvus to a Fly.
Country Dance, A.
Cowper's Three Hares.
From Harvest to January.

Gout and Wings.
Great Britain Through the Ice: Or, Premature
   Patriotism.
Julius Caesar and the Honey-Bee.
Letty's Globe.
Lion's Skeleton, The.
Maggie's Star.
Minnie and Her Dove.
Needles' Lighthouse from Keyhaven,
   Hampshire, The.
Old Ruralities: A Regret.
On a Vase of Gold-Fish.
On Finding a Small Fly Crushed in a Book.
On Seeing a Little Child Spin a Coin of
   Alexander the Great.
On Shooting a Swallow in Early Youth.
On Some Humming-Birds in a Glass Cage.
On the Eclipse of the Moon of October 1865.
Quiet Tide near Ardossan, The.
Rose and Cushie.
Seaside: In and Out of the Season, The.
Steam Threshing-Machine, The.
Summer Night in the Beehive, A.
To a "Tenting" Boy.
Vacant Cage, The.
White Horse of Westbury, The.
Wind on the Corn.

Turner, Darwin T.
Night Slivers.
To Vanity.

Turner, Doris
Fragment Reflection I.
Reckoning A.M. Thursday.

Turner, Elizabeth
Bird's Nest, The.
Canary, The.
How to Write a Letter.
Truth's the Best.
Two Little Miss Lloyds, The.

Turner, Godfrey
Journal of Society, The.
Tattle.

Turner, Nancy Byrd
Death Is a Door.
First Thanksgiving of All.
Immigrants.
Lincoln.
Old Quin Queeribus.
Pop Corn Song, A.
Rivers Remember, The.
They Will Look for a Few Words.
Washington.
When Young Melissa Sweeps.
Wings and Wheels.

Turner, Steve
Christmas Is Really for the Children.

Turner, Walter James
Beneath a thundery glaze, *sel*.
Dancer, The.
Dian, Isis, Artemis, whate'er thy name, *sel*.
Ecstasy.
Epithalamium: "Can the lover share his soul."
Giraffe and Tree.
Hymn to Her Unknown.
I had watched the ascension and decline of the
   moon, *sel*.
I have seen mannequins, *sel*.
If God kept a terrarium, *sel*.
In Time like Glass.
India.
Life and Death.
Lion, The.
Love-song, A: "Beautiful, delicate bright
   gazelle, The."
Men Fade Like Rocks.
Music of a Tree, The.
Navigators, The.
Poetry and Science.
Reflection.
Robber, The.
Romance.

Silence.
Song: "Lovely hill-torrents are."
Spirits walking everywhere, *sel.*
Sun, The.
Talking with Soldiers.
This is the last time, *sel.*
Tragic Love.
What is the meaning of this Ideal, *sel.*
What is this tempest, *sel.*
Word Made Flesh, The.
Turner, William
Turners Dish of Lentten Stuffe or A
    Galymaufery.
Turner, William Price
Alien.
Coronary Thrombosis.
University Curriculum.
Turrini, Peter
As a boy/ I sometimes lifted.
How much longer.
I am not I.
I can understand.
I would like/ to love my enemies.
If I wanted to be satisfied.
No/ that I always wanted to say, The.
Worst is/ that I don't know, The.
Turtiainen, Arvo
Finally I understood Rose's death, *sel.*
Helsinki, *sel.*
Loveliest Poem.
Shoemaker Nikke.
There where the Kulo Saari bridge, *sel.*
Where could I find the words, *sel.*
Tusiani, Joseph
Anticipation.
Rest O Sun I Cannot.
Tusser, Thomas
Upon the Author's First Seven Years' Service.
When harvest is done all thing placed and set,
    sel.
Winds, The.
Tussman, Malka Heifetz
Cellars and Attics.
Dream.
Forgotten.
Homeless.
I Say.
In Spite.
Leaves.
Lord, my God.
My Persecutor.
Out of and Back in.
Saw You among Trees.
Songs of the Priestess.
Spoil.
With Teeth in the Earth.
Tuttle, Stella Weston
Quickening, The.
Tuwhare, Hone
Burial.
Fall of Rain at Miti-Miti, A.
Friend.
Girl in the Park, The.
Heemi.
Lament: "In that strident summer of battle."
Monologue.
Muscle and Bone of Song.
No Ordinary Sun.
Not by Wind Ravaged.
Old Place, The.
Rain.
Ron Mason.
Song in Praise of a Favourite Humming-Top,
    A.
Talk with My Cousin Alone, A.
Tangi.
Time and the Child.
To a Maori Figure Cast in Bronze outside the
    Chief Post Office, Auckland.
Tuwim, Julian [*or* Juljan]
Gypsy Bible, The.

Lodgers.
Mother.
Prayer, A: "I pray Thee O Lord."
Pursuit.
There Is No Country.
"Twain, Mark" (Sameul Langhorne Clemens)
Aged Pilot Man, The.
Emmeline Grangerford's "Ode to Stephen
    Dowling Bots, Dec'd.," *sel.*
Epitaph Placed on His Daughter's Tomb.
He Done His Level Best.
Home without a Cat, A.
Imitation of Julia A. Moore.
Limerick, A: "Man hired by John Smith and
    Co., A."
Twala, James
Biltong.
Twardowski, Samuel
Epitaph for a Dog.
Tweedsmuir, John Buchan, 1st Baron. *See*
    Buchan, John
Tweedy, Henry Hallam
Eternal God, Whose Power Upholds *with*
    music.
O Gracious Father of Mankind.
Twichell, Chase
Abandoned House in Late Light.
Blurry Cow.
Cedar Needles.
Watercress & Ice.
Twig, John
Ballade of the Nurserie, A.
Twiss, Horace
Fashion.
Two Eagles, Gayle
Young Warrior, The.
Tylee, Edward Sydney
Outward Bound.
Tyler, Inez M.
Call to Pentecost, A.
Tyler, Parker
Anthology of Nouns.
Nijinsky.
Tyler, Royall
Anacreontic to Flip.
Gambling.
Hail to the Joyous Day.
Independence Day.
Love Song, A: "By the fierce flames of love
    I'm in a sad taking."
Original Epitaph on a Drunkard.
Widower, The.
Tylor, Edward Burnett *and* **Andrew Lang.**
    See **Lang, Andrew** *and* **Edward Burnett**
    Tylor
Tymnes
Maltese Dog, A.
Tynan, Katharine (Katherine Tynan Hinkson)
Doves, The.
Epitaph, The: "Write on my grave when I am
    dead."
Farewell: "Not soon shall I forget—a sheet."
Flying Wheel, The.
Holy Family.
In Time of Need.
Leaves.
Lux in Tenebris.
Making of Birds, The.
Man of the House, The.
Mater Dei.
Nightingale, The.
Of an Orchard.
Passiontide Communion.
Pink Almond.
Sheep and Lambs.
Slow Spring.
Witch, The.
Tyrtaeus
How Can Man Die Better.
Tyuchev, Fyodor
Spring; a Formal Ode.

Tyutchev, Fyodor Ivanovich
As Ocean's Stream.
As round this earthly globe the oceans pour.
At Vshchizh.
Bestow, O Lord, thy gracious pardon.
Day and Night.
I love the rite of Luther's congregation.
Last Love.
My soul is an Elysium of shades.
Seated there upon the floor.
She was oblivious the livelong day.
Silentium.
There is about these autumn evenings bright.
Through reason Russia can't be known.
When locked in murd'rous toils of wants and
    cares.
Tzara, Tristan
Approach.
Approximate Man.
Bonita.
Death of Guillaume Apollinaire, The.
Doors Have Opened, The.
Drugstore Conscience.
Epidermis of the Night-Time Growth.
Evening.
Fluid.
Highway Single Sun.
Maturity.
Monsieur AA, Antiphilosopher.
Mothers.
Saltimbanques.
Song: "If words were nothing but signs."
Sunday solid lid above the boilings of
    bubbling blood, *sel.*
Tonic.
Volt.
Water Was Carving Out Tall Grills of Girls,
    The.
Way.
Tzu Yeh
Bare branches tremble, The.
I had not fastened my sash over my gown.
It is night again.

U

Uba, George
Firefly.
Gary Gotow.
How Do You Spell "Missile"?: Preliminary
    Instructions in the Nuclear Age.
Old Photo, 1942.
Uberti, Fazio degli
Canzone: His Portrait of His Lady, Angiola of
    Verona.
Uceda, Julia
Time Reminded Me.
2976.
Uchiko, Princess
Spring Day in a Mountain Lodge.
Udall [*or* Udal], Nicholas
I Mun Be Married a Sunday, *sel.*
Minion Wife, A, *sel.*
Udwan, Mamdouh
Casbah, The.
Elegy for a Man Who Died and Died.
Uejima Onitsura. *See* **Onitsura.**
Ugaas, Raage
Like the yu'ub wood bell tied to gelded
    camels that are running away.
Uhland, Ludwig (Johann Ludwig Uhland)
Castle by the Sea, The.
Durand of Blonden.
Hostess' Daughter, The.
Ichabod! The Glory Has Departed.
In a Lovely Garden Walking.
Leaf, A.

Luck of Edenhall, The.
Spirits Everywhere.
Ujvary, Liesl
Everything Has Its Reason.
Important!
Leave Everything the Way It Is.
Ukihashi
Whether I sit or lie.
Ulinover, Miriam
Havdolah Wine.
In the Courtyard.
Ullman, Leslie
Loyalty.
Private Acts.
Running.
Ullmann, Liv
I was born in a small hospital in Tokyo.
Mama says, *sel.*
Ulloa, Yolanda
Ita.
Short Biography of a Washerwoman.
Ulmer, James
For the Little Girl Who Asked Why the
Kitchen Was So Bright.
Uloccanar
What Her Girl Friend Said, Consoling Her
when She Was Distressed by the Town's
Gossip.
What Her Girl Friend Said, the Lover within
Earshot, behind a Fence.
Umakai (Fujiwara no Umakai)
Written When Appointed Commander of the
Western Sea Marches.
Underhill, Evelyn
Introversion.
Supersensual.
Theophany.
Underwood, Wilbur
Cattle of His Hand, The.
To the Brave Soul.
Ungaretti, Giuseppe
Agony.
Feeling of Time.
In Memoriam.
Morning.
Quiet.
Tedium.
Vanity.
Vigil.
Watch, Cima Quattro.
Weightless Now.
Ungo
Eyes blinded by three poisons.
Unik, Pierre
Manless Society, The.
Unoku
Moving/ resting is meaningless.
Untermeyer, Jean Starr
Autumn.
Country of No Lack.
Dew on a Dusty Heart.
False Enchantment.
High Tide.
Lake Song.
Last Plea.
Passionate Sword, The.
Sinfonia Domestica.
Sung on a Sunny Morning.
Untermeyer, Louis
Archibald MacLeish Suspends the Five Little
Pigs, *sel.*
At the Bottom of the Well.
Caliban in the Coal Mines.
Dance of Dust, The.
Dark Chamber, The.
Edgar A. Guest Considers "The Good Old
Woman Who Lived in a Shoe" and the
Good Old Truths Simultaneously, *sel.*
Edna St. Vincent Millay Exhorts Little Boy
Blue, *sel.*
End of the Comedy.

Feuerzauber.
Food and Drink.
Glad Day.
Goliath and David.
Infidelity.
Irony.
John Masefield Relates the Story of Tom,
Tom, the Piper's Son, *sel.*
Koheleth.
Last Words before Winter.
Long Feud.
On Hearing Prokofieff's Grotesque for Two
Bassoons, Concertina and Snare-Drums.
Portrait of a Machine.
Prayer.
Prayer for This House.
Prayer: "God, though [*or* although] this life
is but a wraith."
Questions at Night.
Relativities.
Repentance.
Sagging Bough, The.
Song Tournament: New Style.
Then, the quick plunge into the cool, green
dark, *sel.*
To a Vine-clad Telegraph Pole.
Wallflower to a Moonbeam.
Walter de la Mare Tells the Listener about
Jack and Jill, *sel.*
Wind Gardens.
Unto, Takeuchi. *See* **Takeuchi Unto**
Unzan
Ask Buddha—he doesn't know.
Updike, John
Agatha Christie and Beatrix Potter.
Amish, The.
August, *sel.*
Bendix.
Cars in Caracas, The.
Déjà, Indeed.
Dog's Death.
Ex-Basketball Player.
February 22.
From a Cheerful Alphabet.
Great Scarf of Birds, The.
Hymn to These Newly Abbreviated States.
I Like to Sing Also.
I Missed His Book, I Read His Name.
Idyll: "Within a quad of aging brick."
Insomnia the Gem of the Ocean.
January.
Love Sonnet.
May, *sel.*
Mime.
Minority Report.
Mosquito.
Naked Ape, The.
Note to the Previous Tenants.
October.
Ode, An: "I'm going to write a novel, hey."
Party Knee.
Player Piano.
Recital.
Seagulls.
Seven Stanzas at Easter.
Short Days, The.
Solitaire.
Some Frenchmen.
Sunflower.
Telephone Poles.
There was an old poop from Poughkeepsie,
sel.
3 A.M.
Touchy old gent from Cohasset, A, *sel.*
Upon Shaving Off One's Beard.
V. B. Nimble, V. B. Quick ("V. B.
Wigglesworth wakes at noon").
Vow.
Winter Ocean.
Youth's Progress.

Upham, Thomas Cogswell
Fear Not, Poor Weary One.
Song of the Pilgrims.
Upson, Arthur W.
Failures.
Uraiyur Mutukorran
What the Passersby Said to the Lover Eloping
with the Girl.
Urbina, Luis G.
Ancient Tear, The.
Centaur's Bath, The.
Dayspring.
Our Lives Are Rivers.
Silent Day, The.
Urchard, T.
Truly Rich, The.
Urdang, Constance
Birth.
Birth of Venus.
Changes of Life.
Children, The.
Day the Houses Sank, The.
Invention of Zero, The.
Uriarte, Ivan
Pier.
Rama ("Rama's a bunch of little shops").
Uribe, Armando
I love you and the rosebush.
Urmy, Clarence Thomas
As I Came Down Mount Tamalpais.
Blondel.
Ursell, Geoffrey
Beaver Love.
Uruttiran
Girl Friend Describes the Bull Fight, The.
What She Said to Her Girl Friend, and What
Her Girl Friend Said in Reply.
Usborne, Richard
Epitaph on a Party Girl.
Usher, Leila
I Am the Cat.
Utahania
Accusation.
**U'Tamsi, Felix TchiKaya (Tchicaya U
Tam'si)**
Scorner, The.
Utley, Steven
Local Allosaurus, The.
Uvlunuaq
I Should Be Ashamed.

V

"V., B." *See* **Thomson, James (1834–82)**
Váci, Mihály
Before I Die.
Most-Age, The.
Vakaló, Eléni
But there was/ once/ a time.
Genealogy.
My Father's Eye.
Song of the Hanged.
"Vala, Katri" (Karen Alice Heikel)
Bridge, The.
Child Plays, The.
On the Meadow.
String of Pearls.
Winter Has Come.
Winter Is Here.
Valaitis, Laura
Field Poem, A.
Valdés, Gabriel de la Concepción. *See*
"Plácido"
Valen, Nanine
Fisherman's Hands, The.

Valentine, Edward Abram Uffington
Helen.
Spirit of the Wheat, The.
Valentine, G. D.
Night up There.
Valentine, Jean
After Elegies.
Anaesthesia.
April.
Bride's Hours, A.
December 21st.
Dream Barker.
Field, The.
Forgiveness Dream; Man from the Warsaw
    Ghetto, The.
Knife, The.
Messenger, The.
Orpheus and Eurydice.
Pilgrims.
Sasha and the Poet ("Sasha: I dreamed you
    and he").
Second Dream, The.
Sex.
Silences; a Dream of Governments.
Valeri, Diego
Days, the Months, the Years, The.
Violets in Saint Mark's Square.
Valerio, Anita
I Am Listening: A Lyric of Roots.
Valéry, Paul
Asides.
Caesar.
Friendly Wood, The.
Helen.
Helen, the Sad Queen.
Narcissus.
Pomegranates.
Sylph, The.
To an impervious nothingness they're thinned,
    sel.
Vali, Shamsuddin Mohammad
Beware of my heart: it is.
Cup in hand the bashful beauty.
Do not be faithless to me.
Fire of your anger scalds, The.
I saw the beauty of my love.
Whenever I remember.
Vallana. *See* Villana
Valle, Carmen
Glenn Miller's music is a trunk.
I'm going to break out.
What Is Lived.
Valle, Isabel
Very Minor Poet Speaks, A.
Valle, Victor M.
Food.
Vallejo, César
And don't bother telling me anything.
Anger that breaks a man down into boys,
    The.
Considering Coldly, Impartially.
I have a terrible fear of being an animal.
Masses.
Masses, *sel.*
One pillar holding up consolation.
Pagan Woman.
Poem to Be Read and Sung.
Vallerugo, Ida
We Must Free Ourselves Today.
Valli, Maria
Crows, The.
Vallis, Val
Fishing Season.
Vammelvuo, Anja
Aleksandra Kollontay.
Another Spring, Another Year.
Even the Mirror Dies.
Small Boys.
Van Beck, Fritzi Harmsen. *See* Harmsen
    van Beek, Fritzi
Vance, Thomas H.
Frozen Hero, The.

"Vandegrift, Margaret" (Margaret Thomson
    Janvier)
Little Wild Baby.
Van Den Heever, C. M.
Fallen Zulu Commander, The.
Vandersee, Charles
Spring at Arm's Length.
Van Doren, Mark
Ancient Couple on Lu Mountain, The.
And Did the Animals?
And Then It Rained.
Apple Hell.
April, 1942.
Autonomous.
Burial.
City Songs.
Close Clan, The.
Distant Runners, The.
Donkey.
Dunce Song 6.
Envy the Old.
Escape, The.
Eternity's Low Voice.
Family Prime.
Former Barn Lot.
Ghost Boy.
God of Galaxies, The.
Good Appetite.
He's Coming.
History Lesson.
I Had to Be Secret.
If They Spoke.
Immortal.
Laly, Laly.
Merry-go-round.
Midwife Cat.
Moments He Remembers, The.
Music God.
Needles and Pins.
Old Ben Golliday.
Our Lady Peace.
Praise Doubt.
Praise Him Who Makes Us Happy.
Proper Clay.
Pulse, The.
Runaways, The.
Sad Child's Song, The.
Seven Sleepers, The.
Slowly, Slowly Wisdom Gathers.
That Day.
This Amber Sunstream.
Wait till Then.
When the World Ends.
Where Did He Run To?
Whisperer, The.
Why, Lord ("Why Lord, must something in
    us").
Wind in the Grass.
Winter Tryst.
Young Woman at a Window.
Van Dusen, Ruth B.
Prayer in a Country Church.
Van Duyn, Mona
Ballad of Blossom, The.
Birthday Card for a Psychiatrist.
Causes.
Economics.
Fear of Flying, The.
Leda.
Leda Reconsidered.
Letters from a Father.
Open Letter from a Constant Reader.
Pieta, The, Rhenish, 14th C., The Cloisters.
This seems, in a world where love must take
    its chances, *sel.*
What the Motorcycle Said.
"Wish to Be Believed, The."
Van Dyke, Henry
America for Me.
America's Welcome Home.
Angler's Reveille, The, *sel.*

Angler's Wish, An.
Envoy: "Legend of Felix is ended, the toiling
    of Felix is done, The," *sel.*
Four Things.
Gospel of Labor, The.
Grant us the knowledge that we need, *sel.*
Great River, The.
If All the Skies Were Sunshine.
Jesus, Thou Divine Companion.
Lily of Yorrow, The.
Lost Word of Jesus, A.
Mare Liberum.
Mile with Me, A.
Mother's Birthday, A.
Peace Hymn of the Republic.
Reliance.
Roslin and Hawthornden.
Tennyson.
These Are the Gifts I Ask.
To the Child Jesus.
Veery, The.
Zest of Life, The, *sel.*
Van Eck, Alice
Football Game, A.
Van Hoddis, Jakov
Air Vision, The.
End of the World.
Vannier, Angèle
To Speak I Know Not Where.
Vannoz, Philippine de
Reply to the Verses of M. Lebrun Entitled:
    "My Last Word on Women Poets."
"Vanolis, Bysshe." *See* **Thomson, James
    (1834–1882)**
Vanparanar
Price of Giving Too Much, The.
Woman and Her Dying Warrior, A.
Van Poznak, Joan
Euro-Squawk.
Sun Dance in St. Lucia.
Van Rensselaer, Mariana Griswold
Manners.
Van Rensselaer, Peyton
At Twilight.
Van Sertima, Ivan
Volcano.
Van Slyke, Beren
Shepherds, The.
Van Spanckeren, Kathryn
Muse Poem.
Van Toorn, Peter
Mountain Study.
Shake'n bake Ballad.
Van Troyer, Gene
Axeltree, The.
Van Vliet, Eddy. *See* Vliet, Eddy van
Van Voorhis, Linda Lyon
To a Humble Bug.
Van Vriesland, Victor
Evening.
Van Walleghen, Michael
Driving into Enid.
Van Wyk Louw, N. P. *See* Louw, N. P. van
    Wyk
Van Wynen, Peter
May God Give Strength.
Van Zyl, Tania
Horses of Marini, The.
House, The.
Man with the Hollow Breast, The.
Rope, The.
She Waited.
Two Women.
Várady, Szabolcs
Chairs above the Danube.
Outsider, If There Were Such a Man, An.
Vardhill, Anna Jane
To a Skeleton.

Varela, Blanca
Before the Pacific.
Captain, The.
Nobody will open the door for you.
Things I Say Are True, The.
Vargas, Roberto
Chile.
Vas, István
Anacreontic.
Boccherini's Tomb.
Budapest Elegy.
Catacombs.
Equinoctial.
Etruscan Sarcophagus, The.
Forum Romanum.
Gods.
Grand Finale, The.
History of Lit: A Communication.
Idling.
It Doesn't Count.
Just This.
Ladder, The.
Lion, The.
Mad Town, The.
Nagyszombat, 1704.
Night without Light, A.
On Approaching Fifty.
Once More.
Ports.
Saint Médard.
Tambour.
This Too Is Ars Poetica.
What Is Left?
Vásquez, Ricardo
Maestro's Barber Shop, The.
Vaughan, Henry
Abel's Blood.
As Time One Day by Me Did Pass.
Ascension-Hymn ("Dust and clay").
Bird, The.
Book, The.
Brecon Beacons and the Black Mountains,
  The.
Buriall.
Cock-crowing.
Come, come, what doe I here?
Come then! and while the slow icicle hangs,
  sel.
Constellation, The.
Corruption.
Dawning, The.
Dear, beauteous death! the jewel of the just,
  sel.
Dear Night! this world's defeat, *sel.*
Distraction.
Dwelling-Place, The.
Eclipse, The.
Fragment: "Walk with thy fellow-creatures:
  note the hush."
I Walked [*or* Walkt] the Other Day to Spend
  My Hour.
Incarnation and Passion, The.
Jews, The.
Joy of My Life! While Left Me Here.
Lamp[e], The.
London in 1646.
Love and Discipline.
Man.
Morning Watch, The.
Night, The.
Peace.
Pursuit[e], The.
Queer, The.
Quickness.
Regeneration.
Relapse, The.
Religion.
Retreat[e], The.
Revival, The.
Rhapsody, A.
Rom. Cap. 8 Ver. 19.
Search, The.

Seed Growing Secretly, The.
Shower [*or* Showre], The.
Silence and Stealth of Day[e]s!
Son-Dayes.
Starre, The.
Storm, The.
They Are All Gone into the World of Light.
Timber, The.
To Amoret.
To Amoret Gone from Him.
To His Books.
To the River Isca.
Unprofitablenes.
Upon the Priory Grove, His Usual Retirement.
Vanity of Spirit.
Waterfall [*or* Water-Fall], The.
Winged Heart, A, *sel.*
Winter's Frosty Pangs, *sel.*
World, The.
Vaughan, Henry *and* **Thomas Stanley**
In March birds couple, a new birth, *at.*
Vaughan, Thomas
"So Have I Spent on the Banks of Ysca Many
  a Serious Hour."
Stone, The.
Vaughan-Thomas, Wynford
Farewell to New Zealand.
Hiraeth in N.W.3.
To His Not-so-coy Mistress.
Vaughn, James P.
Four Questions Addressed to His Excellency,
  the Prime Minister.
So?
Three Kings.
Vaughn Williams, Ursula
Penelope.
Vautor, Thomas
Sweet Suffolk Owl, *at.*
Vaux, Thomas, 2d Baron Vaux of Harrowden
Aged Lover Renounceth Love, The.
No Pleasure without Some Pain.
Of a Contented Mind.
Sins of Youth, The.
Vayilanrevan
What She Said.
Vaynshteyn, Berysh
Chilly walls with sharp steel hooks, *sel.*
Division Street, *sel.*
Dogs of Dawn, *sel.*
Harlem—a Negro Ghetto.
Harlem Negroes, *sel.*
Hides.
Junk, *sel.*
Laundry, *sel.*
Lynching, *sel.*
Mangin Street, *sel.*
My Street—Sheepshead Bay.
Negro Geo'ge, *sel.*
Negro Village, *sel.*
New York Everywhere, *sel.*
On the Docks.
On Your Soil, America.
People Who Talk to Themselves, *sel.*
Sailors.
Sheep in New York, *sel.*
Veale, Peter
Bold Troubleshooters.
I put my hat upon my head.
Vedder, Miriam
Epitaph for a Persian Kitten.
Vega, José Luis
Brotherhood.
Conditions.
Erotic Suite.
My love, like the vast majority, *sel.*
Poemlove (Fragment), *sel.*
Vega Carpia, Lope de. *See* **Lope de Vega
  Carpio, Felix**
Veinstein, Alain
Toward the Other.

Veintimilla de Galindo, Dolores
Laments.
Velema
Tip-of-the-Single-Feather.
**Velho de Costa, Maria Maria Isabel Barreno
  Maria Theresa Horta.** *See* **Marias, The
  Three**
Venable, William Henry
Battle Cry.
Founders of Ohio, The.
John Filson.
Johnny Appleseed.
My Catbird.
National Song.
School Girl, The.
Teacher's Dream, The.
Venantius Fortunatus, Saint
Written on an Island off the Breton Coast.
Venkorran
What She Said.
Venmanipputi
What She Said to Her Girl-Friend.
Ventadour, Bernard de
No Marvel Is It.
Ventadour, Marie de. *See* **Marie de
  Ventadour**
Vere, Edward de, 17th Earl of Oxford. *See*
  De Vere, Edward, 17th Earl of Oxford
Veress, Miklós
Self-Portrait at Thirty.
Vergil. *See* **Virgil**
Verhaeren, Emile
Poor, The.
Verhagen, Hans
Cancer.
Hans Verhagen & Son.
Stars.
Veripatiya Kamakkanniyar
Leaf in Love and War, A.
Verlaine, Paul
A la Promenade.
Art Poétique.
Auburn.
Bad Sleeper, A.
Chansons d'Automne.
Clair de Lune.
Clymène, A.
Colloque Sentimental.
Confession, A.
Cortège.
Cythère.
Dans l'Allée.
En Bateau.
Fantoches.
Femme et Chatte.
Il Pleut Doucement sur la Ville.
Lassitude.
Lyric: You Would Have Understood Me.
Mandoline.
Muted.
My God, you have wounded me with love,
  sel.
Ode: To My Lovers.
Pantomime.
Pensionnaires.
Retinue.
Sentimental Conversations.
Sky is up above the roof, The, *sel.*
Slumber dark and deep, *sel.*
Spleen.
Spring.
Thousands and Three.
Vernon, William J.
Out on the Course.
Verplanck, Gulian
"Prophecy."
Verry, Isabel Williams
Alcestis.
**Verstegan [or Verstegen], Richard
  (Richardowlands)**
Lullaby: "Upon my lap my sovereign sits."
Vision of the World's Instability, A.

Very, John
Robbin, The.
Very, Jones
Clouded Morning, The.
Columbine, The.
Cottage, The.
Created, The.
Day of Denial, The.
Dead, The.
Eagles, The.
Earth, The.
Enoch.
Fair Morning, The.
Fugitive Slaves, The.
Garden, The.
Gifts of God, The.
Grave-Yard, The.
Hand and Foot, The.
Health of Body Dependent on Soul.
I Was Sick and in Prison.
Idler, The.
In Him We Live.
Lament of the Flowers, The.
Light from Within, The.
Lost, The.
New Birth, The.
New Man, The.
New World, The.
Old Road, The.
On Finding the Truth.
On the Completion of the Pacific Telegraph.
On Visiting the Graves of Hawthorne and
Thoreau.
Prayer, The: "Wilt Thou not visit me?"
Presence, The.
Slave, The.
Spirit Land, The.
Strangers, The.
Sumach Leaves, The.
To the Canary Bird.
Today.
Tree, The.
Trees of Life, The.
Yourself.
"Vesay, Paul." See Allen, Samuel
Vészi, Endre
Dreaming of the Castle.
Vice, Lisa
Cambodia Witness.
Houston Street.
Pants.
To the Waitress at the Hickory Pit.
Vicente, Gil
Song: "If thou art sleeping, maiden."
Vickers, V. C.
Moon Bird, The.
Swank, The.
Victor, Florence
Contest.
Vicuña, Cecilia
Ideal Woman, The.
Vidal, Peire
For a long time I was bitter.
I suck deep in air come from Provence to
here.
It'll be a long time again before my friends.
Long I looked for what I did not need, then.
Lord Expositor, if I had a horse.
More than a beggar I dare not.
Near to disgust, close to calling quits with
song.
One canso I've made murderously.
Song of Breath.
**Vidame de Chartres. See Chartres, Vidame
de**
Vidya
I praise the disk of the rising sun, sel.
One born to hardship in his place and station,
sel.

Please keep an eye on my house for a few
moments.
You are fortunate, dear friends, that you can
tell.
Vidya (Vijjika)
Friends,/ you are lucky you can talk.
Hiding in the/ cucumber garden.
Say, friend, if all is well still with the bowers,
sel.
Vieira, Luandino
Song for Luanda.
Vieno, Jukka
Land of the White Lily.
Open Your Fist.
We Must Shed our Illusions.
Viereck, George Sylvester
After the Battle.
Viereck, Peter
Blindman's Buff.
Don't Look Now but Mary Is Everybody.
Ennui.
From Ancient Fangs.
Graves Are Made to Waltz On.
Homecoming.
Kilroy.
Love Song to Eohippus.
1912–1952, Full Cycle.
Now Kindness.
Poet.
Tenderness of dignity of souls, The, sel.
To Be Sung.
To Helen of Troy (N.Y.).
Vale from Carthage.
You All Are Static; I Alone Am Moving.
Vigée, Claude
Destiny of the Poet.
Every Land Is Exile.
House of the Living.
Light of Judea.
Phoenix of Mozart, The.
Poetry.
Song of Occident.
Struggle with the Angel, The.
Tree of Death, The.
Wanderer, The.
Vigny, Alfred de
Eva, I agree to love, among creation, all the
creatures!, sel.
Nature.
Vilakazi, B. W.
Because.
I Heard the Old Song.
In the Gold Mines.
Sound of the Horn, The.
Then I'll Believe.
Vilariño, Idea
Everything Is Very Simple.
In Order to Say It.
Siren, The.
There's Nobody.
Vildrac, Charles
After Midnight.
Villa, José Garcia
God, Is, Like, Scissors.
My, Fellowship, with, God.
Way My Ideas Think Me, The.
Villakaviralinar
What the Concubine Said When She Heard
the Wife Complain about the Concubine's
Wiles.
Villana
After he stripped off my clothes.
Villanueva, Alma
I Sing to Myself.
I Was a Skinny Tomboy Kid.
Last Words, The.
Mother, May I?
Of Utterances.
Of/To Man.
There Were Times.
To Jesus Villanueva, with Love.

Witches' Blood.
(Wo)man.
You Cannot Leave.
ZINZ.
Villanueva, Salvador
I would go around biting my nails.
Maybe You Cannot Comprehend.
Temple is full of blood, The.
Villanueva, Tino
Aquellos Vatos.
Pachuco Remembered.
Villatoro, José Luis
Elegy for the Young Corpse.
Villaurrutia, Xavier
Los Angeles Nocturne.
Our Love.
**Villiers, George, 2nd Duke of Buckingham.
See Buckingham, George Villiers, 2nd
Duke of**
Villon, François
Arbor Amoris.
Ballad against the Enemies of France.
Ballad of the Gibbet.
Ballad of the Lords of Old Time.
Ballad of the Women of Paris.
Ballad of Villon and Fat Madge, The.
Ballad Written for a Bridegroom.
Ballad[e] of Dead Ladies.
Ballad[e] of Ladies' Love, Number Two.
Ballade to His Mistress.
Ballat o the Hingit.
Ballat o the Leddies o Langsyne.
Complaint of the Fair Armoress [or
Armouress], The.
Dispute of the Heart and Body of François
Villon, The.
Double Ballad of Good Counsel, A.
Epistle in Form of a Ballad to His Friends.
Epitaph in Form of a Ballad, The.
Fragment on Death, A.
His Mother's Service to Our Lady.
Hold the Wind.
Lament of the Lovely Helmet-Dealer.
No, I Am Not as Others Are.
Old Lady's Lament for Her Youth, The.
Old Woman's Lamentations, An.
Prayer of the Old Woman.
Prayer of the Old Woman, Villon's Mother,
sel.
Quatrain: "François am I, heavy my lot."
Quatrain: "I am François to my great dismay."
Rondel: "Good-by, the tears are in my eyes."
To Death, of His Lady.
Villon's Prayer for His Mother to Say to the
Virgin.
Vinal, Harold
Flight.
Hymnal.
Quest, The.
Vinaver, Stanislav
Cathedral, A.
European Night, The.
Inscription, An: "Over the sheer rocks over
the gorges."
Vincent, Stephen
Anthem: "America, if you were a basketball
court."
Basketball.
Coming Up and Falling Down.
Floor: Five, sel.
Floor: O, sel.
Jealousy.
Mother.
Relationship, The.
Requiem: "I watch the roses float."
Song of This House, The.
Vinner, Shlomo
In the Cabinet.
Jerusalem.
Lullaby: "Sleep now."
Midnight and Ten Minutes.

Need to Love, The.
Parting.
Training on the Shore.
Vinograd, Julia
I Hate Poetry.
Investigation.
Vinz, Mark
Fat Boy, The.
November Song.
Old Doc.
Quilt Song.
Return.
Variations on a Theme.
Wild West.
Violi, Paul
"At the Corner of Muck and Myer."
Index.
Outside Baby Moon's.
Whalefeathers.
Viorst, Judith
Mother Doesn't Want a Dog.
Night Fun.
Since Hanna Moved Away.
Some Things Don't Make Any Sense at All.
Virgil (Publius Vergilius Maro)
Aeneas Sees Italy, *sel.*
Affrayit, I glistnyt of sleip, and stert on feit, *sel.*
Amyd the wod his modir met thame tway, *sel.*
And now Aeneas charges straight at Turnus, *sel.*
And oft the owle with rufull song complaind, *sel.*
And Turnus than, quhar he at erth dyd ly, *sel.*
Arms, and the man I sing, who forc'd by fate, *sel.*
As, sum tyme, dois the curser stert and ryn, *sel.*
As this convine and ordinance was mayd, *sel.*
As when a fragment, from a mountain torn, *sel.*
Attentively he heard us, while we spoke, *sel.*
Batellis [*or* Batalis] and the man I will descrive, *sel.*
Battle of Actium, *sel.*
Boat Race, The, *sel.*
Bot now the haisty, egir, and wild Dido, *sel.*
Boxing Match, The, *sel.*
Care of Bees, The, *sel.*
Corydon and Thyrsis, *sel.*
Dear Sister, my resentment had not been, *sel.*
Destruction of Troy, The, *sel.*
Dido among the Shades, *sel.*
Dido's Hunting, *sel.*
Eneas wonderit the greitnes of Cartaige, *sel.*
Entrance to Hell, The, *sel.*
Exulting in his strength, he seems to dare, *sel.*
Greeks' chieftains, all irked with the war, The, *sel.*
Heaven, the earth, and all the liquid mayne, The, *sel.*
It was the time when, granted from the gods, *sel.*
It was then night: the sound[e] and quiet sleep [*or* slepe], *sel.*
Loe! formest of a rout that followd him, *sel.*
Loud report through Lybian cities goes, The, *sel.*
Lycidas and Moeris, *sel.*
Marcellus, *sel.*
Messiah, The, *sel.*
Now manhood and garbroyls I chaunt, *sel.*
Observe the daily circle of the sun, *sel.*
Onto the hallowit steid bryng in, thai cry, *sel.*
Prelude: "What makes a plenteous harvest," *sel.*
Prince, with wonder, sees the stately tow'rs, The, *sel.*
Prologue to Book VII, The, *sel.*
Queen Dido Rides Out Hunting, *sel.*

Quhen thou art careit to that cuntree, *sel.*
Rang'd on the line oppos'd, Antonius brings, *sel.*
Shepherd's Gratitude, The, *sel.*
Sixth Book of the Aeneis, The, *sel.*
There Charon stands, who rules the dreary coast, *sel.*
They wished [*or* whisted] all, with fixèd face attent, *sel.*
Thir riveris and thir watteris kepit war, *sel.*
Thus fell the King, who yet surviv'd the state, *sel.*
To my prowd foe thus, sister, humblie saye, *sel.*
We Have Paid Enough Long Since in Our Own Blood, *sel.*
Wee leave Creete Country; and our sayls unwrapped uphoysing, *sel.*
Welcome to the Sun, *sel.*
Whom when I saw assembled in such wise, *sel.*
Virgilio, Nicholas
Into the blinding sun.
Virrurru Muteyinanar
What He Said after a Quarrel, Remembering His Wedding Night.
Virtue, Vivian
Hour, The.
Waifs.
Vittorelli, Jacopo
On a Nun.
Vivaldi, Cesare
Mother, I Won't Forget.
September.
To Giovanni.
Voyage.
Wall, The.
Vivanti, Annie
Ego.
Vivian, Mary
Four Scarlet Berries.
Snowdrops.
Vivien, Renée
Litany of Hate, A.
Nocturne: "I love the languor of your sensual lips."
Pillory, The.
Sappho Lives Again.
Toward Lesbos.
Words to My Friend.
Vizenor, Gerald
Anishinabe Grandmothers.
Auras on the Interstates.
Family Photograph.
February Park.
Haiku: "August heat."
Haiku: Seasons in Santa Fe.
Holiday Inn at Bemidji.
Indians at the Guthrie.
Minnesota Camp Grounds.
North to Milwaukee.
Raising the Flag.
Seven Woodland Crows.
Shaman Breaks.
Surrendered Names.
Thumbing Old Magazines.
Tropisms on John Berryman.
Tyranny of Moths.
Unhappy Diary Days.
White Earth.
White Earth Reservation 1980.
Vlek, Hans
Durable Material.
Famine Winter.
Not for Sale.
Vliet, Eddy van
Birth.
Every soldier in the streetcar was a relation, *sel.*
Green. I Rewrite.
In These Exhausting Lowlands.

Old Champagne Glass.
Shoreline Doesn't Change, The.
Stockholm.
Vogel, Alois
Situation.
With Closed Eyes.
Vogel, David
Black Flags Are Fluttering.
Days Were Great as Lakes.
How Can I See You, Love.
In Fine, Transparent Words.
Now I Have Forgotten All.
Our Childhood Spilled into Our Hearts.
Plain, Humble Letters.
When I Was Growing Up.
Vogelsang, Arthur
Americans in an Orange Grove.
Clouds, The.
Drive Imagining.
Feeling That Way Too.
Vogelweide, Walther von der. *See* **Walther von der Vogelweide**
Voigt, Ellen Bryant
At the Movie: Virginia, 1956.
Bat, The.
Blue Ridge.
Daughter.
Exile.
Farm Wife.
Farmer, The.
For My Husband.
For My Mother.
Fugue, A.
January.
Jug Brook.
Landscape, Dense with Trees.
Last Class, The.
Letter from Vermont.
Lotus Flowers, The.
Marriage Poem, A.
Pastoral: "Crouched in the yard."
Rescue.
Short Story.
Spire, The.
Spring, The.
Storm, The.
Sweet Everlasting.
"The Wife Takes a Child."
Tropics.
Victim, The.
Visiting the Graves.
Why She Says No.
Year's End.
Voiture, Vincent
Rondeau: "Lord, I'm done for: now Margot."
Volckmann, Anna Helena
Letter to Mariana Ziegler.
Volf, Leyzer
Coarse Old Maid, The.
I Am Not a Honey-Hearted Child.
Montefiore in Vilna.
Vollmoeller, Karl Gustav
Nocturne in G Minor.
Volponi, Paolo
Another Voice.
Comet, The.
Roman Rooms.
Summer's End.
Tomorrow Is March Already.
Walls of Urbino, The.
Voltaire
Moralist still obstinate replies, The, *sel.*
Volwerk, Leen
Bog.
Staoineag.
Von Aist, Dietmar
Lady Stood, A.
Vondel, Joost van den
Adam's Hymn in Paradise.
Von Greiffenberg, Catharina Regina
Why the Resurrection Was Revealed to Women.

Von Hofmannsthal, Hugo
Travel Song.
Vision, A.
Von Morstein, Petra
1968.
Anthology Poem.
Von Rugge, Heinrich. *See* **Heinrich von Rugge**
Von Salis-Seewis, Johann Gaudenz
Song of the Silent Land.
Von Trimberg, Süsskind
Power of Thought, The.
Virtuous Wife, The.
Why Should I Wander Sadly.
Vories, William M.
Let There Be Light.
Voronca, Ilarie
Quick and the Dead, The.
Seven-League Boots, The.
Voss, J. H.
Who Does Not Love Wine, Women and Song.
Voznesensky, Andrei
Darkmotherscream.
Dead Still.
I Am Goya.
War.
Vrepont, Brian
Apple-Tree, The.
Net Menders, The.
Vriesland, Victor van
Ars Poetica.
Vroman, Leo
Daily Preparations.
Feathers.
February.
Horse of Death, The.
Indian Summer.
Old Miniatures.
River, The.
To Whom This May concern.
Vuckovic, Isabelle
Maturity.
Vuglar, Jenny
Leaving.
Vulgarius, Eugenius
Metrum Parhemiacum Tragicum.
Vyazemsky, Prince P. A.
I have outlived most things and people round me.
Remembrance.
Russian God, The.
Tear, The.
Tears.
To Natalia Nikolaevna Pushkina.

W

"W., A."
Desire's Government.
Dispraise of Love, and Lovers' Follies.
Give Me Leave.
Hopeless Desire Soon Withers and Dies.
In Praise of a Beggar's Life.
In Praise of the Sun.
Ladies' Eyes Serve Cupid Both for Darts and Fire.
To Time.
Upon Visiting His Lady by Moonlight.
Where His Lady Keeps His Heart.
"W., C. A."
To have it out or not? that is the question.
"W., J. J."
Brotherhood.
"W. A. G." *See* **"G., W. A."**
Wabnitz, William S.
Hinds of Kerry, The.

Wachtel, Chuck
Answer, The.
Horror Story Written for the Cover of a Matchbook, A.
Paragraph Made Up of Seven Sentences Which Have Entered My Memory, A.
Sirventes against the Management of the Mammoth Supermarket in Toulouse, A.
Waddell, Jean Percival
Half-Light.
Rhythm.
Wadding [*or* Waddinge], Luke
Christmas Day Is Come.
For Christmas Day.
For Innocents' Day.
For Saint John's Day.
For Saint Stephen's Day.
For Twelfth Day.
On the Circumcision: New Year's Day.
Waddington, James
Genius.
Sonnet to Poesy.
Waddington, Miriam
Advice to the Young.
Cadenza.
Catalpa Tree.
Desert Stone.
Field of Night, The.
Icons.
Investigator.
Lullaby: "Hush dove the summer."
My Lessons in the Jail.
Old Women of Toronto.
Restricted.
Season's Lovers, The.
Survivors, The.
Ten Years and More.
Thou Didst Say Me.
Women's Jail, The.
Wade, Blanche Elizabeth
Song of the Christmas Tree, The.
Wade, Thomas
Winter Shore, The.
Wadsworth, Oliver A.
Over in the Meadow.
Wagenlander, Lydia
Mother's Birthday.
Wagner, Charles Abraham
Three City Cantos.
Wagner, Mary Boyd
Lethal Thought, The.
Wagoner, David
Advice to the Orchestra.
Art of Surrender, The.
Being Herded Past the Prison's Honor Farm.
Best Slow Dancer, The.
Boy Who Became Sky, The.
By a Waterfall.
Calculation, The.
Canticle for Xmas Eve.
Closing Time.
Death of the Moon, The.
Diary.
Elegy for a Forest Clear-Cut by the Weyerhaeuser Company.
Elegy for Yards, Pounds, and Gallons.
Emergency Maker, The.
Feast, The.
Fruit of the Tree, The.
In the Badlands.
Leaving Something Behind.
Looking for Mountain Beavers.
Lost.
Making Up for a Soul.
Man from the Top of the Mind, The.
Man of the House, The.
Marsh Leaf.
Meeting a Bear.
Muse.
My Father's Garden.
News from the Court.

Nine Charms against the Hunter.
On Motel Walls.
Photographing a Rattlesnake.
Poem about Breath.
Poets Agree to Be Quiet by the Swamp, The.
Police Manual, A.
Salmon Boy.
Sharp-Shin.
Shooting of John Dillinger outside the Biograph Theater July 22, 1934, The.
Singing Lesson, The.
Staying Alive.
To a Farmer Who Hung Five Hawks on His Barbed Wire.
Tumbleweed.
Valedictory to Standard Oil of Indiana, A.
Victorian Idyll, A.
Visiting Hour, The.
Walking in a Swamp.
Warning to My Love, A.
Words, The.
Working against Time.
Young Girl with a Pitcher Full of Water, A.
Wagstaff, Blanche Shoemaker
All Paths Lead to You.
Earth Trembles Waiting.
Quiet Waters.
Wah, Fred
Breathe Dust.
Wahl, Jean
Decayed Time.
Evening in the Walls.
Lean Day in a Convict's Suit, A.
Prayer of a Little Hope.
Wain, John
Anniversary.
Apology for Understatement.
Arrival.
Au Jardin des Plantes.
Brooklyn Heights.
Lie Easy in Your Secret Cradle, *sel.*
My Name.
Poem without a Main Verb.
Song about Major Eatherly, A.
This above All Is Precious and Remarkable.
Wainwright, Jeffrey
Fierce Dream, The.
Illumination.
Wainwright, Margaret
O Susanna.
Waite, Arthur Edward
At the End of Things.
Wakarpa
Golden Sea-Otter, The, *sel.*
Wakayama Bokusui
Ah, our kiss—may the sea remain as it is, *sel.*
Arm for a pillow, fragrance of hair, *sel.*
At midday when the sea's visible, *sel.*
At my side.
At times you fall silent, *sel.*
Bird flies away quietly, A, *sel.*
By a window where evening silence falls, *sel.*
By chance I find a strand of your hair, *sel.*
Clouds burn, the sun sets, The, *sel.*
Does its pounding pierce the sun in the sky?, *sel.*
"Don't leave me, ever!" she said.
Eyes closed, you lean on a tree, *sel.*
For Sonoda Saeko, *sel.*
Hill asleep, The.
How forlorn.
How long our kiss was!, *sel.*
How lovely! getting drunk faster than I do, *sel.*
How many mountains and rivers to cross, *sel.*
Huge swells move blue against the winds, *sel.*
I drank yesterday, I drink today, *sel.*
I weep aloud—may my voice, *sel.*

I'm lost in the sea under the shining sun, *sel.*
In front of me the sea lies on its side, *sel.*
In the dark night it's light, *sel.*
In the spring night's fragrant darkness, *sel.*
Leaning on the chest of your seasick young
    mother, *sel.*
Like a bubbling stream.
Lodging the fireflight from a fire, *sel.*
Look at the mountain, *sel.*
Mountain soars and the sea lies on its side,
    The, *sel.*
Mountaintop: as far as I can see, *sel.*
My ship stopped, I've come upon this
    country, *sel.*
My train passes Ono Station, *sel.*
Not speaking many words, *sel.*
On Drinking, *sel.*
On the sea-bed.
Parched throat ashen, while sobering up, *sel.*
Sadly stars fall; two in love have lain side by
    side, *sel.*
Stars in the great sky fall in confusion, *sel.*
Such loneliness! If I could carve in stone, *sel.*
Sucked into the hillside darkness, *sel.*
Sun's light and the water's light muddy one
    color, The, *sel.*
Thousands of white wings wheel in the
    morning wind, *sel.*
Through the blue, blue moonless night, *sel.*
Used to lying together, *sel.*
When you smile, the sea becomes fragrant,
    sel.
White bird cries in a hushed manner, A, *sel.*
White bird—is it not sad?, A, *sel.*
Wholly drunk, I see only, *sel.*
Wakefield, Samuel
    Music of His Steps, The.
Wakeman, John
    Garden, A.
    Love in Brooklyn.
Wakley, Thirza
    An Easter Chick.
    Mouse, The.
    Spring Work at the Farm.
Wakoski, Diane
    Anticipation of Sharks.
    Apology, An.
    Belly Dancer.
    Coda: Greed Part 12—Looking for Beethoven
      in Las Vegas.
    Father of My Country, The.
    Having Replaced Love with Food and Drink.
    Hitchhikers, The.
    I Have Had to Learn to Live with My Face.
    Inside Out.
    Italian Woman.
    Journey.
    Justice Is Reason Enough.
    Mechanic, The.
    My Mother Tries to Visit Me in the Dead of
      Night.
    Night a Sailor Came to Me in a Dream, The.
    No More Soft Talk.
    Patriotic Poem.
    Photos, The.
    Placing a $2 Bet for a Man Who Will Never
      Go to the Horse Races Any More.
    Poet Recognizing the Echo of the Voice, A.
    Ring, The.
    Ringless.
    Sestina from the Home Gardener.
    Sestina to the Common Glass of Beer: I Do
      Not Drink Beer.
    Smudging.
    Summer.
    Thank You for the Valentine.
    Thanking My Mother for Piano Lessons.
    Uneasy Rider.
    Valentine for Ben Franklin Who Drives a
      Truck in California, A.
    Walking Past Paul Blackburn's Apt. on 7th
      St.

Wind Secrets.
You, Letting the Trees Stand as My Betrayer.
Walcott, Derek
    Alba.
    Another Life.
    Codicil.
    Country Club Romance, A.
    Egypt, Tobago.
    Elsewhere.
    Europa.
    Far Cry from Africa, A.
    Fist, The ("The fist clenched round my
      heart").
    For the Altarpiece of the Roseau Valley
      Church, Saint Lucia.
    Force.
    Forest of Europe.
    Fortunate Traveller, The.
    Frederiksted, Dusk.
    Gauguin.
    Glory Trumpeter, The.
    Greece.
    Gulf, The.
    In the middle of the harbour, *sel.*
    Letter from Brooklyn, A.
    Man o' War Bird.
    Man Who Loved Islands, The.
    Marina Tsvetayeva.
    Midsummer.
    Moon.
    Names.
    Nearing La Guaira.
    New World.
    Nights in the Gardens of Port of Spain.
    Oak Inns Creak in Their Joints as Light
      Declines, The.
    Port of Spain.
    Rest, Christ! from tireless war. See, it's
      midsummer, *sel.*
    Roman Outposts.
    Ruins of a Great House.
    Sabbaths, W.I.
    Sea Canes.
    Sea-Chantey, A.
    Season of Phantasmal Peace, The.
    Spoiler's Return, The.
    Tales of the Islands.
    Virgins, The.
    Voice out of the Sabbaths, W.I., A
    Volcano.
    Whale, His Bulwark, The.
    Winding Up.
    Young Wife, The.
Waldheim, Franklin
    Help Wanted.
Waldman, Anne
    After Li Ch'ing-chao.
    Berthe Morisot.
    Canzone: "I crisscross my feelings with a
      view."
    Color of Honey.
    Complaynt.
    Goddess of Wisdom Whose Substance Is
      Desire.
    July 4th.
    Lady Tactics.
    Number Song.
    On Walt Whitman's Birthday.
    Pressure.
    Song: "Time drawes neere."
Waldman, Anne and Ted Berrigan
    And now the book is closed, *sel.*
Waldrop, Keith
    Introducing a Madman.
    Proposition II.
    Song: Paper.
Waldrop, Rosemarie
    Ambition of Ghosts, The.
    Confession to Settle a Curse.
    Morning Has No House.

Relaxed Abalone, The.
Shorter American Memory of the American
    Character According to Santayana.
Waley, Arthur
    Censorship.
    No Discharge.
    Song: "I had a bicycle called "Splendid."
Walford, William W.
    Sweet Hour of Prayer.
Walker, Alice
    African Images.
    Black Mail.
    Burial.
    Chic Freedom's Reflection.
    Early Losses; a Requiem.
    Even as I Hold You.
    Expect Nothing.
    "Good Night, Willie Lee, I'll See You in the
      Morning."
    Green lawn/ a picket fence, *sel.*
    I/ never liked/ white folks, *sel.*
    I Said to Poetry.
    In These Dissenting Times.
    In Uganda an Early King.
    It is true—/ I've always loved, *sel.*
    Medicine.
    My Husband Says.
    New Face.
    Old man in white, An, *sel.*
    On Stripping Bark from Myself.
    Once.
    Revolutionary Petunias.
    So We've Come at Last to Freud.
    Suicide.
    Women.
    Your Soul Shines.
Walker, Annie L.
    Work, for the night is coming.
Walker, Charlie
    St. George.
Walker, Dee Lawrence
    Et Cetera.
Walker, E. M.
    To America, on Her First Sons Fallen in the
      Great War.
Walker, J.
    Love Song of J. Alfred Prufrock, The,.
Walker, James
    Safe.
Walker, Kath
    Dawn Wail for the Dead.
    Then and Now.
    We Are Going.
Walker, Margaret Abigail
    Ballad of the Hoppy-Toad.
    Birmingham.
    Childhood.
    For Andy Goodman—Michael Schwerner—
      and James Chaney.
    For Malcolm X.
    For Mary McLeod Bethune.
    For My People.
    Girl Held without Bail.
    Harriet Tubman.
    Jackson, Mississippi.
    Kissie Lee.
    Lineage.
    Molly Means.
    October Journey.
    Prophets for a New Day.
    Street Demonstration.
    Today.
    We Have Been Believers.
Walker, Paul
    Leaves.
Walker, Ted
    Breakwaters.
    By the Bridge.
    By the Saltings.
    Emigrés, The.
    Estuary.

Heron.
Homing Pigeons.
Lemons.
Mules.
On Scafell Pike.
Skimmers.

Walker, William
High o'er the Hills.

Walker, William Sidney
Too solemn for day, too sweet for night.

Walla, Edna Kingsley
Christmas Eve.

Wallace, Edgar
War.

Wallace, James Cowden
God the Omniscient.

Wallace, Lew
Song: "Wake not, but hear me, love!," *sel.*

Wallace, Robert
Among the Finger Lakes.
Aubade: N.Y.C.
Ballad of the Mouse.
Bird Theater.
Dig for Her the Narrow Bed.
Dog's Song.
Double Play, The.
Fly in December.
Girl Writing Her English Paper, The.
In a Spring Still Not Written Of.
In One Place.
In the Shadows of Early Sunlight.
In Winter.
Problem in History, A.
Snapshot for Miss Bricka Who Lost in the
  Semi-final Round of the Pennsylvania Lawn
  Tennis Tournament, A.
Storm, The.
Under the September Peach.

Wallace, Ronald
At the St. Louis Institute of Music.
Belly Dancer in the Nursing Home, The.
Constipation.
Feline.
Grandmother Grace.
Tunes for Bears to Dance To.

Wallace, William Ross
Hand That Rocks the Cradle Is the Hand That
  Rules the World, The.
What Rules the World.

Wallace, William S.
Song of Snohomish, The.

Wallace-Crabbe, Chris
Ancient Historian.
Citizen.
Dirigible, The.
Love Poem: "Written under Capricorn, a
  land."
Rebel General, The.

Wallach [or Wollach], Yona
Absalom.
All The.
Are These Moods of Mine Memory.
At Sea.
Body, The.
Christina.
Cradle Song: "Imagine lamenting our longing,
  no."
Death; She Was Always Here.
Gentle as Moon on Water.
House Is Empty, The.
I Feel Empty.
Jonathan.
Lola.
Love Poem No. 2.
Never Will I Hear the Sweet Voice of God.
Preannual Poem.
Sebastian.
Splitting the Infinite.
This Poem Should Have Etc.
To Live at the Speed of Biography.
To See Long like El Greco.

Two Gardens.
When the Angels Are Exhausted.
When You're Not a Poet.

Wallada
I wonder: is there no way for us to meet
  again.
If you were just in keeping our pact of love.
To Ibn Zaidun.
Wait till the darkness is deep.

Wallbank, Susan
For her birthday.
Invitation to a Dance.
Why So Many of Them Die.
Woman into Man.

Waller, Edmund
Aid me Bellona, while the dreadful fight, *sel.*
Apologie for Having Loved Before, An.
At Penshurst [Another]
Battel of the Summer-Islands, The.
Chloris and Hilas. Made to a Saraban.
Chloris Farewell.
Dancer, The.
Go [*or* Goe,] Lovely Rose.
Instructions to a Painter.
Of English Verse.
Of His Majesties Receiving the News of the
  Duke of Buckingham's Death.
Of Loving at First Sight.
Of My Lady Isabella Playing on the Lute.
Of the Last Verses in the Book.
On a Girdle.
On the Friendship betwixt Two Ladies.
Puerperium.
Seas are quiet when the winds give o'er, The,
  sel.
Selfe Banished, The.
Song: "Stay Phoebus, stay."
Soul's Dark Cottage, The, *sel.*
Story of Phoebus and Daphne Applied. The.
To a Fair Lady Playing with a Snake.
To a Very Young Lady.
To Amoret.
To Chloris, upon a Favour Received.
To Mr. Henry Lawes, Who Had Then Newly
  Set a Song of Mine in the Year 1635.
To One Married to an Old Man.
To Phyllis.
To the Mutable Fair.
Under a Lady's Picture.
Upon Ben Johnson.
While with a strong and yet a gentle hand,
  sel.

Waller, Janet
Aviemore.

Waller, John Francis
Spinning-Wheel, The.

Wallis, Eleanor Glenn
"Trade" Rat.

Wallis, George B.
Lovely Rivers and Lakes of Maine, The.

Wallis, John
When a twister a-twisting will twist him a
  twist.

Walpole, Henry
Martyrdom of Father Campion.

Walpole, Horace, 4th Earl of Orford
All praise your face, your verses none abuse.
Epitaph on Lady Ossory's Bullfinch, *sel.*
Epitaphs on Two Piping-Bullfinches of Lady
  Ossory's.
Estate and an earldom at seventy-four, An!
On the Translation of Anacreon.
To Lady Anne Fitzpatrick, When about Five
  Years Old, with a Present of Shells, 1772.
To the Gardener at Nuneham.

Walsh, Chad
Invocation: "Great-hearted Christ, importunate
  and mild," *sel.*
My God, My God, Look upon Me, *sel.*
Quintina of Crosses, A.

There Is None to Help, *sel.*
Why Hast Thou Forsaken Me?, *sel.*

Walsh, Christina
Prayer to Isis.
Woman to Her Lover, A.

Walsh, Edward
Kitty Bhan.

Walsh, Ernest
Doctor Bill Williams.
I Played on the Grass with Mary.
Old Fellow.
Serious Poem, A.
Sonnet: "My duchess was the werst she laffed
  she bitte."

Walsh, Marnie
Thomas Iron-Eyes.

Walsh, Thomas
Rare Willie Drowned in Yarrow; or, The
  Water o Gamrie.

Walsh, William
Abigail's Lamentation for the Loss of Mr.
  Harley.
Against Marriage to His Mistress.
Despairing Lover, The.
Love and Jealousy.
Lyce.
Phillis's Resolution.

Walsh, William *and* **Sir George Etherege**
Rivals, at.

Walter, Beatrice
Photograph the Cat Licks, The.

Walter, Howard Arnold
My Creed.

Walter, Nehemiah
Elegiack Verse on . . . Mr. Elijah Corlet,
  An.

Walters, Anna
Hartico.
I Am of the Earth.
I Have Bowed before the Sun.
My Brothers.
Simplicity Aims Circularly.
Teacher Taught Me, A.

Walters, Dorothy
Cinéma Vérité.
Flannery O'Connor.
Two Roads, Etc.

Walters, Lila V.
He Shall Speak Peace unto the Nations.

Walters, Muru
Haka: The Feathered Albatross.

Walters, Winifred Fields
Navajo Signs.

Walther, J. Monika
My Penultimate Speech at a Meeting of Some
  People of Good Will.

Walther von der Vogelweide
Awake!
There Is a Lady ("There is a lady conquering
  with glances").
Translation from Walter von der Vogelweide,
  A.
Under the Lindens [*or* Lime Tree]
With a Rod No Man Alive.

Walton, Eda Lou
Necessary Miracle, A.

Walworth, Clarence A.
Holy God, We Praise Thy Name.

Wan Kin-lau
Title Lost.

Wandor, Michelene
Eve Meets Medusa.
Lilith Re-Tells Esther's Story.

Wang An-shih
By the River.
Confiscating Salt.
Fresh Flowers.
Impromptu; Late Spring at Pan-shan.
Once I was a cow, a horse, *sel.*
Written for My Own Amusement.
Written on the Wall of Pan-shan Temple.

Wang Ch'ang-ling
Castleside Song.
Under the Frontier Post.
Wang Chi
Tell Me Now.
Wang Chia
Shrine Festival.
Wang Chien
Palace Song.
South, The.
Weaving at the Window.
Words of the Newly Wed Wife.
Wang Ch'ing-hui
Now the lotuses in the imperial lake.
Wang Chiu-ssu
Ballad of Selling a Child.
Ballad of the Fatherless Boy.
Chanting Poems.
Floating, floating, the river waters, *sel.*
For Several Days I Have Not Visited the
   Garden Pavilion.
I love the serenity of living in the woods, *sel.*
Quiet Sitting.
Recording My Happiness.
Rising from Sleep.
Song of the Painting of the Long-Life Star.
This crazy man has escaped the world, *sel.*
Thunder.
Today I am a farmer in the fields, *sel.*
Total failure—Master Han Shan, A, *sel.*
You think I am happy, *sel.*
Wang Fu-chih
An Autumn Song.
Bamboo Branch Song.
Miscellany, A.
On Frost.
Withered Willows.
Wang I
Lychee, The.
Wang Jun-hua
Bricks.
Landscape Philosophy.
Outdoor Collections.
Which Chapter.
Which Chapter—A Continuation.
Wang K'ai-yün
Since You Went Away.
Spring Sun.
Wang K'ang-chü
Refuting the "Invitation to Hiding."
Wang Kuo-wei
Drum sounds from the high city wall as the
   lampwick burns, The.
How much has the light thickened outside the
   window, under the green bough?
Mountain temple dim and far away, its back
   against the setting sun, A.
Random Thoughts.
Tune: Immortal at Magpie Bridge.
Who says that in the human world autumn has
   already gone?
Wang P'eng-yün
Brilliant minds were legion by the gate of the
   ancestral kingdom, *sel.*
Climbing to the Peak of Yang-t'ai Mountain
   to View the Ming Tombs.
For thirty years this entire world has looked to
   lung-men, sel.
Wang Seng-ta
To Match the Prince of Lang-yeh's Poem in
   the Old Style.
Wang Shih-chen
After Rain, Visiting the Temple of Heavenly
   Peace.
And what of the journey where the head of
   Wu meets the tail of Ch'u?, *sel.*
At dawn I climb a river tower to its very
   highest storey, *sel.*
Bamboo Branch Song of Han-chia.
Climbing to the Very Top of Swallow Rock
   Once Again, in an Early Morning Rain.

Crossing the River at Kuan-yin Gate after
   Rain.
Crossing the River in Heavy Wind.
Crossing the Yangtze in a Strong Wind.
Echoing Old Man Mu's Poem.
Lamenting for My Wife.
Mooring at Night at Kao-yu.
Mooring at Night at the River Mouth, I Heard
   a Flute.
Mooring in the Rain at Kao-yu.
Most of the houses along the river are those
   of fisherfolk, *sel.*
Over the years hearts have been broken on
   Mo-ling boats, *sel.*
Quatrain at Chen-chou.
Seeing off Editor Wang Chou-tz'u and
   Secretary Lin Shih-lai.
Song of the Ch'in-Dynasty Mirror.
Things Seen.
Thinking of the Past on an Autumn Night at
   Tz'u-jen Temple.
Viewing the Sea from the Li-shuo Pavilion.
When the tide ebbed in the Ch'in-huai,
   autumn after spring, *sel.*
Wang T'ing-hsiang
At Arrow Rapids, the water spashes foam,
   sel.
Climbing to the Top of the City Walls at
   Kan-yü.
Don't ask about the Six Dynasties of the Sui
   Palace, *sel.*
Flowering Tree, The.
I am a man of Chiang-nan, *sel.*
I pluck *heng* -herbs at the Chin-ling riverside,
   sel.
On New Year's Day of the Year *Kuei-ssu*.
Pagoda of Master Chih, The, *sel.*
Song of the Wanderer.
Thousands of mountains, tens of thousands of
   mountains.
Wall Painting by Wu Wei, A, *sel.*
Written in the Office Precincts.
Wang Ts'ai-wei
Since You Went Away.
Written in Response to Wei-yin's Rhymes.
Written in the Mountains.
Wang Ts'an
Tribes of Ching—that's not my home, *sel.*
Western Capital in lawless disorder, The, *sel.*
Wang Wei
At My Country Home in Chung-nan.
Bamboo Mile Lodge, *sel.*
Deer Fence, *sel.*
Duckweed Pond.
Green Stream, A.
Lush, lush, fragrant grasses in autumn green,
   sel.
Meng-ch'eng Hollow, *sel.*
Parting, A.
Seeing Someone Off.
Seeking a Mooring.
Visiting the Temple of Accumulated
   Fragrance.
Weather Newly Cleared.
Weeping for Ying Yao.
Wang Wei, Lady
Hsi.
Wang Yü-ch'eng
Journey to a Village.
Wangara, Malaika Ayo
From a Bus.
Waniek, Marilyn Nelson
Dinosaur Spring.
Herbs in the Attic.
It's All in Your Head.
Light under the Door.
Mama's Promise.
Old Bibles.
Women's Locker Room.
Wanley, Nathaniel
Humaine Cares.

Instead of Incense (Blessed Lord) if wee, *sel.*
Royall Presents.
Sigh, The.
Warburton, R. E. Egerton
Past and Present.
"Ward, Artemus" (Charles Farrar Browne)
Uncle Simon and Uncle Jim.
Ward, Diane
Approximately.
Habit of Energy, The.
Prosperity.
Tender Arc.
Ward, Edward
Ballad on the Taxes, A.
Dialogue between a Squeamish Cotting
   Mechanic and His Sluttish Wife, in the
   Kitchen, *sel.*
Extravagant Drunkard's Wish, The.
Parish Poor-Officers, The, *sel.*
**Ward, Elizabeth Stuart Phelps (Elizabeth
   Stuart Phelps)**
Conemaugh.
Generous Creed, A.
Gloucester Harbor.
Lost Colors, The.
Message, A.
Room's Width, The.
Ward, Kenneth
Investor's Soliloquy.
Ward, May Williams
Wet Summer.
Ward, Nathaniel
Mercury shew'd Apollo, Bartas Book.
Mr. Ward of Anagrams Thus.
Poetry's a gift wherein but few excell.
World's a well strung fidle, mans tongue the
   quill, The.
Ward, Samuel
Proem, A: "When in my walks I meet some
   ruddy lad."
Ward, William Hayes
New Castalia, The.
To John Greenleaf Whittier.
Ware, Eugene
Blizzard, The.
Ware, Eugene Fitch ("Ironquill")
Aztec City, The.
Ballad in "G," A.
He and She.
Manila.
Whist.
Zephyr.
Ware, Henry, Jr.
Great God, the Followers of Thy Son.
Lift Your Glad Voices in Triumph on High.
Warfield, Catherine Anne
Beauregard.
Manassas.
Waring
Myself.
Waring, Anna L.
My Times Are in Thy Hand.
Waring, H. C.
Quite the Cheese.
Warmond, Ellen
Change of Scene.
Warne, Candice
Blackbird Sestina.
Warner, Anna Bartlett ("Amy Lothrop")
Jesus Loves Me, This I Know.
One More Day's Work for Jesus.
We Would See Jesus.
Warner, Charles Dudley
Bookra.
Warner, Eva
Irony of God.
Warner, Rex
Chough.
Palm Trees.
Warner, Sylvia Townsend
Absence, The.

After He Had Gone.
Alarum, The.
Benicasim.
Building in Stone.
Country Thought.
Elizabeth.
Epitaph: "Her grieving parents cradled here."
Epitaph: "I, an unwedded wandering dame."
Epitaph: "I, Richard Kent, beneath these stones."
Epitaph: "John Bird, a laborer, lies here."
Gloriana Dying.
Graveyard in Norfolk.
Green Valley, The.
Killing No Murder.
King Duffus.
Modo and Alciphron.
Nelly Trim.
Rival, The.
Road 1940.
Sad Green.
Sailor, The.
Song from the Bride of Smithfield.
Song: "She has left me, my pretty."
Triumph of Sensibility.

Warner, William
Fate of Narcissus, The, *sel.*
My Mistress.

Warr, Bertram J.
Deviator, The.
On a Child with a Wooden Leg.
Poets in Time of War.
Trees, Who Are Distant.
Working Class.

Warren, Hamilton
Requiem: "Let the mountains stand forth!"

Warren, Hans
Aging Poet, The.
Moorish Frigate: 2, A.
Soap Bubble: 3, A.

Warren, James E., Jr.
Schoolroom: 158–

Warren, Joseph
Free America.

Warren, Mrs. Mercy
Massachusetts Song of Liberty, at.

Warren, Robert Penn
American Portrait: Old Style.
Aubade for Hope.
Ballad of Billie Potts, The.
Bearded Oaks.
Birth of Love.
Blow West wind.
Boy Wandering in Simms' Valley.
Boyhood in Tobacco Country.
Colder Fire, *sel.*
Country Burying (1919).
Covered Bridge.
Debate: Question, Quarry, Dream.
Dragon Country: To Jacob Boehme.
Dream, Dump-Heap, and Civilization.
Evening Hawk.
Evening Hour.
Fall Comes in Back-Country Vermont.
Far West Once.
Flaubert in Egypt.
Founding Fathers, Nineteenth-Century Style, *sel.*
Function of Blizzard.
Garden, The.
Gold Glade.
Heart of Autumn.
Heart of the Backlog.
Heat Lightning.
History among the Rocks, *sel.*
History during Nocturnal Snowfall.
I Can't Even Remember the Name, *sel.*
In Time's concatenation and/ Carnal conventicle, *sel.*
Last Laugh.
Last Meeting.

Letter from a Coward to a Hero.
Letter of a Mother.
Letter to a Friend.
Limited, The.
Little Girl Wakes Early.
Love and Knowledge, *sel.*
Man in the Street.
Mango on the Mango Tree, The, *sel.*
Masts at Dawn.
Muted Music.
Myth on Mediterranean Beach: Aphrodite as Logos.
Natural History.
Nightmare of Mouse.
Notes on a Life to Be Lived.
Old-Time Childhood in Kentucky.
Original Sin; a Short Story.
Owl, The.
Patriotic Tour and Postulate of Joy.
Picnic Remembered.
Pondy Woods.
Pro Sua Vita.
Pursuit.
Rattlesnake Country.
Real Question Calling for a Solution, A.
Remarks of Soul to Body.
Revelation.
Riddle in the Garden.
Rumor Verified.
Seasons.
Sila.
Sister Water.
Small Winter House.
Spider, The.
Summer Rain in Mountains.
Swimming in the Pacific.
Tell Me a Story.
Terror.
There's a Grandfather's Clock in the Hall.
Treasure Hunt.
True Love.
Two Pieces for Suetonius.
Was Not the Lost Dauphin, *sel.*
Watershed.
Way to Love God, A.
Ways of Day.
Wet Hair: If Now His Mother Should Come, *sel.*
What Voice at Moth-Hour.
What was the promise that smiled from the maples at evening?, *sel.*
When the Century Dragged.
Where the Slow Fig's Purple Sloth.
Why You Climbed Up.
Work, *sel.*
Youthful Picnic Long Ago: Sad Ballad on Box.

Warren, Rosanna
Alps.
Daylights.
History as Decoration.
Hunter, *sel.*
Interior at Petworth: From Turner.
Lily.
Mother, *sel.*
Painting a Madonna.
Timarista and Krito, *sel.*
To Max Jacob.
Virgin Pictured in Profile.

Warren, William F.
I Worship Thee, O Holy Ghost.

Warren, Edward Perry. *See* "Raile, Arthur Lyon"

Warrior, Emma Lee
Enemy's Eyes, The.
How I Came to Have a Man's Name.
New Indian Medicine.
Reginald Pugh, The Man Who Came from the Army.

Warsaw, Irene
Slither Tither.

Warsh, Lewis
4/13/79.
Love's Will.
March Wind.
Precious Mettle.

Warton, Joseph
Charms of Nature, The.
Dying Indian, The.
Enthusiast: or, The Lover of Nature, The.
O warm, enthusiastic maid, *sel.*
Ode: To the Nightingale.
Revenge of America, The.
Verses Written at Montauban in France, 1750.
Ye green-robed Dryads, oft at dusky eve, *sel.*

Warton, Thomas, the Younger
Beneath yon ruin'd abbey's moss-grown piles, *sel.*
Come, gentle sleep, death's image though thou art.
Grave of King Arthur, The.
Mother of musings, contemplation sage, *sel.*
On King Arthur's Round Table, at Winchester.
On Leander's Swimming over the Hellespont to Hero.
Pleasures of Melancholy, The.
Sonnet: To the River Lodon.
Sonnet: Written in a Blank Leaf of Dugdale's "Monasticon."
Swallow, for a moment seen, The, *sel.*
To Mr. Gray.
Verses on Sir Joshua Reynolds's Painted Window at New College, Oxford.
Written at Stonehenge.

Washbourne, Thomas
Circulation, The.
Prayer: "What a commanding power."
Upon a Great Shower of Snow That Fell on May-Day, 1654.
Upon a Passing Bell.

Washburn, Archie
Hogan.
Unknown Smoke.

Washburn, Henry Stevenson
Almighty God, Thy Constant Care.
Song of the Harvest.

Waskowsky, Riekus
Essay.
If by Eternity.
Salt Peanuts.
That the Sun Will Rise Tomorrow.

Wassall, Irma
Singing in the Dark.
Stone from the Gods.

Wasserman, Rosanne
Inuit and Seal.

Wastell, Simon
Man's Mortality, *sel.*

Wat, Aleksander
Arithmetic.
Before Breughel the Elder.
By a great, swift water, *sel.*
Disgusted by everything alive I withdrew into the, *sel.*
Flamingo's Dream, A.
If the Word "Exists."
Japanese Archery.
Notes to the Books of the Old Testament.
So now, having fled into the stone world, I was slowly, *sel.*
There Is No Place.
To Be a Mouse.
Willows in Alma-Ata.
X was asked, *sel.*

Watanabe Suiha
Haiku: "Autumn wind:/ Eyes distended."
Haiku: "Noisy cricket, The."
Haiku: "Waves on the ebb."
Haiku: "Wild geese flying."

Waterbury, Jared Bell
I Have Fought the Good Fight.
Sinner, Is Thy Heart at Rest?

Waterman, Cary
Last Game.
Waterman, Nixon
Cheer for the Consumer.
Far from the Madding Crowd.
If We Didn't Have to Eat.
Johnny's Hist'ry Lesson.
Life would be an easy matter, *sel.*
Making a Man.
To Know All Is to Forgive All.
What Have We Done Today?
Whistling Boy.
Watermeyer, G. A.
Harvest Time.
Waters, Michael
American Bandstand.
Among Blackberries.
Anniversary of the Air.
Apples.
Dogs in the Storm.
Drunk with Pavese.
Faithful, The.
Frank Sinatra.
Furniture-Maker, The.
Mystery of the Caves, The.
Mythology.
Negative Space.
Preserves.
Singles.
Stories in the Light, The.
Watkins, Edward
Carrot Crazy.
Figures of Authority.
Watkins, Lucian B.
Star of Ethiopia.
To Our Friends.
Two Points of View.
Watkins, Vernon
Ballad of the Two Tapsters.
Ballad of the Three Coins.
Beaver's Story, The.
Cave-Drawing, The.
Collier, The.
Compost Heap, The.
Cwmrhydyceirw Elegiacs.
Dead Words, The.
Demands of the Muse.
Discoveries.
Earth and Fire.
Feather, The.
Fingernail Sunrise.
Fire in the Snow, The.
Foal.
For a Wine Festival.
Furnace of Colors, The.
Gravestones.
Healing of the Leper, The.
Heron, The.
Hurdy-Gurdy Man in Winter.
Indolence.
Lady with the Unicorn, The.
Mare, The.
Music of Colours: The Blossom Scattered.
Music of Colours—White Blossom.
Napkin and Stone.
Ode to Swansea.
Old Triton Time.
Peace in the Welsh Hills.
Returning from Harvest.
Returning to Goleufryn.
She That Is Memory's Daughter.
Shooting of Werfel, The.
Snow Curlew, The.
Song of the Good Samaritan, The.
Spoils of War, The.
Swendenborg's Skull.
Tine Picture Restored.
Two Decisions.
Waterfalls.
Yew-Tree, The.
Watkyns, Rowland
Antipathy.

Bad company is a disease.
Saul did much care and diligence express.
Strange Monsters.
Upon Christ's Nativity or Christmas.
Worldly Wealth.
Watson, Albert Durrant
Breeze and Billow.
Hymn for Canada, A.
Priest and Pagan.
Soul Lifted.
Watson, Barbara Bellow
Late Light.
Watson, Clyde
Belly and Tubs Went Out in a Boat.
Dilly Dilly Piccalilli.
Do the Baby Cake-Walk.
Huckleberry, Gooseberry, Raspberry Pie.
Hushabye My Darling.
Phoebe in a Rosebush.
Rock, Rock, Sleep, My Baby.
Yip-yap Rattletrap.
Watson, Edward Willard
Absolution.
Watson, Flora Willis
Calendar Rhyme.
Watson, J. Y.
Soldier, The.
Watson, James Wreford ("James Wreford")
Gatineaus, The.
Our Love Shall Be the Brightness.
Sic Transit Gloria Mundi.
Stay, Time.
We Shall Have Far to Go.
Watson, John Whittaker
Beautiful Snow, The.
Watson, Nancy Dingman
Grasshopper Green.
Makers.
Up in the Pine.
Watson, Robert
Blue Whale, The.
Watson, Rosamund Marriott ("Graham R. Tomson"; "R. Armytage")
Ave atque Vale.
Watson, Roy W.
View on Death, A.
Who a Mother Is.
Watson, Sir William
Church Today, The.
Domine Quo Vadis?
Epigram: "When whelmed the altar, priest and creed."
Epitaph, An: "His friends he loved. His direst earthly foes."
God-seeking.
Hope of the World, The.
If I had never known your face at all, *sel.*
Love, *sel.*
Ode in May.
Poet, The, *sel.*
Song: "April, April,/ Laugh thy girlish laughter."
Sovereign Poet, The.
Things That Are More Excellent, The.
Unknown God, The.
Wordsworth's Grave.
Watson, Thomas
Come, Gentle Death!, *sel.*
Go Idle Lines, *sel.*
Here Lieth Love, *sel.*
I Saw the Object, *sel.*
My Love Is Past.
Some that reporte great Alexanders life, *sel.*
Sonnet: "I saw the object of my pining thought."
Speake gentle heart, where is thy dwelling place?, *sel.*
Time, *sel.*
With Fragrant Flowers We Strew the Way, *sel.*

Watson, W. F. N.
Hicche-Hykeres Tale, The.
Watson, Wilfred
Canticle of Darkness.
Emily Carr.
Invocation: "Appear, O Mother, was the perpetual cry."
Lines: I Praise God's Mankind in an Old Woman.
O My Poor Darling.
White Bird, The.
Windy Bishop, The.
Watt, Frederick B.
Inspection, The.
Watt, Lauchlan MacLean
Wind from the West, A.
Watt, T. S.
From My Rural Pen.
Watt, W. W.
Summer Song.
Watten, Barrett
Complete Thought.
Mimesis.
Mode Z.
Plasma.
Position.
Relays.
"X."
Watterman, Catharine H.
Come unto Me, When Shadows Darkly Gather.
Wattles, Willard Austin
Pisgah.
Watts, Alaric Alexander
Austrian Army, An, at.
Watts, Isaac
Adventurous Muse, The.
Almighty Maker God!, *sel.*
Broad Is the Road.
Christ hath a garden walled around.
Church the Garden of Christ, The.
Comparison and Complaint, The.
Cradle Hymn, A.
Day of Judgement [*or* Judgment]; an Ode, The.
Early, my God, without delay.
Edom.
Few Happy Matches.
For the Lord's Day Evening.
Great God, attend while Zion sings.
Hosanna to Christ.
How Doth the Little Busy Bee.
How long, dear Savior, O how long.
Hurry of the Spirits, in a Fever and Nervous Disorders, The.
Incomprehensible, The.
Innocent Play.
Jesus Shall Reign Where'er the Sun.
Kind Deeds.
Look on Him Whom They Pierced, and Mourn.
Love between Brothers and Sisters.
Miracles at the Birth of Christ.
Ninetieth Psalm, The.
Ninety-fifth.
O God, Our Help in Ages Past.
Our God, Our Help in Ages Past.
Our Saviour's Golden Rule.
Passion and Exaltation of Christ, The.
Praise for Mercies Spiritual and Temporal.
Shortness and Misery of Life, The.
Sluggard, The.
Spare Us, O Lord, Aloud We Pray.
Submission to Afflictive Providences.
Sweet Muse, Descend.
There is a land of pure delight.
Through every age, eternal God.
When I Survey the Wondrous Cross.
Where-e'er My Flatt'ring Passions Rove.
Where Nothing Dwelt but Beasts of Prey.
Why Do We Mourn Departing Friends?

Watts, Mabel
Maytime Magic.
Riveter, The.
Yesterday's Paper.
Watts-Dunton, Theodore
Coleridge.
Waugh, Edwin
Cultivate Your Men.
I've Worn My Bits o' Shoon Away.
Man of the Time, The.
Wawra, Karl
Antique Shop in New York.
Capri as Cloud.
Scarecrow in Capri, The.
Wayland, John Elton ("Idas")
Epilogue at Wallack's, An.
Wayman, Tom
Another Poem about the Madness of Women.
Chilean Elegies: 5, The. The Interior.
Picketing Supermarkets.
Wayman in Love.
What Good Poems Are For.
Wayne, Jane O.
Looking Both Ways.
Wazyk, Adam
An Attempt.
Ars Poetica.
Hotel.
Nike.
Pre-Columbian Sculpture, A.
Search, A.
Sketch for a Memoir.
Weare, Meshech
Blasted Herb, The.
Weatherly, Frederic Edward
Holy City, The.
Limerick: "My name's Mister Benjamin
Bunny."
When the Christ Child Came.
Weatherly, Tom
Arroyo.
Canto 5: Coon Fire.
Canto 7: First Thesis.
Coon Fire, sel.
First Monday Scottsboro Alabama.
First Thesis, sel.
Gullfish, sel.
Imperial Thumbprint.
Weaver, John Van Alstyn
Legend.
Webb, Charles Henry ("John Paul")
At the Ball!
Autumn Leaves.
Dum Vivimus Vigilamus.
Gil, the Toreador.
March.
With a Nantucket Shell.
Webb, Francis
Airliner.
Five Days Old.
Gunner, The.
Idyll: "At noon the sun puffed up, outsize."
Papuan Shepherd, A, sel.
Room, The, sel.
Sea, The.
This Runner.
Ward Two.
Webb, Frederick G.
Dash for the Colors, The.
Webb, Mary
Foxgloves.
Green Rain.
Market Day.
Secret Joy, The.
Water-Ousel, The.
Webb, Phyllis
Days of the Unicorns, The.
Imperfect Sestina.
Marvell's Garden.
Poetics against the Angel of Death.
Propositions.

Spots of Blood.
Syllables disintegrate ingrate alphabets, sel.
Tall Tale; or, A Moral Song, A.
"The Time of Man."
To Friends Who Have Also Considered
Suicide.
Webb, Tessa Sweazy
Bright Abandon.
Webb, Thomas Henry Basil
Ancient Prayer, An.
Webbe, Charles
Against Indifference.
Weber, Richard
Elizabeth in Italy.
Envying the Pelican.
In Memoriam I, Elizabeth at Twenty.
Poet's Day, The.
Primer for Schoolchildren, A.
Visit to Bridge House, A.
Webster, Augusta Davies ("Cecil Home")
Oh smooth adder/ who with fanged kisses
changedst my natural blood, sel.
Pine, The.
Well, well, I know the wise ones talk and
talk, sel.
Webster, Daniel
On the Death of My Son Charles.
Webster, H. D. L.
Lorena.
Webster, John
All the Flowers of the Spring, sel.
Call for the Robin Redbreast and the Wren,
sel.
Duchess of Malfi, sels.
Execration against Whores, An, sel.
Hark, Now Everything Is Still, sel.
I am come to make thy tomb, sel.
Madman's Song, The, sel.
What, are you drop't?, sel.
What death?, sel.
What hideous noise was that?, sel.
Yond's the Cardinall's window: This
fortification, sel.
Webster, John and William Rowley
Art Thou Gone in Haste?, sel.
Love Is a Law, sel.
Whither shall I go, sel.
Webster, Mary Morison
Grass.
I Set Aside.
Illi Morituri.
Marriage of Pocahontas, The.
Ox, The.
Quiet of the Dead, The.
Secret, The.
Webster, W. J.
Prick a maiden nether holly.
To His Coy Mistress.
Wedde, Ian
And this is where, sel.
Beautiful Poultry.
Beggar at the Gate, The.
By day and also by night and you are, sel.
Dark Song.
Diesel trucks past the Scrovegni chapel, sel.
Driving into the Storm: The Art of Poetry.
Hardon ("Get One Today").
I imagine the womb as a honeycomb, sel.
"If thy wife is small bend down to her and",
sel.
In time a message back, like this, to say, sel.
It's Time, sel.
King Solomon Vistas.
Land-Mine Casualty Amman 1970, sel.
Madonna, sel.
Paradiso Terrestre, sel.
Power Transformer, sel.
Precocious spring how beautiful you are!, sel.
Right now the elm seeds whisper to the
ground, sel.

That autumn day suddenly broken into, sel.
Those Others.
Wedgefarth, W. Dayton
Bum.
Weeden, Craig
Pizza Joint in Cranston, A.
Right Where He Left Off.
Weeden, Lula Lowe
Dance.
Have You Seen It.
Little Dandelion, The.
Me Alone.
Robin Red Breast.
Stream, The.
Weekes, Nathaniel
Virtues of the cane must now be sung, The,
sel.
When frequent rains, and gentle show'rs
descend, sel.
Weeks, James Eyre
On the Great Fog in London, December 1762.
Weeks, Robert Kelley
Man and Nature.
Medusa.
Song for Lexington, A.
Weeks, Robert Lewis
Appalachian Front.
Weelkes, Thomas
Madrigal: "Ay me, alas, heigh ho, heigh ho!"
Weever, John
De Se.
Wei Ch'eng-pan
Deva-like Barbarian.
Flowers Fill the Palace.
Magnolia Flower, The.
Melody in C.
Mountain Hawthorns.
Song of the Fisherman.
Song of the Jade Tower in Spring.
Speaking of Love.
Wei Chuang
Delight in the High-Flying Orioles.
Deva-like Barbarian.
Echoing Heaven's Everlastingness.
Gazing after the Distant Traveler.
Heaven's Immortal.
Late Rising on Spring Days.
Lotus Leaf Cup.
Magnolia Flower, The.
Manifold Little Hills.
Paying Homage at the Golden Gate.
Pure Serene Music.
Returning to My Distant Home.
River Messages.
Sand of Silk-Washing Stream.
Song of the River City.
Song of the Water Clock at Night.
Song of the Wine Spring.
Speaking of Love.
Taoist Nun, The.
Thoughts of Paradise.
Toast to the Traveler, A.
Tune: Deva-like Barbarian ("People all say the
southland's better").
Tune: Lotus-leaf Cup.
Tune: The Taoist Priestess.
Wei Ying-wu
Sent to the Taoist Holy Man of Ch'üan-chiao.
To Send to Li Tan and Yüan Hsi.
Tune: Flirtatious Laughter.
West Creek at Ch'u-chou.
Wei Yüan
Ah-fu-jung, ah-fu-jung!, sel.
On the Chia-ling River.
"Plant the flower farms", sel.
Remembering the Past at Chin-ling.
Sitting in Meditation at Night, Facing
Hui-shan.

Weichmann, H. E.
Wanting to Air His Thoughts about and Prove
  His Respect for Mademoiselle Weichmann's
  Unusual Talent.
Wanting to Answer Mr. Darnmann's
  Undeserved Civility in the Same
  Rhyme-Scheme.
Weigel, James, Jr.
Egg grew human, The, *sel.*
Farewell, A: "While time hustled."
I should quit this craft, *sel.*
Mouth should launch words gracefully, A,
  sel.
Out of my sleeves ten bones protrude, *sel.*
Translated once, *sel.*
Weigel, Sigrid
Mathematics for the Women's Movement.
Weigl, Bruce
Burning Shit at An Khe.
Harp, The.
Homage to Elvis, Homage to the Fathers.
Man Who Made Me Love Him, The.
1955.
Regret for the Mourning Doves Who Failed to
  Mate.
Romance, A.
Snowy Egret.
Song of Napalm.
Weil, James L.
At a Loss.
Coney Island Life, A.
Weil, Simone
Creatures speak in sounds, *sel.*
Illumination.
Weiman, Andrew
Andy-Diana DNA Letter.
Wein, Jules Alan
Genesis.
Weiner, Hannah
Little Book 107.
Little Book 124.
What if the September flowers hurt.
Weiners, John
Poem for the Insane, A.
Weingarten, Roger
Blue Bog Children.
Ethan Boldt.
Her Apron through the Trees.
History of the World, The.
Night-Blooming Cereus, The.
Shadow Shadow.
Sometimes, at Thirty-Six.
These Obituaries of Rattlesnakes Being Eaten
  by the Hogs.
Two Sons Drowning.
Weinstein, Berish
Executioners.
In the Port.
Railroad Thieves.
Weiser, Conrad
Jehovah, Lord and Majesty.
Weismiller, Edward
To the Woman in Bond Street Station.
Trail, The.
Weiss, David
On the Marshes at Dawn.
Weiss, Neil
Ageing Athlete, The.
Hike, The.
Word, The.
Weiss, Theodore
Another and Another and.
As You Like It.
Barracks Apt. 14.
Clothes Maketh the Man.
Dab of Color, A.
Death of Fathers, The.
Egyptian Passage, An.
Everlasting Once, An.
Fire at Alexandria, The.
Grey and dankish thing, A, *sel.*

Last Day and the First, The.
Letter from the Pygmies, A.
Life of . . . , The.
Moral, The.
Off to Patagonia.
Pair of Shoes, A.
Preface: "Sonja Henie," the young girl."
Saw's Ear, A.
Ten Little Rembrandts.
This narrow stage.
To Forget Me.
Ultimate Antientropy, The.
Web, The.
"Yes, But . . ."
Weissbort, Daniel
Anniversary.
Murder of a Community.
Walking Home at Night.
Weisslitz, E. F.
Baldpate Pond.
Welburn, Ron
Avoidances.
Cecil County.
Eulogy for Populations.
Percussions.
Regenesis.
Welby, Amelia B.
Twilight at Sea.
Welch, Don
Chicken Poem, The.
High Jumper.
Poet in Residence at a Country School.
Spade Scharnweber.
Still Hunting.
To Bear Bryant, Somewhere on That Taller
  Tower.
Vice-President of the Universe, The.
We Used to Play.
Welch, James
Across to the Peloponnese.
Arizona Highways.
Blue like Death.
Christmas Comes to Moccasin Flat.
D-Y Bar.
Day after Chasing Porcupines.
Directions to the Nomad.
Dreaming Winter.
Going to Remake This World.
Grandma's Man.
Harlem, Montana; Just Off the Reservation.
In My First Hard Springtime.
In My Lifetime.
Lady in a Distant Face.
Magic Fox.
Man from Washington, The.
Never Give a Bum an Even Break.
One More Time.
Only Bar in Dixon, The.
Plea to Those Who Matter.
Please Forward.
Renegade Wants Words, The.
Snow Country Weavers.
Surviving.
Thanksgiving at Snake Butte.
Verifying the Dead.
Visit.
Why I Didn't Go to Delphi.
Welch, John
Posting the Letter.
That Night.
White Lilac.
Welch, Lew
After Anacreon, *sel.*
Chicago Poem.
Song of the Turkey Buzzard.
Wobbly Rock.
Welch, Marie De L.
Prelude to Commencement.
Welch, Myra Brooks
Touch of the Master's Hand, The.

Welch, Noel
Anne and the Peacock.
Weldon, Charles
Poem of the Universe, The.
Welish, Marjorie
Careers.
Picture Collection.
Respected, Feared, and Somehow Loved.
Servant in Literature, The.
Street Cries.
Wellen, Edward
Adaption—Year 2000.
Welles, Winifred
Cruciform.
Dogs and Weather.
"God's First Creature Was Light."
Man with a Little Pleated Piano, A.
Old Ellen Sullivan.
River Skater.
Starfish.
Stocking Fairy.
Wellesley, Dorothy, Duchess of Wellington
As Lambs into the Pen.
Asian Desert.
Camels in Persia.
Fire.
First Flight.
Fishing.
Lighthouses.
Lost Lane.
Milk Boy.
Morning After, The.
So I came down the steps to Lenin, *sel.*
Spiritual, the carnal, are one, The, *sel.*
Spring in the Park.
Wellesley, Dorothy, Duchess of Wellington
  (Duchess of Wellington)
Epilogue: "He is not dead nor liveth," *sel.*
Horses.
Wellman, Wade
Onlooker, The.
Vampire's Tryst, The.
Wells, Amos Russel
Ambitious Ant, The.
Considerate Crocodile, The.
Inn That Missed Its Chance, The.
Length of Life, The.
Mothers—and Others.
People's Prayer, The.
Wells, Anna Maria
Cow-Boy's Song, The.
Little Maid, The.
Wells, Carolyn
Bath-Bunny, The, *sel.*
Canner, Exceedingly Canny, A.
Corn-Pone-y, The, *sel.*
Cream-Puffin, The, *sel.*
Diversions of the Re-Echo Club.
Dresscessional, A.
Grandiloquent Goat, The.
How To Tell the Wild Animals.
Limerick: "Tutor who tooted a flute, A."
Marvel, A.
Mince-Python, The, *sel.*
Overworked Elocutionist, An.
Oyster-Crabs.
Poster Girl, The.
Puzzled.
To a Baked Fish.
Universal Favorite, The.
Wells, Faith
More than We Ask.
Wells, Marcus Morris
Holy Spirit, Faithful Guide.
Wells, Robert
Alfred Jewel, The.
Before a Journey.
Sunrise.
Wells, Rollin J.
Growing Old [*or* Growing Older]

Welsh, Anne
Between Seasons.
Many Birds.
Sharpeville Inquiry.
That Way.
Waterfall.
Welsted, Leonard
Invitation, The.
Welt, Bernard
Prose.
Welte, Lou Ann
Those Last, Late Hours of Christmas Eve.
Welty, Eudora
Flock of Guinea Hens Seen from a Car, A.
Wen Cheng-ming
Beneath the Shrine of the Three Loyal Ones,
sel.
Evening Bell from a Misty Temple.
Hearing a Flute on the River Chi.
Mooring My Boat on the Ssu River and
Watching the Moon.
New Year's Eve.
On First Returning from Taking the
Examinations.
Painting a Picture "The Tranquil Boat."
Quiet courtyard fills with greenery, The, *sel.*
Recording My Happiness upon Returning
Home.
Smiling, we set the testing tray before the
hall, *sel.*
Staying Overnight at Spirit-Source Temple.
There was no reason to expect sadness, *sel.*
This little courtyard—the wind is pure, *sel.*
Volumes of books, tea and incense, *sel.*
Walking to the Temple of Precious Light.
While It Was Raining.
Written While Sick.
Year *Chi-wei* (1559), New Year's Day, The.
Year *Hsin-hai* (1551), New Year's Eve, The.
Year *I-mao* (1555), New Year's Eve, The.
Wen-chün, Cho
Song of Snow-white Heads.
Wen T'ing-shih
I diligently concoct my elixir in a crucible of
Himalayan bamboo, *sel.*
Impressions.
Out of the floodgate of stone, just closed, a
three-foot cataract, *sel.*
Written on a Boat in Canton, 1882.
Wen T'ing-yün
Deva-like Barbarian.
Dreaming of the South.
Foreign Woman's Complaint, The.
Hatred of Distant Places.
Jade Butterflies.
Lotus Leaf Cup.
Pacifying the Western Barbarians.
Pure Serene Music.
Returning to my Distant Home.
River Messages.
Song of the Water Clock at Night.
Song of the Wine Spring.
Southern Song, A.
Speaking of Love.
Spirit of the Yellow River, The.
Taoist Nun, The.
Thought of Paradise.
Tune: Deva-like Barbarian ("In her ornate
tower by bright moonlight always she
thinks of him").
Tune: Deva-like Barbarian ("On the
many-leafed bedscreens, gold flickers and
fades").
Tune: Dreaming of the South.
Willow Branches, The.
Wen Yi-tuo
Confession, The.
Wenberi
Wenberi's Song.
Wendt, Ingrid
Newest Banana Plant Leaf, The.
Personal Poem.

Wentworth, William Charles
Land of my birth! though now, alas! no more,
sel.
Weöres, Sándor
Antithin.
As Though It Had Never Been.
At Sixty.
Bleak.
Contraries.
Crossed Wires.
Dream, A.
Dream of Roaming, A.
Earthquake.
Elan.
Ephemeral.
Eternal Evening.
Excerpts from the Modern Tragedy.
Game.
Gate of Teeth, The.
In the Beginning.
Internus.
Landscape with Mountain.
Le Journal.
Lost Parasol, The.
Magnetic.
Monkeyland.
Muttering.
Noise in Darkness.
Owl, The.
Plain, The.
Poem on Theater, A.
Prologue to "The Boatman in the Moon."
Providential.
Queen Tatavane.
Rain.
Seventh Garden, The.
Sonnet Manqué.
Strange City, A.
Stray Dog.
Thule.
Up and Down.
Upwards.
Variations on the Themes of Little Boys.
Vision, A.
Where metalled road invades light thinning
air, *sel.*
Werfel, Franz
Exaltation.
For I Have Done a Good and Kindly Deed.
Litany of the Rooms of the Dead.
Loneliness.
Song of Life, A.
Strangers Are We All upon the Earth.
Teach Us to Mark This, God.
To a Lark in War-Time.
Ye Sorrowers, *sel.*
Wergeland, Henrik Arnold Thaulov
Wall-Flower, The.
Werner, Martina
Monogram 4.
Monogram 23.
Monogram 29.
Wertheimer, Paul
Souls.
Wescott, Glenway
Poet at Night-Fall, The.
Summer Ending, The.
Wesley, Cecil Cobb
As Night Comes On.
Wesley, Charles
Ah! Lovely Appearance of Death!
Come, Thou Almighty King.
During His Courtship.
Easter Hymn.
Father, How Wide Thy Glories Shine.
For His Wife, on Her Birthday.
Free Grace.
Gentle Jesus Meek and Mild.
Hymn: "O thou who camest from above."
Incarnation, The.
Jesus, Lover of My Soul.

Love Divine, All Loves Excelling.
Morning Hymn.
O Thou Eternal Victim Slain.
On Sympathisers with the American
Revolution.
On the Death of His Son.
Sinners, abhor the Fiend, *sel.*
Whole Armour of God, The.
Wrestling Jacob.
Wesley, John
Hymn: "Thou hidden love of God, whose
height."
Rule, A.
Wesley, Samuel (1662–1735)
Monument, The.
Pindaric on the Grunting of a Hog, A.
Wesley, Samuel (1691–1739)
Anacreontic, on Parting with a Little Child.
Epitaph, An: "Here lie I, once a witty fair."
On the Setting Up of Mr. Butler's Monument
in Westminster Abbey.
Wesley-Smith, Peter
Arbuckle Jones.
Ugstabuggle, The.
West, Arthur Graeme
God, How I Hate You.
West, Charles
Autumn in California.
West, Don
My South.
West, Jessamyn
Song of the Settlers.
West, Paul
Cumberbunce, The.
West, Robert A.
Come, Let Us Tune Our Loftiest Song.
Westcott, G. C.
Gobbolino, the Witch's Cat.
Westerfield, Nancy G.
Amortization.
Westmorland, Mildmay Fane, Earl of
In Obitum Ben. Jons.
In Praise of Fidelia.
Occasioned by Seeing a Walk of Bay Trees.
Weston, Mildred
Bleat of Protest.
Central Park Tourney.
Cider Song.
Echo.
Hat Bar.
To a Lady Holding the Floor.
Westrup, J. M.
Best of All.
Flying.
Furry Home, The.
Growing Rhyme, A.
My Little House.
Poor Snail, The.
Vision Clear, The.
Westwood, Thomas
Little Bell.
Mine Host of "The Golden Apple."
Night of Spring.
Wetherald, Ethelwyn
House of the Trees, The.
In April.
Woodland Worship.
Wever, Robert
In a herber [*or* a harbour *or* an arbour] green
[*or* grene], asleep [*or* aslepe] whereas [*or*
where as *or* where] I lay, *sel.*
Wevill, David
Birth of a Shark, The.
Body of a Rook.
In Love.
Irish Hotel.
Monsoon.
Snow.
Spiders.
Wexionius, Olof
On the Death of a Pious Lady.

Wexler, Irving
When Friday nights are lucky, you, *sel.*
Weyburn, Ruby T.
True Apostolate, The.
Weyburn, T. [Ruby T.] *See* **Tobias, Ruby Weyburn**
Whalen, Philip
Denunciation; or, Unfrock'd Again.
Early Spring.
For C.
For Kai Snyder.
For My Father.
Further Notice.
Life in the City: In Memoriam Edward Gibbon.
Literary Life in the Golden West.
Martyrdom of Two Pagans.
Same Old Jazz, The.
Sourdough Mountain Lookout.
Take I, 4:11:58.
Technicalities for Jack Spicer.
10:X:57, 45 Years Since the Fall of the Ch'ing Dynasty.
To the Muse.
25:I:68.
2 Variations: All About Love.
Where or When.
Whalley, George
Affair of Honour.
Night Flight.
We Who Are Left.
Wharton, Thomas Wharton, 1st Marquess of
Lilli Burlero [*or* Lilliburlero]
Wharton, William H.
Ben Milam.
Wheatley, Phillis
Hymn to the Evening, An.
Hymn to the Morning, An.
Liberty and Peace.
Lo! Freedom comes. Th' prescient Muse foretold, *sel.*
No more, America, in mournful strain, *sel.*
On Being Brought from Africa to America.
On Imagination.
On the Death of the Rev. Mr. George Whitefield.
On Virtue.
Should you, my lord, while you pursue my song, *sel.*
Thoughts on the Works of Providence.
To a Gentleman and Lady on the Death of the Lady's Brother and Sister, and a Child of the Name Avis, Aged One Year.
To a Lady on the Death of Her Husband.
To His Excellency, General Washington.
To S.M., a Young African Painter, on Seeing His Works.
To the King's Most Excellent Majesty.
To the Right Honourable William, Earl of Dartmouth.
To the University of Cambridge, in New-England.
Wheeler, Charles Enoch
Adjuration.
Tumult.
Wheeler, Kathleen
New Leaf, A.
Wheeler, Susan
What Memory Reveals.
Wheelock, John Hall
Afternoon: Amagansett Beach.
Amagansett Beach Revisited.
Beethoven.
Black Panther, The.
Dear Men and Women.
Divine Insect, The.
Earth.
Earth ("A planet doesn't explode").
Earth ("Grasshopper, your fairy song").
Elegy: "Gnu up at the zoo, The."
Exile from God.

Far Land, The.
Gardener, The.
Hippopotamothalamion.
Holy Poet, I have heard, *sel.*
House in the Green Well, The.
Love and Liberation.
Night Thoughts in Age.
Nirvana.
Prayer: "Have pity on us, Power just and severe."
Random Reflections on a Summer Evening.
Silence.
Slow Summer Twilight.
Sunday Evening in the Common.
This Quiet Dust.
Triumph of Love.
Valediction: "Glory of soundless heaven, wheel of stars."
Wheelock, Lucy
Song of the Lilies, The.
Wheelwright, John
Canal Street.
Father.
Fish Food.
There Is No Opera like "Lohengrin."
Train Ride.
Why Must You Know?
Wheelwright, John Brooks
Second Ascension of Christ, The, *sel.*
Whetstone, George
Give Me My Work.
Whicher, George Meason
Bacchylides.
Whinery, Verna
This Day is Thine.
Whipple, Lucky
Buckin' Horse Ballet.
Chookaloski Mare.
Whipple, Melvin L.
Open Range.
Voices in the Night.
Whistler, Laurence
Form of Epitaph, A.
Portrait in the Guards, A.
Whitaker, Alexander
Leaving the Dance.
Whitaker, Robert
Out-of-Doors.
Worship.
Whitbread, Thomas
CCC, The ("CCC campers near West Cummington").
Civilities.
Pool, A.
To My Fellow-Mariners, March, '53.
White, Adeline
Autumn Morning.
Christmas Party, The.
Colour.
Over the Fields.
White, Edward Lucas
Genius.
Last Bowstrings, The.
White, Elwyn Brooks
Classic Waits for Me, A.
Commuter.
Critic, *sel.*
Fashions in Dogs.
I Paint What I See.
Listener's Guide to the Birds, A.
Marble-Top.
Red Cow Is Dead, The.
Song of the Queen Bee.
Sweet Reader.
Tennis, The.
Window Ledge in the Atom Age.
White, Gilbert
Naturalist's Summer-Evening Walk, The.
On the Dark, Still, Dry, Warm Weather Occasionally Happening in the Winter Months.
Shower of Cobwebs, A.

White, Harriet R.
Uffia.
White, Henry Kirke
Lo! in the West, fast fades the ling'ring light, *sel.*
Man's Littleness in Presence of the Stars.
To an Early Primrose.
White, James L.
Making Love to Myself.
White, Jon Manchip
Captain, The.
Count Orlo in England.
Orlo's Valediction.
Rout of San Romano, The.
White, Joseph Blanco
Black Is a Soul.
To Night.
White, Lillian Zellhoefer
Hangman's Tree.
White, Richard Edward
Discovery of San Francisco Bay.
White, Terence Hanbury
To Myself, after Forty Years.
Witch's Work Song, The.
White, Vera
You Are on U.S. 40 Headed West.
White, William Allen
Rhyme of the Dream-Maker Man, A.
White-arm
Child listen/ I am singing.
Whitecotton, Moses
Fuller and Warren, at.
Whitehead, Charles
Lamp, The.
Whitehead, James
About a Year After He Got Married He Would Sit Alone in an Abandoned Shack in a Cotton Field Enjoying Himself.
Flood Viewed by the Tourist from Iowa, The.
For Ellen after the Publication of Her Stories.
Good Linemen Live in a Closed World.
He Remembers How He Didn't Understand What Lieutenant Dawson Meant.
How It Seemed to Him Away from Home.
Local Contractor Flees His Winter Trouble and Saves Some Lives in a Knoxville Motel Room, A.
Local Man Goes to the Killing Ground, A.
Local Man Remembers Betty Fuller, A.
Long Tour: The Country Music Star Explains Why He Put off the Bus and Fired a Good Lead Guitar in West Texas.
Narrative Hooper and L.D.O. Sestina with a Long Last Line, The.
Natural Theology, A.
Poem Called Poem.
Visionary Oklahoma Sunday Beer.
Whitehead, Paul
As when two monarchs of the brindled breed, *sel.*
Hunting Song, *sel.*
Whitehead, William
If nature prompts you, or if friends persuade, *sel.*
"Je Ne Sais Quoi," The.
New Night Thoughts on Death; a Parody.
Sweepers, The.
Whiteman, Roberta Hill (Roberta Hill)
Acknowledgement.
Beginning the Year at Rosebud, S.D.
Blue Mountain.
Climbing Gannett.
Depot in Rapid City.
Direction.
Dream of Rebirth.
E Uni Que A The Hi A Tho, Father.
Falling Moon.
Fogbound.
For Heather, Entering Kindergarten.
From the Sun Itself.
Horses in Snow.

In Mosa's Time.
In the Longhouse, Oneida Museum.
In the Madison Zoo.
Leap in the Dark.
Lines for Marking Time.
Midnight on Front Street.
Midwinter Stars.
Nation Wrapped in Stone, A.
Night along the Mackinac Bridge.
Notes for Albuquerque.
One More Sign.
Overcast Dawn.
Patterns.
Reaching Yellow River.
Seal at Stinson Beach.
Sleeping with Foxes.
Song for Healing.
Star Quilt.
Steps.
Swamp.
Variations for Two Voices.
Waiting for Robinson.
Whispers.
White Land, The.
Winter Burn.
Woman Seed Player.

Whiteside, Mary Brent
Carpenter, The.
Who Has Known Heights.

Whitewing, Donna
August 24, 1963—1:00 A.M.—Omaha.
Vegetable, I Will Not Be, A.

Whitfield, James M.
From America.

Whiting, Charles Goodrich
Blue Hills beneath the Haze.
Eagle's Fall, The.
Way to Heaven, The.

Whiting, Lilian
Mystery, The.

Whiting, Nathaniel
Office of Poetry, The, sel.

Whiting, Seymour W.
Alamance.

Whiting, William
Eternal Father, Strong to Save.

Whitman, Ruth
Almost Ninety.
Castoff Skin.
Dan, the Dust of Masada Is Still in My
    Nostrils.
Dead Center.
Flight.
Listening to Grownups Quarreling.
Marriage Wig, The.
Mediterranean.
Sister Pharaoh.
Spring.
Translating.
Watching the Sun Rise over Mount Zion.
Yom Kippur: Fasting.

Whitman, S. W.
October.

Whitman, Sarah Helen
If thy sad heart, pining for human love, sel.
Oft since thine earthly eyes have closed on
    mine, sel.
On our lone pathway bloomed no earthly
    hopes, sel.
When first I looked into thy glorious eyes,
    sel.

Whitman, Walt
Aboard at a Ship's Helm.
Afoot and light-hearted I take to the open
    road, sel.
After an Interval.
After the Sea-Ship.
After the Supper and Talk.
Ah, more than any priest, O soul, we too
    believe in God, sel.
Ah Poverties, Wincings, and Sulky Retreats.

Ah, what can be more stately, sel.
All the Past We Leave Behind with music.
America.
An Evening Lull.
Are you he who would assume a place to
    teach or be a poet here in the States?, sel.
Are You the New Person Drawn toward Me?
Army Corps on the March, An.
As Adam Early in the Morning.
As I Ebb'd with the Ocean of Life.
As I Lay with My Head in Your Lap
    Camerado.
As I Sit Writing Here.
As If a Phantom Caress'd Me.
As Toilsome I Wander'd Virginia's Woods.
Bathe me O God in thee, mounting to thee,
    sel.
Battle of the Bonhomme Richard and the
    Serapis, sel.
Beat! Beat! Drums!
Beautiful Swimmer, The.
Beauty.
Beauty of the Ship, The.
Beginners
Beginning My Studies.
Bivouac on a Mountain Side.
Boston Ballad, A.
Broad-Ax, The, sel.
Broadway.
By That Long Scan of Waves.
By the Bivouac's Fitful Flame.
Carol of Death, The, sel.
Cavalry Crossing a Ford.
Centenarian's Story, The.
Chanting the Square Deific.
Child said, A What is the grass?
Clear Midnight, A.
Come, Said My Soul.
Come Up from the Fields, Father.
Commonplace, The.
Crossing Brooklyn Ferry.
Dalliance of the Eagles, The.
Darest Thou Now O Soul.
Dirge for Two Veterans.
Dismantled Ship, The.
Drayman, The, sel.
Earth, My Likeness.
Ethiopia Saluting the Colors.
Faces.
Facing West from California's Shores.
Farm Picture, A.
Flaunt of the sunshine I need not your bask,
    sel.
For You, O Democracy.
From Montauk Point.
From Paumanok Starting I Fly like a Bird.
From Pent-up Aching Rivers.
Gigantic beauty of a stallion, fresh and
    responsive to my caresses, A, sel.
Give Me the Splendid Silent Sun.
Glimpse, A.
Good-bye My Fancy!
Had I the Choice.
Halcyon Days.
Hand-Mirror, A.
Has Any One Supposed It Lucky to Be
    Born?, sel.
Here the Frailest Leaves of Me.
Heroes, sel.
Houses and rooms are full of perfumes, sel.
Hub for the Universe, A, sel.
Hush'd Be the Camps To-Day.
I Am He That Aches with Love.
I am the poet of the Body and I am the poet
    of the Soul, sel.
I believe a leaf of grass is no less than the
    journey-work of the stars, sel.
I believe in the flesh and the appetites, sel.
I believe in you my soul, sel.
I celebrate myself, and sing myself, sel.
I Hear America Singing.

I hear and behold God in every object, yet
    understand God not in the least, sel.
I Hear and See Not Strips of Cloth Alone.
I Hear It Was Charged against Me.
I Heard You Solemn-sweet Pipes of the
    Organ.
I know I have the best of time and space, sel.
I Saw in Louisiana a Live-Oak Growing.
I Saw the Vision of Armies.
I Sit and Look Out.
I think I could turn and live with animals, sel.
In Cabin'd Ships at Sea.
In Paths Untrodden.
In the swamp in secluded recesses, sel.
Infinity, sel.
Joy, Shipmate, Joy!
Justified Mother of Men, The.
Last Invocation, The.
Little one sleeps in its cradle, The, sel.
Long I Thought That Knowledge Alone
    Would Suffice.
Long, Too Long America.
Mannahatta.
March in the Ranks Hard-Prest, and the Road
    Unknown, A.
Me Imperturbe.
Memories.
Miracles.
Muse in the New World, The, sel.
My Picture-Gallery.
My 71st Year.
My signs are a rain-proof coat, good shoes, a
    staff cut from the woods, sel.
Native Moments.
Night on the Prairies.
No Labor-saving Machine.
Noiseless Patient Spider, A.
Now I will do nothing but listen, sel.
O Captain! My Captain!, sel.
O Hymen! O Hymenee!
O Living Always, Always Dying.
O my body! I dare not desert the likes of you
    in other men and women, nor the likes of
    the parts of you, sel.
Old War-Dreams.
On the Beach at Night.
On the Beach at Night Alone.
Once I Pass'd through a Populous City.
One's-Self I Sing.
Orange Buds by Mail from Florida.
Osceola.
Others May Praise What They Like.
Out of the Cradle Endlessly Rocking.
Ox-Tamer, The.
Passage to India.
Patrolling Barnegat.
Pensive, on Her Dead Gazing, I Heard the
    Mother of All.
Pioneers! O Pioneers!
Poet, The, sel.
Poets to Come.
Prayer of Columbus.
Pure contralto sings in the organloft, The, sel.
Reconciliation.
Recorders Ages Hence.
Respondez!
"Rounded Catalogue Divine Complete, The."
Runaway Slave, The, sel.
Runner, The.
Scented Herbage of My Breast.
Shut Not Your Doors.
Sight in Camp [in the Daybreak Gray and
    Dim], A.
Singer in the Prison, The.
Sleepers, The.
Sometimes with One I Love.
Song for All Seas, All Ships.
Song of the Open Road.
Song of the Redwood-Tree.
Sparkles from the Wheel.
Spirit Whose Work Is Done.
Spontaneous Me.

Spotted hawk swoops by and accuses me, The, *sel.*
Stallion, The, *sel.*
Still Though the One I Sing.
There Was a Child Went Forth, *sel.*
There was a child went forth every day, *sel.*
This Compost.
This is the female form, *sel.*
Thou knowest my years entire, my life, *sel.*
To a Common Prostitute.
To a Locomotive in Winter.
To a President.
To a Stranger.
To Soar in Freedom and in Fullness of Power.
To the Man-of-War-Bird.
To the Pending Year.
To the States.
To Think of Time.
Trickle Drops.
Trippers and askers surround me, *sel.*
Twenty-eight young men bathe by the shore, *sel.*
Untold Want, The.
Vigil Strange I Kept on the Field One Night.
Wallabout Martyrs, The.
Walt Whitman, a kosmos, of Manhattan the son, *sel.*
Washington's Monument, February 1885.
We Two Boys Together Clinging.
When I Heard at the Close of the Day.
When I Heard the Learn'd Astronomer.
When I Peruse the Conquer'd Fame.
When I Read the Book.
When Lilacs Last in the Dooryard Bloom'd, *sel.*
Whispers of Heavenly Death.
Who goes there? hankering, gross, mystical, nude, *sel.*
Whoever You Are Holding Me Now in Hand.
With music strong I come, with my cornets and my drums, *sel.*
Woman Waits for Me, A.
World below the Brine, The.
Wound-Dresser, The.
Wounded Person, The, *sel.*
Yonnondio.
You, Whoever You Are.

Whitney, Adeline D. T.
Peace.

Whitney, Anna Temple
Kneeling Camel, The.

Whitney, Geffrey
Content.

Whitney, Isabella
Do not account that for thine own, *sel.*
Gold savours well, though it be got, *sel.*
In loving, each one hath free choice, *sel.*
Little gold in law will make, A, *sel.*
Present day we cannot spend, The, *sel.*
Seek not man to please, for that, *sel.*
Such poor folk as to law do go, *sel.*

Whitney, Joseph Ernest
Drop of Ink, A.

Whittaker, Frederick
Custer's Last Charge.

Whittemore, Reed
Abbreviated Interviews with a Few Disgruntled Literary Celebrities.
After Some Day of Decision.
Clamming.
Day with the Foreign Legion, A.
Departure, The.
Floridian Museum of Art, A.
Lines on Being Refused a Guggenheim Fellowship.
Love Song: "I know not how to speak to thee, girl (damselle?)."
Only the Dead.
Party, The.
Projection, A.
Radio under the Bed, The.

Recall.
Still Life.
Storm from the East, A.
Summer Concert.
Tarantula, The.
Thinking of Tents.
Treasure, A.
Week of Doodle, A.

Whittier, John Greenleaf
Abraham Davenport.
Adjustment.
All souls that struggle and aspire, *sel.*
All's Well.
Amy Wentworth.
And Thou, O Lord! by whom are seen, *sel.*
Angel of Patience, The.
Angels of Buena Vista, The.
Astræa.
Astraea at the Capitol.
At Last.
At Port Royal.
Autograph, An.
Barbara Frietchie.
Barefoot Boy, The.
Bartholdi Statue, The.
Battle Autumn of 1862, The.
Blessings on thee, little man, *sel.*
Book Our Mothers Read, The, *sel.*
Brewing of Soma, The.
Brown of Ossawatomie.
Burial of Barber.
Burning Drift-Wood.
Cable Hymn, The.
Call of the Christian, The.
Cassandra Southwick.
Centennial Hymn.
Chicago.
Clerical Oppressors.
Corn-Song, The.
Crisis, The.
Dead Feast of the Kol-Folk, The.
Dear Lord and Father of Mankind, *sel.*
Dedication: "I would the gift I offer here," *sel.*
Eternal Goodness, The.
Farewell, The: "Gone, gone—sold and gone."
First-Day Thoughts.
For Righteousness' Sake.
Forgiveness.
Godspeed.
Harvest Hymn, *sel.*
Haschish, The.
Help.
Henchman, The.
Hunters of Men, The.
I know not what the future hath, *sel.*
Ichabod.
Immortal Love, Forever Full.
In Earthen Vessels.
In School-Days.
In the "Old South."
Inscription: "Eagle, stooping from yon snow-blown peaks, The."
John Underhill.
Kallundborg Church.
Kansas Emigrants, The.
King's Missive, The.
Laus Deo!
Le Marais du Cygne.
Lexington.
Life and Love.
Lost Occasion, The.
Make my mortal dreams come true, *sel.*
Maud Muller.
Mother, *sel.*
Mulford.
My Playmate.
My Triumph.
Norembega.
Norsemen, The.
O Thou who bidst the torrent flow, *sel.*
O Thou! Whose Presence Went Before.

Oh for boyhood's painless play, *sel.*
On the Big Horn.
Our Country.
Our Master.
Over-Heart, The.
Palestine.
Pardon, Lord, the lips that dare, *sel.*
Pentucket.
Picture memory brings to me, A, *sel.*
Pipes at Lucknow, The.
Poem: "I love the old melodious lays."
Poor Voter on Election Day, The.
Prelude: "Along the roadside, like the flowers of gold," *sel.*
Proclamation, The.
Prophetess, *sel.*
Pumpkin, The.
St. John.
Shut in from all the world without, *sel.*
Sister, *sel.*
Sisters, The.
Skipper Ireson's Ride.
Snow-Bound; a Winter Idyl [*or* Idyll]
Song of Slaves in the Desert.
Song of the Negro Boatman, *sel.*
Sun that brief December day, The, *sel.*
Swan Song of Parson Avery, The.
Telling the Bees.
Texas.
The *Palatine.*
To John C. Frémont.
To My Old Schoolmaster.
To Pius IX.
To the Thirty-ninth Congress.
To William Lloyd Garrison.
Two Angels, The.
Unwarmed by any sunset light, *sel.*
Vanishers, The.
Vesta.
Vow of Washington, The.
Waiting, The.
Washington's Vow.
What the Birds Said.
Winter Night, *sel.*
Worship.

Whittingham, William
Now Israel May Say, and That Truly.

Whittle, Daniel W
Moment by Moment.

Whittlin, Josef
St. Francis of Assisi and the Miserable Jews.

Whur, Cornelius
Female Friend, The.

Whythorne, Thomas
Now That the Truth Is Tried.

Wickham, Anna
After Annunciation.
Boy and the Dream, The.
Cherry-Blossom Wand, The.
Creatrix.
Dedication of the Cook.
Divorce.
Envoi: "God, thou great symmetry."
Fired Pot, The.
First Thing to Do in a House, The.
Free Intelligence, The.
Fresh Start, The.
Friend Cato.
Gift to a Jade.
Last Round, The.
Marriage, The.
Meditation at Kew.
Nervous Prostration.
Sehnsucht.
Self-Analysis.
Singer, The.
Song: "I was so chill, and overworn, and sad."
Song-Maker, The.
Soul's Liberty.
Tired Woman, The.

To a Crucifix.
To Men.
Vanity.
Weapons.

Wickstrom, Lois
MC ^{2}-E.
Slice of Life, A.

Widdemer, Margaret
As I Lay Quiet.
Awakened War God, The.
Barter.
Bear Hunt, The.
Comfort.
Invisible Playmate, The.
New Victory, The.
Oiseaurie.
Rainuv; a Romantic Ballad from the Early
  Basque.
Rambuncto.
Search.
Secret Cavern, The.
Watcher, The.

Widerberg, Siv
At Annika's Place.
Best?
Once.

Wiebe, Dallas E.
Epilogue: "My bibliography has grown."
L'Elisir d'Amore.

Wieber, Wendy
One, The Other, And.

Wieners, John
Anniversary of Death, An.
Le Chariot.
Moon Poems.
My Mother.
Poem for Museum Goers, A.
Poem for Painters, A.
Poem for the Old Man, A.
Poem for Trapped Things, A.
There Are So Many Fatherless Children
  Around.
Two Years Later.
What Happened?

Wier, Dara
Fear.
Keno.
Late Afternoon on a Good Lake.
Then the Skin Falls Apart.
This Cold Nothing Else.

Wierzynski, Kazimierz
Word to Orphists, A.

Wieseltier, Meir
Again the greyish khaki light descends, *sel.*
Allenby.
And Even if They Live.
Blood flows from my brow, The, *sel.*
Caution Prevents Accidents.
Columns.
Everyone passes under the moon.
Friends.
God's Fire upon Children ("God's fire upon
  cities").
Here in Netanya.
Holy Is the Desire to Proclaim the Existence
  of God.
I Shall Empty My Head like Jam.
Leningrad: Picture Postcard.
Love Poem: Extended Sonnet on the Death of
  Isaac Danziger.
Love Poem: "Greyish yellow is the color of
  the dust."
Note.
On Guard.
+30° C.
Poetry's Buried.
Saul Re-enthroned.
Site.
Take a Look at My Rebels.
Take poems, but don't read them.

Too Short.
Weather, The.

Wigglesworth, Michael
Day of Doom, The.
For Just Men Light Is Sown.
God's Controversy with New-England.
Prayer unto Christ the Judge of the World, A.
Song of Emptiness to Fill up the Empty Pages
  Following, A.
Then to the bar, all they drew near, *sel.*
Welcome, Sweet Rest.

Wightman, Richard
Pilgrim, The.
Servants, The.

Wigson, John
On the Death of Squire Christopher.

Wilberforce, Ernest R.
Just for To-Day.

Wilberforce, Samuel
Impromptu.

Wilborn, Rob
Rag Rug.

Wilbur, Richard
Advice to a Prophet.
After the Last Bulletins.
All These Birds.
Altitudes.
Apology.
April 5, 1974.
Aspen and the Stream, The.
Baroque Wall-Fountain in the Villa Sciarra,
  A.
Beasts.
Beautiful Changes, The.
Bell Speech.
Black November Turkey, A.
Boy at the Window.
Catch, The.
Ceremony.
Christmas Hymn, A.
Cigales.
Cottage Street, 1953.
Death of a Toad, The.
Digging for China.
Epistemology.
Exeunt.
Fire-Truck, A.
First Snow in Alsace.
Folk Tune.
For K. R. on Her Sixtieth Birthday.
For the New Railway Station in Rome.
For the Student Strikers.
Grace.
Grasse: The Olive Trees.
Grasshopper, A.
Hamlen Brook.
He Was.
Hole in the Floor, A.
In a Churchyard.
In the Elegy Season.
In the Field.
In the Smoking-Car.
John Chapman.
Juggler.
Junk.
Lamarck Elaborated.
Late Aubade, A.
Looking into History.
Love Calls Us to the Things of This World.
Loves of the Puppets.
Lying.
Marginalia.
Merlin Enthralled.
Milkweed, A, *sel.*
Mill, The.
Miltonic Sonnet for Mr. Johnson on His
  Refusal of Peter Hurd's Official Portrait, A.
Mind.
Mind-Reader, The.
Museum Piece.
My Father Paints the Summer.

O.
Objects.
On the Eyes of an SS Officer.
On the Marginal Way.
Opposite of Two, The.
Orchard Trees, January.
Pangloss's Song [A Comic-Opera Lyric].
Parable.
Pardon, The.
Part of a Letter.
Piazza di Spagna, Early Morning.
Place Pigalle.
Playboy.
Potato.
Praise in Summer.
Prisoner of Zenda, The.
Proof, The.
Ride, The.
Rillons, Rillettes.
Running.
Seed Leaves.
Shame.
She.
Simile for Her Smile, A.
Simplification, A.
Sleepless at Crown Point.
Some Opposites.
Speech for the Repeal of the McCarran Act.
Star System, The.
Statues.
Still, Citizen Sparrow.
Stone, A, *sel.*
Stop.
Storm in April, A.
Summer Morning, A.
Teresa.
Thyme Flowering among Rocks.
To an American Poet Just Dead.
To the Etruscan Poets.
Transit.
Trolling for Blues.
Two Voices in a Meadow.
Tywater.
Undead, The.
Voice from under the Table, A.
Walking to Sleep.
What is the opposite of a prince?
What is the opposite of two?
What should I tell them?, *sel.*
What's Good for the Soul Is Good for Sales.
Winter Deepening, The.
"World without Objects Is a Sensible
  Emptiness, A."
Writer, The.
Year's End.

Wilcox, Ella Wheeler
Ad Finem.
Answered Prayers.
Art and Heart.
As by Fire.
Attainment.
Beautiful Land of Nod, The.
Belief.
Better, Wiser and Happier.
Communism.
Dawn.
Days grow shorter, the nights grow longer,
  The.
Duet, The.
Faith.
Fault of the Age, The.
Five Little Brothers.
I Love You.
If my vain soul needs blows and bitter losses,
  sel.
Illusion.
Inspiration, An.
Law, The.
Life's Journey.
Life's Scars.
Lifting and Leaning.
Love's Coming.

My Ships.
Optimism.
Peace and Love.
Peace at the Goal.
Price He Paid, The.
Progress.
Queen's Last Ride, The.
Recrimination.
Room beneath the Rafters, The.
Secret Thoughts.
Solitude.
Sunset.
There Comes a Time.
They Say.
Through the Valley.
To know thy bent and then pursue.
True Brotherhood.
Two Glasses, The.
Unanswered Prayers.
Upon the Sand.
Uselessness.
What Love Is.
Whatever Is—Is Best.
Will.
Winds of Fate, The.
World, The.
Worth While.
Year Outgrows the Spring, The.
You Never Can Tell.

Wilczek, Frank
Virtual Particles.

Wild, Peter
Air Raid.
Dog Hospital.
For the El Paso Weather Bureau.
Ice Cream.
Riding Double.
Snakes.
Thomas and Charlie.

Wild, Robert
Epitaph for a Godly Man's Tomb, An.
Iter Boreale.
Poem upon the Imprisonment of Mr. Calamy
    in Newgate, A.

Wilde, J.
Verses to Miss———.

Wilde, Lady Jane Francesca ("Speranza")
Famine Year, The.

Wilde, Oscar
Athanasia.
Ballad of Reading Gaol, The.
By the Arno.
Disciple, The.
E Tenebris.
Fabien Dei Franchi.
For oak and elm have pleasant leaves, sel.
Grave of Shelley, The.
Harlot's House, The.
He did not wear his scarlet coat, sel.
Hélas!
How subtle-secret is your smile! Did you love
    none then? Nay, I know, sel.
Impression du Matin.
In Debtor's Yard the stones are hard, sel.
In Reading Gaol by Reading Town, sel.
Le Jardin, sel.
Les Ballons.
Magdalen Walks.
My Voice.
Portia.
Preface: "Artist is the creator of beautiful
    things, The," sel.
Requiescat.
San Miniato.
Sea is flecked with bars of grey, The, sel.
Sonnet on Hearing the Dies Irae Sung in the
    Sistine Chapel.
Symphony in Yellow.
Theocritus.
Theoretikos.
There is no chapel on the day, sel.

To Milton.
Yet Each Man Kills the Thing He Loves, sel.

Wilde, Richard Henry
Farewell to America, A.
My Life Is like the Summer Rose.
Oh! dearer by far than the land of our birth.
To the Mocking-bird.

Wilder, Amos Niven
De Profundis.
If I Have Lifted Up Mine Eyes to Admire.
Prayer: "Omnipotent confederate of all good."

Wilder, John Nichols
Stand by the Flag.

Wilk, Melvin
Blessing.

Wilkerson, Buck
Saddle Tramp.

Wilkes, Lyall
Nightmare.

Wilkins, William
Engine Driver's Story, The.
Magazine Fort, Phoenix Park, Dublin, The.

Wilkinson, Anne
Adam and God.
Carol: "I was a lover of turkey and holly."
Cautionary Tale, A.
Daily the Drum.
Falconry.
In June and Gentle Oven.
Leda in Stratford, Ont.
Lens.
Nature Be Damned.
Red and the Green, The.
Summer Acres.
Variations on a Theme.

Wilkinson, H. E.
Bread.
Topsy-turvy Land.
What Is It?

Wilkinson, Iris Gulver. *See* "Hyde, Robin"

Wilkinson, Marguerite
Chant Out of Doors, A.
Psalm to the Son, A.

Wilkinson, William Cleaver
At Marshfield, sel.

Will, James
Mountain Sculpture.

Willard, Emma Hart
Rocked in the Cradle of the Deep.

Willard, Nancy
Angels in Winter.
Blake Leads a Walk on the Milky Way.
Foxfire.
How the Hen Sold Her Eggs to the Stingy
    Priest.
In the Hospital of the Holy Physician.
Insects, The.
King of Cats Sends a Postcard to His Wife,
    The.
Lightness Remembered.
Lullaby for Familiars.
Marmalade Man Makes a Dance to Mend Us,
    The.
Night Light.
No-Kings and the Calling of Spirits.
Original Strawberry.
Poem Made of Water.
Questions My Son Asked Me, Answers I
    Never Gave Him.
Saint Pumpkin.
Science Fiction.
Way of Keeping, A.
Wreath to the Fish, A.

Willems, J. Rutherford
Hebrew Letters in the Trees.

William of Shoreham
At Prime Jesus was y-led, sel.

Williams, Bertye Young
Friend Who Just Stands By, The.
Trus' an' Smile.

Williams, Big Joe
President Roosevelt.

Williams, Charles
At the "Ye That Do Truly."
Dream, A.
From a Walking Song.
Kings Came Riding.
Mount Badon.
Night Song for a Child.
Taliessin's Song of the Unicorn.

Williams, Charles Kenneth
Blades.
Combat.
Day for Anne Frank, A.
Downwards.
Floor.
From My Window.
Gas Station, The.
It Is This Way with Men.
Patience Is When You Stop Waiting.
Rampage, The.
Spit.
Still Life.
Tar.
Then the Brother of the Wind.
They Warned Him Then They Threw Him
    Away.
Waking Jed.
World's Greatest Tricycle Rider, The.

Williams, Clarence
Ugly Chile.

Williams, Daniel
We Are the Cenotaphs.

Williams, Edward
Poet's Arbour in the Birchwood, The.

Williams, Eliseus
Heather Flowers.

Williams, Emmett
Like Attracts Like.

Williams, Evelyn M.
Chestnut Buds.

Williams, Francis Howard
Electra.
Song: "Bird in my bower, A."
Walt Whitman.

Williams, Frederick
Eighties, De.

Williams, George. *See* **Awoonor, Kofi**

Williams, Gwyn
Today has it all, sunshine, sel.

Williams, Hazel
Beware of the Poison.
Old Age Come to Us All.

Williams, Hugo
Aborigine.
Butcher, The.
Elaine, sel.
Gladys, sel.
Kirsten, sel.
Noelle, sel.
Some Kisses from The Kama Sutra.
Them, sel.
Tracy & Co., sel.

Williams, John (1761–1818)
Matrimony.
Safari West.
Some Contemplations of the Poor, and
    Desolate State of the Church at Deerfield.

Williams, John (b. 1922)
On Reading Aloud My Early Poems.
Skaters, The.

Williams, John Lloyd
Naming of Private Parts.

Williams, Jonathan
Adhesive Autopsy of Walt Whitman, The.
Anthropophagites See a Sign on NC Highway
    177 That Looks like Heaven, The.
Bitch-Kitty, The.
Distances to the Friend, The.
Fast Ball.

Hermit Cackleberry Brown, on Human
Vanity, The.
Honey Lamb, The.
Little Tumescence, A.
Mrs. Sadie Grindstaff, Weaver and Factotum.
Ovid, Meet a Metamorphodite.
Switch Blade, The; or, John's Other Wife.
Symphony No. 3, in D Minor, *sel.*
Those Troublesome Disguises.
Three Sayings from Highlands, North
Carolina.
Uncle Iv Surveys His Domain from His
Rocker.
Vulnerary, A.

Williams, Kim
Requiem for a River.

Williams, Lucy
Origin of the Skagit Indians, The.

Williams, Lucy Ariel. *See* **Holloway, Lucy
Ariel Williams**

Williams, Max
Empty House, The.

Williams, Miller
After the Revolution for Jesus the Associate
Professor [*or* a Secular Man] Prepares His
Final Remarks.
Aging Actress Sees Herself a Starlet on the
Late Show, The.
Caterpillar, The.
Firebreathers at the Café Deux Magots, The.
For Victor Jara.
Love and How It Becomes Important in Our
Day to Day Lives.
Love Poem: "Six o'clock and/ the sun rises."
On a Photograph of My Mother at Seventeen.
On the Symbolic Consideration of Hands and
the Significance of Death.
Poem for Emily, A.
Rubaiyat for Sue Ella Tucker.
Ruby Tells All.
Sale.
Why God Permits Evil: For Answers to This
Question of Interest to Many Write Bible
Answers Dept. E-7.

Williams, Norman
Tremors at Balvano, The.

Williams, Oscar
Borrower of Salt, The, *sel.*
By Fiat of Adoration.
Dwarf of Disintegration.
Golden Fleece, The.
I Sing an Old Song.
In Postures That Call.
Jeremiad.
Last Supper, The.
Leg in the Subway, The.
Man Coming toward You, The.
Man in That Airplane, The.
Milk at the Bottom of the Sea.
Mirage, The.
On the Couch.
On the Death of an Acquaintance, *sel.*
One Morning the World Woke Up.
Picture Postcard of a Zoo.
Praying Mantis Visits a Penthouse, The ("The
praying mantis with its length of straw").
Seesaw, The.
Shopping for Meat in Winter.
Spring.
Spritely Dead, The.

Williams, Peter
When She Was Here, Li Bo.

Williams, Rhydwen
Baboon, The.

Williams, Robert
On a Woman.

Williams, Roger
Adulteries, murthers, robberies, thefts.
Boast not proud English, of thy birth and
blood.
Course bread and water's most their fare.

Courteous pagan shall condemne, The.
God gives them sleep on ground, on straw.
God Makes a Path.
How busie are the sonnes of men?
I have heard ingenuous Indians say.
If Birds That neither Sow nor Reap.
Indians count of men as dogs, The.
Indians prize not English gold, The.
Mans restlesse soule hath restlesse eyes and
ears.
One step twix't me and death, (twas Davids
speech).
Our English gamesters scorne to stake.
Pagans wild confesse the bonds, The.
They see Gods wonders that are call'd.
Truth is a native, naked beauty; but.
What Habacuck once spake, mine eyes.
When Sun Doth Rise.

Williams, Sarah
Deep Sea Soundings.
Is It True?
Old Astronomer to His Pupil, The.

Williams, Sherley Anne
Driving Wheel.
Empress Brand Trim: Ruby Reminisces, The.
House of Desire, The.
Say Hello to John.

Williams, Shirley
If He Let Us Go Now.
Killing of the Birds, The.

Williams, Sir Charles Hanbury
Monkey, lap-dog, parrot, and her Grace, The,
sel.
Verses: "Poor fellow, what is it to you."

Williams, Tennessee
Carrousel Tune.
Crepe de Chine.
Gold Tooth Blues.
Kitchen Door Blues.
Life Story.
My Love Was Light.
Sugar in the Cane.
You and I.

Williams, Theodore Chickering
Hast Thou Heard It, O My Brother.
My Country, to Thy Shore.
When Thy Heart with Joy O'erflowing.

Williams, Trevor
Girl I Took to the Cocktail Party, The.

Williams, Veronica
Hankering after Truth, A.
I Wish You Had Warned Me.
One Angry Woman.

Williams, Waldo
Daffodil.
In Two Fields.
Summer Cloud, A.

Williams, William ("Pantycelyn")
Guide Me, O Thou Great Jehovah.
I Gaze across the Distant Hills.
Marriage in Eden, The, *sel.*

Williams, William Carlos
Act, The.
Address.
Apology: Why Do I Write Today?
Approach to a City.
Approaching death, *sel.*
Après le Bain.
Arrival.
Artist, The.
At Kenneth Burke's Place.
At the Ball Game.
Ballad of Faith.
Beautiful thing/ I saw you, *sel.*
Between Walls.
Black, black cloud, A.
Botticellian Trees, The.
Bull, The.
Burning the Christmas Greens.
Catholic Bells, The.
Classic Scene.

Clouds, The.
Coda.
Cold Front, A.
Complaint.
Corn Harvest, The, *sel.*
Daisy.
Dance, The.
Danse Russe.
Dawn.
Dead Baby, The.
Death.
Deceptrices, The.
Descent, The.
Descent of Winter, The (Section 10/30).
Drink.
Edward/ Paterson has grown older, *sel.*
El Hombre.
End of the Parade, The.
Episode 17, *sel.*
Fine Work with Pitch and Copper.
First Praise.
Flowers by the Sea.
For Eleanor and Bill Monahan.
Forgotten City, The.
4th of July.
Goodnight, A.
Graceful Bastion, The.
Great Figure, The.
Gulls.
Hard Listener, The.
Haymaking, *sel.*
Hemmed-in Males, *sel.*
High Bridge above the Tagus River at Toledo,
The.
History of Love, A.
Horse Show, The.
Hounded Lovers, The.
House, The.
Hunters in the Snow, The, *sel.*
Illegitimate Things.
Intelligent Sheepman and the New Cars, The.
Iris.
It is far to Assisi, *sel.*
Ivy Crown, The.
January.
January Morning.
Lament: "What face, in the water."
Landscape with the Fall of Icarus, *sel.*
Last Words of My English Grandmother, The.
Le Médecin Malgré Lui.
Lear.
Lighthearted William.
Locust Tree in Flower, The.
Lonely Street, The.
Love Song: "Sweep the house clean."
Manoeuvre, The.
Marriage.
Mental Hospital Garden, The.
Metric Figure.
Nantucket.
Of asphodel, that greeny flower, *sel.*
Ol' Bunk's Band.
On Gay Wallpaper.
Orchestra, The.
Outside/ outside myself/ there is a world, *sel.*
Pastoral: "Little sparrows, The."
Pastoral: "When I was younger."
Paterson lies in the valley under the Passaic
Falls, *sel.*
Peace on Earth.
Philomena Andronico.
Poem: "As the cat."
Poem, The: "It's all in/the sound. A song."
Poem: "On getting a card."
Poor, The.
Porous.
Portrait of a Lady.
Pot of Flowers, The.
Predicter of Famine, The.
Preface: "Rigor of beauty is the quest. But
how will you find beauty when it is
locked," *sel.*

Preface: "To make a start," *sel.*
Proletarian Portrait.
Puerto Rico Song.
Queen-Ann's-Lace.
Raleigh Was Right.
Raper from Passenack, The.
Red Wheelbarrow, The.
Return to Work, The.
Ritualists, The.
River Rhyme.
Rose, The.
Russia.
Savage Beast, The.
Sea-Elephant, The.
Self-Portrait, *sel.*
Semblables, The.
Silence.
Slow Movement.
Smell.
Sort of a Song, A.
Sparrow, The.
Sparrows among Dry Leaves ("The sparrows/
    by the iron fence post").
Spring and All.
Storm, The.
Term, The.
Testament of Perpetual Change, The.
There is a woman in our town, *sel.*
These.
These Purists.
This Is Just to Say.
To.
To a Dead Journalist.
To a Dog Injured in the Street.
To a Friend Concerning Several Ladies.
To a Poor Old Woman.
To a Solitary Disciple.
To an Elder Poet.
To Be Recited to Flossie on Her Birthday.
To Elsie.
To Ford Madox Ford in Heaven.
To Greet a Letter-Carrier.
To Mark Anthony in Heaven.
To Waken an Old Lady.
Tract.
Trala Trala Trala Le-le-la.
Unison, A.
View by Color Photography on a Commercial
    Calendar.
Widow's Lament in Springtime, The.
Willow Poem.
Wind Increases, The.
Yachts, The.
Yellow Flower, The.
Yellow Season, The.
Young Housewife, The.
Young Sycamore.

Williamson, Alan
Friends Who Have Failed.
Recitation for the Dismantling of a Hydrogen
    Bomb.
Robert Lowell: His Death.

Williamson, Bruce
Afternoon in Anglo-Ireland.
For M.
Homage of War.
Thought for My Love, A.

Williamson, Mrs. J. B. *See* **"Scrace,
    Richard."**

Williamson, Roosevelt. *See* **Shahid.**

Willis, John
Verses to Be Repeated by an Attorney
    Leaving His Lodging to Wait upon Judges
    Riding the Circuits from One County to
    Another, Least He Forget Some Necessary
    Thing.

Willis, Love Maria
Father, Hear the Prayer We Offer.

Willis, Nathaniel Parker
Ambition.
April.

Death of Harrison, The.
Declaration, The.
If, in well-bred society, ("hear! hear!"), *sel.*
Leper, The.
Parrhasius.
Some men, 'tis said, prefer a woman fat, *sel.*
Spring.
To Giulia Grisi.
To Helen in a Huff.
To the Lady in the Chemisette with Black
    Buttons.
Torn Hat, The.
Two Women.

Willoby, Henry
To Avisa, *sel.*

Willson, Dixie
Mist and All, The.
Tip-Toe Tail.

Willson, Forceythe
Boy Brittan.
O Keeper of the Sacred Key, *sel.*
Old Sergeant, The.

Wilmot, Frank. *See* **"Maurice, Furnley"**

Wilmot, John, 2d Earl of Rochester. *See*
    Rochester, John Wilmot, 2d Earl of

Wilson, Alexander
Blue-Bird, The.
Fisherman's Hymn, The.
Poet's Corner, The.

Wilson, Antoinette
Wit's End Corner.

Wilson, August
Theme One: The Variations.

Wilson, Charlotte. *See* **Baker, Karle Wilson**

Wilson, Dedie Huffman
Speak to the Sun.

Wilson, Edmund
Drafts of a Quatrain.
Lido, The.
Not Here.
Omelet of A MacLeish, The.
On Editing Scott Fitzgerald's Papers.
Peterhof.
Something for My Russian Friends.
Voice, The.

Wilson, Edward E.
Autumnal Equinox.

Wilson, Edwin H.
Where Is Our Holy Church?

Wilson, Elizabeth A.
Snow Crystals on Meall Glas.

Wilson, Ernest J., Jr.
Mae's Rent Party.
Paternal.

Wilson, Gavin
From the *Caledonian Mercury.*

Wilson, James
Casey's Revenge.

Wilson, James Edward
When I Am Dead.

Wilson, Jane
Willow in a Gale.

Wilson, John (1588–1677)
Armada, 1588, The.

Wilson, John (1591–1667)
Confess We All, before the Lord.
For Lo! My Jonah How He Slumped.
Whoso Would See This Song of Heavenly
    Choice.

Wilson, John (1627?–1696)
Copy of Verses, A.
Rose and the Gauntlet, The.
Sacred Poetry.

Wilson, Keith
Dog Poisoner, The.
Idiot, The.
Lamb, The.
Old Women beside a Church.
One Rose of Stone.
Prayer for Rivers, A.
Twin Aces.

Wilson, Marjorie
From the Train.
Gates to England, The.
Jungle Trees, The.
Lighthouse, The.
Little Things That Happen, The.
Through the Porthole.

Wilson, Mary
Mamzelle.
Oxford in Wartime.

Wilson, Pat
Anchorage, The.
Cuvier Light.
Farewell, The: "And so, one day when the
    tide was away out."
Precious Pearl, The.
Tree, The.

Wilson, Ramona
Bags Packed and We Expected This.
Eveningsong.
Eveningsong 2.
Keeping Hair.
Late in Fall.
Meeting, The.
Overnight Guest.
Reading Indian Poetry.
Spring at Fort Okanogan.
Spring in Virginia.
Summer.

Wilson, Robert
New Brooms, *sel.*
Simplicity's Song, *sel.*

Wilson, Robert Burns
Ballad of the Faded Field.
Battle Song.
It Is in Winter That We Dream of Spring.
Such Is the Death the Soldier Dies.
Sunrise of the Poor, The.
To a Crow.

Wilson, Robert Noble Denison
Elegy in a Presbyterian Burying-Ground.

Wilson, Robley, Jr.
Moving Out.

Wilson, T. P. Cameron ("Tipcuca")
Magpies in Picardy.

Winant, Fran
Christopher Street Liberation Day, June 28,
    1970.
Sacred Grove, A.
To Begin.

Winch, Terence
Bells Are Ringing for Me and Chagall, The.
Comfortable Strangers.
Iron Eyes.
Mysteries.
Success Story.
Them Decade, The.

Winchester, Caleb T.
Lord Our God Alone Is Strong, The.

Winchester, Elhanan
Behold with Joy.

Winchilsea, Anne Finch, Countess of
Enquiry after Peace. A Fragment.
Give me, O indulgent fate!, *sel.*
Greater Trial, The.
Introduction, The: "Did I my lines intend for
    public[k] view."
Jealousie Is the Rage of a Man.
Letter to Daphnis, A.
Nocturnal Reverie, A.
On Myself.
Petition for an Absolute Retreat, A.
Song, A: "Nymph in vain bestows her pains,
    The."
Song of the Cannibals, A.
Song on the South Sea, A.
To Melancholy.
To the Nightingale.
Trail All Your Pikes.

Windhager, Juliane
Children's Carnival.

Confirmation Day.
Fata Morgana.
St. Nicholas.

Wine, Maria
Love Me.
Woman, you are afraid of the forest.

Wingate, Mary
Washington.

Wingfield, Sheila
Winter.
Young Argonauts.

Winkler, Manfred
And So They Withered.
At the Art Exhibit.
Birthday.
Conclusion: "I came to pay you a visit, but
you were sad and I empty-handed."
Evening Closes over Me, The.
I Love What Is Not.
If My Hands Were Mute.
Night after Night I Come to Worship.
One Goes with Me along the Shore.
She.
Somewhere You Exist.
Sun Held in Tender Hands, The.

Winner, Joseph E.
Little Brown Jug, *at.*

Winner, Robert
Banjo, The.
Elegy: "I remember the feel of a hammer."

Winner, Septimus ("Alice Hawthorne")
Coolie Chinee, The.
Lilliputian's Beer Song.
Ten Little Injuns.

Winsor, Frederick
This little pig built a spaceship, *sel.*

Winstanley, Gerrard
Digger's Song, The.

Winstanley, John
Epigram on Florio.
Epigram on the First of April.
Fanny's Removal in 1714.
Inventory of the Furniture of a Collegian's
Chamber, An.
Last Will and Testament, A.
Miss Betty's Singing-Bird.
On a Certain Effeminate Peer.
On a Stingy Beau.
To the Revd. Mr. ——— on His Drinking
Sea-Water.

Wintchevsky, Morris
Child-King, The.
If I Felt Less.

Winter, Mary
Blessing the Hounds.
Lower Forms of Life.

Winter, William
Adelaide Neilson.
Arthur.
Asleep.
I. H. B.
My Queen.
Night Watch, The.
On the Verge.
Passing Bell at Stratford, The.
Unwritten Poems.

Winters, Anne
Key to the City, The.

Winters, Yvor
Apollo and Daphne.
April.
At the San Francisco Airport.
Before Disaster.
California Oaks, The.
Elegy, An: "Noon is beautiful, The: the
perfect wheel."
For the Opening of the William Dinsmore
Briggs Room.
Fragment, A: "I cannot find my way to
Nazareth."
Hawk's Eyes.

Heracles.
Hymn to Dispel Hatred at Midnight.
Inscription for a Graveyard.
John Sutter.
Manzanita, The.
Marriage, The.
Night of Battle.
Nocturne for October 31st, A.
On a View of Pasadena from the Hills.
On Teaching the Young.
Orpheus.
Prayer for My Son, A.
Precision, The.
Quod Tegit Omnia.
Rows of Cold Trees, The.
Sir Gawaine and the Green Knight.
Slow Pacific Swell, The.
Song in Passing, A.
Static Autumn.
Summer Commentary, A.
Theseus: A Trilogy.
Time and the Garden.
To a Military Rifle, 1942.
To Emily Dickinson.
To My Infant Daughter.
To the Holy Spirit.
To the Moon.

Winthrop, Theodore
But Once.

Wintle, Walter D.
Thinking.

Winwar, Frances
Autumn.

Wisdome, Robert
Religious Use of [Taking] Tobacco, *at.*

Wise, Isaac M.
In Mercy, Lord, Incline Thine Ear.

Wise, Joseph
Glory.

Wise, William
After the Party.
Just Three.
My Little Sister.
Rainy Day.
Runaway.

Wishik, Heather
Visitation Rights.

Wiswall, Ichabod
Judicious Observation of That Dreadful
Comet, A.

Witheford, Hubert
Arena, The.
At the Discharge of Cannon Rise the
Drowned.
Barbarossa.
Bondage.
Cactuses, The.
Cloud Burst.
Displacement, The.
Elegy in the Orongorongo Valley.
King of Kings.
Mid Winter.
Snow.
Waters, Indeed, Are to the Palate, Bitter,
The.
What Is Happening Now?
White Goddess.

Wither, George
Ah Me! Am I the Swaine.
Choice, The.
Christmas Carol, A: "So now is come our
joyful'st feast."
Divided Heart, The, *sel.*
For a Musician, *sel.*
For Scholars and Pupils.
Fourth Eclogue, The, *sel.*
Hence, Away, You Sirens, *sel.*
Hymn L: Rocking Hymn, A, *sel.*
Hymne I: Generall Invitation to Praise God,
A, *sel.*

I know that if thou please thou canst provide,
sel.
I Loved a Lass.
It may be 'tis observ'd, I want relations, *sel.*
Lord, Many Times Thou Pleased Art.
Marigold, The.
Philarete Praises Poetry, *sel.*
Shall I Wasting in Despair, *sel.*
Why, silly Man! so much admirest thou, *sel.*
Widow's Hymn, A.

Witherby, Diana
Casualty.

Withers, Carl
Charlie Chaplin went to France, *at.*

Witherspoon, Naomi Long. *See* **Madgett,
Naomi Long**

Witherup, William
Crows.

Withington, Leonard
O Saviour of a World Undone.

Witt, Harold
Dream.
Dreamscape in Kümmel.
First Photos of Flu Virus.
Lanky Hank Farrow.
More Nudes for Florence.
Nude.

Witte, John
Home.

Wittenberg, Ernest
Sub-average *Time* Reader, The.

Wittlin, Jozef
On the Jewish Day of Judgment in the Year
1942 (5703).
To the Jews in Poland.

Wittlinger, Ellen
Second Heart, The.

Woddis, Roger
Ethics for Everyman.
Final Curtain.
Hero, The.
Nothing Sacred.

Wodehouse, E. A.
Afforestation.

Wodehouse, Pelham Grenville
Gourmet's Love-Song, The.
Printer's Error.
Song about Whiskers.
Time like an Ever-rolling Stream.
To William (Whom We Have Missed).

Wohmann, Gabriele
Again Everything Has Gone Quite Well.
Evildoer.
I Am Not a Bug.

Wojahn, David
Another Coast.
Betrayal of Christ in Tucson and Brussels,
The.
Bicycle, The.
Cold Glow: Icehouses.
Cool Nights of October.
Evening Snow.
Floating Houses.
Man Who Knew Too Much, The.
Satin Doll.
Weldon Kees in Mexico, 1965.

Wojtyla, Karol
Marble Floor.
Song of the Brightness of Water.

Wolcot, John. *See* **"Pindar, Peter"**

Wolcott, Roger
Heart Is Deep, The.
Matthew X. 28.

Wolcott, Samuel
Christ for the World! We Sing.
Father! I Own Thy Voice.

Wolf, Leonard
Peasant, The.
Sonnet: "Sits by a fireplace, the seducer
talks."

Wolf, Phyllis
Akawense.
Lac Courte Orielles; 1936.
Manomin.
Midewiwan.
Rolling Thunder.
Wolf, Poor
Poor Wolf Speaks.
Wolf, Robert Leopold
Pagan Reinvokes the Twenty-third Psalm, A.
Wolfe, Aaron R.
Complete in Thee, No Work of Mine.
Parting Hymn We Sing, A.
Wolfe, Charles
Burial of Sir John Moore after [*or* at]
 Corunna, The.
To Mary.
Wolfe, Ffrida
Choosing Shoes.
Four and Eight.
Poppies in the Garden, The.
Wolfe, Gene
Computer Iterates the Greater Trumps, The.
Wolfe, Humbert
A. E. Housman and a Few Friends.
Autumn.
Blackbird, The.
British Journalist, The.
Come! let us draw the curtains, *sel.*
D. H. Lawrence and James Joyce.
Dead Fiddle, The.
Dean Inge.
Denmark.
G. K. Chesterton.
Gray Squirrel, The.
Green Candles.
Hilaire Belloc.
Iliad.
Journey's End.
Lilac, The.
Love Is a Keeper of Swans.
Man.
Things Lovelier.
This Is Not Death.
Tulip.
Wardour Street.
Waters of Life, The.
Zoo, The.
Wolfe, James
Why, Soldiers, Why? at.
Wolfe, Thomas Clayton
Burning in the Night.
Wolfenstein, Alfred
Exodus 1940.
Wolff, Daniel
"Heaven in Ordinarie."
Wolff, David
While We Slept.
Wolfram von Eschenbach
His Own True Wife.
Wolfskehl, Karl
And Yet We Are Here!
From Mount Nebo.
Shekhina[h].
To Be Said at the Seder.
We Go.
Wolker, Jiří
Epitaph: "Here lies the poet Wolker, lover of
 the world."
On This My Sick-Bed Beats the World.
Wolny, P.
Harmonica Man.
Words, like Spiders.
Wolstenholme-Elmy, Elizabeth
Marriage, which might have been a mateship
 sweet, *sel.*
Wong, Nellie
Eat, Eat!
Funeral Song for Mamie Eisenhower.
Have Head, Have Tail.
How a Girl Got Her Chinese Name.

New Romance.
Song of Farewell.
Under Our Own Wings.
Wong, Shawn
Island, An.
Lapis.
Periods of Adjustment.
Wong, Orlando. *See* **Onuora, Oku**
Woo, Merle
Poem for the Creative Writing Class, Spring
 1982.
Subversive, The.
Yellow Woman Speaks.
Wood, A. J.
Rolling John and night together, *sel.*
Wood, Alfred E.
Fight at Dajo, The.
Wood, Clement
Enter the Vampire.
Prayer in Time of Blindness, A.
Wood, Robert Williams
Elk, The Whelk, The.
Pecan, The Toucan, The.
Pen-guin. The Sword-fish, The.
Puffin, The.
Wood, Sallie Burrow
Rain Drops.
Wood, William
Kinds of Shel-fish.
King of waters, the sea shouldering whale,
 The.
Kingly lyon, and the strong arm'd beare, The.
Princely eagle, and the soaring hawke, The.
Trees both in hills and plaines, in plenty be.
Woodberry, George Edward
America to England.
At Gibraltar.
Child, The, *sel.*
Divine Awe, *sel.*
Essex Regiment March.
Homeward Bound, *sel.*
Islands of the Sea, The.
Love's Rosary.
O destined Land, unto thy citadel, *sel.*
O, Inexpressible as Sweet, *sel.*
O Land Beloved, *sel.*
O, Struck beneath the Laurel, *sel.*
On a Portrait of Columbus.
Our First Century.
Rose of Stars, The, *sel.*
Seaward, *sel.*
Secret, The, *sel.*
So Slow to Die, *sel.*
Song of Eros, *sel.*
Sonnets Written in the Fall of 1914.
When First I Saw Her, *sel.*
"Woodbine Willie." *See* **Studdert-Kennedy,**
 Geoffrey Anketell
Woodbourne, Harry
Flute of May, The.
Woodbridge, Benjamin
Upon the Author; by a Known Friend.
Upon the Tomb of the Most Reverend Mr.
 John Cotton.
Woodcock, George
Imagine the South.
Island, The.
Island, The.
Pacifists.
Paper Anarchist Addresses the Shade of
 Nancy Ling Perry.
Poem for Garcia Lorca.
Woodford, Bruce P.
Going Through.
Woodhouse, James
Birmingham and Wolverhampton, *sel.*
Tribulations of an Uneducated Poet in the
 1760's, The, *sel.*
Woodley, F. S.
Beautiful, The.

Woodrow, Constance Davies
To a Vagabond.
Woods, John
Cursing the First Book.
Long-Head Poem, The.
Woods, Margaret Louisa
Father of Life, with songs of wonder, *sel.*
Genius Loci.
Woods, Nancy
I Read a Tight-fisted Poem Once.
Woodward, Charles
Midnight Ramble, The.
Woodworth, Samuel
How dear to my heart are the scenes of my
 childhood, *sel.*
Hunters of Kentucky; or, Half Horse and Half
 Alligator, The.
Loves She Like Me?
Needle, The.
Old Oaken Bucket, The.
Woody, Elizabeth
Black Fear.
Custer Must Have Learned to Dance.
Eagles.
In Impressions of Hawk Feathers Willow
 Leaves Shadow.
Night Crackles.
You Smell like Grandma's Beads.
Wooley, Celia Parker
Refracted Lights.
Woolf, Virginia
Let Us Go, Then, Exploring.
Woolsey, Theodore Dwight
Eclipse of Faith, The.
Woolsey, Sarah Chauncey. *See* **"Coolidge,**
 Susan"
Woolson, Constance Fenimore
Kentucky Belle.
Yellow Jessamine.
"Worcester"
Pastoral; in the Modern Style, A.
Wordsworth, C. W. V.
Song in Praise of Paella.
Wordsworth, Christopher
O Day of Rest and Gladness.
Wordsworth, Dorothy
Address to a Child during a Boisterous Winter
 Evening.
Cottager to Her Infant, The.
He said he had been a soldier.
I gathered mosses in Easedale.
Loving and Liking.
Wordsworth, Elizabeth
Good and Clever.
Wordsworth, William
Admonition to a Traveller.
Affliction of Margaret, The.
Alice Fell; or, Poverty.
Among all lovely things my love had been.
And thus continuing, she said, *sel.*
Anecdote for Fathers.
At the Grave of Burns.
Beetle loves his unpretending track, The, *sel.*
Books, *sel.*
Calais, August 15, 1802.
Cambridge and the Alps, *sel.*
Change Me, Some God, into that Breathing
 Rose.
Character of the Happy Warrior.
Childhood and School-Time, *sel.*
Childless Father, The.
Complaint, A.
Composed at Neidpath Castle, the Property of
 Lord Queensberry, 1803.
Composed by the Seaside, near Calais,
 August, 1802.
Composed by the Side of Grasmere Lake.
Composed near Calais, on the Road Leading
 to Ardres, August 7, 1802.
Composed upon an Evening of Extraordinary
 Splendour and Beauty.

Composed upon Westminster Bridge, September 3, 1802.
Conclusion ("It was a close, warm, breezeless summer night"), *sel*.
Contrast; the Parrot and the Wren, The.
Curious child, who dwelt upon a tract, A, *sel*.
Dear Brook, farewell! To-morrow's noon again, *sel*.
Dear native regions, I foretell.
Decay of Piety.
Despondency Corrected, *sel*.
Discourse of the Wanderer, and an Evening Visit to the Lake, *sel*.
Driven in by autumn's sharpening air, *sel*.
1801.
Elegiac Stanzas.
Elegiac Stanzas Suggested by a Picture of Peele Castle, in a Storm [Painted by Sir George Beaumont]
Expostulation and Reply.
Extempore Effusion [upon the Death of James Hogg], An.
Farmer of Tilsbury Vale, The.
Fidelity.
For I have learned, *sel*.
For thou art with me here upon the banks, *sel*.
Fountain, The.
France, *sel*.
French and the Spanish Guerrillas, The.
Great Men Have Been among Us.
Green Linnet, The.
Hart-Leap Well.
Hast thou then survived, *sel*.
Her Eyes Are Wild.
Here Pause: The Poet Claims at Least This Praise.
High on a mountain's highest ridge, *sel*.
I thought of Thee, my partner and my guide, *sel*.
I Traveled [*or* travell'd] among Unknown Men, *sel*.
I Wandered Lonely as a Cloud.
I Watch, and Long Have Watched.
Idiot Boy, The.
If Thou Indeed Derive Thy Light from Heaven.
Imagination and Taste, How Impaired and Restored, *sel*.
Incident at Bruges.
Incident Characteristic of a Favourite Dog.
Inside of King's College Chapel, Cambridge, *sel*.
It Is a Beauteous Evening [Calm and Free]
It Is Not to Be Thought Of [That the Flood]
It Was an April Morning.
Kitten at Play, The, *sel*.
Laodamia.
Leaves that rustled on this oak-crowned hill, The.
Lesson, The.
Lines Composed a Few Miles above Tintern Abbey on Revisiting the Banks of the Wye during a Tour, July 13, 1798.
Lines Written in Early Spring.
London, 1802 ("Milton! thou should'st be living at this hour").
London, MDCCCII ("O friend! I know not which way I must look").
London, from Hampstead Heath, *sel*.
Louisa.
Lucy Gray; or, Solitude.
Michael.
Most alluring clouds that mount the sky, The.
Most Sweet It Is with Unuplifted Eyes.
Mutability, *sel*.
My Heart Leaps Up [When I Behold]
Near Dover, September 1802.
Night in June, A.
Night-Piece, A.
November, 1806.
Now, whether it were by peculiar grace, *sel*.

Now, while the birds thus sing a joyous song, *sel*.
Nuns Fret Not at Their Convent's Narrow Room.
Nutting.
O joy! that in our embers, *sel*.
O Nightingale! Thou Surely Art.
O there is blessing in this gentle breeze, *sel*.
October 1803.
Ode: Intimations of Immortality from Recollections of Early Childhood.
Ode to Duty.
Ode to Duty.
Oh! what's the matter? what's the matter?, *sel*.
Old Cumberland Beggar, The.
Old Man [*or* Old Man Travelling], An.
On Man, on Nature, and on Human Life, *sel*.
On the Departure of Sir Walter Scott from Abbotsford, for Naples.
On the Extinction of the Venetian Republic.
Our birth is but a sleep and a forgetting, *sel*.
Personal Talk.
Pet Lamb, The.
Pilgrim Fathers, The.
Poet, A!—He Hath Put His Heart to School.
Poet's Epitaph, A.
Prospectus, *sel*.
Quantocks, The.
Residence at Cambridge, *sel*.
Residence in France, *sel*.
Residence in London, *sel*.
Retrospect—Love of Nature Leading to Love of Mankind, *sel*.
Return, *sel*.
Reverie of Poor Susan, The.
Ruth; or, The Influences of Nature.
Salisbury Plain and Stonehenge, *sel*.
School-Time, *sel*.
Scorn not the sonnet; critic, you have frowned.
She Dwelt among the Untrodden Ways, *sel*.
She Was a Phantom of Delight.
Simon Lee.
Simple child, A, *sel*.
Slumber Did My Spirit Seal, A, *sel*.
So Fair, So Sweet, Withal So Sensitive.
Solitary, The, *sel*.
Solitary Reaper, The.
Song at the Feast of Brougham Castle.
Sonnet: Composed after a Journey across the Hamilton Hills, Yorkshire.
Sonnet: Composed while the Author Was Engaged in Writing a Tract Occasioned by the Convention of Cintra.
Sonnet: "England! the time is come when thou shouldst wean."
Sonnet: September, 1815.
Sonnet: September 1, 1802.
Sonnet: There Is a Bondage Worse.
Sonnet: To— — —
Sonnet: To the Lady Beaumont.
Sounding cataract, The/ Haunted me like a passion, *sel*.
Sparrow's Nest, The.
Speak!
Stanzas Written in My Pocket Copy of Thomson's "Castle of Indolence."
Steamboats, Viaducts, and Railways.
Stepping Westward.
Strange Fits of Passion Have I Known.
Summer Vacation, *sel*.
Sunbeam Said, Be Happy, The, *sel*.
Surprised by Joy [Impatient as the Wind]
Tables Turned, The.
There Was a Boy, *sel*.
There was a time when meadow, grove and stream, *sel*.
Thorn, The.
Thought [*or* Thoughts] of a Briton on the Subjugation of Switzerland.

Three Years She Grew in Sun and Shower, *sel*.
'Tis Said That Some Have Died for Love.
To a Butterfly.
To a Child.
To a Skylark ("Ethereal minstrel! pilgrim of the sky").
To a Skylark ("Up with me!").
To a Young Lady.
To H. C.
To Lady Eleanor Butler and the Honourable Miss Ponsonby, Composed in the Grounds of Plas-Newydd, Llangollen.
To My Sister.
To Sleep.
To Sleep ("Fond words have oft been spoken to thee, sleep!").
To Sleep ("O gentle sleep! do they belong to thee").
To the Cuckoo.
To the Daisy.
To the Daisy ("In youth from rock to rock I went").
To the Daisy ("With little here to do or see").
To the [*or* a] Highland Girl of Inversneyde.
To the Men of Kent.
To the Same Flower.
To the Small Celandine.
To Toussaint L'Ouverture.
Trepidation of the Druids, *sel*.
Tribute to the Memory of the Same Dog.
Trosachs, The.
Two April Mornings, The.
Up with me! up with me into the clouds!, *sel*.
Voice of the Derwent, The.
Wanderer, The, *sel*.
Wanderer Recalls the Past, The, *sel*.
Water Fowl.
We Are Seven.
We Poets in Our Youth, *sel*.
Weak Is the Will of Man, His Judgment Blind.
When I Have Borne in Memory.
Where is he, that giddy sprite, *sel*.
Where Lies the Land to Which Yon Ship Must Go ?
Where Lies the Truth? Has Man in Wisdom's Creed.
While Anna's peers and early playmates tread, *sel*.
Wild Duck's Nest , The.
With Ships the Sea Was Sprinkled Far and Nigh.
World Is Too Much with Us, The.
Written in London, September, 1802.
Written in March.
Written in Very Early Youth.
Yarrow Revisited.
Yarrow Unvisited.
Yarrow Visited.
Yes, It Was the Mountain Echo.
Yew Trees.

Work, Henry Clay
Grandfather's Clock.
Marching through Georgia.
Ship That Never Returned, The.
The Year of Jubilee.

Worley, Jeff
Whitley at Three O'Clock.

Worley, Mrs. J. B.
Mighty Hunter, The.

Wormser, Baron
By-Products.
For My Brother Who Died before I Was Born.
Mowing Crew, The.
Piano Lessons.
Poem to the Memory of H. L. Mencken.
Sunday Review Section.

Worsley-Benison, H.
Song of the Engine, The.

Worth, Douglas
Ghetto Summer School.
War Bride.
Worth, Kathryn
Smells.
Worth, Valerie
Acorn.
Chairs.
Christmas Lights.
Christmas Ornaments.
Crickets.
Daisies.
Dinosaurs.
Duck.
Fireworks.
Haunted House.
McDonald's, New Hartford, NY.
Marbles.
Safety Pin.
Shoes.
Zinnias.
Wortman, Denis
God of the Prophets! Bless the Prophets'
Sons.
Today beneath Benignant Skies.
Wotton, Sir Henry
Character of a Happy Life, The.
De Morte.
Dialogue betwixt God and the Soul, A, *at.*
Eternal mover, whose diffused glory.
Hymn to My God in a Night of My Late
Sicknesse, A.
On a Bank [*or* Banck] as I Sat [*or* Sate]
a-Fishing; a Description of the Spring.
On [*or* To] His Mistress, the Queen of
Bohemia.
Tears at the Grave of Sir Albertus Morton.
Upon the Death of Sir Albert Morton's Wife.
Upon the Sudden Restraint of the Earl[e] of
Somerset, Then Falling from Favor [*or*
Favour].
Wotton, Sir John
In Praise of His Daphnis.
In Praise of His Love.
Woty, William
I now solicit not the Muses nine, *sel.*
Lines Written in the Dog-Days.
White Conduit House.
Wrafter, Denis
Old Man to His Scythe, The.
On Hearing a Broadcast of Ceremonies in
Connection with Conferring of Cardinals'
Hats.
Sabbath Reflection.
Wratislaw, Theodore
Eros D'Aute.
To a Sicilian Boy.
Wray, Ruby Marion
You'll Never Know.
Wreford, John R.
Lord, While for All Mankind.
"Wreford James." *See* **Watson, James
Wreford**
Wright, Bruce McM.
African Affair, The.
Journey to a Parallel.
Wright, C. D.
Beautiful Urinals of Paris, The.
Birth of the Cool.
Slag.
Tours.
Wright, Carolyne
Celebration for the Cold Snap.
Custody of the Eyes, The.
Josie Bliss, October 1971.
Under the Sign of Cancer.
Wright, Catharine Morris
Hillside Pause.
Wright, Celeste Turner
Kineo Mountain.
Noblesse Oblige.

Thumbprint.
Yugoslav Cemetery.

Wright, Charles
All day at the window seat, *sel.*
April.
Arkansas Traveller.
Ars Poetica.
Bar Giamaica, 1959-60.
Blackwater Mountain.
California Dreaming.
Chinoiserie.
Clear Night.
Cloud River.
Daughters of Blum, The.
Dead are a cadmium blue, The, *sel.*
Dead Color.
Delta Traveller.
Dog Creek Mainline ("Dog Creek: cat track
and bind splay").
Dog Day Vespers.
Dog Yoga.
Driving through Tennessee.
Edvard Munch.
Equation.
Fever Toy, The.
Firstborn.
Hawaii Dantesca.
Holy Thursday.
Homage to Paul Cézanne.
How strange it is to awake, *sel.*
I have nothing to say about the way the sky
tilts, *sel.*
I'll tell you I never asked for it, *sel.*
Invisible Landscape.
Laguna Blues.
March Journal.
Mount Caribou at Night.
Negatives.
New Poem, The.
Night Journal.
Nightdream.
Nightletter.
Northhanger Ridge.
October.
Other Side of the River, The.
Photographs.
Portrait of the Artist with Hart Crane.
Reunion.
Self-Portrait in 2035.
Sex.
Sitting at Night on the Front Porch.
Smoke.
Snow.
Spider Crystal Ascension.
Stone Canyon Nocturne.
Tattoos.
Two Stories.
Under the rock, in the sand and the gravel
run, *sel.*
Virginia Reel.
Virgo Descending.
Yellow.
You've talked to the sun and moon, *sel.*

Wright, Charles David
Obedience of the Corpse.

Wright, David
Anniversary Approaches, An; of the Birth of
God, *sel.*
Encounter in a Glass.
For George Barker at Seventy.
Invocation to the Goddess.
Images for a Painter.
Grassmere Sonnets.
Kleomedes.
Monologue of a Deaf Man.
Moral Story II.
My countryman, the poet, wears a Stetson,
sel.

My grandfather was an elegant gentleman,
sel.
On the Death of an Emperor Penguin in
Regent's Park, London.
Pastoral: "Afternoon wears on, The."
Rousecastle.
Under the African lintel, Table Mountain, *sel.*
Wright, David McKee
Danny's Wooing.
My Love is the voice of a song, *sel.*
On a shining silver morning long ago, *sel.*
While the Billy Boils.
Wright, Ernest Vincent
When Father Carves the Duck.
Wright, Franz
There.
Wright, Frederick Adams
Letter to the City Clerk.
Wright, George T.
Aquarium.
Wright, Hetty
To an Infant Expiring the Second Day of Its
Birth.
Wedlock; a Satire.
Wright, Ivan Leonard
Want of You, The.
Wright, James
Against Surrealism.
American Twilights, 1957.
Apollo.
Arrangements with Earth for Three Dead
Friends.
As I Step over a Puddle at the End of Winter,
I Think of an Ancient Chinese Governor.
Assignation, The.
At the Executed Murderer's Grave.
At the Slackening of the Tide.
Autumn Begins in Martins Ferry, Ohio.
Beautiful Ohio.
Before the [*or* a] Cashier's Window in a
Department Store.
Blessing, A.
Breath of Air, A.
By a Lake in Minnesota.
Complaint.
Dawn near an Old Battlefield, in a Time of
Peace.
Discoveries in Arizona.
Dream of Burial, A.
Eisenhower's Visit to Franco, 1959.
Evening.
Fear Is What Quickens Me.
For the Marsh's Birthday.
Gesture by a Lady with an Assumed Name,
A.
Girl in a Window, A.
Goodbye to the Poetry of Calcium.
Having Lost My Sons, I Confront the
Wreckage of the Moon: Christmas, 1960.
Honey.
In Memory of Leopardi.
In Ohio.
In Response to a Rumor That the Oldest
Whorehouse in Wheeling, West Virginia,
Has Been Condemned.
Inscription for the Tank.
Jerome in Solitude.
Jewel, The.
Journey, The.
Late November in a Field.
Life, The.
Little Marble Boy.
Living by the Red River.
Love in a Warm Room in Winter.
Lying in a Hammock at William Duffy's Farm
in Pine Island, Minnesota.
Mad Fight Song for William S. Carpenter,
1966, A.
Mantova.
Micromutations.
Milkweed.

Minneapolis Poem, The.
Moral Poem Freely Accepted from Sappho, A.
Mutterings over the Crib of a Deaf Child.
My Grandmother's Ghost.
Names in Monterchi: To Rachel.
Northern Pike.
Note Left in Jimmy Leonard's Shack, A.
Ohio Valley Swains.
Ohioan Pastoral.
Old Age Compensation.
Old Dog in the Ruins of the Graves at Arles, The.
On the Skeleton of a Hound.
Outside Fargo, North Dakota.
Paul.
Poem about Breasts, A.
Poem of Towers, A.
Poems to a Brown Cricket.
Prayer to Escape from the Market Place, A.
Prayer to the Lord Ramakrishna, A.
Presentation of Two Birds to My Son, A.
Private Meeting Place, The.
Quest, The.
Rain.
Raisin, The.
Redwings.
Revelation, The.
Rip.
Saint Judas.
Sappho.
Saying Dante Aloud.
Secret Gratitude, A.
Simon and the Tarantula.
Small Frogs Killed on the Highway.
Snowfall; a Poem about Spring.
Song for the Middle of the Night, A.
Speak.
Stages on a Journey Westward.
Taranto.
Three Sentences for a Dead Swan.
To a Beautiful Pear Tree.
To a Defeated Saviour.
To a Salesgirl, Weary of Artificial Holiday Trees.
To a Troubled Friend.
To Flood Stage Again.
To the Cicada.
To the Evening Star: Central Minnesota.
To the Ghost of a Kite.
To the Muse.
To the Poets in New York.
Trouble.
Twilights.
Two Hangovers.
Two Poems about President Harding.
Two Postures beside a Fire.
Ungathered Apples, The.
Vain Advice at the Year's End.
Verona.
Way to Make a Living, A.
What the Earth Asked Me.
Willy Lyons.
Winter Daybreak above Vence, A.
With a Sliver of Marble from Carrara.
With the Shell of a Hermit Crab.
Written in a Copy of Swift's Poems, for Wayne Burns.
Yes, But.
You and I Saw Hawks Exchanging the Prey.
Your Name in Arezzo.
Youth.
Wright, Jay
Altars and Sacrifice.
Charge, The.
Dead, The.
Death as History.
Homecoming Singer, The.
Invitation to Madison County, An.
Wednesday Night Prayer Meeting.
Wright, Jeff
Flesh Coupon.

Higher Love.
Industrial Size.
Sermon on the Mount.
Stay Beautiful.
Wright, John
Poor Man's Province, The.
Wright, Judith
And Mr. Ferritt.
At Cooloolah.
Australia 1970.
Beanstalk, Meditated Later, The.
Bora Ring.
Brother and Sisters.
Builders, The.
Bull, The.
Bullocky.
Charity lotteries for dream houses, The, *sel.*
Country Dance, *sel.*
Cup, The.
"Dove-Love."
Drought Year.
Egrets.
Eli, Eli.
Extinct Birds.
Flood Year.
Furniture: humble, dependent, *sel.*
Hawthorn Hedge, The.
Ishtar.
Legend.
Lyrebirds.
Night and the Child.
Old Prison, The.
Portrait.
Remittance Man.
Request to a Year.
Sanctuary.
South of My Days.
Storm.
Surfer, The.
Tableau.
Train Journey.
Turning Fifty.
Twins, The.
Two Fires, The.
Wings.
Woman to Child.
Woman to Man.
Wonga Vine.
Wright, Kit
Dad and the Cat and the Tree.
I Don't Like You.
New World Symphony, A.
Wright, Richard
Between the World and Me.
Hokku: In the Falling Snow, *sel.*
Hokku Poems.
I Have Seen Black Hands.
Wright, Sarah E.
To Some Millions Who Survive Joseph E. Mander, Sr.
Until They Have Stopped.
Urgency.
Wright, William Bull
Through his million veins are poured, *sel.*
Wrighton, W. T.
Dearest Spot on Earth, The.
Wroth, [or Wroath], Mary Sidney, Countess of Montgomery
Duke's Song, The, *sel.*
In This Strange Labyrinth How Shall I Turn?, *sel.*
Lindamira's Complaint, *sel.*
Love Leave to Urge, *sel.*
Morea's Sonnet, *sel.*
Pamphilia to Amphilanthus, *sel.*
Pamphilia's Sonnet, *sel.*
Verses of the Talkative Knight, The, *sel.*
When Night's Black Mantle, *sel.*
Wu Chen
Drunk, he leans back in his boat, *sel.*
Fantastic Rock, The.

For action, I chant out loud, for quiet, I just think, *sel.*
In leaf after leaf we seem to hear the sighing of the wind, *sel.*
Inscribed on a Painting of Bamboo.
Leaning on clouds, hugging rocks, slanting every way, *sel.*
Level forest stretching far and wide, A.
Moonlight Bay.
Ni Tsan Poem Following Rhyme-Words of Wu Chen.
To the Tune "Chiu-ch'üan tzu."
West of the village, evening rays linger on red leaves, *sel.*
Wu Chia-chi
At the Ch'ang Family Well, *sel.*
Falling Leaves.
Grain-Barge Wife, The.
In the morning they build embankments against floods, *sel.*
Itinerant trade is the business of petty men, *sel.*
My Hut.
On Virtuous Government—For His Excellency Wang Fu-ssu, Salt Subcontroller of T'ai-chou.
Passing the Retreat of Hsü Ching-po.
Poem: "Beside the road the *wu t'ung* tree," *sel.*
Poem: "I have beaten my sword into an axe," *sel.*
Quatrain: "East of the salt village, low and narrow."
Quatrain: "Old saltman, hair turned white, The."
To Ch'eng Fei-t'ao.
Woman Née Wu, The.
Woman Tung.
Wu Chün
Song of Spring.
Wu Hsi-ch'i
Colophon Written on the Flyleaf of a Book Sent to My Several Friends at Hsi-ling.
Curtain hooks sway gently in the spring breeze.
Tune: A Song to Induce Laughter.
Wu Sheng
An Accident.
Elegy: "Yes, I experienced youth."
Impressions of My Village.
Morning Scene, A.
Rainy Season, The.
Shop, The.
Wild Grass.
Wu T'e-Liang
Night Guards.
Nostalgia.
Sharpshooters.
Wu Ti, [or Ou—ty], Emperor
Autumn Wind, The ("Autumn wind rises; white clouds fly").
Wu Tsao
Bitter rain in my courtyard.
For the Courtesan Ch'ing Lin.
In the Home of the Scholar Wu Su-chiang.
Swallows.
Tune: Bitter Longing.
Tune: Fragrant Wandering: A Song.
Tune: Full River Bed.
Wu Wei-yeh
Ancient Feeling.
Ancient Sentiments.
At the Mountain of the Mysterious Tomb.
At the River Tower Parting from My Younger Brother, Fu-ling.
Autumn Night—Sleepless.
Ballad of Yüan-yüan.
Blocked by Snow.
Broken Lampstand, The.
Climbing P'iao-miao Peak.
Distant Roads.

Fading, sick, again I hear of war, *sel.*
Feelings Come As I Pass through Wu-chiang.
Garden Living.
Impromptu.
Lamenting for My Late Daughter.
Leaving T'u-sung at Dawn.
Passing by Huai-yin I Have Feelings.
Poem of the Western Fields.
Reading the Annals of Emperor Wu of the Han Dynasy.
River Ching flows rapidly, The, *sel.*
Seeing Off Sun Ling-hsiu.
Seeing Off Wang Yüan-chao—Reprise.
Setting Out at Dawn.
Song of Yüan-yüan, The.
Song to the Tune "Perching Crows."
Written in Jest: On "The Old Man Who Rolled with the Punch."

Wu Wen
All day I fret over wind and sand, *sel.*
Bridge of Drifted Fragrance, The, *sel.*
Crane Lodge, *sel.*
From endless rains comes autumn's dusk, *sel.*
Heart that yearns for fame never dies, A, *sel.*
Jasper Cloud Monastery, The.

Wurdemann, Audrey
Text.

Wyatt, Sir Thomas
Absence absenting causeth me to complain.
Accused though I be without desert.
After great storms the calm returns.
Ah, Robin,/ Jolly Robin.
Alas! Madam, for Stealing of a Kiss.
Alas, poor man, what hap have I.
Alas the grief, and deadly woful smart!
All heavy minds.
And if an eye may save or slay.
And Wilt Thou Leave Me Thus?
Answer that ye made to me, my dear, The.
As power and wit will me assist.
At last withdraw your cruelty.
Behold, love, thy power how she despiseth!
Blame Not My Lute for He Must Sound *or* Sownde.
Comfort thyself, my woful heart.
Constancy.
Courtier's Life, The.
Deem as ye list, upon good cause.
Deme as Ye List Uppon Goode Cause.
Disdain Me Not.
Disdain me not without desert.
Divers Doth Use.
Eche man me telleth I chaunge moost my devise.
Epigram: "Enemy of life, decayer of all kind, The."
Epigram: "Face that should content me wonders well, A."
Epigram: "Fruit of all the service that I serve, The."
Epigram: "Lux my fair falcon, and your fellows all."
Epigram: "Sighs are my food, drink are my tears."
Epigram: "Who hath he[a]rd of such[e] cruelty before?"
Epitaph of Sir Thomas Gravener [Knight], An.
Farewell, all my welfare.
Farewell the reign of cruelty.
For want I will in woe I plain.
Forget Not Yet.
Fortune.
Full well it may be seen.
Furious Gun, The.
Give place all ye that doth rejoice.
He is not ded that somtyme hath a fall.
Heart and service to you proffer'd, The.
Heart oppress'd with desperate thought.
Help Me to Seek.
How Should I Be So Pleasant.
I am as I am and so will I be.

I have sought long with steadfastness.
I love, loved, and so doth she.
I see that chance hath chosen me.
If chance assign'd.
If ever man might him avaunt.
If fancy [*or*] fansy would favor.
If in the World There Be More Woe.
If thou wilt mighty be, flee from the rage.
If waker care, if sodayne pale coulor.
If with complaint the pain might be express'd.
In Eternum ("In eternum I was ons determined.").
In faith I wot not what to say.
Is It Possible?
It may be good, like it who list.
It Was My Choice.
Joy so short alas, the pain so near, The.
Knot which first my heart did strain, The.
Lament my losse, my labor, and my payne.
Like as the bird in the cage enclosed.
Like as the swan towards her death.
Lo, how I seek and sue to have.
Longer to muse.
Love doth again.
Lover Complaineth the Unkindness of His Love, The.
Lover Having Dreamed Enjoying of His Love, Complaineth That the Dreame Is Not either Longer or Truer, The.
Lover Rejoiceth the Enjoying of His Love, The.
Lyve thowe gladly, yff so thowe may.
Madame, withouten Many Wordes.
Me list no more to sing.
Mine Own John Poins [*or* Poyntz], *sel.*
Mistrustful minds be moved.
Most wretched heart, most miserable.
My hope, alas, hath me abused.
My Lute and I.
My mother's maids [*or* maydes], when they did sew and spin [*or* sowe and spynne], *sel.*
My Pen, Take Pain a Little Space.
Mye love toke skorne my servise to retaine.
Now all of change.
Now must I learn to live [*or* lerne to lyve] at rest.
O Goodly Hand.
O miserable sorrow, withouten cure.
Pass forth, my wonted cries.
Patience, for I have wrong.
Patience for my device.
Patience of all my smart.
Patience, Though I Have Not.
Piller pearisht is whearto I lent, The.
Process of time worketh such wonder.
Protest, A.
Quondam was I in my lady's grace.
Resignation.
Resound my voyse [*or* voice], ye wodes [*or* woods] that here [*or* hear] me plain.
Restful place, reviver of my smart, The.
Robyn, A/ Joly Robyn.
Rondeau: "What no, perdy! ye may be sure!"
Since love is such that as ye wot.
Since love will needs that I shall love.
Since so ye please to hear me plain.
Since ye delight to know.
Since you will needs that I shall sing.
So unwarely was never no man caught.
Some tyme I fled the fyre that me brent.
Sometime I sigh, sometime I sing.
Sonnet: "Each man me telleth I change most my devise."
Sonnet: "Farewell, love, and all thy laws [*or* lawes] for ever."
Sonnet: "I abide and abide and better abide."
Sonnet: "My love took scorn my service to retain."
Sonnet: "To rail or jest, ye know I use it not."
Sonnet: Whoso List to Hunt [I Know Where Is an Hind]

Sonnet: "You that in love find[e] luck[e] and abundaunce [*or* habundance]"
Spending hand that alway poureth out [*or* powreth owte], A, *sel.*
Spite hath no power to make me sad.
Such hap as I am happed in.
Sufficed not, madame, that you did tear.
Tagus, Farewell.
Take heed betime, lest ye be spied.
That time that mirth did steer my ship.
There was never nothing more me pained [*or* payned].
They Flee [*or* Fle] from Me That Sometime Did Me Seek [*or* Seke]
Tho' I can not your cruelty constrain.
Though this the port, and I thy servant true.
Throughout the World, If It Were Sought.
To cause accord or to agree [*or* aggre].
To His Heart.
To seek each where where man doth live.
To wet your eye withouten tear.
To wish, and want, and not obtain.
V. Innocentia Veritas Viat Fides Circumdederunt Me Inimici Mei.
What death is worse than this.
What meaneth [*or* menethe] this? When I lie [*or* lye] alone.
What nedeth these thretning wordes and wasted wynde?
What Once I Was.
What rage is this? what furor [*or* furour] of what kind [*or* kynd]?
What should [*or* shulde] I say[e]?
What vaileth trouth? or by it to take payn?
What wourde is that that chaungeth not.
When first mine eyes did view and mark.
Where shall I have at mine own will.
Will ye see what wonders love hath wrought.
With Serving Still.
Ye know my heart, my lady dear.
Ye old mule, that thinck your self so fayre.
Your looks so often cast.

Wyche, Marvin, Jr.
And She Was Bad.
Five Sense.
Leslie.
We Rainclouds.

Wycherley, William
Drinking-Song, against All Sorts of Disputes in Drinking, A.
Song: In the Name of a Lover, to His Mistress; Who Said, She Hated Him for His Grey Hairs, Which He Had at Thirty, A.
To a Fine Young Woman.
To a Good Physician.
To a Witty Man of Wealth and Quality; Who, after His Dismissal from Court, Said, He Might Justly Complain of It.
Upon the Most Useful Knowledge, Craft or Cunning, Which Is More Wisdom, as 'Tis Less Wit.

Wygodski, Stanislaw
Going to the North.
Those Betrayed at Dawn.
Voyage.
Winter Journey.

Wylie, Elinor
Address to My Soul.
Atavism.
August.
Beauty.
Birthday Sonnet.
Cold-blooded Creatures.
Confession of Faith.
"Desolation Is a Delicate Thing."
Down to the Puritan marrow of my bones, *sel.*
Eagle and the Mole, The.
Epitaph: "For this she starred her eyes with salt."
Escape.

Farewell, Sweet Dust.
Full Moon.
Full Moon.
Golden Bough.
Hughie at the Inn.
Hymn to Earth.
In our content, before the autumn came, sel.
Innocent Landscape.
Knight Fallen on Evil Days, The.
Lament for Glasgerion.
Let No Charitable Hope.
Little Beauty That I Was Allowed, The, sel.
Little Elegy.
Lodging for the Night, A.
Love Song: "Had I concealed my love."
Madman's Song.
Nebuchadnezzar.
O Virtuous Light.
Parting Gift.
Pebble, The.
Pegasus Lost.
Peregrine.
Peregrine's Sunday Song.
Peter and John.
Pretty Words.
Prophecy.
Sanctuary.
Sea Lullaby.
Simon Gerty.
Sonnet: "How many faults you might accuse
    me of."
Sonnet: "I hereby swear that to uphold your
    house," sel.
Sonnet: "Let us leave talking of angelic
    hosts," sel.
This Corruptible.
To a Book.
Tortoise in Eternity, The.
True Vine.
Velvet Shoes.
Wild Peaches.
"Wyn, Eition."   See Williams, Eliseus
Wynne, Annette
House Cat, The.
I Keep Three Wishes Ready.
Memorial Day.
People Buy a Lot of Things.
Pilgrims Came, The.
Thanksgiving Day.
Wynne, John Huddlestone
Horse and the Mule, The.
Time.
Wyse, Elizabeth
What big heavy doors! sel.

X

"Xariffa."   See Townsend, Mary Ashley
Xenos Palaestes
Requirements ("Not too pallid, as if bleacht").

Y

Ya Hsien
An Opera Songstress.
Common Song, A.
For Ch'iao.
Red Corns.
"Ya-Ka-Nes."   See Harjo, Patty L.
Yabu Kozan
Cowherd, The.
Yadoya Meshimori.   See Yadoyano
    Meshimori
Yadoyano Meshimori
Our poets had best.
When it comes to poets.

Yagi Jukichi
I first saw my face in a dream.
Yaguchi Kensai
End of Winter in a Mountain Village.
Yakamochi (Otomo no Yakamochi)
We were together.
Yakatsugu (Isonokami no Yakatsugu)
Rhyme-Prose on the Small Hills.
Yako, St. J. Page
Year's Ending, The.
Yalan-Shteklis, Miriam
Padlock your garden, my dear, sel.
Yamamoto, Traise
Biting Through.
Diving for Pearls.
In the Van Gogh Room.
Prelude: "Grace comes only after the long
    study of choice."
Yamanoue no Okura.   See Okura
Yamazaki Sokan.   See Sokan
Yamora, Daisy
Song of Hope.
Yanagawa Koran
Coming Home at Night in the Snow.
Yanagawa Seigan
Crier-to-Heaven.
You, whose ancestors in the mighty days.
Yang Chi
After my illness, so hard to be a traveler, sel.
Autumn season comes to the country, The,
    sel.
Describing My Feelings While Living in
    Retirement by the Riverside: Seven Poems
    to the Tune "Ch'ing-p'ing-yüeh."
Eastern neighbor, western neighbor, sel.
Five-Color.
I planned to get drunk to ease my sadness,
    sel.
I've given up poetry—I have no new
    manuscripts, sel.
Just a few feet away, a temple from the Six
    Dynasties, sel.
Meeting My Fellow Countryman, Yü
    Wu-chung.
Nesting among Clouds.
Noble Scholar Playing the Lute, A.
On Seeing a Firefly in My Room.
Painting of Bamboo by Ni Yün-lin, A.
Pitch-Ball, A.
Poem Making Fun of Chi-ti for His Eye
    Illness, A.
Poem on Passing by Hsin-k'ai Lake at
    Kao-yu, A.
Reflections in the river: trembling spring trees,
    sel.
Reviewing the Troops at Kuei-lin.
Selling My Official Robe.
Shut in behind the window, a glittering
    candle, sel.
Spring Dreams.
Springtime Embroidery, sel.
Studio for Listening to the Snow, The.
Submitting a Memorial Requesting Permission
    to Return Home and Care for My Parents.
Suddenly, warm weather, I change to lighter
    clothes, sel.
This place is near Hua-yang Mountain, sel.
This thatched hut, its master returned, sel.
Thousands of flowers, thousands of petals,
    sel.
Three feet of mud in this narrow alley, sel.
Up at the prow, I wash my mouth, dripping
    water on my robe, sel.
Walking in the Country outside T'ai-yüan on
    a Spring Day.
Wild singing and drunken dancing, sel.
Wu Shan-yang, sel.
You remove a jade pendant—to exchange for
    a lute, sel.
Your garden hut stands by the green waters,
    sel.

Yang Fang
Joy of Union, The.
Yang Kuei-fei
Dancing.
Yang Mu
Chi Tzu of Yen Ling Hangs Up His Sword.
Let the Wind Recite.
Loneliness.
MS. Found in a Bottle.
Night Song: How to Defend against Tree
    Shadows, A.
Somewhat.
Sonnet: "I want you to come rushing in the
    rain."
Sonnet: "I want you to come rushing in the
    wind."
Wine Vessels: Two Labels.
Yang Shen
To the Tune "Chao-chün's Sorrow."
To the Tune "Chiang ch'eng tzu."
To the Tune, "Chieh san ch'eng" ("I love the
    spring moon"), sel.
To the Tune "Child at Play."
To the Tune, "Ch'ing-p'ing Yüeh."
To the Tune "Flowers in the Rain."
To the Tune "Heavenly Immortal" ("I
    remember those years when we shared the
    joy of love").
To the Tune "Heavenly Immortal" ("Waves
    wash off the peach blossoms").
To the Tune "Moon Over West River."
To the Tune "New Moon."
To the Tune "Partridge Sky."
To the Tune "Song of the Plum Blossom at
    the River Town."
To the Tune "Spring in Tien Is Fine."
To the Tune "Stopping My Horse to Listen."
To the Tune "The Southerner."
To the Tune "Yellow Oriole" ("Threads of
    rain weave lambent light").
To the Tune "Yellow Oriole" ("Willows
    weave spring sorrow").
To the Tune "Yu hu-lu" ("I love the summer
    moon"), sel.
To the Tune "Yu hu-lu" ("I love the winter
    moon"), sel.
Yang Shih-ch'i
After the rain, the vegetables from your
    garden, sel.
Beyond the temple, a hidden cliff, sel.
Blue Mud Shoal, sel.
Crossing the River.
Dawn: Clear Skies.
Dragon-Tiger Terrace.
Enclosed with a Letter to My Family.
Eulogy on My Own Portrait, A.
Even ordinarily, parting is difficult, sel.
Evening of My Birthday, The.
False words of the Buddhists and Taoists,
    The, sel.
Following the Rhymes of Shao-pao Huang's
    Poem on Being Moved While Visiting the
    Farmers.
Forty li through Chü-yang Pass, sel.
Herdboy returns, none too early, The, sel.
I Was Received in an Early Audience at
    Heaven-Gate.
Inscribed on the Painting "Stabbing a Tiger"
    by Chao Tzu-ang.
I've drawn a salary in the capital for forty
    years now, sel.
Li Hsü of Ch'ien-chou is an old friend of
    mine, sel.
Liang Family Pool, sel.
Natural Stockade at Bamboo Lake, The, sel.
Night Rain: A Wall Collapses.
Night Rain beneath the City Walls of
    P'i-chou.
Not sobered up from my muddy Kao-yang
    drunk, sel.
On the Hall of Precious Virtue.
Palace of Prince Ma, The, sel.

Recording a Dream.
Red Heart Station.
Searching for the Ruins of the Pavilion of the Drunken Old Man.
Sha-ch'eng, "Sand City" ("In former years I passed this city.").
Sha-ch'eng, "Sand City" ("Overlooking the water, a desolate city").
Song of the Merchant's Wife.
White Stone Slope, *sel.*

Yang Tse
Somewhat in the Kingdom of His Majesty, No. 2.

Yang Wan-li
Cold Fly.
Keng-tzu (1180), First Month, Fifth Day, Dawn.
Relaxing in the Evening in My Study.
Sitting at Night on the Moonlit Terrace.

Yang Wei-chen
Bamboo Branch Song of the Seacoast.
Bamboo Branch Song of West Lake.
Horse-Watering Hole, The.
Horseman at the Roadside, The.
Man of Tao-his iron flute plays music, The, *sel.*
Painting Her Nails.
Residence of the Emperors of Ch'en, The.
Song of a Dream Journey over the Vast Sea.
Song of the Merchant's Wife.
Song of the Waterfall at Mount Lu.
Sun sets on Tung-t'ing's waves, *sel.*
This morning the air is fine for Ch'ing-ming, *sel.*
Tu-lu Poem ("Tu-lu, Tu-lu, evil waters running muddy.").
Willow catkins, white as cotton, *sel.*

Yannai
And It Came to Pass at Midnight.

Yao Nai
Government Pond, The.
Pavilion of the Infinite Heavens, The.
Temple in the Hills, A.

Ya'oz-kest, Itamar
Apples.
Children called, The, *sel.*
Flag on the house you dwelled in the wind blows now and then, The, *sel.*
Funeral, The, *sel.*
On the River Lookout.
Quarry.
Railway car, *sel.*
Shot, *sel.*
Suddenly a squeal, *sel.*
Yonder.

Yaso, Saijo. *See* **Saijo Yaso**

Yasu (Asada no Yasu)
Fujiwara no Nakamaro, Governor of Omi, Wrote a Poem on the Two Willows.

Yasuhara Teishitsu. *See* **Teishitsu**

Yasuhide (Bunya Yasuhide)
Grasses and trees, The.

Yates, J. Michael
Again and again I go away from you, *sel.*
I persist in a little fabric between me and the world, *sel.*
Legend : The god in the sun made two men, *sel.*
Wolves say to the dogs, The, *sel.*

Yates, John H.
Model Church, The.

Yates, L. E.
Strange Talk.

Yau, John
Broken Off by the Music.
Genghis Chan: Private Eye.
Instant Coffee.
January 18, 1979.
Kiss, The.
Shimmering Pediment.

Yazykov, N. M.
Elegy: "O money, money, tell me why."
Elegy: "People's wrath finds no expression, The."
Elegy: "Proud freedom's noble inspiration."
Song: "Pour one for me, friend good and true."
Thanksgiving.

Yearsley, Ann
To Mr. ———, an Unlettered Poet, on Genius Unimproved.

Yeatman, Jennette
Exile.

Yeatman, R. J. *and* **W. C. Sellar**
How I Brought the Good News from Aix to Ghent (or Vice Versa).

Yeats, William Butler
Acre of Grass, An.
Adam's Curse.
Aedh Thinks of Those Who Have Spoken Evil of His Beloved.
Aedh Wishes for the Cloths of Heaven.
After Long Silence.
All Things Can Tempt Me.
Among School Children.
An Old Man Stirs the Fire to a Blaze, *sel.*
Ancestral Houses, *sel.*
Apparitions, The.
At Galway Races.
At The Abbey Theatre (Imitated from Ronsard).
At the Grey Round of the Hill.
Ballad of Father Gilligan, The.
Before the World Was Made.
Beggar to Beggar Cried.
Black Tower, The.
Bronze Head, A.
Brown Penny.
Byzantium.
Cap and Bells, The.
Cast a cold eye, *sel.*
Cat and the Moon, The.
Chambermaid's Second Song, The.
Choice, The.
Chosen.
Church and State.
Circus Animals' Desertion, The.
Coat, A.
Cold Heaven, The.
Collarbone of a Hare, The.
Coming of Wisdom with Time, The.
Consolation.
Coole Park and Ballylee, 1931.
Coole Park, 1929.
Cradle Song, A: "Angels are bending, The."
Crazed Girl, The.
Crazy Jane and Jack the Journeyman.
Crazy Jane and the Bishop.
Crazy Jane Grown Old Looks at the Dancers.
Crazy Jane on God.
Crazy Jane on the Day of Judgment.
Crazy Jane on the Mountain.
Crazy Jane Reproved.
Crazy Jane Talks with the Bishop.
Cuchulain Comforted.
Curse of Cromwell, The.
Death.
Death of Cuchulain, The.
Deep-sworn Vow, A.
Dialogue of Self and Soul, A.
Dolls, The.
Down by the Salley Gardens.
Dream of Death, A.
Dreaming of the Bones, The, *sel.*
Drinking Song, A.
Easter, 1916.
Ego Dominus Tuus.
Ephemera.
Everlasting Voices, The.
Fallen Majesty.
Fascination of What's Difficult, The.
Fiddler of Dooney, The.

Fisherman, The.
Folly of Being Comforted, The.
For Anne Gregory.
Four Ages of Man, The.
Fragment: "Locke sank into a swoon."
Friends.
Great Day, The.
Gyres, The.
Hawk, The.
He Hears the Cry of the Sedge.
He Remembers Forgotten Beauty.
He Thinks of His Past Greatness When a Part of the Constellations of Heaven.
Host of the Air, The.
Hosting of the Sidhe, The.
How shall I name you, immortal, mild, proud shadows?
"I Am of Ireland."
I See Phantoms of Hatred and of the Heart's Fullness and of the Coming Emptiness, *sel.*
In Memory of Eva Gore-Booth and Con Markiewicz.
In Memory of Major Robert Gregory.
In the Seven Woods.
Indian upon God, The [*or* an].
Irish Airman Foresees His Death, An.
John Kinsella's Lament for Mrs. Mary Moore.
Lady's Third Song, The, *sel.*
Lake Isle of Innisfree, The.
Lamentation of the Old Pensioner, The.
Lapis Lazuli.
Last Confession, A.
Leaders of the Crowd, The.
Leda and the Swan.
Let All Things Pass Away.
Lines Written in Dejection.
Lonely the Sea-Bird Lies at Her Rest.
Long-legged Fly.
Lover Mourns for the Loss of Love, The.
Lover Tells of the Rose in His Heart, The.
Lullaby: "Beloved, may your sleep be sound."
Mad as the Mist and Snow.
Madness of King Goll, The.
Magi, The.
Man Who Dreamed of Faeryland, The.
Many ingenious lovely things are gone, *sel.*
Memory.
Meru.
Michael Robartes and the Dancer.
Michael Robartes Bids His Beloved Be at Peace.
Model for the Laureate, A.
Mohini Chatterjee.
Moods, The.
Municipal Gallery Revisited, The.
Must we part, Von Hügel, though much alike, *sel.*
My Descendants, *sel.*
My House, *sel.*
My Table, *sel.*
Never Give All the Heart.
New Faces, The.
News for the Delphic Oracle.
Nineteen Hundred and Nineteen.
Nineteenth Century and After, The.
No Second Troy.
Now shall I make my soul, *sel.*
Oil and Blood.
Old Men Admiring Themselves in the Water, The.
On a Political Prisoner.
On Being Asked for a War Poem.
On Hearing That the Students of Our New University Have Joined the Agitation against Immoral Literature.
On Those That Hated *The Playboy of the Western World.*
On Woman.
Pardon, old fathers, if you still remain, *sel.*
Parnell.
Parting.
Paudeen.

People, The.
Pilgrim, The.
Pity of Love, The.
Poet to His Beloved, A.
Politics.
Prayer for My Daughter, A.
Prayer for My Son, A.
Purgatory.
Ragged Wood, The.
Red Hanrahan's Song about Ireland.
Renowned Generations, The.
Reprisals.
Ribh Considers Christian Love Insufficient.
Road at My Door, The, sel.
Rose of the World, The.
Rose Tree, The.
Running to Paradise.
Sad Shepherd, The.
Sailing to Byzantium.
Scholars, The.
Second Coming, The.
Secret Rose, The.
September 1913.
Seven Sages, The.
Sixteen Dead Men.
Solomon and the Witch.
Solomon to Sheba.
Some moralist or mythological poet, sel.
Song of the Happy Shepherd, The.
Song of the Old Mother, The.
Song of Wandering Aengus, The.
Song: "Woman's beauty is like a white, A,"
    sel.
Sorrow of Love, The.
Spilt Milk.
Spur, The.
Stare's Nest by My Window, The, sel.
Statesman's Holiday, The.
Statues, The.
Stolen Child, The.
Swift's Epitaph.
Symbols.
That the Night Come.
Those Images.
Thought from Propertius, A.
Three Hermits, The.
Three Movements.
Three Things.
To a Friend Whose Work Has Come to
    Nothing.
To a Poet, Who Would Have Me Praise
    Certain Bad Poets, Imitators of His and
    Mine.
To a Shade.
To a Squirrel at Kyle-na-no.
To a Young Beauty.
To a Young Girl.
To an Isle in the Water.
To Be Carved on a Stone at Thoor Ballylee.
To Ireland in the Coming Times.
To the Rose upon the Rood of Time.
Tom O'Roughley.
Tower, The.
Travail of Passion, The.
Two Songs from a Play, sel.
Two Songs of a Fool.
Two Trees, The.
Under Ben Bulben.
Upon a Dying Lady.
Upon a House Shaken by the Land Agitation.
Vacillation.
Valley of the Black Pig, The.
Wanderings of Oisin, The.
We galloped over the glossy sea, sel.
What Then?
Wheel, The.
When Helen Lived.
When You Are Old.
Whence Had They Come?
Where My Books Go.
White Birds, The.
Who Goes with Fergus?

Wicked Hawthorn Tree, The.
Wild Old Wicked Man, The.
Wild Swans at Coole, The.
Wind Blows out of the Gates of the Day,
    The, sel.
Wisdom.
Youth and Age.

**"Yehoash" (Solomon Bloomgarden [or
    Blumgarten])**
At the Tomb of Rachel.
Harp of David, The.
Hunting.
Jephthah's Daughter.
Mystery.
Old Song, An.
Prayer, A: "Eternal God, our life is but."
Prophet, The.
Psalm: "Happy is the man whom Thou hast
    set apart."
Shadows.
Song, A: "Song of grass, A,/ A song of
    earth."
Song as Yet Unsung, A.
Strongest, The.
Terror.
Thanksgiving.
That Is All I Heard.
Tool of Fate, The.
Wanderer, The.
Withered Rose, A.
Yang-Se-Fu.

Yellen, Samuel
Personal.

Yen Hsüan
Beautiful Lady Yü, The.
Eight-beat Barbarian Tune.
Immortal at the River.
River Messages.
Sand of Silk-Washing Stream.

Yenser, Stephen
Ember Week, Reseda.

Yeo, Marg
Getting Wise.
Jumping into Joy.
Siren Song.

Yerby, Frank
Calm after Storm.
Fishes and the Poet's Hands, The.
Weltschmerz.
Wisdom.
You Are a Part of Me.

Yeshurun, Avot
Poem on Our Mother, Our Mother Rachel,
    The.
Poem on the Guilt, The.
Poem on the Jews, The.

Yevtushenko, Yevgeny
Birthday.
Colors.
People.
Under the dawn I wake my two-wheel friend,
    sel.
Waiting.

Yi Shun-ting
Dawn Journey.
Leaving the Mountains in the Rain from
    Yellow Dragon Temple.
Passing the Bridge of Immortal Encounter
    Looking for the Sublime Ascent Temple.

Yin O
Apricot Garden in Blossom.
Deva-like Barbarian.
Drunken Gentleman, The.
Flowers Fill the Palace.
Immortal at the River.

Yin Shih
Parting from the Courtier Sung.

Yip Wai-lim
From Old Mrs. Mo of Heng Yang: A Letter
    to My Son, Lo Fu.
Resounding Wall, The.

Story of Wildflowers, The.
Voice of Blooming, The.
Waking Up: A Song.

Yitzchok Leibush Peretz. See **Peretz, Isaac
    Leibush**

Yoldugu
It would be very pleasant to die with a wolf
    woman.

Yolen, Jane
Bluffalo, The.
Caliban's Song.
Death of a Unicorn.
Fossilot, The.
Grandpa Bear's Lullaby.
Homework.
Icarus.
Metamorphosis.
Mother Cat's Purr.
Neptune Rising.

Yomono Akara
Blind-drunk/ New Year caller, A.
Season greeter, The.
Young fiddlehead ferns, The.

Yonathan, Nathan
And the Silver Turns into Night.
Another Poem on Absalom.
South Wind.

Yooku
Stone mortar rushes through the air, The.

York, Eva Rose
I Shall Not Pass This Way Again.

York, Sarah E.
I Am Weary of Straying.

Yosa Buson. See **Buson (Yosa Buson)**

Yosano Akiko
After throwing a parasol to the grass, sel.
Another look like his mixed me up again, sel.
As I am unhappy.
As I wait for you in the grass with lilies, sel.
"At least, at least in his dreams"—so
    thinking, sel.
"At least let it burn just as it burns!"—that
    way I feel, sel.
Bird comes, A/ delicately as a little girl.
Black hair.
Camellia, yes, and plum, yes, sel.
"Can't say that now, you have little spring",
    sel.
For some reason I thought you'd be waiting
    for me, sel.
Girl, twenty—her black hair, The, sel.
Hair, five feet long, sel.
Having changed my tangled hair into Shimada
    style, sel.
Hugging my breasts I lightly kick, sel.
I bathe and step out of the Spring, sel.
I can give myself to her.
"I don't want to take a beautiful bud," said
    the god, sel.
"I must go now, goodbye," said the god of
    night, sel.
I won't let you go, this spring evening turns
    dark, sel.
In my bath.
In the spring dusk I find our next-door
    painter, sel.
Just one room away, from time to time you
    sighed, sel.
Labour Pains.
No camellia.
Not even trying to touch the hot blood-tide,
    sel.
Not speaking of the Way, sel.
Our friend's feet were cold the morning we
    set out, sel.
Saying nothing, asking nothing, sel.
Shall I receive the spring rain dripping on
    swallow wings, sel.
Sliding down two feet of my gossamer sleeve,
    sel.
Spring is short.

"Spring is short! Who says our life's immortal?" I said, *sel.*
Sutra is sour, The.
"The three of us are relatives not doing well", *sel.*
This evening rainfall is merciful, *sel.*
To Kiyomizu, through Gion, *sel.*
To smear poisoned honey on my lips, *sel.*
Wave of coldness, A.
Way morning looks in the plum valley, The, *sel.*
When I reflect on it now, *sel.*
Who shall I tell of the color rouge?, *sel.*
With your other hand support me, *sel.*
Wondering, I touched it with my young lips, *sel.*
Yesterday feels like a thousand years ago, *sel.*
You are ill; let me put my slender arm, *sel.*
You never touch.
"You picked a white chrysanthemum and smiled", *sel.*
You think of him, and so do I; our hearts, *sel.*

Yoshida no Kenko. *See* **Kenko**

Yoshihara Sachiko
Madness.

Yoshimoto (Nijo Yoshimoto)
As the night deepens.
As the old year ends.
In the light of dawn.
In the morning mist.
In the setting sunlight.
Now at long last.
Storm at a House in the Hills, A.

Yoshinobu (Onakatomi Yoshinobu)
Fires lit by the guards, The.
On Evergreen Hill.

Yoshioka Minoru
Coolie.
Holy Girl.
Lilac Garden.
Negative.
Ode to an Old Man.
Past, The.
Pastorale: "Wheels fall innumerably."
Quiet House.
Still Life.

Yoshiro, Ishihara. *See* **Ishihara Yoshiro**

Yoshitada (Sone Yoshitada)
Like a boatman.

Yoshitsune (Fujiwara no Yoshitsune)
Cicada shrieks, The.
No man lives now.

Young, Al
Birthday Poem.
Blues Don't Change, The.
"Boogie with O. O. Gabugah."
Dance for Ma Rainey, A.
Dance for Militant Dilettantes, A.
Dance of the Infidels.
Dancer, The.
Dear Old Stockholm.
For Poets.
Ho.
Identities.
Intimacy.
Kiss.
Lemons, Lemons.
Lester Leaps In.
Loneliness.
Lonesome in the Country.
Moon Watching by Lake Chapala.
Move Continuing, The.
Myself When I Am Real.
Ocean Springs Mississippy, *sel.*
Old O. O. Blues, The.
One West Coast.
Ponce de León: A Morning Walk.
Visiting Day.
W. H. Auden & Mantan Moreland.
Yes, the Secret Mind Whispers.

Young, Andrew
At Arley.
Ba Cottage.
Beauty and Love.
Bee-Orchis, The.
Beech, The.
Black Rock of Kiltearn.
Christmas Day.
Climbing in Glencoe.
Cuckoo.
Cuckoos.
Culbin Sands.
Daisies.
Dead Bird, The.
Dead Crab, The.
Dead Mole, A.
Dead Sheep, The.
Dundonnel Mountains.
Eagle, The.
Echoing Cliff, The.
Fairy Ring, The.
Fallen Tree, The.
Falls of Glomach, The.
Field-Glasses.
Go Now, My Song.
Hard Frost.
Hymn: "Lord, by whose breath all souls and seeds are living."
In December.
In Teesdale.
Last Snow.
Loch Luichart.
Man and Cows.
Mist.
Nightfall on Sedgemoor.
Old Tree, The.
On Middleton Edge.
On the Ridgeway.
Paps of Jura, The.
Prospect of a Mountain.
Round Barrow, The.
Scarecrow, The.
Sheaf, The.
Shepherd's Hut, The.
Snow Harvest.
Song for Autumn.
Stay, Spring.
Suilven.
Wiltshire Downs.
Young Martins, The.

Young, Augustus
Advice of an Efficiency Expert, The.
After Five Years.
Ballad of Fat Margot.
Elegy for a School-Friend.
Heritage.
Last Refuge, The.
Woman, Don't Be Troublesome.

Young, Barbara
I Hear It Said.
World, The.

Young, Clifford
Dominatrix.

Young, David
August at the Lake.
Boxcar Poem, The ("The boxcars drift by").
Death of the Novel, The.
"It's a Whole World, the Body. A Whole World!"—Swami Satchidandanda.
Mandelstam.
Thoughts of Chairman Mao.

Young, Douglas
Caller rain frae abune.
Deid sall ye ligg, and ne'er a memorie.
For a Wife in Jizzen.
Ice-Flumes Owregie Their Ladies.
Last Lauch.
Minnie, I canna caa my wheel.
Steekit, consecrat, fou o fire but fuel, *sel.*
Winter Homily on the Calton Hill.

Young, Edith Lillian
Disappointment—His Appointment.

Young, Edward (1683–1765)
Britannia's daughters, much more fair than nice, *sel.*
Consolation, The, *sel.*
Epigram on Voltaire.
How poor, how rich, how abject, how august, *sel.*
Infidel Reclaimed, The, *sel.*
Life is the desert, life the solitude, *sel.*
Live ever here, Lorenzo?—shocking thought!, *sel.*
Love of praise, howe'er concealed by art, The, *sel.*
One to destroy, is murder by the law.
See commons, peers, and ministers of state, *sel.*
Since Brunswick's smile has authoris'd my muse, *sel.*
These all their care expend on outward show, *sel.*
These labouring wits, like paviours, mend our ways, *sel.*
Thy nature, immortality! who knows?, *sel.*
Tired nature's sweet restorer, balmy Sleep!, *sel.*
Where dwells that wish most ardent of the wise?, *sel.*
Where, thy true treasure? Gold says, "Not in me,", *sel.*
With what, O Codrus! is thy fancy smit?, *sel.*

Young, Edward (b. 1818)
Under the Violets.

Young, Ella
Unicorn, The.

Young, Francis Brett
Atlantic Charter, A.D. 1620-1942.
Atlantic Charter: 1942.
Bête Humaine.
Seascape.

Young, Gary
To Raise a Chimney.

Young, Geoffrey
Rocks and Deals.

Young, George W.
Lips That Touch Liquor.

Young, Ian
At Rochdale.
Double Exposure.
Elephants from the Sea.
Honi Soit Qui Mal Y Pense.
It's no good/ being an actor.
Skull, The.
Sugar-Candy Bird, A.

Young, Jim
Latest Diet, The.

Young, Marguerite
Angels, The.
Death by Rarity.
Noah's Ark.
Speculative Evening.
Whales, The.
Winter Scene.

Young, Ree
Blue Springs, Georgia.
Storyteller, The.

Young, Roland
Flea, The.
Pig, The.

Young, Virginia Brady
Teacher, The.

Young, William
Bells, The, *sel.*
Bridal Pair, The, *sel.*
Conscience-Keeper, The, *sel.*
Flower-Seller, The, *sel.*
Judith.
Pawns, The, *sel.*
Philomel to Corydon.

Young Bear, Ray A.
Another Face.
Before the Actual Cold.

Black Dog.
Celebration.
Coming Back Home.
Cook, The.
Crow-Children Walk My Circles in the Snow,
  The.
Differences.
Emily Dickinson, Bismarck and the
  Roadrunner's Inquiry.
Empty Streams of Autumn.
First Dimension of Skunk, The.
From the Spotted Night.
Grandmother.
I am walking and I.
In Dream: The Privacy of Sequence.
In Missing.
In the First Place of My Life.
King Cobra as Political Assassin, The.
Language of Weather, The.
Last Dream, The.
Listening Rock, The.
My reflection.
Nothing Could Take Away the Bear-King's
  Image.
One Chip of Human Bone.
Personification of a Name, The.
Place of O, The.
Place of V, The.
Poem for Diane Wakoski, A.
Poem for Viet Nam.
Race of the Kingfishers.
Remembrance of a Color inside a Forest, A.
Rushing.
Significance of a Water Animal, The.
Star Blanket.
These Horses Came.
This House.
This little house swallows.
Through the cracks.
Trains Made of Stone.
Wadasa Nakamoon, Vietnam Memorial.
Waiting to Be Fed.
War Walking Near.
Warrior Dreams.
Way the Bird Sat, The.
What We Can.
Wrong Kind of Love.

Youngblood, Sarah
At the Western Shore.
Walking the Beach.

Yü Chi
After Snow-Impromptu.
Following the Rhymes of "Autumn Night
  Song" by Meng Tzu-chou.
Following the Rhymes of Bamboo Branch
  Songs.
Getting on Horseback.
Going to the Ministry with Chao Tzu-ch'i.
Hearing Loom and Shuttle.
Inscribed on a Painting.
Inscribed on the Painting "Solitary Crane."
Late in the Year K'uei-yu.
Little Landscape by Chao Ch'ien-li, A.
Little Landscape by Yen Wen-kuei, A.
Sent to Be Inscribed on the Temple of
  P'u-jun.
Sitting Alone in the Courtyard.
Traveling Early through a Snowy Valley.
What Family?
When I Was Young, I Stopped by a Wine
  Shop in Chi-men.

Yü Hsüan-chi
Advice to a Neighbour Girl.
Answering Li Ying Who Showed Me His
  Poems about Summer Fishing.
At the End of Spring.
Boudoir Lament.
Composed on the Theme "Willows by the
  Riverside."
On a Visit to Ch'ung Chen Taoist Temple.
Poem to the Tune "Riverbank Willows."
Regretful Thoughts.

Rhyming a Friend's Poem.
Rhyming with a Friend.
Sending Spring Love to Tzu-An.
Sent to Wen T'ing-yün on a Winter Night.
Staying in the Mountains in Summer.
To the Minister Liu.

Yü Hu
Thoughts South of the Yangtze.

Yu Kuang-chung
After My Fiftieth Birthday.
An Old Woman in Mongkok.
Cricket and the Machine Gun, The.
Kowloon-Canton Railway, The.
Nostalgia.
Pine Waves.
Sea Offerings.
To a Painter.
White Jade Bitter Melon.

Yu T'ung
Autumn Night, An.
Bananas.
Burning Incense.
Desultory Thoughts on My Old Home.
On Hearing the Chukar.

Yü Wu-ling
Offering Wine.

Yüan Chen
Airing Painful Memories.
Pitcher, The.
Song of the Weaving Woman.

Yüan Hung-tao
Climbing Mount Yang.
Eastern mountains/ and western mountains,
  sel.
On Board a Boat at Chi-ning.
On Receiving My Letter of Termination.
Pei-mang Cemetery.
Record of My Trip to Mount She, A.
"Slowly, Slowly" Poem, The.
Twenty-first Day of the Seventh Month.
Woman's Room in Autumn, A.

Yüan Mei
After half a minute of conversation, *sel.*
Arriving at Hangchou.
As I grow old, and weaker grow my eyes,
  sel.
Ballad of Peach Blossom Spring.
Bird in flight parts from the old wood, The,
  sel.
Busy.
Climbing T'ai Mountain.
Delerium: Jesting at Illness.
Do not say that time once gone can never be
  returned!
Eyes, nose, ears, mouth and mind, *sel.*
Finding Serenity.
Flowers will arrive with spring, *sel.*
Flying Bells.
Fog at Liang-hsiang.
For My Wife: A Poem Written in Sickness.
Happy about Being Old.
I gaze at this, my hometown, *sel.*
I Know Inside.
I write characters in lamplight, *sel.*
In building houses, I'm content with few, *sel.*
In Early Years.
Joy and rage are not caused by things, *sel.*
Leaving My Post to Retire at the Sui Garden.
Long robes, or short, *sel.*
Ma-wei.
Mad Words.
Miscellaneous Feelings in the Sui Garden.
Mocking Spectacles.
Money.
My whole family floats out on the lake, *sel.*
Next Day the Fog Was Even Worse, The.
Night of the Fifteenth, Second Month.
Of all the famous Hangchou sights, *sel.*
Of my flesh and blood, only one remains, *sel.*
Old habits it seems cannot be swept away,
  sel.

Old house from my childhood, The, *sel.*
On the Twenty-First Day of the Fifth Month,
  I Reached Home.
On the Way to Pa-ling.
Once again to see West Lake!
One morning I call for a sedan-chair man, *sel.*
Only Be Willing to Search for Poetry.
Peonies below the stairs, The, *sel.*
Praising Spectacles.
Rain Passes.
Rains Pass.
Returning Home.
Rough Ridge.
Self-Ridicule.
Sleeplessness.
Things Seen.
Things Seen on Spring Days.
Three magnolias, identical, *sel.*
Willow Flowers.
Words from the Goblet of Wisdom.
Writing My Feelings.
Written at the Graveside.
You mustn't laugh at my tall tower, *sel.*

Yubai Sesson. *See* **Sesson Yubai**

Yud, Nachum
Like the Eyes of Wolves.

Yugo
After their bells stopped.

Yuji, Kinoshita. *See* **Kinoshita Yuji**

Yukihira (Ariwara no Yukihira)
I must depart now.
Robe of mist, The.

Yumei, Kambara. *See* **Kambara Yumei**

Yün-feng, Sun
Starting at Dawn.

Yün Shou-p'ing
As old age approaches, *sel.*
As we say farewell to autumn, *sel.*
Autumn Plants, Flowers, Bamboo, Rocks.
Brush in rocks, draw a stream, *sel.*
Early Summer in the Year Jen-tzu.
Early Summer, *Jen-tzu* Year, in Playful
  Imitation of Ts'ao Yün-hsi.
Essence of ink, The, *sel.*
Facing you, on the wall, across from your
  bed, *sel.*
For a hundred miles the west wind carries the
  fragrance of millet, *sel.*
Green Banana Leaves.
Hearing a Flute at Broken Bridge.
Humming My Verse, in My Leisure, beneath
  Blossoming Cassia Trees.
I listen to a waterfall, *sel.*
In a hidden spot on the northern mountain,
  sel.
Inscibed on a Painting of Sailboats on the
  River.
Inscribed on a Painting ("Magic mists twirl
  around the sky").
Inscribed on a Painting ("Who needs a raft
  that can invade the stars?").
Inscribed on a Snowscape.
Inscription for a Painting, An: "A Forest in
  the Frost."
Lament for the Willows outside the City
  Walls, A.
Nature's workings made this gentle place, *sel.*
On a Landscape by Myself.
On a Painting "Ancient Trees and Flowing
  Stream."
On a Painting of Mushrooms.
Painting in the Style of Secretary Kao, A.
Painting of Chrysanthemums in the Boneless
  Style of Hsü Ch'ung-ssu, A.
Painting of Yams, A.
Picture of Village Happiness, A.
Sadness in the Autumn Chambers.
Scorpion's tails, silver hooks, *sel.*
Through the windy valley, *sel.*
Tree and Boulder.
War ships, cold tides, *sel.*

Waterside Village.
Written on the Night of the Twenty-ninth of
   the First Month.
Yung Tzu
Ch'ing-ming Nostalgia.
World of Verna Lisa, The.
Yungman, Moshe
Don't Say.
Encounter in Safed.
Melons.
Messiah, The.
Sacrifice, The.
Yuson, Alfred A.
Midlandfall.
Yusuf, Sa'di
As though you never lived, *sel.*
Departure of '82.
Electricity.
Elegy: The Woods.
Exhaustion.
Fighting Position, A.
Flying.
Guns.
Hamra Night.
Hot Evening, A.
Last train to Barcelona, The, *sel.*
Resurrection.
Room, A.
Sentiment.
State of Fever, A.
Water.
Why does your name continue, *sel.*
Woman, A.
Yuwaku
I think about you & it's like having spirits
   come down on me.
Yuzan
What's life? What's death?
Yvonne
Deborah Lee.
Emma.
Little Girl Blue.
Where She Was Not Born.

Z

"Z., Z."
Here lies a poet—where's the great surprise!
Zabel, Morton Dauwen
Journal to Stella.
Zabolotsky, Nikolai Alekseevich
Face of the Horse, The.
Thistle.
Walk, A.
Zach, Natan
Against Parting.
Against Sadness.
As Sand.
Death Came for Michael Rockinghorse.
Foreign Country, A.
Give Me What the Tree Has.
Harvest Month.
How the Days Passed. Who.
I Hear Something Falling.
In the Course of Time.
In This Deep Darkness ("In this deep heavy
   darkness").
Like Sand.
Listening to Her.
Max Is Dead.
Nameless.
No.
Painter Paints, The.
Peaceful Song, A.
Perhaps It's Only Music.
Poem Too Late, A.
Problem, The.

Prologue to a Poem.
Quiet Light of Flies, The.
Samson's Hair.
Short Winter Tale, A.
Soft Warm Breeze, A.
To Be a Master in Your House.
War Confession.
When God First Said.
When the Last Riders.
Zafar. *See* **Bahadur Shah Zafar**
Zagajewski, Adam
Freedom.
I Talked to a Frenchman.
Verses about Poland.
Zaidi, Mustafa
Life!/ I came to your door like a beggar, *sel.*
Lights were drowned in fog, The, *sel.*
Madhouse.
Vietnam.
Zamora, Bernice
Bearded Lady.
California.
Cat Poem.
Final Dance, The.
Having Drowned.
Notes from a Chicana "COED."
Penitents.
Sonnet, Freely Adapted, for J. R. S.
When We Are Able.
Zamora, Daisy
Letter to a Sister Who Lives in a Distant
   Country.
When We Return.
Zamudio, Adela
Manhood.
To Be Born Male.
Zana
Broken.
Zand, Herbert
Continually.
Gardener, The.
I Have a Wild Desire to Die.
My Poor Exploited Language.
Pain.
Waiting.
Zangwill, Israel
At the Worst.
At the Zoo.
Death's Transfiguration.
Despair and Hope.
Dreams.
Evolution.
In the City.
In the Morgue.
Inexhaustible.
Israel.
Jehovah.
"Might Is Right."
Moses and Jesus.
Seder-Night.
Sundered.
Tabernacle Thought, A.
Theodor Herzl.
To a Pretty Girl.
Vanitas Vanitatum.
Vision.
Why Do We Live?
Yom Kippur.
Zanzotto, Andrea
Ecolgue IV.
From a New Height.
Lorna Slope.
Perfection of Snow, The.
September 13, 1959 (Variation).
Subnarcosis.
To the World.
Zapata, Santiago Mendes. *See* **Mendes**
   Zapata, Santiago
Zappi, Faustina Maratti
To Her Little Son Rinaldo When Sick.

Zaranka, William
Conceit upon the Feet.
Continuation of *The Cook's Tale*, The.
Cropdusting, The.
Cry of the Child, The.
High-toned Old Fascist Gentleman, A.
In the Ladies' Room at the Bus Terminal.
Lovers' Debouchment.
Memories of Aunt Maria-Martha.
Ode: "Mistah Berrybones, you daid?"
Parachuting Thoor Ballylee.
Peruke of Poets.
Quicksands.
Ragout.
Robert Frost's Left-leaning *Trespassers Will*
   Be Shot Sign.
Zarathustra. *See* **Zoroaster**
Zarco, Cyn
Emergency Poem 1973.
Flipochinos.
Lolo died yesterday.
Nights.
Poem in Nueva York.
Saxophonetyx.
Teaching Poetry.
What the Rooster Does before Mounting.
Zarzyski, Paul
Dear Mom.
Zaturenska, Marya Alexandrovna (Mrs.
   Horace Gregory)
Bird and the Muse.
Daisy, The.
Descent of the Vulture, The.
Head of Medusa.
Lovers, The.
Tempest, The.
Variations on a Theme by George Herbert.
White Dress, The.
Woman at the Piano.
Zäunemann, Sidonie Hedwig
Maid's Fortune, A.
Zauq, Sheikh Ibrahim
Hard it was for this garden soil.
If you killed a helpless being, O cruel one.
Since life had brought us we had come.
Weary with life we long for death.
Zavatsky, Bill
Bald.
Ex-Poet, The.
Testament.
Zayyad, Tawfiq
Before Their Tanks.
Here We Will Stay.
Pagan Fires.
Passing Remark.
Salman.
They Know.
Zeb-un-Nissa, Princess
Though I am Laila of the Persian romance.
Zehrd
Woman Cleaning Lentils, The.
Zeidler, Susanna Elisabeth
Verification of the Poetic Talents of Young
   Maidens.
Zeidner, Lisa
Still.
Zeiger, L. L.
Fish, The.
Snack, The.
Zeiger, Lila
Clerihew: "Said Jean Arp's wife to Mary
   Martin."
Clerihew: "When Georges Seurat."
River Rhyme.
Zeitlin, Aaron
Dream about an Aged Humorist, A.
Empty Apartment, The.
Ode to Freedom.
Six Lines.
Ten Groschen.
Text.

To Be a Jew.
Twelve Autumn Lines.
Zeitlin, Israel. *See* **Tiempo, Cesar**
Zekkai Chushin
Impromptu Poem in Yün-chien.
Zelazny, Roger
Dreamscape.
I Used to Think in Lines That Were Irregular
to the Right.
"Zelda" (Zelda Mishkovsky)
Acacia Tree, The.
An Enchanted Bird.
Here's a Woman Lived to an Extreme Old
Age.
I Stood in Jerusalem.
In the Dry Riverbed.
Moon Is Teaching Bible, The.
Wicked Neighbor, The.
With My Grandfather.
"Zelda" (Zelda Schneurson)
Black Rose.
Faint Echo.
Light a Candle.
Merry Imagination, The.
Zeldis, Chayyim
Holy Ones, the Young Ones, The.
Zelk, Zoltán
Alone.
And And.
Cry.
Echo.
Man Falling.
Moment.
More Powerful than the Sea.
October.
Petrified Minute.
Salt and Memory.
Way, The.
Zenchiku, Komparu. *See* **Komparu**
Zenchiku
Zengetsu
Mind, mind, mind—above the Path, *sel.*
Zerbe, Evelyn Arcad
In Memory of My Arab Grandmother.
Zerubavel Gilead
Pomegranate Tree in Jerusalem ("The
pomegranate tree in my garden adorns
itself").
Zetsuzo
Flying Snow Rock.
Zhukovsky, V. A.
Friendship.
March 19, 1823.
Night.
Remembrance.
Song: "Enchantment of my past existence."
Song: "Ring of my true lover, The."
Ziegler, Christiana Mariana von
In Praise of the Male Sex, As Seen by Certain
Females.

Zieroth, Dale
Baptism.
Beautiful Woman.
Hunters of the Deer, The.
Ziety, Ann
O.K.
Zimmer, Paul
Apple Blight.
Blues for Old Dogs.
Day Zimmer Lost Religion, The.
Great Bird of Love over the Kingdom, The.
Julian Barely Misses Zimmer's Brains.
Lester Tells of Wanda and the Big Snow.
Lord Fluting Dreams of America on the Eve
of His Departure from Liverpool.
Phineas Within and Without.
Place, The.
Rollo's Miracle.
Visit from Alphonse, A.
What Zimmer Would Be.
When Angels Came to Zimmer.
Zimmer and His Turtle Sink the House.
Zimmer Drunk and Alone, Dreaming of Old
Football Games.
Zimmer to His Students.
Zimmer's Head Thudding against the
Blackboard.
Zimmer's Street.
Zimmershire Lad, A.
Zimroth, Evan
Front Porch: A Drama Critic Warns of
Clichés.
Planting Children: 1939.
Separations.
Zimunya, Musaemura Bonus
Climbers.
Fighter.
Mountain, The.
Revolution.
To a Detainee.
Zinzendorf, Nikolaus Ludwig, Graf von
For Us No Night Can Be Happier.
Jesu, to Thee My Heart I Bow.
On Earth There Is a Lamb So Small.
Slain Lamb of God.
Zisquit, Linda
Circumcision, The.
Rachel's Lament.
Sabbatical.
Zitz-Halein, Kathinka
Change of Color.
Jeanne Manon Philipon-Roland.
Zolotow, Charlotte
Look.
Missing You.
Moment in Summer, A.
People.
Riddle, A: "Once when I was very scared."
River Winding.
Sandpiper, The.

Spring Wind, The.
Top and the Tip, The.
Zolynas, Al
New Physics, The.
Sailing.
Zoroaster
Sacred Book, The, *at.*
Zosu, Taikyoku. *See* **Taikyoku Zosu**
Zotan
Woodcutter's Hut.
Yomyo Stupa, The.
"Zozimus." *See* **Moran, Michael**
Zuckmayer, Carl
My Death.
Zuiderent, Ad
Appealing to the Imagination.
Gesture of Understanding.
House on the River.
Return to Solitude.
Zuigan
When Master Ungo asked.
Zukofsky, Louis
"A 11" ("River that must turn full after I stop
dying."), *sel.*
"A 4" ("Giant sparkler,/ Lights of the river."),
sel.
Azure.
Blue light is the night harbor-slip, *sel.*
Cars Once Steel and Green, Now Old.
1892-1941.
Expounding the Torah.
From the Head.
Green Leaf that will outlast the winter.
I walk in the old street.
It's hard to see but think of a sea.
Lines of this new song are nothing, The.
Non Ti Fidar.
Not much more than being, *sel.*
Of Dying Beauty.
Ways, The.
Zumpf, Peter
Beginning/ each day.
Neatly/ and well/ ordered.
Quietly/ just for himself.
Tell me,/ you visited.
Zussman, Ezra
At Dante's Grave.
Last, The.
Zweig, Paul
Father.
Zweig, Stefan
Chosen of God, *sel.*
Flowering Without End, *sel.*
Zwicky, Fay
Chosen—Kalgoorlie, 1894, The.
Summer Pogrom.
Zychlinska, Rayzel
Clothes, The.
My Mother's Shoes.
Remembering Lutsky.

SUBJECT INDEX

Entries in the Subject Index contain one or more of the following types of information: first, poems are listed that fall within the particular subject category (for example, **Fireflies***); second, in many cases anthologies are listed that in whole or in part focus on the subject in question; third, anthologies that are mainly translations into English are listed under their appropriate countries or languages; fourth, there may be cross-references to related subjects.*

The categories here range from specific (for example, persons) to general (for example, abstractions such as **Separation***). Some categories, such as* **Love** *are so broad that we have used them only to list anthologies.*

Aachen, Germany
  Aix-La-Chappelle, 1945. Bowers
Aardvarks
  Aardvark, The. Logue
Aaron
  Aaron. Herbert
Abandonment
  Abandoned, The. N'Ait Attik
  Ah Wretched Me, Who Loved a Sparrow
    Hawk. *Unknown*
  Airly Beacon. Kingsley
  Cooking Eggs. Smith
  Cumnor Hall. Mickle
  Death of the Kapowsin Tavern. Hugo
  Empty Backstreet in a Small Southern Town.
    Hummer
  Havana Blues. Carlile
  House on 15th S.W., The. Hugo
  I Dreamt You Went. Freistadt
  John Kinsella's Lament for Mrs. Mary Moore.
    Yeats
  Lady of Miracles. Cassian
  Montana Ranch Abandoned. Hugo
  Presences. Justice
  Rubaiyat for Sue Ella Tucker. Williams
  Second Year, The. Montgomery
  Speaking of Loss. Clifton
  Traveler, The. Mathis
  Valley Blood. Sternlieb
  With a Ring. Porumbacu
Abbey Theatre, Dublin
  At The Abbey Theatre (Imitated from
    Ronsard). Yeats
  Old Woman, Outside the Abbey Theater, An.
    Strong
Abbeys. *See* **Monasteries.**
Abel. *See* **Cain and Abel.**
Abelard and Heloise
  Eloïsa to Abelard. Pope
  Heloise. Frabotta
  Sic et Non. Read
Aberdeen, Scotland
  To Aberdein. Dunbar
Abishag
  Abishag. Glatstein
  Abishag. Spire
Abolitionists
  Douglass. Dunbar
  Runagate Runagate. Hayden
  To W. L. G. on Reading His "Chosen Queen.
    Forten
Aborigines
  Aborigine. Williams

  Bora Ring. Wright
  We Are Going. Walker
Abortion
  Abortion. Ai
  Abortion, The. Sexton
  Abortion, The. Sexton
  Cold Front, A. Williams
  Epitaph on a Child Killed by Procured
    Abortion. *Unknown*
  Illegal Operation, The. Conrad
  Inquest, The. Davies
  Lost Baby Poem, The. Clifton
  Mother, The. Brooks
Abraham
  Abraham. Schwartz
  Abraham and Isaac. Lasker-Schüler
  Abraham and Sarah. Manger
  Abraham in Egypt. Schwartz
  Hagar Leaves Abraham's House. Manger
  Harlot's Catch. Nichols
  Parable of the Old Man and the Young, The.
    Owen
  Sacrifice, The. Bloch
  Sacrifice. Leivick
  Story of Abraham and Hagar, The. Aphek
Absalom
  Absalom. Wallach
  Another Poem on Absalom. Yonathan
  Dispraise of Absalom, The. *Unknown*
  Samson's Hair. Zach
Absence
  Absence. Hoskyns
  Absence. Jago
  Absence. Knies
  Absence. McKay
  Absence. Mew
  Absence, The. Warner
  Alone. De la Mare
  Another Time. Bernstein
  Banks of Claudy, The. *Unknown*
  Birthday. Winkler
  Celadyne's Song. *Fr.* Britannia's Pastorals.
    Browne
  Daisy, The. Tennyson
  Elinda's Glove. Lovelace
  Ellen Taylor. *Unknown*
  For Anne. Cohen
  From the age of the gods. *Fr.* Manyo Shu.
    Kogyoku
  Girl I Left behind Me, The. *Unknown*
  Hello, Hello. Matthews
  Her Going. Kaufman
  Here Awa', There Awa'. *Unknown*
  Hush. St. John

  I could not save the heart. Mir
  I Live Not Where I Love. *Unknown*
  If I Had but Two Little Wings. Coleridge
  Lady Prayeth the Return of Her Lover
    Abiding on the Seas, The. *Unknown*
  Lamenting Maid, The. *Unknown*
  Late Light. Blunden
  "Like as the culver on the bared bough." *Fr.*
    Amoretti. Spenser.
  Love-Letter One. *Unknown*
  Love-Letter Two. *Unknown*
  Million, A. Ratosh
  Never the Time and the Place. Browning
  Out of Sight, Out of Mind. Googe
  Presences. Justice
  Queen of Hearts, The. *Unknown*
  Quite Forsaken. Lawrence
  Selfe Banished, The. Waller
  Separation. Merwin
  Since Hanna Moved Away. Viorst
  Small Moon. Nemerov
  Solitude. Monro
  Song, A: "Absent from thee, I languish still."
    Rochester
  Song: "First month of his absence, The."
    Lewis
  Song: "I walk'd in the lonesome evening."
    Allingham
  Song: "'Tis said that absence conquers love!"
    Thomas
  Speak! Wordsworth
  Splittings. Rich
  Spring, The. *Fr.* The Mistress. Cowley
  To Amoret Gone from Him. Vaughan
  Voice, The. Hardy
  Western Wind. *Unknown*
  Winter Remembered. Ransom
  World Is Not a Pleasant Place to Be, The.
    Giovanni
  See also **Loneliness; Separation.**
Acacia
  Acacia Tree, The. "Zelda"
  Young Acacia, The. Bialik
Academia
  Stacademia. Barlow
  To a Friend, on Her Examination for the
    Doctorate in English. Cunningham
Acadia and Acadians
  Evangeline. Longfellow
  Evangeline. Smith
  In ev'ry thought, in ev'ry wish I own. *Fr.*
    Acadia. Howe
Accidents
  Accident, The. Gasparini

Another Kind of Burning. Fox
Blue-Tail Fly, The. *Unknown*
Clayfeld's Twin. Pack
Cut. Plath
Dying Mine Brakeman, The. Jenks
Elegy for Jane. Roethke
Falling. Dickey
First Love. Olds
Foundered Tram, The. Monro
Henry K. Sawyer. *Unknown*
Holiday Girls. Raymond
Horror Story Written for the Cover of a
 Matchbook, A. Wachtel
Horse Chestnut. Miranda
I Can't Even Remember the Name. *Fr.*
 Ballad: Between the Boxcars. Warren.
It's Here in The. Atkins
Jack and Jill went up the hill. Mother Goose
Jogging Injury, A. Jackson
New York City—1935. Corso
One Thousand Feet of Shadow. Craig
"Out, Out." Frost
Poems about Playmates. Davis
Ruth. McElroy
Sir Smasham Uppe. Rieu
White Dust, The. Gibson
Worker, The. Thomas
See also **Airplane Crashes; Automobile**
 Accidents; Disasters; Railroad Wrecks;
 Shipwrecks.

Accordions
Man with a Little Pleated Piano, A. Welles

Accounting and Accountants
Hardship of Accounting, The. Frost
Poetess, The. Fabiani

Achilles
Achilles Shows Himself in the Battle by the
 Ships. *Fr.* The Iliad. Homer
Achilles with wild fury in his heart. *Fr.* The
 Iliad. Homer
Shield of Achilles, The. Auden

Acorns
Acorn. Worth

Acrobats
Acrobat from Xanadu disdained all nets, The.
 Georgakas
See also **Circus; Gymnastics; Trapeze**
 Artists.

Acrostic (form)
Discovering My Daughter. Stuart
You Are Gorgeous and I'm Coming. O'Hara

Actaeon
Actaeon. Heppenstall
Acteon. *Fr.* Metamorphoses. Ovid
I Would I Were Actaeon. Bewe

Acting and Actors
Aging Actress Sees Herself a Starlet on the
 Late Show, The. Williams
Author to His Booke, The. *Fr.* An Apology
 for Actors. Heywood
Ballade of Dead Actors. Henley
Boy Actor, The. Coward
David Garrick. *Fr.* Retaliation. Goldsmith
"Ej Blot til Lyst." Payne
Garbo Stepping In. Balderston
Helen in Hollywood. Grahn
J. B. Bunner
Movie Actors Scribbling Letters Very Fast in
 Crucial Scenes. Garrigue
Old Trouper, The. *Fr.* Archy and Mehitabel.
 Marquis
Ophelia. Hillman
Santa Claus. Hassall
Strolling Player, The. Rimbaud
Tallulah at the Schubert. Berger
Thespians at Thermopylae, The. Cameron
To a Dead Actress. Sandoval y Zapata
To the Film Industry in Crisis. O'Hara

Adam and Eve
Adam. Dropkin
Adam and Eve. Manger

Adam and Eve. Sisson
Adam in Love. Mitchell
Adam Lay Ibounden *or* Ibowndyn *or*
 Ybounden. *Unknown*
Adam's Curse. Yeats
Adam's Dream. Schwartz
Adam's Footprint. Miller
Adam's Task. Hollander
Age of Innocence. Hough
Ancient History. Sassoon
Apple, The. Rozewicz
As Adam Early in the Morning. Whitman
Begetting of Cain, The. Plutzik
Circle, A. Spencer
Death of the First Man, The. Sullivan
Epigram: "While Adam slept, from him his
 Eve arose." *Unknown*
Eve: Night Thoughts. Jerome
First Wedding in the World, The. Rosenberg
Fisherman, The. Macpherson
Fortunate Fall, The. Alvarez
Good Beasts, The. Barnstone
Imperial Adam. Hope
Jealous Adam. Manger
Marriage in Eden, The. *Fr.* A View of
 Christ's Kingdom. Williams
Naming of the Beasts, The. Sparshott
O favorable spirit, propitious guest. *Fr.*
 Paradise Lost. Milton
O hell! what do mine eyes with grief behold!
 Fr. Paradise Lost. Milton
Paradise. Bloch
Reflection, A. Hood
Reveille. Hughes
Sickness of Adam, The. *Fr.* Adam and Eve.
 Shapiro
So it begins. Adam is in his earth. *Fr.*
 Sonnets. Agee
Strains of Sight. Duncan
Theology. Hughes
There Are No People Song. *Unknown*
Whate'er Has Been. Lanier
When Adam Day by Day. Housman
When Adam Was First Created. *Unknown*
See also **Eve.**

Adams, Henry
Henry Adams. Auden

Adams, John
Twilight's Last Gleaming. Monks

Adams, John Quincy
John Quincy Adams. Benét

Adderley, Julian ("Cannonball")
Cannon Arrested. Harper

Addison, Joseph
Atticus ("Peace to all such! but were there one
 whose fires"). *Fr.* Epistle to Dr.
 Arbuthnot. Pope
To the Earl of Warwick, on the Death of Mr.
 Addison. Tickell

Adobes
Mending the Adobe. Carruth

Adolescence
Adolescence. Levis
Adolescence. Orr
Adolescence—II. Dove
Allegory of the Adolescent and the Adult.
 Barker
Boy Hiding in a Closet. Orlen
Burning Hills. Ondaatje
Child, The. Keithley
Childhood. Rokeah
Confirmation, The. Shapiro
Cruel Boys. Soto
Deck of Cards, A. Mazur
Dedication to Hunger. Glück
Dimpled Cloud, A. Seidel
Epigram: "Most inexplicable the wiles of boys
 I deem." Rhianus
Equation. Wright
First Day at Boarding School. Power
For Example. Ladányi

Great-Aunt Francesca. McLaughlin
Hanging Fire. Lorde
Heaven. Soto
I Remember How She Sang. Penny
In Laddery Street Herself. *Fr.* Forgotten
 Girlhood. Riding
Into Laddery Street. *Fr.* Forgotten Girlhood.
 Riding
Kiss, The. Bogin
Lines to His Son on Reaching Adolescence.
 Logan
Little Girl, My Stringbean, My Lovely
 Woman. Sexton
Month of June: 13½, The. Olds
Mrs. Applebaum's Sunday Dance Class.
 Schultz
1943. McPherson
Nobody. Agard
Pinay. Cerenio
Question, The. Rukeyser
Romance. Turner
September 7. Bass
Sheep Child, The. Dickey
16/53. Piercy
Spade Scharnweber. Welch
Sunrise. Wells
Teen-Ager, A. Snodgrass
There Is a Girl Inside. Clifton
To a Daughter at Fourteen Forsaking the
 Violin. Oles
Two girls of twelve or so at a table.
 Reznikoff
Waiting in Front of the Columnar High
 School. Shapiro
Wild Pitches. Dacey
Young Girls. Souster
Young Ones, The. Jennings

Adonis
Adonis. Doolittle
Cherry-lipped Adonis. *Fr.* Cynthia.
 Barnfield
Death of Adonis, The. Ayres
Infida's Song. *Fr.* Never Too Late. Greene
Venus and Adonis. Shakespeare

Adriatic Sea
I rode one evening with Count Maddalo. *Fr.*
 Julian and Maddalo. Shelley

Adultery
Adultery. Dickey
Adultery at a Las Vegas Bookstore. Liu
An Old Husband Suspects Adultery. Ewart
Elsa Wertman. *Fr.* Spoon River Anthology.
 Masters
Fine joy brings me great happiness. Beatriz
 de Dia
For All Mary Magdalenes. Maksimovic
Friend, because of you I'm filled. *Unknown*
I'll make a tune for dancing, gay and.
 Unknown
In Memory, 1978. Kazantzis
In the Restaurant. *Fr.* Satires of
 Circumstance. Hardy
I've lately been in great distress. Beatrice,
 Countess de Die
Jacob. Ramke
Lauzengiers and the deceitful spies, The.
 Clara d'Anduza
Marriage and Midsummer's Night. Gregg
Nothing to Fear. Amis
Punishment. Heaney
Queen Eleanor's Confession. *Unknown*
Woman's Song, about Men, A. *Unknown*

Advent
Advent. Hartigan
Advent. Kavanagh
Farewell! Advent. Ryman

Adventure and Adventurers
Peregrine. Wylie

Advertising
Advertising Agency Song, The. *Unknown*
Carnation Milk ("Carnation milk is the best in
 the land"). *Unknown*

Double Standard, The. Adams
Hymn in Columbus Circle. Benét
Legend of the Admen, The. Lord
Memorial to the Great Big Beautiful
 Self-sacrificing Advertisers. Ebright
Poem, or Beauty Hurts Mr. Vinal.
 Cummings
Song of the Open Road. Nash
Summer Song. Watt
Faber Book of Useful Verse, The (FaBoUs),
 pp. 203-217. Simon Brett, ed.
See also **Billboards.**

Advice
Good Counsel. *Unknown*

Aegean Sea
Aegean. Simpson
Santorin. Flecker

Aeneas
Aeneas at Washington. Tate
Aeneid, The, *sels.* Virgil

Aeneid, The (Virgil)
Falling Asleep over the Aeneid. Lowell

Aengus
Song of Wandering Aengus, The. Yeats

Aesop
Improvisations on Aesop. Hecht

Africa
Africa. Alexander
Africa. Angelou
Africa. Diop
Africa. Grant
Africa. McKay
Africa. Moorer
Africa. Naudé
African Affair, The. Wright
African Dance. Hughes
African Dream. Kaufman
African Images. Walker
African Things. Cruz
Africa's Plea. Dempster
Africland. La Grone
All That You Have Given Me, Africa. Kanié
Art Market: Leopoldville. Jackson
Blue Tanganyika. Bethune
Bwagamoyo. Bethune
Ceremony. Cumbo
Change Is Not Always Progress. Lee
Comprehensive. Duffy
Congo, The. Lindsay
Coptic Poem ("A Coptic deputation, going to
 Ethiopia"). Durrell
Dawn in the Heart of Africa. Lumumba
Distance. Delius
Driving through New England. Clifton
Elephant of Moissel, hear my pious prayer.
 Fr. Return of the Prodigal Son. Senghor
Far Cry from Africa, A. Walcott
Far from the Beach. Espírito Santo
Green Hills of Africa, The. Fuller
Hand, The. Fawcett
Heritage. Bennett
Heritage. Cullen
Hottentot, The. Pringle
If You Want to Know Me. Sousa
Is This Africa. Dempster
Meaning of Africa, The. Nicol
My Africa. Dei-Anang
Our Voice. Sousa
Return from Luluabourg. Jackson
Sermonette. Reed
Simoom, The. Tupper
Song of the Cape of Good Hope. Schubart
They Clapped. Giovanni
Three Phases of Africa. Parkes
White and the Black, The. Khaketla
Who Knows? Milner-Brown
Wildebeest, The. Daly
Word, The. Dowe
Yes, I Am an African Woman. Foxworth
Penguin Book of South African Verse, The
 (PeSA). Jack Cope *and* Uys Krige, eds.

Poems from Black Africa (PBA). Langston
 Hughes, ed.
*When My Brothers Come Home; Poems from
 Central and Southern Africa* (WMBCH).
 Frank Mkalawile Chipasula, ed.

African Verse
*When My Brothers Come Home; Poems from
 Central and Southern Africa* (WMBCH).
 Frank Mkalawile Chipasula, ed.

Afterlife
Any [*or* Aye], but to die, and go we know
 not where. *Fr.* Measure for Measure.
 Shakespeare

Afternoon
Afternoon. Fritsch
Afternoon. Guggenberger
Afternoon of Grand Old Men. Csoori
Our Barrio. Alurista

Afton River, Scotland
Flow Gently, Sweet Afton. Burns

Afzal Khan
Rise of Shivaji, The. Ghose

Agamemnon
Agamemnon's Tomb. Sitwell
Iphigeneia and Agamemnon. *Fr.* The
 Hellenics. Landor.

Agassiz, Louis
Farewell to Agassiz, A. Holmes
Fiftieth Birthday of Agassiz, The.
 Longfellow

Agincourt, Battle of (1415)
Agincourt. Drayton
Agincourt Carol, The. *Unknown*
Now Entertain Conjecture of a Time. *Fr.*
 King Henry V. Shakespeare.
Stedes ther stumbelyd in that stownde.
 Unknown

Aging
Advice to Colonel Valentine. Graves
Age. Creeley
Aging. Jarrell
All Souls' Night. Cornford
Although I Am Taking Courses in the
 Language. Janowitz
Ambulando. Brasch
An Accident. Wu Sheng
Another Year Come. Merwin
As the old year ends. Yoshimoto
At Bickford's. Stern
Bird. Shotetsu
Black of my hair, The. Teika
But I Am Growing Old and Indolent. Jeffers
Chard Whitlow. Reed
Collector, The. Flynn
Coming of Wisdom with Time, The. Yeats
Contre Jour. Bartlett
Couplet. Hall
Death of the Trackstar. Meissner
Descent, The. Williams
Diary of a Prisoner. Lo Ch'ing
Distraction. Ammons
Don't Grow Old. Ginsberg
Elegy XI: "Ah me, my friend! it will not, will
 not last!" Shenstone
Father William. *Fr.* Alice's Adventures in
 Wonderland. "Carroll"
Fifty. Rexroth
Firstness. Tillinghast
Folly of Being Comforted, The. Yeats
Game Resumed. Lattimore
Garden Moss under Snow. Kaneyoshi
Growing Old. Arnold
Growing Old. Henderson
His Plans for Old Age. Meredith
How Soon Hath Time [the Subtle Thief of
 Youth] Milton
How to Be Old. Swenson
I have made a pledge. Kenko
I Try to Turn In My Jock. Hilton
I welcome the anonymity of the middle years.
 Fr. Letters to Live Poets. Beaver

In a Prominent Bar in Secaucus [One Day]
 Kennedy
In a Town Garden. Mattam
I've reached my seventy-seventh year.
 Gyozan
Jane Austen at the Window. Beer
Journey toward Evening. McGinley
Lament, A: "I have grown old." Shotetsu
Lamentation of the Old Pensioner, The.
 Yeats
Let Me Grow Lovely. Baker
Letter from a Girl to Her Own Old Age, A.
 Meynell
Like as the waves make towards the pebbled
 shore. *Fr.* Sonnets, LX. Shakespeare
Lines Written in Dejection. Yeats
Magician Suspends the Children, The. Oles
Middle Age. Beer
Minuet on Reaching the Age of Fifty, A.
 Santayana
Mirror. Plath
Moon, The. *Fr.* The Moon. Tamesada
More Lovely Grows the Earth. Coleman
More than Fifty. Gilbert
My Son, My Executioner. Hall
Next Day. Jarrell
No Reparation. Brasch
Old Familiar Faces, The. Lamb
Old man now, An. Tonna
Old Pro's Lament, The. Petrie
Old Swimmer, The. Morley
On Approaching Fifty. Vas
On Looking in the Looking Glass. Gardner
On My Fortieth Birthday. Tripp
Only with Radiance. Szécsi
Only Years. Rexroth
Poem: "All the mirrors in the world."
 O'Hara
Poor Relations, The. Smith
Rabbi Ben Ezra. Browning
Reports of Midsummer Girls. Lattimore
Scene from a Dream. Hale
Schiehallion. Cruickshank
Senex. Betjeman
Since all things must end. Tonna
Slightly Old. Rosenthal
Spot-Check at Fifty. Scannell
Stanzas for Music. Byron
Stella's Birth-day, 1718/19. Swift
Still Hunting. Welch
Story, The. Smith
Terminus. Emerson
That time of year thou may'st [*or* maist] in
 me behold. *Fr.* Sonnets, LXXIII.
 Shakespeare
Thirtieth Anniversary Report of the Class of
 '41. Nemerov
Thirty-eight. Smith
To Age. Landor
To Earthward. Frost
To My Dead Father. O'Hara
Touch Football. Driscoll
Trees of the same age. Masayori
Turning Thirty. Pollitt
Veteran Sirens. Robinson
Warning. Joseph
What Lips My Lips Have Kissed. Millay
Whatever It Is. Simmerman
When Aurelia First I Courted. *Unknown*
When forty winters shall besiege thy brow.
 Fr. Sonnets, II. Shakespeare
When Helen first saw wrinkles in her face.
 Fr. Ianthe. Landor
White Dwarf. Ammons
Why My Hair Is Not Gray. Picirantaiyar
Wild Swans at Coole, The. Yeats
Will You Love Me When I'm Old?
 Unknown
Wilt Chamberlain. Knudson
Woman making advances publicly, A.
 Kazantzis

Writ on the Eve of My 32nd Birthday.
  Corso
See also **Middle Age; Old Age.**
Agnosticism
  Biography of an Agnostic. Ginsberg
  Harald, the Agnostic Ale-loving Old Shepherd
    Enemy of the Whisky-drinking Ploughmen
    and Harvesters, Walks over the Sabbath
    Hill to the Shearing. Brown
  Impercipient, The. Hardy
  Three Towns, The. Nemerov
  See also **Doubt.**
Agoraphobia
  Another Poem about the Madness of Women.
    Wayman
Agriculture. *See* **Farming and Farmers;**
  Farmworkers.
Agustini, Delmira
  Market Women. Figueroa-Aymerich
  Words for Delmira Agustini. Storni
"Ahkmatova, Anna"
  Survivor, The. Gallagher
AIDS
  An Alarming New Development. Schreiber
  How to Watch Your Brother Die. Lassell
  Lament: "Your dying was a difficult
    enterprise." Gunn
  Memoir. Moore
  Monologue of a Dying Beast. Ameen
  Sonnet No. 21. Ameen
Air
  Air. Raine
  Blessed Virgin Compared to the Air We
    Breathe, The. Hopkins
  Fresh Air. Koch
  I Hear America Griping. Bishop
  Oxygen. Swift
Air Conditioning
  I Hear America Griping. Bishop
Air Plants
  Air Plant, The. Crane
Air Travel
  Air Travel in Arabia. Johnston
  At the San Francisco Airport. Winters
  Cockpit in the Clouds. Dorrance
  Day Flight. Davis
  First Flight. Wellesley
  Flight Plan. Merchant
  Flying at Night. Kooser
  Flying Friendly Skies. Cassity
  Flying Home from Utah. Swenson
  N.Y. to L.A. by Jet Plane. Dorman
  On Seeing My Birthplace from a Jet Aircraft.
    Pudney
  Our Ground Time Here Will Be Brief.
    Kumin
  Twenty-third Flight. Birney
  Up Silver Stairsteps. Stuart
  See also **Airports.**
Air Warfare
  Air Raid. Wild
  Airstrip in Essex, 1960, An. Hall
  Ascension: 1925, The. Brinnin
  Bombardment. Lawrence
  Bombers, The. Churchill
  Bombers. Day Lewis
  Brother Fire. MacNeice
  Caution Prevents Accidents. Wieseltier
  Ceremony after a Fire Raid. Thomas
  De Civitate Hominum. MacGreevy
  Dead in Europe, The. Lowell
  Death of the Ball Turret Gunner, The. Jarrell
  During a Bombardmant by V-Weapons.
    Fuller
  Eighth Air Force. Jarrell
  Erige Cor Tuum ad Me in Caelum. Doolittle
  Firebombing, The. Dickey
  Front, A. Jarrell
  Fury of Aerial Bombardment, The. Eberhart
  Gods in Vietnam. Redmond
  Gunner, The. Webb

Henry's Understanding. Berryman
Irish Airman Foresees His Death, An. Yeats
Journal. Ciardi
Losses. Jarrell
One of Our Aircraft Failed to Return.
  Saunders
Ops in a Wimpey. *Unknown*
Pilots, Man Your Planes. Jarrell
Radar. Ross
R.A.F. Churchill
Raid, The. Everson
Raider, The. Rodgers
Refusal to Mourn the Death, by Fire, of a
  Child in London, A. Thomas
Reprisals. Yeats
Second Air Force. Jarrell
Soliloquy in an Air-Raid. Fuller
Still Falls the Rain. Sitwell
Stoic; for Laura von Courten, The. Bowers
Thoughts during an Air Raid. Spender
Usual exquisite boredom of patrols, The.
  Popham
War in the Air, The. Nemerov
When a Beau Goes In. Ewart
Words Spoken by Pasternak during a
  Bombing. Akhmadulina
Airline Stewardesses
  Falling. Dickey
Airplane Crashes
  Ceiling Unlimited. Rukeyser
  Dreamers and Flyers. LaBombard
  Man in the Dead Machine, The. Hall
  Two Memorial Poems. Avidan
  When a Beau Goes In. Ewart
Airplanes
  Aeroplane, The. Kirby
  Biplane, The. Orlen
  Cockpit in the Clouds. Dorrance
  Dreamers and Flyers. LaBombard
  Enginngines, The. Goodman
  First Solo. McDonald
  Heavenly Aeroplane, The. *Unknown*
  Jet. Moore
  Night Plane. Frost
  Over the Field. Swenson
  Prayer for a Pilot. Roberts
  Riding in an Airplane. Baruch
  Silver Ships. Meigs
  See also **Aviation and Aviators.**
Airports
  At the San Francisco Airport. Winters
  Flood. Matthews
  Night at an Airport. Ignatow
  Piarco. Roach
  See also **Air Travel.**
Ajanta, India
  Ajanta. Rukeyser
Alabama (ship)
  Roll, *Alabama*, Roll. *Unknown*
Alabama (state)
  Alabama. Fields
  Alabama. Simmons
  Alabama Bus. Hairston
  Alabama Earth. Hughes
  Birmingham 1963. Patterson
  Birmingham Sunday. Hughes
  Craven. Newbolt
  Daybreak in Alabama. Hughes
Alamo
  Defense of the Alamo, The. Miller
  Lament for the Alamo. Guiterman
  Men of the Alamo, The. Roche
Alaric I
  Dirge of Alaric the Visigoth. Everett
Alaska
  Alaska. Fordham
  Alaskan Fragments June 1981—Summer
    Solstice. Rose
  Anchorage. Harjo
  Before Breakup on the Chena outside
    Fairbanks. McElroy

Funny Joke, A. Stokesbury
To Vera Thompson. Haines
Albatrosses
  Albatross. Stoddard
  Celtic Albatross, The. Bold
  Last Straw. Starbuck
  Rime of the Ancient Mariner, The.
    Coleridge
  Sea Change. Masefield
Alcestis
  Alcestis. Verry
Alchemy and Alchemists
  Alchemist, The. Pound
  Philosopher's Stone, The. *Unknown*
Alcoholism and Alcoholics
  Benefits and Abuse of Alcohol, The.
    Eubulus
  Booze Turns Men into Women. Mayer
  Christmas with the Holy Family. Cavin
  Clifton. Larkin
  Englishry. Shepherd
  Hilltop, The. Hugo
  Interview with Doctor Drink. Cunningham
  Lament for Barney Flanagan. Baxter
  Letters & Other Words. Ondaatje
  My Papa's Waltz. Roethke
  Once More O Ye Etc. Reck
  Piss Artist, The. Shepherd
  Reunion. Tawney
  Taoist Huang Has Died of Alcoholism, The.
    Shen Chou
  See also **Drunkards.**
Alder Trees
  Victors, The. Levertov
Ale
  Back and Side Go Bare, Go Bare. *Fr.*
    Gammer Gurton's Needle. Stevenson
  Bring Us In Good Ale. *Unknown*
  On a Quaker's Tankard. Landor
  When Jones's Ale Was New. *Unknown*
Aleichem, Sholom
  Sholom Aleichem. Lieberman
Alexander Jannaeus, King of Judah
  Alexander Jannai. Cavafy
Alexander, Sir William
  Sonnet on Sir William Alexander's Harsh
    Verses after the English Fashion, A.
    James I, King of England
  To Sir William Alexander. Drummond
Alexander the Great
  Alexander the Great. *Unknown*
  How Big Was Alexander? Jones
  In the Year 200 B.C. Cavafy
  On Alexander and Aristotle, on a
    Black-on-Red Greek Plate. Dugan
  Santorin. Flecker
  Speaking Tree, The. Rukeyser
Alfonso X, King of Castile and León
  Alphonso of Castile. Emerson
Alfred the Great
  Alfred the Harper. Sterling
  Ballad of the White Horse, The, *sel.*
    Chesterton
Alhambra, The
  Legend of Alhambra, A. Trench
Ali, Muhammad
  Black Lady in an Afro Hairdo Cheers for
    Cassius. Holmes
Alienation
  Back Again, Home. Lee
  Between Me and Anyone Who Can
    Understand. Scott
  Blight. Emerson
  Chicken-Licken. Angelou
  Childhood. Stanton
  Dirge: "1-2-3 was the number he played but
    today the number came 3-2-1." Fearing
  Effort at Speech between Two People.
    Rukeyser
  Fields, The. Merwin
  Finches. Southwick

First Day at Boarding School. Power
Gerontion. Eliot
Howl. Ginsberg
I Am. Clare
Ibn Battuta. Davis
Invention of New Jersey, The. Anderson
Love Song of J, The Alfred Prufrock. Eliot
Man Missing. Brasch
Mr. Flood's Party. Robinson
Night-blooming Cereus, The. Hayden
On the Apparition of Oneself. Burford
Outcast. McKay
Paperweight, The. Schnackenberg
Poem about People. Pinsky
Refusals. Anderson
Soledad. Hayden
Untitled. Bass
Waste Land, The. Eliot
Wave of coldness, A. Yosano Akiko
Waving of a Hand, The. Merwin
Winter's Cold. Rodgers
World Is Too Much with Us, The.
  Wordsworth

Aliens
Defeat at the Hands of Alien Scholars.
  Boston
Ode to an Alien. Ackerman

All Souls' Day
All Soul's Day. Celan

All Souls' Night
All Hallows Eve. Byer
All Souls' Night. Cornford
On Kingston Bridge. Cortissoz

Allen, Ethan
Green Mountain Boy. Smyth

Allen, Richard
Rt. Rev. Richard Allen. Heard

Allen University
Farewell to Allen University. Heard

Alligators
Alligator, The. Macdonald
Alligator, The. Ravenel
Alligator on the Escalator. Merriam
Purist, The. Nash
See also **Crocodiles.**

Almanacs
Child Reads an Almanac, The ("The child
  reads on; her basket of eggs stands by").
  Jammes

Almond Trees
Almond Blossoms. Netser
Bare Almond-Trees. Lawrence

Alphabet
Aleph Bet, The. Lipshitz
Alphabet, The. Shapiro
Alphabet Came to Me, The. Rothenberg
Letters at School, The. Dodge
Life of the Letters. Borenstein
Vowels. Rimbaud

Alphabet Peoms
A was an archer, who shot at a frog.
  Unknown

Alphabet Poems
A. Stands for Absolutely Anything. *Fr.* The
  Little Ones' A. B. C. Coward
A was an apple pie, B bit it, C cut it.
  Mother Goose
Alphabet, An. Lear
Alphabet of Aristotle, The. Benet
Austrian Army, An. Watts
Curious Discourse That Passed between the
  Twenty-five Letters at Dinner-Time, A.
  Unknown
From a Cheerful Alphabet. Updike
He That Ne'er Learns His ABC. *Unknown*
In Adam's fall/ We sinned all. *Fr.* The New
  England Primer. *Unknown*
Letters of the Book, The. Drachler
Lumberman's Alphabet, The. *Unknown*
Monster Alphabet. Fisher
Primer of the Daily Round, A. Nemerov

Sailors' Alphabet, The. *Unknown*
Sailors' Alphabet, The. *Unknown*
Single-Rhyme Alphabet, A. *Unknown*

Alpheus
Arethusa. Shelley

Alphonsus Rodriguez, Saint
In Honour of St. Alphonsus Rodriguez.
  Hopkins

Alps
Alpine Spirit's Song. Beddoes
Crossing the Alps. *Fr.* The Prelude [or,
  Growth of a Poet's Mind]: Cambridge and
  the Alps. Wordsworth
Hymn before Sunrise, in the Vale of
  Chamouni. Coleridge
Nocturne of the Self-evident Presence.
  MacGreevy
On the Fly-Leaf of Pound's Cantos. Bunting
Schreckhorn, The. Hardy

Alsace, France
First Snow in Alsace. Wilbur

Altar Boys
1955. Weigl
Purpose of Altar Boys, The. Ríos

Altars
Altar, The. Herbert
Mountain Altar, The. O'Higgins

Altgeld, John Peter
Eagle That Is Forgotten, The. Lindsay

Alumni
Blues for an Old Blue. Gibson
Thirtieth Anniversary Report of the Class of
  '41. Nemerov

Amaryllis (mythology)
I Care Not for These Ladies. Campion

Amazons
White Women, The. Coleridge

Ambition
Ambition. Davies
Ambition. Herrick
Ambition. Johnson
Ambition. Kennedy
Ambition. Ray
Chorus: "How dost thou wear and weary out
  thy days." *Fr.* The Tragedie of Philotas.
  Daniel
Mills of the Gods, The. *Unknown*

Ambulances
Resuscitation Team. Fanthorpe

Amen Ra. See **Amon Ra.**

America
America. Dumas
America. Ginsberg
America. McKay
America. Smith
America Is Hard to See. Frost
Anthem: "America, if you were a basketball
  court." Vincent
Balance Sheet with Incident. Born
England. Moore
Heartland. Engle
I Sing of Olaf Glad and Big. Cummings
In the Golden Land. Halpern
Irrational. Lamantia
Let America Be America Again. Hughes
Love in America. Moore
Midlandfall. Yuson
Next to of Course God America I.
  Cummings
O Ship of State. Longfellow
On the Emigration to America [and Peopling
  the Western Country] Freneau
On Your Soil, America. Vaynshteyn
One Thing That Can Save America, The.
  Ashbery
Owed to America. Durrell
Thank You, America. Salamon
Thanksgiving Day. Storm
To America. Leivick
To the Western World. Simpson

Tragic Condition of the Statue of Liberty,
  The. Mayer
Tribute to America. Shelley
Triple Trouble. Saint
"Watch Your Step!" Halpern
See also **United States.**

American Indians. See **Indians, American.**

American Revolution
Battle of the Kegs, The. Hopkinson
Boston in Distress. *Unknown*
Bunker Hill. Calvert
Centenarian's Story, The. Whitman
Concord Hymn. Emerson
Dying Sergeant, The. *Unknown*
Emily Geiger. *Unknown*
God Save the Plough. Sigourney
Green Mountain Boys, The. Bryant
Lafayette to Washington. *Fr.* Valley Forge.
  Anderson
Little Britain. *Unknown*
Molly Pitcher. Richards
New England's Chevy Chase. Hale
On Sympathisers with the American
  Revolution. Wesley
On the Late Engagement in Carles Town
  River. *Unknown*
Paul Revere's Ride (The Landlord's Tale).
  Fr. Tales of a Wayside Inn. Longfellow
Prophecy in Flame. Howard
Rise then, ere ruin swift surprize. *Fr.*
  M'Fingal. Trumbull
Seventy-six. Bryant
Song for Lexington, A. Weeks
Song of Marion's Men. Bryant
Swamp Fox, The. Simms
To the Memory of the Brave Americans.
  Freneau
Yankee Doodle. Bangs
Yankee Doodle. Shuckburg

Americans
American Primitive. Smith
Ave Caesar. Jeffers
Ballad of Abbreviations, A. Chesterton
Boy-Man. Shapiro
I Am an American. Lieberman
I Hear America Singing. Whitman
I, Too, Sing America. Hughes
Inner Part, The. Simpson
On the Circuit. Auden
Oven Loves the TV Set, The. McHugh
What Thou Lovest Well, Remains American.
  Hugo

Amherst, Massachusetts
New England Interlude. DeFrees

Amish, The
Amish, The. Updike

Amnesia
Amnesiac. Plath

Amon Ra
Hymn to Amen Ra, the Sun God. *Unknown*
I Am a Cowboy in the Boat of Ra. Reed

Amputees
Amputee Soldier, The. Dacey
Does It Matter? Sassoon
In the Children's Hospital. "MacDiarmid"
Lament for a Leg. Ormond
Leg, The. Shapiro
Mirage. Sumrall
On Forgetting to Cry. Colvin
Phantom Pain. Chernoff
Question of Energy, A. Sumrall

Amsterdam, Netherlands
Amsterdam Letter. Garrigue
Epigram on the Play-House at Amsterdam.
  Parsons
School Hockey Team in Amsterdam, The.
  Ormsby

Amusement Parks
Coney Island Life, A. Weil
Old Amusement Park. Moore

Anacreon
This is Anacreon's grave. Here lie. Antipater of Sidon
Anarchism and Anarchists
As I lay asleep in Italy. *Fr.* The Mask of Anarchy. Shelley
Paper Anarchist Addresses the Shade of Nancy Ling Perry. Woodcock
Ancestry and Ancestors
Ah, the glorious ancestors. *Unknown*
Ancestors. Randall
Ancestors. Schimmel
Ancestors' Graves in Kurakawa. Kogawa
Ancestral Faces. Brew
Ancient Tear, The. Urbina
And. Creeley
Black Star Line. Dumas
Forebears. Gibbon
Forefathers. Blunden
Gadoshkibos. Burns
Genealogy. Phillips
He comes in solemn state. *Unknown*
Heirloom. Klein
Here, then, I come. *Unknown*
Heredity. Guiterman
Heritage. Bennett
Heritage. Cullen
His Father's Hands. Kinsella
Idea of Ancestry, The. Knight
Illustrious Ancestors. Levertov
In These Dissenting Times. Walker
Lineage. Walker
My Dark Fathers. Kennelly
Pity me, your child. *Unknown*
Planted Heel, The. Quiller-Couch
Pride of Ancestry. Frost
So they appeared before their lord the king. *Unknown*
Song of Ancient Ways, The. Oandasan
Tomb of an Ancestor. Curnow
Voice in the Blood. Bush
Anchorage, Alaska
Anchorage. Harjo
Anchors
Anchor: "Oft I must strive with wind and wave." *Fr.* Riddles (Exeter Book). Cynewulf
Anci
Elegy: "Let day, let night, come no more." Auvaiyar
Elegy: "This bright burning pyre." Auvaiyar
His Welcome. Auvaiyar
André, John
Brave Paulding and the Spy. *Unknown*
Andrea Doria (ship)
Last Words. Hollander
Andromache
Andromache's Lamentation. *Fr.* The Iliad. Homer
Andromache's Wedding. Sappho
Hector. Iremonger
Andromeda
Andromeda. Aldrich
Andromeda. Hopkins
Anemones
To a Wind-Flower. Cawein
Angels
Air[e] and Angels. Donne
And is there care in heaven? and is there love. *Fr.* The Faerie Queene. Spenser
Angel. Merrill
Angel Describes Truth, An. *Fr.* Hymenaei. Jonson.
Angel of Death Is Always with Me, The. Marcus
Angel Surrounded by Paysans. Stevens
Angels. Abse
Angels, The. Eberhart
Angels, The. Lauer
Angels, The. Ramsey
Angels. Szumigalski

Angels, The. Young
Angels in the House. Metz
Angels in Winter. Willard
Angel's Song. Causley
Angel's Visit, The. Field
Café. Baykov
Conversation with an Angel. Barford
From the Coptic. Smith
Galloping Cat, The. Smith
God's Language. Fainlight
How Grand and How Bright. *Unknown*
Images of Angels. Page
Israfel. Poe
It Came upon the Midnight Clear. Sears
Lame Angel. Finkel
Laughing Angel: Reims, The. Socolow
Little East of Jordan, A. Dickinson
Locked Doors. Sexton
Lord, Forgive a Spirit. Stern
Michael. McPherson
My Guardian Angel Stein. Schultz
No Categories! Smith
On a Fifteenth-Century Flemish Angel. Ray
On Angels. Ross
Sonnet: "Bible says Sennacherib's campaign was spoiled, The." Lewis
This is no rune nor riddle. *Fr.* Tribute to the Angels. Doolittle
To an Artist. Burns
Tom's Angel. De la Mare
When Angels Came to Zimmer. Zimmer
Wrestling Jacob. Wesley
Anger
Anger. Creeley
Anger. Lamb
Anger Lay by Me All Night Long. Daryush
Angry Children. Stewart
Death of Poetry, The. Candiani
Even my own heart. Tameko
He That Is Slow to Anger. *Fr.* Proverbs.
Man Arrested in Hacking Death Tells Police He Mistook Mother-in-Law for Raccoon. Ludvigson
On Hurt. Jin
One Angry Woman. Williams
Peppery Man, The. Macy
Poison Tree, A. *Fr.* Songs of Experience. Blake
Red Anger. Smith
Sapphics against Anger. Steele
Snapshot. Kassák
Sulk. Holman
Temper. Fyleman
This Rage. Batisti
What Her Girl Friend Said to Him. Ammuvanar
Winter Moon, The. Kyozo
Woman Talk. Simba
Tygers of Wrath: Poems of Hate, Anger, and Invective (TW). X. J. Kennedy, ed.
See also **Quarrels.**
Angkor Wat, Cambodia
Ank'hor Vat. Devlin
Angola
Augusto Ngangula. Andrade
We Must Return. Neto
When My Brothers Come Home. Santos
Animal Migration
Something Told the Wild Geese. Field
To a Waterfowl. Bryant
Animals
Ad Limina. Campbell
Age of Animals, The. *Unknown*
Allie ("Allie, call the birds in"). Graves
And Did the Animals? Van Doren
Animal Fair. *Unknown*
Animal Kingdom. Clouts
Animal Pictures. Locke
Animal Song. McHugh
Animal Store, The. Field
Animals, The. Jacobsen

Animals, The. Muir
Animals, The. Pastan
Animals in That Country, The. Atwood
At the Zoo. Milne
At the Zoo. Thackeray
Barnyard, The. *Unknown*
Barnyard Melodies. Brooks
Beasts. Wilbur
Beasts and Birds. O'Keeffe
Bestiary, A. Rexroth
Blue Animals, The. Anderson
Burial of the Linnet, The. Ewing
Butterfly's Ball, The. Roscoe
Cage, The. Stephens
Cats Crept Up on Me Slowly. Laird
Christmas Folk-Song, A. Reese
Daydreamers. Davis
Deer among Cattle. Dickey
Dogs and Cats and Bears and Bats. Prelutsky
Double Agent. McHugh
Dumb World, The. Davies
Eau-Forte. Flint
Face of the Horse, The. Zabolotsky
Familiar Friends. Tippett
Feather or Fur. Becker
Fiddle-I-Fee. *Unknown*
Friendly Beasts, The. *Unknown*
Frog Went a-Courtin.' *Unknown*
Giving Rabbit to My Cat Bonnie. Stevenson
Good Morning. Sipe
Heaven of Animals, The. Dickey
Hedge Life. Dickey
How To Tell the Wild Animals. Wells
Hymn to Joy. Cunningham
Infinite Millimeter Manifesto. Arp
Kindness to Animals. *Unknown*
Kingly lyon, and the strong arm'd beare, The. Wood
Laughing Time. Smith
Lion is the [or a] beast to fight, The. Quiller-Couch
Little Things. Stephens
Losing Track. Levertov
Menagerie, The. Moody
Monkeys, The. Moore
Mrs. Malone. Farjeon
My Father Kept a Horse. *Unknown*
Mystical Beast in the Shadows, The. Eberhart
Nell. Knister
News from the Cabin. Swenson
Ovibos, The. Hale
Ox-Tamer, The. Whitman
Pangolin, The. Moore
Parley of Beasts. "MacDiarmid"
Peacock "At Home," The. Dorset
Psalm to the Creatures. Jones
Rabbit as King of the Ghosts, A. Stevens
Rose and Cushie. Turner
Running Lightly over Spongy Ground. Roethke
Self-Pity. Lawrence
Significance of a Water Animal, The. Young Bear
Snakes, Mongooses, Snake-Charmers and the Like. Moore
Stockyard, The. Squire
Take One Home for the Kiddies. Larkin
Talking to Animals. Howes
To the Animal Lover. *Fr.* Bear Song. Rákos.
Tree in the Wood, The. *Unknown*
Turkish Trench Dog, The. Dearmer
Ways of Living Things, The. Prelutsky
What Violins Are Singing in Their Beds of Lard. Arp
Wild Beasts. Stein
Witnesses, The. Kennedy
Wolf Said to Francis, The. Rochelle
World of Darkness. Chatain
Young Stock. Sackville-West

Zoo Manners. Mathias
Fellow Mortals (FM). Roy Fuller, ed.
See also **Death of Animals.**
Animism
Intimate Associations. Baudelaire
Sometimes. Hesse
Anne of Denmark
On Queen Anne's Death. *Unknown*
Anne, Queen of England
New Ballad, A. Mainwaring
Pasquin to the Queen's Statue at St. Paul's.
  Shippen
Queen Anne. *Unknown*
Queen's Speech, The. Mainwaring
To a Good Friend Who Would Prove the
  Fickleness of Women with the Example of
  Queen Anne. Kuntsch
Anniversaries
After the Golden Wedding. Stephen
Anniversary. Kooser
Anniversary. Lattimore
Clayfeld's Anniversary Song. Pack
Golden Wedding, The. Gray
Looking at a Picture on an Anniversary.
  Hardy
Annunciation of the Virgin
Annunciation. *Fr.* La Corona. Donne
Annunciation, The. Muir
Annunciation. Smith
Sonnet:
Annunciation. Belli
Antaeus
Antaeus; a Fragment. Owen
Antaeus (The Prodigious Builders). Dutcher
Antarctica
Antarctic Muse, The. Perry
Traveller's Guide to Antarctica. Stoutenburg
Anteaters
Pangolin, The. Moore
Antelopes
Kob Antelope. *Fr.* Hunter Poems of the
  Yoruba. *Unknown*
"Word" of an Antelope Caught in a Trap,
  The. Sandag
See also **Elands.**
Anthony, Saint
Temptation of Saint Anthony, The. Symons
Temptations of Saint Anthony, The.
  McGinley
Anti-Semitism
How Come the Truck-Loads? Rodriguez
To T. S. Eliot. Litvinoff
Antietam Campaign (1862)
Battle of Antietam Creek, The. *Unknown*
Antigone
Antigone and Oedipus. Ray
Antiques
Antique Shop. Carmer
Chair, Dog, and Clock. Corke
Antonioni, Michelangelo
In Praise of Antonioni. Holden
Antony (Marc Antony)
Antony and Cleopatra. Coulette
Antony to Cleopatra. Lytle
Death of Antony. *Fr.* Antony and Cleopatra.
  Shakespeare
Early in the Morning. Simpson
Tact. Pascal
Antrim *See* **County Antrim, Northern
Ireland.**
Ants
Ant, The. Lovelace
Ant, The. Nash
Ant-Heap, The. Benson
Ant-Hills. "Douglas"
Ant Trap, The. Rosenblatt
Ants. Al-Sa'igh
Ants. Hoberman
Ants. López Velarde
Ants, Although Admirable Are Awfully
  Aggravating. Brooks

Ants at the Olympics, The. Digance
Ants Live Here. Moore
Country Roads. Jacobsen
Departmental. Frost
"Go to the Ant." Sharpless
Haiku: "Ants stopped coming." *Fr.* One
  Hundred Haiku in Free Form. Hosai
Immanent. De la Mare
Ondt and the Gracehoper, The. *Fr.*
  Finnegans Wake. Joyce
Turkey and the Ant, The. *Fr.* Fables. Gay
Antwerp, Belgium
Antwerp: Musée Des Beaux-Arts. Ross
Anxiety
Excrement Poem, The. Kumin
Humaine Cares. Wanley
It's All in Your Head. Waniek
Longing to Be Saved, The. Kumin
Overheard in an Orchard. Cheney
Prognosis. MacNeice
Voyages, The. Orr
Apartheid
Child Who Was Shot Dead by Soldiers at
  Nyanga, The. Jonker
In Bloemfontein. Ross
In the Gold Mines. Vilakazi
Landscape of Violence. Currey
Me, Colored. *Fr.* Tell Freedom.
  Abrahams.
Pass Office Song. *Unknown*
Where the Rainbow Ends. Rive
White and Black, The. Khaketla
Winnie Song. Clifton
*When My Brothers Come Home; Poems from
  Central and Southern Africa* (WMBCH).
  Frank Mkalawile Chipasula, ed.
Apartments
Living in Sin. Rich
Apathy
Celestial Surgeon, The. Stevenson
Chebutykin. Davis
Indifference. Studdert-Kennedy
Musée des Beaux Arts. Auden
Pooh! de la Mare
Revelation, The. *Fr.* The Angel in the
  House. Patmore
There Is None to Help. *Fr.* The Psalm of
  Christ. Walsh
Apes
Artist and Ape. Link
Best Loved of Africa. Danner
First Philosopher's Song. Huxley
Aphrodisiacs
Aphrodisiac, The. McGuckian
In Praise of Cocoa, Cupid's Nightcap.
  Sharpless
Aphrodite
Blue Sleep. Bryher
Myth on Mediterranean Beach: Aphrodite as
  Logos. Warren
Ring Of, The. Olson
See also **Venus (goddess).**
Apocalypse. *See* **End of the World.**
Apollinaire, Guillaume
Death of Guillaume Apollinaire, The. Tzara
Homage to Guillaume Apollinaire. Cendrars
I Am Almost Asleep. Grier
To Guillaume Apollinaire. Brodey
Volt. Tzara
Apollo
Apollo and Daphne. Winters
Archaic Torso of Apollo. Rilke
Before the Statue of Apollo.
  Tchernichowsky
Canticle to Apollo, A. Herrick
Hymn of Apollo. Shelley
Many Are Called. Robinson
Phoebus, Arise. Drummond
Phoebus with Admetus. Meredith
Sacrifice to Apollo, The. Drayton

Song for Apollo. *Fr.* Empedocles on Etna.
  Arnold
Story of Phoebus and Daphne Applied, etc.,
  The. Waller
Translation into the Original. Gilbert
Apostles
Ballad of the Goodly Fere. Pound
Last Supper, The. Williams
Appalachia
Another Kind of Burning. Fox
Appalachian Front. Weeks
Apple Blossoms
Comparison, A. Farrar
Apple Trees and Apples
After Apple-picking. Frost
An Apple Tree and a Pig. Humphreys
Another Sarah. Porter
Apple Blossoms. Parker
Apple Harvest. Leuty
Apple Hell. Van Doren
Apple Orchard in the Spring, An. Martin
Apple Poem. Scannell
Apple Song. Frost
Apples. Kaufman
Apples. *Fr.* Verses for Fruitwomen. Swift
Apples. Waters
Apples in New Hampshire. Gilchrist
Cider Song. Weston
Crossed Apple, The. Bogan
Green Apples. Stone
Love And Work: Apple Picking. Goldensohn
Medlars and Sorb-Apples. Lawrence
Moonlit Apples. Drinkwater
Old Apple Trees. Snodgrass
On Apples. Ross
On Observing a Large Red-Streak Apple.
  Freneau
Orchard. Engels
Paring the Apple. Tomlinson
Pattern Poem with an Elusive Intruder. Döhl
Planting of the Apple-Tree, The. Bryant
Sharing Eve's Apple. Keats
Symposium: Apples, A. Pastan
Tapestry Trees. Morris
Unharvested. Frost
Wood-Pile, The. Frost
Appleseed, Johnny. *See* **Chapman, John.**
Apprentices
Sheffield Apprentice, The. *Unknown*
Apricot Trees and Apricots
Apricot Tree. Isanos
Vegetable Destiny. Cassian
April
April. Clifton
April. Pastan
April. Ray
April. *Fr.* Sonnets of the Months. San
  Gimignano
April. Teasdale
April. Willis
April and Dying. Aldrich
April, 1885. Bridges
April Fantasie. Cortissoz
April, Glengarry. Coxon
April Inventory. Snodgrass
April Rain. Loveman
April Rain Song. Hughes
Aprilly. Taylor
Be Ye in Love with April-Tide. Scollard
Break-up, The. Klein
Day before April, The. Davies
Dutch April. Halpern
Epigram on the First of April. Winstanley
For City Spring. Benét
Home Thoughts from Abroad. Browning
In April. Wetherald
Prayer in April. Hay
Relearning the Language of April. Kumin
Song: "April, April,/ Laugh thy girlish
  laughter." Watson
Song of a Second April. Millay

Spring. Millay
Storm in April, A. Wilbur
West Wind, The. Masefield
Whan that Aprill[e] with his shoures [or shower] soote. Fr. The Canterbury Tales: Prologue. Chaucer

April Fool's Day
First of April, some do say, The. *Unknown*

Aquariums
Aquarium. Wright
At the Aquarium. Eastman
Enormous Aquarium, The. Santos
Sharks at the New York Aquarium. Martin

Aquinas, St. Thomas. See Thomas Aquinas, Saint.

Arab-Israeli Wars
Caution Prevents Accidents. Wieseltier
November '73. Pagis

Arabia
Arabia. Falkner

Arabic Verse
Modern Arabic Poetry; an Anthology (MAP). Salma Khadra Jayyusi, ed.
Modern Poetry of the Arab World (MPAW). Abdullah al-Udhari, ed. *and* tr.

Arabs
Arab Love-Song, An. Thompson
Arab to His Favorite Steed, The. Norton
Arabic Script. Thwaite
Bedouin Song. Taylor
In an Arab Town. Tichy
In Memoriam. Ungaretti

Arachne
Arachne. Kazantzis

Aran Islands, Ireland
Aran Islands. Layton
Arran. *Unknown*

Arawak Indians
Arawak Prologue. McFarlane
Ethnocide. Fergus

Arbor Day
Plant a Tree. Larcom
What Do We Plant [When We Plant the Tree] Abbey
Woodman, Spare That Tree. Morris

Arbus, Diane
To D——, Dead by Her Own Hand. Nemerov

Arbutus
Pink, small and punctual. Dickinson
To a Mayflower. Marshall

Arcadia
On a Picture by Poussin Representing Shepherds in Arcadia. Symonds
Way to Arcady, The. Bunner

Archaeology
Archaeological Picnic, The. Betjeman
Archaeology. Pollitt
Archaeology of Love, The. Murphy
Ashkelon. Rudolf
Barbury Camp. Sorley
Colossus, The. Plath

Archery
Archer, The. Scollard
Archery Instructor. Aldridge
Japanese Archery. Wat
Need to Win, The. Merton

Architecture and Architects
On Sir John Vanbrugh [Architect]. Evans
Eye's Delight: Poems of Art and Architecture (EyDe). Helen Plotz, ed.

Arctic
Ballad of Sir John Franklin, A. Boker
Frozen Fire. McLaren
Immoral Arctic, The. Bishop
Polar Exploration. Spender
Song of the Rejected Woman. Kibkarjuk
Wolf Cry, The. Sarett

Arethusa
Arethusa. Shelley

Argentina
Madwomen of the Plaza de Mayo, The. Mandel

Arguments. See Quarrels.

Ariadne
To Ariadne. Plath

Arion
On a Picture by Michele Da Verona, of Arion as a Boy Riding upon a Dolphin. Ridler

Aristotle
Humanities Lecture. Stafford

Arithmetic
Arithmetic ("Arithmetic is where numbers fly like pigeons in and out of your head"). Sandburg

Arizona
Arizona Village. Davieau
Discoveries in Arizona. Wright
Hitchhiker, The. Ai
Yuma. Phelps

Ark, The
Ararat. Pagis
Gold Glade. Warren
Life-Giving, The. Leithauser
Problem in History, A. Wallace
See also **Noah.**

Arkansas
Little White Schoolhouse Blues. Lennon
My Arkansas. Angelou

Arlington National Cemetery, Virginia
Arlington Cemetery Looking toward the Capitol. Palmer

Armada. See Spanish Armada.

Armenia
Song from Armenia, A. Hill

Armies
All the Same. Arif
Sad Evenings. Arif

Armistice
All That We Try to Do. Orlen
America's Welcome Home. Van Dyke
"And There Was a Great Calm." Hardy
Armistice Day. Freeman
Eternal Return, The. Hillyer
Everyone Sang. Sassoon
Message of Peace, A. Fr. The Arsenal at Springfield. Longfellow
November 1918. Hanson
Peace. Markham
Today Is Armistice, a Holiday. Schwartz
Veterans Day, 1981. Oles
Where Are You Going, Greatheart? Oxenham
See also **Peace.**

Armstrong, Johnie (Scots *fl.* 1530)
Johnie Armstrong. *Unknown*

Armstrong, Louis
Satchmo. Tolson

Armstrong, Neil
White Power Poem. Bishop

Armstrong, William (Scots, *fl.* 1596)
Kinmont Willie. *Unknown*

Army Life
Americans Playing Slow-Pitch Softball at an Airbase near Kunsan, South Korea. Johnson
Boots. Kipling
By the Bivouac's Fitful Flame. Whitman
Cavalry Crossing a Ford. Whitman
Class Incident from Graves. Brownjohn
Danny Deever. Kipling
'Eathen, The. Kipling
Going In to Dinner. Shanks
Gunga Din. Kipling
It Happened Before. Jarman
Mandalay. Kipling
Officers' Mess. Ewart
On Guard. Wieseltier
Spring 1942. Fuller
Stand-to: Good Friday Morning. Sassoon

Oxford Book of War Poetry, The (OBWP). Jon Stallworthy, ed.
See also **Soldiers.**

Arnold, Matthew
Dover Bitch, The. Hecht
Laleham: Matthew Arnold's Grave. Johnson
Pax Paganica. Guiney

Arranged Marriage
In the Season When the World's in Leaf and Flower. Compiuta Donzella

Arrows
Arrow and the Song, The. Longfellow
Arrows. Heyen
Ill-tempered Lover, The, *sel.* MacKay
Song of the Arrow, The. Fr. Gisli, the Chieftain. Crawford
This is the arrow which I, a warrior, shot. Fr. Manyo Shu. Kanamura

Art and Artists
Anecdote of the Jar. Stevens
Anonymous Drawing. Justice
Art. Flax
Art. Melville
Art. Perry
Art. *Unknown*
Art and Heart. Wilcox
Artist, An. Jeffers
Artist, The. Kunitz
Artist, The. *Unknown*
Artist and Ape. Link
Artists East and West. Chang
At a Bach Concert. Rich
At an Exhibition of Historical Paintings, Hobart. Smith
Aunt Jennifer's Tigers. Rich
Biography of a Still LIfe. Eaton
Black Art. Baraka
Conundrum of the Workshops, The. Kipling
Crayons. Chute
Dab of Color, A. Weiss
Drawing Wildflowers. Graham
Epitaph on an Unfortunate Artist. Graves
Four Heads & How to Do Them. Forbes
From the Workshop of Brancusi and Giancometti. Haines
Half an Hour. Cavafy
Hand, The. Fawcett
I cannot bring a world quite round. Fr. The Man with the Blue Guitar. Stevens
I Laughed When the Painter, Caroline. Martin
Japanese Print. Clarke
Keziah. Brooks
Lapis Lazuli. Yeats
L'Art. Feirstein
L'Art, 1910. Pound
Leaf-Makers, The. Stewart
London Pavement Artist. Schevill
Love's Coming. Wilcox
Monet's Lilies Shuddering. Ferlinghetti
Mosaic Worker, The. Peach
Musée des Beaux Arts. Auden
Museum Piece. Wilbur
Ode on a Grecian Urn. Keats
On Seeing the Elgin Marbles. Keats
On the Marriage of Art and Science. Dorman
Painting a Madonna. Warren
Paring the Apple. Tomlinson
Perfect Symbol, The. Johnson
Post-Impressionist Susurration for the First of November, 1983, A. Carruth
Primitives. Randall
Prolific. Matthews
Recital, The. Schwartz
Rockefeller Collection of Primitive Art, The. Johnson
Sculptor, The. Edson
Sovereigns, The. Mifflin
These are the days when birds come back. Dickinson

Thin are, oh Mind!—the colours which delight. *Fr.* The Mind. Swain
To My Son Parker, Asleep in the Next Room. Kaufman
To Pope Julius II. Michelangelo
Trying to Separate. Pack
Upon Umber: Epigram. Herrick
What Is Left? Vas
When I Buy Pictures. Moore
Why I Am Not a Painter. O'Hara
Woman with Gardenia: A Sketch. Hadas
Eye's Delight: Poems of Art and Architecture (EyDe). Helen Plotz, ed.
See also **Artists' Colonies.**

Artemis
Artemis. Davison
Artemis. Deamer
See also **Diana.**

Arthritis
Arthritis. Glading
While Pruning. Partridge

Arthurian Legend
Defense of Guenevere, The. Morris
Epic, The. Tennyson
Grail, The. Keyes
Grave of King Arthur, The. Warton
"Great Unaffected Vampires and the Moon." Smith
King Arthur's Death. *Unknown*
Lady of Shalott, The. Tennyson
Lancelot. Bontemps
Legend of Camelot, A. Du Maurier
Marriage of Sir Gawain, The. *Unknown*
Merlin. Emerson
Merlin. Hill
Morte d'Arthur. Tennyson
Near Avalon. Morris
On King Arthur's Round Table, at Winchester. Warton
Passing of Arthur, The. *Fr.* The Brut. Layamon
Passing of Arthur, The. Squire
Pelleas and Ettarre. *Fr.* Idylls of the King. Tennyson
Prayer ("Pray for my soul. More things are wrought by prayer"). *Fr.* Idylls of the King: The Passing of Arthur. Tennyson
Prophecia Merlini Doctoris Perfecti. *Unknown*
Round Table, The. Mannyng
Salad—After Tennyson. Collins
Sir Gawaine and the Green Knight. Winters
Temptation of Sir Gawain, The. *Fr.* Sir Gawain and the Green Knight. *Unknown*
Wizard of Alderley Edge, The. Coe

Artichokes
Artichoke. Taylor
Private Feast, A. Jerome

Artifacts
Artifact. Purevich
Stone Hammer Poem. Kroetsch

Artificial Insemination
Alchemy. Farooqi
To My Children Unknown, Produced by Artificial Insemination. Kirkup

Artists' Colonies
Hillcrest. Robinson

Ascension Day
Ascension [*or* Ascention] *Fr.* La Corona. Donne
Ascension Thursday. Lewis
Hymne of the Ascension, An. Drummond
Second Ascension of Christ, The. *Fr.* Forty Days. Wheelwright
They Are All Gone into the World of Light. Vaughan

Ash Trees
Tapestry Trees. Morris

Ashbery, John
To John Ashbery. O'Hara

Ashby, Turner
Ashby. Thompson

Ashes
Novena. Swander

Asia
Tears of Pearl, The. Chang Ts'o

Asian-Americans
Susie Wong Doesn't Live Here. Mark
Breaking Silence; an Anthology of Contemporary Asian American Poets (BrSi). Joseph Bruchac, ed.
See also **Chinese, The; Filipinos; Japanese, The.**

Aspen Trees
Aspen and the Stream, The. Wilbur
Aspens. Thomas
Binsey Poplars (Felled 1879). Hopkins
See also **Poplar Trees.**

Asphodels
Of asphodel, that greeny flower. *Fr.* Asphodel, That Greeny Flower. Williams
Snowflake on asphodel, clear ice on rose. Aiken

Aspirations
Keep a Hand on Your Dream. Kennedy

Assassinations and Assassins
Assassination, The. Justice
Assassination. Lee
Assassination Poems. Ridland
Booth Killed Lincoln. *Unknown*
Charles Guiteau. *Unknown*
Claus von Stauffenberg. Gunn
Down in Dallas. Kennedy
For Malcolm: After Mecca. Barrax
In Memory, 1978. Kazantzis
Martyr, The. Melville
On the Duke of Buckingham, Slain by Felton, the 23rd August, 1628. Felltham
Traction: November 22, 1963. Moss
Zolgotz. *Unknown*

Asses. *See* **Donkeys.**

Assyrians
Destruction of Sennacherib, The. Byron

Astaire, Fred
Dream with Fred Astaire. Berkson

Astarte
To Ashtaroth and Bel. Tchernichowsky

Astrology
Astrologer's Song, An. Kipling
Love's Horoscope. Crashaw
Upon Looking at a Book of Astrology. McFadden
Zodiac Rhyme, The. *Unknown*

Astronauts
Astronaut's Widow. Sneyd
Home. Witte
Problems. Scott
Projection, A. Whittemore
So long. *Fr.* For the First Manned Moon Orbit. Dickey
Spacepoem 3: Off Course. Morgan
Stone Stars. Dann
White Power Poem. Bishop

Astronomy and Astronomers
Astronomer's Journal, An. Shore
Astronomers of Mont Blanc, The. Bowers
Blue Glass. Adcock
Copernican System, The. Chatterton
Ex-Queen among the Astronomers, The. Adcock
Gemini Jones. Espy
Greenwich Observatory. Keyes
Microcosmos. Payack
Old Astronomer to His Pupil, The. Williams
Planetarium. Rich
Stargazer, The. *Unknown*
When I Heard the Learn'd Astronomer. Whitman

Astrophysics
Collapsars. McPherson

Atalanta
Atalanta in Calydon, *sels.* Swinburne

Atheism
At the Smithville Methodist Church. Dunn
Impercipient, The. Hardy
Three Towns, The. Nemerov

Athena
Postcards to Athena. Bishop
See also **Minerva.**

Athens, Greece
Look once more ere we leave this specular Mount. *Fr.* Paradise Regained. Milton
Spring Wind, A. Spencer
Timon Curses Athens and Mankind. *Fr.* Timon of Athens. Shakespeare

Athletes
Ageing Athlete, The. Weiss
Athletes. Gibson
Breed of Athletes, The. Euripides
Ex-Basketball Player. Updike
Morning Athletes. Piercy
Runner, The. Whitman
To an Athlete Dying Young. *Fr.* A Shropshire Lad. Housman

Atlanta, Georgia
Atlanta Exposition Ode. Fordham
Litany of [*or* at] Atlanta, A. Du Bois

Atlantic Charter
Atlantic Charter: 1942. Young

Atlantic Ocean
Castaway, The. Cowper
Crossing the Atlantic. Sexton
How Cyrus Laid the Cable. Saxe
Night Storm. Simms
North Atlantic. Sandburg
Seaweed. Longfellow

Atomic Bomb
Actual Vision of Morning's Extrusion. Dugan
At the Bomb Testing Site. Stafford
Atomic Bomb. Tsuchiya Kyutai
Atomic Courtesy. Jacobson
Back Again from Yucca Flats. Kelley
Day after Trinity, The. Oyama
Day I Once Dreamed, The. Arrowsmith
Earth ("A planet doesn't explode"). Wheelock
Flesh. Levy
Gathered at the River. Levertov
Hibakusha's Letter (1955), The. Mura
Hiding Place. Armour
Hiroshima. Beadnell
In the Year 1945 an Original Child Was Born. *Fr.* Original Child Bomb. Merton
Song: "There's no more talk and ease." Beecham
Test, The. Guttenbrunner
U. S. 1946 King's X. Frost
See also **Hiroshima, Japan; Nuclear War.**

Atsumichi, Prince
Elegies for Prince Atsumichi ("Because I do not know where you are"). *Fr.* Fifty-one Tanka. Izumi
Elegies for Prince Atsumichi ("Clearly he would notice: in my eyes"). *Fr.* Fifty-one Tanka. Izumi
Elegies for Prince Atsumichi ("Dead people come to visit tonight"). *Fr.* Fifty-one Tanka. Izumi
Elegies for Prince Atsumichi ("Discard myself—just the thought is bitter"). *Fr.* Fifty-one Tanka. Izumi
Elegies for Prince Atsumichi ("I miss your voice as you talked to me"). *Fr.* Fifty-one Tanka. Izumi
Elegies for Prince Atsumichi ("I wish I could see you like this snow"). *Fr.* Fifty-one Tanka. Izumi
Elegies for Prince Atsumichi ("It would console me to see you"). *Fr.* Fifty-one Tanka. Izumi

Elegies for Prince Atsumichi ("No dreams through the night"). *Fr.* Fifty-one Tanka. Izumi
Elegies for Prince Atsumichi ("One body, but heart shattered into a thousand pieces"). *Fr.* Fifty-one Tanka. Izumi
Elegies for Prince Atsumichi ("Though my heart isn't a summer field"). *Fr.* Fifty-one Tanka. Izumi
Elegies for Prince Atsumichi ("You are gone, and I have nothing unhappy to remember"). *Fr.* Fifty-one Tanka. Izumi

Attaché Cases
Attaché Case, The. Bogin
Atterbury, Francis, Bishop of Rochester
Epitaph: "Meek Francis lies here, friend, without stop or stay." Prior
Attics
Attic, The. Coulette
Herbs in the Attic. Waniek
In a Garret. Allen
In the Attic. Justice
Up There. Auden
Attucks, Crispus
Crispus Attucks. Hayden
Auckland, New Zealand
Northern Building Society Office Showing Police Headquarters, Auckland. Ensing
To a Maori Figure Cast in Bronze outside the Chief Post Office, Auckland. Tuwhare
Auctions
Auction Sale, The. Reed
Bags of Meat. Hardy
To Henry Wright of Mobberley, Esq. on Buying the Picture of Father Malebranche. Byrom
Auden, Wystan Hugh
Auden at Milwaukee. Spender
Auden's Funeral. Spender
In Memory of W. H. Auden. Slavitt
Just a Smack at Auden. Empson
Seeing Auden Off. Booth
Self-Congratulatory Ode on Mr. Auden's Election to the Professorship of Poetry at Oxford. Mason
To Auden on His Fiftieth. Eberhart
To W.H. Auden at 63. Jackson
To Wystan Auden. Grigson
W. H. Auden & Mantan Moreland. Young
Aughrim, Battle of (1691)
After Aughrim. Lawless
Deep red bogs divided. *Fr.* The Battle of Aughrim. Murphy
Green Martyrs. *Fr.* The Battle of Aughrim. Murphy
Rapparees. *Fr.* The Battle of Aughrim. Murphy
Wolfhound. *Fr.* The Battle of Aughrim. Murphy
August
August. Kharik
August. Ray
August. *Fr.* Sonnets of the Months. San Gimignano
August. Swinburne
August. Thaxter
August. Wylie
August Heat. *Unknown*
August Midnight, An. Hardy
August Night. Fritsch
Mid-August at Sourdough Mountain Lookout. Snyder
Augustine, Saint
Saint Augustine. Plunkett
Augustus. *See* Caesar, Augustus.
Auks
Great Auk's Ghost, The. Hodgson
Aunt Jemima
Aunt Jemima of the Ocean Waves. Hayden
Aunts
Aga Khan, The. Orlen

Aunt Jennifer's Tigers. Rich
Aunt Leaf. Oliver
Emma. Yvonne
Family Turn, A. Stafford
Hope. Sleigh
Introduction to Some Poems, An. Stafford
My Aunt. Holmes
Pair of Fireflies, A. Liu
Photo of Emily, The. Ferlinghetti
Satin Doll. Wojahn
To Aunt Rose. Ginsberg
Auschwitz, Poland
Children of Auschwitz. Korzhavin
Dreams of Auschwitz. Slutsky
On the 25th Anniversary of the Liberation of Auschwitz. Mandel
What big heavy doors! *Fr.* Auschwitz. Wyse
Your Attention Please. Porter
Australia
As a Man Walks. Simpson
At Cooloolah. Wright
Australia. Hope
Australia 1970. Wright
Botany Bay. Freeth
Death of Morgan, The. *Unknown*
First of the Emigrants, The. *Unknown*
H.M.S. Glory at Sydney. Causley
Now I'm Easy. Bogle
Short Time. Ewart
Summer Christmas in Australia, A. Sladen
Sydney Cove, 1788. Porter
Visit of Hope to Sydney Cove, near Botany-Bay. Darwin
Wild Colonial Boy, The. *Unknown*
Collins Book of Australian Poetry, The (CBAP). Rodney Hall, ed.
Poetry in Australia (PoAu). T. Inglis Moore, ed.
Austrian Verse
Contemporary Austrian Poetry; an Anthology (CoAuP). Beth Bjorklund, ed. *and* tr.
Authorship and Authors
Absolute and Abitofhell. Knox
After Dilettante Concetti. Traill
Argument of His Book, The. Herrick
Author to Her Book, The. Bradstreet
Boatman, The. Macpherson
Burning Hills. Ondaatje
Cacoëthes Scribendi. Holmes
Canadian Authors Meet, The. Scott
For the Young Who Want To. Piercy
Gas from a Burner. Joyce
George Crabbe. Robinson
Hamlet's Soliloquy Imitated. Jago
I Have Approached. Paton
Lake Isle, The. Pound
Obit on Parnassus. Fitzgerald
On His Books. Belloc
On Some South African Novelists. Campbell
On the Same. Campbell
Poetry Perpetuates the Poet. Herrick
So That's Who I Remind Me Of. Nash
Sonnet: "I know that all beneath the moon decays." Drummond
There Is No Opera like "Lohengrin." Wheelwright
To an Author. Freneau
Upon the Saying That My Verses Were Made by Another. Killigrew
"What hundred books are best, think you?" I said. Bangs
Words, like Spiders. Wolny
Autism
Death of a Son. Silkin
Private Rooms. O Hehir
Automation
All Watched Over by Machines of Loving Grace. Brautigan
Four Quartz Crystal Clocks. Moore
Valedictory to Standard Oil of Indiana, A. Wagoner

Automobile Accidents
After Labor Day. Lea
Auto Wreck. Shapiro
Bystanders. Matthews
Department, The. Grossman
End, The. Olds
My Father; October 1942. Stafford
Obituary. Fearing
Racer's Widow, The. Glück
Solitude. Tranströmer
Spider Web. Dobyns
Whiplash. Matthews
Automobile Racing
Racer's Widow, The. Glück
Automobiles
Abandonment of Autos. Dawe
Ambition. Bishop
As a boy with a richness of needs I wandered. Dyment
At a Low Mass for Two Hot-Rodders. Kennedy
Autobahnmotorwayautoroute. Mitchell
Automobile, The. Edson
Automobile Mechanics. Baruch
Ballad of Faith. Williams
Brides, The. Hope
Buick. Shapiro
Car, The. Creeley
Car Wash. Livingston
Cars in Caracas, The. Updike
Cherrylog Road. Dickey
Dandy Horse, The. *Unknown*
Drive, The. McFatter
Driving. Livingston
Driving to the Beach. Cole
Driving toward the Lac Qui Parle River. Bly
Fugue. Nemerov
Funny the Way Different Cars Start. Baruch
Gas and Hot Air. Bishop
Gesture. Finkel
Jump Cabling. Pastan
Last of the Poet's Car. Connor
Little Car, The. Apollinaire
Maine. Booth
Man on Wheels. Shapiro
Man Who Owned Cars, The. Fried
Meditation on the A30. Betjeman
Moving between Beloit and Monroe. Noll
Ode to a Dead Dodge. McElroy
Pedestrian's Plaint, The. Lucas
Portrait of the Autist as a New World Driver. Murray
Sacred, The. Dunn
Short Days, The. Updike
Song for a Blue Roadster. Field
Southbound on the Freeway. Swenson
This Dim and Ptolemaic Man. Bishop
Thoreau. Jones
Trip, The. Stafford
True Ballad of the Great Race to Gilmore City, The. Hey
Twink Drives Back, in a Bad Mood, from a Party in Massachusetts. Amabile
Autumn
Ambition. Kennedy
Ancient Autumn. Simic
Apple Song. Frost
As autumn wears on. Tamenori
At this year's end too. Munenaga
Automne Malade. Apollinaire
Autumn. Akhmadulina
Autumn. Apollinaire
Autumn. Baratynsky
Autumn. Campbell
Autumn. *Fr.* The Four Seasons in the Mountains. Chang Yü
Autumn. *Fr.* Aella; a Tragycal Enterlude. Chatterton
Autumn. Clare
Autumn. Glatstein
Autumn. Hoatson
Autumn. Hubbell

Autumn. Hulme
Autumn. Junzaburo
Autumn. Leyeles
Autumn. Manger
Autumn. *Fr.* Summer's Last Will and Testament. Nashe
Autumn. Rossetti
Autumn. Scannell
Autumn. Stevens
Autumn. Tagore
Autumn. Untermeyer
Autumn. Winwar
Autumn, Again Grass. Hidalgo
Autumn; an Ode. Gullans
Autumn Birds. Clare
Autumn, Dark Wanderer. Daryush
Autumn Day. Rilke
Autumn Day, An. Thompson
Autumn day its course has run—the Autumn evening falls, The. Brontë
Autumn Evening. Shotetsu
Autumn Fancies. *Unknown*
Autumn has come. Teika
Autumn ("I at my window sit, and see"). *Unknown*
Autumn in the West. Gallagher
Autumn, Iowa City. Thumboo
Autumn Leaves. Thompson
Autumn ("List to the sad wind, drearily moaning"). Thompson
Autumn Morning, An. *Unknown*
Autumn Night. Michizane
Autumn Night. Tanaka Fuyuji
Autumn so soon. Kyoroku
Autumn ("Summer is gone and all the merry noise"). Clare
Autumn ("The sun shines bright, but sadly"). Thompson
Autumn Thoughts. Tucker
Autumn Wind, The. Clare
Autumnal. Dowson
Autumnal Consummation. Stevenson
Autumnal Ode. De Vere
Autumnal Spring Song. Miller
Autumn's Poem. Kim Hyun-sung
Autumnus. Sylvester
Boudoir Feeling. Hsü Ts'an
Burning of the Leaves, The. Binyon
Calvinist Autumnal. Harrod
Chestnut vendor, The. Szelki
Child's Thought of Harvest, A. "Coolidge"
Colour. White
Come! let us draw the curtains. *Fr.* Autumn. Wolfe.
Cry of the crickets, The. Saigyo
Cuckoo called, The. Sanesada
Day in Autumn, A. Thomas
Death of the Flowers, The. Bryant
Dew and the frost, The. Tameuji
Down! Down! Farjeon
Dying Garden, The. Nemerov
Early Autumn. Joben
Early Autumn. Keiun
Early Autumn. *Fr.* Twenty-three Hokku. Onitsura
Early Autumn. Shotetsu
Eggplants Have Pins and Needles, The. Matveyeva
Elul in Galilee. Goldberg
End of Fall, The. Ponge
End of Summer. Kunitz
End of Summer, The. Minty
Epilogue: "Painted autumn overwhelms, The." Falkner
Evening mists in the depths of my heart. *Fr.* Seventy-eight Tanka. Shikishi
Every single thing. Saigyo
Fall, The. Barnes
Fall. Bethell
Fall. Francis
Fall Is Here, The. Linden
Fall, Leaves, Fall. Brontë

Fall of Leaves. Savage
Falling Leaves. Wu Chia-chi
Falltime. Sandburg
Field of Autumn. Lee
Fields, the mountains, The. Tonna
God's World. Millay
Gold Leaves. Chesterton
Harvest Home. Guiterman
Harvest Moon, The. Longfellow
Heaving Roses of the Hedge Are Stirred, The. Dixon
How One Winter Came in the Lake Region. Campbell
Hurrahing in Harvest. Hopkins
I Am the Autumn. Manger
Illuminations. Goldberg
Immortal Autumn. MacLeish
In the Fall. *Fr.* In Memoriam James Joyce. "MacDiarmid"
Indian Summer. Parker
Issues of the Fall. Lea
Lament in Autumn. Stewart
Last Brightness. Goldberg
Late Fall. Altmann
Late in Fall. Wilson
Leaves of the small oaks, The. *Fr.* Twenty-four Tanka. Sanetomo
Long and Lonely Winter, The. Goulder
Maple and Sumach. Day Lewis
Mist and All, The. Willson
Mnemosyne. Stickney
Moon, The. *Fr.* The Moon. Tamesada
Morns are meeker than they were, The. Dickinson
Mountain wind blows, The. Tonna
Mummies, The. Kumin
Name of it is "Autumn," The. Dickinson
Not many days have passed. *Fr.* A Compendium of Good Tanka. Teika
November. Bryant
November Night. Crapsey
O Amber Day, amid the Autumn Gloom. Allison
October. Justice
October Arriving. Simic
Ode to the Spirit of Earth in Autumn. Meredith
Ode to the West Wind. Shelley
Of Autumn. Porumbacu
On autumn nights. *Fr.* Kokin Shu. *Unknown*
On Evergreen Hill. Yoshinobu
On Lake Pend Oreille. Shelton
Only yesterday/ I had thought I must visit. Ietaka
Orchard. Engels
Poem in October. Thomas
Poor is the triumph o'er the timid hare. *Fr.* The Seasons: Autumn. Thomson
Quiet. Ungaretti
Random Thoughts on Autumn. Liang Ch'i-ch'ao
Real Property. Monro
Red in Autumn. Gould
Red Leaves. Tameshige
Rich Days. Davies
Ripe and Bearded Barley, The. *Unknown*
Robin Redbreast. Allingham
Robin sang sweetly. *Unknown*
Scattered Leaves. Henson
September. Fallis
September Midnight. Teasdale
Shape of Autumn, The. Russ
Simple Autumnal. Bogan
Something Told the Wild Geese. Field
Song: "Feathers of the willow, The." Dixon
Song: "Why fadest thou in death." Dixon
Song at the Beginning of Autumn. Jennings
Song for Autumn. Young
Sonnet: Autumn Garden. Campana
Sonnet in Autumn. Petersen

Soon Autumn. Tachihara Michizo
Spring and Fall. Hopkins
Summer Is Gone. *Unknown*
Survivor. MacLeish
Tell Me Not Here [It Needs Not Saying] Housman
Ten Lines: Autumn. Hsiang Yang
That the autumn has come. *Fr.* Eighty-seven Hokku. Buson
That time of year thou may'st [or maist] in me behold. *Fr.* Sonnets, LXXIII. Shakespeare
There is about these autumn evenings bright. Tyutchev
They Say My Verse Is Sad: No Wonder. Housman
They say the rose garden. Dard
Thief, The. Pawsey
To Autumn. Blake
To Autumn. Keats
To the Fringed Gentian. Bryant
Too beautiful for me, but I have to cleave in. *Fr.* Inutsukuba Shu. *Unknown*
Too restless to sleep. Teika
Tourist Death. MacLeish
Vagabond Song, A. Carman
Well do I know that human life is passing. *Fr.* Manyo Shu. Yakamochi
When I see the moonlight pouring. *Fr.* Kokin Shu. *Unknown*
When the Frost Is on the Punkin. Riley
When the moonlight. *Fr.* Kokin Shu. *Unknown*
When the spring comes. *Fr.* Manyo Shu. Nukada
When you think of it. Teika
Wind and Silver. Lowell
Winds of spring, The. Saigyo
Written in Autumn. Cole

Aviation and Aviators
Aging Poet, on a Reading Trip to Dayton, Visits the Air Force Museum and Discovers There a Plane He Once Flew, The. Snyder
Air Field. Siegel
Airstrip in Essex, 1960, An. Hall
Buzz Plane, The. Francis
Darius Green and His Flying-Machine. Trowbridge
Death of the Ball Turret Gunner, The. Jarrell
First Flight. Hoffman
Frightened Flier Goes North, The. Kazantzis
Icarus. Iremonger
Icarus. Spender
Landscape near an Aerodrome, The. Spender
Losses. Jarrell
Lost Pilot, The. Tate
Nocturne for October 31st, A. Winters
Old Pilot, The. Hall
Winged bull trundles to the wired perimeter, The. *Fr.* Flight to Italy. Day Lewis
To an Aviator. Hicky
When a Beau Goes In. Ewart
Wrights' Biplane, The. Frost
See also **Air Travel; Air Warfare; Airports.**
Avignon, France
An Orchard at Avignon. Robinson
Avoca, Ireland
Meeting of the Waters, The. Moore
Avocados
Avocado. Logan
Avon River, Canada
To the Avon River above Stratford, Canada. Reaney
Avon River, England
Ebb Tide, The. Southey
Axes
Axe Handles. Snyder
In a muddy creek. *Unknown*
Ay
Ay: A Gift of Elephants. Mutamociyar
Ay: His Hill. Mutamociyar

Ayr, Scotland
Flow Gently, Sweet Afton. Burns
Azaleas
Azalea, The. *Fr.* The Unknown Eros.
  Patmore
Though I see the white azaleas on the shore.
  Fr. Manyo Shu. *Unknown*
White Azaleas. Kimball
Aztecs
Aztec City, The. Ware
La Noche Triste. Frost
Song of Nezahualcoyotl. *Unknown*

B

Baal
To Ashtaroth and Bel. Tchernichowsky
Baal-Shem-Tov
Baal Shem Tov. Klein
Saint Besht. Manger
Babel, Tower of
From the four corners of the earth. *Fr.* The
  People, Yes. Sandburg
Tower of Babel, The. Crouch
Babies
An Unborn Child. Mahon
At the Washing of My Son. Ray
Babies, The. Strand
Baby. Eastman
Baby, The. *Fr.* At the Back of the North
  Wind. Macdonald
Baby. Oates
Babyhood. *Fr.* Bitter-sweet. Holland
Baby's Drinking Song. Kirkup
Baby's feet, like sea-shells pink, A. *Fr.*
  Étude Réaliste. Swinburne
Bringing Up Babies. Fuller
Candida ("Candida is one today").
  Kavanagh
Candle Has Slept in Its Own Flame, A. Lo
  Chih-ch'eng
Chicago Boy Baby. Sandburg
Child Crying. Thwaite
Child Is Introduced to the Cosmos at Birth,
  The. *Unknown*
Clinic Day. Barnes
Coming and Going. Johnson
Cottager to Her Infant, The. Wordsworth
Cradle Song: "Curled like a hoop in sleep."
  Durrell
Cradle Song: "Sleep, sleep, beauty bright."
  Blake
Dahn the Plug'ole. *Unknown*
Days fail: night broods over afternoon, The.
  Fr. The First Year. Scovell
Dolls, The. Yeats
Errantry. Fitzgerald
Eskimo Baby, An. Diamond
Evening of Montale's Death, The. Stewart
First Step, The. Saxton
Five Days Old. Webb
Frost at Midnight. Coleridge
How Many Days Has My Baby to Play?
  Unknown
How You Were Born. Libera
I am proud of your soft, brown eyes. *Fr.*
  Sunlight: A Sequence for My Daughter.
  Ignatow
In go-cart so tiny. Greenaway
In My Name. Nichols
In the Forest. Bowering
Infant. O Hehir
Infant Joy. *Fr.* Songs of Innocence. Blake
Infant Sorrow. *Fr.* Songs of Experience.
  Blake
Kadia the Young Mother Speaks. Sampter
Little. Aldis

Little Brown Baby. Dunbar
Lucky. Song
Magus, The. Dickey
Man Dancing with a Baby. Stewart
Maternal Despotism; or, The Rights of
  Infants. Graves
Morning Song. Plath
Mother to Her Waking Infant, A. Baillie
Mundus et Infans. Auden
My Baby Has No Name Yet. Nam Jo
My infinite child, hold me to sleep. *Fr.*
  Sunlight: A Sequence for My Daughter.
  Ignatow
Night Dances, The. Plath
Night Feeding. Rukeyser
Now or Never. Moffett
O sleep, my babe, hear not the rippling wave.
  Fr. Phantasmion. Coleridge
On an Infant. Illyés
Peacock's Feather, A. Heaney
Peak and Puke. De la Mare
Photograph of a Baby. Brasch
Poem for Emily, A. Williams
Rampage, The. Williams
Rock-a-bye, baby, thy cradle is green.
  Mother Goose
Sara in Her Father's Arms. Oppen
Six Weeks Old. Morley
Slippery. Sandburg
Song for the Middle of the Night, A. Wright
Song for the Newborn. *Unknown*
Song My. Griffin
Sonnet to a Friend Who Asked, How I Felt
  When the Nurse First Presented My Infant
  to Me. Coleridge
Terrible Infant, A. Locker-Lampson
To a Friend's Child. Barnstone
To Our Daughter. Armitage
To the Newborn. Tóth
Tonversation with Baby, A. Bishop
Unknown Girl in the Maternity Ward.
  Sexton
Verses for a First Birthday. Barker
Way the Baby Slept, The. Riley
Where Is My Butterfly Net? McCord
Young bee falls between my window, A.
  Fr. Brother Jonathan, Brother Kafka.
  O'Sullivan
You're. Plath
See also   **Infant Death.**
Baboons
Baboon. *Unknown*
Baboon. *Fr.* Hunter Poems of the Yoruba.
  Unknown
Baboon, The. Williams
Baboon 2. *Unknown*
Big Baboon, The. Belloc
Theology of Bongwi, the Baboon, The.
  Campbell
Baby-sitting
Baby-Sitting. Clarke
Babysitters, The. Plath
Lullaby: "Than mind a child/ That yelps like
  this/ I'd all day work." *Unknown*
Misnomer. Merriam
Babylon
Babylon. Hodgson
Babylon, O Babylon. Guevara
Harps Hung Up in Babylon. Colton
Bacchus
Bacchus's Opinion of Wine, and Other
  Beverages. *Fr.* Bacchus in Tuscany.
  Redi
Drinking Song, A. *Fr.* Antony and
  Cleopatra. Shakespeare
Great Bacchus: From the Greek. Prior
Hymn to Bacchus, A. Herrick
Triumph of Bacchus and Ariadne. Medici
Bach, Johann Sebastian
Bach. Manner
Dream. Moore
Jesu, Joy of Man's Desiring. Fitzgerald

Living Room, The. Schnackenberg
Theme and Variation. De Vries
Upon Listening to the Third Brandenburg
  Concerto. Fritsch
Bachelors
Bachelor, The/ Gives humblest thanks.
  Unknown
Burial of the Bachelor, The. *Unknown*
Home from work. *Unknown*
I Don't Let the Girls Worry My Mind.
  Unknown
New England Bachelor, A. Eberhart
Two Old Bachelors, The. Lear
Where the Single Men Go in Summer.
  Bourne
Back to Africa Movement
Back to Africa. Bennett
Centenary's Day. Garvey
Bacon, Francis (b. 1910)
Francis Bacon Paints Velázquez's Pope.
  Schmied
Badgers
Badger. Clare
Badgers, The. Phillpotts
Bess My Badger. Hughes
Catch, The. Ghiselin
Six Badgers, The. Graves
Bagels
Bagel, The. Ignatow
Baggage
In the Baggage Room at Greyhound.
  Ginsberg
Bagpipes
Pipes at Lucknow, The. Whittier
Bahamas
Bahamas. Oppen
Baker, Josephine
So Many Feathers. Cortez
Balaam
Balaam. Keble
Balaclava, Crimea
Charge of the Light Brigade, The. Tennyson
Baldness
Bald. Zavatsky
Bald Cavalier, The. *Unknown*
Penalties of Baldness, The. Seaman
Baldwin, James
For James Baldwin. Boyle
Ballads and Folk Songs
American Folk Poetry; an Anthology (AmFP).
  Duncan Emrich, ed.
American Songbag, The (AS). Carl
  Sandburg, ed.
*Common Muse, The; an Anthology of Popular
  British Ballad Poetry, XVth-XXth Century*
  (CoMu). Vivian de Sola Pinto *and* Allan
  Edwin Rodway, eds.
English and Scottish Ballads (EnSB). Robert
  Graves, ed.
English and Scottish Popular Ballads (ESPB).
  Helen Child Sargent *and* George Lyman
  Kittredge, eds.
Faber Book of Ballads, The (FaBoBa).
  Matthew Hodgart, ed.
Oxford Book of Ballads, The (OxBB). James
  Kinsley, ed.
*Oxford Book of English Traditional Verse,
  The* (OBET). Frederick Woods, ed.
Oxford Book of Scottish Verse, The (OxBS).
  John MacQueen *and* Tom Scott, comps.
See also   **Blues (Music); Sea Chanteys.**
Ballet
Ballet Blanc. Pollitt
Dance Script with Electric Ballerina. Fulton
Song of the Ballet. Morton
Balloons
Air Balloon, The. *Fr.* Aerophorion. Pye
Armadillo[—Brazil], The. Bishop
Balloon, The. Kuskin
Balloon Faces. Sandburg
Balloon Man, The. Fyleman

Balloon Man, The. Herbert
Balloon Seller, The. Fleming
Balloons. Pagis
Balloons. Plath
Breaking Out. Ammons
Les Ballons. Wilde
Pop. McFadden
Tragedy. Spargur

Ballrooms
Armadillo[—Brazil], The. Bishop

Balls
Ball Poem, The. Berryman

Ballylee, Ireland
Coole Park and Ballylee, 1931. Yeats
To Be Carved on a Stone at Thoor Ballylee.
　Yeats

Baltimore, Maryland
Incident. Cullen
Streets of Baltimore. *Unknown*

Bamboo
Bamboo. Hagiwara Sakutaro
Bamboo. Plomer
Bamboo Grass. Kagura
Don't cut the bamboo grass under the elm.
　Fr. Manyo Shu. *Unknown*
Hearing the Snow. Kido
If not for the bamboos. Joben

Bananas
Banana. Bell

Bandits. *See* **Crime and Criminals;**
　Highwaymen.

Bands
Band Played On, The. Palmer
Ten Tom-Toms. Fitzpatrick

Bangkok, Thailand
Bangkok. Scott

Bangladesh
Bangladesh. A'Zmi

Banjos
Banjo, The. Winner
Banjo Player, The. Johnson
Song of the Banjo, The. Kipling

Banking and Bankers
Girls Working in Banks. Shapiro
Goody O'Grumpity. Brink
Plot to Assassinate the Chase Manhattan
　Bank, The. Larsen
See also **Financiers.**

Baptism
Baptism. Bell
Jesus, Master, O Discover. *Unknown*
My Baptismal Birthday. Coleridge
On the Baptized Ethiopian. Crashaw
Peacock's Feather, A. Heaney
Testimony, A. Lyon

Bar Kokba, Simon
Bar Kochba. Lazarus

Bar Mitzvah
Bar Mitzvah. Goldemberg

Barbados
Still sparkles here the glory of the west. *Fr.*
　Barbadoes. Chapman
When frequent rains, and gentle show'rs
　descend. *Fr.* Barbados. Weekes

Barbecues. *See* **Picnics and Barbecues.**

Barbers
Ballad of a Barber, The. Beardsley
Barber, barber, shave a pig. Mother Goose
Barber's, The. De la Mare
Barbershop. Gardner
Lyric Barber. Romano
Maestro's Barber Shop, The. Vásquez
New Lady Barber at Ralph's Barber Shop,
　The. Dangel
To a Child Trapped in a Barber Shop.
　Levine
To My Hairdresser. St. Leger

Barcelona, Spain
Dream of Barcelona: My Ancient World.
　Mutsuo

Bards
Good Tradition, The. *Unknown*
Hear the Voice of the Bard! *Fr.* Songs of
　Experience. Blake
I ask, who will buy a poem? O'Heffernan
O Black and Unknown Bards. Johnson
On the Breaking-up of a School. O'Huiginn
Were Not the Gael Fallen. O'Mulconry

Barebone, Praise-God
Praise-God Barebones. Cortissoz

Barges
Hospital Barge at Cérisy. Owen

Barker, George
For George Barker at Seventy. Wright

Barley
Ripe and Bearded Barley, The. *Unknown*

Barmaids
Glass of Beer, A. Stephens

Barns
Barn, The. Berry
Barn, The. Blunden
Barn, The. Heaney
Barn, The. Spender
Barn, The. Thomas
Barn in Winter, The. MacIntosh
Hay Scuttle. Morgan
Human Things. Nemerov

Barons' War (1263-1267)
Against the Baron's Enemies. *Unknown*
Song of Lewes, The. *Unknown*

Barrel Organs. *See* **Hurdy-Gurdies.**

Barry, Thomas
Answer to Thomas Barry, An. Fitzgerald

Bars and Bartenders
Bars. Guillén
D-Y Bar. Welch
Fill Up Those Glasses, Bartender. Bollers
Glass of Beer, A. Stephens
Hilltop, The. Hugo
I Was Sitting in McSorley's. Cummings
I Went into the Maverick Bar. Snyder
Indian Guys at the Bar. Ortiz
Indian Macho. Oliver
Introduction to a Pub in Limerick. Skinner
Lament for Barney Flanagan. Baxter
Man Is Beaten Up, A. Garai
Miss Babian Tending a Bar on the Atlantic
　Coast ("Miss Babian, in this coast bar").
　Tellez
Saturday Night in Woody. Smith
Sway. Johnson

Barters
Barter. Teasdale

Barth, Karl
On the Death of Karl Barth. Clemo

Baseball
Abominable Baseball Bat, The. Kennedy
Analysis of Baseball. Swenson
At the Ball Game. Williams
Babe Ruth. Runyon
Ballad of Dead Yankees, The. Petersen
Ballgame, The. Baraka
Base Stealer, The. Francis
Baseball. Mazur
Baseball. Sherman
Baseball and Writing. Moore
Baseball Canto. Ferlinghetti
Baseball Note. Adams
Baseball's Sad Lexicon. Adams
Basket Catch. Schneider
Casey at the Bat. Thayer
Casey—Twenty Years Later. McDonald
Casey's Revenge. Wilson
Catch. Francis
Clayfeld's Glove. Pack
Clothespins. Dybek
Cobb Would Have Caught It. Fitzgerald
Couplet. Hall
Decline and Fall of a Roman Umpire. Nash
Don Larsen's Perfect Game. Goodman
Double Play, The. Wallace

Dream of a Baseball Star. Corso
Empathy for David Winfield. Shapiro
Enos Slaughter. Havelin
Exercise in Preparation for a Pindaric Ode to
　Carl Hubbell. Schwartz
Extra-Inning Ballgame, The. Johnson
Fan. Lew
Fly Ball. Masters
For Hoyt Wilhelm. Oppenheimer
Heart. *Fr.* Damn Yankees. Adler
History of the Human Body/ Winfield's Infield
　Hit/ The Lassitude of the Infinite, The.
　Nauen
Hits and Runs. Sandburg
Hometown Piece for Messrs. Alston and
　Reese. Moore
How I Learned English. Djanikian
In My Meanest Daydream. Gildner
Instruction. Hilberry
I've Never Written a Baseball Poem. Ritchie
Jackie Robinson. Clifton
July the First. Currie
Kid, The. Bezner
Lady Pitcher, The. MacDonald
Last Baseball Samurai, The. Clark
Let's Go, Mets. Morrison
Letter to Mantsch from Havre. Hugo
Listening to Baseball in the Car. Mazur
Mantle. Heyen
Mystery Baseball. Dacey
Old-fashioned Pitcher, The. Phair
One to Nothing. Kizer
Origin of Baseball, The. Patchen
Pasttime. Grazia
Pitcher. Francis
Poem for Ed "Whitey" Ford, A. Holden
Polo Grounds. Humphries
Right Where He Left Off. Weeden
Roundhouse Voices, The. Smith
Sacrifice Bunt. Jacobs
Sign for My Father, Who Stressed the Bunt.
　Bottoms
Slide, Kelly, Slide. Kelly
Song of Snohomish, The. Wallace
Take Me Out to the Ball Game. Norworth
Umpire, The. Bracker
Umpire, The. Gibson
Villanelle: "You cannot rest behind the plate."
　Feld
Where, O Where? Bracker
World Champions. Smith

Basho (Matsuo Bosho)
Bosho's Old Hut. *Fr.* Thirty-three Hokku.
　Kikaku

Basketball
Anthem: "America, if you were a basketball
　court." Vincent
Basketball. Giovanni
Basketball. Vincent
Basketball: A Retrospective. Dunn
Basketball Season Begins. Krapf
Basketball Star. Fufuka
Charge. Gilbert
Ex-Basketball Player. Updike
Fast Break. Hirsch
Fernando ("Fernando has a basketball").
　Ridlon
First Love. Lindner
Foul Shot. Hoey
I Try to Turn In My Jock. Hilton
In Memory of the Utah Stars. Matthews
Jump Shooter, The. Trudell
Lanky Hank Farrow. Witt
Makin' Jump Shots. Harper
New World in the Morning. German
Nothing but Net. Scheele
Patrick Ewing Takes a Foul Shot. Ackerman

Point Guard. Adoff
Scoring. Cartwright
Take Who Takes You. Gardner
When I Got It Right. Lindner
Wilt Chamberlain. Knudson

Bass, Sam
Sam Bass. *Unknown*

Bastille Day
14 July 1956. Lerner

Bastogne, Battle of (1944–1945)
Battle, The. Simpson

Bath, England
Hearken, Lady Betty, hearken. *Fr.* The New
  Bath Guide. Anstey
If to the Pump Room in the morn we go.
  Fr. The Diseases of Bath; a Satire.
  Unknown

Baths and Bathing
Bath, The. Graham
Bath, The. Snyder
Bathtubs. Lattimore
Before the Bath. Marsh
Centaur's Bath, The. Urbina
Dahn the Plug'ole. *Unknown*
Friday Night after Bathing. Levy
Girls Bathing, Galway 1965. Heaney
Gloire de Dijon. Lawrence
Hammam Name, The. Flecker
Happy Winter, Steamy Tub. Gundersheimer
Hot Bath in an Old Hotel. Rankin
I Wonder What It Feels Like to Be Drowned?
  Graves
In a Warm Bath. Rakosi
Miss Twye. Ewart
My Mother Takes a Bath. Kageyama
Old Man, the Sweat Lodge. George
Pater's Bathe. Parry
Soap, the Oppressor. Johnson
Song of the Bath, The. Gibbs
Sweat, The. NorthSun
That Old Sauna High. Hollo
38 Main Street. Lifshin
Voyage of Jimmy Poo, The. Emanuel
Washing. Drinkwater
Way They Scrub, The. Ross

Bathsheba
Bethsabe's Song. *Fr.* David and Bethsabe.
  Peele

Bats
Bat, The. Jacobs
Bat. Lawrence
Bat, The. Pitter
Bat, The. Roethke
Bat, The. Spear
Bat in the Bedroom, The. Crum
Bat is dun, with wrinkled wings, The.
  Dickinson
Bats, The. Hillyer
Bats. Jarrell
Bats. Smith
Haiku: "As the bat flies." Masaoka Shiki
Intruder, The. Kizer
Mad Hatter's Song, The. *Fr.* Alice's
  Adventures in Wonderland. "Carroll"
Man and Bat. Lawrence
Mind. Wilbur
Seven Mexican Children. Schmidt
To the Bat. King

Battlefields
All That Is Left. Basho
At Vshchizh. Tyutchev
Battle-Field, The. Bryant
Battle of Blenheim, The. Southey
Battlefield. Aldington
Concord Hymn. Emerson
Grass. Sandburg
In Flanders Fields. McCrae
Inscription for Marye's Heights,
  Fredericksburg. Melville
No Man's Land. Bogle
On a Field Trip at Fredericksburg. Smith

On the Spartan Dead at Thermopylae.
  Simonides
Remembering That Island. McGrath
Shiloh; a Requiem. Melville
Sleeper in the Valley, The. *Fr.*
  Eighteen-Seventy. Arthur Rimbaud
They Will Look for a Few Words. Turner
Vergissmeinnicht. Douglas

Battles. *See under name, e.g.,* **Bunker Hill,**
  Battle of

Baucis and Philemon
Philemon and Baucis. *Fr.* Metamorphoses.
  Ovid

Baudelaire, Charles
After a Passage in Baudelaire. Duncan
Ave atque Vale. Swinburne
Baudelaire. Schwartz
Baudelaire in Brussels. Cronin

Baudot, Jean-Paul
Letter to Jean-Paul Baudot, at Christmas.
  Stryk

Bavaria
Lines on Leaving a Scene in Bavaria.
  Campbell
Munich Elegy No. 1. Barker

Bay Trees. *See* **Laurels.**

Bayous
Down the Bayou. Townsend
Shooting Ducks in South Louisiana.
  Tillinghast

Beaches
Afternoon: Amagansett Beach. Wheelock
Amagansett Beach Revisited. Wheelock
At the Slackening of the Tide. Wright
Beach at Evening, The. Ferry
Beach Glass. Clampitt
Beach in August, The. Kees
Beach is beautiful; and there grow, The. *Fr.*
  Manyo Shu. Kuramochi Chitose
Beach Talk. MacCaig
Beach Women, The. Pinsky
Children, the Sandbar, That Summer.
  Rukeyser
Concerning Unnatural Nature: An Inverted
  Form. Summers
Constant, The. Ammons
Deserted Beach. Dallas
Don't cut the shrub on Idemi Beach. *Fr.*
  Manyo Shu. *Unknown*
Dover Beach. Arnold
Driving to the Beach. Cole
East Anglian Bathe. Betjeman
German Shepherd. Livingston
Littoral. Flax
Miramar Beach. *Fr.* To What Strangers,
  What Welcome. Cunningham
On the Beach at Night. Whitman
On the Beach at Night Alone. Whitman
On the Marginal Way. Wilbur
People on This Beach Will Never, The.
  Amichai
Point Shirley. Plath
Prospect Beach. Lipsitz
Recipe for Sand. Brinson Curiel
Sandpiper, The. Thaxter
Skin Divers, The. Starbuck
Small War, A. *Fr.* Poems from Mexico.
  Bernstein
Snow Lies Sprinkled on the Beach, The.
  Bridges
Son and Surf. Strong
Strand at Lough Beg, The. Heaney
Summer Beach. Cornford
Waking from a Nap on the Beach. Swenson
Watch Hill. Scott
Wind Is Blowing West, The. Ceravolo
With Kit, Age 7, at the Beach. Stafford

Beads
Song for Healing, A. LeBrasseur
You Smell like Grandma's Beads. Woody

Beagles
Beagles. Rodgers

Bean, Judge Roy
Roy Bean. *Unknown*

Beans
Shelling Jacobs Cattle Beans. Kumin

Beards
There was an old man with a beard. Lear

Bears
Adventures of Isabel. Nash
Bear, The. Frost
Bear, The. Hughes
Bear, The. Kinnell
Bear, The. Momaday
Bear, The. Stanford
Bear: A Totem Dance As Seen by Raven.
  Blue Cloud
Bear Hunting. Aua
Bear in Bed. Herzberg
Bear on the Delhi Road, The. Birney
Bear Ropin' Buckaroo. Barker
Bear Who Came to Dinner, The.
  Stoutenburg
Bears. Rich
Brown Bear, The. Austin
Dancing Bear, The. Field
Dancing Bear, The. Southey
Destruction. Kyger
Dino Campana and the Bear. Hirsch
Elizabeth's War with the Christmas Bear.
  Dubie
Grandpa Bear's Lullaby. Yolen
Grizzly. Harte
Grizzly Bear. Austin
He comes from the north. *Fr.* Sioux
  Metamorphoses. *Unknown*
In Love with the Bears. Kuzma
In the Summer We Eat. Gay
Infant Innocence. Housman
Lady and the Bear, The. Roethke
Lines Written by a Bear of Very Little Brain.
  Milne
Lost Silvertip. Reed
Meeting a Bear. Wagoner
Part of the Darkness. Gardner
Polar Bear. Kredensor
Self-Portrait, as a Bear. Hall
Shaman/Bear. Endrezze-Danielson
Squaring the Circle. Coxe
Ten Commandments. Kulbak
To the Bear. *Fr.* Bear Song. Rákos
To the Hunter. *Fr.* Bear Song. Rákos
Truro Bear, The. Oliver

Beatniks
Problem in Social Geometry—the Inverted
  Square! Durem

Beatrice Portinari
Sonnet: Of Beatrice de' Portinari, on All
  Saints' Day. Dante

Beaufort, South Carolina
National Cemetery, Beaufort, South Carolina,
  The. Heard

Beaumont, Francis
Epitaph upon My Dear Brother, Francis
  Beaumont, An. Beaumont
On Mr. Francis Beaumont (Then Newly
  Dead). Corbet
To Francis Beaumont. Jonson

Beauty
African Beauty. Olaleye-Oruene
Ah Cloris! That I Now Could Sit. *Fr.* The
  Mulberry Garden. Sedley
Alabama. Fields
Ask Me No More Where Jove Bestows.
  Carew
Barbie Doll. Piercy
Barter. Teasdale
Beautiful. Bixler
Beautiful Changes, The. Wilbur
Beautiful Ohio. Wright
Beautiful Things. Allerton

Beautiful Woman Who Sings, The ("The beautiful woman at Laguna"). Allen
Beautifull Mistress, A. Carew
Beauty. Binyon
Beauty. Cowley
Beauty. "E-Yeh-Shure"
Beauty. Rosenberg
Beauty. Fr. The Passionate Pilgrim. Shakespeare
Beauty. Whitman
Beauty. Wylie
Beauty and Terror. Harford
Beauty as a Shield. Robinson
Beauty Imposes. Neilson
Beauty of Things, The. Jeffers
Beauty, sweet Love, is like the morning dew. Fr. To Delia. Daniel
Beauty's Hands Are Cool. Baker
Behold, O Aspasia! I Send You Verses. Fr. Pericles and Aspasia. Landor
Believe Me, If All Those Endearing Young Charms. Moore
Brittle beauty [or beautie], that nature made so frail[e]. Surrey
Brown Is My Love. Unknown
Changeful Beauty. Unknown
Cold Term. Baraka
Colours of Love, The. Devlin
Common Blessings. Clark
Continental College of Beauty, The. Strand
Craftsman, The. Christian
Death's Warning to Beauty. Unknown
Defiance, The. Flatman
Definition of Beauty, The. Herrick
Delight in Disorder. Herrick
Description of Beauty, A. Daniel
Do Not, Oh, Do Not Prize. Unknown
Each and All. Emerson
Elegy, to an Old Beauty, An. Parnell
Enjoy Thy April Now. Fr. A Description of Beauty. Daniel
Epigram: "Beauty, a silver dew that falls in May." Unknown
Euclid Alone Has Looked on Beauty Bare. Millay
Frailty of Beauty, The. Fr. Alcilia. "C."
Give beauty all her right. Campion
Glory, The. Thomas
Go [or Goe,] Lovely Rose. Waller
Great Breath, The. "Æ"
High waves that come riding across the sea. Raimbaut de Vaqueiras
Holy Poet, I have heard. Fr. Thanks from Earth to Heaven. Wheelock
Hymn to Intellectual Beauty. Shelley
I Love All Beauteous Things. Bridges
Immortal, The. Pickthall
In Beauty May I Walk. Unknown
Independence Day. Smith
Ingrateful [l] Beauty Threatened. Carew
It Is Not Beauty I Demand. Darley
It'll be a long time again before my friends. Vidal
Johannes Agricola in Meditation. Browning
Judith of Bethulia. Ransom
July 31. Jordan
Lady's Dressing Room, The. Swift
Larkinesque. Ryan
Like Snow on the Alps. Dropkin
List, The. Dennis
Lonely Beauty. Fr. The Complaint of Rosamond. Daniel
Lord, I have not time to pray. Fr. Impiety. Magaret
Lord of the Far Horizons. Carman
Loveliness. Fr. Hymns for the Amusement of Children. Smart
Madrigal: "Like the Idalian Queen [e]." Drummond
Miss Summerfest. Firer
My Love in Her Attire. Unknown

My mistress' eyes are nothing like the sun. Fr. Sonnets, CXXX. Shakespeare
1909. Apollinaire
No Images. Cuney
No Second Troy. Yeats
Nonpareil. Prior
O Love, That Dost with Goodness Crown. Chadwick
Ode on a Grecian Urn. Keats
Ode to Beauty. Emerson
Of Dying Beauty. Zukofsky
Oh, her beauty—the tender maid! Its brilliance gives light. Ibnu 'L-Arabi
Old Lady's Lament for Her Youth, The. Villon
On Lucy Countesse of Bedford. Jonson
Peter Quince at the Clavier. Stevens
Pied Beauty. Hopkins
Poem, or Beauty Hurts Mr. Vinal. Cummings
Poet Recognizing the Echo of the Voice, A. Wakoski
Prayer, A: "Each day I walk with wonder." Scollard
Prayer: "Lord, make me sensitive to the sight." Marr
Primer of Plato. Garrigue
Question in a Field. Bogan
Saint Francis and the Sow. Kinnell
Saturday: The Small-Pox. Fr. Six Town Eclogues. Montagu
Scribe, The. De la Mare
She Walks in Beauty. Byron
Song: "Noe more unto my thoughts appeare." Godolphin
Song: "Oh [or O] fair[e] sweet face, oh [or O] eyes celestial[l] bright." Fr. Women Pleased. Fletcher
Sonnet: Beauty on a Western Balcony. Sandoval y Zapata
Sonnet of Black Beauty. Herbert of Cherbury
Stella's Birth-day, 1718/19. Swift
Stolen Pleasure. Drummond
Study in Aesthetics, The. Pound
There Is a Garden in Her Face. Campion
Thing of beauty is a joy forever, A. Fr. Endymion [a Poetic Romance]. Keats
Thou Art Not Fair. Campion
Time stands still, with gazing on her face! Unknown
Tinder, The. Carew
To a Young Beauty. Yeats
To Cynthia, on Concealment of Her Beauty. Kynaston
To Helen. Poe
To His Friend, Promising That Though Her Beauty Fade, Yet His Love Shall Last. Turberville
To the Most Beautiful Lady, the Lady Bridget Manners. Barnes
True Beauty. Beaumont
Unutterable Beauty, The. Studdert-Kennedy
Upon Her Feet. Herrick
Upon the Nipples of Julia's Breast. Herrick
White Pines, Felled 1984. Eberhart
Who Walks with Beauty. Morton
Wishes to His Supposed Mistress[e] Crashaw
With a half-glance upon the sky. Fr. A Character. Tennyson
Woman's Beauty. Fr. Vashti. Abercrombie
World Is Full of Beauty, The. Edwards
"Ye tradeful merchants that, with weary toil." Fr. Amoretti, XV. Spenser
Yes, But. Wright

Beauty and the Beast
Mythics. Chasin

Beauty Pageants
Ms World. March

Beavers
Beaver's Story, The. Watkins

See also **Mountain Beaver.**
Bedford, Lucy Russell, Countess of. See **Russell.**
Bedouins
Of the Azazmeh Too. Guri
Bedrooms
Country Bedroom, The. Cornford
Beds
"Ah bed! the field where joy's peace some do see." Fr. Astrophel and Stella, XCVIII. Sidney
Bed, The. Hope
Bed, The. Shapiro
Bed Time. Davison
Bed without a Woman, A. Souster
Cot, The. Amen
Earthen K'ang, An. Fr. Songs Composed in Prison. Sung Wan
For City Spring. Benét
Formed long ago, yet made today. Mother Goose
Insomnia the Gem of the Ocean. Updike
Land of Counterpane, The. Stevenson
Most beds are beds. Fr. The Bed Book. Plath
My Bed Is a Boat ("My bed is like a little boat"). Stevenson
My Mother and the Bed. Lifshin
Sleepin' at the Foot o' the Bed. Patrick
These are the beds. Fr. The Bed Book. Plath
Translation of Lines by Benserade. Johnson
Beech Trees
Beech, The. Young
Beecher, Henry Ward
Henry Ward Beecher. Phelps
Beef
But hark! a sound is stealing on my ear. Fr. Beer. Calverley
Beekeeping and Bees
Animal, Vegetable and Mineral. Bogan
Apprentice at the Feast, The. Redgrove
Arrival of the Bee Box, The. Plath
As I went owre the Hill o' Hoos. Unknown
Bee, The. Dickey
Bee, The. Fandel
Bee, The. Fr. Sir Francis Drake. Fitz-Geffry
Bee. Kennedy
Bee and the Petunia, The. Hoskins
Bee! I'm expecting you! Dickinson
Bee Meeting, The. Plath
Bee Song. Sandburg
Bee, the Ant, and the Sparrow, The. Cotton
Bee Wassail. Unknown
Bee-Wisp, The. Turner
Beehive. Toomer
Bees, The. Ridge
Bees are black, with gilt surcingles. Dickinson
Bees Awater. Morgan
Browny Bee. Pawsey
Bumble Bee. Brown
Busy yellow bee, after his mighty quest, A. Unknown
Cruelty. Hummer
Daventry Wonder, The. "Agricola"
Dido: Swarming. Spivack
Farmer, The. Voigt
Flesh-Fly and the Bee, The. Patmore
Flowers. Behn
Honey Bee, The. Marquis
Humble-Bee, The. Emerson
Invitation to the Bee. Smith
Julius Caesar and the Honey-Bee. Turner
Legend of the Hive, A. Hawker
Limerick: "There was an old man in a tree." Lear
Mantova. Wright
More Ancient Mariner, A. Carman
My Playmate. Whittier

Near Dusk. Auslander
Observation of a Bee. Goldberg
On a Honey Bee *or* To a Honey Bee.
  Freneau
Opportunity. Graham
Pedigree of honey, The. Dickinson
Riddle: "As I went over Tipple Tyne."
  Unknown
Song of the Queen Bee. White
Song: "What binds the atom together." Dow
Summer Night in the Beehive, A. Turner
Swarm of bees in May, A. *Unknown*
Swarming Bees, The. Laughlin
Telling the Bees. Reese
Telling the Bees. Whittier
Venerable Bee, The. Klein
Virgil: Georgics, Book IV. Schmitz
Wild Bees. Baxter
Young bee falls between my window, A.
  Fr. Brother Jonathan, Brother Kafka.
  O'Sullivan

Beer
Bacchus on Beverages. *Fr.* Bacchus in
  Tuscany. Redi
Ballad of Lager Bier, The. Stedman
Beer. Arnold
Beer. Calverley
Glass of Beer, A. Stephens
Lilliputian's Beer Song. Winner
Sestina to the Common Glass of Beer: I Do
  Not Drink Beer. Wakoski
Under the Anheuser Bush. Sterling
Wine upon beer, I counsel thee. *Unknown*

Beethoven, Ludwig van
Beethoven. Herbert
Beethoven. Ray
Beethoven. Wheelock
Beethoven's Death Mask. Spender
Composer's Winter Dream, The. Dubie
Higgledy-piggledy/ Ludwig van Beethoven.
  Seaman
Ninth Symphony of Beethoven Understood at
  Last as a Sexual Message, The. Rich
On Hearing a Symphony of Beethoven.
  Millay

Beetles
Beetle on the Shasta Daylight. Kaufman
Clickbeetle. Hoberman
Riddle: "Wee man o' leather." *Unknown*
Sense of death is most in apprehension, The.
  Fr. Measure for Measure. Shakespeare
Shrilling locust slowly sheathes, The. *Fr.*
  The Beetle. Riley

Beets
Beets Poem, The. Aal

Begging and Beggars
A-Begging Buttermilk I Will Go. *Unknown*
Beggar, The. Al-Ghuzzi
Beggar, The. Moss
Beggar. Murano Shiro
Beggar, The. *Unknown*
Beggar Boy, The. Alexander
Beggar Maid, The. Tennyson
Beggar Man, The. Aikin
Beggar Woman, The. King
Beggar Woman of Naples, The. Jacob
Beggars. Davidson
Beloved one, my lord. *Fr.* Manyo Shu.
  Unknown
Blind Old Woman. Major
Cante Hondo. Kay
Dialogue in a Dream. Ryokan
Dives and Lazarus ("There was a man in
  olden times"). *Unknown*
Done Begging. Ryokan
Done with a long day's begging. Ryokan
Empty Begging Bowl. Ryokan
Finished Begging. Ryokan
For the Poor Blind Man. Icaza
From Mathnavi Sehrul Bayaan. Hasan
Gaberlunzie Man, The. *Unknown*

Glass of Beer, A. Stephens
Grab-Bag. Jackson
Hark, hark, the dogs do bark. Mother Goose
I am a bard of no regard. *Fr.* The Jolly
  Beggars. Burns
In the Bay of Naniwa. *Fr.* Manyo Shu.
  Unknown
Jolly Beggars, The. Burns
Jovial Beggar, The. *Unknown*
Merry Jovial Beggar, The. Casey
My good sirs. *Fr.* Manyo Shu. *Unknown*
Old Cumberland Beggar, The. Wordsworth
On a Fair Beggar. Ayres
St. Martin and the Beggar. Gunn
Spring come again, after moody. Ryokan
Time: first day of the eighth month. Ryokan
Twins, The. Browning
Wealth; or Song Written for a Beggar. Nazir
West London. Arnold
See also **Homeless, the; Vagabonds.**

Beiderbecke, Bix
For Leon Bismarck Beiderbecke (1903-1931).
  Horovitz

Beirut, Lebanon
Apple for the sea, marble narcissus flower,
  An. *Fr.* Beirut. Darwish
Beirut. Faraz
Beirut. Mahdi
Bread. Darwish
Desert, The. "Adunis"

Belfast, Northern Ireland
Afterlives. Mahon
Ballad to a Traditional Refrain. Craig
Belfast. Revell
Belfast Confetti. Carson
Campaign. Carson
Falls Funeral. Montague
Summer 1969. Heaney
Under the Eyes. Paulin

Belgium
Antwerp and Bruges. Rossetti
Antwerp: Musée Des Beaux-Arts. Ross
Antwerp to Ghent. *Fr.* A Trip to Paris and
  Belgium. Rossetti
Ballad to a Traditional Refrain. Craig
Brussels in Winter. Auden
Incident at Bruges. Wordsworth
On Passing the New Menin Gate. Sassoon

Belief. *See* **Faith.**

Belisarius
Belisarius. Longfellow

Bellbirds
Bell-Birds. Kendall

Belloc, Hilaire
Hilaire Belloc. Wolfe

Bells
Balsham Bells. Prescot
Because this village. Tameyo
Bega. Pickthall
Beleaguered City, The. Longfellow
Belfry, The. Binyon
Bell Speech. Wilbur
Bell-Toll. Reverdy
Bell Too Heavy to Ring. Kryss
Bell Tower. Adams
Bells, The. Poe
Bells. Scott
Bells Are Calling for Me, The. Nagy
Bells of London, The. *Unknown*
Bells of St. Michael. Fordham
Bredon Hill. *Fr.* A Shropshire Lad.
  Housman
Broken Tower, The. Crane
Buoy-Bell, The. Turner
Catholic Bells, The. Williams
Children's Bells, The. Farjeon
Chimes. Meynell
Christchurch Bells. *Unknown*
Christmas Bells. Longfellow
Church Bells, The. Linden
Church Bells. Thompson

Creeds of the Bells. Bungay
Footsteps of Angels. Longfellow
Hark, the bells are ringing. *Fr.* Manyo Shu.
  Unknown
Here We Come A-Haying. Close
Merry Are the Bells. *Unknown*
My gaze comes to rest. Fushimi
Passing Bell, The. Shirley
Pilgrimage. Duggan
Ringers, The. Peck
Ringing the Bells. Sexton
Sabbath Bells. Heard
School-Bell. Farjeon
Skipper Ireson's Ride. Whittier
Starry Night, The. Sexton
Sweet little bell. *Unknown*
Post-horse bells are tinkling, The. *Fr.*
  Manyo Shu. *Unknown*

Belshazzar
Belshazzar's Feast. Bibb
Vision of Belshazzar, The. Byron

Ben Bulben, Ireland
Deserted Mountain, The. *Unknown*
Under Ben Bulben. Yeats

Benbow, Admiral John
Death of Admiral Benbow, The. *Unknown*

Bengal
Agreement. Naheed
Bengal. "Ludhianvi"

Bennett, Susan Eugenia
In Memoriam. Susan Eugenia Bennett.
  Fordham

Benoit, Joan
Joan Benoit. Ferrarelli

Beowulf
Beowulf. Amis
Scott-Moncrieff's Beowulf. Spear

Bergman, Ingmar
Ingmar Bergman's "Seventh Seal." Duncan

Berkeley, George
Fountain, The. Davie

Berkshire, England
Laleham: Matthew Arnold's Grave. Johnson

Berkshire Hills, Massachusetts
Among the Berkshire Hills. Ray
Monument Mountain. Bryant

Berlin, Germany
Over the Wall: Berlin, May 1975. Sisson
Threnody for Berlin—1945. Jarman

Bermuda
Battel of the Summer-Islands, The. Waller
Bermudas. Marvell

Berrigan, Daniel
For Dan Berrigan. Knight

Berry, Raymond
Unitas. Gold

Berryman, John
Ode: "Mistah Berrybones, you daid?"
  Zaranka
Tongue-tied in Black and White. Harper
Tropisms on John Berryman. Vizenor

Bertrand de Born
Near Perigord. Pound
Sestina: Altaforte. Pound

Bestiality
Sheep Child, The. Dickey

Bethlehem
Carol: "When the herd[s] were watching."
  Canton
Christmas Morning. Roberts
How Far Is It to Bethlehem? Chesterton
Long, Long Ago. *Unknown*
O Little Town of Bethlehem. Brooks

Bethune, Mary McLeod
For Mary McLeod Bethune. Walker

Betjeman, Sir John
Betjeman at the Post Office. Sharpless
Betjeman, 1984. Causley

Betrayal
Ballad of Hell, A. Davidson
Donal Og. *Unknown*

I Have Been in Great Distress. Beatrice
Vow-Breaker, The. King
Yet Each Man Kills the Thing He Loves.
  Fr. The Ballad of Reading Gaol. Wilde
Biafra. *See* **Civil War, Nigerian.**
Bialik, Hayyim Nahman
Harangue on the Death of Hayyim Nahman
  Bialik. Tiempo
Bible
And in the 51st Year of That Century, While
  My Brother Cried in the Trench, While My
  Enemy Glared from the Cave. Plutzik
Art of Poetry, An. McAuley
Ballad of Sue Ellen Westerfield, The.
  Hayden
Best of All, The. Crosby
Bible, The. Moorer
Bible is an antique volume, The. Dickinson
Book of Kells, The. Nemerov
Colenso Rhymes for Orthodox Children.
  Harte
From a London Bookshop. *Unknown*
Gospel According to You, The. *Unknown*
Holy Bible, Book Divine. Burton
Inscription on the Flyleaf of a Bible. Abse
Just One Book. *Unknown*
Just the Same To-Day. *Unknown*
Mountain Tops. Moorer
My Mother's Bible. Morris
My Old Bible. *Unknown*
O How Sweet Are Thy Words! Steele
Old Bibles. Waniek
Old Testament Contents. *Unknown*
Old-Testament Gospel. Cowper
Over 2000 Illustrations and a Complete
  Concordance. Bishop
Respectable Burgher, The. Hardy
Scriptures, The. *Fr.* Religio Laici. Dryden.
Sir Walter Scott's Tribute. *Fr.* The
  Monastery. Scott
Thou, Zion, old and suffering. *Fr.* The
  Bible. Levi
Why God Permits Evil: For Answers to This
  Question of Interest to Many Write Bible
  Answers Dept. E-7. Williams
Word of God, The. Flint
Word of God, Across the Ages. Blanchard
Bicycles and Bicycling
Bicycalamity. Peters
Bicycle, The. Rice
Bicycle, The. Wojahn
Bicycle Rider, The. Shapcott
Different Bicycles. Baruch
To a Bicycle. *Unknown*
Under the dawn I wake my two-wheel friend.
  Fr. On a Bicycle. Yevtushenko
Billboards
Song of the Open Road. Nash
Billiards
Clean. Newman
Billington, William
To the Memory of William Billington. Hull
Bingen, Germany
Bingen on the Rhine. Norton
Biochemistry
See also **Bacteria; Genetic Engineering.**
Biography
But now the dentist cannot die. Lang
Art of Biography, The. *Fr.* Clerihews.
  Bentley
Birch Trees
Birch-Tree at Loschwitz, The. Levy
Birch Trees. Moreland
Birches. Frost
Little Birches. Newsome
Student, The. Meinke
Young Birch, A. Frost
Bird Migration. *See* **Animal Migration.**
Bird-watching
Some Tips on Watching Birds. Hudson
Up from the Egg; the Confessions of a
  Nuthatch Avoider. Nash

Birds
Aesthetic. Rosten
Against Starlings. Plumly
Against the white beach. Abutsu
Alas All for a Sparrowhawk I Sigh.
  Unknown
All These Birds. Wilbur
And every bird shew'd in his proper kind.
  Fr. The Owle. Drayton
Answer to a Child's Question. Coleridge
"As When Emotion Too Far Exceeds Its
  Cause." Oden
Balcony with Birds, A. Moss
Be like the Bird. Hugo
Beat Poem by an Academic Poet. Miller
Belfast Lough. *Unknown*
Bird, The. Hoffenstein
Bird. Jung Han-mo
Bird, The. Michelson
Bird, The. Vaughan
Bird at Dawn, The. Monro
Bird came down the walk, A. Dickinson
Bird flies away quietly, A. *Fr.* Forty-four
  Tanka. Wakayama Bokusui
Bird is tangled in a tree, A. Busch
Bird of Passage. Hahn-Hahn
Bird Song, The. Linden
Bird that fell out of the nest, A. Schönwiese
Bird Theater. Wallace
Bird-Window-Flying. Gallagher
Bird with a Broken Wing, The. Butterworth
Bird-witted. Moore
Birds, The. Blake
Birds. Jeffers
Birds. "Llywelyn"
Birds. Miller
Birds, The. Posner
Birds. Stoddard
Birds, The. *Unknown*
Birds and Fishes. Jeffers
Birds at a Mountain Home. Fushimi
Birds' Ball, The. Bardeen
Birds, birds held by long affinity close to
  man's frontiers. *Fr.* Birds. "Perse"
Bird's call this morning was a fine bird call,
  The. *Unknown*
Bird's Nest, The. Drinkwater
Birds' Nests. Clare
Birds' Nests. Seager
Birds' Nests. *Unknown*
Birds of America, The. Broughton
Birds of Killingworth, The (The Poet's Tale).
  Fr. Tales of a Wayside Inn. Longfellow
Birds of Passage. Longfellow
Birds of the Island Palace, The. *Fr.* Manyo
  Shu. Hitomaro
Birds on the School Windowsill, The.
  Dainty
Blind Linnet, The. Buchanan
Blinded Bird, The. Hardy
Blue Booby, The. Tate
Blue Jay, The. Lawrence
Boy and the Shrike, The. Saba
Canticle to the Waterbirds, A. Everson
Cardinals in the Ice Age. Engels
Chaste Arabian Bird, The. Rochester
Cherry Tree. Eastwick
Ching-wei. Ku Yen-wu
Chough. Warner
Come Wary One. Manning-Sanders
Coppersmith. Murphy
Corncrakes. *Fr.* Nature Notes. MacNeice
Cradle Song: "What does little birdie say."
  Tennyson
Dawn. Bottomley
Dead Bird, The. Young
Dead Birds. Kopland
Death of a Bird. Silkin
Death of the Bird, The. Hope
Decoys, The. Auden
Dipper, The. Hesketh

Dream, The. *Fr.* The Book of the Duchesse.
  Chaucer
Each time a wave rolls in. *Fr.* Eighty-seven
  Hokku. Buson
Educated Love Bird, The. Newell
Esyllt. Jones
Exactly. Metz
Examination of Conscience before Going to
  Sleep. Carmi
Extinct Birds. Wright
Faithful Friend, The. Cowper
Fat Budgie, The. Lennon
Firetail's Nest, The. Clare
Fish and Bird. Brinckman
For Stephen Drawing Birds. Rogers
Fossil. Blodgett
Freaks of Fashion. Rossetti
Goldfinch. Engels
Grackle, The ("Grackle's voice is less than
  mellow."). Nash
Great Scarf of Birds, The. Updike
Green Rain. Webb
Ground Birds in Open Country. Plumly
Harbor plovers calling to their friends. *Fr.*
  Fifty-one Tanka. Izumi
Hoopoe Bird, The. Barakat
House was still—the room was still, The.
  Brontë
Human parent chases a crow away, A.
  Onitsura
Impromptu. Wilberforce
In Glencullen. Synge
In Her Song She Is Alone. Swan
In India lives a bird that is unique. *Fr.* The
  Conference of the Birds. Attar
In 62 the Starving Seabirds Reached the
  Center of Lima. Cisneros
Invitation. Behn
Jackdaw of Rheims, The. *Fr.* The Ingoldsby
  Legends. "Ingoldsby"
Japanese Print. Clarke
Joy of the Morning. Markham
Lady Lost. Ransom
Letters from a Father. Van Duyn
Linnet in November, The. Palgrave
Listener's Guide to the Birds, A. White
Little Beach-Bird, The. Dana
Little Bird. Cunningham
Little Bird, The. *Unknown*
Little Birds. Sternberg
Little Bird's Song, A. Rose
Little Morning Music, A. Schwartz
Little Trotty Wagtail. Clare
Lonely-Bird, The. Morris
Lonely the Sea-Bird Lies at Her Rest.
  Yeats
Making of Birds, The. Tynan
Merry Birds. Bennett
Minor Bird, A. Frost
Mirrorment. Ammons
Mistaking birds for leaves. *Fr.* Seventeen
  Hokku. Chiyojo
Moorhen. Logan
More Joy in Heaven. Nemerov
Morning Bird Songs. Tranströmer
My Little Bird. Bunyan
My Little Birds. *Unknown*
Nest Eggs. Stevenson
Nesting Time. Stewart
Never Again Would Birds' Song Be the
  Same. Frost
Night far gone. *Fr.* Manyo Shu.
  Yakamochi
Nightjar, The. Newbolt
Nine Birds. Cummings
1943. Mitchison
No Shop Does the Bird Use.
  Coatsworth
Now that I've built my house. *Fr.* Kokin
  Shu. *Unknown*
O Bird, So Lovely. Golding
October Redbreast, The. Meynell

Of all the birds that sing and fly. *Fr.* Songs about Life and Brighter Things Yet. Hoffenstein
Oh, plovers on the river-shore. *Fr.* Manyo Shu. Kadobe
On a Clear Night. Hurvits
On a Little Bird. Armstrong
On Hearing the Chukar. Yu T'ung
On river flats, too. *Fr.* Manyo Shu. Yakamochi
Out from Its Fine Cage. *Unknown*
Oven Bird, The. Frost
Oystercatchers. Middleton
Parakeet. Clark
Passenger Pigeons. Morgan
People Buy a Lot of Things. Wynne
Pinionjay shits pebbles. *Unknown*
Plovers on the Coast. Kenko
Poet to the Birds, The. Meynell
Presentation of Two Birds to My Son, A. Wright
Pretty Wantons. *Unknown*
Princely eagle, and the soaring hawke, The. Wood
Quatrain: Poet. Emerson
Rivals, The. Stephens
River plovers, The. Eifuku
River plovers crying. *Fr.* Manyo Shu. Yakamochi
Roaring Frost, The. Meynell
Robert of Lincoln. Bryant
Robin, The. Bent
Rooks, The. *Unknown*
Rose, The. Roethke
Sea Birds, The. Brock
Sea Change. Masefield
Season of Phantasmal Peace, The. Walcott
Selfsame Song, The. Hardy
Shore Birds. Gale
Sing On, Blithe Bird. Motherwell
Skylark rises, A. *Fr.* Twenty-one Hokku. Kaya Shirao
Small Is Beautiful. Liu K'o-hsiang
Snowy Heron. Ciardi
Somewhere Is Such a Kingdom. Ransom
Spotted Flycatcher, The. De la Mare
Spring bird—thinking of what?, A. *Fr.* Twenty-seven Hokku. Natsume Seibi
Still Life: Lady with Birds. Prettyman
Storm-Cock's Song, The. "MacDiarmid"
Sympathy. Dunbar
Tails and Heads. Knowles
That Is All I Heard. "Yehoash"
This morning, in the faint light of dawn a pheasant called, lords. *Unknown*
Throstle, The. Tennyson
Titmouse. De la Mare
To a Waterfowl. Bryant
To Paint the Portrait of a Bird. Prévert
To the Man-of-War-Bird. Whitman
To the Redbreast. Bampfylde
To Waken an Old Lady. Williams
Tomtit, The. De la Mare
Trico's Song. *Fr.* Alexander and Campaspe. Lyly
Truth, The. Davies
Two Pewits. Thomas
Unknown Bird, The. Thomas
Up from the Egg; the Confessions of a Nuthatch Avoider. Nash
Vacant Cage, The. Turner
Waders and Swimmers. Plumly
Warbler: leaves hiding it. *Fr.* Twenty-nine Hokku. Taigi
Water Fowl. Wordsworth
Water-Ousel, The. Webb
Waxwings. Francis
When I went to visit. Tsurayuki
Whip-poor-will. Hall
White bird—is it not sad?, A. *Fr.* Forty-four Tanka. Wakayama Bokusui
White Lake, The. *Unknown*

Wind and the Bird, The. *Unknown*
Wind spills plovers, picks them up, The. *Fr.* Seventeen Hokku. Chiyojo
Windhover, The. Hopkins
Winged in Gold. Bowen
Wingtip. Sandburg
Winter Song. Jiménez
Yellowhammer, The. Clare
Young Martins, The. Young
Penguin Book of Bird Poetry, The (PBBP). Peggy Munsterberg, ed.
See also names of birds (e.g., Canaries).
Birds' Nests
Bird's Nest, The. Drinkwater
Birds' Nests. Thomas
Brown Thrush, The. Larcom
Hen's Nest. Clare
In the Night Birds Fell. Chalfi
Nesting Time. Stewart
On a Forsaken Lark's Nest. Blind
Pettichap's Nest, The. Clare
Warning. *Unknown*
Birds of Paradise
Bird of Paradise, The. Davies
Birds of Paradise, The. Bishop
Birmingham, Alabama
Ballad of Birmingham. Randall
Birmingham 1963. Patterson
Birmingham Sunday. Hughes
Birmingham, England
Birmingham. MacNeice
New Navigation, The. Freeth
Birth
Almond Tree, The. Stallworthy
At Birth. Thwaite
Baby Song. Gunn
Before the Birth of One of Her Children. Bradstreet
Birth. Bruck
Birth. Takahashi Shinkichi
Birth. Urdang
Birth. Vliet
Birth in a Narrow Room, The. Brooks
Birth of a Great Man. Graves
Birthdays. Domin
Birthplace. Big Eagle
Born into the world. Tamesuke
Breeze Swept Through, A. Tapahonso
Calliope in the Labour Ward. Feinstein
Christmas and Common Birth. Ridler
Conception. Miles
Definition. Shakely
Ecce Puer. Joyce
First Birth, The. Jones
First Child, Born Out of Breach in Mid-May. *Fr.* The Sheltering Ground. Santos
First childbirth/ her husband feels like. *Unknown*
First Position. *Fr.* Arabesque: Five Poems for Women without Children. Mackey
Gas Lamp. Barnstone
GN Is Happy. Niccolai
How You Were Born. Libera
In My Name. Nichols
It's Time. *Fr.* Earthly: Sonnets for Carlos. Wedde
Labor. Day
Labour. *Fr.* Paedotrophiae; or, The Art of Bringing Up Children. Saint-Marthe
Labour Pains. Yosano Akiko
Love Medley: Patrice Cuchulain. Harper
Mississippi Born. Lomax
On a Child Who Lived One Minute. Kennedy
On the Birth of a Black/Baby/Boy. Knight
Petals of the Tulips, The. Hemschemeyer
Say Hello to John. Williams
Shelter Him in Milk and Meadow. LeSueur
Shift of Emphasis, A. *Fr.* Two Birth Poems. Edmond
Sister Mother. Catri
Sleep Close to Me. Mistral

Squeal. McHugh
To a Child before Birth. Nicholson
To Have a Child These Days. Fuertes
To Insure Survival. Ortiz
To the Nativity. Gonzáles de Eslava
Woman into Man. Wallbank
Naked Astronaut, The: Poems on Birth and Birthdays (NAs). René Graziani, ed.
Birth Control
No, The. Dacey
See also **Abortion; Contraception.**
Birth Defects
Almond Tree, The. Stallworthy
Birthdays
Betsy Jane's Sixth Birthday. Noyes
Between Birthdays. Nash
Birthday, The. Johnson
Birthday, A. Muir
Birthday, A. Rossetti
Birthday. Winkler
Birthday Candle, A. Justice
Birthday Child, The. Fyleman
Birthday Gift, A. Dunn
Birthday Gifts. Asquith
Birthday of but a single pang. Dickinson
Birthday Poem, A. Simmons
Birthday Wishes to a Husband. Moorer
Birthday Wishes to a Minister of the Gospel. Moorer
Birthday Wishes to a Physician. Moorer
Birthdays. Driver
Birthdays. Hoberman
Cherry blossoms. *Fr.* Kokin Shu. Narihira
Coming of Age. Logan
Epitaph: "Here lies Sir Tact, a diplomatic fellow." Steele
Evening of My Birthday, The. Yang Shih-ch'i
Five Years Old. Allen
For His Wife, on Her Birthday. Wesley
For K. R. on Her Sixtieth Birthday. Wilbur
Giant's Cake, A. San Garde
Home. Jaszi
I Awake Crying on My Birthday. K'uang Chou-yi
If We Didn't Have Birthdays. "Seuss"
In Honor of My Husband's Fiftieth Birthday. Hsüeh Shao-hui
Many Happy Returns. Auden
Monday's child is fair of face. Mother Goose
Mother's Birthday. Wagenlander
My Husband's Birthday. Heard
On My Birthday—Sick. Li K'ai-hsien
On My Thirty-third Birthday. Byron
On My Two-Hundredth Birthday. Glatstein
On This Day I Complete My Fortieth Year. Porter
On This Day I Complete My Thirty-sixth Year. Byron
Poem for My Twentieth Birthday. Koch
Poem in October. Thomas
Poem (3.11.66). Hanafi
Short Song of Congratulation, A. Johnson
Sixty-eighth Birthday. Lowell
Stella's Birth-day, 1718/19. Swift
To Mrs. Thrale [on Her Thirty-fifth Birthday]. Johnson
Villanelle of the Mystical Cycle. Leyeles
Naked Astronaut, The: Poems on Birth and Birthdays (NAs). René Graziani, ed.
Birthmarks
Our Island. Katrovas
Birthplaces
Across Kansas. Stafford
Birthplace, The. Heaney
Birthplace. Saffarzadeh
Birthplace Revisited. Corso
Borning Room, The. Harper
Domicilium. Hardy
Bishop, Elizabeth
For Elizabeth Bishop. McPherson

Bismarck, Otto von
Lines on the Death of Bismarck. Chapman
Bison. *See* **Buffaloes.**
Black (color)
Sonnet of Black Beauty. Herbert of
Cherbury
Black Hawk
Black Hawk in Hiding. Keithley
Black Hills (U. S.)
Dreary Black Hills, The. *Unknown*
Black Holes
Collapsars. McPherson
Well of Baln, The. Le Guin
Black Power
Mabrak. "Jerry"
Motto Vision 1971. Malik de Coteau
Black Verse
American Negro Poetry (AmNP). Arna
Bontemps, ed.
Black Poets, The, (BPo). Dudley Randall,
ed.
Black Sister (BlSi). Erlene Stetson, ed.
Book of American Negro Poetry, The
(BANP). James Weldon Johnson, ed.
*Caroling Dusk; an Anthology of Verse by
Negro Poets* (CDC). Countee Cullen, ed.
*Celebrations; a New Anthology of Black
American Poetry* (CNA). Arnold Adoff,
ed.
Collected Black Women's Poetry (CBWP).
Joan R. Sherman, ed.
Forerunners, The: Black Poets in America
(FB). Woodie King, Jr., ed.
I Am the Darker Brother (IDB). Arnold
Adoff, ed.
Jump Bad; a New Chicago Anthology (JB).
Gwendolyn Brooks, ed.
New Black Poetry, The (NBP). Clarence
Major, ed.
Poems from Black Africa (PBA). Langston
Hughes, ed.
Poetry of Black America, The (PoBA).
Arnold Adoff, ed.
Poetry of the Negro 1746-1970, The (PoNe).
Langston Hughes *and* Arna Bontemps, eds.
3000 Years of Black Poetry (TTY). Alan
Lomax *and* Raoul Abdul, ed.
*Watchers and Seekers; Creative Writing by
Black Women* (WS). Rhonda Cobham *and*
Merle Collins, eds.
*When My Brothers Come Home; Poems from
Central and Southern Africa* (WMBCH).
Frank Mkalawile Chipasula, ed.
Blackberries
Blackberry, The. Nicholson
Blackberry Eating. Kinnell
Blackberry-picking. Heaney
Blackberrying. Plath
Blackbirds
All There Is to Know about Adolph
Eichmann. Cohen
Blackbird, The. Drayson
Blackbird. Kopland
Blackbird, The. Mulock
Blackbird, The. Su Shao-lien
Blackbird, The. Tennyson
Blackbird, The. Wolfe
Blackbird Sestina. Warne
Blackbird Singing, A. Thomas
Faithful Blackbird. Jiménez
Ghazel of Unforseen Love. García Lorca
Sing a song of sixpence. Mother Goose
Singing in the Spring. Eastwick
13 Ways of Eradicating Blackbirds. DeFoe
Thirteen Ways of Looking at a Blackbird.
Stevens
Two Little Blackbirds. *Unknown*
Vespers. Brown
Blackouts
Black-Out. Ackland
Black-out, The. Anderson
Blacks
African. Tosh

African Beauty. Olaleye-Oruene
Against Negritude. Corgo
Alabama Bus. Hairston
Allegory in Black. Clark
Anti Apart Hate Art. Clinton
Anti-Racist Person. Prescod
Assembly: Harlem School. Maleska
Assumption about the Harlem Brown Baby.
Fisher
At Guaracara Park. Roach
At Home in Dakar. Danner
Aunt Jemima of the Ocean Waves. Hayden
Ballad of Rudolph Reed, The. Brooks
Ballade des Belles Milatraisses. Jonas
Beautiful Black Women. Baraka
Beautiful Slave, The. Marino
Between Ourselves. Lorde
Between the World and Me. Wright
Beware, Soul Brother. Achebe
Birthday Poem. Young
Black Art. Baraka
Black Boy. Rosten
Black Dada Nihilismus. Baraka
Black Is Black. Macfield
Black Majesty. Cullen
Black Pride. Burroughs
Black Sister. Cumbo
Black Sketches. Lee
Black Study. Harper
Black Tambourine. Crane
Black Woman. Madgett
Black Woman. Morejón
Black Woman Out Dere. Gayle
Blue-eyed Precinct Worker, The. Coulette
Bones of My Father, The. Knight
"Boogie with O. O. Gabugah." Young
Booker T. and W. E. B. Randall
Bottled [New York]. Johnson
Brother Baptis' on Woman Suffrage. Jonas
Carol of the Brown King. Hughes
Centenary's Day. Garvey
Chain, The. Craig
Coal. Lorde
Congo, The. Lindsay
Cordon Negro. Hemphill
Cross. Hughes
Dab of Color, A. Weiss
Dark Symphony. Tolson
Dark Testament. Murray
Dictionary Black. Roots
Different Image, A. Randall
Ego Tripping. Giovanni
Essay on Language. Coleman
Family Jewels. Hemphill
For Black Poets Who Think of Suicide.
Knight
For Both of Us at Fisk. Scott
For de Lawd. Clifton
Freedom Song for the Black Woman, A.
Gregory
From the Dark Tower. Cullen
Generation Gap, The. Saunders
Girl Talk. Griffiths
Good Times. Clifton
Grandfather. Harper
Grandson Is a Hoticeberg, A. Danner
Harlem—a Negro Ghetto. Vaynshteyn
Harlem Dancer, The. McKay
Harlem Negroes. *Fr.* Negroes.
Vaynshteyn
Heritage. Bennett
Heritage. Cullen
High to Low. Hughes
Hometown. Cornish
How Will You Call Me, Brother. Evans
Hush Honey. Saunders
I Am a Black Woman. Evans
I Came to the New World Empty-handed.
Swift
I, Too. Hughes
I, Woman. McClaurin
Identities. Young
If We Must Die. McKay

If You Black Get Back. Clarke
Image in the Mirror. Kenner
In Defense of Black Poets. Rivers
In Salem. Clifton
Incident. Cullen
It is true—/ I've always loved. *Fr.* Once.
Walker
It's Nation Time. Baraka
Jamaican Fisherman. Sherlock
Jesus Was Crucified or: It Must Be Deep.
Rodgers
Ka 'Ba. Baraka
Laundry. *Fr.* Negroes. Vaynshteyn
Lawd, Dese Colored Chillum. Saunders
Lift Every Voice and Sing. Johnson
Like an Orchid in Deep Muddy Water.
Foxworth
Litany of the Dark People, The. Cullen
Little Black Boy, The. *Fr.* Songs of
Innocence. Blake
Little Half-Brother, Little Black Star.
Barlow
Lynching. *Fr.* Negroes. Vaynshteyn
3-31-70. *Fr.* Journal. Jones
Mask, The. McClaurin
Memorial. Sanchez
Merry-go-round. Hughes
Metamorphosis of Aunt Jemima, The.
Childress
Midway. Madgett
Moment Please, A. Allen
Monuments for a Friendly Girl at a Tenth
Grade Party. Stafford
Mr. Z. Holman
Mrs. Johnson Objects. Thompson
Nappy Edges (A Cross Country Sojourn).
Shange
Naturally. Lorde
Negro Geo'ge. *Fr.* Negroes. Vaynshteyn
Negro Poets. Johnson
Negro Servant. Hughes
Negro Speaks of Rivers, The. Hughes
Negro Spirituals. Benét
Negro Village. *Fr.* Negroes.
Vaynshteyn
New Negro, The. McCall
Nigger. Shapiro
Nikki-Rosa [*or* Nikki-Roasa]. Giovanni
No Say. Murray
Nothing Said. Agard
O Daedalus, Fly Away Home. Hayden
Ode in Time of Hesitation, An. Moody
Old Black Joe. Foster
On Being Brought from Africa to America.
Wheatley
Once. Walker
Only in This Way. Burroughs
Plaint. Ford
Poem for Black Hearts, A. Baraka
Poem for Some Black Women. Rodgers
Portrait of a Woman (and a Man). Figueroa
Postcards of the Hanging: 1869. Hudgins
Runaway Slave at Pilgrim's Point, The.
Browning
Sepia Fashion Show. Angelou
She's Free! Harper
Shipmates. Collins
Song: "I am weaving a song of waters."
Bennett
Song: I Want a Witness. Harper
Song: "We raise de wheat." *Unknown*
Sonnet: September 1, 1802. Wordsworth
Sonnet to a Negro in Harlem. Johnson
Southern Cop. Brown
Stars. Hughes
Stereo. Lee
Story of Marie, The. Burkard
Strong Men. Brown
Telephone Conversation. Soyinka
Theme for English B. Hughes
There Are Black. Baca
Tired. Johnson
To a Gone Era. McClaurin

Blacksmiths *(cont.)*

To Some Supposed Brothers. Hemphill
To Soulfolk. Burroughs
To Usward. Bennett
Touché. Fauset
Tripart. Jones
Upstairs Downstairs. Allen
W. W. Baraka
Way It Was, The. Clifton
We Real Cool. Brooks
White House, The. McKay
White Moon. Leivick
Woman Poem. Giovanni
Woman's Issue, A. Atwood
Woman's Song, A. McElroy
Women. Walker
Word, The. Dowe
Yet Do I Marvel. Cullen
You've Got to Learn the White Man's Game.
    Smith
Collected Black Women's Poetry (CBWP).
    Joan R. Sherman, ed.
Watchers and Seekers; Creative Writing by
    Black Women (WS). Rhonda Cobham *and*
    Merle Collins, eds.
When My Brothers Come Home; Poems from
    Central and Southern Africa (WMBCH).
    Frank Mkalawile Chipasula, ed.
See also **anthologies listed under Black**
    Verse.

Blacksmiths
Anchorsmiths, The. Dibdin
Blacksmiths. *Unknown*
Blacksmiths, The. *Unknown*
Blacksmith's Song, The. *Unknown*
Felix Randal. Hopkins
Village Blacksmith, The. Longfellow
Work. Illyés

Blake, William
William Blake Sees God. McFadden

Blasphemy
For All Blasphemers. Benét

Blenheim, Battle of (1704)
Battle of Blenheim, The. Southey
Poem to His Grace the Duke of Marlborough,
    A. *Fr.* The Campaign. Addison

Blessings
Cuckoo is on the mulberry-tree, The.
    Unknown
Far off at that wayside pool we draw.
    Unknown
Fish caught in the trap, The. *Unknown*
Here we come a-caroling. *Unknown*
In the south is a tree with drooping boughs.
    Unknown
Locusts' wings say "throng, throng", The.
    Unknown
Mandarin ducks were in flight. *Unknown*
May Heaven guard and keep you. *Unknown*
On the southern hills grows the nutgrass.
    Unknown
Through a bend in the hillside. *Unknown*

Blindness
All but Blind. De la Mare
Before I got my eye put out. Dickinson
Blind Boy, The. Cibber
Blind Man. Hamburger
Blind Man at the Fair, The. Campbell
Blind Men and the Elephant, The. Saxe
Blind Upholsterer, The. Cook
Blinded Bird, The. Hardy
Blindness of Samson, The. *Fr.* Samson
    Agonistes. Milton
Does It Matter? Sassoon
For Mama. Kendrick
Greeks Are Blinding Polyphemus, The.
    Raba
In the Garden of the Lord. Keller
Like a convalescent, I took the hand.
    Heaney
Question of Art, A. Kendrick

Sight. Gibson
Smoker, The. Huff
Solitude, A. Levertov
Spring, and the Blind Children. Noyes
They Are All Too Kind. Dunn
To Mr. Cyriack Skinner upon His Blindness.
    Milton
Unblinding, The. Lieberman
War Blinded. Dunn

Blizzards
Blizzard, The. Ware

Blocks (toys)
Block City. Stevenson

Blood
Circulation, The. Washbourne
Circulation of the Blood, The. *Fr.* Creation.
    Blackmore
Nowhere, No Trace Can I Discover. Faiz
On a Line in Sandburg. Thomas
Story, A. Mitchell
Temple is full of blood, The. Villanueva

Blue (color)
Blue Booby, The. Tate
Blue Winter. Francis
Exclusive Blue. Francis
Hitchcock Blue. Brock-Broido
Variation on a Sentence. Bogan

Blue Jays
Blue Jay. Francis
Gift. Barrax
Invitation. Behn

Bluebells
Bluebells. Enoch
Bluebells. Ewing

Blueberries
Hermit Picks Berries, The. Kumin

Bluebirds
Blue-Bird, The. Melville
Blue-Bird, The. Wilson
Last Word of a Bluebird, The. Frost
L'Oiseau Bleu. Coleridge

Blues (mood)
Bound No'th Blues. Hughes
Canyon Day Woman Blues. Keams
Chromo. Fabio
Get Up, Blues. Emanuel
It was not death, for I stood up. Dickinson
Kitchen Door Blues. Williams
Mood Indigo. Sadoff
St. Louis Blues. Handy
September Blue. Burford
34 Blues. Patton

Blues (music)
Blues Don't Change, The. Young
Blues Note. Kaufman
Blues Today, The. Jackson
Brass Spittoons. Hughes
Coal Loadin' Blues. *Unknown*
D Blues. Hernton
Depot Blues. *Unknown*
East St. Louis Blues. *Unknown*
Fat Blues. Crowell
Four o'Clock Flower Blues ("four o'clock
    flowers bloom out in the mornin' ").
    Unknown
Gonna Lay My Head Down on Some Railroad
    Line. *Unknown*
Homage to the Empress of the Blues.
    Hayden
I Remember How She Sang. Penny
I Rode Southern, I Rode L & N. *Unknown*
Lowdown Dirty Blues. *Unknown*
Mask, The. McClaurin
Mississippi Blues. *Unknown*
Music, The. Hoagland
Po' Boy Blues. Hughes
Poem for Otis Redding. Thomas
Ragged and Dirty. *Unknown*
Railroad Blues, The. *Unknown*
Ray Charles. Cornish
Special Rider Blues. *Unknown*

To Dinah Washington. Knight
Train Is Off the Track, The. *Unknown*
Weary Blues, The. Hughes
Why I Sing the Blues. King
Worried Life Blues. *Unknown*

Board Games
Argument One: The Lady Shews How She Is
    Foresaken for a Piece of Wood. Johnson
Chinese Checkers. Cohen
Players. Roston

Boarding Houses
Lodger, The. Longley
Mr. Bleaney. Larkin
On Saint-Urbain Street. Acorn

Boasting
Primer Lesson. Sandburg

Boats. *See* **Ferry Boats; Ships; Tugs; Yachts.**

Boats and Boating
Barges on the Hudson. Deutsch
Beginning to Squall. Swenson
Boat Poem. Spencer
Boats at Night. Shanks
Boats in a Fog. Jeffers
Caique. Sikelianos
Excursion, The. Tu Fu
Fine Day for Straw Hats, A. Stimson
Fishing Boats in Martigues. Campbell
Flower-Boat, The. Frost
Freight Boats. Tippett
Hayeswater. *Fr.* The Hayeswater Boat.
    Arnold
Kayak, The. *Unknown*
Last Galway Hooker, The. Murphy
Like the sails spread on the fishing-boats.
    Fr. Manyo Shu. *Unknown*
Long River, The. Hall
Lost. Sandburg
My Boat. Carver
My Plan. Chute
My whole family floats out on the lake. *Fr.*
    Moments of Fullfillment—Writing Down
    Miscellaneous. Yüan Mei
Night Trip across the Chesapeake and After.
    Lea
Old Boat, The. Pratt
Old Ironsides. Holmes
On a Steamer. Baruch
Paper Boats. Tagore
Reliable Service, A. Curnow
Return, Starting Out. Halpern
Riding a Boat on Wu-ling Stream. Tao-chi
Riding in a Motor Boat. Baruch
River Boats, The. Hicky
Traveling by Boat at Shun-ch'ang. Hsü
    Chung-hsing
Trip to Hua-yang Mountain, A. Tao-chi
We are driven to odd attempts; once it would
    not have occurred. *Fr.* Shooting Script.
    Rich
Where Go the Boats? Stevenson

Bobolinks
Bobolinks, The. Cranch
Robert of Lincoln. Bryant

Bodies
Bath, The. Snyder
Body, The. Herrick
Body Is the Victory and the Defeat of
    Dreams, The. Anghelaki-Rooke
Body Work. Goodman
Busts and Bosoms Have I Known. *Unknown*
Case of Ample Ora: Sweetness and Light,
    The. Hadas
Cats like Angels. Piercy
Dear Body. Canan
Dialogue between the Soul and [the] Body, A.
    Marvell
Ecstasy, The. Donne
Ellen West. Bidart
Ellery Street. Ferry
Epidermal Macabre. Roethke

Eye for an Eye, An. Donald
Feast of Stephen, The. Hecht
Fury of Cocks, The. Sexton
Head Itself. Riding
Her True Body. Metz
His Body. McPherson
House in the Heart, The. Nye
Human Geography. Fuertes
I am the poet of the Body and I am the poet
  of the Soul. *Fr.* Song of Myself.
  Whitman
I Expect You Think This Huge Dark Coat.
  Donald
Innocent Breasts, The. Oppenheimer
"It's a Whole World, the Body. A Whole
  World!"—Swami Satchidandanda.
  Young
Life Drawing. Orlen
Married. Halpern
My Daughter Considers Her Body.
  Skloot
Origin of the Praise of God, The. Bly
Our Bodies. Levertov
Prisons. Szabó
Question. Swenson
Soul's Garment, The. Newcastle
Temple of Venus, The. Jenyns
Thoughts on the Shape of the Human Body.
  Brooke
To My Body. Sullivan
To Praise. Bass
Waiting. Cooper
What Is Man's Body? *Unknown*
Zoo of You, The. Freeman
See also **Nudity and Nudists.**
Bodybuilding
  Gathering Strength. Dangel
Boer War
  Bridge-Guard in the Karroo. Kipling
  Christmas Ghost-Story, A. Hardy
  Colonel's Soliloquy, The. Hardy
  Drummer Hodge. Hardy
  Embarcation. Hardy
  Wife in London, A. Hardy
Boethius, Anicius Manlius Severinus
  Boethius at Cavalzero. Macoubrie
Bogotá, Colombia
  In the City of Bogotá. Pape
Bogs
  Bog Queen. Heaney
  Bogland. Heaney
  Kinship. Heaney
  On Learning That Certain Peat Bogs Contain
    Perfectly Preserved Bodies. Ludvigson
  Tollund Man, The. Heaney
Bohemian Life
  Lines for a Worthy Person Who Has Drifted
    by Accident into a Chelsea Revel. Herbert
  Ode to Bohemians. Padgett
  Problem in Social Geometry—the Inverted
    Square! Durem
Boleyn, Anne
  Anne Boleyn. Bibb
  My Dearling. Allen
  Sonnet: Whoso List to Hunt [I Know Where
    Is an Hind]. Wyatt
Bolivia
  Ita. Ulloa
Bolsheviks
  Bolsheviks. Shtoltsenberg
Bombs and Bombing
  Autumn Blitz. Cornford
  Ballad of Birmingham. Randall
  Bomb Incident. Edwards
  Bomb Story (Manchester, 1942). Lea
  Bombed Church. Berridge
  Bomber, The. Gibbs
  Bombers, The. Churchill
  Entertainment of War, The. Fisher
  On a Bomb Heard through a Violin Concerto.
    Chapin
  Picture from the Blitz. Clark

Song of the Bomber. Mannin
See also **Air Warfare.**
Bonaparte, Josephine
  Appearance and Reality. Hollander
Bonaparte, Louis Napoleon. See Napoleon
  III.
Bonaparte, Napoleon. See Napoleon I.
Bondone, Giotto di. See Giotto.
Bones
  Anthem: "Our bones will all be built into the
    runway." Ewart
  Discoveries of Bones and Stones.
    Grigson
  Epitaph on William Jones. *Unknown*
  Hollow Flute, The. Strauss
  Lady's-Maid 's Song, The. Hollander
  Meditation on a Bone. Hope
  Postcard from the Volcano, A. Stevens
  Relic. Hughes
  Self Portrait. Raab
  See also **Skeletons.**
Bonhomme Richard (ship)
  Paul Jones. *Unknown*
Bonneau, Jennette
  Death of a Grandparent. Mrs. Jennette
    Bonneau. Fordham
Bonnivard, Francois de
  Prisoner of Chillon, The. Byron
Bonsai
  Work of Artifice, A. Piercy
Boobies
  Blue Booby, The. Tate
Book Clubs
  Classic Waits for Me, A. White
Book of Kells. See Kells, Book of.
Books
  Against the Evidence. Ignatow
  Author to Her Book, The. Bradstreet
  Bibliomaniac's Prayer, The. Field
  Bibliophile, The. Jacob
  Book, The. Vaughan
  Books Fall Open. McCord
  Bookshop Idyll, A. Amis
  Bookworm, The. Rabinovitch
  Burning a Book. Stafford
  Classic Waits for Me, A. White
  During the Day He Held a Low-level
    Position. Szabo
  Expostulation and Reply. Wordsworth
  Fiction and the Reading Public. Larkin
  Fire at Alexandria, The. Weiss
  House Was Quiet and the World Was Calm,
    The. Stevens
  I've Got a New Book from My Grandfather
    Hyde. Jackson
  Land of Story-Books, The. Stevenson
  Letter to Hitler, A. Laughlin
  Library, The. Huff
  My Life. Jacob
  November Primrose, The. Devlin
  O for a Booke. *Unknown*
  Of Books. Florio
  On His Books. Belloc
  On the Detraction Which Followed upon My
    Writing Certain Treatises. Milton
  Open Sesame. *Unknown*
  Pleasure-Boat, The. Dana
  Reading in War Time. Muir
  Second Volume, The. Bell
  Shut Not Your Doors. Whitman
  Sibrandus Schafnaburgensis. *Fr.* Garden
    Fancies. Browning
  Sonnet: My Friend's Library. Lott
  Study of Reading Habits, A. Larkin
  Tables Turned, The. Wordsworth
  There is no frigate like a book.
    Dickinson
  To a Thesaurus. Adams
  To His Books. Vaughan
  To My Book. Jonson
  Who Hath a Book. Nesbit
  Word, The. Enright

Books of Hours
  Hours, The. Ramsey
Boone, Daniel
  Boone. Mitchell
  Daniel Boone. Benét
  Daniel Boone. Guiterman
  For the Grave of Daniel Boone.
    Stafford
Booth, Edwin
  Sargent's Portrait of Edwin Booth at "The
    Players." Aldrich
Booth, John Wilkes
  Booth Killed Lincoln. *Unknown*
  Pardon. Howe
Booth, William
  General William Booth Enters into Heaven.
    Lindsay
Bootlegging and Bootleggers
  Garbage. Tretheway
Boots
  Fitting. Fowler
Borden, Lizzie
  Lizzie Borden took an axe. *Unknown*
Borders (region), Scotland. See Scottish
  Borders.
Boredom
  All in the Downs. Hood
  It's Eleven O'Clock. Chambers
  Life, friends, is boring. We must not say so.
    Fr. Dream Songs. Berryman
  Nervous Prostration. Wickham
  Someone's Face. Ciardi
  Suffocation. Pastan
  Variations on Southern Themes. Justice
  Yesterday Down at the Canal. O'Hara
Bores
  Arrogance Repressed. Betjeman
  Grandmamma's Birthday. Belloc
  In Extremis. Fishback
  La Donna E Perpetuum Mobile. Edman
  Pooh! De la Mare
  To a Lady Holding the Floor. Weston
Borgia, Lucretia
  Descent of Winter (Section 10/30, The.)
    Williams
  On Seeing a Hair of Lucretia Borgia.
    Landor
Borneo
  Naked in Borneo. Swenson
Bosch, Hieronymus
  Homage to Hieronymus Bosch. MacGreevy
Boston, Massachusetts
  Boston. Robinson
  Boston Burglar, The. *Unknown*
  Boston Toast, A. Bossidy
  Communication to the City Fathers of Boston.
    Starbuck
  For the Union Dead. Lowell
  New Order, The. McGinley
  Public Garden, The. Lowell
  South End. Aiken
  Unhappy Boston. Revere
  Whaddaya Do for Action in This Place?
    Starbuck
  Where the Rainbow Ends. Lowell
Boston Tea Party
  Ballad of the Boston Tea-Party, A. Holmes
  New Song, A. *Unknown*
Boswell, James
  David Hume, Dying, Talks to Boswell. Bold
Bosworth Field, Battle of (1485)
  Richard III's Speech. *Fr.* Bosworth Field.
    Beaumont
Botany Bay, Australia
  Botany Bay. *Unknown*
Botswana
  Protest from a Bushman (Masarwa), A.
    Malikongwa
Bottles
  Beer Bottle. Kooser
Bouillabaisse
  Ballad of Bouillabaisse, The. Thackeray

Bourgeoisie
Bourgeois Are Beasts, The. Guevara
Challenge. Negri
How Beastly the Bourgeois Is. Lawrence
Life Cycle of Common Man. Nemerov
Marriage. Corso
New-fashioned Farmer, The. *Unknown*
Old Brown's Daughter. *Unknown*
Tenebrae. Levertov
Toads. Larkin
Unknown Citizen, The. Auden
Bowles, William Lisle
To the Reverend W. L. Bowles. Coleridge
William Lisle Bowles. *Fr.* English Bards
  and Scotch Reviewers. Byron
Bowling
Genuine Poem, Found on a Blackboard in a
  Bowling Alley in Story City, Iowa.
  Kooser
Boxing and Boxers
Black Lady in an Afro Hairdo Cheers for
  Cassius. Holmes
Blues for Benny Kid Paret. Smith
Boxer. Clancy
Boxers. Armando
Boxer's Face, The. Lucilius
Boxing Match, The. Ignatow
Boxing Match, The. *Fr.* The Aeneid [*or*
  Eneados]. Virgil
Boxing towards My Birth. Driscoll
Buck. Harper
Fancy, The. Benét
Fighter Learns of Hands, A. Ghigna
Fights, The. Acorn
Gallantly within the Ring. Reynolds
Knockout, The. Morrison
Loser, The. Bukowski
My Lord, What a Morning. Cuney
Nonpareil's Grave, The. McMahon
On Hurricane Jackson. Dugan
Seventh Round, The. Merrill
Shadowboxing. Tate
They All Must Fall. Ali
World's Worst Boxer, The. Lucilius
Boyne, Battle of the (1690)
Boyne Water, The. *Unknown*
Dialogue between King William and the Late
  King James on the Banks of the Boyne, A.
  Blount
Boyne, Ireland
Father and Son. Higgins
Boys
American Boyhood, An. Holden
Barefoot Boy, The. Whittier
Blessing on Little Boys. Guiterman
Boy We Want, The. *Unknown*
Boys. Letts
Boy's Song, A. Hogg
Chicago, Summer Past. Snyder
Dark Danny. Eastwick
Extremes. Riley
False Security. Betjeman
First Song. Kinnell
Fräulein Reads Instructive Rhymes. Kumin
Fun with Fishing. Tietjens
George. Belloc
Godfrey Gordon Gustavus Gore. Rands
Hiding. Aldis
It chanced to be our washing day. *Fr.* The
  September Gale. Holmes
My Lost Youth. Longfellow
Oh for boyhood's painless play. *Fr.* The
  Barefoot Boy. Whittier
Portrait of the Boy as Artist. Howes
There Was a Boy ("There was a boy, ye knew
  him well"). *Fr.* The Prelude [*or*, Growth
  of a Poet's Mind]: Books. Wordsworth
Tired Tim. De la Mare
To a Small Boy Standing on My Shoes While
  I Am Wearing Them. Nash
Variations on the Themes of Little Boys.
  Weöres

Woman into Man. Wallbank
See also **Childhood and Children; Youth.**
Bozzaris, Marco
Marco Bozzaris. Halleck
Bradstreet, Anne
Winters close, springs open, no child stirs,
  The. *Fr.* Homage to Mistress Bradstreet.
  Berryman
Upon Mrs. Anne Bradstreet Her Poems.
  Rogers
Upon the Author; by a Known Friend.
  Woodbridge
Brahma
Brahma. Emerson
From listening,/ Siva, Brahma, Indra. Nanak
Brains
Motorcycle Evolution. Payack
Neurophysiologist, The. Post
Brancusi, Constantin
From the Workshop of Brancusi and
  Giancometti. Haines
Thinking of Constantin Brancusi. Schmied
Brazil
August 1964. Gullar
Brazil. *Fr.* Sentences. Harrison
On Hope. Bell
Port of Call: Brazil. Lewis
Subversive. Gullar
Brazilian Verse
*Anthology of Twentieth-Century Brazilian
  Poetry, An* (ATCBP). Elizabeth Bishop
  and Emanuel Brasil, eds.
Bread
An Old Thought for a New Couple.
  Markham
Bread. Burnshaw
Bread. Corey
Bread. Keesing
Bread. Mitchell
Bread. Wilkinson
Bread Is Born. Hébert
Don't Talk to Me about Bread. Markham
Evening Bread. Glatstein
Go Get Some Bread. Guillén
Loaves, The. Everson
Breakfast
Breakfast in Bed (Influenza in War-time).
  McDonald
Eggs for Breakfast. Pawsey
Hospital Breakfast: With Grace After. Nims
It's in the Egg. Rosenblatt
Morning. *Unknown*
Breasts
Breasts. Chernoff
Busts and Bosoms Have I Known. *Unknown*
"Fair bosom! fraught with virtue's richest
  treasure." *Fr.* Amoretti, LXXVI.
  Spenser
I'll Tell You What a Flapper Is. Freeman
Innocent Breasts, The. Oppenheimer
Many Times November Has Come Back.
  Guidacci
Breath
Breath. Dickey
Breath. Strand
Breathing seems much easier at nighttime.
  Fet
Breathless. Noyce
Poem about Breath. Wagoner
Properties of Breath, The. Korelitz
Brébeuf, Jean de
Brébeuf and His Brethren, *sels.* Pratt
Brecht, Bertolt
Of Poor B.B. Brecht
Breeches
It chanced to be our washing day. *Fr.* The
  September Gale. Holmes
Brendan, Saint
Fish at Mass, The. *Unknown*
Voyage, The. *Fr.* The Voyage of St.
  Brendan. MacCarthy

Breughel, Pieter. *See* **Brueghel, Pieter.**
Bricklayers
Bricklayer's Labours, The. Tatersal
Bricks
Brick, The. Roche
Brides
Bride, The. Akhmadulina
Bride of Corinth, The. Goethe
Brides, The. Hope
Bride's Hours, A. Valentine
False Bride, The. *Unknown*
Gladys. *Fr.* Calling Your Name in the Zoo.
  Williams
Lucky bridegroom. Sappho
Picture Bride. Song
Rosy Apple, Lemon or Pear. *Unknown*
Vampire Bride, The. Liddell
Vampire Bride. Stefanile
See also **Weddings.**
Bridges
At Darien Bridge. Dickey
Bridge, The. Staff
Burned Bridge, The. Stone
C. Aragon
Covered Bridge. Coffin
Covered Bridge. Warren
Hours of a Bridge, The. Merwin
Landscape with Tractor. Taylor
Loew's Bridge, a Broadway Idyl. Tucker
Lying on a Bridge. Brock
Manhattan Bridge. *Fr.* New York. Leyeles
Of London Bridge, and the Stupendous Sight,
  and Structure Thereof. Howell
Old Bridge at Florence, The. Longfellow
Painted Bridge, The. Taylor
Pass, The. Logan
Pont Mirabeau. Kennedy
This Place in the Ways. Rukeyser
To Brooklyn Bridge. *Fr.* The Bridge.
  Crane
Bridges, Robert
To R. B. Hopkins
Bridget, Saint
Invocation to Saint Bride. Irvine
Bright, John
John Bright. Gummere
Brighton, England
John Betjeman's Brighton. Ewart
Bristol, England
Bristol. Savage
Last Verses. Chatterton
British Columbia, Canada
Breathe Dust. Wah
Christ Walks in This Infernal District Too.
  Lowry
Imagine: A Town. *Fr.* Steveston. Marlatt
In the Dome Car of the "Canadian." Marty
In the Selkirks. Scott
Trail to Lillooet, The. Johnson
British Empire
Ballad of East and West, The. Kipling
Boots. Kipling
Geography. *Fr.* Songs of Education.
  Chesterton
Gunga Din. Kipling
How cursed that country, how severe its
  doom. *Fr.* An Epistle to the Right Hon.
  Charles James Fox. Maurice
Mandalay. Kipling
National Anthem. Martin
Ode on Lord Macartney's Embassy to China.
  Shepherd
Recessional. Kipling
Song of the Banjo, The. Kipling
Song of Those Who Died, A. McDonald
British Museum, London
British Museum Reading Room, The.
  MacNeice
Homage to the British Museum. Empson
Brittany, France
Hervé Riel. Browning
Scenes from Carnac. Arnold

Broadway, New York City
Broadway. Sandburg
Broadway. Whitman
On Broadway. *Fr.* New York. Leyeles
Upper Broadway. Rich
Brodsky, Joseph
Forest of Europe. Walcott
Brontë, Anne
On the Death of Anne Brontë. Brontë
Brontë, Charlotte
Charlotte Brontë. "Coolidge"
Charlotte Nicholls. Clemo
Sampler from Haworth. Howard
Where, behind Keighley, the road. *Fr.*
Haworth Churchyard. Arnold
Bronx, New York City
Bronx. Drake
Death of the Bronx, The. Bloch
Brooklyn Bridge
Blueprint. Steinman
Granite and Steel. Moore
Photo at the Bridge. Pagis
Roebling, his life and mind reprieved enough.
Fr. The Bridge from Brooklyn. Henri
To Brooklyn Bridge. *Fr.* The Bridge.
Crane
Brooklyn, New York City
Brooklyn Heights. Wain
Cage, The. Montague
Centenarian's Story, The. Whitman
Crossing Brooklyn Ferry. Whitman
My Street—Sheepshead Bay. Vaynshteyn
Brooks and Streams
Ad Henricum Wottonem. Bastard
Border Burn, A. *Fr.* Epistle to Tammus.
Selkirk
Brook, The. Tennyson
Brook, The. Thomas
Brook in February, The. Roberts
Brook in the City, A. Frost
Brook Song. Morse
Brooklet, The. Skipsey
By the Bridge. Walker
Creek, The. Ross
Crossing, The. Blackburn
Dreaming Trout, The. *Fr.* The Flowing
Summer. Bruce
Elegy: "Clear and gentle stream!" Bridges
Farewell, A: "Flow down, cold rivulet, to the
sea." Tennyson
Hamlen Brook. Wilbur
Hill Burns, The. Shepherd
Hurrying Brook, The. Blunden
Hyla Brook. Frost
In a mountain stream. Tsuneyori
Inversnaid. Hopkins
Ladder, The. Baro
Little Stream, A. Thoby-Marcelin
Mountain Brook. Coatsworth
Mountain stream, The. *Fr.* Thirty Tanka.
Shunzei
On His Mistress Drown'd. Spratt
On the North Side of Suilven. MacCaig
Orara. Kendall
Resolve, The. Levertov
River, The. *Unknown*
Rosane. Hahn-Hahn
Runoff. Ammons
Serpent Country. Ammons
Spring, The. Fyleman
Stream, The. Weeden
That Is All I Heard. "Yehoash"
There is a stream, I name not its name. *Fr.*
The Bothie of Tober-na-Vuolich. Clough
There is a stream which rises. Bruchac
Tibur is beautiful, too, and the orchard slopes,
and the Anio. *Fr.* Amours de Voyage.
Clough
To the sound of the wind. Tameko
Water. Snyder
West-running Brook. Frost

Wet. Moore
See also **Rivers.**
Brooks, Van Wyck
Dear Men and Women. Wheelock
Brooms
Brooms. Simic
New Brooms. *Fr.* The Three Ladies of
London. Wilson
Brotherhood
Abou Ben Adhem. Hunt
Ballad of East and West, The. Kipling
Brother, The. Nadson
Brothers, The. Muir
Carver, The. Clifton
Cuba. MacDermot
Dance of Saul with the Prophets, The.
Tchernichowsky
Dark Testament. Murray
Divine Image, The ("To mercy, pity, peace,
and love"). *Fr.* Songs of Innocence.
Blake
Family. Miles
For A' That and A' That ("Is there, for honest
poverty"). Burns
Fraternitas. *Fr.* Deer Sing. Confucius
Gentle Park, A. Herbert
Goliath and David. Untermeyer
He Is My Countryman. Slonimski
I Believe. Tchernichowsky
I Dream a World. Hughes
I Hear It Was Charged against Me. Whitman
In Distrust of Merits. Moore
In the Mourning Time. Hayden
Interracial. Johnson
Like Water down a Slope. Schneour
Little Black Boy, The. *Fr.* Songs of
Innocence. Blake
London Spring. Slonimski
Man unto His Fellow Man. *Fr.* On a Note
of Triumph. Corwin
New Jewish Hospital at Hamburg, The.
Heine
Out of Our Shame. Rosten
Over the utmost hill at length I sped. *Fr.*
The Revolt of Islam. Shelley
Pebble, The. Wylie
Second Rapture, The. Carew
Sonnet of Brotherhood. Mason
Street Scene—1946. Porter
To Edom. Heine
To Life I Said Yes. Grade
True Brotherhood. Wilcox
Tuft of Flowers, The. Frost
When I See Another's Pain. Leib
Where the Rainbow Ends. Rive
Brothers
Bank Thief, The. Farrell
Bear Hunt, The. Widdemer
Big Brother. Roberts
Brothers. Currie
Brothers, The. Muir
Clayfeld's Twin. Pack
Drinking Wine with Yoshiyuki and Being
Very Happy. Ryokan
Five Little Brothers. Wilcox
Flight Shot, A. Thompson
Gathering the Bones Together. Orr
I Cannot Choose but Think upon the Time.
Fr. Brother and Sister. "Eliot"
In the Tree House at Night. Dickey
Lil' Bro'. Fufuka
Little. Aldis
Little Brother's Secret. Mansfield
Memory. Stroud
O, Shmuel My Brother! Halpern
Quarrel, The. Farjeon
This Was My Brother. Gould
To John Lamb, Esq.: Of the South-Sea
House. Lamb
To My Brothers. Keats
To My Dead Brother. Thompson
Twa Brothers, The. *Unknown*

Two in Bed. Ross
Two-Year-Old Has Had a Motherless Week,
The. Shapiro
When, at our Sovereign's command. *Fr.*
Manyo Shu. Yakamochi
World, The. Creeley
You Can Have It. Levine
Brown, Andrew
Rev. Andrew Brown, over the Hill to Rest.
Heard
Brown, John
Brown of Ossawatomie. Whittier
Harpers Ferry. Rodman
How Old Brown Took Harper's Ferry.
Stedman
John Brown. Koopman
October 16: The Raid. Hughes
Portent, The. Melville
Soul and Body of John Brown, The.
Rukeyser
Brown, Mrs. E. Cohrs
Mrs. E. Cohrs Brown. Fordham
Brown, Sterling A.
Br'er Sterling and the Rocker. Harper
Browning, Elizabeth Barrett
To Edward Fitzgerald. Browning
Browning, Robert
Browning. Stevenson
Browning at Asolo. Johnson
Life-long, Poor Browning. Spencer
To Robert Browning. Landor
Bruce, Robert
Bruce, The, *sels.* Barbour
Bruce and the Spider. Barton
Scots Wha Hae [wi' Wallace Bled]. Burns
Roye Robert the Bruss the rayke he avowit,
The. *Fr.* The Buke of the Howlat.
Holland
Try Again. Cook
Bruckner, Anton
Bruckner. Camp
Brueghel, Pieter
Breughel's Winter. De la Mare
Dance, The. Williams
Die Bauernhochzeit. Smithyman
Et Quid Amabo Nisi Quod Aenigma Est.
Sandy
February; the Boy Breughel. Dubie
Hunters in the Snow: Brueghel. Langland
Musée des Beaux Arts. Auden
Numbering at Bethlehem, The. Goldbarth
Pictures from Brueghel, *sels.* Williams
Proportions. Stroud
Skaters. Rutsala
Two Views of a Cadaver Room. Plath
Brummell, Beau (George Bryan Brummell)
Brummell at Calais. Glassco
Brussels, Belgium
Brussels in Winter. Auden
Brutus (Marcus Junius Brutus)
Portrait of Brutus. *Fr.* Julius Caesar.
Shakespeare
Bryan, William Jennings
Bryan, Bryan, Bryan, Bryan. Lindsay
Free Silver. *Unknown*
Bryant, "Bear" (Paul William Bryant)
To Bear Bryant, Somewhere on That Taller
Tower. Welch
Bryant, William Cullen
Bryant. *Fr.* A Fable for Critics. Lowell
Bubbles
Blowing Bubbles. Hillert
Bubbles. Garrett
Bubbles. Sandburg
Fat Lena's Recipe for Crocodile Soup.
Janowitz
Lightness Remembered. Willard
Madrigal. Drummond
Buber, Martin
Martin Buber in the Pub. Harris

Buckingham, George Villiers, 2d Duke of
In the first rank of these did Zimri stand. *Fr.*
Absalom and Achitophel, Pt. I. Dryden
On the Duke of Buckingham. Shirley
On the Duke of Buckingham, Slain by Felton,
the 23rd August, 1628. Felltham
Budapest, Hungary
Brazilian Rain Forest. Illyés
Budapest. Teller
Budapest Elegy. Vas
Wonder Castle, The. Illyés
Buddha and Buddhism
Brief is this mortal life. *Fr.* Manyo Shu.
Yakamochi
Buddha. Melville
Buddha at Kamakura. Kipling
Buddha himself, The. *Unknown*
Buddha preached the twelve divisions.
Ryokan
Buddha's Birthday: April 8, 1819. *Fr.* Oraga
Haru. Issa
Further Advantages of Learning. Rexroth
Looking for Buddha. Jacinto
Lord Buddha is present everywhere. *Fr.*
Ryojin Hisho. Go-Shirakawa
Proofs of Buddha's Existence. *Unknown*
Buffalo Bill (William Frederick Cody)
Buffalo Bill's. Cummings
Buffaloes
Bison, The. Belloc
Bluffalo, The. Yolen
Bone Yard. Barnes
Buffalo. Daniells
Buffalo. Eglington
Buffalo, The. Moore
Buffalo. *Fr.* Hunter Poems of the Yoruba.
Unknown
Buffalo Dusk. Sandburg
Buffalo Skinners, The. *Unknown*
Flower-fed Buffaloes, The. Lindsay
Ghosts of the Buffaloes, The. Lindsay
I thought I saw buffalo. *Fr.* Sioux
Metamorphoses. *Unknown*
Song: "Hear me, ye smokeless skies and
grass-green earth." *Fr.* The Last Bison.
Mair
Song of the Red & Green Buffalo, A.
Unknown
Trail beside the River Platte, The. Heyen
Bugles and Buglers
Call of the Bugles, The. Hovey
Danny Deever. Kipling
Buildings and Builders
About an Excavation. Reznikoff
After the Rebuilding. Booth
Ceaseless flows that beck. *Unknown*
Completion. Dunn
Construction. Shapiro
Dome Poem. Smith
Hammer Falls, Is Falling, The. Boruch
Love Song: I and Thou. Dugan
Midst the fair range of buildings which,
new-reared. *Fr.* A Burlesque Ode, on the
Author's Clearing a New House of Some
Workmen. Keate
On Watching the Construction of a
Skyscraper. Raffel
Our great Sovereign who rules in peace,/
Offspring of the Bright One on high,/
Wills, as a goddess. *Fr.* Manyo Shu.
Unknown
Remodeling the Hermit's Cabin. Chappell
Scaffolding. Heaney
Ting-star is in the middle of the sky, The.
Unknown
To Raise a Chimney. Young
Bukhara, U. S. S. R.
Prayer Rug, The. Kennedy
Bukowski, Charles
You Don't Know What Love Is. Carver
Bulgaria
Two Masks Unearthed in Bulgaria. Meredith

Bull Run, Battles of (1861, 1862)
Battle of Bull Run, The. *Unknown*
Manassas. Warfield
March into Virginia, The. Melville
"Our Left." Ticknor
Run from Manassas Junction, The. *Unknown*
Upon the Hill before Centreville. Boker
Bullets
What the Bullet Sang. Harte
Bullfights and Bullfighters
Bull, A. Qasmi
Bull-Fights. Leivick
Bullard's Song, The. *Unknown*
Bullfight. Holub
Death Invited. Swenson
Girl Friend Describes the Bull Fight, The.
Uruttiran
Goring, The. Plath
Juan Belmonte, Torero. Finkel
Lament for Ignacio Sánchez Mejías. García
Lorca
Matadors, The. Jacobsen
Bulls
Bull, The. Hodgson
Bull, The. Sackville-West
Bull, The. Williams
Bull, The. Wright
Bull Calf, The. Layton
Bull Moses, The. Hughes
Bullfight. Holub
Hoosen Johnny. *Unknown*
Magnificent Bull, The.
Outlaw, The. Heaney
Spilled from a tree-searing wind. *Fr.* Fifteen
Hokku. Shiba Sonome
Three Tall Men, The. *Unknown*
Two Bulls, The. *Fr.* How the Bulls Were
Begotten. *Unknown*
Bundling
New Bundling Song, A. *Unknown*
Bunke, Tamara ("Ita")
Ita. Ulloa
Bunker Hill, Battle of (1775)
Bunker Hill. Calvert
Bunker's Hill, or the Soldier's Lamentation.
Freeth
Bunyan, John
Of John Bunyan's Life. James
Bunyan, Paul
Legend of Paul Bunyan, A. Bourinot
Bureaucracy and Bureaucrats
Anteroom: Geneva. Devlin
Constable Calls, A. Heaney
Departmental. Frost
Frigate Jones, the Pussyfooter ("Frigate Jones
was very slow and fat"). Burke
Pass Office Song. *Unknown*
Unknown Citizen, The. Auden
Burglars
Burglar Bill. "Anstey"
Off to work. *Unknown*
Burial
Burial Detail. Hudgins
Call for the Robin Redbreast and the Wren.
Fr. The White Devil. Webster
Dead Skunk. Eberhart
Earth Buried. Mackenzie
Funeral, A. Rabon
Hearse Song, The. *Unknown*
I Found Her Out There. Hardy
Mummy of a Lady Named Jemutesonekh XXI
Dynasty. James
Sled Burial, Dream Ceremony. Dickey
Urn for Burial, An. *Unknown*
Was it pleasing to my prince's soul? *Fr.*
Manyo Shu. Tamochi
See also Cemeteries; Funerals; Graves.
Burke, Edmund
Here lies our good Edmund, whose genius
was such. *Fr.* Retaliation. Goldsmith

Burlesque. *See* Striptease.
Burma
Burma Hills. Gutteridge
Mandalay. Kipling
Burns, Robert
Hundred years ago this morn, A. *Fr.* Robin
Burns. Massey
Address. Williams
At the Grave of Burns. Wordsworth
Burns. Halleck
Had We Two Met. Landor
Written in the Visitors' Book at the Birthplace
of Robert Burns. Cable
Burr, Aaron
Aaron Burr's Wooing. Stedman
To Aaron Burr, under Trial for High Treason.
Morton
Burr, Theodosia
Theodosia Burr. Terrell
Theodosia Burr: The Wrecker's Story.
Palmer
Burros. *See* Donkeys.
Bus Terminals
In the Baggage Room at Greyhound.
Ginsberg
Buses
Boarding, The. Johnson
B's the Bus. *Fr.* All around the Town.
McGinley
Bus, The. Cohen
Bus Ride. Kandel
Bus Ride. *Fr.* Ferry Ride. Robinson
Last Bus, The. Knox
Waking on a Greyhound. Henry
Way Downtown, The. Hooper
Business and Businessmen
Accountant in His Bath, The ("The accountant
dried his imperfect back"). Mitchell
Any Man to His Secretary. Corke
Between a Contractor and His Wife.
Unknown
Business Is Business. Braley
Dirge: "1-2-3 was the number he played but
today the number came 3-2-1." Fearing
Endurance Test. Balsdon
Executive. Betjeman
My Brother, Beautiful Shinault, That Goat.
Huddle
See also Accounting and Accountants;
Advertising; Banking and Bankers;
Capitalism; Commerce; Financiers;
Insurance.
Butchering and Butchers
Bags of Meat. Hardy
Butcher Shop. Simic
Butcherboy. Schmidt
Fifth Hell, The. *Fr.* The Seven Hells of
Jigoku Zoshi. Rothenberg
Guys of the Volye, *sels.* Vaynshteyn
Leicester Chambermaid, The. *Unknown*
My Father Owns the Butcher Shop.
Unknown
On a Pig's Head. Tomlinson
Psychonaut Sonnets: Jones, The. Goldbarth
Reuben Bright. Robinson
Stockyard, The. Squire
Butler, Samuel (1612-1680)
English Liberal. Taylor
On Butler who can think without rage. *Fr.*
A Satire. Oldham
Buttercups
Buttercup, A. *Unknown*
Buttercups. Thorley
Buttercups. *Unknown*
Buttercups and Daisies. Howitt

Butterflies
Against the morning glories. *Fr.* Thirty-three
  Hokku. Kikaku
Blue-Butterfly Day. Frost
Butterfly comes and takes a butterfly, A. *Fr.*
  Forty-four Hokku. Issa
Butterfly dying right in front, A. *Fr.*
  Twenty-seven Hokku. Natsume Seibi
Butterfly settles on the neckplate, A. *Fr.*
  Eighty-seven Hokku. Buson
Butterflies. *Fr.* Twelve Miscellaneous Poems
  on the Fang Garden. Chang Yü
Butterflies darting. *Fr.* Sixty-four Tanka.
  Saigyo
Butterfly. Armstrong
Butterfly. Fet
Butterfly, The. Hawker
Butterfly, The. James
Butterfly. Lawrence
Butterfly, The. *Fr.* Three Animals. Padgett
Butterfly, The. Rose
Butterfly, The. Scollard
Butterfly. Smith
Butterfly. Tsuboi Shigeji
Butterfly and the Caterpillar, The. Lauren
Butterfly and the Snail, The. *Fr.* Fables.
  Gay
Butterfly: now in front. *Fr.* Seventeen
  Hokku. Chiyojo
Butterfly on Rock. Layton
Butterfly: what's it dreaming of. *Fr.*
  Seventeen Hokku. Chiyojo
By its own wind, a small butterfly. *Fr.*
  Seventeen Hokku. Chiyojo
Coming out of the privy. *Fr.* Eighty-seven
  Hokku. Buson
Corn-grinding Song. *Unknown*
Dandelion: from time to time. *Fr.* Seventeen
  Hokku. Chiyojo
Dead Butterfly, The. Levertov
Dream. Kogon
Evening dusk: flying in the middle. *Fr.*
  Thirty-three Hokku. Kikaku
Example, The. Davies
Flying Blossoms. Davies
Flying Crooked. Graves
For a companion. Shiki
From time to time, a butterfly. *Fr.*
  Seventeen Hokku. Chiyojo
Graceful Bastion, The. Williams
Haiku: "Falling flower, The." Moritake
Haiku: "First butterfly." Takahama Kyoshi
Haiku: "Fluttering, fluttering." *Fr.*
  Thirty-nine Haiku. Shiki
Haiku: "On an onion tuft." Matsumoto
  Takashi
Hoofer, The. Redwing
I was round and small like a pearl. *Unknown*
King of Yellow Butterflies, The. Lindsay
Ode to a Butterfly. Higginson
Of the Boy and Butterfly. Bunyan
On Discovering a Butterfly. Nabokov
On the Butterflies. T'ang Yin
Only butterflies fly in the field. *Fr.*
  Seventy-six Hokku. Basho
Poem on a Sleeping Butterfly. Liu Shih
Roots and Branches. Duncan
Settled on a temple bell and asleep. *Fr.*
  Eighty-seven Hokku. Buson
Sleeping butterfly. *Fr.* Thirty-three Hokku.
  Kikaku
They look/ like newlyweds. Ryota
To a Butterfly. Davies
To a Butterfly. Wordsworth
Will to Live, The. McBride
Wings. Wright
Written on a Boat on the Ch'ien-t'ang River.
  Hung Liang-chi

Buzzards
Buzzard. Daugherty
Pondy Woods. Warren

Song of the Turkey Buzzard. Welch
See also **Vultures.**
Byelorussia
Byelorussia, *sels.* Kulbak.
Byrd, Mary Furman Weston
Mrs. Mary Furman Weston Byrd. Fordham
Byron, George Gordon Noel Byron, 6th
  Baron
Another Letter to Lord Byron. Slavitt
Byron. Coogler
Byron Recollected at Bologna. *Fr.* Italy.
  Rogers
Memorial Verses. Arnold
On the Proposal to Erect a Monument in
  England to Lord Byron. Lazarus
On This Day I Complete My Thirty-sixth
  Year. Byron
Sketch of Lord Byron's Life. Moore
Very like a Whale. Nash
You lived and moved among the best society.
  Fr. Letter to Lord Byron. Auden
Byzantium
Byzantium. Yeats
Sailing to Byzantium. Yeats

C

Cabala
Kabbalists in Safed. Leivick
Modern Kabbalist. Falk
Cabbages
Cabbage. Norman
Skunk Cabbage. Oliver
Cactus
Cactuses, The. Witheford
Night-blooming Cereus, The. Hayden
Cadavers. See **Corpses.**
Cadiz, Spain, Battle of (1596)
Winning of Cales, The. Deloney
Cads
Rain It Raineth, The. Bowen
Caedmon
Caedmon. Levertov
Caedmon. Nicholson
Caesar, Julius
Antony's Oration [over Caesar's Body] *Fr.*
  Julius Caesar. Shakespeare
Ides of March, The. Cavafy
Julius Caesar. Herrick
Rider at The Gate, The. Masefield
Cafés
In a Cafe. Brautigan
In a Café. Dobson
Cain and Abel
Abel. Capetanakis
Abel. Lasker-Schüler
Autobiography. Pagis
Autobiography. Pagis
Begetting of Cain, The. Plutzik
Brothers. Pagis
My Answer. Adamo
Cakes
After the Party. Wise
Chocolate Cake. Payne
Calais, France
Burgesses of Calais, The. Minot
Calcutta, India
Calcutta. Garai
Calder, Alexander
Calder, A. Shapiro
Caliban
Caliban upon Setebos; or, Natural Theology in
  the Island. Browning
California
Across the Bay. Davie
As I Came Down Mount Tamalpais. Urmy
At Carmel. Austin

Barnsley and District. Davie
Beauty and Sadness. Song
Before the Stuff Comes Down. Snyder
Blue Ridge. Voigt
Burning the Small Dead. Snyder
Butter. Schmidt
California Dead. Murray
California Dreaming. Wright
California Hills in August. Gioia
California Oaks, The. Winters
California Phrasebook, The. Schmitz
Californians, The. Spencer
Carmel Point. Jeffers
Changes around the Bay. Palmer
Circumambulation of Mt. Tamalpais. Hoyem
City [San Francisco] Hughes
Clouds of Evening. Jeffers
Como lo Siento. Cervantes
Death Looks Down. Gregg
Elements of San Joaquin, The. Soto
Freeway 280. Cervantes
Grandfather. Stroud
Hay for the Horses. Snyder
In Montecito. Jarrell
Korea Bound, 1952. Childress
Letter from Vermont. Voigt
Lights among Redwood. Gunn
Mission Bay. Koethe
Naming. Stroud
Napa, California. Castillo
Off from Swing Shift. Hongo
Old Graves fell asleep. *Fr.* The Donner
  Party. Keithley
One West Coast. Young
Open Casket. McPherson
Palo Alto; the Marshes. Hass
Report from California. Moyles
Santa Barbara. Browne
Shore. O Hehir
Sleep in the Mojave Desert. Plath
Smudging. Wakoski
Song of the Redwood-Tree. Whitman
Trip: San Francisco. Hughes
Yugoslav Cemetery. Wright
Calligraphy
Calligraphy Practice. Ou-yang Hsiu
My script soars up, flies away, but I'm too
  drunk to know. Chang Wen-t'ao
Song of Cursive Calligraphy. Hsieh Chin
Calliope (muse)
To Calliope. Graves
Calm
He That Is Slow to Anger. *Fr.* Proverbs
Keep Cool. Garvey
Long Boat, The. Kunitz
Whiteness. Leyeles
Calvary. See **Crucifixion, The.**
Calves
Birth of Rainbow. Hughes
Bridestones. Hughes
First Birth, The. Jones
I Would Like You for a Comrade. Parry
March Calf, A. Hughes
Teaching a Dumb Calf. Hughes
Two-headed Calf, The. Gilpin
What Is Veal? *Unknown*
Calvin, John
Calvinist Autumnal. Harrod
Calvinism
Calvin in the Casino. Cassity
Holy Willie's Prayer. Burns
Latest Decalogue, The. Clough
McAndrew's Hymn. Kipling
Mr. Edwards and the Spider. Lowell
Calypso Music
Calypsomania. Brode
Calypso (mythology)
Calypso's Island. MacLeish
Forever Ambrosia. Morley
Ulysses Leaves the Nymph Calypso. *Fr.*
  Odyssey. Homer

Camaraderie
Assurance. Stafford
Comrade in Arms. Moore.
See also **Friendship.**

Cambodia
Dead Soldiers. Fenton
This Kampuchea. Parini

Cambridge, England
Autumn Morning at Cambridge. Cornford
Cambridge and the Cam. *Fr.* The
  Apollyonists. Fletcher
Hic Vir, Hic Est. Calverley
In the Backs. Cornford
Inside of King's College Chapel, Cambridge.
  Fr. Ecclesiastical Sonnets. Wordsworth
Residence at Cambridge. *Fr.* The Prelude
  [or, Growth of a Poet's Mind]
  Wordsworth
Written at Cambridge. Lamb

Cambridge, Massachusetts
I Like My Body. Cummings
Professor Kelleher and the Charles River.
  O'Grady
See also **Harvard University.**

Cambridge University
Autumn Morning at Cambridge. Cornford
Inside of King's College Chapel, Cambridge.
  Fr. Ecclesiastical Sonnets. Wordsworth
On the University of Cambridge's Burning the
  Duke of Monmouth's Picture. Stepney

Cambridgeshire, England
Bedford Level. *Fr.* The Fleece. Dyer
Old Vicarage, Grantchester, The. Brooke

Camden, New Jersey
Narcissus in Camden. Cone

Camden, William
To William Camden. Jonson

Camellias
Camellia drops and spills, A. *Fr.*
  Eighty-seven Hokku. Buson
Into the darkness of an old well. *Fr.*
  Eighty-seven Hokku. Buson

Camelot
Lady of Shalott, The. Tennyson

Camels
Camel. Akhyaliyya
Camel. Brownjohn
Camel, The. Nash
Camels in Persia. Wellesley
Fruit of the Tree, The. Wagoner
Legend of the First Cam-u-el, The.
  Guiterman
Plaint of the Camel, The. *Fr.* The Admiral's
  Caravan. Carryl

Cameras
Camera. Kooser
See also **Photography and Photographers.**

Camões, Luis de
Camoes and the Debt. Andresen
Luis de Camões. Campbell

Campaigns, Political. *See* **Voting and
  Voters.**

Campanula
Bed of Campanula, A. "Crichton"

Campbell, Roy
In Memoriam: Roy Campbell. Currey

Camping
At the Shelter-Stone. Macrow
August on Sourdough, a Visit from Dick
  Brewer. Snyder
Camp Evergreen. Kenyon
Campfire Extinguished. Roseliep
Lochan. Smith
Minnesota Camp Grounds. Vizenor
Night in the Forest. Kinnell
Oh, Lovely Rock. Jeffers
Staying Alive. Wagoner
To Myself, Late, in a Myrtle Grove.
  Peterson

Two Campers in Cloud Country. Plath
What Are You Thinking About? Macmillan

Campuses
Golgotha. Kennedy
See also **Colleges and Universities.**

Canaan
Dream Canaan. Shtoltsenberg

Canada
At the Tourist Center in Boston. Atwood
Can. Lit. Birney
Canada-I-O. *Unknown*
Crossing the Border into Canada. Harjo
Deep Dark River. Roberts
From Colony to Nation. Layton
Let me put it this way. Jonas
Moose, The. Bishop
Only Tourist in Havana Turns His Thoughts
  Homeward, The. Cohen
Tadoussac. Bancroft
Canadian Poetry in English (CaP). Bliss
  Carman, Lorne Pierce, *and* V. B.
  Rhodenizer, eds.
Modern Canadian Verse (MoCV). A. J. M.
  Smith, ed.
New American and Canadian Poetry (NeAC).
  John Gill, ed.
New Oxford Book of Canadian Verse, The
  (NOBC). Margaret Atwood, ed.
*Oxford Book of Canadian Verse in English
  and French, The* (OBCV). A. J. M.
  Smith, ed.
See also **listings for Canadian provinces.**

Canals
Aged Pilot Man, The. "Twain"

Canaries
Canary, The. Nash
Canary, The. Turner
My Canary. Heard
Poor Matthias. Arnold
To the Canary Bird. Very

Canberra, Australia
Canberra in April. Rowland

Cancer (disease)
Bess. Stafford
Cancer. Verhagen
Cancer Cells, The. Eberhart
Cancer's a Funny Thing. Haldane
Death from Cancer. *Fr.* In Memory of
  Arthur Winslow. Lowell
Farewell, A: "While time hustled." Weigel
For the Death of Vince Lombardi. Dickey
Funeral, The. Dubie
Hunter Radiation Center: Halloween.
  Mattison
Memorial. Pinsky
Miss Gee. Auden
On Visiting the M. D. Anderson. Jayyusi
2 November 1982. Bold
Under the Sign of Cancer. Wright
Where Late the Sweet Birds Sang. Crago

Candlemas
Candlemas. Brown
Candlemas Day. Madeleva
If Candlemas Day be fair and bright.
  Unknown
Procession at Candlemas, A. Clampitt
See also **Groundhogs.**

Candles
Candle, A. Suckling
First Fig. Millay
Flame Point. Supervielle
Floating Candles, The. Lea
Little Nancy [or Nanny] Etticoat. Mother
  Goose
Love Expresses with Candle as a Metaphor.
  Tamemasa

Candy
Chocolates. Simpson
Dakota: Five Times Six. Hansen

Cannibalism and Cannibals
Among the Anthropophagi. Nash

Constant Cannibal Maiden, The. Irwin
Flying Dutchman, The. Laforgue
Juan embark'd—the ship got under way. *Fr.*
  Don Juan. Byron
Poe-'em of Passion, A. Lummis
Snack, The. Zeiger

Canning
Haiku: "As bad as a dyer's." *Unknown*
Preserves. Butler

Canoes and Canoeing
Canoe. Anderson
Canoe Song at Twilight. McCully
Deliverance. Crooker
On the great streams the ships may go. *Fr.*
  The Canoe Speaks. Stevenson
Paddling Song. *Unknown*
Song My Paddle Sings, The. Johnson
White Canoe, The. Sullivan

Canonical Hours
Compline. *Fr.* Horae Canonicae. Davie
Matins. Levertov
Prime. *Fr.* Horae Canonicae. Davie
Song for Ishtar. Levertov

Canonicus
Canonicus and Roger Williams. *Unknown*

Canova, Antonio
On the Bust of Helen by Canova. Byron

Caoilte
Caoilte. *Unknown*

Cape Breton Island, Nova Scotia
Cape Breton. Bishop

Cape Cod, Massachusetts
Cape Cod. Santayana
Old Map of Barnstable County. Galvin
Provincetown, *sels.* Dudek
Provincetown, Mass. Shapiro

Cape Horn
Rounding the Horn. *Fr.* Dauber. Masefield

Cape of Good Hope
Rounding the Cape. Campbell

Capital Punishment
Facing the Chair. "MacDiarmid"
There is no chapel on the day. *Fr.* The
  Ballad of Reading Gaol. Wilde
Thoughts on Capital Punishment. McKuen
See also **Executions.**

Capitalism
After They Have Tired of the Brilliance of
  Cities. Spender
Empire Builders. MacLeish
God or Mammon. Cruickshank
Investor's Soliloquy. Ward
Symphony, The. Lanier
See also **Banking and Bankers; Business
  and Businessmen; Financiers.**

Cappadocia
I Knew a Cappadocian. Housman

Caravaggio, Michelangelo Merisi da
In Santa Maria del Popolo. Gunn
My own head. Seen in mirrors. Cleanly axed.
  Fr. Caravaggio Dying, Porto Ercole, July
  1610, Aged 36. Lucie-Smith

Carcassonne, France
Carcassonne. Nadaud

Card Games
Ballad of Rodborough Common, The.
  Joseph
Full House. Garey
Game of Life, The. Saxe
Playing Solitaire. Fortney
Solitaire. Updike

Cardinals (birds)
As a Child Seeing a Cardinal. Gill
Cardinal Bird, The. Gallagher
Cardinals in the Ice Age. Engels
Chimes for Yahya. Merrill
If the Cardinals Were like Us. McPherson

Cargoes
Cargoes. Masefield
See also **Freighters.**

Carib Indians
Cliffs at Manzanilla, The. Carew
Ethnocide. Fergus
Caribbean Islands. *See* **West Indies.**
Caribbean Sea
For the Altarpiece of the Roseau Valley
Church, Saint Lucia. Walcott
See also **West Indies.**
Carlyle, Thomas
Carlyle and Emerson. Schuyler
Thomas Carlyle. *Unknown*
Carmel, California
Carmel Point. Jeffers
Carnac, France
Scenes from Carnac. Arnold
Carnivals
Alone by the Road's Edge. O Hehir
At the Carnival. Spencer
Lost Carnival, The. Chappell
Miss Tourist. "Kitchener"
Pans at Carnival. Beissel
Sunday Night in Santa Rosa. Gioia
Caroline of Ansbach
On Queen Caroline's Deathbed. Pope
Carousels. *See* **Merry-go-rounds.**
Carpe Diem
Advice to My Son. Meinke
Age. Cowley
Alarm, The. Jacob
Apple, The. Plato
Bacchanal. De Vries
Blue Girls. Ransom
Bridal Couch. Lloyd
But love whilst that thou mayst be loved
again. *Fr.* To Delia. Daniel
Careless Gallant, The. Jordan
Carpe Diem. Stead
Come, Shepherds, Come! *Fr.* The Faithful
Shepherdess. Fletcher
Corinna in Vendome. Ronsard
Corinna's Going a-Maying. Herrick
Enjoy Thy April Now. *Fr.* A Description of
Beauty. Daniel
Go [*or* Goe,] Lovely Rose. Waller
Hope, like the hyaena [*or* hyena], coming to
be old. *Fr.* Diana. Constable
Is It Really Worth the While? *Unknown*
Laugh and Be Merry. Masefield
Lesbia. Catullus
Logical Song, A. *Unknown*
Look, Delia, how we esteem the half-blown
rose. *Fr.* To Delia. Daniel
Love's Emblems. Fletcher
My Sweetest Lesbia [Let Us Live and Love].
Campion
Now Sleeps the Crimson Petal. *Fr.* The
Princess. Tennyson
Now the Lusty Spring [Is Here] *Fr.* The
Tragedy of Valentinian. Fletcher
Nymph's Reply to the Shepherd, The.
Ralegh
O [*or* Oh] Mistress Mine [Where Are You
Roaming?] *Fr.* Twelfth Night.
Shakespeare
Passionate Shepherd to His Love, The.
Marlowe
Pluck the Fruit and Taste the Pleasure. *Fr.*
Robert, Second Duke of Normandy.
Lodge
Ponder, Darling, These Busted Statues.
Cummings
Quid Sit Futurum Cras Fuge Quaerere. Prior
Sing We and Chant It. *Unknown*
Sister, Awake! *Unknown*
Song: "Young Philander woo'd me long."
Unknown
Whiles someone did chant this lovely lay,
The. *Fr.* The Faerie Queene. Spenser
Then Lose in Time Thy Maidenhead.
Unknown

Time. Taylor
To A. L. Carew
To Amarantha, That She Would Dishevel Her
Hair. Lovelace
To His Coy Mistress. Marvell
To Phillis. Waller
To the Virgins, to Make Much of Time.
Herrick
Villanelle of the Poet's Road. Dowson
Where Lies the Land [to Which the Ship
Would Go?] *Fr.* Songs in Absence.
Clough
Whole universe is full of God, The. Emre
Young May Moon, The. Moore
Young Men Come Less Often, The—Isn't It
So? Horace
Youth's the Season. *Fr.* The Beggar's
Opera. Gay
See also **"Come Live with Me and Be My
Love."**
Carpenters
At the Sign-Painter's. Carter
Carpenter's Complaint, The. Baugh
Craftsman. Shaw
Carpets. *See* **Rugs.**
Carriages
Carriage from Sweden, A. Moore
"Carroll, Lewis"
Lewis Carroll. Farjeon
Cars. *See* **Automobiles.**
Cartier, Jacques
Jacques Cartier. McGee
Cary, Sir Lucius
To the Immortal Memory and Friendship of
That Noble Pair, Sir Lucius Cary and Sir
Henry Morison. Jonson
Casabianca, Louis
Casabianca. Hemans
Casement, Roger David
Casement's Funeral. *Fr.* The Battle of
Aughrim. Murphy
Cassandra
Cassandra. Bogan
Cassandra. Jeffers
Cassandra. Robinson
Caste Systems, Indian
If caste was what the Creator had in mind.
Kabir
Castile. *See* **Spain.**
Castlereagh, Robert Stewart, 2d Viscount
Epitaph for Castlereagh, An. Byron
Similes for Two Political Characters of 1819.
Shelley
Castles
Castles. Leyeles
Our great Empress. *Fr.* Manyo Shu.
Hitomaro
Visit to Enniskillen, A. O'Huiginn
Castro, Fidel
One Thousand Fearful Words for Fidel
Castro. Ferlinghetti
Waiting for Fidel. Agard
Catalpa Trees
Catalpa Tree. Waddington
Catbirds
Air: "Cat bird singing." Creeley
Cat Heard the Cat-Bird, The. Ciardi
Catechism
New Dial, The. *Unknown*
Caterpillars
Caterpillar. Kitahara Hakushu
Caterpillar, The. *Fr.* Sing-Song. Rossetti
Caterpillar, The. Williams
Cocoon. McCord
Fuzzy Wuzzy, Creepy Crawly. Schulz
How soft a caterpillar steps. Dickinson
Leaf-eater. Kinsella
Only My Opinion. Shannon
Tickle Rhyme, The. Serraillier

Cathedrals
Laughing Angel: Reims, The. Socolow
Meditation. Hecht
Cather, Willa
Biography. Stanton
Catholicism
Catholic Bells, The. Williams
Fierce and brooding holocaust of faith, The.
Fr. Two Poems on the Catholic Bavarians.
Bowers
First Confession. Kennedy
Hind and the Panther, The, *sels.* Dryden
Hippopotamus, The. Eliot
I know a wasted place high in the Alps. *Fr.*
Two Poems on the Catholic Bavarians.
Bowers
Invites Poets and Historians to Write in
Cynthia's Praise. Ayres
Jansenist Journey. Devlin
Lough Derg. Devlin
Pill, The. Clarke
Sonnet: Zone ("You're weary of this ancient
world at last"). Apollinaire
This is no rune nor riddle. *Fr.* Tribute to the
Angels. Doolittle
Anthology of Catholic Poets, An (ACP).
Shane Leslie, ed.
Cats
Ad-dressing of Cats, The. Eliot
Alley Cat School. Asch
Apartment Cats. Gunn
Appeal to Cats in the Business of Love, An.
Flatman
Bad Kittens, The. Coatsworth
Barn is full of mice, The. Rosei
Burning the Cat. Merwin
Cat, The. *Fr.* Sad Memories. Calverley
Cat. Farjeon
Cat. Hamburger
Cat, The. Herford
Cat, The. Kaschnitz
Cat. Kitahara Hakushu
Cat. Miller
Cat. Rosenblatt
Cat, A. Thomas
Cat and the Moon, The. Yeats
Cat and the Weather. Swenson
Cat Ballerina Assoluta. Glen
Cat Goddesses. Graves
Cat Heard the Cat-Bird, The. Ciardi
Cat in Cold Weather, The. Rai San'yo
Cat in the Dovecot. Trainin
Cat in the Snow. Fisher
Cat Kisses. Katz
Cat Merchant, The. Rabon
Cat Morgan Introduces Himself. Eliot
Cat on the Porch at Dusk. Harriman
Cat Who Aspired to Higher Things, The.
Kennedy
Cats, The. Exler
Cats. Farjeon
Cats. Francis
Cats, The. Kees
Cats, The. Klinger
Cats. *Fr.* Nature Notes. MacNeice
Cats and Dogs. Bodecker
Cat's Conscience, A. *Unknown*
Cats Crept Up on Me Slowly. Laird
Cat's Menu. Shaw
Cats of Campagnatica, The. Porter
Cats of Santa Anna, The. Tasso
Cats sleep fat and walk thin. *Fr.* Catalogue.
Moore
Cat's Song, The. *Unknown*
Cheerio My Deario. *Fr.* Archy and
Mehitabel. Marquis
Civilization. Schmidt
Concrete Cat. Charles

Corpse of a Cat, The. Hagiwara Sakutaro
Country Barnyard. Coatsworth
Cruel, Clever Cat. Taylor
Curiosity. Reid
Death of the Cat. Serraillier
Diamond Cut Diamond. Milne
Disturbed, the cat. *Unknown*
Epitaph for a Cat. Bruner
Epitaph for My Cat. Garrigue
Family Cat, The. Fuller
Favourite Cat's Dying Soliloquy, A. Seward
Feline. Wallace
Feline Fine. Lewis
Flying Cat, The. Nye
For I Will Consider My Cat Jeoffry [*or*
   Jeoffrey]. *Fr.* Jubilate Agno. Smart
Four-Paws. Eden
14-Year-Old Convalescent Cat in the Winter,
   A. Ewart
Galloping Cat, The. Smith
Garden-Lion. "Hayes"
Getting Up. Dobyns
Good Morning? Heavenly Madam Ping.
   Harmsen van Beek
Growltiger's Last Stand. Eliot
Gus: The Theatre Cat. Eliot
Haiku: "Stray cat, A." *Fr.* Thirty-nine
   Haiku. Shiki
Hearth. Bacon
Her Seventeenth Winter. Leax
Hoppy. Gibbons
House Cat, The. Wynne
I Am the Cat. Usher
I Like Little Pussy. Taylor
In Honour of Taffy Topaz. Morley
In Memoriam—Leo: A Yellow Cat.
   Sherwood
Inscrutable Cat. Kvitko
Kilkenny Cats, The. *Unknown*
Kitten, A. Farjeon
Kitten, The. Nash
Last Words to a Dumb Friend. Hardy
Lat Take a Cat. *Fr.* The Canterbury Tales:
   The Manciple's Tale. Chaucer
Lavender Kitten, The. Lopez
Lazy Pussy, The. Cox
Leo to His Mistress. Sedgwick
Listening. Fisher
Little Cat Angel, The. Stanfield
Love for a Hare. La Follette
Lullaby for Familiars. Willard
Macavity: The Mystery Cat. Eliot
Milk for the Cat. Monro
Monk and His Pet Cat, The. *Unknown*
Moon. Smith
Mother Cat. Montague
Mother Cat's Purr. Yolen
Mother Tabbyskins. Hart
Music of the Future, The. Herford
My Cats. Smith
My Father Kept His Cats Well Fed.
   Sherman
My Old Cat. Summers
Mysterious Cat, The. Lindsay
Naming of Cats, The. Eliot
Ode on [*or* On] the Death of a Favourite [*or*
   Favorite] Cat, Drowned in a Tub [*or* Bowl]
   of Gold Fishes. Gray
Offering for the Cat, An. Mei Yao-ch'en
Old Cat's Confessions, An. Cranch
Old Cat's Dying Soliloquy, An. Seward
Old Trouper, The. *Fr.* Archy and Mehitabel.
   Marquis
On a Night of Snow. Coatsworth
On a Picture by J. M. Wright, Esq. Southey
Owl and the Pussy-Cat, The. Lear
Pangur Bán. *Unknown*
Paw. Eluard
Peter. Moore
Pinks and a Blue Cat. Hagiwara Sakutaro
Poem: "As the cat." Williams
Poem: "High on a ridge of tiles." Craig

Prize Cat, The. Pratt
Pussy-Cat and Puppy-Dog. McCrea
Pussy Cat, Pussy Cat, where have you been?
   Mother Goose
Retired Cat, The. Cowper
Rum Tum Tugger, The. Eliot
Sad Memories. Calverley
Shadow. Delius
Singing Cat, The. Smith
Skimbleshanks: The Railway Cat. Eliot
Solomon Grundy. Mother Goose
Song of Mehitabel, The. *Fr.* Archy and
   Mehitabel. Marquis
Song of the Jellicles, The. Eliot
Stable Cat, The. Norris
Sunday. Coatsworth
Supper. Keithley
Teacher, The. Young
That Cat. King
Throwing the Racetrack Cats at Saratoga.
   Ray
To a Cat. Coleridge
Tom-Cat, The. Marquis
Tumble, fall, crash, then silence, A. *Fr.*
   Twenty-four Hokku. Kito
Two Cats, The. Coatsworth
Two Songs of a Fool. Yeats
Verses on a Cat. Shelley
Waiting for the Transformation. Minty
Wanted—a Witch's Cat. McGee
Wet Thursday. Kees
What the Gray Cat Sings. Guiterman
When a Cat Is Asleep. Kuskin
Why Did You Go. Cummings
Wildcat was walking. *Unknown*
Cat will Rhyme with Hat; a Book of Poems
   (CRH). Jean Chapman, ed.

Cattle
Bags of Meat. Hardy
Birth of Rainbow. Hughes
Blackleg. Smithyman
Cattle. Skrzynecki
Driving Cattle to Casas Buenas. Campbell
Drove-Road, The. Gibson
Drover, A. Colum
First Birth, The. Jones
From the Gulf. Ogilvie
Herdsman. Pettit
Jersey Cattle. Currey
MacDuff. Tomlinson
Madhav, please, control that cow. Surdas
March Calf, A. Hughes
Names of the Humble, The. Murray
Quiet-eyed Cattle, The. Norris
Residue. McNeill
Victors, The. McNeill
See also **Bulls; Cowboys; Cows; Meat.**

Catullus
"Frater Ave atque Vale." Tennyson
On Catullus. Landor

Caution
Sonnet: Of Caution. Barberini

Cavafy, Constantine P.
Cavafy in Redondo. Jarman
It Was Your Song. Kowit

Cavalcanti, Guido
Sonnet: Comes Often to My Memory. Dante
Sonnet: To Guido Cavalcanti. Dante

Cavalry
Cavalry Crossing a Ford. Whitman
Charge of the Light Brigade, The. Tennyson
Lancer. Housman

Cavemen
Cave-Boy, The. Richards
See also **Primitive Man.**

Caves
Ajanta. Rukeyser
Cave, The. Fairburn
Cavern, The. Tomlinson
Caves. Baker
Secret Cavern, The. Widdemer

Cecilia, Saint
Ode against St. Cecilia's Day. Barker
Song for St. Cecilia's Day. Auden
Song for St, A Cecilia's Day, 1687. Dryden
Celan, Paul
Continually. Zand
On the Death of Paul Celan (A Vindication).
   Mühringer
Upon Re-reading a Poem by Paul Celan.
   Fried
Celandine
Celandine. Thomas
To the Same Flower. Wordsworth
To the Small Celandine. Wordsworth
Celery
Celery. Nash
Little Brown Celery, The. MacBeth
Celibacy. *See* **Bachelors; Spinsters;**
   Virginity.
Cellars
In the Root Cellar. Kumin
John Mouldy. De la Mare
Root Cellar. Roethke
Cellos
Cello, The. Gilder
Celts
Celts, The. Smith
Cemeteries
Air of June Sings, The. Dorn
America's Answer. Lilliard
Ancestors' Graves in Kurakawa. Kogawa
Anniversary. Heine
Anniversary. Weissbort
At the British War Cemetery, Bayeux.
   Causley
At the Jewish Cemetery in Prague. Levertin
Battlefield. Aldington
Black Angel, The. Coulette
Blows the Wind Today. Stevenson
By St. Thomas Water. Causley
Cemetery at Academy, California, The.
   Levine
Cemetery in New Mexico, A. Alvarez
Cemetery Nights. Dobyns
Cemetery of Orange Trees in Crete, The.
   Stern
Chase Henry. Masters
Children among the Tombstones. Hervey
Child's Grave Marker, A. Kooser
Churchyard of St. Mary Magdalene, Old
   Milton. Heath-Stubbs
Cool Tombs. Sandburg
Cows near the Graveyard, The. Nelson
Dancing at Whitsun. Marshall
Elegy in a Presbyterian Burying-Ground.
   Wilson
Elegy Written in a Country Churchyard.
   Gray
Evening Hour. Warren
Friends Beyond. Hardy
Giorno dei Morti. Lawrence
Graves at Elkhorn. Hugo
Gravestones. Watkins
Graveyard, The. Bialik
Graveyard. Coffin
Graveyard, The. *Unknown*
Graveyard by the Sea. Lux
Graveyard in Norfolk. Warner
Graveyard in Queens, A. Montague
Hill, The. *Fr.* Spoon River Anthology.
   Masters
In a Christian Churchyard. Thomson
In a Churchyard. Wilbur
In a Grave-Yard. Braithwaite
In Flanders Fields. McCrae
In the Cemetery. Hardy
In the Churchyard at Cambridge. Longfellow
In the Graveyard. Clarke
In the Old Jewish Cemetery, Prague, 1970.
   Lowbury
Indian Burying Ground, The. Freneau
Inscribed on a Tombstone. Leib

Jewish Cemetery, The. Tiempo
Jewish Cemetery at Newport, The.
  Longfellow
Jewish Cemetery near Leningrad, A.
  Brodsky
Leningrad Cemetary, Winter of 1941. Olds
Levelled Churchyard, The. Hardy
Magnolia. Fordham
Mistress, The. Barton
Mountain Cemetery, The. Bowers
Mowing Crew, The. Wormser
National Cemetery, Beaufort, South Carolina,
  The. Heard
Negro Cemetery Next to a White One, A.
  Nemerov
Ode: "Sleep sweetly in your humble graves."
  Timrod
Ode to the Confederate Dead. Tate
Old Churchyard of Bonchurch, The. Marston
Old Jewish Cemetery in Worms. Kittner
Papermill Graveyard. Belitt
Pei-mang Cemetery. Yüan Hung-tao
Prairie Graveyard. Marriott
Quaker Graveyard, The. Mitchell
Quaker Graveyard in Nantucket, The.
  Lowell
Quatorzain. Timrod
Sarcophagi. Spencer
Soul Longs to Return Whence It Came, The.
  Eberhart
Sunday Graveyard. Stanton
This quiet dust was gentlemen and ladies.
  Dickinson
To the Holy Spirit. Winters
Tomb of Diogenes, The. *Unknown*
Town without a Market, The. Flecker
Tribal Cemetery. Hale
Under bare Ben Bulben's head. *Fr.* Under
  Ben Bulben. Yeats
Variations on Southern Themes. Justice
Visiting Father. Lim
Voices from Things Growing in a
  Churchyard. Hardy
Wrestling Angels. Bottoms
Yugoslav Cemetery. Wright
See also **Burial; Graves.**
Censorship
Censorship. Waley
Invocation: "Senator Smoot (Republican,
  Ut.)." Nash
Letter to a Librarian. Layton
Penal Law. Clarke
Centaurs
Ambuscade. McCrae
Centaur. Jacob
Centaurs, The. Stephens
Centaur's Bath, The. Urbina
Centipedes
Centipede, The. Herbert
Centipede, The. Nash
Centipede, A. *Unknown*
Central America
Day They Cleaned Up the Border El
  Salvador, February, 1981, The. Rose
Volcán; Poems from Central America (Vol).
  Alejandro Murguiá *and* Barbara Paschke,
  eds.
Central Park, New York City
Central Park. Lowell
Central Park Tourney. Weston
Central Park West. Moss
In Central Park. Halpern
Romeo and Juliet in Central Park. Ausländer
Ceremonial Songs (genre)
Battle Song. Macuilxochitl
Child Is Introduced to the Cosmos at Birth,
  The. *Unknown*
Hunting-Song. *Unknown*
Moon-Bone Song, The. *Unknown*
See also **Wedding Songs.**
Ceres. *See* **Demeter.**
Cereus, Night-blooming
Night-blooming Cereus, The. Hayden

Ceylon. *See* **Sri Lanka.**
Cézanne, Paul
Cézanne. Ausländer
Homage to Paul Cézanne. Wright
Oh, You Wholly Rectangular. Cole
Chagall, Marc
Don't Let That Horse. Ferlinghetti
Homage to Chagall. Niatum
Looking at a Chagall Painting. Netser
On the Farther Wall, Marc Chagall. *Fr.*
  Spectator's Guide to Contemporary Art.
  McGinley
Out of the Land of Heaven. Cohen
Painting. Jacobs
Salt and Memory. Zelk
Snow That Falls on Chagall's Village. Kim
  Chun-soo
Chagres River, Panama
Beyond the Chagres. Gilbert
Chairs
Chair, The. Roethke
Chairs. Worth
Grandmother's Old Armchair. *Unknown*
Old Arm-Chair, The. Cook
Rocking Chair, The. Klein
Chaleur Bay, Canada
Phantom Light of the Baie des Chaleurs, The.
  Eaton
Chamberlain, Wilton Norman
Wilt Chamberlain. Knudson
Chameleons
Chameleon, The. Herbert
Lord's Chameleons, The. Klappert
To a Chameleon. Moore
Chamois
Chamois, The. Belloc
Chance. *See* **Fate; Fortune.**
Chancellorsville, Battle of (1863)
Keenan's Charge. Lathrop
Change
Ancient to Ancients, An. Hardy
Beautiful Changes, The. Wilbur
Bricking the Church. Morgan
Change. Knister
Change and Immutability. Scroggie
Change-up. Lee
Changes. Heaney
Disguises. Jennings
Dispossessed. Gould
Fault, The. Lucie-Smith
From today forward. Tamekane
Grandmother Watching at Her Window.
  Merwin
I Feel Sorry for the Garden.
  Farrokhzad
Lamentation of the Old Pensioner, The.
  Yeats
Mutability. Shelley
Mutability. *Fr.* Ecclesiastical Sonnets.
  Wordsworth
Nothing Gold Can Stay. Frost
Ö. Dove
Other Fabrics, Other Mores! Lenngren
Passin Ben Dorain. *Fr.* At the Heich
  Kirk-Yaird. MacKie
Riddles of Change, The. Mnthali
Van Winkle. *Fr.* The Bridge: Powhatan's
  Daughter. Crane
Ways of God to Men, The. *Fr.* Samson
  Agonistes. Milton
Wedding Party. Hall
Western Approaches, The. Nemerov
Where Dunwich Used to Be. *Fr.* By the
  North Sea. Swinburne
Yardley Oak. Cowper
See also **Transience.**
Changelings
Peak and Puke. De la Mare
Channel Islands
Sark. *Fr.* The Garden of Cymodoce.
  Swinburne
Channing, William Henry
Channing. Alcott

Ode Inscribed to W. H. Channing. Emerson
Chanteys. *See* **Sea Chanteys.**
Chanukah. *See* **Hanukkah.**
Chaos
Connoisseur of Chaos. Stevens
I Will Put Chaos into Fourteen Lines.
  Millay
Chaplin, Charlie
Chaplinesque. Crane
Patriotic Ode on the Fourteenth Anniversary
  of the Persecution of Charlie Chaplin.
  Kaufman
Chapman, George
On First Looking into Chapman's Homer.
  Keats
Chapman, John (Johnny Appleseed)
Apple-Barrel of Johnny Appleseed, The.
  Lindsay
Johnny Appleseed. Lindsay
Johnny Appleseed. Venable
Chardin, Jean Baptiste
Still Life. de la Mare
Charity
Charity. Ray
Charity Overcoming Envy. Moore
Excelente Balade of Charitie, An.
  Chatterton
"For Christ's sweet sake, I beg an alms."
  Fr. The Vision of Sir Launfal. Lowell
Good King Wenceslas. *Unknown*
Good Works. *Fr.* The Vision of Piers
  Plowman. Langland
How the Great Guest Came. Markham
Husband and Heathen. Foss
I Shall Not Pass This Way Again. *Unknown*
If I can stop one heart from breaking.
  Dickinson
Karma. Robinson
Offer, An. Guiterman
Tell Him So. *Unknown*
Triple Bension, The. Ray
See also **Philanthropy and Philanthropists.**
Charlemagne
Charlemagne. Longfellow
Charles I, King of England
And why so coffined in this vile disguise.
  Fr. The King's Disguise. Cleveland
By the Statue of King Charles at Charing
  Cross. Johnson
Epigram, to the Household, 1630, An.
  Jonson
Thou from th' enthroned martyrs blood-stain'd
  line. *Fr.* An Elegy upon the Most
  Incomparable King Charles the First.
  King
Vows, The. Marvell
Charles II, King of England
Ballad Called the Haymarket Hectors, A.
  Unknown
Britannia and Raleigh. Ayloffe
Commons' Petition to Charles II, The.
  Rochester
Essay upon Satire, An. Sheffield
History of Insipids, The. Freke
Horation Ode upon Cromwell's Return from
  Ireland. Marvell
Impromptu on Charles II. Rochester
In pious times ere [*or* e'r] priestcraft did
  begin. *Fr.* Absalom and Achitophel, Pt. I.
  Dryden
Me thinks I see our mighty monarch stand.
  Fr. The Royal Angler. *Unknown*
On the Prorogation. *Unknown*
Parliament Dissolved at Oxford, The.
  Unknown
Satire on Old Rowley. *Unknown*
Song: Old Rowley the King. *Unknown*
Tune to the Devonshire Cant, The.
  Unknown
Charles VI, King of France
Glass King, The. Boland
Charles, Prince of Wales
Caernarfon, 2 July 1969. Davies

Charles, Ray
Bishop of Atlanta: Ray Charles, The. Bond
Blues Note. Kaufman
Ray Charles. Cornish
Charles River, Massachusetts
Professor Kelleher and the Charles River.
O'Grady
Charleston, South Carolina
Charleston. Gilder
Charleston. Hayne
Charleston. Timrod
Charleston Garden, A. Bellamann
How He Saved St. Michael's. Stansbury
New Organ, The. Heard
Ode: "Sleep sweetly in your humble graves."
Timrod
On the Late Engagement in Carles Town
River. *Unknown*
Song about Charleston, A. *Unknown*
Charm
What Is Charm? Thomas
Charms (genre)
Charm, A. Dryden
Charm, A. *Unknown*
Charm for Love and Lasting Affection, A.
Unknown
Eastward I Stand, Mercies I Beg. *Unknown*
Enchantment, The. *Fr.* Idylls. Theocritus
Hoping this night my true love to see.
Unknown
Nativity Chant, The. *Fr. Guy Mannering.*
Scott
New moon, new moon, I hail thee!
Unknown
St. Simon and Jude, on you I intrude.
Unknown
Spell of Invisibility, A. Marlowe
Thrice the Brinded Cat Hath Mewed. *Fr.*
Macbeth. Shakespeare
Twist Ye, Twine Ye! Even So. *Fr. Guy
Mannering.* Scott
Witches' Charms, The. *Fr. The Masque of
Queens.* Jonson
Witch's Broomstick Spell, The. *Unknown*
Witch's Spell [*or* Witch's Milking Charm], A.
Unknown
Charon
Charon. MacNeice
Charon's Cosmology. Simic
Dirce. *Fr. Pericles and Aspasia.* Landor
Epigram: "When Bibo thought fit from the
world to retreat." Prior
Lost on a fogbound spit of sand. Auden
There Charon stands, who rules the dreary
coast. *Fr. The Aeneid [or Eneados]*
Virgil
To Dives. Belloc
Chartism
Chartist Chorus, A. Jones
Song for the free—the brave and the free, A.
Fr. Two Chartist Songs. Cooper
Time shall come when wrong shall end, The.
Fr. Two Chartist Songs. Cooper
Chartres, France
Angel with the Sun Dial (Cathedral at
Chartres), The. Busta
Chartres. *Fr. View of the Cathedral.* Henri
Chattahoochee River, Georgia
Song of the Chattahoochee. Lanier
Chatterton, Thomas
Chatterton. Hands
Last Verses. Chatterton
Chaucer, Geoffrey
Chaucer. Brawley
Chaucer. Longfellow
Description of Sir Geoffrey Chaucer, The.
Fr. Greene's Vision. Greene
For a Statue of Chaucer at Woodstock.
Akenside

Lament for Chaucer. Hoccleve
To Chaucer. *Fr. De Regimine Principum.*
Hoccleve
Chaucer, Thomas
On the Departing of Thomas Chaucer.
Lydgate
Cheese
Cheese it is a peevish elf. *Unknown*
O Cheese. Hall
On Mites; to a Lady. Duck
Queen of Cheese. McIntyre
Quite the Cheese. Waring
What a Friend We Have in Cheeses! Cole
Wild Cheese, The. Tate
Chekhov, Anton
Chocolates. Simpson
Like Loving Chekhov. Levertov
Chemical Warfare
Christmas: 1924. Hardy
Dulce et Decorum Est. Owen
News That Stays News. Mariani
Chemistry
Elements, The. Lehrer
Sir Humphry Davy. *Fr.* Clerihews. Bentley
Chénier, André Marie de
André Chénier. Tsvetayeva
Cherry Trees and Cherries
Adjectives. Nadir
As I searched for cherry blossoms. *Fr. A
Compendium of Good Tanka.* Teika
At this late date. Keiun
Blooming everywhere. Tamehide
Blossoms at Evening. Eifuku
Cherries. Schneour
Cherries. Stryk
Cherries are blooming. Joben
Cherries bloom on distant hills. *Fr. A
Compendium of Good Tanka.* Teika
Cherry. Hagiwara Sakutaro
Cherry Blossoms at Shiga, The. Kaneyoshi
Cherry blossoms must have opened. *Fr. A
Compendium of Good Tanka.* Teika
Cherry flowers. *Fr. Kokin Shu. Unknown*
Cherry petals/ like the tears. *Fr. Sixty-four
Tanka.* Saigyo
Cherry-ripe. Herrick
Cherry Tree, The. Gunn
Cherry Trees, The. Thomas
Dawn Cherries. Hezutsu Tosaku
Down from the branches. Hanazono
End of the Third Lunar Month, The.
Kaneyoshi
Gazing at them. *Fr. Sixty-four Tanka.*
Saigyo
I look out today. Ietaka
If there were no such thing. *Fr. Kokin Shu.*
Narihira
In a Town Garden. Mattam
In my mountain home. Tonna
Ladder, The. Vas
Let me take a good look. *Fr. Sixty-four
Tanka.* Saigyo
Loveliest of Trees [the Cherry Now] *Fr. A
Shropshire Lad.* Housman
Moon in the garden. Tamekane
Not a trace is left. Teika
Off at Tatsuta/ white clouds are piling up.
Teika
Person I meet, A. Kenko
So far from springlike. Hanazono
Sprigs of Blossoms. Tamemasa
Those cherry blossoms. Ietaka
Though your season is not over. *Fr. Manyo
Shu. Unknown*
Unaware of the times. Eifuku
Under the Boughs. Baro
What will have become. Tamefuji
Why should my heart. *Fr. Sixty-four Tanka.*
Saigyo
Wild Cherry Tree. Blunden
Won't you please hasten. Tamesada
You know how I long. Munenaga

Chesapeake Bay
Chesapeake. Kennedy
Night Trip across the Chesapeake and After.
Lea
Of Oystermen, Workboats. Smith
Sea Hold, The. Sandburg
Chess
Duel in the Park. Grenelle
Prodigy. Simic
Song of Chess, The. Ibn Ezra
Watching a Game of Chess: Second Series.
Ch'ien Ch'ien-yi
Young Chess Player, The. Sinclair
Chesterton, Gilbert Keith
G. K. Chesterton. Wolfe
Lines to a Don. Belloc
Chestnut Trees
Chestnuts Are Falling, The. Moore
Horse Chestnut. Miranda
Chestnut Trees and Chestnuts
Winds of autumn, The. Basho
Chevy Chase. *See* **Otterburn, Battle of.**
Chicago, Illinois
Bad Old Days, The. Rexroth
Chicago. Harte
Chacago. Lowell
Chicago. Ridge
Chicago. Sandburg
Chicago Exposition Ode. Fordham
Chicago Odyssey, The. Barnes
Chicago Poem. Welch
Chicago, Summer Past. Snyder
Foreigners at the Fair. Brooks
Making Chicago. Schmitz
Navel. Schmitz
On Clark Street in Chicago. Keithley
On the Upside. Murray
Planting Trout in the Chicago River.
Schmitz
Stockyard, The. Squire
To His Chi Mistress. Starbuck
Tonight in Chicago. *Unknown*
U Name This One. Rodgers
Zoo, The. Logan
Jump Bad; a New Chicago Anthology (JB).
Gwendolyn Brooks, ed.
Chicanos
Black Hair. Soto
Kearney Park. Soto
*Contemporary Chicano Poetry; a Critical
Approach to an Emerging Literature* (CCP).
Marta Ester Sánchez, ed.
Fiesta in Aztlán (FIA). Toni Empringham,
ed.
Chickadees
Chickadee, The. Emerson
Chickens
Beautiful Poultry. Wedde
Chicken. *Fr. Hunter Poems of the Yoruba.
Unknown*
Chicken wants, The. *Unknown*
Chook, chook, chook, chook.
Unknown
Darkling Chicken, The. Peters
Final Soliloquy on a Randy Rooster (in a Key
of Yellow). Peters
Five Little Chickens. *Unknown*
Hens, The. Roberts
Henyard Round, The. Hall
Orphan Born. Burdette
Poultries, The. Nash
Song: "Before the barn-door crowing." *Fr.
The Beggar's Opera.* Gay
Way the chicken walks, The. *Unknown*
Child Abuse
Chain. Lorde
Child Beater. Ai
Inquest, The. Davies
Lilith's Child. Francisco
Man Who Made Me Love Him, The. Weigl
Mary Arnold the Female Monster. *Unknown*

Priest attending, found he spoke at times, The. *Fr.* The Borough: Peter Grimes. Crabbe
Whipping, The. Hayden
Child Labor
Child Labor. Gilman
Chimney Sweeper ("A little black thing among the snow"), The. *Fr.* Songs of Experience. Blake
Chimney Sweeper, The ("When my mother died I was very young"). *Fr.* Songs of Innocence. Blake
Death of the Factory Child, The. Prince
Golf Links, The. Cleghorn
Industrial Evils. *Fr.* Malvern Hills. Cottle
Childhood and Children
Aaron Nicholas, Almost Ten. Hale
About Children. McGinley
After a Photo. Herzberg
Age, An. Jensen
Ajax Samples, The. Jensen
Among School Children. Yeats
And the Children. Ackroyd
Anecdote for Fathers. Wordsworth
Armor. Olds
As a boy/ I sometimes lifted. Turrini
Asked, "How old?" a child shows its palm. Issa
Autobiographia Literaria. O'Hara
Baal Shem Tov. Klein
Baby Running Barefoot. Lawrence
Ball Poem, The. Berryman
Ballad of Selling a Child. Wang Chiu-ssu
Barefoot Boy, A. Riley
Barefoot Boy, The. Whittier
Barren. Rachel
Bears. Rich
Beatrix Is Three. Mitchell
Behind Grandma's House. Soto
Behold the child, by Nature's kindly law. *Fr.* An Essay on Man. Pope
Bianca's First Steps in the Arts. Schippers
Birches. Frost
Bitter Withy, The. *Unknown*
Bleeder. Dobyns
Book of Yolek, The. Hecht
Boy and a Roll, A. *Fr.* From the Nursery. Glatstein
Boy at the Window. Wilbur
Boy Thirteen, A. Irish
Boy with a Hammer. Hoban
Boy with His Hair Cut Short. Rukeyser
Boyhood in Tobacco Country. Warren
Boy's Song, A. Hogg
Centaur, The. Swenson
Changing the Children. Kumin
Child, The. Hall
Child in a Blue Linen Dress. Sorrells
Child jumps out of a willow, A. Issa
Child Naming Flowers. Hass
Child Next Door, The ("The child next door has a wreath on her hat"). Fyleman
Child on Top of a Greenhouse. Roethke
Child says, "Nammu, Nammu", A. Issa
Childhood. Cornford
Childhood. Justice
Childhood. Muir
Childhood. Read
Childhood. Rilke
Childhood. Stanton
Childhood Fled. Lamb
Childhood Is the Kingdom Where Nobody Dies. Millay
Childhood's Retreat. Duncan
Children, The. Dickinson
Children, The. Haddad
Children. McPherson
Children. Manhire
Children. Pantiyan Arivutai Nampi
Children. *Fr.* Forgotten Girlhood. Riding
Children. Su Tung-p'o
Children and Sir Nameless, The. Hardy

Children, Children Everywhere. Prelutsky
Children March, The. Riddell
Children of Auschwitz. Korzhavin
Children: Private Ward. *Fr.* In Hospital. Henley
Children, the Sandbar, That Summer. Rukeyser
Children They, The. Mechtel
Children Walking Home from School through Good Neighborhood. Justice
Children's Elegy. *Fr.* Eighth Elegy. Rukeyser
Children's Games. Reisen
Children's Hour, The. Longfellow
Child's First Grief, The. Hemans
Child's Laughter, A. Swinburne
Child's Mirror, A. Herzberg
Child's Sight, The. Sobiloff
Chinatown Games. Lum
Circus Song. Goedicke
Conversation. McCord
Cry of the Children, The. Browning
Cuddle Doon. Anderson
Dark Welcome, The. Baxter
Day You Are Born, The. Song
Days Gone By, The. Riley
Deaf School. Hughes
Deborah Lee. Yvonne
Digging for China. Wilbur
Don't Forget. Berg
Drawing a Banana. Schneider
Earliest Spring. Levertov
Early Supper. Howes
Earth's Children Cleave to Earth. Bryant
Ecce Puer. Joyce
Echo and the Ferry. Ingelow
Efficiency Apartment. Barrax
Elementary Scene, The. Jarrell
Elementary School Classroom in a Slum, An. Spender
Elevation. Morgan
Eleven. MacLeish
Evening. Wright
Ex Ore Infantium. Thompson
False Security. Betjeman
Farm Child. Thomas
Father and Child. Harwood
Favorite Flower, The. Thaxter
Fern Hill. Thomas
Finding a Lucky Number. Soto
First Love. Polito
First Shoe, The. Mhac an tSaoi
First Song. Kinnell
Follower. Heaney
For a Child Expected. Ridler
For the Crèche. *Fr.* Songs of Education. Chesterton
For the War-Children. Read
Foreign Children. Stevenson
Freedom, New Hampshire. Kinnell
Fresh News from the Past. Bell
Frolic. "Æ"
From a Childhood. Rilke
Fruit Plucker, The. Coleridge
Gardeners. Ignatow
Germinal. "Æ"
Get me that bright moon! Issa
Good and Bad Children. Stevenson
Grandchild. Kumin
Haiku: "Children are shouting." *Fr.* One Hundred Haiku in Free Form. Hosai
Haiku: "Making her doll." *Unknown*
Haiku: "Their many children each reading." *Fr.* One Hundred Haiku in Free Form. Hosai
Happy Child, A. Greenaway
Hero, The. Graves
Hide and Seek. Shuttle
Hiding. Aldis
Holy Thursday ("Is this a holy thing to see"). *Fr.* Songs of Experience. Blake

Holy Thursday (" 'Twas on a Holy Thursday, their innocent faces clean"). *Fr.* Songs of Innocence. Blake
Holy Well, The ("As it fell out on a holiday"). *Unknown*
How our child carries them piggyback. Issa
I Am Called Childhood. More
I Don't Like Beetles. Fyleman
I Remember, I Remember. Hood
I Remember, I Remember. Larkin
I scolded my child. *Fr.* Forty-seven Tanka in Three Lines. Ishikawa Takuboku
I Would Like You for a Comrade. Parry
If I Could Only Live at the Pitch That Is near Madness. Eberhart
If not so my children. Abutsu
If you drink the milk of the black cow, Gopal. Surdas
In just-/ spring when the world is mud. *Fr.* Chansons Innocentes. Cummings
In Reference to Her Children, 23 June, 1656. Bradstreet
In School-Days. Whittier
In the Attic. Justice
In the Barrio. Alurista
In the Waiting Room. Bishop
Incident. Cullen
Infancy. Andrade
Infant Innocence. Housman
Infant Joy. *Fr.* Songs of Innocence. Blake
Infant Sorrow. *Fr.* Songs of Experience. Blake
It Was a Special Treat. Tapahonso
Jenny White and Johnny Black. Farjeon
Jest 'fore Christmas. Field
Jim, Who Ran Away from His Nurse, and Was Eaten by a Lion. Belloc
Jo Jo, My Child. *Unknown*
Judeebug's Country. Johnson
Kindergarten. Schmitz
Kirsten. Berrigan
Land of Counterpane, The. Stevenson
Last Child. Kennedy
Laughing Child. Sandburg
Letters to My Daughters, No. 3. Minty
Life-Lesson, A. Riley
Lilliput Levee. Rands
Lines: "Here often, when a child, I lay reclined." Tennyson
Lisa. Carrier
Little Boy, A. Kim Chun-soo
Little Boy Blue. Field
Little Brother, The. Reeves
Little Brother's Secret. Mansfield
Little Dancers, The. Binyon
Little Girl Wakes Early. Warren
Little Girl with Bands on Her Teeth, The. Taggard
Little Girl's Show, A. Su Shao-lien
Little Mute Boy, The. García Lorca
Little Orphant Annie. Riley
Lives of Gulls and Children, The. Nemerov
Living with Children. Miller
Lost Child, The. Reaney
Lost Children, The. Jarrell
Love. Lane
Lullaby: "O! hush thee, my darling, sleep soundly my son." *Unknown*
Lunch with Girl Scouts. Bryan
Magic. Herzberg
Magician Suspends the Children, The. Oles
Mamma! Horne
Many Times November Has Come Back. Guidacci
Memory. Lincoln
Memory of Pinks. Kitahara Hakushu
Methinks 'Tis Pretty Sport. Bastard
Minnie and Winnie. Tennyson
Monterrey Sun. Reyes
More Powerful than the Sea. Zelk

Mrs. Johnson Objects. Thompson
My child, we were two children. Heine
My Daughter. Jalib
My Father in the Night Commanding No.
  Simpson
My Lost Youth. Longfellow
My Parent's House. Morriën
Names, The. Edmond
Next War, The. Graves
Night Thoughts over a Sick Child. Levine
Nikki-Rosa. Giovanni
Nostalgia of the Lakefronts. Giovanni
Nurse's Song. *Fr.* Songs of Experience.
  Blake
Nurse's Song. *Fr.* Songs of Innocence.
  Blake
Observing Children. *Fr.* Sixty-four Tanka.
  Saigyo
Ode on a Distant Prospect of Eton College.
  Gray
Oft, in the Stilly Night. Moore
Oh Come, Little Children. McGinley
Oh for boyhood's painless play. *Fr.* The
  Barefoot Boy. Whittier
Old Crib, The. Tucker
Old Oaken Bucket, The. Woodworth
Old-Time Childhood in Kentucky. Warren
On a Journey. Shohaku
On the Beach at Fontana. Joyce
On the Picture of a Child. Ray
Ontogeny. Ramsey
Our Child. Neruda
Our child, our treasure. Issa
Painting a Madonna. Warren
Parental Recollections. Lamb
Party, The. Whittemore
Party in Winter. Shapiro
Perfect Child, The. Porter
Piano. Lawrence
Picnic, The. Logan
Picture of Little T. C. in a Prospect of
  Flowers, The. Marvell
Poem for the Sandman. Tate
Poem of Distant Childhood. Sousa
Poet and His Songs, The. Longfellow
Prayer for My Daughter, A. Yeats
Puer Aeternus. Raine
Rebecca, Who Slammed Doors for Fun and
  Perished Miserably. Belloc
Retreat[e], The. Vaughan
Ring-a-Ring. Greenaway
Rocking My Child. Mistral
Rustic Childhood. Barnes
Sales Talk for Annie. Bishop
School-Bell. Farjeon
School Globe, The. Reaney
Schoolbus Comes before the Sun, The.
  Currie
Sculpture. *Unknown*
Settlers, The. Hemschemeyer
Ships of Yule, The. Carman
Shy Geordie. Cruickshank
Sick Child, A. Jarrell
Sick Child, The. Stevenson
Sign of Saturn, The. Olds
Sleeping Giant, The. Hall
Somewhere in the House. Michaelis
Son and Surf. Strong
Song for the Middle of the Night, A. Wright
Sonnet in Which I Say My Son Is a Long
  Way Off and Has Been for More Than a
  Year, A. Cisneros
Spitting on Ira Rosenblatt. Hershon
Spring and Fall. Hopkins
Spring rain: a child's hands. Torai
Squatter's Children. Bishop
Startled by the sound. *Fr.* Sixty-four Tanka.
  Saigyo
Stove. Booth
Sugar-Plum Tree, The. Field

Suppose. Cary
Tamerlane. Daley
Testing-Tree, The. Kunitz
Thank God for Little Children. Harper
"The Wife Takes a Child." Voigt
There Was a Boy ("There was a boy, ye knew
  him well"). *Fr.* The Prelude [or, Growth
  of a Poet's Mind]: Books. Wordsworth
There Was a Child Went Forth. Whitman
There Were Some Summers. Lux
Thesis, Antithesis and Nostalgia. Dugan
They Grow Up Too Fast, She Said. O Hehir
This is mine, this is mine. Issa
This Song Shows Me Pictures; Morningside
  Drive, New York City 1950-1960. Oyama
Thoughts on Schoolchildren. Shauqi
Three Poems about Children. Clarke
To a Child. Gardons
To a Child. Montgomery
To a Child. Owen
To a Child. Wordsworth
To a Child Five Years Old. Cotton
To a Child of Quality [Five Years Old, the
  Author Supposed Forty]. Prior
To a Child Running with Outstretched Arms
  in Canyon de Chelly. Momaday
To a Child Trapped in a Barber Shop.
  Levine
To a Dead Childhood. Hinostroza
To a Small Boy Standing on My Shoes While
  I Am Wearing Them. Nash
To Carry the Child. Smith
To H. C. Wordsworth
To My Child Carlino. Landor
To My Four-Year-Old Daughter. Todd
To Myself, after Forty Years. White
Toy Bone, The. Hall
Ts'eekkaayah. TallMountain
Tumbling. *Unknown*
Two girls of twelve or so at a table.
  Reznikoff
Ugly Chile. Williams
Uncle Dog; the Poet at 9. Sward
Under the tree with rice-cake flowers. Issa
Verigin, Moving in Alone. Newlove
Vision of Children, A. Ashe
Waifs. Virtue
Waking in the Dark. Livesay
War of the Worlds, The. Rutsala
Warning to Children. Graves
Wartime Story, A. Scovell
We Are Seven. Wordsworth
We Were Two Pretty Babes. Lamb
What My Child Learns of the Sea. Lorde
What Zimmer Would Be. Zimmer
When I am grown to man's estate.
  Stevenson
When I eat melon. *Fr.* Manyo Shu. Okura
When I Was Six. Cross
When I Was Small. Chénier
When I was very little the lake was blue.
  Kajava
Where Are the Waters of Childhood? Strand
Where Children Live. Nye
Where Knock Is Open Wide. Roethke
Whipping, The. Hayden
Who Knows? Perry
Whole Duty of Children. Stevenson
Why? Boyd
Wise Child, The. Lucie-Smith
Wishes, for Alix. Emanuel
Wishes for My Son. MacDonagh
Woodman, Spare That Tree. Morris
Yet Another Poem about a Dying Child.
  Frame
Your sisters all must stay at home. *Fr.*
  Kokin Shu. Michizane
Youth and Age. Coleridge
Zimmer's Head Thudding against the
  Blackboard. Zimmer
See also **Adolescence; Boys; Death in
  Childhood; Girls; Youth.**

Children's Verse
  Cat Will Rhyme with Hat; a Book of Poems
    (CRH). Jean Chapman, ed.
  Faber Book of Children's Verse, The
    (FaBoCh). Janet Adam Smith, comp.
  Faber Book of Useful Verse, The (FaBoUs),
    pp. 85-104. Simon Brett, ed.
  Golden Numbers (GN). Kate Douglas
    Wiggin *and* Nora Archibald Smith, eds.
  New Treasury of Children's Poetry, A
    (NTCP). Joanna Cole, ed.
  Once upon a Rhyme (OnUR). Sara *and*
    Stephen Corrin, eds.
  *Oxford Book of Children's Verse in America,
    The* (OBCA). Donald Hall, ed.
  Oxford Book of Children's Verse, The
    (OxBChV). Iona *and* Peter Opie, eds.
  Oxford Nursery Rhyme Book, The (OxNR).
    Iona *and* Peter Opie, eds.
  Piping Down the Valleys Wild (PDV).
    Nancy Larrick, ed.
  Poems for Young Children (PYC). Caroline
    Royds, comp.
  *Random House Book of Poetry for Children,
    The* (RHPC). Jack Prelutsky, ed.
  Read-Aloud Rhymes for the Very Young
    (RAR). Jack Prelutsky, comp.
Chile
  All of a Sudden. Jesús
  Teachers, The. Parra
  To Speak of Chile. Gibson
Chilembwe, John
  Before Chilembwe Tree. Mapanje
Chillon Castle, Switzerland
  Prisoner of Chillon, The. Byron
Chimney Sweepers
  Chimney Sweeper ("A little black thing
    among the snow"), The. *Fr.* Songs of
    Experience. Blake
  Chimney Sweeper, The ("When my mother
    died I was very young"). *Fr.* Songs of
    Innocence. Blake
  Chimney-Sweeper's Complaint, The ("A
    chimney—sweepers' boy am I"). Alcock
  "Sooeep!" De la Mare
  Wmffre the Sweep. Humphries
Chimneys
  Chimney-Tops. *Unknown*
  Kitchen Chimney, The. Frost
  To Raise a Chimney. Young
China
  At the Great Wall of China. Blunden
  China. Empson
  Chinese Nightingale, The. Lindsay
  Digging for China. Wilbur
  Great Wall, The. Lucebert
  I Lie on the Chilled Stones of the Great Wall.
    Liu
  Merchants from Cathay. Benét
  Poem: "At night Chinamen jump." O'Hara
  Sea Gypsy, The. Hovey
  Sea Offerings. Yu Kuang-chung
  Song: "I watered my horse at the Long Wall
    caves." Ch'en Lin
  South, The. Wang Chien
  Tears of Pearl, The. Chang Ts'o
  To the Tune "The River Is Red." Ch'iu Chin
  Wall of China, The. Colum
  Watching the Native Country from the
    Border. Lo Fu
  What Is It Makes the Stranger? Hyde
Chinaglia, Giorgio
  Soccer at the Meadowlands. Ackerman
Chinatowns
  Chinatown. Chiang Hsun
  Chinatown Games. Lum
  Chinatown Talking Story. Tsui
  Day of the Parade. Lau
  Disco Chinatown. Kageyama
  My son & I, between *Fu-Sang* and/ Cathay.
    Fr. Sussyissfriin. Dow

Chinaware
Bone China. Lister
No Swan So Fine. Moore
To a Lady on Her Passion for Old China.
   Gay
What Came to Me. Kenyon
Willowware Cup. Merrill
Chinese, The
At a Chinaman's Grave. Lum
Chinaman, The. Rossetti
Chinaman's Chance, A. Chin
Coolie. Yoshioka Minoru
Grandmother Poems. Chin
How a Girl Got Her Chinese Name. Wong
Immigration Act of 1924, The. Mar
Landlord's Wife, The. Chin
Losing Track. Song
Miss Cho Composes in the Cafeteria. Tate
My Father's Martial Art. Liu
My Mother, Who Came from China, Where
   She Never Saw Snow. Mar
Second Nature. Chang
Sweet 'n Sour. Lim
We Are a Young Nation, Uncle. Chin
Yellow Woman Speaks. Woo
Chinese Verse
Among the Flowers; the Hua-chien Chi
   (ATF). Lois Fusek, tr.
Book of Songs, The; the Ancient Chinese
   Classic of Poetry (BoS). Arthur Waley, tr.
Columbia Book of Chinese Poetry, The, from
   Early Times to the Thirteenth Century
   (CoBCP). Burton Watson, ed. *and* tr.
Columbia Book of Later Chinese Poetry, The
   (CoBLCP). Jonathan Chaves, ed. *and* tr.
Isle Full of Noises, The; Modern Chinese
   Poetry from Taiwan (IFON). Dominic
   Cheung, ed. *and* tr.
Japanese Literature in Chinese (JLIC).
   Burton Watson, tr.
Waiting for the Unicorn; Poems and Lyrics of
   China's Last Dynasty, 1644-1911 (WFTU).
   Irving Yucheng Lo *and* William Schultz,
   eds.
Chipmunks
Chipmunk, The. Jarrell
Chipmunk, The. Nash
Chipmunk can't drag it along. Gonzales
Chipmunk was standing. Gonzales
Chipmunk's Day, The. Jarrell
Little Charlie Chipmunk. LeCron
Chirico, Giorgio de
Meeting with Giorgio de Chirico. Schmied
Opinions about the Painter de Chirico.
   Schmied
Chisholm Trail
Old Chisholm Trail, The. *Unknown*
Chocolates
Chocolates. Simpson
Choctaw Indians
Four Choctaw Songs. Barnes
Four Things Choctaw. Barnes
Choking
Daughter. Voigt
Chopin, Frédéric François
Chopin's Minute Waltz. Mayer
Christchurch, New Zealand
Old Provincial Council Buildings,
   Christchurch, The. Curnow
Skeleton of the Great Moa in the Canterbury
   Museum, Christchurch, The. Curnow
Christenings
Kyran's Christening. Nowlan
To C. F. H. on Her Christening-Day. Hardy
See also **Baptism.**
Christianity and Christians
At the Piano. Hudgins
At the Smithville Methodist Church. Dunn
Call to the Strong, The. Merrill
Challenge, The. Kleiser
Christians at War. Kendrick

Clarion-Call, The. *Unknown*
God Wants a Man. *Unknown*
In the Twentieth Century of My Trespass on
   Earth. *Fr.* The Dead Shall Be Raised
   Incorruptible. Kinnell
Is This the Time to Sound Retreat? *Unknown*
Last Words of Don Henriquez, The.
   Schneour
Let Us Cheer the Weary Traveler. *Unknown*
Light of Faith, The. Dupree
Query. McTurk
Saint Patrick's Breastplate. *Unknown*
Sunday Morning. Stevens
New Oxford Book of Christian Verse, The
   (NOCV). Donald Davie, ed.
Treasury of Christian Poetry, The (TrCP).
   Lorraine Eitel, comp.
Christmas
Advent 1966. Levertov
Advent; a Carol. Dickinson
Ah, Christ. *Fr.* Sonnets at Christmas. Tate
All on a Christmas Morning. Coatsworth
Ane Sang of the Birth of Christ, with the
   Tune of Baw Lula Low. Luther
Apple Wassail. *Unknown*
As I Sat on a Sunny Bank. *Unknown*
As I Sat under a Sycamore Tree. *Unknown*
At Christmas-Tide. Ray
Babushka. Thomas
Ballad of the Bread Man. Causley
Ballad of the Epiphany. Dalmon
Barn, The. Coatsworth
BC:AD. Fanthorpe
Before the Paling of the Stars. Rossetti
Bethlehem Town. Field
Birth of Jesus, The. Heard
Bow Down, Mountain. Farber
Boy Shepherds' Simile, The. Bottoms
Brightest and Best of the Sons of the
   Morning. Heber
Burning Babe, The. Southwell
Burning the Christmas Greens. Williams
But hark! The sharp beat of the Afric drum.
   Fr. The Isle of Streams; or, the Jamaica
   Hermit. Hosack
Carnal and the Crane, The. *Unknown*
Carol: "When the herd[s] were watching."
   Canton
Carol for Children, A. Nash
Carol of Patience. Graves
Carol of the Poor Children, The. Middleton
Cause for Wonder, A. *Unknown*
Cherry-Tree Carol, The. *Unknown*
Child's Song of Christmas, A. Pickthall
Christ Climbed Down. Ferlinghetti
Christmas. "Æ"
Christmas. Betjeman
Christmas. Herbert
Christmas. Koh Chang-soo
Christmas. Leib
Christmas 1914. Harding
Christmas at Freelands. Stephens
Christmas at Sea. Stevenson
Christmas Bells. Longfellow
Christmas Carol, A: "Close to a quarter of a
   century since then." Parry-Williams
Christmas Carol, A: "In the bleak
   mid-winter." Rossetti
Christmas Carol, A: "Lacking samite and sable."
   Probyn
Christmas Carol, A: "There's a song in the
   air!" Holland
Christmas Carol: "Three outas from the bleak
   Karoo." Opperman
Christmas Childhood, A. Kavanagh
Christmas Day. Young
Christmas Day in the Workhouse. Sims
Christmas Day Is Come. Wadding
Christmas Day; the Family Sitting. Falkner
Christmas Eve. Moorer
Christmas Eve. Siegel
Christmas Folk-Song, A. Reese

Christmas Hymn. Juana Inés de la Cruz
Christmas Hymn. *Unknown*
Christmas Hymn, A. Wilbur
Christmas in Biafra (1969). Achebe
Christmas in Penang. Leyden
Christmas in the Heart. *Unknown*
Christmas in the Wood. Frost
Christmas Is Really for the Children. Turner
Christmas Morning. Roberts
Christmas Morning I. Freeman
Christmas Mourning. Miller
Christmas 1959 et Cetera. Barrax
Christmas Now Is Drawing Near. *Unknown*
Christmas Party, The. White
Christmas Prayer, A. Macdonald
Christmas Prayer, A. Stevenson
Christmas Revel, A. Dafydd Bach ap Madog
   Wladaidd
Christmas Rhyme, A. Johnson
Christmas Rush, The. Thompson
Christmas Song. Field
Christmas, South, 1866. Tucker
Christmas Story (1980). Arrowsmith
Christmas Times. Johnson
Christmas Verse, A. "Kay"
Computer's First Christmas Card, The.
   Morgan
Cradle Hymn, A. Watts
Cradle Song at Bethlehem. Falconer
Crib, The. Finch
Cultivation of Christmas Trees, The. Eliot
Day before Christmas. Chute
December Fragments. Lattimore
End of the Play, The. *Fr.* Dr. Birch and His
   Young Friends. Thackeray
Eve. Nemerov
Ex Ore Infantium. Thompson
Farewell! Advent. Ryman
Festival of the Nativity, The. De Ledrede
Flight into Egypt, The. *Fr.* For the Time
   Being; a Christmas Oratorio. Auden
For Christmas Day. Wadding
For Us No Night Can Be Happier.
   Zinzendorf
Friendly Beasts, The. *Unknown*
Gloucestershire Wassail. *Unknown*
Groundhog, The. Shaw
Hail, Comly and Clene. *Fr.* The Second
   Shepherd's Play. *Unknown*
Happy Christmas, A. Havergal
Heavenly Stranger, The. Blenkhorn
Here we come a-caroling. *Unknown*
Holy Night. Benson
House of Christmas, The. Chesterton
House of Hospitalities, The. Hardy
How Far Is It to Bethlehem? Chesterton
How Far to Bethlehem? Miller
Hymn: "Lord, when the wise men came from
   far[r]" Godolphin
Hymn [*or* Hymne] on the Nativity [*or*
   Nativitie] of My Saviour, A. Jonson
I Saw a Stable. Coleridge
I Sing of a Maiden. *Unknown*
In Dulci Jubilo. *Unknown*
In Honour of Christmas. *Unknown*
In the Holy Nativity of Our Lord God.
   Crashaw
In the Town. *Unknown*
In the Week When Christmas Comes.
   Farjeon
Incarnation, The. Wesley
Inn That Missed Its Chance, The. Wells
Innkeeper's Wife, The. Sansom
Instead of Neat Inclosures. *Fr.* An Ode of
   the Birth of Our Saviour. Herrick
It Came upon the Midnight Clear. Sears
It was a night in winter. *Fr.* The Witnesses.
   Sansom
Jest 'fore Christmas. Field
Jew at Christmas Eve, The. Shapiro
Jolly Shepherd, The. *Unknown*
Journey Back to Christmas. Dunn

Karma. Robinson
Kid Stuff. Horne
Kings of the East, The. Bates
Krismas Dinnah. Johnson
Led by the light of an unusual star. *Fr.* For the Time Being; a Christmas Oratorio. Auden
Let me tell to you the story. Agnew
Little tree. *Fr.* Chansons Innocentes. Cummings
Long, Long Ago. *Unknown*
Lullaby of the Nativity, A. *Unknown*
Man Exalted. *Unknown*
Masters, in This Hall. Morris
Medieval Poem of the Nativity, A. *Unknown*
Meditation for Christmas, A. Image
Mice in the Hay. Norris
Miracles at the Birth of Christ. Watts
Nativity [*or* Nativitie] *Fr.* La Corona. Donne
Nativity, The. Fordham
Nativity, The. Lewis
Nativity. Montgomery
Nativity, The. *Unknown*
Nativity of Our Lord and Saviour Jesus Christ, The. *Fr.* Hymns and Spiritual Songs. Smart
New Prince, New Pomp. Southwell
Noel. Gilder
Noel; Christmas Eve, 1913. Bridges
Now Is the Time of Christmas. *Unknown*
Now the Most High Is Born. Ryman
O Christmas Night. Selyns
On Christmas Day. Orrery
On Christmas-Day. Traherne
On the Nativity of Our Saviour. Philipott
Outlanders, The. *Fr.* The Earthly Paradise. Morris
Oxen, The. Hardy
Reminder, The. Hardy
Sailor's Carol. Causley
Sailor's Christmas Day, The. *Unknown*
Santa Claus. Nemerov
Shepherds' Carol. Nicholson
Shepherd's Dog, The. Norris
Shepherd's Tale, The. Kirkup
Silver Bells. Hendry
Sing, hey! Sing, hey!/ For Christmas Day. *Unknown*
Sing We Yule. *Unknown*
Six Things for Christmas. May
Softly the Night. *Unknown*
Sonnets at Christmas, *sels.* Tate
Stars in Apple Cores. Shaw
Sweet Was the Song. *Unknown*
Tarragona Wine. McWhirter
Thames Head Wassailers' Song. *Unknown*
Time draws near the birth of Christ, The. *Fr.* In Memoriam A. H. H. Tennyson
This Endris Night. *Unknown*
This Is the Day. *Fr.* Sonnets at Christmas. Tate.
Thou whose birth on earth. *Fr.* Christmas Antiphones. Swinburne
Thoughts of Loved Ones. Fishback
Three Kings, The. Longfellow
To a Young Wretch. Frost
To Christ Our Lord. Kinnell
To Jesus on His Birthday. Millay
To See the Cross at Christmas. Cooper
Upon a Christmas Morning. *Unknown*
Upon Christ's Nativity or Christmas. Watkyns
Visit from St. Nicholas, A. Moore
Week to Christmas, A. *Fr.* Autumn Journal. MacNeice
Welcome Yule. *Unknown*
What the Donkey Saw. Fanthorpe
While Shepherds Watched [Their Flocks by Night] Tate
White Christmas. Rodgers
Widow Brown's Christmas. Trowbridge

Wise Men Ask the Children the Way, The. Heine
Yule Days, The. *Unknown*
Yule Log, The. Hayne
Naked Astronaut, The: Poems on Birth and Birthdays (NAs), pp. 173-192. René Graziani, ed.
Oxford Book of Christmas Poems, The (OBCP). Michael Harrison *and* Christopher Stuart-Clark, eds
Poems of Christmas (PChr). Myra Cohn Livingston, ed.
Christmas Cards
Computer's First Christmas Card, The. Morgan
Christmas Carols
Away in a Manger. Luther
Carol Singers, The. Rhodes
Child's Christmas Carol, A. Chaundler
Christmas Carols. Longfellow
First Nowell, The. *Unknown*
God Rest You [*or* ye] Merry, Gentlemen. Craik
Good King Wenceslas. *Unknown*
I Saw Three Ships Come Sailing In. *Unknown*
It Came upon the Midnight Clear. Sears
O Little Town of Bethlehem. Brooks
Out of Your Sleep Arise and Wake. *Unknown*
Christmas Eve
Canticle for Xmas Eve. Wagoner
Christmas Eve. Cole
Christmas Eve. Day Lewis
Christmas Eve. Walla
Christmas Eve, South, 1865. Tucker
Christmas Ghost, A. Thompson
Oxen, The. Hardy
Visit from St. Nicholas, A. Moore
Christmas Roses
Christmas Rose, The. Day Lewis
Christmas Trees
Burning the Christmas Greens. Williams
Christmas Song, A. *Unknown*
Christmas Tree, A. Burford
Christmas Tree. Cook
Christmas Tree, The. De Savitzsky
Christmas Tree. Fisher
Christmas Tree, The. Moorer
Christmas Tree, The. Morgan
Christmas Tree. Smith
Christmas Tree in the Nursery, The. Gilder
Christmas-Tree Song, A. Bennett
Little Fir Tree, The. Rose
Little tree. *Fr.* Chansons Innocentes. Cummings
Miss Cho Composes in the Cafeteria. Tate
Ten Little Christmas Trees. Bennett
Wild Common, The. Lawrence
Chrysanthemums
As we say farewell to autumn. *Fr.* Chyrsanthemums. Yün Shou-p'ing
Chrysanthemum and the Sword, The. Tu Yeh
Chrysanthemum didn't spill a dewdrop, The. *Fr.* Seventy-six Hokku. Basho
Chrysanthemums. Seymour-Smith
In Hatchobori. *Fr.* Seventy-six Hokku. Basho
In the candlelight in my hand. *Fr.* Eighty-seven Hokku. Buson
Last Chrysanthemum, The. Hardy
Planting Chrysanthemums. Michizane
This white chrysanthemum doesn't have a speck of dust. *Fr.* Seventy-six Hokku. Basho
White chrysanthemum, A. *Fr.* Sixteen Hokku. Miura Chora
Chungking, China
Lyric to Spring. Stilwell
Church of England
Bristol and Clifton. Betjeman

Church of England, The. *Fr.* The Hind and the Panther. Dryden
Church of England's Glory, The. *Unknown*
New Catch in Praise of the Reverend Bishops, A. *Unknown*
Paradox, The. *Unknown*
Pulpit to Be Let, A. *Unknown*
Sentiments, The. *Unknown*
Vicar of Bray, The. *Unknown*
Churches
Angel Unawares, An. *Unknown*
At Church Next Sunday. *Unknown*
Bells of London, The. *Unknown*
Boccherini's Tomb. Vas
Bombed Church. Berridge
Bricking the Church. Morgan
Building in Stone. Warner
Children's Bells, The. Farjeon
Church, The. Piper
Church Going. Larkin
Church on Comiaken Hill, The. Hugo
Church the Garden of Christ, The. Watts
Country Thought. Warner
Dark Churches. *Fr.* A Hymn [*or* Hymne] to Christ, at the Author's Last Going into Germany. Donne
Dedication: "Thou, whose unmeasured temple stands." Bryant
Diary of a Church Mouse. Betjeman
For the Altarpiece of the Roseau Valley Church, Saint Lucia. Walcott
For the Lord's Day Evening. Watts
Good Friday and the Present Crucifixion. Buckley
Greater Friendship Baptist Church, The. Gregory
Hangover Mass. Kennedy
Here We Come A-Haying. Close
Hymn of Dedication. Scantlebury
In a Country Church. Thomas
In Memory of George Whitby, Architect. Betjeman
In Santa Maria del Popolo. Gunn
Inside of King's College Chapel, Cambridge. *Fr.* Ecclesiastical Sonnets. Wordsworth
It Isn't the Church—It's You. *Unknown*
Just like Me. Sinks
Knole. Sisson
Ladies' Aid, The. *Unknown*
Little Rhyme and a Little Reason, A. Anstadt
Manners. Shiffert
Meeting-House Hill. Lowell
My Grandfather's Church Goes Up. Chappell
New England Church, A. Barrett
Old Women beside a Church. Wilson
On Seeing Two Brown Boys in a Catholic Church. Horne
Opening Service, An. Thompson
Pastor Speaks Out, The. Fisher
Poem in Defence of the Decent Ornaments of Christ-Church, Oxon, Occasioned by a Banbury Brother, Who Called Them Idolatries, A, *sels.* *Unknown*
Poor Man and His Parish Church, The. Hawker
Prayer in a Country Church. Van Dusen
Rugby Chapel. Arnold
Saint Maria Maggiore. Fritsch
St. Sophia. Fuller
Some keep the Sabbath [*or* Sunday] going to church. Dickinson
Sunday Afternoon Service in St. Enodoc Church, Cornwall. Betjeman
Sunday Morning, King's Cambridge. Betjeman
Walking on Sunday. Murphy
We Love the Venerable House. Emerson
Wednesday Night Prayer Meeting. Wright
What the Choir Sang about the New Bonnet. Morrison

Winds; words of the wind; rumor of great walls pierced. *Fr.* The Asylum. Carruth

Churchill, John, Duke of Marlborough. *See* **Marlborough, John Churchill, 1st Duke of.**

Churchyards
Elegy Written in a Country Churchyard. Gray
In Carrowdore Churchyard. Mahon
Ode on the Poetical Character. Collins

Cibber, Colley
Cibber! write all thy verses upon glasses. Pope
Quoth Cibber to Pope, tho' in verse you foreclose. Pope

Cicadas
Cicada, The. Green
Cicada. Stoutenburg
Cicada shrieks, The. Yoshitsune
Cigales. Wilbur
Haiku: "Pillow hard as stone!" Kawabata Bosha
Haiku: "So few the cicadas." Masaoka Shiki
Haiku: "Soon to die." Masaoka Shiki
Its sloughed-off shell. Joso
Quietness: piercing the rocks. *Fr.* Seventy-six Hokku. Basho
Clear-toned cicadas have exhausted their voices, The. *Fr.* Seventy-eight Tanka. Shikishi
Though it will die soon. Basho
Tired of sitting indoors all day long. *Fr.* Manyo Shu. Yakamochi
To the Cicada. Wright

Cigarettes
First Cigarette, The. Rolnik
Haiku: "Cigarette is dead, The." *Fr.* One Hundred Haiku in Free Form. Hosai
"Luckies." Gibbons
See also **Smoking.**

Cigars
To a Segar. Low

Cinderella
Cinderella. Jarrell
Cinderella. Sexton
Queen Charming. Hadas

Cinque Ports, England
Cinque Port, A. Davidson
Warden of the Cinque Ports, The. Longfellow

Circe
Circe. De Tabley
Circe. Doolittle
Circe. Gibson
Circe. Hope
Circe. MacNeice
Moly. Gunn
Strayed Reveller, The. Arnold

Circumcision
Circumcision, The. Zisquit
On the Circumsision: New Year's Day. Wadding

Circus
Circus, The. Kaplan
Circus, The. Roberts
Circus; or One View of It, The. Spencer
Circus Parade, The. Pyle
Cirque d'Hiver. Bishop
Hill of Beans, A. Dove
Julia. Rose
Litanies of Julia Pastrana (1832-1860, The. Shapcott
Tell me,/ you visited. Zumpf
What Happens. Jordan
When I Went to the Circus. Lawrence

Cities
Across the Straits. Dobson
Air: "For often my mammy has told." *Fr.* Jack the Giant Queller; an Antique History. Brooke
Approach to a City. Williams

Assistance, The. Blackburn
Aztec City, The. Ware
Barrel-Organ, The. Noyes
Christ Walks in This Infernal District Too. Lowry
Cities and Science. McCord
Cities behind Glass. Hogan
City. Hofshteyn
City, The. Ignatow
City. Stembridge
City, City. Ridlon
City Dump, The. Holman
City in the Sea. Poe
City, Oh, City! Prelutsky
City Rises, The. Cunningham
Complacent Cliff-Dweller, The. Fishback
Countryman's Return, The. Thomas
Dalesman's Litany, The. *Unknown*
Drat my hateful birthday. Sulpicia
Every City. Rokeah
Faces in the Street. Lawson
For, Lord, the Crowded Cities Be. Rilke
Greener Grass. Steele
In the Aging City. Tuqan
Like This. Kassák
Lion Named Passion, A. Hollander
London Town. Johnson
Master City, The. Orente
More Foreign Cities. Tomlinson
Nocturnal Sounds. Cumbo
Pride of Cities. Akhtar-ul-Iman
Roof Garden, The. Moss
Rudolph Is Tired of the City. Brooks
Sing a Song of People. Lenski
Sparkles from the Wheel. Whitman
Strange City, A. Weöres
Thaw in the City. Lipsitz
Tired of Towns. Lang
To Sextus. Martial
Up at a Villa—Down in the City. Browning
White City, The. McKay
Zimmer's Street. Zimmer

Citizenship
Citizen of—the World, A. McDonald

Civil Defense
Civil Defense. Burke

Civil Rights. *See* **Protest, Social.**

Civil War, American
All Quiet along the Potomac. Beers
Army Corps on the March, An. Whitman
Army Correspondent's Last Ride. Townsend
Around the March. Hudgins
As I Lay with My Head in Your Lap Camerado. Whitman
As Toilsome I Wander'd Virginia's Woods. Whitman
Ball's Bluff. Melville
Barbara Frietchie. Whittier
Battle Cry of Freedom, The. Root
Battle Hymn of the [American] Republic, The. Howe
Bivouac on a Mountain Side. Whitman
Blue and the Gray, The. Finch
Bonnie Blue Flag. McCarthy
Brother Green. *Unknown*
By the Bivouac's Fitful Flame. Whitman
By the Potomac. Aldrich
Cannon Park. St. Germain
Cavalry Crossing a Ford. Whitman
Charleston. Timrod
College Colonel, The. Melville
Come Up from the Fields, Father. Whitman
Craven. Newbolt
Dan Ellis's Boys. *Unknown*
Dirge for McPherson, A. Melville
Dixie. Emmett
Driving Home the Cows. Osgood
Ethnogenesis. Timrod
Fare You Well, My Darling. *Unknown*
Farragut. Meredith

For the Union Dead. Lowell
From Trollope's Journal. Bishop
Goin' 'cross the Mountain. *Unknown*
Grant at Appomattox. Claytor
House by the Side of the Road, The. Foss
Hunting Civil War Relics at Nimblewill Creek. Dickey
Huts at Esquimaux, The. Dubie
I Fights Mit Sigel! Robinson
Kearny at Seven Pines. Stedman
Keenan's Charge. Lathrop
Kentucky Belle. Woolson
Killed at the Ford. Longfellow
Little Giffen. Ticknor
Lost Occasion, The. Whittier
Malvern Hill. Melville
March in the Ranks Hard-Prest, and the Road Unknown, A. Whitman
March into Virginia, The. Melville
Marching through Georgia. Work
Meditation, A. Whitman
Memorial: On the Slain at Chickamauga. Melville
Memorial Wreath. Randall
Mower in Ohio, The. Piatt
Music in Camp. Thompson
My Maryland. Randall
Negro Soldier's Civil War Chant. *Unknown*
Ode: "Sleep sweetly in your humble graves." Timrod
Ode to the Confederate Dead. Tate
Portent, The. Melville
Rebel, The. Randolph
Red, White and Red, The. *Unknown*
River Fight, The. Brownell
Robert G. Shaw. Ray
Robert Gould Shaw. Dunbar
Roses of Memory. Gordon
Sambo's Right to Be Kilt. Halpine
Sheridan's Ride. Read
Shiloh; a Requiem. Melville
Sight in Camp [in the Daybreak Gray and Dim], A. Whitman
Spirit Whose Work Is Done. Whitman
Stonewall Jackson's Way. Palmer
Uninscribed Monument on One of the Battle-Fields of the Wilderness, An. Melville
Unsung Heroes, The. Dunbar
Vicksburg. Hayne
Vigil Strange I Kept on the Field One Night. Whitman
Volunteer's Thanksgiving, The. Larcom
When Dey 'Listed Colored Soldiers. Dunbar
When Johnny Comes Marching Home. Gilmore
When the Great Gray Ships Come In. Carryl
When This Cruel War Is Over. Sawyer
Whisperin' Bill. Bacheller
Wound-Dresser, The. Whitman

Civil War, Nigerian
Nigerian Unity/ or Little Niggers Killing Little Niggers. Lee

Civil War, Spanish
And I remember Spain. *Fr.* Autumn Journal. MacNeice
Battle Hymn of the Spanish Rebellion. MacKay
Full Moon at Tierz; before the Storming of Huesca. Cornford
International Brigade Arrives at Madrid, The. Neruda
Italian soldier shook my hand, The. Orwell
Letter from Aragon, A. Cornford
Of what a quality is courage made. *Fr.* Charles Donnelly. MacDonagh
Port Bou. Spender
Spain. Livesay
Spain 1937. Auden
Spanish War, The. "MacDiarmid"
Toledo. Campbell

Two Armies. Spender
See also **Spain.**
Civil Wars, English
It was upon the twilight of that day. *Fr.* The
 Civil Wars. Daniel
King Enjoys His Own Again, The. Parker
On the New Forcers of Conscience Under the
 Long Parliment. Milton
Parliament Soldiers, The. *Unknown*
There Faunus and Sylvanus keep their courts.
 Fr. Cooper's Hill. Denham
To the Lord General Cromwell. Milton
When the Assault Was Intended to the City.
 Milton
Civilization
Dream, Dump-Heap, and Civilization.
 Warren
Invention of New Jersey, The. Anderson
Long-legged Fly. Yeats
Martian Sends a Postcard Home, A. Raine
Meditations for a Savage Child. Rich
Text for These Distracted Times, A. Hall
That Which We Call a Rose. Dransfield
Tired. Johnson
Waste Land, The. Eliot
Clams and Clamming
Clamming. Whittemore
Clams. Ishigaki Rin
Mussels. Oliver
Sonnet to a Clam. Saxe
Clans
Massacre of the Macpherson, The. Aytoun
See also **Culloden, Battle of; Scotland;
 Scottish Highlands.**
Clare. *See* **County Clare, Ireland.**
Clarke, Austin
Visit to Bridge House, A. Weber
Class. *See* **Social Class.**
Claustrophobia
Claustrophobia. O Riordain
Cleanliness
Advantages of Washing, The. *Fr.* The Art
 of Preserving Health. Armstrong
Our fathers, who were wondrous wise.
 Unknown
Clemens, Samuel Langhorne. *See* **"Twain,
 Mark."**
Cleopatra
Alexandrian Kings. Cavafy
Antony and Cleopatra. Coulette
Antony to Cleopatra. Lytle
Cleopatra. "Akhmatova"
Cleopatra. Mackey
Cleopatra. Story
Cleopatra. Swinburne
Cleopatra Dying. Collier
Cleopatra to the Asp. Hughes
Dead Cleopatra lies in a crystal casket. *Fr.*
 Discordants. Aiken
Death of Cleopatra. *Fr.* Antony and
 Cleopatra. Shakespeare
Tact. Pascal
Clergy
Aaron. Herbert
Amorous Temper, An. *Fr.* The Progress of
 Dulness. Trumbull
Ballad of Father Gilligan, The. Yeats
Baucis and Philemon; Imitated from the
 Eighth Book of Ovid. Swift
Birthday Wishes to a Minister of the Gospel.
 Moorer
Bishop Orders His Tomb at Saint Praxed's
 Church, The. Browning
Buddhist Priest, A. Ho Xuan Huong
Character of a Good Parson, The. Dryden
Church of England's Glory, The. *Unknown*
Confessor, The. Belli
Country Clergy, The. Thomas
Country Curate, The. Taylor
Eddi's Service. Kipling

Elegy Written in a Country Churchyard.
 Gray
Excellent New Ballad, Called the Brawny
 Bishop's Complaint, An. Mainwaring
Father Mat. Kavanagh
Fra Lippo Lippi. Browning
Gentle Alice Brown. Gilbert
Good Bishop, A. *Unknown*
Grandfather. Bowering
Habit of Perfection, The. Hopkins
High Priest, The. *Unknown*
If you for orders, and a gown design. *Fr.* A
 Satyr Address'd to a Friend That Is About
 to Leave the University, and Come Abroad
 in the World. Oldham
In Church. *Fr.* Satires of Circumstance.
 Hardy
Irish-American Dignitary. Clarke
Jackdaw of Rheims, The. *Fr.* The Ingoldsby
 Legends. "Ingoldsby"
Let the bells ring, and let the boys sing. *Fr.*
 The Spanish Curate. Fletcher
Lycidas. Milton
Model Sermon, A. *Unknown*
On a Clergyman's Horse Biting Him.
 Unknown
On Hearing a Lady Praise a Certain Rev.
 Doctor's Eyes. Outram
On Those That Deserve It. Quarles
Paradox, The. *Unknown*
Poet vs. Parson. Elliott
Poor Parson, The. *Fr.* The Canterbury Tales:
 Prologue. Chaucer
Preacher's Mistake, The. Doane
Preacher's Vacation, The. *Unknown*
Preachment for Preachers. *Fr.* The Ship of
 Fools. Barclay
Priestcraft and Private Judgement. *Fr.*
 Religio Laici. Dryden
Priestin' of Father John, The. Sheridan
Priest's Lament, The. Benson
Priest's Prayer, A. Bianchi
Problem, The. Emerson
Rival Curates, The. Gilbert
Sea-Chaplain's Petition to the Lieutenants in
 the Ward-Room, for the Use of the
 Quarter-Gallery, A. "T"
Sentiments, The. *Unknown*
Soliloquy of the Spanish Cloister. Browning
Sonnet: Good Spiritual Father, The. Belli
Susan, the constant slave to mop and broom.
 Fr. The Sorrows of Sunday; an Elegy.
 "Pindar"
To the New Ordained. Sheridan
Tom Brainless as Student and Preacher at
 College. *Fr.* The Progress of Dulness.
 Trumbull
Unfrocked Priest, The. Campbell
Upon Bishop Andrewes His Picture before His
 Sermons. Crashaw
Upon Glass: Epigram. Herrick
Vicar, The. *Fr.* The Borough. Crabbe
Vicar, The. *Fr.* Every-Day Characters.
 Praed
Vicar of Bray, The. *Unknown*
Village Parson, The. *Fr.* The Deserted
 Village. Goldsmith
Village Preacher, The. *Fr.* The Deserted
 Village. Goldsmith
Wanted, a Minister's Wife. *Unknown*
Windows, The. Herbert
Witch Doctor. Hayden
See also **Rabbis.**
Clerks
Balance. Schultz
Clerks, The. Robinson
Dolor. Roethke
Report, The. Swan
Song from a Two-Desk Office. Buck
Song of the GPO, A. Hamill

Thirty Bob a Week. Davidson
See also **Office Workers.**
Cleveland, Ohio
Ordinary Evening in Cleveland, An. Turco
Clichés
On a Lover of Books. Grigson
Cliff Dwellers
Testament of Perpetual Change, The.
 Williams
Cliffs
Dover, the Samphire Cliff. *Fr.* King Lear.
 Shakespeare
Clive, Robert
Alarum, The. Warner
Clock, The. Holman
Clock. Monro
Clock in the Square, A. Rich
What I like about Clive. *Fr.* Clerihews.
 Bentley
Clocks
Alarm's Callous Racket, The. Michaelis
Clock on the War, The. al-Qasim
Clocks. Ginsberg
Clocks. Locker
Cuckoo Clock, The. Stanton
Four Quartz Crystal Clocks. Moore
Grandfather's Clock. Work
Lines in Praise of a Self-Chiming Clock.
 Hsüan-yeh
Mr. Coggs. Lucas
Old Clock on the Stairs, The. Longfellow
Old Kitchen Clock, The. Hawkshawe
Speed Track, The. "Peter"
Sun-Dial, The. *Fr.* Melincourt. Peacock
Time Piece. Cole
Twelve. Glatstein
See also **Watches.**
Clonmacnoise, Ireland
Dead at Clonmacnois [*or* Clonmacnoise], The.
 O'Gillan
End of Clonmacnois, The. *Unknown*
Pilgrimage. Clarke
Clonmel, Ireland
In Clonmel Parish Churchyard. Piatt
Clothing
Braid Claith. Fergusson
Brocaded Sash. *Unknown*
Catch, The. Wilbur
Change of Color. Zitz-Halein
Clothes, The. Zychlinska
Clothes Do but Cheat and Cozen Us.
 Herrick
Clothes Make the Man. Conway
Clothes Maketh the Man. Weiss
Delight in Disorder. Herrick
Describing a Suit. Ibrahim
Dresses. Fraser
Fulling Cloth for Clothes. Hsieh Hui-lien
In Praise of Clothes. Jong
Kimono. Graham
Laundry and School Epigrams. Mayer
Lines to an Old Dress. Tucker
My Best Clothes. Netser
My Burned Suit. Farhat
My Love in Her Attire. *Unknown*
New Vestments, The. Lear
Nothing to Wear. Butler
On a Girdle. Waller
On the fine new robes. Tameko
Pink Frock, The. Hardy
Salma. Farhat
Still to Be Neat [Still to Be Drest (*or*
 Dressed)]. *Fr.* Epicoene; or, The Silent
 Woman. Jonson
Think of dress in every light. *Fr.* Achilles.
 Gay
This Shirt. Trías
Though I have silks. *Fr.* Manyo Shu.
 Unknown
Transmigration. McBride
Underwear. Ferlinghetti

Upon Julia's Clothes. Herrick
Upon Julia's Ribband. Herrick
Veiled Land. Gibran
Will the Real Me Please Stand Up?
  Hendricks
Wintah Styles, De. Johnson
Winter Clothes. Kuskin
Written for My Son, and Spoken by Him at
  His First Putting on Breeches. Barber
See also **Jewelry.**

Clouds
Among the Millet. Lampman
As the mountain torrents roar and roar again.
  Fr. Manyo Shu. Hitomaro
Bedouins of the Skies, The. Kenyon
Black, black cloud, A. Williams
Black Cloud, The. Davies
Broken Sky. Sandburg
Cloud, The. Shelley
Cloud clings, The. *Fr.* Manyo Shu.
  Unknown
Cloud Country. Merrill
Cloud-Mobile, The. Swenson
Cloud Parade, The. Jensen
Cloud Shadow. Moore
Cloud Song. Ray
Clouded Morning, The. Very
Clouds. Brooke
Clouds. Levine
Clouds. Schutting
Clouds, The. Williams
Clouds and Clay. Gillies
Clouds from the peak. Tameko
Clouds That Are So Light, The. Thomas
Corn-grinding Song. *Unknown*
Cumulus Clouds. Nelms
Entreaty to the Cloud. Nervo
For the Girls 'cause They Know. Littlebird
I think about you & it's like having spirits
  come down on me. Yuwaku
Low-anchored Cloud. *Fr.* A Week on the
  Concord and Merrimack Rivers. Thoreau
Moon and a Cloud, The. Davies
Night Clouds. Lowell
O cloud that wants to be the sky's arrow.
  Castellanos
O that I were the cloud. *Fr.* Manyo Shu.
  Unknown
Patch of cloud rides the moon tonight, A.
  Fr. Twenty-one Hokku. Boncho
Saw the Cloud Lynx. Makidemewabe
Sea Surface Full of Clouds. Stevens
Sky Pictures. Newsome
Spyglass Conversations. *Unknown*
Trout leaping. Onitsura
Winter. Masayori

Clough, Arthur Hugh
On Arthur Hugh Clough. Swinburne
Thyrsis. Arnold

Clover
Bush clovers must have shed their flowers.
  Fr. A Compendium of Good Tanka. Teika
Clover, The. Riley
Clover. Tabb
Four-Leaf Clover. Higginson
Since the sparse bush clover began to flower.
  Fr. A Compendium of Good Tanka. Teika
Summer's Day, A. Riley
There is a flower that bees prefer. Dickinson
Thoughts on a Pore Joke. Riley

Clowns
Clown, The. Aldis
Clown, The. Hall
Clowns, The. Laforgue
Phantom of the Clouds. Apollinaire
Saltimbanques. Apollinaire
Saltimbanques. Reverdy
See also **Circus.**

Clumsiness
Love Poem: "My clumsiest dear, whose hands
  shipwreck vases." Nims

Coal Mining and Coal Miners
Agape the sooty collier stands. *Fr.* A
  Descriptive Poem, Addressed to Two
  Ladies at Their Return from Viewing the
  Mines, near Whitehaven. Dalton
Avondale Mine Disaster, The. *Unknown*
Blantyre Explosion, The. *Unknown*
Blue Monday. *Unknown*
Brave Collier Lads. *Unknown*
Caliban in the Coal Mines. Untermeyer
Call the Horse, Marrow. *Unknown*
Cleator Moor. Nicholson
Coal Diggin' Blues. *Unknown*
Coal Miner's Goodbye, A. *Unknown*
Coalmen, The. Nagy
Collier, The. Watkins
Collier Lad's Lament, The. *Unknown*
Collier Lass, The. Armstrong
Colliers' March, The. Freeth
Collier's Rant, The. *Unknown*
Collier's Wife, The. Lawrence
Down in a Coal Mine. Geoghegan
Dying Mine Brakeman, The. Jenks
Explosion, The. Larkin
Fourpence a Day. *Unknown*
Gresford Disaster, The. *Unknown*
Grey October. "Critics, The"
Hill above the Mine, The. Cowley
I'll Have a Collier for My Sweetheart.
  Oliver
Jowl, Jowl and Listen. *Unknown*
Los Mineros. Dorn
Meditation on Rhode Island Coal, A. Bryant
Miners. Owen
Miner's Doom, The. *Unknown*
Miner's Helmet, The. MacBeth
Miner's Life, A. *Unknown*
Old Miner, The. *Unknown*
Old Miner's Refrain, The. *Unknown*
Robens' Promised Land. Purdom
That Little Lump of Coal. *Unknown*
Trimdon Grange Explosion, The. Armstrong
Two-Cent Coal. *Unknown*
Two hundred men and eighteen killed.
  Henry

Coatimundi
Coati-Mundi. Smith

Cobblers. *See* **Shoemakers.**

Coca Cola
You Too? Me Too—Why Not? Soda Pop.
  Hollander

Cocaine
Cocaine Lil [and Morphine Sue]. *Unknown*

Cockaigne, Land of
Cockaigne: A Dream. Sissman
Land of Cokaygne, The. *Unknown*

Cockfighting
Cock of the Game, The. *Unknown*

Cockroaches
At Last We Killed the Roaches. Clifton
Aubade: N.Y.C. Wallace
Cockroaches. Starbird
Roach, The. Raven
St. Roach. Rukeyser
Scuttle, scuttle little roach. *Fr.* Nursery
  Rhymes for the Tender-hearted. Morley
To a Humble Bug. Van Voorhis
Whose Scene? Stone

Cocks. *See* **Roosters.**

Cocoa
In Praise of Cocoa, Cupid's Nightcap.
  Sharpless
Saddled Ass, The. La Fontaine

Coconuts
Coconut, The. "Ande"
Coconut. Shimazaki Toson
Green Coconuts: Rio. Durrell

Cody, William. *See* **Buffalo Bill.**

Coffee
Bacchus on Beverages. *Fr.* Bacchus in
  Tuscany. Redi
Hills Brothers Coffee. Tapahonso
Upon Receipt of a Pound of Coffee in 1863.
  Tucker

Coffins
First Coffin Poem. Ignatow

Coins
Money. Nemerov

Cold
Cold. Francis
Cold. Roberts
Cold! Cold!/ Wide Lurg Plain is cold tonight.
  Unknown
Cremation of Sam McGee, The. Service
Dragon Smoke. Moore
Ducks along the reedy shore, The. *Fr.*
  Manyo Shu. Shiki
On the Unusual Cold and Rainie Weather in
  the Summer, 1648. Heath
Pray to What Earth Does This Sweet Cold
  Belong. Thoreau
Snow-Girl. Moritz
So cold is the night. Ryoshun
Song on Enduring the Cold. Ts'ao Ts'ao
There Are Roughly Zones. Frost
Though I lie here. Ryokan
Tramontana at Lerici. Tomlinson
'Twas warm—at first—like us. Dickinson
Twenty Below. Ford
Young Charlottie or, The Frozen Girl.
  Unknown

Colds (illness)
To Bary Jade. Adams

Cole, Thomas
To Cole, the Painter, Departing for Europe.
  Bryant

Coleridge, Samuel Taylor
Bards, The. De la Mare
Coleridge. Thomas
Coleridge. Watts-Dunton
Coleridge Crossing the Plain of Jars; 1833.
  Dubie
Dedicatory Sonnet to S. T. Colerige.
  Coleridge
Most of It, The. Frost
On the Late S. T. Coleridge. Allston
Person from Porlock, A. Thomas
S. T. Coleridge Dismisses a Caller from
  Porlock. Meyer
Thoughts about the Person from Porlock.
  Smith
To Coleridge in Sicily. *Fr.* The Prelude [or,
  Growth of a Poet's Mind]: France.
  Wordsworth
Written on the Anniversary of Our Father's
  Death. Coleridge

Colette (Sidonie Gabrielle Colette)
Cortege for Colette. Garrigue

Colleges and Universities
Claflin's Alumni. Moorer
Dedication Day Poem. Moorer
Fisk is/ a/ negroid/ institution. Scott
Student, The. Moore
To a Visiting Poet in a College Dormitory.
  Kizer
To the University of Cambridge, in
  New-England. Wheatley
Tuskegee. Hill
University. Shapiro
University Curriculum. Turner
Views of the Favorite Colleges. Brinnin
Walk in Würzburg, A. Plomer
What We Teach at Claflin. Moorer
Written at Cambridge. Lamb
You Understand the Requirements. Lifshin
See also **Students.**

Collies
Praise of a Collie. MacCaig

Cologne, West Germany
Cologne. Coleridge
Cologne. Domin

Colonialism
Colonialism ("The colonialist governments").
  Qarshe
Environment. Kearns
Foreign Aid. Kearns
Hottentot, The. Pringle
Triptych. Collymore
United Fruit Co, The. Neruda
Verses on the Prospect of Planting Arts and
  Learning in America. Berkeley
West Indies, The. Montgomery
You Who Occupy Our Land. Margarido
See also **British Empire; Imperialism.**

Colorado
Fifth Season, The. Saner
House in Denver. Ferril
New Story, A. Ortiz

Colors
Distinctions. Tomlinson
Dun-Colour [*or* Dun-Color] Pitter
Furnace of Colors, The. Watkins
Green and the Black, The. Bailey
I Asked the Little Boy Who Cannot See.
  Unknown
I planned to have a border of lavender.
  Goodman
Love Bit, The. Oppenheimer
Paint Box, The. Rieu
Rainbow Writing. Merriam
What Is Orange? O'Neill
What Is Pink? *Fr.* Sing-Song. Rossetti
What Is Red? O'Neill
Without Colors. Kouwenaar
Yellow. McCord

Colosseum, Rome
Coliseum, The. Poe
Colosseum. Norse
Survey of the Amphitheatre, A. Browne

Coltrane, John
After the Rain. Crouch
Dear John, Dear Coltrane. Harper
Here Where Coltrane Is. Harper
In Memoriam John Coltrane. Stillman
John Coltrane: An Impartial Review.
  Spellman
Sopranosound, Memory of John. Bourke

Colts
Its rope broken. Teika
Runaway, The. Frost
See also **Horses.**

Columba, Saint. *See* **Columcille, Saint.**

Columbus, Christopher
Dark foreboding haunts me lest I die, A. *Fr.*
  San Gloria. MacDermot
And of Columbus. Gregory
Columbus. Clough
Columbus. Miller
Columbus. Nash
Columbus. Schiller
Columbus. Sigourney
Columbus. Simpson
Columbus and the Mermaids. Coatsworth
Columbus Day. Durham
Columbus Reaches Juana, 1492. Gustafson
Columbus to Ferdinand. Freneau
Discovery of America, The. Robertson
For Christopher Columbus, sels. Seymour
May 1506 (Christopher Columbus Speaking).
  Scott
Mysterious Biography. Sandburg
On a Portrait of Columbus. Woodberry
Passage to India. Whitman
Prayer of Columbus. Whitman
You, Genoese Mariner. Merwin

Columcille, Saint
Poem in Praise of Colum Cille, A. Forgaill
Saint Colm-Cille and the Cairn of Farewell.
  Irvine
Saint Columba. Johnson
St. Columcille's Island Hermitage. *Unknown*

Comas
Coma. Logue
To the Reader. Jarman

Combs
Comb, The. De la Mare

"Come Live with Me and Be My Love"
Bacchanal. De Vries
Bait, The. Donne
Come, live with me and be my love. *Fr.*
  Two Songs. Day Lewis
Come, live with me and be my love. *Fr.*
  Invocation. Hoffenstein
Daphnis to Ganymede. *Fr.* The Affectionate
  Shepherd. Barnfield
Nymph's Reply to the Shepherd, The.
  Ralegh
Passionate Shepherd to His Love, The.
  Marlowe
Passionate Shepherd to His Love, The.
  Schwartz

Comedians
Epitaph for a Funny Fellow. Bishop
Why That's Bob Hope. Hathaway

Comets
Comet, The. Beddoes
Comet, The. Makai
Comet at Yell'ham, The. Hardy
Comets and Princes. Johnson
Other Night (Comet Kohoutek), The.
  Ackerman
To school till five! and then again we fly.
  Browning

Comic Strips
Brickbat for Krazy Kat, A. Schippers
Farm Implements and Rutabagas in a
  Landscape. Ashbery
Katzenjammer Kids, The. Reaney

Commandments. *See* **Decalogue.**

Commencement Day
Commencement. Carrier

Commerce
Wool Trade, The. *Fr.* The Fleece. Dyer
See also **Barter; Business and
  Businessmen.**

Communes
Six-forty-two Farm Commune Struggle Poem.
  Leifer

Communication
Medusa's Hair Was Snakes. Was Thought,
  Split Inward. Fraser
Who's on First? Schwartz

Communion. *See* **Eucharist.**

Communism
Communism. Fortini
Communism. Wilcox
Epigram: "What is a communist? One who
  hath yearnings." Elliott
For the Cultural Campaign. Jigmed
Full Moon at Tierz; before the Storming of
  Huesca. Cornford
Garland for a Propagandist. Pauker
H——y P——tt. *Unknown*
Kral Majales. Ginsberg
Réveille. Ridge
Stray Prostrations. A'Zmi
This is an ancient waltz. *Fr.*
  Tcheliabtraktrostroi Waltz. Aragon

Commuters
Commuters. Hirsch
See also **Suburbs.**

Companionship
Good Company. Baker
Lullaby: "Lay your sleeping head, my love."
  Auden
On Frozen Fields. Kinnell
Pasture, The. Frost
See also **Friendship.**

Computers
All Watched Over by Machines of Loving
  Grace. Brautigan

Computative Oak. Berman
Computer Iterates the Greater Trumps, The.
  Wolfe
Computer's First Christmas Card, The.
  Morgan
No Holes Marred. Douglass
On National Data Banks. Phillips
Perforated Spirit, The. Bishop
Univac to Univac. Salomon
When we invent a machine to read. *Fr.*
  Hospital Songs. Dann

Concentration Camps
Arbeit Macht Frei. Schmitz
Bird, The. Simpson
Book of Yolek, The. Hecht
Buchenwald, 1945. *Fr.* He Kept On
  Burning. Ai
Camp in the Prussian Forest, A. Jarrell
Cradle Song: "Sleep, my child, my little
  daughter." *Unknown*
Crazed Man in Concentration Camp.
  Gergely
Day for Anne Frank, A. Williams
Desnos Reading the Palms of Men on Their
  Way to the Gas Chambers. Berg
Female War Criminal. Paterson
From Tomorrow On. *Unknown*
Funeral, The. "J"
Funeral Trains. Ishihara Yoshiro
Gift, The. Ciardi
"Lovers of Israel" at the Belzhets Death
  Camp, The. Manger
"More Light! More Light!" Hecht
On the 25th Anniversary of the Liberation of
  Auschwitz. Mandel
Paper Cities. Schnackenberg
Protocols. Jarrell
Starvation Camp near Jaslo. Szymborska
This Urn Contains Earth from German
  Concentration Camps. Lorde
To One Put to Death in a Gas Chamber.
  Marx
What big heavy doors! *Fr.* Auschwitz.
  Wyse
See also **Holocaust; Internment.**

Conception
Immaculate Conception, The. MacRae
Michael. Sheridan
Observation. Herrick
When I Was Conceived. Ryan

Concerts
Summer Band Concert. Smith

Concord, Massachusetts
Concord Hymn. Emerson
Raven, The. Poe

Concrete Poetry. *See* **Shaped Poetry.**

Condors
Condors. Colum

Confederacy
Conquered Banner, The. Ryan
Dixie. Emmett
Dixie. Pike
Lines on the Back of a Confederate Note.
  Jonas
My Maryland. Randall
Ode: "Sleep sweetly in your humble graves."
  Timrod
Ode to the Confederate Dead. Tate
"We Conquer or Die." Pierpont
See also **Civil War, American.**

Confessions
Ancient Lights. Clarke
Confession, The. Wen Yi-tuo
First Confession. Kennedy
Sonnet: Good Spiritual Father, The. Belli

Conformity
Calf-Path, The. Foss
Disillusionment of Ten o'Clock. Stevens
I Never Even Suggested It. Nash

"Let Us Now Praise Famous Men." Day
  Lewis
Much madness is divinest sense. Dickinson
Poetry of Departures. Larkin
Unknown Citizen, The. Auden

Confusion
Confusion. Cruz

Congo River
On the Congo. Martinson

Congreve, William
To My Dear Friend Mr. Congreve [on His
  Comedy Called "The Double-Dealer"].
  Dryden

Connaught, Ireland
Vision of Connaught in the Thirteenth
  Century, A. Mangan

Connecticut
River of Rivers in Connecticut, The. Stevens
Sleeping Giant, The. Hall
Winter without Snow, A. McClatchy

Connecticut River
River of Rivers in Connecticut, The. Stevens

Conquistadors
El Dorado. Ryan

Conrad, Joseph
Conrad. Slonimski

Conscience
Conscience. Ravitch
Conscience. Sherburne
"Love is too young to know what conscience
  is." Fr. Sonnets, CLI. Shakespeare
To His Conscience. Herrick

Conscientious Objectors
Conscientious Objector, The. Shapiro
Memories of West Street and Lepke. Lowell
Supremer Sacrifice, The. "Maurice"
See also **Pacifism and Pacifists.**

Conscription, Military
Crippler, The. Siegel
Selective Service. Forché

Conservation. See Ecology.

Consolation
Consolation. Yeats
Fish Upstairs, The. Dickey
Life-Lesson, A. Riley
Psalm of Life, A. Longfellow
Rainy Day, The. Longfellow

Constable, John
Meditation on John Constable, A. Tomlinson

Constancy. See Fidelity.

Constantine I (Constantine the Great)
Constantine's Vision of the Cross. Fr.
  Elene. Cynewulf

Constantinople, Turkey
Painted whore, the mask of deadly sin, A.
  Lithgow
Verses Written in the Chiosk at Pera,
  overlooking Constantinople. Montagu

Constellations
Bad Craftsmen. Segalen
Cowherd, since parting with the Princess
  Weaver, The. Fr. Manyo Shu. Okura
Famous Archer, The. Park Je-chun
Far far away, the Herdboy Star. Fr.
  Nineteen Old Poems of the Han. Unknown
Great Bear, The. Hollander
Hunter: 20,000 A.D, The. Joron
Imagination of the Retina, The. Compton
La Bagarède. Kinnell
Lion Named Passion, A. Hollander
On Looking Up by Chance at the
  Constellations. Frost
Orion. Rich
Oxherd and the Weaver Maid standing, The.
  Fr. Manyo Shu. Okura
Planetarium. Rich
Pleiades, The. Barnard
Rain-drops, The/ That fall this evening. Fr.
  Manyo Shu. Unknown
Star-Talk. Graves
See also **Sky; Stars.**

Constitution (ship)
Main-Truck; or, A Leap for Life, The.
  Morris
Old Ironsides. Holmes
Resurrection. Blackmur

Consumerism
Cheer for the Consumer. Waterman
In Answer to Your Query. Lazard
Life Cycle of Common Man. Nemerov
Poem, or Beauty Hurts Mr. Vinal.
  Cummings

Contentment
Ah, sweet Content! where is thy mylde
  abode? Fr. Parthenophil and Parthenophe.
  Barnes
Art thou poor, yet hast thou golden slumbers?
  Fr. The Pleasant Comedy of Patient
  Grissell. Dekker
Careless Content. Byrom
Character of a Happy Life, The. Wotton
Choice, The. Pomfret
Content. Campion
Contentment. Cotton
Contentment. Holmes
Contentment. Fr. The Autocrat of the
  Breakfast Table. Holmes
For fifty years I followed an "overturned
  cart." Fr. Songs from Living in the
  Mountains. Huang Tsung-hsi
Garden, The. Marvell
Gift, The. Ochester
Good Company. Unknown
Grongar Hill. Dyer
He that is down needs fear no fall. Fr. The
  Pilgrim's Progress. Bunyan
Heart's Content. Unknown
His Grange, or Private Wealth. Herrick
How Happy the Man. Unknown
How Pleasant Is This Flowery Plain.
  Unknown
Hymn to Contentment, A. Parnell
If I Might Be an Ox. Unknown
Jesu. Herbert
Lake Isle of Innisfree, The. Yeats
Maesia's Song. Fr. Farewell to Folly.
  Greene
My Mind to Me a Kingdom Is. Dyer
Oh, Sweet Content. Davies
Peace. Calverley
Quiet Mind, The. Unknown
Resolve, The. Chudleigh
Squid. Blumenthal
Truly Great. Davies
We May Be Lo', We May Be Poor. Blackah
See also **Happiness.**

Continuity
Continuum. Levertov
Drawn by Stones, by Earth, by Things That
  Have Been in the Fire. Bell
Epilogue: "Years later the girl died." Pastan
Eternal City, The. Ammons
Excrement Poem, The. Kumin
Family Reunion. Kumin
He got his friends to agree to shoot him
  standing against a stone wall. Fr. Leaving
  the Door Open. Ignatow
Heredity. Hardy
In Blackwater Woods. Oliver
Milkweed. Levine
Perennials. Kitchen
Procession at Candlemas, A. Clampitt
This Day. Raab
Untitled Poem. Dugan
Warning of Winter. Bethell
Wreath to the Fish, A. Willard

Contraception
No, The. Dacey
Pill, The. Clarke
To Fine Lady Would-Be. Jonson

Contrariness
I Want to Know. Drinkwater

Convalescence
Among the Narcissi. Plath

Convents
Mountain Convent. Benét
See also **Nuns.**

Conversation
Chocolates. Simpson
La Donna E Perpetuum Mobile. Edman
Little Talk. Fisher
Recreation. Taylor

Conversion
Answer to Thomas Barry, An. Fitzgerald
Call of the Christian, The. Whittier
Christ's Bounty. Unknown
Compel Them to Come In. Dodd
I Met the Master. Unknown
Mr. Davis's Experience. Unknown
Mrs. Saunder's Experience. Unknown
Night, The. Vaughan
On Being Brought from Africa to America.
  Wheatley
Sweetness of Nature, The. Unknown
Vicar of Bray, The. Unknown

Convoys
Jervis Bay, The. Unknown
Kola Run, The. Goodbrand

Cook, Captain James
Five Visions of Captain Cook, sels. Slessor

Cooking and Cooks
Banquet, A. Sotades
Cutting Greens. Clifton
Flutter, flutter go the gourd leaves. Unknown
Haunted Oven, The. Kennedy
Hollandaise. Bryan
How to Eat Alone. Halpern
Men May Talk of Country-Christmasses.
  Massinger
Mr. T. S. Eliot Cooking Pasta. Tornai
Mummy Slept Late and Daddy Fixed
  Breakfast. Ciardi
On a Gentleman Marrying His Cook. Ellis
Some Cook. Ciardi
Squid. Blumenthal
Thanksgiving Magic. Bennett
What's That Smell in the Kitchen? Piercy
Woman Who Loved to Cook, The. Jong

Coole, Ireland
Coole Park and Ballylee, 1931. Yeats
Coole Park, 1929. Yeats
In the Seven Woods. Yeats
Wild Swans at Coole, The. Yeats

Cooper, James Fenimore
Cooper. Fr. A Fable for Critics. Lowell

Cooper, Peter
Peter Cooper. Miller

Copenhagen, Denmark
Non Sum Qualis Eram in Bona Urbe Nordica
  Illa. Hollander

Coral
Coral Grove, The. Percival

Corinth,Greece
Drinking the Sun of Corinth. Elytis
This Wind That Loiters. Elytis

Cork. See County Cork, Ireland.

Corks
Concerning Cork. Bold

Cormac Mac Art
Burial of King Cormac, The. Ferguson

Cormorants
Common Cormorant [or Shag], The.
  Isherwood
Cormorant in His Element, The. Clampitt
Cormorants. Blight
Praise for the Fountain Opened. Cowper
To the Unborn and Waiting Children.
  Clifton

Corn
Corn-Planter. Kenny
Cornfield. Cox
Cornfield, The. Roberts
Cornfield Myth. Goose

Frost in the Corn, The. McAlmon
Guinea Corn. *Unknown*
Last Corn Shock, The. Dresbach
Poem to Be Recited Every 8 Years While
    Eating Unleavened Tamales. *Unknown*
Rainbow, The. *Unknown*
Corncrakes
First Corncrake. Hewitt
Cornwall, England
Back Again for the Holidays. *Fr.*
    Summoned by Bells. Betjeman
Ballad of a Mine, A. Skelton
Lamorna Cove. Davies
March Evening. Strong
Minerals of Cornwall, Stones of Cornwall.
    Redgrove
On the South Coast of Cornwall. Gray
Song of the Western Men, The. Hawker
Trebetherick. Betjeman
Tregardock. Betjeman
Tresco. Grigson
Cornwallis, Charles Cornwallis, 1st Marquis
Cornwallis's Surrender. *Unknown*
Coronado, Francisco Vasquez de
Quivíra. Guiterman
Corpses
Franz. Strand
Hearse Song, The. *Unknown*
Milton by Firelight. Snyder
Old Apple Trees. Snodgrass
Two Views of a Cadaver Room. Plath
Viewing the Body. Snodgrass
Correggio (Antonio Allegri)
Correggio's Cupolas at Parma. De Vere
Man of Taste, The. Parsons
Cortés, Hernán
With Cortez in Mexico. Campbell
Coruña, La, Spain
Burial of Sir John Moore after Corunna, The.
    Wolfe
Cosmetics
Government Injunction. Miles
Maquillage. Symons
Still to Be Neat [Still to Be Drest (*or*
    Dressed)]. *Fr.* Epicoene; or, The Silent
    Woman. Jonson
Cosmology
Cosmology. Gotlieb
Cosmology and Us. Disch
Eppur Si Muove? Hillyer
Man Alone. Levertov
Passage. Levertov
Stick in the Forest, The. Stafford
Tergvinder's Stone. Merwin
When Did the World Begin. Clairmont
See also **Creation.**
Cotswold Hills, England
Adlestrop. Thomas
Dawns I Have Seen. Gurney
High Hills, The. Gurney
Cotton
Cotton. Martinson
Cotton Boll, The. Timrod
Cotton Song. Toomer
Poor Little Johnny. *Unknown*
Roll the Cotton Down. *Unknown*
Snapshots of the Cotton South. Davis
Counterfeiting and Counterfeiters
Dark Girl Dressed in Blue, The. *Unknown*
Counting
Counting-out Rhymes. *Unknown*
Counting-Song. *Unknown*
Counting the Mad. Justice
Making Tens. Hutchinson
Ten Little Dicky-Birds. Baldwin
Country Antrim, Northern Ireland
Grace for Light. O'Neill
Country Dialects
Ech, Sic a Pairish. *Unknown*
From My Rural Pen. Watt
Irish Schoolmaster, The. Sidney

Rustic Song, A. Deane
Swell's Soliloquy. *Unknown*
Country Life
At a Country Hotel. Nemerov
Back to Griggsby's Station. Riley
Before the Thaw. Gill
Boy's Song, A. Hogg
Bright Abandon. Webb
Bull, The. Sackville-West
Childhood. Walker
Cit's Country Box, The. Lloyd
City Clerk, The. Ashe
Cotter's Saturday Night, The. Burns
Country Bedroom, The. Cornford
Country Dance. *Fr.* The Blind Man.
    Wright.
Country Faith, The. Gale
Country Matters. Ewart
Country North of Belleville, The. Purdy
Country of No Lack. Untermeyer
Country Reverie. Coates
Country Summer. Adams
Country Towns. Slessor
Cranberry Song, The. Reynolds
Crunking crane heard high amongst the
    clouds, The. *Fr.* The Country Man.
    Farewell
Dance on Pushback. Still
Digging. Thomas
Directive. Frost
Disappointment, A. Baillie
Dusk in the Country. Martinson
Epic. Kavanagh
Expanded Want Ad, An. Leithauser
Far from the Madding Crowd. Waterman
Farm Picture, A. Whitman
Farrell O'Reilly. Gogarty
Fire of Drift-wood, The. Longfellow
From where dark clouds of curling smoke
    arise. *Fr.* Stoklewath; or, The Cumbrian
    Village. Blamire
Garden, The. Marvell
Garden Living. Wu Wei-yeh
Goin' Back T'morrer. Garland
Grongar Hill. Dyer
Happy Is the Country Life. *Unknown*
Hardweed Path Going. Ammons
Haymaking. Thomas
His Content in the Country. Herrick
How Happy the Man. *Unknown*
How sweet it is, at first approach of morn.
    Fr. The Rising Village. Goldsmith
Impressions of the Countryside. Ito Togai
In Time of "The Breaking of Nations."
    Hardy
Is It Right to Move to the Country? Giudici
Knoxville, Tennessee. Giovanni
Lake Isle of Innisfree, The. Yeats
Lonesome in the Country. Young
Love on the Farm. Lawrence
Lush, lush, fragrant grasses in autumn green.
    Fr. Joys of the Country: Seven Poems.
    Wang Wei
Maguire is not afraid of death, the Church
    will light him a candle. *Fr.* The Great
    Hunger. Kavanagh
Merry Country Lad, The. *Fr.* The Passionate
    Shepherd. Breton
Montana Pastoral. Cunningham
Mountain Greenery. Hart
Names of Horses. Hall
Need of Being Versed in Country Things,
    The. Frost
Noon. Clare
North Country Maid, The. *Unknown*
Not without Beauty. McLeish
Ode on His Majesty's Proclamation. *Fr.* Il
    Pastor Fido. Fanshawe
Old Man of Verona, The. Claudian
Old Squire, The. Blunt
Ox Cart Man. Hall

Philemon and Baucis. *Fr.* Metamorphoses.
    Ovid
Raleigh Was Right. Williams
Reflections on Having Left a Place of
    Retirement. Coleridge
Rudolph Is Tired of the City. Brooks
Rural. Fried
Rural Simplicity. Byron
Rustic Landscape. Snoek
Silent Poem. Francis
Sonnet: To One Who Has Been Long in City
    Pent. Keats
Spraying the Potatoes. Kavanagh
Sweet Country Life, A. *Unknown*
Thank God for the Country! Arnold
"There is no God," the wicked saith. *Fr.*
    Dipsychus. Clough
There Were Some Summers. Lux
Things of the North, The. McOwan
Time allowed for sleep at length elapsed, The.
    Fr. The Life of Hubert. Cole
To Miss Laetitia Van Lewen. Grierson
To My Honour'd Kinsman, John Driden, of
    Chesterton. Dryden
To Penshurst. Jonson
Under the Greenwood Tree. *Fr.* As You
    Like It. Shakespeare
Upper Canadian, The. Reaney
Verses Addressed to a Friend, Just Leaving a
    Favourite Retirement. Henley
Village, The. Gashe
Visit to the Farm, A. Siegel
When This Old Hat Was New. *Unknown*
Wish, The. *Fr.* The Mistress. Cowley
Wish, A. Rogers
County Antrim, Northern Ireland
Carrickfergus. MacNeice
County Cork, Ireland
Attractions of a Fashionable Irish
    Watering-Place, The. Mahony
Groves of Blarney, The. Millikin
County Donegal, Ireland
Glen Lough. Grigson
County Galway, Ireland
Galway. O'Neill
High Island. Murphy
Sailing to an Island. Murphy
Wild Swans at Coole, The. Yeats
County Kerry, Ireland
In Kerry. Synge
County Kildare, Ireland
Lamenting Maid, The. *Unknown*
County Mayo, Ireland
County Mayo. Raftery
County of Mayo, The. Flavell
County Meath, Ireland
Father and Son. Higgins
County Monaghan, Ireland
Shancoduff. Kavanagh
Stony Grey Soil. Kavanagh
County Sligo, Ireland
Lake Isle of Innisfree, The. Yeats
County Waterford, Ireland
God of his goodnes, praysed that he be. *Fr.*
    The Praise of Waterford. *Unknown*
Courage
Abnormal Is Not Courage, The. Gilbert
Any Complaints? Scannell
Baptism. McKay
Barbara Frietchie. Whittier
Be Never Discouraged. Colesworthy
Be Strong. Babcock
Besieged. Schneour
Captain Death. *Unknown*
Charge of the Light Brigade, The. Tennyson
Courage. Brooke
Curfew Must Not Ring Tonight. Thorpe
Dare to Do Right. Taylor
Defiance. Ibn Gabirol
Gallantry. Douglas

Hero, The. Sassoon
If We Must Die. McKay
In an Age of Fops and Toys. *Fr.*
  Voluntaries. Emerson
Inevitable, The. Bolton
Leak in the Dike, The. Cary
Legend. Wright
Lore. Thomas
Masses. *Fr.* España, Aparta de me Este
  Caliz. Vallejo
Naked and Alone and Unwary You Caught
  Me. Franco
No Coward Soul [Is Mine]. Brontë
Red Harlaw. *Fr.* The Antiquary. Scott
Some Notes on Courage. Ludvigson
Song of the Hammer. Guiducci
Strong Men, Riding Horses. Brooks
Who would true valour see. *Fr.* The
  Pilgrim's Progress. Bunyan
You Are the Brave. Patterson

Coureurs de Bois
Coureurs de Bois. Le Pan

Courtiers
Epitaph: "Here lies Sir Tact, a diplomatic
  fellow." Steele
Skelton Laureate, Defender, against Lusty
  Garnesche, Well-beseen Christopher,
  Challenger. Skelton
Toad-Eater, The. Burns

Courtship
Advice, The. Sackville
Advice to the Ladies of London in the Choice
  of Their Husbands. *Unknown*
Arise, Arise. *Unknown*
Bailiff's Daughter of Islington, The.
  Unknown
Ballad of the Oysterman, The. Holmes
Billy Boy. *Unknown*
Call, The. Hall
Cap and Bells, The. Yeats
Carentan O Carentan. Simpson
Change, The. *Fr.* The Mistress. Cowley
Corinna's Going a-Maying. Herrick
Courtship, The. Lyon
Courtship. Strand
Courtship of the Yonghy-Bonghy-Bo, The.
  Lear
Drumming and dancing in the gulley.
  Unknown
Duncan Gray ("Duncan Gray cam here to
  woo"). Burns
Fifteen Boys, or Perhaps Even More.
  Akhmadulina
Frog He Would A-Wooing Go, A. *Unknown*
Grandma's Advice. *Unknown*
He waited for me at the gate-screen, heigh-ho!
  Unknown
I am going to gather the dodder. *Unknown*
I Am No Subject unto Fate. *Unknown*
I beg of you, Chung Tzu. *Unknown*
In the ten-acre field. *Unknown*
Indian Macho. Oliver
It Was a Lover and His Lass. *Fr.* As You
  Like It. Shakespeare
I've won Yasumiko! *Fr.* Manyo Shu.
  Kamatari
Lord Thomas and Fair Annet. *Unknown*
Love in Brooklyn. Wakeman
Love Serviceable. *Fr.* The Angel in the
  House. Patmore
Luck. Shute
Madame, withouten Many Wordes. Wyatt
Marriage. Corso
My Man John. *Unknown*
Nymph's Reply to the Shepherd, The.
  Ralegh
Oh, See How Thick the Goldcup Flowers.
  Fr. A Shropshire Lad. Housman
Oranges. Soto
Out in the bushlands a creeper grows.
  Unknown

Passionate Shepherd to His Love, The.
  Marlowe
Pleasant New Court Song, A. *Unknown*
Plop fall the plums; but there are still seven.
  Unknown
Plum Tree Drops Its Fruit, The. *Unknown*
Polly Perkins. *Unknown*
Pride of Kildare, The. *Unknown*
Quoth John to Joan. *Unknown*
Roger and Dolly. Carey
Sagimusume: The White Heron Maiden.
  Sullivan
Serenade at the Villa, A. Browning
She threw a quince to me. *Unknown*
So often, lady, I have asked you. Raimbaut
  de Vaqueiras
Some One. De la Mare
Song, A: "Fair, sweet and young, receive a
  prize." Dryden
Song: "Love still has something of the sea."
  Sedley
Songs Exchanged between Prince Okuninushi
  and Princess Nunakawa ("The divine prince
  of eight thousand spears/ great ruler of our
  land"). *Fr.* The Kojiki. *Unknown*
Subaltern's Love-Song, A. Betjeman
Think'st Thou to Seduce Me Then. Campion
This crab—where does it come from? *Fr.*
  Manyo Shu. Ojin
Three Knights from Spain. *Unknown*
Time I've Lost in Wooing, The. Moore
To His Mistris Confined. Shirley
Under a hedge the other day. Marcabrun
Vampire's Love Song, The. Keyes
Vampyre, The. Maxwell
What She Said to Her Girl Friend ("O you,
  you wear flowers of gold"). Kapilar
When a King Asks for a Chieftain's Daughter.
  Maturai Marutan Ilanakanar
When I see the meadows greening. *Unknown*
When the Chen and Wei. *Unknown*
Whistle, and I'll Come to Ye My Lad.
  Burns
With you first shown to me. Barnes
Wooing Rogue, The. *Unknown*
See also **Bundling.**

Cousins
My Cousin Agueda [*or* Agatha] López
  Velarde

Coventry, England
I Remember, I Remember. Larkin

Cowboys
As I Walked Out in the Streets of Laredo.
  Unknown
Bear Ropin' Buckaroo. Barker
Bronco Busting, Event #1. Swenson
Bucking Bronco. *Unknown*
Buffalo Skinners, The. *Unknown*
Closing of the Rodeo, The. Smith
Cowboy, The. Antrobus
Cowboy Song. Causley
Cowboy's Christmas Ball, The. Chittendon
Cowboy's Favorite. Nelson
Cowboy's Life, The. Adams
Cowboy's Life Is a Very Dreary Life, The.
  Unknown
Cowboy's Prayer, A. Clark
Cowboy's Prayer, The. Fletcher
Cowboy's Soliloquy, The. McCanless
Cowboy's Toast. Gibford
Cows and Logs. Otto
Dude Wrangler, The. Gardner
Dudes. Johnson
Dying Times, The. Knox
Easy Chairs and Saddle Sores. Knox
El Vaquero. Foote
Git Along Little Dogies. *Unknown*
Gol-Darned Wheel, The. *Unknown*
Greasin' the Miles. Johnson
High-loping Cowboy, The. Fletcher
I Am a Cowboy in the Boat of Ra. Reed
I Ride an Old Paint. *Unknown*

I'm an Old Cowhand. Mercer
I've Got No Use for the Women. *Unknown*
Jack Potter's Courtin'. Barker
Murph and McClop. *Unknown*
New-Chum's First Trip, The. *Unknown*
Old Chisholm Trail, The. *Unknown*
Old Cowman, The. Gibford
Peeler's Lament, The. *Unknown*
Poor Lonesome Cowboy. *Unknown*
Rain on the Range. Barker
Red Whiskey. *Unknown*
Saddle Tramp. Wilkerson
Sierry Petes, The. Gardner
Tenderfoot, The. O'Malley
Texas Cowboy, The. *Unknown*
To Be a Top Hand. Sicking
Vaquero. Dorn
Vaquero. Miller
Way of Speaking, A. Ehrlich
When the Work's All Done This Fall.
  Unknown
Wild Rippling Water, The. *Unknown*
Windy Bill. *Unknown*
Zebra Dun, The. *Unknown*
Cowboy Poetry; a Gathering (CowP). Hal
  Cannon, ed.

Cowper, William
Homage to William Cowper. Davie

Cows
Ah, Yes, I Wrote the "Purple Cow."
  Burgess
Being Herded Past the Prison's Honor Farm.
  Wagoner
Blurry Cow. Twichell
Canadian Herd-Boy, The. Moodie
Cow. McFatter
Cow, The. Nash
Cow, The. O'Dowd
Cow, The. Prelutsky
Cow, The. Roethke
Cow, The. Stevenson
Cow, The. Taylor
Cow, The. *Unknown*
Cow-Boy's Song, The. Wells
Cow Dance. Beaver
Cow in Apple Time, The. Frost
Cow of Our Time, A. Disch
Cow Pissing. Morgan
Cowherd, The. Yabu Kozan
Cows. Reeves
Cows and Logs. Otto
Cows at Night, The. Carruth
Cows near the Graveyard, The. Nelson
Discreet. Flook
Fable of the Speckled Cow. Opperman
Fetching Cows. MacCaig
Four stiff-standers. *Unknown*
Haiku: "Udders dripping." Iida Dakotsu
Herd, The. Cornford
How fleet is air! how many things have
  breath. *Fr.* Mully of Mountown. King
How Many Cows? Henderson
Man and Cows. Young
Midsummer. Scully
Milk-white Moon, Put the Cows to Sleep.
  Sandburg
Milking Time. Roberts
Moo! Hillyer
Moo-Cow-Moo, The. Cooke
Purple Cow, The. Burgess
Range Cow in Winter. Mortensen
Red Cow Is Dead, The. White
Rose and Cushie. Turner
Silver Coin, The. Reeves
Sometime the Cow Kick Your Head. Grossman
To a Sacred Cow. *Unknown*
Trees and Cattle. Dickey
See also **Cattle.**

Coyote (mythological)
Agnes. Tohee
Coyote, Coyote, Please Tell Me. Blue Cloud
Saint Coyote. Hogan

Sweat Song. Blue Cloud
Toe'osh; a Laguna Coyote Story. Silko
Coyotes
Coyote. Harte
Sweat Song. Blue Cloud
Toe'osh; a Laguna Coyote Story. Silko
Crab Apple Trees
Crab Tree, The. Gogarty
Crabbe, George
George Crabbe. Robinson
Crabs
Dead Crab, The. Young
Crabs and Crabbing
Pea crab crawls up my leg, A. *Fr.*
Seventy-six Hokku. Basho
Crab. Adcock
Crab. Dodat
Crabbing. Levine
Crustaceans. Fuller
Dead Crab, The. Young
In the Bay of Naniwa. *Fr.* Manyo Shu.
Unknown
In the wave-bright Naniwa Bay. *Fr.* Manyo
Shu. *Unknown*
Landcrab. Atwood
Lobsters and the Fiddler Crab, The ("The
lobsters came ashore one night"). Forster
With the Shell of a Hermit Crab. Wright
Cracow. *See* **Krakow, Poland.**
Cradle Songs. *See* **Cradle Song** *and* **Lullaby**
in **Title and First Line Index.**
Craftsmanship
Correct Compassion, A. Kirkup
Craftsmen. Sackville-West
Crane, Hart
Fish Food. Wheelwright
Hart Crane. Symons
Homage to Hart Crane. Balakian
Portrait of the Artist with Hart Crane.
Wright
Words for Hart Crane. Lowell
Cranes (birds)
Crane. Kaoru
Crane. Langland
Cranes, The. Po Chü-i
From the broad sea plain. Fushimi
On New Year's dawn. Kikaku
Pet Crane, A. *Unknown*
Song of the Wild Crane: Presented to a
Friend, A. Singde
Cranmer, Thomas
Admire Cranmer! Smith
Cranmer. Sisson
Crashaw, Richard
On the Death of Mr. Crashaw. Cowley
Crazy Horse (Indian Chief)
Crazy Horse Returns to South Dakota.
Elliott
Report to Crazy Horse. Stafford
Sound from the Earth, A. Stafford
Creation
Almighty Maker God! *Fr.* Sincere Praise.
Watts
Beginning and an End, A. Roditi
Beginnings. *Fr.* The Popol Vuh. *Unknown*
Book of How, The. Moore
Caedmon's Hymn. Caedmon
Canticle of Created Things. Francis of Assisi
Chant Out of Doors, A. Wilkinson
Chant to Io. Paraone
Creation, The. *Fr.* Davideis. Cowley
Creation. Fordham
Creation, The. Johnson
Creation. Nicholl
Eve. Flores
Father, thy hand/ Hath reared. *Fr.* A Forest
Hymn. Bryant
Fisherman, The. Macpherson
Genesis. Glatstein
God of the Granite and the Rose! *Fr.*
Reconciliation. Doten

In the beginning God created the heaven and
the earth. *Fr.* Genesis.
Lamentations. Glück
Ode: "Spacious firmament on high, The."
Addison
Old Creation Chant. *Unknown*
Origin of the Skagit Indians, The. Williams
Pulley, The. Herbert
Stately Structure of This Earth, The.
Brewster
These are thy glorious works, Parent of good.
Fr. Paradise Lost. Milton
Thou Art, O God. Moore
Tiger [*or* Tyger], The. *Fr.* Songs of
Experience. Blake
Up from the Bed of the River. *Fr.* The
Creation. Johnson
Whilst I beheld the neck o' th' dove. Cary
Wonderful World, The. Rands
See also **Cosmology.**
Creatures
Allie ("Allie, call the birds in"). Graves
End-of-Summer Poem. Bennett
Feather or Fur. Becker
Little Black Bug. Brown
Little Talk. Fisher
Little Things. Stephens
Mystical Beast in the Shadows, The.
Eberhart
Near Dusk. Auslander
Only My Opinion. Shannon
See also **Animals.**
Creçy, Battle of (1346)
Creçy. Palgrave
Credit. *See* **Installment Buying.**
Cremation
Crematorium, The. Grigson
Fire Burial. McInnis
Crete
Cemetery of Orange Trees in Crete, The.
Stern
Paranoia in Crete. Corso
Crew
Eight Oars and a Coxswain ("Eight oars
compel"). Guiterman
Crew Racing
Boat Race, The. *Fr.* The Aeneid [*or*
Eneados]. Virgil
Crew Cut. McCord
Eight Oars and a Coxswain ("Eight oars
compel"). Guiterman
Racing Eight, A. Cuthbertson
Cricket (game)
At Lord's. Thompson
Brahma. Lang
Extra Inch, The. Sassoon
Game of Cricket, The. Belloc
How McDougal Topped the Score. Spencer
I ran for a catch. Kernahan
When the returning sun begins to smile. *Fr.*
Cricket; an Heroic Poem. Dance
Crickets
Passing shower, A. *Fr.* Manyo Shu.
Unknown
Rainy night, A. *Fr.* Twenty-three Tanka.
Tamekane
As autumn wears on. Tamenori
Black Jewel, The. Merwin
But I Wonder. Fisher
Cricket, The. Bourne
Cricket. Kagura
Cricket, The. Tuckerman
Cricket Kept the House, The. Thomas
Cricket sings on Twelfth-night, The.
Gorbanevskaya
Crickets. McCord
Crickets. Rigsbee
Crickets. Saroyan
Crickets. Worth

Crickets—/ as the cold of the night. *Fr.*
Sixty-four Tanka. Saigyo
Crickets chirp at my bedside, The. *Fr.*
Manyo Shu. *Unknown*
Cruel: under a helmet, a cricket. *Fr.*
Seventy-six Hokku. Basho
Evening moon shines, The. *Fr.* Manyo Shu.
Yuhara
Haiku: "Cricket singing, A." *Fr.* Thirty-nine
Haiku. Shiki
Haiku: "Crickets/ in the corner of the garden."
Fr. Thirty-nine Haiku. Shiki
Haiku: "noisy cricket, The." Watanabe Suiha
In the garden where no one comes. *Fr.*
Seventy-eight Tanka. Shikishi
On Hearing a Cricket in the Boat. Sung Wan
On the Grasshopper and [the] Cricket. Keats
Out in the garden. Tamekane
Poems to a Brown Cricket. Wright
Seeking in my hut. Issa
Song of the Cricket. Lo Fu
Splinter. Sandburg
Spring Cricket. Rodman
Thinker, The. Delius
To a Cricket. Bennett
To the Grasshopper and the Cricket. Hunt
Winter Cricket. Heath-Stubbs
Crime and Criminals
At the Executed Murderer's Grave. Wright
Boston Burglar, The. *Unknown*
Burglar of Babylon, The. Bishop
Bushrangers, The. Harrington
Capture of Edwin Alonzo Boyd, The. Miller
Claude Allen. *Unknown*
Cole Younger. *Unknown*
Crafty Farmer, The. *Unknown*
Death of Ben Hall, The. Ogilvie
Dopefiends Trip. Angulo
Dude Wrangler, The. Gardner
Effort at Speech. Meredith
Father and Son. Ignatow
Flyin' Outlaw, The. Fletcher
Frank James, the Roving Gambler. *Unknown*
Frankie Silvers. Silvers
Gentle Alice Brown. Gilbert
Geordie. *Unknown*
Gilderoy. *Unknown*
He Fell among Thieves. Newbolt
Highwayman, The. Noyes
Hustler, The. *Unknown*
I know some lonely houses off the road.
Dickinson
In the Servants' Quarters. Hardy
Johnie Armstrong. *Unknown*
Johnson-Jinkson. *Unknown*
Las' Rights. Meeks
Lizzie and Joe Catch a Thief. Cordle
Marrying the Hangman. Atwood
Mary Arnold the Female Monster. *Unknown*
Morgan. Harrington
Musgrove. *Unknown*
Ned Christie. Conley
Newgate's Garland. Gay
Peddler and His Wife, The. *Unknown*
Quaker's Meeting, The. Lover
Queen of Hearts, The. Mother Goose
Results of Stealing a Pin, The. *Unknown*
Sam Bass. *Unknown*
Sam Hall. *Unknown*
Shining Night or Dick Daring, the Poacher,
A. *Unknown*
Shooting of Dan McGrew, The. Service
Shooting of John Dillinger outside the
Biograph Theater July 22, 1934, The.
Wagoner
Silver Bells and Golden Spurs. *Unknown*
Since Then. Enright
Streets of Forbes, The. *Unknown*
Taffy was a Welshman, Taffy was a thief.
Mother Goose
Thief's Niece, The. Keithley
Tom Starr. Conley

Tonite I walked out of my red apartment door
on East tenth street's dusk. *Fr.* Mugging.
Ginsberg
Twenty-one Years. *Unknown*
Visited by Thieves. Ryokan
Wild Colonial Boy, The. *Unknown*
See also **Prisons and Prisoners.**

Crimean War
Balaclava. *Unknown*
Charge of the Light Brigade, The. Tennyson
Due of the Dead, The. Thackeray
Song of the Camp, The. Taylor
Sonnet on the Crimean War. Forster

Cripples
Cowboy-Boot Sale. Colvin
Crip. Kirk
Cripple in Sight. Crosson
Cripples. Cassian
Disabled. Owen
Earthquake Somewhere Else, An. Finch
Enid Field: In Memoriam. Maxson
Faithless Nelly Gray. Hood
Mrs. McGrath. *Unknown*
On Forgetting to Cry. Colvin
Questions. Sumrall
Stumpfoot on 42nd Street. Simpson
See also **Handicaps and the Handicapped.**

Criticism and Critics
And now, kind friends, what I have wrote.
Moore
Ballad: "Hundred ballads I have written, A."
Pisan
Behold! in various throngs the scribbling
crew. *Fr.* English Bards and Scotch
Reviewers. Byron
Black Poet, White Critic. Randall
Character of a Critic. *Fr.* The Rosciad.
Churchill
Choice of Weapons, A. Kunitz
Critic, A. Landor
Critic on the Hearth, The. Sissman
Critics, The. Spencer
Eminent Critic. Nims
Essay on Criticism, An. Pope
Hendecasyllabics. Tennyson
Hobbes clearly proves that every creature.
Fr. On Poetry; a Rhapsody. Swift
Lines to a Don. Belloc
Modern Critics. Coleridge
My tune is of troubadours who sing variously.
Peire d'Alvernhe
Narcissus and Some Tadpoles. Daley
Now Muse assist me, aptly to describe. *Fr.*
Dunciad Minor. Hope
On Certain Wits. Nemerov
On Dennis. Pope
On First Looking in on Blodgett's *Keats's
"Chapman's Homer."* Starbuck
Owl-Critic, The. Fields
Pipling. Roethke
Poems by Women. Maraini
Poet and Critic. *Fr.* Musophilus; or, Defence
of All Learning. Daniel
Poet's Fate, The. Hood
Popular. Tennyson
Saturday Review, The. Greenwell
Since Peter of Auvergne once sang.
Montaudon
To a Captious Critic. Dunbar
To a Reviewer Who Admired My Book.
Ciardi
To Certain Critics. Cullen
To Christopher North. Tennyson
To Critics. Herrick
To My Least Favorite Reviewer. Nemerov
Valentine. Hemingway

Crockett, Samuel Rutherford
To S. R. Crockett. *Fr.* Songs of Travel.
Stevenson

Crocodiles
Amphibious Crocodile. Ransom

Crocodile, A. *Fr.* The Last Man. Beddoes
Don't Ever Cross a Crocodile. Starbird
How doth the little crocodile. *Fr.* Alice's
Adventures in Wonderland. "Carroll"
If you should meet a crocodile. *Unknown*
Monkeys and the Crocodile, The. Richards
My Dream. Rossetti
On the Crocodile. Heyrick
Purist, The. Nash
See also **Alligators.**

Crocuses
Crocus, The. Crane
Crocuses, The. Harper
Crocuses. Platt

Cromwell, Oliver
Heroique Stanzas, Consecrated to the Glorious
Memory of His Most Serene and Renowned
Highnesse, Oliver, Late Lord Protector of
This Common-Wealth. Dryden
Horatian Ode upon Cromwell's Return from
Ireland, An. Marvell
On the Late Metamorphosis of an Old Picture
of Oliver Cromwell's. *Unknown*
Three Troopers, The. Thornbury
To the Lord General Cromwell. Milton
While with a strong and yet a gentle hand.
Fr. A Panegyric[k] to My Lord Protector.
Waller

Croquet
Soap Suds. MacNeice

Cross, The
Celtic Cross, The. Magee
Cross, The. Pace
Dream of the Rood, A. Cynewulf
Dream of the Rood, The. *Unknown*
Holy Cross. Leslie
Making of the Cross, The. Everson
To See the Cross at Christmas. Cooper
Trees on a Frosty Night. O Direain
With Mercy for the Greedy. Sexton
See also **Crucifixion, The.**

Crowds
At the Ball Game. Williams
Center of Attention, The. Hoffman
Crowds. Schonborg
I Am the People, the Mob. Sandburg
Vox Populi. *Fr.* The Medal [*or* Medall].
Dryden

Crowns
Coronet, The. Marvell
La Corona. Donne

Crows
Crow that feeds on the rice, A. *Fr.* Manyo
Shu. Takamiya
Crow wipes its beak on young grass, A. *Fr.*
Twenty-one Hokku. Boncho
Laconic crow flies by, A. *Fr.* Forty-four
Hokku. Issa
Carrion crow sat upon an oak, The. Mother
Goose
Caw Caw the Crows Caw Caw. *Unknown*
Composition in Black and White. Pollitt
Crow, The. Creeley
Crow, The. Hoban
Crow. Rosen
Crow, crow, get out of my sight. *Unknown*
Crow in the night, A. Kogon
Crow on the fence. *Unknown*
Crow Resting. Pygge
Crows. McCord
Crows. Piercy
Crows. Simic
Crows. Witherup
Crows in Spring. Clare
Fox and the Crow, The. La Fontaine
Frog and the Crow, The. *Unknown*
Haiku: "Crow wordlessly flew away, A."
Fr. One Hundred Haiku in Free Form.
Hosai
He Asked Them What Did They Know &
They Told Him. *Unknown*

Hoggie dead, A! a hoggie dead! a hoggie
dead! *Unknown*
Hooded Crow, The. McOwan
Hungry Crow, The. Ch'en Wei-sung
In Air. Clarke
Love Poem, A: "That widowed crow."
Kogon
Lucky and Unlucky. Matthews
My Sister Jane. Hughes
Night Crow. Roethke
Night crow calls as if to tell of dawn, The.
Fr. Manyo Shu. *Unknown*
Preparations. Silko
Rooks, The. Browne
Rooks. Sorley
Song of Crows Gleaning the Grain, A. Cha
Shen-hsing
To a Crow. Wilson
To Be or Not to Be. *Unknown*
Twa Corbies, The. *Unknown*
Two More about a Crow, in the Manner of
Zukofsky. *Unknown*
Two Old Crows. Lindsay
What the Weather Does. *Unknown*

Crucifixion, The
At Gesthemane. Kim Chun-soo
Ballad of Trees and the Master, A. Lanier
Calvary. De Brun
Calvary. Robinson
Calvary. Stopple
Crucifixion, The. Fordham
Crucifixion, The. *Unknown*
Crucifying. Donne
Crucifying. *Fr.* La Corona. Donne
Death and Resurrection. Thompson
Dream of the Rood, The. *Unknown*
Early Lynching. Sandburg
Easter. Sisson
Fill High the Bowl. Keble
Garden, The. Beaumont
Good Friday. Brown
Good Friday. Nims
Good Friday. Rossetti
Good Friday [*or* Goodfriday], 1613. Riding
Westward. Donne
Guard of the Sepulcher, A. Markham
Hill, The. Holley
His Are the Thousand Sparkling Rills.
Alexander
His Saviour's Words, Going to the Cross.
Herrick
Hours of the Passion, The. *Unknown*
I should have been too glad, I see.
Dickinson
In the Deep Museum. Sexton
Indifference. Studdert-Kennedy
Leaves of Life, The. *Unknown*
Look on Him Whom They Pierced, and
Mourn. Watts
My God, My God, Look upon Me. *Fr.* The
Psalm of Christ. Walsh
Now Goeth [*or* goth *or* goothe] Sun [*or*
Sunne] under Wood. *Unknown*
On Our Crucified Lord, Naked and Bloody.
Crashaw
Our Saviour's Love. *Unknown*
Passion, The. Knevet
Passion of Jesus, The. *Unknown*
Robin Redbreast. Doane
Seven Virgins, The. *Unknown*
Shield of Achilles, The. Auden
Simon the Cyrenian Speaks. Cullen
Soldiers Bathing. Prince
Sometime during eternity. Ferlinghetti
Sonnet: To Crucify the Son. Miguel de
Guevara
Still Falls the Rain. Sitwell
That Day. Leax
There Is a Green Hill Far Away. Alexander
There Is None to Help. *Fr.* The Psalm of
Christ. Walsh
Thief, The. *Unknown*

Thou Who Createdst Everything. *Unknown*
To the Good Thief. Lewis
Tree. Artaud
Trees on a Frosty Night. O Direain
Uranne. Fordham
Were You There When They Crucified My
  Lord? *Unknown*
When I Survey the Wondrous Cross. Watts
York Play of the Crucifixion, The. *Unknown*
Zone of Death. Everson
See also **Cross, The.**

Cruelty
Cheers, Cheers for Old Cha Cha Ass
  ("Cheers, cheers for old Patchogue High").
  Borawski
Secret of Poetry, The. Anderson

Cruelty to Animals
Bells of Heaven, The. Hodgson
Blinded Bird, The. Hardy
Epigram: "Thy nags (the leanest things
  alive)." Prior
Formal Application. Baker
Gallows, The. Thomas
Nymph Complaining for the Death of Her
  Fawn, The. Marvell
Seven Mexican Children. Schmidt
Snare, The. Stephens
S.P.C.A. Sermon. Hemsley
Thoughts on Capital Punishment. McKuen
To a Little Boy, Who Had Destroyed a Nest
  of Young Birds. *Unknown*

Crum, William
Crum Appointment, The. Moorer

Crusades
Lament for the Sailing of the Crusade.
  D'Aquino
Lepanto. Chesterton

Crusoe, Robinson. *See* **Robinson Crusoe.**

Crystals
Crystals like Blood. "MacDiarmid"

Cuauhtémoc
Space is azure and the mountains bathe. *Fr.*
  Prophecy of Cuauhtémoc. Galván

Cuba
Cuba. MacDermot
Farewell to Cuba. Brooks
I Live in Cuba. Casal
Maceo. Lloréns Torres
On a Monument to Martí. Roberts
On Leaving Cuba, Her Native Land. Gomez
  de Avellaneda
Our Home. Carew

Cuchulain (Irish legendary hero)
Cuchulain Comforted. Yeats
Death of Cuchulain, The. Yeats

Cuckoldry and Cuckolds
Bold *Princess Royal. Unknown*
Captain Glen's Unhappy Voyage to New
  Barbary. *Unknown*
New Song, Called the Frolicsome Sea
  Captain; or, Tit for Tat, A. *Unknown*
Silly Old Man, The. *Unknown*
When Daisies Pied [and Violets Blue]. *Fr.*
  Love's Labour's Lost. Shakespeare
See also **Adultery.**

Cuckoos
As the seasons change. *Fr.* Manyo Shu.
  Yakamochi
Blue Cuckoo. *Fr.* Hunter Poems of the
  Yoruba. *Unknown*
Bowman listens to a cuckoo, A. *Fr.*
  Twenty-one Hokku. Kaya Shirao
Come, then, cuckoo. *Unknown*
Cuckoo, The. Chalmers
Cuckoo, The. Hopkins
Cuckoo, The. Thomas
Cuckoo, The. *Unknown*
Cuckoo. Young
Cuckoo—/ I've yet to hear him. *Fr.*
  Sixty-four Tanka. Saigyo

Cuckoo,/ repeating his cry, The. *Fr.*
  Twenty-three Tanka. Tamekane
Cuckoo Clock, The. Stanton
Cuckoo, cuckoo/ What do you do? *Unknown*
Cuckoo: "In former days my father and
  mother." *Fr.* Riddles (Exeter Book).
  Cynewulf
Cuckoo sings/ at right angles, The. *Fr.*
  Twenty Hokku. Kyorai
Cuckoo Song. Ray
Cuckoo, what are you. *Fr.* Thirty Tanka.
  Shunzei
Cuckoos. Young
Cuckoo's voice lays itself over the water, A.
  Fr. Seventy-six Hokku. Basho
Did the cuckoo pity me in the sky. *Fr.*
  Seventy-eight Tanka. Shikishi
Gowk, The. Soutar
Great Time, A. Davies
Has it flown away. Shunzei
Hearing the Cuckoo on the Nineteenth Day of
  the Third Month. Huang Tsung-hsi
In the leafy tree-tops. *Fr.* Manyo Shu.
  Yakamochi
Ingratitude. Thynne
Koocoo, The. *Unknown*
Lament for the Cuckoo. Alcuin
Late Winter. McAuley
Lone cuckoo, A. *Fr.* Manyo Shu.
  Mushimaro
Nightingale, the organ of delight, The.
  Unknown
O cuckoo, you were born. *Fr.* Manyo Shu.
  Mushimaro
O distant cuckoo. Nagachika
Of the Cuckoo. Bunyan
Of Use. Heywood
On summer nights. *Fr.* Kokin Shu.
  Tsurayuki
Oocuck, The. Richardson
Pallid Cuckoo. Campbell
Riddle: Cuckoo. *Unknown*
Summer [*or* Summer] is icumen [*or* y-comen]
  in. *Unknown*
That cuckoo who sang. *Fr.* Kokin Shu.
  Unknown
Twilight cuckoo, The. *Fr.* Sixty-four Tanka.
  Saigyo
Theory, A. Simic
To the Cuckoo. Townsend
To the Cuckoo. Wordsworth
Well fare the nightingale. *Unknown*

Cucumbers
Cautionary Limerick. *Unknown*
How to Grow Cucumbers. *Fr.* The Task.
  Cowper

Cuernavaca, Mexico
View from the Gorge. Belitt

Cullen, Countee
Countee Cullen. Maleska

Culloden, Battle of (1746)
Lovely Lass o' Inverness, The. Burns
Old Scottish Cavalier, The. Aytoun

Culture
Breakfast for Barbarians, A. MacEwen
Footnote to Enright's "Apocalypse." Bell

Cumberland, Virginia
Cumberland Station. Smith

Cunningham, James Vincent
Terse Elegy for J.V. Cunningham. Kennedy

Cunningham, Merce
Merce Cunningham and the Birds. Mueller
Merce of Egypt. Olson

Cupboards
Cupboard, The. De la Mare

Cupid
Abdelazer, *sel.* Behn
Aeliana's Ditty. *Fr.* Piers Plainness' Seven
  Years' Prenticeship. Chettle
Cupid. *Unknown*
Cupid and my Campaspe played. *Fr.*
  Alexander and Campaspe. Lyly

Cupid Far Gone. Lovelace
Cupid in a Bed of Roses. *Unknown*
Cupid the Ploughboy. *Unknown*
Cupid, thou naughty boy, when thou wert
  loathed. *Fr.* Caelica. Greville
Cupid's Indictment. *Fr.* Galathea. Lyly
Damon and Cupid. Gay
Eros. Bridges
Eros Possessed. Roche
Farewell, sweet boy; complain not of my
  truth. *Fr.* Caelica. Greville
Love in fantastic [*or* fantastique] triumph sate
  [*or* satt] *Fr.* Abdelazer. Behn
Love Sleeping. Plato
Metamorphosis, The. Suckling
O Cupid! Monarch over Kings. *Fr.* Mother
  Bombie. Lyly
O Gentle Love. *Fr.* The Arraignment of
  Paris. Peele
Shoot, false Love, I care not. *Unknown*
Song: "Fool, take up thy shaft again."
  Stanley
To Cupid. Drayton
To the God of Love. Knox
Wounded Cupid, The. Herrick

Curfew
Curfew Must Not Ring Tonight. Thorpe

Curie, Marie
Power. Rich

Curiosity
Curiosity. Reid

Curses
Bagman O'Reilly's Curse. Murray
Cenci's Curse upon His Daughter, The. *Fr.*
  The Cenci. Shelley
Curse, The. Donne
Curse, A. Feldman
Curse. Greacen
Curse, The. Synge
Curse, A. *Unknown*
Curse against the Owner, A. Sutter
Curse for a Nation, A. Browning
Glass of Beer, A. Stephens
Goblin Market. Rossetti
I curse my bearing, childhood, youth. Synge
Nell Flaherty's Drake. *Unknown*
Odell. Stephens
On a Cock at Rochester. Sedley
On Judas Iscariot. Quarles
Rime of the Ancient Mariner, The.
  Coleridge
Sam Hall. *Unknown*
Skin the Goat's Curse on Carey. *Unknown*
Song of the Witches. *Fr.* Macbeth: Thrice
  the Brinded Cat Hath Mewed.
  Shakespeare
Timon Curses Athens and Mankind. *Fr.*
  Timon of Athens. Shakespeare
Travel[l]er's Curse after Misdirection, The.
  Graves
Widow's Curse, The. *Unknown*

Custer, George Armstrong
Custer. Stedman
Custer's Last Charge. Whittaker
General Custer. McKenty
Revenge of Rain-in-the-Face, The.
  Longfellow

Cyclamen
Cyclamen, The. Bates
Cyclamens. "Field"
Sicilian Cyclamens. Lawrence

Cyclops
And so an easier life our Cyclops drew. *Fr.*
  Idylls. Theocritus
Cave we found, but vacant all within, The.
  Fr. Odyssey. Homer
More whyght thou art than primrose leaf my
  Lady Galatee. *Fr.* Metamorphoses. Ovid

Cymon
Cymon and Iphigenia. Dryden

Cynicism
As a Plane Tree by the Water. Lowell

Cynic, The. Tucker
Unfortunate Coincidence. Parker
Cypress Trees
Cypress. Mayröcker
Cypresses, The. Anderson
Cypresses. Francis
Cypresses. Lawrence
Cyprus
Home of Aphrodite, The. *Fr*. Bacchae.
Euripides
Paphos. Durrell
Czechoslovakia
Geography Lesson. Rumens
My Return to Czechoslovakia. Edmond

D

Da Vinci, Leonardo. *See* **Leonardo da
Vinci.**
Dachshunds
Geist's Grave. Arnold
Daedalus
Be Daedalus. Alba
Now in this while gan Daedalus a wearinesse
to take. *Fr*. Metamorphoses. Ovid
Daffodils
Daffodil. Williams
Daffodils. Heffernan
Daffodils. Reese
Daffodils. Ropes
Daffodil's Return. Carman
I Wandered Lonely as a Cloud. Wordsworth
On a Daffodil, the First Flower the Author
Had Seen That Year. Johnson
To Daffodils [*or* Daffadills] Herrick
Daggers
Address to My Malay Krees. Leyden
Dahlias
Dahlias. Colum
Daisies
Buttercups and Daisies. Howitt
Daisies, The. Carman
Daisies. Nowlan
Daisies. Worth
Daisy, The. Tennyson
Daisy. Williams
Daisy, The. Zaturenska
Daisy's Song. Keats
There is a flower, a little flower. *Fr*. The
Daisy. Montgomery
To a Child. Wordsworth
To a Daisy. Meynell
To Daisies, Not to Shut So Soon[e]. Herrick
Dalai Lama
Address to the Dalai Lama. Artaud
Dali, Salvador
Surreal Appetite. McWhirter
Damascus, Syria
Gates of Damascus. Flecker
Damien, Father
Father Damien. Tabb
Molokai. Tranströmer
Pagan Woman. Vallejo
Damnation and the Damned
"Go Bring Me," Said the Dying Fair. Hunter
Ubi Sunt Qui ante Nos Fuerunt? *Unknown*
Damocles
Damocles. Graves
Dams
Big Dam. Moses
Boulder Dam. Sarton
Fish Counter at Bonneville, The. Stafford
Dancing and Dancers
African Dancer. Palés Matos
Almost Dancing. Simmerman
American Bandstand. Waters
Arthur Mitchell. Moore

Artist, The. Williams
At a Pause in a Country Dance. Hardy
At the Treatment Center. Sala
Attic Dance. Ritchings
Ballad of the Ten Casino Dancers. Meireles
Ballet Blanc. Pollitt
Ballroom Dancing Class. McGinley
Band Played On, The. Palmer
Belly Dancer. Wakoski
Best Slow Dancer, The. Wagoner
Boogie Chant and Dance. *Unknown*
Bottled [New York] Johnson
Castanets. Spencer
Cat or Stomp. Tohe
Catch. McKiernan
Celebration. Lopez
Celeste Dancing. Osgood
Circus Dancer, The. Dropkin
Cowboy's Dance Song, The. Adams
Dance, The. Gustafson
Dance. Weeden
Dance, The. Williams
Dance Calls. *Unknown*
Dance Instructions for a Young Girl. Hahn
Dance of the Abakweta. Danner
Dance of the Rain Gods. *Unknown*
Dance on Pushback. Still
Dance Poem. Giovanni
Dance Script with Electric Ballerina. Fulton
Dancer, The. Campbell
Dancer. Scheele
Dancers Exercising. Clampitt
Dancer's Life, A. Justice
Dancing. Yang Kuei-fei
Dancing on the Shore. Hutchinson
Dancing School. Holden
Dem Belly Full. Cogil
Dream Boogie. Hughes
Egyptian Dancer. Tiller
Egyptian Dancer at Shubra. Spencer
Fancy's Knell. Housman
Female Dancer. Camp
Fiddler of Dooney, The. Yeats
Golden Oldie. Mariani
Gratiana Dancing [*or* Dauncing] and Singing.
Lovelace
Harlem Dancer, The. McKay
Her Dancing Days. Adams
Heredity. Howells
Hipsaw! my deaa! you no do like a-me! *Fr*.
Dancing Songs. *Unknown*
I Danced to the Rumble of the Drum.
Burbank
Jimmie's got a goil. Cummings
Kearney Park. Soto
Lasses dance and tread the ground, The. *Fr*.
Manyo Shu. Hitomaro
Leaving the Dance. Whitaker
Lines Written for Gene Kelly to Dance To.
Sandburg
Little Dancers, The. Binyon
Lost Dancer, The. Toomer
Lyrics of the Bon Dance. *Unknown*
Man Dancing with a Baby. Stewart
Marmalade Man Makes a Dance to Mend Us,
The. Willard
Martha Graham. Laughlin
May Day Dancing, The. Nemerov
Merce Cunningham and the Birds. Mueller
Merce of Egypt. Olson
Minuet, The. Dodge
Mrs. Applebaum's Sunday Dance Class.
Schultz
Muse of the many-twinkling feet! whose
charms. *Fr*. The Waltz. Byron
My Papa's Waltz. Roethke
New Platform Dances, The. Mapanje
No Dead Ends. Quirk
Of Dancing. Brownjohn
On a Female Rope-Dancer. *Unknown*
On festal days; or when their work is done.
Fr. The Sugar Cane. Grainger

On Lydia Distracted. Ayres
Orchestra; or, A Poem of Dancing. Davies
Perdita. Coates
Poet to a Dancer, A. Auvaiyar
Powwow 79, Durango. Allen
Quick-Step. Creeley
Rumba. Tallet
Rural Dance about the Maypole, The.
Unknown
Seeing Her Dancing. Heath
Sole heir of virtue, and of beauty both. *Fr*.
Orchestra; or, A Poem[e] of Da[u]ncing.
Davies
Song from a Country Fair. Adams
Sonsito. Cruz
Susie Asado. Stein
Tarantella. Belloc
Things that dance well, exquisitely. *Fr*.
Ryojin Hisho. Go-Shirakawa
Truth Made Breakfast, The. Miller
Tullochgorum. Skinner
Variations on a Theme. Vinz
Watching the Dance. Merrill
We Dance Like Ella Riffs. Rodgers
Wheel, The. Berry
Window, The. Dobyns
Zalka Peetruza. Dandridge
Untune the Sky (UnS). Helen Plotz, ed.
See also **Ballet.**
Dandelions
Dandelion. Conkling
Dandelion: from time to time. *Fr*. Seventeen
Hokku. Chiyojo
Dandelion Puff, The. Robinson
Dandelions. Albee
Dandelions. *Fr*. Nature Notes. MacNeice
Dandelions, The. *Unknown*
Dandelions for Chains ("Dandelions meet me
wherever I am"). Kirsch
Gently, gently, the wind blows. Mizumura
Late Dandelions. Belitt
Little Dandelion, The. Weeden
O Dandelion. *Unknown*
Of Dandelions & Tourists. Rosenblatt
To the Dandelion. Lowell
Who tossed those golden coins. Mizumura
Kazue
Daniel
Handwriting on the Wall, The. Shaw
Dante Alighieri
At Dante's Grave. Zussman
Cradle Song: "Come here, little girl, come
here." Avidan
Dante. Michelangelo
Dante. Ray
Illustration to Dante, An. Adcock
On a Bust of Dante. Parsons
On the "Vita Nuova" of Dante. Rossetti
Saying Dante Aloud. Wright
Sleep, Leopard, Sleep. Avidan
Danube
It Doesn't Count. Vas
Saint Médard. Vas
Danziger, Isaac
Love Poem:
Extended Sonnet on the Death of Isaac
Danziger. Wieseltier
Daphne
Apollo and Daphne. Winters
Daphne. Carman
Daphne. Rodman
Daphne and Apollo. *Fr*. Metamorphoses.
Ovid
Story of Phoebus and Daphne Applied, etc.,
The. Waller
Dare, Virginia
Peregrine White and Virginia Dare. Benét
Darkness
Afraid. De la Mare
And Then Suddenly It's Dark. Quasimodo
Auld Daddy Darkness. Ferguson

Dark, The. Heyen
Darkness. Byron
Darkness. Cattafi
Flowers of Darkness. Davis
His Necessary Darkness. Sullivan
Hymn to Darkness. Norris
In the Dark. Gilboa
In the Hours of Darkness. Flexner
Migration of Darkness, The. Payack
Out in the Dark. Thomas
Out of the Darkness. Armstrong
Phases of Darkness, The. Petrie
Pleasures of Darkness, The. al-Najafi
Three Darks Come Down Together. Francis
Traveling through the Dark. Stafford
While I, with no guide. *Fr.* Ten Tanka.
    Myoe

Darling, Grace Horsley
Grace Darling. *Unknown*

Darwin, Charles
Darwin in 1881. Schnackenberg
Darwinity. Merivale
See also **Evolution.**

Dating
Backing into the Fan Mail (Unreceived).
    Gallup
Blake Mistake, The. Castle
Blind Date. Aiken
Story We Know, The. Collins

Daughters
After Reading *Mickey in the Night Kitchen* for
    the Third Time before Bed. Dove
Beauty of Job's Daughters, The.
    Macpherson
Bells for John Whiteside's Daughter.
    Ransom
Blessing, The. Kizer
Breeze Swept Through, A. Tapahonso
Clayfeld's Daughter Reveals Her Plans. Pack
Daughter, take this amulet. *Fr.* Poem to Her
    Daughter. Msham
Daughterly. Spivack
Daughters of Blum, The. Wright
Dear child, my daughter, who stood. *Fr.*
    Manyo Shu. Otomo no Sakanoe
Discovering My Daughter. Stuart
First Lesson. Booth
Fish Story. Olds
Flower Given to My Daughter, A. Joyce
For Alissa. Cooley
For My Daughter. Kazantzis
For My Daughter. Kees
I am proud of your soft, brown eyes. *Fr.*
    Sunlight: A Sequence for My Daughter.
    Ignatow
I Have Three Daughters. Stone
I see her in my sleep, my red, terrible girl.
    Fr. Three Women. Plath
I See My Girl. Olds
If I Should Ever by Chance. Thomas
Little Girl, My Stringbean, My Lovely
    Woman. Sexton
Little Sleep's-Head Sprouting Hair in the
    Moonlight. Kinnell
Louise on the Door-Step. MacKay
Making the Jam without You. Kumin
Mama and Daughter. Hughes
Marina. Eliot
Missing My Daughter. Spender
Month of June: 13½, The. Olds
More than the gems. *Fr.* Manyo Shu.
    Otomo no Sakanoe
Mothers, Daughters. Kaufman
Mountain, The. Kaufman
My Daughter. Jalib
My Daughter Considers Her Body. Skloot
My daughter must be past ten by now. *Fr.*
    Ryojin Hisho Go-Shirakawa
My infinite child, hold me to sleep. *Fr.*
    Sunlight: A Sequence for My Daughter.
    Ignatow

My mother wept loudly. *Fr.* Tiresias.
    Clarke
My Small Daughter. Huang Tsun-hsien
My Youngest Daughter Getting Up in the
    Morning. Davide
Old Song Resung, An. Graves
On a Nun. Vittorelli
On My First Daughter. Jonson
Only Daughter, The. *Unknown*
Pain for a Daughter. Sexton
Poem for Emily, A. Williams
Poet's Welcome to His Love-begotten
    Daughter, A. Burns
Prayer for My Daughter, A. Yeats
Putting My Daughter to Bed. Li Nan
Rachel. Pastan
Scenario. Reiss
Sent from the Capital to Her Elder Daughter.
    Otomo no Sakanoe
This Morning. Stallworthy
Thoughts about My Daughter before Sleep.
    Hochman
To a Daughter Leaving Home. Pastan
To a Daughter with Artistic Talent. Meinke
To an Infant Daughter. Clare
To My Daughters. Seymour-Smith
To My Infant Daughter. Winters
To Our Daughter. Armitage
Waiting for the Transformation. Minty
Writer, The. Wilbur
*Tangled Vines; A Collection of Mother and
    Daughter Poems* (TV). Lyn Lifshin, ed.

David
Abishag. Glatstein
Abishag. Spire
After Goliath. Amis
David and Goliath. Crouch
David and Goliath. Thompson
David and Jonathan. *Fr.* Davideis. Cowley
David's Lament for Jonathan. Abelard
Death of David, The. Bialik
Goliath and David. Untermeyer
Harp of David, The. Cohen
Harp of David, The. "Yehoash"
King David and King Solomon. Naylor
Like David. Preil
Malcontents, The. *Fr.* Absalom and
    Achitophel, Pt. I. Dryden
O thou, that sitst upon a throne. *Fr.* A Song
    to David. Smart
Song to David, A. Smart
That Harp You Play So Well. Moore
Translating. Whitman

Davidson, John
In Memoriam: John Davidson. Macfie

Davies, Dr. John
Upon Dr. Davies's British Grammar. Howell

Davies, Sir John
Four for Sir John Davies. Roethke

Davis, Angela
Angela Davis. Cobb

Davis, Miles
Miles' Delight ("Miles Davis"). Joans

Davis, Thomas Osborne
Lament for the Death of Thomas Davis.
    Ferguson

Davy, Sir Humphry
Sir Humphry Davy. *Fr.* Clerihews. Bentley

Dawn
Ah, When Will Dawn Begin to Break?
    Halkin
Alba. Walcott
All things have an end. Ietaka
At Dawn. Symons
Break of Day. Neilson
But Venus first. *Fr.* First Dream. Juana
    Inés de la Cruz
Cock-Crow. Thomas
Creatures of Early Morning. Lewis
Dawn. Betjeman
Dawn. Dunbar

Dawn. Ibarbourou
Dawn. Jaccottet
Dawn. Masefield
Dawn. Myles
Dawn. *Fr.* A Season in Hell. Rimbaud
Dawn. *Fr.* Thirty Tanka. Shunzei
Dawn. Stryk
Dawn, The. Tennyson
Dawn. Wilcox
Dawn. Williams
Dawn Blossoms. Eifuku
Dawn of Day. *Fr.* The Shepherd's Pipe.
    Browne
Dawn on the Lievre, The. Lampman
Dawn Walk. Hirsch
Dawncall. Osundare
Dawning. Dixon
Dawn's Carol. Ray
Dawns I Have Seen. Gurney
Daybreak. Longfellow
Daybreak/ On the corn shoots. Onitsura
Death at Daybreak. Aldrich
Deirdre's Song at Sunrise. Maura
Did it not signal. Tameuji
Early Morning, The. Belloc
Early News. Pratt
Earthsleep. Chappell
Edge of Day, The. Lee
First Light. Kinsella
Fourth Floor, Dawn, Up All Night Writing
    Letters. Ginsberg
Frosty Dawn. Rokunyo
Golden-Green Dawn, A. Chalfi
Hark! Hark! the Lark. *Fr.* Cymbeline.
    Shakespeare
Has dawn come so soon? Fushimi
I awoke from sleep. Ietaka
If anyone asks. Tameuji
If one must live in the world. Ryoshun
In dawn's first light. Chikako
In every household. Hanazono
In gold sandals. Sappho
In the broad dawn sky. Ietaka
In the light of dawn. Yoshimoto
Lark Now Leaves His Water [*or* Wat'ry]
    Nest. Davenant
Late Starting Dawn. Brautigan
Little Morning Music, A. Schwartz
Mad Song. Blake
Matins. Levertov
Miraculous Dawn. Parry
Moon in the garden. Tamekane
Moon on a Spring Dawn. Sanetaka
Morning on the St. John's. Cooper
Morning Prayer. Aua
Mountain Haze. Keiun
Mountain Vigil. Fraser
My mind is made up. Tamekane
Night Is Near [*or* Neir] Gone, The.
    Montgomerie
Now from the east. Masahongva
Oath. Sica
Outside my window. Chikako
Owl, The. Thomas
Phoebus, Arise. Drummond
Prayer at Dawn. Poteat
Prelude: "Night was dark, though sometimes a
    faint star, The." *Fr.* The New Day.
    Gilder
Revisit. Engels
Salutation of the Dawn, The. *Unknown*
So much more forlorn. Tamekane
Spring Dawn. Ietaka
Summer Dawn. Morris
Trumpet, The. Thomas
Up from the paddies. Tonna
Very Early. Kuskin
Vision, The. O'Rahilly
What had looked like fires. Ryoshun
When the new day dawns. Ietaka
With no lover's pledge. Ietaka

With the Dawn. Irwin
See also **Morning; Sunrise.**
Dawson, F. W.
Tribute to Capt. F. W. Dawson. Fordham
Day
Day. Mansour
Day and Night. Kvitko
Days. Emerson
Days. Larkin
Sun: Day, The. Schierbeek
Swell My Net Full. *Unknown*
This Day is Thine. Whinery
Wee Davie Daylicht. Tennant
Daydreams
Instruction Manual, The. Ashbery
Mixed Feelings. Ashbery
Remembering Snow. Csoori
Scrut Gets Marty Crowe for Social Studies.
Roberts
Song of Kuk-ook, the Bad Boy, The.
See also **Dreams and Dreaming.**
De Hooch, Pieter
Dutch Interior. Sarton
De la Mare, Walter
Walter de la Mare Tells the Listener about
Jack and Jill. *Fr.* Mother Goose
Up-to-Date. Untermeyer
De Soto, Hernando
Distant Runners, The. Van Doren
New Orleans. Harjo
De Spirito, Tony
Never Be As Fast As I Have Been. Hahn
Deafness
Covering All Bases. Thomas
Deaf. Bunner
Deaf. Higgs
Deaf-and-Dumb School. Delius
Deaf-Mute in the Pear Tree. Page
Deaf School. Hughes
Deafness. Ryan
How to Sign. Stroblas
Mutterings over the Crib of a Deaf Child.
Wright
On His Own Deafness. Swift
To a Deaf and Dumb Little Girl. Coleridge
Dean, James
For James Dean. O'Hara
Death
Vital spark of heavenly flame! Pope
Death and the Dead
Abide with Me. Lyte
Abyss of Death, The. al-Rasafi
Adieu, Farewell, Earth's Bliss[e] *Fr.*
Summer's Last Will and Testament.
Nashe
Afraid! Of whom am I afraid? Dickinson
African Dirge. Chapman
After a Death. Orr
After Death. Rossetti
After Death. Swinburne
After Death in Arabia. Arnold
After death nothing is, and nothing, death.
Fr. Troades. Seneca
After Grave Deliberation. Flynn
After Grief. Plumly
After his weary travels. *Fr.* Manyo Shu.
"Tsuki"
After Lorca. Creeley
After My Grandmother's Death. Roberts
After the Funeral. Thomas
Afternoon Gossip, An. Thompson
Afternoon Sun, The. Cavafy
Afterwards. Hardy
Again a Neighbor Died. *Fr.* Clouds behind
the Forest. Leivick
Age. Landor
Age of the Rubber Seals. al-Haidari
Ah me! How differently th'untutor'd slave.
Fr. A General Description of the West
Indian Islands. Singleton
Ala. Nichols

Alas, Death. Orléans
Alas! 'Tis Very Sad to Hear. Landor
Algonkian Burial. Bailey
All Being Well. Gibson
All the Dead Dears. Plath
All the Death-Room Needs. Hartnett
All the Hills and Vales Along. Sorley
All Things Decay and Die. Herrick
Along the Field as We Came By. *Fr.* A
Shropshire Lad. Housman
Along the path of Iware. *Fr.* Manyo Shu.
Yamakuma
Ambassador, The. Smith
America's Answer. Lilliard
Among Those Killed in the Dawn Raid Was a
Man Aged a Hundred. Thomas
Ancestor, The. Smith
And Again. Evans
And Death Shall Have No Dominion.
Thomas
And the Earth Rebelled. Suhl
And Then Suddenly It's Dark. Quasimodo
Andrée Rexroth. Rexroth
Angel of Death Is Always with Me, The.
Marcus
Angina Pectoris. Moses
Annabel Lee. Poe
Apparitions. Aldrich
Approaching Death. Otsu
Archer, The. Smith
Are there no gods of heaven and earth? *Fr.*
Manyo Shu. *Unknown*
Arrangements with Earth for Three Dead
Friends. Wright
As He Came near Death. Fisher
As I lay asleep in Italy. *Fr.* The Mask of
Anarchy. Shelley
As I Walked Out in the Streets of Laredo.
Unknown
As Long as You're Happy. Myers
As on a Darkling Plain. Taylor
As soone as wee to bee begvnne. *Unknown*
Asians Dying, The. Merwin
Asleep. Owen
At a Loss. Weil
At Daybreak. Sassoon
At Henry's bier let some thing fall out well.
Fr. Dream Songs. Berryman
At His Father's Grave. Ormond
At my side. Wakayama Bokusui
At the Bus Stop: Eurydice. Ferry
At the Ferry. Fanthorpe
At the Wailing Wall. Mathews
Aubade: "I work all day, and get half drunk at
night." Larkin
Aunt Jane. Nowlan
Autumn. De la Mare
Autumnus. Sylvester
Ave atque Vale. *Fr.* Sigismonda and
Guiscardo. Dryden
Any, but to die, and go we know not where.
Fr. Measure for Measure. Shakespeare
Bachelor Hall. Field
Ballad of Dead Yankees, The. Petersen
Ballad of John Cable and Three Gentlemen.
Merwin
Ballad of the Frozen Field, The. Stuart
Barbara. Smith
Barbie Doll. Piercy
Beauty was hers that glowed like autumn
mountains. *Fr.* Manyo Shu. Hitomaro
Because I am human and unable to be near a
god. *Fr.* Manyo Shu. *Unknown*
Because I could not stop for death.
Dickinson
Before a Corpse. Acuña
Before a Funeral. Edmond
Before Death. Quijada Urías
Before I Die. Váci
Before the Birth of One of Her Children.
Bradstreet

Before They Made Things Be Alive They
Spoke. Cuevish
Being Called For. Dobson
Belfast. Revell
Beside a Deathbed. Miller
Beside the Bed. Kavanagh
Beside the Bed. Mew
Bess. Stafford
Between Here and Illinois. Pomeroy
Between Love and Death. Stanford
Beyond. Johnson
Beyond. *Unknown*
Bid me remember, O my gracious Lord. *Fr.*
Death. Coleridge
Bird of Paradise, The. Davies
Birthday. Kavanagh
Birthday Visit. Kavanagh
Black Angel, The. Anghelaki-Rooke
Black Rose. "Zelda"
Black Sun, The. *Fr.* Four Songs. Gatsos
Blind Date. Aiken
Blue Sparks in Dark Closets. Snyder
Body Fished from the Seine. Corso
Book Ends. Harrison
Border, The. Muir
Born into the world. Tamesuke
Bourne, The. Rossetti
Boy and the Deer, The. Peynetsa
Boy Died in My Alley, The. Brooks
Boy Wandering in Simms' Valley. Warren
Brain, within its groove, The. Dickinson
Breath. Dickey
Bride, The. Lawrence
Bridge of Sighs, The. Hood
Broken Tower, The. Crane
Burial, A. Deane
Burial. Tuwhare
Burial. Walker
Burial Detail. Hudgins
Burial of Sir John Moore after Corunna, The.
Wolfe
Burn Out Burn Quick. Reisen
Burying. Herzberg
Bustle in a house, The. Dickinson
By St. Thomas Water. Causley
Call for the Robin Redbreast and the Wren.
Fr. The White Devil. Webster
Call Me Not Dead. Gilder
Cambridge Elegy. Olds
Candle, Lamp & Firefly. Gallagher
Casualty. Heaney
cause: "Brain is wider than the sky, The."
Dickinson
Cemetery in Pernambuco ("Nobody lies in this
earth"). Melo Neto
Cemetery Nights. Dobyns
Channel Firing. Hardy
Charon's Cosmology. Simic
Child-Bride, The. Oates
Child Dying, The. Muir
Child Explains Dying, A. Crum
Childhood Is the Kingdom Where Nobody
Dies. Millay
Children called, The. *Fr.* Ordeal by Fire.
Ya'oz-kest
Choice. al-Maqalih
Choosing a Death. Turner
Choosing to Think of It. Dunn
Christo's. Muldoon
Chronicle. Quijada Urías
City in the Sea *or* The Doomed City, The.
Poe
Cleaning the Fish. Pack
Clear the Way. Montague
Closing Piece. Rilke
Closing Prayer. Patrick
Closing the House. Miller
Clouds Are the First Fatalities, The.
Amichai
Clues to Displaced Persons. Jarman
Cold Green Element, The. Layton

Come Away, Come Away, Death. *Fr.*
  Twelfth Night. Shakespeare
Come Up from the Fields, Father. Whitman
Come, walk with me. Brontë
Coming and Going. Goodman
Complaint of the Grandparents. Justice
Complaint of the Oblivion of the Dead.
  Laforgue
Conception. Miles
Conqueror Worm, The. Poe
Conqueror Worm, The. Poe
Consumptive, The. Thompson
Contemplation of Our State in Our Deathbed.
  Fr. Of the Progresse of the Soule; the
  Second Anniversarie. Donne
Cool Tombs. Sandburg
Coronach. *Fr.* The Lady of the Lake. Scott
Corpse, The. Díaz Mirón
Corpse, The. Ruano
Corpse-bearing. Ashe
Cover Her Face. Kinsella
Cradle Song: "Come here, little girl, come
  here." Avidan
Created Clay. Brown
Créide's Lament for Dínertech. *Unknown*
Cripple, The. Khouri
Cross of Snow, The. Longfellow
Crossing the Bar. Tennyson
Crossing the Water. Plath
Dancing Partners. Child
Dareios. Cavafy
D'Avalos' Prayer. Masefield
David Hume, Dying, Talks to Boswell. Bold
Day concludes burning, The. *Fr.* The Dying
  Gaul. O'Grady
Day in, day out. *Fr.* Manyo Shu. Yosami
Dead, The. Blind
Dead, The. Dudek
Dead, The. *Fr.* Two Guitars. Maxson
Dead, The. Smith
Dead, The. Strand
Dead, The. Very
Dead are a cadmium blue, The. *Fr.* Homage
  to Paul Cézanne. Wright
Dead before Death. Rossetti
Dead Girl. *Fr.* Images. Hajnal
Dead Knight, The. Masefield
Dead Man's Dump. Rosenberg
Dead Ponies. Chamberlain
Dead Witness, The. Al-Haidari
Death. Baratynsky
Death. Bodenheim
Death. Brontë
Death. Fuller
Death. Harjo
Death. Herbert
Death. Kim Chun-soo
Death. Miller
Death. O Riordain
Death. Oppenheim
Death. Pellew
Death. Santos
Death. Scott
Death. Stone
Death. *Unknown*
Death. Williams
Death. Yeats
Death and Co. Plath
Death and the Lady. Adams
Death and the Plowman. Keyes
Death and the River. al-Sayyah
Death-Bed, The. Hood
Death Bed. Kinsella
Death-Bed, The. Sassoon
Death Bed Poem. Jakusho
Death Came for Michael Rockinghorse.
  Zach
Death-Charade. Glatstein
Death Circus, The. Tranter
Death Crown. Morgan
Death Fugue. Celan
Death in Leamington. Betjeman

Death in the Family, A. Manhire
Death in the Home. Moore
Death Invoked. *Fr.* The Emperor of the
  East. Massinger
Death is a dialogue between. Dickinson
Death Is a Door. Turner
Death is all metaphors, shape in one history.
  Fr. Altarwise by Owl-Light. Thomas
Death King, The. Sexton
Death of a Comic Opera Composer. *Fr.*
  Baroque Quatrains. Porter
Death of a Parent, The. Pastan
Death of a Poet. Causley
Death of a Prominent Business Man.
  MacNeice
Death of a Soldier, The. Stevens
Death of a Vermont Farm Woman. Howes
Death of a Whale. Blight
Death of an Old Man, The. Hamburger
Death of David, The. Bialik
Death of Friends, The. Levi
Death of Guillaume Apollinaire, The. Tzara
Death of Moses, The. *Unknown*
Death of Poetry, The. *Unknown*
Death of the Ball Turret Gunner, The. Jarrell
Death of the Bosun's Mate. Johnson
Death of the Craneman, The. Hayes
Death of the Day. Landor
Death of the First Man, The. Sullivan
Death of the Flowers, The. Bryant
Death of the Hired Man, The. Frost
Death of the Shoemaker, The. Dahbur
Death, Said Remco. Schierbeek
Death; She Was Always Here. Wallach
Death sitting, death standing. Koho
Death Snips Proud Men. Sandburg
Death Song, A. Dunbar
Death Song. Hawker
Death Song, A. Morris
Death Song for Owain ab Urien. Taliesin
Death Sonnet I. Mistral
Death Sweet. Beddoes
Death, Thou Hast Seized Me. Luzzatto
Death Was a Woman. Russell
Death Will Come and Will Have Your Eyes.
  Pavese
Deathbed Verse. Jippensha Ikku
Death's the Classic Look. Ciardi
Death's Transfiguration. Zangwill
Death's Warning to Beauty. *Unknown*
Deceased. Corman
Deep Sea Soundings. Williams
Delicate, Plummeting Bodies, The. Dobyns
Delta Traveller. Wright
Departure. Brock
Departure in Middle Age. Mathias
Descending Figure. Glück
Desire and Revenge. Raab
Destruction of Sennacherib, The. Byron
Dew on the leek. *Unknown*
Dialogue. Al-Haidari
"Did You Call Me, Father?" Tucker
"Died. . ." Browning
Digger for Gold, The. Chalfi
Dirge: "1-2-3 was the number he played but
  today the number came 3-2-1." Fearing
Dirge, A: "Why were you born when the
  snow was falling." Rossetti
Dirge in Woods. Meredith
Distance that the dead have gone, The.
  Dickinson
Divers' Death, The. Brackenbury
Divine Rose, That in a Pleasant Garden.
  Juana Inés de la Cruz
Do Not Die. Merwin
Do Not Go Gentle into That Good Night.
  Thomas
Doll, The. Beutler
Doom Ferry. Quiller-Couch
Dragons, The. Komrij
Dream, A. Allingham
Dream Fantasy. "Macleod"

Dream, The ("Last night I had a dream bad
  'cess to my dreaming."). *Unknown*
Drum. Hughes
Drummer Hodge. Hardy
During Wind and Rain. Hardy
Dwellings of Our Dead, The. Adams
Dying. Alvarez
Dying. Menken
Dying. Pinsky
Dying Airman, The. *Unknown*
Dying Away. Meredith
Dying Gaul, The. O'Grady
Dying Girl, The. Fordham
Dying Lover, The. Stoddard
Dying Stockman, The. *Unknown*
Earth out of Earth. *Unknown*
Edge. Plath
Egoist Dead, The. Brewster
Eighty-eight, my head's pure white. Seiko
Elegies for Her Daughter, Ko-Shikibu ("That
  she may know I love her and miss her").
  Fr. Fifty-one Tanka. Izumi
Elegies for Prince Atsumichi ("Dead people
  come to visit tonight"). *Fr.* Fifty-one
  Tanka. Izumi
Elegy: "Death be not proud, thy hand gave
  not this blow." Harington
Elegy: December, 1970, An. Bowers
Elegy: "Fled is the swiftness of all the
  white-footed ones." Auslander
Elegy for a Man Who Died and Died.
  Udwan
Elegy for a School-Friend. Young
Elegy for a Woman of No Importance.
  Al-Mala'ika
Elegy for Alfred Hubbard. Connor
Elegy for His Daughter Ellen. Owen
Elegy for Jack Bowman. Bruchac
Elegy for Jane. Roethke
Elegy for Lyn James. Norris
Elegy for My Father. Strand
Elegy for the Young Corpse. Villatoro
Elegy: "Newspaper appears in the morning,
  The." Al-Wugayyan
Elegy on Gordon Barber. Derwood
Elegy on Mistress Boulstred. Donne
Elegy on the Death of His Mistress Hoor
  Tal'at. Momin
Elegy over a Tomb. Herbert of Cherbury
Elegy: "This bright burning pyre." Auvaiyar
Elegy to Li Shuang-tse. Chiang Hsun
Elegy to the Memory of an Unfortunate Lady.
  Pope
Elegy: "Today, because I am not dead."
  O'Sullivan
Elegy upon His Tomb in Herndon-Hill
  Church, Erected by His Wife, Who Speaks,
  An. Howell
Elegy: "Were you, as old prints have shown."
  Nims
Elegy: "Who keeps the owl's breath? Whose
  eyes desire?" St. John
Ellie Mae Leaves in a Hurry. Klappert
Emperor of Ice-Cream, The. Stevens
Encounters. Faiz
End, The. Owen
End of a Course. Richards
End of life's journey, The. Ghalib
End of Man Is Death, The. Ibn Ezra
Endless Nights of Rain. Pape
Envy. Procter
Epi-strauss-ium. Clough
Epigram: Fatum Supremum. *Unknown*
Epigram: "Life flows to death as rivers to the
  sea." Cunningham
Epilogue: "That death might not be casual."
  Singer
Epistle to a Lady, An. Leapor
Epitaph for a Postal Clerk. Kennedy
Epitaph for My Tomb. Storni
Epitaph: "Here lies the flesh that tried."
  Driscoll

Epitaph: "I lived in those times. For a thousand years." Desnos
Epitaph: "Man who in his life trusts in this world, A." *Unknown*
Epitaph: "My brother is skull and skeleton now." Montgomerie
Epitaph of Nearchos. Ammianus
Epitaph on Elizabeth, L. H. Jonson
Epitaph on M. H., An. Cotton
Epitaph on Master Vincent Corbett, An. Jonson
Epitaph on the Marchioness of Winchester, An. Milton
Epitaph: "This is the end of him, here he lies." Levy
Epitaph upon Husband and Wife Who Died and Were Buried Together, An. Crashaw
Epitaph: "When I put my slate back in the void." Frénaud
Epos. Raba
Eulogy. Nichols
Eve. Rossetti
Even a flaming fire can be snatched. *Fr.* Manyo Shu. Jito
Even Such Is Time. Ralegh
Evensong. Lewis
Everything is only an image. Schönwiese
Examination at the Womb-Door. Hughes
Example, The. Díaz Mirón
Exequy, The. King
Exequy: To Peter Allt. Dobbs
Exile from God. Wheelock
Exit. MacDonald
Exit. Robinson
Extempore Effusion [upon the Death of James Hogg], An. Wordsworth
Extreme Unction. Dowson
Exultation. Hywel ab Owain Gwynedd
Fabius Lind to Comrade Death. Leyeles
Faithful, The. Cooper
Fall Comes in Back-Country Vermont. Warren
Fall Journey. Stafford
Falstaff's Song. Stedman
Farewell to a Jovial Friend. Escoffery
Farmer, Dying. Hugo
Fast Break. Hirsch
Father Death Blues. *Fr.* Don't Grow Old. Ginsberg
Fathers of a Star, The. Herbert
Fear No More the Heat o' the Sun. *Fr.* Cymbeline. Shakespeare
Fearful Death. *Unknown*
Feeling Her End Would Come with Summer's End. Castro
Felix Randal. Hopkins
Fidele, A. Collins
Fifty-four years I've entered. Jisso
Fifty-six years, above Buddhas, Patriarchs. Doyu
Fig for Thee, Oh! Death, A. Taylor
Final Prospect, The. Stach
Fire and Ice. Frost
First Death. Justice
First Death in Nova Scotia. Bishop
First Night, A. Dufault
First of My Lovers, The. Carter
First Snowfall [or Snow-Fall], The. Lowell
Flat One, A. Snodgrass
Flight, The. *Fr.* The Lost Son. Roethke
Flower, A. Nangolo
Flower Market. Reverdy
For a Dead Lady. Robinson
For a Friend. Kooser
For all I know, I myself. *Fr.* Kokin Shu. Tsurayuki
For Andrew. Adcock
For Annie. Poe
For E. McC. Pound
For Michael. Bloom
For My Funeral. Housman
For My Mother. Voigt

For My Younger Brother Shinkei on the Seventeenth Anniversary of His Death. Kan Sazan
For seventy-four years. Kokan Shiren
For Sleep, or Death. Pitter
For the Anniversary of My Death. Merwin
For the Dead Gregorians. Ramírez
For the jewel-like dew. Teika
For Victor Jara. Williams
For Zbigniew Herbert, Summer, 1971, Los Angeles. Levis
Force That through the Green Fuse Drives the Flower, The. Thomas
Forever. O'Reilly
Forsaken, The. Scott
Forsaken Garden, A. Swinburne
Four and fifty years. Dogen
Fourth Poem. Andrade
Fragment on Death, A. Villon
Fragment Sixty-eight: "I envy you your chance of death." Doolittle
Freedom, New Hampshire. Kinnell
Friends Beyond. Hardy
From Old Mrs. Mo of Heng Yang: A Letter to My Son, Lo Fu. Yip Wai-lim
From Scars Where Kestrels Hover. Auden
From the Antique. Rossetti
Full fathom [or fadom] five thy father lies. *Fr.* The Tempest. Shakespeare
Funeral. Bennett
Funeral, The. "J."
Funeral, The. Spender
Funeral Hymn. Howe
Funeral Poem. Baraka
Funeral Song. Hayiaku
Funeral[l], The. Donne
Funerall Song, A. *Unknown*
Futility. Owen
Gallows, The. Thomas
Game of Chance, A. Moss
Garden of Proserpine, The. Swinburne
Gardener, The. Housman
Gardener, The. *Fr.* Novelettes. MacNeice
Ghost Psalms. Kalász
Giorno dei Morti. Lawrence
Glory of the Day Was in Her Face, The. Johnson
Go Down Death. Johnson
Go then, my dove, but now no longer mine. Mather
God, A Poem. Fenton
God of all power and might. *Fr.* In Memoriam, A. C. M. L. Spring-Rice
Going, The. Hardy
Gone. Tucker
Gone on before me. Tonna
Good-bye. Emerson
"Good Night, Willie Lee, I'll See You in the Morning." Walker
Grace to Be Said at the Supermarket. Nemerov
Grandfather Dying. *Fr.* Byelorussia. Kulbak
Grandfather's Sermon and Michael Smith. Markham
Grandmother Grace. Wallace
Grass. Sandburg
Grave, A. Moore
Grave, The. *Unknown*
Graves of a Household, The. Hemans
Graves the rain makes wet and sleek, The. *Fr.* The Stanzas of the Graves. *Unknown*
Gravestone, The. Kassid
Great Man's Death: An Anecdote, The. Maddox
Green Tomatoes. Trudell
Grieving for the Student Abe. Michizane
Gudveig. Berry
Hand That Signed the Paper Felled a City, The. Thomas
Hanging Burley. Miller
Harbach 1944. Pilinszky

Hark, Now Everything Is Still. *Fr.* The Duchess of Malfi. Webster
Harvest. Levine
He Came to Visit Me. Seymour-Smith
He lies unloosened of his white clothes. *Fr.* Manyo Shu. Tanabe Sakimaro
He Remembers How He Didn't Understand What Lieutenant Dawson Meant. Whitehead
He Smelt the Smell of Death within the Marrow. Johnson
Hearse Song, The. *Unknown*
Heart asks pleasure—first, The. Dickinson
Heaven and Hell. Nalungiaq
Heavens revolve both night and day, The. Ghalib
Henry My Son. *Unknown*
Henry's Lament. *Fr.* The Complaint of Rosamond. Daniel
Her Son. Leaf
Here dead lie we because we did not choose. Housman
Here Lies a Lady. Ransom
Highland Mary. Burns
Hill, The. *Fr.* Spoon River Anthology. Masters
Hills of Rest, The. Paine
His Winding-Sheet. Herrick
Holiday Girls. Raymond
Holy Song of the Holy Grocer, The. Leivick
Horse of Death, The. Vroman
Hospital Window, The. Dickey
Hot Summer Sunday. Hendricks
Hour of Death, The. Hemans
Hours, The. Bishop
House. For Sale. Clark
House of Falling Leaves, The. Braithwaite
How changed is here each spot man makes or fills! *Fr.* Thyrsis. Arnold
How Death Comes. *Unknown*
How Did You Die? Cooke
How Great unto the Living Seem the Dead! Heavysege
How It Is. Kumin
How many times these low feet staggered. Dickinson
How Shall We Honor Them? *Unknown*
How Should I Your True Love Know. *Fr.* Hamlet. Shakespeare
How to Kill. Douglas
Hungry Dead, The. Miller
Hut near Desolated Pines. Campbell
Hymn[e] to God My God, In my Sickness[e] Donne
I am of this world. *Fr.* Manyo Shu. *Unknown*
I Ask My Teachers. *Fr.* Concerning Death. Madeleva.
I died for beauty—but was scarce. Dickinson
I enter and find I stand. *Fr.* At Thurgarton Church. Barker
I felt a funeral, in my brain. Dickinson
I Found Her Out There. Hardy
I Have a Rendezvous with Death. Seeger
I have made a pledge. Kenko
I have not told my garden yet. Dickinson
I heard a fly buzz—when I died. Dickinson
I Hoed and Trenched and Weeded. *Fr.* A Shropshire Lad. Housman
I Honour You in Dread. López Velarde
I Know Moonrise. *Unknown*
I Laughed When the Painter, Caroline. Martin
I like a look of agony. Dickinson
I loved her like the leaves. *Fr.* Manyo Shu. Hitomaro
I make a pillow of a rock-root on Mount Kamo. *Fr.* Manyo Shu. Hitomaro
I never lost as much but twice. Dickinson
I Never Shall Love the Snow Again. Bridges
I Picked Up Your Cast Away Hide. Moran
I Tell of Another Young Death. Tiempo

I Thank God I'm Free at Las'. *Unknown*
I Want to Die While You Love Me. Johnson
I wanted to write the lips of sleepers. Gilboa
I Went to Death. *Unknown*
I would like my love to die. Beckett
Ice Cold. O Riordain
If We Must Die. McKay
If you killed a helpless being, O cruel one. Zauq
Ignorance of Death. Empson
Ikons of the Dead, The. Barker
Illi Morituri. Webster
Immortality. "Æ"
Immortality. Ai
Immortality. Mitchell
Impossible, The. Laforgue
Improvisation of the Dead Boy. Andrade
In a Grave-Yard. Braithwaite
In Carrowdore Churchyard. Mahon
In Flanders Fields. McCrae
In life I had a fear of death. Ghalib
In Me. Segal
In Memoriam. Gingell
In Memoriam. Gruffydd
In Memoriam. Longley
In Memoriam Francis Ledwidge. Heaney
In Memoriam M. Tambimuttu. Stanford
In Memoriam of E. B. Clark. Moorer
In Memory of a Friend. Barker
In Memory of Izziddin al-Qalaq. Dahbur
In Memory of Jane Fraser [or Frazer] Hill
In Memory of My Dear Grandchild [Anne Bradstreet] Bradstreet
In my garden. *Fr.* Manyo Shu. Yakamochi
In Sepia. Anderson
In 728, Longing for His Deceased Wife. *Fr.* Manyo Shu. Tabito
In the Cemetery. Hardy
In the end. *Fr.* Kokin Shu. Narihira
In the evening. *Fr.* Manyo Shu. Tajihi
In the House of the Dying. Cooper
In the Moonlight. Hardy
In the Valley of Death. Hanafi
Incident. Baraka
Incident in a Rose Garden. Justice
Indian Burying Ground, The. Freneau
Inevitable. Betjeman
Infinite Debt, The. Bates
Inheritance. *Unknown*
Inscription for a Graveyard. Winters
Inseparable. Marston
Internus. Weöres
Invocation to the Mummy. Artaud
Iona; the Graves of the Kings. Jeffers
Ireland 1972. Durcan
Irish Airman Foresees His Death, An. Yeats
Irony. Untermeyer
Irreconcilables. Gregor
Is all this sorrow? I don't know. *Fr.* Laments on the War Dead. Amichai
Is It Well-Lighted, Papa? Bertram
Is My Team Ploughing [or Plowing]. *Fr.* A Shropshire Lad. Housman
Isaac Leybush Peretz. Halpern
Island, The. Dickey
It Is Five Years Now. Illyés
It Is Her Cousin's Death. Fox
It Is Nearly Summer. Manhire
It Was All Very Tidy. Graves
It was not death, for I stood up. Dickinson
I've seen a dying eye. Dickinson
Johnson Brothers Ltd. Kopland
Journey of the Magi. Eliot
Journey's End. Wolfe
Joy, Shipmate, Joy! Whitman
Just Passing. *Unknown*
Keen Thyself, Poor Wight. Keating
Keys of Morning, The. De la Mare
Kindertotenlieder. Longley
Knight, Death, and the Devil, The. Jarrell
La Chute. Olson
Labasheedy (the Silken Bed). Dhomhnaill

Ladies and Gentlemen, my mother is. *Fr.* Mourning Pictures. Moore
Lads in Their Hundreds, The. *Fr.* A Shropshire Lad. Housman
Lady of Shalott, The. Tennyson
Lament for Barney Flanagan. Baxter
Lament for Lleucu Llwyd. Llywelyn Goch ap Meurig Hen
Lament for Siôn y Glyn. Cothi
Lament for Taramoana. Makere
Lament for Te Iwi—ika. *Unknown*
Lament: "I lie in darkness, as the dead shades gather." Hauroa
Lament of my Father, Lakota. Allen
Lamentation, A. Campion
Lamenting for Kao Ch'ing-ch'iu, Chi-ti. Chang Yü
Lamenting the Dead. P'an Yüeh
Lamp Goes Out, The. Michizane
Land o' the Leal, The. Nairne
Last Confession, A. Yeats
Last Day, The. Seferis
Last Invocation, The. Whitman
Last night that she lived, The. Dickinson
Last Plea. Untermeyer
Last Quatrain of the Ballad of Emmett Till, The. Brooks
Last Rebirth, The. Barks
Last Word: For My Son Yung. Chin Jen-Jui
Last Words. Plath
Last Words of My English Grandmother, The. Williams
Last Words to James Wright. Hugo
Last Years, The. Davies
Lay a garland on my hearse. *Fr.* The Maid's Tragedy. Beaumont
Leaden-eyed, The. Lindsay
Leningrad Cemetary, Winter of 1941. Olds
Lenore. Poe
Lesson, The. Lucie-Smith
Let Me Go Down to Dust. Sarett
Let Me Not Die. Pierce
Let us go to a realm beyond going. Mirabai
Letters of the Dead. Szymborska
Life. Herbert
Life and Death. Turner
Life and death? Shoving a cart. Jittei
Life-Hook. Ibarbourou
Lift Me Higher. Tucker
Lights Out. Thomas
Linen Workers, The. Longley
Lines on a Dead Girl. Thompson
Litany of the Rooms of the Dead. Werfel
Little Boy Blue. Field
Little Death. Thomas
Little Peach, The. Field
Live Flesh. Reverdy
Living, The. *Fr.* Two Guitars. Maxson
Living among the Dead. Matthews
Long neglect has worn away. Brontë
Lord! if in love, though fainting oft, I have tended thy gracious Vine. *Fr.* Last Lines. "Meredith"
Losers. Sandburg
Losses. Jarrell
Lost in dream I slept. Mir
Lost Leader, The. Browning
Louise on the Door-Step. MacKay
Luke Havergal. Robinson
Lycidas. Milton
Lydia Is Gone This Many a Year. Reese
Madam Life's a Piece in Bloom. Henley
Madrigal: "Your love is dead, lady, your love is dead." Thomas
Magician, The. Miranda
Magnolia. Fordham
Man Arrested in Hacking Death Tells Police He Mistook Mother-in-Law for Raccoon. Ludvigson
Man in the Dead Machine, The. Hall

Man is a sacred city built of marvelous earth. *Fr.* The Tragedy of Pompey the Great. Masefield
Man-Moth, The. Bishop
Man of Rain, A. Barbeitos
Man on a Raft. Hervey
March 19, 1823. Zhukovsky
Marina. Eliot
Market Women. Figueroa-Aymerich
Masses. *Fr.* España, Aparta de me Este Caliz. Vallejo
Mater Dolorosa. Barnes
Matter of Urgency. Johnson
Maud. Swander
Maybe Elegies. Csoori
Meanwhile the adversary of God and man. *Fr.* Paradise Lost. Milton
Meeting the British. Muldoon
Meeting the Dead. Ostriker
Memento Mori. Halpern
Memorial. Pinsky
Memorial Poem. Fuller
Memory. Lincoln
Merlin. Hill
Message to a Loved One Dead, A. Heard
Messmates. Newbolt
Mid-Term Break. Heaney
Midnight. Kang
Mill, The. Wilbur
Miners. Owen
Minor Elegy. Lisboa
Mirror, The. Muldoon
Missing. Pudney
Missing. Tabb
Missing. *Unknown*
Missing Dates. Empson
Mongol Libation. Segalen
Monody. Melville
Monte Cassino 1945. Coleman
Monument. Sullivan
"More Light! More Light!" Hecht
Morgue, The. Baxter
Moriturus. "Madelaine"
Mortal creature as I am. *Fr.* Manyo Shu. *Unknown*
Mortality. Devaney
Mortician's Twelve-year-old Son, The. Ai
Mortification. Herbert
Mother. Bland
Mother, The. Pearse
Mother and Poet. Browning
Mother Dies. Saito Mokichi
Mother Goose's Garland. MacLeish
Mother, I Won't Forget. Vivaldi
Mountain Creed. Rae
Mourning for My Teacher Hokuju. Buson
Mourning Poem for the Queen of Sunday. Hayden
Mourning Song. Pearl
Mr. Edwards and the Spider. Lowell
Mr. Over. Smith
Mr. Slimmer's Funeral Verses for the *Morning Argus.* "Adeler"
Mummy of a Lady Named Jemutesonekh XXI Dynasty. James
My Dead. Hosmer
My Death. Smith
My Death. Zuckmayer
My Faces. Raba
My Father; October 1942. Stafford
My Father Today. Hunt
My Father's Death. Foscolo
My Grandfather's Funeral. Applewhite
My Grandmother's Burial Ground. Cook-Lynn
My life closed twice before its close. Dickinson
My Mother's Burying. O Riordain
My prince, graceful as the pliant bamboo. *Fr.* Manyo Shu. Niu
My prince, who bent to me. *Fr.* Manyo Shu. Niu

My Sister. Al-Ghuzzi
My Sister. Nieminen
My Sister's Sleep. Rossetti
My son, you loved telling the story of Prince
  Nata. *Fr.* Twenty-two Quatrains on
  Receiving the Obituary Not. T'ang
  Hsien-Tsu
My Uncle Tum. Ridings
Nature. Longfellow
Necropolis. Shapiro
Nettles, The. Hardy
Never. Fet
New Night Thoughts on Death; a Parody.
  Whitehead
Newly Discovered "Homeric" Hymn, A.
  Olson
Next, Please. Larkin
Night Is Freezing Fast, The. Housman
Night of darkness and of storms!, A. *Fr.*
  Thalaba the Destroyer. Southey
Night of Death, The. Harper
Night-Piece on Death, A. Parnell
No Coward Soul [Is Mine] Brontë
No funeral gloom, my dears, when I am
  gone. Allingham
No help I'll call till I'm put in the narrow
  coffin. O'Rahilly
No Worst, There Is None. Hopkins
North Haven. Booth
Not Dead, but Sleeping. Thompson
Not Thou but I. Marston
Not Waving but Drowning. Smith
Now landed Trader, that, with haughty stare.
  Fr. The Village Patriarch. Elliott
Now, My Usefullness Over. Honig
Now only the moon. Shinkei
Nowhere did I ever meet. Mir
Numskull for eighty-five years!, A. Kogetsu
O All Down within the Pretty Meadow.
  Patchen
O Death, Rock Me Asleep. Boleyn
O death you dark master. Artmann
O My Poor Darling. Watson
O Sanuki of beautiful seaweed. *Fr.* Manyo
  Shu. Hitomaro
Oh! sing unto my roundelay [*or* O! Synge
  untoe mie roundelaie]. *Fr.* Aella; a
  Tragycal Enterlude. Chatterton
O What Is That Sound [Which So Thrills the
  Ear] Auden
Oath, The. Tate
Obedience of the Corpse. Wright
Obit on Parnassus. Fitzgerald
Oblivion. Naji
Ode: "Sleep sweetly in your humble graves."
  Timrod
Ode to Joy. O'Hara
Of De Witt Williams on His Way to Lincoln
  Cemetery. Brooks
Of Death. *Fr.* Antonius. Pembroke
Oh, the autumn foliage. *Fr.* Manyo Shu.
  Jito
Oh, Thou! Who Dry'st the Mourner's Tear.
  Moore
Oh, when this earthly tenement. "Ada"
Oh [*or* O]! Why Should the Spirit of Mortal
  Be Proud? Knox
Old Familiar Faces, The. Lamb
Old man dozed, The. The hospital quietened.
  Fr. Sonnets for a Dying Man. Singer
Old Man Who Is Gone Now, The. Reyes
Old People Speak of Death, The. Troupe
Old Story, An. Robinson
Old yew, which graspest at the stones. *Fr.*
  In Memoriam A. H. H. Tennyson
Omnia Exeunt in Mysterium. Sterling
On a Nun. Vittorelli
On Death. Killigrew
On Death. *Fr.* Measure for Measure.
  Shakespeare

On Finding Out that the One You Slept with
  the Night Before Was Murdered the Next
  Day. Ortleb
On His Deceased Wife. Milton
On looming Mount Hatsuse. *Fr.* Manyo
  Shu. Hitomaro
On Neal's Ashes. Ginsberg
On One Dying in a Convent. Gwynn
On Parting with a Friend. Fordham
On the day my father died a flame-tree. *Fr.*
  Brother Jonathan, Brother Kafka.
  O'Sullivan
On the Death of a Metaphysician. Santayana
On the Death of a Prince; a Meditation.
  Philipott
On the Death of Friends in Childhood.
  Justice
On the Death of Her Mother. Rukeyser
On the Death of His Son Vincent. Hunt
On the Death of His Wife. O'Dalaigh
On the Death of Joseph Rodman Drake.
  Halleck
On the Death of Lisa Lyman. Burt
On the Death of Mr. William Hervey [*or*
  Harvey], *sel.* Cowley
On the Death of Phillips. *Unknown*
On the Death of Robert Lowell. Myles
On the Death of the Rev. Mr. George
  Whitefield. Wheatley
On the Imprint of the First English Edition of
  "The Works of Max Beerbohm."
  Beerbohm
On the mountain is the thorn-elm. *Unknown*
On the Symbolic Consideration of Hands and
  the Significance of Death. Williams
On Time. Milton
One dignity delays for all. Dickinson
One Morning in May; or, The Young Girl Cut
  Down in Her Prime. *Unknown*
One of Wally's Yarns. Masefield
One Who Watches. Sassoon
One X. Cummings
Only the Polished Skeleton. Cullen
Orchids. Minty
Osceola. Whitman
Others may cease to remember. *Fr.* Manyo
  Shu. Yamato-hime
Our comrade, crossing. *Fr.* Manyo Shu.
  Unknown
Our Ernest. "Elmo"
Our lord and prince, ruling in peace. *Fr.*
  Manyo Shu. Okisome no Azumabito
Our prince, pliant as the soft bamboo. *Fr.*
  Manyo Shu. Niu
Out of the Cradle Endlessly Rocking.
  Whitman
Out of the Hitherwhere. Riley
"Out, Out." Frost
Owl, The. Weöres
Pale Blue Casket, The. Pitcher
Pardon, The. Wilbur
Passer Mortuus Est. Millay
Peace. *Fr.* 1914. Brooke
Peace. Hughes
Pedigree of honey, The. Dickinson
People Who Died. Berrigan
Per Iter Tenebricosum. Gogarty
Piazza Piece. Ransom
Pietà. McAuley
Place of Rest, The. "Æ"
Plague Sermon. Heyen
Poem Ended by a Death. Adcock
Poem, A: "Father of all! in Death's relentless
  claim." Holmes
Poem for My Father's Ghost. Oliver
Poem: "If I speak always of the dead." Fa'iq
Poem in the Form of a Coffin-Puller's Song
  ("In life I stroll the capital city."). Miu
  Hsi
Poem in the Form of a Coffin-Puller's Song
  ("What has a life must have a death").
  T'ao Ch'ien

Poem on His Death-Bed. Cynddelw Brydydd
  Mawr
Poem on His Death-Bed. Meilyr Brydydd
Poem to My Death. Burgos
Poet Is Dead, The. Everson
Poet's Wish. Larbaud
Post Mortem. Munby
Postcard from the Volcano, A. Stevens
Posthumous Rehabilitation. Rozewicz
Prayer for the Little Daughter between Death
  and Burial. Scott
Prayer: "Give me a death like Buddha's. Let
  me fall." Moss
Prayer in the Prospect of Death, A. Burns
Prayer to Go to Paradise with the Donkeys,
  A. Francis
Prayer to Mother Mary. Pearse
Precious in the Sight of the Lord. *Unknown*
Preface to Dying. Raba
Preparing for Weather. Oles
Price, The. Davidson
Print of Your Hand, The. Csoori
Private Theater, The. Risi
Progress. "Miraji"
Prophecy. Wylie
Prospice. Browning
Province of Sanuki, renowned for lovely
  seaweed, The. *Fr.* Manyo Shu.
  Hitomaro
Psalm and Lament. Justice
Pure Death. Graves
Quaker Graveyard in Nantucket, The.
  Lowell
Quatorzain. Timrod
Quentin Matsys. Iwaszkiewicz
Question, A. Synge
Racer's Widow, The. Glück
Rain. Thomas
Rainy Mountain Cemetery. Momaday
Raising of Lazarus, The. Clifton
Rata blooms explode, the bow-legged tomcat,
  The. *Fr.* Autumn Testament. Baxter
Ravens. Hughes
Ready. Preston
Reasonable Affliction, A. Prior
Recollection, A. Cornford
Reconciliation. Day Lewis
Reconciliation. Whitman
Reflections, Written on Visiting the Grave of
  a Venerated Friend. Plato
Refusal to Mourn the Death, by Fire, of a
  Child in London, A. Thomas
Rehearsing for Death. Sikelianos
Remembrance. Brontë
Reminiscence, A. Brontë
Remorse. Betjeman
Repentance. Behan
Requiem: "Under the wide and starry sky."
  Stevenson
Requiescat. Arnold
Requiescat. Wilde
Resounding Wall, The. Yip Wai-lim
Resting. Heard
Resurgam. Menken
Resurgam. Pickthall
Resurgam. *Unknown*
Retrieval System, The. Kumin
Reuben, Reuben. Harper
Revel, The. Dowling
Revelation, The. Wright
Rhyme of the Dead Self. Fairburn
Rites for a Demagogue. Thwaite
Rites for Cousin Vit, The. Brooks
River and Death, The. al-Sayyah
Robert Lowell: His Death. Williamson
Ron Mason. Tuwhare
Room, The. Raab
Roundhouse Voices, The. Smith
Ruin, The. *Unknown*
Russian Death. Kvitko
Sacrifice, The. Bidart
Sad Remembrance. Mei Yao-ch'en

Safe in their alabaster chambers. Dickinson
Sailing to Byzantium. Yeats
Saint, Bird, Angel. *Unknown*
St. James Infirmary. *Unknown*
Scream, A. al-Faituri
Sea Canes. Walcott
Sea of Death, The. Hood
Seaman, 1941. Holden
Second Wind. Chappell
Secret, The. Kaneko
Seeds. Oxenham
Self-Portrait in 2035. Wright
Serious and a Curious Night-Meditation, A. Traherne
Setting of the Moon, The. Leopardi
Sew a Pocket. Smith
Shadows. Pastan
Shape of Death, The. Swenson
She Was a Phantom of Delight. Wordsworth
Ship, The. *Unknown*
Ship of Death, The. Lawrence
Should You Go First. Rowswell
Sick Rose, The. *Fr.* Songs of Experience. Blake
Sightseers, The. Muldoon
Silver Swan, The. Gibbons
Simplify Me When I'm Dead. Douglas
Since Amaro died I cannot sleep at night. *Fr.* Kokin Shu. Michizane
Since in Karu lived my wife. *Fr.* Manyo Shu. Hitomaro
Sir Emperour, lorde of al the ground. *Fr.* The Dance of Death. *Unknown*
Sister Lou. Brown
Sitting at Night on the Front Porch. Wright
Sixty-eighth Birthday. Lowell
Skeleton at the Feast, The. Roche
Sled Burial, Dream Ceremony. Dickey
Sleep, The. Browning
Sleep Brought Me Vision. Bishop
Sleep, Leopard, Sleep. Avidan
Sleeper in the Valley, The. Rimbaud
Sleeping at Last. Rossetti
Slim Cunning Hands. De la Mare
Small Square, The. Andresen
Smell of death is so powerful, The. Navarre
Smile, Death. Mew
So Might It Be. Galsworthy
Soliloquy I. Aldington
Soliloquy II. Aldington
Soliloquy on Death. Fiawoo
Some Time at Eve. Hardy
Song in Passing, A. Winters
Song: "Linnet in the rocky dells, The." Brontë
Song of a Girl Journeying to the Country of the Dead. *Unknown*
Song of the Invisible Corpse in the Field. Orr
Song, The: "Oh, foully slighted Ethiope maid!" Thompson
Song: "Oh roses for the flush of youth." Rossetti
Song: "When I am dead, my dearest." Rossetti
Sonnet: And You as Well Must Die, Beloved Dust. Millay
Sonnet: Death's Last Will. Drummond
Sonnet: "He came in silvern armor, trimmed with black." Bennett
Sonnet: "It is not death, that sometime in a sigh." Hood
Sonnet on the Death of Mr. Richard West. Gray
Sonnet: "She took the dappled partridge flecked [*or* fleckt] with blood." Tennyson
Sonnet: "Sweet soul, which in the April of thy years." Drummond
Sonnet: The Death of Virgil. Di Costanzo
Sonnet: "There, on the darkened deathbed, dies the brain." Masefield
Sonnet to My Father. Justice

Sonnet: To Primal Matters. Sandoval y Zapata
Sonnet 21. Goodman
Soon at Last My Sighs and Moans. Ginsberg
Sorrowin.' Ramsbottom
Space Burial. Aldiss
Space in the Air, A. Silkin
Spark's Farewell to Its Clay, The. Mason
Speculation. Nemerov
Spending the Night. Kumin
Spring and Death. Hopkins
Springfield Mountain. *Unknown*
Spritely Dead, The. Williams
Staircase, The. Allen
Stanzas: "I'll not weep that thou art going to leave me." Brontë
Stanzas to———. Brontë
Stations. Hughes
Statue, The. Belloc
Staying Overnight at Blue Cloud Temple. Mo Shih-lung
Still Life. Angelotti
Still Life. Ausländer
Stirrup-Cup, The. Lanier
Strange Meeting. Owen
Stranger, A. Csoori
Strangers Are We All upon the Earth. Werfel
Stratis Thalassinos among the Agapanthi. Seferis
Suave Mari Magno. *Fr.* De Rerum Natura (On the Nature of Things). Lucretius
Subalterns, The. Hardy
Subjects and Arguments for an Act of Desperation. Pagliarani
Suburban. Coursen
Such Instance. Reece
Suffering. Ehrenstein
Sunday before Christmas, The. Csoori
Sunday Morning. Stevens
Sunlight on the Garden, The. MacNeice
Suppose This Moment Some Stupendous Question. Nowlan
Supreme Death. Dunn
Survivor. McGough
Sweet after showers, ambrosial air. *Fr.* In Memoriam A. H. H. Tennyson
Swerve, The. Stafford
Sylvester's Dying Bed. Hughes
Talisman 18. Stern
Tangi. Tuwhare
Tell Me You Wandering Spirits. *Unknown*
Telling the Bees. Reese
Telling the Bees. Whittier
Tenancy, The. Gilmore
Terminus. Emerson
Tetélestai. Aiken
Thanatopsis. Bryant
Thank your engines. *Fr.* The Unhappy Revenge. Swinburne
That Dark Other Mountain. Francis
That Very Night. Hame'iri
That's Life? Bold
"That time of year thou may'st [*or* maist] in me behold." *Fr.* Sonnets, LXXIII. Shakespeare
Then. Rukeyser
Then Sings My Soul. Mariani
There. Wright
There is a land of pure delight. Watts
There is no chapel on the day. *Fr.* The Ballad of Reading Gaol. Wilde
There Is No Death. McCreery
Therefore, We Thank Thee, God. Grossman
There's a certain slant of light. Dickinson
There's been a death in the opposite house. Dickinson
These Bones. Parry-Williams
These eighty-four years. Kangan
They Are All Gone into the World of Light. Vaughan
They lie at rest, our blessed dead. Rossetti

They Never Quite Leave Us. Sangster
Things Dead. Schwob
Things that Will Not Die, The. Sill
Think upon Death. Coleridge
Thinking "Today! Today!" I wait for you. *Fr.* Manyo Shu. Yosami
Third Light, The. Longley
This Day after Yesterday. Booth
This Is a Photograph of Me. Atwood
Thomas Iron-Eyes. Walsh
Though my eyes could see your spirit soar. *Fr.* Manyo Shu. Yamato-hime
Thought of Death, A. Flatman
Thoughts of Phena. Hardy
Thoughts on the Works of Providence. Wheatley
Three Fishers, The. Kingsley
Three images of dying stick in my mind like morbid transfers. *Fr.* Letters to Live Poets. Beaver
Threnody: "Only quiet death." Cuney
Through a Glass, Darkly. Dowling
Tichborne's Elegy. Tichborne
Tie the strings to my life, my Lord. Dickinson
Tiger Bay. *Unknown*
Till my black hair be white. *Fr.* Manyo Shu. "Takahashi"
Time to Die, The. Edwards
Timor Mortis. *Unknown*
'Tis the Last Rose of Summer. Moore
Tithonus. Tennyson
To a Dead Actress. Sandoval y Zapata
To a Deceased Friend. Thompson
To a Gentleman and Lady on the Death of the Lady's Brother and Sister, and a Child of the Name Avis, Aged One Year. Wheatley
To an American Poet Just Dead. Wilbur
To an Athlete Dying Young. *Fr.* A Shropshire Lad. Housman
To-day, taking my last sight of the mallards. *Fr.* Manyo Shu. Otsu
To Death. Gogarty
To Die for Something. Tornai
To His Dead Body. Sassoon
To His Dying Brother, Master William Herrick. Herrick
To know just how He suffered would be dear. Dickinson
To L. H. B. Mansfield
To Laura Phelan: 1880-1906. Stokesbury
To My Dead Brother. Thompson
To My Mother. Fordham
To One in Paradise. Poe
To Perilla. Herrick
To Rise, So Suddenly. Behn
To Robin Redbreast. Herrick
To S. A. Lawrence
To Show My Sons. Lu Yu
To Sir William Alexander. Drummond
To Someone. Kotaro
To the Dead. Bidart
To the Fringed Gentian. Bryant
To the Holy Spirit. Winters
To the Memory of Mr. Oldham. Dryden
To the Reverend Shade of His Religious Father. Herrick
To the Spirit of Monahsetah. DeClue
To the Thoughtful Reader. Meredith
To Think of Time. Whitman
To this land of Tsukushi. *Fr.* Manyo Shu. Okura
To Vera Thompson. Haines
To Vittoria Colonna. Michelangelo
Today, today,/ I wait for him. *Fr.* Manyo Shu. Yosami
Tolerance of Crows, The. Donnelly
Tomb of an Ancestor. Curnow
Transfiguration, The. Herrick
Transparent Man, The. Hecht
Travel Poem, A. Teika

Traveller, A. *Unknown*
Travellers, The. Spires
Triviality, A. Cuney
Truganinny. Rose
Truly do we live on earth? *Unknown*
Truth the Dead Know, The. Sexton
Tune: Song of River City. Su Tung-p'o
Turn Again to Life. Hall
Twa Brothers, The. *Unknown*
Twa Corbies, The. *Unknown*
'Twas just this time, last year, I died.
  Dickinson
'Twas warm—at first—like us. Dickinson
Twilight Musings. Fordham
Two Coffins, The. Field
Two Hearts Divided. Parry
Two hundred men and eighteen killed.
  Henry
Two Mysteries, The. Dodge
Ubi Sunt Qui ante Nos Fuerunt? *Unknown*
Unhappy Diary Days. Vizenor
Unknown Soldier, The. Rose
Unquiet Grave, The. *Unknown*
Unquiet Ones, The. Kunitz
Upbraiding, An. Hardy
Uphill [*or* Up-Hill]. Rossetti
Upon a Dying Lady. Yeats
Upon His Sister-in-Law, Mistress Elizabeth
  Herrick. Herrick
Upon Prue, His Maid. Herrick
Upon the Image of Death. Southwell
Upper Garrison Farm: A Ballad a Lament for
  a Woman Killed by the Soldiery. Shih
  Jun-chang
Vacillation. Yeats
Valley of the Shadow. Galsworthy
Vanity of the World, The. Siôn Cent
Vase, The. Mistral
Verses Written in 1872. Stevenson
Vespers. Mitchell
Vesta. Whittier
Victim No. 48. Darwish
View on Death, A. Watson
Viewing Nara from a Distance in Wind and
  Rain. Fujii Chikugai
Viewing the Body. Snodgrass
Vigil. Meireles
Vigil. Ungaretti
Villagers and Death, The. Graves
Virgo Descending. Wright
Virtue. Herbert
Visiting the Graves. Voigt
Voice, The. Hardy
Voices of Heroes. Gregory
Votive Song. Pinkney
Waiting for the Post. Auchterlonie
Wake of William Orr, The. Drennan
Wanting to Die. Sexton
Warning and Reply. Brontë
Watch, The. Cornford
Watch Them Die. Trudell
Water Island. Moss
Waterfall, The. Vaughan
We Are Passing Away. Edwards
We are travelers along the road. Mir
We Do Lie beneath the Grass. *Fr.* Death's
  Jest Book. Beddoes
We Never Know. Komunyakaa
We Shall Know. *Unknown*
Weary with life we long for death. Zauq
Weaver, The. Pascoli
Wedding-cake face in a paper frill, A. *Fr.*
  Berck-Plage. Plath
Weeping for Hsüeh Tzu-shu.
  Liu-K'o-chuang
Weeping for My Elder in Poetry Shimada.
  Michizane
Weeping for the Priest Gempin. Saga
Welcome, Sweet Rest. Wigglesworth
What Are Years? Moore
What Became of the Family? Johnson
What If Some Little Paine the Passage Have.
  Fr. The Faerie Queene. Spenser

What is that death they boast but a frail
  pageant. *Fr.* The Unhappy Revenge.
  Swinburne
What Shines in Winter Burns. Hummer
What worth to me the seven treasures. *Fr.*
  Manyo Shu. Okura
When, at our Sovereign's command. *Fr.*
  Manyo Shu. Yakamochi
When Death Comes. *Unknown*
When Death to Either Shall Come.
  Bridges
When I Am Dead. Barrie
When I Am Dead. Wilson
When I am dead and some kind soul.
  Bahadur Shah Zafar
When I Die. *Fr.* All Flesh Is Grass.
  Macrow
When I Have Fears [That I May Cease to Be].
  Keats
When I Was Dying. Hathaway
When Mother Died. *Fr.* Twenty-seven
  Hokku. Natsume Seibi
When News of Saichi's Death Arrived.
  Ryokan
When she was alive, now a memory. *Fr.*
  Manyo Shu. Hitomaro
When the Day Comes. Gutiérrez Nájera
When Thou Must Home to Shades of
  Underground. Campion
Where behind the Night Did You Get Lost.
  Kilpi
Where shall the lover rest. *Fr.* Marmion.
  Scott.
Where the Rainbow Ends. Lowell
White Notes. Justice
Who Says. Laaber
Who Was Born Dead. Aleixandre
Why be so proud of this useless, used-up
  body? Kabir
Why should one care to unpack. Mir
Widow's Lament in Springtime, The.
  Williams
Wife a-Lost, The. Barnes
Wife in London, A. Hardy
Wife of Usher's Well, The. *Unknown*
Will of a Man Dying in Exile, The.
  Al-Qasim
Willy Lyons. Wright
Winter. Segal
Winter Solstice—for Frank. Asphodel
Winter Song. Abd al-Sabur
Winter Visit, A. Abse
Winter Walking. Purdy
Wishbone, The. Muldoon
With grass for a pillow, on a journey. *Fr.*
  Manyo Shu. Hitomaro
With Rue My Heart Is Laden. *Fr.* A
  Shropshire Lad. Housman
Within the Veil. Sangster
Witness to Death. Lattimore
Wizard's Funeral, The. Dixon
Woman Mourned by Daughters, A. Rich
Woman Shopping, A. Glover
Words for Delmira Agustini. Storni
World, The. Creeley
Wound, The. "Adunis"
Wounds. Longley
Writing while My Father Dies. Pastan
Written at the Graveside. Yüan Mei
Written in Autumn When Spending the Night
  Near the Grave of His Wife. *Fr.* Thirty
  Tanka. Shunzei
Written on the Anniversary of Our Father's
  Death. Coleridge
Yesterday I chanced to step. Mir
You Rise among Truths. Abd al-Wahid
Young Sailor Cut Down in His Prime, The.
  Unknown
Young Wife, The. Walcott
You've heard that saying brave. Batyushkov
*Chaos of the Night; Women's Poetry and
  Verse of the Second World War* (CN).
  Catherine W. Reilly, ed.

Death in Literature (DL). Robert F. Weir,
  ed.
Oxford Book of Death, The (OBD). D. J.
  Enright, ed.
Death at Sea
Deep Sea. Supervielle
Lament: "We knelt on the rocks by the dark
  green pools." Mayo
Seaman, 1941. Holden
What the Light Was Like. Clampitt
Death in Childhood
Abraham. Bogin
Afraid. De la Mare
After Labor Day. Lea
Airing Painful Memories. Yüan Chen
At the dawn of your life, you ate gruel. *Fr.*
  Mourning for My Son Jun-erh. Cheng
  Hsieh
At the Lake—Remembering My Dead Son,
  Yü. Pien Kung
Autumn Night. Michizane
Babes in the Wood, The. *Unknown*
Ballad of Birmingham. Randall
Bells for John Whiteside's Daughter.
  Ransom
Bewail not much, my parents! me, the prey.
  Lucian
Child Dying, The. Muir
Childless Father, The. Wordsworth
Child's Grave, Hale County, Alabama.
  Simmerman
Child's Wish Granted, The. Lathrop
Christmas Carol: "I walk today, the pain of
  childbirth in each step." Murillo
Dead Boy. Ransom
Dead Child, The. Dowson
Dead Sister, The. Gilman
Death of a Son. Silkin
Death of a Young Son by Drowning.
  Atwood
Death of the Factory Child, The. Prince
Dying Animals, The. Ewart
Dying Child, The. Clare
Dying Child's Request, The. Gould
Dying in the Street. Johnson
Epitaph, An: "His friends he loved. His direst
  earthly foes." Watson
Epitaph: "Last year the child died." Senior
Epitaph on S. P. [Salomon *or* Salathiel Pavy],
  a Child of Queen Elizabeth's Chapel.
  Jonson
Falls Funeral. Montague
February 11, 1977. Morgan
First Death in Nova Scotia. Bishop
Flood Year. Wright
Flower Farm, The. Pape
For Erotion's Grave. Martial
For My Brother Who Died before I Was
  Born. Wormser
For the Children Who Died in a Smallpox
  Epidemic. Ryokan
For the Parents of a Dead Child.
  Ryokan
Funeral. Meyers
Grief fills the room up of my absent child.
  Fr. King John. Shakespeare
Grieving for Tatsuzo: Today Spring Ended.
  Rai San'yo
Home Burial. Frost
I send these along. Munenaga
I stand and gaze at the tomb. *Fr.* Manyo
  Shu. Tanabe Sakimaro
In Memoriam. Alphonse Campbell Fordham.
  Fordham
In Memory of My Dear Grandchild [Anne
  Bradstreet]. Bradstreet
Inquest, The. Davies
Is it children we are killing now? My God.
  Fr. A Recollection of the Night of the
  Fourth. Hugo
Lamenting for My Late Daughter. Wu
  Wei-yeh
Limbo. Heaney

Little Boy Blue. Field
Little Elegy. Kennedy
Little Libbie. Moore
Longings. Cavafy
Lost Children, The. Jarrell
Maiden Unai of Ashinoya, The. *Fr.* Manyo
  Shu. Mushimaro
Massacre of the Innocents. Rózewicz
Maternity. Meynell
Mid-Term Break. Heaney
My beloved brother, born of my own parents.
  Fr. Manyo Shu. Tanabe Sakimaro
My sorrow, Donncha, my thousand-cherished.
  O Heigeartaigh
Night Has a Thousand Eyes, The.
  Bourdillon
Nightmare Begins Responsibility. Harper
1925. *Fr.* To Restore a Dead Child. Honig
O, Shmuel My Brother! Halpern
Of My Dear Son [*or* Deare Sonne], Gervase
  Beaumont. Beaumont
On a Dead Child. Bridges
On a Dead Child. Middleton
On a Dying Boy. Bell
On an Infant Which Died before Baptism.
  Coleridge
On My Dear Grandchild Simon Bradstreet.
  Bradstreet
On My First Daughter. Jonson
On My First Son [*or* Sonne] Jonson
On the Death of Friends in Childhood.
  Justice
On the Death of His Son. Wesley
On the Death of His Younger Sister. *Fr.*
  Twenty Hokku. Kyorai
On the Death of Mistress Mary Prideaux.
  Strode
"Out, Out." Frost
Papa's Letter. *Unknown*
Protocols. Jarrell
Queenie. Fordham
Refusal to Mourn the Death, by Fire, of a
  Child in London, A. Thomas
Request of a Dying Child. Sigourney
Requiescat. Wilde
Return of the Children, The. Kipling
Reuben, Reuben. Harper
Russia's Resentment. Moorer
Seeing Flowers I Remember My Late
  Daughter, Shu. Kao Ch'i
Seven treasures, The. *Fr.* Manyo Shu.
  Okura
Seven types of treasures, The. *Fr.* Manyo
  Shu. Okura
She's dead—but in my grief. *Fr.* Kokin
  Shu. Tsurayuki
Skater in Blue. Parini
Solace. Heard
Spring and Fall. Hopkins
Spring Betrayed. Boulton
Strange Case, The. Ondaatje
Sun is soon to rise as bright, The. *Fr.* Songs
  on the Death of Children. Rückert
Surprised by Joy [Impatient as the Wind]
  Wordsworth
Ten Heawrs a Day. Burgess
There Was a Boy ("There was a boy, ye knew
  him well"). *Fr.* The Prelude [or, Growth
  of a Poet's Mind]: Books. Wordsworth
They look up with their pale and sunken
  faces. *Fr.* The Cry of the Children.
  Browning
Thirteenth Year of *Genroku* [1700], the Year
  My Boy Toshiaki Died, The. *Fr.*
  Twenty-three Hokku. Onitsura
To a Child in Death. Mew
To an Infant. Fordham
To My Daughter Betty. Kettle
Upon a Child That Died. Herrick
Upon Wedlock and Death of Children.
  Taylor

Vesta. Whittier
We Are Seven. Wordsworth
Why I Write Not of Love. Jonson
Wind, The. Kazuko Yamada
Year's End. Voigt
Yet Another Poem about a Dying Child.
  Frame
Death in War. *See* **War Dead.**

Death of Animals
Burial of the Dog. Musgrave
Celestial. Pettit
Cottontail. Bogin
Dead by the Side of the Road, The. Snyder
Dead Horse, The. Meireles
Dead Lamb, A. Curnow
Dead Ponies. Chamberlain
Dead Skunk. Eberhart
Death of a Dog. Bland
Death of a Toad, The. Wilbur
Dog, The. Stern
Dog On the Road. Bernstein
Dog Poisoner, The. Wilson
Draft Horse, The. Frost
Elegy for Delina. Rowe
For a Dead Kitten. Hay
For a Lamb. Eberhart
Gallows, The. Thomas
Goose. Braun
Heaven of Animals, The. Dickey
Hurt Hawks. Jeffers
Interruption to a Journey. MacCaig
Kitten. Herzberg
Kitten, The. Oliver
Lilies, The. Braun
Mare's skeleton in the clearing: another sign
  of life, The. *Fr.* Shooting Script. Rich
Obituary. Parsons
Ode on the Death of a Favourite Cat,
  Drowned in a Tub of Gold Fishes. Gray
Offering for the Cat, An. Mei Yao-ch'en
Old Age Gets Up. Hughes
Pardon, The. Wilbur
Procession. Booth
Sitting Around Waiting for Your Cat to Die.
  Jacobson
Small Frogs Killed on the Highway. Wright
Traveling through the Dark. Stafford
Wellfleet Whale, The. Kunitz
With Stephen in Maine. Plumly

Debauchery
Disabled Debauchee, The. Rochester
Hand-Mirror, A. Whitman
On Gut. Jonson
Short Song of Congratulation [*or* To a Young
  Heir], A. Johnson
Village of Balmaquhapple, The. Hogg

Debt
File-Hewer's Lamentation, The. Mather
If I Should Die Tonight. King
Promissory Note, The. Taylor
Remember. *Unknown*

Decadence
Habitué. Stickney
Modern Fine Lady, The. Jenyns
Modern Fine Lady, The, *sel.* Jenyns
To a Boy-Poet of the Decadence. Seaman

Decalogue
Latest Decalogue, The. Clough
Thoughts on the Commandments. Baker

Decay
As a Plane Tree by the Water. Lowell
Boy Wandering in Simms' Valley. Warren
Consciousness. Nagy
Death of the Kapowsin Tavern. Hugo
Ditty: "If this town should tumble down."
  Beecham
Finding an Old Newspaper in the Woods.
  Morgan
Groundhog, The. Eberhart
Homer Mitchell Place, The. Engels

House on 15th S.W., The. Hugo
House on the Hill, The. Robinson
Ivy Green, The. *Fr.* The Pickwick Papers.
  Dickens
Junk. Wilbur
Lion's Skeleton, The. Turner
Montana Ranch Abandoned. Hugo
Ozymandias [*or* Ozymandias of Egypt*or*
  Sonnet: Ozymandias]. Shelley
Prescription of Painful Ends. Jeffers
Raleigh Was Right. Williams
Range-finding. Frost
Refugee, The. Battcock
Wood-Pile, The. Frost

December
Bon Mot, A. *Unknown*
Daft Days, The. Fergusson
December. Clare
December. Francis
December. Fyleman
December. Heard
December. Kenny
December. Ray
December. *Fr.* Sonnets of the Months. San
  Gimignano
December Blues. Pinsky
December Stillness. Sassoon
I Heard a Bird Sing. Herford
In a Drear-nighted December. Keats
Tree in December. Cane

Deception
Adam, David, Samson, Solomon. *Fr.* The
  Epistle to the God of Love. Pisan
Clerks pretend to be shepherds, and under,
  The. Cardenal
Word of Encouragement, A. Pope

Decisions
Road Not Taken, The. Frost
See also **Free Will.**

Declaration of Independence
Emancipation from British Dependence.
  Freneau

Decorum
Shepherdess, The. Meynell

Deer
Color of Many Deer Running, The. Gregg
Death of a Hind. Maclean
Deer, The. Austin
Deer. Drinkwater
Deer among Cattle. Dickey
Deer at the Red Sea. Sutskever
Deer at the Roadside. *Fr.* Deer on the High
  Hills—a Meditation. Smith
Deer in the Bush. Bloch
Deer in the morning look edgy and lost. *Fr.*
  Twenty-seven Hokku. Natsume Seibi
Deer Isle. Booth
Deer Song. Silko
Doe at Evening, A. Lawrence
Envoy: "On Meall nan Con, the Peak of the
  Dogs." Maclean
Fallow Deer at the Lonely House, The.
  Hardy
Fawn in the Snow, The. Benét
Fawn's Foster-Mother. Jeffers
Four Deer, The. Jones
Hanging Man, The. Plath
How to See Deer. Booth
Hunting-Song. *Unknown*
In the Falling Deer's Mouth. Levien
In this mountain village. Tamesuke
Knole. Sisson
Landscape, Deer Season. Howes
Lowermost leaves, The. Ietaka
Morning Song. Orr
My good sirs. *Fr.* Manyo Shu. *Unknown*
New Jersey White-tailed Deer. Oates
O good friend, dear master. *Fr.* Manyo Shu.
  Unknown
On a summer hill a doe appears. Gomei
Psalm: "In the small beauty of the forest."
  Oppen

Roe Deer. Hughes
Runnable Stag, A. Davidson
Sila. Warren
So loud the deer cries, calling to his mate.
 Fr. Manyo Shu. Yakamochi
Song for the Greenwood Fawn. Salomon
Sonnet: Whoso List to Hunt [I Know Where
 Is an Hind]. Wyatt
Soy Sauce. Snyder
Stags. Montgomerie
Stag of the Ogura Mountain, The. Fr.
 Manyo Shu. Jomei
Traveling through the Dark. Stafford
Two Fawns That Didn't See the Light This
 Spring. Snyder
Two Look at Two. Frost
When I hear deep in the mountains. Fr. A
 Compendium of Good Tanka. Teika
 See also Hunting and Hunters.
Defeat
Beauty of Israel is slain [or slaine] upon thy
 high places, The. Fr. Second Samuel
Heavens, ocean, and all earth, rejoice! Fr.
 The Defeat of the Norsemen. Sedulius
 Scottus
Last Word, The. Arnold
Mighty Runner, A. Robinson
My portion is defeat—today. Dickinson
Russia 1812. Hugo
To the Men Who Lose. Scarborough
Defoe, Daniel
To That Most Senseless Scoundrel, the Author
 of Legion's Humble Address to the Lords.
 Brown
Deformities
Angles. Partridge
Degas, Edgar
Museum Piece. Wilbur
Dehumanization
Applicant, The. Plath
Black Cry. Craveirinha
Circular Roads. Muchemwa
Contrast. Nangolo
Factory Hands, The. Chimedza
Human Remains. Boston
If You Want to Know Me. Sousa
Mamano. Craveirinha
Midnight. Nortje
Nightfall in Soweto. Mtshali
Of Reason and Discovery. Mattera
Tell Me News. Sepamla
To White South Africa. Pieterse
 See also Bureaucracy and Bureaucrats;
 Oppression; Racial Prejudice; Sexism.
Deirdre
Deirdre. Stephens
Deism
Ode: "Spacious firmament on high, The."
 Addison
There is no God, as I was taught in youth.
 Fr. Sonnets. Masefield
Déjà Vu
Encounter in a Glass. Wright
Vision by Sweetwater. Ransom
Dejection
Dejection; an Ode [or A Letter to Sara
 Hutchinson]. Coleridge
Stanzas Written in Dejection [–December
 1818,] near Naples. Shelley
 See also Melancholy.
Delaware River
Across the Delaware. Carleton
Delft, Holland
At Delft. Tomlinson
Courtyards in Delft. Mahon
Delight
Rarely, Rarely, Comest Thou. Shelley
Deliverance
I to the Lord from My Distress. Unknown

Delphi, Oracle of
News for the Delphic Oracle. Yeats
Delvaux, Paul
Homage to Paul Delvaux. Guthrie
Demeter
To Demeter. Fleming
Democracy
Councils. Piercy
Democracy. Fr. Commemoration Ode.
 Monroe
For You, O Democracy. Whitman
Hark! Young Democracy from sleep. Fr.
 Young Democracy. O'Dowd.
On a General Election. Belloc
Thanksgiving (1956). Cummings
 See also Voting and Voters.
Dempsey, William Harrison ("Jack")
Boxing Match, The. Ignatow
Nonpareil's Grave, The. McMahon
Denial
Thin Man, The. Justice
Denmark
Denmark. Wolfe
King Christian. Evald
There Is a Charming Land. Oehlenschläger
Dennis, John
Lines Spoken by the Ghost of John Dennis at
 the Devil Tavern. Gray
Dentistry and Dentists
Hands folded like napkins in my lap.
 Peterson
Next. Koyama
Ode to a Dental Hygienist. Hooton
Dentures
Poet's Farewell to His Teeth, The. Dickey
Denver, Colorado
House in Denver. Ferril
Waltz against the Mountains. Ferril
Department Stores
Fixture, A. Swenson
Hi-Fashion Girl. Equi
Deportation
Deportation. Teller
Deportation Order. Fortini
Three. Fr. Psychoanalysis. Teller
Depression (economic). See Great
 Depression.
Depression (psychological). See Melancholy;
 Mental Illness.
Descartes, René
Descartes. Insingel
Reply to the Shade of Descartes. La Vigne
Theological. Fadiman
Deserts
Death in the Desert, A. Tomlinson
Desert, The. al-Wahaybi
Desert Madness. Leyeles
Desert Shipwreck. Jordan
Drifting Sands and a Caravan. Langworthy
In Scorching Time. Stevens
Logbook of a Lost Caravan. Illyés
Ozymandias [or Ozymandias of Egypt or
 Sonnet: Ozymandias]. Shelley
Simoom, The. Tupper
Sleep in the Mojave Desert. Plath
What Frank, Martha and I Know about the
 Desert. Sadongei
Yuma. Phelps
Desire
Abstinence Sows Sand All Over. Fr.
 Gnomic Verses. Blake
Against winter which advances. Marcabrun
At Mid-Ocean. Bly
Aye Waukin' O! Unknown
Because I had reproached him where he
 failed. Jausbert de Puycibot
Beloved,/ What does it take to put a house in
 order? Fr. Letters from a Married Man.
 Mager
Blueberry Man. Bergman
Courtship. Strand

Desire. "Æ"
Desire. Cornish
Desire. Eddy
Desire. Mackey
Desire is a witch. Day Lewis
Desire Is Dead. Lawrence
Desire makes you. Smith
Desires. Bensley
Early Love. Scott
Epigram: "Beauty, a silver dew that falls in
 May." Unknown
Filling her compact and delicious body. Fr.
 Dream Songs. Berryman
Fire and Ice. Frost
First Love. Clare
For My Husband. Voigt
High on the peak of Mikasa. Fr. Manyo
 Shu. Akahito
I Knew a Woman [Lovely in Her Bones]
 Roethke
I turn you out of doors. Chartier
I'd Want Her Eyes to Fill with Wonder.
 Patchen
Inanna's Song. Unknown
Kaddish. Ginsberg
Long Lines: Youth and Age. Goodman
Love. Baker
Maiden. Kalász
Men with the fire of deep desire. Ghalib
My Past. Cooper
Nature of creation itself, The. Ghalib
No man can utterly fulfill what he has in his
 heart. Aimeric de Belenoi
Older Men. Corn
Our neighbors are so courteous, worthy and
 human! Cardenal
Palmer's Ode, The. Fr. Never Too Late.
 Greene
Phalanstery. Fr. Sketchbook. Ladányi
Rapture, The. Baker
Re-forming the Crystal. Rich
Sea at Evening, The. Laird
Seizure. Sappho
Sex, as they harshly call it. Fr. Two Songs.
 Rich
Shall I come, if I swim? wide are the waves,
 you see. Campion
She Loves. Broumas
Star-Sown. Netser
Sweet softness with which love serves me
 often, The. Guilhem de Cabestanh
"Thou blind man's mark, thou fool's
 self-chosen snare." Fr. Astrophel and
 Stella, CIX. Sidney
This crab—where does it come from? Fr.
 Manyo Shu. Ojin
Tom. Schuyler
Uneasy Rider. Wakoski
Want Bone, The. Pinsky
What is it men in women do require? Fr.
 Several Questions Answered. Blake
White Rose, A. O'Reilly
Wondrous the Merge. Broughton
Yes! hope may with my strong desire keep
 pace. Michelangelo
You Must Have Been a Sensational Baby.
 Norse
 See also Erotic Love; Lust.
Desks
Desks. Smith
Desolation
Desolation. Baratynsky
Ha'nacker Mill. Belloc
Hand That Signed the Paper Felled a City,
 The. Thomas
Last Visit. Finch
More than People. Fr. A Cleared Land.
 Fulton
No Voice of Man. Falconer

Sgurr Nan Gillean. *Fr.* The Cuillin. MacLean
To the pit of my heart I pine. *Fr.* Manyo Shu. Yakamochi

Despair
Against Hope. *Fr.* The Mistress. Cowley
Against winter which advances. Marcabrun
Amagoduka at Glencoe Station. Mtshali
Another While. Rosenfeld
Anyone who swallows foolishly. Pons de Capdueill
Ashes of Life. Millay
At the point of separating out. Marcabrun
Ballad of the Despairing Husband. Creeley
Before Mine Eye. *Fr.* Gascoigne's Memories. Gascoigne
Better Resurrection, A. Rossetti
Canada's Natural Resource. Midnight Sun
Carrion Comfort. Hopkins
Cave of Despair, The. *Fr.* The Faerie Queene. Spenser
Collar, The. Herbert
Cry of the Peoples, The. Brody
Dance of Despair, The. Bialik
Darkling Thrush, The. Hardy
Dead Faith, The. Lea
Delirium in Vera Cruz. Lowry
Despair. Kálnoky
Despair. *Fr.* The Faerie Queene. Spenser
Despairing Lover, The. Walsh
Deva-like Barbarian. Wen T'ing-yün
Die My Shriek. Kushniroff
Divorce of a Lover, The. Gascoigne
Dust Is Upon Us, The. Rashed
Dying in the Street. Johnson
Epistle to the Gentiles. Hayes
House, The. Kailas
Housewife's Lament, The. *Unknown*
How Much Longer? Mezey
I cannot live with you. Dickinson
I see the clear weather darken. Jordan
If Only. Rossetti
In the Silence of Endless Night. Rashed
It was not death, for I stood up. Dickinson
Knife, The. Kaplan
Koheleth. Untermeyer
Leaden Echo and the Golden Echo, The. Hopkins
Lines Written among the Euganean Hills. Shelley
Madrigal. Drummond
Mariana. Tennyson
Miserere, My Maker. *Unknown*
Moses and Jesus. Zangwill
Mountaineer, The. Nathan
My Guests. Faiz
No Worst, There Is None. Hopkins
O dull, cold northern sky. Stevenson
O Heavy Step of Slow Monotony. Toller
O Powers Celestial, with what sophistry. *Fr.* Parthenophil and Parthenophe. Barnes
Raging Generation, The. Mtshali
Redeployment. Nemerov
Remembrance. Slonimski
Renascence. Millay
Reunion. Tawney
Shall the Dead Praise Thee? Macdonald
Sick Rose, The. *Fr.* Songs of Experience. Blake
Song: "My silks and fine array." Blake
Song of Despair. Rangiaho
Stanzas Written in Dejection [–December 1818,] near Naples. Shelley
Tailor, The. "Ansky"
Thick grows that tarragon. *Unknown*
To My Generation. Galai
Tregardock. Betjeman
'Twas Night. *Unknown*
Why Hast Thou Forsaken Me? *Fr.* The Psalm of Christ. Walsh
With a pleasant/ heaviness. Riquier
Work without Hope. Coleridge

You buy some flowers for your table. *Fr.* Poems in Praise of Practically Nothing. Hoffenstein

Destiny. *See* **Fate.**

Destruction
Destruction. Kyger
End of Clonmacnois, The. *Unknown*
For the Record. Rich
I Saw a Broken Town. Allan
Kilcash. *Unknown*
Summer Holiday. Jeffers
Threnody for Berlin—1945. Jarman

Detectives
Operative No. 174 Resigns. Fearing

Detroit, Michigan
Coming Home. Levine
Detroit. Hall
Idea of Detroit, The. Gustafson

Devil. *See* **Satan.**

Devonshire, England
Devonshire Scenes. *Fr.* Tamerton Church-Tower or First Love. Patmore
Devonshire Walk, A. *Fr.* Britannia's Pastorals. Browne
Discontents in Devon. Herrick
Frolic Mariners of Devon, The. *Fr.* Britannia's Pastorals. Browne

Dew
As winds blow over white dewdrops. *Fr.* A Compendium of Good Tanka. Teika
Dew and the frost, The. Tameuji
Dew at the tip of a leaf. *Fr.* A Compendium of Good Tanka. Teika
Dripping dew of the foot-wearying mountain, The. *Fr.* Manyo Shu. Ishikawa
Drop of Dew, A. Halkin
Even the dead leaves. Tameie
In the dripping dew of the foot-wearying mountain. *Fr.* Manyo Shu. Otsu
Is it because autumn dew has collected. *Fr.* A Compendium of Good Tanka. Teika
On a Drop of Dew. Marvell
Over heavy dew. Tamenori
Quick-falling dew. Basho
Warrior walks, A. *Fr.* Eighty-seven Hokku. Buson
White dew,/ come from no one knows where, The. *Fr.* Twenty-three Tanka. Tamekane
White dew: one drop on each prickle. *Fr.* Eighty-seven Hokku. Buson
Wondering, I touched it with my young lips. *Fr.* Thirty-nine Tanka. Yosano Akiko
World of dew, A. Issa
World of dew is, yes, The. Issa

Dewey, George
Dewey and His Men. Rice
Dewey at Manila. Johnson
Dewey in Manila Bay. Risley
Manila. Ware

Diabetes
Day of the Pancreas, The. McFadden

Diana
Hymn to Diana. *Fr.* The Golden Age. Heywood
Hymn to Diana. *Fr.* Cynthia's Revels. Jonson
See also **Artemis.**

Diaries
Lady's Diary, The. Dibdin
Nothing to Write Home About. Brainard
On a Seven-Day Diary. Dugan
Writing. Allingham

Dickens, Charles
Dickens in Camp. Harte

Dickinson, Emily
Altitudes. Wilbur
Because I Could Not Dump. Paterson
Brief History. Briggs
Emily Dickinson. Longley
Emily Dickinson Postage Stamp. Strongin

Emily Dickinson's Sestina for Molly Bloom. Lefcowitz
Houses of Emily Dickinson, The. Rubin
"I Am in Danger—Sir." Rich
Mystery of Emily Dickinson, The. Bell
To Emily Dickinson. Crane
To Emily Dickinson. Winters
Visiting Emily Dickinson's Grave with Robert Francis. Bly
Your Birthday in Wisconsin You Are 140. Berryman

Dictionaries
Aardvark. Fields

Dido
Dido's Hunting. *Fr.* The Aeneid [*or* Eneados]. Virgil
I am that Dido which thou here do'st see. Ausonius

Didrickson, Mildred
Babe Didrikson. Rice

Dieting
Breakfast Song in Time of Diet. King
Diet, The. Burge
I Can't Have a Martini, Dear, but You Take One. Nash
Jack Sprat could eat no fat. Mother Goose

Dikes
Dykes, The. Kipling
Leak in the Dike, The. Cary

Dillinger, John
Shooting of John Dillinger outside the Biograph Theater July 22, 1934, The. Wagoner

Dimples
Where Shall the Baby's Dimple Be. Holland

Diners
At Kresge's Diner in Stonefalls, Arkansas. Hirsch
Meanwhile. Dailey
Whalefeathers. Violi

Dinosaurs
Brontosaurus. Kredenser
Dinosaur Spring. Waniek
Dinosaurs. Stoloff
Dinosaurs. Worth
Local Allosaurus, The. Utley
Long Gone. Prelutsky
So Big! Fatchen
Unfortunately. Katz

Diocletian
Great Diocletian. *Fr.* The Garden. Cowley

Diogenes
Tomb of Diogenes, The. *Unknown*

Dionysus
Ambrosia of Dionysus and Semele, The. Graves
Hail, Dionysos. Randall

Diplomacy and Diplomats
I Had a Duck-billed Platypus. Barrington

Dirigibles
Blimps and Nightingales. Moore
Dirigible, The. Bergengren
Zeppelin. Glaze

Disabilities
Disabled. Owen
Toward Solomon's Mountain; the Experience of Disability in Poetry (TSM). Joseph L. Baird *and* Deborah S. Workman, eds.

Disarmament
This Excellent Machine. Lehmann
See also **Militarism; Pacifism and Pacifists.**

Disasters
Albion Battleship Calamity, The. McGonagall
Ashtabula Disaster, The. Moore
Blantyre Explosion, The. *Unknown*
Dinner Party 1940. Sherlock
Disaster, The. Bennet
Eternal City, The. Ammons
Explosion, The. Larkin

Gresford Disaster, The. *Unknown*
Trimdon Grange Explosion, The. Armstrong

Discipline
Discipline. Herbert
Lesson, The. Mariani

Discontent
Discontented Woman, The. *Unknown*
Evidently Chicken Town. Clarke
Goodnight. Smith
Grumble Family, The. *Unknown*
How to Like It. Dobyns
Inquietude. Murray
Meditation on the A30. Betjeman
Nervous Prostration. Wickham
Spinster. Plath

Discotheques
Chances "R." Ginsberg
Disco Chinatown. Kageyama

Disease
Arteriosclerosis. Glatstein

Dishonor
She Was Poor but She Was Honest.
  Unknown

Disraeli, Benjamin
To Disraeli. Brooks

Distrust
Bird, The. Halpern
Filth of Your Suspicion, The. Schulman

Ditmars, Raymond Lee
Lines to Dr. Ditmars. Robinson

Dives (Bible)
Dives and Lazarus. *Unknown*
On Dives. Crashaw

Diving and Divers
Cold Logic. Hutchinson
Diver, The. Hayden
Diver, The. Howard
Diver, The. Ross
Diver. Simpson
Divers, The. Quennell
Divers' Death, The. Brackenbury
Diving into the Wreck. Rich
Elegy for a Diver. Meinke
Fancy Dive. Silverstein
Fantasia. Livesay
Fine, a Private Place, A. Ackerman
High Diver. Francis
Imagined Description of Myself, in Another
  Scene, An. Bernstein
Springboard, The. Rich

Divining and Diviners
Diviner, The. Heaney

Divorce
Ballad of the Despairing Husband. Creeley
Beginning. Nowlan
Broken Home, The. Merrill
By this he knew she wept with waking eyes.
  Fr. Modern Love. Meredith
Chance Meeting. Griffin
Divorce. Koehn
Divorce. Noll
Divorce Song. *Unknown*
For Starters. McCabe
Getting Out. Mathis
Gift, The. Jarman
He would/ in the case of a divorce. *Fr.*
  Divorce. Ditlevsen
It is not easy. *Fr.* Divorce. Ditlevsen
Jamie Douglas. *Unknown*
People Getting Divorced. Ferlinghetti
Popular Functionary, A. Dibdin
Power of Innocence, The. "H"
Songs of Divorce. Green
Thus piteously Love closed what he begat.
  Fr. Modern Love. Meredith
Victims, The. Olds
Wail of the Divorced. Tucker
Wedding-Ring. Levertov

Doctors. *See* **Physicians.**

Dodo Birds
Dodo. Carlile

Dogs
Age. Tomioka Taeko
Ah, Are You Digging on My Grave? Hardy
An Unromantic Awakening. Thompson
At the Dog Show. Morley
At thieves I bark; at lovers wag my tail.
Back Country. Oates
Ballad of Master McGrath, A. *Unknown*
Bandog, The. De la Mare
Bingo. *Unknown*
Biography. Ondaatje
Bishop Doane on His Dog. Doane
Bliss. Farjeon
Blues for Old Dogs. Zimmer
Bony. Ortiz
Bounce to Fop; an Heroick Epistle from a
  Dog at Twickenham to a Dog at Court.
  Pope
Brave Rover. Beerbohm
Bum. Wedgefarth
Burial of the Dog. Musgrave
Cats and Dogs. Bodecker
Chums. Guiterman
Curate Thinks You Have No Soul, The.
  Lucas
D is for Dog. Davies
Daley's Dorg Wattle. Goodge
Dead "Wessex" the Dog to the Household.
  Hardy
Death. Williams
Death of a Dog. Bland
Denise. Hale
Dog, The. Faber
Dog, The. Herford
Dog, The. Iremonger
Dog. Monro
Dog. Smith
Dog, The. Stern
Dog, The. *Unknown*
Dog in San Francisco, A. Ondaatje
Dogs. Tu Kuo-ch'ing
Dogs and Weather. Welles
Dog's Death, A. Squire
Dog's Death. Updike
Dogs in the Morning Light. Dawe
Dogs of Dawn. *Fr.* Guys of the Volye.
  Vaynshteyn
Donahue's Sister. Gunn
Drifters. Dawe
Early Spring. Whalen
Elegy on the Death of a Mad Dog, An. *Fr.*
  The Vicar of Wakefield. Goldsmith
Epitaph for a Dog. Twardowski
Epitaph on Fop. Cowper
Epitaph on True, Her Majesty's Dog, An.
  Prior
Fashions in Dogs. White
Fidelity. Wordsworth
Flush or Faunus. Browning
Geist's Grave. Arnold
German Shepherd. Livingston
Gift with the Wrappings Off. Counselman
Gone. McCord
Hairy Dog, The. Asquith
How a Puppy Grows. Jackson
I Muse Not. Davison
I Think I Know No Finer Things than Dogs.
  Brent
If Our Dogs Outlived Us. Hines
In the Days of Rin-Tin-Tin. Hoffman
Incident Characteristic of a Favourite Dog.
  Wordsworth
Introduction to Dogs, An. Nash
Jubilate Canis. Jong
Kaiser Dead. Arnold
Letter to the City Clerk. Wright
Lines I Told Myself I Wouldn't Write.
  Mariani
Little Black Dog, The. Reynolds
Little Dog-Angel, A. Holland

Little Dog under the Wagon, The. *Unknown*
Lone Dog. McLeod
Loyal. Matthews
Macinnes's Mountain Patrol. Patey
Madness. Dickey
Malemute Dog, A. O'Cotter
Mother Doesn't Want a Dog. Viorst
My Dog. Bangs
My Dog. Chute
My Dog Dash. Ruskin
My Dog Ponto. Masters
My Dog, Spot. Bennett
My Doggie. Nurton
My Little Dog. MacEwen
Nero. Tanikawa Shuntaro
Night Song. Cornford
Nino, the Wonder Dog. Fuller
Noctambule. Johnston
Obituary. Parsons
Old Blue. *Unknown*
Old Dog in the Ruins of the Graves at Arles,
  The. Wright
Old Dog, New Dog. Lea
Old Mother Hubbard. Martin
Old Tuff. Sicking
One to Grieve, The. Thomas
Overland to the Islands. Levertov
Pardon, The. Wilbur
Popular Personage at Home, A. Hardy
Power of the Dog, The. Kipling
Praise of a Collie. MacCaig
Properties of a Good Greyhound, The.
  Berners
Puppy and I. Milne
Puppy Chased the Sunbeam, The. Eastwick
Pussy-Cat and Puppy-Dog. McCrea
Rags. Cooke
Red Dog, The. Jensen
Roger the Dog. Hughes
Rover. Stafford
Sandra: At the Beaver Trap. Harper
Savage Beast, The. Williams
Sheepdog Trials in Hyde Park. Day Lewis
Shepherd's Dog, The. Norris
Shlup, shlup, the dog. *Fr.* Six Variations.
  Levertov
Sila. Warren
Simon and the Tarantula. Wright
Song of the Mischievous Dog, The. Thomas
Sonnet: To Tartar, a Terrier Beauty.
  Beddoes
Stray Dog. Mish
Stray Dog. Weöres
Sunning. Tippett
Supplication of the Black Aberdeen. Kipling
This Tree. Hathaway
Three Dogs. Brereton
Timon Speaks to a Dog. Hobsbaum
To a Bull-Dog. Squire
To a Dog. Peabody
To a Dog Injured in the Street. Williams
To a Spaniel. Landor
To My Dog "Blanco." Holland
To My Setter, Scout. Seldon
To Our House-Dog Captain. Landor
To robbers furious, and to lovers tame.
  Johnson
To Scott. Letts
Today Was Not. Rosen
Towser Shall Be Tied Tonight. *Unknown*
Tray. Browning
Tribute to the Memory of the Same Dog.
  Wordsworth
Turkish Trench Dog, The. Dearmer
Two Dogs. Kim Chun-soo
Uncle Dog; the Poet at 9. Sward
Victor Dog, The. Merrill
Ye Bruthers Dogg. Anderson
Yoko. Gunn
Your Dog Dies. Carver
See also **individual breeds of dogs (e.g.,**
  Collies).

Dollhouses
Making a Door. Schmitz
Dolls
Doll, The. Beutler
Doll, The. *Fr.* Sonnet Variations. Houston
Doll. Riaz
Dolls, The. Yeats
Russian Doll, The. Shore
Dolphins
Watching for Dolphins. Constantine
Dominican Republic
Cane Fields, The. *Fr.* Parsley. Dove
Palace, The. *Fr.* Parsley. Dove
Parsley. Dove
Don Juan
Aubade: Donna Anna to Juan, Still Asleep.
Howard
Don Giovanni on His Way to Hell. Gilbert
Don Juan, *sels.* Byron
Don Juan. Lawrence
Don Juan in Hell. Baudelaire
How to Tell Juan Don from Another. Lewis
Don Quixote
Bridge of Heraclitus, The. Reavey
Don Quixote. Betts
Don Quixote. Tomer
Donegal. *See* **County Donegal, Ireland.**
Donkeys
Big Friend of the Stones. Orlen
Donkey, The. Chesterton
Donkey, The. Fyleman
Donkey, The. Roethke
Donkey, The. *Unknown*
Donkey. Van Doren
Donkey and the Lapdog, The. La Fontaine
Little Donkey, The. Jammes
Prayer to Go to Paradise with the Donkeys,
A. Francis
To a Young Ass. Coleridge
Turf Carrier on Aranmore. Hewitt
What the Donkey Saw. Fanthorpe
Donne, John
John Donne. Simmons
John Donne's Statue. Bishop
Letter to John Donne, A. Sisson
On Donne's Poetry. Coleridge
To John Donne. Jonson
Upon the Death of My Ever Desired Friend
Doctor Donne Dean of Pauls. King
Donnelly, Charles
Of what a quality is courage made. *Fr.*
Charles Donnelly. MacDonagh
Doorbells
Doorbells. Field
Doors
Delights of the Door, The. Ponge
Door, The. *Fr.* The Quest. Auden
Door, The. Tomlinson
Door Number Four. Pomerantz
Doorway, The. Lin Huan-ch'ang
Lockless Door, The. Frost
Old Essex Door. Hickey
Terrible Door, The. Monro
Dormice
Dormouse, The. Cole
Elf and the Dormouse, The. Herford
Dorset, England
Ad Henricum Wottonem. Bastard
Domicilium. Hardy
Once at Swanage. Hardy
Overlooking the River Stour. Hardy
Roman Road, The. Hardy
Dostoyevsky, Feodor
Dostoevsky. Glatstein
Respectable Burgher, The. Hardy
Three Dostoievskian Masks. Rákos
Doubt
Doubt. Deland
Doubt. Gregh
Doubt. Thompson

Doubter, The. Gilder
Doubter's Prayer, The. Brontë
Dover Beach. Arnold
Father. Ficke
Praise Doubt. Van Doren
Prayer for Living and Dying. La Farge
Prayer of an Unbeliever. Reese
Scholfield Huxley. *Fr.* Spoon River
Anthology. Masters
Skeptic, The. Thompson
Song of Doubt, A. Holland
See also **Agnosticism.**
Douglas, Stephen Arnold
Lecompton's Black Brigade. Halpine
Douglass, Frederick
Douglass. Dunbar
Frederick Douglass. Cornish
Frederick Douglass. Dunbar
Frederick Douglass. Hayden
In Memoriam Frederick Douglass. Bibb
In Memoriam Frederick Douglass. Ray
Welcome to Hon. Frederick Douglass. Heard
Woman at the Washington Zoo, The. Jarrell
Dover, England
Dover Beach. Arnold
Dover, the Samphire Cliff. *Fr.* King Lear.
Shakespeare
Doves
Captive Dove, The. Brontë
Coo-pe-coo. *Unknown*
Dove. Farber
Dove, The. MacColl
Dove Apologizes to His God for Being
Caught by a Cat, The. Eaton
Dove says, Coo, coo, The. Mother Goose
Doves. Falconer
Doves. Schutting
Dove's Loneliness, The. Darley
Flowers Pink with Ebony. Chalfi
High in the afternoon the dove. *Fr.*
Considerations. Smithyman
In the valley shade. Chikako
Jealousie Is the Rage of a Man. Winchilsea
My Easter Dove. Ray
Nature of the Turtle Dove, The. *Fr.* The
Bestiary. *Unknown*
Regret for the Mourning Doves Who Failed to
Mate. Weigl
There Once Was a Dove. Guri
Turtle thus with plaintive crying, The. Gay
Down's Syndrome
Almond Tree, The. Stallworthy
Dinner at the Mongoloid's. Rubin
Jenny. Astrachan
Mongoloid Child Handling Shells on the
Beach, A. Snyder
Dowries
Arise, Arise. *Unknown*
Lass with a Lump of Land. Ramsay
Dowsing
Water-Witch, The. Perry
Dragonflies
Bête Humaine. Young
Dragonfly, The. Bogan
Dragonfly, A. Farjeon
Dragonfly. Jaques
Dragonfly, The. Nemerov
Dragonfly, The. Rand
Dragonfly—unable to get hold of a grass
blade. *Fr.* Seventy-six Hokku. Basho
Dragonfly catches a fly, A. *Fr.* Fifteen
Hokku. Joso
Hunter's Moon. Sandy
Stay, stay, dragonfly! *Fr.* Ryojin Hisho.
Go-Shirakawa
Dragons
Dragon, The. Mullineaux
Fafnir and the Knights. Smith
Gold-tinted Dragon, The. Kuskin
Jabberwocky. *Fr.* Through the
Looking-Glass. "Carroll"

My Dragon. Kennedy
Natural History of Unicorns and Dragons My
Daughter and I Have Known, A. Root
O to Be a Dragon. Moore
Song of the Dragon's Daughter, The. Le
Guin
Tale of Custard the Dragon, The. Nash
Toaster, The. Smith
Drake, Joseph Rodman
On the Death of Joseph Rodman Drake.
Halleck
Drake, Sir Francis
Epigram: On Sir Francis Drake. *Unknown*
Farewell to Sir John Norris and Sir Francis
Drake, A. Peele
To the Noble Sir Francis Drake. Beedome
Upon Sir Francis Drake's Return from His
Voyage about the World, and the Queen's
Meeting Him. *Unknown*
Drama. *See* **Theater.**
Drawing
Life Drawing. Orlen
Woman with Gardenia: A Sketch. Hadas
Drayton, Michael
Funeral Elegy on the Death of His Very Good
Friend, Mr. Michael Drayton. Cokayne
Dreams and Dreaming
African Dream. Kaufman
Afterthoughts. Tachihara Michizo
Again I remember. Ghalib
Against Romanticism. Amis
Ante-natal Dream. Kavanagh
Après un Rêve. Seymour-Smith
Bad Dream. MacNeice
Barber, The. Gray
Beale Street. Hughes
Betrayal. Santos
Birthday Dream, The. Dickey
Brothers, The. Muir
Cave-Boy, The. Richards
Chimera. Howes
Cowboy's Dream, The. Kiskaddon
Cry of the Dreamer, The. O'Reilly
Darkness. Byron
Daybreak. Spender
Directions for Dreamfishing. Johnston
Dream, A. Al-Ghuzzi
Dream, A [*or* The] Allingham
Dream, The. Bogan
Dream, The. Byron
Dream, The. Ignatow
Dream, A. Johnson
Dream, A. *Fr.* The Fall of Hyperion.
Keats
Dream. Miles
Dream, The. Sherburne
Dream. *Unknown*
Dream, A. Weöres
Dream. Witt
Dream about Our Master, William
Shakespeare, The. Plutzik
Dream Barker. Valentine
Dream, Dump-Heap, and Civilization.
Warren
Dream Farmer. Boyer
Dream-Land. Poe
Dream of Fair Women, A. Amis
Dream of Fair Women, The. Dennis
Dream of Roaming, A. Weöres
Dream of the Rood, The. *Unknown*
Dream of the Rood, The. *Unknown*
Dream of wandering in woods with. Howe
Dream-Pedlary. Beddoes
Dream-Ship, The. Field
Dream, The ("Last night I had a dream bad
'cess to my dreaming."). *Unknown*
Dream Time. Thwaite
Dream Variation. Hughes
Dream with Fred Astaire. Berkson
Dream within a Dream, A. Poe

Dream[e], The. Donne
Dreamer of Dreams. Carruth
Dreams. Bloch
Dreams. Daley
Dreams, The. Field
Dreams. Giovanni
Dreams. Herrick
Dreams. Hughes
Dreams. Poe
Dreamscape. Zelazny
Dreamt I Today the Dream of Yesternight.
   Santayana
Echo. Rossetti
El Sueño de la Razón. Cooper
Empire of Dreams. Simic
Epistle to John Hamilton Reynolds. Keats
Even in my dreams. Keiun
Expostulation and Reply. Wordsworth
Eye of Humility, The. Smith
Fierce Dream, The. Wainwright
Fire-Logs. Sandburg
First of All My Dreams, The. Cummings
First one notices. Tamehide
Forgotten Dreams. Silvera
Fourth Street, San Rafael. Berkson
Girl Butterfly Girl. al-Haj
Hammer Falls, Is Falling, The. Boruch
Harlem. Hughes
Harlequin of Dreams, The. Lanier
His Dream of the Sky-Land: A Farewell
   Poem, sel. Li Po
Hold Fast Your Dreams. Driscoll
House in the Wood, The. Jarrell
I Am Being Dragged by Red Dolphins.
   Kormos
I awake from sleep. Kenko
I Dream. Roubaud
I dreamed a dream: I dreamt that I espied.
   Clough
I dreamed I was holding. Fr. Manyo Shu.
   Kasa
I Drink the Wine of Your Dreams. Nieminen
I Have Dreamed of You So Much. Desnos
I may well once more. Tamehide
Illusion. Wilcox
I'm a Dreamer. Cumbo
In My Dreams. Smith
In the far realm of our Lord. Fr. Manyo
   Shu. Yakamochi
In Your Bad Dream. Hugo
It's Comforting. Simmons
Ivory, Coral, Gold, The. Drummond
Kalapuya Prophecy, A. Unknown
Kitchenette Building. Brooks
Land of Dreams, The. Blake
Le Jazz Hot. Hollo
Lesson for Dreamers. Janeczko
Long History of the Short Poem. Hoover
Longing to Be Saved, The. Kumin
Lotos-Eaters, The. Tennyson
Love of the Scorching Wind. Nagy
Mad Scene, The. Merrill
Making the Jam without You. Kumin
Man Asleep in the Desert. Lux
Methought That I Had Broken from the
   Tower. Fr. King Richard III.
   Shakespeare
Miniver Cheevy. Robinson
Mirage. Rossetti
Mowing the Lawn. Bensko
My Dream. Blockcolski
My Dream. Rossetti
My Father's Dream. Boulus
My Little Dreams. Johnson
Night a Sailor Came to Me in a Dream, The.
   Wakoski
Nightmare. Fr. Iolanthe. Gilbert
Nightmares. Fox
No, Love Is Not Dead. Desnos
Nocturne in the Women's Prison. Beneyto
Nun's Priest's Tale, The. Fr. The
   Canterbury Tales. Chaucer

Old Man Dreams, The. Holmes
Old War-Dreams. Whitman
On Dreams. Swift
On Dreams, October 15, 1782. Brydges
On His Deceased Wife. Milton
On My Late Dear Wife. Richardson
On this spring night. Fujwara no Teika
Orchard-Pit, The. Rossetti
Origin of Dreams. Bell
Out of the Frying Pan into the Fire. Henry
Painting of the Butterfly Dream by the Master
   Artist Li Tsai, A. Chu Yün-ming
Peacock Woman, The. Nagy
Pinch of Salt, A. Graves
Prelude to an Evening. Ransom
Prowling the Ridge. Minty
Rain. Murray
Recording a Dream. Yang Shih-ch'i
Rhyme of the Dream-Maker Man, A. White
Rock-a-by Lady, The. Field
Roman in Libya, A. Evans
Scapegoat. Rodgers
Self-Unseeing, The. Hardy
September. Pastan
Sleep-Learning. Fainlight
Song: "Don't Tell Me What You Dreamt Last
   Night." Adams
Song: "It Autumnne was, and on our
   hemisphere." Drummond
Sonnet: "I dreamed that I was thrown from a
   crag." Terrazas
Southern Pacific. Sandburg
Space is azure and the mountains bathe. Fr.
   Prophecy of Cuauhtémoc. Galván
Spider Dream. Hall
Story You Know, A. Strand
Strange Meeting. Owen
Sugar-Plum Tree, The. Field
They Flee from Me That Sometime Did Me
   Seek. Wyatt
This was my dream! I saw a forest. Fr. Bad
   Dreams. Browning
To Dark Eyes Dreaming. Snyder
To-night I am coming. Fr. Manyo Shu.
   Unknown
Tonight Everyone in the World Is Dreaming
   the Same Dream. Litwack
Tropics. Voigt
True to a Dream. Petersen
Undergraduate. Moore
Vanilla Sugar; or, Verse for a "Hallmark"
   Greeting Card. Howard
Vine, The. Herrick
Vision, The. O'Rahilly
Visions, The. Fr. Sonnets to Laura: Songs.
   Petrarch
Vocation. Stafford
Waking. Pyle
Was it that I went to sleep. Komachi
Window Sill, The. Graves
With the Thin Girl. Petri
Within the dream the thought. Ghalib
Wormwood. Kinsella
Wynken, Blynken, and Nod. Field
Yes, wonderful are dreams: and I have
   known. Fr. The Tower of the Dream.
   Harpur
You're So Far Away. Hazeley
Dress. See **Clothing.**
Driftwood
Driftwood. Smythe
Driftwood Dybbuk. Lefcowitz
Fires of Driftwood. MacKay
Drinking
After Getting Drunk, I Scribble Songs and
   Poems. Lu Yu
After we, dear friends, have drunk together.
   Fr. Manyo Shu. Otomo no Sakanoe
Alaskan Drinking Song. Morice
Anacreontic to Flip. Tyler
Auld Lang Syne. Burns
Bacchanal. De Vries

Bacchus's Opinion of Wine, and Other
   Beverages. Fr. Bacchus in Tuscany.
   Redi
Back and Side Go Bare, Go Bare. Fr.
   Gammer Gurton's Needle. Stevenson
Ballad of the Drinker in His Pub. Louw
Ballade of Liquid Refreshment. Bentley
Beer. Arnold
Beer. Calverley
Beer Drops. Boyd
Benefits and Abuse of Alcohol, The.
   Eubulus
Bring the Wine! Li Po
Cap so tall, A. Unknown
Captain Stratton's Fancy. Masefield
Circle, The. Moorer
Circumstance. Bowen
Daft Days, The. Fergusson
Dartmouth Winter-Song. Hovey
Drinking. Chu Yün-ming
Drinking at Night with Yen Kung-mou.
   Shen Chou
Drinking Song. Fr. The Bloody Brother.
   Fletcher
Drinking Song. Sainctonge
Drinking Song. Fr. The School for Scandal.
   Sheridan
Drinking Song. Stephen
Drinking Song, A. Yeats
Drinking Wine. Mo Shih-lung
Drunk Last Night with Friends, I Go to Work
   Anyway. Dow
Drunken Dee, The. Scroggie
Dry. Hoffenstein
England's Triumph. Unknown
Englishry. Shepherd
Epicure, The ("Fill the bowl with rosie
   wine"). Cowley
Face upon [or on] the Floor, The. D'Arcy
Fill the Bowl, Butler! Unknown
Finnegan's Wake. Unknown
Frolic, A. Herrick
Genius and Intemperance. Nicholson
Glass of Beer, A. Stephens
Grape Daiquiri. Koyama
Green Revolutions. Guest
Had We Two Met. Landor
Hangover Mass. Kennedy
Head and Bottle. Thomas
Hilltop, The. Hugo
How lovely! getting drunk faster than I do.
   Fr. Forty-four Tanka. Wakayama Bokusui
Hymn to Bacchus, A. Herrick
I get so drunk, I could be called the Earl of
   Dissipation! Fr. Thirty Poems of Longing
   for People. Chin Nung
If all be true that I do think. Aldrich
Impromptu on a Hangover. P'i Jih-hsiu
In the 2 A.M. Club, a working man's bar.
   Peterson
Indian Macho. Oliver
Inebriety. Crabbe
Interview with Doctor Drink. Cunningham
John Barleycorn. Burns
John Barleycorn's Diary: An Uncoloured
   Picture. McManus
Judged by the Company One Keeps.
   Unknown
Late Rising on Spring Days. Wei Chuang
Lilliputian's Beer Song. Winner
Lips That Touch Liquor. Young
Liquor and Longevity. Unknown
Logical Vegetarian, The. Chesterton
Love. Unknown
Man in the Moon Drinks Clarret, The.
   Unknown
Miniver Cheevy. Robinson
Mint Julep, The. Hoffman
Mr. Flood's Party. Robinson
Ode for a Social Meeting. Holmes
Of Drunkenness. Turberville
Old Keg of Rum, The. Unknown

Drinking Water *(continued)*

Old Wife in High Spirits. "MacDiarmid"
Omnes Gentes Plaudite! *Unknown*
Parting Glass, The. Freneau
Piss Artist, The. Shepherd
Quebec Liquor Commission Store. Klein
R-E-M-O-R-S-E. Ade
Rye Whisky. *Unknown*
Sigh as It Ends. Berryman
Sir John Barleycorn. *Unknown*
Sloe Gin. Heaney
Social Glass, The. Moorer
Song: "Let school-masters puzzle their brain."
 Fr. She Stoops to Conquer. Goldsmith
Song: "Pints and the pistols, the pike-staves
 and pottles, The." Praed
Song: "There's a barrel of porter at Tammany
 Hall." Halleck
Song in a Siege. Heath
Strip Me Naked, or Royal Gin for Ever; a
 Picture. *Unknown*
Tale of Lord Lovell, The. *Unknown*
Tam o' Shanter. Burns
Terence, This Is Stupid Stuff. *Fr.* A
 Shropshire Lad. Housman
There is drink fermented. *Fr.* A Satirical
 Poem about Drink. Jigmed
Two Glasses, The. Wilcox
Up in the Air. Ramsay
Upon Drinking in a Bowl. Rochester
Wassail Song. *Unknown*
Water-Drinker, The. Jonson
We are drunk with wine. *Unknown*
We Be Soldiers Three. *Unknown*
Welcome to Sack, The. Herrick
West Sussex Drinking Song. Belloc
What Thomas an Buile Said in a Pub.
 Stephens
When I Drink I Become the Joy of Faggots.
 Allison
Whenever you drink all night you make.
 Martial
Wholly drunk, I see only. *Fr.* Forty-four
 Tanka. Wakayama Bokusui
Willie Brew'd [*or* Brewed] a Peck o' Maut.
 Burns
Willows, The. Harte
Wine's inebriety. Ghalib
Winter Wish, A. Messinger
Yellow Bittern, The. Mac Giolla Ghunna
See also **Alcoholism and Alcoholics;**
 Drunkards.

Drinking Water
Drinking Fountain. Chute

Driving and Drivers
Drive Imagining. Vogelsang
Drive on the Peninsula, A. Turner
Driver in Italy, The. Christopher
Driving in Oklahoma. Revard
Driving Lesson. Pettit
Fiesta. Hannigan
Functional Poem. Halliday
Limited Access. Brosmer
Looking for a Rest Area. Dunn
Mad Town, The. Vas
Meditation on the A30. Betjeman
Once, Driving West of Billings, Montana.
 Mitchell
See also **Automobiles.**

Drought
Drought, The. Cheng Min
Drought Year. Wright
Dust Bowl. Davis
Poem 1: "What happens here happened to my
 grandfather and my father." Leon
Said Hanrahan. Hartigan
Song in Time of Drought. Péret
Song of a Fisherman, A. Sung Wan
Song of Bitter Drought, A. Cha Shen-hsing
Waiting for the Rain. Mnthali
Wind/ flattening its gaunt furious self against.
 Fr. The Wind Our Enemy. Marriott

Drowning
At the Discharge of Cannon Rise the
 Drowned. Witheford
Ballad of the Oysterman, The. Holmes
Beautiful Swimmer, The. Whitman
Body Fished from the Seine. Corso
Castaway, The. Cowper
Dead Man Dragged from the Sea, The.
 Gardner
Death by Drowning. Brewster
Death of a Young Son by Drowning.
 Atwood
Drowned, The. Bottoms
Drowned, The. Spender
Drowning is not so pitiful. Dickinson
Elegy: "Morning after death on the bar was
 calm." Henderson
Elegy on Gordon Barber. Derwood
Emmeline Grangerford's "Ode to Stephen
 Dowling Bots, Dec'd." *Fr.* The
 Adventures of Huckleberry Finn. "Twain"
Family. Miles
Fish Food. Wheelwright
Full fathom [*or* fadom] five thy father lies.
 Fr. The Tempest. Shakespeare
Having Drowned. Zamora
Jimmy Judge. *Unknown*
Lady in Kicking Horse Reservoir, The.
 Hugo
Lake. Miyoshi Tatsuji
Limbo. Heaney
Lowlands o' [*or* of] Holland, The. *Unknown*
Lycidas. Milton
Mary in the Silvery Tide. *Unknown*
New Ballad of Sir Patrick Spens, The.
 Quiller-Couch
Not Waving but Drowning. Smith
Note Left in Jimmy Leonard's Shack, A.
 Wright
Outlandish Knight, The. *Unknown*
Samuel Allen. *Unknown*
Seaman, 1941. Holden
Secrets. Pack
Skater in Blue. Parini
Swan Swims So Bonny, The. *Unknown*
These Trees Are No Forest of Mourners.
 Jones
This Is a Photograph of Me. Atwood
Under the Boathouse. Bottoms
Villagers. Smith
Walking Out. Adcock
Water Island. Moss

Drug Addiction
Addict, The. Rubin
Aga Khan, The. Orlen
Babylon Revisited. Baraka
Blues for Sister Sally. Kandel
Certain Choices. Shelton
Class of 19——. Dec
Cocaine Lil [and Morphine Sue] *Unknown*
Documentary on Airplane Glue, A.
 Henderson
Drugs Made Pauline Vague. Smith
Ho. Young
Idea of Ancestry, The. Knight
In Praise of Laudanum. Harrison
Junior Addict. Hughes
Kicking the Habit. T'Hooft
Laudanum. *Unknown*
"O. D." Gilbert
Opium-Eater, The. Tucker
Say Goodbye to Big Daddy. Jarrell
Solo for Bent Spoon. Finkel
Street Song. Gunn
Summer Words of a Sistuh Addict. Sanchez
To My Daughter the Junkie on a Train.
 Lorde
Willie the Weeper. *Unknown*

Drugs
Discovery of LSD a True Story, The. Hollo

Drugstores
Drug Store. Shapiro

Druids
Trepidation of the Druids. *Fr.* Ecclesiastical
 Sonnets. Wordsworth

Drums
African Dance. Hughes
Beat! Beat! Drums! Whitman
Distant Drum, The. Hernton
Drummer Hodge. Hardy
Drums. Chosa
Drums/ Then again drums. Seymour
La Chute. Olson
Ode: "I hate that drum's discordant sound."
 Scott of Amwell
Percussions. Welburn
Piano and Drums. Okara
Talking Drums, The. Kyei

Drunkards
Absinthe-Drinker, The. Symons
Alaskan Drinking Song. Morice
Alcoholic. Berryman
Closing Time. Michie
Cynical Portraits. Paul
Drunk in the Furnace, The. Merwin
Drunkard, The. Levine
Drunkards, The. Lowry
Drunkard's Doom, The. *Unknown*
Drunkard's Wife, The. Tucker
Drunken Gentleman, The. Yin O
Drunken Man, The. Orlen
Eclipse. Probst
Elegy for a Diver. Meinke
Epigram: "When Bibo thought fit from the
 world to retreat." Prior
Epitaph: "Stavro's dead. A truant vine."
 Durrell
Extravagant Drunkard's Wish, The. Ward
Face upon [*or* on] the Floor, The. D'Arcy
Falling Down to Bed. NorthSun
Guests are taking their seats, The. *Unknown*
He as O, A. Cummings
Interview with Doctor Drink. Cunningham
John Adkins' Farewell. *Unknown*
Lying in a Yuma Saloon. Barnes
Midnight Ramble, The. Woodward
Miniver Cheevy. Robinson
Mr. Flood's Party. Robinson
Not a Sous Had He Got. *Fr.* The Ingoldsby
 Legends: The Cynotaph. "Ingoldsby"
Note Left in Jimmy Leonard's Shack, A.
 Wright
Of Drunkenness. Turberville
Old Witherington. Randall
Original Epitaph on a Drunkard. Tyler
Pig, The. *Unknown*
Point of No Return. Graves
Red Whiskey. *Unknown*
Resentments Composed because of the Clamor
 of Town Topers Outside My Apartment.
 Knight
Rolling English Road, The. Chesterton
Song-Maker. Endrezze-Danielson
Sweet Will. Levine
There is drink fermented. *Fr.* A Satirical
 Poem about Drink. Jigmed
Where He Hangs His Hat. Lee
Willie's and Nellie's Wish. Moore
Zimmer Drunk and Alone, Dreaming of Old
 Football Games. Zimmer
See also **Alcoholism and Alcoholics.**

Dryads
Dryad Song. Fuller

Dryden, John
Dear John, whoever now takes pen to write.
 Fr. A Letter to John Dryden. McAuley
Panegyric on the Author of "Absalom and
 Achitophel," A. *Unknown*
To Mr. Bays. Sackville

Du Bois, William Edward Burghardt
Booker T. and W. E. B. Randall

For William Edward Burghardt Du Bois on
His Eightieth Birthday. Latimer
On the Death of William Edward Burghardt
Du Bois by African Moonlight and
Forgotten Shores. Rivers

Dublin, Ireland
At the Jaffé Memorial Fountain, Botanic
Gardens. Ormsby
Back to Dublin. Ford
Bewley's Oriental Café, Westmoreland Street.
Durcan
Canal Bank Walk. Kavanagh
Dublin. *Fr.* The Closing Album. MacNeice
Dublin Made Me. MacDonagh
Herbert Street Revisited. Montague
If Ever You Go to Dublin Town. Kavanagh
Lights of Dublin, The. O'Connor
Lines Written on a Seat on the Grand Canal,
Dublin. Kavanagh
Mountown! Thou Sweet Retreat. *Fr.* Mully
of Mountown. King
No Place So Grand. *Unknown*
Rocky Road to Dublin, The. *Unknown*
See also **Easter Rebellion.**

Duchamp, Marcel
Nude Descending a Staircase. Kennedy

Ducks
Can't you see it there. Sogi
Duck, The. Digance
Duck. Donaghy
Duck, The. King
Duck, The. Nash
Duck. Worth
Duck and the Kangaroo, The. Lear
Duck-chasing. Kinnell
Duck in Central Park. Savage
Ducks. Harvey
Ducks' Ditty. *Fr.* The Wind in the Willows.
Grahame
Ducks in the Rain. Tippett
Dusk: Mallards on the Charles River.
Blumenthal
Four Ducks on a Pond. Allingham
I had a duck and the young duck died.
Stodart-Walker
In an evening shower ducks walk around.
Fr. Thirty-three Hokku. Kikaku
Muscovy Drake, The. Lesoro
Nearing Winter. Sandeen
Nell Flaherty's Drake. *Unknown*
New Duckling, The. Noyes
Notorious Glutton, The. Taylor
Peter and Wendy. Garthwaite
Quack, Quack! "Seuss"
Shooting Ducks in South Louisiana.
Tillinghast
Song of the Duck Hunters. Kao Ch'i
That duck, bobbing up. Joso
Three Moves. Logan
Trueblue Gentleman, A. Patchen
Widgeon. Heaney
Wild Duck, The. Masefield
Wild Duck's Nest, The. Wordsworth
Wood Ducks. *Unknown*

Dude Ranches
Time to Stay, a Time to Go, A. Black

Duels
Dowie Houms o' Yarrow, The. *Unknown*
Duel, The. Field
Young Barnswell. *Unknown*

Dulles, John Foster
Just Dropped In. Cole

Dumont, Margaret
To the Lady Portrayed by Margaret Dumont.
Hollander

Dumps
Dump, The. Kuzma
Rural Dumpheap. Cane
Town Dump, The. Nemerov

Dunbar, Paul Laurence
Dunbar. Spencer

For Paul Laurence Dunbar. *Fr.* Four
Epitaphs. Cullen
In Memoriam Paul Laurence Dunbar. Ray
Paul Laurence Dunbar. Corrothers
Paul Laurence Dunbar. Hayden
Paul Laurence Dunbar. Linden

**Dundee, John Graham of Claverhouse, 1st
Viscount (Bonnie Dundee)**
Bonny [*or* Bonnie] Dundee. *Fr.* The Doom
of Devorgoil. Scott

Dunes
Sand Dunes. Frost

Dunkirk, France
Little Boats of Britain, The. Carsley

Duns Scotus
Duns Scotus's Oxford. Hopkins

Dunwich, England
At Dunwich. Thwaite

Dürer, Albrecht
Dürer; Innsbruck, 1495. "Malley"
Face of Dürer, The. Anderson
Knight, Death, and the Devil, The. Jarrell
Steeple-Jack, The. Moore

Duse, Eleonora
Seeing You Stand Once More before My
Eyes. *Fr.* Eleanora Duse. Lowell

Dusk. *See* **Twilight.**

Dust
Common Dust. Johnson
Dust. "Æ"
Dust, The. Hall
Dust. Ropes
Dust. Spire
Dust Is Upon Us, The. Rashed
Dust on Spring Street. Grudin
Praise of Dust, The. Chesterton
This Quiet Dust. Wheelock

Dutch, The
Political Despatch, A. Canning

Dutch Verse
*Dutch Interior; Postwar Poetry of the
Netherlands and Flanders* (DuIn). James
S. Holmes *and* William Jay Smith, eds.

Dutch Wars
Battle of Sole Bay, The. *Unknown*
Fourth Day's Battle, The. *Fr.* Annus
Mirabilis. Dryden
Now van to van the foremost squadrons meet.
Fr. Annus Mirabilis. Dryden
Song Written at Sea in the First Dutch War
(1665), the Night before an Engagement.
Sackville

Duty
Abraham Davenport. Whittier
Do It Now! *Unknown*
Duty. Clough
Duty. *Fr.* Voluntaries. Emerson
Duty, or Truth at Work. Moorer
Ego. Vivanti
Life's Common Duties. Savage
Ode to Duty. Wordsworth
Stopping by Woods on a Snowy Evening.
Frost
Three Fishers, The. Kingsley

Dwarfs
Epitaph on a Dwarf. Frances

E

Eagles
Ailing Eagle, The. Droste-Hülshoff
American Eagle, The. Lawrence
Dalliance of the Eagles, The. Whitman
Dead Eagle, The. Campbell
Eagle, An. Abu Risha
Eagle. Bowker

Eagle, The. *Fr.* Transcripts from Nature.
"Macleod"
Eagle. Skelton
Eagle, The. Tennyson
Eagle, The. Young
Eagle above Us, The. Altamirano
Eagle and the Mole, The. Wylie
Eagle Plain. Francis
Eagle Poem. Harjo
Eagles. Woody
Fire on the Hills. Jeffers
Inability to Depict an Eagle. Eberhart
Mole and the Eagle, The. Hale
Nature of the Eagle, The. *Fr.* The Bestiary.
Unknown
Salmon Drowns Eagle. Lowry
So the struck eagle, stretch'd upon the plain.
Byron
Story of a Well-made Shield, The.
Momaday
To the Eagle. Fordham
Towards the sun, towards the south-west.
Fr. Eagle in New Mexico. Lawrence
White Eagle, The. McDonald

Ears
Colonel, The. Forché

Earth
Advent. Rossetti
Aspects of the World like Coral Reefs.
Bronk
Bog Queen. Heaney
Common Living Dirt, The. Piercy
Competitors, The. Barrax
Dust. "Æ"
Earth. Denis
Earth. Gibran
Earth ("A planet doesn't explode").
Wheelock
Earth and Sky. Euripides
Earth in Spring, The. Halevi
Epitaph on the World. Thoreau
Eye, The. Jeffers
Face. Guillevic
First Psalm, The. Brecht
Funeral March for the Death of the Earth.
Laforgue
God's Grandeur. Hopkins
God's World. Millay
Goodbye to the Poetry of Calcium. Wright
Hymn to Earth. Wylie
I am the poet of the Body and I am the poet
of the Soul. *Fr.* Song of Myself.
Whitman
I never saw a moor. Dickinson
La Guerre. Cummings
Lute Music. Rexroth
Merchant Marine. Miles
Moment Please, A. Allen
O Earth, Sufficing All Our Needs. Roberts
O Earth, Turn! Johnston
O Sweet Spontaneous. Cummings
On Inhabiting an Orange. Miles
Once the Sole Province. Crase
One Foot in Eden. Muir
Overtime. Halpern
Report from a Planet. Lattimore
Song of the Plain. Hajnal
Story of the World, The. Halpern
This Earth. Minthorn
This Newly Created World. *Unknown*
To an Old Lady. Empson
To what shall I compare this world? *Fr.*
Manyo Shu. Manzei
Town Window, A. Drinkwater
Under the Ground. Bacmeister
Under the Hill. Eberhart
Underworld, The. Lavington
Vacation on Earth, A. Disch
Wonderful World, The. Rands
World, The. Faber
World, The. Raine
World, The. Vaughan

World Is Everything That Is the Case, The. Mahon
World Is Full of Beauty, The. Edwards
World's Music, The. "Setoun"
Yes to the Earth. Aleramo
You Can't Go to the Moon There's No Trains. Howard

Earthquakes
Before They Made Things Be Alive They Spoke. Cuevish
Crack in the Wall Holds Flowers. Miller
Earth Tremor in Lugano. Kirkup
Earthquake. Ford
Earthquake. Kokan Shiren
Earthquake. Weöres
Earthquake covered Shansi and Shensi, The. Fr. Earthquake. Li K'ai-hsien
Earthquake of 1886, The. Heard
Hearing of the Earthquake in Kyoto. Rai San'yo
On Catania and Syracuse Swallowed Up by an Earthquake, from the Italian of Filicaja. Seward
Returning Home. Rai San'yo
Ruaumoko—the Earthquake God. Turei
Santa Barbara Earthquake, The. Unknown
Then earthquakes, nature's agonizing pangs. Fr. The Sugar Cane. Grainger
Tremors at Balvano, The. Williams

Easter
African Easter. Nicol
Alleluia! Christ Is Risen Today. Hopkins
Christ Is Risen! Dugan
Christmas Is Really for the Children. Turner
Day of Resurrection, The. John of Damascus
Easter. Kilmer
Easter. Sabin
Easter. Sisson
Easter Beatitudes. Burkholder
Easter Carol. Lovejoy
Easter Carol. Ray
Easter Chick, An. Wakley
Easter Communion. Hopkins
Easter Hymn. Housman
Easter Hymn. Wesley
Easter ("I got me flowers to strew thy way"). Herbert
Easter Light, The. Thompson
Easter Monday. Rossetti
Easter Morn. Heard
Easter Morning. Ammons
Easter Night. Meynell
Easter, 1923. Neihardt
Easter; or, Spring-Time. Moorer
Easter Poem. Raine
Easter Praise. Bennett
Easter ("Rise, heart, thy Lord is risen. Sing his praise"). Herbert
Easter Thought. Cox
Easter Wings. Herbert
If Easter Be Not True. Barstow
Legend of the Easter Eggs, The. O'Brien
Morning, Noon, And. Truax
"Most glorious Lord of Life [or Lyfe]! that on this day." Fr. Amoretti, LXVIII. Spenser
On Easter Day. Thaxter
On Easter Morning. Rexford
Rejoice, Let Alleluias Ring. Schaefer
Resurrection, The. Brooks
Rhyme for Remembering the Date of Easter. Richardson
Seven Stanzas at Easter. Updike
Some Things That Easter Brings. Parrish
That Nature Is a Heraclitean Fire and of the Comfort of the Resurrection. Hopkins
Well Pleaseth Me the Sweet Time of Easter. Bertrans de Born
When Mary thro' the Garden Went. Coleridge
Words for a Resurrection. Kennedy

Easter Island
Easter Island. Scott
Easter Rebellion (1916)
Easter, 1916. Yeats
Lament for the Poets: 1916. Ledwidge
Lament for Thomas MacDonagh. Ledwidge
Rose Tree, The. Yeats
Veterans, The. MacDonagh
Eatherly, Claude R.
Song about Major Eatherly, A. Wain
Eating
Beautiful Meals. Moore
Life would be an easy matter. Fr. If We Didn't Have to Eat. Waterman
Meal, The. Kuskin
O I Have Dined on This Delicious Day. Snyder
When Father Carves the Duck. Wright
See also Food; Gluttony and Gluttons.
Eating Disorders
Ellen West. Bidart
Echo Lake, New Hampshire
Echo Reverie. Ray
Echo (mythology)
Echo's Complaint. Ray
See also Narcissus (mythology).
Echoes
Echo. Clark
Echo. De la Mare
Echo. Saxe
Echo. Fr. Arcadia. Sidney
Echo. Weston
Echo. Zelk
Echoing Cliff, The. Young
Gentle Echo on Woman, A. Swift
Eclipses
December Eclipse. Lockwood
Lunar Eclipse. Mei Yao-ch'en
Moon Eclipse Exorcism. Unknown
Solar Eclipse. Tornai
Spot on the Sun, A. Gar
Total Eclipse. Rosen
Ecology
All the Smoke. Siegel
Baby Ten Months Old Looks at the Public Domain, A. Stafford
Binsey Poplars (Felled 1879). Hopkins
Bungaloid Growth. Ellis
Dead Seal. Purdy
Dogwood Blossoms. Blue Cloud
Flower-fed Buffaloes, The. Lindsay
Gathered at the River. Levertov
Hard Questions. Tsuda
Hymn to Moloch. Hodgson
Inversnaid. Hopkins
Little Things. Stephens
Malediction. Spacks
Martyred Earth, The. Milne
Moss-gathering. Roethke
Mother Earth; Her Whales. Snyder
Mystic River. Ciardi
Plans for Altering the River. Hugo
Poplar Field, The. Cowper
Quid Restat. Beebe
Requiem for a River. Williams
Smokey the Bear Sutra. Unknown
Song of Cove Creek Dam, The. Unknown
Statement on Our Higher Education. Ransom
Stranded Whales, The. Dutton
Then. Levine
To a Young Wretch. Frost
War against the Trees, The. Kunitz
Why the Soup Tastes like the Daily News. Piercy
Woodman, Spare That Tree. Morris
Working against Time. Wagoner
News of the Universe. (NU). Robert Bly, ed.
See also Pollution.
Eczema
Eczema. Slavitt

Eden
Adam Lay Ibounden or Ibowndyn or Ybounden. Unknown
Alas, that ever that speche was spoken. Unknown
Another side, umbrageous grots and caves. Fr. Paradise Lost. Milton
Apple, The. Smith
Brazen Image. Hartigan
Corruption. Vaughan
Descended, Adam to the bower where Eve. Fr. Paradise Lost. Milton
Fall, The. Rochester
Garden, The. Beaumont
Garden, The. Very
Lord God Planted a Garden, The. Gurney
Naming of the Beasts, The. Sparshott
Old Story, An. Lee
One Foot in Eden. Muir
Rose of Eden, The. Phillips
So spake our Mother Eve, and Adam heard. Fr. Paradise Lost. Milton
Spring. Hopkins
Theology. Hughes
What Words Have Passed. Fr. Paradise Lost. Milton
See also Adam and Eve.
Edinburgh, Scotland
Daft Days, The. Fergusson
To the Merchantis of Edinburgh. Dunbar
Editors
Editor Whedon. Fr. Spoon River Anthology. Masters
Editor's Tragedy, The. Hankin
To the Monk Wu-hsia. Mo Shih-lung
Education
Advance of Education, The. Heard
As Joe Gould says in. Cummings
Campus on the Hill, The. Snodgrass
Clerk of Oxford, The. Fr. The Canterbury Tales: Prologue. Chaucer
Elementary School Classroom in a Slum, An. Spender
Frost at Midnight. Coleridge
History of Education. McCord
Indian Education. Louis
Lines to a Don. Belloc
Little learning is a dangerous thing, A. Fr. Essay on Criticism. Pope
On the Prospect of Planting Arts and Learning in America. Berkeley
Poem: "In the earnest path of duty." Forten
Supervising Examinations. Lucy
Sweeper of Ways, The. Nemerov
To Cyriack Skinner ("Cyriack, whose grandsire"). Milton
To David, about His Education. Nemerov
University Examinations in Egypt. Enright
Verses on the Prospect of Planting Arts and Learning in America. Berkeley
Women. Walker
Would you your son should be a sot or dunce. Fr. Tirocinium; or, A Review of Schools. Coper
See also Colleges and Universities; Scholars and Scholarship; Students; Teaching and Teachers.
Edward I, King of England
Death of King Edward I, The. Unknown
Edward II, King of England
This Edward in the Aprill of his age. Fr. Piers Gaveston. Drayton
Edward IV, King of England
King Edward the Fourth and a Tanner of Tamworth. Unknown
Edward VII, King of England
Death of King Edward VII, The. Unknown
Elegy on Albert Edward the Peacemaker. Unknown
New Song on the Birth of the Prince of Wales, A. Unknown

Edwards, Jonathan
After the Surprising Conversions. Lowell
Mr. Edwards and the Spider. Lowell
Theology of Jonathan Edwards, The.
   McGinley
Eels
Ballad of the Electric Eel. Brown
Bucket of Sea-Serpents. Ant
Eel, The. Nash
Electric Eel, The. *Fr.* Three Animals.
   Padgett.
Existential. Heyen
Instructions for Fishing the Eel. Schmitz
Song of Hate for Eels. Guiterman
Strange the formation of the eely race. *Fr.*
   Halieutica. Diaper
Eggs
Beautiful Poultry. Wedde
Egg, The. Bowering
Egg, The. Day
Egg, The. Follain
Egg Boiler, The. Brooks
Eggomania. Lamport
How the Hen Sold Her Eggs to the Stingy
   Priest. Willard
In marble walls [*or* halls] as white as milk.
   Mother Goose
It's in the Egg. Rosenblatt
Little Bits of Soft-boiled Egg. Maschler
Long white barn, A. *Unknown*
Meg's Egg. Hoberman
Motherhood. Calverley
Oak Leaf Plate. Hoberman
Your love is like fire, croons the. Rosei
Egotism
Ego. Siegel
Immoral Proposition, The. Creeley
Megaceph, chosen to serve the State. *Fr.*
   The Devil's Dictionary. Bierce
Travelling Companions. Armour
See also **Individualism.**
Egrets
Egrets. Wright
Residue. McNeill
Snowy Egret. Weigl
Victors, The. McNeill
White Egret, The. Rosen
Wreath for the Suicide Heart, A. McNeill
Egypt
Africa. McKay
Chorus: "Then thus we have beheld." *Fr.*
   Cleopatra. Daniel
Deir El Bahari: Temple of Hatshepsut.
   Enright
Egyptian Tomb, An. Bowles
Egypt's Might Is Tumbled Down. Coleridge
I Am a Cowboy in the Boat of Ra. Reed
Nile, The. Hunt
Ozymandias. Shelley
Pelters of Pyramids. Horne
People of My Country, The. Abd al-Sabur
Sakhara. Ford
Snails. Blodgett
Theodotos. Cavafy
There Is a Dream Dreaming Us. Dubie
Tranquil above the rapids, rocks, and shoals.
   Fr. The Burden of Egypt. Milnes
Witch Going Down to Egypt, A. Chalfi
Written on the Plain of Thebes. Burgon
Eichmann, Adolf
Eichmann. Beecham
For Adolf Eichmann. Levi
Einstein, Albert
Einstein's Exile in an Old Dutch Winter.
   Dubie
Gift to Be Simple, The. Moss
Thomas Hardy Considers the Newly-Published
   Special Theory of Relativity. Aldiss
Eiseley, Loren
Loren Eiseley's Time Passages. Frazier

Eisenhower, Dwight David
Eisenhower's Visit to Franco, 1959. Wright
President in His Country Residence, A.
   Campert
Eisenhower, Mamie Doud
Funeral Song for Mamie Eisenhower. Wong
El Dorado
Eldorado. Poe
El Greco. *See* **Greco, El.**
El Salvador
Collective Shot, A. Suárez Quemain
Day They Cleaned Up the Border El
   Salvador, February, 1981, The. Rose
Dictators, The. Suárez Quemain
They Fell on the Stairway. Durand
Elands
Seele im Raum. Jarrell
Eleanor of Aquitaine
Queen Eleanor's Confession. *Unknown*
Rose of the World, The. Masefield
Electricity
Action of Electricity, The. *Fr.* The Economy
   of Vegetation. Darwin
Electricity Is Funny! Currier
Men against the Sky. Haines
Ohms. Layton
Pylons, The. Spender
Elephants
Address to Mr. Cross, of Exeter 'Change, on
   the Death of the Elephant. Hood
Beside the Line of Elephants. Becker
Blind Men and the Elephant, The. Saxe
Cradle Song of the Elephants. Del Valle
Death of an Elephant, The. Pagnucci
Elephant, The. Asquith
Elephant, The. Belloc
Elephant, The. Falconer
Elephant. Johnson
Elephant, The. Pagis
Elephant. *Fr.* Hunter Poems of the Yoruba.
   Unknown
Elephant Is Slow to Mate, The. Lawrence
Elephant, or the Force of Habit, The.
   Housman
Eletelephony. Richards
Gross innocent. *Fr.* Elephant. Neruda
Holding Hands. Link
Indian Elephant, The. Kaberry
Just Jumbo. Mathias
Oliphaunt. Tolkien
Pete at the Zoo. Brooks
Salute to the Elephant. Apolebieji
Tit for Tat; a Tale. Aikin
To a Dead Elephant. Livingstone
Two Performing Elephants. Lawrence
What She Said. Maturai Ilampalaciriyan
   Centan Kuttanar
What She Said to Her Friend ("The colors on
   the elephant's body"). Kapilar
Elgin Marbles
On Seeing the Elgin Marbles. Keats
Elijah (Bible)
Angel, The. Hayes
"Eliot, George" (Mary Ann Evans Cross)
George Eliot Country. Clampitt
Eliot, Thomas Stearns
Mr. Eliot's Day. Francis
Mr. T. S. Eliot Cooking Pasta. Tornai
T. S. Eliot. Auden
T. S. Eliot. Lowell
To T. S. Eliot. Litvinoff
Vice. Hecht
Elizabeth I, Queen of England
Looking Glass, The. Kipling
With Fragrant Flowers We Strew the Way.
   Fr. The Honourable Entertainment Given to
   the Queen's Majesty in Progress at
   Elvetham, 1591. Watson
Elizabeth II, Queen of England
Greeting to Queen Elizabeth, the Rare White
   Heron of Single Flight, A. Kerekere

Elizabeth I, Queen of England
Elizabeth. Ondaatje
Elizabeth's War with the Christmas Bear.
   Dubie
Songe betwene the Quenes Majestie and
   Englande, A. Birche
Elizabeth, Queen Consort of Henry VII
Rueful Lamentation on the Death of Queen
   Elizabeth, A. More
Elk
Elk at Black Fork Canyon. Sleigh
Ellington, Edward Kennedy (Duke)
Morning Duke Ellington Praised the Lord and
   Six Little Black Davids Tapped Danced
   Unto, The. Dodson
Elliot, Ebenezer
To the Memory of Ebenezer Elliott the
   Corn-Law Rhymer. Furness
Elm Trees
Dilemma of the Elm. Taggard
Drone *v.* Worker. Elliott
Elm's Home, The. Heyen
Fallen Elm, The. Clare
Elopement
Jock of [*or* o'] Hazeldean. Scott
Lochinvar. *Fr.* Marmion. Scott
Lord Ullin's Daughter. Campbell
Skeleton in Armor, The. Longfellow
Elves
Darkling Elves, The. Prelutsky
Dream of Elfland, A. Ray
Elf and the Dormouse, The. Herford
Elf Night. Rogers
For a Mocking Voice. Farjeon
How to Tell Goblins from Elves. Shannon
How to Treat Elves. Bishop
Little Elf, The. Bangs
Man Who Hid His Own Front Door, The.
   MacKinstry
Seven Ages of Elf-hood, The. Field
See also **Fairies.**
Ely, England
Monks of Ely, The. *Unknown*
Emancipation (1863-1865)
Emancipation. Thompson
Emancipation Day. Moorer
Freedom at McNealy's. Thompson
General Robert Smalls. Heard
Hymn, A: "Lord, within thy fold I be."
   Thompson
Laus Deo! Whittier
Proclamation, The. Whittier
Embryos
Dead Embryos. Tóth
Voyages, The. Orr
Woman to Man. Wright
Emerson, Ralph Waldo
Carlyle and Emerson. Schuyler
Emerson. Alcott
Emerson. Dodge
Emerson. Ray
In the Garden. Schmidt
There comes Emerson first, whose rich words,
   every one. *Fr.* A Fable for Critics.
   Lowell
Emigration
Colonization in Reverse. Bennett
Complaint of the Morpethshire Farmer, The.
   Bunting
Emigrant Ship, The. Dalton
Excitement. Bennett
First of the Emigrants, The. *Unknown*
Gin the Goodwife Stint. Bunting
To the New World. Jarrell
Ye Simple Men. Blackie
Emmet, Robert
Oh, Breathe Not His Name! Moore
She Is Far from the Land. Moore
Empedocles
Death and Empedocles 444 B.C. Gregory
Empedocles on Etna. Mallalieu

Emptiness
Carrying On. Nathan
Fall, The. Nathan
House in the Heart, The. Nye
If You Have an Enemy. Skoyles
Lessons. McBride
Old People on the Nursing Home Porch.
   Strand
On Vacation. Creeley
People in These Houses, The. Matthews
Ravel and Unravel. Graham
Stove's Out. Bernstein
Tangier. Dunn
Emus
Emus. Fullerton
Enclosures. See Inclosure Movements.
End of the World
Advice to a Prophet. Wilbur
Black Mesa. Rogers
End of the World, The. Bottomley
End of the World, The. MacLeish
Epitaph Ending in And, The. Stafford
Everyone Knows the World Is Ending.
   Fulton
Fire and Ice. Frost
Fundamental Project of Technology, The.
   Kinnell
LMFBR. Snyder
Once by the Pacific. Frost
Reliable Service, A. Curnow
Song on the End of the World, A. Milosz
Sun and Moon. Macpherson
What If a Much of a Which of a Wind.
   Cummings
When I Awoke. Patterson
See also **Judgment Day.**
Endangered Species
Moschus Moschiferus. Hope
Endurance. See Fortitude.
Endymion
Endymion. Longfellow
Endymion [a Poetic Romance], *sels.* Keats
Fairy Song, A. *Fr.* Endymion. Lyly
I Envy Not Endymion. *Fr.* Aurora.
   Stirling
Oh, Sleep Forever in the Latmian Cave.
   Millay
Phoebe on Latmus. *Fr.* Endimion and
   Phoebe. Drayton
Energy Crisis
Elegy Written in a Country Coal-Bin.
   Morley
Engineers
Engineer, The. Melo Neto
England
Above the Medway. *Fr.* The Vales of the
   Medway. Munby
Adlestrop. Thomas
America to England. Woodberry
And Did Those Feet in Ancient Time. *Fr.*
   Milton. Blake
Anglicized Utopia. Gilbert
Bundle of Truths—A Parody, A. Rodger
By the River Eden. Raine
Calder Valley: At the Top of the Ainleys.
   Cook
Channel Crossing. Barker
Christmas. Betjeman
Corrymeela. "O'Neill"
Distant View of England from the Sea.
   Bowles
Durham. Harrison
1887. Housman
Elegy in a Country Churchyard. Chesterton
England. *Fr.* The Task. Cowper
England. Day
England. Montgomery
England. Moore
England. Newman
England. Salter
England. *Unknown*

England, My England. Henley
England's Sovereigns in Verse. *Unknown*
English Fog, The. *Fr.* The Fleece. Dyer
English Succession, The. *Unknown*
Eureka! Godley
Fair England. Cone
Farewell to England. *Unknown*
Fields from Islington to Marybone, The. *Fr.*
   Jerusalem. Blake
Free Parliament Litany, A. *Unknown*
George III. Lowell
Happy Britannia. *Fr.* The Seasons: Summer.
   Thomson
Home Thoughts from Abroad. Browning
Home Thoughts, from the Sea. Browning
Homes of England, The. Hemans
How Sleep the Brave. Collins
I Have Loved England. *Fr.* The White
   Cliffs. Miller
In Westminster Abbey. Betjeman
International Hymn. Huntington
John of Gaunt Speaks. *Fr.* King Richard II:
   John of Gaunt's Dying Speech.
   Shakespeare
Land, The. Kipling
Land of Hope and Glory. Benson
Last Buccaneer, The. Kingsley
Laurel Axe, The. *Fr.* An Apology for the
   Revival of Christian Architecture in
   England. Hill
London, 1802 ("Milton! thou should'st be
   living at this hour"). Wordsworth
Look for Me on England. Mallalieu
Matlock Bath. Betjeman
Mercian Hymns, *sels.* Hill
Mother England. Thomas
MCMXIV. Larkin
O England, Country of My Heart's Desire.
   Lucas
O My Mother Isle! ("Not yet enslaved, not
   wholly vile"). *Fr.* Ode on the Departing
   Year. Coleridge
Old Vicarage, Grantchester, The. Brooke
On a Political Prisoner. Yeats
On This Island. Auden
On Wenlock Edge. Housman
Princely Ditty in Praise of the English Rose,
   A. Deloney
Properties of the Shires of England, The.
   Unknown
Puck's Song. *Fr.* Puck of Pook's Hill.
   Kipling
Ravenglass Railway Station, Cumberland.
   Nicholson
Remembering England. Bland
Return, The. Kipling
Return, The. Silkin
Rhymed Mnemonic of the Forty Counties of
   England. Monat
Rhyming Prophecy for a New Year. Cooper
Rolling English Road, The. Chesterton
Rule, Britannia! *Fr.* Alfred, A Masque.
   Thomson
Sheffield East End. Cook
Soldier, The. *Fr.* 1914. Brooke
Sonnet: "England! the time is come when thou
   shouldst wean." Wordsworth
Song for England, A. Salkey
Song of Sherwood, A. Noyes
Song to the Men of England. Shelley
South Country, The. Belloc
Summer in England, 1914. Meynell
This Is England. Binyon
To England. Moore
Town Clerk's Views, The. Betjeman
True-born Englishman, The. Defoe
Truth's Complaint over England. Lodge
Ulster. Kipling
Voices against England in the Night. Smith
Whack Fol the Diddle. Kearney

While with a strong and yet a gentle hand.
   Fr. A Panegyric[k] to My Lord Protector.
   Waller
Writing in England Now. O'Connor
You That Love England. Day Lewis
See also **Civil wars, English.**
**England, Church of. See Church of
   England.**
English, The
Bonne Entente. Scott
Britannia's Baby. Lawrence
British Journalist, The. Wolfe
English, The. *Unknown*
English Are Frosty, The. *Fr.* The White
   Cliffs. Miller
Englishman on the French Stage, The.
   Seaman
Fears in Solitude. Coleridge
For the Rain It Raineth Every Day. Graves
How Beastly the Bourgeois Is. Lawrence
In pious times ere [*or* e'r] priestcraft did
   begin. *Fr.* Absalom and Achitophel, Pt. I.
   Dryden
Jobson's Amen. Kipling
Mad Dogs and Englishmen. Coward
Neutral British Gentleman, The. "Kerr"
Observations in a Cornish Teashop. Rexroth
Old England Forever and Do It No More.
   Unknown
Secret People, The. Chesterton
Soldier, The. *Fr.* 1914. Brooke
Solitary Travel. MacNeice
Song to the Men of England. Shelley
Tragic Guilt. Rhys
Two Englishmen. Stewart
Wherever God erects a house of prayer. *Fr.*
   The True-born Englishman. Defoe
Why Should I Care for the Men of Thames?
   Blake
World Is a Bundle of Hay, The. Byron
Ye Mariners of England. Campbell
English Channel
Channel Crossing. Barker
Outlanders, The. Glaze
Envy
Agnodicia, or Ignorance Banished from the
   Presence of Women. Des Roches
Envy. *Fr.* The Faerie Queene. Spenser
See also **Jealousy.**
Epic Poetry
Epic. Kavanagh
Epic, The. Tennyson
Critics say that epics have died out, The. *Fr.*
   Aurora Leigh. Browning
Epictetus
To a Friend. Arnold
Epicureanism
Author Loving These Homely Meats, The.
   Fr. The Scourge of Folly. Davies
Epicure, The ("Fill the bowl with rosie
   wine"). Cowley
Epigrams
Epigrams must be curt, nor seem. Landor
What is an epigram? a dwarfish whole.
   Coleridge
Faber Book of Epigrams and Epitaphs, The
   (FaBoEE). Geoffrey Grigson, ed.
Epiphany. See Twelfth Night.
Equality
Equality. Guiducci
For A' That and A' That ("Is there, for honest
   poverty"). Burns
Woman to Her Lover, A. Walsh
Women's Worth. Pozzo
See also **Social Class.**
Eraikkon
Tiger, The. Kuramakal Ilaveyini
Erie Canal
E-ri-e, The. *Unknown*
Erie Canal, The. Allen

Erie, Lake
Autumn Squall—Lake Erie. Russo
Battle of Erie, The. *Unknown*
Perry's Victory. *Unknown*

Ernst, Max
Max Ernst. Eluard
Max Ernst's Walk. Schmied

Eros. *See* **Cupid.**

Erosion
Where Dunwich Used to Be. *Fr.* By the
North Sea. Swinburne

Erotic Love
After Love. Kumin
Amores (after Ovid). Parini
Ants. López Velarde
Body, Remember. . . Cavafy
Cherrylog Road. Dickey
Courtship. O Hehir
Drunk as drunk on turpentine. Neruda
Elegy, The: "Madam, no more! The time has
come to eat." Hope
Envy of Poor Lovers, The. Clarke
Equilibrists, The. Ransom
Fine, a Private Place, A. Ackerman
Flea, The. Donne
For the Lady of a Physicist. Bishop
Geranium, The. Sheridan
Going to Bed. *Fr.* Elegies. Donne
Goodbye, Sally. Simmons
Half an Hour. Cavafy
His Legs Ran About. Hughes
Hunchback and the Dwarf, The.
Marutanilanakanar
I Care Not for These Ladies. Campion
I Like My Body When It Is With Your Body.
Fr. Sonnets—Actualities. Cummings
Imperfect Enjoyment, The. Rochester
It Fell on a Summer's Day. Campion
Last Confession, A. Yeats
Last Ride Together, The. Browning
Libertine, The. MacNeice
Love and Sleep. Swinburne
Love at Roblin Lake. Purdy
Love Made in the First Age: To Chloris.
Lovelace
Love Poem: "I like/ the feel of your pulsating
fibers." Kageyama
Love Poem: "Last night you would not
come." Logan
Love Poem on Theme by Whitman.
Ginsberg
Lugete O Veneres. Mason
Luminare. Minar
Man and Woman. Lee
Net, The. Rodgers
New Year's Eve. Lawrence
New York, Summer. Gilbert
Night-Piece, to Julia, The. Herrick
No Platonic Love. Cartwright
Now Ain't That Love? Rodgers
Oh! the time that is past. *Unknown*
On the Happy Corydon and Phyllis. Sedley
On the Hill below the Lighthouse. Dickey
Penal Law. Clarke
Poem Unwritten, The. Levertov
Poemlove (Fragment). *Fr.* Erotic Suite.
Vega
Queen-Ann's-Lace. Williams
Rapping Along with Ronda Davis.
Cunningham
Rapture, A. Carew
Recreation. Lorde
Rigs o' Barley, The. Burns
Rondeau after a Transatlantic Telephone Call.
Hacker
Salmon. Graham
Second Story, The. Hummer
Shelley and jazz and lieder and love and
hymn-tunes. *Fr.* Autumn Journal.
MacNeice

Soft, lovely, rose-like lips, conjoined with
mine. *Fr.* Parthenophil and Parthenophe.
Barnes
Song of Dalliance, A. Cartwright
Suzanne. Logan
Swimmer. Francis
Taking the Milk to Grandmother. Kloefkorn
That Day. Sexton
To a Fine Young Woman. Wycherley
To His Dear Friend, Bones. Parini
To Remain. Cavafy
To the Tune "Red Embroidered Shoes."
Huang O
Touching Each Other's Surfaces. Bangs
Tryst [*or* Trysting Place], The. Soutar
Tubes. Mollin
Twenty-Year Marriage. Ai
Uncle Henry. Auden
Upon Julia's Breasts. Herrick
Upon My Lady Carlisle's Walking in
Hampton Court Garden. Suckling
Us. Sexton
Vine, The. Herrick
We Must Make a Kingdom of It. Orr
What He Said after a Quarrel, Remembering
His Wedding Night. Virrurru Muteyinanar
You Ask Why Sometimes I Say Stop. Piercy
See also **Sex.**

Esau
Esau. Kvitko

Escalators
Escalator, The. Glasgow

Escapes
Autumnal Equinox. Wilson
Houdini. Mandel
I'd Leave. Lang
In Snow. Leivick
Manzini; Escape Artist. MacEwen
Methought That I Had Broken from the
Tower. *Fr.* King Richard III.
Shakespeare
On the Roads of Siberia. Leivick
Somewhere Far Away. Leivick
Summer Killer. Broughton

Eschatology. *See* **End of the World.**

Eskimos
Al Capone in Alaska. Reed
Bear Hunting. Aua
Eskimo Baby, An. Diamond
Eskimo Chant. *Unknown*
For an Eskimo. Dalton
Immoral Arctic, The. Bishop
Kayak Song, A. Diamond
Lament for the Dorsets. Purdy
Sila. Warren
Song of the Trout Fisher, The. Ikinilik
Walrus Hunting. Aua

Essex, England
Map of the Western Part of the County of
Essex in England, A. Levertov

Essex, Robert Devereux, 2nd Earl of
Lementable New Ballad upon the Earle of
Essex Death, A. *Unknown*
Young Earl of Essex's Victory over the
Emperor of Germany, The. *Unknown*

Esther, Book of (Bible)
Before the Feast of Shushan. Spencer
Lilith Re-Tells Esther's Story. Wandor
Vashti. Harper

Eternity
Animula. Merwin
Because I could not stop for death.
Dickinson
Chorus Tertius: Of Time; Eternitie. *Fr.*
Mustapha. Greville
Ditty: "If this town should tumble down."
Beecham
Do Not Die. Merwin
Eternal City, The. Ammons
Eternity. Guillevic

Eternity. Heard
Eternity. Herrick
Eternity ("He who binds [*or* bends] to himself
a joy"). *Fr.* Several Questions Answered.
Blake
Face of the Waters, The. Fitzgerald
1st April 1984. Russell
Hallaj's corpse was burnt and when the flame.
Fr. The Conference of the Birds. Attar
If by Eternity. Waskowsky
Infinite, The. Leopardi
Only news I know, The. Dickinson
Our journey had advanced. Dickinson
Passengers. Johnson
Pibroch. Hughes
Where Runs the River. Bourdillon
World, The. Vaughan
See also **Immortality.**

Ethiopia
I Came from Ethiopia. Leyeles
On the Baptized Ethiopian. Crashaw
Rusted Chain, The. Ben Yeshaq
Star of Ethiopia. Watkins

Etiquette
Boy Serving at Table, The. Lydgate
Etiquette. Gilbert
How to Get On in Society. Betjeman
Manners. Van Rensselaer
Manners at Table When Away from Home.
Unknown
Manners [for a Child of 1918] Bishop
Mutual Subjection. *Fr.* Hymns for the
Amusement of Children. Smart
Respectability. Browning
Rude, The. McCloskey
Story of Fidgety Philip, The. Hoffmann
Suppose. Trowbridge
Table Manners. Burgess
Table Manners. *Unknown*
Table Rules for Little Folk[s] *Unknown*
Taste. *Fr.* Hymns for the Amusement of
Children. Smart
Toothsome. Smaridge

Eton College
Ode on a Distant Prospect of Eton College.
Gray

Etruscan Civilization
Cypresses. Lawrence
Etruscan Sarcophagus, The. Vas
Etruscan Warrior's Head. Henze

Eucharist
At Communion. L'Engle
Bread of Heaven, on Thee We Feed. Conder
Bugler's First Communion, The. Hopkins
Communion Hymn. Seaver
General Communion, A. Meynell
In Portugal, 1912. Meynell
Let Us Break Bread Together. *Unknown*
Lines to the Blessed Sacrament. *Unknown*
Love. Herbert
Martha Blake. Clarke
Of the Holy Eucharist. *Unknown*
Receiving Communion. Miller
Sacrament of the Altar, The. *Unknown*
To the Blessed Sacrament. Constable

Euclid
Euclid Alone Has Looked on Beauty Bare.
Millay
Hades and Euclid. Martinson

Europa
Europa. Walcott

Europe
Beyond the Alps. Lowell
Channel Crossing. Barker
Europa. Thayer
Europe and America. Ignatow
European Night, The. Vinaver
Farewell to Europe. Pillen
1945. Cussons
Of Commerce and Society. Hill
To Cole, the Painter, Departing for Europe.
Bryant

Eurydice
Death of Eurydice and Orpheus' Journey to
  Hell, The. *Fr.* Metamorphoses. Ovid
Early Love. Scott
Eurydice. Gregg
Eurydice. Santos
Orpheus and Eurydice. Browning
Orpheus and Eurydice. Valentine
Orpheus to Beasts. Lovelace
Eurynome
Eurynome. Macpherson
Eutaw Springs, South Carolina, Battle of
  (1781)
To the Memory of the Brave Americans.
  Freneau
Euthanasia
Hurt Hawks. Jeffers
To the Mercy Killers. Randall
Evangelism
Evangelize! Crocker
Few ever came to help you speak or sell.
  Fr. The Fragments. Dale
Pilgrims. Stafford
Revivalist in Boston, A. Rich
This Child Is the Mother. Oden
Eve
Adam and Eve. Manger
Adam and Eve. Sisson
Adam's Curse. Yeats
Adam's Dream. Schwartz
Age of Innocence. Hough
Aspects of Eve. Pastan
Brazen Image. Hartigan
Circle, A. Spencer
Eve. Bull
Eve. Flores
Eve. Follain
Eve. Gascoyne
Eve. Hébert
Eve. Hodgson
Eve. Rossetti
Eve am I, great Adam's wife. *Unknown*
Eve and the Apple Tree. Manger
Eve in Reflection. Macpherson
Eve: Night Thoughts. Jerome
Eves Apologie. Lanier
Eve's Birth. Chernin
Eve's Song in the Garden. Gottlieb
First Wedding in the World, The. Rosenberg
Forsake me not thus, Adam, witness Heav'n.
  Fr. Paradise Lost. Milton
Fortunate Fall, The. Alvarez
Good Beasts, The. Barnstone
I Was That Woman. Chatterjee
Imperial Adam. Hope
In bower and field he sought, where any tuft.
  Fr. Paradise Lost. Milton
In the Beginning. Sinason
Jealous Adam. Manger
Lament of Eve, The. *Unknown*
Never Again Would Birds' Song Be the
  Same. Frost
Paradise. Bloch
Reflection, A. Hood
Reveille. Hughes
Rose of Eden, The. Phillips
She. Wilbur
Temptation and Fall of Man, The. *Fr.*
  Genesis. Caedmon
Theology. Hughes
Vision of Eve, The. Ray
Waiting for Lilith. Kessler
See also **Adam and Eve.**
Evening
As day nears its end. Ietaka
At Sunset. Eastwick
Between clouds of fire and clouds of blood.
  Fr. At Evening Time. Bialik
Crickets sang, The. Dickinson
Dusk. Harrison
Dusk. Kaoru

Early Autumn Evening. Rokunyo
Evenen in the Village. Barnes
Evening. Aldington
Evening, An. Allingham
Evening. Ausländer
Evening. Clare
Evening. Doolittle
Evening. *Fr.* New York. Leyeles
Evening. McCrae
Evening. Manger
Evening. Matheson
Evening. Miller
Evening. Sangster
Evening. Stephens
Evening at [*or* on] the Farm. Trowbridge
Evening Bell. Shotetsu
Evening by the Sea. Swinburne
Evening Hymn, An. Ken
Evening Is Coming, The. *Unknown*
Evening Light along the Sound, The. Santos
Evening sun shines, The. Kogon
Evening Tide. Kennedy
Evening Wind, The. Bryant
Evening without Angels. Stevens
Evensong. Lewis
Evensong. Stevenson
February Twilight. Teasdale
Gascoigne's [*or* Gascoygnes] Good-Night.
  Gascoigne
Georgia Dusk. Toomer
Going Under of the Evening Land, The.
  McBride
Grace before Sleep. Teasdale
Home-coming. Adams
Hours. González León
In Evening Air. Roethke
In the dusky light. Tamenori
In the Evening. Lara
In the evening light. Ietaka
Island in the Evening, The. Porter
Lake in the Sky, The. Haines
Late, Last Rook, The. Hodgson
Mist. Gyoko
Morning and Evening. Slonimski
Naturalist's Summer-Evening Walk, The.
  White
Nightfall on Sedgemoor. Young
November Blue. Meynell
O God, whose daylight leadeth down. *Fr.*
  Evening Hymn. Macdonald
Ode to Evening. Collins
Priest's Chant, The. *Fr.* The Faithful
  Shepherdess. Fletcher
Progress of Evening. Landor
Sonnet: "Evening, as slow thy placid shades
  descend." Bowles
Sonnet:
Saturday Evening in the Village. Leopardi
Stopping by Woods on a Snowy Evening.
  Frost
Summer Evening. De la Mare
Summer Evening. Kogon
Summer Grasses in the Fields at Dusk.
  Gyoko
Surprised by Evening. Bly
To the Evening Star. Blake
Vespers. Shepard
Wet Earth. López Velarde
Windmill of Evening, The. Reich
Winter Evening. De la Mare
Winter Evening. Hitoshi
Winter Evening. Lampman
Winter Evening ("Just when our
  drawing-rooms begin to blaze"). *Fr.* The
  Task. Cowper
Winter Nightfall. Bridges
Witnesses. Merwin
See also **Twilight.**
Evening Star
Hesperus. Clare
Lamp in the West, The. Higginson

To the Evening Star. Blake
See also **Venus (planet).**
Evers, Medgar
Medgar Evers. Brooks
Evictions
Oakey Street Evictions, The. Armstrong
See also **Inclosure Movement.**
Evil
Doth then the world go thus, doth all thus
  move? Drummond
Hymn to Evil. Ginsberg
I Sit and Look Out. Whitman
On the Origin of Evil. Byrom
Puritan, The. Shapiro
Pythoness, The. Raine
Evolution
Ballade of Evolution, A. Allen
Chimpanzee, The. Herford
Darwin on Species. *Unknown*
Darwinity. Merivale
Evolution. Blight
Evolution. Smith
Evolution. Swenson
Evolutionary Hymn. Lewis
Love Song to Eohippus. Viereck
Missing Link, The. Herford
Monkeys. Collymore
Motorcycle Evolution. Payack
On Evolution. Ciardi
Progression of the Species. Aldiss
Self-Protection. Lawrence
Similar Cases. Gilman
See also **Extinction; Genetics.**
Ewing, Patrick
Patrick Ewing Takes a Foul Shot. Ackerman
Excrement
Excrement Poem, The. Kumin
Execution
February 1. *Fr.* Fabius Lind's Diary.
  Leyeles
Executions
Among Philistines. Gwynn
Arbitrary Destiny. Desnos
Artemis. Boumi-Pappas
At Iwashiro I tie together branches of a beach
  pine. *Fr.* Manyo Shu. Arima
Ballad of Reading Gaol, The. Wilde
Black and White. Adame
Bride's Toilette, The. Cortissoz
Carpenter's Son, The. *Fr.* A Shropshire
  Lad. Housman
Clever Tom Clinch Going to Be Hanged.
  Swift
Condemned, The. Howland
Croppy Boy, The. *Unknown*
Danny Deever. Kipling
Dunlavin Green. *Unknown*
Eight o'Clock. Housman
Electrocution. Ridge
Epitaph in Form of a Ballad, The. Villon
Example, The. Díaz Mirón
Execution of Cornelius Vane, The. Read
Executioners. Weinstein
He Fell among Thieves. Newbolt
King Charles on [*or* upon] the Scaffold. *Fr.*
  An Horatian Ode upon Cromwell's Return
  from Ireland. Marvell
Krinio. Boumi-Pappas
London Fete, A. Patmore
Louis XVI Goes to the Guillotine. Péret
Mary Hamilton. *Unknown*
"More Light! More Light!" Hecht
Night before Larry Was Stretched, The.
  Unknown
No Speech from the Scaffold. Gunn
On Moonlit Heath and Lonesome Bank. *Fr.*
  A Shropshire Lad. Housman
Queen's Marie, The. *Unknown*
Salute. Halpern
Savage, A. O'Reilly
Shameful Death. Morris

Shlomo Molkho Sings on the Eve of His Burning. Leyeles
Sleepless Nights. Péret
Stranger's Song, The. Hardy
They brought him one morning. *Fr.* A Rhapsody of Old Men. Tsaloumas
Tichborne's Elegy. Tichborne
Voice of Robert Desnos, The. Desnos
Woman's Execution, A. King
See also **Capital Punishment; Hanging.**

Exercise
Exercise ("Get loaded"). Nolan
Exercise ("Just as I stood up"). Nolan
Tea for Two. Nolan

Exile
Andalusian Exile, An. Shauqi
Ballata II: Last Song: from Exile. Cavalcanti
Banished from the Palace. Nakao
Brumana. Flecker
Brunanburg. *Unknown*
Canadian Exile, The. Gerin-Lajoie
Castaway. Nerber
Clinging to this transient life. *Fr.* Manyo Shu. Omi
Dublin. MacNeice
Elegy: "I visit once again." Pushkin
Emigrant Song. "Ansky"
Emigré Jewess. Mistral
Exile. Nasir
Exile. Scott
Exile in Nigeria. Mphahlele
Exile's Reverie, The. Fordham
Exodus to Connacht. O'Meallain
Foreign Land. Delgado
From Exile. Dafydd Benfras
From Exile to Exile. Al-Baraduni
House and Land. Curnow
If I owned all of Alba. Columcille
In Memoriam. Ungaretti
In Snow. Leivick
Irish Reaper's Harvest Hymn. Keegan
Is the Prince of Omi a fisherman? *Fr.* Manyo Shu. Omi
Lark, The. Bernart de Ventadorn
Look, he is superfluous—for of what use was it to be born? *Fr.* Tristium. Ovid
My homeless one, will you ever fly again? *Fr.* To a Jewish Dancer. Markish
New House, A. Brecht
Old Vicarage, Grantchester, The. Brooke
On Not Going Out the Gate. Michizane
On the Roads of Siberia. Leivick
Ovid on the Dacian Coast. Thompson
Pacifists. Woodcock
Paschal Fire, The. MacCarthy
Seafarer. *Unknown*
Somewhere Far Away. Leivick
Song seizes me, but my own vers gives me dolor. Guillaume de Poitiers
Strange land is hard to live in, A. *Fr.* Manyo Shu. Sanu Chigami
To Cordelia. Stansbury
Travelogue for Exiles. Shapiro
Welshman in Exile Speaks, The. Jones
Were it not for the dresses. *Fr.* Manyo Shu. Nakatomi Yakamori
Will of a Man Dying in Exile, The. Al-Qasim
Written in Exile. Raine
Written on My Way into Exile. Han Yü
Your sisters all must stay at home. *Fr.* Kokin Shu. Michizane

Existentialism
As I Step over a Puddle at the End of Winter, I Think of an Ancient Chinese Governor. Wright
Gas Station, The. Williams
Lying quietly on the bed. *Fr.* Leaving the Door Open. Ignatow

Exodus
Exodus. Shapiro

Exodus from Egypt, The. Ezekielos of Alexandria
Flowering Without End. *Fr.* Jeremiah. Zweig
Go Down, Moses. *Unknown*
Parting of the Red Sea, The. *Fr.* Exodus. *Unknown*

Exploring and Explorers
Arabia. Falkner
As when a Scout/ through dark and desert wayes with peril gone. *Fr.* Paradise Lost. Milton
Bermudas. Marvell
Bold Adventures of Captain Ross. *Unknown*
Columbus. Miller
Dolphin's Return, The. *Unknown*
Explorers as Seen by the Natives. Fetherling
For the Grave of Daniel Boone. Stafford
Lady Franklin's Lament for Her Husband. *Unknown*
North Pole Story, A. Smedley
O Pioneers! Bishop
Ode: To the Virginian Voyage. Drayton
On the Discoveries of Captain Lewis. Barlow
Orinoco, 1561, The. *Fr.* The Gilded Man. Ai
Polar Quest, The. Burton
Samuel Hearne in Wintertime. Newlove
Sir Humphrey Gilbert. Longfellow
Sonnet: "There was an Indian, who had known no change." Squire
They made impudent inspection of our coast. *Fr.* The Great South Land. Ingamells
To the Western World. Simpson
Voyage West. MacLeish

Explosions
Explosion, The. Larkin

Exterminators
Exterminator. Stryk

Extinction
Bedtime Story. MacBeth
Conspirators, The. Prokosch
Dodo. Carlile
For a Coming Extinction. Merwin
"Heaven and earth." *Fr.* Manyo Shu. Hitomaro
Moschus Moschiferus. Hope

Extrasensory Perception
ESP. Tem

Extreme Unction
Extreme Unction. Dowson

Eyeglasses
Mocking Spectacles. Yüan Mei
Praising Spectacles. Yüan Mei
Singing, 1977. Fuller

Eyes
After Greece. Merrill
Another transparent skin has grown. *Fr.* Tunnel Visions. Pollak
Celebration for the Cold Snap. Wright
Custody of the Eyes, The. Wright
Elsa's Eyes. Aragon
Eye, The. Herrick
Eye. Nishiwaki Junzaburo
Eye and Tooth. Lowell
Eyes. De la Mare
Eyes. Nicoïdski
Eyes of Night-Time. Rukeyser
First the light cracked. *Fr.* Tunnel Visions. Pollak
Fury of Hating Eyes, The. Sexton
Her Eyes. Ransom
Her voice enters the room. *Fr.* Tunnel Visions. Pollak
I wake to the sound of rain. *Fr.* Tunnel Visions. Pollak
In My Eye. Seymour-Smith
Ladies' Eyes Serve Cupid Both for Darts and Fire. "W."

My Father's Eye. Vakaló
Pretty Twinkling Starry Eyes. *Fr.* The Passionate Shepherd. Breton
Silverhill. Seymour-Smith
Soft Black Eyes. Thompson
There was a man of our town. Mother Goose
Through a Glass Eye, Lightly. Kizer
Today, Again, the Jagged Black Line. Dunn
"When Nature made her chief work, Stella's eyes." *Fr.* Astrophel and Stella, VII. Sidney
Your Eyes Have Their Silence. Barrax

Ezra
So I Said I Am Ezra. Ammons

F

Faces
Epigram: "Face that should content me wonders well, A." Wyatt
Eternal Contour. Smyth
Face in the Mirror, The. Graves
Faces Seen Once. Dickey
Poem about Your Face. Alterman
Self-Portrait. Cassian
Sweet mouth, that send'st a musky-rosed breath. Sylvester
There Is a Garden in Her Face. Campion

Factories
Ah! leave my harp and me alone. *Unknown*
Birmingham and Wolverhampton. *Fr.* The Life and Lucubrations of Crispinus Scriblerus. Woodhouse
Changsha Shoe Factory. Barnstone
Dream after Touring the Tokyo Tokei. Kogawa
Factory Girl, The. Phillips
Factory Girl, The. *Unknown*
Factory Rainbow, A. Saadi
Factory Windows Are Always Broken. Lindsay
Hands. Glasgow
Iron Industry in Birmingham, The. *Fr.* Edge-Hill; or, The Rural Prospect Delineated and Moralised. Jago
Jute Mill Song, The. *Unknown*
Little Factory Girl to a More Fortunate Playmate, The. *Unknown*
"Oh! isn't it a pity, such a pretty girl as I." Robinson
On the Closing of Millom Ironworks. Nicholson
Our Father's Hand. Flint
Song of a Factory Worker, The. Collins
Song of the Factory Girls. *Unknown*

Faerie Queene, The
Vision upon This Conceit of the Fairy Queen, A. *Fr.* Commendatory Verses to Edmund Spenser's Fairy Queen. Ralegh

Failure
Bewick Finzer. Robinson
Clavering. Robinson
Consecration, A. Masefield
Epitaph on a Young Poet Who Died before Having Achieved Success. Lowell
Failure. Goode
Failure. Ray
Failure and Success. Gilder
Failures. Upson
Farmer John. Trowbridge
In the Smoking-Car. Wilbur
Never Say Fail. *Unknown*
Nobody Loses All the Time. Cummings
Ode to Failure. Ginsberg
Success is counted sweetest. Dickinson
To a Friend Whose Work Has Come to Nothing. Yeats
Victory in Defeat. Markham

Fair Isle, Scotland
Fair Isle at Sea—thy lovely name. Stevenson

Fairies
Alice Brand. *Fr.* The Lady of the Lake.
  Scott
Ann and the Fairy Song. *Fr.* A Child's Day.
  De la Mare
Beggar to Mab, the Fairy [*or* Fairie] Queen,
  The. Herrick
Bogeyman, The. Prelutsky
Brownies' Celebration, The. Cox
Changeling, The. Mew
Come unto these yellow sands. *Fr.* The
  Tempest. Shakespeare
Cornish Magic. Durell
Could It Have Been a Shadow? Shannon
Dusk in the Domain. MacKellar
Elf and the Dormouse, The. Herford
Elfin Town. Field
Fairies, The. Allingham
Fairies. Conkling
Fairies. Farjeon
Fairies. Fyleman
Fairies, The. Herrick
Fairies' Farewell, The. Brontë
Fairies Feast, The. Doughty
Fairies Have Never a Penny to Spend, The.
  Fyleman
Fairies of the Caldon-Low, The. Howitt
Fairy Book, The. Gale
Fairy Harpers, The. Dollard
Fairy Song. Keats
Fairy Thorn, The. Ferguson
Fairy Went a-Marketing, A. Fyleman
Fairyland. Tagore
Goblin, The. Fyleman
Goblin Market. Rossetti
Godmother. Morden
Hob Gobbling's Song. Lowell
How to Tell Goblins from Elves. Shannon
How to Treat Elves. Bishop
I'd Love to Be a Fairy's Child. Graves
La Belle Dame sans Merci. Keats
Light-hearted Fairy, The. *Unknown*
Little Elf, The. Bangs
Little Orphant Annie. Riley
Mab the Mistress-Fairy. *Fr.* The Satyr.
  Jonson
Midsummer Night's Dream, A, *sels.*
  Shakespeare
Mr. Moon. Carman
Oberon's Feast. Herrick
Oberon's Palace. Herrick
Of Certain Irish Fairies. Guiterman
On a Nook Called Fairyland. Ray
Overheard on a Saltmarsh. Monro
Plumpuppets, The. Morley
Puk-Wudjies. Chalmers
Queen's Chariot, The. *Fr.* Nymphidia.
  Drayton
Robene and Makyne ("Robene [*or* Robin] sat
  on gude green hill"). Henryson
Shakespeare: The Fairies' Advocate. *Fr.* The
  Plea of the Midsummer Fairies. Hood
She is the fairies' midwife, and she comes.
  Fr. Romeo and Juliet. Shakespeare
Song of Sherwood, A. Noyes
Song of the Ogres. Auden
Squats on a toad-stool under a tree. *Fr.*
  Death's Jest Book. Beddoes
Stocking Fairy. Welles
Stolen Child, The. Yeats
Thomas the Rhymer. *Unknown*
Tim, the Fairy. Livesay
To Mother Fairie. Cary
Very Nearly. Scott-Hopper
Wee Wee Man, The. *Unknown*
When I Was Six. Cross
Where the bee sucks, there suck I. *Fr.* The
  Tempest. Shakespeare
Yesterday in Oxford Street. Fyleman

*Why Am I Grown So Cold? Poems of the
Unknowable* (WSC), pp. 104-121. Myra
  Cohn Livingston, ed.
See also **Elves; Goblins.**

Fairs
Agricultural Show, Flemington, Victoria, The.
  "Maurice"
Ballad-Singer, The. *Fr.* At Casterbridge
  Fair. Hardy
Bartleme Fair. Stevens
Blaydon Races. *Unknown*
Cattle Show. "MacDiarmid"
Dance, The. Williams
Dunmow Flitch of Bacon, The. *Unknown*
Fair at Windgap, The. Clarke
Fair below Helvellyn, The. *Fr.* The Prelude
  [or, Growth of a Poet's Mind]: Residence
  in London. Wordsworth
Fairground. Auden
Former Beauties. *Fr.* At Casterbridge Fair.
  Hardy
Lads in Their Hundreds, The. *Fr.* A
  Shropshire Lad. Housman
One-Night Fair. Price
Sledburn Fair. *Unknown*
Sneaking in the State Fair. Fitzpatrick

Fairy Tales
Counsel. Lewis
Frog Prince, The. Smith
House in the Wood, The. Jarrell
Jack, Afterwards. Dacey
Kinder- und Hausmärchen. Alderson
Kinds of Luck. Reisen
Märchen, The. Jarrell
Märchenbilder. Ashbery
Reading the Brothers Grimm to Jenny.
  Mueller
So They Went Deeper into the Forest.
  Daniells
True Story of Snow White, The. Bennett

Faith
Act of Faith. Trías
After the Burial. Lowell
Apostasy. Aus of Kuraiza
As a Plane Tree by the Water. Lowell
At the Smithville Methodist Church. Dunn
Auguries of Innocence. Blake
Ballad of the Tempest. Fields
Ballad Which Anne Askew Made and Sang
  When She Was in Newgate, The. Askew
Beginnings of Faith, The. Morris
Believe and Take Heart. Spalding
Bishop Blougram's Apology. Browning
Carrion Comfort. Hopkins
Collar, The. Herbert
Common Inference, A. Gilman
Confession. Clifton
Country Faith, The. Gale
Credo. Jeffers
Credo. Robinson
Creed, A. Macleod
Creed, A. Masefield
Creeds. Baker
Death. *Unknown*
Disappointment—His Appointment. Young
Discipline. Herbert
Divine Image, The ("To mercy, pity, peace,
  and love"). *Fr.* Songs of Innocence.
  Blake
Doubt. Jackson
Doubter's Prayer, The. Brontë
Dover Beach. Arnold
"Dream is the thought in the ghost, The."
  Fr. A Faith on Trial. Meredith
Eclipse of Faith, The. Woolsey
Even Such Is Time. Ralegh
Evensong. Stevenson
Every Breath. Pilinszky
Exodus to Connacht. O'Meallain
Faith. Cambridge
Faith. Daley
Faith. Kemble

Faith. *Fr.* An Essay on Man. Pope
Faith. Tabb
Faith. Wilcox
Faith is a fine invention. Dickinson
Faith's Difficulty. Maynard
Faith's Vista. Abbey
For the Sleepwalkers. Hirsch
Generous Creed, A. Ward
God and Yet a Man, A? *Unknown*
God Be in My Head. *Fr.* Sarum Primer.
  Unknown
God's Grandeur. Hopkins
Have Faith. Carpenter
Heaven. Brooke
Highway, The. Gannett
His Litany to the Holy Spirit. Herrick
Homeward Journey, The. Aaronson
Hope Evermore and Believe. Clough
Hound of Heaven, The. Thompson
How the Great Guest Came. Markham
Hymn for Atonement Day. Halevi
Hymn of Saint Thomas in Adoration of the
  Blessed Sacrament, The. Crashaw
Hymn: "Thou hidden love of God, whose
  height." Wesley
Hymn to Tirumal (Visnu). Kirantaiyar
I know not what will befall me: God hangs a
  mist o'er my eyes. *Fr.* Not Knowing.
  Brainard
I never lost as much but twice. Dickinson
I never saw a moor. Dickinson
I Saw Three Ships. Arthur
If This Were Faith. *Fr.* Songs of Travel.
  Stevenson
Impercipient, The. Hardy
In a Country Church. Thomas
In the Hospital. Guiterman
Incomprehensible, The. Watts
Inspiration. Thoreau
Joy and Peace in Believing. Cowper
Lamb, The. *Fr.* Songs of Innocence. Blake
Light Shining out of Darkness. Cowper
Meditation on Communion with God. Halevi
Mock On, Mock On, Voltaire, Rousseau.
  Blake
My Creed. Cary
My Creed. Gilder
My Faith. Acharya
My Faith Looks Up to Thee. Palmer
My Spirit Longeth for Thee. Byrom
Night. *Fr.* Songs of Innocence. Blake
No Coward Soul [Is Mine] Brontë
On Time. Milton
Opportunity. Malone
Optimism. Wilcox
Pagan Isms, The. McKay
Passionate Man's Pilgrimage, The. Ralegh
Poet's Simple Faith, The. Hugo
Possession. *Unknown*
Prayer for Faith, A. Norris
Prayer, A: "Let me do my work each day."
  Ehrmann
Prayer: "Prayer the church's [*or* churches]
  banquet, angels' age." Herbert
Problem, The. Emerson
Rapture Is Coming, The. Phillips
Read, sweet, how others strove. Dickinson
Real Presence. Adair
Recessional. Kipling
Religion and Doctrine. Hay
Retreat[e], The. Vaughan
Rocked in the Cradle of the Deep. Willard
Rugby Chapel. Arnold
Sense and Spirit. Meredith
Shema Yisrael. *Unknown*
Silence. Towne
Song of Faith, A. Holland
Song of the Soul That Knows God by Faith.
  John of the Cross
Song of the Soul that Rejoices in Knowing
  God through Faith. John of the Cross

Sonnet: "I am not moved to love thee, my Lord God." Guevara
Stanzas of the Soul that Suffers with Longing to See God. John of the Cross
Temper, The. Herbert
That which we dare invoke to bless. *Fr.* In Memoriam A. H. H. Tennyson
"There is no God," the wicked saith. *Fr.* Dipsychus. Clough
There Is No Unbelief. Case
Therefore, We Thank Thee, God. Grossman
This World I'd Wish to Leave and God to Serve. Compiuta Donzella
Though Mine Eye Sleep Not. *Fr.* The Dead Sea Scrolls. *Unknown*
Thus man by his own strength to Heaven would soar. *Fr.* Religio Laici. Dryden
Thy Way, Not Mine. Bonar
Tide of Faith, The. *Fr.* A Minor Prophet. "Eliot"
Time of Change, A. O'Rahilly
Tirumal. Katuvan Ilaveyinanar
To a Waterfowl. Bryant
To Be Said at the Seder. Wolfskehl
To God. Herrick
To Him Who Is Feared. Ben Kalir
To Trust. Pozzi
Tree in December. Cane
Triple Bension, The. Ray
Unshrinking Faith. Balhurst
Victory. *Unknown*
Visionary, The. Brontë
Whenever I remember. Vali
You say, but with no touch of scorn. *Fr.* In Memoriam A. H. H. Tennyson
Contemporary Religious Poetry (CRP). Paul Ramsey, ed.

Faith Healers
Faith Healing. Larkin

Faithfulness. *See* Fidelity.

Falcons
Epigram: "Lux my fair falcon, and your fellows all." Wyatt
Falcon, The. Lovelace
Falcon and the Dove, The. Read
Falcons, The. Merwin
Hawking. *Fr.* Polyolbion. Drayton
Lover Compareth Himself to the Painful Falconer, The. *Unknown*
My Mother Would Be a Falconress. Duncan
Timor Mortis. *Unknown*
When the water fowl are found, the falconers hasten. *Fr.* The Parlement [*or* Parliament] of the Thre[e] Ages. *Unknown*
Windhover, The. Hopkins

Falkland, Lucius Cary, Viscount
Falkland at Newbury, 1643. Conway

Fall. *See* Autumn.

Fame
After Publication of Under the Volcano. Lowry
Consider Famous Men, Dai Bach. Davies
Contemporary. Flexner
Fame. Cantus
Fame. Emerson
Fame. Heard
Fame. Mew
Fame and Fortune. *Fr.* The Legend of Robert, Duke of Normandy. Drayton
Fame Makes Us Forward. Herrick
Glory and Enduring Fame. Simms
Greatness. *Unknown*
I'm nobody! Who are you? Dickinson
In an Album. Lowell
Let us now praise famous men. *Fr.* Ecclesiasticus
Love of praise, howe'er concealed by art, The. *Fr.* Love of Fame, the Universal Passion. Young
Ozymandias [*or* Ozymandias of Egypt *or* Sonnet: Ozymandias]. Shelley

Provide, Provide. Frost
Resolve, The. Chudleigh
Settling Some Old Football Scores. Bishop
Stanzas Written on the Road between Florence and Pisa. Byron
There is a tall long-sided dame. *Fr.* Hudibras. Butler
True and False Glory ("To whom our Saviour calmly thus reply'd"). *Fr.* Paradise Regained. Milton
Wish, A. Kemble
See also **Greatness.**

Family Life
Animal Crackers. Morley
Animal House, The. Brechin
Ave Maria. O'Hara
Beneath the Shadow of the Freeway. Cervantes
Brown Family, The. Thibaudeau
Childhood. Stanton
Church Poem. Thomas
Coming Home. Stone
Dedication to Hunger. Glück
Eat, Eat! Wong
Eating Lechon, with My Brothers and Sisters. Cabalquinto
Emerald, The. *Fr.* Up and Down. Merrill
Every Town a Home Town. Kaniyan Punkunran
Eyes, the Blood, The. Meltzer
Familial. Prévert
Family. MacCaig
Family. Tanikawa Shuntaro
Family Court. Nash
Family Pictures. Morris
Family Portrait. Andrade
Family Reunion. Kumin
Family Turn, A. Stafford
Father and Son. Kunitz
Folded Flock, The. Meynell
For My Mother, Feeling Useless. Rankin
From a Childhood. Rilke
Funnel. Sexton
Gemwood. Bell
Good Times. Clifton
Green Family, The. Thibaudeau
House on Buder Street, The. Gildner
Ice Cream. Wild
Idea of Ancestry, The. Knight
In the Old Guerilla War. Pastan
In the Park. Harwood
Landscape of Domestic Life. Graham
Let's Be Merry. Rossetti
Letter to Peter, A. Chiang
Long Island Springs. Moss
Looking for a Country under Its Original Name. McElroy
Love between Brothers and Sisters. Watts
Love Should Grow Up like a Wild Iris in the Fields. Griffin
Mother. Montoya
My Father in the Night Commanding No. Simpson
Nails. Gildner
Nikki-Rosa [*or* Nikki-Roasa]. Giovanni
Nisei Picnic, A. Mura
Old Man Dreams, The. Holmes
Physical Universe. Simpson
Relations. Orerulavanar
Rescued Year, The. Stafford
Retrieval System, The. Kumin
Somerset Dam for Supper, The. Holmes
Sunday Morning. Jenkins
Those Winter Sundays. Hayden
Verandahs. Brissenden
Watch Them Die. Trudell
What Became of the Family? Johnson
When Father Carves the Duck. Wright

Famine
Famine Year, The. Wilde
Flight from Famine: A Ballad. Cheng Hsieh
Hunger. Binyon

Maguire is not afraid of death, the Church will light him a candle. *Fr.* The Great Hunger. Kavanagh
Oh, the flowers of the bignonia. *Unknown*
Oh, what has become of us? *Unknown*

Fancy. *See* Imagination.

Fans
Eagle-Feather Fan, The. Momaday
In Passing. Jonas
Japanese Fan. Kirkup
Present from the Emperor's New Concubine, A. Pan
To a Lady, with a Present of a Fan. Brandling

Farewell
At a Farewell Party for Fujiwara no Yoshino. Junna

Fargo, North Dakota
Outside Fargo, North Dakota. Wright

Farmers and Farming
Haying. Graham

Farming and Farmers
After Winter. Brown
Anxious Farmer, The. Johnson
At a Potato Digging. Heaney
Big field brings a heavy crop, The. *Unknown*
Black Man Talks of Reaping, A. Bontemps
Boy Wandering in Simms' Valley. Warren
Canadian Farmer. Bartole
Code, The. Frost
Come now! the victorious kings. *Unknown*
Cooney Potter. *Fr.* Spoon River Anthology. Masters
Corn-Planter. Kenny
Cotter's Saturday Night, The. Burns
Country Greeting. Steele
Country Hirings. *Unknown*
Country Summer. Adams
Cupid the Ploughboy. *Unknown*
Curse, The. Francis
Death of a Vermont Farm Woman. Howes
Death of the Hired Man, The. Frost
Deserted Homestead, The. Eiseley
Drover, A. Colum
Drumdelgie. *Unknown*
Earth Dweller. Stafford
Eleven. MacLeish
Entailed Farm, The. Glassco
Essay. Mayer
Farewell to the Farm. Stevenson
Farm Child. Thomas
Farm Hands, The. Laing
Farm near Norman's Lane, The. Finnin
Farm Picture, A. Whitman
Farm Wife. Mitchell
Farm Woman: 1942, The. Mitchison
Farmer, The. Herbert
Farmer. Stryk
Farmer, The. Voigt
Farmer and the Farmer's Wife, The. Hiebert
Farmer, Dying. Hugo
Farmers. Percy
Farmer's Boy, The. *Unknown*
Farmer's Son So Sweet, A. *Unknown*
Field and Forest. Jarrell
Field Work. Cockrell
Floodtide. Touré
French Peasants. Gibbon
Frost in the Corn, The. McAlmon
Fruit Rancher, The. Roberts
Gin the Goodwife Stint. Bunting
Go Home. McFatter
God Save the Plough. Sigourney
Ground-Thumping Song. *Unknown*
Hay for the Horses. Snyder
Hayfield, The. *Fr.* The Flowing Summer. Bruce
Haymaking. Thomas
Henyard Round, The. Hall
Hill Farmer Speaks, The. Thomas

His Grange, or Private Wealth. Herrick
Husbandman and Serving-Man, The.
  Unknown
I May Reap. Kavanagh
I Will Go with My Father a-Ploughing.
  Campbell
Improved Farm Land. Sandburg
In the seventh month the fire ebbs. *Unknown*
John Barleycorn. *Unknown*
Lament of the Farm Wife of Wu. Su
  Tung-p'o
Landscape of Domestic Life. Graham
Lark along the Road, A. Tamemasa
Man with the Hoe, The. Markham
Marginal Field, The. Spender
Memoirs of a Spinach-Picker. Plath
Method of Preserving Hay from Being
  Mow-Burnt, or Taking Fire, A. *Fr.*
  Agriculture. Dodsley
Mighty are you, Hou Chi. *Unknown*
Miss Creighton. Taylor
Mother. Heaney
Mowing. Frost
Mowing, The. Roberts
New-fashioned Farmer, The. *Unknown*
Nobody Loses All the Time. Cummings
Now I'm Easy. Bogle
Oliver Johnson Comes Back to Bed the
  Morning after the Ice Storm and Tells His
  Wife Why. Jauss
Ox Cart Man. Hall
Pasture, The. Frost
Peasant and Ox. Shin Dong-jip
Ploughman. Kavanagh
Pretty Ploughboy, The. *Unknown*
Prodigal, The. Bishop
Purpose of Poetry, The. Carter
Putting in the Seed. Frost
Range-finding. Frost
Reapers. Blind
Reapers. Toomer
Retired Farmer. Evans
Retreat of Ita Cagney, The. Hartnett
Rival, The. Warner
Saving the Harvest. Lehmann
Six Badgers, The. Graves
Small Farm, A. Hartnett
Solitary Reaper, The. Wordsworth
Son, The. Torrence
Song of the Banana Man, The. Jones
Sower, The. Blind
Sower, The. Figueroa
Sower, The. Roberts
Spraying the Potatoes. Kavanagh
Times Have Altered, The. *Unknown*
Very sharp, the good shares. *Unknown*
Wheat. Gildner
Wife's Tale, The. Heaney
Yamashiro. Saibara
Faber Book of Useful Verse, The (FaBoUs),
  pp. 36-55. Simon Brett, ed.

Farmworkers
Napa, California. Castillo
They clear away the grass, the trees.
  Unknown
Washing the Coins. Dunn
See also **Migrant Workers.**

Farragut, David Glasgow
Farragut. Meredith
River Fight, The. Brownell

Fashion
Beau's Receipt for a Lady's Dress, The.
  Unknown
Dandy O, The. *Unknown*
Dresssessional, A. Wells
Fashion. Twiss
Lady's Receipt for a Beau's Dress, The.
  Unknown
On English Monsieur. Jonson
Monkey, lap-dog, parrot, and her Grace, The.
  Fr. Isabella; or, The Morning. Williams

Things lately fashionable in the capital. *Fr.*
  Ryojin Hisho. Go-Shirakawa
Time was, an Englishman would join. *Fr.*
  Of Taste; an Essay. Cawthorn
What the Choir Sang about the New Bonnet.
  Morrison
See also **Clothing.**

Fate
Alone up here on the mountain. *Unknown*
Crimson Lute That Comest in the Dawn.
  Juana Inés de la Cruz
Definition of Love, The. Marvell
Design. Frost
Destiny. Arnold
Destiny. Bibb
Destiny. Guglielminetti
Draft Horse, The. Frost
Eros Turannos. Robinson
Eshu, the God of Fate. *Unknown*
Fate. Merwin
Flux. Eberhart
From Prison. Abulafia
Green Enravishment of Human Life. Juana
  Inés de la Cruz
Hap. Hardy
Karma. Robinson
Kore. Creeley
Lachesis. Raine
Murmur. Hecht
Omens. *Unknown*
Poet's Fate, The. Hood
Song: "There's nothing in this gardenous
  world more delightful." Stern
Trojans. Cavafy
Unmanifest Destiny. Hovey
Waiting. Burroughs
What Different Dooms Our Birthdays Bring!
  Fr. Miss Kilmansegg and Her Precious
  Leg. Hood
Whiplash. Matthews
Winds of Fate, The. Wilcox
See also **Fortune.**

Fathers
After Dark. Rich
After Grief. Plumly
All My Pretty Ones. Sexton
American Primitive. Smith
Apples. Waters
Attic, The. *Fr.* The Flowing Summer.
  Bruce
Au Tombeau de Mon Père. McCuaig
Automobile Mechanics. Baruch
Axe Handles. Snyder
Because. McAuley
Becoming a Dad. Guest
Bee, The. Dickey
Beryl. Lifshin
Between Here and Illinois. Pomeroy
But then what do you know about the rights
  of suffocated genitals. *Fr.* Paternal.
  Bettarini
Cage, The. Montague
Childless Father, The. Wordsworth
Christo's. Muldoon
Clayfeld's Daughter Reveals Her Plans. Pack
Clayfeld's Glove. Pack
Clock on Hancock Street. Jordan
Clues to Displaced Persons. Jarman
Colossus, The. Plath
Coming and Going. Johnson
Commander Lowell. Lowell
Composed on a Journey Homeward; the
  Author Having Received Intelligence of the
  Birth of a Son. Coleridge
Copy. *Fr.* Song Sequence. Tomer
Country Ways. *Fr.* Impressions of My
  Father. Masters
Crown of Hatred and Love. Juhász
Dad. Feinstein
Daddy. Clifton

Daddy. Plath
Daddy Fell into the Pond. Noyes
Death of Fathers, The. Weiss
Desk, The. Bottoms
Do Not Go Gentle into That Good Night.
  Thomas
"Dreadful Has Already Happened, The."
  Strand
Economics Lesson. Scotellaro
Efficiency Apartment. Barrax
Elegy for My Father. Moss
Elegy for My Father. Strand
Elegy: "I know but will not tell." Dugan
Equality, Father! Bruck
Europe and America. Ignatow
Eyes of Flesh, The. Hochman
Family Photograph. Vizenor
Father. Frost
Father. Kafka
Father. Lipkin
Father. Livingston
Father and Child. Harwood
Father and Son. Higgins
Father of My Country, The. Wakoski
Father Son and Holy Ghost. Lorde
Father Takes to the Road and Lets His Hair
  Down. Lau
Fathers of Desire. Scott
Father's Story. Roberts
Father's Testament, A. Ibn Tibbon
Figures of Authority. Watkins
First Prelude. Dream in Ohio; the Father.
  Fr. Poem in Progress. Logan
Flag on the house you dwelled in the wind
  blows now and then, The. *Fr.* My
  Father—Is the Root. Ya'oz-kest
Follower. Heaney
Forever Mountain. Chappell
Forgiving My Father. Clifton
From Father to Son. Humphreys
Full Well I Know. Coleridge
Gardener, The. Wheelock
Goodnight Irene. Mariani
Grief. Díaz Mirón
Hank. Tapscott
Havana Blues. Carlile
Heirloom. Klein
His Father's Hands. Kinsella
Holiday. *Fr.* Remembrances. Leivick
Hospital Window, The. Dickey
How My Father Died. Ezekiel
I Remember. Sánchez
I Sit with My Dolls. *Unknown*
In Memoriam. Longley
In the Winter Dark. Gerber
Indian Summer. Hirsch
Irish Cliffs of Moher, The. Stevens
Joe Gillon Hypnotizes His Son. Goldbarth
Johnson Brothers Ltd. Kopland
Keeping the Horses. Scheele
Labasheedy (the Silken Bed). Dhomhnaill
Last Journey. Montague
Letter. Fortini
Letters & Other Worlds. Ondaatje
Letters from a Father. Van Duyn
Lines to His Son on Reaching Adolescence.
  Logan
Lines to My Father. Daiken
Little Father Poem. Bell
Lost Pilot, The. Tate
Love from My Father. Clemmons
Love Poem: "Speak earth and bless me with
  what is richest." Lorde
Magician, The. Ramke
Man Who Finds That His Son Has Become a
  Thief, The. Souster
Man's Song, about His Daughter, A.
  Unknown
Means of Production, The. Hofmann
Meeting the British. Muldoon
Memory of my Father. Kavanagh
Mirror, The. Muldoon

Moss of His Skin, The. Sexton
My Father. Aleixandre
My Father. Berry
My Father. Bialik
My Father. Chalfi
My Father. Guevara
My Father. Rübner
My Father after Work. Gildner
My Father Died This Spring. Kyger
My father has big skin like a soldier's cape.
  Khoury-Gata
My Father in the Night Commanding No.
  Simpson
My Father Kept His Cats Well Fed.
  Sherman
My Father Moved through Dooms of Love.
  Cummings
My Father, My Son. Brinnin
My Father; October 1942. Stafford
My father played the melodion. Fr. A
  Christmas Childhood. Kavanagh
My Father Scything. Hunt
My Father Today. Hunt
My Father, Who's Still Alive. Kozer
My Father's Death. Foscolo
My Father's Martial Art. Liu
My Father's Song. Ortiz
My Father's Wedding. Bly
My Old Man's Dawdling. Illyés
My Papa's Waltz. Roethke
News That Stays News. Mariani
1933. Levine
Not Saying Much. Gregg
Note apropos a Light Breeze and an Elderly
  Couple on a Bench, Together, in the
  National Park at Ram. Kovner
On a Nun. Vittorelli
On My First Son [or Sonne] Jonson
On the Road at Night There Stands the Man.
  Ravikovich
On the Seventh Anniversary of the Death of
  My Father. Pack
Origin of Dreams. Bell
Oui Papa. Malik de Coteau
Out-of-the-Body Travel. Plumly
Pain-Killers. Harrison
Passion. Prospere
Photograph of My Father in His
  Twenty-second Year. Carver
Placing a $2 Bet for a Man Who Will Never
  Go to the Horse Races Any More.
  Wakoski
Poem for My Father, A. Sanchez
Poem for My Father's Ghost. Oliver
Portrait, The. Kunitz
Premonition, The. Roethke
Quoits. Newsome
Rare Rhythms. London
Re-education. Polet
Reformer to His Father, A.
  Simmons
Reggae fi Dada. Johnson
Return, The. MacBeth
Revelation, The. Wright
Russian Cradle Song, A. Nomberg
Second Prelude. Reality in Albuquerque: The
  Son. Fr. Poem in Progress. Logan
Secret, The. Kaneko
Setting Out from Hiroshima, Saying Goodby
  to My Father. Rai San'yo
Shore. O Hehir
Sightseers, The. Muldoon
Silence. Moore
Sometimes, in the Evening. Buddingh'
Starlight. Levine
Story of Lava, The. Evans
Stranger, The. Gelman
Stray Bird's Homeland, A. Liu K'o-hsiang
Sunflowers and Saturdays. Boyd
Swerve, The. Stafford
That Day. Kherdian

There were no hidden motives to his life.
  Ignatow
Those Winter Sundays. Hayden
To Father. Tucker
To My Father. Butler
To My Father. Dmitrova
To My Father. Ray
To the Memory of My Dear and Ever
  Honored Father Thomas Dudley Esq.
  Bradstreet
To the Reverend Shade of His Religious
  Father. Herrick
Two Postures beside a Fire. Wright
Uncle Robert. Morgan
Victims, The. Olds
Visitation Rights. Wishik
Visiting My Father. Rai San'yo
Waking. Maxton
What For. Hongo
When Father Came Home for Lunch. Mitsui
When Father Carves the Duck. Wright
Why Are Daddies So Mean? Chambers
Windharp. Montague
Winter Stars. Levis
Wishbone, The. Muldoon
Woman's Song, about Men, A. Unknown
Woods. MacNeice
Working late. Stimson
Worm, The. Barnstone
Wounds. Longley
Writing while My Father Dies. Pastan
Written on the Anniversary of Our Father's
  Death. Coleridge
Youth. Wright
Zealot without a Face. Dobzynski
Divided Light: Father and Son Poems (DiL).
  Jason Shinder, ed.

Fathers-in-Law
Father-in-Law. Mahon
Fatigue. See **Weariness.**
Fauns
Faun, The. Pound
Faust
Faust. Ashbery
Progress of Faust, The. Shapiro
Prologue in Heaven [or The Chorus of the
  Archangels] Fr. Faust. Goethe
Royalties. Enright
Fawkes, Guy
Gunpowder Plot, The. Unknown
November the Fifth. Clark
Fear
Afraid. De la Mare
Be Fair. Guillevic
Fairy Tale, A. Mackenzie
Fear. Camerino
Fear. Fritsch
Fear. Hajnal
Fear. Peacock
Fear. Simic
Fear Is What Quickens Me. Wright
Fear Test: Integrity of Heroes. Simmons
Fears of the Eighth Grade. Derricotte
Frightened Flier Goes North, The. Kazantzis
Great Fear, The. Oppezzo
I am afraid. Unknown
I Give You Back. Harjo
In Waste Places. Stephens
My Daughter's Ring. Reiss
Ode to Fear. Collins
"Paper Men to Air Hopes and Fears."
  Francis
Patience Is When You Stop Waiting.
  Williams
Same But Different. Collins
Sometimes. Kuzma
Storm Fear. Frost
Terror. Kitahara Hakushu
February
Brook in February, The. Roberts
February. Heath-Stubbs

February. Pasolini
February. Ray
February. Fr. Sonnets of the Months. San
  Gimignano
February Thaw. Dutton
February Twilight. Teasdale
In the month of February. Unknown
Mirror in February. Kinsella
When. Aldis
Federal Bureau of Investigation
Award. Durem
Feet
About Feet. Hillert
Baby's feet, like sea-shells pink, A. Fr.
  Étude Réaliste. Swinburne
Feet. Thompson
Fitting. Fowler
My Mother's Feet. Plumly
To the Foot from Its Child. Neruda
Upon Her Feet. Herrick
Fellowship. See **Brotherhood.**
Feminism
About Women's Liberation. Saucedo
Ain't I a Woman? Truth
Aleksandra Kollontay. Vammelvuo
Another Spring, Another Year. Vammelvuo
Breaking Tradition. Mirikitani
Clubwoman. Smith
Daughters. Astra
Emulation, The. Egerton
Funeral Song for Mamie Eisenhower. Wong
He and She. Ware
Her Sister. O'Neill
Housewife's Lament, The. Unknown
Hypocrite Women. Levertov
I take as my theme, "The Independent
  Woman." Fr. Pro Femina. Kizer
It's in the Name. Tsui
It's No Good! Lawrence
Liberation. Stone
March of the Women, The. Hamilton
Myth. Rukeyser
Ninth Symphony of Beethoven Understood at
  Last as a Sexual Message, The. Rich
Notes from a Chicana "COED." Zamora
On a Fortification at Boston Begun by
  Women. Tompson
Pan, the Pot, the Burning Fire I Have in Front
  of Me, The. Ishigaki Rin
Purple, White and Green, The.
  Morgan-Browne
Rights of Woman, The. Barbauld
Significant Fevers. Fell
Snapshots of a Daughter-in-Law. Rich
Strawberry Moon. Oliver
Subversive, The. Woo
There Is a Woman in This Town. Parker
They lived out in a women's house. Fr. The
  Rime of the Ancient Feminist. Markman
Things Not of This Union. Gregg
To Kate, Skating Better than Her Date.
  Daiches
To the Ladies. Chudleigh
To the Tune "The River Is Red." Ch'iu Chin
To Women. Hugo
Under Our Own Wings. Wong
Woman Defending Herself Examines Her
  Own Character Witness, A. Griffin
Women of My Land. Armstrong
Women's Marseillaise, The. Macaulay
Wonder Woman. Lim
Ain't I a Woman! a Book of Women's Poetry
  from around the World (AIW). Illona
  Linthwaite, ed.
Defiant Muse, The; French Feminist Poems
  from the Middle Ages to the Present
  (DMF). Domna C. Stanton, ed.
Defiant Muse, The; German Feminist Poems
  from the Middle Ages to the Present
  (DMG). Susan L. Cocalis, ed.

Defiant Muse, The; Hispanic Feminist Poems from the Middle Ages to the Present (DMH). Angel Flores *and* Kate Flores, eds.
Defiant Muse, The; Italian Feminist Poems from the Middle Ages to the Present (DMI). Beverly Allen, Muriel Kittel, *and* Keala Jane Jewell, eds.
Early Ripening; American Women's Poetry Now (ER). Marge Piercy, ed.
Faber Book of 20th Century Women's Poetry, The (FaBoWP). Fleur Adcock, ed.
I Hear My Sisters Saying (IHMS). Carol Konek *and* Dorothy Walters, eds.
No More Masks! (NMM). Florence Howe *and* Ellen Bass, eds.
Other Voices, The; Twentieth-Century Women's Poetry in Translation (OV). Joanna Bankier *and others*, eds.

Fences
Barbed Wire Fence Meditates upon the Goldfinch, A. McKay
Fence, A. Sandburg
Fence Wire. Dickey
How to Build a Ha-ha. *Fr.* The English Garden. Mason
Old Fence Post. Hanes
Picket Fence, The. Morgenstern
Pickety fence, The. McCord
See also **Walls.**

Fencing
Fencing School. Manifold
For E. McC. Pound
Idyll: "Within a quad of aging brick." Updike

Fenians
Caoilte. *Unknown*

Ferns
Bracken Hills in Autumn. "MacDiarmid"
Ferns, The. Baro
Tree Ferns. Plumly
Young fiddlehead ferns, The. Yomono Akara

Ferry Boats
Back and Forth. Mitchell
Crossing Brooklyn Ferry. Whitman
Ferry Me across the Water. *Fr.* Sing-Song. Rossetti
Ferryman, The. Nagy
Jolly Young Waterman, The. Dibdin
Recuerdo. Millay
Trip on the Staten Island Ferry, A. Lorde

Fertilizer
Compost. *Fr.* The Sugar Cane. Grainger

Festivals
Green Corn Festival. Harris
On the Cold Food Festival, Entertaining at the Southern Estate. Li K'ai-hsien
Walking Outside the City Walls. Pien Kung

Feuds
Lads of Wamphray, The. *Unknown*
Lord Maxwell's Last Goodnight. *Unknown*
Massacre of the Macpherson, The. Aytoun
Rowan County Crew, The. Day

Fever
Fever. *Fr.* The Dance of Death. Browning
Fever, The. Dobson
Fever 103°. Plath

Fiacre, Saint
Saint Fiacre. Irvine

Fiddlers and Fiddles
At My Wedding. Segal
Clabe Mott. Still
Country Fiddler, The. Montague
Fiddler of Dooney, The. Yeats
First Song. Kinnell
Mountain Whippoorwill, The. Benét
My Fiddle. Kwitko
Nuala's Fiddle. O Canainn
Seven Fiddlers, The. Evans

Take Down the Fiddle, Karl! Neilson
See also **Violins.**

Fidelity
Barbara. Smith
Blame was all. Dard
Born with the Vices. D'Urfey
Chinese Ballad. Mao Tse-tung
Fair Sylvia. *Unknown*
Faithful, The. Waters
Faithful Wife, The. Greenberg
Irish Peasant to His Mistress, The. Moore
Kudzu Spreads Till It Darkens the Brier, The. *Unknown*
Lament of the Border Widow, The. *Unknown*
"Let me not to the marriage of true minds." *Fr.* Sonnets, CXVI. Shakespeare
Love Me Little, Love Me Long. Herrick
Lover Exhorteth His Lady to Be Constant, The. *Unknown*
Meeting. Rossetti
My dear and only love, I pray. Graham
Non Sum Qualis Eram Bonae sub Regno Cynarae [*or* Cynara] Dowson
Oh Count, Where Has Gone. Stampa
Pledge. Rashed
Promise of a Constant Lover, The. *Unknown*
So long as life remains. Dard
Song, A: "Chloris, when I to thee present." *Unknown*
There Is a Lady Sweet and Kind. Ford
Though a time come. *Fr.* Twenty-four Tanka. Sanetomo
Unquiet Grave, The. *Unknown*
Visionary, The. Brontë
When men shall find thy flower [*or* flow'r], thy glory, pass. *Fr.* To Delia. Daniel
Woman. Barrett
Woman, Don't Be Troublesome. Young

Field Athletics
Challenge. Hazo
Pole Vault. Murano Shiro

Field-Glasses
Field-Glasses. Young

Fields and Pastures
Cornfield, The. Roberts
Field-Glasses. Young
Hares at Play. Clare
Immortal. Van Doren
Like a Field Waiting. Chalfi
Lost. Brand
Low Fields and Light. Merwin
Meadow-Field, The. *Fr.* Pleasant Memories. Sangster
Meadows, The. Taylor
Mountain Meadows. Keller
Mower's Song, The. Marvell
Pastoral: "Annette came through the meadows." Ray
Pasture, The. Frost
Pasture, A. Knowles
Pea-Fields, The. *Fr.* Songs of the Common Day. Roberts
Poplar Field, The. Cowper
Return, The. Ostenso
When You Will Walk in the Field. Goldberg
White Fields. Stephens

Fiesole, Italy
In the Old Theatre, Fiesole. Hardy

Fig Trees and Figs
Beware of Figs. Nicophon
Figs. Lawrence
Tapestry Trees. Morris
Where the Slow Fig's Purple Sloth. Warren

Fights
Fist Fight. Cockrell

Figureheads (ship)
Figurehead, The. Adams

Filipinos
Lolo died yesterday. Zarco

Manong Federico Delos Reyes and His Golden Banjo. Robles
Manong Jacinto Santo Tomas. Robles
New Manong, The. Syquia
Pick-up at Chef Rizal Restaurant. Cerenio
Pinay. Cerenio
We who carry the endless seasons. Cerenio
Without Names. Tagami
You Lovely People. Cerenio
See also **Philippines.**

Financiers
New Order of Chivalry, A. Peacock
On a Travelling Speculator. Freneau
See also **Banking and Bankers.**

Finches
Birdsong. Singer
Blind Linnet, The. Buchanan
Finches, The. Shapcott
Green Linnet, The. Wordsworth
110 Year Old House. Ochester
Sometimes goldfinches one by one will drop. *Fr.* I Stood Tiptoe. Keats

Fingers
Bestiary for the Fingers of My Right Hand. Simic
Finger of Necessity. Barks
Now It Is Broccoli. Tagami
Ten Fingers. *Unknown*
This little pig went to market. Mother Goose

Finland
Finland. Graves
Reindeer and Engine. Jacobsen

Finnish Civil War (1918)
There where the Kulo Saari bridge. *Fr.* Ballad of Herman's Rose. Turtiainen

Finnish Verse
Salt of Pleasure: Twentieth-Century Finnish Poetry (SOP). Aili Jarvenpa, tr.

Finns
Kirsten. *Fr.* Calling Your Name in the Zoo. Williams

Finnsburg, Battle of
Battle of Finnsburg, The. *Unknown*

Fionn (legendary king of Fenians)
Praise of Fionn, The. *Unknown*

Fir Trees
Epitaph on a Fir-Tree. Murphy
Fir-Tree, The. Thomas
Tapestry Trees. Morris

Fire
Armies in the Fire. *Fr.* A Child's Garden of Verses. Stevenson.
Banking Coal. Toomer
Barn Fire. Lux
Barnfire during Church. Bly
Brooklyn Theater Fire, The. *Unknown*
Brother Fire. MacNeice
Burning the Small Dead. Snyder
Burnt Child, The. Merwin
Bushfire. Salom
Coal Fire in Winter, A. McGrath
Death of the Horses by Fire. Gallagher
Encountering Fire Again in the Fifth Month. Huang Tsung-hsi
Execration upon Vulcan, An. Jonson
Feeding the Fire. Finkel
Fire and Ice. Frost
Fire at Alexandria, The. Weiss
Fire of London, The. *Fr.* Annus Mirabilis. Dryden
Fire on the Hills. Jeffers
Firelight. Robinson
Fires. Fleming
Fires. Heyen
First Grass. Leivick
Heart Will Have Its Way, The. Efrat
Hotel Fire: New Orleans. Ruffin
Houses Burning; Quebec. Anderson
In Fire. Leivick
Lighting a Fire. Kennedy
Looking West. Stafford

Lumberyard, The. Herschberger
Man and His Wife, A. Redgrove
Marriage of Heaven and Earth, The. Nemerov
Milwaukee Fire, The. *Unknown*
Miramichi Fire, The. *Unknown*
On Hearing That the Market outside the East Gate of the City Has Been Burned Down. Cheng Chen
Prairie Fires. Garland
Sappho. Wright
Scare-Fire, The. Herrick
Some Verses upon the Burning of Our House, July 10th, 1666. Bradstreet
Sourdough mountain called a fire in. *Fr.* Myths and Texts: Burning. Snyder
Street Fire. Halpern
Summer Oracle. Lorde
To Live Here. Eluard
Two Fires, The. Wright
Where Fire Burns. Cardiff
Window Seat, A. Goldbarth

Fire-eaters
Firebreathers at the Café Deux Magots, The. Williams

Fire Engines
Fire-Truck, A. Wilbur
Great Figure, The. Williams

Fire Island
True Account of Talking to the Sun at Fire Island, A. O'Hara
Two Drops. Herbert

Firearms. *See* **Guns.**

Firecats
Earthy Anecdote. Stevens

Firefighters
Firemen. Sutskever
Habeas Corpus Blues, The. Aiken

Fireflies
As I picked it up. Taigi
Come, come, I say. Onitsura
Fire of the Fireflies, The. Hung Sheng
Fireflies. Chao Chih-hsin
Fireflies. Charles
Fireflies. Fawcett
Fireflies. Hall
Fireflies. *Fr.* Transcripts from Nature. "Macleod"
Fireflies. Shohaku
Fireflies in the Garden. Frost
Fireflies over a Marsh. Tamemasa
Firefly, The. McPherson
Firefly, The. Nash
Firefly. Roberts
Glittering, glittering, fireflies in the grass. *Fr.* Miscellaneous Words on the Lake. Tsung Ch'en
Glow-Worm, The. Mercer
Glow-Worm, The. Smith
Glow-Worms. Ropes
Glowworm. Dodat
Haiku: "From the firefly." *Fr.* Thirty-nine Haiku. Shiki
How dreamy-dark it is! *Fr.* The Fireflies. Mair
Huge firefly, undulating, A. *Fr.* Forty-four Hokku. Issa
Lightning Bug. Morgan
Lightning Bugs. Slyman
Making no sound. Shigeyuki
Mower to the Glow-Worms [*or* Glowworms], The. Marvell
My thoughts on the past. Sanetaka
Night-Piece, to Julia, The. Herrick
Oi! oi! firefly, here! *Unknown*
Only over the river, darkness flows: fireflies. *Fr.* Seventeen Hokku. Chiyojo
Under the lower leaves of hydrangea fireflies cluster. *Fr.* Eighty-four Tanka. Teika
Very Minor Poet Speaks, A. Valle
Were I in Trouble. Frost

Fires
Encountering Fire in Early Spring, 1662. Huang Tsung-hsi

Fireworks
Fireworks. Deutsch
Fireworks. Reeves
Fireworks. Worth
Fourth of July Night. Sandburg
July 4th. Swenson
Pinwheel's Song, The. Ciardi

Firpo, Luis
Boxing Match, The. Ignatow

Fish
Although it's cold no clothes I wear. *Unknown*
Aquarium. Wright
At the Aquarium. Eastman
Barracuda. MacInnis
Beginning of an Undergraduate Poem. *Unknown*
Birds and Fishes. Jeffers
Cleaning the Fish. Pack
Description of a Strange (and Miraculous) Fish, A. Parker
Dreaming Trout, The. *Fr.* The Flowing Summer. Bruce
Drinking at the Cave Mouth. Tsung Ch'en
Evolution. Blight
Fish, The. Bishop
Fish. Bourinot
Fish, The. Brooke
Fish, The. Gustafson
Fish. Hoberman
Fish, The. Oliver
Fish. Rosenblatt
Fish. Ross
Fish and Bird. Brinckman
Fish in River: "My house is not quiet, I am not loud." *Fr.* Riddles (Exeter Book). Cynewulf
Fish Story. Carlile
Fish-teeming sea. *Fr.* Amergin's Songs. Amergin
Fishes, The. *Unknown*
Fishes' Evening Song. Ipcar
Flattered Flying Fish, The. Rieu
Flying Fish, The. Cope
Frying Fish. Chan Ch'e
Fun with Fishing. Tietjens
Gar, The. Bell
Goose Fish, The. Nemerov
Great fish's eyes never shut, The. Castellanos
Grunion. Livingston
Heaven. Brooke
How They Brought the Good News by Sea. Farber
Ichthycide. Rosenblatt
Ichthyology. Achterberg
Joy of Fishes, The. Chuang Tzu
King of waters, the sea shouldering whale, The. Wood
Little Fish. Lawrence
Mackerel. Brown
Maldive Shark, The. Melville
Methods of Cooking Trout. *Fr.* The Art of Angling. Barker
Minnows. *Fr.* I Stood Tiptoe [upon a Little Hill]. Keats
Movement of Fish, The. Dickey
Mrs. Busk. Sitwell
Northern Pike. Wright
Pesci Misti. Aaronson
Pike, The. Blunden
Pike. Hughes
Pity. Mills
Returning. Shanley
Robbers came to our house, The. *Unknown*
Sea School. Howes
Snapper, The. Heyen
Sonnet of Fishes. Barker
Starfish. Welles

Three Movements. Yeats
To a Baked Fish. Wells
To a Fish. Hunt
To the Immortal Memory of the Halibut on Which I Dined This Day, Monday, April 26, 1784. Cowper
Trout, The. Montague
Two Fish. Pollitt
Two Fish by a Willow Embankment. Hsü Wei
Watching Fish in the Water. Suemochi
When Howitzers Began. Carruth
White fish graphically move in the water's color. *Fr.* Thirteen Hokku. Raizan
Wreath to the Fish, A. Willard

Fisher, John, Cardinal (Saint John Fisher)
Alas, Alack! De la Mare
Cardinal Fisher. Heywood

Fishing and Fishermen
And Angling, Too. *Fr.* Don Juan. Byron
Angels, The. Eberhart
Anglers, The. Mar
Angler's Invitation, The. Stoddart
Angler's Song, The. *Fr.* The Secrets of Angling. Dennys
Angler's Wish, An. Van Dyke
Are these truly the fisher-maids. *Fr.* Manyo Shu. Tanabe Akiniwa
As inward love breeds outward talk. *Fr.* The Anglers Song. Basse
At the Fishhouses. Bishop
Bait[e], The. Donne
Bait-Gathering. Martin
Beacons of the fishing-boats, The. *Fr.* Manyo Shu. *Unknown*
Big One, The. Cabalquinto
Blackfriars. Farjeon
Bobber. Carver
Boy Fishing, The. Scovell
Cable Ship, The. Martinson
Caller Herrin'. Nairne
Candlelight Fisherman, The. *Unknown*
Canst Thou Draw Out Leviathan with an Hook. Curnow
Careful Angler, The. Stevenson
Casting. Nemerov
Catch, The. Carver
Catch. McKiernan
Caught. Dubois
Cedar River, The. Gibbons
Coracle Fishers, The. *Fr.* The Banks of Wye. Bloomfield
Cormorant boats, The. Tameyo
Crabbing. Levine
Crying Uncle. Hansen
Did You Ever Go Fishing? *Unknown*
Disappointed Shrimper, The. Ropes
Don's Holiday. Hamilton
Drunken Fisherman, The. Lowell
Elver Fishers. Gurney
Father Fisheye. Balakian
Final Trawl, The. Fisher
Finding a Teacher. Merwin
Fish, The. Bishop
Fish, The. Nash
Fish Story. Carlile
Fisher-maids at Shika, The. *Fr.* Manyo Shu. Kimiko
Fisherman, The. Brown
Fisherman, The. Cheng Hsieh
Fisherman, The. Ho Ning
Fisherman. Honei
Fisherman, The. McCord
Fisherman. Setcho
Fisherman, The. Yeats
Fisherman's Story, The. Ray
Fishermen. Bunting
Fishermen's Song. *Unknown*
Fisher's Life, The. *Unknown*
Fishing. Nilsen
Fishing on a Lake at Night. Bly

Fishing Pole, The ("A fishing pole's a curious thing"). Davies
Fishing Season. Vallis
Fishing Song, A. Rands
Fishing the Dream. Delp
Float-rigged strands, The. *Fr.* Sixty-four Tanka. Saigyo
Fly fisherman in Wartime. Bacon
Fly-fishing. *Fr.* Rural Sports. Gay
Fun with Fishing. Tietjens
Gar, The. Bell
Green Stream, A. Wang Wei
Grimsby Fisherman, The. *Unknown*
Grimsby Lads, The. Conolly
Halibut Cove Harvest. Leslie
Heave Away, My Johnny. *Unknown*
Hint for the Incomplete Angler. Smithyman
Hollow, The. Morgan
How They Bite. *Unknown*
Ice-Fishing. Pendleton
In the Deep Channel. Stafford
In the Shadows of Early Sunlight. Wallace
Instruction in the Art. Booth
Instructions for Fishing the Eel. Schmitz
Is it always so bleak a sight? *Fr.* Twenty-four Tanka. Sanetomo
It Is Hard to Catch Trout. Piuvkaq
Jim Desterland. Plutzik
Last Chance, The. Lang
Late Afternoon on a Good Lake. Wier
Master and Man. Newbolt
Memorial for a Fisherman. Bobrowski
Men Fishing in the Arno. Jennings
Navel. Schmitz
Neither Hook nor Line. Bunyan
Net, The. Rolnik
Net Menders, The. Vrepont
Night of rain on the autumn river, A. *Fr.* Miscellaneous Words on the Lake. Tsung Ch'en
Nocturne: Georgia Coast. Hicky
Off to the Fishing Ground. Montgomery
Old Fisherman with Guitar. Brown
Our Biggest Fish. Field
Out Fishin'. Guest
Out Fishing. Howes
Out from Lobster Cove. Reed
Papio. Chock
Pike, The. Bruce
Pike, The. Roethke
Planting Trout in the Chicago River. Schmitz
Priest attending, found he spoke at times, The. *Fr.* The Borough: Peter Grimes. Crabbe
Purse-Seine, The. Jeffers
Rainy Midnight. Gurney
Reading Plato. Graham
Ritualists, The. Williams
Rituals along the Arkansas. Mills
Running the River Lines. Baker
Salmon-fishing. Jeffers
Shoals of Herring, The. MacColl
Side by side. *Fr.* Sixty-four Tanka. Saigyo
Skipper Ireson's Ride. Whittier
Smacksman, The. Larner
Snacks. Tanaka
Sockeye Salmon. Hambleton
Song of the Clear River. Huang T'ing-chien
Song of the Fisherman. Li Hsün
Song of the Fisherman. Sun Kuang-hsien
Song of the Fisherman's Lover. Lloyd
Song of the Full Catch. Skinner
Song of the Trout Fisher, The. Ikinilik
Spending the Night on the River. T'ang Hsien-Tsu
Spring Sea. Tamemasa
Suma fisherman/ may know the ring of the sea breeze, A. Teika
Swell My Net Full. *Unknown*
Though not commanded. *Fr.* Manyo Shu. Okura

Three Fishers, The. Kingsley
Three Jolly Fishermen. *Unknown*
Three Score and Ten. *Unknown*
Trolling for Blues. Wilbur
Trout, The. Montague
What She Said ("The fishermen who go"). Ammuvanar
What's Good for the Soul Is Good for Sales. Wilbur
With the Herring Fishers. "MacDiarmid"
Words Are Never Enough. Bruce
See also **Crabs and Crabbing.**

Fitts, Dudley
Elegy and Flame. Gregory

Fitzgerald, Edward
Appearances. Browning
To E. Fitzgerald. Tennyson
To Edward Fitzgerald. Browning

Fitzgerald, F. Scott
Effervescence and Evanescence. Preston
On Editing Scott Fitzgerald's Papers. Wilson

Flags
Conquered Banner, The. Ryan
Union Jack, The. Kirby

Flags, United States
American Flag, The. Drake
Barbara Frietchie. Whittier
Betsy's Battle Flag. Irving
Centennial Hymn. Whittier
Conquered Banner, The. Ryan
Flag Goes By, The. Bennett
Flower of Liberty, The. Holmes
God Save the Flag. Holmes
I Am the Flag. Jones
I Am What You Make Me ("I am whatever you make me, nothing more"). Lane
Old Flag, The. Bunner
Our Country's Emblem. *Unknown*
Our National Banner. Smith
Song for Our Flag, A. Sangster
Stand by the Flag. Wilder
Star-spangled Banner, The. Key
Stars and Stripes. Fordham
Toast to the Flag, A. Daly
Your Flag and My Flag. Nesbit

Flamingos
Flamingo, The. Barakat
Impossible, The. Al-Bayyati
Song of the Turtle and the Flamingo, The. Fields

Flanders, Belgium
Another Reply to "In Flanders Fields." Armstrong
In Flanders Fields. Claus
In Flanders Fields. McCrae
In Flanders Now. Jaques
Into Battle. Grenfell
Old Houses of Flanders, The. Ford
Reply to "In Flanders Fields." Mitchell

Flapjacks. See Pancakes.

Flattery
Fox and the Crow, The. La Fontaine
Spider and the Fly, The. Howitt
"When my love swears [or sweares] that she is made of truth." *Fr.* Sonnets, CXXXVIII. Shakespeare

Fleas
Flea, The. Donne
Flea, The. Young
Fleas. Appleman
Fleas interest me so much. Neruda
Frog and a Flea, A. Mitchell
Haiku: "I'm looking for a single flea, midnight." *Fr.* One Hundred Haiku in Free Form. Hosai
Harlot's Catch. Nichols
Must be a good day. *Fr.* Forty-four Hokku. Issa
On Donne's Poem "To a Flea." Coleridge
To a Flea in a Glass of Water. Greig

Fletcher, John
To Fletcher Reviv'd. Lovelace
Upon Master Fletcher's Incomparable Playes. Herrick
Upon the Dramatick Poems of Mr. John Fletcher. Cartwright

Flies
Amber Bead, The. Herrick
Blue-Fly, The. Graves
Blue-Tail Fly, The. *Unknown*
Calvus to a Fly. Turner
Cold Fly. Yang Wan-li
Dead Fly. Ní Chuilleanáin
Evening Dance of the Grey Flies. Page
Flesh-Fly and the Bee, The. Patmore
Fly, The. De la Mare
Fly, The. Holub
Fly, The. Ignatow
Fly, The. Nash
Fly, The. Shapiro
Fly Caught in a Cobweb, A. Lovelace
Fly in December. Wallace
Fly That Flew into My Mistress's Eye, A. Carew
Harriet. Lowell
I heard a fly buzz—when I died. Dickinson
Little Fly,/ Thy summers play. *Fr.* Songs of Experience. Blake
Math Class. Livingston
Near Dusk. Auslander
On Finding a Small Fly Crushed in a Book. Turner
Once Musing as I Sat. Googe
Silence. Aubert
Spider and the Fly, The. Howitt
To a Fly, Taken out of a Bowl of Punch. "Pindar"
To a Midge. Nisbet
Truth. Nemerov
Upon a Flie. Herrick

Flight
Bird that fell out of the nest, A. Schönwiese
Dreamers and Flyers. LaBombard
Feel like a Bird. Swenson
Flight. Hsin Mu
Flight. Vinal

Flirtation
Advice to the Ladies. Somervile
Disillusion. Burge
Doris. Congreve
Flirt, The. Davies
O Polly, you might have toy'd and kist. *Fr.* The Beggar's Opera. Gay
Ode, An: "Merchant, to secure his treasure, The." Prior
Rape of the Lock, The. Pope

Flodden Field, Battle of (1513)
Battle of Flodden, The. *Fr.* Scotish Feilde. *Unknown*
Battle, The ("By this, though deep the evening fell"). *Fr.* Marmion. Scott
Then the Provost he uprose. *Fr.* Edinburgh after Flodden. Aytoun

Flood, The
And God saw that the wickedness of man was great. *Fr.* Genesis
Late Passenger, The. Lewis
Noah's Prayer. Gasztold
Noah's Raven. Merwin
Return to Ararat. Halsall

Floods
Beanstalk, Meditated Later, The. Wright
Days of Rain; the Rivers Have Overflowed. Su Tung-p'o
Flood, The. Bell
Flood. Charles
Flood, The. Clare
Flood. McGough
Flood, The. Stanford
Flood Viewed by the Tourist from Iowa, The. Whitehead

Flood Year. Wright
Floods, by nature enemies to land, The. *Fr.*
  Metamorphoses. Ovid
Following the Rhymes of Chiang Hui-shu.
  Su Tung-p'o
Great Wanagan Creek Flood, The. Lowman
No More the Slow Stream. McLaren
River in Spate. MacNeice
Too much/ at one time. *Fr.* Twenty-four
  Tanka. Sanetomo
Wat A Rain. Bloom

Florence, Italy
Above the Arno. Swenson
Bat. Lawrence
Daisies of Florence. Raine
È, the Feasting Florentines. Hoffman
Florence. Landor
More Nudes for Florence. Witt
Old Bridge at Florence, The. Longfellow
Open Window in Florence. Goldberg
Santa Maria del Fiore. Clarke
Sonnet: Autumn Garden. Campana

Florida
At Loxahatchie. Oliver
Clearwater Beach, Florida. Matthews
Florida. Bishop
Florida. Rakosi
Florida Road Workers. Hughes
Floridian Museum of Art, A. Whittemore
Okeechobee. Allison
Okefenokee Swamp. Hicky
Removal, The. *Unknown*
Sharks, Caloosahatchee River. Pape

Florists
Old Florist. Roethke

Flowers
Among the Narcissi. Plath
Arise and Pick a Posy. *Unknown*
As the seasons change. *Fr.* Manyo Shu.
  Yakamochi
Babiaantje, The. Prince
Baby Seed Song. Nesbit
Bachelor's-Buttons. Smith
Bavarian Gentians. Lawrence
Behold, O Man. *Fr.* The Faerie Queene.
  Spenser
Bouquet in Dog Time. Carruth
Buttercups and Daisies. Howitt
Carnation, The ("May this carnation announce
  to you"). Apollinaire
Carnation, The ("May this carnation tell
  you"). Apollinaire
Chanted Calendar, A. *Fr.* Balder. Dobell
Cheddar Pinks. Bridges
Christmas Rose, The. Day Lewis
Chrysanthemums. Seymour-Smith
City, The. Ignatow
Clusters of cold-weather blossoms. *Fr.* In
  Lamplight, Watching My Wife Preparing a
  Flower. Ch'ien Ch'ien-i
Columbine, The. Very
Contemplation upon Flowers, A. King
Cut Flower, A. Shapiro
Cycle. Hughes
Daffodils. Heffernan
Death of the Flowers, The. Bryant
Dislike for Flowers, A. Cadnum
Earliest Spring. Levertov
Even in a strange land I see. *Fr.* Manyo
  Shu. Hasetsukabe Mamaro
Exclusive Blue. Francis
Flower, A. Guadamuz
Flower, The. Herbert
Flower Farm, The. Pape
Flower in the Crannied Wall. Tennyson
Flower-Press, The. Shuttle
Flower-Seller, The ("The flower-seller's fat").
  Farjeon
Flowers. Behn
Flowers. Jaccottet
Flowers, The. Stevenson

Flowers and Men ("Flowers achieve their own
  floweriness and its's a miracle").
  Lawrence
Flowers' Ball, The. King
Flowers by the Sea. Williams
Flowers in the Ward. Neilson
Flower's Name, The. *Fr.* Garden Fancies.
  Browning
Flowers that blow, The. *Fr.* Manyo Shu.
  Okura
For the doubling of flowers is the
  improvement of the gardners talent. *Fr.*
  Jubilate Agno. Smart
Forget-Me-Not, The. *Unknown*
Four and Eight. Wolfe
Fresh Flowers. Wang An-shih
Fury of Flowers and Worms, The. Sexton
Garden. Doolittle
Geranium, The. Roethke
Ghost-Flowers. Higginson
Haiku: "I don't know when." *Fr.* Fifteen
  Haiku. Masaoka Shiki
Hard it was for this garden soil. Zauq
Here's flowers for you. *Fr.* The Winter's
  Tale. Shakespeare
I Hoed and Trenched and Weeded. *Fr.* A
  Shropshire Lad. Housman
I Walked [*or* Walkt] the Other Day to Spend
  My Hour. Vaughan
Idle Flowers, The. Bridges
I'll Twine White Violets. Meleager
In Back of the Real. Ginsberg
Iris. Williams
Kingcups. Sitwell
Lament of the Flowers, The. Very
Life. Herbert
Locust Tree in Flower, The. Williams
Lustre of the flowers, The. Komachi
Meditation for His Mistress[e], A. Herrick
Menace of the Flower, The. Reyes
Mirrorment. Ammons
Morning Compliments. Dayre
Narcissus and chrysanthemum. *Fr.* In
  Lamplight, Watching My Wife Preparing a
  Flower. Ch'ien Ch'ien-i
No camellia. Yosano Akiko
No soothing time for someone who thinks of
  blossoms. *Fr.* Fifty-one Tanka. Izumi
Nosegay Always Sweet, for Lovers to Send
  for Tokens of Love at New Year's Tide, or
  for Fairings, A ("Nosegay, lacking flowers
  fresh,"). Hunnis
O that my father and my mother were flowers.
  Fr. Manyo Shu. Hasetsukabe Kuromasa
On Clarastella walking in Her Garden. Heath
Passing Miscanthus on the Road. Tamesada
Pearly Everlasting, The. Fewster
Peire Salvatge, it's the flowers. Pedro III,
  King of Aragon
Picture of Little T. C. in a Prospect of
  Flowers, The. Marvell
Pimpernel. Cole
Poem: "Geranium, houseleek, laid in oblong
  beds." Gray
Power of the Flowers. Juhász
Pyxidanthera, The. Bristol
Quaker Ladies. Cortissoz
Rape flowers: the moon in the east. *Fr.*
  Eighty-seven Hokku. Buson
Scene on the Banks of the Hudson, A.
  Bryant
Sea Rose. Doolittle
Sketch of Flower. Kim Chun-soo
Slight not these flowers! *Fr.* Manyo Shu.
  Hirotsugu
Soil and Flower. Hsiang Yang
Some Flowers o' the Spring. *Fr.* The
  Winter's Tale: Here's flowers for you.
  Shakespeare
Spring Flowers. *Fr.* The Seasons: Spring.
  Thomson
Spring Flowers from Ireland. MacCarthy

Spring of Cities, The. Rokeah
Sundew, The. Swinburne
Swans, The. Sitwell
Sweet Peas. *Fr.* I Stood Tiptoe [upon a
  Little Hill]. Keats
Tale about a Flower. Somlyó
Tamborillo. Payeras
That you like me not. *Fr.* Manyo Shu.
  Unknown
To a Wind-Flower. Cawein
To Be Continued. Péret
To Blossoms. Herrick
To Daffodils [*or* Daffadills]. Herrick
To Mistress Margery Wentworth. *Fr.* The
  Garlande [*or* Garlands] of Laurell. Skelton
To plant plum-flowers. *Fr.* Kokin Shu.
  Unknown
To Violets. Herrick
Troll's Nosegay, The. Graves
Vlamertinghe; Passing the Château, July
  1917. Blunden
Were these flowers broken off. *Fr.* Manyo
  Shu. *Unknown*
White coral bells upon a slender stalk.
  Unknown
White Gentian, A. Hunt
Why Flowers Change Color. Herrick
Wild Honeysuckle, The. Freneau
Wild Thyme, The. *Fr.* Milton. Blake
Window Boxes ("A window box of pansies").
  Farjeon
With a sudden gust. Tamekane
With fairest flowers,/ Whilst summer lasts.
  Fr. Cymbeline. Shakespeare
Wonga Vine. Wright
Woodspurge, The. Rossetti
You white hydrangeas. Teika

Flute
Spring Night in Lo-Yang—Hearing a Flute.
  Li Po

Flutes
Amateur Flute, The. *Unknown*
Elderberry Flute Song. Blue Cloud
Fairy Flute, The. Fyleman
Flute-Players. Hoyland
Flutist Diviner. Daisen
Lament of the Flutes. Okigbo
Musical Instrument, A. Browning
No flute, The. *Unknown*
Old [*or* Ould] Orange Flute, The. *Unknown*
Shakuhachi. Mitsui
Something Whispered in the *Shakuhachi*.
  Hongo
Tree to Flute. Hajnal

Flying Dutchman (ship)
Flying Dutchman, The. Robinson
Flying Dutchman, The. *Unknown*

Flying Saucers
Go Fly a Saucer. McCord
Saucer Station: Monday-Friday. Goldbarth

Foals
Birth of the Foal. Juhász
Foal. Miller

Fog
Ballad of the Great London Fog. Huang
  Tsun-hsien
Because fog engulfs. *Fr.* Ten Tanka. Myoe
Boats in a Fog. Jeffers
Fog-Horn. Clarke
Haiku: "Morning fog/ one man's got a fire
  going." *Fr.* Thirty-nine Haiku. Shiki
Night Fog, The. Kim Hyun-sung
On the Great Fog in London, December 1762.
  Weeks
Quiet Fog, The. Piercy
River-Fog. Kiyowara Fukuyabu
Sea Fog, The. Jacobsen
Sounding Fog, The. Pulsifer
Tides carry the haze, The. *Fr.* Twenty-one
  Hokku. Kaya Shirao

Folk Songs. *See* **Ballads and Folk Songs.**

Food
Animal Crackers. Morley
Any Part of Piggy. Coward
Author Loving These Homely Meats, The.
  Fr. The Scourge of Folly. Davies
Ballad of Bouillabaisse, The. Thackeray
Butchery. McPherson
Can Zone; or, The Good Food Guide. Lesser
Chicken. *Fr.* Hunter Poems of the Yoruba.
  Unknown
Christmas Dinner. Rosen
Conserves. *Fr.* The Joy of Cooking. Mus
Crunch and Lick. Aldis
Dietary Advice. *Unknown*
Dish for a Poet, A. *Unknown*
Dried Apple Pies. *Unknown*
Elegy, The: "Madam, no more! The time has
  come to eat." Hope
Epigram on Fasting. Swift
Essay on Lunch. Gibson
Fat Boy's Dream, The. McCann
Fire, The. Scott
Fish are at home, at home among their water
  plants, The. *Unknown*
Flutter, flutter go the gourd leaves. *Unknown*
Food. Valle
Food and Drink. Untermeyer
Food of the North. Lawrence
Gastronomy. Morriën
Giving Potatoes. Mitchell
Gourmet's Love-Song, The. Wodehouse
Grace to Be Said at the Supermarket.
  Nemerov
Having Replaced Love with Food and Drink.
  Wakoski
High on the Hog. Fields
Hog Meat. Davis
Hymn to Comus. *Fr.* Pleasure Reconciled to
  Virtue. Jonson
I Had But Fifty Cents. *Unknown*
If We Didn't Have to Eat. Waterman
I'm Hungry! Prelutsky
Invitation to Lubberland, An. *Unknown*
Inviting a Friend to Supper. Jonson
Lemon Pie. Guest
Love Song, A: "By the fierce flames of love
  I'm in a sad taking." Tyler
Miss Foggerty's Cake. *Unknown*
Miss T. De la Mare
Mix a Pancake. Rossetti
Mountown! Thou Sweet Retreat. *Fr.* Mully
  of Mountown. King
My Other Chinee Cook. Stephens
Observations in a Cornish Teashop. Rexroth
Ode to Food. Gray
On Jam. Belloc
On Tomato Ketchup. *Unknown*
Peasant Declares His Love, The. Roumer
Pesci Misti. Aaronson
Renderings and Sunderings of Cobbett's
  "Rural Rides." Leale
Repast. Tiemer-Wille
Rillons, Rillettes. Wilbur
Salad, A. Smith
Sausage. Guest
Song of the Taste. Snyder
Stomach. Norris
Suet Dumpling, The. *Unknown*
Survey of Literature. Ransom
This Is Just to Say. Williams
Those Flapjacks of Brown's. Taylor
Universal Favorite, The. Wells
Watermelons. Simic
When de Co'n Pone's Hot. Dunbar
When good King Arthur ruled this land.
  Mother Goose
When in Rome. Evans
Who Among You Knows the Essence of
  Garlic? Hongo
Witches' Menu. Nikolay

Yellow Butter. Hoberman
See also **Cooking and Cooks; Eating;**
  Gluttony and Gluttons.

Food Poisoning
Dog Shark. *Unknown*

Fools
Compassionate Fool, The. Cameron
Epigram: "Yes, every poet is a fool." Prior
Fool much bit by fleas put out the light, A.
  Lovelace
Fool's Prayer, The. Sill
On a misty day in spring. *Fr.* Manyo Shu.
  Mushimaro
Plays. Landor
To Fool, or Knave. Jonson
Tonversation with Baby, A. Bishop
Upon a Fool. Hoskyns
With a Fool. Heifetz-Tussman
See also **Jesters.**

Football
Alumnus Football. Rice
Autumn Begins in Martins Ferry, Ohio.
  Wright
Bee, The. Dickey
Billy Ray Smith. Nash
Bull-Dog! Porter
Dedicated to F. W. Hemingway
Execution. Hirsch
Fall Practice. Stuart
First Practice. Gildner
Football. Fitzgerald
Football. Mason
Football Game, A. Van Eck
Football Song. Scott
For the Death of Vince Lombardi. Dickey
Friendly Game of Football, A. Dyson
Funky Football. Saunders
Heaps on Heaps. *Fr.* A Match at Football.
  Concanen
In the Beginning Was the. Murchison
In the Pocket. Dickey
Insanity. Dubois
Kicker's Last Steps, The. Meissner
Man from Inversnaid, The. Murray
Marvin Pickett. Glenn
Meeting My Best Friend from the Eighth
  Grade. Gildner
Minneapolis Poem, The. Wright
Notre Dame Victory March, The. Shea
Passer, The. Abbe
Say Goodbye to Big Daddy. Jarrell
Second Half. McCord
Settling Some Old Football Scores. Bishop
Sleeper, The. Field
Ties. Stuart
To the Field Goal Kicker in a Slump. Pastan
Touch Football. Driscoll
Unitas. Gold
Watching Football on TV. Nemerov
Watching the Jets Lose to Buffalo at Shea.
  Swenson
You've Got to Learn the White Man's Game.
  Smith
See also **Soccer.**

Ford, Ed ("Whitey")
Poem for Ed "Whitey" Ford, A. Holden

Ford, Ford Madox
Ford Madox Ford. Lowell
To Ford Madox Ford in Heaven. Williams

Fordham, Alphonse Campbell
In Memoriam. Alphonse Campbell Fordham.
  Fordham

Fordham, Edward
Mr. Edward Fordham. Fordham

Forest Fires
Lost Silvertip. Reed

Foresters
I Have Been a Foster. *Unknown*
Solitary Woodsman, The. Roberts
Song of the Forest Ranger, The. Bashford

Forests
Among the Firs. Lee-Hamilton
Arcana Sylvarum. De Kay
Ballad of Trees and the Master, A. Lanier
Breathing, The. Levertov
By Canoe through the Fir Forest. Dickey
Charnwood Forest. *Fr.* Polyolbion.
  Drayton
Choir Practice. Crosby
Christmas in the Wood. Frost
Dark Forest, The. Thomas
Dark Wood. Wedde
Death in the Woods. Littlebird
Deep in a windless/ wood. Buson
Departure, The. Whittemore
Ecce in Deserto. Beers
English Wood, An. Graves
Ettrick Forest in November. *Fr.* Marmion.
  Scott
Forest. Blackwell
Forest Hymn, A. Bryant
Forest Thoughts. Casement
Gift of Sight. Graves
Glyn Cynon Wood. *Unknown*
Green Roads, The. Thomas
In a Wood. Hardy
In Carpenter's Woods. Stern
In November. Lampman
In the forest, in unexplored. *Fr.* Geography.
  Dransfield
In the Woods. Scott
In Winter in the Woods Alone. Frost
Inscription for the Entrance to a Wood.
  Bryant
Larch Trees. Kitahara Hakushu
Lost. Wagoner
Neighbors. Ammons
Passing of the Forest, The. Reeves
Piney Woods. Cowley
Quilled Quilt, a Needle Bed, A. Leithauser
Sancta Silvarum. Johnson
Silent Wood, A. Siddal
Sleeping in the Forest. Oliver
Solitary Woodsman, The. Roberts
Solitude. Lampman
Solitude. Savage
Solitude Late at Night in the Woods. Bly
Song of the Forest Ranger, The. Bashford
Song, A: "There is ever a song somewhere,
  my dear." Riley
Sonnet Made upon the Groves near Merlou
  Castle. Herbert of Cherbury
Staying Alive. Wagoner
Stopping by Woods on a Snowy Evening.
  Frost
Stump, The. Bly
Waldeinsamkeit. Emerson
Walk, The. Ross
Way Through the Woods, The. Kipling
Wood Carols. Ray
Woodland Mass, The. Dafydd ap Gwilym
Woodland Worship. Wetherald
Woodlands, The. Barnes
Woodlands. Read
Woods. MacNeice

Forges
Casualty. Heaney
Forge, The. Heaney

Forgetfulness
Always. Strand
For the Lame. Clifton
Forgetfulness. Lowell
Keeper, The. Carpenter
Lethe. Doolittle

Forgiveness
Brazen Tongue. Benét
Condemned, The. Gonzáles Martínez
Confessional. Bidart
Forgiveness. Whittier
Hymn to God the Father [or For Forgiveness
  or To Christ], A. Donne
Lord, Have Mercy. Tate

Love. Herbert
Mailman, The. Strand
Outwitted. Markham
Prayer for Forgiveness, A. Aengus the
  Culdee
Prayer to the Virgin. Columcille
Ten Years and More. Waddington

Forks
Fork. Simic

Forsythia
Haiku: "Forsythia blossoms gone." *Fr.*
  Thirty-nine Haiku. Shiki
Haiku: "Summer grass/ way in the distance."
  Fr. Thirty-nine Haiku. Shiki

Fortitude
Don't Quit. *Unknown*
Granma's Words. Palmanteer
If. Kipling
Nevertheless. Moore
Solitude. Wilcox
Winners, The. *Fr.* The Story of the
  Gadsbys. Kipling
Worth While. Wilcox

Fortune
Author, of His Own Fortune, The.
  Harington
Doth then the world go thus, doth all thus
  move? Drummond
Fame and Fortune. *Fr.* The Legend of
  Robert, Duke of Normandy. Drayton
Fate. Spalding
Fortune. Wyatt
Fortune and Virtue. *Fr.* Old Fortunatus.
  Dekker
Fortune Welcomed Me at Last. *Fr.* Unbind
  Your Angered Tresses. Massimi
Fortune's Treachery. Halevi
Hap. Hardy
Here Are Told the Misfortunes of Women.
  Fr. The Book of Fortune's Changes.
  Pisan
Hughie at the Inn. Wylie
Now the golden morn aloft. *Fr.* Ode on the
  Pleasure Arising from Vicissitude. Gray
Of Fortune. *Fr.* Cornelia. Kyd
Rattlesnake Band, The. Conley
Since You Have Clipped the Wings of Fine
  Desire. Morra
To Fortune. More
See also **Fate; Luck.**

Fortunetellers
Crepe de Chine. Williams
Fortune Teller, The. Rifqa
Lady and the Gypsy, The. Scannell
Madre Sofía. Ríos
Spaewife, The. Stevenson

Fossils
Autograph, An. Lowell
Fish in the Stone, The. Dove
Fossil. Blodgett
Fossil, The. Merrill
Fossil, 1975. Lewis
Fossilot, The. Yolen
Fossils. Pagis
Ichthyology. Achterberg

Fountains
Baroque Wall-Fountain in the Villa Sciarra,
  A. Wilbur
Drinking Fountain. Chute
Fountain, The. Davie
Fountain. Jennings
Fountain, The. Lowell
Fountain, The. Wordsworth
Fountains ("Proud fountains, wave your
  plumes"). Sitwell
From Rome, for More Public Fountains in
  New York City. Dugan
Roman Fountain. Bogan

Fourth of July
Brownies' Celebration, The. Cox

Dear Land of All My Love. *Fr.* The
  Centennial Meditation of Columbia.
  Lanier
Fatherland, The. Lowell
Fourth, The. Silverstein
Fourth of July, The. Pierpont
Independence Bell—July 4, 1776. *Unknown*
Independence Day. Berry
July 4th. Swenson
July 4th. Waldman
Rocket in My Pocket, A. *Unknown*

Fox, Charles James
Nelson, Pitt, Fox. *Fr.* Marmion. Scott

Foxes
Abnegation. Rich
Ballad of Red Fox, The. La Follette
Bold Reynard the Fox. *Unknown*
False Fox, The. *Unknown*
Four Little Foxes. Sarett
Fox. Dyment
Fox, The. Parry
Fox. *Fr.* A Bestiary. Rexroth
Fox, The. Scheuer
Fox and the Crow, The. La Fontaine
Fox and the Goose, The. *Unknown*
Fox and the Grapes, The. La Fontaine
Fox Dancing. Knowles
Fox knew well, that before they tore him,
  The. *Fr.* Reynard the Fox. Masefield
Fox's Counsel, The. Llwyd
In the heat haze a fox. *Fr.* Twenty-one
  Hokku. Boncho
Kilruddery Hunt, The. Mozeen
Night of Wind. Frost
Owl and the Fox, The. *Unknown*
Sycophantic Fox and the Gullible Raven, The.
  Carryl
Tasting the Wild Grapes. Oliver
Thought-Fox, The. Hughes
Three Foxes, The. Milne
Vixen, The. Clare
Wily Fox, The. Davies

Foxgloves
Four and Eight. Wolfe
Foxgloves. Webb

France
Between Talcy and Mer. Oles
C. Aragon
Calais, August 15, 1802. Wordsworth
Composed by the Seaside, near Calais,
  August, 1802. Wordsworth
Day in France, A. Holbrook
Declamatory Poem. Jacob
Discoveries of Bones and Stones. Grigson
England. Moore
Evil. Rimbaud
Four Sheets to the Wind and a One-Way
  Ticket to France. Rivers
Fragrance of Night, A. Fargue
Grasse: The Olive Trees. Wilbur
Great Men Have Been among Us.
  Wordsworth
It was a beautiful and silent day. *Fr.* The
  Prelude [or, Growth of a Poet's Mind]:
  Residence in France. Wordsworth
Journey into France, The. *Unknown*
Kings of France. Lincoln
Night Drive. Heaney
Provincia Deserta. Pound
Rioupéroux. Flecker
Rouen. Cannan
St. Aubin d'Aubigne. Dehn
Scenes from Carnac. Arnold
Seamstress at St. Léon. *Fr.* A Journal from
  France. Clarke
Summer Journey. Rodgers
Trees on the Calais Road. Blunden
Verses Written at Montauban in France, 1750.
  Warton
Where We Could Go. Soto
Winter Daybreak above Vence, A. Wright

Francesca, Piero della. *See* **Piero della**
  Francesca.

Francis of Assisi, Saint
In Assisi. Blumenthal
It is far to Assisi. *Fr.* The Garden.
  Williams
Love. Graham
Saint Francis. Bishop
Saint Francis and the Birds. Heaney
Saint Francis and the Sow. Kinnell
Wolf Said to Francis, The. Rochelle

Franco, Francisco
Eisenhower's Visit to Franco, 1959. Wright

Franco-Prussian War
In Time of "The Breaking of Nations."
  Hardy
Poster of Our Dazzling Victory at
  Saarbrucken, A. *Fr.* Eighteen-Seventy.
  Arthur Rimbaud

Franconia Mountains
Lines Written on a Farewell View of the
  Franconia Mountains at Twilight. Ray

Frank, Anne
Day for Anne Frank, A. Williams

Frankenstein
Bride of Frankenstein, The. Field
Frankenstein. Field

Franklin, Aretha
Poem for Aretha. Giovanni

Franklin, Benjamin
On the Death of Benjamin Franklin. Freneau

Franklin, Sir John
Ballad of Sir John Franklin, A. Boker

Fraternity. *See* **Brotherhood.**

Free Will
Road Not Taken, The. Frost

Freedom
Ante-Bellum Sermon, An. Dunbar
Antiquity of Freedom, The. Bryant
Assembly: Harlem School. Maleska
At the Zoo. Zangwill
Battle Hymn of the [American] Republic,
  The. Howe
Brave New World. MacLeish
Cat, The. Kaschnitz
Country Justice, The. Langhorne
Dame Liberty Reports from Travel. Pinkney
Dark Testament. Murray
Deliverance of Argos, The. Dufresnoy
Eagles and Isles. Gibson
Elegy: "Proud freedom's noble inspiration."
  Yazykov
Emancipation. Thompson
For A' That and A' That ("Is there, for honest
  poverty"). Burns
For All. Otto-Peters
Frederick Douglass. Hayden
Freedom [*or* Fredome]. *Fr.* The Bruce.
  Barbour
Freedom. Hughes
Freedom. O Riordain
Freedom. Zagajewski
Freedom a Come Oh! *Unknown*
Freedom of the Hills. Fraser
Freedom's Dawn. Faiz
Fugitive, The. Thompson
Great Escape, The. Roots
Harp That Once through Tara's Halls, The.
  Moore
Hymn of Freedom. Barry
I Thank God I'm Free at Las'. *Unknown*
It Is Not to Be Thought Of [That the Flood].
  Wordsworth
Letter from Italy, to the Right Honourable
  Charles Lord Halifax, A. Addison
Liberty. Éluard
Liberty. Hay
Liberty. MacLeish
Liberty. Matraini
Liberty Tree. Paine
Midway. Madgett

Night in Prison, A. Aleramo
No More Beneath the Oppressive Hand.
   Unknown
Notes for My Son. *Fr.* The Song of
   Lazarus. Comfort
Ode: "God save the Rights of Man!"
   Freneau
Poem: "I love the old melodious lays."
   Whittier
Prayer, A: "Oh, Lord! I lift my heart."
   Thompson
Prayers to Liberty. Shaul
Question, The. Ignatow
Runagate Runagate. Hayden
Shine, Republic. Jeffers
Silkworms, The. Stewart
Song of the Settlers. West
They shut me up in prose. Dickinson
To Althea, from Prison. Lovelace
To My Father. Ray
Tree of Liberty, The. Burns
Trumpet of Liberty, The. Taylor
Twilight of Freedom. Mandelstam
Undertaking, The. Glück
We Must Free Ourselves Today. Vallerugo
When a man hath no freedom to fight for at
   home. Byron

Freemasonry
Level and the Square, The. Morris

Freezers
Hiding Place. Armour

Freighters
Freight Boats. Tippett
See also **Cargoes.**

Frémont, John Charles
To John C. Frémont. Whittier

French, The
Bonne Entente. Scott
Ode: Salute to the French Negro Poets.
   O'Hara
To Henrietta, on Her Departure for Calais.
   Hood

French Revolution
France; an Ode. Coleridge
It was a beautiful and silent day. *Fr.* The
   Prelude [or, Growth of a Poet's Mind]:
   Residence in France. Wordsworth
Jeanne Manon Philipon-Roland. Zitz-Halein
La Tricoteuse. Thornbury
Louis XVI. *Fr.* The French Revolution.
   Blake
Louis XVI Goes to the Guillotine. Péret
Ode: "God save the Rights of Man!"
   Freneau
Sleepless Nights. Péret

French Verse
*Defiant Muse, The; French Feminist Poems
   from the Middle Ages to the Present*
   (DMF). Donna C. Stanton, ed.
Proensa; an Anthology of Troubadour Poetry
   (Pro). Paul Blackburn, comp. *and* tr.;
   George Economou, ed.
*Random House Book of Twentieth-Century
   French Poetry, The* (RHTwFP). Paul
   Auster, ed.
Women Troubadours, The (WT). Meg
   Bogin, ed.

Freud, Sigmund
In Memory of Sigmund Freud. Auden
Jud' Süss Oppenheimer on His First Visit with
   Professor Sigmund Freud. *Fr.*
   Psychoanalysis. Teller
Leap before You Look. Auden
Letter to Sigmund Freud. *Fr.*
   Psychoanalysis. Teller
Mundus et Infans. Auden
Sigmund Freud. Nemerov
Sigmund Freud at the Age of Eighty-Two.
   Fr. Psychoanalysis. Teller
Song: "Don't Tell Me What You Dreamt Last
   Night." Adams
Wayman in Love. Wayman

Friars
Friar and the Nun, The. *Unknown*
Friar Complains, A. *Unknown*
Friars' Enormities. *Unknown*

Friends, Society of
On Barclay's Apology for the Quakers.
   Green
Quaker Widow, The. Taylor

Friendship
After the Quarrel. Dunbar
Around the Corner ("Around the corner I have
   a friend"). Towne
Arrow and the Song, The. Longfellow
As Toilsome I Wander'd Virginia's Woods.
   Whitman
Auld Lang Syne. Burns
Burden, The. Pereira
Epigram: "Lux my fair falcon, and your
   fellows all." Wyatt
Even the rising waters. *Unknown*
Faithful Friend, The. Cowper
Fellowship. *Unknown*
Female Friend, The. Whur
Friend. Brooks
Friend, The. Piercy
Friend, A. Power
Friend Mussunda. Neto
Friend Who Just Stands By, The. William
Friend Who Never Came. Stafford
Friendly Wood, The. Valéry
Friends. Durem
Friends. Goose
Friends. Yeats
Friends Come. Clifton
Friend's Greeting, A. Guest
Friends Who Have Failed. Williamson
Friendship. Craik
Friendship. Silverstein
Friendship. Zhukovsky
Friendship in Perfection. Ramsay
Friendship's Mystery; to My Dearest Lucasia.
   Philips
Gone. Coleridge
Grasshopper, The. Lovelace
Hide-and-Go-Seek. Simmerman
House by the Side of the Road, The. Foss
How splendid he was! *Unknown*
How to Murder Your Best Friend. O Hehir
I Have a Friend. Spencer
I Have Never Forgotten You. Frénaud
I Hear It Said. Young
I Met This Guy Who Died. Corso
I Saw in Louisiana a Live-Oak Growing.
   Whitman
I smell the smell. *Fr.* Kokin Shu.
   Unknown
I Tell of Another Young Death. Tiempo
If You Have a Friend. *Unknown*
In your lamb's wool and cuffs of leopard's
   fur. *Unknown*
Interlude. Smith
I've Gone and Stained with the Color of
   Love. Acorn
Joe's No Saint. Sheridan
La Belle Confidente. Stanley
Late at Night During a Visit of Friends. Bly
Letter to a Friend. Thompson
Losing Track. Song
Love and Friendship. Brontë
Loyalty. Braley
Meeting My Best Friend from the Eighth
   Grade. Gildner
Mile with Me, A. Van Dyke
Modes of the Court, The. *Fr.* The Beggar's
   Opera. Gay
Money and a Friend. *Unknown*
More Girl Than Boy. Komunyakaa
My Familiar. Saxe
My Prayer. O'Connor
New Friends and Old Friends. Parry
Oath of Friendship. Li Po
Of Money. Googe

Of Perfect Friendship. Cheke
Old Familiar Faces, The. Lamb
Old-Long-Syne. *Unknown*
On Parting with Moses ibn Ezra. Halevi
Poem: "I loved my friend." Hughes
Reflection: After Visiting Old Friends.
   Allison
Remembrance. Zhukovsky
Scars Remaining, The. *Fr.* Christabel.
   Coleridge
Song: "Pour one for me, friend good and
   true." Yazykov
Sonnet: Comes Often to My Memory. Dante
Sonnet: To Guido Cavalcanti. Dante
Sweet Loving Friendship. Bellamy
They Say That in the Unchanging Place. *Fr.*
   Dedicatory Ode. Belloc
Three Friends. *Unknown*
Time to Talk, A. Frost
To a Friend. Bowles
To a Friend. Dawson
To a Friend. Gullans
To a Friend. Lowell
To Drink to Friends. Frénaud
To My Excellent Lucasia, on Our Friendship.
   Philips
To My Friend. Thompson
Upon the Sand. Wilcox
Verses Written in 1872. Stevenson
"When to the sessions of sweet silent
   thought." *Fr.* Sonnets, XXX.
   Shakespeare
Without My Friends the Day Is Dark. Ibn
   Ezra
You Opened a Door. Fiore
*Going Over to Your Place; Poems for Each
   Other* (GOYP). Paul B. Janeczko, ed.
*I Like You, If You Like Me; Poems of
   Friendship* (ILY). Myra Cohn Livingston,
   ed.

Frietchie, Barbara
Barbara Frietchie. Whittier

Frisbees
Frisbee. Humphries

Frith, John
From William Tyndale to John Frith.
   Bowers

Frog Prince, The
Frog Prince, The. Smith

Frogs
Aesop's Fable of the Frogs. La Fontaine
After their bells stopped. Yugo
Among floating weeds, frogs. Kashiku
Arms spread, a frog floats. Chiri
Ascend my shoulders, firmly keep thy seat.
   Fr. The Battle of the Frogs and Mice.
   Homer
At daybreak frogs begin. Sensetsu
At human footfalls a frog. Ko'oku
Beside a dewless, noonday mugwort. Santen
Between Leaps. Leithauser
Brown Frog, The. Robinson
Bullfrog. Hughes
Bullfrogs. Evans
By a clump of grass. *Fr.* Forty-four Hokku.
   Issa
Carrying his wife on his back a frog.
   Jokushi
Death of a Naturalist. Heaney
Deep in the bamboo grove. Haritsu
Even the frog's voices. Kogon
Evening shadow: frogs call out. Hoju
Firefly: a frog opens his mouth a bit. *Fr.*
   Forty-four Hokku. Issa
First Song. Kinnell
Folding its hands. Sokan
Friend in the Garden, A. Ewing
Frog, The. Belloc
Frog, The. Carolyn
Frog, The. Fyleman
Frog and a Flea, A. Mitchell

Frog and the Crow, The. *Unknown*
Frog and the Golden Ball, The. Graves
Frog climbs up a willow, A. Kosai
Frog crawls out and rubs his back, A.
  Kyohaku
Frog emerges with its child on its back, A.
  Toyo
Frog has legs, The. Kiju
Frog has lifted a fallen blossom, A. Soha
Frog He Would A-Wooing Go, A.
  Unknown
Frog Hunting. Cooley
Frog looks at me, A. *Fr.* Forty-four Hokku.
  Issa
Frog on the Log, The. Orleans
Frog Prince, The. Smith
Frogs Croaking. Masso
Frog's Fate, A. Rossetti
Frogs in rain—as their croaks rise. Sodo
Frogs play hide-and-seek. *Fr.* Forty-four
  Hokku. Issa
Green Frog at Roadstead, Wisconsin.
  Schevill
Here and there frogs croak. Kikaku
Hidden in water plants, a frog. Ryusui
His mansion in the pool. Dickinson
His tail fell off, but the frog. Bunsoku
Hopping frog, A. Zempo
Hopping frog—is a cat chasing you.
  Suiyu
In an old pond a frog. *Fr.* Eighty-seven
  Hokku. Buson
In spring they croak. *Fr.* Twenty-three
  Hokku. Onitsura
Innocently a frog squats. Senka
Lodging in the puddle from the straw coat.
  Kitsujo
Looking at a passing cloud. *Fr.*
  Eighty-seven Hokku. Buson
Looking like a guide to the Joined Bridge.
  Fuboku
Morning fodder: a frog. Ranchiku
Mountain spring: near the black sleeve, A.
  Sampu
Narrow path: frog, A. Korin
Old pond, An: a frog jumps in. *Fr.*
  Seventy-six Hokku. Basho
On a young rush blade a frog. Shoda
One paddy ceases croaking for a while.
  Kyorai
Out from the moat, a frog. Totaku
Padda Song, The. *Unknown*
Rebels from Fairy Tales. Hill
Right next to a mud turtle a frog. Bunrin
Shifty-eyed, the frog. Ranran
Small Frogs Killed on the Highway. Wright
Sound of rain dripping, The. Tonan
Speckle-black Toad and freckle-green Frog.
  Fr. Thomas à Becket, a Dramatic Comedy.
  Darley
Story Wet as Tears, A. Piercy
Straw-coat vendor saw the frog last year, The.
  Rika
Swimming, a frog looks as if. *Fr.*
  Eighty-seven Hokku. Buson
Thin little frog. Issa
This moonlit evening. Kimpu
Tin Frog, The. Hoban
Tree Frog, The. Moore
Under a tree a frog. Suiko
Undulating, a frog undulates. Hokukon
What can I do?—frog dumped. Ransetsu
When you're depressed, a toad's distant voice
  too. Sora
Where was the monk? Shugen
Wooing Frog, The. Reeves
You hook it, but it's no fun. Kyosui

Frontiers
  Watching the Native Country from the
    Border. Lo Fu

Frost
  Apparently with no surprise. Dickinson

Dew and the frost, The. Tameuji
Frost. Davies
Frost, The. Gould
Frost. Thomas
Frost at Midnight. Coleridge
Frosts Are Coming. Nagy
Go not away, dear heart. *Fr.* Manyo Shu.
  Unknown
Hard Frost. Young
I shall not forget. Teika
Jack Frost. Davis
Jack Frost. Pike
Jack Frost. "Setoun"
Jack Frost. Thaxter
Jack Frost in the Garden. Smeeton
Winter ("What art thou, frost? and whence are
  thy keen stores"). *Fr.* The Seasons:
  Winter. Thomson

Frost, Robert
  For Robert Frost. Kinnell
  Letter to Robert Frost, A. Hillyer
  Of Robert Frost. Brooks
  On the Porch at the Frost Place, Franconia,
    NH. Matthews
  Robert Frost. Lowell
  Robert Frost. *Fr.* Writers. Lowell

Fruit
  Fruits and Vegetables. Saba
  Full, ripe apple, a pear and banana. *Fr.*
    Sonnets to Orpheus. Rilke
  Goblin Market. Rossetti
  Nevertheless. Moore
  Pear, The. Moraes
  This Is Just to Say. Williams
  Tropics in New York, The. McKay

Fry, Elizabeth
  Friendly Address, A. Hood

Fuchsia
  Fuchsia Hedges in Connacht. Colum
  Lodging-House Fuchsias, The. Hardy

Fujiwara no Teika
  Random Thoughts on the Skinkokinshu:
    Fujiwara no Teika. Anzai Hitoshi

Fujiyama
  Ever since heaven and earth were parted. *Fr.*
    Manyo Shu. Akahito
  Fuji. Nooteboom
  Fuji alone. Buson
  Fujiyama/ is quite a sight, The. *Fr.* Two
    Japanese Poems. Gils
  In the capital. Kenko
  Lo! There towers the lofty peak of Fuji. *Fr.*
    Manyo Shu. Mushimaro
  Mount Fuji, Opus 5. Kusano Shimpei
  Mountain Haze. Keiun
  Since heaven and earth parted. *Fr.* Manyo
    Shu. Akahito
  Smoke rising, The. Tamesada
  Tourist Japan. Takenaka Iku
  Trailing on the wind. *Fr.* Sixty-four Tanka.
    Saigyo

Fuller, Margaret
  Margaret Fuller. Alcott
  On the Death of M. D'Ossoli and His Wife,
    Margaret Fuller. Landor

Fun
  Frolic. "Æ"
  Night Fun. Viorst
  Ring-a-Ring. Greenaway
  See also **Play; Pleasure.**

Fundy, Bay of
  Biftek aux Champignons. Beers

Funerals
  After the Funeral. Thomas
  Ah me! How differently th'untutor'd slave.
    Fr. A General Description of the West
    Indian Islands. Singleton
  Alas! England now mourns for her poet that's
    gone. *Fr.* Death and Burial of Lord
    Tennyson. McGonagall

At a Low Mass for Two Hot-Rodders.
  Kennedy
At the hour shaped for him Scyld departed.
  Fr. Beowulf. *Unknown*
Aunt Laura Moves toward the Open Grave of
  Her Father. De Roche
Bells for John Whiteside's Daughter.
  Ransom
Blossom [*or* Blossome], The. Donne
Boy Changed into a Stag Cries Out at the
  Gate of Secrets, The. Juhász
Brown Girl Dead, A. Cullen
Bucolic Funeral. Sierra
Burial. Walker
Burial of a Fisherman in Hydra.
  Schulman
Burial of Sir John Moore after [*or* at]
  Corunna, The. Wolfe
Corpse-bearing. Ashe
Country Burial. Lewis
Country Doctor, The. Carleton
Dead of Winter. Towne
Dead on the War Path. *Unknown*
Detour. Longley
Dirge for McPherson, A. Melville
Dirge without Music. Millay
Do Nothing till You Hear from Me.
  Henderson
Está Muy Caliente. Bowering
Falls Funeral. Montague
Finnegan's Wake. *Unknown*
First Death. Justice
From the Outside. Gwala
Funeral[l], The. Donne
Funeral, The. Dubie
Funeral, The. Hall
Funeral, A. Rabon
Funeral, The. Spender
Funeral, The. *Fr.* Ordeal by Fire.
  Ya'oz-kest
Funeral Pyre, The. *Fr.* Beowulf.
  Unknown
Funeral Song. Kaoru
Ganges, The. Dubie
Grief. Díaz Mirón
I felt a funeral, in my brain. Dickinson
Island Funeral. Stanford
King over Israel. Ravikovich
Lenore. Poe
Lovers, The. Aiken
Milton by Firelight. Snyder
My Father's Funeral. Shapiro
My Grandfather's Funeral. Applewhite
Myris: Alexandria, A.D. 340. Cavafy
Night Funeral in Harlem. Hughes
Old Apple Trees. Snodgrass
Pall-Bearers. Prévert
Pauper's Funeral, The. *Fr.* The Village.
  Crabbe
Queen's Last Ride, The. Wilcox
Requiem after Seventeen Years.
  Ravikovich
Rites for Cousin Vit, The. Brooks
Rites of the Eastern Star. Pommy-Vega
Sarcophagi. Spencer
She Plans Her Funeral. Bowman
Tract. Williams
Twelve Minutes. Hall
Up yonder hill, behold how sadly slow.
  Fr. Night Piece on Death. Parnell
Upon a Funeral. Beaumont
Viewing the Body. Snodgrass
War's End. Ravikovich
Watching TV, the Elk Bones Up on
  Metaphysics. Bensko
Wedding-cake face in a paper frill, A.
  Fr. Berck-Plage. Plath

Furnaces
  Drunk in the Furnace, The. Merwin

Furniture
  Inventory of the Furniture of a Collegian's
    Chamber, An. Winstanley

My Mother's Breakfront. Sternburg
Table, The. DiPalma

G

Gabriel
Sonnet: Annunciation. Belli
Vision of the Blessed Gabriele, The. Shuttle
Galatea
Question, A. Livingston
Galilee, Israel
Elul in Galilee. Goldberg
In Galilee. Butts
Galley Slaves
Song of the Galley-slaves. Kipling
Gallipoli Campaign (1915)
War Story. Stallworthy
Galloway, Scotland
Grey Galloway. Cairncross
Gallows
Tyburn and Westminster. Heywood
See also **Hanging.**
Galoshes
Galoshes. Bacmeister
Upon Julia's Arctics. Taylor
Galuppi, Baldassaro
Toccata of Galuppi's, A. Browning
Galveston, Texas
On Galveston Beach. Howes
Galway. *See* **County Galway, Ireland.**
Gambling and Gamblers
Crapshooters. Sandburg
Deathbed, A. *Fr.* The Journey and
Observations of a Countryman. Hawthorn
Gambling. Tyler
Great Wager, The. Studdert-Kennedy
John Hardy. *Unknown*
Keno. Wier
Off from Swing Shift. Hongo
On a Distant Prospect of an Absconding
Bookmaker. Hamilton
One Time Henry Dreamed the Number.
Long
Placing a $2 Bet for a Man Who Will Never
Go to the Horse Races Any More.
Wakoski
Root Hog or Die. *Unknown*
Shake Hands with Your Bets, Friend.
Thomas
Wise Owl. Goedicke
Games
After Reading *The Great American Marble
Book* and Reflecting on Life's Lessons
Learned at An Early. Cleary
Before Play. *Fr.* Games. Popa
Dunmow Flitch of Bacon, The. *Unknown*
Game after Supper. Atwood
Game of Consequences, A. Dehn
Getting Berries. *Unknown*
Getting Firewood. *Unknown*
Grass Fight. Ryokan
He. *Fr.* Games. Popa
Hide-and-Seek. *Fr.* Games. Popa
Little Girl Blue. "Yvonne"
Lying Down. *Unknown*
Nail, The. *Fr.* Games. Popa
Pac-Man. Dacey
Pieces of Snot. *Unknown*
Playing Bowl-and-Bead. Tate Ryuwan
Playing the Game. Goldowsky
Playing Time. Pappas
Poems for the Game of Silence, *sels.*
Unknown
Rose Thieves, The. *Fr.* Games. Popa
Temari. Ryokan
When he kicked the ball under a plum tree.
Unknown
Yo-Yo King, The. Cohn

This Sporting Life (TSL). Emilie Buchwald
and Ruth Roston, eds.
See also **Card Games; Sports.**
Gandhi, Mohandas Karamchand
In India. Shapiro
Vaticide. O'Higgins
Ganges River, India
Ganges, The. Dubie
Madhav, you'll find none duller than I.
Tulsidas
Oh well born of Benares, I too am born well
known. Ravidas
River of the gods, the act of recalling you.
Tulsidas
Gangs and Gangsters
Black Jackets. Gunn
Blackstone Rangers, The. Brooks
Dogchain Gang, The. Rice
Matadero, Riley and Company. Mariani
Morning They Shot Tony Lopez, Barber and
Pusher Who Went Too Far, 1958, The.
Soto
Gannets
Long-billed Gannets. Emery
See also **Boobies.**
Ganymede
Ganymede. Plomer
Ganymede and Helen. *Unknown*
Jupiter and Ganimede. Heywood
Garages
Detail. Bethell
Garage in Co. Cork, A. Mahon
Garbage and Garbage Men
Dustman, The. Sansom
Dustman, The. *Unknown*
Garbage. Tretheway
Sarah Cynthia Sylvia Stout Would Not Take
the Garbage Out. Silverstein
Town Dump, The. Nemerov
Trash Men, The. Bukowski
García Lorca, Federico
García Lorca. Dudek
Garcia Lorca Murdered in Granada.
Manifold
Poem for Garcia Lorca. Woodcock
Garda, Lake, Italy
"Frater Ave atque Vale." Tennyson
Gardens and Gardening
Abandoned Garden. Kikuchi Gozan
Broken-hearted Gardener, The. *Unknown*
Butterbean Tent, The. Roberts
Charleston Garden, A. Bellamann
Dance Song. Poliziano
Digging In. Piercy
Erica. Bethell
Flowers. Behn
Footprints are gone, The. Tameie
For Jim, Easter Eve. Spencer
Forsaken Garden, A. Swinburne
Garden, The. *Fr.* The Task. Cowper
Garden, The. Grimald
Garden, The. Marvell
Garden, The. Shirley
Garden, The. Strand
Garden, A. Wakeman
Garden, The. Warren
Garden Boy, The. Motaung
Garden Lore. Ewing
Garden of Abu Mahmoud, The. Nye
Garden Song, A. Dobson
Garden Song, A. Sims
Gardener, The. *Fr.* Novelettes. MacNeice
Gardener, The. Symons
Gardener, The. Zand
Gardeners. Ignatow
Gardeners, The. Reid
Gardens. Curry
Gardens Are All My Heart. Triem
Grace for Gardens. Driscoll
H. Milosz
Her Garden. Downie

How to Build a Ha-ha. *Fr.* The English
Garden. Mason
In a Garden. Jennings
In an Abandoned Garden. Nishiwaki
Junzaburo
In my garden. Meiji
In My Garden. *Unknown*
In the garden of spring. *Fr.* Manyo Shu.
Yakamochi
Indolent Gardener, The. Kennedy
Just after Noon with Fierce Shears. Combs
Long Garden, The. Kavanagh
Lord God Planted a Garden, The. Gurney
Lost Garden. "Hale"
Love of Lettuce, The. Piercy
Manor Garden, The. Plath
Monk Kudo Asked Me, "What's Your Haikai
Eye Like?' *Fr.* Twenty-three Hokku.
Onitsura
Mower against Gardens, The. Marvell
Mr. Bidery's Spidery Garden. McCord
Mummies, The. Kumin
My Garden. Brown
My Garden. Davies
My Garden. Lindon
My garden is a pleasant place. Driscoll
My Mother's Garden. Allen
October in the Country: 1983. Simmons
Old Quin Queeribus. Turner
On Addy Road. Swenson
Our Garden. Halpern
Outdoor Anniversary with Maria. Shuttle
Perfect Garden, The. Robertson
Philoctetes. De Tabley
Playing with Fire. Simmons
Pruning. *Fr.* Cyder. Philips
Public Garden, The. Lowell
Pulling Weeds. Chock
Red Seeds Opening in the Shade.
McPherson
Roof Garden, The. Moss
Saint Fiacre. Irvine
Seeds of Love, The. Habergham
Seventh Garden, The. Weöres
She Would Have Roses. Ingraham
Sonnet:
Autumn Garden. Campana
Sowing Seeds. Cornwall
Spring Arithmetic. *Unknown*
Suburban Garden a Nature Reserve.
Shepherd
Summer Garden. "Akhmatova"
Their Lonely Betters. Auden
This Poem Is for Nadine. Janeczko
Time and the Garden. Winters
Trance. Bethell
Vegetable Garden. Lu Yu
Villa d'Este Gardens. Sassoon
Warning of Winter. Bethell
Who Loves a Garden. Jones
Widow's Weeds, A. De la Mare
Gardner, John
Notes for an Elegy: for John Gardner. Pastan
Garfield, James Abram
At the President's Grave. Gilder
Bells at Midnight, The. Aldrich
Charles Guiteau. *Unknown*
On the Death of President Garfield. Holmes
President Garfield. Longfellow
Garfield, John
John Garfield. Christopher
Gargoyles
Gargoyle. Rabbitt
Gargoyle. Sandburg
Gargoyle. Shaw
Garibaldi, Giuseppe
In Front of a Poster of Garibaldi. Moss
Garlic
Counterblast against Garlic, A. *Fr.* Epodes.
Horace
Garlic, The. Meyers
Ode to Garlic. Stafford

Garrick, David
Prologue Spoken [by Mr. Garrick] [at the Opening of the Theatre in Drury-Lane, 1747]. Johnson
Retaliation. Goldsmith

Garrison, William Lloyd
Garrison. Alcott
To William Lloyd Garrison. Whittier
William Lloyd Garrison. Ray

Garters
On a Pair of Garters. Davies

Gasoline Stations
Filling Station. Bishop

Gauguin, Paul
Vor a Gauguin Picture zu Singen. Stein

Gaveston, Piers
This Edward in the Aprill of his age. *Fr.* Piers Gaveston. Drayton

Gawaine, Sir
Sir Gawaine and the Green Knight. Winters
This kyng lay at Camylot upon Krystmasse. *Fr.* Sir Gawain and the Green Knight. *Unknown*

Gazelles
Gazelle, The. Hafiz
Gazelle Calf, The. Lawrence
Gazelles, The. Moore

Geese
As banked clouds. *Fr.* Sixty-four Tanka. Saigyo
Barnacle Geese. Higham
Beating their wings. *Fr.* Kokin Shu. *Unknown*
Cackle, cackle, Mother Goose. *Unknown*
Departing Geese. Yoshida no Kenko
Departing wild geese. *Fr.* Forty-four Hokku. Issa
Difference, The. Gozzano
Forsaking the mists. Ise
Fox and the Goose, The. *Unknown*
Gesse Departing at Early Dusk. Kenko
Goose. Braun
Haiku: "Wild geese flying." Watanabe Suiha
Heart of Autumn. Warren
If I could have my way. Tameyo
In the setting sunlight. Yoshimoto
In the spring haze. *Fr.* Kokin Shu. *Unknown*
Last Scene in the First Act. Piercy
Late at Night. Stafford
Lilies, The. Braun
Night Flight. Whalley
No Matter What, after All, and That Beautiful Word So. Carruth
O for my couriers. *Fr.* Manyo Shu. *Unknown*
Old Grey Goose, The. *Unknown*
On the Grass. Miyoshi Tatsuji
Poem about Poems about Vietnam, A. Stallworthy
Postcard from the Garden. Piercy
Sao Princess/ borrows a new robe of haze, The. Tamesada
Something Told the Wild Geese. Field
Swan and the Goose, The. Aesop
Season has come, The. *Fr.* Manyo Shu. Yakamochi
Three grey geese in a green field grazing. *Unknown*
To a Goose. Southey
We hearing them. *Fr.* Thirty Tanka. Shunzei
When the Rain Raineth. *Unknown*
When the wild goose. *Fr.* Twenty-four Tanka. Sanetomo
Wild Geese. Chipp
Wild geese departing, The. *Fr.* Sixty-four Tanka. Saigyo
Wild geese departing, their wings in white clouds, The. *Fr.* A Compendium of Good Tanka. Teika

Wild geese gone, the cove looks cleared. *Fr.* Forty-four Hokku. Issa
Wild geese leave no trace in the citadel of water, The. *Fr.* Seventy-eight Tanka. Shikishi
Wild geese lured by the autumn wind. *Fr.* A Compendium of Good Tanka. Teika
Wild geese returning, The. Kunimoto
Wild Goose, Wild Goose. Issa

Gehrig, Henry Louis ("Lou")
Babe & Lou. Douskey
To Lou Gehrig. Kieran

Gems
Mine Argosy from Alexandria. *Fr.* The Jew of Malta. Marlowe
Stone Diary, A. Lowther

Generals
Bold General Wolfe. *Unknown*
General, The. Sassoon

Generosity
Elegy: "He has held." Perevin Muruvalar
Kari Sober. Kapilar
This World Lives Because. Ilam Peruvaluti

Genetic Engineering
Progression of the Species. Aldiss

Genetics
Full House. Garey
See also **Evolution.**

Geneva, Switzerland
Geneva. Reid

Genius
Ben Jonson Entertains a Man from Stratford. Robinson
Genius. Menken
Mortified Genius, The. Graeme

Gentians
Bavarian Gentians. Lawrence
Fringed Gentians. Lowell
God made a little gentian. Dickinson
To the Fringed Gentian. Bryant

Geodes
Geode, the troll's melon. *Fr.* In Nine Sleep Valley. Merrill

Geography and Geographers
Geographers. *Fr.* The Ship of Fools. Barclay
Geography. *Fr.* Songs of Education. Chesterton
Geography. Farjeon

Geology
Goodnight. Ciardi
Minerals of Cornwall, Stones of Cornwall. Redgrove
Precambrian [*or* Pre-Cambrian] Shield, The. *Fr.* Towards the Last Spike. Pratt
What Happened Here Before. Snyder

Geometry
Geometry. Dove
Plane Geometry. Rounds
See also **Euclid.**

George I, King of England
Epigram: "King George, observing with judicious eyes." Trapp
Epigram: "King to Oxford sent a troop of horse, The." Browne
Pasquin to the Queen's Statue at St. Paul's. Shippen

George II, King of England
Lilliputian Ode on Their Majesties' Accession, A. Carey
What mean these loud aerial cracks I hear? *Fr.* Bedlam; a Poem on His Majesty's Happy Escape from His German Dominions. *Unknown*

George III, King of England
George III. Lowell
George III Visits Whitbread's Brewery. *Fr.* Instructions to a Celebrated Laureat. "Pindar"

George the Third. *Fr.* The Vision of Judgment. Byron
Saint Peter sat by the celestial gate. *Fr.* The Vision of Judgment. Byron

George IV, King of England
Epitaph on the Late King of the Sandwich Isles. Praed

George V, King of England
"New King Arrives in His Capital by Air. "—Daily Newspaper. Betjeman

George VI, King of England
Praises of King George VI. Ngani

Georgia
Another Small Town in Georgia. Ramke
Coon Hunt, Sixth Month (1955). Lea
Daufuskie. Evans
Georgia Dusk. Toomer
Georgia Towns. Hicky
In a U-Haul North of Damascus. Bottoms
In the Marble Quarry. Dickey
Marching through Georgia. Work
Nocturne: Georgia Coast. Hicky
Purpose of Altar Boys, The. Ríos
Refugee. Madgett
Robert Whitmore. Davis
Roll Call: A Land of Old Folk and Children. Black
Song of the Chattahoochee. Lanier
Talking to the Townsfolk in Ideal, Georgia. Black

Geraniums
Geranium, The. Roethke
Red Geranium and Godly Mignonette. Lawrence
Red Geraniums. Clark

German Verse
Contemporary Austrian Poetry; an Anthology (CoAuP). Beth Bjorklund, ed. *and* tr.
Defiant Muse, The; German Feminist Poems from the Middle Ages to the Present (DMG). Susan L. Cocalis, ed.

Germany
Bingen on the Rhine. Norton
High Germany. Shanks
In Freiburg Station. Brooke
No Offence. Enright
Nuremberg. Longfellow
On a German Tour. Porson
Over the Wall: Berlin, May 1975. Sisson
Pictures of the Rhine. Meredith
Small Park in East Germany: 1969. Mayer
Song of the Cape of Good Hope. Schubart
To Germany. Sorley
Walk in Würzburg, A. Plomer
Ye tourists and travellers, bound to the Rhine. Hood

Germs
Germ, The. Nash
Some Little Bug. Atwell
Things on a Microscope Slide. Kennedy
See also **Bacteria.**

Geronimo
Geronimo. McGaffey

Gethsemane
Agony in the Garden, The. Hemans
Christ's Prayer in Gethsemane. *Unknown*

Gettysburg, Battle of (1863)
Battle of Gettysburg, The. *Fr.* John Brown's Body. Benét
Dickens in Camp. Harte
Gettysburg. Roche
Gettysburg. Stedman
High Tide at Gettysburg, The. Thompson
John Burns of Gettysburg. Harte
Lincoln at Gettysburg. *Fr.* The Gettysburg Ode. Taylor
Sanitary Message, A. Harte

Ghana
Cornfields in Accra. Aidoo

Ghettos
Anglosaxon Street. Birney

Autobiographical. Klein
Back to the Ghetto. Glatstein
Disco Chinatown. Kageyama
Ghetto Twilight. Brody
In the Ghetto. Sonnenschein
Jewish Main Street. Layton
Poor Christian Looks at the Ghetto, A.
  Milosz
Resistance in the Ghetto. Glatstein

Ghosts
All Souls' Night. Cornford
Apparition, The. Donne
Barbarossa. Rückert
By St. Thomas Water. Causley
Chatterton. Hands
Chez Brébant. Durivage
Colonel Fazackerley. Causley
Corporal Stare. Graves
Dark House, The. *Unknown*
Dido among the Shades. *Fr.* The Aeneid [*or*
  Eneados]. Virgil
Distance that the dead have gone, The.
  Dickinson
False Dawn. De la Mare
Father in the Railway Buffet. Fanthorpe
Garden Seat, The. Hardy
Ghost, The. De la Mare
Ghost, The. Lowell
Ghost & Shaman. *Unknown*
Ghost of a Ghost, The. Leithauser
Ghost of the Cargo Boat, The. Neruda
Ghost Story. Thomas
Ghosts. Behn
Ghosts. Jennings
Ghosts. Reid
Greyport Legend, A. Harte
Hallowe'en. Farjeon
Haunted House, The. Hood
Haunted Houses. Longfellow
Horseman, The. De la Mare
I am my father's spirit. *Fr.* Hamlet.
  Shakespeare
In the Night. Roberts
Klabauterwife's Letter. Morgenstern
Listeners, The. De la Mare
Longing for Death because of Feebleness.
  Smith
Midnight. Kang
My Grandmother's Ghost. Wright
My Spirit Will Not Haunt the Mound. Hardy
Oft in the lone church-yard at night I've seen.
  Fr. The Grave. Blair
Old Ghost, The. Beddoes
Ollie McGee. Masters
Our Little Ghost. Alcott
Phantom Horsewoman, The. Hardy
Phantom-Wooer, The. Beddoes
Sally Simpkin's Lament. Hood
Shadwell Stair. Owen
Silent Hill. Snyder
Souls of the Slain, The. Hardy
Southern Mansion. Bontemps
Spritely Dead, The. Williams
Squats on a toad-stool under a tree. *Fr.*
  Death's Jest Book. Beddoes
Suffolk Miracle, The. *Unknown*
Priest attending, found he spoke at times,
  The. *Fr.* The Borough: Peter Grimes.
  Crabbe
Three Ghostesses. *Unknown*
To a Shade. Yeats
Unquiet Grave, The. *Unknown*
Way a Ghost Dissolves, The. Hugo
Welsh Incident. Graves
What beck'ning ghost, along the moonlight
  shade. *Fr.* Elegy to the Memory of an
  Unfortunate Lady. Pope
While some affect the sun, and some the
  shade. *Fr.* The Grave. Blair
Why do we return? Not in the darkened
  rooms. *Fr.* Ghost Voice. Fuller
Why He Was There. Robinson

Wicked Hawthorn Tree, The. Yeats
Wife of Usher's Well, The. *Unknown*
William and Margaret. Mallet
Willis, The. Proudfit
Xenia. Montale
*Why Am I Grown So Cold? Poems of the
  Unknowable* (WSC), Pp. 44-56, 124-142.
  Myra Cohn Livingston, ed.

Giacometti, Albert
From the Workshop of Brancusi and
  Giacometti. Haines
Giants
Bean-Stalk, The. Millay
Being a Giant. Mezey
Hickenthrift and Hickenloop. Kennedy
In the Orchard. Stephens
Sleeping Giant, The. Hall
Gibbon, Edward
Distribution of Honours for Literature.
  Landor
Lausanne. Hardy
Gibbs, Josiah Willard
It was much later in his life he rose. *Fr.*
  Gibbs. Rukeyser
Gibraltar
At Gibraltar. Woodberry
Gibraltar. Blunt
Gibralter. Trench
Gifts and Giving
Accompanying a Gift ("From thy patient, who
  while here"). Moorer
Accompanying a Gift ("One whose love will
  never end"). Moorer
Birthday Gift, A. Dunn
Birthday Gifts. Asquith
For the Lady Olivia Porter; a Present upon a
  New Year's Day. Davenant
Gift. Cohen
Gift. Hemschemeyer
Gift, The. Lourie
Gifts. Snow
How Long Shall I Give? *Unknown*
How to Give. *Unknown*
I've Got a New Book from My Grandfather
  Hyde. Jackson
Little Brother's Secret. Mansfield
Oh, the Ch'i and the Chü. *Unknown*
Roman Presents. Martial
Roman Thank-You Letter, A. Martial
Six Things for Christmas. May
Gilbert, Sir Humphrey
Sir Humphrey Gilbert. Longfellow
Gilbert, Sir William Schwenck
"Everybody Works but Father" as W. S.
  Gilbert Would Have Written It. Burgoyne
Ginkgo Trees
Ginkgoes in Fall. Nemerov
These Green-going-to-Yellow. Bell
Ginsberg, Allen
Blessing a Bride and Groom; a Wedding
  Night Poem. Peters
He. Ferlinghetti
Giotto
Perfect Symbol, The. Johnson
To Giotto. Trimpi
Giraffes
Giraffe, The. *Fr.* Three Animals. Padgett
Giraffe. Smith
Giraffe. *Unknown*
Giraffes Don't Huff. Kuskin
Listen:/ There roams, far away, by the waters
  of Clead. *Fr.* The Giraffe. Gumilev
Mr. Giraffe. LaPage
On the Death of the Giraffe. Hood
Poem Not about a Zebra, A. Hadas
Girdles
On a Girdle. Waller
Woman with Girdle. Sexton
Girls
Child Next Door, The ("The child next door
  has a wreath on her hat"). Fyleman

Extremes. Riley
Felicia Ropps. Burgess
From Our Mary to Me. Fulton
Girl. *Unknown*
In Praise of a Girl. Morus
In the Library. Ochester
Little Jumping Girls, The. Greenaway
Narcissa. Brooks
Ode to a Country Hoyden. "Pindar"
Pretty Girls Just Are. Ogunsiji
Teen-Ager, A. Snodgrass
Violins. *Fr.* Chords. Montale
See also **Adolescence; Childhood and
  Children; Youth.**
Glaciers
Glacier. Nicholson
Glassblowers
Epitaph: "Glassblower lies here at rest, A."
  Morton
Glass Blower, The. Scully
Glasses. *See* **Eyeglasses.**
Glencoe, Scotland
Glencoe. Chesterton
Glencoe. Stewart
Globes
Letty's Globe. Turner
School Globe, The. Reaney
Glossolalia
Gift of Tongues, The. Morgan
Gloucester, Massachusetts
Gloucester Moors. Moody
Gloves
Elinda's [*or* Ellinda's] Glove. Lovelace
Glove, The. Bond
Glove, The. *Fr.* Cynthia's Revels. Jonson
That Glove. Tucker
See also **Mittens.**
Glowworms. *See* **Fireflies.**
Gluttony and Gluttons
Eat-It-All Elaine. Starbird
Glutton [*or* Glutton in the Tavern], The. *Fr.*
  The Vision of Piers Plowman. Langland
Glutton, The. Oakman
Greedy Jane. *Unknown*
Hymn to Comus. *Fr.* Pleasure Reconciled to
  Virtue. Jonson
Mouse and the Cake, The. Cook
Notorious Glutton, The. Taylor
On Gut. Jonson
Vulture, The. Belloc
Gnats
Accidentally. Kumin
Gnat, The. Beaumont
Gnomes
Gnome, The. Behn
Gnus
G stands for Gnu, whose weapons of defence.
  Belloc
Wildebeest, The. Daly
Goats
April. Winters
Care. Murphy
Goat, The. Saba
Goat, The. *Unknown*
Goat Paths, The. Stephens
I Have Got to Stop Loving You. Ai
Smile of the Goat, The. Herford
Goblins
Goblin, The. Fyleman
How to Tell Goblins from Elves. Shannon
Little Orphant Annie. Riley
Overheard on a Saltmarsh. Monro
See also **Elves; Fairies; Ghosts.**
God
Adon 'Olam. *Unknown*
All are but parts of one stupendous whole.
  Fr. An Essay on Man. Pope
All-embracing, The. Faber
All the Hosts of Heaven. Ben Isaac ben
  Abun of Mainz

Ancient Thought, The. Kerr
And in the 51st Year of That Century, While My Brother Cried in the Trench, While My Enemy Glared from the Cave. Plutzik
And Yet. Rhinow
Ballad for Gloom. Pound
Before the Mountains Were Brought Forth. Fr. Later Life. Rossetti
Beginning. Glatstein
Bermudas. Marvell
Berries, The. Heyen
Bible Story. Causley
Birth (al-Maulid). al-Majdhoub
Bitter-sweet. Herbert
Bless Him ("Bless Him, O constant companions"). Unknown
Blessed Be the Holy Will of God. Unknown
Book, The. Drummond
Both Earth and Heaven. Namani
Business Man's Prayer, A. Ludlum
Canticle of Created Things. Francis of Assisi
Child of Loneliness. Gale
Child's Thought of God, A. Browning
Christmas Folk-Song, A. Reese
Colin, you can tell my words are crippled now. Fr. Jerusalem Sonnets. Baxter
Collar, The. Herbert
Contentment. Schlipf
Creation of Light, The. Maura
Creation of the Inaudible, The. Rogers
Creatures speak in sounds. Fr. Random Thoughts on the Love of God. Weil
"Daily with You." Flint
Day after Sunday, The. McGinley
De Profundis. De la Mare
Discipline. Herbert
Divine Abundance. Unknown
Divine Image, The ("To mercy, pity, peace, and love"). Fr. Songs of Innocence. Blake
Do not be faithless to me. Vali
Each in His Own Tongue. Carruth
Easter Wings. Herbert
Ecclesiastes. Mahon
Eclogue: Queen Elizabeth's Day. Davidson
Egocentric. Smith
End of Being, The. Seneca
Eternal Goodness, The. Whittier
Eternal Jew, The. Cohen
Everlasting Love, The. Flint
Eyewitness. Hall
Faith and Sight. King
Father Knows, The. "H."
First Love. Clare
Flower in the Crannied Wall. Tennyson
For Inspiration. Michelangelo
Forest Song. Leslie
Forgotten. Tussman
Friendly Beasts, The. Unknown
Fury of Aerial Bombardment, The. Eberhart
Genesis. Glatstein
Genesis. Jones
God. Bradford
God. Fr. Dawn. Monro
God. Slutsky
God, A Poem. Fenton
God Cares. Casterline
God Everywhere. Ibn Ezra
God Has Pity on Kindergarten Children. Amichai
God Is. Mathias
God is a distant, stately lover. Dickinson
God Is at the Anvil. Sarett
God, Is, Like, Scissors. Villa
God Is Love. Bowring
God Makes a Path. Williams
God No Longer Speaks. Fridman
God of Israel, The. Leyeles
God of Mercy. Molodovsky
God of Might, God of Right. Unknown
God of the Living, The. Ellerton
God Poem. Moss

God, Whom Shall I Compare to Thee? Halevi
God's Electric Power. Linden
God's Funeral. Hardy
God's Grandeur. Hopkins
God's Love. Unknown
God's Mood. Clifton
God's Remembrance. Ledwidge
God's Ways, Not Our Ways. Ray
Great Sad One, The. Greenberg
Guide Me, O Thou Great Jehovah. Williams
Hail, Thou great mysterious Being! Fr. God. McLachlan
He Leadeth Me. Gilmore
He Puts Me to Rest. Ignatow
Heal Me, My God. Halevi
Hidden Weaver, The. Shepard
Higher Pantheism, The. Tennyson
Highest Divinity. Unknown
His Necessary Darkness. Sullivan
His Presence Came Like Sunrise. Cushman
Hitherto and Henceforth. Flint
Holy God, We Praise Thy Name. Walworth
Holy of Holies, The. Chesterton
Hope Thou in God. Heard
Hound of Heaven, The. Thompson
Hunchback, The. Bishop
Hymn of Unity. Unknown
Hymn to God the Father [or For Forgiveness or To Christ], A. Donne
Hymn to the Creator. Clare
I Die because I Do Not Die. Theresa
I Will Look Up. Heard
I wish, God, for some end I do not will. Fr. The Sonnets of Michelangelo. Jennings
If God Exists. Lipska
If We Believed in God. Gibbs
Image of God, The. Aldana
Immanence. Hovey
In the market, in the cloister—only God I saw. Baba Kuhi of Shiraz
In the Valley. Thompson
In Westminster Abbey. Betjeman
Indian upon God, The [or an]. Yeats
Inside God's Eye. Rogers
Invocation, An: "To God, the everlasting, who abides." Symonds
Jehovah. Zangwill
Just the Same To-Day. Unknown
Kingdom of God, The. Rab
Lauds. Berryman
Let Us with a Gladsome Mind. Milton
Light Shining Out of Darkness. Borthwick
Light Shining Out of Darkness. Cowper
Lilies for the Prophet. Al-Mala'ika
Living God, The. Gilman
Living God, The. Ibn Ezra
Lord Is King, The. Unknown
Lord, my God. Tussman
Lord of the World. Unknown
Lost. Muyassar
Love of the Father, The. Unknown
Love Poem: "In your quest or request God is remote." Na mani
Majesty and Mercy of God, The. Grant
Maximus. Lawrence
Mighty Fortress Is Our God, A. Luther
More than We Ask. Wells
Mr. Edwards and the Spider. Lowell
My Father Knows. Tillett
"My Grace Is Sufficient for Thee." Unknown
My Wander-Brother. Glatstein
Mysteries of Life. Tucker
Mystery, The. Amergin
Mystery, The. Hodgson
Name of God Is, The. Hathaway
New God, The. Fr. The New World. Bynner
No Coming to God without Christ. Herrick
No Coward Soul [Is Mine] Brontë
No Time for God. Trott
Noah's Ark. Young

O God, Our Help in Ages Past. Watts
O God, unknown, invisible, secure. Fr. An Invocation. Symonds
O, Thou Eternal One! Derzhavin
Of Gods Omnipotencie. Hume
Offertorium. Fr. Requiem for the Living. Day Lewis
Old Repair Man, The. Johnson
Omnipresence. Hale
On Saturday sailed from Bremen. Fr. The Wreck of the Deutschland. Hopkins
151st Psalm, The. Shapiro
Our God, Our Help in Ages Past. Watts
Paradox, The. Pereira
Passage. Levertov
Perhaps it is God. Teller
Petition. Auden
Physics, A. McHugh
Pied Beauty. Hopkins
Plaint. Elliott
Prayer: "Inmost sense, The." Glatstein
Prayer: "Lord, what a change within us one short hour." Trench
Prayer, A: "Teach me, teach me how." Reisen
Prayer, The: "Wilt Thou not visit me?" Very
Prayer for Every Day. Unknown
Preface, The: "Infinity, when all things it beheld." Fr. God's Determinations. Taylor
Pulley, The. Herbert
Questions of Ethne Alba, The. Unknown
Quite Apart from the Holy Ghost. Mitchell
Rain, Wind and a New City. Niazi
Raise Me Up, Lord. Miguel de Guevara
Recessional. Kipling
Revelation. Markham
Rinsed with Gold, Endless, Walking the Fields. Siegel
St. Patrick's Breastplate. Patrick
Sanctification. Ibn Abithur
Scapegoat. Rodgers
Search, The. Clark
Seeking God. Dowden
Some Verses upon the Burning of Our House, July 10th, 1666. Bradstreet
Song: "My straying thoughts, reduced stay." Collins
Song of the Wind and the Rain. Ibn Gabirol
Songs of Kabir. Kabir
Sonnet: To Crucify the Son. Miguel de Guevara
Sonnet XI: "Is God invisible? This very room." Greeff
Spring and Fall. Hopkins
Stanzas of the Soul that Suffers with Longing to See God. John of the Cross
Still, Still, with Thee. Stowe
Sweet Father. Heifetz-Tussman
Testimony. Rodgers
Then Sings My Soul. Mariani
Third Enemy Speaks. Fr. The Magnetic Mountain. Day Lewis
This Is My Father's World. Babcock
This Moment. Flint
Thou Art Indeed Just, Lord, If I Contend. Hopkins
Thou Great God. Unknown
Though Mine Eye Sleep Not. Fr. The Dead Sea Scrolls. Unknown
Three Towns, The. Nemerov
To a Dark Moses. Clifton
To a God Unknown. Eller
To a Waterfowl. Bryant
To Heaven. Jonson
To Men. Wickham
To Percy Shelley: On the Degrading Notions of Deity. Hunt
To the Nativity. Gonzáles de Eslava
Transcendence. Hovey

Transcendence of God, The. *Fr.* Samson
  Agonistes. Milton
Tree. Artaud
Truant, The. Pratt
True Hymn, A. Herbert
True Knowledge. Panatattu
Twelve Lines about the Burning Bush.
  Ravitch
Twice. Rossetti
Ultimate Problems. Stafford
Under a Wiltshire Apple Tree. De Bary
Unity of God, The. Panatattu
Unknown God, The. Watson
Vestigia. Carman
Voice of God, The. Barnard
Walking with God. Cowper
Walking with God. *Unknown*
Watchmaker God. Lowell
What if the foot, ordain'd the dust to tread.
  Fr. An Essay on Man. Pope
What the Devil Said. Stephens
What Thomas an Buile Said in a Pub.
  Stephens
When God First Said. Zach
When I Was Growing Up. Vogel
When there was nothing, there was God.
  Ghalib
Whose Hand. *Unknown*
Why God Permits Evil: For Answers to This
  Question of Interest to Many Write Bible
  Answers Dept. E-7. Williams
Wish, that of the living whole, The. *Fr.* In
  Memoriam A. H. H. Tennyson
With Deep Repentance for My Wasted Days.
  Stampa
Without Jews. Glatstein
Wolf Bezberider. Shtoltsenberg
Work of Love, The. Sangster
Written in Exile. Raine
Yet Do I Marvel. Cullen
Zebaoth. Lasker-Schüler
Godiva, Lady
Godiva. Tennyson
Godly Casuistry
Godly Casuistry ("The sun had long since in
  the lap"). *Fr.* Hudibras. Butler
Godolphin, Sidney Godolphin, 1st Earl of
Sidney Godolphin. Scollard
Gods and Goddesses
From Mythology. Herbert
God-Maker, Man, The. Marquis
Gods, The. Lee
Gods. Vas
Gods Are Mighty, The. Louw
Hertha. Swinburne
Hymn to Diana. *Fr.* Cynthia's Revels.
  Jonson
Immortal Aphrodite, on your patterned throne.
  Sappho
Murmur. Hecht
No Man, if Men Are Gods. Cummings
Old Gods, The. Muir
Rec Room in Paradise. Clark
River God, The. Smith
Visit of the Gods, The. Schiller
Weather of Olympus, The. Graves
God's Protection
I to the Hills Will Lift Mine Eyes. Rous
Godwin, William
Hard was thy fate in all the scenes of life.
  Roscoe
Goebbels, Joseph
Dr. Joseph Goebbels. *Fr.* The Führer
  Bunker. Snodgrass
Goethe, Johann Wolfgang von
Goethe's Death Mask. Gregg
Memorial Verses. Arnold
Shake, Mulleary, and Go-ethe. Bunner
Sorrows of Werther, The. Thackeray
Gogh, Vincent van. *See* **Van Gogh, Vincent.**
Gogol, Nikolai Vasilyevich
Gogol. Tranströmer

Gold Mining and Gold Miners
Broken-down Digger, The. *Unknown*
Californian, The. *Unknown*
Cleaning Up. Dyson
Cremation of Sam McGee, The. Service
Dow's Flat. Harte
Dreary Black Hills, The. *Unknown*
Gold-Seekers, The. Garland
Golden Gullies of the Palmer, The.
  Unknown
Joe Bowers. *Unknown*
John Sutter. Winters
Look Out Below! Thatcher
Lousy Miner. *Unknown*
Miner's Lament, The. *Unknown*
Mistress of the Matchless Mine. Robertson
National Miner, The. *Unknown*
Oh, My Darling Clementine. Montross
San Francisco Company, The. *Unknown*
Spell of the Yukon, The. Service
Sweet Jane. *Unknown*
When I Went Off to Prospect. *Unknown*
Golden Age
Age of Gold. Metastasio
Golden Age, The. Fenollosa
Golden Age, The. *Fr.* The Faithful
  Shepherd. Guarini
O lovely age of gold! *Fr.* Aminta. Tasso
Verses on the Prospect of Planting Arts and
  Learning in America. Berkeley
Golden Rule, The
Do As You Would Be Done By. Edwards
Goldenrod
Golden Rod, The. Sherman
Goldfinches
Goldfinch. Engels
Mechanism. Ammons
On a Goldfinch Starved to Death in His Cage.
  Cowper
Goldfish
Goldfish, The. Brown
Goldfish. Monro
On a Vase of Gold-Fish. Turner
To Miss––– on the Death of Her Goldfish.
  Meredyth
Goldilocks
In Love with the Bears. Kuzma
Golem
Golem, The. Reich
How They Made the Golem. Colombo
Golf
Afforestation. Wodehouse
Babe Didrikson. Rice
Ball and the Club, The. Lindsay
City of Golf, The. Murray
First Green Heron. Margolis
Golf Links, The. Cleghorn
Golfers. Layton
Golfer's Rubaiyat, The. Boynton
History of Golf—Sort Of, A. Hirsch
I was playing golf that day. *Unknown*
Last Game. Waterman
Lesson from Golf, A. Guest
Mullion. Herbert
One Down. Armour
Public Nuisance, A. Arkell
Seaside Golf. Betjeman
Victory on the Last Green. *Fr.* The Goff; an
  Heroi-comical Poem. Mathison
Goliath
David and Goliath. Crouch
David and Goliath. Thompson
Goliath and David. Untermeyer
Good Friday
Good Friday. Brown
Good Friday. Rossetti
Good Friday. Smith
Good Friday. *Unknown*
Good Friday [*or* Goodfriday], 1613. Riding
  Westward. Donne
Tenebrae. Clarke

Good Hope, Cape of. *See* **Cape of Good**
Hope.
Good Samaritan
Good Samaritan, The. Newman
Man Who Had Fallen among Thieves, A.
  Cummings
Goodman, Benny
"Sure," Said Benny Goodman. Carruth
Gore-Booth, Eva
In Memory of Eva Gore-Booth and Con
  Markiewicz. Yeats
Gorillas
Au Jardin des Plantes. Wain
Best Loved of Africa. Danner
Gospel Music
And the Old Women Gathered. Evans
Gossip
Because people's words are rampant and the
  rumor pains me. *Fr.* Manyo Shu. Tajima
Gossip. Linden
Journal of Society, The. Turner
Noël Tragique. Guthrie
Ornament here, a decoration there, An.
  Unknown
People do gossip. Sappho
People Will Talk. Dodge
Sir, so suspicious. *Unknown*
Tattle. Turner
They Say. Wilcox
See also **Reputation; Rumor.**
Govan, Saint
St. Govan. Prys-Jones
Government
1801. Wordsworth
Government! Nihoniho
Grave and dignified manners. *Unknown*
Politics Kaiso. McTair
Under the Rose. *Unknown*
Goya y Lucientes, Francisco José de
Church of San Antonio de la Florida, The.
  Petrie
In Goya's Greatest Scenes. *Fr.* A Coney
  Island of the Mind. Ferlinghetti
In Goya's Greatest Scenes We Seem to See.
  Ferlinghetti
Grace
Grace. Emerson
Grace Abounding. Ammons
Graces of the Holy Ghost, The. *Unknown*
Love. Herbert
Thy grace, dear Lord's my golden wrack I
  find. *Fr.* Preparatory Meditations before
  My Approach to the Lord's Supper.
  Taylor
Grackles
Grackle, The ("Grackle's voice is less than
  mellow."). Nash
Graf Spee (ship)
Sinking of the *Graf Spee*, The. *Unknown*
Graffiti
From a Lavatory Wall. *Unknown*
Kilroy. Viereck
Men's Room in the College Chapel, The.
  Snodgrass
Observing a Vulgar Name on the Plinth of an
  Ancient Statue. Landor
Sunny Prestatyn. Larkin
Thesis, Antithesis and Nostalgia. Dugan
To Desi as Joe as Smoky the Lover of 115th
  Street. Lorde
Graham, James, Marquess of Montrose
See **Montrose, James Graham, 5th Earl**
and 1st Marquess of.
Graham, Martha
Martha Graham. Laughlin
Grain Elevators
Grain Elevator. Klein
Grammar
How a Girl Was Too Reckless of Grammar
  [by Far]. Carryl

Gramsci, Antonio
Gramsci's Ashes. Pasolini
Grand Pré, Nova Scotia
Low Tide on Grand Pré. Carman
Grand Rapids, Michigan
Grand Rapids. Moore
Grandchildren
Grandchild. Kumin
Granddaughters
Grandmothers. Rich
Grandfathers
Blue Lantern. Song
Careless/ but not fearless. *Fr.* Urn I: Silent
for Twenty-five Years, the Father of My
Mother Advises Me. Lew
Chant Royal. Morgan
Child to His Sick Grandfather, A. Baillie
Gardeners. Ignatow
Grampa. Scott
Grampaw's Smoking Pipe. Hsiang Yang
Grandfather. Barnstone
Grandfather. Bowering
Grandfather. Harper
Grandfather. Henson
Grandfather. Mahon
Grandfather. Martin
Grandfather Dying. *Fr.* Byelorussia.
Kulbak
Grandfather in the Old Men's Home.
Merwin
Grandfathers. Castro
Grandfather's Clock. Work
Grandfather's Last Letter, A. Dubie
Grandpa and the Uncles. *Fr.* Byelorussia.
Kulbak
Great-Grandfather. Downie
Harmonica Man. Wolny
Hot Summer Sunday. Hendricks
I Want to Write a Jewish Poem. Pacernick
In January, 1962. Kooser
I've Got a New Book from My Grandfather
Hyde. Jackson
Late Gothic. Gotlieb
Letters to My Daughters, No. 3. Minty
Links. Cassity
Manners [for a Child of 1918] Bishop
Maple Syrup. Hall
Mendacious Song. Rabon
Mi Abuelo. Ríos
My Grandaddy Mostly with His Knife.
Huddle
My Grandfather's Church Goes Up.
Chappell
Naming. Stroud
On the Photograph of a Man I Never Saw.
Plutzik
Pass It On Grandson. Palmanteer
Pass On, You Lonely Grandfathers. Kharik
Poem for My Grandfather. Jacobs
Poet Imagines His Grandfather's Thoughts on
the Day He Died, The. Lum
Short Story. Voigt
Strikover Rabbi, The. Landau
To Be a Jew. Zeitlin
With My Grandfather. Zelda
Yahrzeit. Schaeffer
Zaydee. Levine
Grandmothers
Afternoon with Grandmother. Huff
Almost Ninety. Whitman
Anishinabe Grandmothers. Vizenor
At My Grandmother's. Malouf
At the Long Island Jewish Geriatric Home.
Graham
Beads, The. Jacinto
Beneath the Shadow of the Freeway.
Cervantes
Beside My Grandmother. Lee
Cupboard, The. De la Mare
Eurynome. Fourtouni
Favorite Flower, The. Thaxter

First Death. Justice
For All My Grandmothers. Brant
For My Grandmother. *Fr.* Four Epitaphs.
Cullen
For My Grandmother, Bridget Halpin.
Hartnett
For My Mother's Mother. McDaniel
From My Mother's House. Goldberg
Grammer's Shoes. Barnes
Grandmamma's Birthday. Belloc
Grandma's Advice. *Unknown*
Grandmother. Allen
Grandmother, The. Berry
Grandmother. Young Bear
Grandmother and Child. Dallas
Grandmother and Grandson. Merwin
Grandmother Grace. Wallace
Grandmother Jackson. Jackson
Grandmother Poems. Chin
Grandmother, Rocking. Merriam
Grandmother Sleeps. Bahe
Grandmothers, The. Oliver
Grandmothers. Rich
Green Rain. Livesay
Growing Old. Henderson
Her Garden. Downie
Housewife's Lament, The. *Unknown*
I'm Making You Up. "Chrystos"
In Cold Storm Light. Silko
In Memory of My Arab Grandmother. Zerbe
It Was a Long Time Before. Silko
It's All the Same. Davis
Last Words of My English Grandmother, The.
Williams
Late Gothic. Gotlieb
Lineage. *Fr.* Elegy. Bidart
Lineage. Walker
Long Time Ago. Silko
Looking for My Old Indian Grandmother in
the Summer Heat of 1980. Glancy
Love Necessitates. Redmond
Minuet, The. Dodge
My Grandmother. Adams
My Grandmother. Ismay
My Grandmother. Shapiro
My Grandmother Washes Her Feet. Chappell
My Grandmother's Ghost. Wright
My Grandmother's Love Letters. Crane
Nechama. Kaufman
Point Shirley. Plath
Recollection. Big Eagle
Returning to Granny. Abi Shaqra
Sestina: "September rain falls on the house."
Bishop
Song for Healing, A. LeBrasseur
Sorrow. Hummer
Strikover Rabbi's Wife, The. Landau
Sunflower Sonnet Number One. Jordan
Taking the Milk to Grandmother. Kloefkorn
Thoughts for My Grandmother. Firestone
To Jesus Villanueva, with Love. Villanueva
To My Grandmother. McGuckian
Victorian Grandmother. Lockwood
When My Grandmother Died. Cornish
Woman of the House, The. Murphy
Written at the Graveside. Yüan Mei
Yonosa House. Smith
You Smell like Grandma's Beads. Woody
Grandparents
Complaint of the Grandparents. Justice
Insight. Goose
Long Island Springs. Moss
Night above the Town. Lux
Granicus, Battle of (334 B.C.)
How We Heard the Name. Dugan
Grant, Ulysses Simpson
Achilles Deatheridge. Masters
Aged Stranger, The. Harte
Death of Grant, The. Bierce
In Memory of General Grant. Abbey
Lee's Parole. Manville
Vanquished. Browne

Grapes
American Vineyard. Cousens
Father and His Children, The. *Unknown*
Grapes Making. Adams
Taste of Purple. Jacobs
Grass
Blade of Grass Sings to the River, The.
Goldberg
Builder of Continents, The. *Fr.* The Stars.
"Ping Hsin"
Cut Grass. Larkin
Former Barn Lot. Van Doren
Grass, The. Bowering
Grass. Corn
Grass. Sandburg
Grass. Webster
Grass Fingers. Grimké
Grassroots. Sandburg
He who burns the sere weeds. *Fr.* Manyo
Shu. *Unknown*
Long Feud. Untermeyer
Lying in the Grass. Gosse
My love-thoughts these days. *Fr.* Manyo
Shu. *Unknown*
Sad Green. Warner
Shearing Grass. Redgrove
Speaks the Whispering Grass. Stuart
Spring Grass. Sandburg
Susuki, growing along the way to my beloved.
Fr. Manyo Shu. *Unknown*
To those who await. Ietaka
Tribute to Grass. Ingalls
Tuft by Tuft. Campert
Voice of the Grass, The. Boyle
Grasshoppers
Airport in the Grass. Kennedy
Explanation of the Grasshopper, An.
Lindsay
Grasshopper, The. Lovelace
Grasshopper, The. McCord
Grasshopper, The. Stanley
Grasshopper, A. Wilbur
Grasshopper Green. Watson
Grasshoppers. Clare
Grasshopper's Song, The. Bialik
High June. Morin
On the Grasshopper and [the] Cricket. Keats
Ondt and the Gracehoper, The. *Fr.*
Finnegans Wake. Joyce
R-P-O-P-H-E-S-S-A-G-R. Cummings
To the Grasshopper and the Cricket. Hunt
Gratitude
Gratitude. Glück
Graves
Ah, Are You Digging on My Grave? Hardy
All Souls. Lawrence
Ample make this bed. Dickinson
At Frost's Grave. Smith
Beach Burial. Slessor
Beneath the Mound. Smith
Bishop Orders His Tomb at Saint Praxed's
Church, The. Browning
Buffel's Kop. Campbell
Burial Detail. Hudgins
Bury Me in a Free Land. Harper
"Childe Roland to the Dark Tower Came."
Browning
Child's Grave, Hale County, Alabama.
Simmerman
Child's Grave Marker, A. Kooser
Coffin-Worm, The. Pitter
Cool Tombs. Sandburg
Cry of the Gravediggers, The. Glatstein
Despair. Levertov
Dig My Grave. *Unknown*
Elegy Written in a Country Churchyard.
Gray
Elizabeth. Warner
Fame. Browning
Father Son and Holy Ghost. Lorde
Form of Epitaph, A. Whistler
G. I. Graves in Tuscany. Hugo

Giorno dei Morti. Lawrence
Grandma Chooses Her Plot at the County
   Cemetery. Ruffin
Grave, The. Blair
Grave, A. Moore
Grave in Ukraine, A. Tchernichowsky
Graves. Muyassar
Graveyard, The. Cooper
Graveyard by the Sea. Lux
I asked the grave-digger, "Do you have."
   Fr. Personal Reflections. Al-Udwani
In the Grave No Flower. Millay
Indian's Grave, The. Mountain
Invocation: "Let me be buried in the rain."
   Johnson
Iona; the Graves of the Kings. Jeffers
Jewish Graveyards, Italy. Levine
Knight's Tomb, The. Coleridge
Lord Cozens Hardy. Betjeman
Maple Syrup. Hall
Meditations on the Sepulchre in the Garden.
   Doddridge
Midnight. Kang
Nettles, The. Hardy
Night of darkness and of storms!, A. *Fr.*
   Thalaba the Destroyer. Southey
Not Any Higher Stands the Grave.
   Dickinson
On a Grave in Christchurch, Hants. Adams
One Rose of Stone. Wilson
Orange Piano, The. St. John
Prehistoric Burials. Sassoon
Relic, The. Donne
Requiescat. Wilde
Sir Walter Scott at the Tomb of the Stuarts in
   St. Peter's. Milnes
Snails. Blodgett
Song for the Burial of My Mother.
   Shimazaki Toson
Sunday Graveyard. Stanton
They're Shifting Father's Grave. *Unknown*
Unquiet Grave, The. *Unknown*
We Do Lie beneath the Grass. *Fr.* Death's
   Jest Book. Beddoes
We do not play on graves. Dickinson
With fairest flowers,/ Whilst summer lasts.
   Fr. Cymbeline. Shakespeare
Yugoslav Cemetery. Wright
Graves, Robert
My Name and I. Graves
Robert Graves. Ewart
Graveyards. See Cemeteries.
Gravity
Gravity. Nims
If Gravity Were Like Weather. Boston
Gray, Thomas
To Mr. Gray. Warton
**Great Britain. See England; Scotland;
Wales.**
Great Depression
Arizona. *Unknown*
Great Lakes
Aubade: Lake Erie. Merton
Great Lakes of Canada, The. Perry
Lake Superior. Goodrich
Lost. Sandburg
Thousand Islands, The. *Fr.* St. Lawrence
   and the Saguenay. Sangster
Greatness
Great Men Have Been among Us.
   Wordsworth
I Think Continually of Those Who Were
   Truly Great. Spender
Let us now praise famous men. *Fr.*
   Ecclesiasticus.
On the Vanity of Earthly Greatness.
   Guiterman
Song about Great Men, A. Hamburger
See also **Fame.**
Greco, El
High Renaissance. Starbuck

Greece
After Greece. Merrill
At Epidaurus. Durrell
At Lindos. Sarton
Corfou. *Fr.* The Ionian Islands. Milnes
Corinna, to Tanagra, from Athens. Landor
England. Moore
Genius of ancient Greece! whose faithful
   steps. *Fr.* The Pleasures of Imagination.
   Akenside
Greece, *sels.* Haygarth
Greece. Walcott
Greek Archipelagoes. Leigh-Fermor
Happening on Aegina. Logan
Islands, The. Doolittle
Isles of Greece, The. *Fr.* Don Juan. Byron
Isles of Greece, The. Capetanakis
Marco Bozzaris. Halleck
Mycenae. Fisher
Nemea. Durrell
On This Day I Complete My Thirty-sixth
   Year. Byron
Remembering Mykenai. Corn
Samos. *Fr.* Scripts for the Pageant. Merrill
Schoolmaster Abroad, The. Seaman
Song of Greece, The. Chiang Hsun
To a Greek Ship in the Port of Dublin.
   Stanford
Tourists on Paros. Ryan
With the Greeks. Nye
World's great age begins anew, The. *Fr.*
   Hellas: Choruses from "Hellas." Shelley
Written after Swimming from Sestos to
   Abydos. Byron
Greed
Covetousness. Idley
Greedy Richard. Taylor
Pardoner's Tale, The. *Fr.* The Canterbury
   Tales. Chaucer
To a Covetous Churl. May
With Mercy for the Greedy. Sexton
Greek Verse
Voices of Modern Greece (VMG). Edmund
   Keeley *and* Philip Sherrard, trs. *and* eds.
Green (color)
Green. Lawrence
Green Eye, The. Merrill
Variables of Green. Graves
Greene, Graham
Muted Screen of Graham Greene, The.
   McGinley
Greene, Nathanael
To the Memory of the Brave Americans.
   Freneau
Greenhouses
Big Wind. Roethke
Child on Top of a Greenhouse. Roethke
Forcing House. Roethke
Greenland
Greenland Whale Fishery, The. *Unknown*
Greenland Winter, A. Diamond
Gudveig. Berry
Greenwich Village, New York City
Autumn Song on Perry Street. Frankenberg
Sad Song about Greenwich Village, A. Park
Gregory, Lady Augusta
Municipal Gallery Revisited, The. Yeats
Gregory, Robert
In Memory of Major Robert Gregory. Yeats
Grenada
Lament for Maurice Bishop. Fergus
Grenville, Sir Richard
First American Sailors, The. Rice
Greyhounds
Ballad of Master McGrath, A. *Unknown*
Greyhound, The. Barakat
Properties of a Good Greyhound, The.
   Berners

Grief
After great pain, a formal feeling comes.
   Dickinson
After the Burial. Lowell
Alone. Finch
Alone in an Inn at Southampton, April the
   25th, 1737. Hill
Among the Grieving One Should Speak
   Softly. Anhava
Ancient Tear, The. Urbina
And Wilt Thou Leave Me Thus? Wyatt
Andrée Rexroth. Rexroth
Annabel Lee. Poe
Away loose-reined careers of poetry! *Fr.* An
   Elegie upon That Reverend. Mr. Thomas
   Shepard. Oakes
Ballad: "He went with another." Mistral
Ballade: "Lone am I, and would be." Pisan
Bereavement. Browning
Bereft. Hardy
Bereft. Heard
Blackbird calls in grief, The. *Unknown*
Blame Not My Lute for He Must Sound *or*
   Sownde. Wyatt
Break, Break, Break. Tennyson
Brooding Grief. Lawrence
Bustle in a house, The. Dickinson
By Now I Am So Tired of Waiting. Stampa
Calm Is the Morn. *Fr.* In Memoriam A. H.
   H. Tennyson
Carousel, The. Oden
Complaint. Wright
Confession. Herbert
Coronach. *Fr.* The Lady of the Lake.
   Scott
Country Woman Elegy. Gibson
Cross of Snow, The. Longfellow
David's Lament for Jonathan. Abelard
Death of the Flowers, The. Bryant
Describes Rationally the Irrational Effects of
   Love. Juana Inés de la Cruz
Deva-like Barbarian. Wen T'ing-yün
Deva-like Barbarian. Yin O
Dirge, A: "Rough wind, that moanest loud."
   Shelley
Eight-beat Barbarian Tune. Yen Hsüan
Elegy on a Lady, Whom Grief for the Death
   of Her Betrothed Killed. Bridges
Exequy, The. King
Farewell to the Court. Ralegh
First Love. Olds
For Annie. Poe
Forsaken. Schneour
Fountain of tears, river of grief. Pisan
Gathering the Bones Together. Orr
Gingerly walked the hare. *Unknown*
Glory of the Day Was in Her Face, The.
   Johnson
Great grief came over me. Aleqaajik
Grief. Achterberg
Grief. Berry
Grief. Browning
Grief. Díaz Mirón
Grief. *Unknown*
Grief and God. Phillips
Grief Plucked Me Out of Sleep. King
Grieving for Tatsuzo: Today Spring Ended.
   Rai San'yo
Home Burial. Frost
Home-Coming. Ehrenstein
Homer. Ehrenstein
I, a Most Wretched Atlas. *Fr.* Homeward
   Bound. Heine
I am of this world. *Fr.* Manyo Shu.
   Unknown
I Heard of Master Kan's Illness but Couldn't
   Get There in Time. Rai San'yo
I Held It Truth. *Fr.* In Memoriam A. H. H.
   Tennyson
I Write Only to Relieve My Inner Grief.
   Colonna

If Ever Hapless Woman Had a Cause.
Pembroke
If in the World There Be More Woe. Wyatt
In the Silent Night. Peretz
In the Time of Trouble. Clark
Invocation, An: "Last night my soul
departed." O Dalaigh
Kilcash. *Unknown*
Kol Nidra. Leiser
Lament for Te Heuheu Herea. Te Heuheu
Tukino
Lamentations. Brody
Like the sedge of Naniwa. *Fr. Manyo Shu.*
Otomo no Sakanoe
Lost Love. Graves
Lycidas. Milton
Memorial I. Lorde
Missing. Tabb
Monody. Melville
Mourning. Marvell
My Buried Friends. *Unknown*
My eyes are dry of tears. Mir
My grief on the ocean. *Unknown*
My heart no longer is. Momin
"My True Love Hath My Heart and I Have
His." Coleridge
No Worst, There Is None. Hopkins
Not even the moon. Chikako
Not Lost, but Gone Before. Norton
Not Thou but I. Marston
Nurse No Long Grief. Gilmore
Oh, Thou! Who Dry'st the Mourner's Tear.
Moore
On Another's Sorrow. *Fr. Songs of
Innocence.* Blake
On His Deceased Wife. Milton
On My First Son [*or* Sonne]. Jonson
On My Late Dear Wife. Richardson
On My Sorrowful Life. Ibn Ezra
One to Grieve, The. Thomas
Plaint of Flowers, A. Sandeen
Receipt to Cure [*or* for] the Vapours, A.
Montagu
Requiescat. Wilde
Reuben Bright. Robinson
Sad Shepherd, The. Yeats
Simply, it is a man who has died. Sordello
Sleepless Night, A. O'Rahilly
Slow, Slow, Fresh Fount. *Fr. Cynthia's
Revels.* Jonson
Solitude. Monro
Someone passes on. Chikako
Song: "When I am dead, my dearest."
Rossetti
Sonnet: "Because my grief seems quiet and
apart." Nathan
Sonnet: "My soul surcharged with grief now
loud complains." Morpurgo
Sonnet on the Death of Mr. Richard West.
Gray
Sorrow. De Vere
Sorrow. Hummer
Sorrow. Lawrence
Sorrow. Phillips
Sorrow Is the Only Faithful One. Dodson
Spell against Sorrow. Raine
Spiritual Isolation. Rosenberg
Spring and Fall. Hopkins
Stanzas: "With tears thy grief thou dost
bemoan." Ibn Gabirol
Stop All the Clocks, Cut Off the Telephone.
Auden
Sweet after showers, ambrosial air. *Fr. In
Memoriam A. H. H.* Tennyson
Swift Floods. Petröczi
Tears. Vyazemsky
Tears, Idle Tears [I Know Not What They
Mean] *Fr. The Princess.* Tennyson
Telling the Bees. Whittier
There Is No Country. Tuwim
Those bitter feelings. Tamekane
Three Seamstresses, The. Peretz

To Laura in Life. *Fr. Sonnets to Laura.*
Petrarch
To One in Paradise. Poe
Unquiet Grave, The. *Unknown*
Valediction: Forbidding Mourning, A.
Donne
Vesta. Whittier
Victory in Defeat. Markham
Visiting My Wife's Grave. *Fr.
Twenty-seven Hokku.* Natsume Seibi
We are like tears of grief. Nazir
Weeping for Ying Yao. Wang Wei
When I See Another's Pain. Leib
When My Dog Died. Littledale
When she was alive, now a memory. *Fr.
Manyo Shu.* Hitomaro
Wherefore should I seek the bud. Bahadur
Shah Zafar
Widow's Lament in Springtime, The.
Williams
Wine and Grief. Ibn Gabirol
Woodspurge, The. Rossetti
You Will See Far. Kirstinä

Grocers
Holy Song of the Holy Grocer, The. Leivick
London Adulterations. *Unknown*
Shopping. Buddingh'
Song against Grocers, The. Chesterton

Groundhogs
Drumlin Woodchuck, A. Frost
Ground Hog Day. Moore
Groundhog, The. Eberhart
Groundhog, The. Shaw
Woodchuck Who Lives on Top of Mt. Ritter.
Simon
Woodchucks. Kumin

Grouse
Blackcock, The. Baillie
Plea for a Plural, A. Lehmann

Guadalajara, Mexico
Instruction Manual, The. Ashbery

Guatemala
Below Mount T'ui K'oy, Home of the Gods,
Todos Santos Cuchumatán, Guatemalan
Highlands. Stroud
Guatemalan *Huipil.* Sosa
Prayer for the Soul of My Country. Castillo
Salon Chronicle. Paredes
That Sleepless Flame. Obregón

Guérin, Maurice de
Maurice de Guérin. Egan

Guernica, Spain
Remembrances of Guernica. Schmied

Guerrillas
French and the Spanish Guerrillas, The.
Wordsworth
Guerilla, The. *Unknown*
Guerrilla. Pieterse
Guerrilla Promise. Nangolo
Guerrilla's Goodbye, A. Heraud
Guerrilla's Word, A. Heraud
Josina, You Are Not Dead. Machel
My Brother: ("My brother is not he who was
born"). *Unknown*
Requiem for the Croppies. Heaney
This Is the Time. Machel
With the Guerrillas. Pile

Guest, Edgar A.
Edgar A. Guest Considers "The Good Old
Woman Who Lived in a Shoe" and the
Good Old Truths Simultaneously. *Fr.
Mother Goose Up-to-Date.* Untermeyer
Lines to a World-famous Poet Who Failed to
Complete a World-famous Poem; or, Come
Clean, Mr. Guest! Nash

Guests
Doorbells. Field
Guest, a guest, A/ And white his horse.
Unknown
High rise the pole-banners. *Unknown*
In the Valley of the Elwy. Hopkins

Inviting a Friend to Supper. Jonson
See also **Hospitality; Visiting and Visitors.**

Guggenheim, John Simon
No Foundation. Hollander

Guilt
Debt, The. Dunbar
Guilty Even if I Were Innocent. Al-Haidari
Guilty Man. Kailas
Oedipus. Muir
Pursuit. Warren
Sacrifice, The. Bidart
Something Left to Say. Soniat
Song about Major Eatherly, A. Wain
Why Would I Have Survived? Bruck

Guinea Hens
Flock of Guinea Hens Seen from a Car, A.
Welty

Guitars
Guitar. García Lorca
Guitarist Tunes Up, The. Cornford
How a Guitar Can Lie on a Chair. Schippers
I cannot bring a world quite round. *Fr. The
Man with the Blue Guitar.* Stevens
On Learning to Play the Guitar. Fraser
On My Old Ramkiekie. Leipoldt
Six Strings, The. García Lorca

Guiteau, Charles J.
Charles Guiteau. *Unknown*

Gulf Stream
Gulf Stream. "Coolidge"

Gulls
Ballet of the Fifth Year, The. Schwartz
Can't you see it there. Sogi
Dirty-billed Freeze Footy, The.
Hemschemeyer
Even gulls appear to feel cold. *Fr.
Twenty-seven Hokku.* Natsume Seibi
Gull, it is said, The. Nakasuk
Gulls. Williams
Gulls and Dreams. Stevenson
Gulls in an äery morrice. Henley
Lives of Gulls and Children, The. Nemerov
Magic Words to Feel Better. Nakasuk
Sea-Birds. Allen
Sea-Gull, The. Howitt
Sea-Gull, The. Nash
Sea-Gull, The. *Unknown*
Sea-ward, white gleaming through the busy
scud. Coleridge
Seagull, The. Dafydd ap Gwilym
Seagull, The. Phylip
Seagulls. Francis
Seagulls. Hubbell
Seagulls. Updike
Song of the Gull. Maruyama Kaoru
Sorrow of Parting. Maruyama Kaoru
Visit from the Sea, A. Stevenson
Wings. Maruyama Kaoru
Winter seagull, A. Shuson

Gum Trees
Gnarled Riverina Gum-Tree, A. Moll
Snow-Gum, The. Stewart

Gunpowder Plot. *See* **Fawkes, Guy.**

Guns
A. E. F. Sandburg
Arms and the Boy. Owen
Channel Firing. Hardy
Cricket and the Machine Gun, The. Yu
Kuang-chung
Defensive Position. Manifold
Grandpa's .45. Ransom
Gun, The. Dobyns
Gun Emplacement. Maruyama Kaoru
Merle Bascom's .22. Hall
Original Sin. Laing
Take a Gun. Price
Technique on the Firing Line. Cassity
There was a little man,/ And he had a little
gun. Mother Goose
Unarmed Combat. *Fr. Lessons of the War.*
Reed

Gustavus II (Gustavus Adolphus), King of Sweden
Battle Hymn. Altenburg
Guthlac, Saint
Death of Saint Guthlac. *Fr.* Guthlac. Cynewulf
Guy Fawkes Day. *See* Fawkes, Guy.
Guyana
First of August. Seymour
Guyana not Ghana. Matthews
Slaves/ Humming in the twilight by the shanty door. Seymour
Gwyn, Nell
Ballad Called the Haymarket Hectors, A. *Unknown*
Gymnastics
Gymnasts, The. Feldman
Parallel Bars. Stockwell
Uneven Parallel Bars. Gary
Watching Gymnasts. Francis
See also Acrobats.
Gypsies
Dino Campana and the Bear. Hirsch
Gipsies, The. "Scrace"
Gipsy, The. Nazir
Gipsy Man. King
Gipsy-Night. Hughes
Gypsies. Field
Gypsies. *Fr.* The Country Justice. Langhorne
Gypsies. Nowlan
Gypsy, The. Thomas
Gypsy Countess, The. *Unknown*
Gypsy Laddie, The. *Unknown*
Idlers, The. Blunden
Isabel. Hovey
Johnny Faa, the Lord of Little Egypt. *Unknown*
Lady and the Gypsy, The. Scannell
Meg Merrilees [*or* Merrilees]. Keats
Men That Don't Fit In, The. Service
On Jessy Watson's Elopement. Fleming
Plaça Santiago, The. *Fr.* The Spanish Gypsy. "Eliot"
Quit now the town, and with a journeying dream. *Fr.* The Spanish Gypsy. "Eliot"
Scholar-Gipsy, The. Arnold
Sea Gypsy, The. Hovey
Song: "Trip it Gipsies, Trip it Fine." *Fr.* The Spanish Gipsy [*or* Gypsy]. Middleton
Where Do the Gipsies Come From? Bashford
Wraggle Taggle Gipsies, The. *Unknown*

H

Habits
Builder's Lesson, A. O'Reilly
Hades
Hades and Euclid. Martinson
Hael, Ifor
Hall of Ifor Hael, The. Evans
Hafiz
To Hafiz. Aldrich
Hagar
Expulsion of Hagar, The. Bibb
Hagar and Ishmael. Lasker-Schüler
Hagar Leaves Abraham's House. Manger
Hagar to Ishmael. Eibel
Haggard, Sir Henry Rider
To R. K. Stephen
Haiku (form)
Absent Friends. *Fr.* Separation. Bloch
As It Was. Mander
Campfire Extinguished. Roseliep
Dreams. Bloch
Outer Space Haiku. Disch

Pied à Terre. Bloch
Senryu. Frazier
They Didn't Hire Him. *Fr.* Hitch Haiku. Snyder
Winter seagull, A. Shuson
Hail
Ballad of the Strange and Wonderful Storm of Hail, A. *Unknown*
Following the wind. Tameko
In a field with scentless winter trees. *Fr.* Twenty-one Hokku. Kaya Shirao
In my native home. Ietaka
In the snow piled. *Fr.* Twenty-three Tanka. Tamekane
Night hailstones fall so hard. *Fr.* Twenty-one Hokku. Kaya Shirao
Starting, then stopping. Tamekane
Hair
Bald. Zavatsky
Black of my hair, The. Teika
Boy with His Hair Cut Short. Rukeyser
Buy me a Kyoto comb, yes, a Kyoto comb! *Unknown*
Combing. Cardiff
"Do it up!" *Fr.* Manyo Shu. Mikata Shami
Everyone says "It's so long—put it up!" *Fr.* Manyo Shu. Mikata no Sami
First Grey Hair, The. Tucker
For Anne Gregory. Yeats
For Muh' Dear. Rodgers
Girl with Long Dark Hair. Gray
Girl's Hair, A. Dafydd ab Edmwnd
Hair. al-Sa'igh
Hair. Silverman
Hair washed,/ she wrings it out. *Unknown*
Haircut. May
Haircut. Shapiro
I will not comb my morning hair. *Fr.* Manyo Shu. *Unknown*
If tied, it would slip off. *Fr.* Manyo Shu. Mikata Shami
Keeping Hair. Wilson
Lady in the Barbershop, The. Rudnik
Maiden and Her Hair, A. Davies
My tangled hair. *Fr.* Manyo Shu. *Unknown*
Oh Who Is That Young Sinner with the Handcuffs on His Wrists? Housman
On Getting a Natural. Randall
On Seeing a Hair of Lucretia Borgia. Landor
Plaits. Tuckett
Rape of the Lock, The. Pope
Song Called "His Hide Is Covered with Hair," The. Belloc
There's even someone combing her hair. *Fr.* Twenty-one Hokku. Kaya Shirao
Those long black tresses. Teika
Washing My Hair. Tadaomi
"What guile [*or* guyle] is this, that those her golden tresses." *Fr.* Amoretti, XXXVII. Spenser
Wrapped Hair Bundles. Tauhindauli
Your Hair. Kim Chun-soo
Your hair comes undone when you put it up. *Fr.* Manyo Shu. Mikata no Sami
Hairdressers
Elaine. *Fr.* Calling Your Name in the Zoo. Williams
Haiti
Haitian Suite. Orr
Hale, Nathan
Nathan Hale. Finch
Nathan Hale. Partridge
Nathan Hale. *Unknown*
Halevi, Judah
If, Jerusalem, I Ever Should Forget Thee. Heine
Haley, Alex
For Kinte. La Grone
Hallam, Arthur Henry
Clevedon Church. Lang

Halloween
Hallowe'en. Behn
Hallowe'en. Farjeon
Halloween. Livingston
Hallowe'en. Moorer
Halloween Witches. Holman
Hist Whist. Cummings
It's Halloween. Prelutsky
Lazy Witch. Livingston
Mr. Macklin's Jack O'Lantern ("Mr. Macklin takes his knife"). McCord
October Magic. Livingston
On Halloween. Fisher
Skeleton Parade. Prelutsky
This Is Halloween. Thompson
What Night Would It Be? Ciardi
Halpern, Moyshe Leyb
Memento Mori. Halpern
Why Not. Halpern
Ham
Messengers. Glück
Notes for a Southern Road Map. McGinley
Smithfield Ham. Smith
Hamer, Fannie Lou
Remembering Fannie Lou Hamer. Davis
Hamlet
Elegy of Fortinbras. Herbert
Hamlet. al-Bayati
Midrash on Hamlet. Landy
Ophelia. Hillman
They All Want to Play Hamlet. Sandburg
Hammocks
Hammock. Horiguchi Daigaku
Hampstead Heath, London
Breath of Hampstead Heath. Thomas
Hamsters
Hamsters. Ridlon
Han-shan
Poem to Han-shan. Stroud
Handball
Day and Night Handball. Dunn
Game Resumed. Lattimore
Handicaps and the Handicapped
Disabled. Owen
Freaks at Spurgin Road Field, The. Hugo
Hunchback in the Park, The. Thomas
Near the School for Handicapped Children. Shapcott
See also Amputees; Birth Defects; Blindness; Cripples; Deafness; Mental Retardation.
Hands
Haiku: "Holding a child's hand intently." *Fr.* One Hundred Haiku in Free Form. Hosai
Hand, The. Moss
Hand, The. Thomas
Hand That Signed the Paper Felled a City, The. Thomas
Hands. Finkel
Hands. Glasgow
Hands, The. Harrison
Hands. Stevenson
I pound the rice. *Fr.* Manyo Shu. *Unknown*
Look to the Back of the Hand. Minty
Love for a Hand. Shapiro
Palm of the Hand. Rilke
Sketch of Hands. Koh Chang-soo
Study: A Hand. Raba
This Living Hand Now Warm and Capable. Keats
Two Hands. Sexton
Wukhand. Keens-Douglas
Your Hand in Mine. Aleixandre
Your Hands. Grimké
Handwriting
Lesson in Handwriting, A. Reid
Writing. Nemerov
Hanging
Clever Tom Clinch Going to Be Hanged. Swift

Constance Kent. *Unknown*
Danny Deever. Kipling
Eight o'Clock. Housman
Epitaph: "They hanged him on a clement
  morning, swung." Scott
Example, The. Díaz Mirón
Geordie. *Unknown*
Hang Me, O Hang Me, and I'll Be Dead and
  Gone. *Unknown*
Hanged Man, The. Simon
Hanging, A. Chipasula
Hanging, The. MacDonald
Hanging of Sam Archer, The. *Unknown*
Jack Hall. *Unknown*
Jeff Buckner. Beddo
Kevin Barry: Died for Ireland, 1st November,
  1920. *Unknown*
Life of the Mannings. *Unknown*
London Fete, A. Patmore
Marrying the Hangman. Atwood
Murder of Maria Marten, The. Corder
Night before Larry Was Stretched, The.
  Unknown
Portent, The. Melville
Receipt to Cure a Love Fit, A. *Unknown*
Sam Hall. *Unknown*
Scaffold, The. Dunqul
Sonnet: Of Why He Is Unhanged. Angiolieri
  da Siena
See also **Executions; Lynching.**

Hanks, Nancy
Nancy Hanks, Mother of Abraham Lincoln.
  Lindsay
Out of the Wilderness. Troubetzkoy

Hansel and Gretel
Hansel and Gretel. Sexton

Hanukkah
Dreidel Song. Rosenzweig
Kindle the Taper. Lazarus
Light Another Candle. Chaikin
Light the Festive Candles. Fisher

Happiness
Anatomy of Happiness, The. Nash
Blessing, A. Wright
Character of a Happy Life, The. Wotton
Choice, The. Pomfret
Cliff Klingenhagen. Robinson
Eskimo Occasion. Rodriguez
Example, The. Davies
Four Things Make Us Happy Here. Herrick
Good Times. Clifton
Happiness. Leonard
Happiness. Sandburg
Happiness Is When. *Fr.* Thirty Tanka.
  Tachibana Akemi
Happiness Makes Up in Height for What It
  Lacks in Length. Frost
Happy Heart, A. Heard
Happy Thought. Stevenson
If You Happy Would Be. Fernández
Joy. Delany
Joy of Fishes, The. Chuang Tzu
L'Allegro. Milton
Moments of happiness, The. Mir
Moments-of-Past-Happiness Quilt, The.
  Spivack
On Frozen Fields. Kinnell
On the South Downs. Teasdale
Rarely, Rarely, Comest Thou. Shelley
Running. Wilbur
Song of Delight. Shao Yung
Starlight. Levine
III, 29. "Descended of an ancient line"
  ("Tyrrhena regum progenies"). *Fr.* Odes.
  Horace
To-day, when people in China, it is said.
  Fr. Manyo Shu. Yakamochi
Today Was Not. Rosen
Waking ("I strolled across/ An open field"),
  The. Roethke
Wish, A. Rogers

Wishes. Harjo
See also **Contentment.**

Harbors and Ports
Cinque Port, A. Davidson
Harbor, The. Sandburg
Harbor Dawn, The. *Fr.* The Bridge:
  Powhatan's Daughter. Crane
In the Lake of Omi. *Fr.* Manyo Shu.
  Unknown
In the Port. Weinstein
Long Harbour, The. Bethell
On the Docks. Vaynshteyn
Outward Bound. Aldrich
Ports. Vas

Hardin, John Wesley
Wes Hardin: From a Photograph. Carver

Harding, Warren Gamaliel
Two Poems about President Harding. Wright

Hardy, Thomas
Heart of Thomas Hardy, The. Betjeman
Luncheon, A. Beerbohm
Scholars. De la Mare
Thomas Hardy. De la Mare

Hares
Cowper's Tame Hare. Nicholson
Cowper's Three Hares. Turner
Dance, The. Davies
Ecclesiastes. Langland
Epitaph on a Hare. Cowper
Hare. Holden
Hare, The. Sisson
Hare and the Tortoise, The. Serraillier
Hare in the Moon, The. Ryokan
Hare in the Snow, The. Rawlinson
Hare in Winter. Piercy
Hares at Play. Clare
Interruption to a Journey. MacCaig
Lullaby: "Hare, Mr. Hare." *Unknown*
Names of the Hare, The. *Unknown*
Poor Wat. *Fr.* Venus and Adonis.
  Shakespeare
Trapped Hare, The. Dowling
Two Songs of a Fool. Yeats
See also **Rabbits.**

Harlem, New York City
Esthete in Harlem. Hughes
Harlem. Hughes
Harlem—a Negro Ghetto. Vaynshteyn
Harlem at Night. Ausländer
Harlem Dancer, The. McKay
Harlem Freeze Frame. Bethune
Harlem Gallery: From the Inside. Neal
Harlem in January. Fields
Harlem Negroes. *Fr.* Negroes. Vaynshteyn
Harlem Shadows. McKay
Harlem Sounds: Hallelujah Corner. Browne
Harlem Sweeties. Hughes
Jitterbugging in the Streets. Hernton
Juke Box Love Song. Hughes
Keep on Pushing. Henderson
Lenox Avenue. Alexander
Night Funeral in Harlem. Hughes
Prime. Hughes
Sketches of Harlem. Henderson
Sonnet to a Negro in Harlem. Johnson
Still Voice of Harlem, The. Rivers
Train Runs Late to Harlem, The. Rivers
Under the Edge of February. Cortez
Walk with de Mayor of Harlem. Henderson
Young Negro Poet. Hernton

Harper's Ferry, West Virginia
Harpers Ferry. Rodman
How Old Brown Took Harper's Ferry.
  Stedman
Narrative. Atkins

Harps and Harpists
Bishop's Harp, The. Mannyng
Dear Harp of My Country. Moore
Harp of Wild and Dream-like Strain. Brontë
Harp That Once through Tara's Halls, The.
  Moore

Harper, The. *Unknown*
Military Harpist, The. Pitter
Minstrel Boy, The. Moore
Ode to David's Harp. Rosenberg
Silence, The. Mac Siomoin

Harpur, Charles
Extinct Birds. Wright

Harrison, Benjamin
Historical Reflections. Hollander

Hartley, Marsden
Vision of Marsden Hartley, The. Haines

Harvard University
I Went to See Irving Babbitt. Eberhart
In and Out, *sel.* Sissman
Ode Recited at the Harvard Commemoration.
  Lowell
To the University of Cambridge, in
  New-England. Wheatley

Harvest
Antique Harvesters. Ransom
August. Fallon
Big field brings a heavy crop, The.
  Unknown
Harvest, The. Al-Khal
Harvest. Anderson
Harvest. Cortissoz
Harvest. Hutchinson
Harvest. Shuford
Harvest and Consecration. Jennings
Harvest Home. *Fr.* King Arthur. Dryden
Harvest Home. Guiterman
Harvest Poem. Fisher
Harvest Song. Campbell
Harvest Song. Toomer
Harvest Song. *Unknown*
Harvest Time. Powers
Harvest Time. Watermeyer
Hay Fever. Hope
Haying. Herbin
Ho, ho, my servants and officers! *Unknown*
Hock-Cart, or Harvest Home, The. Herrick
Hurrahing in Harvest. Hopkins
Potato Harvest, The. Roberts
Praise of Ceres. *Fr.* The Silver Age.
  Heywood
Reaper, The. Allen
Reapers. Blind
Reapers. Toomer
Returning from Harvest. Watkins
Ripe and Bearded Barley, The. *Unknown*
Solitary Reaper, The. Wordsworth
Soon as the harvest hath laid bare the plains.
  Fr. The Thresher's Labour. Duck
Threshing Machine, The. Meynell
Threshing Machine. Szabo
Very sharp, the good shares. *Unknown*
Village people/ will be out picking young
  greens, The. Tameie
Youth Mowing, A. Lawrence

Hashish
Haschish, The. Whittier

Hasidism
Bratslaver to His Scribe, The. Glatstein
Invocation: "Good morning to you, Lord of
  the world!" Levi Yitzhok
Nakhman of Bratslav to His Scribe.
  Glatstein
Saint Besht. Manger

Hate
Beyond Words. Frost
Enslaved. McKay
Epitaph of Nearchos. Ammianus
Fire and Ice. Frost
Fury's Field. Bodker
Hate. Stephens
Hate-Song, A. Shelley
Hatred. Bennett
I Hate Harry. Chaikin
I Saw a Little Girl I Hate. Spilka

Iceball, The. Hathaway
Litany of Hate, A. Vivien
Love and Hate. *Unknown*
On Love. *Fr.* Twenty-three Tanka.
  Tamekane
Soliloquy of the Spanish Cloister. Browning
Song of Hate. Frances
Stone Orchard, The. Oates
To———: "When I loved you, I can't but
  allow." Moore
Transformations. Harjo
Tree of Hatred, The. Moreh
Tygers of Wrath (TW). X. J. Kennedy, ed.

Hats
Alicia's Bonnet. Pullen
At the Millinery Shop. Epstein
Easter Bonnet, The. Thompson
Glass Hat, The. Kálnoky
Hat Bar. Weston
Little Jesus of the Barren, The. Nagy
My Hat. Smith
My Infundibuliform Hat. Adams
My Ol' Stetson. Barton
My Old Straw Hat. Cook
Quangle Wangle's Hat, The. Lear
Saint Wears a Halo, The. "Peter"
When Polly Buys a Hat. Hill

Haunted Houses
Empty House, The. Hoban
Ghost House. Frost
Haunted House. Worth
Haunted Palace, The. Poe
In the Old House. Aiken
Southern Mansion. Bontemps

Hawaii
Above the Falls at Waimea. Johnson
Born was the island. *Unknown*
Kula. a Homecoming. Mark
Leper, The. Ka-'ehu
Mango Tree, The. Chock
Poet Imagines His Grandfather's Thoughts on
  the Day He Died, The. Lum
Twenty-third Flight. Birney
Waikiki. Brooke

Hawks
Ah Wretched Me, Who Loved a Sparrow
  Hawk. *Unknown*
Evening Hawk. Warren
Hawk, The. Brown
Hawk. Hellaakoski
Hawk, The. Knister
Hawk. Turner
Hawk Is a Woman. Flanner
Hawk Nailed to a Barn Door. Blue Cloud
Hawk Roosting. Hughes
Hurt Hawks. Jeffers
In the far realm of our Lord. *Fr.* Manyo
  Shu. Yakamochi
In this distant outpost. *Fr.* Manyo Shu.
  Yakamochi
Old Night Hawk, The. Kiskaddon
Sharp-Shin. Wagoner
Sparrow Hawk, The. Hoban
Sparrow-Hawk, A. *Unknown*
Tamer and Hawk. Gunn
To a Marsh Hawk in Spring. Thoreau
To the Man-of-War-Bird. Whitman
Windhover, The. Hopkins
Wounded Hawk, The. Palmer

Hawthorn
Haw Lantern, The. Heaney
Hawthorn, The. *Unknown*
Hawthorn Hedge, The. Wright
I Bended unto Me. Brown

Hawthorne, Nathaniel
Hawthorne. Alcott
Hawthorne. Longfellow
Hawthorne. *Fr.* A Fable for Critics. Lowell
Hawthorne Garland, A. Fogle

Monody. Melville
On Visiting the Graves of Hawthorne and
  Thoreau. Very
Hayden Planetarium (New York City)
Ode to the Hayden Planetarium. Guiterman
Hayden, Robert
Healing Song. Harper
Haydn, Franz Joseph
To Haydn. Holcroft
Haydon, Benjamin Robert
Great Spirits Now on Earth. Keats
Haze. *See Fog.*
Heads
Head, The. Cendrars
Head Is a Paltry Matter, The. Di Cicco
Thoughts on One's Head. Meredith
Heaney, Seamus
Letter to Seamus Heaney. Longley
Hearne, Samuel
Samuel Hearne in Wintertime. Newlove
Hearst, William Randolph
Doxology. Taylor
Hearts
Heart, The. Ignatow
In the Desert. *Fr.* The Black Riders. Crane
Repose. Marson
To a Bad Heart. Reynolds
To pray for an easy heart is no prayer at all.
  Fr. Autumn Testament. Baxter
Heat
August Heat. *Unknown*
Central Heating System. Spender
Child I carry on my back, The. *Fr.* Fifteen
  Hokku. Shiba Sonome
Cool Web, The. Graves
Floating cloud before my eyes, The. *Fr.*
  Twenty-one Hokku. Kaya Shirao
Heat. Doolittle
Heat. Lampman
Heat. Mackenzie
Heat's so intense I dry my towel, The. *Fr.*
  Fifteen Hokku. Shiba Sonome
Hot is the sun, so hot the birds complain.
  Dabir
In this heat. *Fr.* Twenty Hokku. Kyorai
January. Voigt
Shade-Seller, The. Jacobsen
Sitting at an edge. *Fr.* Eighty-seven Hokku.
  Buson
Heather
Erica. Bethell
Heather Flowers. Williams
Heaven
As Pants the Hart. Tate
As Weary Pilgrim, Now at Rest. Bradstreet
Blessed Damozel, The. Rossetti
Bower of Bliss, The. *Fr.* The Faerie
  Queene. Spenser
By good luck a few days back. Montaudon
Cold Heaven, The. Yeats
Eager he look'd. Another train of years. *Fr.*
  The Columbiad. Barlow
End of the Way, The. Cole
Eternal Light! Binney
Fair is Our Lord's Own City. *Unknown*
Far Land, The. Wheelock
Fiddler's Green. Conolly
For a Lady I Know. *Fr.* Four Epitaphs.
  Cullen
General William Booth Enters into Heaven.
  Lindsay
Glorious Things of Thee Are Spoken.
  Newton
God's Trails Lead Home. Clements
Gradatim. Holland
He Will Give Them Back. "Klingle"
He Would Have His Lady Sing. Dolben
Heaven. Brooke
Heaven. Herbert
Heaven. Moss

Heaven. *Unknown*
Heaven and Hell. Nalungiaq
Heaven-Haven. Hopkins
Heaven, Heaven, Heaven Is the Place.
  Hughes
Heaven is what I cannot reach. Dickinson
Heaven of Animals, The. Dickey
Heavenly City, The. Smith
Hold the Wind. Villon
Holy City, The. Weatherly
Home at Last. Chesterton
Home of the Soul. Gates
Homeland, The. Haweis
Hour of Peaceful Rest, The. Tappan
Hymn for the Close of the Week. Abelard
I ascended to heaven again last week.
  Montaudon
I never saw a moor. Dickinson
I went to heaven. Dickinson
If Thou Indeed Derive Thy Light from
  Heaven. Wordsworth
If to Die. Romilu
Immortal is an ample word. Dickinson
Jerusalem, My Happy Home. *Unknown*
Kubla Khan; or, A Vision in a Dream.
  Coleridge
Land o' the Leal, The. Nairne
Land of the Evening Mirage, The. *Unknown*
Last Landlord, The. Allen
Leave Me, O Love. Sidney
Let Us Go Down, the Long Dead Night Is
  Done. *Fr.* Towards the Source. Brennan
Life Above, the Life on High, The. Theresa
Life after Death. Pindar
Love thou saist. *Fr.* Paradise Lost. Milton
My Ain Countree. Demarest
Nearer Home. Cary
No sooner had th' Almighty ceas't, but all.
  Fr. Paradise Lost. Milton
Nothing in Heaven Functions as It Ought.
  Kennedy
O Mother Dear, Jerusalem. "F. B. P."
O Paradise! O Paradise! Faber
Oh that I was the Bird of Paradise! *Fr.*
  Preparatory Meditations before My
  Approach to the Lord's Supper. Taylor
Other World, The. Stowe
Our Companie in the Next World. *Fr.* Of
  the Progresse of the Soule; the Second
  Anniversarie. Donne
Out of the Hitherwhere. Riley
Paradise. Rossetti
Paradise Lost, *sels.* Milton
Peace. Vaughan
Pieces of Heaven, The. Rogers
Plains of Heaven, The. Goldensohn
Port of Many Ships. Masefield
Report from Paradise. Herbert
Reverence, reverence! *Unknown*
Saint Peter sat by the celestial gate. *Fr.* The
  Vision of Judgment. Byron
Seek Flowers of Heaven. Southwell
Sister Lou. Brown
Song: "It Autumnne was, and on our
  hemisphere." Drummond
Sonnet: To That Fair Kingdom, O My Gentle
  Lord. Boccaccio
Soul's Desire, The. *Unknown*
Stairway up to heaven, The. *Fr.* Manyo
  Shu. *Unknown*
There is a land of pure delight. Watts
They Are All Gone into the World of Light.
  Vaughan
Thy Heaven. Moore
Tired of Towns. Lang
To Heaven. Jonson
True Heaven, The. Hayne
Uphill [*or* Up-Hill]. Rossetti
What Is Heaven? Bailey

What is—"Paradise." Dickinson
White Island; or, The Place of the Blest [or Blessed], The. Herrick

Hebe
Hebe. Lowell

Hebrew
Hebrew of Your Poets, Zion, The. Reznikoff

Hebrides
Beckon Me, Ye Cuillins. Hendrie
Island of Mull.
Island of Rhum, The. Ferguson
Misty Island, The. *Unknown*
Nightmare on Rhum. Macmillan
Skye. Gawsworth
There Are Gods. Riley
View. Munro
Witch, The. *Fr.* Skye. Gibson

Hector
Achilles with wild fury in his heart. *Fr.* The Iliad. Homer
Ballad of Hector in Hades. Muir
Hector. Iremonger

Hedgehogs
Hedgehog, The. Bell
Hedgehog, The. King
Hedgehog. Muldoon
To a Hedgehog. Thompson

Heidelberg, Germany
Garden at Heidelberg. Landor
Thinking of Hölderlin. Middleton

Heine, Heinrich
Heinrich Heine. Lewisohn
Translator to Translated. Pound
Venus of the Louvre. Lazarus

Helen of Troy
Ah, Faustus,/ Now hast thou but one bare hour [or hower] to live. *Fr.* Doctor Faustus. Marlowe
Ganymede and Helen. *Unknown*
Helen. Doolittle
Helen. Valéry
Helen Grown Old. Lewis
Helen like the Rose. *Fr.* The Powers of the Pen. Lloyd
Helen—Old. MacKay
Mythmaking. Spivack
Past ruin'd Ilion Helen lives. *Fr.* Ianthe. Landor
So we were together. *Fr.* Winter Love. Doolittle
To Helen. Poe
Under a Lady's Picture. Waller
Was this the face that launched a thousand ships? *Fr.* Doctor Faustus. Marlowe
White Isle of Leuce, The. Read
White Queen. Fuller

Helicopters
Flight Plan. Merchant

Heliogabalus
Heliogabalus. Hollander

Hell
Arrival in Hell. Huch
Did I hear you ask. *Fr.* Sixty-four Tanka. Saigyo
Dungeon horrible, on all sides round, A. *Fr.* Paradise Lost. Milton
Good Man in Hell, The. Muir
Heaven and Hell. Nalungiaq
Hell is a city much like London. *Fr.* Peter Bell the Third. Shelley
In Hell. Jarman
Jews in Hell, The. Goldemberg
Lament of an Idle Demon. Lister
Nothing in Heaven Functions as It Ought. Kennedy
Pan Cogito's Thoughts on Hell. Herbert
Paradise Lost, *sels.* Milton
Poets of Hell, The. Shapiro
Proof. Milosz
Simon Legree—a Negro Sermon. *Fr.* The Booker Washington Trilogy. Lindsay

Strange Meeting. Owen
There is a place,/ List, daughter! in a black and hollow vault. *Fr.* 'Tis Pity She's a Whore. Ford
To Dives. Belloc
Warm Babies. Preston
Where are you damn'd? *Fr.* Doctor Faustus. Marlowe

Hell's Angels
Black Jackets. Gunn

Heloise. *See* **Abelard and Heloise.**

Helsinki, Finland
Helsinki. *Fr.* Ballad of Herman's Rose. Turtiainen
I Live in Helsinki. Saarikoski

Hemingway, Ernest
To Ernest Hemingway. al-Bayati

Hemlocks
Bonus. Ammons

Hengist
Hengest Cyning. Borges

Henie, Sonja
Sonja Henie Sonnet. Field

Henry II, King of England
King Henry to Rosamond. *Fr.* England's Heroical Epistles. Drayton
Queen Eleanor's Confession. *Unknown*

Henry V, King of England
King Henry Fifth's Conquest of France. *Unknown*

Henry VIII, King of England
Ballade of the Scottyshe Kynge, A. Skelton

Henry, King of England
Henry VIII. *Unknown*
Tudor Portrait. Lattimore
White Ship, The. Rossetti

Henry the Navigator
Portrait of Prince Henry, The. Clouts
Prince Henry the Navigator. Clouts

Hens
Browny Hen, The. Pawsey
Clucking Hen, The. *Unknown*
Cock and the Hen, The. Heywood
Flock of Guinea Hens Seen from a Car, A. Welty
Hen, The. Douglas
Hen. Eluard
Hen, The. Morgenstern
Hen Flower, The. Kinnell
Hen It Is a Noble Beast, The. McGonagall
Hen under Bay-Tree. Pitter
Hens, The. Roberts
Hen's Nest. Clare
Higgledy, piggledy, my black hen. Mother Goose
Motherhood. Calverley
See also **Chickens.**

Heraclitus
From Heraclitus. Dugan
Heraclitus. Cory
That Nature Is a Heraclitean Fire and of the Comfort of the Resurrection. Hopkins

Herbs
Basil. Ruark
Lines with a Gift of Herbs. Lewis
Nosegay Always Sweet, for Lovers to Send for Tokens of Love at New Year's Tide, or for Fairings, A ("Nosegay, lacking flowers fresh,"). Hunnis
Old Man. Thomas

Hercules
Antaeus; a Fragment. Owen
Heracles. Winters

Herding
How Low Is the Lowing Herd. Kelly
Tilly. Joyce
See also **Shepherds and Shepherdesses.**

Hermit Crabs
With the Shell of a Hermit Crab. Wright
Your Name in Arezzo. Wright

Hermits
Black Jess. Dufault
Bushed. Birney
Desire for Hermitage, The. *Unknown*
Eremites, The. Graves
He told the crowd "The devils." *Fr.* A Short Life of the Hermit. Logan
Hermit, The. Bibb
Hermit, The. Bly
Hermit, The. Davies
Hermit, The. Hsü Pên
Hermit and the Soul, The. Ray
Hermit Feng's Residence on the Lake. Hsü Pen
Hermit Marbán, The. *Unknown*
Hermit's Song, A. *Unknown*
Marban, a Hermit Speaks. *Unknown*
Remodeling the Hermit's Cabin. Chappell
Saying Good-Bye to Feng the Hermit. Mo Shih-lung
Shack Poem. Bly
Three Hermits, The. Yeats
To a Hermit in the Mountains. Hsü Pen
Wish of Manchin of Liath, The. *Unknown*

Hero and Leander
Hero and Leander. Marlowe
On a Landscape of Sestos. *Fr.* A Visit to the Art Gallery. Baker
On Leander's Swimming over the Hellespont to Hero. Warton
Subjectivity at Sestos. Hubbard
Written after Swimming from Sestos to Abydos. Byron

Herod the Great
Clap Your Hands for Herod. Hanzlik
Coventry Carol, The. *Unknown*
Herod. Leyeles
Innocents, The. Macpherson
Innocent's Song. Causley

Heroes and Heroines
About the Hero. Ladányi
Ballad of Heroes, A. Dobson
Casabianca. Hemans
Casey at the Bat. Thayer
Commemorative of a Naval Victory. Melville
Critics say that epics have died out, The. *Fr.* Aurora Leigh. Browning
Emily Geiger. *Unknown*
For the Union Dead. Lowell
From Scars Where Kestrels Hover. Auden
Heroes. Creeley
Heroes, The. Simpson
Heroisms. "Marie"
Hervé Riel. Browning
How Sleep the Brave. Collins
I Think Continually of Those Who Were Truly Great. Spender
Man from the Crowd, The. Foss
Molly Pitcher. Richards
New Hunting Song, A. *Unknown*
O What Is That Sound [Which So Thrills the Ear]. Auden
Poem for Heroes, A. Fields
Settling Some Old Football Scores. Bishop
Sinfonia Eroica. James
Song for the Heroes. Comfort
Where Are You Now Superman? Patten
Where, O Where? Bracker
Who'd Be a Hero (Fictional)? Bishop

Heroin. *See* **Drug Addiction.**

Herons
Blue Heron, The. Roberts
Cutting past the front. Hanazono
Evening wind: the water strikes. *Fr.* Eighty-seven Hokku. Buson
Great Blue Heron, The. Kizer
Heron. Booth
Heron, The. Donaghy
Heron, The. Roethke
Heron. Walker

Heron, The. Watkins
Heron in Swamp. Howard
Heron Standing in a River, A. Shotetsu
Herons, The. Ledwidge
In the sleet too, the heron. *Fr.* Thirty-three
    Hokku. Kikaku
Night Heron. Frost
Snowy Heron. Ciardi
Spring breeze. Raizan
Herrick, Robert
To his book's end this last line he'd have
    placed. Herrick
Herring
Caller Herrin.' Nairne
Herrings. *Fr.* Verses for Fruitwomen.
    Swift
Red Herring, The. MacBeth
Smoked Herring, The. Cros
Hervey, William. *See* **Harvey, William.**
Herzl, Theodor
Theodor Herzl. Zangwill
Hess, Dame Myra
Jesu, Joy of Man's Desiring. Fitzgerald
Hiawatha
Give me of your bark, O Birch-tree! *Fr.* The
    Song of Hiawatha. Longfellow
Hiawatha's Photographing. "Carroll"
Song of Hiawatha, The, *sels.* Longfellow
What I Think of Hiawatha. Morris
Hiccups
Charm: Hiccups. *Unknown*
Hicks, Edward
For Edward Hicks. Helwig
Highlands of Scotland. *See* **Scottish**
    Highlands.
Highwaymen
Brennan on the Moor. *Unknown*
Death of Morgan, The. *Unknown*
Execution of Luke Hutton, The. *Unknown*
Highwayman, The. Noyes
Mulberry Mountain. *Unknown*
Rambling Boy, The. *Unknown*
Wild Colonial Boy, The. *Unknown*
Highways. *See* **Roads.**
Hiking and Hikers
Crossing the Alps. *Fr.* The Prelude [or,
    Growth of a Poet's Mind]: Cambridge and
    the Alps. Wordsworth
Hills and Mountains
Above crimson leaves. Teika
Afternoon on a Hill. Millay
Alaskan Mountain Poem #1. Silko
Alpine. Thomas
Alpine Spirit's Song. Beddoes
Among the Finger Lakes. Wallace
Ave Caesar. Jeffers
Childhood and School-Time. *Fr.* The
    Prelude [or, Growth of a Poet's Mind].
    Wordsworth
Circumambulation of Mt. Tamalpais. Hoyem
Climbing in Glencoe. Young
Close-up. Ammons
Dark Hills, The. Robinson
Fable: Mountain and the Squirrel, The.
    Emerson
Golgotha Is a Mountain. Bontemps
Grongar Hill. Dyer
Having Climbed to the Topmost Peak of the
    Incense-Burner Mountain. Po Chü-i
Hike, The. Weiss
Hill, A. Hecht
Hills and the Sea, The. Campbell
In dawn's early glow. Tameie
In the Mountains on a Summer Day. Li Po
In the Selkirks. Scott
Mid-August at Sourdough Mountain Lookout.
    Snyder
Mountain, The. Frost
Mountain Barrier. Su Shao-lien
Mountain sat upon the plain, The. Dickinson
Mountain Talk. Ammons

Mountains. Auden
Mountains, The. De la Mare
Mountains, The. Gibson
Mountains. Larcom
Mountains grow unnoticed, The. Dickinson
Nocturne of the Self-evident Presence.
    MacGreevy
Object Lesson. Henderson
Olives and Mountains. *Fr.* Aurora Leigh.
    Browning
On Middleton Edge. Young
Pennines in April. Hughes
Pilgrimage Song. *Unknown*
Quantocks, The. Wordsworth
Schreckhorn, The. Hardy
Shancoduff. Kavanagh
Sleeping Giant, The. Hall
Survey, A. Stafford
That Dark Other Mountain. Francis
To My Mountain. Raine
To Walk on Hills. Graves
Trosachs, The. Wordsworth
Up to thy summit, Lewesdon, to the brow.
    Fr. Lewesdon Hill. Crowe
Ute Mountain. Tomlinson
With Hands like Leaves. Still
Poems of the Scottish Hills (PoSH). Hamish
    Brown, ed.
See also **Mountain Climbing.**
Hilo, Hawaii
Hongo Store 29 Miles Volcano Hilo, Hawaii,
    The. Hongo
Hinduism
Hymn to Tirumal (Visnu). Kirantaiyar
Indian upon God, The [*or* an]. Yeats
Mahabalipuram. MacNeice
Murukan: His Places. Nakkiranar
Murukan, the Red One. Nakkiranar
Studies at Delhi, 1876. Lyall
Tirumal. Katuvan Ilaveyinanar
Songs of the Saints of India (SSI). John
    Stratton Hawley, ed.
Hippies
False Youth: Autumn: Clothes of the Age.
    Dickey
Hippopotamuses
Dawn Hippo. Clouts
Habits of the Hippopotamus. Guiterman
Hippo, The. Roethke
Hippopotamothalamion. Wheelock
Hippopotamus, The. Belloc
Hippopotamus. Cole
Hippopotamus, The. Eliot
Hippopotamus, The. Nash
Hippopotamus, The. Prelutsky
Hippopotamus's Birthday, The. Rieu
I Had a Hippopotamus. Barrington
I had a hippopotamus; I loved him as a friend.
    Fr. I Had a Hippopotamus. Barrington
To a Blue Hippopotamus. Kay
Trauma. Leithauser
Hips
Homage to My Hips. Clifton
Hirohito, Emperor
Emperor, The. Ryuichi
Hiroshige, Ando
Hiroshige. Perlberg
Hiroshima, Japan
Day after Trinity, The. Oyama
Hiroshima. Beadnell
Hiroshima Bomb, The. Roversi
Hiroshima Exit. Kogawa
Lot's Wife. Gilbert
Monuments of Hiroshima, The. Enright
Shadow of Cain, The. Sitwell
Welcome to Hiroshima. Salter
Hispanic Verse
*Defiant Muse, The; Hispanic Feminist Poems
    from the Middle Ages to the Present*
    (DMH). Angel Flores *and* Kate Flores,
    eds.

Love Poems from Spain & Spanish America
    (LPSS). Perry Higman, ed. *and* tr.
Penguin Book of Caribbean Verse in English,
    The (PBCV). Paula Burnett, ed.
See also **Spanish-American Literature;**
    West Indies.
Hispanics. *See* **Chicanos; Puerto Ricans.**
History and Historians
Again for Hephaistos, the Last Time.
    Howard
Ancient Historian. Wallace-Crabbe
Ancient History. Guiterman
Antiquary, The. Campbell
Belfast. Revell
Cannon Park. St. Germain
Fall of Rome, The. Auden
History. Francis
History. Gregor
History of the World, The. Weingarten
Human Greatness. Barclay
I Shall Laugh Purely. Jeffers
Johnny's Hist'ry Lesson. Waterman
Living Truth, The. Plumpp
Meredith Phyfe. *Fr.* The New Spoon River.
    Masters
On Sir Nathaniel Wraxall the Historian.
    Colman
Our History. Coblentz
Poet Speaks from the Visitors' Gallery, A.
    MacLeish
Shelf Is a Ledge, A. Orr
Streets. Perelman
There was a time when the stars fell like rain.
    Tauhindauli
Untitled Poem. Dugan
What Happened Here Before. Snyder
When All's Said and Done. Ladányi
Written in the Beginning of Mezeray's History
    of France. Prior
Hitchhiking and Hitchhikers
Faces. Ciardi
Hitchhiker, The. Ai
Hitchhikers, The. Wakoski
Poets Hitchhiking on the Highway. Corso
Hitler, Adolf
Executioners. Weinstein
Hitler, frothy-mouth, wooden-head.
    Unknown
Letter to Hitler, A. Laughlin
Hitomaro (Kakinomoto no Hitomaro)
Day in, day out. *Fr.* Manyo Shu. Yosami
Hitomaro. Hitoshi
Thinking "Today! Today!" I wait for you.
    Fr. Manyo Shu. Yosami
Though you say, "Do not grieve!" *Fr.*
    Manyo Shu. Yosami
Ho Chi Minh
On the Death of Ho Chi Minh. Mandel
Hobbes, Thomas
To Mr. Hobs. Cowley
Hoboes. *See* **Vagabonds.**
Hogarth, William
Epitaph on William Hogarth. Johnson
Hogg, James
Extempore Effusion [upon the Death of James
    Hogg], An. Wordsworth
Hogue, La, Battle of (1692)
Hervé Riel. Browning
Holbein, Hans
Fancy Dress. MacKellar
Hölderlin, Friedrich
Elegy for Hölderlin, An. Rifqa
Holiday, Billie (Eleanora Fagan McKay)
Day Lady Died, The. O'Hara
Holidays
Bonne Entente. Scott
Ceremonies for Candlemas[se] Eve. Herrick
Conversation with Washington. Livingston
Holiday. *Fr.* Remembrances. Leivick
Memorial Days. Sadoff

Our Holidays in Poetry (OHIP). Mildred P.
   Harrington *and* Josephine H. Thomas,
   comps
   See also **specific holidays.**
Holland. *See* **Netherlands.**
Holly
   Green Groweth the Holly. *Unknown*
   Holly, The. De la Mare
   Holly against Ivy. *Unknown*
   Holly and Mistletoe. Farjeon
   Holly Tree, The. Southey
   Itum Paradisum all clothed in green.
      Unknown
   Riddle: "Highty, tighty, paradighty, clothed
      [all] in green." *Unknown*
Hollyhocks
   Hollyhock, A. Sherman
   Hollyhocks, The. Betts
Hollywood, California
   Bleed Through. Harjo
   Helen in Hollywood. Grahn
   Hollywood. Shapiro
   Song of Bullets, The. Hagedorn
Holmes, Oliver Wendell
   Holmes. *Fr.* A Fable for Critics. Lowell
Holocaust
   Auschwitz from Colombo. Ranasinghe
   Babi Yar. Ozerov
   Book of Yolek, The. Hecht
   Camp in the Prussian Forest, A. Jarrell
   Children of Auschwitz. Korzhavin
   Desnos Reading the Palms of Men on Their
      Way to the Gas Chambers. Berg
   Eichmann. Beecham
   Epitaphs. Sutskever
   Extermination of the Jews, The. Bell
   From the Corpse Woodpiles, from the Ashes.
      Hayden
   God of Mercy. Molodovsky
   Holocaust. Sklarew
   Holocaust 1944. Ranasinghe
   Home. Gershon
   How? Sutskever
   How They Killed My Grandmother. Slutsky
   Jew's Calendar, A. Gershon
   Lead Plates at the Rom Press, The.
      Sutskever
   Letter from Berlin, A. Stallworthy
   "Lovers of Israel" at the Belzhets Death
      Camp, The. Manger
   "More Light! More Light!" Hecht
   Mother. Tuwim
   Murder of a Community. Weissbort
   My Sister. Kovner
   1980. *Fr.* Poems from a Diary. Sutskever
   Of All My Loves. Kovner
   Ordeal by Fire, *sels.* Ya'oz-kest
   Poem for Anton Schmidt, A. Pillen
   Poor Christian Looks at the Ghetto, A.
      Milosz
   Pripet Marshes, The. Feldman
   Riddle: "From Belsen a crate of gold teeth."
      Heyen
   September Song. Hill
   Shipment to Maidanek. Fogel
   Teaching the Children. Sklarew
   Tending the Garden. Pankey
   That's It. Leyeles
   They. Leib
   This Urn Contains Earth from German
      Concentration Camps. Lorde
   To the Things That Are Immortal. Kovner
   Wall, The. Askenazy
   War against the Jews, The. Stern
   What big heavy doors! *Fr.* Auschwitz.
      Wyse
   Written in Pencil in the Sealed Railway-Car.
      Pagis
Holy Baptism. *See* **Baptism.**
Holy Communion. *See* **Eucharist.**
Holy Family
   Cherry-Tree Carol, The. *Unknown*

Holy Family. Tynan
Stable Straw. Farren
Swiftly Arose. *Fr.* Song of Myself: I believe
   in you my soul. Whitman
Holy Ghost
   His Litany to the Holy Spirit. Herrick
Holy Innocents
   For Innocents' Day. Wadding
Holy Spirit
   Call to Pentecost, A. Tyler
   Graces of the Holy Ghost, The. *Unknown*
   Hymn for Pentecost. Mangan
   Hymn to the Holy Spirit. Langton
   Prayer for Pentecost, A. Brown
Holy Thursday
   Holy Thursday ("Is this a holy thing to see").
      Fr. Songs of Experience. Blake
   Holy Thursday (" 'Twas on a Holy Thursday,
      their innocent faces clean"). *Fr.* Songs of
      Innocence. Blake
Home
   Autumn. Untermeyer
   Blows the Wind Today. Stevenson
   Considerations. Helwig
   Dearest Spot on Earth, The. Wrighton
   Death of the Hired Man, The. Frost
   Empty house, The. *Fr.* Manyo Shu. Tabito
   Exiled. Millay
   Family Prime. Van Doren
   Farewell to My Cottage. Bamford
   Go Home. McFatter
   Going Home. Kenny
   Hame, Hame, Hame. Cunningham
   Hearth and Home. King
   Heart's Content. *Unknown*
   Home. Edwards
   Home. Guest
   Home. Miki Rofu
   Home Is Where There Is One to Love Us.
      Swain
   Home Song. Longfellow
   Home, Sweet Home. Payne
   Home, Sweet Home. *Fr.* Clari, the Maid of
      Milan. Payne
   Home Sweet Home with Variations. Bunner
   Home! You're Where It's Warm Inside.
      Prelutsky
   Homecoming. Thompson
   Hometown. Cabalquinto
   House on the Hill, The. Robinson
   House with Nobody in It, The. Kilmer
   I Have a House. Mühringer
   I Shall Never Go On Bragging. Halpern
   In the Inner City. Clifton
   I've Got a Home in That Rock. Patterson
   Letter from Home, A. Li Nan
   My Ain Fireside. Hamilton
   My Early Home. Clare
   My Old Kentucky Home, [Good Night].
      Foster
   New House, The. Rutsala
   Nightfall, Midwinter, Missouri. *Fr.* Missouri
      Sequence. Coffey
   No Place Like Home. Llawdden
   Old Woman of the Roads, An. Colum
   On a misty day in spring. *Fr.* Manyo Shu.
      Mushimaro
   On the Wide Heath. Millay
   Our House. Thompson
   Pilgrim from the East, The. Kahn
   Prayer for a Little Home, A. Bone
   Prayer for This House. Untermeyer
   Return of the Native, The. Matthews
   Roofs. Kilmer
   Sweet Stay-at-Home. Davies
   Thanksgiving for a Habitat. Auden
   Thanksgiving to God for His House, A.
      Herrick
   Very Nicest Place, The. *Unknown*
   Visiting My Father. Rai San'yo

Welcome Home. Heard
West Wind, The. Masefield
Where He Hangs His Hat. Lee
With her basket, her basket. *Fr.* Manyo
   Shu. Yuryaku
Workman's Home, A. Ince
Zlochov [*or* Zlotchev, My Home]. Halpern
Homecoming
   Dry River Bed. Salkey
   Homecoming. Scott
   Late Return. Markham
Homeless, The
   Bag Woman. Randall
   Bedtime Story. Abse
   By-Blows. Jarman
   Houston Street. Vice
   Hunchback in the Park, The. Thomas
   Miss Rosie. Clifton
   Old Lady under the Freeway, The. O Hehir
   Old Woman of the Roads, An. Colum
   People Who Talk to Themselves. *Fr.* New
      York Everywhere. Vaynshteyn
   Street Musicians. Ashbery
   Three Journeys. Hirsch
   To a Poor Old Woman. Williams
   Two girls of twelve or so at a table.
      Reznikoff
   Waifs. Virtue
Homer
   By Deputy. Adcock
   Cure for Poetry, A.
   Homer. Ehrenstein
   Isaiah and Homer. Leyeles
   Odyssey, The. Lang
   On First Looking into Chapman's Homer.
      Keats
   On Looking into E. V. Rieu's Homer.
      Kavanagh
   Praise of Homer. Chapman
   To Homer. Keats
Homesickness
   Away from Home. *Unknown*
   Ch'ing-ming Nostalgia. Yung Tzu
   City Clerk, The. Ashe
   Don't Walk beside the Big Carriage.
      Unknown
   Guinea Corn. *Unknown*
   Hame, Hame, Hame. Cunningham
   Home Thoughts from Abroad. Browning
   Homesick Blues. Hughes
   I Wonder How My Home Is. *Unknown*
   Lines Written in the Album at Elbingerode, in
      the Hartz Forest. Coleridge
   Lotus Leaf Cup. Wen T'ing-yün
   My Heart Is in Merioneth. *Unknown*
   My Own Hills. Story
   North Country Maid, The. *Unknown*
   Not knowing that the long spring day. *Fr.*
      Manyo Shu. Ikusa
   Of the flaming rose, The. Mir
   Oh, bright Heaven high above. *Unknown*
   Old Vicarage, Grantchester, The. Brooke
   On a Snowy Night Thinking of the Bamboos
      at Home. Michizane
   Outcast. McKay
   Outside Fargo, North Dakota. Wright
   Ripples Sifting Sand. Huang-fu Sung
   Since I was suddenly sent away. *Fr.* Kokin
      Shu. Michizane
   Spraying of the waters, The. *Unknown*
   Still Night Thoughts. Li Po
   Tropics in New York, The. McKay
   Two Trunks. Kuan Kuan
   Unreturning Native, The. Dowling
   We Pick Ferns, We Pick Ferns. *Unknown*
   When mist rises on the seashore. *Fr.* Manyo
      Shu. *Unknown*
   When on my travels I pine for home. *Fr.*
      Manyo Shu. Kurohito
   Willow Branches. Huang-fu Sung
Homesteaders
   Kansas Emigrants, The. Whittier

Homophobia
Little Old Sod Shanty. *Unknown*
Starving to Death on a Government Claim. *Unknown*

Homophobia
Blueberry Man. Bergman
Cafe: 3 A.M. Hughes
Cheers, Cheers for Old Cha Cha Ass ("Cheers, cheers for old Patchogue High"). Borawski
Curing Homosexuality. Everhard
De Ambiente. De La Tierra
Deadly Weapon. Gates
Fairy Straighttalk. Morse
Gay Psalm from Fort Valley, A. Crew
Interface. Anzaldúa
Invisible History. Borawski
My Brother. Parker
Rape Poem, The. Avicolli
Some of our dead are famous, but they would not care. *Fr.* In Time of War. Auden
We Bumped Off Your Friend the Poet. Norse
Where Will You Be? Parker

Homosexuality and Homosexuals
Against Homosexuality. *Fr.* View of the Town, A. In an Epistle to a Friend. Gilbert
Cafe: 3 A.M. Hughes
Chances "R." Ginsberg
Couplets. Barney
Double Exposure. Young
Dream. Dobyns
Feast of Stephen, The. Hecht
For Freckle-faced Gerald. Knight
Good Old Body. Donald
Homosexuality. O'Hara
Love a woman! y'are an ass. Rochester
Magnificat. Roberts
Myself in an Anatomical Chart of Sexual Intercourse. Mutsuo
Old Age of Michelangelo, The. Prince
On the Road to the Sea. Mew
Pick-up at Chef Rizal Restaurant. Cerenio
Sappho Lives Again. Vivien
This Form of Life Needs Sex. Ginsberg
Wholesome. Meredith
Why We Bombed Haiphong. Holden
Woman. Barney
Words for Hart Crane. Lowell
Gay & Lesbian Poetry in Our Time; an Anthology (GLP). Care Morse *and* Joan Larkin, eds.
Penguin Book of Homosexual Verse, The (PeHV). Stephen Coote, ed.

Honduras
Incurable Love, The. Quesada
One Island. Nye

Honey
Bees Awater. Morgan
I eat my peas with honey. *Unknown*

Honey Eaters
Nesting Time. Stewart

Honeymoons
Bridal Piece. Glück
Marriage. Corso

Honeysuckle
Wild Honeysuckle, The. Freneau

Hong Kong
How Hong Kong Was Destroyed. Ravikovich

Honor
If We Must Die. McKay
O lovely age of gold! *Fr.* Aminta. Tasso
On Honour. Mandeville
She Was Poor but She Was Honest. *Unknown*
To Lucasta, Going to the Wars [*or* Warres]. Lovelace
Ulysses and the Siren. Daniel

Hooker, Joseph
Hooker's Across! Boker

Hoopoes
Solitary wayfarer! *Fr.* Nepenthe. Darley

Hoover Dam
Boulder Dam. Sarton

Hope
Anticipation. Brontë
Aspiration. Menken
Aspiration. Ray
At summer eve, when Heaven's ethereal bow. *Fr.* The Pleasures of Hope. Campbell
Aubade for Hope. Warren
"Bottle Should Be Plainly Labeled 'Poison.' " Hay
Dark Testament. Murray
Darkling Thrush, The. Hardy
Door of Hope, The. Moorer
For a Child. Davis
Good Man in Hell, The. Muir
Hold Fast Your Dreams. Driscoll
Hope. Brontë
Hope. Heard
Hope. Herbert
Hope. Howells
Hope. Hughes
Hope. Jarrell
Hope. Thompson
Hope. Tucker
Hope and Fear. Swinburne
Hope Deferred. Thompson
Hope is the thing with feathers. Dickinson
I dwell in possibility. Dickinson
Leaden Echo and the Golden Echo, The. Hopkins
Lines Written among the Euganean Hills. Shelley
Maestro's Barber Shop, The. Vásquez
Message of the March Wind, The. Morris
"Paper Men to Air Hopes and Fears." Francis
Pause of Thought, A. Rossetti
Pleasure of Hope, The. *Fr.* An Essay on Man. Pope
Triple Bension, The. Ray
Work without Hope. Coleridge
See also **Optimism.**

Hope, Bob
Why That's Bob Hope. Hathaway

Hopi Indians
Butterfly Maidens. Lahpu
Death in the Desert, A. Tomlinson

Hopkins, Gerard Manley
Poetry of Gerard Manley Hopkins, The. Gibbon

Horace
After Horace. Godley
Horace. Sargent
On First Looking into Loeb's Horace. Durrell
Truth about Horace, The. Field

Horatius
Horatius. *Fr.* Lays of Ancient Rome. Macaulay

Horn, Cape. *See* **Cape Horn.**

Horse Chestnut Trees
Hampstead; the Horse Chestnut Trees. Gunn

Horse Racing
At Galway Races. Yeats
At Grass. Larkin
Camptown Races, The. Foster
Famous Ballad of the Jubilee Cup, The. Quiller-Couch
Galway Races. *Unknown*
How We Beat the Favourite. Gordon
Jockey, A. Koertge
Morning Track, The. Parone
Morning Workout. Deutsch
Never Be As Fast As I Have Been. Hahn
Placing a $2 Bet for a Man Who Will Never Go to the Horse Races Any More. Wakoski
Tom Fool at Jamaica. Moore

Horseback Riding
Billy Could Ride. Riley
Boy Riding Forward Backward. Francis
Bronco Busting, Event #1. Swenson
Getting on Horseback. Yü Chi
Horse-Watering Hole, The. Yang Wei-chen
Horseback. Kizer
Horseman at the Roadside, The. Yang Wei-chen
How They Brought the Good News from Ghent to Aix. Browning
Night of Spring. Westwood
Polo Ponies Practicing. Stevens
Ride, The. Wilbur
Riding Lesson. Taylor
Stallion. Whitman
Young Horseman. Kassák

Horses
Animal Mood. Teller
Apostrophe to a Dead Friend. Kumin
Arab to His Favorite Steed, The. Norton
At Grass. Larkin
Birth of the Foal. Juhász
Blessing, A. Wright
Bronco Busting, Event #1. Swenson
Buckin' Horse Ballet. Whipple
Buckskin Flats. Eastman
Cariboo Horses, The. Purdy
Celebration: Birth of a Colt. Hogan
"Childe Roland to the Dark Tower Came." Browning
Chookaloski Mare. Whipple
Circus-Postered Barn, The. Coatsworth
Corral, The. Thompson
Crossing the River. Yang Shih-ch'i
Cynthia on Horseback. Ayres
Daniel Webster's Horses. Coatsworth
Dappled Horse, The. Mei Yao-ch'en
Dead Ponies. Chamberlain
Distant Runners, The. Van Doren
Dobbin. Bowering
Draft Horse, The. Frost
Dream of Horses, A. Hughes
Dusk of Horses, The. Dickey
Elegy on the Death of Dobbin, the Butterwoman's Horse, An. Fawkes
Face of the Horse, The. Zabolotsky
Flying Change, The. Taylor
Foal. Miller
Foal, The. Renton
Foal. Watkins
Gallop of Fire, A. Pitt
Ghostly Story. Acorn
Gid dy/ up gid/ dy up. Minor
Gigantic beauty of a stallion, fresh and responsive to my caresses, A. *Fr.* Song of Myself. Whitman
Grace of Geldings in Ripe Pastures, The. Kumin
Gun Teams. Frankau
Haiku: "He washes his horse." Masaoka Shiki
Horse, The. Eguren
Horse, The. Kicknosway
Horse, The. Ponge
Horse. *Fr.* A Bestiary. Rexroth
Horse, The. Royde-Smith
Horse and His Rider, The. Baillie
Horse is loose, The. *Fr.* Manyo Shu. Ojibe Kurome
Horsemen, The. Baro
Horses. Mendes
Horses. Ravitch
Horses. Riedemann
Horses. Thomas
Horses. Wellesley
Horses Aboard. Hardy
Horses Chawin' Hay. Garland
Horse's Head, The. Kennelly
Horses of Marini, The. Van Zyl
Horses of the sea, The. *Fr.* Sing-Song. Rossetti

Horses on the Camargue. Campbell
Horses, The ("Barely a twelvemonth after").
  Muir
Hoss, The. Riley
How They Brought the Good News from
  Ghent to Aix. Browning
How to Choose a Horse. *Unknown*
Huckster's Horse, The. Strong
I like to see it lap the miles. Dickinson
In wild flight. *Fr.* Sioux Metamorphoses.
  Unknown
Incongruity of the Age, Satire on a Miser's
  Horse. Sauda
Inviolable. Hoffman
Is it the horn that, on this holy day. *Fr.* The
  Village Patriarch. Elliott
Johnny's Team. Field
Keeping the Horses. Scheele
Kentucky Belle. Woolson
Love Song to Eohippus. Viereck
Lovers, The. Comfort
Mare, A. Barnes
Mare, The. Watkins
Mares of the Camargue, The. *Fr.* Mirèio.
  Mistral
Mouth of the mare, The. *Fr.* Manyo Shu.
  Unknown
Names of Horses. Hall
Nell. Knister
Nell. *Fr.* A Row of Stalls. Knister
New York City—1935. Corso
Noonday Sun. Jackson
Old Brown Horse, The. Holmes
Old Gray Mare. *Unknown*
Old Horse. Smith
Old Mare, The. Coatsworth
On Buying a Horse. *Unknown*
Pain for a Daughter. Sexton
Paiute Ponies. Barnes
Phar Lap in the Melbourne Museum. Porter
Pinto Mare, A. Smith
Poor Old Horse. *Unknown*
Racing-Man, The. Herbert
Ride, The. Wilbur
Riders' Horses, The ("The riders' spears
  touched heaven"). Gilboa
Riding a One-eyed Horse. Taylor
Riding in the Rain. Kumin
Roan Hunter, The. Harris
Rondeau of the Little Horses. Bandeira
Runaway, The. Frost
Say This of Horses. Moody
Shadow of Himself, The. Renton
She Had Some Horses. Harjo
Silver. Ammons
Stallion, The. Tudur Aled
Stallion. Whitman
Steeds the prince of Minu keeps, The. *Fr.*
  Manyo Shu. *Unknown*
Stout and strong our stallions. *Unknown*
Strawberry Roan, The. Fletcher
Tenderfoot, The. O'Malley
That Little Blue Roan. Kiskaddon
Tim. Montague
To Fido, His Horse. Alfieri
To Ride. Eluard
To the Four Courts, Please. Stephens
Tom Fool at Jamaica. Moore
Track, The. Christopher
Triangular Field, The. Dobyns
Unbridled Now. LeGear
Undertaker's Horse, The. Kipling
War God's Horse Song, The. *Unknown*
War Horse, The. Boland
What a Proud Dreamhorse. Cummings
White Horse, The. Lawrence
White Horse of the Father, White Horse of
  the Son. Root
White Horses. Farjeon
Widdecombe [*or* Widdicombe] Fair.
  Unknown

Wild Horses of Assateague Island, The.
  Bensko
Wild, the Free, The. Byron
Zebra Dun, The. *Unknown*
Hospitality
Ballad of East and West, The. Kipling
Flock the egrets in their flight. *Unknown*
Guest, a guest, A/ And white his horse.
  Unknown
High rise the pole-banners. *Unknown*
Hospitality in Ancient Ireland. *Unknown*
In the south there are lucky fish. *Unknown*
Inviting a Friend to Supper. Jonson
On a Dead Hostess. Belloc
Red bow is unstrung, The. *Unknown*
Yu, yu, cry the deer. *Unknown*
Yussouf. Lowell
See also **Guests.**
Hospitals
At Nuclear Medicine. Partridge
At the Treatment Center. Sala
Balance. Schultz
Benicasim. Warner
Clinics. Bachstein
Cottage Hospital, The. Betjeman
Days Ago. Hai-Jew
Double Semi-Sestina. Starbuck
Emergency Room, The. Fisher
Evening in the Sanitarium. Bogan
Far Cry after a Close Call, A. Howard
Field Hospital, The. Muldoon
Flat One, A. Snodgrass
Flight. Whitman
Happening at Sordid Creek. Porter
Hospital, The. Kavanagh
Hospital. Shapiro
Hospital Breakfast: With Grace After. Nims
Hospital Evening. Harwood
Hospital Observation. Symons
Hospital Waiting-Room, The. Davies
In Hospital. Flecker
In Hospital: Poona, I. Lewis
In the Children's Hospital. "MacDiarmid"
In the Hospital. Guiterman
Malice of Innocence, The. Levertov
Mental Cases. Owen
My Mother and the Touched Old Woman.
  Gildner
Notes for the Chart in 306. Nash
Old Men's Ward. Dean
Operation, The. Snodgrass
Red Cross Nurses. Stewart
Rescue the Dead. Ignatow
Semi-Private Room. Nowlan
Stones, The. Plath
Sunday at the State Hospital. Ignatow
Surgical Ward: Men. Graves
Transfusion. Moore
Tulips. Plath
2 November 1982. Bold
University Hospital, Boston. Oliver
Unknown Girl in the Maternity Ward.
  Sexton
Viaticum. MacCarthy
Visit to a Hospital. Chace
Wait. Steele
Ward Two. Webb
Hot Springs
Atami. Chugan Engetsu
Hotels
At a Summer Hotel. Gardner
At the Algonquin. Moss
At the End of the Affair. Kumin
Black Bull of Aldgate. Tennyson
Conversation Piece. Graves
Dolgelley Hotel, The. Hughes
Finn's Wishes. O'Grady
Holiday Inn at Bemidji. Vizenor
Hotel, The. Abi Shaqra
Hotel Brown Poems, The. Ash
Irish Hotel. Wevill
Lament for Lost Lodgings. McGinley

Savannah, Sleepless. Tillinghast
Stirling's Hotel. *Unknown*
Strand Hotel, Rosslare, The. Liddy
Uphill [*or* Up-Hill]. Rossetti
Written at [*or* in] an Inn at Henley.
  Shenstone
See also **Motels.**
Hottentots
Hottentot, The. Pringle
Houdini, Harry
Houdini. Mandel
Hourglasses
Hourglass [*or* The Houre-Glasse], The ("Do
  but consider this small dust"). Jonson
House Painting
Painters, The. Hemschemeyer
Housekeeping
Housewife, The. Coblentz
Huswifery. Taylor
I Like Housecleaning. Thompson
When Young Melissa Sweeps. Turner
See also **Housewives.**
Houses
Abandoned House, The. Hubbell
Architect. Nicholl
Architectural Masks. Hardy
Buildings, The. Berry
Consecration of the House. Fairbridge
Corner Lot. Bryan
Crack is moving down the wall, The. *Fr.*
  Five Villanelles. Kees
Crayon House. Rukeyser
Deserted House, The. Coleridge
Directive. Frost
Domicilium. Hardy
Empty House, The. De la Mare
Empty House, The. Monro
Empty House, The. Spender
Empty House, The. Williams
Fire. Carpenter
Floating Houses. Wojahn
Floor and the Ceiling, The. Smith
For the Rebuilding of a House. Berry
Ghosts. Jennings
Ground for the Floor. *Unknown*
Haunted House, The. Hood
House, A. Agard
House, The. Bowering
House. Browning
House, The. Nelson
House. O Hehir
House, The. Van Zyl
House, The. Williams
House Blessing. Guiterman
House on the Hill, The. Robinson
House with Nobody in It, The. Kilmer
Houses. Fisher
Housing Starts. Davison
I know some lonely houses off the road.
  Dickinson
I Like Housecleaning. Thompson
Invites His Nymph to His Cottage. Ayres
Invocation: "Silent, about-to-be-parted-from
  house." Levertov
Jeronimo's House. Bishop
Like a cloud haunted by the moon. *Fr.* The
  Third House. Károlyi
Love Song: I and Thou. Dugan
Mending the Adobe. Carruth
My house, I say. But hark to the sunny
  doves. Stevenson
My Little House. Westrup
New House, The. McDougall
New House, The. Thomas
O Blessèd House, That Cheerfully Receiveth.
  Spitta
O Thou Whose Gracious Presence Blest.
  Benson
Old Houses of Flanders, The. Ford
Old Mansion. Ransom
Old Woman of the Roads, An. Colum
On a Picture of Your House. Jones

On Lord Holland's Seat near Margate, Kent.
  Gray On the Hall at Stowey. Tomlinson
Point Shirley. Plath
Post Mortem. Harden
Prayer for This House. Untermeyer
Quebec Farmhouse. Glassco
Roof. Rin
Ruin, The. Tomlinson
Setting the Table. Aldis
Song for a Little House. Morley
Thanksgiving to God for His House, A.
  Herrick
To Penshurst. Jonson
To Saxham. Carew
Vagabond House. Blanding
World, The. Herbert
  See also **Home.**

Housewives
Cooking the Rice. Mechtel
Divine Office of the Kitchen, The. Hallack
Farmer's Bride, The. Mew
Gone Is the Sleepgiver. Shuttle
Housewife, The. Coblentz
Marks. Pastan
Next Day. Jarrell
Suburban Wife's Song. Hutchinson
Vampire Housewife, The. Fainlight
Young Housewife, The. Williams
  See also **Housekeeping.**

Housman, Alfred Edward
Another Epitaph on an Army of Mercenaries.
  "MacDiarmid"
Mr. Housman's Message. Pound

Hubbell, Carl
Exercise in Preparation for a Pindaric Ode to
  Carl Hubbell. Schwartz

Hudson Bay
Empty Threat, An. Frost

Hudson, Henry
Henry Hudson's Quest. Stevenson

Hudson River
Egyptian Passage, An. Weiss
Lordly Hudson, The. Goodman
Mouth of the Hudson, The. Lowell
On the Hudson. Leyeles
Why? Leyeles

Hughes, Langston
Do Nothing till You Hear from Me.
  Henderson
For All Things Black and Beautiful. Rivers
Langston. Evans
Langston Blues. Randall
Langston Hughes. Blockcolski
Reading Walt Whitman. Forbes
Rhetoric of Langston Hughes, The. Danner

Hughes, Ted
Policeman's Lot, A. Cope

Huguenots
Psalm, The: "While Northward the hot sun
  was sinking o'er the trees." Bridges

Human Folly
Whate'er the passion—knowledge, fame, or
  pelf. *Fr.* An Essay on Man. Pope

Human Race. See Mankind.

Hume, David
David Hume, Dying, Talks to Boswell. Bold

Humility
Charity. Bensley
Clod and the Pebble, The. *Fr.* Songs of
  Experience. Blake
Happiest Heart, The. Cheney
He that is down needs fear no fall. *Fr.* The
  Pilgrim's Progress. Bunyan
House by the Side of the Road, The. Foss
Humble Heart, A. Norris
Magnanimous, The. Kay
O Why Should the Spirit of Mortal Be Proud?
  Knox
Resolve, The. Chudleigh
To Show How Humble. *Unknown*

Hummingbirds
Container, The. Corman
Humming Bird, The. Kemp
Humming-Bird. Lawrence
Humming-Bird, The. Tucker
Humming Birds. Sage
Hummingbird. Littlebird
Hummingbird. Piercy
Murmurers, The. Jacobsen
Vision. Eberhart

Humorous Verse
Century of Humorous Verse, 1850-1950, A
  (CenHV). Robert Lancelyn Green, ed.
Faber Book of Comic Verse, The (FaBoCo).
  Michael Roberts *and* Janet Adam Smith,
  eds.
Faber Book of Nonsense Verse, The
  (FaBoNo). Geoffrey Grigson, ed.
Fireside Book of Humorous Poetry, The
  (FiBHP). William Cole, ed.
Moon Is Shining Bright As Day, The.
  (MoShBr). Ogden Nash, ed.
New Oxford Book of English Light Verse,
  The. (NOBL). Kingsley Amis, ed.
Nonsense Anthology, A (NA). Carolyn
  Wells, ed.
Norton Book of Light Verse, The (NBLV).
  Russell Baker, ed.
Oxford Book of American Light Verse, The
  (OBAL). William Harmon, ed.
Oxford Book of Light Verse, The (OxBoLi).
  W. H. Auden, ed.

Hunchbacks
Capes. Goldsmith
Hunchback in the Park, The. Thomas

Hundred Years War
Creçy. Palgrave
King Henry Fifth's Conquest of France.
  Unknown

Hungarian Verse
Face of Creation, The; Contemporary
  Hungarian Poetry (FoC). Jascha Kessler,
  ed.
Modern Hungarian Poetry (MHuP). Miklos
  Vaida, ed.

Hungary
Birth of a Country. Gergely
Confession of Faith. Csanádi
Music of Hungary. Aldrich

Hunger
Bard's Family, A. Peruncittiranar
Colliers' March, The. Freeth
Food-Rioter Banished, The. Thom
For an Obligate Parasite. Dugan
Give Me Three Grains of Corn, Mother.
  Edwards
Hunger. Binyon
Hunger. Samik
Hunger. Stone
Hunger. *Unknown*
Hunger and Thirst. Bishop
Hunger in New York City. Ortiz
Leawood Hall. Jones
Lullaby for the Hungry. Al-Jawahiri
Oh, the flowers of the bignonia. *Unknown*
Oh, what has become of you? *Unknown*
Preawd Tum's Prayer. Ramsbottom
Rainy Night. Michizane
Those Makheta Nights. Chipasula
To starve, or not to starve? that is the
  question. Ireland

Hunt, Leigh
Jenny kiss'd me when we met. *Fr.* A
  Leaden Treasury of English Verse. Dehn
Sonnet: Written on the Day That Mr. Leigh
  Hunt Left Prison. Keats
"Such Stuff as Dreams." Adams
To Leigh Hunt, Esq. Keats

Hunting and Hunters
A-Hunting. Dunbar
After the Night Hunt. Dickey

Ageing Hunter, The. Avane
All in Green Went My Love Riding.
  Cummings
Baboon. *Fr.* Hunter Poems of the Yoruba.
  Unknown
Badger. Clare
Ballad of Red Fox, The. La Follette
Beagles. Rodgers
Bear Hunt, The. Widdemer
Bear Hunting. Aua
Blackwater Mountain. Wright
Blessing the Hounds. Winter
Blow Thy Horn, Hunter. *Unknown*
Blue Cuckoo. *Fr.* Hunter Poems of the
  Yoruba. *Unknown*
Bold Reynard the Fox. *Unknown*
Boy and the Deer, The. Peynetsa
Buffalo. *Fr.* Hunter Poems of the Yoruba.
  Unknown
Buffalo Skinners, The. *Unknown*
Carmen Possum. *Unknown*
Cheerful Horn, The. *Unknown*
Chop, chop they cut the hardwood.
  Unknown
Coon Hunt, Sixth Month (1955). Lea
Death of a Hind. Maclean
December. Francis
Decoys, The. Auden
Deer Hunt. Jerome
Deer Hunt, Salt Lake Valley. Handley
Dido's Hunting. *Fr.* The Aeneid [*or*
  Eneados]. Virgil
Doe. Dow
Dream 2: Brian the Still-Hunter. Atwood
Dressing Game. Schmitz
Duck. Donaghy
Duck Pond at Mini's Pasture, a Dozen Years
  Later, The. Dow
Elk Camp. Carver
Fall. Lea
Festival of the Hunter and the Trees. Char
Fox-Hunters, The. Elliott
Fox knew well, that before they tore him,
  The. *Fr.* Reynard the Fox. Masefield
Good Grease. TallMountain
Hawking. Keiun
Hawking. Shotetsu
Here come the hounds, ting-a-ling. *Unknown*
His team of darkies pull well. *Unknown*
Horse & Rider. Robinson
Hunt. La Follette
Hunt, The. *Fr.* Windsor Forest. Pope
Hunt Is Up, The. *Unknown*
Hunter, The. Nash
Hunter, The. Souster
Hunter of the Prairies, The. Bryant
Hunter Trials. Betjeman
Hunter's Morning. Littlebird
Hunters of the Deer, The. Zieroth
Hunting, The. Lux
Hunting. Sheedy
Hunting for Grouse. Lloyd
Hunting of the Hare, The. Lucas, Duchess
  of Newcastle
Hunting Season. Reidy
Hunting Song. *Fr.* Don Quixote in England.
  Fielding
Hunting Song. Finkel
Hunting-Song. *Unknown*
Hunting Song. *Fr.* Apollo and Daphne.
  Whitehead
Huntress, The. Pesado
Huntsmen, The. De la Mare
I Saw a Jolly Hunter. Causley
It's up Glenbarchan's braes I gaed. Scott
Jacklight. Erdrich
John Peel. Graves
Kilruddery Hunt, The. Mozeen
Kirk Lonegren's Home Movie Taking Place
  Just North of Prince George, with Sound.
  Thesen
Last Hunt, The. Thayer

Lion Hunts. Beer
Lucky day, fifth of the week, A. *Unknown*
Magic Words for Hunting Caribou.
   Unknown
Magic Words for Hunting Seal. *Unknown*
Manlet, The. "Carroll"
Mighty Hunter, The. Worley
Morgante and the Boars. Pulci
My Woodcock. Chalmers
Nine Charms against the Hunter. Wagoner
Nor less the spaniel, skillful to betray. *Fr.*
   Rural Sports. Gay
Nymph Complaining for the Death of Her
   Fawn, The. Marvell
Of the Stalking of the Stag. Seaman
Old Dog, New Dog. Lea
Old Squire, The. Blunt
On His Mistris That Lov'd Hunting.
   Unknown
Our chariots are strong. *Unknown*
Our great prince who orders. *Fr.* Manyo
   Shu. Hitomaro
Our noble prince, child of the Bright One on
   high. *Fr.* Manyo Shu. Hitomaro
Out in the Woods. Arnett
Possibility That Has Been Overlooked Is the
   Future, The. Hartnett
Rabbit Hunter, The. Frost
Rainbow. Huff
Revenge of the Hunted. Ford
Rock Painting. Cope
Rousing Canoe Song, The. Fraser
Runnable Stag, A. Davidson
St. Valentine's Day. *Fr.* The Love Sonnets
   of Proteus. Blunt
Scene after Hunting at Swallowfield in
   Berkshire, A. Davies
See! from the brake the whirring Pheasant
   springs. *Fr.* Windsor Forest. Pope
Shooting. Fairchild
Shooting Crows. Huddle
Shooting Ducks in South Louisiana.
   Tillinghast
Song of the Duck Hunters. Kao Ch'i
Song of the Rejected Woman. Kibkarjuk
Sonnet: "Like [or Lyke] a huntsman after
   weary chase [*or* chace]" *Fr.* Amoretti,
   LXVII. Spenser.
Sonnet: Whoso List to Hunt [I Know Where
   Is an Hind]. Wyatt
Sonnets of the Months: September. San
   Geminiano
Still Hunting. Welch
Stories of Snow. Page
Strange People, The. Erdrich
Target Practice. Finkel
There Faunus and Sylvanus keep their courts.
   Fr. Cooper's Hill. Denham
To Christ Our Lord. Kinnell
Tracking Rabbits: Night. Barnes
Trapped Hare, The. Dowling
Walrus Hunting. Aua
We'll All Go a-Hunting Today. *Unknown*
What Shines in Winter Burns. Hummer
When Autumn smiles, all beauteous in decay.
   Fr. Field Sports. Somervile
When milder autumn summer's heat succeeds.
   Fr. Windsor Forest. Pope
Winter: East Anglia. Blunden
Woodchucks. Kumin
Yolp, Yolp, Yolp, Yolp. *Unknown*

Hurdy-Gurdies
Barrel Organ, The. *Fr.* Homage to
   Mallarmé. Epstein
Barrel-Organ, The. Noyes
Barrel-Organ, The. Symons
Hurdy-Gurdy Man, The. Fleming
Hurdy-Gurdy Man in Winter. Watkins
Lines on Hearing the Organ. Calverley

Huron, Lake
Huron, The. Herschberger

Hurricanes
After the Hurricane. Hazo
Hurricane, The. Crane
Hurricane, The. Freneau
Hurricane, The. Matos
Wasn't That a Mighty Storm? *Unknown*
Husbands
Advice to the Ladies of London in the Choice
   of Their Husbands. *Unknown*
After the Golden Wedding. Stephen
And My Mama Used to Tell Me. *Unknown*
Ballad of the Despairing Husband. Creeley
Brother-in-Law, The. Rubin
First Ode. Des Roches
Husband's Return, The. Thompson
I am sick body and soul. *Fr.* Manyo Shu.
   Kuramochi
Lady Carenza of the lovely, gracious body.
   Alais, Iselda
Letter to Daphnis, A. Winchilsea
Melting, The. Edson
Motet: "O God! I have no husband."
   Unknown
My Husband's Birthday. Heard
Perfect Husband, The. Nash
Prowling the Ridge. Minty
Thalia, you will remember that recently I
   made. *Fr.* The Fair Sex Avenged by the
   Fair Sex, or a New Satire on Husbands.
   De———
That's his specialty. *Unknown*
To My Dear and Loving Husband.
   Bradstreet
Today, today,/ I wait for him. *Fr.* Manyo
   Shu. Yosami
Hutchinson, Anne
Brother Symmes conversed with her on the
   ship. *Fr.* The Covenant of Grace.
   Stanford
Hyacinths
Admonition for Spring. MacKay
Babiaantje, The. Prince
Hyacinths to Feed Thy Soul. *Fr.* The
   Gulistan. Sadi
Water Hyacinth. Kitahara Hakushu
Hyde, Douglas
Burial of An Irish President. Clarke
Hydrangeas
White Hydrangeas. Shotetsu
Hyenas
Hyaenas, The. Kipling
Hyena. *Unknown*
Hyena. *Fr.* Hunter Poems of the Yoruba.
   Unknown
Hyena's Song to her Children. *Unknown*
Hymns
Hymn Tunes, The. Lucie-Smith
American Hymns Old and New (AH). Albert
   Christ-Janer, Charles W. Hughes, *and*
   Carleton Sprague Smith, eds.
Hypocrisy
Address to the Unco Guid, or the Rigidly
   Righteous. Burns
American Heartbreak. Hughes
At dinner, she is hostess, I am host. *Fr.*
   Modern Love. Meredith
Better to live as a rogue and a bum. Mahsati
Confessor, The. Belli
Double Standard, A. Harper
Epistle from Mrs. Yonge to Her Husband.
   Montagu
Ethics for Everyman. Woddis
Holy Willie's Prayer. Burns
Hue and Cry after Fair Amoret, A.
   Congreve
Human Relations. Sisson
Hyena. *Unknown*
Hypocrisy will serve as well. Butler
Hypocrite Women. Levertov
Latest Decalogue, The. Clough
Modes of the Court, The. *Fr.* The Beggar's
   Opera. Gay

Next to of Course God America I.
   Cummings
Soliloquy of the Spanish Cloister. Browning
We Wear the Mask. Dunbar

I

Ibn Ezra, Abraham ben Meir
Rabbi Ben Ezra. Browning
Ibn Ezra, Moses
On Parting with Moses ibn Ezra. Halevi
Ibsen, Henrik
Fox Who Watched for the Midnight Sun, The.
   Dubie
Ibycus
Cranes of Ibycus, The. Lazarus
Icarus
Daedalus. *Fr.* Metamorphoses. Ovid
Icarus. Iremonger
Icarus. Spender
Icarus. Yolen
Landscape with the Fall of Icarus. *Fr.*
   Pictures from Brueghel. Williams
Musée des Beaux Arts. Auden
Now in this while gan Daedalus a wearinesse
   to take. *Fr.* Metamorphoses. Ovid
Waiting for Icarus. Rukeyser
Winged Man. Benét
Wings. Malcohn
Ice
Break-up, The. Klein
Fire and Ice. Frost
Ice. Roberts
Ice-Floes, The. Pratt
Ice River. Baker
Icy. Bacmeister
Late Blossoms in the Cold Mountains.
   Gyoko
Oliver Johnson Comes Back to Bed the
   Morning after the Ice Storm and Tells His
   Wife Why. Jauss
Sleet. MacCaig
Ice Cream
Good Humor Man, The. McGinley
Ice-Cream Man, The. Field
Tableau at Twilight. Nash
Ice Hockey
High Stick. Collins
Hockey. Blaine
Hockey Poem, The. Bly
Rink Keeper's Sestina. Draper
There's This That I Like about Hockey, My
   Lad. Kieran
Ice-Skating. See Skating and Skaters.
Icebergs
Berg, The. Melville
Convergence of the Twain (Lines on the Loss
   of the *Titanic*, The). Hardy
Iceberg, The. Roberts
Imaginary Iceberg, The. Bishop
On the Ice Islands Seen Floating in the
   German Ocean. Cowper
Iceland
Gunnar's Howe above the House at Lithend.
   Morris
Iceland First Seen. Morris
Journey to Iceland. Auden
Letter to Graham and Anna. MacNeice
Thinking of Iceland. Paulin
Icicles
Icicles. Pinsky
To an Icicle. Dickinson
Why are some icicles long, some short? *Fr.*
   Twenty-three Hokku. Onitsura
Idaho
Idaho. *Unknown*

Identity Crisis
2021: Noon: Idaho. Hawkins
Way Out in Idaho. *Unknown*

Identity Crisis
After Love. Kumin
Agony, An. As Now. Baraka
Being Somebody. Honig
Exits and Entrances. Madgett
Give Me Five. Harris
My Son. Stone
Self-Dependence. Arnold
Woman at the Washington Zoo, The. Jarrell

Idleness
Against Whatever It Is That's Encroaching.
  Simic
Breakfast in Bed (Influenza in War-time).
  McDonald
Idler, The ("Idler holds that rose as always
  rose, An."). Jennings
Idling. Vas
Lament of a Slug-a-Bed's Wife. Smith
Sluggard, The. Watts
To My Now Distant But Once Much Loved
  Friend, Mr. Michael White. Logue
See also **Sloth.**

Idolatry
Idols. Burton
Manicheans did no idols make, The. *Fr.*
  Caelica. Greville
Three things there be in man's opinion dear[e]
  Fr. Caelica. Greville
Worship of Cromm Cruaich, The. *Fr.* The
  Voyage of Bran. *Unknown*

Ignorance
Ignorance of the Wise. Arif

Iguanas
Mid-Noon in January. *Fr.* Australian
  Transcripts. "Macleod"

Illegitimacy
Brown Baby Blues. Marson
Elsa Wertman. *Fr.* Spoon River Anthology.
  Masters
Girl's Lamentation, The. Allingham
Poet's Welcome to His Love-begotten
  Daughter, A. Burns
Practical Woman, A. Hardy
Unknown Girl in the Maternity Ward.
  Sexton

Illinois
Blues for Bessie. O'Higgins
Early Illinois Winter, An. Kuo
El-a-noy. *Unknown*
First Song. Kinnell
From the Illinois Shore. Sheridan
Lovers of the Poor, The. Brooks
Making Chicago. Schmitz
On Clark Street in Chicago. Keithley
On the Building of Springfield. Lindsay
On the Upside. Murray
Planting Trout in the Chicago River.
  Schmitz
Zoo, The. Logan

Illiteracy
Illiterate, The. Meredith
Reading Lesson, The. Murphy
Sarah Byng. Belloc

Illness
Adieu, Farewell, Earth's Bliss[e] *Fr.*
  Summer's Last Will and Testament.
  Nashe
Ague. Csoori
Ailing Japanese Monk, The. Hsiang Ssu
Albumen. Rozewicz
Among the Narcissi. Plath
Blossoms bloom, I don't wanna die, but this
  illness. *Fr.* Thirteen Hokku. Raizan
Bout with Burning. Miller
But, O immortals! What had I to plead. *Fr.*
  Hymn to the Supreme Being on Recovery
  from a Dangerous Fit of Illness. Smart
Comfort for the Sick Child. O'Brien

Composed While Ill. *Fr.* Seventy-six
  Hokku. Basho
Convalescence. McAuley
Crying Uncle. Hansen
Daughter's House, A. Richman
Delighted that Jippo Has Come to See Me in
  My Illness. Rai San'yo
Departure. Lim
Dialogue between the Soul and [the] Body, A.
  Marvell
Each Day. Maura
Entreaty. Fitzgerald
Far Cry after a Close Call, A. Howard
Felix Randal. Hopkins
Fever. *Fr.* The Dance of Death. Browning
Flat One, A. Snodgrass
For Deliverance from a Fever. Bradstreet
For My Wife: A Poem Written in Sickness.
  Yüan Mei
Haiku: "This year/ I took sick with the
  peonies." *Fr.* Thirty-nine Haiku. Shiki
Haiku: Written when Sick in Bed ("I keep on
  asking"). *Fr.* Thirty-nine Haiku. Shiki
His Illness. Ibn Gabirol
Household Remedies. *Unknown*
Hymn to God the Father [*or* For Forgiveness
  or To Christ], A. Donne
Hymn to My God in a Night of My Late
  Sicknesse, A. Wotton
I turn and gaze far. *Fr.* Manyo Shu.
  Yamato-hime
In a Time of Sickness. Orpingalik
In Praise of Music in Time of Pestilence.
  Hine
In Sickness Written Soon after the Author's
  Coming to Live in Ireland, upon the
  Queen's Death, October 1714. Swift
Infirmity. Roethke
Invalid's Song. Harata Tangikuku
Judgment, The. Spivack
Land of Counterpane, The. Stevenson
Leave Us Alone. Rozewicz
Letters from a Father. Van Duyn
Librarian, The. Olson
Lion, Leopard, Lady. Le Pan
Medicine. Walker
Mother Dies. Saito Mokichi
Night Nurse Goes Her Round, The. Gray
999 Call. Bartlett
Notes for the Chart in 306. Nash
Nurse's hand taking my pulse, The. *Fr.*
  Forty-seven Tanka in Three Lines.
  Ishikawa Takuboku
Pain did not wish to be indebted. Ghalib
Parting Talk with Seigan, A. Rai San'yo
Personal Values. Howard
Poem: "You are ill and so I lead you away."
  Purdy
Praise of Diseases. Jacopone da Todi
Return: Intensive Care, The. Lea
Scar, The. Hewitt
She was oblivious the livelong day.
  Tyutchev
Should I, a man, die in vain. *Fr.* Manyo
  Shu. Okura
Sickly Face at the Bottom of the Ground.
  Hagiwara Sakutaro
Sisters. McPherson
So long as lasts the span of life. *Fr.* Manyo
  Shu. Okura
Something Left to Say. Soniat
Song of Sickness, A. Tangikuku
Song of the Darkness. Bricuth
Star Trek III. Harteis
Stones, The. Plath
Summer Nights. Halpern
Tableau. Wright
Tear. Kinsella
To Helen. Praed
To Her Little Son Rinaldo When Sick. Zappi
To Mr. William Long, On His Recovery from
  a Dangerous Illness, 1785. Hayley

To Someone. Kotaro
Tuberculosis. Abse
Tulips. Plath
Tunes for Bears to Dance To. Wallace
2 November 1982. Bold
University Hospital, Boston. Oliver
Upon Prudence Baldwin Her Sickness.
  Herrick
Waiting for a Second Time. Tauhindauli
Watch, The. Cornford
Winter Song. Abd al-Sabur
Year's End. Voigt
Your hair comes undone when you put it up.
  Fr. Manyo Shu. Mikata no Sami

Imagination
Attic, The. Coulette
Autumnal Equinox. Wilson
Bedpost, The. Graves
Block City. Stevenson
Bottle, The. Levine
Centaur, The. Swenson
Child Plays, The. Vala
Corsons Inlet. Ammons
Creative Process, The. *Fr.* The Pleasures of
  Imagination. Akenside
Elevation. Morgan
Fancy and Imagination. Ray
Final Soliloquy of the Interior Paramour.
  Stevens
Good Play, A. Stevenson
He Held Radical Light. Ammons
Hold Fast Your Dreams. Driscoll
Imagine. Campert
Land of Counterpane, The. Stevenson
Laser. Ammons
Letter to a Censor. Cherry
Live here for awhile. Kenko
Mad Gardener's Song, The. *Fr.* Sylvie and
  Bruno. "Carroll"
Magnetized. Sze
Merry Imagination, The. Zelda
Mind's Liberty, The. Davies
Mr. Nobody. *Unknown*
Mrs. Alfred Uruguay. Stevens
My Guardian Angel Stein. Schultz
O warm, enthusiastic maid. *Fr.* Ode to
  Fancy. Warton
Oh, Sleep, Fond Fancy. *Unknown*
On Imagination. Wheatley
One Day When We Went Walking. Hobbs
Plain Sense of Things, The. Stevens
Power of Fancy, The. Freneau
Puella Parvula. Stevens
Romance. Turner
Romance of the Living Corpse. Gonzáles
  Martínez
Settlers, The. Hemschemeyer
Ships of Yule, The. Carman
Sick Child, A. Jarrell
Snow Man, The. Stevens
Somewhere. De la Mare
Storyteller, The. Young
Talking with Soldiers. Turner
Tell Me Where Is Fancy [*or* Fancie] Bred.
  Fr. The Merchant of Venice. Shakespeare
To Imagination. Thomas
Toad, The. Oliver
Underwood. Moss
Upon My Lady Carlisle's Walking in
  Hampton Court Garden. Suckling
Walking to Sleep. Wilbur
Warning to Children. Graves
When the Mississippi Flowed in Indiana.
  Lindsay

Imayavarampan Netunceralatan
Where the Lilies Were in Flower. Kumattur
  Kannanar

Immigrants
America Greets an Alien. Montgomery
At a Chinaman's Grave. Lum
Chinatown Talking Story. Tsui

Chinese Camp, Kamloops (circa 1883). Suknaski
Climb Up, The. *Fr.* Kentucky. Schwartz
Elegy for Bella, Sarah, Rosie, and All the Others. Dorman
Europe and America. Ignatow
Fields, The. Merwin
Foreign Soil. Hai-Jew
How I Learned English. Djanikian
I Am the Little Irish Boy. Thoreau
Immigrants. Frost
Immigrants. Turner
Inheritors, The. Geddes
Letter from Mama Dot. D'Aguiar
Mohajir. Riaz
My Father. Dalven
My Guardian Angel Stein. Schultz
My People Came to This Country. Burt
My Polish Grandma. Field
Nechama. Kaufman
No Irish Need Apply. *Unknown*
No Land like Ours. Barrick
On the Docks. Vaynshteyn
On the Emigration to America [and Peopling the Western Country]. Freneau
On Your Soil, America. Vaynshteyn
Prospective Immigrants Please Note. Rich
Speech for the Repeal of the McCarran Act. Wilbur
Swedish Lesson. Sutter
This Was a Wonderful Night. Stern
To the New World. Jarrell
Who Makes the Journey. Song
William and Phyllis. *Unknown*

Immortality
Ambition. Ringelnatz
Arjuna said:/ How shall I in battle against Bhisma. *Fr.* The Bhagavad-Gita. *Unknown*
Because I could not stop for death. Dickinson
Carried Away. Elder
Come away. *Fr.* Dooms-Day. Herbert
Creed, A. Masefield
Darkling I listen; and for many a time. *Fr.* Ode to a Nightingale. Keats
Dear, beauteous death! the jewel of the just. *Fr.* Ascension Hymn. Vaughan
Death. Herbert
Dryad Song. Fuller
Elegy: "Along the tangled path and in the red." Othón
From too much love of living. *Fr.* The Garden of Proserpine. Swinburne
Great Victory, The. Gilbert
His Immortality. Hardy
Human Life; on the Denial of Immortality. Coleridge
Iliad. Wolfe
Immortal. Teasdale
Immortal Mind, The. Byron
Immortality. "Æ"
Immortality. Arnold
Immortality. "Badawi al-Jabal"
Immortality. Dana
Immortality. Jefferson
Immortality. "Minsky"
Immortality. Mitchell
Immortality. Moorer
Immortality. Reese
Invite to Eternity, An. Clare
It is an honorable thought. Dickinson
Joy, Shipmate, Joy! Whitman
Kiss of God, The. Studdert-Kennedy
My Hereafter. De Long
My life closed twice before its close. Dickinson
New Birth, The. Very
Non Omnis Moriar. Gutiérrez Nájera
"Not marble, nor the gilded monuments." *Fr.* Sonnets, LV. Shakespeare

Ode: Intimations of Immortality from Recollections of Early Childhood. Wordsworth
Ode on a Grecian Urn. Keats
Oh, when this earthly tenement. "Ada"
On a misty day in spring. *Fr.* Manyo Shu. Mushimaro
On the Beach at Night. Whitman
On the day of death, when my bier is on the move. Rumi
"One day I wrote her name upon the strand." *Fr.* Amoretti, LXXV. Spenser
Our Dead. Nichols
Poem in Three Parts. Bly
Poet and His Book, The. Millay
Resurrection. Donne
Sailing to Byzantium. Yeats
Shelley's Skylark. Hardy
Song: "Soules joy, now I am gone." Pembroke
Song of Derivations, A. Meynell
There Is No Death. McCreery
There Is No Death. *Unknown*
Thy nature, immortality! who knows? *Fr.* Night Thoughts. Young
Tithonus. Tennyson
To a Gentleman and Lady on the Death of the Lady's Brother and Sister, and a Child of the Name Avis, Aged One Year. Wheatley
To Bring the Dead to Life. Graves
To Inez Milholland. Millay
To This Hill Again. Macmillan
Village Atheist, The. *Fr.* Spoon River Anthology. Masters
Virtue. Herbert
Waterfall [*or* Water-Fall], The. Vaughan
We thirst at first—'tis nature's act. Dickinson
Well, all these seamen—sailors and skippers—they. *Fr.* The End. Corbière
What street is this? Mandelstam
Whispers of Immortality. Eliot
With you, I know, my offering will find grace. *Fr.* Epistle to Elizabeth, Countess of Rutland. Jonson

Imperialism
European Crimes. *Fr.* Gotham. Churchill
Free Up de Lan, White Man. Mutabaruka
Goodbye Nkrumah. DiPrima
Hand, The. Fawcett
Hatred of Men with Black Hair. Bly
Hope. O'Connor
Human Wisdom. Delgado
Imperial. *Fr.* Album Leaves. Fairburn
Imperialists in Retirement. Lucie-Smith
Recessional. Kipling
Remember Suez? Mitchell
Scythians, The. Blok
When London Calls. Daley
Your Pain. Guebuza

Impermanence. *See* **Transience.**

Impotence
Against an Old Lecher. Harington
And Now You're Ready Who While She Was Here. Cunningham
Disabled Debauchee, The. Rochester
Faint Heart. Rufinus Domesticus
Imperfect Enjoyment, The. Rochester
O Dear O. *Unknown*
One Writing against His Prick. *Unknown*
To the Tune "Red Embroidered Shoes." Huang O

Impressionism
Berthe Morisot. Waldman
Monet Refuses the Operation. Mueller

Incantations
Thrice the Brinded Cat Hath Mewed. *Fr.* Macbeth. Shakespeare

Incense
Burning Incense. Yu T'ung

Incest
Chain. Lorde
Christmas with the Holy Family. Cavin
Delgadina. *Unknown*
English Was Only a Second Language. Borawski
Shower, The. Smukler
Sons and Fathers. Mitchell
We built mountain paddies. *Fr.* Manyo Shu. Kinashi no Karu
Wind of Late Summer, The. Stewart

Inclosure Movement
Cottager's Complaint, on the Intended Bill for Enclosing Sutton-Coldfield, The. Freeth
John Clare and the Acts of Enclosure. Curry

Indecision. *See* **Decisions.**

Independence
Even Tho. Nichols
Hour, The. Virtue
Independance. Bennett
Independence Twenty-One. Bennett

Independence Day. *See* **Fourth of July.**

India
Ajanta. Rukeyser
Bear on the Delhi Road, The. Birney
Defence of Lucknow, The. Tennyson
Documentary. Stroud
Evening Walk in Bengal, An. Heber
Gunga Din. Kipling
In India. Shapiro
In Springtime. Kipling
In the Bazaars of Hyderabad. Naidu
India. Coates
Introduction, An: "I don't know politics but I know the names." Das
Lepers Cry. Orlovsky
Mahratta Ghats, The. Lewis
Mandalay. Kipling
Passage to India. Whitman
Postcards from Kodai. Crossley-Holland
Rajpoot Rebels. Lyall
Signature II. Stroud
Suttee, The. Skinner
Painted streets alive with hum of noon, The. *Fr.* The Light of Asia. Arnold.
Golden Tradition, The; an Anthology of Urdu Poetry (GoT). Ahmed Ali, ed. *and* tr.
Penguin Book of Modern Urdu Poetry, The (PBMUP). Mahmood Jamal, ed. *and* tr.
Poems of Love and War from the Eight Anthologies and the Ten Long Poems of Classical Tamil (PLW). A. K. Ramanujan, comp. *and* tr.
Songs of the Saints of India (SSI). John Stratton Hawley, ed.

Indian Summer
Indian Summer. Breban
Indian Summer. Campbell
Indian Summer. Leib
Indian Summer. Moodie
Indian Summer. Tabb
Indian Summer Day on the Prairie, An. Lindsay
Pyre of My Indian Summer, The. Leib
These are the days when birds come back. Dickinson
Vermont: Indian Summer. Booth

Indiana
July in Indiana. Fitzgerald
Sketch for a Morning in Muncie, Indiana. Murray
Valedictory to Standard Oil of Indiana, A. Wagoner

Indians, American
Adulteries, murthers, robberies, thefts. Williams
Aecclesiae et Reipub. Strachey
Alice Corbin Is Gone. Sandburg
American Indian, The. *Unknown*
Arrowy Dreams. Bynner
At Gull Lake; August, 1810. Scott

At the Klamath Berry Festival. Stafford
Ballad of Ira Hayes. La Farge
Bar's Fight, August 28, 1746. Terry
Black Hawk in Hiding. Keithley
Boast not proud English, of thy birth and blood. Williams
Calling One's Own. *Unknown*
Can I Say. Bird
Carrier Indians. Belford
Cattle Thief, The. Johnson
Caughnawaga Beadwork Seller, The. Lighthall
Cherokee, The. Fordham
Christmas Comes to Moccasin Flat. Welch
Church on Comiaken Hill, The. Hugo
Columbus Reaches Juana, 1492. Gustafson
Crazy Horse Returns to South Dakota. Elliott
Dakota: October, 1822, Hunkpapa Warrior. Taylor
Dawn Boy's Song. *Unknown*
Dead on the War Path. *Unknown*
Dying Indian, The. Warton
End of the Indian Poems, The. Plumly
Forsaken, The. Scott
From his wanderings far to eastward. *Fr.* The Song of Hiawatha. Longfellow
Gateway Arch. Cheng Ch'ou-yu
Ghost Dance: August, 1976, The. Jauss
Ghosts of the Buffaloes, The. Lindsay
Go For Broke. Breton
Hiawatha's Childhood. *Fr.* The Song of Hiawatha. Longfellow
I Expected My Skin and My Blood to Ripen. Rose
I love you better than I love my race. *Fr.* Tecumseh. Mair
Immigrants. Turner
In Cold Storm Light. Silko
In the Oregon Country. Stafford
Indian at the Burial-Place of His Fathers, An. Bryant
Indian Burying Ground, The. Freneau
Indian Camp. McFatter
Indian Convert, The. Freneau
Indian Dance. Niven
Indian Hunter, The. Cook
Indian Lass, The. *Unknown*
Indian Maid, The; Demararie, Oct. 27, 1781. Thompson
Indian Names. Sigourney
Indian Reservation: Caughnawaga. Klein
Indian School. Russell
Indian Student; or, Force of Nature, The. Freneau
Indians. Fandel
Indians Come Down from Mixco, The. Asturias
Indian's Welcome to the Pilgrim Fathers, The. Sigourney
Inscription: "Eagle, stooping from yon snow-blown peaks, The." Whittier
It Was a Long Time Before. Silko
Keep a Dime. Swallow
Lamentable Ballad of the Bloody Brook, The. Hale
Last Man Killed by Indians in Kimble County, Texas, The. Angelotti
Last Reservation, The. Learned
Lennox Island. McFadden
Little Mohea, The. *Unknown*
Little Papoose. Conkling
Long Time Ago. Silko
Lovewell's Fight. *Unknown*
Magpie Song. *Unknown*
Meanings in the Pattern, The. Grahn
Memorial Ode. Buck
Mending the Adobe. Carruth
Native, The. Merwin
Natives of America, The. Plato
New Apartment, Minneapolis, The. Hogan
New Mexican Mountain. Jeffers

Of Sitting Bear. *Fr.* The General Mule Poems. Dodd
Ojistoh. Johnson
Old Man, the Sweat Lodge. George
On the Way to the Mission. Scott
Osceola. Whitman
Pocahontas. Thackeray
Poem for Nana. Jordan
Portrait of an Indian. Rashley
Powwow. Snodgrass
Pride, The. Newlove
Prophecy of King Tammany, The. Freneau
Rain Song of the Giant Society. *Unknown*
Red Men, The. Sangster
Remains of an Indian Village. Purdy
Returned to Say. Stafford
Savage, A. O'Reilly
Saying Her Name. Galvin
Song of Greatness, A. *Unknown*
Song of the Ancient People, The. Proctor
Song of the Micmac, The. Howe
Songs in the Garden of the House God. *Unknown*
Sonnet: "There was an Indian, who had known no change." Squire
Speech of the Salish Chief. *Fr.* Damnation of Vancouver. Birney
Spontaneous Requiem for the American Indian. Corso
Thomas Iron-Eyes. Walsh
To the Driving Cloud. Longfellow
Ute Lover, The. Garland
Ute Mountain. Tomlinson
We Are a People. Henson
Winkte. Kenny
Woman Hanging from the Thirteenth Floor Window, The. Harjo
Yonosa House. Smith
Carriers of the Dream Wheel; Contemporary Native American Poetry (CDW). Duane Niatum, ed.
Gathering of Spirit, A; Writing and Art by North American Indian Women (GOS). Beth Brant.
Harper's Anthology of 20th-Century Native American Poetry (HATNAP). Duane Niatum, ed.
New and Old Voices of Wah'kon-tah; Contemporary Native American Poetry (NOVW). Robert K. Dodge *and* Joseph B. McCullough, eds.
Shaking the Pumpkin; Traditional Poetry of the Indian North Americans (STP). Jerome Rothenberg, ed.
Songs from This Earth on Turtle's Back (STE). Joseph Bruchac, ed.
Voices of the Rainbow (VoR). Kenneth Rosen, ed.

Individualism
Game of Life, The. Saxe
Mission of the Flowers, The. Harper
Ode Inscribed to W. H. Channing. Emerson
On Stripping Bark from Myself. Walker
Self-Dependence. Arnold
Silence. Moore
See also **Egotism.**

Indolence. *See* **Idleness; Laziness; Sloth.**

Indonesia
Dead Soldiers. Fenton
Walking down Jalan Thamrin. Brissenden
See also **Borneo.**

Indulgences
Pardoner's Tale, The. *Fr.* The Canterbury Tales. Chaucer

Industrial Revolution
Factory Girl's Come-All-Ye, The. *Unknown*
My Grandfather's Days. *Unknown*
Next day they rambled round the town, and swore. *Fr.* Ramble of the Gods through Birmingham. Bisset
Steam at Sheffield. Elliott

Steam King, The. Mead
Steam Power. *Fr.* The Botanic Garden: The Economy of Vegetation. Darwin
While neighbouring cities waste the fleeting hours. *Fr.* Colebrook Dale. Seward

Industrialization
Cornfields in Accra. Aidoo
Tyrants were/ people. Saarikoski
Valedictory to Standard Oil of Indiana, A. Wagoner

Infant Death
Child Dying, The. Muir
Cruel Mother, The. *Unknown*
Dead Baby, The. Williams
Firstborn, The. Soto
For a Child Born Dead. Jennings
Future Generation. NorthSun
Gill Boy. Schmitz
Home Burial. Frost
Inquest, The. Davies
Lament for Tadhg Cronin's Children. Hartnett
On a Child Who Lived One Minute. Kennedy
On a Dead Babe. Riley
On an Infant Dying as Soon as Born. Lamb
On My First Daughter. Jonson
On My First Son [*or* Sonne]. Jonson
Pietà. McAuley
To an Infant Expiring the Second Day of Its Birth. Wright
We Assume: On the Death of Our Son, Reuben Masai Harper. Harper
See also **Death in Childhood.**

Infanticide
At Devlin's Siding. Boake
Inquest, The. Davies
Mary Hamilton. *Unknown*
Queen's Marie, The. *Unknown*
Runaway Slave at Pilgrim's Point, The. Browning

Infants. *See* **Babies.**

Infidelity
Adultery. Dickey
Along the Field as We Came By. *Fr.* A Shropshire Lad. Housman
Away! Go back to where you spent the night! Surdas
Bianca among the Nightingales. Browning
By day and also by night and you are. *Fr.* Earthly: Sonnets for Carlos. Wedde
By Then You'd Dressed. Oravecz
Caledonia. McElroy
Change Thy Mind since She Doth Change. Essex
Chop-Cherry. Herrick
Clever Skipper, The. *Unknown*
Crowned with flowers, I saw fair Amarillis. *Unknown*
Deposition from Love, A. Carew
Dionysus. Layton
Epistle from Mrs. Yonge to Her Husband. Montagu
First Lawcase, The. *Unknown*
Five on the Riverside Cane, *sels.* Orampokiyar
Frankie Blues. *Unknown*
Host of the Air, The. Yeats
"If thy wife is small bend down to her and." *Fr.* Earthly: Sonnets for Carlos. Wedde
Jilted Nymph, The. Campbell
Kiss ("She came home, smelling of another man"). Tanikawa Shuntaro
Little Musgrave and Lady Barnard. *Unknown*
Little Sparrow. *Unknown*
Madrigal: "Your love is dead, lady, your love is dead." Thomas
Newcomer's Wife, The. Hardy
Non Sum Qualis Eram Bonae sub Regno Cynarae [*or* Cynara]. Dowson

Ode, An: "Now I find thy looks were feigned." *Fr.* Phyllis. Lodge
Of an Heroical Answer of a Great Roman Lady to Her Husband. Harington
Only Jealousy of Emer, The. *Unknown*
Queen Eleanor's Confession. *Unknown*
Resolving Doubts. Dickey
Scrutiny [*or* Scrutinie], The. Lovelace
Song: "Go and catch a falling star." Donne
Song: "Phillis is my only joy." Sedley
Song: "'Tis affection but dissembled." Godolphin
Sonnet: Oh, Think Not I Am Faithful to a Vow! Millay
Stanzas Written in Great Haste in Reply to Some Proposing That Women Are Fickle. Belisarda
Temperaments, The. Pound
Thursday. Millay
Trail to Mexico, The. *Unknown*
Two or Three; a Recipe [*or* Receipt] to Make a Cuckold. Pope
Upon Scobble [Epigram]. Herrick
What Her Girl Friend Said, Seeing Her Friend Suffer in Silent Dignity over Her Husband's Infidelity. Kayamanar
What Her Girl Friend Said, When the Woman Was About to Take Back Her Unfaithful Husband. Orampokiyar
What She Said about Her Unfaithful, Estranged Husband. Netumpalliyattan
What She Said ("As the lovely new flowers"). Allur Nanmullai
What should [*or* shulde] I say[e]. Wyatt
When Daisies Pied [and Violets Blue]. *Fr.* Love's Labour's Lost. Shakespeare
"When my love swears [*or* sweares] that she is made of truth." *Fr.* Sonnets, CXXXVIII. Shakespeare
When We Two Parted. Byron
White-flower is twisted into bast, The. *Unknown*
Who Would Have Thought. *Fr.* The Lover Deceived Writes to His Lady. Howell
Woman's Constancy. Donne
See also **Adultery.**

Inflation
$. Abelardo

Inheritance
Inheritance. *Unknown*
Lines to My Father. Daiken
Michael. Wordsworth
Remonstrance, A. Gerrard
Short Song of Congratulation [*or* To a Young Heir], A. Johnson
To Geron. Jacob

Injustice
Abraham Lincoln Walks at Midnight. Lindsay
And yet not long ago. *Fr.* Vox Populi, Vox Dei. *Unknown*
Anti-Racist Person. Prescod
Epistle to the Emperor Napoleon (1810). Salm-Dyck
I pray you, be not wroth. *Fr.* Vox Populi, Vox Dei. *Unknown*
Injustice. Delarue-Mardrus
Injustice of the Courts. Moorer
Justice Denied in Massachusetts. Millay
"Tired [*or* Tyr'd] with all these, for restful death I cry." *Fr.* Sonnets, LXVI. Shakespeare
See also **Protest, Social.**

Inkwells
To a Post-Office Inkwell. Morley

Innisfree, Ireland
Lake Isle of Innisfree, The. Yeats

Innocence
Auguries of Innocence. Blake
Garden, A. Wakeman
In School-Days. Whittier

Innocence. Kavanagh
Old Whorehouse, An. Oliver
Posting the Letter. Welch
Vanishers, The. Whittier

Inns
Hostess of the Ferry Inn, The. Gwerfyl Mechain
See also **Hotels; Motels.**

Insanity. *See* **Madness; Mental Illness.**

Insects
As the night deepens. Yoshimoto
August Midnight, An. Hardy
Divine Insect, The. Wheelock
Insect Heads. Bly
Insects, The. Willard
Little Black Bug. Brown
Minimal, The. Roethke
Motive for Mercy. Milburn
Nameless One, A. Avison
Not Machines. Redgrove
Plane Geometer. McCord
Tiniest of Lives, The. Chin Jen-Jui
To a Midge. Nisbet

Insomnia
Foreign Fencers. Leyeles
I Need Help. Hirsch
Insomnia. Thomas
Insomnia I. Nemerov
Insomnia the Gem of the Ocean. Updike
One Night. Saba
Savannah, Sleepless. Tillinghast
Sleeplessness. Yüan Mei
Walking to Sleep. Wilbur

Inspiration
If with light head erect I sing. *Fr.* Inspiration. Thoreau
Inspiration. Gibson
Inspiration. Service
Inspiration. Thoreau

Institutionalization
Evening in the Sanitarium. Bogan
In the Ward. Lowell
Institutions. Fox
Martha Nelson Speaks. Bogin
Ringing the Bells. Sexton
Sleepers, The. Kocan
Supremer Sacrifice, The. "Maurice"
To One in Bedlam. Dowson
Transparent Man, The. Hecht
Visitor's Parking. Szumigalski
Waking in the Blue. Lowell

Intellect
All-seeing Intellect, The. *Fr.* The Purple Island. Fletcher
At Woodward's Gardens. Frost
Blue Swallows, The. Nemerov
Brainstorm. Nemerov
Cause: "Brain is wider than the sky, The." Dickinson
Freedom for the Mind. Garrison
Gathering, The. Ammons
Harsh Climate. Simic
Hymn to Intellectual Beauty. Shelley
I Remember Galileo. Stern
In a Hard Intellectual Light. Eberhart
Lobotomy. Pitchford
Mind. Graham
Mind. Wilbur
Mind, Intractable Thing, The. Moore
Mind Is an Enchanting Thing, The. Moore
My Mind [*or* Minde *or* Mynde] to Me a Kingdom [*or* Kyngdome] Is. Dyer
On the Birth of His Son. Su Tung-p'o
Perishing Bird, The. Jones
Pet Panther. Ammons
Reply to the Committed Intellectual. Sparshott
Sonnet: Content and Resolute. Drummond
Thought. Emerson
Wandering Lunatic Mind, The. Carpenter
What if the foot, ordain'd the dust to tread. *Fr.* An Essay on Man. Pope

International Brigade. *See* **Civil War, Spanish.**

Internationalism. *See* **League of Nations; United Nations.**

Internment
Breaking Silence. Mirikitani
Coming Home from Camp. Kaneko
Family Album. Kaneko
In Response to Executive Order 9066: All Americans of Japanese Descent Must Report to Relocation Centers. Okita
Old Photo, 1942. Uba
On the Bus. *Fr.* Camp Notes. Mitsuye Yamada
Relocation. Mura

Interracial Love and Marriage
Ballad: "Altho' a slave me is born and bred." Moreton
Brown Baby Blues. Marson
Obeah Night. Rhys

Inventors
In Tesla's Laboratory. Johnson
Inventors. Blumenthal
Inventor's Wife, The. Corbett
Wrights' Biplane, The. Frost

Investment
Investor's Soliloquy. Ward

Iona, Scotland
Iona. Coxe
Iona; the Graves of the Kings. Jeffers
There Are Gods. Riley

Iowa
Amazing Grace. Hollo
Autumn, Iowa City. Thumboo
Explanation. Hewitt
Images from the Midwest. Belev
Indian Summer. Breban
Iowa. Browne
Iowa City under the Sky of the Mayflower. Espina-Villafan
Iowa Recollected in Tranquility. Jay
Mile Hill. Schmitz
Of Time and River. Romano de Sant'Anna
Old Dubuque. Etter
Possibilities of Snow. Cheng Wen-tao
Snow in Iowa City. Mahapatra
What I Owe Iowa. Longinovic

Iphigenia
Cymon and Iphigenia. Dryden
Iphigeneia and Agamemnon. *Fr.* The Hellenics. Landor

Iran
O Realm Bejewelled. Farrokhzad
When the Sultan Goes to Ispahan. Aldrich

Ireland
Alfrid's Itinerary through Ireland. *Unknown*
Andromeda. Roche
Anglo-Eire Vignette. Stevenson
Anseo. Muldoon
Arran. *Unknown*
Back to Dublin. Ford
Bogland. Heaney
Celts, The. Magee
Clay is the word and clay is the flesh. *Fr.* The Great Hunger. Kavanagh
Cold Irish Earth, The. Skinner
Croppy Boy, The. *Unknown*
Cult of the Celtic, The. Deane
Cushendun. *Fr.* The Closing Album. MacNeice.
Dark Rosaleen. MacWard
Dawning o' the Year, The. Blake
Dear Harp of My Country. Moore
Downfall of the Gael, The. O'Gnive
Dublin. *Fr.* The Closing Album. MacNeice
Dublin Made Me. MacDonagh
Dunlavin Green. *Unknown*
Easter, 1916. Yeats

Eireann. *Fr.* Afternoons with Baedeker.
  Lancaster
Eviction, The. *Fr.* Laurence Bloomfield in
  Ireland. Allingham
Fair Hills of Ireland, The. *Unknown*
Famine Road, The. Boland
Fern Hill. Thomas
General wonder in our land. *Unknown*
Glorious Twelfth, The. Greacen
Go to Old Ireland. *Unknown*
Harp That Once through Tara's Halls, The.
  Moore
Hibernia. Howard-Jones
His Father's Hands. Kinsella
Holy Ground, The. *Unknown*
Hospitality in Ancient Ireland. *Unknown*
Hosting of the Sidhe, The. Yeats
"I Am of Ireland." Yeats
I call the land of Ireland. *Fr.* Amergin's
  Songs. Amergin
If Ever You Go to Rubbu Town. Kavanagh
In Ireland: By the Pool at the Third Rosses.
  Symons
In Memoriam Francis Ledwidge. Heaney
Ireland. Stuart
Ireland. Swift
Ireland Never Was Contented. Landor
Ireland Weeping. Livingston
Ireland with Emily. Betjeman
Irish Cliffs of Moher, The. Stevens
Irish Dancer, The. *Unknown*
Irish Picture, An. Bigg
Irish Skies. Letts
Island, The. Jennett
Kathaleen Ny-Houlahan. Heffernan
Kevin Barry. *Unknown*
Land Called Scotia, The. Donatus
Let Erin Remember the Days of Old. Moore
Little Black Rose. *Unknown*
Lord Crashton: The Absentee Landlord. *Fr.*
  Laurence Bloomfield in Ireland.
  Allingham
Maguire is not afraid of death, the Church
  will light him a candle. *Fr.* The Great
  Hunger. Kavanagh
Many ingenious lovely things are gone. *Fr.*
  Nineteen Hundred and Nineteen. Yeats
Midnight Court, The. Merriman
Minstrel Boy, The. Moore
Mountown! thou sweet retreat from Dublin
  cares. *Fr.* Mully of Mountown. King
Mr. Gunman. Garbutt
Municipal Gallery Revisited, The. Yeats
Nation Once Again, A. Davis
Nightmare leaves fatigue. *Fr.* Autumn
  Journal. MacNeice
No table there is spread. *Fr.* The Image of
  Irelande. Derricke
Numerous Celts. Squire
Oh! blame not the bard, if he fly to the
  bowers. Moore
Oh! where's the slave so lowly. Moore
On a Political Prisoner. Yeats
On the Irish Club. Swift
Once Alien Here. Hewitt
Orange Lily, The. *Unknown*
Our Stars Come from Ireland. Stevens
Parnell. Yeats
Pastoral Ballad by John Bull, A. Moore
Petition of the Orangemen of Ireland, The.
  Moore
Poor Scholar of the 'Forties, A. Colum
Prayer for My Daughter, A. Yeats
Prelude: "Still south I went and west and
  south again." Synge
Red Hanrahan's Song about Ireland. Yeats
Remittance Man. Wright
Requiem for the Croppies. Heaney
Right Heart in the Wrong Place, The.
  Joyce
Rose Tree, The. Yeats
September 1913. Yeats

Shan Van Vocht, The. *Unknown*
Singing School. Heaney
Sixteen Dead Men. Shorter
Sleepless Night, A. O'Rahilly
Small Towns of Ireland, The.
  Betjeman
Soggarth Aroon. Banim
Song: "In Ireland, in Ireland." Morgan
Song to Erin. Fordham
Spenser's Ireland. Moore
Spring Flowers from Ireland.
  MacCarthy
Sweet Innisfallen. Moore
Time of Change, A. O'Rahilly
To Ireland in the Coming Times. Yeats
To My Native Land. Mangan
Traditions. Heaney
Ulster. Kipling
View of the Present State of Ireland, A.
  Blunden
Vision, The. O'Rahilly
Washing the Coins. Dunn
Wearin' o' the Green, The. *Unknown*
Wearing of [*or* Wearin' o'] the Green, The.
  Unknown
Whack Fol the Diddle. Kearney
Wounds. Longley
Written in Ireland. Alcock
Anthology of Irish Literature, An (AnIL).
  David H. Greene, ed.
Book of Irish Verse, The (BIrV). John
  Montague, ed.
Contemporary Irish Poetry (CIP). Anthony
  Bradley, ed.
*Faber Book of Contemporary Irish Poetry,
  The* (FaBCIP). Paul Muldoon, ed.
Irish Poetry after Yeats (IPY). Maurice
  Harmon, ed.
New Irish Poets (NeIP). Devin A. Garrity,
  ed.
New Oxford Book of Irish Verse, The (NOIV).
  Thomas Kinsella, ed. *and* tr.
Treasury of Irish Religious Verse (TIRV).
  Patrick Murray, ed.
See also **Individual Counties listed under
  (e.g.) County Donegal, Ireland;** *also*
  Northern Ireland.
Ireland, Northern. *See* **Northern Ireland.**
Iris (flower)
  Beds of Fleur-de-Lys, The. Gilman
  Blue Flag. Donnelly
  Iris. Williams
  Irises. Colum
  Irises in a Marsh. Tamemasa
  Iris looks exactly like the one in the water,
    The. *Fr.* Seventy-six Hokku. Basho
  White Iris, A. Barrington
Irish, The
  Barney McGee. Hovey
  Boys of Wexford, The. *Unknown*
  Civil Irish and Wild Irish. Mac an Bhaird
  Cult of the Celtic, The. Deane
  Docker. Heaney
  Exiles. O'Connor
  Exodus to Connacht. O'Meallain
  Fighting Race, The. Clarke
  Finnegan's Wake. *Unknown*
  Gaeltacht. Hutchinson
  Hibernia. Howard-Jones
  Insular Celts, The. Carson
  Ireland. Hewitt
  Irish Antiquities. Moore
  Irish Grandmother. Edelman
  Irishman in Coventry, An. Hewitt
  No Irish Need Apply. *Unknown*
  On Behalf of Some Irishmen Not Followers of
    Tradition. "Æ"
  Poor Paddy Works on the Railway.
    Unknown
  Ulsterman, An. Doyle
  Written on the Sense of Isolation in
    Contemporary Ireland. Greacen

Irish Verse
  Anthology of Irish Literature, An (AnIL).
    David H. Greene, ed.
  Book of Irish Verse, The (BIrV). John
    Montague, ed.
  Contemporary Irish Poetry (CIP). Anthony
    Bradley, ed.
  *Faber Book of Contemporary Irish Poetry,
    The* (FaBCIP). Paul Muldoon, ed.
  Irish Poetry after Yeats (IPY). Maurice
    Harmon, ed.
  New Irish Poets (NeIP). Devin A. Garrity,
    ed.
  New Oxford Book of Irish Verse, The (NOIV).
    Thomas Kinsella, ed. *and* tr.
  Treasury of Irish Religious Verse (TIRV).
    Patrick Murray, ed.
Iron
  Humphrey Hardfeature's Descriptions of
    Cast-Iron Inventions. *Unknown*
  Red Iron Ore. *Unknown*
  Scrap Iron. Durgnat
  Some Good Things to Be Said for the Iron
    Age. Snyder
Iron Lungs
  Iron Lung, The. Plumly
Irony
  Sonnet Ending with a Film Subtitle. Hacker
  Tiresias. Garrett
Isaac
  Akedah, The. Megged
  Isaac. Burnshaw
  Isaac. Guri
  Isaac. Holtz
  Isaac. Jacobs
  Parable of the Old Man and the Young, The.
    Owen
  Sacrifice, The. Bloch
  Sacrifice. Leivick
  Story of Isaac. Cohen
Isaiah
  Isaiah and Homer. Leyeles
Ishi
  Ishi. Schierbeek
Ishmael
  Hagar and Ishmael. Lasker-Schüler
  Isaac. Jacobs
  Ishmael. Palmer
Ishtar
  Song for Ishtar. Levertov
Isis
  Isis and the Animals: I. Claus
  Prayer to Isis. Walsh
Islands
  Alaskan Fragments June 1981 — Summer
    Solstice. Rose
  Arran. *Unknown*
  Barred Islands. Booth
  Enviable Isles, The. Melville
  If Once You Have Slept on an Island. Field
  Island, The. Jennett
  Island. Rin
  Islandish. Leyeles
  Lake Isle of Innisfree, The. Yeats
  Letter from an Island. Brinnin
  Love for an Island. Allfrey
  Love Overgrows a Rock. Roach
  On This Island. Auden
  One Island. Nye
  Ragged Island. Millay
  Shore Thing. Hillila
  Sorrow of Love, The. Yeats
  Tristan da Cunha. Campbell
Isle of Man
  Braddan Vicarage. Brown
Isle of Wight, England
  At Farringford. *Fr.* To the Rev. F. D.
    Maurice. Tennyson
  Forsaken Garden, A. Swinburne
  November in the Isle of Wight. *Fr.* Enoch
    Arden. Tennyson

Israel
Banner of the Jew, The. Lazarus
But We Shall Bloom. Guri
Canaan. Spark
Déjà Vu. Kaufman
Desert Wind. Heifetz-Tussman
For Years I Wallowed. Manger
Garden of Abu Mahmoud, The. Nye
Hear, O Israel! Spire
New Ezekiel, The. Lazarus
Pictures at an Exhibition. Rosenbaum
Temple, The. Kahn
Israeli Poetry; a Contemporary Anthology
(IP). Warren Bargad *and* Stanley F.
Chyet, comps. *and* trs.
Modern Hebrew Poetry (MHeP). Bernhard
Frank, ed. *and* tr.

Italian Verse
*Defiant Muse, The; Italian Feminist Poems
from the Middle Ages to the Present* (DMI).
Beverly Allen, Muriel Kittel, *and* Keala
Jane Jewell, eds.
*New Italian Poetry, The, 1945 to the Present;
a Bilingual Anthology* (NItP). Lawrence
R. Smith, ed. *and* tr.
Poems from Italy (PFI). William Jay Smith
and Dana Gioia, eds.

Italians, The
Cigarette for the Bambino. Ewart
Market Day. Roversi
Modern Romans, The. Johnson

Italy
Agrigentum Road, The. Quasimodo
Amours de Voyage, *sels.* Clough
And you, Italy, one day I knelt. *Fr.* Europe.
Larbaud
Apple Trees at Olema, The. Hass
Byron Recollected at Bologna. *Fr.* Italy.
Rogers
Cats of Campagnatico, The. Porter
City of Beggars, The. Hayes
Cypresses. Lawrence
Daisy, The. Tennyson
Driver in Italy, The. Christopher
England. Moore
Fiascherino. Tomlinson
Field Ambulance in Retreat. Sinclair
Florence. *Fr.* Aurora Leigh. Browning
"Frater Ave atque Vale." Tennyson
Good-bye to the Mezzogiorno. Auden
Hotel Paradiso e Commerciale. Brinnin
Immortal glories in my mind revive. *Fr.* A
Letter from Italy [to the Right Honourable
Charles Lord Halifax]. Addison
Italia, Io Ti Saluto. Rossetti
Italian Woman. Wakoski
Italy. Filicaia
Journey. *Fr.* Wright
Letter from Italy, to the Right Honourable
Charles Lord Halifax, A. Addison
Life of. . . , The. Weiss
Lines Written among the Euganean Hills.
Shelley
Memories of Italy (Broken Sestina). Ash
Olives and Mountains. *Fr.* Aurora Leigh.
Browning
On Descending the River Po. Parsons
On the Road to Vicenza. Gustafson
Piano di Sorrento. *Fr.* The Englishman in
Italy. Browning
Poem: "So many pigeons at Columbus."
Gregor
Super Flumina Babylonis. Swinburne
Up at a Villa—Down in the City. Browning
Walking in the 15th Century. Halpern
What I love best in all the world. *Fr.* De
Gustibus. Browning

Itching
Taboo to Boot. Nash

Ithaca, New York
Ithaca. Aal

Ivy
Holly against Ivy. *Unknown*
In Praise of Ivy. *Unknown*
Ivy Green, The. *Fr.* The Pickwick Papers.
Dickens

J

Jack and Jill
Flight of the Bucket, The. Kipling
Jack and Jill. Loomis
Jill, Afterwards. Dacey
Jack and the Beanstalk
Jack, Afterwards. Dacey
Jack and the Beanstalk. Rosen
Jackdaws
Of a Daw. Heywood
Jackrabbits
Jack Rabbit. Stoutenburg
Jackson, Andrew
Andrew Jackson. Keller
Jackson at New Orleans. Rice
Madam Hickory. Larremore
Three Presidents. Bly
Jackson, Helen Hunt
Helen Hunt Jackson. Coolbrith
Jackson, "Hurricane"
On Hurricane Jackson. Dugan
Jackson, Mahalia
When Mahalia Sings. Prettyman
Jackson, Thomas Jonathan (Stonewall)
Dying Words of Stonewall Jackson, The.
Lanier
Stonewall Jackson. Flash
Stonewall Jackson's Way. Palmer
Under the Shade of the Trees. Preston
Jacob
Jacob. Reznikoff
Jacob. Schwartz
Jacob and the Angel. Mitchell
Jacob ("Jacob: a bull among his herd").
Lasker-Schüler
Jacob Studies "The Selling of Joseph" with
His Sons. Manger
Little East of Jordan, A. Dickinson
Patriarch Jacob Meets Rachel, The. Manger
Wrestling Jacob. Wesley
Jacob, Max
To Max Jacob. Warren
Jacobites
Old Scottish Cavalier, The. Aytoun
Jaguars
Second Glance at a Jaguar. Hughes
Jaikur, Iraq
In the Arab Maghreb. Al-Sayyab
Jaikur and the City. Al-Sayyah
Shadows of Jaikur. Al-Sayyab
Jails. *See* **Prisons and Prisoners.**
Jam-and Jelly-Making
Making the Jam without You. Kumin
On Jam. Belloc
Jamaica
Hour, The. Virtue
Independance. Bennett
Independence Twenty-One. Bennett
Jamaica. Simpson
Maroon Girl, The. Roberts
No Man's Land. Escoffery
Our tropic fruits, nurs'd 'neath a torrid sky.
Fr. A Poetical Epistle, from the Island of
Jamaica, to. *Unknown*
Valediction, A: "Before the seas again
divide." Roberts
Jamaica, West Indies
Jamaica Market. Maxwell-Hall
Two-an'-Six. McKay

James I, King of England
To His Late Majesty Concerning the True
Form of English Poetry. Beaumont
James II, King of England
Dialogue between King William and the Late
King James on the Banks of the Boyne, A.
Blount
King James II. *Fr.* The Hind and the
Panther. Dryden
Trick for Tyburn; or, A Prison Rant, A.
Unknown
Upon the King's Voyage to Chatham to Make
Bulwarks against the Dutch. *Unknown*
James IV, King of Scotland
Ballade of the Scottyshe Kynge, A. Skelton
Then the Provost he uprose. *Fr.* Edinburgh
after Flodden. Aytoun
James, Henry
At the Grave of Henry James. Auden
Henry James. Stevenson
Henry James at Newport. Kees
Jacobean. Fadiman
James I, King of England
To His Late Majesty Concerning the True
Form of English Poetry. Beaumont
James II, King of England
Humble Address, The. *Unknown*
Jamestown, Virginia
Burning of Jamestown, The. English
Jamestown. Jarrell
Ode to Jamestown. Paulding
January
January. Gibson
January. Heath-Stubbs
January. Nishiwaki Junzaburo
January. Ray
January. *Fr.* Sonnets of the Months. San
Gimignano
January. Updike
January. Voigt
January. Williams
January 25th. Kumin
On the wind of January. *Unknown*
Janus
Janus. Mason
Japan
Ancestors' Graves in Kurakawa. Kogawa
Buddha at Kamakura. Kipling
Cottage at Chigasaki, The. Blunden
Japan. Hecht
Japanesque. Herford
Letters from Kazuko (Kyoto, Japan—Summer
1980). Lau
Merchant at Yokohama, The. *Fr.* Residential
Rhymes. Edwards
Professor in Nirvana, The. *Fr.* Residential
Rhymes. Edwards
Snow Party, The. Mahon
Untitled. Bass
Walk in Kyoto, A. Birney
*From the Country of Eight Islands; an
Anthology of Japanese Poetry* (FCEI).
Hiroaki Sato *and* Burton Watson, eds. *and*
trs.
Japanese Literature in Chinese (JLIC).
Burton Watson, tr.
Manyoshu, The (Ma). Foreword by Donald
Keene
Penguin Book of Japanese Verse, The
(PeBJV). Geoffrey Bownes *and* Anthony
Thwaite, trs.
*Waiting for the Wind; Thirty-six Poets of
Japan's Late Medieval Age* (WFTW).
Steven D. Carter, tr. *and* ed.
Japanese, The
Breaking Silence. Mirikitani
Coming Home from Camp. Kaneko
Dance Instructions for a Young Girl. Hahn
In a Bar near Shibuya Station, Tokyo. Engle
In Response to Executive Order 9066: All
Americans of Japanese Descent Must
Report to Relocation Centers. Okita

Love Poem: "I like/ the feel of your pulsating fibers." Kageyama
Musmee, The. Arnold
Obon by the Hudson. Oyama
Relocation. Mura
Strings/Himo. Kageyama
Sushi-Okashi and Green Tea with Mitsu Yashima. Robles
This Song Shows Me Pictures; Morningside Drive, New York City 1950-1960. Oyama

Japanese Verse
From the Country of Eight Islands; an Anthology of Japanese Poetry (FCEI). Hiroaki Sato *and* Burton Watson, eds. *and* trs.
Japanese Literature in Chinese (JLIC). Burton Watson, tr.
Manyoshu, The (Ma). Foreword by Donald Keene
Penguin Book of Japanese Verse, The (PeBJV). Geoffrey Bownes *and* Anthony Thwaite, trs.
Waiting for the Wind; Thirty-six Poets of Japan's Late Medieval Age (WFTW). Steven D. Carter, tr. *and* ed.

Jasmine
Yellow Jessamine. Woolson

Jason
Golden Fleece, The. Williams
Old Jason, the Argonaut, The. Glover

Jays
Riddle: Jay: *Higora*. *Unknown*
See also **Blue Jays.**

Jazz
Battle Report. Kaufman
Dear John, Dear Coltrane. Harper
For Leon Bismarck Beiderbecke (1903-1931). Horovitz
Jazz. Brown
Jazz Band in a Parisian Cabaret. Hughes
Jazz Fantasia. Sandburg
Jazzonia. Hughes
Lamda. Tolson
Lester Leaps In. Young
Lester Young. Joans
Mingus. Kaufman
Night above the Town. Lux
Reuben, Reuben. Harper
Satchmo. Tolson
Song thumbed down a cruiser for a ride, A. *Fr.* The Narrator's Trance. Cunningham
There were blood spots on the skirt. *Fr.* The Narrator's Trance. Cunningham
Walking Parker Home. Kaufman

Jealousy
Attempt at Jealousy, An. Tsvetayeva
Dream of Jealousy, A. Heaney
Face upon [or on] the Floor, The. D'Arcy
Fair Margaret and Sweet William. *Unknown*
God sends us from I don't know where. Marcabrun
I Can't Think What He Sees in Her. Herbert
In Oxford City. *Unknown*
Jealous Lovers, The. Hall
Jealous Man, A. Graves
Jealous Wife, The. Scannell
Jealousy. Johnson
Lily of the West, The. *Unknown*
Lord Thomas and Fair Annet. *Unknown*
Love and Jealousy. Greene
Madam if you please. Smart
My Last Duchess. Browning
Other Woman, The. Shore
She Lay Wrapped. Fox
Sheffield 'Prentice, The. *Unknown*
Shooting of Dan McGrew, The. Service
Six Said by the Concubines to Him. Ammuvanar
This Evening When I Spake with Thee, Beloved. Juana Inés de la Cruz
To Clarissa. Nugent

Two Sisters, The. *Unknown*
What if jealousy is just a bad dream? Palmer
Widow's Old Broom, The. *Unknown*
You that are jealous and have a wife. *Unknown*
See also **Envy.**

Jeffers, Robinson
Man-Fate, The. Everson
Poet Is Dead, The. Everson

Jefferson, Thomas
Brave New World. MacLeish
Death of Jefferson, The. Butterworth
Monticello. Sarton
Thomas Jefferson [1743-1826] Benét
Twilight's Last Gleaming. Monks

Jehovah's Witnesses
3-31-70. *Fr.* Journal. Jones

Jellyfish
Jellyfish, A. Moore
Lesson, The. Rubin

Jeremiah (Bible)
Prophet Jeremiah and the Personification of Israel, The. Ben Kalir

Jericho
Jericho. Gouri

Jerome, Saint
Jerome. Jarrell
Leonardo Da Vinci's. Moore
Thunderer, The. McGinley

Jerusalem
Acacia Tree, The. "Zelda"
And Did Those Feet in Ancient Time. *Fr.* Milton. Blake
At the Wailing Wall. Mathews
At the Western Wall. Lefcowitz
By the Waters of Babylon. *Fr.* Hebrew Melodies. Heine
Guide to Jerusalem. Silk
Hierusalem, my happy [or happie] home. *Unknown*
Holy City, The. Weatherly
I Don't Know if Mount Zion. Kovner
I Return unto Zion. *Fr.* Zechariah.
If I Forget Thee. Litvinoff
If, Jerusalem, I Ever Should Forget Thee. Heine
In the Old City. Fichman
Jerusalem. Ausländer
Jerusalem. Halevi
Jerusalem. Kanalenstein
Jerusalem. Slonimski
Jerusalem. Vinner
Jerusalem and the Hour. Husain
Jerusalem in the Snow. Bental
Jerusalem, My Happy Home. *Unknown*
Jerusalem, Port City. Amichai
Longing for Jerusalem. Halevi
Mirrors of Jerusalem, The. Lefcowitz
Prayer for Redemption. *Unknown*
Prisoner's Song of Jerusalem, A. *Unknown*
Shadow of the Old City. Amichai
Sodom's Sister City. Amichai
Wandering Jew Comes to the Wall, The. *Fr.* The Wall of Weeping. Fleg
Who Art Thou, O Great Mountain. Ravikovich
See also **Zion.**

Jesters
Cap and Bells, The. Yeats
Cap and Bells, The. Yeats
Fool's Prayer, The. Sill
Jester's Sermon, The. Thornbury
See also **Fools.**

Jesuits
Brébeuf and His Brethren. Scott
Satires [or Satyrs] upon the Jesuits, *sels.* Oldham

Jesus Christ
Adam and Eve. Sisson
Agraphon. Sikelianos
Airy Christ, The. Smith

All Hail the Power of Jesus' Name. Perronet
And Did Those Feet in Ancient Time. *Fr.* Milton. Blake
Ascension of Our Lord Jesus Christ. *Fr.* Hymns and Spiritual Songs. Smart
At Prime Jesus was y-led. *Fr.* Hours of the Passion. William of Shoreham
Away in a Manger. Luther
Bag, The. Herbert
Ballad of the Bread Man. Causley
Ballad of the Golden Bowl. Hay
Ballad of the Goodly Fere. Pound
Ballade of Illegal Ornaments. Belloc
Barnfloor and Winepress. Hopkins
Benefits of Sorrow. Moorer
Betrayal of Christ in Tucson and Brussels, The. Wojahn
Birth of Jesus, The. Heard
Bitter Withy, The. *Unknown*
Boyhood of Christ, The. Columbanus
Bridegroom of Cana, The. Pickthall
Burning Babe, The. Southwell
But Thee, but Thee, O sovereign Seer of time. *Fr.* The Crystal. Lanier
Calvary. De Brun
Calvary. Robinson
Carol: "Garden and gardener He made." Kinsella
Carol: "Now is the world withdrawn all." Nemerov
Carpenter, The. Whiteside
Christ and the Pagan. Tabb
Christ Child, The. Fordham
Christ Climbed Down. Ferlinghetti
Christ in the Clay-Pit. Clemo
Christ in the Universe. Meynell
Christ, My Beloved. Baldwin
Christ of Judea, look thou in my heart! *Fr.* Credo. Gilder
Christ, the Man. Davies
Christ Walking on the Water. Rodgers
Christmas Rose, The. Day Lewis
Christ's Bounty. *Unknown*
Christ's Descent into Hell. Rilke
Christ's Tear Breaks My Heart. *Unknown*
Church's One Foundation, The. Stone
Coming of Christ, The. *Unknown*
Comrade Jesus. Cleghorn
Coronet, The. Marvell
Coventry Carol. *Unknown*
Credo. Oxenham
Cross Talk. Cusack
Crucified and the Verminous Man, The. Manger
Crucifixion, The. *Unknown*
Crucifixion of the Word. Faraz
Death and Resurrection. Thompson
Deep Spring. *Unknown*
Descent of the Child, The. Mitchell
Despised and Rejected. Bates
Devout Prayer of the Passion, A. *Unknown*
Drunken Fisherman, The. Lowell
Dumbfounding, The. Avison
E Tenebris. Wilde
Earliest Christian Hymn. Clement of Alexandria
Easter. Sisson
Easter Hymn. Housman
Ecce Homo. *Fr.* Miserere. Gascoyne
Ecce Homunculus. Mason
El Greco: Espolio. Birney
Eli, Eli. Wright
Empty Tomb, The. Thompson
Ex Ore Infantium. Thompson
Fairest Lord Jesus. *Unknown*
Father to the Man. Knight
Feet of Judas, The. McClellan
For God While Sleeping. Sexton
For My Brother Jesus. Layton
From Heaven High I Come to You. Luther
Fugitive, The. Meynell
Garden, The. *Fr.* The Task. Cowper

Gentle Jesus Meek and Mild. Wesley
Give Me Jesus. *Unknown*
God? O'Flynn
God is a distant, stately lover. Dickinson
Good Friday. Brown
Great Man, The. Tietjens
Greatest Person in the Universe, The. Marsh
He. Kunitz
He "Had Not Where to Lay His Head."
  Harper
He Is the Lonely Greateness. Rock
He is the way. *Fr.* For the Time Being; a
  Christmas Oratorio. Auden
He Made Us Free. Egan
Hem of His Garment, The. Hamilton
His Are the Thousand Sparkling Rills.
  Alexander
His Monument. Bolton
Holy Cross. Leslie
Holy Night. Jylhä
Holy Well, The ("As it fell out on a
  holiday"). *Unknown*
Hound of Heaven, The. Thompson
Hymn[e] to Christ, at the Author's Last Going
  into Germany, A. Donne
I Met the Master. *Unknown*
I Saw a Peacock with a Fiery Tail. *Unknown*
I Saw a Stable. Coleridge
I Saw the Sun at Midnight, Rising Red.
  Plunkett
I See His Blood upon the Rose. Plunkett
I shall know why—when time is over.
  Dickinson
I Told Jesus. Plumpp
I Wonder as I Wander. *Unknown*
If the Drink. Mason
Immolation. Farren
In the Wilderness. Graves
Incarnate Love. Tillett
Incarnation and Passion, The. Vaughan
Incarnation Poem. Leax
Inner Light, The. Myers
Innumerable Christ, The. "MacDiarmid"
Invocation: "Great-hearted Christ, importunate
  and mild." *Fr.* The Psalm of Christ.
  Walsh
Irony of God. Warner
Jesu. Herbert
Jesukin. Ita
Jesus. McAuley
Jesus and His Mother. Gunn
Jesus and I. Crawford
Jesus Bids Man Remember. *Unknown*
Jesus Borned in Bethlea. *Unknown*
Jesus Christ ("Jesus Christ was a man that
  travelled through the land"). Guthrie
Jesus Contrasts Man and Himself. *Unknown*
Jesus, Lover of My Soul. Wesley
Jesus, My Sweet Lover. *Unknown*
Jesus on the Sabbath. *Unknown*
Jesus Reassures His Mother. *Unknown*
Jesus Reproaches His People. *Unknown*
Jesus Saviour, Pilot Me. Hopper
Jesus Shall Reign Where'er the Sun. Watts
Jesus, Thou Joy of Loving Hearts. Bernard
  of Clairvaux
Jesus to Those Who Pass By. *Unknown*
Joys of Mary, The. *Unknown*
Keening of Mary, The. *Unknown*
Lachrimae Verae. *Fr.* Lachrimae. Hill
Lamb, The. *Fr.* Songs of Innocence. Blake
Last Supper, The. Rilke
Last Words of Don Henriquez, The.
  Schneour
Line of Beauty, The. O'Shaughnessy
Little Cradle Rocks Tonight in Glory, The.
  Unknown
Lo, between the Myrtles Standing. Griffiths
Look once more ere we leave this specular
  Mount. *Fr.* Paradise Regained. Milton
Lord of the Dance. Carter
Lost Word of Jesus, A. Van Dyke

Love. Beaumont
Love. Herbert
Lovely was the death. *Fr.* Religious
  Musings. Coleridge
Luke XI: Blessed Be the Paps Which Thou
  Hast Sucked. Crashaw
Mediator, The. Browning
Messiah, The ("So they in Heav'n their odes
  and vigils tun'd"). *Fr.* Paradise Regained.
  Milton
Moses and Jesus. Zangwill
Mother and Her Son on the Cross, The.
  Unknown
My Song Is Love Unknown. Crossman
Mystic Song, A. *Unknown*
Nails and a Cross. Mason
Nativity, The. Fordham
Never Said a Mumbalin' Word. *Unknown*
New Approach Needed. Amis
New Heaven, New War[re]. Southwell
New Year's Carol. *Unknown*
Night. *Fr.* Songs of Innocence. Blake
Night, the Starless Night of Passion, The.
  Fr. Divine Meditations. Alabaster
No Coming to God without Christ. Herrick
O Christ of Olivet, you hushed the wars. *Fr.*
  The Christ of the Andes. Markham
O Christ, Who Died. Slemp
O Come, All Ye Faithful. *Unknown*
O Little Town of Bethlehem. Brooks
O Master-Workman of the Race. Stocking
On Our Crucified Lord, Naked and Bloody.
  Crashaw
On the Circumsision: New Year's Day.
  Wadding
On the Death of Our Lord. Flecknoe
On the Flesh of Christ. Corrington
On the Swag. Mason
On the Wounds of Our Crucified Lord.
  Crashaw
Once in Royal David's City. Alexander
Our Master. Whittier
Pair of Wings, A. Hawes
Passion and Exaltation of Christ, The. Watts
Passion of Christ, The. Devlin
Peace. Vaughan
Peace, Perfect Peace. Bickersteth
Poem to the Heart of Jesus, A. O'Sullivan
Poet, The. Bynner
Prayer: "O Christ, who in Gethsemane." Ray
Protagonist, The. Hopegood
Quia Amore Langueo. *Unknown*
Quintina of Crosses, A. Walsh
Reality. Havergal
Redemption. Herbert
Rose That Bore Jesu, The. *Unknown*
St. Patrick's Breastplate. Patrick
Salutation to Jesus Christ. Calvin
Search, The. Vaughan
Second Coming, The. Clark
Second Crucifixion, The. Le Gallienne
Second Seeing. Golding
Sheep and Lambs. Tynan
Shine Out, Fair Sun, with All Your Heat.
  Fr. The Masque of the Twelve Months.
  Chapman
Sometime during eternity. *Fr.* A Coney
  Island of the Mind. Ferlinghetti
Son, The. *Fr.* The Temple. Herbert
Song of a Heathen, The. Gilder
Song of Childbirth, The. *Unknown*
Song of Love for Jesus, A. Rolle
Song of the Woman, The. *Fr.* The Voyage
  of Bran. *Unknown*
Song to the Most Holy Name of Jesus.
  Córdova y Bocanegra
Sonnet: "I am not moved to love thee, my
  Lord God." Guevara
Soul of Jesus Is Restless, The. Mitchell
Spring. Hopkins
Stable Straw. Farren
Stars Sang in God's Garden, The. Plunkett

Stigmata. Stoddard
Summer Reflection. Cusack
Sweet after showers, ambrosial air. *Fr.* In
  Memoriam A. H. H. Tennyson
Swet Jesus. Michael of Kildare
Sympathy. Moorer
Temple. Donne
Temple. *Fr.* La Corona. Donne
There Is a Green Hill Far Away. Alexander
There Were Ninety and Nine. Clephane
This Endris Night. *Unknown*
Three Enemies, The. Rossetti
To a Crucifix. Wickham
To Christ. Tuqan
To God the Son. Constable
To Jesus of Nazareth. Knowles
To the Child Jesus. Van Dyke
To the Christians. Adams
To the Nativity. Gonzáles de Eslava
To the Young Man Jesus. Dalton
Trees on a Frosty Night. O Direain
True Apostolate, The. Weyburn
Under Sorrow's Sign. O'Dalaigh
Upon Christ's Nativity or Christmas.
  Watkyns
Virile Christ, A. Boundy
Vision of Ita, The. *Unknown*
Vision of Jesus, The. *Fr.* The Vision of
  Piers Plowman. Langland
Wake the Song of Jubilee. Bacon
Way, the Truth, and the Life, The. Parker
What Christ Is to Us. *Unknown*
When I See on Rood. *Unknown*
When Rooks Fly Homeward. Campbell
While Shepherds Watched [Their Flocks by
  Night]. Tate
Windhover, The. Hopkins
Woman. Barrett
Wonder. Traherne
Word made flesh is seldom, A. Dickinson
Young Poet. O'Higgins
Young Workman, The. Frear

Jewelry
Amber Beads. Brown
Ring, The. Wakoski
Sparrow and Diamond, The. Green
To His Ring, Given to His Lady, Wherein
  Was Graven This Verse, "My Heart Is
  Yours." Turberville
When Diamonds, Nibbling in My Ears.
  Davies
With a Gift of Rings. Graves
See also **Rings.**

Jews
Autobiographical. Klein
Before Passover. Mayne
Crowing of the Red Cock, The. Lazarus
Days of 1978. Stern
Design for Mediæval Tapestry. Klein
Emigré Jewess. Mistral
Evening Jews. Glatstein
Genius, The. Cohen
Hebrew of Your Poets, Zion, The. Reznikoff
Heirloom. Klein
Home. Gershon
Jew, The. Rosenberg
Jew to Jesus, The. Frank
Jewish Cemetery at Newport, The.
  Longfellow
Jewish Girls, The. Lask
Jewish Graveyards, Italy. Levine
Jewish Main Street. Layton
Jews, The. Herbert
Jews, The. Vaughan
Jews at Haifa. Jarrell
Jew's Calendar, A. Gershon
Judaism. Newman
Little Sir Hugh. *Unknown*

"More Light! More Light!" Hecht
Nazis. Sadoff
On the Russian Persecution of the Jews.
　Swinburne
151st Psalm, The. Shapiro
Portrait of a Jew Old Country Style.
　Rothenberg
Rabbi Ben Ezra. Browning
Resistance in the Ghetto. Glatstein
Riddle: "From Belsen a crate of gold teeth."
　Heyen
Scene of a Summer Morning. Feldman
Scraps. Kamenetz
Shirt Poem, The. Stern
Sir Hugh; or, The Jew's Daughter. *Unknown*
Song: "By the wayside." *Fr*. Fall and Exile.
　Jabès
Spit. Williams
Still Small Voice, The. Klein
Story about Chicken Soup, A. Simpson
That Was Then. Gardner
They. Leib
To Russia. Miller
Wandering Jew, The. Bibb
Wandering Jew, The. Bridges
Wandering Jew, The. Mezey
War against the Jews, The. Stern
What Is a Jewish Poem? Sklarew
Without Jews. Glatstein
Worm, The. Barnstone
Yiddish Poet. Jacobs
Yom Kippur 1984. Rich
American Yiddish Poetry (AYP). Benjamin
　Harshaw *and* Barbara Harshaw, eds.
Israeli Poetry; a Contemporary Anthology
　(IP). Warren Bargad *and* Stanley F.
　Chyet, comps. *and* trs.
Modern Hebrew Poetry (MHeP). Bernhard
　Frank, ed. *and* tr.
Penguin Book of Modern Yiddish Verse, The
　(PeBMYV). Irving Howe, Ruth R. Wisse,
　and Khone Shmeruk, eds.
Treasury of Jewish Poetry, A (TrJP). Nathan
　Ausubel *and* Marynn Ausubel, eds
Voices Within the Ark; the Modern Jewish
　Poets (VWA). Howard Schwartz *and*
　Anthony Rudolf, eds

Jew's Harps
Weeping and Wailing. Stern

Jezebel
Men made myths. *Fr*. Jezebel: Her Progress.
　Hanscombe
Song for the Clatter-Bones. Higgins

Jigsaw Puzzles
Jigsaw Puzzles. Schippers

Jito, Empress
Our great Empress. *Fr*. Manyo Shu.
　Hitomaro

Joan of Arc
Good Joan, The. Reese
Jeanne d'Arc. Ludvigson
Joan of Arc. McCrae
Joan of Arc to the Tribunal. Frisch
Maid, The. Roberts
Maid of Arc, The. Bottomley

Job (Bible)
Beauty of Job's Daughters, The.
　Macpherson
Job. Sewell

Jockeys
Old Jockey, The. Higgins
See also **Horse Racing.**

Jogging and Joggers. *See* **Running and
　Runners.**

Johannesburg, South Africa
City Johannesburg. Serote

John XXIII, Pope
Rome Sunday June 1960. Hewitt

John Bull
World Is a Bundle of Hay, The. Byron

John Capystrano, Saint
Capystranus. *Unknown*
John of Austria
Lepanto. Chesterton
John Paul II, Pope
Lolek. Jordan
John, Saint
Peter and John. Wylie
Song to John, Christ's Friend, A. *Unknown*
John the Baptist, Saint
John the Baptist. Simpson
Johnson, Lionel
In Memory of Major Robert Gregory. Yeats
Johnson, Samuel
Doctor Johnson. Jenyns
My Marriage with Mrs. Johnson. Gilbert
To the Oaks of Glencree. Synge
Johnston, James Hugo
James Hugo Johnston. Johnson
Jonah
I to the Lord from My Distress. *Unknown*
Jonah. Huxley
Jonah. *Fr*. Patience. *Unknown*
Jonah's Canticle. Dadelsen
Noah an' Jonah an' Cap'n John Smith.
　Marquis
Ribs and Terrors in the Whale, The. *Fr*.
　Moby Dick. Melville
Jonathan (Bible)
Beauty of Israel is slain [*or* slaine] upon thy
　high places, The. *Fr*. Second Samuel.
Jones, Ebenezer
Incident in the Early Life of Ebenezer Jones,
　Poet, 1828, An. Betjeman
Jones, John Paul
Paul Jones. *Unknown*
Paul Jones—a New Song. *Unknown*
Paul Jones's Victory. *Unknown*
Yankee Man-of-War, The. *Unknown*
Jonson, Ben
Ben Jonson. *Fr*. Sonnets of English
　Dramatic Poets. Swinburne
Elegy on Ben Jonson, An. Cleveland
His Prayer to Ben Jonson [*or* Johnson].
　Herrick
In Obitum Ben. Jons. Westmorland
Ode for Ben Jonson, An. Herrick
Scorne then their censure, who gave out thy
　wit. *Fr*. To the Memory of Ben Johnson.
　Mayne
To Ben Jonson [*or* Johnson]. Carew
To My Dead Friend Ben: Johnson. King
Joplin, Janis
Burying Blues for Janis. Piercy
Joseph (Bible, *O.T.*)
Glimpse of an Open Dream. Avidan
Jacob Studies "The Selling of Joseph" with
　His Sons. Manger
September, the First Day of School.
　Nemerov
Joseph, Saint
Joseph's Suspicion. Rilke
Man of the House, The. Tynan
Joseph (Chief Joseph)
Tribute to Chief Joseph, A. Niatum
Joshua
Joshua Fit De [*or* Fought the] Battle of [*or*
　ob] Jericho. *Unknown*
Joshua's Face. Gilboa
Moses and Joshua. Lasker-Schüler
Journalism
British Journalist, The. Wolfe
Press, The. Elliott
Problems of a Journalist. Kees
Song: "Closes and courts and lanes."
　Davidson
Southern Press, The. Moorer
See also **Magazines; Newspapers.**
Jowett, Benjamin
First come I. My name is Jowett. *Fr*. Balliol
　Rhymes. Beeching
I am the great Professor Jowett. *Unknown*

Joy
After the Second Operation. Goedicke
Answer, The. Teasdale
Birthday, A. Rossetti
Blessing, A. Wright
Bunch of Grapes, The. Herbert
Conjugation. Hubbell
Eternity ("He who binds [*or* bends] to himself
　a joy"). *Fr*. Several Questions Answered.
　Blake
First or Last. Hardy
Got a lover, tell you that. *Unknown*
How full of joy were the days of youth.
　Nazir
Hurrahing in Harvest. Hopkins
In Assisi. Blumenthal
Infant Joy. *Fr*. Songs of Innocence. Blake
Joy. Creeley
Joy. Delany
Joy. Jeffers
L'Allegro. Milton
My lord came to survey. *Fr*. Manyo Shu.
　Mushimaro
Quatrains for Joy. Al-Ghuzzi
Shadow and Sunrise. Ray
To the Lord General Cromwell. Milton
With the coming of clear days. *Unknown*
Woman Talk. Simba
Joyce, James
D. H. Lawrence and James Joyce. Wolfe
Emily Dickinson's Sestina for Molly Bloom.
　Lefcowitz
In the Fall. *Fr*. In Memoriam James Joyce.
　"MacDiarmid"
It was Landor who first said. *Fr*. In
　Memoriam James Joyce. "MacDiarmid"
Poets of Hell, The. Shapiro
Ulysses' Library. Daiches
Judas Iscariot
Descent for the Lost. Child
Historical Judas, The. Nemerov
Judas. Fritsch
Judas. Miller
Judas. *Unknown*
Judas Iscariot. Cullen
Judas Iscariot. Mason
Judas Iscariot. Spender
Judas Sells His Lord. *Unknown*
Realpolitik. Kirschenbaum
Saint Judas. Wright
Judges
Beak, The. Smither
Condemned, The. Gonzáles Martínez
On Ryñeveld, an Unpopular Dutch Judge.
　Unknown
Roy Bean. *Unknown*
When the spring comes. *Fr*. Manyo Shu.
　Nukada
Judgment Day
Abraham Davenport. Whittier
Auguries of Innocence. Blake
Carol for the Last Christmas Eve. Nicholson
Crazy Jane on the Day of Judgment. Yeats
Crowdieknowe. "MacDiarmid"
Day of Judgement, The. Swift
Day of Judgment, The. Buchanan
Day of Judgment, The. Thomas of Celano
Death. Herbert
Death and Resurrection. Croly
Dies Irae. Thomas of Celano
Fifteen Days of Judgment, The. Evans
Heavenly Aeroplane, The. *Unknown*
How long, dear Savior, O how long. Watts
In Dat Great Gittin'-up Mornin'. *Unknown*
Judgement. Herbert
Last Judgment, The. Belli
O may I join the choir invisible. *Fr*. O May
　I Join the Choir Invisible. "Eliot"
Rise and Shine. Lattimore
Second Coming, The. Yeats

Judith (Apocrypha)
Judith. Bibb
Judith. Menken
Judith of Bethulia. Ransom
Judith Recalls Holofernes. Stanton
Jugglers
Draw me nere [or near], draw me nere [or near]. *Unknown*
In one place, flying clubs. *Fr.* Inscribed on Paintings for the People of Hangchow. Hsü Wei
Jenny the Juvenile Juggler. Lee
Juggler, The. Straus
Juggler. Stryk
Juggler. Wilbur
Juggling Jerry. Meredith
Julius Caesar. *See* Caesar, Julius.
July
Fourth, The. Silverstein
Fourth of July, The. Pierpont
July. Ray
July. *Fr.* Sonnets of the Months. San Gimignano
July. Swett
July in Indiana. Fitzgerald
Jumping
Just Watch. Livingston
Little Jumping Girls, The. Greenaway
June
All in June. Davies
And June. . . ? Somlyó
Cut Grass. Larkin
Earth gets its price for what Earth gives us. *Fr.* The Vision of Sir Launfal. Lowell
Full early in the morning. *Unknown*
I Think. Schuyler
In June and Gentle Oven. Wilkinson
June. Feinstein
June. Fisher
June. Fordham
June. Ledwidge
June. MacDonald
June. Pawsey
June. Rand
June. Ray
June. *Fr.* Sonnets of the Months. San Gimignano
June Bracken and Heather. Tennyson
June Morning. McCrae
June Thunder. MacNeice
June Twilight. Masefield
Knee-deep in June. Riley
Mowing, The. Roberts
Night in June, A. Scott
Over his keys the musing organist. *Fr.* The Vision of Sir Launfal. Lowell
What [or And what] Is So Rare as a Day in June? *Fr.* The Vision of Sir Launfal. Lowell
Jungles
At the Edge of the Jungle. Lane
Jungle. Haring
Jungle, The. Lewis
Jungle, The. *Fr.* Thailand Railway. Stow
Jungle Husband, The. Smith
Juniper
Juniper. Francis
Junk and Junkyards
Caravati's Junkyard. Morgan
Caravati's Salvage: Richmond, Virginia. Smith
Cherrylog Road. Dickey
Drunk in the Furnace, The. Merwin
Garbage. Tretheway
In Passing. Jonas
Johnny Spain's White Heifer. Carruth
Junk. *Fr.* New York Everywhere. Vaynshteyn
Junk. Wilbur
Jupiter (god)
Jupiter and Ganimede. Heywood
Jupiter and Ten. Fields

Jupiter (Planet)
Destruction of the Fifth Planet. Aldiss
Justice
All We Ask Is Justice. Linden
Carl Hamblin. *Fr.* Spoon River Anthology. Masters
Country Justice, The. Langhorne
Death of Justice, The. Hawkins
"Guilty or Not Guilty?" *Unknown*
Hidden Justice. Stern
Justice. Hughes
Justice Denied in Massachusetts. Millay
Justice of Men! I Look for You. Castro
Nothing Said. Agard
Rain It Raineth, The. Bowen
They Can't Do That. *Unknown*
To Sir Thomas Egerton. Daniel
Who but the Lord? Hughes
Youth. "Hope"
See also **Injustice.**
Juvenile Delinquency
We Real Cool. Brooks

K

Kabbala. *See* Cabala.
Kabul, Afghanistan
Ford o' Kabul River. Kipling
Kafka, Franz
Letter to Kafka. Stanton
Tribute to Kafka. Dugan
Kalakaua (Hawaiian King)
Praise Song for King Kalakaua. *Unknown*
Kalamazoo, Michigan
Sins of Kalamazoo, The. Sandburg
Kalankaykkanni Narmuticceral
Harvest of War. Kappiyarrukkappiyanar
Kane (Hawaiian God)
O Kane, O Lono of the blue sea. *Unknown*
Water of Kane, The. *Unknown*
Kangaroos
Delicate Mother Kangaroo. Lawrence
Duck and the Kangaroo, The. Lear
Frog and a Flea, A. Mitchell
Hospital Kangaroos, The. Kocan
Kangaroo. Lawrence
Sing-Song of Old Man Kangaroo, The. Kipling
Kansas
Across Kansas. Stafford
Ceremony. Stafford
Crossing Kansas by Train. Justice
Kansas Boy. Lechlitner
Kansas Boys. *Unknown*
Rescued Year, The. Stafford
Stories from Kansas. Stafford
Trail into Kansas, The. Merwin
Kansas City, Kansas and Missouri
Kansas City West Bottoms. Dahlberg
Kapiti Island, New Zealand
Looking at Kapiti. Campbell
Karate
Karate. Plumly
Katharine of Aragón, Queen of England
Ballad for Katharine of Aragon, A. Causley
Catharine of Arragon. Bibb
Katmandu, Nepal
Sestina: Here in Katmandu. Justice
Katsushika Hokumei
Camden Magpie. McCrae
Laughing Hyena, by Hokusai, The. Enright
Katydids
Katydid stops chirping, A. *Fr.* Twenty-one Hokku. Kaya Shirao
From my sleeve a katydid. *Fr.* Fifteen Hokku. Joso

On the road with not a soul. *Fr.* Sixty-four Tanka. Saigyo
To a Caty-did. Freneau
To an Insect. Holmes
Katzenjammer Kids
Katzenjammer Kids, The. Reaney
Kavanagh, Patrick
If Ever You Go to Dublin Town. Kavanagh
November 1967. Durcan
Kayaks
Kayak, The. *Unknown*
Kayak Song, A. Diamond
Kearny, Philip
Kearny at Seven Pines. Stedman
Keaton, Buster
Buster Keaton & the Cops. Keithley
Keats, John
For John Keats, Apostle of Beauty. *Fr.* Four Epitaphs. Cullen
Keats. Longfellow
Keats. Reese
Keats to Fanny Brawne. Masters
October XXIX, 1795. Braithwaite
Ode on a Grecian Urn Summarized. Skirrow
On the Death of Keats. Logan
Peace, peace! he is not dead, he doth not sleep. *Fr.* Adonais; an Elegy on the Death of John Keats. Shelley
Posthumous Keats. Plumly
Rome. Hardy
Sonnet: "Three colours have I known the Deep to wear." Owen
To John Keats. Hunt
To John Keats. Lowell
To John Keats, Poet, at Springtime. Cullen
To Keats: On Reading His Sonnet Written in Chaucer. Reynolds
To the Spirit of Keats. Lowell
Who Kill'd John Keats? Byron
Keller, Helen
Helen Keller. Stedman
Kells, Book of
Book of Kells, The. Colum
Kennedy, John Fitzgerald
Belief. Ammons
Channel U.S.A.—Live. Stoutenburg
Down in Dallas. Kennedy
November Twenty-sixth Nineteen Hundred and Sixty-three. Berry
Seven Houses, The. Brown
Three Presidents. Bly
Traction: November 22, 1963. Moss
Kennedy, Robert Francis
Assassination, The. Justice
Beyond the Presidency. Gibson
Kensington Gardens, London
In Kensington Gardens. Symons
Lines Written in Kensington Gardens. Arnold
Kent, England
In Romney Marsh. Davidson
On Lord Holland's Seat near Margate, Kent. Gray
On the Pilgrim's Way in Kent, as It Leads to the Coldrum Stones. Asphodel
To Penshurst. Jonson
Tunbridge Wells. Rochester
See also **Cinque Ports.**
Kent State University, Ohio
Kent State, May 4, 1970. Goodman
Kentucky
American Portrait: Old Style. Warren
My Fathers Came from Kentucky. Lindsay
My Old Kentucky Home, [Good Night]. Foster
Road in Kentucky, A. Hayden
Walthena. Peck
Kerouac, Jack
I Met This Guy Who Died. Corso
Sunflower Sutra. Ginsberg

Kerry. *See* **County Kerry, Ireland.**
Kew Gardens, London
Barrel-Organ, The. Noyes
Key West, Florida
Hemingway House in Key West, The. Schultz
Idea of Order at Key West, The. Stevens
Keys
Key, The. Jacob
Keys of Morning, The. De la Mare
Liberator, The. Coleman
Skeleton Key. Hollander
Khamsin
Khamsin of Nisan. Goldberg
Kidd, William
Captain Kidd. *Unknown*
Captain Kid's Farewell to the Seas; or, The Famous Pirate's Lament. *Unknown*
Kilcash, Ireland
Kilcash. *Unknown*
Kildare. *See* **County Kildare, Ireland.**
Killi Parananuru
Guide to Patrons, A. Alattur Killar
Killing
How It's Done. Aubert
Kimble County, Texas
Last Man Killed by Indians in Kimble County, Texas, The. Angelotti
Kimonos
Kimono. Graham
Kindness
Gratitude. Glück
Kindly Deed, A. Thompson
Kindness. Plath
Kindness. Tucker
King, Edward
Lycidas. Milton
King Kong
Fay Wray to the King. Rechter
King Lear
Lear. Williams
On Sitting Down to Read "King Lear" Once Again. Keats
Refrain. Salter
King, Martin Luther, Jr.
Alabama Bus. Hairston
Assassination. Lee
Death of Dr. King. Cornish
Funeral of Martin Luther King, Jr., The. Giovanni
In Memoriam: Martin Luther King, Jr. Jordan
King Lives. Boyer
Martin Luther King. Livingston
Martin Luther King, Jr. Brooks
Martin's Blues. Harper
White Weekend. Troupe
King, William, Archbishop of Dublin
Excellent New Song upon His Grace Our Good Lord Archbishop of Dublin, An. Swift
King, William Lyon Mackenzie
W. L. M. K. Scott
Kingfishers
Kingfisher, The. Davies
Kingfisher. Farjeon
Kingfishers, The. Olson
Kings
Abdication of Noman, The. Stoddard
Alexandrian Kings. Cavafy
And Ride in Triumph through Persepolis. *Fr.* Tamburlaine the Great. Marlowe
And welcom now (Great Monarch) to your own. *Fr.* Astraea Redux. Dryden
Chapter of Kings, The. Collins
Coronation. Jackson
Elegy on the Late King of Patagonia, An. Hankin
England's Sovereigns in Verse. *Unknown*
English Succession, The. *Unknown*
Georges, The. Landor

He brought peace to myriad lands. *Unknown*
He goes through his lands. *Unknown*
In Uganda an Early King. Walker
King John and the Abbot of Canterbury. *Unknown*
Kings and Queens of England, The. *Unknown*
King's Epitaph, The. Rochester
Kings of France. Lincoln
Lines on Succession of the Kings of England. *Unknown*
Model for the Laureate, A. Yeats
Oh, gloriously did the king lead. *Unknown*
Oh, great were you, King Wu! *Unknown*
Old King Cole was a merry old soul. Mother Goose
On King Richard the Third, Who Lies Buried under Leicester Bridge. Suckling
Pity me, your child. *Unknown*
Royal Line, The. Hunt
Sesostris. Mifflin
Terrible in his power was King Wu. *Unknown*
Time seems not now beneath his years to stoop. *Fr.* To His Sacred Majesty, a Panegyrick on His Coronation, 1661. Dryden
Yet if his majesty, our sovereign [*or* soveraign] Lord. *Unknown*
See also **individual names of kings.**
Kingston, Jamaica
Back to Hometown Kingston. Berry
Kinsey Report
Kinsey Report. Schutting
Kipling, Rudyard
Ballad, A: "As I was walkin' the jungle round, a-killin' of tigers an' time." Carryl
To R. K. Stephen
Kirk, Henry
To the Poets. *Unknown*
Kisses
Ae Fond Kiss. Burns
After the Kiss. Miki Rofu
Caress, The. Ibarbourou
Cat Kisses. Katz
Dream Kiss, The. Günderode
First Kiss. Holden
First time he kissed me, he but only kissed. *Fr.* Sonnets from the Portuguese. Browning
House, A. Orlen
I Envy Not Endymion. *Fr.* Aurora. Stirling
I Kissed You. *Unknown*
"I never drank of Aganippe well." *Fr.* Astrophel and Stella, LXXIV. Sidney
Jenny Kiss'd [*or* Kissed] Me. Hunt
Keep your kiss to yourself. *Unknown*
Kiss, The. Bogin
Kiss, A. Drummond
Kiss, A. Herrick
Kiss, The. Moore
Kiss, The. *Fr.* The Angel in the House. Patmore
Kiss, The. *Fr.* The House of Life. Rossetti
Kiss, A. Tucker
Kiss, A ("He's my doll!"). *Unknown*
Kiss ("I close my eyes, the world recedes"). Tanikawa Shuntaro
Kisses Desired. Drummond
Kisses Loathesome. Herrick
Kissing Natalia. Grier
Lady, A. Snodgrass
Like the Sea, Kisses. Aleixandre
Poor Is the Life That Misses. *Unknown*
Moth's kiss, first, The! *Fr.* In a Gondola. Browning
To Anthea. Herrick
To Electra. Herrick

What They Do to You in Distant Places. Bell
You Kissed Me. Hunt
Kitchens
Kitchen Range. Saba
Kites
Flying kite, in the spot in the sky, A. *Fr.* Eighty-seven Hokku. Buson
Dragon Song. Park Je-chun
Kite, The. Behn
Kite. McCord
Kite, The. MacEwen
Kite, The. O'Keeffe
Kite, A. *Unknown*
Kite, completed thus, is borne along, The. *Fr.* The Paper Kite. Bowden
Kite-Flying. McKay
Kite for Michael and Christopher, A. Heaney
Kite Is a Victim, A. Cohen
Paper Dragons. Schmeltz
When the wind is gentle. *Fr.* A Kite. Hsü Wei
Kittens
Four-Paws. Eden
Kitten, A. Farjeon
Kitten, The. Nash
Kitten, The. Oliver
Kitten twirls around, A. *Fr.* Forty-four Hokku. Issa
Kitty. McLeod
Kitty. Prentiss
Kitty Cornered. Merriam
Two Little Kittens. Taylor
Klee, Paul
Paul Klee. Haines
Paul Klee. Todd
Klimt, Gustav
Two Paintings by Gustav Klimt. Graham
Knees
Knee, The. Morgenstern
Knife-Grinders
Scissor-Man, The. Nightingale
Sparkles from the Wheel. Whitman
Knight, Etheridge
Hospital/Poem. Sanchez
Knighthood and Knights
Bristowe Tragedie: or, The Dethe of Syr Charles Bawdin. Chatterton
Dead Knight, The. Masefield
Duke of Marlborough, The. *Unknown*
Fafnir and the Knights. Smith
Haystack in the Floods, The. Morris
Knight Knocked at the Castle Gate, The. *Unknown*
Knight Stained from Battle, The. Herebert
La Belle Dame sans Merci. Keats
Lochinvar. *Fr.* Marmion. Scott
New Order of Chivalry, A. Peacock
Outlandish Knight, The. *Unknown*
Sir Eglamour. *Fr.* The Melancholy Knight. Rowlands
Sir Gawaine and the Green Knight. Winters
Sir Roland; a Fragment. Merry
Sir Thopas. *Fr.* The Canterbury Tales. Chaucer
True Knight [*or* True Knighthood], The. *Fr.* The Pastime of Pleasure. Hawes
Wandering Knight's Song, The. Lockhart
Knights of Pythias
For the Good of the Pythian Order. Linden
Knitting
Knitting. Tucker
On a Grey-haired Old Lady Knitting at an Orchestral Concert. "Maurice"
Knives
Dagger, The ("A dagger rests in a drawer"). Borges
Inventory. Stanford
Knife, The. Tillinghast
On the Gift of a Knife. O Dalaigh

Knowledge
Gathering, The. Ammons
I know my soul hath power to know all
  things. *Fr.* Nosce Teipsum: Man. Davies
Know then thyself, presume not God to scan.
  Fr. An Essay on Man. Pope
Little learning is a dangerous thing, A. *Fr.*
  Essay on Criticism. Pope
To David, about His Education. Nemerov
What Is This Knowledge? *Fr.* Nosce
  Teipsum. Davies
Written upon the Top of Ben Nevis. Keats

Knox, George L.
Lines to the Hon. George L. Knox. Bibb

Knoxville, Tennessee
Knoxville, Tennessee. Giovanni

Koalas
Koala. Ross

Koehler, Reinhold
In Memory of Reinhold Koehler. Schmied

Kollontay, Aleksandra
Aleksandra Kollontay. Vammelvuo

Koran
Even from earthly love thy face avert not.
  Jami
Page from the Koran. Merrill

Korean Verse
Anthology of Contemporary Korean Poetry
  (ACKP). Koh Chang-soo, comp.

Korean War
Final Night, The. Sardar J'afri
Korea Bound, 1952. Childress
Ode for the American Dead in Korea.
  McGrath
On a Certain Engagement South of Seoul.
  Carruth

Koreans
Careless/ but not fearless. *Fr.* Urn I: Silent
  for Twenty-five Years, the Father of My
  Mother Advises Me. Lew

Kosciusko, Thaddeus
Koskiusko. Coleridge

Krakow, Poland
Waiting for Death. Gebirtig

Kreisler, Fritz
Fritz. Stern
Poem after Leopardi. Strand

Ku Klux Klan
Ku Klux. Cawein
Ku Klux. Hughes
Night, Death, Mississippi. Hayden
Special Bulletin. Hughes

Kubla Khan
Eulogy of the Sagely Virtue of His Imperial
  Majesty Emperor Shih-tsu, A. Chao
  Meng-fu
Kubla Khan; or, A Vision in a Dream.
  Coleridge
Lamenting the Taoist Wei Kung-yüan. Chao
  Meng-fu

Kumanan
Bard's Family, A. Peruncittiranar

Kutakko Ilanceral Irumporai
Parade, A. Perunkunrur Kilar

Kwan-Yin (Chinese Goddess of Mercy)
Bronze Statuette of Kwan-yin, A. Stork

Kyoto, Japan
Things to Do around Kyoto. Snyder

L

La Hogue, Battle of (1692)
Sea Fight in '92, The. *Unknown*

La Plata, Missouri
Last Look at La Plata, Missouri. Barnes

Labor and Laborers
Artisan, The. Brown
At the Sign-Painter's. Carter
Awakening of the People, The. Massey
Beginning of the Day, The. Lin
  Huan-ch'ang
Bird's-Eye View of the Tool and Die Co.
  Ashbery
Black Money. Gallagher
Carpenter, The. Macdonald
Carpenter, The. Whiteside
Chartist Chorus, A. Jones
Day is o'er! yet pleasure, commerce, gain,
  The. *Fr.* Night. Cleaver
Description of the Morning, A. Swift
Digging. Heaney
Dignity of Labor, The. Bersohn
England and America, 1863. Milnes
England! my persecuted isle. *Fr.* Patriotism.
  Richardson
English Labourer, The. *Unknown*
Epitaph: "John Bird, a laborer, lies here."
  Warner
Equipment. Dunbar
Factory Girl, The. "Bill o' th' Hoylus End"
Factory Girl's Come-All-Ye, The. *Unknown*
Factory Hands, The. Chimedza
Father Is Leaving. Kajava
Feeding Ground. McCarthy
Fellow Workers. "Marie"
Fetchin Water. McKay
Florida Road Workers. Hughes
For Consciousness. Morris
Forgotten Man, The. Markham
Freighting from Wilcox to Globe. *Unknown*
Get Up! Skipsey
Go Down, Old Hannah. *Unknown*
Gospel of Labor, The. van Dyke
Hail, Sabbath! day of mercy, peace, and rest!
  Fr. The Village Patriarch. Elliott
Hay for the Horses. Snyder
Helmet, The. Levine
Horn Blow, The. Tagami
I Hear America Singing. Whitman
Ice Handler. Sandburg
Inspiration. Thoreau
Invisible Work. Gibson
Laborer, The. Chimsoro
Labour. "Marie"
Labour Song. Syme
Labourer, The. Iolo Goch
Labourer's Song, A. Dawson
Labouring Man, The. *Unknown*
Legacy. Kalász
Life-Mosaic. Havergal
Lining Track. *Unknown*
Little Tommy Yesterday. Glasgow
Man Carrying Bale. Monro
Man with the Hoe, The. Markham
Mission Tire Factory, 1969. Soto
Monument. Sullivan
Morning Work. Lawrence
Muckers. Sandburg
My Mother, Who Came from China, Where
  She Never Saw Snow. Mar
Now It Is Broccoli. Tagami
O Son of Man, Thou Madest Known.
  Littlefield
Piece Worker, The. Döltz
Pity Poor Labourers. *Unknown*
Prayer, A: "Let me work and be glad."
  Garrison
Preacher and the Slave, The. Hill
Psalm of Those Who Go Forth before
  Daylight. Sandburg
Raggedy Man, The. Riley
Reapers. Toomer
Réveille. Ridge
Riveter, The. Watts
Road, The. Aiken
Serf, The. Campbell
Servants, The. Wightman

Shoemaker Nikke. Turtiainen
Shovelling Iron Ore. *Unknown*
Sisyphus. Garioch
Six o'Clock. Stickney
Something Has Fallen. Levine
Song: "Child, is thy father dead?" Elliott
Song: "I watered my horse at the Long Wall
  caves." Ch'en Lin
Song for the free—the brave and the free, A.
  Fr. Two Chartist Songs. Cooper
Song of the Builders. Murton
Song of the Low, The. Jones
Song of the Lower Classes, The. Jones
Song of the Rice Workers. *Unknown*
Song of the Shirt, The. Hood
Song to the Men of England. Shelley
Steam King, The. Mead
Stevedore. Collins
Stonehouse. Tagami
Sweepers, The. Whitehead
Thatcher, The. Kennelly
Thinker, The. Braley
This Old Hammer. *Unknown*
This Sun Is Hot. *Unknown*
Three-handed Fugue. Gotlieb
Time shall come when wrong shall end, The.
  Fr. Two Chartist Songs. Cooper
Tired Worker, The. McKay
To Be of Use. Piercy
To Labor. Gilman
Toads. Larkin
Toads Revisited. Larkin
Track-lining Song. *Unknown*
Trade. Martin
Train Runs Late to Harlem, The. Rivers
True Aristocrat, The. Stewart
Twa Weavers, The. Rodger
Unaccompanied. Andrews
Unloading Rails. *Unknown*
Warkin' Mon's Reflections, A. Baron
Way Out in Idaho. *Unknown*
Western Civilization. Neto
What Grandma Knew. Field
What's de Use ob Wukin in de Summer Time
  at All. Johnson
Where could I find the words. *Fr.* Ballad of
  Herman's Rose. Turtiainen
Whisperings for the Unwashed. Thom
Winter Night in Manchester, A. Connell
Women Transport Corps. *Unknown*
Wood-Cutter's Night Song, The. Clare
Word "Silk", The. McCarthy
Work. Block
Work; a Song of Triumph ("Work!/ Thank
  God for the might of it"). Morgan
Work—work—work. *Fr.* The Song of the
  Shirt. Hood
Worker, The. Massey
Worker, The. Thomas
Working Class. Warr
Workman's Home, A. Ince
Wukhand. Keens-Douglas
Young Workman, The. Frear
Saturdays Children: Poems of Work (SaC).
  Helen Plotz, ed.

Labor Unions
Blackleg Miners, The. *Unknown*
Comrade Jesus. Cleghorn
Joe Hill. Hayes
My Master and I. *Unknown*
Old Man's Advice, An. *Unknown*
Talking Union: 1964. Sissman
Union Man. Morgan
See also **Strikes and Strikers.**

Labrador, Canada
North Labrador. Crane

Labyrinthitis
Inner Ear. Hummer

Labyrinths
Labyrinth, The. Muir

Lade, Sir John
Short Song of Congratulation [*or* To a Young
Heir], A. Johnson

Ladybirds
Clock-a-Clay. Clare
Lady Lost. Ransom
Ladybird. Sansom
Ladybird, Ladybird fly away home. Mother
Goose
Ladybug. Anglund
Ladybug. Dodat
Ladybugs. Shumaker
Ladybug's Christmas. Farber
Lines to a Lady-Bird. De Tabley

Lafayette, Marie Joseph, Marquis de
La Fayette. Madison

Lake District, England
Childhood and School-Time. *Fr.* The
Prelude [or, Growth of a Poet's Mind].
Wordsworth
Raised are the dripping oars. *Fr.* The Youth
of Nature: Wordsworth's Country. Arnold

Lakes and Ponds
Among the Finger Lakes. Wallace
Beaver Pond. Marriott
Goose Pond. Kunitz
Lake, A. Beddoes
Lake, The. Coxe
Lake, The. Hughes
Lake, The. Poe
Lake. Simpson
Lake Chelan. Stafford
Lake in the Sky, The. Haines
Lakes. Auden
Lakes. Preil
Lakeshore. Scott
Little Lough, The. Hewitt
Midnight Skaters, The. Blunden
Ode to the Lake of Geneva. Parsons
On Autumn Lake. Ashbery
On Windermere; Bowness Bay and Belle Isle.
Fr. The Prelude [or, Growth of a Poet's
Mind]: Childhood and School-Time.
Wordsworth
Sonnet to Lake Leman. Byron
Spring Pools. Frost
Suicide Pond. McLaughlin
To Ben, at the Lake. McQueen
To Senaca Lake. Percival
Unnamed Lake, The. Scott
Vapour and Blue. Campbell
Winter Lakes, The. Campbell
Winter Pond. Belitt
Young Argonauts. Wingfield

Lalemant, Gabriel
Brébeuf and His Brethren. Scott

Lamb, Charles
This Lime-Tree Bower My Prison. Coleridge

Lambs
Child's Pet, A. Davies
Dead Lamb, A. Curnow
First Sight. Larkin
For a Lamb. Eberhart
Lamb, The. *Fr.* Songs of Innocence. Blake
Lambs at Play. Rossetti
Pallid Cuckoo. Campbell
Pet Lamb, The. Wordsworth
Ravens. Hughes
Sale of the Pet Lamb, The. Howitt
Searching for Lambs. *Unknown*
Wolf and the Lambs, The. Eastwick

Lament
Last Song of the Angel of Bad Luck. Levine

Lamplighters
Lamplighter, The. "O'Sullivan"
Lamplighter, The. *Fr.* A Child's Garden of
Verses. Stevenson
Lamplighter: 1914. Kunitz
Light the Lamps Up, Lamplighter! Farjeon

Lampman, Archibald
Bereavement of the Fields. Campbell

Lampreys
Lamprey, glowing with uncommon fires, The.
Fr. Halieutica. Diaper
To a Young Lady, with Some Lampreys.
Gay

Lancashire, England
Lancashire Winter. Connor
To Saxham. Carew

Lancelot du Lac
Lancelot. Bontemps

Landlords and Landladies
Adieu to My Landlady, An. Farewell
Ballad of the Landlord. Hughes
Behold the Deeds! Bunner
Inn That Missed Its Chance, The. Wells
Landlord's Wife, The. Chin
Landowner, The. Bamford
Redemption. Herbert
Scenery. Joans
Song: "Leaves are still; not a breath is heard,
The." Linton
Telephone Conversation. Soyinka

Landor, Walter Savage
Envoi: "I warmed both hands before the fire
of Life." Lewis
For an Epitaph at Fiesole. Landor
In Memory of Walter Savage Landor.
Swinburne
Landor. Albee
W. S. Landor. Moore

Landscape
Before a Journey. Wells
Communion. Ignatow
Distances. Hugo
Double Mock Sonnet. Hartman
Familiar Landscapes. Raab
Florence. *Fr.* Aurora Leigh. Browning
Iron Landscapes (and the Statue of Liberty).
Gunn
Iron Landscapes (and the Statue of Liberty).
Gunn
Landscape. Horiguchi Daigaku
Landscape. Koh Chang-soo
Landscape. *Fr.* Anna Perenna. Piccolo
Language As Inevitable Metaphor. Idea As
Inevitable Figment. Carruth
Mask. Spender
Midsummer Day in France. *Fr.* Of the Day
Estivall. Hume
New Hampshire. *Fr.* Landscapes. Eliot
Rannoch, by Glencoe. *Fr.* Landscapes.
Eliot
Storm, The. Williams
Summit gain'd how glorious the reward, The.
Fr. The Cruise. Dunbar
Usk. *Fr.* Landscapes. Eliot
View. Munro
Virginia. *Fr.* Landscapes. Eliot

Landslides
Clarity. Ammons

Lang, Andrew
Ballade of Andrew Lang. MacColl

Language
About. Sherry
Aestivation [an Unpublished Poem, by My
Late Latin Tutor]. *Fr.* The Autocrat of the
Breakfast Table. Holmes
Americana IX. Rakosi
Ancient Speech, The. *Fr.* Eileann Chanaidh.
Raine
And the whole earth was of one language, and
of one speech. *Fr.* Genesis.
Anthology of Nouns. Tyler
Antiques. De la Mare
Birth of Sound. Ondaatje
Bonne Entente. Scott
Burning of Paper instead of Children, The.
Rich
Change, The. O'Bruadair

Charles Darwin Pays a Visit, December 1971.
Ondaatje
Clearwater Beach, Florida. Matthews
Coal. Lorde
Cool Web, The. Graves
Could mortal lip divine. Dickinson
Desmet, Idaho, March 1969. Hale
Dirty Word, The. Shapiro
Essay on Language. Coleman
Eve: Night Thoughts. Jerome
For the Mute. Clifton
Fragment: "Language has not the power to
speak what love indites." Clare
Genesis. Higgins
Grafted Tongue, A. Montague
Grammar Lesson. Pastan
Greenwood. Jackson
Hail native language, that by sinews weak.
Fr. At a Vacation Exercise [in the College].
Milton
Hearing Russian Spoken. Davie
Hints on Pronunciation for Foreigners.
Unknown
Hogwash. Francis
Home for Thanksgiving. Merwin
How a Girl Was Too Reckless of Grammar
[by Far]. Carryl
I Speak, I Say, I Talk. Shapiro
In Hungarian. Garai
Language, The. Creeley
Language As Inevitable Metaphor. Idea As
Inevitable Figment. Carruth
Language Lesson, 1976. McHugh
Last One, The. Merwin
Little Girl, Be Careful What You Say.
Sandburg
Loving and Liking. Wordsworth
Makers, The. Nemerov
Moon, Sun, Sleep, Birds, Live. Patchen
Naughty Preposition, The. Bishop
New Style, The. O'Bruadair
Nigger. Sanchez
No Matter What, after All, and That Beautiful
Word So. Carruth
Nothingness. Amir
Of the Manner of Addressing Clouds.
Stevens
On the Way to Language. Palmer
Paradoxes and Oxymorons. Ashbery
Parnassians, The. Merrill
Permanently. Koch
Persephone, 5, Outside. Abbott
Persimmons and Plums. Hodges
Phraseology. Cortez
Post-Impressionist Susurration for the First of
November, 1983, A. Carruth
Precious Moments. Sandburg
Pretty Words. Wylie
Price of Wildness, The. Moffett
Primer Lesson. Sandburg
Report from a Far Place. Stafford
Saxon Legend of Language, The. Fordham
Seduced by Analogy. Perelman
Since When As Ever More. Inada
Singular Singulars, Peculiar Plurals. Espy
Spell against Spelling, The. Starbuck
These Green-going-to-Yellow. Bell
Think'st Thou to Seduce Me Then. Campion
Tilth. Graves
Tip of the Iceberg, The. Blumenthal
To a Thesaurus. Adams
Torn-Word. McGavin
Traditions. Heaney
Tree of Silence, The. Miller
Usk, The. Sisson
Varitalk. Holbrook
Very like a Whale. Nash
Vowels. Rimbaud
Ways of Pronouncing "Ough." *Unknown*
What's the Plural? *Unknown*
When the Wine Was Gone. Aubert

When Water Stands Still It's Stone.
  Kouwenaar
Why English Is So Hard. *Unknown*
Word. Spender
Word World. Perelman
Words. Finch
Words. Harpur
Wreath, A. Illyés
You Have Taken My Language Away.
  Pataki
In the American Tree (IAT). Ron Silliman,
  ed.
"Language" Poetries; an Anthology (LP).
  Douglas Messerli, ed.

Lanterns
Street Lanterns. Coleridge

Laos
Room above the White Rose, The. Stroud

Lapwings
O Lapwing! Blake

Larches
Larch Wood Secrets. Eastwick
Larches. Kitahara Hakushu
Tamarack. McCarthy

Larkin, James
Inscription for a Headstone. Clarke

Larkin, Philip
Larkin. Ruark

Larks
Bunch of Larks, The. Leighton
Caged Skylark, The. Hopkins
Crier-to-Heaven. Yanagawa Seigan
From my little hut. Keiun
Green cornfield. Onitsura
Hark! Hark! the Lark. *Fr.* Cymbeline.
  Shakespeare
In the middle of a plain. *Fr.* Seventy-six
  Hokku. Basho
Lark, A. Tonna
Lark, The. *Unknown*
Lark Ascending, The. Meredith
Lark's Nest, The. Clare
Lo! Here the Gentle Lark. *Fr.* Venus and
  Adonis. Shakespeare
Morning. Eastwick
On a Picture by J. M. Wright, Esq. Southey
Over Salève. Clarke
Praying. Kavanagh
Returning, We Hear the Larks. Rosenberg
Shelley's Skylark. Hardy
Skylark, The. Hogg
Skylark, The. Tennyson
Skylark rises through the dawn, A. *Fr.*
  Twenty-four Hokku. Kito
Skylarks. Hughes
Skylark's Nest, The. Long
To a Lark in War-Time. Werfel
To a Skylark. Shelley
Trying to hide her nestlings, a skylark cries.
  Issa
Upon the Lark and the Fowler. Bunyan
Woodlark, The. Hopkins
See also **Meadowlarks; Skylarks.**

Larsen, Don
Don Larsen's Perfect Game. Goodman

Last Judgment
Last Judgment, The. Belli

Last Rites. *See* **Extreme Unction.**

Last Supper
Anatomy of a Supper. Görgey
Last Supper, The. Al-Khal
Last Supper, The. Prévert
Last Supper, The. Williams

Latin America. *See* **Central America; South
  America; West Indies.**

Latter-Day Saints, Church. *See* **Mormons.**

Lauder, William
To the Editor of Mr. Pope's Works.
  Edwards

Laughter
Child's Laughter, A. Swinburne
Dirty-billed Freeze Footy, The.
  Hemschemeyer
Early Supper. Howes
Her Merriment. Davies
Laugh It Off. Elliot
Laughing Backwards. Hall
Laughing Song. *Fr.* Songs of Innocence.
  Blake
Laughter. Crawford
Laughter. Enoch
Missing You. Zolotow
When You Laugh. Jonker
See also **Mirth.**

Laughton, Charles
Letter to the Actor Charles Laughton
  concerning the Work on the Play "The Life
  of Galileo." Brecht

Laundry and Laundering
Bendix. Updike
Days through Starch and Bluing. Fulton
Dolls' Wash, The. Ewing
Goldfish Wife, The. Hochman
In an Iridescent Time. Stone
Laundry. Smith
Laundry. *Fr.* Negroes. Vaynshteyn
Laundry and School Epigrams. Mayer
Laundryman—/ By his neighbours', The.
  Unknown
Love Calls Us to the Things of This World.
  Wilbur
Mad Scene, The. Merrill
News from the Basement Laundromat.
  Gabbard
Old Ellen Sullivan. Welles
Public Wash House, The. Bold
Saturday Morning at the Laundry. Gilbert
Sheets, The. Steele
Shepherd's Hut, The. Young
Short Biography of a Washerwoman. Ulloa
Storm. Nagy
Thinking Twice in the Laundromat. Elliott
Tubby or not tubby—there's the rub.
  Burnand
Wash-Day. McCrea
Wash Day. Mollin
Washer-Woman, The. Bohanan
Washerwoman, The. *Fr.* The Woman's
  Labour; an Epistle to Mr. Stephen Duck.
  Collier
Washerwoman, The. Fordham
Washing Machine, The. Davies

Laurels
Tapestry Trees. Morris
To Laurels. Herrick

Laurentian Mountains, Canada
Laurentian Shield. Scott

Lavender
I planned to have a border of lavender.
  Goodman
Lavender Bush, The. Fleming
Lavender's Blue. *Unknown*

Law and Lawyers
Merchant Shipping Act, The. *Unknown*

Lawes, Henry
To Mr. H. Lawes on His Airs. Milton
To Mr. Henry Lawes. Philips
To Mr. Henry Lawes, Who Had Then Newly
  Set a Song of Mine in the Year 1635.
  Waller

Lawns
Rolling the Lawn. Empson

Lawrence, David Herbert
D. H. Lawrence and James Joyce. Wolfe

Lawrence, Edward
Sonnet: To Mr. Lawrence. Milton

Lawrence, Thomas Edward
Void, The. *Fr.* The T. E. Lawrence Poems.
  MacEwen

Lawyers and Law
Air: "Fox may steal your hens, sir, A." *Fr.*
  The Beggar's Opera. Gay
Beneath this smooth stone by the bone of his
  bone. *Unknown*
Case at Sessions, A. Landor
Case to the Civilians, A. *Unknown*
Damages, Two Hundred Pounds. Thackeray
Help Wanted. Waldheim
In the Dock. De la Mare
Injustice of the Courts. Moorer
Laws of God, the Laws of Man, The.
  Housman
Lawyers Know Too Much, The. Sandburg
Lawyers' Ways, The. Dunbar
Legal Fiction. Empson
Legal Mouse, A. Moorer
Lizzie and Joe in Court. Cordle
Penal Law. Clarke
To Sir Thomas Egerton. Daniel

Lazarus
Act of Faith. Trías
Dives and Lazarus ("There was a man in
  olden times"). *Unknown*
Raising of the Dead, The. Dobson
When Lazarus left his charnel-cave. *Fr.* In
  Memoriam A. H. H. Tennyson

Lazarus, Emma
Homecoming of Emma Lazarus, The.
  Kinnell

Laziness
Epitaph, An: "Interred [*or* Interr'd] beneath
  this marble stone." Prior
Get Up, Get Up. *Unknown*
I'm Really Not Lazy. Spilka
Lament of a Slug-a-Bed's Wife. Smith
Lazy Man's Song. Po Chü-i
Sluggard, The. Watts

Leadership
God, Give Us Men! Holland
He Who Calls Himself Leader. Halpern
Leaders. *Unknown*
Masters. Amis

League of Nations
League of Nations, The. Siegrist

Leap Year
Leap Yeah Party, De. Johnson

Lear, Edward
Edward Lear. Auden
How Pleasant to Know Mr. Lear. Lear

Lear, King. *See* **King Lear.**

Learning
Father's Testament, A. Ibn Tibbon
On the Prospect of Planting Arts and Learning
  in America. Berkeley
Chiefe use then in man of that he knowes,
  The. *Fr.* Of Human Learning. Greville
Verses on the Prospect of Planting Arts and
  Learning in America. Berkeley

Leaves
Auction. Heyen
Autumn Leaves. Thompson
Autumn Leaves. Webb
Beautiful Dead Leaf. Kotaro
Burning of the Leaves, The. Binyon
Burnt in the fireplace. *Fr.* Eighty-seven
  Hokku. Buson
College of Surgeons, The. Stephens
Come, Little Leaves. Cooper
Even before they fall. *Fr.* Kokin Shu.
  Unknown
Fading-Leaf and Fallen-Leaf. Garnett
Fallen Leaves. Tupper
Fallen Leaves in a Valley. Sogi

Falling Leaves. Ch'iao Lin
Falling Leaves. Wu Chia-chi
Falling Leaves before the Wind. Shotetsu
Falling leaves, making no sound. *Fr.*
   Forty-four Hokku. Issa
Fluttering Leaves. Bennett
Gathering Leaves. Frost
L(a. Cummings
Leaves. Davies
Leaves. Tussman
Leaves. Tynan
Leaves in a Frolic, The. *Unknown*
Leaves like Fish. Cardiff
Leaves Making a Sound as They Fall.
   Shotetsu
Looking Up at Leaves. Howes
Love in Spring. Shotetsu
Markings. Steele
Mountains, darkening, have robbed. *Fr.*
   Eighty-seven Hokku. Buson
November. *Fr.* Forest Leaves in Autumn.
   Keble
November Night. Crapsey
October's Party. Cooper
Pity of the Leaves, The. Robinson
Poem on Falling Leaves. Liu E
Sonnet: Leaves. Barnes
Sweeping Leaves. Ryushu Shutaku
Two Pictures of a Leaf. Bell
Windfall. Scott
See also **Autumn.**

Lebanon
As I Came Down from Lebanon. Scollard
Lebanon. Hawi
On Lebanon. Gray

Leda
Leda. Doolittle
Leda. Van Duyn
Leda and the Swan. Gogarty
Leda and the Swan. Harasymowicz
Leda and the Swan. Yeats
Leda Reconsidered. Van Duyn
People do gossip. Sappho

Ledwidge, Francis
In Memoriam Francis Ledwidge. Heaney

Lee, Robert Edward
Lee to the Rear. Thompson
Lee's Parole. Manville
Robert E. Lee. *Fr.* John Brown's Body.
   Benét
Robert E. Lee. Howe

Leeds, England
Poem for Jacqueline Hill. *Unknown*

Leeuwenhoek, Anton
Microscope, The. Kumin

Legree, Simon
Simon Legree—a Negro Sermon. *Fr.* The
   Booker Washington Trilogy. Lindsay

Legs
Leg, The. Shapiro
Legs, The. Graves
Poem in Which My Legs Are Accepted.
   Fraser
Sailor's Apology for Bow-Legs, A. Hood
Vet's Rehabilitation. Durem

Leicester, Robert Dudley, Earl of
Epitaph on the Earl of Leicester. Ralegh

Leif Ericsson
Story of Vinland, The. *Fr.* Psalm of the
   West. Lanier

Leisure
Hob upon a Holiday ("Hob yawned three
   times and rubbed his eyes"). *Unknown*
Leisure. Davies

Lemmings
Lemmings, The. Masefield

Lemons
Lemon. Satz
Lemon Elegy. Kotaro
Lemons, Lemons. Young

Lenin, Vladimir Ilyich
Lenin. Ladányi
Second Hymn to Lenin. "MacDiarmid"
Skeleton of the Future, The. "MacDiarmid"
So I came down the steps to Lenin. *Fr.*
   Lenin. Wellesley
This is an ancient waltz. *Fr.*
   Tcheliabtraktrostroi Waltz. Aragon

Leningrad, U. S. S. R.
Leningrad. Mandelstam
Leningrad Cemetary, Winter of 1941. Olds
Leningrad: Picture Postcard. Wieseltier

Lent
Lent. Rodgers

Lentils
Woman Cleaning Lentils, The. Zehrd

Leonardo da Vinci
Leonardo Da Vinci's. Moore
Leonardo's Secret. Bly

Leonidas
Death of Leonidas, The. Croly

Leopards
Leopard. Kreps
Leopard. *Fr.* Hunter Poems of the Yoruba.
   Unknown
Lullaby: "Leopard, nocturnal, with eyes
   infernal, The." Rübner
Snow-Leopard, The. Jarrell

Leopold III, King of the Belgians
Moon and the Night and the Men, The.
   Berryman

Lepanto, Battle of (1571)
Lepanto. Chesterton

Leprechauns
Faith, I Wish I Were a Leprechaun. Ritter

Leprosy
Leper, The. Ka-'ehu
Leper, The. Willis

Lesbians *See* **Homosexuality and
   Homosexuals.**

Lesbos, Greece
Night in Lesbos, A. Horton
Sappho Lives Again. Vivien

Lethargy
Lethargy. Justice

Letters
Burning Love Letters. Moss
Children's Letters, The. Livesay
Correspondence School Instructor Says
   Goodbye to His Poetry Students, The.
   Kinnell
Dear Reader. Meinke
Dear wife and bosom friend I hat seen hart.
   Fr. Letters from Vicksburg. Gildner
Dear Wordsworth. Hathaway
Deceased. Corman
Destruction of Letters. Deutsch
Empty at the Heart of Things. Polite
Familiar Letter to Several Correspondents, A.
   Holmes
From a Letter to America on a Visit to
   Sussex: Spring 1942. Cornford
Haiku: "All its advertisements." *Unknown*
Haiku: "Found while spring-cleaning."
   Unknown
Haiku: "Sheltering from rain." *Unknown*
Haiku: "Waiting for his turn." *Unknown*
Haiku: "Winter fly, The." *Unknown*
Hate Mail. Kowit
History of the Human Body/ Winfield's Infield
   Hit/ The Lassitude of the Infinite, The.
   Nauen
How to Write a Letter. Turner
Illiterate, The. Meredith
Jungle Husband, The. Smith
Letter. Blight
Letter, A. Joseph
Letter, The. Tennyson
Letter from a man, A. *Unknown*
Letter from the Mountain Sanitarium.
   Giuliani

Letter in the Present and Present Perfect.
   Menicanti
Letter to a Censor. Cherry
Letter to a Friend. Moore
Letter to a Live Poet, A. Brooke
Letter to an American Visitor. Comfort
Letter to Her Husband, A. Bradstreet
Letter to Jean-Paul Baudot, at Christmas.
   Stryk
Letter to Madame la Marquise de C———.
   Sainctonge
Letter to Paul Celan in Memory, A.
   Rothenberg
Letter to Peter, A. Chiang
Letter to Sigmund Freud. *Fr.*
   Psychoanalysis. Teller
Letter to Tina Koyama from Elliot Bay Park.
   Mitsui
Letters. Campert
Letters. Emerson
Letters from a Father. Van Duyn
Lines Occasioned by the Burning of Some
   Letters. Dixon
Love Letter. Ray
Love-letter, A. Tucker
Love Letter from Mars. Ciardi
Love Letters. Heard
Mother-land'scape (Letters). Harmon
My Grandmother's Love Letters. Crane
Naked Poetry. Cooley
Not going in. *Unknown*
Old letters!/ I was on such familiar terms.
   Fr. Forty-seven Tanka in Three Lines.
   Ishikawa Takuboku
Packet of Letters. Bogan
Parting, without a Sequel. Ransom
Postcards to Athena. Bishop
Postman's Bell Is Answered Everywhere,
   The. Gregory
Praise for an Urn. Crane
Queen Charming. Hadas
Railway Stationery, The. Koch
Reading a Letter from Home. Michizane
Rimbaud Fire Letter to Jim Applewhite.
   Chappell
Seated there upon the floor. Tyutchev
Special Delivery. Montague
Spring Training. Polito
Thank You for Your Letter. Ch'ao Li-houa
Those days I didn't even notice. *Fr.*
   Forty-seven Tanka in Three Lines.
   Ishikawa Takuboku
Wife in London, A. Hardy
Words, like Spiders. Wolny

Lettuce
Love of Lettuce, The. Piercy

Leukemia
Transparent Man, The. Hecht

Levet, Robert
On the Death of Mr. [*or* Dr.] Robert Levet, a
   Practiser in Physic. Johnson

Levita, Eliajah
Epitaph: "Stone cries from the wall, The."
   Unknown

Lewis, Meriwether
On the Discoveries of Captain Lewis.
   Barlow

Lexington and Concord, Battle of
Paul Revere's Ride. Longfellow

Liars. *See* **Lies and Lying.**

Liberace
Liberace. Holden

Liberalism and Liberals
Lost Leader, The. Browning

Liberia
On the Founding of Liberia. *Fr.* Libretto for
   the Republic of Liberia. Tolson

Liberty. *See* **Freedom.**

Liberty Bell
Independence Bell—July 4, 1776. *Unknown*

Liberty, Statue of
Emigrés, The. Walker
Fairest of Freedom's Daughters. Rankin
Iron Landscapes (and the Statue of Liberty).
  Gunn
New Colossus, The. Lazarus
To the Statue. Swenson
Tragic Condition of the Statue of Liberty,
  The. Mayer
Libraries
British Museum Reading Room, The.
  MacNeice
Certified Copy. Deagon
Fire at Alexandria, The. Weiss
Library, The. Huff
November Primrose, The. Devlin
Public Library. Stevenson
Reading Room, The New York Public
  Library. Eberhart
Scholar II. Deane
Sonnet: My Friend's Library. Lott
Libya
Roman in Libya, A. Evans
Lice
Head-lice make merry on my head. *Fr.*
  Ryojin Hisho. Go-Shirakawa
Immortals, The. Rosenberg
Louse Crept Out of My Lady's Shift, A.
  Bottomley
Louse Hunting. Rosenberg
Shih-hou Pointed Out to Me That from
  Ancient Times There Had Never Been a
  Poem on the Subject of Li. Mei
  Yao-ch'en
To a Louse [on Seeing One on a Lady's
  Bonnet at Church] Burns
Lies and Lying
Ancient Custom, An. Steiger
Book of Lies, The. Tate
Cotignac Again ("Cotignac is full of spies").
  Sisson
Golly, How Truth Will Out. Nash
How Lies Grow. Chernoff
Insult before Gift-Giving. Bolton
Liar, The. *Unknown*
Lie, The. Kipling
Lie, The. Ralegh
Lying. Hillyer
Matilda. Belloc
Song: "Lying is an occupation." Pilkington
Tony Baloney ("Tony Baloney is fibbing
  again"). Lee
Uncle Ananias. Robinson
Use of Fiction, The. Nye
Word of Encouragement, A. Pope
Lièvre River, Quebec
Morning on the Lièvre. Lampman
Life
Accident, An. Wu Sheng
Afraid of Life? Rashed
Alas, the days of youth fly past. Insha
All the World's a Stage. *Fr.* As You Like
  It. Shakespeare
Alumnus Football. Rice
And the days are not full enough. Pound
Anyone Lived in a Pretty How Town.
  Cummings
April Inventory. Snodgrass
Arena, The. Witheford
As Much as You Can. Cavafy
As One Who Bears beneath His Neighbor's
  Roof. Hillyer
Ask me not of the heart's. Mir
Bankrupt. Sayres
Be Merry. *Unknown*
Beach in August, The. Kees
Because I Deeply Praised. Sikelianos
Before the Beginning of Years. *Fr.* Atalanta
  in Calydon. Swinburne
Behind me—dips eternity. Dickinson
Behold the child, by Nature's kindly law.
  Fr. An Essay on Man. Pope

Change. Bass
Choice, The. Pomfret
Choruses from "Hellas." *Fr.* Hellas.
  Shelley
Comment. Parker
Consumer's Report, A. Porter
Cut the Grass. Ammons
Dance. Rashed
Days. Larkin
De Morte. Wotton
Do Not Die. Merwin
Dreams. Zangwill
Ego. Vivanti
Epigram: "Life flows to death as rivers to the
  sea." Cunningham
Esthete in Harlem. Hughes
Even at its longest. Tameko
Everything is only an image. Schönwiese
Experience. Harford
Face in the Ceiling, The. Dobyns
Firstness. Tillinghast
Force That through the Green Fuse Drives the
  Flower, The. Thomas
Forget everything you have seen.
  Schönwiese
Four Ages of Man, The. Yeats
Heart's Location, The. Meinke
High Country Weather. Baxter
His Life. Devecseri
Homage to Life. Supervielle
Honey. Wright
Horse Show, The. Williams
Hound, The. Francis
How much had happened on the earth. Mir
Hughie at the Inn. Wylie
Human Seasons, The. Keats
I did see the moth go up. Mir
I drive my carriage from the Upper East Gate.
  Fr. Nineteen Old Poems of the Han.
  Unknown
I Have a Rendezvous with Life. Cullen
I know well this body of mine. *Fr.* Manyo
  Shu. Yakamochi
I Shall Not Pass This Way Again. York
If. Howells
If they really lived. Schönwiese
Illusion. Wilcox
Introduction of the Shopping Cart. Costanzo
Is Life Worth Living? Austin
It's in Your Face. *Unknown*
Last Chapter, The. De la Mare
Last Poem. Berrigan
Last Statement for a Last Oracle. Dugan
Length of Life, The. Wells
Life. Barbauld
Life. Dunbar
Life. Follain
Life. Herbert
Life. Ray
Life. Sill
Life. Treasone
Life. Tucker
Life!/ I came to your door like a beggar. *Fr.*
  Renewal. Zaidi
Life Cycle of Common Man. Nemerov
Life Encompassed. Davie
Life of Man, The. Bacon
Life Sculpture. Doane
Life's a Funny Proposition after All. Cohan
Life's a Game. *Unknown*
Life's Boundary. Ray
Life's Journey. Wilcox
Life's Morning. Lewis
Life's Poor Play. *Fr.* An Essay on Man.
  Pope
Life's Will. Al-Shabbi
Little Song of Life, A. Reese
Live for It. Bass
Lore. Thomas
Lucinda Matlock. *Fr.* Spoon River
  Anthology. Masters
Madrigal:

Madrigal. Drummond
Making a Man. Waterman
May It Be. Pasternak
Meditation at Seventy. Henz
Men Made out of Words. Stevens
Mother to Son. Hughes
Music after Reading. Larbaud
My life had stood—a loaded gun. Dickinson
My Life Is like the Summer Rose. Wilde
My life is the great expanse. Ghalib
My Own Epitaph. Gay
My precious life was spent. Mir
Mysteries of Life. Tucker
Mystery of Life, The. Gambold
Naked I Came. Palladas
Nature. Longfellow
Next, Please. Larkin
None knows since when the sea. Mir
Nothing to Write Home About. Brainard
Now that I am brought to know. *Fr.* Manyo
  Shu. Tabito
Old Adam, The. Levertov
Old Man on the River Bank, An. Seferis
Old Man's Idyl, An. Realf
On Finding the Tree of Life. Dugan
On the Impermanence of Life. *Fr.* Sixty-four
  Tanka. Saigyo
Our life is like a forest, where the sun. *Fr.*
  Sonnets Written in the Orillia Woods.
  Sangster
Our Lives Are Rivers. Urbina
Our lives are Swiss. Dickinson
Pale Blue Casket, The. Pitcher
Pants. Vice
Passage. Levertov
Picture-Show. Sassoon
Pilgrimage, The. Herbert
Playing the Game. *Unknown*
Poem for Trapped Things, A. Wieners
Postscript. Hochman
Psalm of Life, A. Longfellow
Quatrain: "Just life and death make up our
  worldly state." Farhat
Quickness. Vaughan
Rainy Day, The. Longfellow
Responding Voice. Icaza
River of Life, The. Campbell
Road Not Taken, The. Frost
Rock of This Odd Coincidence, The. Schott
Secret Ballgame. Schönwiese
Sergeant, The. Johnson
She should have died hereafter. *Fr.*
  Macbeth. Shakespeare
Ship of Life, The. Al-Najafi
Sic Vita. King
Since life had brought us we had come.
  Zauq
Since the far beginning of heaven and earth.
  Fr. Manyo Shu. Yakamochi
Slavery. Heifetz-Tussman
Slice of Life, A. Wickstrom
Song of Life, A. Werfel
Sonnet: "Lift not the painted veil which those
  who live." Shelley
Sonnet: To Primal Matters. Sandoval y
  Zapata
Sower, The. Blind
Spider Web. Dobyns
Steed of life is galloping fast, The. Ghalib
Steps. O'Hara
Still Here. Hughes
Story, The. Smith
Sum of Life, The. King
Sunday Morning. Stevens
Tears. Reese
Things, The. Aiken
This Life Is All Chequer'd with Pleasures and
  Woes. Moore
To Robert Louis Stevenson. Henley
Tree to Flute. Hajnal
Turn your face and look. Insha
25.40 P.M. (Past Mourning). Simba

Under Sorrow's Sign. O'Dalaigh
Untitled Poem. Dugan
Uphill [or Up-Hill]. Rossetti
Variant, A. Leyeles
Vitae Summa Brevis Spem Nos Vetat
  Incohare Longam. Dowson
Walk, The. Aiken
We Are Transmitters. Lawrence
We hurry on, nor passing note. Dolben
We Love Life Whenever We Can. Darwish
What I Live For. Banks
What Is Lived. Valle
What Is Our Life? A Play of Passion.
  Ralegh
When I Consider Life. Fr. Aureng-Zebe.
  Dryden
Whist. Ware
Who'd have thought it? Fr. Thirty Tanka.
  Shunzei
Wisdom of Life, The. "Al-Akhtal al-Saghir"
You were born; must die; were loved; must
  love. Spender

Lifeguards
Lifeguard, The. Dickey
Liffey (river), Ireland
Anna Livia Plurabelle. Fr. A Mini-Samizdat
  of New River Rhymes. Cole
To the Liffey with the Swans. Gogarty
Light
City Lights. Field
City Limits, The. Ammons
Creation of Light, The. Maura
Dazzle. Roberts
Grace for Light. O'Neill
Hail holy light, ofspring [or offspring] of
  Heav'n first born. Fr. Paradise Lost.
  Milton
Hymn: To Light. Cowley
Light exists in spring, A. Dickinson
Light the Lamps Up, Lamplighter! Farjeon
O Light Invisible, we praise Thee! Fr. The
  Rock. Eliot
O Virtuous Light. Wylie
There's a certain slant of light. Dickinson
When the Light Falls. Kunitz
Lighthouses
Brilliant kernel of the night, The. Fr. The
  Light-Keeper. Stevenson
Cuvier Light. Wilson
Flannan Isle. Gibson
I'd Like to Be a Lighthouse. Field
Lighthouse, The. Wilson
Lighthouse in Maine, A. Mahon
Lighthouse in the Night. Storni
Lighthouses. Wellesley
Needles' Lighthouse from Keyhaven,
  Hampshire, The. Turner
Skerryvore. Stevenson
Lightning
At Great Torrington, Devon. Unknown
Dance-Song of the Lightning. Unknown
Heat Lightning. Warren
Lightning. Tamehide
Lightning: again the sky's morning glow.
  Fr. Thirty-three Hokku. Kikaku
Lightning gets to be terrifying. Fr.
  Twenty-one Hokku. Kaya Shirao
Lightning: in the east yesterday. Fr.
  Thirty-three Hokku. Kikaku
Lightning is a yellow fork. Dickinson
Lightning Rod Salesman, The. Hester
Lightning spills a noise. Fr. Eighty-seven
  Hokku. Buson
Miramichi Lightning. Bailey
Once, Driving West of Billings, Montana.
  Mitchell
She Didn't Even Wave. Ai
Too momentary/ to be called evanescent.
  Teika
Lightning Bugs. See **Fireflies.**
Lilacs
Cut Lilac. Beyer

Lilac, The. Wolfe
Lilacs. Lowell
Rain Games. Beyer
White Lilac. Welch
With Lilacs. Crandall
Lilies
Bulb, A. Munkittrick
Lilies, The. Berry
Lilly in a Christal, The. Herrick
Mariposa Lily, The. Coolbrith
Maudle-in Ballad, A. Unknown
On a Bed of Guernsey Lilies. Smart
On Easter Day. Thaxter
Picking Lilies. Unknown
Lilies of the Valley
Lilies of the Valley. Silkin
White coral bells upon a slender stalk.
  Unknown
Lilith
Anguish'd Doubt Broods over Eden, The.
  Fr. Lilith. Brennan
Lilith. Fainlight
Lilith. Feldman
Lilith. Finkel
Lilith. Gregg
Lilith. Grossman
Lilith. Levi
Waiting for Lilith. Kessler
Limbo
Limbo. Coleridge
Limestone
In Praise of Limestone. Auden
Lincoln, Abraham
Abraham Lincoln. Stoddard
Abraham Lincoln. Taylor
Abraham Lincoln Walks at Midnight.
  Lindsay
Anne Rutledge. Fr. Spoon River Anthology.
  Masters
Booth Killed Lincoln. Unknown
Born without a Chance. Cooke
Cool Tombs. Sandburg
Death of Lincoln, The. Bryant
Emperor of Ice-Cream, The. Stevens
Fire-Logs. Sandburg
Hand of Lincoln, The. Stedman
Honest Abe Lincoln. Shulman
Lincoln. Fletcher
Lincoln. Fr. Commemoration Ode. Monroe
Lincoln. Ray
Lincoln. Turner
Lincoln Monument: Washington. Hughes
Lincoln Statue, The. Collins
Martyr, The. Melville
Master, The. Robinson
O Captain! My Captain! Fr. Memories of
  President Lincoln. Whitman
On the Life-Mask of Abraham Lincoln.
  Gilder
Poetry Is a Destructive Force. Stevens
Remembering Lincoln. Mundorf
Statue, The. Roseveare
They Will Look for a Few Words. Turner
To Abraham Lincoln. Piatt
When Lilacs Last in the Dooryard Bloom'd.
  Fr. Memories of President Lincoln.
  Whitman
Lincolnshire, England
At Lincoln. Adams
Boston, Lincolnshire. Unknown
High Tide on the Coast of Lincolnshire
  (1571), The. Ingelow
Lincolnshire; from the Wolds to the Fens.
  Fr. The Sad Shepherd. Jonson
Lincolnshire's Holland Speaks of Her
  Waterfowl. Fr. Polyolbion. Drayton
Lines: "Here often, when a child, I lay
  reclined." Tennyson
Lind, Fabius
Bolted Room. Leyeles
Disorder. Leyeles

Fabius Lind Is Riding the Wind. Leyeles
Fabius Lind to Comrade Death. Leyeles
Fabius Lind to Fabius Lind. Leyeles
Fabius Lind's Days. Leyeles
Lindbergh, Charles
Lindbergh. Unknown
Linen
Linen Industry, The. Longley
Linnets
Green Linnet, The. Wordsworth
Grey Linnet, The. McCarroll
I Heard a Linnet Courting. Bridges
Linnet, The. De la Mare
Lions
Glove and the Lions, The. Hunt
Jim, Who Ran Away from His Nurse, and
  Was Eaten by a Lion. Belloc
Lion, The. Belloc
Lion, The. Howitt
Lion, The. Nash
Lion, The. Prelutsky
Lion. Smith
Lion. Swenson
Lion. Unknown
Lion, The. Vas
Lion and Albert, The. Edgar
Lion and the Mouse, The. Shteynbarg
Lion and the Wave, The. Allingham
Lion for Real, The. Ginsberg
Lion-Hunt, The. Pringle
Lion Hunts. Beer
Lion's Skeleton, The. Turner
O My Poor Darling. Watson
Song of the Lioness for Her Cub. Unknown
Sunt Leones. Smith
Li Po
Dreaming of Li Po. Tu Fu
Grave of Li Po, The. Huang Ching-jen
On the Subject of Waves. Grier
Three Jewish Boys Write to an Ancient
  Chinese Poet. Teller
Twenty-odd years in doubt. Joju
Lippi, Fra Filippo
Fra Lippo Lippi. Browning
Lipscomb, Eugene
Say Goodbye to Big Daddy. Jarrell
Lisbon, Portugal
Sonnet on Passing the Bridge of Alcantra,
  near Lisbon. Mickle
While you, my friend, from louring wintry
  plains. Fr. Almada Hill: An Epistle from
  Lisbon. Mickle
Lister, Joseph
"Chief, The." Fr. In Hospital. Henley
Literature
Can. Lit. Birney
Canadian Prairies View of Literature, The.
  Donnell
England, Autumn. Brown
Lecture, A. Preil
Literature and Poetry. Jacob
Nocturne: "long arm embossed with gold
  slides from the tree tops, A." Fargue
Principal British Writers. Goodwin
Survey of Literature. Ransom
See also **Authorship and Authors;
  Criticism and Critics.**
Lithuania, U.S.S.R.
Little House in Lithuania, The. Marshak
Summer Pogrom. Zwicky
Vilna. Kulbak
Little Bighorn, Battle of (1876)
Down the Little Big Horn. Brooks
Little Big Horn. McGaffey
Miles Keogh's Horse. Hay
Revenge of Rain-in-the-Face, The.
  Longfellow

Little Red Riding Hood
Red Ridinghood. Alterman
Livingstone, David
Into the Dark. Monette
Lizards
Americans Are Afraid of Lizards. Shapiro
Crumbs. Finkel
Horned Lizard. Molesworth
Justification of the Horned Lizard. Rogers
Lizard, The. Gardner
Lizard. Lawrence
Lizard, The. Murray
Lizard, The. Roethke
Mr. Lizard is Crying. García Lorca
Small Lizard, The. Gregg
Under Creag Mhor. Conn
Witches' Menu. Nikolay
Llamas
In Praise of Llamas. Guiterman
Llama, The. Belloc
One-l lama, the. Nash
Lobsters
Lobster. Sexton
Lobsters and the Fiddler Crab, The ("The
lobsters came ashore one night"). Forster
Lobsters in the Window. Snodgrass
Loch Ness. *See* **Ness, Loch, Scotland.**
Locusts
Coyote and the Locust, The. *Unknown*
Locust, The. *Unknown*
Log Houses
Old Log House. Tippett
Lombardi, Vince
For the Death of Vince Lombardi. Dickey
London, England
About in London. *Fr.* Trivia; or, The Art of
Walking the Streets of London. Gay
Afterlives. Mahon
Ballad of London, A. Le Gallienne
Ballad of the Great London Fog. Huang
Tsun-hsien
Ballad of the Londoner. Flecker
Barrel-Organ, The. Noyes
Bells of London, The. *Unknown*
Breath of Hampstead Heath. Thomas
Composed upon Westminster Bridge,
September 3, 1802. Wordsworth
Country and Town. Morris
Countryman's Return, The. Thomas
Description of a City Shower, A. Swift
Description of London, A. Bancks
Eight o'Clock. Housman
Farewell to Kurdistan. Tonks
Fields from Islington to Marybone, The. *Fr.*
Jerusalem. Blake
Fire of London, The. *Fr.* Annus Mirabilis.
Dryden
Hell is a city much like London. *Fr.* Peter
Bell the Third. Shelley
His Return to London. Herrick
Homage to Wren. MacNeice
Impression de Nuit; London. Douglas
Impression du Matin. Wilde
In the Dials. Henley
Latter-day Geography Lesson. Mason
Let dirty streets be paved with flow'ry green.
Fr. The Comparison. *Unknown*
Lines on the Mermaid Tavern. *Unknown*
London. Davidson
London. *Fr.* Reformation of Manners.
Defoe
London. Johnson
London. Rowland
London at Night. *Fr.* Trivia; or, The Art of
Walking the Streets of London. Gay
London, 1802 ("Milton! thou should'st be
living at this hour"). Wordsworth
London ("I wander through each chartered
street"). *Fr.* Songs of Experience. Blake
London in 1646. Vaughan

London Interior. Monro
London Is a Fine Town. *Unknown*
London Lickpenny. *Unknown*
London Snow. Bridges
London Suburbs. *Fr.* Retirement. Cowper
London Town. Johnson
London versus Epping Forest. *Fr.* Child
Harold. Clare
Love among the Ruins of London. Grainger
New London, The. *Fr.* Annus Mirabilis.
Dryden
New River Head, a Fragment, The. Dower
November Blue. Meynell
Of London Bridge, and the Stupendous Sight,
and Structure Thereof. Howell
Old Song, The. Chesterton
Poor of London, The. Forster
Regent's Park Terrace. Spencer
Satire on London, A. Surrey
Solitude and Reason, in the Village. *Fr.* Of
Solitude. Cowley
Song: "Closes and courts and lanes."
Davidson
Streets of Laredo, The. MacNeice
Sunken Evening [in Trafalgar Square]. Lee
Symphony in Yellow. Wilde
Trivia; or, The Art of Walking the Streets of
London, *sels.* Gay
Tyburn and Westminster. Heywood
Wandsworth Common. Bromwich
West London. Arnold
Which is the way to London Town.
Unknown
Yet London, empress of the northern clime.
Fr. Annus Mirabilis. Dryden
You are now/ In London, that great sea. *Fr.*
Letter to Maria Gisborne. Shelley
Young Wordsworth's London, The. *Fr.* The
Prelude [or, Growth of a Poet's Mind]:
Residence in London. Wordsworth
Londonderry, Northern Ireland
Derry Morning. Mahon
Loneliness
Acquainted with the Night. Frost
Alone. De la Mare
Alone. Manger
Alone by the Road's Edge. O Hehir
At the Turning Point of Life. Illyés
Autobiography. MacNeice
Autumn. Ietaka
Because We Are Not Taken Seriously. Dunn
Bereft. Frost
Bereft. Hardy
Company in Loneliness. *Unknown*
Consider a Move. Ryan
Deep loneliness/ was something I was used to.
Tamemasa
Departure's Girl-Friend. Merwin
Desert Places. Frost
Donal Og. *Unknown*
Dove's Loneliness, The. Darley
Eleanor Rigby. Lennon
Empty at the Heart of Things. Polite
Fable: "Once upon a time/ there was a lonely
wolf." Pilinszky
Fairy Tale. Holub
From the age of the gods. *Fr.* Manyo Shu.
Kogyoku
From this time on. *Fr.* Manyo Shu.
Yakamochi
Fruit of Loneliness. Sarton
Gazing at the sky. Ietaka
Gone on before me. Tonna
Green green, river bank grasses. *Fr.*
Nineteen Old Poems of the Han. *Unknown*
Grievance I. Tu Yeh
He Resigns. Berryman
Here. Manner
Hide-and-Go-Seek. Simmerman
How many times. Tamekane
I Saw in Louisiana a Live-Oak Growing.
Whitman

I Wandered Lonely as a Cloud. Wordsworth
In the loneliness of my heart. *Fr.* Manyo
Shu. Kasa
In this world of ours. Tonna
It Is Five Years Now. Illyés
Kept Indoors on a Winter Evening. Tameko
Knowledge of What Is. Elburg
L(a. Cummings
Lessons. McBride
Loneliness. Carruth
Loneliness. Essex
Loneliness. Faiz
Loneliness. *Fr.* The Hill Wife. Frost
Loneliness. Holman
Loneliness. Nasir
Loneliness. Werfel
Loneliness. Yang Mu
Loneliness. Young
Lonely. Modisane
Lonely. Spire
Lonely Monday. Lewis
Lonely Road. Abrahams
Lonely Woman's Room, The. Hijazi
Lonely World. Linden
Lonesome. Livingston
Looking at it, just thinking about it. *Fr.* A
Compendium of Good Tanka. Teika
Love in the Night. Hanazono
Love Poem, A: "That widowed crow."
Kogon
Mariana. Tennyson
Mnemosyne. Stickney
Most of It, The. Frost
Mr. Flood's Party. Robinson
My loneliness/ I snuggle it up. *Unknown*
On a Fall Night. Ben-Amittai
On the Wide Heath. Millay
One. Rodgers
One lone pine tree. *Fr.* Sixty-four Tanka.
Saigyo
Poem for Some Black Women. Rodgers
Poem: "I loved my friend." Hughes
Political Activist Living Alone. Arrowsmith
Seafarer. *Unknown*
Search. Souster
Secret of Poetry, The. Anderson
Seeing the stars through a willow. *Fr.*
Sixteen Hokku. Miura Chora
Sent to the Hsiu-ts'ai on His Entry into the
Army. Hsi K'ang
Singles. Waters
So lonely am I. Ono no Komachi
Solitude. Monro
Song: "You're wondering if I'm lonely."
Rich
Sorrow. Chu Shu-chen
Spring Night. Teasdale
Stranger in This Land, A. Ashby
Summary. Sanchez
Tell just this one thing. Munenaga
They Ask: Is God, Too, Lonely. Sandburg
To a Friend Shot on a Mexican Bus.
Halpern
To Marguerite—Continued. *Fr.* Switzerland.
Arnold
To my hut overgrown with burdocks. *Fr.* A
Compendium of Good Tanka. Teika
Toy Bone, The. Hall
Trees of the same age. Masayori
Under the Winter Sky. Pilinszky
What Color Is Lonely. Rodgers
What Her Girl Friend Said, Seeing Her Friend
Suffer in Silent Dignity over Her Husband's
Infidelity. Kayamanar
What is the opposite of two? Wilbur
What She Said ("Only the dim-witted say it's
evening"). Milaipperun Kantan
White Light. Gregg
Wife a-Lost, The. Barnes
Wind Blows out of the Gates of the Day,
The. *Fr.* The Land of Heart's Desire.
Yeats

Wind Carol, The. Turco
With him bound by fear. Tamekane
Long Island, New York
Afternoon: Amagansett Beach. Wheelock
Amagansett Beach Revisited. Wheelock
Fire Island. Swenson
Long Island. Powell
Long Island Springs. Moss
On the Island. Sissman
Port Jefferson. Simpson
Longfellow, Henry Wadsworth
Longfellow. Ray
Longfellow's Visit to Venice. Betjeman
Poe and Longfellow. *Fr.* A Fable for
  Critics. Lowell
Shades of Night, The. Housman
Longing
Go Heart, Hurt with Adversity. *Unknown*
Hiraeth. *Unknown*
In a hidden bay. Fushimi
In 728, Longing for His Deceased Wife. *Fr.*
  Manyo Shu. Tabito
Since you, my Lord, were gone. *Fr.* Manyo
  Shu. Iwa no hime
Longshoremen
Docker. Heaney
Lookout Mountain, Battle of (1863)
Battle in the Clouds, The. Howells
On Lookout Mountain. Hayden
Loons
Loon, The. Rand
Loon, The. Street
Running the River Lines. Baker
Three. Coatsworth
Lorelei
Lorelei. Heine
Los Angeles, California
Gary Gotow. Uba
Watts. Rivers
Yellow Light. Hongo
See also **Hollywood, California.**
Loss
Business, The. Creeley
Cambridge Elegy. Olds
Goodnight Irene. Mariani
Horn. Lea
Last Words to James Wright. Hugo
Little Song, A. Hartman
One Art. Bishop
Speaking of Loss. Clifton
Lot (Bible)
Half-way, for One Commandment Broken.
  Housman
His Wife. Kaufman
Lot Later. Nemerov
Lotus
Blow wind of heaven. Henjo
Egyptian Lotus, The. Eaton
Lotos-Eaters, The. Tennyson
Lotus. Huan Fu
Louis XIV, King of France
Eclipse, The. Prévert
Satire upon the French King, A. Brown
Louis XV, King of France
Louis XV. Sterling
Louis XVI, King of France
Louis XVI Goes to the Guillotine. Péret
Louisiana
Aerial View of Louisiana. Mathis
African in Louisiana. Kyei
In Louisiana. Paine
New Orleans. Carruth
Shooting Ducks in South Louisiana.
  Tillinghast
Song for New Orleans, A. Keithley
Vieux Carré. Roberts
L'Ouverture, Toussaint *See* **Toussaint**
  L'Ouverture, Francois Dominique.
Love
Book of Love Poetry, A (BoLoP). Jon
  Stallworthy, ed.

*Dancing the Tightrope; New Love Poems by
  Women* (DT). Barbara Burford, Lindsay
  MacRae, *and* Sylvia Paskin, eds.
English Love Poems (EnLoPo). John
  Betjeman *and* Geoffrey Taylor, eds.
Erotic Poetry (ErPo). William Cole, ed.
Gambit Book of Love Poems, The (GBL).
  Geoffrey Grigson, ed.
Love Is Like the Lion's Tooth (LLLT).
  Frances McCullough, ed.
Love Poems from Spain and Spanish America
  (LPSS). Perry Higman, ed. *and* tr.
*Poems of Love and War from the Eight
  Anthologies and the Ten Long Poems of
  Classical Tamil* (PLW). A. K.
  Ramanujan, comp. *and* tr.
Under All Silences; Shades of Love (UnAS).
  Ruth Gordon, comp.
Lovebirds
Two and One Are a Problem. Nash
Lovelace, Richard
Footnote to a Famous Lyric, A. Guiney
Lowell, Amy
For Amy Lowell. Cullen
Lowell, James Russell
Lowell. *Fr.* A Fable for Critics. Lowell
To John Greenleaf Whittier. Ward
Lowell, Robert
North Haven. Bishop
On the Death of Robert Lowell. Myles
Robert Lowell: His Death. Williamson
This Day after Yesterday. Booth
Lowry, Malcolm
Homage to Malcolm Lowry. Mahon
Loyalty
His Golden Locks Time Hath to Silver
  Turned. *Fr.* Polyhymnia. Peele
Loyalty. Davies
See also **Fidelity.**
Luanda, Angola
Kinaxixi. Neto
Song for Luanda. Vieira
Luck
Coming of Good Luck, The. Herrick
Favour. Fitzgerald
For Good Luck. Ewing
Good Luck and Bad ("Good luck is the gayest
  of all gay girls"). Hay
Jackpot. Graham
Lover Remembereth Such as He Sometimes
  Enjoyed and Showeth How He Would Like
  to Enjoy Her Again, The. Stokesbury
Of Money. Googe
Pain. Södergran
Rumors of the Turning Wheel. Halley
Rune for C, A. Howes
Stupid Old Myself. Hoban
See also **Chance; Fate; Fortune.**
Lucknow, India
Defence of Lucknow, The. Tennyson
Pipes at Lucknow, The. Whittier
Lucretius
Lucretius. Tennyson
Luddites
Framework-knitters Lamentation, The.
  Unknown
Framework-Knitters Petition, The. Briggs
Ode to the Framers of the Frame Bill, An.
  Byron
Lullabies
All the Pretty Little Horses. *Unknown*
Bye, baby bunting. Mother Goose
Cottager to Her Infant, The. Wordsworth
Coventry Carol. *Unknown*
Cradle Song, A. Colum
Evening. *Unknown*
Golden Slumbers. *Fr.* The Pleasant Comedy
  of Patient Grissell [*or* Grissel *or* Grissill].
  Dekker

Hush-a-bye, baby, on the tree-top. Mother
  Goose
Italian Lullaby. *Unknown*
Japanese Lullaby. Field
Lullaby. Kowit
Lullaby for Familiars. Willard
Lullaby: "Lay your sleeping head, my love."
  Auden
Lullaby: Puva, puva, puva. *Unknown*
Lullaby: "Sleep, baby, sleep." *Unknown*
Lullaby: "Someone would like to have you for
  her child." *Unknown*
Mary's Song. Causley
Minnie and Winnie. Tennyson
Mouse's Lullaby, The. Cox
Norse Lullaby. Field
O sleep, my babe, hear not the rippling wave.
  Fr. Phantasmion. Coleridge
On a Quiet Conscience. Charles I, King of
  England
Rock-a-bye, baby, thy cradle is green.
  Mother Goose
Sleep, Baby Boy. *Unknown*
Slumber Song. Ledoux
Song for Susannah: A Lullaby. Hardie
Summer Lullaby, A. Bumstead
Sweet and Low [Sweet and Low]. *Fr.* The
  Princess. Tennyson
Virgin's Lullaby, The. *Unknown*
Wynken, Blynken, and Nod. Field
See also **Cradle Song** *and* **Lullaby** *in Title
  and First Line Index.*

Lumbering and Lumbermen
Again the ancient, meaningless. *Fr.* Myths
  and Texts: Logging. Snyder
At the Cedars. Scott
Bushfeller, The. Duggan
Canada-I-O. *Unknown*
Deep in the Mountain. Saibara
Elegy for a Forest Clear-Cut by the
  Weyerhaeuser Company. Wagoner
Farmer and the Shanty Boy, The. *Unknown*
In Winter in the Woods Alone. Frost
Jim the Splitter. Kendall
Johnny Carroll's Camp. *Unknown*
Little Brown Bulls, The. *Unknown*
Log Jam, The. Drummond
Lumberman's Alphabet, The. *Unknown*
Man Splitting Wood in the Daybreak, The.
  Kinnell
Michigan-I-O. *Unknown*
Once More a-Lumbering Go. *Unknown*
Peter Amberley. Calhoun
Roving Shanty Boy, The. *Unknown*
Saws Were Shrieking, The. Ross
Shanty Boys and the Pine, The. *Unknown*
Suruga Dance. *Unknown*
To a Farmer Who Hung Five Hawks on His
  Barbed Wire. Wagoner
Turner's Camp on the Chippewa. *Unknown*
When the Drive Goes Down. Malloch
Wild Mustard River, The. *Unknown*
Woodman, Spare That Tree. Morris
Woodyards in the Rain. Marriott
Lumumba, Patrice
Lumumba's Grave ("Lumumba was black").
  Hughes
To Patrice Lumumba. Armijo
Lunch
Lunch. Koch
Step Away from Them, A. O'Hara
Lundy's Lane, Battle of (1814)
Battle of Bridgewater, The. *Unknown*
Lungs
Properties of Breath, The. Korelitz
Lungworms
Autobiography of a Lungworm. Fuller

Lust
Against Them Who Lay Unchastity to the Sex of Women. *Fr. Castara.* Habington
Arrowhead Christian Center and No-Smoking Luncheonette. Sylvester
But for Lust. Pitter
Conversion. Hewitt
"Expense of spirit in a waste of shame, The [*or* Th']." *Fr.* Sonnets, CXXIX. Shakespeare
Hares on the Mountain. *Unknown*
In Praise of Beverly. Orlen
Late-flowering Lust. Betjeman
Nine Times a Night. *Unknown*
Once-over, The. Blackburn
Portrait of a Lady. Ryan
Romance, A. Weigl
Senex. Betjeman
Sex without Love. Olds
Sic et Non. Read
Slogan, The. Blackburn
Sunflower Sonnet Number One. Jordan
There Is a Girl Inside. Clifton
To Barba. May
Vine, The. Herrick
What a Time! Blumenthal
Where I'll Be Good. Ryan
See also **Erotic Love; Seduction; Sex.**

Lutes
Blame Not My Lute for He Must Sound *or* Sownde. Wyatt
Crimson Lute That Comest in the Dawn. Juana Inés de la Cruz
I Give up Trying to Learn to Play the Lute. Michizane
I was certain that lute and calligraphy would help my studies. *Fr. Kokin Shu.* Michizane
Listening to the Lute. Jakuan
Of My Lady Isabella Playing on the Lute. Waller
On Seeing Lute Priest Off. Enkei
Sonnet: "My lute, be as thou wast [*or* wert] when thou didst grow." Drummond
When to Her Lute Corinna [*or* Corrina] Sings. Campion

Luther, Martin
Luther to a Bluebottle Fly. *Fr. Imaginary* Sonnets. Lee-Hamilton

Lutheranism
I love the rite of Luther's congregation. Tyutchev

Luxury
Contentment. *Fr. The Autocrat of the Breakfast Table.* Holmes

Lying. *See* **Lies and Lying.**

Lynching
Between the World and Me. Wright
Bird and the Tree, The. Torrence
Black Boy. Rosten
Emmett Till. Emanuel
Eutawville Lynching, The. Moorer
Fourteen Men. Gilmore
Haunted Oak, The. Dunbar
I Saw Them Lynch. Freeman
Local Man Goes to the Killing Ground, A. Whitehead
Lynched Negro. Bodenheim
Lynching, The. McKay
Lynching. Moorer
Lynching. *Fr. Negroes.* Vaynshteyn
Lynching and Burning. St. John
Nice Day for a Lynching. Patchen
Night, Death, Mississippi. Hayden
Plaint. Ford
Postcards of the Hanging: 1869. Hudgins
Retribution. Moorer
So Quietly. Hill
Song for a Dark Girl. Hughes
Swimmers, The. Tate

Lynn, Massachusetts
Bells of Lynn, The. Longfellow

Lynx
Lesser Lynx, The. Rieu
Lynx, The. Eaton
Lynx. Ford
Lynx. Howard

Lyonesse
Sunk Lyonesse. De la Mare
When I Set Out for Lyonnesse. Hardy

Lyrebirds
Lyre-Bird, The. Robinson
Lyrebirds. Wright

Lysergic Acid (LSD)
Discovery of LSD a True Story, The. Hollo

M

M'; Mc *For names beginning thus, see* **Mac.**
Mac Liammóir, Micheál
Micheál Mac Liammóir. Durcan
McClellan, George Brinton
How McClellan Took Manassas. *Unknown*
Victor of Antietam, The. Melville
"MacDiarmid, Hugh" (Christopher Murray Grieve)
To Hugh MacDiarmid. Morgan
McHenry, Fort
Fort McHenry. *Unknown*
Star-spangled Banner, The. Key
Machines
Beautiful Lawn Sprinkler, The. Nemerov
Concrete Mixers. Hubbell
Crane, The. Tomlinson
Egg and the Machine, The. Frost
Horatian Variation. Bacon
Needs. Ammons
Nightmare Number Three. Benét
Portrait of a Machine. Untermeyer
Progress. Lyon
Steam Threshing-Machine, The. Turner
Steamboats, Viaducts, and Railways. Wordsworth
Time for Building, A. Livingston
To a Steam Roller. Moore
Useless Machine. Frénaud
Washing Machine, The. Davies
McKinley, William
Faithful unto Death. Titherington
McKinley. *Unknown*
Zolgotz. *Unknown*
MacLeish, Archibald
On a Flimmering Floom You Shall Ride. Sandburg
MacNeice, Louis
Autobiography. MacNeice
In Carrowdore Churchyard. Mahon
McPherson, James Birdseye
Dirge for McPherson, A. Melville
Mad Song (genre)
Fool's Song. Holcroft
Mad Gardener's Song, The. *Fr. Sylvie and Bruno.* "Carroll"
Mad Song. Blake
Tom o' Bedlam's Song. *Unknown*
Madness
Another Poem about the Madness of Women. Wayman
As other men, so I myself do muse. *Fr. Idea.* Drayton
Bedlamite, The. Mozeen
Bushed. Lillard
Buzzard. Garrett
Counting the Mad. Justice
Crazed Girl, The. Yeats
Deserter, The. Smith
Division. Ratti

Evening in the Sanitarium. Bogan
Flee on Your Donkey. Sexton
For God's sake, let me not go mad. Pushkin
From an Asylum; Kathy Chattle to Her Mother, Ruth Arbeiter. Stevenson
Glass King, The. Boland
Hatters, The. McDonald
Haunted Palace, The. Poe
Heard in a Violent Ward. Roethke
Hoccleve Remembers His Madness. *Fr. The* Complaint. Hoccleve
Hurry of the Spirits, in a Fever and Nervous Disorders, The. Watts
I Am. Clare
In a Dark Time. Roethke
Letter from a State Hospital. Mundorf
Lines Written during a Period of Insanity. Cowper
Local Man Remembers Betty Fuller, A. Whitehead
Mad Gardener's Song, The. *Fr. Sylvie and* Bruno. "Carroll"
Mad Maid's Song, The. Herrick
Mad Song. Blake
Mad Song. *Fr. Poetical Sketches.* Blake
Mad Song. Levertov
Mad Woman of Punnet's Town, The. Strong
Madhouse. Zaidi
Madman, The. Pretorius
Madman's Song, The. *Fr. The Duchess of* Malfi. Webster
Madness. *Fr. The Art of Preserving Health.* Armstrong
Madness. *Fr. The Dance of Death.* Browning
Madness. Yoshihara Sachiko
Madwoman at Rodmell. Roberts
Mental Cases. Owen
Much madness is divinest sense. Dickinson
Nebuchadnezzar. Wylie
On a Painting by Patient B of the Independence State Hospital for the Insane. Justice
Ringing the Bells. Sexton
Seele im Raum. Jarrell
Sonnet Found in a Deserted Madhouse. *Unknown*
There Was a Man and He Was Mad. *Unknown*
To One in Bedlam. Dowson
Tom o' Bedlam's Song. *Unknown*
Vietnamese Girl in the Madhouse, The. Fisher
Visitor's Parking. Szumigalski
Visits to St. Elizabeths. Bishop
You, Doctor Martin. Sexton
See also **Mental Illness.**
Madonnas
Madonna in the Subway, The. Leyeles
Madrid, Spain
Segovia and Madrid. Cooke
Magazines
News of Old Girls. Baines
Talk of the Town, The. Fisher
See also **Journalism; Newspapers.**
Magdalene, Mary. *See* **Mary Magdalene.**
Maggots
Filbert, The. Southey
Magi
Adoration of the Magi, The. Pilling
Camels, the Kings' Camel, The. Norris
Carol of the Brown King. Hughes
Carol of the Three Kings. Merwin
Hymn: "Lord, when the wise men came from far[r]." Godolphin
Journey of the Magi. Eliot
Kings and Stars. Erskine
Kings Came Riding. Williams
Kings of the East, The. Bates
Magi, The. Garrett
Magi, The. Glück

Magi, The. Guthrie
Magi, The. Yeats
Magi in Europe, The. Hawi
Mystic Magi, The. Hawker
Perfect Gift, The. Cooke
Royall Presents. Wanley
Take Frankincense, O God. *Fr.* Holy
   Transportations. Fitz-Geffry
Three Holy Kings from Morgenland. Heine
Three Kings, The. Darío
Three Kings, The. Longfellow
Wise Men Ask the Children the Way, The.
   Heine

Magic
De Cunjah Man. Campbell
For the El Paso Weather Bureau. Wild
Houdini. Mandel
La Belle Dame sans Merci. Keats
Magic Words. *Unknown*
Magical Eraser. Silverstein
Magician, The. Miranda
Magician, The. Ramke
Manzini; Escape Artist. MacEwen
Merlin. Muir
Sermonette. Reed
Testing-Tree, The. Kunitz
Two Magicians, The. *Unknown*
Usk. *Fr.* Landscapes. Eliot

Magnolias
Three magnolias, identical. *Fr.* Moments of
   Fullfillment—Writing Down Miscellaneous.
   Yüan Mei
To a Magnolia Flower in the Garden of the
   Armenian Convent at Venice. Mitchell

Magpies
Camden Magpie. McCrae
Magpie. Davison
Magpies, The. Glover
One for sorrow, two for mirth. *Unknown*
One is a sign of mischief. *Unknown*
One is sorrow, two mirth. *Unknown*

Magritte, René
Things of René Magritte, The. Schmied

Maguire, Hugh, Lord of Fermanagh
Hugh Maguire. O'Hussey
O'Hussey's Ode to the Maguire. O'Hussey

Mahon, Derek
Letter to Derek Mahon. Longley

Mail and Mailmen
Epitaph for a Postal Clerk. Kennedy
Getting the Mail. Kinnell
Hope. Jarrell
Mail Has Come, The. Tucker
Mailman, The. Strand
Night Mail, The. Auden
Night Mail North, The.
   Cholmondeley-Pennell
Postman, The. Al-Haidari
Postman, The. Challis
Postman, The. Sansom
Postman, The. *Unknown*
Postman's Fear, The. al-Maghut
Postman's Knock. Bennett
Siege. Al-Maghut
Too Slow. Morrison

Maine (State)
Brass Tacks. Levertov
Exiled. Millay
For Jean Vincent d'Abbadie, Baron
   St.-Castin. Nowlan
Jake's Wharf. Booth
Kineo Mountain. Wright
Lovely Rivers and Lakes of Maine, The.
   Wallis
Maine. Booth
Maine Lake at Night. Morris
North Haven. Booth
Skunk Hour. Lowell
Somewhere on the Coast of Maine. Long
Stove. Booth
Summer Rentals. Halpern

Vision of Marsden Hartley, The. Haines
Water. Lowell
Why We Always Take Vacations by the
   Water. Sadoff
With Stephen in Maine. Plumly
York Harbor Morning. Garrett

**Maintenon, Françoise, d'Aubigné, Marquise
de**
Portrait of the Consort to Louis XIV.
   Kirschenbaum

Majorca
Andraitx—Pomegranate Flowers. Lawrence

Malachy, Saint
St. Malachy. Merton

Malaga, Spain
Malaga. Hutchinson

Malaiyaman Tirumutikkari
Kari Sober. Kapilar
True Protocol of Poets, The. Kapilar

Malawi
Love Poem for My Country, A. Chipasula
Malawi. Banda
Riddles of Change, The. Mnthali
Those Makheta Nights. Chipasula

Malaysia
Christmas in Penang. Leyden

Malcolm X (Malcolm Little)
Aardvark. Fields
At That Moment. Patterson
El-Hajj Malik El-Shabazz. Hayden
For Malcolm: After Mecca. Barrax
For Malcolm Who Walks in the Eyes of Our
   Children. Troupe
For Malcolm X. Alba
For Malcolm X. Walker
I Remember ("I remember/ January,/ 1968").
   Jackson
It Was a Funky Deal. Knight
Malcolm. Clifton
Malcolm, a Thousandth Poem. Rivers
Malcolm X. Brooks
Malcolm X—an Autobiography. Neal
Poem for Black Hearts, A. Baraka
Portrait of Malcolm X. Knight
Sun Came, The. Knight
They Are Killing All the Young Men.
   Henderson

Maldon, Battle of (991)
Battle of Maldon, The. *Unknown*

Mallards
Dusk: Mallards on the Charles River.
   Blumenthal

Mallarmé, Stéphane
Barrel Organ, The. *Fr.* Homage to
   Mallarmé. Epstein

Malls. *See* Shopping Malls.

Malta
Farewell to Malta. Byron

Man in the Moon
Moon-Man. Hewett

Man-of-War Birds
To the Man-of-War-Bird. Whitman

**Manassas, Battles of. *See* Bull Run, Battles
of.**

Manatees
Manatee, The. Blyton

Manchester, England
Lowly Bard, The. "Forester"
Manchester. Rogerson
Manchester Ship Canal, The. *Unknown*
Winter Night in Manchester, A. Connell

Mandalay, Burma
Mandalay. Kipling

Mandela, Nelson
Echo of Mandela. Mandela
My Country. Mandela
Winnie Song. Clifton

Mandelstam, Osip
Mandelstam. Young
Osip Mandelshtam. Layton

Mandrills
Mandrill, The. Aiken

Mangan, James Clarence
Clarence Mangan. Kinsella
Nameless One, The. Mangan

Mangoes
Mango Tree, The. Chock

Manhattan. *See* New York City.

Manila Bay, Battle of (1898)
Battle of Manila, The. Hovey
Captive Ships at Manila, The. Paul
Manila. Ware
Manila Bay. Hale

Manitoba, Canada
Signature. Livesay
Wilderness Gothic. Purdy

Mankind
All the World's a Stage. *Fr.* As You Like
   It. Shakespeare
As Concerning Man. Radcliffe
Autonomous. Van Doren
Away, Melancholy. Smith
Bliss of man, The (could pride that blessing
   find). *Fr.* An Essay on Man. Pope
Brief Essay on Man. Guiterman
Chorus Sacerdotum. *Fr.* Mustapha.
   Greville
Collective Portrait, The. Finch
Common Dust. Johnson
Contemplations. Bradstreet
Corruption. Vaughan
Day of Judgement, The. Swift
Divine Image, A ("Cruelty has a human
   heart"). *Fr.* Songs of Experience. Blake
Divine Image, The ("To mercy, pity, peace,
   and love"). *Fr.* Songs of Innocence.
   Blake
For a Coming Extinction. Merwin
For A' That and A' That ("Is there, for honest
   poverty"). Burns
For the Record. Rich
Formal Application. Baker
Four Ages of Man, The. Yeats
From Stone to Steel ("From stone to bronze,
   from bronze to steel"). Pratt
Genesis. Jones
Horror Comic. Conquest
Human Clay, The. Abu Madi
Human Form Divine, The. Raine
Human Races, The. Lister
Human Seasons, The. Keats
Human Species, The. Queneau
I know my soul hath power to know all
   things. *Fr.* Nosce Teipsum: Man. Davies
I think I could turn and live with animals.
   Fr. Song of Myself. Whitman
If. Kipling
In Men Whom Men Condemn as Ill. *Fr.*
   Byron. Miller
In the Waiting Room. Bishop
Inquisitors, The. Jeffers
"It Was Wrong to Do This" Said the Angel.
   Fr. The Black Riders. Crane
Last Man, The. Campbell
Let Us Be Frank. Cruickshank
Man. Herbert
Man. Nazir
Man. Vaughan
Man. Wolfe
Man with the Hoe, The. Markham
Mankind and man's world. Tameko
Meditatio. Pound
Men. MacLeish
Monkeys. Collymore
Nature of Man, The. Sisson
Ode on a Distant Prospect of Eton College.
   Gray
On Man. Landor
Pity This Busy Monster, Manunkind.
   Cummings

Placed on this isthmus of a middle state. *Fr.* An Essay on Man. Pope
Pulley, The. Herbert
Sans Equity and sans Poise. *Fr.* Yung Wind. Confucius
Sic Vita. King
Small Comment. Sanchez
Tetélestai. Aiken
Timon Curses Athens and Mankind. *Fr.* Timon of Athens. Shakespeare
Timon Speaks to a Dog. Hobsbaum
To Men. Wickham
To My Son Parker, Asleep in the Next Room. Kaufman
To the Lady Margaret Countesse of Cumberland. Daniel
Truant, The. Pratt
Two Hands. Sexton
Two-Legs. Pagis
We Are the Cenotaphs. Williams
Weak Is the Will of Man, His Judgment Blind. Wordsworth
Were I, who to my cost already am. *Fr.* A Satire against [Reason and] Mankind. Rochester
What would this Man? Now upward will he soar. *Fr.* An Essay on Man. Pope
Wishes of an Elderly Man. Raleigh
Words Made of Water. Singer
World, The. Vaughan
World Is a Bundle of Hay, The. Byron

Mannequins
Mannequins. Epstein

Manners. *See* **Etiquette.**

Mantis. *See* **Praying Mantis.**

Mantle, Mickey
Mantle. Heyen

Maori
Haka: The Feathered Albatross. Walters
It was a wondrous realm beguiled. *Fr.* Ranolf and Amohia. Domett
Land Is Gone, The. *Unknown*
Moment of Truth. Habib
Returning to Yin-ch'eng Early in the Year *Ting-ch'ou.* Tai Piao-yüan
Song of Instruction, A. Te Kooti Rikirangi
To a Maori Figure Cast in Bronze outside the Chief Post Office, Auckland. Tuwhare
"When the Wild Goose Finds Food He Calls His Comrades"—I Ching. Kemp

Maple Sugar and Maple Syrup
Maple Syrup. Hall
Sugar Weather. McArthur
Sugaring, The. Klein
Valley Blood. Sternlieb

Maps
Cartographers, The. Allen
Map, The. Oden
Map, The. Strand
Mapmaker on His Art, The. Nemerov
Mappemounde. Birney
Maps. Thompson
Mermaids. *Fr.* The Atlas. Slessor
Old Map of Barnstable County. Galvin
Private Letter to Brazil, A. Oden

Marathon, Battle of
Persian Version, The. Graves

Marathon (Race)
Strategy for a Marathon. Mueller

Marble
In the Marble Quarry. Dickey
Island Quarry. Crane

Marbles
Marbles. LaBombard
Marbles. Worth
Taxonomical Note. Sutton

Marc Antony. *See* **Antony.**

March
Day before April, The. Davies
Four Little Foxes. Sarett
In March. Martin

Mad Day in March. Levine
March. Coatsworth
March. Crane
March. Housman
March. Ray
March. *Fr.* Sonnets of the Months. San Gimignano
March. *Unknown*
March Snow. McKay
March, Upstate. Bronk
March Weather. Swan
March Wind, The. *Unknown*
March Winds. Lloyd
Not Ideas about the Thing but the Thing Itself. Stevens
Song in March. Simms
Thorn Leaves in March. Merwin
Twilight in Middle March, A. Ledwidge
Unstill Universe. Piccolo
We like March—his shoes are purple. Dickinson
Written in March. Wordsworth

Marching and Marches. *See* **Parades.**

Marduk
Hymn to Marduk, *sels. Unknown*

Margaret, Saint
To Saint Margaret. Constable

Marigolds
How Marigolds Came Yellow. Herrick
Marigold, The. Wither
Marigolds. Driscoll
Marigolds. Graves

Marijuana
Smoking Drugs with Strangers. Bowering

Marin County, California
Clouds of Evening. Jeffers

Marin, John
Marin. Booth

Mariners. *See* **Sailing and Sailors.**

Marines. *See* **United States Marine Corps.**

Marinetti, Filippo
Glass Hat, The. Kálnoky

Marinho, Francisco Chagas
Soccer at the Meadowlands. Ackerman

Marion, Francis
Song of Marion's Men. Bryant
Swamp Fox, The. Simms

Mark Antony. *See* **Antony.**

Markets
In the Bazaars of Hyderabad. Naidu
Linstead Market. *Unknown*
Marketing. Falconer
Orgy (That Is, Vegetable Market, at Sarno). Labriola
Saturday Market ("In Saturday Market, there's eggs a-plenty"). *Fr.* Saturday Market. Mew

Markiewicz, Constance Georgine, Countess
In Memory of Eva Gore-Booth and Con Markiewicz. Yeats

Marlborough, John Churchill, 1st Duke of
False Favorite's Downfall, The. *Unknown*
Poem to His Grace the Duke of Marlborough, A. *Fr.* The Campaign. Addison.
Satirical Elegy on the Death of a Late Famous General, A. Swift

Marley, Bob
Elegy for Bob Marley, An. Matthews

Marlowe, Christopher
Christoper Marlowe. *Fr.* Sonnets of English Dramatic Poets. Swinburne
Christopher Marlowe. *Fr.* To Henry Reynolds, of Poets and Poesy. Drayton
Marlowe. Bayldon

Marmalade
Ode to the Last Pot of Marmalade. "John"

Marpessa
Marpessa's Choice. Ritsos

Marriage
About Marriage. Levertov

Ache of Marriage, The. Levertov
After the Golden Wedding. Stephen
All's Well That Ends Well. *Unknown*
Antiquary. Donne
Any Wife or Husband. Haynes
Any Wife to Any Husband. Browning
April Fool, The. Field
As I am unhappy. Yosano Akiko
At dinner, she is hostess, I am host. *Fr.* Modern Love. Meredith
At Taieri Mouth. Baxter
Auld Robin Gray. Lindsay
Ballad of Calvary Street. Baxter
Ballad of the Despairing Husband. Creeley
Bed, The. Saleh
Bon Mot, A. *Unknown*
Brewer's Man, The. Strong
Bridal Piece. Glück
Bride, The. Akhmadulina
Bride's Hours, A. Valentine
Bride's Song, The. Cory
But That Is Another Story. Justice
By this he knew she wept with waking eyes. *Fr.* Modern Love. Meredith
Caledonia. McElroy
Call It a Good Marriage. Graves
Carry Her over the Water. Auden
Che Fece. Il Gran Rifiuto. Cavafy
Chirp Chirp the Katydids. *Unknown*
Civil Marriage. Bustamante
Clayfeld's Anniversary Song. Pack
Clayfeld's Daughter Reveals Her Plans. Pack
Close the cloth-plant spreads its fibres. *Unknown*
Combat, The. Muir
Come All You Young Ladies and Gentlemen. *Unknown*
Conformers, The. Hardy
Contention betwixt a Wife, a Widow, and a Maid, A. Davies
Crisis, The. Creeley
De Se. Weever
Dead Bride, The. Hill
Decade, A. Lowell
Dedication to Hunger. Glück
Dedication to My Wife, A. Eliot
Degli Sposi. Lesser
Deuce, a Roast of Scraggy Quails, a Bit, The. Berni
Developing a Wife. Taylor
Dialogue between a Squeamish Cotting Mechanic and His Sluttish Wife, in the Kitchen. *Fr.* Nuptial Dialogues. Ward
Double Transformation, The. Goldsmith
Dying Wife to Her Husband, A. Ibn Ezra
Early Thoughts of Marriage. Cotton
Eating. Gibbons
Emerald, The. *Fr.* Up and Down. Merrill
Epigram: "As Thomas was cudgell'd [or cudgel'd] one day by his wife." Swift
Epistle from Mrs. Yonge to Her Husband. Montagu
Epitaph on His Wife. Dryden
Epitaph upon Husband and Wife Who Died and Were Buried Together, An. Crashaw
Epithalamion Made at Lincolnes Inne. Donne
Eros Turannos. Robinson
Eurynome. Macpherson
Family Life. Laing
Family Scene: Mid-Twentieth Century. Pastan
Farmer's Bride, The. Mew
Four Notions of Love and Marriage. Momaday
Get Up and Bar the Door. *Unknown*
Good and Bad Wives. *Unknown*
Goodnight. Smith
Green Mossy Banks of the Lee, The. *Unknown*
Groom's Lament, The. Peterson
Habitation. Atwood

Hail wedded love, mysterious law, true
   source. *Fr.* Paradise Lost. Milton
Hans Breitmann's Party [*or* Barty]. Leland
Hardness Scale, The. Peseroff
He'd Nothing but His Violin. Dallas
His Being Was in Her Alone. Sidney
Home Burial. Frost
Honeymoon. Albert
Housewife's Lament, The. *Unknown*
Husbands and Wives. Hershenson
Hymeneal Song on the Nuptials of the Lady
   Anne Wentworth and the Lord Lovelace,
   An. Carew
Hymeneall Dialogue, An. Carew
I Am Married to Myself. Goodman
I Am Told. Segalen
I Don't Have No Bunny Tail on My Behind.
   Alta
I ride home, I gallop. *Unknown*
I went into the country. *Unknown*
Ideal Husband to His Wife, The. Foss
If Ever I Marry, I'll Marry a Maid.
   Unknown
If I get a horse, my beloved. *Fr.* Manyo
   Shu. *Unknown*
If No One Ever Marries Me. Alma-Tadema
In our old shipwrecked days there was an
   hour. *Fr.* Modern Love. Meredith
In the days when my wife lived. *Fr.* Manyo
   Shu. Hitomaro
In the Hill Country. Jacob
Indian's Bride, The. Pinkney
Jealous Wife, The. Scannell
Joy of Union, The. Yang Fang
Keep a Good Tongue in Your Head. Parker
Lady Carenza of the lovely, gracious body.
   Alais, Iselda
Le Touquet. Jarman
Les Sylphides. MacNeice
Letter. Bergman
Letter to Madame la Marquise de C———.
   Sainctonge
Local News. Merenda
Love and Marriage. Mathew
Love in a Life. Browning
Lucky Marriage, The. Blackburn
Major Macroo. Smith
Man and Wife. Goodman
Man and Wife. Sexton
Man and Wife Is One Flesh. Deagon
Man Who Married Magdalene, The.
   Simpson
Marriage. Clarke
Marriage. Corso
Marriage. Fordham
Marriage. Hall
Marriage. *Unknown*
Marriage, The. Wickham
Marriage. Williams
Marriage, The. Winters
Marriage and Money. *Fr.* The Happy Pair.
   Sedley
Marriage is a lovely thing. Pisan
Marriage Poem, A. Voigt
Marriage Portrait. Applewhite
Marriage Ring, A. Crabbe
Marriage Song. Halevi
Marriage Vow. Linden
Marriage, which might have been a mateship
   sweet. *Fr.* Woman Free.
   Wolstenholme-Elmy
Married and Single Life. *Unknown*
Married Love. Kuan Tao Sheng
Married Love. Rosenberg
Married Love. Santos
Marry the Lass? Greig
Marrying Again. Mei Yao-ch'en
Maternity Gown. Holbrook
Matrimony. Williams
Meditation at Kew. Wickham
Melting, The. Edson
Middle-aged, The. Rich

Midnight Court, The. Merriman
Minion Wife, A. *Fr.* Ralph Roister Doister.
   Udall
Most Like an Arch This Marriage. Ciardi
Most Like an Arch This Marriage. Ciardi
Most vile of beings—man. Oe no Asatsuna
Mother of the Groom. Heaney
My Last Duchess. Browning
My Marriage with Mrs. Johnson. Gilbert
My Mother Shoots the Breeze. Chappell
My Second Marriage to My First Husband.
   Fulton
Nervous Prostration. Wickham
Nesting. Saleh
Newlyweds, The. Criswell
1943. McPherson
No Love, to Love of Man and Wife. Eedes
Nox. Díaz Mirón
Nuptial[l] Song, or Epithalamie [*or*
   Epithalamy], on Sir Clipseby Crew and His
   Lady, A. Herrick
O, love, in your sweet name enough. *Fr.*
   Essay on Marriage. Finch
Ode: "That I have often been in love, deep
   love." "Pindar"
Old Man's Song, about His Wife, The.
   Unknown
Old-Marrieds, The. Brooks
On Giles and Joan. Jonson
On the Marriage of a Virgin. Thomas
One Flesh. Jennings
One Wife for One Man. Aig-Imoukhede
Our Goodman. *Unknown*
Our Ship She Lies in Harbour. *Unknown*
Passionate Shepherd to His Love, The.
   Schwartz
Performance, The. Dickey
Plea for Trigamy, A. Seaman
Portrait: My Wife. Holmes
Prayer for a Marriage, A. Davies
Prince of Wales' Marriage. *Unknown*
Prothalamion. Spenser
Prothalamium. MacDonagh
Proverb reporteth, no man can deny, The.
   Fr. Tom Tyler and His Wife. *Unknown*
Psalm of Marriage. Cary
Reasonable Affliction, A. Prior
Red-haired Man's Wife, The. Stephens
Rejoice, O Bridegroom! *Unknown*
Retort, The. Morris
Rhyme-Prose on the Marriage of Man and
   Woman. Asatsuna
Robertin Tush. *Unknown*
Rosy Apple, Lemon or Pear. *Unknown*
Rural Lass, The. Jemmat
Sacred Ceremony, A. Aston
Sanctum, The. Daly
Sandgate Girl's Lamentation, The. *Unknown*
Second Wife, The. N'Ait Attik
Sign of the Bonny Blue Bell, The. *Unknown*
Silver Wedding. Hodgson
Slave Marriage Ceremony Supplement.
   Unknown
Slice of Wedding Cake, A. Graves
Socrates Snooks. Ludlow
Song Ballet (I Was Sixteen Years of Age).
   Unknown
Song: "In a maiden-time professed." *Fr.* The
   Witch. Middleton
Sonnet Reversed. Brooke
Stumbling. Lourie
Suite for Marriage, A. Ignatow
That I'm Ill Married. *Unknown*
Thick grows the tarragon. *Unknown*
This Evening. Landau
This Winter's Weather It Waxeth Cold.
   Unknown
Three Seamstresses, The. Peretz
Three Seasons. Sparshott
Thus piteously Love closed what he begat.
   Fr. Modern Love. Meredith
To a Bride-to-Be. Barney
To a Lady on Her Marriage. Bell

To Be or Not to Be. Edmunds
To My Dear and Loving Husband.
   Bradstreet
To the Ladies. Chudleigh
To Wed or Not to Wed. Marson
To wed, or not to wed? That is the question.
   Unknown
Together. Lewisohn
True Marriage Is True Love. *Fr.* Two Lives.
   Leonard
Twenty-Year Marriage. Ai
Upon Wedlock and Death of Children.
   Taylor
Wait for Me. Creeley
Washing the Dishes. Morley
Wasp Sex Myth (One). Hollo
Wasp Sex Myth (Two). Hollo
Way Sun Keeps Falling Away from Every
   Window, The. Lifshin
We thought you were a simple peasant.
   Unknown
Wedding-Hymn. Lanier
Wedding Morn. Lawrence
Wedding-Ring. Levertov
Wedding Song. *Unknown*
Wedding-Wind. Larkin
Wedlock; a Satire. Wright
What He Said after a Quarrel, Remembering
   His Wedding Night. Virrurru Muteyinanar
When I Was a Child They Married Me.
   Unknown
While You. Reyna
Whistle o'er the Lave o't. Burns
Whitsun Weddings, The. Larkin
Who Drags the Fiery Artist Down? Day
Why Should a Foolish Marriage Vow. *Fr.*
   Marriage à la Mode. Dryden
Why Should I Be with a Husband Bound?
   Unknown
Wife, The. Creeley
Wife to Husband. Adcock
Wife Who Would a Wanton Be, The.
   Unknown
Wife Wrapt [*or* Wrapped] in Wether's Skin,
   The. *Unknown*
Wild and windy was the day. *Unknown*
Woman to Her Lover, A. Walsh
World Is Really a Sugarplum House in the
   Forest, The. Boyajian
Would It Had Pleased the Lord That I Never
   Was Born. *Unknown*
You were young—but that was scarcely to
   your credit. *Fr.* Monogamy. Gould.
Young Wife, A. Lawrence
Zip, zip the valley wind,/ Bring darkness,
   bringing rain. *Unknown*
Zip, zip the valley wind!/ Nothing but wind
   and rain. *Unknown*
Faber Book of Useful Verse, The (FaBoUs),
   pp. 74-80. Simon Brett, ed.
See also **Wedding Songs; Weddings.**

Mars (god)
Ares. Ehrenstein
God of War, The. Brecht
Mars and Venus. *Fr.* Tullie's Love.
   Greene

Mars (planet)
Love Letter from Mars. Ciardi

Marshes
Bedford Level. *Fr.* The Fleece. Dyer
Fireflies over a Marsh. Tamemasa
Irises in a Marsh. Tamemasa
Marsh, The. Hawley
Marsh, The. Snodgrass
Marsh, New Year's Day, The. Everwine
Marshes of Glynn, The. Lanier
Marshlands. Johnson
Sunrise in Summer. Clare
Wood Thrush Concealed, A. Tamemasa

Martens
Dead Marten, The. Landor

Fisher Cat, The. Eberhart
On My Pretty Marten. Cotton
Martí, José
On a Monument to Martí. Roberts
Martial Arts
My Father's Martial Art. Liu
Martin, Saint
St. Martin and the Beggar. Gunn
Martyrs
Cardinal Fisher. Heywood
City of Slaughter, The. Bialik
Crosses. Faiz
Da Silva Gives the Cue. Blumenthal
Elegy: "I die for Your holy word without
regret." Gomez
Fr. Anselm Williams and Br. Leander
Neville. Smither
Here Followeth the Songe of the Death of Mr.
Thewlis. Unknown
Last Words of Don Henriquez, The.
Schneour
Live here, great heart; and love and dy and
kill. Fr. The Flaming Heart. Crashaw
Marching Litany to Our Martyrs, A.
Mapanje
Martyr, The. Tuqan
Martyrdom. "Learsi"
Martyrdom: A Love Poem. Ramke
Martyrdom of Brébeuf and Lalemant, 16
March 1649, The. Fr. Brébeuf and His
Brethren. Pratt
Martyrdom of Father Campion. Walpole
Martyrdom of Mary, Queen of Scots, The.
Southwell
Père Lalement. Pickthall
Robe of Flame. Sardar J'afri
Song of Four Priests Who Suffered Death at
Lancaster, A. Unknown
Sunt Leones. Smith
Te Martyrum Candidatus. Johnson
Thy Faithful Sons. Eleazar
To the Infant Martyrs. Crashaw
Two Souls. Pickthall
Upon the Infant Martyrs. Crashaw
Vanzetti. Buckmaster
Wake of William Orr, The. Drennan
Wallabout Martyrs, The. Whitman
When the Martyrs Go to Sleep. Darwish
Marvell, Andrew
Marvell's Ghost. Ayloffe
You, Andrew Marvell. MacLeish
Marx, Karl
God Bless Karl Marx. Sisson
Karl Heinrich Marx. Enzensberger
Karl Marx Died 1883 Aged 65. Cisneros
Wayman in Love. Wayman
Mary I, Queen of England
Marigold, The. Forrest
Mary Magdalene
At Glastonbury. Kingsley
For All Mary Magdalenes. Maksimovic
Lent. Rodgers
Man Who Married Magdalene, The.
Simpson
Marie Magdalens Complaint at Christs Death.
Southwell
Mary Magdalene. Lewis
"Multum Dilexit." Coleridge
Palm Leaf of Mary Magdalene. Clarke
To Saint Mary Magdalen. Constable
To St. Mary Magdalen. Hill
Woman. Barrett
Mary, Queen of England
New Ballade of the Marigolde, A. Forrest
Mary Queen of Scots
Doubt of Future Foes, The. Elizabeth I,
Queen of England
Martyrdom of Mary, Queen of Scots, The.
Southwell
Mary, Queen of Scots. Bell

Mary, the Virgin
Against Women's Fashions. Lydgate
Aishah Schechinah. Hawker
Annunciation. Fr. La Corona. Donne
Annunciation, The. Muir
Assumption, The. Beaumont
Assumption. Fallon
At Dawn the Virgin Is Born. Lope de Vega
Carpio
Ballade of Illegal Ornaments. Belloc
Ballade to Our Lady of Czestochowa. Belloc
Ballade which Villon Made. MacDonagh
Bee, The. Hawkins
Blessed Virgin Compared to the Air We
Breathe, The. Hopkins
Carol: The Five Joys of the Virgin.
Unknown
Cherry-Tree Carol, The. Unknown
Devout Man Prays to His Relations, The.
Herebert
Five Joys of Mary, The. Unknown
Gift of God, The. Robinson
Hail, Queen of Heaven. Unknown
Heretic's Pilgrimage, A. Gore-Booth
Hymn to the Virgin Mary. O'Riordan
I call you with honest words. Fr. A Poem to
Mary. Mac Con Brettan
I Have Lighted the Candles, Mary. Patchen
I Sing of a Maiden. Unknown
In the Town. Unknown
Invitation to Mary. O Direain
Irish Reaper's Harvest Hymn. Keegan
Jesus and His Mother. Gunn
Keening of Mary, The. Unknown
Leaves of Life, The. Unknown
Litany to Our Lady. Unknown
Little Hymn to Mary, A. Unknown
Living Room, The. Schnackenberg
Luke XI: Blessed Be the Paps Which Thou
Hast Sucked. Crashaw
Mary Complains to Other Mothers.
Unknown
Mary Is with Child. Unknown
Mary, Mother of Christ. Cullen
Mary, Queen of Heaven. Unknown
Mary, The Mother of Jesus. Gardner
Mary Weeps for Her Child. Unknown
Mary's Dream. Unknown
Mary's Girlhood. Rossetti
Mater Dei. Fallon
Mater Dei. Tynan
Mother and Her Son on the Cross, The.
Unknown
Motherhood. Lee
New Song of Mary, A. Unknown
Now Fade the Rose and Lily-Flower.
Unknown
O Glorious Childbearer. Campbell
O Simplicitas. Fr. Three Songs of Mary.
L'Engle
O Virgin. Unknown
On the Blessed Virgin's Bashfulness.
Crashaw
On the Infancy of Our Saviour. Quarles
Our Lady. Coleridge
Our Lady in the Middle Ages. Faber
Our Lady's Song. Unknown
Penitent Considers Another Coming of Mary,
A. Brooks
Prayer to the Virgin. Columcille
Quaerit Jesum Suum Maria. Crashaw
Quia Amore Langueo. Unknown
Quickening, The. Tuttle
Rosa Mystica. Hopkins
Rose That Bore Jesu, The. Unknown
San Miniato. Wilde
Seven Virgins, The. Unknown
Song of the Woman, The. Fr. The Voyage
of Bran. Unknown
Sonnet: Annunciation. Belli

Star of the Sea. Fr. The Ship of Fools.
Barclay.
Sweet Was the Song. Unknown
To a Seagull. Griffin
To Our Blessed Lady. Constable
To Our Lady. Henryson
To the Blessed Virgin Mary. Griffin
To the Virgin. Lydgate
Villon's Prayer for His Mother to Say to the
Virgin. Villon
Virgin Mary, The. Bowers
Virgin Mary, The. Unknown
Visitation, The. Jennings
We have seen her/ the world over. Fr.
Tribute to the Angels. Doolittle
When Mary thro' the Garden Went.
Coleridge
Maryland
Barbara Frietchie. Whittier
Battle of Baltimore, The. Unknown
Chesapeake. Kennedy
Cumberland Station. Smith
Fort McHenry. Unknown
Harriet Tubman. Walker
Incident. Cullen
Maryland Battalion, The. Palmer
Maryland Resolves. Unknown
Miss Crustacean. Phillips
My Maryland. Randall
Purpose of the Chesapeake & Ohio Canal,
The. Smith
Sometimes I Think of Maryland. Braxton
Through Baltimore. Taylor
Masefield, John
John Masefield Relates the Story of Tom,
Tom, the Piper's Son. Fr. Mother Goose
Up-to-Date. Untermeyer
Masks
Mask, The. Larbaud
Mask of Evil, The. Brecht
On a Celtic Mask by Henry Moore. Gregory
Women and Masks. Devecseri
Masochism
In Francum. Davies
Massachusetts
Bar's Fight, August 28, 1746. Terry
Bells of Lynn, The. Longfellow
Boston. Bossidy
Boston Burglar, The. Unknown
Cape Ann; a View. Brinnin
Concord Hymn. Emerson
Evening in Tyringham Valley. Gilder
For the Union Dead. Lowell
From Gloucester Out. Dorn
In the Waiting Room. Bishop
Men of Sudbury, The. Baker
Monument Mountain. Bryant
New Order, The. McGinley
On a Fortification at Boston Begun by
Women. Tompson
Point Shirley. Plath
Provincetown, sels. Dudek
Provincetown, Mass. Shapiro
Massacre of the Innocents
Clap Your Hands for Herod. Hanzlik
Coventry Carol, The. Unknown
Holy Innocents, The. Lowell
To a Christmas Two-Year-Old. Shaw
Massacres
After you, the killed of the Ukraine. Fr. The
Mound. Markish
And the Earth Rebelled. Suhl
City of Slaughter, The. Bialik
Come with me to the City of Slaughter, come,
enter its courtyards. Fr. In the City of
Slaughter. Bialik
Elegy: "Those reckless hosts rush to the
wells." Baruch of Worms
Last Man Killed by Indians in Kimble
County, Texas, The. Angelotti
On the Slaughter. Bialik
Summer Pogrom. Zwicky

Massada
Never Again, The. Dobzynski
On an autumn night, lying restless, far from
her broken homeland. *Fr.* Massada.
Lamdan
Massey, Gerald
Gerald Massey. Billington
Masts
Choosing a Mast. Campbell
Matadors. *See* **Bullfights and Bullfighting.**
Maternity
Man Who Would Be a Mother, The. Scott
7 October, 1940. Ackland
Mathematics and Mathematicians
Arithmetic ("Arithmetic is where numbers fly
like pigeons in and out of your head").
Sandburg
Invention of Zero, The. Urdang
Mathematician. Boston
Mortifying Mistake, A. Pratt
New Maths. Lehrer
Power of Numbers, The. *Fr.* Davideis.
Cowley
Sines. Queneau
Song of the Screw. *Unknown*
Imagination's Other Place (ImOP). Helen
Plotz, ed.
See also **Arithmetic.**
Matterhorn
High Brow. Fitch
Zermatt: To the Matterhorn. Hardy
Mausoleums
Lines Written in a Mausoleum. Grant
Queen of Heaven Mausoleum. Schmitz
Skeleton of the Future, The. "MacDiarmid"
See also **Cemeteries; Graves; Monuments.**
May
Baby Seed Song. Nesbit
Corinna's Going a-Maying. Herrick
Flute of May, The. Woodbourne
Here We Come a-Piping. *Unknown*
Home Thoughts from Abroad. Browning
Jewish May, The. Rosenfeld
Judgment of the May, The. Dixon
Kalenda Maya. Raimbaut de Vaqueiras
Locust Tree in Flower, The. Williams
Lusty May. *Unknown*
May. Edwards
May. Hovell-Thurlow
May. Linden
May. Neilson
May. Ray
May. Rossetti
May. *Fr.* Sonnets of the Months. San
Gimignano
May. *Unknown*
May and Death. Browning
May Carol. *Unknown*
May Day. Teasdale
May in the Green-Wood. *Unknown*
May Is Building Her House. Le Gallienne
May Morning. Thaxter
May Song. *Unknown*
May 10th. Kumin
May-Time. *Unknown*
May's Invocation after a Tardy Spring. Ray
Moon Shines Bright, The. *Unknown*
O, the Month of May. *Fr.* The Shoemaker's
Holiday. Dekker
Ode in May. Watson
Old May Song. *Unknown*
Padstow Night Song, The. *Unknown*
Poem in May. Hewitt
Poet's Dream, The. *Fr.* The Golden [*or*
Goldyn] Targe. Dunbar
St. Mary's Loch. Faber
Song on [*or* of] May Morning. Milton
May Day
On Mayday we dance. *Unknown*
Mayflower (ship)
Mayflower, The. Ellsworth

Mayflower. O'Reilly
Mayflowers. *See* **Arbutus.**
Mayo. *See* **County Mayo, Ireland.**
Mazepa, Ivan
Mazeppa. Byron
Mead
Honey-Mead: "I am valued by men, fetched
from afar." *Fr.* Riddles (Exeter Book).
Cynewulf
Meadowlarks
Meadow Lark, The. Garland
Meadows. *See* **Fields and Pastures.**
Meadowsweet
Meadowsweet. Allingham
Meat
Any Part of Piggy. Coward
Bags of Meat. Hardy
Butchery. McPherson
Receipt for Stewing Veal, A. Gay
Recipe: Hare. Archestratus
Recipe: Sausage. Axionicus
To Stew a Rump-Steak. *Unknown*
What Is Veal? *Unknown*
Meath. *See* **County Meath, Ireland.**
Mechanics
Misery of Mechanics, The. Booth
Medawar, Peter
Morden Lecture, 1978. Le Guin
Medea
Dress, The. Ravikovich
Jason and Medea. *Fr.* Confessio Amantis.
Gower
Letter to Medea. Novak
Oh smooth adder/ who with fanged kisses
changedst my natural blood. *Fr.* Medea in
Athens. Webster
Medici, Lorenzo de'
Statue of Lorenzo de' Medici, The. Nesmith
Medicine
Calling the Doctor. Holloway
Drinking Song, A. *Unknown*
Mountain Medicine. Long
On Hygiene. Belloc
Plantation Bitters. *Unknown*
See also **Hospitals; Illness; Nurses;
Physicians.**
Meditation
How to Meditate. Kerouac
If you ponder it,/ no obstacle blocks your
path. Nanak
If you ponder it,/ there is mindfulness,
wisdom of mind. Nanak
If you ponder it,/ you find the door of
deliverance. Nanak
Meditation. Hecht
Meditation Rock, The. Mo Shih-lung
Quiet Sitting. Wang Chiu-ssu
Way one ponders it, The. Nanak
Mediterranean Sea
Golden-Green Dawn, A. Chalfi
Mediterranean, The. Tate
Middle of the World. Lawrence
Medusa
Eve Meets Medusa. Wandor
Look, Medusa! Namjoshi
Medusa. Bogan
Medusa. O'Sullivan
Muse as Medusa, The. Sarton
Perseus. Hayden
Remember Medusa? Souza
Statue of Medusa, The. Drummond
Meiklejohn, Alexander
I read your testimony and I thought. *Fr.* To
Alexander Meiklejohn. Beecher
Melampus
Melampus. Meredith
Melancholy
Ah Me! Am I the Swaine. Wither
Artist, The. Kunitz
Authors Abstract of Melancholy, The. *Fr.*
The Anatomy of Melancholy. Burton

Away, Melancholy. Smith
Broken Heart, The. Beedome
Charles Carville's Eyes. Robinson
Completion. Dunn
Dejection. Bridges
Dejection; an Ode [*or* A Letter to Sara
Hutchinson]. Coleridge
Depression. Cope
Earth, Late Choked with Showers, The. *Fr.*
Scilla's Metamorphosis. Lodge
Elk on Mutability, The. Bensko
His Litany to the Holy Spirit. Herrick
If Only. Rossetti
Il Penseroso. Milton
Itylus. Swinburne
Lost. Spender
Melancholia. Bly
Melancholia. Bridges
Melancholia. Plaice
Melancholy. *Fr.* The Nice Valor. Fletcher
Melancholy. Thomas
My Sad Self. Ginsberg
My Spirit Longeth for Thee. Byrom
Naked Seed, The. Lewis
Ode to a Nightingale. Keats
Only with Radiance. Szécsi
Platonick Love. Herbert of Cherbury
Poppies in July. Plath
Pulley, The. Herbert
Reverie. Marquis
Sad Boy, The. Riding
Sad Child's Song, The. Van Doren
She Warns Him. Cornford
Sigh, The. Wanley
Solitude. Traherne
Song:
Why So Pale and Wan, Fond Lover?
Suckling
Stanzas Written in Dejection [–December
1818,] near Naples. Shelley
This Lime-Tree Bower My Prison. Coleridge
Water Is Wide, The. *Unknown*
Wet Evening in April. Kavanagh
What rage is this? what furor [*or* furour] of
what kind [*or* kynd]? Wyatt
World Is Too Much with Us, The.
Wordsworth
Youthful Picnic Long Ago: Sad Ballad on
Box. Warren
See also **Dejection.**
Meleager
Meleager. *Fr.* Metamorphoses. Ovid
Melons
So hot the melons. *Fr.* Twenty Hokku.
Kyorai
Melville, Herman
At Melville's Tomb. Crane
Herman Melville. Aiken
Herman Melville. Auden
Memento Mori
Upon a Dead Man's Head. Skelton
Upon the Image of Death. Southwell
Memnon
Memnon. Scollard
Memorial Day
Bivouac of the Dead, The. O'Hara
Blue and the Gray, The. Finch
Decoration Day. Heard
Decoration Day. Longfellow
How Sleep the Brave. Collins
In Flanders Fields. McCrae
March, The. Squire
May 30, 1893. Bangs
Memorial Day. Anania
Memorial Day. Garrison
Memorial Day. Lent
Memorial Day. Thompson
Memorial Days. Sadoff
O gallant brothers of the generous South.
Fr. Ode for Decoration Day. Peterson
One to destroy, is murder by the law. Young

Memory
After a Journey. Hardy
Afterwards. Hardy
Age of Blue Memory, The. Elytis
Ah, Are You Digging on My Grave? Hardy
Alma Perdida. Larbaud
Ancient to Ancients, An. Hardy
Animals, The. Muir
Apple Fell in the Night and a Wagon
  Stopped, An. McMichael
Aspects. MacCaig
At Ballyshannon, Co. Donegal. Allingham
August from My Desk. Flint
Babiaantje, The. Prince
Bachelor Hall. Field
Bagatelles. Orlen
Barefoot Boy, The. Whittier
Before the Big Storm. Stafford
Ben Alder 1963-1977. Hannigan
Birthplace Revisited. Corso
Blows the Wind Today. Stevenson
Burning Hills. Ondaatje
Cameo, The. Millay
Celandine. Thomas
Cold Glow: Icehouses. Wojahn
Collector, The. Flynn
Companions. Calverley
Considerations. Helwig
Crystals like Blood. "MacDiarmid"
Dear Men and Women. Wheelock
Diary of Days for Adjoa. Kay
Directive. Frost
Dream of Fair Women, The. Dennis
Evocation. Nervo
Face of Creation, The. Orban
Fall Journey. Stafford
Far West Once. Warren
Fire of Drift-wood, The. Longfellow
Firefly. Uba
Flame-Heart. McKay
For Memories. Nishiwaki Junzaburo
For Victor Jara. Williams
Forget Thee? Moultrie
Forgiven Past, The. Riding
Gean Trees, The. Jacob
Generation. Torrevillas
Ghost Psalms. Kalász
Goodnight Irene. Mariani
Grandmothers Land. Oandasan
Green Rain. Livesay
Green Slates. Hardy
Green Valley, The. Warner
Heart, we will forget him! Dickinson
Home-Coming. Ehrenstein
Hours, The. Bishop
House, A. Orlen
How to Like It. Dobyns
Hunting Horns. Apollinaire
I Cannot Forget You. Unknown
I Remember, I Remember. Hood
I remember ("I remember/ watching the
  women."). Anyiam–St. John
I think of when she comes. Fr. Six Poems
  on Remembering. Shen Yüeh
I think of when she sits. Fr. Six Poems on
  Remembering. Shen Yüeh
I think of when she sleeps. Fr. Six Poems
  on Remembering. Shen Yüeh
In Hell. Jarman
In Memory. Pollitt
In scenes paternal, not beheld through years.
  Fr. Eyam. Seward
In the Evening. Cavafy
Intrusion. Levertov
It Was Your Song. Kowit
Journey, The. Ignatow
Just Now. Kooser
Kashmiri Song. Hope
Lament for the O'Neills. Montague
Last Night Your Lost Memory. Faiz
Letter from the Caribbean, A. Howes
Lilacs and the Roses, The. Aragon

Long, Long Be My Heart with Such
  Memories Filled. Moore
Long Winter Night. Ryokan
Look at the bulbul and the rose. Mir
Looking at Pictures to Be Put Away. Snyder
Memories. Horiguchi Daigaku
Memories. Whitman
Memories of Italy (Broken Sestina). Ash
Memories of Verdun. Dugan
Memory. Aldrich
Memory. Brontë
Memory. Deutsch
Memory. Hoyt
Memory. Kitahara Hakushu
Memory. Landor
Memory. Lincoln
Memory. MacCaig
Memory, A. Menken
Memory, A. Mustapää
Memory. Pinkney
Memory. Reverdy
Memory. Rossetti
Memory of Dust and Light. Ortega
Memory of my Father. Kavanagh
Memory System, A. Unknown
Mill, The. Wilbur
Mnemosyne. Stickney
Moments He Remembers, The. Van Doren
Music, When Soft Voices Die. Shelley
My Best Clothes. Netser
My Lost Youth. Longfellow
New Apartment, Minneapolis, The. Hogan
Now I understand. Fr. Sixty-four Tanka.
  Saigyo
O plovers flying over the evening waves. Fr.
  Manyo Shu. Hitomaro
October. Kavanagh
Ode to Michael Goldberg's Birth and Other
  Births. O'Hara
Offering Deep Affection. Ku Hsiung
Oft, in the Stilly Night. Moore
Old Familiar Faces, The. Lamb
Old Memories of Earth. Mason
Old Oaken Bucket, The. Woodworth
Old Times Were the Best, The. Riley
On My Two-Hundredth Birthday. Glatstein
On the Death of Friends in Childhood.
  Justice
Out of the Cradle Endlessly Rocking.
  Whitman
Out to Old Aunt Mary's. Riley
People, The. Creeley
Perennials. Kitchen
Piano. Lawrence
Postscript. Pilinszky
Rain in my ears: impatiently there raps. Fr.
  Essay on Memory. Fitzgerald
Ram Time. Heyen
Recollection. Aldrich
Recuerdo. Allen
Remember the M. Unknown
Remembering. Tóth
Remembrance. Slonimski
Reminiscence. Irwin
Report for Isolda. Ortega
Resurrection. Fearing
Return. Spencer
Reverie of a Mum. Keesing
Rhapsody on a Windy Night. Eliot,
Ring Road. Mangini
School Globe, The. Reaney
Scrapbooks. Giovanni
Self Portrait 4. Ditlevsen
Since. Auden
Since Nine O'Clock. Cavafy
Song: "Place in thy memory, dearest, A."
  Griffin
Special Delivery. Montague
Spirit of the Yellow River. Sun Kuang-hsien

Stanzas: "Black absence hides upon the past."
  Clare
Stitching in Time: Dorothy Ruddick.
  Howard
Tale of the Airly Days, A. Riley
Tears, Idle Tears [I Know Not What They
  Mean]. Fr. The Princess. Tennyson.
Telling the Bees. Whittier
Ten Days Leave. Snodgrass
Then and Now. Murray
They Were Pure Gold. Nieminen
Things Past. Tillinghast
This Memory. Giroux
Time Reminded Me. Uceda
To a Loved One of Other Days. Edwards
Today, today,/ I wait for him. Fr. Manyo
  Shu. Yosami
Tortoise, The. Corman
Touched. Giroux
Tower, The. Yeats
Transformations. Muyassar
Trusting Each Other. Stafford
Tune, A. Symons
Two Old Ladies. Sassoon
Two Years Later. Wieners
Unknown, The. Laughlin
Veterans, The. MacDonagh
Visit to the Author's Paternal Seat, A. Fr.
  The Influence of Local Attachment.
  Polwhele
Voice, The. Hardy
Walls of Ice. Hale
Warning and Reply. Brontë
What Lips My Lips Have Kissed. Millay
What Need Have I for Memory? Johnson
"When to the sessions of sweet silent
  thought." Fr. Sonnets, XXX.
  Shakespeare
Where Are the Waters of Childhood? Strand
Why You Climbed Up. Warren
Woodman, Spare That Tree. Morris
World, The. Rutsala
You stood at a bend. Fr. Manyo Shu.
  Osakabe Ataechikuni

Memphis, Tennessee
Memphis Blues. Brown

Men
Antithin. Weöres
Being with Men. Gregg
Bird Sings to Establish Frontiers, A. Gilbert
Equality. Guiducci
Exorcism of the Straight/Man/Demon.
  Shurin
Experience. Simmons
Feast of Stephen, The. Hecht
Female of the Species, The. Kipling
How Beastly the Bourgeois Is. Lawrence
I Can No Longer Laugh with Real Joy.
  Malfaiera
I Fear No Power a Woman Wields.
  McGaffey
I Quite Like Men. Landesman
I'm Not a Man. Norse
In Praise of the Male Sex, As Seen by Certain
  Females. Ziegler
In the Evening. Lara
It Is This Way with Men. Williams
Male Rage Poem. Di Cicco
Man. Guiducci
Manhood. Zamudio
Memories of Italy (Broken Sestina). Ash
Men Po Men with Glasses. Plantier
Militerotics. Ortleb
Mr. Macklin's Jack O'Lantern ("Mr. Macklin
  takes his knife"). McCord
Mr. Wells. Roberts
On Fatherish Men. Rosselli
Otis. Thomas
Sail and Oar. Graves
Sigh No More, Ladies [Sigh No More]. Fr.
  Much Ado about Nothing. Shakespeare
Some Men. Anderson

Stand, Stately Tavie. *Unknown*
Surgery. Pitchford
Train to Hell, The. Buri
Trying to Talk with a Man. Rich
Twin Aces. Wilson
Wanted—A Man. Stedman
When I am grown to man's estate.
  Stevenson
With Lamp in Hand. Gergely
Women and Men. Sheikh Mumin
Word in Edgeways, A. Tomlinson
Menageries. *See* **Zoos.**
Mencken, Henry Louis
Poem to the Memory of H. L. Mencken.
  Wormser
Menopause
Bloody Pause. Astra
Something to Look Forward To. Piercy
Menstruation
First Menstruation. Bass
Mental Illness
Bill. Kocan
Counting the Mad. Justice
Dementia Praecox. Bishop
Deserter, The. Smith
Diving into the Wreck. Rich
Evening in the Sanitarium. Bogan
Hard Rock Returns to Prison from the
  Hospital for the Criminal Insane. Knight
Kaddish. Ginsberg
Kitchenette Building. Brooks
Lines Written during a Period of Insanity.
  Cowper
Madhouse. Zaidi
Mental Cases. Owen
Mental Hospital Garden, The. Williams
Moon and the Yew Tree, The. Plath
November 1968. Rich
Of Kings and Dukes. Fuller
Poetic Institution. T'Hooft
Ringing the Bells. Sexton
Schizophrenic. Page
Schizophrenics, The. Fuller
Servant to Servants, A. Frost
Simplicity. Simpson
Sleepers, The. Kocan
Third Avenue in Sunlight. Hecht
Villanelle: Man in the Recreation Room, The.
  Harkness
Visit to the Asylum, A. Millay
Witch Burning. Plath
See also **Madness; Psychiatry and**
  Psychiatrists.
Mental Retardation
Black Dog, Red Dog. Dobyns
Bleeder. Dobyns
Halfwit. Dowling
Hospital for Defectives. Blackburn
Idiot, The. Wilson
In the Dome Car of the "Canadian." Marty
Retarded Children Find a World Built Just for
  Them, The. O Hehir
See also **Down's Syndrome.**
Menus
La Carte. Richardson
Mephistopheles. *See* **Satan.**
Mercenaries
Another Epitaph on an Army of Mercenaries.
  "MacDiarmid"
Demon. Faraz
Mercenaries. Faraz
Merchants
Merchant's Joy, The. Lu Yu
Seraph and the Snob, The. Kendall
Turners Dish of Lentten Stuffe or A
  Galymaufery. Turner
See also **Business and Businessmen; Clerks.**
Mercy
Discipline. Herbert
God of Mercy. Molodovsky

I opened the window wide and leaned. *Fr.*
  The Everlasting Mercy. Masefield
Mercy. Harjo
Quality of Mercy [Is Not Strain'd], The. *Fr.*
  The Merchant of Venice. Shakespeare
Merlin
Merlin. Emerson
Merlin and the Gleam. Tennyson
Merlin and the Snake's Egg. Norris
Merlin Enthralled. Wilbur
Prophecia Merlini Doctoris Perfecti.
  Unknown
Mermaid Tavern, London
Lines on the Mermaid Tavern. *Unknown*
Mermaids and Mermen
Clerk Colvill. *Unknown*
Fisherman Writes a Letter to the Mermaid,
  The. Aiken
Forsaken Merman, The. Arnold
Little Fan. Reeves
Loreley, The. Heine
Mermaid, The. King
Mermaid, The. Tennyson
Mermaiden, A. Hennell
Mermaidens, The. Richards
Mermaidens' Vesper-Hymn, The. *Fr.* Syren
  Songs. Darley
Mermaids. *Fr.* The Atlas. Slessor
Mermaids, The. *Fr.* The Faerie Queene.
  Spenser
Merman, The. Tennyson
Moon-Child, The. "Macleod"
Rowing, I reach'd a rock—the sea was low.
  Fr. A Vision of the Mermaids. Hopkins
Sam. De la Mare
Seamen's Distress, The. *Unknown*
Song of the Mermaids and Mermen. *Fr.* The
  Pirate. Scott
Merrimac (ship)
Turtle, The. *Unknown*
See also **Monitor (ship).**
Merry-go-rounds
Carousel, The. Oden
Green Horse, The. Ramke
Merry-go-round. Hughes
Merry-go-round. Jenkins
Merry-go-round. McAuley
Merry-go-round. Rawlinson
Merry-go-round, The. Rilke
Messengers
How They Brought the Good News from
  Ghent to Aix. Browning
Messiah
Advice to a Prophet. Wilbur
Encounter in Safed. Yungman
Hush, Hush. Leib
Instructions for the Messiah. Sklarew
King Shabtai Tsvi. Greenberg
Messiah, The. Yungman
When the Days Grow Long. Bialik
Metaphor
Ballad of Rodborough Common, The.
  Joseph
House, The. Levine
How Metaphor Can Save Your Life.
  Sklarew
Language As Inevitable Metaphor. Idea As
  Inevitable Figment. Carruth
Metaphors. Plath
Overture. Pastan
Spider Web. Dobyns
Very like a Whale. Nash
Want Ad. Boston
What Is a Jewish Poem? Sklarew
Young Housewife, The. Williams
Meteors and Meteorites
Winslow Crater. Bryant
Methodism
Hearken, Lady Betty, hearken. *Fr.* The New
  Bath Guide. Anstey
Religion and the Lower Classes. *Fr.* The
  Methodist. Lloyd

Metric System
Elegy for Yards, Pounds, and Gallons.
  Wagoner
Mexican Verse
Mexican Poetry; an Anthology (MexPo).
  Octavio Paz, comp.; Samuel Beckett, tr.
Mexican War
Angels of Buena Vista, The. Whittier
Fight at [the] San Jacinto, The. Palmer
Maid of Monterey, The. *Unknown*
Monterey. Hoffman
Mexico
At Kino Viejo, Mexico. Ríos
Baja. Stern
Carravagio. Hamill
For *Under the Volcano*. Lowry
In Mexico. Stein
Indians Come Down from Mixco, The.
  Asturias
Instruction Manual, The. Ashbery
Mexican Serenade. Guiterman
Monte Albán. Stroud
Mountain Town—Mexico. Grier
Ponce de León: A Morning Walk. Young
Postcard from Mexico, 16.x.1973. Salkey
Seasons Greetings, Love and Revolution.
  Miles
Sinalóa. Birney
View from the Gorge. Belitt
Visions of Mexico While at a Writing
  Symposium in Port Townsend, Washington.
  Cervantes
Visions of Mexico While at a Writing
  Symposium in Port Townsend, Washington.
  Cervantes
Mexico City
Fire Breather, Mexico City, The. Jacinto
Mexico City, 150 Pesos to the Dollar.
  Mitsui
Mice
Ascend my shoulders, firmly keep thy seat.
  Fr. The Battle of the Frogs and Mice.
  Homer
Ballad of the Mouse. Wallace
Cat and Mouse. Hughes
City Mouse and the Garden Mouse, The. *Fr.*
  Sing-Song. Rossetti
Clock-a-Clay. Clare
Country Mouse and the City Mouse, The.
  Sharpe
Diary of a Church Mouse. Betjeman
Elf and the Dormouse, The. Herford
Exterminator. Stryk
Fieldmouse, The. Alexander
Four III. Cummings
Funeral Oration for a Mouse. Dugan
Furry Home, The. Westrup
Hickory, dickory, dock. Mother Goose
House Mouse, The. Prelutsky
House of the Mouse, The. Mitchell
I Wouldn't. Ciardi
Legal Mouse, A. Moorer
Lion and the Mouse, The. Shteynbarg
Little Black Bug. Brown
Magical Mouse, The. Patchen
Me Up at Does. Cummings
Meadow Mouse, The. Roethke
Message from a Mouse, Ascending in a
  Rocket. Hubbell
Mice. Fyleman
Mice in the Hay. Norris
Midnightmouse, The. Morgenstern
Missing. Milne
Mouse, The. Coatsworth
Mouse, The. Garrigue
Mouse, The. Johnson
Mouse, The. Richards
Mouse, The. Wakley
Mouse and the Cake, The. Cook
Mouse Dinner. Fisher
Mouse Dinners, The. Edson

Mouse in the Wainscot, The. Serraillier
Mouse's Nest. Clare
Mouse's Petition, The. Barbauld
New Strain. Starbuck
On the Eating of Mice. Edson
Snail and the Mouse, The. Richards
Tale of the Upland Mouse and the Burgess
  Mouse, The. Henryson
Three blind mice, see how they run! Mother
  Goose
Three Mice. Cole
To Be a Mouse. Wat
Trapped Mouse. Cunningham
Waltzer in the House, The. Kunitz
Michael, Saint
Sequence for Saint Michael, A. Alcuin
Michaelmas
Michaelmas. Nicholson
Michelangelo Buonarroti
Death-Bed Reflections of Michel-Angelo.
  Coleridge
Love Song of J, The Alfred Prufrock. Eliot
Old Age of Michelangelo, The. Prince
To Giovanni da Pistoia on the Painting of the
  Sistine Chapel, 1509. Michelangelo
With a Sliver of Marble from Carrara.
  Wright
Michigan
Coming Home. Levine
Detroit. Hall
Detroit City. Boyer
End of Summer, The. Minty
Expanded Want Ad, An. Leithauser
Making Music. Minty
That Was Then. Gardner
Microbes
Microbe's Serenade, The. Ade
See also **Bacteria.**
Microscopes
Microscope, The. Kumin
Microscope. Thomas
Virus Poliomyelitis. Gaumond
Midas
Epigram: "Midas, they say, possessed the art
  of old." "Pindar"
King Midas. Moss
King Midas. *Fr.* Metamorphoses. Ovid
Ungrateful Garden, The. Kizer
Middle Age
Ambulando. Brasch
At My Country Home in Chung-nan. Wang
  Wei
Autumnal[l], The. *Fr.* Elegies. Donne
Bloody Pause. Astra
"Dover Beach"—a Note to That Poem.
  MacLeish
Dreaded Road. Abd al-Wahid
End of Summer. Kunitz
First Grey Hair, The. Tucker
From a Correct Address in a Suburb of a
  Major City. Sorrells
Game Resumed. Lattimore
I Am Coming to You. Glatstein
Lady's Complaint, The. Heath-Stubbs
Loved One, The. Hansen
Men at Forty. Justice
Menstruation at Forty. Sexton
Mezzo Cammin. Longfellow
Middle Age. Beer
Middle Age. Rankin
Middle-aged, The. Rich
Middleaged Man, The. Simpson
Minuet on Reaching the Age of Fifty, A.
  Santayana
Next Day. Jarrell
Now or Never. Astra
Ode on Celestial Music. Patten
Phillis's *or* Phyllis's Age. Prior
Professor Waking, The. Tate
Reaching Forty. Abd al-Wahid
Stella's Birth-day, 1718/19. Swift
Thirty-eight. Smith

Middle Ages
Middle Ages, The. Haines
Ode to the Medieval Poets. Auden
Middlesex, England
Middlesex. Betjeman
Pax Paganica. Guiney
Slough. Betjeman
Midgets
Lie Easy in Your Secret Cradle. *Fr.*
  Wildtrack. Wain
Midnight
At Midnight. Kooser
Midnight. Mistral
Midnight. *Fr.* Idyl. Ray
No Time for Poetry. Fields
Twelve. Glatstein
Mignonettes
Pitcher of Mignonette, A. Bunner
Red Geranium and Godly Mignonette.
  Lawrence
Migrant Workers
Pastures of Plenty. Guthrie
See also **Farmworkers.**
Migration
Migration. Lane
To a Waterfowl. Bryant
Milan, Italy
Duomo, Milan. *Fr.* View of the Cathedral.
  Henri
Milan August 1943. Quasimodo
Miracle in Milan. Klinger
Militarism
Cavalier's Song, The. Motherwell
Channel Firing. Hardy
Mrs. Snatcher Thatcher. *Fr.* Jezebel: Her
  Progress. Hanscombe
On the Frequent Review of the Troops.
  "M."
When the Great Gray Ships Come In. Carryl
Military Justice
Danny Deever. Kipling
Military Life. *See* **Army Life.**
Milk and Milking
Drink of Milk, A. Montague
If you wish to live for ever. *Unknown*
Milke before wine, I would 'twere mine.
  Unknown
Milking Time. Roberts
Milkmaid. Lee
Milkmaids
Buxom Young Dairy Maid, The. *Unknown*
To Milk in the Valley Below. *Unknown*
Milkmen
Milkman, The. Sansom
Milkman and His Son, The. Lux
Milkweed
From a Milkweed Pod. Frost
Milkweed. Levine
Milkweed, A. *Fr.* Two Voices in a
  Meadow. Wilbur
Milkweed. Wright
Milkweed Pods in Winter. Mueller
To the Milkweed. Mifflin
Two Voices in a Meadow. Wilbur
Milky Way
McLuhan Transposed. Elgin
Mill, John Stuart
John Stuart Mill. *Fr.* Clerihews. Bentley
Millay, Edna St. Vincent
Edna St. Vincent Millay Exhorts Little Boy
  Blue. *Fr.* Mother Goose Up-to-Date.
  Untermeyer
Millennium
Dawning, The. Vaughan
End, The. Owen
Epitaph Ending in And, The. Stafford
Second Coming, The. Yeats
Miller, Glenn
Glenn Miller's music is a trunk. Valle
Millet, Jean François
Man with the Hoe, The. Markham

Mills and Millers
Dishonest Miller, The. *Unknown*
Mill, A. Allingham
Mill, The. Robinson
Mill, The. Wilbur
Miller, The. Clerk
Miller and His Sons, The. *Unknown*
Miller, Miller. Eastwick
Old Mill, The. English
Old Rustic Mill, The. Johnson
Tact. Robinson
Unfortunate Miller, The. Coppard
Water Mill, The. Doudney
Windmill, The. Lucas
Milton, John
Adventurous Muse, The. Watts
And Did Those Feet in Ancient Time. *Fr.*
  Milton. Blake
In Age. *Fr.* Milton: On the Busts of Milton,
  in Youth and Age. Bowles
In Youth. *Fr.* Milton: On the Busts of
  Milton, in Youth and Age. Bowles
Johannes Milton, Senex. Bridges
Lines Printed under the Engraved Portrait of
  Milton [in Tonson's Folio of the "Paradise
  Lost"]. Dryden
London, 1802 ("Milton! thou should'st be
  living at this hour"). Wordsworth
Milton. Longfellow
Milton. Mifflin
Milton. Ray
Milton by Firelight. Snyder
Milton's Prayer for [*or of*] Patience. Howell
On Mr. Milton's Paradise Lost. Marvell
To Milton. Wilde
Mincemeat
Remembering Mincemeat. MacBeth
Mind. *See* **Intellect.**
Minerals
Crystals like Blood. "MacDiarmid"
Mineral Kingdom. Dupin
Minerals of Cornwall, Stones of Cornwall.
  Redgrove
See also **Metals; Mining and Miners.**
Minerva
To Minerva. Hood
See also **Athena.**
Mining and Miners
Air Shaft. *Fr.* Poems from the Coalfields.
  Healy
Avondale Mine Disaster, The. *Unknown*
Ballad of a Mine, A. Skelton
Blackleg Miners, The. *Unknown*
Burning Mountain. Merwin
Caliban on the Coal Mines. Untermeyer
Christ in the Clay-Pit. Clemo
Coal-Owner and the Pitman's Wife, The.
  Unknown
Collier, The. Watkins
Down in a Coal Mine. Geoghegan
Dreary Black Hills, The. *Unknown*
Drill Man Blues. Sizemore
Durham Lock-out, The. *Unknown*
Dynamite Song. *Unknown*
Explosion, The. Larkin
Hard-working Miner, The. *Unknown*
He Done His Level Best. "Twain"
Hill above the Mine, The. Cowley
I tell him how it used to be in Paguate. *Fr.*
  After the Pow-Wow. Littlebird
I'm Only a Broken-down Miner. *Unknown*
Lament while Descending a Shaft. *Unknown*
Magaiça. Sousa
Mamana Saquina. Craveirinha
Miner Boy, The. *Unknown*
Miners. Owen
Mother Wept. Skipsey
Oh, Give Me the Hills. *Unknown*
Only a Miner. *Unknown*
Photos of a Salt Mine. Page
Plodder Seam, The. *Unknown*

Ramon. Harte
Scenes in a Silver Mine. *Fr.* Thirty Tanka.
    Tachibana Akemi
Stars Are Twinkling, The. Skipsey
Tramp Miner's Song. *Unknown*
Where shall the eyes a darkness find. *Fr.*
    Back in the Return. Menai
White Dust, The. Gibson
See also **Coal Mining and Coal Miners;**
    Gold Mining and Gold Miners.

Ministers. *See* **Clergy.**

Mink
Thanksgiving Dinner during Pelting Season.
    Moran

Minnesota
Blessing, A. Wright
By a Lake in Minnesota. Wright
Driving toward the Lac Qui Parle River. Bly
Ice. Ai
Lying in a Hammock at William Duffy's Farm
    in Pine Island, Minnesota. Wright
Minneapolis Poem, The. Wright
Minnesota Camp Grounds. Vizenor
Minnesota Thanksgiving. Berryman
Pine Point, You Are. Henry

Minotaur
Minotaur. Fisher

Minstrels
Deor's Lament. *Unknown*
Minstrel, The. Goethe
Minstrel, The. Skipsey
Minstrel Boy, The. Moore
Minstrel's Lot, The. Rogerson
Oh! sing unto my roundelay [*or* O! Synge
    untoe mie roundelaie]. *Fr.* Aella; a
    Tragycal Enterlude. Chatterton
Sonnet: "O! how my poet's-spirit doth it vex."
    Lott
Widsith, the Minstrel. *Fr.* Widsith.
    Unknown

Miracles
Cana. Merton
Getting Inside the Miracle. Shaw
Jesus Himself. Burton
Leave the Miracle to Him. Allan
Miracles. Aiken
Miracles. Whitman
Miracles Real Miracles. Jacob
On the Miracle of Loaves. Crashaw
On the Miracle of Multiplied Loaves.
    Crashaw
Religion. Vaughan
Sonnet: To the Admirable Transubstantiation
    of the Roses into the Marvellous Image of
    Our Lady of Guadalupe. Sandoval y
    Zapata

Mirages
Beauty. "Badawi al-Jabal"
Dark Mirage. "Badawi al-Jabal"
Fata Morgana. Windhager
Into My Heart [an Air That Kills]. *Fr.* A
    Shropshire Lad. Housman.

Mirrors
Bad Mirror. Jandl
Beware: Do Not Read This Poem. Reed
Furniture: humble, dependent. *Fr.* Habitat.
    Wright
Image in a Mirror. Goodman
In a Glass-Window for Inconstancy. Herbert
    of Cherbury
Infinity Effect at the Hôtel Soubise. Corn
Lady Who Offers Her Looking-Glass to
    Venus, The. Prior
Looking-Glass, A. Carew
Looking Glass, The. Kipling
Man and His Image, The. La Fontaine
Mirror, The. Chan Ch'e
Mirror. Chimako
Mirror. Plath
Mirror Poems, The. Derricotte

Mirrors, The. Andresen
Mirrors, no one yet has really described. *Fr.*
    Sonnets to Orpheus. Rilke
Moments of Vision. Hardy
On His Mistress Looking in a Glass. Carew
On Looking in the Looking Glass. Gardner
Poem: "All the mirrors in the world."
    O'Hara
Reflection. Smith
Reflections. MacNeice
Seeing for a Moment. Levertov
Shadows in the Water. Traherne
To My Dead Father. O'Hara

Mirth
Eskimo Occasion. Rodriguez
Hock-Cart, or Harvest Home, The. Herrick
L'Allegro. Milton
Lyric to Mirth, A. Herrick
To Cyriack Skinner ("Cyriack, whose
    grandsire"). Milton
To Live Merrily, and to Trust to Good
    Verses. Herrick
See also **Laughter.**

Misanthropy
Complete Misanthropist, The. Bishop
Eagle and the Mole, The. Wylie

Miscarriages
Country Woman Elegy. Gibson
Dead Embryos. Tóth
Flowers. Fraser
For a Woodscolt Miscarried. Corrington
Vow, The. Hecht

Misfortune
Hymn to Adversity. Gray
Ode on the Pleasure Arising from Vicissitude.
    Gray
Shrubbery, The. Cowper
We Are Lowly. Nicoll

Mishima, Yukio
Mysterious East. Cole

Misogyny
Gentle Echo on Woman, A. Swift
Love a woman! y'are an ass. Rochester
Misogynist, The. Morgan
Tho' You May Boast You're Fairer.
    Unknown
Upon Some Women. Herrick
Warning, A. Patmore

Missionaries
Africa. Moorer
Cry for Light, A. *Unknown*
Fr. Anselm Williams and Br. Leander
    Neville. Smither
From Greenland's Icy Mountains. Heber
He is coming, Adzed-Head. *Unknown*
Let Me Go Back. Albright
Magalu. Johnson
Martyrdom of Brébeuf and Lalemant, 16
    March 1649, The. *Fr.* Brébeuf and His
    Brethren. Pratt
Memorial to a Missionary. Sinclair
Missionary, The. Linden
Missionary Hymm. Burke
Missionary Visits Our Church in Scranton,
    The. Parini
Path of the Padres, The. Osborne
Père Lachaise. Pickthall
Two Souls. Pickthall
Your Mission. Gates

Mississippi (State)
Birthday Poem. Young
Church Burning: Mississippi. Emanuel
Jackson, Mississippi. Walker
Mississippi Born. Lomax
Mississippi Mornings. Dent
Night, Death, Mississippi. Hayden

Mississippi River
Down the Mississippi. Fletcher
Down the Yellowstone, the Milk, the White
    and Cheyenne. *Fr.* The River. Lorentz
River, The. *Fr.* The Bridge: Powhatan's
    Daughter. Crane

Missouri (State)
Childhood. Justice
Last Look at La Plata, Missouri. Barnes
Meet Me in St. Louis, Louis. Sterling
Porpoise, The. Pape
Sunday Dreamer's Guide to Yarrow,
    Missouri, A. Barnes
When I Was Conceived. Ryan

Missouri, River
Foreclosure. Brown

Mist
As the mist clears away. Tamehide
Autumn mists/ don't rise up this morning!
    Fr. Kokin Shu. *Unknown*
I thought it was mist. Tamehide
In dawn's early glow. Tameie
Kythans. McGavin
Mist. Man
Mist. Thoreau
Mist. Young
Mist and All, The. Willson
Sao Princess/ has donned her new robe of
    haze, The. Tameuji
Spring Moon Concealed, The. Tamemasa
See also **Fog.**

Mistletoe
Mistletoe. De la Mare
Mistletoe, The. Prelutsky
Mistletoe. Tucker
Mistletoe Bough, The. Bayly
Under the Mistletoe. Cullen

Mitchell, Arthur
Arthur Mitchell. Moore

Mites
Mite, The. Merrill

Mithridates the Great
Mithridates. Emerson

Mittens
Mitten Song, The. Allen
This Little House Is Sugar. Hughes
See also **Gloves.**

Mnemonics
Faber Book of Useful Verse, The (FaBoUs).
    Simon Brett, ed.

Moas
Skeleton of the Great Moa in the Canterbury
    Museum, Christchurch, The. Curnow

Mobile Bay, Battle of
Bay Fight, The. Brownell
Craven. Newbolt
Farragut. Meredith

Mockingbirds
Bird at Night. Hamilton
Bird-witted. Moore
Lament of a Mocking-Bird. Kemble
Mocking-Bird, The. Clarke
Mocking Bird, The. Hayne
Mocking-Bird, The. Lanier
Mocking Bird, The. Stanton
Mocking-Bird, The. Stockard
Mockingbird, The. Jarrell
Mockingbird of Mockingbirds, The.
    Levertov
My Mocking Bird. Heard
To the Mock-Bird. Fordham
To the Mocking-Bird. Pike

Models
Life Drawing. Orlen
Mannequins. Kaléko
Noelle. *Fr.* Calling Your Name in the Zoo.
    Williams
Ode to a Model. Nabokov

Moderation
Counsel of Moderation, A. Thompson

Modern Man
Christ I Wudint Know Normal if I Saw It
    When. Bissett
Common Man, The. Smith
Dirge: "1-2-3 was the number he played but
    today the number came 3-2-1." Fearing
Every Thing. Monro

Face in the Ceiling, The. Dobyns
Flying Deeper into the Century. Di Cicco
Glengormley. Mahon
Life Cycle of Common Man. Nemerov
Lost Parents. Ferlinghetti
Make Love Not War. Nemerov
Net and the Sword, The. Le Pan
Quiet Desperation. Simpson
Season 'Tis, My Lovely Lambs, The.
    Cummings
Unknown Citizen, The. Auden
Wasp Sex Myth (One). Hollo
Wasp Sex Myth (Two). Hollo
We're OK. Fuertes
Who's Who. Auden

Modesty
"Sure," Said Benny Goodman. Carruth

Moles
All but Blind. De la Mare
Back to Base. Joseph
Blue Moles. Plath
Dead Mole, A. Young
Eagle and the Mole, The. Wylie
Mole and the Eagle, The. Hale
Mole makes his pole redhot. Alonzo
    Gonzales
Moles. Stafford
Unfortunate Mole, The. Kennedy

Molkho, Shlomo
Shlomo Molkho Sings on the Eve of His
    Burning. Leyeles

Momin, Momin Khan
There was a young man who was famed
    among. Momin

Mona Lisa
Mona Leo. McKenty
Mona Lisa. Pater

Monaghan. See **County Monaghan, Ireland.**

Monasteries
All alone in my little cell. *Unknown*
December. Snyder
Jasper Cloud Monastery, The. Wu Wen
Lament over the Ruins of the Abbey of Teach
    Molaga. *Unknown*
On Rising at Dawn and Seeing the Mountains.
    Hung Sheng
Passing the Night at the Monastery of Eternal
    Peace. Hung Sheng
Reader, The. Merton
Semblables, The. Williams
Sonnet: Written in a Blank Leaf of Dugdale's
    "Monasticon." Warton
Stanzas from the Grande Chartreuse. Arnold
See also **Monks.**

Monday
On a Monday Morning. Tawney

Monet, Claude
Monet Refuses the Operation. Mueller
Monet's Lilies Shuddering. Ferlinghetti
Monet's "Waterlilies." Hayden

Money
America. Dumas
American Change. Ginsberg
American Primitive. Smith
Basic. Durem
Behaviour of Money. Spencer
Christmas Bills. Hatton
Dialogue. Nemerov
Economics. Van Duyn
Fantasy of an African Boy. Berry
Fatigue. Belloc
Gold. Hood
Hardship of Accounting, The. Frost
How Five and Twenty Shillings Were
    Expended in a Week. *Unknown*
Investor's Soliloquy. Ward
Jolly Shilling, The. *Unknown*
Lines Composed at Hope Ranch. Clark
Lines on the Back of a Confederate Note.
    Jonas
Lyric[k] for Legacies. Herrick

Marriage and Money. *Fr.* The Happy Pair.
    Sedley
Memento Vitae. McHugh
Money. Armour
Money. Davies
Money. Nemerov
Money. Sisson
Money. Yüan Mei
Money and a Friend. *Unknown*
Money Cry, The. Davison
Money Gets the Mastery. Herrick
Money Is What Matters. *Unknown*
Money Isn't Everything! Hammerstein
Money Makes the Mirth. Herrick
Montefiore. Bierce
My Purse. *Unknown*
Of Money. Googe
Parley with His Empty Purse, A. Randolph
Reckoning, The. Roethke
To Their Excellencies the Lords Justices of
    Ireland, the Humble Petition of Frances
    Harris, Who Must Starve, and Die a Maid
    if It Miscarries. Swift
Worry about Money. Raine

Mongolia
For the Cultural Campaign. Jigmed

Mongolism. See **Down's Syndrome.**

Mongooses
Mon-Goos, The. *Fr.* Child's Natural
    History. Herford

Monitor (ship)
Utilitarian View of the *Monitor's* Fight, A.
    Melville

Monkeys
At Woodward's Gardens. Frost
Autumn Cove. Li Po
Before the Monkey's Cage. Becker
Colobus Monkey. *Fr.* Hunter Poems of the
    Yoruba. *Unknown*
Monkey, The. Buddingh'
Monkey. Shotetsu
Monkeyland. Weöres
Monkeys. Colum
Monkeys, The. Moore
Monkeys on Mt. Hiei. Shiffert
Red Monkey. *Fr.* Hunter Poems of the
    Yoruba. *Unknown*
Ship of Rio, The. De la Mare
Sonnet on a Monkey, A. Fleming
Three Wise Monkeys, The. Davis
When You Talk to a Monkey. Bennett

Monks
At Shoraku-ji in Omi, First Poem of the Year.
    Kishun Ryuki
At the Mountain of the Mysterious Tomb.
    Wu Wei-yeh
Bothered by Something. Ryokan
Carthusians. Dowson
Elegy for the Monastery Barn. Merton
Monk and His Pet Cat, The. *Unknown*
Monks at Ards, The. Maybin
My one aim, to be a wandering monk.
    Ryokan
Pangur Bán. *Unknown*
Pilgrimage. Clarke
Soliloquy of the Spanish Cloister. Browning
Trappists. Artaud
Weak Monk, The. Smith
See also **Clergy; Monasteries.**

Monmouth, James Scott, Duke of
Advice to the Painter. Prior
Dutchess of Monmouth's Lamentation for the
    Loss of Her Duke, The. *Unknown*
England's Darling; or, Great Britain's Joy and
    Hope on That Noble Prince James, Duke of
    Monmouth. *Unknown*
Hue and Cry after Blood and Murder, A.
    Unknown

In pious times ere [*or* e'r] priestcraft did
    begin. *Fr.* Absalom and Achitophel, Pt. I.
    Dryden
On the University of Cambridge's Burning the
    Duke of Monmouth's Picture. Stepney

Monmouth, Battle of (1778)
Battle of Monmouth, The. English
Molly Pitcher. Richards

Monogamy
What a Time! Blumenthal

Monsters
Attack of the Crab Monsters. Raab
Chimera, The. Mombert
Demons. Césaire
Father and Mother. Kennedy
Kraken, The. Tennyson
Monster, The. Lunde
Scylla and Charybdis. *Fr.* Odyssey.
    Homer
Sheep Child, The. Dickey
Amazing Monsters (AmMo). Robert Fisher,
    ed.

Mont Blanc
Hymn before Sunrise, in the Vale of
    Chamouni. Coleridge
Mont Blanc. Shelley

Mont-Saint-Michel
Discoveries of Bones and Stones. Grigson

Montana
Christmas Comes to Moccasin Flat. Welch
Degrees of Gray in Philipsburg. Hugo
Elegy to the Sioux. Dubie
Harlem, Montana; Just Off the Reservation.
    Welch
Lady in Kicking Horse Reservoir, The.
    Hugo
Map of Montana in Italy, A. Hugo
Montana Eclogue. Stafford
Montana Pastoral. Cunningham
Montana Wives. Haste
Mount Caribou at Night. Wright
Rosebud. Anderson

Montefiore, Moses
Montefiore in Vilna. Volf

Monterrey, Mexico
Monterey. Hoffman
Monterrey Sun. Reyes

Montgomery, Richard
Montgomery at Quebec. Scollard

Months
Four Sweet Months, The. Herrick
Garden Year, The. Coleridge
Inst., Ult., and Prox. Herbert
Labours of the Months. *Unknown*
Marjorie's Almanac. Aldrich
Mask of Mutability, The. *Fr.* The Faerie
    Queene. Spenser
Months, The. Chaucer
Months, The. Rossetti
Months, The. *Unknown*

Montreal, Quebec
Bonne Entente. Scott
Montreal. Klein
O God! O Montreal! Butler

**Montrose, James Graham, 5th Earl and 1st
    Marquess of**
Execution of Montrose, The. Aytoun

Monuments
Cenotaph, The. Mew
Church Monuments. Herbert
Concord Hymn. Emerson
For the Union Dead. Lowell
Inscription for Marye's Heights,
    Fredericksburg. Melville
Lines Written on a Seat on the Grand Canal,
    Dublin. Kavanagh
Monument, The. Bishop
Monuments. Hollander
Pro Patria. Carrier
Washington Monument by Night. Sandburg

Moods
  Mood Indigo. Sadoff
Moon
  Above the Dock. Hulme
  After his tryst. Teika
  Ah, the Sea of Grebes!/. Ietaka
  Another Full Moon. Fainlight
  Apollo 8. Berryman
  As I look, the moon has moved West. *Fr.*
    Eighty-four Tanka. Teika
  As I sit worn and weary. *Fr.* Manyo Shu.
    Unknown
  As swift as the moon. Tonna
  As the night wears on. Tamekane
  Astolfo Visits the Moon. *Fr.* Orlando
    Furioso. Ariosto
  At Night. Trakl
  Auctioneer. Sandburg
  Autumn ("But see the fading many-colour'd
    woods"). *Fr.* The Seasons: Autumn.
    Thomson
  Aware. Lawrence
  Bay at Shiga, The. Ietaka
  Beating their wings. *Fr.* Kokin Shu.
    Unknown
  Blossoms at Their Height. Kaneyoshi
  Bright bright!/ bright bright bright! *Fr.* Ten
    Tanka. Myoe
  Cat and the Moon, The. Yeats
  Charming the Moon. DenBoer
  Chase, The. Davies
  Clair de Lune. Verlaine
  Cold moon: a white sheet. *Fr.* Twenty-one
    Hokku. Kaya Shirao
  Cold-night Moon—In the Manner of Meng
    Tung-yeh. Huang Tsung-hsi
  Complaint of the Moon in the Provinces.
    Laforgue
  Cooler than the wind. Tameyo
  Crescent Moon. D'Annunzio
  Crescent Moon. Renton
  Crow in the night, A. Kogon
  Dead Girl. *Fr.* Images. Hajnal
  Death of the Moon, The. Wagoner
  Did it not signal. Tameuji
  Did it perhaps. Joben
  Dirge for Two Veterans. Whitman
  Early Darkness. Illyés
  Even on the Loveliest of Nights. Khomsky
  Evening. Aldington
  First Walk on the Moon. Swenson
  Flying. Westrup
  Following the wind. Tameko
  From the outer gate. Teika
  Full Moon. De la Mare
  Full Moon. Hayden
  Full Moon. Wylie
  Full Moon in Malta. Asphodel
  Full Moon, Rising. Holden
  Full Moon; Santa Barbara. Teasdale
  Glow and beauty of the stars, The. Sappho
  Golden Bird, The. Ingamells
  Golden Moonrise. Braithwaite
  Half Moon. García Lorca
  Harvest Moon, The. Longfellow
  Hazy moon has detached itself, The. *Fr.*
    Twenty-seven Hokku. Natsume Seibi
  Horseman, The. De la Mare
  How Sweet the Moonlight Sleeps. *Fr.* The
    Merchant of Venice. Shakespeare
  How to Reach the Moon. Pomerantz
  Hymn to Diana. *Fr.* Cynthia's Revels.
    Jonson
  I See the Moon. *Unknown*
  I shall not forget. Teika
  I wish I could tell. Tamesuke
  In Dispraise of the Moon. Coleridge
  In Mornigan's park there is a deer. *Unknown*
  In the hazy night. Fushimi
  In their seasons. Tameko
  Instamatic The Moon February 1973.
    Morgan

  Is it not time now. Go-Komatsu
  Is the Moon Tired? Rossetti
  Isuzu River—/ like a mirror left behind.
    Tameie
  It was long ago. Chikako
  It Was the Lovely Moon. Freeman
  Lady Moon. Milnes
  Landing on the Moon. Swenson
  Little Moon, The. Longfellow
  Lunar Baedeker. Loy
  Man in the Moon, The. Riley
  Man in the Moon, The. *Unknown*
  Man in the moon was caught in a trap, The.
    Unknown
  Match with the Moon, A. Rossetti
  Meditations on the Moon. Allen
  Milk-white Moon, Put the Cows to Sleep.
    Sandburg
  Moon. Artaud
  Moon, The. Creeley
  Moon, The. Davies
  Moon, The. Dickinson
  Moon, The. Gyoko
  Moon. Horovitz
  Moon, The. *Fr.* The Moon. Tamesada
  Moon/ Have you met my mother? Kuskin
  Moon above the clouds doesn't look like the
    moon, The. *Fr.* Fifty-one Tanka. Izumi
  Moon and a Cloud, The. Davies
  Moon and the Yew Tree, The. Plath
  Moon at evening, The. Kogon
  Moon at heaven's center. *Fr.* Eighty-seven
    Hokku. Buson
  Moon Boat. Pomerantz
  Moon-Come-Out. Farjeon
  Moon Dips in the Puddle's Flow, The.
    Khomsky
  Moon Eclipse Exorcism. *Unknown*
  Moon from a Boat, The. Gyoko
  Moon in a Winecup, The. Shen Chou
  Moon-Man. Hewett
  Moon Rises, The. García Lorca
  Moon rising white, A. *Unknown*
  Moon Shadow. Bowering
  Moon shines bright, The. In such a night as
    this. *Fr.* The Merchant of Venice.
    Shakespeare
  Moon Sings, The. *Unknown*
  Moon Song, Woman Song. Sexton
  Moon-Witches. Hughes
  Moonlight. De la Mare
  Moonlight. Nazir
  Moonlight in the Forest. Hellaakoski
  Moonlight on Lake Sydenham. MacDonald
  Moonlight remains, The. Gyoko
  Moonrise. Hopkins
  Moonrise. Lawrence
  Moon's the North Wind's Cooky, The.
    Lindsay
  Moonset. Newbolt
  Moonset, Gloucester, December 1, 1957, 1:58
    A.M. Olson
  Moontan. Strand
  Mr. Moon. Carman
  Net of Moon, The. Mitchell
  New Moon, The. Blunden
  New Moon. Lawrence
  Night Light. Willard
  Night of the First Full Moon. Liang
    Ch'i-ch'ao
  Night Song. Cornford
  Not even the moon. Chikako
  Not even waiting. Tameyo
  Now at long last. Yoshimoto
  Now only the moon. Shinkei
  O Lady Moon. Rossetti
  O moon at dawn. Tameyo
  Oh! Look at the Moon. Follen
  On a spring night. Tameuji
  On Aesthetics, More or Less. Dufault
  On Leaping over the Moon. Traherne
  On the Telescopic Moon. Drennan

  Orb. Kumin
  Pellucid moon, The. Gyoko
  Phases of the Moon. *Fr.* One Word More.
    Browning
  Poetic Thought. *Unknown*
  Prayer by Moonlight. Swartz
  Prayer to the Young Moon. *Unknown*
  Proposition. Guillén
  Rays of the autumn moon, The. *Fr.* Kokin
    Shu. Tsurayuki
  Re-birth. *Unknown*
  Riddle 29: The Moon and the Sun. *Unknown*
  Set now,/ and I too will go below. *Fr.* Ten
    Tanka. Myoe
  Setting of the Moon, The. Leopardi
  Silver. De la Mare
  Since the moon resides. Tameuji
  Singing of the Moon. Mommu
  Singing on the Moon. Hughes
  So long. *Fr.* For the First Manned Moon
    Orbit. Dickey
  Song for Ishtar. Levertov
  Song for the Moon. Al-Mala'ika
  Song: "Make this night loveable." Auden
  Song of the Moon, A. McKay
  Sonnet of the Moon, A. Best
  Spring Moon Concealed, The. Tamemasa
  Starlight. Downie
  Summer Moon. Tamemasa
  Sun and Moon. Macpherson
  They Went to the Moon Mother. *Unknown*
  This Lunar Beauty. Auden
  Thoughts on the Sight of the Moon. Knight
  To a Solitary Disciple. Williams
  To Akashi's strand/ I came in hope of finding.
    Tameie
  To an Old Lady. Empson
  To-and-Fro of Saint Theresa. Reyes
  To the Moon. Hardy
  To the Moon. Leopardi
  To the Moon. Leopardi
  To the Moon. Shelley
  To the Moon. Smith
  To the Moon. Winters
  Tonight the Moon Fell. Chalfi
  Touching the line from a fishing pole. *Fr.*
    Seventeen Hokku. Chiyojo
  Turn of the Moon. Graves
  View. Armantrout
  Vision of Moonlight, A. Ray
  Waiting for Love in Vain. Tonna
  Waning Moon, The. Shelley
  Was/Man. Gotlieb
  We wait for the moon. *Fr.* Manyo Shu.
    Nukada
  Welcome to the Moon. *Unknown*
  When I look up and gaze. *Fr.* Manyo Shu.
    Yakamochi
  When I see the moonlight pouring. *Fr.*
    Kokin Shu. *Unknown*
  When you think of it. Teika
  Who Knows if the Moon's. Cummings
  Wind and Silver. Lowell
  Wind and the Moon, The. Macdonald
  Window Frames the Moon, The. Mar
  Winter Moon. Hughes
  Winter Moon. Jaccottet
  Winter Moon after a Rain, The. Tamesada
  "With how sad steps, O [*or* Oh] Moon, thou
    climb'st the skies!" *Fr.* Astrophel and
    Stella, XXXI. Sidney
  Working late. Stimson
  Yawning and praising the moon. *Fr.*
    Twenty-four Hokku. Kito
  You Made It Rain. Saunders
  Young May Moon, The. Moore
Moonflowers
  Evening Faces. Keiun
  To the Moonflower. Betts
Moore, Henry
  On a Celtic Mask by Henry Moore. Gregory
  Reclining Figure. Hall

Moore, Sir John
Burial of Sir John Moore after [*or* at]
Corunna, The. Wolfe
Moore, Thomas
On Thomas Moore's Poems. *Unknown*
Recollections of "Lalla Rookh." Trowbridge
To Thomas Moore. Byron
Will you come to the bower I have shaded for
you? *Fr.* A Reply to Lines by Thomas
Moore. Landor
Moors (geography)
Barren Moors, The. Channing
Gloucester Moors. Moody
Ilkla Moor. *Unknown*
Rannoch Moor. MacGregor
Moors (people)
War Song of the Saracens. *Fr.* Hassan.
Flecker
Morality Plays
Very fownder and begynner of owr fyrst
creacyon, The. *Fr.* Mankind. *Unknown*
Morandi, Giorgio
With Giorgio Morandi in Bologna. Schmied
More, Sir Thomas
Friend, on This Scaffold Thomas More Lies
Dead. Cunningham
Morgan, John Hunt
Kentucky Belle. Woolson
Morgan, Sir Henry
Morgan. Stedman
Morison, Sir Henry
To the Immortal Memory and Friendship of
That Noble Pair, Sir Lucius Cary and Sir
Henry Morison. Jonson
Morisot, Berthe
Berthe Morisot. Waldman
Mormons
Fire and Ice. Pettit
Marching to Utah. *Unknown*
Nauvoo. Taylor
Morning
Aubade: Lake Erie. Merton
Awake, mine eyes, see Phoebus bright
arising. *Unknown*
Awaking. Spender
Ballad of the Morning Streets. Baraka
Barefoot Days. Field
Beginning of the Day, The. Lin
Huan-ch'ang
Bleak. Weöres
Blocked by thick branches. Tamekane
Break[e] of Day. Donne
Calm Morning at Sea. Teasdale
Cock. Amir
Cocoa Morning. Kaufman
Convalescence. Coward
Courtier's Good-Morrow to His Mistress,
The. *Unknown*
Creature. Rákos
Dawn Walk. Hirsch
Daybreak. Longfellow
Description of the Morning, A. Swift
Dew. Maiden
Dog Poem, A. Farooqi
Early Morn. Davies
Early Morning, The. Belloc
Early Morning Meadow Song. Dalmon
Early Rising. Saxe
"Full many a glorious morning have I seen[e]"
Fr. Sonnets, XXXIII. Shakespeare
Gascoigne's Good-Morrow. Gascoigne
Glory, The. Thomas
Good Morrow. *Fr.* The Rape of Lucrece.
Heywood
Hark! Hark! the Lark. *Fr.* Cymbeline.
Shakespeare
Hymn: "Framer of the earth and sky."
Ambrose
I arise and see. Hanazono
Impression du Matin. Wilde
In the Morning. Fox

In the morning mist. Yoshimoto
In the Naked Bed, in Plato's Cave. Schwartz
January Morning, A. Lampman
January Morning. Williams
June Morning. McCrae
Lauds. Auden
Love Calls Us to the Things of This World.
Wilbur
Matin Hymn. Heard
Matinal. McQueen
Matins. Levertov
Mattens. Herbert
May All Earth Be Clothed in Light.
Hitchcock
Morn. Heard
Morning. Anis
Morning. Blake
Morning. Carlyle
Morning. Martínez de Navarrete
Morning. Ungaretti
Morning, about six, as I look at the rim of the
hill. *Unknown*
Morning and Evening. Slonimski
Morning at the Window. Eliot
Morning Light, The. Simpson
'Morning, Morning. Mathew
Morning on the Shore. Campbell
Morning Prayer. Nash
Morning Scene, A. Wu Sheng
Morning Song. DeClue
Morning Song. Orr
Morning Song. Teasdale
Morning Sounds. Farooqi
Morning Star. Pavese
Morning Stillness. Demus
Morning Sun. MacNeice
Morning Watch, The. Vaughan
Morning Work. Lawrence
My ruminations/ are still far from exhausted.
Ietaka
9:00 A.M. Oravecz
No Time for Poetry. Fields
November Morning Near Abingdon. Larbaud
October Morning. Bethell
On the Bright Side. Revard
On the River Lookout. Ya'oz-kest
Opening a little the wheeled door at the back,
I look out. *Unknown*
Out for a morning meal a little crow,
drenched with dew. *Unknown*
Pheasant. Rákos
Phoebus, Arise. Drummond
Poem about Morning. Meredith
Poet's Dream, The. *Fr.* The Golden [*or*
Goldyn] Targe. Dunbar
Prayer for Dreadful Morning. Root
Reveille. *Fr.* A Shropshire Lad. Housman
Satyr's Song. *Fr.* The Faithful Shepherdess.
Fletcher
Singing-Time. Fyleman
Sister, Awake! *Unknown*
Song Form. Baraka
Spring Morning. Lin Huan-ch'ang
Star-Sown. Netser
Summer Morning, A. Field
Summer Morning, A. Wilbur
Sun [*or* Sunne] Rising, The. Donne
Sunday Morning. MacNeice
Sung on a Sunny Morning. Untermeyer
Sunlight Shining of Red Leaves. Masayori
To Morning. Blake
Turning. Finch
Upon Phillis Walking in a Morning before
Sun-Rising. Cleveland
Very Early. Kuskin
Village people/ will be out picking young
greens, The. Tameie
Waking from Sleep. Bly
Wayside Station, The. Muir
Wet Morning. Frame
What Do I Care for Morning. Johnson
Will there really be a morning? Dickinson

Year's at the Spring, The. *Fr.* Pippa Passes.
Browning
Yonder. Ya'oz-kest
Morning-Glories
Haiku: "Morning-glories' white continues to
bloom." *Fr.* One Hundred Haiku in Free
Form. Hosai
Morning-Glories. Rokunyo
Morning glories: a single flower. *Fr.*
Eighty-seven Hokku. Buson
Morocco
Marrakech. Currey
Morris, William
Rondel: "Behold the works of William
Morris." *Unknown*
Morrison, Norman
Norman Morrison. Mitchell
Mortality
All the Flowers of the Spring. *Fr.* The
Devil's Law Case. Webster
April Mortality. Adams
Because I could not stop for death.
Dickinson
Black Faced Sheep, The. Hall
Cloud Chamber, The. Sze
Dead Fly. Ní Chuilleanáin
Death the Consequence of the Fall. *Fr.* The
State of Innocence. Dryden
Epitaph of Graunde [*or* La Graunde] Amoure,
The. *Fr.* The Pastime of Pleasure.
Hawes
Fear No More the Heat o' the Sun. *Fr.*
Cymbeline. Shakespeare
Fire in My Meditation Burned. Ainsworth
Life and Death. *Fr.* The Christian's Reply to
the Philosopher. Davenant
Little Sleep's-Head Sprouting Hair in the
Moonlight. Kinnell
Lullaby: "Lay your sleeping head, my love."
Auden
Man That Lives, The. *Unknown*
Man's Life. Hammond
Meditation of a Mariner. Auchterlonie
Mimnermus in Church. Cory
Murmur. Hecht
My Midnight Meditation. King
Oh [*or* O]! Why Should the Spirit of Mortal
Be Proud? Knox
Omnia Somnia. Sylvester
On a Child Who Lived One Minute.
Kennedy
On a Similar Occasion for the Year 1792.
Cowper
On the Vanity of Man's Life. *Unknown*
People. Yevtushenko
Piazza Piece. Ransom
Picture of Little T. C. in a Prospect of
Flowers, The. Marvell
Quickness. Vaughan
Respice Finem. Proctor
Rueful Lamentation on the Death of Queen
Elizabeth, A. More
Shortness and Misery of Life, The. Watts
Sic Vita. King
So, pure and dutiful, she sought that place.
Fr. The Mahabharata. *Unknown*
Stanzas Subjoined to the Yearly Bill of
Mortality of the Parish of All Saints,
Northampton; for the Year 1787. Cowper
Submission to Afflictive Providences. Watts
Sunlight on the Garden, The. MacNeice
Tetélestai. Aiken
Virtue. Herbert
Vitae Summa Brevis Spem Nos Vetat
Incohare Longam. Dowson
What's the Life of a Man? *Unknown*
World a hunting is, The. Drummond
Morticians. See **Undertakers.**
Mosby, John Singleton
Mosby at Hamilton. Cawein
Moses
Angels Came a-Mustering, The. *Unknown*

Burial of Moses, The. Alexander
Burning Bush, The. Nicholson
Death of Moses, The. *Unknown*
Deuteronomy. Bringhurst
Go Down, Moses. *Unknown*
Moses' Account. Fuest
Moses and Jesus. Zangwill
Moses and Joshua. Lasker-Schüler
Moses on Mount Nebo. Regelson
Murder of Moses, The. Shapiro
Our Teacher Moses. Glatstein
Pharao's Daughter. Moran
Soliloquy of One of the Spies Left in the
   Wilderness, A. Hopkins

Mosquitoes
Mosquito whirs each time, A. *Fr.*
   Eighty-seven Hokku. Buson
At my house small mosquitoes. *Fr.*
   Seventy-six Hokku. Basho
Baja. Stern
I Hate Mosquitoes. Shu Wei
Just one mosquito raises a fuss. *Fr.*
   Forty-four Hokku. Issa
Many mosquitoes bloated with blood. *Fr.*
   Twenty-nine Hokku. Taigi
Mosquito, The. Jones
Mosquito, The. Lawrence
Mosquito. Updike
Mosquito-buzz. Buson
Mosquitoes came in, and while the two. *Fr.*
   Thirteen Hokku. Raizan.
Sound of the rain, The. *Fr.* Twenty-nine
   Hokku. Taigi
They sucked me to their satisfaction. *Fr.*
   Inutsukuba Shu. *Unknown*

Moss
Moss-gathering. Roethke

Motels
In the Motel. Kennedy
On Motel Walls. Wagoner
Report from K9 Operator Rover on the Motel
   at Grand Island. Stafford
Soliloquy in a Motel. Gibson
Star Motel. Berkson
See als **Hotels.**

Mothers
Adversary, The. McGinley
Affliction of Margaret, The. Wordsworth
After Reading *Mickey in the Night Kitchen* for
   the Third Time before Bed. Dove
Apples. Kaufman
As Long as You're Happy. Myers
At My Mother's Bedside. Masters
Autumn. Untermeyer
Awful Mother, The. Griffin
Bad Mother, The. Griffin
Ballad of an Old Woman. Collymore
Be strong like a mansion built. *Fr.* Manyo
   Shu. Sakatabe Obitomaro
Because. McAuley
Belief. Miles
Birdless Country. Shimazaki Toson
Blessing, The. Kizer
Boy Changed into a Stag Cries Out at the
   Gate of Secrets, The. Juhász
Boy's Mother, A. Riley
Bravest Battle, The. Miller
Breaking Silence. Mirikitani
Buckdancer's Choice. Dickey
Canine Mother. Maraini
Carpenter's Wife, The. *Unknown*
Certain True Woords Spoken Concerning One
   Benet Corbett after Her Death. Corbett
Child Bearers, The. Sexton
Child Taken from the Mother, The. Pratt
Children of a Grieved Mother. Abi Shaqra
Coconut, The. Shimazaki Toson
Confession to Settle a Curse. Waldrop
Cradle Song: "Sleep, my child, my little
   daughter." *Unknown*
Cruel Mother, The. *Unknown*

Dear Mother. Leaf
Decision, The. *Fr.* The Unwed Mother.
   Bélot
Disquieting Muses, The. Plath
Distances. Gallagher
Distress. Griffin
Division of Parts, The. Sexton
Dragonfly-Mother, The. Levertov
Each Bird Walking. Gallagher
Earthquake. Heifetz-Tussman
Emma. Yvonne
Escorting My Mother Home.
   Rai San'yo
Even in a strange land I see. *Fr.* Manyo
   Shu. Hasetsukabe Mamaro
Evening Snow. Wojahn
External Element, The. McFadden
First Love. Dorcey
First Love. Hemschemeyer
Footnote to John II: 4. Mason
For an Obligate Parasite. Dugan
For My Mother. Bass
For My Mother. Glück
For My Mother. Voigt
For My Mother: Genevieve Jules Creeley.
   Creeley
For Shirley. Panek
Foundling, The. Alterman
From a New Height. Zanzotto
From an Asylum; Kathy Chattle to Her
   Mother, Ruth Arbeiter. Stevenson
From Old Mrs. Mo of Heng Yang: A Letter
   to My Son, Lo Fu. Yip Wai-lim
From the House of Yemanjá. Lorde
Grandchild. Kumin
Gray Woods Exploding, The. Birney
Hand That Rocks the Cradle Is the Hand That
   Rules the World, The. Wallace
Her Oak. Heifetz-Tussman
Here We Are. Jodorowsky
Home and Mother. Ramsey
Home Burial. Frost
Horse Show, The. Williams
"How's My Boy?" Dobell
I See My Girl. Olds
I Should Be Ashamed. Uvlunuaq
I Used to Watch You, Sleeping. *Fr.* My
   Mother's Birthday. Raine
In Memory of My Mother. Kavanagh
In the Ocean. Goedicke
Inheritance, The. Hawkins
Interior. Colum
Intruder, The. Kizer
Jessie Mitchell's Mother. Brooks
Kaddish. Ginsberg
Kineo Mountain. Wright
Lacking Sense, The. Hardy
Ladies and Gentlemen, my mother is. *Fr.*
   Mourning Pictures. Moore
Ladybird. Jonker
Lament to My Mother, A. Mhone
Late Mother, The. MacDonald
Legacy. Kalász
Let's Talk, Mother. Bruck
Letter to My Mother. Quasimodo
Lineage. *Fr.* Elegy. Bidart
Lines to Mother. Stein
Lonely Mother, The. Johnson
Look. Levine
Lost Children, The. Jarrell
Mama. Anyiam-St. John
Mama and Daughter. Hughes
Mary Complains to Other Mothers.
   Unknown
Men Tell and Talk. Francisco
Metamorphoses. Fuller
Miracle, The. Hawkins
Morning Song. Plath
Mother. Bland
Mother, The. Claus
Mother. Dow
Mother, The. Gardons

Mother. Heard
Mother. Helburn
Mother. Jong
Mother. Kelleher
Mother. Montoya
Mother. Morejón
Mother. Nagase Kiyoko
Mother, The. Palmer
Mother. Ramsey
Mother, The. Snodgrass
Mother. Vincent
Mother and Poet. Browning
Mother and Son. Heyen
Mother Dies. Saito Mokichi
Mother, Home, Heaven. Brown
Mother, I Am. Clifton
Mother, I Won't Forget. Vivaldi
Mother o' Mine. Kipling
Mother of the Groom. Heaney
Mother to Son. Hughes
Mother with Child. Keeshig-Tobias
Mothers. Auvaiyar
Mothers. Figueroa-Aymerich
Mothers. Giovanni
Mothers. Kakkai Patiniyar Naccellaiyar
Mothers. Kavarpentu
Mothers. Maturaipputan Ilanakanar
Mothers. Punkanuttiraiyar
Mothers: A Meditation. Brosmer
Mothers—and Others. Wells
Mother's Birthday. Wagenlander
Mothers, Daughters. Kaufman
Mother's Day. Castle
Mother's Day. Sala
Mother's Habits. Giovanni
Mother's Joy, A. Maxwell
Mother's List of Duties, A. Ponmutiyar
Mother's Love. Clapp
Mother's Nerves. Kennedy
Mother's Recall. Fordham
Mother's Song, The. *Unknown*
Mother's Voice. Creeley
Must Be the Season of the Witch. Alurista
My father has big skin like a soldier's cape.
   Khoury-Gata
My Mother. Campbell
My Mother. Ledwidge
My Mother. Mezey
My Mother. Wieners
My Mother and the Bed. Lifshin
My Mother on an Evening in Late Summer.
   Strand
My Mother Pieced Quilts. Acosta
My Mother Takes a Bath. Kageyama
My Mother Tries to Visit Me in the Dead of
   Night. Wakoski
My Mother Was Always Dressed. Luttinger
My Mother Would Be a Falconress. Duncan
My Mother's Body. Piercy
My Mother's Breakfront. Sternburg
My Mother's Feet. Plumly
My Mother's Garden. Allen
My Mother's Novel. Piercy
My Mother's Prayer. O'Kane
My Mother's Voice. Tucker
My Nightingale. Ausländer
My Trundle Bed. Baker
My Young Mother. Cooper
Names. Neef-Uthoff
Nancy Hanks, Mother of Abraham Lincoln.
   Lindsay
Night Feeding. Rukeyser
Nobody Knows but Mother. Morrison
Nothing to Say. Griffiths
Now It Is Broccoli. Tagami
Now or Never. Moffett
Oh, that my dear mother. *Fr.* Manyo Shu.
   Tsumori Okurusu
Old Arm-Chair, The. Cook
Old Ladies. Dromgoole
Old Mother Hubbard. Martin
Olga Poems. Levertov

On Mother's Day. Fisher
On the Death of Her Mother. Rukeyser
On the Receipt of My Mother's Picture out of
  Norfolk. Cowper
One Who Struggles, The. Toller
Patches. Shelton
Perfect Mother, The. Griffin
Photo of Emily, The. Ferlinghetti
Picture memory brings to me, A. *Fr. My
  Trust.* Whittier
Poem for My Mother. Fox
Poems. Gildner
Praise Song for My Mother. Nichols
Prayer to My Mother. Pasolini
Put Your Mother on the Ceiling. Pape
Queen Charming. Hadas
Question, The. Rukeyser
Reading Mother, The. Gillilan
Recollection. Govan
Reflections. Barrows
Reunion. Herzberg
Revelation. Gregory
Revelation. Warren
Revenge Fable. Hughes
Reverie of a Mum. Keesing
Riddle in the Garden. Warren
Rock Me to Sleep, [Mother] Allen
Ruth. McElroy
Saw You among Trees. Tussman
Second Heart, The. Wittlinger
She Didn't Even Wave. Ai
She Would Have Roses. Ingraham
She'd Say. Davey
Sick Child, The. Stevenson
Sister Mother. Catri
Sitting. Griffin
Somebody's Mother. Brine
Song for the Burial of My Mother.
  Shimazaki Toson
Song of the Old Mother, The. Yeats
Song: Thoughts of a Traveler on the Chikuma
  River. Toson
Sonnet to My Mother. Barker
Sonnet to My Mother, A. Heine
Stabat Mater. Hunt
Survivors, The. Hemschemeyer
Taint. Socolow
Teeth. Griffin
That There Should Be Laughter. Banda
There was an old woman who lived in a shoe.
  Mother Goose
Tissue. Griffin
To Mainz! Krechel
To Mother. Drown
To My Mother. Colonna
To My Mother. Fordham
To My Mother. Poe
To My Mother. Ray
To My Mothers. Ammer
To Someone. Kotaro
To the Anxious Mother. Malangatana
To the Mothers. Toller
Trying On for Size. Dorcey
Upon a Young Mother of Many Children.
  Herrick
Variations on Southern Themes. Justice
Violets for Mother. Kaneko
Way It Is, The. Oden
What Frank, Martha and I Know about the
  Desert. Sadongei
What'll the Neighbours Say? Kerr
When a Girl Looks Down. Smith
When Mother Reads Aloud. *Unknown*
Which Loved Best? "Allison"
Whipping, The. Hayden
Who a Mother Is. Watson
Who can find a virtuous woman? for her price
  is far above rubies. *Fr. Proverbs.*
With the ships all in trim. *Fr. Manyo Shu.*
  Mariko Omaro
Woman Back in the Kitchen, The. Ingraham
Words from a Bottle. Lee

Written when the Poet Was Seventy-six. *Fr.*
  Thirty Tanka. Shunzei
Your Mother. Cornish
*Tangled Vines; a Collection of Mother and
  Daughter Poems* (TV). Lyn Lifshin, ed.

Mother's Day
Hand That Rocks the Cradle Is the Hand That
  Rules the World, The. Wallace
Mother's Day. Becker
Mothers of Men, The. Miller

Mothers-in-Law
His Mother-in-Law. Parke
Man Arrested in Hacking Death Tells Police
  He Mistook Mother-in-Law for Raccoon.
  Ludvigson
"Mother-in-Law Is Cruel." Cheng Hsieh
Prince Robert. *Unknown*
Unexpected Pleasure, An. *Unknown*
Unrecorded Speech. Adams

Moths
Book Moth: "A moth ate a word. To me it
  seemed." *Fr.* Riddles (Exeter Book).
  Cynewulf
Confusion. Cruz
Ghost Moth, The. Edmond
Great Moth, The. Gittings
Lying Awake. Snodgrass
Moth, The. Al-Najafi
Moth, A. Baildon
Moth, The. De la Mare
Moth-Song. Cortissoz
Moth-Terror. De Casseres
Moths, The. Jackson
Moths, The. O Riordain
Near Dusk. Auslander
Thunder Moth. Miyoshi Tatsuji
Tyranny of Moths. Vizenor
Warning, The. Crapsey

Motion Pictures
About Motion Pictures. Darr
At a Private Showing in 1982. Kumin
Ave Maria. O'Hara
Curse of the Cat Woman. Field
Day with the Foreign Legion, A.
  Whittemore
Déjà, Indeed. Updike
Documentary. Stroud
Film, A. Goldbarth
Frankenstein. Field
Horror Movie. Moss
If Life's a Lousy Picture, Why Not Leave
  before the End. McGough
Image of Leda, An. O'Hara
Ingmar Bergman's "Seventh Seal." Duncan
Movie-Going. Hollander
Movies, The. Gilbert
Movies for the Home. Moss
Newsreel. Day Lewis
Newsreel. *Fr.* Shooting Script. Rich
Old Movies. Cotton
Star & Garter Theater. Schmitz
This world/ is amazingly flat.
  Gorbanyevskaya
To the Film Industry in Crisis. O'Hara
Triple Feature. Levertov
Village Cinema, The. Grochowiak
Watching War Movies. Stryk
Where Are You Now Superman? Patten
Why I Like Movies. Jones

Motley, John Lothrop
In Memory of John Lothrop Motley. Bryant

Motor Boats
Riding in a Motor Boat. Baruch

Motorcycles and Motorcycling
Motorbike, A. Hughes
Motorcycle. Pray
Motorcycle Irene. Spence
Motorcycle Racer Thinks of Quitting.
  Butcher
On the Move. Gunn

Unsettled Motorcyclist's Vision of His Death,
  The. Gunn
What the Motorcycle Said. Van Duyn

Mount Olivet
Up to Mount Olivet. *Fr.* Divine Meditations.
  Alabaster

Mount Saint Helens, Washington
Loo-wit. Rose

Mount Tamalpais
Circumambulation of Mt. Tamalpais. Hoyem

Mount Vernon, Virginia
Monument and the Shrine, The. Logan
Mount Vernon, the Home of Washington.
  Day
Visiting Mount Vernon and Paying Homage at
  George Washingon's Burial Vault. K'ang
  Yu-wei

Mountain Beavers
Looking for Mountain Beavers. Wagoner

Mountain Climbing
Alpine. Thomas
Climb in Torridon. Macrow
Climber Surveys His Mountain, The. Ouston
Climbing in Glencoe. Young
Climbing Rope, The. Stuart
Climbing T'ai Mountain. Yüan Mei
Climbing the Mountain. Chiang Hsun
Climbing the peaks of Tsukuba. *Fr.* Manyo
  Shu. Mushimaro
Climbing Zero Gully. Morley
David. Birney
De Gustibus. Hankin
Doing the Dubhs. *Unknown*
Finding a Poem. Merriam
Flower Herding on Mount Monadnock.
  Kinnell
How Small Is Man. Blackie
In Memoriam. Gingell
Last Defile, The. Carmichael
Last of the Grand Old Masters, The. Patey
Lines. Smith
Lost Leader, The. Fraser
Marriage on a Mountain Ridge. Conn
Mountain Creed. Rae
Mountain Days. Fraser
Mountaineering Bus. McOwan
My lord came to survey. *Fr.* Manyo Shu.
  Mushimaro
O Aa the Manly Sports. Annand
On a Cold Day I Climbed Tiger Hill With
  Professor Ho. Mo Shih-lung
On Falling. *Fr.* Men on Ice. Greig
On Looking at an Old Climbing Photograph.
  Fraser
On Scafell Pike. Walker
One Thousand Feet of Shadow. Craig
Pitch Seven. Brown
Scottish Mountaineering Club Song, The.
  Stott
Sestina: Here in Katmandu. Justice
Spring Mountain Climb. Eberhart
Story, A. Stafford
Three Girls on a Buttress. Nisbet
What Called Me to the Heights. Pilkington
Wingwalking in Oregon. Peterson

Mountain Lions
Last Mountain Lion on Maple Crest
  Mountain, The. Meinke
Mountain Lion. Lawrence

Mountains
As spring has come when the mist trails. *Fr.*
  Manyo Shu. Kamo Taruhito
I Love Mountains. Ho Shao-chi
In the land of Koshi. *Fr.* Manyo Shu.
  Yakamochi
Lofty beyond the mountains. *Fr.* Manyo
  Shu. Ikenushi
Mount Kagu strove with Mount Miminashi.
  Fr. Manyo Shu. Tenji
Mountaintop: as far as I can see. *Fr.*
  Forty-four Tanka. Wakayama Bokusui

On the peak of Mimiga of fair Yoshinu. *Fr.* Manyo Shu. Temmu

Though many are the lofty mountains. *Fr.* Manyo Shu. Tajihi Kunihito

See also **Hills and Mountains.**

Mourning

At the Draper's. Hardy

Ballad: "He went with another." Mistral

Ballade: "Lone am I, and would be." Pisan

Because limits are set. *Fr.* A Compendium of Good Tanka. Teika

Bustle in a house, The. Dickinson

Consoling Wu Te-cheng on the Death of His Son. Shen Chou

Cuckoo, The. Thomas

Dark house, by which once more I stand. *Fr.* In Memoriam A. H. H. Tennyson

Elegy for My Father. Moss

Every Day. MacCaig

Fifth Day, The. Kilpi

Gray Light, The. Leyeles

Here shift the scene, to represent. *Fr.* Verses on the Death of Doctor Swift [D.S.P.D., Occasioned by Reading a Maxim in Rochefoucauld]. Swift

John Kinsella's Lament for Mrs. Mary Moore. Yeats

Joyce: By Herself and Her Friends. Grenfell

Kaddish. Ginsberg

Lament: "Even beauty must die! That which subdues both gods and mortals." Schiller

Lament for Tadhg Cronin's Children. Hartnett

Like the yu'ub wood bell tied to gelded camels that are running away. Ugaas

Lost Love. Graves

Lovely White Flowers. Cavafy

Minyan, The. Myers

Morning. Mahdi

Morning sky was overcast, The. *Fr.* Manyo Shu. *Unknown*

Mourn for Yourself. Keating

Mourning Pablo Neruda. Bly

Mourning-Song for Rangiaho, A. Herea

My Father's Memorial Day. Amichai

Not to Be Born. Sutton

Oh! sing unto my roundelay [*or* O! Synge untoe mie roundelaie]. *Fr.* Aella; a Tragycal Enterlude. Chatterton

On My First Son [*or* Sonne]. Jonson

Seven treasures, The. *Fr.* Manyo Shu. Okura

Song: "When I am dead, my dearest." Rossetti

Sonnet on the Death of Mr. Richard West. Gray

Sorrow. Lawrence

Sun is soon to rise as bright, The. *Fr.* Songs on the Death of Children. Rückert

Surprised by Joy [Impatient as the Wind] Wordsworth

Tam Cari Capitis. MacNeice

Thou Ling'ring Star. Burns

To Joshua. Ellis

Unquiet Grave, The. *Unknown*

Valediction: Forbidding Mourning, A. Donne

Valediction Forbidding Mourning, A. Rich

Wake of William Orr, The. Drennan

World of dew is, The. Issa

Yahrzeit. Jaffe

You could sit there with the stains on your shoes. *Fr.* Home Burial. Frost

See also **Funerals; Grief.**

Mouths

Her Mouth. Aldington

Movies. *See* **Motion Pictures.**

Moving and Movers

Almost Grown. Ai

In a U-Haul North of Damascus. Bottoms

Moving. McFatter

Moving. Steele

Moving In. Engle

Moving In. Miles

New House, The. Rutsala

Note to the Previous Tenants. Updike

October 1. Shapiro

Photograph of Haymaker, 1890. Holden

Removal from Terry Street, A. Dunn

Mowing and Mowers

Hay-Time; or, The Constant Lovers. A Pastoral. Relph

Haymaking. Thomas

Lost. Brand

Lying in the Grass. Gosse

Mower, The. *Unknown*

Mower against Gardens, The. Marvell

Mower's Song, The. Marvell

Mowing. Frost

Mowing, The. Roberts

Needs. Ammons

Old Field Mowed, An. Meredith

Reapers. Toomer

Scythe Song. Lang

Scything. Dowling

Tuft of Flowers, The. Frost

Youth Mowing, A. Lawrence

Mozambique

Guerilla, The. *Unknown*

Here We Were Born. Santos

My Brother: ("My brother is not he who was born"). *Unknown*

Mozart, Wolfgang Amadeus

Corner Knot, The. Graves

Mozart's Grave. Mowrer

Mud

Mud. Boyden

Muddy Puddle, The. Lee

Muffins

Aunt Nerissa's Muffin. Irwin

Muffs

On an Old Muff. Locker-Lampson

See also **Gloves; Mittens.**

Muhammad

Birth (al-Maulid). Al-Majdhoub

Lilies for the Prophet. Al-Mala'ika

Mulberry Trees

Tapestry Trees. Morris

Mules

Cool Mule. Schreiber

Kicking Mule, The. *Unknown*

Mule, The. Merrill

Mules. Walker

My Father Washes His Hands. Chappell

My Sweetie's a Mule in the Mine. *Unknown*

Mummies

In the Museum. Gardner

Invocation to the Mummy. Artaud

Land of Metamorphoses, The. Daumal

Mummy of a Lady Named Jemutesonekh XXI Dynasty. James

Punishment. Heaney

Tollund Man, The. Claus

Tollund Man, The. Heaney

Wanting a Mummy. McPherson

Mumps

Mumps. Roberts

Munch, Edvard

Edvard Munch. Wright

Munch's Scream. Hall

Murder and Murderers

Ashland Tragedy, The. Adams

Assassination. Lee

Autumnal Equinox. Wilson

Babylon; or, The Bonnie Banks o' Fordie. *Unknown*

Bad Man Ballad. *Unknown*

Ballad of a Barber, The. Beardsley

Ballad of Reading Gaol, The. Wilde

Ballad of William Bloat, The. *Unknown*

Bonny Earl of Murray, The. *Unknown*

Cheerful Chilterns, The. Sidgwick

Constance Kent. *Unknown*

Constant Farmer's Son, The. *Unknown*

Crime Club. Kees

Cruel Mother, The. *Unknown*

Dance a Ghost. "Chrystos"

Death of Samuel Adams, The. *Unknown*

Delia Holmes ("Delia, Delia, why didn't you run?"). Ruff

Dog Poisoner, The. Wilson

Edwin in the Lowlands Low. *Unknown*

Ella Speed. *Unknown*

Ellen Flannery. *Unknown*

Farewell to Barn and Stack and Tree. *Fr.* A Shropshire Lad. Housman

Florella; or, The Jealous Lover. *Unknown*

For Andy Goodman—Michael Schwerner—and James Chaney. Walker

For the One Who Would Take Man's Life in His Hands. Schwartz

Fragment from the Elizabethans. Bridges-Adams

Frankie Blues. *Unknown*

Ghost Story. Pack

Gosport Tragedy, The. *Unknown*

Great Palaces of Versailles, The. Dove

He Fell among Thieves. Newbolt

Hitchhiker, The. Ai

Hugh of Lincoln. *Unknown*

I Should Be Ashamed. Uvlunuaq

If it were done when 'tis done, then 'twere well. *Fr.* Macbeth. Shakespeare

If Justice Moved. Sellers

Inquest, The. Davies

It is the cause, it is the cause, my soul. *Fr.* Othello. Shakespeare

John Adkins' Farewell. *Unknown*

John Hardy. *Unknown*

Johnson-Jinkson. *Unknown*

Kid, The. Ai

Lady Isabella's Tragedy, The. *Unknown*

Life of the Mannings. *Unknown*

Little Musgrave and Lady Barnard. *Unknown*

Little Sir Hugh. *Unknown*

Loose Woman. Kennedy

Lord Randal. *Unknown*

Lula Vires. *Unknown*

McCaffery. *Unknown*

Man Arrested in Hacking Death Tells Police He Mistook Mother-in-Law for Raccoon. Ludvigson

Man He Killed, The. Hardy

Mary in the Silvery Tide. *Unknown*

Murder of Goins, The. *Unknown*

Murder of Maria Marten, The. Corder

Murdered Girl Is Found on a Bridge, The. Hayman

Murderer, The. Petrie

Murderer, The. Smith

On the Duke of Buckingham, Slain by Felton, the 23rd August, 1628. Felltham

Pearl Bryan. *Unknown*

Peddler and His Wife, The. *Unknown*

Poem for Jacqueline Hill. *Unknown*

Poor Ellen Smith. *Unknown*

Poor Omie. *Unknown*

Porphyria's Lover. Browning

Pretty Polly. *Unknown*

Prince Robert. *Unknown*

Revolutionary Petunias. Walker

Robin Hood's Death. *Unknown*

Rose Connoley. *Unknown*

Sacrifice of a Virgin in the Mayan Ball Court. Dubie

Sam Hall. *Unknown*

Scenery. Joans

Shooting, The. Tohe

Shooting of Dan McGrew, The. Service

Silvery Tide, The. *Unknown*

Sir Hugh; or, The Jew's Daughter. *Unknown*

Southern Cop. Brown

Stab, The. Harney

Summer Killer. Broughton
To an Avenue Sport. Collins
To the Spirit of Monahsetah. DeClue
Two Sisters, The. *Unknown*
Under the Green Ceiling. Dobyns
Wake of William Orr, The. Drennan
Wexford Girl, The ("My tender parents
   brought me here"). *Unknown*
Young Hunting. *Unknown*
Murfreesboro, Battle of (1862–1863)
Battle of Murfreesboro, The. Cornwallis
Muses
Admonition to the Muse. Taylor
Angel with Horn. Szécsi
I now solicit not the Muses nine. *Fr.* A
   Mock Invocation to Genius. Woty
Invocation to the Muse. Ray
Mock Translation from the Greek. Dugan
Muse, The. Davies
Muse. Wagoner
Muse in the New World, The. *Fr.* Song of
   the Exposition. Whitman
Saint Harmony my patroness. Goodman
To the Muses. Blake
Museums
Antwerp: Musée Des Beaux-Arts. Ross
At the National Gallery. Kazantzis
Floridian Museum of Art, A. Whittemore
Historical Museum, Manitoulin Island.
   Mueller
Homage to the British Museum. Empson
In a Country Museum. Beer
In Galleries. Jarrell
In the Egyptian Museum. Lewis
In the Local Museum. De la Mare
In the Museum. Gardner
Leaving the Tate. Adcock
Municipal Gallery Revisited, The. Yeats
Musée des Beaux Arts. Auden
Museum of the Second Creation, The.
   McPherson
Museum Piece. Wilbur
Museums. MacNeice
National Gallery, The. MacNeice
Night in the Royal Ontario Museum, A.
   Atwood
Our Bias. Auden
Pitt-Rivers Museum, Oxford, The. Fenton
Saturday under the Sky. Soto
Tutankhamen. Dickey
Mushrooms
Autumn Mushrooms. Mackenzie
Fairy Ring, The. Young
Gathering Mushrooms. Muldoon
Morels. Smith
Mushroom Hunting in Late August,
   Peterborough, N.H. Blumenthal
Mushrooms. Dowling
Mushrooms. Plath
On a Painting of Mushrooms. Yün
   Shou-p'ing
Toadstool Wood, The. Reeves
Toadstools. Fleming
Wild Mushroom, The. Snyder
Music and Musicians
Abt Vogler. Browning
Accompanist, The. Matthews
Apocalypse. Enright
At a Bach Concert. Rich
At the Band Concert. Brinnin
Bach. Manner
Bagpipe Music. MacNeice
Bard. Bantock
Barrel-Organ, The. Noyes
Battle Report. Kaufman
Blind men, blind men. *Unknown*
Blind Musician, The. Taha
Blues Note. Kaufman
Brain Drain. "Mighty Chalkdust"
Cadenza. Hughes
Calyx of the Oboe Breaks, The. Aiken

Cello, The. Gilder
Choral Symphony Conductor. Coates
Church-Music[k]. Herbert
Country Dance. Baugh
Daybreak in Alabama. Hughes
Dead Musicians. Sassoon
Dear John, Dear Coltrane. Harper
Don. McNeill
Entertainment Industry, The. *Fr.* The Vision
   of Piers Plowman. Langland
Epitaph upon the Celebrated Claudy Phillips,
   Musician, Who Died Very Poor, An.
   Johnson
Evening Musicale. McGinley
Festival in Fishing Village No. 25. Park
   Je-chun
Fiddler of Dooney, The. Yeats
Flute-Players. Hoyland
For the spiritual musick is as follows. *Fr.*
   Jubilate Agno. Smart
Free Thoughts on Several Eminent
   Composers. Lamb
Fritz. Stern
Fugue, A. Voigt
Garden of Song, The. Ibn Ezra
German Organ. Artaud
Guide to the Symphony. Kees
Guitarist Tunes Up, The. Cornford
Harlem Sounds: Hallelujah Corner. Browne
Harper, The. *Unknown*
Hearing Flutes along the Road in the Autumn
   Night. Fuyutsugu
Here Where Coltrane Is. Harper
Hex on the Mexican X, A. McCord
How High the Moon. Jeffers
Hugging the Jukebox. Nye
Hymn of Pan. Shelley
I Was Fair Beat. Garioch
In a Music-Hall. Davidson
In Commendation of Music. Strode
In Memory of Bryan Lathrop. Masters
In Praise of Music in Time of Pestilence.
   Hine
It's All in Your Head. Waniek
Jazz Fantasia. Sandburg
Johann Joachim Quantz's Five Lessons.
   Graham
Juke Box Love Song. Hughes
Lamda. Tolson
Lament for the O'Neills. Montague
Lark Now Leaves His Water [*or* Wat'ry]
   Nest. Davenant
Late Stravinsky Listening to Late Beethoven.
   Spender
L'Envoi: "Now in a thought, now in a
   shadowed word." Robinson
Lester Leaps In. Young
Lives of the Great Composers. Gioia
Lost Chord, A. Procter
Lyre Player, The. George
Make Music with Your Life. O'Meally
Meet the Supremes. Trinidad
Military Harpist, The. Pitter
Mr. Brunt. Siegel
Music. Dunbar-Nelson
Music. Emerson
Music. Heard
Music. Herrick
Music ("Down the quiet eve"). *Fr.* In
   Hospital. Henley
Music in Camp. Thompson
Music Lessons. Oliver
Music Makers, The. Buddingh'
Music of the Future, The. Herford
Musical Instrument, A. Browning
Musician. Bogan
Musician of Saint-Merry, The. Apollinaire
My father played the melodion. *Fr.* A
   Christmas Childhood. Kavanagh
Narnian Suite. Lewis
New Music. Harwood

Ninth Symphony of Beethoven Understood at
   Last as a Sexual Message, The. Rich
Nuala's Fiddle. O Canainn
Oh fine, oh lovely! *Unknown*
Old Fisherman with Guitar. Brown
Old Gramophone Records. Kirkup
Old Guitar, The. Hollander
Old Story Is Retold, An. Hollander
On Hearing a Symphony of Beethoven.
   Millay
On Hearing Mrs. Woodhouse Play the
   Harpsichord. Davies
On Music. Landor
On the Death of Phillips. *Unknown*
Orchestra. Saner
Orchestra, The. Williams
Orpheus. Roberts
Orpheus with His Lute [Made Trees]. *Fr.*
   King Henry VIII. Shakespeare
Other Great Composers, The. Ash
Overture. Pastan
Percussions. Welburn
Perfect Orchestra, The. Ray
Peter Quince at the Clavier. Stevens
Piano. Lawrence
Piano. Shapiro
Piano after War. Brooks
Piano and Drums. Okara
Piano Player Explains Himself, The.
   Grossman
Piano Practice. Moss
Piper, A [*or* The]. "O'Sullivan"
Piping Down the Valleys Wild. *Fr.* Songs of
   Innocence. Blake.
Recital. Updike
River Water Music. Eberhart
Rock 'n' Roll. Frost
Romance. Artaud
Romance. Stern
Rubinstein Staccato Etude, The. Dett
Saxophonetyx. Zarco
Schumann's Sonata in A Minor. Thaxter
Second Violinist's Son, The. Greger
Selfsame Song, The. Hardy
Shooting Script, A. Heaney
Singers to Come. Meynell
Song, A: "Music, thou queen of souls, get up
   and string." Randolph
Song of the Banjo, The. Kipling
Songs, The. Bell
Sonnet: "My lute, be as thou wast [*or* wert]
   when thou didst grow." Drummond
Soul. Graham
Spanish Johnny. Cather
Spirits Unchained. Kgositsile
Street Music. Angell
Supermarket in Guadalajara, Mexico, A.
   Levertov
Supremes, The. Jarman
Syringa. Ashbery
Tambour. Vas
Telemann to A.C. Chasin
Ten Tom-Toms. Fitzpatrick
Thanking My Mother for Piano Lessons.
   Wakoski
There'd be an orchestra. *Fr.*
   Thousand-and-First Ship. Fitzgerald
This Is Our Music. Leong
Three Musicians, The. Beardsley
To———. Braithwaite
To His Friend Master R.L., In Praise of
   Music and Poetry. Barnfield
To Lucasta. Lovelace
To Melody. Allen
To Music. Herrick
To Music Bent Is My Retired Mind.
   Campion
To the One of Fictive Music. Stevens
Toccata of Galuppi's, A. Browning
Trenchtown Rock. Marley
Two Musicians, The. Ray

Unrelenting Flood. Matthews
Valentine for Ben Franklin Who Drives a
  Truck in California, A. Wakoski
Victor Dog, The. Merrill
Violinist, The. Lampman
Vow. Updike
We Dance Like Ella Riffs. Rodgers
Weeping and Wailing. Stern
When de Saints Go Ma'chin' Home. Brown
When I take the *koto*, sobs break forth. *Fr.*
  Manyo Shu. *Unknown*
Untune the Sky (UnS). Helen Plotz, ed.
Music Festivals
  Woodstock. Mitchell
Music Halls
  In a Music-Hall. Davidson
Music Lessons
  To a Daughter at Fourteen Forsaking the
    Violin. Oles
Musk Oxen
  Arctic Ox, The. Moore
  Long River, The. Hall
  See also **Ovibos.**
Muslims
  Hush Honey. Saunders
Mussels
  There's Life in a Mussel; a Meditation.
    Farewell
Mustaches
  Mustacheless Bard, A. Coogler
Mutiny
  Captain, The. Tennyson
Mysticism
  Kabbalist, The. Eibel
  Mystic, The. Rice
  Waiting for the Transformation. Minty
  *Tongues of Fire; an Anthology of Religious
    and Poetic Experience* (TOF). Karen
    Armstrong, ed.
Mythology
  Bath in Pylos, The. Devecseri
  Boy Who Became Sky, The. Wagoner
  Daedalus. Sikelianos
  Europa. Walcott
  Interruption. Cavafy
  Ionic. Cavafy
  Ithaka. Cavafy
  Kaisarion. Cavafy
  On Acrocorinth. Sikelianos
  One of Their Gods. Cavafy
  Sabrina. *Fr.* Comus; a Masque Presented at
    Ludlow Castle. Milton
  Salmon Boy. Wagoner
  Story of Phoebus and Daphne Applyed, The.
    Waller
  Tithonus. Tennyson

N

Nabokov, Vladimir
  Nabokov's Death. Matthews
Nagasaki, Japan
  Wedding Day at Nagasaki. Hall
Nagyszombat, Battle of (1704)
  Nagyszombat, 1704. Vas
Nalli
  Price of Giving Too Much, The. Vanparanar
Names
  Adam's Task. Hollander
  American Names. Benét
  Angel of Death, The. *Unknown*
  Career Women Who Marry Today. Pastor
  Changeling VIII. Gunnars
  Choosing a Name. Lamb
  Crow, Straight Flier, but Dark. Firestone
  Dirty Work on the Appellation Trail. Cole
  Empty Dwelling Places. Patchen

Family Name, The. Lamb
"Heaven and earth." *Fr.* Manyo Shu.
  Hitomaro
How a Girl Got Her Chinese Name. Wong
Ill Met by Zenith. Nash
In America. Sheridan
Indian Names. Sigourney
It's in the Name. Tsui
John. Elliott
Liberty. Éluard
Lovely Rivers and Lakes of Maine, The.
  Wallis
Makers, The. Nemerov
Michael. Sheridan
Miss M. F. H. E. I. I. Jones. Kuskin
Mutual Problem. Cole
My Name. Wain
My Name and I. Graves
Name, A. Chernoff
Names, The. Edmond
Nomen. Madgett
Nomenclature. Benét
Song for My Name. Hogan
Song to the Most Holy Name of Jesus.
  Córdova y Bocanegra
True Name. Bonnefoy
Unfamiliar Quartet. Benét
Well-intentioned Question, The. Rose
What do I care if my name. *Fr.* Manyo Shu.
  Otomo no Sakanoe
With her basket, her basket. *Fr.* Manyo
  Shu. Yuryaku
See also **Place Names.**
Nampi Netunceliyan
  Elegy: "He has held." Perevin Muruvalar
Namur, Belgium
  English Ballad, on the Taking of Namur by
    the King of Great Britain, 1695, An. Prior
Nantucket, Massachusetts
  Nantucket. Williams
  Phenomenal Survivals of Death in Nantucket.
    Glück
  Quaker Graveyard in Nantucket, The.
    Lowell
  Wisdom. Teasdale
  Wood Song. Teasdale
**Napier, Robert Cornelis, 1st Baron Napier of
  Magdala**
  Lost Colors, The. Ward
Naples, Italy
  Literature and Poetry. Jacob
  Naples. Rogers
  Naples Again. Freeman
  Napoli Again. Hugo
  Nocturne: "long arm embossed with gold
    slides from the tree tops, A." Fargue
  To Naples. Mallalieu
Napoleon I
  Advice to a Raven in Russia [December,
    1812]. Barlow
  Buonaparte. Tennyson
  Epistle to the Emperor Napoleon (1810).
    Salm-Dyck
  Exile at Rest, The. Pierpont
  Feelings of a Republican on the Fall of
    Bonaparte. Shelley
  Funeral of Napoleon I. Hagarty
  Incident of the French Camp. Browning
  Lines Written on Hearing the News of the
    Death of Napoleon. Shelley
  March to Moscow, The. Southey
  Napoleon. De la Mare
  Napoleon and the British Sailor. Campbell
  October 1803. Wordsworth
Napoleon III
  Poster of Our Dazzling Victory at
    Saarbrucken, A. *Fr.* Eighteen-Seventy.
    Arthur Rimbaud
Napoleonic Wars
  Advice to a Raven in Russia [December,
    1812]. Barlow

Banks of the Nile, The. *Unknown*
Battle of the Baltic. Campbell
Buonaparte. Tennyson
Burial of Sir John Moore after [*or* at]
  Corunna, The. Wolfe
Fears in Solitude. Coleridge
Incident of the French Camp. Browning
November, 1806. Wordsworth
Plains of Waterloo, The. *Unknown*
Russia 1812. Hugo
There was a sound of revelry by night. *Fr.*
  Childe Harold's Pilgrimage. Byron
To the Men of Kent. Wordsworth
Year 1812, The. Davie
Nara, Japan
  City of Nara of good blue clay, The. *Fr.*
    Manyo Shu. Ono no Oyu
Narcissism
  Laus Virginitatis. Symons
  Love Affair, The. Edson
  Narcissus. Efrat
Narcissus (flower)
  Among the Narcissi. Plath
  Two Voices in a Meadow. Wilbur
  Window Ledge in the Atom Age. White
Narcissus (mythology)
  Farewell to Narcissus. Horan
  Fate of Narcissus, The. *Fr.* Albion's
    England. Warner
  Narcissus. Gullans
  Narcissus. Petersen
Narcotics. *See* Drug Addiction.
Nash, Richard (Beau Nash)
  On Mr. Nash's Picture at Full Length.
    Brereton
Nasturtiums
  Big Nasturtiums, The. Hale
Nationalism
  On National Vanity. McFarlane
Nativity, The. *See* Christmas.
Naturalists
  Death of a Naturalist. Heaney
  Naturalist's Summer-Evening Walk, The.
    White
Nature
  All Nature Has a Voice to Tell. Lawson
  All That's Past. De la Mare
  All the Scenes of Nature Quicken. Smart
  All Things Bright and Beautiful. Alexander
  Almighty Maker God! *Fr.* Sincere Praise.
    Watts
  And what if all Nature ratify this merciless
    outrage? *Unknown*
  Animal, Vegetable and Mineral. Bogan
  Assynt. Gilchrist
  At Nature's Shrine. Ray
  Beatus Vir. Le Gallienne
  Blue Horses. Roberson
  Book, The. Drummond
  Bring me the sunset in a cup. Dickinson
  By Frazier Creek Falls. Snyder
  Change and Immutability. Scroggie
  Chant Out of Doors, A. Wilkinson
  Comparison and Complaint, The. Watts
  Contemplations. Bradstreet
  Corsons Inlet. Ammons
  Cosmic Fabric, The. Polonsky
  Creative Force. Hadden
  Cut the Grass. Ammons
  Dauncing (bright Lady) then began to bee.
    Fr. Orchestra; or, A Poem[e] of
    Da[u]ncing. Davies
  Design. Frost
  Dislike of Nature. Tozaburo
  Dry Loaf. Stevens
  Each and All. Emerson
  Enough. Finkel
  Eternity of Nature, The. Clare
  Expostulation and Reply. Wordsworth
  Fall of Rome, The. Auden

Father, thy hand/ Hath reared. *Fr.* A Forest Hymn. Bryant
Field of Light, A. Roethke
For My Grandmother, Bridget Halpin. Hartnett
Give Me the Splendid Silent Sun. Whitman
Glory of Nature, The. Tennyson
God of the Granite and the Rose! *Fr.* Reconciliation. Doten
God's Grandeur. Hopkins
God's World. Keeling
God's World. Millay
Grandfather's Last Letter, A. Dubie
Gravelly Run. Ammons
Green Symphony. Fletcher
Grongar Hill. Dyer
Happy Swain, The. Philips
Heptonstall Old Church. Hughes
Highland Loves. McOwan
Holding the Mirror Up to Nature. Nemerov
How to See Deer. Booth
I taste a liquor never brewed. Dickinson
In a Wood. Hardy
In Blackwater Woods. Oliver
In the Fields. Mew
Instability. Ray
Inward Morning, The. Thoreau
Lachesis Net. Mustapää
Lines Written in Early Spring. Wordsworth
Long spring day, The. *Fr.* Manyo Shu. Ikusa
Loving and Liking. Wordsworth
Lowest Trees Have Tops, the Ant her Gall, The. Dyer
Marban, a Hermit Speaks. *Unknown*
Memories of a Dorset Childhood in the 1730's. *Fr.* The Life of Hubert. Cole.
Minimal, The. Roethke
Miracle, The. De la Mare
Mont Blanc. Shelley
Mower against Gardens, The. Marvell
Nature. Longfellow
Nature. Stone
Nature. Thoreau
Nature and the Poets. *Fr.* The Minstrel. Beattie
Nature Be Damned. Wilkinson
Nature Is. Prelutsky
Nature one hour appears a thing unsexed. *Fr.* Contemplation. Thompson
Nature's Lineaments. Graves
Nature's Minor Chords. Ray
Nature's Questioning. Hardy
Nature's Uplifting. Ray
Neighbors. Ammons
Nocturnal Reverie, A. Winchilsea
Ode: "Spacious firmament on high, The." Addison
Ode to the Spirit of Earth in Autumn. Meredith
Of the Day Estivall. Hume
On a Bank [*or* Banck] asl I Sat [*or* Sate] a-Fishing; a Description of the Spring. Wotton
On the Religion of Nature. Freneau
On the Uniformity and Perfection of Nature. Freneau
Oneness of the Philosopher with Nature, The. Chesterton
Oracle. Finkel
Out-of-Doors. Whitaker
Over-Heart, The. Whittier
Pause. Bethell
Persistence of Nature in Our Lives, The. Hudgins
Pied Beauty. Hopkins
Poets Love Nature. Clare
Possession. *Unknown*
Prayer, A: "O Earth, O dewy mother, breathe on us." Lampman

Prayer, A: "Teach me, Father, how to go." Markham
Prayer, A: "Tend me my birds, and bring again." Gale
Prelude: "Along the roadside, like the flowers of gold." *Fr.* Among the Hills. Whittier
Prelude: "Still south I went and west and south again." Synge
Proem: "There is no rhyme that is half so sweet." Cawein
Quiet Work. Arnold
Rainy Summer, The. Meynell
Regeneration. Vaughan
River Water Music. Eberhart
Rondel: "World is taking off her clothes, The." Kennedy
Rooftop, The. Gunn
St. Philip and St. James. *Fr.* Hymns and Spiritual Songs. Smart
Second Wisdom. Robinson
Since I, by My Good Fortune, Return to Look On. Gambara
Sky is low, the clouds are mean, The. Dickinson
Sky's unresting cloudland, that with varying play, The. *Fr.* The Testament of Beauty. Bridges
Sofa, The. *Fr.* The Task. Cowper
Song Tournament: New Style. Untermeyer
Spring Mountain Climb. Eberhart
Sweetness of Nature, The. *Unknown*
Tables Turned, The. Wordsworth
Thanatopsis. Bryant
That Nature Is a Heraclitean Fire and of the Comfort of the Resurrection. Hopkins
These are thy glorious works, Parent of good. *Fr.* Paradise Lost. Milton
This Is My Father's World. Babcock
This Too Is Ars Poetica. Vas
Thistle. Kilpi
Thou Art, O God. Moore
Thought-Fox, The. Hughes
Three Kingdoms of Nature, The. Lessing
To Mr. Henry Lawes. Philips
To the River Isca. Vaughan
To Walk Abroad. Traherne
Vegetable Loves. *Fr.* The Botanic Garden: The Loves of the Plants. Darwin
Vestigia. Carman
Walk, A. Zabolotsky
What if the foot, ordain'd the dust to tread. *Fr.* An Essay on Man. Pope
"When I consider everything that grows." *Fr.* Sonnets, XV. Shakespeare
When I Reflect on Nature's Cruelty. Themerson
Wilderness, The. Raine
Wind in the Pine. Sarett
Wish, that of the living whole, The. *Fr.* In Memoriam A. H. H. Tennyson
Wonderful World, The. Rands
Word, The. Realf
Work without Hope. Coleridge
Year's at the Spring, The. *Fr.* Pippa Passes. Browning
Youth of a Poet, The. *Fr.* The Minstrel. Beattie
Book of Nature Poems, A (BoNaP). William Cole, comp.
Room for Me and a Mountain Lion (RFM). Nancy Larrick, ed.

Nautilus (shell)
Chambered Nautilus, The. *Fr.* The Autocrat of the Breakfast Table. Holmes

Nauvoo, Illinois
Nauvoo. Taylor

Navaho Indians
Dawn Boy's Song. *Unknown*
Navajo, The. Coatsworth
War God's Horse Song, The. *Unknown*

Naval Battles
Battle of Actium. *Fr.* The Aeneid [*or* Eneados]. Virgil
Burnt Ship, A. Donne
Casabianca. Hemans
Commemorative of a Naval Victory. Melville
Fourth Day's Battle, The. *Fr.* Annus Mirabilis. Dryden
Now van to van the foremost squadrons meet. *Fr.* Annus Mirabilis. Dryden
Song Written at Sea in the First Dutch War (1665), the Night before an Engagement. Sackville
Word's gone out, and now they spread the main, The. *Fr.* The Spanish Descent. Defoe
Oxford Book of Sea Songs, The (OxBSS). Roy Palmer, ed.

Navarino, Battle of (1827)
Battle of Navarino, The. *Unknown*
Glorious Victory of Navarino! The. *Unknown*

Navels
Definition. Shakely

Navy, France
Ballad for a Boy, A. Cory
Hervé Riel. Browning

Navy, Great Britain
Admirals All. Newbolt
Ballad for a Boy, A. Cory
Battle of Sole Bay, The. *Unknown*
Captain, The. Tennyson
Captain Death. *Unknown*
Chief Petty Officer. Causley
Famous Fight at Malago; or, The Englishmen's Victory over the Spaniards, The. *Unknown*
Heart of Oak. Garrick
Instructions to a Painter. Waller
Joyful [*or* Joyfull] New Ballad, A. Deloney
Midshipman, The. Falconer
Second Advice to a Painter, The. Marvell
"Soldier an' Sailor Too." Kipling
Third Advice to a Painter, The. Marvell
Victory. *Unknown*
Ye Mariners of England. Campbell
Oxford Book of Sea Songs, The (OxBSS). Roy Palmer, ed.

Navy, Netherlands
Famous Sea-Fight, A. Looke

Navy, Spain
Famous Sea-Fight, A. Looke

Navy, United States
Bay Fight, The. Brownell
Blood Is Thicker than Water. Rice
Farragut. Meredith
Fleet at Santiago, The. Russell
Homing, The. Rooney
Men behind the Guns, The. Rooney
Naval Photograph: 25 October 1942: What the Hand May Be Saying. Bottoms
Old Ironsides. Holmes
River Fight, The. Brownell
Running the Batteries. Melville
Strong Swimmer, The. Benét
When the Great Gray Ships Come In. Carryl

Nazis
Albert Speer. Snodgrass
Death Camp. Klepfisz
Dr. Joseph Goebbels. *Fr.* The Führer Bunker. Snodgrass
Invisible History. Borawski
"More Light! More Light!" Hecht
Mother. Tuwim
Nazis. Sadoff
On the Eyes of an SS Officer. Wilbur
Poem for Putzi Hanfstaengel. Paterson
Poem Touching the Gestapo. Heyen
White Rose: Sophie Scholl 1921-1943, The. Mumford
Years Later. Lerner

Nebraska
Biography. Stanton
Kinkaiders, The. *Unknown*
Pornography, Nebraska. McPherson
Wild Pigs. Kooser
Nebuchadnezzar
Nebuchadnezzar. Wylie
Warm Babies. Preston
Needles
Old Mother Twitchett had [*or* has] but one
eye. Mother Goose
Nefertiti
Queen Nefertiti. *Unknown*
Negro Spirituals
Negro Spiritual. Trott
O Black and Unknown Bards. Johnson
Negroes. *See* **Blacks.**
Neighbors
Body, The. Bronk
Friend. Holman
Good Neighbors. Justus
Letter on the Lake, A. Dennis
Neighbors. Evans
Neighbors. Hoberman
Neighbors. Spencer
Neighbors. Tate
Portrait by a Neighbor. Millay
Song, A: "Good neighbour, why do you look
awry?" *Unknown*
Summer. Stryk
This and That. Davis
What Thou Lovest Well, Remains American.
Hugo
Winter Saint. Ammons
Nelson, Horatio Nelson, Viscount
Admirals All. Newbolt
Ballad of the Good Lord Nelson, A. Durrell
Death of Nelson, The. *Unknown*
1805. Graves
England Expects? Seaman
Grand Conversation on Brave Nelson.
Unknown
Nelson's Death. *Unknown*
Nelson's Death and Victory. *Unknown*
New Song on the Total Defeat of the French
Fleet, A. *Unknown*
Second of August. *Unknown*
Trafalgar. Palgrave
Nepal
Sestina: Here in Katmandu. Justice
Neptune (god)
Neptune Rising. Yolen
Neri, Filippo de'. *See* **Philip Neri, Saint.**
Nero
Ave! Nero Imperator. Osborne
Neruda, Pablo
Last Letter to Pablo. Lowther
Mourning Pablo Neruda. Bly
Ness, Loch, Scotland
Monster, The. Lowbury
Nessie. Hughes
Nests. *See* **Birds' Nests.**
Netanya, Israel
Here in Netanya. Wieseltier
Netherlands
Character of Holland, The. Marvell
Description of Holland. Butler
Dutch April. Halpern
Dutch Picture, A. Longfellow
Dutch Seacoast. *Fr.* The Atlas. Slessor
Einstein's Exile in an Old Dutch Winter.
Dubie
Leak in the Dike, The. Cary
Lowlands o' [*or* of] Holland, The. *Unknown*
Netherlands, The. Coleridge
Political Despatch, A. Canning
To———: "I gaze upon a city." Hood
Dutch Interior; Postwar Poetry of the
Netherlands and Flanders (DuIn). James
S. Holmes *and* William Jay Smith, eds.

Nettles
Nettles in May. Bowen
Tall Nettles. Thomas
Nevada
Celebration 1982. Meyette
Nevada. Gurney
Vacation. Stafford
You Are on U.S. 40 Headed West. White
New Brunswick, Canada
Banks of the Gaspereaux, The. *Unknown*
Biftek aux Champignons. Beers
Saint John, The. Clarke
New Deal
CCC, The ("CCC campers near West
Cummington"). Whitbread
New England
Air Raid. Wild
Late Comer. Hastings
Lilacs. Lowell
New England. Percival
New England. Robinson
New England Interlude. DeFrees
New England Is New England Is New
England. Green
New England Sampler, A. Brinnin
New England, Springtime. Dubie
Praise of New England. Chubb
River Water Music. Eberhart
Uppon the First Sight of New England, June
29, 1638. Tillam
With hearts revived in conceit, new land and
trees they eye. *Fr.* Good News from New
England. Johnson
New Guinea
New Guinea. McAuley
New Hampshire
Black Faced Sheep, The. Hall
Flower Herding on Mount Monadnock.
Kinnell
Freedom, New Hampshire. Kinnell
Mushroom Hunting in Late August,
Peterborough, N.H. Blumenthal
New Hampshire. *Fr.* Landscapes. Eliot
New Hampshire. Hall
On the Porch at the Frost Place, Franconia,
NH. Matthews
Spring in New Hampshire. McKay
Town of Hill, The. Hall
New Jersey
April One. Ostriker
Corsons Inlet. Ammons
In a Prominent Bar in Secaucus [One Day].
Kennedy
Invention of New Jersey, The. Anderson
Jersey Bait Shack. Balakian
Jersey Marsh, The. Galler
Legend. Weaver
New Jersey. Bennett
New Jersey White-tailed Deer. Oates
Paterson, *sels.* Williams
Sandy Hook. Houghton
Toward the Verrazano. Dunn
New Jersey (State)
Preface: "Rigor of beauty is the quest. But
how will you find beauty when it is
locked." *Fr.* Paterson. Williams
New Mexico
At Mexican Springs. Tohe
Back Again from Yucca Flats. Kelley
I tell him how it used to be in Paguate. *Fr.*
After the Pow-Wow. Littlebird
I Went into the Maverick Bar. Snyder
It Was a Special Treat. Tapahonso
New Mexican Mountain. Jeffers
Old Women beside a Church. Wilson
Progress. Agnew
Sand Painters, The. Belitt
Sound of Morning in New Mexico, The.
Kelley
When the Fairies. Dorn

New Orleans, Battle of (1815)
Battle of New Orleans, The. English
Jackson at New Orleans. Rice
To the Defenders of New Orleans. Drake
New Orleans, Louisiana
Ballade des Belles Milatraisses. Jonas
Girod Street Cemetery: New Orleans. Morris
Letter from the Vieux Carre. Russell
New Orleans. Carruth
New Orleans. Harjo
Song for New Orleans, A. Keithley
Vieux Carré. Roberts
New Year
All thro' the Year. *Unknown*
Another Year Is Dawning. Havergal
At the coming of the New Year. *Fr.* Manyo
Shu. Funado
At the New Year. Patchen
At the Portal. Havergal
Auld Lang Syne. Burns
Backward—Forward. *Unknown*
Both my child. Teitoku
Confidence. *Unknown*
Even as the snow falls to-day. *Fr.* Manyo
Shu. Yakamochi
Facing the New Year. Pearse
For a fresh start. *Fr.* Oraga Haru. Issa
For the Lady Olivia Porter; a Present upon a
New Year's Day. Davenant
"Go Forward." "G."
God Is Faithful. Havergal
Here we come a-caroling. *Unknown*
Hymn for the Eve of the New Year. Gerondi
"I Am with Thee." Allen
In Lieu of a Preface to *The Great*
Commonwealth Book. K'ang Yu-wei
Last Day of the Year (New Year's Eve), The.
Droste-Hülshoff
Last Day of the Year; or, New Year's Eve,
The. Linden
Lessons of the Year. *Unknown*
Lord, Make a Regular Man out of Me.
Guest
New House. Rai San'yo
New Leaf, A. Wheeler
New Time. *Unknown*
New Year. Al-Mala'ika
New Year, The. Cotton
New Year. Harada
New Year, The. Homer-Dixon
New Year, The. *Unknown*
New Year Carol, A. *Unknown*
New Year Wish, A. Havergal
New Year Wish, A. *Unknown*
New yeares, expect new gifts: Sister, your
Harpe. Jonson
New Year's Carol. *Unknown*
New Year's Day. Lowell
New Year's Day. Rai San'yo
New Years Day at the Official Lodge.
Michizane
New Year's Day—Following the Rhymes of
Inspector Luan-chiang. Pien Kung
New Year's Eve. Berryman
New Year's Eve. Hardy
New Year's Eve. Liu E
New Year's Eve. Wen Cheng-ming
New Year's Eve in the Year *Keng-tzu*. Chu
Hsiao-tsang
New Year's Morning; or, the First Day of the
Year. Linden
New Year's Poem. Avison
New Year's Promise, A. *Unknown*
New Year's Wish, A. "S."
New Year's Wishes. Havergal
Old and New. *Unknown*
Old Year, The. Clare
Old Year, The. Thompson
Old Year and the New, The. Flint
On this New Year's Day. *Fr.* Manyo Shu.
Fujii Moroai

Opening Year, The. *Unknown*
Passing of the Old Year. Fordham
Prayer for the New Year, A. *Unknown*
Ring Out, Wild Bells. *Fr.* In Memoriam A.
   H. H. Tennyson
Season greeter, The. Yomono Akara
Sitting Up with My Wife on New Year's Eve.
   Hsü Chün-ch'ien
There was no reason to expect sadness. *Fr.*
   Lines Written on New Year's Day. Wen
   Cheng-ming
To the Countesse of Bedford, on New-Yeares
   Day. Donne
To the New Year. Thompson
Written on New Year's Eve. Rai San'yo
Year Ahead, The. Powers
Year *Chi-wei* (1559), New Year's Day, The.
   Wen Cheng-ming
Year *Hsin-hai* (1551), New Year's Eve, The.
   Wen Cheng-ming
Year *I-mao* (1555), New Year's Eve, The.
   Wen Cheng-ming
Year's End. Wilbur
Year's first day, The. *Fr.* Thirty-three
   Hokku. Kikaku

New York City
Arrival, New York Harbor. Peters
Aspects of Robinson. Kees
At the Battery Sea-Wall. Laube
B Negative. Kennedy
Back on Times Square, Dreaming of Times
   Square. Ginsberg
Birthday Memorial to Seventh Street, A.
   Lorde
Bleat of Protest. Weston
Bottled [New York]. Johnson
Chelsea. Long
City Roofs. Towne
Curse, A. Feldman
Day in the City, A. Sissman
Early Dutch. Palen
East River. Thomas
Epistrophe. Baraka
Evening. *Fr.* New York. Leyeles
Give Me the Splendid Silent Sun. Whitman
Grave for New York, A. "Adunis"
Harlem at Night. Ausländer
High Wind at the Battery. Pomeroy
Houston Street. Vice
I Am New York City. Cortez
I Awoke with the Room Cold. Piercy
I'd rather listen to a flute. Hoffenstein
Imprisoned, The. Fitzgerald
In the Subway ("Rush hour"). *Fr.* New
   York. Leyeles
In the Subway ("Wall, A"). *Fr.* New York.
   Leyeles
In the Subway ("Walled-in"). *Fr.* New
   York. Leyeles
Iron Landscapes (and the Statue of Liberty).
   Gunn
January 30. *Fr.* Fabius Lind's Diary.
   Leyeles
John Garfield. Christopher
Jottings of New York. McGonagall
Junk. *Fr.* New York Everywhere.
   Vaynshteyn
Junkie with a Flute in the Rain, A. Fisher
Key to the City, The. Winters
Last Impression of New York. Mason
Letter to N. Y. Bishop
Loew's Bridge, a Broadway Idyl. Tucker
Madison Square. *Fr.* New York. Leyeles
Manhattan. Beer
Manhattan. Hart
Manhattan Bridge. *Fr.* New York. Leyeles
Manhattan Lullaby. Field
Manhattan Menagerie. Cherwinski
Mannahatta. Whitman

Metropolitan Nightmare. Benét
My City. Johnson
My Sad Self. Ginsberg
Negro Geo'ge. *Fr.* Negroes. Vaynshteyn
New York. Leyeles
New York. Logan
New York. Moore
New York City. Abbe
New York City—1935. Corso
New York Everywhere. *Fr.* New York
   Everywhere. Vaynshteyn
New York in a Jewish Mood. Teller
New York Landscapes. Teller
Night. *Fr.* New York. Leyeles
Obon by the Hudson. Oyama
On Broadway. *Fr.* New York. Leyeles
On Your Soil, America. Vaynshteyn
Owed to New York. Newton
Review from Staten Island. Oden
School Days in New Amsterdam. Guiterman
Seventh Avenue. Rukeyser
Sidewalks of New York, The. Blake
Skyscrapers of the Financial District Dance
   with Gasman, The. Piercy
Slogan, The. Blackburn
Snow. Chiang
Speakers, Columbus Circle. Souster
Step Away from Them, A. O'Hara
Steps. O'Hara
Stone, The. Blackburn
Stumpfoot on 42nd Street. Simpson
Sunday on Riverside Drive. Ausländer
These Green-going-to-Yellow. Bell
This Song Shows Me Pictures; Morningside
   Drive, New York City 1950-1960. Oyama
Times-Square-Shoeshine-Composition.
   Angelou
To New York. Sédar-Senghor
Towering life of the towering city, The. *Fr.*
   Here Lives the Jewish People. Leivick
Tulips and Addresses. Field
Twenty-third Street Runs into Heaven.
   Patchen
Under. Bowering
Upper Broadway. Rich
Walking the New York Bedrock Alive in the
   Sea of Information. Snyder
Wall Street. *Fr.* New York. Leyeles
Washington Heights, 1959. Blumenthal
Whitman in Black. Berrigan
Winter Sketches. Reznikoff
See also **Bronx, Brooklyn** *and* **Queens.**

New York (state)
Among the Finger Lakes. Wallace
E-ri-e, The. *Unknown*
Erie Canal, The. Allen
Getting a Poem in the Rain. Lourie
Grandfather. Harper
Long Island Springs. Moss
Mother and Son. Heyen
Pearl Harbor Day 1970. Lourie
Sestina d'Inverno. Hecht
State of Nature, A. Hollander
Summer in a Small Town. Gregg

New Yorker, The (magazine)
Talk of the Town, The. Fisher

New Zealand
East Coast Journey. Baxter
Farewell to New Zealand. Vaughan-Thomas
Foxes, The. Frame
Instead of an Interview. Adcock
It was a wondrous realm beguiled. *Fr.*
   Ranolf and Amohia. Domett
Landfall in Unknown Seas. Curnow
Last Moriori, The. Smithyman
Muscle and Bone of Song. Tuwhare
Te Rangi Hiroa/ Buck. Smithyman
Uneasy Resident. Johnson
Waitomo. Smithyman
Warlike of the Isles, The. *Unknown*

*Anthology of Twentieth-Century New Zealand
   Poetry, An* (ATNZ). Vincent O'Sullivan,
   comp.
Penguin Book of New Zealand Verse, The
   (PeNZ). Ian Wedde *and* Harvey
   McQueen, eds.
Newark, New Jersey
Ballgame, The. Baraka
Newark, for Now (68). Rodgers
Newfoundland, Canada
Gazeteer of Newfoundland. Harrington
North Labrador. Crane
Pleasant Life in Newfoundland, The.
   Hayman
Wreckers' Prayer, The. Roberts
Newgate Prison, London
Friendly Address, A. Hood
Newman, John Henry, Cardinal
Cardinal Newman. Rossetti
News
New Republic Is Infuriated at the News
   Coverage, The. Starbuck
News of Old Girls. Baines
Newspapers
After the Last Bulletins. Wilbur
British Journalist, The. Wolfe
Carl Hamblin. *Fr.* Spoon River Anthology.
   Masters
Country Press. Dobson
Daisy Fraser. *Fr.* Spoon River Anthology.
   Masters
Editor Whedon. *Fr.* Spoon River Anthology.
   Masters
Extras. Burton
Finding a Yiddish Paper on the Riverside
   Line. Spacks
Finding an Old Newspaper in the Woods.
   Morgan
Haiku: "Small rural newspaper, The." *Fr.*
   One Hundred Haiku in Free Form. Hosai
Headline History. Plomer
It Is Dangerous to Read Newspapers.
   Atwood
News. Schmitz
Newsboy. Layton
Personal Column. Paulin
Southern Press, The. Moorer
Sunday Review Section. Wormser
To a Dead Journalist. Williams
Yesterday's Paper. Watts
See also **Journalism; Magazines.**
Newton, Sir Isaac
All–intellectual eye, our solar round. *Fr.* To
   the Memory of Sir Isaac Newton.
   Thomson
Newton. *Fr.* The Prelude [or, Growth of a
   Poet's Mind]: Residence at Cambridge.
   Wordsworth
Newton to Einstein. Chappell
Sir Isaac Newton. *Unknown*
Niagara Falls
Niagara Falls Nocturne. Gasparini
Public Aid for Niagara Falls. Bishop
Nicaragua
Ecology. Cardenal
Houses Were Left Full of Smoke, The.
   Rugama
June 10. Rodriguez
Past Will Not Return, The. Coronel Urtecho
Pier. Uriarte
Song of Hope. Yamora
Nigeria
Anthropology: Cricket at Kano. Brown
Safari West. Williams
See also **Civil War, Nigerian.**
Night
Above in the clear. Tamenori
Acquainted with the Night. Frost
All things have an end. Ietaka
Ancient Thought, The. Kerr
As the night deepens. Yoshimoto

As the night grows late. Kogon
Ashes. *Fr.* Games. Popa
At the Mid Hour of Night. Moore
Auld Daddy Darkness. Ferguson
Autumn Night. Tanaka Fuyuji
Ballad of London, A. Le Gallienne
Battle, A. Crawford
Beautiful is the moon-lit night. *Fr.* Manyo
    Shu. Yotsuna
Beautiful Night, A. Beddoes
Beneath a clear sky. Hanazono
Check. Stephens
Clearly I see the pebbles in the water. *Fr.*
    Manyo Shu. *Unknown*
Cuckoo calls out, A. Tameie
Dark Stag, The. Crawford
Day and Night. Kvitko
Day Is Done, The. Longfellow
Day That I Have Loved. Brooke
Distant View of the Sea, A. Tamekane
Eternal Evening. Weöres
Evening. Doolittle
Evening Snow. Tamekane
Falling Asleep. Sassoon
Fields, the mountains, The. Tonna
Flowers of Darkness. Davis
Four Glimpses of Night. Davis
From a clump of grass. Kogon
God's Dark. Martin
Good Night. Hugo
Good Night, Good Night. Lee
Has it grown so late? Tonna
Hotel in Paris. Trudell
Hour of Magic, The. Davies
Hymn to Night. Cane
Hymn to Night, A. Michelson
Hymn to the Evening, An. Wheatley
Hymn to the Night. Longfellow
I Love the Night. Edwards
I wish I could tell. Tamesuke
If night takes the form of a whale and.
    Fraire
In the Dark None Dainty. Herrick
In the Night. Jennings
In the valley shade. Chikako
Interim. Delany
Light the Lamps Up, Lamplighter!
    Farjeon
Love Poem, A: "Night has fallen, The."
    Eifuku
Madrigal: "Unhappie Light." Drummond
Marichi. Rexroth
Meeting at Night. Browning
Melrose Abbey. *Fr.* The Lay of the Last
    Minstrel. Scott
Middle of the Night, The. Kuskin
Midnight. Bethell
Midnight. Lampman
Midnight. Masefield
Midnight Prayer. Bialik
Moonlight. Nazir
Moonlit Apples. Drinkwater
Mother Night. Johnson
Night. Benét
Night. *Fr.* Songs of Innocence. Blake
Night. Camerino
Night. *Fr.* The Shadow of Night. Chapman
Night. Hayes
Night. Heard
Night. Heavysege
Night. Hébert
Night. Hoberman
Night. Hubbell
Night. Ibn Gabirol
Night. Jeffers
Night. Kenji
Night, The. Leuty
Night. *Fr.* New York. Leyeles
Night. Lovelace
Night. Radcliffe
Night. Shuntaro

Night. Sutu
Night. Teasdale
Night, The. Vaughan
Night. Zhukovsky
Night and the Pines. Scott
Night, Be Mood to Me. *Fr.* From the
    Nursery. Glatstein
Night Comes. De Regniers
Night Crackles. Woody
Night deepens, the sound of water trickling,
    The. *Fr.* Seventy-eight Tanka. Shikishi
Night Hymns on Lake Nipigon. Scott
Night in June, A. Scott
Night in Prison, A. Aleramo
Night Is Near [*or* Neir] Gone, The.
    Montgomerie
Night of Spring. Westwood
Night-Piece. Patterson
Night-Piece, A. Wordsworth
Night-Piece, to Julia, The. Herrick
Night Snow. Kogon
Night up There. Valentine
Night Will Never Stay, The. Farjeon
Nightfall. Davies
Nights along the River. Sullivan
No Difference in the Dark. Herrick
Nocturnal Reverie, A. Winchilsea
Nocturnal Sketch, A. Hood
Nocturnal Sounds. Cumbo
Nocturne: "Listening for the sound." Lane
Nocturne: "Red flame flowers bloom and die,
    The." Garstin
Nocturne: "This cool night is strange."
    Bennett
Noises in the Night. Middleton
Now Winter Nights Enlarge. Campion
O Daedalus, Fly Away Home. Hayden
Old Girl, The. Lenhart
On a Calm Summer's Night. Nicholson
On a Fall Night. Ben-Amittai
On the Night in Question. Goedicke
Out in the Dark. Thomas
Outside Baby Moon's. Violi
Pine Tree Tops. Snyder
Questions at Night. Untermeyer
Rhapsody on a Windy Night. Eliot
Rhapsody, Written at the Lakes in
    Westmorland, A. Brown
Silent Night, The. Linden
Silver. De la Mare
So Beautiful Is the Tree of Night. Hanson
Song for Past Midnight. Lehmann
Song: "Make this night loveable." Auden
Sound of Night, The. Kumin
Spaces inside Sleep, The. Desnos
Spring Night. *Fr.* Twelve Miscellaneous
    Poems on the Fang Garden. Chang Yü
Spring Night. Hagiwara Sakutaro
Spring Night. Su Tung-p'o
Starlight Thought. *Fr.* A Group of Musings.
    Ray
Still Life. Whittemore
Summer Moon. Tamemasa
Summer Night, A. Arnold
Summer Night. Kogon
Suns, planets, stars, in glorious array. *Fr.*
    Night. Daley
Though men say/ An autumn night is long.
    Fr. Manyo Shu. *Unknown*
Thu Sun: Night. Schierbeek
Time Exposures. Rukeyser
To Night. Beddoes
To Night. Shelley
To Night. White
To Night, the Mother of Sleep and Death.
    Symonds
Tom's Garland: Upon the Unemployed.
    Hopkins
Too restless to sleep. Teika
Two Tramps in Mud Time. Frost
Wait till the darkness is deep. Wallada
Waiting for Love in Vain. Tonna

Walking at Night. Hare
Walking Late. Montague
Watchman, The. Kingsley
Watchman, What of the Night? Swinburne
What is it/ that is senseless to lament.
    Tameyo
When All the World's Asleep. Posey
Wild Goose Lingering on an Inlet. Shinkei
Winter Moon. Tameshige
Winter Night, A. Barnes
Winter Night. Fairburn
Winter Night, A. Thompson
With him bound by fear. Tamekane
See also **Evening.**

Nightclubs
Jazz Band in a Parisian Cabaret. Hughes
Jazzonia. Hughes
Night Club. MacNeice
Night Club. Scott

Nightingales
As it fell upon a day. *Fr.* The Affectionate
    Shepherd. Barnfield
Bianca among the Nightingales. Browning
Canadian Rossignol, The. Thomson
Early Nightingale. Clare
Fields Abroad with Spangled Flowers, The.
    Unknown
Haiku: "On the snow." Kawabata Bosha
Happy Nightingale, The. *Unknown*
Hast Thou Heard the Nightingale? Gilder
My Nightingale. Ausländer
Nightingale, The. Clare
Nightingale, The. Coleridge
Nightingale, The. Tynan
Nightingale near the House, The. Monro
Nightingales. Bridges
No cloud, no relique of the sunken day. *Fr.*
    The Nightingale. Coleridge
O Nightingale! Thou Surely Art.
    Wordsworth
Ode to a Nightingale. Keats
Ode: To the Nightingale. Warton
Out from Its Fine Cage. *Unknown*
Philomela. Arnold
Philomela. Ransom
Pig and the Nightingale, The. Shteynbarg
Riddle: Nightingale. *Unknown*
Semichorus II: "There the voluptuous
    nightingales." *Fr.* Prometheus Unbound.
    Shelley
Sparrow-Hawk, A. *Unknown*
To a Nightingale. Drummond
To the Nightingale. Winchilsea
Upon the boughs and tops of trees. *Fr.*
    Philomela, the Nightingale. Hannay
When I was in a summer valley. *Fr.* The
    Owl and the Nightingale. De Guildford

Nightmares
Apology for Bad Dreams. Jeffers
In Your Bad Dream. Hugo
Nightmare Inspection Tour for American
    Generals. Ruark
Original Sin; a Short Story. Warren
See also **Dreams.**

Nihilism
Shapelessness, The. Nagy
Upon Nothing. Rochester

Nijinsky, Vaslav
Friends. Ashbery
Nijinsky. Tyler

Nike
Ballad of the Bayonet, A. Bryll
Nike. Bryll

Nile, Battle of the (1798)
New Song on the Total Defeat of the French
    Fleet, A. *Unknown*

Nile (river)
Chorus: "Then thus we have beheld." *Fr.*
    Cleopatra. Daniel
Nile, The. Hunt
River Nile, The. LaMers

Niobe
Niobe. Ray
Nixon, Richard Milhous
Campaign Promise. Taylor
Final Curtain. Woddis
Nkrumah, Kwame
Goodbye Nkrumah. DiPrima
Noah
And Did the Animals? Van Doren
Ballad of Mrs. Noah, The. Duncan
Ballad of the Flood. Muir
Flood, The. Mak
Hammer, Ring. *Unknown*
History of the Flood, The. Heath-Stubbs
Late Passenger, The. Lewis
Life-Giving, The. Leithauser
Missing Link, The. Herford
New Noah, The. "Adunis"
Noah. Bloch
Noah. Brown
Noah. Daniells
Noah an' Jonah an' Cap'n John Smith.
   Marquis
Noah at Sea. Rantala
Noah's Ark. Young
Noah's Flood. *Fr.* Genesis. Caedmon
Noah's Song. Jones
Parley of Beasts. "MacDiarmid"
Proust on Noah. Silberschlag
Wine and Water. *Fr.* The Flying Inn.
   Chesterton
Nobility
My Lord Tomnoddy. Brough
Noises
Ears Hear. Hymes
Noises in the Night. Middleton
Noon
Noon. Clare
Noonday Thought. *Fr.* A Group of Musings.
   Ray
Noontide. *Fr.* Idyl. Ray
Norfolk, England
Horsey Gap. *Unknown*
Normandy, Invasion of
Carentan O Carentan. Simpson
Norris Dam, Tennessee
Norris Dam. Rodman
North, The
North/South. Mariani
North Carolina
Cottonmouth Country. Glück
It's a debatable land. The winds are variable.
   Fr. Report from the Carolinas. Bevington
North, Christopher (John Wilson)
To Christopher North. Tennyson
North Dakota
August from My Desk. Flint
Outside Fargo, North Dakota. Wright
North, Frederick, Earl of Guilford and Baron
   North
Lord North's Recantation. *Unknown*
North Haven, Maine
North Haven. Booth
North Pole
From the North Pole. Galai
90 North. Jarrell
North Wind
Awake! *Fr.* The Song of Solomon.
Blow, Northern Wind. *Unknown*
Exile in Nigeria. Mphahlele
Moon's the North Wind's Cooky, The.
   Lindsay
Northwind. Baro
Northamptonshire, England
Sunrise in Summer. Clare
Northern Ireland
Brandy Glass, The. MacNeice
Carrickfergus. MacNeice
Derry. Deane
Letter to Seamus Heaney. Longley
Lisnagade. *Unknown*

Northern Ireland: Two Comments. Deane
Of Difference Does It Make. Paulin
Settlers. Paulin
Strand at Lough Beg, The. Heaney
Ulster. Kipling
Ulster Twilight, An. Heaney
Whatever You Say Say Nothing. Heaney
See also counties listed under, e.g **County**
   Tyrone, Northern Ireland.

Northern Lights. *See* **Aurora Borealis.**

Northumberland, England
Alnwick Castle. Halleck
At Elsdon. Chatt
Elsdon. Downie
Northwest Territories, Canada
I persist in a little fabric between me and the
   world. *Fr.* The Great Bear Lake
   Meditations. Yates
Trees at the Arctic Circle. Purdy
Noses
Dong with a Luminous Nose, The. Lear
Hairs in My Nose, The. Boyajian
My Nose. Aldis
Nose, The. Smith
Of One That Had a Great Nose. Turberville
Of Tyndarus, That Frumped a Gentlewoman.
   Unknown
Smell. Williams
There's a man with a nose. *Fr.* The Devil's
   Dictionary. Bierce
To My Nose. Forrester
Nostalgia
After a Journey. Hardy
Anseo. Muldoon
Bagatelles. Orlen
Break, Break, Break. Tennyson
Certain Bend, A. Stafford
Clayfeld's Glove. Pack
Closed Doors. Thorson
Daffodils. Heffernan
Deserted Home, A. Lysaght
Desultory Thoughts on My Old Home. Yu
   T'ung
Dreaming of the South. Huang-fu Sung
Driving through Tennessee. Wright
Family Album, A. Brody
Farewell: "Not soon shall I forget—a sheet."
   Tynan
Farewell to Leyden's lonely bound. *Fr.* On
   Leaving Holland. Akenside
Flood. Matthews
For a Suicide, a Little Early Morning Music.
   Ruark
Home No More Home to Me. Stevenson
House, A. Orlen
I Remember, I Remember. Larkin
Immortal at the River. Ku Hsiung
Indian Summer. Hirsch
Irish Skies. Letts
Landscape, Dense with Trees. Voigt
Leaving Inishmore. Longley
Lines Written in the Album at Elbingerode, in
   the Hartz Forest. Coleridge
Miniver Cheevy. Robinson
Moon behind the Hill, The. *Unknown*
My Other Me. Litchfield
No Denying. Ladányi
Nostalgia. Lawrence
Nostalgia. Lowell
Nostalgia. Ramke
Nostalgia. Wu T'e-Liang
Nostalgia. Yu Kuang-chung
Nostalgia of the Lakefronts. Justice
Oh, Give Us Back the Days of Old.' Neale
Old Familiar Faces, The. Lamb
Old Furniture. Hardy
Old-Long-Syne. *Unknown*
Old Man at the Window, The. Harvey
Old Movies. Cotton

One day when I was a child, long ago.
   Paley
Other Side of the River, The. Wright
Out to Old Aunt Mary's. Riley
Piano. Lawrence
Player Piano, The. Jarrell
Premonition, The. Roethke
Raleigh Was Right. Williams
Range-finding. Frost
Retreat[e], The. Vaughan
Soliloquy on a Southern Strand. Montague
Song: "I had a bicycle called "Splendid."
   Waley
Song of the Autumn Wind. Liu Ch'e
Soy Sauce. Snyder
Sweep. Jones
Tears, Idle Tears [I Know Not What They
   Mean]. *Fr.* The Princess. Tennyson
Thinking about the Past. Justice
Toy Bone, The. Hall
Twenty Years Ago. Lawrence
What Came to Me. Kenyon
When This Old Hat Was New. *Unknown*
Where a Roman Villa Stood, above Freiburg.
   Coleridge
Written at Night, after Dreaming That I Had
   Returned to My Old Home. Li Tz'u-ming
You Were Still the Sun's There. Csoori
Nothingness
Double. Armantrout
Neither Here nor There. Rodgers
Nothing. Sherry
Sestina: "Is this the object." Kroll
See also **Nihilism.**
Notre Dame Cathedral
Cathedral in the Thrashing Rain. Kotaro
Notre Dame. Mandelstam
Notre Dame, University of
Notre Dame Victory March, The. Shea
Nottingham, England
Nottamun Town. *Unknown*
Nova Scotia, Canada
By Cobequid Bay. Fraser
First Death in Nova Scotia. Bishop
Louisburg. *Unknown*
Low Tide on Grand Pré. Carman
Poem: "About the size of an old-style dollar
   bill." Bishop
To Cordelia. Stansbury
Words Are Never Enough. Bruce
Novels
Who'd Be a Hero (Fictional)? Bishop
November
Beautiful Ruined Orchard, The. Berrigan
Ettrick Forest in November. *Fr.* Marmion.
   Scott
In November. Aldrich
In November. Lampman
Late November. Santos
Late November in a Field. Wright
Mist and All, The. Willson
My November Guest. Frost
Nearing Winter. Sandeen
November. Bridges
November. Bryant
November. Cary
November. *Fr.* Sonnets to the Seasons.
   Coleridge
November. Harvey
November. Hughes
November. Leyeles
November. Manger
November. Pascoli
November. Ray
November. *Fr.* Sonnets of the Months. San
   Gimignano
November. Stoddard
November in the Isle of Wight. *Fr.* Enoch
   Arden. Tennyson
November Night. Crapsey
November Song. Vinz

Nuclear Accidents *(cont.)*
November Surf. Jeffers
November through a Giant Copper Beech.
   Honig
There's Nothing like the Sun. Thomas
Nuclear Accidents
Atomic Pantoum. Meinke
Three Mile Island. Owen
See also **Radiation and Radiation Sickness.**
Nuclear Energy
Black Mesa. Rogers
Tar. Williams
Nuclear War
Advice to a Prophet. Wilbur
After the War. Garbovsky
Before the Day of Wrath. *Fr.* Four Poems
   from the Strontium Age. Johnson
Blue Alert. Merriam
Disaster. Jin
Fall 1961. Lowell
Fifteen Million Plastic Bags. Mitchell
Fundamental Project of Technology, The.
   Kinnell
How Do You Spell "Missile"?: Preliminary
   Instructions in the Nuclear Age. Uba
How to Survive Nuclear War. Kumin
Nuclear wind, when wilt thou blow. *Fr.* A
   Leaden Treasury of English Verse. Dehn
On Passing by Those Icy Stones (and Yes,
   Columbia!). Bunch
Song about Major Eatherly, A. Wain
Survivors, The. Hine
Wedding Day at Nagasaki. Hall
Welcome to Hiroshima. Salter
When the Vacation Is Over for Good. Strand
Your Attention Please. Porter
See also **Atomic Bomb; Radiation and
   Radiation Sickness.**
Nudity and Nudists
"Gross, Coarse, Hideous" (Police Description
   of My Pictures). Lawrence
Landscape as a Nude. *Fr.* Frescoes for Mr.
   Rockefeller's City. MacLeish
Naked and the Nude, The. Graves
Naked in Borneo. Swenson
Nude Descending a Staircase. Kennedy
Nudes. Howell
Nudities. Spire
Playboy. Wilbur
To His Mistress Going to Bed. *Fr.* Elegies.
   Donne
Woman with Gardenia: A Sketch. Hadas
Number Poems (genre)
Cardinal Ideograms. Swenson
Numbers
Accountant in His Bath, The ("The accountant
   dried his imperfect back"). Mitchell
One, two,/ Buckle my shoe. Mother Goose
2000. Smith
Nuns
Ballad of a Nun, A. Davidson
Carmelite. Murray
February 4. *Fr.* Fabius Lind's Diary.
   Leyeles
Felixstowe; or, The Last of Her Order.
   Betjeman
Fixture, A. Swenson
For the Sisters of the Hôtel Dieu. Klein
Friar and the Nun, The. *Unknown*
Heaven-Haven. Hopkins
I am a young girl, gay. *Unknown*
Intercessors. Clarke
Lady That in the Prime. Milton
Motet: "I am a young girl." *Unknown*
Motet: "I am merry,/ Pretty, pleasing."
   Unknown
My Parents, as If Enemies. *Unknown*
Now That I'm Young. *Unknown*
Nuns at Eve. Brinnin
Nuns in the Wind. Rukeyser
Portrait of a Nun. Jones

Taoist Nun, The. Hsüeh Chao-yün
Taoist Nun, The. Li Hsün
Vestal, The. *Fr.* Eloisa to Abelard. Pope
See also **Convents.**
Nuremberg, Germany
Nuremberg. Longfellow
Nursery Rhymes
Goosey Goosey Gander—by Various Authors.
   French
"Pussy, Pussy Baudrons." Morley
Nurses
Malice of Innocence, The. Levertov
Negro Heroines. Moorer
Night Nurse Goes Her Round, The. Gray
Nurse believed the sick man slept, The.
   Brontë
Nurse's Song. *Fr.* Songs of Innocence.
   Blake
Staff-Nurse: New Style. *Fr.* In Hospital.
   Henley
Staff-Nurse: Old Style. *Fr.* In Hospital.
   Henley
Terrible Infant, A. Locker-Lampson
Wound-Dresser, The. Whitman
Nursing Homes
Nursing Home. Spacks
Old People on the Nursing Home Porch.
   Strand
Nymphs
Centaur's Bath, The. Urbina
Nymph Complaining for the Death of Her
   Fawn, The. Marvell
Oread. Doolittle
Overheard on a Saltmarsh. Monro
Rape of Mensola, The. *Fr.* Nymphs of
   Fiesole. Boccaccio
Sabrina. *Fr.* Comus; a Masque Presented at
   Ludlow Castle. Milton
To the Water Nymphs, Drinking at the
   Fountain. Herrick
Water Lady, The. Hood

O

Oafs
What Kind of a Guy Was He? Nemerov
Yes, What? Francis
Oak Trees
At the Woodpile. Henri
Autumn Scene. Dowling
Bearded Oaks. Warren
Brave Old Oak, The. Chorley
California Oaks, The. Winters
Computative Oak. Berman
Heart of Oak. Lüders
I Saw in Louisiana a Live-Oak Growing.
   Whitman
Oak, The. Tennyson
Spring Oak. Kinnell
Tapestry Trees. Morris
To an Oak Tree. *Fr.* Waverley. Scott
To the Oaks of Glencree. Synge
Yardley Oak. Cowper
Oases
Green, Green Is El Aghir. Cameron
Oasis of Sidi Khaled, The. Blunt
See also **Deserts.**
Oates, Joyce Carol
When she lived near St. Lawrence. *Fr.* A
   Mini-Samizdat of New River Rhymes.
   Cole
Oates, Titus
Ballad upon the Popish Plot, A. Gadbury
Panegyric upon Oates, A. Duke
Tragi-Comedy of Titus Oates, The.
   Unknown

Oban, Scotland
End of the Season on a Stormy Day—Oban.
   Smith
Obesity
Blank Verse for a Fat Demanding Wife.
   Lindsey
Case of Ample Ora: Sweetness and Light,
   The. Hadas
Fat Blues. Crowell
Fat Boy, The. Vinz
Fat Boy's Dream, The. McCann
Fat Lady Travels, The. Smith-Bowers
Fat Mama at Swenson's. Briefs
Fat Men, The. Dabydeen
Good Old Body. Donald
Invitation. Nichols
Perils of Obesity, The. Graham
Things to Say When You Quit Smoking.
   Blossom
Whistle, Daughter, Whistle. *Unknown*
Zimmershire Lad, A. Zimmer
Obscenity
Finger of Necessity. Barks
Obscene Caller, The. Fein
See also **Pornography.**
Observatories
Greenwich Observatory. Keyes
See also **Astronomy and Astronomers.**
Obsessions
Juliet. Belloc
Occult, The
Diehard. Moffett
Séance. King
Why Am I Grown So Cold? Poems of the
   Unknowable (WSC). Myra Cohn
   Livingston, ed.
Occupations
Foreplay of the Alphabet. Gray
No Money in Art. Gustafson
Vocation. Tagore
Ocean. *See* **Sea.**
O'Conaire, Padraic
Padraic O'Conaire, Gaelic Storyteller.
   Higgins
O'Connell, Daniel
Dead Tribune, The. MacCarthy
O'Connor, Flannery
Flannery O'Connor. Walters
O'Connor, Rory
Grave of Rury, The. Rolleston
They are the spit of virtue now. *Fr.* Civil
   War. Clarke
October
Ambition. Kennedy
Boys in October. Layton
Chestnut vendor, The. Szelki
Especially When the October Wind. Thomas
Harvest Home. Guiterman
In the Month of Green Fire. Himmell
Late October. Carleton
Mallee in October. Hudson
Now Blue October. Nathan
October. Fordham
October. Frost
October. Justice
October. Kavanagh
October. Ray
October. Rossetti
October. *Fr.* Sonnets of the Months. San
   Gimignano
October. Teller
October. Thomas
October. Updike
October. Zelk
October Arriving. Simic
October Elegy. Gibson
October in Tennessee. Malone
October Is Here. Linden
October Journey. Walker
October Poem. Tamura Ryuichi

October's Bright Blue Weather. Jackson
October's Party. Cooper
Poem in October. Thomas
Tregardock. Betjeman
Vagabond Song, A. Carman

Octopuses
Earth-Ocean. Apollinaire
Octopus. Al-Gosaibi
Octopus. Hilton
Octopus, The. "MacDiarmid"
Octopus, The. Merrill
Octopus, The. Nash

Odysseus. *See* **Ulysses.**

Oedipus
Antigone. Sophocles
Antigone and Oedipus. Ray
Incantation to Oedipus. *Fr.* Oedipus.
  Dryden
Myth. Rukeyser
Oedipus. Blackburn
Oedipus. Muir

Oenone
Oenone's Complaint. *Fr.* The Arraignment
  of Paris. Peele

Offa, King of Mercia
Princes of Mercia were badger and raven,
  The. *Fr.* Mercian Hymns. Hill

Office Workers
Any Man to His Secretary. Corke
Back Again, Home. Lee
Dolor. Roethke
Love in Brooklyn. Wakeman
Report, The. Swan
Return to Work, The. Williams
Song from a Two-Desk Office. Buck
Stenographers, The. Page
What Grandma Knew. Field
See also **Clerks; Secretaries.**

Officers, Military
Base Details. Sassoon

Ogres
Ogres and Pygmies. Graves
See also **Monsters; Trolls.**

O'Hara, Frank
Frank O'Hara. Berrigan

Ohio
At the Executed Murderer's Grave. Wright
Autumn Begins in Martins Ferry, Ohio.
  Wright
Beautiful Ohio. Wright
By the Beautiful Ohio. LaBombard
Founders of Ohio, The. Venable
In Response to a Rumor That the Oldest
  Whorehouse in Wheeling, West Virginia,
  Has Been Condemned. Wright
Ohioan Pastoral. Wright
Taking the Train Home. Matthews
Waders and Swimmers. Plumly
Yes, But. Wright

Ohio River
When I asked for fish in the restaurant facing
  the Ohio River. *Fr.* Whiffs of the Ohio
  River at Cincinnati. Sandburg

Oisin
Bathing of Oisin's Head, The. *Unknown*
History. Liddy
Oisin in the Land of Youth. Comyn
Praise of Fionn, The. *Unknown*
Wanderings of Oisin, The. Yeats

O'Keeffe, Georgia
O'Keeffe Retrospective. Swenson

Okinawa, Japan
Okinawa Kanashii Monogatari. Kudaka
Picture of Okinawa, A. Schmitz

Oklahoma
Captive Stone, The. Barnes
Driving into Enid. Van Walleghen
Oklahoma Rt. 66. Naranjo-Morse
Poem near Midway Truck Stop. Henson

Race Riot, Tulsa, 1921. Olds
Starving to Death on a Government Claim.
  Unknown

Old Age
Acre of Grass, An. Yeats
Advice to the Old Beaux. Sedley
After a Long Time in the Provinces, I
  Returned to My Old School in My Late
  Years. Saba
After Touch. Clausen
Against Winter. Feinstein
Age. Jones
Age. Landor
Age in Prospect. Jeffers
Aged Fisherman. Bynner
Aged Lover Renounceth Love, The. Vaux
Ago. Jennings
Alas! 'Tis Very Sad to Hear. Landor
Almost Ninety. Whitman
Almswomen. Blunden
Already old age is wrinkling my. Sappho
Ancient to Ancients, An. Hardy
Apology. Niatum
April Inventory. Snodgrass
As I grow old, and weaker grow my eyes.
  Fr. Moments of Fullfillment—Writing
  Down Miscellaneous. Yüan Mei
As old age approaches. *Fr.* A Lament for
  Myself. Yün Shou-p'ing
As the night wears on. Tamekane
At Fifteen I Went Off to the Army.
  Unknown
At noon I watch the sun shine. *Fr.* Little
  Diary on Growing Old. Betocchi
At the Doors. Der Nistor
Auspex. Lowell
Autumn. Wolfe
Autumnus. Sylvester
Baucis and Philemon. Hoskins
Bean Eaters, The. Brooks
Bedtime Story, A. Mezey
Before my back was bent I was eloquent.
  Fr. Hateful Old Age. *Unknown*
Belly Dancer in the Nursing Home, The.
  Wallace
Bent. Carter
Beware of age. *Fr.* The Regrets. Sisson
Birthday, The. Johnson
Black and glossy as a bee and curled was my
  hair. Ambapali
Blue Springs, Georgia. Young
Boarding, The. Johnson
Body of John. Mason
Boys, The. Holmes
Bulldozers. Dec
Cattle Sale. Salom
Centenarian's Story, The. Whitman
Chaperon, The. Bunner
Chard Whitlow. Reed
Childhood. Cornford
Chough, The. Reaney
City Pigeons. Chasin
Come On in, the Senility Is Fine. Nash
Comfort. Widdemer
Coming of Wisdom with Time, The. Yeats
Complaint of the Grandparents. Justice
Crows, The. Bogan
Cry of an Aged One, The. Fraser
Daguerreotype Taken in Old Age. Atwood
Danny Murphy. Stephens
Days Ago. Hai-Jew
Dear Men and Women. Wheelock
Death Invoked. *Fr.* The Emperor of the
  East. Massinger
Disturb me not, oh bouyant youths!
  Unknown
Do Not Go Gentle into That Good Night.
  Thomas
Don't, Don't. Huan Fu
Dream. Shotetsu
Dust to Dust. De la Mare
Each Bird Walking. Gallagher

Elegy: "Extinguished are my years of carefree
  laughter." Pushkin
Emancipation. *Unknown*
Emeritus, The. Nathan
Envy the Old. Van Doren
Faded Face, The. Hardy
Failure. Lattimore
Fall. Bethell
Fall. Smith
Falling Teeth. Shih Jun-chang
Father. Lipkin
Father William. *Fr.* Alice's Adventures in
  Wonderland. "Carroll"
Femme Agée. Edmond
First Meditation. *Fr.* Meditations of an Old
  Woman. Roethke
First Poem of the Year. Kishun Ryuki
Flying Wheel, The. Tynan
Folding Fan, The. Cohoe
For an Octogenarian. Turner
Forerunners, The. Herbert
Fountain, The. Wordsworth
Fresh Flowers. Wang An-shih
From the Crag. Leib
Gather Ye Rosebuds. Fowler
Generations. Eörsi
George. Randall
Gerontion. Eliot
Gold Leaves. Chesterton
Golden Age. Hammond
Good Old Days. Mitchell
Grand Finale. Layton
Grandfathers [*or* After a Line by John Peale
  Bishop], The. Justice
Grandmother, Rocking. Merriam
Grey Woman. Cardiff
Grow Old Along with Me. *Fr.* Rabbi Ben
  Ezra. Browning
Growing Old. Arnold
Growing Old. Fraser
Haiku: "In the old man's eyes." Takahama
  Kyoshi
Happy about Being Old. Yüan Mei
Harmonica Man. Wolny
He Never Expected Much. Hardy
Heads in the Women's Ward. Larkin
Healing. Reisen
Here's a Woman Lived to an Extreme Old
  Age. "Zelda"
His Golden Locks Time Hath to Silver
  Turned. *Fr.* Polyhymnia. Peele
How Old Are You? Fritsch
How to Be Old. Swenson
Hut near Desolated Pines. Campbell
I Am Growing Old. Johnson
I Followed a Path. Parker
I give Thee thanks, my King. O Brolchain
I have outlived most things and people round
  me. Vyazemsky
I Know Inside. Yüan Mei
I Look into My Glass. Hardy
I Strove with None. *Fr.* The Last Fruit Off
  an Old Tree. Landor
I Used to Watch You, Sleeping. *Fr.* My
  Mother's Birthday. Raine
Ice, The. Gibson
If I Ever Grow Old: Grim and Gleeful
  Resolutions. Nauen
If I had known. *Fr.* Kokin Shu. *Unknown*
I'm Here. *Fr.* Meditations of an Old
  Woman. Roethke
Imaginary Translation. Hacker
In Age. *Fr.* Milton: On the Busts of Milton,
  in Youth and Age. Bowles
In Respect of the Elderly. Peacock
In the end I find. *Fr.* Kokin Shu. Narihira
In the turn of the world. *Fr.* The Turn of the
  World. Sitwell

In Time of Gold. Doolittle
In times yet to come. Munenaga
Infirmity. Roethke
It Is Too Late. Fr. Morituri Salutamas.
 Longfellow
Jane Seagrim's Party. Nathan
Lament of the Lovely Helmet-Dealer. Villon
Lamentation of the Old Pensioner, The.
 Yeats
Last Chapter, The. De la Mare
Last Leaf, The. Holmes
Last Words of My English Grandmother, The.
 Williams
Late-flowering Lust. Betjeman
Leaden Echo and the Golden Echo, The.
 Hopkins
Let Me Grow Lovely. Baker
Letter. Bergman
Letter from a Girl to Her Own Old Age, A.
 Meynell
Letters from a Father. Van Duyn
Life's Golden Sunset. Linden
Litany for Old Age, A. Harsen
Little Boy and the Old Man, The. Silverstein
Little Old Lady in Lavender Silk, The.
 Parker
Long Hill, The. Teasdale
Long Time a Child. Coleridge
Love and Friendship. Brontë
Man Who Became Old, The. Ríos
Man's Going Hence. Fr. Human Life.
 Rogers
Medicine. Walker
Meditation. Hecht
Millie's Date. Abse
Minuet on Reaching the Age of Fifty, A.
 Santayana
Miscellaneous Poems on Growing Old, sels.
 Yüan Mei
Miss Creighton. Taylor
Miss Euphemia. Ransom
Moccasins of an Old Man, The. Carden
Model Church, The. Yates
Moonlight. Teasdale
Mr. Flood's Party. Robinson
Muttering. Weöres
My Love Is Young. Birney
My sins in their completeness. O Brolchain
Nature. Longfellow
Near Death. Pixner
New Day. Madgett
Night Thoughts in Age. Wheelock
No charm can stay, no medicine can assuage.
 Landor
Nod. De la Mare
Ode to an Old Man. Minoru
Of Growing Old. Enright
Old Adam, The. Levertov
Old Age. Füst
Old Age. Glatstein
Old Age. Keary
Old Age. Morris-Jones
Old Age. Tennyson
Old Age Come to Us All. Williams
Old Age in His Ailing. Melville
Old Age Pensioner, The. Campbell
Old Age Sticks. Cummings
Old Black Men. Johnson
Old Couple, The. Green
Old Couple. Simic
Old Crabbed Men. Reeves
Old Dan'l. Strong
Old Familiar Faces, The. Lamb
Old Folk, The. Ditlevsen
Old Freedman, The. Thompson
Old Habitant, An. Call
Old I Am. Bosman
Old Jockey, The. Higgins
Old Ladies. Dromgoole
Old Lady's Lament for Her Youth, The.
 Villon
Old Man, The. Fisher

Old Man. Henry
Old Man. Jennings
Old Man [or Old Man Travelling], An.
 Wordsworth
Old Man at the Window, The. Harvey
Old Man Dreams, The. Holmes
Old Man He Courted Me, An. Unknown
Old Man Stirs the Fire to a Blaze, An. Fr.
 The Wanderings of Oisin. Yeats
Old Man, the Sweat Lodge. George
Old Man's Comforts and How He Gained
 Them, The. Southey
Old Man's Song, about His Wife, The.
 Unknown
Old Man's Thoughts, An ("Lonelier still than
 last year"). Fr. Eighty-seven Hokku.
 Buson
Old Man's Winter Night, An. Frost
Old Man's Wish, The. Pope
Old Men, The. Corman
Old Men, The. De la Mare
Old Men, The. Feldman
Old Men, The. Kipling
Old Men. Nash
Old Men Admiring Themselves in the Water,
 The. Yeats
Old, old/ To live on, wretched to behold.
 Fr. The Men That Once Were. Gruffydd
Old People Dozing. Levertov
Old People on the Nursing Home Porch.
 Strand
Old Seawoman. LeClaire
Old though I am. Fr. Thirty Tanka.
 Shunzei
Old Wife in High Spirits. "MacDiarmid"
Old Wife Speaks, The. Mayer
Old Woman, The. Campbell
Old Woman, An. Jones
Old Woman. Smith
Old Woman, The. Swirszczynska
Old Woman Awaiting the Greyhound Bus.
 Niatum
Old Woman of the Roads. Colum
Old Women of Toronto. Waddington
Older American, The. Clarke
On a Photograph of My Mother at Seventeen.
 Williams
On a Winter Day Drinking Wine at a Friend's
 House in the Country. I Nagashiro
On Ageing. Angelou
On Growing Old. Masefield
Once I Played and Danced in My Parents'
 Kingdom.
One Flesh. Jennings
Over the Hill to the Poor-House. Carleton
Parable of the Old Man and the Young, The.
 Owen
Pass we the ills, which each man feels or
 dreads. Fr. Solomon on the Vanity of the
 World. Prior
Pause for Breath, A. Hughes
Peekaboo, I Almost See You. Nash
Phone Call to Rutherford. Blackburn
Piazza Piece. Ransom
Pigeon-Feeders in Battery Park, The.
 Altrocchi
Planting a Wood. Baratynsky
Poem: "Old man in the crystal morning after
 snow." Schwartz
Poet Laments the Coming of Old Age, The.
 Sitwell
Poor Old Fat Woman. Donald
Portrait of a Very Old Man. Carsley
Portrait of an Old Man. Mitterer
Portrait of the Artist as a Prematurely Old
 Man. Nash
Promise of Peace. Jeffers
Prospect of the Future, The. Linden
Provide, Provide. Frost
Purpose of Poetry, The. Carter

Quatrain: "My foolish heart keeps beckoning
 to me." Farhat
Rabbi Ben Ezra. Browning
Rare Rhythms. London
Reflecting on the Aging-Process. Peters
Remarks of Soul to Body. Warren
Requiem, A: "My father listening to opera,
 that's me." Ignatow
Retirement. Unknown
Sailing to Byzantium. Yeats
Sair Fyel'd, Hinny. Unknown
Seas are quiet when the winds give o'er, The.
 Fr. Of The Last Verses in the Book.
 Waller.
Second Madrigal, The. Swirszczynska
Self-Portrait. Thomas
Senex. Betjeman
Setting of the Moon, The. Leopardi
Seventies, The. Johnson
She Does Not Remember. Swirszczynska
She, to Him. Hardy
Silly Old Man, The. Unknown
Silver Threads among the Gold. Rexford
Simon Lee. Wordsworth
Sixty-eighth Birthday. Lowell
Smell of Old Newspapers Is Always Stronger
 after Sleeping in the Sun, The. Lowery
So long as lasts the span of life. Fr. Manyo
 Shu. Okura
So What. Appleman
Sometimes, in the Evening. Buddingh'
Song: "Age is when to a man." Beckett
Song for September. Fitzgerald
Song from a Country Fair. Adams
Song of a Woman Abandoned by the Tribe.
 Unknown
Song of the Old Woman. Unknown
Span of Life, The. Frost
Spur, The. Yeats
Stabat Mater. Hunt
Still Life. Angelotti
Stone on the Hilltop, The. Lu Yu
Strokes. Stafford
Survivor. MacLeish
Survivor, The. Thomas
Swan Song. Marcus
Tear. Kinsella
Temporal. Jonas
Terminus. Emerson
"That time of year thou may'st [or maist] in
 me behold." Fr. Sonnets, LXXIII.
 Shakespeare
Tithonus. Tennyson
To a Poor Old Woman. Williams
To Age. Landor
To an Old Gentlewoman That Painted Her
 Face. Turberville
To an Old Lady. Empson
To have grown old. Teika
To Mother. Drown
To One Being Old. Mitchell
To Perilla. Herrick
To the Reader. Jarman
To Waken an Old Lady. Williams
Too Late. Ludlow
Tower, The. Yeats
Tuba. Marcus
Turn from Self. Macdonald
Twenty Golden Years Ago. Mangan
Two Old Men Look at the Sea. Hervey
Ulysses. Tennyson
Uselessness. Wilcox
Very Old Man. Henry
Very Old Woman, A. Eshleman
Waiting for a Second Time. Tauhindauli
Warning. Joseph
Watching a Child Watching a Witch. Fr.
 Derivations. Joseph
Weeksville Women. Loftin
Welcome Eild. Unknown

When I Am Old. Mason
When I See Old Men. Souster
When the Sword of Sixty Comes Nigh His
   Head. Firdausi
When They Grow Old. Ralph
When We That Now Ha' Childern Wer
   Childern. Barnes
When winter is gone and spring comes. *Fr.*
   Manyo Shu. *Unknown*
When You Are Old. Yeats
Whom the Gods Love. Bruner
Widower in the Country, The. Murray
Wishes of an Elderly Man. Raleigh
Written in a Carefree Mood. Lu Yu
Written when He Was Well Over Eighty.
   Fr. Thirty Tanka. Shunzei
Young and Old. *Fr.* The Water Babies.
   Kingsley
Young Old Young Old. Elburg
Youth and Age. Coleridge
Youth and Age on Beaulieu River, Hants.
   Betjeman
Zeke. Strong
See also **Pensions; Retirement.**
Old Ironsides. *See* **Constitution (ship).**
Oldham, John
To the Memory of Mr. Oldham. Dryden
Olive Trees and Olives
An Olive Tree in Corfu. Busta
Elul in Galilee. Goldberg
Grasse: The Olive Trees. Wilbur
Oleaster, The. Graves
Olive, The. *Unknown*
Olive Tree, The. Baring-Gould
Olive Trees. Spencer
Oliver Cromwell
I saw him dead, a leaden slumber lyes [*or*
   lies] *Fr.* A Poem upon the Death of
   Oliver Cromwell. Marvell
Oliver Twist
Oliver Twist. Philip
Olympics
Boomerang. Cram
Joan Benoit. Ferrarelli
Omar Khayyám
In a Copy of Omar Khayyám. Lowell
O'Neill, Owen Roe
Lament for the Death of Eoghan Ruadh
   O'Neill. Davis
O'Neill, Shane
Shane O'Neill's Cairn. Jeffers
Onions
Man in the Onion Bed, The. Ciardi
Onion, The. Gibson
Onyons. *Fr.* Verses for Fruitwomen. Swift
Peeling Onions. Rich
Recipe: Onions. Philemon
Traveling Onion, The. Nye
Ontario, Canada
Battle of Bridgewater, The. *Unknown*
Burning Hills. Ondaatje
Capital Square. Anderson
Country North of Belleville, The. Purdy
Crossing Ontario. Grenier
Giant's Tomb in Georgian Bay. "Hale"
Stranded in My Ontario. Everson
Temagami. Lampman
Tick Picking in the Quetico. Johnson
Wilderness Gothic. Purdy
Winter Night: Mount Royal. Klein
Ontario, Lake
Thought of Lake Ontario, A. Ray
Opera
Aux Italiens. "Meredith"
Carmen. Levy
Das Liebesleben. Gunn
Faust. Ashbery
Il Janitoro. Ade
Ill Met by Zenith. Nash
Lohengrin. Payne
Matinees. Merrill

Rigoletto. Levy
Tannhauser. Levy
Tannhäuser. Payne
Ophelia
Ballad of Another Ophelia. Lawrence
Ophelia. Rimbaud
Opium
Evanishings. Tucker
Opium-Eater, The. Tucker
Willie the Weeper. *Unknown*
Opossums
Carmen Possum. *Unknown*
Oppenheimer, Joseph Süss
Jud' Süss Oppenheimer on His First Visit with
   Professor Sigmund Freud. *Fr.*
   Psychoanalysis. Teller
Jud' Süss Tells about Them and about
   Himself. *Fr.* Psychoanalysis. Teller
Opportunity
Opportunity. Braley
Opportunity. Graham
Opportunity. Ingalls
Opportunity. Machiavelli
Opportunity. Malone
Opportunity. *Fr.* The Rape of Lucrece.
   Shakespeare
Opportunity. Sill
Secret Ballgame. Schönwiese
Today. Carlyle
Oppression
Burning of Paper instead of Children, The.
   Rich
Commission. Pound
Determination. Clarke
Great Insohreckshan, Di. Johnson
Hamlet in Russia, A Soliloquy. Pasternak
I Was Washing Outside in the Darkness.
   Mandelstam
Last Statement. Mayakovsky
Man with the Hoe, The. Markham
Of Reason and Discovery. Mattera
Oppression. Hughes
Waiting Inside. Ignatow
You Ask Me. Mutabaruka
See also **Apartheid; Dehumanization;**
   Sexism; Slavery; Tyranny.
Optimism
Away, Melancholy. Smith
Optimism. Wilcox
Say Not the Struggle Nought Availeth.
   Clough
Try the Uplook. *Unknown*
When the clouds' swoln bosoms echo back
   the shouts of the many and strong. *Fr.* In
   Tenebris. Hardy
Year's at the Spring, The. *Fr.* Pippa Passes.
   Browning
See also **Hope.**
Oracles
Hebrew Sibyl, The. Fainlight
Oracle. Finkel
Oracles, The. Housman
Orange (color)
What Is Orange? O'Neill
Orange Trees and Oranges
Cemetery of Orange Trees in Crete, The.
   Stern
Orange. Ferland
Orange blossoms that came. *Fr.* Kokin Shu.
   Unknown
Oranges. Soto
Red-Gold Rain, The. Sitwell
Smudging. Wakoski
Tapestry Trees. Morris
While I waited and wondered. *Fr.* Manyo
   Shu. Yakamochi
Wild orange tree, The. Ietaka
Oratory
Overworked Elocutionist, An. Wells
Orchards
An Orchard at Avignon. Robinson

Good-by and Keep Cold. Frost
I Have an Orchard. *Fr.* The Tragedy of
   Dido. Marlowe
In an Old Orchard. Dufault
Lost Orchard, The. Masters
My Orcha'd in Linden Lea. Barnes
Of an Orchard. Tynan
Old Apple Trees. Snodgrass
Orchard. Doolittle
Orchard, The. Ehrlich
Orchard. Engels
Orchard Trees, January. Wilbur
Through Ruddy Orchards. Oliver
Orchids
Bee-Orchis, The. Young
Orchids. Roethke
Order
Cantica: Our Lord Christ: Of Order. Francis
   of Assisi
Idea of Order at Key West, The. Stevens
Oregon (state)
Fish Counter at Bonneville, The. Stafford
Grand Ronde Valley, The. Higginson
Lines Written in Oregon. Nabokov
Men against the Sky. Haines
Oregon Winter. McGahey
Wingwalking in Oregon. Peterson
Orestes (mythology)
Essay. Waskowsky
Organ-grinders. *See* **Hurdy-gurdies.**
Organs and Organists
German Organ. Artaud
New Organ, The. Heard
Organist, The. Stevens
Wesley in Heaven. Brown
Origami
Origami for Two. Dominick
Original Sin
Adam Lay Ibounden *or* Ibowndyn *or*
   Ybounden. *Unknown*
Alas, that ever that speche was spoken.
   Unknown
Corruption. Vaughan
Ha! Original Sin. Nash
Original Sin; a Short Story. Warren
Orioles
An Oriole at Dawn. Li Meng-yang
To hear an oriole sing. Dickinson
Orion
Famous Archer, The. Park Je-chun
Orion (constellation)
Hunter: 20,000 A.D, The. Joron
Orion. Cendrars
Orion. Rich
Oriskany, Battle of (1777)
Battle of Oriskany, The. Helmer
Orkney Islands
Above Ben Loyal. Ball
In Orknay. Fowler
Lion Gate. Rich
Oronsay, Scotland
Saint Colm-Cille and the Cairn of Farewell.
   Irvine
Orphans
Babes in the Wood, The. *Unknown*
Bitter sight—/ I watch and my tears. *Fr.*
   Twenty-four Tanka. Sanetomo
Children's Elegy. *Fr.* Eighth Elegy.
   Rukeyser
Little Orphant Annie. Riley
Orphan, The. *Unknown*
Orphan Boy, The. *Unknown*
Orphan Girl, An. Linden
Orphan's Song, The. Dobell
Readen ov a Head-Stwone. Barnes
Orpheus
Death of Eurydice and Orpheus' Journey to
   Hell, The. *Fr.* Metamorphoses. Ovid
Lament of Orpheus, The. Kormos
Orpheus. Davie
Orpheus. Herrick

Orpheus. Tichy
Orpheus. Winters
Orpheus and Eurydice. Browning
Orpheus and Eurydice. Valentine
Orpheus in Greenwich Village. Gilbert
Orpheus in the Underworld. Gascoyne
Orpheus to Beasts. Lovelace
Orpheus to Woods. Lovelace
Power of Music, The. Lisle
Thus Sung Orpheus to His Strings. *Unknown*

Orr, Robert
High Stick. Collins

Osmond, Marie
To Marie Osmond. Skelley

Ostriches
Bedraggled Ostrich. Takamura Kotaro
He "Digesteth Harde Yron." Moore
Ostrich is a Silly Bird, The. Freeman

Ottawa, Ontario
Capital Square. Anderson

Ottawa River
Deep Dark River. Roberts

Otterburn, Battle of (1388)
Battle of Otterburn [*or* Oterborne], The.
   Unknown
Chevy Chase. *Unknown*

Otters
Giant Otters. Mac Low
Otter, The. Heaney
Otter, An. Hughes
Possibility That Has Been Overlooked Is the
   Future, The. Hartnett

Ouija Boards
For My Husband. Voigt
Life like the periodical not yet. *Fr.* The
   Book of Ephraim. Merrill
Voices from the Other World. Merrill

Outlaws. *See* **Crime and Criminals.**

Ovenbirds
Oven Bird, The. Frost

Ovibos
Ovibos, The. Hale
See also **Musk Oxen.**

Ovid (Publius Ovidius Naso)
Ovid on the Dacian Coast. Thompson
Written in an Ovid. Prior

Owain Gwynedd, Prince of North Wales
Triumphs of Owen, The. Gray

Owen, Wilfred
Wilfred Owen's Photographs. Hughes

Owls
Amused at My Own Figure while Traveling.
   Fr. Thirty-three Hokku. Kikaku
Aziola, The. Shelley
Bird of Night, The. Jarrell
Come, doleful owl, the messenger of woe.
   Unknown
Eyes. Davies
Father and Child. Harwood
From a Printed Bill, Fixed in the Beak of One
   in a Group of Five Stuffed Owls in the
   Shop Window of a Bird Stuffer, at
   Richmond, Yorkshire. *Unknown*
"Good Night," Says the Owl. Crum
Great Brown Owl, The. Browne
Hail to Thee, Blithe Owl. Lardner
If the Owl Calls Again. Haines
In the Eyes of a Screech Owl. Tozaburo
Leaves that rustled on this oak-crowned hill,
   The. Wordsworth
Materialized into an Owl. Oliver
Of all the gay birds that e'er I did see.
   Unknown
Owl, The. De la Mare
Owl. Dufault
Owl/ you/ my frightful friend. Mühringer
Owl. Rokwaho
Owl, The. Smith
Owl, The. Tennyson
Owl, The. Thomas

Owl/ whose home was in the hemlock, The.
   Unknown
Owl and the Fox, The. *Unknown*
Owl and the Pussy-Cat, The. Lear
Owl-Critic, The. Fields
Owl in the Rabbi's Barn, The. Jaffe
Owls. Snodgrass
Owl's Bedtime Story, The. Jarrell
Questioning Faces. Frost
Rhyme-Prose on the Owl. Chia Yi
Sea Owl. Smith
Snow Owl. Smith
Song of the Owl, The. Munkittrick
There came a gray owl at sunset. *Unknown*
There was an old owl lived in an oak.
   Unknown
When I was in a summer valley. *Fr.* The
   Owl and the Nightingale. De Guildford
White Owl, The. *Fr.* Love in a Valley.
   Meredith
Wise Old Owl, A. Richards
You look at me, a hut or cage contains. *Fr.*
   Sagesse. Doolittle

Oxen
Crossing the Plains. Miller
I have an ox but its tail is missing. Shitago
I Have Twelve Oxen. *Unknown*
If I Might Be an Ox. *Unknown*
My Ox Duke. Dyer
Old Ox, The. Hamilton
Ox, The. Webster
Ox-Tamer, The. Whitman
Oxen, The. Hardy
Oxen: Ploughing at Fiesole. Tomlinson
Song of Praise for an Ox. Sutskever
Too tired to move fast. Teika
White Oxen. Simpson
Windy Bill. *Unknown*
Winter ("Drooping, the labourer-ox"). *Fr.*
   The Seasons: Winter. Thomson

Oxford, England
Above the High. Grigson
By Magdalen Bridge, Oxford. Hopkins
Christ Church Meadows, Oxford. Hall
Duns Scotus's Oxford. Hopkins
Epigram on the Refusal of the University of
   Oxford to Subscribe to His Translation of
   Homer. Cowper
How changed is here each spot man makes or
   fills! *Fr.* Thyrsis. Arnold
Letter, A. Quiller-Couch
Oxford. Douglas
Oxford. Johnson
Oxford Bells. Hopkins
Oxford in Wartime. Wilson
Oxford Is a Stage. Nolan
Oxford Nights. Johnson
Philomela. Ransom
Pitt-Rivers Museum, Oxford, The. Fenton
Scholar-Gipsy, The. Arnold
Spires of Oxford, The. Letts
To Oxford. Hopkins
To Oxford. Russell
Trent Again, The. *Fr.* Polyolbion.
   Drayton

Oysters
Hoity-Toity Oyster, The. *Fr.* A Fable in
   Two Languages. Pratt
Oyster Shell. Kambara Yumei
Oystering. Howard
Oysters. Swift
Pearls plucked,/ the oyster shells. *Fr.*
   Sixty-four Tanka. Saigyo
Walrus and the Carpenter, The. *Fr.* Through
   the Looking-Glass. "Carroll"
Wildflowers. Howard

Ozark Mountains
Caves. Baker

P

Pacific Ocean
Eye, The. Jeffers
Facing West from California's Shores.
   Whitman
On Teaching the Young. Winters
Once by the Pacific. Frost
Pacific Sonnets, *sels.* Barker
Prayer to the Pacific. Silko
Remembering That Island. McGrath
Slow Pacific Swell, The. Winters

Pacifism and Pacifists
Breakthrough. Sinclair
Christmas Eve under Hooker's Statue.
   Lowell
Conscientious Objector, The. Shapiro
Dooley Is a Traitor. Michie
Dove, The. MacColl
For the Minority. Peterson
I Sing of Olaf Glad and Big. Cummings
In the one-two domestic goose one-two
   one-two step. *Fr.* New Wings for Icarus.
   Beissel
Memories of West Street and Lepke. Lowell
See also **Conscientious Objectors.**

Pack, Robert
North/South. Mariani

Paganism and Pagans
Christ and the Pagan. Tabb
First and Last Man. McTell
Plain of Adoration, The. *Unknown*

Pain
After-Glow of Pain, The. Thompson
After great pain, a formal feeling comes.
   Dickinson
Credential, A. Hobsbaum
Flat One, A. Snodgrass
Flower, The. Creeley
I heard a fly buzz—when I died. Dickinson
I Sit and Look Out. Whitman
If my vain soul needs blows and bitter losses.
   Fr. The Christian's New-Year Prayer.
   Wilcox
Is it not sure a deadly pain. *Unknown*
Joy of every drop, The. Ghalib
Much madness is divinest sense. Dickinson
My Toe. Holman
My Uninvited Guest. Smith
Never Admit the Pain. Gilmore
90 North. Jarrell
Pain. "Æ"
Pain. Gonzáles Martínez
Pain. Hand
Pain. Henry
Pain. Södergran
Pain. Zand
Pain for a Daughter. Sexton
Pain—has an element of blank. Dickinson
Pain Is My Brother. Hand
Pain-Killers. Harrison
Personal Opinion, A. Ravikovich
Phantom Pain. Chernoff
Prayer for Pain. Neihardt
Process. O'Donnell
Security. O'Donnell
Solitude. Wilcox
Splittings. Rich
There is a languor of the life. Dickinson
There is a pain—so utter. Dickinson
To Be. Gutiérrez Nájera
Villanelle: "It is the pain, it is the pain,
   endures." Empson
Woman Talk. Simba
Woodworm, The. Fusinato

Paine, Thomas
 God Save Great Thomas Paine. Mather
 On Mr. Paine's Rights of Man. Freneau
Painting and Painters
 After two sittings, now our Lady State. *Fr.*
  The Last Instructions to a Painter. Marvell
 After Whistler. Plumly
 An Old Picture. Nemerov
 Andrea del Sarto. Browning
 Anonymous Drawing. Justice
 Another November. Plumly
 Artist, The. Kunitz
 At Luca Signorelli's Resurrection of the
  Body. Graham
 Backgrounds to Italian Paintings: Fifteenth
  Century. Ridler
 Beauty and Sadness. Song
 Cardinal's Dog, The. Glassco
 Dance, The. Williams
 Detail from an Annunciation by Crivelli.
  Dobson
 Dutch Interior. Sarton
 Early Unfinished Sketch. Clarke
 Elegiac Stanzas. Wordsworth
 Face, A. Browning
 Face upon [or on] the Floor, The. D'Arcy
 Fra Lippo Lippi. Browning
 Framed. Harris
 Giovanni da Fiesole on the Sublime; or, Fra
  Angelico's "Last Judgment." Howard
 How to Paint a Perfect Christmas. Holub
 I Paint What I See. White
 Images for a Painter. Wright
 In an Artist's Studio. Rossetti
 In Santa Maria del Popolo. Gunn
 Joan Brown, about Her Painting. Fraser
 Landscape in a Pot. Lo Ch'ing
 Large Bad Picture. Bishop
 Laughing Hyena, by Hokusai, The. Enright
 Man with the Hoe, The. Markham
 Meditation on John Constable, A. Tomlinson
 Monet Refuses the Operation. Mueller
 Most Expensive Picture in the World, The.
  Nemerov
 Musée des Beaux Arts. Auden
 Museum Piece. Wilbur
 My Madonna. Service
 My own head. Seen in mirrors. Cleanly axed.
  Fr. Caravaggio Dying, Porto Ercole, July
  1610, Aged 36. Lucie-Smith
 Nightmare. *Fr.* The Botanic Garden: The
  Loves of the Plants. Darwin
 O that I'd had. *Fr.* Manyo Shu. Mononobe
  Furumaro
 Old Paintings on Italian Walls. Raine
 On a Fifteenth-Century Flemish Angel. Ray
 On a Painting by Patient B of the
  Independence State Hospital for the Insane.
  Justice
 On a Picture by Michele Da Verona, of Arion
  as a Boy Riding upon a Dolphin. Ridler
 On Her Portrait. Juana Inés de la Cruz
 Order for a Picture, An. Cary
 Paint Box, The. Rieu
 Painted Head. Ransom
 Painted Passages. Harada
 Painter, The. Ashbery
 Painter Who Pleased Nobody and Everybody,
  The. Gay
 Painter's Mistress, The. Flecker
 Painting. Jacobs
 Painting a Madonna. Warren
 Painting Entitled Love and the Pilgrim, A.
  O'Brien
 Painting the Gate. Swenson
 Painture. Lovelace
 Paul Klee. Haines
 Pictor Ignotus. Browning
 Poem: "About the size of an old-style dollar
  bill." Bishop
 Poem by a Perfectly Furious Academician.
  Brooks

 Poem, The: "Painter of Dante's awful
  ferry-ride, The." Deutsch
 Politics of Rich Painters, The. Baraka
 Portrait of a Cree. "Hale"
 Portrait of Prince Henry, The. Clouts
 Proportions. Stroud
 Recollection, A. Bishop
 Ryder. Haines
 Sir Joshua Reynolds. Blake
 Sketchbook Ashes of Jehoshaphat, The.
  Dubie
 Technique. Eaton
 To Cole, the Painter, Departing for Europe.
  Bryant
 To Giovanni da Pistoia on the Painting of the
  Sistine Chapel, 1509. Michelangelo
 To Paint the Portrait of a Bird. Prévert
 To S.M., a Young African Painter, on Seeing
  His Works. Wheatley
 Unpraised Picture, An. Burton
 White Fox. Shepard
 Why I Am Not a Painter. O'Hara
 Winter Landscape. Berryman
Paleontology
 Imitation of Julia A. Moore. "Twain"
 See also **Dinosaurs; Evolution; Extinction;
  Fossils.**
Palestine
 In Galilee. Butts
 On Jordan's Bank. Byron
 Palestine. Whittier
 To Those Palestinians Martyred in Foreign
  Lands. Faiz
 See also **Israel.**
Palm Sunday
 Donkey, The. Chesterton
 Willow-Boughs, The. Block
Palm Trees
 Palm House, Botanic Gardens. Hetherington
 Palm Tree, The. Abd-ar-Rahman I
 Palm Trees. Warner
 Royal Palm. Crane
 Song of the Palm. Robinson
Pan (god)
 God of Sheep, The. *Fr.* The Faithful
  Shepherdess. Fletcher
 Hymn of Pan. Shelley
 Hymn to Pan. *Fr.* Endymion [a Poetic
  Romance] Keats
 Musical Instrument, A. Browning
 My Last Duchess. Browning
 Pan in Wall Street. Stedman
 Pan Piping. Plato
 Pans Anniversarie. Jonson
 Pan's Syrinx. *Fr.* Midas. Lyly
 Syrinx. Merrill
Panama
 Beyond the Chagres. Gilbert
 Panama. Jones
 Panama. Roche
Panama Canal
 Song of Panama, A. Runyon
Pancakes
 Mix a Pancake. Rossetti
 Pancake Collector, The. Prelutsky
 Those Flapjacks of Brown's. Taylor
Pandas
 Panda, The. *Fr.* Animals That Stand in
  Dreams. Elliott
Pansies
 Pansy. Newsome
Pantheism
 Higher Pantheism, The. Tennyson
 Higher Pantheism in a Nutshell, The. *Fr.*
  The Heptalogia. Swinburne
 It Is a Beauteous Evening [Calm and Free]
  Wordsworth
 One, The. Kavanagh
Panthers
 In the Night. Roberts
 Panther, The. Nash

Papacy
 To Pius IX. Whittier
 To Pope Julius II. Michelangelo
 See also **Catholicism.**
Paperclips
 Paperclips. Kennedy
Paperweights
 Paperweight, The. Schnackenberg
Parachuting *See* **Sky Diving and Sky Divers.**
Parades
 Flag Goes By, The. Bennett
 Parade. *Fr.* A Circus Garland. Field
 Whirring, A. Aldan
 See also **Marching and Marches.**
Paradise. See **Heaven.**
Paradise Lost
 On Mr. Milton's Paradise Lost. Marvell
 See also **Milton, John.**
Parakeets
 Parakeet, The. Sinclair
Paralysis
 If my legs cannot move. Morrison
 Tingle, The. Kirk
Paranoia
 Tryst. Merriam
 Tunnel, The. Strand
 Widow, The. Ludvigson
Parenthood
 Adam. Hecht
 Anacreontic, on Parting with a Little Child.
  Wesley
 Any Time. Stafford
 Becoming a Dad. Guest
 Censorship. Ciardi
 Childless. MacNamee
 Door and Window Bolted Fast. Leib
 Expectant Father, The. Ai
 Father Poem. Oppenheimer
 For a Child Expected. Ridler
 For Sapphires. Rodgers
 Fruit of the Flower. Cullen
 Gift, The. Jarman
 Heart's Needle. Snodgrass
 I am slowly dying, water evaporating. *Fr.*
  Summer Solstice. Bowering
 I See My Girl. Olds
 I Sleep to the Patter of the Rain. Anhava
 Living among the Dead. Matthews
 My Son. Kailas
 On My First Daughter. Jonson
 On My First Son [or Sonne]. Jonson
 On the Birth of His Son. Su Tung-p'o
 Parents. Buckley
 Parents. Meredith
 Poet's Welcome to His Love-begotten
  Daughter, A. Burns
 Prayer for My Daughter, A. Yeats
 Secret Laughter. Morley
 Separate Parties. Stuart
 Sleep, My Child. Aleichem
 Sonnet to a Friend Who Asked, How I Felt
  When the Nurse First Presented My Infant
  to Me. Coleridge
 They Grow Up Too Fast, She Said. O Hehir
 Upon Wedlock and Death of Children.
  Taylor
 What My Child Learns of the Sea. Lorde
 "When forty winters shall besiege thy brow."
  Fr. Sonnets, II. Shakespeare
 Which Shall It Be? Beers
 Wishes for My Son. MacDonagh
Parents
 Ancestral Poem. Senior
 At Misaka, the Pass of the Gods. *Fr.* Manyo
  Shu. Kamutobe Kooshio
 Death of a Parent, The. Pastan

Driving My Parents Home at Christmas. Bly
For My Son, Noah, Ten Years Old. Bly
How I regret it now. *Fr.* Manyo Shu.
   Udobe Ushimaro
I leave my father and mother behind. *Fr.*
   Manyo Shu. Hasetsukabe Hitomaro
Le Touquet. Jarman
Never can I forget the words. *Fr.* Manyo
   Shu. Hasetsukabe Inamaro
Sleeping, The. Emanuel
Though I tried to forget, as I came. *Fr.*
   Manyo Shu. Akino Osamaro
Unquiet Ones, The. Kunitz

Paret, Benny ("Kid")
Memory of Boxer Benny (Kid) Paret, The.
   Lima

Pari
Farewell to Pari's Hill. Kapilar
His Hill. Kapilar
Memory of the Hill, A. Kapilar
Pari! Pari! they cry. Kapilar
Pari's Green Land, Remembered. Kapilar
Pari's Hill Is Partial to Dancers. Kapilar
That Month. Pari
Waterfalls and Liquor ("Waterfalls
   sounded."). Kapilar

Paris, France
Ballad of Bouillabaisse, The. Thackeray
Epistle to the Right Honourable William
   Pulteney, Esq. Gay
Four Sheets to the Wind and a One-Way
   Ticket to France. Rivers
Garden, The. Prévert
Homeless. Aragon
In a Station of the Metro. Pound
In the World's Heart. Cendrars
In Vain. Prévert
Le Sacré-Coeur. Mew
Mourning Letter from Paris, A. Rivers
No Grounds for Prosecution. Breton
104 Boulevard Saint-Germain. Pitchford
Paris. Symons
Paris; This April Sunset Completely Utters.
   Cummings
Pont Mirabeau. Kennedy
Public Holiday: Paris. Horner
Sunflower. Breton
Too Bad for Me. Aragon
Two X. Cummings
Unromantic Song. Brode
What People Say about Paris. Koch
Woman's Execution, A. King
Zone. Apollinaire

Parker, Charlie
Mellowness and Flight. Barlow
Requiem for "Bird" Parker. Corso
Walking Parker Home. Kaufman
Yardbird's Skull. Dodson

Parks
Back to Life. Gunn
City Park. Campert
Crossing the Park. Moss
Definition of Nature. Redmond
Lines Written in Kensington Gardens.
   Arnold
London versus Epping Forest. *Fr.* Child
   Harold. Clare
On the Fine Arts Garden, Cleveland. Atkins
Park. Ignatow
Public Garden, The. Lowell
South End. Aiken
Upon the Priory Grove, His Usual Retirement.
   Vaughan

Parliament (Great Britain)
And now a fig for the lower house. Carey
Free Parliament Litany, A. *Unknown*
On the New Forcers of Conscience Under the
   Long Parliment. Milton
Wilfred Owen's Photographs. Hughes

Parma, Italy
Correggio's Cupolas at Parma. De Vere
Naples. Rogers

Parmigianino
Self-Portrait in a Convex Mirror. Ashbery

Parnell, Charles Stewart
Parnell. Yeats

Parodies
Brand-X Anthology of Poetry, The (BXAP).
   William Zaranka, ed.
Faber Book of Parodies, The (FaBoPa).
   Simon Brett, ed.
*Parodies; an Anthology from Chaucer to
   Beerbohm—and After* (Par). Dwight
   Macdonald, ed.
Understanding Poetry (UnPo). Cleanth
   Brooks *and* Robert Penn Warren, eds.

Parrots
Gossip, The. Halpern
Little Miss and Her Parrot. Marchant
My name is Parrot, a byrd of paradise. *Fr.*
   Speak [*or* Speke], Parrot. Skelton
"Not home! Not home!" *Fr.* Twenty-seven
   Hokku. Natsume Seibi
Parakeet. Clark
Parrot, The. Campbell
Parrot, The. Flecker
Parrot, The. Lucie-Smith
Parrot, The. Tablada
Parrots, The. Gibson
Poor Poll. Bridges
"Psittachus Eois Imitatrix Ales ab Indis."
   Sitwell
Reflections on the Death of a Parrot. Jacinto

Parsifal. *See* Arthurian Legend.

Parthenon
On Seeing the Elgin Marbles. Keats
Parthenon, The. Heath-Stubbs

Parties
After the Party. Wise
Cap so tall, A. *Unknown*
Cricket is in the hall, The. *Unknown*
Dancers Inherit the Party, The. Finlay
False Security. Betjeman
Feckless Dinner Party, The. De la Mare
Love Feast, The. Auden
Office Party. McGinley
Party, The. Avison
Party, The. Dunbar
Party, The. Sala
Party in Winter. Shapiro
Rose on My Cake, The. Kuskin
Sopping lies the dew. *Unknown*

Parting
Adieu. Tucker
Ae Fond Kiss. Burns
After He Had Gone. Warner
After the Supper and Talk. Whitman
Against Parting. Zach
And Wilt Thou Leave Me Thus? Wyatt
At the San Francisco Airport. Winters
Bequest of His Heart, A. Scott
Bi-Lingual. Paskin
Bright Was the Morning. D'Urfey
Childe Harold's Farewell to England. *Fr.*
   Childe Harold's Pilgrimage. Byron
Chilterns, The. Brooke
Chloris Farewell. Waller
Corydon's Farewell, on Sailing in the Late
   Expedition Fleet. *Unknown*
Deva-like Barbarian. Ho Ning
Deva-like Barbarian. Sun Kuang-hsien
Difficulty of Parting, The. Hsüeh Chao-yün
Dreadful order, The. *Fr.* Manyo Shu.
   Mononobe Akimochi
End Is Now, The. "Madelaine"
End Song. Tan'ee
Esyllt. Jones
Even as I Hold You. Walker
Fare Thee Well. Byron
Farewell, The:
It Was A' for Our Rightfu' King. Burns

Farewell to Juliet ("I see you, Juliet, still,
   with your straw hat"). *Fr.* The Love
   Sonnets of Proteus: Farewell to Juliet.
   Blunt
Farewell, Unkind! Farewell! to me, no more a
   father! *Unknown*
Farewell, A: "With all my will, but much
   against my heart." *Fr.* The Unknown
   Eros. Patmore
Gazing after the Distant Traveler. Wei
   Chuang
Gesture, The. Libbey
Good-bye My Fancy! Whitman
Goodbye. Bloch
Goodbye. Lewis
Heaven's Immortal. Huang-fu Sung
His Parting from Her. *Fr.* Elegies. Donne
I must depart now. Yukihira
I Will Not Let Thee Go. Bridges
I Will Write. Graves
If He Let Us Go Now. Williams
In the service of/ My mighty Lord. *Fr.*
   Manyo Shu. Yakamochi
Kathleen Mavourneen. Crawford
Leave-taking, A. Swinburne
Leaving. Vuglar
Lines Written Immediately after Parting from
   a Lady. Brydges
Lotus Leaf Cup. Wei Chuang
Lucasia, Rosania and Orinda Parting at a
   Fountain, July 1663. Philips
Maid of Athens [Ere We Part]. Byron
Mountain Hawthorns. Niu Hsi-chi
My life closed twice before its close.
   Dickinson
Oath. Sica
Odeon. Amir
On Fanny Godwin. Shelley
On His Mistress Going from Home.
   Unknown
On His Mistresse Going to Sea. Cary
On Leaving Cuba, Her Native Land. Gomez
   de Avellaneda
Orinda to Lucasia Parting, October, 1661, at
   London. Philips
Our Captain Cried All Hands. *Unknown*
Parting, The. Heard
Parting. *Fr.* Twenty-four Hokku. Kito
Parting. Thomas
Parting, A. Wang Wei
Parting as Descent. Berryman
Parting at Morning. Browning
Parting in Wartime. Cornford
Parting Kiss, The. Heard
Parting with Lucasia; a Song. Philips
Parting, without a Sequel. Ransom
Paying Homage at the Golden Gate. Sun
   Kuang-hsien
Poem of Parting. *Fr.* Twenty Hokku.
   Kyorai
Sad Parting. Maruyama Kaoru
Seamen and Soldiers' Last Farewell to Their
   Dearest Jewels, The. *Unknown*
Since that parting. Mibu Tadamine
Since there's [*or* ther's] no help[e], come let
   us kiss[e] and part. *Fr.* Idea. Drayton
Song of the Water Clock at Night. Sun
   Kuang-hsien
Song of the Wine Spring. Sun Kuang-hsien
Song: "Sweetest love, I do not go[e]."
   Donne
Taking Leave of a Friend. Li Po
Taoist Nun, The. Sun Kuang-hsien
There Is No Word for Goodbye.
   TallMountain
To His Lady. Henry VIII, King of England
To Lucasta, Going to the Wars [*or* Warres].
   Lovelace
To William Roe. Jonson
Toast to the Traveler, A. Sun Kuang-hsien
Toast to the Traveler, A. Wei Chuang

Upon [His] Leaving His Mistress. Rochester
Waterloo Station. Norman
Weary Lot Is Thine, A. *Fr.* Rokeby. Scott
When It Came Time. Amir
When We Two Parted. Byron
Winter. Wingfield
Winter's Tale, A. Lawrence
Partridges
Another Song of the Same Woman, to Some
   Partridges, Sent to Her Alive. Pinar
On Some Partridges Sent to Her Alive. Pinar
Pasadena, California
On a View of Pasadena from the Hills.
   Winters
Passion
Slumbering Passion. Heard
Passivity
I Never Even Suggested It. Nash
Passover
Angel, The. Hayes
Holiday. *Fr.* Remembrances. Leivick
Passover Eve. Kruger
Seder, 1944. Torberg
Still Small Voice, The. Klein
Past
There was an end to hearts and rhymes.
   Hollander
Why have I locked myself inside. Hollander
Pasternak, Boris
Last Year's Discussion: The Nobel Russian.
   McGinley
1976. *Fr.* Poems from a Diary. Sutskever
Pastoral Verse
Bucolic. Rae
Nymph's Reply to the Shepherd, The.
   Ralegh
Passionate Shepherd to His Love, The.
   Marlowe
Pastoral Poesy. Clare
To Make a Pastoral; a Receipt. *Unknown*
Pastures. See **Fields and Pastures.**
Pater, Walter
Gemlike Flame, The. Lister
Paterson, New Jersey
Paterson, *sels.* Williams
Preface: "Rigor of beauty is the quest. But
   how will you find beauty when it is
   locked." *Fr.* Paterson. Williams
Paths
Footpath. Ngatho
Patience
Disappointment, The. Taylor
His Answer. Thompson
My own heart let me more have pity on.
   Hopkins
Owl, The. Davison
Patience. Horne
Patience Is When You Stop Waiting.
   Williams
Patience, Though I Have Not. Wyatt
Sonnet: "Patience, hard thing! the hard thing
   but to pray." Hopkins
Third Wonder, The. Markham
Waiting. Burroughs
Waiting Both. Hardy
Patients
In Hospital, *sels.* Henley
Mental Cases. Owen
Old Men's Ward. Dean
See also **Hospitals; Illness;**
   Institutionalization; Mental Illness.
Patriarchy
Fat Blues. Crowell
History of Lesbianism, A. Grahn
Woman like Me, A. Myles
Patrick, Saint
At Saint Patrick's Purgatory. O'Dala
Bard's Chant. *Fr.* Saint Patrick for Ireland.
   Shirley
March. McFadden
Praise of Fionn, The. *Unknown*

Saint Patrick. Leslie
St. Patrick's Breastplate. Patrick
White Lake, The. *Unknown*
Patriotic Songs, American
America. Smith
America for Me. Van Dyke
America the Beautiful. Bates
As Down a Lone Valley. Dwight
Battle Cry of Freedom, The. Root
Battle Hymn of the [American] Republic,
   The. Howe
Hail, Columbia. Hopkinson
Land of the Free. Hosking
Song for Our Flag, A. Sangster
Star-spangled Banner, The. Key
Yankee Doodle. Shuckburg
See also **Patriotic Songs, Confederate.**
Patriotic Songs, Canadian
Hymn for Canada, A. Watson
Patriotic Songs, Confederate
My Maryland. Randall
Patriotic Songs, English
Heart of Oak. Garrick
Rule, Britannia! *Fr.* Alfred, A Masque.
   Thomson
Patriotic Songs, French
Marseillaise, The. Rouget de Lisle
Patriotic Songs, Italian
Garibaldi Hymn, The. Mercantini
Patriotism
America for Me. Van Dyke
As One Non-Combatant to Another. Orwell
Barbara Frietchie. Whittier
Better Way. Coolidge
Bleat of Protest. Weston
Breathes There the [or a] Man [with Soul So
   Dead]. *Fr.* The Lay of the Last Minstrel.
   Scott
Celebrations. Clarke
Columbia. *Unknown*
Composed by the Seaside, near Calais,
   August, 1802. Wordsworth
Dear Harp of My Country. Moore
Dulce et Decorum Est. Owen
England, My England. Henley
England! my persecuted isle. *Fr.* Patriotism.
   Richardson
Fatherland, The. Lowell
Flag Goes By, The. Bennett
Great Britain Through the Ice: Or, Premature
   Patriotism. Turner
Hame, Hame, Hame. Cunningham
Harbour, The. Letts
Harp That Once through Tara's Halls, The.
   Moore
Homes of England, The. Hemans
I Am an American. Lieberman
I Have Loved England. *Fr.* The White
   Cliffs. Miller
I Hear America Singing. Whitman
I Vow to Thee, My Country. Spring-Rice
In an Age of Fops and Toys. *Fr.*
   Voluntaries. Emerson
In Westminster Abbey. Betjeman
Invasion. Duggan
Italy. Filicaia
Kid Has Gone to the Colors, The. Herschell
Killers That Run, The. Cohen
Loyalty to the Flag. Moorer
Marseillaise, The. Rouget de Lisle
Minority Report. Updike
Native Land. Lermontov
New Colossus, The. Lazarus
Next to of Course God America I.
   Cummings
MCMXIV. Larkin
O land of mine where I was bred. Tolstoy
Patriot, The. Milne
Pro Patria Mori. Moore

Soldier, The. *Fr.* 1914. Brooke
101 Patriotic Poems (OPP).
Patrons
Miserly Patron, A. *Unknown*
To Pope Julius II. Michelangelo
Paul, Saint
Our Two Worthies. Ransom
Saul, Afterward, Riding East. Brinnin
To St. Peter and St. Paul. Constable
Pawnbrokers and Pawnshops
New Order of Chivalry, A. Peacock
Pawnshop Window. Grenville
Street Window. Sandburg
Payne, D. A.
Dedicated to the Right Rev'd D. A. Payne.
   Fordham
Peace
A. E. F. Sandburg
"And There Was a Great Calm." Hardy
Bugle Song of Peace. Clark
Cessation of War. Collins
Easter. Nemerov
Enquiry after Peace. A Fragment.
   Winchilsea
Even During War. *Fr.* Letter to the Front.
   Rukeyser
For I Dipped [*or* Dipt] into the Future. *Fr.*
   Locksley Hall. Tennyson
Forty Years Peace. Sivan
He Shall Speak Peace. Clark
He Shall Speak Peace unto the Nations.
   Walters
How Sweet the Night. Bates
In Distrust of Merits. Moore
Lark, The. *Unknown*
Legend of Versailles, A. Tolson
Lotos-Eaters, The. Tennyson
Man unto His Fellow Man. *Fr.* On a Note
   of Triumph. Corwin
My Penultimate Speech at a Meeting of Some
   People of Good Will. Walther
Not Marching Away to Be Killed. Fuller
Ode on His Majesty's Proclamation. *Fr.* Il
   Pastor Fido. Fanshawe
Ode to Peace. Fordham
Pax. Lawrence
Peace. *Fr.* 1914. Brooke
Peace. De la Mare
Peace. Edman
Peace. Herbert
Peace. Hopkins
Peace. Jonas
Peace. Longley
Peace. Markham
Peace. Vaughan
Peace of Wild Things, The. Berry
Peace Poem. Maturai Velacan
Pleading Voices. Katav
Poet Questions Peace, The. *Fr.* Euthymiae
   Raptus; or, The Teares of Peace.
   Chapman
Prince of Peace His Banner Spreads, The.
   Fosdick
Reconciliation. Whitman
Reign of Peace, The. Starck
Season of Phantasmal Peace, The. Walcott
Shalom Aleichem. *Unknown*
Song for Simeon, A. Eliot
Peace, Isabel
Lines to Mrs. Isabel Peace. Fordham
Peach Trees and Peaches
Going for Peaches, Fredericksburg, Texas.
   Nye
I asked a thief to steal me a peach. Blake
Peach Tree with Fruit. Colum
Wild Peaches. Wylie
Peacocks
Eight-Beat Barbarian Tune. Sun Kuang-hsien
Fragment: "Mark you how the peacock's
   eye." Hopkins

Peacocks. Roberts
Verses under a Peacock Portrayed in Her Left Hand. Greene
What is it more eyes doth wear. *Unknown*
Pear Trees and Pears
Haiku: "Pear blossoms." Mizuhara Shuoshi
Haiku: "Peeling pears/ sweet juice drips." *Fr.* Thirty-nine Haiku. Shiki
Pear Tree. Doolittle
Pear Tree, The. Millay
Pears. Pastan
Peeling Pears at Midnight. Lo Fu
Sadness and Still Life. Ramke
Stone Orchard, The. Oates
Study of Two Pears. Stevens
Tapestry Trees. Morris
That Broad and Spreading Sweet Pear. *Unknown*
Pearl Diving
Diving for Pearls. Yamamoto
Pearl Harbor
Day of Pearl Harbor, The. *Fr.* A Brief History of Imbecility. Takamura Kotaro
Pearls
Precious Pearl, The. Thompson
Precious Pearl, The. Wilson
Peas
I eat my peas with honey. *Unknown*
In the Pea Patch. Kumin
Peasants
Exiles. "Æ"
French Peasants. Gibbon
Grandpa and the Uncles. *Fr.* Byelorussia. Kulbak
I Am the Mountainy Singer. Campbell
Market Day. Roversi
Nobleman and Thresherman, The ("Nobleman lived in a valley of late."). *Unknown*
Peasant. Merwin
Peasant Poet, The. Clare
Peasants, The. Lewis
To His Father on Praising the Honest Life of the Peasant. E'tesami
Winter at Night in the Old Hut. *Fr.* Byelorussia. Kulbak
Pedantry
On the Edition of Mr. Pope's Works with a Commentary and Notes. Edwards
Purist, The. Nash
To the Editor of Mr. Pope's Works. Edwards
Tongue-Doughty Pedant. Edwards
See also **Scholarship and Scholars.**
Peddling and Peddlers
Fine Knacks for Ladies. *Unknown*
Lace Pedlar, The. Morin
Negro Peddler's Song, A. Johnson
New Brooms. *Fr.* The Three Ladies of London. Wilson
Oysters. Swift
Pedlar Jim. Hoare
Pedlar's Caravan, The. Rands
Peele Castle, England
Elegiac Stanzas. Wordsworth
Peeping Toms. *See* **Voyeurism.**
Peewees or Peewits. *See* **Pewees *or* Pewits.**
Pelicans
Frigate Pelican, The. Moore
Pelicans. Jeffers
Reason for the Pelican, The. Ciardi
Penelope (mythology)
No Easy Harbour. Hartigan
Penelope. Dubé
Penelope. Harrison
Penelope's Despair. Ritsos
Prayer: "Fabric I must keep mended. Rend." Graham
World as Meditation, The. Stevens
Penguins
On the Death of an Emperor Penguin in Regent's Park, London. Wright

Penguin, A. Herford
Penguin on the Beach. Miller
View from Here, The. Stafford
Peninsular War
Burial of Sir John Moore after [*or* at] Corunna, The. Wolfe
Pennsylvania
All the Smoke. Siegel
Driving through Coal Country in Pennsylvania. Holden
Missionary Visits Our Church in Scranton, The. Parini
Pennsylvania Places. Daly
Pennsylvania Winter Indian 1974. Littlebird
Pittsburgh. Bynner
Prophecy in Flame. Howard
Snake Hill. Parini
Penshurst, England
To Penshurst. Jonson
Pensions
On Seeing an Officer's Widow Distracted. Barber
Pluralist and Old Soldier, The. Collier
See also **Retirement.**
Pentagon (building)
March 2, The. Lowell
Pentagonia. Bates
Pentecost
Call to Pentecost, A. Tyler
Dominica Pentecostes. De Vere
Hymn for Pentecost. Mangan
Pentecost. Coats
Peonies
In the dark garden at night. *Fr.* Twenty-one Hokku. Kaya Shirao
Peony in a wide garden. *Fr.* Eighty-seven Hokku. Buson
White peonies about to collapse. *Fr.* Twenty-seven Hokku. Natsume Seibi
Peppertrees
Scenes from the Life of the Peppertrees. Levertov
Perception
Charles on Fire. Merrill
Communion. Ignatow
Distances. Hugo
ESP. Tem
Idea of Order at Key West, The. Stevens
Poem: "All the mirrors in the world." O'Hara
Seeing for a Moment. Levertov
Snow Man, The. Stevens
Thirteen Ways of Looking at a Blackbird. Stevens
We Continue. Merwin
Windows. Dickey
Percivale. *See* **Parsifal.**
Percy, Sir Henry
Battle of Otterburn [*or* Oterborne], The. *Unknown*
Chevy Chase. *Unknown*
Perets, Yitskhok Leybush
Yitskhok Leybush Perets. Halpern
Perfection
Sunflower Sonnet Number Two. Jordan
Perry, Oliver Hazard
On the Death of Commodore Oliver H. Perry. Brainard
Perry's Victory. *Unknown*
Perry's Victory—A Song. *Unknown*
Persecution
From the Corpse Woodpiles, from the Ashes. Hayden
Persephone
Garden of Proserpina, The. *Fr.* The Faerie Queene. Spenser
Garden of Proserpine, The. Swinburne
Gardens of Proserpine, The. Cassity
Hymn to Proserpine. Swinburne
Kore. Creeley
Proserpine at Enna. Bottrall

Perseus
Medusa. O'Sullivan
Perseus. Baxter
Perseus. Hayden
Perseus. MacNeice
Perseverance
After. Ryan
Ants at the Olympics, The. Digance
Cost of Pretending, The. Davison
Excelsior. Longfellow
Keep a-Goin'. Stanton
Nevertheless. Moore
Pluck Wins. *Unknown*
Plug. Cooke
Psalm of Life, A. Longfellow
Reeds in the Loch Sayis, The. *Unknown*
Say Not the Struggle Nought Availeth. Clough
Ulysses. Tennyson
Persia. *See* **Iran.**
Persian Wars
On the Spartan Dead at Thermopylae. Simonides
Persian Version, The. Graves
Salamis. *Fr.* The Persians. Aeschylus
Peru
Death of Atahuallpa, The. Larbaud
History of Peru. Delgado
Imperfect Times. Delgado
Of History More Like Myth. Garrigue
Peru; the New Poetry (Per). David Tipton, ed.
Peruncattan
Elegy: "Young will not wear it, The." Kutavayir Kirattanar
Peruvaluti, King
Your bards are wearing lotuses. Nettimaiyar
Pessimism
Epitaph on a Pessimist. Hardy
Of Misery. Howell
Pessimist, The. King
Sum of Life, The. King
There Are Bad Times Just around the Corner. Coward
Violent Storm. Strand
What Do People Do? Leyeles
Worried Skipper, The. Irwin
Petakh Tikva, Israel
Old Ice Factory in Petakh Tikva, The. Amichai
Peter Rabbit
Peter Rabbit. McPherson
Peter, Saint
Domine, Quo Vadis? *Unknown*
Domine Quo Vadis? Watson
In the Servants' Quarters. Hardy
Look, The. Browning
Meaning of the Look, The. Browning
Peter and John. Wylie
St. Peter. Rossetti
To St. Peter and St. Paul. Constable
Peter the Great
Song of History: Peter the Great. Sakuma Shozan
Peterloo Massacre (1819)
Mask [*or* Masque] of Anarchy, The. Shelley
Song to the Men of England. Shelley
Petra, Jordan
Air Travel in Arabia. Johnston
Pedra. Burgon
Petrarch
Petrarch. Carducci
Petrels
Stormpetrel. Murphy
To see the petrel cropping in the farmyard. *Fr.* Sonnets for a Dying Man. Singer
Pets
Bess My Badger. Hughes
Child's Pet, A. Davies
Disaster. Calverley
Epitaph on a Hare. Cowper

Geist's Grave. Arnold
If You. Creeley
In the far realm of our Lord. *Fr.* Manyo
　Shu. Yakamochi
Meadow Mouse, The. Roethke
Monk and His Pet Cat, The. *Unknown*
My Doggie. Nurton
Nero. Tanikawa Shuntaro
Parakeet. Clark
Praise of a Collie. MacCaig
Retrieval System, The. Kumin
Two Songs of a Fool. Yeats

Pewees [*or* Pewits]
Two Pewits. Thomas

Peyote
Peyote Vision. Blockcolski
Tarahumara Herbs ("Tarahumara Indians have
　come down, The"). Reyes

Pheasants
Darting over the cedar brakes. *Fr.* Manyo
　Shu. Yakamochi
Echoing with the cries. *Fr.* Manyo Shu.
　Yakamochi
Golden Pheasants Flying. Csoori
Obscure Pleasure of the Indistinct, The.
　Ramke
Pheasant. Nishiwaki Junzaburo
Pheasant. Plath
Pheasant. Rákos
See! from the brake the whirring Pheasant
　springs. *Fr.* Windsor Forest. Pope

Philadelphia, Pennsylvania
Philadelphia. Kipling
Philadelphia ("Philadelphia is a handsome
　town"). *Unknown*
South Street. Silvera

Philanthropy and Philanthropists
Disagreeable Man, The. Gilbert
Lines on Being Refused a Guggenheim
　Fellowship. Whittemore
Offer, An. Guiterman
See also **Charity.**

Philately
Philatelic Lessons: The German Collection.
　Spingarn
Philatelist Royal. Graves

Philip, King (American Indian Chief)
King Philip's Last Stand. Scollard

Philiphaugh, Battle of (1645)
Battle of Philiphaugh, The. *Unknown*

Philipon-Roland, Jeanne Manon
Jeanne Manon Philipon-Roland. Zitz-Halein

Philippines
Blue Tropic. Cabalquinto
Flower Vendor, The. Cabalquinto
See also **Filipinos.**

Phillips, Wendell
Wendell Phillips. Alcott
Wendell Phillips. Ray

Philomela
Philomela. Arnold
Philomela. Ransom
Philomela. Ritsos

Philosophy and Philosophers
Department, The. Grossman
Dissatisfaction with Metaphysics. Empson
Excommunication, The. Ravitch
Homage to the Philosopher. Deutsch
In Defense of Metaphysics. Tomlinson
Looking at Old Note-Books. Sisson
Makhno's Philosophers. Manifold
Metaphysical Amorist, The. Cunningham
Metaphysics. Herford
Mock On, Mock On, Voltaire, Rousseau.
　Blake
Moorlands of the Not. *Unknown*
On Philosophers. *Unknown*
On the Death of a Metaphysician. Santayana
Philosopher, The. Foss
Philosopher, The. Sill
Philosopher and Her Father, The. Brooks

Philosopher and the Birds, The. Murphy
Philosophers, The. Edson
Philosophy, the great and only heir. *Fr.* To
　the Royal Society. Cowley
Poetry and Philosophy. *Fr.* An Eclogue to
　Mr. Johnson. Randolph
Positivists, The. Collins
Stacademia. Barlow
To a Maid Demure. Sill
To an Old Philosopher in Rome. Stevens
To the Royal Society. Cowley
Voltaire at Ferney. Auden

Phoebus Apollo. *See* **Apollo.**

Phoenix
News of the Phoenix. Smith
O Blest Unfabled Incense Tree. *Fr.*
　Nepenthe. Darley
Phoenix, The. Abu Madi
Phoenix, The. J. V. Cunningham
Phoenix, The. Megged
Phoenix, The. Nash
Phoenix, bird of terrible pride. *Fr.*
　Mutations of the Phoenix. Read
Phoenix Self-born, The. *Fr.* Metamorphoses.
　Ovid

Photocopying
Certified Copy. Deagon

Photography and Photographers
Baby Pictures of Famous Dictators. Simic
Camera. Kooser
Chinese Camp, Kamloops (circa 1883).
　Suknaski
City Afternoon. Ashbery
City Lights: I Took That Picture. Albert
Daguerreotype Taken in Old Age. Atwood
Family Album, A. Brody
Family Man, A. Kumin
Family Portraits. Tucker
Family Scene: Mid-Twentieth Century.
　Pastan
Floor. Williams
Hardness Scale, The. Peseroff
Hiawatha's Photographing. "Carroll"
History of Photography, A. Goldbarth
I Am Not a Camera. Auden
In Front of a Japanese Photograph. Peck
In the Field. Jung Han-mo
Le Touquet. Jarman
Lines on a Young Lady's Photograph Album.
　Larkin
Looking at a Photograph on My Forty-Fourth
　Birthday. Dennis
Mary Ackerman, 1938. Glancy
Middle of a War, The. Fuller
Naval Photograph: 25 October 1942: What the
　Hand May Be Saying. Bottoms
Negatives. Wright
Old Photo, 1942. Uba
Photo of Emily, The. Ferlinghetti
Photo of the Author with a Favorite Pig.
　Matthews
Photograph, The. Drake
Photograph. May
Photograph. Prettyman
Photograph in a Stockholm Newspaper for
　March 13, 1910. Coles
Photograph of My Room. Forché
Photographer. Booth
Photographer, The. Simpson
Photographing a Rattlesnake. Wagoner
Photos, The. Wakoski
Portrait. Osbey
Sensationalism. Levis
Shooting the Horses. Mordecai
Six Young Men. Hughes
Suite of Six Pieces for Siskind, A. Logan
This Is a Photograph of Me. Atwood
View by Color Photography on a Commercial
　Calendar. Williams

Physical Handicaps
Handicapped Children Swimming. Browne
*Toward Solomon's Mountain; the Experience
　of Disability in Poetry* (TSM). Joseph L.
　Baird *and* Deborah S. Workman, eds.

Physicians
Archaic Song of Dr. Tom the Shaman.
　Unknown
Arthur Ridgewood, M.D. Davis
Better Way, The. Leaf
Birthday Wishes to a Physician. Moorer
"Chief, The." *Fr.* In Hospital. Henley
Cold Front, A. Williams
Correct Compassion, A. Kirkup
Country Doctor, The. Carleton
Doctor Who Sits at the Bedside of a Rat, The.
　Miles
Doctors' Row. Aiken
Doctor's Story, The. Carleton
House-Surgeon. *Fr.* In Hospital. Henley
Le Médecin Malgré Lui. Williams
Ol' Doc' Hyar. Campbell
Old Doc. Vinz
On Hygiene. Belloc
On the Death of Mr. [*or* Dr.] Robert Levet, a
　Practiser in Physic. Johnson
Remedy Worse than the Disease, The. Prior
To a Good Physician. Wycherley
To Doctor Empiric[k]. Jonson
See also **Medicine; Nurses.**

Physics and Physicists
After Reading a Child's Guide to Modern
　Physics. Auden
First and Second Law. Flanders
First Rainfall. Lightman
New Physics, The. Zolynas
Physicist's Purpose, The. Marcus
Song of the Screw. *Unknown*

Pianos
Investment, The. Frost
Piano. Lawrence
Piano, The. Lawrence
Piano at Evening. Palea
Piano Lessons. Wormser
Player Piano. Updike
Recital, The. Schwartz
Visitor, The. Ruark

Picasso, Pablo
Father, The. Lattimore
Remembrances of Guernica. Schmied

Pickles
Meditation for a Pickle Suite. Dillard
Ode on [*or* to] a Jar of Pickles. Taylor

Picnics and Barbecues
Archaeological Picnic, The. Betjeman
Georgia Dusk. Toomer
Picnic, The. Aldis
Picnic. Lofting
Picnic at the Beach. Johnson, Jr.
Picnic Day. Field
Picnic: the Liberated. Holman
Picnics. *Unknown*
Rhyming with Tzu-yu's "Treading the Green.
　Su Tung-p'o

Pico della Mirandola, Giovanni
Pico della Mirandola. Mason

Pies
Lemon Pie. Guest
Melton Mowbray Pork Pie, A. Le Gallienne

Pigeons
Fly. Merwin
Homing Pigeons. Walker
Leave Them Alone. Kavanagh
Mrs. Peck-Pigeon. Farjeon
On Seeing a Pigeon Make Love. Hunt
Pigeon, A. Claus
Pigeons, The. Bennett
Pigeons. Moore
Pigeons. Reid
Trinity Place. McGinley

Pigs
An Apple Tree and a Pig. Humphreys
Animals Are Passing from Our Lives.
  Levine
Ego. Siegel
Feed. Knister
For the Eating of Swine. Jones
Greedy Little Pig, The. Pawsey
Hare and the Pig, The. Bridgman
Hog at the Manger. Farber
Hog-calling Competition. Bishop
I Had a Little Pig. *Unknown*
Judged by the Company One Keeps.
  Unknown
Little Pig, The. Landau
Little Piggies, The. Hood
Mary Middling. Fyleman
Moly. Gunn
Morgante and the Boars. Pulci
Ode to a Pig while His Nose Was Being
  Bored. Southey
Ode to the Pig: His Tail. Brooks
Pig. Eluard
Pig, The. Nash
Pig. Popa
Pig, The. *Unknown*
Pig, The. Young
Pig and the Nightingale, The. Shteynbarg
Pig Is Never Blamed, A. Deutsch
Pig Song. Atwood
Pig-Tale, A. *Fr.* Sylvie and Bruno
  Concluded. "Carroll"
Pigs, The. Lehmann
Pigs, The. Poulsson
Pigs, The. Taylor
Pindaric on the Grunting of a Hog, A.
  Wesley
Poor Man's Pig, The. Blunden
Roasted Sucking Pig. *Unknown*
Rumors of the Turning Wheel. Halley
St. Anthony and His Pig; a Cantata. Forrest
Saint Francis and the Sow. Kinnell
Seven Little Pigs. *Unknown*
Sow of Feeling, The. Fergusson
There Was a Small Pig Who Wept Tears.
  Lobel
This little pig went to market. Mother Goose
Three Little Pigs, The. Gatty
Transubstantiation. Geddes
Unknown Color, The. Cullen
View of a Pig. Hughes
Wild Boar and the Ram, The. *Fr.* Fables.
  Gay
Wild Pigs. Kooser

Pike, Zebulon Montgomery
Death of General Pike, The. Osborn

Pike (fish)
Pike, The. Bruce
Pike. Hughes
Song of the Pike. Sato Haruo

Pilgrim Fathers
Boston Hymn. Emerson
Children of Light. Lowell
Courtship of Miles Standish, The.
  Longfellow
First Proclamation of Miles Standish, The.
  Preston
Landing of the Pilgrim Fathers [in New
  England], The. Hemans
Mayflower, The. Ellsworth
Pilgrim Fathers, The. Bacon
Pilgrim Fathers, The. Pierpont
Upon the First Sight of New England, June
  29, 1638. Tillam
Word of God to Leyden Came, The. Rankin

Pilgrimages and Pilgrims
At Saint Patrick's Purgatory. O'Dala
Bullocky. Wright
Carcassonne. Nadaud
Christmas Creek. Kendall
End of the Way, The. Cole

O California. Murguía
O Weary Pilgrims. *Fr.* The Growth of Love.
  Bridges
Palmer, The. *Fr.* The Vision of Piers
  Plowman. Langland
Passionate Man's Pilgrimage, The. Ralegh
Pilgrim, The. Wightman
Pilgrim, The. Yeats
Pilgrimage. Clarke
Pilgrimage, The. Herbert
Pilgrim's Problem. Lewis
Pilgrims' Sea Voyage and Seasickness, The.
  Unknown
Pilgrim's Song. Ingemann
Seekers, The. Masefield
Uphill [*or* Up-Hill]. Rossetti
Way to Jerusalem, The. *Unknown*
Who would true valour see. *Fr.* The
  Pilgrim's Progress. Bunyan

Pilots
Fleet Fighter. FitzRoy
John Douglas White. Ferrett
My Brother Flies Over Low. Huddle
Prayer for a Pilot. Roberts
Sonnet: Zone ("You're weary of this ancient
  world at last"). Apollinaire
When He Is Flying. FitzRoy
Zone. Apollinaire
See also **Air Warfare**.

Pindar
Pindar. Antipater of Sidon
Poem Beginning with a Line by Pindar, A.
  Duncan

Pine Island, Minnesota
Lying in a Hammock at William Duffy's Farm
  in Pine Island, Minnesota. Wright

Pine Trees
Aspects of the Pines. Hayne
At Sasanami/ the pines are just as they were.
  Tameuji
Cutting Beetle-Blighted Ponderosa Pine.
  Holden
Foxtail Pine. Snyder
I had never guessed. Teika
O solitary pine, how many. *Fr.* Manyo Shu.
  Ichihara
Pine, The. Webster
Pine at Timber-Line, The. Monroe
Pine Gum. Ross
Pines, The. Lippmann
Pines, The. Spofford
Poem on a Little Pine, A. Hsieh Chin
Quilled Quilt, a Needle Bed, A. Leithauser
Snowing of the Pines, The. Higginson
Southern Pines. Bishop
Up in the Pine. Watson
White Pines, Felled 1984. Eberhart
Within the sacred fence. Ryoshun

Ping-pong
Unsound Condition. Armour

Pinkham, Lydia
Lydia Pinkham. *Unknown*

Pioneers
American History. Moses
Arrival, The. *Fr.* The Emigrant.
  McLachlan
Axe of the Pioneer, The. Crawford
Ballad of William Sycamore, The. Benét
Boys of Sanpete County, The. *Unknown*
Camp within the West, The. Quinn
Crossing the Plains. Miller
End of Steel. Saunders
Face to Face. Rich
For Jean Vincent d'Abbadie, Baron
  St.-Castin. Nowlan
Gateway Arch. Cheng Ch'ou-yu
Grandfather. Bowering
Great-Aunt Rebecca. Brewster

Handcart Song, The. *Unknown*
I love you better than I race my race. *Fr.*
  Tecumseh. Mair
Pioneer Woman. Crawford
Pioneers. Clark
Pioneers. Garland
Pioneers! O Pioneers! Whitman
St. George. Walker
Settler, The. Street
Settler in the olden times went forth, A. *Fr.*
  The Creek of the Four Graves. Harpur
Tempest, The. Smith
Tittery-Irie-Aye. *Unknown*
Westward Ho! Miller
What noble courage must their hearts have
  fired. *Fr.* The Rising Village. Goldsmith
Where the Pelican Builds. Foott
Wilderness Theme. Mudie
Women of the West, The. Evans

Pipers
Piper, A [*or* The]. "O'Sullivan"
Piping Down the Valleys Wild. *Fr.* Songs of
  Innocence. Blake

Piracy and Pirates
Captain Kidd. *Unknown*
Captain Kid's Farewell to the Seas; or, The
  Famous Pirate's Lament. *Unknown*
Captain Stratton's Fancy. Masefield
Captain Ward and the *Rainbow*. *Unknown*
Derelict. Allison
Dutch Picture, A. Longfellow
Execution of Five Pirates for Murder.
  Unknown
Flying Cloud, The. *Unknown*
Last Buccaneer, The. Kingsley
Morgan. Stedman
Murder of a Spanish Lady by a Pirate. Dana
Pirate Don Durk of Dowdee, The. Meigs
Pirate Story. Stevenson
Pirates' Fight, The. *Fr.* The Legend of
  Ghost Lagoon. Schull
Rhyme of the Three Captains, The. Kipling
Sir Andrew Barton. *Unknown*

Pitcher, Molly
Molly Pitcher. Richards
Molly Pitcher. Sherwood

Pittsburgh, Pennsylvania
Fort Duquesne. Plimpton
Pittsburgh. Bynner

Pity
Compassionate Fool, The. Cameron
God's Pity. Driscoll
She Is More to Be Pitied than Censured.
  Gray
Sonnet XXIX: Pity Me Not [Because the
  Light of Day]. Millay

Pius XII, Pope
Eugenio Pacelli. Neilson

Pius IX, Pope
To Pius IX. Whittier

Pixies. *See* **Fairies.**

Pizarro, Francisco
Revenge of America, The. Warton

Pizza
Answer, The. Wachtel

Place Names
American Names. Benét
American Traveller, The. "Kerr"
Indian Names. Sigourney
Localities. Sandburg
Names from the War. Catton
Pennsylvania Places. Daly

Plague
Adieu, Farewell, Earth's Bliss[e] *Fr.*
  Summer's Last Will and Testament.
  Nashe
Coming of the Plague, The. Kees
Plague Sermon. Heyen
Tarantula or the Dance of Death. Hecht

Plains. *See* **Prairies.**

Planets
Jupiter uninhabited. Jandl
On Passing by Those Icy Stones (and Yes, Columbia!). Calder

Plants
Air Plant, The. Crane
Beware, My Successor. Eiseley
Bracken Hills in Autumn. "MacDiarmid"
Cuttings ("Sticks-in-a-drowse droop over sugary loam"). Roethke
Cuttings ("This urge, wrestle, resurrection of dry sticks"). Roethke
Green Things Growing. Craik
House Plants. McFadden
Houseplant. Napier
Jubilate Herbis. Farber
Moss-gathering. Roethke
Nevertheless. Moore
Rooftop, The. Gunn
Root Cellar. Roethke
Spike of Green, A. Baker
Sundew, The. Swinburne
Woman with Flower. Madgett
Woodspurge, The. Rossetti
See also **Flowers, Trees,** *etc.*

Plath, Sylvia
Babysitters, The. Plath
Cottage Street, 1953. Wilbur
On the Death of Sylvia Plath. Herzberg
Requiem for Sylvia Plath. Frezza
Sylvia's Death. Sexton
Your face broods from my table, Suicide. *Fr.* Dream Songs. Berryman

Plato
Spirit of Plato. *Unknown*
What Then? Yeats

Platonic Love
Against Platonick Love. *Unknown*
No Platonic Love. Cartwright

Platte River
Trail beside the River Platte, The. Heyen

Plattsburgh, Battle of (1814)
Battle of Plattsburg, The. *Unknown*
Battle of Plattsburg Bay, The. Scollard

Platypuses
I Had a Duck-billed Platypus. Barrington
Platypus, The. Herford

Play
At the Playground. Stafford
Behind Grandma's House. Soto
Boy with a Hammer. Hoban
Chinatown Games. Lum
Frolic. "Æ"
Hide and Seek. Shuttle
Hop, Skip, and Jump. Snyder
I Am Called Childhood. More
In High Spirits. Ryokan
Innocent Play. Watts
Land of Counterpane, The. Stevenson
Land of Story-Books, The. Stevenson
Laughing Child. Sandburg
Length of Days. Bonar
Nurse's Song. *Fr.* Songs of Innocence. Blake
Ring-a-Ring. Greenaway
Roller Skates. Farrar
Voyage of Jimmy Poo, The. Emanuel

Playhouses. *See* **Theater and Theaters.**

Playmates
Invisible Playmate, The. Widdemer

Pleasure
Canzone: "Consider the three functions of the tongue." Hacker
Goblin Market. Rossetti
Poems of Solitary Delights. Tachibana

Pleiades
Pleiades, The. Coatsworth

Plowing and Plowmen
All Jolly Fellows That Follow the Plough. *Unknown*

Follower. Heaney
Frightened Ploughman, The. Clare
Harry Ploughman. Hopkins
Horse, The. Kicknosway
I Will Go with My Father a-Ploughing. Campbell
On the Plough-Man. Quarles
Painful Plough, The. *Unknown*
Ploughboy, The. Clare
Ploughing on Sunday. Stevens
Ploughman, The. *Unknown*
Ploughman at the Plough. Golding
Ploughman, in Imitation of Milton, The. Jones
Plower, The. Colum
Plowman, The. Knister
Plowman's Song. Knister
Seed. Bosman
Sod-Breaker, The. Stringer
To a Schoolboy. *Unknown*

Plum Trees and Plums
Ancient Plum Tree at the K'ai-hsien Buddhist Monastery, An. Ch'ü Ta-chün
Blossoming plum. Teika
Blossoms of plum. Teika
Empty house, The. *Fr.* Manyo Shu. Tabito
For white plum blossoms. *Fr.* Eighty-seven Hokku. Buson
In dawn's first light. Chikako
In my dream said a plum-blossom. *Fr.* Manyo Shu. Tabito
In my garden fall the plum-blossoms. *Fr.* Manyo Shu. Tabito
In the light of dawn. Yoshimoto
Little Jack Horner. Mother Goose
Oh, when will this night end. *Fr.* Manyo Shu. *Unknown*
On an evening/ aglow with the crimson. Tamekane
Plum, A. Leib
Plum Blossoms Late at Night. Shinkei
Plum Blosssoms. Michizane
Plum flowers/ blooming crimson. *Fr.* Twenty-three Tanka. Tamekane
Plum fragrance startles me again and again. *Fr.* Fifty-one Tanka. Izumi
Plum Scent through a Window closed against the Snow. Shotetsu
Plum Tree, The. Reaney
Plum Tree by the House, The. Gogarty
Plum's Heart, The. Soto
Scent of plum flowers, The. Tamekane
This Is Just to Say. Williams
This stream that. *Fr.* Kokin Shu. Ise
'Tis the White Plum Tree. Neilson
To a Poor Old Woman. Williams
Word *Plum,* The. Chasin
You bloom/ with a color and fragrance. *Fr.* Kokin Shu. Tsurayuki

Plumbing and Plumbers
Difference, The. King
Elegy for Alfred Hubbard. Connor
Murie Sing. Campbell

Plymouth, England
For an Age of Plastics. Plymouth. Davie
Hardy's Plymouth. Grigson
Marble-streeted Town, The. Hardy

Poaching and Poachers
Lincolnshire Poacher, The. *Unknown*
Nottinghamshire Poacher, The. *Unknown*

Pocahontas
Capt. Smith and Pocahontas. Bibb
Marriage of Pocahontas, The. Webster
Pocahontas. Thackeray
Pocahontas to Her English Husband, John Rolfe. Allen
Wearied arm, and broken sword. *Fr.* Pocahontas. Thackeray

Poe, Edgar Allan
Goblin Goose, The. *Unknown*

Mysteries. Winch
Poe and Longfellow. *Fr.* A Fable for Critics. Lowell
Poe's Cottage at Fordham. Boner
Walt Whitman at the Reburial of Poe. Christopher

Poetic Meter
Hendecasyllabics. Tennyson

Poetics
As for Poets. Snyder
Great Poems, The. Kuzma
House, The. Levine
Later Note on Letter 15, A. *Fr.* The Maximus Poems. Olson
Lot of Night Music, A. Hecht
Poem Made of Water. Willard
Poem: "This poem is not addressed to you." Justice
Toward a Poetic Art. Queneau
Variations on a Text by Vallejo. Justice
Zimmer to His Students. Zimmer

Poetry and Poets
Ecstatic Occasions, Expedient Forms; 65 Leading Contemporary Poets Select and Comment on Their Poems (EOEF). David Lehman, ed.
Heath Introduction to Poetry, The (HeIP). Joseph de Roche, ed.
How Does a Poem Mean? (HoPM). John Ciardi *and* Miller Williams, eds.
Introduction to Poetry, An (InPK). X. J. Kennedy, ed.
Introduction to Poetry, An (InPS). Louis Simpson, ed.
Modern Poems; an Introduction to Poetry (MoP). Richard Ellman *and* Robert O'Clair, eds.
Norton Anthology of American Literature, The (NAAL). Nina Baym *and others,* eds.
Norton Anthology of English Literature, The (NAEL). M. H. Abrams, general ed.
Norton Anthology of Modern Poetry, The (NoAM). Richard Ellman *and* Robert O'Clair, eds.
Norton Anthology of World Masterpieces, The (NAWM). Maynard Mack, general ed.
Norton Introduction to Poetry, The (NIP). J. Paul Hunter, ed.
Poetspeak; in Their Work, about Their Work (Psk). Paul B. Janeczko, comp.
Practical Imagination, The; an Introduction to Poetry (PrIm). Northrop Frye, Sheridan Baker, *and* George Perkins
Singular Voices; American Poetry Today (SV). Stephen Berg, ed.
Understanding Poetry (UnPo). Cleanth Brooks *and* Robert Penn Warren, eds.
Western Wind; an Introduction to Poetry (WeW). John Frederick Nims, ed.
See also **names of individual poets.**

Pogroms. *See* **Massacres.**

Poker
My Poker Girl. Masson
Root Hog or Die. *Unknown*
Twin Aces. Wilson

Pokuttelini
Young Chieftain, A. Auvaiyar

Poland
Beast That Rode the Unicorn, The. Meyer
Good sir, whose powers are these? *Fr.* Hamlet. Shakespeare
In northern climes where furious tempests blow. *Fr.* The Diet of Poland, A Satire. Defoe
Korets Landscape. Segal
To the Jews in Poland. Wittlin
Verses about Poland. Zagajewski

Police and Police Stations
Action Rhyme. Adams
Award. Durem
Bobby Blue. Drinkwater

Constable Calls, A. Heaney
Definition for Blk/Children. Sanchez
Idiot, The. Randall
Lust. Matthews
Negro Hero. Brooks
P.C. Plod versus the Dale St. Dog Strangler.
  McGough
Peeler and the Goat, The. *Unknown*
Poem to a Nigger Cop. Hamilton
Police Station Ditties. Beerbohm
Policeman's Lot, A [*or* The] *Fr*. The Pirates
  of Penzance. Gilbert
Precinct Station, The. Simpson
Southern Cop. Brown
26th Precinct Station. Simpson
Two X. Cummings
Who but the Lord? Hughes

Police States
Age of Snow, The. Kalász
All of a Sudden. Jesús
August 1964. Gullar
Augusto Ngangula. Andrade
Begging A.I.D. Rubadiri
Blood River Day. Brutus
Curfew Breakers, The. Chimsoro
From the Outside. Gwala
If I Leave Here Alive. Mahaka
Letter No. 18. Brutus
Love Poem for My Country, A. Chipasula
Malawi. Banda
"More Light! More Light!" Hecht
Poem Touching the Gestapo. Heyen
Political Prisoner, The. Kunene
Somehow We Survive. Brutus
Sounds Begin Again, The. Brutus
Subversive. Gullar
When This Carnival Finally Closes. Mapanje
See also **Nazis.**

Politics and Politicians
As I strole the city, oft I. *Fr*. The Legion
  Club. Swift
Bryan, Bryan, Bryan, Bryan. Lindsay
Campaign, The. Miles
Canopus. Taylor
Civil Service, The. *Fr*. The Vision of Piers
  Plowman. Langland
Daughters of the Horseleech, The. Kunitz
Dead Statesman, A. Kipling
Dodger, The. *Unknown*
Eisenhower's Visit to Franco, 1959. Wright
Election 1960. Baxter
Election Reflection. Jones
Election Speech for the Presidency of the
  United States of Chinamerica. Avidan
Elegy in a Country Churchyard. Chesterton
Epigram: "Midas, they say, possessed the art
  of old." "Pindar"
Epitaph on the Politician Himself. Belloc
Gaelic is the conscience of our leaders. *Fr*.
  A Farewell to English. Hartnett
Get to Hell Outa Here. "Mighty Sparrow"
Hibiscus and Salvia Flowers. Lawrence
Killers That Run, The. Cohen
Legend of Versailles, A. Tolson
London Sad London. *Unknown*
Misconception, A. Lowell
Next to of Course God America I.
  Cummings
On a General Election. Belloc
On Watching Politicians Perform at Martin
  Luther King's Funeral. Knight
Political Meeting. Klein
Politician, A. Cummings
Politics. Yeats
Rebel's Progress. Earley
Senior Members. Lucy
Similes for Two Political Characters of 1819.
  Shelley
Tall Hat. Daley
This, the last ornament among the peers.
  Belloc

Time's Changes. *Fr*. The Art of Politics.
  Bramston
To a Noisy Politician. Freneau
To My Honour'd Kinsman, John Driden, of
  Chesterton. Dryden
Tory Pledges. Moore
W. L. M. K. Scott
Wharton ("Wharton! the scorn and wonder of
  our days"). *Fr*. Epistle to Sir Richard
  Temple. Pope
What the Moon Saw. Lindsay
Faber Book of Political Verse, The (FaBoPV).
  Tom Paulin, ed.

Pollock, Jackson
Squeeze Play. *Fr*. Spectator's Guide to
  Contemporary Art. McGinley

Pollution
All the Smoke. Siegel
Country Stars. Meredith
Rural Dumpheap. Cane
Urban Pollution. *Fr*. The Art of Preserving
  Health. Armstrong
White Trash. Hall
See also **Ecology.**

Polo
Polo Ponies Practicing. Stevens

Polyandry
One Wife for One Man. Aig-Imoukhuede

Pomegranates
Pomegranate, The. Dudek
Pomegranate. Harada

Pompadour, Marquise de
Pompadour, The. Thornbury

Pompeii, Italy
At Pompeii. *Fr*. Ode to Naples. Shelley
Girl of Pompeii, A. Martin
Listening Nydia. Ray
On First Looking into Michael Grant's *Cities
  of Vesuvius*. Ewart
Volcanoes. Akhmadulina

Ponds. *See* **Lakes and Ponds.**

Ponies
Blessing, A. Wright
Hey! My Pony! Farjeon
Hunter Trials. Betjeman

Pony Express
Pony Express, The. Thompson

Pool (game)
8-Ball at the Twilite. Baker
Kelly. Hershon
Madhouse, The. Carter
Rotation. Bond

Poorhouses
Over the Hill to the Poor-House. Carleton

Popcorn
Pop Corn Song, A. Turner

Pope, Alexander
Mr. Pope. Tate
Mr. Pope's Welcome from Greece. Gay
On the Death of Mr. Pope. *Unknown*
On the Edition of Mr. Pope's Works with a
  Commentary and Notes. Edwards
Spoken Extempore on the Death of Mr. Pope.
  Unknown
To the Editor of Mr. Pope's Works.
  Edwards

Poplar Trees
Binsey Poplars (Felled 1879). Hopkins
Poplar Field, The. Cowper
Poplar Tree. Colum
Poplars, The. Garrison
Poplars. Leuty
Poplars. Reed
Poplars, The. Trotter
Poplar's Shadow, The. Swenson
Tapestry Trees. Morris
See also **Aspen Trees.**

Poppies
Farewell Ballad of Poppies, A. Brudne
In the Poppy Field. Stephens
November Poppies. Corke

Ode to the Poppy. Oneil
Poppies. McPherson
Poppies. Ropes
Poppies in July. Plath
Poppies in October. Plath
Poppies in the Garden, The. Wolfe
Poppies in the Wheat. Jackson
Poppy. Fritsch

Porcupines
Friend. Moore
Porcupine, The. Kinnell

Pornography
Being Aware. Cooper
Ode to Pornography. Anderson
Saturday Afternoon at the Movies. Logan
See also **Obscenity.**

Porter, Cole
Parodies of Cole Porter's "Night and Day."
  Lardner

Portland, Maine
My Lost Youth. Longfellow

Portraits
Against Portraits. Tomlinson
Dorothy Q. Holmes
Enemy's Portrait, The. Hardy
Faded Pictures. Moody
"Formerly a Slave." Melville
His Picture. *Fr*. Elegies. Donne
How do you like what you have. *Fr*.
  Portraits and Repetition. Stein
In an Artist's Studio. Rossetti
Inventory. Ladányi
Kinsman, A. Miller
Likeness, A. Browning
My Last Duchess. Browning
On His Portrait. Cowper
On Mr. Nash's Present of His Own Picture at
  Full Length. Chesterfield
On the Portrait of a Woman about to Be
  Hanged. Hardy
On the Receipt of My Mother's Picture out of
  Norfolk. Cowper
Poem: "I do not want only." Thibaudeau
Portrait by Alice Neel. Kramer
Portrait of a Lady in the Exhibition of the
  Royal Academy. *Fr*. Every-Day
  Characters. Praed
Rembrandt's Late Self-Portraits. Jennings
Self-Portrait at Thirty. Veress
Self-Portrait in a Convex Mirror. Ashbery
Sonnet on a Family Picture. Edwards
Tudor Portrait. Lattimore
Unwanted. Field
See also **Painting and Painters.**

Ports. *See* **Harbors and Ports.**

Portugal
Camoes and the Debt. Andresen

Porvaikkopperunar Killi
King Killi in Combat. Cattantaiyar
Woman in Love with a Captive King, A.
  Nakkannaiyar

Poseidon. *See* **Neptune.**
Possums. *See* **Opossums.**
Postmen. *See* **Mail and Mailmen.**

Potatoes
Giving Potatoes. Mitchell
Poème de Terre; or, Love Song to a Potato.
  Little
Potato. Wilbur
Potatoes. Donnell
Potatoes' Dance, The. Lindsay
Spraying the Potatoes. Kavanagh

Potomac, River
All Quiet along the Potomac. Beers
By the Potomac. Aldrich
By the Potomac. Aldrich
Evening on the Potomac. Hovey

Pottery and Potters
Drawn by Stones, by Earth, by Things That
  Have Been in the Fire. Bell
For Marsha. Hoyos

Pound, Ezra
Another Canto. Morton
Cage, The. Berryman
Epistle to the Rapalloan. MacLeish
Ezra Pound. Lowell
Ezry. MacLeish
On the Fly-Leaf of Pound's Cantos. Bunting
Pound at Spoleto. Ferlinghetti
Rainuv; a Romantic Ballad from the Early
  Basque. Widdemer
Talking of Ezra Pound and long-dead pantos.
  Fr. Fisbo. Nichols

Poverty
Alice Fell; or, Poverty. Wordsworth
All Things Be Dear but Poor Mens Labour;
  or, The Sad Complaint of Poor People.
  Unknown
And yet not long ago. *Fr.* Vox Populi, Vox
  Dei. *Unknown*
Bad Old Days, The. Rexroth
Bard's Family, A. Peruncittiranar
Bean Eaters, The. Brooks
Between a Contractor and His Wife.
  Unknown
By numbers here from shame or censure free.
  Fr. London: A Poem in Imitation of the
  Third Satire of Juvenal. Johnson
Christmas Day in the Workhouse. Sims
Christmas Eve, South, 1865. Tucker
Christmas 1970. Milligan
Country Justice, The. Langhorne
Dry Loaf. Stevens
Dry River Bed. Salkey
Elementary School Classroom in a Slum, An.
  Spender
Evening Faces. Keiun
Face of Poverty. Smith
Facts. Davies
Far from the Beach. Espírito Santo
Farewell at the Hour of Parting. Neto
Food-Rioter Banished, The. Thom
For A' That and A' That ("Is there, for honest
  poverty"). Burns
Forgotten Man, The. Markham
Furnished Lives. Silkin
Gaffer Gray. Holcroft
Gin the Goodwife Stint. Bunting
Gleaner, The. Taylor
Good Times. Clifton
"Guilty or Not Guilty?" *Unknown*
Happy Workhouse and the Good Effects of
  Industry, The. *Fr.* The Fleece. Dyer
Heap of Rags, The. Davies
His Throne Is with the Outcast. Lowell
Holy Thursday ("Is this a holy thing to see").
  Fr. Songs of Experience. Blake
Holy Thursday (" 'Twas on a Holy Thursday,
  their innocent faces clean"). *Fr.* Songs of
  Innocence. Blake
I an I Alone; or Goliath. Smith
I pray you, be not wroth. *Fr.* Vox Populi,
  Vox Dei. *Unknown*
I was born in a beggar family. Tulsidas
In the attic, at night, a poor man sits. *Fr.*
  Songs of a Poor Man. Kulbak
I've Worn My Bits o' Shoon Away. Waugh
Kitchenette Building. Brooks
Lady Poverty, The. Meynell
Leawood Hall. Jones
Legacy. Kalász
Life and Adventure of Bob Thin, The. *Fr.*
  Bob Thin; or, the Poorhouse Fugitive.
  Linton
Lives of Famous Men, The. Gilbert
London ("I wander through each chartered
  street"). *Fr.* Songs of Experience. Blake
Lovers of the Poor, The. Brooks
Luck's Shining Child. Garrett
May poverty, without offence, approach. *Fr.*
  The Complaints of Poverty. James
Mrs. Evans Fach, You Want Butter Again.
  Davies

My Song. Bialik
No New Music. Crouch
Now landed Trader, that, with haughty stare.
  Fr. The Village Patriarch. Elliott
On cold nights. *Fr.* Manyo Shu. Okura
On Hope. Bell
On the night when the rain beats. *Fr.* Manyo
  Shu. Okura
One Time Henry Dreamed the Number.
  Long
Orphan Girl, The. *Unknown*
Over the Hill to the Poor-House. Carleton
Palaces of Gold. Rosselson
Parley with His Empty Purse, A. Randolph
Poor, The. *Fr.* The Country Justice.
  Langhorne
Poor, The. Sosa
Poor, The. Williams
Poor for Our Sakes. Smith
Poor Girl's Meditation, The. *Unknown*
Poor Man's Province, The. Wright
Poor of London, The. Forster
Poverty. Simic
Poverty. Traherne
Poverty, in Imitation of Milton. Jones
Poverty Knock. *Unknown*
Praise for Mercies Spiritual and Temporal.
  Watts
Pray Remember the Poor. Smart
Preawd Tum's Prayer. Ramsbottom
Priest attending, found he spoke at times,
  The. *Fr.* The Borough: Peter Grimes.
  Crabbe
Proletarian Portrait. Williams
Rags and tatters, rags and tatters. Ryokan
Red Wig, The. *Unknown*
Reminder, The. Hardy
Rich and Poor; or, Saint and Sinner.
  Peacock
Sale of the Pet Lamb, The. Howitt
She Was Poor but She Was Honest.
  Unknown
Shoofly, The. O'Hare
Slum Dwelling, A. *Fr.* The Borough.
  Crabbe
Small Paths. Roland-Holst
Song: "Child, is thy father dead?" Elliott
Song: "Leaves are still; not a breath is heard,
  The." Linton
Song of the Low, The. Jones
Song, A: "While a thousand fine projects are
  planned ev'ry day." *Unknown*
Sonnet: Of Why He Would Be a Scullion.
  Angiolieri da Siena
Starving to Death on a Government Claim.
  Unknown
Street Musicians. Ashbery
Strictly for Posterity. Simic
Sunrise of the Poor, The. Wilson
Ten Heawrs a Day. Burgess
Third Wonder, The. Markham
Thirty Bob a Week. Davidson
Timothy Winters. Causley
To a Poor Old Woman. Williams
To a Red-headed Do-good Waitress. Dugan
To Be Poor. Orban
To the Four Courts, Please. Stephens
Twa Weavers, The. Rodger
Village life, and every care that reigns. *Fr.*
  The Village. Crabbe
We Live in a Rickety House. McLachlan
We May Be Lo', We May Be Poor. Blackah
West London. Arnold
What You Goin' to Do When the Rent Comes
  'Round? Sterling
When I stop to think. Kogon
Whisperings for the Unwashed. Thom
Wind and Rain. Michizane
Winter. Synge
Worry about Money. Raine
Ye Simple Men. Blackie

Power
Song: I Want a Witness. Harper

Prague, Czechoslovakia
My Return to Czechoslovakia. Edmond
Prague, January 1964. Bachmann
Prague Spring. Harrison

Prairie Dogs
Prairie-Dog Town. Austin

Prairies
America the Beautiful. Bates
Canadian Prairies View of Literature, The.
  Donnell
Horizontal World. Saunders
My Prairies. Garland
Nebraska. Swan
Open Range. Whipple
Prairie. Bates
Prairie Birth. Coates
Prairie Graveyard. Marriott
Prairie Water Colour, A. Scott
Prairie Waters by Night. Sandburg
Prairies, The. Bryant
Stories from Kansas. Stafford
To make a prairie it takes a clover and one
  bee. Dickinson
West of Chicago. Dimoff
Wind of the Prairie. Howes
Woodlot, The. Clampitt

Praxiteles
Spoken by Venus on Seeing Her Statue Done
  by Praxiteles. *Unknown*

Prayer
Abide with Me. Lyte
Abundant is the year, with much millet, much
  rice. *Unknown*
After the Rain. Collier
Answered Prayers. Wilcox
Are You You? Cook
Ask, and Ye Shall Receive. Havens
Barbarian Prayer. Csoori
Be With Me, Lord. *Fr.* Diary of an Old
  Soul. Macdonald
Because We Do Not See. *Unknown*
Bestow, O Lord, thy gracious pardon.
  Tyutchev
Child's Prayer, A. Tabb
Child's Prayer, A. *Unknown*
Christ./ May I die at night. Lowell
Christ's Bounty. *Unknown*
Communion. Spicer
Conversation of Prayer, The. Thomas
Cowboy's Prayer, A. Clark
Cowboy's Prayer, The. Fletcher
Dark Scent of Prayer, The. Drachler
Day by Day the Manna Fell. Conder
Death Bed, The. Cuney
Divine Office of the Kitchen, The. Hallack
During His Courtship. Wesley
E Tenebris. Wilde
Ethick. *Fr.* The Testament of Beauty.
  Bridges
Evening Hymn, An. Ken
Evening Prayer, An. Kendall
Evening Prayer. Ray
Exhortation to Prayer. Cowper
Fool's Prayer, The. Sill
Forme of Prayer, A. Quarles
Fragrant the Prayer. *Unknown*
Gascoigne's [*or* Gascoygnes] Good-Night.
  Gascoigne
Glory to Thee, My God, This Night. Ken
God bless this food, and bless us all.
  Unknown
God is great and God is good. *Unknown*
Grace for a Child. Herrick
Gray Light, The. Leyeles
Great God, let all my tuneful pow'rs.
  Heginbothom
Great God, Thou giver of all good.
  Unknown

Heaven which art in Heaven Our Father in Heaven. *Fr.* Footnote to the Lord's Prayer. Smith
Heavenly Father, bless this food. *Unknown*
Here, then, I come. *Unknown*
His Litany to the Holy Spirit. Herrick
His Prayer for Absolution. Herrick
His Prayer to Ben Jonson [*or* Johnson]. Herrick
Holy Willie's Prayer. Burns
Home from Praying. Rolnik
Housewife, The. Coblentz
Huswifery. Taylor
Hymn of Freedom. Barry
Hymn to God the Father [*or* For Forgiveness *or* To Christ], A. Donne
I Dare Not Pray to Thee. Baring
I lie down with God, and may God lie down with me. *Unknown*
I Thank Thee, Lord. *Unknown*
In Westminster Abbey. Betjeman
Jesus Tender Shepherd. Duncan
Keep On Praying. Lyon
Larger Prayer, The. Cheney
Lark, The. *Unknown*
Leave It with Him. *Unknown*
Let the Roots Speak. Al-Khal
Like crystal through the mountains. *Fr.* Manyo Shu. Kanamura
Litanie, The, *sels.* Donne
Lord, Hear My Prayer. Clare
Lord, Make a Regular Man out of Me. Guest
Matins, or Morning Prayer. Herrick
Matthew, Mark, Luke and John. *Unknown*
Morning Prayer. Mac An Bhaird
Mountain Drive. Gogan
My Father's Voice in Prayer. Nottage
My Prayer. Bonar
My Prayer. *Unknown*
My Times Are in Thy Hand. Waring
Night Prayer. *Unknown*
Now I Lay me Down to Sleep. *Unknown*
Now I wake and see the light. Pullen
O come, our Lord and Saviour. *Unknown*
O Master, Let Me Walk with Thee. Gladden
Of course I prayed. Dickinson
Offertory. Deane
Old Saint's Prayer, The. Thompson
Old Shepherd's Prayer. Mew
Our God, Our Help in Ages Past. Watts
Out of the Deep. Thompson
Pagan Prayer. Brown
Pagan Prayer. Spaziani
Paths of Prayer, The. Roditi
Payments. O Hehir
Peace Hymn of the Republic. Van Dyke
People's Prayer, The. Wells
People's Sabbath Prayer, The. Elliott
Poet Prays, The. Crowell
Poet's Prayer. Love
Poet's Prayer, The. Philipps
Poet's Prayer, The. *Unknown*
Poor Women in a City Church. Heaney
Pray! Arnold
Pray—Give—Go. Flint
Prayer: "As I walk through the streets." Flint
Prayer, A: "Be thou my vision, O Lord of my heart." *Unknown*
Prayer: "Come let us also raise our hands to pray." Faiz
Prayer, A: "Father in Heaven! from whom the simplest flower." Hemans
Prayer: "Give me a death like Buddha's. Let me fall." Moss
Prayer: "I ask good things that I detest." Stevenson
Prayer, A: "Let me do my work each day." Ehrmann
Prayer: "Let us leave our island woods grown dim and blue." "Æ"

Prayer, A: "Lord, not for light in darkness do we pray." Drinkwater
Prayer: "Lord, what a change within us one short hour." Trench
Prayer: "Master, they say that when I seem." Lewis
Prayer: "O Christ, who in Gethsemane." Ray
Prayer: "Oh! that mine eye might closed be." Ellwood
Prayer: "Prayer the church's banquet, Angel's age." *Fr.* The Temple. Herbert
Prayer, A: "To Thy continual Presence, in me wrought." Channing
Prayer: "What a commanding power." Washbourne
Prayer, The: "Wilt Thou not visit me?" Very
Prayer before Birth. MacNeice
Prayer for All Poets at This Time. Edman
Prayer for Forgiveness, A. Aengus the Culdee
Prayer for Guidance. *Fr.* The Tibetan Book of the Dead. *Unknown*
Prayer for My Daughter, A. Yeats
Prayer for My Son, A. Yeats
Prayer for This House. Untermeyer
Prayer in Darkness, A. Chesterton
Prayer of a Pagan Woman. Gogan
Prayer Service in an English Church. Bly
Prayer to the Virgin. Columcille
Prayers, The. Schwartz
Prayers in a Temple. Al-Khal
Prizefighter's Prayer, The. Caprani
Psalms. Segal
Qui Laborat, Orat. Clough
Quiet Hour, The. Bowman
Recessional. Kipling
Right Use of Prayer, The. De Vere
Rocked in the Cradle of the Deep. Willard
School Days. Babcock
Scribe's Prayer, The. Guiterman
Scribe's Prayer, The. Service
Sentinel, The. *Unknown*
Shall the Dead Praise Thee? Macdonald
Song for Simeon, A. Eliot
Sonnet: "Bible says Sennacherib's campaign was spoiled, The." Lewis
Stanzas: On Prayer. Milosz
Stone Too Can Pray. Aiken
Supplication. Masters
Sweet Hour of Prayer. Walford
Taste of Prayer, The. Seager
Temple, The. Sisson
Teresa of Avila. Jennings
Thanksgiving to God for His House, A. Herrick
There Are Gains for All Our Losses. Stoddard
To Begin the Day. *Unknown*
To Heaven. Jonson
Two Prayers, The. Gillies
Two Went Up into the Temple to Pray. Crashaw
Unanswered Prayers. Wilcox
Unuttered Prayer. Heard
We thank Thee for the morning light. *Unknown*
We thank Thee, Lord, for this our food. *Unknown*
What Is Prayer? Montgomery
When I Had Need of Him. Kiser
When Ol' Sis' Judy Pray. Campbell
Wherefore Hidest Thou Thy Face, and Holdest Me for Thine Enemie? *Fr.* Emblems. Quarles
While now I lay me down to sleep. *Fr.* Sleep. Farren
Wish of Manchin of Liath, The. *Unknown*
Without Ceremony. Miller

Praying Mantis
Don't Sit under the Apple Tree with Anyone Else but Me. Pack
Haiku: "Praying mantis drops with a thud, A." *Fr.* One Hundred Haiku in Free Form. Hosai
Mantis. McCord
Praying Mantis. Hoberman

Preaching and Preachers
At the Piano. Hudgins
Let Us Cheer the Weary Traveler. *Unknown*
Mourning Poem for the Queen of Sunday. Hayden
Music of His Steps, The. Wakefield
On Hearing a Lady Praise a Certain Rev. Doctor's Eyes. Outram
Southern Pulpit, The. Moorer
Theology of Jonathan Edwards, The. McGinley
Three Preachers, The. MacKay
Vicar of Bray, The. *Unknown*
See also **Clergy**.

Predestination
Disappointment—His Appointment. Young
God Is Working His Purpose Out. Ainger
God's Plans. Smith
Life and the Weaver. Dewar
Our Father's Plan. Flint
Predestination and Free Will. *Fr.* The State of Innocence. Dryden
Subalterns, The. Hardy
Western Approaches, The. Nemerov

Prefontaine, Steve
Prefontaine. Ghigna

Pregnancy
After Annunciation. Wickham
Annunciation, The. Pritam
Belly Woman's Lament. Allen
Buddha in the Womb, The. Jong
Cell Lay Inside Her Body, The. *Fr.* A Patching Together. Edmond
Child Waters. *Unknown*
Cravings during Pregnancy. *Fr.* Paedotrophiae; or, The Art of Bringing Up Children. Saint-Marthe
Died of Love. *Unknown*
Early Pregnancy. Shuttle
Emergency at 8. Hewitt
Expectant Mother. Shuttle
First Pregnancy. Alta
I loved/ secretly. *Fr.* Carmina Burana. *Unknown*
I Wish, I Wish. *Unknown*
Labour of the Brain, Ballad of the Body. Forman
Maritimes. Shuttle
Maternity Gown. Holbrook
Meeting, The. Spivack
Men Tell and Talk. Francisco
Metaphors. Plath
Night Watch. Magid
Now Jentil Belly Down. *Unknown*
Now That I Am Forever with Child. Lorde
Poem for J. Berry
Poem Wondering If I'm Pregnant. Fraser
Portrait of a Pregnant Woman. Jones
Pregnancy. McPherson
Pregnant Woman. Jonker
Sarah Hazard's Love Letter. Ellis
Sister. n'Ait Attik
Song for Bringing a Child into the World. *Unknown*
Song of a Woman in Labor. *Unknown*
Song of Cradle-making. Skinner
To a Child Born in Time of Small War. Sorrells
Trouble. Wright
Voyages, The. Orr
With Child. Taggard
Woman to Child. Wright
Youth Mowing, A. Lawrence

Prejudice
Hunters of Men, The.   Whittier
Moderation.   *Fr.* Hymns for the Amusement
   of Children.   Smart
Paki Go Home.   Bannerji
Prejudice.   Moorer
Town and Country.   Riley
You Will Be Hearing from Us Shortly.
   Fanthorpe
See also   **Racial Prejudice; Sexism**.
Presbyterianism and Presbyterians
Elegy in a Presbyterian Burying-Ground.
   Wilson
On the New Forcers of Conscience Under the
   Long Parliment.   Milton
Presbyterian Wedding, The.   *Unknown*
Presbyterians, The.   *Fr.* The Hind and the
   Panther.   Dryden
Presence
Assurance.   Stafford
Presents.   **See Gifts and Giving.**
Presidency, The (U.S.)
Historical Reflections.   Hollander
Our Presidents.   *Unknown*
President Roosevelt.   Williams
Presidents, The.   Moorer
Presidents of the United States.   *Unknown*
To the States.   Whitman
Woodrow Wilson.   Jeffers
Pride
Be not proud of your sweet body.
Do Not, Oh, Do Not Prize.   *Unknown*
Godolphin Horne.   Belloc
Naturally.   Lorde
Of all the causes which conspire to blind.
   Fr. Essay on Criticism.   Pope
Ozymandias [*or* Ozymandias of Egypt *or*
   Sonnet: Ozymandias].   Shelley
Primer Lesson.   Sandburg
Proper Pride.   Lawrence
Song: "One day the god of fond desire."
   Thomson
Priests.   **See Clergy.**
Prillerman, Byrd
Sister Johnson's Speech.   Johnson
To Professor Byrd Prillerman.   Johnson
Primitive Man
Tollund Man, The.   Heaney
See also   **Cavemen.**
Primroses
Primrose, The.   Herrick
To an Early Primrose.   White
Prince Edward Island, Canada
Acadian Lane.   St. John
Lennox Island.   McFadden
Princes and Princesses
Another Prince Is Born.   Mitchell
Duke Is the Lad to Frighten a Lass, The.
   Moore
Everymaid.   Oxenham
Our great prince who orders.   *Fr.* Manyo
   Shu.   Hitomaro
Prince of Wales' Marriage.   *Unknown*
Royal Princess, A.   Rossetti
To an Island Princess.   Stevenson
Princeton, Battle of (1777)
Trenton and Princeton.   *Unknown*
Princeton, New Jersey
April One.   Ostriker
Printing and Printers
Charlotte, Her Book.   Bartlett
Composed in the Composing Room.   Adams
Country Press.   Dobson
Gas from a Burner.   Joyce
Pan in Battle.   *Unknown*
Printer, The.   Pastan
Printers.   Glover
Printer's Error.   Wodehouse
Prior, Matthew
Senex to Matt. Prior.   *Fr.* Two Epigrams.
   Stephen

Prisoners of War
Hospital Prison Ship, The.   *Fr.* The British
   Prison Ship.   Freneau
Pilots, The.   Levertov
Prisoner of War.   Lutz
Tending the Garden.   Pankey
Prisons and Prisoners
Ballad of Reading Gaol, The.   Wilde
Been in the Pen So Long.   *Unknown*
Bell-Man, The.   Herrick
Blood River Day.   Brutus
Boston Burglar, The.   *Unknown*
Botany Bay.   *Unknown*
Captivity.   Rogers
Cell Song.   Knight
Cells.   Bennett
Certain Mercies.   Graves
Chain Gang Blues.   *Unknown*
Child in Prison, A.   O'Dalaigh
Christmas 1962.   Mariah
Clonmel Jail.   *Unknown*
Cloudy Day.   Baca
Coming of Age in the County Jail.   Revard
Convict, The.   Frisch
Convict of Clonmel, The.   *Unknown*
Convict Song, The.   Cruickshank
Decayed Time.   Wahl
Down in the Valley.   *Unknown*
Female Prisoners—Boggo Road.   Thurston
Flower, A.   Guadamuz
Flowering Bars, The.   Donnelly
For Freckle-faced Gerald.   Knight
For oak and elm have pleasant leaves.   *Fr.*
   The Ballad of Reading Gaol.   Wilde
Forest of Europe.   Walcott
From an Inmate Rule Book.   Bruchac
Gaol Song, The.   *Unknown*
Girl Held without Bail.   Walker
Glance, A.   *Unknown*
Great Escape, The.   Adamo
Hanging, A.   Chipasula
Hard Rock Returns to Prison from the
   Hospital for the Criminal Insane.   Knight
He did not wear his scarlet coat.   *Fr.* The
   Ballad of Reading Gaol.   Wilde
He Sees Through Stone.   Knight
Hospital Prison Ship, The.   *Fr.* The British
   Prison Ship.   Freneau
Humours of the King's Bench Prison, a
   Ballad, The.   Howard
Idea of Ancestry, The.   Knight
If I Leave Here Alive.   Mahaka
If you see my mother, partner, tell her pray
   for me.   Maze
In Jail.   Corretjer
In Prison.   Rai Mikisaburo
In Prison.   Smith
In the Cage.   Lowell
In the Prison Pen.   Melville
In the Tank.   Gunn
King's Last Words, A.   Ceraman Kanaikkal
   Irumporai
Lean Day in a Convict's Suit, A.   Wahl
Letter from Pretoria Central Prison.   Nortje
Letter No. 18.   Brutus
Limbo.   *Unknown*
Line-up, The.   Swift
Little Bird I Am, A.   Guyon
Locked up within the prison I.   Mir
Loyalty Confin'd.   L'Estrange
Memories of West Street and Lepke.   Lowell
Miscellaneous Poems Written While in Jail.
   Ch'ien Ch'ien-i
Motet: "I am merry,/ Pretty, pleasing."
   Unknown
My mother's phantom hovers here.   *Fr.*
   Behind Bars.   Tuqan
Night in Prison, A.   Aleramo
No Word.   Goldensohn
O Death, Rock Me Asleep.   Boleyn
Of the flaming rose, The.   Mir

Officer's Prison Camp Seen from a Troop
   Train, An.   Jarrell
Oh Who Is That Young Sinner with the
   Handcuffs on His Wrists?   Housman
Oil Painting.   Martínez
Old Prison, The.   Wright
On the Island.   Brutus
One Year.   Sardar J'afri
Owslebury Lads, The.   *Unknown*
Partial Accounts.   Meredith
Pen Pal.   Dennis
Poem: "Nothing is more cruel than to see."
   Sa'id
Political Prisoner, The.   Kunene
Portland County Jail.   *Unknown*
Prison House, The.   Paton
Prisoned in Windsor, He Recounteth His
   Pleasure There Passed.   *Fr.* Windsor
   Castle.   Surrey
Prisoner, The.   Plomer
Prisoner of Chillon, The.   Byron
Prisoners, The.   Hayden
Prison's Stream, The.   Abi Shaqra
Requiem 1935-1940, *sels.*   "Akhmatova"
Singer in the Prison, The.   Whitman
Soldier Boy's Dream, The.   Tucker
Somehow We Survive.   Brutus
Song of a Prison Guard.   Mphande
Song of the Turnkey, The.   Smith
Songs That Cannot Be Silenced.   Hien Luong
Sonnet: The Cell.   Thelwall
Sounds Begin Again, The.   Brutus
Southern Road.   Brown
Spring.   Hogan
Station Master, The.   Kolatkar
Still, let my tyrants know, I am not doomed
   to wear.   *Fr.* The Prisoner.   Brontë
Stir the Wallaby Stew.   *Unknown*
Stop Press.   Cendrars
Street Kid.   Niatum
Surveillances.   Paulin
Sympathy.   Dunbar
There Are Black.   Baca
There is no chapel on the day.   *Fr.* The
   Ballad of Reading Gaol.   Wilde
To Althea, from Prison.   Lovelace
Visit to the Juvenile Penitentiary.   Gail
Visiting Day.   Young
Where Is the Guard?   Al-Najafi
White Tiger Battalion, The.   Sahara
   Morizumi
Wind at Your Door, The.   Fitzgerald
Woman in Love with a Captive King, A.
   Nakkannaiyar
Women's Jail, The.   Waddington
Words from Hell.   Helwig
Written in Prison.   Ch'ien Ch'ien-yi
You Ask Me.   Mutabaruka
Privacy
Sexual Privacy of Women on Welfare.   Lane
See also   **Solitude.**
Privateers
Honour of Bristol, The.   Price
New Song on the *Blandford* Privateer, A.
   Unknown
Sea Song, A.   *Unknown*
Prizefighting and Prizefighters
Prizefighter's Prayer, The.   Caprani
Procne
Procne.   Quennell
Procrastination
Delay.   Bates
Loss in Delay.   Southwell
When I Get Time.   Masson
Prodigal Son
Dead Poet in the Mountains.   Guttenbrunner
He who tears his heart out of his breast at
   night reaches for the rose.   Celan
Moment after the Rain.   Ebner
Prodigal, The.   Bishop
Prodigal Son, The.   Busta

Progress
For the Cultural Campaign. Jigmed
LMFBR. Snyder
Pity This Busy Monster, Manunkind. Cummings
Plans for Altering the River. Hugo
Progress. Lyon
Progress. Wilcox
Similar Cases. Gilman
To the Wheel of Progress. Linden

Prometheus
Now I know I never shall. *Fr.* Prometheus on His Crag. Hughes
Prometheus. Byron
Prometheus. Mastoraki
Prometheus. Swift
Prometheus Unbound. Shelley
Wail of Prometheus Bound, The. *Fr.* Prometheus Bound. Aeschylus

Promises
Pledge. Rashed

Pronunciation
Literary Squabble, A. Planché

Propertius, Sextus
Ghost, The. Lowell
Note on Propertius I.5. Adcock

Property
Fire. Carpenter
Soul's Liberty. Wickham

Prophecy and Prophets
Beauty Too of Twisted Trees, A. Sherlock
Great Book, The. Dadelsen
I Am Told. Segalen
Kalapuya Prophecy, A. *Unknown*
Light—My Word. Halpern
Mother Shipton's Prophecies. Hindley
Prophecy. Césaire
Prophecy, A. Ginsberg
Prophet, The. Lermontov
Prophet, The. Pushkin
Prophets for a New Day. Walker
Space is azure and the mountains bathe. *Fr.* Prophecy of Cuauhtémoc. Galván
Word, The. Kahn
See also **Oracles.**

Proserpina *or* **Proserpine.** *See* **Persephone.**

Prospectors. *See* **Gold Mining and Miners.**

Prostitution and Prostitutes
All-Nite Donuts. Goldbarth
As You Leave Me. Knight
Beautiful Young Nymph Going to Bed, A. Swift
Belle de Jour. Melly
Black Magdalens. Cullen
Comrades in Arms: Conversation Piece. *Unknown*
Curtain Curtain. Breton
Daisy Fraser. *Fr.* Spoon River Anthology. Masters
Dino. *Fr.* Times Square Poems. Lassell
Execration against Whores, An. *Fr.* The White Devil. Webster
Fille de Joie: Congo. Jackson
For a Masseuse and Prostitute. Rexroth
Gas Station, The. Williams
Going Rate, The. *Fr.* Times Square Poems. Lassell
Greasy Spoon Blues. Gasparini
Great Favourite Song, Entitled The Sailor's Hor npipe, A. *Unknown*
Hey, women, spotted with typhus and riddled with rakes of fingers. Markish
Ho. Young
Hustlers. Cooper
Impression du Matin. Wilde
In Response to a Rumor That the Oldest Whorehouse in Wheeling, West Virginia, Has Been Condemned. Wright
"In These Houses of Swift Easy Women." Osbey

Injustice. Delarue-Mardrus
Man and Woman Absolutely White, A. Breton
Man Who Married Magdalene, The. Simpson
Net, The. Rodgers
Old Lady's Lament for Her Youth, The. Villon
Old Whore Speaks to a Young Poet, The. Smith
Old Whorehouse, An. Oliver
Prostitute, too, The. *Unknown*
Ruined Maid, The. Hardy
Saigon Bar Girls, 1975. Komunyakaa
Scarlet Woman, The. Johnson
She Is More to Be Pitied than Censured. Gray
Simon Judson. *Fr.* Bordello. Turco
Song of the Tart. Kaneko Mitsuharu
Sweet Ethel. Piper
Things a prostitute likes. *Fr.* Ryojin Hisho. Go-Shirakawa
To a Courtesan a Thousand Years Dead. Eldridge
Violent Space, The. Knight

Protest, Social
Advice to a Prophet. Wilbur
After the Industrial Revolution, All Things Happen at Once. Bly
Alabama Bus. Hairston
Alabama Centennial. Madgett
America. Ginsberg
And yet not long ago. *Fr.* Vox Populi, Vox Dei. *Unknown*
And you'll say a nation totters. *Fr.* Civil Riot. Cole
April 1962. Goodman
Bad Old Days, The. Rexroth
Ballad of Birmingham. Randall
Burning of Paper instead of Children, The. Rich
Chic Freedom's Reflection. Walker
Chile. Griffin
Cinque. Hale
Comments. Kenner
Custer Lives in Humbolt County. Hale
Death to Van Gogh's Ear! Ginsberg
Eighties, De. Williams
Environment. Kearns
First Fight. Then Fiddle. Brooks
For My People. Walker
For the Student Strikers. Wilbur
Free Silver. *Unknown*
Girl Held without Bail. Walker
Harlem. Hughes
Hi De Buckras Hi! Nichols
How Beastly the Bourgeois Is. Lawrence
I am waiting for my case to come up. *Fr.* Oral Messages. Ferlinghetti
I pray you, be not wroth. *Fr.* Vox Populi, Vox Dei. *Unknown*
If We Must Die. McKay
Jim Crow Cars. Moorer
Just Instinct and Brute Reason. *Unknown*
Just Taking Note. Scott
Labourer's Wife, A. *Fr.* To the Street Piano. Davidson
Latest Decalogue, The. Clough
Lovers of the Poor, The. Brooks
March 1, The. Lowell
March 2, The. Lowell
Memorial Day. Miles
Memories of West Street and Lepke. Lowell
Montgomery. Cornish
Much madness is divinest sense. Dickinson
No More. Clark
Norman Morrison. Mitchell
Ode Inscribed to W. H. Channing. Emerson
Of Late. Starbuck
On a Recent Protest against Social Conditions. Posner
Paki Go Home. Bannerji

Peace Walk. Stafford
Picketing Supermarkets. Wayman
Plot to Assassinate the Chase Manhattan Bank, The. Larsen
Reflection in Red. Onuora
Revolutionary Poets. Mutabaruka
Rich and Poor; or, Saint and Sinner. Peacock
Season 'Tis, My Lovely Lambs, The. Cummings
Secret People, The. Chesterton
Song of the Shirt, The. Hood
Song to the Men of England. Shelley
Stand Up! Lawrence
Strange Hells. Gurney
Street Demonstration. Walker
Thanks to Industrial Essex. Davie
Thirty Bob a Week. Davidson
Two X. Cummings
Un-American Investigators. Hughes
Unlawful Assembly. Enright
Until They Have Stopped. Wright
We Shall Overcome. *Unknown*
Women on the Road to Pine Gap. Poussard
Forerunners, The: Black Poets in America (FB). Woodie King, Jr., ed.

Protestants
At the Protestant Museum. Maxton
Spot the Ball. Ormsby
Survivors. Ormsby

Proust, Marcel
Hymn to Proust. Ewart
Proust on Noah. Silberschlag

Provence, France
Cocooning, The. *Fr.* Mirèio. Mistral.
Grasse: The Olive Trees. Wilbur
I suck deep in air come from Provence to here. Vidal

Providence, Rhode Island
Things to Do in Providence. Berrigan

Psyche (mythology)
Mythics. Chasin
Ode to Psyche. Keats

Psychiatry and Psychiatrists
Analyst. Fisher
Some Terms. *Fr.* Essay on Psychiatrists. Pinsky
Their Speech, Compared with Wisdom and Poetry. *Fr.* Essay on Psychiatrists. Pinsky
See also **"Mental Illness.**

Psychoanalysis and Psychoanalysts
Analysands. Randall
Ballad of the Oedipus Complex. Durrell
Curing Homosexuality. Everhard
Interrogator, The. Jennings
Jud' Süss Oppenheimer on His First Visit with Professor Sigmund Freud. *Fr.* Psychoanalysis. Teller
Notes from an Analyst's Couch. Probst
Psychoanalysis. Ewart

Psychological Testing
Ptarmigan, The. *Unknown*

Pterodactyls
Pterodactyl, The. Farmer

Puberty
Puberty Tree, The. Thomas

Publishing
Publisher's Party. McGinley
Stop Press. Cendrars

Pudding
Little Pudding. Roberts
Pudding Charms. Cole
When good King Arthur ruled this land. Mother Goose

Puddles
Watch Your Step—I'm Drenched. Mitchell

Puerto Ricans
You're Nothing but a Spanish Colored Kid.
  Luciano
Inventing a Word; an Anthology of
  Twentieth-Century Puerto Rican Poetry
  (InW). Julio Marzań, ed.

Puerto Rico
African Things. Cruz
Why I Can't Write a Poem about Lares.
  Silén

Pumpkins
Mr. Macklin's Jack O'Lantern ("Mr. Macklin
  takes his knife"). McCord
Pumpkin, The. Graves
Pumpkin. Morgan
Pumpkins. Cotton
Saint Pumpkin. Willard

Punctuation
What Hath Man Wrought Exclamation Point.
  Bishop

Punishment
Bitter Withy, The. *Unknown*
Punishment. Heaney
Whipping, The. Hayden

Puns
Feline Fine. Lewis

Puppets and Puppeteers
Puppeteers, The. Tadamichi
Street Performers, 1851. Tiller
Puppets which perform before the curtains,
  The. *Fr.* Inscribed on Paintings for the
  People of Hangchow. Hsü Wei
Young Master's Account of a Puppet Show.
  Marchant

Puppies
Buying a Puppy. Norris
Puppy and I. Milne
Tamarindo Puppy, The. Pomerantz
Vern. Brooks

Purcell, Henry
Henry Purcell. Hopkins

Puritans and Puritanism
After the Surprising Conversions. Lowell
On Those That Deserve It. Quarles
Praise-God Barebones. Cortissoz
Puritan, The. Shapiro
Zealous Puritan, The. *Unknown*
See also **Calvinism.**

Pushers
Street Song. Gunn
See also **Drug Addiction.**

Pushkin, Aleksandr Sergeyevich
Natalya Nikolayevna Goncharov. Coles
Pushkin. "Akhmatova"

Pussy Willows
Pussy Willows. Fisher

Pygmalion.
O gracious gods, take compassion. *Fr.* The
  Metamorphosis of Pygmalion's Image.
  Marston
Pygmalion's Statue Comes to Life. *Fr.*
  Metamorphoses. Ovid

Pygmies
Ogres and Pygmies. Graves

Pym, John
Pyms Anarchy. Jordan

Pyramids
Innovator, The. Benét
Pelters of Pyramids. Horne
Pyramis; or, The House of Ascent. Hope

Pyramus and Thisbe
Epitaph of Pyramus and Thisbe. Cowley
Pyramus and Thisbe. Saxe

Pythons
Python, The. Belloc

Q

Quail
California Quail in January. Jumper
Quail in Autumn. Smith

Quakers *See* **Friends, Society of.**

Quarrels
Accusation. Utahania
After a Fruitless Argument. Ishikawa
  Takuboku
After the Quarrel. Dunbar
After the Quarrel. Thompson
City Eclogue. "J."
Defiance, The. Behn
Domestic Quarrel. McInerney
Domestic Storm, A. Thompson
Early Evening Quarrel. Hughes
Malcontents, The. *Fr.* Absalom and
  Achitophel, Pt. I. Dryden
No More Fighting. Jin
Quarrel, The. Farjeon
Quarrel, The. Heard
Quarrel, The. Swenson
Repulse, The. Stanley
Sword of Li Ling, The. Lo Ch'ing
To One That Pleaded Her Own Want of
  Merit. Stanley
When Thou Did Thinke I Did Not Love.
  Ayton
Words! Words! Fauset
See also **Anger.**

Quarries
Green Slates. Hardy
Passage Rite. Caddy
Rockferns. Nicholson

Quebec (city), Canada
At Quebec. Blewett
Brave Wolfe. *Unknown*
Houses Burning; Quebec. Anderson
Quebec. Ray

Quebec (province), Canada
Bonne Entente. Scott
Dawn on the Lievre, The. Lampman
Indian Reservation: Caughnawaga. Klein
Nicolas Gatineau. Bourinot
Off Rivière du Loup. Scott
On Autumn Lake. Ashbery
Quebec Farmhouse. Glassco
Sunset at Les Éboulements, A. Lampman
Wednesday at North Hatley. Gustafson

Queen Anne's Lace
Queen Anne's Lace. Newton
Queen-Ann's-Lace. Williams

Queens
Australian Dream, The. Campbell
Queen Mother to New Queen. Graves
Queen of the Nile, The. Smith
Queens. *See also* individual names of queens.
See also *individual names of queens.*

Questions
Why? De la Mare

Quests
Credo. Gale
Desire. "Æ"
I found Thee in my heart, O Lord. *Fr.* New
  Hymns for Solitude. Dowden
If There Had Anywhere Appeared. Trench
Lord, If Thou Art Not Present. Gray
O Thou/ God of all long desirous roaming.
  Fr. The Song of the Pilgrims. Brooke
O Thou who bidst the torrent flow. *Fr.*
  Hymn from the French of Lamartine.
  Whittier

Prayer: "Bear with me, Master, when I turn
  from Thee." Pierce
Pursuit. Warren
Quest, The. Scudder
Search. Widdemer
Seeker in the Night, A. Coates
Sight and Insight. Slater
To-Morrow. Lope de Vega Carpio
World's Desire, The. Benét

Quilts
In a Country Museum. Beer
Looking at Quilts. Piercy
My Mother Pieced Quilts. Acosta
Patchwork Quilt, The. Fleming
Quilt, The. Levis
Quilt, The. Newsome
Quilt Song. Vinz
Spare Quilt, The. Bishop

Quince Trees and Quinces
As for the Quince. Dhomhnaill

Quivira
Quivíra. Guiterman

R

Ra. *See* **Amon-Ra.**

Rabbis
Baal Shem Tov. Klein
Bratslaver to His Scribe, The. Glatstein
Bratzlav Rabbi to His Scribe, The. Glatstein
Hear and Be Stunned. Glatstein
Nakhman of Bratslav to His Scribe.
  Glatstein
Rabbi, The. Morgenstern
Rabbi Ben Ezra. Browning
Rabbi Yom-Tob of Mayence Petitions His
  God. Klein
Strikover Rabbi, The. Landau
Sunday Shtetl. Glatstein

Rabbits
Big Rabbit goes to see his baby. *Unknown*
Bunny Rabbit. *Unknown*
Cottontail. Bogin
Giving Rabbit to My Cat Bonnie. Stevenson
Hare and the Pig, The. Bridgman
Love for a Hare. La Follette
My New Rabbit. Gould
Myxomatosis. Larkin
Rabbit, The. King
Rabbit, The. Roberts
Rabbit. Robinson
Rabbit, The. *Unknown*
Rabbit Cry. Lucie-Smith
Skippets, the Bad One. Bradley
Snare, The. Stephens
Song of the Rabbits outside the Tavern, The.
  Coatsworth
Timid Bunnies. Kirby
Toad and the Rabbit, The. Martin
Topsy-Turvy Land. Stone
White Season. Frost
See also **Hares.**

Rabelais, François
In Memory of Francois Rabelais. Moritz

Rabi, Isidor Isaac
People. Kennedy
Who Ordered That? Stewart

Rabies
Elegy on the Death of a Mad Dog, An. *Fr.*
  The Vicar of Wakefield. Goldsmith

Raccoons
Diary of a Raccoon. Bennett
Holding a Raccoon's Jaw. Schnackenberg
Mill Valley. Livingston
Raccoon. *Fr.* A Bestiary. Rexroth
Raccoon on the Road. Brennan

Raccoon Poem. Palmer
Raccoons. Fisher
Rachel
  At the Tomb of Rachel. "Yehoash"
  Like Rachel. Ravikovich
  Patriarch Jacob Meets Rachel, The. Manger
  Rachel's Lament. Zisquit
Rachmaninov, Sergei
  Rachmaninov. Seymour-Smith
Racial Prejudice
  Against Negritude. Corgo
  Amagoduka at Glencoe Station. Mtshali
  American History. Harper
  Backlash Blues, The. Hughes
  Ballad of Rudolph Reed, The. Brooks
  Birmingham Sunday. Hughes
  Black Mother. Cruz
  Black Poet, White Critic. Randall
  Black Truth. Agard
  Boccherini's Tomb. Vas
  Children's Rhymes. Hughes
  Circles. Sandburg
  Coming Home from Camp. Kaneko
  Communication to Nancy Cunard, A. Boyle
  Contrast. Nangolo
  Coon Hunt, Sixth Month (1955). Lea
  Cordon Negro. Hemphill
  Corruption. Simoko
  Creation, According to Coyote, The. Ortiz
  Crispus Attucks McCoy. Brown
  Cross. Hughes
  Day in a Long Hot Summer, A. Kageyama
  Defeat. Bynner
  Dream Boogie. Hughes
  Everybody but Me. Burroughs
  Family Album. Kaneko
  Family Jewels. Hemphill
  Farewell at the Hour of Parting. Neto
  Grandfather. Harper
  Gulf, The. Walcott
  Harlem. Hughes
  Harlem, Montana; Just Off the Reservation. Welch
  Hatred of Men with Black Hair. Bly
  Home. Sepamla
  I Fight Back. Allen
  I Love. Chimsoro
  I Saw as a Child. Mandela
  Immigration Act of 1924, The. Mar
  In Bloemfontein. Ross
  In re Solomon Warshawer. Klein
  In the Matter of Two Men. Corrothers
  Incident. Cullen
  Island. Hughes
  It is true—/ I've always loved. *Fr.* Once. Walker
  Justiniano Lamé Has Been Killed. Durham
  Kinky Hair Blues. Marson
  Little Black Boy, The. *Fr.* Songs of Innocence. Blake
  Little White Schoolhouse Blues. Lennon
  Look Back. Arnett
  Lover's Question, A. Baldwin
  Melting Pot, The. Randall
  Merry-go-round. Hughes
  Moment Please, A. Allen
  Monangamba. Jacinto
  Montgomery. Cornish
  1974. Hacker
  No Irish Need Apply. *Unknown*
  Oh God Forbid. Greenfield
  Old Lem. Brown
  On Seeing Two Brown Boys in a Catholic Church. Horne
  Once. Walker
  Parasitosis. Davis
  Poem about My Rights. Jordan
  Poem for the Young White Man Who Asked Me How I, an Intelligent, Well-read Person, Could Believe in the War between Races. Cervantes
  Poem in Black and White, A. Serote

Politeness. Marson
Postcards of the Hanging: 1869. Hudgins
Power. Lorde
Prejudice. Johnson
Raging Generation, The. Mtshali
Runaway Slave at Pilgrim's Point, The. Browning
Searching, The. Cobb
Slim Greer. Brown
Southern Cop. Brown
Status Quo. Dismond
Stereo. Lee
Sure You Can Ask Me a Personal Question. Burns
Tableau. Cullen
Telephone Conversation. Soyinka
There's Somethin'. Small
Tiger. McKay
To White South Africa. Pieterse
Tripart. Jones
Ultimate Equality. Durem
Upstairs Downstairs. Allen
Vietnam #4. Major
Warming Up for the Real Thing. Rudolph
We Call Them Greasers. Anzaldúa
Where I Am. Santos
Where? When? Which? Hughes
White and the Black, The. Khaketla
White House, The. McKay
With All Deliberate Speed. Lee
With the Herring Fishers. "MacDiarmid"
Woodtick. Kogawa
You've Got to Be Taught. Hammerstein
See also **Apartheid.**
Racing. *See* **Automobile Racing; Crew Racing; Horse Racing; Track Athletics.**
Racism
  Alabama Bus. Hairston
  Black Sampson, The. Heard
  From the Corpse Woodpiles, from the Ashes. Hayden
  Policeman Cleared in Jaywalking Case. Harris
  To an Expatriate Friend. Morris
  Uncle Rube on the Race Problem. Thompson
  Uncle Rube to the Young People. Thompson
Rackham, Arthur
  Inscription for Arthur Rackham's Rip Van Winkle. Flecker
Radar
  Radar. Ross
Radcliffe, James, 3d Earl of Derwentwater
  Lord Derwentwater. *Unknown*
Radiation and Radiation Sickness
  Celebration 1982. Meyette
  Hunter Radiation Center: Halloween. Mattison
  Three Mile Island. Owen
  See also **Nuclear Accidents; Nuclear War.**
Radio
  Dinner Party 1940. Sherlock
  In Memory of Radio. Baraka
  Kay-You-Enn-Aye Radio, Iowa. Augustin
  Major Bowes' Diary. Baraka
  Mr. Vachel Lindsay Discovers Radio. Hoffenstein
  Radio. O'Hara
  Radio under the Bed, The. Whittemore
  Umbilical. Merriam
  War of the Worlds, The. Rutsala
  Wireless. Bennett
Radishes
  Daikon Song. Rai Kyohei
Raffles
  Midweek. Miles
Ragworts
  Ragwort, The. Clare
Railroad Wrecks
  Ashtabula Disaster, The. Moore
  Wreck of the Royal Palm, The. *Unknown*

Railroads
  Asleep at the Switch. Hoey
  Burying Ground by the Ties. *Fr.* Frescoes for Mr. Rockefeller's City. MacLeish
  Calling Trains. *Unknown*
  Crossing. Booth
  Depot, The. Turco
  Echo Canyon. *Unknown*
  Engine Driver's Story, The. Wilkins
  Engineer's Story, The. *Unknown*
  For Esther. Plumly
  Henry K. Sawyer. *Unknown*
  In Texas Grass. Troupe
  I've Been Workin' on the Railroad. *Unknown*
  Jay Gould's Daughter. *Unknown*
  Melodic Trains. Ashbery
  Metropolitan Railway, The. Betjeman
  Night Journey. Roethke
  Observation Car. Hope
  Observation Car and Cigar. Stafford
  Old Section Boss, The. *Unknown*
  Oxford and Hampton Railway, The. *Unknown*
  Parting in Wartime. Cornford
  Railroad Bill. *Unknown*
  Railroad Blues, The. *Unknown*
  Railroad Cars Are Coming, The. *Unknown*
  Railway Junction, The. De la Mare
  Railway Stationery, The. Koch
  River, The. *Fr.* The Bridge: Powhatan's Daughter. Crane
  Rock Island Line, The. *Unknown*
  Sister on the Tracks, A. Hall
  Stop. Wilbur
  To a Locomotive in Winter. Whitman
  Train Song. Siebert
  Trains. Tippett
  Travel. Millay
  Utah Iron Horse, The. *Unknown*
  Way Out in Idaho. *Unknown*
  What's the Railroad to Me? Thoreau
  Wreck of the Royal Palm, The. *Unknown*
  See also **Trains.**
Railway Stations
  Adlestrop. Thomas
  At Euston. Harbord
  Cumberland Station. Smith
  Looking for the Melungeon. Smith
  Pennsylvania Station. Hughes
  Ravenglass Railway Station, Cumberland. Nicholson
  Striking. Calverley
Railway Travel
  Faintheart in a Railway Train. Hardy
  From a Railway Carriage. Stevenson
  I Rode Southern, I Rode L.&N. *Unknown*
  Rock away, passenger, in the Third Class. *Unknown*
Rain
  About in London. *Fr.* Trivia; or, The Art of Walking the Streets of London. Gay
  After the Shower. Lampman
  All Night I Heard. Moffatt
  And Then It Rained. Van Doren
  April. Clifton
  April Rain. Loveman
  April Rain Song. Hughes
  August Rain. Bly
  Autumn Poem, An. Kogon
  Autumn Rain. Lawrence
  Autumn Rain. Rexroth
  Beautiful, seen through holes. Issa
  Biography of Southern Rain. Patchen
  Can only a spring rain so drench. *Fr.* Manyo Shu. *Unknown*
  Cloud, The. Shelley
  Cloud Burst. Witheford
  Cold Irish Earth, The. Skinner
  Conversation with Rain. Gunn
  Crimson Leaves. Joben
  Daisies and Grasses. *Unknown*

Dance of the Rain, The. Marais
Dance of the Rain Gods. *Unknown*
Dark and Falling Summer, The. Schwartz
Dark gray clouds, The. Belting
Deluge. Clare
Description of a City Shower, A. Swift
Drops of pattering rain, The. Jakuren
Drought Breaks, The. Adcock
Drums. Chosa
Even the showers/ fall, then stop. Tonna
Evening downpour: clutching grass blades.
　Fr. Eighty-seven Hokku. Buson
Evening shower, An. Eifuku
Fall of Rain at Miti-Miti, A. Tuwhare
Female Rain. Tohe
First Rain. Gar
First Rainfall. Lightman
Fishermen. Preil
For the Rain It Raineth Every Day. Graves
Fragment: Rain. Shelley
Green Rain. Webb
Haiku: "Fall rains/ scum collecting on." *Fr.*
　Thirty-nine Haiku. Shiki
Haiku: "It's been raining for days." *Fr.* One
　Hundred Haiku in Free Form. Hosai
Hours of the spring night are not many, The.
　Fr. Kokin Shu. Michizane
How can it be. Tamesuke
How they sting! *Fr.* Ten Tanka. Myoe
Hung low with clouds. Kogon
I cannot accept. Saigyo
I Saw God Wash the World. Stidger
I thought it was mist. Tamehide
If one is not used. Kenko
In a patch of sky. Teika
In front of my eyes. Chikako
In the Middle of August. Hirsch
In the mountain stream. Tameyo
Is it a shower of rain? Saigyo
It Will Pour. Leyeles
It's Raining. Apollinaire
It's raining, but you say, "Go away!" *Fr.*
　Ryojin Hisho. Go-Shirakawa
June Thunder. MacNeice
Let no rain fall to drench me through. *Fr.*
　Manyo Shu. *Unknown*
Like rain it sounded till it curved. Dickinson
Little Rain, The. Tu Fu
Little Raindrops. Hawkshawe
London Rain. MacNeice
Long-wished-for rain has fallen, The. *Fr.*
　Manyo Shu. Yakamochi
Male Rain. Tohe
Man in the Rain, The. Brock
May rain: in front of a wide river. Buson
May rain: paddy by paddy. *Fr.* Eighty-seven
　Hokku. Buson.
May rain: the muddy water thrusts. *Fr.*
　Eighty-seven Hokku. Buson
Monsoon. Wevill
Moods of Rain. Scannell
Moon after rain—who's that! Buson
Mountain Rain. Ho Shao-chi
Now Comes the Good Rain Farmers Pray for
　(and). Cummings
Ode on Contemplating Clapham Junction.
　Fr. Herman Moon's Hourbook. Middleton
On an evening/ aglow with the crimson.
　Tamekane
On my way back home. Tameie
Out in the garden. Tamekane
Out of Midsummer's Blazing Most Not Night.
　Cummings
Pines along the Coast. Tameko
Prayer for Rain. Jama
Prayer for Rain. *Unknown*
Rain, The. Creeley
Rain, The. Davies
Rain. DiPasquale
Rain. Evans

Rain. Henson
Rain. Junzaburo
Rain. McCrea
Rain. Nabokov
Rain. Nishiwaki Junzaburo
Rain. Riley
Rain. Stevenson
Rain. Stoutenburg
Rain. Thomas
Rain. Tuwhare
Rain, The. *Unknown*
Rain. Weöres
Rain after a Vaudeville Show. Benét
Rain at Wildwood. Swenson
Rain beats on me, I make a shelter, The. *Fr.*
　Manyo Shu. *Unknown*
Rain Clouds. Long
Rain-drops, The/ That fall this evening. *Fr.*
　Manyo Shu. *Unknown*
Rain Drops. Wood
Rain Has Silver Sandals, The. Justus
Rain in Ohio. Oliver
Rain in Summer. Longfellow
Rain in the Pine Grove, The. D'Annunzio
Rain in the Southwest. Kelley
Rain It Raineth, The. Bowen
Rain on Castle Island. Kitahara Hakushu
Rain on the Cumberlands. Still
Rain on the Roof. Frame
Rain, rain, go away. Mother Goose
Rain (Rapa Nui), The. Neruda
Rain Says, The. Cheng Ch'ou-yu
Rain Song. Al-Sayyab
Rain Song, The. Rogers
Rain, The (" 'twas in Koolau I met with the
　rain"). *Unknown*
Raindrops. Fisher
Raindrops drip down, The. Teika
Raindrum. Osundare
Rainpoem. Dransfield
Rains. Césaire
Rains. Hajnal
Rains Pass. Yüan Mei
Rainy Day. Wise
Rainy Morning. Rivera-Avilés
Rainy Nights. Thompson
Rainy Season. Kan Sazan
Rainy Season, The. Wu Sheng
Rainy Summer, The. Meynell
Reading in Fall Rain. Bly
Reprieve. Cormack
Rhyme of Rain. Holmes
"Right Here the Other Night Something."
　Cummings
Ruinous Rains. Fu Hsien
Running out of the nets. Buson
Sailing in the Rain. Hsiang Yang
Sestina: "September rain falls on the house."
　Bishop
Seven Rainy Months. Plomer
Sheets of rain, The. Tameko
Shower, The. Vaughan
Shower comes up, A. Abutsu the Nun
Showers. Chute
Showers are falling. Tameko
Showers go on, The. Tamesuke
Signs of Rain. Jenner
Song of the Rain. McCrae
Sound of Rain, The. Evans
South Texas Summer Rain. Gonzales
Sower, The. Figueroa
Spring rain:/ A man lives here. Buson
Spring rain:/ Telling a tale as they go. Buson
Spring Rain. Chute
Spring rain falls, unknown to the cow's eyes.
　Fr. Thirteen Hokku. Raizan
Spring rain: I put my foot out of the
　footwarmer. *Fr.* Thirteen Hokku.
　Raizan
Spring rain: small clams. *Fr.* Eighty-seven
　Hokku. Buson

Spring rain: telling stories. *Fr.* Eighty-seven
　Hokku. Buson
Spring rains weaving. *Fr.* Kokin Shu. Ise
Squirrel in the Rain. Frost
Sudden Shower. Okubo Shibutsu
Summer Rain. Merriam
Summer Rain. Tillinghast
Take pity on me! Munenaga
Thunderstorm in South Dakota. Boyle
Thunderstorm in Town, A. Hardy
To Walk in Warm Rain. McCord
Tropic Rain. Stevenson
Voices of the Rain. Ray
Waiting for Love in Vain. Tonna
Way Through, The. Levertov
Weather, The. Wieseltier
Weather[s]. Hardy
Wet Thursday. Kees
Wet Weather. Low
Who Likes the Rain? Bates
Winter Moon after a Rain, The. Tamesada
Winter Poem, A. Tameie
Winter Rain. Rossetti

Rain-in-the-Face
On the Big Horn. Whittier
Revenge of Rain-in-the-Face, The.
　Longfellow

Rainbows
Bubbles. Sandburg
Colour-Scheme. Baugh
Door, The. Strong
Great Time, A. Davies
In a Double Rainbow. Littlebird
In a patch of sky. Teika
Legend. Wright
My Heart Leaps Up [When I Behold].
　Wordsworth
Prisms. Dacey
Rainbow, The. Davies
Rainbow, The. Hopkins
Rainbow, The. McCord
Rainbow, The. *Fr.* The Angel in the House.
　Patmore
Rainbow, The. *Fr.* Sing-Song. Rossetti
Red and blue and delicate green. *Unknown*
Watergaw, The. "MacDiarmid"

Rainey, Gertrude (Ma)
Dance for Ma Rainey, A. Young

Ralegh, Sir Walter
Britannia and Raleigh. Ayloffe
Call on Sir Walter Raleigh, A. Piatt
Epitaph: On Sir Walter Rawleigh at His
　Execution. *Unknown*
Lady Ralegh's Lament. Lowell
Sir Walter Rauleigh His Lamentation.
　Unknown

Rameau, Jean Philippe
On an Air of Rameau. Symons

Rams. *See* **Sheep.**

Ramses II, King
Ozymandias [*or* Ozymandias of Egypt *or*
　Sonnet: Ozymandias]. Shelley

Ranches
Lines Composed at Hope Ranch. Clark
Montana Ranch Abandoned. Hugo
Cowboy Poetry; a Gathering (CowP). Hal
　Cannon, ed.

Rape
Adaption—Year 2000. Wellen
Bride of Frankenstein, The. Field
Deceptions. Larkin
Exodus. Probst
Head-Rape, The. Thomas
Jewish Girls, The. Lask
Rape. Pickard
Rape. Rabbitt
Rape of Mensola, The. *Fr.* Nymphs of
　Fiesole. Boccaccio
Rape Poem, The. Avicolli
Raper from Passenack, The. Williams

Raphael Santi
Raphael. Ray

Raskolnikov
Three Dostoievskian Masks. Rákos

Rastafarianism
Dem Belly Full. Cogil
Mabrak. "Jerry"

Rathel, James M.
In Memory of James M. Rathel. Heard

Rationalism
Mock On, Mock On, Voltaire, Rousseau.
Blake
On the Triumph of Rationalism. Ainger
See also **Reason.**

Rats
Assailant. Raven
Hello. Nye
How to Exterminate Rats. *Fr*. The Sugar
Cane. Grainger
Pied Piper of Hamelin, The. Browning
Rat, The. Davies
Rat, The. Leale
Rat Riddles. Sandburg
Rats. Tu Kuo-ch'ing
Rat's Legs, The. Edson
Reapers. Toomer
Song of a Rat. Hughes
"Trade" Rat. Wallis
What Became of Them? *Unknown*

Rattlesnakes
Crotalus. Harte
Photographing a Rattlesnake. Wagoner

Ravenna, Italy
Ravenna. MacNeice

Ravens
Advice to a Raven in Russia [December,
1812]. Barlow
Garden, The. Pound
Raven, The. Coleridge
Raven, The. Poe
Raven, The. Rich
Ravens. Hughes
Sycophantic Fox and the Gullible Raven, The.
Carryl
Three Ravens, The. *Unknown*
True Facts of the Case, The. Euwer
Twa Corbies, The. *Unknown*

Reading and Readers
Breakfast with Gerard Manley Hopkins.
Brode
But What Is the Reader to Make of This?
Ashbery
During the Day He Held a Low-level
Position. Szabo
Eastern hills—dense and lush. *Fr*. Reading
Books. Rai San'yo
Fiction and the Reading Public. Larkin
House Was Quiet and the World Was Calm,
The. Stevens
Large Red Man Reading. Stevens
Learning to Read. Harper
Old Susan. De la Mare
On Reading Aloud My Early Poems.
Williams
On Reading Poems to a Senior Class at South
High. Berry
Poem: "This poem is not addressed to you."
Justice
Proverbial Philosophy: Of Reading.
Calverley
Reading Walt Whitman. Forbes
Study of Reading Habits, A. Larkin
There is no frigate like a book. Dickinson
This morning, splendid breeze and sunlight.
Fr. Reading Books. Rai San'yo
To the Reader. Levertov
Winter Night, Reading Books. Kan Sazan

Real Estate
Condo Girl. Equi

Realism
In the American Tree (IAT). Ron Silliman,
ed.
*New Italian Poetry, The, 1945 to the Present;
a Bilingual Anthology* (NItP). Lawrence
R. Smith, ed. *and* tr.

Reality
Angel Surrounded by Paysans. Stevens
Graffiti for a Particle Accelerator. Masters
Not Ideas about the Thing but the Thing
Itself. Stevens
Seeing for a Moment. Levertov
Quest for Reality (QFR). Yvor Winters *and*
Kenneth Fields, eds.

Reaping and Reapers
Solitary Reaper, The. Wordsworth

Reason
Eclipse of Faith, The. Woolsey
Mock On, Mock On, Voltaire, Rousseau.
Blake
On the Triumph of Rationalism. Ainger
Once Musing as I Sat. Googe
Reason. Miles
Reason and Imagination. *Fr*. Milton.
Blake
To Hell with Commonsense. Kavanagh
See also **Intellect.**

Rebellions and Rebels
Croppy Boy, The. McBurney
Croppy Boy, The. *Unknown*
Great Insohreckshan, Di. Johnson
Popular Negro Song, A. *Unknown*
Requiem for the Croppies. Heaney
Rising in the North, The. *Unknown*
Song of the King of the Eboes. *Unknown*
Take a Look at My Rebels. Wieseltier
Ulster. Kipling
See also **Revolution.**

Rebirth
After Grief. Plumly
Ascension-Hymn ("Dust and clay").
Vaughan
Baptism. McKay
Flower, The. Herbert
For Life I Had Never Cared Greatly. Hardy
I Walked [*or* Walkt] the Other Day to Spend
My Hour. Vaughan
Last Rebirth, The. Barks
Let Me Begin Again. Levine
Masses. *Fr*. España, Aparta de me Este
Caliz. Vallejo
Onset, The. Frost
Renascence. Millay
Saint Francis and the Sow. Kinnell

Rebuilding
Eternal City, The. Ammons

Recipes
Ballad of Culinary Frustration. McGinley

Reconciliation
My Heart Atones. López Velarde
My Mother Really Knew. Lum
Quarrel, The. Aiken
Sunshine after Cloud. Heard

Reconstruction, United States
Mr. Johnson's Policy of Reconstruction.
Halpine
To the Thirty-ninth Congress. Whittier

Record Players
Conversations from Childhood: the Victrola.
Langland
Gramophone, The. Reaney

Red
All in Red. Mathias
What Is Red? O'Neill

Red Jacket
Red Jacket. Halleck

Red Riding Hood. *See* **Little Red Riding
Hood.**

Red Sea
Deer at the Red Sea. Sutskever
Night in the Red Sea, A. Lyall

Parting of the Red Sea, The. *Fr*. Exodus.
Unknown

Redbirds. *See* **Cardinals.**

Redding, Otis
Poem for Otis Redding. Thomas

Redemption
All My Luve, Leave Me Not. *Unknown*
Ballad of Barnaby, The. Auden
Carol: "Now is the world withdrawn all."
Nemerov
Done Is a Battle. Dunbar
Father, Thy word is past, man shall find
grace. *Fr*. Paradise Lost. Milton
Free Grace. Wesley
Garden, The. Beaumont
God's Grandeur. Hopkins
He who would acclaim Cleanness in becoming
style. *Fr*. Cleanness. *Unknown*
Hound of Heaven, The. Thompson
"I Am the Way." Meynell
Lift Up Your Heads, Rejoice! Lynch
Love. Herbert
"Most glorious Lord of Life [*or* Lyfe]! that on
this day." *Fr*. Amoretti, LXVIII.
Spenser
Out of Your Sleep Arise and Wake.
Unknown
Pulley, The. Herbert
Redemption. *Fr*. The Temple. Herbert
Regeneration. Vaughan
Requests. Dolben
Truth from Above, The. *Unknown*
World, The. Herbert

Redwings
Redwings. Wright

Redwood Trees. *See* **Sequoia Trees.**

Reeds
Always in the past. Tameie
Cold Reeds around the Inlet. Joben
In the thick grasses. Tonna
Reeds in the Loch Sayis, The. *Unknown*
When one looks at it. Tamekane

Refugees
Address to the Refugees. Brinnin
Arab Refugee, The. Al-Bayati
Fugitive, The. Al-Bayati
My Polish Grandma. Field
Refugees. Grade
Refugees, The. Jarrell
Refugees. MacNeice
Refugees, The. Read
Road to Pengya, The. Tu Fu
Two Refugees. Marcus

Reggae
Reflection in Red. Onuora

Regret
Eyes of My Regret, The. Grimké
False Though She Be. Congreve
I was not to know. *Fr*. Manyo Shu.
Unknown
In a creek in Muko Bay. *Fr*. Manyo Shu.
Unknown
In the scramble to get away. *Fr*. Manyo
Shu. Udobe Ushimaro
On my lofty ship. *Fr*. Manyo Shu.
Unknown
On the beach where you sleep. *Fr*. Manyo
Shu. *Unknown*
Once. Batterham
Retreat[e], The. Vaughan
Sonnet: "In minds pure glasse when I my
selfe behold." Drummond
Text. Wurdemann
When autumn is here. *Fr*. Manyo Shu.
Unknown
You who journey to Shiragi. *Fr*. Manyo
Shu. *Unknown*

Reims, France
Laughing Angel: Reims, The. Socolow

Reincarnation
From the start there's no. Sensai
How long the stars. Nansen
Pre-Existence. Hayne
Reincarnation. McRae
Transformations. Hardy
We Have Been Here Before. Bishop
Your chance of human birth. Kabir

Reindeer
Reindeer and Engine. Jacobsen
Rigorists. Moore

Rejection
Dream about Sunsets. Hébert
Farewell, Ungrateful Traitor. *Fr.* The
   Spanish Friar [*or* Fryar]. Dryden
Hate Mail. Kowit
I Lov'd Thee Once. Ayton
If even now/ in the midst of rejection.
   Eifuku
Locksley Hall. Tennyson
Look, Delia, how we esteem the half-blown
   rose. *Fr.* To Delia. Daniel
Meditation on a Bone. Hope
Song of Regret. Pan
What Saundra Said about Being Short. Hall

Relativity
Thomas Hardy Considers the Newly-Published
   Special Theory of Relativity. Aldiss

Religion
After Lorca. Creeley
Antichrist, or the Reunion of Christendom; an
   Ode. Chesterton
Bangkok. Scott
Bishop's See, The. *Unknown*
Boom! Nemerov
Brébeuf and His Brethren. Scott
Church Going. Larkin
Church Poem. Thomas
Church's One Foundation, The. Stone
Day after Sunday, The. McGinley
Did I not tell you, avoid the path. Mir
Dim, as the borrow'd beams of moon and
   stars. *Fr.* Religio Laici. Dryden
Garden of Love, The. *Fr.* Songs of
   Experience. Blake
Gray Squirrel, The. Wolfe
Higher Pantheism in a Nutshell, The. *Fr.*
   The Heptalogia. Swinburne
Hippopotamus, The. Eliot
Holy Fair, The. Burns
How to Start a War. McGinley
Humbly. López Velarde
I'm ceded—I've stopped being theirs.
   Dickinson
Indian Convert, The. Freneau
Lay Preacher Ponders, The. Davies
Matlock Bath. Betjeman
Mock On, Mock On, Voltaire, Rousseau.
   Blake
Moses and Jesus. Zangwill
My Church ("My church has but one
   temple"). "G."
Old [*or* Ould] Orange Flute, The. *Unknown*
"Onward Christian Soldiers!" Davis
Preacher and the Slave, The. Hill
Private Judgement Condemned. *Fr.* The
   Hind and the Panther. Dryden
Problem, The. Emerson
Religion. Vaughan
Religion Back Home. Stafford
Respectable Burgher, The. Hardy
Semblables, The. Williams
Some keep the Sabbath [*or* Sunday] going to
   church. Dickinson
Soul of Jesus Is Restless, The. Mitchell
Southern Pulpit, The. Moorer
Sunday Morning. Stevens
"They." Sassoon
Thus man by his own strength to Heaven
   would soar. *Fr.* Religio Laici. Dryden
To Caelia. *Unknown*
Tradition. *Fr.* Religio Laici. Dryden

Transcendentalism. *Unknown*
Vicar of Bray, The. *Unknown*
We Live in a Rickety House. McLachlan
Wednesday Night Prayer Meeting. Wright
When Mahalia Sings. Prettyman
Wisdom. Yeats
With Mercy for the Greedy. Sexton
Written in Exile. Raine
Year of Our Lord two thousand one hundred
   and seven, The. *Fr.* An Ecclesiastical
   Chronicle. Heath-Stubbs
See also **Faith.**

Religious Life
Affliction ("When first thou didst entice to
   thee my heart"). Herbert
Contentment. *Fr.* Christian Ethics.
   Traherne
Created, The. Very
Decay of Piety. Wordsworth
December. Snyder
Fire Burns Low, The. Leax
Gospel According to You, The. *Unknown*
Harder Task, The. *Unknown*
Huswifery. Taylor
Joy and Peace in Believing. Cowper
One Thing Needful, The. Reich
Resurgam. Bitton
Take Time to Be Holy. Longstaff
To a Young Gentle-Woman, Councel
   Concerning Her Choice. Crashaw
To the Countesse of Bedford, on New-Yeares
   Day. Donne
Walking with God. Cowper
What God Hath [*or* Has] Promised! Flint
Whole Armour of God, The. Wesley
See also **Clergy; Convents; Monasteries;
   Monks; Nuns; Rabbis.**

Religious Verse
Anthology of Catholic Poets, An (ACP).
   Shane Leslie, ed.
Best-Loved Religious Poems, The (BLRP).
   James Gilchrist Lawson, ed.
Contemporary Religious Poetry (CRP). Paul
   Ramsey, ed.
Earth Is the Lord's, The (EaLo). Helen
   Plotz, comp.
New Oxford Book of Christian Verse, The
   (NOCV). Donald Davie, ed.
*Tongues of Fire; an Anthology of Religious
   and Poetic Experience* (TOF). Karen
   Armstrong, ed.
Treasury of Christain Poetry, The (TrCP).
   Lorraine Eitel, ed.
Treasury of Irish Religious Verse (TIRV).
   Patrick Murray, ed.
Treasury of Jewish Poetry, A (TrJp). Nathan
   Ausubel *and* Marynn Ausubel, eds.
*Treasury of Poems for Worship and Devotion,
   A* (TrPWD). Charles L. Wallis, ed.
World's Great Religious Poetry, The
   (WGRP). Caroline Miles Hill, ed.

Religious Wars
Christians at War. Kendrick

Rembrandt, Harmenszoon van Rijn
Rembrandt's Late Self-Portraits. Jennings

Remorse
At Sunset. Sangster
Brazen Tongue. Benét
Eternal Lord! Eased of a Cumbrous Load.
   Michelangelo
God, to whom we look up blindly. *Fr.* The
   Poet's Journal. Taylor
Hymn to God the Father [*or* For Forgiveness
   or To Christ], A. Donne
Last Prayer, A. Jackson
Mea Culpa. "Carbery"
Pagan Reinvokes the Twenty-third Psalm, A.
   Wolf
Prayer in the Prospect of Death, A. Burns
Prayer, A: "When I look back upon my life
   nigh spent." Macdonald

Remorse is memory awake. Dickinson
Resolution. O'Donnell
Ruins. Strand
Tichborne's Elegy. Tichborne
'Tis not by guilt the onward sweep. *Fr.* The
   Fool's Prayer. Sill

Renaissance
Exodus from a Renaissance Gallery. Acton
Renaissance. Avrett

Repentance
Advent. Kavanagh
Airman's Breastplate, The. Gogarty
Answer to Thomas Barry, An. Fitzgerald
As Pants the Hart. Tate
Ash Wednesday. Rossetti
At Saint Patrick's Purgatory. O'Dala
Away Vane World. Montgomerie
Ballade which Villon Made. MacDonagh
Day of Judgment, The. Thomas of Celano
Deeply repentant of my sinful ways. Stampa
Discipline. Herbert
Forsake me not thus, Adam, witness Heav'n.
   Fr. Paradise Lost. Milton
Hymn to God the Father, A. Jonson
Joyce's Repentance, The. *Unknown*
Keen Thyself, Poor Wight. Keating
Latter Day Psalms. Ashby
Lifting of the Cloud, The. McDonagh
Lord Will Happiness Divine, The. Cowper
O Lord, I Come Pleading. Lawson
Pilgrim, The. Kennelly
Poem to the Heart of Jesus, A. O'Sullivan
Psalm LXXIV: "O God, why hast thou cast us
   off for ever?" Pembroke
Reconciliation. "Æ"
Relapse, The. Vaughan
Repentance. Behan
Rock of Ages. Toplady
Self-Acquaintance. Cowper
So Little and So Much. Oxenham
With Deep Repentance for My Wasted Days.
   Stampa

Reptiles
Prayer for Reptiles. Hubbell

Reputation
Good Name, A. *Fr.* Othello. Shakespeare
See also **Fame; Gossip; Rumor.**

Rescues
Macinnes's Mountain Patrol. Patey

Reservations, Indian
Big Fun. Burns
Indian Reservation: Caughnawaga. Klein
New Direction, The. Mitchell
Pine Point, You Are. Henry
Reginald Pugh, the Man Who Came from the
   Army. Warrior
Reservation Girls. NorthSun
Up & Out. NorthSun

Resorts
Salford Bridge That Popular Resort of the
   Great Unwashed. Billington
Saratoga Ending. Kees

Restaurants
Ballad of Bouillabaisse, The. Thackeray
Eat and Walk. Hall
I Had But Fifty Cents. *Unknown*
La Carte. Richardson
Lines on the Mermaid Tavern. *Unknown*
McDonald's, New Hartford, NY. Worth
Obscure Pleasure of the Indistinct, The.
   Ramke

Resurrection, The
And with what body do they come?
   Dickinson
Because He Lives. Lathrop
Christ Is Arisen. *Fr.* Faust. Goethe
Christ's Resurrection and Ascension.
   Doddridge

Empty Tomb, The. Thompson
Evolution. Porter
For They Shall See God. Shaw
Guard of the Sepulcher, A. Markham
Hymn for Easter Morn. Neale
I Have Labored Sore. *Unknown*
"Most glorious Lord of Life [*or* Lyfe]! that on this day." *Fr.* Amoretti, LXVIII. Spenser
Not in Vain. *Unknown*
Resurrection, The. Brooks
Seven Stanzas at Easter. Updike
That Nature Is a Heraclitean Fire and of the Comfort of the Resurrection. Hopkins
That Thou Art Nowhere to Be Found. *Fr.* Diary of an Old Soul. Macdonald
Triumph. Stearns

Retirement
Day of my double birth, if such the year. *Fr.* Lines Written at Bridgewater, 27 July 1797. Thelwall
Death. Byatt
Fruits of Retirement, The. Camp
Garden, The. Marvell
Lamentation of the Old Pensioner, The. Yeats
Retirement, The. Norris
Swineherd. Ni Chuilleanáin
Teacher, The. Fisher
Tomorrow. Collins
See also **Old Age; Pensions.**

Reunions
All Legendary Obstacles. Montague
Auld Lang Syne. Burns
Dis Long Time, Gal. *Unknown*
Eating Lechon, with My Brothers and Sisters. Cabalquinto
Face to Face. Rich
Family Reunion. Kumin
Father and Son. Kunitz
How It Seemed to Him Away from Home. Whitehead
Over and Over Again. MacCaig
Renewal by Her Element. Devlin
Return, The. Dickinson
Reunion. Wright
Sailor's Wife, The. Mickle
Semele Recycled. Kizer

Revenants. See Ghosts.

Revenge
Achilles with wild fury in his heart. *Fr.* The Iliad. Homer
Aunt Sponge and Aunt Spiker. Dahl
Enslaved. McKay
Heroic Vengeance. *Fr.* Samson Agonistes. Milton
I Shall Not Care. Teasdale
I Woke Up. Revenge. Poulin
If Justice Moved. Sellers
Kissie Lee. Walker
Laily Worm and the Machrel of the Sea, The. *Unknown*
Oh [*or* O], how comely it is, and how reviving. *Fr.* Samson Agonistes. Milton
Pied Piper of Hamelin, The. Browning
Revenge. Rashed
Revenge. Tucker
Revenge of Rain-in-the-Face, The. Longfellow
Wild Boar and the Ram, The. *Fr.* Fables. Gay
William Taylor. *Unknown*

Revere, Paul
Paul Revere's Ride (The Landlord's Tale). *Fr.* Tales of a Wayside Inn. Longfellow

Revivalism
Gettin de Spirit. Marson
Revival. Garrett
Revivalist in Boston, A. Rich
See also **Evangelism; Religion.**

Revolution
Abu. Randall

And. Gonsalves
Coup-clock Clicks, The. Meeks
Exhortation: Summer, 1919. McKay
For My People. Walker
For Saundra. Giovanni
For the Last Time, Fire. Scott
Great Day, The. Yeats
June 10. Rodriguez
Letter to the Revolution. Griffin
Meditation on the Lake. García Laviana
Militant. Hughes
My Poem. Giovanni
O! Start a Revolution. Lawrence
Pentecost. Ai
Poem: "Come, brother, and tell me your life." Rebelo
Radical War Song, A. Macaulay
Revolutionaries, The. *Unknown*
Revolutionary Dreams. Giovanni
Revolutionary Poets. Mutabaruka
Roses and Revolutions. Randall
Royal Princess, A. Rossetti
This Is the Time. Machel
Tryptych for Jan Bockelson, A. Simon
Warning. Hughes

Revolutionary War, American. See American Revolution.

Reynolds, Sir Joshua
Retaliation. Goldsmith
Sir Joshua Reynolds. Blake

Rhinoceroses
Rhinoceros, The. Belloc
Rhinoceros, The. Coninck
Rhinoceros, The. Nash

Rhode Island
Canonicus and Roger Williams. *Unknown*
Rhode Island. Meredith
Roger Williams. Butterworth

Rhythm
Bass Culture. Johnson
Teaching My Students Prosody. Rogoff

Ribbons
On a Girdle. Waller

Rice
I pound the rice. *Fr.* Manyo Shu. *Unknown*
Manomin. Wolf
Mist clears away, The. Hanazono
Price of Rice, The. Shu Wei
Song of the Rice Workers. *Unknown*
Stalks of rice. *Fr.* Kokin Shu. Tsurayuki
Stopping by Saigyo's Willow. *Fr.* Seventy-six Hokku. Basho

Richard I (Richard Coeur de Lion), King of England
Coeur de Lion to Berengaria. Tilton

Richard II, King of England
King Richard II, sels. Shakespeare.

Richard III, King of England
King Richard III, sels. Shakespeare.
On King Richard the Third, Who Lies Buried under Leicester Bridge. Suckling
Richard III's Speech. *Fr.* Bosworth Field. Beaumont
Tudor Rose, The. *Fr.* The Ship of Fools. Barclay

Richard, Earl of Cornwall
Song of Lewes, The. *Unknown*

Richardson, Samuel
To the Author of Clarissa. Edwards

Riches. See Wealth.

Riddles
Anchor: "Oft I must strive with wind and wave." *Fr.* Riddles (Exeter Book). Cynewulf
Bishop of Canterbury, The. *Unknown*
Book Moth: "A moth ate a word. To me it seemed." *Fr.* Riddles (Exeter Book). Cynewulf
Captain Wedderburn's Courtship. *Unknown*

Cuckoo: "In former days my father and mother." *Fr.* Riddles (Exeter Book). Cynewulf
Devil's Nine Questions, The. *Unknown*
Fish in River: "My house is not quiet, I am not loud." *Fr.* Riddles (Exeter Book). Cynewulf
Four stiff-standers. *Unknown*
From house to house he goes. *Unknown*
Honey-Mead: "I am valued by men, fetched from afar." *Fr.* Riddles (Exeter Book). Cynewulf
Horn: "Time was when I was weapon and warrior." *Fr.* Riddles (Exeter Book). Cynewulf
I have a little sister, they call her Peep-Peep. Mother Goose
I Have a Young Sister. *Unknown*
I'm called by the name of a man. *Unknown*
In marble walls [*or* halls] as white as milk. Mother Goose
In Spring I look gay. *Unknown*
Little Nancy [*or* Nanny] Etticoat. Mother Goose
Long white barn, A. *Unknown*
Man in the wilderness asked [of] me [*or* said to me], The [*or* A]. Mother Goose
Old Mother Twitchett had [*or* has] but one eye. Mother Goose
Olive, The. *Unknown*
Present to a Lady, A. *Unknown*
Riddle: "As I went over London Bridge." *Unknown*
Riddle: "As I went over Tipple Tyne." *Unknown*
Riddle: "At the end of my yard there is a vat." *Unknown*
Riddle: "Highty, tighty, paradighty, clothed [all] in green." *Unknown*
Riddle: "I am within as white as snow." *Unknown*
Riddle: I washed my face in water. *Unknown*
Riddle: "It is in the rock, but not in the stone." *Unknown*
Riddle: "Land was white, The." *Unknown*
Riddle: "On yonder hill there is a red deer." *Unknown*
Riddle, A: "'Twas in heaven pronounced, and 'twas muttered in hell." Fanshawe
Riddle: "Wee man o' leather." *Unknown*
Riddle: "White bird featherless/ Flew from Paradise." *Unknown*
Riddle: "White bird floats down through the air, A." *Unknown*
Riddles Wisely Expounded. *Unknown*
Swan, The: "Clothes make no sound when I tread ground." *Fr.* Riddles (Exeter Book). Cynewulf
Weathercock, The: "I puff my breast out, my neck swells." *Fr.* Riddles (Exeter Book). Cynewulf
Wheat, The. *Unknown*

Rifles
A. E. F. Sandburg
Unarmed Combat. *Fr.* Lessons of the War. Reed

Riley, James Whitcomb
Options. "Henry"

Rimbaud, Arthur
Aeterna Poetae Memoria. MacLeish
Birds in the Night. Cernuda
Death of Rimbaud. Fisher
Prelude LVI: "Rimbaud and Verlaine, precious pair of poets." *Fr.* Preludes for Memnon; or, Preludes to Attitude. Aiken
Response to Rimbaud's Later Manner. Moore
Rimbaud Fire Letter to Jim Applewhite. Chappell
To Rimbaud. Besseisso

Rin-Tin-Tin
In the Days of Rin-Tin-Tin. Hoffman
Rings
Double Jade Ring Grievance. Chang Ts'o
Emerald, The. *Fr.* Up and Down. Merrill
Jet Ring Sent, A. Donne
Ring, The. Mariani
Ring, The. Wakoski
Wedding-Ring. Levertov
With a Gift of Rings. Graves
Riots
Gulf, The. Levertov
Harlem Riot, 1943. Murray
House-Top, The. Melville
Litany of [*or* at] Atlanta, A. Du Bois
Mr. Roosevelt Regrets. Murray
New Dance, A. Anderson
Old Woman Remembers, An. Brown
On Riots. Leslie
Riot. Brooks
Riot, A. Linden
To a Friend in Love during the Riots.
  Parsons
Risorgimento
To Pius IX. Whittier
Ritsos, Yannis
After Reading the Poetry of Yannis Ritsos.
  Mayröcker
Four Attempts at Definition. Jandl
Rituals
From Delphi. Charmoy
Simple Rituals. Sublett
Rivera, Diego
I Paint What I See. White
Rivers
Above the Medway. *Fr.* The Vales of the
  Medway. Munby
Apostrophe to the Parret. Burrington
At Takase Mountain. Tamekane
Ballad of a Springtime River: Presented to
  Wang the Elder, A. Hung Liang-chi
Baptism. Zieroth
Blade of Grass Sings to the River, The.
  Goldberg
Blue-Hole, The. Bell
Brazos River, The. *Unknown*
By the Beautiful Ohio. LaBombard
By the Potomac. Aldrich
By the River Eden. Raine
Call of the River Nun, The. Okara
Clear and Cool. *Fr.* The Water Babies.
  Kingsley
Clever River, The. Shteynbarg
Course of the Tavy, The. *Fr.* Britannia's
  Pastorals. Browne
Death and the River. al-Sayyah
Deep Dark River. Roberts
Downstream. Kinsella
Dream Variation [*or* Variations]. Hughes
Easy River, they call it. Tamekane
Estuary. Kaoru
Flow Gently, Sweet Afton. Burns
Globeflowers on a Riverbank. Tameie
Going to the Water. Hobson
"Good-bye," said the river, "I'm going
  downstream." Nemerov
Green River. Bryant
Growing River, The. Bennett
I like to see it lap the miles. Dickinson
Ice River. Baker
In the Deep Channel. Stafford
In the mountain stream. Tameyo
Isuzu River. Rai San'yo
Isuzu River—/ like a mirror left behind.
  Tameie
Kibune River—/ the rocky waves of its
  rapids. *Fr.* Thirty Tanka. Shunzei
Like Ghosts of Eagles. Francis
Long River, The. Hall
Lord of the River. *Fr.* Nine Songs.
  Unknown

Low Tide on Grand Pré. Carman
Maiden and River. Fordham
Max Schmitt in a Single Scull. Lattimore
Meditation at Oyster River. Roethke
Mother to Son. Hughes
Negro Speaks of Rivers, The. Hughes
Nicolas Gatineau. Bourinot
On the Congo. Martinson
On the Rouge. Souster
Our Lives Are Rivers. Urbina
Ox-Bow. Davie
Rapid, The. Sangster
Rapids at Night. Scott
Requiem For The Sumpul. Durand
Río Grande de Loíza. Burgos
River, The. *Fr.* The Bridge: Powhatan's
  Daughter. Crane
River. Locke
River. Soupault
River Afram. Opoku
River and Death, The. al-Sayyah
River God, The. Sitwell
River God, The. Smith
River God's Song. Ridler
River in the Meadows, The. Adams
River Is a Piece of Sky, The. Ciardi
River Lynher, The. *Fr.* Survey of Cornwall.
  Carew
River of Oblivion. Reyes
River of Rivers in Connecticut, The.
  Stevens
River Rhyme. Williams
River Roads. Sandburg
River Song. Brewster
River Sound Remembered. Merwin
Rivers. Storer
Rivers Arise; a Fragment. Milton
Rivers Come to the Hall of Proteus for the
  Marriage of the Thames and the Medway,
  The. *Fr.* The Faerie Queene. Spenser
Rivers Remember, The. Turner
Sailing upon the River. *Fr.* The Borough.
  Crabbe
Saint John, The. Clarke
Serpent Country. Ammons
Skykomish River Running. Hugo
Slip, The. Berry
Small Is Beautiful. Liu K'o-hsiang
"So Have I Spent on the Banks of Ysca Many
  a Serious Hour." Vaughan
Song of the Chattahoochee. Lanier
Song of the Southern Country. Ou-yang
  Chiung
Sonnet: To the River Otter. Coleridge
Stanzas to the Po. Byron
This Solitude of Cataracts. Stevens
To the River Isca. Vaughan
To the River Itchin, near Winton. Bowles
Tree Celebrates the River, The. Goldberg
Trent Again, The. *Fr.* Polyolbion. Drayton
Tweed Visited, The. Bowles
Two Rivers. Emerson
Vigilance. Breton
Virginia. *Fr.* Landscapes. Eliot
Walking to Bellrock. Ondaatje
Way to the Sea, The. Lerner
Weeds. Su Shao-lien
When the Drive Goes Down. Malloch
Where Go the Boats? Stevenson
Where the water. *Fr.* Thirty Tanka.
  Shunzei
Wide Mizzoura, The. *Unknown*
Wilderness Rivers. Coatsworth
Yellow River. Fei Ma
Yoshino River/ with kerria blossoming.
  Ietaka
See also **Brooks and Streams.**

Roaches. *See* **Cockroaches.**
Roads
Afoot and light-hearted I take to the open
  road. *Fr.* Song of the Open Road.
  Whitman
Beauty and Sadness. Song
Bound No'th Blues. Hughes
City Highway. Teller
Como lo Siento. Cervantes
Florida Road Workers. Hughes
Fork of the Road, The. Renton
Freeway 280. Cervantes
Highway, The. Merwin
Landscape. Teller
Leaving Mendota, 1956. Locke
Merritt Parkway. Levertov
Old River Road. Keysner
Old Roads. Ní Chuilleanáin
On the Ridgeway. Young
Path, The. Thomas
Post-Roads. *Fr.* The Atlas. Slessor
Road, The. Aiken
Road, The. Johnson
Road, The. Muir
Road, The. Orr
Road in Kentucky, A. Hayden
Road Not Taken, The. Frost
Roads. Brown
Roads. Field
Roads Go Ever On and On. Tolkien
Roadways. Masefield
Rolling English Road, The. Chesterton
Roman Road, The. Hardy
Song of the Open Road. Nash
Song of the Open Road. Whitman
Way Through the Woods, The. Kipling
You Are on U.S. 40 Headed West. White
See also **Streets.**
Rob Roy
Rob Roy. *Unknown*
Robbers. *See* **Crime and Criminals.**
Robert I, Duke of Normandy
Legend of Robert, Duke of Normandy, The,
  sel. Drayton
Robert I *or* **Robert the Bruce, King of
  Scotland.** *See* **Bruce, Robert.**
Roberts, Elizabeth Madox
For Elizabeth Madox Roberts. Lewis
Robeson, Paul
Paul Robeson. Brooks
Robespierre, Maximilien Marie Isidore
Robespierre and Mozart as Stage. Lowell
Robin Hood
Archer, The. Scollard
Birth of Robin Hood, The. *Unknown*
Bold Pedlar and Robin Hood, The. *Unknown*
Death of Robin Hood, The. *Unknown*
Gest of Robyn Hode, A. *Unknown*
In Sherwood lived stout Robin Hood.
  Unknown
Jolly Pinder of Wakefield, The. *Unknown*
Little John a Begging. *Unknown*
Robin Hood. Keats
Robin Hood and Allen [*or* Allin] -a-Dale.
  Unknown
Robin Hood and Guy of Gisborne. *Unknown*
Robin Hood and Little John. *Unknown*
Robin Hood and Maid Marian. *Unknown*
Robin Hood and Queen Katherine. *Unknown*
Robin Hood and the Bishop. *Unknown*
Robin Hood and the Bishop of Hereford.
  Unknown
Robin Hood and the Curtal Friar. *Unknown*
Robin Hood and the Monk. *Unknown*
Robin Hood and the Potter. *Unknown*
Robin Hood and the Tanner. *Unknown*
Robin Hood and the Three Squires.
  Unknown
Robin Hood and the Tinker. *Unknown*
Robin Hood Newly Revived. *Unknown*

Robins

Robin Hood Rescuing Three Squires.
  Unknown
Robin Hood Rescuing Will Stutly. *Unknown*
Robin Hood's Chase. *Unknown*
Robin Hood's Death. *Unknown*
Robin Hood's End. *Unknown*
Robin Hood's Golden Prize. *Unknown*
Robin Hood's Progress to Nottingham.
  Unknown
Sherwood. Noyes
Song of Sherwood, A. Noyes

Robins

All on a Christmas Morning. Coatsworth
Catch. Mother Goose
Driven in by autumn's sharpening air. *Fr.*
  The Redbreast. Wordsworth
Epitaph on a Free but Tame Redbreast.
  Cowper
Epitaph on a Robin Redbreast, An. Rogers
First Robin, The. Leveridge
Gay Robin Is Seen No More. Bridges
I am called by name of man. *Unknown*
Kill a robin or a wren. *Unknown*
Little Cock Robin. *Unknown*
Little Robin Redbreast. *Unknown*
North wind doth blow, The. Mother Goose
Opposition. Lanier
Pinto Mare, A. Smith
Robbin, The. Very
Robin, The. Alma-Tadema
Robin, The. Clare
Robin, The. Daniel
Robin, A. De la Mare
Robin, The. Scott
Robin is the one, The. Dickinson
Robin Redbreast. Allingham
Robin Redbreast. Doane
Robin Redbreast. Kunitz
Robin Redbreast's Testament. *Unknown*
Robin's call has stumbled on a rock, A. *Fr.*
  Fifteen Hokku. Shiba Sonome
Tampa Robins. Lanier
Fowls of heaven, The. *Fr.* The Seasons:
  Winter. Thomson
Warning. *Unknown*
Welcome, little Robin. *Unknown*
What Robin Told. Cooper
Why the Robin's Breast Was Red. Randall

Robinson Crusoe

Amsterdam. Jammes
Crusoe in England. Bishop

Robinson, Edwin Arlington

T. R. Hall

Robinson, Jackie

Jackie Robinson. Clifton

Robinson, Smokey

Motown/ Smokey Robinson. Hagedorn

Robots

Man from the Top of the Mind, The.
  Wagoner
Ybba. Malcohn

Rock Lilies

Rock-Lily. Robinson

Rockefeller Center, New York City

I Paint What I See. White

Rockets

Enough. Masson
See also **Space and Space Travel.**

Rocking Chairs

Rocking Chair, The. Klein

Rocks. See **Stones and Rocks.**

Rocky Mountains

David. Birney
Moonrise in the Rockies. Higginson
On Recrossing the Rocky Mountains after
  Many Years. Frémont

Rodeos

Bronco Busting, Event #1. Swenson
Bull Rider's Advice, The. Evans
Closing of the Rodeo, The. Smith
Dear Mom. Zarzyski

Going to the Shawnee Rodeo. Bell
Sierry Petes, The. Gardner
Two of a Kind. Schild
Young Fellers. Munn

Roethke, Theodore

Lines for Roethke Twenty Years after His
  Death. Niatum
Poet on the Island, The. Murphy
Roethke Plain. Brinnin
Theodore Roethke Foots It. Berry

Roland

In wrath and grief away the Paynims fly. *Fr.*
  The Song of Roland. *Unknown*
Too-late Born, The. MacLeish

Roller-Coasters

Flight of the Roller Coaster. Souster

Roller Skating

Roller Rink. Adcock
Roller Skates. Farrar
Skating in Pleasant Hill, Ohio. Iddings
We're Racing, Racing down the Walk.
  McGinley

Roman Catholicism See **Catholicism.**

Romanticism

Miniver Cheevy. Robinson

Rome, Italy

Aeneas built, in days of yore. *Fr.* Roman
  History in Rhyme. Goodwin
Amours de Voyage, *sels.* Clough
Boy from Rome, Da. Daly
Epithalamium: "In the streets the crowds go
  about their business." Halpern
Humble Beginnings. Beddoes
Marcellus. *Fr.* The Aeneid [*or* Eneados].
  Virgil
On First Looking into Michael Grant's *Cities
  of Vesuvius.* Ewart
Piazza di Spagna, Early Morning. Wilbur
Roma. Rutilius
Roma Aeterna. Crapsey
Roman Roman, A. Del Monte
Rome. Cunningham
Rome. Hardy
Rome: Building a New Street in the Ancient
  Quarter. Hardy
Rome by Metella's Tomb. *Fr.* Childe
  Harold's Pilgrimage. Byron
Rome, Conqueror, Conquered. Sylvester
Rome Remember. Keyes
Rome ("Rome disappoints me much"). *Fr.*
  Amours de Voyage. Clough
Rome ("The City which thou seest no other
  deem"). *Fr.* Paradise Regained. Milton
Tautology. Risi
Thief, The. Kunitz
Thou stranger, which for Rome in Rome here
  seekest. *Fr.* Ruins of Rome. Du Bellay
Trinità dei Monti. Risi
Two in the Campagna. Browning
Villa Sciarra: Rome. Curtis
What, though oblivion in her sable shroud.
  Fr. Ancient and Modern Rome. Keate

Romeo and Juliet

Play, The. *Fr.* The Sentimental Bloke.
  Dennis
Silver Dagger, The. *Unknown*

Romney Marsh, England

In Romney Marsh. Davidson

Roofing and Roofers

Tar. Williams
Thatcher. Heaney
Thatcher, The. Kennelly

Rooks

Black Rook in Rainy Weather. Plath

Rooming Houses. See **Boarding Houses.**

Roosevelt, Franklin Delano

Danish Wit. Hollander
President Roosevelt. Williams

Roosevelt, Theodore

Man! A. Scollard

T. R. Hall
Three Presidents. Bly

Roosters

Bantams in Pine-Woods. Stevens
Bonny Grey, The. *Unknown*
Chanticleer. Irvin
Clock, The. Moto
Cock. Amir
Cock and the Hen, The. Heywood
Cock-Crow. Currey
Cock-throwing. Lluellyn
Dawn in the Cockloft. Tablada
Escaping a dog, a rooster flaps. *Fr.*
  Twenty-four Hokku. Kito
Gamecock. Dickey
Henyard Round, The. Hall
Idol in the Porch, The. Tablada
Nun's Priest's Tale, The. *Fr.* The
  Canterbury Tales. Chaucer
On a Cock at Rochester. Sedley
On a Fall Night. Ben-Amittai
Roosters. Bishop
Roosters. Coatsworth
Song: "Before the barn-door crowing." *Fr.*
  The Beggar's Opera. Gay
To Be or Not to Be. *Unknown*
Weaving the Morning. Melo Neto
See also **Chickens.**

Rosamond (Rosamond Clifford)

Henry's Lament. *Fr.* The Complaint of
  Rosamond. Daniel
King Henry to Rosamond. *Fr.* England's
  Heroical Epistles. Drayton

Rosary

Rosary, The. Rogers

Rose, Peter Edward

Last Baseball Samurai, The. Clark

Roses

Act, The. Williams
All Night by the Rose. *Unknown*
And Thou, Expectant. Nervo
Cast Rose. *Fr.* Images. Hajnal
Cliff Rose, The. Fewster
Divine Rose, That in a Pleasant Garden.
  Juana Inés de la Cruz
Elect. Bethell
Garden. Doolittle
Go [*or* Goe,] Lovely Rose. Waller
Go not too near a house of rose. Dickinson
How Roses Came Red. Herrick
I Am Rose. Stein
In a moment/ The roses have faded. *Fr.*
  Four Lyrics for Sibilla Aleramo. Campana
Landscape as Metal and Flowers. Scott
Little Rose Tree, The. Field
Love and Friendship. Brontë
Love's Emblem. Clare
Memory of a Rose. Koh Chang-soo
Midsummer's Rose, A. Kilpi
My Pretty Rose Tree. *Fr.* Songs of
  Experience. Blake
Mystery, The. Hodgson
Of a Rose, a Lovely Rose. *Unknown*
One Perfect Rose. Parker
Red, Red Rose, A. Burns
Rose, The. Gaumond
Rose, The. Hammond
Rose, The. Howell
Rose, The. Roethke
Rose-Bud, The. Broome
Rose Family, The. Frost
Rose in the Afternoon. Joseph
Rose of Eden, The. Phillips
Rose, Oh Pure Contradiction. Rilke
Roses. Eliot
Roses of Saadi, The. Desbordes-Valmore
Roses on the Breakfast Table. Lawrence
Said the Rose. Miles
Sea Rose. Doolittle
Sick Rose, The. *Fr.* Songs of Experience.
  Blake

Song: "What is there hid in the heart of a rose." Noyes
Sonnet: To the Admirable Transubstantiation of the Roses into the Marvellous Image of Our Lady of Guadalupe. Sandoval y Zapata
Southern Gothic. Justice
Sweet Violets. *Unknown*
'Tis the Last Rose of Summer. Moore
To a Withered Rose. Bangs
To Roses in the Bosom[e] of Castara. *Fr.* Castara. Habington
To the Rose. *Fr.* Hymns of Astraea. Davies
To the Rose; a Song. Herrick
To the Rose upon the Rood of Time. Yeats
White Rose, A. O'Reilly
Wild Roses. Newsome

Rosh Hashanah
Feast of the Ram's Horn. Shapiro
Tashlich. Kovner
This is the autumn and our harvest. *Fr.* New Year's. Reznikoff
Written When Appointed Commander of the Western Sea Marches. Umakai

Ross, Betsy
Betsy's Battle Flag. Irving

Rothko, Mark
Sleeping, The. Emanuel

Rouen, France
Rouen. Cannan

Roundheads (English Political Party)
Character of a Roundhead, The. *Unknown*

Rousseau, Henri
Henri Rousseau Style, The. Edmond

Rousseau, Jean Jacques
Mock On, Mock On, Voltaire, Rousseau. Blake
Rousseau in His Day. Davie

Rowe, Crystal
Crystal Rowe. Glenn

Rowing and Rowers
Eton Boating Song. Cory
Football and Rowing—an Eclogue. Godley
Max Schmitt in a Single Scull. Lattimore
Morning, A. Strand
Rowers, The. Benét
Rowing Early. Peck
See also **Crew Racing.**

Royal Society
Philosophy, the great and only heir. *Fr.* To the Royal Society. Cowley

Royalty
End of a Dynasty, The. Herbert
Epitaph on the Late King of the Sandwich Isles. Praed
Georges, The. Landor
On a Royal Demise. Hood
Royal Princess, A. Rossetti
See also **Kings; Princes and Princesses; Queens.**

Rubens, Peter Paul
Women of Rubens, The. Szymborska

Rugs
Amish Rug, An. Longley
Figure in the Carpet, The. Camp
Prayer Rug, The. Kennedy
Turkish Carpet, The. Durcan

Ruins
At a Ruined Croft. Manson
Barbury Camp. Sorley
Boy Wandering in Simms' Valley. Warren
Corner Stone, The. De la Mare
Crooked bank still winds to something new, The. *Fr.* A Voyage to Tintern Abbey. Davies
Death of the Kapowsin Tavern. Hugo
Grapevine, The. Brockman
Hast Thou Not Seen an Aged Rifted Tower. Coleridge
House on the Hill, The. Robinson

House That Was, The. Binyon
Jade Flower Palace. Tu Fu
Love among the Ruins. Browning
Love among the Ruins of London. Grainger
Melrose Abbey. *Fr.* The Lay of the Last Minstrel. Scott
Netley Abbey. Bowles
Netley Abbey; Midnight. Sotheby
Nettles. Munro
Newstead Abbey. Byron
On a Ruined House in a Romantic Country. *Fr.* Sonnets Attempted in the Manner of Contemporary Wr. Coleridge
On a Stupendous Leg of Granite, Discovered Standing by Itself in the Deserts of Egypt, with the Inscription Inserted Below. Smith
Ozymandias [*or* Ozymandias of Egypt *or* Sonnet: Ozymandias]. Shelley
Rain, The. Dafydd ap Gwilym
Ravaged Villa, The. Melville
Remains of an Indian Village. Purdy
Roman Temple, A. Abu Risha
Ruin, The. *Unknown*
Ruined House, A. Aldington
Ruins. Teller
Silence. Hood
Sonnet Written in Tintern Abbey, Monmouthshire. Gardner

Rum
Captain Stratton's Fancy. Masefield

Rumor
Buzz Buzz, the Blue Flies. *Unknown*
Combat. Williams
Rumor Verified. Warren
Virginia Reel. Wright
See also **Fame; Gossip; Ruputation**.

Running and Runners
At Guaracara Park. Roach
Birthday on the Beach. Nash
Crystal Rowe. Glenn
Finish, The. Hoffman
His Running My Running. Francis
Homage to the Runner. *Fr.* The Escape into You. Bell
Interview with a Winner. Finkle
Joan Benoit. Ferrarelli
Jogger from Schönbrunn, The. Jandl
Mighty Runner, A. Robinson
Morning Athletes. Piercy
Night Runner's Prayer. Reidy
On the Tomb of Kalamachius, the Jogger. Richman
Out on the Course. Vernon
Photograph, The. Drake
Prefontaine. Ghigna
Runner, The. Whitman
Running. Wilbur
Sometimes Running. Ciardi
Song of the Ungirt Runners, The. Sorley
Strategy for a Marathon. Mueller
This Runner. Webb

Russell, Lucy, Countess of Bedford
To Lucy, Countesse of Bedford, with Mr. Donnes Satyres. Jonson

Russia
Advice to a Raven in Russia [December, 1812]. Barlow
Epilogue: "There I learned how faces fall apart." *Fr.* Requiem 1935-1940. "Akhmatova"
Hamlet in Russia, A Soliloquy. Pasternak
I Was Washing Outside in the Darkness. Mandelstam
Last Statement. Mayakovsky
Leningrad. Mandelstam
Less Nonsense. Herbert
Moscow Night, End of December 1934. Leyeles
Requiem 1935-1940, *sels.* "Akhmatova"
Rostov. Fraser
Russia. Blok

Russia. Dole
Russia. Halkin
Russia. Williams
Russian Death. Kvitko
Russian God, The. Vyazemsky
Soviet Union, The. Berryman
Stalin Epigram, The. Mandelstam
To Russia. Miller
To Spencer. Turberville
Voronezh. "Akhmatova"
White-Hot Blizzard, The. Ratushinskaya
Why Do You Write about Russia? Simpson

Russian Revolution
History of the Revolution. Saarikoski
Makhno's Philosophers. Manifold
Sons of Our Sons, The. Ehrenburg

Russian Verse
Age Ago, An; a Selection of Nineteenth-Century Russian Poetry (AAA). Alan Myers, comp. *and* tr.

Russians, The
To Parker. Turberville

Rustum
Then Sohrab with is sword smote Rustum's helm. *Fr.* Sohrab and Rustum. Arnold

Ruth
Ruth. Hood

Ruth, George Herman ("Babe")
Babe & Lou. Douskey
Babe Ruth. Runyon

Rutledge, Anne
Anne Rutledge. *Fr.* Spoon River Anthology. Masters

Rydal Water, England
Sunrise on Rydal Water. Drinkwater

Ryder, Albert Pinkham
Ryder. Haines

S

Sabbath
First Cigarette, The. Rolnik
Home from Praying. Rolnik
It's good, it's good not to shield the heart this way. Markish
Kabbalists in Safed. Leivick
Keep Ye Holy Sabbath Rest. *Unknown*
Light a Candle. Zelda
Light and Rejoicing to Israel. *Unknown*
Marketplace sleeps, its booths like skulls, The. Markish
Outgoing Sabbath. *Unknown*
Princess Sabbath. Heine
Queen Sabbath. Bialik
Sabbath. Glatstein
Sabbath. Haan
Sabbath Hours. Leyeles
Sabbath, My Love. Halevi
Sabbath of Rest, A. Luria
Some keep the Sabbath [*or* Sunday] going to church. Dickinson
Son-Dayes. Vaughan
Song of the Sabbath. Molodowsky
Summer Sabbath. Sampter
Sunday. Herbert
Sunday Morning. MacNeice
Thou Beautiful Sabbath. *Unknown*
Welcome, Queen Sabbath. Schneour
See also **Sunday.**

Sacajawea
One Who Skins Cats, The. Allen
Sa-cá-ga-we-a. Proctor

Sacco-Vanzetti Case
Justice Denied in Massachusetts. Millay
Sacco-Vanzetti. Halpern
Vanzetti. Buckmaster

Sacraments *See* Baptism; Eucharist; Extreme Unction; Marriage.

Sacré-Coeur, Le
Le Sacré-Coeur. Mew

Sacrifices
Abundant is the year, with much millet, much rice. *Unknown*
Ah, the glorious ancestors. *Unknown*
Big field brings a heavy crop, The. *Unknown*
He comes in solemn state. *Unknown*
Little Boy Lost, A. Blake
Look at the foothills of Mount Han. *Unknown*
Messenger, The. Horovitz
Murukan: His Places. Nakkiranar
Sacrifice. Leivick
Scapegoat. Rodgers
So they appeared before their lord the king. *Unknown*
They clear away the grass, the trees. *Unknown*
Thick grows the star-thistle. *Unknown*
Tollund Man, The. Heaney
Truly, those southern hills. *Unknown*
We bring our offerings. *Unknown*
Wild-duck are on the Ching, The. *Unknown*

Sade, Donatien Alphonse François, Marquis
Marquis de Sade, The. Breton

Sadism
Andrew Rose. *Unknown*
Captain James. *Unknown*

Sadness
At Fifteen I Went Off to the Army. *Unknown*
At the bidding of my great Sovereign. *Fr.* Manyo Shu. Yakamochi
Broken Heart. Ray
Cries of crickets, The. Ietaka
Did it perhaps. Joben
Dolor. Roethke
Early Autumn. Joben
Early Autumn. Keiun
Feelings Wakened by a Mirror. Po Chü-i
For the jewel-like dew. Teika
Good Night, World. Glatstein
Hunger Fell upon Us, A. Glatstein
I Am the Train of Sadness. Qabbani
In Mourning for the Summer. Tachihara Michizo
In the evening light. Ietaka
Kol-Nidre. Halpern
Last Betrayal, The. Gozzano
Light Furs, Fat Horses. Po Chü-i
Looking at the moon, I feel sad. *Fr.* A Compendium of Good Tanka. Teika
Miss Blues'es Child. Hughes
Ms Understood. Springer
Now that I am brought to know. *Fr.* Manyo Shu. Tabito
On and on, going on and on. *Fr.* Nineteen Old Poems of the Han. *Unknown*
River Messages. Wei Chuang
Sad. Nishiwaki Junzaburo
Sad Boy, The. Riding
Sad Song. *Unknown*
Sadness of the lifeless sand. *Fr.* Forty-seven Tanka in Three Lines. Ishikawa Takuboku
Shadow and Sunrise. Ray
Small Night-Music. Glatstein
Sometimes. Prelutsky
Song of Sorrow. *Unknown*
To Akashi's strand/ I came in hope of finding. Tameie
Traveler's Moon, The. Po Chü-i

Safety Pins
Safety Pin. Worth

Sailing and Sailors
Adieu My Lovely Nancy. *Unknown*

Alarmed Skipper, The. Fields
All through the windless night the clipper rolled. *Fr.* Dauber. Masefield
Anchor. Maruyama Kaoru
Arion. Pushkin
Ballad of the Tempest. Fields
Bay of Biscay, The. *Unknown*
Becalmed. Blight
Belly and Tubs Went Out in a Boat. Watson
Bermudas. Marvell
Birlinn Chlann-Raghnaill. MacDonald
Blooming Sally. *Unknown*
Blow Ye Winds. *Unknown*
Boat Song. Ray
British Man-of-War, A. *Unknown*
Burial of the Dane, The. Brownell
Canada-I-O. *Unknown*
Captain Bunker. *Unknown*
Captain Reece. Gilbert
Cheerily Man. *Unknown*
Chief Petty Officer. Causley
Child and the Mariner, The. Davies
Choosing Craft. Swenson
Christmas at Sea. Stevenson
Commemorative of a Naval Victory. Melville
Crowd, The. Masefield
Dance the Boatman. *Unknown*
Drowned Sailor. Shaw
Early, Early in the Spring. *Unknown*
Enoch Arden. Tennyson
Evening on the Broads. Swinburne
Female Sailor, The. *Unknown*
Fiddler's Green. Roberts
Fife Tune. Manifold
Fifteen Ships on Georges Banks. *Unknown*
Forty Singing Seamen. Noyes
Girls around Cape Horn, The. *Unknown*
Good Play, A. Stevenson
Greenland Whale Fishery, The. *Unknown*
Grey Funnel Line, The. Tawney
Haul Away, My Rosy. *Unknown*
Heaving the Lead Line. *Unknown*
Hell's Pavement. Masefield
Hervé Riel. Browning
Homeward Bound. Allingham
"How's My Boy?" Dobell
Hugging the Shore. Tucker
Ibn Battuta. Davis
If you my dear mother, had e'er been at sea. *Fr.* India Guide, The; or, Journal of a Voyage to the East Indies in 1780. Dallas
In Praise of Seafaring Men, in Hopes of Good Fortune. Grenville
Indian Lass, The. *Unknown*
Into the Wind. Petoskey
I've served my country nine and twenty years. *Fr.* An Humble Wish; off Porto-Sancto, March 29, 1779. Thompson
Jack Robinson. *Unknown*
Jolly Soldier. *Unknown*
Jovial Marriner; or, The Sea-Man's Renown, The. Playford
Just as the Tide Was a-Flowing. *Unknown*
Lament for the Sailing of the Crusade. D'Aquino
Last Chantey, The. Kipling
Life on the Ocean Wave, A. Sargent
Lightning Flash, The. *Unknown*
Longshore Intellectual. Lucy
Lowlands o' [or of] Holland, The. *Unknown*
McAndrew's Hymn. Kipling
Manchester Ship Canal, The. *Unknown*
Mariners' Carol. Merwin
Mariner's Dream, The. Dimond
Masts at Dawn. Warren
Men behind the Guns, The. Rooney
Merchant Marine. Miles
Messmates. Newbolt
My Galley. Petrarch

My ship stopped, I've come upon this country. *Fr.* Forty-four Tanka. Wakayama Bokusui
Naval Photograph: 25 October 1942: What the Hand May Be Saying. Bottoms
New Ballad of Sir Patrick Spens, The. Quiller-Couch
No, I'm not Byron, it's my role. Lermontov
O Minume Bay, chosen by all Yashima's shipmen. *Fr.* Manyo Shu. Tanabe Sakimaro
O Sailor, Come Ashore. Rossetti
Ode for a Master Mariner Ashore. Guiney
Off Rivière du Loup. Scott
Offshore. Booth
Old Deep Sing-Song. Sandburg
Old Sailor Looking at a Container Ship. Carson
Old Song Re-sung, An. Masefield
On the Congo. Martinson
On Weathering Gales. Ritchie
One of Wally's Yarns. Masefield
Over Bright Summer Seas. Hillyer
Overboard. Swenson
Paddy, Get Back. *Unknown*
Pat Cloherty's Version of *The Maisie*. Murphy
Pleasant and Delightful. *Unknown*
Poem to Show the Trouble That Befell Him When He Was at Sea, A. Prys
Poor Jack. Dibdin
Putting to Sea. Bogan
Rambling Sailor, The. Mew
Red Iron Ore,. *Unknown*
Reuben Ranzo. *Unknown*
Rime of the Ancient Mariner, The. Coleridge
Rosemary Lane. *Unknown*
Rounding the Horn. *Fr.* Dauber. Masefield.
Rude Boreas. *Unknown*
Sail, The. Lermontov
Sailboat, Your Secret. Francis
Sailing. Zolynas
Sailing in the Rain. Hsiang Yang
Sailing, Sailing. Burr
Sailing, Sailing. Morrison
Sailing to an Island. Murphy
Sailor. Hughes
Sailor, The. MacDonald
Sailors. Vaynshteyn
Sailors' Alphabet, The. *Unknown*
Sailor's Wife, A. Bernhardt
Salem. Lowell
Sally Free and Easy. Tawney
Sapphics: At the Mohawk-Castle, Canada. Morris
Saucy Sailor, The. *Unknown*
Saylors for My Money. Parker
Sea, The. "Cornwall"
Sea Dialogue, A. Holmes
Sea Fever. Masefield
Sea Gypsy, The. Hovey
Sea-Voyage from Tenby to Bristol, A. Philips
Seafarer. MacLeish
Seafarer, The. *Unknown*
Seaman, 1941. Holden
Sensitive Sydney. Irwin
Seumas Beg. Stephens
Sheep. Davies
Shepherdess and the Sailor, The. *Unknown*
Shipman, The. *Fr.* The Canterbury Tales: Prologue. Chaucer
Shipmen, The. Hunnis
Song for All Seas, All Ships. Whitman
Song of the Lamp. Masefield
Song of the Sail. Maruyama Kaoru
Sounding. Ferne
Sunfish Races. Preston
Tacking Ship Off Shore. Mitchell

Tempest, The. *Unknown*
Tilting Sail. Illyés
To a Seaman Dead on Land. Boyle
To Sea. *Fr. Death's Jest Book.* Beddoes
To Stay. Mühringer
Two Anchors, The. Stoddard
Vacationer. Gibson
Wet Sheet and a Flowing Sea, A.
  Cunningham
What the Red-haired Bo'sun Said. Souter
Where Lies the Land [to Which the Ship
  Would Go?] *Fr. Songs in Absence.*
  Clough
While at Nigitazu we await the moon. *Fr.*
  Manyo Shu. Nukada
William Taylor. *Unknown*
Wind Sou'west, The. *Unknown*
Wynyard Sailor. Mathew
Yacht for Sale. MacLeish
Yachts, The. Williams
Ye Mariners of England. Campbell
Young Allan. *Unknown*
Young Sailor Cut Down in His Prime, The.
  Unknown
American Sea Songs and Chanteys (AmSS).
  Frank Shay, ed.
Moods of the Sea (MOS). George C. Solley
  and Eric Steinbaugh, eds.
Oxford Book of Sea Songs, The (OxBSS).
  Roy Palmer, ed.
St. Agnes' Eve
St. Agnes' Eve. Tennyson
St. Cecilia's Day
Song for St, A Cecilia's Day, 1687. Dryden
See also **Cecilia, Saint.**
Saint Cloud, France
Saint Cloud. Scott
St. Croix (river), Canada
Border River. Bailey
St. David's Day
In Honour of St. David's Day. *Unknown*
St. John's Day
For Saint John's Day. Wadding
St. Lawrence River
On the rapids of the St. Lawrence. Ray
St. Louis, Missouri
Meet Me in St. Louis, Louis. Sterling
Saint Lucia
For the Altarpiece of the Roseau Valley
  Church, Saint Lucia. Walcott
St. Maria Maggiore
Saint Maria Maggiore. Fritsch
St. Mark's Eve
Eve of Saint Mark, The. Keats
St. Patrick's Day
Paschal Fire, The. MacCarthy
Wearing of the Green. Fisher
St. Paul's Cathedral
Homage to Wren. MacNeice
Saint Peter's Church, Rome
Marble Floor. Wojtyla
Sir Walter Scott at the Tomb of the Stuarts in
  St. Peter's. Milnes
St. Stephen's Day
For Saint Stephen's Day. Wadding
St. Stephen's Day. Hewitt
St. Valentine's Day. *See* **Valentine's Day.**
Saints
Mrs. Malone. Farjeon
Nameless Saints, The. Hale
Sainthood. O'Flynn
Saints. Garrett
Vision of the Blessed Gabriele, The. Shuttle
Salads
Universal Favorite, The. Wells
Salamis, Battle of (480 B.C.)
Salamis. *Fr.* The Persians. Aeschylus
Salem, Massachusetts
Salem. Lowell
Salem. Stedman
Salem, Massachusetts. Muir

Salem Witch, A. Clarke
Sales Clerks. *See* **Clerks.**
Salesmen
One Foot in the Door. Elder
Salesman Is an It That Stinks Excuse, A.
  Cummings
Salisbury, England
In a Cathedral City. Hardy
Salmon
Salmon Courage. Philip
Salmon Drowns Eagle. Lowry
Sockeye Salmon. Hambleton
Weir Bridge. Fallon
Salt
Confiscating Salt. Wang An-shih
Ode to Salt. Neruda
Photos of a Salt Mine. Page
Salt. Francis
What She Said ("The fishermen who go").
  Ammuvanar
Salt Lake City, Utah
Salt Lake City. Carruth
Saltus, Thaddeus
To Rev. Thaddeus Saltus. Fordham
Salvation
Bhil woman tasted them, plum after plum,
  The. Mirabai
"Go Bring Me," Said the Dying Fair. Hunter
Go to where my loved one lives. Mirabai
Ubi Sunt Qui ante Nos Fuerunt? *Unknown*
Zion's Sons and Daughters. *Unknown*
Salvation Army
General William Booth Enters into Heaven.
  Lindsay
Karma. Robinson
Roll the Chariot. *Unknown*
Samarkand
Journey in the Orient. Spaziani
Samos, Greece
Samos. *Fr.* Scripts for the Pageant. Merrill
Samson
Among Philistines. Gwynn
Blindness of Samson, The. *Fr.* Samson
  Agonistes. Milton
Come, come, no time for lamentation now.
  Fr. Samson Agonistes. Milton
General Truths. *Fr.* Samson, Our Hero.
  Avidan
Loosely from the Latin. Galef
Love Letter. Gregory
My Samsons. Guri
Oh [*or* O], how comely it is, and how
  reviving. *Fr.* Samson Agonistes. Milton
Samson. Gilboa
Samson's Hair. Zach
Ways of God to Men, The. *Fr.* Samson
  Agonistes. Milton
San Francisco, California
City [San Francisco]. Hughes
Idea of San Francisco, The. Gustafson
Pan-Asian Holiday Tour. Syquia
San Francisco. Roberts
San Francisco Poem. Logan
Trip: San Francisco. Hughes
Sancho Panza
Sancho. Collin
Sancho Panza's Homecoming. Yoshiro
Sanctuaries
Sanctuary. Boothroyd
Sand
Baby's Baking. Stein
Castles in the Sand. Baker
Culbin Sands. Young
Grain of Sand, A. Harper
I dug and dug amongst the snow. Rossetti
Recipe for Sand. Brinson Curiel
We Lying by Seasand. Thomas
Sand, George
George Sand. Parker
To George Sand. Reinsberg-Düringsfeld

Sandpipers
Certain Sandpiper, A. Kennedy
Sandpiper. Bishop
Sandpiper, The. Bynner
Sandpiper, The. Frost
Sandpiper, The. Thaxter
Sandpiper, The. Zolotow
Sandpipers. Egerton
Summer's Early End at Hudson Bay.
  Carruth
Sanitary Engineering
They're Shifting Father's Grave. *Unknown*
See also **Sewers.**
Santa Barbara, California
Santa Barbara. Browne
Santa Claus
Boy Who Laughed at Santa Claus, The.
  Nash
Mrs. Kriss Kringle. Thomas
Saint Nicholas. Moore
Santa Claus. De la Mare
Santa Claus. *Unknown*
Visit from St. Nicholas, A. Moore
Santa Fe Trail
Old Santa Fe Trail, The. Burton
Santayana, George
For George Santayana. Lowell
To an Old Philosopher in Rome. Stevens
Santiago de Cuba, Battle of (1898)
Charge at Santiago, The. Hayne
Deeds of Valor at Santiago. Scollard
Santiago. Janvier
Spain's Last Armada. Rice
Sappho
Last Song of Sappho, The. Leopardi
Sappho. Cope
Sappho. Najmájer
Sappho's Last Song. Pompili
Sappho's Tomb. Stringer
Summer Matures. Johnson
Sarah
Adage Concerning a Man and an Old Book,
  An. Shtern
Days of Sarah, The. Galai
Sarah. Schwartz
Sarai. Sherman
Women's Songs ("For poor brides who were
  servant girls"). Molodovsky
Sarajevo, Yugoslavia
Sarajevo. Durrell
Saratoga, New York
Field of the Grounded Arms, The. Halleck
Sarto, Andrea del
Andrea del Sarto. Browning
Saskatchewan, Canada
Breathe Dust. Wah
Double-headed Snake, The. Newlove
From the North Saskatchewan. Mandel
Verigin, Moving in Alone. Newlove
Sassafras
Sassafras. Peck
Satan
Address to the Deil. Burns
After Reading the Life of Mrs. Catherine
  Stubbs in Isaac Ambrose's "War with the
  Devils." Hann
But he his wonted pride. *Fr.* Paradise Lost.
  Milton
Copy of an Intercepted Despatch from His
  Excellency Don Strepitoso Diabolo.
  Moore
Dark Angel, The. Johnson
Devil, A. Herbert
Devil in Texas, The. *Unknown*
Devil's Bag, The. Stephens
Epilogue: "Truly, my Satan, thou art but a
  dunce." *Fr.* The Gates of Paradise.
  Blake
Hell in Texas. *Unknown*
Knight Fallen on Evil Days, The. Wylie
Lament of an Idle Demon. Lister

Litany to Satan. Baudelaire
Lucifer in Starlight. Meredith
Lucifer in the Train. Rich
Man's Amazement. *Unknown*
Meanwhile the adversary of God and man.
  Fr. Paradise Lost. Milton
Miniatures. Kiss
Overthrow of Lucifer, The. *Fr.* The Purple
  Island. Fletcher
Prologue in Heaven [*or* The Chorus of the
  Archangels]. *Fr.* Faust. Goethe
Sinners, abhor the Fiend. *Fr.* The Horrible
  Decree. Wesley
Tale of the Fly, The. Halpern
Limits of the sphere of dream, The. *Fr.*
  Faust. Goethe
Three Enemies, The. Rossetti
To an Artist. Burns
Whale, The. *Fr.* Physiologus. *Unknown*

Satie, Erik
Angel. Merrill
Erik Satie. Bernlef
Satie, at the End of Term. Curtis

Satiric Verse
Maturity. Owen
Anthology of Poems on Affairs of State:
  Augustan Satirical Verse (APAS). George
  deF. Lord, ed.
Oxford Book of Satirical Verse, The (OBSV).
  Geoffrey Grigson, ed.

Saturday
Saturday under the Sky. Soto
Sonnet: Saturday Evening in the Village.
  Leopardi
See also **Sabbath.**

Saudi Arabia
In Memory, 1978. Kazantzis

Saul
Dance of Saul with the Prophets, The.
  Tchernichowsky
King Saul. Horvitz
Saul. Alterman
Saul. Gilboa
Saul. Lasker-Schüler
Saul Re-enthroned. Wieseltier
Beauty of Israel is slain [*or* slaine] upon thy
  high places, The. *Fr.* Second Samuel.

Saunas. *See* **Baths and Bathing.**

Sausage
Recipe: Sausage. Axionicus
Sausage. Guest

Savannah, Georgia
About Savannah. *Unknown*
Savannah. Burroughs
Savannah, Sleepless. Tillinghast

Savonarola, Girolamo
Savonarola ("Savonarola looks more grim
  today"). Beerbohm

Sayigh, Taufiq
To Taufiq Sayigh. al-Rayyes

Scallions
Scallions just washed white in this cold. *Fr.*
  Seventy-six Hokku. Basho

Scarecrows
Lonely Scarecrow, The. Kirkup
Mr. Scarecrow. Braine
Rainy Nights. Thompson
Scarecrow, The. De la Mare
Scarecrow, The. Franklin
Scarecrow, The. Young
Scarecrow in Capri, The. Wawra
Waka on Zen Sitting. Dogen

Scheherazade
Scheherazade. Burford

Schoenberg, Arnold
Ode to Arnold Schoenberg. Tomlinson

Scholarship and Scholars
Academic Curse; an Epitaph. Court
Andrew M'Crie. Murray
Baccalaureate. McCord
Binni the Meshuggener. Siegel

Emeritus, The. Nathan
End of April, The. Murray
Epigram: "Gold priests, wooden chalices."
  Unknown
Epilogue: "My bibliography has grown."
  Wiebe
For Scholars and Pupils. Wither
Giles Johnson, Ph.D. Davis
Going to School. Shapiro
Grammarian's Funeral, A. Browning
He That Never Read a Line. *Unknown*
If, Jerusalem, I Ever Should Forget Thee.
  Heine
Imaginary Translation. Hacker
Lines on Being Refused a Guggenheim
  Fellowship. Whittemore
Lines to a Don. Belloc
Miniature. Phillpotts
Of the Manner of Addressing Clouds.
  Stevens
Poor Scholar. Cheng Hsieh
Poor Scholar, The. Ibn Chasdai
Poor Scholar of the 'Forties, A. Colum
Professor Gratt. Hall
Scholar, The. Clarke
Scholar, The. Cornford
Scholar Complains, The. *Unknown*
Scholar-Gipsy, The. Arnold
Scholar I. Deane
Scholar II. Deane
Scholars, The. Yeats
Scholar's Life, The. *Unknown*
Schools. *Fr.* The Borough. Crabbe
Sons of Our Sons, The. Ehrenburg
Talmud Student, The. Bialik
To a Friend, on Her Examination for the
  Doctorate in English. Cunningham
Two men wrote a lexicon, Liddell and Scott.
  Unknown
See also **Pedantry; Students; Teaching and
  Teachers.**

Scholl, Sophie
White Rose: Sophie Scholl 1921-1943, The.
  Mumford

School
Anseo. Muldoon
Classroom in October. Lieberman
Cruel Boys. Soto
Dancing School. Holden
Description of a Good Boy, The. Dixon
Desk, The. Bottoms
Distracted the Mother Said to Her Boy.
  Harrison
Ecole St. Luc. Fraser
Elementary School Classroom in a Slum, An.
  Spender
Examination, The. Thompson
First Day at Boarding School. Power
First Practice. Gildner
Ghetto Summer School. Worth
Goodbye to Regal. Huws
How a Girl Got Her Chinese Name. Wong
In School-Days. Whittier
In School-Days. Whittier
Janie Swecker and Me and Gone with the
  Wind. Huddle
Johnny's Hist'ry Lesson. Waterman
Kindergarten. Schmitz
Last Lesson of the Afternoon. Lawrence
Lines to an Old School-House. Thompson
Meeting the British. Muldoon
Memories of the Village School. Bashir
Model School, Inchicore. Kinsella
Mortifying Mistake, A. Pratt
Negro Schools, The. Moorer
Nobody. Agard
Ode on a Distant Prospect of Clapham
  Academy. Hood
On Reading Poems to a Senior Class at South
  High. Berry
Our School Now Closes Out. Dumas
Overworked Elocutionist, An. Wells

School-Bell. Farjeon
School Cadets. Elder
School Children, The. Glück
School Days. Stafford
School Report, A. Hunt
Schoolboys in Winter. Clare
Schools. *Fr.* The Borough. Crabbe
Schools and Schoolmasters. Flanzbaum
Schoolyard in April. Koch
Shapes, Vanishings. Taylor
Small Boy, Dreaming, A. Herzing
Student, The. Moore
Though the New Teacher Is a Trifle Odd.
  Fr. Word from the Hills. Moore
Thoughts on Schoolchildren. Shauqi
Tom Brainless as Student and Preacher at
  College. *Fr.* The Progress of Dulness.
  Trumbull
Tree of Knowledge, The. Moorer
Unhappy Schoolboy, The. *Unknown*
Vanishers, The. Whittier
Zimmer's Head Thudding against the
  Blackboard. Zimmer
See also **Colleges and Universities.**

Schoolmasters. *See* **Teaching and Teachers.**

Schubert, Franz
Schubertiana. Tranströmer

Schwartz, Delmore
I can't get him out of my mind, out of my
  mind. *Fr.* Dream Songs. Berryman
This world is gradually becoming a place.
  Fr. Dream Songs. Berryman

Science and Scientists
Apprentices. Munro
Assembling the Model. Payack
Bright New Missouri. Sneyd
Calling the Scientists Home. Rose
Can You Hear Me, Thinktank Two? Disch
Counting Sheep. Edson
Cytogenetics Lab. Day
Dr. Sigmund Freud Discovers the Sea Shell.
  MacLeish
Full House. Garey
Horrid Voice of Science, The. Lindsay
In Sobieski's Shield. Morgan
Laboratory Poem. Merrill
Letter to Alex Comfort. Abse
Loren Eiseley's Time Passages. Frazier
MC^2-E. Wickstrom
Meditations for a Savage Child. Rich
Morden Lecture, 1978. Le Guin
Neural Folds. Day
Neutrinos. Perry
Ode to Terminus. Auden
On an Engraving by Casserius. Hope
On Passing by Those Icy Stones (and Yes,
  Columbia!). Bunch
On the Marriage of Art and Science.
  Dorman
Oxford Street Museum. Lockwood
Poetry and Science. Turner
Problems. Scott
Purist, The. Nash
Revelation. Keesing
Science, the agile ape, may well. Patmore
Science/Fiction. Marcus
Slice of Life, A. Wickstrom
Sonnet to Science. Poe
Thermodynamics. Marcus
To Science. Poe
Toad, The. Oliver
Under dream interrogation. Calder
V. B. Nimble, V. B. Quick ("V. B.
  Wigglesworth wakes at noon"). Updike
When we invent a machine to read. *Fr.*
  Hospital Songs. Dann
*Burning with a Vision; Poetry of Science and
  the Fantastic* (BwV). Robert Frazier, ed.

*Burning with a Vision; Poetry of Science and
  the Fantastic* (BwV). Robert Frazier, ed.
Imagination's Other Place (ImOP). Helen
  Plotz, ed.
Science Fiction
  Discovery of the New World. Revard
  Gran Mal. Rantala
  Neurophysiologist, The. Post
  On Science Fiction. Disch
  Science Fiction. Amis
  Science Fiction. Willard
  Science/Fiction. Marcus
Scilly Islands
  Tresco. Grigson
Scopes Trial
  Bryan's Last Battle. *Unknown*
  See also **Evolution.**
Scorpions
  Playing House. Gilbert
  Scorpion, The. Plomer
Scotland
  Ballade of the Scottyshe Kynge, A. Skelton
  Birks of Aberfeldy, The. Burns
  Breathes There the [*or* a] Man [with Soul So
    Dead]. *Fr.* The Lay of the Last Minstrel.
    Scott
  Caledonia. Powell
  Cotter's Saturday Night, The. Burns
  Highland Mary. Fordham
  Inchcape Rock, The. Southey
  Lochinvar. *Fr.* Marmion. Scott
  Lord Ullin's Daughter. Campbell
  Massacre of the Macpherson, The. Aytoun
  Melrose Abbey. *Fr.* The Lay of the Last
    Minstrel. Scott
  Scotland. Gray
  Scotland Small? "MacDiarmid"
  Scotland's Winter. Muir
  Sic Transit Gloria Scotia. "MacDiarmid"
  Soldier, The. Watson
  Upon the Death of the Viscount of Dundee.
    Dryden
  Vision, The. Defoe
  Golden Treasury of Scottish Poetry, The
    (GoTS). "Hugh MacDiarmid," ed.
  Oxford Book of Scottish Verse, The (OxBS).
    John MacQueen *and* Tom Scott, eds.
  Poems of the Scottish Hills (PoSH). Hamish
    Brown, ed.
Scots, The
  Border Ballad. *Fr.* The Monastery. Scott
  Gathering, The. *Fr.* Towards the Last Spike.
    Pratt
  Genealogical Reflection. Nash
  Nature herself doth Scotchmen beasts confess.
    Fr. The Rebel [*or* Rebell] Scot. Cleveland
  Scotland 1941. Muir
Scott, Sir Walter
  Green Breeks. Dunn
  On the Departure of Sir Walter Scott from
    Abbotsford, for Naples. Wordsworth
  Sir Walter Scott at the Tomb of the Stuarts in
    St. Peter's. Milnes
  Yarrow Revisited. Wordsworth
  Young Lochinvar. *Unknown*
Scottish Borders
  Dreary Change, The. Scott
  Ettrick Forest in November. *Fr.* Marmion.
    Scott
  Flowers of the ForestThe. Elliot
  Village of Balmaquhapple, The. Hogg
Scottish Highlands
  In the Highlands. Stevenson
  Ode on the Popular Superstitions of the
    Highlands of Scotland, An. Collins
  Poems of the Scottish Hills (PoSH). Hamish
    Brown, ed.
Scottsboro Case
  Communication to Nancy Cunard, A. Boyle
  Scottsboro, Too, Is Worth Its Song. Cullen

They Are Ours. Magil
Trial, The. Rukeyser
Screams
  Landscape of Screams. Sachs
  Munch's Scream. Hall
  Scream, A. Abse
Scribes
  Scribe, The. *Unknown*
  See also **Secretaries; Stenographers.**
Sculpture and Sculptors
  Children and Sir Nameless, The. Hardy
  Convert, The. Danner
  Crack, The. Goldman
  Etruscan Warrior's Head. Henze
  Homage to David Smith. Haines
  Museum-Piece. Brown
  "Night" in the Medici Chapel. Michelangelo
  No Swan So Fine. Moore
  O God! O Montreal! Butler
  On Seeing the Elgin Marbles. Keats
  On the Bust of Helen by Canova. Byron
  Praxiteles and Phryne. Story
  Reclining Figure. Hall
  Sculptor, The. Edson
  Sculptor's Vision, The. Ray
  Statue, The. Fuller
  Statues, The. Yeats
  Tireles Sculptor, The. Ray
  Tulip. Wolfe
Sea
  Ah, the Sea of Grebes!/. Ietaka
  All Day I Hear The Noise of Waters. Joyce
  Am I the son my father and mother cherish.
    Fr. Manyo Shu. Yakamochi
  At Melville's Tomb. Crane
  At Sainte-Marguerite. Stickney
  At the Seaside. Stevenson
  Aunt Zillah Speaks. Palmer
  Ayii, Ayii,/ I walked on the ice of the sea.
    Unknown
  Ayii, Ayii/ The great sea has set me in
    motion. *Unknown*
  Beach Glass. Clampitt
  Beautiful Sea, The. Tucker
  Bones. Sandburg
  Break, Break, Break. Tennyson
  By the Sea. Dixon
  By the Sea. Rossetti
  By the Sea on a Winter Day. Koh
    Chang-soo
  City in the Sea *or* The Doomed City, The.
    Poe
  Coming Homeward out of Spain. Googe
  Coming Suddenly to the Sea. Dudek
  Comparatives. Momaday
  Dancing Sea, The. *Fr.* Orchestra; or, A
    Poem[e] of Da[u]ncing. Davies
  Dark Sea. Maruyama Kaoru
  Deep, The. Brainard
  Distant View of the Sea, A. Tamekane
  Do the vast oceans die? *Fr.* Manyo Shu.
    Unknown
  Dover Beach. Arnold
  Down from the Country. Blight
  Earth-Ocean. Apollinaire
  East Anglian Bathe. Betjeman
  Enigmas. Neruda
  Evening by the Sea. Swinburne
  Extinction of Plankton. Tozaburo
  Eye, The. Jeffers
  Feeling from the Sea, A. Burkard
  Fine Day for Straw Hats, A. Stimson
  Flowers by the Sea. Williams
  Frozen Ocean, The. Meynell
  Grave, A. Moore
  Gravedigger, The. Carman
  Graveyard by the Sea. Lux
  Ground-Swell, The. Pratt
  Had I the Choice. Whitman
  Haiku: "Sea becomes light, a window is open,
    The." *Fr.* One Hundred Haiku in Free
    Form. Hosai

Hall of Ocean Life. Hollander
Her Heards Be Thousand Fishes. *Fr.* Colin
  Clout's Come Home Again. Spenser
High Tide. Untermeyer
Hills and the Sea, The. Campbell
I never saw a moor. Dickinson
I Will Go Back to the Great Sweet Mother.
  Fr. The Triumph of Time. Swinburne
Idea of Order at Key West, The. Stevens
In Horse Latitudes. Pollitt
Iphione. Irwin
Kraken, The. Tennyson
Last Chantey, The. Kipling
Life on the Ocean Wave, A. Sargent
Lines on the Sea. Laing
Listening to Beethoven on the Oregon Coast.
  Carlile
Maggie and Milly and Molly and May.
  Cummings
Main-Deep, The. Stephens
Man Whom the Sea Kept Awake, The. Bly
Marin. Booth
Marina. Hardison
Marine Biology. Efrat
Maritimes. Shuttle
Naskeag. Corn
Neither Out Far nor In Deep. Frost
New Ballad of Sir Patrick Spens, The.
  Quiller-Couch
November Surf. Jeffers
Now is it pleasant in the summer-eve. *Fr.*
  The Borough. Crabbe
O Billows Bounding Far. Housman
Ocean, The. Moschus
Ocean Is like a Wreath, The. Kuapakaa
Ode to the Sea. Baker
Off Cape Leeuwen. Joseph
Off the beach at dusk. Kenko
Offshore Breeze. Acorn
On a Steamer. Baruch
On the Beach at Fontana. Joyce
On the Shore. Meriluoto
On This Island. Auden
Once at Swanage. Hardy
Once by the Pacific. Frost
Open Sea, The. Meredith
Oread. Doolittle
Pines along the Coast. Tameko
Plague of Dead Sharks. Dugan
Point Shirley. Plath
Prayer to the Pacific. Silko
Resting my eyes on the bay of Miho. *Fr.*
  Manyo Shu. Masuhito
Sailor's Prayer, A. Morris
Sappho's Last Song. Pompili
Sea, The. "Cornwall"
Sea, The. Guillevic
Sea, The. Lawrence
Sea, The. *Fr.* Nature Notes. MacNeice
Sea. Shin Dong-jip
Sea, The. Webb
Sea and Ourselves at Cape Ann, The.
  Ferlinghetti
Sea and the Hills, The. Kipling
Sea at Evening, The. Laird
Sea Birds, The. Brock
Sea-Chill. Guiterman
Sea Dirge, A. "Carroll"
Sea Fever. Masefield
Sea-Grief. O'Reilly
Sea-Limits, The. Rossetti
Sea Offerings. Yu Kuang-chung
Sea Promenade, A. Pasolini
Sea retains such images, The. *Fr.* Europe.
  Dudek
Sea Song, A. Dolben
Sea Song. Holland
Sea Surface Full of Clouds. Stevens
Sea Things. MacEwen
Seafarer, The. *Unknown*
Sea's Spell, The. Spalding
Seascape. Bishop

Seascape. Spender
Seascape. Young
Seashell. Efrat
Shell, The. Stephens
Shore. Miller
Silences. Pratt
Song for All Seas, All Ships. Whitman
Sound of the Sea, The. Longfellow
Spring Sea. Tamemasa
Surf. Morrison
Thalassa. Larbaud
Thalassa. MacNeice
Through the blue, blue moonless night. *Fr.*
   Forty-four Tanka. Wakayama Bokusui
Tide Rises, the Tide Falls, The. Longfellow
Time of the Sea. Reverdy
To the Sea. Larkin
Training. Demetrio
Until I Saw the Sea. Moore
Uses of Ocean, The. Seaman
Waking from a Nap on the Beach. Swenson
Wanderer's Song, A. Masefield
Water. Lowell
Waves Gleam in the Sunshine, The. *Fr.*
   Songs to Seraphine. Heine
Where Tide. Booth
Wind and Wave. Stoddard
Winter Ocean. Updike
Winter Views Serene. *Fr.* The Borough.
   Crabbe
World below the Brine, The. Whitman
Yachts, The. Williams
You Can Have It. Levine
You Will Know When You Get There.
   Curnow
American Sea Songs and Chanteys (AmSS).
   Frank Shay, ed.
Moods of the Sea (MOS).   George C. Solley
   and Eric Steinbaugh, eds.
Oxford Book of Sea Songs, The (OxBSS).
   Roy Palmer, ed.
Oxford Book of Sea Songs, The (OxBSS).
   Roy Palmer, ed.
See also **Sailing and Sailors.**
Sea Battles. *See* **Naval Battles.**
Sea Chanteys
Sea-Chantey, A. Walcott
Wide Mizzoura, The. *Unknown*
American Sea Songs and Chanteys (AmSS).
   Frank Shay, ed.
Oxford Book of Sea Songs, The (OxBSS).
   Roy Palmer, ed.
Sea Creatures
Sadomasochistic Satisfactions of Seafood,
   The. Ewart
Sea Gulls. *See* **Gulls.**
Sea Hawks
Sea-Hawk. Eberhart
Sea Monsters and Sea Serpents
Kraken, The. Tennyson
Sea Monster. Merwin
Sea Serpent, The. Irwin
Sea Serpent Chantey, The. Lindsay
Sea Shells. *See* **Shells.**
Sea Voyages. *See* **Voyages.**
Seacoasts. *See* **Shores.**
Seafaring and Seafarers
I rode one evening with Count Maddalo. *Fr.*
   Julian and Maddalo. Shelley
Pilgrims' Sea Voyage and Seasickness, The.
   Unknown
See also **Sailing and Sailors.**
Seals
Dancing Seal, The. Gibson
Dead Seal. Purdy
Dead Seal near McClure's Beach, The. Bly
Ice-Floes, The. Pratt
Magic Words for Hunting Seal. *Unknown*
Performing Seal, The. *Fr.* A Circus
   Garland. Field
Seal. Smith

Seal Rock. Pollitt
Seals at High Island. Murphy
Seals in Penobscot Bay, The. Hoffman
Seals, Terns, Time. Eberhart
Spring Fiord. *Unknown*
Seamstresses
Three Seamstresses, The. Peretz
Seashore. *See* **Shores.**
Seasickness
Channel Passage, A. Brooke
Pilgrims' Sea Voyage and Seasickness, The.
   Unknown
Seasons
Acceleration near the Point of Impact. Oates
Against Seasons. Mezey
Autumn. *Fr.* The Four Seasons in the
   Mountains. Chang Yü
Autumn. *Fr.* Aella; a Tragycal Enterlude.
   Chatterton
Come Not the Seasons Here. Pratt
Common Poem, A. Rodgers
Eskimo Chant. *Unknown*
Fall, Leaves, Fall. Brontë
Four Seasons, The. Prelutsky
Four Seasons of the Year, The. Bradstreet
Human Seasons, The. Keats
Hymn on the Seasons, A. *Fr.* The Seasons.
   Thomson
If Only. Rossetti
In Due Season. Auden
In the Elegy Season. Wilbur
In their seasons. Tameko
Januar: by this fire I warme my handes.
   Unknown
January Man. Goulder
Let the Wind Recite. Yang Mu
Mask of Mutability, The. *Fr.* The Faerie
   Queene. Spenser
Metamorphosis. Stevens
Muted Music. Warren
November. *Fr.* A Suit of Nettles. Reaney
Pencil and Paint. Farjeon
Rhyme-Prose on the Small Hills. Yakatsugu
Round the Year. Patmore
Season Song. *Unknown*
Seasons, The. Holcroft
Seasons, The. Humphries
Seasons. Warren
Seasons of the Soul. Tate
Seasons Their Asterisks and Their Pawns.
   Arp
Solace. Delany
Spring. *Fr.* The Four Seasons in the
   Mountains. Chang Yü
Still. Meriluoto
Summer. *Fr.* The Four Seasons in the
   Mountains. Chang Yü
Summer Dawn. Morris
Through the Year. Cutler
To Autumn. Keats
What Her Girl Friend Said to Her.
   Kovatattan
What She Said ("Bird and Beast").
   Nannakaiyar
Wheel, The. Yeats
When Daisies Pied [and Violets Blue]. *Fr.*
   Love's Labour's Lost. Shakespeare
When spring comes. *Unknown*
Winter. *Fr.* The Four Seasons in the
   Mountains. Chang Yü
Winter's Onset from an Alienated Point of
   View. Dugan
Year Outgrows the Spring, The. Wilcox
Seattle, Washington
Letter to Tina Koyama from Elliot Bay Park.
   Mitsui
Seaweed
Kelp. Dauenhauer
Sea-Weed. Lawrence
Sea-Weed, The. Pullen
Seaweed. Longfellow

Seaweeds. McPherson
Tuft of Kelp, The. Melville
Second Coming
Earth Breaks Up. *Fr.* Christmas-Eve and
   Easter-Day. Browning
See also **Millennium.**
Second World War. *See* **World War II.**
Secrecy and Secrets
Canal Bank, The. Stephens
Winter: My Secret. Rossetti
Secretaries
Girl Friday. Equi
Scribe, The. De la Mare
Secretary, The. Redgrove
Stenographers, The. Page
See also **Scribes.**
Sectarianism
Fragment of an Anti-Papist Ballad. *Unknown*
Your Church and Mine. Lord
Security
Abide with Me. Lyte
Hitherto and Henceforth. Flint
I to the Hills Will Lift Mine Eyes. Rous
Ninetieth Psalm, The. Watts
Old Woman of the Roads, An. Colum
Reckoning, The. Roethke
Safety. *Fr.* 1914. Brooke
Seduction
Abroad as I Was Walking. *Unknown*
Amyntas Led Me to a Grove. *Fr.* The Dutch
   Lover. Behn
As I Walked through the Meadows.
   Unknown
Dark-eyed Gentleman, The. Hardy
Down by the Riverside. *Unknown*
Fair Singer, The. Marvell
Foggy Dew, The. *Unknown*
Fragment, A: "In Cloe's chamber, she and I."
   Bancks
In the Meadow There's a Dead Deer.
   Unknown
Invites His Nymph to His Cottage. Ayres
It Fell on a Summer's Day. Campion
Leicester Chambermaid, The. *Unknown*
Posy of Thyme, The. *Unknown*
Rosemary Lane. *Unknown*
Seduction. Giovanni
Seduction. Hall-Evans
Seventeen Come Sunday. *Unknown*
She Bewitched Me. Burbidge
Solitary Canto to Chloris the Disdainful, A.
   Smith
Under a hedge the other day. Marcabrun
Volatile Kerryman, The. O'Sullivan
Seeds
Baby Seed Song. Nesbit
Cabinet of Seeds Displayed, A. Nemerov
I Hoed and Trenched and Weeded. *Fr.* A
   Shropshire Lad. Housman
If a seed is there. *Fr.* Kokin Shu.
   Unknown
In Scorching Time. Stevens
Little Seeds. Minarik
Red Seeds Opening in the Shade.
   McPherson
Seed, The. Fisher
Seed Leaves. Wilbur
Seed Shop, The. Stuart
Seeds. Reeves
Ten Lines: On Seed. Hsiang Yang
Self
As long as I remained asleep. Bahadur Shah
   Zafar
Birthday Gift, A. Dunn
Day Glo Question of Identity, The. Miller
Dialogue of Self and Soul, A. Yeats
I celebrate myself, and sing myself. *Fr.*
   Song of Myself. Whitman
I know I have the best of time and space.
   Fr. Song of Myself. Whitman

Integrity. Rich
Just Looking, Thank You. Nathan
Let Me Tell You about Myself. Tomioka
  Taeko
Maggie and Milly and Molly and May.
  Cummings
Me. De la Mare
My Inside-Self. Field
Myself. Menken
See You Soon. Tomioka Taeko
Self-Mastery. Ray

Self-Pity
Self-Pity. Lawrence
Tichborne's Elegy. Tichborne

Self-Reliance
My Place. Ignatow

Self-Righteousness
Holy Willie's Prayer. Burns

Selfishness
Cherries. Stryk
Legend of the Northland, A. Cary
Pliant the horn bow. *Unknown*

Semele
Ambrosia of Dionysus and Semele, The.
  Graves
Semele Recycled. Kizer

Senegal
Double Take at Relais de L'Espadon. Davis
On the Way to Dakar. Cendrars

Senility
Senile. Folk

Sennacherib, King of Assyria
Destruction of Sennacherib, The. Byron
Parting at Morning. Browning

Sensuality
Canzone: "Consider the three functions of the
  tongue." Hacker

Seoul, Korea
Leaving Seoul; 1953. Lew

Separation
Above the High. Grigson
Ae Fond Kiss. Burns
Ancient Couple on Lu Mountain, The. Van
  Doren
At Parting. Ridler
At the San Francisco Airport. Winters
Auf Wiedersehen. Hayes
Ballad of the Despairing Husband. Creeley
Before a Journey. Wells
Before Sleep. Ridler
Blessed Damozel, The. Rossetti
Brazos River, The. *Unknown*
Casablanca Time Again. Howard
Corona. Hacker
Deep Gratitude. Niu Chiao
Deep rolls the thunder. *Unknown*
Definition of Love, The. Marvell
Departure, The. Steele
Drunk among the Flowers. Mao Wen-hsi
Earthquake. Heifetz-Tussman
Epistle to Miss [*or* Miss Teresa] Blount, on
  Her Leaving the Town after the Coronation.
  Pope
Even the Mirror Dies. Vammelvuo
Excuse of Absence, An. Carew
Exile. Dowson
Fare Thee Well. Byron
Father's Testament, A. Ibn Tibbon
Fatima. Tennyson
First Winter. Harada
Flowers of the Forest, The. Elliot
Foreign Woman's Complaint, The. Wen
  T'ing-yün
Forsaken. Schneour
Good-bye My Fancy! Whitman
Hatred of Distant Places. Wen T'ing-yün
He Resigns. Berryman
He Would Not Stay for Me; and Who Can
  Wonder? Housman
He's Gone Away. *Unknown*
I am now so weary with waiting. Stampa

I have had not one word from her. Sappho
I let the incense grow cold. Li Ch'ing-chao
I took leave of my beloved one evening: how
  I wish. At Taliq
I was not to know. *Fr.* Manyo Shu.
  Unknown
I Will Write. Graves
In a creek in Muko Bay. *Fr.* Manyo Shu.
  Unknown
In the Golden Land. Halpern
In the Last Few Moments Came the Old
  German Cleaning Woman. Cooper
In the spring meadow. *Fr.* Manyo Shu.
  Unknown
In the Year 4 after Father. Meriluoto
It's Already Autumn. Pagliarani
Jade Butterflies. Wen T'ing-yün
Kashmiri Song. Hope
Last Ride Together, The. Browning
Let the Wind Blow High or Low. *Unknown*
Letter to Her Husband, Absent upon Public
  Employment, A ("as loving hind. . .").
  Bradstreet
Like Loving Chekhov. Levertov
Like the Touch of Rain. Thomas
Long Boat, The. Kunitz
Magnolia Flower, The. Wei Chuang
Meeting, The. Rukeyser
Message. Ginsberg
Miss You. Cory
Molly of the North Country. *Unknown*
Moving Out. Wilson
My Best Clothes. Netser
My Johnny. *Unknown*
My life closed twice before its close.
  Dickinson
My Lord has departed. *Fr.* Manyo Shu.
  Iwa no Hima
O oriole, yellow bird. *Unknown*
On Parting with Moses ibn Ezra. Halevi
On the beach where you sleep. *Fr.* Manyo
  Shu. *Unknown*
On the Departure Platform. Hardy
Orinda to Lucasia. Philips
Out of Sight, Out of Mind. Googe
Pacifying the Western Barbarians. Wen
  T'ing-yün
Painful Love Song, A. Amichai
Parting. Halevi
Parting. *Fr.* A Chaste Maid in Cheapside.
  Middleton
Parting in Wartime. Cornford
Partings. Jewsbury
Paying Homage at the Golden Gate. Wei
  Chuang
Poem Unwritten, The. Levertov
Portrait of a Lady. Eliot
Pure Serene Music. Wei Chuang
Retreat[e], The. Vaughan
Returning to My Distant Home. Wei Chuang
Sale. Williams
Sand of Silk-Washing Stream. Ku Hsiung
Sand of the Silk-Washing Stream. Hsüeh
  Chao-yün
Saw You among Trees. Tussman
Semele Recycled. Kizer
Sence You Went Away. Johnson
Separation. Bianchi
Separation, A. Cory
Separation. Merwin
Separation on the River Kiang. Li Po
Separations. Zimroth
Since there's [*or* ther's] no help[e], come let
  us kiss[e] and part. *Fr.* Idea. Drayton
Song of the Water Clock at Night. Wen
  T'ing-yün
Song of the Wine Spring. Wen T'ing-yün
Southern Song, A. Wen T'ing-yün
Spirit of the Yellow River, The. Wen
  T'ing-yün
Splittings. Rich
Spring of Joy Is Dry, The. *Unknown*

Stones. Kumin
Story of Bitter Tea, The. Lo Ch'ing
Strange. Burnshaw
Sundered. Barford
Sundered. Zangwill
Taoist Nun, The. Wei Chuang
Terrible Door, The. Monro
Thick sea-pine, The. *Fr.* Manyo Shu.
  Hitomaro
To Her in Absence; a Ship. Carew
To His Lady. Henry VIII, King of England
To Lucasta, Going to the Wars [*or* Warres].
  Lovelace
To meet my love. *Fr.* Manyo Shu.
  Unknown
Trying to Separate. Pack
Unquiet Ones, The. Kunitz
Upon Your Leaving. Knight
V-Letter. Shapiro
Valediction, A: "Bid me not go where neither
  suns nor show'rs." Cartwright
Villanelle: "Every day our bodies separate."
  Hacker
Western Wind. *Unknown*
What should [*or* shulde] I say[e]. Wyatt
When autumn is here. *Fr.* Manyo Shu.
  Unknown
When We Two Parted. Byron
When You Go Away. Merwin
Wife's Lament, The. *Unknown*
Willow Branches, The. Wen T'ing-yün
Within the Dream You Said. Larkin
Without Mercy. Nagy
Woodchucks. Kumin
Year after year I have watched. Li
  Ch'ing-chao
You who journey to Shiragi. *Fr.* Manyo
  Shu. *Unknown*

Sepoy Rebellion
Defence of Lucknow, The. Tennyson

September
Another September. Kinsella
Artist on Penmaenmawr, The. Turner
For Nicholas, Born in September. Perry
Pont-y-Wern. *Fr.* Ambarvalia. Clough
September. Fallis
September. Howitt
September. Kyger
September. Pastan
September. Ray
September. *Fr.* Sonnets of the Months. San
  Gimignano
September Afternoon. Carpenter
September [Days Are Here]. Jackson
September in Australia. Kendall
Sonnet: September, 1815. Wordsworth
Tell Me Not Here [It Needs Not Saying].
  Housman

Sequoia Trees
Kind. Ammons
Lights among Redwood. Gunn
Redwoods, The. Simpson
Thumbprint. Wright

Serenity
Finding Serenity. Yüan Mei

Serfs. *See* **Slavery.**

Sermons
Model Sermon, A. *Unknown*

Servants
Buttons. De la Mare
Country Hirings. *Unknown*
Country Statutes. *Unknown*
Domestics. Cumbo
Elegy: "Nor Hammond's love nor Shenstone's
  was sincere." Maclaurin
Familiar Faces, Long Departed. Hillyer
Husbandman and Serving-Man, The.
  Unknown
In an Old House. Brown
Nani. Ríos

Odour, The. Herbert
Old-Time Service. *Fr.* A Fayned Fancy
betweene the Spider and the Gowte.
Churchyard
Serving Maid, The. Munby
Summer Morning, A. Wilbur
To His Maid Prew. Herrick
To Their Excellencies the Lords Justices of
Ireland, the Humble Petition of Frances
Harris, Who Must Starve, and Die a Maid
if It Miscarries. Swift
Upon Prue, His Maid. Herrick
Upstairs Downstairs. Allen
When in Rome. Evans

Service (plant)
Life of Service, The. Davie
Shadbush. Rainsford

Service Stations. *See* **Gasoline Stations.**

Sestina (form)
At Kresge's Diner in Stonefalls, Arkansas.
Hirsch
Blackbird Sestina. Warne
Double Semi-Sestina. Starbuck
Emily Dickinson's Sestina for Molly Bloom.
Lefcowitz
Farm Implements and Rutabagas in a
Landscape. Ashbery
Figures of Authority. Watkins
Floating Houses. Wojahn
Grandmother Grace. Wallace
Imperfect Sestina. Webb
Island in the Evening, The. Porter
Jill, Afterwards. Dacey
Magician Suspends the Children, The. Oles
Morning on the St. John's. Cooper
Murmurers, The. Jacobsen
Naked Poetry. Cooley
Nani. Ríos
Painter, The. Ashbery
Quintina of Crosses, A. Walsh
Rink Keeper's Sestina. Draper
Sestina: Altaforte. Pound
Sestina: Here in Katmandu. Justice
Sestina: "September rain falls on the house."
Bishop
Sestina d'Inverno. Hecht
Sestina in Time of Winter. Anderson
Sestina of the Tramp-Royal. Kipling
Sestina to the Common Glass of Beer: I Do
Not Drink Beer. Wakoski
Sestina with Refrain. Shapcott
Tatiana Kalatschova. Logan
Tide Turning. Nims

Seven Deadly Sins
Dance of the Sevin Deidly Synnis, The.
Dunbar

Seven Years War
Admiral Byng. *Unknown*

Severn River, England
Seven Fiddlers, The. Evans
Severn, The. *Fr.* The Baron's War.
Drayton
Danube to the Severn gave, The. *Fr.* In
Memoriam A. H. H. Tennyson

Sewall, Samuel
Samuel Sewall. Hecht

Sewers
Municipal. Kipling
See also **Sanitary Engineering.**

Sewing
Balgu Song. *Unknown*
Delia Very Angry. *Unknown*
Embroidery. Crystal
Huswifery. Taylor
Leave the Thread with God. *Unknown*
My Mother Pieced Quilts. Acosta
Needle, The. Woodworth
Seamstress at St. Léon. *Fr.* A Journal from
France. Clarke
See also **Seamstresses.**

Sex
Against Coupling. Adcock
Ballatetta. Pound
Bathing. Boyes
Blank Verse for a Fat Demanding Wife.
Lindsey
Blue Bottle. Hampl
Blundering. Schutting
Brickster, The. *Unknown*
Cats like Angels. Piercy
Censorship. Ciardi
End of the Weekend, The. Hecht
Fair Ursly, in a merry mood. Cruceius
Fall Practice. Stuart
First Time, The. Shapiro
Fury of Cocks, The. Sexton
Glutton, The. Graves
Haven't I said that part of having intercourse.
Fr. Hmmmm. Scalapino
How can I help myself, as one woman said to
me about wanting. *Fr.* Hmmmm.
Scalapino
"How can you say you have no bedclothes?"
Unknown
I like gayety and horsing around. Montaudon
I think I'll wash my testicles with care.
Unknown
I would like it if people knew this song.
Guillaume de Poitiers
I'd Have You, Quoth He. *Unknown*
If. Lane
I'm going to make a vers boys,. good
enough? Guillaume de Poitiers
Kaddish. Ginsberg
Kinsey Report. Schutting
Late Aubade, A. Wilbur
Let's Not Think about That. Landesman
Lingam and the Yoni, The. Hope
Lion, The. Vas
Little Tumescence, A. Williams
Long John Brown and Little Mary Bell.
Blake
May I Feel Said He. Cummings
Mower, The. *Unknown*
Mr. Muscle-On. Kicknosway
Myself in an Anatomical Chart of Sexual
Intercourse. Mutsuo
Myself with a Glory Hole. Mutsuo
Naked Poetry. Cooley
Not the Arms Race. Abrams
One Man Down. Ai
One Writing against His Prick. *Unknown*
Our Love Is Made, Your Heavy Head.
Fowler
Out in the bushlands a creeper grows.
Unknown
Poem Unwritten, The. Levertov
Poet Loves a Mistress, but Not to Marry,
The. Herrick
Poetess's Bouts-Rimés, The. *Unknown*
Post-Coitum Tristesse: A Sonnet. Leithauser
Question, The. Rukeyser
Rubaiyat for Sue Ella Tucker. Williams
Sand of Silk-Washing Stream. Ou-yang
Chiung
Second Story, The. Hummer
Sex. Valentine
Sex. Wright
Sex, as they harshly call it. *Fr.* Two Songs.
Rich
Sex without Love. Olds
She Lays ("She lays each beautifully mooned
finger"). Peacock
Siren Song. Yeo
So much bad food and worse liquor, friends.
Guillaume de Poitiers
Source, The. Stallworthy
Strong Thighs astride My Chest. Griffin
Summer Killer. Broughton
Sun, The. Hummer
That "old last act"! *Fr.* Two Songs. Rich
That They Were at the Beach. Scalapino

To Hell with Your Fertility Cult. Snyder
Toward a Better Love. Dalton
Tracks. Montague
Trooper's Horse, The. *Unknown*
Wanton Seed, The. *Unknown*
Wayman in Love. Wayman
What Every Boy Knows. Antler
Why Can't I Leave You? Ai
With the Thin Girl. Petri
Woman Moving with You in Coitus, The.
Stefan
Words from Hell. Helwig
World of Expectations, The. Goldbarth
You Ask Why Sometimes I Say Stop. Piercy
See also **Erotic Love; Homosexuality and
Homosexuals; Lust; Sexuality; Voyeurism.**

Sexism
Advice to Young Ladies. Hope
Ballad of the Dreamy Girl. Roseveare
Barbie Doll. Piercy
Paper Matches. Jiles
Poem for Jacqueline Hill. *Unknown*
Poet Recognizing the Echo of the Voice, A.
Wakoski
Snapshots of a Daughter-in-Law. Rich
Sunday Afternoon. Bangs
What cruel laws depress the female kind.
Fr. Hypatia. Tollet

Sexual Abuse
Rapunzel. Kicknosway

Sexual Exploitation
Ballad: "Altho' a slave me is born and bred."
Moreton
Being Aware. Cooper
For Hollis Sigler. Equi
James Bond Movie, The. Swenson
Poem: "Clitoris is a kind of brain, A."
Notley
To Female Duties Clorinda Scorned.
Massimi

Sexuality
Almond Blossoms. Netser
Annus Mirabilis. Larkin
Cats like Angels. Piercy
Courage, a Tale. Gunn
Cry Faugh! Graves
Early Love. Scott
From Pent-up Aching Rivers. Whitman
Monologue of a Dying Beast. Ameen
Sonnet No. 22. Ameen
Tom. Schuyler
When I Drink I Become the Joy of Faggots.
Allison
White. Buckley
You Ask Why Sometimes I Say Stop. Piercy

Seymour, Edward, Duke of Somerset. *See*
Somerset, Edward Seymour, Duke of.

Seymour, Jane
Death of Queen Jane, The. *Unknown*

Shadbush. *See* **Service (plant).**

Shadows
Child and the Shadow, The. Jennings
Could It Have Been a Shadow? Shannon
Countershadow, The. Booth
Escape. Johnson
Follow Thy Fair Sun [Unhappy Shadow].
Campion
For the Little Girl Who Asked Why the
Kitchen Was So Bright. Ulmer
Harbor, The. Engels
Her Shadow. Pullen
Hide-and-Seek Shadow. Hillert
I Heard a Noise and Wishèd for a Sight.
Unknown
Lecture upon the Shadow, A. Donne
Look. Zolotow
My Shadow. Stevenson
Nocturne Varial. Alexander
Noonday Sun and the Shade, The.
Al-Maghut

On the Croun o Bidean. Annand
Poor Shadow. Orleans
Shadow, The. De la Mare
Shadow. Polet
Shadowless Man, The. Challis
Shadows. Hubbell
Shadows. Pastan
Shadows. Plarr
Shadows, The. Sherman
Shadows among the Ettrick Hills. Addison
Stopping by Shadows. Fulton
Swan and Shadow. Hollander
Tenebris. Grimké

Shadwell, Thomas
Thomas Shadwell the Poet. *Fr.* Absalom and Achitophel: Part II. Dryden

Shaftesbury, Anthony Ashley Cooper, 1st Earl of
Ballad upon the Popish Plot, A. Gadbury
Dutchess of Monmouth's Lamentation for the Loss of Her Duke, The. *Unknown*
Hypocrite, The. Caryll
In pious times ere [*or* e'r] priestcraft did begin. *Fr.* Absalom and Achitophel, Pt. I. Dryden
Of these the false Achitophel was first. *Fr.* Absalom and Achitophel, Pt. I. Dryden

Shaka
Birth of Shaka, The. Mtshali

Shakespeare, William
"A Midsummer Night's Dream" in Regent's Park. May
Archy Confesses. *Fr.* Archy and Mehitabel. Marquis
At Shakespeare's Grave. Browne
At the Mermaid Inn. Hildreth
Before Rereading Shakespeare's Sonnets. Moore
Ben Jonson Entertains a Man from Stratford. Robinson
Brush Up Your Shakespeare. Porter
By Deputy. Adcock
Charms of Nature, The. Warton
Cynicus to W. Shakspere. *Fr.* Two Epigrams. Stephen
Dream about Our Master, William Shakespeare, The. Plutzik
Guilielmus Rex. Aldrich
On Shakespeare. Milton
Quotation from Shakespeare with Slight Improvements, A. "Carroll"
Romeo and Juliet in Central Park. Ausländer
Shake, Mulleary, and Go-ethe. Bunner
Shakespeare. Arnold
Shakespeare. Blood
Shakespeare. Ray
Shakespeare Dead. Holland
Thing Is Sex, Ben, The. *Fr.* Tomorrow Is My Birthday. Masters
To an Artist, to Take Heart. Bogan
To Shakespeare. Crane
To Shakespeare. Edwards
To Shakespeare. Kemble
To the Memory of My Beloved Master [*or* the Author, Mr.] William Shakespeare and What He Hath Left Us. Jonson
To the Reader. Jonson
True Genius. *Fr.* Shakespeare; an Epistle to David Garrick, Esq. Lloyd
Upon the Lines and Life of the Famous Scenic Poet, Master William Shakespeare. Holland
When I Read Shakespeare. Lawrence

Shamans
Morning Star Man. Keithley

Shame
In Palo Alto. Johnson
Mystic Pig, The. Katrovas
Shame. Wilbur
Tears of Shame. Sardar J'afri
Veil, The. Johnson

Shamrocks
Shamrock, The. Egan

Shannon (river)
Feeding a Child. Dhomhnaill
Parthenogenesis. Dhomhnaill
Race, The. Dhomhnaill
Shannon Estuary Welcoming the Fish, The. Dhomhnaill

Shannon (ship). *See* **Chesapeake (ship).**

Shaped Poetry
Altar, The. Herbert
Andy-Diana DNA Letter. Weiman
Carnation, The ("May this carnation announce to you"). Apollinaire
Christmas Tree, A. Burford
Clobber the Lobber. Lamport
Computer's First Christmas Card, The. Morgan
Concrete Cat. Charles
Dead of Winter. Towne
Do not come down the ladder. Howe
Easter Wings. Herbert
Forsythia. Solt
400-Meter Freestyle. Kumin
Fury Said to a Mouse. *Fr.* Alice's Adventures in Wonderland. "Carroll"
Grasshopper, The. McCord
Hang Up the Baby's Stocking! *Unknown*
Headrock. Coffey
I. Cummings
Into the Wind. Petoskey
It's Raining. Apollinaire
Like Attracts Like. Williams
Little Car, The. Apollinaire
Ludicrous Stick. Darragh
Marriage. Solt
Moonshot Sonnet. Solt
Night Practice. Swenson
O/ Holy/ Wood. Madeleva
Oil. Mayer
Overboard. Swenson
Owl/ whose home was in the hemlock, The. *Unknown*
Pattern Poem with an Elusive Intruder. Döhl
Pillar of Fame, The. Herrick
Rain Down. Solt
Running rings. Howe
Seal. Smith
Semen. Paley Francescato
Sharpbreasted Snake, The. Oliver
Skeleton Key. Hollander
Spinning Yarns, Relatively Speaking. Payack
State of Nature, A. Hollander
Swan and Shadow. Hollander
Wild Crab. Solt
Winslow Crater. Bryant
Women. Swenson
You Too? Me Too—Why Not? Soda Pop. Hollander

Shapiro, Karl
V-Letter to Karl Shapiro in Australia. Rodman

Sharecroppers
Share-Croppers. Hughes

Sharks
About the Teeth of Sharks. Ciardi
Birth of a Shark, The. Wevill
Envoi, L': "My towers at last! These rovings end." Melville
Maldive Shark, The. Melville
Sea Offerings. Yu Kuang-chung
Shark, The. Douglas
Shark, The. Pratt
Sharks. Kaneko Mitsuharu
Sharks at the New York Aquarium. Martin
Shark's Parlor, The. Dickey
Spirit of Wrath, The. Heyen

Shaving
Upon Shaving Off One's Beard. Updike

Shaw, George Bernard
Epitaph for G. B. Shaw. Beerbohm

Shaw, Robert Gould
For the Union Dead. Lowell
My Hero. Brawley
Ode in Time of Hesitation, An. Moody
Ode, on the Unveiling of the Shaw Memorial on Boston Common, May 31st, 1897, An. Aldrich
Robert G. Shaw. Ray
Robert Gould Shaw. Dunbar

Shays's Rebellion
Radical Song of 1786, A. Honeywood

Sheep
Ariel. Campbell
Baa, baa, black sheep, have you any wool? Mother Goose
Black Faced Sheep, The. Hall
Bleat of Protest. Weston
Child's Pet, A. Davies
Dead Sheep, The. Young
Death of a Ram. Sedulius Scottus
Derby Ram, The. *Unknown*
Happy. Fowler
How Low Is the Lowing Herd. Kelly
Lambs of Grasmere, 1860, The. Rossetti
Poor Mailie's Elegy. Burns
Shearing, The. *Unknown*
Sheep. Davies
Sheep. Francis
Sheep. Hoffenstein
Sheep. Porter
Sheep, The. Taylor
Sheep Fair, A. Hardy
Sheep in New York. *Fr.* New York Everywhere. Vaynshteyn
Wild Boar and the Ram, The. *Fr.* Fables. Gay

Sheepshearing
Banks of the Condamine, The. *Unknown*
Click Go the Shears, Boys. *Unknown*
Flash Jack from Gundagai. *Unknown*
How to Shear Sheep. *Fr.* The Fleece. Dyer
Shearer's Song, The. *Unknown*
Sheep Shearing. *Unknown*

Sheets
Song of the Sheet. *Unknown*

Sheffield, England
Sheffield East End. Cook

Shelley, Percy Bysshe
Fishes and the Poet's Hands, The. Yerby
Grave of Shelley, The. Wilde
Lines Written in a Blank Leaf of the Prometheus Unbound. Beddoes
Memorabilia. Browning
Percy Shelley. Bishop
Rome. Hardy
Shelley's Skylark. Hardy
To Percy Shelley: On the Degrading Notions of Deity. Hunt
To Shelley. Tabb

Shells
Curious child, who dwelt upon a tract, A. *Fr.* The Excursion. Wordsworth
Chambered Nautilus, The. *Fr.* The Autocrat of the Breakfast Table. Holmes
Conch. Queneau
Dr. Sigmund Freud Discovers the Sea Shell. MacLeish
Enchanted Shell, The. Ray
From Table Isle. *Unknown*
Frutta di Mare. Scott
Horn. Lea
Lonely Shell, The. Perry
Lower Forms of Life. Winter
Mantelpiece of Shells, A. Todd
On Some Shells Found Inland. Stickney
Paper Nautilus, The. Moore
Poem about a Seashell. Crosby
Sea Shell. Lowell
Seashell. Efrat
Secrets. Pack

Shell, The. Stephens
Shell Secrets. *Unknown*
Shells. Raine
Some Small Shells from the Windward
    Islands. Swenson
Striped Shell, A. Dallas
To Lady Anne Fitzpatrick, When about Five
    Years Old, with a Present of Shells, 1772.
    Walpole

Shenandoah River and Shenandoah Valley
Portent, The. Melville
Wide Mizzoura, The. *Unknown*

Shepherds and Shepherdesses
Black Faced Sheep, The. Hall
Come, Shepherds, Come! *Fr.* The Faithful
    Shepherdess. Fletcher
Coridon and Phillis. *Fr.* Perimedes [*or*
    Perimedes, the Blacksmith]. Greene
Coy Shepherdess; or, Phillis and Amintas,
    The. *Unknown*
Eclogue: "Late 'twas in June, the fleece when
    fully grown." *Fr.* The Shepherd's
    Garland. Drayton
Green Shepherd, The. Simpson
Harpalus' Complaint of Phillida's Love.
    Unknown
How Pleasant Is This Flowery Plain.
    Unknown
In Praise of His Love. Wotton
In the Cheviots. Lindsay
Lincolnshire Shepherd, A. *Unknown*
Little Bo-Peep has lost her sheep. Mother
    Goose
Long, Long Ago. *Unknown*
Lyric from a Play, A. *Unknown*
Merry Country Lad, The. *Fr.* The Passionate
    Shepherd. Breton
Michael. Wordsworth
Moonlight. Scattered Clouds. *Fr.* The
    Farmer's Boy. Bloomfield
Nod. De la Mare
Nymph's Reply to the Shepherd, The.
    Ralegh
Old Shepherd's Prayer. Mew
Once I Was a Shepherd Boy. *Unknown*
Passionate Shepherd to His Love, The.
    Marlowe
Priest's Chant, The. *Fr.* The Faithful
    Shepherdess. Fletcher
Sheepherder, The. Sarett
Shep'erd Bwoy, The. Barnes
Shepherd, The. *Fr.* Songs of Innocence.
    Blake
Shepherd, The. Gilmore
Shepherd, The. *Fr.* The Prelude [or, Growth
    of a Poet's Mind]: Retrospect—Love of
    Nature Leading to Love of Mankind.
    Wordsworth
Shepherd and His Flock, The. Mtshali
Shepherd and Shepherdess. Hennell
Shepherd and the Shepherdess, The.
    Unknown
Shepherd Boy, The. Clare
Shepherd Boy, The. Heine
Shepherd Left Behind, The. Meigs
Shepherd Speaks, The. Erskine
Shepherd Who Stayed, The. Garrison
Shepherdess, The. Meynell
Shepherdess, The. Meynell
Shepherdess and the Sailor, The. *Unknown*
Shepherds, The. Van Slyke
Shepherds' Carol. Nicholson
Shepherd's Ode, The. *Fr.* Tullie's Love.
    Greene
Shepherd's Song at Christmas. Hughes
Shepherd's Tale, The. Kirkup
Shepherd's Wife's Song, The. *Fr.* Greene's
    Mourning Garment. Greene
Tenth Eclogue, The. *Fr.* The Shepherd's
    Garland. Drayton
Tom Farley. Thiele

Tuesday; or, the Ditty. *Fr.* The Shepherd's
    Week. Gay
Unknown Shepherd's Complaint, The.
    Barnfield
While Shepherds Watched [Their Flocks by
    Night]. Tate
Ya Se Van Los Pastores. Fitts
Young Shepherd Bathing His Feet. Clarke
Sheppard, W. H.
Dedicated to Dr. W. H. Sheppard. Johnson
Sheridan, Philip Henry
Sheridan at Cedar Creek. Melville
Sheridan's Ride. Read
Sherman, General William Tecumseh
Marching through Georgia. Work
Sherman. Gilder
Sherman's in Savannah. Holmes
Shetlands
Shetland, Hill Dawn. Munro
Shields
Copper Song, The. Fraser
Goldyn Targe, The. Dunbar
Shiloh, Battle of (1862)
Battle of Shiloh, The. *Unknown*
Drummer Boy of Shiloh, The. *Unknown*
Shiloh; a Requiem. Melville
Ships
Aboard at a Ship's Helm. Whitman
After the Sea-Ship. Whitman
Battle of the *Bonhomme Richard* and the
    Serapis. *Fr.* Song of Myself. Whitman
Beauty of the Ship, The. Whitman
Birlinn Chlann-Raghnaill. MacDonald
Boats in a Fog. Jeffers
Camouflaged Troop-Ship. Lowell
Cargoes. Masefield
Derelict, The. Foote
Derelict, The. Kipling
Derelict. Pullen
Dismantled Ship, The. Whitman
Down Below. Aiken
Dutch Ship. Rai San'yo
Fire of Drift-wood, The. Longfellow
Freighter. Ruddick
Frightening. Lewis
Gallant Ship, The. Scott
Garden of Ships, The. Stewart
Ghost of the Cargo Boat, The. Neruda
I saw a ship a-sailing. Mother Goose
Liner She's a Lady, The. Kipling
Main-Truck; or, A Leap for Life, The.
    Morris
Marina. Eliot
My Brigantine. *Fr.* The Water Witch.
    Cooper
Night Boat. Brown
Nocturne of the Wharves. Bontemps
North Ship, The. Larkin
Ocean Liner. Koh Chang-soo
Off Rivière du Loup. Scott
Oil. Snyder
Old Ships, The. Flecker
Passer-by, A. Bridges
Ports. Vas
She Is Far from the Land. Hood
Ship, The. Squire
Ship That Never Returned, The. Work
Ships, The. Bell
Ships of Yule, The. Carman
Silver Ships. Meigs
Sir Andrew Barton. *Unknown*
Song for All Seas, All Ships. Whitman
Sucked into the hillside darkness. *Fr.*
    Forty-four Tanka. Wakayama Bokusui
Tacking Ship Off Shore. Mitchell
Trooship, The. Johnson
Wanderer, The. Masefield
Where Go the Boats? Stevenson
Where Lies the Land to Which Yon Ship
    Must Go? Wordsworth
Oxford Book of Sea Songs, The (OxBSS).
    Roy Palmer, ed.

Oxford Book of Sea Songs, The (OxBSS).
    Roy Palmer, ed.
See also **Boats; Yachts.**
Shipwrecks
Aeolian Harp, The. Melville
Alec Yeaton's Son. Aldrich
As we go fast, rowing the huge ship. *Fr.*
    Manyo Shu. Hanishi Mitoshi
At Parting. Ho Sun
Banks of Newfoundland ("Oh may you bless
    your happy lot that lies secure on shore"),
    The. *Unknown*
Berg, The. Melville
Castaway, The. Cowper
Convergence of the Twain (Lines on the Loss
    of the *Titanic*, The). Hardy
Diving into the Wreck. Rich
Dream of Wrecks, A. *Fr.* King Richard III.
    Shakespeare
Etiquette. Gilbert
Final Moments, The. *Fr.* The Titanic. Pratt
Full Fathom Five. *Fr.* The Tempest.
    Shakespeare
Grace Darling. *Unknown*
"How's My Boy?" Dobell
In Wintry Midnight, o'er a Stormy Main.
    Petrarch
Inchcape Rock, The. Southey
Isle of Man Shore, The. *Unknown*
Last Words. Hollander
Loss of the *Amphitrite*. *Unknown*
Loss of the *Due Dispatch*, The. *Unknown*
Loss of the *Evelyn Marie*, The. *Unknown*
Mail Boat, *Leinster*, The. *Unknown*
New Ballad of Sir Patrick Spens, The.
    Quiller-Couch
Ode to a Lost Cargo in a Ship Called *Save*.
    Craveirinha
On Saturday sailed from Bremen. *Fr.* The
    Wreck of the *Deutschland*. Hopkins
Picking Rushes. *Unknown*
Posted. Masefield
Rain, and a flurry of wind shaking the pear's
    white blossom. *Fr.* Twenty-one Sonnets.
    Stead
Sea, The. Stoddard
Second Mate, The. O'Brien
Ship That Went Down, The. Menken
Shipwreck. Fordham
Silk Merchant's Daughter, The. *Unknown*
Skipper Ireson's Ride. Whittier
Song of the Negro on the Ferry. Craveirinha
Three Fishers, The. Kingsley
Three Score and Ten. *Unknown*
Tribute to a Lost Steamer. Fordham
Unseaworthy Ship, The. Smith
White Ship, The. Rossetti
Wreck, The. De la Mare
Wreck of the *Northfleet*, The. *Unknown*
Wrecked Boat on the River Shore. Chiang
    Lu
Shirts
Shirt. Simic
Shiva
Shiva. Jeffers
Shoemakers
Amendis to the Telyouris and Sowtaris for the
    Turnament Maid on Thame, The. Dunbar
At His Father's Grave. Ormond
Cobbler, The. *Unknown*
Death of the Shoemaker, The. Dahbur
Female. al-Ghuzzi
I Am. Leib
Jeremy Hobbler. *Unknown*
Shoe Shop. Sutter
Shoemaker Nikke. Turtiainen
Shoemaker's Holiday, The, *sels.* Dekker
Shoes
Boots and Shoes. McCrea
Cartload of Shoes, A. Sutskever

Choosing Shoes. Wolfe
Fitting. Fowler
Folding Fan, The. Cohoe
Grammer's Shoes. Barnes
Moccasins of an Old Man, The. Carden
My Mother's Shoes. Zychlinska
My Shoes. Simic
Nature Morte. Fowler
No Taker for the Small Shoes. Roe
Sale. Miles
Shoe Shop. Sutter
Shoes. Worth
Sneakers. Herzberg
Teresa's Red Adidas. Janeczko
To a Pair of Egyptian Slippers. Arnold
Unusual Shoelaces. Kennedy
Velvet Shoes. Wylie

Shoplifting
Shoplifters. Stanton

Shopping and Shops
Christmas Rush, The. Thompson
Christmas Shopping. MacNeice
Country Store, The. *Unknown*
Garage Sale. Shapiro
I shop in the streets of my hometown with/
my family. *Fr.* Letters to Live Poets.
Beaver
Junk Shop, The. Coulette
My Father's Store. Finkelstein
Shop, The. Wu Sheng
Shopping for Midnight. Murray
Supermarket in California, A. Ginsberg
To a Salesgirl, Weary of Artificial Holiday
Trees. Wright
Winds Are Bleak, Stars Are Bright. *Fr.* The
Victoria Markets Recollected in
Tranquillity. "Maurice"

Shopping Malls
Day Begins at Governor's Square Mall.
Stokesbury

Shores
Address to the Vacationers at Cape Lookout,
An. Stafford
At Carmel Highlands. Lewis
At the Seaside. Stevenson
Birds and Fishes. Jeffers
"But Still in Israel's Paths They Shine."
Revard
By Cobequid Bay. Fraser
By the Pacific Ocean. Miller
By the Saltings. Walker
Cliff-Top, The. Bridges
Coastline. Feinstein
Corsons Inlet. Ammons
Earliness at the Cape. Deutsch
East Coast—Canada. Brewster
Fisher's Boy, The. Thoreau
Giant's Tomb in Georgian Bay. "Hale"
Headland. Ghiselin
I pray you, let us roam no more. *Fr.* Odes
to Nea. Moore
Low Fields and Light. Merwin
Meditation at Oyster River. Roethke
Moonlight Night: Carmel. Hughes
Morning at Point Dume. Swenson
Morning on the Shore. Campbell
On the Beach at Fontana. Joyce
Once by the Pacific. Frost
Pines and the Sea, The. Cranch
Provincetown, Mass. Shapiro
Salt Flats, The. Roberts
Seaside: In and Out of the Season, The.
Turner
Seaweeds. McPherson
Shore. Miller
Shore, The. St. John
Shore Scene. Logan
Shoreline. Barnard
Some Sound Advice from Singapore. Ciardi
Suffolk. *Fr.* By the North Sea. Swinburne
Tide Turning. Nims
To the Sea. Larkin

We Lying by Seasand. Thomas
Winter Shore, The. Wade
See also **Beaches.**

Shorter, James A.
Bishop James A. Shorter. Heard

Show Business. *See* **Acting and Actors;**
Motion Pictures; Theater and Theaters.

Shrews
Masked Shrew, The. Gardner
Shrew, The. Nash
Small, Smaller. Hoban

Shrimp
Shrimp, A! Black thing as widow's crape.
Fr. The Shrimp. Browne

Shrines
Before Gion Shrine, determined to drive away
poverty. *Fr.* Miscellaneous Songs of the
Four Seasons East of the Kamo. Nakajima
Soin
Dangling sacred cords. Tameie
Deep in the family shrine. *Fr.* Twenty
Hokku. Kyorai
Kehi Shrine. Kagura
Shrine of General Pien, The. Chu Yün-ming
Sonetto XXXV: To Guido Orlando.
Cavalcanti
Written on Visiting the Shrine of the Minister
of the Right Sugawara no Michizane. Rai
San'yo
See also **Mausoleums; Monuments.**

Shropshire, England
On Wenlock Edge [the Wood's in Trouble].
Fr. A Shropshire Lad. Housman

Shrouds
Shroud. Brown

Siberia
In Snow. Leivick
In the Hamlet. Sutskever
Message to Siberia. Pushkin
On the Roads of Siberia. Leivick
Siberia. Mangan

Sibyl
Sibyl, The. LaBombard

Sicily
Almond Blossom. Lawrence
Bare Almond-Trees. Lawrence
On Catania and Syracuse Swallowed Up by an
Earthquake, from the Italian of Filicaja.
Seward

Sickness. *See* **Illness.**

Siddons, Mrs. Sarah
As When a Child. Lamb

Sideshows
Sideshow: Julia the Lion Woman. Rose

Sidmouth, Henry Addington, Viscount
Similes for Two Political Characters of 1819.
Shelley

Sidney, Sir Philip
An Epitaph on Sir Philip Sidney. James I,
King of England
Epitaph on Sir Philip Sidney. Ralegh
On Sir Philip Sidney. *Fr.* An Elegy, or
Friend's Passion for His Astrophil [or
Astrophel]. Royden
Such skill, matcht with such courage as he
had. *Fr.* Astrophel. Spenser
To Elizabeth, Countess of Rutland. Jonson

Sierra Nevada Mountains
Ascent to the Sierras. Jeffers
Strength through Joy. Rexroth

Siestas
Mad Dogs and Englishmen. Coward

Sight
Eye and Tooth. Lowell
On the Speed of Sight. DiZazzo
Sight. Gibson

Signorelli, Luca
At Luca Signorelli's Resurrection of the
Body. Graham

Silence
After Long Silence. Yeats

Answerers. Stafford
Approaching Silence, The. Illyés
Burke and Wills. Barratt
Colloquy of Silences, A. Heffernan
Elected Silence. Sassoon
Gift. Cohen
Night Song at Amalfi. Teasdale
Pastourelle. Hayes
Patience Is When You Stop Waiting.
Williams
Precept of Silence, The. Johnson
Sea of Silence Exhales Secrets, The. Bialik
Second Poem the Night-Walker Wrote, The.
Goethe
Silence. Cummings
Silence. Hood
Silence. Moore
Silence. Turner
Silence. Williams
Silences. Pratt
Silent Day, The. Urbina
Silent Piano, The. Simpson
Sonnet—Silence. Poe
To Silence. Beddoes
To Silence. Moore
Velvet Shoes. Wylie

Silk
Liao-ling. Po Chü-i
Song of the Venetian Silk-Spinners.
Unknown
Quilted silk from Tsukushi, The. *Fr.* Manyo
Shu. Manzei
Upon Julia's Clothes. Herrick

Silkweed
Silkweed. Savage

Silkworms
Silkworms, The. Stewart
Silkworms my mother rears, The. *Fr.*
Manyo Shu. Hitomaro

Silva, Antonio José da
Da Silva Gives the Cue. Blumenthal

Silver
Silver. De la Mare

Simhath Torah
Simchas Torah. Rosenfeld
Simhat Torah. Gordon
This Feast of the Law. *Unknown*

Similes. *See* **Metaphor.**

Simon of Cyrene
Simon the Cyrenian Speaks. Cullen

Simplicity
Familiar Epistle, A. Murry
Ode to Simplicity. Collins
Still to Be Neat [Still to Be Drest (or
Dressed)]. *Fr.* Epicoene; or, The Silent
Woman. Jonson
They. Bell
'Tis the Gift To Be Simple. *Unknown*
To Simplicity. *Fr.* Sonnets Attempted in the
Manner of Contemporary Wr. Coleridge
Wreath, A. Herbert

Sin
Adam Lay Ibounden *or* Ibowndyn *or*
Ybounden. *Unknown*
Ah, Christ. *Fr.* Sonnets at Christmas. Tate
All My Luve, Leave Me Not. *Unknown*
And Forgive Us Our Trespasses. Behn
At Sunset. Sangster
Attend, Young Friends, While I Relate.
Unknown
Authour's Dreame, The. *Fr.* Argalus and
Parthenia. Quarles
Biothanatos. Beaumont
Blasphemies, The. MacNeice
Christ Complains to Sinners. *Unknown*
Cinderella. Saunders
Corruption. Vaughan
First Confession. Kennedy
Girl's Lamentation, The. Allingham
Ha! Original Sin. Nash

High Windows. Larkin
I Stood upon a High Place. *Fr.* The Black Riders. Crane
If I Could Shut the Gate against My Thoughts. *Unknown*
Jehovah Our Righteousness. Cowper
Lord, Have Mercy. Tate
Love. Herbert
Lure, The. O'Reilly
Luxury of Sin. Oates
No more of talk where God or Angel Guest. *Fr.* Paradise Lost. Milton
Of man's first disobedience, and the fruit. *Fr.* Paradise Lost. Milton
Oh, If They Only Knew! Mapes
Original Sin; a Short Story. Warren
Penitent, The. Taylor
Portrait of the Artist as a Prematurely Old Man. Nash
Sin. Herbert
Snow White and the Seven Deadly Sins. Gwynn
Stains. Garrison
Sting of Death, The. Scott
There Was One I Met upon the Road. Crane
"They that have power to hurt, and will do none." *Fr.* Sonnets, XCIV. Shakespeare
Two Questions, The. Meynell
Undo! *Unknown*
Unpardonable Sin, The. Lindsay
Vision of Sin, The. Tennyson
When rising from the bed of death. Addison
Young People Who Delight in Sin. *Unknown*
See also **Original Sin, Seven Deadly Sins.**

Singing and Singers
Aim Was Song, The. Frost
Alabama. Fields
All Which Isn't Singing Is Mere Talking. Cummings
Ancient Speech, The. *Fr.* Eileann Chanaidh. Raine
And the Old Women Gathered. Evans
Arrival at the Waldorf. Stevens
Autumn Song on Perry Street. Frankenberg
Buckdancer's Choice. Dickey
Cino. Pound
City Singers, The. Owen
Everyone Sang. Sassoon
Fair Singer, The. Marvell
Gratiana Dancing [or Dauncing] and Singing. Lovelace
How to the Singer Comes the Song? Gilder
Hugging the Jukebox. Nye
Hymn to Priapus. Lawrence
I Am the Mountainy Singer. Campbell
I Hear America Singing. Whitman
I Remember How She Sang. Penny
Idea of Order at Key West, The. Stevens
M., Singing. Bogan
Mourning Poem for the Queen of Sunday. Hayden
Navaho Sings. Benally
No Possum, No Sop, No Taters. Stevens
O Black and Unknown Bards. Johnson
Old Women Still Sing, The. Rowell
On Clarastella Singing. Heath
Piano. Lawrence
Poem for a Singer. Acorn
Silver Swan, The. Gibbons
Singers to Come. Meynell
Singing in the Spring. Eastwick
Singing Lesson, The. Wagoner
Singing on the Moon. Hughes
Singing-Time. Fyleman
So Sat the Muses. *Fr.* Caelia. Browne
Solitary Reaper, The. Wordsworth
Song Making. Teasdale
Threnody: "Let happy throats be mute." Hayes
Throat Song: The Whirling Earth. Rose

To a Lady Who Did Sing Excellently. Herbert of Cherbury
To Constantia Singing. Shelley
Tommy Tucker. Mother Goose
Tullochgorum. Skinner
Upon Julia's Voice. Herrick
Wayfaring. Icaza
When Malindy Sings. Dunbar
Who Bids Us Sing? Carpenter
Yiddish. Herzberg
Yonosa House. Smith
Untune the Sky (UnS). Helen Plotz, ed.
See also **Tenors.**

Sinkholes
Sinkholes. McFatter

Sioux Indians
Dakota: October, 1822, Hunkpapa Warrior. Taylor
Elegy to the Sioux. Dubie
Ghost Dance: August, 1976, The. Jauss
Rosebud. Anderson
Sioux, The. Field

Sirens (mythology)
Mermaidens' Vesper-Hymn, The. *Fr.* Syren Songs. Darley
Nearing Again the Legendary Isle. *Fr.* The Magnetic Mountain. Day Lewis
Siren Song. *Fr.* Songs of the Transformed. Atwood
Sirens, The. Manifold
Sirens' Song, The. *Fr.* The Inner Temple Masque. Browne
Ulysses and the Siren. Daniel

Sisera
His Mother. Guri

Siskind, Aaron
Suite of Six Pieces for Siskind, A. Logan

Sisters
Dirty-billed Freeze Footy, The. Hemschemeyer
Elder Sister, The. Olds
Family. Tanikawa Shuntaro
Goblin Market. Rossetti
In go-cart so tiny. Greenaway
Little. Aldis
Love. Kinsella
My Sisters. Kushner
Olga Poems. Levertov
Our Silly Little Sister. Aldis
Sisters. Farjeon
Sisters. McPherson
Sisters. Roberts
Triolet against Sisters. McGinley
Two Sisters, The. *Unknown*
We built mountain paddies. *Fr.* Manyo Shu. Kinashi no Karu

Sistine Chapel
To Giovanni da Pistoia on the Painting of the Sistine Chapel, 1509. Michelangelo

Sisyphus
Sisyphus. Garioch
Sisyphus. Miles

Sitting Bull
Song of Sitting Bull. *Unknown*

Sitwell, Dame Edith
Thin Façade for Edith Sitwell, A. Brinnin

Skateboarding and Skateboarders
Sidewalk Racer, The. Morrison
See also **Roller-skating.**

Skating and Skaters
Black Water and Bright Air. Carrier
Boys of These Men Full Speed. Rukeyser
Fast. Tagliabue
Ice. Bottoms
Ice-Skaters. Olson
Midnight Skaters, The. Blunden
On Cedar Lake, 1957. Brin
On the Frozen Lake. *Fr.* The Prelude [or, Growth of a Poet's Mind]: Childhood and School-Time. Wordsworth
Rink Keeper's Sestina. Draper

River Skater. Welles
Skate. Blossom
Skater, The. Roberts
Skater in Blue. Parini
Skaters, The. Fletcher
Skaters. Rutsala
Skaters, The. Williams
Skating. Asquith
Skating. Dacey
Skating. Kipling
Skating after School. Crooker
So through the darkness and the cold we flew. *Fr.* The Prelude [or, Growth of a Poet's Mind]: Childhood and School-Time. Wordsworth
Sonja Henie Sonnet. Field
Three children sliding on the ice. Gay
To Kate, Skating Better than Her Date. Daiches
Wings and Wheels. Turner
Winter Piece. Gozzano
Woman Skating. Atwood
See also **Roller-skating.**

Skeletons
All That Is Left. Hartnett
Lion's Skeleton, The. Turner
To a Skeleton. Vardhill
See also **Bones.**

Skelton, John
John Skelton. Graves

Skepticism. *See* **Doubt.**

Skiing and Skiers
Aviemore. Waller
Away she flies and he follows. *Fr.* Anglo-Swiss, or a Day among the Alps. Plomer
International Ski-Flying Championship, Oberstorf. Ritchie
Remembering You. Kumin
Ski Song of the U.S. Army's Tenth Mountain Division. Levitt
Skibomber, The. Steingesser
Skier. Francis
Skiing Home at Dusk. Parini
Song of the Ski, The. MacDonald
T-Bar. Page
Transit. Rich
Winter Trees. Diekmann

Skin
Eczema. Slavitt
Epiderm. Dransfield
Flesh. Rice
Skin. Achterberg

Skin Diving
Haiti: Skin Diving. Shore

Skulls
Perfect. "MacDiarmid"
Scientist, The. Burroway
Sparrow's Skull, The. Pitter
To a Skull. Jones
Upon a Dead Man's Head. Skelton
Yardbird's Skull. Dodson
See also **Bones.**

Skunks
Dead Skunk. Eberhart
Skunk, The. Coffin
Skunk, The. Dow
Skunk, The. Heaney
Skunk Hour. Lowell

Sky
Battle, A. Crawford
Broken Sky. Sandburg
How to Write a Poem about the Sky. Silko
I never saw a moor. Dickinson
Irish Skies. Letts
Lullaby, a Farewell, A. Dorman
Ode: "Spacious firmament on high, The." Addison
Sky, The. Roberts
Sky, The. Stoddard
Sky Picture. Ray

Sky went before me wherever I went, The.
  Kajava
Skycoast. Hazo
Sky's unresting cloudland, that with varying
  play, The. *Fr.* The Testament of Beauty.
  Bridges
We will watch the Northern Lights.
  Unknown
Winter Heavens. Meredith
See also **Constellations; Stars.**
Sky Diving and Sky Divers
  Divers. Ghigna
  Hazard's Optimism. Meredith
  Parachutist, The. Anderson
  Skydivers, The. Murphy
Skye, Isle of, Scotland
  Beckon Me, Ye Cuillins. Hendrie
  Skye. Gawsworth
  Warning, A. Nicolson
Skylarks. *See* **Larks.**
Skyscrapers
  Building a Skyscraper. Tippett
  Monadnock, The. Fletcher
  On Watching the Construction of a
    Skyscraper. Raffel
  Skyscraper. Lee
  Skyscrapers. Field
  Skyscrapers of the Financial District Dance
    with Gasman, The. Piercy
  Storms and Towers. Leyeles
Slander
  Buzz, buzz the bluebottles. *Unknown*
  Ornament here, a decoration there, An.
    Unknown
Slaughter, Enos
  Enos Slaughter. Havelin
Slaughter of the Innocents. *See* **Massacre of
  the Innocents.**
Slaughterhouses
  Guys of the Volye, *sels.* Vaynshteyn
  Hides. Vaynshteyn
  Sheep in New York. *Fr.* New York
    Everywhere. Vaynshteyn
  Point, greatly enlarged, The. *Fr.* A
    Technical Supplement. Kinsella
Slavery
  Address to Ethiopia. Thompson
  Adolescence—I. Dove
  African Chief, The. Bryant
  African Dirge. Chapman
  Ah me! How differently th'untutor'd slave.
    Fr. A General Description of the West
    Indian Islands. Singleton
  All the Slaves. Lux
  American History. Harper
  And can the muse reflect her tear-stain'd eye.
    Fr. Jamaica, a Poem in Three Parts,
    Written in That Island in the Year 1776.
    Unknown
  Ballad: "Altho' a slave me is born and bred."
    Moreton
  Ballad of Nat Turner, The. Hayden
  Beautiful Slave, The. Marino
  Black Woman. Morejón
  Bondage. "Innsley"
  Breath in My Nostrils. Jeffers
  Captain Barton's Distress on Board the
    Lichfield. *Unknown*
  Chant-Pagan. Kipling
  Creole Slave-Song, A. Thompson
  Dark Testament. Murray
  Death of Slavery, The. Bryant
  Early Losses; a Requiem. Walker
  Emancipation Day. Moorer
  Enslaved. McKay
  Farewell, The: "Gone, gone—sold and gone."
    Whittier
  Favorite Slave's Story, The. Thompson
  First of August. Seymour
  Flying Cloud, The. *Unknown*
  Folklore. Dabydeen

"Formerly a Slave." Melville
Frederick Douglass. Hayden
From America. Whitfield
Fugitive, The. Thompson
Fugitive Slaves, The. Very
Fugitive Slave's Apostrophe to the North Star,
  The. Pierpont
Go Down, Moses. *Unknown*
Great Escape, The. Roots
Hearing Men Shout at Night on MacDougal
  Street. Bly
High in the Air Exposed. Southey
Hold Your Mad Hands. Southey
House Slave, The. Dove
House-Slave, The. Morris
Hunters of Men, The. Whittier
Husband's Return, The. Thompson
I Love My Master. Morejón
If me want for go in a Ebo. *Fr.*
  Work-Songs. *Unknown*
If You Want to Know Me. Sousa
In Bondage. McKay
Independence. Faleti
Jack and Dinah Want Freedom. *Unknown*
John Cherokee. *Unknown*
Letter from Phillis Wheatley, A. Hayden
Liberty for All. Garrison
Lines: "From fair Jamaica's fertile plains."
  "Ada"
Middle Passage. Hayden
Miss Geeta. Reckord
Mother Dark. Pereira
Must Be Freed. Moorer
My Great-Grandfather's Slaves. Berry
My Name Was Legion. Swift
No more, America, in mournful strain. *Fr.*
  To the Right Honourable William, Earl of
  Dartmouth. Wheatley
No More Auction Block. *Unknown*
Old Cabin, The. Dunbar
On Being Brought from Africa to America.
  Wheatley
On festal days; or when their work is done.
  Fr. The Sugar Cane. Grainger
On Liberty and Slavery. Horton
Peonage System, The. Moorer
Prayer, A: "Oh, Lord! I lift my heart."
  Thompson
Primitive, The. Lee
Promises of Freedom. *Unknown*
Runagate Runagate. Hayden
Runaway Slave, The. *Fr.* Song of Myself.
  Whitman
Runaway Slave at Pilgrim's Point, The.
  Browning
Safari West. Williams
Serf, The. Campbell
She's Free! Harper
Simon Legree—a Negro Sermon. *Fr.* The
  Booker Washington Trilogy. Lindsay
Slave, The. Oppenheim
Slave Auction, The. Harper
Slave Chase, The. *Unknown*
Slave Quarters. Dickey
Slave Singing at Midnight, The. Longfellow
Slave Song. Dabydeen
Slaves. *Fr.* The Sugar Cane. Grainger
Slaves/ Humming in the twilight by the shanty
  door. Seymour
Slave's Dream, The. Longfellow
Song of the Galley-slaves. Kipling
Song to the Runaway Slave. *Unknown*
Song: "We raise de wheat." *Unknown*
Strong Men. Brown
Suffer, Poor Negro! Diop
Sweet Meat Has Sour Sauce; or, The
  Slave-Trader in the Dumps. Cowper
Sympathy. Dunbar
Those Who Lost Everything. Diop
Time-Piece, The. *Fr.* The Task. Cowper
Tink dere is a God in a top. *Fr.*
  Work-Songs. *Unknown*

To a Dark Girl. Bennett
To Sir Toby. Freneau
To the First of August. Plato
To William Wilberforce, Esq. Cowper
Trellie. Jeffers
Victim, The. Mphande
Virtues of the cane must now be sung, The.
  Fr. Barbados. Weekes
West Indies, The. Montgomery
While the noon-lustre o'er the land is spread.
  Fr. Barbadoes. Chapman
White Man's Burden, The. Kipling
Wild Negro Bill. *Unknown*
Winter Twilight, Glowing Black and Gold,
  The. Schwartz
Witnesses, The. Longfellow
Woman's Song, A. McElroy
Wounded Person, The. *Fr.* Song of Myself.
  Whitman
Sleds
  Sledding Song, A. Schlichter
  See also **Sleighs.**
Sleep
  At Night. Cornford
  Care-Charmer Sleep. *Fr.* Fidessa, More
    Chaste than Kind. Griffin
  Care-charmer sleep[e], son[ne] of the sable
    night. *Fr.* To Delia. Daniel
  Care-charming Sleep [Thou Easer of All
    Woes]. *Fr.* The Tragedy of Valentinian.
    Fletcher
  Cares of Majesty, The. *Fr.* King Henry IV,
    Pt. II. Shakespeare
  Come, sleep. *Fr.* The Woman-Hater.
    Beaumont
  "Come sleep! O sleep, the certain knot of
    peace." *Fr.* Astrophel and Stella, XXXIX.
    Sidney
  Conversation at the Bend in the Road.
    Al-Haidari
  Country of Water. Ames
  Covers. Giovanni
  Cuddle Doon. Anderson
  Early Rising. Saxe
  Falling Asleep. Sassoon
  Flash Sleep. Frazier
  For Sleep, or Death. Pitter
  Hour of Sleep, The. Ellis
  If Once You Have Slept on an Island. Field
  If You Can't Eat You Got To. Cummings
  In Sleep. Burton
  Insomnia. Bishop
  Insomnia. Tabb
  Just about Asleep Together. Peacock
  Laura Sleeping. Cotton
  Lonely Are the Fields of Sleep. Baldwin
  Lullaby: "Beloved, may your sleep be sound."
    Yeats
  Nod. De la Mare
  Pains of Sleep, The. Coleridge
  Rock-a-by Lady, The. Field
  Rocked in the Cradle of the Deep. Willard
  Sacrament of Sleep, The. Oxenham
  Silverly. Lee
  Sleep. Brown
  Sleep, The. Browning
  Sleep. *Fr.* Arcadia. Sidney
  Sleep, The. Strand
  Sleep. Trakl
  Sleep and Poetry. Keats
  Sleep, My Child. Aleichem
  Sleep, Silence' Child. Drummond
  Sleep Sweet. Gates
  Sleep Watch. Henson
  Sleeper, The. Clouts
  Sleeper, The. De la Mare
  Sleeping Outdoors. Chute
  Slumber Song. Ledoux
  Somnia. Gong
  Song: "Let not the sluggish sleep." *Unknown*
  Song: "See, how like twilight slumber falls."
    Cotton

Sugar-Plum Tree, The. Field
To Sleep. Fleming
To Sleep. Keats
To Sleep. Osgood
To Sleep. Smith
To Sleep ("Fond words have oft been spoken
   to thee, sleep!"). Wordsworth
To Sleep ("O gentle sleep! do they belong to
   thee"). Wordsworth
Variation on the Word *Sleep*. Atwood
Walking to Sleep. Wilbur
Watching You Sleep under Monet's Water
   Lilies. Ruark
We are not wholly blest who use the earth.
   Fr. Dreamland. Mair
Weep [*or* Weepe] You No More [Sad
   Fountains]. *Unknown*
When All the World's Asleep. Posey
When the Eye of Day Is Shut. Housman
Where You Go When She Sleeps. Hummer
Wynken, Blynken, and Nod. Field

Sleepwalking. See Somnambulism.

Sleighs
Phantoms of the Steppe. Pushkin
Possible Salvation of Continuous Motion,
   The. Rogers
Sleighride. Anderson
See also **Sleds.**

Sligo. *See* County Sligo, Ireland.

Sloth
Lament of a Slug-a-Bed's Wife. Smith
Sluggard, The. Watts

Sloths
Sloth, The. Roethke
Sloth, The. Romanes

Slough, England
Slough. Betjeman

Slugs
Slug in Woods. Birney

Slums
Childhood. Latimore
"Dangerous Condition": Sign on Inner-City
   House. Atkins
Elementary School Classroom in a Slum, An.
   Spender
Feeding the Lions. Jordan
Get the Gasworks. Ignatow
In the Barrio. Alurista
In the Slums. Campbell
Judeebug's Country. Johnson
Letter in Winter. Patterson
Lovers of the Poor, The. Brooks
On Saint-Urbain Street. Acorn
Our Barrio. Alurista
Pressure Drop. Onuora
Rat, The. Davies
Reckoning A.M. Thursday. Turner
Reflections in a Slum. "MacDiarmid"
Scenery. Joans
"Summertime and the Living." Hayden
To the New Annex to the Detroit County Jail.
   Thomas

Smallpox
Lizzie Discourses on the Small-Pox. Cordle

Smalls, Robert
General Robert Smalls. Heard

Smart, Christopher
To Christopher Smart. Stroud

Smells
Alien. Hayes
Cologne. Coleridge
Epitaph on the Fart in the Parliament House.
   Hoskyns
Lady's Dressing Room, The. Swift
Now, I cannot tell. Tsurayuki
Odors. Leib
Old Movies. Cotton
Sense of Smell, The. MacNeice
Smell. Williams
Smells. Worth

Smiles
Growing Smiles. *Unknown*
Having seen your smile. *Fr.* Manyo Shu.
   Yakamochi
Hustle and Grin. *Unknown*
Judy-One. Lee
Keep Smiling. *Unknown*
Let Us Smile. Nesbit
Philosophy. Dunbar
Simile for Her Smile, A. Wilbur
Smile, The. Blake
Smile, A. *Unknown*
Smile. *Unknown*
Trus' an' Smile. Williams
Try Smiling. *Unknown*
You Smiled. O'John

Smith, Adam
Adam Smith. *Fr.* Clerihews. Bentley

Smith, Bessie
Blues for Bessie. O'Higgins
Homage to the Empress of the Blues.
   Hayden
Last Affair: Bessie's Blues Song. Harper

Smith, Billy Ray
Billy Ray Smith. Nash

Smith, David
Homage to David Smith. Haines

Smith, John
Capt. Smith and Pocahontas. Bibb
John Smith's Approach to Jamestown. Hope
Last Meeting of Pocahontas and the Great
   Captain, The. Preston
Noah an' Jonah an' Cap'n John Smith.
   Marquis

Smith, Joseph
Nauvoo. Taylor

Smoke
All the Smoke. Siegel
On the Closing of Millom Ironworks.
   Nicholson
Song of the Smoke, The. DuBois

Smoking
Burying Uncle Salomon. Avidan
Hotel. Apollinaire
On Giving Up Smoking. *Fr.* A
   Looking-Glass for Smokers. Spooner
Smoker, The. Huff

Smugglers
Smuggler's Song, A. *Fr.* Puck of Pook's
   Hill. Kipling
Smuggler's Victory, The. *Unknown*

Snails
After Tempest. MacKaye
Butterfly and the Snail, The. *Fr.* Fables.
   Gay
Considering the Snail. Gunn
For a Five-Year-Old. Adcock
Haiku: "Warm and snug." Hara Sekitei
Haughty Snail-King, The. Lindsay
Housekeeper, The. Bourne
Little Snail. Conkling
Poor Snail, The. Westrup
Remembering with Feeling. *Fr.*
   Twenty-three Hokku. Onitsura
Snail. Drinkwater
Snail. Eybers
Snail. García Lorca
Snail. *Fr.* Songs of Childhood. García
   Lorca
Snail, The. Giusti
Snail. Hughes
Snail, The. Lovelace
Snail, The. Reeves
Snail and the Mouse, The. Richards
Snails. Liagarang
Snail's Derby, A. Lee-Hamilton
Snail's Lesson, The. Thompson
Snail's Pace. Fisher
To a Snail. Moore
Upon the [*or* a] Snail. Bunyan

Well! Hello down there. Issa
Widow's Yard, The. Gardner

Snakebites
Snakebite. James

Snakes
Black Snake, The. Hubbell
Boy and the Snake, The. Lamb
Breaking Green. Ondaatje
Close to Home. Steele
Cocker of Snooks, A. Gotlieb
Contest Snake, The. Cheng Hsieh
Copperhead, The. Bottoms
Copperhead, The. Gregg
Dying Viper, A. "Field"
Grass Snake and Fish. Illyés
Green and Yellow. *Unknown*
Haiku: "Snake, killed, A." *Fr.* One Hundred
   Haiku in Free Form. Hosai
Haiku: "Snake fled, The." Takahama Kyoshi
He drank enough. *Fr.* Snake. Lawrence
Horned Snake, The. Oliver
In a Garden. Babcock
In the Snake Park. Plomer
In winter in my room. Dickinson
Lizards and Snakes. Hecht
Medallion. Plath
Mountain Bride. Morgan
Narrow fellow in the grass, A. Dickinson
On a Little Boy's Endeavouring to Catch a
   Snake. Foxton
Photographing a Rattlesnake. Wagoner
Pit Viper. Momaday
Pit Viper. Starbuck
Prologue: Moments in a Glade. Stephens
Python, The. Belloc
Rattler, Alert. Ghiselin
Reveille. Hughes
Rural Carrier Stops to Kill a Nine-Foot
   Cottonmouth, The. Hummer
Serpent, The. Roethke
Sharpbreasted Snake, The. Oliver
Silent Snake, The. *Unknown*
Slither Tither. Warsaw
Snake. Abse
Snake, The. Berry
Snake. Lawrence
Snake. Roethke
Snake Skin. Beser
Snake Trying, The. Ross
Snakebite. James
Snakecharmer. Plath
Snakes of September, The. Kunitz
Song of the Cannibals, A. Winchilsea
Springfield Mountain. *Unknown*
Summer. Wakoski
Swamp Nocturne. Césaire
Time We Climbed Snake Mountain, The.
   Silko
To a Fair Lady Playing with a Snake. Waller
To a Fine Young Woman. Wycherley
To the Snake. Levertov
Variations on Southern Themes. Justice
Victory, A. Smith
Viper, The. Belloc
Viper, The. Pitter

Sneezing
Scratching your eyebrows, sneezing. *Fr.*
   Manyo Shu. *Unknown*
Sneeze. Kumin
Sneeze on a Monday, You Sneeze for Danger.
   Unknown
Sound of My Sneezing Nose, The. Te
   Whetu

Snipes
Snipe in the Marshes, A. Tamemasa
To the Snipe. Clare
Up from the paddies. Tonna

Snoring
Snoring Bedmate, The. *Unknown*

Snorkeling and Snorkelers
Snorkeling in the Caribbean. Doom

Snow

Above Ohara/ the fallen snow has piled up. Munenaga
Age of Snow, The. Kalász
Angels in Winter. Willard
As day fades away. Hanazono
Atami. Chugan Engetsu
Beautiful Snow, The. Watson
Because You Asked about the Line between Prose and Poetry. Nemerov
Blizzard, The. Ware
Blocked by Snow. Wu Wei-yeh
Brindabella. Stewart
Calendar Rhyme. Watson
Could it be I wait. Teika
Dafydd ap Gwilym Resents the Winter. Humphries
Dawn Snow. Huang Ching-jen
Dawn Walk. Hirsch
Desert Places. Frost
Drove-Road, The. Gibson
Dust of Snow. Frost
Early Snow. Lo Fu
Eight o'Clock. Housman
Even as it falls. Gyoko
Evening Snow. Tamekane
Falling of the Snow, The. Souster
Faun Sees Snow for the First Time, The. Aldington
Feathers of Snow. Unknown
Fields, the mountains, The. Tonna
Fire in the Snow, The. Watkins
First Snow. Allen
First Snow. Kooser
First Snow in Alsace. Wilbur
First Snow on an Airfield. Ciardi
First Snowfall [or Snow-Fall], The. Lowell
For Snow. Farjeon
Function of Blizzard. Warren
Ghosts. Munkittrick
Grasses and trees, The. Yasuhide
Grasses and trees, When. Keiun
Haiku: "Snow fades into the river, The." Fr. One Hundred Haiku in Free Form. Hosai
Having met you as in a dream. Fr. Manyo Shu. Unknown
Hearing the Snow. Kido
In the broad dawn sky. Ietaka
In the snow piled up. Tamekane
In the Snowfall. Mechain
It Fell in the City. Merriam
It sifts from leaden sieves. Dickinson
It snowed yesterday. Fr. Manyo Shu. Akahito
It was I who did command. Fr. Manyo Shu. Fujiwara
Jane's Village. Koh Chang-soo
Kate and I. Tarrant
Landscape. Purdy
Late Winter Snow. Turner
Lester Tells of Wanda and the Big Snow. Zimmer
London Snow. Bridges
Long Lines. Goodman
Magnificent snow/ Has fallen here at my place. Fr. Manyo Shu. Temmu
Metaphysic of Snow. Finkel
Monticello. Hass
More It Snows, The. Milne
Mountain winds, The. Tamesuke
Night Snow. Kogon
Night Snow. Po Chü-i
Now even the sound. Tameyo
On a Night of Snow. Coatsworth
On a Snowy Night. Koh Chang-soo
On the leaves of the bamboo-grass. Unknown
Once in a Lifetime, Snow. Murray
Onset, The. Frost
Patch of Old Snow, A. Frost
Phantoms of the Steppe. Pushkin

Plum blossoms are hard to make out. Fr. A Compendium of Good Tanka. Teika
+30° C. Wieseltier
Presence of Snow. Cane
Remembering Snow. Csoori
Revival. Crow
Rondel: "Beautiful snow falls on a bed, A." Dacey
See, It Begins to Come Down. Szabo
Snow. Artaud
Snow. Chiang
Snow. Ch'ü Ta-chün
Snow. Crapsey
Snow. De la Mare
Snow/ blue/ eyes. Grenier
Snow, The. Hall
Snow. Kuskin
Snow. MacNeice
Snow. Malouf
Snow. Nagy
Snow. Pomeroy
Snow. Rosselli
Snow. Sexton
Snow. Stone
Snow. Thomas
Snow. Witheford
Snow Anthology. Bourinot
Snow covers the slopes, covers the slopes. Fr. A Sequence/ 28 Separate Poems. Grenier
Snow Crystals on Meall Glas. Wilson
Snow Curlew, The. Watkins
Snow-Flakes. Longfellow
Snow-Flakes, The. Thompson
Snow Harvest. Young
Snow in October. Nelson
Snow in Spring. Eastwick
Snow in the Suburbs. Hardy
Snow in Town. Mark
Snow Man, The. Stevens
Snow on the Mountain at Dusk. Shotetsu
Snow Print Two: Hieroglyphics. Esbensen
Snow Signs. Tomlinson
Snow Song. Ray
Snow Song. Shne'ur
Snow-Storm, A. Carducci
Snow-Storm, The. Emerson
Snow Storm, The. Fordham
Snow Storm, The. Millay
Snow That Falls on Chagall's Village. Kim Chun-soo
Snow toward Evening. Cane
Snowbanks North of the House. Bly
Snowfall. Bernard
Snowfall. Carducci
Snowfall, The. Gwerfyl Mechain
Snowfall, The. Justice
Snowfall: Four Variations. Amabile
Snowfall in the Afternoon. Bly
Snowfish, The. Field
Snowflake, The. De la Mare
Snowflakes. Behrend
Snowflakes. Chute
Snowflakes. Dodge
Snowflakes Sail Gently Down, The. Okara
Snowman, The. Adams
Snowman. McCord
Snowsong. Priessnitz
Snowstorm. Clare
Snowy Mountains. Tsung Ch'en
Soft Snow. Blake
Spring Snow. Chugan Engetsu
Spring Snow. Matthews
Spring Snow and Tui. Bethell
Stopping by Woods on a Snowy Evening. Frost
Stories of Snow. Page
Storm. Oliver
Storm Fear. Frost
Storm in April, A. Wilbur
Sun that brief December day, The. Fr. Snow-bound; a Winter Idyl. Whittier

There Blooms No Bud in May. De la Mare
There's Snow on the Fields. Rossetti
To a Snowflake. Thompson
Tons of snow have fallen in my village. Fr. Manyo Shu. Temmu
Traveling Early through a Snowy Valley. Yü Chi
Tread not the snow. Fr. Manyo Shu. Mikata Shami
Upon a Great Shower of Snow That Fell on May-Day, 1654. Washbourne
Vanishing Point, The. Davison
Velvet Shoes. Wylie
Village Snowfall. Tamemasa
Wednesday at North Hatley. Gustafson
When All the World Is Full of Snow. Bodecker
White Fields. Stephens
White snow fills the lakeside village. Fr. Miscellaneous Words on the Lake. Tsung Ch'en
White snow which lies so deep, The. Fr. Manyo Shu. Yakamochi
Why Does It Snow? Richards
Winter. De la Mare
Winter. Menashe
Winter's Tale. Farber
Yonder in the plum-tree. Fr. Manyo Shu. Unknown
See also **Snowflakes.**

Snow White

Snow White and the Seven Dwarfs. Sexton
True Story of Snow White, The. Bennett

Snowdrops

Snowdrop. De Bary
Snowdrop, The. Fordham
Snowdrop. Hughes
Snowdrops. Evans
Snowdrops. MacBeth
Snowdrops. Tadema
Snowdrops. Vivian

Snowflakes

Snowflake, The. De la Mare
Snowflake on asphodel, clear ice on rose. Aiken
Snowflakes. Nemerov
Snowflakes. Sansom
Watering the Horse. Bly

Snowmen

Boy at the Window. Wilbur
Snowman, The. Page

Soap

Naughty Soap Song. Aldis
Soap Suds. MacNeice
Soap, the Oppressor. Johnson

Soccer

Bewteis of the Fute-Ball, The. Unknown
Dangers of Foot-ball, The. Fr. Trivia; or, The Art of Walking the Streets of London. Gay
Eureka! Godley
Football and Rowing—an Eclogue. Godley
Soccer at the Meadowlands. Ackerman
Stanley Matthews. Ross

Social Class

Dignity of Labor, The. Bersohn
False Security. Betjeman
For a Lady I Know. Fr. Four Epitaphs. Cullen
Garden, The. Pound
Maud Muller. Whittier
Modest Wit, A. Osborn
Old Woman, Outside the Abbey Theater, An. Strong
Red Wig, The. Unknown
Song of the Lower Classes, The. Jones
Topography. Facknitz
When Adam Delved. Unknown
Without and Within. Lowell
Working Class. Warr
See also **Snobbery.**

Social Protest. *See* **Protest, Social.**

Social Workers
Feeding the Lions. Jordan

Socialism
Confession of Faith. Csanádi
Emigrant Song. "Ansky"
Hibiscus and Salvia Flowers. Lawrence
Socialism, I Say. Erb
To a Woman Socialist. Reisen
Why I Voted the Socialist Ticket. Lindsay
Yiddish Speaking Socialists of the Lower East
   Side. Sanders

Socrates
Reply of Socrates, The. Thomas
Socrates' Death. Jackson

Sodom
And there came two angels to Sodom at even.
   Fr. Genesis.
Lot Later. Nemerov
Lot's Wife. "Akhmatova"
Sodom. Grade
This Place Rumord to Have Been Sodom.
   Duncan

Softball
Americans Playing Slow-Pitch Softball at an
   Airbase near Kunsan, South Korea.
   Johnson
Casey's Daughter at the Bat. Graham
Missoula Softball Tournament. Hugo
Night Game in Menomonie Park, A. Firer
Softball Dreams. Kevorkian
Spiel. Johnson

Soldiers
Achilles Deatheridge. Masters
Aged Stranger, The. Harte
Air Sentry, The. Barrington
All Day It Has Rained. Lewis
All the Hills and Vales Along. Sorley
American Soldier, The. Freneau
Amputee Soldier, The. Dacey
And to Private Ball it came. *Fr.* In
   Parenthesis. Jones
Another Epitaph on an Army of Mercenaries.
   "MacDiarmid"
Anthem for Doomed Youth. Owen
Apologia pro Poemate Meo. Owen
Aristocrats. Douglas
Arms and the Boy. Owen
Army Corps on the March, An. Whitman
As Toilsome I Wander'd Virginia's Woods.
   Whitman
Back in the States. Stimson
Ballad for the Unknown Soldier. Taylor
Ballad of a General. Snoek
Ballad of East and West, The. Kipling
Band Played Waltzing Matilda, The. Bogle
Banks of Claudy, The. *Unknown*
Banks of the Nile, The. *Unknown*
Base Details. Sassoon
Battle, The. Simpson
Before Action. Gellert
Bingen on the Rhine. Norton
Bivouac of the Dead, The. O'Hara
Black Regiment, The. Boker
Black Truth. Agard
Bold Dragoon, A. *Unknown*
Bold Dragoon, The. *Unknown*
Bonnets So Blue. *Unknown*
Boots. Kipling
Border Ballad. *Fr.* The Monastery. Scott
Breakfast. Gibson
British Grenadiers, The. *Unknown*
Budmouth Dears. *Fr.* The Dynasts. Hardy
By the Bivouac's Fitful Flame. Whitman
Call to Arms. Tso Yen-nien
Canadians. Gurney
Cavalry Crossing a Ford. Whitman
Centenarian's Story, The. Whitman
Champs d'Honneur. Hemingway
Chant-Pagan. Kipling
Charge of the Light Brigade, The. Tennyson

Charlie He's My Darling. Burns
Christmas Night of '62. McCabe
Cloth-plant on that high mound, The.
   Unknown
Cold. Coffey
Cool Web, The. Graves
Cry from the Canadian Hills, A. Leveridge
Danny. Cowley
Danny Deever. Kipling
Dardanelles 1916. Fallon
Death of a Warrior, The. Mastoraki
Deserter, The. Housman
Dirge for a Soldier. Boker
Disabled. Owen
Dreamers. Sassoon
Drummer Hodge. Hardy
Dug-out, The. Sassoon
Dulce et Decorum Est. Owen
Eighth Air Force. Jarrell
Elegy for a Dead Soldier. Shapiro
Endless Nights of Rain. Pape
Enemy Action. Cruikshank
Epistle from a Half-Pay Officer in the Country
   to His Friend in London, An. Pack
Epitaph on a Soldier. Barton
Execution of Cornelius Vane, The. Read
Exposure. Owen
Fable of the War, A. Nemerov
Fallen, The. Scott
Farewell, The:
It Was A' for Our Rightfu' King. Burns
Fathers, The. Sassoon
Fife Tune. Manifold
Firmly set are the rabbit nets. *Unknown*
Flowers of the ForestThe. Elliot
For My Torturer, Lieutenant D——. Djabali
For Our Soldiers Who Fell in Russia. Fortini
For Soldiers. Gifford
For those men night was a more bitter day.
   Fr. Heroic and Elegiac Song for the Lost
   Second Lieute. Elytis
Forgive Me, Sire. Cameron
General, The. Sassoon
General's Death, The. O'Connor
Georgia Volunteer, A. Townsend
Girl I Left behind Me, The. *Unknown*
Glory of Women. Sassoon
Guard at the Binh Thuy Bridge, The.
   Balaban
Gunga Din. Kipling
Gunner. Jarrell
Haltersick's Song. *Fr.* Horestes. Pickering
   (or Pikerying)
Happy Warrior, The. Read
Harmonics. Moody
Headwaters of the Lung River. Hsü Ts'an
Here dead lie we because we did not choose.
   Housman
High Germany. *Unknown*
His furs of lamb's wool so glossy! *Unknown*
History of My Heart. Pinsky
Homage to a Government. Larkin
How can you plead that you have no wraps?
   Unknown
How few of us are left, how few! *Unknown*
How Sleep the Brave. Collins
I Am the Very Model [*or* Pattern] of a
   Modern Major-General. *Fr.* The Pirates of
   Penzance. Gilbert
I Climb That Barren Ridge. *Unknown*
I climb that wooded hill. *Unknown*
I Heard a Soldier. Trench
If you draw a bow, draw a strong one. *Fr.*
   On the Border, First Series. Tu Fu
In an Age of Fops and Toys. *Fr.*
   Voluntaries. Emerson
In Barracks. Sassoon
In Flanders Fields. McCrae
In the Army. Fujita Koshiro
Insensibility. Owen
Into Battle. Grenfell

Irish Airman Foresees His Death, An. Yeats
It Was the Last of the Parades. Simpson
Jester in the Trench, The. Gellert
Jewish Conscript, The. Frank
Jimmy's Enlisted; or, The Recruited Collier.
   Unknown
Johnny, I Hardly Knew Ye. *Unknown*
Kid Has Gone to the Colors, The. Herschell
Lament for a Cornish Soldier. Herbertson
Lancashire Lads. *Unknown*
Lancer. Housman
Last Poem. Donnelly
Little Giffen. Ticknor
Lofty Lane. Gerard
Louse Hunting. Rosenberg
Lullaby, A: "For wars his life and half a
   world away." Jarrell
McCaffery. *Unknown*
Man He Killed, The. Hardy
March in the Ranks Hard-Prest, and the Road
   Unknown, A. Whitman
Men behind the Guns, The. Rooney
Men in Green. Campbell
Men Who March Away. *Fr.* The Dynasts.
   Hardy
Mental Cases. Owen
Minister of War. *Unknown*
Mother's List of Duties, A. Ponmutiyar
Mrs. McGrath. *Unknown*
My Lord's Gone to Service. *Unknown*
New Mistress, The. *Fr.* A Shropshire Lad.
   Housman
Nocturne: "Be thou at peace this night."
   Davison
Nostalgia. Shapiro
O What Is That Sound [Which So Thrills the
   Ear]. Auden
Ode for the American Dead in Korea.
   McGrath
Ode: "I hate that drum's discordant sound."
   Scott of Amwell
Officers' Mess (1916). Monro
Old Battalion, The. *Unknown*
Old Souldier of the Queens, An. *Unknown*
Old Timers. Sandburg
On a Soldier Fallen in the Philippines.
   Moody
One of the Regiment. Le Pan
Orphan Boy, The. *Unknown*
Over the Top with Pershing. Fitzgerald
Parthians, The ("He look't and saw what
   numbers numberless"). *Fr.* Paradise
   Regained. Milton
Peasants, The. Lewis
Plains of Waterloo, The. *Unknown*
Poem for Anton Schmidt, A. Pillen
Poem of the Conscripted Warrior. "Nogar"
Portrait in the Guards, A. Whistler
Portrait: The Freedom Fighter. Jonas
Private of the Buffs; or, The British Soldier in
   China. Doyle
Procession. Hofshteyn
Prolonged Sonnet: When the Troops Were
   Returning from Milan [*or* When The
   Troops Were Returning from Milan].
   Albizzi
Rambling Soldier, The. *Unknown*
Rebel, A. Fletcher
Recall. Whittemore
Recessional. Kipling
Recruit, The. Housman
Recruiting Drive. Causley
Recruiting Sergeant, The. *Unknown*
Repression of War Experience. Sassoon
Return, The. Kipling
Richard III's Speech. *Fr.* Bosworth Field.
   Beaumont
Royal Light Dragoon, The. *Unknown*
Send-off, The. Owen
Sergeant-Major Money. Graves
Shillin' a Day. Kipling
Show, The. Owen

Sight in Camp [in the Daybreak Gray and Dim], A. Whitman
Sir Dilberry Diddle, Captain of Militia. *Unknown*
Snowy Morning, 1940. Cruikshank
Soldier, The. *Fr.* 1914. Brooke
Soldier, A. Frost
Soldier, The. Krige
Soldier, A. Suckling
Soldier Boy's Dream, The. Tucker
Soldier from the Wars Returning. Housman
Soldier Going to the Field, The. Davenant
Soldier Rest! [Thy Warfare O'er]. *Fr.* The Lady of the Lake. Scott
Soldier That Has Seen Service, The. *Unknown*
Soldier: Twentieth Century. Rosenberg
Soldiers. *Unknown*
Soldiers Bathing. Prince
Soldier's Death, A. *Fr.* The Atheist's Tragedy. Tourneur
Soldier's Dream, The. Campbell
Soldier's Farewell to Manchester, The. *Unknown*
Soldiers on the Platform. Cornford
Soldier's Prayer, A. Freeman
Soldier's Song. *Unknown*
Song of the Banjo, The. Kipling
Song of the Camp, The. Taylor
Sons of War. Al-Qasim
Souldiers Farewel to His Love, The. *Unknown*
Sound of the Drum, The. *Unknown*
Speak. Wright
Spires of Oxford, The. Letts
Spring Offensive. Owen
Strange Meeting. Owen
Street Sounds to the Soldiers' Tread, The. Housman
Subalterns, The. Hardy
Tambourine song for Soldiers Going into Battle. Hind bint Utba
Tears. Thomas
Ten Days Leave. Snodgrass
There Was an Old Soldier. *Unknown*
"They." Sassoon
They beat their drums with a loud noise. *Unknown*
Things that Make a Soldier Great, The. Guest
Three Troopers, The. Thornbury
Threnode for Young Soldiers Killed in Action. Bairacli-Levy
To a Comrade in Arms. Lewis
To Billy, My Son. Bax
To Lucasta, Going to the Wars [*or* Warres]. Lovelace
To Richard, My Son. Bax
To the Veterans of the Abraham Lincoln Brigade. Taggard
To you, brave warrior, starting for the Land of Kara. *Fr.* Manyo Shu. Tajihi Takanushi
Tommy. Kipling
Trooper's Horse, The. *Unknown*
Troops, The. Sassoon
Two Armies. Spender
Unknown Soldier, The. Lewis
Unknown Soldier, The. Rose
Vergissmeinnicht. Douglas
Veteran, The. Blunden
Volunteer, The. Asquith
Volunteer, The. Cutler
Volunteer, The. *Unknown*
War Blinded. Dunn
War Song of Dinas Vawr, The. *Fr.* The Misfortunes of Elphin. Peacock
Warren's Address at Bunker Hill [*or* to the American Soldiers]. Pierpont
We Pick Ferns, We Pick Ferns. *Unknown*

We recruits have our commanders to send us off. *Fr.* On the Border, First Series. Tu Fu
What plant is not faded? *Unknown*
What the Servants Said to Him, as He Returned Home. Maturaittamilkkuttan Katuvan Mallanar
When Johnny Comes Marching Home. Gilmore
When the Assault Was Intended to the City. Milton
When the War Is Over. Merwin
Whisperin' Bill. Bacheller
Why, Soldiers, Why? Wolfe
Widow at Windsor, The. Kipling
Working Party, A. Sassoon
Wound-Dresser, The. Whitman
Young Lady Dancing with Soldier. Allfrey
Young Warrior, A. Ponmutiyar
Poems of Love and War from the Eight Anthologies and the Ten Long Poems of Classical Tamil (PLW). A. K. Ramanujan, comp. *and* tr.
See also **War.**

Solipsism
Argent Solipsism. Blake
Complaint on Solipsism. Illyés
Good Creatures, Do You Love Your Lives. Housman

Solitude
Acquainted with the Night. Frost
Alone. Holden
Anticipation of Sharks. Wakoski
Autobiographia Literaria. O'Hara
Beautiful Lady Yü, The. Sun Kuang-hsien
Cloth-plant grew till it covered the thorn bush, The. *Unknown*
Compensation. Jeffers
Desert Places. Frost
Deviator, The. Warr
Eagle and the Mole, The. Wylie
Elected Silence. Sassoon
Garden, The. Marvell
Garden, The. Strand
Goat Paths, The. Stephens
Good Hours. Frost
Hatred of Distant Places. Wen T'ing-yün
Hermit, The. Bly
How to Eat Alone. Halpern
Hymn on Solitude. Thomson
I Am. Clare
I Met My Solitude. Replansky
I wish to go away and live. Ghalib
I'm Alone in the Evening. Rosen
In November. Lampman
Inniskeen Road: July Evening. Kavanagh
Invocation: "Earth, ocean, air, belovèd brotherhood!" *Fr.* Alastor; or, The Spirit of Solitude. Shelley
Keziah. Brooks
Lake Isle of Innisfree, The. Yeats
Lisa. Carrier
Manifold Little Hills. Mao Hsi-chen
Maud. Swander
Mid-August at Sourdough Mountain Lookout. Snyder
Morning, A. Strand
Most of It, The. Frost
Mountain Hawthorns. Wei Ch'eng-pan
9:00 A.M. Oravecz
Not a soul is left. Teika
On Looking into Henry Moore. Livesay
One Song, The. Strand
Other Great Composers, The. Ash
Paying Homage at the Golden Gate. Wei Chuang
Peter Grimes at Aldeburgh. *Fr.* The Borough: Peter Grimes. Crabbe
Poem: "Eager note on my door said "Call me," The." O'Hara
Poems of Solitary Delights. Tachibana

Prelude: "Still south I went and west and south again." Synge
Pure Serene Music. Wen T'ing-yün
Quiet. Pickthall
Rain. Thomas
Remodeling the Hermit's Cabin. Chappell
Retirement. Cowper
Singles. Waters
Sitting Alone in the Courtyard. Yü Chi
Six Winter Privacy Poems. Bly
Small Moon. Nemerov
Soledad. Hayden
Solitariness. *Fr.* Arcadia. Sidney
Solitary, The. Teasdale
Solitary Reaper, The. Wordsworth
Solitude. De la Mare
Solitude. Fairburn
Solitude. Keats
Solitude. Lampman
Solitude. *Fr.* The Search after Happiness. More
Solitude. Peterson
Solitude. Rilke
Solitude. Tranströmer
Solitude. Wilcox
Song of the Water Clock at Night. Wei Chuang
Spirit of the Yellow River. Sun Kuang-hsien
Sun Moon Kelp Flower or Goat. Gregg
There is a charm in solitude that cheers. Clare
There was a poet whose untimely tomb. *Fr.* Alastor; or, The Spirit of Solitude. Shelley
Things That Happen Where There Aren't Any People. Stafford
Thrice Happy He. Drummond
Under a Wiltshire Apple Tree. De Bary
Wants. Larkin
Woman Alone. Levertov
Wood-Cutter's Night Song, The. Clare

Solomon
I chanced to see one day. Mir
On Woman. Yeats
Solomon. Heine
Solomon and the Witch. Yeats
Solomon to Sheba. Yeats

Solstices
Toward the Solstice. Rich

Somer, Sir Henry
Balade and Roundel to Master Somer. Hoccleve

Somersaults
Somersaults. Prelutsky

Somerset, Edward Seymour, Duke of
On Edward Seymour, Duke of Somerset. *Unknown*

Somerset, England
Apostrophe to the Parret. Burrington
Nightfall on Sedgemoor. Young
Quantocks, The. Wordsworth
Seen from the Quantocks. *Fr.* This Lime Tree Bower My Prison. Coleridge

Somnambulism
For the Sleepwalkers. Hirsch
Sleepwalking. Achterberg
Somnambulist. Hervey

Somoza Debayle, Anastasio
Death of Somoza, The. Mejía Sánchez

Son
Childhood Fled. Lamb

Songs
So! Reisen

Sonnets
Enigma, An. Poe
In Magic Words. Moore
Nuns Fret Not at Their Convent's Narrow Room. Wordsworth
On a Magazine Sonnet. Loines
On the Sonnet. Keats

Scorn not the sonnet; critic, you have frowned. Wordsworth
Single Sonnet. Bogan
Sonnet upon Sonnets, A. Burns
Sonnet, The: "What is a sonnet? 'Tis the pearly shell." Gilder
Sonneteering Made Easy. Botsford
Velvet Sonneteers, The. MacInnes
What the Sonnet Is. Lee-Hamilton

Sonora Desert
Requiem for Sonora. Shelton

Sons
Affliction of Margaret, The. Wordsworth
Almond Tree, The. Stallworthy
Ancient Couple on Lu Mountain, The. Van Doren
Axe Handles. Snyder
Basketball. Vincent
Bee, The. Dickey
Birth of a Son. Hunt
Birthday. Yevtushenko
Blaming Sons. T'ao Ch'ien
Boy Changed into a Stag Cries Out at the Gate of Secrets, The. Juhász
Brat, tied up, The. Issa
Breaking a branch off my cherry tree. Kikaku
Breakings. Taylor
Daedalus. Reid
Death of a Son. Silkin
Each Bird Walking. Gallagher
For a Father. Cronin
For My Father. Potts
For their son who wears his first *hakama*. Shido
For You, My Son. Gregory
From Father to Son. Humphreys
From Old Mrs. Mo of Heng Yang: A Letter to My Son, Lo Fu. Yip Wai-lim
Gemwood. Bell
H. Milosz
He ties him to a breezy tree. Issa
In the Winter Dark. Gerber
It Comes during Sleep. Dow
Joe Gillon Hypnotizes His Son. Goldbarth
Look. Levine
Lost Son, The. Roethke
Lullaby: "O my son, born on a winter's morn." Noho-mai-te-Rangi
Mothers of Sons. Saunders
My Mother Would Be a Falconress. Duncan
My Only Son. Halpern
My son must be twenty by now. *Fr.* Ryojin Hisho. Go-Shirakawa
My Sons Have Grown to Manhood. Anhava
No fields, no house, one poor scholar. *Fr.* Shortly after I Married, I Had to Go into Mourning. Rai San'yo
Notes for My Son. *Fr.* The Song of Lazarus. Comfort
On My First Son [*or* Sonne]. Jonson
On the Birth of His Son. Su Tung-p'o
On the Death of His Son. Wesley
On the Death of My Son Charles. Webster
Prayer for My Son, A. Winters
Prayer for My Son, A. Yeats
Second Prelude. Reality in Albuquerque: The Son. *Fr.* Poem in Progress. Logan
Son, The. Torrence
Sonnet to My First Born. Fordham
Starlight. Levine
Sympathy, a Welcome, A. Berryman
Then Sohrab with is sword smote Rustum's helm. *Fr.* Sohrab and Rustum. Arnold
To Billy, My Son. Bax
To My Child Carlino. Landor
To My Son. Byron
To My Unborn Son. Thorne
To Richard, My Son. Bax
Two Postures beside a Fire. Wright
Two Prayers, The. Gillies
Wayward Son, The. Linden

Wild Pitches. Dacey
Wishes for My Son. MacDonagh
World Is with Me, The. Hood
Yesterday. Merwin
Young Man Thinks of Sons, The. Mason
Divided Light: Father and Son Poems (DiL). Jason Shinder, ed.

Sophocles
To a Friend. Arnold

Sorcerers
Our Sorcerers. Cornford

Sorrow
And this/ is all there is. *Fr.* Manyo Shu. Yakamochi
Bad Season Makes the Poet Sad, The. Herrick
Braes of Yarrow, The. Logan
Come, Ye Disconsolate. Moore
Dark Song. Ammons
Depths of Sorrow, The.
Desolate. Massey
"Desolation Is a Delicate Thing." Wylie
Echoing Heaven's Everlastingness. Mao Wen-hsi
Ettrick. Scott
Eyes of Dark Sorrow, The. Rashed
Girl's Song. *Unknown*
Had Sorrow Ever Fitter Place. *Fr.* Hymen's Triumph. Daniel
Harp of Sorrow, The. Clifford
I Saw My Lady Weep. *Unknown*
I Sit and Look Out. Whitman
Immortal at the River. Mao Wen-hsi
In my garden. *Fr.* Manyo Shu. Yakamochi
Lost Love. Graves
Love Again. Reverdy
Oh! sing unto my roundelay [*or* O! Synge untoe mie roundelaie]. *Fr.* Aella; a Tragycal Enterlude. Chatterton
On a Picture by J. M. Wright, Esq. Southey
On Another's Sorrow. *Fr.* Songs of Innocence. Blake
Rainy Day, The. Longfellow
Shrubbery, The. Cowper
Sorrow. Noshiwaki Junzaburo
Sorrow. Shin Dong-jip
Sorrow Is the Only Faithful One. Dodson
Spell against Sorrow. Raine
Stormy Night in Autumn. Chu Shu-chen
Stretch of Cloud over Mount Wu, A. Mao Wen-hsi
Tailor Called Sorrow, A. Alver
Tenth Eclogue, The. *Fr.* The Shepherd's Garland. Drayton
They Say My Verse Is Sad: No Wonder. Housman
To Two Bereaved. Ashe
Troubled Woman. Hughes
With Rue My Heart Is Laden. *Fr.* A Shropshire Lad. Housman
See also **Grief.**

Soul
All Hallows Eve. Byer
Anastasis. Smythe
Animal Song. McHugh
Animula. Merwin
Any Soul to Any Body. Monkhouse
Be still, my soul, be still; the arms you bear are brittle. *Fr.* A Shropshire Lad. Housman
Caged Skylark, The. Hopkins
Commentary Applied to Spiritual Things. John of the Cross
Dead Waters. Gutiérrez Nájera
Dialogue between the Resolved Soul and Created Pleasure, A. Marvell
Dialogue between the Soul and [the] Body, A. Marvell
Dialogue of Self and Soul, A. Yeats

Difference between despair, The. Dickinson
Doubts. Brooke
Ecstasy, The. Donne
Falconer of God, The. Benét
Green River, The. Douglas
Hadrian's Address to His Soul When Dying. Hadrian
I Know My Soul. McKay
Indian Burying Ground, The. Freneau
Invention of Comics, The. Baraka
Lie, The. Ralegh
Lost, One Soul. McIntosh
Love Calls Us to the Things of This World. Wilbur
Most souls, 'tis true, but peep out once an age. *Fr.* Elegy to the Memory of an Unfortunate Lady. Pope
My Book. Ackermann
My soul is an Elysium of shades. Tyutchev
Noiseless Patient Spider, A. Whitman
Octopus, The. "MacDiarmid"
On a Drop of Dew. Marvell
Palladium. Arnold
Peace. Vaughan
Poor soul, in this thy flesh what dost thou know? *Fr.* Of the Progresse of the Soule; the Second Anniversarie. Donne
Rebirth. Machado
Scorpion. Smith
Sea Change. Masefield
Self-Judgment. Lask
Song of the Soul That Knows God by Faith. John of the Cross
Soul, The. Cawein
Soul, The. Dana
Soul selects her own society, The. Dickinson
Soul, thou must seek thyself in Me. Theresa
Soul's Courts, The. Ray
Soul's Desire, The. *Unknown*
Speculation. Nemerov
Virtue. Herbert
What Are Years? Moore
Wineglass, The. Baratynsky

Sound
Ear, The. MacNeice
Hermit Wakes to Bird Sounds, The. Kumin
Hurlygush. Lindsay
Nocturnal Sounds. Cumbo
Overheard. Levertov
Sound of Night, The. Kumin
Sounds. Tanikawa Shuntaro

Soup
January. Sendak

South, The
Alas! for the South. Coogler
Appeal to My Countrywomen, An. Harper
At Bessemer. Levine
Childhood. Walker
Day in a Long Hot Summer, A. Kageyama
Dixie. Pike
First Families Move Over! Nash
Georgia Dusk. Toomer
Invitation to Madison County, An. Wright
It is true—/ I've always loved. *Fr.* Once. Walker
It's a debatable land. The winds are variable. *Fr.* Report from the Carolinas. Bevington
Legacy: My South. Randall
My South. West
North/South. Mariani
Once. Walker
Snapshots of the Cotton South. Davis
Southern Mansion. Bontemps
Southern Road, The. Randall
Southern Ships and Settlers. Benét
Southerner, The. Shapiro
Variations on Southern Themes. Justice
When the Mint Is in the Liquor. Ousley
Why Are Daddies So Mean? Chambers
Made Thing, The; an Anthology of Contemporary Southern Poetry (MT). Leon Stokesbury, ed.

South Africa
Attend my fable if your ears be clean. *Fr.* The Wayzgoose. Campbell
Beauty of My Land Peers Warily, The. Brutus
Birth of Moshesh, The. Bereng
Brief Thunder at Sharpeville. Nortje
City Johannesburg. Serote
Guess Who! Roots
In the Gold Mines. Vilakazi
Letter from Pretoria Central Prison. Nortje
Midnight. Nortje
Nightfall in Soweto. Mtshali
Offering to the Storm. Césaire
On Some South African Novelists. Campbell
On the Island. Brutus
Pass Office Song. *Unknown*
Poem, A: "What is there that we can do or say." Mphahlele
Soliloquy: South Africa. Nortje
Soweto. Sepamla
There's an Unknown River in Soweto. Mandela
Penguin Book of South African Verse, The (PeSA). Jack Cope *and* Uys Krige, eds.
South African War. *See* **Boer War.**
South America. *See* **Brazilian Verse; Peru.**
South Carolina
Battle of Charleston Harbor, The. Hayne
Brother Jonathan's Lament for Sister Caroline. Holmes
Carolina. Timrod
Charleston. Gilder
Charleston. Hayne
Charleston. Timrod
Crum Appointment, The. Moorer
It's a debatable land. The winds are variable. *Fr.* Report from the Carolinas. Bevington
Ode: "Sleep sweetly in your humble graves." Timrod
South Carolina to the States of the North. Hayne
South Dakota
Crazy Horse Returns to South Dakota. Elliott
Dakota Badlands. Landeweer
South Sea Islands
Fun with Fishing. Tietjens
South Wind
Awake! *Fr.* The Song of Solomon.
Moon's the North Wind's Cooky, The. Lindsay
South Wind laid his moccasins aside, The. *Fr.* Malcolm's Katie. Crawford
Southern Cross, The (constellation)
Southern Cross. Melville
Southey, Robert
Dedication: "Bob Southey! You're a poet— poet-laureate." *Fr.* Don Juan. Byron
Vision of Judgment, The. Byron
Southpaws
Southpaw. Mueller
Soviet Union. *See* **Russia.**
Soweto, South Africa
Midnight. Nortje
Nightfall in Soweto. Mtshali
Soweto. Sepamla
There's an Unknown River in Soweto. Mandela
Soy Sauce
Soy Sauce. Snyder
Space and Space Travel
Achieving Perspective. Rogers
Apollo 8. Berryman
Autosonic Door. Thompson
Canopus. Taylor
Christmas 1959 et Cetera. Barrax
Corruption of Metals. Dorman
Far Trek. Brady
First Walk on the Moon. Swenson

How Strange It Is. Lewis
Lighting the Colony. Tem
Lure, The. Sneyd
Message from a Mouse, Ascending in a Rocket. Hubbell
Moonwalk. Engels
On Shooting Particles beyond the World. Eberhart
Post Early for Space. Henniker-Heaton
Soft Landings. Sergeant
Space Shuttle. Ackerman
Spacepoem 3: Off Course. Morgan
This little pig built a spaceship. *Fr.* The Space Child's Mother Goose. Winsor
Unknown Shores. Thomas
Walk on the Moon. Momaday
Spain
And I remember Spain. *Fr.* Autumn Journal. MacNeice
Cordoba. Mendelssohn
Feller I Know, A. Austin
García Lorca: A Photograph of the Granada Cemetery, 1966. Levis
Lost Fan, Hotel Californian, Fresno, 1923. Levis
Monserrat. Collin
Plaça Santiago, The. *Fr.* The Spanish Gypsy. "Eliot"
Poem for Garcia Lorca. Woodcock
Port Bou. Spender
Quit now the town, and with a journeying dream. *Fr.* The Spanish Gypsy. "Eliot"
Recollections of a Day's Journey in Spain. Southey
Spain. Guillevic
Spain. Symons
You Hated Spain. Hughes
Spanish-American Verse. *See* **Hispanic Verse.**
Spanish-American War
Breath on the Oat. Taylor
Deeds of Valor at Santiago. Scollard
Dewey at Manila. Johnson
No Hint of Stain. *Fr.* An Ode in Time of Hesitation. Moody
Ode in Time of Hesitation, An. Moody
On a Soldier Fallen in the Philippines. Moody
Surrender of Spain, The. Hay
Unmanifest Destiny. Hovey
Spanish Armada
Armada, The. Macaulay
Armada, 1588, The. Wilson
Joyful [or Joyfull] New Ballad, A. Deloney
Sailor's Only Delight, The. *Unknown*
Sir Francis Drake; or, Eighty-eight. *Unknown*
Spanish Civil War. *See* **Civil War, Spanish.**
Spanish Succession, War of the
Battle of Blenheim, The. Southey
Poem to His Grace the Duke of Marlborough, A. *Fr.* The Campaign. Addison
Word's gone out, and now they spread the main, The. *Fr.* The Spanish Descent. Defoe
See also **Blenheim, Battle of.**
Spanish Verse
Love Poems from Spain & Spanish America (LPSS). Perry Higman, ed. *and* tr.
Spankings
Whipping, The. Hayden
Sparrows
Baby sparrows. Kikaku
Because You Asked about the Line between Prose and Poetry. Nemerov
Bee, the Ant, and the Sparrow, The. Cotton
City Sparrow. Mayhall
Dead Sparrow, The. Cartwright

Did You Ever Hear an English Sparrow Sing? Johnston
Fringilla Melodia, The. Hirst
"Good brother Philip, I have borne you long." *Fr.* Astrophel and Stella, LXXXIII. Sidney
Haiku: "I know the footsteps of the sparrow." *Fr.* One Hundred Haiku in Free Form. Hosai.
Haiku: "Sparrows scurrying." Ishida Hakyo
Haiku: "Sparrows all at once are gone, The." *Fr.* One Hundred Haiku in Free Form. Hosai
Hedge-Sparrows and House-Sparrows. Fuller
I let the sparrows play. *Fr.* Forty-four Hokku. Issa
Icehouse in Summer, The. Nemerov
little cock sparrow sat on a tree, A. *Unknown*
Mr. and Mrs. Spikky Sparrow. Lear
Song of the Reed Sparrow, The. *Unknown*
Sparrow, The. Williams
Sparrow and Diamond, The. Green
Sparrow Bathing. Ono Tozaburo
Sparrow Flock. Tozaburo
Sparrow goes in and out of jail, A. *Fr.* Forty-four Hokku. Issa
Sparrow in the Zoo, The. Nemerov
Sparrow in Winter. Takahashi Shinkichi
Sparrow's Fall, The. Harper
Sparrow's Feather, A. Barker
Sparrows' friendship breaks up. *Fr.* Forty-four Hokku. Issa
Spring day: a sparrow sand-bathing in my garden. *Fr.* Twenty-three Hokku. Onitsura
They've All Gone South. Miller
Upon the Death of His Sparrow; an Elegie. Herrick
Sparta, Greece
Death of Leonidas, The. Croly
In Sparta. Cavafy
On the Spartan Dead at Thermopylae. Simonides
Sparta. Sikelianos
To the Lacedemonians. Tate
Spas
Though many were the hot springs. *Fr.* Manyo Shu. Akahito
Tunbridge Wells. Rochester
Spastics
Song for My Son. Davis
Spastic Child. Miller
Subterfuge. Miller
Speech
Apology for a Short Speech, An. Al-Bayati
Effort at Speech between Two People. Rukeyser
My Voice. Guglielminetti
Overworked Elocutionist, An. Wells
See also **Screams; Talk.**
Spelling
I before E. *Unknown*
Principal and Principle. *Unknown*
Spelling Bees
Banananananananana. Cole
Spender, Stephen
To Stephen Spender. Corsellis
Spenser, Edmund
To Spenser. Reynolds
Upon Master Edmund Spenser. Beaumont
Vision upon This Conceit of the Fairy Queen, A. *Fr.* Commendatory Verses to Edmund Spenser's Fairy Queen. Ralegh
Spenser, Edmund ("Colin Clout")
To the Most Excellent and Learned Shepherd, Colin Clout. *Fr.* Chloris. Smith
Sphinx
Myth. Rukeyser
Sphinx, The. Brownell
Sphinx, The. Emerson
Sphinx Speaks, The. Saltus

Spider Webs
Spider Web. Dobyns
Spiders
Arachne. Cooke
Arachne. Empson
Broken, The. Merwin
Design. Frost
Discoveries in Arizona. Wright
Geese, The. Graham
I Would Visit Him in the Corner. Rios
Image, The. Fuller
In the Woman Arms of the Ground. Rios
Incey Wincey Spider. *Unknown*
Mr. Edwards and the Spider. Lowell
Mrs. Spider. Livingston
Noiseless Patient Spider, A. Whitman
Parson's Pleasure. Higgs
Shower of Cobwebs, A. White
Spider. Basho
Spider, The. Coffin
Spider, The. Eberhart
Spider. Farber
Spider. Farooqi
Spider, The. Littleton
Spider, The. Michizane
Spider and the Fly, The. Howitt
Spider and the Ghost of the Fly, The.
  Lindsay
Spider Dream. Hall
Spider holds a silver ball, The. Dickinson
Spider, World-Spinner. Hall
Spiders. Ackerman
Study of a Spider, The. De Tabley
Tarantula. O Hehir
To a Spider. Southey
To the Spider. Russell
To the Spider in the Crevice behind the Toilet
  Door. Sutherland
Upon a Spider Catching a Fly. Taylor
Spies
Childhood of a Spy. Davis
Foreign Agents. "Ludhianvi"
On Spies. Jonson
Spinning and Spinners
House. Saibara
My Mother Spinning. Olds
Song of the Venetian Silk-Spinners.
  Unknown
Spinning Wheel, The. Klein
Summer Spinning. Saibara
Spinoza, Baruch
Excommunication, The. Ravitch
Spinsters
Coarse Old Maid, The. Volf
Daily Round of the Spinster. Castellanos
Eleanor Rigby. Lennon
Furniture-Maker, The. Waters
I'll Marry Not at All. *Unknown*
Mezzo Cammin. Moffett
Miss Gee. Auden
My Aunt. Holmes
My Mother's Sister. Day Lewis
1955. Weigl
Old Ladies, The. Ellis
Old Maid's Song. *Unknown*
Singles. Waters
Some Foreign Letters. Sexton
Spinster. Plath
Spinster's Lullaby. Miller
Three Sisters. De la Mare
Upon Himself. Herrick
Waiting, the Hallways under Her Skin Thick
  with Dreamchildren. Lifshin
Spiritualists
Plain Song. Raine
Spirituals
Go Down, Moses. *Unknown*
Negro Spiritual. Trott
Negro Spirituals. Benét
O Black and Unknown Bards. Johnson
Swing Low, Sweet Chariot. *Unknown*

Spittoons
Brass Spittoons. Hughes
Spohr, Ludwig
Violinist, The. Lampman
Sports
First Practice. Gildner
Frisbee. Humphries
Heaps on Heaps. *Fr.* A Match at Football.
  Concanen
In the Spring. Hall
We Used to Play. Welch
Where fair Sabrina's wand'ring currents flow.
  Fr. The Bowling-Green. Somervile
American Sports Poems (ASP). R. R.
  Knudson *and* May Swenson, comps.
This Sporting Life (TSL). Emilie Buchwald
  and Ruth Roston, eds.
See also **Athletes; Games;** *and names of*
  individual sports.
Spring
Abishag. Fichman
Above the cascade running [*or* tumbling] down
  the rocks. *Fr.* Manyo Shu. Shiki
Admonition for Spring. MacKay
After Dark Vapours. Keats
All over the meadow. *Fr.* Manyo Shu.
  Takata
Among Old Houses. Dallas
Among the Myriad Voices of the Spring.
  Santayana
Answer to a Child's Question. Coleridge
April. Teasdale
April. Thompson
April. Wright
April, 1885. Bridges
April 5, 1974. Wilbur
April Rain Song. Hughes
As Spring the Winter Doth Succeed.
  Bradstreet
At my mountain home. Tonna
Autumnal Spring Song. Miller
Baby Seed Song. Nesbit
Backward Spring, A. Hardy
Bee! I'm expecting you! Dickinson
Blossoming plum. Teika
Budding Spring. Lindsay
Budding-Time Too Brief. Stein
Butterflies. *Fr.* Twelve Miscellaneous Poems
  on the Fang Garden. Chang Yü
Chanted Calendar, A. *Fr.* Balder. Dobell
Cherry Blossoms at Shiga, The. Kaneyoshi
Cloud, The. Shelley
Cold Spring, A. Bishop
Come, Love, Let's Walk. *Unknown*
Coming. Larkin
Coming of Spring, The. Perry
Coming of Spring, The. Ray
Darling! Because My Blood Can Sing.
  Cummings
Days Too Short. Davies
Delight in the High-Flying Orioles. Mao
  Wen-hsi
Depression before Spring. Stevens
Dying Child, The. Clare
Eager Spring. Bottomley
Earliest Spring. Levertov
Early Spring. Bibb
Early Spring. Keyes
Earth in Spring, The. Halevi
Easter; or, Spring-Time. Moorer
Echoing [*or* Ecchoing] Green, The. *Fr.*
  Songs of Innocence. Blake
Enkindled Spring, The. Lawrence
Even the bird calls. Tamekane
Even the frog's voices. Kogon
Farewell Frost; or, Welcome the Spring.
  Herrick
February's Forgotten Mitts. Knister
Fight of the Year, The. McGough
First Day of Spring, The. Pien Kung

First Julep, The. Carman
First Sight. Larkin
First Spring Day, The. Rossetti
First Spring Morning. Bridges
For Jane Myers. Glück
For, lo, the winter is past. *Fr.* The Song of
  Solomon.
For Spring. Jones
Four Little Foxes. Sarett
Four Sweet Months, The. Herrick
From today forward. Tamekane
Georgian Spring. Campbell
Gesse Departing at Early Dusk. Kenko
Good-by My Winter Suit. Bodecker
Green Song. Booth
Hark! Hark! the Lark. *Fr.* Cymbeline.
  Shakespeare
Here We Come a-Piping. *Unknown*
Home Thoughts from Abroad. Browning
Hope and Faith. Peretz
How Many Heavens. Sitwell
Huge gate and its heavy doors, A. *Fr.*
  Eighty-seven Hokku. Buson
I crossed the spring mountains. Tsurayuki
I dreaded that first robin, so. Dickinson
Ice has vanished—don't be left behind. *Fr.*
  Fifteen Hokku. Shiba Sonome
Idyl of Spring, An. Ray
If I could have my way. Tameyo
If only the world. Tonna
Immortal Springtime and Its Tokens. *Fr.*
  Grandeza Mexicana. Balbuena
In a Spring Still Not Written Of. Wallace
In a Town Garden. Mattam
In dawn's first light. Chikako
In front of my eyes. Chikako
In just-/ Spring when the world is mud.
  Cummings
In my mountain home. Tonna
In Springtime. Kipling
In the fields of spring. *Unknown*
In the Spring. *Fr.* Locksley Hall. Tennyson
In the tranquil sun of spring. *Fr.* Manyo
  Shu. Yakamochi
It's Spring Returning, It's Spring and Love.
  Unknown
It's the start of spring, they say. *Fr.* A
  Compendium of Good Tanka. Teika
June. Ledwidge
Last Snow. Young
Late Spring, A. Scully
Late Spring: A Heaving, a Turning. Gill
Laughing Song. *Fr.* Songs of Innocence.
  Blake
Lawyer's Invocation to Spring, The.
  Brownell
Lenten Is [*or* Ys] Come [with Love to
  Toune]. *Unknown*
Letter to His Friend Isaac, A. Halevi
Light exists in spring, A. Dickinson
Lines Written in Early Spring. Wordsworth
Little Madness in the spring, A. Dickinson
Love Likened to Clouds. Tamesada
Lumber of Spring. Ridler
Lyric to Spring. Stilwell
Magdalen Walks. Wilde
Magic Piper, The. Marsh
Manifold Little Hills. Ho Ning
May 10th. Kumin
Miracle. Bailey
Miss Euphemia. Ransom
Moon in the garden. Tamekane
Moorburn in Spring. *Unknown*
Mountain winds, The. Tamesuke
My mind is made up. Tamekane
Natural Theology, A. Whitehead
New Hampshire. *Fr.* Landscapes. Eliot
Northern Spring, A. Baro
Not in Heaven. Smith
Now fades the last long streak of snow. *Fr.*
  In Memoriam A. H. H. Tennyson

Now the Lusty Spring [Is Here] *Fr.* The Tragedy of Valentinian. Fletcher
Ode on the Spring, An. Gray
Ode to Spring. Brooks
Off at Tatsuta/ white clouds are piling up. Teika
On a Bank [*or* Banck] asl I Sat [*or* Sate] a-Fishing; a Description of the Spring. Wotton
On an evening/ aglow with the crimson. Tamekane
On spring fields there was only snow. *Fr.* Fifty-one Tanka. Izumi
On the fine new robes. Tameko
On this spring night. Fujwara no Teika
One Morning When the Rain-Birds Call. Roberts
Page's Road Song, A. Percy
Prayer for This Day. Flanner
Prayer in Spring, A. Frost
Question, The. Shelley
Relearning the Language of April. Kumin
Response. Bethell
Return to Spring. Mastin
Rising sun casts the same light, The. *Fr.* Eighty-four Tanka. Teika
Robe of haze is wet at its hem, A. *Fr.* Inutsukuba Shu. *Unknown*
Rondel: "World is taking off her clothes, The." Kennedy
Round and round time turns. Tamekane
Sadness in Spring. *Unknown*
Saint-Henri Spring. Acorn
Screw Spring. Hoffman
Seed Leaves. Wilbur
Seeing Spring Off. K'ang Yu-wei
Shapes of swallows. Kogon
Sixth-Month Song in the Foothills. Snyder
Small Pavilion. *Fr.* To Dispel the Cold: Two Poems on Spring. Hung Liang-chi
Snow is all gone, The. Tameshige
So cold is this spring. Masayori
Song of Spring. Keats
Song of Spring. Wu Chün
Song of the Wine Spring. Mao Wen-hsi
Soote Season, The. Surrey
Sparrows twitter, The. Hanazono
Sprin' Fevah. Dandridge
Spring, The. Barnes
Spring. *Fr.* Songs of Innocence. Blake
Spring. Bye
Spring, The. Carew
Spring. *Fr.* The Four Seasons in the Mountains. Chang Yü
Spring, The. *Fr.* The Mistress. Cowley
Spring. Hogan
Spring. Hopkins
Spring. Kuskin
Spring. Larkin
Spring. *Fr.* The Biglow Papers: 2d Series, No. VI. Lowell
Spring. Millay
Spring. Ridge
Spring. Rodgers
Spring. Rossetti
Spring. Stewart
Spring. Still
Spring. Tucker
Spring. Willis
Spring; a Formal Ode. Tyuchev
Spring Air. Derwood
Spring and All. Williams
Spring and Death. Hopkins
Spring and Fall. Hopkins
Spring at Arm's Length. Vandersee
Spring at Fort Okanogan. Wilson
Spring at Nant Dywelan. Jones
Spring come again, after moody. Ryokan
Spring Coming. Ammons
Spring Doggerel. Coghill
Spring Goeth All in White. Bridges
Spring Has Come. *Unknown*

Spring has come again, The. Ghalib
Spring in New Hampshire. McKay
Spring in the Land. Rübner
Spring in Virginia. Wilson
Spring in War-Time. Teasdale
Spring Is. Katz
Spring Is a Looping-free Time. Robbins
Spring Is at Work with Beginnings of Things. Rose
Spring is coming, spring is coming. *Unknown*
Spring is like a perhaps hand. Cummings
Spring Landscape. La Follette
Spring Morning, A. Clare
Spring Morning. Cornford
Spring Morning. Lawrence
Spring Night. *Fr.* Twelve Miscellaneous Poems on the Fang Garden. Chang Yü
Spring night. *Fr.* Thirty Tanka. Shunzei
Spring Nocturne. Liessin
Spring Oak. Kinnell
Spring of Cities, The. Rokeah
Spring Poem, A. Chikako
Spring Pools. Frost
Spring Quiet. Rossetti
Spring Season of Muddy Roads. Brodsky
Spring Song. Carman
Spring Song. Fallon
Spring Song, A. Howitt
Spring Song. Nahum
Spring Song. O'Brien
Spring Song, A. *Unknown*
Spring Song of the Birds. James I, King of Scotland
Spring, the Sweet Spring. *Fr.* Summer's Last Will and Testament. Nashe
Spring, the Travelling Man. Letts
Spring Voices. MacNeice
Spring Was Begging to Be Born. Tate
Spring Will Come, The. Lowry
Spring's Arrival. *Unknown*
Spring's Delights. Ashby-Sterry
Stay, Spring. Young
Sunny Spring. Hagiwara Sakutaro
Sweet o' the Year, The. Meredith
Thaw. Thomas
Thaw in the City. Lipsitz
There Will Come Soft Rains. Teasdale
Things Seen on Spring Days. Yüan Mei
This is the time when fresh, green leaves. Mir
Those cherry blossoms. Ietaka
Thou hearest the nightingale begin the song of spring. *Fr.* Milton. Blake
Though I know in time. *Fr.* Kokin Shu. Tsurayuki
To be in a place for spring and not have lived its winter. *Fr.* Brother Jonathan, Brother Kafka. O'Sullivan
To Bring Spring. Keithley
To John Keats, Poet, at Springtime. Cullen
To My Sister. Wordsworth
To Spring. Blake
To Spring. Smith
To the Spring Sun. Laughton
Trico's Song. *Fr.* Alexander and Campaspe. Lyly
Twilight in Middle March, A. Ledwidge
Vernal Equinox. Johnston
Waking Up. *Unknown*
Welcome to Spring. Thompson
Well Pleaseth Me the Sweet Time of Easter. Bertrans de Born
When a thousand birds. *Fr.* Kokin Shu. *Unknown*
When, after holing up for winter, the spring comes. *Fr.* Manyo Shu. Nukada
When daffodils begin to peer. *Fr.* The Winter's Tale. Shakespeare
When Daisies Pied [and Violets Blue] *Fr.* Love's Labour's Lost. Shakespeare

When faces called flowers float out of the ground. Cummings
When, loosened from the winter's bonds. *Fr.* Manyo Shu. Nukada
When Spring came,/ Leaves grew with a green fresh. *Unknown*
When spring comes. *Fr.* Thirty Tanka. Shunzei
When the hills of spring. *Fr.* Manyo Shu. "Owari"
When the Hounds of Spring [Are on Winter's Traces]. *Fr.* Atalanta in Calydon. Swinburne
When the spring comes. *Fr.* Manyo Shu. Nukada
When with the first month comes the spring. *Fr.* Manyo Shu. Ki
Winding Pond. *Fr.* To Dispel the Cold: Two Poems on Spring. Hung Liang-chi
Winter's Cold. Rodgers
Written in March. Wordsworth
Year's at the Spring, The. *Fr.* Pippa Passes. Browning
Year's Awakening, The. Hardy
Yellow Violet, The. Bryant

Springfield, Illinois
On the Building of Springfield. Lindsay
Springfield, Massachusetts
Arsenal at Springfield, The. Longfellow
Springfield, Ohio
Riot, A. Linden
Springs
Enchanted Spring, The. Darley
Spring, The. Fyleman
Spruce Trees
Proud Little Spruce Fir. Kirby
Spruce. George
Squash (fruit)
Squash in Blossom. Francis
Squash (sport)
After a Game of Squash. Albert
Civilities. Whitbread
Game Resumed. Lattimore
Squid
Squid. Blumenthal
Squirrels
Abandoned House, The. Hubbell
Curliest Thing, The. *Unknown*
Fable: Mountain and the Squirrel, The. Emerson
Gray Squirrel, The. Wolfe
Migration of the Grey Squirrels, The. Howitt
Mr. Squirrel. Julian
My Little Neighbor. Mason
On a Squirrel Crossing the Road in Autumn, in New England. Eberhart
Sacrifice of a Red Squirrel. Langland
Squirrel, The. Barakat
Squirrel, The. Howell
Squirrel, The. Howitt
Squirrel, The. Nash
Squirrel, The. *Unknown*
Squirrel in the Rain. Frost
Squirrel near Library. Taggard
To a Squirrel at Kyle-na-no. Yeats
Whisky Frisky. *Unknown*
Sri Lanka
Auschwitz from Colombo. Ranasinghe
Ceylon. Junzaburo
Coppersmith. Murphy
Letters & Other Worlds. Ondaatje
Stagecoaches
Is it the horn that, on this holy day. *Fr.* The Village Patriarch. Elliott
Jolly Waggoner, The. *Unknown*
Stairs
Halfway Down. Milne
On the Banisters. Gibbs
Stairs. Herford

Stalin, Joseph
Less Nonsense. Herbert
Stalin. Lowell
Stalin Epigram, The. Mandelstam
Stamp Collecting. *See* **Philately.**
Standish, Miles
Courtship of Miles Standish, The.
Longfellow
Stanford, Frank
Elegy for Frank Stanford. Lux
Stanley, Sir Henry Morton
Stanley Meets Mutesa. Rubadiri
Starfish
Daybreak. Kinnell
Secrets. Pack
Starfish, The. Coffin
Starfish. Welles
Stark, John
Marching Song of Stark's Men, The. Hale
Starlings
Against Starlings. Plumly
Manoeuvre, The. Williams
Plague of Starlings, A. Hayden
Starling, The. Buchanan
Stars
Ah! Why, because the Dazzling Sun. Brontë
Asteroid Lil. Sneyd
Baby Toes. Sandburg
Beauty of the Stars, The. Ibn Ezra
Bright Star, Would I Were Steadfast as Thou
Art! Keats
Canopus. Taylor
Choose Something like a Star. Frost
Counting. Johnson
Country Stars. Meredith
Daisies. Young
Darkness. Campbell
Diving into the Wreck. Rich
Dying Lamp, The. Li Chien
El Hombre. Williams
Elk Uncovers the Heavens, The. Bensko
Es Stehen Unbeweglich. Heine
Escape at Bedtime. Stevenson
Evening Star. Barker
Fallen Star, The. Darley
Falling Star, The. Teasdale
From the Milky Way. Laaber
Great Bear, The. Hollander
I sat in my chamber yesternight. Graves
I see the golden hunter go. *Fr.* Songs of the
Sea-Children. Carman
If the Stars Should Fall. Allen
Imagination of the Retina, The. Compton
In the Field. Wilbur
It Is the Stars That Govern Us. Magee
Kitchen Window. MacDonald
La Plata, Missouri: Clear November Night.
Barnes
Lost Lane. Wellesley
Lucifer in Starlight. Meredith
Man's Littleness in Presence of the Stars.
White
Martial Cadenza. Stevens
My Star. Browning
North Star, The. Morris-Jones
Nova. Jeffers
"Nox Nocti Indicat Scientiam." *Fr.* Castara.
Habington
On the Beach at Night. Whitman
Once you shone among the living as the
morning star. Plato
One Reason for Stars. Butler
Partial View of a Supernova. Garey
Planetarium. Rich
Pleiades, The. Coatsworth
Pole Star, The. Coslett
Procession. Booth
Song: "How sweet I roam'd from field to
field." Blake
Speculation. Nemerov

Star, The. Redpath
Star, The. Taylor
Star Drifter Grounded, The. Boston
Star Drill. Moore
Star-Gazer. MacNeice
Star Song. Ray
Star-Talk. Graves
Starbirth. Goldbarth
Starlight. Meredith
Starlight Night, The. Hopkins
Starry Host, The. *Fr.* God and the Soul.
Spalding
Stars, The. Dodge
Stars. Hayden
Stars. Moss
Stars. Soto
Stars. Takenaka Iku
Stars. Teasdale
Stars Are Glittering in the Frosty Sky, The.
Heavysege
Stars glowed red in leaf-still weather, The.
Fet
Stars, I Have Seen Them Fall. Housman
Stars in Apple Cores. Shaw
Stars of the superior class. *Fr.* The Stars.
Smart
Stars over the Dordogne. Plath
Stars Wheel in Purple. Doolittle
Summer Stars. Sandburg
Suns in a skein, the uncut stones of night.
Fr. Mythological Sonnets. Fuller
To the Evening Star. *Fr.* Poetical Sketches.
Blake
To the Evening Star. Campbell
Waiting Both. Hardy
When I Heard the Learn'd Astronomer.
Whitman
When Sun Doth Rise. Williams
Winter Heavens. Meredith
Wishing Poem. *Unknown*
You Learned the Stars. Jackson
See also **Astronomy and Astronomers;
Astrophysics; Constellations; Sky.**

Statistics
Meditation on Statistical Method.
Cunningham

Statue of Liberty. *See* **Liberty, Statue of.**

Statues
After Plotinus. Stafford
Angels, The. Eberhart
Archaic Torso of Apollo. Rilke
By the Statue of King Charles at Charing
Cross. Johnson
Christmas Eve under Hooker's Statue.
Lowell
Colossus, The. Plath
Duke of York's Statue, The. Landor
Etruscan Statue. Raab
Figures, The. Creeley
Frozen Hero, The. Vance
Green Mountain Boy. Smyth
Haiku: "Carved into Buddha's form." *Fr.*
One Hundred Haiku in Free Form. Hosai
I Carried Statues. Nagy
Letter to Statues. Brinnin
Marble Statuette Harpist. Allen
O God! O Montreal! Butler
On a Statue of Sir Arthur Sullivan. Hamilton
Only Statues Don't Shy Away. Gar
Ozymandias [*or* Ozymandias of Egypt *or*
Sonnet: Ozymandias]. Shelley
Rider Victory, The. Muir
Spanish Lions, The. McGinley
Statue, The. Creeley
Statue, The. Grilikhes
Statue, The. Roseveare
Statue of Lorenzo de' Medici, The. Nesmith
Statue of Medusa, The. Drummond
Statues. Nagy
Statues. Raine

Statues. Wilbur
Statues, The. Yeats
Statues in the Public Gardens, The.
Nemerov
Tale of the Assyrian Statue. Al-Buraikan
Venus of Milo, The. Ray
Wayside Virgin, The. Mitchell
Steak
Thoughts of Loved Ones. Fishback
Steam Baths. *See* **Baths and Bathing.**
Steam Rollers
To a Steam Roller. Moore
Steam Shovels
Steam Shovel. Malam
Steamers. *See* **Ships.**
Steel
Bar of steel—it is only, A. *Fr.* Smoke and
Steel. Sandburg
My Father's Garden. Wagoner
Prayers of Steel. Sandburg
Smoke and Steel, *sels.* Sandburg
See also **Iron.**
Steel Bands
Pans at Carnival. Beissel
Steeples
Steeple-Jack, The. Moore
To a Solitary Disciple. Williams
Steers. *See* **Oxen.**
Stein, Gertrude
They Don't Speak English in Paris. Nash
Stenographers
Stenographers, The. Page
See also **Scribes; Secretaries.**
Stepfathers and Stepmothers
Second Madrigal, The. Swirszczynska
She Does Not Remember. Swirszczynska
Stephen, Saint
Feast o' Saint [*or* St.] Stephen, The. Sawyer
Feast of Stephen, The. Nichols
St. Stephen's Day. Dickinson
Sterne, Laurence
Epitaph on Laurence Sterne. Garrick
Stevedores. *See* **Longshoremen.**
Stevens, Wallace
So Long? Stevens. *Fr.* Dream Songs.
Berryman
Stevenson, Robert Louis
Apparition. *Fr.* In Hospital. Henley
Still Lifes
Biography of a Still Life. Eaton
Still Life. Williams
Stockholm, Sweden
Dear Old Stockholm. Young
Old Champagne Glass. Vliet
Stockholm. Vliet
Stockmen
Andy's Gone with Cattle. Lawson
Ballad of the Drover. Lawson
Dying Stockman, The. *Unknown*
Harry Pearce. Campbell
Man from Snowy River, The. Paterson
My Mate Bill. Gibson
Sick Stockrider, The. Gordon
Stoicism
Old Stoic, The. Brontë
Stoic. Durrell
Stonecutters
To the Stone-Cutters. Jeffers
Stonehenge, England
In Love, at Stonehenge. *Fr.* The Angel in
the House. Patmore
Salisbury Plain and Stonehenge. *Fr.* Guilt
and Sorrow. Wordsworth
Stonehenge. *Fr.* Polyolbion. Drayton
Stonehenge. *Fr.* The Seven Wonders of
England. Sidney
To My Friend, Dr. Charleton, on His Learned
and Useful Works; and More Particularly

This of Stone-Heng, by Him Restored to the True Founders. Dryden
Written at Stonehenge. Warton

Stones and Rocks
Apologia pro Vita Sua. Ammons
Beach Stones. Moore
Black Rock of Kiltearn. Young
Crag, The. Pagaza
Crystals like Blood. "MacDiarmid"
Cutting Edge, The. Levine
Detail, The. Corman
Devastation. Russell
Hard, but you can polish it. *Fr.* Things. Justice
How happy is the little stone. Dickinson
I've Got a Home in That Rock. Patterson
Minerals of Cornwall, Stones of Cornwall. Redgrove
Mossy Stane, The. Nicoll
Mountain Sculpture. Will
Naskeag. Corn
Path among the Stones, The. Kinnell
Rock Climbing. Cooper
Serenity in Stones, The. Ortiz
Silica Carbonate Rock. Berry
Stanes. Glen
Stone, The. Blackburn
Stone. Justice
Stone. Simic
Stone, The. Vaughan
Symbolum. Goethe
Tergvinder's Stone. Merwin
This Is My Rock. McCord
Thyme Flowering among Rocks. Wilbur
To the Stone-Cutters. Jeffers
Two Voices in a Meadow. Wilbur
Why Stone Does Not Sing by Itself. Endrezze-Danielson

Stonington, Battle of
Battle of Stonington on the Seaboard of Connecticut, The. Freneau

Stony Point, Battle of (1779)
Storming of Stony Point, The. Guiterman
Wayne at Stony Point. Scollard

Storms
Approach of the Storm, The. *Unknown*
Ballad of the Tempest. Fields
Beginning to Squall. Swenson
Black Cloud, The. Davies
Brainstorm. Nemerov
City-Storm. Monro
Eastern Tempest. Blunden
Epitaph Ending in And, The. Stafford
Equinox, The. Heyward
First Things First. Auden
First Winter Storm. Everson
Found in a Storm. Stafford
Gale in April. Jeffers
Golden Hour, The. *Fr.* Lalla Rookh. Moore
Hatteras Calling. Aiken
Hurricane, The. Freneau
In Cold Storm Light. Silko
In the pines, a storm. Tameko
It. Snyder
It sounded as if the streets were running. Dickinson
It Will Pour. Leyeles
Late Light. Blunden
Little Exercise at 4. A.M. Bishop
Lord Ullin's Daughter. Campbell
Low Barometer. Bridges
Mightier Storms than This. Santayana
Miriam Tazewell. Ransom
Monsoon History. Lim
New Year's Blizzard, The. Su Tung-p'o
Night Storm. Simms
Offering to the Storm. Césaire
On a Sea-Storm nigh the Coast. Steere
Safe. Walker
Snow-Storm, The. Emerson
Snow Storm, The. Fordham

Spring Storm. Miller
Storm, The. Jennings
Storm, The. Patmore
Storm, The. Shanks
Storm, The. Voigt
Storm, The. Wallace
Storm, The. Williams
Storm. Wright
Storm at Sea, A. *Unknown*
Storm Cone, The. Kipling
Storm Fear. Frost
Storm from the East, A. Whittemore
Storm in April, A. Wilbur
Storm in Summer, A. Blunt
Storm is over, the land hushes to rest, The. Bridges
Storm Warning. Moss
Storm Warnings. Rich
Storm Windows. Nemerov
Stormy Night in Autumn. Chu Shu-chen
Summer Storm. Johnson
Sword, The. Anis
Tempest, The. Smith
Tempest, The. *Unknown*
Tempest, The. Zaturenska
That Is All I Heard. "Yehoash"
Thunder mutters louder & more loud, The. Clare
Thunderstorm, A. Lampman
Thunderstorm in Town, A. Hardy
Tornado. Stafford
Traveler, The. Anis
Vision of the Sea, A. Shelley
West Palm Beach Storm, The. *Unknown*
Wet Night, A. Ryan
Wind begun to knead [or rock] the grass, The. Dickinson
Wind begun to rock the grass, The. Dickinson
Wind Took Up the Northern Things, The. Dickinson
See also **Blizzards.**

Story Poems
Best Loved Story Poems (BeLS). Walter E. Thwing, ed.
Modern Ballads and Story Poems (MoBS). Charles Causley, ed.
100 More Story Poems (OnMSP). Elinor Parker, ed.
Oxford Book of Narrative Verse, The (OBNV). Iona Opie *and* Peter Opie, eds.
Story Poems, New and Old (StPo). William Cole, ed.

Storytelling and Storytellers
Devil's Advice to Story-Tellers, The. Graves
Kinder- und Hausmärchen. Alderson
Lost Anchors. Robinson
Martha. De la Mare
Mythology. Thompson
No, no! I say,/ But still you command. *Fr.* Manyo Shu. Shihi
Request Number. Sprod
So They Went Deeper into the Forest. Daniells
Story Tellers Summer, 1980. Francisco
To Juan at the Winter Solstice. Graves

Stowe, Harriet Beecher
Greeting. Ray
Harriet Beecher Stowe. Dunbar

Strafford, Thomas Wentworth, 1st Earl of
Epitaph on the Earl of Strafford. Cleveland

Strangers
Both Strangers. al-Zahawi
Encounter in a Glass. Wright
L'étrangère. Milosz
Robert, Who Is Often a Stranger to Himself. Brooks
Stranger, A. Csoori
What Is It Makes the Stranger? Hyde

Strasbourg, France
O Strassburg. *Unknown*

Strawberries
Millions of Strawberries. Taggard
Original Strawberry. Willard
Strawberries. Morgan
Strawberries in November. Neilson
Strawberry, The. Johnson
Strawberry Shrub, The. Millay
Wild Strawberries. Graves
Wild strawberries/ fatten. Moore
Wild Strawberry. Kenny

Strawberry Jam
Strawberry Jam. Justus

Streams. *See* **Brooks and Streams.**

Street Performers
Fire Breather, Mexico City, The. Jacinto
Street Musicians. Ashbery

Streetcars
Burned Bridge, The. Stone
Foundered Tram, The. Monro
Halsted Street Car. Sandburg
Riding on a Streetcar with My Father. Larkin

Streets
Manhole Covers. Shapiro
Prayer: "As I walk through the streets." Flint
Step Away from Them, A. O'Hara
Street, The. Baro
See also **Roads.**

Strength
Be Strong. Babcock
Strength for To-Day. *Unknown*

Strikes and Strikers
Case for the Miners, The. Sassoon
Durham Lock-out, The. *Unknown*
Owslebury Lads, The. *Unknown*
Resignation; an Ode to the Journeyman Shoemakers, sel. "Pindar"
Strike. Belli
Strike, The. *Unknown*
Striking Times. *Unknown*

String
Henry King, Who Chewed Bits of String, and Was Early Cut Off in Dreadful Agonies. Belloc
See also **Rope.**

Striptease
Stripper, The. Probst
Why Rosalie Did It. Miller

Strokes
Ojisan after the Stroke; Three Notes to Himself. Koyama
Paralytic. Plath
Parting. Ammons
Resurrection of the Right Side. Rukeyser
Stroke. Lowery
Strokes. Stafford

Struwwelpeter
Fräulein Reads Instructive Rhymes. Kumin

Stuart, Charles Edward (The Young Pretender)
O'er the Water to Charlie. Burns
Old Scottish Cavalier, The. Aytoun
Will He No Come Back Again? *Unknown*

Stuart, James Ewell Brown ("Jeb")
Obsequies of Stuart. Thompson

Stuart, James Francis Edward (The Old Pretender)
New Song Entitled the Warming Pan, A. *Unknown*

Students
Campus on the Hill, The. Snodgrass
Correspondence School Instructor Says Goodbye to His Poetry Students, The. Kinnell
Discontented Student, The. Tucker
For the Student Strikers. Wilbur
Freshmen. Spacks
Heathen Pass-ee, The. Hilton
In a Spring Still Not Written Of. Wallace
Indian Student; or, Force of Nature, The. Freneau

School Girl, The.   Venable
Schoolboy, The.   *Fr.* Songs of Experience.
   Blake
September, the First Day of School.
   Nemerov
Straying Student, The.   Clarke
Student.   Miles
Student, The.   Moore
Student, The.   *Unknown*
Theme for English B.   Hughes
To the University of Cambridge, in
   New-England.   Wheatley
Tokyo Imperial University Students.   Nakano
   Shigeharu
University Examinations in Egypt.   Enright
Vulture and the Husbandman, The.   Hilton

Stuttering
Stutterer.   Dugan

Stuyvesant, Peter
Peter Stuyvesant's New Year's Call.
   Stedman

Submarines
Diesel and Shale.   Tawney
Mare Liberum.   Van Dyke
U-24 Anchors off New Orleans.   Cassity

Suburban Life
Inspiration.   Knox

Suburbs
Decks.   Phillips
Housewife.   Miles
In the Suburbs.   Simpson
London Suburbs.   *Fr.* Retirement.   Cowper
Long Island Springs.   Moss
Middlesex.   Betjeman
Northern Suburb, A.   Davidson
Sacred Objects.   Simpson
Slough.   Betjeman
Snow in the Suburbs.   Hardy
Soliloquy in the Suburbs, A.   *Unknown*
Suburb, The.   Stevenson
Suburban Song.   Riddell
Suburban Sonnet.   Harwood
Suburban Wife's Song.   Hutchinson
Three-handed Fugue.   Gotlieb
To an American Poet Just Dead.   Wilbur
Ways of Conquest.   Levertov

Subways
Boy Who Smells like Cocoa, A.   Hershon
Curse, The.   Hollander
Going Uptown to Visit Miriam.   Cruz
In a Station of the Metro.   Pound
In the Subway.   *Fr.* New York.   Leyeles
Métro Balard-Charenton.   Handke
Metropolitan Railway, The.   Betjeman
Once-over, The.   Blackburn
One Year to Life on the Grand Central
   Shuttle.   Lorde
Queen, The.   Pitchford
Rapid Transit.   Agee
Sing a Song of Subways.   Merriam
Subway, The.   Tate
Subway Rush Hour.   Hughes
Subway Wind.   McKay
Things to Do If You Are a Subway.   Katz
Tubes.   Mollin
Tunnel, The.   *Fr.* The Bridge.   Crane
Underground, The.   Boas
Virginal, A.   Pound
"Watch Your Step!"   Halpern

Success
After Publication of Under the Volcano.
   Lowry
Back to Griggsby's Station.   Riley
Don't Quit.   *Unknown*
Failure and Success.   Gilder
Farmer John.   Trowbridge
Game of Life, The.   Saxe
If.   Kipling
It Couldn't Be Done.   Guest
Kindly Unhitch That Star, Buddy.   Nash
Names.   Enright

Robert Whitmore.   Davis
Success!   Braley
Success.   *Unknown*
Success is counted sweetest.   Dickinson
Success Story.   Winch
Thy Best.   Cole
To a Friend Whose Work Has Come to
   Nothing.   Yeats
Will.   Wilcox
Winners, The.   *Fr.* The Story of the
   Gadsbys.   Kipling

Sudan
Fuzzy-Wuzzy.   Kipling

Suez Canal
Reflexions on the Seizure of the Suez, and on
   a Proposal to Line the Banks of That Canal
   with Bill.   Nemerov

Suffering
After.   Grayson
Alajire, we ask you to be patient.
All-sufficient Christ, The.   Lubke
Amen.   Browning
And Yet.   Sloan
Bridge, The.   Vala
Convinced by Sorrow.   *Fr.* The Cry of the
   Human.   Browning
Guide and Friend.   *Unknown*
How Can I Smile?   Hodgdon
I Do Not Ask Thee, Lord.   *Unknown*
I Have Always Found It So.   Bell
Jesus Understands.   *Unknown*
May God Give Strength.   Van Wynen
Musée des Beaux Arts.   Auden
Our Light Afflictions.   *Unknown*
Revelation.   Cook
School of Sorrow, The.   Hamilton
Security.   Sangster
Some Time We'll Understand.   Cornelius
Song of Agony.   Lemos
Suffering.   Nobile
There is no chapel on the day.   *Fr.* The
   Ballad of Reading Gaol.   Wilde
Warp and Woof.   Halbisch
Whipping, The.   Hayden
Wind Suffers of Blowing, The.   Riding
Winter Has Come.   Vala
See also **Pain.**

Suffern, New York
House with Nobody in It, The.   Kilmer

Suffolk, England
Evening by the Sea.   Swinburne
Peter Grimes at Aldeburgh.   *Fr.* The
   Borough: Peter Grimes.   Crabbe
Suffolk.   *Fr.* By the North Sea.   Swinburne
Suffolk Shore, The.   *Fr.* The Borough.
   Crabbe
Where Dunwich Used to Be.   *Fr.* By the
   North Sea.   Swinburne

Suffolk, William de la Pole, Duke of
Now is the fox drevin to hole! hoo to hym,
   hoo, hoo!   *Unknown*

Suffrage.   *See* **Voting and Voters; Woman
   Suffrage.**

Sugar
Little Brother's Secret.   Mansfield
Rehearsal.   Dabydeen
Sugar Cane.   Charles

Sugar Cane
Virtues of the cane must now be sung, The.
   Fr. Barbados.   Weekes

Suibhne, King
I perched for rest, and imagined.   *Fr.*
   Sweeney Astray.   Heaney
I stirred wet sand and gathered myself.   *Fr.*
   Sweeney Redivivus.   Heaney
Sweeney kept going until he reached the
   church at/ Swim-two-birds.   *Fr.* Sweeney
   Astray.   Heaney
Sweetness of Nature, The.   *Unknown*

Suicide
Advice of an Efficiency Expert, The.   Young

After the Surprising Conversions.   Lowell
Autumn.   Shapcott
Ballade of Suicide, A.   Chesterton
Beaver Moon—The Suicide of a Friend.
   Oliver
Before Suicide.   "Ludhianvi"
Bridge of Sighs, The.   Hood
Call It a Good Marriage.   Graves
Caroline of Edinboro' Town.   *Unknown*
Cartwheels.   Smith
Center of Attention, The.   Hoffman
Citizen's Dissertation on His Neighborhood,
   A.   Shlonsky
Death of Lovers, The.   Baudelaire
Despairing Lover, The.   Walsh
Dispute over Suicide, A.   *Unknown*
Edge.   Plath
Elegy for a Schoolmate.   O'Sullivan
Epigram: "When would-be suicides in purpose
   fail."   Hood
Ever since the day he started.   *Fr.* Manyo
   Shu.   Minaka
Faithless Nelly Gray.   Hood
Felo de Se.   Blackburn
Felo de Se.   Scannell
Fish Food.   Wheelwright
For Black Poets Who Think of Suicide.
   Knight
Good Creatures, Do You Love Your Lives.
   Housman
Hanged Man, The.   Simon
Hardy Perennial.   Eberhart
Hart Crane.   Symons
He got his friends to agree to shoot him
   standing against a stone wall.   *Fr.* Leaving
   the Door Open.   Ignatow
How It Is.   Kumin
I Am Going to Sleep.   Storni
I Am Going to Sleep (Suicide Poem).   Storni
Immigration Act of 1924, The.   Mar
In Memoriam.   Ungaretti
Is It Well-Lighted, Papa?   Bertram
Japanese Girl with Red Table.   Dobyns
Jewish Girls, The.   Lask
Justice Is Reason Enough.   Wakoski
Lady Lazarus.   Plath
Lament for Those Who Hanged Themselves,
   A.   Cheng Chen
Leap, The.   Dickey
Mill, The.   Robinson
My desolation does begin to make.   *Fr.*
   Antony and Cleopatra.   Shakespeare
Newcomer's Wife, The.   Hardy
Of Late.   Starbuck
Of One Self-slain.   Towne
Of Suicide.   Berryman
On the Death of Francisco López Merino.
   Borges
On the Suicide of the Refugee W. B.   Brecht
On the Threshold.   *Unknown*
Passion.   Prospere
Poem on the Suicide of My Teacher.   Stroud
Poor Shammes of Berditchev, The.   Ratner
Portrait, The.   Kunitz
Résumé.   Parker
Richard Cory.   Robinson
Sacrifice, The.   Bidart
Second Year, The.   Montgomery
Seeing Off a Friend.   Dobyns
Sentiment.   Chatterton
She Was Poor but She Was Honest.
   Unknown
Shooting, The.   Tohe
Shot? So Quick, So Clean an Ending?   *Fr.* A
   Shropshire Lad.   Housman
Six Feet Under.   Hale
Song for a Suicide.   Hughes
Springboard, The.   MacNeice
Still Life.   Angelotti
Suicide.   *Fr.* In Hospital.   Henley
Suicide.   Lowell
Suicide, The.   MacNeice

Suicide, The. Oates
Suicide. Stevenson
Suicide. Walker
Suicide in [the] Trenches. Sassoon
Suicide of Atzesivano Disciple of Buddha,
   The. Sikelianos
Suicide off Egg Rock. Plath
Suicide's Note. Hughes
Then both ourselves and seed at once to free.
   Fr. Paradise Lost. Milton
To be, or not to be, that is the question. Fr.
   Hamlet. Shakespeare
To D——, Dead by Her Own Hand.
   Nemerov
To Friends Who Have Also Considered
   Suicide. Webb
To Helen in a Huff. Willis
To this world, farewell. Fr. The Love
   Suicides at Sonezaki. Chikamatsu
   Monzaemon
Two Views of a Cadaver Room. Plath
Wanting to Die. Sexton
Way Down, The. Sandeen
Weeds. Su Shao-lien
Who travels by the wearie wandring way.
   Fr. The Faerie Queene. Spenser
Wilhelm Stekel Gives Up Life. Fr.
   Psychoanalysis. Teller
Winter Drought. Ryan
Woman Hanging from the Thirteenth Floor
   Window, The. Harjo
X, Oh X. Simpson

Sullivan, John L.
John L. Sullivan Enters Heaven. Frost

Sumac
Sumach Leaves, The. Very

Summer
As imperceptibly as grief. Dickinson
At a Summer Hotel. Gardner
August. Thaxter
Beginning, The. Stevens
Calm. Hass
Comfort of the Fields. Lampman
Country Summer. Adams
Ear Is Not Deaf. Dayton
End of Summer. Kunitz
End of Summer, The. Millay
End-of-Summer Poem. Bennett
Fair Summer Droops. Fr. Summer's Last
   Will and Testament. Nashe
First of summer, lovely sight. Unknown
For Summer's Here. Barnett
Four Sweet Months, The. Herrick
Full early in the morning. Unknown
Ghetto Summer School. Worth
Gold Medal. Soupault
Harvest, The. Henderson
He lights a lamp at such an awkward spot.
   Fr. Inutsukuba Shu. Unknown
Heat. Lampman
Here's flowers for you. Fr. The Winter's
   Tale. Shakespeare
High Summer. Jones
High Summer on the Mountains. Davies
Impression of Early Summer, An. Hagiwara
   Sakutaro
In Fields of Summer. Kinnell
In Mourning for the Summer. Tachihara
   Michizo
In the Middle of August. Hirsch
Indian Summer at Land's End. Kunitz
It's summer; then. Onitsura
Knoxville, Tennessee. Giovanni
Late Summer. Kinoshita Yuji
Lines Written in the Dog-Days. Woty
Loch Ossian. Scroggie
Long Summer. Lee
Love. Browning
Love's Rebel. Surrey
Midsummer. Kinsella
Midsummer. Scully
Midsummer. Trowbridge

Midsummer Noon in the Australian Forest, A.
   Harpur
Midsummer Song, A. Gilder
Misericordia. Mead
Musings. Barnes
My Father Paints the Summer. Wilbur
Now summer's come. Fr. Kokin Shu.
   Unknown
Of the Day Estivall. Hume
On a Wet Summer. Bampfylde
Rainy Summer, The. Meynell
Schoolboy, The. Fr. Songs of Experience.
   Blake
"Shall I compare thee to a summer's day?"
   Fr. Sonnets, XVIII. Shakespeare
Soote Season, The. Surrey
Spring has passed away. Fr. Manyo Shu.
   Jito
Spring having passed. Tamesada
Summer. Asch
Summer. Fr. The Four Seasons in the
   Mountains. Chang Yü
Summer. Kulbak
Summer. Rossetti
Summer. Soto
Summer. Wilson
Summer Countries, The. Rago
Summer Dawn. Morris
Summer Day in the Mountains. Li Po
Summer Days. Call
Summer Days. Daniells
Summer Evening. De la Mare
Summer Farm. MacCaig
Summer Haloed. Csoori
Summer ("Home from his morning task the
   swain retreats"). Fr. The Seasons:
   Summer. Thomson
Summer Idyll. Barker
Summer Images. Clare
Summer in England, 1914. Meynell
Summer Magic. Hill
Summer Malison, The. Hopkins
Summer Matures. Johnson
Summer Morning, A. Field
Summer night/ I close my eyes. Tsurayuki
Summer Rentals, The. Halpern
Summer Sabbath. Sampter
Summer Song. Watt
Summer Stars. Sandburg
Summer Storm. Montague
Summer Wind. Bryant
Summer Wisteria. Shotetsu
Summer's Day, A. Hume
Summer's End. Volponi
"Summertime and the Living." Hayden
Taking the Cool to Forget Summer.
   Tamemasa
That Summer. Treece
That Was Summer. Ridlon
There Were Some Summers. Lux
These are the days when birds come back.
   Dickinson
Throstle, The. Tennyson
To Summer. Blake
Too tired to move fast. Teika
Touring. Morton
Wet Summer. Ward
Winter Saint. Ammons

Sumner, Charles
Charles Sumner. Ray

Sumter, Fort, South Carolina
Fight at Sumter, The. Unknown
On Fort Sumter. Unknown
Sumter. Brownell
Sumter. Stedman
Sumter's Band. Simmons
Twilight on Sumter. Stoddard

Sun
Autumn sunlight, The. Shotetsu
Cock-crowing. Vaughan
Dream, or the Type of the Rising Sun, A.
   Adams

Even in the heat. Fr. Manyo Shu.
   Unknown
Fair sun, if you would have me praise your
   light. Fr. Diana. Constable
February Sun. Rodenko
First Sunshine. Okopenko
Follow Thy Fair Sun [Unhappy Shadow].
   Campion
Forecast. Miles
Give Me the Splendid Silent Sun. Whitman
Hint from Voiture. Shenstone
Hot is the sun, so hot the birds complain
   Dabir
Hymn of Apollo. Shelley
Hymn to the Sun. Percy
I'll tell you how the sun rose. Dickinson
In Praise of the Sun. "W."
Indian Summer Day on the Prairie, An.
   Lindsay
It will not shine again. Brontë
Metric Figure. Williams
Monterrey Sun. Reyes
Morning Sun. MacNeice
Narcolepsy. Owen
Noonday Sun and the Shade, The.
   Al-Maghut
Nova. Jeffers
November. Harvey
Ode to the Sun. Bibb
One Morning. Hanlo
Phoebus, Arise. Drummond
Poem to the Sun ("All the Cattle are resting in
   the fields"). Unknown
Poem to the Sun ("The boats sail upstream
   and downstream alike"). Unknown
Puppy Chased the Sunbeam, The. Eastwick
Riddle: "On yonder hill there is a red deer."
   Unknown
Riddle 29: The Moon and the Sun. Unknown
Seeing through the Sun. Hogan
Some say the sun is a golden earring.
   Belting
Song for the Sun That Disappeared behind the
   Rainclouds.
Song: "I'd much rather sit there in the sun."
   Krauss
Song: "Stay Phoebus, stay." Waller
Sonnet: "Lamp of heaven's crystal hall that
   brings the hours." Drummond
Spot on the Sun, A. Gar
Summer Sun. Stevenson
Sun, The. Davis
Sun, The. Drinkwater
Sun, The. Sexton
Sun, The. Fr. Ode to the Setting Sun.
   Thompson
Sun, The. Turner
Sun after Rain. Farber
Sun and Moon. Macpherson
Sun: Day, The. Schierbeek
Sun-Flower, The. Greenwell
Sun God, The. De Vere
Sun Held in Tender Hands, The. Winkler
Sun Is Good, The. Leib
Sun [or Sunne] Rising, The. Donne
Sunbeams. Trainin
Sunbeams Diagonally. Khomsky
Sunlight on the Garden, The. MacNeice
Sunning. Tippett
Sun's Perpendicular Rays, The. Mansel
Sun's Travels, The. Stevenson
Sun, his journey ending in the west, The.
   Fr. Diana. Constable
There's Nothing like the Sun. Thomas
Thu Sun: Night. Schierbeek
To the Sun. Bachmann
To the Sun from a Flower. Gezelle
True Account of Talking to the Sun at Fire
   Island, A. O'Hara
Two Drops. Herbert
Welcome to the Sun. Fr. The Aeneid [or
   Eneados]. Virgil

Sunburn
Some Sound Advice from Singapore. Ciardi
Sunday
Aside. Dugan
Bliss of Sunday, The. Nagy
Break-up, The. Nagy
Coati-Mundi. Smith
God Made a Trance. *Unknown*
O Day of Rest and Gladness. Wordsworth
Poor Man's Sunday Walk, The. MacKay
Sabbath Bells. Heard
Sabbath Sonnet. Hemans
Sunday. Coatsworth
Sunday. Herbert
Sunday. Miles
Sunday Afternoon. Levine
Sunday Evenings. Hollander
Sunday Morning. Jenkins
Sunday Morning. MacNeice
Sunday Morning. Stevens
Sunday Night Walk. Souster
Those Winter Sundays. Hayden
When You Have Forgotten Sunday: The Love
  Story. Brooks
See also **Sabbath.**
Sundews
Sundew, The. Swinburne
Sundials
Epigram: "I who by day am function of the
  light." Cunningham
I am a sundial. Ordinary words. Belloc
I am a sundial, turned the wrong way round.
  Belloc
Motto for a Sundial. *Unknown*
On a Sundial. Belloc
On the Needle of a Sundial. Quarles
Rhyme of the Sun-Dial, A. Scott
Sunflowers
Ah! Sun-Flower ("Ah! Sun-flower, weary of
  time"). *Fr.* Songs of Experience. Blake
Sun-Flower, The. Greenwell
Sunflower, The. Montale
Sunflower. Rübner
Sunflower. Updike
Sunflower Sutra. Ginsberg
Sunflowers in October. Fritsch
Sunrise
Ant Sun, The. *Fr.* Herman Moon's
  Hourbook. Middleton
Dark Stag, The. Crawford
Earliness at the Cape. Deutsch
Fingernail Sunrise. Watkins
Hymn to the Morning, An. Wheatley
Hymn to the Sun. *Unknown*
Hymn to the Sunrise. *Unknown*
Idyl: Sunrise. Ray
I'll tell you how the sun rose. Dickinson
Lever de Rideau. Bethell
Out of the Sea, Early. Swenson
Plainview: 3. Momaday
Reveille. *Fr.* A Shropshire Lad. Housman
Revisit. Engels
Scent of plum flowers, The. Tamekane
Still-Life. Daryush
Sun [*or* Sunne] Rising, The. Donne
Sunrise. King
Sunrise. *Fr.* Idyl. Ray
Sunrise. Wells
Sunrise in Summer. Clare
Sunrise Thought. *Fr.* A Group of Musings.
  Ray
Sunrise Trumpets. Auslander
Watching the Sun Rise over Mount Zion.
  Whitman
Sunset
Acceptance. Frost
Afterglow. Borges
Afterglow, The. Ray
Allie ("Allie, call the birds in"). Graves
At Sunset. Ray
Between clouds of fire and clouds of blood.
  Fr. At Evening Time. Bialik

Cader Idris at Sunset. Turner
Crickets sang, The. Dickinson
Dark Hills, The. Robinson
Datur Hora Quieti. Scott
Descend, Fair Sun! *Fr.* The Masque of the
  Middle Temple and Lincoln's Inn.
  Chapman
Distant View of the Sea, A. Tamekane
Dreary Change, The. Scott
Evening Sun, The. Brontë
Great Breath, The. "Æ"
Haiku: "Sky blazing/ as I go down the gravel
  path." *Fr.* Thirty-nine Haiku. Shiki
Hesperos, you bring home all the bright dawn
  disperses. Sappho
How the old mountains drip with sunset.
  Dickinson
I saw the sun set in clouds. *Fr.* Manyo Shu.
  Tenji
Idyl: Sunset. Ray
I'll tell you how the sun rose. Dickinson
In just the same way. Eifuku
Mediterranean. Whitman
Mise en Scène. Fitzgerald
Of the Going Down of the Sun. Bunyan
On Its Way. Swenson
Paris; This April Sunset Completely Utters.
  Cummings
Silence. Hame'iri
Sun is almost down, The. Tamekane
Sun must be setting, The. Tamesuke
Sundown. Adams
Sunset. Bayldon
Sunset. Bialik
Sunset, The. Burgess
Sunset. Fordham
Sunset. Longfellow
Sunset. Moore
Sunset. *Fr.* Idyl. Ray
Sunset. Wilcox
Sunset at Les Éboulements, A. Lampman
Sunset over the Aegean. *Fr.* The Corsair.
  Byron
Sunset Picture. Ray
Sunset Thought. *Fr.* A Group of Musings.
  Ray
Sunset Wings. Rossetti
Sunsets. Sandburg
With night coming on. Tamekane
You Will Know When You Get There.
  Curnow
Superior, Lake
Lake Superior. Goodrich
Lake Superior. Niedecker
Supermarkets
Grace to Be Said at the Supermarket.
  Nemerov
Picketing Supermarkets. Wayman
Supermarket in California, A. Ginsberg
Supernatural
Ballad of Hell, A. Davidson
Cold blows the blast—the night's obscure.
  Fr. Maid of the Moor, The; or, The
  Water-Fiends. Colman
Cremation of Sam McGee, The. Service
Green Candles. Wolfe
Kilmeny. *Fr.* The Queen's Wake. Hogg
Kingdom of God, The. Thompson
La Belle Dame sans Merci. Keats
Low Barometer. Bridges
Pied Piper of Hamelin, The. Browning
Pocomania. Sherlock
Raven, The. Poe
Shadows in the Water. Traherne
Skeleton in Armor, The. Longfellow
Sonnet: Supernatural Beings. Ewart
Strange Tree. Roberts
Ulalume. Poe
*Why Am I Grown So Cold? Poems of the
  Unknowable* (WSC). Myra Cohn
  Livingston, ed.

Superstition
Chorus Quintus: Tartarorum. *Fr.* Mustapha.
  Greville
Evil Eye, The. Ciardi
Johnny's Pet Superstition. Thompson
See a pin and pick it up. *Unknown*
Silver Coin, The. Reeves
Superstition. Karibo
Superstitions. Johnson
Voices in the Night. Whipple
Supper
Animal Crackers. Morley
Early Supper. Howes
Setting the Table. Aldis
Surfing and Surfers
From the Wave. Gunn
Song of Surfing on the Bore. Cheng Hsieh
Surfer, The. Wright
Surfers at Santa Cruz. Goodman
Surgery
Correct Compassion, A. Kirkup
Hard Rock Returns to Prison from the
  Hospital for the Criminal Insane. Knight
In the Operating Room. Nowlan
Surgical Ward: Men. Graves
See also **Medicine; Physicians**.
Surrealism
Against Surrealism. Wright
Surrealism in the Middle Ages. Lamantia
English and American Surrealist Poetry
  (EAS). Edward B. Germain, ed.
Poetry of Surrealism, The; an Anthology
  (POS). Michael Benedikt, ed. *and* tr.
Survival
Anchorage. Harjo
How to Survive Nuclear War. Kumin
Instinct of Self-Preservation, The. Balestrini
Phenomenal Survivals of Death in Nantucket.
  Glück
Staying Alive. Wagoner
Surviving. Ismay
Survivor, The. Cook
Swimming Lesson, The. Oliver
Susanna
Peter Quince at the Clavier. Stevens
Susanna and the Elders. Crapsey
Susanna and the Elders. Gilbert
Susannah and the Elders. *Unknown*
Sussex, England
Green Sussex. *Fr.* Prologue to General
  Hamley. Tennyson
Puck's Song. *Fr.* Puck of Pook's Hill.
  Kipling
South Country, The. Belloc
West Sussex Drinking Song. Belloc
See also **Cinque Ports.**
Suttee
Suttee, The. Skinner
Sutter, John
John Sutter. Winters
Swallows
Blue Swallows, The. Nemerov
Children's Song, The. *Unknown*
Even swallows seem to have no time. *Fr.*
  Thirty-three Hokku. Kikaku
In the Cathedral Close. Dowden
Itylus. Swinburne
My Swallows. Stern
O Master Masons. Toller
O My Swallows! Toller
On Shooting a Swallow in Early Youth.
  Turner
Sand Martin, The. Clare
Shapes of swallows. Kogon

Sixth-Month Song in the Foothills. Snyder
Swallow, The. Cowley
Swallow, The. Nash
Swallow has erased a rainbow, A. *Fr.*
    Thirty-three Hokku. Kikaku
Swallow Song. Pickthall
Swallow Tails. Robinson
Swallows. Ferril
Swallows. Wu Tsao
Swallow's Flight, The. Levy
Swallows over the Camp. Krige
Swallows, when your wings are full grown.
    Unknown
To a Swallow. Bishop
To the Swallow. Cowper
To the Swallows of Viterbo. Ruark
Upon the Swallow. Bunyan

Swamps
Alligator, The. Ravenel
Bogland. Heaney
I May, I Might, I Must. Moore
Suburban Swamp. Parini
Swamp Nocturne. Césaire
Walking in a Swamp. Wagoner

Swans
Bereaved Swan, The. Smith
Black Swan, The. Jarrell
Dying Swan, The. Tennyson
Dying Swan, The. *Unknown*
Elementary Scene, The. Jarrell
His Swans. Grigson
Leda. Doolittle
Leda and the Swan. Yeats
Love the Wild Swan. Jeffers
No Swan So Fine. Moore
Riddle: Mute Swan. *Unknown*
Siesta of a Hungarian Snake. Morgan
Silver Swan, The. Gibbons
Sitting Pretty. Fishback
Sonnet 7: "I've found out why, that day, that
    suicide." Berryman
Swan. Lawrence
Swan. Lowbury
Swan and Shadow. Hollander
Swan and the Goose, The. Aesop
Swan Bathing, The. Pitter
Swan swam over the sea. *Unknown*
Swan, The: "Clothes make no sound when I
    tread ground." *Fr.* Riddles (Exeter Book).
    Cynewulf
Swans. Durrell
Swans, The. Sitwell
Swans. Speyer
Swan's Feet, The. Scovell
Swans Mating. Longley
To the Liffey with the Swans. Gogarty
Wild Swans at Coole, The. Yeats
Within the night, above the dark. *Fr.* Swans
    at Night. Gilmore
Wring the Swan's Neck. Gonzáles Martínez

Swansea, Wales
Ode to Swansea. Watkins

Sweatshops
Sweatshop, The. Rosenfeld

Sweden
Autobiography. Akesson
Carriage from Sweden, A. Moore
Evening Walk. Akesson
Sonnet upon a Swedish Cottage. Carr
Swedish Lesson. Sutter

Swift, Jonathan
Day will come, when't shall be said, The.
    Fr. The Life and Character of Dean Swift.
    Swift
Here shift the scene, to represent. *Fr.* Verses
    on the Death of Doctor Swift [D.S.P.D.,
    Occasioned by Reading a Maxim in
    Rochefoucauld]. Swift
Hypocrite Swift. Bogan
Lines on Swift's Ancestors. Pope
Sermon on Swift, A. Clarke

Swift. Schwartz
Swift's Epitaph. Yeats
Tryst in Brobdingnag, A. Rich

Swimming and Swimmers
Above These Cares. Millay
Ballade of Boys Bathing. Rolfe
Bathers, The. Shapiro
Bathing Song. Ridler
Black Water and Bright Air. Carrier
Come On In. *Unknown*
Diver, The. Herbin
First Lesson. Booth
400-Meter Freestyle. Kumin
Friend asks why I swim, A. *Fr.* Sixty-four
    Caprices for a Long-Distance Swimmer:
    Notes on Swimming 100 Miles. Lynch
Greg Hoffman. Glenn
Handicapped Children Swimming. Browne
I saw him beat the surges under him. *Fr.*
    The Tempest. Shakespeare
Idea of a Swimmer. Bloch
In the Ocean. Goedicke
Inner Tube. Ondaatje
Into Fish. Nelms
It's Great When You Get In. O'Neill
Lakeshore. Scott
Led by the Hebrew School Rabbi. Baumel
Lifeguard, The. Dickey
Lone Bather. Klein
Medals and Money: A Re-evaluation.
    Lamblin
Morning at Point Dume. Swenson
Morning Swim. Kumin
Nude Swim, The. Sexton
Of Swimming in Lakes and Rivers. Brecht
Old Swimmer, The. Morley
Old Swimmin'-Hole, The. Riley
On Being Much Better Than Most and Yet
    Not Quite Good Enough. Ciardi
Our Silly Little Sister. Aldis
Questions of Swimming, 1935. Davison
Reunion: Swimming, The. Meissner
Swimmer. Francis
Swimmer, The. Ransom
Swimmer's Chant, The. Spelius
Swimmer's Moment, The. Avison
Swimming. Higgins
Swimming. Scollard
Swimming by Night. Merrill
Swimming Chenango Lake. Tomlinson
Swimming in the Pacific. Warren
Swimming Lesson, The. Oliver
Then, the quick plunge into the cool, green
    dark. *Fr.* Swimmers. Untermeyer
To Swim, to Believe. Kumin
Under the Boathouse. Bottoms
Upon Boys Diverting Themselves in the
    River. Foxton
Voice in the Garden, A. Hill
Written after Swimming from Sestos to
    Abydos. Byron
Yellow-belly, yellow-belly, come and take a
    swim. *Unknown*
See also **Surfing and Surfers.**

Swinburne, Algernon Charles
If. Collins

Swings
At the Playground. Stafford
Backyard Swing. Hale
Swing, The. Osborn
Swing, The. Stevenson
Swing Song, A. Allingham
Swinging. Thompson
Walnut Tree, The. McCord

Switzerland
Alpine Spirit's Song. Beddoes
Great St. Bernard, The. Rogers
Have you the Giesbach seen? a fall. *Fr.*
    Mari Magno. Clough
Lausanne. Hardy
Mont Blanc. Shelley

Such soft ideas all my pains beguile.
    Montagu
Switzerland. Godley
Switzerland. Thwaite
Switzerland 1938-1965. Teller
Terrace at Berne, The. Arnold
Turn we to survey. *Fr.* The Travel[l]er; or,
    A Prospect of Society. Goldsmith
View by Color Photography on a Commercial
    Calendar. Williams

Swordfish
Marvel, The. Douglas

Swords
End of Clonmacnois, The. *Unknown*
Silver Clasp. *Unknown*
Sword. Kagura

Sydney, Australia
Sydney and the Bush. Murray
Visit of Hope to Sydney Cove, near
    Botany-Bay. Darwin

Symbols. *See* **Metaphor; Similes.**

Sympathy
Sympathy. Moorer

Synagogues
Cry for a Disused Synagogue in Booysens.
    Hirsch
Odors. Leib

Synge, John Millington
Homage to John Millington Synge.
    O Direain
In Memory of Major Robert Gregory. Yeats
Memory, A. Strong
Municipal Gallery Revisited, The. Yeats

Syphilis
Pangloss's Song [A Comic-Opera Lyric].
    Wilbur
See also **Veneral Disease.**

Syria
Still this, still that I would! all I surmise.
    Lithgow

Syrinx. *See* **Pan.**

T

Tabor, Elizabeth McCourt
Mistress of the Matchless Mine. Robertson

Tadpoles
Sher Imdad Ali's Tadpole. Farooqi
Tadpole, The. Gould

Tagore, Sir Rabindranath
Taghore. Al-Ghuzzi

Tagus River, Spain and Portugal
Tagus, Farewell. Wyatt

Tahiti
To an Island Princess. Stevenson
Vor a Gauguin Picture zu Singen. Stein

Tailors
Amendis to the Telyouris and Sowtaris for the
    Turnament Maid on Thame, The. Dunbar
Tailor, The. "Ansky"
Tailor. Farjeon
Tailor, The. Leftwich

Taj Mahal
Oh! thou—whose great imperial mind could
    raise. *Unknown*
Taj, The. Keene

Takatur Erinta Perunceral Irumporai
Battle Scene. Aricil Kilar

Taliesin
I Am Taliesin. I Sing Perfect Metre.
    Unknown
Taliesin, sel. Hovey
Taliessin's Song of the Unicorn. Williams

Talk
Talk. Stalker
See also **Speech.**

Talmage, S. K.
Lines on the Death of the Rev. S. K.
Talmage. Tucker
Talmud, The
Monish. Peretz
Pilpul. Kamenetz
Talmud, The. Frug
Talmud Student, The. Bialik
Tamerlane
Tamburlaine the Great, *sels.* Marlowe
Tammuz
Death of Tammuz, The. Tchernichowsky
Tammuz. Alterman
Tanagers
Scarlet Tanager, The. Benton
Scarlet Tanager, The. Mason
Tangier, Morocco
Tangier: Hotel Rif. Thomas
Tanguy, Yves
Yves Tanguy. Eluard
Tanks (vehicle)
Army, The. Hagiwara Sakutaro
Tannhäuser
Tannhauser. Levy
Taos, New Mexico
House in Taos, A. Hughes
New Mexican Mountain. Jeffers
Tapestries
Aunt Jennifer's Tigers. Rich
Beyond the Tapestries. Farber
Offering of the Heart Tapestry from Arras,
XV Century, The. Humphries
Tapestry, The. Nemerov
Tapestry. Simic
Unicorn and the Lady, The. Garrigue
Tara, Ireland
Harp That Once through Tara's Halls, The.
Moore
Tara Is Grass. *Unknown*
Taranto, Italy
Taranto. Wright
Tarantulas
Discoveries in Arizona. Wright
Tasman, Abel
Landfall in Unknown Seas. Curnow
Tasmania
Truganinny. Rose
Van Dieman's Land. *Unknown*
Taste
Ode to Garlic. Stafford
Tattoos
Pornography, Nebraska. McPherson
Tattooed Man, The. Hayden
Taverns
At the Cantina. Soto
Bard's Reformation, The. Bamford
Closed Door, The. Al-Faituri
Closing Time. Wagoner
8-Ball at the Twilite. Baker
Glass of Beer, A. Stephens
Lady of the Ferry Inn. Mechain
Lines on the Mermaid Tavern. *Unknown*
Old Wife in High Spirits. "MacDiarmid"
Rank. Kirstein
Singles. Waters
Tavern, The. Robinson
Tavernkeeper, The. Cheng Hsieh
Taxes
Ballad on the Taxes, A. Ward
Black Hole of Calcutta, The. Elliott
Caged Rats. Elliott
Inventory, in Answer to the Usual Mandate
Sent by a Surveyor of the Taxes, Requiring
a Return of the Number of Horses,
Servants, Carriages, etc., Kept, The.
Burns
New Song on the Birth of the Prince of
Wales, A. *Unknown*
Tax Return. *Unknown*

Taxidermy
From a Printed Bill, Fixed in the Beak of One
in a Group of Five Stuffed Owls in the
Shop Window of a Bird Stuffer, at
Richmond, Yorkshire. *Unknown*
Owl-Critic, The. Fields
Taxis
After Anacreon. *Fr.* Taxi Suite. Welch
Taxis. Field
Taxis, The. MacNeice
Tayside, Scotland
Rannoch Moor. MacGregor
Tea
Drinking Tea. Chang Ts'o
How to Get On in Society. Betjeman
Legend of Tea, The. Chang Ts'o
Pot of Tea. Griffin
Story of Bitter Tea, The. Lo Ch'ing
To the Hosts: A Reply. Chang Ts'o
Twinings Orange Pekoe. Moffett
See also **Teahouses**.
Teaching and Teachers
April Inventory. Snodgrass
Backing into the Fan Mail (Unreceived).
Gallup
Blake Mistake, The. Castle
Campus on the Hill, The. Snodgrass
Correspondence School Instructor Says
Goodbye to His Poetry Students, The.
Kinnell
Creature in the Classroom, The. Prelutsky
Distracted the Mother Said to Her Boy.
Harrison
Education. Lee
Emeritus, n. Coulette
Farewell, My Latin Master. Plaice
First Day of Teaching. Overstreet
For an Early Retirement. Hall
Freshmen. Spacks
Golgotha. Kennedy
Grouchy Good Night to the Academic Year,
A. Pauker
Hedge Schoolmaster, A. Fallon
History of Education. McCord
I Went to See Irving Babbitt. Eberhart
Irish Schoolmaster, The. Hood
Kiss, The. Bogin
Late Tutorial. Buckley
Learning. Simpson
Lessons in Parsing. Husain
Letter to a Substitute Teacher. Gildner
Miss Norma Jean Pugh. O'Neill
Mr. Brunt. Siegel
No teacher I of boys or smaller fry. Ramsay
Off to Patagonia. Weiss
Pedagogical Principles. Amoss
Poor Scholar of the 'Forties, A. Colum
Prayer of a Beginning Teacher. Dunnam
Prayer of a Teacher. Littlewort
Professor's Song, A. Berryman
Purist, The. Nash
Schoolmaster, The. *Unknown*
Schoolmaster Abroad with His Son, The.
Calverley
Schools and Schoolmasters. Flanzbaum
Servant in Literature, The. Welish
Shapes, Vanishings. Taylor
Teacher, The. Hill
Teachers, The. Parra
Teacher's Dream, The. Venable
Teaching Staff Disbanded, The. Rónay
Teaching Swift to Young Ladies. Dickey
To Dr. Swift on His Birthday, 30th November
1721. Johnson
To My Children. Guerrini
Village Schoolmaster, The. *Fr.* The
Deserted Village. Goldsmith
What Schoolmasters Say. Seymour-Smith
"When the Students Resisted, a Minor Clash
Ensued." Knight
See also **Scholars and Scholarship**.

Teahouses
White Conduit House. Woty
See also **Tea**.
Teamsters
How the Fire Queen Crossed the Swamp.
Ogilvie
See also **Trucks and Truckers**.
Tears
Absolutely Ordinary Rainbow, An. Murray
Burning Bright. Morrison
By this he knew she wept with waking eyes.
Fr. Modern Love. Meredith
Flow Not So Fast. Dowland
Flow, O My Tears! *Unknown*
Hymn: "Drop, drop, slow tears." Fletcher
I Saw My Lady Weep. *Unknown*
I Weep. Grimké
It's such a little thing to weep. Dickinson
Man in the Onion Bed, The. Ciardi
Maxim Revised, A. *Unknown*
Peeling Onions. Rich
Rain. Lindsay
Slow, Slow, Fresh Fount. *Fr.* Cynthia's
Revels. Jonson
Sowing of Tears, A. Jaccottet
Tear [*or* The Teare], The. Crashaw
Tear, The. López Velarde
Tear, The. Vyazemsky
Tears. Browning
Tears. Reese
Tears. Sitwell
Tears. Vyazemsky
Tears, Flow No More. Herbert of Cherbury
Tears, Idle Tears [I Know Not What They
Mean]. *Fr.* The Princess. Tennyson
Twicknam *or* Twickenham Garden. Donne
Valediction: Of Weeping, A. Donne
Wasted Sympathy, A. Howells
Weep [*or* Weepe] You No More [Sad
Fountains]. *Unknown*
Technology
Bright New Missouri. Sneyd
Fundamental Project of Technology, The.
Kinnell
Lighting the Colony. Tem
MC²-E. Wickstrom
Most-Age, The. Váci
Old Whim Horse, The. Dyson
Steam Engine; or, The Power of the Flame,
The, *sels.* Baker
Telephone Poles. Updike
Ybba. Malcohn
Tecumseh
Fall of Tecumseh, The. *Unknown*
Tecumseh, *sels.* Mair
Teddy Bears
My Teddy Bear. Chute
My Teddy Bear. Hillert
Teenagers
Tracy & Co. *Fr.* Calling Your Name in the
Zoo. Williams
Teeth
Dentologia; a Poem on the Diseases of the
Teeth and Their Proper Remedies, *sels.*
Brown
Good Riddance to Bad Rubbish O at Last.
Goodman
Poet's Farewell to His Teeth, The. Dickey
Thirty white horses upon a red hill. Mother
Goose
To have it out or not? that is the question.
"W."
To Women, to Hide Their Teeth, if They Be
Rotten or Rusty. Herrick
Twenty white horses on a red hill. *Unknown*
Your Teeth. López Velarde
See also **Dentistry and Dentists; Dentures;
Smiles; Toothaches**.
Tel Aviv, Israel
Weather, The. Wieseltier

Telegraph
On the Completion of the Pacific Telegraph. Very
To a Vine-clad Telegraph Pole. Untermeyer
Telephones
"Are You Still There." Harjo
Business Life, The. Ignatow
Central. Kooser
Dial Tone, The. Nemerov
Eletelephony. Richards
Goodbye Forever. Morrison
Hot Line. Dunann
I Am a Victim of Telephone. Ginsberg
Long Distance. Stafford
Obscene Caller, The. Fein
On Seeing a Torn Out Coin Telephone. Robbins
Rondeau after a Transatlantic Telephone Call. Hacker
Simultaneously. Ignatow
Telephone Poles. Updike
Television
Anchors Weighed. McMillan
Death. Byatt
Electric Cop, The. Cruz
Going Home to Mayo, Winter, 1949. Durcan
Great Annelid Worm, A. Hawkins
Jimmy Jet and His TV Set. Silverstein
Metaphysical Shock while Watching a TV Cartoon. Rice
Mousemeal. Nemerov
New Republic Is Infuriated at the News Coverage, The. Starbuck
Not-so-good Earth, The. Dawe
Robin Hood. *Fr.* Speaking of Television. McGinley
Television. Fei Ma
TV Blooper Spotter. Skelley
Utopia TV Store. Chernoff
Watching Television. Bly
Way of Life, A. Nemerov
Wife Who Smashed Television Gets Jail. Durcan
Winning of the TV West, The. Alexander
Tell, William
Archer, The. Scollard
Archery. De la Mare
Temperance
Have Courage, My Boy, to Say No! Hilton
John Barley-Corn, My Foe. Adams
Temperance. *Unknown*
Temperance Song. *Unknown*
We Live in a Rickety House. McLachlan
Temptation
All Things Can Tempt Me. Yeats
Dialogue between the Resolved Soul and Created Pleasure, A. Marvell
John Barleycorn's Diary: An Uncoloured Picture. McManus
Lure, The. O'Reilly
Quip, The. Herbert
Ten Commandments
Latest Decalogue, The. Clough
Ten Commandments, The. *Unknown*
Tenby, Wales
Gereint ab Erbin. *Unknown*
In Praise of Tenby. *Unknown*
Never Tell. *Unknown*
Tennessee
Hills of Sewanee, The. McClellan
Knoxville, Tennessee. Giovanni
October in Tennessee. Malone
Shiloh; a Requiem. Melville
Street Scene—1946. Porter
Tennessee Valley Authority
Norris Dam. Rodman
Tennis
At the Tennis Club. Martin
Ballade of Lawn Tennis, A. Adams
Clobber the Lobber. Lamport

Dark Eyes at Forest Hills. Martin
In the Spring. Hall
Lawn-Tennisonian Idyll, A. *Unknown*
Love. Muth
Midnight Tennis Match, The. Lux
Miraculously, through prayer to Saint Anthony. *Fr.* Adulescentia. Fitzgerald
Old Pro's Lament, The. Petrie
Old Tennis Player. Brooks
Olympic Girl, The. Betjeman
On the Tennis Court at Night. Kinnell
Preparedness. Lamport
Prothalamion. Kumin
Snapshot for Miss Bricka Who Lost in the Semi-final Round of the Pennsylvania Lawn Tennis Tournament, A. Wallace
Tennis. Avison
Tennis, The. White
Tennis in San Juan. Denney
Tennis in the City. Higgins
Watching Tennis. Heath-Stubbs
Tennyson, Alfred Tennyson, 1st Baron
Alas! England now mourns for her poet that's gone. *Fr.* Death and Burial of Lord Tennyson. McGonagall
Footnote to Tennyson. Bullett
Tennyson. Aldrich
Tennyson. Coates
Tennyson. Van Dyke
Tennyson's Poems. Heard
Tenors
Schmaltztenor! Branch
Tents
Silken Tent, The. Frost
Thinking of Tents. Whittemore
Teresa, Saint. *See* **Theresa, Saint.**
Termites
Termite, The. Nash
Termites. Chock
Terns
Arctic Tern in a Museum. Newsome
Gracious Goodness. Piercy
Seals, Terns, Time. Eberhart
Terror
Study in Terror, A. Tamura Ryuichi
Terrorism and Terrorists
Mr. Gunman. Garbutt
Tesla, Nikola
In Tesla's Laboratory. Johnson
Texas
Barbara's Land Revisited—August 1978. Hobson
Crêpes Flambeau. Gallagher
Defeat. Bynner
Devil in Texas, The. *Unknown*
Down in Dallas. Kennedy
East Texas. Stokesbury
Hell in Texas. *Unknown*
Homage to Texas. Graves
In Blanco County. Fowler
Lament for the Alamo. Guiterman
Lasca. Desprez
Texas. Lowell
Texas Ranger, The. Boswell
That Texan Cattle Man. Miller
Wes Hardin: From a Photograph. Carver
Texas Revolution
Valor of Ben Milam, The. Scollard
See also **Alamo.**
Thackeray, William Makepeace
Adsum. Stoddard
Thames (river), England
Bab-Lock-Hythe. Binyon
Lover to the Thames of London, to Favour [*or* Favor] His Lady Passing Thereon, The. Turberville
My eye descending from the Hill, surveys. *Fr.* Cooper's Hill. Denham
Old Summerhouse, The. De la Mare
Rivers. Storer

Rivers Come to the Hall of Proteus for the Marriage of the Thames and the Medway, The. *Fr.* The Faerie Queene. Spenser
Thames, The. Hutchinson
Thankfulness
Grace for Light. O'Neill
Thanksgiving
Blessings That Remain, The. Flint
Child's Grace, A. Burns
Child's Prayer, A. *Unknown*
First Thanksgiving of All. Turner
For the rosebud's break of beauty. *Fr.* A Thanksgiving. Larcom
God, You Have Been Too Good to Me. Stork
Grace. Emerson
Grace, A. Tiplady
Grace and Thanksgiving. Gould
Grace at Evening. Guest
Grace at Evening. Poteat
Grace for a Child. Herrick
Gratitude. Lermontov
Gratitude. McGee
Harvest Home. Alford
Hymn: "For Summer's bloom and Autumn's blight." *Fr.* Bitter-sweet. Holland
Hymn: "Lord, by whose breath all souls and seeds are living." Young
Hymn of Gratitude. *Unknown*
I Have a Roof. Jackson
I Thank You God for Most This Amazing. Cummings
In Thankfull Remembrance for My Dear Husband's Safe Arrivall Sept. 3, 1662. Bradstreet
Lovely Things. Sarson
Morning Thanksgiving. Drinkwater
Most Acceptable Gift, The. Claudius
Not Alone for Mighty Empire. Merrill
Ol'Tunes, The. Dunbar
Poet's Grace, A. Burns
Prayer before Meat. Harsen
Prayer for Thanksgiving, A. Auslander
Prayer for the Great Family. Snyder
Signs of the Times. Dunbar
Thankfulness. Procter
Thanksgiving. Best
Thanksgiving. Coates
Thanksgiving. Eastwick
Thanksgiving. Herrick
Thanksgiving. Moorer
Thanksgiving. Morgan
Thanksgiving. Morris
Thanksgiving, A. Newman
Thanksgiving. Oxenham
Thanksgiving. Sangster
Thanksgiving Day. Storm
Thanksgiving Magic. Bennett
Thanksgiving to God for His House, A. Herrick
Things I Miss, The. Higginson
Thy Name We Bless and Magnify. Power
To the Spirit Great and Good. Hunt
We Thank Thee. *Unknown*
Thanksgiving Day
De Day befo' Thanksgibin'. Johnson
First Thanksgiving, The. Prelutsky
Good Thanksgiving, A. Robinson
Harvest Hymn. *Fr.* For an Autumn Festival. Whittier
Minnesota Thanksgiving. Berryman
Story of Lovers Leap, The. Johnson
Thanksgiving Day. Bangs
Thanksgiving Dinner during Pelting Season. Moran
Thanksgiving, Growing Older. Doreski
Thanksgiving in Boston Harbor, The. Butterworth
Thanksgiving Magic. Bennett
Thanksgiving (1956). Cummings
Volunteer's Thanksgiving, The. Larcom

Thatcher, Margaret
Mrs. Snatcher Thatcher. *Fr.* Jezebel: Her
Progress. Hanscombe
Theater and Theaters
At the Theater. Field
At the Theater. Herbert
Curtain! Dunbar
Elegy in a Theatrical Warehouse. Fearing
Epilogue at Wallack's, An. Wayland
Identities. Young
Ode to Himsel[f]e ("Come leave the loathed
stage"). Jonson
Old Woman, Outside the Abbey Theater, An.
Strong
Playhouse Key, The. Field
Poem on Theater, A. Weöres
Rehearsal, The. Gregory
Saved. *Unknown*
Theft. *See* **Crime and Criminals.**
Theocritus
Theocritus. Fields
Theocritus. Wilde
Written on a Fly-Leaf of Theocritus.
Thompson
Theology
Burning Bush, The. Nicholson
He preached upon "Breadth" till it argued him
narrow. Dickinson
Here stood Hypocrisy, in sober brown. *Fr.*
The Triumph of Infidelity. Dwight
Man on the dubious waves of error toss'd.
Fr. Truth. Cowper
Presbyterian Church Government ("Synods are
whelps of the Inquisition"). *Fr.* Hudibras.
Butler
Respectable Burgher, The. Hardy
Theologians. De la Mare
Thera (island), Greece
Santorin. Flecker
Theresa, Saint, of Avila
Conversation in Avila. McGinley
Flaming Heart, The. Crashaw
Flaming Heart, The, *sels.* Crashaw
Hymn to the Name and Honour [*or* Honor] of
the Admirable Saint[e] T[h]eresa, A, *sels.*
Crashaw
Mould of Castile. Clemo
Teresa. Wilbur
Thermopylae, Battle of
On the Spartan Dead at Thermopylae.
Simonides
Thermopylae. Cavafy
Thermopylae. Thwaites
Theseus
Labyrinth, The. Muir
Theseus: A Trilogy. Winters
Theseus and Ariadne. Graves
See also **Minotaur.**
Thieves
Stealing. Tozaburo
See also **Crime and Criminals.**
Thinness
Thin Man, The. Justice
Third World
Economics. Van Duyn
Remember Haiti, Cuba, Vietnam. Salkey
Underdeveloped Country, An. Enright
Thirst
Green, Green Is El Aghir. Cameron
Hunger and Thirst. Bishop
I Am Crying from Thirst. Lopez
We drink with palms cupped. Tsurayuki
See also **Hunger.**
Thistles
Looking at a Dry Canadian Thistle Brought In
from the Snow. Bly
Roadside thistle, eager, The. Basho
Thistle. Kilpi
Thistle. Zabolotsky
Thistledown. Monro
Thistles. Hughes

Thomas à Becket, Saint
Becket's Diadem. *Unknown*
Murder of Saint Thomas of Kent, The.
Unknown
Thomas à Kempis
Thomas à Kempis. Bowker
Thomas à Kempis. Reese
Thomas Aquinas, Saint
Dumb Oxen. *Fr.* Of Mary. Madeleva
Thomas in the Fields. Moyles
Thomas, Dylan
Cwmrhydyceirw Elegiacs. Watkins
Elegy for Dylan Thomas. Sitwell
Thomas, Edward
To Edward Thomas. Lewis
Thomas, George Henry
Thomas at Chickamauga. Sherwood
Thomas, Saint
Hymn of Saint Thomas in Adoration of the
Blessed Sacrament, The. Crashaw
Thomas the Rhymer (Thomas of Erceldoune)
Thomas the Rhymer [*or* Rimer]. *Unknown*
Thomson, James (1700-1748)
Ode Occasioned by the Death of Mr.
Thomson. Collins
Thomson, Tom
Tom Thomson. Bourinot
Thoreau, Henry David
Men of Sudbury, The. Baker
On Visiting the Graves of Hawthorne and
Thoreau. Very
Tears in Spring. Channing
Thoreau. Alcott
Thoreau. Jones
Thoreau's Flute. Alcott
Thought at Walden, A. Ray
To Thoreau on Rereading Walden. Gardner
Thought
Climate of Thought, The. Graves
Mind Is an Enchanting Thing, The. Moore
On the Flightiness of Thought. *Unknown*
See also **Intellect; Reason.**
Thousand Islands, New York and Ontario
Thousand Islands, The. *Fr.* St. Lawrence
and the Saguenay. Sangster
Three Henrys, War of the. *See* **War of the
Three Henrys.**
Three Kings *or* **Three Wise Men.** *See* **Magi.**
Three Mile Island, PA
Three Mile Island. Owen
Thrushes
And what now, wood thrush. Ietaka
Bring your first song. Ietaka
Brown Thrush, The. Larcom
Come In. Frost
Cuckoo calls out, A. Tameie
Darkling Thrush, The. Hardy
I had lost myself. Tameie
I Have Taken a Thrush. O'Sullivan
Proud Songsters. Hardy
Reminder, The. Hardy
So many nights. Fushimi
Throstle, The. Tennyson
Thrush, The. Austin
Thrush before Dawn, A. Meynell
Thrushes. Hughes
Thrush's Nest, The. Clare
Thrush's Song, The. *Unknown*
Veery-Thrush, The. Taylor
What the Thrush Says. Scott-Hopper
Thumbs
Thumbs. Silverstein
Who Am I? Holman
Thunder
Black Cloud, The. Davies
Giant Thunder. Reeves
If the thunder rolls for a while. *Fr.* Manyo
Shu. Hitomaro
June Thunder. MacNeice

Like the flash and roar near the clouds of
heaven. *Fr.* Manyo Shu. *Unknown*
Song of the Thunder. *Unknown*
Thunder. Wang Chiu-ssu
Thunder My Brother. Heifetz-Tussman
Thyme
Thyme Flowering among Rocks. Wilbur
Wild Thyme. Sambrook
Ticonderoga, Battle of (1775)
On the Defeat at Ticonderoga or Carilong.
Unknown
Surprise at Ticonderoga, The. Stansbury
Tides
High Tide on the Coast of Lincolnshire
(1571), The. Ingelow
Low Tide on Grand Pré. Carman
Tide Rises, the Tide Falls, The. Longfellow
Tide Turning. Nims
Tides, The. Bryant
Tides. Stafford
We wait for the moon. *Fr.* Manyo Shu.
Nukada
Where Tide. Booth
Tigers
Ballad of the Ferocious Tiger. Hsü Pen
Ballad of the Righteous Tiger, A. Sung Wan
Bengal Tiger, The. Spence
Dying tiger—moaned for drink, A.
Dickinson
How brave the peasant who lives beside the
lake. *Fr.* Song of Catching Tigers. Hsü
Chung-hsing
O Have You Caught the Tiger? Housman
There Was a Young Lady of Niger.
Monkhouse
Tiger, The. Belloc
Tiger, The. *Fr.* Songs of Experience.
Blake
Tiger. Hope
Tigers of Nanzen-ji, The. Leithauser
Tightrope Walkers. *See* **Acrobats.**
Till, Emmett
Emmett Till. Emanuel
Last Quatrain of the Ballad of Emmett Till,
The. Brooks
Time
Acceleration near the Point of Impact. Oates
Alas, the days of youth fly past. Insha
All the World's a Stage. *Fr.* As You Like
It. Shakespeare
All's Not That Simple. Shalom
And What though Winter Will Pinch Severe.
Fr. Old Mortality. Scott
Angel-Thief, The. Holmes
Another Year Come. Merwin
Anyone Lived in a Pretty How Town.
Cummings
As I Walked Out One Evening. Auden
As You Came from the Holy Land. Ashbery
August. MacNeice
Awake! for morning in the bowl of night.
Fr. The Rubáiyát of Omar Khayyám of
Naishápúr. Khayyám
Away, away, O breeze of the spring. Insha
Billows in love's stormy sea, The. Insha
Birth of Time, The. Heard
Birthday Verses Written in a Child's Album.
Lowell
Birthright. Drinkwater
Burnt Norton. *Fr.* Four Quartets. Eliot
Certain Years. Orban
Changes to Corinna, The. Herrick
Chronology. Cassity
Cities and Thrones and Powers. *Fr.* Puck of
Pook's Hill. Kipling
Clock in the Square, A. Rich
Collected Time. Laaber
Continental Crossing. Thompson
Counting the Beats. Graves
Creatures of Early Morning. Lewis
Days. Emerson

Days. Larkin
Days, the Months, the Years, The. Valeri
Dear Men and Women. Wheelock
"Devouring Time, blunt thou the lion's paws [lyons pawes]." Fr. Sonnets, XIX. Shakespeare
Digging. Thomas
During Wind and Rain. Hardy
Earliest before sunrise. Howe
Earthly Illusion. Leighton
End of a Century. Follain
Epilogue: "Time is a thing." Spender
Estuary, The. Fairburn
Eternity's Speech against Time. Fr. Mustapha: Chorus Tertius: Of Time; Eternitie. Greville
Even Such Is Time. Ralegh
Excerpts from the Modern Tragedy. Weöres
Express Train. Kraus
Fatalities. Ackerman
Father Father Son and Son. Swan
Feeling of Time. Ungaretti
Flying Change, The. Taylor
Force That through the Green Fuse Drives the Flower, The. Thomas
Four Preludes on Playthings of the Wind. Sandburg
Four Quartz Crystal Clocks. Moore
Gold Watch. Kavanagh
Gone in the Wind. Mangan
Growing Up. Behn
Harvest to Seduce, A. Cane
Headlands, 2365. Simon
His Golden Locks Time Hath to Silver Turned. Fr. Polyhymnia. Peele
His Poetry [or Poetrie] His Pillar. Herrick
Hour-Glass, The. Herrick
How on Solemn Fields of Space. Daryush
I Put the Tip of the Pen to the Paper. Gilboa
I Saw from the Beach. Moore
In a Prominent Bar in Secaucus [One Day]. Kennedy
In a Rose Garden. Bennett
In the Fleeting Hand of Time. Corso
In Time. Graves
Isle of the Long Ago, The. Taylor
Ladder, The. Vas
Lamentation of the Old Pensioner, The. Yeats
Last Leaf, The. Holmes
Leave Him Now Quiet. Stickney
Leisure. Davies
Life. Herbert
Light Year, The. Ridland
"Like as the waves make towards the pebbled shore." Fr. Sonnets, LX. Shakespeare
Limited. Sandburg
L'Imprévisibilité. Hippius
Mankind and man's world. Tameko
Marjorie's Almanac. Aldrich
Moment. Creeley
Moment Please, A. Allen
Months, The. Rossetti
Nature, That Washed or Washt Her Hands in Milk[e]. Ralegh
New Guinea Time. Johnson
Noise That Time Makes, The. Moore
Nothing Gold Can Stay. Frost
Nymph's Reply to the Shepherd, The. Ralegh
O Heavy Step of Slow Monotony. Toller
Of Time and Us. Bunch
Old Clock on the Stairs, The. Longfellow
Old Furniture. Hardy
Old Triton Time. Watkins
On Time. Hughes
On Time. Milton
On Wenlock Edge [the Wood's in Trouble]. Fr. A Shropshire Lad. Housman

Ozymandias [or Ozymandias of Egypt or Sonnet: Ozymandias]. Shelley
Palindrome. Mueller
Polo Grounds. Humphries
Prayer for the New Year, A. Storey
Prelude LVI: "Rimbaud and Verlaine, precious pair of poets." Fr. Preludes for Memnon; or, Preludes to Attitude. Aiken
Quatrain: "I've learnt to laugh now at adversity." Farhat
Quatrain: "Time promises, should I in that confide?" Farhat
Quietude. Ladányi
Quod Tegit Omnia. Winters
Rhapsody on Time. Simon
River of Life, The. Campbell
Road, The. Muir
Rome, Conqueror, Conquered. Sylvester
Scraps of Time. Linden
Sheep Fair, A. Hardy
So, So. Clerke
Song: "Let it be forgotten, as a flower is forgotten." Teasdale
Sonnet: Time and Account. Miguel de Guevara
Sorrow. Dickinson
Sound of Water. Ortega
Stillness. Flecker
Sun-Dial, The. Fr. Melincourt. Peacock
Sunshade, The. Hardy
Tahiti. Johnson
Temporary Facts. Stafford
There Isn't Time. Farjeon
This Solitude of Cataracts. Stevens
Thistledown. Fr. Sings Harry. Glover
Tide Rises, the Tide Falls, The. Longfellow
Time. Creeley
Time. Curnow
Time. Herbert
Time. Hodgson
Time. Ibarbourou
Time. Roubaud
Time. Shelley
Time. Fr. Hecatompathia; or, Passionate Century of Love. Watson
Time. Wynne
Time and Eternity. Bunyan
Time and Tide. Lamarre
Time, cruel time, come and subdue that brow. Fr. To Delia. Daniel
Time Is the Mercy of Eternity. Rexroth
Time; or, How the Line about Chagall's Lovers Disappears. Miller
Time Passes. Kitahara Hakushu
Time Passes. Lister
Time, Real and Imaginary. Coleridge
Time time said old King Tut. Marquis
Time, You Old Gypsy Man. Hodgson
Timers. Arnstein
Time's Bright Sand. Finch
Time's Dedication. Schwartz
Time's No Grammar. Kalász
Time's Song. Praed
To His Coy Mistress. Marvell
To His Watch, When He Could Not Sleep. Herbert of Cherbury
To Think of Time. Whitman
Trumpet, The. Ehrenburg
Unbeseechable, The. Cornford
Uncle Time. Scott
Upon Time. Herrick
Vanishing Point, The. Davison
Walk, The. Aiken
Weaver, The. Burleigh
What Did I Lose? Sun Yü-tang
What Is Time? Marsden
"When I do count the clock that tells the time." Fr. Sonnets, XII. Shakespeare
"When I have seen by Time's fell hand defaced." Fr. Sonnets, LXIV. Shakespeare
Who Was It, Tell Me. Heine

Wilderness. Seymour-Smith
Words in Time. MacLeish
Yesterday. Chesterman
You, Andrew Marvell. MacLeish
Timoshenko, Semyon Konstantinovich
Timoshenko. Keyes
Tinkers
Tinker Man. Unknown
Tintern Abbey
Tintern Abbey. Fr. Chepstow: A Poem. Davies
Tiresias
Judgement of Tiresias, The. Jacob
My mother wept loudly. Fr. Tiresias. Clarke
Tiresias. Garrett
Tisha Ba'Ab
Dirge for the Ninth of Ab. Unknown
Titanic (ship)
Convergence of the Twain (Lines on the Loss of the Titanic, The). Hardy
Final Moments, The. Fr. The Titanic. Pratt
Great Titanic. Unknown
I Sing of Shine. Knight
Tithonus
Tithonus. Tennyson
Titian (Tiziano Vecellio)
From Titian's "Bacchanal" in the Prado at Madrid. Moore
Titmice
Titmouse. De la Mare
See also Chickadees.
Titus (Roman Emperor)
Titus and Berenice. Heath-Stubbs
Toads
Adman into Toad. Polite
At the Garden Gate. McCord
Death of a Toad, The. Wilbur
Song of the Toad, The. Burroughs
Speckle-black Toad and freckle-green Frog. Fr. Thomas à Becket, a Dramatic Comedy. Darley
Spring Song. Finkel
Toad, A. Allen
Toad, The. Coatsworth
Toad, The. Oliver
Toad and the Rabbit, The. Martin
Toad Song. Brennan
Warty Bliggens, the Toad. Fr. Archy and Mehitabel. Marquis
Toasters
Toaster, The. Smith
Toaster Time. Merriam
Tobacco
Blest leaf! whose aromatic gales dispense. Fr. A Pipe of Tobacco. Browne
From a Tobacco Wrapper. Unknown
Hanging Burley. Miller
I'll Never Use Tobacco. Unknown
Letter to Madame la Marquise de S[imiane], on Sending Her Tobacco. C———.
Make three fourths of a cross, and a circle complete. Unknown
Ode to Tobacco. Calverley
On Tobacco. Cotton
On Tobacco. Pestel
Says the Miner to the Mucker. Unknown
Tobacco. Freneau
Tobacco is a filthy weed. Unknown
Tobacco Plant. Gurney
Tobacco ("Tobacco is a dirty weed."). Hemminger
Tobey, Mark
Mark Tobey's Legacy. Schmied
Toes
Hairy Toe, The. Unknown
If my legs cannot move. Morrison
Moses. Unknown
My Toe. Holman
See also Feet.

Tokyo, Japan
Dream after Touring the Tokyo Tokei.
Kogawa
Ending, The. Engle
Toledo, Spain
High Bridge above the Tagus River at Toledo,
The. Williams
Toledo. Campbell
Toller, Ernst
In Memoriam: Ernst Toller. Auden
Tollund Man
Tollund Man, The. Claus
Tollund Man, The. Heaney
Tombs. *See* **Cemeteries; Graves;**
Mausoleums.
Tone, Wolfe
Wolfe Tone. Clarke
Tongues
Canzone: "Consider the three functions of the
tongue." Hacker
Tongue. Marcus
Tongue, The. Strong
Tools
Hammer, A. Guillevic
His Request. O'Sullivan
Toothaches
Meditation upon the Toothache, A. Lerner
See also **Teeth.**
Toothbrushes
My Six Toothbrushes. McGinley
Torah, The
Angels Came a-Mustering, The. *Unknown*
Expounding the Torah. Zukofsky
Pilpul. Kamenetz
Simhat Torah. Gordon
Talmud Student, The. Bialik
This Feast of the Law. *Unknown*
Tories
Tory Pledges. Moore
Tornadoes
News of the Occluded Cyclone. Fulton
Sherman Cyclone, The. *Unknown*
Terrestrial Magnetism. Fulton
Tornado, The. Césaire
Tornado, The. Russell
Tupelo Destruction, The. *Unknown*
Toronto, Ontario
Nights Passed on Ward's Island, Toronto
Harbour. Fetherling
Often I sit in the sun and brooding over the
city, always. *Fr.* Civil Elegies. Lee
Tortillas
Consecration of the Corn Tortilla.
Castorrivas
Tortoises
Baby Tortoise. Lawrence
Desert Tortoise. Baylor
Elegy for the Giant Tortoises. Atwood
Hare and the Tortoise, The. Serraillier
Meditations of a Tortoise Dozing under a
Rosetree Near a Beehive at Noon While a
Dog Scampers About and a Cuckoo Calls
from a Distant Wood. Rieu
Night Thought of a Tortoise Suffering from
Insomnia on a Lawn. Rieu
To My Tortoise Chronos. Lee-Hamilton
Tortoise Family Connections. Lawrence
Tortoise Gallantry. Lawrence
Tortoise-Shell. Lawrence
Tortoise Shout. Lawrence
Torture
Ala. Nichols
For My Torturer, Lieutenant D——. Djabali
No Need for Nuremberg. Marx
On Hearing That Torture Was Suppressed
throughout the Austrian Dominions.
Bampfylde
Poet's Counsel ("You come from the line of a
Cola king"), A. Kovur Kilar
Things That Are Worse than Death. Olds

Toulouse-Lautrec, Henri de
Comedy of Art: Henri de Toulouse Lautrec,
The. Howard
Mule Team and Poster. Justice
Note to R. H. from Strongsville. Hugo
Tourism and Tourists
For the Stranger. Forché
Importer, An. Frost
Manners. Shiffert
Niagara Falls. Dugan
Permanent Tourists, The. Page
Thief, The. Kunitz
Tourist. Al-Maghut
Tourist and the Town, The. Rich
Tourists. Moss
Trading Post—Winslow, Arizona. Meyette
Trials of a Tourist. Tibble
Virgins, The. Walcott
Toussaint L'Ouverture, François Dominique
To Toussaint L'Ouverture. Wordsworth
Toussaint L'Ouverture. Ray
Toussaint L'Ouverture. Robinson
Towns
Another Small Town in Georgia. Ramke
Be'mi'ster. Barnes
Good Town, The. Muir
It's the Little Towns I Like. Lux
Purpose of Altar Boys, The. Ríos
Small Towns. Murguía
Steeple-Jack, The. Moore
Up at a Villa—Down in the City. Browning
See also **Cities; Villages.**
Toys
Block City. Stevenson
Cirque d'Hiver. Bishop
Land of Counterpane, The. Stevenson
Little Boy Blue. Field
Lost Teddy Bear, The. Johnson
Mrs. Indiarubber Duck. Carter
My Toys. McCrea
Orange Bears, The. Patchen
Ships of Yule, The. Carman
Tin Frog, The. Hoban
Tin Toys. Gar
Toys. Sutskever
Toys Talk of the World, The. Pyle
Track Athletics
Death of the Trackstar. Meissner
From the Greek Anthology. Krinagoras
High Jumper. Welch
Hurdler. Butcher
Kind of Thanks, A. *Fr.* From the XXIII
Summer Olympics, the Poet as Report.
Fischer
Mighty Runner, A. Robinson
Notes on a Track Meet. McCord
Pole Vaulter. Evans
Runner. Auden
Runner, The. Whitman
Sluggard, The. Lucilius
Sprinters, The. Murchison
Standing Broad Jump, The. Frost
Tractors
Drive a Tractor. *Unknown*
New Farm Tractor. Sandburg
Traction Engine, The. Auden
Trafalgar, Battle of (1805)
Night of Trafalgar, The. *Fr.* The Dynasts.
Hardy
Trafalgar. Palgrave
Victory. *Unknown*
Traffic
Before Disaster. Winters
Traffic Accidents. *See* **Automobile Accidents.**
Traherne, Thomas
Of Thomas Traherne and the Pebble Outside.
Clouts

Trains
All I'd wanted was to get on a train. *Fr.*
Forty-seven Tanka in Three Lines.
Ishikawa Takuboku
Blurry Cow. Twichell
By Rail through the Earthly Paradise, Perhaps
Bedfordshire. Levertov
California Zephyr, The. Kroll
Casey Jones. *Unknown*
Departure. Reverdy
Empties Coming Back. Ponciano
Engine Driver, The. "O."
Express, The. Spender
Faintheart in a Railway Train. Hardy
Freight Train, The. Bennett
From a Railway Carriage. Stevenson
Funeral Trains. Ishihara Yoshiro
Goat, The. *Unknown*
Hold-up. MacNeice
Holiday Train, The. Thompson
I like to see it lap the miles. Dickinson
In a Train. Bly
In the Dome Car of the "Canadian." Marty
In the Train. Thomson
Jim Crow Cars. Moorer
Journey, The. Clarke
Landscape as Metal and Flowers. Scott
Limited. Sandburg
Modern Dragon, A. Bennett
Mystic Moment. Tate
Night Journey. Roethke
Night Mail North, The.
Cholmondeley-Pennell
Night Train. Stoutenburg
North Philadelphia, Trenton, and New York.
Lattimore
Ode: "Lend me thy great noise, thy powerful,
gentle gait." Larbaud
Old Station of Cahors, The. Larbaud
Orient Express, The. Jarrell
Praises of the Train. Segooa
Punishment for a Wayward Train. Jacinto
Railroad Cars Are Coming, The. *Unknown*
Railroad Thieves. Weinstein
Red Letters. McBride
Regent's Park Terrace. Spencer
Reindeer and Engine. Jacobsen
Rhyme of the Rail[s]. Saxe
Siding near Chillicothe, A. Lattimore
Sister on the Tracks, A. Hall
Song of a Train. Davidson
Song of the Engine, The. Worsley-Benison
Song of the Train. McCord
This Train ("This train is bound for glory, this
train"). *Unknown*
To a Locomotive in Winter. Whitman
Track. Tranströmer
Train, The. Brownjohn
Train, The. Coleridge
Train, The. Machado
Train, The. *Unknown*
Train: Abstraction. Taggard
Train Song. Siebert
Train to Dublin. MacNeice
Train Tune. Bogan
Trains. Shepherd
Trains. Tippett
Travel. Millay
Travelling Backward. Baro
Vacation. Stafford
Western Town. Shapiro
See also **Railroads.**
Traitors. *See* **Treason and Traitors.**
Tramps. *See* **Vagabonds.**
Transformation
Frog Prince, The. Smith
Metamorphosis. Yolen
Transformations. Hardy

Transience
Adieu, Farewell, Earth's Bliss[e]. *Fr.*
  Summer's Last Will and Testament.
  Nashe
After the Revolution for Jesus the Associate
  Professor [*or* a Secular Man] Prepares His
  Final Remarks. Williams
Along the Field as We Came By. *Fr.* A
  Shropshire Lad. Housman
Ancestors. Habib
Apple, The. Plato
As I Walked Out One Evening. Auden
Before a Corpse. Acuña
Blue Girls. Ransom
Break, Break, Break. Tennyson
Breathing Space July. Tranströmer
Changes to Corinna, The. Herrick
Corinna's Going a-Maying. Herrick
Do not say that time once gone can never be
  returned! *Fr.* Moments of Fullfillment—
  Writing Down Miscellaneous. Yüan Mei
Epilogue: "Years later the girl died." Pastan
Even Such Is Time. Ralegh
Fear No More the Heat o' the Sun. *Fr.*
  Cymbeline. Shakespeare
Grandmother Watching at Her Window.
  Merwin
Groundhog, The. Eberhart
Haka: The Feathered Albatross. Walters
In this world is there. *Fr.* Kokin Shu.
  Unknown
La Chute. Olson
March Journal. Wright
Nothing Gold Can Stay. Frost
Now is Past. Clare
"Nox Nocti Indicat Scientiam." *Fr.* Castara.
  Habington
Nymph's Reply to the Shepherd, The.
  Ralegh
On a Stupendous Leg of Granite, Discovered
  Standing by Itself in the Deserts of Egypt,
  with the Inscription Inserted Below. Smith
On the Vanity of Earthly Greatness.
  Guiterman
Our Revels Now Are Ended. *Fr.* The
  Tempest. Shakespeare
Ozymandias [*or* Ozymandias of Egypt*or*
  Sonnet: Ozymandias]. Shelley
Palinode, A. Bolton
Passing of the Forest, The. Reeves
Pont Mirabeau. Kennedy
Response. Bethell
Road, The. Muir
Ruin, The. *Unknown*
"Shall I compare thee to a summer's day?"
  Fr. Sonnets, XVIII. Shakespeare
Sic Vita. King
Sonnet: "I know that all beneath the moon
  decays." Drummond
Sunlight on the Garden, The. MacNeice
Sweet Will. Levine
Temporary Facts. Stafford
This Day. Raab
Those Hours When Happy Hours Were My
  Estate. Millay
Time. Bethell
To Blossoms. Herrick
To Daffodils [*or* Daffadills]. Herrick
To Dianeme. Herrick
To the Stone-Cutters. Jeffers
Trying to Name What Doesn't Change. Nye
Virtue. Herbert
Waka on Impermanence. Dogen
We are helpless in this world. *Fr.* Manyo
  Shu. Okura
What If a Day [or a Month or a Year].
  Campion
See also **Change.**
Translations and Translators
Each poet with a different talent writes. *Fr.*
  An Essay on Translated Verse.
  Roscommon

Lesson in Translation, A. Preil
On First Looking into Chapman's Homer.
  Keats
On the Translation of Anacreon. Walpole
On Tom Moore's Translation of Anacreon.
  Erskine
Translation. Lesser
Translations. Rich
Translator to Translated. Pound
Transportation, Penal
Moreton Bay. *Unknown*
Trapeze Artists
Man on the Flying Trapeze, The. *Unknown*
Trapping and Trappers
Hare in Winter. Piercy
Little Random Creatures, The. *Unknown*
Meeting Trappers on the Road in Heavy
  Snow. Li K'ai-hsien
Snare, The. Stephens
Staying Overnight on the Banks of
  Embroidered River. Li K'ai-hsien
Trash. *See* **Garbage and Garbage Men.**
Traubel, Helen
I Like to Sing Also. Updike
Traveling and Travelers
Cranes fly calling towards Sakurada Fields.
  Fr. Manyo Shu. Kurohito
Drawn on by moonlight. *Fr.* Twenty-three
  Tanka. Tamekane
Driving toward the Lac Qui Parle River. Bly
Even if one has. Ryoshun
Far Trek. Brady
Frightened Flier Goes North, The. Kazantzis
From a Railway Carriage. Stevenson
Frontier, The. Hewitt
Gemwood. Bell
Good-Night. Thomas
He passes the inn. Tamekane
Hitch Haiku. Snyder
Home Leave. Howes
How many mountains and rivers to cross.
  Fr. Forty-four Tanka. Wakayama Bokusui
How marvelous a fellow. *Fr.* Manyo Shu.
  Unknown
I am on a journey. *Fr.* Manyo Shu.
  Unknown
I drank yesterday, I drink today. *Fr.*
  Forty-four Tanka. Wakayama Bokusui
Ibn Battuta. Davis
Ijajee's Story. DeClue
Journey into France, The. *Unknown*
Last Farewell, The. Miyazawa Kenji
Lonely Traveller, The. Brew
Lunch. Koch
Man Walking through the Snow, A.
  Shotetsu
Melodic Trains. Ashbery
Movies for the Home. Moss
Moving between Beloit and Monroe. Noll
My friend, you are setting out. *Fr.* Manyo
  Shu. *Unknown*
Night Boat. Brown
Night Journey. Roethke
Night Song of a Traveller. Tachihara
  Michizo
Night Train. Hagiwara Sakutaro
No shelter in sight. Teika
North Philadelphia, Trenton, and New York.
  Lattimore
Not That Far. Miller
October Journey. Walker
Old Walking Song, The. Tolkien
On a journey and lonesome, I see below a
  hill. *Fr.* Manyo Shu. Kurohito
On a Trip. Hagiwara Sakutaro
On Descending the River Po. Parsons
On Tatsuta Hill. *Fr.* Manyo Shu.
  Mushimaro
On the beach of Iwashiro. *Fr.* Manyo Shu.
  Arima

On the Circuit. Auden
On the Road through Chang-te. Sun
  Yün-feng
On the road to Yamashiro. *Fr.* Manyo Shu.
  Unknown
Over 2000 Illustrations and a Complete
  Concordance. Bishop
Passing Miscanthus on the Road. Tamesada
Passing the shore of Minume. *Fr.* Manyo
  Shu. Hitomaro
Questions of Travel. Bishop
Railway Junction, The. De la Mare
River, The. *Fr.* The Bridge: Powhatan's
  Daughter. Crane
Sestina of the Tramp-Royal. Kipling
Silver. Juhász
Six on the Desert Ways. Otalantaiyar
Song: Thoughts of a Traveler on the Chikuma
  River. Toson
Spencer the Rover. *Unknown*
Stepping Westward. Wordsworth
Moon as your guide, The. *Fr.* Seventy-six
  Hokku. Basho
There Are So Many Ways of Going Places.
  Thompson
They Clapped. Giovanni
To My Fellow-Mariners, March, '53.
  Whitbread
Travel. Gyoko
Travel. Millay
Travel. Stevenson
Travel Poem, A. Teika
Traveler. Kenji
Travelers/ are all up and on their way, The.
  Abutsu the Nun
Traveling past a Market Town. Shotetsu
Traveller, The. Berryman
Traveller Has Regrets, The. Fraser
Travellers. Adcock
Travelling. Graddon
Travelling Companions. Armour
Trip, The. Stafford
Unexplorer, The. Millay
Uphill [*or* Up-Hill]. Rossetti
What Her Girl Friend Said, Consoling Her
  when She Was Distressed by the Town's
  Gossip. Uloccanar
What Her Girl Friend Said to Him, Trying to
  Dissuade Him from His Long Journey.
  Unknown
What She Said ("Forest animals walk there").
  Kapilar
When the new day dawns. Ietaka
Wonderful is the sea. *Fr.* Manyo Shu.
  Unknown
World's Wanderers, The. Shelley
Oxford Book of Travel Verse, The (OBTV).
  Kevin Crossley-Holland, ed.
Treason and Traitors
Ballad of Christmas, A. De la Mare
If Justice Moved. Sellers
This *Humanist* Whom No Beliefs Constrained.
  Cunningham
Treasures
Spanish Waters. Masefield
Treaties
Hand That Signed the Paper Felled a City,
  The. Thomas
Tree of Life
Last Statement for a Last Oracle. Dugan
On Finding the Tree of Life. Dugan
Tree Toads. *See* **Toads.**
Trees
Advice to a Forest. Bodenheim
All That Time. Swenson
Although I Remember the Sound. Huff
And So They Withered. Winkler
Autumn Fancies. *Unknown*
Autumnal Spring Song. Miller
Bare Almond-Trees. Lawrence
Bare Arms of Trees, The. Tagliabue

Be Different to Trees. Davies
Binsey Poplars (Felled 1879). Hopkins
Birches. Frost
Black Walnut Tree, The. Oliver
Bound. Roethke
Brocades left at the treetops ceased to be,
   The. *Fr.* Seventy-eight Tanka. Shikishi
Buds. Coatsworth
Chestnut Avenue at Alton House, The.
   Tomlinson
Child's Song in Spring. Nesbit
City Tree, The. Crawford
City Trees. Millay
Complicity. Gallagher
Dogwood Blossoms. Blue Cloud
Every Time I Climb a Tree. McCord
Fallen Elm, The. Clare
Fallen Tree, The. Young
Felled Plane Tree, The. Hajnal
Fir Tree. Brown
Five-Fingered Maple, The. Brown
Foreign Soil. Hai-Jew
Forester's Song. Coppard
Gathered at the River. Levertov
Good Company. Baker
Great-great Grandma, Don't Sleep in Your
   Treehouse Tonight. Kennedy
Green Grass Growing All Around, The.
   Unknown
Haiku: "Against the broad sky." Takahama
   Kyoshi
Hampstead; the Horse Chestnut Trees. Gunn
Happy Tree, The. Gould
He Praises the Trees. *Unknown*
Heart of the Tree, The. Bunner
House of the Trees, The. Wetherald
Hurrah for Trees! Nagy
I Consider the Tree. Buber
In One Place. Wallace
In the Ringwood. Kinsella
Injured Maple. Everson
Into the Tree. Milosz
Jacaranda. Livingston
Jungle Trees, The. Wilson
Juniper. Duggan
Keeping Things Whole. Strand
Larch Trees. Kitahara Hakushu
Laurel Tree, The. Simpson
Learning by Doing. Nemerov
Lines to a Tree. Teller
London Trees. Nethercliff
Long Island. Bell
Maidenhair Tree, The. Curry
Mango Tree, The. Chock
Mountain Tree, The. Connell
Music of a Tree, The. Turner
Nest, The. Bell
New Year for Trees, The. Schwartz
No Ordinary Sun. Tuwhare
November through a Giant Copper Beech.
   Honig
Old Tree, The. Young
On a Tree Fallen across the Road. Frost
On the day my father died a flame-tree. *Fr.*
   Brother Jonathan, Brother Kafka.
   O'Sullivan
On the Life of Trees. Jandl
On Trees. Dugan
Orchard Trees, January. Wilbur
Out on Kara Cape. Tameko
Over empty limbs. Tamekane
Paradigm. Deutsch
Pastoral, A: "Wise old apple tree in spring,
   The." Hillyer
Plant a Tree. Larcom
Planting Trees. Friedlaender
Pruned Tree, The. Moss
Roots. Ginsberg
Rowan, The. Jacob
Second Shadow. Roethke
Snow-Gum, The. Stewart
Some Trees. Ashbery

Song of the Open Road. Nash
Song to a Tree. Markham
Sound of Trees, The. Frost
South Seas. Pavese
Strange Tree. Roberts
Stump, The. Bly
Sweeney Praises the Trees. *Unknown*
Tall Trees. Mathias
Tapestry Trees. Morris
Tenebris. Grimké
Then. Levine
These Trees Are No Forest of Mourners.
   Jones
They. Bell
This Tree. Hathaway
This Way Only. Harford
Three Drawings. Ladányi
To Sycamores. Herrick
Tree. Artaud
Tree, The. Björnson
Tree, The. Ehrenburg
Tree, The. Very
Tree and the Lady, The. Hardy
Tree at My Window. Frost
Tree Celebrates the River, The. Goldberg
Tree Design, A. Bontemps
Tree-Felling, Upper Junction Road.
   Turner
Tree in the Garden, The. Chandler
Tree of Liberty, The. Burns
Tree Old Woman. Makidemewabe
Tree Party. MacNeice
Tree Sleeps in the Winter, The. Russell
Tree Surgeon. Herzberg
Tree to Flute. Hajnal
Trees. Coleridge
Trees. Hughes
Trees. Kilmer
Trees. Nemerov
Trees, The. Larkin
Trees, The. Rich
Trees. Schutting
Trees and Cattle. Dickey
Trees and Evening Sky. Momaday
Trees Are Down, The. Mew
Trees at Night. Johnson
Trees at the Arctic Circle. Purdy
Trees both in hills and plaines, in plenty be.
   Wood
Trees in the Garden. Lawrence
Trees Lose Parts of Themselves Inside a
   Circle of Fog. Ponge
Trees, Who Are Distant. Warr
Tulip Tree. Sitwell
Twenty Lines to a Tree. Teller
War against the Trees, The. Kunitz
What Do We Plant [When We Plant the
   Tree]. Abbey
When Mary Goes Walking. Chalmers
When the plum-blossoms are gone. *Fr.*
   Manyo Shu. Sakiko
Willow-Man, The. Ewing
Winter Trees. Plath
Wood Music. King
Woodman, Spare That Tree. Morris
Yes! I have seen the ancient oak. *Fr.* The
   Brereton Omen. Hemans
Yew Trees. Wordsworth
See also names of tree species.
Trelawny, Sir Jonathan
Song of the Western Men, The. Hawker
Trench Warfare
Aftermath. Sassoon
Anthem for Doomed Youth. Owen
Attack. Sassoon
Counter-Attack. Sassoon
Dug-out, The. Sassoon
Exposure. Owen
Great War, The. Scannell
In Parenthesis,*sels.* Jones
In the Trench. Gellert
It's a Queer Time. Graves

Rear-Guard, The. Sassoon
Winter Warfare. Rickword
Trenton, Battle of (1776)
At the Grave of Walker. Miller
Battle of Trenton, The. *Unknown*
Trenton and Princeton. *Unknown*
Washington by the Delaware. Miller
Trieste, Italy
Three Streets. Saba
Trilobites
Lay of the Trilobite, The. Kendall
Trinidad and Tobago
Brain Drain. "Mighty Chalkdust"
Fortunate Traveller, The. Walcott
Piarco. Roach
Port of Spain. Walcott
Returning to Store Bay. Howes
Spoiler's Return, The. Walcott
Tell Me Again. Keens-Douglas
Yankees Back, The. "Mighty Sparrow, The"
Trinity, The
Feast of the Most Holy Trinity. De Vere
Trinity, The. *Unknown*
Triolet (form)
Early Supper. Howes
First Photos of Flu Virus. Witt
How Great My Grief. Hardy
To a Fat Lady Seen from the Train.
   Cornford
Triolet against Sisters. McGinley
Triolet: "When first we met we did not
   guess." Bridges
Tristan da Cunha (islands)
Tristan da Cunha. Campbell
Tristram and Isolde
Tristram of Lyonesse,*sel,* Swinburne
Tristram's End. Binyon
Trystan and Esyllt. *Unknown*
Troilus and Cressida
Testament of Cresseid, The. Henryson
Troilus and Cressida, *sels.* Dryden
Troilus and Cressida, *sels.* Shakespeare
Troilus and Criseyde [*or* Criseide], *sels.*
   Chaucer
Trojan War
Aegean. Simpson
Leda and the Swan. Yeats
Menelaus and Helen. Brooke
Palladium. Arnold
Return, The ("The veteran Greeks came
   home"). Muir
Trojan Horse, The. Drummond
Trojans. Cavafy
Why They Waged War. Bishop
See also **Troy.**
Trolleys. *See* **Streetcars**.
Trolls
Her-zie. Smith
Kallundborg Church. Whittier
Stone Troll, The. Tolkien
Troll, The. Prelutsky
Trossachs, The (Scotland)
Trossachs, The. Wordsworth
Troubadours
Proensa; an Anthology of Troubadour Poetry
   (Pro). Paul Blackburn, comp. *and* tr.;
   George Economou, ed.
Women Troubadours, The (WT). Meg
   Bogin, ed.
Trout
Hamlen Brook. Wilbur
It Is Hard to Catch Trout. Piuvkaq
Sanctuary, The. Nemerov
Trout, The. Montague
Trout. Turner
Troy
Troy. Flower
Troy. Muir
Troy Depicted. *Fr.* The Rape of Lucrece.
   Shakespeare
See also **Trojan War.**

Trucks and Truckers
Country Trucks. Shannon
Song of the Truck. Frankel
Trucker, A. Gunn
Trucks. Tippett
Water-Truck, The. Lane
Why Log Truck Drivers Rise Earlier than
  Students of Zen. Snyder
Trujillo Molina, Rafael Leonidas
Cane Fields, The. *Fr.* Parsley. Dove
Palace, The. *Fr.* Parsley. Dove
Trumpets
How High the Moon. Jeffers
Lewis Has a Trumpet. Kuskin
Trust
Clear and loud. *Fr.* Manyo Shu. Hitomaro
Hymn of Trust, A. Sargent
Truth
Duty, or Truth at Work. Moorer
Goddess, The. Levertov
Hankering after Truth, A. Williams
Here, in This Little Bay. *Fr.* The Unknown
  Eros. Patmore
History of Truth, The. Auden
Leaders of the Crowd, The. Yeats
Lie, The. Ralegh
Lying. Wilbur
Meaning and Truth. Themerson
On Finding the Truth. Very
Red Beard, A. Leyeles
Robe of Flame. Sardar J'afri
Song of the Bald Eagle. *Unknown*
Standing on Tiptoe. Cameron
Tell all the truth but tell it slant. Dickinson
Therefore I Must Tell the Truth. Torlino
To Truth. *Fr.* Solomon. *Unknown*
Truth. "Æ"
Truth. Duggan
Truth. Heard
Truth, The. Joans
Truth, The. Lampman
Truth. Lloyd
Truth. McKay
Truth. Masefield
Truth. Riaz
Truth is as old as God. Dickinson
Truth Never Dies. *Unknown*
Truth Suppressed, The. Moorer
Truth, Sojourner
Ain't I a Woman? Truth
Oriflamme. Fauset
Sojourner Truth. *Fr.* Stars. Hayden
Stars. Hayden
Truxtun, Thomas
Truxton's Victory. *Unknown*
Tuberculosis
Consumptive, The. Thompson
Open up, Gate. *Fr.* Clouds behind the
  Forest. Leivick
Sanatorium. Leivick
Tuberculosis. Abse
Tuberoses
Tuberose. Block
Tubman, Harriet
Harriet Tubman. Walker
I Like to Think of Harriet Tubman. Griffin
Runagate Runagate. Hayden
Tugboats
Deep Sea Tug. Robertson
East River. Thomas
Tugs. Tippett
Tulip Trees
Tulip Tree. Sitwell
Tulips
Mimesis. Somlyó
Stately Lady, The. Sandstrom
To a Bed of Tulips. Herrick
Tulips. Colum
Tulips. Plath
Tulips and Addresses. Field

Tumbleweeds
Tumbleweed. Carden
Weeds. Stanford
Turkey
In the Turkish Ward. Balakian
Thoughts of Loved Ones. Fishback
Turkeys
Black November Turkey, A. Wilbur
Soliloquy of a Turkey. Dunbar
Table-Birds. Mackenzie
Turkey, A. Claus
Turkey is dancing near the rocks, A.
  Unknown
Turner, Dennis
Fast Break. Hirsch
Turner, Joseph Mallord William
Turner's Sunrise. Bevington
Turner, Lana
Poem: "Lana Turner has collapsed!" O'Hara
Turner, Mrs. Bishop
Resting. Heard
Turner, Nat
Ballad of Nat Turner, The. Hayden
Nat Turner. Allen
Remembering Nat Turner. Brown
Turnips
Mr. Finney's Turnip. *Unknown*
Swedes. Thomas
Turtle Doves
High in the pine-tree. *Unknown*
Turtledoves. Glatstein
See also **Doves**.
Turtles
Big Turtle, A. *Unknown*
Haiku: "I release a turtle." *Fr.* One Hundred
  Haiku in Free Form. Hosai
Haiku: "In a pond of silence a turtle." *Fr.*
  One Hundred Haiku in Free Form. Hosai
Little Turtle, The. Lindsay
Living Tenderly. Swenson
Mud Turtle, The. Nemerov
Snapper, The. Heyen
Tony the Turtle ("Tony was a turtle"). Rieu
Tortoise, The. Corman
Tortoise in Eternity, The. Wylie
Turtle. Lowell
Turtle, The. Nash
Turtle's Song, The. *Unknown*
Zimmer and His Turtle Sink the House.
  Zimmer
See also **Tortoises**.
Tuscany
Journey, The. Wright
Tuskegee Institute
Tuskegee. Hill
Twain, Mark
Last Laugh. Warren
"Twain, Mark" (Samuel Langhorne Clemens)
When the Mississippi Flowed in Indiana.
  Lindsay
Tweed (river), Scotland and England
Tweed Visited, The. Bowles
Twelfth Night
Ballad of the Epiphany. Dalmon
For Twelfth Day. Wadding
Old Christmas Morning. Helton
Twelfth Night. Booth
Twickenham, England
Twicknam *or* Twickenham Garden. Donne
Twilight
As day fades away. Hanazono
Autumn Dusk. Eifuku
Back to Life. Gunn
By the Margin of the Great Deep. "Æ"
Children's Hour, The. Longfellow
Crimson Leaves. Joben
Day That I Have Loved. Brooke
Dusk. Apollinaire
Dusk. Grimké
Dusk. Lopez-Penha
Dusk in the Country. Martinson

Dusk of Horses, The. Dickey
Evening Light along the Sound, The. Santos
Evening sunlight, The. Eifuku
From my little hut. Keiun
Georgia Dusk. Toomer
Going Under of the Evening Land, The.
  McBride
Half Past Four, October. Hajnal
Home-coming. Adams
I sit idly here. Chikako
In the gloom of dusk. Tamehide
Invisible Landscape. Wright
Lark, A. Tonna
Last weak rays, The. Kogon
Near Dusk. Auslander
On the Road at Dusk. Hanazono
Sparrows twitter, The. Hanazono
Twilight. Guggenberger
Twilight at Sea. Welby
Twilight Calm. Rossetti
Twilight in Middle March, A. Ledwidge
When the Day Comes. Gutiérrez Nájera
Winter Twilight. Elliot
Winter Twilight, A. Grimké
Winter Twilight. Lipsitz
See also **Evening; Sunset**.
Twins
Twins. Escoffery
Twins. Graves
Twins, The. Leigh
Twins. Matthews
Twins, The. Shapiro
Twins, The. Wright
Tyndale, William
From William Tyndale to John Frith.
  Bowers
Typing and Typists
Back from the Word-Processing Course, I Say
  to My Old Typewriter. Blumenthal
Learning to Type. O Hehir
Please Excuse Typing. Boothroyd
Typewriter Revolution, The. Enright
Tyranny
Epitaph on a Tyrant. Auden
Foreign Ruler, A. Landor
Human Debasement; a Fragment. Rushton
If You Ask Me Who I Am. Guebuza
In New South Wales, as I plainly see. *Fr.*
  The Devil and the Governor. Forster
Lindedi Singing. Banda
Poem of João, The. Sousa
Poem, A: "What is there that we can do or
  say." Mphahlele
Protea. Mattera
Rain and the Tyrants. Supervielle
Song to the Men of England. Shelley
Tyrone. *See* **County Tyrone, Northern
Ireland**.

U

Uccello, Paolo
Rout of San Romano, The. White
Uccello. Corso
UFOs. *See* **Flying Saucers**.
Uganda
In Uganda an Early King. Walker
Kaleidoscope, The. Gill
Ugliness
Deformed Mistress, The. Suckling
John, Tom, and James. Ross
Ukraine, U.S.S.R.
Zlochov [*or* Zlotchev, My Home]. Halpern
Ukrainians
Young Ukrainians. Shtoltsenberg
Ulysses
Last Words. *Fr.* Ithaca: The Palace at Four
  A.M. Howard

Lotos-Eaters, The. Tennyson
Odysseus. Fallon
Odysseus. Guri
Odysseus. Merwin
Odysseus in Phaeacia. Devecseri
Odyssey, The. Lang
Old Ships, The. Flecker
Strayed Reveller, The. Arnold
Ulysses. Graves
Ulysses. Saba
Ulysses. Tennyson
Ulysses and the Siren. Daniel
Ulysses Leaves the Nymph Calypso. *Fr.*
  Odyssey. Homer
Voyage. Kormos
World as Meditation, The. Stevens

Umbrellas
Days I've got. *Unknown*
Elf and the Dormouse, The. Herford
My New Umbrella. Hutchinson
Umbrella, The. Stanford
Umbrellas. Esbensen

Uncle Tom's Cabin
Eliza in Uncle Tom's Cabin. Bibb
She's Free! Harper

Uncles
Bobby's First Poem. Gale
Lolo died yesterday. Zarco
Magician, The. Miranda
My Uncle. Corbett
My Wicked Uncle. Mahon
Nobody Loses All the Time. Cummings
Uncle. Graham
Uncle. Levine
Uncle Avram Pastures the Horses. *Fr.*
  Byelorussia. Kulbak
Winter at Night in the Old Hut. *Fr.*
  Byelorussia. Kulbak

Underground Railroad
Runagate Runagate. Hayden

Underhill, John
John Underhill. Whittier

Undertakers
Undertakers' Club, The. *Unknown*

Underwear
Underwear. Ferlinghetti

Unemployment
Between an Unemployed Artist and His Wife.
  Unknown
Brother, Can You Spare a Dime? Harburg
Homely Advice to the Unemployed.
  Laycock
Muckers. Sandburg
Prayer: "God, I need a job because I need
  money." Dugan
Tiempo Muerto. Alonso
Tom's Garland: Upon the Unemployed.
  Hopkins
Trinity Place. McGinley
Unemployment/Monologue. Jordan

Unicorns
Days of the Unicorns, The. Webb
I Stood in the Maytime Meadows. *Unknown*
Inhuman Henry. Housman
Late Passenger, The. Lewis
Oh this is the animal that never was. *Fr.*
  The Unicorn. Rilke
Taliessin's Song of the Unicorn. Williams
Unicorn, The. *Fr. Nepenthe.* Darley
Unicorn, The. Komrij
Unicorn, The. Pitter
Unicorn, The. Rieu
Unicorn. Smith
Unicorn, The. Young
Unicorn and the Lady, The. Garrigue
Unicornis Tale, The. *Fr. The Talis of the
  Fyve Bestis. Unknown*

Union of Soviet Socialist Republics. *See*
  Russia

Unions, Labor. *See* **Labor Unions.**

Unitas, John
Unitas. Gold

United Nations
Just Dropped In. Cole

United States
America. *Fr. The Torch-Bearers.* Bates
America. Creeley
America. Ginsberg
America. McKay
America. Newlove
America. Smith
America. Whitman
America a Prophecy. Blake
America Bleeds. Lewis
America for Me. Van Dyke
America the Beautiful. Bates
America the Beautiful. Rice
American Eagle, The. Lawrence
American Letter. MacLeish
American Lights, Seen from Off Abroad.
  Berryman
American Names. Benét
Brooklyn Heights. Wain
Columbia. *Unknown*
Coming Back to America. Dickey
Das Kapital. Baraka
Dear Land of All My Love. *Fr. The
  Centennial Meditation of Columbia.*
  Lanier
Dreaming America. Oates
Empire Builders. MacLeish
1492. Lazarus
From My Lai the Thunder Went West. Ryan
From Paumanok Starting I Fly like a Bird.
  Whitman
Gift Outright, The. Frost
Great Society, The. Bly
Hail, Columbia. Hopkinson
I am waiting for my case to come up. *Fr.*
  Oral Messages. Ferlinghetti
I Hear America Singing. Whitman
I, Too. Hughes
I Went into the Maverick Bar. Snyder
In the States. Stevenson
Inner Part, The. Simpson
International Hymn. Huntington
Invocation: "American muse, whose strong
  and diverse heart." *Fr. John Brown's
  Body.* Benét
Land of the Free. Hosking
Land of the Free. MacLeish
Land That We Love. Gilder
Land Where Hate Should Die, The.
  McCarthy
Lion's Cub, The. Thompson
Lyric: "From now on kill America out of your
  mind." Agee
Map of My Country. Holmes
Melting Pot, The. Randall
Men. MacLeish
Meredith Phyfe. *Fr. The New Spoon River.*
  Masters
Minority Report. Updike
Mrs. Trollope in America. Bevington
My Blackness Is the Beauty of This Land.
  Jeffers
My Country, to Thy Shore. Williams
New Colossus, The. Lazarus
Next to of Course God America I.
  Cummings
Night Journey. Roethke
Nobody Lives on Arthur Godfrey Boulevard.
  Costanzo
N.Y. to L.A. by Jet Plane. Dorman
O Beautul, My Country. Hosmer
Ode Recited at the Harvard Commemoration.
  Lowell
Oh Mother of a Mighty Race. Bryant
On the Prospect of Planting Arts and Learning
  in America. Berkeley
Our Country. Thoreau
Parting of the Ways, The. Gilder
Passage to India. Whitman
Peace Hymn of the Republic. Van Dyke

Plain-Chant for America. Chapin
Poem of the Forty-eight States, A. Koch
Poem, or Beauty Hurts Mr. Vinal.
  Cummings
Serpent Knowledge. *Fr. An Explanation of
  America.* Pinsky
Shine, Perishing Republic. Jeffers
Sleep, My Child. Aleichem
Then and Now. Harper
To My Son Parker, Asleep in the Next Room.
  Kaufman
To the States. Whitman
To the Western World. Simpson
Toast to the Flag, A. Daly
United States, The. Goethe
United States of America We, The. Abrams
Unmanifest Destiny. Hovey
Verses on the Prospect of Planting Arts and
  Learning in America. Berkeley
Voice of America, 1961, The. Liddy
Vow, A. Ginsberg
What Happened Here Before. Snyder
Yonder. Eberhart
Gift Outright, The; America to Her Poets
  (GOA). Helen Plotz, ed.
101 Patriotic Poems (OPP).

Unity
Cutting Greens. Clifton

Universe
Christ in the Universe. Meynell
Imagine Grass. Skinner
Ode on Zero. Pettingell
Physical Universe. Simpson
Universe, The. Miller

Universities. *See* **Colleges and Universities.**

Unknown Soldier
Elegy for an Unknown Soldier. Baxter
Infinite Debt, The. Bates
Unknown, The. Laughlin
Unknown Soldier, The. Rose
Unknown Soldiers. *Fr. The New Spoon
  River.* Masters
Unknown Warrior Speaks, The. Smith

Urbino, Italy
Walls of Urbino, The. Volponi

Urdu Poetry
*Golden Tradition, The; an Anthology of Urdu
  Poetry* (GoT). Ahmed Ali, ed. *and* tr.
Penguin Book of Modern Urdu Poetry, The
  (PBMUP). Mahmood Jamal, ed. *and* tr.

Uriel
Uriel. Emerson

Ursa Major
Great Bear, The. Hollander
Ursa Major. Kirkup

Usury
Gombeen, The. Campbell
With Usura. *Fr. Cantos.* Pound

Utah
From the Salt Lake City Airport—82. Harjo
Marching to Utah. *Unknown*
Salt Lake City. Carruth

Ute Indians
Ute Mountain. Tomlinson

Utopia
Anglicized Utopia. Gilbert
Pantisocracy. Coleridge
Utopia. Szymborska

V

Vacation
Any Time. Stafford
Back Again for the Holidays. *Fr.
  Summoned by Bells.* Betjeman
First vacation day, A. Schutting
I'm Going to Rocky Island. *Unknown*

In the Motel. Kennedy
July Wakes. Pomfret
Lake Chemo. Rowe
Movies for the Home. Moss
On Vacation. Creeley
Vacation. Stafford
Vacation on Earth, A. Disch
Vacation Time. Hutt
Vacuum Cleaners
Vacuum, The. Nemerov
Vagabonds
African Tramp, The. Haresnape
Communion of Saints: The Poor Bastard
 under the Bridge. Ponsot
Despised and Rejected. Bates
Drifters. Dawe
Drifter's Song. Leino
Dying Hobo, The. *Unknown*
Every Shuiler Is Christ. Campbell
Freeborn Man. MacColl
Jay Gould's Daughter. *Unknown*
Joys of the Road, The. Carman
Nocturne: "Song of a blackbird in my ears."
 Leino
November. Hughes
Old Woman of the Roads, An. Colum
People Who Talk to Themselves. *Fr. New
 York Everywhere.* Vaynshteyn
Raggedy Man, The. Riley
River, The. *Fr. The Bridge: Powhatan's
 Daughter.* Crane
Road to Vagabondia, The. Burnet
Sestina of the Tramp-Royal. Kipling
Song of the Open Road. Whitman
Sundowner, The. Neilson
Things of the Spirit. Mason
To a Vagabond. Woodrow
Trampwoman's Tragedy, A. Hardy
Two Hoboes. *Unknown*
Two Tramps in Mud Time. Frost
Vagabond, The. Stevenson
Vagabonds, The. Trowbridge
Wanderers. Calverley
Wanderer's Song, A. Masefield
When window-lamps had dwindled, then I
 rose. *Fr. The Wanderer.* Brennan
Valentine's Day
St. Valentine. Moore
To Clarastella on St. Valentines Day
 Morning. Heath
To His Valentine. Drayton
Tomorrow Is Saint Valentine's Day. *Fr.
 Hamlet.* Shakespeare
Valentine. Hall
Valentine. Hemingway
Valentine, A. Richards
Valentine. Silverstein
Valentine, A. Thompson
Valentines to My Mother, 1880. Rossetti
Valkyries
Fatal Sisters, The. Gray
Song of the Valkyries, The. *Unknown*
Valparaiso, Battle of (1866)
Battle of Valparaiso, The. *Unknown*
Vampires
But thou, false infidel! shall writhe. *Fr. The
 Giaour.* Byron
La Belle Morte. Aiken
Undead, The. Wilbur
Vampire, The. Kipling
Vampire, The. Rebolledo
Voices Answering Back: The Vampires.
 Raab
Vampires in Verse, The; an Anthology
 (VVA). Steven Moore, ed.
Van Doren, Mark
Ballad of Remembrance, A. Hayden
Van Gogh, Vincent
Birds of Arles, The. Fisher
Farewell to Van Gogh. Tomlinson
In the Van Gogh Room. Yamamoto
Vincent Van Gogh. Smith

Vancouver, British Columbia
Christ Walks in This Infernal District Too.
 Lowry
Vancouver Lights. Birney
Vancouver Island, British Columbia
Lairdless Place, The. Archer
Vandalism
Desk, The. Bottoms
Vanderbilt, Gloria
Poor Kid. Cole
Vane, Sir Henry (1613-62)
To Sir Henry Vane the Younger. Milton
Vanity
Evening Out, The. Nash
Flesh and the Spirit, The. Bradstreet
Goose, affected, empty, vain, A. *Fr. The
 Goose and the Swans.* Moore
Man and His Image, The. La Fontaine
On a Stupendous Leg of Granite, Discovered
 Standing by Itself in the Deserts of Egypt,
 with the Inscription Inserted Below. Smith
On National Vanity. McFarlane
On the Vanity of Earthly Greatness.
 Guiterman
Our God, Our Help in Ages Past. Watts
Ozymandias [*or* Ozymandias of Egypt*or*
 Sonnet: Ozymandias]. Shelley
Palinode, A. Bolton
Proud Maisie ("Proud Maisie is in the
 wood"). *Fr. The Heart of Midlothian.*
 Scott
Song of Emptiness to Fill up the Empty Pages
 Following, A. Wigglesworth
Spider and the Fly, The. Howitt
To Vanity. Turner
Vanity. Ungaretti
Vanity of All Worldly Things, The.
 Bradstreet
Vanity of Spirit. Vaughan
Verses under a Peacock Portrayed in Her Left
 Hand. Greene
See also **Pride.**
Vashti
Before the Feast of Shushan. Spencer
Vashti. Harper
Vaudeville
Death of the Vaudevillian, The. Sanders
Vaudeville. Kirstein
Vaughan, Henry
At the Grave of Henry Vaughan. Sassoon
To Henry Vaughan. Smith
Vaughn, Robert Boardman
In Memory of the Unknown Poet, Robert
 Boardman Vaughn. Justice
Veeries
Veery, The. Van Dyke
Veery-Thrush, The. Taylor
Vegetables
For Instance. McAlmon
Fruits and Vegetables. Saba
Mummies, The. Kumin
Potato. Wilbur
Say It with Vegetables. Snoek
Swedes. Thomas
Vegetables. Farjeon
Young Lettuce. Kopland
See also *names of specific vegetables.*
Vegetarians
Logical Vegetarian, The. Chesterton
Velázquez, Diego Rodríguez de Silva y
Francis Bacon Paints Velázquez's Pope.
 Schmied
Juan de Pareja: Painted by Velazquez. Long
Rokeby Venus, The. Conquest
Venereal Disease
Buck's Elegy, The. *Unknown*
Young Sailor Cut Down in His Prime, The.
 Unknown
See also **Syphilis.**
Vengeance
Famine Year, The. Wilde

Venice, Italy
Doves of Venice, The. Hutton
From a Venetian Sequence. Naudé
Heat Spell in Venice. Goldberg
I stood in Venice on the Bridge of Sighs.
 Fr. Childe Harold's Pilgrimage. Byron
Music in Venice. Simpson
On the Extinction of the Venetian Republic.
 Wordsworth
Saint Maria Maggiore. Fritsch
Gondola that glides, The. *Fr. The Motets.*
 Montale
Toccata of Galuppi's, A. Browning
Venetian Fragment. Hergouth
Venice. Longfellow
Venice. Symons
Violets in Saint Mark's Square. Valeri
Water-Colour of Venice, A. Durrell
Venus (goddess)
Birth of Venus. Urdang
Evening Star, The. *Fr. Moon-Bone Song [or
 Cycle].*
Infida's Song. *Fr. Never Too Late.*
 Greene
Invocation: "Appear, O Mother, was the
 perpetual cry." Watson
Mars and Venus. *Fr. Tullie's Love.*
 Greene
Prayer to Venus. *Fr. The Faerie Queene.*
 Spenser
Queen of Paphos, Erycine, The. *Unknown*
Spoken by Venus on Seeing Her Statue Done
 by Praxiteles. *Unknown*
Venus and Adonis. Browne
Venus and Adonis. Shakespeare
Venus of the Salty Shell. Devlin
Venus Transiens. Lowell
See also **Aphrodite.**
Venus of Milo (statue)
Venus of the Louvre. Lazarus
Venus (planet)
But Venus first. *Fr. First Dream.* Juana
 Inés de la Cruz
Hesperus. Clare
Morning Star, The. Brontë
Perspective. *Fr. The Angel in the House.*
 Patmore
Venus Poised. López
See also **Evening Star.**
Veracruz, Mexico
Beach at Veracruz, The. Bowering
Veracruz. Hayden
Verdi, Giuseppe
Barrel-Organ, The. Noyes
Verdun, Battle of (1916)
Memories of Verdun. Dugan
Vergil. *See* **Virgil.**
Verlaine, Paul
Birds in the Night. Cernuda
Prelude LVI: "Rimbaud and Verlaine,
 precious pair of poets." *Fr. Preludes for
 Memnon; or, Preludes to Attitude.* Aiken
Vermont
Fall Comes in Back-Country Vermont.
 Warren
Mating the Goats. Barnstone
Pearl Harbor Day 1970. Lourie
Poem to Explain Everything about a Certain
 Day in Vermont, A. Taggard
Vermont: Indian Summer. Booth
Versailles, France
No Swan So Fine. Moore
Pompadour, The. Thornbury
Versailles. Rich
Veterans
Aby Kirly, the War Hero. Halpern
By-Products. Wormser
Memorial to the Vicars of Urswick. Curry
Survivor, The. Cook
See also **Soldiers.**

Veterans' Day *or* **Armistice Day.** *See*
  Armistice.
Vice. *See* Evil; Sin.
Vicksburg Campaign (1862–63)
  Before Vicksburg. Boker
  Dear wife and bosom friend I hat seen hart.
    Fr. Letters from Vicksburg. Gildner
  Running the Batteries. Melville
Victoria, Queen of England
  1887. Housman
  Much Distressed. *Unknown*
  On the Jubilee of Queen Victoria. Tennyson
  Queen Victoria. *Unknown*
  Sidera Cadentia. Ford
  To the Queen of the British Government.
    Linden
  Widow at Windsor, The. Kipling
Victory
  Conquerors. Treece
Vienna, Austria
  Empire Clock, The. Spencer
  Vienna. Porter
Vienna, Siege of (1683)
  Carrouse to the Emperor, the Royal Pole, and
    the Much-wronged Duke of Lorrain, A.
    Unknown
Vietnam
  Advent 1966. Levertov
  Altars in the Street, The. Levertov
  Asians Dying, The. Merwin
  Bring the War Home. Matthews
  Burning Shit at An Khe. Weigl
  Butter. Schmidt
  "Containing Communism." Cobb
  Driving through Minnesota during the Hanoi
    Bombings. Bly
  Facing It. Komunyakaa
  Fare Thee Well. Siegel
  From My Lai the Thunder Went West. Ryan
  Gods in Vietnam. Redmond
  Grey October. "Critics, The"
  Guard at the Binh Thuy Bridge, The.
    Balaban
  Homecoming. Dawe
  How Much Longer? Mezey
  Ia Drang Valley. Komunyakaa
  In the Mourning Time. Hayden
  Junglegrave. Anderson
  Kilroy. McCarthy
  Lan Nguyen; the Uniform of Death, 1971.
    Mura
  Memo. Lynch
  Nam. Lowery
  National Security. MacLeish
  Negro Soldier's Viet Nam Diary, A. Martin
  Nerves. *Fr.* Tour of Duty. Huddle
  Norman Morrison. Mitchell
  Operation Memory. Lehman
  Poem for Viet Nam. Young Bear
  Poem to My Sister, Ethel Ennis, Who Sang
    "The Star-spangled Banner" at the Second
    Inauguration of Richard Milhous Nixon.
    Jordan
  Ponsonby/Remuera/My lai. Mitchell
  Problems. Scott
  Somewhere near Phu Bai. Komunyakaa
  Song My. Griffin
  Song of Napalm. Weigl
  Starlight Scope Myopia. Komunyakaa
  Teeth Mother Naked at Last, The. Bly
  Tenebrae. Levertov
  To Whom It May Concern. Mitchell
  Up Rising. *Fr.* Passages. Duncan
  Vapor Trail Reflected in the Frog Pond.
    Kinnell
  Vietnam. Faraz
  Vietnam. Major
  Vietnam. Zaidi
  Vietnam #4. Major
  Voice from Danang. Redshaw

  Wadasa Nakamoon, Vietnam Memorial.
    Young Bear
  Waking in the Dark. Livesay
  What Were They Like? Levertov
  Women in Vietnam, The. Paley
  Words. *Fr.* Tour of Duty. Huddle
Vikings
  Battle of Maldon, The. *Unknown*
  Christmas in England ("Heap on more
    wood!—the wind is chill") Time. *Fr.*
    Marmion. Scott
  Skeleton in Armor, The. Longfellow
  Vikings, The ("Bitter the wind tonight").
    Unknown
Villages
  Crown of Hatred and Love. Juhász
  Elegy: "Yes, I experienced youth." Wu
    Sheng
  Impressions of My Village. Wu Sheng
  Our Village—by a Villager. Hood
  So Let Me Have My Fun. Palazzeschi
  Sonnet:
    Saturday Evening in the Village. Leopardi
  Steeple-Jack, The. Moore
  Villages. Govoni
  See also **Towns.**
Villanelle (form)
  Amnesia. Lehman
  Canticle for Xmas Eve. Wagoner
  Chateau Papineau. Harrison
  Do Not Go Gentle into That Good Night.
    Thomas
  Ellie Mae Leaves in a Hurry. Klappert
  Freaks at Spurgin Road Field, The. Hugo
  House on the Hill, The. Robinson
  Missing Dates. Empson
  Obsessions. Levertov
  One Art. Bishop
  Runes for an Old Believer. Humphries
  Story We Know, The. Collins
  Crack is moving down the wall, The. *Fr.*
    Five Villanelles. Kees
  Unknown, The. Davidson
  Villanelle: "It is the pain, it is the pain,
    endures." Empson
  Villanelle: "It's all a trick, quite easy when
    you know it." Skeat
  Villanelle: "Proud inclination of the flesh."
    Laing
  Villanelle at Sundown. Justice
  Villanelle of Marguerites. Dowson
  Villanelle of Sunset. Dowson
  Villanelle of the Mystical Cycle. Leyeles
  Waking, The. Roethke
  Want Bone, The. Pinsky
  Women in Love. Justice
Villon, François
  Ballad of François Villon, A. Swinburne
  Ballade which Villon Made. MacDonagh
  Exile. Stroud
Vilna, Poland
  Like Groping Fingers. Sutskever
  Secret Town, The. Sutskever
  Vilna. Kulbak
  We Survive! Glick
Vinci, Leonardo da. *See* **Leonardo da Vinci.**
Vines
  Tapestry Trees. Morris
Vinland
  Story of Vinland, The. *Fr.* Psalm of the
    West. Lanier
Violence
  Be punctual then to know. *Fr.* The Art of
    Wenching. *Unknown*
  Beating, The. Stanford
  Bloody Sire, The. Jeffers
  Great Palaces of Versailles, The. Dove
  Law in the Country of the Cats. Hughes
  Man Is Beaten Up, A. Garai
  Militerotics. Ortleb

  Sereno. Lea
  Snowy Egret. Weigl
  Street Fight. Monro
  To the Spirit of Monahsetah. DeClue
  Under the Green Ceiling. Dobyns
  Why We Bombed Haiphong. Holden
Violets
  Coming by a mountain path. *Fr.* Seventy-six
    Hokku. Basho
  How Violets Came Blue. Herrick
  Not content, the violets have dyed. *Fr.*
    Fifteen Hokku. Shiba Sonome
  On a Violet in Her Breast. Stanley
  Sea Violet. Doolittle
  Sonnet: "I had no thought of violets of late."
    Nelson
  Spring Poem, A. Chikako
  Sweet Violets. *Unknown*
  To Violets. Herrick
  Violets. Kate Louise
  Violets. Moultrie
  Violets. Ropes
  Violets have withered. *Fr.* Fifteen Hokku.
    Shiba Sonome
  Violets in Thaumantia's Bosome. Sherburne
  White Violet. Osborne
  Yellow Violet, The. Bryant
Violins
  My Fiddle. Riley
  Old Violin, The. Egan
  On Sivori's Violin. Osgood
  Out-of-the-Body Travel. Plumly
  Violin's Complaint, The. Thayer
Virgil
  Sonnet: The Death of Virgil. Di Costanzo
  Virgil's Tomb. Rogers
Virgin Islands
  Skin Diving in the Virgins. Brinnin
  Virgins, The. Walcott
Virgin Mary. *See* **Mary, the Virgin.**
Virginia
  Abandoned, Overgrown Cemetery in the
    Pasture near Our House, An. Orr
  As Toilsome I Wander'd Virginia's Woods.
    Whitman
  Blossom. Plumly
  Caravati's Salvage: Richmond, Virginia.
    Smith
  Carry Me Back to Old Virginny. Bland
  Farewell, The: "Gone, gone—sold and gone."
    Whittier
  I went to the valley. Clifton
  Jamestown. Jarrell
  Leafless Trees, Chickahominy Swamp.
    Smith
  Life-long, Poor Browning. Spencer
  Low Fields and Light. Merwin
  Monticello. Sarton
  Monument and the Shrine, The. Logan
  Night Trip across the Chesapeake and After.
    Lea
  Ode:
    To the Virginian Voyage. Drayton
  On a Field Trip at Fredericksburg. Smith
  Perspective and Limits of Snapshots, The.
    Smith
  Snowy Egret. Weigl
  Virginia. *Fr.* Landscapes. Eliot
  Virginians of the Valley, The. Ticknor
  Wide Mizzoura, The. *Unknown*
Virginity
  Advice to Lovers. *Fr.* The Oeconomy of
    Love; a Poetical Essay. Armstrong
  Alas How Long ("Alas how long shall I and
    my maidenhead lie"). *Unknown*
  Beware Fair Maide. Sylvester
  Blow Away the Morning Dew. *Unknown*
  Broomfield Hill, The. *Unknown*
  Dialogue after Enjoyment. Cowley
  Envoi to Poem to the Virgin. Terracina
  First Time, The. Newlove

Honour. Cowley
In Bertram's Garden. Justice
In Praise of Virginity. Hroswitha
Inscription on a Chemise. *Fr.* The Thousand and One Nights. *Unknown*
Lady Carenza of the lovely, gracious body. Alais, Iselda
My Little Love Lies on the Ground. Paraske
On the Marriage of a Virgin. Thomas
Song: "Where shall Celia fly for shelter." Smart
Temperance and Virginity. *Fr.* Comus; a Masque Presented at Ludlow Castle Milton.
To His Lady, Who Had Vowed Virginity. Davison
Truè Maid, A. Prior
Twa Magicians, The. *Unknown*
Virgin Pictured in Profile. Warren
Whistle, Daughter, Whistle. *Unknown*
Within an Emerald. Díaz Mirón

Virtue
Virtue. Herbert

Viruses
First Photos of Flu Virus. Witt

Vishnu
Gita Govinda, The, *sels.* Jayadeva
Hymn to Tirumal (Visnu). Kirantaiyar

Vision
Another transparent skin has grown. *Fr.* Tunnel Visions. Pollak
First the light cracked. *Fr.* Tunnel Visions. Pollak
Her voice enters the room. *Fr.* Tunnel Visions. Pollak
I wake to the sound of rain. *Fr.* Tunnel Visions. Pollak
Today, Again, the Jagged Black Line. Dunn
Tonight I Stood Looking. Dunn

Visiting and Visitors
Doorbells. Field
House with Two Doors. Gonzáles Martínez
One Poet Visits Another. Davies
Visit. Ammons

Vivaldi, Antonio
Vivaldi. Schwartz

Vocations. See Occupations.

Vogler, Georg Joseph
Abt Vogler. Browning

Voices
London ("I wander through each chartered street"). *Fr.* Songs of Experience. Blake
Three Voices. Tamura Ryuichi
Upon Julia's Voice. Herrick
Voices. Dauenhauer
What Voice at Moth-Hour. Warren
See also **Screams; Speech; Talk.**

Volcanoes
But lo! The reaking surface of the vale. *Fr.* A General Description of the West Indian Islands. Singleton
Futurist Aviator Speaks to His Father, Vulcan, The. Marinetti
Hongo Store 29 Miles Volcano Hilo, Hawaii, The. Hongo
In awful ruins Ætna thunders nigh. *Unknown*
Listening Nydia. Ray
Loo-wit. Rose
Peace. Lawrence
Romance. Turner
Soufrière. Salkey
Then earthquakes, nature's agonizing pangs. *Fr.* The Sugar Cane. Grainger
Volcano. Van Sertima
Volcanoes. Akhmadulina

Volleyball
Volleyball Match, The. Pearlman

Voltaire, François Marie Arouet de
Mock On, Mock On, Voltaire, Rousseau. Blake

Shopping in Ferney with Voltaire. Kumin
Voltaire at Ferney. Auden

Voodoo
Women's Locker Room. Waniek

Voting and Voters
Ballot, The. Pierpont
Deliverance. Harper
Give Us the Right to Vote! Döltz
Negro Ballot, The. Moorer
Poll. Roberson
Poor Voter on Election Day, The. Whittier
See also **Woman Suffrage.**

Vowels
A E I O U. Swift
On the Vowels—a Riddle. Swift

Voyages
Christmas at Sea. Stevenson
Crossing the Atlantic. Sexton
First Night at Sea. Berryman
Helena Embarks for Palestine. *Fr.* Elene. Cynewulf
North Ship, The. Larkin
Ode: To the Virginian Voyage. Drayton
Pat Cloherty's Version of *The Maisie*. Murphy
St. Andrew's Voyage to Mermedonia. *Fr.* Andreas. *Unknown*
Seafarer, The. *Unknown*
Seafarer, The. *Unknown*
Setting Off. Rifqa
What Is. Cummings
What triumph moves on the billows so blue? Lewis

Voyageurs
Voyageur. Rashley

Voyeurism
Close under here, I watched two lovers once. *Fr.* The Beaches. Hyde
Fiend, The. Dickey
Girl in a Window, A. Wright
Peeper, The. Davidson
Peeping Tom. Hope
Second Story, The. Hummer
That They Were at the Beach. Scalapino
Voyeur. Hardy

Vuillard, Edouard
Interior with Mme. Vuillard and Son. Fraser

Vulcan
Execration upon Vulcan, An. Jonson
Futurist Aviator Speaks to His Father, Vulcan, The. Marinetti
Shield of Achilles, The. Auden
To Vulcan. Herrick

Vultures
Mythical Journey, The. Muir
Still, Citizen Sparrow. Wilbur
Under the Vulture-Tree. Bottoms
Vulture, The. Belloc
Vulture. Jeffers
Vulture. *Fr.* A Bestiary. Rexroth
Vulture! Vulture in Your Mountains. Tchernichowsky
See also **Buzzards.**

W

Wagner, Richard
Tannhauser. Levy
Wagner. Brooke

Wagon Trains
Oregon Trail, The. Guiterman
See also **Prairie Schooners.**

Wagtails
Little Trotty Wagtail. Clare

Wailing Wall, The
At the Wailing Wall. Mathews

Waiters and Waitresses
Contrary Waiter, The. Parker

Crêpes Flambeau. Gallagher
Dumpy and obese—a woman. *Fr.* Written in a Public Restaurant. Efrat
Epitaph on a Waiter. McCord
Somewhere Else. Rankin
To a Junior Waiter. Herbert
To a Red-headed Do-good Waitress. Dugan
To the Waitress at the Hickory Pit. Vice

Waiting Rooms
In the Counselor's Waiting Room. Sellers
In the Waiting Room. Bishop
Waiting-Room, The. Fulton
Waiting Rooms. Nemerov

Wakes
Finnegan's Wake. *Unknown*
Willie's Lyke-Wake. *Unknown*

Waking
Let Me Get Up Early. Guillevic
Waking, The. Roethke
Waking from Sleep. Bly
Wide Awake. Livingston
World Awoke Me, The. Devecseri

Walden Pond, Massachusetts
Walden in July. Junkins

Waldenses
Day Zimmer Lost Religion, The. Zimmer

Wales
Artist on Penmaenmawr, The. Turner
Cader Idris at Sunset. Turner
Dafydd ap Gwilym Resents the Winter. Humphries
Days That Have Been. Davies
For My Ancestors. Humphries
Grongar Hill. *Fr.* Looking Back. Dyer
Hiraeth in N.W.3. Vaughan-Thomas
On the Welsh Marches. Stone
Peace in the Welsh Hills. Watkins
Pont-y-Wern. *Fr.* Ambarvalia. Clough
Wales Visitation. Ginsberg
We Who Were Born. Lewis
Welsh Incident. Graves
Welsh Landscape. Thomas
Oxford Book of Welsh Verse in English, The (OBWVE). Gwyn Jones, comp.
See also **Welsh, The.**

Waley, Arthur
Homage to Arthur Waley. Kees

Walker, William
At the Grave of Walker. Miller

Walking
How to Walk in a Crowd. Hershon
Jump or Jiggle. Beyer
Long walk, A. Grenier
Long Walk before the Snows Began, A. Bly
Long Walks in the Afternoon. Gibson
One Day When We Went Walking. Hobbs
Stepping Westward. Wordsworth
Velvet Shoes. Wylie
Walk, A. Zabolotsky
Walking West. Stafford

Wall Street, New York City
Pan in Wall Street. Stedman
Skyscrapers of the Financial District Dance with Gasman, The. Piercy
Wall Street. *Fr.* New York. Leyeles

Wallace, Sir William
Burning of the Barns of Ayr, The. *Fr.* The Wallace. Henry the Minstrel
Gude Wallace. *Unknown*
Wallace, The, *sels.* Henry the Minstrel

Wallflowers
Wall-Flower, The. Wergeland

Walls
Grongar Hill. Dyer
Mending Wall. Frost
Old Grey Wall, The. Carman
Stone Walls. Lippmann
Wall, The. Deguy
Wall, The. Gascoyne

Wall, The. Phelps
Wall, The. Vivaldi
Wall of China, The. Colum
Walls. Cavafy
See also **Fences.**
Walnut Trees and Walnuts
Basket of Walnuts, A. MacBeth
Bye Baby Walnut. Farber
Riddle: "I am within as white as snow."
Unknown
Shriving, The. Carter
Walpole, Robert, 1st Earl of Orford
Character of Sir Robert Walpole, The. Swift
Walruses
Smile of the Walrus, The. Herford
Walrus Hunting. Aua
Walton, Izaak
Ike Walton's Prayer. Riley
Retirement, The. *Fr.* To Mr. Izaak Walton.
Cotton
Waltzing
My Papa's Waltz. Roethke
Wanderlust
Afoot and light-hearted I take to the open
road. *Fr.* Song of the Open Road.
Whitman
How Old Is My Heart. *Fr.* The Wanderer.
Brennan
In Praise of Seafaring Men, in Hope of Good
Fortune. *Unknown*
Land I Came Thro' Last, The. *Fr.* The
Wanderer. Brennan
Long Gone. Brown
Poetry of Departures. Larkin
Sea Fever. Masefield
Ulysses. Tennyson
Vagabond Song, A. Carman
Wakeful in the Township. Riddell
Wander-Lovers, The. Hovey
Wanderer, The. Auden
Wang Wei
Note to Wang Wei. Berryman
War
Absolution. Sassoon
Advent 1966. Levertov
Advice to a Prophet. Wilbur
After the Killing. Randall
Aftermath. Sassoon
Against the Age. Simpson
Age of the Rubber Seals. al-Haidari
Air: "What a charming thing's a battle!" *Fr.*
The Recruiting Serjeant. Bickerstaffe
All, All of a Piece Throughout. *Fr.* The
Secular Masque. Dryden
All Day It Has Rained. Lewis
All Quiet along the Potomac. Beers
And to Private Ball it came. *Fr.* In
Parenthesis. Jones
Apologia pro Poemate Meo. Owen
Ares. Ehrenstein
Aristocrats. Douglas
Armies Enter Cuailnge, The. *Fr.* The Táin.
Unknown
Arms and the Boy. Owen
Around the Campfire. Hudgins
Arsenal at Springfield, The. Longfellow
As One Non-Combatant to Another. Orwell
At alarming bell daybreak, before. *Fr.* Site
of Ambush. Ní Chuilleanáin
Attack. Sassoon
August 1914. Rosenberg
Awakened War God, The. Widdemer
Barrage. Aldington
Battle, The. Simpson
Battle-Field, The. Bryant
Battle Hymn of the [American] Republic,
The. Howe
Battle of Blenheim, The. Southey
Battle Scene. Aricil Kilar
Beat! Beat! Drums! Whitman
Before the Last Battle. *Fr.* The Táin.
Unknown

Bivouac of the Dead, The. O'Hara
Bloody Sire, The. Jeffers
Boots. Kipling
Breakfast. Gibson
Burial of Sir John Moore after [*or* at]
Corunna, The. Wolfe
But We Shall Bloom. Guri
Carrickfergus. MacNeice
Censorship. Waley
Chances, The. Owen
Channel Firing. Hardy
Chariot Wheel, A. Auvaiyar
Christmas Letter Home. Fraser
Chronicler, The. Bergman
Civil War. Shanly
Come to the Stone. Jarrell
Consolation in War. Mumford
Corporal Stare. Graves
Counting Small-boned Bodies. Bly
Cricket and the Machine Gun, The. Yu
Kuang-chung
Crucifix, The. Read
Daughters of War. Rosenberg
Dead Musicians. Sassoon
Dead Witness, The. Al-Haidari
Demon. Faraz
Deserted Village, The. "Hyde"
Deserter, The. Housman
Dialogue. Al-Haidari
Disabled. Owen
Distressed Men of War. *Unknown*
Do Not Weep, Maiden, for War Is Kind.
Fr. War Is Kind. Crane
Does It Matter? Sassoon
Dover Beach. Arnold
Driving Home the Cows. Osgood
Dry Loaf. Stevens
Dulce et Decorum Est. Owen
During a Bombardment by V-Weapons.
Fuller
During the War. Bell
Early in the Morning. Simpson
Earth. Wheelock
Eighth Air Force. Jarrell
Elegy on Gordon Barber. Derwood
Escape. Graves
Every Day. Bachmann
Execution of Cornelius Vane, The. Read
Explosion, The. Larkin
Exposure. Owen
Fable of the War, A. Nemerov
Facts. Bustamante
"Faith and Practice." Balaban
Familial. Prévert
Feast of Blood, The. *Fr.* The Art of War.
Fawcett
Fife Tune. Manifold
Fighting South of the Ramparts. *Unknown*
First Snow in Alsace. Wilbur
Five Minutes after the Air Raid. Holub
Floral Invasions. Hsiang Yang
Flowers of the Forest, The. Elliot
For Soldiers. Gifford
For those men night was a more bitter day.
Fr. Heroic and Elegiac Song for the Lost
Second Lieute. Elytis
Foreign Woman's Complaint, The. Wen
T'ing-yün
Fortunes of War, I Tell You Plain, The.
Unknown
Fury of Aerial Bombardment, The. Eberhart
Futility. Owen
Fuzzy-Wuzzy. Kipling
Gallantry. Douglas
General, The. Sassoon
God of us who kill our kind! *Fr.* A Prayer
of the Peoples. MacKaye
God of War, The. Brecht
Graves the rain makes wet and sleek, The.
Fr. The Stanzas of the Graves. *Unknown*
Gun Teams. Frankau

Hame, Hame, Hame. Cunningham
Harvest of War. Kappiyarrukkappiyanar
Henry before Agincourt: October 25, 1415.
Lydgate
Hooded in angry mist, the sun goes down.
Fr. Nightfall. Asquith
Horses, The ("Barely a twelvemonth after").
Muir
How to Kill. Douglas
How to Start a War. McGinley
Hugh Maguire. O'Hussey
I Have a Rendezvous with Death. Seeger
I have been/ Three separate times, in war.
Fr. What Is Truth? Manning
I Sing of Olaf Glad and Big. Cummings
I Sit and Sew. Nelson
I was playing golf that day. *Unknown*
In Distrust of Merits. Moore
In the Dordogne. Bishop
In the sixth month all is bustle. *Unknown*
In Time of "The Breaking of Nations."
Hardy
Insensibility. Owen
Into Battle. Grenfell
Invocation: "There is no balm on earth."
Thomas
Irish Airman Foresees His Death, An. Yeats
It's a Queer Time. Graves
Jagged are the rocks. *Unknown*
Jeannette and Jeannot. Jefferys
Jewish Conscript, The. Frank
Judging Distances. *Fr.* Lessons of the War.
Reed
Jumper. Harrison
Just an Old Sweet Song. MacDonagh
King, majestic and glorious, The. *Unknown*
Lan Nguyen; the Uniform of Death, 1971.
Mura
Last War, The. Amis
Leaf in Love and War, A. Veripatiya
Kamakkanniyar
Legion, The. Graves
Letter to an American Visitor. Comfort
Life at War. Levertov
Lullaby: "Though the world has slipped and
gone." Sitwell
Macadam Road Remembers, The. Csukás
Man He Killed, The. Hardy
Manila. Ware
March into Virginia, The. Melville
Marching. Rosenberg
Meeting in the Forest, A. Jylhä
Memories of a Lost War. Simpson
Men of Ch'ing are in P'eng, The. *Unknown*
Mental Cases. Owen
Mercenaries. Faraz
Mid-Ocean in War-Time. Kilmer
Mightiest of all heights is the Peak.
Unknown
Montcalm and Wolfe. *Unknown*
Mothers. Maturaipputan Ilanakanar
Mrs. McGrath. *Unknown*
Munich Elegy No. 1. Barker
My Company. Read
National Security. MacLeish
Nerves. *Fr.* Tour of Duty. Huddle.
Next War, The. Graves
Next War, The. Owen
Night of Trafalgar, The. *Fr.* The Dynasts.
Hardy
Nightingales Are Not Singing. Dor
1935. Benét
No Man Knows War. Rolfe
None saw their spirits' shadow shake the
grass. *Fr.* Dead Man's Dump.
Rosenberg
Northern Legion, A. Read
Now with a general peace the world was
blest. *Fr.* Astraea Redux. Dryden
O. T.'s Blues. Cuney
Ode: "I hate that drum's discordant sound."
Scott of Amwell

Oh, It's Nine Years Ago I Was Digging in the Land. *Unknown*
Old Man and Jim, The. Riley
Old War-Dreams. Whitman
On the Lawn at the Villa. Simpson
On the March. Aldington
On the Suicide of the Refugee W. B. Brecht
One-and-Twenty. *Unknown*
One Morning the World Woke Up. Williams
One Morning We Brought Them Order. Lee
Orion. Cendrars
Out of Our Shame. Rosten
Pacifying the Western Barbarians. Wen T'ing-yün
Parable of the Old Man and the Young, The. Owen
Parade, A. Perunkunrur Kilar
Peasants, The. Lewis
People Went to War, The. Jacinto
Permanence of the Young Men, The. Soutar
Picciola. Newell
Poets in Time of War. Warr
Ponsonby/Remuera/My lai. Mitchell
Portrait: The Freedom Fighter. Jonas
Prayer after World War. Sandburg
Prayer during Battle. Hagedorn
Prayer for Light. Coblentz
Prayer for the Age. Broomell
Prayer from 1936, A. Sassoon
Prey to Prey. Rowbotham
Prince of Peace His Banner Spreads, The. Fosdick
Prologue to a Poem. Zach
Protest in the Sixth Year of Ch'ien Fu, A. Ts'ao Sung
Quintana Lay in the Shallow Grave of Coral. Shapiro
Recalling War. Graves
Refugees, The. Read
Repression of War Experience. Sassoon
Respondez! Whitman
Send-off, The. Owen
Sestina: Altaforte. Pound
Sharpshooters. Wu T'e-Liang
Show, The. Owen
Sick Nought, The. Jarrell
Sing, Brothers, Sing! Rodgers
Soldiers Bathing. Prince
Song: "Pints and the pistols, the pike-staves and pottles, The." Praed
Song in a Siege. Heath
Sonnet to Britain. Aytoun
Sons of Our Sons, The. Ehrenburg
Spring 1942. Fuller
Spring Offensive. Owen
Stone God, The. Meriluoto
Story of Wildflowers, The. Yip Wai-lim
Strange Meeting. Owen
Strange Meeting. Owen
Strength through Joy. Rexroth
Summer in England, 1914. Meynell
Sunset Horn. O'Higgins
Sweetness of Nature, The. *Unknown*
Tamborillo. Payeras
Tapestry of the Great Fear. Aragon
Ten Thousand Miles. *Unknown*
There Was a Crimson Clash of War. Crane
There where the sun first dwelt. *Fr.* Heroic and Elegiac Song for the Lost Second Lieute. Elytis.
"They." Sassoon
Three Little Girls. Aldington
.303. Douglas
To Germany. Sorley
To Lucasta, Going to the Wars [*or* Warres]. Lovelace
To the Mothers. Toller
Too-late Born, The. MacLeish
Torn widow's veil. *Fr.* Songs of Sorrow (Spring 1918). Kajava
Trees on the Calais Road. Blunden
Triumphs of Owen, The. Gray

Tupac Amaru Relegated. Cisneros
Two Armies. Spender
Unarmed Combat. *Fr.* Lessons of the War. Reed
Unoccupied Zone, The. Aragon
Unpardonable Sin, The. Lindsay
Unseen Fire. Currey
Valley of the Black Pig, The. Yeats
Vergissmeinnicht. Douglas
Virgins, in vain you labour to prevent. *Fr.* Tamburlaine the Great. Marlowe
Voices of Heroes. Gregory
War. Ish-Kishor
War. Langland
War! Lawson
War. Li Po
War. Voznesensky
War Comes. Schneour
War Is Kind, *sels.* Crane.
War Is the Statesman's Game. *Fr.* Queen Mab. Shelley
War Party. Grant
War Poetry. *Fr.* Blenheim. Philips
War Song. Davidson
War Song of Dinas Vawr, The. *Fr.* The Misfortunes of Elphin. Peacock
War Song to Englishmen, A. *Fr.* King Edward the Third. Blake
Warriors go forth, The. *Fr.* Manyo Shu. Kanamura
Watch, Cima Quattro. Ungaretti
Watching War Movies. Stryk
We bring out our carts. *Unknown*
We plucked the bracken, plucked the bracken. *Unknown*
We were glad together in gladsome meads. *Fr.* The Rhyme of Joyous Garde. Gordon
We Who Are Left. Whalley
What the Orderly Dog Saw. Ford
When Banners Are Waving. *Unknown*
While We Slept. Wolff
White Horse, The. Tu Fu
Who died on the wires, and hung there, one of two. *Fr.* The Silent One. Gurney
Why Should Vain Mortals Tremble. Niles
Willow Branches, The. Wen T'ing-yün
Winds; words of the wind; rumor of great walls pierced. *Fr.* The Asylum. Carruth
Winter Warfare. Rickword
Without Benefit of Declaration. Hughes
Women at the Corners Stand, The. Golding
Words. *Fr.* Tour of Duty. Huddle
Wounds. Longley
Chaos of the Night; Women's Poetry and Verse of The Second World War (CN). Catherine W. Reilly, ed.
Men Who March Away; Poems of the First World War (MMA). I. M. Parsons, ed.
Oxford Book of War Poetry, The (OBWP). Jon Stallworthy, ed.
Poems of Love and War from the Eight Anthologies and the Ten Long Poems of Classical Tamil (PLW). A. K. Ramanujan, comp. *and tr.*
War and the Poet (WaaP). Richard Eberhart *and* Selden Rodman, eds.
War Poets, The (WaP). Oscar Williams, ed.
See also **Soldiers** *and names of specific wars and battles.*

War Casualties
Voluntary Mutilation. Follain
War Casualties
Air-Raid Casualties: Ashridge Hospital. Ledward
Blossom. Plumly
Carentan O Carentan. Simpson
Casualties. Cornford
Casualty. Witherby
Dear wife and bosom friend I hat seen hart. *Fr.* Letters from Vicksburg. Gildner
Disabled. Owen
Field Hospital, 1945. Fodor

From My Window. Williams
Futility. Owen
March in the Ranks Hard-Prest, and the Road Unknown, A. Whitman
Mental Cases. Owen
My Sons Have Grown to Manhood. Anhava
Nightmare Inspection Tour for American Generals. Ruark
Nocturn at the Institute. McElroy
Now with a still wind in his quiet hair. *Fr.* Heroic and Elegiac Song for the Lost Second Lieute. Elytis
Sestina with Refrain. Shapcott
Soldier Is Home, The. Neilson
"They." Sassoon
To the Memory of Gavin Wilson (Boot, Leg and Arm Maker). Galloway
War Blinded. Dunn
War Casualty in April. Bellerby
Wound-Dresser, The. Whitman
Wounds. Longley
See also **Soldiers**.

War Dead
Among the Grieving One Should Speak Softly. Anhava
Another Epitaph on an Army of Mercenaries. "MacDiarmid"
Anthem for Doomed Youth. Owen
Arm in Arm. Simpson
Armistice. Dehn
As the Team's Head-Brass. Thomas
Astronomy. Housman
At the British War Cemetery, Bayeux. Causley
Ballad of Heroes, A. Dobson
Base Details. Sassoon
Beach Burial. Slessor
Blue and the Gray, The. Finch
Burial in Flanders, The. Nichols
By the Wood. Nichols
Cenotaph, The. Mew
Certain Dead. Haines
Charge of the Light Brigade, The. Tennyson
Classic Encounter. "Caudwell"
Come Up from the Fields, Father. Whitman
Concord Hymn. Emerson
Coronach. *Fr.* The Lady of the Lake. Scott
Corpses in the Wood. Toller
Dead Man's Dump. Rosenberg
Dead, The ("Blow out, you bugles, over the rich dead!"). *Fr.* 1914. Brooke
Dead, The ("These hearts were woven"). *Fr.* 1914. Brooke
Death in Spring, A. Gilboa
Death of a Soldier, The. Stevens
Death of the Ball Turret Gunner, The. Jarrell
Decoration Day. Heard
Devil's Advice to Story-Tellers, The. Graves
Diameter of the Bomb Was Thirty Centimeters, The. Amichai
Drummer Hodge. Hardy
Due of the Dead, The. Thackeray
Dulce et Decorum Est. Owen
1887. Housman
Elegy for a Dead Soldier. Shapiro
Elegy for an Unknown Soldier. Baxter
End, The. Owen
Epitaph: "Underneath this wooden cross there lies." *Fr.* Elegy for a Dead Soldier. Shapiro
Facing It. Komunyakaa
Farewell, The:
It Was A' for Our Rightfu' King. Burns
Fighting Race, The. Clarke
Flat One, A. Snodgrass
For the Fallen. Binyon
For the Union Dead. Lowell
Full Tide. Tomoana
Futility. Owen
G. I. Graves in Tuscany. Hugo
Gallantry. Douglas

Game of Cards. Aichinger
Grass. Sandburg
Greater Love. Owen
Gunner. Jarrell
He was a fine young man. The first day he
  was born. *Fr.* Heroic and Elegiac Song
  for the Lost Second Lieute. Elytis.
Henry's Understanding. Berryman
Here dead lie we because we did not choose.
  Housman
Hero, The. Sassoon
Holy Innocents, The. Lowell
Homecoming. Dawe
Horse Did Not Come Back, The. Erumai
  Veliyanar
How Sleep the Brave. Collins
Hunting Civil War Relics at Nimblewill
  Creek. Dickey
In Flanders Fields. McCrae
In Memoriam (Easter, 1915). Thomas
In Memoriam Francis Ledwidge. Heaney
In Memory of Basil, Marquess of Dufferin
  and Ava. Betjeman
In the distance crystal bells ring out. *Fr.*
  Heroic and Elegiac Song for the Lost
  Second Lieute. Elytis
Inscription for Marye's Heights,
  Fredericksburg. Melville
Irish Airman Foresees His Death, An. ·Yeats
Is all this sorrow? I don't know. *Fr.*
  Laments on the War Dead. Amichai
Island, The. Dickey
Johnny, I Hardly Knew Ye. *Unknown*
Killed in Action. Bairacli-Levy
Lamentation, A. Campion
Landscape with Figures. Douglas
Leningrad Cemetary, Winter of 1941. Olds
Life. Follain
Losses. Jarrell
Lost Pilot, The. Tate
Man He Killed, The. Hardy
March, The. Squire
Masses. Vallejo
Memo. Lynch
Memorial in Aachen. Richter
Memorial Wreath. Randall
Messmates. Newbolt
Minstrel Boy, The. Moore
Mother and Poet. Browning
Mothers. Kakkai Patiniyar Naccellaiyar
Mothers. Punkanuttiraiyar
My Luve's in Germany. *Unknown*
National Cemetery, Beaufort, South Carolina,
  The. Heard
New Song Called the *Victory*, A. *Unknown*
MCMXIV. Larkin
No Man's Land. Bogle
November '73. Pagis
Now that his fatherland has darkened on
  earth. *Fr.* Heroic and Elegiac Song for the
  Lost Second Lieute. Elytis
Ode for the American Dead in Korea.
  McGrath
Ode: "Sleep sweetly in your humble graves."
  Timrod
Ode to the Confederate Dead. Tate
Of what a quality is courage made. *Fr.*
  Charles Donnelly. MacDonagh
On a Field Trip at Fredericksburg. Smith
On a Photo of Sgt. Ciardi a Year Later.
  Ciardi
On a Soldier Fallen in the Philippines.
  Moody
On a Soldier Killed in the Great War. Parry
On Passing the New Menin Gate. Sassoon
On the idle hill of summer. *Fr.* A
  Shropshire Lad. Housman
On the Spartan Dead at Thermopylae.
  Simonides
Pensive, on Her Dead Gazing, I Heard the
  Mother of All. Whitman
Photographs: A Vision of Massacre. Harper

Plaque in the Reading Room for My
  Classmates Killed in Korea, The. Reeve
Pro Patria. Carrier
Protocols. Jarrell
Rouge Bouquet. Kilmer
Sight in Camp [in the Daybreak Gray and
  Dim], A. Whitman
Six Young Men. Hughes
Slain. Crosland
Soldier in the Park, The. Riddell
Soldier Rest! [Thy Warfare O'er]. *Fr.* The
  Lady of the Lake. Scott
Song of the Camp, The. Taylor
Song of Those Who Died, A. McDonald
Sons of War. Al-Qasim
Spires of Oxford, The. Letts
Spoilers and the Spoils, The. Sherwin
Spring Betrayed. Boulton
Strange Meeting. Owen
Sun, bronze voice, and holy etesian wind.
  Fr. Heroic and Elegiac Song for the Lost
  Second Lieute. Elytis
Tending the Garden. Pankey
Those Who Died for Their Country. *Fr.*
  Nine Songs. *Unknown*
Threnode for Young Soldiers Killed in
  Action. Bairacli-Levy
To Billy, My Son. Bax
To His Love. Gurney
To My Brother. Bogan
To Richard, My Son. Bax
Ultima Ratio Regum. Spender
Uncle Robert. Morgan
Unknown Soldier, The. Rose
Unknown Soldiers. *Fr.* The New Spoon
  River. Masters
Vergissmeinnicht. Douglas
Vigil Strange I Kept on the Field One Night.
  Whitman
Volunteer, The. Asquith
War. Langland
War Tribunal. Daryush
Wartime Maternity Ward, A. Edwards
We Never Know. Komunyakaa
We Soldiers of All Nations Who Lie Killed.
  Agee
When You See Millions of the Mouthless
  Dead. Sorley
Widows' Rice. Okkur Macattanar
Wife in London, A. Hardy
Woman and Her Dying Warrior, A.
  Vanparanar
Young Dead Soldiers, The. MacLeish
*Chaos of the Night; Women's Poetry and
  Verse of the Second World War (CN).*
  Catherine W. Reilly, ed.

War of 1812
Banks of Champlain, The. *Unknown*
Battle of Bridgewater, The. *Unknown*
Battle of New Orleans, The. *Unknown*
James Bird. *Unknown*
Star-spangled Banner, The. Key
Ye Parliament of England. *Unknown*
War of the Grand Alliance
Hervé Riel. Browning
Warblers
Warbler escapes next door, A. *Fr.*
  Twenty-four Hokku. Kito
Birds called warblers are fancy mountain
  birds, The. *Unknown*
Haiku: "Reed-warbler, The." Mizuhara
  Shuoshi
Happy Bird, The. Clare
I mistook a warbler for a sparrow. *Fr.*
  Eighty-seven Hokku. Buson
I see the shadow of a warbler. *Fr.*
  Twenty-four Hokku. Kito
Warbler's voice, The. *Fr.* Twenty-three
  Tanka. Tamekane
Warbler. Hitoshi
Warbler, what are you afraid of? *Fr.*
  Twenty-four Hokku. Kito

When the spring comes. *Fr.* Manyo Shu.
  Nukada
Where the spring mist slowly drifts. *Fr.*
  Manyo Shu. *Unknown*
Warburton, William
Tongue-Doughty Pedant. Edwards
Ward, John
Captain Ward and the *Rainbow*. *Unknown*
Warren, Joseph
Death of Warren, The. Sargent
Wars of the Roses
Song at the Feast of Brougham Castle.
  Wordsworth
Wars of the Roses, The. *Unknown*
Warsaw Ghetto
History Teacher in the Warsaw Ghetto Rising.
  Paterson
Poor Christian Looks at the Ghetto, A.
  Milosz
Stone and the Blade of Grass in the Warsaw
  Ghetto, The. Scheinert
Warsaw, Poland
Conversation with a Countryman. Slonimski
Sketch for a Memoir. Wazyk
Ten Groschen. Zeitlin
Willows in Alma-Ata. Wat
Warwickshire, England
Dwindling Forest of Arden, The. *Fr.*
  Polyolbion. Drayton
Washing
As day nears its end. Ietaka
Old Ellen Sullivan. Welles
Public Wash House, The. Bold
See also **Baths and Bathing.**
Washing Machines
Our Washing Machine. Hubbell
See also **Laundry and Laundering.**
Washington, Booker Taliaferro
Alabama Earth. Hughes
Booker T. and W. E. B. Randall
Monuments for a Friendly Girl at a Tenth
  Grade Party. Stafford
Notable Dinner, A. Moorer
Our Noble Booker T. Washington. Linden
To See Ol' Booker T. Johnson
Washington, George
Advice to a Raven in Russia [December,
  1812] Barlow
Cameo No. II. Jordan
February 22. Updike
George Washington. Benét
George Washington. Ingham
Leetla Giorgio Washeenton. Daly
Mount Vernon. *Unknown*
Never to see a nation born. *Fr.* Under the
  Old Elm. Lowell
Patriotic Poem. Wakoski
Rivers Remember, The. Turner
To His Excellency, General Washington.
  Wheatley
Visiting Mount Vernon and Paying Homage at
  George Washingon's Burial Vault. K'ang
  Yu-wei
Washington. *Fr.* Ode to Napoleon Bounaparte.
  Byron
Washington. *Fr.* Under the Old Elm.
  Lowell
Washington. *Fr.* Commemoration Ode.
  Monroe
Washington. Turner
Washington in Love. Berryman
Which Washington? Merriam
Young Washington. Guiterman
Washington (State)
Age, An. Jensen
American Landscape with Clouds & a Zoo.
  Anderson
Bobber. Carver
Fish Counter at Bonneville, The. Stafford
Letter with a Black Border. McPherson

Mid-August at Sourdough Mountain Lookout. Snyder
Sourdough mountain called a fire in. *Fr.* Myths and Texts: Burning. Snyder
White Center. Hugo

Washington, D.C.
Aeneas at Washington. Tate
Homage to Paul Mellon, I. M. Pei, Their Gallery, and Washington City. Meredith
July in Washington. Lowell
View of the Capitol from the Library of Congress. Bishop

Washington Monument
Monument and the Shrine, The. Logan
Washington Monument by Night. Sandburg
Washington's Monument, February 1885. Whitman
Washington's Monument. *Unknown*

Washington Square, New York City
Villanelle of Washington Square. Roberts

Wasp (ship, War of 1812)
Ocean-Fight, The. *Unknown*

Wasps
How to Catch Wasps. *Fr.* Cyder. Philips
New Hampshire, February. Eberhart
Upon a Wasp Chilled [*or* Child] with Cold. Taylor
Wasp, The. Davidson
Wasp, The. Hine
Wasp, The. *Fr.* Transcripts from Nature. "Macleod"
Wasp, The. Oates
Wasps. Aldis
Wasps' Nest, The. MacBeth

Watches
Girl in the Hall, The. Stone
Gold Watch. Kavanagh
Mr. Coggs. Lucas
Tide and Time. McGouch
To His Watch. Hopkins
To His Watch, When He Could Not Sleep. Herbert of Cherbury
Watch, The. Cornford
Watch, The. Swenson
Watch Repair. Simic
Watchmaker's Shop, The. *Unknown*
See also **Clocks.**

Water
Clear water has no front or back. *Fr.* Seventeen Hokku. Chiyojo
Come, Happy Children,. *Unknown*
Desire of Water, The. Jarman
Diviners, The. Oliver
Drink of Water, A. Heaney
Drinking Fountain. Chute
Gift of Water, The. Garland
Glass Town, The. Reid
Green, Green Is El Aghir. Cameron
I go on, and the clear water meets me again. *Fr.* Seventeen Hokku. Chiyojo
I raise my hands, and the clear water. *Fr.* Seventeen Hokku. Chiyojo
Imitation of Water. Melo Neto
Inscription for a Wayside Spring. Cornford
Like Water down a Slope. Schneour
On the North Side of Suilven. MacCaig
Poem Made of Water. Willard
Poet's Counsel, The. Soupault
Sound of Water. O'Neill
There is a stream that flowed before the first beginning. *Fr.* Water. Raine
To Drink. Mistral
To the Revd. Mr. ——— on His Drinking Sea-Water. Winstanley
Tumbling water breaks upon the rocks, The. *Fr.* Manyo Shu. *Unknown*
Water. Conkling
Water. Crossland
Water. Larkin
Water. Lowell
Water. Norris

Water Carrier, The. Montague
Water Song. Ibn Gabirol
Water spurting out of a pump, The. *Fr.* Forty-seven Tanka in Three Lines. Ishikawa Takuboku
Water without Sound. Heifetz-Tussman
Well Water. Jarrell
Wetness. Eluard
Word of Water, The. Mayo
Zuni Derivations. *Unknown*

Water Lilies
Lotus Flowers, The. Voigt
Monet's Lilies Shuddering. Ferlinghetti
Monet's "Waterlilies." Hayden
Water-Lily, The. Tabb

Water Ouzels
Water Ouzel. Matchett

Waterbeds
Insomnia the Gem of the Ocean. Updike

Watercolors
Watercolor of Grantchester Meadows. Plath

Waterfalls
American Falls. Keeler
At the Cascade. Ray
By a Waterfall. Wagoner
By Frazier Creek Falls. Snyder
By the Waterfall. Adler
Cataract of Lodore, The. Southey
Falls of Glomach, The. Young
Fragment: "Cataract, whirling to the precipice, The." Clare
From its sources which well. *Fr.* The Cataract of Lodore. Southey
Have you the Giesbach seen? a fall. *Fr.* Mari Magno. Clough
It was a hard thing to undo this knot. Hopkins
Someone must be. *Fr.* Kokin Shu. Narihira
Under the Waterfall. Hardy
Viewing the Waterfall at Mount Lu. Li Po
Waterfall. Heaney
Waterfall [*or* Water-Fall], The. Vaughan
Waterfall. Welsh
Waterfalls and Liquor ("Waterfalls sounded."). Kapilar

Waterford. *See* **County Waterford, Ireland.**

Waterfowl
Duck Pond at Mini's Pasture, a Dozen Years Later, The. Dow
Lincolnshire's Holland Speaks of Her Waterfowl. *Fr.* Polyolbion. Drayton.
Pair, A. Swenson
To a Waterfowl. Bryant
To a Waterfowl. Hall
Water Fowl. Wordsworth
Willets, The. Swenson
See also **Ducks; Geese; Swans.**

Watergate
Final Curtain. Woddis
See also **Mitchell, Martha; Nixon, Richard Milhous.**

Waterloo, Battle of
Plains of Waterloo, The. *Unknown*
There was a sound of revelry by night. *Fr.* Childe Harold's Pilgrimage. Byron

Watermelons
Ode to the Watermelon. Neruda
Watermelons. Simic

Watteau, Jean-Antoine
Watteau's Coloration ("Watteau's color: atmospheric May."). Gesswein

Watts, Isaac
For the Bicentenary of Isaac Watts. Nicholson

Watts, Los Angeles, California
Watts. Kaufman
Watts. Rivers

Waugh, Evelyn
Elegy: E. W. Sissman

Waves
As if it were a relic. Tsurayuki

"Dover Beach"—a Note to That Poem. MacLeish
Each time they break. Kaneyoshi
From the Wave. Gunn
How Everything Happens. Swenson
I awoke from sleep. Ietaka
Main-Deep, The. Stephens
Seasonless waves/ of the Izumi River, The. Teika
There Are Big Waves. Farjeon
Waves of the great sea, The. *Fr.* Twenty-four Tanka. Sanetomo
White Horses. Pawsey

Wayne, Anthony
Wayne at Stony Point. Scollard

Wealth
Back to Griggsby's Station. Riley
Beverly Hills, Chicago. Brooks
Bewick Finzer. Robinson
Description of an American Billionaire. Gail
Even as the raven, the crow, and greedy kite. *Unknown*
Lord Finchley. Belloc
Mornin's Mornin, The. Brennan
On Dives. Crashaw
Quatrain: "O gold, a deep contempt for you I own." Farhat
Rich and Poor; or, Saint and Sinner. Peacock
Richard Cory. Robinson
Short Song of Congratulation [*or* To a Young Heir], A. Johnson
To a Millionaire. Lampman
Worldly Wealth. Watkyns
Your Riches Taught Me Poverty. Dickinson

Weariness
Closing Door, The. Pozzi
I Am So Good. Aleramo
I am Weary, Mother. Tucker
Tired Tim. De la Mare
Weariness. Tucker
What am I to do? Ietaka

Weasels
Dead Weasel, A. Helwig
Don't Ever Seize a Weasel by the Tail. Prelutsky
Weasel, The. *Unknown*

Weather
Bones of Incontention, The. Cohen
Border Forecast, A. Landles
Crow on the fence. *Unknown*
English Fog, The. *Fr.* The Fleece. Dyer
English Weather. Cope
If the robin sings in the bush. *Unknown*
Weather Forecast. Lamarque
Weather Forecasters. Kilpi
Weather of Olympus, The. Graves
Weather Rhymes. Brown
Weather Wisdom. *Unknown*
Weather[s]. Hardy
Wild geese, wild geese, ganging to the sea. *Unknown*
Wild Iron. Curnow
Winter's Onset from an Alienated Point of View. Dugan
Faber Book of Useful Verse, The (FaBoUs), pp. 31-37. Simon Brett, ed.

Weathervanes
Upon the Weathercock. Bunyan
Weathercock. Jennings
Weathercock, The: "I puff my breast out, my neck swells." *Fr.* Riddles (Exeter Book). Cynewulf

Weaving and Weavers
Carpet-Weavers' Lament, The. *Unknown*
Coaxin.' Ramsbottom
Factory Girl, The. "Bill o' th' Hoylus End"
Funny Rigs of Good and Tender-hearted Masters. *Unknown*

General Ludd's Triumph. *Unknown*
Life and Adventure of Bob Thin, The. *Fr.*
   Bob Thin; or, the Poorhouse Fugitive.
   Linton
Life and the Weaver. Dewar
Linen Weaver, The. *Unknown*
New Bury Loom, The. *Unknown*
Poor Cotton Weaver, The. *Unknown*
Poverty Knock. *Unknown*
Rug of Woven Magic. Benally
Shurat Weaver's Song, The. Laycock
Song of a Silesian Weaver. Aston
Tapestry Weavers, The. Chester
Ten Heawrs a Day. Burgess
This is the cloth I wove for my lord. *Fr.*
   Manyo Shu. Hitomaro
Weaver, The. Pascoli
Weaver, The. *Unknown*
Weaver and the Factory Maid, The.
   Unknown

Webster, Daniel
Daniel Webster's Horses. Coatsworth
Ichabod. Whittier
Why did all manly gifts in Webster fail?
   Emerson

Webster, John
John Webster. Swinburne
John Webster. *Fr.* Sonnets of English
   Dramatic Poets. Swinburne
Whispers of Immortality. Eliot

Wedding Songs
Away to Twiver, Away, Away! *Unknown*
Beauty, Arise! *Fr.* The Pleasant Comedy of
   Patient Grissell [or Grissel or Grissill].
   Dekker
Bridal Song. *Fr.* The Masque of the Middle
   Temple and Lincoln's Inn. Chapman
Bridal Song ("Cynthia, to thy power"). *Fr.*
   The Maid's Tragedy. Beaumont
Bridal Song ("Hold back thy hours"). *Fr.*
   The Maid's Tragedy. Beaumont
Epithalamion: "Ye learned sisters which have
   oftentimes." Spenser
Epithalamium: "Come, virgin tapers of pure
   wax." Crashaw
Epithalamium: "We have found our peace,
   and move with a turning globe." Fairburn
Epithalamy to Sir Thomas Southwell and His
   Lady, An. Herrick
Gwan! Gwan! Cry the Fish Hawks.
   Unknown
I Mun Be Married a Sunday. *Fr.* Ralph
   Roister Doister. Udall
Nuptial Hymn. *Fr.* The Period of Mourning.
   Peacham
Phoenix and the Turtle, The. Shakespeare
Sergeant's Weddin', The. Kipling
Song for a Country Wedding. Smith

Weddings
Anxiously chirps the cicada. *Unknown*
At last the beef appears in sight. *Fr.* The
   Collier's Wedding. Chicken
At My Wedding. Segal
Below fair Peebles, on the river's side. *Fr.*
   A Marriage betwixt Scrape, Monarch of the
   Maunders, and Blobberlips, Queen of the
   Gypsies. Pennecuik
Betrothed. Bogan
Black Wedding Song, A. Brooks
Bride's Hours, A. Valentine
Coach-wheels crunch, The. *Unknown*
Companion of her lord till death. *Unknown*
"Fair, fair," cry the ospreys. *Unknown*
Fast bundled is the firewood. *Unknown*
Gorgeous in their beauty. *Unknown*
Here they gallop pak, pak. *Unknown*
High spurt the waters of that fountain.
   Unknown
I Am Married to Myself. Goodman
In the south is an upturning tree. *Unknown*
In the wicker fish-trap by the bridge.
   Unknown

Lochinvar. *Fr.* Marmion. Scott
Marriage. Corso
Mulberry on the lowland, how graceful!, The.
   Unknown
My Father's Wedding. Bly
My lord is all a-glow. *Unknown*
Now the magpie had a nest. *Unknown*
Over the southern hill so deep. *Unknown*
Slim and fine is the axle-pin of a coach.
   Unknown
Splendid woman and upstanding, A.
   Unknown
Swoop flies that falcon. *Unknown*
There Should Have Been. Lea
There was a girl with us in our carriage.
   Unknown
Thick grows that southernwood. *Unknown*
To the Last Wedding Guest. Gregory
Tribute to the Bride and Groom, A.
   Thompson
Waiting For Breakfast, While She Brushed
   Her Hair. Larkin
Wedding Party. Hall
Whitsun Weddings, The. Larkin
Wind and rain, chill, chill! *Unknown*
Written on Yün-lang's Nuptial Day. Ch'en
   Wei-sung
See also **Marriage**.

Weeds
Bindweed, The. De la Mare
My Aunt. Hughes
Tumbleweed. Wagoner

Weeping. *See* Tears.

Weight Lifting
My Father Toured the South. Nichols
Pumping Iron. Ackerman
Weight Room, The. Rabbitt

Welfare
Can I Say. Bird
Feeding the Lions. Jordan
Sexual Privacy of Women on Welfare. Lane

Wellington, Arthur Wellesley, 1st Duke of
Lamentation on the Death of the Duke of
   Wellington. *Unknown*
Warden of the Cinque Ports, The.
   Longfellow

Wellington, New Zealand
Wellington. Johnson

Wells
At Grandfather's. Bates
Cleaning the Well. Chappell
In the land of Azuma. *Fr.* Manyo Shu.
   Mushimaro
Jacob's Well. *Unknown*
Personal Helicon. Heaney
Well, The. Brown
Well, The. La Parra
Well, The. Seymour
Well Water. Jarrell
What mystery pervades a well! Dickinson

Welsh, The
Tragic Guilt. Rhys
Oxford Book of Welsh Verse in English, The
   (OBWVE). Gwyn Jones, comp.
See also **Wales.**

Wentworth, Thomas, Earl of Strafford
Epitaph on the Earl of Strafford. Cleveland

Werewolves
Beasts. Wilbur
Were-Wolf. Hawthorne

Werfel, Franz
Shooting of Werfel, The. Watkins

Wessex, England
Wessex Heights. Hardy

West Indies
Jamaican Bus Ride. Tessimond
O Carib Isle! Crane
Tales of the Islands. Walcott
*Penguin Book of Caribbean Verse in English,
   The* (PBCV). Paula Burnett, ed.

West, Mae
Mae West. Field

West, Richard
Sonnet on the Death of Mr. Richard West.
   Gray

West (United States)
An Opera Songstress. Ya Hsien
Arizona Nature Myth. Michie
Gateway Arch. Cheng Ch'ou-yu
Goin' Back T'morrer. Garland
Hitch Haiku. Snyder
Horse Thief, The. Benét
Let the Rest of the World Go By. Brennan
Man's Vocation Is Nobody's Business, A.
   Galvin
On the Emigration to America [and Peopling
   the Western Country]. Freneau
One more rendezvous. *Fr.* The Song of Jed
   Smith. Neihardt
Out Where the West Begins ("Out where the
   hand-clasp's a little stronger"). Chapman
Spanish Johnny. Cather
Stages on a Journey Westward. Wright
Sunset from Omaha Hotel Window.
   Sandburg
Texas Ranger, The. Boswell
Westering. Kane
Western Magic. Austin
Western Wagons. Benét
Westward Ho! Miller
Wild West. Vinz
19 New American Poets of the Golden Gate
   (NPGG). Philip Dow, ed.

West Virginia
Harpers Ferry. Rodman
How Old Brown Took Harper's Ferry.
   Stedman
In Response to a Rumor That the Oldest
   Whorehouse in Wheeling, West Virginia,
   Has Been Condemned. Wright
Mad Fight Song for William S. Carpenter,
   1966, A. Wright
Narrative. Atkins
Written at the White Sulphur Springs. Key

West Wind
Ode to the West Wind. Shelley
To the Western Wind. Halevi
To the Western Wind. Herrick
West Wind, The. Masefield
Western Wind. *Unknown*

Westminster Abbey
In Westminster Abbey. Betjeman
On First Entering Westminster Abbey.
   Guiney
Refusal, A. Hardy

Weston, Louise B.
Mrs. Louise B. Weston. Fordham

Weston, Rebecca
Mrs. Rebecca Weston. Fordham

Weston, Samuel
Rev. Samuel Weston. Fordham

Whales and Whaling
Abduction, The. Kunitz
Al Capone in Alaska. Reed
And God created the great whales, and each.
   Fr. Paradise Lost. Milton
Autumn. Carpenter
Balena, The. Unknown
Bill the Whaler. Lawson
Blackfish Poem. Acorn
Blow Ye Winds in the Morning. *Unknown*
Blue Whale, The. Watson
Cachalot, The, *sels.* Pratt.
Cordial Advice. *Unknown*
Daybreak/ whales trumpet. *Fr.* Sixteen
   Hokku. Kyotai
Death of a Whale. Blight
For a Coming Extinction. Merwin
Greenland Voyage; or, The Whale Fisher's
   Delight, The. *Unknown*
Greenland Whale Fishery, The. *Unknown*

Greenland Whale Fishery, The. *Unknown*
Hunting of Whales, The. Prévert
Leviathan. Merwin
Norway. Dubie
Poem Begun in the Haro Strait When I Was 28 and Finished When I Was 38. McPherson
Psalm: "Whale, says Jonah, is the war and its black-outs, The." Dadelsen
Ribs and Terrors in the Whale, The. *Fr.* Moby Dick. Melville
Shooting Whales. Strand
Spouting Whale. Takamura Kotaro
Stranded Whales, The. Dutton
To explain the nature of fishes in craft of verse. *Fr.* Physiologus: The Whale. *Unknown*
Waterwitch, The. *Unknown*
Wellfleet Whale, The. Kunitz
Whale. Benét
Whale, The. *Fr.* The Progress[e] of the Soul[e] Donne
Whale, The. *Fr.* The Bestiary. *Unknown*
Whale, His Bulwark, The. Walcott
Whale Songs. Ackerman
Whales, The. Young
Whales off Wales, The. Kennedy
Whales Weep Not! Lawrence
Wharves
Bight, The. Bishop
Jake's Wharf. Booth
Wheat
Sheaves, The. Robinson
Spirit of the Wheat, The. Valentine
Wheat. Glancy
Wheat, The. *Unknown*
Wheatley, Phillis
Letter from Phillis Wheatley, A. Hayden
Wheelbarrows
Red Wheelbarrow, The. Williams
Wheelchairs
Disabled. Owen
I Am Mama Bear. Davis
Way Downtown, The. Hooper
Wheeler, Joseph
Wheeler at Santiago. Gordon
Wheeling, West Virginia
In Response to a Rumor That the Oldest Whorehouse in Wheeling, West Virginia, Has Been Condemned. Wright
Wheelock, Eleazar
Eleazar Wheelock. Hovey
Wheels
Figured Wheel, The. Pinsky
Whippoorwills
Mountain Whippoorwill, The. Benét
Whip-poor-will. Hall
Whippoorwill this/ moonday into. Cummings
Whiskey
John Barleycorn. *Unknown*
Rye Whiskey. *Unknown*
Whistler, James Abbott McNeill
After Whistler. Plumly
Limerick: "There's a combative artist named Whistler." Rossetti
To Whistler, American. Pound
Whistling
Whistling. Prelutsky
White, Peregrine
Peregrine White and Virginia Dare. Benét
White Sulphur Springs, West Virginia
Written at the White Sulphur Springs. Key
Whitefield, George
On the Death of the Rev. Mr. George Whitefield. Wheatley
Thoughts on the Works of Providence. Wheatley
Whitman, Walt
Adhesive Autopsy of Walt Whitman, The. Williams
Cape Hatteras. *Fr.* The Bridge. Crane

Let us tunnel. *Fr.* Letters to Walt Whitman. Johnson
Ode to Walt Whitman. García Lorca
Old Walt. Hughes
On Walt Whitman's Birthday. Waldman
Pact, A. Pound
Reading Walt Whitman. Forbes
Supermarket in California, A. Ginsberg
To Walt Whitman. MacInnes
Tribute of Grasses, A. Garland
Walt Whitman. Carnevali
Walt Whitman. Honig
Walt Whitman. Morris
Walt Whitman. Robinson
Walt Whitman. Williams
Walt Whitman at Bear Mountain. Simpson
Walt Whitman at the Reburial of Poe. Christopher
Whitman. Levis
Whitsunday. *See* **Pentecost.**
Whittier, John Greenleaf
Mr. Whittier. Scott
To John Greenleaf Whittier. Ward
To Whittier. Heard
White Magic; an Ode. Braithwaite
Whittier. Dunbar
Whittier. *Fr.* A Fable for Critics. Lowell
Whittier. Sangster
Widecombe Fair
Widdecombe [*or* Widdicombe] Fair. *Unknown*
Widows and Widowers
At first I was given centuries. Atwood
Brisk Young Widow, A. *Unknown*
Contention betwixt a Wife, a Widow, and a Maid, A. Davies
Courtship, The. Lyon
Free woman, A. At last free! Sumangala
I am a widow, robed in black, alone. Pisan
Lament of the Border Widow, The. *Unknown*
On His Deceased Wife. Milton
On Seeing an Officer's Widow Distracted. Barber
Portrait of a Widow. Strauss
Preparing for Weather. Oles
Reasons for and against Marrying Widows. Selyns
To a Lady on the Death of Her Husband. Wheatley
Upon the Death of Sir Albert Morton's Wife. Wotton
War Widow. Noël-Paton
Widow, The. Southey
Widow in Wintertime, A. Kizer
Widow Perez, The. Soto
Widow under a New Moon. Clark
Widower, The. Tyler
Widowhood. Heifetz-Tussman
Widows. Masters
Widow's Lament. *Fr.* Shih Ching. *Unknown*
Widow's Lament in Springtime, The. Williams
Wigs
Bald Cavalier, The. *Unknown*
Wilberforce University
Golden Jubilee of Wilberforce. Linden
To the Conference. Linden
Wilberforce. Heard
Wilberforce, William
To William Wilberforce, Esq. Cowper
Wilde, Oscar
Arrest of Oscar Wilde at the Cadogan Hotel, The. Betjeman
Dead Poet, The. Douglas
Message, A. Ives
Wildebeests. *See* **Gnus.**
Wilderness
Dark foreboding haunts me lest I die, A. *Fr.* San Gloria. MacDermot

Above Pate Valley. Snyder
Among High Hills. Soutar
Bushed. Birney
Call of the Wild, The. Service
Do You Fear the Wind? Garland
En Route. Scott
Inversnaid. Hopkins
Laurentian Shield. Scott
Lonely Land, The. Smith
North, The. McKinnon
Okeechobee. Allison
Oreads. Raine
Peace of Wild Things, The. Berry
Precambrian [*or* Pre-Cambrian] Shield, The. *Fr.* Towards the Last Spike. Pratt
Requiem for Sonora. Shelton
Rocky Acres. Graves
Staying Alive. Wagoner
There was a time on this fair continent. *Fr.* Tecumseh. Mair
Wildflowers
Buttercups and Daisies. Howitt
Ghost-Flowers. Higginson
Kind. Ammons
Peppergrass. Plumly
Queen-Ann's-Lace. Williams
Violet Bank, A. *Fr.* A Midsummer Night's Dream. Shakespeare
Wild Flower's Song. Blake
Wildflower. Plumly
Woodspurge, The. Rossetti
Wilhelm, Hoyt
For Hoyt Wilhelm. Oppenheimer
William III, King of England (William of Orange)
Dialogue between King William and the Late King James on the Banks of the Boyne, A. Blount
Duchess of York's Ghost, The. *Unknown*
Impartial Inspection, The. *Unknown*
Mourners, The. Higgons
New Song of an Orange, A. *Unknown*
On the Late Metamorphosis of an Old Picture of Oliver Cromwell's. *Unknown*
Panegyric, A. *Unknown*
Shash, The. *Unknown*
Upon the King's Return from Flanders. Hall
William IV, King of England
Royal Adventurer, The. Freneau
Williams, Arthur Clement
In Memory of Arthur Clement Williams. Bibb
Williams, Roger
Canonicus and Roger Williams. *Unknown*
Roger Williams. Butterworth
Williams, Theodore Samuel ("Ted")
Dream of a Baseball Star. Corso
Kid, The. Bezner
Williams, William Carlos
Doctor Bill Williams. Walsh
Elegy for W. C. W., the Lovely Man, An. *Fr.* Dream Songs. Berryman
Letter to William Carlos Williams, A. Rexroth
Nuances of a Theme by Williams. Stevens
Phone Call to Rutherford. Blackburn
To William Carlos Williams. Kinnell
Williams: An Essay. Levertov
Willow Trees
At the Ferry in Kuwana. *Fr.* Seventeen Hokku. Chiyojo
Bent Willows. Li Chien
Green willow's quiet, A. *Fr.* Seventeen Hokku. Chiyojo
Haiku: "They've cut down the willow." *Fr.* Thirty-nine Haiku. Shiki
Sauchs in the Reuch Heuch Hauch, The. "MacDiarmid"
Song, A: "My head on moss reclining." *Unknown*

To tangle or untangle a willow. *Fr.*
Seventeen Hokku. Chiyojo
To the Willow-Tree. Herrick
Willow, The. Tu Fu
Willow Branches. Sun Kuang-hsien
Willow flows away, The. *Fr.* Seventeen
Hokku. Chiyojo
Willow in a Gale. Wilson
Willow Poem. Williams
Willows, The. Eaton
Willows. Langland
Willows of Massachusetts, The. Levertov
Wills
E. K.'s Will. Csoori
Extraordinary Will. Jackett
In the Twentieth Century of My Trespass on
Earth. *Fr.* The Dead Shall Be Raised
Incorruptible. Kinnell
Last Will and Testament, A. Winstanley
Mira's Will. Leapor
Wilson, Woodrow
Woodrow Wilson. Jeffers
Wiltshire, England
Houseless Downs, The. *Fr.* The Shepherds'
Song, Sung before Queen Anne, on the
Wiltshire Downs, 11 June 1613. Ferebe
Prehistoric Burials. Sassoon
Wiltshire Downs. Young
Winchester, England
On King Arthur's Round Table, at
Winchester. Warton
Winchester, Virginia
Sheridan's Ride. Read
Wind
Address to a Child during a Boisterous Winter
Evening. Wordsworth
Aim Was Song, The. Frost
At Sasanami/ the pines are just as they were.
Tameuji
Autum: "Wind—tapped like a tired man,
The." Dickinson
Beggar Wind, The. Austin
Big Wind. Roethke
Blow, Blow, Thou Winter Wind. *Fr.* As
You Like It. Shakespeare
Candlelight Fisherman, The. *Unknown*
Cars Once Steel and Green, Now Old.
Zukofsky
Contrary Wind, A. Ho Shao-chi
Cooler than the wind. Tameyo
Desire. Eddy
Dirge, A: "Rough wind, that moanest loud."
Shelley
Echoing high/ in the tips of the pines.
Fushimi
Even a breeze may fail me. *Fr.* Manyo Shu.
Kagami
Even the night wind. Eifuku
Evening Wind, The. Bryant
Evening windstorm, An. Fushimi
Following the wind. Tameko
Four Winds, The. Lüders
Hearing the Wind at Night. Swenson
High Wind at the Battery. Pomeroy
I Have a Young Sister. *Unknown*
I Saw the Wind Today. Colum
I waited and I. *Fr.* Manyo Shu. Nukada
January. Williams
Least it could do, The. Ryoshun
Little Wind. Greenaway
March Wind, The. Henderson
Mid-Country Blow. Roethke
Mistral. Howes
Mountain Hut in a Storm. Tamekane
Mountain Wind. Loots
Mountain wind blows, The. Tonna
Night Wind, The. Field
North Wind, The. Graddon
"Not a leaf shall stay." Tameuji
O Thirsty Wind. *Unknown*
Over heavy dew. Tamenori

Rags. Thurman
Scattering blossoms. Eifuku
Sheets of rain, The. Tameko
Simoom, The. Tupper
Sleepless at Crown Point. Wilbur
Snow-Storm, The. Emerson
Some Notes on the Wind. Görgey
Song of the Four Winds, The. *Fr.* The
Misfortunes of Elphin. Peacock
Song of the Wind. Niazi
Song to the Wind, A. Taliesin
Sound of the Wind, The. *Fr.* Sing-Song.
Rossetti
South Wind. Sassoon
Spring Wind, The. Zolotow
Spring wind: over the river bank comes a
bull's voice. *Fr.* Thirteen Hokku. Raizan
Strong Wind, A. Clarke
Summer Breeze. *Unknown*
Summer Wind. Bryant
Sun Has Set, The. Brontë
Theory of Wind, A. Goldbarth
There came a wind like a bugle. Dickinson
Through the chinks. *Fr.* Koka Shu.
Unknown
To the sound of the wind. Tameko
To the Wind. Palacio
Traveling past a Market Town. Shotetsu
Unknown Wind, The. "Macleod"
Villain, The. Davies
Waiting for the Wind. Finkel
Weather of Olympus, The. Graves
Western Wind. *Unknown*
What If a Much of a Which of a Wind.
Cummings
What the Winds Bring. Stedman
When evening falls, the autumn wind rustles.
Fr. A Compendium of Good Tanka. Teika
When the east wind blows. Michizane
When the Wind. Deguy
When the wind blows. Mibu Tadamine
When the wind is in the east. Mother Goose
When the Wind Is Strong. Tanikawa
Shuntaro
Who Has Seen the Wind? *Fr.* Sing-Song.
Rossetti
Wind. Brown
Wind, The. Dafydd ap Gwilym
Wind, The. Graddon
Wind, The. Hughes
Wind, The. Reeves
Wind, The. Rendall
Wind, The. Stephens
Wind, The. Stevenson
Wind/ flattening its gaunt furious self against.
Fr. The Wind Our Enemy. Marriott
Wind and the Bird, The. *Unknown*
Wind and the Moon, The. Macdonald
Wind at Penistone, The. Davie
Wind begun to knead the grass, The.
Dickinson
Wind blew: for you, The. *Fr.* Manyo Shu.
Kagami
Wind Blows out of the Gates of the Day,
The. *Fr.* The Land of Heart's Desire.
Yeats
Wind in a Frolic, The. Howitt
Wind in the Grass. Van Doren
Wind Is Blind, The. Meynell
Wind is rustling, The. Munenaga
Wind is wild tonight, The. *Unknown*
Wind of an Evening Shower. Shotetsu
Wind Song. Sandburg
Wind that rose, A. Dickinson
Wind That Shakes the Rushes, The. Clare
Wind that sweeps down Ikaho, The. *Fr.*
Manyo Shu. *Unknown*

Wind Took Up the Northern Things, The.
Dickinson
Wind-Wolves. Sargent
Winds. McCrae
Winds, The. Tusser
Wind's Lament, The. Morris-Jones
Wind's Work. Moore
Windy Nights. Stevenson
Winter wind: pebbles in a plowed field. *Fr.*
Eighty-seven Hokku. Buson
With a sudden gust. Tamekane
See also **East Wind; North Wind; South
Wind; West Wind.**
Windflowers. *See* **Anemones.**
Windhovers. *See* **Falcons.**
Windmills
At the Art Exhibit. Winkler
Mill, The. Heyen
Stone. Amir
Windmill, The. Longfellow
Windmill, The. Lucas
Windmill on the Cape. Sieller
Window Boxes
Window Boxes ("A window box of pansies").
Farjeon
Window Washers
Fall, The. Nathan
Window Washer. Simic
Windows
Factory Windows Are Always Broken.
Lindsay
Torn Windows, No Paper. Keijo Shurin
Window, The. Aiken
Window Cleaner, The. Fleming
Window Washer. Simic
Windows. Dickey
Windows, The. Herbert
Windows in Providence. Barnstone
Windsor Castle
When Windsor walls sustain'd my wearied
arm. Surrey
Windsor Forest, England
Lines Written in Windsor Forest. Pope
Thy forests, Windsor! and thy green retreats.
Fr. Windsor Forest. Pope
Wine
Awake, My Soul. *Fr.* Wine-Songs. Ibn
Ezra
Bacchus. Emerson
Bacchus's Opinion of Wine, and Other
Beverages. *Fr.* Bacchus in Tuscany.
Redi
Bring Me the Cup. *Fr.* Wine-Songs. Ibn
Ezra
Bring the Wine! Li Po
Bubbling Wine. Abu Zakariya
Circumstance. Bowen
Drink, Friends. *Fr.* Wine-Songs. Ibn Ezra
Drinking Wine. Mo Shih-lung
Drinking Wine: Second Series. Ch'ien
Ch'ien-yi
Epicure, The ("Fill the bowl with rosie
wine"). Cowley
Five Arabic Verses in Praise of Wine.
Unknown
Fly, The. Ayres
In a Wine Cellar. Daley
Instead of wasting thoughts on unavailing
things. *Fr.* Manyo Shu. Tabito
Let's make sake, strong and clear, from early
rice. *Unknown*
Logic. *Unknown*
Ode in the Praise of Sack, An. *Unknown*
On Drinking. *Fr.* Forty-four Tanka
Wakayama Bokusui.
On Hearing That San-p'ing's Newly Brewed
Chrysanthemum Wine Is Ready to Drink.
Pien Kung
Poem on Drinking Wine with the
Degree-Holder Ku. Ch'ien Ch'ien-i

Rather than worry. *Fr.* Manyo Shu. Tabito

Trip to Mountain West Village, A. Lu Yu

Under Leafy Bowers. Al-Harizi

Welcome to Sack, The. Herrick

Wine. Lebensohn

Wine Bowl. Doolittle

Wine upon beer, I counsel thee. *Unknown*

Wineglass, The. Baratynsky

Wine's inebriety. Ghalib

With the bounteous wine the doughty warrior blesses. *Fr.* Manyo Shu. Yuhara

You Serve the Best Wines Always, My Dear Sir. Martial

Wings

What the Wing Says. Swanger

Wings. Fisher

Wingspan. Cattafi

Winnipeg, Manitoba

Signature. Livesay

Winslow, John Ancrum

Eagle and Vulture, The. Read

Winter

After the Leaves Fall. Kim Chun-soo

Alone. De la Mare

Ancestor of the Hunting Heart. Haines

Ancient Music. Pound

As I looked, winter came. *Fr.* Seventy-eight Tanka. Shikishi

Ballad of the Oysterman, The. Holmes

Before Sunrise in Winter. Sill

Birches. Frost

Birds at Winter Nightfall. Hardy

Bitter Winter. Fortini

Blue Horses. Roberson

Blue Winter. Francis

Calm Winter Sleep. Corke

Child's Winter Evening, A. John

Clear Winter. Reverdy

Cold Blows the Wind. Hamilton

Cold Fear. Roberts

Cold in the Grass. Kenko

Cold Reeds around an Inlet. Tameshige

Colonial Set. Bailey

Come with Me into Winter's Disheveled Grass. Swenson

Coming of the Cold, The. Roethke

Coming of Winter, The. Laforgue

Comparison, A. Farrar

Could it be I wait. Teika

Dartmouth Winter-Song. Hovey

Days in White. Bachmann

Dead of winter: crows are black. *Fr.* Eighty-seven Hokku. Buson

Death of the Flowers, The. Bryant

December. Kenny

Dirge for the Year. Shelley

Down swept the chill wind from the mountain peak. *Fr.* The Vision of Sir Launfal. Lowell

Early Illinois Winter, An. Kuo

Emmonsail's Heath in Winter. Clare

End of the Street, The. Haines

Evening Walk in Winter. Bethell

Exposure. Owen

February Twilight. Teasdale

First month of winter: cold air comes. *Fr.* Nineteen Old Poems of the Han. *Unknown*

First Winter. Harada

Function of Winter, The. Parini

Garden Moss under Snow. Kaneyoshi

Gone Were but the Winter Cold. Cunningham

Good Hours. Frost

Haiku: "Early winter." Naito Meisetsu

Helen. Valéry

Hillside Thaw, A. Frost

How One Winter Came in the Lake Region. Campbell

Hugh Maguire. O'Hussey

I bring you news. *Unknown*

I Walked [*or* Walkt] the Other Day to Spend My Hour. Vaughan

Ice. Bottoms

Ice. Roberts

Ice River. Baker

Icicles. Pinsky

In a Remote Korean Village. Koh Chang-soo

In Defense of Felons. Mezey

In my mountain hamlet. Muneyuki

In the broad dawn sky. Ietaka

In the snow piled up. Tamekane

In the Wood. Mathias

In Winter. Dunbar

In Winter. Wallace

In Winter's Dusk. *Fr.* On Winter Evenings; 1912. Hofshteyn

January 25th. Kumin

Kept Indoors on a Winter Evening. Tameko Lalique. Porter

Long Walk before the Snows Began, A. Bly

Love. Browning

March 1st. Spivack

Midnight. Lampman

Midwinter. Trowbridge

Midwinter Thaw. Pratt

Midwinter Warm. Stone

My Winter Past. Grier

New Year's Days. Standish

New Year's [*or* Year] Song. Hughes

Night is cold on the Great Bog, The. *Fr.* Toward Winter. *Unknown*

Night Is Freezing Fast, The. Housman

No noise is here, or none that hinders thought. *Fr.* The Task: A Winter Walk at Noon. Cowper

No Possum, No Sop, No Taters. Stevens

No storm, but the forest is drumming. *Fr.* Frost, the Red-nosed. Nekrasov

"Not a leaf shall stay." Tameuji

Now Winter Nights Enlarge. Campion

Ode to Winter. Campbell

Old Man's Winter Night, An. Frost

Old Winter. Noel

On a Winter Evening. Koh Chang-soo

On the Dark, Still, Dry, Warm Weather Occasionally Happening in the Winter Months. White

Onset, The. Frost

Orchard Trees, January. Wilbur

Outside. Chesterman

Over empty limbs. Tamekane

Persia. Sackville-West

Poem of the Frost and Snow. Morris

Poet in Winter. Lucie-Smith

Procession. Booth

Remembering Snow. Csoori

Robin, The. Daniel

Sayings from the Northern Ice. Stafford

Scene on the Banks of the Hudson, A. Bryant

Schoolboys in Winter. Clare

Sestina d'Inverno. Hecht

Signs of Winter. Clare

Six Winter Privacy Poems. Bly

Skiing Home at Dusk. Parini

Sledding Song, A. Schlichter

Sleet rattles on the leaves. *Fr.* Twenty-four Tanka. Sanetomo.

Sliab Cua, dark and broken, is full of wolf packs. *Fr.* Toward Winter. *Unknown*

Snow-Flakes. Longfellow

Snow Man, The. Stevens

Snow on the Mountain at Dusk. Shotetsu

Snow toward Evening. Cane

Snowdrop. Hughes

Snowstorm: At a Gathering at Chang Chu-fu's House. Tsung Ch'en

Snowy Day, A. *Unknown*

So much more forlorn. Tamekane

Something Told the Wild Geese. Field

Song: "I'd much rather sit there in the sun." Krauss

Song: "Lovely hill-torrents are." Turner

Song in the Cold Season. Morse

Song of Winter, A. Pfeiffer

Song of Winter, A. *Unknown*

Star-Talk. Graves

Stopping by Woods on a Snowy Evening. Frost

Storm. Oliver

Summer and Winter. Shelley

Summer Is Gone. *Unknown*

Surprised by Winter. Michizane

Thaw. Thomas

These. Williams

Those Winter Sundays. Hayden

To the Maiden in the East. Thoreau

To Winter. Blake

Tree Sleeps in the Winter, The. Russell

Tumultuous winter sky all day. *Fr.* Seventy-eight Tanka. Shikishi

Turning. Finch

Under the Winter Sky. Pilinszky

Up in the Air. Ramsay

Velvet Shoes. Wylie

Want and winter are upon us. *Fr.* Toward Winter. *Unknown*

Warning of Winter. Bethell

We are shattered and battered, engulfed. *Fr.* Toward Winter. *Unknown*

When Icicles Hang by the Wall. *Fr.* Love's Labour's Lost. Shakespeare

White Fields. Stephens

Wind piercing, hill bare, hard to find shelter. *Fr.* Winter. *Unknown*

Winter. Akhmadulina

Winter. Al-Maghut

Winter. *Fr.* Eclogues. Barclay.

Winter. Blyton

Winter. *Fr.* The Four Seasons in the Mountains. Chang Yü

Winter. De la Mare

Winter. Donaghy

Winter. Douglas

Winter. Hughes

Winter. Landor

Winter. Mair

Winter. Rossetti

Winter. Synge

Winter blast. Mukai Kyorai

Winter Burn. Hill

Winter Climb. Eunaich

Winter Days. Abbey

Winter Days. Owen

Winter Deepening, The. Wilbur

Winter Evening. De la Mare

Winter Evening. Lampman

Winter Evening. Teller

Winter Fairyland in Vermont. Osgood

Winter Garden. Gascoyne

Winter Has Come. *Unknown*

Winter in Lower Canada. *Fr.* The Emigrant. O'Grady

Winter in the Fens. Clare

Winter Joys. Graddon

Winter Lakes, The. Campbell

Winter Landscape. Berryman

Winter Love. Jennings

Winter Memories. Thoreau

Winter moon. *Fr.* Ten Tanka. Myoe

Winter Morning. Smith

Winter: My Secret. Rossetti

Winter Night, A. Barnes

Winter Night, A. Thompson

Winter Night, Reading Books. Kan Sazan

Winter ("Now, when the cheerless empire of the sky"). *Fr.* The Seasons. Thomson

Winter Pause: Mt. Liberty, N.H. Robbins

Winter Piece, A. Bryant

Winter Poem, A. Tameie

Winter Portrait. Southey

Winter Remembered. Ransom

Winter Scene. Young

Winter Shore, The. Wade
Winter Song. Daiches
Winter Time. *Fr.* A Child's Garden of
    Verses. Stevenson
Winter Twilight, A. Grimké
Winter [*or* Wynter] Wakeneth All [*or* Al] My
    Care. *Unknown*
Winter without Snow, A. McClatchy
Wintering. Plath
Winter's Tale, A. Thomas
Winter's Troops. *Fr.* Winter. Cotton
Winterward. Stafford
Words of Finn, The. *Unknown*
World Winter. Birney
Year's End. Wilbur

Winters, Yvor
    To Yvor Winters, 1955. Gunn

Wisconsin
    For the Death of Vince Lombardi. Dickey
    La Crosse at Ninety Miles an Hour. Eberhart

Wisdom
    Coming of Wisdom with Time, The. Yeats
    For This Is Wisdom. *Fr.* The Teak Forest.
      "Hope"
    Happy Is the Man. *Fr.* Proverbs
    Lost Genius, The. Piatt
    On Wisdom. Hakuin
    Voyage, The. Sisson
    Wisdom. Sobiloff
    Wisdom is the finest beauty of a person.
    Word to the Wise, A. Duer
    See also **Reason.**

Wise Men. *See* **Magi.**

Wishes
    Bunches of Grapes. De la Mare
    Counsel. Lewis
    I Keep Three Wishes Ready. Wynne
    My Inside-Self. Field
    Penny Wish, A. Thompson
    Rathers. Austin
    Reflections at Dawn. McGinley
    Richard Roe and John Doe ("Richard Roe
      wished himself Solomon."). Graves
    Sonnet: "Guido, I wish that you and Lapo and
      I." Dante
    Wish, The. Friday
    Wish. Thompson
    Wishes. Rogers
    Wishes. *Unknown*
    Wishing. Allingham
    Wishing. Saxe

Wisteria
    Clear is the bottom of the lake. *Fr.* Manyo
      Shu. Yakamochi
    Haiku: "Before the/ red blossoms." *Fr.*
      Fifteen Haiku. Masaoka Shiki
    Haiku: "If I were to paint." *Fr.* Fifteen
      Haiku. Masaoka Shiki
    Haiku: "If you stick the stems." *Fr.* Fifteen
      Haiku. Masaoka Shiki
    Haiku: "Last year in spring." *Fr.* Fifteen
      Haiku. Masaoka Shiki
    Haiku: "Sprays of wisteria, The/ arranged in
      the vase/ are so short." *Fr.* Fifteen Haiku.
      Masaoka Shiki
    Haiku: "Sprays of wisteria/ arranged in a
      vase—/ the blossoms hang down." *Fr.*
      Fifteen Haiku. Masaoka Shiki
    Haiku: "Sprays of wisteria/ arranged in a
      vase—/ one cluster." *Fr.* Fifteen Haiku.
      Masaoka Shiki
    Haiku: "These wisterias." *Fr.* Fifteen Haiku.
      Masaoka Shiki
    Haiku: "When I look/ at the wisteria
      blossoms/ I think of long ago." *Fr.*
      Fifteen Haiku. Masaoka Shiki
    Haiku: "When I look/ at wisteria blossoms/ I
      want to get out." *Fr.* Fifteen Haiku.
      Masaoka Shiki
    I put aside a story. *Fr.* Twenty-one Hokku.
      Kaya Shirao

    Summer Wisteria. Shotetsu
    Wisteria in the Rain. Gyoko

Wit
    Ode: Of Wit. Cowley

Witchcraft and Witches
    Against Witches. *Unknown*
    Ballad of the Harp-Weaver, The. Millay
    Ballad of the Hoppy-Toad. Walker
    Diving into the Wreck. Rich
    Eight Witches. Lee
    Expelling Witches. Chiang Shih-ch'üan
    Fable: "Pity the girl with crystal hair."
      Aiken
    Fatal Sisters, The. Gray
    Hag-ridden. Graves
    Hag, The ("The hag is astride"). Herrick
    Her Kind. Sexton
    Her Strong Enchantments Failing. Housman
    Hey-How for Hallowe'en. *Unknown*
    In Salem. Clifton
    Incantation to Oedipus. *Fr.* Oedipus.
      Dryden
    Invention of White People, The. Silko
    Korf's Enchantment. Morgenstern
    Lincolnshire; from the Wolds to the Fens.
      Fr. The Sad Shepherd. Jonson
    Look out! Look out, boys! Clear the track!
      Fr. The Broomstick Train. Holmes
    Molly Means. Walker
    Mother Maudlin the Witch. *Fr.* The Sad
      Shepherd. Jonson
    November 1968. Rich
    Queen Nefertiti. *Unknown*
    Ride-by-Nights, The. De la Mare
    Riverman, The. Bishop
    Song of Wandering Aengus, The. Yeats
    Sorcerer, Mr. Wells, The, *sel.* Gilbert
    Sorceress, The! Lindsay
    Tam o' Shanter. Burns
    Thrice the Brinded Cat Hath Mewed. *Fr.*
      Macbeth. Shakespeare
    Two Witches, The. Graves
    Uncle Mells and the Witches' Tree. Roberts
    Wanted—a Witch's Cat. McGee
    What is the opposite of a prince? Wilbur
    When All the World Is Young. Kingsley
    Wind on the Hills, The. Shorter
    Witch, The. Coleridge
    Witch, The. Ilott
    Witch, The. Tynan
    Witch-Bride, The. Allingham
    Witch Burning. Plath
    Witch of Coös, The. Frost
    Witch of East Seventy-second Street, The.
      Bishop
    Witch, The! The Witch! Farjeon
    Witchcraft. Naranjo-Morse
    Witchcraft: New Style. Abercrombie
    Witchcraft Woman. Naranjo-Morse
    Witches. Hughes
    Witches' Charms, The. *Fr.* The Masque of
      Queens. Jonson
    Witches' Menu. Nikolay
    Witches' Ride, The. Kuskin
    Witch's Ballad, The. Scott
    Witch's Cat, The. Serraillier
    Witch's Life, The. Sexton
    Witch's Spell [*or* Witch's Milking Charm], A.
      Unknown
    Witch's Work Song, The. White
    Wizard of Alderley Edge, The. Coe
    Wizards. Mó
    *Why Am I Grown So Cold? Poems of the
      Unknowable* (WSC), pp. 24-42, 170-185.
      Myra Cohn Livingston, ed.

Wittgenstein, Ludwig Josef Johann
    Philosopher and the Birds, The. Murphy

Wives
    After the Golden Wedding. Stephen

    Aged Wino's Counsel to a Young Man on the
      Brink of Marriage, The. Kennedy
    Alive or Not. Purdy
    Are there no gods of heaven and earth? *Fr.*
      Manyo Shu. *Unknown*
    Auld Robin Gray. Lindsay
    Ballad of the Despairing Husband. Creeley
    Berry Picking. Layton
    Brewer's Man, The. Strong
    By the Boat House, Oxford. Stevenson
    Cinnamon Peeler, The. Ondaatje
    Clear and loud. *Fr.* Manyo Shu. Hitomaro
    Contention betwixt a Wife, a Widow, and a
      Maid, A. Davies
    Double Transformation, The. Goldsmith
    Dream, The. "Bendo"
    Exequy, The. King
    Farm Wife. Voigt
    For Fran. Levine
    For My Lover, Returning to His Wife.
      Sexton
    For My Wife: A Poem Written in Sickness.
      Yüan Mei
    Fox and the Hare, The. *Unknown*
    Free Union. Breton
    Grass of Kasuga Moor. *Fr.* Kokin Shu.
      Unknown
    Hill Wife, The. Frost
    His Half-Breed Wife. Seale
    Housewife's Lament, The. *Unknown*
    I loved her like the leaves. *Fr.* Manyo Shu.
      Hitomaro
    I Married in My Youth a Wife. Cunningham
    In the evening. *Fr.* Manyo Shu. Tajihi
    In the spring meadow. *Fr.* Manyo Shu.
      Unknown
    In Uganda an Early King. Walker
    Johnny Sands ("There was a man named
      Johnny Sands, who married Betty Hague").
      Unknown
    Jug Brook. Voigt
    Julia. Rose
    Melting, The. Edson
    My dear wife loved my arm. *Fr.* Manyo
      Shu. Tabito
    My Old Wife's a Good Old Cratur.
      Unknown
    Next Day. Jarrell
    O that I'd had. *Fr.* Manyo Shu. Mononobe
      Furumaro
    October. Spacks
    Of Scolding Wives and the Third Day Ague.
      Selyns
    Old Flame, The. Lowell
    Old Poem. *Unknown*
    On His Deceased Wife. Milton
    On My Wife's Birth-Day. Smart
    On the Death of His Wife. O'Dalaigh
    Our Wives. Galassi
    Peter, Peter, pumpkin eater. Mother Goose
    Poor Man's Work Is Never Done, A.
      Unknown
    Retreat of Ita Cagney, The. Hartnett
    Sad Remembrance. Mei Yao-ch'en
    Sailors' Wives, The. *Unknown*
    Scholar's Wife, The. Mernit
    Seamen's Wives' Vindication, The.
      Unknown
    Since in Karu lived my wife. *Fr.* Manyo
      Shu. Hitomaro
    Sweet 'n Sour. Lim
    That wife of mine. *Fr.* Manyo Shu.
      Wakayama Mimaro
    Thick sea-pine, The. *Fr.* Manyo Shu.
      Hitomaro
    This Evening. Landau
    Till my black hair be white. *Fr.* Manyo Shu.
      "Takahashi"
    Tinker's Wife. Kavanagh
    To the Ladies. Chudleigh
    To this land of Tsukushi. *Fr.* Manyo Shu.
      Okura

Toiler's Wife, The. Hull
Upon the Death of Sir Albert Morton's Wife.
  Wotton
When Adam Was First Created. *Unknown*
When evening comes. *Fr.* Manyo Shu.
  Yakamochi
While the leaves of the bamboo rustle. *Fr.*
  Manyo Shu. *Unknown*
Who Drags the Fiery Artist Down? Day
Wife a-Lost, The. Barnes
Wife a-Prais'd, A. Barnes
Wife of Winter's Tale, The. Browne
Wife won/ and she never, The. *Unknown*
Wife's Lament. *Unknown*
Wish for a Young Wife. Roethke
Wives in the Sere. Hardy
Words of the Newly Wed Wife. Wang
  Chien
Young Housewife, The. Williams
See also **Marriage.**
Wolfe, James
  Bold General Wolfe. *Unknown*
  Brave Wolfe. *Unknown*
  Death of Wolfe, The. *Unknown*
Wollstonecraft, Mary
  Hard was thy fate in all the scenes of life.
    Roscoe
Wolsey, Thomas, Cardinal
  Colin Clout, *sels.* Skelton
  Such a prelate, I trow. *Fr.* Why Come Ye
    Not to Court. Skelton
Wolves
  Fable: "Once upon a time." Pilinszky
  Four Mountain Wolves. Silko
  He was an old wolf, no teeth, his tail all but
    bare. *Fr.* Sioux Metamorphoses.
    Unknown
  Howling of Wolves, The. Hughes
  Lobo. Lillard
  Poem about a Wolf Maybe Two Wolves, A.
    Unknown
  Wolf, The. Al-Haj
  Wolf. Blue Cloud
  Wolf, The. Durston
  Wolf. *Fr.* A Bestiary. Rexroth
  Wolf and the Lambs, The. Eastwick
  Wolf and the Stork, The. La Fontaine
  Wolf Cry, The. Sarett
  Wolf Girl Speaks, The. Springer
  Wolf Said to Francis, The. Rochelle
  Wolves. Haines
  Wolves in the Zoo. Nemerov
  Wolves' voices harmonize. *Fr.* Fifteen
    Hokku. Joso
Woman Suffrage
  Brother Baptis' on Woman Suffrage. Jonas
  See also **Voting and Voters.**
Wombats
  Wombat, The. Nash
Women
  Against Blame of Woman. Desmond
  Against Women. *Unknown*
  Agatha Christie and Beatrix Potter. Updike
  And blessed be the women who get you
    through. *Fr.* The Hallowing of Hell.
    Morgan
  Another Poem about the Madness of Women.
    Wayman
  Answer to a Man's Question, "What Can I Do
    about Women's Liberation?" Griffin
  As Joe Gould says in. Cummings
  At the Theater. Herbert
  Beach Women, The. Pinsky
  Beautiful Black Women. Baraka
  Beautiful Woman Who Sings, The ("The
    beautiful woman at Laguna"). Allen
  Because I had reproached him where he
    failed. Jausbert de Puycibot
  Belly Dancer. Wakoski
  Beneath the Shadow of the Freeway.
    Cervantes

Black Sister. Cumbo
Black Woman. Madgett
Black Woman Out Dere. Gayle
Bookshop Idyll, A. Amis
Brave at Home, The. Read
Breaking Tradition. Mirikitani
Butcher's Wife, The. Erdrich
Cachikel Woman. Meneses
Canyon Day Woman Blues. Keams
Changes. Bulwer-Lytton
Charming Woman, The. Sheridan
Colours of Love, The. Devlin
Combing. Cardiff
Creatrix. Wickham
Darby and Joan. Honeywood
Dear Old Stockholm. Young
Dear World. Allen
December: Of Aphrodite. Merwin
Declaimer, The. Baker
Dedication of the Cook. Wickham
Dispraise of Absalom, The. *Unknown*
Divine Office of the Kitchen, The. Hallack
Don't Call Me Mama. Stewart
Don't Call Me Sir Call Me Strong. Tsui
Dream-Language of Fergus, The.
  McGuckian
Dressed to Kill. Major
Drinking Song. *Fr.* The School for Scandal.
  Sheridan
Duplicity of Women, The. Lydgate
Elaine. *Fr.* Calling Your Name in the Zoo.
  Williams
Energetic Women. Lawrence
Epigram on Woman, An. Ayres
Essay on Woman, An. Leapor
Eve-Song. Gilmore
Eye for an Eye, An. Donald
Farm Wife. Mitchell
Father of Women, A. Meynell
Female Friend, The. Whur
Female God, The. Rosenberg
Female of the Species, The. Kipling
50 on 50. Meinke
Fine Young Folly. *Fr.* The Queen of
  Aragon. Habington
For love no time has she, or inclination. *Fr.*
  The Modern Fine Lady. Jenyns
Four Women. Simone
Frailty Is Not My Name. Ismay
Freedom Song for the Black Woman, A.
  Gregory
Friend Cato. Wickham
From an Old House in America. Rich
From Sappho to myself, consider the fate of
  women. *Fr.* Pro Femina. Kizer
From the Monkey House and Other Cages:
  Monkey II. Klepfisz
Garment of Good Ladies, The. Henryson
Gentle Echo on Woman, A. Swift
Gentlemen. Laforgue
Girl. *Unknown*
Gladys. *Fr.* Calling Your Name in the Zoo.
  Williams
Glass of Beer, A. Stephens
Glory of Women. Sassoon
Green Grow the Rashes, O. Burns
Grinding Vibrato. Cortez
Hamtramck: The Polish Women. Derricotte
Hand That Rocks the Cradle Is the Hand That
  Rules the World, The. Wallace
Health, A. Pinkney
Heart of a Woman, The. Johnson
Her Sister. O'Neill
His Mother-in-Law. Parke
Hot Dog Poem, The. Barnes
House of Mercy, A. Smith
Hush Honey. Saunders
Hypocrite Women. Levertov
I Am a Black Woman. Evans
I Am Not That Woman. Naheed
I, Being Born a Woman and Distressed.
  Millay

I Knew a Woman [Lovely in Her Bones].
  Roethke
I Know a Lady. Thomas
I Never Even Suggested It. Nash
I Shall Not Die for Thee. *Unknown*
I Was That Woman. Chatterjee
I, Woman. McClaurin
If the heart of a man is deprest [*or* depressed]
  with cares. *Fr.* The Beggar's Opera.
  Gay
I'll Tell You What a Flapper Is. Freeman
Impossible to Trust Women. *Unknown*
In Celebration of My Uterus. Sexton
In her first passion woman loves her lover.
  Fr. Don Juan. Byron
In Her Praise. Graves
In Librum. Davies
In the land of Azuma. *Fr.* Manyo Shu.
  Mushimaro
In the Old Guerilla War. Pastan
In the Person of Womankind (In Defense of
  Their Inconstancy). Jonson
It'll be a long time again before my friends.
  Vidal
It's No Good! Lawrence
I've Got the Giggles Today. Herbert
I've heard the talk. Guillaume de Poitiers
January 18, 1979. Yau
Jewish Woman, The. Kolmar
Josina, You Are Not Dead. Machel
Kirsten. *Fr.* Calling Your Name in the Zoo.
  Williams
Korean Woman Seated by a Wall, A.
  Meredith
Kwa Mama Zetu Waliotuzaa. Sanchez
Labourer's Wife, A. *Fr.* To the Street
  Piano. Davidson
Ladies, The. Kipling
Ladies of Bygone Days, The. Orban
Lady. Laforgue
Lady/ I clear myself toward you. Bertrans de
  Born
Lady, Lady. Spencer
Lady's Dressing Room, The. Swift
Lady's-Maid 's Song, The. Hollander
Lark, The. Bernart de Ventadorn
Lay Your Arms Aside. Ferriter
Letter to My Sister. Spencer
Lieder. Castro
Like the sedge of Naniwa. *Fr.* Manyo Shu.
  Otomo no Sakanoe
Looking Out. Chasin
Lord Walter's Wife. Browning
Lords of Creation, The. *Unknown*
Lost and Given Over. Brady
Love a woman! y'are an ass. Rochester
Love of the Scorching Wind. Nagy
Lure, The. O'Reilly
Mabel Kelly. Carolan
Man, Man, Man. *Unknown*
Man's Woman, A. Davies
Mast Year, The. McGuckian
Maxim Revised, A. *Unknown*
Mean Drunk Poem. Thesen
Meditation at Kew. Wickham
Metamorphoses. Fuller
Moments-of-Past-Happiness Quilt, The.
  Spivack
Most Beautiful Woman at My Highschool
  Reunion, The. Bissert
Mother. Montoya
Mr. McGregor's Garden. McGuckian
My Lady Carenza of the lovely body.
  Unknown
My Mother's Sister. Day Lewis
My Sisters, O My Sisters. Sarton
Mynstrelles Songe: "Angelles bee wrogte to
  bee of neidher kynde." *Fr.* Aella; a
  Tragycal Enterlude. Chatterton
Negro Woman. Alexander
New York Woman, The. Sissman
Next Day. Jarrell

No Images. Cuney
No Say. Murray
No Second Troy. Yeats
Noelle. *Fr. Calling Your Name in the Zoo.*
  Williams.
Nude Descending a Staircase. Kennedy
Nursery, The. Howe
Ode to a Beautiful Woman. Clark
Of Women. Edwards
Of Women. *Fr. The Thousand and One*
  Nights. Unknown
Of Women No More Evil. *Unknown*
Oh, oh, you will be sorry for that word!
  Millay
Old Woman, The. Campbell
Old Women of Toronto. Waddington
On Being a Woman. Parker
On the Watergate Women. Morgan
On Woman. Yeats
One Angry Woman. Williams
One canso I've made murderously. Vidal
Other Fabrics, Other Mores! Lenngren
Otis. Thomas
Pan, the Pot, the Burning Fire I Have in Front
  of Me, The. Ishigaki Rin
Pants. Vice
Patterns. Lowell
Peacock Woman, The. Nagy
Peggy Browne. Carolan
Pioneer Woman. Crawford
Planetarium. Rich
Poem about My Rights. Jordan
Poem for Some Black Women. Rodgers
Portrait d'une Femme. Pound
Portrait of a Lady. Williams
Prayer for My Daughter, A. Yeats
Prayer to the White Lady. Nagy
Quarry, The. Kálnoky
Queen-Ann's-Lace. Williams
Raising the Flag. Vizenor
Rape. Larkin
Rassa, I rise. Bertrans de Born
Rhyme of My Inheritance. Larkin
Sail and Oar. Graves
Serious Merriment of Women, The.
  Goedicke
She. Roethke
She. Roots
She. Wilbur
She Is Not Mute. Chan Ch'e
She Walked Unaware. MacDonogh
She Was a Phantom of Delight. Wordsworth
She's Free! Harper
Smothered Fires. Johnson
Snapshots of a Daughter-in-Law. Rich
Song: "Go and catch a falling star." Donne
Song: "He who offends a woman."
  Machiavelli
Song: "Ladies, though to your conquering
  eyes." *Fr. The Comical Revenge.*
  Etherege
Song: Promoting Women's Rights, A. Ch'iu
  Chin
Song: "Woman's face is full of wiles, A."
  Gifford
Sonnet: Dolce Stil Novo. Ewart
Starling, take wing and go. Marcabrun
Subjection of Women, The. Clarke
Sun Was Slumbering in the West, The.
  Hood
Susie Wong Doesn't Live Here. Mark
Sweet softness with which love serves me
  often, The. Guilhem de Cabestanh
Tame Cat. Pound
Tell Me. Mordecai
That Reminds Me. Nash
That Women Are but Men's Shadows.
  Jonson
Their Plan. Roots
Them. *Fr. Calling Your Name in the Zoo.*
  Williams
There Has to Be a Jail for Ladies. Merton

There Is a Girl Inside. Clifton
They say a man dies. *Fr. Songs.* Crow
Thoughts after Ruskin. Mitchell
Three Poems for Women. Griffin
To a Dark Girl. Bennett
To a Pretty Girl. Zangwill
To Caelia. *Unknown*
To Kate, Skating Better than Her Date.
  Daiches
To Some Supposed Brothers. Hemphill
To Women. Hugo
To Women, as Far as I'm Concerned.
  Lawrence
Tracy & Co. *Fr. Calling Your Name in the*
  Zoo. Williams
Transit. Rich
Tribute, The. *Fr. The Angel in the House.*
  Patmore
Triolet: "All women born are so perverse."
  Bridges
Troubled Woman. Hughes
True love/ warms my heart. Cercamon
Trust in Women. *Unknown*
Twicknam *or* Twickenham Garden. Donne
Two Parents, The. "MacDiarmid"
Two Strange Worlds. Pereira
Two Women. Willis
Upon Some Women. Herrick
Vampire, The. Kipling
Volcanic Venus. Lawrence
Washer-Woman, The. Bohanan
Way It Was, The. Clifton
We the Women. Nichols
Weeksville Women. Loftin
What Women Are Not. *Unknown*
Why Do We Love. Rudyerd
Why, Some of My Best Friends Are Women.
  McGinley
Wife's Tale, The. Heaney
Wings of a Wild Goose, The. Chrystos
Wish, A. Lerner
Woman. Barrett
Woman. "Chrystos"
Woman! Ibarbourou
Woman. Layton
Woman. Malangatana
Woman. *Fr. Samson Agonistes.* Milton
(Wo)man. Villanueva
Woman Hanging from the Thirteenth Floor
  Window, The. Harjo
Woman Is a Worthy Thing, A. *Unknown*
Woman is by aptitude. *Fr. Against Women.*
  Unknown
Woman Is of Man the Best. Lope de Vega
  Carpio
Woman Is Talking to Death, A. Grahn
Woman Me. Angelou
Woman, Mother of Man. *Fr. God, Our*
  Lady. Michel
Woman of Three Cows, The. *Unknown*
Woman Poem. Giovanni
Woman Recipe. Moraes
Woman Waits for Me, A. Whitman
Woman Who Understands, The. Appleton
Woman Work. Angelou
Woman's Answer to "The Vampire," A.
  Blake
Woman's Song, A. McElroy
Women. Bogan
Women. Cartwright
Women. Heath
Women. Swenson
Women and Men. Sheikh Mumin
Women are at their best. *Fr. Ryojin Hisho.*
  Go-Shirakawa
Women at the Corners Stand, The. Golding
Women in Love. Justice
Women in Old Parkas, The. TallMountain
Women in Vietnam, The. Paley
Women of Dan Dance with Swords in Their
  Hands to Mark the Time When They Were
  Warriors, The. Lorde

Women Open Cautiously. Lee
Women Who Cook. Skeen
Women Who Hate Me, The. Allison
Wonder Woman. Lim
Yellow Woman Speaks. Woo
Young Acacia, The. Bialik
Ain't I a Woman! a Book of Women's Poetry
  from around the World (AIW). Illona
  Linthwaite, ed.
Black Sister; Poetry by Black American
  Women, 1746-1980 (BlSi). Erlene Stetson,
  ed.
Book of Women Poets from Antiquity to Now,
  A (BoWoP). Aliki Barnstone *and* Willis
  Barnstone, eds.
Bread and Roses; an Anthology of Nineteenth-
  and Twentieth-Century Poetry by Women
  Writers (BrRo). Diana Scott, comp.
Chaos of the Night; Women's Poetry and
  Verse of the Second World War (CN).
  Catherine W. Reilly, ed.
Collected Black Women's Poetry (CBWP).
  Joan R. Sherman, ed.
Dancing the Tightrope; New Love Poems by
  Women (DT). Barbara Burford, Lindsay
  MacRae, *and* Sylvia Paskin, eds.
Defiant Muse, The; French Feminist Poems
  from the Middle Ages to the Present
  (DMF). Donna C. Stanton, ed.
Defiant Muse, The; German Feminist Poems
  from the Middle Ages to the Present
  (DMG). Susan L. Cocalis, ed.
Defiant Muse, The; Hispanic Feminist Poems
  from the Middle Ages to the Present
  (DMH). Angel Flores *and* Kate Flores,
  eds.
Defiant Muse, The; Italian Feminist Poems
  from the Middle Ages to the Present (DMI).
  Beverly Allen, Muriel Kittel, *and* Keala
  Jane Jewell, eds.
Early Ripening; American Women's Poetry
  Now (ER). Marge Piercy, ed.
Faber Book of 20th Century Women's Poetry,
  The (FaBoWP). Fleur Adcock, ed.
Gathering of Spirit, A; Writing and Art by
  North American Indian Women (GOS).
  Beth Brant, ed.
I Hear My Sisters Saying; Poems by
  Twentieth-Century Women (IHMS). Carol
  Konek *and* Dorothy Walters, eds.
No More Masks! An Anthology of Poems by
  Women (NMM). Florence Howe *and* Ellen
  Bass, eds.
Other Voice, The; Twentieth-Century
  Women's Poetry in Translation (OV).
  Joanna Bankier, *and others,* eds.
Penguin Book of Women Poets, The (PBWP).
  Carol Cosman, Joan Keefe, *and* Kathleen
  Weaver, eds.
Watchers and Seekers; Creative Writing by
  Black Women (WS). Rhonda Cobham *and*
  Merle Collins, eds.
Women Poets in English, The (WPE). Ann
  Stanford, ed.
Women Poets of the World (WPOW). Joanna
  Bankier *and* Deirdre Lashgari, eds.
Women Troubadours, The (WT). Meg
  Bogin, ed.
See also **Daughters; Feminism; Girls;**
  Mothers.

Wood
Chopping Wood. Smith
Dark Wood. Wedde
Old Boards. Bly
Wood-Pile, The. Frost
Woodworker's Ballad. Palmer
Workbox, The. Hardy

Wood, Grant
Grant Wood's American Landscape. Scott

Woodchucks *See* **Groundhogs.**

Woodcocks
My Woodcock. Chalmers
Woodpeckers
Legend of the Northland, A. Cary
Woodpecker, The. Ni Tsan
Woodpecker, The. Roberts
Woodpecker, The. Sambrook
Woodpecker in Disguise. Hallock
Woods. *See* **Forests.**
Woodstock, New York
Woodstock. Mitchell
Wool
Braid Claith. Fergusson
Woolf, Virginia
Virginia Woolf, Etc. Peri Rossi
Woolworth Building, New York City
Storms and Towers. Leyeles
Worcestershire, England
At Arley. Young
Words
All the Words. Hanscombe *and* Suniti
Namjoshi
Alphabet for Auden. Duffy
Coal. Lorde
Could mortal lip divine. Dickinson
Feelings about Words. O'Neill
Greenwood. Jackson
Heloise. Frabotta
I Search Again for a Word Today. Faiz
Idle Words. Landor
Last Words. Pastan
Like Ghosts of Eagles. Francis
Louisiana Perch. Padgett
Lyric for Legacies. Herrick
Meditation at Lagunitas. Hass
Moon, Sun, Sleep, Birds, Live. Patchen
My Words. Hathaway
Ö. Dove
Permanently. Koch
Price of Wildness, The. Moffett
Report from a Far Place. Stafford
Rune. Rukeyser
Second Story, The. Hummer
Some Words Which, Up until Now, Had
Remained Mysteriously Forbidding for Me.
Eluard
Threes. Sandburg
Tip of the Iceberg, The. Blumenthal
Torn-Word. McGavin
Two Words; a Wedding. Nichol
Word. Spender
Word is dead, A. Dickinson
Words. Hay
Words. Plath
Words That Speak of Death. Eldan
See also **Language.**
Wordsworth, William
Bards, The. De la Mare
Dear Wordsworth. Hathaway
Dedication: "Bob Southey! You're a poet—
poet-laureate." *Fr.* Don Juan. Byron
He Lived amidst th' Untrodden Ways.
Coleridge
Here Pause: The Poet Claims at Least This
Praise. Wordsworth
Lost Leader, The. Browning
Memorial Verses. Arnold
On a Portrait of Wordsworth by B. R.
Haydon. Browning
Raised are the dripping oars. *Fr.* The Youth
of Nature: Wordsworth's Country. Arnold
Resolution of Dependence. Barker
Some of Wordsworth. Landor
Sonnet, A: "Two voices are there: one is of
the deep." Stephen
To the Poet Wordsworth. Hemans
To William Wordsworth. Coleridge
To Wordsworth. Clare
To Wordsworth. Coleridge
To Wordsworth. Landor
To Wordsworth. Shelley

William Wordsworth. Keyes
William Wordsworth (1770-1850). Ewart
With Wordsworth at Rydal. Fields
Wordsworth's Grave. Watson
Work. *See* **Labor and Laborers.**
Work Songs
American Folk Poetry (AmFP). Duncan
Emrich, ed.
World. *See* **Earth.**
World Federation
For I Dipped [*or* Dipt] into the Future. *Fr.*
Locksley Hall. Tennyson
See also **United Nations.**
World War I
Aftermath. Sassoon
America's Answer. Lilliard
America's Welcome Home. Van Dyke
"And There Was a Great Calm." Hardy
Another Reply to "In Flanders Fields."
Armstrong
Anthem for Doomed Youth. Owen
Anzac Cove. Gellert
Apologia pro Poemate Meo. Owen
August 1914. Rosenberg
"Blighters." Sassoon
Break of Day in the Trenches. Rosenberg
But sweet sister death has gone debauched
today and stalks. *Fr.* In Parenthesis.
Jones
Calligram, 15 May 1915. Apollinaire
Camouflaged Troop-Ship. Lowell
Channel Firing. Hardy
Christmas 1914. Harding
Christmas Eve in France. Fauset
Christmas: 1924. Hardy
Cold. Coffey
Coming of War; Actaeon, The. Pound
Corpses in the Wood. Toller
Counter-Attack. Sassoon
Dardanelles 1916. Fallon
Disabled. Owen
Dulce et Decorum Est. Owen
Epicedium. Miller
Eternal Return, The. Hillyer
Everyone Sang. Sassoon
Farmer Remembers the Somme, The. Palmer
For All We Have and Are. Kipling
Futility. Owen
Going and Staying. Hardy
Great War, The. Scannell
Gun Teams. Frankau
In Flanders Fields. McCrae
In Flanders Now. Jaques
In Memoriam (Easter, 1915). Thomas
In Memoriam Francis Ledwidge. Heaney
In the Dordogne. Bishop
In Time of "The Breaking of Nations."
Hardy
Jezreel. Hardy
Little Car, The. Apollinaire
Little Song of the Maimed. Péret
Mail Boat, *Leinster*, The. *Unknown*
Mail Call. Bensko
Miners. Owen
Next War, The. Owen
MCMXIV. Larkin
November 1918. Hanson
On Being Asked for a War Poem. Yeats
On Passing the New Menin Gate. Sassoon
Over the Top with Pershing. Fitzgerald
Parable of the Old Man and the Young, The.
Owen
Passport. *Fr.* Invasion. Teller
Peace. *Fr.* 1914. Brooke
Pity of It, The. Hardy
Private, A. Thomas
Rear-Guard, The. Sassoon
Reply to "In Flanders Fields." Mitchell
Repression of War Experience. Sassoon
Reprisals. Yeats

Rouen. Cannan
Rouge Bouquet. Kilmer
Send-off, The. Owen
Sergeant-Major Money. Graves
Show, The. Owen
Silent One, The. Gurney
Silver Jubilee. Griffith
Soissons. Douglas
Soldier, The. *Fr.* 1914. Brooke
Sonnets Written in the Fall of 1914.
Woodberry
Spring Offensive. Owen
Summer in England, 1914. Meynell
There died a myriad. *Fr.* Hugh Selwyn
Mauberley. (Life and Contacts). Pound
There Is. Apollinaire
These fought in any case. *Fr.* Hugh Selwyn
Mauberley. (Life and Contacts). Pound
These Men. Gellert
To a Conscript of 1940. Read
To the United States of America. Bridges
Towards Lillers. Gurney
Veteran of the Great War, A. Bensko
Vlamertinghe; Passing the Château, July
1917. Blunden
War Story. Stallworthy
While Marching Around to Attract Shells.
Apollinaire
Wounds. Longley
Zonnebeke Road, The. Blunden
Men Who March Away (MMA). I. M.
Parsons, ed.
World War II
Aristocrats. Douglas
Ballad of the D-Day Dodgers. *Unknown*
Beach Burial. Slessor
Bird, The. Simpson
Black-out. Jeffers
Breaking. Allan
Camp in the Prussian Forest, A. Jarrell
Carentan O Carentan. Simpson
Chez-Nous. Austin
Children's Crusade 1939. Brecht
Christmas 1942. Irvin
D-Dawn. McGarvey
Day of Pearl Harbor, The. *Fr.* A Brief
History of Imbecility. Takamura Kotaro
Death Camp. Klepfisz
Death of an Aircraft. Causley
Death of the Ball Turret Gunner, The. Jarrell
Deep Sea Tug. Robertson
Deluge 1939, The. Lewis
Eighth Air Force. Jarrell
El Alamein. Crow
El Alamein Revisited. Macnab
Epitaphs. Sutskever
Exodus 1940. Wolfenstein
Field Hospital, 1945. Fodor
Firebombing, The. Dickey
Footnote to Enright's "Apocalypse." Bell
Fourth Act. Jeffers
Grand Finale, The. Vas
Guita Bruner. Guevara
Harbach 1944. Pilinszky
Here war is harmless like a monument. *Fr.*
Sonnets from China. Auden
Hitler, frothy-mouth, wooden-head.
Unknown
In Distrust of Merits. Moore
In Westminster Abbey. Betjeman
Incident on a Front Not Far from Castel di
Sangro. Brown
Jervis Bay, The. *Unknown*
Kilroy. Viereck
Kola Run, The. Goodbrand
Landscape with Figures. Douglas
Lead Plates at the Rom Press, The.
Sutskever
Leningrad Cemetary, Winter of 1941. Olds
Less Nonsense. Herbert
Lilacs and the Roses, The. Aragon
Little Boats of Britain, The. Carsley

Losses. Jarrell
Man unto His Fellow Man. *Fr.* On a Note
  of Triumph. Corwin
Milan August 1943. Quasimodo
Moon and the Night and the Men, The.
  Berryman
Nerves. "Sagittarius"
Night of Battle. Winters
Nike. Wazyk
1916. Lauer
Notes for a Movie Script. Holman
On the Eyes of an SS Officer. Wilbur
Ops in a Wimpey. *Unknown*
Picture of Okinawa, A. Schmitz
Pilots, Man Your Planes. Jarrell
Remembering That Island. McGrath
Reverie of a Mum. Keesing
Scyros. Shapiro
Second Air Force. Jarrell
September 1, 1939. Auden
Sergeant, The. Johnson
Sinking of the *Graf Spee*, The. *Unknown*
Spring 1942. Fuller
Spring Offensive, 1941. Biggs
Still Falls the Rain. Sitwell
Stoic; for Laura von Courten, The. Bowers
Streets of Laredo, The. MacNeice
Sunday: New Guinea. Shapiro
That's It. Leyeles
This Was My Brother. Gould
Timoshenko. Keyes
To a Conscript of 1940. Read
To Any Member of My Generation. Barker
Vale from Carthage. Viereck
Vergissmeinnicht. Douglas
War. Langland
War against the Jews, The. Stern
Wartime Dawn, A. Gascoyne
Watching War Movies. Stryk
Welcoming Party, A. Montague
White Rose: Sophie Scholl 1921-1943, The.
  Mumford
World War II. Field
World War II. Hughes
*Chaos of the Night, Women's Poetry and
  Verse of the Second World War* (CN).
  Catherine W. Reilly, ed.

Worms
Autobiography of a Lungworm. Fuller
Christmas Dinner. Rosen
Earthworm, The. Martinson
Fishing Song, A. Rands
Fury of Flowers and Worms, The. Sexton
Night Crawler. Bodecker
Old Shellover. De la Mare
Our little kinsmen after rain. Dickinson
Periphrastic Insult, Not a Banal, A.
  Cunningham
Seeing the Light. Gar
Sick Rose, The. *Fr.* Songs of Experience.
  Blake
Tell Me Little Woodworm. Milligan
This Is an African Worm. Danner
To a Worm Which the Author Accidentally
  Trode Upon. Hawkins
Two Sad. Cole
Wee Little Worm, A. Riley
Woodworm, The. Fusinato
Worm, The. Bergengren
Worms. Leyeles

Wormwood
Tall Ambrosia. Thoreau

Worry
"Don't worry!" he says. *Unknown*

Worship
All Hail the Power of Jesus' Name. Perronet
As Spring the Winter Doth Succeed.
  Bradstreet
At Mass. Lindsay
First-Day Thoughts. Whittier
Gascoigne's Good-Morrow. Gascoigne

Go, Heart, unto the Lamp of Licht.
  Unknown
Hosanna to Christ. Watts
Hymn: "Lord, when the wise men came from
  far[r]" Godolphin
In the First Cave. Mayne
Jordan. Herbert
O my Lord, if I worship you from fear of
  Hell. Al-Adawiyya
On Christmas-Day. Traherne
Pied Beauty. Hopkins
Some keep the Sabbath [*or* Sunday] going to
  church. Dickinson
Song to David, A. Smart
Sunday. Herbert
Temper, The. Herbert
True Hymn, A. Herbert
Water and Worship: An Open-Air Service on
  the Gatineau River. Avison
Worship. Whittier
Ye holy Angels bright. *Fr.* A Psalm of
  Praise. Baxter
See also **Churches; Prayer; Religion.**

Wounded Knee, Battle of (1890)
I Expected My Skin and My Blood to Ripen.
  Rose

Wren, Sir Christopher
Homage to Wren. MacNeice
Sir Christopher Wren. *Fr.* Clerihews.
  Bentley

Wrens
Dove says, Coo, coo, The. Mother Goose
Jenny Wren. Davies
Kill a robin or a wren. *Unknown*
Little Lady Wren. Robinson
Little Wren, A. Thompson
Looking at a Dead Wren in My Hand. Bly
Mrs. Jenny Wren. Bennett
Warning. *Unknown*
Wren, The. *Unknown*

Wrestling and Wrestlers
Antaeus; a Fragment. Owen
Sleeping Wrestler. Mutsuo
Sumo Wrestlers. Kirkup
Winning wrestler leaves, The. *Fr.*
  Twenty-four Hokku. Kito
Two Wrestlers. Francis
Wrestlers. *Fr.* Polyolbion. Drayton
Wrestling. Fraser
Wrestling The Beast. Adoff
Young Wrestlers. Butcher

Wright, James
Last Words to James Wright. Hugo

Wright, Richard
Mourning Letter from Paris, A. Rivers
To Richard Wright. Rivers

Writing and Writers
About This Book. Mechthild of Magdeburg
Ama Credo. Reckord
Amateur Thinks, An. Themerson
Ars Poetica? Milosz
Ars Poetica. Tornai
Ars Poetica. Wright
As for Poets. Snyder
At a Reading. McClatchy
Ballad of the Dreamy Girl. Roseveare
Because We Are Not Taken Seriously. Dunn
Blue Spruce. Halliday
Burning Hills. Ondaatje
Canadian Prairies View of Literature, The.
  Donnell
City Lights: I Took That Picture. Albert
Cognition, Language, Poetry. Nagy
Compound Eye, The. Davison
Dawn. Stryk
Dragons, The. Komrij
Eve of Easter. Mayer
False Youth: Autumn: Clothes of the Age.
  Dickey
Fiction-Makers, The. Stevenson
First Step, The. Cavafy

For the Christian Reader. Hoyers
Future Work. Adcock
High Poetic Circles. Ewart
I Am. Leib
I Have Lived This Way for Years and Do Not
  Wish to Change. Blumenthal
I Make Poems, Gentlemen! Fuertes
I shall make a vers about/ nothing.
  Guillaume de Poitiers
I write because not to write is a breach of
  faith. *Fr.* A Simple Act (Story Two: My
  House). Brant
Impromptu. Kalász
In form most people look to Sung and Yuan
  models. *Fr.* Twenty-seven Quatrains
  Discussing Poetry. Rai San'yo.
Introduction: "To be a writer and write
  things." Ashbery
Invocation, An: "My claw is tired of
  scribing!" Columcille
Last Night I Felt a Poem on My Lips. Korn
Like a convalescent, I took the hand.
  Heaney
Lit. Crit. Logue
Literary Manners I. Jacob
Literary Manners II. Jacob
Love Poem, A: "In sad revery." Tameko
Madly Singing in the Mountains. Po Chü-i
Makers, The. Nemerov
Making Poetry. Stevenson
Marginalia. Somlyó
Means of Production, The. Hofmann
Moonshine. Murphy
Movement along the Frieze. Knox
My Latest Publication. Capern
My Mother's Novel. Piercy
My Sisters, O My Sisters. Sarton
Neighbors. *Fr.* Poets. Rolnik
Next Poem, The. Gioia
No Denying. Ladányi
Non Omnis Moriar. Gutiérrez Nájera
Not Allowed to Write. Fuertes
Pen, The. Fordham
Poem of Pathos. Rozewicz
Poem: "This poem is not addressed to you."
  Justice
Poem with Capital Letters, A. Cooper
Poems by Women. Maraini
Poems We Can Understand. Hoover
Poetess, The. Fabiani
Poetical Economy. Graham
Poetry. Fridman
Poetry. "Peter"
Poetry. Sutskever
Poets. Boyle
Post-Impressionist Susurration for the First of
  November, 1983, A. Carruth
Reading the Books Our Children Have
  Written. Smith
Record, The. Preil
Rereading Old Writing. Ferry
Reunion. Wright
Romance. Stern
Rondeau: "Lord, I'm done for: now Margot."
  Voiture
Sacred Objects. Simpson
Sines. Queneau
Testament. Zavatsky
That I be a writer? Absolutely not! *Fr.*
  Resolution. Masanés
To a Japanese Poet. Stryk
To a Political Poet. Heine
To a Young Poet Who Fled. Logan
To Himself. Jouve
To the Gentile Poet. Leib
Twenty-some years and I've finished my
  book. *Fr.* Random Thoughts on the
  Writing of History. Rai San'yo
Variations on a Text by Vallejo. Justice
Voice. Padgett

Wanting to Air His Thoughts about and Prove His Respect for Mademoiselle Weichmann's Unusual Talent. Weichmann
Wanting to Answer Mr. Darnmann's Undeserved Civility in the Same Rhyme-Scheme. Weichmann
We have such plain faces. *Fr.* Poets. Rolnik
With Exultation, As We Can! Leivick
Woman Poet, The. Kolmar
Work, The. *Fr.* Dante Études. Duncan
Work. Jouve
Writer, The. Wilbur
Writing. Cronin
Writing. Jooris
Yiddish Poets. Leivick
Zimmer to His Students. Zimmer
In the American Tree (IAT). Ron Silliman, ed.
See also **Handwriting.**

Wyatt, Sir Thomas
Death of Wyatt, The. Surrey
In Praise of Wyatt's Psalms. Surrey
In the rude age when seyence was not so rife. Surrey
Note on Wyatt, A. Amis
Wyatt Resteth Here. Surrey

Wye (river), Wales and England
Meandering Wye. *Fr.* The Banks of Wye. Bloomfield

Wyoming
Accountability. Stafford
Cutting Wood on Shell Creek. Ehrlich
Old Photo, 1942. Uba
Orchard, The. Ehrlich
Sheepherder, The. Sarett
Snow Country. Etter
Way of Speaking, A. Ehrlich

Wyspianski, Stanislaw
To Stanislaw Wyspianski. Mansfield

X

X-Rays
Röntgen Photograph. Eybers
Walk in Würzburg, A. Plomer
X-Ray. Ray
X-Ray. Speyer

Xantippe
Xantippe. Levy

Xenophanes
Xenophanes. Emerson

Y

Yachts
Yachts, The. Williams
Yachts on the Nile. Spencer
See also **Boats.**

Yaks
Yak, The. Belloc
Yak, The. Prelutsky
Yak, The. Sheard

Yale University
Bull-Dog! Porter

Yangtze River
Inscribed on the Painting "River in Autumn." Ni Tsan

Yankees (New York baseball team)
Ballad of Dead Yankees, The. Petersen
Baseball and Writing. Moore

Yarrow *or* **Yarrow Water, Scotland**
Braes of Yarrow, The. Logan

Yarrow Revisited. Wordsworth
Yarrow Visited. Wordsworth

Years
What Are Years? Moore

Yeats, John Butler
John Butler Yeats. Foster

Yeats, William Butler
After W. B. Yeats. Chesterton
Circus Animals' Desertion, The. Yeats
Death of Yeats, The. Barker
Earth, receive an honoured guest. *Fr.* In Memory of W. B. Yeats. Auden
To W. B. Yeats Who Says That His Castle of Ballylee Is His Monument. Gogarty
Under Ben Bulben. Yeats
William Yeats in Limbo. Keyes

Yellow
New Colour in the Colour of Sunlight, A. Niazi
Symphony in Yellow. Wilde
Yellow. McCord
Yellow Light. Hongo

Yesenin, Sergey
Death of the Epileptic Poet Yesenin, The. Boyajian

Yew Trees
Fallen Yew, A. Thompson
Moon and the Yew Tree, The. Plath
Old yew, which graspest at the stones. *Fr.* In Memoriam A. H. H. Tennyson
Yew Trees. Wordsworth

Yiddish
Finding a Yiddish Paper on the Riverside Line. Spacks
Move On, Yiddish Poet. Glatstein
Where the Cedars. Glatstein
Yiddish. Herzberg
Yiddish. Sutskever
Yiddish Poet. Jacobs
Yiddish Speaking Socialists of the Lower East Side. Sanders

Yiddish Verse
American Yiddish Poetry (AYP). Benjamin Harshaw *and* Barbara Harshaw, eds.
Penguin Book of Modern Yiddish Verse, The (PeBMYV). Irving Howe, Ruth R. Wisse, *and* Khone Shmeruk, eds.

Ying Yao
Weeping for Ying Yao. Wang Wei

Yom Kippur
Day of Atonement. Myers
Kol Nidra. Leiser
On the Day of Atonement. Amichai
Riding Westward. Shapiro
To Raja Rao. Milosz
Yom Kippur. Bloch
Yom Kippur. Chaet
Yom Kippur. Day
Yom Kippur. Pastan
Yom Kippur. Zangwill
Yom Kippur: Fasting. Whitman

York, England
Coldness, The. Silkin

Yorkshire, England
In Teesdale. Young
Inside the Cave. Grigson
Ode to the Yorkshire Dales. Buddingh'
Sonnet: Composed after a Journey across the Hamilton Hills, Yorkshire. Wordsworth
Sound of Matter, The. Bernlef
Uncle Carl: A Home Movie. Bernlef

Yoruba
I-Tie-All-My-People-Together. Cliff

Young, Brigham
Nauvoo. Taylor

Young, Lester
Lester Leaps In. Young
Lester Young. Joans

Young Men's Christian Association
Y. M. C. A, The. Linden

Young Pretender, The. *See* **Stuart, Charles Edward.**

Younger, Cole
Cole Younger. *Unknown*

Youth
A'Chuilionn. Hutchison
Anthem for Doomed Youth. Owen
Aquellos Vatos. Villanueva
At Majority. Rich
At the Doors. Der Nistor
Ballade of Lost Objects. McGinley
Barefoot Boy, The. Whittier
Bedtime Story, A. Mezey
Birches. Frost
Boy's Song, A. Hogg
Cherries. Schneour
Daedalus. Reid
Deceptrices, The. Williams
Dedication to the Generation Knocking at the Door. Davidson
Description of Beauty, A. Daniel
Don't Trust Anyone over Thirty. Szabo
Down by the Salley Gardens. Yeats
Elegy: "Yes, I experienced youth." Wu Sheng
English Schoolboy, The. *Fr.* The Play of the Weather. Heywood
Exit. MacDonald
Farm Child. Thomas
Father William. *Fr.* Alice's Adventures in Wonderland. "Carroll"
For Freckle-faced Gerald. Knight
For My Son on the Highways of His Mind. Kumin
Furniture. Harris
Green Apples. Randall
He who in his youth. *Fr.* The Prelude [or, Growth of a Poet's Mind]: Books. Wordsworth
Her Dancing Days. Adams
How Soon Hath Time [the Subtle Thief of Youth]. Milton
How to Be Old. Swenson
I Saw from the Beach. Moore
In a herber [or a harbour or an arbour] green [or grene], asleep [or aslepe] whereas [or where as or where] I lay. *Fr.* Lusty Juventus. Wever
In a Spring Still Not Written Of. Wallace
In an Age of Fops and Toys. *Fr.* Voluntaries. Emerson
In Memoriam F. A. S. Stevenson
Intimations of Sublimity. *Fr.* The Prelude [or, Growth of a Poet's Mind]: School-Time. Wordsworth
Lines to Do with Youth. Bynner
Little Boy and the Old Man, The. Silverstein
Lost Shipmate, The. Roberts
My Gang. Kerouac
My Lost Youth. Longfellow
My Rival. Kipling
October Redbreast, The. Meynell
Ode on a Distant Prospect of Eton College. Gray
Old Age Sticks. Cummings
Old Man at the Window, The. Harvey
Old Man's Comforts and How He Gained Them, The. Southey
Old Swimmin'-Hole, The. Riley
On Reading Aloud My Early Poems. Williams
Our Youth. Ashbery
Out to Old Aunt Mary's. Riley
Parable of the Old Man and the Young, The. Owen
Piazza Piece. Ransom
Poem: "There I could never be a boy." O'Hara
Poet at Seventeen, The. Levis
Reports of Midsummer Girls. Lattimore
Rock Me to Sleep, [Mother]. Allen
Schiehallion. Cruickshank

Schoolboy, The. *Fr.* Songs of Experience. Blake
Seventeen. Holden
Short Song of Congratulation [*or* To a Young Heir], A. Johnson
Since Nine O'Clock. Cavafy
Snake Hill. Parini
Stanzas Written on the Road between Florence and Pisa. Byron
Talmud Student, The. Bialik
There Are Gains for All Our Losses. Stoddard
There Was a Boy ("There was a boy, ye knew him well"). *Fr.* The Prelude [or, Growth of a Poet's Mind]: Books. Wordsworth
To Youth. Heard
To Youth. Landor
Trees They Do Grow High, The. *Unknown*
Unemployment/Monologue. Jordan
We Real Cool. Brooks
What Saundra Said about Being Short. Hall
"What You See Is Me." Gibbs
When I Was Twenty. Carman
When I Was Young. Llywelyn-Williams
Young and Old. *Fr.* The Water Babies. Kingsley
Young Girl. Huch
Young Old Young Old. Elburg
Young Ones, Flip Side, The. Emanuel
Youth. Cloud
Youth. "Hope"
Youth. Hughes
Youth. Johnson
Youth. Neruda
Youth and Age. Coleridge
Youth and Age on Beaulieu River, Hants. Betjeman
Youth Mowing, A. Lawrence
Youth Sings a Song of Rosebuds. Cullen
Youth's the Season. *Fr.* The Beggar's Opera. Gay

Yugoslavia
And Forgetful of Europe. Grigson
Crew Practice on Lake Bled, in Jugoslavia. Scully
Dubrovnik Poem (Emilio Tolentino). Rudolf
Sarajevo. Durrell
Seventh Eclogue. Radnóti

Yukon Territory
Cremation of Sam McGee, The. Service
Law of the Yukon, The. Service
Spell of the Yukon, The. Service

Z

Zacchaeus
On Zacchaeus. Quarles

Zambia
Leader, The. Livesay

Zapata, Emiliano
Pentecost. Ai

Zebras
Zebra. "Dinesen"
Zebra. *Unknown*
Zebra Stallion. *Unknown*
Zebras, The. Campbell

Zen Buddhism
December. Snyder
New World in the Morning. German
Zen Poems of China & Japan; the Crane's Bill (ZPCJ). Lucien Stryk, Takashi Ikemoto, *and* Taigan Takayama, eds.

Zenobia
Goodbye, Zenobia. Salih

Zeppelins. *See* **Dirigibles.**

Zeus
Europa. Plomer
Hymn to Zeus. *Fr.* Agamemnon. Aeschylus
Leda and the Swan. Yeats
Zeus, whoever Zeus may be, if he. Aeschylus

Zevi, Shabbetai
King Shabtai Tsvi. Greenberg

Zimbabwe
Black and White. Adame
Revolution. Zimunya

Zinnias
Zinnias. Worth

Zion
By the Waters of Babylon. *Fr.* Hebrew Melodies. Heine
Hebrew of Your Poets, Zion, The. Reznikoff
Kadia the Young Mother Speaks. Sampter
Last Words of Don Henriquez, The. Schneour
Light and Rejoicing to Israel. *Unknown*
My Heart Is in the East. Halevi
Ode to Zion. Halevi
Promised Land, The. Sampter
Song: "There stands a lonely pine-tree." Heine
Through These Pale Cold Days. Rosenberg
To the Western Wind. Halevi

Zionism
Hatikvah—a Song of Hope. Imber
Road, The. Schneour
Theodor Herzl. Zangwill
Those Zionists. Del Monte
Zionist Marching Song. Imber

Zipcodes
Hymn to These Newly Abbreviated States. Updike

Zodiac
Signs of the Zodiac, The. Brewer
Zodiac Song, The. Ruskin

Zola, Émile
Zola. Robinson

Zoos
At the Zoo. Milne
At the Zoo. Thackeray
Au Jardin des Plantes. Wain
Elephant. Johnson
False Country of the Zoo. Garrigue
In the Snake Park. Plomer
Jaguar, The. Hughes
Lion. Swenson
Lion and Albert, The. Edgar
Menagerie, The. Moody
On the Death of an Emperor Penguin in Regent's Park, London. Wright
Picture Postcard of a Zoo. Williams
Van Amburgh's Menagerie ("Van Amburgh is the man that goes with all the shows"). *Unknown*
Zoo, The. Logan
Zoo in the City, The. Allen

Zulus
Birth of Shaka, The. Mtshali
Fallen Zulu Commander, The. Van Den Heever
Lalela Zulu. *Unknown*
Weep Not for a Warrior. Mtshali
Zulu Girl, The. Campbell